Go beyond the
with the companion website for the
Funding Sources for Children and Youth Programs

Dig in deeper with expanded resources,
putting more grants dollars within reach

*Perfect for use in the classroom or as a tool for professional
grant seeking, the website features*:

- **Remote and site-wide access**
- **Broad range of up-to-date funding opportunities**
- **Cost-effective plans**

Subscriptions available for institutions, organizations and individuals

https://www.grantselect.com

Other books in the GRANTS Series:
Directory of Biomedical and Health Care Grants
Directory of Research Grants
Operating Grants for Nonprofit Organizations
Funding Sources for Community and Economic Development
Funding Sources for K-12 Education
Directory of Grants in the Humanities

Press
West Lafayette, Indiana

GRANTS Series

FUNDING SOURCES FOR CHILDREN AND YOUTH PROGRAMS

10th Edition

Edited by
Louis S. Schafer, Ed.S.

Littleberry
Press
West Lafayette, Indiana

Every effort has been made to ensure that all the information in this book is accurate at the time of publication; however, Littleberry Press neither endorses nor guarantees the content of external links referenced in this book.

If you have questions or comments about this book, or need information about licensing, custom editions, or special sales, please contact Littleberry Press. For academic/corporate purchases, please contact the Ingram Content Group: (615) 793-5000 or visit www.ingramcontent.com.

Published by Littleberry Press LLC
1048 B Sagamore Pkwy W, #48
West Lafayette, IN 47906
www.littleberrypress.com
765-237-3390
info@littleberrypress.com

Distributed by Ingram Content Group
1 Ingram Blvd.
La Vergne, TN 37086 USA
(615) 793-5000

First published 2002, 10th Edition 2021
ISBN 978-1-940750-14-9
ISBN-10 1-9407501-4-8

Editor: Louis S. Schafer, Ed.S.
Book design: Anita Schafer
Editorial assistance: Kira Axsiom and Andrea Axsom
Production: Littleberry Press and IngramSpark
Contributors: Kira Axsiom, Andrea Axsom, Zahraa Ouyoun, Anita Schafer, Louis S. Schafer
Cover image: Betelgejze via iStockPhoto.com

Printed and bound in the United States of America

At Littleberry Press, we publish a collection of books that reflect on real events and people and books that help educators and nonprofit personnel achieve their goals.

CONTENTS

Introduction   vii

How to Use This Directory   viii

Government and Organization Acronyms   xi

Grant Programs   1

Index: Subject Headings   453

Index: Program Types   603

Index: Geographic   675

INTRODUCTION

The entry into the world of grantseeking and grantsmanship is not usually a direct one. Many researchers, students, and nonprofit workers acquire those skills along the way, funding projects and education by learning-by-doing and writing grant proposals. What is considered to be a "soft" skill actually helps to keep the doors open, the lights on, and programs running. Every grant writer, new and experienced, learns quickly that all the grant writing proficiency in the world does not matter unless you have someone or some organization to send your proposal. In order to ask for the money, you must have someone to ask.

For four decades the GRANTS Database and its print complements, including the annual *Funding Sources for Children and Youth Programs*, have provided the grant community with current, accurate information regarding funding for children and youth programs and projects, scholarships, fellowships, conferences, and internships. To meet increased information needs, the GRANTS Database, researched and edited by members of the GrantSelect editorial staff, has grown significantly. This 10th edition of the annual *Funding Sources for Children and Youth Programs* offers factual and concise descriptions of more than 2,500 funding programs. With this new edition both experienced and novice grantseekers will be better able to target only the most applicable programs for their funding needs.

Funding Sources for Children and Youth Programs

The *Funding Sources for Children and Youth Programs* features listings that offer non-repayable funding for projects in medicine, the physical and social sciences, the arts and humanities, education, community and economic development, and parks and recreation programs. Listings in the main section of *Funding Sources* contain annotations describing each program's focuses and goals, program requirements explaining eligibility, funding amounts, deadlines, sponsor name and address, contact information, and the sponsor's web address. Grantseekers with access to the Internet can use the addresses to locate further information about the organizations and their application procedures. Internet addresses are also provided, when available. Some of the grant programs listed in the main section have geographic restrictions for applicants.

Indexes. The Subject Index of *Funding Sources* lists all program titles—with accession numbers—under their applicable subject terms. Other indexes follow, including the Grants by Program Type Index, which lists 44 program categories, such as Basic Research, Fellowships, Travel Grants, etc., with the grants that fall within their scope; and the Geographic Index, which lists programs that have state, regional, or international focus. See "How to Use This Directory" on pages viii to xiii for sample index entries.

Using the *Funding Sources* for Grantseeking

By using the *Funding Sources for Children and Youth Programs*, grantseekers can match the needs of their particular programs with those sponsors offering funding in the researchers' area of interest. The information listed here is meant to eliminate the costs incurred by both grantseekers and grantmakers when inappropriate proposals are submitted. However, because the GRANTS database is updated daily basis, with program listings continually added, deleted, and revised, grantseekers using this directory may also search the GRANTS database online through *GrantSelect* (www.grantselect.com).

All new and revised information within *Funding Sources* has been taken from (1) sponsors' updates of previously published program statements, (2) questionnaires sent to sponsors whose programs were not listed in previous editions, or (3) other materials published by the sponsor and furnished to Littleberry Press. Updated information for U.S. government programs includes new and revised program information published in the *Federal Register*, the *NIH Guide*, published by the National Institutes of Health; and the *NSF E-Bulletin*, a monthly publication of the National Science Foundation. Included in this edition are identifying document numbers from the NIH and NSF publications. Located at the ends of the program descriptions in certain entries, the numbers indicate the ongoing NIH program number (PA) or the request for applications number (RFA). For programs of the National Science Foundation, the *NSF Bulletin* number appears. This information will help users identify the programs when seeking additional information from program staff.

While Littleberry Press has made every effort to verify that all information is both accurate and current within the confines of format and scope, the publisher does not assume and hereby disclaims any liability to any party for loss or damages caused by errors or omissions in *Funding Sources*, whether such errors or omissions result from accident, negligence, or any other cause. Questions should be directed to the Editor at Littleberry Press via email at editor@littleberrypress.com.

HOW TO USE THIS DIRECTORY

The *Funding Sources for Children and Youth Programs* is designed to allow the user quick and easy access to information regarding funding in a researcher's specific area of interest. *Funding Sources* is composed of a main section, Grant Programs, which lists grant programs in alphabetical order, and three indexes: the Subject Index, the Grants by Program Type Index, and the Geographic Index.

GRANT PROGRAMS

Each listing in this section consists of the following elements: an annotation describing each program's focus and goals, requirements explaining eligibility, funding amounts, application and renewal dates, sponsor information, contact information, and Internet address.

GRANT TITLE——— **Paul G. Allen Family Foundation Grants**   4298 ———ACCESSION NUMBER

The single foundation, created through the consolidation of Allen's six previous foundations (The Allen Foundation for the Arts, The Paul G. Allen Charitable Foundation, The Paul G. Allen Foundation for Medical Research, The Paul G. Allen Forest Protection Foundation, The Allen Foundation for Music, and The Paul G. Allen Virtual Education Foundation), will continue to focus on the Allen family's philanthropic interests in the areas of arts and culture, youth engagement, community development and social change, and scientific and technological innovation. The Arts and Culture Program fosters creativity and promotes critical thinking by helping strong arts organizations become sustainable and supporting projects that feature innovative and diverse artistic forms. ———GRANT DESCRIPTION

The Youth Engagement Program improves the way young people learn by supporting organizations that use innovative teaching strategies and provide opportunities for children to address issues relevant to their lives. The Community Development and Social Change Program promotes individual and community development by supporting initiatives and organizations that provide access to resources and opportunities. The Scientific and Technological Innovation Program advances promising scientific and technology research that has the potential to enhance understanding and stewardship of the world in which we live. Organizations may only receive one grant per year. Organizations must not have any delinquent final reports due to any of the Paul G. Allen Foundations for previous grants. Grantseekers are encouraged to apply through the online application process, where basic organizational and project information will be requested. Guidelines are available online.

REQUIREMENTS——— *Requirements* 501(c)3 tax-exempt organizations, status from the Internal Revenue government entities, and IRS-recognized tribes are eligible. Eligible organizations must be located in, or serving populations of, the Pacific Northwest, which includes Alaska, Idaho, Montana, Oregon, and Washington.

RESTRICTIONS——— *Restrictions* In general, the foundation will not consider requests for general fund drives, annual appeals, or federated campaigns; special events or sponsorships; direct grants, scholarships, or loans for the benefit of specific individuals; projects of organizations whose policies or practices discriminate on the basis of race, ethnic origin, sex, creed, or sexual orientation; contributions to sectarian or religious organizations whose principle activity is for the benefit of their own members or adherents; loans or debt retirement; projects that will benefit the students of a single school; general operating support for ongoing activities; or projects not aligned with the foundation's specified program areas. 509(a) private foundations are ineligible.

APPLICATION/
DUE DATE ——— *Date(s) Application Is Due* Mar 31; Sep 30.

Contact Grants Administrator, (206) 342-2030; fax: (206) 342-3030; ———CONTACT
email: info@pgafamilyfoundation.org

INTERNET ADDRESS ——— *Internet* http://www.pgafamilyfoundation.org

Sponsor Paul G. Allen Family Foundation ———SPONSOR INFORMATION
505 Fifth Ave S, Ste 900
Seattle, WA 98104

SUBJECT INDEX

The most effective way to access specific funding programs is through the Subject Index. This index lists the subject terms with applicable grants program titles – and their accession numbers – alphabetically under each term. Terms were assigned to target the specific area of research designated in the description of each program. Cross-references are used to link subjects and assist the user in finding specific grant information.

Following are general guidelines that can make your search of this index more successful. First, check under the specific topic of interest rather than a more general term. For instance, if you are interested in chemical engineering, look under "Chemical Engineering" rather than "Engineering." Items indexed under "Engineering" indicate funding in broad areas of engineering.

Use general headings when you want grants covering broader areas or if you can't find a specific topic. For example, many grants list funding for humanities research, health programs, or science and technology. To find these grants use such headings

as "Humanities," "Medical Programs," "Science," or "Technology." For additional grant information on more specific humanities research opportunities, such as in American History or Cultural Anthropology, also check under the topics "United States History" and "Anthropology, Cultural."

Many of the grant programs provide funding for research-related scholarships, faculty fellowships, dissertations, undergraduate education, conferences, or internships. If grant funds are designated for specific disciplines, you will find the items under the specific subject. Scholarships and fellowships are also listed under the terms "Native American Education," "African Americans (Student Support)," "Hispanic Education," "Minority Education," and "Women's Education."

Grants concerning study of a particular country are listed under the name of the country. Grants concerning the history, literature, art and language of a country are listed under the name of the country also, e.g., "Chinese Art" and "Chinese Language/ Literature."

SUBJECT TERM ——————— **Education**

A.L. Mailman Family Foundation Grants, 5

AAAS Science & Technology Policy Fellowships - Health, Education & Human Services, 22

AARP Andrus Foundation Grants, 104

Abbott Laboratories Fund Grants, 125

ACIE Host University Edmund S. Muskie/Freedom Support Act Graduate Fellowships, 156

ACT Awards, 189

Akonadi Foundation Anti-Racism Grants, 351 ——————— PROGRAM TITLE

Akron Community Foundation Grants, 352

Albert and Margaret Alkek Foundation Grants, 370

Albuquerque Community Foundation Grants, 379

Alcoa Foundation Grants, 380

Alcon Foundation Grants Program, 382

GEOGRAPHIC INDEX

This index lists programs that have state, regional, or international geographic focus. The Geographic Index is arranged by state, followed by Canadian programs, then by international programs by country, and lists grant program titles and their corresponding accession numbers.

COUNTRY——————————— **United States**

Alabama ——————————————————————————————— STATE

3M Fndn Grants, 2

Alabama Humanities Fndn Grants Program, 368

Arkema Inc. Fndn Science Teachers Program, 705

CDC Injury Control Research Centers Grants, 1198

PROGRAM TITLE——————— DOE Experimental Program to Stimulate Competitive Research (EPSCoR), 1653

Hill Crest Fndn Grants, 2293

Linn-Henley Charitable Trust Grants, 2777

NOAA Community-Based Restoration Program (CRP) Grants, 3843

Southern Company's Longleaf Pine Reforestation Fund, 4726

PROGRAM TYPE INDEX

This index is broken into 44 categories according to the type of program funded:

- Adult Basic Education
- Adult/Family Literacy Training
- Awards/Prizes
- Basic Research
- Building Construction and/or Renovation
- Capital Campaigns
- Centers: Research/Demonstration/Service
- Citizenship Instruction
- Community Development
- Consulting/Visiting Personnel
- Cultural Outreach
- Curriculum Development/Teacher Training
- Demonstration Grants
- Development (Institutional/Departmental)
- Dissertation/Thesis Research Support
- Educational Programs
- Emergency Programs
- Endowments
- Environmental Programs
- Exchange Programs
- Exhibitions, Collections, Performances, Video/Film Production
- Faculty/Professional Development
- Fellowships
- General Operating Support
- Graduate Assistantships
- Grants to Individuals
- International Exchange Programs
- International Grants
- Job Training/Adult Vocational Programs
- Land Acquisition
- Matching/Challenge Funds
- Materials/Equipment Acquisition (Computers, Books, Tapes, etc.)
- Preservation/Restoration
- Professorships
- Publishing/Editing/Translating
- Religious Programs
- Scholarships
- Seed Grants
- Service Delivery Programs
- Symposia, Conferences, Workshops, Seminars
- Technical Assistance
- Training Programs/Internships
- Travel Grants
- Vocational Education

GOVERNMENT & ORGANIZATION ACRONYMS

AAAAI	American Academy of Allergy Asthma and Immunology
AAAS	American Association for the Advancement of Science
AACAP	American Academy of Child and Adolescent Psychiatry
AACN	American Association of Critical Care Nurses
AACR	American Association of Cancer Research
AAFCS	American Association of Family and Consumer Sciences
AAF	American Architectural Foundation
AAFP	American Academy of Family Physicians Foundation
AAFPRS	American Academy of Facial Plastic and Reconstructive Surgery
AAP	American Academy of Pediatrics
AAR	American Academy in Rome
AAS	American Antiquarian Society
AASL	American Association of School Libraries
AAUW	American Association of University Women
ABA	American Bar Association
ACC	Asian Cultural Council
ACF	Administration on Children, Youth and Families
ACLS	American Council of Learned Societies
ACM	Association for Computing Machinery
ACE	American Council on Education
ACMP	Amateur Chamber Music Players
ACS	American Cancer Society
ADA	American Diabetes Association
ADHF	American Digestive Health Foundation
AF	Arthritis Foundation
AFAR	American Federation for Aging Research
AFOSR	Air Force Office of Scientific Research
AFUD	American Foundation for Urologic Disease
AFUW	Australian Federation of University Women
AGS	American Geriatrics Society
AHA	American Heart Association
AHAF	American Health Assistance Foundation
AFHMR	Alberta Heritage Foundation for Medical Research
AHRQ	Agency for Healthcare Research and Quality
AICR	American Institute for Cancer Research
AIIS	American Institute for Indian Studies
AJA	American Jewish Archives
AJL	American Jewish Libraries
ALA	American Library Association
ALISE	Association for Library and Information Science Education
AMNH	American Museum of Natural History
AMS	American Musicological Society
ANL	Argonne National Library
ANS	American Numismatic Society
AOA	American Osteopathic Association
AOCS	American Oil Chemists' Society
APA	American Psychological Association
APAP	Association of Performing Arts Presenters
APEAL	Asian Pacific Partners for Empowerment and Leadership
APS	Arizona Public Service
APSA	American Political Science Association
ARIT	American Research Institute in Turkey
ARO	Army Research Office
ASA	American Statistical Association
ASCSA	American School of Classical Studies at Athens
ASECS	American Society for Eighteenth-Century Studies
ASF	American-Scandinavian Foundation
ASHA	American Speech-Language-Hearing Association
ASHRAE	American Society of Heating, Refrigerating, and Air Conditioning Engineers
ASME	American Society of Mechanical Engineers
ASNS	American Society for Nutritional Sciences
ASPRS	American Society of Photogrammetry and Remote Sensing
ASTA	American String Teachers Association
ATA	Alberta Teachers Association
AWHONN	Association of Women's Health, Obstetric, and Neonatal Nurses
AWU	Associated Western Universities
AWWA	American Water Works Association
BA	British Academy
BBF	Barbara Bush Foundation
BCBS	Blue Cross Blue Shield
BCBSM	Blue Cross Blue Shield of Michigan
BCBSNC	Blue Cross Blue Shield of North Carolina
BWF	Burroughs Wellcome Fund
CBIE	Canadian Bureau for International Education
CCF	Catholic Community Foundation
CCF	Common Council Foundation
CCFF	Canadian Cystic Fibrosis Foundation
CCFF	Christopher Columbus Fellowship Foundation
CDC	Centers for Disease Control and Prevention
CDECD	Connecticut Department of Economic and Community Development
CDI	Children's Discovery Institute
CEC	Council for Exceptional Children
CEF	Chemical Educational Foundation
CES	Council for European Studies
CF	The Commonwealth Fund
CFF	Cystic Fibrosis Foundation
CFFVR	Community Foundation for the Fox Valley Region
CFKF	Classic for Kids Foundation
CFNCR	Community Foundation for the National Capital Region
CFPC	College of Family Physicians of Canada

CFUW	Canadian Federation of University Women
CHCF	California Health Care Foundation
CHEA	Canadian Home Economics Association
CICF	Central Indiana Community Foundation
CIES	Council for International Exchange of Scholars
CIUS	Canadian Institute of Ukrainian Studies
CLA	Canadian Lung Association
CLF	Canadian Liver Foundation
CMS	Centers for Medicare and Medicaid Services
CNCS	Corporation for National and Community Service
CRI	Cancer Research Institute
CTCNet	Community Technology Centers Network
DAAD	Deutscher Akademische Austauschdienst (German Academic Exchange Service)
DHHS	Department of Health and Human Services
DOA	Department of Agriculture
DOC	Department of Commerce
DOD	Department of Defense
DOE	Department of Energy
DOI	Department of the Interior
DOJ	Department of Justice
DOL	Department of Labor
DOS	Department of State
DOT	Department of Transportation
EFA	Epilepsy Foundation of America
EIF	Entertainment Industry Foundation
EPA	Environmental Protection Agency
ESF	European Science Foundation
ETS	Educational Testing Service
FCAR	Formation de Chercheurs et L'Aide a la Recherche
FCD	Foundation for Child Development
FDA	Food and Drug Administration
FIC	Fogarty International Center
GAAC	German American Academic Council
GCA	Garden Club of America
GEF	Green Education Foundation
GNOF	Greater New Orleans Foundation
HAF	Humboldt Area Foundation
HBF	Herb Block Foundation
HHS	Health and Human Services
HHMI	Howard Hughes Medical Institute
HRSA	Health Resources and Services Administration
HUD	Department of Housing and Urban Development
ICC	Indiana Campus Compact
IIE	Institute of International Education
IRA	International Reading Association
IRC	International Rescue Committee

IREX	International Research and Exchanges Board
IUCP	Indiana University Center on Philanthropy
IYI	Indiana Youth Institute
JDF	Juvenile Diabetes Foundation International
JMO	John M. Olin Foundation
JSPS	Japan Society for the Promotion of Science
KFC	Kidney Foundation of Canada
LISC	Local Initiatives Support Corporation
LSA	Leukemia Society of America
MFRI	Military Family Research Institute
MHRC	Manitoba Health Research Council
MLA	Medical Library Association
MLB	Major League Baseball
MMA	Metropolitan Museum of Art
MMS	Massachusetts Medical Society
MSSC	Multiple Sclerosis Society of Canada
NAA	Newspaper Association of America
NAACP	National Association for the Advancement of Colored People
NAGC	National Association for Gifted Children
NAPNAP	National Association of Pediatric Nurse Associates and Practitioners
NARSAD	National Alliance for Research on Schizophrenia and Depression
NASA	National Aeronautics and Space Administration
NASE	National Association for the Self-Employed
NASM	National Air and Space Museum
NATO	North Atlantic Treaty Organization
NCCAM	National Center for Complementary and Alternative Medicine
NCFL	National Center for Family Literacy
NCI	National Cancer Institute
NCIC	National Cancer Institute of Canada
NCRR	National Center for Research Resources
NCSS	National Council for the Social Studies
NEA	National Education Association
NEH	National Endowment for the Humanities
NEI	National Eye Institute
NFID	National Foundation for Infectious Diseases
NFL	National Football League
NFWF	National Fish and Wildlife Foundation
NGA	National Gardening Association
NHGRI	National Human Genome Research Institute
NHLBI	National Heart, Lung and Blood Institute
NHSCA	New Hampshire State Council on the Arts
NIA	National Institute on Aging
NIAF	National Italian American Foundation
NIAAA	National Institute on Alcohol Abuse and Alcoholism
NIAF	National Italian American Foundation
NIAID	National Institute of Allergy and Infectious Diseases
NIAMS	National Institute of Arthritis and Musculoskeletal Skin Diseases

NICHD	National Institute of Child Health and Human Development
NIDA	National Institute on Drug Abuse
NIDCD	National Institute on Deafness and Other Communication Disorders
NIDCR	National Institute of Dental and Craniofacial Research
NIDDK	National Institute of Diabetes, and Digestive and Kidney Diseases
NIDRR	National Institute on Disability and Rehabilitation Research
NIEHS	National Institute of Environmental Health Sciences
NIGMS	National Institute of General Medical Sciences
NIH	National Institutes of Health
NIJ	National Institute of Justice
NIMH	National Institute of Mental Health
NINDS	National Institute of Neurological Disorders and Strokes
NINR	National Institute of Nursing Research
NIOSH	National Institute for Occupational Safety and Health
NIST	National Institute of Standards and Technology
NJSCA	New Jersey State Council on the Arts
NKF	National Kidney Foundation
NL	Newberry Library
NLM	National Library of Medicine
NMF	National Medical Fellowships, Inc.
NMSS	National Multiple Sclerosis Society
NNEDVF	National Network to End Domestic Violence Fund
NOAA	National Oceanic and Atmospheric Administration
NRA	National Rifle Association
NRC	National Research Council
NSERC	Natural Sciences and Engineering Research Council of Canada
NSF	National Science Foundation
NSTA	National Science Teachers Association
NYCH	New York Council for the Humanities
NYCT	New York Community Trust
NYFA	New York Foundation for the Arts
NYSCA	New York State Council on the Arts
OAH	Organization of American Historians
ODKF	Outrigger Duke Kahanamoku Foundation
OJJDP	Office of Juvenile Justice and Delinquency Prevention
ONF	Oncology Nursing Foundation
ONR	Office of Naval Research
OREF	Orthopaedic Research and Education Foundation
ORISE	Oak Ridge Institute for Science and Education
OSF	Open Society Foundation
PAS	Percussive Arts Society
PCA	Pennsylvania Council on the Arts
PDF	Peace Development Fund
PDF	Parkinson's Disease Foundation
PhRMA	Pharmaceutical Research and Manufacturers of American Foundation
PHSC	The Photographic Historical Society of Canada
PSEG	Public Service Enterprise Group
RCF	Richland County Foundation
RCPSC	Royal College of Physicians and Surgeons of Canada
RSC	Royal Society of Canada
RWJF	Robert Wood Johnson Foundation
SAMHSA	Substance Abuse and Mental Health Services Administration
SLA	Special Libraries Association
SME	Society of Manufacturing Engineers
SOCFOC	Sisters of Charity Foundation of Cleveland
SORP	Society of Biological Psychiatry
SSHRC	Social Sciences and Humanities Research Council of Canada
SSRC	Social Science Research Council
STTI	Sigma Theta Tau International
SVP	Social Venture Partners
SWE	Society of Women Engineers
TAC	Tennessee Arts Commission
TOMF	Tucson Osteopathic Medical Foundation
TRCF	Three Rivers Community Fund
TSYSF	Teemu Selanne Youth Sports Foundation
UPS	United Parcel Service
USHMM	United States Holocaust Memorial Museum Research Institute
USIA	United States Information Agency
USAID	United States Agency for International Development
USDA	United States Department of Agriculture
USFA	United States Fencing Association
USGA	United States Golf Association
USIP	United States Institute of Peace
USTA	United States Tennis Association
UUA	Unitarian Universalist Association
WAWH	Western Association of Woman Historians
WHO	Women Helping Others

1st Source Foundation Community Involvement Grants   1

Established in 1952 in Indiana and administered by the 1st Source Bank, the Foundation supports community foundations, youth clubs and organizations involved with television, education, health, and human services. The Foundation provides support to organizations working in the following areas: social welfare and human services; education; culture and the arts; and community, civic and neighborhood involvement. Giving is primarily centered in Indiana, and the major type of funding given is for general operating support. Since there are no specific applications forms required or deadlines with which to adhere, applicants should send a letter of request detailing the project and the amount of funding needed. Most recent awards have ranged from $500 to $60,000. There are two annual deadline for application submissions: April 25 and September 25.
Requirements: Any 501(c)3 serving the residents of Indiana communities where 1st Source Banks are located are eligible to apply.
Geographic Focus: Indiana
Date(s) Application is Due: Apr 25; Sep 25
Amount of Grant: 500 - 60,000 USD
Contact: Renée Fleming, Director; (574) 235-2790 or (574) 235-2119
Internet: www.1stsource.com/about-us/community-involvement
Sponsor: 1st Source Foundation
100 N Michigan Street, P.O. Box 1602
South Bend, IN 46601-1630

1st Touch Foundation Grants   2

Established by Derek L. Lee in 2006 in an effort to help his daughter, Jada, giving is centered around the testing and researching of Leber's Congenital Amaurosis (LCA), an extremely rare disease which causes severe vision loss and blindness. The Foundation's primary long-range mission is to help researchers find a cure and eradicate this disease. It will also continue to provide grants for higher education, and help children and youth organizations within its local communities. There are no specific guidelines, application forms, or deadlines with which to adhere, so applicants should contact the Foundation office directly.
Geographic Focus: All States
Contact: Derrek Lee, Director; (415) 421-0535 or (818) 501-4421
Sponsor: 1st Touch Foundation
16030 Ventura Boulevard, Suite 240
Encino, CA 91436

2 Depot Square Ipswich Charitable Foundation Grants   3

In December of 2005, Ipswich Co-operative Bank established the 2 Depot Square Ipswich Charitable Foundation with an initial contribution of $200,000. Charitable giving has been a cornerstone of the Bank's business philosophy for many years. The Foundation plays a vital role in supporting economic development and improving the quality of life in the communities that it serves. The Foundation focuses its giving in the following areas: economic and community empowerment—includes programs which focus on the promotion and development of access to safe and affordable housing, and programs which support community revitalization efforts; youth development—initiatives that encourage youth through social, educational, athletic or cultural programs; arts and culture—programs and organizations which provide art and cultural programs that enrich communities; and health and human services—organizations which strive to enhance the health and well-being of children and families in its communities. The Grant Committee meets in April and November. Completed applications are due April 1st and November 1st.
Requirements: The Foundation awards funds to non-profit organizations based in Ipswich and the surrounding communities. Applications for grants will only be accepted from qualified 501(c)3 or 501(c)1 organizations.
Geographic Focus: Massachusetts
Date(s) Application is Due: Apr 1; Nov 1
Contact: Tammy Roeger; (978) 462-3106; fax (978) 462-1980; tammy.roeger@ifs-nbpt.com
Internet: www.institutionforsavings.com/site/charitable_2depot_about.html
Sponsor: 2 Depot Square Ipswich Charitable Foundation
2 Depot Square
Ipswich, MA 01938-1914

3 Dog Garage Museum Tours   4

Established in 2007 in Pennsylvania, 3 Dog Garage offers educational tours to K-12 students and adults. Founder Ross Myers got his start in the old car hobby at an early age, and his father had antique Fords which now comprise part of his 3 Dog Garage collection. Despite its value to history, the 3 Dog Garage has deliberately kept a low profile and is not well known by the general public or even by most car enthusiasts. The collection is housed in a facility in Boyertown, Pennsylvania, that its founder has turned into a museum, open for educational tours by appointment. Those interested should contact the office directly.
Geographic Focus: All States
Contact: Teresa Hasson, (610) 473-7007; 3dg@comcast.net
Internet: www.3dog.org/
Sponsor: 3 Dog Garage
15 South Madison Street
Boyertown, PA 19512-2206

3M Company Foundation Community Giving Grants   5

The 3M Company Foundation supports organizations involved with arts and culture, K-12 education, higher education, the environment, and health and human services. Special emphasis is directed toward programs designed to help prepare individuals and families for success. Fields of interest are: arts; arts education; business education; disaster relief, preparedness, and services; economics; elementary and secondary education; employment training; engineering; environmental causes; family services; federated giving programs; health care; higher education; human services; mathematics; minorities; science programs; youth development; and youth, services. Types of support include: building construction and renovation, capital campaigns, curriculum development, employee matching gifts, general operating support, in-kind gifts, program development, and scholarship funds. The foundation utilizes an invitational Request For Proposal (RFP) process for organizations located in Minneapolis and St. Paul, Minnesota, and Austin, Texas. Application forms are not required.
Requirements: Established 501(c)3 tax-exempt organizations in all 3M communities are eligible.
Restrictions: The 3M Company Foundation does not accept unsolicited proposals in St. Paul/Minneapolis, Minnesota, and Austin, Texas. No support for religious organizations, conduit agencies, political groups, fraternal organizations, social groups, or veteran organizations. No funding for hospitals, K-12 schools, military organizations, animal-related organizations, or disease-specific organizations. No grants to individuals, or for endowments, emergency operating support, advocacy and lobbying efforts, fundraising events and associated advertising, travel, publications, start-up needs, non -equipment, debt reduction, conferences, athletic events, or film or video production; no loans or investments.
Geographic Focus: Alabama, Alaska, Arkansas, California, Connecticut, Georgia, Hawaii, Illinois, Indiana, Iowa, Kentucky, Massachusetts, Michigan, Minnesota, Missouri, Nebraska, New York, Ohio, South Carolina, South Dakota, Texas, Utah, Wisconsin
Contact: Cynthia F. Kleven, Manager of Corporate Contributions; (651) 733-0144 or (651) 736-8146; fax (651) 737-3061; cfkleven@mmm.com
Internet: www.3m.com/3M/en_US/gives-us/community/
Sponsor: 3M Company Foundation
3M Center, Building 225-01-S-23
Saint Paul, MN 55144-1000

3M Company Foundation Health and Human Services Grants   6

Parallel to its Foundation, the 3M Company makes charitable contributions to nonprofit health and human services organizations directly. Support is given on a national basis. Most giving is initiated through a Request for Proposal process that allows the company to focus our giving and maximize results. Areas of interest for Health and Human Services include: to increase resiliency in youth through prevention efforts from early childhood to 12th grade; and to build and sustain healthy communities. Types of support include: building and renovation; capital campaigns; donated equipment; donated land; donated products; employee volunteer services; general operating support; in-kind gifts; internship funds; program development; seed money; technical assistance; and use of facilities. The Company also reaches out to bring assistance and help communities prepare for disaster.
Restrictions: No support is offered for: political, fraternal, social, veterans, or military organizations, propaganda or lobbying organizations; religious organizations not of direct benefit to the entire community; animal-related organizations; or disease-specific organizations. No grants are given to individuals, or for electronic media promotion or sponsorships, athletic events, non-3M equipment, endowments, emergency needs, conferences, seminars, workshops, symposia, fund raising or testimonial events, travel, or film or video production; no cause-related marketing.
Geographic Focus: Alabama, Alaska, Arkansas, California, Connecticut, Georgia, Hawaii, Illinois, Indiana, Iowa, Kentucky, Massachusetts, Michigan, Minnesota, Missouri, Nebraska, New Jersey, New York, Ohio, South Carolina, South Dakota, Texas, Utah, Wisconsin
Contact: Cynthia F. Kleven, Manager of Corporate Contributions; (651) 733-0144 or (651) 736-8146; fax (651) 737-3061; cfkleven@mmm.com
Internet: www.3m.com/3M/en_US/gives-us/
Sponsor: 3M Company Foundation
3M Center, Building 225-01-S-23
Saint Paul, MN 55144-1000

4imprint One by One Charitable Giving   7

4imprint's One by One charitable giving program is based on the company's culture and our team members' belief that nonprofit organizations are important and the work they do makes this world a better place. Each business day 4imprint gives two worthy organizations $500 in promotional products. Nonprofits can select any product at the web site for a donation. Applications will be reviewed by the one by one committee. All decisions will be based on geographic location, programming diversity, charitable diversity, value and merit of cause, and audience served.
Requirements: In order to apply for a donation an individual must be employed by or be a member of the Board of Directors for a 501(c)3 organization, a school, a registered Canadian charity/society or a religious organization. Applicants must be at least 18 years of age. There are no deadline dates, however you should submit your application a minimum of 2 months before you need the items. Applicants can select more than one product. If your organization is chosen for a donation, you may split your donation between two and three different products. If the total amount exceeds the $500 donation, the recipient is expected to pay the difference.

Restrictions: In order to help as many organizations as possible, 4imprint can only grant one donation per year to a particular organization. The donation must be used within 30 days of the date that you were selected.
Geographic Focus: All States, Canada
Amount of Grant: Up to 500 USD
Contact: Cheryl Sina, Corporate Giving Specialist; (877) 446-7746; onebyone@4imprint.com
Internet: onebyone.4imprint.com/
Sponsor: 4imprint
101 Commerce Street
Oshkosh, WI 54901

7-Eleven Corporate Giving Grants 8

Since 1927, 7 Eleven has been dedicated to making life more convenient for its customers. Today, with nearly 10,000 locations across the U.S., the Corporation continues to lead through service, no matter how big the challenge. From strengthening communities through signature outreach programs to stepping up during the COVID-19 pandemic with vital supplies and aid, 7 Eleven is making a big impact. The 7-Eleven Corporate Giving program provides support to organizations in communities where 7-Eleven operates stores. In general, support is provided at the local level for police, school and youth sports programs and community events. It supports programs and projects in the area of education, with emphasis on workforce development, language education, and programs to assist at-risk and economically disadvantaged individuals. Other areas of interest include multicultural understanding, safety, health and wellness, crime prevention, community revitalization, and hunger. Types of support include: specific project support; overall program support; and special event support. Applicants should begin the process by contacting the Community Relations Department directly.
Requirements: 7-Eleven charitable contributions support: 501(c)3 not-for-profit organizations and government agencies, such as public schools, libraries or police departments; organizations and initiatives that support communities where 7-Eleven operates stores; organizations and initiatives that support its strategic focus areas (safety, education, health and wellness, and community revitalization projects).
Restrictions: 7-Eleven charitable contributions do not support: religious or political organizations; general operating, multi-year commitments or capital, building or endowment campaigns; sponsorships for individuals; or organizations that discriminate on the basis of race, religion, sex or national origin.
Geographic Focus: All States, American Samoa, District of Columbia, Guam, Marshall Islands, Northern Mariana Islands, Puerto Rico, U.S. Virgin Islands
Amount of Grant: 1,000 - 2,500 USD
Contact: Community Relations Manager; (972) 828-7480 or (800) 255-0711; fax (972) 828-8972
Internet: corp.7-eleven.com/corp/sustainability#corp_csr_people
Sponsor: 7-Eleven
1722 Routh Street, Local 199, P.O. Box 711
Dallas, TX 75221

100 Club of Arizona Financial Assistance Grants 9

The mission of the 100 Club of Arizona is to provide financial assistance to families of public safety officers and firefighters who are seriously injured or killed in the line-of-duty, and to provide resources to enhance their safety and welfare. Aid is also extended to officers and firefighters who are called to active duty military. The Club pays a one-time benefit of $10,000 to $15,000 to surviving families of public safety officers and firefighters killed while on duty. In addition, $5,000 is available for non-line of duty deaths, $500 per month is available for line of duty injury, and $500 one-time assistance is available to on duty injury.
Requirements: Financial assistance is provided to the families of public safety officers and firefighters upon death or serious injury; aid is also extended to officers and firefighters who are called to active duty military. Assistance is extended to volunteer and/or reserve officers/firefighters only when the incident occurs while he/she is on duty. To request assistance for a public safety officer or firefighter, the appropriate form must be completed by a supervisor or by human resource personnel.
Geographic Focus: Arizona
Amount of Grant: Up to 18,000 USD
Contact: Angela Harrolle; (602) 485-0100 or (877) 564-6100; fax (480) 242-1715; angela@100club.org
Internet: www.100club.org/financial-assistance/
Sponsor: 100 Club of Arizona
333 North 48th Street, Suite 100
Phoenix, AZ 85008

100 Club of Dubuque 10

The 100 Club of Dubuque will provide financial aid to the families of those brave men and women who proudly serve Dubuque County in the capacity of police officer, deputy sheriff, firefighter, EMS provider, volunteer firefighter, volunteer EMS provider and park ranger. In addition to funds being paid for someone killed in the line of duty, funds may also be paid to the family of someone who has a loved one who dies while on duty.
Requirements: Benefits are paid to surviving family members of fallen heroes in Dubuque, Iowa.
Geographic Focus: Iowa
Amount of Grant: Up to 15,000 USD
Contact: Dennis Avenarius, Director; (563) 583-1323; dennis3122@msn.com
Internet: 100clubofdubuque.org/
Sponsor: 100 Club of Dubuque
2250 Fawnview Drive
Dubuque, IA 52002

100% for Kids - Utah Credit Union Education Foundation Major Project Grants 11

The Major Project Grant is a one-time grant intended for substantial funding of specific, innovative, classroom-level endeavors based on credit union principles. This includes multi-class projects that impact individual classroom instruction. Items purchased with grant money belong to the school. Priority will be given to grants which cover core curriculum materials that will be used by and for the kids. Grants are reviewed on a quarterly basis. Once a Grant request is received, teachers will be notified of acceptance or denial within approximately 45 days of the end of the quarter.
Requirements: Applicant must be a public school teacher within the state of Utah, grades K-12. Teachers will not be awarded more than one grant per school year. Equipment purchased with grant money is property of the school. All recipients agree to submit an Accountability Form within 90 days of receipt of awarded funds.
Restrictions: Grants in the following categories are not eligible: incentives/rewards; field trips & travel costs; artist-in-residence; teachers' aides/staffing; stipends for time/salaries; plants and furniture; disposable items; training, conferences, or seminars; audio enhancement systems; or character education.
Geographic Focus: Utah
Date(s) Application is Due: Mar 30; Jun 30; Sep 30; Dec 31
Amount of Grant: 1,000 - 10,000 USD
Contact: Elizabeth White, Chairperson; (801) 972-3400 or (800) 662-8684; liz@utahscreditunions.org or foundation@ulcu.com
Internet: www.100percentforkids.org/
Sponsor: 100% for Kids - Utah Credit Union Education Foundation
455 East 500 South, Suite 400
Salt Lake City, UT 84111

100% for Kids - Utah Credit Union Education Foundation Mini Grants 12

The 100% for Kids - Utah Credit Union Education Foundation seeks to improve education in Utah by enhancing and expanding classroom-level resources and programs. Mini Grants are intended for a classroom level project. This grant will assist teachers with the out of pocket expense during a school year. Priority will be given to grants which cover core curriculum materials that will be used by and for the kids. The deadline is the last day of each month. Mini-Grants are generally reviewed on a monthly schedule.
Requirements: Applicant must be a public school teacher within the state of Utah, grades K-12. Teachers will not be awarded more than one grant per school year. All recipients agree to submit an Accountability Form within 90 days of receipt of awarded funds. Project must meet a need and justify the amount of funding requested. Project must directly involve and benefit students.
Restrictions: The following requests will not be funded: Character Education items and programs; requests for rewards or incentives; requests for teaching salaries or guest speaking fees; construction and/or building costs; shipping and handling fees; installation and labor fees; grant applications submitted by principals; or funding for furniture and storage items. The maximum amount for books for an individual classroom is $350. The maximum for manipulatives and other miscellaneous supplies is $350.
Geographic Focus: Utah
Date(s) Application is Due: Jan 31; Feb 28; Mar 31; Apr 30; May 31; Jun 30; Jul 31; Aug 31; Sep 30; Oct 31; Nov 30; Dec 31
Amount of Grant: 50 - 1,000 USD
Contact: Elizabeth White, Chairperson; (801) 972-3400 or (800) 662-8684; liz@utahscreditunions.org or foundation@ulcu.com
Internet: www.100percentforkids.org/
Sponsor: 100% for Kids - Utah Credit Union Education Foundation
455 East 500 South, Suite 400
Salt Lake City, UT 84111

100% for Kids - Utah Credit Union Education Foundation School Grants 13

The School Grant is a one-time grant intended for substantial funding of specific, innovative, classroom-level endeavors based on credit union principles. This includes multi-class projects that impact individual classroom instruction. Items purchased with grant money belong to the school. Priority will be given to grants which cover core curriculum materials that will be used by and for the kids. Grants are reviewed on a quarterly basis. Once a Grant request is received, teachers will be notified of acceptance or denial within approximately 45 days of the end of the quarter. Grants range from $1,000 to $5,000.
Requirements: Applicant must be a public school teacher within the state of Utah, grades K-12. Teachers will not be awarded more than one grant per school year. Items purchased with grant money belong to the school. All recipients agree to submit an Accountability Form within ninety days of receipt of awarded funds.
Restrictions: Grants in the following categories are not eligible: incentives/rewards; field trips & travel costs; artist-in-residence; teachers' aides/staffing; stipends for time/salaries; plants and furniture; disposable items; training, conferences, or seminars; audio enhancement systems; or character education.
Geographic Focus: Utah
Date(s) Application is Due: Mar 30; Jun 30; Sep 30; Dec 31
Amount of Grant: 1,000 - 5,000 USD
Contact: Elizabeth White, Chairperson; (801) 972-3400 or (800) 662-8684; liz@utahscreditunions.org or foundation@ulcu.com
Internet: www.100percentforkids.org/
Sponsor: 100% for Kids - Utah Credit Union Education Foundation
455 East 500 South, Suite 400
Salt Lake City, UT 84111

520 Charitable Foundation Grants 14

The 520 Charitable Foundation, established in Nashua, New Hampshire, supports programs that benefit children and youth, elementary and secondary education, neighborhood revitalization, and the family. Most recent awards have ranged from $100 up to a maximum of $40,000. Generally, funding will support general operations and program development. Since there are no specified annual deadlines or application formats, interested applicants should begin the process by contacting the grants office directly via telephone or in writing.

Requirements: Any 501(c)3 organization supporting the residents of Nashua, New Hampshire, are eligible to apply.
Geographic Focus: New Hampshire
Amount of Grant: Up to 40,000 USD
Contact: Cynthia Herweck, Trustee; (603) 882-8786 or (603) 566-3966
Sponsor: 520 Charitable Foundation
4 Crestwood Lane
Nashua, NH 03062

786 Foundation Grants   **15**
The 786 Foundation, established in 1990 and currently administered by the BMO Harris Bank, has the following primary fields of interest: education, the environment, natural resource development, housing and shelter for the poor, human and social service programs, and YMHA/YMCAs. Giving is designated throughout Wisconsin, and typically comes in the form of curriculum development, general operating support, matching funds, and scholarship endowments. There are no specific application forms or deadlines with which to adhere, and applicants should begin by contacting the Foundation in writing.
Requirements: All 501(c)3 organizations either based in or serving residents of Wisconsin are eligible to apply. There is also some giving outside of Wisconsin.
Geographic Focus: All States
Amount of Grant: Up to 50,000 USD
Samples: Camp Manito-Wish, Boulder Junction, Wisconsin, $50,000 - support of the construction of the North Bath House; Kemp Natural Resources, Woodruff, Wisconsin, $25,000 - support of professional development and scholarships; Huntington Valley Little League, Huntington, California, $25,000 - general operating support.
Contact: Jennifer Ridley-Hanson, Vice President; (608) 232-2009 or (414) 815-3915
Sponsor: 786 Foundation
P.O. Box 2980
Milwaukee, WI 53201-2980

A-T Children's Project Grants   **16**
The A-T Children's Project strives to assist respected scientists in developing a clearer understanding of ataxia-telangiectasia. The Project is determined to find a timely cure, or life-improving treatments, for this serious disease. Grant awards are made through a careful and detailed selection process. The members of the Scientific Advisory Board examine each proposal and make their independent recommendations to its Board of Directors which then votes on each proposed project. Proposals from junior investigators, from scientists in related disciplines, and from individuals with innovative new ideas for A-T research are particularly encouraged, as are laboratories and teams working together from industry as well as teaching universities. The Project provides competitive grant awards for basic and translational research grants related to A-T. One- and two-year projects are funded up to a maximum total direct cost of $75,000 per year. Grants of $75,000 per year, however, are rare; grants in the $25,000 to 50,000 per year range are much more common. Budgets for up to $150,000 for a two-year project are acceptable.
Requirements: Proposals from junior investigators, from scientists in related disciplines, and from individuals with innovative new ideas for A-T research are particularly encouraged, as are laboratories and teams working together from industry as well as teaching universities. A Letter of Intent is not required. However, prior to submission of a full-length proposal, applicants seeking Scientific Advisory Board input may submit a Letter of Intent directly to the A-TCP Science Coordinator. This letter (not to exceed two pages) should include a brief abstract describing the proposed research, specific aims and an estimated budget. Applicants must submit an electronic copy of their Proposal in either MSWord or PDF formats to grants@atcp.org.
Restrictions: The sponsor does not pay for administrative overhead and indirect costs. The sponsor does not pay for institutional construction or renovation; purchase of major capital equipment other than directly needed for proposed experiments; office equipment or furniture; travel (except as required to perform the project); tuition fees; journal subscriptions; dues or memberships; and printing or publishing costs.
Geographic Focus: All States
Date(s) Application is Due: Mar 1; Sep 1
Amount of Grant: Up to 150,000 USD
Contact: Cynthia Rothblum-Oviatt, PhD, Science Coordinator; (703) 765-1223 or (954) 481-6611; fax (954) 725-1153; cynthia@atcp.org or grants@atcp.org
Internet: www.communityatcp.org/page.aspx?pid=3538
Sponsor: A-T Children's Project
5300 W. Hillsboro Boulevard, Suite 105
Coconut Creek, FL 33073

A-T Children's Project Post Doctoral Fellowships   **17**
The A-T Children's Project strives to assist respected scientists in developing a clearer understanding of ataxia-telangiectasia. Post doctorals with one year experience or less post degrees are eligible and must be nominated for this award by their principal investigator (PI). Any interested PI who would like to nominate a new post doc for the A-T Post Doctoral Fellowship Award must send a Letter of Intent to the A-T Children's Project. This letter (not to exceed two pages) should include a brief abstract describing the proposed research, specific aims and an estimated budget. Fellowship award applications are subject to the same conditions and guidelines as the Project's regular investigator initiated grants. However, the level of funding will be in the range of $30,000 to $40,000 per year for two years.
Restrictions: The sponsor does not pay for administrative overhead and indirect costs. The sponsor does not pay for institutional construction or renovation; purchase of major capital equipment other than directly needed for proposed experiments; office equipment or furniture; travel (except as required to perform the project); tuition fees; journal subscriptions; dues or memberships; and printing or publishing costs.
Geographic Focus: All States

Date(s) Application is Due: Mar 1; Sep 1
Amount of Grant: 30,000 - 40,000 USD
Contact: Cynthia Rothblum-Oviatt, Science Coordinator; (703) 765-1223 or (954) 481-6611; fax (954) 725-1153; cynthia@atcp.org or grants@atcp.org
Internet: www.communityatcp.org/page.aspx?pid=3539
Sponsor: A-T Children's Project
5300 W. Hillsboro Boulevard, Suite 105
Coconut Creek, FL 33073

A. Alfred Taubman Foundation Grants   **18**
The A. Alfred Taubman Foundation was established in Michigan in 1979. It was named for Adolf Alfred Taubman, an American entrepreneur and philanthropist, known for conceptualizing and pioneering the concept of shopping mall, an emerging trend in the global arena. The combination of his brilliance and sincerity shaped the emergence of shopping centers around the world. His imaginative vision transformed many lives along with his own; his is the story of a man who rose from rags to riches. Born to a low class immigrant family in Michigan, he started working at a young age alongside receiving his education. He developed his sophisticated sense of design and space during his architectural studies. He started from a small real estate development firm and through his insight in merchandising and retailing, he became a shopping mall magnate, with an enormous enterprise under his name which is worth billions of dollar. He incorporated his ideas to build incredible retail stores, hotels, enclosed malls and shopping centers all around the world. Apart from being a successful businessman, he was also a leading philanthropist who donated large sums of money for various health, education and art causes. His generous contributions supported various medical researches and helped in imparting education to several underprivileged sections of the society. He was a man of immense dedication towards his work and his life journey is an inspiration for everyone. Today, the Foundation named in his honor gives primarily in Michigan and New York. Its primary fields of interest include: basic and emergency aid; crime prevention; disease control and research; elementary and secondary education; higher education; Judaism; museums; natural resources; nonprofits; performing arts; reproductive health care; and special population support. Most often, support is given for general operations. Applicants should submit: a detailed description of project; the amount of funding being requested; and a list of additional sources and amount of support. There are no specified annual application submission deadlines.
Requirements: any 501(c)3 organization serving residents of Michigan or New York are eligible to apply.
Geographic Focus: Michigan, New York
Amount of Grant: 1,000 - 100,000 USD
Contact: Gayle T. Kalisman, President; (248) 258-6800 or (248) 258-7200
Sponsor: A. Alfred Taubman Foundation
200 East Long Lake Road, Suite 180
Bloomfield Hills, MI 48304-2336

A.C. and Penney Hubbard Foundation Grants   **19**
In 1969, A.C. and Penney Hubbard had no inkling that the garden they would create at their home north of Baltimore would become recognized as one of the finest in Maryland. Today, the Hubbard garden contains a fine and vast horticultural variety that is artistic and cohesive throughout the year. These two acres, restructured to create multiple terraces and filled with sculpture, are themselves living sculpture. The garden has figured in all seasons of the Hubbards' lives. From the garden of young parents with three small children, to a recreational space for family activities, to an idyllic setting for a wedding, to a poolside gathering spot for grandchildren, the garden is a prominent figure in family life. The Hubbards established the A.C. and Penney Hubbard Foundation in 1986, with giving primarily in Maryland and Wyoming. Its major fields of interest include support for: art museums; arts and culture; basic emergency assistance; communication media; elementary and secondary education; higher education; human services; music; natural resources; community nonprofits; performing arts; residential adult shelters; and sports. Grants typically take the form of: annual campaign support; continuing support; financial sustainability; general operating support; program development; and re-granting. There are no annual deadlines, and applications are accepted at any time.
Requirements: Any 501(c)3 supporting the residents of Maryland or Wyoming are eligible.
Geographic Focus: Maryland, Wyoming
Amount of Grant: Up to 20,000 USD
Samples: Baltimore Education Scholarship Trust, Baltimore, Maryland, $15,955 - annual campaign support; Byrn Mawr School, Baltimore, Maryland, $4,063 - general operating support; Baltimore Museum of Art, Baltimore, Maryland, $3,000 - general operating support.
Contact: A.C. Hubbard, President; (410) 825-8221
Sponsor: A.C. and Penney Hubbard Foundation
1408 Walnut Hill Lane
Baltimore, MD 21204-3662

A.L. Mailman Family Foundation Grants   **20**
The A.L. Mailman Family Foundation focuses on improving the systems and policies that impact very young children and their families. The foundation's quest is to make quality early experiences the norm, so that ALL children are primed for success. From its founding in 1980, the Foundation has maintained its focus on early care and education, inspired by the belief that positive early experiences lay the foundation for future learning. The foundation funds the creation and dissemination of curricula, materials or tools that promote quality; advocacy and strategic communication to inform and build public will; applied research designed to inform policy and improve practice; and funder collaboratives to expand its own learning and broaden its sphere of influence. There are five categories of funding: System Wide Change; Resources and Development; Advocacy; Policy-Based Research; Communications; and Funder Collaboratives. Under the System-Wide Change

program area grants promote coordinated, comprehensive, continuous systems of care for young children. Relative to this, for example, the foundation has funded: the promotion of policies that support comprehensive systems of early care and education; the examination and development of financing mechanisms to sustain quality and accessible services; the improvement of teacher preparation systems; and the creation of strategic plans for mental health services for children from birth to age 3. Under the Resource Development program area, grants focus on the development of tools and training materials to improve quality of care and inform stakeholders. Relative to this, for example, the foundation has funded the development of: a resource guide on working with children affected by trauma; infant/toddler materials for home visitors; a training video for a clinical infant behavioral assessment scale; the revised materials for the Family Child Care Environment Rating Scale. Grants made in the Advocacy program area focus on the development and implementation of various strategies to inform the public about early childhood issues and promote public will to increase early investments for young children and their families. Relative to this, for example, the foundation has funded: the recruitment, training and engagement of new champions for early childhood issues; the strengthening of organizational capacity to address issues of children from birth to age 3; and the education and training of state advocates on current communication research and strategies. Grants made in the Policy-Based Research program area use research and survey findings to promote the development of quality early childhood systems. Relative to this, the foundation has funded: assessment of current practices and needs; translation of research to inform practice and policy; and knowledge synthesis and development of policy-related materials. Grants made in the Communications program area focus on communications strategies in order to bring public attention to the needs of young children. Relative to this, for example, the foundation has funded: research of new approaches and strategies to communicate the needs of young children and the importance of early investments; communication of knowledge to inform the field and build public will; and dissemination and distribution of grantee materials, tools and products. The application process begins with the submission of a letter of inquiry, accepted on a rolling basis, and the submission of a full proposal upon invitation. The Foundation board meets in April and October to authorize grants. Proposals should be sent to the foundation by June 15 for fall review and by January 15 for spring review. Letters of inquiry should be submitted by May 1 for fall proposals and by December 1 for spring proposals.
Restrictions: Grants do not support direct service organizations, childcare centers and schools, locally focused organizations, individuals, capital campaigns and endowments, scholarships, general operating expenses or deficit reduction, or organizations or projects outside of the United States.
Geographic Focus: All States
Date(s) Application is Due: Jan 15; Jun 15
Amount of Grant: 5,000 - 50,000 USD
Samples: Algebra Project for Math Talk. Cambridge, Massachusetts, $10,000 - general operating support (2018); Joe Dimaggio Children's Hospital, Hollywood, Florida, $25,000 - general operating support (2018); Women One, Alexandria, Virginia, $19,000 - general operating support (2018).
Contact: Bobbie Enright; (914) 683-8089; fax (914) 686-5519; info@mailman.org
Sponsor: A.L. Mailman Family Foundation
707 Westchester Avenue
White Plains, NY 10604

A.L. Spencer Foundation Grants 21

The A.L. Spencer Foundation was established in Pittsburgh, Pennsylvania, in 1999, with the primary interest of supporting: camps; community recreation; elementary and secondary education; health programs; hospital care; human service organizations; in-patient medical care; sports and recreation; and youth development. Funding is provided for a wide array of purposes, including: capacity building; technical assistance; capital and infrastructure; staff development; general operating support; professional training; and program development. The Foundation's major geographic focus is the State of Pennsylvania, though some funding has also been given in Florida. Most recently, awards have ranged as high as $52,500. There are no specified annual deadlines, and would-be applicants should forward a letter of application which includes the overall need, a program budget, and a copy of the 501(c)3 IRS determination letter.
Requirements: 501(c)3 organizations serving the residents of Pennsylvania or Florida are eligible to apply.
Geographic Focus: Florida, Pennsylvania
Amount of Grant: Up to 52,500 USD
Samples: YMCA of Greater Pittsburgh, Pittsburgh, Pennsylvania, $52,500 - general operating support; Bethesda Hospital Foundation, Boynton Beach, Florida, $50,000 - general operating support.
Contact: David G. Martin, President; (412) 768-6011
Sponsor: A.L. Spencer Foundation
P.O. Box 609
Pittsburgh, PA 15230-9738

AAAS/Subaru SB&F Prize for Excellence in Science Books 22

The AAAS/Subaru SB&F Prize for Excellence in Science Books celebrates outstanding science writing and illustration for children and young adults. The prizes, established in 2005, are meant to encourage the writing and publishing of high-quality science book for all age groups. Solely supported by Subaru since their inception, the prizes recognize recently published works that are scientifically sound and foster an understanding and appreciation of science in young readers. Prizes will be awarded in the following categories: Children's Science Picture Book (prize to author and illustrator); Middle Grades Science Book (prize to author); Young Adult Science Book (prize to author); and Hands-On Science Book (prize to author). The annual deadline is September 5. A judging panel made up of scientists, experts in the field of science literature, librarians, and AAAS staff, will assess the entries based on these several criteria.
Geographic Focus: All States, American Samoa, District of Columbia, Guam, Marshall Islands, Northern Mariana Islands, Rhode Island, U.S. Virgin Islands

Contact: Kira E. Mock, Program Manager; (202) 326-6617 or (202) 326-6700; fax (202) 289-4950; kmock@aaas.org
Internet: www.sbfonline.com/Subaru/Pages/PrizesHome.aspx
Sponsor: American Association for the Advancement of Science
1200 New York Avenue NW
Washington, D.C. 20005-3920

AACAP Educational Outreach Program for Child and Adolescent 23
Psychiatry Residents

The Educational Outreach Program (EOP) funding provides the opportunity for up to 50 child and adolescent psychiatry residents to receive a formal overview to the field of child and adolescent psychiatry, establish child and adolescent psychiatrists as mentors and experience the AACAP Annual Meeting. Participants will be exposed to the breadth and depth of the field of child and adolescent psychiatry, including research opportunities, access to mentors, and various networking opportunities. Participation in this program provides up to $1,000 for travel expenses, which includes airfare, hotel, and meals (maximum $75/day).
Requirements: Applicants must: be child and adolescent psychiatry residents at the time of the AACAP Annual Meeting; be currently enrolled in a residency program in the United States; be residents in their first or second year of child fellowship training are eligible (Triple Boarders in their fourth or fifth year of training in their triple board programs are eligible); either be members of the AACAP or have a membership application pending at the time of application; and attend all AACAP Annual Meeting events specified by AACAP.
Geographic Focus: All States
Date(s) Application is Due: Jul 12
Amount of Grant: Up to 1,000 USD
Contact: Ashley Partner, (202) 966-7300, ext. 117; fax (202) 966-2891; apartners@aacap.org
Internet: www.aacap.org/cs/residents/eop-capfellows
Sponsor: American Academy of Child and Adolescent Psychiatry
3615 Wisconsin Avenue, NW
Washington, D.C. 20016-3007

AACAP Educational Outreach Program for General Psychiatry Residents 24

The Educational Outreach Program (EOP) for General Psychiatry residents provides the opportunity for up to 20 general psychiatry residents to receive a formal overview to the field of child and adolescent psychiatry, establish child and adolescent psychiatrists as mentors and experience the AACAP Annual Meeting. Participants will be exposed to the breadth and depth of the field of child and adolescent psychiatry, including research opportunities, access to mentors, and various networking opportunities. Participation in this program provides up to $1,500 for travel expenses to the AACAP Annual Meeting.
Requirements: Applicants must: be general psychiatry residents at the time of the AACAP Annual Meeting; be currently enrolled in a residency program in the United States; be residents in their first, second or third year of general psychiatry training (Triple Boarders in their first, second or third year of training in their triple board programs are eligible); either be members of the AACAP or have a membership application pending at the time of application; and attend all AACAP Annual Meeting events specified by AACAP.
Geographic Focus: All States
Date(s) Application is Due: Jul 12
Amount of Grant: Up to 1,500 USD
Contact: Ashley Partner, (202) 966-7300, ext. 117 or (202) 587-9663; fax (202) 966-2891; apartner@aacap.org or training@aacap.org
Internet: www.aacap.org/cs/residents/eop-generalresidents
Sponsor: American Academy of Child and Adolescent Psychiatry
3615 Wisconsin Avenue, NW
Washington, D.C. 20016-3007

AACAP George Tarjan Award for Contributions in Developmental Disabilities 25

The AACAP George Tarjan Award for Contributions in Developmental Disabilities recognizes a child and adolescent psychiatrist and Academy member who has made significant contributions in a lifetime career or single seminal work to the understanding or care of those with mental retardation and developmental disabilities. These contributions must have national and/or international stature and clearly demonstrate lasting effects. The contributions may be in areas of teaching, research, program development, direct clinical service, advocacy or administrative commitment. A cash prize of up to $1,000 will be awarded. The award winner will be recognized at a Distinguished Awards Luncheon and make an Honors Presentation about his or her work during the AACAP Annual Meeting.
Requirements: Nomination letters must be accompanied by a CV for the individual nominated.
Geographic Focus: All States
Date(s) Application is Due: Apr 30
Amount of Grant: 1,000 USD
Contact: Bryan King; (202) 966-7300; bking@aacap.org or clinical@aacap.org
Internet: www.aacap.org/cs/distinguishedmembers
Sponsor: American Academy of Child and Adolescent Psychiatry
3615 Wisconsin Avenue, NW
Washington, D.C. 20016-3007

AACAP Irving Philips Award for Prevention 26

The AACAP Irving Philips Award for Prevention recognizes a child and adolescent psychiatrist and Academy member who has made significant contributions in a lifetime career or single seminal work to the prevention of mental illness in children and adolescents. These contributions must have national and/or international stature and clearly demonstrate lasting effects. The contributions may be in the areas of teaching, research, program development, direct clinical service, advocacy or administrative commitment. The award pays $2,500 to the winner and a $2,000 donation to a prevention program or center of the awardee's choice. The award winner will be recognized at a Distinguished Awards Luncheon and make an Honors Presentation about his or her work during the AACAP Annual Meeting.

Requirements: Nomination letters must be accompanied by a CV for the individual nominated.
Geographic Focus: All States
Date(s) Application is Due: Apr 30
Amount of Grant: 4,500 USD
Contact: James Hudziak; (202) 966-7300; jhudziak@aacap.org or clinical@aacap.org
Internet: www.aacap.org/cs/distinguishedmembers
Sponsor: American Academy of Child and Adolescent Psychiatry
3615 Wisconsin Avenue, NW
Washington, D.C. 20016-3007

AACAP Jeanne Spurlock Lecture and Award on Diversity and Culture   27

The Jeanne Spurlock Lecture and Award on Diversity and Culture reflects the spirit of the nomination for outstanding contributions to diversity and culture and in some way encourages individuals from diverse cultural backgrounds to become child and adolescent psychiatrists. Nominees should be individuals who have made contributions in the areas of social awareness including: civil rights; spirituality and/or religion; social welfare; public information; scientific research; education and mentoring; and the arts (literature, theatre, music, painting, sculpture or photography). The award includes an honorarium of $2,500, with the award winner being recognized at a Distinguished Awards Luncheon where he or she will make an honors award presentation about his or her work during the AACAP Annual Meeting.

Geographic Focus: All States
Date(s) Application is Due: Apr 30
Amount of Grant: 2,500 USD
Contact: Adriano Boccanelli, Clinical Practice Manager; (202) 966-7300, ext. 133; fax (202) 966-9518; aboccanelli@aacap.org or clinical@aacap.org
Internet: www.aacap.org/cs/distinguishedmembers
Sponsor: American Academy of Child and Adolescent Psychiatry
3615 Wisconsin Avenue, NW
Washington, D.C. 20016-3007

AACAP Jeanne Spurlock Research Fellowship in Substance Abuse and   28
Addiction for Minority Medical Students

The Jeanne Spurlock Research Fellowship in Substance Abuse and Addiction for Minority Medical Students offers a unique opportunity for minority medical students to explore a research career in substance abuse in relation to child and adolescent psychiatry, gain valuable work experience, and meet leaders in the child and adolescent psychiatry field. The fellowship opportunity provides up to $4,000 for 12 weeks of summer research under a child and adolescent psychiatrist researcher/mentor. The research training plan must provide for significant contact between the student and the mentor and for exposure to state-of-the-art drug abuse and addiction research. The plan should include program planning discussions, instruction in research planning and implementation, regular meetings with the mentor, laboratory director, and the research group, and assigned readings. Research assignments may include responsibility for part of the observation or evaluation, developing specific aspects of the research mechanisms, conducting interviews or tests, use of rating scales, and psychological or cognitive testing of subjects.

Requirements: All fellowship participants must attend the AACAP Annual Meeting. Applications are considered from African-American, Native American, Alaskan Native, Mexican American, Hispanic, Asian, and Pacific Islander students in accredited U.S. medical schools.
Geographic Focus: All States
Date(s) Application is Due: Feb 15
Amount of Grant: Up to 4,000 USD
Contact: Ashley Partner; (202) 966-7300, ext. 117; fax (202) 966-2891; apartner@aacap.org or training@aacap.org
Internet: www.aacap.org/cs/students/opportunities/SpurlockResearch
Sponsor: American Academy of Child and Adolescent Psychiatry
3615 Wisconsin Avenue, NW
Washington, D.C. 20016-3007

AACAP Junior Investigator Awards   29

The AACAP Junior Investigator Award offers two awards of up to $30,000 a year for two years for child and adolescent psychiatry junior faculty (assistant professor level or equivalent). The program is intended to facilitate innovative research. The research may be basic or clinical in nature but must be relevant to our understanding, treatment and prevention of child and adolescent mental health disorders. The award also includes the cost of attending the AACAP Annual Meeting for five days.

Requirements: Recipients are required to submit a poster or oral presentation on his or her research for the AACAP's Annual Meeting. Applicants must: be board eligible or certified in child and adolescent psychiatry; have a doctoral level degree and be in a faculty or independent research position; and have an on-site mentor who has had experience in the type of research that is being proposed that will normally include work with children and adolescents. Candidates must either be AACAP members or have a membership application pending (not paid by the award).
Restrictions: Applicants who have served as Principal Investigator on an NIH R01 grant are not eligible.
Geographic Focus: All States
Date(s) Application is Due: Mar 1
Amount of Grant: Up to 30,000 USD
Contact: Alyssa Sommer, Research Coordinator; (202) 966-7300, ext. 157; fax (202) 364-5925; asommer@aacap.org or research@accap.org
Internet: www.aacap.org/cs/root/research_and_training_awards/aacap_junior_investigator_awards
Sponsor: American Academy of Child and Adolescent Psychiatry
3615 Wisconsin Avenue, NW
Washington, D.C. 20016-3007

AACAP Life Members Mentorship Grants for Medical Students   30

The Life Members Mentorship Grants for Medical Students (MGM) provides the opportunity for seven medical students to attend the AACAP Annual Meeting and receive an introduction into the field of child and adolescent psychiatry through the AACAP Mentorship Program. MGM recipients also participate in programs sponsored by the Life Members, which is a group of the oldest and most distinguished members of AACAP, all having been members for at least 30 years. Many of those in this group served as AACAP leadership and also pioneered many of the significant discoveries and developments in the field of child and adolescent psychiatry. Partnered with the Mentorship Program, this program provides participants with networking opportunities, exposure to varying specialties, and interaction with Life Members. Participation in this program provides up to $1,000 for travel expenses to the AACAP Annual Meeting, which includes airfare, hotel, and meals (maximum $75/day).

Requirements: Applicants must be enrolled in a medical school in the United States at the time of the AACAP Annual Meeting. Recipients are required to: share the AACAP recruitment video with fellow medical students in their program within the six months following the Annual Meeting; and write a follow-up report on the experience that they would be encouraged to submit to their program's listserve and/or website and share a copy of this with AACAP. Participants must: be in good standing at their medical school; and attend all AACAP Annual Meeting events specified by AACAP.
Geographic Focus: All States
Date(s) Application is Due: Jul 12
Amount of Grant: Up to 1,000 USD
Contact: Ashley Partner, (202) 966-7300, ext. 117 or (202) 587-9663; fax (202) 966-2891; apartner@aacap.org or training@aacap.org
Internet: www.aacap.org/cs/students/opportunities/life_members_mentorship_grants_for_medical_students
Sponsor: American Academy of Child and Adolescent Psychiatry
3615 Wisconsin Avenue, NW
Washington, D.C. 20016-3007

AACAP Mary Crosby Congressional Fellowships   31

The Mary Crosby Congressional Fellowships program is designed to educate policy makers and Congressional staff about child and adolescent psychiatry, and to foster awareness of children's mental health issues. This experience will allow the Fellow to develop a keen understanding of how public policy affects patient care, education, and health insurance issues. The AACAP Mary Crosby Congressional Fellow will be placed with a Congressional office or Committee where they will gain invaluable experience as they assist in the development of legislative and public policy initiatives. The award includes an $85,000 stipend, up to $3,000 in relocation or moving expenses, and health insurance for the length of the fellowship program.

Requirements: Successful applicants must: be an AACAP member; be a PGY-4 psychiatry resident or beyond; have completed training in or be scheduled to complete training in one of the child and adolescent psychiatry programs (CAP training program, Combined General Psychiatry/CAP Program, or Triple Board Program); have a demonstrated interest in public policy issues; exhibit an interest in applying medical and scientific knowledge to the resolution of public policy issues; and be a U.S. citizen or permanent resident.
Geographic Focus: All States
Amount of Grant: 85,000 - 88,000 USD
Contact: Ashley Partner, (202) 966-7300, ext. 117; fax (202) 966-2891; apartner@aacap.org or training@aacap.org
Internet: www.aacap.org/cs/root/legislative_action/2008_congressional_fellowship_program
Sponsor: American Academy of Child and Adolescent Psychiatry
3615 Wisconsin Avenue, NW
Washington, D.C. 20016-3007

AACAP Pilot Research Award for Attention-Deficit Disorder   32

The AACAP Pilot Research Award for Attention Disorders, supported by The Elaine Schlosser Lewis Fund, offers $15,000 for child and adolescent psychiatry residents and junior faculty who have an interest in beginning a career in child and adolescent mental health research. By providing one award to a child and adolescent psychiatry junior faculty member or resident for pilot research on attention disorders, the AACAP supports a young investigator at a critical stage, encouraging a future career in child and adolescent psychiatry research. The recipient has the opportunity to submit a poster presentation on his or her research for AACAP's Annual Meeting, and present at the Elaine Schlosser Lewis Luncheon.

Requirements: Candidates must be board eligible, certified in child and adolescent psychiatry, or enrolled in a child psychiatry residency or fellowship program. Candidates must also have a faculty appointment in an accredited medical school or be in a fully accredited child and adolescent psychiatry clinical research or training program.
Restrictions: At the time of application, candidates may not have more than two years experience following graduation from residency/fellowship training. Candidates must not have any previous significant, individual research funding in the field of child and adolescent mental health. These include the following: NIMH/NIH Funding (Small Grants, T Award or R-01) or similar foundation or industry research funding.
Geographic Focus: All States
Date(s) Application is Due: Apr 29
Amount of Grant: 15,000 USD
Contact: Ashley Partner; (202) 966-7300, ext. 117; fax (202) 364-5925; apartner@aacap.org
Internet: www.aacap.org/cs/root/research_and_training_awards/pilot_research_award_for_attention_disorder_for_a_junior_faculty_or_child_psychiatry_resident_supported_by_the_elaine_schlosser_lewis_fund
Sponsor: American Academy of Child and Adolescent Psychiatry
3615 Wisconsin Avenue, NW
Washington, D.C. 20016-3007

AACAP Rieger Psychodynamic Psychotherapy Award   33

The AACAP Rieger Psychodynamic Psychotherapy Award recognizes the best published or unpublished paper, written by an AACAP member that addresses the use of psychodynamic psychotherapy in clinical practice and fosters development, teaching, and practice of psychodynamic psychotherapy within child and adolescent psychiatry. Papers that express a novel hypothesis, raise questions about existing theory, or integrate new neuroscience and developmental psychotherapy research with psychodynamic principles may be nominated. Unpublished, new papers and papers published within the last three years may be submitted by their authors. Published papers may be nominated by any member of the AACAP. Authors may be senior or junior faculty members or residents. Delivery of the winning paper will be made at the AACAP Annual Meeting Honors Presentation.

Geographic Focus: All States
Date(s) Application is Due: Apr 30
Amount of Grant: 4,500 USD
Contact: Tim Dugan, Co-Chair; (202) 966-7300; fax (202) 966-2891; tdugan@aacap.org or clinical@aacap.org
Efrain Bleiberg, Co-Chair; (202) 966-7300; fax (202) 966-2891; ebleiberg@menninger.edu or clinical@aacap.org
Internet: www.aacap.org/cs/awards/riegerpsychotherapy
Sponsor: American Academy of Child and Adolescent Psychiatry
3615 Wisconsin Avenue, NW
Washington, D.C. 20016-3007

AACAP Rieger Service Program Award for Excellence   34

The AACAP Rieger Service Program Award for Excellence recognizes innovative programs that address prevention, diagnosis, or treatment of mental illnesses in children and adolescents, and serve as model programs to the community. This award of $4,500 is shared among the awardee and his or her service program. The award winner will be recognized at a Distinguished Awards Luncheon and make an Honors Presentation about his or her work during the AACAP Annual Meeting.

Requirements: Nomination letters must be accompanied by a CV and any support materials for the individual or organization nominated.
Geographic Focus: All States
Date(s) Application is Due: Apr 30
Amount of Grant: 4,500 USD
Contact: Kaye McGinty, Co-Chair; (202) 966-7300; fax (202) 966-2891; kmcginty@aacap.org or clinical@aacap.org
Mark Chenven, Co-Chair; (202) 966-7300; fax (202) 966-2891; mchenven@aacap.org or clinical@aacap.org
Internet: www.aacap.org/cs/distinguishedmembers
Sponsor: American Academy of Child and Adolescent Psychiatry
3615 Wisconsin Avenue, NW
Washington, D.C. 20016-3007

AACAP Robert Cancro Academic Leadership Award   35

The AACAP Cancro Academic Leadership Award recognizes a currently serving General Psychiatry Training Director, Medical School Dean, CEO of a Training Institution, Chair of a Department of Pediatrics or Chair of a Department of Psychiatry for his or her contributions to the promotion of child and adolescent psychiatry. Named in honor of Robert Cancro, M.D., Chairman at New York University, this award offers a $2,000 honorarium to the awardee. The award is presented in even-numbered years. Nominations for the award may be made by Child and Adolescent Training Directors or Division Directors and must include a CV for the individual nominated. The recipient of this award will receive a plaque and be recognized at the AACAP Annual Meeting in San Francisco, CA. The award recipient will be honored at the Distinguished Awards Luncheon, Residency Program Directors Luncheon, and will provide an Honors Presentation on his or her work during the Annual Meeting.

Requirements: Nominations must include a CV for the individual nominated
Geographic Focus: All States
Date(s) Application is Due: Apr 30
Amount of Grant: 2,000 USD
Contact: Jeffrey Hunt, Co-Chair; (202) 966-7300; fax (202) 966-2891; jhunt@aacap.org or training@aacap.org
Howard Liu; (202) 966-7300; fax (202) 966-2891; hliu@aacap.org or clinical@aacap.org
Internet: www.aacap.org/cs/distinguishedmembers
Sponsor: American Academy of Child and Adolescent Psychiatry
3615 Wisconsin Avenue, NW
Washington, D.C. 20016-3007

AACAP Sidney Berman Award for the School-Based Study and   36
Intervention for Learning Disorders and Mental Ilness

The AACAP Sidney Berman Award for the School-Based Study and Treatment of Learning Disorders and Mental Illness recognizes an individual or program that has shown outstanding achievement in the school-based study or delivery of intervention for learning disorders and mental illness. A cash prize of $4,500 will be awarded. The award winner will be recognized at a Distinguished Awards Luncheon and make an Honors Presentation about his or her work during the AACAP Annual Meeting.

Requirements: Nomination letters must be accompanied by a CV for the individual nominated or program information.
Geographic Focus: All States
Date(s) Application is Due: Apr 30
Amount of Grant: 4,500 USD

Contact: Sheryl Kataoka, Co-Chair; (202) 966-7300; fax (202) 966-2891; skataoka@aacap.org or clinical@aacap.org
Shashank Joshi; (202) 966-7300; fax (202) 966-2891; sjoshi@aacap.org or clinical@aacap.org
Internet: www.aacap.org/cs/distinguishedmembers
Sponsor: American Academy of Child and Adolescent Psychiatry
3615 Wisconsin Avenue, NW
Washington, D.C. 20016-3007

AACAP Simon Wile Leadership in Consultation Award   37

The Simon Wile Leadership in Consultation Award recognizes innovative programs that address prevention, diagnosis, or treatment of mental illnesses in children and adolescents, and serve as model programs to the community. This award of $4,500 is shared among the awardee and his or her service program. Nomination letters must be accompanied by a CV and any support materials for the individual or organization nominated. The recipient will be recognized at a Distinguished Awards Luncheon and make an Honors Presentation about his or her work during the AACAP Annual Meeting.

Requirements: Practicing child and adolescent psychiatrists are eligible for nomination.
Geographic Focus: All States
Date(s) Application is Due: Apr 30
Amount of Grant: 500 USD
Contact: Kaye McGinty, Co-Chair; (202) 966-7300; fax (202) 966-2891; kmcginty@aacap.org or clinical@aacap.org
Mark Chenven, Co-Chair; (202) 966-7300; fax (202) 966-2891; mchenven@aacap.org or clinical@aacap.org
Internet: www.aacap.org/cs/distinguishedmembers
Sponsor: American Academy of Child and Adolescent Psychiatry
3615 Wisconsin Avenue, NW
Washington, D.C. 20016-3007

AACAP Summer Medical Student Fellowships   38

AACAP Summer Medical Student Fellowships offer a chance for medical students to explore a career in child and adolescent psychiatry, gain valuable work experience, and meet leaders in the child and adolescent psychiatry field. The fellowship opportunity provides up to $3,500 for 12 weeks of clinical or research training under a child and adolescent psychiatrist mentor. Fellowship stipends will be distributed in two installments. Upon receipt of the fellowship, $2,500 will be sent to the student's mentor to be disbursed at the onset of the summer fellowship. Upon meeting all program requirements, the last installment will be sent directly to the recipient and will be pro-rated according to the total amount of time spent completing the fellowship. Fellowships lasting the full 12 weeks will receive the maximum amount. Participants are required to attend the AACAP Annual Meeting. The application deadline for this fellowship is February 15.

Requirements: Applicants must be students enrolled in accredited U.S. medical schools.
Geographic Focus: All States
Date(s) Application is Due: Feb 15
Amount of Grant: 3,500 USD
Contact: Ashley Partner, (202) 966-7300, ext. 117; fax (202) 966-2891; apartner@aacap.org or training@aacap.org
Internet: www.aacap.org/cs/students/summerfellowship
Sponsor: American Academy of Child and Adolescent Psychiatry
3615 Wisconsin Avenue, NW
Washington, D.C. 20016-3007

AACAP Systems of Care Special Program Scholarships   39

The American Academy of Child and Adolescent Psychiatry (AACAP) is pleased to announce the opportunity for child and adolescent psychiatry residents to apply for the 2012 Systems of Care Special Program Scholarship. The Special Program is a day-long event that explores the psychological, psychosocial and psycho-educational needs of children and adolescents as manifest in their experiences in the schools. Policy and best practice considerations will be reviewed as regards health promotion, screening, assessment and treatment intervention for students and student groups, with the goal of advancing the knowledge, skills and attitudes of child psychiatrists and other mental health providers so that they can better function as service providers and systems consultants for youth and their school systems. The scholarship includes $750 for travel expenses to the AACAP's 59th Annual Meeting. This includes airfare, hotel, and meals, maximum $75 per day.

Geographic Focus: All States
Date(s) Application is Due: Jul 12
Amount of Grant: 750 USD
Contact: Adriano Boccanelli, Clinical Practice Assistant; (202) 966-7300, ext. 133 or (202) 587-9671; fax (202) 966-2891; aboccanelli@aacap.org or clinical@aacap.org
Internet: www.aacap.org/cs/root/medical_students_and_residents/residents/2012_systems_of_care_special_program_scholarship
Sponsor: American Academy of Child and Adolescent Psychiatry
3615 Wisconsin Avenue, NW
Washington, D.C. 20016-3007

A and B Family Foundation Grants   40

The A and B Family Foundation was established in Illinois in 1999 by Kenneth D. Alpart, founder and managing partner of the Alpart Trading Company, whose line of business includes Federal Government and federally-sponsored credit agencies primarily engaged in guaranteeing, insuring, or making loans. The Foundation's activities include: youth entrepreneurship education; job and career exposure; academic enrichment; and sports. There is no specific application or deadline with which to adhere, and initial contact should be made in written form.

Requirements: Support is offered to 501(c)3 organizations serving the Cook County, Illinois, region.
Geographic Focus: Illinois
Amount of Grant: 1,000 - 20,000 USD
Contact: Kenneth D. Alpart, President; (312) 388-1698 or (312) 341-0615
Sponsor: A and B Family Foundation
111 West Jackson Boulevard, Suite 1300
Chicago, IL 60604

Aaron Foundation Grants   41

The Aaron Foundation, established in California in 1987 by the Aaron Mortgage Corporation, supports programs for children and youth, health care facilities, and human services agencies. Giving is primarily centered in the Bakersfield, California, region. Applicants should submit: a copy of current year's organizational budget and/or project budget; a copy of IRS Determination Letter; a detailed description of project and amount of funding requested; a statement of the problem that the project will address; and a brief history of organization and description of its mission.
Requirements: The proposed project must benefit the residents of Bakersfield, California.
Geographic Focus: California
Date(s) Application is Due: Nov 30
Contact: Hal E. Aaron, Trustee; (661) 322-6353; fax (661) 322-6120
Sponsor: Aaron Foundation
651 H Street, Suite 100
Bakersfield, CA 93304-1305

Aaron Foundation Grants   42

Established in Massachusetts in 1951, the Aaron Foundation awards grants to eligible nonprofit organizations in its areas of interest, including: arts and culture; health care; higher education; Jewish services and temples; health care; social services; and youth. There are no application deadlines or forms with which to adhere. Applicants should submit: results expected from proposed grant; a copy of IRS Determination Letter; copy of most recent annual report/audited financial statement or 990; a listing of board of directors, trustees, officers and other key people and their affiliations; and a copy of current year's organizational budget and/or project budget.
Requirements: Connecticut, Massachusetts, and Rhode Island nonprofit organizations are eligible to apply.
Restrictions: Individuals are ineligible to apply.
Geographic Focus: Connecticut, Massachusetts, Rhode Island
Amount of Grant: 1,000 - 100,000 USD
Samples: Beth Israel Deaconess Medical Center, Boston, Massachusetts, $50,000 - to support a capital campaign; United Way of Massachusetts Bay, Boston, Massachusetts, $90,000 - for the annual campaign.
Contact: Avram J. Goldberg, Trustee; (617) 695-1300 or (617) 695-1946
Sponsor: Aaron Foundation
225 Franklin Street, Suite 1450
Boston, MA 02110

AASA Urgent Need Mini-Grants   43

Disadvantaged students from every size school district continue to struggle against the odds. Their lives are shaped, as never before, by crushing social and economic hardships. School system leaders have no more control over these forces than children do. Developing a mini-grant program was seen as an opportunity by AASA to help superintendents address some of these needs born of hardship where no other resources appear available. Since 2002, the AASA Urgent Need Mini-Grant Program has helped school districts meet health, social service, academic and/or related family needs of individual disadvantaged children. Some examples are: enrichment — academic, or life-enhancing opportunities that could not otherwise be provided; urgent medical or dental care; eyeglasses, prescriptions and hearing aids; emergency clothing, food, shelter, supplies, furniture and fuel; and emergency transportation or child care.
Geographic Focus: All States, American Samoa, District of Columbia, Guam, Marshall Islands, Northern Mariana Islands, Puerto Rico, U.S. Virgin Islands
Amount of Grant: 500 - 5,000 USD
Contact: Bernadine Futrell, Director, Awards and Collaborations; (703) 875-0717 or (703) 528-0700; fax (703) 841-1543; bfutrell@aasa.org or awards@aasa.org
Internet: www.aasa.org/content.aspx?id=5618
Sponsor: American Association of School Administrators
1615 Duke Street
Alexandria, VA 22314

AAUW International Project Grants   44

International Project Grants are intended to provide fellows the opportunity to develop knowledge and skills that will directly benefit their home countries. To support the continuation of fellows' work after they return home, AAUW will award a limited number of International Project Grants of $5,000 to $7,000 to those who held an AAUW International Fellowship within the last ten years. The grants provide support for community-based projects that benefit women and girls in the fellow's home country. Applications may be submitted online between August 1 and January 15, and are available at the AAUW website. Awards range from $5,000 to $7,000.
Requirements: Applicants must be citizens in a country other than the U.S. They must also have completed an AAUW International Fellowship within the last ten years. Proposed projects must be implemented in the applicant's home country, and have a direct, positive impact on women and girls. The applicant must be the primary director of the project, with controlling programmatic, administrative, fiscal, and editorial responsibility for the project's implementation.

Restrictions: Funds are not available for the following: salaries or stipends for primary director, project directors, or permanent positions, or to reimburse employees; tuition; higher education scholarships for students and participants; personal expenses (shelter, vehicle, insurance); building funds, construction, or renovations; previous expenditures, deficits, or loans (in existence at time of grant award); purchase of equipment; overhead or general operating expenses for any organization or nonprofit organization; creating or providing grants to other organizations; entertainment; travel expenses (unless directly related to project activities); copyright or attorney fees; or fundraising activities.
Geographic Focus: All Countries
Date(s) Application is Due: Jan 15
Amount of Grant: 5,000 - 7,000 USD
Contact: Gloria Blackwell, Vice President of Fellowships, Grants and Global Programs; (202) 785-7700 or (800) 326-2289; fax (202) 872-1425; grants@aauw.org or blackwellg@aauw.org
Internet: www.aauw.org/what-we-do/educational-funding-and-awards/international-projects-grants/ipg-application/
Sponsor: American Association of University Women
1310 L Street NW, Suite 1000
Washington, D.C. 20005

Abbott Fund Access to Health Care Grants   45

Abbott's Access to Health Care programs seek innovative solutions to improve and expand access to health care services for disadvantaged populations. Specific areas of focus include cardiovascular health, diabetes, nutrition, maternal and child health and neonatal care. Many Abbott Fund programs are engaged in closing gaps in ethnic and minority communities, promoting health and nutrition education for families, training health workers, and improving delivery of health services. Complete and submit the Abbott Fund online grant application, posted when available. It should include your organization's Federal Tax ID. At times when the Abbott Fund is accepting unsolicited grant applications, it will acknowledge receipt of an online application via email. The Fund will notify an applicant of its decision on a funding request within six to eight weeks.
Requirements: Grants are made to tax-exempt organizations supporting access to health care.
Restrictions: The Abbott Fund does not accept unsolicited grant applications for projects outside the United States. Contributions will not be made to individuals; for-profit entities; purely social organizations; political parties or candidates; sectarian religious organizations; advertising; symposia, conferences, and meetings; ticket purchases; memberships; business-related purposes; volunteer efforts of non-Abbott employees; or marketing sponsorships.
Geographic Focus: Arizona, California, Illinois, Kansas, Massachusetts, Michigan, New Jersey, New York, North Carolina, Ohio, Puerto Rico, Texas, Utah, Virginia
Amount of Grant: 20,000 - 100,000 USD
Contact: Mary K. Moreland, Executive Vice President; (224) 667-6100 or (866) 298-9699
Internet: www.abbottfund.org/tags/access
Sponsor: Abbott Fund
100 Abbott Park Road, Department 379, Building 6D
Abbott Park, IL 60064-3500

Abbott Fund Community Engagement Grants   46

The Abbott Fund Community Engagement Grant program is active in communities around the world where Abbott has a significant presence. It pursues local partnerships and creative programs that address unmet needs of a community. Emphasis is placed on improving access to health care and promoting science education. The program also supports major civic, arts and other cultural institution programming, primarily in the Chicago metropolitan area where Abbott is headquartered. Complete and submit the Abbott Fund online grant application, posted when available. It should include your organization's Federal Tax ID. At times when the Abbott Fund is accepting unsolicited grant applications, it will acknowledge receipt of an online application via email. The Fund will notify an applicant of its decision on a funding request within six to eight weeks.
Requirements: Grants are made to tax-exempt organizations supporting company operating areas in Arizona, California, Illinois, Kansas, Massachusetts, Michigan, New Jersey, New York, North Carolina, Ohio, Puerto Rico, Texas, and Virginia, and Utah. It also supports the communities of: Abingdon, England; Brockville, Canada; Campoverde, Italy; Clonmel, Ireland; Cootehill, Ireland; Delkenheim, Germany; Kanata, Canada; Katsuyama, Japan; Ludwigshafen, Germany; Queenborough, England; Rio de Janeiro, Brazil; Sligo, Ireland; and Zwolle, the Netherlands.
Restrictions: Contributions will not be made to individuals; for-profit entities; purely social organizations; political parties or candidates; sectarian religious organizations; advertising; symposia, conferences, and meetings; ticket purchases; memberships; business-related purposes; volunteer efforts of non-Abbott employees; or marketing sponsorships.
Geographic Focus: Arizona, California, Illinois, Kansas, Massachusetts, Michigan, New Jersey, New York, North Carolina, Ohio, Puerto Rico, Texas, Utah, Virginia, Brazil, Canada, Germany, Ireland, Italy, Japan, Netherlands, United Kingdom
Amount of Grant: 10,000 - 100,000 USD
Contact: Mary K. Moreland, Executive Vice President; (224) 667-6100 or (866) 298-9699
Internet: www.abbott.com/responsibility/social-impact/community-engagement.html
Sponsor: Abbott Fund
100 Abbott Park Road, Department 379, Building 6D
Abbott Park, IL 60064-3500

Abbott Fund Global AIDS Care Grants   47

Abbott has been a significant contributor to the fight against HIV/AIDS for more than two decades. Since 2000, Abbott and the Abbott Fund have invested $225 million in grants and product donations targeted to resource poor countries most impacted by HIV/AIDS. The focus of these efforts includes expanding access to care, testing and treatment; strengthening HIV/AIDS health care systems; preventing mother-to-child transmission; and supporting children and families affected by HIV/AIDS. In addition, Abbott and the

Abbott Fund have helped pioneer innovative model programs to combat the disease. For example, we helped build the Baylor International Pediatric AIDS Initiative's first pediatric outpatient clinic in Romania in 2001 that has served an average of 600 patients per year. The clinic has reduced pediatric HIV mortality rates by more than 90 percent. Today Baylor has replicated the Romania model in additional clinics throughout Africa and now serves nearly 60,000 children and young people with HIV – including those at two clinics built by and supported by the Abbott Fund in Malawi and Tanzania.
Requirements: Grants are made to tax-exempt organizations supporting global HIV/AIDS programs.
Restrictions: Contributions will not be made to individuals; for-profit entities; purely social organizations; political parties or candidates; sectarian religious organizations; advertising; symposia, conferences, and meetings; ticket purchases; memberships; business-related purposes; volunteer efforts of non-Abbott employees; or marketing sponsorships.
Geographic Focus: Arizona, California, Illinois, Kansas, Massachusetts, Michigan, New Jersey, New York, North Carolina, Ohio, Puerto Rico, Texas, Utah, Virginia
Amount of Grant: 10,000 - 100,000 USD
Contact: Mary K. Moreland, Execitive Vice President; (224) 667-6100 or (866) 298-9699
Internet: www.abbott.com/responsibility/social-impact/access-to-healthcare.html
Sponsor: Abbott Fund
100 Abbott Park Road, Department 379, Building 6D
Abbott Park, IL 60064-3500

Abbott Fund Science Education Grants   48
The world urgently needs people who are well-trained in science and technology, and the Abbott Fund is committed to doing its part to address this challenge. Serving as a catalyst by stimulating community investment and engagement, Abbott's investment in science education: engages and inspires students, families and teachers in scientific exploration in out-of-school informal settings; encourages young people to be more proficient in science and attracts more scientists to the field; and builds strong partnerships that are systemic, replicable and sustainable for multiple years and multiple locations. Complete and submit the Abbott Fund online grant application, posted when available. It should include your organization's Federal Tax ID. At times when the Abbott Fund is accepting unsolicited grant applications, it will acknowledge receipt of an online application via email. The Fund will notify an applicant of its decision on a funding request within six to eight weeks.
Requirements: Grants are made to tax-exempt organizations supporting company operating areas in Arizona, California, Illinois, Kansas, Massachusetts, Michigan, New Jersey, New York, North Carolina, Ohio, Puerto Rico, Texas, and Virginia, and Utah. It also supports the communities of: Abingdon, England; Brockville, Canada; Campoverde, Italy; Clonmel, Ireland; Cootehill, Ireland; Delkenheim, Germany; Kanata, Canada; Katsuyama, Japan; Ludwigshafen, Germany; Queenborough, England; Rio de Janeiro, Brazil; Sligo, Ireland; and Zwolle, the Netherlands.
Restrictions: Contributions will not be made to individuals; for-profit entities; purely social organizations; political parties or candidates; sectarian religious organizations; advertising; symposia, conferences, and meetings; ticket purchases; memberships; business-related purposes; volunteer efforts of non-Abbott employees; or marketing sponsorships.
Geographic Focus: Arizona, California, Illinois, Kansas, Massachusetts, Michigan, New Jersey, New York, North Carolina, Ohio, Puerto Rico, Texas, Utah, Virginia, Brazil, Canada, Germany, Ireland, Italy, Japan, Netherlands, United Kingdom
Amount of Grant: 20,000 - 100,000 USD
Contact: Mary K. Moreland, Executive Vice President; (224) 667-6100 or (866) 298-9699
Internet: www.abbott.com/responsibility/social-impact/science-education.html
Sponsor: Abbott Fund
100 Abbott Park Road, Department 379, Building 6D
Abbott Park, IL 60064-3500

Abby's Legendary Pizza Foundation Grants   49
As a company, Abby's Legendary Pizza Foundation contributes to many community-based events and programs. Non-profits such as the Children's Miracle Network, the American Cancer Society, the Alzheimer's Association, and many others benefit from the Foundation's partnership as a business that cares about local people and causes. Typically, the Foundation provides support for: athletics, sports, and amateur leagues; child development; and higher education. The Foundation also supports most local high schools in its hometown communities throughout the states of Oregon and Washington. There are no identified annual deadlines for application submission, and interested parties should contact their local Abby's Legendary Pizza. Most recently, awards have ranged from $25 to $5,000.
Requirements: 501(c)3 non-profits either located in, or serving the residents of, Abby's Legendary Pizza communities should apply.
Geographic Focus: Oregon, Washington
Amount of Grant: 25 - 5,000 USD
Contact: Mills Sinclair, President; (541) 689-0091
Internet: abbys.com/fundraising/
Sponsor: Abby's Legendary Pizza Foundation
1970 River Road
Eugene, OR 97404

ABC Charities Grants   50
ABC Charities, formerly known as ADE Charities, is based in Indianapolis, Indiana, and primarily offers its support to organizations that maintain a home for destitute, abandoned, neglected, and dependent children, as well as to Christian organizations, including missions. Its major fields of interest include: children and youth; Christian agencies and churches; higher education; human and social services; Protestant agencies and churches; and residential/custodial care facilities. Although ABC's geographic stated focus is in Indiana, the Foundation has also given grants in Ohio, Alabama, Florida, Arizona, Texas, and Tennessee.
Geographic Focus: Alabama, Arizona, Florida, Indiana, Ohio, Tennessee, Texas

Amount of Grant: Up to 120,000 USD
Samples: Baptist Children's Home, Valparaiso, Indiana, $1,200; Campus Crusade for Christ, Orlando, Florida, $2,200; Urban Foundation, Indianapolis, Indiana, $60,000.
Contact: D. Michael Hockett, Director; (317) 862-7325; fax (317) 862-7325
Sponsor: ABC Charities
8250 Woodfield Crossing Boulevard, Suite 300, P.O. Box 39026
Indianapolis, IN 46239-0026

Abeles Foundation Grants   51
Established in New Mexico in 2002, the Abeles Foundation is an organization that provides general operating support in the areas of elementary and secondary education, public foundations, higher education, and the performing arts in the Albuquerque and Santa Fe areas. The Foundation makes gifts to organizations based on their interactions within the community. There is no formal application required or specified annual deadlines. Applicants should contact the Foundation directly. Awards range up to about $1,200.
Restrictions: No grants are made to individuals and applicant's organization must be a qualified 501(c)3 organization.
Geographic Focus: New Mexico
Amount of Grant: Up to 1,200 USD
Contact: Richard A. Abeles, President; (505) 988-1115; fax (505) 984-2040; rick@abeles.net
Sponsor: Abeles Foundation
3730 Old Santa Fe Trail
Santa Fe, NM 87505-4573

Abell-Hanger Foundation Grants   52
The Abell-Hanger Foundation makes grants to nonprofit Texas organizations, other than private foundations, that are involved in such undertakings for the public and society benefit, including: arts, cultural, and humanities; education; health; human services; and religion. Types of support include general operating support, continuing support, annual campaigns, capital campaigns, building construction/renovation, equipment acquisition, endowment funds, program development, seed funds, scholarship funds, research grants, and matching funds. Block scholarship grants are made only to institutions of higher education located in Texas. Recipient colleges and universities are free to administer the grants. Education grants are limited generally to institutions of higher education, including religious institutions (Baptist, Christian, Lutheran, Methodist, and Presbyterian). Applicants must seek funding for the same proposal from various sources because sole sponsorship of programs is rarely undertaken. Grant requests are considered and awarded throughout each year. The trustees prefer to consider only one request per applicant each fiscal year. Unsuccessful proposals may not be resubmitted for at least 12 months. Applicant organizations that have never received funding from the foundation should request a pre-proposal questionnaire; the trustees will review the request to determine whether it warrants a complete proposal.
Requirements: Applicant organizations must be located in Texas and be 501(c)3 tax-exempt. National organizations with significant operations in, or providing material benefits to the citizens of, Texas will be considered based on the degree of operations/benefits within the state.
Restrictions: The Foundation does not fund grants, scholarships, or fellowships for individuals.
Geographic Focus: Texas
Date(s) Application is Due: Jan 11; May 10; Oct 11
Amount of Grant: 10,000 - 500,000 USD
Samples: West Texas Food Bank, Odessa, Texas, $100,000 - for general operating support (2020); YMCA of Midland, Midland, Texas, $50,000 - for general support (2020); The Way Retreat Center, Midland, Texas, $25,000 - for general operating support (2020).
Contact: Mark Palmer; (432) 684-6655; fax (432) 684-4474; ahf@abell-hanger.org
Internet: abell-hanger.org/our-process/#grant-guidelines
Sponsor: Abell-Hanger Foundation
112 Corporate Drive, P.O. Box 430
Midland, TX 79702-0430

Abell Foundation Education Grants   53
The Foundation supports efforts to provide quality instruction and leadership, promote professional development, develop effective curricula (pre-school through 12th grade) through pilot projects, improve the transition to college and work, increase community involvement, enhance basic skills and further literacy enrichment. After-school activities and intramural sports with academic components have received on-going support to help fill gaps in the extra-curricular programming. In recognition of the pivotal role of quality teaching and leadership, the Foundation also supports recruitment and retention efforts, teacher training, and principal recruitment. Areas of interest include: public school reform/ new schools and charter schools; high school and middle school reform; early childhood education; K-12 curriculum development; literacy enrichment; teacher recruitment and training; technology education; career and technology education programs; advanced academic/gifted and talented programming; post-graduate remediation curriculum; access to higher education institutions; alternative schools/programs, particularly high schools; principal recruitment, development and retention; transition from high school to community college and to two-and four-year colleges; and after-school, weekend, and summer programs.
Requirements: 501(c)3 organizations serving Maryland communities, especially in the Baltimore area, may apply. The foundation prefers grantees that show strong fiscal management, their project's benefit to the community, ability to achieve goals, unique work, and other sources of financial support.
Restrictions: The Foundation does not fund educational programs at higher education institutions, medical facilities, individual scholarships, fellowships, annual operating expenses, sponsorships, deficit financing, endowments, travel or memberships.
Geographic Focus: Maryland
Date(s) Application is Due: Jan 4; Mar 1; May 3; Jul 1; Oct 15
Amount of Grant: 1,000 - 250,000 USD

Samples: Baltimore Corps, Baltimore, Maryland, $79,000 - to fund an internship program (2020); Baltimore Education Research Consortium (BERC), Baltimore, Maryland, $200,000 - to support general operating costs (2020); Baltimore Kids Chess League, Baltimore, Maryland, $40,000 - to support the new virtual chess platform (2020).
Contact: Robert C. Embry, Jr., President; (410) 547-1300; fax (410) 539-6579; abell@abell.org
Internet: www.abell.org/programareas/education.html
Sponsor: Abell Foundation
111 S Calvert Street, Suite 2300
Baltimore, MD 21202-6174

Abington Foundation Grants 54

The Abington Foundation awards grants to Ohio nonprofit organizations serving Cuyahoga County in its areas of interest, including pre-primary and higher education, geriatric healthcare and nursing, the promotion or sustenance of individual and family economic independence, and cultural activities. Priority is given to funding requests for specific programs or projects that represent critical periods in a child's development from birth to age five, and to early adolescence, ages ten through fifteen. Requests for endowment or general operating support are discouraged. Foundation staff is available for consultation during the proposal preparation process.
Requirements: Ohio nonprofit organizations serving Cuyahoga County are eligible.
Geographic Focus: Ohio
Date(s) Application is Due: May 1; Sep 1; Dec 1
Amount of Grant: 5,000 - 50,000 USD
Samples: Cleveland Public Theatre, Cleveland, Ohio, $15,000 - to support the Brick City after school and summer arts program (2018); Montclair Art Museum, Cleveland, Ohio, $30,000 - to support the Pilot an Artist in Residence program (2018); University Circle Incorporated, Cleveland, Ohio, $50,000 - for the development of the Cozad-Bates House Interpretive Center (2018).
Contact: Cristin Slesh, Consultant; (216) 621-2901 or (216) 621-2632; fax (216) 621-8198; cslesh@fmscleveland.com
Internet: www.fmscleveland.com/abington/grant-philosophy.cfm
Sponsor: Abington Foundation
1422 Euclid Avenue, Suite 966
Cleveland, OH 44115-1952

Abney Foundation Grants 55

The foundation makes grants for innovative and creative projects, and to programs that are responsive to changing community needs in the areas of health, social service, education, and cultural affairs in South Carolina. The foundation's primary focus is on higher education. All requests must be in writing and in accordance with foundation guidelines, which are available upon request, and from the website. Applicants may submit a Letter of Intent (LOI) briefly describing the project before submitting a proposal in order to find out if their ideas are potentially supported by the foundation.
Requirements: Agencies applying for funds should be serving the citizens of South Carolina.
Restrictions: The foundation does not generally fund requests for operating expenses.
Geographic Focus: South Carolina
Date(s) Application is Due: Nov 15
Amount of Grant: 5,000 - 100,000 USD
Samples: Anderson College (Anderson, SC)—for scholarships, $100,000; Anderson College (Anderson, SC)—to establish a scholarship fund, $100,000.
Contact: David C. King; (864) 964-9201; fax (864) 964-9209; info@abneyfoundation.org
Internet: www.abneyfoundation.org/guideline.htm
Sponsor: Abney Foundation
100 Vine Street
Anderson, SC 29621-3265

ABS Foundation Grants 56

ABS–American Building Supply is a manufacturer and wholesale distributor of quality door, millwork, and hardware products for both residential and commercial applications. Established in California in 2003, the ABS Foundation funds programs in areas of company operations in California, Nevada, Arizona, Washington, Georgia, Colorado, Texas, North Carolina, and Hawaii. Its primary fields of interest include: the arts; education; human services; and youth development. Types of support include capital campaigns, endowments, and general operations. Applicants should contact the Foundation directly to request an application. There are no specified annual deadlines, and grant amounts typically range from $1,000 to $5,000.
Geographic Focus: California, Colorado, Georgia, Hawaii
Amount of Grant: 1,000 - 5,000 USD
Samples: Palama Settlement, Honolulu, Hawaii, $5,000 - art and culture programs; Aquarium of the Pacific, Long Beach, California, $5,000 - youth activities; Red Rocks Community College, Lakewood, Colorado, $2,000 - general operations.
Contact: Mark C. Ballantyne, President; (916) 503-4100; fax (916) 503-4180
Sponsor: ABS Foundation
8360 Elder Creek Road, P.O. Box 276227
Sacramento, CA 95827-6227

Abundance Foundation International Grants 57

The Abundance Foundation makes grants to organizations aligned with its mission to improve global health through education, economic empowerment and health systems strengthening. It is focused on programs that unlock the potential of local communities particularly in Africa, Central America and Haiti. Its grantee partners train, support and empower local leaders to create new capabilities that result in lasting improvement in quality of life. In addition to direct grant funding that allows for upscaling of successful existing programs, the Foundation raise awareness about local leaders whose vision and heroism are creating positive change in their communities.

Geographic Focus: All States, Haiti
Contact: Stephen Kahn; (510) 841-4123; fax (510) 841-4093; info@abundancefound.org
Internet: www.abundancefound.org/grants/
Sponsor: Abundance Foundation
127 University Avenue
Berkeley, CA 94710-1616

Abundance Foundation Local Community Grants 58

The Abundance Foundation is a Non-Profit 501(c)3 Public Charity established in California in 2004. The Foundation makes grants in the San Francisco Bay Area to support youth development, the arts and education. Its current partners train, support and empower local leaders to create new capabilities and lasting improvement in quality of life. Though no specific deadlines are listed, applicants should begin by contacting the Foundation offices directly.
Geographic Focus: California
Contact: Stephen Kahn; (510) 841-4123; fax (510) 841-4093; info@abundancefound.org
Internet: www.abundancefound.org/grants/
Sponsor: Abundance Foundation
127 University Avenue
Berkeley, CA 94710-1616

ACCF Dennis and Melanie Bieberich Community Enrichment Fund Grants 59

The Dennis and Melanie Bieberich Community Enrichment Fund was established in Adams County, Indiana, in 2002. Melanie Bieberich, daughter of Gene and Norma Clark, was raised and attended school in Madison County, Indiana. Melanie and Dennis "Denny" were married in 1973 and have lived in rural Decatur ever since. Denny is the son of Roy and Phyllis Bieberich and is a life-long resident of Adams County. He and Melanie are the parents of two children: Amber and Todd. The couple is active in St. Mark's United Methodist Church, serving the church on various committees. Melanie served as a board member of the Adams/Wells Crisis Center and has been active on various boards throughout the years. A 36 year employee at Decatur Bank and Trust Company/First Merchants Bank, and having served as president for over 25 years, Denny currently serves as Senior Executive Officer and FMB board member. He has been involved in Youth for Christ, Adams County Economic Development Corporation, Adams County Economic Development Commission, Adams Central Elementary School Building Corporation, and the Adams County Community Foundation Finance Committee, with past board memberships of various community organizations. The Enrichment Fund named in their honor is used to provide financial support to the organizations they have served in the community. The quarterly deadlines for application submission are the second Wednesday of January, April, July, and October.
Requirements: Applicants must support businesses, educational programs, the arts, health care, and residents of Adams County, Indiana.
Geographic Focus: Indiana
Date(s) Application is Due: Jan 10; Apr 11; Jul 11; Oct 10
Amount of Grant: Up to 5,000 USD
Contact: Coni Mayer; (260) 724-3939; fax (260) 724-2299; accf@adamscountyfoundation.org
Internet: www.adamscountyfoundation.org/funds/m/bieberich-dennis-melanie-community-enrichment-fund-unrestricted
Sponsor: Adams County Community Foundation
102 N. Second Street
Decatur, IN 46733

ACCF John and Kay Boch Fund Grants 60

The John and Kay Boch Fund was established in Adams County, Indiana, in 1996. John is a retired postmaster in Decatur, while Kay is the owner/operator of the popular Kiddie Shop, located on Second Street across from the Decatur Daily Democrat offices. Both have long remained leaders of philanthropic giving throughout Adams County. Growing the fund to over $4,000,000 nephew Robert Boch oversees the investment and the distribution of the grants. A portion of the interest generated from this fund is awarded to non-profit organizations to benefit the youth and residents of the county. Funds are distributed by an all-volunteer Foundation Grants Committee and approved by the Board of Directors of the Foundation and the executor of John and Kay Boch, Incorporated. Quarterly deadlines for application submission are the second Thursday of January, April, July, and October.
Requirements: To be eligible for this grant, applicant 501(c)3 organizations must offer programs that support the residents of Adams County, Indiana.
Geographic Focus: Indiana
Date(s) Application is Due: Jan 11; Apr 12; Jul 12; Oct 11
Amount of Grant: Up to 5,000 USD
Contact: Coni Mayer; (260) 724-3939; fax (260) 724-2299; accf@adamscountyfoundation.org
Internet: www.adamscountyfoundation.org/funds/m/boch-john-kay-fund-scholarship-grants
Sponsor: Adams County Community Foundation
102 N. Second Street
Decatur, IN 46733

ACCF Marlene Bittner Memorial Community Enrichment Fund Grants 61

The Marlene Bittner Memorial Community Enrichment Fund was established in 2015. It was named in honor of Marlene K. Bittner of Decatur, born on March 6, 1938, in Adams County to the late Robert K. and Parilee L. (Pressler) Johnson. Marlene was a member of St. Peter Lutheran Church. She retired from North Adams Community Schools as Treasurer/Executive School Secretary for the district. The scholarship serves as an annual tribute to Marlene's support of youth, education, and her service to this community. Quarterly deadlines are the second Wednesday of January, April, July, and October.
Requirements: To be eligible for this grant, 501(c)3 applicant organizations must offer programs that support the residents of Adams County, Indiana.
Geographic Focus: Indiana

Date(s) Application is Due: Jan 10; Apr 11; Jul 11; Oct 10
Amount of Grant: Up to 5,000 USD
Contact: Coni Mayer; (260) 724-3939; fax (260) 724-2299; accf@adamscountyfoundation.org
Internet: www.adamscountyfoundation.org/funds/m/bittner-marlene-memorial-community-enrichment-fund-unrestricted
Sponsor: Adams County Community Foundation
102 N. Second Street
Decatur, IN 46733

ACCF of Indiana Angel Funds Grants   **62**
The Adams County Community Foundation created the Angel Funds in 2000 after noting a significant number of memorial contributions were designated to national organizations. However, when families were given the opportunity to keep their money local, they preferred this option. There are eight options available for the Funds: Arthritis; Alzheimer/Dementia; Diabetes; Heart; Hospice; Kidney; Lung; and Cancer. There are no annual deadlines for application submission.
Requirements: Recipients of the Angel Funds should be current or former residents of Adams County, Indiana.
Geographic Focus: Indiana
Contact: Coni Mayer; (260) 724-3939; fax (260) 724-2299; accf@adamscountyfoundation.org
Internet: www.adamscountyfoundation.org/funds/m/angel-funds-field-of-interest
Sponsor: Adams County Community Foundation
102 N. Second Street
Decatur, IN 46733

ACCF of Indiana Anonymous Community Enrichment Fund Grants   **63**
Anonymous Community Enrichment Fund was established in the Adams County Community Foundation in 2008. The Fund provides support to Adams County nonprofit organizations that serve Adams County residents. Organizations should submit a grant request within the guidelines set by the ACCF. This fund is especially helpful as it changes with the times and needs of the community. This award distribution is at the discretion of the ACCF Board of Directors. Quarterly deadlines are the second Wednesday of January, April, July, and October.
Requirements: To be eligible for this grant, applicant organizations must offer programs that support the residents of Adams County, Indiana.
Geographic Focus: Indiana
Date(s) Application is Due: Jan 10; Apr 11; Jul 11; Oct 10
Contact: Coni Mayer; (260) 724-3939; fax (260) 724-2299; accf@adamscountyfoundation.org
Internet: www.adamscountyfoundation.org/funds/m/anonymous-community-enrichment-fund-unrestricted
Sponsor: Adams County Community Foundation
102 N. Second Street
Decatur, IN 46733

ACCF of Indiana Bank of Geneva Heritage Fund Grants   **64**
In the late 1980s, several Adams County community leaders convened to develop the vision of a community foundation to serve the residents of the community. With the inspiration of the Portland, Jay County Foundation and the financial, administrative, and legal boost from Lilly Endowment Foundation, the dream of the Adams County Community Foundation was formed. As early as 1885, Charles D. Porter put a large burglar-proof safe in his drug store and rendered what accommodation he could to those whose business required them to handle large sums of money. In 1889, Porter started the Geneva Bank. When the building for the Bank was completed in 1893, the original Bank of Geneva was organized. This Fund awards numerous grants annually, all with the mission of improving the lives of residents of Adams County. Quarterly deadlines are the second Wednesday of January, April, July, and October.
Requirements: Applicants must support businesses, educational programs, the arts, health care, and residents of Adams County, Indiana.
Geographic Focus: Indiana
Date(s) Application is Due: Jan 10; Apr 11; Jul 11; Oct 10
Amount of Grant: Up to 5,000 USD
Contact: Coni Mayer; (260) 724-3939; fax (260) 724-2299; accf@adamscountyfoundation.org
Internet: www.adamscountyfoundation.org/funds/m/bank-of-geneva-heritage-fund-unrestricted
Sponsor: Adams County Community Foundation
102 N. Second Street
Decatur, IN 46733

ACCF of Indiana Berne Ready Mix Community Enrichment Fund Grants   **65**
The Adams County Community Foundation and supporting organization, John and Kay Boch, award numerous grants annually. Specifically, the Berne Ready Mix Community Enrichment Fund was formed by the Gene and Nancy Subler family in 2013. Areas of primary interest include: children and youth; community and economic development; elementary and secondary education; community development; and parks and recreation. Money awarded from the various funds helps to enrich and enhance the quality of life throughout Adams County, Indiana. Grants awarded annually help both businesses and the communities in which it serves. Quarterly deadlines are the second Wednesday of January, April, July, and October.
Requirements: Applicants must support businesses, educational programs, or residents of Adams County, Indiana.
Geographic Focus: Indiana
Date(s) Application is Due: Jan 10; Apr 11; Jul 11; Oct 10
Amount of Grant: 200 - 5,000 USD
Contact: Coni Mayer; (260) 724-3939; fax (260) 724-2299; accf@adamscountyfoundation.org

Internet: www.adamscountyfoundation.org/funds/m/berne-ready-mix-community-enrichment-fund-unrestricted
Sponsor: Adams County Community Foundation
102 N. Second Street
Decatur, IN 46733

ACCF of Indiana First Merchants Bank / Decatur Bank and Trust Fund Grants   **66**
In the late 1980s, several Adams County community leaders convened to develop the vision of a community foundation to serve the residents of the community. With the inspiration of the Portland, Jay County Foundation and the financial, administrative, and legal boost from Lilly Endowment Foundation, the dream of the Adams County Community Foundation was formed. Established in 1967, the Decatur Bank and Trust Company was the second such lending institution to be established since the collected history of Decatur, with the Main Office located on Thirteenth Street in that community. This Fund awards numerous grants annually, all with the mission of improving the lives of residents of Adams County. Quarterly deadlines are the second Wednesday of January, April, July, and October.
Requirements: Applicants must support businesses, educational programs, the arts, health care, and residents of Adams County, Indiana.
Geographic Focus: Indiana
Date(s) Application is Due: Jan 10; Apr 11; Jul 11; Oct 10
Amount of Grant: Up to 5,000 USD
Contact: Coni Mayer; (260) 724-3939; fax (260) 724-2299; accf@adamscountyfoundation.org
Internet: www.adamscountyfoundation.org/funds/m/bank-first-merchants-bank-decatur-bank-trust-fund-unrestricted
Sponsor: Adams County Community Foundation
102 N. Second Street
Decatur, IN 46733

ACCF of Indiana Michael Basham Community Enrichment Fund Grants   **67**
In the late 1980s, several Adams County community leaders convened to develop the vision of a community foundation to serve the residents of the community. With the inspiration of the Portland, Jay County Foundation and the financial, administrative, and legal boost from Lilly Endowment Foundation, the dream of the Adams County Community Foundation was formed. Michael J. Basham was born in Decatur in 1959 to James C. and Ellen K. Basham. He lived in Adams County his entire life, except when he attended Purdue University. Growing up he was blessed with outstanding athletic abilities, playing Little League at Hanna Nuttman Park, Pony League at Worthman Field and football and basketball at many different venues. As he got older he acquired a tremendous appreciation for nature, enjoying walking and biking the trails of Adams County. He loved gardening, growing beautiful flowers and landscaping his home. He assisted others at the community garden by helping stake out plots and tilling plots for other gardeners. Mike died unexpectedly at the age of 51 from a bicycle accident that resulted in a skull fracture with a brain hemorrhage, an injury that could have been prevented by wearing a bicycles helmet. The family's prayer is that, upon hearing this information, people will become more cognizant of the importance of wearing helmets when biking. Since Mike loved helping others he would be pleased to know that his story might help someone else avert such a tragedy. The Michael Basham Community Enrichment Fund named in his honor awards numerous grants annually, all with the mission of improving the lives of residents of Adams County. Quarterly deadlines are the second Wednesday of January, April, July, and October.
Requirements: Applicants must support businesses, educational programs, the arts, health care, and residents of Adams County, Indiana.
Geographic Focus: Indiana
Date(s) Application is Due: Jan 10; Apr 11; Jul 11; Oct 10
Amount of Grant: Up to 5,000 USD
Contact: Coni Mayer; (260) 724-3939; fax (260) 724-2299; accf@adamscountyfoundation.org
Internet: www.adamscountyfoundation.org/funds/m/basham-michael-basham-community-enrichment-fund-unrestricted
Sponsor: Adams County Community Foundation
102 N. Second Street
Decatur, IN 46733

ACCF of Indiana Ron and Susie Ballard Community Enrichment Fund Grants   **68**
Ron Ballard began his lifelong career of repairing automobiles during his senior year at Bellmont High School while enrolled in the Industrial Cooperative Training Program. He remained employed in the collision repair field until 1979, at which time he opened R.B.'s Body Shop at his residence. In 1988 he moved the business to U.S. 27 South in Decatur, and in April 2003, he purchased property at 1027 Southampton Drive (behind the Back 40 Restaurant). Ron holds a Masters Degree in refinishing from PPG Industries, attaining that level after fourteen years of training and study. He is still an active member of the ICT Advisory Board at BHS. Ron was also one of the founding board members for the Boys and Girls Club of Decatur. In February of 2008, Ron formed a partnership with a company in England and recently launched Wren Turbines U.S.A. The company designs and builds miniature turbine engines for use in the modeling and filming industries. The Ron and Susie Ballard Community Enrichment Fund will be used to provide financial support to the organizations of their interest in this community. Quarterly deadlines are the second Wednesday of January, April, July, and October.
Requirements: Applicants must support businesses, community development, educational programs, or residents of Adams County, Indiana.
Geographic Focus: Indiana
Date(s) Application is Due: Jan 10; Apr 11; Jul 11; Oct 10
Contact: Coni Mayer; (260) 724-3939; fax (202) 265-1662; accf@adamscountyfoundation.org
Internet: www.adamscountyfoundation.org/funds/m/ballard-ron-susie-community-enrichment-fund-unrestricted

Sponsor: Adams County Community Foundation
102 N. Second Street
Decatur, IN 46733

ACCF Ralph Biggs Memorial Community Enrichment Fund Grants   69

Ralph E. Biggs was a loving husband, father, grandfather, brother and friend. He was an avid golfer, an outdoors man, private pilot and entrepreneur. He attended Purdue University where he graduated with a Masters in Business Administration and an Undergraduate Degree in Agricultural Economics. Ralph came to Decatur in the fall of 1962 to work for Clark Smith at Ideal Suburban Homes. Eventually, after founding GKB Enterprises in 1980 along with Steve Kreigh, he developed 43 communities in Northeast Indiana and Ohio. Through Biggs, Inc. he developed 32 apartment complexes and managed 2,700 apartment homes. Ralph also developed Cross Creek Golf Course, Eagle Glen Golf Course, and Blackford County Country Club. He was one of the founders of Rural Rental Housing Association and a member of the Fort Wayne Home Builders Association for 44 years where he received numerous Spike Awards. The Ralph Biggs Memorial Community Enrichment Fund was established in 2011 to provide support to local organizations that serve Decatur, Indiana. Its flexibility allows that a different organization can be served each year. Quarterly deadlines are the second Wednesday of January, April, July, and October.
Requirements: Applicants must be 501(c)3 organizations serving the residents of Decatur, Indiana.
Geographic Focus: Indiana
Date(s) Application is Due: Jan 10; Apr 11; Jul 11; Oct 10
Amount of Grant: Up to 5,000 USD
Contact: Coni Mayer; (260) 724-3939; fax (260) 724-2299; accf@adamscountyfoundation.org
Internet: www.adamscountyfoundation.org/funds/m/biggs-ralph-memorial-community-enrichment-fund-unrestricted
Sponsor: Adams County Community Foundation
102 N. Second Street
Decatur, IN 46733

ACF Abandoned Infants Assistance Grants   70

The Abandoned Infants Assistance program provides support for the development,implementation and operation of projects to demonstrate strategies and approaches to: prevent abandonment of infants and young children, particularly those who have been perinataly exposed to a dangerous drug and those with the human immunodeficiency virus (HIV) or who have been perinatally exposed to the virus; identify and address needs of those abandoned infants, especially those with AIDS; assist these children to reside with their biological families, if possible or in foster care; recruit train health and social services personnel foster care families and residential care providers to meet the needs of abandoned infants and children who are at risk abandonment; carry out residential care programs and foster families; and provide technical assistance and training to providers to meet the needs of this population.
Requirements: Eligible applicants include: state governments; private institutions of higher education; special district governments; public housing authorities; Indian housing authorities; Native American tribal organizations (other than Federally recognized tribal governments); nonprofits that do not have a 501(c)3 status with the IRS, other than institutions of higher education; city or township governments; small businesses; independent school districts; nonprofits having a 501(c)3 status with the IRS, other than institutions of higher education; for profit organizations other than small businesses; Native American tribal governments (Federally recognized); unrestricted (i.e., open to any type of entity above); county governments; and public and state controlled institutions of higher education.
Restrictions: Applications from individuals (including sole proprietorships) and foreign entities are not eligible and will be disqualified from competitive review and from funding under this announcement.
Geographic Focus: All States
Contact: Jan Shafer, Division of Program Innovation; (202) 205-8172; jan.shafer@acf.hhs.gov
Internet: www.acf.hhs.gov/cb/resource/abandoned-infants-assist
Sponsor: Administration for Children and Families
8th Floor, 1250 Maryland Avenue, SW
Washington, D.C. 20024

ACF Adoption Opportunities Grants   71

The Adoption Opportunities program provides discretionary funds for projects designed to eliminate barriers to adoption and help find permanent families for children who would benefit from adoption, particularly children with special needs. The major programs areas, as mandated by the legislation, are: the development and implementation of a national adoption and foster care data gathering and analysis system; the development and implementation of a national adoption information exchange system; the development and implementation of an adoption training and technical assistance program; increasing the placements in adoptive families of minority children who are in the foster care and have the goal of adoption with a specials emphasis on recruitment of minority families; post-legal adoption services for families who have adopted children with special needs including day treatment and respite care; support the placement of children in kinship care arrangements, pre-adoptive, or adoptive homes; study the efficacy of state contracting with public and private agencies (including community-based and other organizations); increase the number of older children adopted from foster care, emphasizing several child specific recruitment strategies (media campaigns to inform the public of the needs of older children available for adoption; training personnel in older children's needs and recruiting families to adopt older children); to improve efforts to eliminate interjurisdictional adoption barriers; study manner in which interstate placements are financed; best practice recommendations for inter and intra state adoptions and how State definitions of special needs differentiate and/or group similar categories of children; and research adoption outcomes and factors that affect these outcomes.

Requirements: Eligible applicants include: for profit organizations other than small businesses; Native American tribal governments (Federally recognized); county governments; Native American tribal organizations (other than federally recognized tribal governments); state governments; nonprofits that do not have a 501(c)3 status with the IRS, other than institutions of higher education; city or township governments; and nonprofits having a 501(c)3 status with the IRS, other than institutions of higher education.
Geographic Focus: All States
Contact: Matthew McGuire, Child Welfare Program Specialist, Division of Program Innovation; (202) 205-8172; matthew.mcquire@acf.hhs.gov
Internet: www.acf.hhs.gov/cb/resource/adoption-opportunities
Sponsor: Administration for Children and Families
8th Floor, 1250 Maryland Avenue, SW
Washington, D.C. 20024

ACF American Indian and Alaska Native Early Head Start Expansion Grants   72

The Administration for Children and Families solicits applications from public or private non-profit organizations, including community-based and faith-based organizations, or for-profit agencies that wish to compete for funds that are available to provide American Indian and Alaska Native Early Head Start Expansion services to infants, toddlers, pregnant women, and their families. An estimated ten (10) grants will be awarded, ranging from $500,000 to $5,000,000. Electronically submitted applications must be submitted no later than 11:59 p.m., ET, on March 13.
Requirements: Eligible applicants include: independent school districts; small businesses; state governments; for profit organizations other than small businesses; public housing authorities/Indian housing authorities; public and state controlled institutions of higher education; nonprofits that do not have a 501(c)3 status with the IRS, other than institutions of higher education; county governments; nonprofits having a 501(c)3 status with the IRS, other than institutions of higher education; Native American tribal organizations (other than federally recognized tribal governments); city or township governments; Native American tribal governments (federally recognized); and private institutions of higher education. Faith-based and community organizations that meet the eligibility requirements are also eligible.
Geographic Focus: All States
Date(s) Application is Due: Mar 13
Amount of Grant: 500,000 - 5,000,000 USD
Contact: Shawna Pinckney, Program Officer; (888) 242-0684 or (202) 401-9200; fax (202) 205-4891; ohstech@reviewops.org
Internet: www.acf.hhs.gov/ecd/early-learning/ehs-cc-partnerships
Sponsor: Administration for Children and Families
Portals Building, 1250 Maryland Avenue, SW
Washington, D.C. 20024

ACF Basic Center Program Grants   73

The Administration for Children and Families, through its Basic Center Program, supports organizations and communities that work every day to put an end to youth homelessness, adolescent pregnancy, and domestic violence. FYSB's Runaway and Homeless Youth (RHY) program is accepting applications for the Basic Center Program (BCP). The purpose of the BCP is to provide temporary shelter and counseling services to youth who have left home without permission of their parents or guardians, have been forced to leave home, or other homeless youth who might otherwise end up in the law enforcement or in the child welfare, mental health, or juvenile justice systems. Funds ranging from $50,000 to $200,000 are available, with nearly one hundred grants given annually. Priority will be given to private entities that have experience in providing shelter and services to runaway, homeless and street youth. The deadline for electronic applicants is June 13.
Requirements: Eligible applicants include: Native American tribal organizations (other than Federally recognized tribal governments); public and state controlled institutions of higher education; county governments; nonprofits that do not have a 501(c)3 status with the IRS, other than institutions of higher education; state governments; public housing authorities/Indian housing authorities; Native American tribal governments (federally recognized); special district governments; city or township governments; independent school districts; nonprofits having a 501(c)3 status with the IRS, other than institutions of higher education; and private institutions of higher education.
Geographic Focus: All States
Date(s) Application is Due: Jun 13
Amount of Grant: 50,000 - 200,000 USD
Contact: Gloria Watkins, Program Officer; (202) 205-9546; gloria.watkins@acf.hhs.gov
Internet: www.acf.hhs.gov/fysb/programs/runaway-homeless-youth/programs/basic-center-program
Sponsor: Administration for Children and Families
118 Q Street NE
Washington, D.C. 20002-2132

ACF Child Abuse Prevention and Treatment Act Discretionary Funds Grants   74

The discretionary fund activities funded by the Child Abuse Prevention and Treatment Act (CAPTA) support a variety of activities, including research and demonstration projects on the causes, prevention, identification, assessment and treatment of child abuse and neglect, the development and implementation of evidence-based training programs, technical assistance to grantees and communities through national resource centers and the Child Welfare Information Gateway. Grants are provided to State and local agencies and organizations as well as university- and hospital-affiliated programs. Funds have also supported contracts for cross-site evaluations, technical assistance to grantees, the biennial National Conference on Child Abuse and Neglect, various publications most notably the User Manual Series, Congressionally mandated studies, and Interagency Agreements to support multi-agency efforts at the Federal level.

Requirements: Eligible applicants include: nonprofits having a 501(c)3 status with the IRS, other than institutions of higher education; Native American tribal governments (federally recognized); special district governments; private institutions of higher education; public and state controlled institutions of higher education; Native American tribal organizations (other than federally recognized tribal governments); city or township governments; independent school districts; for profit organizations other than small businesses; public housing authorities/Indian housing authorities; county governments; nonprofits that do not have a 501(c)3 status with the IRS, other than institutions of higher education; small businesses; and state governments.
Geographic Focus: All States
Contact: Jan Shafer, Division of Program Innovation; (202) 205-8172; jan.shafer@acf.hhs.gov
Internet: www.acf.hhs.gov/cb/resource/capta-discretionary-grants
Sponsor: Administration for Children and Families
8th Floor, 1250 Maryland Avenue, SW
Washington, D.C. 20024

ACF Child Welfare Training Grants 75

The Child Welfare Training program upgrades the skills, knowledge and qualifications of prospective and current child welfare agency staff and supports special projects for training personnel to work in the field of child welfare. These discretionary grants are awarded to public and private non-profit institutions of higher learning and are designed to assist State child welfare agencies in developing a stable and highly skilled workforce for providing effective child welfare services. Further, the Child Welfare Discretionary Grant Projects develop and maintain a strong University- Public Agency Partnership toward the goal of identifying and developing the appropriate staff competencies.
Requirements: Eligible applicants include: Native American tribal organizations (other than Federally recognized tribal governments); public and state controlled institutions of higher education; county governments; nonprofits that do not have a 501(c)3 status with the IRS, other than institutions of higher education; state governments; public housing authorities/ Indian housing authorities; Native American tribal governments (federally recognized); special district governments; city or township governments; independent school districts; nonprofits having a 501(c)3 status with the IRS, other than institutions of higher education; and private institutions of higher education.
Geographic Focus: All States
Contact: Jan Shafer, Division of Program Innovation; (202) 205-8172; jan.shafer@acf.hhs.gov
Internet: www.acf.hhs.gov/cb/resource/cw-training
Sponsor: Administration for Children and Families
8th Floor, 1250 Maryland Avenue, SW
Washington, D.C. 20024

ACF Community-Based Child Abuse Prevention (CBCAP) Grants 76

Community-Based Child Abuse Prevention (CBCAP) programs were established by Title II of the Child Abuse Prevention and Treatment Act Amendments of 1996 and most recently reauthorized by the CAPTA Reauthorization Act of 2010 (P.L. 111-320). The purpose of the CBCAP program is: to support community-based efforts to develop, operate, expand, enhance, and coordinate initiatives, programs, and activities to prevent child abuse and neglect and to support the coordination of resources and activities to better strengthen and support families to reduce the likelihood of child abuse and neglect; and to foster understanding, appreciation and knowledge of diverse populations in order to effectively prevent and treat child abuse and neglect. Programs can also finance the development of a continuum of preventive services through public-private partnerships, financing the start-up, maintenance, expansion, or redesign or child abuse prevention programs, maximizing funding through leveraging funds, and financing public education activities that focus on the promotion of child abuse prevention.
Requirements: Eligible applicants include: small businesses; state governments; county governments; Native American tribal governments (federally recognized); public and state controlled institutions of higher education; public housing authorities/Indian housing authorities; nonprofits that do not have a 501(c)3 status with the IRS, other than institutions of higher education; Native American tribal organizations (other than federally recognized tribal governments); for profit organizations other than small businesses; special district governments; nonprofits having a 501(c)3 status with the IRS, other than institutions of higher education; city or township governments; independent school districts; and private institutions of higher education.
Geographic Focus: All States
Contact: Jan Shafer, Division of Program Innovation; (202) 205-8172; jan.shafer@acf.hhs.gov
Internet: www.acf.hhs.gov/cb/resource/cbcap-state-grants
Sponsor: Administration for Children and Families
8th Floor, 1250 Maryland Avenue, SW
Washington, D.C. 20024

ACF Community-Based Child Abuse Prevention Tribal and Migrant DiscretionaryGrants 77

The purpose of the Community-Based Child Abuse Prevention (CBCAP) Tribal and Migrant Discretionary funding s to provide financial support to selected Tribes, Tribal organizations, and migrant programs for child abuse prevention programs and activities that are consistent with the goals outlined by Title II of the Child Abuse Prevention and Treatment Act (CAPTA). This legislation specifies that one percent of the available funding from Title II will be reserved to fund Tribes, Tribal organizations and migrant programs. The goal of the programs and activities supported by these funds is to prevent the occurrence or recurrence of abuse or neglect within the Tribal and migrant populations. The funds support more effective and comprehensive child abuse prevention activities and family support services that will enhance the lives and ensure the safety and well-being of migrant and Native American children and their families. Some examples of programs that are funded include parenting education and family support services. Grantees are strongly encouraged to implement evidence-based and evidence-informed programs and practices that reflect the unique cultural characteristics and needs of their communities. The funds must also be used to support an evaluation of the programs and services funded by the grant. Finally, programs funded should develop stronger linkages with the Community-Based Child Abuse Prevention Program (CBCAP) State Lead Agency funded under Title II of CAPTA.
Requirements: Eligible applicants include: small businesses; state governments; county governments; Native American tribal governments (federally recognized); public and state controlled institutions of higher education; public housing authorities/Indian housing authorities; nonprofits that do not have a 501(c)3 status with the IRS, other than institutions of higher education; Native American tribal organizations (other than federally recognized tribal governments); for profit organizations other than small businesses; special district governments; nonprofits having a 501(c)3 status with the IRS, other than institutions of higher education; city or township governments; independent school districts; and private institutions of higher education.
Geographic Focus: All States
Contact: Jan Shafer, Division of Program Innovation; (202) 205-8172; jan.shafer@acf.hhs.gov
Internet: www.acf.hhs.gov/cb/resource/cbcap-state-grants
Sponsor: Administration for Children and Families
8th Floor, 1250 Maryland Avenue, SW
Washington, D.C. 20024

ACF Early Care and Education Research Scholars: Child Care Research Scholars 78

Funds for Child Care Research Scholars grants are available to support dissertation research on child care policy issues in partnership with State Child Care and Development Fund (CCDF) lead agencies. Since 2000, Congress has appropriated about $10 million per year of CCDF discretionary funds to be used for child care research and evaluation. These funds have supported projects that add to our knowledge about the efficacy of child care subsidy policies and programs in supporting employment and self-sufficiency outcomes for parents, and providing positive learning and school readiness outcomes for children. Previously funded Child Care Research Scholars have made significant contributions to the child care policy research field. To ensure that research is responsive to the changing needs of low-income families, partnerships between the graduate student, their mentor and the State CCDF lead agency are essential. This partnership ensures the research will be policy-relevant and is the foundation that fosters skills necessary to build the graduate student's career trajectory of successful partnership-building and contributions to the policy and scientific communities. An estimated six (6) grants will be awarded, ranging from $20,000 to $25,000. Electronically submitted applications must be submitted no later than 11:59 p.m., ET, on April 10.
Requirements: Eligible applicants include: public and state controlled institutions of higher education; state governments; nonprofits having a 501(c)3 status with the IRS, other than institutions of higher education; Native American tribal governments (federally recognized); nonprofits that do not have a 501(c)3 status with the IRS, other than institutions of higher education; public housing authorities/Indian housing authorities; special district governments; county governments; private institutions of higher education; Native American tribal organizations (other than federally recognized tribal governments); independent school districts; and city or township governments. Faith-based and community organizations that meet the eligibility requirements are also eligible to receive awards under this funding opportunity announcement.
Geographic Focus: All States
Date(s) Application is Due: Apr 10
Amount of Grant: 20,000 - 25,000 USD
Contact: Ann Rivera, Program Officer; (202) 401-5506 or (202) 401-9220; fax (202) 205-3598; ann.rivera@acf.hhs.gov
Internet: www.acf.hhs.gov/opre/research/project/child-care-research-scholars
Sponsor: Administration for Children and Families
330 C Street, SW
Washington, D.C. 20201

ACF Early Care and Education Research Scholars: Head Start Graduate Student Research Grants 79

The Head Start Graduate Student Research grant program is designed to build research capacity in and knowledge of effective early childhood interventions with low-income children and families. The grant program does this by providing support for dissertation research conducted by graduate students working in partnership with local Head Start or Early Head Start programs. Many former grantees have become leading researchers who continue to conduct research that informs and improves Head Start/Early Head Start, other early childhood intervention practices, and our understanding of low-income populations. The immediate goals of the grant program are to: support the completion of high quality research projects directed at the current concerns of Head Start and Early Head Start programs and policy makers; encourage research with Head Start and Early Head Start populations; promote mentor-student relationships that provide project supervision in the field and support students' professional development; emphasize the importance of developing working research partnerships with Head Start and Early Head Start programs, thereby increasing the effectiveness of the applied research work; and support active communication, networking and collaboration among the group of grantee graduate students, their mentors and other prominent researchers in the field. An estimated six (6) grants will be awarded, ranging from $20,000 to $25,000. Electronically submitted applications must be submitted no later than 11:59 p.m., ET, on April 21.
Requirements: Eligible applicants include: public and state controlled institutions of higher education; state governments; nonprofits having a 501(c)3 status with the IRS, other than institutions of higher education; Native American tribal governments (federally recognized); nonprofits that do not have a 501(c)3 status with the IRS, other than institutions of higher education; public housing authorities/Indian housing authorities;

special district governments; county governments; private institutions of higher education; Native American tribal organizations (other than federally recognized tribal governments); independent school districts; and city or township governments. Faith-based and community organizations that meet the eligibility requirements are also eligible to receive awards under this funding opportunity announcement.
Geographic Focus: All States
Date(s) Application is Due: Apr 21
Amount of Grant: 20,000 - 25,000 USD
Contact: Wendy DeCourcey, Federal Project Officer; (202) 260-2039 or (202) 401-9220; fax (202) 205-3598; wendy.decourcey@acf.hhs.gov
Internet: www.acf.hhs.gov/opre/research/project/head-start-graduate-student-research-program
Sponsor: Administration for Children and Families
330 C Street, SW
Washington, D.C. 20201

ACF Ethnic Community Self Help Grants   80
The Administration for Children and Families, Office of Refugee Resettlement invites the submission of applications for funding under the Ethnic Community Self-Help (ECSH) Program. The goal of this program is to support Ethnic Community-Based Organizations (ECBOs) in providing refugee populations with critical services to assist them in becoming integrated members of American society. Under the ECSH Program, the following three main objectives must be implemented: to strengthen ECBOs' provision of culturally and linguistically appropriate services to refugees within five years after their initial resettlement; to support ECBOs' organizational development and engagement in capacity building by encouraging their collaboration with established refugee service providers and mainstream organizations; and to support ECBOs in promoting community building and civic participation by refugee individuals and refugee community members. Electronically submitted applications must be submitted no later than 11:59 p.m., ET, on May 30. Approximately thirteen grants will be awarded, ranging from $100,000 to $200,000.
Requirements: This Funding Opportunity Announcement (FOA) is open only to Ethnic Community-Based Organizations (ECBOs). For the purposes of this FOA, the Office of Refugee Resettlement considers an ECBO as a non-profit organization whose board of directors is comprised of at least 60 percent current and/or former refugees. The applicant must demonstrate that at the time of submission its board of directors is comprised of at least 60 percent current and/or former refugees. Faith-based and community organizations that meet the eligibility requirements are eligible to receive awards under this funding opportunity announcement.
Geographic Focus: All States
Date(s) Application is Due: May 30
Amount of Grant: 100,000 - 200,000 USD
Contact: Zahra Cheema, Program Officer; (202) 401-5676 or (202) 401-9246; fax (202) 401-5487; zahra.cheema@acf.hhs.gov
Internet: www.acf.hhs.gov/orr/programs/ethnic-community-self-help
Sponsor: Administration for Children and Families
Mary E. Switzer Building, 330 C Street, SW
Washington, D.C. 20201

ACF Family Strengthening Scholars Grants   81
The Family Strengthening Scholars grant program is designed to build research capacity in the healthy marriage/responsible fatherhood field (HM/RF). These grants are to support dissertation research on HM/RF policy issues and are meant to build capacity in the research field to focus research on questions that have direct implications for HM/RF decision-making and program administration. They are intended to focus particularly on underserved/understudied populations, such as low-income families and minority population, utilize rigorous methodology and help inform the development of future intervention research. The specific goals of the Family Strengthening Scholars grants are: to address issues of significant relevant to policy decisions related to low-income families in order further the HM/RF field; to directly support graduate students' engagement in HM/RF research; to foster mentoring relationships between faculty members and graduate students who are pursuing doctoral-level research in the HM/RF field; and to encourage active communication, networking and collaboration among graduate students, their mentors, and other senior family strengthening researchers. An estimated three (3) grants will be awarded, ranging from $10,000 to $25,000. Electronically submitted applications must be submitted no later than 11:59 p.m., ET, on May 10.
Requirements: Eligible applicants include: private institutions of higher education; and public and State controlled institutions of higher education.
Geographic Focus: All States
Date(s) Application is Due: May 20
Amount of Grant: 10,000 - 25,000 USD
Contact: Kathleen Mccoy, Program Officer; (202) 401-5436 or (202) 401-9220; fax (202) 205-3598; kathleen.mccoy@acf.hhs.gov
Internet: www.acf.hhs.gov/opre/research/project/family-strengthening-scholars
Sponsor: Administration for Children and Families
330 C Street, SW
Washington, D.C. 20201

ACF Head Start and/or Early Head Start Grantee - Clay, Randolph,   82
    and Talladega Counties, Alabama
The Administration for Children and Families solicits applications from local public or private non-profit organizations, including faith-based organizations or local for-profit organizations, that wish to compete for funds that are available to provide a high-quality, comprehensive birth-to-five program incorporating both Head Start and Early Head Start funding, or to provide for Head Start only or Early Head Start only, to children and families residing in Clay, Randolph, and Talladega Counties, Alabama. Funds in the amount of

$1,870,755 annually will be available to provide Head Start and/or Early Head Start program services to eligible children and their families. The deadline for applicants is April 3.
Requirements: Applicants should propose a design or designs that best address the needs of the proposed service area. Applicants have flexibility in determining the appropriate number of children to be served by the various program options (center-based, home-based, or combination) and program designs (hours per day, days per week, weeks per year). Preference will be given to applicants who can demonstrate efficient management of several or all of the service areas.
Restrictions: Grantees are required to meet a non-Federal share of the project costs, in accordance with section 640(b) of the Head Start Act. Grantees must provide at least 20 percent of the total approved cost of the project.
Geographic Focus: Alabama
Date(s) Application is Due: Apr 3
Amount of Grant: 1,870,755 USD
Contact: Shawna Pinckney, Program Officer; (888) 242-0684; OHSTech@reviewops.org
Internet: www.acf.hhs.gov/ohs/funding
Sponsor: Administration for Children and Families
Portals Building, 1250 Maryland Avenue, SW
Washington, D.C. 20024

ACF Head Start and/or Early Head Start Grantee - St. Landry Parish, Louisiana   83
The Administration for Children and Families solicits applications from local public or private non-profit organizations, including faith-based organizations or local for-profit organizations, that wish to compete for funds that are available to provide Head Start and/or Early Head Start services to children and families residing in St. Landry Parish, Louisiana. Funds in the amount of $7,641,447 annually will be available to provide Head Start program services to eligible children and their families. The deadline for applicants is April 3.
Requirements: Applicants should propose a design or designs that best address the needs of the proposed service area. Applicants have flexibility in determining the appropriate number of children to be served by the various program options (center-based, home-based, or combination) and program designs (hours per day, days per week, weeks per year). Preference will be given to applicants who can demonstrate efficient management of several or all of the service areas.
Restrictions: Grantees are required to meet a non-Federal share of the project costs, in accordance with section 640(b) of the Head Start Act. Grantees must provide at least 20 percent of the total approved cost of the project.
Geographic Focus: Louisiana
Date(s) Application is Due: Apr 3
Amount of Grant: 7,641,447 USD
Contact: Shawna Pinckney, Program Officer; (888) 242-0684; OHSTech@reviewops.org
Internet: www.acf.hhs.gov/ohs/funding
Sponsor: Administration for Children and Families
Portals Building, 1250 Maryland Avenue, SW
Washington, D.C. 20024

ACF Infant Adoption Awareness Training Program Grants   84
On October 17, 2000 the U.S. Congress, under Public Law 103-310, amended the Public Health Services Act to authorize specific activities pertaining to Infant Adoption Awareness (title XII, Subtitle A). The legislation requires the Secretary of the Department of Health and Human Services (DHHS) to award grants to adoption organizations to develop and implement programs to train the designated staff of eligible health centers in providing adoption information and referral to pregnant women on an equal basis with all other courses of action included in nondirective counseling for pregnant women. The term eligible health centers means public and nonprofit private entities that provide health services to pregnant women. The legislation also requires the Secretary to establish a set of best-practice guidelines to which the DHHS-funded training programs will adhere in providing training to staff of eligible health centers.
Requirements: Eligible applicants include: public and state controlled institutions of higher education; small businesses; special district governments; nonprofits having a 501(c)3 status with the IRS, other than institutions of higher education; county governments; for profit organizations other than small businesses; state governments; public housing authorities/Indian housing authorities; nonprofits that do not have a 501(c)3 status with the IRS, other than institutions of higher education; city or township governments; Native American tribal organizations (other than federally recognized tribal governments); Native American tribal governments (federally recognized); independent school districts; and private institutions of higher education. Faith-based and community organizations that meet the eligibility requirements are also eligible to receive awards under this funding opportunity announcement.
Geographic Focus: All States
Contact: Jan Shafer, Division of Program Innovation; (202) 205-8172; jan.shafer@acf.hhs.gov
Internet: www.acf.hhs.gov/cb/resource/adoption-awareness-traning
Sponsor: Administration for Children and Families
8th Floor, 1250 Maryland Avenue, SW
Washington, D.C. 20024

ACF Marriage Strengthening Research & Dissemination Center Grants   85
The Administration for Children and Families (ACF) is soliciting applications for the establishment of a Marriage Strengthening Research & Dissemination Center. The grantee will oversee a 60-month plan that aims to form a nexus between basic and applied research and evaluation on marriage and families in the United States and programmatic approaches to supporting healthy marriages and families, especially approaches fundable by the federal Healthy Marriage and Relationship Education (HMRE) program. The Center will contribute to the research/evaluation base relevant to marriage/relationships

(including current and future relationships among youth) and HMRE programs/practices; build and support capacity for demographic trends and practice-focused research and evaluation; and translate and disseminate emerging research and evaluation. The Center will be expected to have a primary focus on economically disadvantaged populations and other under-studied population groups. The Center also will be expected to actively engage a range of stakeholders, including researchers, evaluators, practitioners, program officials and policymakers, throughout the course of the project. The application due date is July 11.
Requirements: Eligible applicants include: state governments; county governments; city or township governments; special district governments; independent school districts; public and state controlled institutions of higher education; Native American tribal governments (federally recognized); public housing authorities and/or Indian housing authorities; Native American tribal organizations (other than federally recognized tribal governments); nonprofits having a 501(c)3 status with the IRS, other than institutions of higher education; nonprofits that do not have a 501(c)3 status with the IRS, other than institutions of higher education; private institutions of higher education; for profit organizations other than small businesses; and small businesses.
Restrictions: Applications from individuals (including sole proprietorships) and foreign entities are not eligible and will be disqualified from competitive review and from funding under this announcement.
Geographic Focus: All States
Contact: Samantha Illangasekare, Program Officer; (202) 401-5692 or (202) 401-9333; samantha.illangasekare@acf.hhs.gov
Internet: ami.grantsolutions.gov/index.cfm?switch=foa&fon=HHS-2018-ACF-OPRE-PR-1372
Sponsor: Administration for Children and Families
330 C Street, SW
Washington, D.C. 20201

ACF National Human Trafficking Hotline Grants **86**

The overall purpose of this project is to support the Administration for Children and Families in its efforts to: describe the activities, procedures, and organization of the National Human Trafficking Hotline (NHTH) program, including staff training, staff capacity, and service delivery; describe the customer service of the NHTH, for example who contacts the NHTH, and what information or assistance do they seek; describe the immediate outcomes of the NHTH, specifically with regard to experiences of callers and users; and explore the creation of one or more new performance measures, to enable NHTH to explain its activities and accomplishments in an ongoing way to stakeholders. The Administration for Children and Families, Office on Trafficking in Persons announces that funds will be available for the NHTH program. With these funds, the NHTH program seeks to support the operation of a dedicated, toll-free, 24-hour, seven days a week, every day of the year U.S. national telephone and online communication system with trained and experienced human trafficking advocates that provide services and assistance to victims of severe forms of labor and sex trafficking in persons. Multi-lingual services and assistance for foreign and domestic victims must include crisis intervention, information and referrals to anti-trafficking and/or direct victim services programs, temporary lodging and/or housing resources, and access to other emergency assistance. The overall goals of the NHTH program are: to operate the National Human Trafficking Hotline, a 24/7 U.S national telephone and online communication hotline system with experienced and trained anti-trafficking advocates; to increase the identification and protection of victims of severe forms of human trafficking; to provide information and service referrals to human trafficking victims using a trauma-informed, victim-centered approach, and in a timely manner; and to notify law enforcement agencies of potential cases of human trafficking as well as instances when a trafficking victim is in imminent danger, and document emerging trafficking schemes to assist in the detection and investigation of trafficking cases. One award will be approved, ranging from $800,000 to $1,500,000. Electronically submitted applications must be submitted no later than June 10, with an estimated program start date of September 30.
Requirements: The National Human Trafficking Hotline (NHTH) program must: work cooperatively with law enforcement and other key stakeholders to support appropriate notification and interventions on behalf of potential victims in distress; have the capacity to receive and process requests in multiple formats (i.e. text, chat, email, and telephonically); and take reasonable measures to safeguard protected personally identifiable information.
Geographic Focus: All States
Date(s) Application is Due: Jun 10
Amount of Grant: 800,000 - 1,500,000 USD
Contact: Ann Rivera, Program Officer; (202) 401-5506 or (202) 401-9220; fax (202) 205-3598; ann.rivera@acf.hhs.gov
Internet: www.acf.hhs.gov/opre/research/project/evaluation-of-the-national-human-trafficking-hotline-program
Sponsor: Administration for Children and Families
330 C Street, SW
Washington, D.C. 20201

ACF Native American Social and Economic Development Strategies for Alaska Grants **87**

Within the Department of Health and Human Services (HHS), ANA serves all Native Americans, including federally recognized tribes, American Indian and Alaska Native organizations, Native Hawaiian organizations and Native populations throughout the Pacific Basin (including American Samoa, Guam, and the Commonwealth of the Northern Mariana Islands). The ANA, within the Administration for Children and Families (ACF), announces the availability of funds for new community-based projects under the ANA Social and Economic Development Strategies for Alaska-SEDS-AK. This Funding Opportunity Announcement (FOA) is focused on community-driven projects designed to grow local economies, strengthen Alaskan Native families, including the preservation of Alaskan Native American cultures, and decrease the high rate of current challenges caused by the lack of community-based businesses, and social and economic infrastructure in Alaskan Native communities. Awards will range from $50,000 to $200,000, and the annual application deadline is April 24.
Requirements: Eligible applicants include Federally recognized Indian Tribes; consortia of Indian Tribes; incorporated non-Federally recognized Tribes; incorporated non-profit, multi-purpose, community-based Indian organizations; urban Indian centers; National or regional incorporated non-profit Native American organizations with Native American community-specific objectives; Alaska Native villages, as defined in the Alaska Native Claims Settlement Act and/or non-profit village consortia; incorporated non-profit Alaska Native multi-purpose, community-based organizations; non-profit Alaska Native Regional Corporations/Associations in Alaska with village-specfic projects; non-profit native organizations in Alaska with village-specific projects; public and non-profit private agencies serving Native Hawaiians; public and private non-profit agencies serving native peoples from Guam, American Samoa, or the Commonwealth of the Northern Mariana Islands (the populations served may be located on these islands or in the United States); tribally controlled community colleges, tribally controlled post-secondary vocational institutions, and colleges and universities located in Hawaii, Guam, American Samoa, or the Commonwealth of the Northern Mariana Islands which serve Native Pacific Islanders; and non-profit Alaska Native community entities or tribal governing bodies (Indian Reorganization Act or Traditional Councils) as recognized by the Bureau of Indian Affairs. Faith-based and community organizations that meet eligibility requirements are eligible to receive awards under this funding opportunity announcement.
Restrictions: Individuals, foreign entities, and sole proprietorship organizations are not eligible to compete for, or receive, awards made under this announcement.
Geographic Focus: All States
Date(s) Application is Due: Apr 24
Amount of Grant: 50,000 - 200,000 USD
Contact: Carmelia Strickland, Director; (202) 401-6741; fax (202) 690-7441; carmelia.strickland@acf.hhs.gov or anacomments@acf.hhs.gov
Tim Chappelle; (202) 401-4855; fax (202) 690-7441; tim.chappelle@acf.hhs.gov
Internet: www.acf.hhs.gov/ana/resource/2016-active-grants-in-social-and-economic-development-strategies-alaska
Sponsor: Administration for Children and Families
370 L'Enfant Promenade SW, Aerospace Center, 2nd Floor-West
Washington, D.C. 20447

ACF Native Youth Initiative for Leadership, Empowerment, and Development Grants **88**

The Administration for Native Americans (ANA), within the Administration for Children and Families (ACF), announces the availability funds for the Native Youth I-LEAD. This program will emphasize a comprehensive, culturally-appropriate approach to ensure that all young Native people can thrive and reach their full potential by fostering Native youth resilience, capacity building, and leadership. Native Youth I-LEAD will specifically focus on implementation of community programs that promote Native youth resiliency and foster protective factors such as connections with Native languages and Elders, positive peer groups, culturally-responsive parenting resources, models of safe sanctuary, and reconnection with traditional healing. Projects will also promote Native youth leadership development through the establishment of local models to instill confidence in Native youth of their value and potential, preparation of older youth to be role models for younger peers, and activities that foster leadership and skills-building. In addition, it is intended that Native youth must be actively involved during the planning and implementation phases of the projects to ensure that they are responsive to the needs of Native youth in the communities to be served and to ensure that youth remain engaged throughout the project period. The awards will range from $100,000 to $300,000, and the application deadline is April 24.
Requirements: Non-profit organizations representing American Indians, Alaska Natives, Native Hawaiians, and other Native American Pacific Islanders, including American Samoa, Guam, and the Commonwealth of the Northern Mariana Islands are eligible applicants under this announcement. This includes: Native American tribal governments (Federally recognized); nonprofits having a 501(c)3 status with the IRS, other than institutions of higher education; and Native American tribal organizations (other than Federally recognized tribal governments).
Restrictions: Applications from individuals (including sole proprietorships) and foreign entities are not eligible and will be disqualified from competitive review and from funding under this announcement.
Geographic Focus: All States
Date(s) Application is Due: Apr 24
Amount of Grant: 100,000 - 300,000 USD
Contact: Carmelia Strickland, Director; (202) 401-6741; fax (202) 690-7441; carmelia.strickland@acf.hhs.gov
Tim Chappelle; (202) 401-4855; fax (202) 690-7441; tim.chappelle@acf.hhs.gov
Internet: www.acf.hhs.gov/ana/grants/funding-opportunities
Sponsor: Administration for Children and Families
370 L'Enfant Promenade SW, Aerospace Center, 2nd Floor-West
Washington, D.C. 20447

ACF Promoting Safe and Stable Families (PSSF) Program Grants **89**

The discretionary fund activities funded by the Promoting Safe and Stable Families (PSSF) Program are meant to develop a coordinated and integrated service system that builds on the strengths of families and communities; emphasize collaborative approaches, early identification of issues and the delivery of prevention, intervention and support services; prevent child abuse and neglect, protect children from further abuse, and promote permanency for children within their own families or with kinship or adoptive families; and strengthen families and remove barriers to child safety, permanency and well-being.

Requirements: Eligible applicants include: for profit organizations other than small businesses; Native American tribal governments (Federally recognized); county governments; Native American tribal organizations (other than federally recognized tribal governments); state governments; nonprofits that do not have a 501(c)3 status with the IRS, other than institutions of higher education; city or township governments; and nonprofits having a 501(c)3 status with the IRS, other than institutions of higher education.
Geographic Focus: All States
Contact: Jan Shafer, Division of Program Innovation; (202) 205-8172; jan.shafer@acf.hhs.gov
Internet: www.acf.hhs.gov/cb/resource/pssf-program
Sponsor: Administration for Children and Families
8th Floor, 1250 Maryland Avenue, SW
Washington, D.C. 20024

ACF Refugee Career Pathways Grants   90

The Office of Refugee Resettlement within the Administration for Children and Families invites eligible entities to submit competitive grant applications for the Refugee Career Pathways program. Through the RCP Program ORR will provide funding to implement projects assisting refugees to qualify for licenses and certifications necessary to attain employment and improve self-sufficiency. Allowable activities will include case management, training and technical assistance, specialized English language training, and mentoring. Grantees may also provide refugee participants with financial assistance for costs related to the establishment or re-establishment of credentials, such as obtaining educational credits or enrollment in required certification programs. Grantees are encouraged to collaborate with professional associations, universities, and others with expertise in this area to facilitate career opportunities in ways that supplement, rather than supplant, existing services. Electronically submitted applications must be submitted no later than 11:59 p.m., ET, on June 2. Twelve grants will be awarded, ranging from $150,000 to $250,000.
Requirements: Eligible applicants include: public and state controlled institutions of higher education; state governments; nonprofits having a 501(c)3 status with the IRS, other than institutions of higher education; Native American tribal governments (federally recognized); nonprofits that do not have a 501(c)3 status with the IRS, other than institutions of higher education; public housing authorities/Indian housing authorities; special district governments; county governments; private institutions of higher education; Native American tribal organizations (other than federally recognized tribal governments); independent school districts; and city or township governments. Faith-based and community organizations that meet the eligibility requirements are also eligible to receive awards under this funding opportunity announcement.
Geographic Focus: All States
Date(s) Application is Due: Jun 2
Amount of Grant: 150,000 - 250,000 USD
Contact: Anastasia Brown, Program Officer; (202) 401-4559 or (202) 401-9246; fax (202) 401-5487; anastasia.brown@acf.hhs.gov
Internet: www.acf.hhs.gov/orr/refugees
Sponsor: Administration for Children and Families
Mary E. Switzer Building, 330 C Street, SW
Washington, D.C. 20201

ACF Refugee Health Promotion Grants   91

The Refugee Health Promotion Grant is now available to states, Wilson/Fish agencies, and state designees that serve refugees, with a special focus on recent arrivals and those that have been in the country two years or less, but still continue to face serious challenges with regards to access to health and mental health services. The RHP program is part of the Division of Refugee Health. The goal of the RHP program is to incorporate a framework of health services from arrival to self-sufficiency, ranging from attending health orientation and education classes, to accessing health services, and obtaining affordable ongoing health care. Within this framework, and differing from the PHG, there is a special emphasis placed on: health literacy; access to health and emotional wellness services, and access to affordable health care beyond the initial services provided upon arrival into the United States. The Refugee Health Promotion Grant is awarded to applicants who can adequately demonstrate their ability to incorporate health equity through a comprehensive, statewide approach, by supporting and streamlining activities that promote health and emotional wellness for refugees and other eligible applicants. Electronically submitted applications must be submitted no later than 11:59 p.m., ET, on March 24. Approximately 45 grants will be awarded, ranging from $75,000 to $200,000.
Requirements: Eligible applicants include: the state government agency that is responsible for the refugee program under 45 CFR 400.5 or such agency's designee or the state government agency responsible for the refugee health program as evidenced by ORR's review of the State Plan; and an agency that has statewide responsibility for an alternative to the state-administered program in lieu of the state under a Wilson/Fish grant authorized by section 412(e)7 of the INA or such agency's designee. Faith-based and community organizations that meet the eligibility requirements are eligible to receive awards under this funding opportunity announcement.
Restrictions: Eligible entities may only submit one application per state or designate one entity to apply on its behalf.
Geographic Focus: All States
Date(s) Application is Due: Mar 24
Amount of Grant: 75,000 - 200,000 USD
Contact: Henley Porter, Program Officer; (202) 401-5585 or (202) 401-9246; fax (202) 401-5487; henley.porter@acf.hhs.gov
Internet: www.acf.hhs.gov/orr/programs/preventive-health
Sponsor: Administration for Children and Families
Mary E. Switzer Building, 330 C Street, SW
Washington, D.C. 20201

ACF Runaway and Homeless Youth Training and Technical   92
Assistance Center Grants

The Family and Youth Services Bureau (FYSB) supports a national Training and Technical Assistance effort designed to enhance and promote the continuous evidence based quality improvement of services with a focus on the social and emotional well being of children, youth and families served by FYSB funded runaway and homeless youth grantees. The Bureau expects to award one cooperative agreement to enhance the programmatic and administrative capacities of public and private agencies to provide services to the targeted populations. Applicants will be expected to provide evidence of their ability to provide services to all grantees of the Administration of Children and Families (ACF) Federal geographic regional locations. Applicants must serve all ten ACF Federal Regions and may include subcontractors to provide services that will cover the regional multi-State areas. This funding opportunity is a 36 month project with five 12-month budget periods. The award will range from $1.5 million to $2.1 million. The deadline for all application materials is June 13.
Requirements: Eligible applicants include: Native American tribal organizations (other than Federally recognized tribal governments); nonprofits that do not have a 501(c)3 status with the IRS, other than institutions of higher education; public and State controlled institutions of higher education; private institutions of higher education; and nonprofits having a 501(c)3 status with the IRS, other than institutions of higher education.
Restrictions: Applications from individuals (including sole proprietorships) and foreign entities are not eligible and will be disqualified from competitive review and from funding under this announcement.
Geographic Focus: All States
Date(s) Application is Due: Jun 13
Amount of Grant: 1,500,000 - 2,100,000 USD
Contact: Gloria Watkins, Program Officer; (202) 205-9546; gloria.watkins@acf.hhs.gov
Internet: www.acf.hhs.gov/fysb/programs/runaway-homeless-youth/programs/rhyttac
Sponsor: Administration for Children and Families
118 Q Street NE
Washington, D.C. 20002-2132

ACF Social and Economic Development Strategies Grants   93

Grant awards made under this Funding Opportunity Announcement are for projects that promote economic and social self sufficiency for American Indians, Alaska Natives, Native Hawaiians, and other Native American Pacific Islanders from American Samoa, Guam, and Commonwealth of the Northern Mariana Islands. ANA is particularly interested in projects designed to grow local economies, strengthen Native American families, and decrease the high rate of social challenges caused by the lack of community-based business, and social and economic infrastructure. ANA has identified two major program areas of interest for this funding opportunity announcement, which include social development and economic development. In the area of social development, of most interest are proposals that improve: human services; community living; early childhood development; youth development; community health; arts and culture; safety and security; nutrition and fitness; and the strengthening of families. In the area of economic development, of most interest are proposals that improve: economic stability; economic competitiveness; agriculture; infrastructure; emergency preparedness; subsistence; and commercial trade. Awards will range from $100,000 to $400,000, and the current application deadline is April 24.
Requirements: Eligible applicants include Federally recognized Indian Tribes; consortia of Indian Tribes; incorporated non-Federally recognized Tribes; incorporated non-profit, multi-purpose, community-based Indian organizations; urban Indian centers; National or regional incorporated non-profit Native American organizations with Native American community-specific objectives; Alaska Native villages, as defined in the Alaska Native Claims Settlement Act and/or non-profit village consortia; incorporated non-profit Alaska Native multi-purpose, community-based organizations; non-profit Alaska Native Regional Corporations/Associations in Alaska with village-specfic projects; non-profit native organizations in Alaska with village-specific projects; public and non-profit private agencies serving Native Hawaiians; public and private non-profit agencies serving native peoples from Guam, American Samoa, or the Commonwealth of the Northern Mariana Islands (the populations served may be located on these islands or in the United States); tribally controlled community colleges, tribally controlled post-secondary vocational institutions, and colleges and universities located in Hawaii, Guam, American Samoa, or the Commonwealth of the Northern Mariana Islands which serve Native Pacific Islanders; and non-profit Alaska Native community entities or tribal governing bodies (Indian Reorganization Act or Traditional Councils) as recognized by the Bureau of Indian Affairs. Faith-based and community organizations that meet eligibility requirements are eligible to receive awards under this funding opportunity announcement. Grantees must provide at least 20 percent of the total approved cost of the project.
Restrictions: Individuals, foreign entities, and sole proprietorship organizations are not eligible to compete for, or receive, awards made under this announcement.
Geographic Focus: All States, American Samoa, Guam, Marshall Islands, Northern Mariana Islands
Date(s) Application is Due: Apr 24
Amount of Grant: 100,000 - 400,000 USD
Contact: Carmelia Strickland, Director; (202) 401-6741; fax (202) 690-7441; carmelia.strickland@acf.hhs.gov
Tim Chappelle; (202) 401-4855; fax (202) 690-7441; tim.chappelle@acf.hhs.gov
Internet: www.acf.hhs.gov/ana/programs/seds
Sponsor: Administration for Children and Families
370 L'Enfant Promenade SW, Aerospace Center, 2nd Floor-West
Washington, D.C. 20447

ACF Street Outreach Program Grants 94

The mission of the Street Outreach Program is to support the organizations and communities that work every day to put an end to youth homelessness, adolescent pregnancy and domestic violence. Primarily, the Street Outreach Program enables organizations around the country to help young people get off the streets. To that end, the program promotes efforts by its grantees to build relationships between street outreach workers and runaway, homeless and street youth. Grantees also provide support services that aim to move youth into stable housing and prepare them for independence. The program's ultimate goal is to prevent the sexual abuse or exploitation of young people living on the streets or in unstable housing. Overall, street outreach programs provide services directly or by collaborating with other agencies. In particular, street outreach programs work closely with other organizations that work to protect and treat young people who have been or are at risk of sexual abuse or exploitation. Street outreach services include the following: street-based education and outreach; access to emergency shelter; survival aid; individual assessments; trauma-informed treatment and counseling; prevention and education activities; information and referrals; crisis intervention; and follow-up support. Approximately fifteen (15) to twenty (20) awards will be approved, ranging from $90,000 to $200,000 each. The annual application deadline is April 10.

Requirements: Eligible applicants include: state governments; public and state controlled institutions of higher education; special district governments; Native American tribal organizations (other than Federally recognized tribal governments); public housing authorities/Indian housing authorities; independent school districts; city or township governments; Native American tribal governments (Federally recognized); county governments; nonprofits that do not have a 501(c)3 status with the IRS, other than institutions of higher education; and nonprofits having a 501(c)3 status with the IRS, other than institutions of higher education.

Geographic Focus: All States

Date(s) Application is Due: Apr 10

Amount of Grant: 90,000 - 200,000 USD

Contact: Oluwatoyin Akintoye; (202) 205-7745; oluwatoyin.akintoye@ACF.hhs.gov

Internet: www.acf.hhs.gov/fysb/resource/sop-fact-sheet

Sponsor: Administration for Children and Families

118 Q Street NE

Washington, D.C. 20002-2132

ACF Sustainable Employment and Economic Development Strategies Grants 95

The Administration for Native Americans (ANA) supports economic development in Native American communities through the provision of discretionary grants to tribal governments and native-serving non-profit organizations. The current economic climate has increased ANA's focus on developing employment opportunities and business creation in native communities, resulting in this special funding initiative to promote Sustainable Employment and Economic Development Strategies (SEEDS). In an effort to reduce unemployment and stimulate local economies, ANA, within the Administration for Children and Families, announces the availability of funds for community-based projects that will foster economic development through the creation of small businesses and sustainable job growth. One of ANA's primary goals is to promote economic self-sufficiency for American Indians, Native Hawaiians, Alaskan Natives, and Native American Pacific Islanders, including American Samoa Natives. In pursuit of this goal, four priorities that ANA will promote through the SEEDS initiative are: creation of sustainable employment opportunities; professional training and skill development that increases participants' employability and earning potential; creation and development of small businesses and entrepreneurial activities; and a demonstrated strategy and commitment to keeping the jobs and revenues generated by project activities within the native communities being served. Improving access to employment opportunities and supporting small businesses will enhance local economies, enable more tribal members to acquire and maintain gainful employment, and improve the long-term financial health of tribal members and their families.

Requirements: Eligible applicants include Federally recognized Indian Tribes; consortia of Indian Tribes; incorporated non-Federally recognized Tribes; incorporated non-profit, multi-purpose, community-based Indian organizations; urban Indian centers; National or regional incorporated non-profit Native American organizations with Native American community-specific objectives; Alaska Native villages, as defined in the Alaska Native Claims Settlement Act and/or non-profit village consortia; incorporated non-profit Alaska Native multi-purpose, community-based organizations; non-profit Alaska Native Regional Corporations/Associations in Alaska with village-specfic projects; non-profit native organizations in Alaska with village-specific projects; public and non-profit private agencies serving Native Hawaiians; public and private non-profit agencies serving native peoples from Guam, American Samoa, or the Commonwealth of the Northern Mariana Islands (the populations served may be located on these islands or in the United States); tribally controlled community colleges, tribally controlled post-secondary vocational institutions, and colleges and universities located in Hawaii, Guam, American Samoa, or the Commonwealth of the Northern Mariana Islands which serve Native Pacific Islanders; and non-profit Alaska Native community entities or tribal governing bodies (Indian Reorganization Act or Traditional Councils) as recognized by the Bureau of Indian Affairs. Faith-based and community organizations that meet eligibility requirements are eligible to receive awards under this funding opportunity announcement. Awards will range from $100,000 to $400,000, and the annual application deadline is April 6.

Restrictions: Individuals, foreign entities, and sole proprietorship organizations are not eligible to compete for, or receive, awards made under this announcement.

Geographic Focus: All States

Date(s) Application is Due: Apr 24

Amount of Grant: 100,000 - 400,000 USD

Contact: Carmelia Strickland, Director; (202) 401-6741; fax (202) 690-7441; carmelia.strickland@acf.hhs.gov or anacomments@acf.hhs.gov

Tim Chappelle; (202) 401-4855; fax (202) 690-7441; tim.chappelle@acf.hhs.gov

Internet: www.acf.hhs.gov/ana/resource/sustainable-employment-and-economic-strategies

Sponsor: Administration for Children and Families

370 L'Enfant Promenade SW, Aerospace Center, 2nd Floor-West

Washington, D.C. 20447

ACF Transitional Living Program and Maternity Group Homes Grants 96

The Family and Youth Services Bureau (FYSB) is forecasting a funding opportunity announcement for the Transitional Living Program (TLP) and for Maternity Group Homes (MGH) for a five year project period. The TLP and MGH projects will work to implement, enhance, and/or support promising intervention strategies for the effective transition of homeless youth (for the purposes of MGH projects, homeless youth and their dependent child(ren)) to self-sufficiency. Both projects must provide safe, stable, and appropriate shelter for up to 21 months and comprehensive services that supports the transition of homeless youth to stable living. More than 100 awards will be funded, ranging from $100,000 to $194,726. Electronically submitted applications must be submitted no later than 11:59 p.m., ET, on June 13.

Requirements: Eligible applicants include: public housing authorities/Indian housing authorities; special district governments; Native American tribal governments (Federally recognized); nonprofits having a 501(c)3 status with the IRS, other than institutions of higher education; private institutions of higher education; independent school districts; public and state controlled institutions of higher education; county governments; nonprofits that do not have a 501(c)3 status with the IRS, other than institutions of higher education; Native American tribal organizations (other than Federally recognized tribal governments); city or township governments; and state governments.

Geographic Focus: All States

Date(s) Application is Due: Jun 13

Amount of Grant: 100,000 - 194,726 USD

Contact: Angie Webley, Program Officer; (202) 401-5490; aAngie.webley@acf.hhs.gov

Internet: www.acf.hhs.gov/fysb/grants

Sponsor: Administration for Children and Families

118 Q Street NE

Washington, D.C. 20002-2132

ACF Tribal Maternal, Infant, and Early Childhood Home Visiting Program: Development and Implementation Grants 97

This funding opportunity announcement (FOA) provides funds for the Tribal Maternal, Infant, and Early Childhood Home Visiting Grant Program (Tribal MIECHV) Development and Implementation Grants. Funds will support 5-year grants (cooperative agreements) between ACF and federally-recognized Indian tribes (or a consortium of Indian tribes), tribal organizations, or urban Indian organizations to: conduct community needs assessments; develop the infrastructure needed for widespread planning, adopting, implementing, expanding, enhancing, and sustaining of evidence-based maternal, infant, and early childhood home visiting programs; and provide high-quality evidence-based home visiting services to pregnant women and families with young children aged birth to kindergarten entry. Home visiting programs are intended to promote outcomes such as improved maternal and prenatal health, infant health, and child health and development; reduced child maltreatment; improved parenting practices related to child development outcomes; improved school readiness; improved family socio-economic status; improved coordination of referrals to community resources and supports; and reduced incidence of injuries, crime, and domestic violence. The goals of the Tribal MIECHV program are to support healthy, happy, successful American Indian and Alaska Native (AIAN) children and families through a coordinated, high-quality, evidence-based home visiting strategy, and to continue to build the evidence base for home visiting in tribal communities. An estimated four awards will range from $100,000 to $400,000 each, and the application deadline is March 23.

Requirements: This FOA is intended for tribal entities that do not have prior experience with implementing evidence-based home visiting models, performance measurement systems, and rigorous evaluation. Eligible applicants include: nonprofits having a 501(c)3 status with the IRS, other than institutions of higher education; Native American tribal organizations (other than Federally recognized tribal governments; and Native American tribal governments (Federally recognized).

Restrictions: Applications from individuals (including sole proprietorships) and foreign entities are not eligible and will be disqualified from competitive review and from funding under this announcement.

Geographic Focus: All States

Date(s) Application is Due: Mar 23

Amount of Grant: 100,000 - 400,000 USD

Contact: Moushumi Beltangady, Program Officer; (202) 260-3613; fax (202) 401-0981; tribal.homevisiting@acf.hhs.gov

Tim Chappelle, Office of Grants Management; (202) 401-4855; fax (202) 690-7441; tim.chappelle@acf.hhs.gov or tichappelle@acf.hhs.gov

Internet: www.acf.hhs.gov/ecd/home-visiting/tribal-home-visiting

Sponsor: Administration for Children and Families

330 C Street SW

Washington, D.C. 20201

ACF Tribal Maternal, Infant, and Early Childhood Home Visiting Program: Implementation and Expansion Grants 98

This funding opportunity announcement (FOA) provides funds for the Tribal Maternal, Infant, and Early Childhood Home Visiting Program (Tribal MIECHV) Implementation and Expansion Grants. Funds will support 5-year grants (cooperative agreements) between the Administration for Children and Families (ACF) and federally-recognized Indian tribes (or a consortium of Indian tribes), tribal organizations, or urban Indian organizations that are currently operating an evidence-based home visiting program and propose to sustain and/or expand their established infrastructure for home visiting services in tribal communities. The primary goals of the Tribal MIECHV program include: supporting the development of happy, healthy, and successful American Indian and Alaska Native (AI/AN) children and families through a coordinated home visiting strategy that addresses critical maternal and child health, development, early learning, family support, and child abuse and neglect prevention needs; implementing high-quality, culturally-relevant, evidence-based home visiting programs in AI/AN communities; expanding the evidence base around home visiting interventions with Native populations; and supporting and strengthening cooperation and coordination and promoting linkages among various programs that serve pregnant women, expectant fathers, young children, and families, resulting in coordinated, comprehensive early childhood systems in grantee communities. An estimated twenty awards will range from $250,000 to $1,000,000 each, and the application deadline is March 23.

Requirements: Eligible applicants include: nonprofits having a 501(c)3 status with the IRS, other than institutions of higher education; Native American tribal organizations (other than Federally recognized tribal governments; and Native American tribal governments (Federally recognized).

Restrictions: Applications from individuals (including sole proprietorships) and foreign entities are not eligible and will be disqualified from competitive review and from funding under this announcement.

Geographic Focus: All States
Date(s) Application is Due: Mar 23
Amount of Grant: 250,000 - 1,000,000 USD
Contact: Moushumi Beltangady, Program Officer; (202) 260-3613; fax (202) 401-0981; tribal.homevisiting@acf.hhs.gov
Tim Chappelle, Office of Grants Management; (202) 401-4855; fax (202) 690-7441; tim.chappelle@acf.hhs.gov or tichappelle@acf.hhs.gov
Internet: www.acf.hhs.gov/ecd/home-visiting/tribal-home-visiting
Sponsor: Administration for Children and Families
330 C Street SW
Washington, D.C. 20201

ACF Unaccompanied Refugee Children Grants   99
The Office of Refugee Resettlement, a Division of Children's Services under the Unaccompanied Refugee Minors program (ORR/DCS/URM) provides child welfare services and benefits to children eligible for placement, services and benefits. As it exists today, the Unaccompanied Refugee Minors (URM) program provides such youth with the same range of child welfare benefits and services available to other foster children, including services identified in a State's plans under titles IV-B and IV-E of the Social Security Act, such as associated independent living benefits and services. The existing program is funded through grants to states and is subject to state child welfare laws and regulations. This Alternative Transitional Services for Unaccompanied Refugee Minors (ATS URM) project will provide time-limited transitional placement, benefits and services to assist eligible older youth to obtain the skills necessary for economic self-sufficiency and independent living, as quickly as possible. A range of possible placement options are anticipated. Placements provided to youth under the age of 18 must be licensed according to state/local licensing regulations. Major program activities will include: work readiness training; job placement; and retention in a supportive environment. Beneficiaries will include older youth eligible for services, including but not limited to Special Immigrant Juveniles and trafficking victims. Two awards are anticipated, ranging from $700,000 to $2,000,000. Electronically submitted applications must be submitted no later than 11:59 p.m., ET, on June 2.

Requirements: Beneficiaries must be oriented towards entering the work force and obtaining independence in a short period of time. Eligible applicants include: private institutions of higher education; nonprofits having a 501(c)3 status with the IRS, other than institutions of higher education; and nonprofits that do not have a 501(c)3 status with the IRS, other than institutions of higher education. Faith-based and community organizations that meet the eligibility requirements are eligible to receive awards under this funding opportunity announcement.

Geographic Focus: All States
Amount of Grant: 700,000 - 2,000,000 USD
Contact: Shawna Pinckney, Program Officer; (888) 242-0684; OHSTech@reviewops.org
Internet: www.acf.hhs.gov/orr/programs/ucs
Sponsor: Administration for Children and Families
Mary E. Switzer Building, 330 C Street, SW
Washington, D.C. 20201

ACF Voluntary Agencies Matching Grants   100
The Voluntary Agencies Matching Grant program is an alternative to public cash assistance providing services to help ORR-eligible populations (refugees, asylees, Cuban and Haitian entrants, certain Amerasians from Vietnam, Victims of Severe Forms of Trafficking, and Special Immigrant Visa Holders (SIVs) to become economically self-sufficient within 120 to 180 days of program eligibility. Services required under this program include, but are not limited to, case management, employment services, maintenance assistance and cash allowance, and administration. Self-sufficiency must be achieved without accessing public cash assistance. Enrollment is available to all ORR-eligible populations meeting the minimum employability requirements as defined under the Program Guidelines; however, enrollment must occur within 31 days of becoming eligible to ensure adequate services are provided and self-sufficiency is achieved and maintained within the period of eligibility. Client services provided through MG include, but are not limited to, case management, employment services, housing and utilities, food, transportation, cash allowance, health and medical, English language training, social adjustment, and other support services. Electronically submitted applications must be submitted no later than 11:59 p.m., ET, on June 30. An estimated nine grants will be awarded, ranging from $1,000,000 to $26,400,000.

Requirements: Eligible applicants are: Church World Service and/or Immigration and Refugee Program, New York, New York; Domestic and Foreign Missionary Society

of the Protestant Episcopal Church of the U.S.A., New York, New, York; Ethiopian Community Development Council, Inc./Refugee Resettlement Program, Arlington, Virginia; Hebrew Immigrant Aid Society/Refugee and Immigrant Services, Silver Spring, Maryland; International Rescue Committee/Resettlement, New York, New York; Lutheran Immigration and Refugee Service, Baltimore, Maryland; U.S. Conference of Catholic Bishops, Washington, D.C; U.S. Committee for Refugees and Immigrants, Arlington, Virginia; and World Relief Corporation of National Association of Evangelicals/Refugee and Immigration Programs, Baltimore, Maryland. Faith-based and community organizations that meet the eligibility requirements are also eligible to receive awards under this funding opportunity announcement.

Geographic Focus: All States
Date(s) Application is Due: Jun 30
Amount of Grant: 1,000,000 - 26,400,000 USD
Contact: Henley Porter; (202) 619-0257 or (202) 401-9246; fax (202) 401-5487
Internet: www.acf.hhs.gov/orr/programs/matching-grants/about
Sponsor: Administration for Children and Families
Mary E. Switzer Building, 330 C Street, SW
Washington, D.C. 20201

Achelis and Bodman Foundation Grants   101
The Achelis and Bodman Foundation was formed in 2015 through the merger of The Achelis Foundation and The Bodman Foundation. These foundations had been run jointly for many years, but the merger brought with it certain operational and administrative efficiencies. Each year the Foundation makes approximately $5 million in grants. Although the Foundation is relatively small, it supports a broad variety of institutions rather than choosing to focus narrowly on one or two fields. In part this reflects the richness of New York's not-for-profit sector, with hundreds of strong potential grantees.

Requirements: Nonprofit organizations based in New York City and northern New Jersey that are tax-exempt under Section 501(c)3 of the Internal Revenue Code and fall within the program areas of the Foundation are welcome to submit an inquiry or proposal letter by email. An initial inquiry to The Achelis and Bodman Foundation should include only the following items: a proposal letter that briefly summarizes the history of the project, need, objectives, time period, key staff, project budget, and evaluation plan; latest annual report; latest complete audited financial statements; and an IRS 501(c)3 tax-exemption letter.

Restrictions: The Foundation generally does not make grants for the following purposes or program areas: nonprofit organizations outside of New York and New Jersey; annual appeals, dinner functions, and fundraising events; endowments and capital campaigns; loans and deficit financing; direct grants to individuals; individual day-care and after-school programs; housing; organizations or projects based outside the U.S; small art, dance, music, and theater groups; individual K-12 schools (except charter schools); national health and mental health organizations; government agencies; or nonprofit organizations significantly funded or reimbursed by government agencies.

Geographic Focus: New Jersey, New York
Amount of Grant: Up to 300,000 USD
Samples: Hospital for Special Surgery; New York, New York; $80,000 - to support a research project personalizing treatment for children affected by juvenile dermatomyositis (2019). Classic Stage Company; New York, New York; $20,000 - for general operating support (2019).
Contact: John B. Krieger, Executive Director; (212) 644-0322; fax (212) 759-6510; info@AchelisBodman.org or application@achelisbodman.org
Internet: achelisbodman.org/guidelines/
Sponsor: Achelis and Bodman Foundation
420 Lexington Avenue Suite 2803 New York, NY
New York, NY 10170

Achelis Foundation Grants   102
Elisabeth Achelis was born in Brooklyn Heights in 1880. She used her inheritance from her father Fritz Achelis, who was President of the American Hard Rubber Company, to establish the Achelis Foundation in 1940 to aid and contribute to charitable, benevolent, educational and religious uses and purposes for the moral, ethical, physical, mental and intellectual well-being and progress of mankind; to aid and contribute to methods for the peaceful settlement of international differences; to aid and contribute to the furtherance of the objects and purposes of any charitable, benevolent, educational or religious institution or agency; and to establish and maintain charitable, benevolent and educational institutions and agencies. The Achelis Foundation shares trustees, staff, office space, and even a website with the Bodman Foundation which has a similar mission and geographic area of concentration (both foundations give in New York City, while the Bodman Foundation also gives in New Jersey). Funding is concentrated in six program areas: arts and culture; education; employment; health; public policy; and youth and families. Most recent awards have ranged from $10,000 to $200,000, though typical awards average $20,000 to $50,000.

Requirements: 501(c)3 organizations based in New York City that fall within the foundation's areas of interest are welcome to submit an inquiry or proposal letter by regular mail (initial inquiries by email or fax are not accepted, nor are CDs, DVDs, computer discs, or video tapes). An initial inquiry to the foundation should include only the following items: a proposal letter that briefly summarizes the history of the project, need, objectives, time period, key staff, project budget, and evaluation plan; the applicant's latest annual report and complete set of audited financial statements; and the applicant's IRS 501(c)3 tax-exemption letter. Applications may be submitted at any time during the year. Each request is reviewed by staff and will usually receive a written response within thirty days. Those requests deemed consistent with the interests and resources of the foundation will be evaluated further and more information will be requested. Foundation staff may request a site visit, conference call, or meeting. All grants are reviewed and approved by the Trustees at one of their three board meetings in May, September, or December.

Restrictions: The foundation generally does not make grants for the following purposes or program areas: nonprofit organizations outside of New York; annual appeals, dinner functions, and fundraising events; endowments and capital campaigns; loans and deficit financing; direct grants to individuals; individual day-care and after-school programs; housing; organizations or projects based outside the U.S; films or video projects; small art, dance, music, and theater groups; individual K-12 schools (except charter schools); national health and mental health organizations; and government agencies or nonprofit organizations significantly funded or reimbursed by government agencies. Limited resources prevent the foundations from funding the same organization on an ongoing annual basis.
Geographic Focus: New York
Amount of Grant: 10,000 - 200,000 USD
Samples: American Ballet Theatre, New York, New York, $25,000 - general operating support; East Harlem School at Exodus House, New York, New York, $25,000 - general operating support (2014; International Center for the Disabled, New York, New York, $25,000 - to support the ReadyNow program.
Contact: John B. Krieger; (212) 644-0322; fax (212) 759-6510; main@achelis-bodman-fnds.org
Internet: www.achelis-bodman-fnds.org/guidelines.html
Sponsor: Achelis Foundation
767 Third Avenue, 4th Floor
New York, NY 10017-2023

Ackerman Foundation Grants **103**
The Ackerman Foundation was established as a charitable trust in 1992 by James F. Ackerman, a local entrepreneur and philanthropist. As an Indianapolis based organization, grants are made predominately to central Indiana organizations as well as a few national medical research institutions. Specifically, the foundation focuses on Indiana cultural institutions and organizations benefiting health and human services, community development, and education. Grant requests will be considered for both operating fund purposes and as capital campaigns. The foundation does not have grant application forms. To be considered for assistance, an organization should write a brief one or two page letter describing its proposal. The Trustees of the foundation meet semi-annually on the business day that falls on or closest to June 15 and December 15.
Requirements: Established under the laws of the State of Indiana, the foundation considers grant proposals from eligible organizations which are tax exempt under the United States Internal Revenue Service Code section 501(c)3.
Restrictions: The foundation does not make grants to individuals.
Geographic Focus: Indiana
Date(s) Application is Due: May 15; Nov 15
Amount of Grant: 500 - 100,000 USD
Samples: Conner Prairie Museum, Fishers, Indiana, $1,000 - general operating support; Elevate Indy, Indianapolis, Indiana, $15,000 - general operating support; Providence Cristo Rey High School, Indianapolis, Indiana, $10,000 - general operating support.
Contact: John F. Ackerman; (317) 663-0205; fax (317) 663-0215; jdisbro@cardinalep.com
Internet: ackermanfoundation.com/
Sponsor: Ackerman Foundation of Indiana
8801 River Crossing Boulevard, Suite 320
Indianapolis, IN 46240

ACL Alternatives to Guardianship Youth Resource Center Grants **104**
The Administration on Disabilities (AoD) seeks to fund one five-year grant to create an Alternatives to Guardianship Youth Resource Center. Research shows the majority (57 percent) of people with Intellectual and Developmental Disabilities (ID/DD) ages 18 to 22 receiving publicly funded services have guardians. The Center will work to divert high school students with ID/DD away from guardianship to less restrictive decisional supports. The target audience for this information includes youth with ID/DD, parents and caregivers of high school students with ID/DD, special education teachers, education administrators, advocates, vocational rehabilitation counselors, guidance counselors, and school district officials. As a result of funding this Center, AoD expects that: 1.) More students with ID/DD will have more decisional options, such as Powers of Attorney, supported-decision-making (SDM), joint bank accounts, bill paying services, and medical or educational release forms, on completion of high school; 2.) Fewer young adults with I/DD will be subject to guardianship; 3.) The public will become more knowledgeable of alternatives to guardianship; and 4.) Youth will become more independent by gaining job experience and personal responsibilities. Award amounts typically range from $250,000 to $300,000.
Requirements: Applications will be submitted online. Eligible applicants include Private institutions of higher education; Native American tribal organizations (other than Federally recognized tribal governments); Independent school districts; Public and State controlled institutions of higher education; Nonprofits having a 501(c)3 status with the IRS; and Nonprofits that do not have a 501(c)3 status with the IRS.
Restrictions: Foreign entities are not eligible to compete for, or receive, awards made under this announcement.
Geographic Focus: All States
Date(s) Application is Due: Jun 29
Amount of Grant: 250,000 - 300,000 USD
Contact: Katherine Cargill-Willis; (202) 401-4634; katherine.cargill-Willis@acl.hhs.gov
Internet: www.grants.gov/web/grants/view-opportunity.html?oppId=324349
Sponsor: U.S. Department of Health and Human Services
330 C Street SW
Washington, D.C. 20201

ACL Disability and Rehabilitation Research Projects Program: Independent Living Transition Services for Youth and Young Adults Grants **105**
The purpose of the Disability and Rehabilitation Research Projects (DRRP), funded through the Disability and Rehabilitation Research Projects and Centers Program, is to plan and conduct research, demonstration projects, training, and related activities, including international activities, to develop methods, procedures, and rehabilitation technology that maximize the full inclusion and integration into society, employment, independent living, family support, and economic and social self-sufficiency of individuals with disabilities, especially individuals with the most severe disabilities, and to improve the effectiveness of services authorized under the Rehabilitation Act of 1973, as amended (Rehabilitation Act). This particular DRRP priority is a joint-funding collaboration between the National Institute on Disability, Independent Living, and Rehabilitation Research (NIDILRR) and the Independent Living Administration (ILA), both within the Administration for Community Living (ACL). The DRRP grant to be made under this priority will conduct research to generate evidence-based practices for services provided by Centers for Independent Living (CILs) to facilitate the transition of youth with significant disabilities from racial and ethnic minority backgrounds who were eligible for individualized education programs and who have completed their secondary education or otherwise left school. The amount given for this award is typically $1,293,390.
Requirements: Applications will be submitted online via the ACL website. Applicants under this priority must propose to conduct research to: (1) systematically identify promising practices for facilitating the transition of youth and young adults with significant disabilities from minority backgrounds, (2) develop at least two manualized transition interventions for youth and young adults with significant disabilities from minority backgrounds, and (3) assess the feasibility and efficacy of the transition interventions for youth and young adults with significant disabilities from minority backgrounds. Applicants must also include a plan of dissemination, training, and technical assistance services to CILs, regarding services to facilitate the transition of youth and young adults with significant disabilities from racial and ethnic minority backgrounds to post-secondary life. To help ensure the relevance of the research-based knowledge generated by this grant, CILs must be substantially involved in the design and implementation of the proposal, including all research, development, dissemination, training, and technical assistance activities. Minority entities are the only applicants that are eligible to apply for this grant opportunity. Section 21(b)(2)(A) of the Rehabilitation Act authorizes NIDILRR and ILA to make awards to minority entities and Indian tribes to carry out activities authorized under Titles II and VII of the Act, respectively. A minority entity is defined as a historically black college or university (a part B institution, as defined in section 322(2) of the Higher Education Act of 1965, as amended), a Hispanic-serving institution of higher education, an American Indian tribal college or university, or another institution of higher education whose minority student enrollment is at least 50 percent.
Restrictions: Foreign entities are not eligible to compete for, or receive, awards made under this announcement.
Geographic Focus: All States
Date(s) Application is Due: Aug 19
Amount of Grant: 1,293,390 USD
Contact: Marlene Spencer, Grantor Contact; (202) 401-4634; Marlene.spencer@acl.hhs.gov
Internet: www.grants.gov/web/grants/view-opportunity.html?oppId=316634
Sponsor: U.S. Department of Health and Human Services
330 C Street SW
Washington, D.C. 20201

ACL Neonatal Abstinence Syndrome National Training Initiative Grant **106**
The Administration on Intellectual and Developmental Disabilities (AIDD), Administration on Disabilities (AOD), Administration for Community Living (ACL), U.S. Department of Health and Human Services (HHS) announces the availability of Fiscal Year 2019 funds to award, on a competitive basis, a three year National Training Initiative (NTI) cooperative agreement to University Centers for Excellence in Developmental Disabilities Education, Research, and Service (UCEDDs). AOD anticipates awarding one neonatal abstinence syndrome (NAS) training agreement to pay for the federal share of this initiative. Funds will be used to support the implementation of a NAS training program. HHS is committed to ending the crisis of opioid addiction and overdose in America. This training initiative is intended to identify, and train practitioners in, emerging knowledge and evidence-based practices in screening, monitoring and care for children diagnosed with neonatal abstinence syndrome (NAS), or suspected of being impacted by related trauma exposure. This proposed opportunity seeks to address the gaps in access and delivery of quality services to children diagnosed with NAS. The desired performance outcomes include: (1) Increased collaboration and coordination among federal, state and local entities addressing NAS. (2) Increase in trauma-informed care in prevention and treatment services for neonates, families and caregivers. Evaluation of the results will be collected from practioners, trainees, families, UCEDD network partners and governmental agencies via customer satisfaction survey data collected pre and post interventions. Award amounts are typically worth $452,199.
Requirements: Applications will be submitted online via the ACL website. Section 151(b) of the DD Act states that from appropriations authorized under section 156(a) (1) and reserved under section 156(a) (2), grants shall be made to UCEDDs to carry out National Training Initiative grants. Entities eligible to apply for funds under this funding opportunity announcement are the 67 current AIDD grantees that are designated UCEDDs. Applications from other entities not designated as a current UCEDD by 2018 will not be reviewed.
Restrictions: Foreign entities are not eligible to compete for, or receive, awards made under this announcement.
Geographic Focus: All States
Date(s) Application is Due: Aug 20
Amount of Grant: 452,199 USD
Contact: Pamela O'Brien, Grantor Contact; (202) 401-4634; Pamela.O'Brien@acl.hhs.gov
Internet: www.grants.gov/web/grants/view-opportunity.html?oppId=313068

Sponsor: U.S. Department of Health and Human Services
330 C Street SW
Washington, D.C. 20201

ACL Rehabilitation Research and Training Center (RRTC) on 107
Employment of Transition-Age Youth with Disabilities Grants

The purpose of the RRTCs, which are funded through the Disability and Rehabilitation Research Projects and Centers Program, is to achieve the goals of, and improve the effectiveness of, services authorized under the Rehabilitation Act through well-designed research, training, technical assistance, and dissemination activities in important topical areas as specified by NIDILRR. These activities are designed to benefit people with disabilities, family members, rehabilitation service providers, policymakers and other research stakeholders. The purpose of this particular RRTC is to conduct research, training, technical assistance, and related activities to contribute to improved employment outcomes of transition-age youth with disabilities. Award amounts typically range from $850,000 to $875,000.
Requirements: Applications will be submitted online via the ACL website. Eligible applicants include states; public or private agencies, including for-profit agencies; public or private organizations, including for-profit organizations, IHEs; and Indian tribes and tribal organizations.
Restrictions: Foreign entities are not eligible to compete for, or receive, awards made under this announcement.
Geographic Focus: All States
Date(s) Application is Due: May 24
Amount of Grant: 850,000 - 875,000 USD
Contact: Patricia Barrett, Grantor Contact; (202) 401-4634; Patricia.Barrett@acl.hhs.gov
Internet: www.grants.gov/web/grants/view-opportunity.html?oppId=311514
Sponsor: U.S. Department of Health and Human Services
330 C Street SW
Washington, D.C. 20201

ACMP Foundation Community Music Grants 108

Awards provide funding to community arts organizations in support of ongoing programs that offer musicians of all ages the opportunity to play and be coached in chamber music. Community Music grants to organizations serving pre-college players favor programs for students of intermediate level and above. Grants ranging from $1,500 to $2,500 are generally made in support of scholarship aid and program staff salaries. This funding often makes it possible for students to experience chamber music for the first time. Community Music grants also support ongoing programs for adults at all levels of expertise in chamber music.
Restrictions: ACMP does not provide funding for the following: individual or group lessons in instrumental technique; choral or orchestral programs or performances; guest artist performances or travel; activities intended for audience development; general administration; or fundraising events.
Geographic Focus: All States, All Countries
Date(s) Application is Due: Apr 23
Amount of Grant: 3,000 USD
Samples: Baltimore Symphony Orchestra, Baltimore, Maryland, $3,000 - general operating support; I Cambristi (Tutti Cambristi), Brussels, Belgium, $2,000 - general operating support; New Horizons International Music Association, Philomath, Oregon, $3,000 - general operating support.
Contact: Jennifer Clarke, Executive Director; (212) 645-7424; fax (212) 741-2678; acmpfoundation@acmp.net or jclarke@acmp.net
Internet: acmp.net/sites/default/files/Community%20Music%20Program%20 Guidelines%20REV%202.6.18_1.pdf
Sponsor: Associated Chamber Music Players Foundation
1133 Broadway, Suite 810
New York, NY 10010-2007

Active Living Research Grants 109

Active Living Research has funded over 230 projects examining environmental and policy strategies that can promote daily physical activity for children and families across the United States. Many of these studies place special emphasis on research related to children of color and lower-income children who are at highest risk for obesity. Grants and award amounts vary by year.
Requirements: Requirements vary from one Call for Proposals to the next, and can all be found on the Active Living Research website. Grantees with projects funded for more than 12 months are required to submit an annual and a final report. The annual report is due one month after the completion of the first 12 months of your project, and the final report is due one month after the final project end date.
Restrictions: The program does not provide support for international activities, or for institutions in other countries.
Geographic Focus: All States
Contact: James F. Sallis, Program Director; (858) 246-2783; ALR@ucsd.edu
Internet: activelivingresearch.org/grantsearch/projects
Sponsor: Active Living Research
9500 Gilman Drive
La Jolla, CA 92093-0631

Acuity Charitable Foundation Grants 110

The Acuity Charitable Foundation was established in 2003 with a major donation from the Acuity Mutual Insurance Company. The foundation primarily supports Sheboygan, Wisconsin, organizations involved with arts and culture, elementary and secondary education, engineering, health care, cancer, and youth development. Types of support include general operating support, program development, and sponsorships. Though formal application forms are not required, proposals should be submitted using the organization's letterhead. There are

no deadlines, and applicants should submit the entire proposal, which should include: need for the project, group being served, evaluation process, and necessary funding.
Requirements: 501(c)3 organizations based in or serving residents of Sheboygan, Wisconsin, can apply.
Geographic Focus: Wisconsin
Amount of Grant: Up to 125,000 USD
Samples: Aurora Health Foundation, Aurora, Wisconsin, $125,000 - general operating support; Feeding America, Milwaukee, Wisconsin, $68,200 - general operating support; Mental Health America, Sheboygan, Wisconsin, $83,810 - general operating support.
Contact: Carli R. Miller, (920) 458-9131
Sponsor: Acuity Charitable Foundation
2800 South Taylor Drive, P.O. Box 58
Sheboygan, WI 53082-0058

ADA Foundation Samuel Harris Children's Dental Health Grants 111

The American Dental Association Foundation Samuel Harris Children's Dental Health Grants provides funding to programs that are designed to improve and maintain children's oral health through outreach, primary prevention, and education. The program currently focuses on funding parent and caregiver education programs to prevent early childhood caries, also known as baby bottle tooth decay, by circumventing primary oral bacterial infection before it can take hold. See the website for the complete request for proposal, application materials, and deadlines.
Requirements: Proposals are accepted from nonprofit 501(c)3 organizations and government agencies for community-based oral health and prevention education programs for parents and caregivers of infants in the United States and its territories.
Restrictions: The Foundation does not accept unsolicited proposals outside of its request for proposal programs announced via their website.
Geographic Focus: All States
Amount of Grant: Up to 5,000 USD
Contact: Cristina Garcia, Grants Administrator; (312) 440-2547, ext. 2763; fax (312) 440-3526; garciac@ada.org or adaf@ada.org
Internet: www.ada.org/applyforassistance.aspx#harris
Sponsor: American Dental Association Foundation
211 East Chicago Avenue
Chicago, IL 60611-2616

Adam Don Foundation Grants 112

Adam Don was born in 1969, the youngest of three children. From an early age, he had a twinkle in his eye that reflected equal parts joie de vivre and mischief. Adam attended the University of Texas at Austin where he was a member of the Sigma Alpha Mu fraternity and The Silver Spurs, a service and spirit honor society that cares for the University of Texas mascot and engages in philanthropy on campus and in the greater Austin community. He graduated from the University of Texas with a degree in accounting. The Adam Don Foundation was formed in March, 2005 immediately after the mountain bike accident that resulted in Adam Don's untimely death at the age of thirty-five. Throughout his life, Adam demonstrated leadership skills, charisma, and humor. Shortly after his death in 2005, he was posthumously awarded the "Outstanding Achievement Award" by Edward Don and Company. The award has since been renamed The Adam Don Outstanding Achievement Award and is given annually to a member of the Edward Don and Company sales force. In order to honor his life and preserve his memory, the Foundation was formed with the broad mission of helping to make life better for young people. There are no formal applications to submit, and no particular deadlines with which to adhere. Most recently, the Adam Don Foundation has focused its support on three unique organizations with programs focused on making life better for young people in Lake County, Illinois.
Geographic Focus: Illinois
Amount of Grant: Up to 25,000 USD
Contact: Robert E. (Bob) Don, Co-Chair; (708) 883-8080; info@adamdon.org
Internet: adamdon.com/index.html
Sponsor: Adam Don Foundation
9801 Adam Don Parkway
Woodridge, IL 60517

Adams-Mastrovich Family Foundation Grants 113

Mary Adams Balmat established the Adams-Mastrovich Family Foundation in 1957. Born in 1898 in Lead, South Dakota, she married William Emory Adams II in 1927. He was a prominent businessman in Deadwood, South Dakota, as well as its mayor for six terms during the 1920s. The couple maintained residences in both South Dakota and California. Their home in Deadwood now belongs to the local Historic Preservation Commission. Over the years Mary shared her resources with education, the performing arts, institutions of higher learning, Roman Catholic parishes, hospitals, museums and libraries, as well as programs for battered women and an organization serving delinquent teenage boys. The Foundation continues to support these same organizations today, primarily throughout South Dakota and Los Angeles County, California. Types of funding include: building and renovation, ongoing operating support, equipment purchase, program development, and support of scholarship funds. Applications must be submitted through ab online grant application form, with the annual submission deadline June 30. The Board meets in September for final decision-making. Average grant size range from $5,000 to $20,000, with between 30 and 40 awards each year totaling more than $1.5 million annually.
Requirements: 501(c)3 organizations located in, or serving residents of, South Dakota or Los Angeles County, California, are eligible to apply. Grants to religious organizations and their affiliates are made only to organizations that are a part of or affiliated with the Roman Catholic Church.
Restrictions: The foundation will not consider funding requests for the following: political campaigns or lobbying activities; fundraising campaigns; endowment campaigns;

individuals; travel for groups or individuals; conferences, seminars, workshops, or symposia; or benefits or fundraisers. No capital requests will be considered unless solicited by the Foundation's advisory board.
Geographic Focus: California, South Dakota
Date(s) Application is Due: Jun 30
Amount of Grant: Up to 100,000 USD
Contact: Halsey H. Halls, Vice President; (612) 667-9084 or (612) 316-4112
Internet: www.wellsfargo.com/private-foundations/adams-mastrovich-family-foundation
Sponsor: Adams-Mastrovich Family Foundation
P.O. Box 53456, MAC S4101-22G
Phoenix, AZ 85072-3456

Adams and Reese Corporate Giving Grants 114
At Adams and Reese, the Corporation takes pride in giving back to its communities and believes success is directly related to the prosperity and the quality of life within the communities it serves. Its corporate philanthropy program, HUGS (Hope, Understanding, Giving, and Support) was founded in 1988 by Partner, Mark Surprenant. Since its inception, the firm has devoted financial resources and thousands of volunteer hours to offer assistance to those in need. A fundamental commitment to volunteerism is the deep-rooted characteristic of the corporation. Primary activities include grants in support of health, youth development, and human services. Fields of interest are: general charitable giving, operating support, health care organizations, legal services, social services, and youth programs.
Requirements: Regions of grant application eligibility include: Birmingham and Mobile, Alabama; Jacksonville, Sarasota, St. Petersburg, Tallahassee, and Tampa, Florida; Baton Rouge and New Orleans, Louisiana; Jackson, Mississippi; Columbia, South Carolina; Chattanooga, Memphis, and Nashville, Tennessee; Houston, Texas; and Washington, D.C.
Geographic Focus: Alabama, District of Columbia, Florida, Louisiana, Mississippi, South Carolina, Tennessee, Texas
Contact: Mark C. Surprenant, Liaison Partner; (504) 581-0213 or (504) 581-3234; fax (504) 566-0210; mark.surprenant@arlaw.com
Internet: www.adamsandreese.com/community/
Sponsor: Adams and Reese Corporation
701 Poydras Street, Suite 4500
New Orleans, LA 70139-7755

Adams County Community Foundation Grants 115
The Adams County Community Foundation was established in October of 2007 as a Pennsylvania corporation to succeed the Adams County Foundation, which for 22 years had operated as a trust-based community foundation. The Foundation is a public charity that the IRS has determined to be a 501(c)3 organization. The purpose of this Foundation is to inspire people and communities to build and distribute charitable funds for good, for Adams County, forever. After one year of operation, the foundation had acquired nine funds established by individual people or families, members of the Foundation's Board of Directors, groups of business people, a local charity and by a visionary patriot from the 1700s. The Foundation's assets are managed by a professional investment company hired by the Board of Directors and overseen by the Foundation's Investment & Finance Committee. From these funds, distribution of grants is made to qualified, local charities who demonstrate that they are meeting community needs. With a 16 member Board of Directors, Adams County Community Foundation serves as a good steward of the monies of our donors and demonstrates accountability, transparency, confidentiality, compassion, inclusiveness and excellence in its work. The foundation gives to organizations that assist, promote and improve the moral, mental, social and physical well-being of area residents. Fields of interest include: arts; Christian agencies and churches; community and economic development; education; and health organizations. Annual grant applications must be received on or before March 15.
Requirements: Applicants must serve residents living in Adams County, Pennsylvania.
Geographic Focus: Pennsylvania
Date(s) Application is Due: Mar 15
Contact: Lisa Donohoe, Director of Community Programs; (717) 337-0060 or (717) 337-3353; fax (717) 337-1080; info@adamscountycf.org or lisa@adamscountycf.org
Internet: www.adamscountycf.org/grants-scholarships/grants/
Sponsor: Adams County Community Foundation
25 South Fourth Street, P.O. Box 4565
Gettysburg, PA 17325-2109

Adams Family Foundation I Grants 116
The Adams Family Foundation I, founded in 1993, offers support primarily in Tennessee and the southeastern portion of the United States. Its major fields of interest include: the arts, children and youth services, Christian agencies and churches, elementary and secondary education programs, and human services. The primary type of funding is general operating support. There are no specific deadlines with which to adhere, and applicants should forward a request by letter outlining the project and a detailed budgetary need. Most grants are in the neighborhood of $500 to $10,000, though occasionally reach as high as $100,000.
Requirements: Any 501(c)3 that is located in, or offers support to Tennessee or the southeastern portion of the United States is eligible to apply.
Geographic Focus: Tennessee
Amount of Grant: Up to 100,000 USD
Samples: Adams Memorial Library, Woodbury, Tennessee, $25,000 - general operating fund; Middle Tennessee Christian School, Murfreesboro, Tennessee, $33,500 - general operating fund; Special Kids, Murfreesboro, Tennessee, $6,000 - general operating fund.
Contact: Robert G. Adams, Trustee; (615) 890-2020 or (615) 896-0374; fax (615) 890-0123
Sponsor: Adams Family Foundation I
2217 Battleground Drive
Murfreesboro, TN 37129-6006

Adams Family Foundation II Grants 117
The Adams Family Foundation, established in 1993 by the founder of the Murfreesboro-based National Health Care L.P. and National Health Investors, is primarily interested in supporting: boys and girls clubs; Boy Scouts of America; children and youth services; Christian agencies and churches; human service organizations; and secondary education. Funding is typically in the form of general operating support. Grants are usually in the $250 to $100,000 range, although occasionally somewhat higher. There are no particular deadlines, and applicants should approach the Foundation initially by letter describing their program and specifying an amount needed.
Requirements: 501(c)3 organizations serving the residents of the general Murfreesboro, Tennessee, region are eligible.
Geographic Focus: Tennessee
Amount of Grant: 250 - 200,000 USD
Samples: Child Advocacy, Murfreesboro, Tennessee, $1,500 - general operating support; Special Kids, Murfreesboro, Tennessee, $15,000 - general operating support; National Tennis Foundation, Alpharetta, Georgia, $34,000 - general operating support.
Contact: W. Andrew Adams, Trustee; (615) 848-2638 or (615) 848-0171
Sponsor: Adams Family Foundation II
801 Mooreland Lane
Murfreesboro, TN 37128-4634

Adams Family Foundation of Nora Springs Grants 118
The Adams Family Foundation of Nora Springs, Iowa, is a private foundation dedicated to enhancing the quality of community life in Nora Springs and the surrounding community. Upon Johns' passing, the Adams Family Foundation expanded the scholarship program and began providing charitable grants for projects that benefit the local community. Today, its mission is to provide scholarships, fund programs that promote excellence in education, and provide grants for projects that enhance the quality of life in Nora Springs and the surrounding community. The Foundation places high priority on the following: projects that address a community based need, demonstrate broad-based community support, and provide benefits to the community at large; and projects that show the organization's ability to leverage funding and support from other sources (grant request applications should clearly show all matching funds for projects. applicant organization and staff's capacity to achieve the desired result is important. Sustainable projects without additional long-term financial commitments from the Foundation are highly encouraged. Particular areas of interest include: community nonprofit program development funds, K-12 school program and teacher development, arts and culture, and environmental programs.
Requirements: Grants are made for charitable purposes to local organizations that are tax-exempt under Section 501(c)3 of the Internal Revenue Code, or other qualified tax exempt organizations such as governmental agencies and schools under Section 170(c)1 of the Internal Revenue Code.
Restrictions: The Foundation will not award grants: to individuals or for-profit businesses; for advocacy or for political purposes; or for debt incurred or purchases made prior to grant award notification.
Geographic Focus: Iowa
Contact: Ron Hoel; (641) 749-2334 or (641) 330-0400; mrhoel@omnitelcom.com
Deb O'Banion, Board Member; (641) 749-2445 or (641) 425-5779
Internet: www.citynorasprings.com/adams-family-foundation.html
Sponsor: Adams Family Foundation of Nora Springs
215 Tenth Street, Suite 1300
Des Moines, IA 50309

Adams Family Foundation of Ohio Grants 119
The Adams Family Foundation was established in Muskingum County, Ohio, with the intent of providing financial awards to local organizations that have the mission of supporting the residents of Muskingum County. Its primary areas of interest include community services, human services, family, and religious organizations. Grants are typically given for general operating support. There are no specific application materials or annual deadlines identified, and interested parties should contact the Foundation directly by way of a brief letter outlining the need and budgetary requirements.
Requirements: 501(c)3 organizations serving the residents of Muskingum County, Ohio, are eligible to apply.
Geographic Focus: Ohio
Contact: Robert Gregory Adams, Presiident; (740) 826-4154 or (740) 390-3368
Sponsor: Adams Family Foundation
165 West Main Street
New Concord, OH 43762

Adams Family Foundation of Tennessee Grants 120
The Adams Family Foundation, established in Tennessee in 2006, provides grants to individuals for family services, cemetery and burial needs, and for the prevention of domestic violence in the Paris, Tennessee, region. Its primary fields of interest have been identified as: agriculture and food; education; and youth development programs. There are no application forms or deadlines with which to adhere, and those in need should forward a letter of request directly to the Foundation office. Most recently, awards have ranged from $1,000 to $6,000.
Geographic Focus: Tennessee
Amount of Grant: 1,000 - 6,000 USD
Samples: Henry County Helping Hand, Paris, Tennessee, $6,000 - general operation support; Caring Hearts Fund, Paris, Tennessee, $2,000 - general operation support; Tomorrow's Hope Pregnancy Medical Clinic, Paris, Tennessee, $1,000 - general operation support.
Contact: David E. Sullivan, Director; (731) 642-2940 or (731) 642-2752
Sponsor: Adams Family Foundation
1101 East Wood Street, P.O. Box 909
Paris, TN 38242-0909

Adams Legacy Foundation Grants 121

The Adams Legacy Foundation was established in 2005 to foster a commitment to philanthropy in the founder's heirs and succeeding generations. It is a family foundation which seeks to leverage its investments for the future. The Foundation's primary goal is to create supportive relationships with dynamic non-profit organizations to enable them to build their capacity and assist them in accomplishing their core programs. In pursuit of this goal, it will consider supporting facilities expansion projects, ongoing operation and program expenses, and leadership development and/or organization improvement initiatives. It will also consider program related investments, matching grants and endowments. The Foundation utilizes a two-stage grant application process. Letters of Inquiry (LOIs) are due no later than November 1. All LOIs will be responded to by December 15. Those organizations invited to submit full grant applications will be given the official form and will be expected to return the completed application and all supporting documentation (in both electronic and hard copy versions) to the Foundation office no later than February 1. Installment grants of up to three years maximum with be considered. Target funding areas include central and southern California, as well as central Ohio. The maximum grant amount is $25,000.
Requirements: Organizations applying for grants must be based in the United States of America. Any 501(c)3 organization which believes its mission is a match for the Foundation is welcome to submit a Letter of Inquiry. Grants must be leveraged for the future (i.e., create a base upon which the Organization can build).
Geographic Focus: California, Ohio
Date(s) Application is Due: Feb 1
Amount of Grant: 1,500 - 25,000 USD
Samples: Assistance League of Long Beach, Long Beach, California, $10,000 - operation School Bell uniform program; Colin Powell Academy for Success, Long Beach, California, $20,000 - computer lab to run MIND Research Institute Math curriculum and Common Core assessments; Friends of IHP at Walter Reed Middle School, Studio City, California, $1,500 - curriculum development.
Contact: Blair Carty, Executive Director; (562) 431-0011; bcarty@adamslegacyfoundation.org
Internet: www.adamslegacyfoundation.org/products.html
Sponsor: Adams Legacy Foundation
P.O. Box 1957
Los Alamitos, CA 90720-1957

Adams Rotary Memorial Fund A Grants 122

Established in Indiana, the Adams Rotary Memorial Fund A offers funding in Howard County, Indiana, with a primary goal to support handicapped children throughout the county. With this in mind, its primary fields of interest include: children and youth services; alleviation of disabilities; and money to support families who have a family member with a disability. Money supports philanthropy and volunteerism, and is given to individual applicants. There are no application deadlines or specific formats, and those in need should begin by contacted the Fund trustee directly.
Geographic Focus: Indiana
Contact: Glenn Grundmann, Trustee; (317) 464-8212 or (574) 282-8839
Sponsor: Adams Rotary Memorial Fund
224 N. Main Street
Kokomo, IN 46901

Adelaide Breed Bayrd Foundation Grants 123

The Adelaide Breed Bayrd Foundation supports programs and projects of nonprofit organizations serving the Boston, Massachusetts, area with emphasis on the Malden community. Areas of interest include: adult and continuing education; aging centers and services; arts; children and youth services; community and economic development; education; family services; health care; health organizations; hospitals (general), human services; libraries and library science; residential and custodial care; and hospices. The Foundation funds annual campaigns, building and renovation, capital campaigns, emergency requests, equipment, program development, and scholarship funds. Grants have been awarded in the past to support public libraries, hospitals, and the Girl Scouts. The foundation accepts the Associated Grant Makers (AGM) Common Proposal Form available from the AGM website; however an application form is not required. Applicants should submit the following: a copy of their IRS Determination Letter; copies of their most recent annual report, audited financial statements, and 990; a detailed description of their project and the amount of funding requested; and a copy of their organizational or project budget for the current year. Proposals should be submitted before the second Tuesday in February. Awardees will be notified in April or May.
Requirements: 501(c)3 organizations serving the Boston, Massachusetts area are eligible. Preference will be given to organizations serving the community of Malden, Massachusetts.
Restrictions: The foundation does not support the following categories: requests from individuals; the performing arts (except for certain educational programs); matching or challenge grants; demonstration projects; conferences; publications; research or endowment funds; or loans.
Geographic Focus: Massachusetts
Amount of Grant: 1,000 - 150,000 USD
Contact: C. Henry Kezer, President; (781) 324-1231
Sponsor: Adelaide Breed Bayrd Foundation
350 Main Street, Suite 13
Malden, MA 02148-5023

Adelaide Christian Home For Children Grants 124

The Adelaide Christian Home For Children provides support to evangelical Christian organizations serving children and youth, with priority given to local California ministries. Its primary fields of interest include: Christian agencies and churches; education; human services; religion; and youth development. Target populations are children, the economically disadvantaged; and single parents. Interested parties should be aware that there is a formal application. Though there are no specified annual deadlines, the board does meet in both January and September to decide funding awards.
Geographic Focus: California
Amount of Grant: Up to 120,000 USD
Samples: Agape Pregnancy Center, San Clemente, California, $10,000 - general operating support for programs serving women facing a crisis pregnancy situation; Christian Missions in Many Lands, Spring Lake, New Jersey, $119,000 - financial assistance to church workers and missionaries; Verdugo Pines Bible Camp, Wrightwood, California, $30,000 - camp and conference center for young people and adults.
Contact: Sherry Parsons, Director; (949) 361-1346
Sponsor: Adelaide Christian Home For Children
122 Avenida Del Mar
San Clemente, CA 92672

Adidas Corporation General Grants 125

The Adidas Corporation supports nonprofits nationwide in its areas of interest, including: sports within a social context; children and youth programs; elementary and secondary education; preventive health projects (preferably sports related); and relief efforts. Forms of Corporate giving include: cash donations; products; equipment; services; and know-how. There are no application deadlines; the board meets monthly. Proposals should be submitted at least two months before funding is needed. Proposals should include articles written about the applicant organization and be one to ten pages in length.
Requirements: Any U.S.-based 501(c)3 is eligible to apply.
Restrictions: In order to comply with core values, the Corporation does not utilize Corporate Giving for the following purposes: private pursuits; political parties, associations and representatives of advocacy groups; organizations that discriminate by race, creed, gender, sexual orientation, age, religion or national origin; cultural projects in association with film, music and theater sponsoring; religious causes; research projects; or advertising and promotion.
Geographic Focus: All States, American Samoa, District of Columbia, Guam, Marshall Islands, Northern Mariana Islands, Puerto Rico, U.S. Virgin Islands
Contact: Committee Supervisor; (971) 234-2300, ext. 4032
Internet: www.adidas-group.com/en/sustainability/people/community-engagement/
Sponsor: Adidas Corporation
5055 North Greely Avenue
Portland, OR 97217

Adobe Foundation Action Grants 126

The Adobe Foundation's Action Grants focus on creativity in education, focusing on: the use of digital technology in schools; and commitment to community, including arts-education programs, environmental issues, homelessness, services for low-income families, and technology for people with disabilities. The program provides one-year general operating grants and program support through a competitive online application process. Letters of intent are accepted year round. Application information and forms are available through the website.
Requirements: Following are criteria for education grants: K-12 public schools and school districts; nonprofit organizations that serve children in grades K-12; providing direct service to students or that prepare teachers at all levels; and emphasizing low-achieving, economically disadvantaged students and/or those who are not succeeding with traditional methods. Nonprofit organizations and schools located throughout the world are eligible.
Geographic Focus: All States, All Countries
Date(s) Application is Due: Jan 1; Jul 1
Amount of Grant: 10,000 - 40,000 USD
Contact: Michelle Crozier, Director, Corporate Responsibility; (408) 536-6000 or (408) 536-3993; fax (408) 537-6000; community_relations@adobe.com
Internet: www.adobe.com/corporate-responsibility/community/action-teams.html
Sponsor: Adobe Foundation
345 Park Avenue
San Jose, CA 95110-2704

Adobe Foundation Community Investment Grants 127

Adobe supports strategic programs and partnerships that help make its communities better, stronger, and more vibrant places to live, work and do business. Adobe's focus areas for giving and grants programs are designed to: increase Adobe's impact in the community through support of more organizations; and strengthen Adobe's role as a corporate partner by creating deeper, stronger, and richer partnerships. The Adobe Community Investment Grant program provides multi-year (with annual review), comprehensive support, including cash, software, volunteers, and facilities use through an Adobe-initiated, RFP application process. Grant amounts are at least $20,000 and can be for up to three years. Organizations selected become Adobe Community Investment Partners and are required to sit out one year after the grant ends before reapplying.
Requirements: Adobe is currently accepting grant proposals in the following communities: San Jose/Silicon Valley, California (southern San Mateo County, Santa Clara County, southern Alameda County); San Francisco, California; Seattle/King County, Washington; and Ottawa, Ontario, Canada.
Geographic Focus: California, Washington, Canada
Amount of Grant: Up to 20,000 USD
Contact: Michelle Crozier, Director, Corporate Responsibility; (408) 536-6000 or (408) 536-3993; fax (408) 537-6000; community_relations@adobe.com
Internet: www.adobe.com/corporate-responsibility/community.html#Community%20giving%20programs
Sponsor: Adobe Foundation
345 Park Avenue
San Jose, CA 95110-2704

Adobe Foundation Hunger and Homelessness Grants 128

Adobe supports strategic programs and partnerships that help make its communities better, stronger, and more vibrant places to live, work and do business. Adobe's focus areas for giving and grants programs are designed to: increase Adobe's impact in the community through support of more organizations; and strengthen Adobe's role as a corporate partner by creating deeper, stronger, and richer partnerships. Specifically, the Hunger and Homelessness grants program directs grants towards services and programs that reduce hunger and homelessness and/or provide affordable housing. This primarily includes food banks, shelters and other direct services to homeless or at-risk individuals.

Requirements: Adobe is currently accepting grant proposals in the following communities: San Jose/Silicon Valley, California (southern San Mateo County, Santa Clara County, southern Alameda County); San Francisco, California; Seattle/King County, Washington; and Ottawa, Ontario, Canada.

Restrictions: Adobe does not support indirect services or programs that focus primarily on workforce development.

Geographic Focus: California, Washington, Canada

Contact: Michelle Crozier, Director, Corporate Responsibility; (408) 536-6000 or (408) 536-3993; fax (408) 537-6000; community_relations@adobe.com

Internet: www.adobe.com/corporate-responsibility/community/community-fund.html

Sponsor: Adobe Foundation

345 Park Avenue

San Jose, CA 95110-2704

Adolph Coors Foundation Grants 129

The Coors Foundation supports organizations that promote the western values of self-reliance, personal responsibility, and integrity. The foundation believes these values foster an environment where entrepreneurial spirits flourish and help Coloradans reach their full potential. High priority is placed on programs that help youth to prosper, that encourage economic opportunities for adults, and that advance public policies that uphold traditional American values. Traditional areas of support include one-on-one mentoring programs, job training, and a variety of self-help initiatives. The foundation also has an interest in bringing integrative medicine into the medical mainstream. In each of its giving areas, the foundation seeks evidenced-based results. Civic and cultural programs attracting the Foundation's attention are typically those that enhance our culture and heritage, that demonstrate our creativity as a people and that are likely to be of economic benefit to and broadly used by the communities they serve. Past grants have supported boys and girls clubs and inner-city health programs. Types of support include building funds, general operating budgets, seed money, and special projects. The foundation has moved to an online screening and application system which is accessible from the foundation website. Application deadlines are March 1, July 1, and November 1.

Requirements: All applicants must be classified as 501(c)3 organizations by the Internal Revenue Service and must operate within the United States.

Restrictions: The foundation does not provide support for the following expenses or entities: organizations primarily supported by tax-derived funds; conduit organizations that pass funds to non-exempt organizations; organizations with two consecutive years of operating loss; K-12 schools or the ancillary programs and projects of those schools; individuals; research projects; production of films or other media-related projects; historic renovation; churches or church projects; museums or museum projects; animals or animal-related projects; preschools, day-care centers, nursing homes, extended-care facilities, or respite care; deficit funding or retirement of debt; special events, meetings, or seminars; purchase of computer equipment; adaptive sports programs; and national health organizations. Organizations applying for start-up funding must have been in operation for at least one full year.

Geographic Focus: All States

Date(s) Application is Due: Mar 1; Jul 1; Nov 1

Contact: Jeanne Bistranin, Program Officer; (303) 388-1636; fax (303) 388-1684

Internet: www.coorsfoundation.org/Process/index.html

Sponsor: Adolph Coors Foundation

4100 E Mississippi Avenue, Suite 1850

Denver, CO 80246

Adray Foundation 130

The Adray Foundation, which was established in Michigan in 1983, offers support for athletic programs with an emphasis on hockey leagues. Types of support include endowments, equipment purchase, and general operations. There are no specific application formats or deadlines with which to adhere, and applicants should begin by forwarding a letter of request to the Foundation. An average size grant is typically $10,000.

Geographic Focus: Michigan

Samples: Adray Community Hockey League, Trenton, Michigan, $10,000 - support of community hockey activities; HFCC Foundation, Dearborn, Michigan, $10,000 - support for scholarships.

Contact: Joseph M. McGlynn, Director; (248) 540-2300; fax (248) 645-2690

Sponsor: Adray Foundation

300 E. Long Lake Road, Suite 200

Bloomfield Hills, MI 48304-2376

Advance Auto Parts Corporate Giving Grants 131

The Advance Auto Parts Corporate Giving program was founded on the belief that good business is more than just selling merchandise. Since the company was founded in 1932, it has been guided by the following principles, known as the Advance Values: inspire and build the self-confidence and success of every Team Member; serve customers better than anyone else and help them succeed; and grow the business and profitability with integrity. While the corporation understands that there are a variety of worthy causes in every community, to maximize its giving and make the greatest possible impact, Advance has chosen to focus its charitable efforts on serving those in need through support of the following four impact areas: health – improving the health and well-being of others; education – helping people reach their potential by providing educational opportunities; at-risk children and families – helping children and families to assure their critical needs are met through comprehensive, community-based programs; and disaster relief – providing timely support to those impacted by disasters such as earthquakes, hurricanes, floods and other natural disasters.

Geographic Focus: All States

Contact: Elisabeth Eisleben, Investor Relations Department Contact; (919) 227-5466 or (540) 362-4911; fax (540) 561-1448; elisabeth.eisleben@advance-auto.com or invrelations@advance-auto.com

Internet: corp.advanceautoparts.com/about/public.asp

Sponsor: Advance Auto Parts Corporate Giving

2635 East Millbrook Road

Raleigh, NC 27604

AEGON Transamerica Foundation Education and Financial Literacy Grants 132

The AEGON Transamerica Foundation will consider favorably grants to established organizations with reputations for excellence and cost-effectiveness. The Foundation's Education and Literacy grant initiative is interesting in supporting programs with a mission to provide knowledge and to expand individual's capabilities; especially in the areas of financial literacy where programs empower individuals to gain the knowledge and skills to build financial security and personal success through financial education and planning. Types of support include continuing support, matching funds, operating budgets, employee-related scholarships, and special projects. Contributions are normally made on a year-to-year basis with no assurance of renewal of support. In certain cases, pledges may be considered for periods not exceeding three years.

Requirements: Nonprofit organizations within the Foundation's focus areas and mission, and that are designated for a community where there is a significant employee presence are eligible. Requests can be directed to the attention of the AEGON Transamerica Foundation at one of the following locations: Louisville, Kentucky; Atlanta, Georgia; Baltimore, Maryland; Bedford, Texas; Cedar Rapids, Iowa; Exton, Pennsylvania; Harrison, New York; Little Rock, Arkansas; Los Angeles, California; Plano, Texas; and St. Petersburg, Florida.

Restrictions: Individuals, as well as the following types of organizations or programs are not eligible to receive grants from the Foundation: athletes or athletic organizations; conferences, seminars or trips; courtesy or goodwill advertising; fellowships; fraternal organizations; K-12 school fundraisers or events; political parties, campaigns or candidates; religious or denominational organizations except for specific programs broadly promoted and available to anyone and free from religious orientation; or social organizations.

Geographic Focus: Arkansas, California, Florida, Georgia, Iowa, Kentucky, Maryland, New York, Pennsylvania, Texas

Amount of Grant: 1,000 - 50,000 USD

Contact: Gregory Tucker, Foundation Contact; (443) 475-3017 or (319) 355-8511; fax (319) 398-8030; greg.tucker@transamerica.com or shaegontransfound@aegonusa.com

Margaret Sherry, Foundation Contact; (213) 742-5134 or (213) 742-2111; margaret.sherry@transamerica.com or shaegontransfound@aegonusa.com

Internet: www.transamerica.com/about_us/aegon_transamerica_foundation.asp

Sponsor: AEGON Transamerica Foundation

6400 C St SW

Cedar Rapids, IA 52499-3210

AEGON Transamerica Foundation Health and Wellness Grants 133

The AEGON Transamerica Foundation will consider favorably grants to established organizations with reputations for excellence and cost-effectiveness. The Foundation's Health and Welfare Grants initiative is interested in supporting programs committed to improving the condition of the human body through nutrition, housing for the homeless, disease prevention and other support services. Types of support include continuing support, matching funds, operating budgets, employee-related scholarships, and special projects. Contributions are normally made on a year-to-year basis with no assurance of renewal of support. In certain cases, pledges may be considered for periods not exceeding three years.

Requirements: Nonprofit organizations within the Foundation's focus areas and mission, and that are designated for a community where there is a significant employee presence are eligible. Requests can be directed to the attention of the AEGON Transamerica Foundation at one of the following locations: Louisville, Kentucky; Atlanta, Georgia; Baltimore, Maryland; Bedford, Texas; Cedar Rapids, Iowa; Exton, Pennsylvania; Harrison, New York; Little Rock, Arkansas; Los Angeles, California; Plano, Texas; and St. Petersburg, Florida.

Restrictions: Individuals, as well as the following types of organizations or programs are not eligible to receive grants from the Foundation: athletes or athletic organizations; conferences, seminars or trips; courtesy or goodwill advertising; fellowships; fraternal organizations; K-12 school fundraisers or events; political parties, campaigns or candidates; religious or denominational organizations except for specific programs broadly promoted and available to anyone and free from religious orientation; or social organizations.

Geographic Focus: Arkansas, California, Florida, Georgia, Iowa, Kentucky, Maryland, New York, Pennsylvania, Texas

Amount of Grant: 1,000 - 50,000 USD

Contact: Gregory Tucker, Foundation Contact; (443) 475-3017 or (319) 355-8511; fax (319) 398-8030; greg.tucker@transamerica.com or shaegontransfound@aegonusa.com

Margaret Sherry, Foundation Contact; (213) 742-5134 or (213) 742-2111; margaret.sherry@transamerica.com or shaegontransfound@aegonusa.com

Internet: www.transamerica.com/about_us/aegon_transamerica_foundation.asp

Sponsor: AEGON Transamerica Foundation

6400 C St SW

Cedar Rapids, IA 52499-3210

Aetna Foundation Regional Health Grants 134

The Aetna Foundation's Regional Grants fund community wellness initiatives that serve those who are most at risk for poor health - low-income, underserved or minority populations. A healthy diet and regular exercise can help prevent obesity and many chronic conditions. Grants will target communities where healthy food can be difficult to buy, and where social and environmental factors may limit people's ability to be physically active. Types of projects the Foundation seeks to support include: school-based or after-school nutrition and fitness programs that help children learn healthy habits at an early age; community-based nutrition education programs for children and families; efforts to increase the availability or affordability of fresh fruits and vegetables in communities; and community gardening and urban farming activities for children and families. Funding ranges from $25,000 to $40,000.

Requirements: 501(c)3 tax-exempt organizations in regionally designated communities are eligible, including: Phoenix, Arizona; Los Angeles, San Diego, Fresno, and San Francisco, in California; Connecticut; Miami and Tampa, Florida; Atlanta, Georgia; Chicago, Illinois; Maine; New Jersey; New York, New York; Charlotte, North Carolina; Cleveland and Columbus, Ohio; Philadelphia and Pittsburgh, Pennsylvania; Nashville and Memphis, Tennessee; Dallas, Houston, Austin, and San Antonio, in Texas; Washington, D.C; Baltimore, Maryland; Northern Virginia; and Washington State.

Restrictions: The Foundation generally does not fund: endowment or capital costs, including construction, renovation, or equipment; direct delivery of reimbursable health care services; basic biomedical research; grants or scholarships to individuals; work for which results and impact cannot be measured; advertising; golf tournaments; advocacy, political causes or events; sacramental or theological functions of religious organizations; operational expenses; or existing deficits.

Geographic Focus: Arizona, California, Connecticut, District of Columbia, Florida, Georgia, Illinois, Maine, Maryland, New Jersey, New York, North Carolina, Ohio, Pennsylvania, Tennessee, Texas, Virginia, Washington

Date(s) Application is Due: Sep 15

Amount of Grant: 25,000 - 50,000 USD

Contact: Melenie O. Magnotta, Grants Manager; (860) 273-1012 or (860) 273-0123; fax (860) 273-7764; aetnafoundation@aetna.com

Internet: www.aetna-foundation.org/foundation/apply-for-a-grant/regional-grants/index.html

Sponsor: Aetna Foundation

151 Farmington Avenue

Hartford, CT 06156-3180

Aetna Foundation Summer Academic Enrichment Grants 135

Through its Summer Academic Enrichment Grants program, the Aetna Foundation provides academic and cultural enrichment opportunities to thousands of at-risk, Hartford-area students. Grants have been made to such organizations as Boys and Girls Club of Hartford, Center City Churches, ConnectiKids, Dance Connecticut, Organized Parents Make a Difference, and many others. In Hartford, a $250,000 Aetna Foundation investment is supporting a local education fund (LEF) designed to improve student retention and achievement

Requirements: 501(c)3 tax-exempt organizations in Hartford, Connecticut, are eligible.

Restrictions: The Foundation generally does not fund: endowment or capital costs, including construction, renovation, or equipment; direct delivery of reimbursable health care services; basic biomedical research; grants or scholarships to individuals; work for which results and impact cannot be measured; advertising; golf tournaments; advocacy, political causes or events; sacramental or theological functions of religious organizations; operational expenses; or existing deficits.

Geographic Focus: Connecticut

Amount of Grant: 500 - 5,000 USD

Contact: Melenie O. Magnotta, Grants Manager; (860) 273-1012 or (860) 273-0123; fax (860) 273-7764; aetnafoundation@aetna.com

Internet: www.aetna.com/about-aetna-insurance/aetna-foundation/aetna-grants/connecticut-grants-education.html

Sponsor: Aetna Foundation

151 Farmington Avenue

Hartford, CT 06156-3180

A Friends' Foundation Trust Grants 136

The Foundation, founded as the Hubbard Foundation in 1959 by philanthropist Frank M. Hubbard, primarily serves central Florida, though funds are also distributed in North Carolina, South Carolina, Missouri, Tennessee, California, and Puerto Rico. Support typically is given for: annual campaigns; capital and infrastructure funds; continuing education; emergency; equipment purchase; general operations; land acquisition; and program development. Grants typically range from $5,000 to $35,000, though some higher amounts have been given. There are no specific application formats or deadlines with which to adhere, and applicants should send a letter of request to the Foundation address listed.

Requirements: Applicants must be 501(c)3 organizations serving the residents of central Florida.

Geographic Focus: Alabama, California, Florida, Missouri, North Carolina, Puerto Rico, South Dakota, Tennessee

Amount of Grant: 5,000 - 35,000 USD

Samples: Home At Last Project, Windemere, Florida, $5,000 - general operating support; Glenville Community Development Club, Glenville, North Carolina, $1,000 - general operating support; Citizens Against Domestic Violence, Camdenton, Missouri, $5,000 - general operating support.

Contact: L. Evans Hubbard, (609) 274-6834; ehubbard@cfl.rr.com

Sponsor: A Friends' Foundation Trust

P.O. Box 1501

Pennington, NJ 08534-1501

A Fund for Women Grants 137

A Fund For Women, a component fund of The Madison Community Foundation was established in 1993 to improve the lives of girls and women in the local community. The fund provides grants to women and girls in the community that enhance education, employment and self-esteem. All grants are driven by the overall goal of helping women and children learn self-reliance and reach self-sufficiency. Under that umbrella, the Fund focuses on the following four key areas of need: keeping elderly or disabled women in their homes, or in community settings; providing services to victims of domestic abuse; helping women achieve economic self sufficiency and increase their earning potential; and reducing homelessness for women and girls. AFFW is particularly interested in innovative programs and services that will reach women and girls from diverse backgrounds in urban, suburban or rural Dane County. Proposals should indicate how the project or program will help connect women or girls to a support network or community that will help them to overcome emotional, social, intellectual, spiritual, occupational and/or physical barriers to self-sufficiency. Applications are due annually by July 1, at 4:30 p.m.

Requirements: Applicants must be non-profit organizations (exempt from Federal income taxes under section 501(c)3 of the Internal Revenue Code), schools, governmental bodies, or under the supervision of such a group. Projects must focus on women and girls in Dane County.

Geographic Focus: Wisconsin

Date(s) Application is Due: Jul 1

Amount of Grant: 2,000 - 25,000 USD

Contact: Jan Gietzel, Executive Director; (608) 441-0630; fax (608) 232-1772; kwoit@madisoncommunityfoundation.org or affw@madisoncommunityfoundation.org

Internet: www.affw.org/grants/apply.php

Sponsor: A Fund for Women

2 Science Court, P.O. Box 5010

Madison, WI 53705-0010

AGFT A Gift for Music Grants 138

A Gift For Music is a nationally recognized, award winning program, founded on the idea that all students, regardless of their socioeconomic status, should have access to the life changing benefits of a quality music education. Each student we serve receives over 150 contact hours with instructors per year through group classes, private lessons, summer camps and ensemble rehearsals. A Gift For Music currently serves 400 Central Florida students each year in its after-school programs at various elementary schools and in its Saturday Orchestra program at Edgewater High School.

Requirements: This program is available to students at the following Central Florida schools: Academic Center For Excellence, Eccleston Elementary School, Forsyth Woods Elementary School, Lake Silver Elementary School, Lake Weston Elementary School, Riverdale Elementary School, Ventura Elementary School, Winegard Elementary School, and Edgewater High School. Those who are interested in being part of the program can contact A Gift for Music through the form on their website.

Geographic Focus: Florida

Contact: Chad McClellan, Program Manager; (407) 318-3128; fax (407) 318-3124; Chad@agiftforteaching.org or Music@agiftforteaching.org

Internet: www.agiftformusic.org/about-us/

Sponsor: A Gift for Teaching

6501 Magic Way, Building 400C

Orlando, FL 32809

AGFT Pencil Boy Express 139

Pencil Boy Express is a Free Teacher Supply Store on wheels that visits different public schools in Central Florida for teachers to shop for essential tools their students need to succeed. Shopping is open from Monday-Saturday. More information on the program is available on the AGFT website.

Requirements: All items distributed through A Gift For Teaching (AGFT) are strictly for student and classroom use only. Items may NOT be taken for personal use, sold, bartered, traded, or donated elsewhere. All full-time instructional personnel from K-12 Orange County Public Schools (OCPS) schools with more than 60% of students in Free and Reduced Lunch Program (FRLP) may shop at AGFT twice between September-December. Instructional personnel includes classroom/general education teachers, media specialists, guidance counselors, nurses, principals, assistant principals, and deans. There will be a limited number of orders available each day. Once they are full, teachers may try again the following day. Items can be ordered at the in-person store or online.

Restrictions: Select items are restricted by grade level. Charter schools, Head Start programs and schools not on the eligible school list will not be able to shop. A Gift For Teaching (AGFT) serves public schools in Orange and Osceola Counties and is unable to service private schools.

Geographic Focus: Florida

Contact: Jane Thompson, President; (407) 318-3123; fax (407) 318-3124; jane@agiftforteaching.org or info@agiftforteaching.org

Internet: www.agiftforteaching.org/teachers/pencil-boy-express/

Sponsor: A Gift for Teaching

6501 Magic Way, Building 400C

Orlando, FL 32809

Agnes M. Lindsay Trust Grants 140

The Agnes M. Lindsay Trust makes grants to nonprofit organizations in the states of Maine, Massachusetts, New Hampshire, and Vermont to improve the quality of life for residents. Areas of interest include: oral health; special needs; blind, deaf and learning disabled; elderly; children's homes; youth organizations; youth and family services; homeless shelters; soup kitchens; food pantries; summer enrichment programs; and camps. Grant proposals are reviewed on a monthly basis, grants average $1,000 to $15,000. Camping applications must be submitted by March 1 and range from $1,000 to $4,000.

Requirements: 501(c)3 Maine, Massachusetts, New Hampshire, and Vermont tax-exempt organizations are eligible to apply for funding. To begin the application process, submit a letter of inquiry prior to submitting a full proposal for funding. In addition to basic information about the organization, include a brief outline of statement of need and a project budget. Grant proposals should contain: proposal summary document (available at Trust website); narrative of the organization and description of need; financial statements for last two years or Form 990; budget for capital expenditures; estimates or quotes obtained; and IRS Determination letter.
Restrictions: The Trust does not fund: endowments, public entities, awarded to individuals, municipalities, libraries, museums, sectarian organizations, or capital grants to private schools. The Trust very rarely provides funding for operating or program support.
Geographic Focus: Maine, Massachusetts, New Hampshire, Vermont
Date(s) Application is Due: Mar 1
Amount of Grant: 1,000 - 5,000 USD
Samples: Castleton Community Seniors, Castleton, Vermont, $2,000 - construction of a van shelter (2019); Child Care of the Berkshires, North Adams, Massachusetts, $5,000 - to assist in converting a single-use lavatory into an enlarged, accessible lavatory on the second floor of the Haskins facility (2019); Liberty House, Manchester, New Hampshire, $5,000 - support extensive renovations (2019).
Contact: Susan E. Bouchard, Administrative Director; (603) 669-1366 or (603) 488-1213; fax (603) 665-8114; admin@lindsaytrust.org
Internet: www.lindsaytrust.org/grant-center-1
Sponsor: Agnes M. Lindsay Trust
15 Constitution Drive, Suite 1A, Office 102
Bedford, NH 03110

AHC R.E.A.C.H. Grants   **141**
The Arkansas Humanities Council invites grant applications from kindergarten through twelfth-grade public schools within Arkansas. Not-for-profit organizations may apply for a Raising Education Achievement and Competence in the Humanities (R.E.A.C.H.) grant if they are working collaboratively with a local school and/or school district and the school is the primary beneficiary. The deadline for submission is the first day of each month (except December). Up to $2,000 is available for each award.
Requirements: The project must have a strong humanities component and must include one or more of the following: language studies, history, anthropology, archeology, social studies, ethics, English language arts, English as a Second Language (ESL), English Language Learners (ELL), and literacy. The applicant school must be located in Arkansas.
Geographic Focus: Arkansas
Date(s) Application is Due: Jan 1; Feb 1; Mar 1; Apr 1; May 1; Jun 1; Jul 1; Aug 1; Sep 1; Oct 1; Nov 1
Amount of Grant: Up to 2,000 USD
Contact: Jama Best, Executive Director; (501) 353-0349; jbest@arkansashumanitiescouncil.org
Internet: arkansashumanitiescouncil.org/how-to-apply-for-a-grant/
Sponsor: Arkansas Humanities Council
1400 W Markham Street Suite 400
Little Rock, AR 72201

Ahearn Family Foundation Grants   **142**
Established in Connecticut in 1994, the Ahearn Family Foundation limits its giving to the Hartford County, Connecticut, region, particularly the Hartford inner city. Its primary field of interest is urban community development in the areas of health care, children and youth, libraries, housing, families, and scholarship endowments. Application forms are required, and annual deadlines are April 15, July 15, October 15, and January 15. Grants range from $500 to $3,000.
Requirements: Any 501(c)3 organization serving the residents of Hartford County, Connecticut, can apply.
Geographic Focus: Connecticut
Date(s) Application is Due: Jan 15; Apr 15; Jul 15; Oct 15
Amount of Grant: 500 - 3,000 USD
Samples: Connecticut Children's Medical Center, Hartford, Connecticut, $2,000 - support for the whale program; Hartford Youth Scholars Foundation, Hartford, Connecticut, $2,500 - purchase of graphic calculators; Village of Families and Children, Hartford, Connecticut, $3,000 - purchase of manditory school uniforms for at-risk students.
Contact: Terrence O. Ahearn, Chairperson; (860) 249-9104
Sponsor: Ahearn Family Foundation
P.O. Box 37
Manchester, CT 06045-0037

AHS Foundation Grants   **143**
Established in Minnesota in 1968, the AHS Foundation offers funding primarily in California, Hawaii, Minnesota, New Jersey, and Ohio. The Foundation's main purpose is support for the relief of poverty and the advancement of education, religion, and community issues. Its primary fields of interest include: the arts; Catholic agencies and churches; Christian agencies and churches; education; human services; performing arts; Protestant agencies and churches; and federated giving programs. Types of support are building and renovations, capital campaigns, endowments, general operations, and program development. Application forms are not required, and interested groups should forward a detailed description of the project, as well as a budget request. There is no specified annual deadline, although the board typically meets in July. Most recent awards have ranged from $5,000 to $30,000.
Restrictions: No grants are offered to individuals, and no loans are considered.
Geographic Focus: California, Hawaii, Minnesota, New Jersey, Ohio
Amount of Grant: 5,000 - 30,000 USD
Samples: Interfaith Working Group, Los Angeles, California, $30,000 - religious purposes; Maui Nui Botanical Gardens, Kahalui, Hawaii, $7,500 - protection of native plants; Mill Valley School Community Foundation, Mill Valley, California, $14,000 - school improvement.

Contact: Thomas Wright, Secretary Treasurer; (612) 667-1784
Sponsor: AHS Foundation
90 South 7th Street, Suite 5300
Minneapolis, MN 55402-4120

Aid for Starving Children Emergency Aid Grants   **144**
For over thirty years Aid For Starving Children has been dedicated to helping children and families in need across four continents. Their focus has been feeding programs, building clean water systems, supporting children's homes for AIDS, orphans and victims of abuse, as well as providing shipments of medicines and medical supplies to hospitals and clinics in underprivileged regions across the globe. For these grants, ASC provides Emergency Aid to communities experiencing widespread hunger, social unrest, natural disasters, and other horrific conditions. Currently, Aid for Starving Children provides aid to families in Ethiopia, South Sudan, Malawi, and Somalia.
Requirements: More information for who is eligible for aid under this grant can be found on the Aid for Starving Children website.
Geographic Focus: Ethiopia, Malawi, Somalia, South Sudan
Contact: Jeff Baugham, Secretary/Treasurer; (800) 514-3499; info@aidforstarvingchildren.org
Internet: aidforstarvingchildren.org/emergencyaid.php
Sponsor: Aid for Starving Children
P.O. Box 2156
Windsor, CA 95492

Aid for Starving Children Health and Nutrition Grants   **145**
For over thirty years, Aid For Starving Children has been dedicated to helping children and families in need across four continents. Their focus has been feeding programs, building clean water systems, supporting children's homes for AIDS, orphans and victims of abuse, as well as providing shipments of medicines and medical supplies to hospitals and clinics in underprivileged regions across the globe. For these grants, ASC provides invaluable shipments of lifesaving medicines and medical supplies to their partners in Haiti, the Philippines, and Nicaragua.
Requirements: More information for who is eligible for aid under this grant can be found on the Aid for Starving Children website.
Geographic Focus: Haiti, Nicaragua, Philippines
Contact: Jeff Baugham, Secretary/Treasurer; (800) 514-3499; info@aidforstarvingchildren.org
Internet: aidforstarvingchildren.org/health-nutrition.php
Sponsor: Aid for Starving Children
P.O. Box 2156
Windsor, CA 95492

Aid for Starving Children Homes and Education Grants   **146**
For over thirty years Aid For Starving Children has been dedicated to helping children and families in need across four continents. Their focus has been feeding programs, building clean water systems, supporting children's homes for AIDS, orphans and victims of abuse, as well as providing shipments of medicines and medical supplies to hospitals and clinics in underprivileged regions across the globe. For these grants, ASC supports housing programs, schools, vocational training, and tuition assistance programs in Kenya, Uganda, and Zambia.
Requirements: More information for who is eligible for aid under this grant can be found on the Aid for Starving Children website.
Geographic Focus: Kenya, Uganda, Zambia
Contact: Jeff Baugham, Secretary/Treasurer; (800) 514-3499; info@aidforstarvingchildren.org
Internet: aidforstarvingchildren.org/homes-education.php
Sponsor: Aid for Starving Children
P.O. Box 2156
Windsor, CA 95492

Aid for Starving Children Water Projects Grants   **147**
For over thirty years, Aid For Starving Children has been dedicated to helping children and families in need across four continents. Their focus has been feeding programs, building clean water systems, supporting children's homes for AIDS, orphans and victims of abuse, as well as providing shipments of medicines and medical supplies to hospitals and clinics in underprivileged regions across the globe. In Africa, thousands of children die every year due to illnesses from drinking contaminated water. Especially in rural areas, access to clean drinking water is extremely problematic for poor families. Few homes have piped water or a well and even fewer families can afford to buy clean water. Instead, they get water for drinking, cooking and cleaning from an open source like a river or pond that is polluted by animal remains, parasites and human waste. Not only is the water dangerous for human consumption, it also needs to be brought to the home, which is traditionally the women's and children's responsibility. So it is not uncommon for women and children to spend hours walking through the heat to the water source and carrying heavy jerry cans back. For these grants, ASC provides members of various Women's "Self-Help" groups in Kenya with large clean water tanks which allow mothers and their children to store and maintain access to disease-free drinking water year-round. These groups consist of between eight and ten mothers living in a small village setting.
Requirements: More information for who is eligible for aid under this grant can be found on the Aid for Starving Children website.
Geographic Focus: Kenya
Contact: Jeff Baugham, Secretary/Treasurer; (800) 514-3499; info@aidforstarvingchildren.org
Internet: aidforstarvingchildren.org/special-projects.php
Sponsor: Aid for Starving Children
P.O. Box 2156
Windsor, CA 95492

Air Products Foundation Grants 148

The Air Products Foundation builds meaningful relationships with charitable organizations that share the values inherent in the Air Products' higher purpose and enhance the Company's positive relations with employees, communities, customers, and shareholders. Air Products' higher purpose is rooted in: attracting and engaging talented and motivated employees; strengthening the quality of life in our host communities; and promoting collaboration among people of different cultures and backgrounds. Using the mission as a guide, the Foundation supports programs in the Lehigh Valley headquarters community, in Air Products host communities throughout the United States, in global locations where Air Products has employees and operations, at colleges and universities where it is strategically engaged, and through employee-directed matching gifts programs. The annual application submission deadline is June 1

Requirements: 501(c)3 nonprofit organizations in company-operating areas are eligible. Nonprofits must serve children, adults, families, and groups. To be eligible for consideration for the Lehigh Valley Grants program, the proposal must serve the greater Lehigh Valley that includes Allentown Bethlehem and Easton area of Pennsylvania.

Restrictions: Grants are not made to/for individuals, sectarian or denominational organizations, political candidates or activities, veterans organizations, organizations receiving United Way support, labor groups, elementary or secondary schools, capital campaigns of national organizations, hospital operating expenses, national health organizations, or goodwill advertising.

Geographic Focus: All States, All Countries

Date(s) Application is Due: Jun 1

Contact: Laurie Hackett, Lehigh Valley Grants Program Manager; (610) 481-2978; gostlelj@airproducts.com

Robert Episcopo, U.S. Field Grants Program Manager; (610) 481-2978

Pete Snyder, International Grants program Manager; (610) 481-2978

Brian McCourt, Talent Grants Program Manager; (610) 481-2978

Internet: www.airproducts.com/Company/Sustainability/corporate-citizenship/investing-in-our-communities-with-charitable-giving-philanthropy.aspx

Sponsor: Air Products Foundation

7201 Hamilton Boulevard

Allentown, PA 18195-1501

AKF Grants for Children 149

All of AKF's financial assistance programs are available to children who are living with kidney failure and whose household incomes qualify them for AKF assistance. In addition, their Summer Enrichment Program provides financial assistance to help children with kidney disease or kidney failure attend specialty camps and other local summer programs of their choice. AKF begins accepting applications for the Summer Enrichment Program each year in early April.

Requirements: AKF will review your household income, reasonable expenses and liquid assets before granting assistance.

Geographic Focus: All States

Contact: Patient Grants Coordinator; (800) 795-3226; patientservice@kidneyfund.org

Internet: www.kidneyfund.org/financial-assistance/information-for-patients/#grants_for_children

Sponsor: American Kidney Fund

11921 Rockville Pike, Suite 300

Rockville, MD 20852

Akron Community Foundation Arts and Culture Grants 150

In addition to honoring its fund holders' individual wishes, the Akron Community Foundation gives strength to big ideas, vulnerable populations, and targeted regions with an array of high-impact initiatives and grants. First, through grants and special projects, the Foundation's Community Fund focuses on four key areas: arts and culture; health and human services; civic affairs; and education. In the area of arts and culture, the Foundation supports Summit County activities that include: summer dance performances in the parks; cultural festivals in every neighborhood; and the Cleveland Orchestra under the stars at Blossom Music Center. Since 2000, the Foundation has directed more than $8 million in competitive grants to such efforts. There are five distinct characteristics that all grantees have in common: organizational strength exhibited via efficient and effective management that significantly improves the County; collaborative efforts that have systematic impact on individuals, families, and neighborhoods; accountability to the highest standards of ethics, integrity, service and fiduciary responsibility; efforts that build governance, management, financial, and organizational capacities of nonprofit agencies and the sector as a whole; and organizations whose missions promote equality and inclusiveness. Applications in this area are accepted each year from March 1 through the April 1 deadline.

Requirements: IRS 501(c)3 nonprofits supporting the residents of Summit County, Ohio, are eligible to apply.

Restrictions: The Foundation generally does not make grants for: endowments; scholarships; direct financial support to individuals; religious organizations for religious purposes; or private non-operating foundations. In accordance with its grant-making priorities, the Foundation generally does not fund: newly established nonprofit organizations that duplicate existing services; curriculum development for schools; disease-specific programs; economic development initiatives already being addressed by the Fund for Our Economic Future; programs at parochial schools that benefit only their students; and multi-year awards.

Geographic Focus: Ohio

Date(s) Application is Due: Apr 1

Amount of Grant: 100 - 100,000 USD

Contact: Diane Schumaker, Scholarships and Grants Administrator; (330) 436-5615 or (330) 376-8522; fax (330) 376-0202; dschumaker@akroncf.org

Teresa LeGrair, Director of Community Investment; (330) 436-5626 or (330) 376-8522; fax (330) 376-0202; tlegrair@akroncf.org

Internet: www.akroncf.org/Initiatives/ArtsCulture.aspx

Sponsor: Akron Community Foundation

345 West Cedar Street

Akron, OH 44307-2407

Akron Community Foundation Education Grants 151

n addition to honoring its fund holders' individual wishes, the Akron Community Foundation gives strength to big ideas, vulnerable populations, and targeted regions with an array of high-impact initiatives and grants. First, through grants and special projects, the Foundation's Community Fund focuses on four key areas: arts and culture; civic affairs; health and human services; and education. In the area of education, the Foundation supports Summit County individual schools, school systems, education leaders, nonprofit innovators, parents and community members to identify the best opportunities for investing in its children's future. Focusing on programs that align with Summit Education Initiative's Cradle to Career continuum, the Foundation board awards grants to programs that concentrate on key transition points in a student's education, including: kindergarten readiness; third grade reading; eighth grade math; and college readiness. In addition, it focuses a portion of its funding specifically on early learning programs that prepare children from birth to age 5 to succeed. Since 2000, the Foundation has directed more than $7.8 million in competitive grants to such education efforts as: early learning and kindergarten readiness; literacy initiatives; and vocational and continuing education. There are five distinct characteristics that all grantees have in common: organizational strength exhibited via efficient and effective management that significantly improves the County; collaborative efforts that have systematic impact on individuals, families, and neighborhoods; accountability to the highest standards of ethics, integrity, service and fiduciary responsibility; efforts that build governance, management, financial, and organizational capacities of nonprofit agencies and the sector as a whole; and organizations whose missions promote equality and inclusiveness. Applications in this area are accepted each year from November 15 through the December 15 deadline.

Requirements: IRS 501(c)3 nonprofits supporting the residents of Summit County, Ohio, are eligible to apply.

Restrictions: The Foundation generally does not make grants for: endowments; scholarships; direct financial support to individuals; religious organizations for religious purposes; or private non-operating foundations. In accordance with its grant-making priorities, the Foundation generally does not fund: newly established nonprofit organizations that duplicate existing services; curriculum development for schools; disease-specific programs; economic development initiatives already being addressed by the Fund for Our Economic Future; programs at parochial schools that benefit only their students; and multi-year awards.

Geographic Focus: Ohio

Date(s) Application is Due: Dec 15

Amount of Grant: 100 - 100,000 USD

Contact: Diane Schumaker, Scholarships and Grants Administrator; (330) 436-5615 or (330) 376-8522; fax (330) 376-0202; dschumaker@akroncf.org

Teresa LeGrair, Director of Community Investment; (330) 436-5626 or (330) 376-8522; fax (330) 376-0202; tlegrair@akroncf.org

Internet: www.akroncf.org/Initiatives/Education.aspx

Sponsor: Akron Community Foundation

345 West Cedar Street

Akron, OH 44307-2407

Akron Community Foundation Health and human services Grants 152

In addition to honoring its fund holders' individual wishes, the Akron Community Foundation gives strength to big ideas, vulnerable populations, and targeted regions with an array of high-impact initiatives and grants. First, through grants and special projects, the Foundation's Community Fund focuses on four key areas: arts and culture; civic affairs; health and human services; and education. In the area of arts and culture, the Foundation supports residents who are most vulnerable to the economy to meet their basic needs, including food, clothing, shelter, and safety from abuse. Its initiatives encourage systemic improvements in the accessibility and availability of each. Since 2000, the Foundation has made approximately $8 million in competitive grants to programs that address: food, clothing and shelter needs; preventative health care and health education; substance abuse, public health, and mental health; and social and legal aid services. There are five distinct characteristics that all grantees have in common: organizational strength exhibited via efficient and effective management that significantly improves the County; collaborative efforts that have systematic impact on individuals, families, and neighborhoods; accountability to the highest standards of ethics, integrity, service and fiduciary responsibility; efforts that build governance, management, financial, and organizational capacities of nonprofit agencies and the sector as a whole; and organizations whose missions promote equality and inclusiveness. Applications in this area are accepted each year from September 1 through the October 1 deadline.

Requirements: IRS 501(c)3 nonprofits supporting the residents of Summit County, Ohio, are eligible to apply.

Restrictions: The Foundation generally does not make grants for: endowments; scholarships; direct financial support to individuals; religious organizations for religious purposes; or private non-operating foundations. In accordance with its grant-making priorities, the Foundation generally does not fund: newly established nonprofit organizations that duplicate existing services; curriculum development for schools; disease-specific programs; economic development initiatives already being addressed by the Fund for Our Economic Future; programs at parochial schools that benefit only their students; and multi-year awards.

Geographic Focus: Ohio

Date(s) Application is Due: Oct 1

Amount of Grant: 100 - 100,000 USD

Contact: Diane Schumaker, Scholarships and Grants Administrator; (330) 436-5615 or (330) 376-8522; fax 330; dschumaker@akroncf.org

Teresa LeGrair, Director of Community Investment; (330) 436-5626 or (330) 376-8522; fax (330) 376-0202; tlegrair@akroncf.org

Internet: www.akroncf.org/Initiatives/HealthHumanServices.aspx

Sponsor: Akron Community Foundation

345 West Cedar Street

Akron, OH 44307-2407

ALA Alex Awards   153

The American Library Association's Alex Awards are given to ten books written for adults that have special appeal to young adults, ages 12 through 18. The winning titles are selected from the previous year's publishing. Awards were first given annually beginning in 1998. The titles were selected by the YALSA Adult Books for Young Adults Task Force from the previous year's publishing and were part of the Adult Books for Young Adults Project, which explored the role of adult books in the reading lives of teenagers and was funded by the Margaret Alexander Edwards Trust. Edwards was a young adult specialist for many years at the Enoch Pratt Library in Baltimore. Her work is described in her book Fair Garden and the Swarm of Beasts, and over the years she has served as an inspiration to librarians who serve young adults. With the approval of the Trust, the task force appointed to develop and implement the project named the awards the Alex Awards after Edwards, who was called Alex by her friends. The major sponsor of the Alex Awards continues to be the Margaret Alexander Edwards Trust. Booklist is also a sponsor.

Requirements: Eligible applicants must be published in the calendar year prior to the announcement and come from a publisher's adult list. Eligible books can include works of joint authorship and editorship, and can be books published in another country in English or in the United States in translation. Books must be selected from genres that have special appeal to young adults. Books can be suggested for the award through an online application on the ALA website.

Geographic Focus: All States, All Countries

Date(s) Application is Due: Dec 31

Samples: C.A. Fletcher, Edinburgh, Scotland - Awarded for their book, "A Boy and His Dog at the End of the World" (2020); Temi Oh, London, United Kingdom - Awarded for their book, "Do You Dream of Terra-Two?" (2020); Angie Cruz, Pittsburgh, Pennsylvania - Awarded for their book, "Dominicana" (2020).

Contact: Tammy Dillard-Steels, Staff Liaison; (312) 280-4391 or (800) 545-2433; fax (312) 440-9374; tdillard@ala.org or ala@ala.org

Internet: www.ala.org/awardsgrants/alex-awards

Sponsor: American Library Association

225 N. Michigan Avenue

Chicago, IL 60601

ALA ALSC Distinguished Service Award   154

The Distinguished Service Award is intended to honor an individual member of the Association for Library Service to Children (ALSC) who has made significant contributions to, and an impact on, library service to children and the Association for Library Service to Children. The recipient receives $1,000 and an engraved pin at the ALSC Membership Meeting during ALA Annual Conference. This award is given out on an annual basis.

Requirements: The nominee and the individual making the nomination must be personal members of ALSC as well as ALA. Individuals nominated my be chosen from any facet of library services to children. The nominee may be a practicing librarian in a public or school library, a library or information science educator, a member of the library press, or an editor or other employee of a publishing house. The individual may be retired. Nominations will be submitted online through a form found on the ALA website.

Restrictions: Organizational members are not eligible.

Geographic Focus: All States

Date(s) Application is Due: Dec 1

Amount of Grant: 1,000 USD

Samples: Claudette S. McLinn, Inglewood, California, $1,000 - Awarded to founder and Executive Director of the Center for the Study of Multicultural Children's Literature (CSMCL) and long-time literacy consultant, advocate, and speaker on library services to children and culturally diverse children's literature (2020).

Contact: Jordan Dubin; (312) 280-2163; fax (312) 440-9374; jdubin@ala.org or ala@ala.org

Internet: www.ala.org/awardsgrants/alsc-distinguished-service-award

Sponsor: American Library Association

225 N. Michigan Avenue

Chicago, IL 60601

ALA Amazing Audiobooks for Young Adults Award   155

The aim of the American Library Association's Amazing Audiobooks for Young Adults Award is to select, annotate, and present for publication an annual list of notable audio recordings significant to young adults from those released in the past two years. Each year's submissions for consideration must have been produced or released within the 24 months previous to the list's release at Midwinter. The recommended titles must address the wide scope of interests and concerns of listeners between 12 and 18. This award is given out on an annual basis.

Requirements: Selected works must include appeal of content to any or all potential listeners between 12 and 18 years old. While the list as a whole addresses the interests and needs of young adults ranging in age from 12 to 18, individual titles may appeal to parts of that range rather than to its whole. Material need not be "family friendly," or appeal to the youngest common denominator of adults. Adapted materials must remain true to, expand, or complement the original work. The criteria against which any particular audiobook should be judged as a candidate for a final list of annual recommendations by YALSA include effective use of voices, music, sound effects, and language, appropriateness of material for audio presentation, suitability of match between performer and text, possible expansion of

audience of young adults for a text that has not been readily accessible in its print format to its target audience, and professional production quality. Correct pronunciation of all text words is required; however, a title would not necessarily be disqualified if an error is deemed by the Committee to be minor when evaluating the recording as a whole. Clarity of recording and Informative packaging is required. Curricular suitability can be a positive consideration but is not a requirement for inclusion. Works can be nominated using the online application form on the ALA website.

Geographic Focus: All States, All Countries

Date(s) Application is Due: Dec 1

Samples: Emily Henry, Cincinnati, Ohio - Awarded for their work "A Million Junes" read by Julia Whelan (2018); Matt de la Peña, Brooklyn, New York - Awarded for their work "Ball Don't Lie" read by Dion Graham (2018); Adam Mansbach and Alan Zweibel - Awarded for their work "Benjamin Franklin You've Got Mail" read by Nick Podehl, Tom Parks, and Lauren Ezzo (2018).

Contact: Nichole O'Connor, Staff Liaison; (800) 545-2433, ext. 4387; fax (312) 440-9374; noconnor@ala.org or ala@ala.org

Internet: www.ala.org/awardsgrants/amazing-audiobooks-young-adults

Sponsor: American Library Association

225 N. Michigan Avenue

Chicago, IL 60601

ALA Amelia Bloomer Book List Award   156

The Amelia Bloomer Project, a committee of the Feminist Task Force of the Social Responsibilities Round Table, compiles the Amelia Bloomer List, an annual annotated book list (or bibliography) of well-written and well-illustrated books with significant feminist content, intended for young readers (ages birth through 18). A few years ago, a book by Shana Carey introduced nineteenth-century feminist activist Amelia Bloomer to the picture-book crowd. Published in 2000, YOU FORGOT YOUR SKIRT, AMELIA BLOOMER! uses humor and history to bring the life and work of this pioneering newspaper editor, feminist thinker, public speaker, and suffragist to a new generation. In the spirit of Amelia Bloomer, the Feminist Task Force of the Social Responsibilities Round Table of the American Library Association proudly announced in 2002 the first annual Amelia Bloomer List, a bibliography of appealing feminist books for young readers from birth to 18. Books eligible for this award must have been published in the United States during the 18 months prior to the selection in January of each year. Set from prehistoric times to the present, these books, both fiction and nonfiction, provide role models of stong, capable, creative women. They introduce children growing up in the South during the Civil Rights Movement, photographers on the cutting edge of their times, young women surviving in today's Afghanistan, and pioneers in the fields of flyinig and space exploration. Others feature girls who outwit dragons, create petroglyphs to save a tribe, and train to win battles. From a picture book using bear hair and other earthen materials in its illustrations to a biography written in graphic-novel format, these books show girls and women exploring exciting ways to solve practical dilemmas through the courage of their convictions. All of them spur the imagination and expand the limits of dreams while confronting traditional female stereotypes. And best of all, these books are fun reading! This award is given out on an annual basis. The list of nominated titles will be available online and distributed to ALA-ODLOS, FTF, and Booklist at the close of Midwinter Meeting. Other print and non-print media will be used to publicize the list, such as magazines directed at children and teens, women, families, and library professionals.

Requirements: A book must have a copyright date during the current calendar year or have been published from July to December of the previous calendar year to be considered for the list. A book originally published outside the United States will be considered according to its U.S. publication year. Books must be distributed in the United States to be considered for the list. Books which are revisions of previously published titles will be considered if the revision is to such an extent as to make the book substantially different from the previous edition. Any book which was discussed at any point during the previous year is not eligible for nomination the following year. The Amelia Bloomer Project accepts field nominations from members of the reading public. These suggestions will be passed on to committee members, who will read the books and determine whether or not they should be officially nominated for the list. Field nominations are accepted each year between March 1st and September 30th.

Geographic Focus: All States

Date(s) Application is Due: Sep 30

Samples: Frank Murphy - Awarded for book "A Boy Like You" illustrated by Kayla Harren (2020); Traci Sorell, Wagoner, Oklahoma - Awarded for book "At the Mountain's Base" illustrated by Weshoyot Alvitre (2020); Libby Babbott-Klein - Awarded for book, "Baby Feminists" illustrated by Jessica Walker (2020).

Contact: Jordan Dubin, Awards Coordinator; (800) 545-2433 ext. 5839; fax (312) 440-9374; jdubin@ala.org or ala@ala.org

Internet: www.ala.org/awardsgrants/amelia-bloomer-book-list

Sponsor: American Library Association

225 N. Michigan Avenue

Chicago, IL 60601

ALA Baker and Taylor/YALSA Collection Development Grants   157

To award $1,000 for collection development to YALSA members who represent a public library and who work directly with young adults ages 12 to 18. Up to two grants will be awarded annually. Each application will be judged on the basis of: the degree of need for additional materials for young adults; the degree of the current collection's use and the specificity of examples used; the soundness of the rationale for the selection of materials; the quality of the description of the benefits this grant will bring to young adults; and the degree to which the applicant's approach to collection development aligns with the principles in The Future of Library Services for and with Teens: A Call to Action.

Requirements: All applicants must be current members of ALA/YALSA at the time of application.

Geographic Focus: All States, Canada

Date(s) Application is Due: Dec 1
Amount of Grant: 1,000 USD
Contact: Nichole O'Connor, Program Officer for Events and Conferences; (800) 545-2433, ext. 4387 or (312) 280-4390; fax (312) 280-5276; noconnor@ala.org or ala@ala.org
Internet: www.ala.org/yalsa/awardsandgrants/bwi
Sponsor: American Library Association
225 N. Michigan Avenue
Chicago, IL 60601

ALA Baker and Taylor Summer Reading Program Grant   158

The Baker and Taylor Summer Reading Program Grant is designed to encourage outstanding summer reading programs by providing financial assistance, while recognizing ALSC members for outstanding program development. Each application will be judged on the plan and outline submitted for a theme-based summer reading program in a public library. The committee encourages innovative proposals involving children with physical or mental disabilities. The award of $3,000 is given out each year. Winners will be announced via a press release on the ALSC website.

Requirements: The applicant must plan and present an outline for a theme-based summer reading program in a public library. The program must be open to all children (birth -14 years). The committee also encourages innovative proposals involving children with physical or mental disabilities. Applicants must be personal members of ALSC as well as ALA. Programs must take place at a public library. The online application can be found on the ALA website.
Restrictions: Organizational members are not eligible.
Geographic Focus: All States
Date(s) Application is Due: Nov 30
Amount of Grant: 3,000 USD
Samples: Homewood Public Library, Homewood, Alabama, $3,000- Presented to build inclusivity and literacy through hands-on sensory programming in the library and outreach, collection development, and community partnerships with organizations that serve youth with special needs (2020).
Contact: Jordan Dubin, Awards Coordinator; (800) 545-2433 ext. 5839; fax (312) 440-9374; jdubin@ala.org or ala@ala.org
Internet: www.ala.org/awardsgrants/baker-taylor-summer-reading-program-grant
Sponsor: American Library Association
225 N. Michigan Avenue
Chicago, IL 60601

Alabama Humanities Foundation Major Grants   159

Alabama Humanities Foundation Major Grants fund a broad range of projects. Formats include public discussion programs, such as workshops, reading and discussion, lecture and discussion, and other community forums which encourage scholar and audience dialogue. They may be supplemented by other formats such as media items or exhibitions. The three essential components of successful grant proposals are active public participation, strong humanities content, and the direct involvement of humanities scholars. Projects often include, but are not limited to the following: Traveling exhibits; Conferences and symposia; Festivals; Lecture programs; Interpretive readings; Teacher workshops; Book discussions; Radio broadcasts; Documentary films; Digital media. Up to a maximum of $7,500 in outright funds are available.
Requirements: All proposed projects should connect the public with the humanities at no cost and must be accessible. Programs should be geared toward a diverse audience and must allow for differing points of view. All projects must be open to the general public and should not be limited to members of a specific organization, scholars, or a campus community. Applicants must ensure that one or more humanities disciplines are central to the project and that humanities themes and topics are adequately explored and interpreted. Major Grant projects must include at least one primary scholar, in addition to the project director, who is integrally involved in both the planning and implementation of the project. Applicants are required to submit an evaluation plan that is appropriate for assessing the project's identified goals. Evaluations are meant to gather the feedback necessary to improve future programming. Grantees must summarize evaluation results as part of the final reporting process to AHF. Organizations must submit a final report through AHF's Online Grant Management System no later than 60 days after the grant period end date. Major grants require a 1:1 cost share match, including cash and in-kind contributions. Project events must take place a minimum of 60 days after the submission deadline. AHF awards all grants on a quarterly basis. Applicants are required to create an account through AHF's Online Grant Management System and must submit a Letter of Intent (LOI) online at least four weeks before the submission deadline. All applicants must obtain a DUNS number to qualify for funding.
Restrictions: Grants are not awarded to individuals or to out-of-state applicants without the support of an in-state fiscal agent. AHF does not fund projects that: promote a course of action or advocacy; discriminate against persons or groups; support individual research or scholarship; support permanent planning, construction, or restoration; result in permanent acquisition of equipment; or realize a profit or result in a free-standing publication. AHF will not fund multiple projects from the same organization at the same time. Line items eligible for applicant cost share but ineligible to receive funding from AHF include the following: Administrative costs; Ongoing operating costs; Audience travel expenses Audience food and beverages; Teacher stipends; Institutional acquisitions; Equipment purchases; Free-standing publications; Construction or restoration; Indirect costs.
Geographic Focus: Alabama
Date(s) Application is Due: Mar 15; Jun 15; Sep 15; Dec 15
Amount of Grant: Up to 7,500 USD
Samples: Coleman Center for the Arts, York, Alabama - supports an exhibit and program series to celebrate the vital role of African-American music in American and international culture and history (2019); Mobile Creole Cultural and Historical Preservation Society, Mobile, Alabama - supports a digitization workshop at the Mobile Public Library (2019); Tennessee Valley Jazz Society, Huntsville, Alabama - supports the Evolution of African-

American Gospel Music in Alabama, a part of the Evolution of Black Music in Alabama Educational and Concert Series that explores the history of spirituals, gospel, blues, and jazz music and their impact on world arts and cultures (2019).
Contact: Graydon Rust, Grants Director; (205) 558-3997 or (205) 558-3980; fax (205) 558-3981; grust@alabamahumanities.org or info@alabamahumanities.org
Internet: www.alabamahumanities.org/grants/
Sponsor: Alabama Humanities Foundation
1100 Ireland Way, Suite 202
Birmingham, AL 35205

ALA Best Fiction for Young Adults Award   160

The Best Fiction for Young Adults Award considers books, recommended for ages 12-18, that meet the criteria of both good quality literature and appealing reading for teens. The list comprises a wide range of genres and styles, including contemporary realistic fiction, fantasy, horror, science fiction and novels in verse. YALSA's Best Fiction for Young Adults (BFYA) Committee evolved from a committee established under the School Libraries Section of ALA, which was charged with producing a list of 1930s "Best Books for Young People." The committee has undergone several changes of focus and names over the years, including the Book Selection Committee (1954), and later the Committee for the Selection of Significant Adult Books for Young People (1963). It became the Best Books for Young Adults Committee (BBYA) in 1966. As publishing for the young adult market grew exponentially (over 2,000 titles per year in 2008) and seven other YALSA selection and award lists for young adults were created since its inception, Best Books for Young Adults was restructured and named Best Fiction for Young Adults by the YALSA Board of Directors at the midwinter meeting.
Requirements: The Committee considers any fiction title published for a teen audience from September 1 of the previous calendar year through December 31 of the current calendar year. The chair is responsible for verifying the eligibility of all nominated titles. A book originally published outside the United States will be considered according to its U.S. publication year. Books published outside of the United States are not eligible unless a U.S. edition is available. "Best" is defined as: of the highest quality, excellence, or standing. As applied to teen fiction, this means that YALSA's BFYA Committee looks for outstanding titles of fiction that are of interest and value to teenagers. Titles are selected for their demonstrated or probable appeal to the personal reading tastes of young adults. However, appeal and popularity are not synonymous. Titles from a series should be considered on their individual merits. In addition to the question of appeal, committee members should consider the following when assessing titles: language, plot, style, setting, dialog, characterization, and design.
Restrictions: Publishers, authors, agents, or editors may not nominate their own titles.
Geographic Focus: All States
Date(s) Application is Due: Nov 1
Contact: Cheryl Malden, Program Officer; (800) 545-2433 ext. 3247 or]; fax (312) 440-9374; cmalden@ala.org or ala@ala.org
Internet: www.ala.org/awardsgrants/best-fiction-young-adults
Sponsor: American Library Association
225 N. Michigan Avenue
Chicago, IL 60601

ALA Bookapalooza Grants   161

The core purpose of the Association for Library Service to Children (ALSC) is creating a better future for all children through libraries. The Association believes that: in every library, children come first; the importance of high quality children's service with adequate materials and resources; collections, services, resources, and staff reflect the communities they serve; the library's physical space reflects the developmental needs of children; and children and their families are served by a variety of non-traditional programs and activities in off-site locations. With this in mind, Bookapalooza Grants offer select libraries a collection of materials that will help transform their collection, and provide the opportunity for these materials to be used in their community in creative and innovative ways. Each application is judged on the following criteria: degree of need in the community and need of the library where the materials will be used; extent to which the materials will improve service to children in the community; the plan for using the materials in a creative and innovative way; and the clarity and effectiveness of the statement of need. This award is given out on an annual basis.
Requirements: Applicants must be personal members of ALSC as well as ALA. Libraries must be located in the U.S. The application is available at the ALA website. Shipping and handling charges for shipment of the Bookapalooza collection are the responsibility of the libraries selected. For the purpose of estimating shipping costs, winning collections are anticipated to weigh as much as 600 pounds and include as many as 12 cartons. Shipping rates may range from $200 - $500 when shipped at book rate.
Restrictions: Organizational members are not eligible to apply.
Geographic Focus: All States
Date(s) Application is Due: Feb 1
Samples: Bezhigoogahbow Library, Cass Lake, Minnesota - Awarded to help build the library's children's collection where it is much needed; David A. Howe Public Library, Wellsville, New York - Awarded to supplement library's youth materials, as well as establish a rotating outreach collection for youth; Nora Sparks Warren Library, Pauls Valley, Oklahoma - Awarded to attract more youth and families to the library and to increase the variety and frequency of their story times and other children's programs.
Contact: Jordan Dubin, Awards Coordinator; (800) 545-2433 ext. 5839; fax (312) 440-9374; jdubin@ala.org or ala@ala.org
Internet: www.ala.org/awardsgrants/bookapalooza-program
Sponsor: American Library Association
225 N. Michigan Avenue
Chicago, IL 60601

ALA Booklist Editors' Choice Books for Youth Awards 162

Committed to providing a broad selection of outstanding books that mixes popular appeal with literary excellence, the Books for Youth editorial staff annually selects a number of titles as representative of the year's outstanding books for public-library collections. Its scope has been intentionally broad, and Booklist has attempted to find books that combine literary, intellectual, and aesthetic excellence with popular appeal. The Books for Youth editorial staff has chosen the titles as best-of-the-year fiction, nonfiction, and picture books.
Requirements: Books for this award are chosen by the Booklist Books for Youth editors and therefore nominations are not accepted for this award.
Geographic Focus: All States, Canada
Date(s) Application is Due: Feb 28
Contact: Cheryl Malden, Program Officer; (800) 545-2433 ext. 3247; fax (312) 440-9374; cmalden@ala.org or ala@ala.org
Internet: www.ala.org/awardsgrants/booklist-editors-choice-books-youth
Sponsor: American Library Association
225 N. Michigan Avenue
Chicago, IL 60601

ALA Bound to Stay Bound Books Scholarships 163

The Bound to Stay Bound Books (BTSB) Scholarships provide financial assistance in the form of four $7,500 annual awards for the education of men and women who intend to pursue an MLS or advanced degree and who plan to work in the area of library service to children. This work may be serving children up to and including the age of 14 in any type of library. The scholarship is made possible by the ALSC through the generous contributions of Bound to Stay Bound Books, Incorporated. This award is given out on an annual basis.
Requirements: Applicants must be citizens of the U.S. or Canada. Each scholarship will be granted to four/two candidates whose educational and personal qualifications indicate fitness for professional preparation at the graduate level in the field of library work with children. Factors considered are academic excellence, leadership qualities and a desire to work with children in any type of library. A Personal Statement describing career interests and goals, and a commitment to library service to children must be included with the application. The recipients will be expected to accept positions after graduation in the field of library service to children for at least one year. These positions shall be in the United States or Canada, or in a library provided for dependents of military personnel of the United States or Canada. Within a year of graduation, each recipient is expected to submit to the Association for Library Service to Children a letter from an institution's director or personnel department verifying appointment as a children's librarian. If the recipient does not complete this requirement, for any reason within the recipient's control, the scholarship money must be refunded. Failure to fulfill requirements will result in forfeiture, or repayment of scholarship monies. Bound to Stay Bound scholarship money will be paid directly to the school. Applications must include a completed online application (found on the ALA website), three references, and official academic transcripts from institutions where you received your bachelors degree.
Restrictions: The applicant may not have earned more than 12 semester hours toward an MLS/MLIS prior to June 1 of the year awarded.
Geographic Focus: All States, Canada
Date(s) Application is Due: Mar 1
Amount of Grant: 7,500 USD
Samples: Keshia Latrice-Carol Nash-Johnson, San Jose, California, $7,500 - Awarded to to pursue an MLS or advanced degree and who plan to work in the area of library service to children; Megan Ashley Hoak, Valdosta, Georgia, $7,500 - Awarded to pursue an MLS or advanced degree and who plan to work in the area of library service to children; Melissa Sue Wise, Denton, Texas, $7,500 - Awarded to pursue an MLS or advanced degree and who plan to work in the area of library service to children.
Contact: Elizabeth Serrano; (312) 280-2164; fax (312) 440-9374; eserrano@ala.org or ala@ala.org
Internet: www.ala.org/awardsgrants/bound-stay-bound-books-scholarship-0
Sponsor: American Library Association
225 N. Michigan Avenue
Chicago, IL 60601

ALA BWI Collection Development Grant 164

The BWI Collection Development Grant awards YALSA members who represent a public library and work directly with young adults ages 12 to 18. Up to two awards of $1,000 each are given on an annual basis.
Requirements: This award is available to YALSA members who represent a public library and who work directly with young adults ages 12 to 18. All applicants must be current personal members of ALA/YALSA at the time the application is submitted. Each application will be judged on the basis of the degree of need for additional materials for young adults, the degree of the current collection's use and the specificity of examples used, the soundness of the rationale for the selection of materials, the quality of the description of the benefits this grant will bring to young adults, and the degree to which the applicant's philosophy reflects the concepts identified in Directions for Library Service to Young Adults. All entries must include the application form provided by the Young Adult Library Services Association and a Description Statement that is no more than 1,000 words and double-spaced. Entries should be models of clarity and completeness. Each candidate must submit a one-page report to the YALSA Office within six months of receiving the grant. This report should contain details on how this award has impacted the grant recipient's collection of materials for young adults. This report may or may not be considered for publication.
Geographic Focus: All States
Date(s) Application is Due: Dec 1
Amount of Grant: 1,000 USD
Samples: Jeanie Austin, Champaign, Illinois, $1,000 - Award to a PhD candidate with the iSchool at UIUC; Katelyn Marsh, West Brookfield, Massachusetts, $1,000 - Awarded to Library Director/Teen Services Librarian at Merriam-Gilbert Public Library.
Contact: Cheryl Malden, Program Officer; (800) 545-2433 ext. 3247; fax (312) 440-9374; cmalden@ala.org or ala@ala.org
Nichole Gilbert; (800) 545-2433 ext. 4387; fax (312) 440-9374; ngilbert@ala.org or ala@ala.org
Internet: www.ala.org/awardsgrants/awards/168/apply
Sponsor: American Library Association
225 N. Michigan Avenue
Chicago, IL 60601

ALA Children's Literature Legacy Award 165

The Legacy Award honors an author or illustrator whose books, published in the United States, have made, over a period of years, a substantial and lasting contribution to literature for children through books that demonstrate integrity and respect for all children's lives and experiences. The award consists of a citation and is given out on an annual basis. From 1954 to 2018, this award was known as the Laura Ingalls Wilder Medal.
Requirements: Nominees are selected by the Committee members, and therefore you cannot apply to this award. Authors/illustrators may be nominated posthumously. Some portion of the nominee's active career in books for children must have occurred in the twenty-five years prior to nomination. Citizenship or residence of the potential nominee is not to be considered. The nominee must have worked on more than one book. First publication of these books does not have to be in the United States, but they must have been published in the United States at some point in time. At least some of the books by the potential nominee need to have been available to children for at least ten years. "A substantial and lasting contribution" means that the books, by their nature (and/or number), occupy an important place in literature for American children and that over the years children have read the books and that the books continue to be requested and read by children. In addition to the criteria implicit in the terms and definitions, the committee may wish to consider whether some or all of the books are exceptionally notable and leading examples of the genre to which they belong, or that some or all of the books have established a new type or kind of book or new trends in books available to children. The committee, in making its selection of nominees, ought to be aware of the entire body of work for children of the potential nominee and may base its decision for nomination on the total body of work for children or on those portions of the total body of work which are of a substantial and lasting nature.
Geographic Focus: All States, All Countries
Date(s) Application is Due: Dec 31
Samples: Kevin Henkes, New York City, New York - Awarded for his "legacy of work full of honest emotion and insight, warm and gentle humor, and playful, nuanced illustrations" (2020).
Contact: Jordan Dubin, Awards Coordinator; (800) 545-2433 ext. 5839; fax (312) 440-9374; jdubin@ala.org or ala@ala.org
Internet: www.ala.org/awardsgrants/childrens-literature-legacy-award
Sponsor: American Library Association
225 N. Michigan Avenue
Chicago, IL 60601

ALA Coretta Scott King-John Steptoe Award for New Talent 166

The Coretta Scott King - John Steptoe Award for New Talent was established to affirm new talent and to offer visibility to excellence in writing and/or illustration which otherwise might be formally unacknowledged within a given year within the structure of the two awards given annually by the Coretta Scott King Book Awards Committee. These books affirm new talent and offer visibility to excellence in writing or illustration at the beginning of a career as a published book creator. The award includes a plaque and an acceptance speech at the Coretta Scott King Book Awards Breakfast at ALA Annual Conference. This award is given out on an annual basis.
Requirements: The author or illustrator must live in the U.S. or maintain dual residency/citizenship. The book must be published in the range of January - December 1 of the year preceding the year the award is given as indicated by the copyright date printed in the book. An author may receive this award one time. Awardees are expected to attend Coretta Scott King Book Awards Breakfast during ALA Annual Conference to deliver acceptance speech. The book must meet the following criteria: portray some aspect of the black experience, past, present, or future; written/illustrated by an African American; an original work; meet established standards of quality writing for youth (clear plot, well drawn characters, suitable for young adults); and written for preschool to grade 4, grades 5 through 8, or grades 9 through 12. Particular attention will be paid to titles which seek to motivate readers to develop their own attitudes and behaviors as well as comprehend their personal duty and responsibility as citizens in a pluralistic society. Awards will be submitted online through the ALA website.
Restrictions: The winner(s)' published works cannot exceed three in number. An author or illustrator who has already received or has just been selected to win one of the Coretta Scott King Book Awards in the current year is not eligible for the John Steptoe Award for New Talent.
Geographic Focus: All States
Date(s) Application is Due: Dec 1
Samples: Tiffany D. Jackson, Brooklyn, New York- Awarded the Author Award for their book, "Monday's Not Coming" (2019); Oge Mora, Providence, Rhode Island- Awarded the Illustrator Award for their book, "Thank You, Omu!" (2019).
Contact: Amber Hayes; (312) 280-2140; fax (312) 440-9374; ahayes@ala.org or ala@ala.org
Internet: www.ala.org/awardsgrants/coretta-scott-king-john-steptoe-award-new-talent
Sponsor: American Library Association
225 N. Michigan Avenue
Chicago, IL 60601

ALA Coretta Scott King-Virginia Hamilton Award for Lifetime Achievement 167

The Coretta Scott King - Virginia Hamilton Award for Lifetime Achievement is named in memory of beloved children's author Virginia Hamilton. The annual award is presented in even years to an African American author, illustrator or author/illustrator for a body of his or her published books for children and/or young adults, and who has made a significant

and lasting literary contribution. In odd years, the award is presented to a practitioner for substantial contributions through active engagement with youth using award winning African American literature for children and/or young adults, via implementation of reading and reading related activities/programs. A medal and check for $1,500 is presented to the winner during the Coretta Scott King Awards Breakfast at the ALA Annual Conference.
Requirements: For the author and/or illustrator recipients: The recipient must be an African American author or illustrator. Recipients may be joint authors, joint illustrators, or joint author/illustrators. Recipients must be living by deadline of nomination date. Authors or illustrators must have residence in the United States. and the majority of the books in the body of work must be available in the United States at the time of the nomination deadline. The body of work selected must represent distinguished writing and/or illustrations by and about the African American experience for children and/or young adults, and the body of work selected has made a substantial contribution to children's and/or young adult literature about the African American experience over a period of years. The body of work must meet established standards of high quality writing and/or illustration for youth. Committee members may also pay particular attention to bodies of work whose interpretation consistently motivates youth readers to stretch their imagination and thinking, which denote exceptional examples of specific types of literature, and that represent trend-setters, innovations, or fresh explorations of themes or topics or perspectives in African American literature for children and/or young adult. The body of work must include at least one CSK Award winner (Author, Illustrator, New Talent winner, or Honor Book for either category). For practitioner recipients: The recipient must be a practicing youth advocate whose productive activities, work, or career engages students in the reading of award winning African American literature for children and young adults. The recipient needs to have made a significant contribution to champion youth reading and engagement with award winning African American literature. Committee will consider the applicant's level of dedication to the promotion of reading and implementation of various reading /reading related programs, depth of involvement, impact of their work, and overall amount of time committed to such service. Preference will be given to the applicant whose service in this area has been significant over a period of years, rather than those whose accomplishments, though highly visible, are more limited in duration. The recipient must be living by deadline of nomination date. Recipients of the award in either year must attend the Coretta Scott King Book Awards Breakfast during ALA Annual Conference and deliver acceptance speech. Applications will be submitted online through the ALA website.
Geographic Focus: All States
Date(s) Application is Due: Dec 2
Amount of Grant: 1,500 USD
Samples: Dr. Pauletta Brown Bracy, Durham, North Carolina, $1,500 - Awarded for successfully merging scholarship and service with publications such as "Libraries, Literacy and African American Youth" (co-edited with Sandra Hughes Hassell and Casey H. Rawson) as well as her work with the Coretta Scott King Book Awards and with workshops and conferences dedicated to promoting African American books for children and teens (2019).
Contact: Amber Hayes; (312) 280-2140; fax (312) 440-9374; jamundsen@ala.org or ala@ala.org
Internet: www.ala.org/awardsgrants/coretta-scott-king-virginia-hamilton-award-lifetime-achievement
Sponsor: American Library Association
225 N. Michigan Avenue
Chicago, IL 60601

ALA Coretta Scott King Book Donation Grant 168

The Coretta Scott King Book Donation Grant was created to help build collections and bring books into the lives of children in latchkey, preschool programs, faith-based reading projects, homeless shelters, charter schools and underfunded libraries. Approximately 300 books by African American authors and illustrators are given out every year. Applications are judged based on the following criteria: the degree of need in the community; the demonstrated need of the institution applying for the materials; the extent to which the materials will improve service to children and youth in the community; the extent to which the materials will be used to promote positive self-image of African American children and youth and/or broaden the worldview of children and youth; the clarity and effectiveness of the statement of need; and the clarity and effectiveness of the plan to make the materials available in their community, including the demonstrated ability of the applicant agency to implement their proposal.
Requirements: Any agency that serves children or youth may apply. This includes, but is not limited to schools, libraries, social service agencies, prisons, detention centers, churches or other religious organizations, and institutions of higher education. Grant recipients are required to submit a brief follow up report by March 31st of the following year. To assure agencies and institutions receive age appropriate books, the committee reserves the right to divide a single grant among two or more agencies or institutions. Applications will be submitted online through the ALA website.
Restrictions: Shipping and handling are the responsibility of the institution selected to receive the materials. Materials must be claimed within one month of notification of the donation. Recipients agree to accept all materials offered. Institutions may receive materials no more than once every five years.
Geographic Focus: All States
Date(s) Application is Due: Feb 1
Samples: Lawrence Memorial Library, Windsor, North Carolina- Awarded to help build collections and bring books into the lives of children; Mayaguez Children's Library, Mayaguez, Puerto Rico- Awarded to help build collections and bring books into the lives of children; W.R. Saffold Community Resource Center, Britton's Neck, South Carolina- Awarded to help build collections and bring books into the lives of children.
Contact: Cheryl Malden, Program Officer; (800) 545-2433 ext. 3247; fax (312) 440-9374; cmalden@ala.org or ala@ala.org
Internet: www.ala.org/awardsgrants/coretta-scott-king-book-donation-grant
Sponsor: American Library Association
225 N. Michigan Avenue
Chicago, IL 60601

ALA Fabulous Films for Young Adults Award 169

The purpose of the Fabulous Films for Young Adults list is to identify for collection developers a body of films relating to a theme that will appeal to young adults in a variety of settings. Selection criteria consistent with the Library Bill of Rights shall be applied throughout the selection process. Titles chosen are of acceptable quality and are effective in their presentation. Selection criteria is based on technical qualities, content, utilization, and overall effect. The nomination suggestion form is available at the website.
Requirements: To be considered for the list, films must be currently available for purchase in the United states. The film must be relevant in a noteworthy way to the chosen theme. In general, a whole series will not be included on the list. Individual titles from a series may be nominated and included. At the chair's discretion, the committee may consider multi-part programs. All segments must be previewed. Titles that are re-edited or re-released must contain a significant amount of new material to qualify for consideration and will be treated as new titles. Titles may be nominated by committee members as well as from the field. Field nominations must be confirmed by a committee member. To be nominated, a title must have been viewed by at least one committee member. Committee members are encouraged to solicit the opinions of young adults on titles being considered for nomination. Nominations for titles to be considered must fill out a suggestion form which can be found on the ALA website.
Restrictions: Film makers, distributors, or producers may not nominate their own productions. They may request that a particular title be viewed by a committee member for list consideration.
Geographic Focus: All States
Date(s) Application is Due: Dec 1
Contact: Jordan Dubin; (800) 545-2433 ext. 5839; fax (312) 440-9374; jdubin@ala.org
Internet: www.ala.org/awardsgrants/fabulous-films-young-adults
Sponsor: American Library Association
225 N. Michigan Avenue
Chicago, IL 60601

ALA Great Books Giveaway Competition 170

Each year the Young Adult Library Services Association (YALSA) offce receives about 1,200 newly published books, videos, CDs, and other materials targeted toward young adults. Publishers and producers submit copies for selection committees to review and nominate. YALSA believes these materials should be passed along to schools, public libraries, or institutions in need. This award is given out on an annual basis.
Requirements: Applicants must be personal members of YALSA and ALA. Selection criteria is based on: the degree of need in the community, school, public library, or institution where the library is located; how service would be improved for young adults in the community; the clarity and effectiveness of the statement of need; the age of the nonfiction collection in the application; and the currency and completeness of the institution's board approved collection development policy, including the materials selection policy, with procedures for handling challenges. Applications will be submitted online through the ALA website.
Restrictions: The recipient of the materials is responsible for shipping costs. For purposes of estimating shipping costs, winning collections have weighed as much as 2,000 lbs. and included as many as 75 cartons. Shipping ranges from $800 - $1,200. ALA organizational members and previous winners are not eligible.
Geographic Focus: All States
Date(s) Application is Due: Dec 1
Samples: Tyler Public Library, Tyler, Texas - Awarded to assist in the expansion of their young adult media collection.
Contact: Cheryl Malden, Program Officer; (800) 545-2433 ext. 3247; fax (312) 440-9374; lsmith@ala.org or ala@ala.org
Internet: www.ala.org/awardsgrants/great-books-giveaway-competition
Sponsor: American Library Association
225 N. Michigan Avenue
Chicago, IL 60601

ALA Innovative Reading Grant 171

The Innovative Reading Grant, established in 2006, supports the planning and implementation of a unique and innovative program for children (K-9th grade) which motivates and encourages reading, especially with struggling readers. The project or reading program should promote the importance of reading, facilitate the learners' literacy development, and be supported by current reading research, practice, and policy. The grant includes $2,500 and is given out on an annual basis.
Requirements: The reading program must be specifically designed for children (grades K-9) in the school library setting. Projects will be judged on the potential to measure and evaluate the impact and reading improvement for its learners, potential to impact student learning (especially reading), originality of project and methodology, and the potential for replication of the program. Applicants should demonstrate an ability to undertake and successfully complete the project, and should include a timeline, budget, and clarity of purpose in their project plan. Research should be evidence-based and scholarly in nature. The grant recipient may be required to present a program at the ALA Annual and/or at a future AASL Conference AFTER the study has been completed and the results known. Recipients may be required to write an article for Knowledge Quest that delineates their reading incentive project and demonstrate their successes, trials, and recommendations for improving so others can replicate the project. Applications will be submitted online through the ALA website.
Restrictions: The program must encourage innovative ways to motivate and involve children in reading. Existing commercial programs will not be considered.
Geographic Focus: All States
Date(s) Application is Due: Feb 1
Amount of Grant: 2,500 USD
Samples: Stefanie Throndson, New Hampton, Iowa, $2,500- Awarded to allow New Hampton Elementary third-graders to increase their nonfiction reading comprehension

along with having students become aware of global issues through texts, field trips, and hands-on experiences (2020).

Contact: Allison K. Cline; (312) 280-4385; fax (312) 440-9374; acline@ala.org or ala@ala.org
Internet: www.ala.org/awardsgrants/innovative-reading-grant
Sponsor: American Library Association
225 N. Michigan Avenue
Chicago, IL 60601

ALA John Newbery Medal   172

The Newbery Medal is awarded annually by the Association for Library Service to Children, a division of the American Library Association, to the author of the most distinguished contribution to American literature for children published in the previous year. In 1921, Frederic G. Melcher proposed the award to the American Library Association meeting of the Children's Librarians' Section and suggested that it be named for the eighteenth-century English bookseller John Newbery. The idea was enthusiastically accepted by the children's librarians, and Melcher's official proposal was approved by the ALA Executive Board in 1922. In Melcher's formal agreement with the board, the purpose of the Newbery Medal was stated as follows: "To encourage original creative work in the field of books for children. To emphasize to the public that contributions to the literature for children deserve similar recognition to poetry, plays, or novels. To give those librarians, who make it their life work to serve children's reading interests, an opportunity to encourage good writing in this field." The Newbery Award thus became the first children's book award in the world. Its terms, as well as its long history, continue to make it the best known and most discussed children's book award in this country. Today the Medal is administered by the Association for Library Service to Children, a division of ALA. The annual award winner receives a bronze medal and honorees, if any, receive a plaque. This award is given out on an annual basis.
Requirements: The Medal shall be awarded annually to the author of the most distinguished contribution to American literature for children published by an American publisher in the United States in English during the preceding year. There are no limitations as to the character of the book considered except that it be original work. Honor books may be named. These shall be books that are also truly distinguished. The Award is restricted to authors who are citizens or residents of the United States. Committee members will consider, in their deliberations, the Interpretation of the theme or concept; Presentation of information including accuracy, clarity, and organization; Development of a plot; Delineation of characters; Delineation of a setting; and Appropriateness of style. Committee members must consider excellence of presentation for a child audience. ALSC membership is not a requirement to submit your work. To submit your work, mail one copy of your book to the Committee Chair (the address can be requested through the ALA website). If you wish, you may attach a cover letter with your contact information to your final work. There is no submission form to fill out (besides address request), nor an entry fee for the Newbery Medal.
Restrictions: The book must be a self-contained entity, not dependent on other media (i.e., sound or film equipment) for its enjoyment.
Geographic Focus: All States
Date(s) Application is Due: Dec 31
Contact: Jordan Dubin, Awards Coordinator; (800) 545-2433 ext. 5839; fax (312) 440-9374; jdubin@ala.org or ala@ala.org
Internet: www.ala.org/awardsgrants/john-newbery-medal-2
Sponsor: American Library Association
225 N. Michigan Avenue
Chicago, IL 60601

ALA Louise Seaman Bechtel Fellowship   173

Louise Seaman Bechtel (1894–April 12, 1985) was an American editor, critic, author, and teacher of young children. Named in her honor, the Louise Seaman Bechtel Fellowship is designed to allow qualified children's librarians to spend a month or more reading and studying at the Baldwin Library of the George A. Smathers Libraries, University of Florida, Gainesville. The Baldwin Library contains a special collection of 85,000 volumes of children's literature published mostly before 1950. Awardees are given $4,000 to support their study and are recognized at the membership meeting during ALA Annual Conference. This award is given out on an annual basis.
Requirements: Candidates must have the following qualifications to be considered: current personal membership with ALSC and ALA; working in direct service to children, or retired members who complete their careers in direct service to children, for a minimum of eight years; have a graduate degree from an ALA-accredited program; and willing to write a report about their study. If selected, retired Fellowship winners would agree to present a minimum of three public programs based on their research project to children in libraries or schools following the completion of their Fellowship period. The online application for this award is available on the ALA website.
Restrictions: Organizational members of ALA and ALSC are not eligible to apply.
Geographic Focus: All States, Canada
Date(s) Application is Due: Oct 1
Amount of Grant: 4,000 USD
Contact: Jordan Dubin; (800) 545-2433 ext. 5839; jdubin@ala.org or ala@ala.org
Internet: www.ala.org/awardsgrants/louise-seaman-bechtel-fellowship
Sponsor: American Library Association
225 N. Michigan Avenue
Chicago, IL 60601

ALA MAE Award for Best Literature Program for Teens   174

The MAE Award for Best Literature Program for Teens honors a Young Adult and Library Services Association (YALSA) member for developing an outstanding reading or literature program for young adults. The MAE Award for Best Literature Program for Teens is sponsored by the Margaret A. Edwards Trust. Winners receive $500 and an additional $500

for their library. Edwards was a well-known and innovative young adult services librarian at Enoch Pratt Free Library in Baltimore for more than 30 years. Her trust has supported many initiatives from YALSA, including the Alex Awards for adult books with teen appeal and all five rounds of the Excellence in Library Service to Young Adults project. This award is given out on an annual basis.
Requirements: All applicants must be current personal members of ALA/YALSA at the time the application is submitted. The purpose of the reading or literature program must be to bring young adults and books together and to encourage the development of life-long reading habits. The program must be specifically designed for and targeted at reaching young adults. All or part of the program must have taken place in the twelve months preceding the award deadline date. The applicant must work directly with young adults and be a personal member of the Young Adult Library Services Association. Nonwinning entries may be resubmitted in subsequent years if the program is current and ongoing and if a new application that updates the documentation is submitted. Entries should be models of clarity and completeness. Applications will be submitted online through the ALA website.
Geographic Focus: All States
Date(s) Application is Due: Dec 1
Amount of Grant: 1,000 USD
Samples: Lauri Vaughan, San Jose, California, $1,000 - Awarded to Upper school campus librarian at The Harker School for the development and success of their program, ReCreate Reading.
Contact: Nichole O'Connor, Staff Liaison; (800) 545-2433, ext. 4387; fax (312) 440-9374; noconnor@ala.org or ala@ala.org
Internet: www.ala.org/awardsgrants/mae-award-best-literature-program-teens
Sponsor: American Library Association
225 N. Michigan Avenue
Chicago, IL 60601

ALA Margaret A. Edwards Award   175

The Margaret A. Edwards Award, established in 1988, honors an author, as well as a specific body of his or her work, that have been popular over a period of time. It recognizes an author's work in helping adolescents become aware of themselves and addressing questions about their role and importance in relationships, society, and in the world. The award includes a cash prize of $1,000 plus an appropriate citation. This award is given out on an annual basis.
Requirements: The award will be given annually to an author (may be an individual or a co-author). The author must be living at the time of the nomination. In the case of co-authors, one must be living. If an author continues to write books of interest and appeal to young adults then he or she may receive more than once as warranted (as long as it is not more frequently than every six years.) The title or titles must be in-print at the time of nomination. Only those titles of an author's work which meet the criteria of the award will be cited over a period of time. This means that the book or books must have been published in the United States no less than five years prior to the first meeting of the current Margaret A. Edwards Award Committee at the Midwinter Meeting. The five year period is stipulated so that the book or books have had enough time to filter down, i.e., reach a wide level of distribution, and to be accepted by young adults. The book must have been accepted by young adults as an authentic voice that continues to illuminate their experiences and emotions(means that the book or books have become a literary cornerstone for young adults), giving insight into their lives. The book or books should enable them to understand themselves, the world in which they live, and their relationship with others and with society. The book or books must be in print at the time of the nomination. The author will be required to attend the event to accept the award and to make a short acceptance speech. The committee making its selection of nominees must be aware of the entire range of books for young adults and will take into account the following: Does the book(s) help adolescents to become aware of themselves and to answer their questions about their role and importance in relationships, society and in the world? Is the book(s) of acceptable literary quality? Does the book(s) satisfy the curiosity of young adults and yet help them thoughtfully to build a philosophy of life? Is the book(s) currently popular with a wide range of young adults in many different parts of the country. And finally, do the book or book(s) serve as a "window to the world" for young adults?
Geographic Focus: All States
Date(s) Application is Due: Jun 1
Amount of Grant: 1,000 USD
Samples: M.T. Anderson, Cambridge, Massachusetts, $1,000 - Author of "Feed" and "The Astonishing Life of Octavian Nothing, Traitor to the Nation" (2019).
Contact: Cheryl Malden, Program Officer; (800) 545-2433 ext. 3247; fax (312) 440-9374; cmalden@ala.org or ala@ala.org
Internet: www.ala.org/awardsgrants/margaret-edwards-award
Sponsor: American Library Association
225 N. Michigan Avenue
Chicago, IL 60601

ALA May Hill Arbuthnot Honor Lecture Award   176

The May Hill Arbuthnot Honor Lecture Award is a unique collaboration between several groups of people—the committee, the chosen lecturer, the ALSC staff and Board of Directors, and the host site coordinators. The result is an opportunity to celebrate and add to the knowledge and scholarship in the field of children's literature. Publication in Children and Libraries: The Journal of the Association for Library Service to Children ensures the lecture will be a lasting contribution that is available to a broad audience. The winning lecturer will receive a $1,000 honorarium. Suggestions for lecturers are welcomed from both ALSC members and the ALSC award committee. The Lecturer is announced at the Youth Media Awards Press Conference at Midwinter Meeting. The host site is announced at the ALSC Membership Meeting in the summer. ALSC established the lecture series in 1969 with sponsorship from Scott, Foresman and Company. The lectureship is now funded by the ALSC May Hill Arbuthnot Honor Lecture Endowment, and administered by ALSC. May Hill Arbuthnot (1884-1969) was born in Mason City, IA, and graduated from the University of

Chicago in 1922, receiving her master's degree in 1924 from Columbia University. Along with educator William Scott Gray, she created and wrote the Curriculum Foundation Readers—better known as the "Dick and Jane" series—for children published by Scott, Foresman and Company (now Pearson Scott Foresman). Her greatest contribution to children's literature, however, was her authorship of Children and Books, the first edition of which was published in 1947. In 1927, she joined the faculty of Case Western Reserve University, and there she met and married Charles Arbuthnot, an economics professor. She also served as editor of both Childhood Education and Elementary English. Her other works include The Arbuthnot Anthology of Children's Literature and Children's Books Too Good to Miss.

Requirements: The lecturer may be an author, critic, librarian, historian, or teacher of children's literature from any country. A school library, department of education in college or university, or a children's library system may be considered as host for the lecture. The lecturer shall prepare a paper considered to be a significant contribution to the field of children's literature. This paper is delivered as a lecture each April, and is subsequently published in Children and Libraries, the journal of the Association for Library Service to Children. It is suggested that all formal nominations be submitted via email, fax, and/or U.S. mail. Nominations should include: name; professional title/occupation; biographical sketch; justification for consideration; and major publications. Anyone may apply to host the lecture, particularly ALSC member organizations or institutions.

Restrictions: Those serving on the Arbuthnot Selection Committee may not be selected as either lecturer or host during the term of their service on the committee.

Geographic Focus: All States, All Countries
Date(s) Application is Due: Dec 31
Amount of Grant: 1,000 USD
Samples: Neil Gaiman, Menomonie, Wisconsin, $1,000 - Awarded for his prolific works of prose, poetry, film, journalism, comics, song lyrics, and drama (2019).
Contact: Jordan Dubin, Awards Coordinator; (312) 280-2163 or (800) 545-2433 ext. 5839; fax (312) 440-9374; jdubin@ala.org or ala@ala.org
Internet: www.ala.org/awardsgrants/may-hill-arbuthnot-honor-lecture-award
Sponsor: American Library Association
225 N. Michigan Avenue
Chicago, IL 60601

ALA Michael L. Printz Award   177

The Michael L. Printz Award is an award for a book that exemplifies literary excellence in young adult literature. When the Newbery Award began, people probably asked, "Who is John Newbery?" After 75 years of Newbery Awards, "everyone knows the name." So that everyone will recognize the name of this new award as quickly as possible, some background information may prove helpful. "Mike," as he was known to his friends and colleagues, was a school librarian at Topeka West (KS) High School for many years and retired from teaching in 1994. Until his untimely death in 1996, he worked as a marketing consultant for Econo-Clad Books. Mike was active in YALSA and served on the Best Books for Young Adults Committee and the Margaret A. Edwards Award Committee. He had a passion for books and reading. Finding the right book for the right student at the right time was not just a slogan to Mike-he lived it. He also appreciated the authors who wrote books for young adults and demonstrated this by initiating an author-in-residence program at his high school. One of those authors was Chris Crutcher, who became a close friend. Chris recalls the quiet times he spent with Mike talking with him about his vision of young adult literature and its place in kid's lives and says, "The ache I feel [upon hearing of Mike's death] is my wish that he could have accepted for himself what he so readily gave to us, readers and writers alike; a place to stand in the circle of the joy and heartache that is storytelling." YALSA has created a place, a circle if you will, for Mike to stand and be recognized- that place is the Michael L.Printz Award. This award is given out on an annual basis.

Requirements: The award-winning book may be fiction, nonfiction, poetry or an anthology. Books must have been published between January 1 and December 31 of the year preceding announcement of the award. Field nominations must be seconded by a committee member. To be eligible, a title must have been designated by its publisher as being either a young adult book or one published for the age range that YALSA defines as "young adult," i.e., 12 through 18. Works of joint authorship or editorship are eligible. The award may be given posthumously provided the other criteria are met. Books previously published in another country are eligible (presuming an American edition has been published during the period of eligibility). Both field and Committee nominations will be accepted for books that meet the published criteria. Nominations will be submitted online through the ALA website.

Restrictions: Publishers, authors, or editors may not nominate their own titles. Adult books are not eligible.
Geographic Focus: All States, All Countries
Date(s) Application is Due: Dec 31
Samples: Elizabeth Acevedo, Washington, D.C. - Awarded for their book, "The Poet X" (2019).
Contact: Jordan Dubin, Awards Coordinator; (800) 545-2433 ext. 5839; fax (312) 440-9374; jdubin@ala.org or ala@ala.org
Internet: www.ala.org/awardsgrants/michael-l-printz-award
Sponsor: American Library Association
225 N. Michigan Avenue
Chicago, IL 60601

ALA Mildred L. Batchelder Award   178

This award honors Mildred L. Batchelder, a former executive director of the Association for Library Service to Children, and a believer in the importance of good books for children in translation from all parts of the world. She began her career working at Omaha (NE) Public Library, then as a children's librarian at St. Cloud (MN) State Teachers College, and subsequently as librarian of Haven Elementary School in Evanston, IL. She eventually joined the ranks of the American Library Association in 1936. Batchelder spent 30 years with ALA, working as an ambassador to the world on behalf of children and books, encouraging and promoting the translation of the world's best children's literature. Her life's work was to

eliminate barriers to understanding between people of different cultures, races, nations, and languages. This award, established in her honor in 1966, is a citation awarded to an American publisher for a children's book considered to be the most outstanding of those books originally published in a foreign language in a foreign country, and subsequently translated into English and published in the United States. ALSC gives the award to encourage American publishers to seek out superior children's books abroad and to promote communication among the peoples of the world. The award includes a plaque and is given out on an annual basis. The award winner attends the ALSC Award Presentation Ceremony during ALA Annual Conference to accept plaque and give acceptance speech. Honorees will also attend to accept plaque.

Requirements: The Mildred L. Batchelder Award shall be made to an American publisher for a children's book considered to be the most outstanding of those books originating in a country other than the United States and in a language other than English during the preceding year. Specifically, these terms encompass traditionally translated books (originally published in a language other than English in a country other than the United States and subsequently published in English the United States) as well as non-traditionally translated books. This includes, but is not limited to, books translated first in other countries, books written originally in another language but previously unpublished, and books originally published in a different format and language; e.g. a selection from an anthology. Primary attention must be directed to the text. Picture books should be considered only if the text is substantial and at least as important as the pictures. The translation should be true to the substance (e.g., plot, characterization, setting) and flavor of the original work and should retain the viewpoint of the author. Reflection of the style of the author and of the original language are assets unless in the translation these reflections result in awkwardness in style or lack of clarity for children. The book should not be unduly "Americanized." The book's reader should be able to sense that the book came from another country. The textual qualities to be evaluated will vary depending on the content and type of the book being considered.

Geographic Focus: All States
Date(s) Application is Due: Dec 31
Samples: Enchanted Lion Books, Brooklyn, New York- Awarded for the book "Brown" written by Håkon Øvreås, illustrated by Øyvind Torseter, and translated from the Norwegian by Kari Dickson (2020).
Contact: Jordan Dubin, Awards Coordinator; (800) 545-2433, ext. 5839; fax (312) 440-9374; jdubin@ala.org or ala@ala.org
Internet: www.ala.org/awardsgrants/awards/3/apply
Sponsor: American Library Association
225 N. Michigan Avenue
Chicago, IL 60601

ALA Notable Children's Books Awards   179

Each year, a committee of the Association for Library Service to Children (ALSC) identifies the best of the best in children's books for the Notable Children's Books Awards. According to the Notables Criteria, "notable" is defined as: Worthy of note or notice, important, distinguished, outstanding. As applied to children's books, notable should be thought to include books of especially commendable quality, books that exhibit venturesome creativity, and books of fiction, information, poetry and pictures for all age levels (birth through age 14) that reflect and encourage children's interests in exemplary ways. The annual recognition of titles is made via publication of the list on the ALSC web site, in Booklist magazine, and announcement of the list in a press release.

Requirements: Considered books must have children (birth through age 14) as a potential audience and must have been published in the United States during the year preceding the Midwinter Meeting at which the selection is made. This means that the book was published in that year, was available for purchase in that year, and has a copyright date no later than that year. A book might have a copyright date prior to the year under consideration but, for various reasons, was not published until the year under consideration. There is no limitation as to format. A book may be in hard or paper covers, spiral bound, in portfolio, etc. It is expected that books will have a collective unity of story-line, theme, or concept developed through text or pictures or a combination thereof. Evaluating criteria for this award are literary quality; originality of text and illustration; clarity and style of language; excellence of illustration; excellence of design and format; subject matter of interest and value to children; and the likelihood of acceptance by children. Applicants must submit two copies of their book— one to the ALSC Office and one to the committee chair— by the deadline in order to be considered. According to ALSC policy, the current year's Newbery, Caldecott, Belpré, Sibert, Geisel, and Batchelder Award and Honor books automatically are added to the Notable Children's Books list.

Geographic Focus: All States
Date(s) Application is Due: Dec 31
Samples: Carlos Aponte, Jersey City, New Jersey - Awarded in the Younger Readers category for their book, "Across the Bay" (2020); Lori Alexander, Tucson, Arizona - Awarded in the Middle Readers category for their book, "All in a Drop: How Antony van Leeuwenhoek Discovered an Invisible World" (2020); Larry Dane Brimner, San Diego, California - Awarded in the Older Readers category for their book, "Accused! The Trials of the Scottsboro Boys: Lies, Prejudice, and the Fourteenth Amendment" (2020).
Contact: Jordan Dubin, Awards Coordinator; (800) 545-2433 ext. 5839; fax (312) 440-9374; jdubin@ala.org or alscawards@ala.org
Internet: www.ala.org/awardsgrants/notable-childrens-books
Sponsor: American Library Association
225 N. Michigan Avenue
Chicago, IL 60601

ALA Notable Children's Recordings Awards   180

Each year, a committee of the Association for Library Service to Children (ALSC) identifies the best of the best in children's recordings for the Notable Children's Recordings Awards. According to the Notables Criteria, "notable" is defined as: Worthy of note or notice, important, distinguished, outstanding. Recordings are evaluated on the following criteria:

respects young people's intelligence and imagination; exhibits venturesome creativity; in exemplary ways reflects and encourages the natural interest of children and young adolescents (birth to age 14); depicts excellence through the effective use of voices, music, sound effects, and language; maintains high standards in aesthetic and technical aspects; and adapted materials remain true to, expand, or complement the original work. The annual recognition of titles is made via publication of the list on the ALSC web site, in Booklist magazine, and announcement of the list in a press release.
Requirements: The Notable Recordings List is developed annually from recordings for children released in the United States during the preceding year. There are no limitations as to the number of titles nor the type of recordings included on the list. The committee, in its deliberations, is to consider only the recordings eligible for the List which were released in the year preceding the Midwinter meeting during which the selections are made, are currently available through a U.S. distributor, are available on audiotape and/or compact disc, and are produced in English. This requirement does not limit the use of words or phrases in another language where appropriate in context. Applicants must submit two copies of their recording— one to the ALSC Office and one to the committee chair— by the deadline in order to be considered. ALSC membership is not a requirement to submit your work and there is not an entry fee for the Notable Children's Recordings.
Geographic Focus: All States
Date(s) Application is Due: Oct 30
Contact: Jordan Dubin, Awards Coordinator; (800) 545-2433 ext. 5839; fax (312) 440-9374; jdubin@ala.org or alscawards@ala.org
Internet: www.ala.org/awardsgrants/notable-childrens-recordings
Sponsor: American Library Association
225 N. Michigan Avenue
Chicago, IL 60601

ALA Notable Children's Videos Awards 181

Each year, a committee of the Association for Library Service to Children (ALSC) identifies the best of the best in children's Videos for the Notable Children's Videos Awards. According to the Notables Criteria, "notable" is defined as: Worthy of note or notice, important, distinguished, outstanding. In identifying notability in videos/DVDs for children, notable should be thought to include videos/DVDs for all age levels (through age 14) of especially commendable quality that demonstrate respect for the child's intelligence and imagination; the video/DVD should, in exemplary ways, reflect and encourage the interests of children. The annual recognition of titles is made via publication of the list on the ALSC web site, in Booklist magazine, and announcement of the list in a press release.
Requirements: To be eligible for consideration, a video/DVD must have children as a potential audience; must have been released in the immediate year preceding the Midwinter Meeting at which the selections are made; can be feature length (but not theatrically released) or an episode in a series; can be based on another medium (except a filmstrip transfer) or made for another medium (i.e. television); should be available for use in homes and public libraries; should be in original format; and must be in English. "In English" means that the committee considers only a video or DVD published in English. This requirement does not limit the use of words or phrases in another language where appropriate in context. Criteria used in evaluation are Utilization of media, Technicality, Organization and appropriate treatment of material, Authenticity, and Subject matter of interest and value to children. The videos/DVDs should make effective use of the special techniques of the medium and should be technically well done with clear and appropriate use of sound and visuals to create a unified artistic whole. Adaptations of material originally produced in the other mediums should remain true to, expand, or complement the original work in some way, as well as meet general criteria for excellence. Applicants must submit a Submission Form and two copies of their book— one to the ALSC Office and one to the committee chair— by the deadline in order to be considered. The Notable Children's Video list will include the Carnegie Medal Award winner.
Geographic Focus: All States
Date(s) Application is Due: Dec 31
Contact: Jordan Dubin, Awards Coordinator; (800) 545-2433 ext. 5839; fax (312) 440-9374; jdubin@ala.org or alscawards@ala.org
Internet: www.ala.org/awardsgrants/notable-childrens-videos
Sponsor: American Library Association
225 N. Michigan Avenue
Chicago, IL 60601

ALA Odyssey Award for Excellence in Audiobook Production 182

The Odyssey Award for Excellence in Audiobook Production will be given to the producer of the best audiobook produced for children and/or young adults, available in English in the United States. The annual award winner receives a bronze medal and honorees, if any, receive a plaque. This award is given out on an annual basis.
Requirements: The committee is only considering recordings released between November 1st of the previous year and October 31st of the current year. Applcations should include an Information Verification Submission Form (found on the ALA website) and a copy of of the recording, which should both be sent to the committee chair. ALSC membership is not a requirement to submit your work and there is not an entry fee for the Odyssey Award.
Geographic Focus: All States
Date(s) Application is Due: Oct 31
Samples: Courtney Summers, Canada - Awarded for the audio recording of their book, "Sadie" (2019).
Contact: Jordan Dubin, Awards Coordinator; (800) 545-2433 ext. 5839; fax (312) 440-9374; jdubin@ala.org or ala@ala.org
Internet: www.ala.org/awardsgrants/odyssey-award-excellence-audiobook-production
Sponsor: American Library Association
225 N. Michigan Avenue
Chicago, IL 60601

ALA Penguin Random House Young Readers Group Award 183

The Penguin Random House Young Readers Group Award, made possible by an annual gift from Penguin Young Readers Group, provides a $600 stipend to up to four children's librarians to attend their first ALA Annual Conference. This award is given out on an annual basis.
Requirements: Applicants must be personal members of ALSC and ALA. They must also work directly with children in elementary and/or middle schools or public libraries, have less than ten years of experience as a librarian, and have no previous attendance at an ALA Conference. Each applicant will be judged on their involvement in ALSC, as well as any other professional or educational association of which the applicant was a member, officer, chairman, etc. They will also be judged on new programs or innovations started by the applicants at the library in which they work and their library experience. Applicants should complete the application form, describe the library program in which they work, and provide their supervisor's supporting statement. Applications will be submitted online through the ALA website.
Restrictions: Organizational members of ALA and ALSC are not eligible.
Geographic Focus: All States
Date(s) Application is Due: Oct 1
Amount of Grant: 600 USD
Samples: Amalia Butler, Maplewood, New Jersey, $600 - Awarded to children's librarian at Maplewood Memorial Library (2020); Carla Davis, Portland, Oregon, $600 - Awarded to employee in Youth Service Department at Multnomah County Library (2020); Jennifer Minehardt, New York City, New York, $600 - Awarded to member of ALSC Children and Technology Committee and employee at New York Public Library (2020).
Contact: Jordan Dubin, Awards Coordinator; (800) 545-2433 ext. 5839; fax (312) 440-9374; jdubin@ala.org or ala@ala.org
Internet: www.ala.org/awardsgrants/penguin-random-house-young-readers-group-award
Sponsor: American Library Association
225 N. Michigan Avenue
Chicago, IL 60601

ALA Popular Paperbacks for Young Adults Awards 184

The Popular Paperbacks for Young Adults Awards are meant to encourage young adults to read for pleasure by presenting to them lists of popular or topical titles which are widely available in paperback and which represent a broad variety of accessible themes and genres. This award is given out on an annual basis.
Requirements: Titles must be in print and available in paperback. Both young adult and adult titles may be considered. Popularity is more important than literary quality. Both fiction and non-fiction may be considered. Copyright dates are not a consideration. A book which has appeared on a previous Popular Paperbacks list can be selected after 5 years have passed since it last appeared on the list. Each committee will have the latitude to select its own topics (this will ensure the inclusion of timely topics, currently fashionable subjects, and fads) but as a matter of course certain perennially popular genres, topics or themes should be considered. Some examples are: adventure, autobiography/biography/diaries, best sellers, fantasy, graphic novels, historical fiction, horror, humor, music, mystery, new voices, romance, science fiction, short stories, sports, suspense, and thrillers. Standard selection criteria consistent with the ALA Library Bill of Rights shall be applied. Librarianship focuses on individuals, in all their diversity, and that focus is a fundamental value of the Young Adult Library Services Association and its members. Diversity is, thus, honored in the Association and in the collections and services that libraries provide to young adults. Members will submit nominations for this list to the Chair that include author, title, publisher, year of publication, price and a brief annotation specifying those qualities the member finds noteworthy. The Chair will merge the nominations into the form of a ballot for distribution to the Committee. Only titles receiving "yes" votes from a majority of Committee members will remain on the list for discussion at Annual. The nomination form can be found online at the ALA website.
Restrictions: Nominations from authors or publishers for their own titles are not eligible for the list.
Geographic Focus: All States
Date(s) Application is Due: May 1
Contact: Jordan Dubin, Awards Coordinator; (800) 545-2433 ext. 5839; fax (312) 440-9374; jdubin@ala.org or ala@ala.org
Internet: www.ala.org/awardsgrants/popular-paperbacks-young-adults
Sponsor: American Library Association
225 N. Michigan Avenue
Chicago, IL 60601

ALA PRIME TIME Family Reading Time Grants 185

Created by the Louisiana Endowment for the Humanities (LEH) in 1991, PRIME TIME Family Reading Time is an award-winning reading, discussion, and storytelling series based on illustrated children's books. National expansion is made possible through a grant from the National Endowment for the Humanities(NEH) and is a cooperative endeavor with the ALA Public Programs Office. PRIME TIME is designed specifically for under-served families with children aged 6 to 10. Pre-reading activities are also available for pre-school children aged 3 to 4. The program helps low-income, low-literate families bond around the act of reading and talking about books. It models and encourages family reading and discussion of humanities topics, and aids parents and children in selecting books and becoming active public library users. This grant is given out on an annual basis.
Requirements: Statewide organizations including state libraries, state humanities councils, centers for the book, and library associations are invited to apply. For the first time, applications are also invited from library systems. The application form can be found on the ALA website and may be completed electronically, but must be printed and mailed with the other materials listed.
Geographic Focus: All States
Date(s) Application is Due: Nov 1
Contact: Jordan Dubin; (800) 545-2433 ext. 5839; fax (312) 440-9374; jdubin@ala.org or ala@ala.org

Internet: www.ala.org/awardsgrants/awards/165/apply
Sponsor: American Library Association
225 N. Michigan Avenue
Chicago, IL 60601

ALA Quick Picks for Reluctant Young Adult Readers Award 186

The Quick Picks for Reluctant Young Adult Readers Award list is for young adults (ages 12-18) who, for whatever reasons, do not like to read. The purpose of this list is to identify titles for recreational reading, not for curricular or remedial use. This award is given out on an annual basis.
Requirements: Anyone may nominate an appropriate title. Each nomination must be submitted on an official form that can be found on the ALA website. Field nominations require a second from a Quick Picks committee member. If no committee member seconds the field nomination, the title is dropped from consideration.
Restrictions: Nominations from authors or publishers for their own titles are not eligible for the list.
Geographic Focus: All States
Date(s) Application is Due: Nov 30
Contact: Jordan Dubin, Awards Coordinator; (800) 545-2433 ext. 5839; fax (312) 440-9374; jdubin@ala.org or ala@ala.org
Internet: www.ala.org/awardsgrants/quick-picks-reluctant-young-adult-readers
Sponsor: American Library Association
225 N. Michigan Avenue
Chicago, IL 60601

ALA Rainbow Project Book List Award 187

The The Rainbow Project Book List Award is a list of recommended books dealing with gay, lesbian, bisexual, transgender, and questioning issues and situations for children up to age 18. Originally a joint project between the Gay, Lesbian, Bisexual, and Transgender Roundtable and the Social Responsibilities Round Table, the Rainbow Book List presents an annual bibliography of quality books with significant and authentic GLBTQ content. The award is given out on an annual basis.
Requirements: Books considered for the bibliography are to have been published in the United States, within the assigned calendar year or between July 1 and December 31 of the previous calendar year. We invite recommendations for this bibliography from anyone not affiliated with the author or the publisher of the proposed book. A short statement explaining the book's merit should accompany the recommendation. Complete information about the jury process, as well as the suggestion form, is available at the Rainbow Book List blog.
Restrictions: Recommendations for books to consider will not be accepted from the publisher of a proposed book, agents or representatives of the author, or anyone else who may stand to gain directly from the recommendation of the book.
Geographic Focus: All States
Date(s) Application is Due: Oct 31
Samples: Little Bee Books- Awarded for their book, "Our Little Rainbow" (2020); Brad Meltzer and Christopher Eliopoulos- Awarded for their book, "I am Billie Jean King" (2020); Fleur Pierets and Fatinha Ramos- Awarded for their book, "Love Around the World" (2020).
Contact: Jordan Dubin, Awards Coordinator; (800) 545-2433 ext. 5839; fax (312) 440-9374; jdubin@ala.org or ala@ala.org
Internet: www.ala.org/awardsgrants/rainbow-project-book-list
Sponsor: American Library Association
225 N. Michigan Avenue
Chicago, IL 60601

ALA Randolph Caldecott Medal 188

The Caldecott Medal was named in honor of nineteenth-century English illustrator Randolph Caldecott. It is awarded annually by the Association for Library Service to Children, a division of the American Library Association, to the artist of the most distinguished American picture book for children. The winner receives a bronze medal and honorees, if any, receive a plaque. Medalist and honorees will attend the Newbery/Caldecott Banquet during the ALA Annual Conference. The medalist will present an acceptance speech. Honorees will accept plaques, without a speech. This award is given out on an annual basis.
Requirements: The Medal shall be awarded annually to the artist of the most distinguished American picture book for children published by an American publisher in the United States in English during the preceding year. There are no limitations as to the character of the picture book except that the illustrations be original work. Honor books may be named. These shall be books that are also truly distinguished. The award is restricted to artists who are citizens or residents of the United States.
Geographic Focus: All States
Date(s) Application is Due: Dec 31
Samples: Kadir Nelson, Los Angeles, California - Awarded for their book, "The Undefeated" written by Kwame Alexander (2020).
Contact: Cheryl Malden, Program Officer; (800) 545-2433 ext. 3247; fax (312) 440-9374; cmalden@ala.org or ala@ala.org
Internet: www.ala.org/awardsgrants/awards/6/apply
Sponsor: American Library Association
225 N. Michigan Avenue
Chicago, IL 60601

ALA Robert F. Sibert Informational Book Medal Award 189

The Robert F. Sibert Informational Book Medal Award honors the most distinguished informational book published in English in the preceding year for its significant contribution to children's literature. The award winning aurthor and illustrator receives a bronze medal. Honorees, if any, receive a plaque. This award is given annually.
Requirements: ALSC membership is not a requirement to submit your work. "Informational books" are defined as those written and illustrated to present, organize, and interpret documentable, factual material. Honor books may be named. They are books that are also truly distinguished.

The award may be given posthumously. In identifying the most distinguished informational book for children from the preceding year, committee members consider important elements and qualities: Excellent, engaging, and distinctive use of language; Excellent, engaging, and distinctive visual presentation; Appropriate organization and documentation; Clear, accurate, and stimulating presentation of facts, concepts, and ideas; Appropriate style of presentation for subject and for intended audience; Supportive features (index, table of contents, maps, timelines, etc); and Respectful and of interest to children. The book must be a self-contained entity, not dependent on other media for enjoyment. The award winner and honorees, if any, attend the ALSC Award Presentation Program during the ALA Annual Conference. Only the award winning author and illustrator prepares and delivers an acceptance speech. One copy of the book must be sent to the committee chair for it to be considered; the address form can be found on the ALA website. If you wish, you may attach a cover letter with your contact information to your final work. There is no entry fee for the Sibert Medal.
Restrictions: Folktales and other traditional literature are not eligible. There are no other limitations as to the character of the book providing it is an original work. The award is restricted to authors, author/illustrator, co-authors, or author and illustrator named on the title page who are citizens or residents of the United States. ALL authors and illustrators credited on the title page must meet award eligibility criteria. The award is restricted to original work first published in the United States.
Geographic Focus: All States
Date(s) Application is Due: Dec 31
Samples: Kevin Noble Maillard, Manhattan, New York - Awarded for their book "Fry Bread: A Native American Family Story" illustrated by Juana Martinez-Neal (2020).
Contact: Jordan Dubin, Awards Coordinator; (800) 545-2433 ext. 5839; fax (312) 440-9374; jdubin@ala.org or ala@ala.org
Internet: www.ala.org/awardsgrants/robert-f-sibert-informational-book-medal
Sponsor: American Library Association
225 N. Michigan Avenue
Chicago, IL 60601

ALA Sara Jaffarian School Library Award for Exemplary 190
Humanities Programming

The purpose of the Sara Jaffarian School Library Award is to recognize, promote and support excellence in humanities programming in elementary and middle school libraries that serve children K-8. To promote and encourage other school libraries interested in developing outstanding humanities programs, a professional development/training opportunity will be presented by the ALA Public Programs Office, in consultation with the Public and Cultural Programs Advisory Committee and the American Association of School Librarians. An annual award of $5,000 is given, in addition to the promotion of the winner as a model program and training opportunity for other school libraries. Sara Jaffarian, a retired school librarian, was a longtime ALA member. She began her career as a librarian in the public school system of Quincy, Massachusetts. She later served as the Director of Libraries for the Greensboro Public Schools in North Carolina and the Supervisor of Libraries for the Seattle Public Schools in Washington. In 1961, she returned to her home state to design and develop a school library program in Lexington, Massachusetts, where she became the Coordinator of Instructional Materials and Services. Ms. Jaffarian received her undergraduate degree in social studies at Bates University and her library science degree at Simmons College. She also held a master's of education from Boston University. Sara Jaffarian had a long history of leadership in the library profession. She held numerous offices and committee appointments, including ALA Councilor, board member and recording secretary of the American Association of School Librarians (AASL), member of the Newbery-Caldecott Awards Committee, and president of the Massachusetts Association of School Librarians. Under her leadership, an Encyclopedia Britannica School Library Award was given to the Lexington Public Schools in 1964.
Requirements: Any elementary or middle school (public or private) library or any school library program in the U.S. that serves children in any combination of grades K-8 is eligible. Selection of the winner is based on the following criteria: excellence, appeal and innovation of program content and presentation; impact, as evidenced by involvement and awareness of parents, administrators and community leaders (letters of support of the nomination are encouraged); evidence of collaborative relationships in developing the programming (e.g., parents, teachers, administrators, humanities scholars, community groups); relationship of the programming to the curriculum and evidence of a curriculum component for classroom treatment of the humanities theme(s) or topic(s) emphasized in the program; and replicability of the programming and the winner's willingness to participate in a conference program or online meeting to showcase the winner as a model for excellence for other school libraries. Applications will be submitted online through the ALA website.
Geographic Focus: All States
Date(s) Application is Due: May 6
Amount of Grant: 5,000 USD
Samples: Friends Seminary, New York City, New York, $5,000- Awarded for exhibit on the Greensboro Sit-In.
Contact: Colleen Barbus; (312) 280-3277; fax (312) 440-9374; cbarbus@ala.org or ala@ala.org
Internet: www.ala.org/awardsgrants/sara-jaffarian-school-library-program-award-exemplary-humanities-programming
Sponsor: American Library Association
225 N. Michigan Avenue
Chicago, IL 60601

ALA Schneider Family Book Awards 191

The Schneider Family Book Awards honor an author or illustrator for a book that embodies an artistic expression of the disability experience for child and adolescent audiences. Three annual awards consisting of $5000 and a framed plaque will be given annually in each of the following categories: birth through grade school (age 0-10), middle school (age 11-13) and teens (age 13-18). The book must portray some aspect of living with a disability or

that of a friend or family member, whether the disability is physical, mental or emotional. This award is given out on an annual basis. The deadline for nominations is December 1. *Requirements:* The person with the disability may be the protagonist or a secondary character. As for the definition of "disability," Dr. Schneider has intentionally allowed for a broad interpretation. By her wording, the book "must portray some aspect of living with a disability, whether the disability is physical, mental, or emotional." This allows each committee to decide on the qualifications of particular titles. The books must be published in English. The award may be given posthumously. Term of eligibility extends to publications from the preceding year. In terms of content, the books may be fiction, biography, or other form of nonfiction. They must portray the emotional, mental, or physical disability as part of a full life, not as something to be pitied or overcome. Representation of characters with disabilities should be realistic avoiding exaggeration or stereotypes. The person with the disability should be integral to the presentation, not merely a passive bystander. The theme must be appropriate for and respectful of the intended audience age. Information on the disability must be accurate. The book's style should be engaging with distinctive use of language for plot and character development and setting delineation. The book should be judged on its own merit as a self-contained entity, not as part of a series, and irrespective of supportive materials such as a CD or other supplemental material. If the book has illustrations, text and images should complement each other, with differentiated contrast between text, pictures, and background; format and typeface must be of age appropriate size, clearly readable, and free of typographical errors; and layout should be easy to follow enhancing the flow of the story or information. Applications will be submitted online through the ALA website; in addition, copies of the nominated book should be mailed to the Program Officer and to each of the Schneider Family Book Awards Jury members. *Restrictions:* Books with death as the main theme are generally disqualified. Books previously discussed and voted on are not eligible in the future.
Geographic Focus: All States
Date(s) Application is Due: Dec 1
Amount of Grant: 5,000 USD
Samples: Sonia Sotomayor, New York City, New York, $5,000 - Awarded in the Young Children category for their book "Just Ask!" illustrated by Rafael López (2020); Lynne Kelly, Houston, Texas, $5,000 - Awarded in the Middle Grade category for their book, "Song for a Whale" (2020); Alison Gervais, $5,000 - Awarded in the Teen Category for their book, "The Silence Between Us" (2020).
Contact: Cheryl Malden, Program Officer; (800) 545-2433 ext. 3247; fax (312) 440-9374; cmalden@ala.org or ala@ala.org
Internet: www.ala.org/awardsgrants/schneider-family-book-award
Sponsor: American Library Association
225 N. Michigan Avenue
Chicago, IL 60601

ALA Scholastic Library Publishing Award 192
The Scholastic Library Publishing Award is presented to a librarian whose "unusual contribution to the stimulation and guidance of reading by children and young people" exemplifies outstanding achievement in the profession. The award includes $1,000 and a 24k gold-framed citation. This award is given out on an annual basis. The annual deadline for nominations is February 1. *Requirements:* Nominees will be evaluated on their clear statement documenting the specific contribution and its impact on children, the methods used to measure the contribution, the quality and scope of the contribution and its impact, and the unusualness of the contribution/how easily another professional could reproduce it with similar results. Applications will be submitted online through the ALA website.
Geographic Focus: All States
Date(s) Application is Due: Feb 1
Amount of Grant: 1,000 USD
Samples: Jennifer McQuown, West Palm Beach, Florida, $1,000 - Awarded to Youth Services Manager of the Mandel Public library for her outstanding contributions to the field of literacy (2020).
Contact: Cheryl Malden, Program Officer; (800) 545-2433, ext. 3247; fax (312) 440-9374; cmalden@ala.org or ala@ala.org
Internet: www.ala.org/awardsgrants/scholastic-library-publishing-award
Sponsor: American Library Association
225 N. Michigan Avenue
Chicago, IL 60601

Alaska Airlines Corporation Career Connections for Youth Grants 193
Alaska Airlines believes in strengthening and supporting the communities our employees, neighbors and guests call home. Partnering with nonprofit organizations, the airline provides in-kind donations and sponsorships for fundraising events that enable organizations to build strong foundations and continue to do great work in the communities served by Alaska Airlines. In one key area, Alaska Airlines believes in the importance of expanding opportunity for young people. They support nonprofit organizations that engage young people furthest from opportunity to achieve their future career goals. They accept requests for in-kind transportation and sponsorships for fundraising events for 501(c)3 nonprofit organizations. Limited resources necessitate focused giving in these communities, and support is generally granted on a one-time basis.
Requirements: The airline generally supports organizations on a one-time basis, and asks that organizations submit requests at least six weeks prior to the event. Applications will be submitted online via the Alaska Airlines website. Once submitted, all requests are personally reviewed.
Restrictions: Requests that are not eligible include: Groups that discriminate on the basis of race, color, creed, religion, national origin, alienage or citizenship status, age, sex, sexual orientation, gender identity or expression, marital status, disability, protected veteran status, genetic information, or any other basis protected by applicable law; Capital projects; Endowments or Private Foundations; Rotary; Golf Tournaments; Guilds; Individual requests

(must be a 501c3 nonprofit request); Multi-year commitment or automatic renewal grants; Organizations whose prime purpose is to influence legislation; Pageants; Pass-through donations (organizations raising funds for other nonprofits); Prizes for incentives; Publicly or privately funded educational institutions; Religious, political or fraternal organizations; Scholarships; School auctions, PTA events, booster clubs, graduation parties are not eligible; Sports team events; Silent Auctions and online Auctions; Memorials; Walks/Runs without employee engagement; Support in areas without Alaska Airlines/Horizon service.
Geographic Focus: Alaska, Oregon, Washington, Canada, Mexico
Contact: Tim R. Thompson, Executive Director; (907) 266-7230 or (800) 252-7522; fax (907) 266-7229; tim.thompson@alaskaair.com
Internet: www.alaskaair.com/content/about-us/social-responsibility/corporate-giving
Sponsor: Alaska Airlines Corporation
4750 Old International Airport Road
Anchorage, AK 99502

Alaska Airlines Foundation LIFT Grants 194
The Alaska Airlines Foundation's LIFT grants focus on young people where Alaska Airlines has a significant presence in Alaska, California, Hawaii, Oregon and Washington – especially those in underserved communities in these states. Working closely with community partners, the Alaska Airlines Foundation will focus on programs, partnerships and initiatives that inspire, empower, mentor, engage and equip young people to connect to career opportunities and to imagine what's possible. The Alaska Airlines Foundation is partnering with organizations with a clear vision on equipping the next generation of leaders with the knowledge, skills and to provide pathways for success. The Alaska Airlines Foundation generally provides grants that range from $5,000 to $20,000. The Alaska Airlines Foundation reviews applications three times a year.
Requirements: Grants are designed to fund and enhance a new or current program provided by a 501(c)3 organization. The Foundation is supporting nonprofit organizations located in Alaska, California, Hawaii, Oregon, and Washington, where Alaska Airlines has a significant presence. Preference for grant decisions is toward supporting young people between about the ages of 10 and 20. Programs should focus on at least one or more of the following: Career exploration and career connected learning experiences; Mentorships; Soft skills, critical thinking, empowerment, job training and leadership development; and Advanced degree or Career and Technical Certification or preparation and support. The average grant will be based on numbers of young people served, geographic reach, organizational capacity, size of operating budget, demonstrated impact, and specific program budget. Funds should be spent within one year of grant award. Applications will be submitted online at the Alaska Airlines Foundation wesbite.
Restrictions: Due to regulatory considerations and the Foundation's funding focus, the following entities and activities are not eligible for funding from The Alaska Airlines Foundation: Nonprofit organizations without a current 501(c)3 exempt status; Political, labor, and fraternal organizations; Religious organizations without a secular community designation; Hospitals and medical research institutions; Individuals; Universities and academic research institutions; Conferences or symposia; Individual schools, school districts, or Parent Teacher Associations; Multi-year grants; Capital campaigns; Exhibitions and performances; Individual sports teams and sports tournaments; One-time volunteer events not connected to a program curriculum; Trips and travel; Contests; Festivals and parades; Sponsorship of fundraising or other events including tables; Advertising; Tickets to events; and Supply drives.
Geographic Focus: Alaska, California, Hawaii, Oregon, Washington
Date(s) Application is Due: Mar 30; Jul 31; Sep 30
Amount of Grant: 5,000 - 20,000 USD
Contact: Tim R. Thompson, Executive Director; (907) 266-7230 or (800) 252-7522; fax (907) 266-7229; tim.thompson@alaskaair.com
Internet: www.alaskaair.com/content/about-us/social-responsibility/alaska-airlines-foundation
Sponsor: Alaska Airlines Foundation
4750 Old International Airport Road
Anchorage, AK 99502

Alaska Children's Trust Conference/Training Sponsorship 195
To support the exchange of information and professional development of individuals working towards ensuring children and families live in safe, stable and nurturing communities, Alaska Children's Trust provides a limited number of sponsorship grants for conferences or trainings. Applicants can apply for up to $1,000. Funds can be used for venues, equipment rental, food, scholarships, outreach materials, or other supplies needed for the conference trainings.
Requirements: Any individual, organization (nonprofit, religious, or tribal), community/ neighborhood associations or coalition is eligible to apply. No 501(c)3 status is required. Only one grant per organization per year.
Restrictions: These grants do not support individual training or attendance to a conference.
Geographic Focus: Alaska
Amount of Grant: Up to 1,000 USD
Contact: Trevor Storrs, President and CEO; (907) 248-7676; tstorrs@alaskachildrenstrust.org
Internet: www.alaskachildrenstrust.org/conferencesponsorships
Sponsor: Alaska Children's Trust
3201 C Street, Suite 110
Anchorage, AK 99503

Alaska Community Foundation Afterschool Network Engineering Mindset Mini-Grant 196
he Alaska Afterschool Network's mission is to support, strengthen, and advocate for quality Out-of-School-Time (OST) programs and activities for children, youth, and families throughout Alaska. The Alaska Afterschool Network (The Network) is a program of Alaska Children's Trust. The Network is dedicated to expanding access to productive out-of-school science, technology, engineering, and mathematics (STEM) learning programs by

improving existing programs and creating new ones. The ability for students to successfully participate in the global workplace depends on their exposure to high quality STEM opportunities. OST STEM can almost double the amount of time some students have to question, tinker, learn, and explore STEM topics, and as such are uniquely effective at reducing achievement gaps. The more students participate in STEM learning opportunities out-of-school, the more interested they become in STEM subjects and majors.
Requirements: Eligible applicants include: Out-of-School Time programs that meets with a consistent group on an ongoing basis throughout the grant cycle. Only applicants who send a complete application will be considered. The Network will require all Engineering Mindset Mini-Grantees to participate in a STEM quality improvement initiative. The Network will utilize the Dimensions of Success (DoS) tool for the assessment phase of the quality improvement process. Each grantee will receive at least two in-person DoS observations (subject to change based off COVID-19 health mandates). This will provide the Network a statewide data snapshot of STEM program quality. Grantees will be expected to prepare a Final Report of Grant Impact following the conclusion of the grant cycle. This report must include: Number of youths reached during grant cycle and the ratio of males and females; Number of new female youth the program has recruited and engaged; A demonstration that youth have effectively developed an engineering mindset.
Restrictions: Only one mini-grant will be awarded per organization.
Geographic Focus: Alaska
Date(s) Application is Due: Aug 28
Amount of Grant: Up to 3,000 USD
Contact: Stefanie O'Brien, Program Officer of Grants & Scholarships; (907) 274-6710 or (907) 334-6700; fax (907) 334-5780; sobrien@alaskacf.org or grants@alaskacf.org
Internet: alaskacf.org/blog/grants/alaska-afterschool-network-engineering-mindset-mini-grant/
Sponsor: Alaska Community Foundation
3201 C Street, Suite 110
Anchorage, AK 99503

Alaska Community Foundation Anchorage Schools Foundation Grant **197**
The Anchorage Schools Foundation (ASF) is a field of interest fund of The Alaska Community Foundation. It was created by a dedicated group of volunteers who are passionate about supporting projects that enhance the success of students in the Anchorage School District (ASD). The ASF Fund provides small grants to accelerate academic achievements, test new ideas, and support innovative projects.
Requirements: Eligible applicants include school professionals such as principals, teachers, nurses, counselors, administrators, certified staff, and students sponsored by certified staff. Projects supported through the ASF grant program should reflect an innovative or creative approach to education; impact multiple students; and demonstrate sustainability if start-up funds are requested. Past grants have included awards to purchase classroom supplies, recreational equipment and uniforms, books, technology, instruments, emergency needs and material needs that support enhanced student success.
Restrictions: Grant funds may not be awarded to individuals. Requested funds should not supplant or replace ASD funds but can be used to support existing efforts to bring additional innovation or creativity. Please note: requests for salary support, transportation costs, and stipends are not eligible. If you are a current recipient of an Anchorage Schools Foundation grant, all reports must be complete before you will be eligible to be considered for another grant.
Geographic Focus: Alaska
Date(s) Application is Due: Nov 5
Amount of Grant: 100 - 500 USD
Contact: Stefanie O'Brien, Program Officer of Grants & Scholarships; (907) 274-6710 or (907) 334-6700; fax (907) 334-5780; sobrien@alaskacf.org or grants@alaskacf.org
Internet: alaskacf.org/blog/grants/asf-grant-cycle/
Sponsor: Alaska Community Foundation
3201 C Street, Suite 110
Anchorage, AK 99503

Alaska Community Foundation Children's Trust Tier 1 Community Based Child Abuse and Neglect Prevention Grants **198**
The mission of Alaska Children's Trust (ACT) is to improve the status of children in Alaska by generating funds and committing resources to eliminate child abuse and neglect. ACT is the statewide catalyst for empowering communities to be leaders in the prevention of child abuse and neglect. For nearly two decades, ACT has provided organizations and communities with the support to build safe, stable and nurturing environments for Alaska's children. ACT was first created by the Alaska State Legislature in 1988 and received initial funding in 1996. In 2010, ACT became an independent 501(c)3 nonprofit. Today, ACT's assets total more than $11 million, which has allowed them to invest over $5 million in communities aimed at strengthening families, protecting children and developing healthy communities.
Requirements: Applications are accepted from qualified 501(c)3 nonprofit organizations, or equivalent organizations located in the state of Alaska. Equivalent organizations may include tribes, local or state governments, schools, or Regional Educational Attendance Areas. Organizations that have received past awards and are in good standing are eligible to apply. Applicants with open ACT grants must be current on all grant reporting. Alaska Children's Trust considers as a priority grants that support an approach of primary prevention and strengthening families. Key components of the primary prevention and strengthening families approach include: Promoting community inclusion; promoting healthy parenting skills and strengthening families; addressing social determinants that create an environment that leads to CAN; providing support and services that are universal; focusing on existing strengths and promoting continued growth and development; fostering parent leadership and empowering parents to identify resources, support and strategies to help them parent more effectively; incorporating the understanding of Adverse Childhood Experiences study (i.e. reduce trauma and build resiliency); and support evidence based or promising practices.
Restrictions: Applications from organizations with outstanding grant reports will not be accepted. Individuals, for-profit, 501(c)(4) or (c)(6) organizations, non-Alaska based organizations, and federal government agencies are not eligible for competitive grants. Applicants with open ACT grants that are past due on any grant reports will not be considered for funding. Applications for religious indoctrination or other religious activities, endowment building, deficit financing, fundraising, lobbying, electioneering and activities of political nature will not be considered. Nor will proposals that promote discrimination based on race, gender, marital status, sexual preference, age, disability, creed or ethnicity. Funds cannot be used for expenses incurred prior to the grant award.
Geographic Focus: Alaska
Date(s) Application is Due: Aug 7
Amount of Grant: Up to 10,000 USD
Contact: Stefanie O'Brien, Program Officer of Grants & Scholarships; (907) 274-6710 or (907) 334-6700; fax (907) 334-5780; sobrien@alaskacf.org or grants@alaskacf.org
Internet: alaskacf.org/blog/grants/the-alaska-childrens-trust/
Sponsor: Alaska Community Foundation
3201 C Street, Suite 110
Anchorage, AK 99503

Alaska Community Foundation Children's Trust Tier 1 Parenting and Child Development Educational Grants **199**
The mission of Alaska Children's Trust (ACT) is to improve the status of children in Alaska by generating funds and committing resources to eliminate child abuse and neglect. The Alaska Children's Trust (ACT) supports a two-generation methodology in our work to ensure children grow up in safe, stable and nurturing environments. ACT recognizes parents are their children's first and most important teachers, and that investment in strong parenting is a critical strategy for ensuring that all children grow up thriving. In partnership with the State of Alaska, Alaska Children's Trust (ACT) is soliciting proposals to provide access to high-quality parenting and child development educational programs (i.e. parenting classes) in 13 identified communities. The goal of the funding is to help equip parents with the knowledge, skills and tools they need to be successful.
Requirements: Grantees are expected to utilize evidence based or informed and culturally responsive parent education, with a focus on measurable gains. A family centered approach recognizes the usefulness of a range of subject, in addition to parenting classes; including financial literacy, leadership skills, goal setting, stress reduction, systems navigation, traditional and cultural practices, and other skill builders provided to parents that will promote resilience. Applications are accepted from qualified 501(c)3 nonprofit organizations, or equivalent organizations located in the state of Alaska. Equivalent organizations may include tribes, local or state governments, schools, or Regional Educational Attendance Areas. Organizations that have received past awards and are in good standing are eligible to apply. Applicants with open ACT grants must be current on all grant reporting. Organizations who receive funding through other ACT grant opportunities are eligible to apply for this funding.
Restrictions: Applications from organizations with outstanding grant reports will not be accepted.
Geographic Focus: Alaska
Date(s) Application is Due: Nov 16
Amount of Grant: 5,000 - 25,000 USD
Contact: Trevor Storrs, Alaska Children's Trust President and CEO; (907) 248-7676 or (907) 334-6700; tstorrs@alaskachildrenstrust.org
Internet: alaskacf.org/blog/grants/alaska-childrens-trust-tier-1-parenting-child-development-educational-programs/
Sponsor: Alaska Community Foundation
3201 C Street, Suite 110
Anchorage, AK 99503

Alaska Community Foundation Children's Trust Tier 2 Innovation Grants **200**
The mission of Alaska Children's Trust (ACT) is to improve the status of children in Alaska by generating funds and committing resources to eliminate child abuse and neglect. Children's Trust Tier 2 Innovation Grants were created to stimulate the development and adoption of groundbreaking approaches and technologies to prevent child abuse and neglect. Innovation is either introducing something new or infusing a current product/program with more resources to strengthen its reach and impact. It is usually driven and supported through data. It is compelled by an organization's desire to understand and meet the ever-changing needs and challenges of the people they are serving while trying to prevent child abuse and neglect. As a catalyst for change, ACT has introduced the Innovative Grants to stimulate new ways of preventing child abuse and neglect and strengthen the current methods that have proven successful.
Requirements: The Children's Trust Tier 2 Innovation Grants supports new and innovative ideas that would prevent child abuse and neglect and current programs could have a greater impact with more support. Applications are accepted from qualified 501(c)3 nonprofit organizations, or equivalent organizations located in the state of Alaska. Equivalent organizations may include tribes, local or state governments, schools, or Regional Educational Attendance Areas. Organizations that have received past awards and are in good standing are eligible to apply. Applicants with open ACT grants must be current on all grant reporting. Alaska Children's Trust considers as a priority grants that support an approach of primary prevention and strengthening families. Key components of the primary prevention and strengthening families approach include: Promoting community inclusion; promoting healthy parenting skills and strengthening families; addressing social determinants that create an environment that leads to CAN; providing support and services that are universal; focusing on existing strengths and promoting continued growth and development; fostering parent leadership and empowering parents to identify resources, support and strategies to help them parent more effectively; incorporating the understanding of Adverse Childhood Experiences study (i.e. reduce trauma and build resiliency); and support evidence based or promising practices.

Restrictions: Applications from organizations with outstanding grant reports will not be accepted. Individuals, for-profit, 501(c)4 or (c)6 organizations, non-Alaska based organizations, and federal government agencies are not eligible for competitive grants. Applicants with open ACT grants that are past due on any grant reports will not be considered for funding. Applications for religious indoctrination or other religious activities, endowment building, deficit financing, fundraising, lobbying, electioneering and activities of political nature will not be considered. Nor will proposals that promote discrimination based on race, gender, marital status, sexual preference, age, disability, creed or ethnicity. Funds cannot be used for expenses incurred prior to the grant award.
Geographic Focus: Alaska
Amount of Grant: 10,000 - 50,000 USD
Contact: Trevor Storrs, Alaska Children's Trust President and CEO; (907) 248-7676 or (907) 334-6700; tstorrs@alaskachildrenstrust.org
Internet: alaskacf.org/blog/grants/alaska-childrens-trust-tier-2-innovation-grants/
Sponsor: Alaska Community Foundation
3201 C Street, Suite 110
Anchorage, AK 99503

Alaska Community Foundation Cordova Community Foundation Grants   201
The Cordova Community Foundation (CCF), an Affiliate of The Alaska Community Foundation (ACF), seeks applications from qualified, tax-exempt 501(c)3 organizations (or equivalents, such as Tribal entities, schools, and faith-based organizations) that support charitable organizations and programs in Cordova. Grants will promote healthy communities and support a broad range of community needs, including: compassionate health care; innovative education; community enrichment; active enjoyment of the natural environment; and arts and cultural expression.
Requirements: Evaluation criteria include, but are not limited to: the overall merit of the project; the ability of the organization to successfully complete the project; the clarity and measurability of the project's goal; the feasibility of the time frame given for completion of the project; and the number of people served. Preference will be given to applications which have the potential to benefit a broad range of Cordova area residents. Applications should detail measurable and achievable outcomes and demonstrate other sources of support, collaboration, and/or cooperation. Applications should also address the sustainability of the proposed program or project for which funding is desired.
Restrictions: Ineligible organizations or activities include: individuals, for-profit, 501(c)4, 501(c)6, and non Alaska based organizations, private or family foundations, state and federal government agencies, and ad hoc groups without a tax exempt legal status are not eligible for competitive grants. Applications for religious indoctrination or other religious activities, endowment building, deficit financing, fundraising, lobbying, electioneering, or activities of political nature will not be considered, nor will proposals for ads, sponsorships, or special events (e.g. fundraisers), and any proposals which discriminate as to race, gender, marital status, sexual preference, age, disability, creed, or ethnicity.
Geographic Focus: Alaska
Date(s) Application is Due: Jan 8
Amount of Grant: 500 - 1,000 USD
Contact: Julie Reynolds, Cordova Community Foundation Program Manager; (907) 334-6700; jreynolds@alaskacf.org or grants@alaskacf.org
Internet: alaskacf.org/blog/grants/cordova-community-foundation-small-grant-program/
Sponsor: Alaska Community Foundation
3201 C Street, Suite 110
Anchorage, AK 99503

Alaska Community Foundation Cordova Community Foundation Mini-Grants   202
The Cordova Community Foundation (CCF), an Affiliate of The Alaska Community Foundation (ACF), seeks applications from qualified, tax-exempt 501(c)3 organizations (or equivalents, such as Tribal entities, schools, and faith-based organizations) that support charitable organizations and programs in Cordova. Grants will promote healthy communities and support a broad range of community needs, including: compassionate health care; innovative education; community enrichment; active enjoyment of the natural environment; and arts and cultural expression.
Requirements: Evaluation criteria include, but are not limited to: the overall merit of the project; the ability of the organization to successfully complete the project; the clarity and measurability of the project's goal; the feasibility of the time frame given for completion of the project; and the number of people served.
Geographic Focus: Alaska
Date(s) Application is Due: Jul 13
Amount of Grant: 500 - 1,200 USD
Contact: Julie Reynolds, Cordova Community Foundation Program Manager; (907) 334-6700; jreynolds@alaskacf.org or grants@alaskacf.org
Internet: alaskacf.org/blog/grants/cordova-community-foundation-mini-grant-program/
Sponsor: Alaska Community Foundation
3201 C Street, Suite 110
Anchorage, AK 99503

Alaska Community Foundation GCI Suicide Prevention Grant   203
The Alaska Community Foundation offers the GCI Suicide Prevention grant program with the goal of funding projects and organizations that will help reduce rates of suicide in Alaska and promote mental wellness through strengthened community and personal connections. Organizations seeking project or operational support are encouraged to apply. Preference will be given to projects that are located in rural Alaska or programs that reach rural communities in Alaska (defined as outside of Anchorage, Fairbanks and Juneau), and which are focused on activities that will: Result in long term change by creating family, school and community support systems; Help grow or support programs that have already demonstrated success in

Alaska or in small communities in the Lower 48; Support programs that have been embraced and that will be sustained by the community; Support work that is happening on multiple levels including prevention, intervention, and crisis response; Conceived or managed by local entities or by and entity that demonstrates a willingness to work with the local community or be advised and/or guided by local planning; Reflects Alaska cultural considerations.
Requirements: Eligible applicants include: 501(c)3 nonprofit or equivalent organizations located in the state of Alaska. Equivalent organizations may include tribes, schools, churches, local government agencies and programs. Preference will be given to projects that: empower Alaskans to work together to promote community wellness; demonstrate measurable results, accountability, cultural sensitivity, and unify communities; will impact communities that might not have easy access to suicide prevention support programs; focus on at least one of the following areas as a way to decrease suicide in Alaska: Addressing generational trauma; Veteran connectedness (means restriction and gun safety, increased connectivity to treatment services, youth coalitions, primary prevention, support for those already doing this work in communities, building on past successes, support of needs assessments, community mobilization, and high-risk populations). Awardees will be required to complete two (2) progress reports that include images documenting their projects and attain photo releases of those recognizable in the images. A final report is due 30 days following completion of the project and no later than one year plus 30 days after the grant award date. All reports are completed in ACF's online grant system using the same profile login and password used to apply for the grant. Failure to complete final reports on time may impact an organization's ability to receive future funding from ACF.
Restrictions: Examples of ineligible activities include: paying for operating activities such as staff training required to perform one's job; staff time; technology (laptop, iPad); and memberships in organizations and/or annual fees. Individuals and projects outside Alaska are not eligible for funding. Applicants may select only one capacity building activity to be accomplished at a time with Strengthening Organizations grant funding. Ineligible applicants include individuals; for profit, 501(c)4 or (c)6 organizations; non-Alaska based organizations; and state or federal government agencies. Ineligible projects include religious indoctrination or other religious activities; endowment building; deficit financing; lobbying; electioneering and activities of political nature; proposals for ads; sponsorships for special events; direct fundraising, including hiring a grant writer; reimbursement of pre-award costs; construction; purchase of real property; pass-through funding or other financial assistance to nonprofits; activities that have the potential to support terrorism; core government or organizational services; any proposals that discriminate as to race, gender, marital status, sexual orientation, age, disability, religion, creed or ethnicity; direct program costs; and personnel costs.
Geographic Focus: Alaska
Date(s) Application is Due: Jul 15
Amount of Grant: Up to 30,000 USD
Contact: Stefanie O'Brien, Program Officer of Grants & Scholarships; (907) 274-6710 or (907) 334-6700; fax (907) 334-5780; sobrien@alaskacf.org or grants@alaskacf.org
Internet: alaskacf.org/blog/grants/gci-suicide-prevention-grant/
Sponsor: Alaska Community Foundation
3201 C Street, Suite 110
Anchorage, AK 99503

Alaska Community Foundation Jack and Nona Renn Anchorage Football Fund   204
In memory of Jack Renn and in honor of the decades of service he and his wife, Nona, gave to high school sports, Nona is creating this fund to help Anchorage school football teams succeed now and in the future. Jack Renn served as an on-field football official from 1981-2015 in local and state games and tournaments and then kept the clock from 2015-2017. Jack recruited Nona as the first female chain gang official for Alaska high school football. He was instrumental in initiating girls' flag football in the Anchorage School District, including training coaches.
Requirements: Anchorage School District High School football and flag football teams are eligible for this grant. If the football or flag football team has a booster club with 501(c)3 status with the IRS or PTA, they may apply on behalf of the team. Funds are to be used for the purchase of team equipment including gear, pads, shoes, helmets, jerseys, etc. to benefit the entire team. Prior to receiving grant funds, each team must perform a community service project.
Geographic Focus: Alaska
Date(s) Application is Due: Sep 30
Amount of Grant: Up to 4,975 USD
Contact: Stefanie O'Brien, Program Officer of Grants & Scholarships; (907) 274-6710 or (907) 334-6700; fax (907) 334-5780; sobrien@alaskacf.org or grants@alaskacf.org
Internet: alaskacf.org/blog/grants/jack-and-nona-renn-anchorage-football-flag-football-fund/
Sponsor: Alaska Community Foundation
3201 C Street, Suite 110
Anchorage, AK 99503

Alaska Community Foundation Kenai Peninsula Foundation Grant   205
The Kenai Peninsula Foundation (KPF), an Affiliate of The Alaska Community Foundation (ACF), seeks applications from qualified, tax exempt 501(c)3 organizations (or equivalents, such as Tribal entities, schools, and faith-based organizations) that support charitable organizations and programs in the central Kenai Peninsula area. Grants may support a broad range of community needs, including but not limited to health and wellness, education, the great outdoors, arts and culture, and community development.
Requirements: Preference will be given to applications which have the potential to impact a broad range of central Kenai Peninsula area residents. Applications should detail measurable and achievable outcomes and demonstrate other sources of support, collaboration, and/or cooperation. Applications should also address the sustainability of the proposed program or project for which funding is desired. Evaluation criteria include, but are not limited to: the overall merit of the project; the ability of the organization to successfully complete the project; the clarity and measurability of the project's goal; the feasibility of the time frame given for completion of the project; and the number of people served.

Restrictions: Ineligible organizations or activities include: individuals, for-profit, 501(c)4, 501(c)6, and non Alaska based organizations, private or family foundations, state and federal government agencies, and ad hoc groups without a tax exempt legal status are not eligible for competitive grants. Applications for religious indoctrination or other religious activities, endowment building, deficit financing, fundraising, lobbying, electioneering, or activities of political nature will not be considered, nor will proposals for ads, sponsorships, or special events (e.g. fundraisers), and any proposals which discriminate as to race, gender, marital status, sexual preference, age, disability, creed, or ethnicity.
Geographic Focus: Alaska
Date(s) Application is Due: Apr 15
Amount of Grant: Up to 1,000 USD
Contact: Hadassah Knight, Kenai Peninsula Foundation Program Manager; (907) 334-6700; fax (907) 334-5780; hknight@alaskacf.org or grants@alaskacf.org
Internet: alaskacf.org/blog/grants/kpf-grant-program/
Sponsor: Alaska Community Foundation
3201 C Street, Suite 110
Anchorage, AK 99503

Alaska Community Foundation Ketchikan Community Foundation Grant　206

The Ketchikan Community Foundation (KCF), an Affiliate of The Alaska Community Foundation (ACF), seeks applications from qualified, tax exempt 501(c)3 organizations (or equivalents, such as Tribal entities, schools, and faith-based organizations) that support charitable organizations and programs in the Ketchikan area. During this grant cycle, awards will be made for projects that support youth.
Requirements: Preference will be given to applicants who have not been funded in the current three-year cycle and to projects which have the potential to impact a broad range of Ketchikan area residents. Applications should detail measurable and achievable outcomes and demonstrate other sources of support, collaboration, and/or cooperation. Applications should also address the sustainability of the proposed program or project for which funding is desired. Please note if partial funding will still allow your organization to achieve success in your grant project. Evaluation criteria include but are not limited to: the overall merit of the project, the ability of the organization to successfully complete the project, the clarity and measurability of the project's goal, the feasibility of the time frame given for completion of the project, and the number of people served.
Restrictions: Ineligible organizations or activities include: individuals, for-profit, 501(c)4, 501(c)6, and non-Alaska based organizations, private or family foundations, state and federal government agencies, and ad hoc groups without a tax-exempt legal status are not eligible for competitive grants. Applications for religious indoctrination or other religious activities, endowment building, deficit financing, fundraising, lobbying, electioneering, or activities of political nature will not be considered, nor will proposals for ads, sponsorships, or special events (e.g. fundraisers), and any proposals which discriminate as to race, gender, marital status, sexual preference, age, disability, creed, or ethnicity.
Geographic Focus: Alaska
Date(s) Application is Due: Feb 6
Amount of Grant: 500 - 7,000 USD
Contact: Emily Chapel, Ketchikan Community Foundation Program Director; (907) 334-6700; echapel@alaskacf.org or grants@alaskacf.org
Internet: alaskacf.org/blog/grants/2020-kcf-grant-program/
Sponsor: Alaska Community Foundation
3201 C Street, Suite 110
Anchorage, AK 99503

Alaska Community Foundation Petersburg Community Foundation Annual Grant　207

The Petersburg Community Foundation (PCF), an Affiliate of The Alaska Community Foundation (ACF), seeks applications from qualified, tax exempt 501(c)3 organizations (or equivalents, such as: Tribal entities, schools, and faith-based organizations) that are based in or serve the community of Petersburg. PCF grants support a broad range of charitable community needs in these areas: health and wellness, education, the great outdoors, arts and culture, animal welfare, community development, and many other charitable activities that benefit the Petersburg community.
Requirements: Preference will be given to applications which have the potential to impact a broad range of Petersburg area residents. Applications should detail measurable and achievable outcomes and demonstrate other sources of support, collaboration, or clearly articulate the need for the proposed project/program and how the community will be impacted through it. Thoughtful applications that concisely identify why it's important for this project/program to be funded this year will be appreciated by the PCF Grants Committee. Evaluation criteria include, but are not limited to: the overall merit of the project; the ability of the organization to successfully complete the project; the clarity and measurability of the project's goal; the feasibility of the time frame given for completion of the project; and the number of people served.
Restrictions: Ineligible organizations or activities include: individuals, for-profit, 501(c)4, 501(c)6, and non Alaska based organizations, private or family foundations, state and federal government agencies, and ad hoc groups without a tax exempt legal status are not eligible for competitive grants. Applications for religious indoctrination or other religious activities, endowment building, deficit financing, fundraising, lobbying, electioneering, or activities of political nature will not be considered, nor will proposals for ads, sponsorships, or special events (e.g. fundraisers), and any proposals which discriminate as to race, gender, marital status, sexual preference, age, disability, creed, or ethnicity.
Geographic Focus: Alaska
Date(s) Application is Due: Apr 1
Amount of Grant: Up to 10,000 USD

Contact: Joni Johnson, Petersburg Community Foundation Program Manager; (907) 334-6700; jjohnson@alaskacf.org or grants@alaskacf.org
Internet: alaskacf.org/blog/grants/petersburgcf-annual-grant-program/
Sponsor: Alaska Community Foundation
3201 C Street, Suite 110
Anchorage, AK 99503

Alaska Community Foundation Petersburg Community Foundation Mini-Grants　208

The Petersburg Community Foundation (PCF), an Affiliate of The Alaska Community Foundation (ACF), seeks applications from qualified, tax exempt 501(c)3 organizations (or equivalents, such as Tribal entities, schools, and faith-based organizations) that support charitable organizations and programs in the Petersburg area. Mini-grants may support a broad range of community needs, including but not limited to health and wellness, education, the great outdoors, arts and culture, and community development.
Requirements: Preference will be given to applications which have the potential to impact a broad range of Petersburg area residents. Applications should detail measurable and achievable outcomes and demonstrate other sources of support, collaboration, and/or cooperation. Applications should also address the sustainability of the proposed program or project for which funding is desired. Evaluation criteria include, but are not limited to: the overall merit of the project; the ability of the organization to successfully complete the project; the clarity and measurability of the project's goal; the feasibility of the time frame given for completion of the project; and the number of people served.
Restrictions: Ineligible organizations or activities include: individuals, for-profit, 501(c)4, 501(c)6, and non Alaska based organizations, private or family foundations, state and federal government agencies, and ad hoc groups without a tax exempt legal status are not eligible for competitive grants. Applications for religious indoctrination or other religious activities, endowment building, deficit financing, fundraising, lobbying, electioneering, or activities of political nature will not be considered, nor will proposals for ads, sponsorships, or special events (e.g. fundraisers), and any proposals which discriminate as to race, gender, marital status, sexual preference, age, disability, creed, or ethnicity.
Geographic Focus: Alaska
Date(s) Application is Due: Oct 1
Amount of Grant: Up to 500 USD
Contact: Holli Flint, Petersburg Community Foundation Program Manager; (907) 334-6700; hflint@alaskacf.org or grants@alaskacf.org
Internet: alaskacf.org/blog/grants/2018-pcf-mini-grant-program/
Sponsor: Alaska Community Foundation
3201 C Street, Suite 110
Anchorage, AK 99503

Alaska Community Foundation Seward Community Foundation Grant　209

The Seward Community Foundation (SCF), an Affiliate of The Alaska Community Foundation (ACF), seeks applications from qualified, tax exempt 501(c)3 organizations (or equivalents, such as: Tribal entities, schools, and faith-based organizations) that are based in or serve the communities of Seward and/or Moose Pass. SCF grants support a broad range of charitable community needs in the areas of: health and wellness, education, the great outdoors, arts and culture, animal welfare, community development, and many other charitable activities that benefit Seward and Moose Pass communities.
Requirements: Preference will be given to applications which have the potential to impact a broad range of Seward/Moose Pass area residents. Applications should detail measurable and achievable outcomes and demonstrate other sources of support, collaboration, or clearly articulate the need for the proposed project/program and how the community will be impacted through it. Thoughtful applications that concisely identify why it's important for this project/program to be funded this year will be appreciated by the SCF Grants Committee. Evaluation criteria include, but are not limited to: the overall merit of the project; the ability of the organization to successfully complete the project; the clarity and measurability of the project's goal; the feasibility of the time frame given for completion of the project; and the number of people served.
Restrictions: Ineligible organizations or activities include: individuals, for-profit, 501(c)4, 501(c)6, and non Alaska based organizations, private or family foundations, state and federal government agencies, and ad hoc groups without a tax exempt legal status are not eligible for competitive grants. Applications for religious indoctrination or other religious activities, endowment building, deficit financing, fundraising, lobbying, electioneering, or activities of political nature will not be considered, nor will proposals for ads, sponsorships, or special events (e.g. fundraisers), and any proposals which discriminate as to race, gender, marital status, sexual preference, age, disability, creed, or ethnicity.
Geographic Focus: Alaska
Date(s) Application is Due: Feb 21
Amount of Grant: 1,000 - 10,000 USD
Contact: Amy Hankins, Seward Community Foundation Program Manager; (907) 334-6700; ahankins@alaskacf.org
Internet: alaskacf.org/blog/grants/scf-grant-program/
Sponsor: Alaska Community Foundation
3201 C Street, Suite 110
Anchorage, AK 99503

Alaska Conservation Foundation Youth Mini Grants　210

The Youth Mini Grant program aims to support youth-led projects that address conservation issues in Alaska. These include climate change, community health, racial and social inequity, and sustainable economies. The Youth Mini Grant Program aims to empower youth leaders as they invest in their communities, become mentors, and delve into issues of social justice impacting Alaska's cultures, communities, and well-being.

Requirements: Youth ages 15-25 are eligible to apply for grant awards. Applicants to the Youth Mini Grant Program must be Alaska based, or if attending school elsewhere, have an Alaska focused project. Applicant must find a fiscal sponsor in the form of one of the following: 501(c)3 nonprofit organization; federally recognized tribe; public school; church; or other equivalent organizations. In addition to a fiscal sponsor, successful applicants will also have an adult mentor/sponsor.
Geographic Focus: Alaska
Date(s) Application is Due: Feb 28; Apr 30
Amount of Grant: Up to 500 USD
Contact: Anna Dalton, Grants Manager; (907) 433-8213; fax (907) 274-4145; adalton@ alaskaconservation.org or grants@alaskaconservation.org
Internet: alaskaconservation.org/community-resources/grant-opportunities/youth-mini-grant/
Sponsor: Alaska Conservation Foundation
1227 W. 9th Avenue, Suite 300
Anchorage, AK 99501

Alaska State Council on the Arts Cultural Collaboration Project Grants   211
Alaska State Council on the Arts Cultural Collaboration Project Grants are matching awards of up to $6,000 in support of high-quality arts and cultural programs for youth that emphasize skill acquisition and direct participation in settings outside of the school day/year. There are two annual deadlines for application submission: June 1 and December 1.
Requirements: Eligible programs provide regularly scheduled sessions over an extended period of time. Nonprofit organizations, schools, or school districts are eligible to apply. Applicants may apply for funding for the same project for up to three consecutive years, demonstrating in successive years that the project is pursuing other funding sources. It is expected that the request amount will decrease over the three-year period. In the initial application state that the project is expected to be a three-year project and outline the successive year's plans. A new application will need to be made for each of the three years stating which year the project is in.
Restrictions: A school or organization may receive only one Cultural Collaboration grant per year.
Geographic Focus: Alaska
Date(s) Application is Due: Jun 1; Dec 1
Amount of Grant: Up to 6,000 USD
Contact: Laura Forbes, Program Director; (907) 269-6682 or (907) 269-6610; fax (907) 269-6601; laura.forbes@alaska.gov
Internet: arts.alaska.gov/cultural-collaborations
Sponsor: Alaska State Council on the Arts
161 Klevin Street, Suite 102
Anchorage, AK 99508-1506

Alaska State Council on the Arts Youth Cultural Heritage Fast Track Grants   212
Youth Cultural Heritage (YCH) is a program of the Alaska State Council on the Arts, with funding support from Rasmuson Foundation. The program supports youth-based projects and activities which enable children and youth to use the arts to approach, understand, express and share their cultural heritage. The program is inclusive of all Alaska's ethnic cultures and residents. Funding priority is given to cultural heritage groups and organizations who face challenges or barriers for receiving grants. The program is envisioned as network and capacity-building, as well as granting in the YCH Fast-track, Project, and Alumni categories of grants. The over-arching goals of the Youth Cultural Heritage Program are as follows: strengthen Alaska children and youth's cultural knowledge and self-awareness; support direct, creative development opportunities for Alaska children and youth to engage with artists and culture bearers; engage citizens around cultural heritage; bridge culture and communities; and create greater cross-cultural understanding and empathy.
Requirements: Alaska 501(c)3, tax exempt youth-serving organizations, schools, tribal organizations, libraries, and other arts/cultural organizations are eligible to receive grants within the program, or to fiscally sponsor otherwise eligible community groups. A completed application consists of the application cover with certification, a two-page project narrative, the project budget form, and attachments. If you are working with a fiscal sponsor, please complete and include the Fiscal Sponsor Information with certification, as well.
Geographic Focus: Alaska
Contact: Laura Forbes, Program Director; (907) 269-6682 or (907) 269-6610; fax (907) 269-6601; laura.forbes@alaska.gov
Internet: arts.alaska.gov/arts-education-grants
Sponsor: Alaska State Council on the Arts
161 Klevin Street, Suite 102
Anchorage, AK 99508-1506

**ALA Sullivan Award for Public Library Administrators Supporting   213
   Services to Children**
The Sullivan Award for Public Library Administrators Supporting Services to Children is given to an individual who has shown exceptional understanding and support of public library service to children, while having general management, supervisory, or administrative responsibility that includes public library service to children. The award consists of a commemorative gift and 24k gold framed citation. This award is given out on an annual basis.
Requirements: Applications must include the nominee's brief career summary, educational background, memberships and participation in professional organizations, publications/productions/presentations, and other significant contributions. Applications will be submitted online through the ALA website.
Geographic Focus: All States
Date(s) Application is Due: Feb 1
Samples: Alice Knapp, Stamford, Connecticut - Awarded to the President of Ferguson Library (2020).

Contact: Cheryl Malden, Program Officer; (800) 545-2433 ext. 3247; fax (312) 440-9374; cmalden@ala.org or ala@ala.org
Internet: www.ala.org/awardsgrants/sullivan-award-public-library-administrators-supporting-services-children
Sponsor: American Library Association
225 N. Michigan Avenue
Chicago, IL 60601

ALA Teen's Top Ten Awards   214
The Teen's Top Ten Awards is a "teen choice" list, where teens nominate and choose their favorite books of the previous year. This award is given out on an annual basis.
Requirements: Any book of teen interest, fiction or nonfiction, adult or young adult, published during the previous year is eligible for the Teens' Top Ten. All applications must be submitted electronically on this official application form. All applicants must be current, personal members of YALSA at the time of application. All applicants must agree to a 2 year term and maintain membership in YALSA throughout their term. Any teen across the country can suggest a book for TTT by filling out the public nomination form. They nominate titles throughout the year and vote on their nominations and the nominations from the public to determine the 25 official TTT nominations. Nominations are posted on Support Teen Literature Day, the Thursday of National Library Week, and teens across the country vote on their favorite titles each year. Readers ages twelve to eighteen will vote online in August and September; the winners will be announced during Teen Read Week. Book nominations must be submitted with the application form and four sample Teen Reviews. The application form can be found online at the ALA website.
Geographic Focus: All States
Date(s) Application is Due: Sep 18
Samples: Kurt Dinan, Cincinnati, Ohio - Awarded for their book, "Don't Get Caught" (2018); Leopoldo Gout, New York City, New York - Awarded for their book, "Genius: The Game" (2018); Marissa Meyer, Tacoma, Washington - Awarded for their book, "Heartless" (2018).
Contact: Jordan Dubin, Awards Coordinator; (800) 545-2433 ext. 5839; fax (312) 440-9374; jdubin@ala.org or ala@ala.org
Internet: www.ala.org/awardsgrants/teens-top-ten
Sponsor: American Library Association
225 N. Michigan Avenue
Chicago, IL 60601

ALA Theodor Seuss Geisel Award   215
The Theodor Seuss Geisel Award, established in 2004, is given annually to the author(s) and illustrator(s) of the most distinguished contribution to the body of American children's literature known as beginning reader books published in the United States during the preceding year. The winning author and illustrator each receive a bronze medal. Honorees, if any, receive a plaque.
Requirements: Award winner(s) and honorees must attend the ALSC Award Presentation Program during the ALA Annual Conference. The award winning author and illustrator each prepare and deliver an acceptance speech. Honorees, if any, accept a plaque, but does not deliver a speech. ALSC membership is not a requirement to submit your work. There are no limitations as to the character of the book considered except that it will be original and function successfully as a book for beginning readers. Honor Books may be named. These shall be books that are also truly distinguished. Subject matter must be intriguing enough to motivate the child to read. The book may or may not include short "chapters." New words should be added slowly enough to make learning them a positive experience. Words should be repeated to ensure knowledge retention. Sentences must be simple and straightforward. There must be a minimum of 24 pages. Books may not be longer than 96 pages. The illustrations must demonstrate the story being told. The book creates a successful reading experience, from start to finish. The plot advances from one page to the next and creates a "page-turning" dynamic. To apply, one copy of the book must be mailed to the ALA/ALSC Office and one must be mailed to the Award Committee Chair. If the applicant wishes, they may attach a cover letter with their contact information to the final work. There is not a submission form to fill out or an entry fee for the Geisel Award. More specific information on how to submit a book can be found on the ALA website.
Restrictions: The Award is restricted to author(s) and illustrator(s) who are citizens or residents of the United States.
Geographic Focus: All States
Date(s) Application is Due: Dec 31
Samples: James Yang, Brooklyn, New York - Awarded for their book, "Stop! Bot!" (2020).
Contact: Jordan Dubin, Awards Coordinator; (800) 545-2433 ext. 5839; fax (312) 440-9374; jdubin@ala.org or alscawards@ala.org
Internet: www.ala.org/awardsgrants/theodor-seuss-geisel-award
Sponsor: American Library Association
225 N. Michigan Avenue
Chicago, IL 60601

Alavi Foundation Education Grants   216
The Alavi Foundation is a private not-for-profit organization devoted to the promotion and support of Islamic culture and Persian language, literature and civilization. Since its inception in 1973, the Foundation has been an independent charitable organization based in the United States. The Foundation has been promoting projects for over 30 years by financially supporting charitable and philanthropic causes through educational, religious, and cultural programs. It supports nine (9) core areas: grants to colleges and universities; donations to Persian schools; donations and loans to Islamic organizations; free distribution of Islamic books; donations for disaster relief; support for the arts; scholarly research; interfaith dialogue and religious pluralism; and student loans.

Requirements: The Foundation's contributions are limited only to public charities that are tax exempt under IRS ruling.
Geographic Focus: All States
Contact: Program Contact; (212) 944-8333; fax (646) 619-4272; info@alavifoundation.org
Internet: alavifoundation.us/grantprograms/
Sponsor: Alavi Foundation
650 5th Avenue, Suite 2406
New York, NY 10019-6108

ALA William C. Morris Debut YA Award   217

The William C. Morris YA Debut Award, first awarded in 2009, honors a debut book published by a first-time author writing for teens and celebrating impressive new voices in young adult literature. The work cited will illuminate the teen experience and enrich the lives of its readers through its excellence, demonstrated by compelling, high quality writing and/or illustration; the integrity of the work as a whole; and its proven or potential appeal to a wide range of teen readers. The award's namesake is William C. Morris, an influential innovator in the publishing world and an advocate for marketing books for children and young adults. Bill Morris left an impressive mark on the field of children's and young adult literature. He was beloved in the publishing field and the library profession for his generosity and marvelous enthusiasm for promoting literature for children and teens. This award is given out on an annual basis.
Requirements: The award and honor book winner(s) must be authors of original young adult works of fiction in any genre, nonfiction, poetry, a short story collection, or graphic work. The award winner(s) must not have previously published a book for any audience. Books previously published in another country, however, may be considered if an American edition has been published during the period of eligibility. Works of joint authorship are eligible, but only if all contributors meet all other criteria. For example, graphic works created by an author and an illustrator are eligible, but only if both contributors have never published before. Books must have been published between January 1 and December 31 of the year preceding announcement of the award. The short list may consist of up to five titles. The award may be given posthumously provided the other criteria are met. To be eligible, a title must have been designated by its publisher as being either a young adult book or one published for the age range that YALSA defines as "young adult," i.e., 12 through 18. The winning title must exemplify the highest standards of young adult literature and must be well written. The book's components [story, voice, setting, accuracy, style, characters, design, format, theme, illustration, organization, etc.] should be of high merit. Popularity is not the criterion for this award, nor is the award based on the message or content of the book. Nominations will be submitted both by the field and the committee; more information on how to submit can be found on the ALA website.
Restrictions: Publishers, authors, agents, or editors may not nominate their own titles. Books published for adults or for younger children are not eligible. Edited works and anthologies are not eligible.
Geographic Focus: All States
Date(s) Application is Due: Dec 1
Samples: Adib Khorram, Kansas City, Missouri - Awarded for their book, "Darius the Great Is Not Okay" (2019).
Contact: Jordan Dubin, Awards Coordinator; (800) 545-2433 ext. 5839; fax (312) 440-9374; jdubin@ala.org or ala@ala.org
Internet: www.ala.org/awardsgrants/william-c-morris-debut-ya-award
Sponsor: American Library Association
225 N. Michigan Avenue
Chicago, IL 60601

ALA YALSA Presidential Citation Award   218

The YALSA Presidential Citation Award is meant to highlight excellence among members of YALSA as well as library supporters who have provided outstanding service to the association or profession of young adult librarianship. The citation may consist of a plaque, letter, or object of recognition. No monetary award will be connected with the citation. This award is given out at the discretion of the president.
Requirements: The citation may be given to an individual or group that meets one or more of the following criteria: Significant impact on the association or the profession, Strategic and compelling advancement of the association or profession, Exemplary or innovative service, Levels of effort well beyond normal volunteer commitment and leadership, and Accomplishments that are significant and don't meet the criteria of other YALSA awards. Nominations may be submitted to the YALSA Board of Directors at any time.
Geographic Focus: All States
Date(s) Application is Due: Dec 31
Contact: Cheryl Malden, Program Officer; (800) 545-2433 ext. 3247; fax (312) 440-9374; cmalden@ala.org or ala@ala.org
Internet: www.ala.org/awardsgrants/yalsa-presidential-citation
Sponsor: American Library Association
225 N. Michigan Avenue
Chicago, IL 60601

Albert and Ethel Herzstein Charitable Foundation Grants   219

The Charitable Foundation was established by Albert and Ethel Herzstein, whose lives symbolized the American dream and the importance of living life to its fullest. They embraced the American spirit and ideals which encourage self-sufficiency and the free enterprise system, but did not forget the importance of helping those who, due to circumstances, were unable to help themselves. Today, the Foundation pursues a mission to support free enterprise, strengthen families, preserve heritage, educate individuals and communities, and provide second chances where appropriate, encouraging individuals to realize their potential and ability to achieve their highest quality of life. Preference will be given to grant requests from organizations in the Houston area or within the state of Texas. Proposals are accepted year-round through the Herzstein Foundation's Online Application.

Requirements: Grants are made to qualified nonprofit organizations with preference given to those in Texas. The Foundation accepts applications on a rolling basis and only accepts one application per grantee per year. Applications will be submitted online through the Foundation website.
Restrictions: Lobbying of individual directors by grant applicants may result in adverse consideration of grant application. Organizations submitting proposals should limit their request to no more than one in any twelve month period. Grants are made only to qualified non-profit organizations. The Foundation does not make grants to individuals.
Geographic Focus: Texas
Samples: American Red Cross, Texas - Awarded to contribute to Disaster Cycle Services and replenish the funds that have been used in response to house fires and natural disasters in our region (2019); Big Brothers Big Sisters Lone Star, Texas - Awarded to provide children facing adversity with strong and enduring, professionally supported, one-to-one relationships (2019); Bridges to Life, Texas - Awarded to connect communities with prisons to reduce the recidivism rate, reduce the number of crime victims, and enhance public safety (2019).
Contact: L. Michael Hajtman, President; (713) 681-7868; fax (713) 681-3652; albertandethel@herzsteinfoundation.org
Internet: herzsteinfoundation.org/application-guidelines/
Sponsor: Albert and Ethel Herzstein Charitable Foundation
6131 Westview Drive
Houston, TX 77055-5421

Albert E. and Birdie W. Einstein Fund Grants   220

The Albert E. and Birdie W. Einstein Fund awards grants primarily in Florida for the arts and cultural programs; education; and human services, including children and youth services, churches and Jewish services, and families. Awards typically range from $1,000 to $100,000. Visit the website for guidelines and a downloadable application.
Requirements: 501(c)3 nonprofits that support organizations in Florida may apply.
Restrictions: The types of grants that the Foundation does not make include: individuals or individual research; general operating expenses; programs outside the State of Florida; and organizations that do not hold a 501(c)3 designation.
Geographic Focus: Florida
Amount of Grant: 1,000 - 100,000 USD
Contact: Joyce M. Boyer, Director; (305) 587-3033; contact@alberteinsteinfund.com
Internet: alberteinsteinfund.com/
Sponsor: Albert E. and Birdie W. Einstein Fund
P.O. Box 372279
Satellite Beach, FL 32937

Albertsons Companies Foundation Nourishing Neighbors Grants   221

Albertsons Companies Foundation funds organizations that strengthen the neighborhoods it serves. On a regional basis, the Foundation funds organizations that impact the lives of its employees and customers. On a national basis, it funds only organizations working in the area of Childhood Hunger through the Hunger Is Campaign. An RFP is released on an annual basis by invitation only. Regionally, areas of charitable giving include health and hunger relief (food banks, churches, and other community-based relief groups); health and nutrition (medical services, flu shots, health screening for diseases such as diabetes and heart disease); and education and development of youth (academic excellence or nurturing efforts). Submit requests in writing and include information about the organization's goals, accomplishments, evaluation plans, leadership, and finances. Requests are accepted throughout the year.
Requirements: Tax-exempt organizations in Arizona, Arkansas, California, Colorado, Delaware, Florida, Georgia, Idaho, Illinois, Indiana, Iowa, Kansas, Louisiana, Maine, Maryland, Massachusetts, Michigan, Minnesota, Mississippi, Missouri, Montana, Nebraska, Nevada, New Hampshire, New Jersey, New Mexico, North Dakota, Oklahoma, Oregon, Pennsylvania, South Dakota, Tennessee, Texas, Utah, Vermont, Washington, Wisconsin, and Wyoming are eligible. Applicants must pass an online eligibility test. Preference will be given to requests that offer volunteerism opportunities.
Restrictions: The Foundation generally does not fund: individuals or for-profit organizations; political organizations or activities; religious organizations for religious purposes; capital or building campaigns; advocacy programs; meetings, conferences or workshops; sports teams or athletic competitions; other foundations or granting organizations; or fundraising dinners, galas, and events.
Geographic Focus: Arizona, Arkansas, California, Colorado, Delaware, Florida, Georgia, Idaho, Illinois, Indiana, Iowa, Kansas, Louisiana, Maine, Maryland, Massachusetts, Michigan, Minnesota, Mississippi, Missouri, Montana, Nebraska, Nevada, New Hampshire, New Jersey, New Mexico, North Dakota, Oklahoma, Oregon, Pennsylvania, South Dakota, Tennessee, Texas, Utah, Vermont, Washington, Wisconsin, Wyoming
Contact: Christy Duncan Anderson, Community Relations Manager; (877) 932-7948 or (208) 395-6200; fax (208) 395-4382; Christy.Duncan-Anderson@safeway.com
Internet: national.albertsonscompaniesfoundation.org/get-funded/
Sponsor: Albertsons Companies Foundation
11555 Dublin Canyon Way
Pleasanton, CA 94588

Albert W. Cherne Foundation Grants   222

The Albert W. Cherne Foundation was established in Minneapolis, Minnesota, in 1968. Currently, the Foundation awards grants to nonprofit organizations, primarily in Minnesota, for general operating support, continuing support, and annual campaigns in its areas of interest. These primary fields of interest include: arts and culture; adult basic education; literacy; elementary and secondary education; children and youth services; higher education; historic preservation; human rights; legal services; public safety; right to life; services for the disabled; and human services. Interested parties should begin by sending a letter of inquiry, which will be followed by a formal invitation to apply. There are no specific annual deadlines.

Requirements: Grants support nonprofit organizations primarily in the five-county metropolitan area of Minneapolis and Saint Paul, Minnesota, though awards are also given across the United States.

Restrictions: Grants do not support veterans, fraternal, or labor organizations; religious purposes; conduit organizations; civil rights/social action groups; mental health counseling; specific-disease organizations; housing programs; individuals; capital improvements; or endowment funds.

Geographic Focus: All States

Amount of Grant: 1,000 - 250,000 USD

Samples: Colby College, Waterville, Maine, $50,000 - for program support (2019); Grace Church, Eden Prairie, Minnesota, $21,000 - for program support (2019); Living Hope Church, Winchester, Wisconsin, $7,000 - for program support (2019).

Contact: Elizabeth B. Cherne, President; (952) 239-5344; fax (952) 944-3070

Sponsor: Albert W. Cherne Foundation

P.O. Box 46117

Eden Prarie, MN 55344

Albert W. Rice Charitable Foundation Grants   223

The Albert W. Rice Charitable Foundation was established in 1959 to support and promote quality educational, human services and health care programming for underserved populations. Special consideration is given to charitable organizations that serve the people of Worcester, Massachusetts and its surrounding communities. Grant requests for general operating support or program support are encouraged. From time to time, the foundation may consider capital requests. The majority of grants from the Rice Foundation are 1 year in duration. On occasion, multi-year support is awarded. Awards amounts typically range between $10,000 and $25,000.

Requirements: Applicants must have 501(c)3 tax-exempt status. Applications will be submitted online through the Bank of America website. A grant report is required within 1 year of the grant application date, regardless of whether all of the funds have been spent.

Restrictions: The foundation does not support requests from individuals, organizations attempting to influence policy through direct lobbying, or any political campaigns.

Geographic Focus: Massachusetts

Date(s) Application is Due: Jul 1

Amount of Grant: 10,000 - 25,000 USD

Samples: Worcester Public Library, Worcester, Massachusetts, $15,000 - Awarded for Major Renovations To The Main Branch Of The Worcester Public Library (2018); African Community Education Program, Worcester, Massachusetts, $15,000 - Awarded for General operations of the organization (2018); Worcester Youth Center, Worcester, Massachusetts, $15,000 - Awarded for General Operations of the Organization (2018).

Contact: Michealle Larkins, Philanthropic Administrator; (866) 778-6859; ma.grantmaking@ustrust.com

Internet: www.bankofamerica.com/philanthropic/foundation/?fnId=44

Sponsor: Albert W. Rice Charitable Foundation

225 Franklin Street, 4th Floor, MA1-225-04-02

Boston, MA 02110

Alcatel-Lucent Technologies Foundation Grants   224

The Alcatel-Lucent Foundation is the philanthropic arm of Alcatel-Lucent and it leads the company's charitable activities. With a focus on volunteerism, the Foundation's mission is to support the commitment of Alcatel-Lucent to social responsibility by serving and enhancing the communities where its employees and customers live and work. To accomplish its mission, the Foundation manages grants and employee volunteerism on a global level. It receives its income from the corporation - Alcatel-Lucent - whose name it bears. However, legally the Foundation is an independent, charitable, non-profit and private entity and is governed by its own board of trustees that is separate from the corporate board of directors. Global Foundation grants are dedicated to the main focus areas of the Foundation and are managed by the Foundation.

Requirements: Giving is on an international basis.

Geographic Focus: All States, All Countries

Amount of Grant: 500 - 5,000 USD

Contact: Bishalakhi Ghosh, Executive Director; +91-99-58418547 or +91-22-66798700; fax +91-22-26598542; bishalakhi.ghosh@alcatel-lucent.com

Internet: www.alcatel-lucent.com/wps/portal/foundation

Sponsor: Alcatel-Lucent Technologies Foundation

600 Mountain Avenue, Room 6F4

Murray Hill, NJ 07974-2008

Alden and Vada Dow Fund Grants   225

Alden B. Dow sought to create quality in all that he did. Whether designing a building, talking to a friend or spending time with his family, quality was a constant. The son of Herbert and Grace Dow, he graduated from Midland High School. After visiting Japan, where he stayed in Frank Lloyd Wright's Imperial Hotel, in 1923 he attended the University of Michigan to study engineering in preparation to enter his father's company, Dow Chemical. But after three years, Dow left to study architecture at Columbia University and graduated in 1931. Dow married Vada Bennett in 1931. Together with their children, Alden and Vada Dow first established the charitable foundation in 1960 to benefit the city of Midland and its surrounding communities. Today, the Alden and Vada Dow Family Foundations are made up of two grant making entities: the Alden and Vada Dow Fund and The Vada B. Dow Charitable Unitrust. The Foundations make grants in Central and Northern Michigan, with a particular focus on Midland, Bay, and Saginaw Counties. The mission of the Alden and Vada Dow Fund is to enhance the quality of life in the State of Michigan, through the funding of programs in the areas of: the arts; the environment; elementary and secondary education; health; human services; and youth programs. First time applicants that meet the eligibility requirements are asked to submit a request in writing

outlining their proposal before sending a formal grant request using the Foundation's grant guidelines. All full proposals should follow the grant guidelines and include all requested information and attachments. No additional copies are needed. The Fund has two funding cycles each year.: all proposals should be fully submitted by February 15 for consideration during the spring cycle and by August 15 for consideration during the fall cycle. The average grant amount awarded range from $3,000 to $20,000. There were exceptional cases wherein the Fund has awarded amount in larger amounts based on the need of the organization.

Requirements: The Alden and Vada Dow Fund support organizations that are tax exempt under Section 501(c)3 of the Internal Revenue Service Code and are not classified as private foundations under section 509(a) of the Code. Organizations may also submit proposals through a sponsoring organization, if the sponsor has 501(c)3 status, is not a private foundation under 509(a) and provides written authorization confirming its willingness to act as a fiscal sponsor

Restrictions: Organizations may only receive one grant within a twelve-month period.

Geographic Focus: Michigan

Date(s) Application is Due: Feb 15; Aug 15

Amount of Grant: 3,000 - 20,000 USD

Contact: Michael Lloyd Dow, President; (517) 839-7444; info@abdow.org

Internet: www.avdowfamilyfoundation.org/

Sponsor: Alden and Vada Dow Fund

315 Post Street

Midland, MI 48640-2658

Aldi Corporation Smart Kids Grants   226

The ALDI Corporation offers Smart Kids Grants that support schools in promoting and encouraging student health and wellness. Funding may be used for programs, projects, and events that focus on education, the arts, physical activity, and nutrition. Awards typically range from $100 to $5,000. Public, private, charter, and home schools, as well as 501(c)3 nonprofit organizations, are welcome to apply. Applications should be submitted using the online and, which are accepted February 1 through December 15 each year. Requests should be submitted at least six weeks prior to the event to be held.

Requirements: Eligible applicants are public and private kindergarten through grade 12 schools and nonprofit 501(c)3 organizations that benefit children in the geographic areas where ALDI conducts business. Qualified applicants must be located near ALDI stores, offices, or warehouses in: Alabama; Arkansas; California; Connecticut; Delaware; Washington, D.C; Florida; Georgia; Illinois; Indiana; Iowa; Kansas; Kentucky; Louisiana; Maryland; Massachusetts; Michigan; Minnesota; Mississippi; Missouri; Nebraska; New Hampshire; New Jersey; New York; North Carolina; Ohio; Oklahoma; Pennsylvania; Rhode Island, South Carolina; Tennessee; Texas; Vermont; Virginia; West Virginia; and Wisconsin.

Geographic Focus: Alabama, Arkansas, California, Connecticut, Delaware, District of Columbia, Florida, Georgia, Illinois, Indiana, Iowa, Kansas, Kentucky, Louisiana, Maryland, Massachusetts, Michigan, Minnesota, Mississippi, Missouri, Nebraska, New Hampshire, New Jersey, New York, North Carolina, Ohio, Oklahoma, Pennsylvania, Rhode Island, South Carolina, Tennessee, Texas, Vermont, Virginia, West Virginia, Wisconsin

Date(s) Application is Due: Dec 15

Amount of Grant: 100 - 5,000 USD

Contact: Corporate Giving Manager; (630) 879-8100; giving@aldi.us

Internet: corporate.aldi.us/en/corporate-responsibility/aldi-smart-kids/

Sponsor: Aldi Corporation

1200 North Kirk Road

Batavia, IL 60510

Alexander Graham Bell Parent and Infant Financial Aid Grants   227

AG Bell is working globally to ensure that people who are deaf and hard of hearing can hear and speak by providing many resources for those who are deaf and their families. The Alexander Graham Bell Parent & Infant Financial Aid Program aids families of infants and toddlers under the age of 4 who are pursuing a spoken language outcome for their child. The deadline to apply is September 27th.

Requirements: This program requires documentation of a pre-lingual bilateral hearing loss in the moderately-severe to profound range and use of listening and spoken language.

Geographic Focus: All States

Date(s) Application is Due: Sep 27

Contact: Emilio Alfonso-Mendoza, Executive Director; (202) 337-5220; fax (202) 337-8314; financialaid@agbell.org

Internet: www.agbell.org/Connect#financial-aid

Sponsor: Alexander Graham Bell Association for the Deaf

3417 Volta Place NW

Washington, D.C. 20007

Alexander Graham Bell Preschool-Age Financial Aid Grants   228

AG Bell offers financial aid programs for families at every stage of raising their child. The Alexander Graham Bell Preschool Financial Aid program is for families of preschool-age children who are learning Listening and Spoken Language. Awards help families with many expenses including auditory support services, speech-language therapy, preschool tuition, etc. Award amounts vary and are made once a year. The deadline to apply is July 5th.

Requirements: Applicants are required to provide documentation of a pre-lingual bilateral hearing loss in the moderately-severe to profound range and use of listening and spoken language.

Geographic Focus: All States

Date(s) Application is Due: Jul 5

Contact: Emilio Alfonso-Mendoza; (202) 337-5220; financialaid@agbell.org

Internet: www.agbell.org/Connect#financial-aid

Sponsor: Alexander Graham Bell Association for the Deaf

3417 Volta Place NW

Washington, D.C. 20007

Alex Stern Family Foundation Grants 229

The Alex Stern Family Foundation awards grants to North Dakota and Minnesota nonprofits in its areas of interest, which include: arts and culture; child welfare; the elderly; alcohol abuse; community affairs; family and social services; education; minorities; hospices; and cancer research. Types of support include: general operating support; continuing support; annual campaigns; building construction and renovation; equipment acquisition; emergency funds; program development; scholarship funds; research; and matching funds. The annual deadlines for submission are March 31 and August 31. Applications are reviewed in June and November. Most recent awards have ranged from $1,000 up to $20,000.

Requirements: Moorhead, Minnesota and Fargo, North Dakota nonprofit organizations are eligible to apply.

Restrictions: Grants are not awarded to individuals or for endowments.

Geographic Focus: Minnesota, North Dakota

Date(s) Application is Due: Mar 31; Aug 31

Amount of Grant: 1,000 - 20,000 USD

Samples: Churches United for the Homeless, Moorhead, Minnesota, $10,000, general operating support (2018); Community of Care, Fargo, North Dakota, $4,000, volunteer program (2018).

Contact: Donald L. Scott; (701) 271-0263 or (701) 237-0170; donlscott@yahoo.com

Dan Carey, Trustee; (701) 412-1937 or (701) 271-0263; danc@visionbanks.com

Internet: www.alexsternfamilyfoundation.org/services.html

Sponsor: Alex Suitern Family Foundation

4141 28th Avenue South

Fargo, ND 58104-8468

ALFJ Astraea U.S. and International Emergency Fund 230

The Astraea Lesbian Foundation for Justice works for social, racial, and economic justice in the U.S. and internationally. Their grantmaking and philanthropic advocacy programs help lesbians and allied communities challenge oppression. Astraea provides rapid response emergency grants to organizations faced with an unforeseeable organizing opportunity or immediate political emergency.

Requirements: Applicants should send a one page letter of inquiry to be certain their project is appropriate for Astraea. Inquiries should include information about the organization, a description of the emergency, and a budget summary of how the funds would be used.

Geographic Focus: All States, All Countries

Contact: Namita Chad; (212) 529-8021; fax (212) 982-3321; nchad@astraeafoundation.org

Internet: www.astraeafoundation.org/apply/

Sponsor: Astraea Lesbian Foundation for Justice

116 East 16th Street, 7th Floor

New York, NY 10003

ALFJ International Fund Grants 231

Astraea's primary purpose is to advance the economic, political, educational, and cultural well-being of lesbians. Astraea raises and distributes funds to organizations, individuals, and projects that promote a feminist perspective advancing the social, political, economic, educational, and cultural well-being of lesbians and all women and girls. Programs and policies will be supported that actively work to eliminate those forms of oppression based on sexual orientation, class, race, age, physical and mental ability, religious affiliation, and all other factors that affect lesbians and gay men in the United States and internationally. It also partners with LGBTQI groups who have limited access to funding, prioritizing support for lesbian, bisexual, and queer women, trans and gender non-conforming people, and/or intersex people; and communities that have been historically marginalized within LGBTQI movements. Organizations may apply for general support or project support. Applications are accepted in English, Spanish, French, Chinese and Russian. Letters of inquiry are accepted May and the end of August.

Requirements: Groups must be based in Latin America, the Caribbean, Asia, the Pacific, Eastern Europe, the former Soviet Republics, the Middle East, and Africa.

Restrictions: Astraea Foundation generally does not fund government agencies or organizations with budgets above $500,000.

Geographic Focus: All States

Date(s) Application is Due: Aug 30

Amount of Grant: Up to 10,000 USD

Contact: Namita Chad, Associate Director of Programs; (212) 529-8021; fax (212) 982-3321; namita@astraeafoundation.org or grants@astraeafoundation.org

Internet: www.astraeafoundation.org/apply/international-fund/

Sponsor: Astraea Lesbian Foundation for Justice

116 East 16th Street, 7th Floor

New York, NY 10003

ALFJ International Social Change Opportunity Fund Grants 232

Astraea's Social Change Opportunity Fund provides grants a dedicated stream of funding for timely legal, policy and institutional change campaigns. Grants are generally provided in three areas: technical assistance; travel and peer-to-peer learning; and historic convenings. Applications are accepted in English, Spanish, French, Chinese and Russian. the Foundation makes grants with the support of our International Advisory Board, a body of nearly 40 LGBTQI activists who are connected to LGBTQI and feminist movements globally and inform its grant making strategies and decisions. Letters of inquiry are accepted May and the end of August.

Requirements: One page letters of inquiry should be sent to the program officer. Information should include information about the organization, the purpose of the request, and a budget summary of how the funds would be used.

Restrictions: Although any organization that fits the funding criteria may apply, Astraea prioritizes current Astraea grantee partners.

Geographic Focus: All States, All Countries

Date(s) Application is Due: Aug 30

Contact: Namita Chad; (212) 529-8021; fax (212) 982-3321; nchad@astraeafoundation.org

Internet: www.astraeafoundation.org/apply/international-fund/

Sponsor: Astraea Lesbian Foundation for Justice

116 East 16th Street, 7th Floor

New York, NY 10003

Alfred E. Chase Charitable Foundation Grants 233

The Alfred E. Chase Charity Foundation was established in 1956 to support and promote quality educational, human services, and health care programming for underserved populations. Special consideration is given to charitable organizations that serve the people of the city of Lynn and the North Shore of Massachusetts. The majority of grants from The Alfred E. Chase Charity Foundation are one year in duration. On occasion, multi-year support is awarded. Award amounts typically range from $10,000 to $30,000.

Requirements: Applicants must have 501(c)3 tax-exempt status. Grant requests for general operating support or program support are encouraged. Small, program-related capital expenses may be included in general operating or program requests. Applications will be submitted online through the Bank of America website. A grant report is required within 1 year of the grant application date, regardless of whether all of the funds have been spent.

Restrictions: The foundation does not support requests from individuals, organizations attempting to influence policy through direct lobbying, or any political campaigns.

Geographic Focus: Massachusetts

Date(s) Application is Due: May 1

Amount of Grant: 10,000 - 30,000 USD

Samples: Neighborhood Of Affordable Housing (NOAH), East Boston, Massachusetts, $25,000 - Awarded for the North Shore Regional Partnership Foreclosure Education Center/TNSRP; Horizons for Homeless Children Inc., Roxbury, Massachusetts, $25,000 - Awarded for Northeast Region Playspace program; Chelsea Collaborative Inc., Chelsea, Massachusetts, $20,000 - Awarded for Chelsea Works: Year Round Youth Employment program.

Contact: Michealle Larkins, Philanthropic Administrator; (866) 778-6859; ma.grantmaking@bankofamerica.com or ma.grantmaking@ustrust.com

Internet: www.bankofamerica.com/philanthropic/foundation/?fnId=35

Sponsor: Alfred E. Chase Charitable Foundation

225 Franklin Street

Boston, MA 02110

Alfred J Mcallister and Dorothy N Mcallister Foundation Grants 234

The foundation was established in 2000 and gives primarily in the Greater Lafayette area in Indiana. Giving has been focused on animals and wildlife, educational programs and human services in the immediate community. Grants typically range up to $50,0000.

Requirements: Unsolicited requests for funds and applications are not accepted. The foundation has a preference for giving in the immediate area of Lafayette, Indiana. Send a letter of inquiry via mail to determine if the foundation will consider entertaining a request.

Geographic Focus: Indiana

Amount of Grant: Up to 50,000 USD

Samples: Jefferson High School Golden Bronchos Club (Lafayette, Indiana) - $200,000; Lafayette School Corporation (Lafayette, Indiana) - $89,500; Wildcat Wildlife Foundation (Lafayette, Indiana) - $50,000; YWCA (Lafayette, Indiana) - $41,500; Wabash Center, Inc. (Lafayette, Indiana) - $35,000; Ivy Tech Foundation (Lafayette, Indiana) - $34,000; Tippecanoe County Historical Association (Lafayette, Indiana) - $ 25,750 Niches Land Trust Corp (Lafayette, Indiana) - $ 20,000 Tippecanoe County Parks Department (Lafayette, Indiana) - $18,700; Food Finders Food Bank (Lafayette, Indiana) - $10,750; Sagamore Council Boy Scouts (Lafayette, Indiana) - $8,000; Lafayette Adult Reading Academy Capital Fund (Lafayette, Indiana) - $7,000

Contact: Charles Max Layden, (765) 742-7646; fax (765) 742-0983

Sponsor: Alfred J Mcallister and Dorothy N Mcallister Foundation

2310 N 725 E

Lafayette, IN 47905

A Little Hope Grants 235

A Little Hope is a not-for-profit publicly supported charitable foundation, recognized by the IRS under 501(c)3, which grants funds to organizations that provide bereavement support services and grief counseling to children and teens who have experienced the death of a parent, sibling or loved one. Strong preference is given to applicants who demonstrate a commitment to the use of community trained volunteers, whose programs demonstrate multicultural competence in addressing children and adolescent's bereavement needs, and whose programs are likely to be replicable in other communities. Grant applications are by invitation only and are processed during the month of October each year.

Requirements: To be considered, email (no telephone calls): the name of your program, your website address, the name of your executive director, and the name of the program director, including their credentials. No other information is needed or will be processed. Do not send letters of inquiry or any other materials unless they have been requested by A Little Hope.

Restrictions: No other organizations are authorized to solicit RFP's or information on our behalf.

Geographic Focus: All States, American Samoa, District of Columbia, Guam, Marshall Islands, Northern Mariana Islands, Puerto Rico, U.S. Virgin Islands

Contact: Tanhya Vancho Schimel, Vice President and Secretary; (203) 581-1011; granting@alittlehope.org or info@alittlehope.org

Internet: www.alittlehope.org/granting

Sponsor: A Little Hope

20 Sterling Road

South Armonk, NY 10504

Allan C. and Lelia J. Garden Foundation Grants   236

The mission of the Allan C. and Lelia J. Garden Foundation is to support charitable organizations in Georgia that maintain, care and educate orphan or underprivileged children. It is also the Foundation's intent to support organizations that provide medical, dental, hospital care, nursing and treatment of crippled or physically handicapped children. Award amounts typically range from $2,000 to $50,000 and are primarily one year in duration. On occasion, multi-year support is awarded.

Requirements: Applicants must have 501(c)3 tax-exempt status and serve residents of Ben Hill, Irwin, and Wilcox Counties in Georgia. Applications will be submitted online through the Bank of America website. Applicants will be notified of grant decisions by letter within 3 to 4 months after the deadline. A grant report is required within 1 year of the grant application date, regardless of whether all of the funds have been spent.

Restrictions: The foundation does not support requests from individuals, organizations attempting to influence policy through direct lobbying, or any political campaigns.

Geographic Focus: Georgia
Date(s) Application is Due: Jun 1
Amount of Grant: 2,000 - 50,000 USD
Samples: Murphy-Harpst Childrens Centers, Cedartown, Georgia, $25,000 - Awarded for general operating support; Hephzibah Ministries, Macon, Georgia, $25,000 - Awarded for support of the Positive Parenting to Prevent Maltreatment program; Communities in Schools of Fitzgerald-Ben Hill County, Fitzgerald, Georgia, $15,000 - Awarded for general operating support.
Contact: Mark S. Drake, Vice President; (404) 264-1377; ga.grantmaking@bankofamerica.com or mark.s.drake@bofa.com
Internet: www.bankofamerica.com/philanthropic/foundation/?fnId=97
Sponsor: Allan C. and Lelia J. Garden Foundation
P.O. Box 1802
Providence, RI 02901-1802

Allegis Group Foundation Grants   237

The Allegis Group Foundation helps causes that align to its mission: education - providing individuals with life skills to reach their full potential; strengthening the workforce - career development and access to employment for under-served adults; and employee engagement - supporting causes that its employees are passionate about. The Foundation awards grants to support organizations providing services or programs in the areas of education, health, and underprivileged children. Types of support have most recently included: general operating support; program development; and scholarship funds. Giving is national in scope, with an emphasis on Baltimore, Maryland.

Requirements: The Foundation will consider one online application submission once a year per organization. Organizations should build in all requests for funding into one annual grant request. This includes both program funding and event sponsorship requests. Organizations should include the following as part of their grant request: organizational overview, programmatic information if earmarked for a specific initiative, opportunities for employee engagement, expected outcomes and plan for reporting project results, and 501(c)3 documentation.

Geographic Focus: All States
Date(s) Application is Due: Mar 31; Jun 30; Sep 30; Dec 31
Amount of Grant: Up to 40,000 USD
Contact: Paul J. Bowie; (410) 579-3509 or (410) 579-3000; CSR@AllegisGroup.com
Internet: www.allegisgroup.com/en/about/application-details-ag-foundation
Sponsor: Allegis Group Foundation
7301 Parkway Drive
Hanover, MD 21076-1159

Allen Foundation Educational Nutrition Grants   238

Established in 1975 by agricultural chemist William Webster Allen and based in Midland, Michigan, the Allen Foundation makes grants to projects that benefit human nutrition in the areas of education, training, and research. Priorities include training programs for children and young adults to improve their health and development; training programs for educators and demonstrators concerned with good nutritional practices; programs for the education and training of mothers during pregnancy and after the birth of their children, so that good nutritional habits can be formed at an early age; and programs that aid in the dissemination of information regarding healthful nutrition practices. The Allen Foundation will consider requests from the following: hospitals or medical clinics; social, religious, fraternal, or community organizations; private foundations; and K-12 public, parochial or private schools. Preference may be given to proposals that include matching funds from the institution or other partners including in-kind contribution. Third party contribution to matching funds such as computer or software donated from a company may be included. Interested organizations should begin by taking the online eligibility quiz. Applications are also available online. The annual deadline is December 31, though proposals are reviewed throughout the year.

Requirements: 501(c)3 tax-exempt organizations nationwide may apply. In certain circumstances, the foundation will consider requests from the following: hospitals or medical clinics; social, religious, fraternal, or community organizations; private foundations; and K-12 public, parochial, or private schools.

Geographic Focus: All States
Date(s) Application is Due: Dec 31
Amount of Grant: 5,000 - 250,000 USD
Contact: Dale Baum, Secretary; (989) 832-5678 or (979) 695-1132; fax (989) 832-8842; dbaum@allenfoundation.org or Lucille@allenfoundation.org
Internet: www.allenfoundation.org/commoninfo/aboutus.asp
Sponsor: Allen Foundation
P.O. Box 1606
Midland, MI 48641-1606

Alliance for Strong Families and Communities Grants   239

The Alliance for Strong Families and Communities provides services to nonprofit child and family serving and economic empowerment organizations. The organization provides member agencies and interested groups with technical assistance, grants, and program planning tools to help build and amplify their voices in the civic arena. Its primary grant award interest areas include: basic and emergency aid; child welfare; Christian-based support programs; community and economic development; community improvement; economic development; family services; human services; mental health care; out-patient medical care; shelter and residential care; special population support; and youth development. Its targeted populations include: children and youth; economically disadvantaged; and low-income and poor. These awards typically come in the form of program development, research and evaluation; and technical assistance. The annual application deadline is May 30.

Requirements: Application are accepted from member organizations only.
Geographic Focus: All States
Date(s) Application is Due: May 30
Amount of Grant: Up to 80,000 USD
Samples: BakerRipley, Houston, Texas, $78,030 - support of human services program operation; Family Foundations, Jacksonville, Florida, $75,000 - general operating support; Grace Hill Settlement House, St. Louis, Missouri, $75,000 - community and economic development program support.
Contact: Lenore Schell, Senior Vice President of Strategic Business Innovation; (414) 359-1040 or (800) 221-3726; fax (414) 359-6721
Internet: www.alliance1.org/web/resources/Funding/web/resources/funding.aspx?hkey=6b062362-4133-4b44-9a46-f72248d6c113
Sponsor: Alliance for Strong Families and Communities
648 North Plankinton Avenue, Suite 425
Milwaukee, WI 53203

Alliant Energy Foundation Community Giving for Good Sponsorship Grants   240

The Alliant Energy Foundation Community Giving for Good sponsorships support community events and programs closely aligned with our community goals. Sponsorships typically range from $250-$2,000. Funds come from Alliant Energy.

Requirements: Events and programs must align with one of our strategic focus areas and projects Alliant funds. Programs must directly impact Alliant Energy customers and communities. Organizations are eligible for one sponsorship per calendar year. Please apply at least 60 days prior to the start of your event or program.

Restrictions: The foundation does not fund contributions to individuals; energy assistance projects; ads in programs, door prizes, raffle tickets, dinner tables, golf outings, or sponsorships of organized sports teams or activities; religious, fraternal, or social clubs; endowments; fiscal agents; fraternal or social clubs; religious institutions whose main purpose is to promote a specific faith, creed or religion and/or direct resources to advocate for a specific ideology; endowments; registration or participation fees for individuals or teams for fundraising events; or books, magazines, or professional journal articles.

Geographic Focus: Iowa, Wisconsin
Amount of Grant: 250 - 2,000 USD
Contact: Julie Bauer; (608) 458-4483 or (866) 769-3779; foundation@alliantenergy.com
Internet: www.alliantenergy.com/CommunityAndStewardship/CommunitySupport/CommunityGivingPrograms/GivingforGoodSponsorships
Sponsor: Alliant Energy Foundation
4902 North Biltmore Lane, Suite 1000
Madison, WI 53718-2148

Alloy Family Foundation Grants   241

Martin K. Alloy was the founder and chairman of Stanley Martin Homes in 1966, which is one of the Washington, D.C., area's most recognized names in new home construction and development, with over 10,000 families living in Virginia and Maryland communities. The Alloy Family Foundation was established by Martin K. Alloy in Reston, Virginia, in 2005, with its major geographic focus being the states of Maryland, Virginia, and Washington, D.C. The Foundation's primary fields of interest include: community and economic development; public and parochial school education; higher education; homeless and homeless shelters; housing development; housing and neighborhood rehabilitation; human services; shelter and residential care; and youth development. Types of awards include: general operating support; annual support; and program development. There are no specified annual deadlines, so interested organizations should begin by submitting a detailed description of project and amount of funding requested. Most recent awards have ranged from $500 to $31,000.

Requirements: Any 501(c)3 organization serving the residents of Maryland, Virginia, and Washington, D.C., are welcome to apply.

Geographic Focus: District of Columbia, Maryland, Virginia
Amount of Grant: Up to 40,000 USD
Samples: Flint High School, Oakton, Virginia, $2,500 - for general support (2018); Friendship Circle, Potomac, Maryland, $500 - for general support (2018); Northwestern University, New York, New York, $104 - for education (2018).
Contact: Martin K. Alloy, President; (703) 964-5000
Sponsor: Alloy Family Foundation
11710 Plaza America Drive, Suite 1100
Reston, VA 20190-4771

Allstate Corporate Giving Grants   242

Allstate is a company of energized people with great ideas. The Corporate Giving program is committed to supporting the communities where company employees live and work by contributing to programs where its experience, partnership and leadership will have the greatest impact. The company offers financial support to a variety of programs and organizations throughout the country that help create strong and vital communities.

Requirements: The Allstate Corporation makes grants to nonprofit, tax-exempt groups under Section 501(c)3 of the Internal Revenue Code.
Geographic Focus: All States
Contact: Executive Director; (847) 402-5000 or (847) 402-5502; fax (847) 326-7517; allfound@allstate.com
Internet: www.allstate.com/social-responsibility/social-impact/corporate-contributions.aspx
Sponsor: Allstate Corporation
2775 Sanders Road, Suite F4
Northbrook, IL 60062

Allstate Corporate Hometown Commitment Grants 243

Allstate takes a special interest in the greater Chicagoland community, the company's hometown for more than 75 years. The corporation is particularly invested in this community because it recognizes that a thriving hometown is critical to Allstate's success. The company recruits local talent, relies on local infrastructure, and depends on the city's vibrancy to ensure that its associates have a rich quality of life. By supporting organizations that build strong Chicagoland communities, the company contributes to the city's position as a center of global culture, education and business.
Requirements: The Allstate Corporation makes grants to Chicago area nonprofit, tax-exempt groups under Section 501(c)3 of the Internal Revenue Code.
Geographic Focus: Illinois, Indiana
Contact: Director; (847) 402-5000 or (847) 402-5502; allfound@allstate.com
Internet: www.allstate.com/social-responsibility/corporate/corporate-giving.aspx
Sponsor: Allstate Corporation
2775 Sanders Road, Suite F4
Northbrook, IL 60062

Allstate Foundation Safe and Vital Communities Grants 244

Established in 1952, The Allstate Foundation is an independent, charitable organization made possible by subsidiaries of The Allstate Corporation. The Foundation is dedicated to fostering safe and vital communities where people live, work and raise families. We strive to foster communities that are economically strong, crime-free, and give residents a sense of belonging and commitment. Our Safe and Vital Communities funding priorities are: teen safe driving - helping to save young lives and instill a lifetime of safe driving attitudes and behaviors; catastrophe response - rebuilding lives after a natural disaster strikes; and neighborhood revitalization - nurturing safe, strong, and healthy communities. Proposals are accepted throughout the year, though the regional grant proposal deadline is May 31. The average grant amount ranges from $5,000 to $20,000 for regional grants.
Requirements: The Allstate Foundation makes grants to nonprofit, tax-exempt organizations under Section 501(c)3 of the Internal Revenue Code, or be a municipal, state or federal government entity.
Restrictions: The Foundation does not support the following: individuals; fundraising events, sponsorships; capital and endowment campaigns; equipment purchase unless part of a community outreach program; athletic events; memorial grants; athletic teams, bands, and choirs; organizations that advocate religious beliefs or restrict participation on the basis of religion; groups or organizations that will re-grant the Foundation's gift to other organizations or individuals; scouting groups; private secondary schools; requests to support travel; grant requests for production of audio, film, or video; multiyear pledge requests; or non-domestic (international) causes.
Geographic Focus: All States
Date(s) Application is Due: May 31
Amount of Grant: 5,000 - 20,000 USD
Contact: Vicky Dinges, Vice President of Corporate Social Responsibility; (847) 402-5600 or (847) 402-7893; fax (847) 326-7517; allfound@allstate.com
Internet: www.allstatefoundation.org/grant-focus-areas
Sponsor: Allstate Foundation
2775 Sanders Road, Suite F4
Northbrook, IL 60062-6127

Allstate Foundation Tolerance, Inclusion, and Diversity Grants 245

Established in 1952, The Allstate Foundation is an independent, charitable organization made possible by subsidiaries of The Allstate Corporation. The Foundation believes that in order for a community to be strong, it has to recognize and value all of its members. That's why the Foundation is committed to programs that bring tolerance, inclusion, and value to people of all backgrounds regardless of ethnicity, sexual orientation, gender, age or physical challenges. Its Tolerance, Inclusion, and Diversity funding priorities are: teaching tolerance to youth and fostering a generation free of bias and intolerance; and alleviating discrimination by encouraging communities to be free of prejudice. Proposals are accepted throughout the year, though the regional grant proposal deadline is May 31. The average grant amount ranges from $5,000 to $20,000 for regional grants.
Requirements: The Allstate Foundation makes grants to nonprofit, tax-exempt organizations under Section 501(c)3 of the Internal Revenue Code, or be a municipal, state or federal government entity.
Restrictions: The Foundation does not support the following: individuals; fundraising events, sponsorships; capital and endowment campaigns; equipment purchase unless part of a community outreach program; athletic events; memorial grants; athletic teams, bands, and choirs; organizations that advocate religious beliefs or restrict participation on the basis of religion; groups or organizations that will re-grant the Foundation's gift to other organizations or individuals; scouting groups; private secondary schools; requests to support travel; grant requests for production of audio, film, or video; multiyear pledge requests; or non-domestic (international) causes.
Geographic Focus: All States
Amount of Grant: 5,000 - 20,000 USD
Contact: Vicky Dinges, Vice President of Corporate Social Responsibility; (847) 402-5600 or (847) 402-7893; fax (847) 326-7517; allfound@allstate.com

Internet: www.allstatefoundation.org/grant-focus-areas
Sponsor: Allstate Foundation
2775 Sanders Road, Suite F4
Northbrook, IL 60062-6127

Alpha Natural Resources Corporate Giving 246

The Alpha Natural Resources Corporate Giving program makes contributions to nonprofit organizations involved with helping children and families, improving education, strengthening arts and culture programs, and providing social services to those in need of health care and emergency fuel. Its primary fields of interest include: aging centers and services; the arts; children's services; primary education; secondary education; the environment; family services; food services; health care; higher education; housing and shelter; human services; substance abuse prevention; and youth development. Types of support given include: annual campaigns, product donations; employee volunteer services; scholarships; general operating support; and matching funds.
Requirements: Applicants must be 501(c)3 organizations located in, or serving the residents of, areas in which Alpha Natural Resources operates. These include selected regions of Kentucky, Illinois, Pennsylvania, Virginia, and West Virginia.
Geographic Focus: Illinois, Kentucky, Pennsylvania, Virginia, West Virginia
Amount of Grant: Up to 20,000 USD
Contact: Corporate Giving Administrator; (276) 619-4410
Internet: Alpha Natural Resources Corporate Giving
Sponsor: Alpha Natural Resources
1 Alpha Place, P.O. Box 16429
Bristol, VA 24209

Altria Group Positive Youth Development Grants 247

Philip Morris USA has had a focus on positive youth development since the creation of its Youth Smoking Prevention department in 1998. Today that program has evolved to Underage Tobacco Prevention, and Altria's tobacco operating companies invest in a range of programs to support its goals of helping reduce underage tobacco use. As part of these efforts, the Group's tobacco operating companies have become a leading funder of positive youth development in the U.S. These investments focus on organizations and programs that emphasize kids' strengths, promote positive behaviors, connect youth with caring adults and enhance community-based resources for kids. These programs are designed to help kids develop the confidence and skills they need to avoid risky behaviors, such as underage tobacco use. The Group's tobacco companies also support adolescent tobacco cessation programs. Its tobacco operating companies' funding supports organizations that: provide evidence-based programs for kids like mentoring, life skills education and substance abuse prevention curricula; help national youth-serving organizations reach more young people, improve program quality and better measure their impact; help community leaders align youth programs and policies; and conduct research on effective positive youth development programs.
Requirements: Unsolicited applications are generally not accepted. The company utilizes an invitation process for giving, which is the result of a letter of inquiry.
Geographic Focus: All States
Date(s) Application is Due: Feb 20
Amount of Grant: 10,000 - 75,000 USD
Contact: Grants Administrator; (804) 274-2200
Internet: www.altria.com/en/cms/Responsibility/investing-in-communities/programs/positive_youth_development/default.aspx
Sponsor: Altria Group
6601 West Broad Street
Richmond, VA 23230-1723

Alvah H. and Wyline P. Chapman Foundation Grants 248

The Alvah H. and Wyline P. Chapman Foundation was created in 1967 to honor and memorialize Alvah H. and Wyline P. Chapman and to perpetuate their charity and concern for others. The trustees and members of the foundation are the direct descendants (and spouses) of Alvah H. and Wyline P. Chapman, including their children, Alvah H. Chapman, Jr. and Wyline C. Sayler. Current fields of interest include: the arts, children and youth services, Christian agencies and churches, civil rights, racial relations, education, family services, homelessness, human services, literature, medical care, rehabilitation, performing arts, orchestras, science, and substance abuse prevention. Types of support offered by the Foundation are: building and renovation, capital campaigns, continuing support, emergency funds, endowments, and general operating support. The two annual deadlines for applications are April 15 and October 15.
Requirements: Applicants should submit the following: copy of IRS Determination Letter; copy of most recent annual report/audited financial statement/990; listing of board of directors, trustees, officers and other key people and their affiliations; detailed description of project and amount of funding requested; and a copy of current year's organizational budget and/or project budget.
Geographic Focus: Florida
Date(s) Application is Due: Apr 15; Oct 15
Contact: Alan Sayler, Chairperson; (727) 580-2728; vsayler@saylerfamily.com
Sponsor: Alvah H. and Wyline P. Chapman Foundation
P.O. Box 55398
St. Petersburg, FL 33732-5398

Ama OluKai Foundation Grants 249

Preserving, protecting and celebrating the cultural heritage and Aloha spirit in Hawai'i is the mission of the Ama OluKai Foundation. The Ama OluKai Foundation targets programs that are directly designed to educate and serve Hawaiian communities. The Foundation's goal is to partner with organizations that promote the Hawaiian culture and heritage from its ancestral past to present day. Primary funding interests include: Supporting endemic organizations whose efforts are directed towards the development of quality communities and individuals in Hawai'i; Preserving the rich traditions and lessons from the past, with emphasis on the arts, sciences, language, customs, morals, physical activities and educational outreach; Supporting organizations that perpetuate the Aloha spirit.

Requirements: The Foundation offers grants to 501(c)3 non-profit organizations located in Hawai'i. Grants will be awarded to organizations participating directly with the community.

Restrictions: Organizations that re-grant, outsource or redistribute to other non-profits or beneficiaries are not eligible.

Geographic Focus: Hawaii

Contact: Dan McInerny; fax (808) 748-0835; Info@amaolukaifoundation.org

Internet: www.amaolukaifoundation.org/grant-request/

Sponsor: Ama OluKai Foundation

3023 B Loomis Street

Honolulu, 96822

Amelia Sillman Rockwell and Carlos Perry Rockwell Charities Fund Grants 250

The Amelia Sillman Rockwell and Carlos Perry Rockwell Charities Fund was established in 1962 to support and promote quality educational, human-services, and health-care programming for underserved populations. Special consideration is given to charitable organizations that serve children or the elderly. Grant requests for general operating support are strongly encouraged. Program support will also be considered. Small, program-related capital expenses may be included in general operating or program requests. The majority of grants from the Rockwell Charities Fund are one year in duration; on occasion, multi-year support is awarded. Applicants must apply online at the grant website. Applicants are strongly encouraged to do the following before applying: review the downloadable state application procedures for additional helpful information and clarifications; review the downloadable online-application guidelines at the grant website; review the foundation's funding history (link is available from the grant website); review the online application questions in advance; and review the list of required attachments. These will generally include: a list of board members, financial statements (audited, reviewed, or compiled by independent auditor); an organization summary; a list of other funding sources; an IRS Determination letter; and other required documents. All attachments must be uploaded in the online application as PDF, Word, or Excel files. The application deadline for the Rockwell Charities Fund is 11:59 p.m. on February 1. Applicants will be notified of grant decisions before May 31.

Requirements: Applicants must have 501(c)3 tax-exempt status.

Restrictions: The trust does not support requests from individuals, organizations attempting to influence policy through direct lobbying, or any political campaigns.

Geographic Focus: Massachusetts

Date(s) Application is Due: Feb 1

Samples: Elizabeth Stone House, Jamaica Plains, Massachusetts, $10,000, general operating support; First Congregational Church, South Windsor, Connecticut, $1,000, for favored charity of Rockwell; Rogerson Communities, Boston, Massachusetts, $10,000, Adult Day Health Programs.

Contact: Miki C. Akimoto, Vice President; (866) 778-6859; miki.akimoto@baml.com

Internet: www.bankofamerica.com/philanthropic/fn_search.action

Sponsor: Amelia Sillman Rockwell and Carlos Perry Rockwell Charities Fund

225 Franklin Street, 4th Floor, MA1-225-04-02

Boston, MA 02110

Ameren Corporation Community Grants 251

The corporation awards grants in Ameren Illinois and Ameren Missouri service areas to programs in arts and culture, civic affairs, public safety, housing, higher education, services for youth and the elderly, and the environment. Types of support include annual campaigns, building construction and renovation, capital campaigns, challenge/matching grants, conferences and seminars, equipment acquisition, federated giving, general operating support, multi-year support, project development, seed money, and sponsorships. Applicants should provide the following information on the nonprofit's letterhead: organization's mission and how the project addresses its mission; program description and expected outcomes; fundraising goal and current funding status; the organization's budget and audited financial statements; tax status determination letter; roster of governing board and executive staff; and specific amount requested. Nonprofits in the Saint Louis, Missouri, metropolitan area should send applications to Ameren Corporate Contributions at the office listed. Nonprofits in the Springfield, Illinois, metropolitan area should send applications to Ameren Public Affairs, 607 E Adams Street, C1301, Springfield, Illinois 62739.

Requirements: Illinois and Missouri tax-exempt organizations in Ameren service areas are eligible.

Restrictions: Grants do not support individuals or political, religious, fraternal, veteran, social, or similar groups. Ameren cannot donate electric or natural gas service.

Geographic Focus: Illinois, Missouri

Amount of Grant: 5,000 - 75,000 USD

Contact: Otie Cowan; (314) 554-4740; fax (314) 554-2888; ocowan@ameren.com

Internet: www.ameren.com/CommunityMembers/CharitableTrust/Pages/Corporationcharitabletrust.aspx

Sponsor: Ameren Corporation

P.O. Box 66149, MC 100

Saint Louis, MO 63166-6149

American Electric Power Corporate Grants 252

American Electric Power's Community Relations goal is to support and play an active, positive role in communities where its people live and work. Providing financial support to non-profit organizations within its service territories is just one way AEP works toward this goal. Contributions are made principally in the areas of education, the environment, and human services, such as hunger, housing, health, and safety. Priority is based on the perceived overall benefit to communities in the company's service area. In the area of

education, preference is given to grades pre-K through 12 in the fields of science, technology and math. Multi-year commitments to capital campaigns generally do not exceed five years. AEP and its employees provide strong support to many annual United Way campaigns within our service territory; therefore, additional support to United Way agencies is limited.

Requirements: 501(c)3 nonprofit organizations, state or political subdivision, government-owned or operated college or university, or exempt operating foundation in Arkansas, Indiana, Kentucky, Louisiana, Michigan, Ohio, Oklahoma, Tennessee, Texas, Virginia and West Virginia are eligible. Grant-seekers should first approach their local AEP operating company.

Restrictions: Grants are not awarded to religious, fraternal, service, and veteran organizations, except for nonsectarian social service activities available to the broader community; organizations with a purpose that is solely athletic in nature; or to individuals.

Geographic Focus: Arkansas, Indiana, Kentucky, Louisiana, Michigan, Ohio, Oklahoma, Tennessee, Texas, Virginia, West Virginia

Contact: Markee Osborne, Grants Administrator; (614) 716-1000; mlosborne@aep.com

Internet: www.aep.com/community/givingback

Sponsor: American Electric Power

1 Riverside Plaza, 23rd Floor

columbus, OH 43215-2372

American Electric Power Foundation Grants 253

The American Electric Power Foundation is funded by American Electric Power and its utility operating units. The Foundation provides a permanent, ongoing resource for charitable initiatives involving higher dollar values and multi-year commitments in the communities served by AEP and initiatives outside of AEP's 11-state service area. The Foundation focuses on improving lives through education from early childhood through higher education in the areas of science, technology, engineering and math and by meeting basic needs for emergency shelter, affordable housing and the elimination of hunger. Other foundation support may be offered to protect the environment, support healthcare and safety, and enrich life through art, music and cultural heritage. The following focus areas will be eligible for consideration by the Foundation: improving lives through education from early childhood through higher education, with an emphasis in the areas of STEM (science, technology, engineering and mathematics); providing basic human services in the areas of hunger and housing to assure that people have the necessities to build successful lives; and enriching the overall vitality of the community and to improving the environment and people's lives. There are six deadlines for application submission each year: February 28; April 30; June 30; August 31; October 31; and December 31.

Requirements: 501(c)3 nonprofit organizations, state or political subdivision, government-owned or operated college or university, or exempt operating foundations in Arkansas, Indiana, Kentucky, Louisiana, Michigan, Ohio, Oklahoma, Tennessee, Texas, Virginia and West Virginia are eligible. Grant-seekers should first approach their local AEP operating company.

Restrictions: Organizations and activities not eligible include: individuals; religious organizations, unless they are proposing non-sectarian social service activities that are available to the broad community; fraternal and veterans organizations; programs that are solely athletic in nature and not connected to broader community or developmental goals; economic development programs; organizations that, either through constitution or written policy, discriminate against others on the basis of political affiliation, religious belief, age, disability, ethnicity, gender, gender identity, national origin, race or sexual orientation; or certain supporting organizations.

Geographic Focus: Arkansas, Indiana, Kentucky, Louisiana, Michigan, Ohio, Oklahoma, Tennessee, Texas, Virginia, West Virginia

Date(s) Application is Due: Feb 28; Apr 30; Jun 30; Aug 31; Oct 31; Dec 31

Amount of Grant: 15,000 - 100,000 USD

Contact: Markee Osborne, Foundation Administrator; (614) 716-1000; mlosborne@aep.com

Internet: www.aep.com/community/givingback

Sponsor: American Electric Power Foundation

1 Riverside Plaza, 23rd Floor

Columbus, OH 43215-2372

American Express Charitable Fund Scholarships 254

The American Express Charitable Fund Scholarship program awards four-year college scholarships of up to $4,000 to children of employees of American Express and its subsidiaries. The program is administered by Scholarship America.

Requirements: Scholarships are awarded on a national basis to family members of employees in areas of company operations, with emphasis on: the State of Arizona; Los Angeles and San Francisco, California; Washington, D.C.; southern Florida; Atlanta, Georgia; Chicago, Illinois; Boston, Massachusetts; Greensboro, North Carolina; New York, New York; Philadelphia, Pennsylvania; Dallas and Houston, Texas; and Salt Lake City, Utah.

Geographic Focus: Arizona, California, District of Columbia, Florida, Georgia, Illinois, Massachusetts, New York, North Carolina, Pennsylvania, Texas, Utah

Amount of Grant: Up to 4,000 USD

Contact: Mary Ellen Craig, Director; (212) 640-5660

Internet: about.americanexpress.com/csr/e-driven.aspx

Sponsor: American Express Charitable Fund

200 Vesey Street, 48th Floor

New York, NY 10285-1000

American Honda Foundation Grants 255

The American Honda Foundation (AHF) engages in grant making that reflects the basic tenets, beliefs and philosophies of Honda companies, which are characterized by the following qualities: imaginative, creative, youthful, forward-thinking, scientific, humanistic and innovative. AHF supports youth education with a specific focus on the STEM (science, technology, engineering and mathematics) subjects in addition to the environment. Funding priorities are identified as youth education, specifically in the areas of science, technology, engineering, mathematics, the environment, job training and literacy. Awards range from $20,000 to $75,000 over a one-year period.

Requirements: Nonprofit charitable organizations classified as a 501(c)3 public charity by the Internal Revenue Service, public school districts, and private/public elementary and secondary schools are eligible to apply. Pass through organization applications are acceptable. To be considered for funding organizations must have two years of audited financial statements examined by an independent CPA for the purpose of expressing an opinion if gross revenue is $500,000 or more. If gross revenue is less than $500,000, and the organization does not have audits, it may submit two years of financial statements accompanied by an independent CPA's review report instead. Organizations may only submit one request in a 12-month period. This includes colleges and universities with several departments/outreach programs.

Restrictions: The foundation does not consider proposals for service clubs, arts and culture, health and welfare issues, research papers, social issues, medical or educational research, trips, attempts to influence legislation, advocacy, annual funds, hospital operating funds, student exchanges, marathons, sponsorships, political activities, conferences, or fundraising events.
Geographic Focus: All States
Date(s) Application is Due: Feb 1; May 1; Aug 1
Amount of Grant: 20,000 - 75,000 USD
Contact: Grants Manager; (310) 781-4090; fax (310) 781-4270; ahf@ahm.honda.com
Internet: corporate.honda.com/america/philanthropy.aspx?id=ahf
Sponsor: American Honda Foundation
1919 Torrence Boulevard, 100-1W-5A
Torrance, CA 90501-2746

American Indian Youth Running Strong Grants 256
Established in Virginia in 1990, American Indian Youth Running Strong's program involvement reaches far and wide. With its longstanding partnerships in Indian Country, the program works to create sustainable change in Native communities. Its primary focus areas include: safe housing; basic needs; culture and language preservation; emergency assistance programs; organic gardens and food; schools and youth centers; women''s health; and seasonal programs. Though it implements its own programs, the group also supports independent groups who align with its mission, such as nonprofits, community centers, and grassroots projects. Its targeted population groups include: American Indians; children and youth; economically disadvantaged people; indigenous peoples; and low-income and poor. Awards average about $10,000.
Requirements: Applications must support Native Americans or indigenous people, and originate from a 501(c)3 organization.
Geographic Focus: All States
Amount of Grant: Up to 75,000 USD
Samples: Oglala Sioux Tribe Partnership for Housing, Pine Ridge, South Dakota, $40,000 - support of a housing development project; Catawba Cultural Preservation Project, Rock Hill, South Carolina, $10,000 - support of a cultural awareness effort; North Kohala Community Resource Center, Hawi, Hawaii, $10,000 - support of a community improvement project.
Contact: Cassandra R. Chee-Tom (Diné), Grants Administrator; (703) 317-9881; fax (703) 317-9690; info@IndianYouth.org
Internet: indianyouth.org/programs
Sponsor: American Indian Youth Running Strong
8301 Richmond Highway, Suite 200
Alexandria, VA 22309

American Psychiatric Foundation Call for Proposals 257
APF support allows organizations across the country to make a difference through unique educational, informational and outreach initiatives that promote the early recognition and treatment of mental illness and encourage leadership in the field of psychiatry. The Call for Proposals program is intended to fund public education programs, as well as information and outreach initiatives that promote the early recognition and treatment of mental illness. Up to $750,000 in grant funds are available over the course of three years. Average grants are in the $50,000 range. Grant making under this program has been temporarily suspended while a new Call for Proposals is being developed. Contact the office for further updates.
Requirements: Organizations that have been in existence for at least two years and currently maintain a 501(c)3 charitable status and American Psychiatric Association District Branches and subsidiaries. Organizations need not be mental health programs.
Geographic Focus: All States
Amount of Grant: Up to 100,000 USD
Contact: Paul T. Burke, Executive Director; (703) 907-8518 or (703) 907-8512; fax (703) 907-7851; pburke@psych.org or apf@psych.org
Internet: www.psychfoundation.org/GrantAndAwards/Grants/CallforProposals.aspx
Sponsor: American Psychiatric Foundation
1000 Wilson Boulevard, Suite 1825
Arlington, VA 22209

American Psychiatric Foundation Typical or Troubled School 258
Mental Health Education Grants
The Grant Program (also known as Típico o Problemático in Spanish) provides funding to implement the Typical or Troubled School Mental Health educational model in communities nationwide. Community organizations, high schools and school districts are eligible to receive funding. The educational program is designed for school personnel (teachers, coaches guidance counselors, etc.) to raise their awareness of mental disorders in teens. The program focuses on promoting the importance of early recognition and treatment, recognizing the early warning signs of mental health problems, and encouraging action and appropriate referral to a mental health professional. Grant support is as follows: for implementation in two to four high schools, $1,000; for implementation in five or more high schools, $2,000.

Geographic Focus: All States
Date(s) Application is Due: Mar 30
Amount of Grant: Up to 2,000 USD
Contact: Paul T. Burke, Executive Director; (703) 907-8518 or (703) 907-8512; fax (703) 907-7851; pburke@psych.org or apf@psych.org
Internet: www.psychfoundation.org/GrantAndAwards/Grants/TypicalorTroubled.aspx
Sponsor: American Psychiatric Foundation
1000 Wilson Boulevard, Suite 1825
Arlington, VA 22209

American Savings Foundation After School Grants 259
The American Savings Foundation supports organizations and programs that improve the quality of life for residents of the communities served by the Foundation, with a special emphasis on the needs of children, youth, and families. Through grants and scholarships, the foundation supports people and organizations in Connecticut. Areas of interest include human services—programs that provide direct services, including prevention and intervention programs, and economic and community development projects; arts and culture—museums, theaters, music, and art programs in our area; and education—direct service programs that enhance and enable academic achievement, tutoring programs, reading readiness, mentoring, school retention programs, and programs that support adult literacy. In the area of After School Grants, support covers a wide range of youth development programs that are conducted outside of the school hours, in the afternoon, evening, on weekends or holidays. The site may be a school building, or any community based facility. The Foundation will only consider funding for programs that incorporate best-practice elements of high quality after school programs, including: youth development activities that include project based learning; academic support and enrichment; homework help and tutoring; recreation activities; a focus on outreach to enroll under-served youth populations; and keeping youth involved and engaged on a regular basis. The size of grants will depend on several factors, including the scope and goals of the program, funding history with the Foundation, and support from other funding sources. The Foundation will consider funding programs for any of the following purposes: support new programs or new sites for existing programs; expand slots in existing programs to serve more youth; support existing programs to maintain high quality services; or support existing programs to improve quality by implementing high quality program elements. Some funds may be used for program supplies, including sports equipment, educational software, art materials, and the like. The annual deadline for grant applications is April 5.
Requirements: 501(c)3 tax-exempt organizations in the Foundation's 64-town service area in Connecticut are eligible to apply.
Restrictions: Grants will not be made for capital improvements, such as space renovations, or for purchasing computers for computer labs.
Geographic Focus: Connecticut
Date(s) Application is Due: Apr 5
Samples: Neighborhood Housing Services of Waterbury, Waterbury, Connecticut, $9,491 - support of an after school and academic enrichment program (2018); New Britain Youth Museums, New Britain, Connecticut, $23,092 - support of an after-school program that encourages middle school girls who love science to explore STEM careers (2018); Palace Theater, Waterbury, Connecticut, $15,000 - support of an after-school theatre arts program designed to enhance language arts and theater appreciation for high school youth (2018).
Contact: Maria Sanchez, Director of Grantmaking and Community Investment; (860) 827-2556; fax (860) 832-4582; msanchez@asfdn.org or info@asfdn.org
Internet: www.asfdn.org/after-school-grants-howto.php
Sponsor: American Savings Foundation
185 Main Street
New Britain, CT 06051

American Savings Foundation Capital Grants 260
The American Savings Foundation supports organizations and programs that improve the quality of life for residents of the communities served by the Foundation, with a special emphasis on the needs of children, youth, and families. Through grants and scholarships, the foundation supports people and organizations in Connecticut. Areas of interest include human services—programs that provide direct services, including prevention and intervention programs, and economic and community development projects; arts and culture—museums, theaters, music, and art programs in our area; and education—direct service programs that enhance and enable academic achievement, tutoring programs, reading readiness, mentoring, school retention programs, and programs that support adult literacy. The Foundation considers select proposals for capital grants. Past grants have included funding for one-time capital expenses as well as for large capital campaigns. The proposal process consists of two steps: organizations must first submit a Letter of Intent to the Foundation; selected projects will then be invited to submit a full proposal. If invited, an organization will be sent the capital proposal guidelines.
Requirements: 501(c)3 tax-exempt organizations in the Foundation's 64-town service area in Connecticut are eligible to apply.
Restrictions: Do not use the program proposal guidelines posted on the website.
Geographic Focus: Connecticut
Amount of Grant: Up to 200,000 USD
Samples: Friendship Service Center, New Britain, Connecticut, $106,861 - final payment towards the Howey House Apartments, a permanent supporting project which provides 10 to 12 one bedroom units for chronically homeless individuals (2018); Mattatuck Museum, Waterbury, Connecticut, $65,000 - first payment towards a campaign gift of $250,000 for a building expansion that will expand educational opportunities for children, families, and adults (2018); Hospital for Special Care, New Britain, Connecticut, $150,000 - support the construction of a new day treatment center for children diagnosed with autism spectrum disorders (2018).

Contact: Maria Sanchez, Director of Grantmaking and Community Investment; (860) 827-2556; fax (860) 832-4582; msanchez@asfdn.org or info@asfdn.org
Internet: www.asfdn.org/capital-grants.php
Sponsor: American Savings Foundation
185 Main Street
New Britain, CT 06051

American Savings Foundation Program Grants   **261**
The American Savings Foundation supports organizations and programs that improve the quality of life for residents of the communities served by the Foundation, with a special emphasis on the needs of children, youth, and families. Through grants and scholarships, the foundation supports people and organizations in Connecticut. Areas of interest include human services—programs that provide direct services, including prevention and intervention programs, and economic and community development projects; arts and culture—museums, theaters, music, and art programs in our area; and education—direct service programs that enhance and enable academic achievement, tutoring programs, reading readiness, mentoring, school retention programs, and programs that support adult literacy. In the area of Program Grants, the Foundation supports new programs, as well as existing programs where the support will enhance, strengthen, expand, or improve services. Primarily, the Foundation is interested in funding collaborative programs, and also in providing matching funds to leverage new dollars into the community. Proposals may be submitted at any time, though there are two annual deadlines: January 18 and July 12.
Requirements: 501(c)3 tax-exempt organizations in the Foundation's 64-town service area in Connecticut are eligible to apply.
Restrictions: Grants are not typically made for general operating support or for endowment funds. Religious institutions are not eligible, except for non-sectarian activities that benefit the community at-large. The Foundation does not award funding directly to individuals.
Geographic Focus: Connecticut
Date(s) Application is Due: Jan 18; Jun 12
Samples: Brass City Harvest, Waterbury, Connecticut, $27,000 - support for a community food program in Waterbury that increases access to fresh produce, and teaches adults and youth about nutrition and healthy eating (2018); Building Hope Together, New Britain, Connecticut, $20,000 - a citywide effort to coordinate housing, employment and homelessness prevention strategies and services for individuals and families (2018); Connecticut Radio Information System, Windsor, Connecticut, $15,000 - a program that produces and broadcasts readings to individuals with visual disabilities (2018).
Contact: Maria Sanchez, Director of Grantmaking and Community Investment; (860) 827-2556; fax (860) 832-4582; msanchez@asfdn.org or info@asfdn.org
Internet: www.asfdn.org/program-grants howto.php
Sponsor: American Savings Foundation
185 Main Street
New Britain, CT 06051

American Schlafhorst Foundation Grants   **262**
The American Schlafhorst Foundation, which was established in 1987, awards grants to eligible North Carolina nonprofit organizations in its areas of interest, including: arts and culture; botanical gardens; children and youth; community college education; the elderly; elementary and secondary education; employment; health care; higher education; hospital care; housing development; museums; science; and social services delivery. Types of support include: building construction and renovation; equipment acquisition; general operating support; research; scholarships; and seed money funding. There are no specific annual application deadlines, so interested parties should begin by contacting the Foundation directly with a proposed concept. Most recently, awards have ranged from $10,000 to $25,000.
Requirements: 501(c)3 tax-exempt organizations serving the greater Charlotte, NC, area are eligible.
Restrictions: Individuals are not eligible.
Geographic Focus: North Carolina
Contact: Dan W. Loftis, Wxecutive Director; (704) 554-0800; info@schlafhorst.com
Sponsor: American Schlafhorst Foundation
8801 South Boulevard, P.O. Box 240828
Charlotte, NC 28224-0828

American Woodmark Foundation Grants   **263**
The American Woodmark Foundation, formed in 1995 in Virginia, is the major vehicle by which American Woodmark Corporation makes its charitable donations. Currently, the Foundation supports organizations involved with education at all levels, domestic violence, housing, and public safety. Types of support include: annual campaigns; building construction and renovation; capital campaigns; continuing support; curriculum development; equipment purchase; and general operating support. The Foundation will forward a formal application upon request. Though there are no specified deadlines, the Board meets four times each year, in January, April, July, and October.
Requirements: Applicants must: have tax-exempt status under Section 501(c)3; be classified as public charities; and be located in a community where American Woodmark Corporation has a facility. This includes company operations in: Kingman, Arizona; Jackson and Toccoa, Georgia; Grant County, Indiana; Monticello and Hazard, Kentucky; Cumberland, Maryland; Tahlequah, Oklahoma; Humboldt, Tennessee; Winchester-Frederick County, Clarke County and Orange; Virginia; and Moorefield, West Virginia.
Geographic Focus: Arizona, Georgia, Indiana, Kentucky, Maryland, Oklahoma, Tennessee, Virginia, West Virginia
Contact: Brenda DuPont, Director; (540) 665-9129
Internet: americanwoodmark.com/about/giving-back
Sponsor: American Woodmark Foundation
3102 Shawnee Drive
Winchester, VA 22601-4208

Amerigroup Foundation Grants   **264**
Helping to create healthy communities is the cornerstone of the Amerigroup Foundation's mission. The objective is to serve as a national resource that fosters an environment where there is a continuum of education, access and care, all of which improve the health and well-being of the financially vulnerable and uninsured Americans. The Foundation primarily provides grants in the form of general support, but program development and sponsorships are also available to qualified non-profit organizations. Most recently, grants have ranged from $250 to $35,000.
Requirements: 501(c)3 non-profits are eligible to apply from the following states: Arizona, California, Colorado, Connecticut, Florida, Georgia, Indiana, Kansas, Kentucky, Louisiana, Maine, Maryland, Massachusetts, Missouri, Nevada, New Hampshire, New Jersey, New Mexico, New York, Ohio, South Carolina, Tennessee, Texas, Virginia, Washington, West Virginia, and Wisconsin.
Restrictions: Funding is unavailable for: projects or organizations that offer a direct benefit to the trustees of the Foundation or to employees or directors of Amerigroup; projects or organizations that might in any way pose a conflict with Amerigroup's mission, goals, programs, products or employees; projects or organizations that do not benefit a broad cross section of the community; individuals; political parties, candidates or lobbying activities; benefits, raffles, souvenir programs, trips, tours or similar events; for-profit entities, including start-up businesses.
Geographic Focus: Arizona, California, Colorado, Connecticut, Florida, Georgia, Indiana, Kansas, Kentucky, Louisiana, Maine, Maryland, Massachusetts, Missouri, Nevada, New Hampshire, New Jersey, New Mexico, New York, Ohio, South Carolina, Tennessee, Texas, Virginia, Washington, West Virginia, Wisconsin
Amount of Grant: 250 - 35,000 USD
Samples: College of William and Mary, Williamsburg, Virginia, $35,000 - general operations; Nature Discovery Center, Bellaire, Texas, $10,000 - general operations; Snohomish County Human Services, Everett, Washington, $30,000 - general operations.
Contact: Grants Manager; (757) 490-6900 or (757) 962-6468; fax (757) 222-2360
Internet: www.realsolutions.com/company/pages/Foundation.aspx
Sponsor: Amerigroup Foundation
4425 Corporation Lane
Virginia Beach, VA 23462-3103

AMERIND Community Service Project Grants   **265**
AMERIND Risk Management Corporation's Community Service program seeks to advance the community aspect of AMERIND's vision to Protect Tribal Families First. Funding limitations for small community service projects include: housing fairs will receive a standard $500 per event; youth activities, including graffiti paint-outs, community clean-up, meth awareness will range from $100 (less than 100 participants) to $250 (more than 100 participants); and health fairs will receive a standard $250. The AMERIND Outreach Committee meets once every month to discuss funding requests received by organizations.
Requirements: Requests for AMERIND contributions must meet of the following criteria; the project must address a demonstrated need in a Native American community in which AMERIND has a presence; the project must provide an opportunity for Native Americans to make learning about fire safety and home safety fun; or the project must support a project or program involving fire safety and/or home safety, business related or other related area to expand, improve and protect the lifestyles of Native Americans and their families.
Restrictions: Powwows and rodeos are considered advertising and are not funded. AMERIND does not contribute to: individual requests; trip expenses; organizations that charge a fee or dues; lobbying organizations; or political organizations.
Geographic Focus: All States
Contact: Mike Jennings, Chief Financial Officer; (505) 404-5000 or (800) 352-3496; fax (505) 404-5001; outreach@amerind-corp.org
Internet: www.amerind-corp.org/index.php/about-amerind/community-outreach/community-service-projects
Sponsor: AMERIND Risk Management Corporation
502 Cedar Drive
Santa Ana Pueblo, NM 87004

Amica Companies Foundation Grants   **266**
The Amica Companies Foundation has a mission to harness the power of enduring relationships to help individuals, families and communities become economically independent and strong. Understanding this, the Foundation provides support to programs that align with its charitable giving mission statement. These programs may fall under the following categories: basic needs and community development; education; health; arts and culture; and community and public affairs. Interested parties should submit a proposal via the Foundation's online application system. The review process can take up to eight weeks. When a decision has been made, applicants will receive an email notification.
Requirements: The Foundation supports qualified, federal tax-exempt 501(c)3 organizations, as defined by the Internal Revenue Service Code. Grants are generally restricted to community-based organizations serving Rhode Island residents.
Restrictions: The Foundation generally does not provide support to: capital campaigns; building restorations; or general operating expenses.
Geographic Focus: Rhode Island
Contact: Meredith Gregory, Charitable Giving Coordinator; (800) 622-6422, ext. 2100; fax (401) 334-4241; AmicaCoFoundations@amica.com
Internet: www.amica.com/en/about-us/in-your-community/charitable-grants.html
Sponsor: Amica Companies Foundation
100 Amica Way
Lincoln, RI 02865-1167

Amica Insurance Company Community Grants 267

The Amica Insurance Company Citizenship Grant program financially supplements employee volunteer efforts. This program provides annual grants of up to $1,000 maximum to community groups in which Amica employees are involved. The corporation's Matching Gift Fund program offers employee-matching grants of up to $1,000 maximum to elementary and secondary schools, two-year colleges and four-year colleges, and universities and college level graduate schools. The company makes corporate donations to health organizations, hospitals, libraries, schools, museums, and other deserving institutions. Recent recipients include the American Heart Association, the Miami Project to Cure Paralysis, and The Nature Conservancy.

Geographic Focus: Arizona, California, Colorado, Connecticut, Georgia, Illinois, Maine, Maryland, Massachusetts, Michigan, Minnesota, Nevada, New Hampshire, New Jersey, New York, North Carolina, Ohio, Oregon, Pennsylvania, Rhode Island, South Carolina, Tennessee, Texas, Virginia, Washington, Wisconsin

Amount of Grant: Up to 1,000 USD

Contact: Meredith Gregory, Charitable Giving Coordinator; (800) 622-6422, ext. 2100; fax (401) 334-4241

Internet: www.amica.com/en/about-us/in-your-community/corporate-citizenship.html

Sponsor: Amica Insurance Company

100 Amica Way

Lincoln, RI 02865-1167

Amica Insurance Company Sponsorships 268

Amica Insurance Company Sponsorships are payments to a for-profit or not-for-profit organization for which Amica will receive promotional, advertising and/or marketing value. A sponsorship is an event that increases Amica's name awareness and brand identity in the local market. Amica considers sponsorships from a wide range of organizations and encourages creativity and innovation to develop partnerships that are of mutual benefit. Sponsorship proposals will also be evaluated for: positive exposure of the Amica brand; tangible benefits associated with the partnership; attendance at the event; ability to reach targeted audiences and build relationships through engagement; and potential for long-term, sustainable partnerships or relationships. Amica generally supports: art and entertainment festivals; healthy living events (healthy food events, marathons, triathlons, etc.); auto shows; home shows; sports teams and events; and events that are based in states where Amica has local offices.

Requirements: Events that occur within the Amica Company areas of operation are eligible to request funding.

Restrictions: Amica generally does not support; national events; advertising not tied to a sponsorship; entry fees for a run or walk; sponsorships for an individual or team competing in an event; charitable fundraisers; religious or political organizations; underwriting of conferences and seminars; and governmental and quasi-governmental agencies or organizations.

Geographic Focus: Arizona, California, Colorado, Connecticut, Georgia, Illinois, Maine, Maryland, Massachusetts, Michigan, Minnesota, Nevada, New Hampshire, New Jersey, New York, North Carolina, Ohio, Oregon, Pennsylvania, Rhode Island, South Carolina, Tennessee, Texas, Virginia, Washington, Wisconsin

Contact: Meredith Gregory, Charitable Giving Coordinator; (800) 622-6422, ext. 2100; fax (401) 334-4241; SponsorshipRequest@amica.com

Internet: www.amica.com/en/about-us/in-your-community/sponsorships.html

Sponsor: Amica Insurance Company

100 Amica Way

Lincoln, RI 02865-1167

Amway Corporation Contributions 269

The Amway Corporation gives primarily in areas of company operations, including: Buena Park and Lakeview, California; Norcross, Georgia; Honolulu, Hawaii; Arlington, Texas; and Kent, Washington, with emphasis on the greater Grand Rapids, Michigan, area, and in Africa, Asia, Australia, Europe, and Latin America. Its primary area of interests include: at-risk children and families; the arts; children services; developmentally disables; disaster preparedness; health care; and nutrition. Major types of support offered are general operations and in-kind gifts. A formal application is required, and the annual deadlines are January 1 and November 1. Final notification is within sixty days of the deadline.

Restrictions: No support for fraternal organizations or school athletic teams, bands, or choirs, political, legislative, or lobbying organizations. No grants to individuals, or for travel, scholarships, religious projects, sports or fundraising events, movie, film, or television documentaries, general awareness campaigns, marketing sponsorships, cause-related marketing, or advertising projects; no in-kind gifts for conferences or conventions, personal use, distribution at an expo, fair, or event, family reunions, or sports fundraising events.

Geographic Focus: All States

Date(s) Application is Due: Jan 1; Nov 1

Contact: Corporate Giving Manager; (616) 787-7000; contributions@amway.com

Internet: www.amway.com/about-amway/campaigns-and-sponsorships

Sponsor: Amway Corporation

5101 Spaulding Plaza, SE

Ada, MI 49355-0001

Anchorage Schools Foundation Grants 270

The Anchorage Schools Foundation is a field of interest fund of The Alaska Community Foundation. It was created by a dedicated group of volunteers who are passionate about supporting projects that enhance the success of students in the Anchorage School District. The fund has attracted donors and partners including Rasmuson Foundation, Alyeska Pipeline Service Co., Anchorage Community Land Trust, CIRI, Credit Union 1, ExxonMobil, Ignite Anchorage, Koahnic Broadcast Corporation, Municipal Light & Power, TOTE, Wells Fargo, individual teachers, and school staff.

Requirements: Eligible applicants include ASD school professionals, such as principals, teachers, nurses, counselors, administrators, and other certified staff.

Geographic Focus: Alaska

Date(s) Application is Due: Nov 5

Amount of Grant: 100 - 500 USD

Contact: Stefanie O'Brien, Program Officer of Grants and Scholarships; (907) 274-6710 or (907) 334-6700; fax (907) 334-5780; sobrien@alaskacf.org

Internet: alaskacf.org/blog/grants/asf-grant-cycle/

Sponsor: Anchorage Schools Foundation

201 C Street, Suite 110

Anchorage, AK 99503

Anderson Foundation Grants 271

Established in Ohio in 1949, the Anderson Family Foundation Trust gives grants in the greater Toledo, Ohio, region, including Maumee and Columbus. Giving also to organizations located within the areas of the Anderson plants in the following states: Champaign, Illinois; Delphi, Lafayette, and Dunkirk, Indiana; and Albion, Potterville, Webberville, and White Pigeon, Michigan. The Foundation's primary fields of interest include: agriculture; arts; children and youth services; education; the environment; government and public administration; higher education; human services; religion; secondary school education; and federated giving programs. Types of support include: annual campaigns; building and renovation programs; capital campaigns; conferences and seminars; emergency funds; general operating support; matching/challenge grants; program development; publications; research; scholarship funds; and seed money. Specific application forms are not required, and board decisions are made on the 3rd Monday of the month in March, June, September, and December. Grant amounts range up to $100,000 on occasion, though most average between $5,000 and $10,000.

Requirements: Nonprofit 501(c)3 agencies in Ohio, Illinois, Indiana, and Michigan serving areas of company operation are eligible to apply.

Restrictions: No support is available for private foundations, public high schools, or elementary schools. No grants are given to individuals, or for endowment funds, travel, or building or operating funds for churches or elementary schools.

Geographic Focus: Illinois, Indiana, Michigan, Ohio

Date(s) Application is Due: Feb 28; May 30; Aug 30; Nov 30

Amount of Grant: Up to 100,000 USD

Samples: Chance for Change Foundation, Toledo, Ohio, $5,000 - human services; DeKalb County Fair Association, DeKalb, Indiana, $5,000 - agriculture ($5,000); Camp Tecumseh, Brookston, Indiana, $5,000 - human services.

Contact: Fredi Heywood; (419) 243-1706 or (419) 893-5050; fax (419) 242-5549; fredi@toledocf.org

Sponsor: Anderson Foundation

480 W. Dussel Drive, P.O. Box 119

Maumee, OH 43537-0119

Andrew Family Foundation Grants 272

The Andrew Family Foundation is a private, philanthropic organization that will consider proposals from public, non-profit organizations under IRS Section 501(c)3 to support projects and organizations that foster individual growth and enhance communities through education, humanitarian efforts, and the arts. Funding primarily in the Illinois with a special interest in the Cook County region. The types of support available include: annual campaigns; building/renovation; capital campaigns; general/operating support; scholarship funds. There is no deadline date when applying for funding. Qualified grant proposals will be reviewed by the Andrew Family Foundation Grant Making Committee prior to quarterly board meetings. The committee will make a recommendation to the Board of Directors of the Foundation.

Requirements: 501(c)3 tax-exempt organizations are eligible to apply for funding. To begin the application process, take the Eligibility Quiz to confirm that you qualify for a grant from the foundation. Upon successful completion of the Eligibility Quiz, you will be invited to complete an online Letter of Inquiry. The Board will review your Letter of Inquiry and may invite you to submit a Full Application for review. Generally, the Board meets in February, May, August and November of each year.

Restrictions: The foundation does not provide funds: to individuals; taxable corporations; religious programs; political organizations; and other private foundations.

Geographic Focus: Illinois

Contact: Connor Humphrey, Grants Administrator; (708) 460-1288 or (602) 828-8471; fax (602) 385-3267; aff@inlignwealth.com or Connor.Humphrey@GenSpring.com

Internet: online.foundationsource.com/andrew/board2.htm

Sponsor: Andrew Family Foundation

14628 John Humphrey Drive

Orland Park, IL 60462

Anheuser-Busch Foundation Grants 273

Support is provided almost exclusively to causes that are located in communities in which the company has manufacturing facilities. Contributions are made for education, health, social services, minorities and youth, cultural enrichment, and environmental protection programs. Types of support include capital grants, employee matching gifts, equipment and material acquisition, general operating support, and donated products. Full proposals are accepted throughout the year.

Requirements: 501(c)3 tax-exempt organizations in corporation operation areas can apply, which includes California, Colorado, Florida, Georgia, Hawaii, Kentucky, Massachusetts, Missouri, New Hampshire, New Jersey, New York, Ohio, Oklahoma, Texas, and Virginia.

Restrictions: Grants are not made to individuals; political, social, fraternal, religious, or athletic organizations; or hospitals for operating funds.

Geographic Focus: California, Colorado, Florida, Georgia, Hawaii, Kentucky, Massachusetts, Missouri, New Hampshire, New Jersey, New York, Ohio, Oklahoma, Texas, Virginia
Amount of Grant: 25,000 - 100,000 USD
Contact: Assistant Manager; (314) 577-2453; fax (314) 557-3251
Internet: anheuser-busch.com/index.php/our-responsibility/community-our-neighborhoods/
Sponsor: Anheuser-Busch Foundation
One Busch Place
Saint Louis, MO 63118-1852

Anna Fitch Ardenghi Trust Grants 274

The Anna Fitch Ardenghi Trust was established in 1981 to support and promote quality educational, cultural, human services, and health care programming for underserved populations living in New Haven, Connecticut. Special preference is given to charitable organizations that focus on the arts or youth-related programming. Award amounts typically range from $1,000 to $6,000, and are typically one year in duration.
Requirements: 501(c)3 organizations serving the residents of New Haven, Connecticut, are eligible to apply. Applicants must have a principal office located in the city of New Haven, Connecticut. Applications will be submitted online through the Bank of America website. Applicants will be notified of grant decisions by letter within 2 to 3 months after the proposal deadline. A grant report is required within 1 year of the grant application date, regardless of whether all of the funds have been spent.
Restrictions: Grant requests for capital projects will not be considered. Applicants will not be awarded a grant for more than 3 consecutive years.
Geographic Focus: Connecticut
Date(s) Application is Due: Jun 15
Amount of Grant: 1,000 - 6,000 USD
Samples: Connecticut Players Foundation Inc., New Haven, Connecticut, $6,000 - Awarded for Long Wharf Theatre Arts Education Programs; Architecture Resource Center Inc., New Haven, Connecticut, $5,000 - Awarded for The Design Connection Partnership-year 6; FISH of Greater New Haven Inc., New Haven, Connecticut, $5,000 - Awarded for Grocery Delivery Program.
Contact: Amy R. Lynch, Philanthropic Client Manager; (860) 244-4870; ct.grantmaking@bankofamerica.com or amy.r.lynch@bofa.com
Internet: www.bankofamerica.com/philanthropic/foundation/?fnId=27
Sponsor: Anna Fitch Ardenghi Trust
P.O. Box 1802
Providence, RI 02901-1802

Anne Arundel Women Giving Together Regular Grants 275

Anne Arundel Women Giving Together (AAWGT) funds programs that improve the quality of life for women and families in Anne Arundel County. AAWGT is a Fund of the Community Foundation of Anne Arundel County. Grants from a minimum of $5,000 up to a maximum of $20,000 are awarded for outstanding programs. Proposals are accepted from local nonprofits in three broad areas directed toward economically-disadvantaged women, families, and children: education, health and welfare, and prevention of/treatment for violence and abuse. Applications are due each year by January 31st.
Requirements: Any 501(c)3 organization serving the residents of Anne Arundel County, Maryland, is eligible to apply.
Restrictions: No support for political activities or political action committees, programs that primarily provide transportation, programs that fund housing development or rental assistance, programs requiring adherence to or acceptance of a particular religious belief or requiring participation in a religious service or activity, or organizations that discriminate by race, creed, gender, sexual orientation, age, religion, disability or national origin. No grants to individuals, or for organizational endowments, capital improvements, deficit reduction, purchase of tickets, event sponsorship, or annual drives.
Geographic Focus: Maryland
Date(s) Application is Due: Jan 31
Amount of Grant: 5,000 - 20,000 USD
Samples: Annapolis Immigration Justice Network, Annapolis, Maryland, $20,000 - for its Legal Fund/Family Preservation Project (2020); The Light House, Inc., Annapolis, Maryland, $20,000 - for a Family Assistance Program (2020); Services from the Heart, Annapolis, Maryland, $10,000 - for a Backpack Buddies Program and food backpacks (2020).
Contact: Susan Cook, Grants Committee Chair; giving@givingtogether.org
Internet: givingtogether.wildapricot.org/grants-overview
Sponsor: Anne Arundel Women Giving Together
914 Bay Ridge Road, Suite 220
Annapolis, MD 21403-3919

Anne J. Caudal Foundation Grants 276

The Anne J. Caudal Foundation was established in 2007 to benefit disabled veterans of any time or of any branch of the United States armed forces and to perpetuate the recognition or memory of their accomplishments or sacrifice in time of war or otherwise. Special consideration is given to organizations that serve disabled veterans in New Jersey. Grant requests for general operating support are strongly encouraged. Program support will also be considered. Small, program-related capital expenses may be included in general operating or program requests. The majority of grants from the Caudal Foundation are one year in duration. On occasion, multi-year support is awarded. Application materials are available for download from the grant website. The application deadline for the Anne J. Caudal Foundation is July 1. Applicants are encouraged to review the state application guidelines for additional helpful information and clarification before applying. Applicants are also encouraged to view the foundation's funding history (link is available at the grant website). Applicants will be notified of grant decisions before August 15.
Requirements: Applicants must have 501(c)3 tax-exempt status.

Restrictions: The foundation does not support requests from individuals, organizations attempting to influence policy through direct lobbying, or any political campaigns.
Geographic Focus: All States
Date(s) Application is Due: Jul 1
Samples: United States Wounded Soldiers Foundation, Dallas, Texas, $12,500; Our Military Kids, McLean, Virginia, $12,500; Jewish Family Service of New Jersey, Wayne, New Jersey, $12,500.
Contact: Maryann Clemente, Vice President; (646) 855-0786; maryann.clemente@baml.com
Internet: www.bankofamerica.com/philanthropic/fn_search.action
Sponsor: Anne J. Caudal Foundation
One Bryant Park, NY1-100-28-05
New York, NY 10036

Annie Gardner Foundation Grants 277

Ed Gardner was one of the wealthiest men in all of Kentucky at the time of his death in 1958. Despite having only an eighth grade education, Gardner literally worked his way up from a lowly position as a day-wage painter, to the owner of a paint store, to a successful bank president. Gardner is probably best known for his stately home, Edana Locus; "Edana" is a joining of Ed's name with that of Ana, his wife, and "Locus" is the Latin word for "place." Upon Gardner's death, he left $12 million in a memorial foundation, in honor of his wife. The Annie Gardner Foundation is intended to help needy families and aid in education throughout Graves County, Kentucky. With that in mind, awards are given to assist in rent, medical care, clothing, and other day-to-day personal necessities. Grants are given directly to the individual in need, and between $800,000 and $1,000,000 is handed out annually. An application form is required, and can be secured by contacting the Foundation office directly. The annual deadline for submission is July 1.
Requirements: Individuals in need of assistance, who are residents of Grave County, Kentucky, may apply.
Geographic Focus: Kentucky
Date(s) Application is Due: Jul 1
Amount of Grant: 100 - 10,000 USD
Samples: Mayfield Graves Company, Needline, Mayfield, Kentucky, $5,000, - help with food contributions within the community, (2019).
Contact: Nancy H. Sparks, Director; (270) 247-5803
Sponsor: Annie Gardner Foundation
620 South 6th Street
Mayfield, KY 42066-2316

Ann L. and Carol Green Rhodes Charitable Trust Grants 278

Ann Rhodes and her mother Carol Green Rhodes were both very supportive of the local arts throughout their lives. Ann was also an animal-lover who fed the wild animals that came into her backyard each night. Their Charitable Trust was established in 2010 to honor their love of theater and the local community. The Trust supports charitable organizations focused on the arts, museums open to the public, theaters and other performing arts organizations, organizations whose primary purpose is to support the arts, organizations providing human services; and occasional support for animal-related charitable organizations. Ann Rhodes requested that preference be given to organizations that she supported in her lifetime. Grants are typically between $500 and $300,000.
Requirements: Applicants must have 501(c)3 tax-exempt status and serve residents of Tarrant County, Texas. Eligibility to re-apply for a grant award from the Ann L. and Carol Green Rhodes Charitable Trust requires organizations to skip 1 grant cycle (1 year) before submitting a subsequent application. Applications will be submitted online through the Bank of America website. A grant report is required within 1 year of the grant application date, regardless of whether all of the funds have been spent.
Restrictions: The Trust does not support requests from individuals, organizations attempting to influence policy through direct lobbying, or any political campaigns.
Geographic Focus: Texas
Date(s) Application is Due: Mar 1
Amount of Grant: 500 - 300,000 USD
Samples: Amphibian Productions, Fort Worth, Texas, $100,000 - Awarded for General Operations of Amphibian Stage Productions (2018); Casa Mañana, Fort Worth, Texas, $100,000 - Awarded for General support of Casa Manana programming and operations which includes Broadway and Children's series and education and outreach programs (2018); Circle Theatre Inc., Fort Worth, Texas, $100,000 - Awarded for general operations of the organization (2018).
Contact: Kelly Garlock, Philanthropic Client Manager; (800) 357-7094; tx.philanthropic@bankofamerica.com or tx.philanthropic@ustrust.com
Internet: www.bankofamerica.com/philanthropic/foundation/?fnId=19
Sponsor: Ann L. and Carol Green Rhodes Charitable Trust
P.O. Box 831041
Dallas, TX 75283-1041

Ann Ludington Sullivan Foundation Grants 279

The Ann Ludington Sullivan Foundation was established by Annie Sullivan, an attorney in Chapel Hill, North Carolina, in Michigan in 1996. The Foundation's expressed purpose is to support residents of North Carolina and Michigan, though support is also offered nationwide. The Foundation's primary fields of interest include: addiction services; arts and culture; Christianity; communication media; diseases and conditions; elementary and secondary education; environmental justice; family services; food banks; higher education; human services; individual liberties; international development; legal services; and natural resources. That support typically comes in the form of general operating support, and the Foundation's target populations include: academics; economically disadvantaged; low-income; and the poor. The largest portion of recent grants have been directed toward

education. The initial approach should be a letter of application, and there are no specified deadlines. Recent awards have ranged up to a maximum of $5,000.
Requirements: 505(c)3 organizations supported the target populations in Michigan and North Carolina are eligible to apply, as well as those in other states.
Geographic Focus: All States, Michigan, North Carolina
Amount of Grant: Up to 5,000 USD
Samples: Blue Ribbon Mentor, Chapel Hill, North Carolina, $500 - general operating support; Roanoke College, Salem, Virginia, $4,000 - general operating support; Albion College, Albion, Michigan, $1,000 - general operating support.
Contact: Annie L. Sullivan, President; (919) 942-0727
Sponsor: Ann Ludington Sullivan Foundation
203 Lake Manor Road
Chapel Hill, NC 27516-4322

Anthony Munoz Foundation Straight A Student Campaign Grants 280
Established in Cincinnati, Ohio, in 2002, the Anthony Munoz Foundation was founded by former football player who played with the Cincinnati Bengals from 1980 to 1992. In 1998, he was inducted into the Pro Football Hall of Fame. The foundation supports children of all races and socio-economic backgrounds through the planning and executing of impact programs and the funding of youth-related charities. Through its Straight "A" Student program, awards are available that recognize students in the greater Cincinnati metropolitan tri-state area who pursue academic excellence and athletic achievement, and play an active role in the community while possessing a strong ambition, a winning attitude, and the ability to overcome adversity. One male and one female applicant will receive a $2,000 grant towards their continuing education; 16 finalists will receive a $500 grant.
Requirements: Students must attend a high school in the tri-state Cincinnati, Ohio, are of Ohio, Indiana, and Kentucky.
Geographic Focus: Indiana, Kentucky, Ohio
Amount of Grant: 500 - 2,000 USD
Contact: Andy Danner; (513) 772-4900; fax (513) 772-4911; info@munozfoundation.org
Internet: www.munozfoundation.org/default.asp?contentID=18
Sponsor: Anthony Munoz Foundation
8919 Rossash Road
Cincinnati, OH 45236-1209

Antone and Edene Vidinha Charitable Trust Grants 281
Before turning 30, Antone "Kona" Vidinha, Jr. was the sheriff for the Koloa district on the Island of Kauai, a post his father had held. Later, he became captain of police when the county centralized its law enforcement. Vidinha served as Kauai's chief executive from 1967 to 1972. He took office with the title of chairman and chief executive of Kauai County in 1967, but the title was changed to mayor during his tenure in office. Along the way, land investments made him wealthy, and Vidinha shared this wealth through charities. One of his favorites, reportedly, was a program of scholarships for needy University of Hawaii students from Kauai. He died in 1976 at the age of 73. Meanwhile, Edene Vidinha was born in 1905 and was raised in Koloa, Kauai, where she first attended Koloa School. She transferred to Kawaiahao Seminary in Honolulu, graduated from Kauai High School, and received her teaching certificate from Normal School in 1926. Returning to Kauai to teach, Edene's first assignment was at Huleia School; and later at Koloa School, where she retired thirty-seven years later. Edene died in 1988. The Antone and Edene Vidinha Charitable Trust was established to benefit the people of Kauai. Following Edene's death, a Distribution Committee, composed of officers of the Trustee and community members, was organized to carry out the charitable intent of the Trust. Today, grants are awarded to qualified tax exempt, 501(c)3 charitable organizations on Kauai or serving the residents of Kauai. By trust provisions, contributions are awarded in four major fields: churches on the Island of Kauai (no on-going maintenance projects); hospitals that benefit Kauai residents; health organizations which benefit the people of Kauai; and educational scholarships to colleges or universities in the State of Hawaii for Kauai students. Types of support include: building and renovation; equipment; general operating support; program development; and scholarship funds. Grants range from $2,000 to $80,000, and applications are due on December 1 each year.
Requirements: 501(c)3 nonprofit organizations in Hawaii are eligible to apply. The Trust places a special emphasis on the island of Kauai.
Restrictions: The Trust does not award grants or scholarships to individuals, nor for endowments, multiple-year pledges, or on-going maintenance projects at churches.
Geographic Focus: Hawaii
Date(s) Application is Due: Dec 1
Amount of Grant: 2,000 - 80,000 USD
Contact: Paula Boyce, c/o Bank of Hawaii; (808) 694-4945; paula.boyce@boh.com Elaine Moniz, Trust Specialist; (808) 694-4944; elaine.moniz@boh.com
Internet: www.boh.com/philanthropy/grants/antone-edene-vidinha-charitable-trust
Sponsor: Antone and Edene Vidinha Charitable Trust
Bank of Hawai'i, Foundation Administration Department 758
Honolulu, HI 96813

AOCS Thomas H. Smouse Memorial Fellowship 282
The Thomas H. Smouse Memorial Fellowship is awarded to a graduate student doing research in areas of interest to AOCS. The award includes a $10,000 stipend, plus $5,000 for travel to professional meetings and research expenditures related to the student's graduate program. Self nominations are welcomed.
Requirements: Individuals must be scholastically outstanding with interests and involvement outside the academic discipline.
Geographic Focus: All States, All Countries
Date(s) Application is Due: Oct 15
Amount of Grant: 15,000 USD

Contact: Barb Semeraro; (217) 693-4804; fax (217) 693-4849; barbs@aocs.org
Silvana Martini; (435) 797-8136; fax (435) 797-2379; silvana.martini@usa.edu
Internet: www.aocs.org/Membership/content.cfm?ItemNumber=938
Sponsor: American Oil Chemists' Society
2710 South Boulder
Urbana, IL 61802-6996

APAP All-In Grants 283
The Association of Performing Arts Presenters (APAP) and MetLife Foundation continue a long-standing partnership to offer a new program All-In: Re-imagining Community Participation. The program goal is to support innovative strategies that target the full spectrum of community members from all generations and populations in community-based performing arts programs. One-year grants of up to $25,000 are awarded to current APAP-member presenting organizations in support of promising new approaches to community engagement through the performing arts. Interested applicants should contact APAP for further details. APAP is a non-profit 501(c)3 national-service and advocacy organization dedicated to bringing artists and audiences together. APAP's membership roll of nearly 2,000 represents a growing number of self-presenting artists, leading performing-arts centers, municipal and university performance facilities, nonprofit performing-arts centers, and culturally-specific organizations as well as artist agencies, managers, touring companies, and national consulting practices that serve the field. MetLife Foundation was established in 1976 to continue MetLife's longstanding tradition of corporate contributions and community involvement. The Foundation's commitment to building a secure future for individuals and communities worldwide is reflected in its dedication to empowering older adults, preparing young people and building livable communities.
Requirements: APAP-member presenting organizations are eligible to apply.
Geographic Focus: All States
Amount of Grant: Up to 25,000 USD
Samples: Arts Midwest, Minneapolis, Minnesota, $25,000 - to expand the dialogue between American communities and contemporary Muslim societies through the arts; International Festival of Arts and Ideas, New Haven, Connecticut, $25,000 - the portable Pop-Up Arts Village will travel to select neighborhoods to encourage new participation in the festival; Lied Center of Kansas, Lawrence, Kansas, $25,000 - Issue Theater, for middle school audiences, uses the performing arts as a tool to facilitate discussions about issues faced by today's youth.
Contact: Laura Benson, Professional Development Associate; (888) 820-2787 or (202) 207-3852; fax (202) 833-1543; lbenson@artspresenters.org or info@artspresenters.org
Internet: www.apap365.org/KNOWLEDGE/GrantPrograms/Pages/All-In.aspx
Sponsor: Association of Performing Arts Presenters
1211 Connecticut Avenue, Northwest, Suite 200
Washington, D.C. 20036

Appalachian Community Fund LGBTQ Fund Grants 284
These grants are dedicated to expanding resources for LGBTQ organizing efforts in Appalachian communities. The LGBTQ fund is primarily focused on growing LGBTQ communties' institutional resources, building capacity in LGBTQ efforts, and assisting organizational development. Special priority will be given to new and emerging efforts, particularly among LGBTQ youth.
Requirements: Organizations wishing to apply must: work in the Appalachian counties of Tennessee, Kentucky, Virginia, and/or West Virginia. For organizations based outside the region, the proposal must include a specific work plan for the Appalachian portion of the work; have their 501(c)3 tax exempt status or a fiscal sponsor that is a 501(c)3 organization; be community-led, community-driven, and community-based; strive for change at a systemic level, instead of or in addition to one person at a time; demonstrate an understanding of forms of oppression, especially racism; and have strong local community leadership representative of and accountable to the organization's constituency.
Restrictions: ACF does not fund: profit-making organizations; electoral lobbying for initiatives or public office; individual efforts; major capital projects; or social services organizations (unless they demonstrate some analysis and strategies to challenge the systems that lead to the problem).
Geographic Focus: Kentucky, Tennessee, Virginia, West Virginia
Amount of Grant: Up to USD
Contact: Margo Miller, Executive Director; (865) 523-5783; fax (865) 240-3298; margo@appalachiancommunityfund.org or grants@appalachiancommunityfund.org
Internet: appalachiancommunityfund.org/grant/lgbtq-fund/
Sponsor: Appalachian Community Fund
1405 East Magnolia Avenue
Knoxville, TN 37917

Appalachian Regional Commission Business Development Revolving 285
Loan Fund Grants
The Appalachian Regional Commission supports a variety of activities to promote entrepreneurship and business development in the Appalachian Region. These activities help diversify the Region's economic base, develop and market strategic assets, increase the competitiveness of existing businesses, foster the development and use of innovative technologies, and enhance entrepreneurial activity. ARC entrepreneurship and business development activities include: giving entrepreneurs greater access to capital, including support for microcredit programs, revolving loan funds, and development venture capital funds; educating and training entrepreneurs through youth education programs and adult training initiatives; encouraging sector-based strategies to maximize the economic strengths of local communities; and providing strategic support for business incubators and other forms of technical assistance. Business development revolving loan funds (RLFs) in particular are pools of money used by grantees for the purpose of making loans to create and retain jobs.

As loans are repaid, money is returned to the fund and made available for additional loans. ARC has long used revolving loan funds as an effective tool of economic development.
Requirements: States, and through states, public bodies and private nonprofit organizations are eligible to apply.
Restrictions: Generally, ARC grants are limited to 50% of project costs.
Geographic Focus: Alabama, Georgia, Kentucky, Maryland, Mississippi, New York, North Carolina, Ohio, Pennsylvania, South Carolina, Tennessee, Virginia, West Virginia
Contact: Jill Wilmoth, Budget and Program Specialist; (202) 884-7668 or (202) 884-7700; fax (202) 884-7691; jwilmoth@arc.gov
Internet: www.arc.gov/funding/BusinessDevelopmentRevolvingLoanFundGrants.asp
Sponsor: Appalachian Regional Commission
1666 Connecticut Avenue NW, Suite 700
Washington, D.C. 20009-1068

Appalachian Regional Commission Education and Training Grants   286
Education and training are driving forces behind Appalachia's economic growth, preparing students and workers to compete successfully in the world economy. ARC education and training activities focus on a range of issues including workforce skills, early childhood education, dropout prevention, and improved college attendance. Strategies include: supporting the development and expansion of workforce training and vocational education programs; supporting local and regional efforts that raise the levels of educational achievement and attainment for all students; supporting programs that increase college-going rates; supporting the development of access to early childhood education programs; and supporting dropout prevention programs. The ARDA includes as eligible for funding under Section 205 the following types of projects: assessments of training and job skill needs for an industry; development of curricula and training methods, including electronic learning or technology-based training; identification of training providers and the development of partnerships between the industry and educational institutions, including community colleges; development of apprenticeship programs; development of training programs for workers, including dislocated workers; and development of training plans for businesses. Other types of projects, however, that meet the general eligibility criteria may also be considered for funding.
Requirements: States, and through states, public bodies and private nonprofit organizations are eligible to apply.
Restrictions: Generally, ARC grants are limited to 50% of project costs.
Geographic Focus: Alabama, Georgia, Kentucky, Maryland, Mississippi, New York, North Carolina, Ohio, Pennsylvania, South Carolina, Tennessee, Virginia, West Virginia
Contact: Jill Wilmoth, Budget and Program Specialist; (202) 884-7668 or (202) 884-7700; fax (202) 884-7691; jwilmoth@arc.gov
Internet: www.arc.gov/program_areas/index.asp?PROGRAM_AREA_ID=11
Sponsor: Appalachian Regional Commission
1666 Connecticut Avenue NW, Suite 700
Washington, D.C. 20009-1068

Appalachian Regional Commission Entrepreneurship and   287
  Business Development Grants
The Appalachian Regional Commission supports a variety of activities to promote entrepreneurship and business development in the Appalachian Region. These activities help diversify the Region's economic base, develop and market strategic assets, increase the competitiveness of existing businesses, foster the development and use of innovative technologies, and enhance entrepreneurial activity. ARC entrepreneurship and business development activities include: giving entrepreneurs greater access to capital, including support for microcredit programs, revolving loan funds, and development venture capital funds; educating and training entrepreneurs through youth education programs and adult training initiatives; encouraging sector-based strategies to maximize the economic strengths of local communities; and providing strategic support for business incubators and other forms of technical assistance.
Requirements: States, and through states, public bodies and private nonprofit organizations are eligible to apply.
Restrictions: Generally, ARC grants are limited to 50% of project costs.
Geographic Focus: Alabama, Georgia, Kentucky, Maryland, New York, North Carolina, Ohio, Pennsylvania, South Carolina, Tennessee, Virginia, West Virginia
Contact: Jill Wilmoth, Budget and Program Specialist; (202) 884-7668 or (202) 884-7700; fax (202) 884-7691; jwilmoth@arc.gov
Internet: www.arc.gov/program_areas/index.asp?PROGRAM_AREA_ID=14
Sponsor: Appalachian Regional Commission
1666 Connecticut Avenue NW, Suite 700
Washington, D.C. 20009-1068

Appalachian Regional Commission Health Care Grants   288
Access to comprehensive, affordable health care is vital to social and economic growth in the Appalachian Region. The Appalachian Regional Commission's health projects focus on community-based efforts to encourage health-promotion and disease-prevention activities. Strategies include: using best practices in public health to develop targeted approaches to wellness and disease prevention; supporting partnerships that educate children and families about basic health risks; using telecommunications and other technology to reduce the high cost of health-care services; and encouraging the development and expansion of health professional education services within the Region. ARC health care grants have helped provide equipment for hospitals and rural clinics, training for health care professionals, and support for community-based health education activities. ARC also works with other organizations to address the high incidence of life-threatening diseases in the Region, as in its ongoing partnership with the Centers for Disease Control and Prevention in diabetes and cancer education, prevention, and treatment programs in the Region's distressed counties.
Requirements: States, and through states, public bodies and private nonprofit organizations are eligible to apply.

Restrictions: Generally, ARC grants are limited to 50% of project costs.
Geographic Focus: Alabama, Georgia, Kentucky, Maryland, Mississippi, New York, North Carolina, Ohio, Pennsylvania, South Carolina, Tennessee, Virginia, West Virginia
Contact: Jill Wilmoth, Budget and Program Specialist; (202) 884-7668 or (202) 884-7700; fax (202) 884-7691; jwilmoth@arc.gov
Internet: www.arc.gov/program_areas/index.asp?PROGRAM_AREA_ID=16
Sponsor: Appalachian Regional Commission
1666 Connecticut Avenue NW, Suite 700
Washington, D.C. 20009-1068

Appalachian Regional Commission Housing Grants   289
The Appalachian Regional Commission provides funds for basic infrastructure services, including water and sewer facilities, that enhance economic development opportunities or address serious health issues for residential customers. ARC supports projects that stimulate the construction or rehabilitation of housing for low- and moderate-income residents. ARC housing grants fund planning, technical services, and other preliminary expenses of developing housing projects, as well as demolition and necessary site improvements, including excavation, land fills, land clearing and grading; and infrastructure improvements, such as water and sewer system construction.
Requirements: States, and through states, public bodies and private nonprofit organizations are eligible to apply.
Restrictions: Generally, ARC grants are limited to 50% of project costs.
Geographic Focus: Alabama, Georgia, Kentucky, Maryland, New York, North Carolina, Ohio, Pennsylvania, South Carolina, Tennessee, Virginia, West Virginia
Contact: Jill Wilmoth, Budget and Program Specialist; (202) 884-7668 or (202) 884-7700; fax (202) 884-7691; jwilmoth@arc.gov
Internet: www.arc.gov/funding/arcprojectgrants.asp
Sponsor: Appalachian Regional Commission
1666 Connecticut Avenue NW, Suite 700
Washington, D.C. 20009-1068

Ar-Hale Family Foundation Grants   290
Established in Ohio in 1990, the Ar-Hale Family Foundation (formerly the Ar-Hale Foundation) is dedicated to supporting philanthropic and religious initiatives that personally impact the lives of families and children. Support is given primarily to communities where American Trim does business and in the communities where American Trim shareholders reside. The Foundation's major fields of interest include the support of: athletics and sports (primarily baseball); Catholic agencies and churches; Christian agencies and churches; K-12 education; family services; health care programs and access; higher education; human services; performing arts; and YMCAs and YWCAs. Many types of funding is offered, including: annual campaigns; building and renovation support; capital campaigns; consulting services; continuing support; curriculum development; emergency funds; endowments; fellowships; film, video, and radio production; general operating support; management development; capacity building; challenge support; program development; scholarships to individuals; seed money; and technical assistance. There are no annual deadlines, and most recent awards have ranged from $250 to $20,000.
Requirements: Non-profit organizations located in, or serving the residents, the following areas may apply: Louisville, Kentucky; Allen, Auglaize, and Shelby counties in Ohio; the cities of Dayton and Lima, Ohio; Shawnee, Oklahoma; and Erie, Pennsylvania.
Restrictions: No support is offered for political organizations.
Geographic Focus: Kentucky, Ohio, Oklahoma, Pennsylvania
Amount of Grant: 250 - 20,000 USD
Contact: Arlene F. Hawk, President; (419) 331-1040; dprueter@cox.net
Sponsor: Ar-Hale Family Foundation
P.O. Box 210
Lima, OH 45802-0210

Arizona Commission on the Arts Learning Collaboration Grant   291
Arts Learning Collaboration Grants enhance the work of school-based arts teaching and learning programs through collaborative projects taking place in-school, after-school, or during summer/inter-session and in-services in one of the following three categories: planning for future project planning, curriculum development, evaluation, resource development; professional development for training and learning for certified arts educators, classroom teachers, administration, teacher/artist teams; and student learning for sequential, hands-on learning in, though, and/or about the arts.
Requirements: Eligible applicants are Arizona PreK-12 schools or school districts. Whether it's a collaboration between teachers or departments within a school, between multiple schools within a district, or between a school and a community arts resource, the Arts Learning Collaboration Grant is available to help advance arts learning.
Restrictions: Nonprofit arts organizations are not eligible.
Geographic Focus: Arizona
Date(s) Application is Due: May 30
Amount of Grant: 1,500 - 2,500 USD
Contact: Anastasia Freyermuth, Arts Learning and Special Projects Coordinator; (602) 771-6529 or (602) 771-6501; fax (602) 256-0282; afreyermuth@azarts.gov or info@azarts.gov
Internet: azarts.gov/grant/arts-learning-collaboration-grant/
Sponsor: Arizona Commission on the Arts
417 West Roosevelt Street
Phoenix, AZ 85003-6501

Arizona Commission on the Arts Youth Arts Engagement Grant   292
Administered by the Arizona Commission on the Arts Youth Arts Council, the Youth Arts Engagement Grant is a funding opportunity for projects that support young people's stories and ideas through creative expression. Applicants can request the following flat grant amounts: $500, $1,000, $1,500. Funds may be distributed to individuals, Arizona non-

profit organizations or public schools, or individuals/collaboratives with a fiscal sponsor. Grant funds may be used for any of the following (this list is not comprehensive): artist, consultant, and other fees; materials or supplies; travel costs; technology; space/rental fees; and documentation. The annual application deadline is March 19.

Requirements: Arizona arts organizations, collaboratives, youth councils, clubs or similar organizations that are majority youth-led (20 years-old and under). An adult's role is as an ally or accomplice supporting and ensuring youth leadership and shared decision making. Eligible applicants must: be under the age of 20; propose a project that is majority youth-led; and propose a project that provides an artistic experience for the direct benefit of young people under the age of 20 in Arizona.

Geographic Focus: Arizona
Date(s) Application is Due: Mar 19
Amount of Grant: 500 - 1,500 USD
Contact: Elisa Radcliffe, Arts Learning Manager; (602) 771-6528; fax (602) 256-0282; eradcliffe@azarts.gov or info@azarts.gov
Internet: azarts.gov/grant/youth-arts-engagement/
Sponsor: Arizona Commission on the Arts
417 West Roosevelt Street
Phoenix, AZ 85003-6501

Arizona Foundation for Women Deborah G. Carstens Fund Grants 293

Arizona Foundation for Women funds projects and programs that enhance the lives of Arizona women and children. They educate others about the barriers facing women and children and involve members of the community in efforts to remove those barriers. The Deborah G. Carstens Fund provides grants to not-for-profit organizations that motivate and empower girls and women to take responsibility for their economic lives by developing skills, building self-esteem and identifying challenges that impede their success.

Geographic Focus: Arizona
Contact: Nancy A. Dean, Executive Director/President; (602) 532-2800; fax (602) 532-2801
Internet: www.azfoundationforwomen.org/
Sponsor: Arizona Foundation for Women
2828 North Central Avenue
Phoenix, AZ 85004

Arizona Foundation for Women General Grants 294

Arizona Foundation for Women funds projects and programs that enhance the lives of Arizona women and children. They educate others about the barriers facing women and children and involve members of the community in efforts to remove those barriers. Current types of programs supported include: the Men's Anti-violence Network (M.A.N); Emergency Crisis Transportation; Medical Services for Victims of Domestic Violence; ASU Hispanic Mother-Daughter Program; and the Arizona Coalition on Adolescent Pregnancy and Parenting (ACAPP). The Foundation's General Grant program provides funding to address identified unmet needs of women and girls. Grant funding focuses upon innovative and/or model primary prevention programs.

Requirements: Programs must address social change so that women and girls may live free from fear and violence, attain self-reliance and achieve social equity.
Restrictions: Operational funding is not available.
Geographic Focus: Arizona
Contact: Nancy A. Dean, Executive Director/President; 602-532-2800; fax 602-532-2801
Internet: www.azfoundationforwomen.org/
Sponsor: Arizona Foundation for Women
2828 North Central Avenue
Phoenix, AZ 85004

Arizona State Library LSTA Collections Grants 295

The Arizona State Library, Archives, and Public Records Agency (State Library) offers libraries the opportunity to apply for grant funding. Collections projects support exemplary stewardship of library collections in a variety of formats; as well as facilitate access to, discovery of, and use of those collections. Collections Grant programs and activities include: access to electronic books; creating, providing, and informing about databases of periodical and reference resources; materials for the visually impaired or those with other disabilities; Arizona Memory Projects; cataloging, access to, and promotion of Arizona governmental publications; online job and career materials; historic Arizona newspapers access; and print materials for tribal and rural libraries. Collections Grants should address these LSTA priorities: establishment or enhancement of electronic and other linkages and improved coordination among and between libraries and entities for the purpose of improving the quality of and access to library and information services; and the development of library services that provide all users access to information through local, state, regional, national and international collaborations and networks.

Requirements: All public libraries recognized by the State Library, including museum libraries, are eligible to apply for LSTA funds. To be eligible to receive LSTA funds in Arizona, all libraries must meet the following criteria: be open to the public at least 750 hours per year, with regular, posted hours; provide core library services, such as borrowing privileges and computer use, free of charge to all residents within the library's service area.

Geographic Focus: Arizona
Date(s) Application is Due: Mar 1
Contact: Mary Villegas, (602) 926-3600; mvillegas@azlibrary.gov
Internet: www.azlibrary.gov/lsta/documents/pdf/13guidelines.pdf
Sponsor: Arizona State Library
1700 W Washington, Suite 300
Phoenix, AZ 85007-2935

Arizona State Library LSTA Community Grants 296

The Arizona State Library, Archives, and Public Records Agency (State Library) offers libraries the opportunity to apply for grant funding. Community Grant program and activities include: job assistance and training; small business development; community referral; civic engagement; and legal information. Community Grants should address these LSTA priorities: develop public and private partnerships with other agencies and community-based organizations; target library services to individuals of diverse geographic, cultural, and socioeconomic backgrounds, to individuals with disabilities, and to individuals with limited functional literacy or information skills; and target library and information services to persons having difficulty using a library and to under-served urban and rural communities including children from families with incomes below the poverty line.

Requirements: All public libraries recognized by the State Library, including museum libraries, are eligible to apply for LSTA funds. To be eligible to receive LSTA funds in Arizona, all libraries must meet the following criteria: be open to the public at least 750 hours per year, with regular, posted hours; provide core library services, such as borrowing privileges and computer use, free of charge to all residents within the library's service area.

Geographic Focus: Arizona
Date(s) Application is Due: Mar 1
Contact: Dale Savage, (602) 926-3988; dsavage@azlibrary.gov
Internet: www.azlibrary.gov/lsta/documents/pdf/13guidelines.pdf
Sponsor: Arizona State Library
1700 W Washington, Suite 300
Phoenix, AZ 85007-2935

Arizona State Library LSTA Learning Grants 297

The Arizona State Library, Archives, and Public Records Agency (State Library) offers libraries the opportunity to apply for grant funding. Learning Grant programs and activities include: early literacy programs; youth and adult reading programs; information literacy classes and resources; and programming for youth and adults. Learning Grants should address these LSTA priorities: expand services for learning and access to information and educational resources in a variety of formats, in all types of libraries, for individuals of all ages in order to support such individuals' needs for education, lifelong learning, workforce development, and digital literacy skills; target library services to individuals of diverse geographic, cultural, and socioeconomic backgrounds, to individuals with disabilities, and to individuals with limited functional literacy or information skills; and target library and information services to persons having difficulty using a library and to under-served urban and rural communities including children from families with incomes below the poverty line.

Requirements: All public libraries recognized by the State Library, including museum libraries, are eligible to apply for LSTA funds. To be eligible to receive LSTA funds in Arizona, all libraries must meet the following criteria: be open to the public at least 750 hours per year, with regular, posted hours; provide core library services, such as borrowing privileges and computer use, free of charge to all residents within the library's service area.

Geographic Focus: Arizona
Date(s) Application is Due: Mar 1
Contact: Holly Henley, Grants Administrator; (602) 926-3366; hhenley@azlibrary.gov
Internet: www.azlibrary.gov/lsta/documents/pdf/13guidelines.pdf
Sponsor: Arizona State Library
1700 W Washington, Suite 300
Phoenix, AZ 85007-2935

Arkema Foundation Grants 298

The Arkema Inc. Foundation, through philanthropic grants and gifts to local social, cultural and educational organizations, enhances the quality of life in the communities where we do business. The Foundation also supports science and science education at all levels. For those seeking grant support, the Foundation invites letters of inquiry throughout the year. These letters can be up to two pages in length, and should include: a brief description of the program or project; the amount of funding requested; and proof of non-profit status. Most recently, grants have ranged from $500 to $35,000. Though there are no specified deadlines, the Board meets to review applications in March, June, September, and December.

Requirements: Non-profit organizations serving residents in the following regions may apply: Mobile County, Alabama; the Kentucky counties of Graves, Livingston, Lyon, Marshall, McCracken, Carroll, Gallatin, Trimble, and Jefferson; Wayne County, Michigan; the Minnesota counties of Dodge, Mower, and Steele; the New Jersey counties of Burlington, Camden, Gloucester, and Salem; the New York counties of Genesee and Livingston; the Pennsylvania counties of Berks, Bucks, Chester, Delaware, Montgomery, and Philadelphia; Shelby County, Tennessee; and the Texas counties of Jasper, Newton, Jefferson, Orange, Harris, and Brazos.

Restrictions: No support for veterans', fraternal, labor, or sectarian religious organizations, or sports teams is offered. Furthermore, funding is not provided to individuals (except for employee-related scholarships), or for endowments, special projects, research, publications, conferences, courtesy advertising, entertainment promotions, event sponsorships, public education, athletic competitions, or political causes or campaigns.

Geographic Focus: Alabama, Kentucky, Michigan, Minnesota, New Jersey, New York, Pennsylvania, Tennessee, Texas
Contact: Diane Milici; (215) 419-7735 or (610) 205-7000; diane.milici@arkema.com
Internet: www.arkema-americas.com/en/social-responsibility/local-programs/arkema-inc.-foundation/index.html
Sponsor: Arkema Foundation
900 First Avenue
King of Prussia, PA 19406-1308

Arkema Foundation Science Teachers Grants 299

The goal of the Science Teachers Program is to bring Arkema scientists and local teachers together to spark an interest in science among elementary school students. Additionally, the program aims to make teachers more expert when teaching science. Funded by the Arkema Foundation, the program is run in communities in which Arkema has manufacturing operations. The majority of students who benefit from the program come from socioeconomically disadvantaged homes. The program is generally an intensive week-long session for elementary and secondary school teachers. Armed with innovative science experiment kits and the guidance of chemical engineers and scientists, teachers learn new and fascinating ways to illustrate scientific concepts. Scientific topics explored include life, earth and physical science and technology. A formal application is not required, and interested parties should begin by forwarding a letter of inquiry no longer than two pages. The Board meets to review applications in March, June, September, and December.
Requirements: Teachers in grades 3 through 6 employed in the following geographic areas may participate: Mobile County, Alabama; the Kentucky counties of Graves, Livingston, Lyon, Marshall, McCracken, Carroll, Gallatin, Trimble, and Jefferson; Wayne County, Michigan; the Minnesota counties of Didge, Mower, and Steele; the New Jersey counties of Burlington, Camden, Gloucester, and Salem; the New York counties of Genesee and Livingston; the Pennsylvania counties of Berks, Bucks, Chester, Delaware, Montgomery, and Philadelphia; Shelby County, Tennessee; and the Texas counties of Jasper, Newton, Jefferson, Orange, Harris, and Brazos.
Restrictions: No support for veterans', fraternal, labor, or sectarian religious organizations, or sports teams is offered. Furthermore, funding is not provided to individuals (except for employee-related scholarships), or for endowments, special projects, research, publications, conferences, courtesy advertising, entertainment promotions, event sponsorships, public education, athletic competitions, or political causes or campaigns.
Geographic Focus: Alabama, Kentucky, Michigan, Minnesota, New Jersey, New York, Pennsylvania, Tennessee, Texas
Amount of Grant: 500 USD
Contact: Diane Milici; (215) 419-7735 or (610) 205-7000; diane.milici@arkema.com
Internet: www.arkema-americas.com/en/social-responsibility/local-programs/science-teacher-program/
Sponsor: Arkema Foundation
900 First Avenue
King of Prussia, PA 19406-1308

Armstrong McDonald Foundation Children and Youth Grants 300

The Armstrong McDonald Foundation was incorporated in the State of Nebraska in 1986. The mission of the Foundation is to continue the philanthropic ideals and goals of James M. McDonald, Sr. through prudent and impartial review of all qualifying grant requests received annually to insure that awards are made to soundly conceived and operated non-profit organizations. For its Children and Youth category, the Foundation is looking for projects submitted by BSA, GSA, Boys and Girls Clubs and Teen Challenge type organizations that are related to their mission or for improvement to their facilities and equipment, such as games, computers and renovations. The Foundation provides a formal downloadable application which is to be completed by all applicants approved for submission of a grant request. All required application materials need to be received on or before September 15.
Requirements: The Armstrong McDonald Foundation will only accept unsolicited grant requests from those IRS approved non-profits listed on the Pre-Approved for Grant Submission List. Please note that this list will be updated annually in December with additions and/or deletions. All other IRS approved non-profits desiring to submit a grant request to this foundation must meet the following three qualifications: be incorporated in either the State of Arizona or Nebraska; have a physical office located in their state of incorporation; and spend any awarded grant funds within their state of incorporation.
Restrictions: Grants do not support advocacy organizations, individuals, international organizations, political organizations, or state and local government agencies. The foundation does not fund capital campaigns, salaries/stipends, and multi-year projects. Organization must have received a grant from the foundation within the last five years unless it is located within the states of Arizona or Nebraska. No organization east of the Mississippi is eligible for a grant.
Geographic Focus: Arizona, Nebraska
Date(s) Application is Due: Sep 15
Amount of Grant: 1,000 - 80,000 USD
Contact: Laurie L. Bouchard, President; (520) 878-9627; fax (520) 797-3866; info@ArmstrongMcDonaldFoundation.org
Internet: www.armstrongmcdonaldfoundation.org/cat.html
Sponsor: Armstrong McDonald Foundation
P.O. Box 70110
Tucson, AZ 85737-0110

Armstrong McDonald Foundation Special Needs Grants 301

The Armstrong McDonald Foundation was incorporated in the State of Nebraska in 1986. The mission of the Foundation is to continue the philanthropic ideals and goals of James M. McDonald, Sr. through prudent and impartial review of all qualifying grant requests received annually to insure that awards are made to soundly conceived and operated non-profit organizations. With its Special Needs category, the Foundation has sent disabled kids to camp; made playgrounds handicapped accessible and friendly; purchased specialized equipment for licensed care facilities for the disabled and mentally retarded; contributed toward the training of dogs for the visually impaired and restricted mobility seniors, adults, and youth; assisted with purchase of equipment to be used by or for the disabled (wheelchairs, ramps, shower facilities); publication of new books and distribution of Braille textbooks; underwrote sport recreation meets for the disabled and mentally retarded; assisted with the costs of providing media services for the blind; and contributed to the costs of providing multiple services to the hearing impaired. The Foundation provides a formal downloadable application which is to be completed by all applicants approved for submission of a grant request. All required application materials need to be received on or before September 15.
Requirements: The Armstrong McDonald Foundation will only accept unsolicited grant requests from those IRS approved non-profits listed on the Pre-Approved for Grant Submission List. Please note that this list will be updated annually in December with additions and/or deletions. All other IRS approved non-profits desiring to submit a grant request to this foundation must meet the following three qualifications: be incorporated in either the State of Arizona or Nebraska; have a physical office located in their state of incorporation; and spend any awarded grant funds within their state of incorporation.
Restrictions: Grants do not support advocacy organizations, individuals, international organizations, political organizations, or state and local government agencies. The foundation does not fund capital campaigns, salaries/stipends, and multi-year projects. Organization must have received a grant from the foundation within the last five years unless it is located within the states of Arizona or Nebraska. No organization east of the Mississippi is eligible for a grant.
Geographic Focus: Arizona, Nebraska
Date(s) Application is Due: Sep 15
Amount of Grant: 1,000 - 80,000 USD
Contact: Laurie L. Bouchard, President; (520) 878-9627; fax (520) 797-3866; info@ArmstrongMcDonaldFoundation.org
Internet: www.armstrongmcdonaldfoundation.org/cat.html
Sponsor: Armstrong McDonald Foundation
P.O. Box 70110
Tucson, AZ 85737-0110

Arthur Ashley Williams Foundation Grants 302

The Arthur Ashley Williams Foundation was established in Holliston, Massachusetts, in February of 1954. Today, its primary areas of interest include: religious, educational, charitable, scientific, literary, testing for public safety, fostering national or international amateur sports competition (as long as it doesn't provide athletic facilities or equipment), or the prevention of cruelty to children or animals. The Foundation awards grants to charitable organizations to help improve quality of life for those seeking assistance from these charitable organizations. Grant requests will be considered for program support, seed money, challenge grants, and capital improvements. Awards generally range up to a maximum of $10,000.
Requirements: To apply for a grant, applicants must be non-profit 501(c)3 organizations or public schools.
Restrictions: The Foundation will not fund political or sectarian activities.
Geographic Focus: All States
Amount of Grant: Up to 10,000 USD
Samples: Bosom Buddies Breast Cancer, Naples, Florida - general operating support, $10,000 (2018); Canaan FAST Squad, Canaan, New Hampshire - general operating support, $1,000 (2018); Cape Vineyard Community Church, Cape Coral, Florida - discretionary funding, $2,000 (2018).
Contact: Eugene R. Liscombe, Program Contact; (508) 520-2728 or (508) 533-8633; eliscombe@lpcpas.com
Sponsor: Arthur Ashley Williams Foundation
379 Underwood Street, P.O. Box 6280
Holliston, MA 01746-1562

Arthur E. and Josephine Campbell Beyer Foundation Grants 303

The Arthur E. and Josephine Campbell Beyer Foundation was established in Indiana in 1969, with giving centered in the Noble County region. The Foundation's primary fields of interest include: arts, culture, and humanities; education; the environment and animals; health care; human services; public and society benefit; and religion. Grants are offered in the form of scholarship funding and general operations. Since there are no application forms required, applicants should submit personal contact information in writing, along with a detailed description of the project, the primary contact person, and budgetary needs. The annual deadline for full proposal submission is May 1. Most recent amounts have ranged from $1,000 to $6,000.
Requirements: There are no geographic restrictions; however, the trust has a practice of primarily supporting organizations in Noble County, Indiana.
Geographic Focus: Indiana
Date(s) Application is Due: May 1
Amount of Grant: 1,000 - 6,000 USD
Contact: Jenny King; (260) 461-6458; fax (260) 461-6678; jennifer.i.king@wellsfargo.com
Internet: www.wellsfargo.com/private-foundations/beyer-foundation
Sponsor: Arthur E. and Josephine Campbell Beyer Foundation
1 West 4th Street, 4th Floor, MAC D4000-041
Winston-Salem, NC 27101-3818

Arthur M. Blank Family Foundation AMB West Community Fund Grants 304

Through the AMB West Community Fund, the Arthur M. Blank Family Foundation makes grants to nonprofit organizations that seek to support high quality of life for residents of Montana, particularly in Park and Gallatin Counties. The Foundation directs most of its funding to children birth to five years old and their parents/caregivers. By investing in opportunities that support proven and innovative interventions and/or enhancement that gets young children ready to learn, the Foundation hopes to improve long-term outcomes for Park and Gallatin counties and the State of Montana. The Foundation is particularly interested in opportunities that lend themselves to scale in support of a high quality early childhood development, youth empowerment and development, wellness, and youth suicide prevention. Program approaches should first look to benefit those young children who live in high need communities. Interested parties should begin by sending a concept query to the Foundation office. Applications are by invitation only.

Requirements: 501(c)3 organizations serving the residents of Montana are eligible to apply. The AMB West Community Fund supports creative approaches and innovative programs that improve outcomes for children and families, particularly in Park and Gallatin Counties. The Fund will only consider supporting organizations that can demonstrate the ability to foster community cooperation and collaboration. Nonprofit organizations focused on advocacy or policy changes are eligible to apply and must demonstrate how their activities hold promise for large-scale systemic change
Restrictions: The Foundation does not make grants: directly to individuals; for scholarships; or to support houses of worship or religious activity.
Geographic Focus: Montana
Amount of Grant: Up to 300,000 USD
Samples: Community Health Partners and Park County Health Department, Livingston, Montana, $283,500 (over three years) - challenge grant for the Babies Plus program and expansion of the Connect Referral Network (2019); Montana Community Foundation, Helena, Montana, $25,000 - to mobilize the private sector in Montana creating a statewide network of early childhood champions to elevate early care as a critical workforce and economic issue (2019); Little Rangers Learning Center, West Yellowstone, Montana, $5,000 - support of the Teaching and Learning Through Innovative Service program (2019).
Contact: John Bare, Senior Vice President for Programs; (404) 367-2100; jbare@ambfo.com
Internet: blankfoundation.org/initiative/amb-west-philanthropies/#tab2
Sponsor: Arthur M. Blank Family Foundation
3223 Howell Mill Road, NW
Atlanta, GA 30327

Arthur M. Blank Family Foundation American Explorers Grants   305
Created by The Arthur M. Blank Family Foundation, in partnership with Atlanta Public Schools, community-based organizations and the North Carolina Outward Bound School (NCOBS), American Explorers is a comprehensive leadership development program giving youth from Atlanta's Historic Westside communities pathways to leadership. Through a collection of programs and hands-on learning experiences, American Explorers become change agents, educators, community builders, entrepreneurs and stewards of their communities. The American Explorers leadership development program involves year-round opportunities and activities for participants to engage in school and community service projects, leadership cultivation, and collaborative experiences. Participation requires youth to meet annual benchmarks and to identify ways in which they can improve their Circles of Influence.
Requirements: 501(c)3 organizations serving the residents of Atlanta, Georgia, are eligible to apply.
Restrictions: The Foundation does not make grants: directly to individuals; for scholarships; or to support houses of worship or religious activity.
Geographic Focus: Georgia, North Carolina
Amount of Grant: 5,000 - 1,200,000 USD
Samples: The Scholarship Academy, Atlanta, Georgia, $37,500 - to provide college preparatory services to American Explorers with emphasis on applying for financial aid; North Carolina Outward Bound School, Asheville, North Carolina, $1,191,341 - to provide summer expeditionary learning opportunities for up to 160 high school students in Atlanta's Westside neighborhoods.
Contact: John Bare, Senior Vice President for Programs; (404) 367-2100; jbare@ambfo.com
Internet: blankfoundation.org/initiative/american-explorers/#tab1
Sponsor: Arthur M. Blank Family Foundation
3223 Howell Mill Road, NW
Atlanta, GA 30327

Arthur M. Blank Family Foundation Art of Change Grants   306
The Arthur M. Blank Family Foundation recognizes that a thriving arts community contributes immeasurably to Atlanta's economic and social vitality. The arts also inspire and engage young people in ways that spark academic and social success. Through its Art of Change program, the Foundation seeks partners that aim to broaden audiences, promote sustainability and vitality of the Arts in the Atlanta Metropolitan Area. Interested parties should begin by sending a concept query to the Foundation office. Applications are by invitation only.
Requirements: 501(c)3 organizations serving the residents of Atlanta, Georgia, are eligible to apply.
Restrictions: The Foundation does not make grants: directly to individuals; for scholarships; or to support houses of worship or religious activity.
Geographic Focus: Georgia
Samples: Atlanta Ballet, Atlanta, Georgia, $23,750 - general operating funds; Aurora Theatre, Lawrenceville, Georgia, $25,000 - general operating funds; Springer Opera House, Columbus, Georgia, $23,775 - general operating funds.
Contact: Lea Bond, Program Director and Grants Administrator; (404) 367-2100; lbond@ambfo.com
Internet: blankfoundation.org/initiative/art-of-change/
Sponsor: Arthur M. Blank Family Foundation
3223 Howell Mill Road, NW
Atlanta, GA 30327

Arthur M. Blank Family Foundation Atlanta Falcons Youth Foundation Grants   307
The Atlanta Falcons Youth Foundation is an affiliated fund of the Arthur M. Blank Family Foundation and invests in innovative approaches to increase time kids spend in physical activity and to give more children access to fresh fruits and vegetables. Since 2002, the foundation has awarded more than $20 million in grants to non-profit organizations serving children across Georgia. As a leader in the Georgia SHAPE initiative, AFYF is helping Georgia elementary schools reach more than 350,000 students through the Power Up for 30 program, which adds 30 minutes of physical activity during the school day. In partnership with the Atlanta Falcons Youth Foundation, Good Sports will be donating equipment to Georgia organizations serving low-income children. AFYF is especially interested in innovations that change the lives of children who traditionally are most likely to miss out

or opt out of physical activity. Instead of prescribing particular types of physical activity, AFYF challenges partners to deliver activities that the kids want to do.
Requirements: Community organizations or schools in Georgia must apply through the Good Sports web site. Schools must apply through the Let's Move Salad Bar online portal at Let's Move Salad Bars to Schools.
Restrictions: The foundation does not provide funding for events, individuals, government agencies, municipalities, or parochial or private schools.
Geographic Focus: Georgia
Amount of Grant: Up to 20,000 USD
Samples: Bearings Bike Shop, Atlanta, Georgia, $20,000 - operating support, enabling the organization to offer kids an opportunity to earn a bike of their own as well as the environment to develop skills and keep that bike in working order; Community Farmers Markets, Atlanta, Georgia, $20,000 - to build and test a bicycle produce cart that will be used to promote local food along the Beltline, in Westside neighborhoods and community events that currently lack a local food option; East Point Velodrome Association, Atlanta, Georgia, $5,000 - for the 2018 Youth Cycling League, providing 900 rider days of participation to youth ages 8-16 from across Metro Atlanta.
Contact: Lea Bond, Program Director and Grants Administrator; (404) 367-2100
Internet: blankfoundation.org/initiative/atlanta-falcons-youth-foundation/
Sponsor: Arthur M. Blank Family Foundation
3223 Howell Mill Road, NW
Atlanta, GA 30327

Arthur M. Blank Family Foundation Atlanta United Foundation Grants   308
Through the arthur M. Blank Foundation, the Atlanta United Foundation strives to make the game of soccer accessible and inclusive for individuals across the state of Georgia. Through the global game of soccer, the Foundation's grant programs stress the importance of physical fitness while building a supportive culture of play and sportsmanship. Atlanta United's community efforts focus on the basic need for access and inclusion. Its primary goal is to create opportunities that make it possible for individuals across the state to use the beautiful game as a positive catalyst for change in the community. Whether it's a team receiving new equipment that they otherwise wouldn't be able to afford, or giving a child an opportunity of a lifetime, the Foundation strives to create deep ripples of change in the community through soccer. AUF accepts Letters of Inquiry (LOI) for Program Grants, Play Spaces, Pitches, and Fields and Equipment Donations. AUF does not accept unsolicited proposals. Based on a review submission, AUF will determine whether to invite a full proposal.
Requirements: AUF makes grants to nonprofit organizations that show promise for extending soccer programs and participation to children and adults who would not otherwise get to participate. The LOI should be a two- or three-page document that explains the project, the population that will be served, the time line for implementation and a cost estimate.
Geographic Focus: All States
Amount of Grant: Up to 100,000 USD
Samples: Fugees Family, Scottsdale, Georgia, $80,000 - support for the Fugees Family Soccer Program, an innovative program that combines soccer with rigorous academic standards and wraparound services to improve the lives of refugee children and their families; The Father Christmas Cup, Norcross, Georgia, $6,000 - sponsorship of the tournament on 12/16/2017 at Atlanta Silverbacks Park o/b/o Atlanta United to benefit a family or families who have recently suffered the loss of a parent; Square Feet Studio, Atlanta, Georgia, $6,012 - to conduct technical advisory sessions with each of the four finalists in Atlanta United's The Next Great Pitch project.
Contact: John Bare, Senior Vice President for Programs; (404) 367-2100; jbare@ambfo.com
Internet: www.atlutd.com/community/atlanta-united-foundation
Sponsor: Arthur M. Blank Family Foundation
3223 Howell Mill Road, NW
Atlanta, GA 30327

Arthur M. Blank Family Foundation Inspiring Spaces Grants   309
The Arthur M. Blank Foundation believes that young people, families, and entire communities need healthy, green, inspiring places to grow and develop. The Foundation seeks partners with a passion for parks and green space. Through these partners, it aims to preserve and enhance a new generation of safe, clean, accessible parks and community green spaces. Parks and community green spaces offer social, ecological, and economic benefits to residents and visitors alike. Through this initiative, the Foundation and the Atlanta Falcons Youth Foundation have partnered with the Georgia's State Park system and the Georgia Association of Physician Assistants (GAPA) to sponsor Rx for Fitness. Through the new Rx for Fitness program, physician assistants can prescribe healthy hikes in the great outdoors, and patients can turn in their prescriptions for free park passes. Interested parties should begin by sending a query letter to the Foundation office. Applications are by invitation only.
Requirements: 501(c)3 organizations serving the residents of Atlanta, Georgia, are eligible to apply.
Restrictions: The Foundation does not make grants: directly to individuals; for scholarships; or to support houses of worship or religious activity.
Geographic Focus: Georgia, New York
Amount of Grant: Up to 1,000,000 USD
Samples: Friends of the High Line, New York, New York, $10,000 - general operating funds; Montana Community Foundation, Helena, Montana, $50,000 - for the Montana Wildfire Relief Fund; Atlanta Botanical Garden, Atlanta, Georgia, $1,000,000 - or the water mirror and stairs in Storza Woods as part of the Nourish and Flourish Campaign.
Contact: John Bare, Senior Vice President for Programs; (404) 367-2100; jbare@ambfo.com
Internet: blankfoundation.org/initiative/inspiring-spaces/#tab1
Sponsor: Arthur M. Blank Family Foundation
3223 Howell Mill Road, NW
Atlanta, GA 30327

Arthur M. Blank Family Foundation Molly Blank Fund Grants 310

Molly Blank lived her life, in word and deed, consistent with her favorite quote: "I expect to pass through this world but once. Any good thing, therefore, that I can do or any kindness that I can show to any fellow creature, let me do it now. Let me not defer nor neglect it; for I shall not pass this way again." Her goals accomplished, Molly, mother of Michael Blank and Arthur M. Blank, died January 7, 2015, in Atlanta, at the age of 99. Molly Graff Blank was born on May 21, 1915, in New York, the daughter of Austrian immigrant parents Louis Graff and Celia Hoffman Graff. From the start, family and friends say she had an insatiable curiosity to try new things - and do them her way. As the only Jewish girl in her Girl Scout troop, for example - and at a time when Jews were not openly embraced - she became a troop leader and counselor. She also had a thirst for knowledge, becoming an avid reader and, in her later years, an intrepid traveler. Molly enjoyed family, art, dance and philanthropy throughout her life, but might best be remembered as an independent thinker and self-made businesswoman who, after being widowed at a young age, raised two sons and took control of the family business, Home Depot, turning it into a thriving operation that was later sold to a large retail conglomerate. The Arthur M. Blank Family Foundation Molly Blank Fund focus of investments are on programs that address the interests Molly Blank supported in her lifetime, including at-risk youth, arts and culture, and Jewish causes emphasizing social justice and interfaith coalitions.
Requirements: 501(c)3 organizations serving the residents of Atlanta, Georgia, are eligible to apply.
Restrictions: The Fund does not make grants: directly to individuals; for scholarships; or to support houses of worship or religious activity.
Geographic Focus: All States
Amount of Grant: Up to 225,000 USD
Samples: Atlanta Jewish Film Festival, Atlanta, Georgia, $225,000 - sponsorship of the annual film festival 2018-2020, community engagement and year-round programming; Jewish Home Life Communities, Atlanta, Georgia, $45,000 - to provide financial support to older adults in need of home care services for which no, or insufficient, public or other financial assistance is available; Camp Twin Lakes, Atlanta, Georgia, $45,000 - to help fund the Camper Scholarship program.
Contact: John Bare, Senior Vice President for Programs; (404) 367-2100; jbare@ambfo.com
Internet: blankfoundation.org/initiative/the-molly-blank-fund/
Sponsor: Arthur M. Blank Family Foundation
3223 Howell Mill Road, NW
Atlanta, GA 30327

Arthur M. Blank Family Foundation Mountain Sky Guest Ranch Fund Grants 311

The Mountain Sky Guest Ranch Fund is an affiliated fund of the Arthur M. Blank Family Foundation. The Fund has contributed more than $3.5 million to local nonprofits since Arthur M. Blank, co-founder of the Home Depot, owner of the Atlanta Falcons, MLS Atlanta, and chairman of PGA Tour Superstore, acquired the ranch in 2001. The Fund pays particular focus on programs that develop young stewards of land and wildlife through education and outdoor experiences, including innovations that introduce youth to area natural resources, as well as programs that provide children, birth to five, with quality opportunities that will prepare them for successful lifelong development. Preference will be given to innovations that expand opportunities for participation beyond current levels in Park and Gallatin counties. The Fund seeks creative approaches to expanding opportunity and does not intend to fund existing programs at their current levels of participation. The Fund is interested in opportunities that incorporate two or more nonprofit organizations working together in service of a common goal. Preference will be given to approaches that serve the rural areas of Park and Gallatin counties.
Requirements: 501(c)3 organizations serving the residents of Montana are eligible to apply.
Restrictions: The Foundation does not make grants: directly to individuals; for scholarships; or to support houses of worship or religious activity.
Geographic Focus: Montana
Contact: Whitney Lane; (404) 367-2100; wlane@ambfo.com
Internet: www.mountainsky.com/
Sponsor: Arthur M. Blank Family Foundation
3223 Howell Mill Road, NW
Atlanta, GA 30327

Arthur M. Blank Family Foundation Pathways to Success Grants 312

Through its Pathways to Success initiative, the Arthur M. Blank Family Foundation seeks to expand education opportunities in ways that open new pathways to success in school and in life. The Foundation supports in-school innovations and out-of-school initiatives that provide powerful learning and mentoring experiences, encourage and guide youth to pursue rigorous post-secondary programs and offer useful information about what it takes to gain access to and persist in high-quality post-secondary education and training. Interested parties should begin by sending a concept query to the Foundation office. Applications are by invitation only.
Requirements: 501(c)3 organizations serving the residents of Atlanta, Georgia, are eligible to apply.
Restrictions: The Foundation does not make grants: directly to individuals; for scholarships; or to support houses of worship or religious activity.
Geographic Focus: Georgia
Amount of Grant: 75,000 - 2,000,000 USD
Samples: Girls Who Code, Atlanta, Georgia, $300,000 (over three years) - to grow local Atlanta programming to reach over 1400 Black and Latina girls to be competitive in the tech talent pipeline, with over 400 girls participating in a summer career program (2018); The Black Teacher Collaborative, Atlanta, Georgia, $100,000 (over two years) - to support a three-year teacher development program for 80 APS teachers that provides differentiated, racial identity-focused and culturally affirming training and development for Black teachers serving predominantly Black student populations (2018); Community Foundation of Greater Atlanta, Atlanta, Georgia, $2,050,000 (over three years) - to expand grassroots and grass-tops community organizations, educational advocacy, and stakeholder engagement efforts throughout the city to expand and support high-quality school leadership pipelines for Atlanta (2018).

Contact: John Bare, Senior Vice President for Programs; (404) 367-2100; jbare@ambfo.com
Internet: blankfoundation.org/initiative/pathways-to-success/#tab2
Sponsor: Arthur M. Blank Family Foundation
3223 Howell Mill Road, NW
Atlanta, GA 30327

Arthur M. Blank Family Foundation Pipeline Project Grants 313

The Arthur M. Blank Family Foundation's Pipeline Project seeks to increase the number of low-income, preK-12 students in Atlanta, Fulton County and DeKalb County demonstrating demand for and proficiency in STEAM subjects. The Pipeline Project believes in learning by doing and seeks to use experiential, hands-on programs to draw more students into the pipeline. In pursuit of the long-term goal of more students earning post-secondary certification and degrees in STEAM (science, technology, engineering, art, and mathematics) fields, The Pipeline Project will invest in innovations that disrupt the status quo for under-served preK-12 students. The Project is especially interested in emerging programs that succeed in reaching youth who would otherwise have little meaningful access to hands-on STEAM programs. It is through these classrooms, after-school and summer experiences that The Pipeline Project seeks to build both the supply of and the demand for STEAM programs among low-income youth and their families. By fostering peer learning and exchange through the collection of Pipeline Project partner organizations, AMBFF seeks to build a network of practitioners with influence sufficient enough to shift the direction of policy and the allocation of resources toward students who are not served by the current system. For after-school and summer programs, the Project will consider requests for three types of support: grants; equipment; and human capital. Prior to applying, interested parties should submit an online questionnaire, which are due by September 15, October 15, November 11, and December 1. If invited to apply, final submissions are due by September 29, October 29, December 1, and December 11.
Requirements: The Pipeline Project seeks proposals from nonprofit organizations, community groups and classroom teachers delivering hands-on STEAM programming to preK-12 youth attending public schools in Atlanta, Fulton County, and DeKalb County who would not otherwise be served. Organizations must primarily serve low income children and those underrepresented in STEAM fields.
Restrictions: The Foundation does not make grants: directly to individuals; for scholarships; or to support houses of worship or religious activity.
Geographic Focus: Georgia
Date(s) Application is Due: Sep 29; Oct 29; Dec 1; Dec 11
Samples: Power My Learning Greater Atlanta Region, Atlanta, Georgia, $233,000 - to pilot the Coca-Cola Company High School Young Entrepreneurs program at Washington High School and support the expansion of Power My Learning into Metro Atlanta middle schools; Mount Vernon Institute for Innovation, Atlanta, Georgia, $13,200 - to host a two-day event to cultivate the emerging Atlanta STEAM network and provide design thinking training to Pipeline Projects grantees in order to improve their program service delivery; Netcentric Campaigns, Washington, D.C., $50,000 - to design and launch a networking campaign that brings together nonprofit executives, educators, funders and influencers in order to accelerate opportunity in the STEAM education sector.
Contact: Ayana Gabriel, Senior Program Officer; (404) 367-2100; agabriel@ambfo.com
Internet: blankfoundation.org/initiative/pathways-to-success/#tab3
Sponsor: Arthur M. Blank Family Foundation
3223 Howell Mill Road, NW
Atlanta, GA 30327

Arts Council of Greater Lansing Young Creatives Grants 314

The Young Creatives Grant was established to support and increase access to arts education for under-served youth ages 5-17. Funded by the Arts Council of Greater Lansing through its Arts Advancement Endowment Fund and the Michigan State University Federal Credit Union, this program provides grants of up to $1,500 to selected organizations to provide scholarships for children with financial need to attend classes and programs or funds to support free arts/cultural programming with an educational focus targeting under-served youth. The annual deadline for application submission is August 1. Decisions will be announced by December 1.
Requirements: Applicants may only apply for funds in one of the two provided categories, not both. Applicant organization must: be located in the greater Lansing area, with a majority of the organization's programming dedicated to arts and cultural projects (first priority will be given to arts and culture organizations with arts and culture as a sole mission); be a Michigan public or private not-for-profit corporation as evidenced by an Internal Revenue Service 501(c)3 letter of determination or a copy of the Articles of Incorporation as filed with the State of Michigan, Department of Commerce; have a legal address and physically operate within the tri-county region (Ingham, Eaton, or Clinton counties); and be current members in good standing of the Arts Council of Greater Lansing.
Geographic Focus: Michigan
Date(s) Application is Due: Aug 1
Amount of Grant: Up to 1,500 USD
Samples: All of the Above Hip Hop Academy, Lansing, Michigan, $1,500 - to present scholarships to students (2019); Lansing Art Gallery and Education Center, Lansing, Michigan, $1,500 - to fund Spring Break and Summer Art Camps (2019).
Contact: Taylor Haslett, Executive Director; (517) 372-4636; fax (517) 484-2564; Taylor@lansingarts.org or info@lansingarts.org
Internet: www.lansingarts.org/programs/grants
Sponsor: Arts Council of Greater Lansing
1208 Turner Street
Lansing, MI 48906

ASCAP Foundation Grants 315

The ASCAP Foundation is dedicated to nurturing the music talent of tomorrow, preserving the legacy of the past and sustaining the creative incentive for today's creators through a variety of educational, professional, and humanitarian programs and activities which serve the entire music community. Grants are awarded to eligible nonprofit organizations engaged in educational programs for aspiring songwriters and composers. Grant awards average $3,000.
Requirements: 501(c)3 organizations engaging in music education and talent development are eligible.
Restrictions: The foundation does not consider requests for general operating support or annual giving campaigns, capital purposes, endowments, deficit operations, recordings, or performance or production funding. Grants are not awarded to purchase advertisements or donate equipment.
Geographic Focus: All States
Amount of Grant: Up to 5,000 USD
Contact: Grants Administrator; (212) 621-6219 or (212) 621-6588; fax (212) 595-3342; ascapfoundation@ascap.com or info@ascapfoundation.com
Internet: www.ascapfoundation.org/grants.aspx
Sponsor: ASCAP Foundation
1 Lincoln Plaza
New York, NY 10023

Aspen Community Foundation Grants 316

The Aspen Community Foundation awards grants to 501(c)3 nonprofits that serve the residents of Pitkin, Garfield, and west Eagle Counties of Colorado in its areas of interest, including: health and human services (particularly with respect to children and families); education programs that develop thoughtful, self-sufficient citizens who contribute to their communities; and strengthening community to promote positive community integration, inter-ethnic understanding, citizen responsibility, volunteerism, and the capacity of communities to solve problems. Types of support include technical assistance, capital grants, general operating support, continuing support, program development, seed grants, and matching funds. Organizations applying for projects that have not previously received funds from the foundation should review their proposals with the program director in advance of submission.
Requirements: The foundation supports 501(c)3 organizations that enhance the quality of life in Pitkin, Garfield, and west Eagle counties of Colorado.
Restrictions: The foundation does not consider grants for projects that have been completed or that will be held prior to the allocations decisions; deficits, retirement of debt, or endowments; religious purposes; political campaigns or organizations that publicly take political positions; medical research; organizations primarily supported by tax-derived funding; or conduit organizations. The foundation does not give priority to applications for hospital equipment; conferences; sports/recreational groups; civic, environmental, or media projects; or arts and culture groups.
Geographic Focus: Colorado
Amount of Grant: 1,000 - 100,000 USD
Contact: Tamara Tormohlen, Executive Director; (970) 925-9300; fax (970) 920-2892; info@aspencommunityfoundation.org
Internet: www.aspencommunityfoundation.org/grant-making/apply-for-a-grant-through-acfs-competitive-cycle/
Sponsor: Aspen Community Foundation
110 East Hallam Street, Suite 126
Aspen, CO 81611

Assisi Foundation of Memphis Capital Project Grants 317

The foundation supports organizations in its areas of interest, including health and human services—promote the health and well-being of the Mid-South community and help the health care system respond more effectively to community needs; education and literacy—projects/programs that build organizational capacity of provider agencies, provide professional development to service providers, promote collaboration among provider agencies, and leverage resources (local, state, and federal); social justice/ethics—projects/programs that strengthen ethical values among Mid-South citizens and promote social justice leading to a better understanding of and a more effective response to economic or social threats to the community; and cultural enrichment and the arts—projects/programs that foster an appreciation of the arts in the Greater Memphis community. Religious organizations seeking funding for religious programs also are eligible. Typical capital projects include: building - new construction, addition to existing facility, or renovation; technology - Information Management System installation/upgrade, computer hardware, audio-visual equipment/systems; and furnishings/equipment. Typically, payment of capital project grants is made when the organization begins the construction/renovation. Specific terms and schedule of payments will be based upon the scope of the project, amount of award, duration of the project, and completion of required reporting at appropriate intervals.
Requirements: The Foundation makes grants only to organizations that are classified as tax-exempt under Section 501(c)3 of the Internal Revenue Code and as public charities under Section 509(a) of that Code. The Foundation uses its resources for charitable endeavors that advance the well-being of people and institutions located in Shelby, Fayette, and Tipton Counties in Tennessee; Crittenden County, Arkansas; and Desoto County, Mississippi.
Restrictions: Grants are not made for individuals, national fundraising drives, projects that address the needs of only one congregation, tickets for benefits, political organizations or candidates for public office, lobbying activities, recurring budget deficits, or tournament fees and/or travel for athletic competitions.
Geographic Focus: Arkansas, Mississippi, Tennessee
Date(s) Application is Due: Feb 15; May 17; Aug 16; Nov 15
Contact: Jan Young, Executive Director; (901) 684-1564; jyoung@assisifoundation.org
Internet: www.assisifoundation.org/capitalproject.html
Sponsor: Assisi Foundation of Memphis
515 Erin Drive
Memphis, TN 38117

Assisi Foundation of Memphis General Grants 318

The foundation supports organizations in its areas of interest, including health and human services—promote the health and well-being of the Mid-South community and help the health care system respond more effectively to community needs; education and literacy—projects/programs that build organizational capacity of provider agencies, provide professional development to service providers, promote collaboration among provider agencies, and leverage resources (local, state, and federal); social justice/ethics—projects/programs that strengthen ethical values among Mid-South citizens and promote social justice leading to a better understanding of and a more effective response to economic or social threats to the community; and cultural enrichment and the arts—projects/programs that foster an appreciation of the arts in the Greater Memphis community. Religious organizations seeking funding for religious programs also are eligible. Deadlines are set to coordinate with quarterly meetings of the Board of Directors of the Foundation.
Requirements: The Foundation makes grants only to organizations that are classified as tax-exempt under Section 501(c)3 of the Internal Revenue Code and as public charities under Section 509(a) of that Code. The Foundation uses its resources for charitable endeavors that advance the well-being of people and institutions located in Shelby, Fayette, and Tipton Counties in Tennessee; Crittenden County, Arkansas; and Desoto County, Mississippi.
Restrictions: Grants are not made for individuals, national fundraising drives, projects that address the needs of only one congregation, tickets for benefits, political organizations or candidates for public office, lobbying activities, recurring budget deficits, or tournament fees and/or travel for athletic competitions.
Geographic Focus: Arkansas, Mississippi, Tennessee
Date(s) Application is Due: Feb 15; May 17; Aug 16; Nov 15
Amount of Grant: Up to 20,000 USD
Contact: Jan Young, Executive Director; (901) 684-1564; jyoung@assisifoundation.org
Internet: www.assisifoundation.org/generalgrants.html
Sponsor: Assisi Foundation of Memphis
515 Erin Drive
Memphis, TN 38117

Assisi Foundation of Memphis Mini Grants 319

A limited number of Mini-Grants are considered annually for consulting services, training, and other items that meet specific criteria. For these grants, the benefit to the organization or to the community served should be clearly identified and easily evaluated. The proposal should increase management efficiency, program capacity or quality of services provided by the organization. All requests must be clearly related to the organization's current long-range plan or be part of an effort to develop such a plan. Projects that require continued funding or ongoing maintenance and support should have future sources of this support documented.
Requirements: The Foundation makes Mini Grants only to organizations that are classified as tax-exempt under Section 501(c)3 of the Internal Revenue Code and as public charities under Section 509(a) of that Code. The Foundation uses its resources for charitable endeavors that advance the well-being of people and institutions located in Shelby, Fayette, and Tipton Counties in Tennessee; Crittenden County, Arkansas; and Desoto County, Mississippi. Organizations should provide some matching commitment to the project through either cash or the dedication of other resources.
Restrictions: Grants are not made for individuals, national fundraising drives, projects that address the needs of only one congregation, tickets for benefits, political organizations or candidates for public office, lobbying activities, recurring budget deficits, or tournament fees and/or travel for athletic competitions. Normal overhead expenses and staff salaries are not considered as matching resources. Purchase or replacement of equipment for administrative purposes, that is part of the normal requirements for the operation of the organization and not related to the organization's long-range plan, will not be considered.
Geographic Focus: Alabama, Mississippi, Tennessee
Date(s) Application is Due: Feb 15; May 17; Aug 16; Nov 15
Amount of Grant: Up to 1,500 USD
Contact: Jan Young, Executive Director; (901) 684-1564; jyoung@assisifoundation.org
Internet: www.assisifoundation.org/minigrants.html
Sponsor: Assisi Foundation of Memphis
515 Erin Drive
Memphis, TN 38117

AT&T Foundation Community Support and Safety 320

The AT&T Foundation is pivotal in enriching and strengthening the diverse communities it serves. The Foundation supports nonprofit organizations and programs that foster inclusion and create opportunities for diverse populations. Through its Civic and Community program, approximately $29 million annually is contributed to support programs that enhance education by integrating new technologies and increasing learning opportunities, improve economic development through technology and local initiatives, provide vital assistance to key community-based organizations, support cultural institutions that make a community unique, and advance the goals and meet the needs of diverse populations. Within AT&T's service region, the Foundation consistently reaches ethnic and racial minority groups with its grant-making at levels surpassing these groups' proportion of in-region population. In addition, AT&T is committed to supporting underserved populations including women, seniors, youth, people with disabilities and low-income families. Interested parties should begin by forwarding a letter of inquiry to the Foundation office, outlining the proposed program or project in a brief one- to two-page letter.
Requirements: The Foundation makes grants to 501(c)3 tax-exempt, nonprofit organizations nationally, with emphasis on California, District of Columbia, Florida, Minnesota, and Texas.
Restrictions: No support is offered for: religious organizations not of direct benefit to the entire community; for political, discriminatory, or disease-specific organizations; medical clinics; or research. No grants are given: directly to individuals (except for employee-related disaster grants). Funding is not available for: capital campaigns; endowment funds; goodwill

ads; ticket or dinner purchases; sports programs or events; cause-related marketing; or product donations.

Geographic Focus: All States

Contact: Nicole Anderson, President; (210) 821-4105; foundation@att.com

Internet: about.att.com/content/csr/home/frequently-requested-info/social.html

Sponsor: AT&T Foundation

208 S. Akard Street, Suite 100

Dallas, TX 75202

AT&T Foundation Education Grants 321

AT&T Foundation Aspire program is a $100 million initiative to address high school success and college and workforce readiness. This program is AT&T's most significant education initiative to date, and one of the largest corporate commitments ever to address student curriculum outcomes and workforce preparation. The program includes four key components: high school retention and preparing students for college and/or the workforce; job shadowing for more than 100,000 students; commissioning the next chapter of major research on the high school dropout issue and solutions by directly engaging educational practitioners; and underwriting 100 community dropout-prevention summits. Interested parties should begin by forwarding a letter of inquiry to the Foundation office, outlining the proposed program or project in a brief one- to two-page letter.

Requirements: Qualifying applicants include: school districts and school district foundations; charter school foundations and private school foundations; and nonprofit organizations that work on-site with public and private education institutions or that work with public and private education institutions on a project basis and have 501(c)3 public charity status.

Restrictions: No support is offered for: religious organizations not of direct benefit to the entire community; for political, discriminatory, or disease-specific organizations; medical clinics; or research. No grants are given: directly to individuals (except for employee-related disaster grants). Funding is not available for: capital campaigns; endowment funds; goodwill ads; ticket or dinner purchases; sports programs or events; cause-related marketing; or product donations.

Geographic Focus: All States

Contact: Nicole Anderson, President; (210) 821-4105; foundation@att.com

Internet: about.att.com/csr/home/society/education.html

Sponsor: AT&T Foundation

208 S. Akard Street, Suite 100

Dallas, TX 75202

AT&T Foundation Health and Human Services Grants 322

The AT&T Foundation is pivotal in enriching and strengthening the diverse communities it serves. The Foundation supports nonprofit organizations and programs that foster inclusion and create opportunities for diverse populations. Through its Health and Welfare program, approximately $35 million is contributed annually to support: economically challenged; health and health care access; urban families; and ethnic and racial minority groups. In addition, AT&T is committed to supporting underserved populations including women, seniors, youth, people with disabilities and low-income families. Interested parties should begin by forwarding a letter of inquiry to the Foundation office, outlining the proposed program or project in a brief one- to two-page letter.

Requirements: The Foundation makes grants to 501(c)3 tax-exempt, nonprofit organizations nationally, with emphasis on California, District of Columbia, Florida, Minnesota, and Texas.

Restrictions: No support is offered for: religious organizations not of direct benefit to the entire community; for political, discriminatory, or disease-specific organizations; medical clinics; or research. No grants are given: directly to individuals (except for employee-related disaster grants). Funding is not available for: capital campaigns; endowment funds; goodwill ads; ticket or dinner purchases; sports programs or events; cause-related marketing; or product donations.

Geographic Focus: All States

Contact: Nicole Anderson, President; (210) 821-4105; foundation@att.com

Internet: about.att.com/content/csr/home/frequently-requested-info/social.html

Sponsor: AT&T Foundation

208 S. Akard Street, Suite 100

Dallas, TX 75202

ATA Inclusive Learning Communities Grants 323

The Alberta Teachers' Association offers grants of up to $2,000 to help fund innovative projects designed to build inclusive learning communities. An inclusive learning community is defined as a community based on the principles of respect for diversity, equity and human rights. Such communities foster and support the intellectual, social, physical, emotional and spiritual development of each child. Inclusive learning communities are characterized by cooperation, caring and respect. In addition, they are committed to promoting racial harmony; gender equity; First Nations, Metis, and Inuit education; the alleviation of poverty; peace and global education; the prevention of violence; and respect for all people. Applications and other report forms are available at the ATA website, and may be sent electronically.

Requirements: Applicants must be active or associate members of the ATA. Projects must meet the following criteria: focus on education or communication and advance knowledge, develop skills and foster inclusive behavior among students, school staffs, and the community; advance the mission of public education by helping students to develop a foundation of learning; become citizens of a democratic society, and reach their full potential; reflect the principles of diversity, equity, and human rights; and be sustainable to students and/or teachers. Preference will be given to projects in which stakeholders are involved in the planning.

Restrictions: One-half of the grant will be paid when the grant application is approved. The balance of the grant is paid after the project is completed and the recipient has submitted an accounting and evaluation report explaining how well the project achieved its intended outcomes, how effective the implementation process was, and how the project might be

improved in the future. Grants will not be awarded for the purpose of sponsoring one-time events that are not linked to a broader action plan or purchasing materials (such as textbooks and capital equipment) or services that can ordinarily be obtained using school funds.

Geographic Focus: Canada

Date(s) Application is Due: Apr 30

Amount of Grant: Up to 2,000 CAD

Contact: Robert Mazzotta, Grants Contact; (780) 447-9400 or (800) 232-7208; fax (780) 455-6481; robert.mazzotta@ata.ab.ca

Internet: www.teachers.ab.ca/For%20Members/Programs%20and%20Services/Grants%20 Awards%20and%20Scholarships/Pages/Grants%20Supporting%20Inclusive%20 Learning%20Communities.aspx

Sponsor: Alberta Teachers Association

11010 142nd Street NW

Edmonton, AB T5N 2R1 Canada

ATA Local Community Relations Grants 324

The Alberta Teachers Association offers Community Relations Grants to locals undertaking activities that profile public education and show teachers as active and concerned citizens. Locals that qualify receive a base grant of $250, plus $1 per member. Examples of activities funded are available in the community relations grants booklet at the ATA website. The Association also works with the Alberta division of the Canadian Mental Health Association (CMHA) to promote mental health, discourage the negative stigma often associated with mental illness, and provide teachers with information resources to help them support students with mental health needs. Locals are encouraged to use their CR grants for activities that promote the mental health of children and youth. Such activities would double their grant so that they are eligible for up to $500, plus $2 per member, for community relations projects relating to mental health issues. Applicants should address questions and submit proposals to the contact person.

Geographic Focus: Canada

Date(s) Application is Due: Apr 1

Amount of Grant: Up to 500 CAD

Contact: Philip McRae, Executive Staff Officer; (800) 232-7208; philip.mcrae@ata.ab.ca

Internet: www.teachers.ab.ca/For%20Members/Programs%20and%20Services/Grants%20 Awards%20and%20Scholarships/Pages/Local%20Community%20Relations%20Grants.aspx

Sponsor: Alberta Teachers Association

11010 142nd Street NW

Edmonton, AB T5N 2R1 Canada

Atkinson Foundation Community Grants 325

Community grants are awarded to agencies located within San Mateo County, California, or serving residents of the county, with primary emphasis on the North County and Coastside areas. International grants are awarded to nonprofits in Latin America. The goals of the program are to provide opportunities for people to reach their highest potential and to improve the quality of their lives; and to foster the efforts of individuals and families to become socially, economically, and physically self-sufficient. Program priorities are to support nonprofit agencies that serve children, youth, and families; the elderly and the ill; immigrants; the disadvantaged, needy, and homeless; the mentally and physically disabled; and those suffering from drug, alcohol, or physical abuse. Priority also will be given to programs that provide basic human social, physical, and economic services; secondary, vocational, and higher education; adult literacy and basic skills; planning and health education; respite and child care; rehabilitation and job training; counseling; and community enrichment, including environmental conservation. Types of support include general operating support, continuing support, program development, seed grants, scholarship funds, and technical assistance. It is suggested that organizations contact the Foundation by phone prior to submission of an online grant request to ascertain whether or not the request is within current guidelines.

Requirements: International grants are awarded to organizations working in the Caribbean, Central America, and Mexico; domestic grants are awarded in San Mateo County, CA. 501(c)3 tax-exempt organizations are eligible but those serving residents of San Mateo County, California, are given preference.

Restrictions: The fund does not make grants to organizations without proof of tax-exempt status; grants to organizations chartered outside the United States; grants, scholarships, or loans to individuals; grants designed to influence legislation; grants for doctoral study or research; grants for travel to conferences or events; grants for media presentations; donations to annual campaigns or special fund-raising events; sponsorship of sports groups; or grants to national or statewide umbrella organizations.

Geographic Focus: California, Antigua & Barbuda, Bahamas, Barbados, Belize, Costa Rica, Cuba, Dominica, Dominican Republic, El Salvador, Grenada, Guatemala, Haiti, Honduras, Jamaica, Mexico, Nicaragua

Date(s) Application is Due: Feb 1; May 1; Aug 1; Nov 1

Amount of Grant: 5,000 - 15,000 USD

Contact: Stacey Angeles, Grants Manager; (415) 561-6540, ext. 245; sangeles@pfs-llc.net

Internet: www.atkinsonfdn.org/

Sponsor: Atkinson Foundation

1660 Bush Street, Suite 300

San Francisco, CA 94109

Atlanta Foundation Grants 326

The Atlanta Foundation was created by a resolution adopted on February 1, 1921, by the Board of Directors of the Fourth National Bank of Atlanta under which the bank was named as sole Trustee. The purpose of the Foundation is to assist charitable and educational institutions located in Fulton County or DeKalb County, Georgia that promote education or scientific research; advance care for the sick, aged, or helpless; improve living conditions;

provide recreation for all classes; and such other charitable purposes as will improve the mental, moral, and physical life of the inhabitants of Fulton and DeKalb counties regardless of race, color, or creed. The foundation's board meets in April and October. The foundation assists with funding of program grants and operating projects. Requests must be received by March 1 or September 1 to be considered.
Requirements: Nonprofit 501(c)3 organizations in Georgia's DeKalb and Fulton Counties may apply for grant support.
Restrictions: Grants are not awarded to individuals or for scholarships, fellowships, or loans.
Geographic Focus: Georgia
Date(s) Application is Due: Mar 1; Sep 1
Amount of Grant: 2,500 - 50,000 USD
Contact: Mike Donnelly, Trustee; (888) 234-1999; grantadministration@wellsfargo.com
Internet: www.wellsfargo.com/private-foundations/atlanta-foundation
Sponsor: Atlanta Foundation
3414 Peachtree Road, 5th Floor, MC GA8023
Atlanta, GA 30326

Atlanta Women's Foundation Pathway to Success Grants   327

The Atlanta Women's Foundation awards grants to southern nonprofits to encourage projects that empower women and girls. The Foundation supports efforts to promote economic justice, end all forms of violence, and develop alternatives to homelessness and other effects of poverty. Types of support include start-up and operating costs, conferences, fund-raising efforts that show a significant return, films, and small equipment. Specifically, the Pathway to Success program has the primary goals of: job creation; reduction in poverty; and eliminating barriers to employment for women in metro Atlanta. Under the Women's Pathway to Success Program, ten nonprofit organizations will receive grants of $30,000 for the first year and then $50,000 annually for four-years to provide the critical combination of services needed to move women to economic self-sufficiency. This combination of services includes access to workforce training and development, microenterprise development, childcare, financial literacy, and employment opportunities for women at or below 200% of the federal poverty level. The annual deadline for application submissions is May 6.
Requirements: Southern nonprofits serving one or more of the following counties: Barrow, Bartow, Butts, Carroll, Cherokee, Clayton, Cobb, Cowetta, DeKalb, Douglas, Fayette, Forsyth, Fulton, Gwinnett, Hall, Henry, Newton, Paulding, Pickens, Rockdale, Spalding, and/or Walton are eligible.
Restrictions: Grants are not awarded for endowments, debt reduction, religious groups, building funds, or large equipment (e.g., vehicles).
Geographic Focus: Georgia
Date(s) Application is Due: May 6
Amount of Grant: 5,000 - 25,000 USD
Contact: DiShonda Hughes, Mission Director; (404) 577-5000, ext. 104; fax (404) 589-0000; dhughes@atlantawomen.org or info@atlantawomen.org
Internet: atlantawomen.org/what-we-do/grants/womens-pathway-to-success-program/
Sponsor: Atlanta Women's Foundation
50 Hurt Plaza, Suite 401
Atlanta, GA 30303

Atlanta Women's Foundation Sue Wieland Embracing Possibility Award   328

In 2006, Sue Wieland and her husband John made a $1 million gift to the Atlanta Women's Foundation. That generosity continues to be honored with the annual Sue Wieland Embracing Possibility Award. The award is a special grant of $10,000 given annually to a grantee partner organizations. The selected organization demonstrates outstanding ability to make significant change in the lives of women and girls through their ongoing work and by using an example of one individual that the organization sees as a shining example of their program.
Geographic Focus: Georgia
Amount of Grant: 10,000 USD
Contact: DiShonda Hughes, Mission Director; (404) 577-5000, ext. 104; fax (404) 589-0000; dhughes@atlantawomen.org
Internet: atlantawomen.org/what-we-do/grants/sue-wieland-embracing-possibility-award/
Sponsor: Atlanta Women's Foundation
50 Hurt Plaza, Suite 401
Atlanta, GA 30303

Atlas Insurance Agency Foundation Grants   329

The Atlas Insurance Agency Foundation is a Hawaii Domestic Non-Profit Corporation filed on July 9, 2002. The Foundation is a family-centered, full-service insurance agent dedicated to strengthening families and fostering the healthy development of children. The Foundatiion works with those most in need throughout the State of Hawaii – meeting them where they are, connecting them with the resources they need, and helping them envision and plan a future in which they can live successfully in the community. There are no specified deadlines or application formats, and interested organizations should contact the office before beginning the application process.
Requirements: Any 501(c)3 in Hawaii that is aligned with the Atlas Insurance interest areas is eligible to apply.
Geographic Focus: Hawaii
Amount of Grant: Up to 100,000 USD
Contact: Colbert M. Matsumoto, Agent; (808) 533-8787
Internet: atlasinsurance.com/
Sponsor: Atlas Insurance Agency Foundation
820 Mililani Street, Suite 300
Honolulu, HI 96813

Atwood Foundation General Grants   330

The Atwood Foundation was established for the benefit of the people of Anchorage, Alaska and vicinity, particularly the young people, through assisting financially in the initiation, completion and maintenance of non-profit organizations of the fine arts, journalism, history and other civic enterprises.
Requirements: The Atwood Foundation awards grants to non-profit 501(c)3 organizations serving Anchorage residents and visitors. Their areas of focus are the arts, journalism, history, the military community and related activities that engage families and educate youth. They also support post secondary journalism education at the University of Alaska, Anchorage and scholarships at Alaska Pacific University. In order to apply, the following is required on an application: a brief history of organization; services provided; description of beneficiaries; purpose of the grant request; description of how the funds will be used. If grant is for a specific project, then describe further: description of project; identify need for the project; current status of the project; total timeline for implementation. Before applying for the first time, please call and consult with Atwood Foundation at least two weeks before the deadline.
Geographic Focus: Alaska
Date(s) Application is Due: Feb 14; May 15; Aug 14
Amount of Grant: Up to 150,000 USD
Samples: Alaska Aviation Museum, Anchorage, Alaska, $13,000 - support of Capital Equipment programs (2020).
Contact: Ira Perman, Executive Director; (907) 274-4900; atwoodfoundation@gmail.com
Internet: atwoodfoundation.org/grants.html
Sponsor: Atwood Foundation
301 W. Northern Lights. Boulevard, Suite 440
Anchorage, AK 99503

Aunt Kate Foundation Grants   331

The Aunt Kate Foundation was founded in the State of Missouri in 1989, with a primary geographic focus of Maryland and Missouri. The Foundation's major fields of interest include: Christianity; domestic violence shelters; elementary and secondary education; human services; Presbyterianism; Protestantism; supportive housing; and youth development. Typically, awards are given in the form of general operating support. Most recently, these awards have ranged from $500 to $3,000. A formal application is required, though there are no specified annual deadlines for submission. Interested organizations should begin by contacting the Foundation directly.
Requirements: Any 501(c)3 organization serving the residents of either Maryland or Missouri are welcome to apply.
Geographic Focus: Maryland, Missouri
Amount of Grant: 500 - 3,000 USD
Samples: Holt Internation, Eugene, Oregon, $1,000 - for charitable actions (2018); Moberly's Women Connection, Moberly, Oregon, $1,000 - for public charity (2018); Moberly Public School Foundation, Moberly, Oregon, $2,000 - for general support (2018).
Contact: Elizabeth C. Fleming, President; (704) 367-0935
Sponsor: Aunt Kate Foundation
338 South Sharon Amity Road, P.O. Box 318
Charlotte, NC 28211-2806

Austin Community Foundation Grants   332

The Austin Community Foundation has a competitive grants cycle in which grant requests from organizations in Austin and surrounding areas are reviewed and may receive funding from the Foundation's unrestricted fund or from donor-advised funds. The Foundation grants funds for projects and programs that address community needs in the areas of: arts and culture; education and training; community development and community service; environment; health; human services; recreation, and animal-related services. Foundation encourages grant requests for projects or programs that: are likely to have a substantial impact on the quality of life of a significant number of people in the community; propose practical ways to address community issues and problems; leverage other sources of support (i.e., funds or volunteers); stimulate others to participate in addressing community problems; are innovative, a new initiative, or an enhancement of a program; assist non-profit organizations to maximize effective management; are cooperative efforts and minimize or eliminate duplication of services; and are sustainable over time. The Foundation accepts grant requests submitted through its online application process.
Requirements: Texas 501(c)3 and 170(b)(1)a(vi) tax-exempt organizations located in the central Texas area, including Travis County, are eligible.
Restrictions: Faxed requests will not be accepted. In general, the Foundation does not grant funds for: unrestricted general operating expenses; the use of and payment for services of a fiscal agent; endowment funds; religious organizations for religious purposes; fund raising activities or events (i.e., annual fund drives, telephone solicitations, benefit tickets); umbrella funding organizations that intend to distribute funds at their own discretion; political lobbying or legislative activities; or individuals.
Geographic Focus: Texas
Contact: Meagan Anderson Longley, Director of Grants and Scholarships; (512) 220-1412 or (512) 472-4483; fax (512) 472-4486; mlongley@austincf.org
Internet: www.austincommunityfoundation.org/?nd=grants_intro
Sponsor: Austin Community Foundation
4315 Guadalupe, Suite 300, P.O. Box 5159
Austin, TX 78763

Austin S. Nelson Foundation Grants   333

The primary purpose of the Austin S. Nelson Foundation is to support charitable interests throughout Alberta, Canada. Its major interest areas include: medical research; religious organizations and agencies, community services, and human services. In the area of medicine, it will provide funding for pediatrics, palliative care, cancer research, cerebral

palsy, heart disease, diabetes, lung disease, kidney disorders, leukemia, multiple sclerosis, Alzheimer disease, and severe burns. It also supports Christian organizations and Anglican churches. Other areas of giving includes support for organizations that help the blind, physically disabled children, animal welfare, emergency shelters, crisis intervention services, the poor, alcohol and drug abuse, young offenders, crime prevention, mental health, domestic violence victims, abused children, and sexual assault victims. Though there are no specified annual deadlines, grant decisions are made primarily in November. Interested applicants should contact the Foundation by mail.
Geographic Focus: Canada
Contact: Director
Sponsor: Austin S. Nelson Foundation
4825 89th Street
Edmonton, AB T6E5L3 Canada

Autauga Area Community Foundation Grants   **334**
The Autauga Area Community Foundation (AACF) is a public foundation which links charitable resources with community needs and opportunities. Each year, the Foundation awards grants to nonprofits offering projects and programs in Autauga County that, in the opinion of AACF's Advisory Committee, will improve the quality of life in the community. While many factors are considered, priority is given to proposals that meet the following criteria: programs that address issues affecting Autauga County; seed grants to initiate promising new projects addressing underlying causes of community problems; expanding programs representing innovative and efficient approaches to serving community needs and opportunities; programs that maximize resources and leverage other monies; projects reflecting the cooperative efforts of multiple agencies within the community; and programs that can demonstrate funding plans for the continuation of the project beyond initial funding by the AACF. The maximum grant award is $2500, with the average grant ranging from $500 to $1000. Applications will be accepted online.
Requirements: Nonprofits located in, or serving the residents of, Autauga County are eligible.
Restrictions: Grants are not awarded to: individuals, fundraising events, or capital campaigns.
Geographic Focus: Alabama
Date(s) Application is Due: Mar 8
Amount of Grant: Up to 2,500 USD
Contact: Caroline Montgomery Clark, Vice President, Community Services; (334) 264-6223; fax (334) 263-6225; cacfgrants@bellsouth.net
Internet: www.cacfinfo.org/aacf/grants.html
Sponsor: Autauga Area Community Foundation
434 N. McDonough Street
Montgomery, AL 36104

Autism Speaks Norma and Malcolm Baker Recreation Grants   **335**
Autism Speaks is dedicated to promoting solutions, across the spectrum and throughout the life span, for the needs of individuals with autism and their families. Norma and Malcolm Baker Recreation Program funding supports recreational programs demonstrating the ability to reach a wide age range of individuals on the spectrum and have true, measurable impact on the lives of those who participate and their loved ones. Program must also demonstrate the ability to grow and replicate best practices with other partners in their community, state, or region within the following categories of service delivery: Adult Services – recreation/respite specifically for adults focusing on life, health and community; Employment – finding and maintaining meaningful employment with skills to succeed in the workplace; Physical Fitness and Sports – athletics and team sports, health and wellness programs; Summer Camps – day/overnight programs offering therapeutic activities, sports, arts and technology; or Swimming and Water Safety – swimming and water safety specifically for individuals with autism.
Requirements: All service providers are eligible to apply.
Geographic Focus: All States, District of Columbia
Date(s) Application is Due: Mar 5
Contact: Serena Selkin, sselkin@autismspeaks.org
Internet: www.autismspeaks.org/autism-grants-service-providers
Sponsor: Autism Speaks
1 East 33rd Street, 4th Floor
New York, NY 10016

Avery-Fuller-Welch Children's Foundation Grants   **336**
The Avery-Fuller-Welch Children's Foundation (formerly the Avery-Fuller Children's Center) was originally established in 1914 with bequests from the estates of Mary A. Avery and her brother, Orlando P. Fuller. At that time, the Children's Center operated a facility in San Francisco providing aid to handicapped children. The foundation was renamed to honor Whiting Welch for his many years of dedicated service as President of the Foundation. Today, giving focuses on early intervention and professional guidance to children with physical, behavioral, emotional, and learning challenges. Primary fields of interest, therefore, include: adult day care; child welfare; family services; health and health care; human services; and mental health care. Annual application deadlines are February 22, May 15, August 15, and November 15. All applications should be submitted by the service provider on behalf of a single child and all grants are paid directly to said provider.
Requirements: Grants are limited to services provided to residents of the following Bay Area counties: Alameda, Contra Costa, Marin, San Francisco, and San Mateo, all in California.
Restrictions: Grants are not made for groups of children, preliminary evaluations, orthodontia, eye glasses, or routine eye care. Grants are not made for annual appeals, capital requests, sectarian religious purposes, for conferences and events, or to cover deficits.
Geographic Focus: California
Date(s) Application is Due: Feb 12; May 14; Aug 13; Nov 12
Amount of Grant: Up to 20,000 USD

Samples: Fransisco Rocco, San Francisco, California, $31,200 - support for occupational and physical therapy program (2019); Literacy and Language Center, San Francisco, California, $8,200 - remedial education services (2019); Boys and Girls Clubs, San Francisco, California, $20,504 - support for psychotherapy services (2019).
Contact: Amy Freeman; (415) 561-6540, ext. 224; fax (415) 561-5477; afreeman@pfs-llc.net Derek Aspacher, Executive Director; (415) 561-6540 or 415.561.6540 ext. 249; fax (415) 561-5477; daspacher@pfs-llc.net
Internet: www.afwchildrensfoundation.org/for-grantseekers/application-procedures/
Sponsor: Avery-Fuller-Welch Children's Foundation
1660 Bush Street, Suite 300
San Francisco, CA 94109-5308

Avery Dennison Foundation Education Grants   **337**
The vision of the Avery Dennison Foundation is to inspire human promise toward a more intelligent and sustainable world. This vision drives the Avery Dennison Foundation mission to advance the causes of education and sustainability in the communities where Avery Dennison employees live and work. In cooperation with organizations that receive grants, the Foundation also encourages corporate employees to engage in local community investment opportunities and, through volunteer work, bring the same spirit of invention and innovation found at the heart of our company's success. Grantmaking in education provides funding for educational improvements to elementary, secondary, post-secondary and/or vocational schools; and focuses on STEM (science, technology, engineering and mathematics) or graphic and visual arts educational efforts. These grants direct services to populations who are traditionally underserved because of gender, socioeconomic status or geography.
Restrictions: Grants do not support: organizations that discriminate against a person or a group on the basis of age, political affiliation, race, national origin, ethnicity, gender, disability, sexual orientation or religious belief; individuals (scholarships, stipends, fellowships, travel grants, etc); for-profit organizations or ventures; government agencies; sponsorships (sports teams, fundraising initiatives); religious groups for religious purposes; or political organizations, candidates, ballot measure or other political activities; and institutional endowments.
Geographic Focus: All States, Brazil, China, India
Amount of Grant: Up to 1,300 USD
Contact: Alicia Procello Maddox, President; (626) 304-2000; fax (626) 304-2192
Internet: www.averydennison.com/en/home/about-us/averydennisonfoundation.html
Sponsor: Avery Dennison Foundation
150 N Orange Grove Boulevard
Pasadena, CA 91103

Avery Family Trust Grants   **338**
The Avery Family Trust was established in Tulsa, Oklahoma, in 1999, with the expressed purpose of supporting a variety of programs, including: arts and culture; domesticated animals; music; opera; orchestras; performing arts; children and youth; and elementary and secondary performing arts education. Typically, funds are provided for general operating support, performing arts presentations and productions, and program development. Most recent funding awards have ranged from $2,500 to as much as $300,000. There are no specified application deadlines, and interested organizations should submit a letter of application which includes: a detailed description of the project; the amount of funding requested; and a copy of IRS Determination Letter.
Requirements: Any 501(c)3 organization supporting the residents of Tulsa, Oklahoma, is eligible to apply.
Geographic Focus: Oklahoma
Amount of Grant: 2,500 - 300,000 USD
Samples: Animal Rescue Foundation, Tulsa, Oklahoma, $2,000 - for its annual fund (2018); Chamber Music Tulsa, Tulsa, Oklahoma, $2,000 - for its annual fund (2018); Meals on Wheels, Tulsa, Oklahoma, $2,000 - for its annual fund (2018).
Contact: Etta May Avery, Trustee; (918) 742-7191 or (918) 493-2002
Sponsor: Avery Family Trust
1259 E. 26th Street
Tulsa, OK 74114-2603

Avery Foundation Grants   **339**
The Avery Foundation was established in Philadelphia, Pennsylvania, in 1991, with the expressed purpose of providing support for the arts, education, health organizations and medical research, and human services. With that in mind, the Foundation's primary fields of interest include: arts and culture; diseases; elementary and secondary education; higher education; hospital care; and human services. Typically, funding is provided for general operating support, program development, research, and evaluation of research. Most recent awards have ranged from $10,000 to $20,000. There are no specified annual deadlines for submission, so interested organizations should forward a letter describing the program in need and the amount requested.
Requirements: Any 501(c)3 organization or educational institution serving the residents of Philadelphia are eligible to apply.
Geographic Focus: Pennsylvania
Amount of Grant: 10,000 - 20,000 USD
Samples: Drexel University, Philadelphia, Pennsylvania, $20,000 - general operating support (2019); Franklin Institute, Philadelphia, Pennsylvania, $15,000 - general operating support (2019); Kimmel Center, Philadelphia, Pennsylvania, $10,304 - general operating support (2019).
Contact: William J. Avery, Trustee; (215) 855-8591 or (215) 855-4336
Sponsor: Avery Foundation
417 Gwynedd Valley Road
Gwynedd Valley, PA 19437-0136

Avista Foundation Education Grants 340

The Avista Foundation focuses its giving on grants that strengthen communities and enhance the quality of lives of the people served by Avista Utilities or the Alaska Light and Power Company. One area of emphasis is in K-12 education, particularly in the fields of science, math and technology, as well as higher education (including scholarships). Key examples of support include: providing college scholarships for engineering, IS and the crafts to address utility's future workforce gap; increasing the pipeline of kids seeking engineering and technical careers by enhancing interest in math, science and technology; and providing opportunities for under-served kids to seek a college education. Applications should be submitted online.

Requirements: Applicants must be an IRS 501(c)3 organization serving the residents of Avista Utilities. Eligible regions include: eastern Washington; Goldendale and Stevenson, Washington; northern Idaho; southwestern Oregon; La Grande, Oregon; eastern Montana; and the city and borough of Juneau, Alaska.

Restrictions: The Foundation does not support: individuals; team or extra-curricular school events; trips or tours; religious organization; fraternal organization; memorial campaigns; national health organizations (or their local affiliates); or research/disease advocacy groups.

Geographic Focus: Alaska, California, Idaho, Montana, Oregon, Washington

Contact: Kristine Meyer, Executive Director; (509) 495-8156; kristine.meyer@avistacorp.com or contributions@avistacorp.com

Internet: www.avistafoundation.com/home/pages/default.aspx

Sponsor: Avista Foundation

P.O. Box 3727

Spokane, WA 99220-3727

Avista Foundation Vulnerable and Limited Income Population Grants 341

The Avista Foundation focuses its giving on grants that strengthen communities and enhance the quality of lives of the people served by Avista Utilities or the Alaska Light and Power Company. One area of emphasis is support for vulnerable and limited income populations, with the Foundation providing assistance to those on limited incomes and support for initiatives to reduce poverty. Key examples include: easing the burden of energy prices to customers most in need; providing an enhanced level of support to senior and more vulnerable customers; providing energy conservation education to senior, vulnerable and limited income customers; and supporting community-wide safety net services for basic needs costs.

Requirements: Aside from individuals, applicants should be an IRS 501(c)3 organization serving the residents of Avista Utilities. Eligible regions include: eastern Washington; Goldendale and Stevenson, Washington; northern Idaho; southwestern Oregon; La Grande, Oregon; eastern Montana; and the city and borough of Juneau, Alaska.

Restrictions: The Foundation does not support: individuals; team or extra-curricular school events; trips or tours; religious organization; fraternal organization; memorial campaigns; national health organizations (or their local affiliates); or research/disease advocacy groups.

Geographic Focus: Alaska, California, Idaho, Montana, Oregon, Washington

Contact: Kristine Meyer, Executive Director; (509) 495-8156; kristine.meyer@avistacorp.com or contributions@avistacorp.com

Internet: www.avistafoundation.com/home/pages/default.aspx

Sponsor: Avista Foundation

P.O. Box 3727

Spokane, WA 99220-3727

B.F. and Rose H. Perkins Foundation Community Grants 342

In 1882, B.F. Perkins came to Sheridan, Wyoming, from Philadelphia in a covered wagon. He homesteaded south of town in 1885, founded the Bank of Commerce in 1893, and became its president for twenty-six years. He was elected Mayor of Sheridan, and also invested in various real estate in the region. Since 1933, the youth of the community have benefited from his generosity. From its small beginnings in 1943 the Perkins' Trust has grown into a multi-million dollar Foundation, a ladder built by trusted and qualified people whose work and dedication has and will continue to help all eligible Sheridan County youth reach their goals. The B.F. and Rose H. Perkins Foundation welcomes qualifying graduates and residents of Sheridan County High Schools to apply for educational loans or medical expenses. The Foundation funds medical, dental care, eye glasses, and hearing aids for children and young adults from ages one to 20 that have resided in Sheridan County for minimum of one year and show a financial need based on the family's last year's tax return. The Foundation considers community type grants that fit the criteria of education and/or medical assistance for the youth of Sheridan County. The Foundation requests that all applicants complete an online application. These applications are also available at the Foundation Office.

Requirements: To be eligible for educational loans the student must be a Sheridan County High School graduate under the age of 21, with one year minimum residency and a minimum 2.5 grade point average. The student's financial need is based on supporting documents, the family's last tax return.

Geographic Focus: Wyoming

Contact: Bobbi Neeson, Foundation Manager; (307) 674-8871; fax (307) 674-8803

Internet: www.perkinsfoundation.org/medical-program.html

Sponsor: B.F. and Rose H. Perkins Foundation

45 East Loucks, Suite 110, P.O. Box 1064

Sheridan, WY 82801

Babcock Charitable Trust Grants 343

The Babcock Charitable Trust was established in Pennsylvania in 1957, by way of a donation from Fred C. and Mary A. Babcock. The Trust's primary purpose has always been to support both education and health care throughout the states of Pennsylvania and Florida, although they occasionally give outside of this primary region. With that in mind, the Trust's specified fields of interest include: children and youth services; education; health care programs; higher education; and religion. Application forms are not required, and there are no specific deadlines. Applicants should provide, in written form, a brief overview or history of their organization, a mission statement, a detailed description of the project proposed, and an amount of funding requested. The amount of funding ranges up to $25,000.

Geographic Focus: Florida, Maryland, Massachusetts, New York, Pennsylvania, Wisconsin

Amount of Grant: Up to 25,000 USD

Samples: Allegheny Parks Foundation, Pittsburgh, Pennsylvania, $10,000 - general operating funds; Ellen and Richard Cuda Family Foundation, E. Orleans, Massachusetts, $25,000 - general operating funds; Grove City College, Grove City, Pennsylvania, $20,000 - general operating funds.

Contact: Courtney B. Borntraeger, Treasurer; (412) 351-3515

Sponsor: Babcock Charitable Trust

1105 N. Market Street, Suite 1300

Wilmington, DE 19801

Back Home Again Foundation Grants 344

Based in Indianapolis, Indiana, the Back Home Again Foundation offers funding in the areas of: animal welfare; the arts; children's services and programs; food services; health organizations; higher education; human services; museums; performing arts; and recreational programming. Since there are no specific application forms or deadlines with which to adhere, applicants should contact the office directly with a description of their program or project, and a detailed budget. Grants range from $1,500 to $30,000.

Geographic Focus: Indiana

Amount of Grant: 1,500 - 30,000 USD

Samples: Dance Kaleidoscope, Indianapolis, Indiana, $30,000 - general operating costs.

Contact: Randolph H. Deer, Secretary; (317) 844-2886

Sponsor: Back Home Again Foundation

5846 West 73rd Street

Indianapolis, IN 46268

Bainum Family Foundation Grants 345

Stewart and Jane Bainum founded what is now the Bainum Family Foundation in 1968. It was first known as The College Foundation and later as the Commonweal Foundation. Today, the Bainum Family Foundation continues to combine proven expertise with a passion for helping the whole child by going beyond academics to help them thrive. The Foundation awards grants to eligible nonprofit organizations serving disadvantaged youth in the area comprising the corridor between Baltimore, MD, and Washington, D.C. It also offers some assistance to elementary education, educational research, and some health care causes. Programs include Partners in Learning (address low literacy skills of economically disadvantaged children), community assistance grants (i.e., after-school tutoring, parenting classes, and shelters for the homeless or abused women), and learning disabilities support program (special education services to economically disadvantaged children). Contact the office for application procedures.

Requirements: 501(c)3 tax-exempt organizations serving disadvantaged youth in the corridor between Baltimore, Maryland, and Washington, D.C., are eligible to apply.

Geographic Focus: District of Columbia, Maryland, Virginia

Amount of Grant: Up to 25,000 USD

Contact: Shantelice White, Director of Grants Management; (240) 450-0000; fax (240) 450-4115

Internet: bainumfdn.org/what-we-do/

Sponsor: Bainum Family Foundation

7735 Old Georgetown Road, #1000

Bethesda, MD 20814

Ball Brothers Foundation Organizational Effectiveness/Executive Mentoring Grants 346

Ball Brothers Foundation, in collaboration with the Indiana Youth Institute, is pleased to announce funding for up to two grants per year to youth-serving organizations who wish to re-energize their organization in the areas of strategic planning, evaluation and/or assessment, marketing, board training, fundraising, technology planning, and volunteer recruitment and retention. In addition each organization may apply for up to one year of assistance from an experienced executive mentor working with an organization's executive director or key staff member. In each instance, the organization will be offered up to 120 hours of Professional Nonprofit Coaching and/or 120 hours of Executive Mentoring.

Requirements: The requests are limited to nonprofit youth serving organizations in 6 counties in East Central Indiana, including: Delaware, Madison, Henry, Randolph, Jay and Blackford counties. There must be a: demonstrated need for the service and a willingness to have the request assessed by representatives to determine the focus of the consultation, coaching, and mentoring; and commitment to follow through, including timely responses to requests for information from assigned coaches, with a final product that is produced and the coaching process as the result of the service provided.

Restrictions: The Foundation will not support: direct assistance to individuals or scholarships; applications coming from outside of Indiana; booster organizations; on-going salary requests of staff personnel to support an organization; services that the community-at-large should normally underwrite (i.e. roads, bus transportation, etc.0; capital building projects; research projects (except for philanthropic studies); or unsolicited proposals (all requests must begin with a preliminary proposal).

Geographic Focus: Indiana

Date(s) Application is Due: May 1

Contact: Donna Munchel, Executive Assistant; (765) 741-5500; fax (765) 741-5518; donna.munchel@ballfdn.org or info@ballfdn.org

Internet: www.ballfdn.org/index/applying-for-grant/types-of-grants.asp

Sponsor: Ball Brothers Foundation

222 South Mulberry Street

Muncie, IN 47305

Baltimore Community Foundation Building Stronger Neighborhoods Regionwide Grants 347

The Baltimore Community Foundation seeks to advance the ideals of a welcoming environment, open access and civic engagement - with all of its privileges and responsibilities - in every area of community life. BCF believes in a strengthened network of neighborhoods where people choose to live due to the high quality of life and welcoming environment they offer. BCF focuses its investments in supporting informed citizen action, which is at the core of neighborhood revitalization. Neighborhood grants focus on: mobilization projects that will get more neighbors involved in the community; leadership projects that build new leaders or improve existing leadership for the neighborhood; and youth leadership projects targeted at addressing issues in the community that impact Baltimore youth. Mobilization grants range from $1,000 to $5,000; leadership grants are up to a maximum of $5,000 (with a 25% match required); and youth leadership awards range from $5,000 to $10,000. The applications are open on a rolling-basis.
Requirements: Eligibility varies by grant type. Generally, funding is for resident-led projects and community-based organizations that include resident leadership and that address a community need. Groups in Baltimore City and Baltimore County may apply. Applicants for Leadership Grants must have 501(c)3 nonprofit status. Applicants for Youth Leadership and Mobilization grants may apply with a nonprofit fiscal agent if they do not have 501(c)3 status.
Restrictions: The foundation does not usually make grants for annual fund campaigns; operating support, except for start-up; religious or sectarian purposes; campaigns for capital to which the foundation can contribute no more than a small fraction of the total need; or individuals.
Geographic Focus: Maryland
Amount of Grant: Up to 10,000 USD
Contact: Maya Smith, Program Officer; (410) 332-4172, ext. 142 or (410) 332-4171; fax (410) 837-4701; msmith@bcf.org or neighborhoodgrantsprogram@bcf.org
Internet: bcf.org/for-grantseekers/grants/
Sponsor: Baltimore Community Foundation
11 East Mount Royal Avenue, 2nd Floor
Baltimore, MD 21202

Baltimore Community Foundation Children's Fresh Air Society Fund Grants 348

The mission of the Children's Fresh Air Society Fund is to provide disadvantaged and disabled Metropolitan Baltimore children the benefits of a summer camp experience. Grants are made in the form of camperships; that is, scholarships equal to the amount of normal camp fees and tuition. The next application deadline is February 1st, and applicants can apply for a maximum of $5,000.
Requirements: Organizations (or their fiscal agents) serving the Baltimore area that qualify as public charities under section 501(c)3 of the Internal Revenue Code. Charitable organizations that operate a day or residential camp program are eligible to apply for a grant.
Restrictions: Grants from the Fund are not intended to provide core operating support.
Geographic Focus: Maryland
Date(s) Application is Due: Feb 1
Amount of Grant: Up to 5,000 USD
Contact: Maya Smith, Grants Administrator; (410) 332-4172, ext. 142 or (410) 332-4171; fax (410) 837-4701; msmith@bcf.org
Internet: bcf.org/for-grantseekers/grants/childrens-fresh-air-society-fund/
Sponsor: Baltimore Community Foundation
11 East Mount Royal Avenue, 2nd Floor
Baltimore, MD 21202

Baltimore Community Foundation Mitzvah Fund for Good Deeds Grants 349

The Mitzvah Fund for Good Deeds, established at the Baltimore Community Foundation in 2012, is designed to provide mini-grants to nonprofit organizations to facilitate their good works in neighborhoods and schools when funding from other sources is not available. The purposes to which Mitzvah Fund monies may be applied are broadly defined. Examples might include: $250 to a recreation center to purchase bats, balls, and bases for a summer softball league; $500 to a senior center to purchase art supplies for activities for an adult daycare program; or $1,000 to an elementary school to purchase musical instruments for an after-school music program. Typically, awards range from $250 to $2,500. Proposals are accepted on a rolling basis.
Requirements: Organization must: have 501(c)3 nonprofit status or a fiscal agent; serve the Baltimore area; not discriminate on the basis of race, creed, national origin, color, physical handicap, gender or sexual orientation; have a total budget less than $250,000; apply for a project whose budget is no more than $10,000.
Restrictions: The Mitzvah Fund does not make grants for: start-up organizations; capital campaigns, building construction, renovations or other capital projects; individuals; multiple years; institution of higher education; or projects that do not serve the Baltimore community.
Geographic Focus: Maryland
Amount of Grant: 250 - 2,500 USD
Contact: Maya Smith, Program Officer; (410) 332-4172, ext. 142 or (410) 332-4171; fax (410) 837-4701; msmith@bcf.org or grants@bcf.org
Internet: bcf.org/for-grantseekers/grants/mitzvah-fund-for-good-deeds/
Sponsor: Baltimore Community Foundation
11 East Mount Royal Avenue, 2nd Floor
Baltimore, MD 21202

Baltimore Ravens Corporate Giving 350

The Baltimore Ravens Corporate Giving program offers charitable contribution support of team memorabilia to nonprofit organizations directly, and provides player, staff, and coach appearances. The grant maker has identified the following areas of interest: the Community Quarterback Award program, which salutes Maryland volunteers who exhibit exceptional leadership, dedication and commitment to bettering their local communities;

the Champions Athlete of the Week, a program that recognizes the athletic achievements of Baltimore area youth and promotes local high school athletics; and the Ravens High School Coach of the Week program, which honors a Baltimore-area high school football coach who makes a significant impact on his or her athletes. Applications are limited to one request per organization during any given year. Although there is a rolling deadline, applicants are urged to submit requests a minimum of six weeks prior to any event.
Requirements: Support is given primarily to 501(c)3 organizations established in areas of company operations in Maryland.
Geographic Focus: Maryland
Amount of Grant: Up to 10,000 USD
Contact: Heather Darney; (410) 701-4000; heather.darney@ravens.nfl.net
Internet: www.baltimoreravens.com/community/programs
Sponsor: Baltimore Ravens Corporate Giving
1 Winning Drive
Owings Mills, MD 21117-4776

Baltimore Ravens Foundation Play 60 Grants 351

The Baltimore Ravens Foundation is committed to improving, encouraging and enabling the healthy development of youth in the Baltimore area, as well as other parts of the State of Maryland. To that end, the Foundation is executing the Ravens Play 60 Grant, which provides funding of up to $5,000 to qualifying nonprofit organizations that create and/or continue programs or projects promoting physical fitness and nutrition education. The grant program continues the Foundation's commitment to increasing physical activity among area youth and seeks to encourage healthy youth activities. Applications will be accepted from April 1 through June 15th each year, with decisions made by the end of June and awards announced by July 22nd.
Requirements: The Baltimore Ravens Foundation will consider funding requests that meet the following criteria: organizations that submit requests must be a 501(c)3 organization; programs or projects must be directed at youth (5 to 18 years of age) and must promote physical fitness and/or nutrition education; nonprofits must illustrate a programming component with measurable goals in order to be considered; programs or projects must take place in Maryland; and all applications must be submitted via hard copy mail. Application contact will be notified via email once the application has been received.
Restrictions: Through the Ravens Play 60 Grant, the Foundation will not consider funding for the construction of buildings/fields/etc.
Geographic Focus: Maryland
Date(s) Application is Due: Jun 15
Amount of Grant: Up to 5,000 USD
Contact: Heather Darney, Foundation Director; (410) 701-4000; heather.darney@ravens.nfl.net
Internet: www.baltimoreravens.com/news/community/ravens-foundation.html
Sponsor: Baltimore Ravens Foundation
1 Winning Drive
Owings Mills, MD 21117-4776

Baltimore Ravens Foundation Scholarships 352

The Baltimore Ravens Foundation established the Scholarship program to enable local youth to continue their education on a collegiate level. The team has a long-standing history of service to local communities, and this fund supports those who do the same. In addition, this renewable scholarship will be based on financial need and academic achievement. Five $5,000 scholarship will be given to high school seniors who attend Baltimore City, Baltimore County, or Carroll County public high schools. Applications are accepted each year through the March 1st deadline.
Requirements: Applications will be accepted from high school seniors who attend Baltimore City, Baltimore County, or Carroll County public high schools. Applicants must also be U.S. citizens or permanent residents. Applicants must have a cumulative GPA of 3.0 or higher.
Geographic Focus: Maryland
Date(s) Application is Due: Mar 1
Amount of Grant: 5,000 USD
Contact: Heather Darney, Foundation Director; (410) 701-4000; heather.darney@ravens.nfl.net
Internet: www.baltimoreravens.com/news/community/ravens-foundation.html
Sponsor: Baltimore Ravens Foundation
1 Winning Drive
Owings Mills, MD 21117-4776

Baltimore Ravens Foundation Youth Football Grants 353

The Baltimore Ravens Foundation Youth Football Grant program provides apparel grants to qualifying nonprofit youth football teams. Youth tackle football and flag football teams in Maryland are eligible to apply for an apparel grant containing over $1,000 in Under Armour jerseys, cleats or accessories. Packages include: twenty-five jerseys; twenty-five cleats; eight footballs; twenty-five mouth guards; and twenty-five receiving gloves. Online applications will be accepted each year from February 22 through March 23, with awards being announced by the end of May and apparel distribution in August.
Requirements: Baltimore area youth football programs are eligible to apply.
Geographic Focus: Maryland
Date(s) Application is Due: Mar 23
Contact: Heather Darney, Foundation Director; (410) 701-4000; heather.darney@ravens.nfl.net or RavensRISE@ravens.nfl.net
Internet: www.baltimoreravens.com/news/community/ravens-foundation.html
Sponsor: Baltimore Ravens Foundation
1 Winning Drive
Owings Mills, MD 21117-4776

Bank of America Charitable Foundation Basic Needs Grants   354
Individuals continue to struggle to provide basic necessities for their families. Bank of America Charitable Foundation Basic Human Services philanthropic support is focused on helping these individuals at their point of need, from immediate human needs such as food and shelter, to addressing financial wellness and stability issues facing low-income communities such as access to benefits and resources. Primary areas of interest include: hunger relief and food access; emergency shelter and short-term housing; and transitioning individuals and families to financial stability. The application period for this funding is May 31 through June 25.
Requirements: To be considered for support, a qualifying nonprofit organizations must: have a tax-exempt status by the Internal Revenue Service and not classified as a private foundation; and be based in and serve communities in markets listed at the web site.
Restrictions: The following categories are ineligible for funding: individuals, including those seeking scholarships or fellowship assistance; political, labor, fraternal organizations, or civic clubs; religious organizations (for example, churches and synagogues); individual pre-K through 12 schools (public or private); Pre-Sixth Form/College (London, UK); sports, athletic events, or athletic programs; travel-related events, including student trips or tours; development or production of books, films, videos, or television programs; memorial campaigns; national health organizations (or their local affiliates) or research/disease advocacy groups; and colleges and universities.
Geographic Focus: All States
Date(s) Application is Due: Jun 25
Contact: Anne M. Finucane, Foundation Chairperson/Chief Marketing Officer; (617) 434-9410 or (800) 218-9946; anne.m.finucane@bankofamerica.com
Internet: about.bankofamerica.com/en-us/global-impact/charitable-foundation-funding.html#fbid=UPRWWGl7jHn
Sponsor: Bank of America Charitable Foundation
100 North Tryon Street
Charlotte, NC 28255

Bank of America Charitable Foundation Community Development Grants   355
Housing remains a pressing issue in communities across the country. In response, the Bank of America Charitable Foundation funds programs focused on foreclosure counseling and mitigation, real-estate owned disposition and affordable housing. In conjunction, the Foundation supports financial education and coaching as well as other financial empowerment programs that help individuals become more financially capable and that lead to long-term neighborhood stability. Recognizing that large organizations, such as arts institutions and hospitals, act as economic catalysts in communities, the Foundation funds programs that help advance overall community revitalization. The current grant period for this funding is May 4 through May 29.
Requirements: To be considered for support, a qualifying nonprofit organizations must: have a tax-exempt status by the Internal Revenue Service and not classified as a private foundation; and be based in and serve communities in markets listed at the web site.
Restrictions: The following categories are ineligible for funding: individuals, including those seeking scholarships or fellowship assistance; political, labor, fraternal organizations, or civic clubs; religious organizations (for example, churches and synagogues); individual pre-K through 12 schools (public or private); Pre-Sixth Form/College (London, UK); sports, athletic events, or athletic programs; travel-related events, including student trips or tours; development or production of books, films, videos, or television programs; memorial campaigns; national health organizations (or their local affiliates) or research/disease advocacy groups; and colleges and universities.
Geographic Focus: All States
Date(s) Application is Due: May 29
Contact: Anne M. Finucane, Foundation Chairperson/Chief Marketing Officer; (617) 434-9410 or (800) 218-9946; anne.m.finucane@bankofamerica.com
Internet: about.bankofamerica.com/en-us/global-impact/charitable-foundation-funding.html#fbid=et98gPSg-6s/hashlink=housing
Sponsor: Bank of America Charitable Foundation
100 North Tryon Street
Charlotte, NC 28255

Bank of America Charitable Foundation Matching Gifts   356
The Bank of America Charitable Foundation Matching Gifts program encourages employee giving by offering a way to double – up to $5,000 per person each calendar year – employees' cash or securities contributions to their favorite charitable organizations and thus improve their communities. Annually, the Bank of America Charitable Foundation provides more than $25 million in matching gifts on behalf of employee donations.
Requirements: Charitable organizations in the United States must be tax-exempt under section 501(c)3 of the Internal Revenue Code and not be classified as a private foundation. Charitable Organizations located in England or Wales must be registered with the Charity Commission. Charitable organizations outside of the United States, England or Wales must be qualified as eligible for donations from CAFAmerica.
Restrictions: The Bank of America Charitable Foundation does not: match charitable gifts to private, family or donor advised funds, or gifts to political or fraternal organizations; or match charitable gifts that benefit students directly or that result in an employee receiving a benefit, including tuition or sponsorships.
Geographic Focus: All States, American Samoa, District of Columbia, Guam, Marshall Islands, Northern Mariana Islands, Puerto Rico, U.S. Virgin Islands, Canada, United Kingdom
Date(s) Application is Due: Mar 31
Amount of Grant: Up to 5,000 USD
Contact: Anne M. Finucane, Foundation Chairperson/Chief Marketing Officer; (617) 434-9410 or (800) 218-9946; anne.m.finucane@bankofamerica.com

Internet: about.bankofamerica.com/en-us/global-impact/matching-gifts-features-and-eligibility.html#fbid=wq9wE7VdEpC
Sponsor: Bank of America Charitable Foundation
100 North Tryon Street
Charlotte, NC 28255

Bank of America Charitable Foundation Student Leaders Grants   357
The Bank of America is committed to supporting the development of the next generation of neighborhood leaders by investing in and cultivating future leaders. Successful applicants will attend an eight week paid summer internship program with select community organizations for Student Leaders, so they can experience first-hand how they can help shape their communities now and in the future. To maximize the experience, Student Leaders will participate in a leadership program with local Bank of America executives. Applications for our Neighborhood Excellence Student Leaders awards are accepted beginning January 1 through February 20.
Requirements: Applicants must be: a citizen or a legal permanent resident of the United States; a junior or senior in high school; a student in good standing at his/her school located in one of the participating markets; able to commit to an 8-week (35-hours per week) internship with a nonprofit organization (to be determined) in the summer; able to participate in a series of leadership and community service activities with local Bank of America executives. Participating markets are listed online. Application is made online.
Restrictions: Bank of America associates or members of their immediate family are not eligible for nomination.
Geographic Focus: All States
Date(s) Application is Due: Feb 23
Contact: Anne M. Finucane, Foundation Chairperson/Chief Marketing Officer; (617) 434-9410 or (800) 218-9946; anne.m.finucane@bankofamerica.com
Internet: about.bankofamerica.com/en-us/what-guides-us/student-leaders.html#fbid=et98gPSg-6s
Sponsor: Bank of America Charitable Foundation
100 North Tryon Street
Charlotte, NC 28255

Bank of America Charitable Foundation Volunteer Grants   358
Bank of America employees volunteer thousands of hours globally in our neighborhoods each year. In fact, more than 3,000 charitable organizations benefit from the Foundation's employees' dedication each year. To honor those who give their time and service to causes important to them, the Bank of America Charitable Foundation awards grants, which are up to $500 per employee for each calendar year and are made in the name of the employee, to eligible charitable organizations. An unrestricted grant is made to any eligible nonprofit organization for which an employee or retiree has committed substantial volunteer hours within a calendar year. For 50 hours of volunteer time within a calendar year, Bank of America Charitable Foundation will give a $250 grant; for 100 hours of volunteer time within a calendar year, the grant is $500. Employee hour registration must be completed by January 31 after the year in which the hours were volunteered. Organizations must verify hours by May 15 after the year in which the hours were volunteered.
Requirements: Charitable organizations in the United States must be tax-exempt under section 501(c)3 of the Internal Revenue Code and not be classified as a private foundation. Charitable Organizations located in England or Wales must be registered with the Charity Commission. Charitable organizations outside of the United States, England or Wales must be qualified as eligible for donations from CAFAmerica. Employees must complete an application and have the recipient organization verify the hours.
Geographic Focus: All States, American Samoa, District of Columbia, Guam, Marshall Islands, Northern Mariana Islands, Puerto Rico, U.S. Virgin Islands, Canada, United Kingdom
Date(s) Application is Due: Jan 31
Amount of Grant: 250 - 500 USD
Contact: Anne M. Finucane, Foundation Chairperson/Chief Marketing Officer; (617) 434-9410 or (800) 218-9946; anne.m.finucane@bankofamerica.com
Internet: about.bankofamerica.com/en-us/global-impact/volunteer-grants-features-and-eligibility.html#fbid=2SvmqQPvBb7
Sponsor: Bank of America Charitable Foundation
100 North Tryon Street
Charlotte, NC 28255

Bank of America Corporation Sponsorships   359
Through its regional U.S. sponsorships, the Bank of America Corporation supports the economic, social and cultural life of the places where its customers live and work. The Corporation provide an extensive program of arts and sports sponsorships to help maintain vibrant, healthy communities. This includes underwriting art exhibitions, events and performances that require private funding to make them a reality. Its regional sports sponsorship investments include the Bank of America Chicago Marathon, Major League Baseball, and Bank of America 500.
Requirements: To be considered for support, a qualifying nonprofit organizations must: have a tax-exempt status by the Internal Revenue Service and not classified as a private foundation; and be based in and serve communities in markets listed at the web site.
Restrictions: The following categories are ineligible for funding: individuals, including those seeking scholarships or fellowship assistance; political, labor, fraternal organizations, or civic clubs; religious organizations (for example, churches and synagogues); individual pre-K through 12 schools (public or private); Pre-Sixth Form/College (London, UK); sports, athletic events, or athletic programs; travel-related events, including student trips or tours; development or production of books, films, videos, or television programs; memorial campaigns; national health organizations (or their local affiliates) or research/disease advocacy groups; and colleges and universities.
Geographic Focus: All States

Contact: Anne M. Finucane, Chairperson/Chief Marketing Officer; (617) 434-9410 or (800) 218-9946; anne.m.finucane@bankofamerica.com
Internet: about.bankofamerica.com/en-us/global-impact/find-grants-sponsorships.html?cm_mmc=EBZ-CorpRep-_-vanity-_-EE01LT0021_Vanity_foundation-_-Enterprise#fbid=p61CUWomU3z
Sponsor: Bank of America Corporation
100 North Tryon Street
Charlotte, NC 28255

Bank of Hawaii Foundation Grants 360

The Bank of Hawaii Foundation has a steadfast commitment to strengthening communities in the areas it serves. The Foundation focuses on programs and projects which provide significant impact within low and moderate income communities. In addition to financial support, the Foundation partners with community organizations, providing technical assistance and advisory services to non-profit organizations, mobilizing employee volunteers, and collaborating with business partners to leverage resources and investments. The Foundation's primary interests generally fall within the following categories: community development, including financial literacy, asset building, and economic development; education, with an emphasis on financial literacy and increasing disadvantaged children's access to high-quality educational opportunities; human services, with an emphasis on addressing basic needs such as food, shelter, health, and clothing; arts and culture, with an emphasis on programs that integrate the arts into children's education or increase children's access to major arts partners; and Foundation-initiated special projects. This focus includes partnering with community development organizations whose programs are designed to strengthen low and moderate income communities, which might include: community development non-profits with a focus on affordable housing, economic development, revitalization of low- and moderate-income areas, and community development services; community development corporations and community development financial institutions; and public policy advocacy groups that broadly impact low- and moderate-income communities. The Foundation board meets four times annually. Proposals must be completed by the 15th of January, April, July, and October.
Requirements: To qualify for support, an organization must be a tax-exempt public charity, as determined by Internal Revenue Code Section 501(c)3. The Foundation generally prefers to fund well-established organizations (i.e. generally those which have been in existence for at least ten years) with multiple and dedicated sources of revenue. The Foundation seeks partners with a record of strong fiscal management and successful grant and contract management. The Foundation may also invite certain organizations which do not fall within its focus areas to apply for grants.
Restrictions: The Foundation generally does not support general operating expenses, deficit budgets, general fundraising campaigns, religious purposes, individuals, trips and tours, and charities that redistribute funds to other charitable organizations, except in the case of recognized United Way-type organizations. Requests are limited to one per year per organization.
Geographic Focus: Hawaii
Date(s) Application is Due: Jan 15; Apr 15; Jul 15; Oct 15
Amount of Grant: Up to 25,000 USD
Samples: Cathedral of Saint Andrew, Honolulu, Hawaii, $5,000 - restoration of the Aeolian Pipe Organ; Child and Family Service, Ewa Beach, Hawaii, $19,156 - general operating support; East Hawaii Cultural Center, Hilo, Hawaii, $6,000 - general operating support for low- to moderate-income youth and their families.
Contact: Elaine Moniz; (808) 694-4944; fax (808) 694-4006; elaine.moniz@boh.com
Carol Tom; (808) 694-4525; fax (808) 694-4006; carol.tom@boh.com
Internet: www.boh.com/philanthropy/grants/bank-of-hawaii-foundation
Sponsor: Bank of Hawaii Foundation
P.O. Box 3170, Dept. 758
Honolulu, HI 96802-3170

Bank of the Orient Community Giving 361

In 1971, Bank of the Orient opened its headquarters in the heart of San Francisco's Financial District to serve the banking needs of the Asian-American community. During the past half-decade, the Bank has continued to provide financial support and assistance to help local communities grow and prosper. Since the beginning of its establishment, Bank of the Orient's tradition has been to provide highly personalized service and demonstrate commitment to its customers. Starting from its first year of business, Bank of the Orient has actively provided staff time, encouragement, and financial assistance to a variety of community organizations. Over the years, Bank of the Orient has continued this tradition of neighborhood involvement. Its main areas of interest are: groups that assist the elderly to lead active and independent lives; organizations that serve economically underprivileged youth; and groups building affordable housing for low-income families. There is no specific application format, and interested parties should begin by contacting the customer service office on the mainland.
Geographic Focus: California, Hawaii
Contact: Customer Service Office; (415) 781-6565 or (415) 338-0831; fax (415) 398-8949; info@bankorient.com
Internet: www.bankorient.com/about-us/community/
Sponsor: Bank of the Orient
765 Bishop Street
Honolulu, HI 96813

Barrasso, Usdin, Kupperman, Freeman, and Sarver Corporate Grants 362

Barrasso, Usdin, Kupperman, Freeman, and Sarver are dedicated to giving back to the community of New Orleans, Louisiana. Through its partnerships the Corporation makes charitable contributions to educational institutions and nonprofit organizations involved with arts and culture, health care, and youth development. Primary fields of interest include: the arts; education; health care; legal services; and youth development. Types of support are employee volunteer programs, general operations funding, pro bono services, program development, and contributions to scholarship funds. There are no no specified application materials or deadlines, and interested groups should contact the corporate giving office.
Requirements: Limited to schools and 501(c)3 organizations either in, or serving, the New Orleans region.
Geographic Focus: Louisiana
Contact: Steven W. Usdin, Corporate Giving Manager; (504) 589-9700 or (504) 589-9734; fax (504) 589-9701; info@barrassousdin.com
Internet: www.barrassousdin.com/about-probono.html
Sponsor: Barrasso, Usdin, Kupperman, Freeman, and Sarver
909 Poydras Street, 24th Floor
New Orleans, LA 70112-4053

Baton Rouge Area Foundation Community Coffee Fund Grants 363

The Baton Rouge Area Foundation Community Coffee Fund is a corporate Donor Advised Fund that seeks to support innovative programs that will measurably improve the results of pre-kindergarten through twelfth grade education. Applicants can apply for competitive grants through its online system, which is also used to track applications and gather follow-up material from grantees.
Requirements: Only nonprofits that are registered as 501(c)3 organizations working in the service region of East and West Baton Rouge Parish, East and West Feliciana, Ascension, Livingston, Iberville and Pointe Coupee are eligible to apply for grants.
Geographic Focus: Louisiana
Contact: John G. Davies, President and CEO; (225) 387-6126; fax (225) 387-6153; jdavies@braf.org
John Spain, Executive Vice-President; (225) 387-6126; fax (225) 387-6153; jspain@braf.org
Internet: www.braf.org/index.cfm/page/4/n/8
Sponsor: Baton Rouge Area Foundation
402 North Fourth Street
Baton Rouge, LA 70802

Baton Rouge Area Foundation Every Kid a King Fund Grants 364

Every Kid a King Fund was established by Jim and Dana Bernhard and the Shaw Group in 2010 with the purpose of supporting non-profits in Louisiana, focusing on the Greater Baton Rouge Area, that meet the immediate needs of disadvantaged children in the areas of welfare, health, and education. The Every Kid a King Fund advisory board meets on a quarterly basis to review grant requests in the program areas of human services, healthcare, education, safety and wellness. It will provide grants that have an immediate impact on disadvantaged children. Application deadlines are January 1, April 1, July 1, and October 1. Notification of awards will be given April 1, July 1, September 1, and January 1.
Requirements: The Fund will primarily support nonprofit organizations in the greater communities of Baton Rouge, Louisiana, with future growth throughout the state of Louisiana. The organization must have a non-discriminatory policy. It must demonstrate that it manages its business wisely and that an appropriate percentage of the grant will go to programs rather than administration. Organizations eligible for funding should have values consistent with those of the original donor founders, including the following values: a top priority of everyone is to honor commitments, both personally and professionally; the workplace atmosphere is one of openness and fairness where everyone communicates directly and honestly, and is governed by the same rules; a goal of everyone is to grow, personally and professionally, and to contribute to the achievement of the organization; the importance of innovation is recognized and peak performers are rewarded; and the value of excellence in product quality, customer service and financial performance is stressed.
Geographic Focus: Louisiana
Date(s) Application is Due: Jan 1; Apr 1; Jul 1; Oct 1
Contact: John G. Davies, President and CEO; (225) 387-6126; fax (225) 387-6153; jdavies@braf.org
John Spain, Executive Vice-President; (225) 387-6126; fax (225) 387-6153; jspain@braf.org
Internet: www.braf.org/index.cfm/page/4/n/2
Sponsor: Baton Rouge Area Foundation
402 North Fourth Street
Baton Rouge, LA 70802

Baton Rouge Area Foundation Grants 365

The Baton Rouge Area Foundation seeks to enhance the quality of life for all citizens of Baton Rouge, Louisiana. The foundation concentrates on projects and programs in the areas of community development, education, environment, health and medical, and religion. Applicants should call the office to determine if their project or program is consistent with the foundation's goals before sending an application.
Requirements: Only nonprofits that are registered as 501(c)3 organizations working in the service region of East and West Baton Rouge Parish, East and West Feliciana, Ascension, Livingston, Iberville and Pointe Coupee are eligible to apply for grants.
Geographic Focus: Louisiana
Contact: John G. Davies, President and CEO; (225) 387-6126; fax (225) 387-6153; jdavies@braf.org
John Spain, Executive Vice-President; (225) 387-6126; fax (225) 387-6153; jspain@braf.org
Internet: www.braf.org/index.cfm/page/4/n/8
Sponsor: Baton Rouge Area Foundation
402 North Fourth Street
Baton Rouge, LA 70802

Batters Up USA Equipment Grants 366

Batters Up USA provides free baseball and/or softball equipment, primarily bats, balls, tee ball sets, helmets, catcher's gear, and bases to local organizations to support the start up of new programs or to assist existing programs to grow. The organization serves boys and girls recreational programs up to age 13. Batters Up USA will provide the safety-type baseballs

and softballs so that the games may be played without gloves and to minimize the risk of ball impact injuries. Equipment will be provided on an as-available basis; first come, first served. *Requirements:* A grant application form is available on the website. Grant applications may be submitted on a year round basis. Equipment quantities are based on the size of the program and are subject to availability. Priority is given to those programs serving a high percentage of youth in need such as inner-city and after-school programs. Batters Up has contributed to many such programs run by Parks Departments, Schools, Boys and Girls Clubs, YMCA's Police Athletic Leagues, independent local leagues, Little League, and the other organized youth baseball/softball organizations. The organization also supports the American Baseball Federation Basic after-school reading/baseball program with equipment and reading materials.
Geographic Focus: All States
Contact: Jess Heald, Executive Director; playballusa@msn.com
Internet: www.battersupusa.org/Equipment.html
Sponsor: Batters Up USA, Inc.
1014 Paseo Bufalo
Taos, NM 87571

Batts Foundation Grants 367
Established in 1988, the Batts Foundation supports organizations involved with arts and culture, K-12 and higher education, disease, and human services. Types of support include: annual campaigns, building and renovation; capital campaigns; continuing support; operating support; endowments; matching grants; program development; and scholarship funding. Grants will be awarded primarily in the western Michigan area, particularly the communities of Huron, Zeeland, and Grand Rapids. There are no application forms or deadlines with which to adhere, and applicants should begin by submitting a one page letter summarizing the project.
Requirements: Michigan nonprofit organizations are eligible.
Restrictions: Individuals are ineligible.
Geographic Focus: Michigan
Amount of Grant: 250 - 25,000 USD
Contact: Robert Batts, Director; (616) 956-3053; jsand@battsgroup.com
Sponsor: Batts Foundation
3855 Sparks Drive SE, Suite 222
Grand Rapids, MI 49546-2427

Baxter International Corporate Giving Grants 368
As a complement to its Foundation, the Baxter Corporation makes charitable contributions to nonprofit organizations directly. Primary fields of interest include: disaster preparedness and services; elementary and secondary education; employment services; the environment; health care and health care rights; health organizations; hemophilia; immunology; kidney diseases; mathematics; patients' rights; science; teacher training and education; and youth services. Types of support include: conferences and seminars; curriculum development; donated products; employee volunteer services; general operating support; in-kind and matching gifts; and sponsorships. Support is given primarily in areas of company operations.
Geographic Focus: All States, All Countries
Amount of Grant: Up to 500,000 USD
Contact: Department Chair; (224) 948-2000
Internet: www.sustainability.baxter.com/community-support/
Sponsor: Baxter International Corporation
1 Baxter Parkway
Deerfield, IL 60015-4625

Baxter International Foundation Grants 369
The Baxter International Foundation's grant program is focused on increasing access to healthcare worldwide. The foundation funds initiatives that improve the access, quality and cost-effectiveness of healthcare. Grants awarded most recently fulfilled local needs to increase access to dental care, mental health, and other healthcare services for children, the uninsured, veterans, and the elderly. Funding often comes in the form of salary support and general operations. Focusing on these priorities, the foundation's primary concern is on communities where Baxter has a corporate presence. In Illinois, grants are restricted to Lake, McHenry and Cook counties. The foundation also funds programs throughout the U.S., Asia, Australia, Canada, Europe, Latin America and Mexico.
Requirements: U.S. nonprofits in Lake, McHenry and Cook counties of Illinois are eligible to apply. Internationally, the following regions are eligible to apply: U.S., Asia, Australia, Canada, Europe, Latin America, and Mexico.
Restrictions: In general, The Baxter International Foundation does not make grants to: capital and endowment campaigns (includes requests for infrastructure of any kind, equipment, vehicles, etc.); disease or condition-specific organizations or programs; educational grants/continuing professional education scholarships; educational institutions, except in instances where a grant would help achieve other goals, such as increasing community-based direct health services or the skills and availability of community health-care providers, in areas where there are Baxter facilities; general operating support or maintenance of effort; hospitals; individuals, including scholarships for individuals; lobbying and political organizations; magazines, professional journals, documentary, film, video, radio or website productions; medical missions; organizations seeking travel support for individuals or groups, medical missions or conferences; organizations soliciting contributions for advertising space, tickets to dinners, benefits, social and fund-raising events, sponsorships and promotional materials; organizations with a limited constituency, such as fraternal, veterans or religious organizations; research.
Geographic Focus: All States, Illinois, All Countries
Date(s) Application is Due: Jan 21; Apr 13; Jul 13; Sep 29
Amount of Grant: Up to 100,000 USD

Samples: Access OC, Laguna Hills, California, $49,400 - to support the hiring of a case manager for a new case management program to work with referred patients in Orange County so they can reduce co-morbidities and obtain needed specialty surgeries at their outpatient surgery center; BraveHearts, Harvard, Illinois, $40,000 - to support the salary of a new Volunteer Coordinator needed for all 3 programs within the organization; Kenosha Community Health Center, Kenosha, Wisconsin, $100,000 - upport the hiring of two case managers to be located at the local non-profit agency.
Contact: Foundation Contact; (847) 948-4605; fdninfo@baxter.com
Internet: www.baxter.com/about_baxter/sustainability/international_foundation/grants_program.html
Sponsor: Baxter International Foundation
One Baxter Parkway
Deerfield, IL 60015-4633

Bay and Paul Foundations PreK-12 Transformative Learning Practices Grants 370
The Bay and Paul Foundations' overall mission is to foster and accelerate initiatives that prepare agents of change working to strengthen our social compact and develop authentic solutions to the challenges of this pivotal century. In the broad and inclusive domain of PreK-12 Transformative Learning Practices the Foundations support initiatives that prepare students and educators working together to build transformative learning environments that contribute to strengthening civil society. These grants increasingly feature the visible elevation and authorization of youth voice and agency. The Foundations see education for sustainability and social justice as an integrative driver of school transformation, most often rooted in place-, project-, and problem-based practice and research, and utilizing systems thinking, critical friendship, and critical pedagogy. The Foundation no longer accepts unsolicited proposals; all full proposals will be by invitation only and are considered stage two of a two-part process. Applicants may submit an online funding inquiry (OFI) related to one or more of its current program areas.
Requirements: Nonprofits in Connecticut, Massachusetts, Maine, New Hampshire, New Jersey, New York, Rhode Island, and Vermont are eligible.
Restrictions: Grants do not support requests for endowments, building campaigns, building construction or maintenance, sectarian religious programs, books or studies, individual scholarships or fellowships, loans, travel, film, television or video productions, programs consisting primarily of conferences, for annual fund appeals, or to other than publicly recognized charities. First time grants for K-12 arts-in-education programs and K-12 science and math programs are currently geographically restricted to the New York City metropolitan area.
Geographic Focus: Connecticut, Maine, Massachusetts, New Hampshire, New Jersey, New York, Rhode Island, Vermont
Contact: Rebecca Adamson; (212) 663-1115; fax (800) 839-1754; info@bayandpaul.org
Internet: bayandpaulfoundations.org/areas-of-focus/prek-12-transformative-learning-practices/index.html
Sponsor: Bay and Paul Foundations
17 West 94th Street, 1st Floor
New York, NY 10025

Bay Area Community Foundation Arenac Community Fund Grants 371
The Bay Area Community Foundation offers several opportunities for grant funding for a registered 501(c)3 organization or government entity. Twice a year, the Foundation awards grants in Bay and Arenac counties through its online application process. The Arenac Community Fund will accept grant applications for projects and programs which impact Arenac County. Interested parties should begin by taking the online eligibility quiz and, if eligible, should then contact the office to discuss their idea. If the project is deemed to be a good fit, the Foundation will provide the applicant with a password for its online application portal. There are two annual deadlines for submission: the second Monday in March; and the third Monday in September.
Requirements: 501(c)3 organizations serving the Arenac County, Michigan, area are eligible to apply. Evidence of 501(c)3 status should be submitted with grant requests.
Restrictions: The Foundation will not typically make grants for the following unless designated by a donor: capital campaigns; existing obligations, debts, or liabilities; endowments; individuals; fund raising events.
Geographic Focus: Michigan
Date(s) Application is Due: Mar 9; Sep 21
Amount of Grant: Up to 5,000 USD
Contact: Joni King; (989) 893-4438; jonik@bayfoundation.org or bacfnd@bayfoundation.org
Internet: www.bayfoundation.org/index.php/nonprofits-side/grant-programs
Sponsor: Bay Area Community Foundation
1000 Adams Street, Suite 200
Bay City, MI 48708

Bay Area Community Foundation Arenac County Healthy 372
Youth/Healthy Seniors Fund Grants
The Bay Area Community Foundation offers several opportunities for grant funding for a registered 501(c)3 organization or government entity. Twice a year, the Foundation awards grants in Bay and Arenac counties through its online application process. The Arenac County Healthy Youth/Healthy Seniors Fund will accept grant applications for projects and programs that benefit the health and wellness of Arenac County residents. Interested parties should begin by taking the online eligibility quiz and, if eligible, should then contact the office to discuss their idea. If the project is deemed to be a good fit, the Foundation will provide the applicant with a password for its online application portal. There are two annual deadlines for submission: the second Monday in March; and the third Monday in September.
Requirements: 501(c)3 organizations serving the Bay County, Michigan, area are eligible to apply. Evidence of 501(c)3 status should be submitted with grant requests.
Restrictions: The Foundation will not typically make grants for the following unless designated by a donor: capital campaigns; existing obligations, debts, or liabilities; endowments; individuals; fund raising events.
Geographic Focus: Michigan

Date(s) Application is Due: Mar 9; Sep 21
Amount of Grant: Up to 5,000 USD
Contact: Joni King; (989) 893-4438; jonik@bayfoundation.org or bacfnd@bayfoundation.org
Internet: www.bayfoundation.org/index.php/nonprofits-side/grant-programs
Sponsor: Bay Area Community Foundation
1000 Adams Street, Suite 200
Bay City, MI 48708

Bay Area Community Foundation Auburn Area Chamber of Commerce   373
    Enrichment Fund Grants
The Bay Area Community Foundation offers several opportunities for grant funding for a registered 501(c)3 organization or government entity. Twice a year, the Foundation awards grants in Bay and Arenac counties through its online application process. The Auburn Area Chamber of Commerce Enrichment Fund is to support and enhance Western Bay County through culture and the arts, civic improvement and beautification, health and human services, education/social enrichment, recreation and the environment, and other aspects which lend to improving the quality of life in the community. Interested parties should begin by taking the online eligibility quiz and, if eligible, should then contact the office to discuss their idea. If the project is deemed to be a good fit, the Foundation will provide the applicant with a password for its online application portal. There are two annual deadlines for submission: the second Monday in March; and the third Monday in September.
Requirements: 501(c)3 organizations serving the Bay County, Michigan, area are eligible to apply. Evidence of 501(c)3 status should be submitted with grant requests.
Restrictions: The Foundation will not typically make grants for the following unless designated by a donor: capital campaigns; existing obligations, debts, or liabilities; endowments; individuals; fund raising events.
Geographic Focus: Michigan
Date(s) Application is Due: Mar 9; Sep 21
Amount of Grant: Up to 5,000 USD
Contact: Joni King; (989) 893-4438; jonik@bayfoundation.org or bacfnd@bayfoundation.org
Internet: www.bayfoundation.org/index.php/nonprofits-side/grant-programs
Sponsor: Bay Area Community Foundation
1000 Adams Street, Suite 200
Bay City, MI 48708

Bay Area Community Foundation Bay County Healthy   374
    Youth/Healthy Seniors Fund Grants
The Bay Area Community Foundation offers several opportunities for grant funding for a registered 501(c)3 organization or government entity. Twice a year, the Foundation awards grants in Bay and Arenac counties through its online application process. The Bay County Healthy Youth/Healthy Seniors Fund supports projects and programs that benefit the health and wellness of Bay County residents. Interested parties should begin by taking the online eligibility quiz and, if eligible, should then contact the office to discuss their idea. If the project is deemed to be a good fit, the Foundation will provide the applicant with a password for its online application portal. There are two annual deadlines for submission: the second Monday in March; and the third Monday in September.
Requirements: 501(c)3 organizations serving the Bay County, Michigan, area are eligible to apply. Evidence of 501(c)3 status should be submitted with grant requests.
Restrictions: The Foundation will not typically make grants for the following unless designated by a donor: capital campaigns; existing obligations, debts, or liabilities; endowments; individuals; fund raising events.
Geographic Focus: Michigan
Date(s) Application is Due: Mar 9; Sep 21
Amount of Grant: Up to 5,000 USD
Contact: Joni King; (989) 893-4438; jonik@bayfoundation.org or bacfnd@bayfoundation.org
Internet: www.bayfoundation.org/index.php/nonprofits-side/grant-programs
Sponsor: Bay Area Community Foundation
1000 Adams Street, Suite 200
Bay City, MI 48708

Bay Area Community Foundation Civic League Endowment Fund Grants   375
The Bay Area Community Foundation offers several opportunities for grant funding for a registered 501(c)3 organization or government entity. Twice a year, the Foundation awards grants in Bay and Arenac counties through its online application process. The Civic League Endowment Fund supports Bay County programs that provide services to women, children, and families. Interested parties should begin by taking the online eligibility quiz and, if eligible, should then contact the office to discuss their idea. If the project is deemed to be a good fit, the Foundation will provide the applicant with a password for its online application portal. There are two annual deadlines for submission: the second Monday in March; and the third Monday in September. Applications for this program are only available during the first grant cycle of the year.
Requirements: 501(c)3 organizations serving the Bay County, Michigan, area are eligible to apply. Evidence of 501(c)3 status should be submitted with grant requests.
Restrictions: The Foundation will not typically make grants for the following unless designated by a donor: capital campaigns; existing obligations, debts, or liabilities; endowments; individuals; fund raising events.
Geographic Focus: Michigan
Date(s) Application is Due: Mar 9
Amount of Grant: Up to 5,000 USD
Contact: Joni King; (989) 893-4438; jonik@bayfoundation.org or bacfnd@bayfoundation.org
Internet: www.bayfoundation.org/index.php/nonprofits-side/grant-programs
Sponsor: Bay Area Community Foundation
1000 Adams Street, Suite 200
Bay City, MI 48708

Bay Area Community Foundation Community Initiative Fund Grants   376
The Bay Area Community Foundation offers several opportunities for grant funding for a registered 501(c)3 organization or government entity. Twice a year, the Foundation awards grants in Bay and Arenac counties through its online application process. The Community Initiative Fund supports projects and programs which benefit Bay County. Examples of past grant areas include, but are not limited to: arts and culture, education, environment, recreation, human services, and health and wellness. Interested parties should begin by taking the online eligibility quiz and, if eligible, should then contact the office to discuss their idea. If the project is deemed to be a good fit, the Foundation will provide the applicant with a password for its online application portal. There are two annual deadlines for submission: the second Monday in March; and the third Monday in September.
Requirements: 501(c)3 organizations serving the Bay County, Michigan, area are eligible to apply. Evidence of 501(c)3 status should be submitted with grant requests.
Restrictions: The Foundation will not typically make grants for the following unless designated by a donor: capital campaigns; existing obligations, debts, or liabilities; endowments; individuals; fund raising events.
Geographic Focus: Michigan
Date(s) Application is Due: Mar 9; Sep 21
Amount of Grant: Up to 5,000 USD
Contact: Joni King; (989) 893-4438; jonik@bayfoundation.org or bacfnd@bayfoundation.org
Internet: www.bayfoundation.org/index.php/nonprofits-side/grant-programs
Sponsor: Bay Area Community Foundation
1000 Adams Street, Suite 200
Bay City, MI 48708

Bay Area Community Foundation Dow CommunityGives   377
    Youth Service Program Grants
The Bay Area Community Foundation offers several opportunities for grant funding for a registered 501(c)3 organization or government entity. Thanks to funding from Dow, the Bay Area Community Foundation is able to offer $1,000 grants to youth groups in Bay and Arenac counties. Applicants should drop off, email, or fax a short application that will indicate the volunteer activity and how the applicant will use the grant money.
Requirements: Eligible groups are ages K-12 associated with a school, government entity, or 501(c)3 organization. To earn the grant, the group leader must fill out a short application and, if approved, lead the group in a volunteer activity in the community.
Restrictions: The Foundation will not typically make grants for the following unless designated by a donor: capital campaigns; existing obligations, debts, or liabilities; endowments; individuals; fund raising events.
Geographic Focus: Michigan
Amount of Grant: 1,000 USD
Contact: Joni King; (989) 893-4438; jonik@bayfoundation.org or bacfnd@bayfoundation.org
Kirsten Hellebuyck, Program Officer; (989) 893-4438; kirstenh@bayfoundation.org or bacfnd@bayfoundation.org
Internet: www.bayfoundation.org/index.php/nonprofits-side/grant-programs#dowcommunitygives
Sponsor: Bay Area Community Foundation
1000 Adams Street, Suite 200
Bay City, MI 48708

Bay Area Community Foundation Elizabeth Husband Fund Grants   378
The Bay Area Community Foundation offers several opportunities for grant funding for a registered 501(c)3 organization or government entity. Twice a year, the Foundation awards grants in Bay and Arenac counties through its online application process. The Elizabeth Husband Fund supports Bay County programs that provide holiday season activities. Examples of such activities are, but not limited to: food baskets, clothing, and children's toys. Interested parties should begin by taking the online eligibility quiz and, if eligible, should then contact the office to discuss their idea. If the project is deemed to be a good fit, the Foundation will provide the applicant with a password for its online application portal. Though the Foundation has two annual deadlines for grant application submission (the second Monday in March and the third Monday in September), applications for this particular fund are only available during the second grant cycle of the year.
Requirements: 501(c)3 organizations serving the Bay County, Michigan, area are eligible to apply. Evidence of 501(c)3 status should be submitted with grant requests.
Restrictions: The Foundation will not typically make grants for the following unless designated by a donor: capital campaigns; existing obligations, debts, or liabilities; endowments; individuals; fund raising events.
Geographic Focus: Michigan
Date(s) Application is Due: Sep 21
Amount of Grant: Up to 5,000 USD
Contact: Joni King; (989) 893-4438; jonik@bayfoundation.org or bacfnd@bayfoundation.org
Internet: www.bayfoundation.org/index.php/nonprofits-side/grant-programs
Sponsor: Bay Area Community Foundation
1000 Adams Street, Suite 200
Bay City, MI 48708

Bay Area Community Foundation Human Services Fund Grants   379
The Bay Area Community Foundation offers several opportunities for grant funding for a registered 501(c)3 organization or government entity. Twice a year, the Foundation awards grants in Bay and Arenac counties through its online application process. The Human Services Fund supports programs in Bay County that assist and/or empower individuals and families to prevent, alleviate, or better cope with crisis, change, or stress. Priority will be given to organizations working to meet the basic needs of area children and infants. Interested parties should begin by taking the online eligibility quiz and, if eligible, should then contact the office to discuss their idea. If the project is deemed to be a good fit, the

Foundation will provide the applicant with a password for its online application portal. The Foundation has two annual deadlines for grant application submission: the second Monday in March; and the third Monday in September.
Requirements: 501(c)3 organizations serving the Bay County, Michigan, area are eligible to apply. Evidence of 501(c)3 status should be submitted with grant requests.
Restrictions: The Foundation will not typically make grants for the following unless designated by a donor: capital campaigns; existing obligations, debts, or liabilities; endowments; individuals; fund raising events.
Geographic Focus: Michigan
Date(s) Application is Due: Mar 9; Sep 21
Amount of Grant: Up to 5,000 USD
Contact: Joni King; (989) 893-4438; jonik@bayfoundation.org or bacfnd@bayfoundation.org
Internet: www.bayfoundation.org/index.php/nonprofits-side/grant-programs
Sponsor: Bay Area Community Foundation
1000 Adams Street, Suite 200
Bay City, MI 48708

Bay Area Community Foundation Leslie L. Squires Foundation Grants 380
The Bay Area Community Foundation offers several opportunities for grant funding for a registered 501(c)3 organization or government entity. Twice a year, the Foundation awards grants in Bay and Arenac counties through its online application process. The Leslie L. Squires Foundation supports projects that specifically benefit children or adults with cognitive or physical disabilities in Bay County. Interested parties should begin by taking the online eligibility quiz and, if eligible, should then contact the office to discuss their idea. If the project is deemed to be a good fit, the Foundation will provide the applicant with a password for its online application portal. There are two annual deadlines for submission: the second Monday in March; and the third Monday in September.
Requirements: 501(c)3 organizations serving the Bay County, Michigan, area are eligible to apply. Evidence of 501(c)3 status should be submitted with grant requests.
Restrictions: The Foundation will not typically make grants for the following unless designated by a donor: capital campaigns; existing obligations, debts, or liabilities; endowments; individuals; fund raising events.
Geographic Focus: Michigan
Date(s) Application is Due: Mar 9; Sep 21
Amount of Grant: Up to 5,000 USD
Contact: Joni King; (989) 893-4438; jonik@bayfoundation.org or bacfnd@bayfoundation.org
Internet: www.bayfoundation.org/page19627.cfm
Sponsor: Bay Area Community Foundation
1000 Adams Street, Suite 200
Bay City, MI 48708

Bay Area Community Foundation Nathalie Awrey Memorial Fund Grants 381
The Bay Area Community Foundation offers several opportunities for grant funding for a registered 501(c)3 organization or government entity. Twice a year, the Foundation awards grants in Bay and Arenac counties through its online application process. The Nathalie Awrey Memorial Fund supports projects and programs that benefit physically challenged children under the age of 18 who are residents of Bay County. Grants are awarded to programs to support physically challenged children with movement, vision, hearing, or health issues that have created barriers in fully participating in society. Interested parties should begin by taking the online eligibility quiz and, if eligible, then contact the office to discuss their idea. If the project is deemed to be a good fit, the Foundation will provide the applicant with a password for its online application portal. The Foundation has two annual deadlines for grant application submission: the second Monday in March; and the third Monday in September.
Requirements: 501(c)3 organizations serving the Bay County, Michigan, area are eligible to apply. Evidence of 501(c)3 status should be submitted with grant requests.
Restrictions: The Foundation will not typically make grants for the following unless designated by a donor: capital campaigns; existing obligations, debts, or liabilities; endowments; individuals; fund raising events.
Geographic Focus: Michigan
Date(s) Application is Due: Mar 9; Sep 21
Amount of Grant: Up to 5,000 USD
Contact: Joni King; (989) 893-4438; jonik@bayfoundation.org or bacfnd@bayfoundation.org
Internet: www.bayfoundation.org/index.php/nonprofits-side/grant-programs
Sponsor: Bay Area Community Foundation
1000 Adams Street, Suite 200
Bay City, MI 48708

Bay Area Community Foundation Semiannual Grants 382
The Bay Area Community Foundation offers several opportunities for grant funding for a registered 501(c)3 organization or government entity. Twice a year, the Foundation awards grants in Bay and Arenac counties through its online application process. Semiannual Grants provide funding for projects related to: arts and culture; education and youth; the environment; health and wellness; human services; recreation; and community initiatives. Interested parties should begin by taking the online eligibility quiz and, if eligible, should then contact the office to discuss their idea. If the project is deemed to be a good fit, the Foundation will provide the applicant with a password for its online application portal. There are two annual deadlines for submission: the second Monday in March; and the third Monday in September.
Requirements: 501(c)3 organizations serving the Bay County, Michigan, area are eligible to apply. Evidence of 501(c)3 status should be submitted with grant requests.
Restrictions: The Foundation will not typically make grants for the following unless designated by a donor: capital campaigns; existing obligations, debts, or liabilities; endowments; individuals; fund raising events.

Geographic Focus: Michigan
Date(s) Application is Due: Mar 9; Sep 21
Amount of Grant: Up to 5,000 USD
Contact: Joni King; (989) 893-4438; jonik@bayfoundation.org or bacfnd@bayfoundation.org
Internet: www.bayfoundation.org/index.php/nonprofits-side/grant-programs
Sponsor: Bay Area Community Foundation
1000 Adams Street, Suite 200
Bay City, MI 48708

Bayer Fund Community Development Grants 383
The Bayer Fund Community Development programs support target grades K-12, under-served students, and under-resourced communities primarily through the categories of youth development, performing arts, and public safety.
Requirements: Organizations eligible to apply for grants in this funding program include: organizations who hold a 501(c)3 tax exempt status and have been operating as such for a minimum of two years; organizations who are units of government under Section 170(c)(1), such as public schools, libraries, villages and municipalities; nonprofits that are experienced, reputable, and financially sound; organizations located within approximately 55 miles of an eligible Bayer community and the program must serve where a Bayer site is located. All applicants must be invited to apply for a grant from Bayer Fund.
Restrictions: Bayer Fund will not fund: endowments; debt retirements; political, labor and fraternal organizations; consumer or governmental lobbying or advocacy; veterans' organizations; benefits, dinners, advertisements; promotion of religious beliefs; trade or business associations; grants for individual aid or personal support; activities that directly support marketing programs; projects in which Bayer Fund or Bayer has a financial interest, or from which either one could derive a financial benefit; organizations that could purchase, dispense or prescribe Bayer products, or their affiliated foundations; organizations that do not comply with Bayer's non-discrimination policy; or infrastructure costs of organizations.
Geographic Focus: Arizona, California, Hawaii, Idaho, Illinois, Indiana, Iowa, Louisiana, Massachusetts, Michigan, Minnesota, Mississippi, Missouri, Nebraska, New Jersey, North Carolina, North Dakota, Pennsylvania, Puerto Rico, Texas, Washington
Date(s) Application is Due: Feb 28; Aug 31
Contact: Albert Mitchell, President; (314) 694-4391; GRANTquestions@bayer.com
Internet: www.fund.bayer.us/grant/2016/1/1/communitydevelopment
Sponsor: Bayer Fund
800 N Lindbergh Boulevard
Saint Louis, MO 63167

Bayer Fund STEM Education Grants 384
Bayer Fund STEM Education Grants support high-quality educational programming by nonprofit organizations that enable access to knowledge and information and empower students and teachers in communities around the nation, with a focus on furthering STEM education. This includes, but is not limited to, in-school programs, technical training programs, and academic programs that enrich or supplement school programs.
Requirements: The educational programs Bayer Fund supports target grades K-12 and under-served students and take place during the school day. Organizations eligible to apply for grants in this funding program include: organizations who hold a 501(c)3 tax exempt status and have been operating as such for a minimum of two years; organizations who are units of government under Section 170(c)(1), such as public schools, libraries, villages and municipalities; nonprofits that are experienced, reputable, and financially sound; organizations located within approximately 55 miles of an eligible Bayer community and the program must serve where a Bayer site is located. All applicants must be invited to apply for a grant from Bayer Fund.
Restrictions: Bayer Fund will not fund: endowments; debt retirements; political, labor and fraternal organizations; consumer or governmental lobbying or advocacy; veterans' organizations; benefits, dinners, advertisements; promotion of religious beliefs; trade or business associations; grants for individual aid or personal support; activities that directly support marketing programs; projects in which Bayer Fund or Bayer has a financial interest, or from which either one could derive a financial benefit; organizations that could purchase, dispense or prescribe Bayer products, or their affiliated foundations; organizations that do not comply with Bayer's non-discrimination policy; or infrastructure costs of organizations.
Geographic Focus: Arizona, California, Hawaii, Idaho, Illinois, Indiana, Iowa, Louisiana, Massachusetts, Michigan, Minnesota, Mississippi, Missouri, Nebraska, New Jersey, North Carolina, North Dakota, Pennsylvania, Puerto Rico, Texas, Washington
Date(s) Application is Due: Feb 28; Aug 31
Contact: Albert Mitchell, President; (314) 694-4391; GRANTquestions@bayer.com
Internet: www.fund.bayer.us/grant/2016/7/1/education
Sponsor: Bayer Fund
800 N Lindbergh Boulevard
Saint Louis, MO 63167

Baystate Financial Charitable Foundation Grants 385
While Baystate Financial Charitable Foundation is proud to help plan for a better future, it is also interested in taking its talent and knowledge into less fortunate communities. Founded in 1999, the Baystate Financial Charitable Foundation was designed to bring assistance to the many children's charities within its communities. Its primary goal is to raise money and awareness in order to make a positive impact in the day to day lives of children in need. The Foundation seeks to support charities which promote and improve quality of life for disadvantaged children and families. It will give to programs that strengthen the family unit and parent-child relationships and promote youth development. The Foundation has a primary mission of contributing to programs that support the needs of children and families in communities in which it does business. There are no specified deadlines, and interested applicants should begin by sending an email to the Foundation office.

Requirements: The Foundations offers support to 501(c)3 organizations serving: Massachusetts residents of Boston, Holyoke, Marshfield, Osterville, South Dennis, Southborough, Wakefield, and Wellesley; Connecticut residents of West Hartford and Westport; Maine residents of Falmouth; Vermont residents of Colchester; New Hampshire residents of Nashua and Exeter; and Rhode Island residents of East Providence.
Geographic Focus: Connecticut, Maine, Massachusetts, New Hampshire, Rhode Island, Vermont
Contact: Robin Trovato, Executive Director; (617) 585-4590 or (617) 585-4500; baystatefoundation@yahoo.com or rtrovato@baystatefinancial.com
Internet: www.baystatefinancial.com/copy-of-why-baystate-financial
Sponsor: Baystate Financial Charitable Foundation
200 Clarendon Street, 19 & 25th Floors
Boston, MA 02116

BBF Florida Family Literacy Initiative Grants 386
As Governor of Florida, Jeb Bush made education and strengthening families a top priority, beginning with his initiative in family literacy. Today, Jeb Bush's commitment to families and education lives strong within the programs of the Florida Family Literacy Initiative, a program of the Volunteer USA Foundation. This Initiative supports a network of Family Literacy academies which help adults become workforce ready through classes that encompass reading, math, parenting skills, and GED instruction; helps children start school ready to excel; and perpetuates lifelong learning as a family value to be passed on through the generations. The initiative awards one-year grants to enhance existing literacy instructional programs in Florida so that a complete family literacy program can be created and will tie family literacy education to cutting-edge reforms in K-12 education. Applications and guidelines are available online.
Requirements: Florida nonprofit literacy programs are eligible.
Geographic Focus: Florida
Amount of Grant: Up to 125,000 USD
Samples: Family Literacy Academy of Apopka, Apopka, Florida, $63,000 - to provide age-appropriate Children's Education, Adult education, Parent Education and Parent and Child Together Time through classes, speakers, workshops, and in-home activities; Family Literacy Academy of Palm Beach County, Delray Beach, Florida, $60,000 - to provide a twenty-hour a week program in which parents and children, birth through age 5, attend the same elementary school as their siblings.
Contact: Roxann R. Campbell, Director of Programs; (850) 562-5300; fax (850) 224-6532; Roxann.Campbell@volunteerusafund.org
Internet: www.barbarabushfoundation.com/site/c.jhLSK2PALmF/b.4425703/k.FC7B/The_Florida_Family_Literacy_Initiative.htm
Sponsor: Barbara Bush Foundation for Family Literacy
1201 15th Street NW, Suite 420
Washington, D.C. 20005

BBF Maine Family Literacy Initiative Implementation Grants 387
The program is designed to support the development and/or improvement of family literacy throughout the State of Maine. Family literacy programs must provide adult literacy, early childhood, parenting and inter-generational literacy services to families with at least one adult reading at less than a 12th grade level and at least one child between the ages of birth and eight who is at risk of being unprepared for starting school. A distinctive feature of each recipient program is the collaboration among the various groups that provide services to adults, children and families. Grants of up to $25,000 are available for the implementation or expansion of comprehensive family literacy programs in year two and three of the grant cycle. These will be awarded based on design, performance, and approval of a panel of Maine experts on literacy.
Requirements: Eligible applicants for these grants include: local education agencies, correctional agencies, community-based organizations, public or non-profit agencies or a consortium of these agencies located in Maine who have been in existence for two or more years, have demonstrated fiscal accountability, and have a literacy program that has operated for at least two years.
Geographic Focus: Maine
Date(s) Application is Due: Mar 16
Samples: Maine School Administration District #22, Hampden, Maine, $5,000—to support the planning of a family literacy program partnership between The Leroy Smith School and Head Start; Broadreach Family and Community Services, Belfast, Main, $25,000—to support Project Life, which will build on existing partnerships to integrate and strengthen current programs and launch a family literacy program, increasing learning success for community's most in need families; University of Southern Maine, Portland, Maine, $25,000—to support Kennedy Park Family Literacy as it broadens the support of English Language Learners to include families with children from birth to age eight and includes the integration of technology to support literacy learning.
Contact: Rebecca V. Dyer; (352) 365-9845; fax (352) 365-9845; becky@mainefamilyliteracy.com
Internet: www.mainefamilyliteracy.com/grants/
Sponsor: Barbara Bush Foundation for Family Literacy
1201 15th Street NW, Suite 420
Washington, D.C. 20005

BBF Maine Family Literacy Initiative Planning Grants 388
The program is designed to support the development and/or improvement of family literacy throughout the State of Maine. Family literacy programs must provide adult literacy, early childhood, parenting and inter-generational literacy services to families with at least one adult reading at less than a 12th grade level and at least one child between the ages of birth and eight who is at risk of being unprepared for starting school. A distinctive feature of each recipient program is the collaboration among the various groups that provide services to adults, children and families. Applicants may submit a proposal for a Planning Grant of up to $5,000 for the exploration and planning of future family literacy programs for year one.

Requirements: Eligible applicants for these grants include: local education agencies, correctional agencies, community-based organizations, public or non-profit agencies or a consortium of these agencies located in Maine who have been in existence for two or more years, have demonstrated fiscal accountability, and have a literacy program that has operated for at least two years.
Geographic Focus: Maine
Date(s) Application is Due: Mar 16
Amount of Grant: Up to 5,000 USD
Contact: Rebecca V. Dyer; (352) 365-9845; fax (352) 365-9845; becky@mainefamilyliteracy.com
Internet: www.mainefamilyliteracy.com/grants/
Sponsor: Barbara Bush Foundation for Family Literacy
1201 15th Street NW, Suite 420
Washington, D.C. 20005

BBF Maryland Family Literacy Initiative Implementation Grants 389
The mission of the Barbara Bush Foundation for Family Literacy is: to establish literacy as a value in every family in America by helping every family in the nation understand that the home is the child's first school, that the parent is the child's first teacher, and that reading is the child's first subject; and to break the inter-generational cycle of illiteracy, by supporting the development of family literacy programs where parents and children can learn and read together. Founded by Doro Bush Koch and Tricia Reilly Koch in 2003, the Foundation's Maryland Family Literacy Initiative supports nonprofit organizations, public school systems, municipal agencies and educational institutions working to improve family literacy rates across the state of Maryland. Between $40,000 and $50,000 is given for up to ten programs annually for Implementation Grants. Grantees are announced each spring at the Maryland Celebration of Reading, a special event sponsored by the Maryland Family Literacy Initiative.
Requirements: Applicants must be a nonprofit or public organization in the state of Maryland.
Geographic Focus: Maryland
Amount of Grant: 40,000 - 50,000 USD
Samples: Board of County Commissioners of Frederick County, Frederick, Maryland, $50,000 - to allow the Family Partnership of Frederick County to continue its successful LIFE (Literacy is Fundamental for Everyone) program at its 2 family support center sites in Frederick and Emmitsburg; Harford County Public Library, Belcamp, Maryland, $49,735 - to provide weekly story times for preschool classes at three Title 1 elementary schools as well as in-class lending libraries and Story Sacks for home use; Ready at Five, Halethorpe, Maryland, $40,000 - to develop and pilot a parent engagement and family literacy component for its highly successful Vocabulary Improvement and Oral Language Enrichment through Stories (VIOLETS) curriculum for English Language Learning families.
Contact: Benita Somerfield, Executive Director; (202) 955-6183; fax (202) 955-8084
Kiev Richardson, Program Officer; (202) 263-4781; fax (202) 955-8084; krichardson@cfncr.org
Internet: www.barbarabushfoundation.com/site/c.jhLSK2PALmF/b.4425723/k.1021/The_Maryland_Family_Literacy_Initiative.htm
Sponsor: Barbara Bush Foundation for Family Literacy
1201 15th Street NW, Suite 420
Washington, D.C. 20005

BBF Maryland Family Literacy Initiative Planning Grants 390
The mission of the Barbara Bush Foundation for Family Literacy is: to establish literacy as a value in every family in America by helping every family in the nation understand that the home is the child's first school, that the parent is the child's first teacher, and that reading is the child's first subject; and to break the inter-generational cycle of illiteracy, by supporting the development of family literacy programs where parents and children can learn and read together. Founded by Doro Bush Koch and Tricia Reilly Koch in 2003, the Foundation's Maryland Family Literacy Initiative supports nonprofit organizations, public school systems, municipal agencies and educational institutions working to improve family literacy rates across the state of Maryland. Up to $5,000 is given for Planning Grants each year. Grantees are announced each spring at the Maryland Celebration of Reading, a special event sponsored by the Maryland Family Literacy Initiative.
Requirements: Applicants must be a nonprofit or public organization in the state of Maryland.
Geographic Focus: Maryland
Amount of Grant: Up to 5,000 USD
Samples: Baltimore City Health Department, Baltimore, Maryland, $5,000 - to provide funding for the Baltimore City Health Department to plan Reading For Health, a program that will integrate and coordinate family literacy services into an existing continuum of care for at-risk women in Baltimore; Literacy Council of Carroll County, Westminster, Maryland, $5,000 - to plan the development of the Each One Teach One Family program; Enterprise Community Partners, Columbia, Maryland, $5,000 - to develop partnerships to identify and address the educational and literacy needs of parents in the families of the children it serves, thus moving the program toward a comprehensive family literacy model.
Contact: Benita Somerfield, Executive Director; (202) 955-6183; fax (202) 955-8084
Kiev Richardson, Program Officer; (202) 263-4781; fax (202) 955-8084; krichardson@cfncr.org
Internet: www.barbarabushfoundation.com/site/c.jhLSK2PALmF/b.4425723/k.1021/The_Maryland_Family_Literacy_Initiative.htm
Sponsor: Barbara Bush Foundation for Family Literacy
1201 15th Street NW, Suite 420
Washington, D.C. 20005

BBF National Grants for Family Literacy 391
Founded by Barbara Bush in 1989, the Barbara Bush Foundation for Family Literacy supports the development and expansion of family literacy programs across the United States. Grants are awarded on a competitive basis to nonprofit organizations, correctional institutions, homeless shelters, schools and school districts, libraries as well as community and faith-based agencies. The Foundation's grant-making program seeks to develop or expand projects designed to

support the development of literacy skills for adult primary care givers and their children. A total of approximately $650,000 will be awarded; no grant request should exceed $65,000.
Requirements: Funding opportunities are available to: nonprofit organizations, public school districts, and other agencies across the United States to improve the literacy skills of parents and their children. In order to be considered eligible for a grant, an organization must meet the following criteria: must have current nonprofit or public status and have been in existence for two or more years as of the date of the application; must have maintained fiscal accountability; and must operate an instructional literacy program that has been in existence for at least 2 years, and includes one or more of the following components - literacy for adults, parent education, pre-literacy or literacy instruction for children pre-k to grade 3, and, intergenerational literacy activities.
Geographic Focus: All States
Amount of Grant: 50,000 - 65,000 USD
Contact: Kiev Richardson; (202) 263-4781; fax (202) 955-8084; krichardson@cfncr.org
Benita Somerfield, Executive Director; (202) 955-6183; fax (202) 955-8084
Internet: www.barbarabushfoundation.com/site/c.jhLSK2PALmF/b.4425435/k.544A/Current_Funding_Opportunities.htm
Sponsor: Barbara Bush Foundation for Family Literacy
1201 15th Street NW, Suite 420
Washington, D.C. 20005

BCBSM Foundation Community Health Matching Grants 392

The program focuses on access to care for the uninsured and under insured. The program's purpose is to encourage nonprofit community based organizations to form partnerships with health care organizations, research organizations, or governmental agencies to develop and rigorously evaluate new ways of increasing access to care for the under and uninsured, in Michigan. The program offers up to $50,000 per year for two years, contingent on a 25% match.
Requirements: Nonprofit 501(c)3 organizations based in Michigan are eligible. Nonprofits do not need a firm commitment of matching support prior to the submission of the proposal [letters from potential funding partners are encouraged, indicating their support for the project and interest in possible funding partnership(s)]. Proposals must include a rigorous evaluation of the outcome of the initiative in accomplishing its objectives (preferably an independent or university-based evaluation).
Restrictions: In-kind contributions are not accepted as a match. Grants under this program do not pay for the cost of equipment (e.g., personal computers), hardware or software. The BCBSM Foundation does not provide support to for?profit organizations or individuals associated with organizations not located in Michigan.
Geographic Focus: Michigan
Amount of Grant: Up to 100,000 USD
Samples: TahLeekah Partee, Pine Rest Christian Mental Health Services, $75,000 - Hope and Healing for Uninsured Youth in Grand Rapids; Michigan League for Human Services, Ingham County, $45,000 - Kids Count in Michigan; Community Church of Douglas, Allegan County, $99,692 - The Provision of Community Nursing.
Contact: Nora Maloy, Dr.P.H., Senior Program Officer; (313) 225-8706; fax (313) 225-7730; foundation@bcbsm.com
Internet: www.bcbsm.com/foundation/grant.shtml
Sponsor: Blue Cross Blue Shield of Michigan Foundation
600 East Lafayette Boulevard
Detroit, MI 48226-2998

Beacon Society Jan Stauber Grants 393

The mission of the Society is to provide needed financial assistance to persons and organizations proposing literacy projects and other educational experiences that will introduce young people to Sherlock Holmes. The program's primary goals include: encouraging young people to read; introducing more young people to Sherlock Holmes; providing needed financial support in the form of grants to support projects introducing more young people to Sherlock Holmes; reaching out to non-Sherlockians and encourage and help them through financial assistance to develop such projects; and to honor Jan Stauber's work introducing young people to Sherlock Holmes (that's her picture above). Applications for funding may be sent at any time, but must be received by May 1 each year. The maximum amount for a funding request is $500.
Requirements: Target audiences include: elementary, middle school, and upper school teachers (both public and private); librarians (school, public libraries, etc.); Sherlockians active in organizations involving young people (Cub Scouts, Brownies, Girl Scouts, Boy Scouts, Camp Fire USA, YMCA, etc.); and Sherlockian Societies, and other such persons and entities.
Restrictions: No funds may be used for paying wages, salaries, stipends, living or travel expenses, honoraria, or catering.
Geographic Focus: All States, American Samoa, Guam, Northern Mariana Islands, Puerto Rico, U.S. Virgin Islands, Canada
Date(s) Application is Due: May 1
Amount of Grant: Up to 500 USD
Contact: Susan Z. Diamond, (315) 637-0609; szdiamond@comcast.net
Internet: beaconsociety.com/index.php/awards/the-jan-stauber-grant-winners/jan-stauber-grant
Sponsor: Beacon Society
100 Van Cortlandt Avenue
Staten Island, NY 10301

Beckman Coulter Foundation Grants 394

Beckman Coulter has a long-standing commitment to its Community Relations program. Within the program, Beckman Coulter associates strive to improve its local communities through a wide range of engagement activities that includes (but is not limited to): service projects; toy drives; blood drives; and walks, runs and bike rides. The Community Relations program also serves as a vehicle that encourages associates to work toward fulfilling the corporate vision of advancing healthcare for every person through our associate-driven fundraising activities that supports science, science education and healthcare-related research to help fight diseases. Since the Foundation is not currently accepting unsolicited applications, interested organization should begin by contacting the Foundation with a concept. If invited, grant applications are reviewed by the Foundation's staff on a regular basis. Each request is evaluated to determine its eligibility and conformity to the Beckman Coulter Foundation's giving guidelines.
Requirements: Organizations seeking funding should submit a letter of concept providing the following information: full legal name of the organization; brief description of the organization (including a mission statement and services provided); amount requested; and a description of how the funds will be used. Additional attachments should include: history of previous support by Beckman Coulter; description of any involvement by Beckman Coulter employees; statement as to why you consider Beckman Coulter an appropriate donor; and a list of governing board members.
Restrictions: The Foundation does not support the following: advertising; awards and recognition programs; beauty or talent contests; capital or building campaigns, including new construction or renovations; for-profit organizations; fraternal, labor, or veteran's organizations and activities; fund-raisers; galas, banquets, or dinners; golf tournaments; indirect costs, media productions (e.g. radio, T.V., film, webcast, publications); meetings, conferences, workshops, forums, summits and symposiums; organizations that discriminate on the basis of race, color, sex, sexual orientation, marital status, religion, age, national origin, veteran's status, or disability; private foundations; political organizations, campaigns and activities; religious organizations or groups; or sports affiliated activities.
Geographic Focus: All States, American Samoa, District of Columbia, Guam, Marshall Islands, Northern Mariana Islands, Puerto Rico, U.S. Virgin Islands
Contact: Marci Raudez, Senior Specialist, Foundation and Community Relations; (714) 961-6672 or (714) 961-6338; mfraudez@beckman.com
Internet: beckmancoulterfoundation.org/grant/
Sponsor: Beckman Coulter Foundation
250 South Kraemer Boulevard, E1.SE.03
Brea, CA 92821

Bee Conservancy Sponsor-A-Hive Grants 395

Bees offer a wonderful way for children and communities to learn about science, ecology, agriculture, societal structure, mutual cooperation, and even history – all by caring for and observing the activity of bees maintained on an on-site bee house. Sponsor-a-Hive is an innovative materials grant program designed by the Bee Conservancy to strategically install honey bees, solitary bees and their homes where they can bolster local bee populations, advance science and environmental education, and pollinate locally grown food. The annual deadline for application materials is December 4, with successful applicants notified by December 29.
Requirements: Eligibility requirements include: being located in the United States; has an IRS 501(c)3 tax-exemption letter or a NCES school ID number; and has been in existence for at least one year. Applicants must represent one of the following types of organizations: grade school, middle school, or high school; college or university; tribal education agency; environmental center; or a food bank or community garden that does not charge a membership fee.
Geographic Focus: All States, American Samoa, District of Columbia, Guam, Marshall Islands, Northern Mariana Islands, Puerto Rico, U.S. Virgin Islands
Date(s) Application is Due: Dec 4
Contact: Guillermo Fernandez; (646) 389-6025; sponsorahive@thehoneybeeconservancy.org
Rebecca Louie; (646) 389-6025; sponsorahive@thehoneybeeconservancy.org
Internet: thebeeconservancy.org/sponsor-a-hive-eligibility/
Sponsor: Bee Conservancy
1732 1st Avenue, #28748
New York, NY 10028

Bella Vista Foundation GSS Healthy Living Grants 396

The GGS Healthy Living program supports organizations that enable youth to thrive and live up to their full potential by building resiliency, promoting healthy coping strategies and positive decision-making, and preventing unhealthy behaviors. These grants fund programs that: work with students facing adversity, particularly those who may be homeless and/or in the foster care system; employ sound youth development and trauma-informed practices; use dedicated curricula in their programming; have leadership and program staff who reflect the communities they serve; and focus on anti-bullying, mentoring (peer and adult), personal development and empowerment, mental health, general health, substance use prevention, and/or school gardens.
Requirements: These grants fund organizations serving at-promise middle and/or high school students in Marin and San Francisco counties.
Geographic Focus: California
Amount of Grant: Up to 50,000 USD
Samples: 18 Reasons, San Fransisco, California, $20,000 - to provide the Cooking Matters program to San Francisco youth (2019); A Home Within, San Fransisco, California, $20,000 - for support of volunteer clinician outreach and recruitment to increase the number of foster youth served in San Francisco County (2019); At The Crossroads, San Fransisco, California, $40,000 - to provide street outreach and counseling for homeless youth in San Francisco (2019).
Contact: Jonny Moy, Grants Manager; (415) 561-6540, ext. 216; jmoy@pfs-llc.net
Internet: www.bellavistafoundation.org/program-areas/ggs-healthy-living/
Sponsor: Bella Vista Foundation
1660 Bush Street Suite 300
San Francisco, CA 94109

Bella Vista Foundation Pre-3 Grants 397

The Pre-3 Support program focuses on building resiliency among families facing adversity or trauma by helping parents and caregivers cope with toxic stress. Programs covered are those that build connections between parents/caregivers, their communities, and supportive local services; infuse trauma-informed practices into their work with parents/caregivers; foster a safe and supportive environment that builds parents'/caregivers' self-confidence; provide opportunities for parents/caregivers to gain parenting education, training, and support; and utilize research-based practice and ongoing measurement and monitoring to continuously improve programs.

Requirements: Early childhood grants support public charities located in California's San Francisco, Marin, San Mateo, and Santa Clara counties.

Restrictions: Grants will not be made to or for the arts, sectarian religious purposes, individuals, or benefit events, and will only be made for medical research, health care, publications, or video production under special circumstances and only in the early childhood development focus area. The foundation does not make multiyear grants.

Geographic Focus: California, Oregon

Amount of Grant: Up to 100,000 USD

Samples: Buckelew Programs, San Rafael, California, $85,000 - for Healthy Families Marin, a program that integrates home visiting services and a support group with medical care for pregnant women and new parents (2019); Canal Alliance, San Rafael, California, $30,000 - to support Latina mothers in the Canal District through birth coaches (Compañeras) and connections to other resources (2019); Grail Family Services, San Jose, California, $40,000 - to support Birth & Beyond Family Empowerment parenting programs for parents of young children in East San Jose (2019).

Contact: Jonny Moy; (415) 561-6540, ext. 216; fax (415) 561-6477; jmoy@pfs-llc.net

Internet: www.bellavistafoundation.org/program-areas/pre-3-support/

Sponsor: Bella Vista Foundation

1660 Bush Street Suite 300

San Francisco, CA 94109

Bella Vista Foundations GSS Early Literacy Grants 398

The GGS Early Literacy program promotes literacy for children, including acquisition of reading, writing, and comprehension skills, and application of literacy skills to critical thinking and self-expression. The grants fund programs that are entirely dedicated to early literacy programming, with strong evaluation methods in place and a proven record of effectiveness.

Requirements: The GSS grants fund organizations serving at-promise students from preschool through third grade in Marin and San Francisco counties.

Geographic Focus: California, Oregon

Amount of Grant: Up to 50,000 USD

Samples: Bridge the Gap College Prep, Sausalito, California, $40,000 - to support literacy and social emotional learning programs for Marin City youth (2019); Springboard Collaborative, San Fransiso, California, $40,000 - for support of Springboard's literacy program in San Francisco (2019); Jamestown Community Center, San Fransiso, California, $35,000 - for after-school literacy programs in three Mission District elementary schools (2019).

Contact: Jonny Moy, Grants Manager; (415) 561-6540, ext. 216; jmoy@pfs-llc.net

Internet: www.bellavistafoundation.org/program-areas/ggs-early-literacy/

Sponsor: Bella Vista Foundation

1660 Bush Street Suite 300

San Francisco, CA 94109

Belvedere Community Foundation Grants 399

The mission of the Belvedere Community Foundation is to: preserve and enhance the quality of life in Belvedere, California; form an endowment fund with contributions from all of its citizens; and provide grants to support projects and volunteers working to enhance the quality of life throughout the community. Grants are targeted at supporting: preservation and enhancement to historically important structures, as well as the natural beauty of the community; positive community interaction; educational opportunities, particularly those focused on stewardship of natural resources and awareness of cultural heritage; healthy living, particularly as it pertains to the benefits of an active lifestyle; funds for emergency preparedness and public safety; seed funding for new community based projects or to aid projects launched by other locally based, non profits aligned with the goals of the Foundation; and crisis funding to existing community based programs in times of urgent need. The Foundation has two online grant cycles per year, with deadlines on March 1 and September 1. Grant requests should be submitted by the beginning of the relevant grant cycle and all applicants will receive a response within 60 days.

Requirements: Any 501(c)3 organization supporting the residents of Belvedere, California, are eligible to apply. The Belvedere Community Foundation requests that grantees provide public recognition of Belvedere Community Foundation's grant support in their newsletters, in the media, and wherever else appropriate. The Belvedere Community Foundation looks most favorably upon applications with matching funding sources, especially when a project is beyond Belvedere city limits, and generally does not make multi-year commitments or grants to projects located outside of the greater Tiburon Peninsula area.

Geographic Focus: California

Date(s) Application is Due: Mar 1; Sep 1

Amount of Grant: Up to 10,000 USD

Contact: Sue Hoeschler, President; (415) 435-3695; info@belvederecommunityfoundation.com

Internet: belvederecommunityfoundation.com/grant-information/

Sponsor: Belvedere Community Foundation

P.O. Box 484

Belvedere, CA 94920

Belvedere Cove Foundation Grants 400

The Belvedere Cove Foundation considers grant requests for a variety of sailing-related activities in Northern California. Youth activities may include, but are not limited to: learn-to-sail programs; competitive and high school sailing teams; individual sailors traveling and competing; individuals pursuing learning programs through sailing; and other programs that get youth on the water. Adult programs may include, but are not limited to: competitive pursuits such as long-duration campaigns (Olympic, match racing, and other); programs focused on increasing sailors' access to the water; and benefit related sailing programs (fundraising for health, medical and other purposes). All grant applications should be submitted through Belvedere Cove Foundation's website.

Requirements: Any 501(c)3 organization serving the residents of northern California is eligible to apply.

Geographic Focus: California

Contact: Dan Buckstaff; (415) 273-1510; dan.buckstaff@belvederecove.org

Internet: www.belvederecovefoundation.org/financial-assistance

Sponsor: Belvedere Cove Foundation

P.O. Box 150180

San Rafael, CA 94915-0180

Belvedere Cove Foundation Scholarships 401

The mission of the Belvedere Cove Foundation is to provide financial assistance to worthy sailors so that they can learn to sail, teach sailing or have the opportunity to compete in major regional and international regattas or enroll in sailing instruction and training programs to help propel them to the top of the sport of sailing. Each year, the Foundation considers scholarship requests for sailing-related activities for individual youth under the age of 18, such as: Learn-to-Sail programs; and High School Sailing team members.

Requirements: Any youth living in northern California whose family's financial situation precludes him or her from fully participating in a sailing program should apply.

Geographic Focus: California

Contact: Dan Buckstaff; (415) 273-1510; dan.buckstaff@belvederecove.org

Internet: www.belvederecovefoundation.org/financial-assistance

Sponsor: Belvedere Cove Foundation

P.O. Box 150180

San Rafael, CA 94915-0180

Ben B. Cheney Foundation Grants 402

Ben B. Cheney Foundation supports projects in communities where the Cheney Lumber Company was active. These areas include: Tacoma, Pierce, southwestern Washington, southwestern Oregon with a focus on Medford, portions of Del Norte, Humboldt, Lassen, Shasta, Siskiyou, and Trinity counties in California. The Foundation's goal is to improve the quality of life in those communities by making grants to a wide range of activities including: Charity (programs providing for basic needs such as food, shelter, and clothing); Civic (programs improving the quality of life in a community as a whole such as museums and recreation facilities); Culture (programs encompassing the arts); Education (programs supporting capital projects and scholarships, primarily for fourteen pre-selected colleges and universities in the Pacific Northwest); Elderly (programs serving the social, health, recreational, and other needs of older people); Health (programs related to providing health care); Social Services (programs serving people with physical or mental disabilities or other special needs); Youth (programs helping young people to gain the skills needed to become responsible and productive adults). Ben B. Cheney Foundation prefers to fund projects that: develop new and innovative approaches to community problem; facilitate the improvement of services or programs; invest in equipment or facilities that will have a long-lasting impact on community needs. The Foundation's application process always begins with a two to three page proposal letter. The process is the same for past grantees and new grant seekers. There are no deadlines. The Foundation accepts proposal letters throughout the year. It may take six to nine months from the receipt of a proposal letter to consideration of a grant application by the Board of Directors.

Requirements: Ben B. Cheney Foundation makes grants to private, nonprofit organizations that have received their 501(c)3 status from the IRS and that qualify as public charities. In special circumstances proposals from governmental organizations are allowed.

Restrictions: Ben B. Cheney Foundation generally does not make grants for: general operating budgets, annual campaigns, projects which are primarily or normally financed by tax funds, religious organizations for sectarian purposes, basic research, endowment funds, individuals, produce books, films, videos, conferences, seminars, attendance, individual student, or student groups raising money for school related trips.

Geographic Focus: California, Oregon, Washington

Amount of Grant: Up to 300,000 USD

Samples: Kitsap Mental Health Services, Bremerton,Washington, $50,000 - build Keller House for residential and outpatient programs; Ocean Shores Friends of the Library, Oceans Shores, Washington $4,000 - support the conference for Nonprofit Leaders in SW Washington to enhance fundraising; Hoover Elementary PTO, Medford, Oregon, $1,260 - provide the last monies needed to complete the new Boundless community playground at the school; Catholic Community Services, Tacoma, Washington, $40,000 - support operations of the downtown emergency shelter.

Contact: Bradbury F. Cheney; (253) 572-2442; info@benbcheneyfoundation.org

Internet: www.benbcheneyfoundation.org

Sponsor: Ben B. Cheney Foundation

3110 Ruston Way, Suite A

Tacoma, WA 98402-5307

Ben Cohen StandUp Foundation Grants 403

The Ben Cohen StandUp Foundation supports organizations, programs and people that advance equality. Its mission is to raise awareness of the long-term, damaging effects of bullying and to raise funds to support those doing real-world work to stop it. The Foundation generally prefers to make smaller, more frequent grants ($10,000 or less) but will consider all requests within its means and mission.

Requirements: Nonprofit organizations in the United States and the United Kingdom are eligible to apply. To be considered for a grant from the Foundation in the U.S., you must be designated a 501(c)3 public charity. Requests are reviewed twice a year (July and December), and grants are awarded to support work that helps stop bullying, helps those hurt by bullying and/or helps increase equality and diversity in sports. U.S. deadlines are June 30 and November 30. To be considered for a grant from the Foundation in the U.K., you have to be an organization, charitable or non-charitable in the U.K. that is carrying out work that is in furtherance of the Foundation's charitable objectives. U.K. deadlines are March 31 and October 31. Qualified applicants must use the required form found at the Foundation's website.
Restrictions: The Ben Cohen StandUp Foundation does not support requests for event or conference sponsorship, for performances, films or movie productions.
Geographic Focus: All States, United Kingdom
Date(s) Application is Due: Mar 31; Jun 30; Oct 31; Nov 30
Amount of Grant: Up to 10,000 USD
Contact: Grants Administrator; info@standupfoundation.com
Internet: www.standupfoundation.com/grants/requesting-funding/
Sponsor: Ben Cohen StandUp Foundation, Inc.
154 Krog Street, Suite 100
Atlanta, GA 30307

Benton Community Foundation - The Cookie Jar Grant 404
The Benton Community Foundation - The Cookie Jar Grant was established by women in the Benton County area to fund programs that empower women. The Cookie Jar is a collaboration of women working together to create a stronger community where women and girls are empowered to reach their full potential. Priority is given to programs that improve the overall health or well-being of women and/or girls in Benton County. Priority is also given to programs that: reach as many people as possible; are run by a collaboration of non-profit organizations; and have multiple sources of funding for their project.
Requirements: Organizations should submit the grant application to the Foundation to include the following information: their organizational information and contacts; a summary of their program with amount requested; program details, such as how the program will benefit women or girls in Benton County; the program's anticipated timeline; the organization's top three goals for the project and how they plan to meet them; budget details; and a list of the organization's board of directors.
Restrictions: Foundation grant programs generally do not fund: ongoing operating expenses; individuals; special events such as parades, festivals and sporting events; debt or deficit reduction.
Geographic Focus: Indiana
Date(s) Application is Due: Sep 15
Amount of Grant: 4,000 USD
Contact: Ashley Bice; (765) 884-8022; fax (765) 884-8023; ashley@bentoncf.org
Internet: www.bentoncf.org/cookiejar.html
Sponsor: Benton Community Foundation
P.O. Box 351
Fowler, IN 47944

Benton Community Foundation Grants 405
The Foundation grants address the broad needs of Benton County residents. Funding is allocated in the following categories: civic affairs; cultural affairs; education; health and safety; and social services. Priority is given to programs that: reach as many people as possible; improve the ability of the organization to serve the community over the long term; serve Benton County residents; are run by a collaboration of nonprofit organizations; and have multiple sources of funding for the project.
Requirements: Grant requests are accepted year-round. Applicants are encouraged to contact the Foundation prior to submitting a request to confirm that the project is appropriate for Foundation funding. To make a request of $750 or less, organizations should submit a letter of application which includes a description of the organization, statement of the problem or need being addressed, explanation of the project, estimated expenses, timeframe for completion, and the amount being requested. Grant decisions are made within 30 days of application. Organizations requesting more than $750 are encouraged to contact the Foundation to discuss the proposed project/program prior to submitting an application. They will then complete the Community Grant Application. Grant decisions are made within 90 days of application.
Restrictions: Benton Community Foundation generally does not fund: political organizations or candidates; endowments; ongoing operating expenses; individuals; special events such as parades, festivals, and sporting events; debt or deficit reduction; or projects funding in a previous year, unless invited to resubmit.
Geographic Focus: Indiana
Date(s) Application is Due: Aug 1
Contact: Ashley Bice, Executive Director; (765) 884-8022; fax (765) 884-8023; ashley@bentoncf.org or info@bentoncf.org
Internet: www.bentoncf.org/grants_community.html
Sponsor: Benton Community Foundation
P.O. Box 351
Fowler, IN 47944

Benwood Foundation Community Grants 406
Funding is to provide opportunities for creativity and innovation on the part of organizations in the community. The Community Grantmaking area will also provide support for Capital Campaigns. Organizations contemplating a Capital Campaign and desiring Foundation support are encouraged to discuss the campaign with a Foundation staff prior to making application. Capital support to an organization will not exceed $250,000 for any campaign.
Requirements: Applications will only be considered from charities organized under Section 509(a)1 or 509(a)2 of the Internal Revenue Code. Programs must benefit the communities of Hamilton County, Tennessee. Grants presently are not being considered for supporting organizations organized under Section 509(a)3. Faxed or electronically submitted applications are not accepted.
Restrictions: Organizations may apply only one time in a twelve-month period. The foundation does not fund individuals; endowments; debt reduction; political organizations or causes; fundraising events; general operating expenses; multi-year grants; grants outside of Hamilton County; Allied Arts agencies (except for capital campaigns); United Way agencies (except for capital campaigns).
Geographic Focus: Tennessee
Date(s) Application is Due: Mar 1; Sep 1
Amount of Grant: Up to 50,000 USD
Contact: Lauren Boehm, Communications and Community Grant Officer; (423) 267-4311; fax (423) 267-9049; lboehm@benwood.org
Internet: www.benwood.org/community.htm
Sponsor: Benwood Foundation
736 Market Street, Suite 1600
Chattanooga, TN 37402

Bernard and Audre Rapoport Foundation Arts and Culture Grants 407
Bernard and Audre Rapoport Foundation supports artistic and cultural programs, especially those that encourage participation, and enrich the lives of children and disadvantaged members of the community. Education and cultivation of new and young patrons is encouraged. The primary focus of the Foundation is on programs that benefit children and youth in Waco and McLennan County, Texas. Proposals that fall outside of this geographical focus are considered as long as they offer imaginative, and when possible, long-range solutions to the problems of the most needy members of society, and ideally solutions that can be replicated in other communities.
Requirements: Program seeking funding must be a catalyst for change and promote both individual competence and social capacity.
Restrictions: Bernard and Audre Rapoport Foundation only supports organizations that are nonprofit 501(c)3 tax-exempt.
Geographic Focus: All States
Date(s) Application is Due: Jun 15; Aug 15
Amount of Grant: 4,000 - 250,000 USD
Samples: Waco Symphony, Waco, Texas, $5,572 - equipment and furniture for new development office.
Contact: Carole Jonesr; (254) 741-0510; fax (254) 741-0092; carole@rapoportfdn.org
Internet: www.rapoport-fdn.org/
Sponsor: Bernard and Audre Rapoport Foundation
5400 Bosque Boulevard, Suite 245
Waco, TX 76710

Bernard and Audre Rapoport Foundation Community Building and Social Service Grants 408
The Foundation seeks to build communities that improve the quality of life for all citizens and foster the growth and development of children. The Foundation encourages programs that build grassroots neighborhood networks, provide job training and job opportunities for the unemployed and under-employed, or provide a comprehensive safety net of social services for the least-advantaged citizens. The primary focus of the Foundation is on programs that benefit children and youth in Waco and McLennan County, Texas. Proposals that fall outside of this geographical focus are considered as long as they offer imaginative, and when possible, long-range solutions to the problems of the most needy members of society, and ideally solutions that can be replicated in other communities.
Requirements: Program seeking funding must be a catalyst for change and promote both individual competence and social capacity.
Restrictions: Bernard and Audre Rapoport Foundation only supports organizations that are nonprofit 501(c)3 tax-exempt.
Geographic Focus: All States
Date(s) Application is Due: Jun 15; Aug 15
Amount of Grant: 4,000 - 250,000 USD
Samples: Planned Parenthood of Central Texas, Waco, Texas, $60,000 - general support; ISD Education Foundation, Waco, Texas, $4,500 - new teacher grants. Waco Tech, Waco, Texas, $25,000 - after school program.
Contact: Carole Jones; (254) 741-0510; fax (254) 741-0092; carole@rapoportfdn.org
Internet: www.rapoport-fdn.org/
Sponsor: Bernard and Audre Rapoport Foundation
5400 Bosque Boulevard, Suite 245
Waco, TX 76710

Bernard and Audre Rapoport Foundation Democracy and Civic Participation Grants 409
Bernard and Audre Rapoport Foundation supports efforts both to make government more responsive and to encourage citizens to take an active interest and role in political life. The Foundation promotes intergovernmental cooperation as well as initiatives that broaden citizen awareness of public policy issues and alternatives, build skills necessary for political leadership, and provide opportunities for community service. The primary focus of the Foundation is on programs that benefit children and youth in Waco and McLennan County, Texas. Proposals that fall outside of this geographical focus are considered as long as they offer imaginative, and when possible, long-range solutions to the problems of the most needy members of society, and ideally solutions that can be replicated in other communities.
Requirements: Program seeking funding must be a catalyst for change and promote both individual competence and social capacity.
Restrictions: Bernard and Audre Rapoport Foundation only supports organizations that are nonprofit 501(c)3 tax-exempt.

Geographic Focus: All States
Date(s) Application is Due: Jun 15; Aug 15
Amount of Grant: 4,000 - 250,000 USD
Samples: Alliance for Justice, Washington, D.C., $10,000 - general support; Central Texas Senior Ministry, Waco, Texas, $10,000 - meals on wheels program.
Contact: Carole Jones; (254) 741-0510; fax (254) 741-0092; carole@rapoportfdn.org
Internet: www.rapoport-fdn.org/
Sponsor: Bernard and Audre Rapoport Foundation
5400 Bosque Boulevard, Suite 245
Waco, TX 76710

Bernard and Audre Rapoport Foundation Education Grants   410
Bernard and Audre Rapoport Foundation is interested in the broad area of education but with a special concern for early learning up to and through the elementary years. Other areas of interest include adult education and training initiatives, and programs that enhance the capabilities of teachers and other professionals in public schools. The primary focus of the Foundation is on programs that benefit children and youth in Waco and McLennan County, Texas. Proposals that fall outside of this geographical focus are considered as long as they offer imaginative, and when possible, long-range solutions to the problems of the most needy members of society, and ideally solutions that can be replicated in other communities.
Requirements: Program seeking funding must be a catalyst for change and promote both individual competence and social capacity.
Restrictions: Bernard and Audre Rapoport Foundation only supports organizations that are nonprofit 501(c)3 tax-exempt.
Geographic Focus: All States
Date(s) Application is Due: Jun 15; Aug 15
Amount of Grant: 4,000 - 250,000 USD
Samples: WISD Education Foundation, Waco, Texas, $125,000 - daycare facility; Child Development Resources, Williamsburg, Virgina, $31,000 - expand 1-2-3 reading program; Marlin Public Library, Marlin, Texas, $6,000 - general support.
Contact: Carole Jones; (254) 741-0510; fax (254) 741-0092; carole@rapoportfdn.org
Internet: www.rapoport-fdn.org/
Sponsor: Bernard and Audre Rapoport Foundation
5400 Bosque Boulevard, Suite 245
Waco, TX 76710

Bernard and Audre Rapoport Foundation Health Grants   411
Bernard and Audre Rapoport Foundation seeks to improve the quality and delivery of healthcare services to all citizens, especially to women, children, and those who do not have access to conventional medical resources. Community-based outreach initiatives such as immunization programs are of interest to the Foundation. The primary focus of the Foundation is on programs that benefit children and youth in Waco and McLennan County, Texas. Proposals that fall outside of this geographical focus are considered as long as they offer imaginative, and when possible, long-range solutions to the problems of the most needy members of society, and ideally solutions that can be replicated in other communities.
Requirements: Program seeking funding must be a catalyst for change and promote both individual competence and social capacity.
Restrictions: Bernard and Audre Rapoport Foundation only supports organizations that are nonprofit 501(c)3 tax-exempt.
Geographic Focus: All States
Date(s) Application is Due: Jun 15; Aug 15
Amount of Grant: 4,000 - 250,000 USD
Samples: University of Texas Health Science Center, Houston, Texas, $20,000 - stroke research; Potter's Vessel Ministry, Waco, Texas, $10,000 - new health care provider; Planned Parenthood of Central Texas, Waco, Texas, $60,000 - general support.
Contact: Carole Jones; (254) 741-0510; fax (254) 741-0092; carole@rapoportfdn.org
Internet: www.rapoport-fdn.org/
Sponsor: Bernard and Audre Rapoport Foundation
5400 Bosque Boulevard, Suite 245
Waco, TX 76710

Bernard F. and Alva B. Gimbel Foundation Criminal Justice Grants   412
The Bernard F. and Alva B. Gimbel Foundation was incorporated in 1943 as a private, family foundation. The Foundation's donors had wide ranging philanthropic interests and the Foundation's original giving guidelines were defined broadly: grants were to be used for charitable, scientific or educational purposes. The Foundation's areas of interest have evolved over the years and are currently more narrowly defined. The Foundation's funding in the area of criminal justice is focused on efforts to promote fair and effective criminal justice policies, to reduce recidivism, and to improve public safety. Among these are sentencing reform initiatives including repeal of mandatory minimum sentencing laws and increased use of alternatives to incarceration. In most cases, the Foundation seeks to fund general operating costs, direct services programs, and advocacy efforts.
Requirements: Grants are made only to tax-exempt 501(c)3 organizations. The Foundation's support for direct services programs is limited to those operating in New York City.
Restrictions: The Foundation does not make grants to: individuals; direct service programs outside of New York City; individual schools; short-term educational programs and workshops; mentoring programs; after-school and summer programs; youth development programs.
Geographic Focus: New York
Amount of Grant: 30,000 - 100,000 USD
Samples: Citizens' Committee for Children, New York, New York, $50,000 - support of Juvenile Justice Initiatives; MFY Legal Services, New York, New York, $40,000 - support of the Workplace Justice Project; National Center for Access to Justice, New York, New York, $50,000 - general operating support.

Contact: Leslie Gimbel, President; (212) 684-9110; fax (212) 684-9114
Internet: www.gimbelfoundation.org/FundingRestrictionsandPriorities.htm
Sponsor: Bernard F. and Alva B. Gimbel Foundation
271 Madison Avenue, Suite 605
New York, NY 10016

Bernau Family Foundation Grants   413
The Bernau Family Foundation was founded in 1995 by Theodore and Ruth Bernau from the estate of the late William A. Bernau. William trained and educated German and Polish immigrants to value the work ethic. He then employed many of them as skilled technicians at Universal Manufacturing Company in Irvington, New Jersey. The Bernau Family Foundation exists to promote the long term improvement of individual lives and the development of positive leadership. Its vision is of a society in which everyone is a healthy, active, contributing member who feels the civic responsibility to continue learning, to teach and mentor the young, and to encourage one another to grow in the grace and faith of Jesus Christ. The Foundation's primary areas of interest include: education services; elementary and secondary education; European football; family services; human services; public affairs; public policy; reading promotion; and sports and recreation.
Requirements: Except in a few circumstances, grants are currently limited to programs and projects that will impact the communities in the following geographic areas: Moneta, Virginia; Fort Worth, Texas; Chicago, Illinois; Hartford, Connecticut; New York, New York; and Provo, Utah. Grants will be made only to those entities designated by the I.R.S. as public charities or nonprofit organizations.
Geographic Focus: Connecticut, Illinois, Maryland, New York, Tennessee, Texas, Utah, Virginia
Amount of Grant: Up to 15,000 USD
Contact: Theodore G. Bernau; (410) 857-6169 or (540) 719-0985; bernauff@gmail.com
Internet: www.bernauff.org/
Sponsor: Bernau Family Foundation
P.O Box 916
Hardy, VA 24101

Best Buy Children's Foundation @15 Community Grants   414
Best Buy Children's Foundation Community Grants Program selects nonprofit organizations from across the United States with initiatives to make technology opportunities more accessible to teens. In 2011, Best Buy Children's Foundation gave $2 million in Community Grants. Applications are accepted once a year in the Summer and grants are issued in the Fall.
Requirements: Best Buy will seek applications from organizations that have current 501(c)3 tax status and are serving a diverse population of teens and providing teens with access to opportunity through technology. Funding must: serve a diverse population in local or regional communities; build academic, leadership and life skills in early adolescents (primarily ages 13-17); show positive results against a demonstrated community need; reach at-risk children in working families.
Restrictions: Organization must be located and serve within the United States.
Geographic Focus: All States
Date(s) Application is Due: Jul 1
Contact: Stephanie Woods, Community Relations Manager; (612) 291-6108; fax (612) 292-4001; communityrelations@bestbuy.com
Internet: www.bestbuy-communityrelations.com/community_grants.htm
Sponsor: Best Buy Children's Foundation
7601 Penn Avenue S.
Richfield, MN 55423

Best Buy Children's Foundation @15 Scholarship   415
Best Buy's @15 Scholarship Program is pleased to award $1,000 scholarships to 1,099 students living in the U.S. and Puerto Rico who will be entering college in the fall after their high school graduation. Scholarships are awarded to students in grades 9-12 who demonstrate academic achievements, volunteer efforts and work experience. As part of its teen platform, Best Buy and Best Buy Children's Foundation are focused on opportunities to help teen students prepare for a brighter future with dollars for college tuition. With the inception of the scholarship program in 1999, Best Buy has now provided nearly $19.7 million in scholarship funds to help 15,438 students attend college.
Requirements: Scholarships are awarded to students in grades 9-12 who demonstrate academic achievements, volunteer efforts and work experience.
Geographic Focus: All States, Puerto Rico
Contact: Stephanie Woods, Community Relations Manager; (612) 291-6108; fax (612) 292-4001; communityrelations@bestbuy.com
Internet: www.bestbuy-communityrelations.com/scholarship.htm
Sponsor: Best Buy Children's Foundation
7601 Penn Avenue S.
Richfield, MN 55423

Best Buy Children's Foundation @15 Teach Awards   416
The @15 Teach Award program helps schools serving grades 7-12 meet their technology needs. Teens (ages 13-18) who are registered on www.at15.com can nominate their school to win a Teach@15 Award. Teen members can vote once a day for 15 days for one nomination. Every 15 days, Best Buy will award 3 schools with Best Buy Gift Cards based on member votes. The school with the most votes will win $1,500, second most votes wins $1,000 and third most votes wins $500.
Requirements: Must be an accredited non-profit junior or senior public, private, parochial, magnet and charter high schools (serving any grades 7-12). All schools must be 501(c)3 certified nonprofit. All schools must be located in the United States. Nominations must be made by Members of the @15 Site.

Restrictions: Home schools, pre-K schools/programs, after-school programs, colleges, universities and vocational-technical schools are not eligible
Geographic Focus: All States
Amount of Grant: 500 - 1,500 USD
Contact: Stephanie Woods, Community Relations Manager; (612) 291-6108; fax (612) 292-4001; communityrelations@bestbuy.com
Internet: www.bestbuy-communityrelations.com/teach_awards.htm
Sponsor: Best Buy Children's Foundation
7601 Penn Avenue S.
Richfield, MN 55423

Best Buy Children's Foundation National Grants   417
Best Buy Children's Foundation strengthens communities by supporting organizations that empower teens to thrive. Best Buy Children's Foundation National Grants Fund supports initiatives with a national focus committed to funding programs that will help teens excel in school, engage in their communities, and develop life and leadership skills.
Requirements: To receive funding organizations must be a nonprofit 501(c)3 certified organization; serve a national audience; have a national distribution plan in place; provide positive experiences that will empower early adolescents (primarily ages 12-17) to excel in school, engage in their communities, and develop life and leadership skills.
Restrictions: Best Buy Children's Foundation National Grant Fund will not support: organizations not certified as 501(c)3 by the IRS; organizations more frequently than annually (not including TagTeam Awards); individuals; schools (please refer to Teach@15 Program); general operating expenses; product requests; endowments; fraternal organizations or social clubs; units of government or quasi-governmental agencies; labor organizations or political campaigns; organizations designed primarily for lobbying; for-profit organizations or travel programs; fundraising dinners, testimonials, conferences or similar events; sole support of operating or advertising expenses; religious organizations for religious purposes; health, medical, or therapeutic programs or living subsidies; athletic teams or events; multi-year requests (grants must be reviewed/made annually).
Geographic Focus: All States
Contact: Stephanie Woods, Community Relations Manager; (612) 291-6108; fax (612) 292-4001; communityrelations@bestbuy.com
Internet: www.bestbuy-communityrelations.com/national_grants.htm
Sponsor: Best Buy Children's Foundation
7601 Penn Avenue S.
Richfield, MN 55423

Best Buy Children's Foundation Twin Cities Minnesota Capital Grants   418
Best Buy Children's Foundation considers proposals from nonprofit organizations that serve a 7-county metro area, provide access to opportunities for teens through technology, and add vibrancy to the Twin Cities area. Applications are reviewed on a quarterly basis. Nonprofits must submit a letter of inquiry including general description of the campaign by February 1st. Organizations will be contacted within 30 days and advised as to whether or not a full proposal will be accepted. If accepted, nonprofits should submit immediately through the on-line process. Accepted capital requests will be presented at the Q1 Foundation meeting, generally in April. Site visits may be conducted between April and June with final decisions announced after the Q2 meeting, generally in July.
Requirements: Best Buy Children's Foundation will only consider capital requests in the 7-county Metro area only. Nonprofits must have received past program support from the Foundation.
Restrictions: Best Buy Children's Foundation Twin Cities Minnesota Capital Grants will not fund: organizations not certified as 501(c)3 by the IRS; organizations more frequently than annually (not including TagTeam Awards); individuals; schools (please refer to Teach@15 Program); general operating expenses; product requests; endowments; fraternal organizations or social clubs; units of government or quasi-governmental agencies; labor organizations or political campaigns; organizations designed primarily for lobbying; for-profit organizations or travel programs; fundraising dinners, testimonials, conferences or similar events; sole support of operating or advertising expenses; religious organizations for religious purposes; health, medical, or therapeutic programs or living subsidies; athletic teams or events; multi-year requests (grants must be reviewed/made annually).
Geographic Focus: Minnesota
Date(s) Application is Due: Feb 1; May 1; Aug 1; Nov 1
Contact: Stephanie Woods, Community Relations Manager; (612) 291-6108; fax (612) 292-4001; communityrelations@bestbuy.com
Internet: www.bestbuy-communityrelations.com/twin_cities.htm
Sponsor: Best Buy Children's Foundation
7601 Penn Avenue S.
Richfield, MN 55423

Better Way Foundation Grants   419
Formerly Alpha Omega Foundation, the Better Way Foundation was established in Florida in 1994. Giving is centered geographically in California, Indiana, Minnesota, Washington, and Tanzania. For the most part, the Foundation supports programs designed to provide holistic and cost-effective development opportunities to young children and families. Special emphasis is directed toward programs designed to improve early childhood outcomes. Its primary fields of interest include: Catholic agencies and churches; early childhood education; family services; health care; higher education; human services; and nutrition. Types of funding support includes: capital campaigns; general operating support; program development; research; and scholarship funding. Application forms are not required, and there are no annual deadlines. Funding amounts range up to $200,000.
Requirements: Unsolicited full proposals are not accepted. Organizations interested in presenting an idea for funding must submit a brief letter of inquiry.
Geographic Focus: California, Indiana, Minnesota, Washington, Tanzania

Amount of Grant: Up to 200,000 USD
Contact: Matthew Rauenhorst, (952) 656-4597 or (952) 656-4806; info@betterwayfoundation.org
Sponsor: Better Way Foundation
10350 Bren Road West
Minnetonka, MN 55343-9014

BibleLands Grants   420
The organization was founded to support Christian missions in the lands of the Bible. The program awards grants to hospitals and schools in the Middle Eastern areas, including Egypt, Lebanon, Israel, and Palestine. BibleLands supports schools and colleges that offer good quality Christian-based education for children whose families could not otherwise afford it.
Requirements: Projects must be Christian led.
Restrictions: Grants are not made to individuals or to projects outside of the Middle East.
Geographic Focus: Egypt, Israel, Lebanon, Palestinian Authority, Palestinian Territory
Contact: Jeremy Moodey, Chief Executive; 01494 897 950; fax 01494 897 951; info@biblelands.org.uk or jeremy.moodey@biblelands.org.uk
Internet: www.biblelands.org.uk/news/latest_grants.htm
Sponsor: BibleLands
24 London Road West
Amersham, HP7 0EZ United Kingdom

Bierhaus Foundation Grants   421
Established in 1950 in Indiana, the Bierhaus Foundation offer funding in its areas of interest, including: education; health organizations; human services; and Protestant agencies and churches. With a geographic focus throughout the State of Indiana, funding is most often offered in the form of ongoing operations. Typically, grants range from $4,000 to $40,000. Applicants should begin the process by contacting the Foundation office by either letter or telephone, offering a detailed description of the project and amount of money being sought. There are no specific deadlines.
Requirements: 501(c)3 organizations either in, or serving the residents of, Indiana can apply.
Geographic Focus: Indiana
Amount of Grant: 4,000 - 40,000 USD
Samples: Vincennes University, Vincennes, Indiana, $28,805 - general operating support; Aurthur Foundation, Bruceville, Indiana, $5,000 - general operating support; Wabash Valley Christian Academy, Vincennes, Indiana, $4,000 - general operating support.
Contact: Jayne Young, President; (812) 882-0990
Sponsor: Bierhaus Foundation
P.O. Box 538
Vincennes, IN 47591

Bikes Belong Foundation Paul David Clark Bicycling Safety Grants   422
The Bikes Belong Foundation, launched in 2006, is a separate, complementary organization to the Bikes Belong Coalition, an organization sponsored by the U.S. bicycle industry. The foundation's focus is on bicycle-safety projects and children's bicycle programs. The foundation offers three distinct grant programs: the REI Grant Program; Bikes Belong Research Grants; and the Paul David Clark Bicycling Safety Fund. The latter is geared toward advocacy efforts to improve bicycling safety. The fund is named for Paul David Clark, one of more than 600 U.S. cyclists killed in motor vehicle collisions and accidents in 2005. Paul was an avid cyclist who loved the outdoors. An attorney, he provided pro bono service to nonprofit conservation groups, including the Natural Resources Defense Council and the Trust for Public Land. In the wake of the accident, Bikes Belong teamed with Paul's brother, Blair, to create a fund to support projects that increase bicycle safety, particularly in northern California. The fund's mission is two-fold: to encourage motorists to be more aware of bicyclists; and to compel motorists and cyclists to respectfully share the road. Interested applicants are encouraged to contact the foundation for information on funding availability and how to apply.
Geographic Focus: All States
Samples: Community Cycling Center, Portland, Oregon, $10,000; Freiker, Boulder, Colorado, $10,000; NorCal High School Mountain Bike League, Petaluma, California, $10,000.
Contact: Zoe Kircos; (303) 449-4893 ext. 5; fax (303) 442-2936; zoe@bikesbelong.org
Sponsor: Bikes Belong Foundation
207 Canyon Boulevard. Suite 202
Boulder, CO 80302

Bikes Belong Foundation REI Grants   423
The Bikes Belong Foundation, launched in 2006, is a separate, complementary organization to the Bikes Belong Coalition, an organization sponsored by the U.S. bicycle industry. The foundation's focus is on bicycle-safety projects and children's bicycle programs. It offers three distinct grant programs: the Paul David Clark Bicycling Safety Fund; Bikes Belong Research Grants; and the REI Grant Program, a partnership with Recreational Equipment, Inc. (REI). The latter provides grants to communities working to improve their bicycle programs, outreach, and infrastructure. In 2011 Bikes Belong was pleased to offer REI Bicycling Design Best Practices Grants. These grants provide funding to cities whose leaders participate in the Green Lane Project and specifically support improvements to the bicycling environment based on experiences from study tours and workshops. Interested applicants are encouraged to visit the grant web for details on future funding availability.
Requirements: In the current initiative, city leaders are required to participate in the Green Lane Project tours and workshops in order for the city to be eligible.
Geographic Focus: All States
Amount of Grant: Up to 25,000 USD
Samples: Los Angeles, California, $17,000 - for the city of Los Angeles' Bicycle Repair Station Business Improvement Program; San Francisco, California, $25,000 - to fund green pavement treatments of sections of The Wiggle, a critical bicycle route that connects

downtown San Francisco with neighborhoods to the west; Pittsburgh, Pennsylvania, $23,000 - Liberty Avenue Green Bike Lanes.
Contact: Zoe Kircos; (303) 449-4893 ext. 5; fax (303) 442-2936; zoe@bikesbelong.org
Internet: www.bikesbelong.org/bikes-belong-foundation/foundation-grants/
Sponsor: Bikes Belong Foundation
207 Canyon Boulevard. Suite 202
Boulder, CO 80302

Bikes Belong Grants   424
Sponsored by the U.S. bicycle industry, the Bikes Belong Coalition has the mission of putting more people on bicycles more often. Bikes Belong grants fund important and influential projects that leverage federal funding and build momentum for bicycling in communities across the U.S. These projects include bike paths, lanes, and routes, as well as bike parks, mountain-bike trails, BMX facilities, and large-scale bicycle-advocacy initiatives. Bikes Belong grants fall into two application categories: facility applications and advocacy applications. The Bikes Belong Coalition usually offers two to three grant cycles per year (see the Schedules and Deadlines section of the website for current deadline dates). Application guidelines and downloadable applications are available at the website. Organizations should submit their completed applications along with a cover letter and any required supporting materials in one pdf file via email by the deadline date. See application guidelines for more detailed instructions.
Requirements: Nonprofit organizations whose missions are bicycle- and/or trail-specific and city, state, regional, and federal agencies are eligible to apply for facility grants. Government entities are encouraged to align with a local bicycle-advocacy group that will help develop and advance the project or program. Only organizations whose primary mission is bicycle advocacy are eligible to apply for advocacy grants. New organizations who have not yet received their nonprofit status may submit an application with the assistance of another nonprofit that has agreed to serve as their fiscal sponsor. In the facility category, the coalition will consider funding construction costs and matching funds. The coalition is particularly interested in projects that serve a range of age and ability levels and that reach the "interested but concerned" riders - those who would bicycle more but don't because of safety issues. Eligible facility requests include bike paths, lanes, trails, and bridges; end-of-trip facilities such as bike racks, parking and storage; mountain-bike facilities; bike parks; and BMX facilities. Preferred advocacy projects include large-scale, innovative, replicable initiatives that significantly increase ridership and improve conditions for bicycling in big U.S. cities. Eligible projects include programs that transform city streets (such as Ciclovias), innovative pilot projects, and initiatives that have a significant political impact. Advocacy projects should demonstrate a reasonable degree of measuring success and of future sustainability.
Restrictions: Bikes Belong will not fund individuals and rarely awards grants to organizations and communities that have received Bikes Belong funding within the past three years. Bikes Belong will NOT consider facility applications for the following types of funding: feasibility studies, master plans, policy documents, or litigation; signs, maps, and travel; trailheads, information kiosks, benches, and restroom facilities; bicycles, helmets, tools, and other accessories or equipment; events, races, clinics/classes, or bicycle rodeos; bike recycling, repair, or earn-a-bike programs; or projects in which Bikes Belong is the sole or primary funder. Bikes Belong will NOT consider advocacy project applications for the following types of funding: general operating costs; staff salaries, except where used to support a specific advocacy initiative; rides and event sponsorships; planning and retreats; or bicycles, helmets, tools, and accessories or equipment.
Geographic Focus: All States
Amount of Grant: Up to 10,000 USD
Samples: Atlanta Bicycle Coalition, Atlanta, Georgia, $10,000 - to connect two segments of existing bike lanes along a popular corridor with the goals of increasing safety and accessibility while making riding an appealing transportation option on campus and throuout the city; San Francisco Bicycle Coalition Education Fund, San Francisco, California, $10,000 - to plan and design three priority crosstown bikeways; Livable Memphis, Memphis, Tennessee, $10,000 - to help construct a two-mile separated bike trail to connect Overton Park with the Shelby Farms Park Greenline, in order to link parks, a low-income neighborhood, multiple businesses, and a local community center to provide an easy and safe transporation option.
Contact: Zoe Zircos, Grants Manager; (303) 449-4893, ext. 5; fax (303) 442-2936; zoe@bikesbelong.org or grants@bikesbelong.org
Internet: www.bikesbelong.org/grants/apply-for-a-grant/grant-seekers-guide/
Sponsor: Bikes Belong Coalition
P.O. Box 2359
Boulder, CO 80306

Bill and Melinda Gates Foundation Agricultural Development Grants   425
The Agricultural Development Program supports projects that enable small farmers in developing countries to break the cycle of hunger and poverty, to sell what they grow or raise, increase their incomes, and make their farms more productive and sustainable. Previously funded initiatives include projects that employ a collaborative and comprehensive approach to agricultural development; provide small farmers with the supplies and support they need to succeed; address the needs of women farmers; help small farmers profit from their crops; use science and technology to develop crops that can thrive; gather and analyze data to improve decision-making; encourage greater investment and involvement in agricultural development; and encourage policy and advocacy efforts that accelerate progress against the world's most acute poverty. Additional information on each agricultural development initiative can be found on the website. New proposals are considered, as well as expansion of existing initiatives currently funded by the Foundation.
Requirements: Proposals should aim to help the world's poorest people lift themselves out of hunger and poverty. The Foundation seeks proposals that: are able to produce measurable results;

use preventive approaches; promise significant and long-lasting change; leverage support from other sources; and accelerate or are in accordance with work the Foundation already supports.
Restrictions: The majority of funding is made to organizations that are independently identified by Foundation staff. Unsolicited proposals are not accepted. Proposals must be made through 501(c)3 or other tax-exempt organizations. The Foundation is unable to make grants directly to individuals. The Foundation will not fund projects addressing health problems in developed countries; political campaigns and legislative lobbying efforts; building or capital campaigns; or projects that exclusively serve religious purposes.
Geographic Focus: All Countries
Contact: Sam Dryden; (206) 709-3400 or (206) 709-3140; info@gatesfoundation.org
Internet: www.gatesfoundation.org/agriculturaldevelopment/Pages/default.aspx
Sponsor: Bill and Melinda Gates Foundation
P.O. Box 23350
Seattle, WA 98102

Bill and Melinda Gates Foundation Emergency Response Grants   426
The Foundation supports effective relief agencies and local organizations that respond quickly to people's most pressing needs in challenging conditions. The Foundation is interested in proposals that deliver food and clean water; improve sanitation; provide medical attention and shelter; prevent or minimize outbreaks of disease; and support livelihoods through cash-for-work programs. The Foundation currently supports people affected by the global food crisis; people in Sri Lanka and Pakistan displaced by political unrest and violence; victims of the earthquake in Haiti; communities affected by Typhoon Ketsana in the Philippines and Vietnam; and a consortium of leading humanitarian aid organizations.
Requirements: Relief agencies must have extensive experience and local relationships and be able to deliver help within days, when needs are most crucial. The Foundation also funds organizational capacity-building and explores learning opportunities to reinforce emergency response capabilities.
Restrictions: The majority of funding is made to organizations that are independently identified by Foundation staff. Unsolicited proposals are not accepted. Proposals must be made through 501(c)3 or other tax-exempt organizations. The Foundation is unable to make grants directly to individuals. The Gates Foundation will not fund:projects addressing health problems in developed countries; political campaigns and legislative lobbying efforts; building or capital campaigns; or projects that exclusively serve religious purposes.
Geographic Focus: All Countries
Contact: Emergency Response Coordinator; (206) 709-3140; info@gatesfoundation.org
Internet: www.gatesfoundation.org/topics/Pages/emergency-response.aspx
Sponsor: Bill and Melinda Gates Foundation
P.O. Box 23350
Seattle, WA 98102

Bill and Melinda Gates Foundation Policy and Advocacy Grants   427
The Foundation supports proposals that do one or more of the following: promote awareness of global development issues; advocate for least-advantaged populations; draw international attention and commitment; identify and promote powerful solutions; work towards additional and more effective investments; and are capable of lasting progress against global hunger and poverty.
Requirements: The Foundation seeks proposals that are able to produce measurable results; use preventive approaches; promise significant and long-lasting change; leverage support from other sources; and accelerate or are in accordance with work the Foundation already supports.
Restrictions: The majority of funding is made to organizations that are independently identified by our staff. Unsolicited proposals are not accepted. Proposals must be made through 501(c)3 or other tax-exempt organizations. The Foundation is unable to make grants directly to individuals. The Gates Foundation will not fund: projects addressing health problems in developed countries; political campaigns and legislative lobbying efforts; building or capital campaigns; or projects that exclusively serve religious purposes.
Geographic Focus: All Countries
Contact: Geoff Lamb, Global Policy and Advocacy; (206) 709-3140; info@gatesfoundation.org
Internet: www.gatesfoundation.org/global-development/Pages/overview.aspx
Sponsor: Bill and Melinda Gates Foundation
P.O. Box 23350
Seattle, WA 98102

Bill and Melinda Gates Foundation Water, Sanitation and Hygiene Grants   428
Poor sanitation causes severe diarrhea, which kills 1.5 million children each year. Smart investments in sanitation can reduce disease, increase family incomes, keep girls in school, help preserve the environment, and enhance human dignity. The Foundation is looking to work with partners in an effort to expand affordable access to sanitation. Detailed information is available at the Foundation website.
Requirements: The Gates Foundation seeks proposals that are able to produce measurable results; use preventive approaches; promise significant and long-lasting change; leverage support from other sources; and accelerate or are in accordance with work the foundation already supports.
Restrictions: The majority of funding is made to organizations that are independently identified by Foundation staff. Unsolicited proposals are not accepted. Proposals must be made through 501(c)3 or other tax-exempt organizations. The Foundation is unable to make grants directly to individuals. The Gates Foundation will not fund projects addressing health problems in developed countries; political campaigns and legislative lobbying efforts; building or capital campaigns; or projects that exclusively serve religious purposes.
Geographic Focus: All States, All Countries
Contact: Kellie Sloan; (206) 709-3140; info@gatesfoundation.org
Internet: www.gatesfoundation.org/watersanitationhygiene/Pages/home.aspx
Sponsor: Bill and Melinda Gates Foundation
P.O. Box 23350
Seattle, WA 98102

Bill Graham Memorial Foundation Grants   **429**

The Bill Graham Memorial Foundation, was formed in January of 2008 in memory of the legendary rock impresario, Bill Graham, a rock impresario and concert promoter who operated the influential counter cultural rock music venues Fillmore West and Fillmore East during the 1970s. He also worked with such acts as Jefferson Airplane, Janis Joplin, and the Grateful Dead. The foundation is a public charity that is funded through individual and corporate contributions and grants. The mission of the Foundation is the giving of grants primarily in the areas of music, the arts and education, while also supporting social work, environmental protection, and spiritual and compassionate projects in our community. In this spirit, The Bill Graham Memorial Foundation seeks to assist those whose needs are oftentimes not served by larger philanthropic organizations. The mission includes education and outreach programs, the establishment of a museum and of an annual community award, the Bill Graham Awards. The geographic scope is primarily but not absolutely limited to the Bay Area and Northern California. The majority of grants given are in the range of $1,500 to $2,500, and the maximum cap is $4,500 for a single grant. The annual application deadline is September 15.
Requirements: Any 501(c)3 organization supporting residents of San Francisco Bay and Northern California are eligible to apply.
Geographic Focus: California
Date(s) Application is Due: Sep 15
Amount of Grant: Up to 4,500 USD
Contact: Bonnie Simmons, Executive Director; (510) 654-4720; bon@billgrahamfoundation.org
Internet: www.billgrahamfoundation.org/guidelines.html
Sponsor: Bill Graham Memorial Foundation
1563 Solano Avenue, PMB 300
Berkeley, CA 94707-2116

Bindley Family Foundation Grants   **430**

Established in 1997 in Indiana, the Bindley Family Foundation gives primarily in the Indianapolis metropolitan area. Its primary fields of interest include children, education, and health service organizations. There are no specific application forms or deadlines, and applicants should begin by contacting the foundation to offer an overview of their program, project, and budgetary needs. Funding generally is offered in the form of operating support or scholarship endowments. Grants typically range from $2,000 to $15,000, though a small number are significantly higher.
Geographic Focus: Illinois, Indiana
Amount of Grant: 2,000 - 50,000 USD
Samples: Brebeuf Preparatory School, Indianapolis, Indiana, $48,213 - for operating support and scholarships; School on Wheels, Indianapolis, Indiana, $10,000 - operating support; Northwestern University, Evanston, Illinois, $7,500 - for operating expenses.
Contact: James F. Bindley, Executive Director; (317) 704-4770
Sponsor: Bindley Family Foundation
8900 Purdue Road, Suite 500
Indianapolis, IN 46268-3150

Bingham McHale LLP Pro Bono Services   **431**

The Bingham Greenebaum Doll firm is committed to the communities it serves, including: Indianapolis, Jasper, Evansville, and Vincennes, Indiana; Louisville, Frankfort, and Lexington, Kentucky; and Cincinnati, Ohio. This commitment includes sharing legal services with those who cannot afford legal assistance on their own. As attorneys, the firm recognizes that it has a special responsibility to provide legal services to the underprivileged within the communities where its attorneys work and live. low income families
Requirements: Residents of communities that the Bingham Greenebaum Doll firm serves are eligible.
Geographic Focus: Indiana
Contact: Partners and Associates; (317) 635-8900; fax (317) 236-9907
Internet: www.bgdlegal.com/aboutus/xprGeneralContent2.aspx?xpST=CommunityService
Sponsor: Bingham McHale LLP Pro Bono Program
2700 Market Tower, 10 W. Market Street
Indianapolis, IN 46204-4900

Biogen Foundation General Donations   **432**

Biogen corporate philanthropic activities are closely aligned with its mission to increase disease awareness, improve patient access to care, and help patients with unmet medical needs. Toward this mission, the Biogen Foundation provides general donations by collaborating with various patient, medical, and scientific organizations to support organizations' missions that improve the health of the patient community.
Requirements: Donations may be requested by patient, medical, and scientific 501(c)3 organizations that support Biogen's mission.
Restrictions: Biogen will not offer donations with the intent of, directly or indirectly, implicitly or explicitly, influencing or encouraging the recipient to purchase, prescribe, refer, sell, arrange for the purchase or sale, or recommend any Biogen product.
Geographic Focus: All States
Contact: Kathryn Bloom, Senior Director, Public Affairs; (617) 914-1299 or (866) 840-1146; fax (617) 679-2617; grantsoffice@biogen.com
Internet: grantsoffice.biogen.com/general-donations
Sponsor: Biogen Foundation
225 Binney Street
Cambridge, MA 02142

Blackford County Community Foundation - WOW Grants   **433**

The Blackford County Community Foundation - WOW Grants offer funding for projects that encourage, educate, and enlighten women and/or children. Applicants may be individuals, groups, or organizations.

Requirements: Applicants should submit the following items to the Foundation: cover page; project narrative with a detailed description of the project, including timeline and results expected; and a detailed budget. All grant recipients will be required to give a brief report about their project at the spring meeting.
Restrictions: The following are not eligible for funding: operating deficits, post-event or after the fact situations; special fundraising events, including endowment campaigns; political endeavors and propaganda; and profit-making enterprises and/or projects for personal gain.
Geographic Focus: Indiana
Date(s) Application is Due: Feb 1
Amount of Grant: 100 - 2,500 USD
Samples: Divorce Care for Kids, $2,500; Career Carnival, $150; Community and Family Services, Women, Infants, and Program for Girls: Making a Better You, $700.
Contact: Patricia Poulson; (765) 348-3411; fax (765) 348-4945; ppoulson@blackfordcounty.org
Internet: www.blackfordcofoundation.org/pages.asp?Page=Women%20of%20Worth&PageIndex=411
Sponsor: Blackford County Community Foundation
121 North High Street
Hartford City, IN 47348

Blackford County Community Foundation Grants   **434**

The Blackford County Community Foundation and its supporting organizations award numerous grants annually. Primary areas of interest include: community and economic development; education; community services planning and coordination; and human services. The Foundation has quarterly deadlines for submitting applications on January 31, March 31, June 30, and September 30.
Requirements: Applicants must contact the Executive Director to determine if their project is suitable for the funding. If the organization is asked to submit a formal proposal, it must consider the following criteria: purpose and definition of the project or program; background of the request office; officers and staff personnel of requesting organization; financial information and budgets; evaluation results; and how the project will be affected if funding is not received. The Foundation will judge the proposal on its merit, priority, and substantive quality.
Restrictions: The Blackford County Community Foundation generally does not fund: profit-making enterprises; political activities; operating budgets of organizations, except for limited experimental or demonstration periods; sectarian or religious organizations operated primarily for the benefit of their own members; endowment purposes; capital grants to building campaigns will only be made when there is evidence that such support is vital to the success of a program meeting priority needs of the community. Grants are not awarded for endowment purposes.
Geographic Focus: Indiana
Date(s) Application is Due: Jan 31; Mar 31; Jun 30; Sep 30
Contact: Patricia D. Poulson, Executive Director; (765) 348-3411; fax (765) 348-4945; ppoulson@blackfordcounty.org or foundation@blackfordcounty.org
Internet: blackfordcofoundation.org/Grants
Sponsor: Blackford County Community Foundation
121 North High Street
Hartford City, IN 47348

Black Hills Corporation Grants   **435**

The corporation is committed to improving the quality of life in the communities it serves. Through corporate contributions and employee contributions and voluntarism, the company assumes a leadership role in community-building. Major areas that have received funding in the past include: human services; civic and community development; education; arts and culture; and environment. Grant awards are considered in the corporation service areas, which include South Dakota, Iowa, Nebraska, Wyoming, Kansas, and Colorado.
Requirements: Nonprofit organizations offering services in South Dakota where the corporation operates are eligible.
Restrictions: While the committee judges each request on its own merits, the following requests are less likely to be approved than others: organizations that do not serve the Black Hills Corporation service territory; organizations and programs primarily designed to influence legislation; religious organizations for religious purposes; grants to individuals or organizations that are not designated by the IRS to be 501(c)3 nonprofits; proposals for conferences, seminars, or festivals; individual or group trips, tours, or pageants; single disease research programs; endowment campaigns; requests to fund deficit operating expenses; and athletic sponsorships.
Geographic Focus: South Dakota
Contact: Marsha Nichols; (605) 721-1844 or (605) 721-1700; bhc@bh-corp.com
Internet: www.blackhillscorp.com/giveguide.htm
Sponsor: Black Hills Corporation
P.O. Box 1400
Rapid City, SD 57709

Blanche and Irving Laurie Foundation Grants   **436**

The Blanche and Irving Laurie Foundation was established in 1983 by New Brunswick philanthropist Irving Laurie. The foundation makes charitable gifts to institutions and nonprofits in broad areas of interest, including the arts, especially theater and music; education; health care; social services; and needs and concerns of the Jewish community. Capital grants, operating support grants, grants for programs/projects, and scholarships are awarded. Applicants should submit seven copies of a written proposal containing the following items: copies of the most recent annual report, audited financial statement, and 990; a detailed description of the project and amount of funding requested; and a copy of the current year's organization budget and/or project budget. The foundation's board meets quarterly to evaluate proposals. Final notification occurs within three to four months from submission. Typically, awards range from $500 to $150,000.

Requirements: Nonprofit organizations in New Jersey are eligible to apply, as well as others from around the United States.

Restrictions: Giving is primarily concentrated in New Jersey. The foundation does not support medical research.

Geographic Focus: All States, New Jersey, New York

Amount of Grant: 500 - 150,000 USD

Samples: Aid the Hungry, Inc; New Providence, New York, $500 - general operating support (2018). Music for All Seasons; Scotch Plaines, New Jersey, $15,000 - general operating support, (2018).

Contact: Laura Baron, President; (908) 614-8333 or (908) 371-1777

Sponsor: Blanche and Irving Laurie Foundation

P.O. Box 53

Roseland, NJ 07068-5788

Blandin Foundation Expand Opportunity Grants   437

The Blandin Foundation's vision for its work is to be the premier partner for building healthy rural communities, grounded in strong economies, where burdens and benefits are widely shared. This vision drives the Foundation's priorities, including areas of focus for grant-making. Expand Opportunity Grants is an evolving area of work in which the Blandin Foundation seeks to blend educational attainment, economic opportunity and broader inclusion in rural Minnesota communities, so all residents have greater opportunities to prosper. Emphasis is on work that moves beyond traditional approaches and that increases impact through a synergistic approach. Roughly 75% of Foundation grants will be made in this focus area. Priority will be given to projects that demonstrate: a strategy involving inter-relationships between economy, education and inclusivity; and clear outcomes such as expanded enterprises and entrepreneurship, increased educational or economic success for populations that have faced historical barriers, and expanded relationships between educational systems, employers and parents.

Requirements: Grants will be made to organizations with a nonprofit 501(c)3 tax exempt status. Units of government may also apply for a grant, but only if the purpose of the grant request goes beyond the normal limits of expected government services and taxpayer responsibility. Grant proposals greater than $50,000 should be received by: March 15 for review in June, September 15 for review in December, and December 15 for review in March. Quick Response grants (less than $50,000), BCLP Quick Start grants and Itasca County Area community donations may be submitted at any time.

Restrictions: The Blandin Foundation does not make grants directly to individuals, except in the case of its Educational Awards Program. Funding does not support: grants outside the state of Minnesota; religious activities; medical research; publications, films or videos; travel grants for individuals or groups; camping and athletic programs; ordinary government services; grants to individuals; grants solely intended to influence legislation.

Geographic Focus: Minnesota

Date(s) Application is Due: Mar 15; Sep 15; Dec 15

Amount of Grant: Up to 250,000 USD

Contact: Wade Fauth, Grants Director; (218) 327-8706 or (218) 326-0523; fax (218) 327-1949; bfinfo@blandinfoundation.org

Internet: www.blandinfoundation.org/grants/grants-detail.php?intResourceID=5

Sponsor: Blandin Foundation

100 North Pokegama Avenue

Grand Rapids, MN 55744

Blandin Foundation Invest Early Grants   438

Invest Early, launched in the fall of 2005, seeks to reach children under the age of five who, due to income or other factors, may be at risk of entering kindergarten without those early skills which are so critical to success in school. Invest Early combines the resources of childhood educators, health and human services professionals, health care professionals, family development specialists, and others to provide a comprehensive program of early childhood care and education services. Some of the services offered through Invest Early include: infant/toddler/preschool programs; parent education; adult basic education (ABE); mental health support; wrap-around childcare; home visits; and transportation.

Requirements: The program is available to qualifying children and their families throughout Itasca County and works in partnership with local school districts, federal, state and county programs, and non-profit resources.

Geographic Focus: Minnesota

Contact: Wade Fauth, Grants Director; (218) 327-8706 or (218) 326-0523; fax (218) 327-1949; bfinfo@blandinfoundation.org

Internet: www.blandinfoundation.org/resources/case-studies-detail.php?intResourceID=130

Sponsor: Blandin Foundation

100 North Pokegama Avenue

Grand Rapids, MN 55744

Blandin Foundation Itasca County Area Vitality Grants   439

The Blandin Foundation's vision for its work is to be the premier partner for building healthy rural communities, grounded in strong economies, where burdens and benefits are widely shared. This vision drives the Foundation's priorities, including areas of focus for grant-making. Itasca County Area Vitality Grants carry on the legacy and commitments of businessman and Blandin Foundation founder Charles K. Blandin to his adopted hometown of Grand Rapids, Minnesota, and surrounding communities. These are grants available only for cultural and social services activities that directly benefit the communities of Itasca County and the neighboring communities of Blackduck, Northome, Hill City and Remer, Minnesota. Low priority is placed on large capital grants, recreation and community amenities. Priority will be given to projects that demonstrate: clear articulation of strategies and outcomes that will strengthen the local community, with particular consideration given to proposals that build the capacity of distressed populations to live in greater dignity; cost-effective service

delivery strategies, including collaboration with organizations addressing similar issues; and community support and sustainability evidenced by significant matching contributions.

Requirements: Grants will be made to organizations with a nonprofit 501(c)3 tax exempt status. Units of government may also apply for a grant, but only if the purpose of the grant request goes beyond the normal limits of expected government services and taxpayer responsibility. Grant proposals greater than $50,000 should be received by: March 15 for review in June, September 15 for review in December, and December 15 for review in March. Quick Response grants (less than $50,000), BCLP Quick Start grants and Itasca County Area community donations may be submitted at any time.

Restrictions: The Blandin Foundation does not make grants directly to individuals, except in the case of its Educational Awards Program. Funding does not support: grants outside the state of Minnesota; religious activities; medical research; publications, films or videos; travel grants for individuals or groups; camping and athletic programs; ordinary government services; grants to individuals; grants solely intended to influence legislation.

Geographic Focus: Minnesota

Date(s) Application is Due: Mar 15; Sep 15; Dec 15

Amount of Grant: Up to 250,000 USD

Contact: Wade Fauth, Grants Director; (218) 327-8706 or (218) 326-0523; fax (218) 327-1949; bfinfo@blandinfoundation.org

Internet: www.blandinfoundation.org/grants/grants-detail.php?intResourceID=5

Sponsor: Blandin Foundation

100 North Pokegama Avenue

Grand Rapids, MN 55744

Blockbuster Corporate Contributions   440

Blockbuster is committed to supporting the communities that its members and employees call home. It does this through outreach programs and partnerships designed to deliver measurable, positive results — on both national and local levels. Wherever possible, Blockbuster incorporates cash contributions with volunteerism and in-kind donations to achieve maximum impact.

Requirements: The company will consider requests from non-profit organizations that meet one or more of the following project *Requirements:* has film/video industry focus; impacts children/families; supports a particular Blockbuster business objective, i.e., employment; and/or, has clearly defined and measurable goals. Requests are reviewed monthly. National initiatives should mailed to the address noted below.

Restrictions: Blockbuster does not donate to the following causes, events or activities: religious organizations; sporting events; political parties, candidates or issues, and fraternal orders; endowment or capital campaigns (building funds); requests for funding or scholarships for individuals; or, independent film or video productions.

Geographic Focus: All States

Contact: Contribution Program Manager; (972) 548-8736

Internet: www.blockbuster.com/corporate/corporateGivingGuideLines

Sponsor: Blockbuster LLC

3000 Redbud Boulevard

McKinney, TX 75069

Blossom Fund Grants   441

The Blossom Fund is a private, independent foundation, which was established in 1994 and supports non-profit 501(c)3 organizations. The Fund makes grants in the following areas: economic justice for women; girls programs; support for local cultural and educational activities; and programs for youth promoting use of outdoor space. The Fund supports the community and grassroots efforts of women in the Boston area, Central America, and Mexico including programs that encourage the social or economic development of women, girls, and their communities. The Fund also supports community-based educational and cultural projects in Brookline, Boston, and Cambridge including projects: promoting increased community use of local libraries and/or enabling libraries to serve as centers for community activities; in the public schools that build skills or foster ongoing associations promoting cooperation among students, educators, parents and members of the local community; and promoting active participation in musical activities that foster community-based live musical performances. Finally, the Fund supports programs for youth that increase the use and awareness of Boston area outdoor resources including projects promoting increased access to and use of public space including parks, sanctuaries, urban wilds, rivers, lakes and harbors. Such projects should foster cooperative work and stewardship in public open spaces. Type of support strategies include: programmatic support; seed funding; start-up money; and occasional operating support. Grant typically range from $2,000 to $20,000, and are renewable upon reapplication. Preference is given to organizations with small annual budgets. There are two annual deadlines for invited applicants: September 15 and March 15.

Requirements: All proposed projects must serve Massachusetts residents of Boston, Brookline, and/or Cambridge. Projects promoting women's economic development may also serve Central America and Mexico.

Restrictions: The Blossom Fund does not fund organizations that have access to other, more-traditional funding sources. It does not fund individuals or programs that assist only a few individuals.

Geographic Focus: Massachusetts, Belize, Costa Rica, El Salvador, Guatemala, Honduras, Mexico, Nicaragua, Panama

Date(s) Application is Due: Mar 15; Sep 15

Amount of Grant: 2,000 - 20,000 USD

Contact: Colleen Berlo; (617) 622-2216 or (617) 523-6531; cberlo@lwcotrust.com

Amy Domini, Trustee; (617) 622-2240 or (617) 523-6531; adomini@lwcotrust.com

Internet: www.blossomfund.org/

Sponsor: Blossom Fund

230 Congress Street

Boston, MA 02110

Blue Cross Blue Shield of Minnesota Foundation - Healthy Children: Growing Up Healthy Grants　　442

The Growing Up Healthy Grants engage community health, early childhood development, housing and environmental organizations, and other community partners to nurture the healthy growth and development of children birth to five years and their families. Through this focus area, the Blue Cross Blue Shield (BCBS) of Minnesota Foundation has improved the quality of housing, reduced children's exposure to harmful chemicals, increased readiness for kindergarten, and increased children's access to healthy foods and safe places to play. Planning grants up to $25,000 are available. Through the planning process, funded organizations and their community partners develop a shared vision of how to improve and protect the health of children through place-based projects (neighborhood, town, region) that address health and at least two of the three determinants: early childhood education, housing, and the environment. At the end of the planning period grantees that have developed a community vision, supported by a written implementation plan, may apply for implementation funding for a period of up to three years. To receive an implementation grant, projects must show broad-based community support, demonstrate innovative approaches and articulate how these approaches will result in healthier communities and children. Letter of inquiry/application instructions, previously funded projects, and an instructional webinar are available at the Foundation website.

Requirements: The Foundation encourages a wide range of organizations to apply for funding, including community- and faith-based organizations; health, environmental, housing, early childhood and civic groups; mutual assistance associations; state, county and municipal agencies; tribal governments and agencies; professional associations or collaboratives; and policy and research organizations. Applicants must be located in Minnesota or serve Minnesotans. Eligible applicants include units of government as those designated as 501(c)3 nonprofit organizations. Organizations are required contact the Foundation to discuss their project idea. Based on the outcome of the conversation, they may then be asked to submit a letter of inquiry with supporting information.

Restrictions: The Foundation is unable to provide funding for the following: individuals; lobbying, political or fraternal activities; legal services; sports events and athletic groups; religious purposes; clinical quality improvement activities; biomedical research; capital purposes (building, purchase, remodeling or furnishing of facilities); equipment or travel, except as related to requests for program support; endowments; fundraising events or development campaigns; retiring debt or covering deficits; payment of services or benefits reimbursable from other sources; supplanting funds already secured for budgeted staff and/or services; or long-term financial support.

Geographic Focus: Minnesota
Amount of Grant: Up to 25,000 USD
Contact: Jocelyn Ancheta, Program Officer; (866) 812-1593 or (651) 662-2894; fax (651) 662-4266; Jocelyn_L_Ancheta@bluecrossmn.com
Internet: bcbsmnfoundation.com/pages-grantmaking-initiative-Healthy_Children?oid=13827
Sponsor: Blue Cross Blue Shield of Minnesota Foundation
1750 Yankee Doodle Road, N159
Eagan, MN 55122

Blue Cross Blue Shield of Minnesota Foundation - Healthy Neighborhoods: Connect for Health Challenge Grants　　443

The Foundation is expanding its focus on the health of neighborhoods and their residents. Social networks like neighborhoods help build trust, reduce isolation, and make it more likely that neighbors will work together to take action on issues affecting their neighborhood. Strong connections to friends and neighbors make people more likely to be involved in their communities, perform better in school, and live longer, healthier lives. The application is available through the Foundation's online process system. A detailed list of previously funded projects is also posted on the website.

Geographic Focus: Minnesota
Samples: The Family Partnership, Minneapolis, Minnesota, Native American Somali Peacemakers, to build a healthier community by empowering Native American and Somali youth to develop leadership skills and collaborate together on public safety and crime prevention in their communities, $100,000; Appetite for Change, Minneapolis, Minnesota, support for community cooks to bring families together to cook healthy food, share knowledge, and explore how food can create health, wealth, and social change, $20,000; Dispute Resolution Center, St. Paul, Minnesota, project to build relationships among diverse families living in public housing by creating safe spaces to talk about the challenge of community living, $20,000.
Contact: Jocelyn Ancheta, Program Officer; (866) 812-1593 or (651) 662-2894; fax (651) 662-4266; Jocelyn_L_Ancheta@bluecrossmn.com
Internet: bcbsmnfoundation.com/pages-grantmaking-initiative-Healthy_Neighborhoods?oid=13830§ion=details
Sponsor: Blue Cross Blue Shield of Minnesota Foundation
1750 Yankee Doodle Road, N159
Eagan, MN 55122

Blue Grass Community Foundation Clark County Fund Grants　　444

The Blue Grass Community Foundation is part of a network of foundations that meet the National Standards for operational quality, donor service and accountability in the community foundation sector. The Clark County Fund was established to encourage local philanthropy and to raise charitable dollars for the good of Clark County. The Fund's primary fields of interest include: arts and culture; health care and health care access; general community development; environmental projects; human services; elementary and secondary education; and social services. The Fund makes annual competitive grants of up to $10,000 to Clark County nonprofit organizations.

Requirements: Nonprofit organizations, schools and exempt government entities serving Clark County, Kentucky, are eligible to apply.

Geographic Focus: Kentucky
Amount of Grant: Up to 10,000 USD
Contact: Barbara Fischer, Director of Nonprofit Services; (859) 721-2344 or (859) 225-3343; fax (859) 243-0770; bfischer@bgcf.org
Internet: www.bgcf.org/community-funds/clark-county/
Sponsor: Blue Grass Community Foundation
499 East High Street, Suite 112
Lexington, KY 40507

Blue Grass Community Foundation Early Childhood Education and Literacy Grants　　445

The Blue Grass Community Foundation's Literacy and Early Childhood Education grant program is offered to charitable organizations serving Anderson, Bourbon, Fayette, Franklin, Harrison, Jessamine, Madison, Montgomery, Scott, or Woodford counties of Kentucky. Projects and programs should be focused on literacy and early childhood education. Suggested awards should range from $2,500 to $10,000.

Requirements: Qualified charitable organizations serving Anderson, Bourbon, Fayette, Franklin, Harrison, Jessamine, Madison, Montgomery, Scott and/or Woodford Counties are eligible to apply for funding for projects that focus early childhood education and/or literacy (including programs for English Language Learners).

Geographic Focus: Kentucky
Amount of Grant: Up to 10,000 USD
Samples: William Wells Brown Elementary School, Lexington, Kentucky, $19,000 - to facilitate the transition to virtual learning for educators and students (2020); Child Care Council of Kentucky, Inc., Lexington, Kentucky, $10,000 - to provide virtual services and adjust to the challenges of the pandemic (2020); Lexington Public Library Foundation, Lexington, Kentucky, $10,000 - to provide virtual services and adjust to the challenges of the pandemic (2020).
Contact: Kristen Tidwell, Grants and Scholarships Coordinator; (859) 721-2347 or (859) 225-3343; fax (859) 243-0770; kristen@bgcf.org
Internet: www.bgcf.org/grant-opportunities/
Sponsor: Blue Grass Community Foundation
499 East High Street, Suite 112
Lexington, KY 40507

Blue Grass Community Foundation Fayette County Fund Grants　　446

The Blue Grass Community Foundation is part of a network of foundations that meet the National Standards for operational quality, donor service and accountability in the community foundation sector. The Fayette County Fund was established to encourage local philanthropy and to raise charitable dollars for the good of Fayette County. The Fund's primary fields of interest include: arts and culture; health care and health care access; general community development; environmental projects; human services; elementary and secondary education; and social services. The Fund makes annual competitive grants of up to $10,000 to Fayette County nonprofit organizations.

Requirements: Nonprofit organizations, schools and exempt government entities serving Fayette County, Kentucky, are eligible to apply.

Geographic Focus: Kentucky
Amount of Grant: Up to 10,000 USD
Contact: Barbara Fischer, Director of Nonprofit Services; (859) 721-2344 or (859) 225-3343; fax (859) 243-0770; bfischer@bgcf,org
Internet: www.bgcf.org/community-funds/fayette-county/
Sponsor: Blue Grass Community Foundation
499 East High Street, Suite 112
Lexington, KY 40507

Blue Grass Community Foundation Franklin County Fund Grants　　447

The Blue Grass Community Foundation is part of a network of foundations that meet the National Standards for operational quality, donor service and accountability in the community foundation sector. Franklin County is home of the Capital of Kentucky, and is centrally located 54 miles east of Louisville and 29 miles west of Lexington. The region is steeped in rich historical heritage, old world ambiance, and a very special brand of famous Southern hospitality. To stroll its downtown district and visit historic homes provides a step back in time. More than anything, the love for Franklin County by it's residents can be shown through their efforts to give back to the community. The Franklin County Fund was established to encourage local philanthropy and to raise charitable dollars for the good of Franklin County. The Fund's primary fields of interest include: arts and culture; health care and health care access; general community development; environmental projects; human services; elementary and secondary education; and social services. The Fund makes annual competitive grants of up to $10,000 to Franklin County nonprofit organizations.

Requirements: Nonprofit organizations, schools and exempt government entities serving Franklin County, Kentucky, are eligible to apply.

Geographic Focus: Kentucky
Amount of Grant: Up to 10,000 USD
Contact: Barbara Fischer, Director of Nonprofit Services; (859) 721-2344 or (859) 225-3343; fax (859) 243-0770; bfischer@bgcf,org
Internet: www.bgcf.org/community-funds/franklin-county/
Sponsor: Blue Grass Community Foundation
499 East High Street, Suite 112
Lexington, KY 40507

Blue Grass Community Foundation Harrison County Fund Grants 448

The Blue Grass Community Foundation is part of a network of foundations that meet the National Standards for operational quality, donor service and accountability in the community foundation sector. The Harrison County Fund was established in 2002 to encourage local philanthropy and to raise charitable dollars for the good of Harrison County. The Fund's primary fields of interest include: arts and culture; health care and health care access; general community development; environmental projects; human services; elementary and secondary education; and social services. The Fund makes annual competitive grants of up to $10,000 to Harrison County nonprofit organizations.

Requirements: Nonprofit organizations, schools and exempt government entities serving Harrison County, Kentucky, are eligible to apply.

Geographic Focus: Kentucky

Amount of Grant: Up to 10,000 USD

Contact: Barbara Fischer, Director of Nonprofit Services; (859) 721-2344 or (859) 225-3343; fax (859) 243-0770; bfischer@bgcf.org

Internet: www.grantselect.com/editor/view_grant/120575

Sponsor: Blue Grass Community Foundation

499 East High Street, Suite 112

Lexington, KY 40507

Blue Grass Community Foundation Hudson-Ellis Grants 449

The Hudson-Ellis Fund was established at Blue Grass Community Foundation for the good of Boyle County through a bequest by Lottie Ellis. Lottie Ellis lived her entire life in Danville, Kentucky. When she died in 1999 at the age of 91, she made a gift to her home town that will live forever. Miss Ellis, a former bookkeeper, lived a quiet, simple, modest life. She was an avid reader. For the last ten years of her life, she was unable to leave her house in downtown Danville, but looked forward to weekly visits from the Boyle County Library's book mobile. Few were aware that she'd inherited $4 million from a long-time friend named T. Yates Hudson, Jr. The Hudson-Ellis Discretionary Fund makes annual competitive grants of up to $10,000 to Boyle County nonprofits. The annual deadline for application submission is July 17.

Requirements: Nonprofit organizations, schools and exempt government entities serving Boyle County are eligible to apply.

Geographic Focus: Kentucky

Date(s) Application is Due: Jul 17

Amount of Grant: Up to 10,000 USD

Samples: Wilderness Trace Child Development Center, Danville, Kentucky, $10,000 - to upgrade playground equipment (2019); Family Services Association of Boyle County, Danville, Kentucky, $10,000 - for emergency housing assistance for residents of Boyle County (2019); Danville-Boyle Early Childhood Alliance, Danville, Kentucky, $10,000 -for a community action plan (2019).

Contact: Kristen Tidwell, Grants and Scholarships Coordinator; (859) 721-2347 or (859) 225-3343; fax (859) 243-0770; kristen@bgcf.org

Internet: www.bgcf.org/grant-opportunities/

Sponsor: Blue Grass Community Foundation

499 East High Street, Suite 112

Lexington, KY 40507

Blue Grass Community Foundation Madison County Fund Grants 450

The Blue Grass Community Foundation is part of a network of foundations that meet the National Standards for operational quality, donor service and accountability in the community foundation sector. Indian trader John Findley, Daniel Boone, and four others first came into the area that is now Madison County in 1769 on a hunting and exploring expedition. In 1774, the Transylvania Company, led by Judge Richard Henderson of North Carolina, purchased 20,000,000 acres of land west of the Appalachians (including present-day Madison County) from the Cherokee Nation. Daniel Boone was hired to cut a trail through the Cumberland Gap and establish a settlement on the Kentucky River. The Madison County Fund was established to encourage local philanthropy and to raise charitable dollars for the good of Madison County. The Fund's primary fields of interest include: arts and culture; health care and health care access; general community development; environmental projects; human services; elementary and secondary education; and social services. The Fund makes annual competitive grants of up to $10,000 to Madison County nonprofit organizations.

Requirements: Nonprofit organizations, schools and exempt government entities serving Madison County, Kentucky, are eligible to apply.

Geographic Focus: Kentucky

Amount of Grant: Up to 10,000 USD

Contact: Barbara Fischer, Director of Nonprofit Services; (859) 721-2344 or (859) 225-3343; fax (859) 243-0770; bfischer@bgcf.org

Internet: www.bgcf.org/community-funds/madison-county/

Sponsor: Blue Grass Community Foundation

499 East High Street, Suite 112

Lexington, KY 40507

Blue Grass Community Foundation Magoffin County Fund Grants 451

The Blue Grass Community Foundation is part of a network of foundations that meet the National Standards for operational quality, donor service and accountability in the community foundation sector. The Magoffin County Fund was established to encourage local philanthropy and to raise charitable dollars for the good of Magoffin County. The Fund's primary fields of interest include: arts and culture; health care and health care access; general community development; environmental projects; human services; elementary and secondary education; and social services. The Fund makes annual competitive grants of up to $10,000 to Magoffin County nonprofit organizations.

Requirements: Nonprofit organizations, schools and exempt government entities serving Magoffin County, Kentucky, are eligible to apply.

Geographic Focus: Kentucky

Amount of Grant: Up to 10,000 USD

Contact: Barbara Fischer, Director of Nonprofit Services; (859) 721-2344 or (859) 225-3343; fax (859) 243-0770; bfischer@bgcf.org

Internet: www.bgcf.org/community-funds/magoffin-county/

Sponsor: Blue Grass Community Foundation

499 East High Street, Suite 112

Lexington, KY 40507

Blue Grass Community Foundation Morgan County Fund Grants 452

The Blue Grass Community Foundation is part of a network of foundations that meet the National Standards for operational quality, donor service and accountability in the community foundation sector. In February 2012, Morgan County was torn apart by a devastating tornado. Businesses and homes were destroyed. The entire town of West Liberty was affected. After months of hard work and perseverance, the community started looking towards the future of Morgan County. The Foundation for Morgan County was officially formed in January 2013 as a geographic component fund of Blue Grass Community Foundation. A local Board of Advisors has been working diligently on a development plan to grow charitable giving in Morgan County. An endowed fund to serve the future needs of the nonprofits in the community and a fund to support local small businesses have been established. Today, the Foundation Fund encourages local philanthropy and raising charitable dollars for the good of Morgan County. The Fund's primary fields of interest include: arts and culture; health care and health care access; general community development; environmental projects; human services; elementary and secondary education; and social services. The Fund makes annual competitive grants of up to $10,000 to Morgan County nonprofit organizations.

Requirements: Nonprofit organizations, schools and exempt government entities serving Morgan County, Kentucky, are eligible to apply.

Geographic Focus: Kentucky

Amount of Grant: Up to 10,000 USD

Contact: Barbara Fischer, Director of Nonprofit Services; (859) 721-2344 or (859) 225-3343; fax (859) 243-0770; bfischer@bgcf.org

Internet: www.bgcf.org/community-funds/morgan-county/

Sponsor: Blue Grass Community Foundation

499 East High Street, Suite 112

Lexington, KY 40507

Blue Grass Community Foundation Rowan County Fund Grants 453

The Blue Grass Community Foundation is part of a network of foundations that meet the National Standards for operational quality, donor service and accountability in the community foundation sector. In April 2014, the RCCFG announced it was accepting applications from nonprofit organizations in Rowan County for the distribution of its first $5,000 on grants. This money came to the RCCF as a challenge grant from ARC and the Appalachia Rural Development Philanthropy Initiative – ARDPI for reaching its goal of $10,000 for the Rowan County Community Fund permanent endowment fund. Currently, the Fund's primary fields of interest include: arts and culture; health care and health care access; general community development; environmental projects; human services; elementary and secondary education; and social services. The Fund makes annual competitive grants of up to $5,000 to Rowan County nonprofit organizations.

Requirements: Nonprofit organizations, schools and exempt government entities serving Rowan County, Kentucky, are eligible to apply.

Geographic Focus: Kentucky

Amount of Grant: 500 - 5,000 USD

Contact: Barbara Fischer, Director of Nonprofit Services; (859) 721-2344 or (859) 225-3343; fax (859) 243-0770; bfischer@bgcf.org

Internet: www.bgcf.org/community-funds/rowan-county/

Sponsor: Blue Grass Community Foundation

499 East High Street, Suite 112

Lexington, KY 40507

Blue Grass Community Foundation Woodford County Fund Grants 454

The Blue Grass Community Foundation is part of a network of foundations that meet the National Standards for operational quality, donor service and accountability in the community foundation sector. The Woodford County Community Fund embraces these values as guides for its work: to be accountable to the community and transparent in how it manages and uses resources; to build partnerships with public and private groups so that together residents can do more for Woodford County; to empower residents, especially youth, to be advocates for creative ways to enhance the quality of life and economic opportunities in Woodford County; and to encourage a sense of responsibility and contribution to community well-being among all residents and organizations. Today, the Fund's primary fields of interest include: arts and culture; health care and health care access; general community development; environmental projects; human services; elementary and secondary education; and social services. The Fund makes annual competitive grants of up to $10,000 to woodford County nonprofit organizations.

Requirements: Nonprofit organizations, schools and exempt government entities serving Woodford County, Kentucky, are eligible to apply.

Geographic Focus: Kentucky

Amount of Grant: Up to 10,000 USD

Contact: Barbara Fischer, Director of Nonprofit Services; (859) 721-2344 or (859) 225-3343; fax (859) 243-0770; bfischer@bgcf.org

Internet: www.bgcf.org/community-funds/woodford-county/

Sponsor: Blue Grass Community Foundation
499 East High Street, Suite 112
Lexington, KY 40507

Blue Mountain Community Foundation Discretionary Grants   455
The Blue Mountain Community Foundation administers charitable funds to benefit people of the Blue Mountain Area. Most of the money for discretionary grants is designated by donors for use by agencies serving Walla Walla County. The Foundation's grant making policies are generally directed toward the fields of social and community services, the arts and humanities, education and health. This opportunity is intended to assist nonprofit organizations in the service areas identified above in continuing to operate during and beyond the pandemic, and to enable them to readjust so that they may reopen or expand programming when it is allowable to do so. The deadline to apply is February 8th.
Requirements: Tax-exempt 501(c)3 charitable organizations in the Foundation's service area, namely Umatilla, Walla Walla, Garfield, and Columbia counties. In limited cases, other charitable entities are considered at the Foundation's sole discretion.
Restrictions: Grants usually will not be made for the following: programs outside the Blue Mountain Area, operating expenses, annual fund drives, field trips, travel to or in support of conferences. No grants will be made for sectarian religious purposes nor to influence legislation or elections.
Geographic Focus: Oregon, Washington
Date(s) Application is Due: Feb 8
Contact: Kol Medina, Executive Director; (509) 529-4371; fax (509) 529-5284; kol@bluemountainfoundation.org or bmcf@bluemountainfoundation.org
Internet: www.bluemountainfoundation.org/grants/grantinfo/
Sponsor: Blue Mountain Community Foundation
22 East Poplar Street, Suite 206, P.O. Box 603
Walla Walla, WA 99362-0015

Blue Mountain Community Foundation Garfield County Health Foundation Fund Grants   456
The Blue Mountain Community Foundation administers charitable funds to benefit people of the Blue Mountain Area. Most of the money for discretionary grants is designated by donors for use by agencies serving Walla Walla County. The Foundation's grant making policies are generally directed toward the fields of social and community services, the arts and humanities, education and health. Regarding the Garfield County Health Foundation Fund specifically, awards are made to support programs and organizations that promote the health and wellness of the citizens of the County. The annual deadline to apply is March 1st.
Requirements: Tax-exempt 501(c)3 charitable organizations in the Foundation's service area, namely Columbia, Garfield and Walla Walla counties in Washington, and Umatilla County in Oregon, may apply. In limited cases, other charitable entities are considered at the Foundation's sole discretion.
Restrictions: Grants usually will not be made for the following: programs outside the Blue Mountain Area, operating expenses, annual fund drives, field trips, travel to or in support of conferences. No grants will be made for sectarian religious purposes nor to influence legislation or elections.
Geographic Focus: Oregon, Washington
Date(s) Application is Due: Mar 1
Contact: Greer Buchanan, Grants Manager; (509) 529-4371; fax (509) 529-5284; greer@bluemountainfoundation.org or bmcf@bluemountainfoundation.org
Internet: www.bluemountainfoundation.org/grants/grantinfo/
Sponsor: Blue Mountain Community Foundation
22 East Poplar Street, Suite 206, P.O. Box 603
Walla Walla, WA 99362-0015

Blue Mountain Community Foundation Warren Community Action Fund Grants   457
The Blue Mountain Community Foundation administers charitable funds to benefit people of the Blue Mountain Area. Most of the money for discretionary grants is designated by donors for use by agencies serving Walla Walla County. The Foundation's grant making policies are generally directed toward the fields of social and community services, the arts and humanities, education and health. Through the Warren Community Action Fund, grants are made to support programs that improve the quality of life in the community focusing on the specific areas of health, education, basic human needs, children and youth, agricultural education and training, historic preservation, scientific programs, arts and recreation, and the environment. Requests for support for capital, project or program, and general operating support will be considered. Of particular interest are projects and organizations about which there is consensus in the community, demonstrated by financial and other support received from other sources. The deadline to apply is May 1st.
Requirements: The Warren Community Action Fund considers requests from charitable 501(c)3 organizations, public agencies and religious organizations, including churches. The primary area of focus for grants is Dayton, Columbia County and northern Walla Walla County, particularly Waitsburg.
Restrictions: Grants usually will not be made for the following: programs outside the Blue Mountain Area, operating expenses, annual fund drives, field trips, travel to or in support of conferences. No grants will be made for sectarian religious purposes nor to influence legislation or elections.
Geographic Focus: Oregon, Washington
Date(s) Application is Due: May 1
Contact: Greer Buchanan, Grants Manager; (509) 529-4371; fax (509) 529-5284; greer@bluemountainfoundation.org or bmcf@bluemountainfoundation.org
Internet: www.bluemountainfoundation.org/grants/grantinfo/
Sponsor: Blue Mountain Community Foundation
22 East Poplar Street, Suite 206, P.O. Box 603
Walla Walla, WA 99362-0015

Blue River Community Foundation Grants   458
The Blue River Community Foundation is a community-based philanthropic organization that identifies, promotes, supports, and manages programs that will enhance the quality of life in Shelby County, Indiana, for this generation and future generations. To this end, the Foundation has established five areas of interest for the competitive grant making program: community and civic—support for community programs designed to improve life in Shelby County; arts and culture—support for programs and facilities that offer widespread opportunities for participation and appreciation; education—support for programs at all levels of education; health—support for the promotion of health and well-being for Shelby County residents; and social services—support of human service organization programs. Organizations interested in submitting a grant request should first submit the grant interest form found on the website. If the grant request meets the Foundation's funding guidelines, the organization will be invited to submit a formal Grant Application Form. Grant applications may be submitted at any time, but will only be reviewed during the next upcoming grant cycle.
Requirements: Any 501(c)3 organization serving the residents of Shelby County, Indiana, may apply.
Geographic Focus: Indiana
Date(s) Application is Due: Feb 1; Jun 1; Oct 1
Contact: Lynne Ensminger, Program Director; (317) 392-7955; fax (317) 392-4545; lensminger@blueriverfoundation.com or brf@blueriverfoundation.com
Internet: blueriverfoundation.com/main.asp?SectionID=6&TM=34321.26
Sponsor: Blue River Community Foundation
54 W Broadway Street, Suite 1, P.O. Box 808
Shelbyville, IN 46176

Blumenthal Foundation Grants   459
In 1924, I.D. Blumenthal was a traveling salesman in need of repair to his car's radiator. A local tinsmith in Charlotte, North Carolina, repaired the radiator with a "magic powder". Impressed with the product, I.D. teamed with the tinsmith and Solder Seal became the first product of the Radiator Specialty Company. The Blumenthal Foundation was founded in 1953 and was endowed with the success of the Radiator Specialty Company. The Foundation focuses the majority of its grants on programs and projects that have an impact on Charlotte, and the state of North Carolina. The philanthropic efforts of the Foundation are focused in nine areas of grant making: arts, science and culture; civic and community; education; environment; foundation affiliates; health; Jewish institutions and philanthropies; religious and interfaith; and social sciences. The foundation believes that basic operational funding for non-profits is just as important, if not more so, than support for special programs or projects; consequently, grants are provided for seed money, annual operating costs, capital campaigns, conferences and seminars, special projects, and endowments. Interested organizations may click the Grant Guidelines link at the website for detailed submission instructions. Applications must be mailed. There are no deadlines, and requests are accepted on an ongoing basis. The Board of Trustees meets quarterly to consider grant applications.
Requirements: 501(c)3 organizations and institutions that serve the city of Charlotte and the State of North Carolina in the Foundation's areas of interest are eligible to apply.
Restrictions: Grants are not made to individuals for any purpose.
Geographic Focus: North Carolina
Contact: Philip Blumenthal, Director; (704) 688-2305; fax (704) 688-2301; foundation@gunk.com or foundation@gunk.com
Internet: www.blumenthalfoundation.org/BFGrantListings.htm
Sponsor: Blumenthal Foundation
P.O. Box 34689
Charlotte, NC 28234-4689

BMW of North America Charitable Contributions   460
BMW of North America funds charitable programs that benefit society in the areas of education, road-traffic safety, and the environment. The corporation supports education at all levels and specifically focuses on the following: intercultural learning for K-12 students and their teachers; automotive technology, mechanics, and career and repair programs in high schools, technical schools, and community colleges; and research in the areas of safety design, ergonomics, and new materials. In the area of road traffic safety, the corporation supports driver-education programs geared at teenagers and new drivers; basic auto-maintenance programs for women; consumer education on general road-safety issues; and programs to promote the safety of children and young people on the road. In the area of the environment, BMW is committed to sustainable development and focuses grant making on the following: conservation/preservation of natural resources, in particular park lands and waterways; research and promotion of alternative fuels; and environmental education for K-12 students. In general, grants are awarded for specific projects rather than for general operating support, although some operating and capital grants are given consideration. Interested organizations may download application instructions and guidelines at the grant website. Organizations wishing to be considered for a grant must submit an application; telephone solicitations will not considered.
Requirements: 501(c)3 charities or 501(c)9 organizations are eligible to apply.
Restrictions: The corporate giving program does not support non-tax-exempt organizations; individuals; religious organizations for religious purposes; political candidates or lobbying organizations; organizations with a limited constituency, such as fraternal, labor, or veterans groups; travel by groups or individuals; national or local chapters of disease-specific organizations; national conferences, sports events, and other one-time, short-term events; sponsorships or advertising; anti-business groups; team sponsorships or athletic scholarships; or organizations outside the United States or its territories.
Geographic Focus: All States
Contact: Grants Coordinator; (201) 307-4000; fax (201) 307 3607
Internet: www.bmwgroup.com/en/verantwortung/gesellschaftliches-engagement.html#

Sponsor: BMW Group of North America
300 Chestnut Ridge Road
Woodcliff Lake, NJ 07677-7731

Bodenwein Public Benevolent Foundation Grants 461

The Bodenwein Public Benevolent Foundation was established in 1938 under the will of Theodore Bodenwein, owner and publisher of The Day newspaper, to support and promote quality educational, cultural, human-services, and health-care programming for underserved populations. The Foundation specifically serves the people of Greater New London County where The Day has a substantial circulation. The majority of grants from the Bodenwein Public Benevolent Foundation are one year in duration; on occasion, multi-year support is awarded. Awards amounts typically range from $150 to $60,000, although the most recently awarded grants have been worth an average of $5,000.

Requirements: Applicant organizations must serve the people of East Lyme, Groton, Ledyard, Lyme, Montville, Mystic, New London, North Stonington, Old Lyme, Salem, Stonington, or Waterford, Connecticut. Payments may be made to any organization under the laws of the state of Connecticut. Applications will be submitted online through the Bank of America website. A grant report is required within 1 year of the grant application date, regardless of whether all of the funds have been spent.

Restrictions: The foundation does not support requests from individuals, organizations attempting to influence policy through direct lobbying, or any political campaigns.

Geographic Focus: Connecticut

Date(s) Application is Due: Nov 15

Amount of Grant: 150 - 60,000 USD

Samples: New London Homeless Hospitality Center Inc., New London, Connecticut, $5,000 - Awarded for Help Center (2018); New London Rotary Foundation Inc., New London, Connecticut, $5,000 - Awarded for Campaign for the Pavilion at Ocean Beach Park (2018); New London Community Meal Center Inc., New London, Connecticut, $5,000 - Awarded for General Operating Support (2018).

Contact: Amy R. Lynch, Philanthropic Client Manager; (860) 244-4870; ct.grantmaking@bankofamerica.com or amy.r.lynch@bofa.com

Internet: www.bankofamerica.com/philanthropic/foundation/?fnId=50

Sponsor: Bodenwein Public Benevolent Foundation
P.O. Box 1802
Providence, RI 02901-1802

Boeing Company Contributions Grants 462

The Boeing U.S. contributions program welcomes applications in five focus areas: education; health and human services; arts and culture; civic; and the environment. Primary fields of interest include: arts; elementary and secondary education; the environment; family services, prevention of domestic violence; health care; public affairs; public safety; substance abuse programs; and general human services. The largest single block of charitable contributions goes toward supporting programs and projects related to education. Boeing also looks for innovative initiatives that promote the economic well-being of the community and neighborhood revitalization. Boeing invests in programs that promote participation in arts and cultural activities and experiences, programs that increase public understanding of and engagement in the processes and issues that affect communities and programs that protect and conserve the natural environment. Boeing accepts applications for cash grants, in-kind donations, and services.

Requirements: To apply for support you must be a U.S. based IRS 501(c)3 qualified charitable or educational organization or an accredited K-12 educational institution. U.S. grant guidelines and applications are available online.

Restrictions: Grants do not support: an individual person or families; adoption services; political candidates or organizations; religious activities, in whole or in part, for the purpose of further religious doctrine; memorials and endowments; travel expenses; nonprofit and school sponsored walk-a-thons, athletic events and athletic group sponsorships other than Special Olympics; door prizes or raffles; U.S. hospitals and medical research; school-affiliated orchestras, bands, choirs, trips, athletic teams, drama groups, yearbooks and class parties; general operating expenses for programs within the United States; organizations that do not follow our application procedures; follow-on applications from past grantees that have not met our reporting requirements or satisfactorily completed the terms of past grants; fundraising events, annual funds, galas and other special-event fundraising activities; advertising, t-shirts, giveaways and promotional items; documentary films, books, etc; debt reduction; dissertations and student research projects; loans, scholarships, fellowships and grants to individuals; for-profit businesses; gifts, honoraria, gratuities; capital improvements to rental properties.

Geographic Focus: Alabama, Arizona, California, Colorado, District of Columbia, Florida, Georgia, Hawaii, Illinois, Kansas, Maryland, Missouri, Nevada, New Mexico, Ohio, Oklahoma, Oregon, Pennsylvania, South Carolina, Texas, Utah, Washington, Australia, Canada

Contact: Antoinette Bailey, (312) 544-2000; fax (312) 544 - 2082

Internet: www.boeing.com/companyoffices/aboutus/community/charitable.htm

Sponsor: Boeing Company Contributions
100 North Riverside
Chicago, IL 60606-1596

Bollinger Foundation Grants 463

The Bollinger Foundation provides grants in the form of Grants and scholarships to surviving members of families in which a parent worked in the fields of community development, housing, or economic development. Grants also support children's education, including but not limited to grants toward special educational needs, school materials, and college tuition. The foundation invites nominations of eligible families for grants. Guidelines and nomination form are available online.

Requirements: Families must be nominated to receive grants.

Geographic Focus: All States

Date(s) Application is Due: May 3

Amount of Grant: Up to 5,000 USD

Contact: Ann Seely, c/o IEDC; (202) 942-9476; fax (202) 223-4745; aseely@iedconline.org

Internet: www.bollingerfoundation.org

Sponsor: Bollinger Foundation
734 15th Street NW, Suite 900
Washington, D.C. 20005

Bothin Foundation Grants 464

The Bothin Foundation helps to build the capacity of nonprofits with grants for durable capital investments. The Foundation makes capital grants to social service, education, arts, and environmental nonprofit organizations that provide direct services to: disadvantaged children and youth (ages 0 to 24), low-income families, and people with disabilities. The Foundation also supports K-12 schools exclusively serving children with learning differences. The Foundation accepts online proposals during specified submission windows in the fall, spring, and summer.

Requirements: Grants are made to public charities operating under an IRS 501(c)3 status or fiscally sponsored by a 501(c)3 organization serving residents of San Francisco, Marin, Sonoma, and San Mateo counties in California.

Restrictions: Grants are not made to individuals, for endowment drives, medical research, general operating expenses, films and other media presentations, religious organizations, conferences, program support, or to educational institutions other than those directly serving the learning and developmentally disabled. The foundation will consider grant applications from the same organization only after three full years have elapsed since the last grant.

Geographic Focus: California

Date(s) Application is Due: Feb 19; Aug 6; Nov 6

Contact: Jennifer Perez Brown; (415) 561-6540, ext. 255; fax (415) 561-6477; jbrown@pfs-llc.net

Internet: www.bothinfoundation.org/

Sponsor: Bothin Foundation
1660 Bush Street, Suite 300
San Francisco, CA 94109

BP Foundation Grants 465

The BP Foundation is a charitable organization that helps communities around the world by supporting: science, technology, engineering and math (STEM) education (except in countries where basic literacy is an issue); enterprise development, jobs training and sustainable community projects; programs that further the understanding of and foster practical means of addressing global environmental issues; and emergency humanitarian relief. Of particular interest are the areas of: basic and emergency aid; community and economic development; disaster relief; elementary and secondary education; the environment; foundations endowments; higher education; human services; international development; job training; natural resources; STEM education; and sustainable development.

Requirements: National and international (in areas where BP operates) nonprofit organizations are entitled to apply. Regions include: United States; Australia; Canada; China; all of Europe; Japan; Philippines; Singapore; and the United Kingdom.

Restrictions: The Foundation does not accept unsolicited proposals, but rather reviews requests submitted by BP businesses around the world.

Geographic Focus: All States, Austria, Belgium, Canada, China, Denmark, Estonia, Finland, France, Germany, Greece, Hong Kong, Ireland, Italy, Japan, Luxembourg, Mexico, Netherlands, Norway, Philippines, Poland, Portugal, Russia, Singapore, Spain, Sweden, Switzerland, United Kingdom

Contact: Tara Harrison, Executive Director; (281) 366-2000

Internet: www.bp.com/en_us/united-states/home/community/bp-foundation.html

Sponsor: BP Foundation
501 Westlake Park Boulevard, 25th Floor
Houston, TX 77079-2604

Bradley-Turner Foundation Grants 466

Incorporated as the W.C. and Sarah H. Bradley Foundation in Georgia in 1943, the Bradley-Turner Foundation uses contributions from the company's success to support the community and region through many different programs and facilities funded in whole or in part by foundation donations. The foundation has a special interest in endeavors related to family and children services, education, religion (Baptist, Christian, interdenominational, Methodist, Presbyterian, Salvation Army, and United Methodist), health, and culture and the arts. Major focus is placed on the vitality and quality of life in Columbus, Georgia, though compelling programs beyond the city's boundaries will also be considered. The foundation is particularly interested in projects that have a broad base of community support. There are no application forms. Applicants are asked to submit a letter of three to five pages describing the project. Grants are reviewed quarterly, in February, May, August, and November, when the board meets.

Requirements: IRS 501(c)3 tax-exempt organizations in Georgia are eligible. Heavily focuses on the southern region of the United States, but the Foundation is not solely limited to this area. It has also donated in Massachusetts, Illinois, and Colorado.

Restrictions: Grants are not made to individuals or to for-profit businesses or corporations.

Geographic Focus: Georgia

Amount of Grant: 2,500 - 300,000 USD

Contact: Phyllis Wagner, Executive Secretary; (706) 571-6040; fax (706) 571-3408

Internet: www.wcbradley.com/about/overview

Sponsor: Bradley-Turner Foundation
1017 Front Avenue, P.O. Box 140
Columbus, GA 31902-0140

Bradley C. Higgins Foundation Grants 467

The Bradley C. Higgins Foundation was established in Massachusetts in 1961, with its primary fields of interest identified as: arts and culture; education; health and health care; and human services. In the majority of instances, awards are given for either general operating support or program development. Interested parties should begin by forwarding a letter of interest to the Foundation office, explaining their overall program and general budgetary needs. A copy of the IRS determination letter should also be included. There are no annual deadlines. Approximately a dozen awards are approved annually, ranging from $500 to $30,000.
Requirements: Support is limited to Massachusetts-based 501(c)3 organizations.
Geographic Focus: Massachusetts
Amount of Grant: 500 - 30,000 USD
Samples: Boothbay Railway Village Museum, Boothbay, Maine, $20,000 - support for general operating expenses (2019); Cotuit Athletic Association, Cotuit, Massachusetts, $5,000 - support for general operating expenses (2019); Willard House and Clock Museum, Worcester, Massachusetts, $30,000 - support for the preservation of the Higgins Armor Collection (2019).
Contact: Sumner B. Tilton, Jr., Chairperson; 508-459-8087 or (508) 459-8000; fax (508) 459-8300; stilton@fletchertilton.com
Sponsor: Bradley C. Higgins Foundation
370 Main Street, 12th Floor
Worcester, MA 01608-1779

Brian G. Dyson Foundation Grants 468

The Foundation, established in Atlanta in 1994 by former Coca-Cola Bottling executive, Brian G. Dyson, offers funding to community foundations, higher education, and federated programs in the Atlanta region and throughout Georgia. Grants typically range up to $20,000, and funding supports general operating costs. There are no specific guidelines, application formats, or deadlines with which to adhere, and initial contact should be made in writing.
Requirements: Applicants must be colleges, public or private schools, or other non-profit organizations located within the state of Georgia.
Geographic Focus: Georgia
Amount of Grant: Up to 20,000 USD
Contact: Brian G. Dyson, Director; (404) 364-2940
Sponsor: Brian G. Dyson Foundation
3060 Peachtree Road NW, Suite 1465
Atlanta, GA 30305-2241

Bridgestone Americas Trust Fund Grants 469

The Bridgestone Americas Trust supports programs and projects of nonprofit organizations in the areas of education, child welfare, and the environment and conservation in communities where the company has operations. While primary consideration is given to organizations and causes related to the three major focus points, the Fund recognizes the importance and value in supporting all types of civic, community and cultural activities. Assistance is regularly given for: community and neighborhood improvements; civil rights and equal opportunity; voter registration and education; job training; performing arts programs; public radio and television; cultural programs; non-academic libraries; and museums. Types of support include: annual campaigns; building/renovation; capital campaigns; continuing support; donated equipment; emergency funds; employee matching gifts; employee-related scholarships; endowments; exchange programs; fellowships; general/operating support; matching/challenge support; program development; research; scholarship funds; and sponsorships. Applications must be submitted in writing and should include a description of the organization (two-page maximum) and its record of accomplishment, objectives of the program, whom the program benefits, and proposed method to evaluate the program's success; amount sought from the trust in relation to the total need; exactly how trust fund money would be used; copy of IRS 501(c)3 confirmation letter; list of board of directors and their professional affiliations; previous year's financial report; current year's operating budget; Form 990; list of other contributors and the amount of their donations; and copy of recent audit if available. Proposals are reviewed upon receipt.
Requirements: IRS 501(c)3 nonprofit tax-exempt organizations in all states are eligible to apply. Schools, governmental agencies, community nonprofits, civic organizations are included. Grant proposals should be completed online.
Restrictions: It is essential that all organizations receiving grants be equal opportunity employers who will operate their programs in support of equal opportunity objectives. Contributions will not be made to groups that discriminate on the basis of race, color, religion, gender, mental or physical disabilities, sexual orientation, national origin, age, citizenship, veteran/reserve/national guard status, or other protected status; partisan political organizations; or groups limited to members of a single religious organization.
Geographic Focus: All States
Amount of Grant: 50 - 50,000 USD
Contact: Dolores Bernice; (615) 937-1415 or (615) 937-1000; fax (615) 937-1414
Internet: www.bridgestoneamericas.com/en/corporate-social-responsibility/community/trust-fund-application
Sponsor: Bridgestone Americas Trust Fund
535 Marriott Drive
Nashville, TN 37214-5092

Bright Promises Foundation Grants 470

The Bright Promises Foundation's primary activities are identifying the most pressing unmet needs of disadvantaged children in Illinois; calling for individuals, foundations, agencies, legislators, parents and the media to join the foundation in supporting these needs; soliciting grant applications and making grants that support these needs; attracting volunteers and funds to the foundation; and recognizing important role models with awards. Currently, the Bright Promises Foundation's focus is promoting better health among low-income and other at-risk children between the ages of 8-12. The Bright Promises

Foundation initiated a four-year grant program called Healthy Children/Healthy Adults: Promoting Health through Better Nutritional Choices. The program responds to the escalating problem of childhood obesity in the state of Illinois. Now in its third year, the Foundation has so far paid and pledged $481,646 to community-based multi-purpose agencies to promote better health among low-income and other at-risk children between the ages of 8-12. The foundation revisits its focus every four years to ensure relevancy.
Requirements: Grant applications are considered annually from a pool of invited applicants. Proposals are evaluated based on criteria including measurable goals and objectives, and sustainability after Bright Promises Foundation funding ends. Grantees are required to report at least twice each year on their measurable objectives, and project coordinators from the Bright Promises Foundation board of directors conduct site visits with staff during the application process and during the grant year.
Geographic Focus: Illinois
Samples: Centers for New Horizons, "Healthy Children/Healthy Adults Project," Chicago, Illinois - program includes nutrition classes delivered to children, parents and staff as well as menu planning, budgeting, food preparation and cooking, developing a working community garden and a peer education program where students will learn to be leaders in their school and to promote health and nutrition school-wide; Children's Home + Aid, "Community Schools Student Health Fitness Project," Austin, Illinois - the program serves 125 children at Howe Elementary School to provide them the foundation for a lifetime of healthy eating and exercise habits; Erie Neighborhood House, "Super H - Healthy Kids Make Happy Kids Project," Chicago, Illinois - the bi-monthly club for children and their parents includes education about the nutritional value of chosen "super foods" and how to prepare them, field trips, staff training and hands-on activities.
Contact: Iris Krieg, Executive Director; (312) 704-8260; info@brightpromises.org
Internet: www.brightpromises.org/OurPrograms/Grants/
Sponsor: Bright Promises Foundation
333 N. Michigan Avenue, Suite 510
Chicago, IL 60601

Brinker International Corporation Charitable Giving 471

The objective of Brinker International Corporation's Charitable Giving is to support programs and projects that are affiliated with children and families, arts, civic organizations, and university related educational programs. Organizations requesting donations must submit the following information on the organization's official letterhead: exact amount requested and the specific purpose for the donation briefly summarized on 1 to 2 typewritten pages; information about your organization, including proof of 501(c)3 status; information, if any, concerning past or current involvement of Brinker International employees. All requests for cash or in-kind donations are reviewed on an ongoing basis.
Requirements: 501(c)3 nonprofit organizations are eligible to apply. A request must be submitted at least 6 weeks prior to an event.
Restrictions: The Brinker International charitable giving program typically does not support the following: individuals seeking aid, including those individuals independently raising money for a non-profit organization; political organizations or candidates; religious organizations or programs; capital campaigns; corporate United Way programs; conferences, seminars, reunions, and pageants; donations for incentive or appreciation events; or sports teams seeking support for travel, equipment, fundraisers, etc.
Geographic Focus: All States, American Samoa, District of Columbia, Guam, Marshall Islands, Northern Mariana Islands, Puerto Rico, U.S. Virgin Islands
Contact: Charitable Giving Coordinator; (972) 980-9917; fax (972) 770-5977
Internet: www.brinker.com/company/community-matters
Sponsor: Brinker International Corporation
3000 Olympus Boulevard
Dallas, TX 75019

Bristol-Myers Squibb Foundation Independent Medical Education Grants 472

For Bristol Myers Squibb to be seen as a worldwide leader in supporting innovative, high quality medical education that closes gaps in HCP knowledge. To advance excellence in global healthcare through expertise in medical education and strategic support of evidence-based educational activities in Bristol Myers Squibb disease areas of focus that measure improvements in professional competence, performance, and patient outcomes.
Requirements: Corporate Giving includes funds or in-kind support provided by BMS to eligible third-party organizations for educational, healthcare-related, scientific, community, public policy, patient advocacy or charitable purposes. Some examples are charitable donations to non-profit organizations, support of medical education programs, corporate sponsorships, fellowships, and corporate memberships.
Restrictions: BMS will not provide funding to: support the start up or establishment of a non-profit organization; an organization's specific day-to-day operational expenses, such as salaries or rent; requests through Corporate Giving from lobbying organizations; support an event that has already occurred; or support entertainment or recreational activities.
Geographic Focus: All States
Contact: John L. Damonti, President; (800) 831-9008 or (212) 546-4000; fax (212) 546-9574; grantsandgiving@bms.com or bms.foundation@bms.com
Internet: www.bms.com/about-us/responsibility/IME.html
Sponsor: Bristol-Myers Squibb Foundation
430 E. 29th Street, 14th Floor
New York, NY 10016

British Columbia Arts Council Youth Engagement Program Grants 473

The British Columbia Arts Council Youth Engagement Pilot Grant program provides support to eligible organizations taking innovative and inspiring approaches to engaging British Columbia's young people with professional artists and arts experiences, as participants in the artistic process or as the primary audiences for works of art. Funding assistance through this program will support exemplary approaches to youth engagement and the development of programming at various stages of implementation, including both new projects and the enhancement or expansion of existing programming initiatives. Applications are encouraged from eligible organizations across the province engaging children and youth in innovative projects that involve professional artists. Eligible projects include new initiatives, including the research and development of pilot projects, as well as enhancements or expansion of existing programs. Funding is available for projects of up to two years duration. All applicants, especially new applicants, are urged to discuss their request with Council staff prior to submission. The annual deadline date for application submission is January 15.

Requirements: In order to be eligible for support through this program, an eligible applicant must: be an organization assisted by the British Columbia Arts Council in recent years through operating or discipline-specific project programs; and demonstrate the need for financial assistance, as defined by Council policy. An eligible project must: have the engagement of children and youth, as audiences and/or as creative participants, at its core; include professional artists; compensate artists and other professional practitioners by paying fees at industry standards and adhere to international intellectual property rights standards.

Restrictions: Awards are not available for: general operating activity; project phases that have begun prior to the application deadline; capital expenditures (construction, renovation, or purchase of property or equipment); fundraising; start-up costs or seed money; feasibility studies; international travel costs of foreign artists visiting British Columbia; travel to international symposia; conferences or competitions; the creation or preparation of performances and/or exhibitions for competitions; projects that are secondary to other purposes (e.g. fundraising events, conventions, or family, religious or community celebrations); subsistence to artists or curators; projects or activities that are funded through other programs of the British Columbia Arts Council or its third party delivery partners; or projects taking place outside British Columbia.

Geographic Focus: Canada
Date(s) Application is Due: Jan 15
Amount of Grant: Up to 27,000 CAD
Samples: Island Mountain Arts Society, British Columbia, Canada, $27,000 - to support youth engagement programs relating to arts (2019); Vancouver Poetry House Society, Vancouver, Canada, $6,400 - to support youth engagement programs relating to arts (2019); 2 Rivers Remix Society, British Columbia, Canada, $12,000 - to support youth engagement programs relating to arts (2019).
Contact: Anissa Paulsen; (236) 478-2560; fax (250) 387-4099; Anissa.Paulsen@gov.bc.ca
Internet: www.bcartscouncil.ca/program/youth-engagement-program/
Sponsor: British Columbia Arts Council
1st Floor, 800 Johnson Street
Victoria, BC V8W 1N3 Canada

Brookdale Foundation Relatives as Parents Grants   474
The Brookdale Foundation Relatives as Parents program (RAPP) awards seed grants to community-based organizations to develop services for grandparents and other relatives acting as surrogate parents, in addition to state agencies planning to offer such services. Currently RAPP provides extensive services, primarily to relative caregivers caring for children outside the foster care system, in 44 states, the District of Columbia, and Puerto Rico. As part of their program, they conduct the National Orientation and Training Conference and provide technical assistance through site bulletins, a listserv, annual newsletter, conference calls and webchats to facilitate opportunities for networking and information exchange. Programs and funding vary by state. Additional information is available at the website. The deadline for applications is June 13.
Requirements: The RAPP Local RFP is available to interested organizations that have a 501(c)3 or equivalent tax exempt status. Organizations from all across the country are eligible to apply.
Geographic Focus: All States, American Samoa, District of Columbia, Guam, Marshall Islands, Northern Mariana Islands, Puerto Rico, U.S. Virgin Islands
Date(s) Application is Due: Jun 13
Contact: Valerie Hall; (201) 836-4602; fax (201) 836-4382; vah@brookdalefoundation.org
Internet: www.brookdalefoundation.org/index.html
Sponsor: Brookdale Foundation
300 Frank W. Burr Boulevard, Suite 13
Teaneck, NJ 07666

Brown County Community Foundation Grants   475
The Brown County Community Foundation strives to enhance the lives of the citizens and organizations of the community. It is a non-profit enterprise that seeks to provide the mechanism through which those who desire to help others in the community may carry out their philanthropy. By supporting charitable organizations in broad areas of community need - education, social services, health care, arts and humanities, and environment - it helps build a stronger, healthier Brown County. In general, grants shall be made for capital purposes only, not for operating expenses. Grant applications are generally available in April. Applications are due late May, with decisions announced in late June or early July. Most recently, awards have ranged from $1,500 to $18,000.
Requirements: Evidence of nonprofit tax status must be submitted with all applications. Proposals must serve the residents of Brown County, Indiana.
Restrictions: Preference is generally given to requests that demonstrate the most urgent and immediate need for funding or satisfy an identifiable community need. Grants are ordinarily made for one year only. The Foundation rarely provides the entire support of a project. Grants are not generally available for those agencies and institutions that are funded primarily through tax support.
Geographic Focus: Indiana
Date(s) Application is Due: May 10
Amount of Grant: 1,500 - 18,000 USD

Samples: Brown County Historical Society, Nashville, Indiana, $5,480 - used for a video system for the public meeting room in the new History Center; Brown County Literacy Coalition, Nashville, Indiana, $3,126 - for the implementation of Ready To Learn, a project aimed at fostering development of cognitive ability in children; Indiana Raptor Center, Nashville, Indiana, $18,000 - for a quality used vehicle for transportation to programs.
Contact: Larry Pejeau; (812) 988-4882; fax (812) 988-0299; larry@bccfin.org
Internet: browncountygives.org/bcgives/895-2/
Sponsor: Brown County Community Foundation
91 West Mound Street, Unit 4
Nashville, IN 47448

Brown Foundation Grants   476
The Brown Foundation distributes funds for public charitable purposes, principally for support, encouragement and assistance to education, community service and the arts. The Foundation's current emphasis is in the field of public education at the primary and secondary levels with focus on supporting non-traditional and innovative approaches designed to improve public education primarily within the State of Texas. The visual and performing arts remain an area of interest. The Foundation also focuses on community service projects which serve the needs of children and families. The Foundation is interested in funding projects which fulfill one or more of the following criteria: addressing root causes of a concern rather than treating symptoms; serving as a catalyst to stimulate collaborative efforts by several sectors of the community; resulting in a long-lasting impact on the situation beyond the value of the grant itself; reflecting and encouraging sound financial planning and solid management practices in administration of the project. Proposals should be submitted a minimum of 4 months before funds are required.
Requirements: 501(c)3 tax-exempt organizations, public charities, and units of government are eligible.
Restrictions: Grants are not made to individuals. Only one application within a twelve month period will be considered. No proposal from an organization previously funded by the Foundation will be considered unless a full and timely report of expenditure of the previous grant has been submitted. The Foundation does not expect to support: grants to religious organizations for religious purposes; testimonial dinners, fundraising events or marketing events; grants intended directly or indirectly to support candidates for political office or to influence legislation; grants to other private foundations; grants to cover past operating deficits or debt retirements.
Geographic Focus: Texas
Contact: Nancy Pittman, Executive Director; (713) 523-6867; fax (713) 523-2917; bfi@brownfoundation.org or mbasurto@brownfoundation.org
Internet: www.brownfoundation.org/Guidelines.asp
Sponsor: Brown Foundation
P.O. Box 130646
Houston, TX 77219-0646

Brown Rudnick Charitable Foundation Community Grants   477
The Brown Rudnick Charitable Foundation's mission is to bring the energy and interests of Brown Rudnick volunteers together with opportunities and resources to create positive social change. To maximize its effect, the Foundation Directors chose to focus on inner-city education in Boston, Providence, Hartford, New York, Washington D.C., Orange County and London, United Kingdom. Since 2001, hundreds of grants have been made and collaborative efforts undertaken, in each of these cities consistent with this initiative. Created to support front-line educators who often do not have a voice in funding decisions, the Foundation's Community Grants subsidize small, concrete projects, which will improve inner-city education within the coming year in the cities where Brown Rudnick has its offices. Although the amount of these grants may seem modest, the Foundation has found that the connections that they foster, the activities they encourage and the energy they create, have the potential to unleash countless contributions to improving inner-city education in the communities where we live and work. The Foundation shall generally consider grant applications monthly and award grants in an amount totaling not more than $2,000 in any one month.
Requirements: Eligible 501(c)3 nonprofit organizations in the following areas can apply: Boston, Massachusetts; Hartford, Connecticut; New York, New York; Washington, D.C; Providence, Rhode Island; Orange County, California; and London, England.
Geographic Focus: California, Connecticut, District of Columbia, Massachusetts, New York, Rhode Island
Amount of Grant: Up to 2,000 USD
Samples: Forest Elementary School, Ridgewood, New York, $2,000 - supports the purchase of mini iPads for use in English as a Second Language (ESL) classrooms (2020); Brooklyn Arbor Elementary, Brooklyn, New York, $2,000 - to allow the children at Brooklyn Arbor Elementary School to participate in a 10-week bilingual soccer program to provide a safe and rich environment for children in 1st- and 2nd-grade (2020); Children's Friend, Providence, Rhode Island, $2,000 - to help purchase culturally authentic West African and Latin American musical instruments for 75 – 100 students enrolled in the school's Introduction to Music course (2020).
Contact: Jeffrey L. Jonas, President; (617) 856-8125 or (617) 856-8577; fax (617) 289-0434; jjonas@brownrudnick.com or center@brownrudnick.com
Internet: www.brownrudnickcenter.com/foundation/community-grant
Sponsor: Brown Rudnick Charitable Foundation
One Financial Center
Boston, MA 02111

Brunswick Foundation Dollars for Doers Grants   478
Established in 1957, the Brunswick Foundation is a 501(c)3 charitable organization that enhances the interests of its employees and the communities in which they live and work, as well as supporting causes and projects that complement the business interests of Brunswick Corporation. The Dollars for Doers program recognizes the volunteer efforts of Brunswick

employees by issuing grants to 501(c)3 organizations. The foundation awards grants to nonprofit organizations for which an individual employee or group of employees has completed volunteer work, such as serving on a Board of Directors or participating in a fundraising event.
Requirements: IRS 501(c)3 organizations in Alabama, Arizona, Connecticut, Florida, Georgia, Illinois, Indiana, Kentucky, Louisiana, Maryland, Michigan, Minnesota, Mississippi, Nebraska, North Carolina, Oklahoma, Oregon, South Carolina, Tennessee, Texas, Washington, and Wisconsin are eligible.
Restrictions: Grants are not made to religious organizations for religious purposes; for any form of political activity; to veterans groups, fraternal orders, or labor groups; for loans of any kind; or for trips, tours, dinners, tickets, or advertising.
Geographic Focus: Alabama, Arizona, Connecticut, Florida, Georgia, Illinois, Indiana, Kentucky, Louisiana, Maryland, Michigan, Minnesota, Mississippi, Nebraska, North Carolina, Oklahoma, Oregon, South Carolina, Tennessee, Texas, Washington, Wisconsin
Contact: B. Russell Lockridge; (847) 735-4467 or (847) 735-4700; fax (847) 735-4765
Internet: www.brunswick.com/company/community/brunswickfoundation.php
Sponsor: Brunswick Foundation
1 North Field Court
Lake Forest, IL 60045-4811

Brunswick Foundation Grants   479
The Brunswick Foundation Grant Program awards direct donations to 501(c)3 organizations that enhance marine, fitness, bowling or billiards activities and related industry interests, or any other Brunswick business interest. The foundation also supports programs where Brunswick Corporation employees volunteer and efforts to provide a higher education for children of employees. Types of support include employee-matching gifts, general operating budgets, building construction and renovation, capital campaigns, special projects, research, and continuing support. Requests for guidelines must be in writing, or applicants may submit a letter describing the purpose of the organization and the request.
Requirements: IRS 501(c)3 organizations in Alabama, Arizona, Connecticut, Florida, Georgia, Illinois, Indiana, Kentucky, Louisiana, Maryland, Michigan, Minnesota, Mississippi, Nebraska, North Carolina, Oklahoma, Oregon, South Carolina, Tennessee, Texas, Washington, and Wisconsin are eligible.
Restrictions: Grants are not made to religious organizations for religious purposes; for any form of political activity; to veterans groups, fraternal orders, or labor groups; for loans of any kind; or for trips, tours, dinners, tickets, or advertising.
Geographic Focus: Alabama, Arizona, Connecticut, Florida, Georgia, Illinois, Indiana, Kentucky, Louisiana, Maryland, Michigan, Minnesota, Mississippi, Nebraska, North Carolina, Oklahoma, Oregon, South Carolina, Tennessee, Texas, Washington, Wisconsin
Date(s) Application is Due: Mar 22
Amount of Grant: 500 - 2,000 USD
Contact: B. Russell Lockridge; (847) 735-4467 or (847) 735-4700; fax (847) 735-4765
Internet: www.brunswickcorp.com
Sponsor: Brunswick Foundation
1 North Field Court
Lake Forest, IL 60045-4811

Bryan Adams Foundation Grants   480
The Bryan Adams Foundation was set up in 2006 by the musician and photographer Bryan Adams, in order to improve the quality of people's lives around the world. The Foundation aims to achieve this by providing financial help and support to those people who are committed to bettering the lives of other people, by providing grants to finance specific projects. The Foundation seeks to protect the most vulnerable or disadvantaged individuals in society. It aims particularly to advance education and learning opportunities for children and young people worldwide, believing that an education is the best gift that a child can be given. The Foundation's area of support is broad and far-reaching, enabling grants to be given for projects supporting the elderly, victims of war and natural disasters, and those suffering from mental or physical illness. Applicant should send an email with the purpose of their project and budgetary needs.
Requirements: The Trustees generally do not make grants in response to unsolicited applications and do not normally make grants to individuals.
Geographic Focus: All States, All Countries
Contact: Bryan Adams, Trustee; foundation@bryanadams.com
Internet: www.thebryanadamsfoundation.com/index.php?target=grants
Sponsor: Bryan Adams Foundation
440 Strand
London, WC2R 0QS

Burlington Industries Foundation Grants   481
This is a company-sponsored foundation, giving primarily in areas of company operations in North Carolina, South Carolina, and Virginia. The foundation supports organizations involved with arts and culture, education, health, youth development, community development, and civic affairs.
Requirements: 501(c)3 organizations in Burlington communities (North Carolina, South Carolina, and Virginia), are eligible for grant support. Requests for funding must be accompanied by: proof of 501(c)3 tax-exempt status; description of the organization and its objective; justification for the project; evidence that the organization is well established; information about the organization's reputation, efficiency, management ability, financial status and sources of income.
Restrictions: No support for: sectarian or denominational religious organizations, national organizations, private secondary schools, historic preservation organizations, individuals (except for employees in distress), conferences, seminars, workshops, endowments, outdoor dramas, films, documentaries, medical research, loans.
Geographic Focus: North Carolina, South Carolina, Virginia

Amount of Grant: 1,000 - 50,000 USD
Samples: Greensboro Day School, Greensboro, NC, $12,450; United Way of Alamance County, Burlington, NC, $3,000; Independent College Fund of North Carolina, Raleigh, NC, $15,000.
Contact: Delores Sides, Executive Director; (336) 379-2903; delores.sides@itg-global.com
Sponsor: Burlington Industries Foundation
P.O. Box 26540
Greensboro, NC 27415-6540

Burton D. Morgan Foundation Hudson Community Grants   482
Burton D. Morgan and his family moved to Hudson in the late 1950s because Burt was starting a new business, Morgan Adhesives Company, in Stow and Mrs. Morgan's ancestors were among the early Hudson settlers. The Morgans have been dedicated to supporting projects in Hudson that contribute to the health and vibrancy of the community. The Foundation supports a wide array of Hudson projects in the fields of arts and culture, education, and the civic arena, but also seeks to work with Hudson organizations in the fields of entrepreneurship and entrepreneurship education in order to experiment with innovative ideas to advance the field. There are three annual deadlines for application submission requesting more than $20,000: February 1, May 1, and September 1. There are three annual deadlines for submission of grants requesting $20,000 or less: February 15, May 15, and September 15. When the deadline falls on a Saturday, Sunday, or holiday, the online Application will be due by 5:00 pm on the next business day.
Requirements: Grants are made to organizations recognized as tax-exempt under the Internal Revenue Service code section 501(c)3 which are not private foundations.
Restrictions: The Foundation does not usually make multi-year grants and does not ordinarily consider grants to annual fund drives, to units of government, or to organizations and institutions which are primarily tax supported, including state universities. The Foundation no longer makes grants to arts, mental health, and social service organizations and programs.
Geographic Focus: Ohio
Date(s) Application is Due: Feb 1; Feb 15; May 1; May 15; Sep 1; Sep 15
Contact: Deborah D. Hoover, President; (330) 665-1630 or (330) 655-1660; fax (330) 655-1673; dhoover@bdmorganfdn.org or admin@bdmorganfdn.org
Internet: www.bdmorganfdn.org/hudson-community
Sponsor: Burton D. Morgan Foundation
22 Aurora Street
Hudson, OH 44236

Burton D. Morgan Foundation Youth Entrepreneurship Grants   483
The Burton D. Morgan Foundation supports youth education programs for elementary, middle, and high school students with a focus on the free enterprise system, financial literacy and entrepreneurship. The Foundation values programs that inspire students to become financially independent and fiscally responsible and to envision a future that includes the highest educational attainment possible. To achieve these goals, teachers must receive the necessary training to incorporate entrepreneurial thinking and economic concepts into coursework and extracurricular activities. While not every student will become an entrepreneur, every student will benefit from learning about entrepreneurship and, thereby, be better equipped to chart their own futures. The Foundation also believes that Northeast Ohio youth entrepreneurship programs will benefit from networking and collaborating and that students will be best served by the creation of educational pathways from one educational level to another. There are three annual deadlines for application submission requesting more than $20,000: February 1, May 1, and September 1. There are three annual deadlines for submission of grants requesting $20,000 or less: February 15, May 15, and September 15. When the deadline falls on a Saturday, Sunday, or holiday, the online Application will be due by 5:00 pm on the next business day.
Requirements: Grants are made to organizations recognized as tax-exempt under the Internal Revenue Service code section 501(c)3 which are not private foundations. The Foundation's geographic preferences complement its program and project focus by targeting: entrepreneurship-related programs in Summit County, Ohio, and surrounding counties, known collectively as the Northeast Ohio region; and Hudson, Ohio-based nonprofit organizations.
Restrictions: The Foundation does not usually make multi-year grants and does not ordinarily consider grants to annual fund drives, to units of government, or to organizations and institutions which are primarily tax supported, including state universities. The Foundation no longer makes grants to arts, mental health, and social service organizations and programs.
Geographic Focus: Ohio
Date(s) Application is Due: Feb 1; Feb 15; May 1; May 15; Sep 1; Sep 15
Contact: Deborah D. Hoover, President; (330) 665-1630 or (330) 655-1660; fax (330) 655-1673; dhoover@bdmorganfdn.org or admin@bdmorganfdn.org
Internet: www.bdmorganfdn.org/youth-entrepreneurship
Sponsor: Burton D. Morgan Foundation
22 Aurora Street
Hudson, OH 44236

Bush Foundation Event Scholarships   484
The Bush Foundation believes in the power of events to inspire, equip and connect people to think bigger and think differently about what is possible in their communities. To that end, the Foundation offers scholarships for individuals from its region to attend national events and conferences, where they can: step out of their daily routines; build new connections both within the region and beyond; develop leadership skills; be inspired to think bigger and think differently about their work; and contribute their voices and perspectives to national conversations.
Requirements: Applicants must have lived or worked at least one continuous year immediately prior to the application deadline in Minnesota, North Dakota, South Dakota, or one of the 23 Native nations that shares the same geography.
Geographic Focus: Minnesota, North Dakota, South Dakota

Contact: Erin Dirksen, Grants Manager; (651) 227-0891; fax (651) 297-6485; edirksen@ bushfoundation.org or communications@bushfoundation.org
Internet: www.bushfoundation.org/fellowships/event-scholarships
Sponsor: Bush Foundation
101 Fifth Street East, Suite 2400
Saint Paul, MN 55101

Bush Foundation Event Sponsorships   485

The Bush Foundation dedicates a limited amount of funds every year to sponsor select events that inspire, equip and connect people to think bigger and think differently about what's possible in their communities and to lead more effectively. The Foundation awards up to $50,000 to select events that fall into one of the following categories: events that bring together a wide variety of people across sectors, geographies and cultural communities to experience engaging programming and discussions that inspire, equip or connect them to more effectively lead change; events that strengthen foundation and nonprofit networks in the region; and events that advance the Foundation's strategic initiatives, particularly those that build capacity and momentum toward specific goals. The Foundation is currently focused on four areas, and may fund events related to work involving: community creativity; education; native nation building; and social business ventures. There are three rounds of funding each year, with deadlines of February 1, May 31, and August 23.
Requirements: Organizations that are LLCs, 501(c)3 public charities, and government entities (including schools) are eligible for event sponsorships. Groups of organizations, such as coalitions or collaboratives, are also eligible to apply, but only one organization may receive the grant or contract. Strong preference will be given to events that take place in the Foundation's region of Minnesota, North Dakota, South Dakota, and the 23 Native nations that share the same geography. Event sponsorship funds must be spent in full three months following the date of the event.
Restrictions: The Foundation generally does not sponsor issue-specific events that are not related to its four strategic initiatives (listed above). Finally, it does not generally do not sponsor fundraisers. Event sponsorship funds may not be used retroactively.
Geographic Focus: Minnesota, North Dakota, South Dakota
Date(s) Application is Due: Feb 1; May 31; Aug 23
Contact: Erin Dirksen; (651) 227-0891; fax (651) 297-6485; edirksen@bushfoundation.org
Internet: www.grantselect.com/editor/view_grant/116384
Sponsor: Bush Foundation
101 Fifth Street East, Suite 2400
Saint Paul, MN 55101

Bushrod H. Campbell and Adah F. Hall Charity Fund Grants   486

Established in Massachusetts in 1956, the Bushrod H. Campbell and Adah F. Hall Charity Fund awards grants to organizations in the Boston area devoted to basic needs for the elderly, education for under-served youth, social services for vulnerable populations, projects relating to medicine and medical research, health care, hospitals, the blind and deaf, and certain discretionary projects. Grants are also awarded countrywide for projects addressing population control. Types of support include: capital grants; general operating grants; program grants' and research grants. There are four quarterly deadlines each year for online application submission: January 15, April 15, August 15, and October 15. Grant awards typically range from $5,000 to $10,000.
Requirements: Tax-exempt organizations located within Boston and neighboring communities and U.S. tax-exempt organizations devoted to population control are eligible.
Restrictions: Grants are not awarded to individuals. The Fund does not typically support direct medical care or public policy advocacy.
Geographic Focus: Massachusetts
Date(s) Application is Due: Jan 15; Apr 15; Aug 15; Oct 15
Amount of Grant: 5,000 - 10,000 USD
Samples: Strong Women, Strong Girls, Pittsburgh, Pennsylvania, $5,000 - general operating support (2019); Boston Health Care Homeless Program, Boston, Massachusetts, $10,000 - support for the Life Essentials Fund (2019); Artists For Humanity, Boston, Massachusetts, $10,000 - support of the Youth Arts Enterprise program (2019).
Contact: Rita Goldberg, Grants Manager; (617) 557-9766 or (617) 557-9766; fax (617) 227-7940, ext. 775; rgoldberg@hembar.com
Gioia C. Perugini; (617) 557-9777 or (617) 557-9766; gperugini@hembar.com
Internet: hembar.com/client_services/bushrod-h-campbell-and-adah-f-hall-charity-fund
Sponsor: Bushrod H. Campbell and Adah F. Hall Charity Fund
75 State Street, 16th Floor
Boston, MA 02109

Byerly Foundation Grants   487

The Byerly Foundation intends to respond to opportunities that address the following focus areas in order of priority: education; economic development; and community life. The Foundation will concentrate on the development and awarding of grants in education. Some of these will be major in scope, requiring significant planning and execution over a period of several years. Other grants will fund educational projects/programs of less complexity. The Foundation will assign a higher priority to programs that: offer creative responses to the community's most pressing needs and concerns; demonstrate cooperation or collaboration among (two or more) agencies or program providers; maximize the impact of modest grants as well as those of significant size; leverage other funding through the use of matching grants; and projects that will become self-sustaining without requiring ongoing funding from the Foundation.
Requirements: Organizations determined as charitable under Section 501(c)3 of the Internal Revenue Code, public entities or other charitable, educational or cultural organizations may submit proposals to the Foundation. All activities funded must benefit residents of the Hartsville, South Carolina, area.

Restrictions: The foundation does not ordinarily fund: individuals; sectarian religious programs; debts or existing obligations; lobbying or political campaigns; technical or specialized research; intermediate organizations; fundraising; teams or events; and advertising or memorials.
Geographic Focus: South Carolina
Amount of Grant: Up to 1,500,000 USD
Samples: Coker College, Hartsville, South Carolina, $1,500,000 - a multi-year grant to help support athletics and resident life; Hartsville Middle School, Hartsville, South Carolina, $1,500,000 - a three-year award for a program aimed at enhancing the chances of success for students considered at risk in the middle school environment (20017); Darlington County First Steps, Hartsville, South Carolina, $16,350 - provides in-home education to support learning during summer months for children about to enter kindergarten.
Contact: Richard Puffer; (843) 383-2400; fax (843) 383-0661; byerlyfdn@yahoo.com
Internet: www.byerlyfoundation.com/grant-making/
Sponsor: Byerly Foundation
101 North 2nd Street
Hartsville, SC 29550

C.F. Adams Charitable Trust Grants   488

Charles Francis Adams created the C. F. Adams Charitable Trust in 1987. He was a direct descendant of John Adams, the second President of the United States, and John Quincy Adams, the sixth President. He was an avid sailor, dedicated civic leader and respected businessman. The primary objectives of the C.F. Adams Charitable Trust are to: encourage Downeast Maine communities to work together to preserve their local cultural heritage, improve their quality of life, adapt to a changing environment, and achieve a sustainable economy; promote innovative broad-based efforts to engage families in meeting the mental health needs of children in Massachusetts and to emphasize the extraordinary therapeutic benefits of the arts; and expand public awareness of the Adams family legacy and to preserve its unique heritage. Types of support include: general operating support; income development; management development; capacity building; and program development. Applicants should begin by forwarding a brief letter containing a detailed description of the project and the amount of funding requested. Recent grants have ranged from $750 to $75,000. The Trust currently commits up to $400,000 per year in Massachusetts to children's mental health and arts therapy programs that fall within the priorities outlined above.
Requirements: Giving is primarily in eastern Massachusetts and down east Maine.
Restrictions: No grants are given to individuals.
Geographic Focus: Maine, Massachusetts
Amount of Grant: 750 - 75,000 EUR
Samples: Adolescent Consultation Services, Cambridge, Massachusetts, $30,000 - Massachusetts Alliance of Juvenile Court Clinics; Hand In Hand Mano En Mano, Milbridge, Maine, $22,000 - operating support; Quoddy Tides Foundation, Eastport, Maine, $30,000 - operating support.
Contact: James H, Lowell, Trustee; (617) 422-0064; info@cfadamstrust.org
Internet: www.cfadamstrust.org/index.html
Sponsor: C.F. Adams Charitable Trust
141 Tremont Street, Suite 200
Boston, 02111-1209

C.H. Robinson Worldwide Foundation Grants   489

Over the last century, C.H. Robinson has established a tradition of giving back to its employees and communities. In 2005, C.H. Robinson created the C.H. Robinson Foundation to provide philanthropic support to communities in which it operates well into the future, through all types of economic and business climates. The Foundation is committed to ensuring that its communities continue to be great places to live and work, and through its employee match programs and grants, the Foundation provides support to hundreds of organizations each year. Giving priorities support organizations that can offer employee engagement opportunities and focus on programs which: expand educational success for at-risk youth; prevent hunger and provide food assistance; expand and improve access to affordable housing; support immediate living needs for people in crisis; and focus on areas of health (research, prevention, and treatment). Most often, awards are given in support of capital campaigns, infrastructure, general operations, program development, scholarships, seed funding, and technical assistance. Grants typically range from $1,000 to $25,000.
Requirements: The Foundation supports organizations that are located within the Minneapolis-St. Paul metropolitan area, greater Minnesota, and surrounding states.
Restrictions: No support is offered for political organizations or religious organizations not of direct benefit to the entire community.
Geographic Focus: Illinois, Indiana, Iowa, Kentucky, Michigan, Minnesota, Ohio, Pennsylvania, Wisconsin
Amount of Grant: Up to 25,000 USD
Samples: Action for Healthy Kids, Chicago, Illinois, $250 - general operating support; Boys and Girls Club of Twin Cities, St. Paul, Minnesota, $15,000 - general operating support; Camp Quality USA, Stow, Ohio, $250 - general operating support.
Contact: Kristi Nichols, (952) 683-3432 or (952) 683-2800; foundation@chrobinson.com
Internet: www.chrobinson.com/en/us/About-Us/CHRobinson/Corporate-Responsibility/Foundation/
Sponsor: C.H. Robinson Worldwide Foundation
401 East Eighth Street, Suite 319
Sioux Falls, SD 57103-7031

Cabot Corporation Foundation Grants   490

The goal of Cabot Corporation Foundation is to support community outreach objectives, with priority given to science and technology, education, and community and civic improvement efforts in the communities where the company has major facilities or operations. Types of support include capital grants, challenge grants, employee matching gifts, fellowships, general support, professorships, project support, research, scholarships,

and seed money. The board meets in January, April, July, and October to consider requests. Applications must be received at least 30 days before a board meeting.
Requirements: The Foundation supports only nonprofit 501(c)3 tax-exempt organizations in areas of company operation. Modest support is available for international organizations that qualify under U.S. tax regulations.
Restrictions: Contributions are not made to individuals; fraternal, political, athletic or veterans organizations; religious institutions; capital and endowment campaigns; sponsorships of local groups/individuals to participate in regional, national, or international competitions, conferences or events; advertising sponsorships; or Tickets or tables at fundraising events.
Geographic Focus: Georgia, Illinois, Louisiana, Massachusetts, New Mexico, Pennsylvania, Texas, West Virginia, Belgium, Canada, China, Switzerland, United Kingdom
Amount of Grant: 2,000 - 75,000 USD
Contact: Cynthia L. Gullotti, Program Manager; (617) 345-0100; fax (617) 342-6312; Cynthia_Gullotti@cabot-corp.com or cabot.corporation.foundation@cabotcorp.com
Internet: www.cabot-corp.com/About-Cabot/Corporate-Giving
Sponsor: Cabot Corporation Foundation
Two Seaport Lane, Suite 1300
Boston, MA 02210-2019

Cadillac Products Packaging Company Foundation Grants 491
Established in Michigan in 1985, the Cadillac Products Packaging Company Foundation offers its grant support to both higher education and youth development programs in the State of Indiana and Phoenix, Arizona. Funding typically comes in the form of general operating support. Since there are no specific application forms or annual deadlines, applicants should forward a letter to the office describing the need and outlining the budget. Grant amounts range up to about $10,000.
Requirements: Any 501(c)3, community college, or 4-year institution serving the residents of Indiana or the Phoenix area are welcome to apply.
Geographic Focus: Arizona, Indiana
Amount of Grant: Up to 10,000 USD
Contact: Roger K. Williams, Treasurer; (248) 879-5000 or (800) 837-0055
Sponsor: Cadillac Products Packaging Company Foundation
5800 Crooks Road
Troy, MI 48098-2830

Caesars Foundation Grants 492
Founded as Harrah's Foundation in Nevada in 2002, giving is in the area of company operations. The foundation supports programs designed to help older individuals live longer, healthier, and more fulfilling lives; promote a safe and clean environment; and improve the quality of life in communities where Caesars operates. Fields of interest include: aging centers and services; Alzheimer's disease; developmentally disabled services; the environment; food distribution programs; food services; health care; patient services; higher education; hospitals; human services; mental health services; public affairs; public safety; nutrition; and youth services. Types of support being offered include: building and renovation; capital campaigns; continuing support; general operating support; program development; research; scholarship funding; and sponsorships. There are no specific deadlines or application forms. Caesars Foundation Trustees meet on a quarterly basis, typically around the second week of each quarter. Check with your nearest Caesars Entertainment property for deadlines. The foundation generally funds programs and projects of $10,000 or more.
Requirements: Eligible organizations are 501(c)3 nonprofits operating programs in the communities where Caesars employees and their families live and work. Applying organizations must also: demonstrate diversity by providing services and volunteer opportunities to all without regard to race, ethnicity, gender, religion, sexual orientation, identity or disability; illustrate strong leadership that will significantly strengthen communities in which Caesars operates; show sound administrative and financial condition; provide opportunities for Caesars staff involvement as volunteers and/or opportunity to serve on Board of Directors; and, provide branding opportunities and openly support Caesars Foundation in a public forum.
Restrictions: The Foundation is not designed to react to last-minute requests or event sponsorships—plan the timing of your proposal accordingly. Caesars Foundation does not accept requests for in-kind contributions.
Geographic Focus: Arizona, California, Illinois, Indiana, Iowa, Louisiana, Mississippi, Missouri, Nevada, New Jersey, North Carolina, Pennsylvania
Amount of Grant: 10,000 USD
Samples: Atlantic Cape Community College Foundation, Atlantic City, New Jersey, $75,000 - general operating support; Calumet College of St. Joseph, Whiting, Indiana, $60,000 - construction of new student center building; University of Chicago Medical Center, Chicago, Illinois, $50,000 - research and development.
Contact: Gwen Migita, Community Affairs; (702) 880-4728 or (702) 407-6358; fax (702) 407-6520; caesarsfoundation@caesars.com
Internet: www.caesarsfoundation.com/
Sponsor: Caesars Foundation
1 Caesars Palace Drive
Las Vegas, NV 89109-8969

California Arts Council Statewide Networks Grants 493
The Statewide Networks Program (SN) is a California Arts Council (CAC) partnership with culturally specific, multicultural, and discipline-based statewide and regional arts networks and service organizations. Its goal is to promote the public value of the arts in communities by strengthening and expanding an organization's delivery of services to its constituents through communications, professional development opportunities, networking and arts advocacy. For this purpose, SN supports new approaches or expansions to an organization's work in the areas of organizational capacity and community building through advocacy, thus fostering an environment where all California cultures are represented. SN grants will be based on a ranking system and will range between $5,000 and $20,000.
Requirements: Statewide and regional culturally specific, multicultural, and discipline-based arts networks and service organizations are eligible to apply. Applicant organizations must have at least a two-year track record of developing its field and providing services to its constituent base (individual artists and/or arts organizations). All grant recipients must provide a dollar-for-dollar (1:1) match. The cash match may be from corporate or private contributions, local or federal government, or earned income. Other State funds cannot be used as a match. A combination of cash and in-kind contributions may be used to match CAC request.
Restrictions: SN requests cannot exceed an organization's total income based on its last completed budget. The Council does dot fund: previous grantee organizations that have not completed grant requirements (progress and final reports, final invoice, etc.); continuation of current work or previously funded SN projects; for-profit organizations; non-arts service organizations; indirect costs of schools, community colleges, colleges, or universities; trust or endowment funds; programs not accessible to the public; projects with religious or sectarian purposes; organizations or activities that are part of the curricula base of schools, colleges, or universities; purchase of equipment, land, buildings, or construction (capital outlay expenditures); out of state travel activities; hospitality or food costs; or expenses incurred before the starting or after the ending date of the contract.
Geographic Focus: California
Date(s) Application is Due: Mar 16
Amount of Grant: 5,000 - 20,000 USD
Contact: Lucero Arellano, SN Program Specialist; (916) 322-6338 or (916) 322-6555; fax (916) 322-6575; larellano@cac.ca.gov
Internet: www.cac.ca.gov/programs/sn.php
Sponsor: California Arts Council
1300 I Street, Suite 930
Sacramento, CA 95814

California Arts Council Technical Assistance Grants 494
The California Arts Council offers technical assistance in a variety of forms. Technical assistance funds are used to support development opportunities and activities that bring the Arts to the broadest constituency. The California Arts Council partners with national services organizations, individual consultants and other technical assistance providers to conduct organizational needs assessments and cultural resource surveys to assist in strengthening the infrastructure of local arts agencies. The California Arts Council has provided scholarships and/or travel assistance to conferences.
Requirements: California non-profit 501(c)3 arts organizations are eligible to apply.
Restrictions: This program does not fund scholarships for pursuing undergraduate or graduate education. Artists may not receive more than one grant within a 12 month period. An applicant may not apply for funding for the same activity, project or program. An applicant may not apply for projects or activities that were previously funded under this grant. The Program does not fund: programs for children; administrative or indirect costs; construction; recreational programs; underwriting an event; construction or renovations; activities or programs outside of California; or start-up costs for a small business.
Geographic Focus: California
Amount of Grant: 500 - 1,000 USD
Contact: Lucy Mochizuki, Contract and Procurement Administration; (916) 322-6337 or (916) 322-6555; fax (916) 322-6575; lmochizuki@cac.ca.gov
Internet: www.cac.ca.gov/programs/ta.php
Sponsor: California Arts Council
1300 I Street, Suite 930
Sacramento, CA 95814

California Endowment Innovative Ideas Challenge Grants 495
California Endowment was founded in 1996 as a result of Blue Cross of California's creation of its for-profit subsidiary, WellPoint Health Networks. The Endowment is a private, California-focused, grant-making foundation that advocates for health and health equity. It does this by raising awareness, by expanding access to affordable, high-quality health care for underserved communities, and by investing in fundamental improvements for the health of all Californians. The Endowment supports the statewide Health Happens Here campaign and is currently engaged in a ten-year, one-billion dollar Building Healthy Communities plan. As a part of this strategy, the Endowment's Innovative Ideas Challenge (IIC) grant-making program solicits ideas that can be classified as disruptive innovations. A disruptive innovation is one that brings to market products and services that are more affordable and, ultimately, higher in quality. It improves a product or service in ways that the market does not expect, typically by being lower priced or being designed for a different set of consumers. Proposed ideas should address either emerging or persistent health-related issues impacting underserved California communities. Interested organizations should initially submit 500-word descriptions of their idea through the Endowment's online system. These are due by 5 p.m. Pacific time on May 1st (deadline dates may vary from year to year). Applicants whose ideas are accepted will be asked to submit a full proposal. Further guidance and clarification in the form of downloadable PDFs and an FAQ are available at the Endowment website.
Requirements: California 501(c)3 nonprofits may apply. Awarded projects will demonstrate the following characteristics: be transformative and disruptively innovative; benefit California's underserved individuals and communities; demonstrate cultural and linguistic competency; build partnerships and encourage collaboration; address persistent and/or emerging health challenges; demonstrate organizational capacity to carry out work; have measurable outcomes; and align with one of the 10 Outcomes and/or 4 Big Results of the Endowment's Building Healthy Communities plan.
Restrictions: Funds may not be used for the following purposes: to carry on propaganda or otherwise attempt to influence any legislation; to influence the outcome of any public election or to carry on any voter registration drive; to make any grant which does not comply

with Internal Revenue Code Section 4945(d)3 or 4; for fees for any services resulting in substantial personal benefit including membership, alumni dues, subscriptions, or tickets to events or dinners; for capital for building acquisition or renovation; for operating deficits or retirement of debt; for scholarships, fellowships, or grants to individuals; for government and public agencies; or for direct services or core/general operating support.
Geographic Focus: California
Date(s) Application is Due: May 1
Samples: Sacramento Community Clinic Consortium, Inc., Sacramento, California, $273,737; Roadtrip Nation, Costa Mesa, California, $500,000—healthy youth developmehnt; The Smiley Group, Los Angeles, California, $100,000.
Contact: Grants Administration Team; (213) 928-8646 or (818) 703-3311; fax (213) 928-8801; tcegrantreports@calendow.org or questions@calendow.org
Internet: www.calendow.org/grants/
Sponsor: California Endowment
1000 North Alameda Street
Los Angeles, CA 90012

Callaway Foundation Grants 496
The Callaway Foundation awards grants for the benefit of projects and people in LaGrange and Troup County, Georgia. Areas of interest, include: arts and entertainment; elementary, higher, and secondary education; libraries; health and hospitals; community funds; care for the aged; community development; historic preservation; and church support. Types of support include: annual campaigns; building construction and renovation; capital campaigns; continuing support; equipment acquisition; general operating support; land acquisition, and matching support. Preference is given to enduring construction projects and capital equipment. The Foundation Board meets four times per year in January, April, July, and October. Grant requests and applications are due on the last day of the month preceding the meetings.
Requirements: IRS 501(c)3 nonprofit organizations in LaGrange and Troup County, Georgia are eligible to apply. Letters of request should briefly cover all aspects of the project, including complete financial planning and costs involved. Copies of budgets and current financial statements should also be included. An application form is available at the Foundation's website.
Restrictions: Grants are usually not made for loans, debt retirement, endowment or operating expenses. Requests from churches located outside Troup County, Georgia, are not considered.
Geographic Focus: Georgia
Date(s) Application is Due: Mar 31; Jun 30; Sep 30; Dec 31
Amount of Grant: 1,000 - 4,000,000 USD
Samples: Chattahoochee Valley Art Museum, LaGrange, GA, $59,000—for operating support; Georgia Cities Foundation, Atlanta, GA, $367,772—for Downtown Revitalization Fund; LaGrange College, LaGrange, GA, $4,000,000—for library building and renovation.
Contact: H. Speer Burdette III; (706) 884-7348; fax (706) 884-0201; hsburdette@callaway-foundation.org
Internet: www.callawayfoundation.org/grant_policies.php
Sponsor: Callaway Foundation
209 Broome Street, P.O. Box 790
La Grange, GA 30241

Cal Ripken Sr. Foundation Grants 497
Cal Ripken Sr. Foundation provides grants to eligible youth organizations, schools, Boys and Girls Clubs, local governments and community non-profits groups that meet our eligibility requirements, in order to support the growth of youth baseball and softball, as well as promote character education. Cal Ripken Sr. Foundation awards grants for multiple initiatives including: baseball/softball equipment grants to organizations and schools that serve disadvantaged children; public youth ball field renovation matching grants to local government departments of parks and recreation, nonprofit organizations, and/or established community baseball or softball leagues; baseball/softball league development or expansion grants in the form of cash grants to community recreation programs run by local governments, Boys and Girls Clubs, public schools with after school and/or summer programming, and/or established community baseball for baseball/softball league development and expansion; Quickball grants to grow baseball and softball at a grassroots level through the game of Quickball; funding grants for baseball/softball programs to help Boys and Girls Clubs hire baseball/softball activity specialists, purchase baseball/softball equipment and apparel, and finance related costs such as league dues, tournament fees and playing field rental fees; camp sponsorship grants to support chosen high school student-athletes (students entering sophomore or junior years who participate on a baseball/softball team in a public school system) to attend a baseball camp to develop their skills and networks; and tournament sponsorship grants to provide selected youth teams, especially those that serve under-resourced populations, an opportunity to attend a baseball/softball tournament.
Geographic Focus: All States
Samples: Boys and Girls Club, Burlington, Vermont, $3,514 non-cash assistance - baseball equipment; Baltimore Orioles Limited Partnership, Baltimore, Maryland, $5,115 non-cash assistance - baseball equipment; Boys and Girls Club of Tampa Bay Inc., Tampa, Florida, $8,597 non-cash assistance and $49,926 cash assistance - baseball equipment.
Contact: Steve Salem; (410) 823-0808; fax (410) 823-0850; info@ripkenfoundation.org
Internet: www.ripkenfoundation.org/
Sponsor: Cal Ripken Sr. Foundation
1427 Clarkview Road, Suite 100
Baltimore, MD 21209

Calvin Johnson Jr. Foundation Mini Grants 498
The Calvin Johnson Jr. Foundation accepts applications to support individual K-12 teachers with the resources for original innovative Science, Technology, Engineering, and Math (STEM) projects, or STEM tutorial programs targeting football athletes. The Foundation mini-grant is named in honor of Calvin's mother, Dr. Arica Johnson, for her dedicated

service to the disciplines of Science, Technology, Engineering, and Math education. Teachers can apply for up to $750 of financial support to enhance instruction in these areas of education. Recipients will be evaluated on their potential benefit to students, project originality, creativity and innovation, implementation of research-based strategies, effective use of resources, and alignment with the vision and mission of the Foundation. Applications should be postmarked by the annual April 24 deadline.
Requirements: The mini-grant is open to all full-time K-12 educators in Metro-Detroit and Metro Atlanta surrounding areas
Geographic Focus: Georgia, Michigan
Date(s) Application is Due: Apr 24
Amount of Grant: Up to 750 USD
Contact: Calvin Johnson Jr., President; (404) 308-0312; fax (770) 969-8579; cjjrf@bigplaycj.com or cjjrf81@yahoo.com
Internet: calvinjohnsonjrfoundation.org/
Sponsor: Calvin Johnson Jr. Foundation
P.O. Box 1015
Tyrone, GA 30290

Camille Beckman Foundation Grants 499
The Camille Beckman Foundation was established by Susan Camille, an artist who grew up in rural Idaho. The daughter of an agriculture teacher, she became immersed in the studies of flowers, herbs and perfume at a young age. After moving to Europe and living as a painter and potter in her 20s, Susan came back to Idaho with a vision for a family company that could benefit women while creating a romantic, beautiful experience for customers. Soon, Susan felt compelled to provide and create opportunities for other children around the world. Realizing her business could be a tool for social change, the Camille Beckman Foundation was realized in 1995. Throughout the years the foundation has contributed to over 120 organizations, building the foundations of tomorrow for our youth and fellow mankind. Today, the Foundation supports disadvantaged children, financially disadvantaged elderly persons, the homeless, and persons with disabilities. The foundation will also provide funding to qualified charities offering training experience and education to allow targeted people to become more productive and self-sufficient. Typically, funding is given for both general operating support and program support. Its interest areas of support include: elementary and secondary education; agriculture; arts and culture; arts education; emergency aid; cancer research; community health care; food assistance; families; food banks; housing development; human services; in-patient medical care; out-patient medical care; pancreatic disease; and visual arts. Most recent awards have ranged up to as much as $50,000. There are no specified annual deadlines to apply.
Requirements: Any 501(c)3 organization supporting the residents of the State of Idaho can apply.
Geographic Focus: Idaho
Amount of Grant: Up to 50,000 USD
Samples: Caring Hearts, Hands of Hope, Boise, Idaho, $50,000 - assistance to disadvantaged individuals; Idaho Foodbank Warehouse, Boise, Idaho, $40,000 - general operating support; Unconditional Life, Boise, Idaho, $20,000 - support for a summer camp for kids.
Contact: Susan Camille Roghani, President; (208) 344-7150
Internet: camillebeckman.com/pages/our-story-purpose
Sponsor: Camille Beckman Foundation
175 S. Rosebud Lane
Eagle, ID 83616-4500

Campbell Foundation Grants 500
The Campbell Foundation was established in Portland, Oregon, in 1993, by J. Duncan Campbell, founder and retired former chairman of the Campbell Group, a full-service timberland investment management company. Prior to forming the Campbell Group, Campbell was a tax manager for Arthur Andersen in Portland, Oregon, where he served many of the large public and private forest products companies. Currently, the Foundation has the expressed purpose of providing support to: child welfare programs; other foundations; higher education; human services; and museums. Most recent awards have ranged from $200 to $368,000. Interested applicants should submit a detailed description of project and amount of funding requested in letter format.
Requirements: Any 501(c)3 supporting residents of Portland, Oregon, and its surrounding suburbs may apply.
Geographic Focus: All States
Amount of Grant: Up to 400,000 USD
Samples: A Circle of Friends, Sisters, Oregon, $10,250 - general operating support (2018); Caldera, Portland, Oregon, $7,500 - general operating support (2018); Door of Hope Church, Portland, Oregon, $11,500 - general operating support (2018).
Contact: Cynthia A. Campbell, Director; (503) 281-6633
Sponsor: Campbell Foundation
841 SW Gaines Street, Unit 2304
Portland, OR 97239

Campbell Soup Foundation Grants 501
Since 1953, the Campbell Soup Foundation has provided financial support to local champions that inspire positive change in communities throughout the United States where Campbell Soup Company employees live and work. The Foundation places particular emphasis on Camden, New Jersey, birthplace of Campbell's flagship soup business and world headquarters. The Campbell Soup Foundation focuses its giving on four key areas: hunger relief-supporting food bank organizations in the communities of operation; wellness-addressing the health of consumers in the communities where they live; education-leveraging the Campbell brand portfolio to support educational programs; community revitalization-enhancing the quality of life in the communities that Campbell operates in. The Foundation only considers applications that meet the following criteria:

the proposal must fit one of the key focus areas; the organization must display strong and effective leadership; the proposed plan must be clear and compelling, with measurable and sustainable commitments expressed in terms of real results; the proposed activity must be sufficiently visible to leverage additional support from other funding sources. The Campbell Soup Foundation now hosts only one funding cycle per year, in the fall. The funding cycle is typically four months in length, and runs July through October.

Requirements: The Foundation limits grants to nonprofit organizations which are tax-exempt under Section 501(c)3 of the Internal Revenue Code. Grants are made to institutions that serve: Camden and East Brunswick, New Jersey; Bakersfield, California; Dixon, California; Stockton, California; Bloomfield and Norwalk, Connecticut; Downers Grove, Illinois; Ferndale and Grand Rapids, Michigan; Maxton, North Carolina; Napoleon and Willard, Ohio; Denver and Downingtown, Pennsylvania; Paris, Texas; Richmond, Utah; Everett, Washington; and Milwaukee, Wisconsin. Organizations do not need to be located in these communities in order to qualify for funding. However, the programs to be funded must serve these communities. Proposals must be submitted electronically. Proposals should be prepared in a concise, narrative form, without extensive documentation.

Restrictions: Grants are not made to the following: organizations that are based outside the United States and its territories; individuals; organizations that limit their services to members of one religious group or whose services propagate religious faith or creed; political organizations and those having the primary purpose of influencing legislation of/or promoting a particular ideological point of view; units of government; events and sponsorships; sports related events, activities and sponsorships. Organizations may not submit the same or similar proposals more than once in a Foundation fiscal year (July 1 through June 30). Proposals submitted via regular mail will not be reviewed.

Geographic Focus: Arizona, Arkansas, California, Connecticut, Florida, Georgia, Illinois, Indiana, Massachusetts, Minnesota, New Jersey, North Carolina, Ohio, Oregon, Pennsylvania, Texas, Utah, Wisconsin

Date(s) Application is Due: Nov 3

Contact: Grant Administrator; (856) 342-6423 or (800) 257-8443; fax (856) 541-8185; community_relations@campbellsoup.com

Internet: www.campbellsoupcompany.com/about-campbell/corporate-responsibility/campbell-soup-foundation/

Sponsor: Campbell Soup Foundation
1 Campbell Place
Camden, NJ 08103-1701

Caplow Applied Science (CappSci) Children's Prize 502

The CappSci Children's Prize is an open web-based competition focused on under-five child survival with eligibility extending to everyone, individuals and organizations, across the world. Through CappSci's entrepreneurial and scientific approaches, the program is ensuring that more children under the age of five survive and thrive. The Children's Prize seeks the best and most effective project that proposes to save the greatest number of children's lives. One recipient will be awarded the $250,000 prize to directly execute their proposed project, within a two year period. Proposals will be judged according to how many lives they propose to save, how credible the plan and the proposer are, how directly the funds can be applied, the probability of success and the ease of verification. The online application must be received by June 12.

Requirements: The Children's Prize is available to anyone. Proposals will be accepted from non-profits (charities), for profits (companies), government programs, academic institutions, and individuals aged 18 years or older.

Geographic Focus: All States

Date(s) Application is Due: Jun 12

Amount of Grant: 250,000 USD

Contact: Aleyda K. Mejia, Director of Global Health & Social Ventures; (305) 776-0902 or (786) 558-9738; fax (786) 269-2266; aleyda@cappsci.org or childrensprize@cappsci.org

Internet: www.childrensprize.org/

Sponsor: Caplow Applied Science
3439 Main Highway, Suite 2
Miami, FL 33133

Cargill Corporate Giving Grants 503

Cargill's purpose is to be the global leader in nourishing people. Cargill measures their performance through engaged employees, satisfied customers, profitable growth and enriched communities. Corporate giving is one important way Cargill works to enrich the 1,000 communities where they conduct business. With 149,000 employees in 63 countries, Cargill people are working everyday to nourish the lives of those around us. The Cargill Citizenship Fund provides strategic grants to organizations serving communities where Cargill has a presence. The Fund provides direct grants for regional, national and global partnerships and provides matching grants for selected local projects supported by our businesses. Cargill seeks to build sustainable communities by focusing our human and financial resources in three areas: Nutrition and Health-support for programs and projects that address long-term solutions to hunger, increase access to health education and/or basic health care in developing and emerging countries, and improve youth nutrition and wellness; Education-support for innovative programs that improve academic achievement, develop logic and thinking skills, promote leadership development, and/or increase access to education for socio-economically disadvantaged children. Cargill also supports mutually beneficial partnerships with selected higher education institutions; Environment-support for projects that protect and improve accessibility to water resources; promote biodiversity conservation in agricultural areas; and educate children about conservation and/or proper sanitation. Application and additional guidelines are available at: www.cargill.com/wcm/groups/public/@ccom/documents/document/doc-giving-funding-app.pdf

Requirements: Applicants must have 501(c)3 status or the equivalent; and they must be located in communities where Cargill has a business presence. Only under special circumstances

will Cargill consider general operating or capital support. Organizations requesting capital or operating support should contact the Cargill Citizenship Fund staff before applying.

Restrictions: Cargill will not fund: organizations without 501(c)3 status or the equivalent; organizations that do not serve communities where Cargill has a business presence; individuals or groups seeking support for research, planning, personal needs or travel; public service or political campaigns; lobbying, political or fraternal activities; benefit dinners or tickets to the same; fundraising campaigns, walk-a-thons, or promotions to eliminate or control; specific diseases; athletic scholarships; advertising or event sponsorships; religious groups for religious purposes; publications, audio-visual productions or special broadcasts; endowments; medical equipment.

Geographic Focus: All States, Albania, Algeria, Andorra, Angola, Armenia, Austria, Azerbaijan, Belarus, Belgium, Benin, Bosnia & Herzegovina, Botswana, Bulgaria, Burkina Faso, Burundi, Cameroon, Cape Verde, Central African Republic, Chad, Comoros, Congo, Democratic Republic of, Congo, Republic of the, Cote d' Ivoire (Ivory Coast), Croatia, Cyprus, Czech Republic (Czechia), Denmark, Djibouti, Egypt, Equatorial Guinea, Eritrea, Estonia, Eswatini (Swaziland), Ethiopia, Finland, France, Gabon, Gambia, Georgia, Germany, Ghana, Greece, Guinea, Guinea-Bissau, Holy See (Vatican City State), Hungary, Iceland, Ireland, Italy, Kenya, Kosovo, Latvia, Lesotho, Liberia, Libya, Liechtenstein, Lithuania, Luxembourg, Madagascar, Malawi, Mali, Malta, Mauritania, Mauritius, Moldova, Monaco, Montenegro, Morocco, Mozambique, Namibia, Netherlands, Niger, Nigeria, North Macedonia, Norway, Poland, Portugal, Romania, Russia, Rwanda, San Marino, Sao Tome & Principe, Senegal, Serbia, Seychelles, Sierra Leone, Slovakia, Slovenia, Somalia, South Africa, Spain, Sudan, Sweden, Switzerland, Turkey, Ukraine, United Kingdom

Amount of Grant: 500 - 100,000 USD

Contact: Stacey Smida; (952) 742-4311; fax (952) 742-7224; stacey_smida@cargill.com

Internet: www.cargill.com/about/community/corporate-giving

Sponsor: Cargill Corporation
P.O. Box 5650
Minneapolis, MN 55440-5650

Cargill Foundation Education Grants 504

The Foundation seeks to fulfill its mission to prepare the next generation for success in school, work and life by investing in organizations and programs that demonstrate leadership and effectiveness in educating socio-economically disadvantaged children and eliminating barriers to their educational success. Through the Foundation, it contributes nearly $4 million annually to youth education programs. With this program, the Foundation supports STEM programs that: increase equitable access to STEM, teacher effectiveness and STEM proficiency for students in grades K-12. STEM organizations of interest: are community organizations serving low-income populations with a high proportion of youth grades K -12; ensure equitable access to STEM; are organizations with hands-on interactive programming/curriculum that improve the understanding of STEM topics; will provide teachers with professional development or access to STEM resources and knowledge to improve student persistence in STEM; and are nonprofits that integrate programs that encourage interest in STEM for post-secondary education and potential careers in STEM fields. College and Career Readiness Organizations of interest: are community organizations serving low income populations with a high proportion of youth in grades 7-12; will increase high school graduation and post-secondary enrollment; are programs that have an emphasis on goal planning, problem solving, and/or awareness with post-secondary application process for students and parents; and will facilitate collaboration/ alignment between high school and post-secondary curriculum to increase college readiness, academic achievement and/or engagement.

Requirements. Grant applicants invited to submit a formal proposal are required to provide a logic model illustrating underlying program theory and linkages between program components and expected outcomes.

Restrictions: Only education programs operating in Minneapolis and its northern and western suburbs are eligible.

Geographic Focus: Minnesota

Date(s) Application is Due: Aug 28

Contact: Stacey Smida; (952) 742-4311; fax (952) 742-7224; stacey_smida@cargill.com

Internet: www.cargill.com/worldwide/usa/cargill-foundation/index.jsp

Sponsor: Cargill Foundation
P.O. Box 5650
Minneapolis, MN 55440-5650

Caring for Colorado Foundation Sperry S. and Ella Graber Packard Fund for 505
Pueblo Grants

The Sperry S. and Ella Graber Packard Fund for Pueblo Grants program has a primary focus of support for children, youth, and families in the Pueblo, Colorado, region. To be considered for a grant, all prospective Packard Fund for Pueblo applicants – including current grantees – must submit a Letter of Inquiry (LOI). The LOI should be no more than two pages in length. If an invitation to apply is extended, grant seekers should register for access to the online grants portal. Applications should be submitted online prior to the annual deadline of January 6.

Requirements: Caring for Colorado will consider applications from and awards to organizations who benefit Colorado and are: charitable nonprofit organizations with tax-exempt classification from the Internal Revenue Service; or tax-supported institutions including state and local governments and schools.

Geographic Focus: Colorado

Date(s) Application is Due: Jan 6

Amount of Grant: Up to 30,000 USD

Samples: Steelworks Center of the West, Pueblo, Colorado, $10,000 - general operating support (2019); Pueblo Diversified Industries, Pueblo, Colorado, $20,000 - general support

for much-needed lifting equipment for PDI in the area of service to our individuals with diverse abilities as well as the safety need of a lift in the manufacturing area (2019); Colorado Farm to Table, Pueblo, Colorado, $7,500 - to help feed the hungry in Pueblo County with fresh, free produce at no cost to those receiving it (2019).
Contact: Jennifer Lobb, Grants Specialist; (720) 524-0770; fax (720) 524-0787; jlobb@caringforcolorado.org or info@caringforcolorado.org
Internet: caringforcolorado.org/grants/packard-fund-for-pueblo-grants/
Sponsor: Caring for Colorado Foundation
1635 West 13th Avenue, Suite 303
Denver, CO 80204

Carl B. and Florence E. King Foundation Grants 506

The lives of Carl B. and Florence E. King were marked by warmth, compassion, and generosity. As they prospered, they believed in giving back. With gracious benevolence, they dedicated themselves to the betterment of individuals, communities, and society through informed giving. Today, the Carl B. and Florence E. King Foundation honors their memory, continues their tradition, and builds upon their vision. The Foundation is principally interested in the following areas: aging population; arts, culture, and history; children and youth; education; the indigent; and to strengthen non-profit capacity. The Foundation awards grants twice each year. Applicants must first submit a letter of inquiry, and then a full grant proposal only upon invitation. For the Spring cycle, the deadline for submitting a letter of inquiry is December 15, with invited full proposals due by February 28. For the Fall cycle, the deadline for submitting a letter of inquiry is June 15, with invited full proposals due by August 31.
Requirements: The Foundation distributes grants only to entities that serve residents of Arkansas and Texas. Within Texas, the Foundation is principally interested in n five counties in North Texas and 38 counties in West Texas. Within Arkansas, the Foundation focuses on the 32 counties in southern and eastern portions of the state. Each area has slightly distinct guidelines. Applicants must also have a letter of determination from the Internal Revenue Service acknowledging tax-exempt status as described in Section 501(c)3 of the Internal Revenue Code.
Restrictions: The Foundation does not award grants: to individuals; to organizations or programs that do not serve residents of our geographic focus areas in Texas or Arkansas; to organizations that are not tax exempt; for general operating support, annual fund drives, or funds to offset operating losses (including retiring debt incurred to cover operating losses); to create endowments; toward balls, events, or galas benefiting charitable organizations; to efforts to treat or cure a single disease or condition; to church or seminary construction, or religious programs (other than social service-based initiatives); toward the cost of hosting or attending professional conferences or symposia, or participating in amateur sports competitions or similar activities.
Geographic Focus: Arkansas, Texas
Date(s) Application is Due: Feb 28; Aug 31
Amount of Grant: Up to 100,000 USD
Samples: Family Endeavors, San Antonio, Texas, $135,000 - support of Veterans Homeless Prevention Services and short-term emergency assistance fund through the Veteran's Administration; Delta Community Development and Law Center, Little Rock, Arkansas, $50,000 - support of community building work offered by the Five Neighborhoods Coalition; Child Care Group, Dallas, Texas, $50,000 - support of an overhaul of the website and integration of program platforms.
Contact: Michelle D. Monse, President; (214) 750-1884; fax (214) 750-1651; michellemonse@kingfoundation.com or info@kingfoundation.com
Internet: www.kingfoundation.com/Grants/King-Foundation-Grants.aspx
Sponsor: Carl B. and Florence E. King Foundation
2929 Carlisle Street, Suite 222
Dallas, TX 75204

Carl M. Freeman Foundation FACES Grants 507

Founded in 2000 in Delaware, FACES stands for Freeman Assists Communities with Extra Support. The FACES program is designed to find and fund the smaller, overlooked projects in it's neighborhoods. The grants are limited to Montgomery County nonprofit organizations with operating budgets of $750,000 or less and Sussex County nonprofit organizations with operating budgets of $500,000 or less. Funding applications are available in six areas of interest: arts and culture; education; the environment; health and human services; housing: and other (this may include anything an applicant feels does not fit in the above categories, for example spaying cats and dogs. Additional guidelines and applications are available at the website.
Requirements: 501(c)3 tax-exempt organizations in Montgomery and Sussex County are eligible. Nonsectarian religious programs also are eligible.
Restrictions: Grants will not be distributed to: individuals; political associations or candidates; organizations that would disperse the funding to others; organizations that discriminate by race, creed, gender, sexual orientation, age, religion, disability or national origin.
Geographic Focus: Delaware, Maryland, West Virginia
Contact: Melissa Rizer, Grants Administrator; (302) 436-3555 or (302) 436-3015; melissa@freemanfoundation.org or info@freemanfoundation.org
Internet: carlmfreemanfoundation.org/grants
Sponsor: Carl M. Freeman Foundation
31556 Winterberry Parkway
Selbyville, DE 19975

Carl M. Freeman Foundation Grants 508

The Carl M. Freeman Foundation has historically emphasized it's support in the following communities: Montgomery County, Maryland; Sussex County, Delaware; and the Eastern Panhandle of West Virginia . Funding is available for a wide variety of community organizations, having supported everything from arts organizations and hunger centers to educational and health related organizations. To simplify the application process, funding applications are available in six areas of interest: arts and culture; education; environment; health and human services; housing; other (this may include anything you feel does not fit in the above categories, for example spaying cats and dogs). Additional guidelines and applications are available at the website.
Requirements: 501(c)3 tax-exempt organizations in Maryland, Delaware and West Virginia are eligible. Nonsectarian religious programs also are eligible.
Restrictions: Grants will not be distributed to: individuals; political associations or candidates; organizations that would disperse the funding to others; organizations that discriminate by race, creed, gender, sexual orientation, age, religion, disability or national origin.
Geographic Focus: Delaware, Maryland, West Virginia
Amount of Grant: 5,000 - 30,000 USD
Contact: Melissa Rizer, Grants Administrator; (302) 436-3555; melissa@freemanfoundation.org
Internet: www.freemanfoundation.org/carl/CarlMFreemanFoundation/Grants/GrantGuidelines/tabid/181/Default.aspx
Sponsor: Carl M. Freeman Foundation
31556 Winterberry Parkway
Selbyville, DE 19975

Carl R. Hendrickson Family Foundation Grants 509

The Carl R. Hendrickson Family Foundation was established in 1991 to support and promote quality education, human-services, and health-care programming for under-served populations. Carl R. Hendrickson was a Chicago entrepreneur who, along with his father and brothers, built the Hendrickson Trucking Company. Carl and his wife, Agnes, had one child, Virginia, who followed in her father's footsteps by leading the family business and by serving as President of the Hendrickson Foundation. The Hendricksons prided themselves on their entrepreneurial spirit, having been in the forefront of the trucking business by inventing the tandem truck. They encouraged others to embrace their entrepreneurial spirit as well and to pursue philanthropic objectives. Reflecting the Hendrickson family's strong Christian faith, special consideration is given to charitable organizations that help individuals meet their basic needs while also addressing their spiritual needs. Preference is given to organizations or programs that approach their mission from an entrepreneurial perspective. The majority of grants from the Family Foundation are one year in duration. Applicants with organizational budgets of $10 million or less may apply for grants of $10,000 up to $50,000 for program or general operating support. For program support, the request may not be more than 30% of the program's budget.
Requirements: Applicants must have 501(c)3 tax-exempt status. Applicants must demonstrate a strong connection with the Carl R. Hendrickson Family Foundation's entrepreneurial spirit. Applications will be submitted online through the Bank of America website. A grant report is required within 1 year of the grant application date, regardless of whether all of the funds have been spent.
Restrictions: In general, grant requests for individuals, endowment campaigns or capital projects will not be considered. The foundation does not support requests from individuals, organizations attempting to influence policy through direct lobbying, or any political campaigns.
Geographic Focus: Illinois
Date(s) Application is Due: Jul 31
Amount of Grant: 10,000 - 50,000 USD
Samples: Bartlett Learning Center Inc., Bartlett, Illinois, $29,953 - Awarded for Occupational Therapy Equipment (2018); Bethany Christian Services, Palos Heights, Illinois, $25,000 - Awarded for Addressing the Distress of Post-Traumatic Stress program (ADOPTS) (2018); Giant Steps Illinois Inc., Lisle, Illinois, $20,000 - Awarded for Giant Steps Canopy Adult Program for adults with autism spectrum disorders (2018).
Contact: Srilatha Lakkaraju, Philanthropic Client Manager; (312) 828-8166 or (866) 752-2127; ilgrantmaking@bankofamerica.com or ilgrantmaking@ustrust.com
Internet: www.bankofamerica.com/philanthropic/foundation/?fnId=109
Sponsor: Carl R. Hendrickson Family Foundation
135 South LaSalle Street, IL4-135-14-19
Chicago, IL 60603

Carl W. and Carrie Mae Joslyn Trust Grants 510

Grants support activities providing services to resident children, elderly, and the disabled in El Paso County, Colorado. Areas of interest include education, medical care, rehabilitation, children and youth services, and aging centers and services. Types of support include general operating support, annual campaigns, building construction and renovation, equipment acquisition, endowment funds, and program development. Application must be in writing and must specifically describe the use of the funds. Grants are not sustaining and new applications must be submitted semiannually for renewal.
Requirements: Nonprofit organizations located in, or serving the residents of, El Paso County, Colorado, are eligible.
Restrictions: Grants are not made to individuals or for research, scholarships, fellowships, loans, or matching gifts.
Geographic Focus: Colorado
Date(s) Application is Due: Apr 30; Oct 31
Amount of Grant: 500 - 15,000 USD
Samples: Pikes Peak Hospice, Colorado Springs, Colorado, $5,000; Silver Key Senior Services, Colorado Springs, Colorado, $5,000; Saint Marys High School, Colorado Springs, Colorado, $3,000.
Contact: Susan Bradt Laabs, Grants Administrator; (719) 227-6435 or (719) 227-6439; fax (719) 2276448
Sponsor: Carl W. and Carrie Mae Joslyn Charitable Trust
Trust Department, P.O. Box 1699
Colorado Springs, CO 80942

Carnegie Corporation of New York Grants   511

The Carnegie Corporation of New York provides research, study, and support for projects to improve government at all levels, to increase public understanding of social policy issues, to equalize opportunities for minorities and women, and to increase participation in political and civic life. Also supported are projects that promote electoral reform; education reform from early childhood through higher education; early childhood development; and urban school reform. The foundation will also fund research on the increasing availability and success of after-school and extended service programs for children and teenagers, particularly those in urban areas, that promote high academic achievement. Dissemination of best practices in teacher education will also be emphasized. There is no formal procedure for submitting a proposal. To apply under any of the corporation's grantmaking programs, applicants should submit a full proposal that describes the project's aims, duration, methods, amount of financial support required, and key personnel. The board meets four times a year, in October, February, April, and June.

Requirements: Only full proposals that have been invited for submission will be considered. After a letter of inquiry has been reviewed, applicants may be invited via email to submit a full proposal.

Restrictions: Grants are not made for construction or maintenance of facilities or endowments. The Corporation does not generally make grants to individuals except through the Carnegie Scholars Program, that supports the work of select scholars and experts conducting research in the foundation's fields of interest.

Geographic Focus: All States

Amount of Grant: Up to 4,000,000 USD

Samples: Massachusetts Institute of Technology, Cambridge, Massachusetts, $1,000,000 - international peace and security; Center for Better Schools, Portsmouth, Rhode Island, $650,000 - strengthening teaching and human capital; Citizen Schools, Boston, Massachusetts, $500,000 - strengthening education.

Contact: Nicole Howe Buggs, Grants Manager; (212) 371-3200; fax (212) 754-4073; externalaffairs@carnegie.org

Internet: www.carnegie.org/grants/grantseekers/

Sponsor: Carnegie Corporation of New York

437 Madison Avenue

New York, NY 10022

Carrie S. Orleans Trust Grants   512

Carrie Sybil Orleans was the wife of Morris J. Orleans. Carrie and Morris traveled extensively together during their lifetime. After her husband's death, Carrie continued in the same manner, but always regarded Dallas as her home. The Carrie S. Orleans Trust was established in 1948 under the will of Carrie Orleans for the purpose of purchasing food and clothing for the poor and needy of Dallas County without regard to race, creed or color. Per Mrs. Orleans' request, distributions are always made immediately following Thanksgiving Day. Award amounts typically range from $1,000 to $10,000. Grants from the Carrie S. Orleans Trust are 1 year in duration.

Requirements: Grants are only awarded to organizations for the purchase of food and clothing for the poor and needy of Dallas County, Texas. Applications will be submitted online through the Bank of America website. A grant report is required within 1 year of the grant application date, regardless of whether all of the funds have been spent.

Geographic Focus: Texas

Date(s) Application is Due: Aug 1

Amount of Grant: 1,000 - 10,000 USD

Samples: North Texas Food Bank, Dallas, Texas, $10,000 - Awarded for Purchase of food for the poor and needy of the greater Dallas area (2018); Sharing Life Community Outreach, Mesquite, Texas, $10,000 - Awarded for Client Choice Food Pantry: Meeting low-income client needs (2018); First Presbyterian, Dallas, Texas, $10,000 - Awarded for Food Programs for At-Risk Children and Their Families (2018).

Contact: Kelly Garlock, Philanthropic Client Manager; (800) 357-7094; tx.philanthropic@bankofamerica.com or tx.philanthropic@ustrust.com

Internet: www.bankofamerica.com/philanthropic/foundation/?fnId=149

Sponsor: Carrie S. Orleans Trust

P.O. Box 831041

Dallas, TX 75283-1041

Carroll County Community Foundation Grants   513

The Carroll County Community Foundation funds initiatives that improve the quality of life for citizens of Carroll County, Indiana. The Foundation's grant program emphasizes change-oriented issues, with the following areas of interest: health and medical; social services; education; cultural affairs; civic affairs; and community beautification. Proposals: must strive to anticipate the changing needs of the community and be flexible in responding to them; must be change-oriented and problem-solving in nature with emphasis on "seed" money or pilot project support rather than for ongoing general operating support; support innovative efforts and projects that offer far-reaching gains and widespread community results; may coordinate with other funders and donors where possible, including using matching or challenge grant techniques; closely relate and coordinate with the programs of other sources for funding such as the government, other foundations, and associations; and achieve certain objectives such as become more efficient, increase fund-raising capabilities, and deliver better products. Grants will be made only to organizations: whose programs benefit the residents of the county, with preference given to those projects with high visibility in the community; which provide for a responsible fiscal agent and adequate accounting procedures, with preference given to those projects that generate revenue and/or have plans that sustain the project.

Requirements: A letter of inquiry to the Foundation is required as a pre-qualification. The letter should contain a brief statement of the applicant's needs for assistance, estimate of total cost of the project, and enough factual information to enable the Foundation to determine whether or not the application falls within the guidelines of its grants program. After the organization has received a response to apply for a grant, the grantee will then fill out the online application and submit ten copies of the application and all attachments to the Foundation for approval. Organizations should refer to the Foundation website for further information.

Restrictions: The Foundation typically does not award grants for: normal operating expenses and/or salaries; individuals; seminars or trips except where there are special circumstances which will benefit the larger community; sectarian religious purposes but can be made to religious organizations for general community programs; endowment purposes of recipient organizations; projects which have been proposed by individuals or organizations responsible to advisory bodies or persons; new projects and/or equipment purchased prior to the grant application being approved.

Geographic Focus: Indiana

Date(s) Application is Due: Sep 6

Samples: Burlington Community Park, replacement and updating park playground equipment, $4,500; Book Readers and Horn Blowers, Delphi Elementary School, $1,000; Delphi Public Library, Delphi, IN, digital media lab report, $1,000.

Contact: Ron Harper, President; (765) 454-7298 or (800) 964-0508; ron@cfhoward.org

Internet: cfcarroll.org/newsite/grantprogram.shtml

Sponsor: Carroll County Community Foundation

215 West Sycamore Street

Kokomo, IN 46901

Case Foundation Grants   514

The Case Foundation, created by Steve Case and Jean Case in 1997, invests in people and ideas that can change the world. The Foundation creates and supports initiatives that leverage new technologies and entrepreneurial approaches to drive innovation in the social sector and encourage individuals to get involved with the communities and causes they care about.

Geographic Focus: All States, District of Columbia, Puerto Rico

Contact: Program Director; (202) 467-5788; fax (202) 775-8513

Internet: befearless.casefoundation.org/finding-fearless/grants-prizes

Sponsor: Case Foundation

1717 Rhode Island Avenue NW, 7th Floor

Washington, D.C. 20036

Cash 4 Clubs Sports Grants   515

Cash 4 Clubs is a sports funding scheme which gives clubs a unique chance to apply for grants to improve facilities, purchase new equipment, gain coaching qualifications, and generally invest in the sustainability of their club. The Cash 4 Clubs scheme is funded by Betfair and is supported by SportsAid, the charity for sports people. Betfair and SportsAid have worked in partnership for a number of years and both organizations understand the importance of community sport in promoting an active lifestyle and stimulating local pride. Three tiers of grants at £250, £500 and £1,000 which are awarded on a discretionary basis twice a year. There are no deadlines for submitting grant applications. Clubs are welcome to apply at any time and they will be considered at the next committee panel meeting.

Requirements: Any sports club that is registered with its sports' National Governing body or local authority can apply. No preference is given to types of sport or the age of people involved with the club, but the sponsor does look for sports clubs that play an active role in the community. Sport is a great way for the community to get together socially and get active and keep fit at the same time. Clubs can apply by filling out the required online form at the sponsor's website.

Geographic Focus: United Kingdom

Amount of Grant: 250 - 1,000 GBP

Samples: Broxbourne Rowing Club, Hertfordshire; Cottenham Roller Hockey Club, Cambridge; Pitsford Pirates Windsurfing Club, Northampton; Nottingham Outlaws BMX Club; Bangladesh Football Association (UK), Tower Hamlets; Croydon School of Gymnastics, Croydon; Marske Junior Badminton Club; Newcastle Wrestling Club, Tyne and Wear; Cartmel Valley Baseball Club; King's Lynn Field Archers; Strabane Sigersons Gaelic Athletic Association, County Tyrone; Aboyne Canoe Club, Aberdeenshire.

Contact: Laura Eddie, National Awards Manager; 020 7273 1975; mail@sportsaid.org.uk

Internet: www.cash-4-clubs.com/

Sponsor: SportsAid

3rd Floor, Victoria House

London, GLONDON WC1B 4SE United Kingdom

Cass County Community Foundation Grants   516

The Cass County Community Foundation (CCCF) assists donors in building enduring sources of charitable assets to promote education, enhance humanity, and advance community development throughout Cass County. The Foundation has the following areas of interest: education; human services; and community development. All applications are reviewed by a committee comprised of CCCF Board members and other volunteers from the community. Non-profit organizations whose projects directly impact the lives of Cass County residents are eligible to apply.

Requirements: The grant application is available online and is also available at the Foundation office. Grant seekers should include their organizational, financial, and project information, and submit seven copies of the application packet to the Foundation. Applicants are encouraged to participate in the free grant writing workshop available each spring.

Restrictions: Public schools, while non-profit, are not 501(c)3 and therefore are not eligible. The Foundation will not consider grants for: existing obligations; services supported by tax dollars; individuals or travel expenses; repeat funding; on-going operating expenses; advocacy; religious purposes or affiliations; or loans or endowments.

Geographic Focus: Indiana

Date(s) Application is Due: Jul 1

Amount of Grant: 5,000 - 14,000 USD

Samples: Galveston, IN, fire department equipment modernization; $5,000; Royal Center, IN, volunteer fire department emergency generator; $5,000; Salvation Army, security and alarm system, ADA compliant restrooms for new building; $14,250.

Contact: Deanna Crispen, Executive Director; (574) 722-2200; fax (574) 753-7501; D.C.rispen@casscountycf.org or info@casscountycf.org

Internet: casscountycf.org/page/Competitive-Grants-Cycle-id-24
Sponsor: Cass County Community Foundation
417 North Street, Suite 102, P.O. Box 441
Logansport, IN 46947

Castle Foundation Grants 517

The Castle Foundation was established in 1952 with financial backing from A.M. Castle and Company, an Oak Brook, Illinois, based metal supplier. Giving is centered primarily in the Midwestern states of Illinois, Wisconsin, Indiana, Missouri, Michigan, and Ohio, with the Foundation's major fields of support being: elementary and secondary education; higher education; human services; community development, and community services. Types of financial support are: general operations; program development; and re-granting programs. A formal application is not required, and interested parties should send a written request letter to the Foundation office. Most recent awards have ranged from $100 to $10,000. There are no specified annual deadlines, and applications are accepted on a rolling basis.
Requirements: 501(c)3 organizations, colleges and universities, and K-12 school districts throughout Illinois, Wisconsin, Indiana, Missouri, Michigan, and Ohio are eligible to apply.
Geographic Focus: Illinois, Indiana, Michigan, Missouri, Ohio, Wisconsin
Amount of Grant: 100 - 10,000 USD
Samples: Elmhurst College, Elmhurst, Illinois, $3,500 - general operating support; Ohio State University, Columbus, Ohio, $3,000 - general operating support; Kohl Children's Museum, Chicago, Illinois, $4,000 - general operating support.
Contact: Anita Panganiban, Treasurer; (847) 349-2598 or (847) 349-2510
Sponsor: Castle Foundation
1420 Kensington Road, Suite 220
Oak Brook, IL 60523-2143

Castle Foundation Grants 518

The Castle Foundation was established in Utah in 1953, with support going to programs throughout the state. The Foundation's primary fields of interest include: arts and culture; child welfare; elementary and secondary education; human services; health; and higher education. Types of support include: equipment purchases; general operations; program development; and scholarship endowments. An application form is required and guidelines are available upon request. Interested parties should submit four copies, with each including: a detailed description of project and amount of funding requested; a copy of IRS Determination Letter; and a copy of current year's organizational budget and/or project budget. Most recent awards have ranged from $1,000 to $20,000. Though there are no specific application deadlines, be aware that the board meets twice annually, in May and November.
Requirements: 501(c)3 organizations serving the residents of Utah are eligible to apply.
Geographic Focus: Utah
Amount of Grant: 1,000 - 20,000 USD
Samples: Women's Resource Center, University of Utah, Salt Lake City, Utah, $19,500 - general operating support; Kostopulos Dream Foundation, Salt Lake City, Utah, $4,000 - general operating support; Prevent Child Abuse, Ogden, Utah, $3,500 - general operating support.
Contact: Michael I. Poulter, Trust Manager; (503) 275-4327
Sponsor: Castle Foundation
P.O. Box 3168
Portland, OR 97208-3168

Castle Industries Foundation Grants 519

The Castle Industries Foundation was established in Princeton, Wisconsin, by a personal holding company. The Foundation's primary fields of interest include: elementary and secondary education; youth organizations; conservation; and religious organizations. Giving is limited to Fond du Lac, Wisconsin, and its surrounding counties of Sheboygan, Dodge, Green Lake, Winnebago, and Calumet. An application is required, and should include a detailed description of project and amount of funding requested. Most recent awards have ranged from $100 to $1,000.
Requirements: 501(c)3 organizations serving the residents of Fond du Lac, Wisconsin, and its surrounding counties are eligible to apply.
Geographic Focus: Wisconsin
Amount of Grant: 100 - 1,000 USD
Contact: Craig E. Castle, Director; (920) 293-4208
Sponsor: Castle Industries Foundation
West 1544 County Highway J
Princeton, WI 54968-0357

Catherine Holmes Wilkins Foundation Charitable Grants 520

The Catherine Holmes Wilkins Charitable Foundation was created in trust to provide charitable grants to qualified medical research and social service agencies in the Puget Sound region. Organizations must operate within or significantly affect the residents of the Greater Seattle region: Tacoma to Everett, Seattle, and the Eastside. Funding priorities include medical research (medical and academic centers conducting research and training in areas such as cancer, heart disease, and mental illness); physically or mentally disabled (community nonprofit organizations providing direct social services to people with physical or mental disabilities who are primarily low-income or destitute); and humanitarian services (community-based programs providing immediate support to those in need with a particular emphasis on services for abused women and children). Preference will be given to projects rather than ongoing operating expenses. When funding capital campaigns, preference will be given to smaller campaigns where modest contributions may have an impact. Average grant size ranges from $2,000 to $10,000 per year. Grants are awarded in three grant cycles per year: the second Monday of March (spring cycle), the fourth Friday of June (summer cycle), and the second Friday of October (fall cycle).

Requirements: 501(c)3 nonprofit organizations that operate within or significantly affect the residents of the greater Seattle/Puget Sound region (Tacoma to Everett, Seattle, and the Eastside) are eligible. Applicant organizations not related to medical research must have annual operating budgets of less than $1 million. Larger organizations that have received two Wilkins grants within the last five years may re-apply for support. After receiving three consecutive grants from the Wilkins Foundation, applicants may not reapply for two years (24 months). Applications will be submitted online through the Bank of America website. A grant report is required within 1 year of the grant application date, regardless of whether all of the funds have been spent.
Restrictions: Grants will not be considered for individuals or for scholarships; organizations which have been declined for funding twice in the previous five years; or debt retirement or to meet operation deficits.
Geographic Focus: Washington
Date(s) Application is Due: Mar 8; Jun 25; Oct 8
Amount of Grant: 2,000 - 10,000 USD
Samples: Northwest Kidney Centers, Seattle, Washington, $10,000 - Awarded for Eastside research suite (2018); University of Washington Foundation, Seattle, Washington, $10,000 - Awarded for Cardiac Sarcoidosis research (2018); Aces of Diamonds, Duvall, Washington, $5,000 - Awarded for Uplifting Women and Kids Program - General Operations (2018).
Contact: Keri Healey, Grants Consultant; (206) 604-5374; keri@kerihealey.com or wa.grantmaking@bankofamerica.com
Internet: www.bankofamerica.com/philanthropic/foundation/?fnId=137
Sponsor: Catherine Holmes Wilkins Charitable Foundation
800 5th Avenue, P.O. Box 24565, WA1-501-33-23
Seattle, WA 98124-0565

Cause Populi Worthy Cause Grants 521

The main purpose of the Worthy Cause marketing grant is to enhance the visibility, online presence, community engagement and fund raising aspects of qualifying nonprofit institutions. Cause Populi, LLC will provide grants of up to $50,000 per project to qualifying non-profits. Grant applications and awards will be reviewed on a monthly basis. The grant is awarded as a matching in-kind donation to the selected non-profit institution(s), and may only be applied towards services provided by Cause Populi. Typical projects funded by the grant would include website redevelopment services, event management and promotion, marketing campaign services, social networking campaigns, etc. The grant award may be applied towards a specific project, or a group of related projects. Applicants may attach documentation describing the project in detail. The deadline for grant applications is the 21st day of each month. Applications will be reviewed upon submission, and awards will be made on a first-come, first-serve basis until the monthly award funds have been allocated. Applications received after this date may be deferred to a future award cycle.
Requirements: Donated services will be distributed under this program to qualifying organizations only, not to individuals. This donation is only available to nonprofits with 501(c)3 designation. The grant award and services may not be transferred, donated or resold.
Geographic Focus: All States, All Countries
Amount of Grant: Up to 50,000 USD
Contact: Eduardo J. Alarcon, CEO; (305) 913-4604; ealarcon@causepopuli.com
Internet: causepopuli.com/marketing-services-grant-for-non-profits/
Sponsor: Cause Populi
201 S. Biscayne Boulevard
Miami, FL 33131

CCFF Christopher Columbus Awards 522

The Christopher Columbus Awards is a national, community-based science, technology, engineering and math (STEM) program for middle school students. The program challenges the students to work in teams of three to four, with an adult coach, to identify a problem in their community and apply the scientific method to create an innovative solution to that problem. All participating teams will receive certificates of participation and judges' feedback. Semifinalist teams will receive judges' feedback and T-shirts. Finalist teams will receive improvement grants, and the teams and coaches will receive a six-day trip to Walt Disney World for National Championship Week, and will be eligible to receive U.S. Saving Bond prizes.
Requirements: The competition is open to sixth- through eighth-graders working in teams of three or four. Each team must choose an adult to serve as coach and adviser. Teams do not need to be school-based; entries also can come from extra-curricular groups such as 4-H Clubs, Girls Scouts and Boy Scouts, YMCAs and YWCAs, and home-school settings.
Geographic Focus: All States
Date(s) Application is Due: Feb 7
Amount of Grant: Up to 25,000 USD
Contact: Judith M. Shellenberger, Executive Director; (315) 258-0090; fax (315) 258-0093; judithmscolumbus@cs.com
Internet: www.christophercolumbusawards.com/
Sponsor: Christopher Columbus Fellowship Foundation
110 Genesee Street, Suite 390
Auburn, NY 13021

CCFF Community Grant 523

The $25,000 Columbus Foundation Community Grant is an additional opportunity for one finalist team to take its project to a higher level. In conjunction with a community partner, the student team uses the grant money to make part or all of its ideas a reality in the community over the course of the year following the competition. The grant is dedicated to encouraging young explorers to grow as individuals and to gain a sense of accomplishment. The grant project is designed to provide a unique opportunity for young people to see hope where there is a problem, and develop confidence in their abilities to change an unacceptable

situation. Adult community leaders play an important role by administering the grant money and providing the team with guidance. The grant brings young people and adults together to create a brighter future for all of us.
Geographic Focus: All States
Amount of Grant: 25,000 USD
Contact: Judith M. Shellenberger; (315) 258-0090; fax (315) 258-0093; judithmscolumbus@cs.com
Internet: www.columbusfdn.org/christophercolumbus/index.php
Sponsor: Christopher Columbus Fellowship Foundation
110 Genesee Street, Suite 390
Auburn, NY 13021

CDC David J. Sencer Museum Student Field Trip Experience 524

The large-school-group field trip experience is available for groups of 10-40 seventh-twelfth graders and to home-schooled groups. During the field trip which will last approximately two hours, students will learn about the Centers of Disease Control and Prevention (CDC)'s history, current work in preventing disease and promoting health, and detailed information about various infectious diseases. Upon arrival to the David J. Sencer CDC Museum, the group will be greeted and oriented to CDC on the Global Symphony platform. The Global Symphony is a media installation featuring four, three-minute stories that describe in depth CDC's contributions to the elimination of polio, the investigation of Legionnaire's disease, the battle to stem the rise of obesity in the United States, and the study of how humans, animals, and the environment interact in the spread of Ebola. Following the orientation, students will be divided into two smaller groups. One group will tour the exhibit area while the other group watches "Behind Closed Doors," a video about CDC. Approximately 40 minutes later the groups will trade places. Tours include the current temporary exhibit and CDC Museum's permanent History of CDC exhibit. Through the context of the History of CDC exhibit, students will learn about infectious and chronic diseases studied at CDC; the bacteria, viruses and risk behaviors that cause diseases; and prevention methods like immunization and healthy lifestyles. Following the guided tour and video presentation, students will have the opportunity to try on a Biosafety Level 4 lab suit and explore the exhibit area independently. Tour requests may be submitted online at the program website (given above). A complete list of attendees' names must also be submitted via the given fax number or first listed email address. Please note the tour is not scheduled until the teacher receives a confirmation email. Teachers are encouraged to visit the program website for more information about current exhibits. The David J. Sencer CDC Museum is a Smithsonian Institution Affiliate, which provides access to unique programming, content and expertise, and provides a network and forum for the CDC Museum to showcase itself on a national stage and at a national level.
Requirements: One chaperone for every 10 students is encouraged. Teachers are encouraged to bring a camera to take pictures of students as they try on Biosafety suits; however cameras are only allowed in the museum area. Teachers are expected to download and review museum behavior expectations with students and to print and read the driving directions and parking instructions. Teachers and chaperones are expected to be active chaperones and to model proper behavior by refraining from talking during the tours, using a cell phone, or bringing food and beverages into the the museum space. After the visit, teachers are asked to complete and return an evaluation form.
Restrictions: Group Size: 10-40 (including chaperones)
Geographic Focus: All States
Contact: Judy Gantt, Curator; (404) 639-0830 or (404) 639-0831; fax (404) 639-0834; museum@cdc.gov or judy.gantt@cdc.hhs.gov
Internet: www.cdc.gov/museum/tours/student.htm
Sponsor: Centers for Disease Control and Prevention
1600 Clifton Road
Atlanta, GA 30333

CDC Disease Detective Camp 525

The Centers for Disease Control and Prevention (CDC)'s Disease Detective Camp (DDC) is an educational program started by CDC's David J. Sencer Museum in 2005 as a mechanism for developing an academic, public-health-day-camp curriculum for state and county health departments. The DDC camp is offered to upcoming high school juniors and seniors and is held at CDC's headquarters in Atlanta, Georgia at no charge. The museum will offer two one-week sessions each summer. The CDC Disease Detective Camp curriculum is based on contextual and situated-cognition learning principles. By learning through hands-on activities and seminars, high school juniors and seniors at the conclusion of the camp will be able to: identify five careers within public health; demonstrate an understanding of basic epidemiology terms; calculate basic epidemiologic rates given an outbreak scenario and data; recognize how infectious and chronic diseases are tracked in the United States; and understand the role of public health law in protecting the public's health in the United States. Over the course of five days, campers will take on the role of disease detectives and learn first-hand how the CDC safeguards the nation's health. Teams will probe a disease outbreak using epidemiologic and laboratory skills and report their findings to a group of CDC scientists. Activities may include short lectures by CDC experts, a mock press conference in the CDC press room, and a look behind the scenes of CDC. The application process for the current DDC is posted the preceding December at the DDC website. Future plans for DDC includes creating a curriculum toolkit for local health departments seeking to offer a similar camp experience. Due to the popularity of this camp, there are more interested students then the program can accommodate. For this reason, interested students must apply (parents are encouraged to help interested students with the application, but not apply for them). Applications will be made available at the DDC website in December or parents and students may call the second phone listed above to have an application mailed. Camp participants are selected in two phases. Applicants are first selected based on their answers to the essay questions on the application and on the recommendation form. The second phase consists of slots assigned through a lottery system. Twenty-seven high-school juniors and seniors will be selected for each camp session. The David J. Sencer CDC Museum is a Smithsonian Institution Affiliate, which provides access to unique programming, content and expertise, and provides a network and forum for the CDC Museum to showcase itself on a national stage and at a national level.
Requirements: The CDC Disease Detective Camp is open to motivated students who will be high-school juniors or seniors. Applicants must be 16 years old by the first day of the camp in order to comply with CDC's laboratory safety requirements. There is no cost associated with attending the CDC Disease Detective Camp, but campers will need to pay for their own lunches. Non-Atlanta residents may apply for the camp, but are responsible for providing their own accommodations and transportation. Campers in past years have stayed with family friends or relatives in Atlanta. Most attendees are from the Atlanta area, but out-of-state students also attend every year. This is a wonderful opportunity to make friends from other schools!
Geographic Focus: All States
Contact: Judy Gantt, Curator; (404) 639-0830 or (404) 639-0831; fax (404) 639-0834; museum@cdc.gov or judy.gantt@cdc.hhs.gov
Internet: www.cdc.gov/museum/camp/index.htm
Sponsor: Centers for Disease Control and Prevention
1600 Clifton Road
Atlanta, GA 30333

CDI Interdisciplinary Research Initiatives Grants 526

The Children's Discovery Institute (CDI) is a world-class center for pediatric research and innovation created to encourage researchers to ask bold questions and take bold risks to uncover answers. By funding the work of creative scientists and clinicians in collaborative, multi-disciplinary research aimed at some of the most devastating childhood diseases and disorders, CDI will accelerate the realization of better treatments, cures, and preventions. Interdisciplinary Research Initiatives (II) provide funds for highly innovative and novel projects in need of initial start-up funding to enable procurement of other independent support. Up to $150,000 per year for up to three years is available for Washington University faculty seeking to embark on novel projects in need of initial start-up funding to enable procurement of other independent support. Projects should strive to bring investigators from multiple disciplines together to identify targets for improved diagnosis, prevention or other treatment of a pediatric health problem relevant to the goals of the CDI.
Requirements: Proposals will be accepted from Washington University faculty and postdoctoral trainees. Preference will be given to faculty members prior to achieving tenure, to teams of investigators from multiple disciplines, and to multi-investigator projects to develop interactive research groups. Preference will also be given to projects with potential for acquisition of new knowledge/translational impact and scientific experience; and to programs synergistic with Washington University and St. Louis Children's Hospital. Letters of intent must be submitted by August 1. For investigators invited to submit a proposal, applications will be due on October 15.
Geographic Focus: Missouri
Date(s) Application is Due: Oct 15
Amount of Grant: Up to 450,000 USD
Contact: Angela Mayer (Corless); (314) 286-2711; CDI@kids.wustl.edu
Internet: www.childrensdiscovery.org/Grants/FundingMechanismsDueDates.aspx
Sponsor: Children's Discovery Institute
660 S. Euclid Avenue
St. Louis, MO 63110

CEC Clarissa Hug Teacher of the Year Award 527

The Council for Exceptional Children is an international community of professionals who are the voice and vision of special and gifted education. CEC's mission is to improve, through excellence and advocacy, the education and quality of life for children and youth with exceptionalities and to enhance the engagement of their families. The CEC Clarissa Hug Teacher of the Year Award recognizes a CEC member (teacher or related service provider) who currently provides direct services to students with exceptionalities. The CEC Clarissa Hug Teacher of the Year is an outstanding member of the profession whose work exemplifies the best in special education teaching. His or her work reflects significant, documented educational success for students, continued professional development, and the highest standards of educational quality. Nominations may be made by a CEC-affiliated organization (state or provincial unit, chapter, division, or subdivision), individual (CEC member, principal, fellow teacher or colleague, student, parent, self), educational organization (school, parent group, etc.), or community group. The Award recipient will: be recognized and receive a commemorative plaque at an awards ceremony during the CEC Convention and Expo; be invited to attend the CEC Convention and Expo compliments of CEC (CEC will cover the recipient's registration, meals, hotel, and airfare/mileage); be an honored guest and speaker at the Teacher of the Year Brunch at the CEC Convention and Expo; receive a $500 cash award; be featured in a press release and in CEC Today, CECs member e-newsletter; be profiled in TEACHING Exceptional Children and Exceptional Children; be featured on CECs Web site; represent CEC before members of Congress and the administration; represent CEC at the annual National Teacher Hall of Fame Selection Committee, typically held in early March, when invited; act as a CEC spokesperson for the media; and speak at CEC unit conferences.
Requirements: The nominee must: be a CEC member in good standing currently and for at least the previous three years (dating from application deadline date); currently provide direct services to students with exceptionalities; hold professional certification in the area in which he or she provides services; and engage in work consistent with CECs mission statement, as stated above.
Geographic Focus: All States, Canada
Date(s) Application is Due: Oct 19
Amount of Grant: 500 USD
Contact: Andrea Elkin, (703) 620-3660; awards@cec.sped.org or andreae@cec.sped.org

Internet: www.cec.sped.org/Content/NavigationMenu/AboutCEC/Awards/Professional/default.htm
Sponsor: Council for Exceptional Children
2900 Crystal Drive, Suite 1000
Arlington, VA 22202-3557

CEC J.E. Wallace Wallin Special Education Lifetime Achievement Award   528
The CEC J. E. Wallace Wallin Special Education Lifetime Achievement Award recognizes an individual who has made continued and sustained contributions to the education of children and youth with exceptionalities. Nominations may be made by an individual or a CEC-affiliated organization (state/provincial unit, chapter, division, or subdivision). The Award recipient will: be recognized and receive a commemorative plaque at an awards ceremony during the CEC Convention and Expo; be invited to present an educational session at the annual convention; receive a $500 cash award; be featured in a press release and in CEC Today, CEC's member e-newsletter; act as a CEC spokesperson; be profiled on CEC's Web site; and be profiled in TEACHING Exceptional Children and Exceptional Children.
Requirements: The nominee must have a prominent reputation nationally or internationally and have made significant contributions to the education of children with exceptionalities in two or more of the following areas: publications; research; development of new concepts, approaches, or programs; improved psychological or educational evaluation procedures; improved administrative procedures; practical application of improved teaching techniques; and dynamic leadership. Nominations can be accepted from individuals or from a CEC unit (federation, branch, chapter, division, or subdivision). Only one nomination will be accepted from each CEC unit.
Restrictions: Posthumous nominations are not accepted.
Geographic Focus: All States, Canada
Date(s) Application is Due: Oct 19
Amount of Grant: 500 USD
Contact: Andrea Elkin, (703) 620-3660 or (888) 232-7733; fax (703) 264-9494; awards@cec.sped.org or andreae@cec.sped.org
Internet: www.cec.sped.org/Content/NavigationMenu/AboutCEC/Awards/Professional/default.htm
Sponsor: Council for Exceptional Children
2900 Crystal Drive, Suite 1000
Arlington, VA 22202-3557

CEC Yes I Can! Awards   529
The Yes I Can! Awards recognize the accomplishments of children and youth with exceptionalities. Thousands of children and youth have been recognized since the program's inception. CEC will select 21 winners for their outstanding achievements in: academics; arts; athletics; school and community activities; self-advocacy; technology; and transition. Each Award winner will: be invited to attend a special awards ceremony and celebration at the CEC Convention and Expo, and to participate in a special field trip; receive two nights' accommodations at a convention-affiliated hotel; receive a statue designed by nationally renowned sculptor Michael Naranjo; receive a letter of congratulations from the CEC President; be featured in CEC Today, CECs member e-newsletter; be featured on CEC's Web site; and may be called upon by CEC to share his or her story to promote the Yes I Can! Awards program and to generally advocate for children and youth with exceptionalities.
Requirements: Candidates must be 2–21 years of age when they are nominated, and the nominee must have an identified disability. Each candidate may be nominated in only one category.
Restrictions: Posthumous nominations are not accepted.
Geographic Focus: All States, Canada
Date(s) Application is Due: Oct 26
Contact: Andrea Elkin, (703) 620-3660 or (703) 264-9481; fax (703) 264-9494; awards@cec.sped.org or andreae@cec.sped.org
Internet: www.cec.sped.org/Content/NavigationMenu/AboutCEC/YesICanFoundation/default.htm
Sponsor: Council for Exceptional Children
2900 Crystal Drive, Suite 1000
Arlington, VA 22202-3557

Central Pacific Bank Foundation Grants   530
The CPB Foundation's mission is to help strengthen Hawaii communities by creating opportunities for our youth and fostering social progress.
Requirements: To be eligible for funding, the organization must be: a registered 501(c)3; in existence for at least two years; and in stable financial condition. All prospective grant applicants must submit an online application (see website).
Geographic Focus: Hawaii
Date(s) Application is Due: Jun 30; Sep 28
Amount of Grant: Up to 150,000 USD
Samples: Baldwin High School Foundation, Kahului, HI, $2,500; Helping Hands Hawaii, Honolulu, HI, $10,000; Friends of the Future, Kamuela, HI, $5,000; Hoala School 1067, Wahiawa, HI, $10,000.
Contact: Grants Administrator; (808) 544-0500; CPBFoundation@centralpacificbank.com
Internet: www.centralpacificbank.com/About-CPB/Works-For-You/Serving-Our-Community/CPB-Foundation.aspx
Sponsor: Central Pacific Bank Foundation
P.O. Box 3590
Honolulu, HI 96811

CenturyLink Clarke M. Williams Foundation Matching Time Grants   531
CenturyLink's vision is to improve lives, strengthen businesses and connect communities by delivering advanced technologies and solutions with honest and personal service. CenturyLink extends this vision through the CenturyLink Clarke M. Williams Foundation, a 501(c)3 organization dedicated to contributing to endeavors that improve the well-being and overall quality of life for people throughout CenturyLink's communities. Named after

CenturyLink's founder Clarke M. Williams, the Foundation is endowed by CenturyLink to support community initiatives that encourage our employees to use their time, talents and resources to strengthen the communities in which they live and work. The Foundation supports programs designed to enrich the lives of children in pre-kindergarten through 12th grade education. Special emphasis is directed toward programs designed to effectively use technology to improve pre-k through 12th grade public school instruction; promote innovative models to strengthen pre-k through 12th grade public school education; improve the skills and leadership of educators and parents; promote innovative early childhood education; and promote diversity awareness and cultural competency. Employees who volunteer 40 or more hours in a six month period for a 501(c)3 organization in good standing with the IRS can earn a $500 grant for that organization. Employees may earn two grants per year to support the agencies and causes about which they are passionate.
Requirements: Eligible are 501(c)3 nonprofit organizations located in the CenturyLink service areas.
Restrictions: The Foundation does not provide support for political organizations, private foundations, pass-through organizations, or organizations that receive 3 percent or more funding from the United Way. No grants are given to individuals (except for Qwest Teacher Grants), or for scholarships, sectarian religious activities, capital campaigns, chairs, endowments, general operating support for single-disease health groups, or goodwill advertising.
Geographic Focus: Wyoming
Amount of Grant: Up to 500 USD
Contact: Grants Manager; (800) 839-1754 or (314) 340-5768; community_relations@centurylink.com
Internet: www.centurylink.com/aboutus/community/foundation.html
Sponsor: CenturyLink Clarke M. Williams Foundation
100 Centurylink Drive
Monroe, LA 71203-2041

CFF First- and Second-Year Clinical Fellowships   532
The Cystic Fibrosis Foundation offers competitive clinical fellowships for up to five years for physicians interested in cystic fibrosis and other chronic pulmonary and gastrointestinal diseases of children, adolescents, and adults. The intent of this award is to encourage specialized training early in a physician's career and to prepare well-qualified candidates for careers in academic medicine. Training must take place in one of the foundation's accredited centers and must provide thorough grounding in diagnostic and therapeutic procedures, comprehensive care, and cystic fibrosis-related research. All first- and second-year programs must commit a significant portion (at least 30 percent over two years) to research training. Fellows funded by other sources for their first year of training may apply to the foundation for subsequent training support. Third-year fellowships are available for additional basic and/or clinical research training. Research fellowships are also available from the foundation to support physicians beyond the fellowship experience; salary will be commensurate with experience.
Requirements: Applicants must be U.S. citizens or have permanent U.S. resident visas, and must have completed pediatric training and be eligible for board certification in pediatrics by the time the fellowship begins. Candidates with prior training in internal medicine may also apply but must have completed at least two years of an approved adult pulmonary or GI fellowship; be jointly sponsored by the departments of medicine and pediatrics; and be willing to commit at least 75 percent of their time to cystic fibrosis and related problems of young adults.
Geographic Focus: All States
Date(s) Application is Due: Oct 2
Amount of Grant: 47,600 - 49,250 USD
Contact: Office of Grants Management; (800) 344-4823 or (301) 951-4422; fax (301) 951-6378; grants@cff.org
Internet: www.cff.org/research/ForResearchers/FundingOpportunities/TrainingGrants/
Sponsor: Cystic Fibrosis Foundation
6931 Arlington Road, 2nd Floor
Bethesda, MD 20814

CFF Leroy Matthews Physician-Scientist Awards   533
In honor of Dr. LeRoy Matthews' dedication and commitment to cystic fibrosis (CF) research and care, the Cystic Fibrosis Foundation (CFF) announces the Physician Scientist Award named in his memory. Awards will provide up to six years of support for outstanding newly trained pediatricians and internists (MDs and MD/PhDs) to complete sub-specialty training, develop into independent investigators, and initiate research programs. Institutional and individual grants are available. Support ranges from a $48,000 stipend, plus $10,000 for research and development for year one, up to a $76,000 stipend, plus $15,000 for research and development for year six.
Requirements: U.S. citizenship or permanent resident status is required.
Restrictions: Indirect costs are not allowed.
Geographic Focus: All States
Date(s) Application is Due: Sep 11
Amount of Grant: 48,000 - 86,000 USD
Contact: Office of Grants Management; (800) 344-4823 or (301) 951-4422; fax (301) 951-6378; grants@cff.org
Internet: www.cff.org/research/cystic_fibrosis_foundation_grants/research_grants
Sponsor: Cystic Fibrosis Foundation
6931 Arlington Road, 2nd Floor
Bethesda, MD 20814

CFF Research Grants   534
Grants are offered by the Cystic Fibrosis Foundation in support of high-quality research projects ranging from basic cellular and metabolic mechanisms to therapy of cystic fibrosis and related chronic and recurrent pulmonary and gastrointestinal diseases of childhood. These grants are broadly oriented to the support of projects for developing and initially

testing new hypotheses and/or new methods, or those being applied to problems of cystic fibrosis for the first time. The intent of this award is to enable the investigator to collect sufficient data to compete successfully for long-term support from NIH. Interested individuals are encouraged to contact the foundation for guidelines and/or to discuss the potential relevance of their work to the objectives of this program. Support is available for $90,000 per year (plus 8% indirect costs) for a period of two years, at which time a grant may be competitively renewed for an additional year of funding.
Requirements: Investigators who seek support from the Foundation under these funding mechanisms must submit a Letter of Intent (LOI). Applications may be submitted by established investigators or new investigators starting their independent research careers but may not represent support for continuation of a line of research already established by the applicant.
Geographic Focus: All States
Date(s) Application is Due: Sep 11
Amount of Grant: Up to 90,000 USD
Contact: Office of Grants Management; (800) 344-4823 or (301) 951-4422; fax (301) 951-6378; grants@cff.org
Internet: www.cff.org/research/ForResearchers/FundingOpportunities/ResearchGrants/
Sponsor: Cystic Fibrosis Foundation
6931 Arlington Road, 2nd Floor
Bethesda, MD 20814

CFF Third-, Fourth-, and Fifth-Year Clinical Fellowships 535
The Cystic Fibrosis Foundation offers competitive clinical fellowships for up to five years for physicians interested in cystic fibrosis and other chronic pulmonary and gastrointestinal diseases of children, adolescents, and adults to encourage specialized training early in a physician's career and to prepare well-qualified candidates for careers in academic medicine. The third-, fourth-, and fifth-year fellowship award offers support for additional intense basic and/or clinical research training related to cystic fibrosis. Up to $68,250 may be awarded: $58,250 for stipend and $10,000 for research costs.
Requirements: Applicants and sponsors must submit proposals of the research studies to be undertaken and other specialized training that will be offered during this year. Preference will be given to applicants whose training was supported by the foundation.
Restrictions: Recipients who do not enter a career of academic medicine will be subject to payback provisions. Indirect costs are not allowed.
Geographic Focus: All States
Date(s) Application is Due: Sep 11
Amount of Grant: 58,250 - 68,250 USD
Contact: Office of Grants Management; (800) 344-4823 or (301) 951-4422; fax (301) 951-6378; grants@cff.org
Internet: www.cff.org/research/ForResearchers/FundingOpportunities/TrainingGrants/
Sponsor: Cystic Fibrosis Foundation
6931 Arlington Road, 2nd Floor
Bethesda, MD 20814

CFFVR Appleton Education Foundation Grants 536
The Appleton Education Foundation (AEF) seeks to improve the well being of children, teachers and community by enhancing the quality of education within the Wisconsin, Appleton Area School District. AEF role is to fund initiatives that fall outside the school budget. Grants are available up to $500 for a single classroom or up to $1,500 for multiple classes, disciplines or schools. Grant application is available online.
Requirements: Any educator employed by the Wisconsin, Appleton Area School District or any community member in partnership with an educator is eligible to apply for a grant.
Restrictions: Generally, equipment alone does not qualify for a grant. Equipment required to complete a project or implement a program that meets the mission of the Foundation will be considered. Equipment upgrades are considered on an individual basis.
Geographic Focus: Wisconsin
Date(s) Application is Due: Apr 10; Nov 10
Contact: Julie Krause, Executive Director; (920) 832-1517; jkrause@cffoxvalley.org
Internet: www.cffoxvalley.org/Page.aspx?pid=415
Sponsor: Community Foundation for the Fox Valley Region
4455 West Lawrence Street, P.O. Box 563
Appleton, WI 54912-0563

CFFVR Basic Needs Giving Partnership Grants 537
Supported by the U.S. Oil Open Fund for Basic Needs within the Community Foundation and the J.J. Keller Foundation, the partnership assists established charitable organizations with successful programs that address root causes of poverty. Available forms of support include: capacity building; general operating support; project support; project analysis & advocacy. A single organization may request up to $15,000 per year for three years, and collaborative proposals may request up to $100,000 per year for three years. Multiple years of support will be considered only if there is a compelling case for multi-year funding and the project clearly demonstrates how progression shall occur over time.
Requirements: Eligible applicants are well-established charitable organizations that are exempt from federal income taxes under the Internal Revenue Code and have been in operation for a minimum of three years. Wisconsin organizations must serve residents in Outagamie, Calumet, Waupaca, Shawano, or northern Winnebago counties.
Restrictions: Grants from the Basic Needs Giving Partnership will not support the following: technology projects; capital campaigns or building projects; organizational set-up costs; annual fund drives or endowments; lobbying for specific legislation; activities that occur before funding is awarded; organizations with past-due or incomplete grant reports.
Geographic Focus: Wisconsin
Date(s) Application is Due: Feb 15; Sep 15

Contact: Martha Hemwall, Community Engagement Officer; (920) 830-1290, ext. 26; mhemwall@cffoxvalley.org
Internet: www.cffoxvalley.org/Page.aspx?pid=400
Sponsor: Community Foundation for the Fox Valley Region
4455 West Lawrence Street, P.O. Box 563
Appleton, WI 54912-0563

CFFVR Clintonville Area Foundation Grants 538
Clintonville Area Foundation (CAF) grants are awarded from unrestricted funds to support specific projects or new programs for which a moderate amount of grant money can make an impact on an area of need. Grants are made for a broad range of purposes to a wide variety of charitable organizations in the focus areas of health, education and community development.
Requirements: Wisconsin organizations eligible to receive grants from the Community Foundation for the Fox Valley Region are those determined by the IRS to be public charities. This encompasses most charitable, scientific, social service, educational and religious organizations described as IRS 501(c)3 of the tax code, as well as government agencies. Organizations that are not public charities may apply through a fiscal sponsor. Organizations must serve residents of the Clintonville area. The grant application form is available at the CFFVR website.
Restrictions: CAF grants typically will not fund: general operating expenses not related to the proposed project; annual fund drives or fundraising events; endowment funds; programs with a sectarian or religious purpose that promote a specific journey of faith; major capital projects such as the acquisition of land or buildings; medical research; travel for individuals or groups such as bands, sports teams or classes; activities that occur before funding is awarded; organizations with past-due or incomplete grant reports.
Geographic Focus: Wisconsin
Date(s) Application is Due: Dec 15
Amount of Grant: 3,000 USD
Contact: Jenny Goldschmidt; (715) 823-7125, ext. 2603; clintonvillefoundation@gmail.com
Todd Sutton, Grants Officer; (920) 830-1290; tsutton@cffoxvalley.org
Internet: www.cffoxvalley.org/Page.aspx?pid=557
Sponsor: Community Foundation for the Fox Valley Region
4455 West Lawrence Street, P.O. Box 563
Appleton, WI 54912-0563

CFFVR Clintonville Area Foundation Grants 539
Clintonville Area Foundation (CAF) grants are awarded from unrestricted funds to support specific projects or new programs for which a moderate amount of grant money can make an impact on an area of need. Grants are made for a broad range of purposes to a wide variety of charitable organizations in the focus areas of health, education and community development. The Foundation is interesting in supporting: creative new activities or services—new programs, one-time projects, events, exhibits, studies or surveys; enhancement or strengthening of existing activities—projects to enhance, expand or strengthen the range, quantity and/or quality of an organization's programs and services; small capital investments—items that are directly related to program delivery or service to clients, such as a refrigerator for a food pantry or equipment to comply with ADA requirements. Grant applications are available online.
Requirements: Wisconsin 501(c)3 nonprofit organizations that serve the residents of the Clintonville area are eligible. General questions can also be directed to the CAF Grants Committee Chair or the Foundation.
Restrictions: The Clintonville Area Foundation will not generally fund the following: general operating expenses not related to the proposed project; annual fund drives or fundraising events; endowment funds; programs with a sectarian or religious purpose that promote a specific journey of faith; major capital projects such as the acquisition of land or buildings; medical research; travel for individuals or groups such as bands, sports teams or classes; activities that occur before funding is awarded; organizations with past-due or incomplete grant reports.
Geographic Focus: Wisconsin
Date(s) Application is Due: Dec 31
Contact: Jenny Goldschmidt, CAF Grants Committee Chair; (715) 823-7125, ext. 2603; clintonvillefoundation@gmail.com
Todd Sutton; (920) 830-1290, ext. 28; tsutton@cffoxvalley.org
Internet: www.cffoxvalley.org/Page.aspx?pid=415
Sponsor: Community Foundation for the Fox Valley Region
4455 West Lawrence Street, P.O. Box 563
Appleton, WI 54912-0563

CFFVR Environmental Stewardship Grants 540
The Environmental Stewardship Fund was established by the Community Foundation in 2006 to support the Wisconsin, Fox Valley-area charitable organizations and projects that further the conservation of nature and enhance education about and enjoyment of the natural world. Funding priority is given to projects that: strengthen the connection between the people and the land; further environmental values; have a wide impact; are visible and inspiring; match groups with similar aspirations.
Requirements: Wisconsin 501(c)3 tax-exempt organizations serving residents of Outagamie, Calumet, Waupaca, Shawano and northern Winnebago counties are eligible to apply. The grant application form is available at the CFFVR website.
Restrictions: Projects that will not be funded: major capital expenses; ongoing operating expenses unrelated to the proposed project; annual fund drives or fund-raising events; recurring events; endowment funds; conference fees; lobbying; activities that occur before funding is awarded; organizations with past-due or incomplete grant reports.
Geographic Focus: Wisconsin
Amount of Grant: 5,000 USD

Samples: Wisconsin League of Conservation Voters, $2,000—a Green Bay based organizer will educate members of Fox Valley environmental groups on such tools as working with the media and advocating with legislators to further a conservation agenda endorsed by more than 80 Wisconsin environmental and conservation groups; Town of Greenville Pebbleidge Park, $2,250—shoreline planting will accompany a 2.5-acre prairie in this 13-acre park on Design Drive; Appleton Area School District, $3,000—Author Paul Fleischman will present three days of classroom workshops on the diversity and nature themes in his book Seedfolks.
Contact: David Horst; (920) 830-1290, ext. 24; dhorst@cffoxvalley.org
Internet: www.cffoxvalley.org/Page.aspx?pid=347
Sponsor: Community Foundation for the Fox Valley Region
4455 West Lawrence Street, P.O. Box 563
Appleton, WI 54912-0563

CFFVR Frank C. Shattuck Community Grants 541
The Frank C. Shattuck Community Fund supports new or supplements existing services for youth and the elderly and benefits education, the arts and health care in Winnebago and Outagamie counties of Wisconsin. Funding is available for programs, capital expenses or operating expenses of qualifying charitable organizations. Grants to projects may be either one-time payments or multi-year commitments. Application forms are available online.
Requirements: Wisconsin 501(c)3 organizations that serve residents in Outagamie or northern Winnebago counties are eligible to apply. To begin the application process, submit the following prior to the application deadline: grant application form; list of the organization's governing board members, including their professional or community affiliation; current year (board-approved) operating budget.
Restrictions: The Shattuck Fund will not typically support the following: grants for religious or political purposes; grants to support endowment funds of organizations; travel for individuals or groups such as bands, sports teams or classes; reimbursement for previously incurred expenses.
Geographic Focus: Wisconsin
Date(s) Application is Due: Mar 1; Sep 1
Contact: Shelly Leadley; (920) 830-1290, ext. 34; sleadley@cffoxvalley.org
Internet: www.cffoxvalley.org/Page.aspx?pid=339
Sponsor: Community Foundation for the Fox Valley Region
4455 West Lawrence Street, P.O. Box 563
Appleton, WI 54912-0563

CFFVR Infant Welfare Circle of Kings Daughters Grants 542
Organizations submitting a grant application to the Infant Welfare Circle must serve residents in Outagamie, Calumet or Winnebago counties of Wisconsin. Preference is given to programs or projects that serve children or young adults. General operating grants are available up to $3,000.
Requirements: Wisconsin 501(c)3 non-profit organizations that serve residents in Outagamie, Calumet or Winnebago counties are eligible to apply. Grant proposal should include the following information: Submit the following prior to the application deadline: public charity name, address, phone number, email address and contact person; description of organization mission; description of program or project for which funding is requested (include timeline, people to be served, community need to be addressed, project goals/anticipated results); project budget, amount of funding requested from Infant Welfare Circle and rationale for Circle assistance, and date needed; agency revenue and expense report for previous fiscal year; revenue and expense budget for current year; list of organization's officers and directors.
Geographic Focus: Wisconsin
Date(s) Application is Due: Sep 30
Amount of Grant: 3,000 USD
Contact: Grants Officer; (920) 830-1290; fax (920) 830-1293; info@cffoxvalley.org
Internet: www.cffoxvalley.org/Page.aspx?pid=415
Sponsor: Community Foundation for the Fox Valley Region
4455 West Lawrence Street, P.O. Box 563
Appleton, WI 54912-0563

CFFVR Jewelers Mutual Charitable Giving Grants 543
Through philanthropy, Jewelers Mutual Insurance Company aspires to achieve a lasting and positive impact on the Fox River Valley. Jewelers Mutual strives to be a responsible corporate citizen and a valued employer by supporting critical needs of the community. Priority areas for giving are: organizations in which Jewelers Mutual employees are actively involved; organizations that address needs in the following areas: basic needs (food, shelter, clothing), as well as programs that reduce/eliminate the root causes of poverty (such as literacy, affordable housing, job training); positive youth development and education; health and wellness, particularly diabetes, cancer, mental health, and affordable access for the disadvantaged; and the vitality of the Fox River area, including gifts to libraries, police or fire departments, parks, the arts, and preservation of the local environment. Letters of request may be sent to the Community Foundation for the Fox Valley Region.
Requirements: 501(c)3 organizations that serve residents of the Fox River Valley are eligible.
Geographic Focus: Wisconsin
Contact: Shelly Leadley, Donor Relations Officer; (920) 830-1290; SLeadley@cffoxvalley.org
Internet: www.jewelersmutual.com/information.aspx?id=4305
Sponsor: Community Foundation for the Fox Valley Region
4455 West Lawrence Street, P.O. Box 563
Appleton, WI 54912-0563

CFFVR Mielke Family Foundation Grants 544
Mielke Family Foundation grants, enhance the quality of life for residents of Appleton and, Shawano, Wisconsin. Priority areas of giving are: projects that primarily serve individuals residing within either the Appleton Area School District or the Shawano School District; special events, start-up expenses of projects expected to become self-sustaining, studies

to determine future courses of action or needs, enrichment programs, or actions to meet similar objectives. Application forms are available online at the Community Foundation for the Fox Valley Region website.
Requirements: Applicants must: be a nonprofit 501(c)3 or qualifying tax-exempt organization; be able to demonstrate, to the satisfaction of the Foundation, that it has the capability to complete the proposed project.
Restrictions: The Mielke Family Foundation typically will not support: transportation costs for individuals or groups such as bands, sports teams or classes; general operating expenses not related to the proposed project; deficits incurred for past activities; programs or needs that do not serve residents in the Appleton Area School District or the Shawano Area School District. The Foundation typically prefers not to engage in long-term grant commitments.
Geographic Focus: Wisconsin
Contact: Cathy Mutschler, Community Engagement Officer; (920) 830-1290, ext. 27; fax (920) 830-1293; cmutschler@cffoxvalley.org
Internet: www.cffoxvalley.org/Page.aspx?pid=415
Sponsor: Community Foundation for the Fox Valley Region
4455 West Lawrence Street, P.O. Box 563
Appleton, WI 54912-0563

CFFVR Myra M. and Robert L. Vandehey Foundation Grants 545
The Myra M. and Robert L. Vandehey Foundation's mission is support the charitable interests of the Myra and Robert Vandehey family. Areas of interest include: education; children and youth; health care and; family services. Funding opportunities are limited to nonprofit organizations that serve residents in the Fox Cities or Keshena areas of Wisconsin. Contact the Vice President for CFFVR prior to submitting a request to verify that the need aligns with current priorities. Unsolicited grant requests are not accepted from organizations not previously awarded support. Applications may be submitted at any time, and no application form is required.
Requirements: Wisconsin 501(c)3 nonprofit organizations that serve residents in the Fox Cities or Keshena are eligible for funding.
Restrictions: No grants to individuals.
Geographic Focus: Wisconsin
Samples: Fox Valley Technical College Foundation, Appleton, WI, $20,000—educational grant; Boys & Girls Clubs of the Fox Valley, Appleton, WI, $25,000—youth development grant; Nami Fox Valley, Inc., $10,000—mental health and crisis intervention grant.
Contact: Cathy Mutschler; (920) 830-1290, ext. 29; cmutschler@cffoxvalley.org
Internet: www.cffoxvalley.org/Page.aspx?pid=415
Sponsor: Community Foundation for the Fox Valley Region
4455 West Lawrence Street, P.O. Box 563
Appleton, WI 54912-0563

CFFVR Project Grants 546
Project grants, support specific projects or new programs for which a moderate amount of grant money can make a significant impact on an area of need. Grants are made for a broad range of purposes to a wide variety of charitable organizations in the focus areas of arts and culture, community development, education, environment, health and human services. Organizations eligible to apply must serve residents in Outagamie, Calumet, Shawano, Waupaca or northern Winnebago counties. Grants for specific projects typically are for no more than $10,000 for one year.
Requirements: Wisconsin 501(c)3 tax-exempt organizations serving residents of Outagamie, Calumet, Waupaca, Shawano and northern Winnebago counties are eligible to apply. The grant application form is available at the CFFVR website.
Restrictions: Project grants typically will not fund the following: general operating expenses not related to the proposed project; annual fund drives or fund raising events; endowment funds; programs with a sectarian or religious purpose that promote a specific journey of faith; major capital projects such as the acquisition of land or buildings; medical research; travel for individuals or groups such as bands, sports teams or classes; activities that occur before funding is awarded; health and safety equipment; playground equipment; organizations with past-due or incomplete grant reports.
Geographic Focus: Wisconsin
Date(s) Application is Due: Feb 1; Aug 1
Amount of Grant: 10,000 USD
Samples: Child Care Resource and Referral, $2,000—to provide at-risk families with young children increased access to supportive community services; Community Clothes Closet, $10,000—to purchase a used cargo van to provide a means of picking up donated clothing; Northeast Wisconsin Land Trust, $4,000—to acquire supplies and equipment necessary to fully implement a newly created land stewardship program.
Contact: Todd Sutton; (920) 830-1290, ext. 28; fax (920) 830-1293; tsutton@cffoxvalley.org
Internet: www.cffoxvalley.org/Page.aspx?pid=343
Sponsor: Community Foundation for the Fox Valley Region
4455 West Lawrence Street, P.O. Box 563
Appleton, WI 54912-0563

CFFVR Robert and Patricia Endries Family Foundation Grants 547
The Robert & Patricia Endries Family Foundation was established for the benefit of people in need, primarily in the Brillion area but with some consideration to the Fox Valley, Lakeshore and Northeastern areas of Wisconsin. Priority areas of giving include: the vitality of the Brillion area; the disadvantaged, particularly the disabled, homeless, low income, single parents, troubled youth, or the chronically or mentally ill; health and human services, particularly diabetes, cancer, cerebral palsy, Alzheimer's disease, kidney disease, or mental health; religious causes or organizations with a spiritual purpose; sports or arts programming and, or sponsorships. Grants are considered for capital campaigns and, or specific capital improvements for the above priority organizations. Gifts will be directed to specific programs or opportunities, not to general operations (with exception for those organizations

the foundation has had a long-established relationship with). Matching or challenge gifts are also encouraged, to motivate additional giving by others. Organizations that support needs outside of the Brillion area or that do not yet have an established relationship with the foundation should contact the foundation prior to submission of a formal request.

Requirements: Wisconsin 501(c)3 charitable organizations are eligible to apply. Contact Foundation directly to begin the application process.

Restrictions: The Foundation will not typically support the following: gifts to political organizations or causes; gifts to organizations that are not pro-life supporters or that lack sensitivity to promoting human life in any form (unborn or born); gifts to organizations affiliated with or in support of cloning or embryonic stem-cell research; grants to organizations that receive significant public/government funding; reimbursement for previously incurred expenses.

Geographic Focus: Wisconsin
Date(s) Application is Due: Jan 1; Apr 1; Oct 1
Contact: Shelly Leadley, Grants Manager; (920) 830-1290, ext. 34; sleadley@cffoxvalley.org
Internet: www.cffoxvalley.org/Page.aspx?pid=415
Sponsor: Community Foundation for the Fox Valley Region
4455 West Lawrence Street, P.O. Box 563
Appleton, WI 54912-0563

CFFVR Schmidt Family G4 Grants 548

The Schmidt Family G4 grants provide funding to improve the quality of life of those most in need in the Fox Valley, Wisconsin region, with a focus on at-risk youth and self-sufficiency for women. This goal will be accomplished by seeking to address immediate needs and to affect meaningful change in the following areas: at-risk youth—especially those with a physical or mental illness, those who have experienced abuse or those who have significant financial need; adult self-sufficiency—with a priority on issues that affect the stability and independence of women, as well as literacy, job skills training and transitional living for all. The G4 Committee prefers: not to be the sole funder for most projects it considers, unless the amount requested is small and/or a one-time request; to support specific projects or new programs for which a moderate amount of grant money can make a significant impact on an area of need and sustainability. A broad array of requests will be considered, including capital campaigns, existing programs or recurring events as long as they fall within the other listed giving guidelines. Grant awards will typically not exceed $15,000. To assist with the educational aspect of this fund, a formal application is required (available online). Prior to submitting an application, organizations are strongly encouraged to contact Cathy Mutschlerto, discuss the potential proposal and process. Complete and submit the application prior to the March 1, October 1 deadlines.

Requirements: IRS 501(c)3 nonprofit organizations, as well as government agencies are eligible to apply for funding. Organizations that are not public charities may apply through a fiscal sponsor. Organizations must serve Fox Valley residents, particularly in Outagamie, Calumet or northern Winnebago counties of Wisconsin.

Restrictions: The G4 Fund typically will not support the following: organizations that have received funding from the G4 Committee in the most recent 20 months; multi-year requests; programs with a sectarian or religious purpose that promote a specific journey of faith; travel for individuals or groups such as bands, sports teams or classes; reimbursement for previously incurred expenses; endowment funds; fund-raising events; requests from organizations with past-due or incomplete grant reports; a program or need previously declined unless the organization is invited back by the committee; programs or needs that do not serve Fox Valley residents, particularly Outagamie, Calumet or northern Winnebago counties.

Geographic Focus: Wisconsin
Date(s) Application is Due: Mar 1; Sep 1
Amount of Grant: 15,000 USD
Contact: Cathy Mutschler; (920) 830-1290, ext. 29; cmutschler@cffoxvalley.org
Internet: www.cffoxvalley.org/Page.aspx?pid=340
Sponsor: Community Foundation for the Fox Valley Region
4455 West Lawrence Street, P.O. Box 563
Appleton, WI 54912-0563

CFFVR Shawano Area Community Foundation Grants 549

Shawano Area Community Foundation works to preserve and improve the quality of life in Shawano, Wisconsin and, the surrounding area, including communities having economic, educational, cultural and recreational ties with the area. Grant applications are available online.

Requirements: Wisconsin 501(c)3 non-profits in or serving surrounding area of Shawano are eligible to apply.

Geographic Focus: Wisconsin
Date(s) Application is Due: Oct 1
Amount of Grant: 5,000 USD
Samples: City of Shawano/County Library, Shawano, WI, $3,000—reading machine for visually impaired; Shawano Oral Health Fund, Shawano, WI, $1,500—program support for seecond grade children in Shawano County; St. John's Trinity Lutheran Church, Shawano, WI, $1,000—food purchase grant.
Contact: Susan Hanson; (715) 253-2580; shawanofoundation@granitewave.com
Internet: www.cffoxvalley.org/Page.aspx?pid=412
Sponsor: Community Foundation for the Fox Valley Region
4455 West Lawrence Street, P.O. Box 563
Appleton, WI 54912-0563

CFFVR Women's Fund for the Fox Valley Region Grants 550

The Women's Fund provides grants for programs that inspire women and girls to flourish personally, economically and professionally. Grants have been distributed to programs supporting the following areas: arts & culture; physical and mental health; economic, self-sufficiency; education; parenting and child care; violence prevention. The Women's Fund believes that no project is too small or too new to be considered. Innovative approaches and projects with limited access to other funding are encouraged. Collaborative efforts are welcome. Grant applicants should address one or more of these funding priorities as they relate to women and girls: promotes economic self-sufficiency; improves safely from violence; provides opportunities to develop life skills; promotes physical and/or mental health; enhances dignity and self-worth; promotes leadership development; provides opportunities for artistic development and/or exposure to the arts; provides gender-specific solutions to problems facing women and girls; creates an environment that encourages social change. To apply submit a letter of interest by the deadline.

Requirements: To be eligible for a grant, the project must be consistent with the Women's Fund mission; benefits women and girls in the Wisconsin, Fox Valley region; organization must be a tax-exempt, not-for-profit organization under the Internal Revenue Code, section 501(c)3.

Restrictions: The Women's Fund will not fund: individuals, endowments, government agencies (however educational institutions may qualify), projects with a religious focus, and political parties, candidates or partisan activities.

Geographic Focus: Wisconsin
Date(s) Application is Due: Mar 15
Contact: Becky Boulanger, Program Director; (920) 830-1290, ext. 17; bboulanger@cffoxvalley.org or grants@womensfundfvr.org
Internet: www.cffoxvalley.org/Page.aspx?pid=415
Sponsor: Community Foundation for the Fox Valley Region
4455 West Lawrence Street, P.O. Box 563
Appleton, WI 54912-0563

CFF Winter Park Community Grants 551

Winter Park Community Grants, a signature initiative of the Winter Park Community Foundation at Central Florida Foundation, seeks to award three one-time capability building and/or programmatic grants to eligible public, private or faith-based entities located in or serving Winter Park, Florida. CFF is most interested in ideas for unique projects that can increase the capability of a nonprofit or its programs. For capability building projects, a strong preference is shown towards technology, program materials, location and space modification, staff training, and community collaboration. Less weight is given to proposals for marketing or strategic plans or staff positions. And, the grant does not need to cover the full cost of the project.

Geographic Focus: Florida
Amount of Grant: Up to 50,000 USD
Contact: Sandy Vidal, Vice President of Community Strategies and Initiatives; (407) 872-3050; fax (407) 425-2990
Internet: cffound.org/receive/cff_grants/#grant28
Sponsor: Central Florida Foundation
800 North Magnolia Avenue, Suite 1200
Orlando, FL 32803

CFGR Community Impact Grants 552

The Community Foundation for a Greater Richmond is committed to improving the quality of life for residents of metropolitan Richmond. Competitive grant making focuses on building or enhancing the resources of the charitable sector to address: basic human needs for children and families who are impoverished; child and youth development, with an emphasis on young people who are at moderate or high risk of experiencing problems in school, in their social interactions, or with lifestyle choices; community development that promotes affordable housing and safe neighborhoods; opportunities to broadly enrich family and community life; and collaborative models of service, volunteerism, and community leadership development. Community Impact grants support nonprofits whose strategies and outcomes align with the Foundation's four focus areas: cultural vibrancy, economic prosperity, educational success, and health and wellness. Generally, projects undertaken in collaboration with other nonprofits receive a higher priority. These may include requests that address unmet or emerging community needs or allow for program expansion or enhancement. Collaborations that include current recipient organizations or that minimize duplication of services will be considered. The foundation will give preference to those organizations that seek to develop or enhance their work through a cohesive regional strategy. Guidelines are available online. Optional grant writing and submission workshops are available each year in January. The deadline for completed proposals is February 21. Awards typically range from $15,000 to $50,000.

Requirements: Proposals will be accepted from 501(c)3 charitable organizations located in the metropolitan Richmond and Central Virginia. This includes: the cities of Colonial Heights, Hopewell, Petersburg and Richmond, as well as the counties of Chesterfield, Goochland, Hanover, Henrico, and Powhatan.

Geographic Focus: Virginia
Date(s) Application is Due: Feb 21
Amount of Grant: 15,000 - 50,000 USD
Contact: Charles Dyson, Director of Data & Customer Support; (804) 409-5637 or (804) 330-7400; fax (804) 330-5992; cdyson@cfrichmond.org or info@cfrichmond.org
Internet: www.cfrichmond.org/Grantseekers/What-We-Fund/Community-Impact-Grants
Sponsor: Community Foundation for a Greater Richmond
3409 Moore Street, P.O. Box 76495
Richmond, VA 23230

CFGR Jenkins Foundation Grants 553

The inspiration for the Jenkins Foundation is found in the story of Annabella Ravenscroft Jenkins, a 19th century pioneer who opened her home to wounded soldiers during the Civil War. Her concern for the medically underserved led to the establishment of Retreat Hospital for the Sick, which provided health care on a sliding fee scale. Today, the Jenkins Foundation embodies that same spirit of compassion and caring in its work, applying her

vision to modern day challenges. Currently, the Foundation is committed to expanding access to community-based services through programs and organizations that have the potential to make a significant impact on the quality of health, especially for the youth in its local area. The Foundation's primary goal is to promote community health by supporting access to the following: primary care; mental health care; oral health care; and health education and prevention services. Current key focus areas are: substance abuse treatment and prevention; violence prevention; and unintended pregnancy prevention. Generally, grants of up to $80,000 will be awarded. The Foundation uses an online application process for nonprofits seeking support through the competitive grants program. There are two proposal cycles each year. For the first cycle, a pre-proposal is due April 22, with the completed application deadline being May 22. For the second cycle, a pre-proposal is due October 5, with the completed applications due on November 5.
Requirements: Proposals are accepted from 501(c)3 charitable organizations, which serve the residents of the City of Richmond and the counties of Chesterfield, Hanover, Henrico, Goochland, and Powhatan.
Geographic Focus: Virginia
Date(s) Application is Due: May 22; Nov 5
Amount of Grant: Up to 80,000 USD
Contact: Eric Clay, Senior Program Officer; (804) 409-5647 or (804) 330-7400; fax (804) 330-5992; eclay@cfrichmond.org or info@cfrichmond.org
Internet: www.cfrichmond.org/Partnering-with-Us/For-Nonprofits/Community-Investments/Jenkins-Foundation
Sponsor: Community Foundation for a Greater Richmond
3409 Moore Street, P.O. Box 76495
Richmond, VA 23230

CFGR SisterFund Grants   554
The Community Foundation for a Greater Richmond SisterFund invests in local nonprofits engaged in helping African American women and girls chart a positive future for themselves through gains in education, workforce, leadership development, and health. SisterFund provides a forum for philanthropic minded African American women to pool our time, talent, and treasure to support organizations that are working to transform the lives of African American women and girls in the Greater Richmond Metro Region. Members contribute a minimum of $1,100 to participate in an investment pool to be awarded to a nonprofit selected through an application process. Sisterfund seeks to make investments in nonprofit, community-based organizations engaged in impacting African American women and girls to have a positive future specifically through gains in education, workforce, leadership development, and health. Typical grant size is $20,000. The application period begins in early May, with the deadline being the first Friday in June.
Requirements: To be eligible to apply for a SisterFund grant, your organization must be a nonprofit 501(c)3 organization that serves the residents of the City of Richmond, and/or the counties of Chesterfield, Hanover, Henrico, Goochland, and/or Powhatan.
Restrictions: The Foundation cannot accept applications from: individual religious institutions; private foundations; colleges and universities; or individuals or scholarship applicants. Funding will not support: debt reduction or operational deficits; endowments or memorials; bridge funding or interim financing; partisan, political or legislative activities; or legal expenses.
Geographic Focus: Virginia
Date(s) Application is Due: Jun 4
Amount of Grant: Up to 20,000 USD
Contact: Charles Dyson, Director of Data and Customer Support; (804) 409-5637 or (804) 330-7400; fax (804) 330-5992; cdyson@cfrichmond.org or info@cfrichmond.org
Internet: www.cfrichmond.org/Partnering-with-Us/For-Nonprofits/Community-Investments/SisterFund-Grants
Sponsor: Community Foundation for a Greater Richmond
3409 Moore Street, P.O. Box 76495
Richmond, VA 23230

CFGR Ujima Legacy Fund Grants   555
The Community Foundation for a Greater Richmond Ujima Legacy Fund supports projects in the Richmond region that will positively impact youth and young adults, ages 12 to 21 years, with emphasis on under-served youth populations. The Fund is a giving circle that provides a forum for civic-minded African American men to increase their philanthropic presence and impact in the Metro Richmond community. Members contribute a minimum of $1,100 to participate in an investment pool that is then awarded to at least one nonprofit selected through an application process. The Fund seeks to support nonprofits that empower youth through education related initiatives. This may include, but is not limited to: after-school and out-of-school time programming; career development; college preparation; entrepreneurship; financial literacy; literacy; mentoring; technology training; and tutoring. Funding may be used for program support or specific projects. Consideration will also be given to capacity building requests to strengthen the infrastructure and increase the program capacity of start-up or established organizations that serve the target demographic. One or two grants of up to $20,000 maximum are awarded each year. The annual deadline is the first Friday in September.
Requirements: To be eligible to apply for a Ujima Legacy Fund grant, your organization must be a nonprofit 501(c)3 organization that serves the residents of the City of Richmond, and/or the counties of Chesterfield, Hanover, Henrico, Goochland and/or Powhatan.
Restrictions: The Foundation cannot accept applications from: individual religious institutions; private foundations; colleges and universities; or individuals or scholarship applicants. Funding will not support: debt reduction or operational deficits; endowments or memorials; bridge funding or interim financing; partisan, political or legislative activities; or legal expenses.
Geographic Focus: Virginia
Date(s) Application is Due: Sep 4

Amount of Grant: Up to 20,000 USD
Contact: Charles Dyson, Director of Data & Customer Support; (804) 409-5637 or (804) 330-7400; fax (800) 330-5992; cdyson@cfrichmond.org or info@cfrichmond.org
Internet: www.cfrichmond.org/Partnering-with-Us/For-Nonprofits/Community-Investments/Ujima-Legacy-Fund-Grants
Sponsor: Community Foundation for a Greater Richmond
3409 Moore Street, P.O. Box 76495
Richmond, VA 23230

CFKF Instrument Matching Grants   556
The Classics for Kids Foundation (CFKF) was created in 1997 in response to the decline of support for string programs around the country. CFKF aims to bridge the funding gap and enhance school music programs by providing matching grants for beautiful new stringed instruments. CFKF strengthens strings programs through matching grants, which encourage partnership with local philanthropy. Students with beautiful new instruments are more engaged, tend to practice more, and participate longer in their strings programs. Applications are accepted quarterly.
Requirements: All applicants must have nonprofit status. Grants are limited to programs serving children kindergarten through grade 12. The grant award will never exceed 50% of total instrument cost. Stringed instruments that can be requested include violins, cellos, violas, double basses, ukuleles, and guitars.
Restrictions: Grants are not made to individuals.
Geographic Focus: All States, District of Columbia
Date(s) Application is Due: Mar 31; Jun 30; Sep 30; Dec 31
Contact: Michael Reynolds; (508) 740-8331; info@classicsforkids.org
Internet: classicsforkids.org/apply-for-a-grant/
Sponsor: Classics for Kids Foundation
P.O. Box 5977
Holliston, MA 01746

CFNEM Women's Giving Circle Grants   557
Community Foundation for Northeast Michigan Women's Giving Circle grants are intended to help regional women and girls in the areas of: aging; sports and recreation; maternity and child rearing; family; health issues and research; crisis prevention; trauma alleviation; and education. The foundation looks for projects that prevent community problems, benefit the greatest number of people, help deliver new services or make existing services more efficient, enhance collaboration among organizations, promote youth development, address emerging community needs, try a new approach to a persistent problem, or encourage people to develop new skills and help themselves. The maximum award amount is $2,000, and the annual deadline for application submission is July 1.
Requirements: IRS 501(c)3 nonprofit organizations, schools, churches (for non-sectarian purposes), cities, townships, and other governmental units serving the four-county area of Alcona, Alpena, Montmorency, and Presque Isle in northeast Michigan are eligible to apply. Public and parochial schools in the counties of Alcona, Alpena, and Montmorency must use the Youth Advisory Council application.
Restrictions: Grants are not given to individuals, except for awards or scholarships from designated donor funds.
Geographic Focus: Michigan
Date(s) Application is Due: Jul 1
Amount of Grant: Up to 2,000 USD
Contact: Laurie Nugent, Program Director; (989) 354-6881 or (877) 354-6881; fax (989) 356-3319; lnugent@cfnem.org
Internet: www.cfnem.org/grants/womens-giving-circle-grants/
Sponsor: Community Foundation for Northeast Michigan
100 N. Ripley, Suite F, P.O. Box 495
Alpena, MI 49707-0495

CFNEM Youth Advisory Council Grants   558
The Community Foundation for Northeast Michigan Youth Advisory Council (YAC) is a group of area grant makers that recommends award amounts for youth projects and programs. YAC members are generally eighth through twelfth graders within the foundation's service area. YAC funds originated from matching grants made by the W.K. Kellogg Foundation. Through grantmaking, YAC members are directly involved in philanthropy. At the same time, they learn about skills necessary for negotiation, communication, team work, conflict resolution, and leadership. Area non-profit organizations can apply for up to $2,500. YAC Grant application deadlines are January 15 and October 15.
Requirements: Regular grant requests require the applicant to make a three-minute presentation about their project. IRS 501(c)3 nonprofit organizations, schools, churches (for non-sectarian purposes), cities, townships, and other governmental units serving the four-county area of Alcona, Alpena, Montmorency, and Presque Isle in northeast Michigan are eligible to apply.
Restrictions: Grants are not given to individuals, except for awards or scholarships from designated donor funds.
Geographic Focus: Michigan
Date(s) Application is Due: Jan 15; Oct 15
Amount of Grant: Up to 2,500 USD
Contact: Laurie Nugent, Program Director; (989) 354-6881 or (877) 354-6881; fax (989) 356-3319; lnugent@cfnem.org
Internet: www.cfnem.org/grants/youth-advisory-council-grants.html
Sponsor: Community Foundation for Northeast Michigan
100 N. Ripley, Suite F, P.O. Box 495
Alpena, MI 49707-0495

Changemakers Innovation Awards 559

The Changemakers Innovation Awards recognize the best social change strategies that emerge from open competitions hosted online every two months. Each competition cycle identifies and refines solutions to a pressing global problem. Winners will be those entries that best address systemic impact, tipping point, replication, sustainability, and innovation. Awards include a cash prize for each winner chosen by vote on the online community. Entries must be submitted in English. Guidelines and nomination forms are available online. Deadlines vary for each contest.

Requirements: To be eligible to win, all project teams/organizations (with the exception of local governments and universities) must enclose a current income statement and a balance sheet. These financial statements need not be audited. Individual who are partnering with an organization to implement the work must submit a copy of the partnering organization's income financial statement. Individuals without an organizational partner are exempt from the filing requirement.

Geographic Focus: All States, All Countries
Amount of Grant: Up to 5,000 USD
Contact: Awards Director
Internet: www.changemakers.com/innovations
Sponsor: Changemakers
1700 North Moore Street, Suite 2000
Arlington, VA 22209

Chapman Charitable Foundation Grants 560

At Chapman, the ongoing business mission includes supporting the non-profit community through innovation, service and charity. The corporation accomplishes this mission through its corporate endeavors by striving to provide non-profit agencies with comprehensive coverage at the most reasonable price. Likewise, since its inception in 2000, the Chapman Charitable Foundation has donated over $6.75 million dollars to more than 470 California based Social Service Agencies. Primarily, the foundation supports organizations involved with education, forest conservation, health, human services, and religion. Particular fields of interest include: children and youth services, foster care, Christian agencies and churches, education (all levels), the environment, health care access, health care clinics and centers, hospitals, human services, and religion. Applicants should begin by contacting the Foundation with a one-page letter of inquiry. The foundation utilizes a Recommendation Committee to select potential grantees. Application forms are not required.

Geographic Focus: California
Amount of Grant: Up to 150,000 USD
Samples: AIDS Healthcare Foundation, Los Angeles, California, $10,000 - general operations; Michael Pourson Ministries, San Rafael, California, $108,000 - support programs; Pachamana Alliance, San Francisco, California, $36,000 - general operations.
Contact: Mari Perez, Grants Coordinator; (626) 405-8031; fax (626) 405-0585; mperez@chapmanins.com or info@chapmanins.com
Internet: www.chapmanins.com/about/foundation
Sponsor: Chapman Charitable Foundation
265 North San Gabriel Boulevard
Pasadena, CA 91107-3423

Chapman Family Charitable Trust Grants 561

The Chapman Family Charitable Trust was established in 1994 in Georgia, with a geographic focus in the states of South Carolina and New York. The independent foundation's primary focus is on educational programs, museum support, children and youth services, and religion. Its main fields of interest include: children and youth services, Christian agencies and churches, education (all levels), support of community foundation operation, and museums. Though there are no application forms, applicants should forward the entire proposal in letter format. There are no annual deadlines.

Geographic Focus: New York, South Carolina
Amount of Grant: Up to 30,000 USD
Contact: Laura Pease, Grants Administrator; (404) 607-5291
Sponsor: Chapman Family Charitable Trust
5033 Wittering Drive
Columbia, SC 29206-2922

Chapman Family Foundation 562

The Chapman Family Foundation was established in 1983 by a donation from Joseph F. Chapman III, former Chief General Counsel for the Governor's Office of the State of Florida as well as Chief Counsel for the Florida State Road Board. The Foundation's primary purpose is the support of human services, youth and children's services, education, and community services. Current fields of interest are: children and youth services, Christian agencies and churches, education (all levels), early childhood education, health organizations, human services, marine science, and youth development services. There are no specific application forms and no annual deadlines. The geographic focus is Panama City, Florida, and applicants should forward a letter of inquiry to the Foundation office.

Requirements: 501(c)3 organization located in, or supporting the residents of, Paname City, Florida, are eligible to apply. Occasionally, the Foundation will support applicants outside of this region of Florida to other portions of the state.

Geographic Focus: Florida
Amount of Grant: Up to 250,000 USD
Samples: First United Methodist Church, Panama City, Florida, $205,000 - general operations; Bay High School, Panama City, Florida, $100,675 - general operations; University of Florida Foundation, Gainesville, Florida, $1,000 - general fund support.
Contact: Jeannette B. Chapman, Director; (850) 769-8981
Sponsor: Chapman Family Foundation
1002 W. 23rd Street, Suite 400
Panama City, FL 32405-3683

Charles Crane Family Foundation Grants 563

The Charles Crane Family Foundation was formed in 1991 by Charles Crane, a Baltimore County real estate investor. Crane died in 1994, and since that time the Foundation has continued to support the work of the Associated Jewish Federation of Baltimore and Mercy Medical Center, two institutions that Crane held in high regard. In addition, the Foundation devotes 70% to 80% of its remaining funds to support Jewish education in Maryland, mostly in greater Baltimore, and 20% to 30% to encourage violence prevention programs to benefit Baltimore and Maryland youth. The Foundation Board of Directors meets three to four times a year. The deadline for submitting a proposal for a violence prevention program is October 15; for a Jewish education program is February 15.

Requirements: Ten copies of the text of the proposal and two copies of the financials should be addressed to the Foundation.

Geographic Focus: Maryland
Date(s) Application is Due: Feb 15; Oct 15
Samples: ACHIM, Brooklyn, New York, $15,000 - for general operating support (2018); Acts 4 Youth, Baltimore, Maryland, $25,000 - for general support (2018); Alternative Directions Inc., Baltimore, Maryland, $10,000 - for general support (2018).
Contact: Larry Ziffer, President; (410) 358-0680 or (410) 580-4410; Lziffer@CraneFdn.org
Internet: www.thecranefoundation.org/application.html
Sponsor: Charles Crane Family Foundation
6225 Smith Avenue
Baltimore, MD 21209-3600

Charles Delmar Foundation Grants 564

Established in 1957, the Foundation supports organizations involved with inter-American studies, higher, secondary, elementary, and other education, underprivileged youth, the disadvantaged, the aged, the homeless and housing issues, general welfare organizations, and fine and performing arts. Giving primarily in the Washington, D.C. area in the U.S., and in Europe and South America. There are no specific deadlines with which to adhere. Contact the Foundation for further application information and guidelines.

Restrictions: No grants to individuals, or for building or endowment funds, or matching gifts; no loans.

Geographic Focus: District of Columbia, Maryland, Virginia, West Virginia, Albania, Andorra, Argentina, Armenia, Austria, Azerbaijan, Belarus, Belgium, Bolivia, Bosnia & Herzegovina, Brazil, Bulgaria, Chile, Colombia, Croatia, Cyprus, Czech Republic (Czechia), Denmark, Ecuador, Estonia, Finland, France, Georgia, Germany, Greece, Guyana, Holy See (Vatican City State), Hungary, Iceland, Ireland, Italy, Kosovo, Latvia, Liechtenstein, Lithuania, Luxembourg, Malta, Moldova, Monaco, Montenegro, Netherlands, North Macedonia, Norway, Paraguay, Peru, Poland, Portugal, Romania, Russia, San Marino, Serbia, Slovakia, Slovenia, Spain, Sweden, Switzerland, Turkey, Ukraine, United Kingdom
Amount of Grant: 500 - 10,000 USD
Contact: Mareen D. Hughes, President; (703) 534-9109
Sponsor: Charles Delmar Foundation
5205 Leesburg Pike, Suite 209
Falls Church, VA 22041-3858

Charles H. Hall Foundation 565

The Charles H. Hall Foundation was established in 2007 to support and promote educational, health and human services, religious, and arts and cultural programming for underserved populations. Special consideration is given to programs whose purpose is the prevention of cruelty to children or animals. Grants will be considered for specific programs or projects with preference given to organizations that provide direct services. Grant size may range from $5,000-$20,000. Grants from the Charles H. Hall Foundation are 1 year in duration. Applicants will not be awarded a grant for more than 3 consecutive years.

Requirements: The Foundation specifically serves organizations based in Berkshire, Hampden, Hampshire, or Franklin Counties, Massachusetts. The foundation does not support requests from individuals, organizations attempting to influence policy through direct lobbying, or any political campaigns.

Restrictions: The foundation does not support requests from individuals, organizations attempting to influence policy through direct lobbying, or any political campaigns.

Geographic Focus: Massachusetts
Date(s) Application is Due: Dec 1
Amount of Grant: 5,000 - 20,000 USD
Samples: Community Action Pioneer Valley Inc., Greenfield, Massachusetts, $15,000 - Awarded for Center for Self-Reliance Food Pantries (2018); Rise Above Foundation Inc., Northbridge, Massachusetts, $10,000 - Awarded for Activities for Foster Youth (2018); Berkshire Arts and Technology Charter School, Adams, Massachusetts, $10,000 - Awarded for 1:1 Computer Initiative for High School Students (2018).
Contact: Caitlin Arnold, Philanthropic Client Manager; (860) 244-4872; ct.grantmaking@bankofamerica.com or caitlin.arnold@bofa.com
Internet: www.bankofamerica.com/philanthropic/foundation/?fnId=77
Sponsor: Charles H. Hall Foundation
200 Glastonbury Boulevard, Suite #200, CT2-545-02-03
Glastonbury, CT 06033-4056

Charles H. Pearson Foundation Grants 566

The Charles H. Pearson Foundation Fund was established in 1922 to support and promote quality educational, human-services, and health-care programming for underserved populations. In the area of education, the fund supports academic access, enrichment, and remedial programming for children, youth, adults, and senior citizens that focuses on preparing individuals to achieve while in school and beyond. In the area of health care, the fund supports programming that improves access to primary care for traditionally underserved individuals, health education initiatives and programming that impact at-risk populations, and medical research. In the area of human services the fund tries to meet evolving needs of communities. Currently the fund's focus is on (but is not limited to) youth development, violence prevention, employment, life-skills attainment, and food programs. Grant requests for general operating support are strongly encouraged. Program support will also be considered. Small, program-related capital expenses may be included in general operating or program requests. The majority of grants from the Pearson Fund are one year in duration; on occasion, multi-year support is awarded. Applicants must apply online at the grant website. Applicants are strongly encouraged to do the following before applying: review the downloadable state application procedures for additional helpful information and clarifications; review the downloadable online-application guidelines at the grant website; review the foundation's funding history (link is available from the grant website); review the online application questions in advance; and review the list of required attachments. These will generally include: a list of board members, financial statements (audited, reviewed, or compiled by independent auditor); an organization summary; a list of other funding sources; an IRS Determination letter; and other required documents. All attachments must be uploaded in the online application as PDF, Word, or Excel files. The application deadline for the Charles H. Pearson Foundation Fund is 11:59 p.m. on July 1. Applicants will be notified of grant decisions before September 30.

Requirements: Applicants must have 501(c)3 tax-exempt status.

Restrictions: In general, capital requests are not advised. The fund does not support endowment campaigns, events such as galas or award ceremonies, and costs of fundraising events. The fund does not support requests from individuals, organizations attempting to influence policy through direct lobbying, or any political campaigns.

Geographic Focus: Massachusetts

Date(s) Application is Due: Jul 1

Samples: United Way of Massachusetts Bay, Boston, Massachusetts, $36,000,; Berklee College of Music, Boston, Massachusetts, $25,000, Berklee City Music Faculty Outreach Program to help underserved youth in the Boston Public Schools; Community Legal Services and Counseling Center, Cambridge, Massachusetts, general operating support to provide free legal services and affordable mental health services to underserved families and individuals.

Contact: Michealle Larkins, Vice President; (866) 778-6859; michealle.larkins@baml.com

Internet: www.bankofamerica.com/philanthropic/fn_search.action

Sponsor: Charles H. Pearson Foundation Fund

225 Franklin Street, 4th Floor, MA1-225-04-02

Boston, MA 02110

Charles Lafitte Foundation Grants 567

The foundation is committed to helping groups and individuals foster lasting improvement on the human condition by providing support to education, children's advocacy, medical research, and the arts. Children's advocacy grants support organizations working to improve the quality of life for children, particularly in relation to child abuse, literacy, foster housing, hunger, and after-school programs. Education grants support innovative programs that work to resolve social service issues, address the needs of students with learning disabilities, provide technology and computer-based education, offer leadership skills education, and support at-risk students. Colleges and universities also receive support for research and conferences. The foundation's medical issues and research grants support healthcare studies, with emphasis on cancer research and treatment, children's health, health education, and promoting healthy living and disease prevention. Art grants support emerging artists and educational art programs.

Requirements: 501(c)3 tax-exempt organizations are eligible. The Foundation does not respond to unsolicited submissions, so submit a letter of inquiry prior to preparing an application.

Restrictions: Political organizations or religious-based programs are not supported.

Geographic Focus: All States

Samples: Girl Scouts of the Jersey Shore, $200,000. Bridge of Books Foundation, $2,500. Hand in Hand, $10,000. Jersey Shore University Medical Center, $700,000.

Contact: Jennifer Vertetis, President; jennifer@charleslafitte.org

Internet: charleslafitte.org/grants/overview/

Sponsor: Charles Lafitte Foundation

29520 2nd Ave SW

Federal Way, WA 98023

Charles N. and Eleanor Knight Leigh Foundation Grants 568

The Charles N. and Eleanor Knight Leigh Foundation was established in Florida in 1985, with the major purpose of awarding grants for youth, education, the environment, and social service organizations. The Foundation's primary fields of interest include: arts and culture; community and economic development; and education. In most cases, support takes the form of general operation funding, program development, and seed money, and it is given throughout southern Florida and in the State of North Carolina. Though unsolicited requests are not accepted, interested parties should approach the Foundation in writing explaining their need in a one-page letter and wait for an invitation to apply. Most recent awards have ranged from $1,500 to $10,000, with approximately twenty to twenty-five grants given annually.

Geographic Focus: Florida, North Carolina

Amount of Grant: 1,500 - 10,000 USD

Samples: Alhambra Orchestra, Coconut Grove, Florida, $5,000 - general operating support (2019); Cane Elementary School, LaGrange, Georgia, $10,000 - general fund support (2019); The Salvation Army, Orange City, Florida, $1,500 - general operating support (2019).

Contact: Pam Admire, Administrator; (305) 444-6121; fax (305) 444-5508; info@sullivanadmire.com or pam.admire@sullivanadmire.com

Sponsor: Charles N. and Eleanor Knight Leigh Foundation

255 Ponce de Leon Boulevard, Suite 320

Coral Gables, FL 33134

Charles Nelson Robinson Fund Grants 569

The Charles Nelson Robinson Fund was established in 1970 to support and promote quality educational, human services, and health care programming for underserved populations in Hartford, Connecticut. Grants from the Robinson Fund are 1 year in duration. Applicants will not be awarded a grant for more than 3 consecutive years. Award amounts typically range from $1,000 to $15,000.

Requirements: Applicant organizations must have 501(c)3 tax-exempt status and have a principal office located in the city of Hartford, Connecticut. Applications will be submitted online through the Bank of America website. A grant report is required within 1 year of the grant application date, regardless of whether all of the funds have been spent.

Restrictions: Grant requests for capital projects will not be considered. The fund does not support requests from individuals, organizations attempting to influence policy through direct lobbying, or any political campaigns.

Geographic Focus: Connecticut

Date(s) Application is Due: Feb 15

Amount of Grant: 1,000 - 15,000 USD

Samples: Almada Lodge-Times Farm Camp Corporation, Andover, Connecticut, $15,000 - Awarded for Inclusive Overnight Summer Camp (2018); Camp Courant Inc., Hartford, Connecticut, $12,000 - Awarded for 2018 Camp Courant Camperships (2018); YWCA of Hartford, Hartford, Connecticut, $10,000 - Awarded for Young Women's Leadership Corps (YWLC) (2018).

Contact: Amy R. Lynch, Philanthropic Client Manager; (860) 244-4870; ct.grantmaking@bankofamerica.com or amy.r.lynch@bofa.com

Internet: www.bankofamerica.com/philanthropic/foundation/?fnId=72

Sponsor: Charles Nelson Robinson Fund

200 Glastonbury Boulevard, Suite # 200, CT2-545-02-05

Glastonbury, CT 06033

Charlotte and Joseph Gardner Foundation Grants 570

The Charlotte and Joseph Gardner Foundation was established in New York in 1981, with a primary interest in offering financial support in the New York City metro area. The Foundation's major fields of interest have always been human services, sports, and recreation. Grants are given to both individuals and nonprofit organizations. Most recently, awards have ranged from $3,600 to $12,000. A formal application is not required, and there are no specific annual deadlines for submission. Interested parties should begin by contacting the Foundation office directly.

Geographic Focus: New York

Amount of Grant: 3,600 - 12,000 USD

Samples: Friends of the High Line, New York, New York, $4,000 - general operations; Advanced Research Foundation, New York, New York, $12,000 - general operations; Youth Renewal Fund, New York, New York, $3,600 - general operations.

Contact: Danielle Gardner, President; (212) 366-4833

Sponsor: Charlotte and Joseph Gardner Foundation

230 West 41st Street, Suite 1500

New York, NY 10036

Charlotte Martin Foundation Youth Grants 571

The Charlotte Martin Foundation is a private, independent foundation dedicated to enriching the lives of youth in the areas of athletics, culture, and education and also to preserving and protecting wildlife and habitat. In the area of Youth, the foundation seeks to ensure opportunities for all youth, particularly the underserved and economically disadvantaged, to develop their skills in education, creative and cultural expression and athletics in ways that ultimately promote their habits of lifelong learning and their ability to make strong and lasting contributions to their respective communities. In regards to Youth Athletics, the foundation is interested in supporting a wide variety of sports programs and equipment for both boys and girls where youth populations are underserved (with special interest in supporting girls' sports; (limited investment in) facilities that are used primarily by youth; after school and off-hours sports programs making better use of existing facilities; and, programs that get younger children introduced to the value of sports. In regards to Youth Culture, the foundation will support projects that utilize active participation of young people in music, art, dance, literature, especially projects where youth are engaged in the production of an art form or event and projects that celebrate the heritage and cultural diversity of a community. For Youth Education grants, the foundation will support: programs in or out of the classroom, after school, weekends and summer; student-directed or inquiry-based learning where students have a clear role in designing and evaluating projects and learning activities; and, programs that promote skills for critical thinking, problem-solving and applied learning including but not limited to inquiry-based science, technology, engineering and environmental education.

Requirements: Washington, Oregon, Idaho, Montana, and Alaska nonprofit organizations are eligible. "Youth" is defined as children in kindergarten through high school, ages six to eighteen. Projects must focus on young people as the primary participants or beneficiaries.

Restrictions: The foundation does not support: large capital investment projects (e.g. track renovation, swimming pools, tennis courts, lockers, gymnasium renovation, bleachers); transportation to tournaments; fitness equipment and activities (e.g. treadmills, weight rooms); playgrounds or playground equipment; admission subsidies or purchase of tickets for events; trips to conferences; international exchange programs; passive participation by youth; artists in residence programs; children's testing or test preparation; purchase of computers or textbooks; programs whose goals are primarily social services; pre-Kindergarten programs; curriculum development; programs for college students.

Geographic Focus: Alaska, Arizona, Idaho, Montana, Oregon, Washington

Date(s) Application is Due: Apr 30; Sep 30

Amount of Grant: Up to 100,000 USD

Contact: Rebekah Wadadli, (800) 839-1821; rwadadli@foundationsource.com

Internet: www.charlottemartin.org/programs.htm
Sponsor: Charlotte Martin Foundation
P.O. Box 1733
Seattle, WA 98111

Charlotte R. Schmidlapp Fund Grants 572

The Foundation Office at Fifth Third Bank is committed to making a significant impact on programs and initiatives that create strong, vibrant communities and provide pathways to opportunity. Through the Foundation Office, the visions of individuals, families and institutions are realized, and legacies are attained by allocating the resources of their respective foundations in support of innovative programs and organizations in our communities. The Charlotte R. Schmidlapp Fund was established in Ohio in 1908. The fund supports initiatives that empower and assist women and girls in achieving self sufficiency. Grants are given for the relief of sickness, suffering, distress, and for the care of young children, the aged, or the helpless and afflicted. Funding is also available for the promotion of education, to improve living conditions, and/or the good and welfare of the state/nation in emergencies. An organization interested in submitting a grant proposal should first submit a Letter of Inquiry (LOI) using the link at the website. LOIs are accepted from October 1 through December 31 each year. The Foundation Office will review each LOI and may contact the applying organization about further discussion of the proposal, which may include a site visit. Each organization will receive either an email declining the inquiry or an invitation to submit a full application online. An invitation to apply will include the foundation funding source, recommended request amount, and a deadline for receipt of the application. The Fifth Third Bank Foundation Office will submit completed applications to the respective Foundation Board or Committee for final review and approval or declination. Grant seekers should allow six to twelve months for the grant making process. In general, the Foundation prefers awarding grants for one year. Most recent awards have ranged from $5,000 to $250,000.
Requirements: Nonprofit organizations that operate in the Greater Cincinnati region and are designated under section 501(c)3 and subsections 509(a)1 or 509(a)2 by the Internal Revenue Service are eligible to apply for a grant.
Restrictions: Nonprofits may apply only once within any 12-month period. The following are ineligible to apply: individuals; individual churches (except for proposals regarding an affiliated school); publicly supported entities such as public schools, government or government agencies; supporting organizations designated 509(a)3 by the IRS; walks, runs, dinners, galas, luncheons and other event sponsorship requests; athletic, band, and other school booster clubs; or startup funding for new programs or organizations (usually not a funding priority). A waiting period of three years is required for prior grant recipients receiving $10,000 or more from any funding source administered by the Fifth Third Bank Foundation Office. This period will begin as of the first payment on the grant.
Geographic Focus: Ohio
Amount of Grant: 5,000 - 250,000 USD
Contact: Heidi B. Jark, Managing Director; (513) 534-7001 or (513) 579-5300
Internet: www.53.com/content/fifth-third/en/personal-banking/about/in-the-community/foundation-office-at-fifth-third-bank.html
Sponsor: Charlotte R. Schmidlapp Fund
38 Fountain Square Plaza, MD 1090CA
Cincinnati, OH 45202

Chassé Youth Leaders Fund Grants 573

As part of the Chassé Cheer For The Cause initiative, Chassé created a fund of $1,000,000 to help youth cheer organizations cover the costs of their uniforms, apparel, accessories and shoes, and to help eliminate financial roadblocks that make cheerleading inaccessible to some families. Eligible youth cheerleading organizations can apply for a chance to receive up to 10% off of their order subtotal of Chassé products. Grant recipients are selected based on eligibility, and funds are available on a first-come, first-serve basis. The fund allows for $1,000,000 worth of grants to be awarded. Once that fund has been exhausted, no more grants will be awarded for the calendar year.
Requirements: Any youth cheerleading organization in good standing, with a U.S. mailing address, serving members aged five years to 15 years old. Eligible organizations include, but are not limited to: church and recreational groups, school squads, and community youth football and cheerleading leagues. Retail stores or team sponsors are not eligible to apply. Each team, individual or organization must fill out an application on his or her own. Individuals that are part of an eligible organization may apply, as long as they provide all information that is required on the application. You must provide a physical mailing address for your organization. P.O. Boxes will not be accepted a mailing address. It is recommended that you apply at least six to eight weeks before you need to have your gear delivered.
Restrictions: Only organizations with a U.S. mailing address are eligible for grants at this time. Chassé Youth Leaders Fund Grants cannot be combined with any other offers available from Chassé distributors, including, but not limited to, free shipping, packages and free gifts.
Geographic Focus: All States
Contact: Brita Bolane, Vice President; (800) 299-7822; youthleadersfund@chassecheer.com
Internet: www.chassecheer.com/grant/
Sponsor: Chassé Cheer
12375 World Trade Drive
San Diego, CA 92128

Chatham Athletic Foundation Grants 574

The Chatham Athletic Foundation (CAF) is a nonprofit organization created to promote youth athletics and help increase safety in youth athletics by providing funding to local non-profit organizations, schools and Chatham Township and Borough governments. Grant requests must support the mission of CAF and directly benefit youth athletics in grades K-8 in the Chathams. If awarded, the grant funding will pay for the costs of the project including, but not limited to, equipment, supplies, construction, labor, etc. The Chatham Athletic Foundation typically considers proposals from $1,000 up to $5,000.
Requirements: Single or multipurpose athletic projects in Chatham Borough and/or Chatham Township may apply. Submissions should include evidence that the project addresses a significant need with clearly defined objectives, and a cost-effective budget. Higher consideration may be given to projects that impact multiple sports and a large number of youth athletics. If your grant request project requires approval from the Borough Council, Township Committee, Board of Ed, Recreation, etc., such approval must be provided with the application.
Geographic Focus: New Jersey
Date(s) Application is Due: May 15
Amount of Grant: 1,000 - 5,000 USD
Contact: Bob Budlow, Grants Administrator; (973) 701-0194; grants@chathamathleticfoundation.org or theboard@chathamathleticfoundation.org
Internet: www.chathamathleticfoundation.org/grants.html
Sponsor: Chatham Athletic Foundation
P.O. Box 568
Chatham, NJ 07928

CHC Foundation Grants 575

The foundation awards general operating grants to southeastern Idaho nonprofit organizations in its areas of interest, including children and youth, community development, natural resource conservation and protection, and social services. There are two granting sessions each year, in the spring and fall. Applicants should submit a letter of inquiry; the foundation will invite full proposals.
Requirements: 501(c)3 southeastern Idaho nonprofit organizations may apply. Under the rules of the Internal Revenue Service, CHC Foundation makes grants only to publicly supported, tax-exempt, nonprofit organizations and institutions and public agencies.
Restrictions: The Foundation does not make grants to: religious groups or churches; political or legislative action groups; national or interstate regional organizations; other charitable foundations; or projects that are already completed. Further, the Foundation does not support: individual participation in trips, tours, workshops, contests, or competitions; specialized training; scholarships; operating expenses of organizations (for example, salaries, fees, rents, and honorariums); annual fund drives; advertising charitable benefits; general activities not clearly linked to specific charitable objectives; or projects that deliver basic educational services.
Geographic Focus: Idaho
Date(s) Application is Due: Mar 15; Sep 1
Amount of Grant: 750 - 150,000 USD
Contact: Ralph Isom, (208) 522-2368; info@chcfoundation.net
Internet: www.chcfoundation.net/grants
Sponsor: CHC Foundation
245 North Placer Avenue, P.O. Box 1644
Idaho Falls, ID 83403-1644

Cheryl Spencer Memorial Foundation Grants 576

The Cheryl Spencer Memorial Foundation was established in March of 1975, and is located in Dedham, Massachusetts, with the expressed purpose of supporting a number of causes. Today, these include: anti-discrimination; diseases and illnesses; higher education; elementary and secondary education; the environment; hospital care; in-patient medical care; international development; international peace and security; Judaism; community nonprofits; physical rehabilitation; special populations; specialty hospital care; and theology. Currently, awrds are centered in the three states of Massachusetts, New York, and Florida, and is generally aimed at re-granting and program development. There are no specified annual deadlines or application formats, so interested parties should forward a letter outlining the proposed program, and provide a program budget and proof of federal non-profit status. Most recent grants have ranged as high as $160,000.
Requirements: Any 501(c)3 organization serving the residents of New York, Massachusetts, and Florida is eligible to apply.
Geographic Focus: Florida, Massachusetts, New York
Amount of Grant: Up to 160,000 USD
Samples: Combined Jewish Philanthropies of Boston, Boston, Massachusetts, $160,000 - general program development support; American Society of the University of Haifa, New York, New York, $120,400 - general program development support; Brigham and Women's Hospital, Boston, Massachusetts, $21,000 - general program development support.
Contact: Aaron Spencer, Trustee; (617) 323-9200; fax (617) 323-4252; mail@unos.com
Sponsor: Cheryl Spencer Memorial Foundation
100 Charles Park Road
West Roxbury, MA 02132-4985

Chesapeake Bay Trust Environmental Education Grants 577

The Chesapeake Bay Trust Environmental Education Grants program is designed to engage Maryland pre-k through 12 grade students in activities that raise awareness and participation in the restoration and protection of the Chesapeake Bay and its rivers. Applicants can request funds in two different tracks: Environmental Literacy Program Track - applicants may request from $35,000 to $50,000 per year for three years ($105,000 to $150,000 total (the Trust anticipates making 1-2 awards in this track); and Meaningful Watershed Educational Experience Track - applicants may request up to $35,000 for one year (the Trust anticipates making 5 to 10 awards in this track). Letters of Intent are due by October 5, with final applications due by December 2. The Trust is piloting an online grants management system to improve ease of the application process, and if awarded, grant management.
Requirements: The Trust welcomes requests from the following organizations: municipal and county agencies and school districts; public and independent higher educational

institutions; 501(c)3 private nonprofit organizations; soil/water conservation districts & resource conservation and development councils. The strongest proposals will show committed partnerships that provide funding, technical assistance, or other in-kind services to support the successful implementation of the project.
Restrictions: The Trust does not fund the following: endowments, deficit financing, individuals, building campaigns, annual giving, research, fund raising or venture capital; mitigation or capital construction activities such as structural erosion control measures; political lobbying; reimbursement for a project that has been completed or materials that have been purchased; projects and programs located outside of Maryland; budget items that are considered secondary to the project's central objective. These items include, but are not limited to, food and refreshments, t-shirts and related materials, cash prizes, cameras and video equipment, and microscopes; funding is generally restricted to projects on public property, property owned by non-profit organizations, community-owned property, and property with conservation easements, unless otherwise specified in a grant program.
Geographic Focus: Maryland
Date(s) Application is Due: Oct 16
Amount of Grant: Up to 50,000 USD
Contact: Jamie Baxter; (410) 974-2941, ext. 105; fax (410) 269-0387; jbaxter@cbtrust.org
Internet: www.cbtrust.org/site/c.miJPKXPCJnH/b.7634923/k.7463/Environmental_Education.htm
Sponsor: Chesapeake Bay Trust
60 West Street, Suite 405
Annapolis, MD 21401

Chesapeake Bay Trust Mini Grants 578

The Chesapeake Bay Trust offers mini grants to promote public participation and awareness in the protection and restoration of the Chesapeake Bay and its tributaries in the state of Maryland. The trust seeks to fund efforts that are having a measurable impact on improving the Bay, its habitat and its water quality. The program awards up to $5,000 for projects that address one or more of the trust's grant making priorities. The majority of Mini Grant applications are submitted by schools for field experiences and on-the ground student service projects. However, organizations and agencies may also submit grants for small projects and public awareness initiatives. Groups working in Maryland's portions of the Chesapeake Bay and Youghlogheny River watersheds may apply for funding through this program. A request can be submitted at any time during the year.
Requirements: Request will not be considered when the application is submitted without sufficient time to review the application. Schools and nonprofits in the Maryland Chesapeake Bay area are eligible.
Restrictions: Grants do not support advertising campaigns, annual campaigns, capital campaigns, computer hardware/software acquisition, debt retirement, emergency funding, facilities, fellowships, general support, indirect costs, leveraging funds, loans, maintenance, membership campaigns, mortgage reduction, multiyear grants, professorships, scholarships, or travel expenses.
Geographic Focus: Maryland
Date(s) Application is Due: Jan 11; Aug 10
Amount of Grant: Up to 5,000 USD
Contact: Kacey Wetzel; (410) 974-2941, ext. 104; fax (410) 269-0387; kwetzel@cbtrust.org
Internet: www.cbtrust.org/site/c.miJPKXPCJnH/b.5457547/k.28ED/Mini_Grant.htm
Sponsor: Chesapeake Bay Trust
60 West Street, Suite 405
Annapolis, MD 21401

Chesapeake Bay Trust Outreach and Community Engagement Grants 579

The Outreach and Community Awareness Grant program seeks to increase public awareness and public involvement in the restoration and protection of the Bay and its rivers. In light of the Trust's commitment to the advancement of diversity in its grant-making and environmental work, the Trust strongly encourages grant applications for projects that increase awareness and participation of communities of color in the restoration and protection of the watershed. Available funding will range between $5,000 to $20,000. All eligible projects should be a component of a clearly defined plan to engage communities, raise awareness and ultimately change citizen behaviors. The strongest proposals will show committed partnerships that provide funding, technical assistance, or other in-kind services to support the successful implementation of the project. Applications must be received via the online grants system, available at the Chesapeake Bay Trust website.
Requirements: The Trust welcomes requests from the following Maryland organizations: 501(c)3 private nonprofit organizations; faith-based organizations; community associations; service, youth, and civic groups; municipal, county, regional, state, federal public agencies; soil/water conservation districts & resource conservation and development councils; forestry boards & tributary teams; public and independent higher educational institutions.
Restrictions: The Trust does not fund the following: endowments, deficit financing, individuals, building campaigns, annual giving, research, direct mail fund raising, or venture capital; mitigation or capital construction activities such as structural erosion control measures; political lobbying; reimbursement for a project that has been completed or materials that have been purchased; projects and programs located outside of Maryland; budget items that are considered secondary to the project's central objective. These items include, but are not limited to, cash prizes, cameras and video equipment, and microscopes. Funding is generally restricted to projects on public property, property owned by non-profit organizations, community-owned property, and property with conservation easements, unless otherwise specified in a grant program. Projects should be completed within approximately one year upon receipt of the grant award.
Geographic Focus: Maryland
Amount of Grant: 5,000 - 20,000 USD
Contact: Kacey Wetzel; (410) 974-2941, ext. 104; fax (410) 269-0387; kwetzel@cbtrust.org
Internet: www.cbtrust.org/site/c.miJPKXPCJnH/b.5457559/k.402C/Outreach_and_Community_Engagement.htm
Sponsor: Chesapeake Bay Trust
60 West Street, Suite 405
Annapolis, MD 21401

Chicago Board of Trade Foundation Grants 580

The Chicago Board of Trade Foundation provides grant support to organizations in the metropolitan Chicago, Illinois, area in its areas of interest. Those areas of interest include: arts and culture, including libraries and museums; education, including higher education, adult basic education and literacy training; science and technology; health care, including mental health services, cancer research, and rehabilitation; child and youth development; minorities; the economically disadvantaged; wildlife; and media and communication. Grants are awarded for general operating support, continuing support, annual campaigns, capital campaigns, and endowments. An online application form is required. The board meets during the first quarter annually to consider requests. The annual application deadline is October 31.
Requirements: All organizations requesting support must: be tax-exempt under Section 501(c)3 of the Internal Revenue Code; demonstrate that they do not restrict services or discriminate in any form on the basis of race, religion, ethnic origin or sexual orientation; have significant interest in the areas of youth, education, seniors, wildlife, or social and human services; be administered in and dedicated to the benefit of the Chicago area; and not contribute funds to ancillary organizations.
Restrictions: The CBOT Foundation generally does not fund the following: organizations without tax-exempt status; exclusionary organizations; private foundations; operating or capital expenses; individuals; political candidates and lobbying organizations; religious, fraternal, social or other membership organizations providing services to their own constituencies; memorials, endowments or multi-year pledges; fundraising efforts to benefit other organizations; fundraising activities related to individual sponsorships (e.g., walk-athons, marathons); special events, such as conferences, symposia and sports tournaments; athletic teams; or video/film production.
Geographic Focus: Illinois
Date(s) Application is Due: Oct 31
Contact: Dawn Andersen; (312) 789-8225 or (312) 435-3456; fax (312) 341-3306
Internet: www.cbotfoundation.org/application.html
Sponsor: Chicago Board of Trade Foundation
141 West Jackson Boulevard, Suite 1404
Chicago, IL 60604-2992

Chicago Community Trust Arts and Culture Grants: Improving Access to Arts Learning Opportunities 581

Arts learning grants seek to provide measurable benefits to students that have inequitable access to these essential opportunities. Elementary-age children can seldom advocate on their own behalf or vote with their feet if the programs provided are mediocre. High school students, by contrast, are quick to vote with their feet if activities are not engaging—and often pursue less constructive alternatives. This funding priority will support programs that will increase and strengthen arts opportunities for underserved children. Within this priority are two specific initiatives: Arts Infusion Initiative for High-Risk Teens and the College Pathways Initiative. The Arts Infusion Initiative currently consists of 15 grant recipients working in high-risk settings with teens who have had encounters with the criminal justice system, experienced school disciplinary action and reside in the federally-designated Comprehensive Anti-Gang Initiative (CAGI) communities. Grant recipients use resources related to the Chicago Public Schools (CPS) Guide for Teaching and Learning in the Arts and stress social/emotional learning skills associated with conflict resolution. Knowledge-sharing occurs through the Arts Infusion Initiative blog and monthly professional development sessions. Expertise is provided by the CPS Office of Arts Education and the Loyola University College of Fine and Performing Arts. Proposals will be solicited directly from specific organizations. There will be no RFP process in the Arts Infusion Initiative. For the College Pathways Initiative, Proposals in this area should provide structured opportunities for students, primarily from disadvantaged backgrounds, to explore advanced performance experience and training that will expose them to post-secondary options. The long-term goal is to build these programs in every artistic discipline for students from neighborhood CPS high schools. Proposals are due on January 5.
Requirements: The Trust funds nonprofit agencies with evidence of tax-exempt status under Section 501(c)3 of the Internal Revenue Code that are not classified as private foundations. The Trust also accepts applications from agencies that operate under a nonprofit fiscal sponsor. Organizations must be located within and/or primarily serving residents of Cook County, except for regional, statewide or national projects or research that may benefit a substantial portion of Cook County residents. Organizations must also be non-discriminatory in the hiring of staff or in providing services on the basis of race, religion, gender, sexual orientation, age, national origin or disability.
Restrictions: The Trust will not provide grants for: scholarships; individuals; sectarian purposes (programs that promote or require a religious doctrine); support of single-disease oriented research, treatment or care; the sole purpose of writing, publishing, producing or distributing audio, visual or printed material; the sole purpose of conducting conferences, festivals, exhibitions or meetings; or, reducing operating deficits or liquidating existing debt.
Geographic Focus: Illinois
Date(s) Application is Due: Jan 5
Contact: Suzanne Connor, Senior Program Officer; sconnor@cct.org
Internet: cct.org/apply/funding-priorities/arts#priority3
Sponsor: Chicago Community Trust
111 East Wacker Drive, Suite 1400
Chicago, IL 60601

Chicago Neighborhood Arts Program Grants 582

The Neighborhood Arts Program is a multi-year program which encourages and supports the presentation of high quality instructional arts programs benefiting youth, senior citizens, and people with disabilities in Chicago's low-to-moderate income neighborhoods. Individual artists of all disciplines with demonstrated teaching experience are eligible to receive funding up to $4,000.

Requirements: Individual artists of all disciplines with demonstrated teaching experience are eligible to apply.
Geographic Focus: Illinois
Amount of Grant: Up to 4,000 USD
Contact: Meg Duguid; (312) 744-9797 or (312) 744-5000; meg.duguid@explorechicago.org
Internet: www.cityofchicago.org/city/en/depts/dca/provdrs/grants.html
Sponsor: Chicago Department of Cultural Affairs
121 N. LaSalle Street
Chicago, IL 60602

Chick and Sophie Major Memorial Duck Calling Contest Scholarships 583

Honoring the memories of Stuttgart's legendary champion duck callers and duck calls makers, Chick and Sophie Major, the competition began in 1974 with a single $500 scholarship given to the winner. During its history, the renowned contest has awarded $60,000 in scholarships to young duck callers attending 32 different colleges and universities in thirteen different states. The contest is associated with the World's Champion Duck Calling Contest and will take place on the Main Street Stage beside the Stuttgart Chamber of Commerce. The first-place winner will receive $2,000, second place will receive $1,000, 3rd place will receive $750, and 4th place will receive $500.

Requirements: The contest is open to any current high school senior graduating in the current year. The only other requirement is the ability to call a duck.
Geographic Focus: All States
Date(s) Application is Due: Nov 25
Amount of Grant: 500 - 2,000 USD
Contact: Dixie Holt; (501) 208-0949 or (870) 364-2551; deholt@windstream.net
Brenda Cahill, Committe Member; (501) 208-0949; bdcahills@aol.com
Internet: www.stuttgartarkansas.org/scholarship-contest.html
Sponsor: Stuttgart Arkansas Chamber of Commerce
507 S. Main Street, P.O. Box 1500
Stuttgart, AR 72160

Children's Brain Tumor Foundation Research Grants 584

The Children's Brain Tumor Foundation (CBTF), a national not-for-profit organization, was founded in 1988 by a group of dedicated parents, physicians and friends to improve the treatment, quality of life, and long-term outlook for children with brain and spinal cord tumors through research, support, education, and advocacy. The number one priority of CBTF is the awarding of grants for research into the causes of and effective treatments for pediatric brain and spinal cord tumors. When funding is available, the grant cycle begins in the spring of the year. Investigators from the U.S. and Canada should submit a pre-application form to be reviewed by an expert panel. Based on this initial review, a selected group of applicants will then be invited to submit a full proposal.

Requirements: Funding is currently restricted to principal investigators at institutions within the United States.
Restrictions: The Foundation does not award grants to individuals or to private foundations, and does not fund debt reduction, capital improvements, or travel expenses. Overhead expenses are not to exceed 10 percent of the total project cost.
Geographic Focus: All States
Amount of Grant: Up to 150,000 USD
Contact: Stacy Wagner, President; (212) 448-9494; swagner@cbtf.org or info@cbtf.org
Internet: cbtf.org/scientific-research-grants-and-clinical-fellowships/
Sponsor: Children's Brain Tumor Foundation
1460 Broadway
New York, NY 10036

Children's Trust Fund of Oregon Foundation Grants 585

The mission of the Children's Trust Fund of Oregon Foundation (CTFO) is to foster healthy child development and to support efforts to protect children in Oregon through strategic investments in local, proven or evidence-based child abuse prevention programs. To achieve this goal, CTFO awards grants to programs which can demonstrate their impact in preventing child abuse in Oregon. CTFO prioritizes grants for programs or program components which nurture and protect children by strengthening families and providing parents and caretakers with the education, skills and resources for healthy child development. The annual deadline for applications is April 1, and awards typically range up to a maximum of $20,000. Potential applicants should begin by contacting the grant office.

Requirements: Oregon public and private nonprofit organizations are eligible.
Geographic Focus: Oregon
Date(s) Application is Due: Apr 1
Amount of Grant: Up to 20,000 USD
Contact: Rajan Mehndiratta; (503) 222-7102; fax (503) 222-6975; prevention@ctfo.org
Internet: ctfo.org/index.php?s=Grants
Sponsor: Children's Trust Fund of Oregon Foundation
1785 NE Sandy Boulevard, Suite 270. P.O. Box 14694
Portland, OR 97293

Children's Trust Fund of Oregon Foundation Small Grants 586

Children's Trust Fund of Oregon Foundation Small Grants program of the Children's Trust Fund of Oregon Foundation (CTFO) allows CTFO to quickly and easily support private nonprofit organization applicants with grants of up to $1,000 for one time projects that provide a unique contribution to child abuse prevention. Some examples of projects or activities suitable for Small Grants include conference sponsorships, special one-time media events, family support events, public awareness and education campaigns and other similar events. These examples are not all inclusive but indicate the type of projects appropriate for Small Grants. The application process is designed to give the applicant an answer within four to six weeks of receipt.

Requirements: Any public or private charitable non-profit offering services in the State of Oregon or an individual contractor performing a service that benefits children and families in the state is eligible.
Restrictions: Specific requests that are not eligible for Small Grants include: emergency needs or loans for individuals; tuition support for individuals; support for religious based activities; capital support; endowments; general fund drives or annual appeals; operational deficits; and lobbying or influencing elections or legislation.
Geographic Focus: Oregon
Amount of Grant: Up to 1,000 USD
Contact: Rajan Mehndiratta; (503) 222-7102; fax (503) 222-6975; prevention@ctfo.org
Internet: ctfo.org/index.php?s=Grants
Sponsor: Children's Trust Fund of Oregon Foundation
1785 NE Sandy Boulevard, Suite 270. P.O. Box 14694
Portland, OR 97293

Children's Tumor Foundation Young Investigator Awards 587

Founded in 1978, the Children's Tumor Foundation is a non-profit organization committed to identifying effective drug therapies for neurofibromatosis type 1 (NF1), neurofibromatosis type 2 (NF2) and Schwannomatosis, and to improving the lives of those living with these disorders. The Young Investigator (YIA) Awards program provides two-year awards for young scientists early in their careers, bringing them into the NF field and helping to establish them as independent investigators. Though a number of YIAs have made significant research findings and made notable publications the main function of the YIA program has been as a 'seeding mechanism' for researchers who went on to secure larger grants from NIH and CDMRP NFRP. Fellowship amounts range from $32,000 to $54,000, depending upon: level of training at the time of the application; and the request year (1st or 2nd).

Requirements: Applicants must be one of the following: a postdoctoral fellow (MD, PhD, or equivalent) but no more than seven years past the completion of their first doctoral degree; or a graduate student pursuing an MD, PhD, or equivalent.
Geographic Focus: All States
Amount of Grant: 32,000 - 54,000 USD
Contact: Patrice Pancza, Research Program Director; (212) 344-7291 or (212) 344-6633; fax (212) 747-0004; ppancza@ctf.org or grants@ctf.org
Internet: www.ctf.org/CTF-Awards-Grants-and-Contracts/CTF-Young-Investigator-Award/
Sponsor: Children's Tumor Foundation
120 Wall Street, 16th Floor
New York, NY 10005

Chilkat Valley Community Foundation Grants 588

The Chilkat Valley Community Foundation uses proceeds from its growing community permanent fund to award yearly grants to worthwhile programs in the Chilkat Valley. These grants are intended to support organizations and programs in the community that serve the needs of people in such areas as health, education, human services, arts and culture, youth, environment, and community development. Applications are being accepted for the following three (3) categories: operating support; new program and special projects; and capital campaigns. Funding for projects during this grant cycle will range from $500 to $3,500. Most recent awards have ranged from $500 to $2,000. The annual deadline for application submission is September 30.

Requirements: Applications are accepted from qualified 501(c)3 nonprofit organizations, or equivalent organizations located in the state of Alaska and serving the Chilkat Valley region. Equivalent organizations may include tribes, local or state governments, schools, or Regional Educational Attendance Areas. Operating Support Grants may be awarded to sustainable organizations in amounts not to exceed 10% of the organization's secured cash annual budget. Capital Grants may be awarded as the local match to another funding source. New Program and Special Project Grants may be awarded for programs and projects that are not undertaken on an annual basis. A grant requesting $1,000 or more is a challenge grant at a ratio of 1:1 (grantees must raise $1 to receive $1). Grants of $500 to $999 do not require a match. The recipient's match must be raised within twelve months of the award notification and must be raised from at least five (5) different donors.
Geographic Focus: Alaska
Date(s) Application is Due: Sep 30
Amount of Grant: 500 - 3,000 USD
Samples: Becky's Place Haven of Hope, Haines, Alaska, $2,000 - operating support; Children's Reading Foundation, Haines, Alaska, $999 - support of the Play With Purpose program; Haines Animal Rescue Kennel, Haines, Alaska, $1,250 - spay and neuter assistance program.
Contact: Ricardo Lopez, Program Officer; (907) 274-6707 or (907)766-6868; fax (907) 334-5780; rlopez@alaskacf.org
Mariko Sarafin, Senior Program Associate; (907) 249-6609 or (907) 334-6700; fax (907) 334-5780; msarafin@alaskacf.org
Internet: chilkatvalleycf.org/projects/
Sponsor: Chilkat Valley Community Foundation
P.O. Box 1117
Haines, AK 99827

ChLA Article Award 589

The ChLA Article Award is given annually by the Children's Literature Association to recognize outstanding articles focusing on a literary, historical, theoretical, or cultural examination of children's texts and/or children's culture. Eligible articles must be written in English exclusively by the author(s) or translator(s) whose name(s) appear(s) on the article and must have been published during the year under consideration. Articles should provide

new insights into the field, making a distinct or significant scholarly contribution to the understanding of children's literature.
Restrictions: Reprints of previously published articles are not eligible.
Geographic Focus: All States
Date(s) Application is Due: Oct 1
Contact: Tammy Mielke; (630) 571-4520; fax (708) 876-5598; info@childlitassn.org
Internet: www.childlitassn.org/article-award
Sponsor: Children's Literature Association
1301 W. 22nd Street, Suite 202
Oak Brook, IL 60523

ChLA Book Award   590

The Children's Literature Association Book Award is given annually to recognize outstanding book-length contributions to children's literature history, scholarship, and criticism. Eligible titles must be published, book-length works on the history of and/or scholarship or criticism on children's literature, written in English exclusively by the author(s) whose name(s) appear on the title page, and bearing an original copyright date of the year under consideration. Anthologies or festschriften, reference works, and textbooks; honors papers, masters theses, and doctoral dissertations, unless reworked as a book; and reprints or new editions of previously published books are not eligible.
Requirements: Nominations for the Book Award are welcome from any current ChLA member.
Geographic Focus: All States
Contact: Kim Reynolds; (630) 571-4520; fax (708) 876-5598; info@childlitassn.org
Internet: www.childlitassn.org/book-award
Sponsor: Children's Literature Association
1301 W. 22nd Street, Suite 202
Oak Brook, IL 60523

ChLA Carol Gay Award   591

Nominations for the ChLA Carol Gay Award should be submitted by a ChLA faculty member on behalf of the undergraduate student author. A cover letter must accompany the submission and provide an endorsement of the paper and explain the faculty member's familiarity with the student's work. Please include both the member's and the student's email and street addresses on the cover letter only. Submissions will be forwarded from the ChLA office to the members of the Carol Gay Award Committee and read blind (without the accompanying cover letter). Papers must be original and show evidence of scholarly research and include a bibliography with more than the primary works included. They should conform to MLA style and should be no fewer than 8 pages and no more than 15 pages including notes and works cited. Award winners will receive a $200 prize, a certificate, and a complimentary year's membership to the Association. With the author's permission, the award winning essay may also be posted on the ChLA website. The recipient is also offered the opportunity to present the winning essay during a session at the annual ChLA conference and to receive his/her award during the awards banquet. If the winner attends the conference, a complimentary banquet ticket is also awarded, and conference registration is waived. Submissions should be submitted electronically. The deadline is February 1, annually for a paper written during the previous year.
Restrictions: Senior theses are not eligible. Only two submissions per ChLA faculty member will be accepted.
Geographic Focus: All States
Date(s) Application is Due: Feb 1
Amount of Grant: 200 USD
Contact: Committee Chair; (630) 571-4520; fax (708) 876-5598; info@childlitassn.org
Internet: www.childlitassn.org/carol-gay-award
Sponsor: Children's Literature Association
1301 W. 22nd Street, Suite 202
Oak Brook, IL 60523

ChLA Edited Book Award   592

The ChLA Edited Book Award is given annually by the Children's Literature Association to recognize an essay collection that makes a distinct or significant contribution to our understanding of youth literature from a literary, cultural, historical or theoretical perspective. To be eligible, works must be published, book-length, edited collections written in English exclusively by the authors whose names appear in the list of contributors and the editor(s) whose name(s) appear on the title page. These works must also bear the copyright date of the year under consideration. Biographical studies and studies of films or other media texts are eligible.
Restrictions: New editions of previously published books and volumes with a primarily pedagogical focus are not eligible.
Geographic Focus: All States
Contact: Donelle Ruwe; (630) 571-4520; fax (708) 876-5598; info@childlitassn.org
Internet: www.childlitassn.org/edited-book-award
Sponsor: Children's Literature Association
1301 W. 22nd Street, Suite 202
Oak Brook, IL 60523

ChLA Faculty Research Grants   593

ChLA Faculty Research Grants have a combined maximum fund of up to $5,000 per year, and individual awards may range from $500 to $1,500, based on the number and needs of the winning applicants. The grants are awarded for proposals dealing with criticism or original scholarship with the expectation that the undertaking will lead to publication and make a significant contribution to the field of children's literature in the area of scholarship or criticism. In honor of the achievement and dedication of Dr. Margaret P. Esmonde, proposals that deal with critical or original work in the areas of fantasy or science fiction for children or adolescents will be awarded the Margaret P. Esmonde Memorial Grant. Applications will be evaluated based upon the quality of the proposal and the potential of

the project to enhance or advance Children's Literature studies. Funds may be used for—but are not restricted to—research-related expenses such as travel to special collections or purchasing materials and supplies. Proposals should be received via email by the annual February 1 deadline, with the application window beginning on January 1.
Requirements: Recipients must either be members of the Children's Literature Association or join the association before they receive any funds. Grantees should acknowledge ChLA in any publication resulting from the grant.
Restrictions: The awards may not be used for obtaining advanced degrees, for researching or writing a thesis or dissertation, for textbook writing, or for pedagogical projects.
Geographic Focus: All States
Date(s) Application is Due: Feb 1
Amount of Grant: 500 - 1,500 USD
Contact: Grant Administrator; (630) 571-4520; fax (708) 876-5598; info@childlitassn.org
Internet: www.childlitassn.org/faculty-research-grant
Sponsor: Children's Literature Association
1301 W. 22nd Street, Suite 202
Oak Brook, IL 60523

ChLA Graduate Student Essay Awards   594

The ChLA Graduate Student Essay awards are comprised of both a PhD level award and a separate master's level award. Award winners receive a $200 prize, a certificate, and a complimentary year's membership to the Association. Recipients are also offered the opportunity to present their winning essays during a session at the annual ChLA conference and to receive their awards during the awards banquet. If the winner attends the conference, a complimentary banquet ticket is also awarded, and conference registration is waived. A student may only win the PhD level award or the Master's level award one time. A cover letter should accompany the submission and provide an endorsement of the paper and explain the faculty member's familiarity with the student's work. Submissions should be submitted electronically.
Requirements: Nominations should be submitted by a faculty member on behalf of the graduate student author. Submissions should demonstrate familiarity with previous scholarship and should contain original, distinctive ideas. They should be at least 10 pages in length and should not exceed 25 pages, including notes and works cited. They should conform to MLA style.
Restrictions: Graduate students may not nominate themselves or other graduate students.
Geographic Focus: All States
Amount of Grant: 200 USD
Contact: Committee Chair; (630) 571-4520; fax (708) 876-5598; info@childlitassn.org
Internet: www.childlitassn.org/graduate-student-essay-awards
Sponsor: Children's Literature Association
1301 W. 22nd Street, Suite 202
Oak Brook, IL 60523

ChLA Hannah Beiter Diversity Research Grants   595

The Diversity Research Grant, initiated in 2013 and approved by the board for disbursement beginning in 2014, is a grant to support research related to children's and young adult cultural artifacts (including media, culture, and texts) about populations that have been traditionally underrepresented or marginalized culturally and/or historically. Applications for this grant are to be considered annually and will be awarded as warranted. Awards will range from $500 to $1000, depending upon the winning proposal's projected budgetary considerations. Each grant will be awarded with the expectation that the undertaking will lead to publication and make a significant contribution to the field of children's literature scholarship or criticism. Within two years of receiving the grant, the recipient will be asked to submit a paper proposal based upon the project for presentation at a ChLA annual conference. Funds may be used for - but are not restricted to -research-related expenses such as travel to special collections, subvention funds, or purchasing materials and supplies. The annual deadline for receiving the application is midnight, February 1.
Requirements: Applications will be evaluated based upon the quality of the proposal and the potential of the project to enhance or advance Children's Literature studies. Winners must be members of the Children's Literature Association before they receive any funds. Winners must acknowledge ChLA in any publication or other presentation resulting from the grant.
Restrictions: The awards may not be used for obtaining advanced degrees, for researching or writing a thesis or dissertation, for textbook writing, or for pedagogical projects.
Geographic Focus: All States
Date(s) Application is Due: Feb 1
Amount of Grant: 500 - 1,000 USD
Contact: Grant Administrator; (630) 571-4520; fax (708) 876-5598; info@childlitassn.org
Internet: www.childlitassn.org/diversity-research-grant
Sponsor: Children's Literature Association
1301 W. 22nd Street, Suite 202
Oak Brook, IL 60523

ChLA Hannah Beiter Graduate Student Research Grants   596

The Hannah Beiter Graduate Student Research Grants were established to honor the memory of Dr. Hannah Beiter, a long-time supporter of student participation in the Children's Literature Association. The Beiter Grants have a combined maximum fund of up to $5,000 per year, and individual awards may range from $500 to $1,500, based on the number and needs of the winning applicants. The grants are awarded for proposals of original scholarship with the expectation that the undertaking will lead to publication or a conference presentation and contribute to the field of children's literature criticism. The award may be used to purchase supplies and materials (e.g., books, videos, equipment), as research support (photocopying, etc.), or to underwrite travel to special collections or libraries. Proposals should be received via email by the annual February 1 deadline, with the application window beginning on January 1.

Requirements: Award recipients must either be members of the Children's Literature Association or join the association before they receive any funds.

Restrictions: Beiter grant funds are not intended as income to assist in the completion of a graduate degree (e.g., applied to tuition), but as support for research that may be related to the dissertation or master's thesis.

Geographic Focus: All States
Date(s) Application is Due: Feb 1
Amount of Grant: 500 - 1,500 USD
Contact: Grant Administrator; (630) 571-4520; fax (708) 876-5598; info@childlitassn.org
Internet: www.childlitassn.org/beiter-graduate-student-research-grant
Sponsor: Children's Literature Association
1301 W. 22nd Street, Suite 202
Oak Brook, IL 60523

ChLA Mentoring Award   597

The Children's Literature Association is pleased to announce the ChLA Mentoring Award. The award recognizes excellence in mentoring taking place within the ChLA and extending beyond the boundaries of the mentor's own university. Awardees will have contributed in significant ways to enhancing others' scholarship and/or professional careers within the field of children's literature over a substantial period of time. Such mentorship may take place in a variety of contexts, including but not limited to organizational committee work, journal or other professional editing work, ChLA discussions of teaching and/or career-building, and informal contacts. Nominations are due electronically by February 1.

Requirements: Nomination packets will be assembled by a nominator who has decided to spearhead this task and to solicit additional material from others who may be interested in furthering the nomination; packets should contain 3-5 letters and a cover sheet with the name and contact information of the nominee and the nominator. Packets should total no more than 10 pages in length, excluding cover sheet. At least two letters must come from people who have never been students or departmental colleagues of the nominee, and all nomination letters must come from current ChLA members. The award will be adjudicated by the ChLA Board and will consist of a framed certificate presented at the annual ChLA conference. Winners will also be presented with a folder containing the letters written on their behalf.

Geographic Focus: All States
Date(s) Application is Due: Feb 1
Contact: Committee Chair; (630) 571-4520; fax (708) 876-5598; info@childlitassn.org
Internet: www.childlitassn.org/mentoring-award
Sponsor: Children's Literature Association
1301 W. 22nd Street, Suite 202
Oak Brook, IL 60523

ChLA Phoenix Award   598

The Children's Literature Association, an organization of teachers, scholars, librarians, editors, writers, illustrators, and parents interested in encouraging the serious study of children's literature, created the Phoenix Award as an outgrowth of the Association's Touchstones Committee. The award, given to a book originally published in the English language, is intended to recognize books of high literary merit. The Phoenix Award is named after the fabled bird who rose from its ashes with renewed life and beauty. Phoenix books also rise from the ashes of neglect and obscurity and once again touch the imaginations and enrich the lives of those who read them. The recipient of the Award has been chosen each year since 1985 by an elected committee of ChLA members that considers nominations made by members and others interested in promoting high critical standards in literature for children. Honor books were instituted in 1989 but have not been named every year.

Geographic Focus: All States
Contact: Lisa Rowe Faustino; (630) 571-4520; fax (708) 876-5598; info@childlitassn.org
Internet: www.childlitassn.org/phoenix-award
Sponsor: Children's Literature Association
1301 W. 22nd Street, Suite 202
Oak Brook, IL 60523

ChLA Phoenix Picture Book Award   599

Established by the ChLA Board in 2010, the Phoenix Picture Book Award is a companion to the original Phoenix Award and recognizes a picture book published twenty years previously that did not win a major award at that time, but that the committee has determined to be of lasting value. The award is innovative, for unlike most picture book awards, it will honor not only the illustrator, but also the author (if they are two separate people). Books are considered not only for the quality of their illustrations, but for the way pictures and text work together to tell a story (whether fact or fiction). Wordless books are judged on the ability of the pictures alone to convey a story.

Geographic Focus: All States
Contact: Andrea Schwenke Wyile; (630) 571-4520; fax (708) 876-5598; info@childlitassn.org
Internet: www.childlitassn.org/phoenix-picture-book-award
Sponsor: Children's Literature Association
1301 W. 22nd Street, Suite 202
Oak Brook, IL 60523

Christensen Fund Regional Grants   600

The fund (TCF) focuses its grantmaking on maintaining the biological and cultural diversity of the world by focusing on four geographic regions: the greater South West (Southwest United States and Northwest Mexico); Central Asia and Turkey; the African Rift Valley (Ethiopia); and Northern Australia and Melanesia. Grants within these programs are generally directed to organizations based within those regions or, where appropriate, to internationally based organizations working in support of people and institutions on the ground. In general, grants are one year or less; currently grants up to two years are by invitation only.

Requirements: 501(c)3 nonprofit organizations and non-USA institutions with nonprofit or equivalent status in their country of origin are eligible. Partnerships or associations with USA-based nonprofit organizations are preferred.

Restrictions: The fund does not make grants directly to individuals but rather assists individuals through institutions qualified to receive nonprofit support with which such individuals are affiliated.

Geographic Focus: All States
Amount of Grant: Up to 200,000 USD
Contact: Grants Administrator; (415) 644-1600; fax (415) 644-1601; info@christensenfund.org
Internet: www.christensenfund.org/index.html
Sponsor: Christensen Fund
260 Townsend Street
San Francisco, CA 94107

Christine and Katharina Pauly Charitable Trust Grants   601

The Christine and Katharina Pauly Charitable Trust was established in 1985 to support and promote quality educational, health and human services programming for underserved populations in Springfield, Missouri and the surrounding SW Missouri region. Special consideration is given to charitable organizations that serve the needs of children and organizations that serve the needs of older adults. The Christine and Katharina Pauly Charitable Trust was created under the wills of Ms. Hazel Katharina Pauly and Ms. Frieda Christine Oleta Pauly. The majority of grants from the Pauly Trust are 1 year in duration. Award amounts typically range from $2,000 to $18,000.

Requirements: Applicants must have 501(c)3 tax-exempt status and serve Springfield, Missouri and the surrounding Southwest Missouri region. Applications will be submitted online through the Bank of America website. A grant report is required within 1 year of the grant application date, regardless of whether all of the funds have been spent.

Restrictions: The Fund will consider requests for general operating support only if the organization's operating budget is less than $1 million. In general, grant requests for individuals, endowment campaigns or capital projects will not be considered. The trust does not support requests from individuals, organizations attempting to influence policy through direct lobbying, or any political campaigns.

Geographic Focus: Missouri
Date(s) Application is Due: Sep 1
Amount of Grant: 2,000 - 18,000 USD
Samples: Boys and Girls Clubs of Springfield - Henderson Unit, Springfield, Missouri, $10,000 - Awarded for Education Beyond the Classroom; Boy Scouts Ozark Trails Council, Springfield, Missouri, $8,000 - Awarded for Scoutreach, Latino Scouting Initiative, and Assistance to Individuals; Ozark Counseling Center, Springfield, Missouri, $6,000 - Awarded for Children's therapy program.
Contact: Tony Twyman, Senior Philanthropic Client Manager; (816) 292-4342; mo.grantmaking@bankofamerica.com or tony.twyman@bofa.com
Internet: www.bankofamerica.com/philanthropic/foundation/?fnId=6
Sponsor: Christine and Katharina Pauly Charitable Trust
231 South LaSalle Street, IL1-231-10-05
Chicago, IL 60697

Christopher Ludwick Foundation Grants   602

The Foundation is named for Christopher Ludwick (1720-1801), Baker General of the Army of the United States during the American Revolution. His bequest of $13,000 was to provide a trust 'for the schooling and education gratis, of poor children of all denominations, in the city and liberties of Philadelphia, without exception to the country, extraction, or religious principles of their parents or friends...' The trust has grown to almost $5,000,000, and grants amounting to approximately $200,000 are awarded each year. Applications are accepted between February 1 and February 28. Grant awards typically range from $2,500 to $20,000.

Requirements: Applicants must use the application form provided on this website and follow the instructions set forth therein.

Geographic Focus: Pennsylvania
Date(s) Application is Due: Feb 28
Amount of Grant: 2,500 - 20,000 USD
Contact: Trina Vaux, Secretary; (610) 525-4517 or (314) 418-2643; info@ludwickfoundation.org
Internet: www.ludwickfoundation.org/about.htm
Sponsor: Christopher Ludwick Foundation
16 N. Bryn Mawr Avenue, P.O. Box 1313
Bryn Mawr, PA 19010-3379

CHT Foundation Education Grants   603

The CHT Foundation was established in 2005 by the family of William O. Taylor of Boston, former publisher of The Boston Globe, and his wife, Sally P. Coxe, a native of Philadelphia. The Foundation has three main areas of interest: education, the environment, and projects that enhance historic preservation. The grants are confined to the Commonwealth of Massachusetts. The Trustees have a strong geographic preference for projects serving the cities of Boston and New Bedford, and rarely make grants for projects serving communities outside those two cities. In the area of Education, the Foundation focus is on the support of programs for pre-school through elementary school age children, with emphasis on early learning, literacy, civics and the teaching of history. Awards typically range from $1,000 to $10,000. While there are no restrictions on grants for capital purposes or general operations, the Foundation prefers to fund project-specific requests. Grant applications must be received by end of business on July 1.

Requirements: Applicants are asked to submit the following: a cover letter signed by the Executive Director or Board President; the Philanthropy Massachusetts Common Proposal

Cover Sheet; a short proposal (no more than four pages) detailing the organization and the request for funding; a detailed organizational budget, and, if requesting project support, a detailed project budget; and a copy of the letter of determination from the Internal Revenue Service confirming the 501(c)3 tax exempt status of the organization.
Restrictions: Multi-year requests will not be considered.
Geographic Focus: Massachusetts
Date(s) Application is Due: Jul 1
Amount of Grant: 1,000 - 10,000 USD
Contact: Rita Goldberg; (617) 227-7940, ext. 775 or (617) 557-9766; rgoldberg@hembar.com
Gioia C. Perugini; (617) 557-9777 or (617) 557-9766; gperugini@hembar.com
Internet: hembar.com/client_services/cht-foundation
Sponsor: CHT Foundation
75 State Street, 16th Floor
Boston, MA 02109

CICF Clare Noyes Grant 604
The Central Indiana Community Foundation Clare Noyes Grant provides funding for high quality ballet performances for the public and ballet education programs for youth in Indianapolis and surrounding counties. Proposals are accepted in the months of February and July, and applications are available on the Foundation's website.
Geographic Focus: Indiana
Amount of Grant: 1,000 - 15,000 USD
Contact: Liz Tate; (317) 634-2423, ext. 175; fax (317) 684-0943; liz@cicf.org
Internet: www.cicf.org/examples-of-named-funds
Sponsor: Central Indiana Community Foundation
615 North Alabama Street, Suite 119
Indianapolis, IN 46204-1498

CICF Howard Intermill and Marion Intermill Fenstermaker Grants 605
The Central Indiana Community Foundation Intermill Fenstermaker Grant exists to support programs for children and youth with disabilities. See the website's Grantseeker's Guide for a specific description of the Fenstermaker Grant. Proposal are accepted in the months of February and July, and the application is available on the Foundation's website.
Geographic Focus: Indiana
Amount of Grant: 1,000 - 15,000 USD
Contact: Liz Tate; (317) 634-2423, ext. 175; fax (317) 684-0943; liz@cicf.org
Internet: www.cicf.org/examples-of-named-funds
Sponsor: Central Indiana Community Foundation
615 North Alabama Street, Suite 119
Indianapolis, IN 46204-1498

CICF Indianapolis Foundation Community Grants 606
CICF's mission is to inspire, support, and practice philanthropy, leadership, and service in the community. Proposed programs should align with any of the Foundation's Seven Elements of a Thriving Community: basic needs; economic stability; health and wellness; education; vitality and connectivity of neighborhoods and communities; arts and culture; and the environment. The application and grant request detail form are available online. Applications are accepted during the months of February and July.
Requirements: CICF welcomes grant applications from charitable organizations that are tax exempt under section 501(c)3 of the Internal Revenue Code, and from governmental agencies. New projects or organizations with pending 501(c)3 status may submit an application with the assistance of a fiscal sponsor. Grant inquiries and proposals will be prioritized using the following criteria: organizations that serve primarily Marion County residents; organizations with a demonstrable track record; programs serving populations disadvantaged due to income, age, ethnicity, language, education, disability, transportation or other adverse conditions; project/program ideas must be fully developed; and projects that strongly connect to existing community initiatives (e.g. the Blueprint to End Homelessness, Indianapolis Cultural Development Initiative, and Family Strengthening Coalition). Application information is available online.
Geographic Focus: Indiana
Contact: Liz Tate, Vice President for Grants; (317) 634-2423, ext. 175; fax (317) 684-0943; liz@cicf.org or program@cicf.org
Internet: www.cicf.org/the-indianapolis-foundation
Sponsor: Central Indiana Community Foundation
615 North Alabama Street, Suite 119
Indianapolis, IN 46204-1498

CICF John Harrison Brown and Robert Burse Grant 607
The purpose of the Central Indiana Community Foundation Brown and Burse Grant is to support academic and moral values for deserving youth in the Indianapolis area. Proposals are accepted in the months of February and July, and applications are available on the Foundation's website. Organizations are encouraged to call the Foundation before submitting their proposal to be certain it is appropriate for funding.
Geographic Focus: Indiana
Amount of Grant: 1,000 - 5,000 USD
Contact: Liz Tate; (317) 634-2423, ext. 175; fax (317) 684-0943; liz@cicf.org
Internet: www.cicf.org/examples-of-named-funds
Sponsor: Central Indiana Community Foundation
615 North Alabama Street, Suite 119
Indianapolis, IN 46204-1498

CICF Summer Youth Grants 608
The Central Indiana Community Foundation Summer Youth Grants provide grants, coordinates professional development opportunities, and disseminates community information to support summer programs serving Marion County youth. The program is designed to make the grant process easier for charitable organizations by using a single application form. Since 1995, SYPF-Indianapolis has awarded more the $29 million in grants to support summer youth programs.
Requirements: Applicants should carefully analyze their project in terms of needs assessment, program emphasis, start and end dates, budget development, recruiting of staff, length of program day, participating ages, safety, the program's site, and collaborations with other programs. Applicants are encouraged to call the Foundation to discuss their proposal in advance. They are also encouraged to review the application and the program guide at the Foundation's website.
Geographic Focus: Indiana
Contact: Mary Johnson, Grants Associate; (317) 634-2423, ext. 554
Internet: www.summeryouthprogramfund-indy.org/contact/
Sponsor: Central Indiana Community Foundation
615 North Alabama Street, Suite 119
Indianapolis, IN 46204-1498

CICF Women's Grants 609
The Central Indiana Community Foundation Women's Grants (CICFWG) create options and opportunities for women and girls in central Indiana through distribution of grants to organizations serving to women and girls. This branch of the Foundation seeks to be the most influential funding organization creating transformative and sustainable change for women and girls. Current funding priorities are caregiving; domestic violence; insufficient income; needs of girls; health; economic empowerment; and self-development. Grants are flexible and adapt to meet the current needs of the community.
Requirements: Applicants must be nonprofit organizations serving women and girls in the following Indiana counties: Boone; Hamilton; Hancock; Hendricks; Johnson; Marion; Morgan; and Shelby. Applicants should review the online guidelines, then contact the Grants Officer for a current application.
Geographic Focus: Indiana
Contact: Julie Koegel, Grants Officer; (317) 293-7006; juliekoegel@sbcglobal.net
Jennifer Pope Baker, Director; (317) 634-2423, ext. 127; jenniferp@cicf.org
Internet: www.cicf.org/womens-fund-of-central-indiana
Sponsor: Central Indiana Community Foundation
615 North Alabama Street, Suite 119
Indianapolis, IN 46204-1498

Cigna Civic Affairs Sponsorships 610
The Cigna Civic Affairs program coordinates the charitable giving and volunteer activities of Cigna and its people, with the overall goal of demonstrating Cigna's commitment to being a socially responsible and responsive corporate citizen. One of the ways Civic Affairs fulfills this mission is through the Cigna Civic Affairs Sponsorships program. These sponsorships support charitable events and activities that enhance the health of individuals and families and the well-being of communities. Its strategy for achieving healthy outcomes around the globe is driven by: promoting wellness—to help individuals and families take ownership of their own health; expanding opportunities—to make health information and services available to everyone; developing leaders—to leverage the education and hands-on life experience that promote personal and professional growth; and embracing communities—to encourage collaborative and sustainable problem-solving approaches.
Geographic Focus: All States
Amount of Grant: 5,000 - 50,000 USD
Contact: Jill Holliday (860) 226-2094 or (866) 865-5277; jill.holliday@cigna.com
Internet: secure16.easymatch.com/cignagive/applications/agency/?Skip=LandingPage&ProgramID=3
Sponsor: Cigna Corporation
1601 Chestnut Street, TL06B
Philadelphia, PA 19192-1540

CIGNA Foundation Grants 611
The Cigna Foundation has identified four areas for grant consideration: health and human services, education, community and civic affairs, and culture and the arts. Health and education are of primary concern and receive priority. Under education, priority is placed on public secondary education, higher education for minorities, and adult basic education/literacy. The foundation also considers requests from U.S. cultural, educational, and public policy organizations that have international components. Requests are accepted and reviewed throughout the year. Consideration will be given to requests for general operating support, program development, annual campaigns, conferences and seminars, fellowships, scholarship funds and employee-related scholarships, and matching gifts and funds.
Requirements: Organizations with 501(c)3 tax-exempt status are eligible.
Restrictions: The foundation will not consider applications for grants to individuals, organizations operating to influence legislation or litigation, political organizations, or religious activities. In general, the foundation will not consider applications from organizations receiving substantial support through the United Way or other CIGNA-supported federated funding agencies; hospitals' capital improvements; or research, prevention, and treatment of specific diseases.
Geographic Focus: All States
Amount of Grant: 5,000 - 50,000 USD
Contact: Jill Holliday; (860) 226-2094 or (866) 865-5277; jill.holliday@cigna.com
Internet: www.cigna.com/aboutus/cigna-foundation
Sponsor: Cigna Foundation
1601 Chestnut Street, TL06B
Philadelphia, PA 19192-1540

Cincinnati Bell Foundation Grants 612

The Cincinnati Bell Foundation awards grants to Ohio organizations in support of elementary and secondary school programs that improve education for disadvantaged youths, such as mentoring or tutoring programs. Grants also support: arts and culture; social services; colleges and universities; and local civic and cultural groups. Types of support include: capital grants; challenge/matching grants; organizational development grants; general operating grants; and program development grants. There are no application deadlines; grant notification is made quarterly.

Requirements: 501(c)3 nonprofit organizations in the Cincinnati Bell service area are eligible. Giving primarily in northern Kentucky, the greater Cincinnati, Ohio, area, and in other cities in which the company has a significant corporate presence.

Geographic Focus: Kentucky, Ohio

Contact: Public Affairs Director; (513) 397-7545 or (513) 565-2210

Internet: www.cincinnatibell.com/about-us/in-the-community

Sponsor: Cincinnati Bell Foundation

201 E 4th Street

Cincinnati, OH 45202

Cincinnati Milacron Foundation Grants 613

The Cincinnati Milacron Foundation awards grants, gifts, and loans to eligible Michigan and Ohio nonprofit organizations in its areas of interest, including the arts, community development, higher education, youth programs, and religion. Types of support include annual campaigns, building/renovations, general operations, and seed money. Grants are awarded for one year and are renewable.

Requirements: Michigan and Ohio 501(c)3 nonprofit organizations are eligible.

Restrictions: Grants are not made to individuals.

Geographic Focus: Michigan, Ohio

Amount of Grant: 5,000 - 200,000 USD

Contact: George G. Price, (513) 487-5912; fax (513) 487-5586

Sponsor: Cincinnati Milacron Foundation

2090 Florence Avenue

Cincinnati, OH 45206-2484

Circle K Corporation Contributions Grants 614

Circle K strives to be a good corporate citizen by improving the quality of life in the communities in which it serves. The corporation's charitable support targets two key areas: youth-at-risk and education. Other fields of interest include: boys clubs; cerebral palsy; community and economic development; food services; girls clubs; housing; and youth development. Types of support include general operating funds, in-kind support, and sponsorships. Additionally, Circle K has been a national sponsor of United Cerebral Palsy (UCP) since 1984, giving hope and encouragement to thousands of children and adults with cerebral palsy and other disabilities. Circle K also facilitates an employee volunteer group, which lends time to company-sponsored community activities.

Requirements: Giving is primarily centered in areas of company operations in Alabama, Arizona, Arkansas, California, Colorado, Florida, Georgia, Illinois, Iowa, Indiana, Kentucky, Michigan, Mississippi, Nevada, New Mexico, North Carolina, Ohio, Oklahoma, Oregon, Pennsylvania, South Carolina, Tennessee, Texas, and Washington.

Geographic Focus: Alabama, Arizona, Arkansas, California, Colorado, Florida, Georgia, Illinois, Indiana, Iowa, Kentucky, Michigan, Mississippi, Nevada, New Mexico, North Carolina, Ohio, Oklahoma, Oregon, Pennsylvania, South Carolina, Tennessee, Texas, Washington

Contact: Contributions Manager; (602) 728-8000

Internet: www.circlek.com/CircleK/AboutUs/CommunityService.htm

Sponsor: Circle K Corporation

P.O. Box 52085

Phoenix, AZ 85072-2085

Cisco Systems Foundation San Jose Community Grants 615

The Cisco Foundation was established in 1997 by a gift from Cisco. Cisco and the Cisco Foundation partner with nonprofits, non-governmental organizations (NGOs), and community-based organizations to carry out many of our Corporate Social Responsibility programs. Currently, the Foundation supports Cisco's efforts to team with nonprofit and non-governmental organizations around the world to develop technology-based solutions in our investment areas. The Foundation focuses this work on underserved communities and looks for solutions that harness the power of the Internet and communications technology. Cisco focuses its social investments in areas where our cash, technology and people can make the biggest impact - education, economic empowerment, and critical human needs.

Requirements: 501(c)3 nonprofit organizations both in the United States and in foreign countries are eligible to apply.

Restrictions: Grants do not support athletic events, capital building campaigns, conferences, fundraising events, sponsorships, general operating expenses, religious or political groups, scholarships, individual schools or school systems, or start-up projects.

Geographic Focus: All States, All Countries

Amount of Grant: Up to 50,000 USD

Samples: Crossroads Foundation, Tuen Mun, Hong Kong, $19,426 - for a flip camera project (2018); Habitat for Humanity Quebec, Montreal, Canada, $10,000 - for building projects (2018); Habitat for Humanity Great Vancouver, Burnaby, Canada, $10,000 - for building projects (2018).

Contact: Chuck Robbins, Executive Director; (408) 526-4000; ciscofoundation@cisco.com

Internet: csr.cisco.com/pages/cisco-foundation

Sponsor: Cisco Foundation

170 West Tasman Drive

San Jose, CA 95134-1706

Citizens Bank Charitable Foundation Grants 616

The Citizens Bank Charitable Foundation looks for opportunities where moderate funding can affect significant results in the communities they serve. Priority consideration is given to programs that: fight hunger and reduce food insecurity; encourage the development of innovative responses to basic human needs; promote fair housing and focus on community issues of neighborhood development and economic self-sufficiency; support the availability of quality, cost-effective, community-based health care, particularly for low-income families and children who are at risk; promote new ways to provide a quality education to populations that are under-served, including job training; teach money management through financial literacy programs that provide individuals and businesses with the tools needed to be fiscally healthy; promote availability and accessibility in the area of culture and the arts; and promote citizen participation in the development of new and workable solutions for improving and maintaining a healthy environment. Charitable grants are usually for capital funding (to build or renovate a facility) or implementation of a specific program.

Requirements: 501(c)3 organizations that support the residents of Rhode Island, Connecticut, Delaware, Massachusetts, New Hampshire, New Jersey, New York, and Vermont are eligible to apply. Priority is given to those projects which: provide direct service to low- or moderate-income populations; are one year in duration; demonstrate a plan for long-term sustainability and potential to be replicated; and are focused on addressing a specific unmet need or issue.

Restrictions: Grants do not support annual appeals, general operating funds, individuals, single disease or issue research organizations, religious organizations for religious purposes, labor or fraternal or veterans groups, political organizations or projects, operating deficits, underwriting of conferences and seminars, governmental public agencies, endowments, annual operating support, historic preservation, trips and tours, payment on bank loans, advertising, public or private education institutions, or fund-raising events.

Geographic Focus: Connecticut, Delaware, Massachusetts, New Hampshire, New Jersey, New York, Pennsylvania, Rhode Island, Vermont

Amount of Grant: 1,000 - 100,000 USD

Contact: Steven Sylvan, Senior Vice President; (781) 471-1481 or (877) 228-6155; fax (401) 456-7366; steven.sylven@citizensbank.com or community@citizensbank.com

Internet: www.citizensbank.com/community/contributions.aspx

Sponsor: Citizens Bank Charitable Foundation

One Citizens Plaza, 870 Westminster Street

Providence, RI 02903

Citizens Savings Foundation Grants 617

In 1998, the Citizens Savings Foundation was established and funded with 300,000 shares of CFS Bancorp, Inc. stock. The primary purpose of the Foundation is to promote charitable and educational activities within the meaning of Section 501(c)3 of the Internal Revenue Code of 1986, within Lake and Porter counties in the State of Indiana and Cook, Will and DuPage counties in the State of Illinois and their neighboring communities. To that end, the Foundation: makes awards, grants or other distributions designed to expand home ownership opportunities and provide access to affordable housing; supports youth development programs to improve life options through education and work skills; and supports community organizations that contribute to the quality of life. There are no specified annual application deadlines, and interested parties should begin by contacting the Foundation office with a two- to three-page preliminary application.

Geographic Focus: Illinois, Indiana

Amount of Grant: Up to 5,000 USD

Contact: Thomas F. Prisby, CEO; (219) 836-2960 or (630) 323-9732

Sponsor: Citizens Savings Foundation

707 Ridge Road

Munster, IN 46321-1611

City of Oakland Cultural Funding Grants 618

The Cultural Funding program awards grants to Oakland-based individuals and nonprofit organizations. Organization Project Support grants support Oakland-based nonprofit organizations producing art activities in Oakland that culminate in a local public outcome for the benefit of the community. Individual Artist Project grants support Oakland resident individual artists producing art activities in Oakland that culminate in a local public outcome for the benefit of the community. Art in the Schools grants support quality, hands-on arts experiences in school settings to educate students about the process of creating and producing arts; support and enhance the classroom curriculum; and support arts residencies on the school site before, during, or after school hours. The January 6 application deadline is for organizations and individual artists; the January 13 deadline is for art in the schools. Guidelines are available online.

Requirements: Oakland-based individuals and nonprofit organizations are eligible to apply.

Geographic Focus: California

Date(s) Application is Due: May 16

Contact: Denise Pate, Cultural Funding Coordinator; (510) 238-7561 or (510) 238-2103; fax (510) 238-6341; dpate@oaklandnet.com

Internet: www2.oaklandnet.com/government/o/CityAdministration/d/Economic Development/o/CulturalArtsMarketing/DOWD000729

Sponsor: City of Oakland

One Frank H Ogawa Plaza, 9th Floor

Oakland, CA 94612

CJ Foundation for SIDS Program Services Grants 619

The CJ Foundation for SIDS offers two types of grants to support services related to the following areas of interest: SIDS (Sudden Infant Death Syndrome), SUID (Sudden Unexpected Infant Death), and Infant Safe Sleep. Program Services Grants, which are the first type, are generally for amounts greater than $5,000 and are offered by invitation only. Program Services Mini-Grants (formerly known as Express Grants) are the second type.

These are for $5,000 or less and may be applied for without invitation. The purpose of the foundation's program-services grants is to support activities that promote safe sleep for infants, educate about SIDS risk reduction, and provide grief support for parents and others who have experienced the sudden, unexpected death of an infant. The grants support the following types of activities: conferences and meetings; training and workshops; community awareness events; production, purchase, and distribution of educational, bereavement, and resource materials; support groups; peer support; counseling; support of staff and consultants who implement education initiatives or provide bereavement services; and newsletter production and distribution. Interested applicants should contact the Assistant Executive Director (see contact section) to request application materials. Submission deadline for the mini-grants is September 26 (deadlines may vary from year to year).
Requirements: The applicant must demonstrate that services relating to SIDS, SUID, and/ or Infant Safe Sleep are an established part of the organization's services.
Restrictions: Projects exclusively serving perinatal and/or neonatal death will not be considered. Data collection and analysis for Fetal Infant Mortality Review (FIMR) and Child Death Review (CDR) will not be considered. The foundation does not provide grants to organizations that discriminate, in policy or practice, against people based on their age, race, color, creed or gender. In general the CJ Foundation does not support the following types of requests: loans; budget requests greater than 100% of the applicant's operating budget; grants to individuals; dues; operating deficits; book publication; capital improvements/building project; chairs or professorships; endowments, annual fund drives, direct mail solicitation, or fundraising events; purchase of advertising space; purchase of products such as t-shirts, cribs, crib sheets, and sleep slacks; activities to influence legislation or support candidates for political office; and re-granting.
Geographic Focus: All States
Date(s) Application is Due: Sep 26
Amount of Grant: 500 - 5,000 USD
Samples: Association of SIDS and Infant Mortality Programs, East Lansing, Michigan, $5,000; Baptist Memorial Healthcare Foundation and NEA Baptist Charitable Foundation, Jonesboro, Arkansas, $2,852; Council for Children & Families, Seattle, Washington, $5,000.
Contact: Wendy Jacobs, Assistant Executive Director, Programs & Grants; (866) 314-7437 or (551) 996-5111; fax (551) 996-5326; wendy@cjsids.org or info@cjsids.org
Internet: www.cjsids.org/grants/grants-overview.html
Sponsor: CJ Foundation for SIDS
30 Prospect Avenue
Hackensack, NJ 07601

Clara Abbott Foundation Need-Based Grants   620
To promote personal financial responsibility, the Foundation provides financial consulting, financial education classes, and monetary financial assistance for personal needs. Assistance is based on financial hardship and is provided for basic needs as a last resource. The Clara Abbott Foundation's definition of financial hardship is any situation that threatens the family's ability to provide basic living needs, such as food, utilities and rent. Additionally, the Foundation may provide financial assistance for expenses due to natural disaster, major health problems of a family member, special needs children and cases of abuse.
Requirements: To receive a financial grant to help meet basic living needs, the following criteria must be met: current employee of Abbott with at least one year of service (or one year from date of Abbott acquisition) and working a minimum of 20 hours per week; retiree of Abbott; spouse of deceased employee/retiree (until remarried); dependent child of deceased employee/retiree until age 23 for students, age 19 otherwise; special-needs children will not lose eligibility based on age; or employee who is under a disability program (sponsored by Abbott). All applicants must be enrolled in a health plan.
Geographic Focus: All States
Contact: Lisa Marie Lillge, Grant Coordinator; (847) 937-1090 or (800) 972-3859; fax (847) 938-6511; AskClara@abbott.com
Internet: clara.abbott.com/financial-assistance/
Sponsor: Clara Abbott Foundation
1505 S White Oak Drive
Waukegan, IL 60085

Clara Blackford Smith and W. Aubrey Smith Charitable Foundation Grants   621
The Clara Blackford Smith and W. Aubrey Smith Charitable Foundation was established in 1978. Mrs. Smith was a well-known benefactor of health care. The foundation was established under her will to support and promote quality education, health-care, and human-services programming for underserved populations. Special consideration is given to charitable organizations that serve the people of Grayson County, Texas. The majority of grants from the Smith Charitable Foundation are one year in duration; on occasion, multi-year support is awarded. Award amounts typically range from $250 to $200,000. Award applications are accepted twice a year.
Requirements: Applicants must have 501(c)3 tax-exempt status and must serve the people of Grayson County, Texas. Applications will be submitted online through the Bank of America website. A grant report is required within 1 year of the grant application date, regardless of whether all of the funds have been spent.
Restrictions: The foundation does not support requests from individuals, organizations attempting to influence policy through direct lobbying, or any political campaigns.
Geographic Focus: Texas
Date(s) Application is Due: Jan 1; Aug 1
Amount of Grant: 250 - 200,000 USD
Samples: Denison Isd, Denison, Texas, $200,000 - Awarded for The Smith Auditorium at the new Denison High School campus; Denison Community Foundation, Denison, Texas, $75,000 - Awarded for Smith Committee Discretionary Funds; City of Denison, Denison, Texas, $60,000 - Awarded for Major renovation and improvements project for the Denison Public Library Building.

Contact: Kelly Garlock, Philanthropic Client Manager; (800) 357-7094; tx.philanthropic@ bankofamerica.com or tx.philanthropic@ustrust.com
Internet: www.bankofamerica.com/philanthropic/foundation/?fnId=68
Sponsor: Clara Blackford Smith and W. Aubrey Smith Charitable Foundation
901 Main Street, 19th Floor, TX1-492-19-11
Dallas, TX 75202-3714

Claremont Community Foundation Grants   622
The Claremont Community Foundation (CCF) was founded in 1989 at the urging of the Claremont city council. At that time, the council was unable to support all the worthy organizations that approached it for funding. Therefore, the council along with the City Manager, decided to work with other concerned citizens to form an organization that could effectively address the needs of many organizations throughout Claremont and its surrounding areas. For nearly 30 years Claremont Community Foundation has provided support for hundreds of programs and organizations that serve Claremont and the local surrounding communities. Grants are awarded through donor-advised funds, established by individuals or groups for a specific purpose, through fundraising efforts, or through the Community Impact and Arts Funds. CCF Grants benefit education, youth and family services, seniors, musicians, artists, the art appreciating public, developmentally and physically disabled children and adults, historical and cultural preservation, animal welfare, healthcare, and the natural environment. Claremont Community Foundation Grants are primarily awarded to support programs and projects in two fields of interest: community impact, and the arts. Historically, individual grant award amounts have averaged $1,000 to $5,000, and in some cases, more. Starting in 2019, the Foundation began offering grants up to $30,000. In addition, it will be awarding a limited number of $50,000 super grants. The annual application submission deadline is November 1.
Requirements: Nonprofit organizations serving the greater Los Angeles, California, metropolitan area may submit proposals.
Geographic Focus: California
Date(s) Application is Due: Nov 1
Amount of Grant: Up to 50,000 USD
Contact: Aurelia Brogan, Executive Director; (909) 398-1060; fax (909) 624-6629; ccf-info@claremontfoundation.org
Internet: claremontfoundation.org/grants-overview/
Sponsor: Claremont Community Foundation
205 Yale Avenue
Claremont, CA 91711

Claremont Savings Bank Foundation Grants   623
Since 1907 Claremont Savings Bank has been committed to serving the needs in the communities where it does business. Monetary donations or sponsorship, in-kind donations or promotional items and volunteer support can be requested. It is the Claremont Savings Bank Foundation's practice to support non-profit groups as a whole. While donations to individuals do not qualify, Claremont Savings Bank may instead elect to contribute directly to the organization. Primary areas of interest include: arts and culture; civic projects; social services; affordable housing; health; minorities; community nonprofits; K-12 education; the environment; and families. The Foundation was developed to fund: projects, programming, and capital expenditures, with the understanding that there is no promise or expectation on annual funding to any organization. The Foundation will consider multi-year pledge requests, however, this practice must be limited and monitored carefully. The sizes of grants generally range from $500 to $5,000. The annual deadline for application submission is May 10.
Requirements: Any 501(c)3 supporting the following New Hampshire communities are eligible to apply: Claremont; Charlestown; or West Lebanon. Additionally, any nonprofit serving the broader New Hampshire counties of Sullivan and Windsor are eligible. Finally, grant awards and donations are also available in the Vermont community of Springfield.
Restrictions: The Foundation does not support: individuals; for profit businesses; government agencies; travel; political organizations; campaigns or candidates; lobbying' or religious purposes.
Geographic Focus: New Hampshire, Vermont
Date(s) Application is Due: May 10
Amount of Grant: 500 - 5,000 USD
Contact: Carolyn Mackenzie, Executive Assistant to the President; 603-542-7711 or 603-690-2713; fax 603-542-5432; cmackenzie@claremontsavings.com
Internet: www.claremontsavings.com/foundation-guidelines-and-criteria.html
Sponsor: Claremont Savings Bank Foundation
145 Broad Street, P.O. Box 1600
Claremont, NH 03743

Clarence T.C. Ching Foundation Grants   624
Founded in 1967 by businessman, developer and philanthropist Clarence T.C. Ching, the Foundation exists to fulfill Ching's vision of helping people in need. Today, as a charitable, private 501(c)3 organization, the Foundation annually donates monies to public and private educational institutions, health, and social service organizations in Honolulu, Hawaii. The Foundation's Mission Statement includes four goals: to assist in the care of the needy, the destitute, the sick and the aged; to provide scholarship aid and assistance, without regard to amount or need and in the form of grants and loans, to those who demonstrate the capacity and desire to improve themselves or develop their capabilities; to provide financial grants to qualified persons, associations and institutions for research and study in all fields, including but not limited to the natural sciences, social sciences, art, literature and music for the advancement of knowledge and culture; and to assist hospitals and other public charitable or educational institutions which qualify as and are treated as tax-exempt organizations, whether supported wholly or in part by private endowment or by donations or by public taxation, with monetary contributions to defray their cost of operation and other proper expenses incurred by them. Types of support available are: scholarship funds; general

operating support; and building and renovation. Grant applications are accepted year round with two application submission deadlines: January 31 and July 31.

Requirements: Nonprofit 501(c)3 organizations in Honolulu, Hawaii, are eligible for funding. When applying for a grant include the following in with the proposal: copy of IRS determination letter; detailed description of project; amount of funding requested; and listing of additional sources and amount of support. Five (5) copies of the proposal should be submitted.

Restrictions: The Foundation will not consider grant applications for: projects outside of the State of Hawaii; projects for which matching funds are borrowed (loans); individuals; political organizations or candidates; ordinary government services; publications, films, or videos; commercial and business development; conferences and seminars; benefit events (table sales or golf tournaments); annual fund drives; or endowments.

Geographic Focus: Hawaii
Date(s) Application is Due: Jan 31; Jul 31
Amount of Grant: 500 - 70,000 USD
Samples: Mediation Center of the Pacific, Honolulu, Hawaii, $250,000 - building renovations (2021); Helping Hands Hawaii, Honolulu, Hawaii, $250,000 - assistance for families in need (2020); Habitat Maui, Lahaina, Hawaii, $35,000 - affordable homes (2020).
Contact: Tertia Freas, Executive Director; (808) 521-0344; admin@chingfoundation.org
Internet: www.clarencetcchingfoundation.org/grant-making
Sponsor: Clarence T.C. Ching Foundation
1001 Bishop Street, Suite 770
Honolulu, HI 96813

Clark and Ruby Baker Foundation Grants   625

The Clark and Ruby Baker Foundation was established to address a number of charitable concerns. The Baker family cared deeply about the Methodist Church and founded the Foundation to support Methodist affiliated, higher educational institutions in rural or small towns; charitable organizations that serve infirm, deserving, and aged ministers; economically disadvantaged and deserving children; and orphans and orphanages. The Foundation also provides support to charitable organizations that extend financial aid to the sick and infirm receiving medical treatment in any hospital or clinic in the state of Georgia. Capital support may be considered for the following purposes: for construction of educational facilities at a college or university; for clinics and hospitals; for libraries; and for any building with a charitable use. Grants from the Clark and Ruby Baker Foundation are primarily one year in duration; on occasion, multi-year support is awarded. Award amounts typically range from $2,000 to $25,000.

Requirements: Applicants must have 501(c)3 tax-exempt status and serve communities in the state of Georgia. Applications will be submitted online through the Bank of America website. A grant report is required within 1 year of the grant application date, regardless of whether all of the funds have been spent.

Restrictions: The foundation does not support requests from individuals, organizations attempting to influence policy through direct lobbying, or any political campaigns.

Geographic Focus: Georgia
Date(s) Application is Due: Jun 1
Amount of Grant: 2,000 - 25,000 USD
Samples: Murphy-Harpst Children's Centers, Cedartown, Georgia, $18,000 - Awarded for General operations of the organization (2018); United Methodist Childrens Home of North Georgia Conference Inc., Tucker, Georgia, $18,000 - Awarded for Fostering Hope Project (2018); Methodist Home of the South Georgia Conference, Macon, Georgia, $17,000 - Awarded for HOPE Foster Care Program (2018).
Contact: Mark S. Drake, Vice President; (404) 264-1377; ga.grantmaking@bankofamerica.com or mark.s.drake@bofa.com
Internet: www.bankofamerica.com/philanthropic/foundation/?fnId=94
Sponsor: Clark and Ruby Baker Foundation
P.O. BOX 40200 FL9-300-01-16
Jacksonville, FL 32203-0200

Clark County Community Foundation Grants   626

Since 1999, the Clark County Community Foundation has awarded over $3.6 million to nonprofits serving Clark County. It would be hard to find a Clark County nonprofit that has not received much-need support through its competitive grantmaking program. Funded projects include a five-year pilot program to provide preventive dental care in Clark County schools; support for a free clinic serving the uninsured; and initiatives to increase the number of students who take advanced placement classes at Clark County High School.

Requirements: Clark County, Kentucky, nonprofit organizations are eligible.
Geographic Focus: Kentucky
Date(s) Application is Due: Mar 15; May 15
Amount of Grant: 5,000 - 10,000 USD
Contact: Kassie Branham; (859) 225-3343; fax (859) 243-0770; kbranham@bgcf.org
Internet: bgcf.org/learn/community-funds/clark-county-community-foundation/
Sponsor: Clark County Community Foundation
499 East High Street, Suite 112
Lexington, KY 40507

Clark Electric Cooperative Grants   627

Established in Wisconsin in 2004, the Clark Electric Cooperative (initially known as the Adler-Clark Electric Community Commitment Foundation) offers grants in Clark County, Wisconsin. It supports athletics and amateur leagues, fire prevention and control, education, food banks, food services, health care, human services, public libraries, and recreation programs, as well as support for rewiring dairy farms. Types of support include: equipment purchase; general operations; and program development. A formal application is required, and the annual deadline has been identified as December 1. Funding amounts range from $500 to $3,000.

Geographic Focus: Wisconsin

Date(s) Application is Due: Dec 1
Amount of Grant: 500 - 3,000 USD
Contact: Mike Ruffs; (715) 267-6188 or (800) 272-6188; mruff@cecoop.com
Internet: www.cecoop.com/
Sponsor: Clark Electric Cooperative
1209 West Dall-Berg Road
Greenwood, WI 54437

Claude A. and Blanche McCubbin Abbott Charitable Trust Grants   628

The Claude A. and Blanche McCubbin Abbott Charitable Trust offers grants primarily in the states of Florida and Maryland. Its identified fields of interest include Catholic agencies and churches, as well as human services. Awards typically come in the form of general operating funds. There are no specified application forms or annual deadlines, and interested parties should begin by contacting the Trust to discuss the program and needed budget support. Grant amounts have typically ranged from $100 to $2,000.

Geographic Focus: Florida, Maryland
Amount of Grant: 100 - 2,000 USD
Samples: Children's Cancer Foundation, Baltimore, Maryland, $1,000 - for general operations; Florida Studio Theatre, Sarasota, Florida, $500 - for general operations; Foundation for Baltimore County Public Library, Baltimore, Maryland, $500 - for general operations.
Contact: Christine Wells, Trustee; (410) 788-1890
Sponsor: Claude A. and Blanche McCubbin Abbott Charitable Trust
6400 Baltimore National Pike No. 105
Catonsville, MD 21228

Clayton Baker Trust Grants   629

The Clayton Baker Trust, established in 1960, awards grants to Maryland nonprofit organizations for programs targeting the disadvantaged, with an emphasis on the needs of children. Grants are awarded nationally in the areas of: environmental protection; population control; arms control; and nuclear disarmament. Types of support include: capital and infrastructure; general operating support; seed grants; program development; systems reform; and special projects. There are three annual deadlines for application submission: April 5, August 5, and December 5.

Requirements: Nonprofit organizations supporting residents in Maryland are eligible to apply. The Association of Baltimore Area Grantmakers Common Grant Application Form is required.

Restrictions: Grants do not support the arts, research, higher educational institutions, individuals, building construction/renovation, or endowment funding.

Geographic Focus: Maryland
Date(s) Application is Due: Apr 5; Aug 5; Dec 5
Amount of Grant: 2,000 - 100,000 USD
Samples: Association of Baltimore Area Grantmakers, Baltimore, Maryland, $11,250 - general operating support (2018); New Leaders Maryland, Baltimore, Maryland, $45,000 - general operating support (2018); Arts Education in Maryland Schools, Baltimore, Maryland, $23,000 - general operating support (2018).
Contact: John Powell, Jr., Executive Director; (410) 837-3555; fax (410) 837-7711
Sponsor: Clayton Baker Trust
2 East Read Street, Suite 100
Baltimore, MD 21202

Clayton F. and Ruth L. Hawkridge Foundation Grants   630

The Clayton F. and Ruth L. Hawkridge Foundation was established in Massachusetts in 2002. The Foundation was intended to honor the memory of Clayton F, Hawkridge, long-time president of the Hawkridge Brothers Company, distributors of steel and aluminum products throughout New England. The Foundation's primary fields of interest include: arts and culture; elementary and secondary education; human services; and special needs students. Typically, funding is provided for general operating support and program development. Typically, awards average around $5,000. There are no specific application deadlines.

Geographic Focus: Connecticut, Maine, Massachusetts, New Hampshire, New York, Rhode Island, Vermont
Amount of Grant: 4,000 - 6,000 USD
Samples: Concord Chorale, Concord, New Hampshire, $4,000 - general operating support (2019); Judge Baker Children's Center, Roxbury Crossing, Massachusetts, $5,000 - general operating support (2019); Kurn Hattin Home, Westminster, Vermont, $5,000 - general operating support (2019).
Contact: Walter Angoff, Co-Trustee; (888) 866-3275
Sponsor: Clayton F. and Ruth L. Hawkridge Foundation
P.O. Box 1802
Providence, RI 02901-1802

Clayton Fund Grants   631

The Clayton Fund Trust was established in Texas in 1952, with a primary mission of offering aid to the needy, especially children, the environment, family planning, education, agriculture, and arts and culture. With that in mind, the Fund's current fields of interest have evolved to include: arts and culture; child welfare; diseases; education (both elementary and secondary); family planning; foundation support; higher education; human services; and natural resources. Awards typically take the form of general operating support, program development, continuing support, building campaigns, and endowment funds. Most recent awards have ranged from $5,000 to $200,000.

Requirements: Giving is limited to 501(c)3 organizations that support the residents of Texas, Maryland, and New York.

Restrictions: Grants are not given directly to individuals.
Geographic Focus: Maryland, New York, Texas
Amount of Grant: 5,000 - 200,000 USD

Samples: Boys and Girls of Austin Area, Houston, Texas, $60,000 - general operating support (2018); Communities in School, Houston, Texas, $25,000 - general operating support (2018); Teensmart International, Houston, Texas, $55,000 - general operating support (2018).
Contact: William Garwood, President; (713) 216-1453
Sponsor: Clayton Fund
712 Main Street 11th Floor North
Houston, TX 77002

Cleo Foundation Grants 632

The Cleo Foundation board meets once each year to support public charities in San Francisco, San Benito, Mendocino, and southern Monterey counties. The Foundation's primary interest is supporting organizations that benefit at-risk and/or low-income children, youth, and adults. Typically, support is offered for academic enrichment, outdoor education, and hospice care. The Foundation is most interested in programs that can make good use of relatively small grants. Types of support include: building construction and renovation; capital campaigns; continuing support; operating support; and program development. Invitations to submit an online application will be issued in early summer. Invited applications are due twelve weeks before the annual board meeting.
Requirements: 501(c)3 organizations in San Francisco, San Benito, Mendocino, and southern Monterey counties in California may apply.
Geographic Focus: California
Amount of Grant: 1,000 - 20,000 USD
Samples: Anderson Valley Education Foundation, Boonville, California, $10,000 - for summer internship program (2020); Community Foundation for Monterey County, Monterey, California, $10,000 - to support CASA of Monterey County (2020); Epicenter of Monterey, Salinas, California, $10,000 - provides virtual tutoring for high school and college students (2020).
Contact: ennifer Perez Brown; (415) 561-6540 ext. 255; fax (415) 561-6477; jbrown@pfs-llc.net
Internet: www.cleofoundation.org/for-grantseekers/application-procedures/
Sponsor: Cleo Foundation
1660 Bush Street, Suite 300
San Francisco, CA 94109

Cleveland Browns Foundation Grants 633

The Cleveland Browns Foundation supports the northeast Ohio community by funding programs that improve the lives of disadvantaged children. The foundation's four major focus areas are education, arts and culture, health, and career development as they relate to children. There are no application deadlines. All sponsorships and financial requests should be submitted in writing at least six (6) weeks in advance of an event. All donation requests should be submitted online.
Requirements: Northern Ohio nonprofit organizations are eligible to apply.
Restrictions: Organizations and causes that will not be considered for funding include fund-raising, sponsorship events, or donation requests; religious organizations for sectarian religious purposes; general or annual operation expenses; capital or building funds; or staff salaries or stipends.
Geographic Focus: Ohio
Contact: Dee Bagwell Haslam, President; (440) 891-5063; fax (440) 891-7529
Internet: www.clevelandbrowns.com/community/in-kind-support.html
Sponsor: Cleveland Browns Foundation
76 Lou Groza Boulevard
Berea, OH 44017

Cleveland Foundation Higley Fund Grants 634

The primary focus for responsive grant making in the Higley Fund program is project-based support for basic human needs with a particular interest in food, housing, education/training, health, and crisis intervention in Cuyahoga County. Grants typically range from $10,000 to $25,000. The annual deadlines for applications are March 1 and August 1.
Requirements: The Cleveland Foundation makes most of its grants to tax-exempt (private agencies classified as 501(c)3 organizations) public charities as defined by the Internal Revenue Service. Some grants are also made to government agencies. The foundation requires all potential grant applicants to submit a grant inquiry, outlining basic information about the proposed project. Grant inquiries can be submitted at any time. If it is determined that your project fits the foundation's guidelines, you will be asked within a few weeks to submit a full application. It is recommended to submit one inquiry per proposed project. Grants are awarded on a quarterly basis.
Restrictions: Grants will not be awarded to/for: individuals; for-profit organizations; endowment campaigns, annual appeals, or membership drives; religious organizations for religious purposes; travel for individuals or groups when travel is the proposal's primary focus; community services such as police and fire protection; staff positions for government agencies; capital projects for hospitals, nursing homes, or institutions of higher education; publications, audiovisual projects, or video productions, however, consideration may be given when they fall within a promising project.
Geographic Focus: Ohio
Date(s) Application is Due: Mar 1; Aug 1
Amount of Grant: 10,000 - 25,000 USD
Contact: Stephen Caviness; (216) 615-7254 or (216) 861-3810; scaviness@CleveFdn.org
Internet: www.clevelandfoundation.org/grants/affiliated-funds/
Sponsor: Cleveland Foundation
1422 Euclid Avenue, Suite 1300
Cleveland, OH 44115

Cleveland Foundation Lake-Geauga Fund Grants 635

The Lake-Geauga Fund of the Cleveland Foundation was established in 1986 in response to the number of key institutions in the two counties that had long-range impact on the region. The fund was developed by individuals with an interest and passion in supporting growth of

the region and addressing unique needs in Lake and Geauga counties. Both are classified as rural counties with a substantial amount of open space and cultivated farmland. The fund is guided by an advisory committee of residents who have a knowledge and passion for their communities. As a supplement to the Foundation's enhanced process, organizations can now apply directly to the Lake-Geauga Fund one time per year by responding to the Request for Proposal. Applications are accepted online each year with a September 29 deadline.
Requirements: The Cleveland Foundation makes most of its grants to tax-exempt (private agencies classified as 501(c)3 organizations) public charities as defined by the Internal Revenue Service. Some grants are also made to government agencies. The foundation requires all potential grant applicants to submit a grant inquiry, outlining basic information about the proposed project. Grant inquiries can be submitted at any time. If it is determined that your project fits the foundation's guidelines, you will be asked within a few weeks to submit a full application. It is recommended to submit one inquiry per proposed project. Grants are awarded on a quarterly basis.
Restrictions: Grants will not be awarded to/for: individuals; for-profit organizations; endowment campaigns, annual appeals, or membership drives; religious organizations for religious purposes; travel for individuals or groups when travel is the proposal's primary focus; community services such as police and fire protection; staff positions for government agencies; capital projects for hospitals, nursing homes, or institutions of higher education; publications, audiovisual projects, or video productions, however, consideration may be given when they fall within a promising project.
Geographic Focus: Ohio
Date(s) Application is Due: Sep 29
Amount of Grant: Up to 100,000 USD
Samples: Catholic Charities Corporation, Cleveland, Ohio, $28,718 - support of a workplace-based resource program for Geauga County; Center for Community Solutions, Cleveland, Ohio, $55,470 - support of the Geauga Income Collaborative program; Friends of James A. Garfield National Historic Site, Cleveland, Ohio, $25,000 - support of a marketing and technology upgrade for the Garfield Centennial and the 2016 Republican National Convention.
Contact: Stephen Caviness; (216) 615-7254 or (216) 861-3810; scaviness@CleveFdn.org
Internet: www.clevelandfoundation.org/grants/lake-geauga/
Sponsor: Cleveland Foundation
1422 Euclid Avenue, Suite 1300
Cleveland, OH 44115

Cleveland Foundation Legacy Village Lyndhurst Community Fund Grants 636

The purpose of the Legacy Village Lyndhurst Community Fund is primarily to support philanthropic and other charitable purposes in Lyndhurst its contiguous communities and the South Euclid-Lyndhurst public schools. It is the intent of the funds to primarily benefit the South Euclid-Lyndhurst Public Schools and various programs and not-for-profit organizations serving the residents of the City of Lyndhurst and its contiguous communities. The fund will award multiple grants ranging from $250 to $5,000. The annual deadlines for application submission are March 1 and August 1.
Requirements: The Cleveland Foundation makes most of its grants to tax-exempt (private agencies classified as 501(c)3 organizations) public charities as defined by the Internal Revenue Service. Some grants are also made to government agencies. The foundation requires all potential grant applicants to submit a grant inquiry, outlining basic information about the proposed project. Grant inquiries can be submitted at any time. If it is determined that your project fits the foundation's guidelines, you will be asked within a few weeks to submit a full application. It is recommended to submit one inquiry per proposed project.
Restrictions: Grants will not be awarded to/for: individuals; for-profit organizations; endowment campaigns, annual appeals, or membership drives; religious organizations for religious purposes; travel for individuals or groups when travel is the proposal's primary focus; community services such as police and fire protection; staff positions for government agencies; capital projects for hospitals, nursing homes, or institutions of higher education; publications, audiovisual projects, or video productions, however, consideration may be given when they fall within a promising project.
Geographic Focus: Ohio
Date(s) Application is Due: Mar 1; Aug 1
Amount of Grant: 250 - 5,000 USD
Contact: Stephen Caviness, Program Officer; (216) 615-7254 or (216) 861-3810
Internet: www.clevelandfoundation.org/grants/affiliated-funds/
Sponsor: Cleveland Foundation
1422 Euclid Avenue, Suite 1300
Cleveland, OH 44115

Cleveland H. Dodge Foundation Grants 637

The Cleveland H. Dodge Foundation awards grants to support projects and programs of educational and charitable nonprofit organizations concerned with the training and development of youth. It is the policy of the Foundation to give priority to institutions and agencies in New York City with programmatic activities in the following categories: those which help underprivileged youth build good character and sound values; those with innovative programs that focus on early childhood education; and those supported by both the Founder and his descendants that continue to perform effective services. Types of support include: building and renovation; equipment acquisition; endowment funds; and matching funds.
Requirements: IRS 501(c)3 nonprofit organizations serving New York City, as well as national programs, are eligible.
Restrictions: The Foundation makes grants only to established institutions. It does not: support individuals through scholarship or other aid; support institutions dealing mainly with medical research, health care or health care training; generally support independent schools, colleges and universities excepting those that the Foundation has consistently supported over a long period of time, or to match gifts made under matching gift plans; make loans; manage programs or projects; or make grants to endowment.

Geographic Focus: All States
Date(s) Application is Due: Jan 15; Apr 15; Sep 15
Amount of Grant: 100 - 25,000 USD
Contact: William D. Rueckert, Executive Director; (212) 972-2800; fax (212) 972-1049; info@chdodgefoundation.org
Internet: www.chdodgefoundation.org/guidelines.shtml
Sponsor: Cleveland H. Dodge Foundation
420 Lexington Avenue, Suite 2331
New York, NY 10170

Clinton County Community Foundation Grants 638

The Clinton County Community Foundation is a catalyst for stimulating and funding initiatives that improve the quality of life for citizens of Clinton County. The Foundation Grants address needs that generally fall into the following categories: health and medical; social services; education; cultural affairs; civic affairs; and community beautification.
Requirements: All applicants must receive pre-qualification prior to submitting an application by submitting a letter of inquiry to the Program Director. The letter should contain a brief statement of the applicant's needs for assistance, estimate of total cost of project, and enough information to enable the Foundation to determine if the application falls within the guidelines of its grants program. If the grant application is decided, organizations must submit one original application, plus ten copies required for review by the grantmaking committee with the following information included: grant application with the cover page; project budget; board list; evidence of board approval; 501(c)3 letter; year-end audit or financial statement; current month and year-to-date financial statement; and when applicable, three estimates must be included, one from a Clinton County business. The organization may be contacted for additional information, an interview with the grant making committee, or a possible site visit, and the time period which a grant decision will likely be made.
Geographic Focus: Indiana
Date(s) Application is Due: May 6; Sep 7
Contact: Kim Abney; (765) 454-7298 or (800) 964-0508; kim@cfhoward.org
Internet: www.cfclinton.org/grant_seekers_cl.html
Sponsor: Clinton County Community Foundation
215 West Sycamore Street
Kokomo, IN 46901

CMS Historically Black Colleges and Universities (HBCU) Health Services Research Grants 639

The purpose of the Historically Black Colleges and Universities (HBCU) Health Services Research Grant program is to support researchers in implementing health services research activities to meet the needs of diverse CMS beneficiary populations. The goals of the grant program are to: encourage HBCU health services researchers to pursue research issues which impact the Medicare, Medicaid, and SCHIP (State Children's Health Insurance Program) programs; assist CMS in implementing its mission focusing on health care quality and improvement for its beneficiaries; assist HBCU researchers by supporting extramural research in health care capacity development activities for the African American communities; increase the pool of HBCU researchers capable of implementing the research, demonstration, and evaluation activities of CMS; and assist in fostering inter-university communication and collaboration regarding African American health disparity issues. Funding is available for grants to implement research related to health care delivery and health financing issues affecting African American communities, including issues of access to health care, utilization of health care services, health outcomes, quality of services, cost of care, health and racial disparities, socioeconomic differences, cultural barriers, managed care systems, and activities related to health screening, prevention, outreach, and education.
Requirements: To be eligible for grants under this program, an organization must be an HBCU (Historically Black College or University) and meet one of the following three *Requirements:* offer a Ph.D. or Master's Degree program in one or more of the following disciplines - Allied Health, Gerontology, Health Care Administration, Health Education, Health Management, Nursing, Nutrition, Pharmacology, Public Health, Public Policy, Social Work; have a School of Medicine; or have a member of the National HBCU Network for Health Services and Health Disparities. All proposals should describe research to be conducted with relevance to the CMS Medicare, Medicaid, and SCHIP programs and which area of Healthy People is served by this project. Applications must be submitted electronically.
Restrictions: Grant funds may not be used for any of the following: to provide direct services to individuals except as explicitly permitted under the grant solicitation; to match any other Federal funds; to provide services, equipment, or supports that are already the legal responsibility of another party under Federal law.
Geographic Focus: All States
Date(s) Application is Due: Jul 18
Amount of Grant: 200,000 - 250,000 USD
Contact: Linda Gmeiner, Grants Management Specialist; (410) 786-9954 or (410) 786-3000; linda.gmeiner@cms.hhs.gov
Internet: www.cms.gov/Research-Statistics-Data-and-Systems/Research/Research DemoGrantsOpt/Historically_Black_Colleges_and_Universities.html
Sponsor: Centers for Medicare and Medicaid Services
7500 Security Boulevard, Room C2-21-15
Baltimore, MD 21244-1850

CMS Research and Demonstration Grants 640

The general purpose of the Centers for Medicare and Medicaid Services' (CMS) research and demonstration grant program is to conduct and support projects to develop, test, and implement new health care financing and payment policies and to evaluate the impact of the agency's programs on its beneficiaries, providers, States, and other customers and partners. The scope of the agency's activities embraces all areas of health care: costs, access, quality, service delivery models, and financing and payment approaches. Generally, the Agency's extramural research and demonstration activities, such as evaluations, demonstration implementation, and research studies, are funded through contracts. CMS awards grants and cooperative agreements under certain specific, focused programs.
Requirements: The following themes represent the agency's current priorities in research. Note that all projects must fall into the agency's statutory authorities to operate and improve Medicare, Medicaid, and other CMS programs and activities: monitoring and evaluating CMS programs; strengthening medicaid, the State Children's Health Insurance Program (SCHIP), and other state programs; expanding beneficiaries' choices and availability of managed care options; developing FFS payment and service delivery systems; improving quality of care and performance under CMS programs; improving the health of our beneficiary population; prescription drugs; and building research capacity. An application kit is available online.
Restrictions: Applicants are expected to contribute towards the project costs. Generally five percent of the total project costs is considered acceptable. CMS rarely approves grants or cooperative agreements for research or demonstration projects in which the Federal Government covers 100 percent of the project's costs. The budget may not include costs for construction or remodeling or for project activities that take place before the applicant has received official notification of our approval of the project.
Geographic Focus: All States
Amount of Grant: 25,000 - 1,000,000 USD
Contact: Linda Gmeiner, Grants Management Specialist; (410) 786-9954 or (410) 786-3000; linda.gmeiner@cms.hhs.gov
Internet: www.cms.gov/Research-Statistics-Data-and-Systems/Research/Research DemoGrantsOpt/index.html?redirect=/ResearchDemoGrantsOpt/04_Other_CMS-Grant_Opportunities.asp
Sponsor: Centers for Medicare and Medicaid Services
7500 Security Boulevard, Room C2-21-15
Baltimore, MD 21244-1850

CNCS AmeriCorps Indian Tribes Planning Grants 641

AmeriCorps planning grants provide up to $75,000 for a one-year period to provide support to an Indian Tribe for the development of an AmeriCorps program that will engage AmeriCorps members in order to address pressing community problems. Planning grant recipients are expected to be better prepared to compete for an AmeriCorps program grant in the following grant cycle. Planning grants may not be used to support AmeriCorps members. An AmeriCorps member is an individual (recruited by an AmeriCorps grant program) who is enrolled in an approved national service position and engages in community service. Members may receive a living allowance and other benefits while serving. Upon successful completion of their service members receive a Segal AmeriCorps Education Award from the National Service Trust. CNCS is targeting AmeriCorps funding in the Education, Disaster Services, Economic Opportunity and Veterans and Military Families Focus Areas. Applications are due May 30.
Requirements: Applicants must be a federally recognized Indian Tribe, band, nation, or other organized group or community, including any Native village, Regional Corporation, or Village Corporation.
Restrictions: Planning grants may not be used to support AmeriCorps members. Project start dates may not occur prior to the date of award. Organizations that have been convicted of a Federal crime are not eligible to apply. Indian Tribe applicants must not have previously received an AmeriCorps grant.
Geographic Focus: All States
Date(s) Application is Due: May 30
Amount of Grant: Up to 75,000 USD
Contact: Vielka Garibaldi, Director for Grants Review Operations; (202) 606-7508 or (202) 606-6886; americorpsgrants@cns.gov
John Gomperts, Director, AmeriCorps State and National; (202) 606-6790 or (202) 606-5000; americorpsgrants@cns.gov
Internet: www.nationalservice.gov/build-your-capacity/grants/funding-opportunities/2013/americorps-indian-tribes-planning-grants
Sponsor: Corporation for National and Community Service
1201 New York Avenue, NW
Washington, D.C. 20525

CNCS AmeriCorps NCCC Project Grants 642

Modeled after the Civilian Conservation Corps of the 1930s and the U.S. military, AmeriCorps NCCC (National Civilian Community Corps) was enacted in 1993 as a demonstration program and is currently a full-time, team-based, ten-month residential program for men and women ages 18–24. While NCCC teams resemble their CCC predecessors, who also functioned under rugged conditions for prolonged periods and engaged in strenuous conservation, wildfire-fighting, flood-control, and disaster-relief projects, the NCCC was not created to be a public-work-relief program, but rather was designed to help communities meet self-identified needs through service projects. The stated mission of AmeriCorps NCCC is "to strengthen communities and develop leaders through direct team-based national and community service." NCCC service projects normally last six to eight weeks and address community needs in the following program areas: natural and other disasters; infrastructure improvement; environmental stewardship and conservation; energy conservation; and urban and rural development. AmeriCorps NCCC has five regional campuses located in Perry Point, Maryland; Denver, Colorado; Sacramento, California; Vicksburg, Mississippi; and Vinton, Iowa. These campuses are the hubs from which AmeriCorps NCCC operates and deploys corps members in teams of eight to twelve to service projects around the country. Each campus serves as a headquarters for its multi-state region and can lodge and feed its entire regional corps, which ranges in size from 150 to 500 members. The staffs at the campuses support both the corps members and project sponsors as they engage in service activities. Members are given a living allowance of approximately $4,000 for 10 months of service; housing; meals; limited medical benefits; up to $400 a month for childcare if eligible; member uniforms; and become eligible for the Segal AmeriCorps Education Award upon successful completion of the program.

Requirements: The following organizations are eligible to apply for NCCC resources: non-profits, secular and faith based; local municipalities; state governments; federal government; national or state parks; Indian tribes; and schools. Projects must be capable of using at least one full team of eight to twelve members effectively. Transportation and some basic tools will be provided by the NCCC; however, project sponsors are required to provide materials, specialized tools, orientation, training, and technical supervision.

Geographic Focus: All States

Contact: Kate Raftery, Director, Office of AmeriCorps NCCC; (202) 606-6706

Erma Hodge, Executive Assistant

Internet: www.nationalservice.gov/programs/americorps/americorps-nccc

Sponsor: Corporation for National and Community Service

1201 New York Avenue, NW

Washington, D.C. 20525

CNCS AmeriCorps State and National Grants 643

AmeriCorps State and National is the broadest of the AmeriCorps programs and, like other programs administered by the Corporation for National and Community Service (the Corporation), has recently been expanded under the Edward Kennedy Serve America Act (SAA). The SAA increases the annual number of persons volunteering in the Corporations's programs from 75,000 to 250,000 by 2017 and incorporates five new service corps into AmeriCorps State and National: a Clean Energy Corps to encourage energy efficiency and conservation; an Education Corps to help increase student engagement, achievement and graduation; a Healthy Futures Corps to improve health care access; a Veterans Service Corps to enhance services for veterans; and a Opportunity Corps. AmeriCorps State and National engages its volunteers (members) with local sponsors in direct service and capacity-building to address critical community needs, usually under the arrangement that AmeriCorps covers expenses of the volunteers and the sponsor covers costs of the program. Sponsors are expected to design service activities for AmeriCorps teams of eight to twelve members serving full- or part-time for one year or during the summer. Sample service activities include tutoring and mentoring youth, providing job-placement assistance to unemployed individuals, addressing childhood obesity through in-school and after-school physical activities, and weatherizing and retrofitting housing units for low-income households. AmeriCorps State and National Grants cover a wide range of grants. National opportunities are announced through Notices at the AmeriCorps website or at www.grants.gov. Regional funding opportunites are announced through the various AmeriCorps State Commissions, which are governor-appointed agencies that have direct accountability for local AmeriCorps programs in each state. Types of grants may include the following: Competitive State Grants, Professional Corps Grants, EAP (Educational Award Program) Fixed grants and Non-EAP Full-Time Fixed grants. A brief breakdown of these follows. Competitive State Grants are awarded to fund a portion of program costs and members' living allowance. Professional Corps Grants are awarded to pay a portion of program costs to place AmeriCorps members as teachers, health care providers, police officers, engineers, or other professionals in communities where there is a documented shortage of such professionals. EAP Fixed Grants are awarded to applicants that apply for a small fixed-amount grant and use their own or other resources for the majority of members' living allowance and program costs. (EAPs may enroll less-than-full-time members.) Non-EAP Full-time Fixed-amount Grant are awarded to applicants who apply for a fixed amount per Member Service Year (MSY) and use their own or other resources for the remaining cost of the program. Additionally, AmeriCorps State and National offers a "fit-finder" tool at their website which will help organizations match their program or project to the right State and National grant and will then take them directly to the latest applicable Notice for that grant. The fit-finder lists available types of State and National grants as follows: State Grants; National Direct Grants; EAP Grants; and Indian Tribe Grants. (The fit finder is located at www.americorps.gov/fitfinder/index.html.) As with types of grants offered, methods of applying may also vary, depending on the sponsor's program or project scope. Single-state applicants must contact their State Commission for instructions and deadlines (contact information for all the State Commissions is available at the AmeriCorps website). Single state applicants must apply directly to their State Commission. State Commissions then forward the projects they select to the Corporation to compete for funding. Organizations proposing to operate in more than one state or organizations operating in states and territories without Commissions must apply directly to the Corporation. (Multi-state applicants are also required to consult with the State Commission of each state in which they plan to operate prior to application submission.) Indian Tribes may apply through their State Commissions, or directly to the Corporation (the Corporation sets aside one percent of grant funds to support programs operated by Indian Tribes). State commissions, multi-state applicants, and Indian Tribes are encouraged to send an email to americorpsgrants@cns.gov, stating intent to apply. Commission sub-applicants should not provide this information. The Corporation requires applicants to submit applications electronically via the Corporation's web-based application system, eGrants. Applicants should draft the application as a word processing document, then copy and paste the document into eGrants no later than 10 days before the deadline. The Corporation may consider an application after the deadline, but only if the applicant submits a letter explaining the extenuating circumstance which caused the delay. The letter must be sent to LateApplications@cns.gov within the 24-hour period following the deadline. Late applications are evaluated on a case-by-case basis. If extenuating circumstances make the use of eGrants impossible, applicants may send a hard copy of the application to the contact information given in the Notice. Hard copy applications must include a cover letter detailing the circumstances that make it impossible to submit via e-Grants. Grant awards are typically awarded for three years, with funding in annual increments. Grantees will be eligible for non-competitive continuation funding in the second and third year contingent

on satisfactory performance, compliance, and availability of appropriations. In awarding funds, CNCS considers continuation grants first, followed by new and re-competing grants.

Requirements: Eligible organizations are as follows: public or private nonprofit organizations, including faith-based and other community organizations; institutions of higher education; government entities within states or territories (e.g., cities, counties); Indian Tribes; labor organizations; partnerships and consortia; and intermediaries planning to subgrant funds awarded. Applicants must register with the Central Contractor's Registry (CCR) and include a Dun and Bradstreet Data Universal Numbering System (DUNS) number on their application. These may be obtained at no cost by calling the DUNS number request line at (866) 705-5711 or by applying online. The website indicates a 24-hour email turnaround time on requests for DUNS numbers; however, the Corporation suggests registering at least 30 days in advance of the application due date. AmeriCorps State and National Grants have varying match requirements. There is no match requirement for fixed-amount grants. Cost reimbursement grants (non-fixed-amount) are required to match at 24 percent for the first three-year funding period. Starting with year four, the match requirement gradually increases every year to 50 percent by year ten. (Living allowances or salaries provided to Professional Corps AmeriCorps members do not count toward the matching requirement.) Indian Tribal Government programs are subject to the same matching requirements for fixed-amount and cost reimbursement grants. However, Tribal governments may under some circumstances apply for a Tribal waiver. Under certain circumstances, applicants may qualify to meet alternative matching requirements that increase over the years to 35 percent instead of 50 percent. To qualify, applicants must demonstrate that the proposed program is either located in a rural county or in a severely economically distressed community as defined in the Application Instructions. Applicants that plan to request an alternative match schedule must submit a request at least 60 days prior to the application deadline.

Restrictions: The Corporation will encourage organizations that have never received funding from them or AmeriCorps to apply for the grants described in their Notices. The general practice is to award no more than 50 member slots for new grantees. Organizations that have been convicted of a Federal crime are disqualified from receiving these grants. Grants under this program, except for fixed-amount and EAP grants, are subject to the applicable Cost Principles under Office of Management and Budget (OMB) Circulars A-21 (2 CFR part 220), A-122 (2 CFR part 230), or A-87 (2 CFR part 225) and the Uniform Administrative Requirements for grants under A-102 (45 CFR part 2541) or A-110 (45 CFR 2543 or 2 CFR part 21).

Geographic Focus: All States

Date(s) Application is Due: Jan 18

Amount of Grant: 6,400 - 159,600 USD

Samples: Citizen Schools, Inc., Boston, Massachusetts, $2,781,979 - to deploy full-time AmeriCorps members to narrow the achievement gap by expanding the learning day in intensive extended-day programs that partner with high-need middle schools across seven states; Duluth Public Schools, Duluth, Minnesota, $1,033,200 - to engage AmeriCorps members to make a measurable difference in reducing Minnesota's drop-out rate by providing evidence-based supports to students in grades 6 - 10; Reading Partners, Oakland, California, $530,000 - to request 40 members who will operate reading centers at under-resourced elementary schools where trained volunteers provide 1:1 literacy tutoring to struggling readers.

Contact: Vielka Garibaldi, Director for Grant Review Operations; (202) 606-7508 or (202) 606-6886; americorpsgrants@cns.gov

Internet: www.nationalservice.gov/programs/americorps/americorps-state-and-national

Sponsor: Corporation for National and Community Service

1201 New York Avenue, NW

Washington, D.C. 20525

CNCS AmeriCorps State and National Planning Grants 644

AmeriCorps is a funding stream of the Corporation for National and Community Service (the Corporation) and includes the national-service programs AmeriCorps Vista, AmeriCorps NCCC, and AmeriCorps State and National. The latter is the broadest of the AmeriCorps programs and, like the rest, has recently been expanded under the Edward Kennedy Serve America Act of 2009 (SAA), which proposes an increase from 75,000 to 250,000 annual volunteers. The SAA incorporates five new service corps into the AmeriCorps State and National program: a Clean Energy Corps to encourage energy efficiency and conservation; an Education Corps to help increase student engagement, achievement and graduation; a Healthy Futures Corps to improve health care access; a Veterans Service Corps to enhance services for veterans; and an Opportunity Corps. The ultimate purpose of the AmeriCorps State and National program is to engage AmeriCorps volunteers (members) with local sponsors in direct service and capacity building to address critical community needs, usually under a cost-sharing arrangement where AmeriCorps covers expenses of the volunteers and the sponsor covers costs of the program. AmeriCorps planning grants support sponsors in developing candidate programs to engage AmeriCorps members in evidence-based interventions to solve community problems. Planning-grant recipients are expected to be better prepared to compete for an AmeriCorps program grant in the following grant cycle. Planning grants may not be used to support AmeriCorps members. Planning-grant project periods last up to one year in duration. The process of competing for federal funding in general is as follows. Types of funding offered by federal programs are set forth in the program's enabling legislation. Grant competitions for a program's funding tend to follow congressional budget and appropriations cycles (as well as multi-year funding cycles in some cases) and are announced through various Notices which provide details, guidelines, and deadlines for the competition. Notices are posted at AmeriCorp's and www.grants.gov websites. A subscription link is also provided at these sites for prospective applicants to be notified via email of upcoming grant competitions. In addition to statutory priorities, the Corporation determines priorities to focus each grant competition. Priorities are drawn from among the Corporation's strategic service areas which include education, healthy futures, environmental stewardship, veterans and military families, economic opportunity, and disaster preparedness (with special consideration given to activities that support and engage veterans and military families). Additionally Congress has set a goal that 10% of AmeriCorps funding should support encore service programs. To meet this target, the Corporation encourages programs that plan to engage a significant number of participants age fifty-five and older to apply. Sponsors that propose to operate an AmeriCorps program in one state only must contact the appropriate State Commission for application materials and must submit their application through that Commission. (State Commissions are organizations appointed by state governors to assume accountability for all AmeriCorps projects within their state.) Contact information for all the State Commissions is available at the AmeriCorps and Corporation websites. Sponsors that propose to operate in more than one state should apply directly to the Corporation. However, multi-state planning applicants must consult with the State Commission of each state in which the organization plans to operate an AmeriCorps program prior to application submission. Grant applications are submitted via eGrants, the Corporation's web-based system for grant application and management. Generally a series of technical assistance calls or workshops will be offered before the application is due. The dates of these will be posted at the Corporation's website. Applications are due no later than 5 p.m. eastern time on the deadline date. Prospective applicants must create an account at the eGrant website (link available at the Corporation website). Applicants are advised to do this at least three weeks prior to the application-submission deadline. Applicants are advised to draft the application as a word-processing document, then copy and paste the document into eGrants no later than ten days before the deadline. If extenuating circumstances make electronic submission impossible, applicants should send a hard copy of their application via overnight carrier (non-U.S. Postal Service because of security–related delays in receiving mail from the U.S. Postal Service). Hard-copy applications must include a cover letter detailing the circumstances that make it impossible to submit via e-Grants. Late applications may be accepted only if the applicant submits a letter via email to LateApplications@cns.gov within the 24-hour period following the deadline explaining the extenuating circumstance which caused the delay. Late applications are evaluated on a case-by-case basis. Application and other deadlines may vary from competition to competition. Prospective applicants are encouraged to verify current deadline dates. Notices of Intent are generally requested rather than required and are used to help the Corporation plan the review process.

Requirements: Eligible applicants include public or private nonprofit organizations (including faith-based and other community organizations); institutions of higher education; government entities within states or territories (e.g., cities, counties); Indian Tribes; labor organizations; partnerships and consortia; and intermediaries planning to subgrant funds awarded. Applicants must provide 24% of the total project cost in cash or in-kind. Indian Tribal Government programs are subject to the same matching requirements but may submit a waiver request. This must be done at least 60 days before the AmeriCorps application is due. Instructions are available by emailing TribalMatchWaiver@cns.gov. Applicants must include a Dun and Bradstreet Data Universal Numbering System (DUNS) number on their applications and register with the Central Contractor's Registry (CCR). The DUNS number does not replace an Employer Identification Number (EIN). DUNS numbers may be obtained at no cost by calling the DUNS number request line at (866) 705-5711 or by applying online: fedgov.dnb.com/webform. The website indicates a 24-hour email turnaround time; however, the Corporation suggests registering at least 30 days in advance of the application due date.

Restrictions: Project start dates may not occur prior to the date of award. Organizations that have been convicted of a Federal crime are not eligible to apply. Single-state planning applicants must not have previously received an AmeriCorps State grant. Multi-state planning applicants must not have previously received a multi-state AmeriCorps grant. Applicants may have received funding through Learn and Serve America, AmeriCorps NCCC or Vista, and Senior Corps. Corporation grants are subject to the Cost Principles and Uniform Administrative Requirements under the applicable Office of Management and Budget (OMB) Circulars. Also, awards will be subject to the law(s) under which the award is made.

Geographic Focus: All States

Date(s) Application is Due: Jan 18

Amount of Grant: Up to 50,000 USD

Contact: Vielka Garibaldi, Director for Grant Review Operations; (202) 606-7508 or (202) 606-6886; americorpsgrants@cns.gov

John Gomperts, Director, AmeriCorps State and National; (202) 606-6790 or (202) 606-5000; americorpsgrants@cns.gov

Internet: www.nationalservice.gov/programs/americorps/americorps-state-and-national

Sponsor: Corporation for National and Community Service

1201 New York Avenue, NW

Washington, D.C. 20525

CNCS AmeriCorps VISTA Project Grants 645

AmeriCorps VISTA is a national-service program of the Corporation for National and Community Service (the Corporation) which oversees a variety of programs including other AmeriCorps programs, SeniorCorps programs, and Learn and Serve America programs. Designed specifically to fight poverty, VISTA was authorized in 1964 as Volunteers in Service to America. The program was incorporated into the AmeriCorps network of programs in 1993. VISTA supports efforts to alleviate poverty by encouraging volunteers (members), ages 18 years and older, from all walks of life, to engage in a year of full-time service with a sponsoring organization (sponsor) to create or expand programs designed to bring individuals and communities out of poverty. Under this arrangement, the Corporation places a team of VISTA members with a sponsor; the sponsor funds local operating and logistics costs of the project while the Corporation covers member and certain sponsor costs as follows: a biweekly living allowance for members; a Segal AmeriCorps Education Award or post-service stipend for members; health coverage for members; a moving allowance for members relocating to serve; liability coverage for members under the Federal Employees Compensation Act and the Federal Torts Claims Act; childcare (for income-eligible members); FICA; payroll services (members receive their paychecks directly from AmeriCorps VISTA); training in project management and leadership for

VISTA members and project supervisors; and assistance for sponsors to recruit VISTA members. Applications for VISTA resources are handled by Corporation State Offices which are federal offices staffed by federal employees in the states. (A list of the offices along with their contact information is available at the AmeriCorps website.) Applying for VISTA resources is a two-step process. As step one, the organization must submit a VISTA Concept Paper. If the concept paper is accepted, the organization must, as step two, submit a VISTA Project Application. Applicants will receive their project-application materials when their concept paper has been approved. The length of the application process varies, but the average length of time from the initial contact to a final decision is three to five months. Both concept papers and project applications are usually submitted using eGrants, the Corporation's web-based system for applications. Organizations must visit the eGrant website (link available at the AmeriCorps website) to create an account prior to submitting concept papers. Organizations that cannot submit using eGrants may submit a paper copy. The forms are included in the downloadable Concept-Paper Instructions document at the AmeriCorps website. As of this writing, VISTA is giving priority to new projects that focus on the areas of housing, financial literacy, and employment.

Requirements: Public organizations such as nonprofit private organizations, Indian Tribes, state and local government organizations, and institutions of higher education can apply to be VISTA sponsors. Eligible nonprofit private organizations are not limited to those with IRS 501(c)3 status, but rather all organizations with IRS 501(c) status that focus on anti-poverty community development. Project sponsors are encouraged (but not required) to provide a financial match; however they must be able to direct the project, supervise the volunteers, and provide necessary administrative support to complete the goals and objectives of the project. Projects must be developed in accordance with all four of the VISTA Core Principles: Anti-Poverty Focus, Community Empowerment, Sustainable Solutions, and Capacity Building. All VISTA resources must be used to create, expand, or enhance projects that lift people out of poverty. Additionally, the Corporation has identified, in its strategic plan, six focus areas for funding: Economic Opportunity; Education; Healthy Futures; Veterans and Military Families; Disaster Services; and Environmental Stewardship. All new VISTA project development must fall within these six focus areas. As of this writing, the Corporation will direct most VISTA resources to the Economic Opportunity and Education focus areas; however, the Corporation will also address the other focus areas, according to the ability of Corporation State Offices to identify opportunities in those areas that can have a direct impact on breaking the cycle of poverty.

Restrictions: Organizations that focus solely on advocacy and lobbying are not eligible. Key legislation and regulations governing the VISTA program are as follows: the Domestic Volunteer Service Act (as amended by Public Law 113-13, April 2009); the National Service Trust Act (as amended by Public Law 113-13, April 2009); the Edward M. Kennedy Serve America Act (Public Law 113-13, April 2009); and the Code of Federal Regulations, Title 45, Parts 1206, 1210-1211, 1216-1220, 1222, and 1226.

Geographic Focus: All States

Contact: Mary Strasser, Director; (202) 606-6943 or (202) 606-5000

Kathy Little, Program Assistant; (202) 606-6852 or (202) 606-5000

Internet: www.nationalservice.gov/programs/americorps/americorps-vista

Sponsor: Corporation for National and Community Service

1201 New York Avenue, NW

Washington, D.C. 20525

CNCS Foster Grandparent Projects Grants 646

The Foster Grandparent Program (FGP) began in 1965 as a national demonstration effort to show how low-income persons aged sixty or over have the maturity and experience to establish a personal relationship with children having either exceptional or special needs. Originally established under the Economic Opportunity Act of 1964 the FGP was operated first as an employment program and eventually as a stipended volunteer program under various federal offices and agencies. Currently RSVP is administered through the Corporation for National and Community Service (the Corporation)'s Senior Corps program. Dual purposes of the RSVP are to provide part-time volunteer service opportunities for income-eligible persons ages fifty-five and over and to give supportive person-to-person assistance in health, education, human-services, and related settings to help address the physical, mental, and emotional needs of special/exceptional-needs infants, children, or youth. The Corporation accepts FGP grant applications only when new funding is available or when it is necessary to replace an existing sponsor. In addition, eligible agencies or organizations may, under a Memorandum of Agreement with the Corporation, receive technical assistance and materials to aid in establishing and operating a non-federally-funded FGP project using local funds. Notices for nationwide competitions for new FGP grants are posted at www.grants.gov and at the Corporation and Senior Corps websites. (Subscription links for receiving RSS feeds on new funding opportunities are also available at the websites.) Notices for applicants to replace a sponsor are advertised locally through Corporation State Offices. (A list of the offices along with their contact information is available at the Corporation website.) Grant applications are submitted through the Corporation's eGrants system. For more information, interested applicants may download the FGP Handbook from the Senior Corps and Corporation websites or contact their Corporation State Office.

Requirements: The Corporation awards grants to public agencies, Indian tribes, and secular or faith-based private non-profit organizations in the United States that have authority to accept and the capacity to administer a Foster Grandparent project. The FGP requires a non-federal share of 10% of the total project cost. FGP projects are generally expected and required to be on-going. FGP sponsors may apply for continued funding from the Corporation.

Restrictions: The total of cost reimbursements for Foster Grandparents, including stipends, insurance, transportation, meals, physical examinations, uniforms if appropriate, and recognition must be equal to at least 80 percent of the Corporation's Federal share of the grant. (Federal and non-Federal resources, including excess non-Corporation resources, can be used to make up this sum.) Key legislative pieces regulating and enabling the FGP

have been the Economic Opportunity Act of 1964, Title Six of the Older Americans Act (1969), the Domestic Volunteer Service Act (DVSA) of 1973, the National and Community Service Trust Act (1993), 45 C.F.R. § 1216 (non-displacement of contracts and employed workers), the Edward Kennedy Serve America Act, and 45 C.F.R. § 2551. FGP funding generally requires an Office of Management and Budget (OMB) audit.
Geographic Focus: All States
Amount of Grant: 250,000 USD
Contact: Wanda Carney; (202) 606-6934 or (202) 606-5000
Dr. Erwin Tan, Director of Senior Corps; (202) 606-6867
Internet: www.nationalservice.gov/build-your-capacity/grants/managing-senior-corps-grants
Sponsor: Corporation for National and Community Service
1201 New York Avenue, NW
Washington, D.C. 20525

CNCS School Turnaround AmeriCorps Grants **647**
The School Turnaround AmeriCorps program supports the placement of a dedicated cadre of AmeriCorps members from the Corporation for National and Community Service (CNCS) in persistently underachieving schools across the country. These AmeriCorps members will be serving in schools implementing school turnaround interventions as required by Department of Education's (ED) School Improvement Grant (SIG) program or as required through Elementary and Secondary Education Act (ESEA) flexibility. Members will help keep students on track to graduate by working to increase student academic achievement, attendance and high school graduation rates; improve college and career readiness; and provide college enrollment assistance and advisement. School Turnaround AmeriCorps will be supported by an initial investment of $15 million in public funds from both agencies and leverage an anticipated $18 million in grantee match funding during a three-year cycle. In addition, AmeriCorps members who complete their service in the program will qualify for a Segal AmeriCorps Education Award, which could total $1.5 million a year for all participants.
Requirements: The program supports organizations that serve low-performing schools around the country, including those in rural areas, and expands on the efforts of Together for Tomorrow, an initiative between ED, CNCS, and the White House Office of Faith-based and Neighborhood Partnerships.
Geographic Focus: All States
Contact: School Turnaround Coordinator; (202) 606-5000 or (800) 942-2677
Internet: www.nationalservice.gov/programs/americorps/school-turnaround-americorps
Sponsor: Corporation for National and Community Service
1201 New York Avenue, NW
Washington, D.C. 20525

CNCS Senior Corps Retired and Senior Volunteer Program Grants **648**
The Retired and Senior Volunteer Program (RSVP), one of the largest volunteer efforts in the nation, has matched local problems with older adults who are willing to help since 1971. Each year nearly 430,000 older adults (ages fifty-five and over) provide community service through more than 740 locally-sponsored RSVP projects. RSVP volunteers serve through nonprofit and public organizations (local sponsors) to organize neighborhood watch programs, tutor children and teenagers, renovate homes, teach English to immigrants, teach computer software applications, help people recover from natural disasters, serve as museum docents—and do whatever else their skills and interests lead them to do to meet the needs of their community. While RSVP volunteers do not receive any monetary incentive or stipend, they may be reimbursed for certain out-of-pocket costs associated with their service activities. In addition, RSVP volunteers receive accident, personal-liability, and excess-automobile insurance, as well as community recognition. Currently RSVP is administered through the Corporation for National and Community Service (the Corporation)'s Senior Corps program. The Corporation solicits applications for new Senior Corps grants (new projects or new sponsors) only when funding is available. The Corporation will notify the public when new grants are being accepted by posting Notices of Funding Availability (NOFA) or Notices of Funding Opportunity (NOFO) at the Senior Corps and Corporation websites and at www.grants.gov. (Subscription links for receiving RSS feeds on new funding opportunities are also available at these websites.) The application process for an RSVP grant begins with submission of a concept paper which will be used to select applicants who will then be invited to submit a full application. Applicants apply through the Corporation's online eGrants system, the link to which is available at the website. Use of eGrants requires setting up an account; the Corporation strongly recommends that applicants create their accounts at least three weeks prior to the submission deadline. Concept papers and full applications must be received by the Corporation by 5:00 p.m. (eastern standard time) on the applicable deadline in order to be considered. (Exceptions may apply under special circumstances; documentation is required.) Deadline dates may vary from funding opportunity to funding opportunity; organizations are encouraged to always verify current deadline dates. For more information, interested applicants may download the RSVP Handbook from the Corporation and Senior Corps websites or contact their Corporation State Office (a list of the state offices along with their contact information is available at the Corporation website).
Requirements: Eligible applicants include public agencies (e.g. state and local agencies and other units of government), non-profit organizations (both faith-based and secular), institutions of higher education, and Indian Tribes. New applicants may propose only to establish a new RSVP project in a geographic area unserved by a current RSVP grantee. Matching is required as follows: new RSVP applicants must budget and raise ten percent of their total project budget in year one, twenty percent in year two, and thirty percent in year three and subsequent years (if the grant is renewed beyond three years). All applications must include a Dun and Bradstreet Data Universal Numbering System (DUNS) number. The DUNS number does not replace the Employer Identification Number. DUNS numbers may be obtained at no cost by calling the DUNS number request line at (866) 705-5711 or by applying online. Either way, the Corporation suggests registering at least 30 days in advance of the application due date. Key programmatic requirements to consider are as follows. At a minimum, 20 percent of a sponsor's or project's RSVP volunteers must be placed in assignments to recruit other community volunteers, thus expanding the capacity of local non-profits to meet their missions. Additionally, all RSVP volunteers must be placed in assignments that address one or more of the 16 categories of community needs identified in the Domestic Volunteer Service Act as "Programs of National Significance (PNS)." In particular the Corporation is interested in supporting the following volunteer activities: providing in-home, non-medical independent-living support to those in need of extra help, including frail seniors, veterans of recent conflicts, and their caregivers; assisting children and youth to succeed academically through provision of mentoring, tutoring, and other assistance to remain in school; and enhancing energy efficiency at home through weatherization of homes, energy audits, or connecting people to related resources and information.
Restrictions: Key legislative pieces regulating and enabling the RSVP have been the Economic Opportunity Act of 1964, Title Six of the Older Americans Act (1969), the Domestic Volunteer Service Act (DVSA) of 1973, the National and Community Service Trust Act (1993), 45 C.F.R. § 1216 (non-displacement of contracts and employed workers), the Edward Kennedy Serve America Act, and 45 C.F.R. § 2551. FGP funding generally requires an Office of Management and Budget (OMB) audit.
Geographic Focus: All States
Date(s) Application is Due: Feb 22
Amount of Grant: 60,000 - 80,000 USD
Contact: Dr. Erwin Tan; (202) 606-6867 or (800) 424-8867; PNS@cns.gov
Vielka Garibaldi, Director for Grant Review Operations; (202) 606-6886
Internet: www.nationalservice.gov/build-your-capacity/grants/managing-senior-corps-grants
Sponsor: Corporation for National and Community Service
1201 New York Avenue, NW
Washington, D.C. 20525

CNCS Social Innovation Grants **649**
The CNCS Social Innovation Fund is authorized by the Edward M. Kennedy Serve America Act and is administered by the Corporation for National and Community Service (the Corporation), a federal agency that engages more than five million Americans as volunteers through well-known national-service programs like Senior Corps, AmeriCorps, and Learn and Serve America. The Social Innovation Fund is primarily concerned with advancing social innovation as a key strategy for solving critical social challenges. The program's goal is to identify and help spread those innovative and potentially transformative approaches that have been developed at the local level to solve community problems. An approach is considered transformative if it not only produces strong impact, but also if it: has the potential to affect how the same challenge is addressed in other communities; addresses more than one critical community challenge concurrently; or produces significant cost savings through gains in efficiency. The operating model of the Social Innovation Fund is distinguished by four key elements: reliance on intermediaries with strong skills and track records of success in selecting, validating, and growing high-impact nonprofit organizations; assuring participation from the non-federal stake-holders by requiring each federal dollar be matched 1:1 with money from non-federal sources not only by the intermediaries but also by their subgrantees; requiring that all intermediaries engage each of their subgrantees in formal evaluations of program performance and impact; and requiring each grantee to commit to knowledge sharing and other initiatives that advance social innovation more generally in the nonprofit sector. The SIF makes grant awards of between $1 million and $10 million per year for up to five years to grantmaking intermediaries, selected through a rigorous, open competition. Intermediaries match their federal grants dollar-for-dollar and with those combined funds they then: host open, evidence-based competitions to select nonprofits implementing innovative program models; invest in expanding the capabilities and impact of the nonprofits they select; and support those nonprofits through rigorous evaluation of their programs.
Requirements: Applicants must be an eligible grantmaking institution or partnership in existence at the time of the application. Providing grants to nonprofit community organizations should be central to the applicant's mission and should be clearly reflected in the organization's promotional materials and annual operating budget. Core operations must include conducting open competitive grant competitions, negotiating specific grant requirements with grant recipients; and overseeing and monitoring performance of grant recipients. By statute Social Innovation Fund intermediaries must operate either as geographically-based or as issue-based grantmakers. A geographically-based intermediary will address one or more priority issues withing a single geographic location. An issue-based intermediary will address a single priority issue in multiple geographic locations. At the time of submission, applicants must demonstrate through a letter or other form of documentation that they have either cash-on-hand or commitments (or a combination thereof) toward meeting 50 percent of their first year matching funds.
Restrictions: Intermediaries must distribute at least 80 percent of awarded federal funds to subgrantees, run an open competition that is available to eligible nonprofit organizations beyond the intermediary's own existing grant portfolio or network, and provide sufficient public notice of the availability of Social Innovation Fund subgrants to eligible nonprofit community organizations. Given that innovation funds currently exist in the Departments of Education and Labor to invest specifically in evidence-based programs in education and job training, the Corporation does not intend to make Social Innovation Fund awards to programs in these areas unless they clearly propose a solution to an unmet need as identified in consultation with both Departments. The funding mechanism for Social Innovation Fund awards is a cooperative agreement that provides for substantial involvement by the Corporation with the intermediaries as they carry out approved activities. The assigned Corporation program officer will confer with the grantee on a regular and frequent basis to develop and/or review service delivery and project status, including work plans, budgets, periodic reports, evaluations, etc. In particular the Corporation anticipates having substantial involvement in developing and approving subgrantee selection plans; developing and approving subgrantee evaluation plans; documenting subgrantee growth plans; and documenting and sharing

lessons learned through a Corporation-sponsored learning community. Grants under the Social Innovation program are subject to the Cost Principles and Uniform Administration Requirements under the applicable Office of Management and Budget (OMB) Circulars.
Geographic Focus: All States
Date(s) Application is Due: Mar 27
Amount of Grant: 1,000,000 - 5,000,000 USD
Contact: Vielka Garibaldi, Director for Grant Review Operations; (202) 606-5000 or (202) 606-3223; info@cns.gov or innovation@cns.gov
Internet: www.nationalservice.gov/about/programs/innovation.asp
Sponsor: Corporation for National and Community Service
1201 New York Avenue NW
Washington, D.C. 20525

CNO Financial Group Community Grants   650
As a company, the CNO Financial Group provides financial support for a number of causes that contribute to the well-being of its communities. As individuals, company personnel invest time and talents in the same causes. Corporate contributions focus on early childhood programs, children-at-risk, and early-childhood education through post-secondary education. Grants support literacy programs, early intervention, and economics education for high-risk students. Interested applicants should contact the office for further direction on guidelines and how to apply.
Geographic Focus: All States
Date(s) Application is Due: Oct 1
Amount of Grant: 1,500 - 10,000 USD
Contact: Carrie Jost, Grant Contact; (312) 396-7673 or (317) 817-3768; fax (317) 817-2179; Carrie.Jost@cnoinc.com
Internet: www.cnoinc.com/about-cno/in-the-community
Sponsor: CNO Financial Group
11825 North Pennsylvania Street
Carmel, IN 46032

Coleman Foundation Entrepreneurship Education Grants   651
Business ownership and the creation of for-profit business ventures are central to the Coleman Foundation definition of entrepreneurship. This perspective inherently involves accepting and managing risk, exercising significant personal control and contains the potential for personal reward. It is a narrower perspective than free enterprise and does not focus on intrapreneurship or social entrepreneurship. The Foundation believes that the principles of self-determination, independence and individual initiative are characteristics essential to the development of entrepreneurs and their pursuit of self-employment. It promotes entrepreneurship as a career option and field of study for individuals of all ages and strives to improve the relevance impact of entrepreneurship education programs. The Foundation has recently established a more focused impact framework for grantmaking in its entrepreneurship program area. The Entrepreneurship Education Impact Plan (see website) has curricular and co-curricular components. Within the curriculum, strategies aim to foster development of core skills and the promotion of entrepreneurship as interdisciplinary learning. The Plan also seeks to improve the quality and quantity of experiential activities across disciplines that develop applied knowledge and experiences in self-employment. Potential grantees should look to this Entrepreneurship Impact Plan for the type of strategies the Foundation is looking to fund. The Foundation has also been promoting the concept of a Pathway for entrepreneurship exploration and education.
Requirements: Grants are made only to 501(c)3 or 509(a)1 nonprofit organizations that are not private foundations. The Foundation's primary geographic focus is the Midwest region, particularly the State of Illinois and the Chicago metropolitan area. Entrepreneurship education, one of the foundation's core initiatives, has been funded nationally. Other program initiatives are only occasionally considered outside of the primary geographic area. Only programs within the United States will be considered, which excludes all international programs. Applicants should submit a letter of inquiry first; LOIs are accepted throughout the calendar year. The Foundation will advise you if a full proposal should be submitted for further review. Proposals are presented by Foundation staff and approved by the Board at quarterly meetings, usually in February, May, August and November.
Restrictions: The program does not fund for-profit businesses, individuals, individual scholarships, advertising books, tickets, equipment purchases (including computer hardware or software), or advertising. General solicitations and annual appeals will not be considered.
Geographic Focus: Illinois, Indiana, Iowa, Michigan, Ohio, Wisconsin
Amount of Grant: 50,000 - 250,000 USD
Samples: Accion Chicago, Chicago, Illinois, $200,000 - to support the creation of The Hatchery, a food business incubator in East Garfield Park; Beloit College, Beloit, Wisconsin, $100,000 - capital project request completes an effort that was begun in 2003; North Central College, Naperville, Illinois, $90,000 - to support arts business program elements for faculty, students and artists.
Contact: Rosa Berardi; (312) 902-7120; fax (312) 902-7124; rberardi@colemanfoundation.org
Lisa Torres, Grants Manager; (312) 902-7120, ext. 105; fax (312) 902-7124; ltorres@colemanfoundation.org or info@colemanfoundation.org
Internet: www.colemanfoundation.org/what_we_fund/entrepreneurship/
Sponsor: Coleman Foundation
651 West Washington Boulevard, Suite 306
Chicago, IL 60661

Colgate-Palmolive Company Grants   652
Nonprofit organizations with IRS tax-exempt status located primarily in the U.S. tristate area of New York, New Jersey, and Connecticut and in locations of foreign subsidiaries may apply for support of programs that are directed toward youth, women, minorities, education, health and welfare, culture and arts, and civic and community activities. Priority

will be given to programs that address the educational needs of youth and minorities. Types of support include program grants, scholarships, general support grants, multiyear support, and employee matching gifts. Proposals are accepted at any time and should include information on the organization, purpose of request, proof of tax-exempt status, and current operating budget.
Geographic Focus: All States
Amount of Grant: Up to 1,000,000 USD
Samples: American Public Health Association, Washington, D.C., $1,000,000 - for program support; Boys and Girls Club of Milwaukee, Milwaukee, Wisconsin, $1,000 - to implement a youth credit union run by and for members; Star Seekers 4-H Club, Bartlett, Illinois, $1,000 - to form a sister club for residents of a learning center for disabled children.
Contact: Sally Phills; (212) 310-2166 or (212) 310-2000; fax (212) 310-2873
Internet: www.colgate.com/app/Colgate/US/Corp/CommunityPrograms/DonationPolicy.cvsp
Sponsor: Colgate-Palmolive Company
300 Park Avenue
New York, NY 10022

Colin Higgins Foundation Courage Awards   653
Colin Higgins, acclaimed screenwriter, director, and producer of films such as Harold and Maude and 9 to 5, established the Colin Higgins Foundation in 1986 to further his humanitarian goals. Each year, the Colin Higgins Foundation salutes, celebrates, and fosters courage in the face of adversity and discrimination by awarding grants to individuals who are: lesbian, gay, bisexual, transgender, or questioning (LGBTQ) youth (through age 21) who have bravely stood up to hostility and intolerance based on their sexual orientation and triumphed over bigotry; lesbian, gay, bisexual, and transgender (LGBT) adults who have made strong impact in the lives of LGBTQ youth or the overall LGBT movement; or allies of any age working to end homophobia and discrimination against the LGBTQ communities. Each Colin Higgins Youth Courage Award winners receive a grant of $10,000 and are honored during Pride weekend on an all-expenses paid trip to New York or Los Angeles. Honorees will also receive an expense-paid trip to the National Gay and Lesbian Task Force Creating Change Conference. Two or three awards will be made each year. Online nominations are available at the website.
Restrictions: Self-nominations are not accepted. Awards are open to U.S. citizens only.
Geographic Focus: All States
Date(s) Application is Due: Mar 2
Amount of Grant: 10,000 USD
Contact: Christine Coleman, Director of Communications; (415) 561-6400 or (415) 561-6300; fax (415) 561-6401; info@colinhiggins.org or info@tides.org
Internet: www.colinhiggins.org/courageawards/index.cfm
Sponsor: Colin Higgins Foundation
1014 Torney Avenue
San Francisco, CA 94129-1704

Collective Brands Foundation Grants   654
The Collective Brands Foundation invests financially in non-profit organizations that align with the Foundation's focus areas. Priority is given to organizations that provide involvement opportunities for team members and employees of Collective Brands, Inc. The Foundation may also consider sponsorships from charitable organizations in the following areas: Eastern Kansas, including Topeka, Lawrence and the Kansas City metropolitan area; New York City; Lexington, Massachusetts and the Greater Boston area; Denver, Colorado; Redlands, California; and Brookville, Ohio.
Requirements: The Collective Brands Foundation will consider requests for monetary grants from 501(c)3 non-profit organizations that manage programs in at least one of the following areas: women's preventative health; children's physical activity and fitness, improving the lives of children and youth in need; preserving the environment; and supporting industry in the United States. Applications must be submitted online at the Foundation's website.
Restrictions: Grants will not be awarded to religious organizations for projects that are sectarian and do not benefit a broad community base. Also, the Foundation will not award grants to: individuals; political causes, candidates or legislative lobbying efforts; or for capital campaigns, debt reduction, travel or conferences.
Geographic Focus: All States
Date(s) Application is Due: Aug 15
Amount of Grant: Up to 3,000 USD
Contact: Michele Gray; (877) 902-4437; grants@greaterhorizons.org
Internet: www.collectivebrands.com/foundation
Sponsor: Collective Brands Foundation
3231 SE 6th Avenue
Topeka, KS 66607

Collective Brands Foundation Payless Gives Shoes 4 Kids Grants   655
The Payless Gives 4 Kids grant supports non-profit organizations serving children with coupons for free, new shoes at Payless. Payless Gives 4 Kids supports organizations in the United States, Canada, Puerto Rico, and Latin America. Applications are accepted every fall and are available at the program's website.
Requirements: 501(c)3 non-profit organizations that serve children within 100 miles of a Payless store are eligible to apply. Applicants must participate in an eligibility quiz and are required to supply the following information: organization information and mission; services and description of services provided to children, as well as an example of a child applicant organization has helped; number of coupons organization can deliver, the process for determining who receives coupons and transportation assistance to be provided; Payless or Collective Brands affiliation; and any additional tax information.
Restrictions: Organizations without a 501(c)3 status or who are more than 100 miles from a Payless ShoeSource are not eligible to apply.

Geographic Focus: All States
Samples: Covenant House Alaska, Anchorage, Alaska - coupons for new shoes for children in need; Catholic Charities of Fairfield County, Inc., Bridgeport, Connecticut - coupons for new shoes for children in need.
Contact: Michele Gray; (877) 902-4437; grants@greaterhorizons.org
Internet: www.paylessgives.com/about.php?page=about_the_program-what_its_about
Sponsor: Collective Brands Foundation
3231 SE 6th Avenue
Topeka, KS 66607

Collective Brands Foundation Saucony Run for Good Grants 656

The Saucony Run for Good grants are focused on improving the lives of children by helping to prevent and reduce childhood obesity by informing the public about its cause and prevention, as well as providing funding to optimize the impact and success of community organizations that promote running and healthy lifestyle programs for youth. The following are a list of priorities the awards should address: utilization of running participation for health and/or well-being in children; serves youth populations not traditionally exposed to running programs; and demonstrates support and inspiration in creating a program that exemplifies Saucony Run for Good's mission of improving the lives of children through running.
Requirements: Eligible applicants must be a 501(c)3 organization serving participants 18 years of age or younger. Proposals must demonstrate the grantee will conduct programs that increase participation in running in order to positively impact the lives of participants. In addition to these requirements, applications must provide proof of tax exempt status from the IRS. If a grant is awarded, grantees must submit proof of performance and demonstrate funds were used for the proposed program. Applications are available at Saucony Run for Good's website, but hard copies must be mailed to: Saucony Run for Good Foundation (please see address below). The proposal must not be more than four 8.5" x 11" typed pages.
Restrictions: Organizations that do not have a 501(c)3 status or serve participants that are 18 years of age or older are not eligible to apply for this program. Also, employees of Saucony, Inc., Collective Brands, Inc., and/or any affiliates are not elliglbe to apply and/or receive grants. Grants may not be used to cover any expenses incurred prior to the award date of the grant. Only one application per organization may be submitted.
Geographic Focus: All States
Date(s) Application is Due: Jun 13; Dec 13
Amount of Grant: Up to 10,000 USD
Samples: AWARE, Inc., Juneau, Alaska - providing running programs for youth in Southeast Alaska; New York Road Runner's Foundation, New York, New York - supporting low-income, at-risk youth with a nutrition and fitness program.
Contact: Michele Gray, Director of Community Investments; (877) 902-4437; grants@greaterhorizons.org or runforgood@saucony.com
Internet: www.sauconyrunforgood.com/
Sponsor: Collective Brands Foundation
3231 SE 6th Avenue
Topeka, KS 66607

Collins C. Diboll Private Foundation Grants 657

The Collins C. Diboll Private Foundation awards grants to Louisiana nonprofit organizations in the areas of higher education, human services, and youth programs. The Foundation's primary field of interest include: Catholic churches and agencies; education; higher education; human services; art museums; and protestant agencies and churches. Types of support include: building construction and renovation; capital campaigns; endowment funds; and general operating support. Typical grants range from $500 up to a maximum of $200,000. There are no identified annual deadlines for submission, though a formal application is required. Applicants should also submit a detailed description of the project and the amount of funding requested, along with a copy of an IRS determination letter.
Requirements: Louisiana nonprofit organizations are eligible.
Restrictions: Individuals are not eligible to apply.
Geographic Focus: Louisiana
Amount of Grant: 500 - 200,000 USD
Samples: Tulane University, Center for Infectious Diseases, New Orleans, Louisiana, $100,000 - for research purposes; National World War II Museum, New Orleans, Louisiana, $50,000 - in support of the China-Burma-India Display Gallary; New Orleans Botanical Garden Foundation, New Orleans, Louisiana, $125,000 - rennovations for the CT Parker Building and the City Park.
Contact: Donald W. Diboll, Chairperson; (504) 582-8103 or (504) 582-8250
Sponsor: Collins C. Diboll Private Foundation
201 Saint Charles Avenue, 50th Floor
New Orleans, LA 70170-5100

Collins Foundation Grants 658

The Collins Foundation is an independent, private foundation that was created in 1947 by Truman W. Collins, Sr., and other members of the Collins family. The Foundation exists to improve, enrich, and give greater expression to humanitarian endeavors in the state of Oregon, and to assist in improving the quality of life in the state. As a general-purpose, responsive grant maker, the Foundation serves people in urban and rural communities across Oregon through its grants to nonprofit organizations working for the common good. The Foundation's broad areas of interest include: arts and humanities; children and youth; community welfare; education; the environment; health and science; and religion. Most recent awards have ranged from as little as $3,000 to a maximum of $400,000. There are no identified annual submission deadlines for applications.
Requirements: Grants are made to 501(c)3 nonprofit agencies domiciled in Oregon. The proposed project must directly benefit the citizens of Oregon.

Restrictions: Grants are not made to individuals or to organizations sponsoring requests intended to be used by or for the benefit of an individual. Grants normally are not made to elementary, secondary, or public higher education institutions; or to individual religious congregations. Grants normally are not made for development office personnel, annual fundraising activities, endowments, operational deficits, financial emergencies, or debt retirement. The Foundation will consider only one grant request from the same organization in a twelve month period, unless an additional request is invited by the Foundation.
Geographic Focus: Oregon
Amount of Grant: 3,000 - 400,000 USD
Samples: Artists Repertory Theatre, Portland, Oregon, $150,000 - support a season of plays, and reconfigure production areas and increase staffing to accommodate resident arts organizations; Children's Center of Clackamas County, Oregon City, Oregon, $25,000 - to enhance follow-up support services for children who have been abused and their non-offending family members in Clackamas County; Albina Opportunities Corporation, Portland, Oregon, $100,000 - to expand advisory and loan services to underserved women- and minority-owned small businesses in low- to moderate-income areas in Portland.
Contact: Cynthia G. Addams, Executive Vice President; (503) 227-7171; fax (503) 295-3794; information@collinsfoundation.org
Internet: www.collinsfoundation.org/submission-guidelines
Sponsor: Collins Foundation
1618 South West First Avenue, Suite 505
Portland, OR 97201

Colonel Stanley R. McNeil Foundation Grants 659

The Colonel Stanley R. McNeil Foundation was established in 1993 to support and promote quality educational, human services and health care programming for underserved populations. Special consideration is given to charitable organizations that serve the needs of children. Colonel Stanley R. McNeil and his wife, Merna McNeil, created the Colonel Stanley R. McNeil Foundation as a perpetual charitable grantmaking trust with Bank of America, N.A. as trustee. During their lifetimes, the McNeils were actively involved in their local church and community. Colonel McNeil also served on a number of boards, including Lake Bluff Children's Home and Ravenswood Hospital. Although the McNeils had no children, they were strong supporters of children's causes. The Foundation is particularly interested in funding programs or organizations that focus on children's causes, start-up initiatives within the human services or arts and cultural arenas, and health care. Award amounts typically range from $500 to $125,000. To better support the capacity of nonprofit organizations, multi-year funding requests are considered. There are two application deadlines annually.
Requirements: Illinois nonprofit organizations serving the Chicago metropolitan area are eligible. Grant requests for naming opportunities that honor the donors — Colonel McNeil and his wife, Merna — are strongly encouraged. Applications will be submitted online through the Bank of America website. A grant report is required within 1 year of the grant application date, regardless of whether all of the funds have been spent.
Restrictions: The Foundation will consider requests for general operations only if the organization's operating budget is less than $1 million. In general, grant request for individuals, endowment campaigns or capital projects will not be considered.
Geographic Focus: Illinois
Date(s) Application is Due: Feb 1; Jun 1
Amount of Grant: 500 - 125,000 USD
Samples: Children's Home and Aid Society of Illinois, Chicago, Illinois, $25,000 - Awarded for Children's Home and Aid Mitzi Freidheim Englewood Child and Family Center (2018); Center on Halsted, Chicago, Illinois, $25,000 - Awarded for Center on Halsted Case Management for LGBTQ Youth Experiencing Homelessness in Chicagoland (2018); Woodstock Institute, Chicago, Illinois, $25,000 - Awarded for Expanding Higher Education Opportunities for Illinois Children (2018).
Contact: Srilatha Lakkaraju, Philanthropic Client Manager; (312) 828-8166; ilgrantmaking@bankofamerica.com or ilgrantmaking@ustrust.com
Internet: www.bankofamerica.com/philanthropic/foundation/?fnId=84
Sponsor: Colonel Stanley R. McNeil Foundation
P.O. Box 1802
Providence, RI 02901-1802

Colorado Health Foundation Family, Friend and Neighbor Caregiver Supports Grants 660

Family, friend and neighbor caregivers bring many strengths to the support of children including caring relationships, the warmth of a home environment, flexibility and – typically – affordability for the families they serve. Now more than ever, family, friend and neighbor caregivers are being called upon to support families as essential workers continue to report to work and hosts of licensed child care sites are closing. At the Foundation, the staff believes that regardless of child care setting, caregivers should have supports for their own well-being, opportunities to grow their knowledge of child development and access to resources to support healthy child development in support of the social-emotional development of the young children they provide care for. The Colorado Health Foundation Family, Friend and Neighbor Caregiver Supports Grants opportunity will support family, friend and neighbor caregivers to build their networks, increase access to information and resources and provide professional development in support of building stable, responsive relationships with the children in their care. Examples of organizations considered for funding: community-based nonprofits; community colleges; community-based coalitions; early childhood councils; family resource centers; local institutions who are viewed by community as trusted partners; and public libraries. The annual deadlines for application submission are February 15 and June 15.
Requirements: gible applicants for this opportunity include community-based organizations, community-based coalitions or public agencies that work with family, friend and neighbor caregivers serving Coloradans living on low income and those historically experiencing

less power and privilege. Applicants are eligible to apply for up to two years of support. Proposed projects must reflect the Foundation's cornerstones, as its work is grounded in serving Coloradans who have-low income and historically have had less power or privilege, putting health equity at the center of everything the Foundation does, and being informed by the community and those it exists to serve. To be considered for funding, organizations must meet the following criteria: align with the Foundation's cornerstones and promote conditions for healthy social-emotional development and resilience of young children; establish the ability to outreach and engage the family, friend and neighbor caregiver population and utilize strong social and community networks; ensure capacity to offer culturally relevant program infrastructure and services; and include family, friend and neighbor caregivers and/or families who serve in advisory and/or co-designer roles.
Geographic Focus: Colorado
Date(s) Application is Due: Jun 15
Contact: Sara Guillaume, Senior Director of Grantmaking; (303) 953-3672 or (303) 953-3600; fax (303) 322-4576; sguillaume@coloradohealth.org or funding@coloradohealth.org
Sarah Bradshaw, Grants Manager; (303) 953-3654 or (303) 953-3600; fax (303) 322-4576; sbradshaw@coloradohealth.org or funding@coloradohealth.org
Internet: www.coloradohealth.org/funding-opportunities/funding-opportunity-family-friend-and-neighbor-caregiver-supports
Sponsor: Colorado Health Foundation
1780 Pennsylvania Street
Denver, CO 80203

Colorado Interstate Gas Grants 661
Nonprofits in communities served by the company are eligible to apply for grants in the categories of education, including early child development, K-12, and higher education; civic; health and welfare; minorities; cultural programs; environmental programs, particularly those focusing on air quality; and youth groups that concentrate on improving areas where CIG employees live and work. The company also supports special event sponsorships, corporate memberships, joint projects with other organizations, and employee participation in volunteer activities.
Requirements: Colorado, Wyoming, Texas, Utah, and Kansas 501(c)3 tax-exempt organizations where the company has pipelines are eligible.
Geographic Focus: Colorado, Kansas, Texas, Utah, Wyoming
Date(s) Application is Due: Aug 1
Amount of Grant: 200 - 20,000 USD
Contact: Richard Wheatley; (713) 420-6828; ichard_Wheatley@K inderMorgan.com
Internet: webapps.elpaso.com/PortalUI/DefaultKM.aspx?TSP=CIGD
Sponsor: Colorado Interstate Gas Company
P.O. Box 1087
Colorado Springs, CO 80944

Colorado Trust Health Equity Investment Grants 662
Periodically, the Colorado Trust has the opportunity to provide one-time or time-limited funding aimed at addressing specific needs among programs and initiatives that align with its health equity vision. This includes program-related investments, in which a low- or no-interest loan or equity stake is provided as financing in lieu of a more traditional grant, with the goal of a earning a future return on the investment. Such returns are then added to the Trust's future grant making capacity, increasing its ability to help improve the health and well-being of Coloradans.
Requirements: The following types of organizations are eligible to apply for grants: nonprofit organizations that are exempt under Section 501(c)3 of the Internal Revenue Code and are classified as not a private foundation under Section 509(a); independent sponsored projects of a nonprofit 501(c)3 organization acting as a fiscal agent; government and public agencies.
Restrictions: The Trust asks for proposals through a Request for Proposal process, rather than accepting unsolicited proposals. Announcements of Requests for Proposals are posted at the website. Grant seekers also may register with the Trust to receive notification of new funding opportunities. The Colorado Trust does not make grants for the following: political campaigns or voter registration drives; capital funding for the purchase, construction or renovation of any facilities or other physical infrastructure; operating deficits or retirement of debt; indirect allocations (excluding fiscal agent fees); religious purposes.
Geographic Focus: Colorado
Amount of Grant: Up to 2,000,000 USD
Samples: Senior Housing Options, Denver, Colorado, $650,000 - funding to help redevelop a senior housing facility in downtown Denver that provides 111 apartment units, all of which are Section 8 housing and predominantly serve low-income Coloradans with disabilities (2018); Urban Land Conservancy, Denver, Colorado,, $1,500,000 - support for the Metro Denver Impact Facility, which will be used to acquire and develop urban properties in underserved Denver communities (2018).
Contact: Jenice Whitehead, Grants Management Specialist; (888) 847-9140 or (303) 837-1200; fax (303) 839-9034; jenice@coloradotrust.org
Michele Chader, Grants Management Specialist; (888) 847-9140 or (303) 837-1200; fax (303) 839-9034; michele@coloradotrust.org
Internet: www.coloradotrust.org/what-we-do/funding-areas
Sponsor: Colorado Trust
1600 Sherman Street
Denver, CO 80203-1604

Columbus Foundation Traditional Grants 663
The Columbus Foundation's Traditional Grants program creates quality opportunities and meets community need by focusing on two areas: Disadvantaged Children funds programs and projects that meet the diverse needs of at-risk children (priority will be given to programs and projects that are in the home, build relationships with the family, and create a support network around and for the families of disadvantaged children; and

Developmental Disabilities funds programs and projects that address the needs of children and adults with physical or cognitive disabilities that impair functions or behavior and that occurred before a person reaches the age of 22 (blindness/visual impairments and deafness/hearing impairments are not considered within this category). If you are implementing your project in a Columbus City School building, or collaborating with the district on a project, and asked to submit a full application, you must request a letter of endorsement from the Office of Development. The annual application deadline is the first Friday in February.
Requirements: Central Ohio, tax-exempt public charities under Section 501(c)3 of the Internal Revenue Service Code may submit grant requests. If you are implementing your project in a Columbus City School building, or collaborating with the district on a project, and asked to submit a full application, you must request a letter of endorsement from the Office of Development. Letter of Intent deadlines are twice a year on the first Friday in February and September.
Restrictions: Operating support will only be considered when the applicant demonstrates continuous innovation that enhances services.
Geographic Focus: Ohio
Date(s) Application is Due: Feb 5
Contact: Emily Savors, Director; (614) 251-4000; fax (614) 251-4009; esavors@columbusfoundation.org or contactus@columbusfoundation.org
Internet: columbusfoundation.org/nonprofit-center/grant-opportunities/columbus-foundation-grants/traditional-grants
Sponsor: Columbus Foundation
1234 East Broad Street
Columbus, OH 43205-1453

Community Foundation for Greater Atlanta Frances Hollis Brain Foundation Fund Grants 664
Happily married for 68 years, David Brain and Frances Hollis Brain were high school sweethearts from Cleveland, Ohio. During their life together, their love, support and care for each other was obvious to everyone they met and they prized a balance of family, community, church and self. Their family lived in Baltimore, Boston and Kentucky, but a common thread was always the spirit of giving. They believed that those who are blessed with resources have a responsibility to share them with those who are less fortunate. David and Frances created the Frances Hollis Brain Foundation in 1993 as a tangible expression of their values and to encourage future generations of the family to make a difference through philanthropy. Inspired by this lifetime legacy of giving by David and Frances Brain, the Frances Hollis Brain Foundation Fund supports nonprofits that benefit vulnerable and under-served communities. The Fund addresses primary needs – clothing, education, food, healthcare and shelter – to enhance the well-being of individuals living in the metro Atlanta counties of Cobb, DeKalb, Fulton and Gwinnett. The Fund also continues to further its mission in Kentucky at the Blue Grass Community Foundation and in Maine at the Maine Community Foundation.
Requirements: To apply for a grant organizations must: be located and providing services within the Foundation's 23-county service area; spend funds within the 23-county service area; be classified by the U.S. Internal Revenue Service under Section 501(c)3 of the I.R.S. code as a nonprofit, tax-exempt organization, donations to which are deductible as charitable contributions under Section 170(c)2 and the I.R.S. determination must be current; be registered with the Georgia Secretary of State as a nonprofit; have a minimum two-year operating history after the date of receipt of its 501(c)3 classification; have annual operating expenses greater than $100,000 as reflected in the most recently filed IRS form 990; have at least one full-time paid employee (paid minimum wage or more, working 2,080 hours or more) for the 12 months prior to submitting a Letter of Intent; and have a current written strategic or business plan for the whole organization that covers at least 24 months which includes the organization's entire current fiscal year.
Geographic Focus: Georgia
Date(s) Application is Due: Apr 5
Contact: Erin Drury Boorn, Senior Philanthropic Officer; (404) 588-3188 or (404) 688-5525; fax (404) 688-3060; eboorn@cfgreateratlanta.org
Internet: cfgreateratlanta.org/nonprofits/available-grants/frances-hollis-brain-foundation-fund/
Sponsor: Community Foundation for Greater Atlanta
191 Peachtree Street NE, Suite 1000
Atlanta, GA 30303

Community Foundation for Greater Atlanta Managing For Excellence Award 665
In 1984, the Community Foundation launched its annual Managing for Excellence Award. Each year, local organizations are invited to compete for the prize. This award is presented to an organization that exhibits outstanding nonprofit management. The redesign includes a more robust award package for winners, year-round exposure for the winners to create connections with potential donors and other individuals of influence and presentation as an industry leader at nonprofit events in the community. Winners will be selected from two budget categories (organizations with budgets between under $2,000,000 and organizations with budgets above $2,000,000) and will receive: $75,000 to each of the two winners (an increased from the previous award amount of $25,000); consulting services by Boston Consulting Group; a press release; inclusion in the Foundation's Extra Wish booklet, sent to all Foundation donors; a donor breakfast featuring the Managing for Excellence Winners, hosted by Alicia Philipp and sponsored by The Boston Consulting Group; special events throughout the year featuring Managing for Excellence winners, including a facilitated conversation for donors and connections with professional advisors; recognition at specific Foundation donor events; and a sponsored table at the Association of Fundraising Professionals National Philanthropy Day.
Requirements: To be eligible to receive the Award organizations must: have received at least one discretionary grant during the past ten years from one of the Foundation's discretionary programs; be located and providing services within the 23-county service area; spend funds within the 23-county service area; be classified by the U.S. Internal Revenue Service under

Section 501(c)3 of the I.R.S. code as a nonprofit, tax-exempt organization, donations to which are deductible as charitable contributions under Section 170(c)2 and the I.R.S. determination must be current; be registered with the Georgia Secretary of State as a nonprofit; have a minimum two-year operating history after the date of receipt of its 501(c)3 classification; have annual operating expenses greater than $100,000; have at least one full-time paid employee (paid minimum wage or more, working 2,080 hours or more) for the 12 months prior to submitting a Letter of Intent; and have a current written strategic or business plan for the whole organization that covers at least 24 months which includes the organization's entire current fiscal year.
Geographic Focus: Georgia
Date(s) Application is Due: Jan 18
Amount of Grant: 75,000 USD
Contact: Lauren Jeong, Program Associate; (404) 333-0229 or (404) 688-5525; fax (404) 688-3060; ljeong@cfgreateratlanta.org or excellence@cfgreateratlanta.org
Internet: cfgreateratlanta.org/nonprofits/available-grants/managing-for-excellence/
Sponsor: Community Foundation for Greater Atlanta
191 Peachtree Street NE, Suite 1000
Atlanta, GA 30303

Community Foundation for Greater Atlanta Metropolitan Extra Wish Grants   666

The Community Foundation of Greater Atlanta's An Extra Wish program provides monetary contributions for specific expenses, not staff or general operations, that contribute in a clear way to the success of organizations and the populations they serve. The Foundation's experience shows that most Extra Wish grants from donor advised funds fall between $500 and $3,500. In the past, the most successful wishes were requests for items that directly help program participants, rather than organizational operating equipment. The Foundation has found the more creative and innovative requests have a better chance of receiving support from a Community Foundation donor. Eligible requests include: resources for program participants or organizations; capital items; and services. The annual application deadlines is June 21.
Requirements: For this program, an organization must be located and providing services within the Foundation's 23-county service area. Other eligibility requirements vary by grant program, but common criteria for nonprofits to meet are: have a multi-year written strategic or business plan for the whole organization that includes measureable goals and methods to assess effectiveness; receive funding from at least three different sources such as individuals, foundations, corporations, faith-based organizations and government; have a minimum two-year operating history after receiving its 501(c)3 classification; have audited financial statements for the past two to three completed fiscal years (for organizations with annual budgets greater than $250,000); have at least one full-time paid employee; have a Board of Directors with representation from the community served and a committee structure with diverse areas of expertise; and be registered with the Georgia Secretary of State as a nonprofit.
Geographic Focus: Georgia
Date(s) Application is Due: Jun 21
Amount of Grant: 500 - 3,500 USD
Contact: Hannah Klemm, Program Assistant; (404) 588-3210 or (404) 688-5525; fax (404) 688-3060; hklemm@cfgreateratlanta.org or extrawish@cfgreateratlanta.org
Internet: cfgreateratlanta.org/nonprofits/available-grants/extra-wish/
Sponsor: Community Foundation for Greater Atlanta
191 Peachtree Street NE, Suite 1000
Atlanta, GA 30303

Community Foundation for Greater Atlanta Spark Clayton Grants   667

The Spark Clayton Fund (formerly the Clayton Fund) of the Community Foundation for Greater Atlanta was established in 1992 to bring together donors, nonprofits, and community members to make philanthropy happen in Clayton County. The Clayton Fund was the first Local Fund of the Community Foundation. It offers an annual grant making program, as well as philanthropic learning opportunities and community awareness activities – all with the goal of building philanthropy and strengthening nonprofit organizations in Clayton County. Organizations receive grants for general operating support, which gives grantees the ability to use funds where they are most needed. The Letter of Intent (LOI) is the first step in the application process. Clayton Fund Advisory Committee and program staff will then review all LOIs and invite organizations to submit final applications.
Requirements: To apply for a grant organizations must: be located and providing services within the Clayton County service area; spend funds within the Clayton County service area; be classified by the U.S. Internal Revenue Service under Section 501(c)3 of the I.R.S. code as a nonprofit, tax-exempt organization, donations to which are deductible as charitable contributions under Section 170(c)2 and the I.R.S. determination must be current; be registered with the Georgia Secretary of State as a nonprofit; have at least one full-time paid employee (paid minimum wage or more, working 2,080 hours or more) for the 12 months prior to submitting a Letter of Intent; and have a current written strategic or business plan for the whole organization that covers at least 24 months which includes the organization's entire current fiscal year.
Geographic Focus: Georgia
Contact: Lita Ugarte Pardi, Director; (404) 526-1131 or (404) 688-5525; fax (404) 688-3060; lpardi@cfgreateratlanta.org
Internet: cfgreateratlanta.org/nonprofits/available-grants/spark-clayton/
Sponsor: Community Foundation for Greater Atlanta
191 Peachtree Street NE, Suite 1000
Atlanta, GA 30303

Community Foundation for Greater Atlanta Spark Newton Grants   668

Newton County, centrally located between the cities of Atlanta, Augusta and Athens, is uniquely positioned for positive expansion and growth. Newton County's strong industrial base continues to grow the level of employment and the local economy. Arts, culture and recreation also play a large role in attracting newcomers to the area. The Spark Newton Fund (formerly the Newton Fund) of the Community Foundation for Greater Atlanta was established in 2000 to bring together donors, nonprofits and community members to make philanthropy happen in Newton County. The Newton Fund offers an annual grant making program, philanthropic learning opportunities, community awareness activities and an annual volunteer service award, the Pat Patrick "Big Heart" Award. Organizations receive grants for general operating support, which gives grantees the ability to use funds where they are most needed. The Letter of Intent (LOI) is the first step in the application process. Newton Fund Advisory Committee and program staff will then review all LOIs and invite organizations to submit final applications.
Requirements: To apply for a grant organizations must: be located and providing services within the Newton County service area; spend funds within the Newton County service area; be classified by the U.S. Internal Revenue Service under Section 501(c)3 of the I.R.S. code as a nonprofit, tax-exempt organization, donations to which are deductible as charitable contributions under Section 170(c)2 and the I.R.S. determination must be current; be registered with the Georgia Secretary of State as a nonprofit; have at least one full-time paid employee (paid minimum wage or more, working 2,080 hours or more) for the 12 months prior to submitting a Letter of Intent; and have a current written strategic or business plan for the whole organization that covers at least 24 months which includes the organization's entire current fiscal year.
Geographic Focus: Georgia
Contact: Lita Ugarte Pardi, Director; (404) 526-1131 or (404) 688-5525; fax (404) 688-3060; lpardi@cfgreateratlanta.org
Internet: cfgreateratlanta.org/nonprofits/available-grants/spark-newton/
Sponsor: Community Foundation for Greater Atlanta
191 Peachtree Street NE, Suite 1000
Atlanta, GA 30303

Community Foundation for Greater Atlanta Strategic Restructuring Fund Grants 669

The Community Foundation for Greater Atlanta is committed to building strong, collaborative nonprofits within the 23-county region. The Foundation holds a common inquiry with other funders and nonprofits to find the best practices to assess, negotiate, implement and evaluate partnership models between nonprofit organizations. The purpose of the Strategic Restructuring Fund is to provide funds and/or management consulting services to support nonprofits as they assess, negotiate, design and/or implement substantive strategic restructuring efforts that seek to promote more effective operations and high-performing programs based on community needs and assets. Currently, the Foundation offers funding in three different stages of a partnership: Partnership Assessment, in which organizations assess their readiness and suitability as potential partners and examine the different types of partnership models; Readiness and Negotiation, in which organizations will examine the pre-existing relationship, if any, between specific potential partners; and Design and/or Implementation, in which organizations finalize the details of their partnership (from timeline to steering committee to changes in staffing structures) and, if appropriate, receive funds to implement their partnership plan.
Requirements: To apply for a grant organizations must: be located and providing services within the Foundation's 23-county service area; spend funds within the 23-county service area; be classified by the U.S. Internal Revenue Service under Section 501(c)3 of the I.R.S. code as a nonprofit, tax-exempt organization, donations to which are deductible as charitable contributions under Section 170(c)2 and the I.R.S. determination must be current; be registered with the Georgia Secretary of State as a nonprofit; have a minimum two-year operating history after the date of receipt of its 501(c)3 classification; have annual operating expenses greater than $100,000 as reflected in the most recently filed IRS form 990; have at least one full-time paid employee (paid minimum wage or more, working 2,080 hours or more) for the 12 months prior to submitting a Letter of Intent; and have a current written strategic or business plan for the whole organization that covers at least 24 months which includes the organization's entire current fiscal year.
Geographic Focus: Georgia
Date(s) Application is Due: Apr 5; Sep 13
Contact: Lita Pardi, Senior Program Officer; (404) 526-1131 or (404) 688-5525; fax (404) 688-3060; lpardi@cfgreateratlanta.org@cfgreateratlanta.org
Internet: cfgreateratlanta.org/nonprofits/available-grants/strategic-restructuring-fund/
Sponsor: Community Foundation for Greater Atlanta
191 Peachtree Street NE, Suite 1000
Atlanta, GA 30303

Community Foundation for Greater Buffalo Competitive Grants   670

The Community Foundation for Greater Buffalo (CFGB) is a public charity holding more than 800 different charitable funds, large and small, established by individuals, families, nonprofit agencies and businesses to benefit Western New York. Since 1919, the Foundation has served the needs of it's community and the wishes of it's donors through personalized service, financial stewardship, local expertise, and community leadership. The Foundation is committed to making grants that maximize impact on the eight counties of Western New York in four main areas of interest: strengthening the region as a center for architecture, arts, and culture; protecting and restoring significant environmental resources and promoting equitable access; increasing racial and ethnic equity; and improving educational achievement for students living in low-income households. Awards typically range up to $25,000.
Requirements: Applicants must be 501(c)3 not-for-profit organizations located or delivering services within the eight counties of Western New York, including: Allegany, Cattaraugus, Chautauqua, Erie, Genesee, Niagara, Orleans, and Wyoming counties.
Restrictions: The Foundation will not consider competitive funding for: endowments; religious purposes; schools not registered with the New York State Education Department; attendance at or sponsorship of fundraising events for organizations; annual events or festivals; any partisan political activity. Funds from the foundation cannot be used to

support or oppose a candidate for political office. The Foundation will not consider more than one application at a time from any organization.

Geographic Focus: New York

Amount of Grant: 1,000 - 25,000 USD

Samples: Family Help Center, Buffalo, New York, $20,000 - to support Best Practices Mentoring (2019); Journey's End Refugee Services, Buffalo, New York, $15,000 - to support an alternative high school program for refugee youth (2019); Buffalo Niagara Waterkeeper, Buffalo, New York, $20,000 - to support the Volunteer Ambassador program (2019).

Contact: Darren Penoyer; (716) 852-2857, ext. 206; fax (716) 852-2861; darrenp@cfgb.org

Internet: www.cfgb.org/nonprofits/grants/community-foundation/

Sponsor: Community Foundation for Greater Buffalo

726 Exchange Street, Suite 525

Buffalo, NY 14210

Community Foundation for Greater Buffalo Garman Family Foundation Grants   671

The Community Foundation for Greater Buffalo (CFGB) is a public charity holding more than 800 different charitable funds, large and small, established by individuals, families, nonprofit agencies and businesses to benefit Western New York. Since 1919, the Foundation has served the needs of it's community and the wishes of it's donors through personalized service, financial stewardship, local expertise, and community leadership. Garman Family Foundation grants offer one cycle per year with a focus on organizations addressing mental health, physical wellness, and education of individuals with a preference for women and children. The annual deadline for application submission is September 14. The maximum amount of funding that can be requested is $50,000. On a very limited basis, the Garman Family Foundation will offer the opportunity for two-year support with second year support contingent upon outcomes from year one.

Requirements: Applications must be submitted electronically online through the Community Foundation for Greater Buffalo's Foundant Grant Lifecycle manager. Applicants must be 501(c)3 not-for-profit organizations located or delivering services within the eight counties of Western New York, including: Allegany, Cattaraugus, Chautauqua, Erie, Genesee, Niagara, Orleans, and Wyoming counties.

Restrictions: The Foundation will not consider competitive funding for: endowments; religious purposes; schools not registered with the New York State Education Department; attendance at or sponsorship of fundraising events for organizations; annual events or festivals; any partisan political activity. Funds from the foundation cannot be used to support or oppose a candidate for political office. The Foundation will not consider more than one application at a time from any organization.

Geographic Focus: New York

Date(s) Application is Due: Sep 14

Amount of Grant: Up to 50,000 USD

Contact: Jean McKeown; (716) 852-2857, ext. 204; fax (716) 852-2861; jeanm@cfgb.org

Alexandra Warner; (716) 852-2857, ext. 213; fax (716) 852-2861; alexandraw@cfgb.or

Internet: www.cfgb.org/nonprofits/grants/garman-family-foundation/

Sponsor: Community Foundation for Greater Buffalo

726 Exchange Street, Suite 525

Buffalo, NY 14210

Community Foundation for Greater Buffalo Josephine Goodyear Foundation Grants   672

The Community Foundation for Greater Buffalo (CFGB) is a public charity holding more than 800 different charitable funds, large and small, established by individuals, families, nonprofit agencies and businesses to benefit Western New York. Since 1919, the Foundation has served the needs of it's community and the wishes of it's donors through personalized service, financial stewardship, local expertise, and community leadership. The Josephine Goodyear Foundation traces its roots back to 1912 when Mrs. Frank Goodyear donated funds to build the Josephine Goodyear Convalescent Home on Main Street in Williamsville, New York. The home housed disadvantaged women and children and provided pre-operative services to prepare them for the rigors of early surgery and to provide post-surgery recovery. After World War II, with the development of antibiotics, the need for such services was greatly reduced. The property was then sold, and the foundation was established. The Josephine Goodyear Foundation Fund now funds approximately 50 annual grants totaling about $300,000. Grant decisions are made at Advisory Council meetings held in May and September of each year by our Contributions Committee. The mission calls for assistance to non-profit agencies which help "indigent women and children, particularly with their physical needs". Applications are accepted from tax-exempt organizations in two pages or less with deadline dates of April 15 and August 15 each year.

Geographic Focus: New York

Date(s) Application is Due: Apr 15; Aug 15

Amount of Grant: Up to 20,000 USD

Contact: Ted Walsh, Program Officer; (716) 853-3820 or (716) 852-2857; fax (716) 852-2861

Internet: www.cfgb.org/nonprofits/grants/josephine-goodyear-foundation/

Sponsor: Community Foundation for Greater Buffalo

726 Exchange Street, Suite 525

Buffalo, NY 14210

Community Foundation for Greater Buffalo Niagara Area Foundation Grants   673

The Community Foundation for Greater Buffalo (CFGB) is a public charity holding more than 800 different charitable funds, large and small, established by individuals, families, nonprofit agencies and businesses to benefit Western New York. Since 1919, the Foundation has served the needs of it's community and the wishes of it's donors through personalized service, financial stewardship, local expertise, and community leadership. The Niagara Area Foundation (NAF) was established in 2000 by a group of Niagara County individuals in the private and nonprofit sectors who felt a major charity-oriented philanthropic void existed in

Niagara County. Members of the NAF Council represent the whole of Niagara County and are committed to county-wide philanthropic efforts. The NAF is committed to supporting programs that will have maximum positive impact on Niagara County in the following categories: health; human services; arts; civic needs; community development; education; and the environment. The maximum grant available is $10,000.

Requirements: Applicants must be 501(c)3 not-for-profit organizations located or delivering services within Niagara County.

Restrictions: The Foundation will not consider competitive funding for: endowments; religious purposes; schools not registered with the New York State Education Department; attendance at or sponsorship of fundraising events for organizations; annual events or festivals; any partisan political activity. Funds from the foundation cannot be used to support or oppose a candidate for political office. The Foundation will not consider more than one application at a time from any organization.

Geographic Focus: New York

Amount of Grant: Up to 10,000 USD

Samples: Buffalo Hearing and Speech, Buffalo, New York, $7,918 - support of the Early Childhood Program at the John Pound Early Childhood Center (2019); Leadership Niagara, Niagara Falls, New York, $8,000 - support for Leadership for the Youth of Niagara Communities (2019); Youth Mentoring Services of Niagara County, Lockport, New York, $10,000 - support for STEM Education programs (2019).

Contact: Darren Penoyer; (716) 852-2857, ext. 206; fax (716) 852-2861; darrenp@cfgb.org

Internet: www.cfgb.org/nonprofits/grants/niagara-area-foundation/

Sponsor: Community Foundation for Greater Buffalo

726 Exchange Street, Suite 525

Buffalo, NY 14210

Community Foundation for Greater Buffalo Ralph C. Wilson, Jr. Legacy Fund Grants   674

The Community Foundation for Greater Buffalo (CFGB) is a public charity holding more than 800 different charitable funds, large and small, established by individuals, families, nonprofit agencies and businesses to benefit Western New York. Since 1919, the Foundation has served the needs of it's community and the wishes of it's donors through personalized service, financial stewardship, local expertise, and community leadership. The Ralph C. Wilson, Jr. Foundation established endowment funds at the Community Foundation for Greater Buffalo to provide annual support for programs and initiatives that reflect the personal passions of Wilson. These areas of support are: caregivers, community assets, design and access, and youth sports. The grants made from these Legacy Funds held at the Community Foundation are distinct from the grants made by the Ralph C. Wilson, Jr. Foundation directly. In most cases, the grants made from these Funds at the Community Foundation serve to support localized projects across the western New York region, for which a smaller grant can make all the difference. In some cases, it may also provide an opportunity to test out ideas and programs on a smaller, pilot level. Grant requests should range between $10,000 and $25,000 for Caregivers, Community Assets and Youth Sports. Design and Access requests should range between $10,000 and $50,000.

Requirements: Applicants must be 501(c)3 not-for-profit organizations located or delivering services within the eight counties of Western New York, including: Allegany, Cattaraugus, Chautauqua, Erie, Genesee, Niagara, Orleans, and Wyoming counties.

Restrictions: The Foundation will not consider competitive funding for: endowments; religious purposes; schools not registered with the New York State Education Department; attendance at or sponsorship of fundraising events for organizations; annual events or festivals; any partisan political activity. Funds from the foundation cannot be used to support or oppose a candidate for political office. The Foundation will not consider more than one application at a time from any organization.

Geographic Focus: New York

Amount of Grant: 10,000 - 50,000 USD

Samples: Alzheimer's Association, Western New York Chapter, Buffalo, New York, $25,000 - support for caregiver program (2019); Buffalo and Erie County Botanical Gardens Society, Buffalo, New York, $25,000 - support for botanical gardens assets (2019); Canisius College, Buffalo, New York, $25,000 - support for youth sports programs (2019).

Contact: Darren Penoyer; (716) 852-2857, ext. 206; fax (716) 852-2861; darrenp@cfgb.org

Alexandra Warner, (716) 852-2857; fax (716) 852-2861; alexandraw@cfgb.org

Internet: www.cfgb.org/nonprofits/grants/ralph-wilson-legacy/

Sponsor: Community Foundation for Greater Buffalo

726 Exchange Street, Suite 525

Buffalo, NY 14210

Community Foundation for Greater Buffalo Ralph C. Wilson, Jr. Youth Sports COVID-19 Fund Grants   675

The Community Foundation for Greater Buffalo (CFGB) is a public charity holding more than 800 different charitable funds, large and small, established by individuals, families, nonprofit agencies and businesses to benefit Western New York. Since 1919, the Foundation has served the needs of it's community and the wishes of it's donors through personalized service, financial stewardship, local expertise, and community leadership. The Ralph C. Wilson, Jr. Foundation created the Youth Sports and Recreation COVID-19 Fund to provide a source of funding to western New York Youth Sport and Recreation Organizations or youth-serving organizations that offer alternative and safe youth sport and recreation activities during the summer of 2020 through the end of the pandemic. The grants made from the Ralph C. Wilson, Jr. Youth Sports and Recreation COVID-19 Fund held at the Community Foundation for Greater Buffalo are distinct from the grants made by the Ralph C. Wilson, Jr. Foundation directly. Structured similarly to the Ralph C. Wilson Jr., Youth Sport Legacy Fund, the Youth Sports and Recreation COVID-19 Fund aims to position organizations to offer alternative and safe youth sport and recreation programming. Grant monies may be used to defray the cost of creating safe programming for youth sport and recreation including the purchase of PPE, implementation of disinfection strategies, activation of alternative programming such as play kit and equipment distributions, street

by street play and sport time, sandlot game days and nights and socially distanced sport stations within local parks. This opportunity provides grants of up to $25,000 to youth sports or youth serving organizations. The annual deadline is June 26.
Requirements: Applicants must be 501(c)3 not-for-profit organizations located or delivering services within the eight counties of Western New York, including: Allegany, Cattaraugus, Chautauqua, Erie, Genesee, Niagara, Orleans, and Wyoming counties. Requests must provide youth sport and recreation programming during the summer of 2020 through the spring of 2021.
Restrictions: The Foundation will not consider competitive funding for: endowments; religious purposes; schools not registered with the New York State Education Department; attendance at or sponsorship of fundraising events for organizations; annual events or festivals; any partisan political activity. Funds from the foundation cannot be used to support or oppose a candidate for political office. The Foundation will not consider more than one application at a time from any organization.
Geographic Focus: New York
Date(s) Application is Due: Jun 26
Amount of Grant: Up to 25,000 USD
Contact: Bridget Niland; (716) 852-2857; fax (716) 852-2861; bridgetn@cfgb.org
Internet: www.cfgb.org/nonprofits/grants/the-ralph-c-wilson-jr-youth-sports-covid-19-fund/
Sponsor: Community Foundation for Greater Buffalo
726 Exchange Street, Suite 525
Buffalo, NY 14210

Community Foundation for Kettering Grants 676

Projects and activities supported by the Community Foundation for Kettering benefit residents of the Greater Kettering area. The foundation generally makes grants to support start-up or new projects currently not addressed by existing organizations, or special efforts by existing organizations to undertake unique activities or projects. Primary areas of interest include: education; art and culture; community development; and children and youth programs. There are two annual application deadlines; October 2 and April 1.
Requirements: To be eligible for a grant, an organization must: be recognized as a 501(c)3 tax-exempt nonprofit, according to the Internal Revenue Code, and be established for at least two years and have a track record of sustainability; benefit the citizens in the Greater Dayton Region, (Montgomery, Miami, Greene, Darke, Preble and Warren (north) counties); have a diversity/inclusion policy; demonstrate systemic collaboration; and address needs that are not met fully by existing organizational or community resources.
Restrictions: The Foundation generally does not award discretionary grants for: general organizational operations and ongoing programs, operational deficits or reduced or lost funding; individuals, scholarship, travel; religious/sectarian causes; fundraising drives; special events; political activities; public or private schools; endowment funds; hospitals and universities for internal programs; matching grants (unless local dollars are needed to fulfill a condition for a state or federal grant); neighborhood or local jurisdiction projects; newly organized not-for-profit organizations; or publications, scientific, medical or academic research projects, research papers.
Geographic Focus: Ohio
Date(s) Application is Due: Apr 1; Oct 2
Contact: Janice McLefresh, Donor Relations Officer; (937) 225-9971 or (937) 222-0410; fax (937) 222-0636; jmclefresh@daytonfoundation.org
Internet: www.daytonfoundation.org/grntfdns.html
Sponsor: Community Foundation for Kettering
40 North Main Street, Suite 500
Dayton, OH 45423

Community Foundation for San Benito County Grants 677

The Foundation serves donors, advances philanthropy and achieves impact by supporting the work of nonprofit organizations. The Foundation continuously monitors the San Benito County community to understand the nature of need, the forces of change, available resources and the capacity for growth. The Foundation provides funding to support impactful programs within and across the following areas of interest: arts and culture; education and youth; health and social services; agriculture and environment; community enhancement; economic development. Application deadlines are announced on the Foundation's website.
Requirements: Selection criteria and priorities are as follows: projects or services which respond to a demonstrated need within San Benito County; effective use and greatest impact of grant funds; initiatives to solve significant community issues; collaboration and coordination of service delivery; demonstrate a level of cooperation with other organizations, including leveraging financial and in-kind support from other groups and individuals; strengthening organizational capacity; addressing diverse community interests; organizational or program sustainability; organizations with demonstrated financial need; and unduplicated services. Awards are generally up to $40,000. Major projects or initiatives over $40,000 must be preliminarily discussed with Foundation staff.
Restrictions: In general the following are not funded: organizations that discriminate on the basis of age, disability, ethnic origin, gender, race or religion; grants to individuals; fraternal or service organizations, unless in support of specific programs open to or benefiting the entire community; salaries and other operating expenses of schools and public agencies; fundraising events such as annual campaigns, walk-a-thons, tournaments, fashion shows, dinners and auctions; organizations and programs designed to support political activities; organizations located outside San Benito County unless for a specific program benefiting residents within San Benito County; pay off existing obligations or enable funding of reserve accounts; endowment funds; and scholarships, fellowships, travel grants and academic, technical or specialized research.
Geographic Focus: California
Samples: Chamberlain's Mental Health Services, Gilroy, California, $100,000 - behavioral management programs for functionally impaired preschool children; SB Collaborative for Homeless Services, Santa Barbara, California, $5,000 - homeless information data program required to enable future HUD funding; and Seniors Council (Foster Grandparents), San Benito, California, $6,159 - support of seniors mentoring and tutoring program for at-risk youth.
Contact: Grants Manager; (831) 630-1924; fax (831) 630-1934; info@cffsbc.org
Internet: www.cffsbc.org/grantoverview.php
Sponsor: Community Foundation for San Benito County
829 San Benio Street, Suite 200
Hollister, CA 95023

Community Foundation for San Benito County Martin Rajkovich Children's Fund Grants 678

The Foundation is pleased to announce available Grants through the Martin Rajkovich Children's Fund. This bequeathed fund is permanently endowed through the Foundation and designated to benefit critically or chronically ill children living in San Benito County. Grants will be used to enhance the quality of life and well-being of a child by providing extra support that is not available or open to the family. It is the lasting wish of the donor that this special fund brings joy and comfort to the sick child and their family.
Requirements: The criteria for eligible children: must be under nineteen years of age; the child must live in San Benito County; and must be under a doctor's care with a critically ill or chronic illness. The fund will consider support including, but not limited to, the following: equipment and accessories to enhance quality of life; special therapeutic treatments outside of the medical field; transportation, respite care, family counseling; and special recreational travel arrangements. To refer a child for Grant consideration, contact the Foundation directly or submit a A Child Referral Form which is available at the Foundation's website.
Restrictions: The Foundation respects the privacy of all children and families. All medical information is confidential and consent is given by the child's parent(s) or guardian(s).
Geographic Focus: California
Contact: Grants Manager; (831) 630-1924; fax (831) 630-1934
Internet: www.cffsbc.org/fund_martinrajkovich.php
Sponsor: Community Foundation for San Benito County
829 San Benio Street, Suite 200
Hollister, CA 95023

Community Foundation for SE Michigan Chelsea Community Foundation Capacity Building Grants 679

The Chelsea Community Foundation is a permanent community endowment with assets in excess of $2.5 million thanks to strong local support and prudent financial management. The Chelsea Community Foundation is guided by Chelsea's civic leaders who care deeply about the community. To-date, more than $1.6 million has been awarded to local nonprofits to address emerging community needs and opportunities. The Civic Foundation of Chelsea was formed in 1981 to coordinate the efforts of various individuals and entities in serving the needs of the community. Another organization, The Foundation for Community Care, was established by the Chelsea Community Hospital to provide financial assistance for patients in need of health care services and lacking insurance or the ability to pay, and for other philanthropic needs not typically part of a hospital's operating budget. In 1994, the two Foundations merged into the Chelsea Foundation, and in 1995 it became an affiliate fund of the Community Foundation for Southeast Michigan. This affiliation offered access to the larger Community Foundation's resources while permitting the flexibility to make sure Chelsea's needs would be met from the proceeds of a well-managed permanent endowment with community-minded donors and advisors. The application is on a rolling-basis, and the process takes about three months.
Requirements: Organizations must be 501(c)3 nonprofit organizations in the Chelsea area with leadership development and capacity-building activities. Organizations must have an independent certified financial audit.
Geographic Focus: Michigan
Amount of Grant: 1,000 - 5,000 USD
Samples: SRSLY, Chelsea, Michigan - to support students remotely during COVID-19 (2020); Chelsea Senior Center, Chelsea, Michigan - to ensure senior citizens are getting the needed care during the COVID-19 crisis (2020); Chelsea School District, Chelsea, Michigan - to support Chelsea education (2020).
Contact: Surabhi Pandit, Senior Program Officer; (313) 961-6675, ext. 123; fax (313) 961-2886; spandit@cfsem.org or spandit@cfsem.org
Internet: cfsem.org/special-opportunities/chelsea-community-foundation/apply/
Sponsor: Community Foundation for SE Michigan
333 W Fort Street, Suite 2010
Detroit, MI 48226-3134

Community Foundation for SE Michigan Chelsea Community Foundation General Grant 680

The Chelsea Community Foundation is a permanent community endowment with assets in excess of $2.5 million thanks to strong local support and prudent financial management. The Chelsea Community Foundation is guided by Chelsea's civic leaders who care deeply about the community. To-date, more than $1.6 million has been awarded to local nonprofits to address emerging community needs and opportunities. The Civic Foundation of Chelsea was formed in 1981 to coordinate the efforts of various individuals and entities in serving the needs of the community. Another organization, The Foundation for Community Care, was established by the Chelsea Community Hospital to provide financial assistance for patients in need of health care services and lacking insurance or the ability to pay, and for other philanthropic needs not typically part of a hospital's operating budget. In 1994, the two Foundations merged into the Chelsea Foundation, and in 1995 it became an affiliate fund of the Community Foundation for Southeast Michigan. This affiliation offered access to the larger Community Foundation's resources while permitting the flexibility to make sure Chelsea's needs would be met from the proceeds of a well-managed permanent endowment with community-minded donors and advisors. The award varies from $5,000 to $25,000 and has deadlines on February 15th and August 15th.

Requirements: Organizations must have an independent certified financial audit.
Geographic Focus: Michigan
Date(s) Application is Due: Feb 15; Aug 15
Amount of Grant: 5,000 - 25,000 USD
Samples: SRSLY, Chelsea, Michigan - to support students remotely during COVID-19 (2020); Chelsea Senior Center, Chelsea, Michigan - to ensure senior citizens are getting the needed care during the COVID-19 crisis (2020); Chelsea School District, Chelsea, Michigan - to support Chelsea education (2020).
Contact: Surabhi Pandit; (313) 961-6675, ext. 123; fax (313) 961-2886; spandit@cfsem.org
Internet: cfsem.org/special-opportunities/chelsea-community-foundation/apply/
Sponsor: Community Foundation for SE Michigan
333 W Fort Street, Suite 2010
Detroit, MI 48226-3134

Community Foundation for SE Michigan Detroit Auto Dealers Association   681
Charitable Foundation Fund Grants
The Detroit Auto Dealers Association Charitable Foundation Fund is a fund of Community Foundation for Southeast Michigan. It was established in 1998 by the Detroit Auto Dealers Association, a trade association representing more than 250 automobile dealers and 240 dealerships in metropolitan Detroit. Grants support worthy programs which improve and enhance the lives of children and youth. Approximately ten awards ranging from $10,000 to $50,000 are awarded annually.
Requirements: The Foundation supports programs and projects that improve life in southeast Michigan, specifically in the seven-county service area of Wayne, Oakland, Macomb, Monroe, Washtenaw, St. Clair and Livingston. Eligible organizations: are a 501(c)3 tax-exempt organization, a government entity, a school district or a university; have headquarters (or a local partner) located in the seven-county service area; serve residents in the seven-county service area; have Board and/or the CEO approval to submit a proposal; and have a current certified financial audit. Nonprofit organizations in the fields of human service, education, arts and culture, environment, recreation, health and public affairs are eligible.
Restrictions: All final reports due to the Foundation for previous grants must be submitted before applying. Requests for sectarian religious programs, individuals, and funding for deficits or other previously incurred obligations are not eligible. The fund does not fund awards to host or sponsor events. Those who receive funding from Charity Preview are ineligible.
Geographic Focus: Michigan
Date(s) Application is Due: Oct 1
Amount of Grant: 10,000 - 50,000 USD
Contact: Surabhi Pandit; (313) 961-6675, ext. 123; fax (313) 961-2886; spandit@cfsem.org
Internet: cfsem.org/special-opportunities/detroit-auto-dealers-association/
Sponsor: Community Foundation for SE Michigan
333 W Fort Street, Suite 2010
Detroit, MI 48226-3134

Community Foundation for SE Michigan Head Start Innovation Fund   682
The Innovation Fund awards competitive grants to Head Start providers, as well as strategic support for system-wide needs, such as oversight of a monthly Learning Network, creation and administration of a common enrollment campaign, comprehensive data collection, and provision of collaborative access to shared resources, such as quality training. The Innovation Fund leverages and supports a $48 million, 5-year federal investment in Head Start programs in Detroit following a rebidding process in 2013, as well a similar recompetition effort that occurred in the outlying counties in 2016. The supporters of the Innovation Fund, saw that these rebidding competitions were a moment of key change in the system locally, and want to be supportive of both new providers and existing providers as they transition to a new model of Head Start that provides more full day options for parents as well as more slots for younger children.
Geographic Focus: Michigan
Samples: Matrix Human Services, Detroit, Michigan, $150,000 - focused on agencies serving children in the city of Detroit, strengthen programmatic offerings related to recompetition of federal Head Start funds (2018); Oakland Livingston Human Services Agency, Pontiac, Michigan, $100,000 - to launch new teacher recruitment and retention strategies leveraging its Trauma Smart trained staff to support teachers and candidates in Oakland and Livingston counties experiencing significant personal trauma (2018); Starfish, Detroit, Michigan, $150,000 - to improve classroom assessment scoring system (CLASS) scores and address teacher recruitment and retention (2018).
Contact: Kamilah Henderson, Senior Program Officer; (313) 961-6675; fax (313) 961-2886; khenderson@cfsem.org
Internet: cfsem.org/initiative/headstart/
Sponsor: Community Foundation for SE Michigan
333 W Fort Street, Suite 2010
Detroit, MI 48226-3134

Community Foundation for SE Michigan Livingston County Grants   683
The Community Foundation for Livingston County is a permanent community endowment established to improve the public well-being and quality of life in Livingston County by: providing leadership in identifying and addressing community needs and opportunities and attracting and managing charitable gifts and bequests primarily in the form of permanent endowments Using the assets to make prudent and creative grants to address emerging community needs in a wide-range of charitable activities. The Community Foundation for Livingston County has awarded more than $900,000 through more than 150 grants to support and improve public well-being and quality of life in the areas of economic development, human services, arts, civic affairs, education, health and the environment in Livingston County. Since its inception, the Community Foundation for Livingston County has established 19 funds to recognize individuals and businesses in Livingston County,

growing the foundation's endowment to more than $1 million. The award ranges from $5,000 to $25,000, and there are two annual deadlines on February 15th and August 15th.
Requirements: Project must impact Livingston County.
Geographic Focus: Michigan
Date(s) Application is Due: Feb 15; Aug 15
Amount of Grant: 5,000 - 25,000 USD
Samples: Livingston County United Way, Livingston County, Michigan, $10,000 -will support United Way's COVID-19 Relief Fund (2020); Ann Arbor Spark, Ann Arbor, Michigan, $10,000 -p to leverage additional resources for small businesses in Livingston County to help cover immediate fixed expenses and alleviate employee layoff and business viability once the stay in place orders are lifted (2020); St. Joseph Mercy Livingston, Howell, Michigan, $15,000 -to help with COVID-19 relief (2020)
Contact: Katie Brisson; (313) 961-6675; fax (313) 961-2886; scholarships@cfsem.org
Internet: cfsem.org/special-opportunities/community-foundation-livingston-county/apply/
Sponsor: Community Foundation for SE Michigan
333 W Fort Street, Suite 2010
Detroit, MI 48226-3134

Community Foundation for SE Michigan Renaissance of Values Scholarships   684
The Community Foundation for Southeast Michigan supports the future by investing in the education of its young people through scholarship programs. The Renaissance Of Values Scholarships are for graduating eighth graders from Cornerstone Schools and Everest Academy to attend the first year in private high school. Two non-renewable scholarships in the amount up to $6,000 are provided. Application materials are available at each school, and the annual deadline for applications is March 15th.
Requirements: The candidate must be graduating from Cornerstone Schools or Everest Academy in the spring and be accepted for entrance into an accredited, private, preparatory/high school. Candidates must also demonstrate a strong commitment to family, friends and the greater community, active participation, as part of his or her family, in an organized Christian religious congregation during the past two years, and participation in an activity that required personal service to others either in the school or in a local religious organization during the past two years. Candidates must also have a strong academic performance achieving a class rank in the top 20% or the equivalent and an indication of financial need by completing the Financial Information Form.
Restrictions: Dependents of employees of the Community Foundation for Southeast Michigan, members of the Board of Trustees of the Foundation, the Advisory Committee of Renaissance of Values Scholarship Program as well as dependents of employees of Cornerstone Schools or Everest Academy and dependents of the scholarship selection committee are ineligible for scholarship consideration.
Geographic Focus: Michigan
Date(s) Application is Due: Mar 15
Amount of Grant: 6,000 USD
Contact: Surabhi Pandit, Senior Program Officer; (313) 961-6675, ext. 123; fax (313) 961-2886; scholarships@cfsem.org or spandit@cfsem.org
Internet: cfsem.org/scholarships/scholarship-opportunities/
Sponsor: Community Foundation for SE Michigan
333 W Fort Street, Suite 2010
Detroit, MI 48226-3134

Community Foundation for SE Michigan Southeast Michigan Immigrant   685
and Refugee Funder Collaborative Grant
The Community Foundation for Southeast Michigan in partnership with other community groups and neighborhood associations throughout the region, has been supporting immigrants and refugees for decades. As the need for support continues to evolve, nonprofits are working hard to effectively deploy resources, such as conducting "know your rights" campaigns; providing direct human services and referrals; serving as a hub for community activities; providing direct legal services, and much more. The current total investment in the Southeast Michigan Immigrant and Refugee Funder Collaborative is $500,000 over two years — a small figure compared with the overall need. But it is an important first step in bringing the philanthropic community together to strategically address the needs of immigrants and refugees in our region. Applications are due on July 21st.
Geographic Focus: Michigan
Date(s) Application is Due: Jul 21
Samples: Chaldean American Ladies of Charity, Detroit, Michigan, $30,000 - to support an immigrant and refugee leadership program in the metro Detroit area, in collaboration with the International Institute of Metropolitan Detroit (2020); Detroit Hispanic Development Corporation, Detroit Michigan, $40,000 - to support the Detroit Latino Coalition, a group comprised of organizations and individual leaders committed to strengthening and unifying the Latino voice in southwest Detroit, in collaboration with We the People Michigan (2020); Freedom House, Detroit, Michigan, $30,000 - to enhance immigration legal services for asylum seekers, asylees, and resettled refugees, in collaboration with the Southwest Detroit Immigrant and Refugee Center and Samaritas (2020).
Contact: Surabhi Pandit; (313) 961-6675, ext. 123; spandit@cfsem.org
Internet: cfsem.org/initiative/immigrants-refugees/
Sponsor: Community Foundation for SE Michigan
333 W Fort Street, Suite 2010
Detroit, MI 48226-3134

Community Foundation for SE Michigan Youth Leadership Grant   686
The Community Foundation's Youth Leadership project was established in 1991 with a $1 million challenge grant from the W.K. Kellogg Foundation. These funds established an endowed youth fund that would, in perpetuity, involve young people in reviewing grant proposals from organizations that benefit youth in southeast Michigan. For more than 20 years,

our middle school- and high school-aged youth advisors have recommended 196 youth-serving grants totaling more than $1.3 million. These grants have had a real impact on growing youth leaders at nonprofit organizations across the region. The awards range from $2,500 to $20,000.
Requirements: Candidates must be local nonprofit organizations or school districts proposing a project that will either involve youth in the development of the program or will build opportunities for youth leaders.
Geographic Focus: Michigan
Amount of Grant: 2,500 - 20,000 USD
Samples: Neutral Zone, Ann Arbor, Michigan, $19,450 - to develop a youth leadership team to guide the agency-wide use of restorative practices, and help train other youth organizations to replicate a sense of belonging and mattering (2020); Detroit Horse Power, Detroit, Michigan, $10,000 - to establish a Youth Leadership Council (2020).
Contact: Surabhi Pandit; (313) 961-6675, ext. 123; fax (313) 961-2886; spandit@cfsem.org
Internet: cfsem.org/special-opportunities/youth-leadership/
Sponsor: Community Foundation for SE Michigan
333 W Fort Street, Suite 2010
Detroit, MI 48226-3134

Community Foundation for the Capital Region Grants   687
The Community Foundation for the Capital Region awards grants to eligible New York nonprofit organizations through the administration of more than 260 charitable funds, established by donors to meet their philanthropic objectives and address current and future needs. The Foundation's primary fields of interest include: art and music therapy; basic and remedial instruction; child welfare; disasters and emergency management; elder abuse; employment; the environment; graduate and professional education; health and health care; HIV/AIDS; home health care; homeless services; medical education; music; nursing care; and senior services. Types of support include: fund raising; operating support; capital grants; seed money; technical assistance; and program development. Grants may be held for a maximum of three years. Applicants should submit a letter of inquiry that describes the organization, the program, and the amount sought. Full applications are by invitation.
Requirements: New York 501(c)3 tax-exempt organizations serving Albany, Rensselaer, Schenectady, or Saratoga Counties are eligible.
Geographic Focus: New York
Amount of Grant: 2,500 - 30,000 USD
Contact: Jackie Mahoney, Program Director; (518) 446-9638; fax (518) 446-9708; Jmahoney@cfcr.org, or info@cfcr.org
Internet: www.cfcr.org/grantmaking/grantmaking.htm
Sponsor: Community Foundation for the Capital Region
6 Tower Place, Executive Park Drive
Albany, NY 12203-3725

Community Foundation for the National Capital Region   688
**   Community Leadership Grants**
The Community Foundation for the National Capital Region has a particular interest in supporting groups in the metropolitan Washington, D.C., area working in the following issue areas: violence prevention; education; community building; cross-cultural or cultural partnership building; family literacy; and healthcare and dental services for underprivileged children, youth, and families. Types of support include general operating support, program development, technical assistance, and program evaluation. Approximately 30 to 40 grants per year are awarded following a Request-for-Proposal cycle, which occurs "several times per year." Letters of inquiry (three-page maximum) must meet the listed application deadlines.
Requirements: 501(c)3 nonprofits in the metropolitan Washington region, including the District of Columbia, northern Virginia, and suburban Maryland may submit letters of inquiry. Applicants must represent a neighborhood, citywide, or regional coalition effort, with one nonprofit organization serving as project sponsor.
Geographic Focus: District of Columbia, Maryland, Virginia
Contact: Dawnn Leary, Senior Philanthropic Services Officer; (202) 973-2519 or (202) 955-5890; fax (202) 955-8084; dleary@cfncr.org or info@cfncr.org
Internet: thecommunityfoundation.org/what-we-do/grantmaking/
Sponsor: Community Foundation for the National Capital Region
1201 15th Street NW, Suite 420
Washington, D.C. 20005

Community Foundation of Abilene Future Fund Grants   689
The Future Fund Grants focus on the needs of children and youth. Future Fund awards a minimum of $15,000 in grants each year. Most grants are in the $5,000 range, although smaller and larger grants will be considered. Chances of funding increase if the project: proposes a practical solution to a youth or children's issue; promotes volunteer participation in the community; is responsive to changing or emerging community needs; leverages or generates other funding or resources; promotes cooperation among nonprofit agencies without duplicating efforts; or addresses prevention as well as assistance for a problem. Consideration is also given to the capability of the agency and its staff and volunteers to achieve expected results, the adequacy and professionalism of the budget, and the support and cooperation of agencies involved in similar projects. Applications are available at the Foundation website, and are accepted at any time.
Requirements: Future Fund will consider funding for special projects and equipment needs for programs that directly serve children and/or youth in the community. Future Fund welcomes proposals from any nonprofit organization in Abilene with an IRS tax-exempt status.
Restrictions: Funding is not available for the following: medical or scholarly research; maintenance expenses; membership fees; ticket sales for charitable fundraising events; church related activities unless they involve children in the entire community; travel for groups, such as school classes, clubs or sports teams; participation in out of town camps;

projects, programs or events that have been completed or items that have already been purchased; capital debt reduction; individuals; political projects.
Geographic Focus: Texas
Amount of Grant: 1,000 - 10,000 USD
Contact: Courtney Vletas, Grants Director; (325) 676-3883, ext 102; cvletas@cfabilene.org
Internet: cfabilene.org/future-fund
Sponsor: Community Foundation of Abilene
500 Chestnut, Suite 1634, P.O. Box 1001
Abilene, TX 79604

Community Foundation of Bartholomew County Heritage Fund Grants   690
The goal of the Heritage Fund's grant program is to achieve the maximum impact with the available resources. The Fund will consider grant applications that: are change-orientated and problem-solving in nature; strive to anticipate the changing needs of the community and to be flexible in responding to them; address the needs of a significant number of community residents and provide the greatest benefit per dollar granted; encourage support from the community by using matching, challenge and other grant techniques; have a broad funding base, with additional support being sought from the government, foundations, associations and other funders; enable grant recipients to achieve certain objectives such as capacity building, and/or increasing efficiency, effectiveness and fundraising capabilities; request technical assistance or specialized help with projects that respond to community needs; or positively impact the Heritage Fund's Areas of Initiative.
Requirements: Grants are made to not-for-profit organizations whose programs benefit the residents of Bartholomew County, Indiana.
Restrictions: Funding is not available for the following: individuals; events, performances, seminars or trips unless there are special circumstances which will benefit the community; individual school needs; faith based organizations unless the project in question is not religious in nature, is not restricted based on faith, and involves no faith based proselytizing; or agency endowments.
Geographic Focus: Indiana
Date(s) Application is Due: Mar 1; Jun 1; Sep 1; Dec 1
Amount of Grant: Up to 3,000 USD
Contact: Lynda J. Morgan, Program Officer; (812) 376-7772; fax (812) 376-0051; lmorgan@heritagefundbc.org
Internet: www.heritagefundbc.org/grants/process_guidelines_deadlines.php
Sponsor: Community Foundation of Bartholomew County
538 Franklin Street, P.O. Box 1547
Columbus, IN 47202-1547

Community Foundation of Bartholomew County James A. Henderson   691
**   Award for Fundraising**
The Henderson Award recognizes the invaluable role volunteer fundraisers play in advancing the quality of life within Bartholomew County, Indiana. Not-for-profit organizations in the county are invited to nominate volunteers who have performed outstanding fundraising for their organizations. A committee will review the nominations and select the person to be honored. The committee will consider such criteria as innovation, sustainability, creativity, effectiveness, effort, ability to engage others, outreach to new donors, etc. Generally the amount raised will not be a major factor in the scoring. Efforts will be made to recognize unsung heroes in fundraising. The successful nominee will be recognized at the Heritage Fund's Annual Report to the Community. He/she will receive a small gift and the nominating organization will receive a $2,500 grant in honor of the winner. The nomination form is available at the website.
Geographic Focus: Indiana
Date(s) Application is Due: Mar 23
Amount of Grant: 2,500 USD
Contact: Lynda J. Morgan, Program Officer; (812) 376-7772; fax (812) 376-0051; lmorgan@heritagefundbc.org
Internet: www.heritagefundbc.com/grants/award_james_henderson.php
Sponsor: Community Foundation of Bartholomew County
538 Franklin Street, P.O. Box 1547
Columbus, IN 47202-1547

Community Foundation of Bartholomew County Women's Giving Circle   692
The Women's Giving Circle of Bartholomew County (WGCBC) seeks to empower women givers and make a positive change in the lives of women and families in Bartholomew County. The WGCBC is a participating membership fund managed by Heritage Fund – the Community Foundation of Bartholomew County. Each year the membership of the WGCBC will vote at the spring Annual Meeting on grant proposals submitted to the membership, following guidelines set out by the Guiding Circle. These grant recommendations will be made to the Heritage Fund Board of Directors for final approval. The application is available at the website.
Requirements: The WGCBC seeks to support programs that make a significant impact on women and their families. The Circle encourage submission of requests for new, emerging and diverse programs with goals to improve the lives of women and families. In addition, it also recognizes the value of existing programs which could be enhanced, updated or broadened for increased impact. All requests must be for programs which address the following focus areas: self sufficiency for women - providing women and their families with the tools necessary to become self-sufficient. Including but not limited to, providing access to opportunities for education and mentoring; job application and interview skills; health issues; developing the knowledge and skills to make informed effective financial decisions; early childhood education - providing young learners with an opportunity to begin school ready to learn; parental support - including but not limited to helping parents and caregivers create a healthy, supportive family environment, providing for the needs of families who

are caring for children with physical, mental, emotional or other types of challenges, and families dealing with the challenges of raising teens; and women in crisis - including but not limited to, providing women in unsafe situations the support to establish a productive life; dealing with homeless causes; women who are faced with the challenges of providing support for elderly parents and ill spouses. Grants are made to Bartholomew County nonprofit organizations, or to qualifying organizations that provide a responsible fiscal agent.
Restrictions: Grants will not be made for any of the following: individuals; general operating costs; scholarships; individual school needs; agency endowments; events, performances, seminars or trips unless there are special circumstances which will benefit the community; faith-based organizations unless the project in question is not religious in nature, is not restricted based on faith, and involves no faith-based proselytizing.
Geographic Focus: Indiana
Date(s) Application is Due: Feb 17
Amount of Grant: Up to 5,000 USD
Contact: Lisa Shafran, Grant Contact; (812) 376-7772; lshafran@heritagefundbc.org
Internet: www.heritagefundbc.org/donors/campaigns/womensgivingcircle/womensgivingcircle.php
Sponsor: Community Foundation of Bartholomew County
538 Franklin Street, P.O. Box 1547
Columbus, IN 47202-1547

Community Foundation of Boone County - Women's Grants   693
The mission of the Community Foundation of Boone County - Women's Grants is to support the Helping Hands Emergency Women's Shelter and to provide grants to Boone County organizations that promote intellectual, physical, emotional, social, economic, and spiritual growth for women of all ages.
Requirements: Organizations should fill out the online application with specific information including the organization and its nonprofit status, a description of the project and amount requested, with a timeline, equipment needed, and the organization's board of directors.
Geographic Focus: Indiana
Amount of Grant: Up to 10,000 USD
Contact: Barb Schroeder, Program Director; (317) 873-0210 or (765) 482-0024; fax (317) 873-0219; barb@communityfoundationbc.org
Internet: communityfoundationbc.org/womens_fund.html
Sponsor: Community Foundation of Boone County
60 East Cedar Street
Zionsville, IN 46077

Community Foundation of Boone County Grants   694
The Community Foundation of Boone County Grants provides funding in the following areas: arts/culture; community development; education; elderly; health; human services; youth; environment; and recreation. Applications for grants of $10,000 or less should be submitted on the Short Form located on the website, while applications for more than $10,000 should follow instructions in the Content and Format section of the website. Awards will be made to nonprofit organizations exempt from federal taxation under section 501(c)3 of the Internal Revenue Code. Grants may be allowed to individuals and to non-501(c)3 organizations if there is documented charitable activity benefiting or serving the residents of Boone County, or if the Community Foundation is acting as fiscal agent for the project or program.
Requirements: Grant proposals for over $10,000 must include the following format: abstract or executive summary; description of organization; statement of problem or need; objectives; proposed solution; materials/equipment; staff; facilities; evaluation; budget and its explanation; and appendices. Organizations should review the Foundation website for specific proposal submission instructions.
Restrictions: Non-allowable expenses include support of pre-award costs (i.e., project costs generated during the preparation of a proposal for the same project); existing general fund operating expenses; regular salaries of pre-award permanent staff (unless overload compensation is justified during the life of the funded project); international travel; first-class air fare; luxury accommodations; hospitality for purposes other than those directly related to meeting program objectives as defined in the proposal; alcohol; and indirect or regular existing administrative costs (e.g., telephone, utilities, general maintenance, etc.) of the applicant organization.
Geographic Focus: Indiana
Date(s) Application is Due: Jan 24; Mar 28; May 30; Aug 1; Oct 3; Nov 21
Samples: Lebanon Area Boys and Girls Club for the SCORE (Scholarship, Citizenship, Organization, Responsibility, Effort) Mentoring Program for high risk youth, $9,995; Youth As Resources Program of United Way of Central Indiana, $5,000 in support of youth-led volunteer community service projects, where young people are exposed to philanthropy and the needs of their community; Otterbein United Methodist Church, $10,000 for the What's For Lunch Program, providing more than 400 lunches for needy families.
Contact: Barbara J. Schroeder, Program Director; (317) 873-0210 or (765) 482-0024; fax (317) 873-0219; barb@communityfoundationbc.org
Internet: www.communityfoundationbc.org/grants.html
Sponsor: Community Foundation of Boone County
60 East Cedar Street
Zionsville, IN 46077

Community Foundation of Crawford County   695
The mission of the Community Foundation of Crawford County (CFCC) is to offer philanthropic grant making and estate planning with the professional and financial expertise needed to engage, affect, and inspire charitable giving for the community of Crawford County, Indiana. The CFCC currently manages more than $6 million in endowed funds. These funds benefit the community through donor advised, field of interest, restricted and unrestricted grants, and scholarship funds. There are two annual grant cycle deadlines: one in early December and one in early June. Typically, awards range up to a maximum of $10,000.

Requirements: Any 501(c)3 organization serving the residents of Crawford County, Indiana, are eligible to apply.
Geographic Focus: Indiana
Date(s) Application is Due: Jun 4; Dec 3
Amount of Grant: Up to 10,000 USD
Contact: Christine Harbeson, Executive Director; (812) 365-2900; charbeson@cf-cc.org
Internet: www.cf-cc.org/grants.html
Sponsor: Community Foundation of Crawford County
4030 East Goodman Ridge Road, Box D
Marengo, IN 47140

Community Foundation of Eastern Connecticut General Southeast Grants   696
Within its geographic area, comprising the 42 towns of eastern Connecticut, the community foundation awards grants to assist charitable, educational, and civic institutions; promote health and general welfare; support environmental programs; provide human care services for the needy; secure the care of children and families; encourage artistic and cultural endeavors; and initiate planning of appropriate projects within these areas. High-priority programs include those that strengthen families; improve access to area resources, especially for underserved populations; encourage residents to participate in the cultural life of the community; demonstrate collaborative efforts and inclusive practices; reinforce best practices or show innovative approaches; and add to the general well being of the community. Types of support include building and renovation, equipment, emergency funds, program development, conferences and seminars, publication, seed grants, scholarship funds, technical support, and scholarships to individuals. Foundation grants have ranged from $1,000 to $25,000 in recent years, with most grants in the $5,000 to $15,000 range. Proposals may be submitted between April 1 and November 15 each year.
Requirements: Grants must be for the benefit of residents of East Lyme, Groton, Ledyard, Lyme, Montville, New London, North Stonington, Old Lyme, Salem, Stonington and Waterford. Preference is given to programs that: are collaborative in nature; are regional in scope; promote systems change; are rooted in evidence-based, solution-oriented approaches; serve lower-income communities; seek to eliminate racism and societal inequities; incorporate the voices of clients, consumers and youth in planning; include specific, measurable outcomes; and affect positive change over the long term.
Restrictions: The foundation does not consider requests for direct financial assistance to individuals; religious or sectarian programs; political or lobbying purposes; fundraising events; or debt retirement. Applications requesting support of normal operating expenses will not be considered.
Geographic Focus: Connecticut
Date(s) Application is Due: Jan 13
Amount of Grant: 5,000 - 30,000 USD
Samples: Planned Parenthood of Southern New England, New England, Connecticut, $25,000 - to provide healthcare access to low income adults (2020); The Arc Eastern Connecticut, Norwich, Connecticut, $20,000 - to provide support services to those with disabilities (2020); New London Homeless Hospitality Center, New London, Connecticut, $25,000 - to support the operation of the shelter and services to the homeless (2020).
Contact: Jennifer O'Brien, Program Director; (860) 442-3572 or (877) 442-3572; fax (860) 442-0584; jennob@cfect.org
Internet: www.cfect.org/Nonprofits/Apply-for-a-Grant/Apply-for-Our-Southeast-General-Fund-Grant
Sponsor: Community Foundation of Eastern Connecticut
68 Federal Street
New London, CT 06320

**Community Foundation of Eastern Connecticut Northeast Women and   697
Girls Grants**
The Community Foundation of Eastern Connecticut's Northeast Women and Girls Fund aims to remove the inequities that block women from self-sustainability and improve the quality of life for all women and girls living in Northeast Connecticut. The Foundation aims to achieve this by focusing on three priority areas, including: empowerment and personal development programs that help women and girls overcome personal obstacles and take positive control of their lives - areas of focus include, but are not limited to, mentoring programs, life skills, connecting to the community, and confidence-building; positive health and well-being programs that promote good physical and mental health practices and healthy lifestyles - areas of focus for such programs may include the whole being (mind, body, soul, nutrition, exercise, etc.), the prevention of high risk behaviors and relationship violence, and the encouragement of supportive networks; and economic independence programs that include, but are not limited to, access to education, full-time employment, vocational skills, career development, affordable childcare, housing, and building financial literacy skills. The deadline to apply is October 1st.
Requirements: IRS tax-exempt organizations serving Brooklyn, Canterbury, Eastford, Hampton, Killingly, Plainfield, Pomfret, Putnam, Sterling, Thompson, and Woodstock are eligible to apply for this funding. Collaboration between service providers is highly encouraged.
Restrictions: The foundation does not consider requests for direct financial assistance to individuals; religious or sectarian programs; political or lobbying purposes; fundraising events; or debt retirement. Applications requesting support of normal operating expenses will not be considered.
Geographic Focus: Connecticut
Date(s) Application is Due: Oct 1
Amount of Grant: Up to 3,000 USD
Samples: Windham-Tolland 4-H Camp, Windham, Connecticut, $750 - to fund those with limited family financial means to be able to attend camp (2019); Planned Parenthood of Southern New England, New England, Connecticut, $1,595 - to support health services for low-income women in Northeast Connecticut (2019); The Arc Eastern Connecticut,

Norwich, Connecticut, $2,500 - to fund "Voices" Empowerment Group for Women with Intellectual and Developmental Disabilities to teach women about healthy behaviors and how to develop good decision-making skills to prevent abuse and exploitation (2019).
Contact: Deb Battit; (860) 442-3572 or (877) 442-3572; fax (860) 442-0584; deb@cfect.org
Internet: www.cfect.org/ForGrantseekers/Howtoapplyforgrants/tabid/319/Default.aspx
Sponsor: Community Foundation of Eastern Connecticut
68 Federal Street
New London, CT 06320

Community Foundation of Eastern Connecticut Norwich Women and Girls Grants   698

The Community Foundation of Eastern Connecticut Norwich Women and Girls Fund was established to harness the vitality of women living and working in the region for the purpose of uplifting other women and girls who face challenges in their lives. The Fund is currently focusing on three program areas: advancing family economic security; preventing teen pregnancy and sexually transmitted diseases; and promoting healthy relationships and safe environments for women and girls. Grants are awarded up to $5,000.
Requirements: The Norwich area Women and Girls Fund supports programs that benefit women and girls in Norwich, Bozrah, Colchester, Franklin, Griswold, Lebanon, Lisbon, Preston, Sprague, and Voluntown.
Restrictions: The foundation does not consider requests for direct financial assistance to individuals; religious or sectarian programs; political or lobbying purposes; fundraising events; or debt retirement. Applications requesting support of normal operating expenses will not be considered.
Geographic Focus: Connecticut
Amount of Grant: Up to 5,000 USD
Samples: Madonna Place, Norwich, Connecticut, $2,500 - to support programs offered at the facility (2019); Safe Futures, Norwich, Connecticut, $3,500 - to provide short-term safe living programs to victims (2019); St. Vincent de Paul, Norwich, Connecticut, $2,500 - to remove barriers to economic security helping women on their path to self-sufficiency (2019).
Contact: Jennifer O'Brien; (860) 442-3572 or (877) 442-3572; fax (860) 442-0584; jennob@cfect.org
Internet: www.cfect.org/Nonprofits/Apply-for-a-Grant/Apply-for-Our-Norwich-Area-Women-Girls-Fund-Grants
Sponsor: Community Foundation of Eastern Connecticut
68 Federal Street
New London, CT 06320

Community Foundation of Eastern Connecticut Norwich Youth Grants   699

Norwich Youth Grants support youth development programs and services for economically and socially disadvantaged Norwich youth, to help fill the gap in services left by the closing of the YMCA of Southeastern CT in Norwich. This grant opportunity aligns with our Empower Youth and Basic Needs & Rights strategic priorities. We are able to offer this grant opportunity due to the generous legacy gifts of Grace & Lewis Sears and Jeannette Frisbie. The award ranges from $5,000 to $10,000 and the deadline to apply is January 13th.
Requirements: Programs must: enhance quality early childhood education and intervention services; support mentoring programs that encourage relationships between youth and caring adults; support access to programs that promote mental and physical health as well as those that address disconnected youth; enhance educational opportunities in science, literacy, arts and culture, especially for those that use experiential learning; support post-secondary education access and job readiness.
Restrictions: The foundation does not consider requests for direct financial assistance to individuals; religious or sectarian programs; political or lobbying purposes; fundraising events; or debt retirement. Applications requesting support of normal operating expenses will not be considered.
Geographic Focus: Connecticut
Date(s) Application is Due: Jan 13
Amount of Grant: 5,000 - 15,000 USD
Samples: Children's Museum of Southeastern Connecticut, Norwich, Connecticut, $10,000 - support of the Star Lab and Force in Motion curriculum (2020); High Hopes Therapeutic Riding, Norwich, Connecticut, $5,000 - in support of the Horse Sense program (2020); Safe Futures, Norwich, Connecticut, $2,000 - support for the Kelly Middle School Healthy Relationships Program (2020).
Contact: Deb Battit; (860) 442-3572 or (877) 442-3572; fax (860) 442-0584; deb@cfect.org
Internet: www.cfect.org/Nonprofits/Apply-for-a-Grant/Apply-for-Our-Norwich-Youth-Fund-Grants
Sponsor: Community Foundation of Eastern Connecticut
68 Federal Street
New London, CT 06320

Community Foundation of Eastern Connecticut Ossen Fund for the Arts Grants   700

Offered in partnership with the Jeffrey P. Ossen Family Foundation, these grants are designed to support arts education for the students of Natchaug, W.B. Sweeney, Windham Center and North Windham elementary schools in the Town of Windham. The applications are accepted on a rolling-basis.
Requirements: Applicants generally must: be 501(c)3 charitable organizations, schools, municipal or governmental agencies, or partner with a nonprofit fiscal agent; and serve one or more of the 42 communities in Eastern Connecticut.
Restrictions: The Community Foundation does not provide funding for capital or endowment campaigns, litigation costs, religious programming, endowment campaigns, deficit funding or debt retirement. It does not typically make grants for special events.
Geographic Focus: Connecticut
Contact: Sharon Haight; (860) 442-3572; fax (860) 442-0584; sharonhgt@gmail.com
Internet: www.cfect.org/Nonprofits/Apply-for-a-Grant/Apply-for-Our-Ossen-Fund-for-the-Arts-Grants
Sponsor: Community Foundation of Eastern Connecticut
68 Federal Street
New London, CT 06320

Community Foundation of Eastern Connecticut Southeast Area Women and Girls Grants   701

The Community Foundation of Eastern Connecticut Southeast Women and Girls Fund is currently focusing on four program areas: preventing teen pregnancy and sexually-transmitted diseases; preventing domestic violence and supporting its victims; aiding elderly, low-income New London women to remain in their homes; and helping women to enter or re-enter the workforce. The annual deadline for application submission is October 1st, and the award ranges from $2,000 to $10,000.
Requirements: The Southeast area Women and Girls Fund supports programs that serve women and girls in the towns of East Lyme, Groton, Ledyard, Lyme, Montville, New London, North Stonington, Old Lyme, Salem, Stonington, and Waterford.
Restrictions: The foundation does not consider requests for direct financial assistance to individuals; religious or sectarian programs; political or lobbying purposes; fundraising events; or debt retirement. Applications requesting support of normal operating expenses will not be considered.
Geographic Focus: Connecticut
Date(s) Application is Due: Oct 1
Amount of Grant: 2,000 - 10,000 USD
Samples: New London Senior Center, New London, Connecticut, $9,400 - to provide seniors with emergency funding (2019); Planned Parenthood of Southern New England, New England, Connecticut, $4,000 - to fund New London Peer to Peer Teen Engagement Program (2019); New London Youth Affairs, $3,500 - to fund the COOL (Careers of our Lives) program (2019).
Contact: Jennifer O'Brien, Program Director; (860) 442-3572 or (877) 442-3572; fax (860) 442-0584; jennob@cfect.org
Internet: www.cfect.org/Nonprofits/Apply-for-a-Grant/Apply-for-Our-Southeast-Area-Women-Girls-Fund-Grants
Sponsor: Community Foundation of Eastern Connecticut
68 Federal Street
New London, CT 06320

Community Foundation of Eastern Connecticut Windham Area Women and Girls Grants   702

The Community Foundation of Eastern Connecticut Windham Women and Girls fund aims to remove the inequities that block women from self-sustainability and improve the quality of life for all women and girls living in the greater Windham area. The program's four priority areas include: reducing domestic violence; enhancing youth development; improving elderly services; and increasing economic security. Most recent awards range from $2,000 and $5,000. The deadline to apply is October 1st.
Requirements: The Windham area Women and Girls Fund supports programs that benefit women and girls in the greater Windham area including Ashford, Chaplin, Columbia, Coventry, Mansfield, Scotland, Stafford, Union, Willington, and Windham/Willimantic.
Restrictions: The foundation does not consider requests for direct financial assistance to individuals; religious or sectarian programs; political or lobbying purposes; fundraising events; or debt retirement. Applications requesting support of normal operating expenses will not be considered.
Geographic Focus: Connecticut
Date(s) Application is Due: Oct 1
Amount of Grant: 2,000 - 5,000 USD
Samples: Covenant Soup Kitchen, Willimantic, Connecticut, $2,500 - to provide food assistance to women and children (2019); Windham Area Interfaith Ministry, Windham, Connecticut, $5,000 - support of the Women and Children's Fund (2019); Windham Region No Freeze Project, Windham, Connecticut, $2,500 - to offer a warm, safe space for women to sleep, shower, and be connected to services (2019).
Contact: Jennifer O'Brien, Program Director; (860) 442-3572 or (877) 442-3572; fax (860) 442-0584; jennob@cfect.org
Internet: www.cfect.org/Nonprofits/Apply-for-a-Grant/Apply-for-Our-Windham-Area-Women-Girls-Fund-Grants
Sponsor: Community Foundation of Eastern Connecticut
68 Federal Street
New London, CT 06320

Community Foundation of Grant County Grants   703

The Community Foundation of Grant County Grants address the needs of Grant County in the fields of community development, education, and health and human services. Nonprofit organizations, coalitions, community associations, and other civic groups may apply if they provide services within the county. The project must be located in or directly serve the people in Grant County, and meet all other criteria in the guidelines and application. All proposals must be received by the Foundation on the last Friday in April, July, October, and January, with committee reviews in May, August, November, and February.
Requirements: The Board will only accept written proposals for consideration after an applicant has first consulted with the Foundation's staff to find if the project is suitable for funding. The organization should keep the following guidelines in mind when preparing their written proposal: the project's purpose; whether the Foundation will be the sole funder; how many will be served or affected by the project, if there is a broad base of support for it, or if services are duplicated by another source; if an important need has been shown; whether the objectives are realistic and measurable; is there a viable plan for future support; who the key people are and if they are available for the long-term; and if all financial information is included and makes sense.
Restrictions: To be eligible for a grant, the project must be located in or directly serve the people and natural resources in Grant County, Indiana. Funding is not available for: profit making enterprises; political activity; operating budgets, except for limited experimental or demonstration periods; salaries; sectarian or religious purposes; endowment purposes

unless for special promotions and/or matching challenges; multi-year funding requests; or capital improvements to church owned facilities or properties.

Geographic Focus: Indiana

Contact: Sherrie Stahl; (765) 662-0065; fax (765) 662-1438; sstahl@comfdn.org

Internet: www.comfdn.org/grants.htm

Sponsor: Community Foundation of Grant County

505 West Third Street

Marion, IN 46952

Community Foundation of Greater Chattanooga Grants 704

The Community Foundation of Greater Chattanooga encourages and invests in creative and long-term solutions to improve Hamilton County, Tennessee, and the lives of its citizens. The foundation supports programs and projects that target root causes of problems, foster individual and family self-sufficiency, work to combat discrimination, benefit larger rather than smaller numbers of people, create long-term impact, recognize that prevention is more cost-efficient than treatment, commit venture capital to promising but untried ideas that have a reasonable chance of success. The foundation is committed to earmarking 60 percent of its earnings to grants that address good beginnings for children with a strong interest in race relations and literacy. The grants committee meets three times each year to consider grant requests. The deadline to apply is February 26th.

Requirements: IRS 501(c)3 or 501(c)4 organizations in Tennessee providing services to Hamilton County or to Hamilton County residents are eligible.

Restrictions: The foundation will not make grants to or for religious activities; private schools; operating support for existing programs; multiyear commitments; individuals; endowment campaigns; conference expenses, memberships, or tickets to events; state, regional, or national organizations; political candidates or organizations; veterans and fraternal organizations; advertising and telephone solicitations; feasibility studies; or fund-raising expenses. Low priority will be given to requests from or to public agencies for mandated services; replacement of government funding; unnecessary duplication of services already provided by other agencies; multiyear grants for unsolicited requests; federated fund drives; or capital campaign requests in excess of $25,000.

Geographic Focus: Tennessee

Amount of Grant: Up to 15,000 USD

Samples: Catholic Charities of East Tennessee, Knoxville, Tennessee, $2,800 - to support the office of immigration services (2018); Chattanooga Chamber Foundation, Chattanooga, Tennessee, $10,000 - for economic prosperity programs (2018); The Enterprise Center, Chattanooga, Tennessee, $4,000 - to support internal programs (2018).

Contact: Robin Posey, Director of Programs; (423) 265-0586; fax (423) 265-0587; rposey@cfgc.org or info@cfgc.org

Internet: cfgc.org/nonprofits/apply-for-a-grant/

Sponsor: Community Foundation of Greater Chattanooga

1400 Williams Street

Chattanooga, TN 37408

Community Foundation of Greater Fort Wayne - Community Endowment 705
and Clarke Endowment Grants

The Foundation encourages projects or programs that are developed in consultation with other agencies and planning groups that increase coordination and cooperation among agencies and reduce unnecessary duplication of services. Preference is given to projects or programs that: address priority community concerns; encourage more effective use of community resources; test or demonstrate new approaches and techniques in the solution of community problems; are intended to strengthen the management capabilities of agencies; promote volunteer participation and citizen involvement in community affairs. Contact program staff for current guidelines and deadlines. The deadlines listed are for concept letters, with final invited proposals due by dates provided by the Foundation.

Requirements: Nonprofit organizations in Allen County, Indiana, are eligible to apply. Applicants should mail hardcopies of the application package including the following: concept letter fact sheet; the original concept letter; a detailed program budget or agency budget; current financial statements; a copy of the organization's 501(c)3 IRS determination letter; and a list of the board of directors and their principal affiliations.

Restrictions: Grants do not support: annual fund drives; operating deficits or after-the-fact support; endowment funds, except for endowment-building matching grants for funds held at the Community Foundation; direct or grassroots lobbying; religious purposes; hospitals, medical research, or academic research; public, private, or parochial educational institutions except in special situations when support is essential to projects/programs that meet critical community needs; governmental agencies, including public school systems, except in special situations when support is essential to projects/programs that meet critical community needs; limited, special interest organizations except when such support significantly benefits the disadvantaged; and funding for sponsorships, special events, commercial advertising, films or videos, television programs, conferences, group uniforms, or group trips.

Geographic Focus: Indiana

Date(s) Application is Due: Jan 9; Apr 9; Jul 9

Samples: Salvation Army of Fort Wayne (Fort Wayne, Indiana)—for remodeling of building, $50,000; United Way of Allen County (Fort Wayne, Indiana)—for diversity and special urban initiatives, $100,000; Local Education Fund (Fort Wayne, IN)—for training materials, $38,314.

Contact: Annette Smith; (260) 426-4083; fax (260) 424-0114; asmith@cfgfw.org

Internet: www.cfgfw.org/

Sponsor: Community Foundation of Greater Fort Wayne

555 East Wayne Street

Fort Wayne, IN 46802

Community Foundation of Greater Fort Wayne - Edna Foundation Grants 706

The Edna Foundation Fund was established to help financially support agencies in Allen County that are dedicated to promoting human services, child development, and the arts. This fund typically awards four to five grants a year, ranging from $1,000 to $5,000. The deadlines listed are for concept letters, with final invited proposals due by dates provided by the Foundation.

Requirements: Nonprofit organizations in Allen County, Indiana area are eligible to apply. To apply for funding, complete the Grant Guidelines and Procedures Concept Letter. The Concept Letter should include a cover letter indicating the grant request is for The Edna Foundation Grant.

Restrictions: Grants do not support: annual fund drives; operating deficits or after-the-fact support; endowment funds, except for endowment-building matching grants for funds held at the Community Foundation; direct or grassroots lobbying; religious purposes; hospitals, medical research, or academic research; public, private, or parochial educational institutions except in special situations when support is essential to projects/programs that meet critical community needs; governmental agencies, including public school systems, except in special situations when support is essential to projects/programs that meet critical community needs; limited, special interest organizations except when such support significantly benefits the disadvantaged; and funding for sponsorships, special events, commercial advertising, films or videos, television programs, conferences, group uniforms, or group trips.

Geographic Focus: Indiana

Date(s) Application is Due: Jan 9; Apr 9; Jul 9; Oct 3

Amount of Grant: 1,000 - 5,000 USD

Contact: Annette Smith; (260) 426-4083; fax (260) 424-0114; asmith@cfgfw.org

Internet: www.cfgfw.org/grants/grant_acctapp.html

Sponsor: Community Foundation of Greater Fort Wayne

555 East Wayne Street

Fort Wayne, IN 46802

Community Foundation of Greater Fort Wayne - John S. and James L. Knight 709
Foundation Donor-Advised Grants

The Community Foundation of Greater Fort Wayne administers the Knight Foundation Donor-Advised Grants. The Knight Foundation invests in communities where the Knight brothers owned newspapers to add focus on fostering informed, engaged communities. Knight believed approaches that put residents at the center of their communities are powerful ways to achieve social change, and engaged communities are better places to live, work, and play. Grant requests should address one of the following four focus areas: creating new opportunities for community participation; supporting and developing community leadership; creating spaces for engagement; and providing leadership in understanding engagement in communities. Possible examples include: provide leadership skills to youth and young professionals; support virtual and physical spaces where social interacting, public deliberation, and community action thrive; and enhance the role of citizens in local problem solving.

Requirements: Applicants should submit the online grant proposal form to the Community Foundation, along with the following information: the grantee's name and contact information; a proposal summary; a detailed proposal narrative that describes the name of the project and the organization, why it is a good fit for the Knight Foundation, and how the organization will measure and communicate the results of their work; a project budget; list of the board of directors; and the IRS letter of determination letter.

Geographic Focus: Indiana

Contact: Annette Smith; (260) 426-4083; fax (260) 424-0114; asmith@cfgfw.org

Internet: www.cfgfw.org/grants/grant_acctapp.html

Sponsor: Community Foundation of Greater Fort Wayne

555 East Wayne Street

Fort Wayne, IN 46802

Community Foundation of Greater Greensboro Community Grants 708

The Community Foundation of Greater Greensboro is a local, charitable giving organization with a proven history of making a real difference right here in Greater Greensboro. Since its founding in 1983, it has granted over $330 million to hundreds of nonprofits and have received over $440 million in contributions. It offers unbiased guidance on charitable giving that is informed by its firsthand knowledge of emerging needs and opportunities in its community. The Community Foundation of Greater Greensboro awards community grants from unrestricted and field-of-interest funds, as allocated by the Board of Directors, to support a wide range of community issues.

Requirements: Applicant must be a 501(c)3 nonprofit organization located in or serving the Greater Greensboro area. Requests cannot be used for expenses already incurred. Typically, multi-year grant applications are not considered in this grant program. Public schools or other public agencies will typically not receive grants through this program, although they may be involved as partners in funded efforts. Grants are not awarded to individuals. If your organization has previously received a grant from the Community Grants Program, a grant report form for that grant must be submitted before a new proposal can be considered. Requests may not exceed $5,000 and cannot be used for expenses already incurred.

Restrictions: Request cannot be used for expenses already incurred. Typically, multi-year grant applications are not considered in this grant program. Public schools or other public agencies will typically not receive grants through this program, although they may be involved as partners in funded efforts. Grants are not awarded to individuals.

Geographic Focus: North Carolina

Amount of Grant: Up to 5,000 USD

Contact: Connie Leeper, Manager; (336) 790-6613; cleeper@cfgg.org

Internet: cfgg.org/grantseekers/nonprofits-community-groups/community-grants/#how-to-apply

Sponsor: Community Foundation of Greater Greensboro

330 S. Greene Street, Suite 100

Greensboro, NC 27401

Community Foundation of Greater Greensboro Teen Grantmaking Council Grants   709

The Teen Grantmaking Council (TGC) is an opportunity for high school age youth across greater Greensboro to gain leadership experience, meet area youth, voice opinions, and make a difference by making grants to youth-directed projects that address community issues. The Council is designed to train young leaders to make decisions about which youth projects in the community will receive money. With support from local and national funders and consultants, the Community Foundation engages youth in philanthropy, as grant makers, grant seekers, and participants in youth-led projects.

Requirements: TGC uses the following guidelines for awarding grants: your project must have a positive impact on elementary to high school youth in Guilford County; your project must be planned by youth (grades 6-12) and/or adults and carried out/led by youth (grades 6-12) only; each group must have an adult advisor and a sponsoring organization. This sponsor organization can be a community group affiliated with a school, church, or other nonprofit organization. The sponsoring organization must be a nonprofit organization. The grant check will be mailed to this organization.

Geographic Focus: North Carolina
Contact: Connie Leeper, Manager; (336) 790-6613; cleeper@cfgg.org
Internet: cfgg.org/initiatives/teen-grantmaking-council/#how-to-apply
Sponsor: Community Foundation of Greater Greensboro
330 S. Greene Street, Suite 100
Greensboro, NC 27401

Community Foundation Of Greater Lafayette Grants   710

The Community Foundation of Greater Lafayette Grants help meet the ever-changing needs of the community. Funding priorities include education, children/youth, health, diversity, physical environment, and arts and culture. Charitable organizations that serve Tippecanoe and the surrounding counties are eligible to apply. Most grants are awarded to nonprofit organizations that are located in and serve Tippecanoe County. Priority is given to projects that reach as many people as possible; improve the ability of organizations to serve the community over the long-term; serve the Greater Lafayette area; and are run by non-profit organizations. Grant seekers are encouraged to contact the Foundation office to be certain their proposal is appropriate for consideration. Proposal deadlines are listed according to dollar amount request, so grant seekers should carefully review the website to judge when to submit their proposal.

Requirements: Organizations should submit the following information along with the online application: contact and background information for the organization; a concise narrative about the project; amount requested from the foundation; and a project budget. Also included is a board of directors list; project estimates/bids; and financial statements. Applicants may be asked for further information or a site visit to clarify the request.

Restrictions: The Foundation does not fund: programs that are sectarian or religious in nature; political organizations or candidates; endowments; ongoing operating expenses; government agencies or public institutions; programs that taxpayers would normally support; individuals; special events (i.e. parades, festivals, sporting activities, fundraisers); programs already completed; multi-year grants; debt or deficit reduction; and projects funded in a previous year (unless invited to resubmit).

Geographic Focus: Indiana
Date(s) Application is Due: Apr 1; Sep 1; Dec 1
Contact: Cheryl Ubelhor, Program Director; (765) 742-9078; fax (765) 742-2428; info@cfglaf.org or cheryl@cfglaf.org
Internet: www.glcfonline.org/grantseekers/index.htm
Sponsor: Community Foundation of Greater Lafayette
300 Main Street, Suite 100
Lafayette, IN 47901

Community Foundation of Henderson County Community Grants   711

Grantmaking interest areas of the Community Foundation of Henderson County Community Grants program are arts and culture, civic affairs, conservation, education, health, human services, and animals. Projects are encouraged that promote cooperation among organizations without duplicating services; promote volunteer involvement; demonstrate practical approaches to current community issues; enhance or improve organizations that serve people whose needs are not met by existing services and encourage independence, self-sufficiency, and effectiveness; and emphasize prevention. Types of support include equipment acquisition, program development, seed grants, publication, curriculum development, scholarships, technical assistance, and matching funds. The foundation favors projects that affect a broad segment of the population, are relevant to overall community needs and available resources, are pilot programs that can clearly be used as a model for others, have reasonable prospects for future support, and move the community to a higher cultural awareness. Grants are ordinarily made for one year only. There are four annual deadlines: March 1, June 1, and September 1, December 1.

Requirements: IRS 501(c)3 organizations in Henderson County in North Carolina are eligible.
Restrictions: Unrestricted funds normally will not be used for programs outside Henderson County unless directly benefiting the area; routine operating support for ongoing programs; annual fund campaigns; religious or political purposes; individuals (including scholarships); organizations whose primary function is to allocate funds to other charitable organizations or projects; research; lobbying; second- or multiyear funding; conferences, seminars, and other short-term events; travel; non-tax-exempt 509(a)91 and 170B(1)(a) organizations under IRS codes; augmenting endowments; underwriting for fund-raising events and performances; or loans.

Geographic Focus: North Carolina
Date(s) Application is Due: Mar 1; Jun 1; Sep 1; Dec 1
Amount of Grant: 500 - 2,000 USD
Contact: Lee Henderson-Hill, Senior Program Officer; (828) 697-6224; fax (828) 696-4026; lhenderson-hill@cfhcforever.org or info@cfhcforever.org
Internet: www.cfhcforever.org/grant-scholarships/grant-funding-for-nonprofits/community-grants

Sponsor: Community Foundation of Henderson County
401 N. Main Street, Suite 300
Hendersonville, NC 28792

Community Foundation of Howard County Grants   712

The Community Foundation of Howard County Grants fund initiatives that improve the quality of life for citizens of Howard County. The Foundation addresses needs that generally fall into the following categories: health and medical; social services; education; cultural affairs; civic affairs; and community beautification. The Foundation uses the following evaluation criteria: does the project fit the purpose of the organization; is there an established need for the project; how well the project's purpose has been defined; does it fit with the Foundation's guidelines; and what kind of impact the project will have on the community.

Requirements: All applicants must receive pre-qualification prior to submitting an application. A letter of inquiry addressed to the Program Director should contain a brief statement of the applicant's need for assistance, estimate of total cost of project, and enough information so that the Foundation can determine whether the application falls within the guidelines of its grants program. The organization may then submit the online application with the following information: the grant application and cover page; project budget; copy of IRS determination 501(c)3 letter; current month and year-to-date financial statement; year-end financial statements; itemized list of board members; and evidence of board approval.

Restrictions: The Foundation does not award grants for: normal operating expenses and/or salaries; individuals; seminars or trips; sectarian religious purposes; endowment purposes of recipient organizations; projects which have been proposed by individuals or organizations responsible to advisory bodies or persons; and new projects and/or equipment which were purchased prior to the grant application being approved.

Geographic Focus: Indiana
Date(s) Application is Due: Mar 5; May 7; Sep 3; Nov 5
Contact: Kim Abney; (765) 454-7298 or (800) 964-0508; kim@cfhoward.org
Internet: www.cfhoward.org/grants.html
Sponsor: Community Foundation of Howard County
215 West Sycamore Street
Kokomo, IN 46901

Community Foundation of Jackson County Classroom Education Grants   713

Teachers often have great ideas of how to engage their students on various topics. But they may find that budget constraints may prevent those ideas. The Classroom Education Grant was designed to help fund highly creative, low cost ideas. Teachers who want to explore new means, methods and bold initiatives are encouraged to apply for this grant opportunity. Any classroom teacher in the following schools or school systems may apply: Brownstown Central; Crothersville; Medora; Seymour; and Jackson County Parochial Schools. The proposal form and samples of previously funded projects are available at the website.

Restrictions: Seminars, continued education, or travel requests will not be funded.
Geographic Focus: Indiana
Date(s) Application is Due: Nov 5
Amount of Grant: 50 - 250 USD
Contact: Lori Miller, Development Associate; (812) 523-4483; fax (812) 523-1433
Internet: www.cfjacksoncounty.org/classroomgrants.php
Sponsor: Community Foundation of Jackson County
107 Community Drive
Seymour, IN 47274

Community Foundation of Jackson County Seymour Noon Lions Club Grant 714

The Seymour Noon Lions Club offers an annual grant opportunity for Jackson County. Grants are available in the areas of speech, eye care, hearing, diabetes and youth. Grant proposal applications are due mid-to-late February each year, and are located at the website.

Requirements: Grant proposals must include four copies of the completed proposal form using only the space provided. Applicants must also include four copies of the budget, a list of current governing board members; and a copy of their 501(c)3 IRS determination letter.

Geographic Focus: Indiana
Date(s) Application is Due: Feb 13
Contact: Grant Contact; (812) 523-4483; fax (812) 523-1433
Internet: www.cfjacksoncounty.org/lions.php
Sponsor: Community Foundation of Jackson County
107 Community Drive
Seymour, IN 47274

Community Foundation of Jackson Hole Youth Philanthropy Grants   715

Through this program, students at local high schools discuss, debate and deliberate about strategies for community impact. They meet with applicant organizations and award grants to nonprofits at an annual awards party. Applying for a Youth Philanthropy grant is a great way to introduce your organization to local youth and to help young people understand nonprofits in our community and who they serve. Grants vary from $500 to $4,000, and the deadline to apply is December 27th.

Requirements: To be eligible for funding, an organization must be a 501(c)3, governmental entity, or other IRS recognized charitable entity serving Teton County, Wyoming. Grant funds must be used in Teton County, Wyoming.

Geographic Focus: Wyoming
Date(s) Application is Due: Dec 27
Contact: Shelby Read; (307) 739-1026; fax (307) 734-2841; sread@cfjacksonhole.org
Internet: www.cfjacksonhole.org/apply/grant-programs/youth-philanthropy-program/
Sponsor: Community Foundation of Jackson Hole
255 East Simpson Street, P.O. Box 574
Jackson, WY 83001

Community Foundation of Louisville AIDS Project Fund Grants   **716**

The Community Foundation of Louisville is unique, in that it responds to the evolving needs and opportunities in the community. There is no set agenda, and no pre-determined recipients. Field of Interest Funds support organizations working within a specific geographic region or toward a specific purpose. The Community Foundation makes grants to the most appropriate and effective organizations working in areas such as arts and culture, education, youth, health, and human services. The AIDS Project Fund, administered by the Community Foundation, was created by the dissolution of a separate nonprofit organization, and it provides grants to support HIV prevention, education, and testing. Eligible organizations may apply to receive a grant award of up to $20,000.

Requirements: Eligible organizations include those that are: headquartered in Jefferson County, Kentucky (if based outside of the county, then the organization must demonstrate that a majority of beneficiaries are located in Jefferson County, Kentucky); and classified as a 501(c)3 public charity in good standing (organizations with a pending application for 501(c)3 status may apply with proof of Form 1023 receipt from the IRS).

Geographic Focus: Kentucky
Amount of Grant: Up to 20,000 USD
Contact: Deja Jackson; (502) 585-4649; fax (502) 855-6173; dejaj@cflouisville.org
Internet: www.cflouisville.org/grants-partnerships/field-of-interest-grants/
Sponsor: Community Foundation of Louisville
325 W Main Street, Suite 1110, Waterfront Plaza, West Tower
Louisville, KY 40202

Community Foundation of Louisville Anna Marble Memorial Fund for   **717**
Princeton Grants

The Community Foundation of Louisville is unique, in that it responds to the evolving needs and opportunities in the community. There is no set agenda, and no pre-determined recipients. The Anna Marble Memorial Fund for Princeton, administered by the Community Foundation, was established by Anna Marble, in support of charitable groups helping the residents of Princeton, Kentucky. Eligible organizations may apply to receive a grant award of up to $20,000. Letters of Intent (LOIs) are due by July 8, and the deadline for invited applications is August 15 at 4:00 pm.

Requirements: Eligible organizations include those that are: headquartered in Jefferson County, Kentucky (if based outside of the county, then the organization must demonstrate that a majority of beneficiaries are located in Jefferson County, Kentucky); and classified as a 501(c)3 public charity in good standing (organizations with a pending application for 501(c)3 status may apply with proof of Form 1023 receipt from the IRS).

Geographic Focus: Kentucky
Date(s) Application is Due: Aug 15
Amount of Grant: 100 - 20,000 USD
Contact: Chelsea VanHook; (502) 855-6963; fax (502) 585-4649; chelseav@cflouisville.org
Internet: www.cflouisville.org/grants-partnerships/
Sponsor: Community Foundation of Louisville
325 W Main Street, Suite 1110, Waterfront Plaza, West Tower
Louisville, KY 40202

Community Foundation of Louisville Boyette and Edna Edwards Fund Grants   **718**

The Community Foundation of Louisville is unique, in that it responds to the evolving needs and opportunities in the community. There is no set agenda, and no pre-determined recipients. Field of Interest Funds support organizations working within a specific geographic region or toward a specific purpose. The Community Foundation makes grants to the most appropriate and effective organizations working in areas such as arts and culture, education, youth, health, and human services. The Boyette and Edna Edwards Fund, administered by the Community Foundation, was established with what remained of the Lucille E. Crosby Charitable Trust to honor her parents with annual grants that support the needs of children in Jefferson County. Typically, eligible organizations may apply to receive a grant award of up to $20,000.

Requirements: Eligible organizations include those that are: headquartered in Jefferson County, Kentucky (if based outside of the county, then the organization must demonstrate that a majority of beneficiaries are located in Jefferson County, Kentucky); and classified as a 501(c)3 public charity in good standing (organizations with a pending application for 501(c)3 status may apply with proof of Form 1023 receipt from the IRS).

Geographic Focus: Kentucky
Amount of Grant: Up to 20,000 USD
Contact: Deja Jackson; (502) 585-4649; fax (502) 855-6173; annemc@cflouisville.org
Internet: www.cflouisville.org/grants-partnerships/field-of-interest-grants/
Sponsor: Community Foundation of Louisville
325 W Main Street, Suite 1110, Waterfront Plaza, West Tower
Louisville, KY 40202

Community Foundation of Louisville C. E. and S. Endowment for the Parks   **719**
Fund Grants

The Community Foundation of Louisville is unique, in that it responds to the evolving needs and opportunities in the community. There is no set agenda, and no pre-determined recipients. The C. E. and S. Endowment for the Parks Fund, administered by the Community Foundation, was created to provide support for the maintenance of children's play areas in California and Cherokee Parks, and to support research, development or implementation of other enhancements to parks in Jefferson County, Kentucky. Eligible organizations may apply to receive a grant award of up to $20,000. Letters of Intent (LOIs) are due by July 8, and the deadline for invited applications is August 15 at 4:00 pm.

Requirements: Eligible organizations include those that are: headquartered in Jefferson County, Kentucky (if based outside of the county, then the organization must demonstrate that a majority of beneficiaries are located in Jefferson County, Kentucky); and classified as a 501(c)3 public charity in good standing (organizations with a pending application for 501(c)3 status may apply with proof of Form 1023 receipt from the IRS).

Geographic Focus: Kentucky
Date(s) Application is Due: Aug 15
Amount of Grant: 100 - 20,000 USD
Contact: Chelsea VanHook; (502) 855-6963; fax (502) 585-4649; chelseav@cflouisville.org
Internet: www.cflouisville.org/grants-partnerships/
Sponsor: Community Foundation of Louisville
325 W Main Street, Suite 1110, Waterfront Plaza, West Tower
Louisville, KY 40202

Community Foundation of Louisville CHAMP Fund Grants   **720**

The Community Foundation of Louisville is unique, in that it responds to the evolving needs and opportunities in the community. There is no set agenda, and no pre-determined recipients. The CHAMP Fund, administered by the Community Foundation, was created in order to provide opportunities for organizations that serve children, the disadvantaged, the underprivileged, or the elderly to attend University of Louisville athletic games. Eligible organizations may apply to receive a grant award of up to $10,000. Letters of Intent (LOIs) are due by July 8, and the deadline for invited applications is August 15 at 4:00 pm.

Requirements: Eligible organizations include those that are: headquartered in Jefferson County, Kentucky (if based outside of the county, then the organization must demonstrate that a majority of beneficiaries are located in Jefferson County, Kentucky); and classified as a 501(c)3 public charity in good standing (organizations with a pending application for 501(c)3 status may apply with proof of Form 1023 receipt from the IRS).

Geographic Focus: Kentucky
Date(s) Application is Due: Aug 15
Amount of Grant: 100 - 10,000 USD
Contact: Chelsea VanHook; (502) 855-6963; fax (502) 585-4649; chelseav@cflouisville.org
Internet: www.cflouisville.org/grants-partnerships/
Sponsor: Community Foundation of Louisville
325 W Main Street, Suite 1110, Waterfront Plaza, West Tower
Louisville, KY 40202

Community Foundation of Louisville Children's Memorial Marker Fund Grants   **721**

The Community Foundation of Louisville is unique, in that it responds to the evolving needs and opportunities in the community. There is no set agenda, and no pre-determined recipients. The Children's Memorial Marker Fund, administered by the Community Foundation, was created in order to provide funds to erect memorial markers on the unmarked graves of children in Jefferson County, Kentucky. Eligible organizations may apply to receive a grant award of up to $10,000. Letters of Intent (LOIs) are due by July 8, and the deadline for invited applications is August 15 at 4:00 pm.

Requirements: Eligible organizations include those that are: headquartered in Jefferson County, Kentucky (if based outside of the county, then the organization must demonstrate that a majority of beneficiaries are located in Jefferson County, Kentucky); and classified as a 501(c)3 public charity in good standing (organizations with a pending application for 501(c)3 status may apply with proof of Form 1023 receipt from the IRS).

Geographic Focus: Kentucky
Date(s) Application is Due: Aug 15
Amount of Grant: 100 - 10,000 USD
Contact: Chelsea VanHook; (502) 855-6963; fax (502) 585-4649; chelseav@cflouisville.org
Internet: www.cflouisville.org/grants-partnerships/
Sponsor: Community Foundation of Louisville
325 W Main Street, Suite 1110, Waterfront Plaza, West Tower
Louisville, KY 40202

Community Foundation of Louisville Delta Dental of Kentucky Fund Grants   **722**

The Community Foundation of Louisville is unique, in that it responds to the evolving needs and opportunities in the community. There is no set agenda, and no pre-determined recipients. The Delta Dental of Kentucky Foundation, administered by the Community Foundation, was created in 2004 in order to support projects and nonprofit organizations that promote dental health and dental education. Eligible organizations may apply to receive a grant award of up to $10,000. Letters of Intent (LOIs) are due by July 8, and the deadline for invited applications is August 15 at 4:00 pm.

Requirements: Eligible organizations include those that are: headquartered in Jefferson County, Kentucky (if based outside of the county, then the organization must demonstrate that a majority of beneficiaries are located in Jefferson County, Kentucky); and classified as a 501(c)3 public charity in good standing (organizations with a pending application for 501(c)3 status may apply with proof of Form 1023 receipt from the IRS).

Geographic Focus: Kentucky
Date(s) Application is Due: Aug 15
Amount of Grant: 100 - 10,000 USD
Contact: Chelsea VanHook; (502) 855-6963; fax (502) 585-4649; chelseav@cflouisville.org
Internet: www.cflouisville.org/grants-partnerships/
Sponsor: Community Foundation of Louisville
325 W Main Street, Suite 1110, Waterfront Plaza, West Tower
Louisville, KY 40202

Community Foundation of Louisville Dr. W. Barnett Owen Memorial   **723**
Fund for the Children of Louisville and Jefferson County Grants

The Community Foundation of Louisville is unique, in that it responds to the evolving needs and opportunities in the community. There is no set agenda, and no pre-determined recipients. Field of Interest Funds support organizations working within a specific geographic region or toward a specific purpose. The Community Foundation makes grants to the most appropriate and effective organizations working in areas such as arts and culture, education, youth, health, and human services. The Dr. W. Barnett Owen Memorial Fund

for the Children of Louisville and Jefferson County, administered by the Community Foundation, was established by Dr. Albert P. Williams to honor the memory of Dr. Owen, a children's health care activist. Owen was instrumental in establishing the Kosair Children's Hospital in Louisville, when polio was the scourge of adolescence. The Fund supports children and youth health and other programs. Eligible organizations may apply to receive a grant award of up to $20,000.
Requirements: Eligible organizations include those that are: headquartered in Jefferson County, Kentucky (if based outside of the county, then the organization must demonstrate that a majority of beneficiaries are located in Jefferson County, Kentucky); and classified as a 501(c)3 public charity in good standing (organizations with a pending application for 501(c)3 status may apply with proof of Form 1023 receipt from the IRS).
Geographic Focus: Kentucky
Amount of Grant: Up to 20,000 USD
Contact: Deja Jackson; (502) 585-4649; fax (502) 855-6173; dejaj@cflouisville.org
Internet: www.cflouisville.org/grants-partnerships/field-of-interest-grants/
Sponsor: Community Foundation of Louisville
325 W Main Street, Suite 1110, Waterfront Plaza, West Tower
Louisville, KY 40202

Community Foundation of Louisville Education Grants 724
The Community Foundation's Fund for Louisville is unique, in that it responds to the evolving needs and opportunities in the community. There is no set agenda, and no pre-determined recipients. In the area of Education, the fund supports: educational policy; and reform and delivery at all attainment levels, including out-of-school, adult education, and vocational education. The grant program is supported primarily by two funds, including: the Winston N. and Nancy H. Bloch Educational Fund; and the Madi and Jim Tate Fund. Eligible organizations may apply to receive a grant award of up to $20,000. The Letter of Intent (LOI) submission deadline is July 8, with invited organizations submitting final applications by August 15 at 4:00 pm.
Requirements: Eligible organizations include those that are: headquartered in Jefferson County, Kentucky (if based outside of the county, then the organization must demonstrate that a majority of beneficiaries are located in Jefferson County, Kentucky); and classified as a 501(c)3 public charity in good standing (organizations with a pending application for 501(c)3 status may apply with proof of Form 1023 receipt from the IRS).
Geographic Focus: Kentucky
Date(s) Application is Due: Aug 15
Amount of Grant: 100 - 20,000 USD
Contact: Chelsea VanHook; (502) 855-6963; fax (502) 585-4649; chelseav@cflouisville.org
Internet: www.cflouisville.org/grants-partnerships/
Sponsor: Community Foundation of Louisville
325 W Main Street, Suite 1110, Waterfront Plaza, West Tower
Louisville, KY 40202

Community Foundation of Louisville Fund 4 Women and Girls Grants 725
The Community Foundation of Louisville is unique, in that it responds to the evolving needs and opportunities in the community. There is no set agenda, and no pre-determined recipients. The Fund 4 Women and Girls, administered by the Community Foundation, was established by Women 4 Women, Inc., a not-for-profit organization which aims to bring about positive social change by addressing existing issues confronting women and bringing these particular issues to a proper level of awareness in the community. In order to accomplish this goal, Women 4 Women offers their various resources to chosen community organizations and assists them in building adequate channels of communication to enhance their capacity to solve social and economic problems affecting women. Typically, eligible organizations may apply to receive a grant award of up to $20,000. Letters of Intent (LOIs) are due by July 8, and the deadline for invited applications is August 15 at 4:00 pm.
Requirements: Eligible organizations include those that are: headquartered in Jefferson County, Kentucky (if based outside of the county, then the organization must demonstrate that a majority of beneficiaries are located in Jefferson County, Kentucky); and classified as a 501(c)3 public charity in good standing (organizations with a pending application for 501(c)3 status may apply with proof of Form 1023 receipt from the IRS).
Geographic Focus: Kentucky
Date(s) Application is Due: Aug 15
Amount of Grant: 100 - 20,000 USD
Contact: Chelsea VanHook; (502) 855-6963; fax (502) 585-4649; chelseav@cflouisville.org
Internet: www.cflouisville.org/grants-partnerships/
Sponsor: Community Foundation of Louisville
325 W Main Street, Suite 1110, Waterfront Plaza, West Tower
Louisville, KY 40202

Community Foundation of Louisville Human Services Grants 726
The Community Foundation's Fund for Louisville is unique, in that it responds to the evolving needs and opportunities in the community. There is no set agenda, and no pre-determined recipients. In the area of human services, the fund supports organizations that provide direct social services to assist families, children, and youth. The grant program is supported primarily by three funds: the Affordable Housing Fund; the Boyette and Edna Edwards Fund; and the Dr. W. Barnett Owen Memorial Fund. Eligible organizations may apply to receive a grant award of up to $20,000. Applications are available on July 7 each year and may be submitted online only. The annual deadline for submission is August 21 at 4:00 pm.
Requirements: Eligible organizations include those that are: headquartered in Jefferson County, Kentucky (if based outside of the county, then the organization must demonstrate that a majority of beneficiaries are located in Jefferson County, Kentucky); and classified as a 501(c)3 public charity in good standing (organizations with a pending application for 501(c)3 status may apply with proof of Form 1023 receipt from the IRS).

Geographic Focus: Kentucky
Date(s) Application is Due: Aug 15
Amount of Grant: 100 - 20,000 USD
Contact: Chelsea VanHook; (502) 855-6963; fax (502) 585-4649; chelseav@cflouisville.org
Internet: www.cflouisville.org/grants-partnerships/
Sponsor: Community Foundation of Louisville
325 W Main Street, Suite 1110, Waterfront Plaza, West Tower
Louisville, KY 40202

Community Foundation of Louisville Madi and Jim Tate Fund Grants 727
The Community Foundation of Louisville is unique, in that it responds to the evolving needs and opportunities in the community. There is no set agenda, and no pre-determined recipients. Field of Interest Funds support organizations working within a specific geographic region or toward a specific purpose. The Community Foundation makes grants to the most appropriate and effective organizations working in areas such as arts and culture, education, youth, health, and human services. The Madi and Jim Tate Fund, administered by the Community Foundation, was established by Edith Terry "Madi" Tate to support the education of disadvantaged students, with priority given to Louisville's African American community. Madi's husband, Jim, was president of the Falls City Brewing Company in Louisville. Eligible organizations may apply to receive a grant award of up to $20,000.
Requirements: Eligible organizations include those that are: headquartered in Jefferson County, Kentucky (if based outside of the county, then the organization must demonstrate that a majority of beneficiaries are located in Jefferson County, Kentucky); and classified as a 501(c)3 public charity in good standing (organizations with a pending application for 501(c)3 status may apply with proof of Form 1023 receipt from the IRS).
Geographic Focus: Kentucky
Amount of Grant: Up to 20,000 USD
Contact: Deja Jackson; (502) 855-6948 or (502) 585-4649; fax (502) 855-6173; dejaj@cflouisville.org
Internet: www.cflouisville.org/grants-partnerships/field-of-interest-grants/
Sponsor: Community Foundation of Louisville
325 W Main Street, Suite 1110, Waterfront Plaza, West Tower
Louisville, KY 40202

Community Foundation of Louisville We Day Kentucky Grants 728
The Community Foundation can play a vital and unique role in supporting partners and groups creating good in the community. By assisting others not-yet-incorporated through fiscal sponsorship, the Foundation allows change agents to test the viability of charitable efforts, support collective impact initiatives, and create space for collaborations and partnerships that can extend the services provided and collectively increase community good. Specifically, "We" is a movement that brings people together and gives them the tools to change the world. Today "we" includes millions of passionate youth, women and men working together to shift the world from 'me' to 'we.' This program develops engaged citizens by bringing passion, inspiration, and support for local and global service learning and service leadership to all students in Kentucky.
Geographic Focus: Kentucky
Contact: Chelsea Pending VanHook; (502) 855-6982; chelseav@cflouisville.org
Internet: www.cflouisville.org/grants-partnerships/supporting-sponsorships/
Sponsor: Community Foundation of Louisville
325 W Main Street, Suite 1110, Waterfront Plaza, West Tower
Louisville, KY 40202

Community Foundation of Louisville Winston N. and 729
Nancy H. Bloch Educational Fund Grants
The Community Foundation of Louisville is unique, in that it responds to the evolving needs and opportunities in the community. There is no set agenda, and no pre-determined recipients. Field of Interest Funds support organizations working within a specific geographic region or toward a specific purpose. The Community Foundation makes grants to the most appropriate and effective organizations working in areas such as arts and culture, education, youth, health, and human services. The Winston N. and Nancy H. Bloch Educational Fund, administered by the Community Foundation, was created by Mary C. Jones in memory of her son and daughter-in-law to help children learn by providing non-traditional classroom resources. Eligible organizations may apply to receive a grant award of up to $20,000.
Requirements: Eligible organizations include those that are: headquartered in Jefferson County, Kentucky (if based outside of the county, then the organization must demonstrate that a majority of beneficiaries are located in Jefferson County, Kentucky); and classified as a 501(c)3 public charity in good standing (organizations with a pending application for 501(c)3 status may apply with proof of Form 1023 receipt from the IRS).
Geographic Focus: Kentucky
Amount of Grant: Up to 20,000 USD
Contact: Deja Jackson; (502) 585-4649; fax (502) 855-6173; dejaj@cflouisville.org
Internet: www.cflouisville.org/grants-partnerships/field-of-interest-grants/
Sponsor: Community Foundation of Louisville
325 W Main Street, Suite 1110, Waterfront Plaza, West Tower
Louisville, KY 40202

Community Foundation of Louisville Youth Philanthropy Council Grants 730
The Community Foundation can play a vital and unique role in supporting partners and groups creating good in the community. By assisting others not-yet-incorporated through fiscal sponsorship, the Foundation allows change agents to test the viability of charitable efforts, support collective impact initiatives, and create space for collaborations and partnerships that can extend the services provided and collectively increase community good. To ensure the ability to effectively sponsor efforts, each opportunity is assessed individually considering alignment of expertise, resources, project needs and opportunity

for impact. The Louisville Youth Philanthropy Council (LYPC) provides a diverse team of up to 35 high school students (public, private and parochial) from Jefferson County, and those contiguous to it, with a hands-on experience in grant-making and philanthropy during a 16-week program on Saturdays during the school year (September through March). These grants fund a program that seeks to educate local high school students about philanthropy and inspire them through hands-on experiences to become community leaders.
Requirements: Any 501(c)3 organization or school supporting the residents of the Louisville region is eligible to apply.
Geographic Focus: Kentucky
Contact: Chelsea VanHook, Program Officer; (502) 855-6982; chelseav@cflouisville.org
Internet: www.cflouisville.org/grants-partnerships/supporting-sponsorships/
Sponsor: Community Foundation of Louisville
325 W Main Street, Suite 1110, Waterfront Plaza, West Tower
Louisville, KY 40202

Community Foundation of Madison and Jefferson County Grants 731
The Community Foundation of Madison and Jefferson County offers more than one hundred permanent funds to help finance projects in Jefferson County. Specific funds are dedicated to the following fields of interest: assist developmentally disabled children; encourage local artistic talent and community participation in the arts; aid and encourage the development of youth in the Southwestern school district; protect and improve the environment; and help children learn how to be good pet owners. Preference will be given to proposals for/that: capital needs beyond an applicant's capabilities and means; one-time projects; seed money for pilot projects; with the greatest benefit per dollar granted; reach a broad segment of the community with needed services that are presently not provided; address priority community concerns by making a significant improvement to the community; are change-oriented and problem-solving in nature; financially support by other organizations and individuals, including board members; have the potential of leveraging additional grants from other sources such as government and other foundations. There is one annual grant cycle each year, opening on June 1 and closing in early August.
Requirements: A preliminary proposal/letter of intent is required. If applicants are approved, the final proposal is due one month later. Grants are only made to 501(c)3 charities or 509(a) agencies. All communications should be directed to the President/CEO. No representative, either staff or volunteer, from an organization is to contact members of the Foundation's grants committee or board of directors regarding grant related information. Deviations from this policy are reported to the grant review committee.
Restrictions: Funding is not available for the following: annual appeals or membership contributions; ongoing operating expenses or regular programming of well established agencies; programs/equipment that were committed to prior to the grant application period; debt reduction; political purposes; religious purposes or programs requiring religious participation; support of public or private educational institutions or government agencies except in special situations where support is essential to projects/programs that meet critical community needs; or travel expenses for individuals or groups.
Geographic Focus: Indiana
Date(s) Application is Due: Aug 3
Amount of Grant: Up to 25,000 USD
Samples: Friends of the Ohio Theatre, Madison, Indiana, $25,000 - to provide a matching grant opportunity for their Raise the Roof campaign; Historic Eleutherian College, Madison, Indiana, $10,000 - to support the organization's capital campaign for strategic planning and board development; Jefferson County Youth Shelter, Madison, Indiana, $3,820 - to replace worn carpet in the upstairs bedrooms of the shelter.
Contact: Bill Barnes; (812) 265-3327; fax (812) 273-0181; info@cfmjc.org or bill@cfmjc.org
Internet: www.cfmjc.org/grants.php
Sponsor: Community Foundation of Madison and Jefferson County
416 West Street, Suite B
Madison, IN 47250

Community Foundation of Morgan County Grants 732
The Community Foundation of Morgan County offers matching grants and arts grants. Matching grants require that the grant applicant must raise an amount at least equal to what they are requesting on their application. Arts grants require no matching funds. The Community Foundation of Morgan County welcomes grant applications from Morgan County non-profit organizations or groups. Occasionally, the CFMC has approved grant applications from organizations whose headquarters are located outside the county if a significant number of persons who will be served reside in Morgan County. The Foundation aims to support creative approaches to community needs and problems by making grants which will benefit a wide range of people. Applicants are encouraged to attend grant writing seminars given by the Foundation. The application is available at the website.
Requirements: Selection criteria for the Matching and Arts Grants will include, but are not limited to: innovative solutions to a significant community issue; impact on the community; ability to carry out the project, and how the project will increase community awareness of the identified funding priority and the Foundation.
Geographic Focus: Indiana
Date(s) Application is Due: Sep 7
Samples: Morgan County Public Library, Martinsville, Indiana, $1,700 - support for Bridging the Wireless Access Gap; Artesian Little League, Martinsville, Indiana, $2,000 - funding for field improvements; Brooklyn STEM Academy, Mooresville, Indiana, $9,498 - support for the Sprouting Community Gardens program.
Contact: Ed Kominowski, Executive Director; (765)-813-0003 or (317) 831-1232; fax (317) 831-2854; ekominowski@cfmconline.org or info@thecfmconline.org
Internet: cfmconline.org/grants/
Sponsor: Community Foundation of Morgan County
56 North Main Street
Martinsville, IN 46151

Community Foundation of Muncie and Delaware County - Kitselman Grants 733
The Community Foundation of Muncie and Delaware County - Kitselman Grants award funding to the following areas: fine arts (music, dance, theatre, and art), recreation, children, and the history of East Central Indiana. The Kitselman Advisory Board meets one or more times each year to review applications and make recommendations to the Board of Directors of The Community Foundation, which makes the final selection of grant recipients. Kitselman applications are reviewed in the first quarter of each year, so applicants are requested to submit their application materials by December 31st of each year. Most grants are significant, usually in excess of $25,000.
Requirements: Organizations interested in receiving grants from the Fund must submit an application through the Community Foundation, using the Community Foundation's Kitselman Fund Grant online application. Applicants should explain how their proposal will fulfill the purposes for which the Fund was established and/or relate to the Fund's areas of focus. In addition to the application, organizations must include their mission statement, a board of directors list, financial statements, their tax exempt IRS letter, and a letter of endorsement from their Board President, Principal, or Chief Executive Officer. They should also include project goals and objectives; implementation plan; project budget including expected revenue; in-kind contributions; and other grants; staff involved in project; community benefits; method of evaluation; and an explanation of how the proposal will fulfill the purpose for which the fund was established and/or relate to the Fund's area of focus. The Kitselman Advisory Board may ask applicants to submit an application addendum containing additional information that will assist the Advisory Board in making its recommendations.
Geographic Focus: Indiana
Date(s) Application is Due: Dec 31
Amount of Grant: Up to 25,000 USD
Contact: Suzanne Kadinger, Program Officer; (765) 747-7181; fax (765) 289-7770; skadinger@cfmdin.org or info@cfmdin.org
Internet: www.cfmdin.org/main/grant-seekers/
Sponsor: Community Foundation of Muncie and Delaware County
201 East Jackson Street
Muncie, IN 47305

Community Foundation of Muncie and Delaware County Maxon Grants 734
The Community Foundation of Muncie and Delaware County Maxon Grants give back to the community by supporting worthy causes in Delaware County. Organizations are notified within eight weeks whether they have been funded.
Requirements: In addition to the online application, organizations must submit the following: the grant application cover sheet; the organization's mission statement; a list of the board of directors with their affiliations; a copy of the organization's Federal IRS tax exemption letter; and a letter of endorsement from the Board President, Principal or Chief Executive Officer. They must also submit a brief proposal that provides; project goals and objectives; implementation plan; project budget including expected revenue, in-kind contributions and other grants; staff involved in project; community benefits; and the organization's method of evaluation.
Geographic Focus: Indiana
Date(s) Application is Due: Jul 30
Amount of Grant: 5,000 - 15,000 USD
Contact: Suzanne Kadinger, Program Officer; (765) 747-7181; fax (765) 289-7770; skadinger@cfmdin.org or info@cfmdin.org
Internet: www.cfmdin.org/main/grant-seekers/
Sponsor: Community Foundation of Muncie and Delaware County
201 East Jackson Street
Muncie, IN 47305

Community Foundation of Randolph County Grants 735
The Community Foundation of Randolph County seeks to bring people and resources together to enrich the lives of Randolph County, Indiana residents. The Foundation makes grants to increase the capacity of Randolph County's not-for-profit organizations to respond effectively to the needs of the community. In general, the Foundation prefers funding for: start-up costs for new programs; one-time projects or needs; capital needs beyond an applicant's capabilities and means. The Foundation also funds projects in the areas of arts and culture, civic and community development, education and libraries, environmental and historical preservation, health and human services, youth; and the elderly.
Requirements: The Foundation makes grants to tax-exempt 501(c)3 organizations operating or proposing to operate programs for the benefit of Randolph County residents. Proposals shall include: completed application cover; one original and 10 copies of completed application; one list of your organization's/agency's officers or governing body; one copy of your federal tax exemption 501(c)3 letter; one copy of your last financial statement showing income and expenses (annual report); one copy of the total project budget; one copy of all pertinent supporting information. Applications can be obtained by contacting the Foundation office or downloading the form from the Foundation's website. Application forms should be mailed or delivered to the Foundation's office, since applications cannot be submitted online.
Restrictions: The Foundation will usually not fund: individuals other than scholarships; organizations for religious or sectarian purposes; make-up of operating deficits, post-event or after-the-fact situations; endowment campaigns; for any propaganda, political or otherwise, attempting to influence legislation or intervene in any political affairs or campaigns; services such as fire, police, schools, parks, etc. that are the responsibility of government and tax supported. However, the Foundation occasionally supports special projects of these agencies.
Geographic Focus: Indiana
Date(s) Application is Due: Mar 31; Sep 30
Contact: Ruth Mills; (765) 584-9077; fax (765) 584-7710; rmills@cfrandolphcounty.org
Internet: cfrandolphcounty.org/cfrc/jsp/GrantCenter/ApplicationForms/main.jsp

Sponsor: Community Foundation of Randolph County
213 South Main Street
Winchester, IN 47394

Community Foundation of Southern Indiana Grants 736

The Community Foundation supports a wide variety of educational opportunities, civic projects and provided equipment and activities that benefit all ages in Floyd and Clark County. Areas of funding interest include arts and culture; community development; education; environment; health; human services; recreation; and youth development. Funding will encourage programs that enhance cooperation and collaboration among organizations in Floyd and Clark County. The application and supporting materials are available at the Foundation website.

Requirements: Organizations with 501(c)3 status in or serving Floyd and Clark counties may apply.

Restrictions: The Foundation does not typically fund any of the following: annual appeals; endowment funds, membership contributions or fundraising events; existing obligations, loans or debt retirement; long-term operating support; multi-year grants or repeat funding; medical, scientific or academic research; operating and construction costs at schools, universities and private academies unless there is significant opportunity for community use or collaboration; projects that promote a particular religion or construction projects of churches and other religious institutions; political campaigns, advocacy or direct lobbying efforts by 501(c)3 organizations; services commonly regarded as the responsibility of governmental agencies, such as fire and police protection; and travel for individuals, bands, sports teams, classes and similar groups.

Geographic Focus: Indiana
Date(s) Application is Due: Sep 1
Amount of Grant: Up to 5,000 USD
Contact: Crystal Gunther, Grants and Programs Officer; (812) 948-4662; fax (812) 948-4678; cgunther@cfsouthernindiana.com
Internet: www.cfsouthernindiana.com/Default.aspx?sitemapid=40
Sponsor: Community Foundation of Southern Indiana - Floyd and Clark County
4104 Charlestown Road
New Albany, IN 47150

Community Foundation of St. Joseph County African American Community Grants 737

The purpose of the African American Community Grant is to enhance the lives of African Americans in St. Joseph County by providing funds for initiatives that build capacity, influence whole system improvements, and achieve tangible long-term progress. Primary consideration will be given to programs addressing these priorities: education; arts; leadership development; and the special challenges facing African American males. Up to $25,000 may be requested. Multi-year funding for exceptional programs and projects may be considered.

Requirements: Ideally, AACF grants will go to 501(c)3 organizations for projects that pursue clearly defined outcomes, and have potential for high impact. In addition to the online application, all candidates must submit the following: up to a two page proposed narrative; a detailed project budget; current board roster with officers identified; and proof of nonprofit status. See the grant website for detailed information.

Restrictions: Grants are not made to fund: routine operating expenses for established programs; conference attendance/training (unless presented as a necessary component of a larger program or objective); development and fundraising-related expenses or events; annual appeals or membership contributions; travel for bands, sports teams, classes, and similar groups; computers (unless presented as a necessary component of larger program or objective); endowments; individuals, directly; debt retirement and back taxes; post-event or after-the-fact situations; political activity.

Geographic Focus: Indiana
Date(s) Application is Due: Mar 1; Oct 1
Amount of Grant: 25,000 USD
Contact: Angela Butiste; (574) 232-0041; fax (574) 233-1906; angela@cfsjc.org
Internet: www.cfsjc.org/initiatives/aacf/aacf_grants.html
Sponsor: Community Foundation of St. Joseph County
205 W Jefferson Boulevard, P.O. Box 837
South Bend, IN 46624

Community Foundation of St. Joseph County Special Project Challenge Grants 738

The Special Project Challenge Grants assist public and other 501(c)3 agencies in their efforts to serve community needs. For every $1 raised by the chosen agency, the Community Foundation will match $1. The foundation encourages projects in the following areas: community development and urban affairs; health and human services; parks, recreation, and environment; and youth and education.

Requirements: In additional to the online application, all applicants must submit the following materials online: up to a two page proposal narrative; a detailed project budget; current board roster with officers identified; fiscal year income statement; proof of nonprofit status. Application materials must be submitted via email to grants@cfsjc.org in word processing format (narrative or budget) or Microsoft Excel (budget). Hard copy applications are no longer accepted.

Restrictions: Grants are not made to fund: operational phases of established programs; endowment campaigns; religious organizations for religious purposes; individuals directly; development or public relations activities (e.g. literature, videos, etc.); retirement of debts; camperships; annual appeals or membership contributions; travel for bands, sports teams, classes, etc; j) computers (unless presented as a necessary component of larger program or objective); and post-event or after-the-fact situations.

Geographic Focus: Indiana
Date(s) Application is Due: Mar 1; Oct 1
Contact: Angela Butiste; (574) 232-0041; fax (574) 233-1906; angela@cfsjc.org

Internet: www.cfsjc.org/grants/sproj/special_project_grants.html
Sponsor: Community Foundation of St. Joseph County
205 W Jefferson Boulevard, P.O. Box 837
South Bend, IN 46624

Community Foundation of Switzerland County Grants 739

The Community Foundation of Switzerland County is a nonprofit organization created to make Switzerland County a better place to live for present and future generations. The Foundation gives priority to applications that focus on the basic needs of the community (food, housing, shelter, health care, clothing, personal care, and transportation). The Foundation also welcomes applications for other programs and projects that benefit Switzerland County. Organizations may request up to $5,000. Applications are reviewed monthly; there are no deadlines. The application and additional guidelines are available at the website.

Requirements: Any organization with a 501(c)3 or any organization that provides a program with charitable intent or has a fiscal agent is eligible to apply.

Geographic Focus: Indiana
Amount of Grant: Up to 5,000 USD
Contact: Pam Acton; (812) 427-9160; fax (812) 427-4033; pacton@cfsci.org
Internet: www.cfsci.org/
Sponsor: Community Foundation of Switzerland County
303 Ferry Street, P.O. Box 46
Vevay, IN 47043

Community Foundation of Wabash County Grants 740

The goal of the Community Foundation of Wabash County Grants is to enrich the quality of life in Wabash County, Indiana, by responding to emerging and changing needs of the community. It also seeks to support existing organizations and institutions through grants in support of the following categories: arts and culture; community and civic development; education; environment; health and human services; and recreation. Types of support include: building or renovation; continuing support; curriculum development; endowments; equipment; general operating support; matching/challenge support; program development; program evaluation; scholarship funds; scholarships to individuals; seed money; and technical assistance.

Requirements: Proposals are accepted from organizations serving Wabash County that are defined as tax exempt under Section 501(c)3 of the IRS code or have comparable status and charitable causes. Grant selection is judged on program focus; program design; benefits; reach; and organizational profile. In addition to the online application, organizations must submit the completed cover sheet, proposal budget, a list of member of the organization's current staff and governing board; current year-end financial statement; and copy of the tax exempt IRS letter. Eight copies of the application and attached documentation are then submitted to the Foundation office for review.

Restrictions: The following are not eligible for funding: national organizations (except for local chapters serving Wabash County); annual fund campaigns; or programs or products produced for resale. Faith-based organizations may apply for program funding, provided there is not a requirement to participate in religious instruction and/or take part in religious activities.

Geographic Focus: Indiana
Date(s) Application is Due: Mar 15; Jul 15; Nov 15
Amount of Grant: Up to USD
Samples: Lighthouse Missions, holiday food baskets: $5,000; North Manchester Parks & Recreation "Keeping Indoor Fitness Fun" After School Program: $2,000; Wabash County Hospital Foundation (85 Hope Free Medical Clinic) $9,500.
Contact: Cathy McCarty; (260) 982-4824; fax (260) 982-8644; cathy@cfwabash.org
Internet: www.cfwabash.org/nonprofits-grant-information/guidelines.html
Sponsor: Community Foundation of Wabash County
218 East Main Street
North Manchester, IN 46962-0098

Community Foundation of Western Massachusetts Grants 741

The general objectives of the community foundation's grant making are to serve a wide range of western Massachusetts community development interests in the areas of the arts, education (including adult basic education and literacy programs), environment, health, housing, and human services; encourage creative and collaborative responses to existing and emerging problems or opportunities; and leverage additional support for programs from other private and public funding sources. The foundation supports capital campaigns, building/renovations, equipment, endowment funds, program development, conferences and seminars, publication, seed money, fellowships, scholarship funds and scholarships to individuals, technical assistance, and matching funds. Proposals are considered at the distribution committee meetings held four times each year and should be received by the first Monday of February, May, August, and/or November. Applicants are encouraged to call the foundation for guidelines.

Requirements: Proposals from western Massachusetts nonprofit organizations, including Hampden, Hampshire, and Franklin Counties, should include the name of the organization; an application; a one-page description of the need, project, and personnel for the project; 501(c)3 and 509(a) determination letters; names and affiliations of the governing board; and a copy of operating budget and/or recent organization audit.

Restrictions: Grants are not usually made to or for individual recipients, including scholarships or loans; operating budget items in general; influencing specific legislation or election campaigns; religious or sectarian purposes; private secondary/private higher education except for programs that serve community needs with a high priority; endowments; fundraising events; academic or medical research; replacement of governmental or other funding except for grants bridging periods before anticipated funding; requests for multiyear funding; or applications for the same project less than one year apart.

Geographic Focus: All States

Date(s) Application is Due: Mar 31; Jun 1; Oct 1
Amount of Grant: Up to 100,000 USD
Contact: Nicole Bourdon, Program Officer; (413) 732-2858; fax (413) 733-8565; grants@communityfoundation.org or nbourdon@communityfoundation.org
Internet: www.communityfoundation.org
Sponsor: Community Foundation of Western Massachusetts
333 Bridge Street
Springfield, MA 01103

**Community Foundation Serving Riverside and San Bernardino Counties   742
  Impact Grants**
The Community Foundation Serving Riverside and San Bernardino Counties awards grants aimed at meeting the needs and enhancing the lives of individuals in California's Riverside and San Bernardino Counties. The Community Impact Fund was established by The Community Foundation to meet the needs of each community served by the Foundation, as determined by our grants committee and with final approval by our full Board of Directors. The grants are awarded through a competitive grant process each year. Funding categories include health and human services—promoting access to healthcare for all residents and helping individuals and families obtain basic services for an improved quality of life; youth and families—enhancing opportunities that promote academic achievement and positive youth development and developing family support services that foster learning and growth; arts and culture—encouraging creative expression and providing opportunities for enjoyment of cultural activities and art forms; civic and public benefit—building a sense of community and promoting civic participation. Preference is given to projects that are perceived as a high need in the community being served; fill a gap in service; benefit a large number of residents; enhance collaboration and/or make the delivery of services more effective and efficient; have clear objectives and can document successful outcomes; expand successful programs to serve additional residents or new geographic areas within the two counties; serve remote areas or areas that have received little funding from the foundation. Contact the office for application deadlines and forms.
Requirements: Nonprofit, public benefit organizations with evidence of tax-exempt status under Section 501(c)3 of the Internal Revenue Code and nor classified as a private foundation are eligible to apply.
Restrictions: Grants are generally not made for on-going operating expenses; retroactive funding for cost already incurred; paying off deficits or existing obligations; endowment, capital fund, or annual fund appeals; capital projects, i.e. construction of new buildings; direct support of individuals; sectarian programs or fraternal organizations; event sponsorships; research or development activities; school or college-based extracurricular activities; partisan activities; or re-granting purposes.
Geographic Focus: California
Date(s) Application is Due: Feb 25
Amount of Grant: Up to 10,000 USD
Contact: Celia Cudiamat, Vice President of Grants; (951) 241-7777; fax (909) 684-1911; ccudiamat@thecommunityfoundation.net or grant-info@thecommunityfoundation.net
Internet: www.thecommunityfoundation.net/grants/grants/grant-schedule/15-grants/51-the-community-foundation-s-community-impact-fund
Sponsor: Community Foundation Serving Riverside and San Bernardino Counties
3700 Sixth Street, Suite 200
Riverside, CA 92501

Community Memorial Foundation Responsive Grants   743
The Community Memorial Foundation encourages public and private endeavors in Illinois by nurturing the formation of creative initiatives and innovative funding strategies. Collaborative efforts may include participation with nonprofit organizations, governments, schools, and the business sector. In general, the Foundation gives preference to organizations that reach underserved segments of the population. A broad range of funding includes service delivery programs for vulnerable populations, start-up funds, building construction/renovation, project support, general operating support, and educational programs. Generally, the Foundation does not consider more than one proposal from any one institution and favors funding non-capital programs. There are two annual deadlines for application submission: 5:00 pm on March 31 and September 30. Most recent awards have ranged from $10,000 to $400,000.
Requirements: 501(c)3 organizations located in the Illinois communities of Argo, Bridgeview, Broadview, Brookfield, Burr Ridge, Clarendon Hills, Countryside, Darien, Downers Grove, Hickory Hills, Hinsdale, Hodgkins, Indian Head Park, Justice, La Grange, La Grange Park, Lyons, McCook, North Riverside, Oak Brook, Riverside, Stickney, Summit, Westchester, Western Springs, Westmont, Willow Springs, and Willowbrooks may apply.
Restrictions: Grants are not awarded to: organizations that limit services to any one religious group or members of a specific sectarian perspective; organizations that as a substantial part of their activities attempt to influence legislation, or directly or indirectly participate in and/or intervene in political organizations, political campaigns or lobbying groups; individuals; organizations that illegally discriminate on the basis of race, gender, sexual orientation, creed, age or national origin; tickets to dinners or advertising space in program books or other publications; endowments; or cost of in-patient care.
Geographic Focus: Illinois
Date(s) Application is Due: Mar 31; Sep 30
Amount of Grant: 10,000 - 400,000 USD
Samples: Advocate Charitable Foundation, Downers Grove, Illinois, $25,000 - to improve care coordination and access to recovery support through Linkage-to-Care program; Catholic Charities of the Archdiocese of Chicago, Chicago, Illinois, $35,000 - basic need services at St. Blase Service Center; The Community House, Hinsdale, Illinois, $80,000 - support of intensive outpatient psychotherapy program and expanded services.
Contact: Nanette Silva; (630) 654-4729; fax (630) 654-3402; info@cmfdn.org

Internet: www.cmfdn.org/responsive-grants
Sponsor: Community Memorial Foundation
15 Spinning Wheel Road, Suite 326
Hinsdale, IL 60521

Con Edison Corporate Giving Civic Grants   744
Con Edison is committed to supporting programs that offer youth, ages 8-18 years old, the skills and opportunities for lifelong civic engagement. The Corporation seeks to create interest in the democratic process by providing young people with the skills necessary to voice their opinions, affect policy changes, and remain civically engaged throughout their lives. It awards grants for specific projects rather than for general operating support. The corporate giving application process is open from March 1 to October 1. Requests for support are accepted at any time during this time period, and grants are made on a rotating basis.
Requirements: Con Edison makes grants to tax-exempt nonprofit organizations as defined under Section 501(c)3 of the U.S. Internal Revenue Code that serve the residents within its areas of operation. Organizations must be nonsectarian and nondenominational to receive support.
Restrictions: Con Edison does not award grants for reducing debts or past operating deficits. Con Edison does not reduce or donate costs of gas and electric services. Further, Con Edison does not award grants to: private foundations; individuals; labor groups; organizations with programs operating principally outside Con Edison's service area; media and literacy projects not connected to an institution or organization; houses of worship, although requests will be considered from religion-affiliated organizations whose activities benefit the overall community and do not support any religious doctrine; or public schools.
Geographic Focus: New York
Date(s) Application is Due: Oct 1
Contact: Walter Shay; (212) 460-2188; fax (212) 460-3730; ShayW@coned.com
Internet: www.coned.com/Partnerships/civics.asp
Sponsor: Con Edison Corporation
4 Irving Place, Room 1650-S
New York, NY 10003-3502

Cone Health Foundation Grants   745
The Cone Health Foundation invests in the development and support of activities, programs, and organizations that measurably improve the health of those in the greater Greensboro, North Carolina area. The Foundation awards grants to eligible not-for-profit organizations, government agencies, public schools and academic and/or research institutions, directing resources to four funding priorities: access to necessary health services with particular emphasis on eliminating the barriers often encountered by people in need; adolescent pregnancy prevention; HIV/AIDS and other sexually transmitted infections; and mental health and substance abuse. Current applications and guidelines are available online.
Requirements: In addition to meeting our funding priorities, your organization must serve people in the greater Greensboro area and fall into one of the following categories: not-for-profit organization; government agency; public school; or academic and/or research institution.
Restrictions: The Foundation does not support: activities that exclusively benefit the members of sectarian or religious organizations; annual fund drives; political campaigns or other partisan political activity; direct financial assistance to meet the immediate needs of individuals; endowments; or retirement of debt.
Geographic Focus: North Carolina
Contact: Antonia Monk Reaves, Senior Program Director; (336) 832-9555; fax (336) 832-9559; antonia.reaves@conehealth.com
Sandra Welch Boren; (336) 832-9555; fax (336) 832-9559; sandra.boren@conehealth.com
Internet: www.conehealthfoundation.com/home/for-grantseekers/
Sponsor: Cone Health Foundation
721 Green Valley Road, Suite 102
Greensboro, NC 27408

CONSOL Energy Academic Grants   746
Through its grant program, the CONSOL Energy Corporation supports employees and their families in its communities of operation. Its overall mission is to become a vital part of the communities where it is located. The Corporation strives to be involved in activities that enjoy wide community support and that benefit the most people, and specifically focus its efforts in the areas of public safety, youth organizations, community organizations, and arts and culture. It the area of academics, CONSOL Energy recognizes the significance in supporting education, as today's youth are tomorrow's future. Not only are monetary contributions made to educational institutions and programs, but the Corporation values opportunities to interface with today's youth. Through programs such as Junior Achievement and The Challenge Program, it is able to educate students on the energy industry as well as prepare them for possible job opportunities. CONSOL Energy partners with numerous local school districts, colleges and universities and youth athletic organizations throughout Pennsylvania, Ohio, West Virginia and Virginia.
Restrictions: CONSOL Energy does not fund: sectarian or denominational religious organizations; individuals; fraternal organizations; organizations outside of the company's service areas; profit-making entities; or individual disease-related fundraising organizations.
Geographic Focus: Ohio, Pennsylvania, Virginia, West Virginia
Contact: Kate O'Donovan, Director of Public Affairs; (724) 485-3097 or (724) 503-8223; kateo'donovan@consolenergy.com
Internet: www.consolenergy.com/about-us/corporate-responsibility/consol-in-the-community.aspx
Sponsor: CONSOL Energy
1000 Consol Energy Drive
Canonsburg, PA 15317-6506

CONSOL Youth Program Grants 747

Through its grant program, the CONSOL Energy Corporation supports employees and their families in its communities of operation. Its overall mission is to become a vital part of the communities where it is located. The Corporation strives to be involved in activities that enjoy wide community support and that benefit the most people, and specifically focus its efforts in the areas of public safety, youth organizations, community organizations, and arts and culture. It the area of youth programs, CONSOL Energy is investing in the future of organizations that promote the growth and continued success of children and youth. The Corporation contributes to organizations that give children and young adults the opportunity to pursue their interest in athletics, agriculture, civic engagement, outdoor recreation, and the arts.

Restrictions: CONSOL Energy does not fund: sectarian or denominational religious organizations; individuals; fraternal organizations; organizations outside of the company's service areas; profit-making entities; or individual disease-related fundraising organizations.

Geographic Focus: Ohio, Pennsylvania, Virginia, West Virginia
Contact: Kate O'Donovan, Director of Public Affairs; (724) 485-3097 or (724) 503-8223; kateo'donovan@consolenergy.com
Internet: www.consolenergy.com/about-us/corporate-responsibility/consol-in-the-community.aspx
Sponsor: CONSOL Energy
1000 Consol Energy Drive
Canonsburg, PA 15317-6506

Cooke Foundation Grants 748

On June 1, 1920, the forerunner of the Cooke Foundation, Limited, the Charles M. and Anna C. Cooke Trust, was created by Anna C. Cooke. The purpose of the Trust was: "to assure in some measure the continuance of, and also to extend and expand, all worthy endeavors for the betterment and welfare of this community and other communities by gifts and donations to the United States of America, any State, Territory, or any political subdivision thereof, and to corporations now or here after organized and operated exclusively for religious, charitable, scientific, or educational purposes, or for the prevention of cruelty to children or animals..." Today, the Cooke Foundation supports worthy endeavors in the community that the family feels will make a significant difference in the betterment and welfare of the people of Hawaii. Grants are awarded primarily for: culture and the arts; social services; education; programs for youth and the elderly; humanities; health; and the environment. Organizations receiving grants must be located in Hawaii or serve the people of Hawaii. Preference will be given to requests from Oahu. Types of support include general operating support, capital campaigns, building and renovations, program development, seed money, and matching funds.

Requirements: Grant making is limited to the state of Hawaii.
Restrictions: Grants are not made to individuals, churches, or religious organizations, or for endowment funds, scholarships, or fellowships.
Geographic Focus: Hawaii
Date(s) Application is Due: Mar 1; Sep 1
Amount of Grant: 5,000 - 50,000 USD
Samples: Lyman House Memorial Museum, Hilo, Hawaii, $50,000 - to support the Island Heritage Center (2018); Hanahauoli School, Honolulu, Hawaii, $50,000 - support of a youth program (2018); Hale Kipa, Honolulu, Hawaii, $50,000 - support for a new home for Hale Kipa (2018).
Contact: Daisy Chung, Program Officer; (808) 566-5524 or (888) 731-3863; fax (808) 521-6286; D.C.hung@hcf-hawaii.org or foundations@hcf-hawaii.org
Internet: www.cookefoundationlimited.org/grant-seekers
Sponsor: Cooke Foundation
827 Fort Street Mall
Honolulu, HI 96813-4317

Cooper Tire and Rubber Foundation Grants 749

The Cooper Tire and Rubber Foundation is a company-sponsored organization that awards grants on a national basis in its areas of interest, including museums, the arts, elementary and secondary education, higher education, and youth-oriented programs. Requests should include a detailed description of the project, the amount requested, and a brief history of the organization and its mission. Submit a letter of intent prior to submitting an entire application. There are no identified annual deadlines or application forms.

Geographic Focus: All States
Contact: Grants Administrator; (419) 423-1321; fax (419) 424-4108
Internet: us.coopertire.com/
Sponsor: Cooper Tire and Rubber Foundation
701 Lima Avenue
Findlay, OH 45840

Corina Higginson Trust Grants 750

The Corina Higginson Trust makes grants to organizations based in or benefiting the greater Washington Metropolitan area. The Trust's goals are: to increase opportunities for individuals for the purpose of improvement and development of their capabilities; to provide relief of the poor, distressed, and underprivileged; to promote social welfare by organizations designed to accomplish any of the above purposes or to lessen neighborhood tensions; to enhance opportunities for education about the arts and about the environment; and to eliminate prejudice and discrimination; or to defend civil rights secured by law. The two-step process of application requires: submission of a Letter of Intent (LOI); and, if invited, submission of a full proposal. There are two annual deadlines for LOIs: the first Friday in January; and the first Friday in July. Typical grant awards are about $5,000.

Requirements: 501(c)3 District of Columbia, Maryland, and Virginia nonprofit organizations are eligible.
Restrictions: Grants do not support individuals, fixed assets, religious organizations, medical or health-related programs, endowment funds to individual schools, or scholarship funds.
Geographic Focus: District of Columbia, Maryland, Virginia

Date(s) Application is Due: Mar 1; Sep 1
Amount of Grant: 5,000 - 10,000 USD
Contact: Adrienne Farfalla; (301) 292-5665; fax (301) 292-1070; info@corinahigginsontrust.org
Internet: www.corinahigginsontrust.org/instructionsforloi.html
Sponsor: Corina Higginson Trust
2001 Bryan Point Road
Accokeek, MD 20607

Cornell Lab of Ornithology Mini-Grants 751

Celebrate Urban Birds at the Cornell Lab of Ornithology invites organizations and educators to apply for mini-grants to help fund neighborhood events in communities everywhere. All applicants (even if they do not win funds to carry out their events) will receive free materials and training. Winning applicants will: hold a Celebrate Urban Birds event; introduce the public/youth to birds; do the 10-minute Celebrate Urban Bird observation with the people in their group, at their event, and report back to the Lab of Ornithology, either by paper forms or on-line; distribute Celebrate Urban Birds kits (with posters, seeds for planting, and more); integrate the arts; integrate gardening/habitat creation; and get people outside. Mini-grants average $100 to $500. Organizations working with underserved communities are strongly encouraged to apply.

Geographic Focus: All States
Date(s) Application is Due: Dec 15
Amount of Grant: 100 - 500 USD
Contact: Program Coordinator; (607) 254-2455; fax (607) 254-2111; urbanbirds@cornell.edu
Internet: www.birds.cornell.edu/celebration/community/minigrants/mini-grants-2012
Sponsor: Cornell Lab of Ornithology
159 Sapsucker Woods Road
Ithaca, NY 14850

Countess Moira Charitable Foundation Grants 752

The Countess Moira Charitable Foundation was established in 2000 with its mission being "to aid the well-being of youth anywhere in the World" by supporting charitable organizations that focus on the betterment of youth. Qualified organizations may submit inquiries for operating program, endowment and capital funding needs that support the mission of the foundation. There are no deadlines; inquiries will be accepted throughout the year.

Requirements: The foundation will only consider unsolicited inquiries from organizations in the New York tri-state area, or national organizations that may also utilize funds in the broader international arena. Grants will only be made to 501(c)3 nonprofit organizations. Initial contact should be made via email (see below) before making a formal grant proposal.
Restrictions: Do not send unsolicited inquiries or grant proposals via paper mail to the foundation's mailing address as these will not be considered at all. Grants will not be given for events or fundraisers nor to individuals.
Geographic Focus: Connecticut, New Jersey, New York
Contact: Carolyn Gray, President/Chairperson; inquiries@countessmoirafdn.org
Internet: sites.google.com/a/countessmoirafdn.org/countessmoirafoundation/
Sponsor: Countess Moira Charitable Foundation
P.O. Box 8078
Pelham, NY 10803

Courtney S. Turner Charitable Trust Grants 753

The Courtney S. Turner Charitable Trust was created (under a will dated August 25, 1978) for the furtherance and development of public charitable and educational purposes. Courtney S. Turner was born March 1st, 1896 in Atchison, Kansas to C.F.A. and Georgia Pierce Turner, two of the Atchison's pioneer residents. Mr. Turner attended Atchison Public Schools and earned his first dime at the age of 6 as a substitute carrier for the Atchison Globe. He then had a distinguished career in the military and later achieved great success in both finance and real estate. He returned to Atchison in 1968, where he spent the remaining 18 years of his life. He was well known in the community for his philanthropic contributions throughout the city. The legacy of his charitable trust continues to play an important role in the development and growth of the Atchison, Kansas area. All grants are 1 year in duration.

Requirements: Applications will only be accepted from 501(c)3 organizations in the Atchison, Kansas community area. The trust prefers to give grants for specific purposes (buildings, capital equipment and programs) to be completed in a fixed number of short years. Only a limited number of grants will be considered for operational expenses. On multi-year requests, the trustees will consider only one-year requests at a time. Applications will be submitted online through the Bank of America website. A grant report is required within 1 year of the grant application date, regardless of whether all of the funds have been spent.
Restrictions: The trust does not support requests from individuals, organizations attempting to influence policy through direct lobbying, or any political campaigns.
Geographic Focus: Kansas
Date(s) Application is Due: Sep 30
Contact: Tony Twyman, Senior Philanthropic Client Manager; (816) 292-4342; mo.grantmaking@bankofamerica.com or tony.twyman@bofa.com
Internet: www.bankofamerica.com/philanthropic/foundation/?fnId=313
Sponsor: Courtney S. Turner Charitable Trust
231 South LaSalle Street, IL1-231-10-05
Chicago, IL 60697

Covenant Educational Foundation Grants 754

The Covenant Educational Foundation offers funding for projects or programs in the arts, health organizations, or human services. Giving is primarily in the North Carolina area. There is no application, but organizations may send a summary of the project in essay form as an initial approach.

Requirements: Applicants must be from the North Carolina area.

Geographic Focus: North Carolina
Date(s) Application is Due: Apr 30
Amount of Grant: 250 - 5,500 USD
Samples: Kidsville News, Fayetteville, North Carolina, $5,500 - improve youth literacy; American Cancer Society, Greenville, North Carolina, $3,000 - help families affected with cancer; American Red Cross, Fayetteville, North Carolina, $250 - help families affected by storm.
Contact: Gardner H. Altman, Sr., President; (910) 484-0041 or (910) 323-5717
Sponsor: Covenant Educational Foundation
P.O. Box 234
White Oak, NC 28399

Covenant Foundation of Brentwood Grants 755

The Covenant Foundation is primarily interested in supporting churches, religious agencies, missionaries, and programs that serve the needy. Types of support include the following: project support; seed money; equipment; and general operating support. Funding is primarily limited to Tennessee. There are no specific applications or deadlines. Interested applicant should send a letter of intent.
Requirements: Only 501(c)3 organizations based in Tennessee should apply.
Geographic Focus: Tennessee
Amount of Grant: 100 - 3,000 USD
Samples: Rockhouse Way, Brentwood, Tennessee, $36,000 - ministry support; Prayer Breakfast Nashville, Franklin, Tennessee, $500 - prayer breakfast donation; Fellowship Bible Church, Brentwood, Tennessee, $100 - church support; Refugee support, Nashville, Tennessee, $265 - groceries for refugee family.
Contact: Donald G. Albright, President; (615) 376-4786 or (615) 373-4693
Sponsor: Covenant Foundation of Brentwood
1815 Cromwell Drive, P.O. Box 1822
Brentwood, TN 37024-1822

Covenant to Care for Children Crisis Food Pantry Giving 756

The Board and Staff members of Covenant to Care for Children (CCC) are dedicated and caring people who give generously of their time and talents. They are a diverse group who share one goal—a strong wish to make the world a better place for kids and families. For more than 25 years, CCC workers have teamed with volunteers from the Asylum Hill and Kensington Congregational churches to deliver fresh food and staples to families in greater Hartford and New Britain. CCC works in cooperation with the Department of Children and Families (DCF). Crisis Food Pantry volunteers field calls from D.C.F social workers when a needy family has been identified. Using a food list created by a dietician, the pantry volunteers assemble and deliver enough food for one week.
Geographic Focus: Connecticut
Contact: Catherine Haugh, Program Coordinator; (860) 243-1806; fax (860) 243-0100; chaugh@covenanttocare.org
Internet: covenanttocare.org/portfolio-items/food/
Sponsor: Covenant to Care for Children
1477 Park Street, 2A
Hartford, CT 06106

Covenant to Care for Children Critical Goods Grants 757

Covenant to Care for Children (CCC) works to mobilize and channel the generosity of caring and faithful people to advocate for, mentor, and provide direct assistance to Connecticut's children and youth who are neglected, abused, or at-risk. The organization's vision is to create a future where all Connecticut children have caring families and safe places to live. The Critical Goods program facilitates family preservation and reunification through the placement of required goods in the homes of client families. Where possible, CCC also aids efforts to place children and youth in foster care and independent living through the placement of required goods. In order to accomplish this, the Program collects high quality new and used furniture, appliances, clothing and infant items from individuals and corporate donors and redistributes it to families in need.
Requirements: By appointment, the Critical Goods Coordinator picks up furniture, toys, clothing, and other goods from donor homes and businesses.
Restrictions: The Program does not accept drop-side cribs, and will dispose of them if they are included with additional furniture.
Geographic Focus: Connecticut
Contact: Catherine Haugh; (860) 243-1806; fax (860) 243-0100; chaugh@covenanttocare.org
Internet: covenanttocare.org/portfolio-items/critical-goods/
Sponsor: Covenant to Care for Children
1477 Park Street, 2A
Hartford, CT 06106

Covenant to Care for Children Enrichment Fund Grants 758

The Covenant to Care for Children's (CCC) Enrichment Fund is a children's advocacy program that helps respond to the less ordinary requests to meet special needs for the support, care and nurturing of youth and children in crisis. This program provides a fund designed to accept designated donations for those special expense needs of children. Social workers can request these funds for the needs of children that are not met by State Government departments, other agencies, or CCC's Adopt a Social Worker Program. Funding examples include summer camp, haircuts, lessons, art, music, sports, tutoring, bikes, or special books. Additional information is available at the website.
Geographic Focus: Connecticut
Contact: Catherine Haugh; (860) 243-1806; fax (860) 243-0100; chaugh@covenanttocare.org
Internet: covenanttocare.org/portfolio-items/cef/
Sponsor: Covenant to Care for Children
1477 Park Street, 2A
Hartford, CT 06106

Covidien Partnership for Neighborhood Wellness Grants 759

Covidien Partnership for Neighborhood Wellness Grants support community projects that increase access to quality, affordable healthcare; benefit people suffering from a specific disease for which treatment options are not affordable or readily available; provides assistance that has a significant impact on the health of the community; or support development of new treatments or new approaches to prevention. Funding requests may vary in range and depth, and should aim to: increase access to quality, affordable healthcare; build capacity to increase services; provide education and awareness, with an emphasis on prevention; provide medical professionals with additional tools to address specific health needs; raise money for capital campaigns for building clinics or healthcare facilities in impoverished communities; fund local community health centers or clinics to augment their medical staff, diagnostic tests and treatments or disease prevention and education initiatives; and fund consumer education related to specific diseases or medical conditions. Grants are made twice a year. Additional information about grant submission and deadlines is available at the Covidien website.
Requirements: Applicants are required to take an online eligibility quiz before submitting a grant request.
Restrictions: The following grant requests are excluded from funding: partisan political organizations, committees or candidates for public office or public office holders; religious organizations in support of their sacramental or theological functions; labor unions; endowments; capital campaigns (although capital campaigns for building clinics or healthcare facilities in impoverished communities are considered); requests for multi-year support; organizations whose prime purpose is to influence legislation; testimonial dinners; for-profit publications or organizations seeking advertisements for promotional support; individuals; fraternities, sororities, etc; or gala dinners, golf fundraisers and other special events.
Geographic Focus: All States
Contact: Teresa Hacunda; (508) 261-8000; Teresa.Hacunda@covidien.com
Internet: www.covidien.com/covidien/pages.aspx?page=AboutUs/socialresponsibility/Giving
Sponsor: Covidien Healthcare Products
15 Hampshire Street
Mansfield, MA 02048

Cralle Foundation Grants 760

The foundation awards grants in the areas of education and higher education, children and youth services, community development, human services, and museums to Kentucky nonprofits. Emphasis is given to nonprofits serving residents of Louisville. Types of support include: building and renovation; capital campaigns; continuing support; endowments; equipment; operating support; matching and challenge support; program development; scholarship funds; and seed money. Interested organizations should initially send a letter requesting an application form. Applicants should submit four copies of their application. Application deadlines are March 1 and September 1. The foundation's board meets in April and October.
Requirements: Nonprofit organizations in Kentucky are eligible.
Restrictions: No grants to individuals.
Geographic Focus: Kentucky
Date(s) Application is Due: Mar 1; Sep 1
Amount of Grant: 5,000 - 50,000 USD
Samples: Maryhurst School, Louisville, KY, $40,250 - for Seven Challenges Program; Blessings in a Backpack, Louisville, KY, $25,000 - for students at Portland Elementary; Family and Children's Place, Louisville, KY, $25,000 - for operating support.
Contact: James Crain, Jr.; (502) 581-1148; fax (502) 581-1937; jcrain37@bellsouth.net
Sponsor: Cralle Foundation, Inc.
614 West Main Street, Suite 2500
Louisville, KY 40202-4252

Crane Foundation General Grants 761

Created in 1951, the Crane Foundation is a non-profit corporation organized exclusively to make charitable contributions for religious, educational and scientific purposes, including institutions that qualify as tax exempt under section 501(c)3 of Internal Revenue Code. As part of the Foundation, the Crane Company offers a program for Matching Gifts to educational institutions. Any employee with at least one year of service may receive a 100% match on their donation up to a maximum of $5,000 per year.
Requirements: Any 501(c)3 organization in the U.S. may apply.
Geographic Focus: All States
Amount of Grant: 1,000 - 10,000 USD
Contact: Foundation Administrator; (201) 585-0888 or (203) 363-7300; crfdn@craneco.com
Internet: www.craneco.com/about/corporate-ethics/default.aspx#crane-fund
Sponsor: Crane Foundation
140 Sylvan Avenue
Englewood Cliffs, NJ 07632

Crane Fund for Widows and Children Grants 762

The Vergona Crane Company was founded by Joseph Vergona III, and the Crane Foundation Fund for Widows and Children was established in his honor to make contributions to charitable organizations that provide direct assistance to underserved populations in the communities where Crane operates. Grants have supported the Red Cross and Salvation Army, as well as efforts to help the homeless, abused and disabled children, runaways, and those with mental health problems. Grants also go to universities to pay for scholarships for disadvantaged students. Application may be made by contacting the office or local Crane operating facilities.
Geographic Focus: All States
Amount of Grant: 1,000 - 10,000 USD
Contact: Grants Administrator; (201) 585-0888 or (203) 363-7300; cfwc@craneco.com

Internet: www.craneco.com/about/corporate-ethics/default.aspx#crane-fund
Sponsor: Crane Foundation
140 Sylvan Avenue
Englewood Cliffs, NJ 07632

Crane Fund Grants 763

The Vergona Crane Company was founded by Joseph Vergona III, and the Crane Foundation Fund was established in his honor in 1914 as a private charitable trust. The Fund grants aid to former employees of the Crane Company (or their dependents) who by reason of age or physical disability are unable to be self-supporting and are in need of assistance. The Fund is administered by a Board of Trustees and a Pension Committee, both appointed by Crane Company's Board of Directors. Application may be made by contacting the office or local Crane operating facilities.
Geographic Focus: All States
Amount of Grant: 1,000 - 10,000 USD
Contact: Grants Administrator; (201) 585-0888 or (203) 363-7300; cranefund@craneco.com
Internet: www.craneco.com/Category/33/The-Crane-Fund.html
Sponsor: Crane Foundation
140 Sylvan Avenue
Englewood Cliffs, NJ 07632

Crayola Champion Creatively Alive Children Grants 764

The Crayola Champion Creatively Alive Children program provides grants for innovative, creative leadership team building within elementary schools. The plan should address specific needs and interests of your professional learning community. Consider how you'd create the team, craft a common vision, chart a strategic plan, change behaviors, build creative confidence, teach design thinking, align new National Arts Standards with Common Core or your state's standards, embed creativity into the school culture, and use professional development, peer observation, and coaching to implement the plan. Each grant-winning school (up to twenty grants awarded) receives $2,500 and Crayola products valued at $1,000 to develop an art-infused education creative capacity-building professional development program. The annual deadline for submissions is June 20. Finalists are contacted by end of September.
Requirements: In collaboration with the National Association of Elementary School Principals (NAESP), Crayola offers up to twenty grants for schools in the United States or Canada.
Restrictions: The applications will only be accepted from principals who are members of NAESP.
Geographic Focus: All States, Canada
Date(s) Application is Due: Jun 20
Amount of Grant: 1,000 - 3,500 USD
Samples: Regency Park Elementary, Pittsburgh, Pennsylvania, $3,500 - support of the Art 'n Bots program; Santo Nino Regional Catholic School, Santa Fe, New Mexico, $3.500 - support of the Art of Our Elders Helps Create Future program; White County Central Elementary, Judsonia, Arkansas, $3,500 - support of the Artistic Habits of Mind program.
Contact: Anita DeChellis, (800) 272-9652; fax (610) 515-8781; creativelyalive@crayola.com
Internet: www.crayola.com/for-educators/ccac-landing/grant-program.aspx
Sponsor: Binney and Smith Corporation
1100 Church Lane, P.O. Box 431
Easton, PA 18044-0431

Credit Suisse Foundation Education Grants 765

The Credit Suisse Foundation's aim is to enable more people to participate in political and economic life by awarding grants for training and education. The Foundation allocates the resources to three global initiatives in the areas of education and micro-finance and manages the Disaster Relief Fund. Launched in 2008, the Global Education Initiative partners' programs have aimed to break down barriers of access to education and to improve the quality of educational opportunities for school-aged children in selected countries throughout the world. The Initiative has developed strong partnerships over the past and the Foundation believes it has made a real impact, reaching over 100,000 students in over 400 schools in 38 countries. Over the past five years more than 15,000 teachers have been trained in subjects ranging from Science, Technology, Engineering, and Math (STEM) and IT to child-friendly teaching methodologies. Based on this success, Credit Suisse is launching a Signature program within the Education Initiative focusing on Financial Education for Girls, to be fully rolled out by the end of the year by its partners, Plan UK and Aflatoun. The Foundation will continue to work with a few of its Global Education Initiative partners in support of education programs in various regions.
Geographic Focus: All States, All Countries
Contact: Director; (212) 325-2000 or (212) 325-2389; americas.corporatecitizenship@credit-suisse.com
Internet: www.credit-suisse.com/us/en/about-us/corporate-responsibility/initiatives/education/about.html
Sponsor: Credit Suisse Foundation
One Madison Avenue, 3rd Floor
New York, NY 10010-3629

Cresap Family Foundation Grants 766

The Cresap Family Foundation was established in 2012, upon the final sale of the family's business, Premium Beers of Oklahoma, one of the largest Anheuser-Busch distributorships in the United States. Though the foundation may be fairly newly-launched, the family's spirit of giving dates as far back as 1968 when a self-made auto dealer purchased a little Anheuser-Busch distributorship in Bartlesville, Oklahoma. The Foundation's primary fields of interest include: animal welfare; arts and humanities; education; health and wellness; and youth and families. Most recent awards have ranged from $1,000 to $50,000. A Letter of Intent summarizing the project for funding should be submitted through an online

application process by the April 1 deadline. Full applications will be by invitation, and must be received by July 15.
Requirements: The Trustees invite proposals from 501(c)3 organizations. Preference will be given to organizations in Central Oklahoma and counties in Northeast Oklahoma, which include: Craig, Delaware, Mayes, Nowata, Osage, Ottawa and Washington.
Geographic Focus: Oklahoma
Date(s) Application is Due: Jul 15
Amount of Grant: 1,000 - 50,000 USD
Samples: Oklahoma Contemporary Arts Center, Oklahoma City, Oklahoma, $10,000 - general operating support (2018); County of Craig-Vinita School District 65, Vinita, Oklahoma, $68,133 - general operating support (2018); National Cowboy and Western Heritage Museum, Oklahoma City, Oklahoma, $25,000 - general operating support (2018).
Contact: Kari Blakley, Executive Director; (405) 755-5571 or (406) 781-9413; fax (405) 755-0938; kblakley@fmiokc.com
Internet: www.cresapfoundation.org/grants-and-giving/
Sponsor: Cresap Family Foundation
2932 NW 122nd Street, Suite D
Oklahoma City, OK 73120

Crescent Porter Hale Foundation Grants 767

The Crescent Porter Hale Foundation places emphasis on organizations engaged in Catholic endeavors, with preference given to organizations in the San Francisco Bay area counties of Alameda, Contra Costa, Marin, San Francisco, and San Mateo. Areas considered desirable for funding include: organizations devoted to Catholic elementary and high school; education in the fields of art and music; agencies serving disadvantaged and at-risk youth; and help for families and the elderly. Applications for capital funds, scholarship funds, and requests for special projects, as well as for general operating program support, will be considered. The Foundation will consider other worthwhile programs that can be demonstrated as serving broad community purposes, leading toward the improvement of quality of life. Agencies serving disadvantaged youth, the disabled, or the elderly are of particular interest. Organizations wishing to apply should complete the online process, indicating the nature of the program and/or the specific project for which funding is sought. Grant requests in the amount of $15,000 and above will be given priority consideration.
Requirements: To be eligible for consideration, organizations must meet the following criteria: be a corporate non-profit organization; qualify for tax exemption by the State of California; be an organization to which contributions are deductible by donors for income tax purposes, generally of the type described in Section 501(c)3 of the Internal Revenue Code; be classified as a non-private foundation pursuant to the 1969 Tax Reform Acts; and conduct an annual financial audit in accordance with approved accounting practices.
Restrictions: Individuals are ineligible. Healthcare-related, research, or postgraduate education programs are ineligible.
Geographic Focus: California
Amount of Grant: 5,000 - 250,000 USD
Contact: Hollyann Vickers; (415) 561-6540, ext. 234; fax (415) 561-5477; hvickers@pfs-llc.net
Internet: www.crescentporterhale.org/for-grantseekers/
Sponsor: Crescent Porter Hale Foundation
1660 Bush Street, Suite 300
San Francisco, CA 94109

Crystelle Waggoner Charitable Trust Grants 768

Born to a ranching family, Crystelle Waggoner raised cattle and thoroughbred horses. A patron of the arts and supporter of medical charities during her lifetime, she established a 50-year trust to benefit charitable organizations in the arts and social services. Award amounts are typically between $1,000 to $150,000.
Requirements: Applicants must have 501(c)3 tax-exempt status. Preference is given to organizations, operating in, or serving Tarrant County. Charitable organizations must have been in existence before January 24, 1982. Eligibility to re-apply for a grant award from the Crystelle Waggoner Charitable Trust requires organizations to skip 1 grant cycle (1 year) before submitting a subsequent application. Applications will be submitted online through the Bank of America website. A grant report is required within 1 year of the grant application date, regardless of whether all of the funds have been spent.
Restrictions: The trust does not support requests from individuals, organizations attempting to influence policy through direct lobbying, or any political campaigns.
Geographic Focus: Texas
Date(s) Application is Due: Aug 1
Amount of Grant: 1,000 - 150,000 USD
Samples: National Cowgirl Museum and Hall of Fame, Fort Worth, Texas, $150,000 - Awarded for Capital Campaign: Second Floor Renovation (2019); New Key School Inc., Fort Worth, Texas, $100,000 - Awarded for Planting Seeds Capital Campaign - Deepening the Roots of Learning (2019); Kimbell Art Foundation, Fort Worth, Texas, $75,000 - Awarded for The Lure of Dresden: Bellotto at the Court of Saxony (2019).
Contact: Kelly Garlock, Philanthropic Client Manager; (800) 357-7094; tx.philanthropic@bankofamerica.com or tx.philanthropic@ustrust.com
Internet: www.bankofamerica.com/philanthropic/foundation/?fnId=12
Sponsor: Crystelle Waggoner Charitable Trust
P.O. Box 831041
Dallas, TX 75283-1041

Cudd Foundation Grants 769

The Cudd Foundation awards grants to eligible nonprofit organizations in its areas of interest, including arts, culture, performing arts, children and youth, education, environment, health care, historic preservation, and social services. Types of support include annual campaigns, capital campaigns, continuing support, curriculum development, emergency

grants, endowments, program development, research, and scholarship funds. The listed application deadline is for letters of interest; full proposals are by invitation only.
Requirements: Louisiana, Oklahoma, California, and New Mexico 501(c)3 nonprofit organizations are eligible to apply.
Geographic Focus: California, Louisiana, New Mexico, Oklahoma
Amount of Grant: 250 - 222,088 USD
Samples: Bayou District Foundation, New Orleans, Louisiana, $500 - education and development; Caldera Arts Organization, Agoura Hills, California, $5,000 - art programs; Rio Grande School, Santa Fe, New Mexico, $6,000 - educational support.
Contact: Amanda Cudd Stuermer; (505) 986-8416; fax (505) 986-8427; cuddfdn@aol.com
Sponsor: Cudd Foundation
P.O. Box 1980
El Prado, NM 87529

CUNA Mutual Group Foundation Community Grants 770

The CUNA Mutual Group Corporation and its Foundation makes grants to programs and organizations that are of benefit to its subsidiaries. Giving is limited to communities in which associates reside and programs that are of benefit to: Fort Worth, Texas; Madison, Wisconsin; and Waverly, Iowa. Priority areas include: at-risk youth; education; urban and civic services; human services; and the arts. A few multi-year grants will be awarded. The committee gives preference to programs in which associates and their families are involved, and those involving more than just monetary funding. There are no application deadlines for grants up to $5,000. For larger grants, allow at least six weeks before board meetings in February, May, and September. The foundation also offers Credit Union Movement Grants. Funding requests are accepted from credit union organizations to support their charitable causes. The foundation also offers Employee Involvement Grants. The Dollars for Doers program provides cash grants to 501(c)3 nonprofit organizations in which current and retired employees, and current board members, make a significant volunteer investment and a financial donation. Foundation grant requests will be reviewed on a rolling basis throughout the year but must be received at least 45 days before the meeting in which it will be reviewed.
Requirements: 501(c)3 organizations located in, or serving the residents of, the following communities are eligible: Fort Worth, Texas; Madison, Wisconsin; and Waverly, Iowa.
Restrictions: The committee will not consider grants for individuals; political parties, candidates, and partisan political campaigns; professional associations; operating expenses for organizations receiving United Way funding; or religious groups for religious purposes.
Geographic Focus: Iowa, Texas, Wisconsin
Amount of Grant: 2,500 - 20,000 USD
Contact: Beth Cutler, Community Relations Leader; (608) 231-7755 or (800) 356-2644, ext. 7755; fax (608) 236-7755; beth.cutler@cunamutual.com
Internet: www.cunamutual.com/about-us/cuna-mutual-group-foundation
Sponsor: CUNA Mutual Group Foundation
5910 Mineral Point Road
Madison, WI 53705

Curtis Foundation Grants 771

The Curtis Foundation, based in Raleigh, North Carolina, supports a wide array of causes, including: abuse prevention; basic and emergency aid; Christianity; diseases and conditions; domesticated animals; equal opportunity in education; graduate and professional education; higher education; human services; international development; Methodism; news and public information; community nonprofits; public policy; reproductive health care; shelter and residential care; special population support; and youth development programs. The Foundation's geographic focus is the State of North Carolina. Applicants should submit the following in letter format: copy of IRS Determination Letter; a brief history of organization and description of its mission; and a detailed description of project and amount of funding requested. Although there are no specified deadlines, applicants should submit their proposal at least six months prior to the requested disbursement date.
Requirements: Any 501(c)3 supporting residents of North Carolina are eligible to apply.
Geographic Focus: North Carolina
Amount of Grant: Up to 100,000 USD
Samples: University of North Carolina at Chapel Hill, Chapel Hill, North Carolina, $110,000 - general operating support; Edenton Street United Methodist Church, Raleigh, North Carolina, $76,000 - general operating support; Food Bank of Central and Eastern Nort Carolina, Raleigh, North Carolina, $15,000 - general operating support.
Contact: Donald W. Curtis, President; (919) 781-6119
Sponsor: Curtis Foundation
P.O. Box 20443
Raleigh, NC 27619-0443

Cystic Fibrosis Lifestyle Foundation Individual Recreation Grants 772

The Cystic Fibrosis Lifestyle Foundation (CFLF) was founded in 2003 by Brian Callanan. From an early age Brian knew he wanted to help others who struggled with the challenges of living with CF. Through his personal experience he learned the importance and value of exercise, recreation and positive mindset for his health. The intent in approving an Individual Recreation Grant request is to encourage activities that physically challenges both the body and the lungs. Priority is given to grant requests of greater duration (i.e., 6-month gym membership or seasonal activity is more favorable than a one-week activity). Typically, Individual Recreation Grants are for up to $500. Application forms can be found at the website.
Restrictions: Purchase of equipment (i.e. treadmills, elliptical, etc.) is not typically funded by CFLF, although exceptions are occasionally made for extenuating circumstances.
Geographic Focus: All States
Amount of Grant: Up to 500 USD
Contact: Erin Evans, Program Coordinator; (802) 310-3176 or (802) 310-5983; fax (802) 877-2034; erin@cflf.org or grants@cflf.org

Internet: www.cflf.org/content_page/individual-recreation-grants
Sponsor: Cystic Fibrosis Lifestyle Foundation
P.O. Box 1344
Burlington, VT 05402

Cystic Fibrosis Lifestyle Foundation Loretta Morris Memorial Fund Grants 773

The Cystic Fibrosis Lifestyle Foundation (CFLF) was founded in 2003 by Brian Callanan. From an early age Brian knew he wanted to help others who struggled with the challenges of living with cystic fibrosis. Through his personal experience he learned the importance and value of exercise, recreation and positive mindset for his health. The Loretta Morris Fund was established in 2010 in her honor. Grants are available for dance, horseback riding, golf and swimming/aquatics. Other recreation requests will be considered. California residents are given preference. Recreation Grants are for up to $500.
Requirements: Applications must be completed by the person with cystic fibrosis. If a child is unable to write the parent or guardian may transcribe for them, but the words must come from the child.
Geographic Focus: All States
Amount of Grant: Up to 500 USD
Contact: Erin Evans, Program Coordinator; (802) 310-3176 or (802) 310-5983; fax (802) 877-2034; erin@cflf.org or grants@cflf.org
Internet: www.cflf.org/content_page/loretta-morris-fund-recreation-grants
Sponsor: Cystic Fibrosis Lifestyle Foundation
P.O. Box 1344
Burlington, VT 05402

Cystic Fibrosis Lifestyle Foundation Mentored Recreation Grants 774

The Cystic Fibrosis Lifestyle Foundation (CFLF) was founded in 2003 by Brian Callanan. From an early age Brian knew he wanted to help others who struggled with the challenges of living with CF. Through his personal experience he learned the importance and value of exercise, recreation and positive mindset for his health. This support can provide greater access and motivation for recipients to get out and have fun in their current interests. CFLF awards grants for up to $500 for pre-approved recreation activities for people with cystic fibrosis. Incorporating a mentor with your recreation activity provides an additional $500 (maximum) in order for the chosen recreation mentor to participate in the activities with the recipient. Application forms can be found at the website.
Requirements: Mentors must be at least 25 years old, and ideally have an established familiarity with the child and family applying for the grant. They may be a family member (other than parent) or a friend of the family.
Restrictions: Purchase of equipment (i.e. treadmills, elliptical, etc.) is not typically funded by CFLF, although exceptions are occasionally made for extenuating circumstances.
Geographic Focus: All States
Amount of Grant: Up to 1,000 USD
Contact: Erin Evans, Program Coordinator; (802) 310-3176 or (802) 310-5983; fax (802) 877-2034; erin@cflf.org or grants@cflf.org
Internet: www.cflf.org/content_page/mentor-recreation-grants
Sponsor: Cystic Fibrosis Lifestyle Foundation
P.O. Box 1344
Burlington, VT 05402

Cystic Fibrosis Lifestyle Foundation Peer Support Grants 775

The Cystic Fibrosis Lifestyle Foundation (CFLF) was founded in 2003 by Brian Callanan. From an early age Brian knew he wanted to help others who struggled with the challenges of living with cystic fibrosis. Through his personal experience he learned the importance and value of exercise, recreation and positive mindset for his health. The intent of the Peer Support Grant option is to allow recipients the opportunity to include a friend in their activity of choice. The Foundation feels that by offering a partnership in the recreation grant activity that there is often more excitement and motivation, thus creating positive feelings toward staying active. A Peer Support is a less formal companion that participates in activities with the applicant. Up to $500 may be added to the grant to cover the costs for this person. If applying for a grant with peer support, the maximum dollar amount may not exceed $1,000, ($500 for the applicant and $500 for the peer). Because the grant is offering to cover recreation expenses for both the recipient and a peer, it will be expected that the Peer Support person be involved for the duration of the activity.
Restrictions: Purchase of equipment (i.e. treadmills, elliptical, etc.) is not typically funded by CFLF, although exceptions are occasionally made for extenuating circumstances.
Geographic Focus: All States
Amount of Grant: Up to 1,000 USD
Contact: Erin Evans, Program Coordinator; (802) 310-3176 or (802) 310-5983; fax (802) 877-2034; erin@cflf.org or grants@cflf.org
Internet: www.cflf.org/content_page/peer-support-grants
Sponsor: Cystic Fibrosis Lifestyle Foundation
P.O. Box 1344
Burlington, VT 05402

D. W. McMillan Foundation Grants 776

The D.W. McMillan Foundation, established in Alabama in 1956, supports organizations involved with children and youth services, health care, health organizations, homelessness, hospitals, human services, mental health and crisis services, residential and custodial care, hospices, people with disabilities, and the economically disadvantaged population. Giving is primarily centered in the states of Alabama and Florida. There are no specific deadlines, though applicants should submit proposals well before the annual board meeting on December 1. Applicants should begin by contacting the Foundation with a letter of inquiry. Final notification of awards are given by December 31 each year.

Geographic Focus: Alabama, Florida
Date(s) Application is Due: Nov 1
Samples: Department of Human Resources, Escambia County, Alabama, $160,000 - general operations; Appleton Volunteer Fire Department, Brewster, Alabama, $5,000 - general operations; Baptist Hospital, Pensacola, Florida, $30,000 - general operations.
Contact: Ed Leigh McMillan II, Treasurer; (251) 867-4881
Sponsor: D.W. McMillan Foundation
329 Belleville Avenue
Brewton, AL 36426-2039

Dana Brown Charitable Trust Grants 777

Dana Brown was a well-known personality in St. Louis due in part to his many appearances on television representing Safari brand coffee and sharing his latest adventures while on safari in Africa. He was an extraordinarily successful entrepreneur and philanthropist. Originally from West Virginia, Mr. Brown adopted St. Louis as his home and had a deep affection for the region and many of the institutions that have made this area great. Established in Missouri in 1994, the Dana Brown Charitable Trust awards grants to eligible Missouri nonprofit organizations. The primary purpose of the trust is to provide for the health, education and welfare of underprivileged and economically disadvantaged children in the St. Louis, Missouri metropolitan area. With that as its focus, the Foundation's current areas of interest include: animal welfare; wildlife and the environment; children and youth; health care; education; and human services. Types of support provided include: annual campaigns; building and renovation; capital campaigns; general operating support; and challenge grants. A formal application is required, with annual deadline dates identified as February 15, May 15, August 15, and November 15.
Requirements: Missouri nonprofit organizations are eligible. Preference is given to requests from the greater Saint Louis metropolitan area.
Restrictions: Grants will not be made directly to individuals. In addition, the Trustees wish to make grants directly to the charitable organizations that will utilize the funds and, therefore, generally will not consider requests of Supporting Organizations. Grants will not be awarded for feasibility studies. Multi-year grants will be considered, but the fulfillment of immediate needs will generally be preferred over long-term possibilities.
Geographic Focus: Missouri
Date(s) Application is Due: Feb 15; May 15; Aug 15; Nov 15
Amount of Grant: 5,000 - 250,000 USD
Samples: Saint Louis Zoo Foundation, Saint Louis, Missouri, $250,000 - general operations; Little Bit Foundation, Saint Louis, Missouri, $5,200 - support of the Saint Louis Journal Giving Guide; Center of Creative Arts, Saint Louis, Missouri, $25,000 - general operations.
Contact: Kimberly Livingston; (314) 418-2643 or (314) 505-8204; kimberly.livingston@usbank.com
Internet: www.danabrowncharitabletrust.org/rules.html
Sponsor: Dana Brown Charitable Trust
P.O. Box 387
St. Louis, MO 63166

Daniel and Nanna Stern Family Foundation Grants 778

The Daniel and Nanna Stern Family Foundation was established in 2006, with the expressed interest in providing support primarily to programs in New York City. The Foundations major fields of interest include: the arts; education; hospitals; film and video; television; and performing arts centers. Though a formal application is required, interested applicants should begin by forwarding a letter to the Foundation office, offering a detailed description of the project, the amount of funding requested, contact information, and copies of both the IRS determination letter and most recent audit. No annual deadlines for submission have been identified. Most recent awards have ranged from $50,000 to $150,000.
Requirements: Any 501(c)3 organization located in, or serving the residents of, New York City are eligible to apply.
Geographic Focus: New York
Amount of Grant: 50,000 - 150,000 USD
Samples: Allen-Stevenson School, New York, New York, $150,500 - general operating support; Carter Burden Center for the Aging, New York, New York, $48,000 - general operating support; Film Society of Lincoln Center, New York, New York, $50,000 - general operating support for the arts.
Contact: Anne Colucci, (212) 610-9006 or (212) 610-9054
Sponsor: Daniel and Nanna Stern Family Foundation
650 Madison Avenue, 26th Floor
New York, NY 10022-1029

Daniels Fund Amateur Sports Grants 779

Bill Daniels was a visionary business leader whose compassion for people, and unwavering ethics and integrity earned him respect throughout his life. He grew up during the Great Depression, served his nation as a decorated fighter pilot, and became a driving force in establishing the cable television industry. Bill's passion for helping others inspired him to create the Daniels Fund to extend his legacy of generosity far beyond his lifetime. The Daniels Fund provides grants to nonprofit organizations in Colorado, New Mexico, Utah, and Wyoming that fit within its eight distinct funding areas. Specifically, the Amateur Sports fund sprouted out of Bill's love for sports and knowledge from personal experience that participation in sports and the influence of quality coaches could change the direction of a young person's life for the better. This particular funding mechanism has the goal to allow youth to experience the benefits of participating in sports programs and give elite amateur athletes the opportunity to participate in national and international competition. There are two strategies to accomplish this by providing: youth sports access; and competition. The Fund accepts grant applications any time during the year; there are no submission deadlines. Awards range as high as $500,000.

Requirements: The Daniels Fund makes grants for specific programs or projects, general operating support, or capital campaigns. The organization applying must be classified by the Internal Revenue Service as a 501(c)3 or have governmental equivalence. Eligible nonprofit organizations must provide programs or services in Colorado, New Mexico, Utah, or Wyoming (though unsolicited applications are not currently being accepted in New Mexico or Utah). Organizations with a nationwide impact and large institutions (such as a university or school district) should contact the office before applying. Before starting the online application process, the sponsor strongly encourages all eligible applicants to call first. The Daniels Fund is rarely the sole provider of funds for a project, and encourages applicants to develop a variety of individual, government, and private funding sources.
Restrictions: The fund generally will not support medical or scientific research; arts, cultural, and museum programs; environmental stewardship programs; historic preservation projects; candidates for political office; sponsorships, tables, or tickets for special events or fundraising events; endowments; fiscal sponsorships; or debt retirement.
Geographic Focus: Colorado, New Mexico, Utah, Wyoming
Amount of Grant: Up to 500,000 USD
Samples: Casper Boxing Club, Casper, Wyoming, $75,00- - General Operating Support (2018).
Contact: Kristin Todd, Executive Vice President; (303) 393-7220 or (877) 791-4726; fax (720) 941-4201; grantsinfo@danielsfund.org or ktodd@danielsfund.org
Internet: www.danielsfund.org/index.php/Grants/funding-areas/Sports
Sponsor: Daniels Fund
101 Monroe Street
Denver, CO 80206

Daniels Fund Drug and Alcohol Addiction Grants 780

Bill Daniels was a visionary business leader whose compassion for people, and unwavering ethics and integrity earned him respect throughout his life. He grew up during the Great Depression, served his nation as a decorated fighter pilot, and became a driving force in establishing the cable television industry. Bill's passion for helping others inspired him to create the Daniels Fund to extend his legacy of generosity far beyond his lifetime. The Daniels Fund provides grants to nonprofit organizations in Colorado, New Mexico, Utah, and Wyoming that fit within its eight distinct funding areas. Specifically, the Drug and Alcohol Addiction fund was a way Bill wanted to educate and provide hope to others, since he suffered from alcoholism and embraced sobriety after seeking treatment and talked openly about his ongoing recovery. This particular funding mechanism has the goal of helping adults and youth with drug and alcohol addiction challenges achieve and maintain stability. There are two strategies to accomplish this by providing: prevention; and treatment and recovery. The Fund accepts grant applications any time during the year; there are no submission deadlines. Awards range as high as $500,000.
Requirements: The Daniels Fund makes grants for specific programs or projects, general operating support, or capital campaigns. The organization applying must be classified by the Internal Revenue Service as a 501(c)3 or have governmental equivalence. Eligible nonprofit organizations must provide programs or services in Colorado, New Mexico, Utah, or Wyoming (though unsolicited applications are not currently being accepted in New Mexico or Utah). Organizations with a nationwide impact and large institutions (such as a university or school district) should contact the office before applying. Before starting the online application process, the sponsor strongly encourages all eligible applicants to call first. The Daniels Fund is rarely the sole provider of funds for a project, and encourages applicants to develop a variety of individual, government, and private funding sources.
Restrictions: The fund generally will not support medical or scientific research; arts, cultural, and museum programs; environmental stewardship programs; historic preservation projects; candidates for political office; sponsorships, tables, or tickets for special events or fundraising events; endowments; fiscal sponsorships; or debt retirement.
Geographic Focus: Colorado, New Mexico, Utah, Wyoming
Amount of Grant: 500,000 USD
Samples: Face It Together, Denver, Colorado, $345,000 - Start up and General Operating Support for Addiction Recovery (2018); A Way Out Inc., Aspen, Colorado, $75,000 - Addiction Recovery Engagement (2018); Mile High Council on Alcoholism and Drug Abuse, Aurora, Colorado, $67,500 - Substance Abuse Rehab (2018).
Contact: Kristin Todd, Grants Program and Operations, (303) 393-7220 or (877) 791-4726; fax (720) 941-4201; grantsinfo@danielsfund.org or ktodd@danielsfund.org
Internet: www.danielsfund.org/index.php/Grants/funding-areas/Addiction
Sponsor: Daniels Fund
101 Monroe Street
Denver, CO 80206

Daniels Fund Early Childhood Education Grants 781

Bill Daniels was a visionary business leader whose compassion for people, and unwavering ethics and integrity earned him respect throughout his life. He grew up during the Great Depression, served his nation as a decorated fighter pilot, and became a driving force in establishing the cable television industry. Bill's passion for helping others inspired him to create the Daniels Fund to extend his legacy of generosity far beyond his lifetime. The Daniels Fund provides grants to nonprofit organizations in Colorado, New Mexico, Utah, and Wyoming that fit within its eight distinct funding areas. Specifically, the Early Childhood Education fund was inspired after Bill saw the need for healthy, safe, and nurturing early childhood experiences in the home and beyond. He wanted to ensure early childhood education started children on a path to success. This particular funding mechanism has the goal to ensure Kindergarten readiness through an improved early childhood system. There are three strategies to accomplish this by providing: teacher/leadership quality; program quality; and parental engagement. The Fund accepts grant applications any time during the year; there are no submission deadlines. Awards range as high as $500,000.
Requirements: The Daniels Fund makes grants for specific programs or projects, general operating support, or capital campaigns. The organization applying must be classified

by the Internal Revenue Service as a 501(c)3 or have governmental equivalence. Eligible nonprofit organizations must provide programs or services in Colorado, New Mexico, Utah, or Wyoming (though unsolicited applications are not currently being accepted in New Mexico or Utah). Organizations with a nationwide impact and large institutions (such as a university or school district) should contact the office before applying. Before starting the online application process, the sponsor strongly encourages all eligible applicants to call first. The Daniels Fund is rarely the sole provider of funds for a project, and encourages applicants to develop a variety of individual, government, and private funding sources.
Restrictions: The fund generally will not support medical or scientific research; arts, cultural, and museum programs; environmental stewardship programs; historic preservation projects; candidates for political office; sponsorships, tables, or tickets for special events or fundraising events; endowments; fiscal sponsorships; or debt retirement.
Geographic Focus: Colorado, New Mexico, Utah, Wyoming
Amount of Grant: 500,000 USD
Samples: Bright by Three, Denver, Colorado, $125,000 - General Operating Support for evidence-based learning tools (2018); Colorado Statewide Parent Coalition, Westminster, Colorado, $125,000 - Provides Assisting School Outcomes (2018); Invest in Kids, Denver, Colorado, $125,000 - General Operating Support for early childhood interventions (2018).
Contact: Kristin Todd, Grants Program and Operations; (303) 393-7220 or (877) 791-4726; fax (720) 941-4201; grantsinfo@danielsfund.org or ktodd@danielsfund.org
Internet: www.danielsfund.org/index.php/Grants/funding-areas/ECE
Sponsor: Daniels Fund
101 Monroe Street
Denver, CO 80206

Daniels Fund Homeless and Disadvantaged Grants 782
Bill Daniels was a visionary business leader whose compassion for people, and unwavering ethics and integrity earned him respect throughout his life. He grew up during the Great Depression, served his nation as a decorated fighter pilot, and became a driving force in establishing the cable television industry. Bill's passion for helping others inspired him to create the Daniels Fund to extend his legacy of generosity far beyond his lifetime. The Daniels Fund provides grants to nonprofit organizations in Colorado, New Mexico, Utah, and Wyoming that fit within its eight distinct funding areas. Specifically, the Homeless and Disadvantaged fund is aligned with Bill's great compassion for people struggling to meet basic human needs which, in turn, fueled his desire to help them get back on their feet. In essence, he wanted to offer disadvantaged individuals and families a hand-up and spark their motivation to reenter the workforce. This particular funding mechanism has the goal to assist homeless individuals and families achieve and maintain self-sufficiency without the need for public assistance. There are two strategies to accomplish this by providing: transitional housing and supportive services; and emergency services for those in crisis. The Fund accepts grant applications any time during the year; there are no submission deadlines. Awards range as high as $500,000.
Requirements: The Daniels Fund makes grants for specific programs or projects, general operating support, or capital campaigns. The organization applying must be classified by the Internal Revenue Service as a 501(c)3 or have governmental equivalence. Eligible nonprofit organizations must provide programs or services in Colorado, New Mexico, Utah, or Wyoming (though unsolicited applications are not currently being accepted in New Mexico or Utah). Organizations with a nationwide impact and large institutions (such as a university or school district) should contact the office before applying. Before starting the online application process, the sponsor strongly encourages all eligible applicants to call first. The Daniels Fund is rarely the sole provider of funds for a project, and encourages applicants to develop a variety of individual, government, and private funding sources.
Restrictions: The fund generally will not support medical or scientific research; arts, cultural, and museum programs; environmental stewardship programs; historic preservation projects; candidates for political office; sponsorships, tables, or tickets for special events or fundraising events; endowments; fiscal sponsorships; or debt retirement.
Geographic Focus: Colorado, New Mexico, Utah, Wyoming
Amount of Grant: Up to 500,000 USD
Samples: Greeley Transitional House, Greeley, Colorado, $25,000 - support of the city's transitional housing program for homeless (2018); Honor Bell Foundation, Englewood, Colorado, $50,000 - support of the Senior Veteran's program (2018); Climb Wyoming, Cheyenne, Wyoming, $100,000 - general operating support (2018).
Contact: Kristin Todd, Grants Program and Operations; (303) 393-7220 or (877) 791-4726; fax (720) 941-4201; grantsinfo@danielsfund.org or ktodd@danielsfund.org
Internet: danielsfund.org/grants/funding-areas/homeless-disadvantaged
Sponsor: Daniels Fund
101 Monroe Street
Denver, CO 80206

Daniels Fund K-12 Education Reform Grants 783
Bill Daniels was a visionary business leader whose compassion for people, and unwavering ethics and integrity earned him respect throughout his life. He grew up during the Great Depression, served his nation as a decorated fighter pilot, and became a driving force in establishing the cable television industry. Bill's passion for helping others inspired him to create the Daniels Fund to extend his legacy of generosity far beyond his lifetime. The Daniels Fund provides grants to nonprofit organizations in Colorado, New Mexico, Utah, and Wyoming that fit within its eight distinct funding areas. Specifically, the Education Reform fund was inspired out of Bill's strong conviction that every student deserves a quality education that provides relevant real-world experiences. He believed free enterprise principles — like competition and choice — have the power to achieve systemic reform and foster excellent schools. This particular funding mechanism has the goal to elevate student achievement through an improved K-12 education system. There are three strategies to accomplish this by providing: reform/school choice; teacher/leadership quality; and

parental engagement. The Fund accepts grant applications any time during the year; there are no submission deadlines. Awards range as high as $500,000.
Requirements: The Daniels Fund makes grants for specific programs or projects, general operating support, or capital campaigns. The organization applying must be classified by the Internal Revenue Service as a 501(c)3 or have governmental equivalence. Eligible nonprofit organizations must provide programs or services in Colorado, New Mexico, Utah, or Wyoming (though unsolicited applications are not currently being accepted in New Mexico or Utah). Organizations with a nationwide impact and large institutions (such as a university or school district) should contact the office before applying. Before starting the online application process, the sponsor strongly encourages all eligible applicants to call first. The Daniels Fund is rarely the sole provider of funds for a project, and encourages applicants to develop a variety of individual, government, and private funding sources.
Restrictions: The fund generally will not support medical or scientific research; arts, cultural, and museum programs; environmental stewardship programs; historic preservation projects; candidates for political office; sponsorships, tables, or tickets for special events or fundraising events; endowments; fiscal sponsorships; or debt retirement.
Geographic Focus: Colorado, New Mexico, Utah, Wyoming
Amount of Grant: 500,000 USD
Samples: Alliance for Choice in Education, Denver, Colorado, $100,000 - Wyoming Scholarships (2018). Education Reform Now Inc., Denver, Colorado, $40,000 - pursuit of education policies that enable students to obtain a competitive education (2018).
Contact: Kristin Todd, Grants Program and Operations; (303) 393-7220 or (877) 791-4726; fax (720) 941-4201; grantsinfo@danielsfund.org or ktodd@danielsfund.org
Internet: www.danielsfund.org/index.php/Grants/funding-areas/K-12
Sponsor: Daniels Fund
101 Monroe Street
Denver, CO 80206

Daniels Fund Youth Development Grants 784
Bill Daniels was a visionary business leader whose compassion for people, and unwavering ethics and integrity earned him respect throughout his life. He grew up during the Great Depression, served his nation as a decorated fighter pilot, and became a driving force in establishing the cable television industry. Bill's passion for helping others inspired him to create the Daniels Fund to extend his legacy of generosity far beyond his lifetime. The Daniels Fund provides grants to nonprofit organizations in Colorado, New Mexico, Utah, and Wyoming that fit within its eight distinct funding areas. Specifically, the Youth Development fund was created out of Bill's support of character-building programs that help youth become confident, patriotic, and independent. He wanted kids to develop personal accountability and responsibility. He also wanted them to understand the value of money, the free enterprise system, and that success is earned through hard work. This particular funding mechanism has the goal to help youth develop character and gain the necessary life skills to become successful adults. There are three strategies to accomplish this by providing: career and technical education; civics education; and financial literacy and free enterprise. The Fund accepts grant applications any time during the year; there are no submission deadlines. Awards range as high as $500,000.
Requirements: The Daniels Fund makes grants for specific programs or projects, general operating support, or capital campaigns. The organization applying must be classified by the Internal Revenue Service as a 501(c)3 or have governmental equivalence. Eligible nonprofit organizations must provide programs or services in Colorado, New Mexico, Utah, or Wyoming (though unsolicited applications are not currently being accepted in New Mexico or Utah). Organizations with a nationwide impact and large institutions (such as a university or school district) should contact the office before applying. Before starting the online application process, the sponsor strongly encourages all eligible applicants to call first. The Daniels Fund is rarely the sole provider of funds for a project, and encourages applicants to develop a variety of individual, government, and private funding sources.
Restrictions: The fund generally will not support medical or scientific research; arts, cultural, and museum programs; environmental stewardship programs; historic preservation projects; candidates for political office; sponsorships, tables, or tickets for special events or fundraising events; endowments; fiscal sponsorships; or debt retirement.
Geographic Focus: Colorado, New Mexico, Utah, Wyoming
Amount of Grant: 500,000 USD
Samples: Center for American Values Inc., Pueblo, Colorado, $125,000 - Youth Educational Outreach: Civics, Ethics, and Character Development (2018); Year One Inc., DBA Mile High Youth Corps, Denver, Colorado, $50,000 - Construction and Healthcare Job Training Programs (2018).
Contact: Kristin Todd, Vice President, Grants Program and Operations; (303) 393-7220 or (877) 791-4726; fax (720) 941-4201; grantsinfo@danielsfund.org or ktodd@danielsfund.org
Internet: www.danielsfund.org/index.php/Grants/funding-areas/YouthDevelopment
Sponsor: Daniels Fund
101 Monroe Street
Denver, CO 80206

David Alan and Susan Berkman Rahm Foundation Grants 785
The David Alan and Susan Berkman Rahm Foundation was established by a pair of prominent attorneys in New York, New York, in 1997. Today, the Foundation concentrates its efforts in the support of: art and culture; children and youth programs; general operating support; higher education; and religion. Typically, funding is given for general operating support, program development, research, and research evaluation. The geographic focus is New York City, and most recent awards have ranged up to nearly $12,000. There are no specified application deadlines, and interested organizations should forward an email letter outlining a detailed description of project or organization, and the amount of funding requested.
Geographic Focus: New York
Amount of Grant: Up to 12,000 USD

Contact: Susan B. Rahm, President; (212) 348-9551 or (212) 831-4442
Sponsor: David Alan and Susan Berkman Rahm Foundation
1125 Park Avenue
New York, NY 10128-1243

David and Barbara B. Hirschhorn Foundation Education and Literacy Grants   786
The David and Barbara B. Hirschhorn Foundation makes grants to improve the lives of families and children and cultivate a level playing field through expanding educational opportunity and addressing human needs. Established in 1986, the Foundation funds primarily in the Baltimore metropolitan area, and supports Jewish and secular initiatives in its four program areas: education and literacy; summer camping; human services; and intergroup understanding. In the area of Education and Literacy, the goal is to equip children and adults with the academic and literacy skills necessary to be productive and contributing members of society. Of particular interest are adult and family literacy programs, and outreach programs that introduce children and families to the joy of reading. There are no specified annual deadlines, so the Foundation accepts applications on a rolling basis. Grants generally range in size from $5,000 to $25,000, though most recent awards have ranged from $10,000 to $500,000.
Requirements: 501(c)3 non-profit organizations are eligible to apply. To begin the application process submit a letter of inquiry to the Foundation, no longer then 3 pages long. The initial application should include the following: information about the programs(s) for which funding is requested; need, purpose, activities, and evaluation plan of the proposed program(s); program budget (including sources of anticipated income as well as expenditure) and timeline; dollar amount of funding requested. Information about your organization: history, mission, and key accomplishments; information on Board members and key staff; current institutional operating budget (including major sources of revenue as well as expenditures); copy of IRS tax status determination letter or information about your fiscal agent.
Restrictions: The Foundation generally does not provide support for individual public, parochial or independent schools. No support available for: scholarships to individuals; unsolicited proposals for academic, scientific, or medical research; direct mail, annual giving, membership campaigns, fundraising and commemorative events.
Geographic Focus: Maryland
Amount of Grant: 10,000 - 500,000 USD
Samples: Beth Tfiloh Congregation, Baltimore, Maryland, $500,000 - a five-year award for an endowment, proceeds from which will provide scholarships for students at Beth Tfiloh Dahan Community School; CHARM: Voices of Baltimore Youth, Baltimore, Maryland, $20,000 - support for the Writers in School program; Turning Pages, Baltimore, Maryland, $10,000 - support for a program to encourage incarcerated fathers to read with their children.
Contact: Lara A. Hall, Senior Program Officer; (410) 347-7104 or (410) 347-7201; fax (410) 347-7210; info@blaufund.org
Internet: www.blaufund.org/foundations/davidandbarbara_f.html#one
Sponsor: David and Barbara B. Hirschhorn Foundation
One South Street, Suite 2900
Baltimore, MD 21202

David and Barbara B. Hirschhorn Foundation Summer Camping Grants   787
The David and Barbara B. Hirschhorn Foundation makes grants to improve the lives of families and children and cultivate a level playing field through expanding educational opportunity and addressing human needs. Established in 1986, the Foundation funds primarily in the Baltimore metropolitan area, and supports Jewish and secular initiatives in its four program areas: education and literacy; summer camping; human services; and intergroup understanding. In the area of Summer Camping, the goal is to help disadvantaged children gain access to exceptional summer camp and summer learning experiences. Priority is given to programs with strong track records that take advantage of the summer as a time for fun, learning and enrichment. There are no specified annual deadlines, so the Foundation accepts applications on a rolling basis. Grants generally range in size from $5,000 to $25,000, though most recent awards have ranged up to $100,000.
Requirements: 501(c)3 non-profit organizations are eligible to apply. To begin the application process submit a letter of inquiry to the Foundation, no longer then 3 pages long. The initial application should include the following: information about the programs(s) for which funding is requested; need, purpose, activities, and evaluation plan of the proposed program(s); program budget (including sources of anticipated income as well as expenditure) and timeline; dollar amount of funding requested. Information about your organization: history, mission, and key accomplishments; information on Board members and key staff; current institutional operating budget (including major sources of revenue as well as expenditures); copy of IRS tax status determination letter or information about your fiscal agent.
Restrictions: No support available for: scholarships to individuals; unsolicited proposals for academic, scientific, or medical research; direct mail, annual giving, membership campaigns, fundraising and commemorative events.
Geographic Focus: Maryland
Amount of Grant: 5,000 - 100,000 USD
Samples: Digital Harbor Foundation, Baltimore, Maryland, $15,000 - support for the STEM Summer Maker Camp; Dyslexia Tutoring Program, Baltimore, Maryland, $30,000 - general operating support for the summer camp program; Parks and People Foundation for Baltimore Recreation and Parks, Baltimore, Maryland, $40,000 - a support for Super Kids Camp 2018 and 2019.
Contact: Lara A. Hall, Senior Program Officer; (410) 347-7204 or (410) 347-7201; fax (410) 347-7210; info@blaufund.org
Internet: www.blaufund.org/foundations/davidandbarbara_f.html#two
Sponsor: David and Barbara B. Hirschhorn Foundation
One South Street, Suite 2900
Baltimore, MD 21202

David and Betty Sacks Foundation Grants   788
David Sacks was a physician and a true renaissance man. He was an accomplished musician, sculptor and active amateur athlete. He passed away in 1998. After grants are made to specific named benefactors, additional distributions will be made exclusively to 501(c)3 charities for the performing arts, the fine arts and educational purposes, with the balance to be distributed for general charitable purposes including religious, scientific, literary or educational purposes or for the prevention of cruelty to children or animals. In addition, grants may be awarded to support sport competitions. Grants typically range between $3,000 and $10,000.
Requirements: Only amateur sports organizations as defined in section 501(j) of the Internal Revenue Code may request support for equipment or facilities. Eligibility to re-apply for a grant award from the David and Betty Sacks Foundation requires organizations to skip 1 grant cycle (1 year) before submitting a subsequent application. Applications will be submitted online through the Bank of America website. A grant report is required within 1 year of the grant application date, regardless of whether all of the funds have been spent.
Restrictions: The trust does not support requests from individuals, organizations attempting to influence policy through direct lobbying, or any political campaigns.
Geographic Focus: Texas
Date(s) Application is Due: Feb 1
Amount of Grant: 3,000 - 10,000 USD
Samples: Youth Orchestras of San Antonio, San Antonio, Texas, $5,145 - Awarded for General Operation of the Organization (2018); Boys and Girls Clubs of San Antonio, San Antonio, Texas, $5,145 - Awarded for program and vehicle expenses only (2018); Children's Chorus of San Antonio, San Antonio, Texas, $1,470 - Awarded for Neighborhood Choirs at Boys and Girls Club of San Antonio (2018).
Contact: Debra Goldstein Phares, Philanthropic Client Director; (800) 357-7094; tx.philanthropic@bankofamerica.com or tx.philanthropic@ustrust.com
Internet: www.bankofamerica.com/philanthropic/foundation/?fnId=146
Sponsor: David and Betty Sacks Foundation
P.O. Box 831
Dallas, TX 75283-1041

David and Laura Merage Foundation Grants   789
The David and Laura Merage Foundation is a private foundation based in Englewood, Colorado, that was founded in 2003. The Foundation's philanthropic investments are focused on social change and result in children, families and communities improving the quality and circumstances of their lives. Primary areas of interest include Jewish organization, children and youth programs, the family, and community nonprofits. Typical awards range up to a maximum of $50,000. There are no specific application submission deadlines or formats, and interested parties should begin by contacting the Foundation with a Letter of Inquiry (LOI).
Requirements: Any 501(c)3 organization supporting programs aligned with the Foundation mission is eligible.
Geographic Focus: All States
Amount of Grant: Up to 50,000 USD
Samples: Clyfford Still Museum, Denver, Colorado, $1,000 - general operating support (2018); Denver Jewish Day School, Denver, Colorado, $5,000 - general operating support (2018); Maui Preparatory Academy, Lahaina, Hawaii, $1,500 - general operating support (2018).
Contact: Sue Renner, Executive Director; (303) 789-2664; fax (303) 789-2696
Internet: www.merage.org/about-us/david-laura-merage-foundation/
Sponsor: David and Laura Merage Foundation
18 Inverness Place East
Englewood, CO 80112

David M. and Marjorie D. Rosenberg Foundation Grants   790
The David M. and Marjorie D. Rosenberg Foundation was established in Pennsylvania in 1993. David Rosenberg attended Penn State at University Park and graduated with a bachelor of science degree in health and human development. He also attended the Howard University School of Law and received his juris doctor degree. In 2012, he and his wife, Marjorie Rosenberg, made the Penn State Brandywine Laboratory for Civic and Community Engagement possible by making a generous donation. The lab encourages leadership among students and develops scholarship in the community while promoting citizenship on a local-to-global level. The Rosenbergs also founded the David and Marjorie Rosenberg Trustee Scholarship and the Rosenberg Family Trustee Scholarship for students enrolled at Penn State Brandywine. The Rosenberg Foundation is a civic and social organization assisting a wide variety of non-profits with the primary focus in the areas of character development and children and youth. Giving is primarily in Pennsylvania, with some awards going to California. The Foundation's primary fields of interest include: child welfare; diseases; elementary and secondary education; higher education; hospital care; human services; Judaism; and community nonprofits. There are no identified annual deadlines, and most recent awards have ranged from $50 to $90,000.
Requirements: 501(c)3 organizations serving residents of Pennsylvania, District of Columbia, and California are eligible to apply.
Geographic Focus: California, District of Columbia, Pennsylvania
Amount of Grant: 250 - 90,000 USD
Samples: American Red Cross, Philadelphia, Pennsylvania, $500 - general operating support; Children's Hospital Foundation, Philadelphia, Pennsylvania, $84,334 - general operating support; Special Olympics, Morristown, Pennsylvania, $26,000 - general operating support.
Contact: Marjorie D. Rosenberg, Trustee; (610) 458-4175
Sponsor: David M. and Marjorie D. Rosenberg Foundation
893 Parkes Run Lane
Villanova, PA 19085-1124

David Robinson Foundation Grants   791

Founded in 1992 by David Robinson, a former National Basketball Association center who played his entire career for the San Antonio Spurs, the David Robinson Foundation awards grants to Texas nonprofit organizations in its areas of interest. Those areas include: alumni relations; diseases; agriculture; education; higher education; family services; single parents; social services; and spirituality. The majority of grants are awarded in the San Antonio area. Interested parties should begin by contacting the Foundation with an explanation of their program.

Requirements: Texas nonprofit organizations are eligible. Contributes only to pre-selected organizations.
Geographic Focus: Texas
Amount of Grant: Up to 50,000 USD
Samples: Silver Spurs Alumni Association, Austin, Texas, $500 - general operating support; Bridge Avenue Church of Christ, Welsaco, Texas, $1,500 - general operating support.
Contact: David Robinson; (210) 473-9542 or (210) 561-2668; drfoundation@express-news.net
Sponsor: David Robinson Foundation
1150 N. Loop 1604 West, Suite 108, Box 505
San Antonio, TX 78248

Daviess County Community Foundation Advancing Out-of-School Learning Grants   792

The Daviess County Community Foundation, in partnership with Regional Opportunity Initiatives, is making $25,000 available for out-of-school learning programs aligning with the following After School STEM Standards: the program creates an inspiring STEM learning environment for all youth; STEM resources, equipment, and supplies support STEM learning; the STEM program engages families, schools, and community; staff receive professional development that increase their confidence and ability to facilitate STEM learning; activities inspire and engage youth in STEM learning; the program provides opportunities for youth to learn STEM content, skills, and knowledge; and the program utilizes a variety of data to measure the impact of its STEM program. The annual deadline for application submissions is December 5. Funding requests will be accepted from June 12 through the August 1 deadline.

Requirements: The letter of inquiry is the required first step in submitting funding requests. Nonprofits that have submitted a letter of inquiry and been invited to submit a full proposal must attend one of the orientation sessions. The Foundation welcomes proposals from nonprofit organizations that are deemed tax-exempt under sections 501(c)3 and 509(a) of the Internal Revenue Code and from governmental agencies serving the County of Daviess, Indiana. Proposals from nonprofit organizations not classified as a 501(c)3 public charity may be considered provided the project is charitable and supports a community need.
Restrictions: Funding is not available for the following: religious organizations for strictly religious purposes; political parties or campaigns; endowment creation or debt reduction; operating costs (not directly related to the proposed project or program); capital campaigns; annual appeals or membership contributions; travel requests for groups or individuals such as bands, sports teams, or classes. Not more than 20% of any grant request may be for personnel costs, office supplies, or other operating costs. Operating costs for any organization must be directly related to the project or program for which funding is being requested.
Geographic Focus: Indiana
Date(s) Application is Due: Dec 5
Contact: Mary E. Smith, Regional Director; (812) 254-9354; fax (812) 254-9355; mary@daviesscommunityfoundation.org
Internet: www.communityfoundationalliance.org/grant/advancing-school-learning-grant-opportunity/
Sponsor: Daviess County Community Foundation
320 East Main Street, P.O. Box 302
Washington, IN 47501

Daviess County Community Foundation Recreation Grants   793

The Daviess County Community Foundation considers proposals for grants on a yearly cycle, which begins each May. At the start of each cycle, a notice is mailed to nonprofit organizations that have applied for grants in the past, have received grants in the past, or have otherwise requested notification of the start of each cycle. Grants in the area of Recreation includes projects aimed at improving and promoting recreational and leisure activities, parks, and community sporting events and activities. Samples of previously funded projects are available at the website.

Requirements: The letter of inquiry is the required first step in submitting funding requests. Nonprofits that have submitted a letter of inquiry and been invited to submit a full proposal must attend one of the orientation sessions. The Foundation welcomes proposals from nonprofit organizations that are deemed tax-exempt under sections 501(c)3 and 509(a) of the Internal Revenue Code and from governmental agencies serving the County of Daviess, Indiana. Proposals from nonprofit organizations not classified as a 501(c)3 public charity may be considered provided the project is charitable and supports a community need.
Restrictions: Funding is not available for the following: religious organizations for strictly religious purposes; political parties or campaigns; endowment creation or debt reduction; operating costs (not directly related to the proposed project or program); capital campaigns; annual appeals or membership contributions; travel requests for groups or individuals such as bands, sports teams, or classes. Not more than 20% of any grant request may be for personnel costs, office supplies, or other operating costs. Operating costs for any organization must be directly related to the project or program for which funding is being requested.
Geographic Focus: Indiana
Contact: Mary E. Smith, Regional Director; (812) 254-9354; fax (812) 254-9355; mary@daviesscommunityfoundation.org
Internet: www.daviesscommunityfoundation.org/program-areas
Sponsor: Daviess County Community Foundation
320 East Main Street, P.O. Box 302
Washington, IN 47501

Daviess County Community Foundation Youth Development Grants   794

The Daviess County Community Foundation considers proposals for grants on a yearly cycle, which begins each May. At the start of each cycle, a notice is mailed to nonprofit organizations that have applied for grants in the past, have received grants in the past, or have otherwise requested notification of the start of each cycle. Grants in the area of Youth Development include activities that strengthen the family unit, help children grow and develop, foster youth sports and athletics, support the YMCA, and support daycare-related issues. Samples of previously funded projects are available at the website.

Requirements: The letter of inquiry is the required first step in submitting funding requests. Nonprofits that have submitted a letter of inquiry and been invited to submit a full proposal must attend one of the orientation sessions. The Foundation welcomes proposals from nonprofit organizations that are deemed tax-exempt under sections 501(c)3 and 509(a) of the Internal Revenue Code and from governmental agencies serving the County of Daviess, Indiana. Proposals from nonprofit organizations not classified as a 501(c)3 public charity may be considered provided the project is charitable and supports a community need.
Restrictions: Funding is not available for the following: religious organizations for strictly religious purposes; political parties or campaigns; endowment creation or debt reduction; operating costs (not directly related to the proposed project or program); capital campaigns; annual appeals or membership contributions; travel requests for groups or individuals such as bands, sports teams, or classes. Not more than 20% of any grant request may be for personnel costs, office supplies, or other operating costs. Operating costs for any organization must be directly related to the project or program for which funding is being requested.
Geographic Focus: Indiana
Contact: Mary E. Smith, Regional Director; (812) 254-9354; fax (812) 254-9355; mary@daviesscommunityfoundation.org
Internet: www.daviesscommunityfoundation.org/program-areas
Sponsor: Daviess County Community Foundation
320 East Main Street, P.O. Box 302
Washington, IN 47501

Dayton Foundation Dayton Youth Enrichment Fund Grant   795

The Dayton Youth Enrichment Fund was established to help broaden perspectives, peak curiosity and inspire a love of learning and exploration by providing support for nonprofit organizations to help youth participate in outside summer enhancement programs or camps. Camps can be in any geographic area and should give students the chance to grow in leadership, music, arts, STEM and a variety of academic and technology skills.

Requirements: Camps should be accredited by the American Camping Association (ACA) or by a comparable accrediting agency. Before submitting an application, nonprofit organizations should identify students in their programs and match them with camps that best fit their needs.
Restrictions: This grant is not designed to fund any summer camps that your organization may offer.
Geographic Focus: Ohio
Amount of Grant: Up to 3,300 USD
Contact: Tania Arseculeratne, Community Engagement Officer; (937) 225-9966; fax (937) 222-0636; tarseculeratne@daytonfoundation.org
Internet: www.daytonfoundation.org/grntfdns.html#dayton
Sponsor: Dayton Foundation
1401 S. Main Street, Suite 100
Dayton, OH 45409

Dayton Foundation Grants   796

The Dayton Foundation awards grants to a full spectrum of 501(c)3 tax-exempt nonprofit organizations - from social service to the arts to health and the environment - based upon worthy community efforts and the greatest community need. Generally grants are awarded to help launch new projects not addressed by existing organizations or to support special efforts of already-established not-for-profit organizations in the Miami Valley. The Foundation gives priority to projects that meet one or more of the following criteria: provides for more efficient use of community resources; promotes coordination, cooperation and sharing among organizations and reduces the duplication of services in the community; tests or demonstrates new approaches and techniques for solving important community problems; promotes volunteer participation and citizen involvement in community affairs; and strengthens not-for-profit agencies and institutions by reducing operating costs, increasing public financial support and/or improving internal management. Letters of Intent are to be submitted through the LOI online system.

Requirements: Programs considered for discretionary support are located primarily in Montgomery, Miami, Greene, Darke and Preble counties. Eligible organizations must be: recognized as a 501(c)3 tax-exempt nonprofit organization, according to the Internal Revenue Code; benefit the citizens in the Dayton/Greater Miami Valley region; have a diversity/inclusion policy; and, address needs that are not met fully by existing organizational or community resources.
Restrictions: Generally, discretionary grants are not awarded for: general organizational operations; individuals; scientific, medical or academic research; operational deficits; religious/sectarian causes; scholarships or travel; fundraising drives; special events; political activities; public or private schools, endowment funds. Also, multi-year commitments rarely are considered.
Geographic Focus: Ohio
Date(s) Application is Due: Apr 1; Oct 2
Contact: Michelle Brown, Program Officer; (937) 225-9965 or (937) 222-0410; fax (937) 222-0636; mbrown@daytonfoundation.org or info@daytonfoundation.org
Internet: www.daytonfoundation.org/how2app.html
Sponsor: Dayton Foundation
1401 S. Main Street, Suite 100
Dayton, OH 45409

Dayton Foundation Huber Heights Grants 797

Projects and activities supported by the Huber Heights Foundation must benefit residents of the greater Huber Heights area. The Huber Heights Foundation has one grant cycle per year. Interested applicants should contact the office for further details.

Requirements: Applicants must be recognized as tax-exempt organizations under Section 501(c)3 of the Internal Revenue Code. The Huber Heights Foundation, a fund of The Dayton Foundation, generally makes grants to support start up or new projects in the areas of the arts and humanities, education and youth, conservation and the environment, health and social services and citizenship. These projects or programs are ones that are not currently being addressed by existing organizations, or they are special efforts by existing organizations to undertake unique activities or projects.

Geographic Focus: Ohio

Contact: Lucy Baker; (937) 225-9960 or (937) 222-0410; lbaker@daytonfoundation.org

Internet: www.daytonfoundation.org/grntfdns.html#huber

Sponsor: Dayton Foundation

1401 S. Main Street, Suite 100

Dayton, OH 45409

Dayton Foundation Rike Family Scholarships 798

The Dayton Foundation provides unmatched services, resources, support and counsel to help individuals achieve their charitable giving goals; we assist other nonprofits by funding important initiatives and offering our expertise to help them operate more effectively; and build a better community by identifying important issues and bringing together the people and organizations who can solve them. The Rike family established this scholarship fund at The Dayton Foundation in 1987 to make awards to one or more private K-8 schools in the Greater Dayton Region. Awards are made on a biennial basis and cover a period of two school years. The size of awards varies from $1,500 to $1,900 annually.

Requirements: Applicants must be a private school, accredited by the State of Ohio and offer a general course of studies within Montgomery or Greene counties.

Geographic Focus: Ohio

Amount of Grant: 1,500 - 1,900 USD

Contact: Marie Arias; (937) 225-9964 or (937) 222-0410; marias@daytonfoundation.org

Internet: www.daytonfoundation.org/grntfdns.html#rike

Sponsor: Dayton Foundation

1401 S. Main Street, Suite 100

Dayton, OH 45409

Dayton Foundation Vandalia-Butler Grants 799

The Dayton Foundation provides unmatched services, resources, support and counsel to help individuals achieve their charitable giving goals; we assist other nonprofits by funding important initiatives and offering our expertise to help them operate more effectively; and build a better community by identifying important issues and bringing together the people and organizations who can solve them. The Vandalia-Butler Grants support charitable endeavors benefiting the citizens of Vandalia and Butler Township. The Foundation's Board of Trustees awards grants to qualified local non-profit organizations.

Requirements: Nonprofit organizations that benefit citizens in the Vandalia-Butler community may apply to the Vandalia-Butler Foundation. The Vandalia-Butler Foundation is a fund of The Dayton Foundation. To be eligible for a grant, an organization must be recognized as tax-exempt under Section 501(c)3 of the Internal Revenue Code, be nondiscriminatory and address needs that are not met fully by existing organizational or community resources.

Geographic Focus: Ohio

Contact: Jean Maychack, President; (937) 898-4460 or (937) 222-0410; info@vandalia-butlerfoundation.org or jean@van-con.com

Internet: www.daytonfoundation.org/grntfdns.html#vandalia

Sponsor: Dayton Foundation

1401 S. Main Street, Suite 100

Dayton, OH 45409

Dayton Foundation VISIONS Endowment Fund Grants 800

VISIONS Grant Committee is chaired by a member of the Vandalia-Butler Foundation Education Fund Advisory Committee. The additional committee members are representatives from the school district and the community at large. Grants are categorized as: district-wide initiatives; grade-level curriculum-based experiences; or individual teachers' classroom programs.

Requirements: The VISIONS Endowment Fund accepts grant requests from any teacher or staff member in the Vandalia-Butler City School System for a project or program for the students in a particular school or classroom. No request is "too large" or "too small." Grant applications may be received at any time during the year.

Geographic Focus: Ohio

Contact: Jean Maychack, President; (937) 222-0410; info@visionsendowmentfund.org or jean@van-con.com

Internet: www.daytonfoundation.org/grntfdns.html#visions

Sponsor: Dayton Foundation

1401 S. Main Street, Suite 100

Dayton, OH 45409

Dayton Power and Light Company Foundation Signature Grants 801

The Dayton Power and Light Company Foundation introduced its Signature Grant program in 2013 to provide nonprofit organizations the opportunity to request funding for larger projects, including but not limited to capital projects. Signature Grants are aimed at special projects (such as a new or innovative program) and long-time partners in the Dayton community efforts. The Foundation commitment for a Signature Grant is for a one-year period. Requests for multi-year grants will be reviewed annually. There will be at least two Signature Grants given each year, one at the $100,000+ level and one at the $50,000+ level.

Requirements: 501(c)3 organizations in the greater Dayton, Ohio, area are eligible.

Geographic Focus: Ohio

Amount of Grant: 50,000 - 200,000 USD

Samples: Culture Works, Dayton, Ohio, $100,000 - to provide matching funds for Power2Give, an online crowd funding initiative empowering individual donors to give directly to a variety of local arts, science and history projects; Dayton Children's Hospital, Dayton, Ohio, $50,000 - to provide car seats and bike helmets to the community and mobile sanitation stations for the safety of hospital staffers and patients; K-12 Gallery for Young People, Dayton, Ohio, $120,000 - to fund new building renovations and to support youth educational programs.

Contact: Ginny Strausburg; (937) 259-7925; fax (937) 259-7923; ginny.strausburg@dplinc.com

Internet: www.dpandl.com/about-dpl/who-we-are/community-investments/#DPLFoundation

Sponsor: Dayton Power and Light Company Foundation

1065 Woodman Drive, P.O. Box 1247

Dayton, OH 45432

Dayton Power and Light Foundation Grants 802

The Dayton Power and Light Foundation was established in 1985 reinvest in the communities it serves and contribute to the improvement of the overall quality of life. The Foundation focuses its contributions in the following strategic contribution areas: economic development - creating an engaged, vibrant, welcoming community that is seen as a great place to live and work; arts and culture - heightening the impact of arts and local culture in our communities; health and human services - to improve the quality of life for all; and education: - improving educational access and outcomes. Direct donations are also made to civic, cultural, and health and welfare organizations that do not participate in community funds, such as United Way or community chests, but serve a real need. Requests should be made via the online application format, and should include a description of the history, structure, purpose, and program of the organization and a summary of the support needed and how it will be used. The annual deadline is October 1

Requirements: 501(c)3 organizations in the greater Dayton, Ohio, area are eligible. This includes a twenty-four county service area surrounding the city (see map at the website for specific details).

Restrictions: The foundation prefers not to support: capital campaigns; college fund-raising associations; conduit organizations; endowment or development funds; fraternal, labor, or veterans organizations; hospital operating budgets; individual members of federated campaigns; individuals; national organizations outside the DP&L service territory; religious organizations; sports leagues; or telephone or mass-mail solicitations. Grants are rarely made to tax-supported institutions.

Geographic Focus: Ohio

Date(s) Application is Due: Oct 1

Amount of Grant: 1,000 - 20,000 USD

Contact: Ginny Strausburg; (937) 259-7925; fax (937) 259-7923; ginny.strausburg@dplinc.com

Internet: www.waytogo.com/cc/cc.phtml

Sponsor: Dayton Power and Light Company Foundation

1065 Woodman Drive, P.O. Box 1247

Dayton, OH 45432

Deaconess Community Foundation Grants 803

The foundation awards grants to eligible Ohio nonprofit organizations in its areas of interest, including health, education, welfare, community, and social service activities. Proposals that are of greatest interest to the Foundation are those that have the strongest fit to the mission statement and that have some or all of the following characteristics: projects that have specific measurable outcomes and a tangible ability to evaluate results and measure success; projects that are supported by other funding sources; and projects that have identified potential for ongoing support beyond the life of the grant. Application information is available online.

Requirements: Only qualified non-profit organizations located in Cuyahoga County which are classified by the Internal Revenue Code as tax-exempt 501(c)3 organizations are eligible for funding consideration.

Restrictions: Grant requests for the following will not be considered: individuals, governmental agencies or any other organization that is not a tax exempt 501(c)3 organization; internal operations and capital campaigns of churches; research projects; or endowments. Grant funds may not be used to carry on propaganda or otherwise attempt to influence legislation, participate in, or intervene in, any political campaign on behalf of or in opposition to any candidate for public office, or to conduct, directly or indirectly, any voter registration drive (within the meaning of Section 4945(d)2 of the Internal Revenue Code).

Geographic Focus: Ohio

Date(s) Application is Due: Jan 15; May 15; Sep 15

Samples: Achievement Centers for Children, Highland Hills, Ohio, $20,000 - program support for Family Support Services for children with disabilities and their families; The Center For Nonprofit Excellence, Cleveland, Ohio, $75,000 - program support for Building Nonprofit Excellence in 2013 which includes Needs Assessments and BVU's Consulting Center for nonprofits with missions that are aligned with D.C.F.

Contact: Deborah Vesy, President; (216) 741-4077; fax (216) 741-6042; dvesy@deacomfdn.org

Internet: www.deacomfdn.org/guidelines.html

Sponsor: Deaconess Community Foundation

7575 Northcliff Avenue, Suite 203

Brooklyn, OH 44144

Deaconess Foundation Advocacy Grants   804

The Deaconess Foundation's community capacity building initiative will include a series of investments designed to make the well-being of low-income children a civic priority. In its initial year, the Foundation will allocate nearly $400,000 to build the region's capacity for aligned work. The advocacy grants are part of Deaconess' evolving community capacity building strategy, which builds on the Foundation's work in recent years to assist individual child-focused organizations to become stronger and more effective agents of positive change for children. Deaconess Foundation intends to award approximately 10 organizations with grants of up to $15,000. This first round of advocacy grants is meant to spark much-needed advocacy on behalf of children, and to help the Foundation learn more about agencies pursuing this important work.

Requirements: Organizations that are eligible to apply for Deaconess Foundation's advocacy grants include: nonprofits whose primary mission is related to health/well-being of children and youth; nonprofits whose primary mission is related to impacting policy through advocacy, community organizing and/or convening; and networks with a designated nonprofit fiscal agent. Organizations from outside the St. Louis metropolitan area may propose a project; however, projects must have primary impact within Deaconess Foundation's giving area: St. Louis City and St. Louis County in Missouri, and St. Clair and Madison Counties in Illinois.

Geographic Focus: Illinois, Missouri
Date(s) Application is Due: Jun 3
Amount of Grant: Up to 15,000 USD
Contact: Rev. Starsky D. Wilson, President; (314) 436-8001; fax (314) 436-5352; starskyw@deaconess.org or info@deaconess.org
Internet: www.deaconess.org/CongregationalHealthGrants_17.aspx
Sponsor: Deaconess Foundation
211 N Broadway, Suite 1260
Saint Louis, MO 63102

Dean Foods Community Involvement Grants   805

Dean Foods community support efforts are focused in three main areas: health/nutrition (including hunger); education/arts; and environmental stewardship and conservation. It supports worthy organizations both at the corporate level and locally through its network of processing facilities nationwide. Preference is given to supporting and participating in a meaningful way with a limited number of organizations that support these three focus areas, rather than spreading limited resources more broadly. Specifically, funding goes to programs that provide direct service to individuals and communities in need. The corporation places special emphasis on supporting organizations that assist children, particularly at-risk children or children with disabilities, or that are dedicated to serving their needs. As a point of contact, the corporate headquarters requests that no phone calls be made regarding its giving programs.

Requirements: 501(3)3 tax-exempt organizations are eligible. Applications must provide background information on the organization as well as how it relates to the mission of Dean Foods. The corporation supports initiatives only in the communities in which they operate and where employees live and work.

Geographic Focus: All States
Samples: North Texas Food Bank, Dallas, Texas, $50,000 - supporting childhood hunger and nutrition programs (2018); National FFA Foundation, Indianapolis, Indiana, $22,700 - supporting the national scholarship program (2018); Food Armor, Madison, Wisconsin, $10,000 - supporting dairy stewardship (2018).
Contact: Stuart R. Hueber; (214) 303-3400 or (214) 303-3442; fax (214) 303-3499
Internet: www.deanfoods.com/our-company/about-us/corporate-responsibility.aspx
Sponsor: Dean Foods Foundation
2515 McKinney Avenue, Suite 1200
Dallas, TX 75201

Dean Foundation Grants   806

Established in 1961, the Dean Foundation of Colorado Springs, Colorado, supports a number of community nonprofits and educational programs. Primary areas of interest include: K-12 education; higher education; national history; environmental and conservation organizations; literacy; animal welfare; and children and youth programs. Typical awards range as high as $25,000. There are no specific annual deadlines or application formats. Interested parties should forward a letter of interest outlining the need, budget, and proof of nonprofit status.

Requirements: Any 501(c)3 supporting residents in Arizona, Colorado, Delaware, New Jersey, New York, North Carolina, Ohio, or Washington are eligible to apply.
Geographic Focus: Arizona, Colorado, Delaware, New Jersey, New York, North Carolina, Ohio, Washington
Amount of Grant: Up to 25,000 GBP
Samples: Seattle Waldorf School, Seattle, Washington, $25,000 - general operating support (2018); Rock Mountain Women's Film Festival, Colorado Springs, Colorado, $16,000 - general operating support (2018); Delaware Historical Society, Wilmington, Delaware, $6,000 - general operating support (2018).
Contact: Leatrice D. Elliman, President; (302) 655-4838 or 719) 630-1186
Sponsor: Dean Foundation
102 North Cascade Avenue, Suite 400
Colorado Springs, CO 80903

Dean Witter Foundation Education Grants   807

The Dean Witter Foundation makes grants to launch and expand innovative conservation and K-12 education programs. The mission of the Dean Witter Foundation K-12 education grant-making program is to help all students develop their full potential and to invest in innovative initiatives to enhance and improve student learning. The Foundation funds promising academic projects that are replicable across educational institutions; cultivate meaningful advances in the delivery of curriculum; inspire educational leaders to improve schools; and are evidence-based. Specific areas of current interest include: leadership; effective education; literacy; science, technology, engineering, arts, and math (STEAM); and graduation rate improvement.

Requirements: The Foundation accepts grant proposals from tax-exempt charitable institutions as defined under Section 501(c)3 of the Internal Revenue Code on a continuing basis. The Foundation does not have a standard application form. Applicants should send one complete proposal to the Consultant with the following elements: cover letter; specific request; personnel information; organizational information; financial information; and addenda.

Restrictions: The Foundation does not: accept funding requests from individuals or award loans, scholarships and grants to specific individuals; assume any obligation to provide continuing support to grantee programs; make grants for annual fundraising events, operating deficits, and capital campaigns; or support sectarian religious activities or sectarian religious facilities.

Geographic Focus: California, Colorado, Washington
Samples: Bellevue Schools Foundation, Bellevue, Washington, $15,000 - to support mental health initiatives and programs (2020); Fifth Avenue Theatre, Seattle, Washington, $10,000 - to support digital arts education programs serving K-12 students in Washington state (2020); Friends of Casterlin Elementary School, Blocksburg, California, $20,000 - for technology, curriculum, classroom materials and enrichment opportunities for high school students and for the Third Teacher position (2020).
Contact: Kenneth J. Blum; (415) 981-2966; fax (415) 981-5218; admin@deanwitterfoundation.org
Internet: www.deanwitterfoundation.org/funding-guidelines.php
Sponsor: Dean Witter Foundation
P.O. Box 6106
San Rafael, CA 94903

Dearborn Community Foundation City of Aurora Grants   808

The City of Aurora Grant Program awards grants to not-for-profit organizations for projects that directly benefit the residents of the City of Aurora. Grants from organizations such as fire departments and emergency units may take priority over other grant requests. Entities that provide specific services for the City of Aurora are also eligible to apply. Examples of the types of services include: economic development, EMS, historic preservation, housing, technical assistance, transportation and youth services.

Requirements: Grants are awarded only to organizations whose programs benefit the residents of Dearborn County, Indiana and which provide for a responsible fiscal agent and adequate accounting procedures. All questions relating to available scholarship/educational grant opportunities should be directed to the D.C.F Program Director.

Restrictions: The grant review process for some grant programs takes up to three months from the grant application due date. Applicants should plan accordingly when considering the date of the project and the date of the grant submission. It is strongly suggested that all applicants consult the Foundation before submitting a grant application to ensure eligibility. Grants are not made to the following: individuals; endowment creation; travel expenses; sustain ongoing programs or projects; salaried/contracted positions; support political parties, campaigns, or issues; sectarian religious purposes; debt reduction of recipient organizations; programs, expenses and/or equipment committed to prior to the grant award date.

Geographic Focus: Indiana
Date(s) Application is Due: Mar 1
Contact: Denise Sedler; (812) 539-4115; fax (812) 539-4119; dsedler@dearborncf.org
Internet: www.dearborncf.org/grants/G_Aurora.aspx
Sponsor: Dearborn Community Foundation
322 Walnut Street
Lawrenceburg, IN 47025

Dearborn Community Foundation City of Lawrenceburg Community Grants   809

The City of Lawrenceburg has allocated grant funds specifically for not-for-profit organizations that provide a benefit, direct or indirect, to the Lawrenceburg community and Dearborn County. The Dearborn Community Foundation will administer this program. The program consists of two phases, Phase I: applications requesting $5,000 or less will be accepted and considered as long as funds are available. Phase II: applications requesting $5,001 - $100,000 will be accepted to the grant application deadlines. Applications will be considered as long as funds are available. The application and specific guidelines are available at the website.

Restrictions: Funding is not available for the following: individuals; endowment creation; travel expenses; sustain ongoing programs or projects; salaried/contracted positions; political parties, campaigns, or issues; sectarian religious purposes; debt reduction of recipient organizations and programs, expenses and/or equipment committed to prior to the grant award date.

Geographic Focus: Indiana
Date(s) Application is Due: Mar 6; Jun 5; Sep 11
Amount of Grant: 5,000 - 100,000 USD
Contact: Denise Sedler; (812) 539-4115; fax (812) 539-4119; dsedler@dearborncf.org
Internet: www.dearborncf.org/grants/G_Lawrence.aspx
Sponsor: Dearborn Community Foundation
322 Walnut Street
Lawrenceburg, IN 47025

Dearborn Community Foundation City of Lawrenceburg Youth Grants   810

The City of Lawrenceburg Youth Grants are made to not-for-profit organizations for programs that directly benefit youth from birth to the age of 18. Half of the total funding available is allocated to benefit youth programs where 75% of the youth reside in the Lawrenceburg School Corporation area, while the other half is allocated for programs that benefit 95% of the youth residing in Dearborn County. Applicants must provide the percentage of youth residing in Lawrenceburg and Dearborn County for their program participants. The application and additional guidelines are available at the website.

Requirements: Grants are awarded only to nonprofit organizations whose programs benefit Dearborn County residents. If they are not nonprofits, organizations must provide for a responsible fiscal agent and adequate accounting procedures. Submitted grant applications shall contain one original application and ten copies.

Restrictions: Any school corporation or school sponsored organization wishing to apply for City of Lawrenceburg Youth Grant funds must first apply for funding through the school's respective Endowment Corporation or Education Foundation. Documentation verifying the Endowment Corporation/Education Foundation's decision must accompany the completed City of Lawrenceburg Youth Grant Program application materials. Select programs/teams, those that allow participation of a few children when other organizations are available to offer the same recreational opportunities, are not eligible to apply. Funding is not provided to support political parties, campaigns, or issues; sectarian religious purposes that do not support the general public; debt reduction of recipient organizations; and programs, expenses and/or equipment committed to prior to the grant award date.
Geographic Focus: Indiana
Date(s) Application is Due: Mar 6; Jun 5; Sep 11
Amount of Grant: 10,000 USD
Contact: Denise Sedler; (812) 539-4115; fax (812) 539-4119; dsedler@dearborncf.org
Internet: www.dearborncf.org/grants/G_Youth.aspx
Sponsor: Dearborn Community Foundation
322 Walnut Street
Lawrenceburg, IN 47025

Decatur County Community Foundation Large Project Grants 811
The Decatur County Community Foundation (DCCF) encourages, manages, and distributes charitable contributions to improve the quality of life of Decatur County, Indiana residents, now and in the future. The Foundation places high priority to funding projects which are: new and innovative projects or programs, including start-ups; projects which Foundation funds can be used as match, seed money or challenge grant funding from other donors; projects which will make a significant impact in the community; projects which act as a catalyst for action and community participation. The Large Project Community Grants are reviewed twice a year.
Requirements: Each applicant is required to submit a letter of intent to see if the project complies with general guidelines. No application will be sent without a letter of intent. Form letters will neither be reviewed nor acknowledged. Upon acceptance, the applicant will receive a grant application packet. The grant committee will review the completed packet. A member of that committee may contact the applicant or request a site visit. The committee's recommendations are forwarded to the Foundation's Board of Directors, who will make final funding decisions. The Board may choose to fund the grant as written, fund part of the grant or provide no funding at all. All applicants are notified in writing regarding funding decisions.
Restrictions: The Foundation will not fund: individual and team travel expenses; multi-year or long term funding; the creation of an endowment; programs that fall appropriately under government funding; annual appeals; projects considered part of the school curriculum; attendance to conferences or seminars; annual campaigns; projects where the Foundation is the sole funder; or advertising. The Foundation will also not fund: political activities; make-up operating deficits; post event or after the fact situations; ongoing operating expenses; debt reduction; or religious organizations strictly for religious purposes.
Geographic Focus: Indiana
Date(s) Application is Due: Feb 15; Sep 15
Amount of Grant: Up to 15,000 USD
Contact: Sharon Hollowell; (812) 662-6364; fax (812) 662-8704; sharon@dccfound.org
Internet: www.dccfound.org/grants.html
Sponsor: Decatur County Community Foundation
101 E Main Street, Suite 1, P.O. Box 72
Greensburg, IN 47240

Decatur County Community Foundation Small Project Grants 812
The Decatur Foundation Small Project Grants fund organizations seeking a grant of $1,500 or less. The grant must demonstrate that it meets one or more of the following categories and criteria: youth and family enrichment - promote or provide for positive growth and development of young people or strengthen families; community development/civic engagement - promote the development of an increased quality of life within the community and foster stronger relationships among individuals or groups; cultural life - add to or enhance the variety of artistic and cultural opportunities available to all; education - demonstrate an ability to help residents gain knowledge and the skills necessary to better themselves either economically or socially, or focus on ways to allow citizens to develop skills; and health and recreation - demonstrate the ability to help residents develop healthy lifestyles. Highest priority will be given to innovative programs or projects that: include start-up costs, publicity, or specialized equipment; provide direct services to individuals or groups; enhance or enable participation by individuals or groups. Grant applications are accepted at any time. Applications received by the 10th of the month will be reviewed in the following month by the Board of Directors. The application and additional guidelines are available at the website.
Requirements: Organizations seeking grants should be a 501(c)3 nonprofit entity, an educational institution or a governmental entity. If they are not, the organization must find a qualified agency or entity to act as the fiscal agent.
Restrictions: Funding will not be considered for the following: political activities; make-up operating deficits; post-event or after the fact situations; debt reduction; or religious organizations for strictly religious purposes.
Geographic Focus: Indiana
Amount of Grant: Up to 1,500 USD
Contact: Sharon Hollowell, Executive Director; (812) 662-6364; sharon@dccfound.org
Internet: www.dccfound.org/grants.html

Sponsor: Decatur County Community Foundation
101 E Main Street, Suite 1, P.O. Box 72
Greensburg, IN 47240

DeKalb County Community Foundation - Garrett Hospital Aid Foundation Grants 813
The DeKalb County Community Foundation administers the Garrett Hospital Aid Foundation Grants, which award funding to nonprofit organizations that serve residents of Garrett, Indiana. Grant proposals are accepted in January of each year and grants are awarded at the recommendation of the Garrett Hospital Aid Foundation board of directors.
Requirements: Organization should submit the online application to the DeKalb Foundation for consideration. They should include the organization's name and contact information, a description of their project and why they need it, in addition to a first and second priority they would consider.
Restrictions: The Foundation only funds projects in Garrett, Indiana.
Geographic Focus: Indiana
Date(s) Application is Due: Jan 1
Amount of Grant: 200 - 800 USD
Samples: DeKalb Association for the Developmentally Disabled, job training to prepare individuals for workforce and independent living, $250; Junior Achievement programs serving Garrett School District, $500; St. Martin's Healthcare Clinic, medical and dental services, $800.
Contact: Rosie Shinkel, Program Manager; (260) 925-0311; rshinkel@dekalbfoundation.org
Internet: www.dekalbfoundation.org/g_garrett.php
Sponsor: DeKalb County Community Foundation
650 West North Street
Auburn, IN 46706

DeKalb County Community Foundation - Literacy Grant 814
The DeKalb County Literacy Grant was created to support adult and children's literacy opportunities in DeKalb County, Indiana. The Grant also advocates the importance of literacy to the community and encourages community members to become involved by committing resources to address literacy needs. Grants are awarded based on how a program addresses literacy needs and the ability of grantees to deliver their service in a cost-effective manner.
Requirements: Nonprofit organizations that provide literacy programs are encouraged to: submit a one-page letter of intent describing your program(s) and who you serve; include a specific dollar request; and specify that your request is for the DeKalb County Literacy Fund. Submit the letter between August 1 and August 31, with grants awarded in September. Applicants are also encouraged to call the Foundation office to discuss their ideas for a request.
Geographic Focus: Indiana
Samples: Butler Public Library, Auburn, IN: literacy program aimed at preschool children which provides bags of books that can be taken home, $300; J.E. Ober Elementary, Auburn, IN: new program "Tool Time" that will work with students in the Response to Intervention groups which are struggling with reading and are below grade level, $500; Eckhart Public Library, Auburn, IN: Book Buddies summer sessions in 2011 for parents and children participating in the Friends Mission Table at Auburn Presbyterian, $500.
Contact: Rosie Shinkel, Program Manager; (260) 925-0311; rshinkel@dekalbfoundation.org
Internet: www.dekalbfoundation.org/g_literacy.php
Sponsor: DeKalb County Community Foundation
650 West North Street
Auburn, IN 46706

DeKalb County Community Foundation Grants 815
The DeKalb County Community Foundation Grants support programs for DeKalb County, Indiana citizens that address today's needs and prepare for tomorrow's challenges. Grant guidelines are intentionally broad in order to meet the community's ever-changing charitable needs. Grants are awarded for charitable programs and projects in the following areas of interest: art and culture; community development; education; environment; health and human services; and youth development. Grants are also available for the general operating expenses of organizations that address local charitable needs. Applicants are encouraged to contact the Foundation before submitting a proposal to be certain it follows the grant guidelines. They are also encouraged to attend a free one hour workshop to help them understand the Foundation's grant process and learn basic proposal writing tips. The Foundation gives priority to grant proposals for programs/projects that: will be completed within one year of receiving a grant; strengthen the grant seeking organization; directly relate to the grant seeker's mission; project a high degree of community impact; benefit many local people; and are proactive rather than reactive.
Requirements: After reviewing the grant guidelines, applicants will fill out the online proposal form. Applicants should include their contact information, financial information, a brief summary of the request, their organization's mission statement, and a detailed explanation of the benefits they'll receive from the grant. They should also include their operating expenses, total budget, and their source of funds. Applicants will then email the proposal form to the Foundation contact person or mail a printed copy to the Foundation address.
Restrictions: Grants are less likely to be awarded for: repeat funding for a program/project that has received a Foundation grant within the last two years; or a funding debt. The Foundation grants to religious organizations for charitable purposes but does not award grants for religious purposes.
Geographic Focus: Indiana
Date(s) Application is Due: Jul 1
Amount of Grant: 500 - 7,000 USD
Samples: American Red Cross of Northeast Indiana, disaster services for DeKalb County; $2,500; St. Martin's Healthcare, operating expenses for medical clinic; $7,000; DeKalb County Council on Aging, exercise equipment; $2,500; Community Care Food Pantry, food pantry/garage infrastructure construction and new commercial freezer/refrigerator equipment; $3,000.

Contact: Rosie Shinkel; (260) 925-0311; rshinkel@dekalbfoundation.org
Internet: www.dekalbfoundation.org/g_grantmaking.php
Sponsor: DeKalb County Community Foundation
650 West North Street
Auburn, IN 46706

DeKalb County Community Foundation VOICE Grant   816
The DeKalb County Community Foundation's VOICE Grant is a grant making student advisory group in the DeKalb County area. VOICE (Views, Organizations, Improvements, Changes, Examples) meets once a month during the school year to learn about the community and its charitable needs. Grant proposals are submitted to Foundation's office. VOICE members then evaluate the proposals against their mission and grant focus, then make funding recommendations to the Foundation's Board of Directors. Once grant decisions are made, notification letters are sent to all applicants within 45 days.
Requirements: Organizations should complete the online application, submitting their organization's name and contact information, financial information, and summary of their request. They should also submit their organization's mission statement, a detailed explanation of how the grant would benefit the organization, its total budget, and other funding sources.
Restrictions: The application is available online, but must be printed and mailed to the Foundation office.
Geographic Focus: Indiana
Date(s) Application is Due: Mar 1; Oct 1
Amount of Grant: 500 - 1,250 USD
Samples: Early Learning Ministry - Beyond the Bell, enrichment activities for Beyond the Bell aftercare program, $500; Farmers and Hunters Feeding the Hungry, butchering fees to process donated meat from hunters and farmers, $1,000; Mad Anthony's Children's Hope House, overnight stays and related services for families, $1,250.
Contact: Rosie Shinkel, Program Manager; (260) 925-0311; rshinkel@dekalbfoundation.org
Internet: www.dekalbfoundation.org/dekalbsvoice.php
Sponsor: DeKalb County Community Foundation
650 West North Street
Auburn, IN 46706

Delaware Community Foundation Grants   817
The Delaware Community Foundation supports organizations and programs throughout the State of Delaware that address a wide range of community needs, including, but not limited to, health and human services, the arts, humanities and culture, the environment, housing and community development. The foundation awards capital grant and program grants. Capital grants are for construction, major renovation or repair of buildings and/or the purchase of land; and also may include requests for equipment purchases. Capital grants typically range from $5,000 to $20,000, with a maximum award of $25,000. Equipment grants generally range from $2,000 to $7,000, with a maximum award for families, $1,250.
Requirements: IRS 501(c)3 non-profit organizations in Delaware are eligible to apply. Grant proposals must be submitted on the appropriate D.C.F application form (capital projects or equipment). One application per organization will be accepted. Application forms may be obtained from the D.C.F office or at the D.C.F website.
Restrictions: Ineligible for support: endowment; debt reduction; religious organizations for sectarian purposes (though projects that serve the entire community, regardless of religious affiliation, are eligible for support); annual fundraising campaigns or general operating expenses; projects completed before June 30; sports clubs or leagues; educational institutions; purchase of vehicles; and individuals.
Geographic Focus: Delaware
Amount of Grant: 2,000 - 25,000 USD
Contact: Sarah Hench Grunewald, Vice President of Community Engagement and Programs; (302) 504-5267 or (302) 571-8004; fax (302) 571-1553; sgrunewald@delcf.org
Internet: www.delcf.org/grants/
Sponsor: Delaware Community Foundation
100 West 10th Street, Suite 115, P.O. Box 1636
Wilmington, DE 19899

Delaware Valley Fairness Project Teacher Assistance Grants   818
The Delaware Valley Fairness Project is a 501(c)3 non-profit organization incorporated in Pennsylvania. Its mission is to make life a little more fair for people – especially children – most affected by poverty. The Project acts on its mission by providing resources to schools serving children in impoverished neighborhoods and by providing support in the form of life-skills education, part-time jobs and emergency financial assistance to the families of the students in those schools. A good education is the best hope for a child to escape the cycle of poverty and an enriching school-life and a nurturing home-life are both needed for the child to receive that good education. The Project assists teachers and schools by providing resources for projects that stimulate creativity, broaden skills, foster social-emotional and character development, or make for innovative learning experiences. Projects focused on financial literacy, health and wellness, care for the planet, or libraries and literacy are of particular interest. Priority is given to projects, programs and activities benefiting disadvantaged youth. Applications may be submitted each fall term, typically between September 1st and November 15th, and each spring term, typically between February 1st and April 30th. Decisions on applications are made at least once per month. Preference is given to applicants who have not received an award during the current school-year. Applications for a classroom project should not exceed $500.
Requirements: Teachers and staff in any pre-K – 12 grade school in southeastern Pennsylvania or southern New Jersey are eligible to apply.
Restrictions: The Project does not fund equipment requests, such as printers, computers, or general classroom supplies.
Geographic Focus: Pennsylvania

Date(s) Application is Due: Apr 30; Nov 15
Amount of Grant: Up to 500 USD
Contact: Edward J. Riehl, President; (215) 341-9188; info@dvfairness.org
Internet: dvfairness.org/teacher-assistance/
Sponsor: Delaware Valley Fairness Project
133 North Bread Street, C3
Philadelphia, PA 19106

Dell Scholars Program Scholarships   819
Dell Scholars demonstrate their desire and ability to overcome barriers and to achieve their goals. Applicants will be evaluated on their individual determination to succeed; future goals and plans to achieve them; ability to communicate the hardships they have overcome or currently face; self motivation in completing challenging coursework; and demonstrated need for financial assistance. Students may apply directly through the Scholar website.
Requirements: To be eligible to apply for the Dell Scholarship, applicants must: participate in a Michael and Susan Dell Foundation approved college readiness program for a minimum of two of the last three years; graduate from an accredited high school this academic year; earn a minimum of a 2.4 GPA; demonstrate need for financial assistance; plan to enter a bachelor's degree program at an accredited higher education institution in the fall directly after their graduation from high school; and be a citizen or permanent resident of the U.S.
Restrictions: Applications faxed, mailed, or emailed to the Michael and Susan Dell Foundation will not be considered. The official Dell Scholars Application can only be found at this web site and must be submitted on-line during the specified application period. Email attachments will not be opened.
Geographic Focus: All States
Date(s) Application is Due: Jan 15
Contact: Dell Scholar Contact; 800-294-2039; apply@dellscholars.org
Internet: www.dellscholars.org/Criteria.aspx
Sponsor: Michael and Susan Dell Foundation
P.O. Box 163867
Austin, TX 78716-3867

Del Mar Foundation Community Grants   820
The Del Mar Foundation is a 501(c)3 California nonprofit public benefit corporation dedicated to promoting civic pride and community cohesiveness, acquiring and preserving open space, improving beaches and parks, raising and granting funds, and sponsoring diverse cultural programs and community events in Del Mar. The Foundation gives preference to projects, activities, and direct provision of services to, for, and within Del Mar that fit within and further its mission, and to Del Mar organizations that do not have ready access to other sources of funding. Priority is given to not-for-profit entities. The Foundation is also willing to support organizations in other ways, such as providing organizational fundraising and marketing expertise as well as seed funding for fundraising and other on-going activities. The application process is ongoing, with not annual deadlines.
Requirements: Organizations supporting the residents of Del Mar, California, are eligible to apply.
Geographic Focus: California
Contact: Bob Gans, President; (858) 635-1363; bgans@delmarfoundation.org or grants@DelMarFoundation.org
Internet: www.delmarfoundation.org/grants.html
Sponsor: Del Mar Foundation
225 9th Street, P.O. Box 2913
Del Mar, CA 92014-2550

Delmarva Power and Light Company Contributions   821
The Delmarva Power and Light Company Contributions (formerly known as the Conectiv Corporate Giving program) offers support primarily in areas of company operations in Delaware and Maryland, although giving is also to national organizations. The Company makes charitable contributions to nonprofit organizations involved with education, the environment, health care, housing, public safety, youth development, and the military. Therefore, its primary fields of interest include: disasters and emergency management; education; environment; health; heart and circulatory system diseases; housing development; public utilities; scouting programs; and youth development. Types of support offered include general operations and sponsorships. Although a formal application is required, interested parties should begin by forwarding an email detailing the program in need.
Requirements: Nonprofit organizations in both Delaware and Maryland, within the regions of company operations, are welcome to apply.
Geographic Focus: Delaware, Maryland
Contact: Matt Likovich; (410) 860-6203; matthew.likovich@delmarva.com
Internet: www.delmarva.com/community-commitment
Sponsor: Delmarva Power and Light Company
401 Eagle Run Road, P.O. Box 17000
Wilmington, DE 19886-7000

Delmarva Power and Light Company Mini-Grants   822
Through its Education Mini-Grant program, Delmarva Power and Light Company provides classroom teachers with grants of up to $500 to support innovative projects that are geared toward energy-related issues. This might include (but is not limited to): wise energy use; local conventional and alternative energy resources; and energy-related science content and electric safety. Grants can be used for purchasing materials, conducting special lessons, taking field trips and implementing special classroom projects that are not usually funded by school districts.
Requirements: Grant awards are available to public and private school teachers in kindergarten through twelfth grade and special education in Kent and Sussex counties in Delaware and in Cecil, Harford, and the Eastern Shore counties in Maryland.

Geographic Focus: Delaware, Maryland
Amount of Grant: Up to 500 USD
Contact: Matt Likovich; (410) 860-6203; matthew.likovich@delmarva.com
Internet: www.delmarva.com/community-commitment
Sponsor: Delmarva Power and Light Company
401 Eagle Run Road, P.O. Box 17000
Wilmington, DE 19886-7000

Delta Air Lines Foundation Community Enrichment Grants   **823**
Established in 1968 as Delta's company-managed giving system, the Delta Air Lines Foundation contributes more than $1 million annually in endowed funds to deserving organizations and programs. Community Enrichment focuses on promoting Delta's presence in the community through involvement and participation in volunteer, civic, and social activities. It also encourages consciousness, awareness, and consideration for community needs and focuses on developing a higher level of sensitivity towards supporting an improved quality of life for others in the communities where we live and work. Supporting Community Enrichment helps Delta establish its position as a corporate citizen and confirms our license to operate in our communities. Once an application is received, applicants should allow up to three months before review.
Requirements: For proposals which meet the foundation's area of focus, priority will be given to: programs meeting compelling needs in communities where Delta has a presence; proposals that exhibit clear, reasonable goals, and measurable outcomes; distinctive projects where the foundation's involvement will leave a legacy; projects that include collaboration or cooperation with other nonprofit organizations; projects that offer opportunities for Delta employee involvement. The foundation Board of Trustees reviews and approves funding in March, June, September, and November. The deadline for receiving completed proposals is the first day of each of these months.
Restrictions: The foundation will generally not consider: individual applicant's request for support of personal needs; religious activities; political organizations or campaigns; specialized single-issue health organizations; annual or automatic renewal grants; general operating expenses; endowment campaigns; capital campaigns; multi-year commitments; fraternal organizations, professional associations, or membership groups; fundraising events such as benefits; charitable dinners, or sporting events.
Geographic Focus: All States
Date(s) Application is Due: Mar 1; Jun 1; Sep 1; Nov 1
Contact: Foundation Administrator; (404) 715-5487 or (404) 715-2554; fax (404) 715-3267
Internet: www.delta.com/about_delta/community_involvement/delta_foundation/
Sponsor: Delta Air Lines Foundation
P.O. Box 20706, Department 979
Atlanta, GA 30320-6001

Delta Air Lines Foundation Youth Development Grants   **824**
Established in 1968 as Delta's company-managed giving system, the Delta Air Lines Foundation contributes more than $1 million annually in endowed funds to deserving organizations and programs. Delta's Youth Development Grants recognize today's young people as tomorrow's leaders. As such, the Foundation supports organizations that focus on keeping young people interested in math and science and helping them develop leadership skills and positive self esteem. Once an application is received, applicants should allow up to three months before review.
Requirements: For proposals which meet the foundation's area of focus, priority will be given to: programs meeting compelling needs in communities where Delta has a presence; proposals that exhibit clear, reasonable goals, and measurable outcomes; distinctive projects where the foundation's involvement will leave a legacy; projects that include collaboration or cooperation with other nonprofit organizations; projects that offer opportunities for Delta employee involvement. The foundation Board of Trustees reviews and approves funding in March, June, September, and November. The deadline for receiving completed proposals is the first day of each of these months.
Restrictions: The foundation will generally not consider: individual applicant's request for support of personal needs; religious activities; political organizations or campaigns; specialized single-issue health organizations; annual or automatic renewal grants; general operating expenses; endowment campaigns; capital campaigns; multiyear commitments; fraternal organizations, professional associations, or membership groups; fundraising events such as benefits; charitable dinners, or sporting events.
Geographic Focus: All States
Date(s) Application is Due: Jun 1; Sep 1; Nov 1
Contact: Foundation Administrator; (404) 715-5487 or (404) 715-2554; fax (404) 715-3267
Internet: www.delta.com/about_delta/community_involvement/delta_foundation/
Sponsor: Delta Air Lines Foundation
P.O. Box 20706, Department 979
Atlanta, GA 30320-6001

Dept of Ed Fund for the Improvement of Education—Partnerships   **825**
   in Character Education Pilot Projects
Applicants to this program may apply for a grant to design and implement a character education program that is able to be integrated into classroom instruction and is consistent with state academic content standards, and carried out in conjunction with other education reform efforts.
Requirements: Eligible applicants under this program are: a state education agency in partnership with one or more local education agencies (LEAs); an SEA in partnership with one or more LEAs and nonprofit organizations or entities, including an institution of higher education (IHE); an LEA or consortium of LEAs; or an LEA or LEAs in partnership with one or more nonprofit organizations or entities, including an IHE.
Geographic Focus: All States
Contact: Sharon Burton, (202) 205-8122; fax (202) 260-7767; sharon.burton@ed.gov

Sponsor: U.S. Department of Education
400 Maryland Avenue SW, Room 3E212, FB-6
Washington, D.C. 20202-6450

Dermody Properties Foundation Capstone Award   **826**
The Capstone gift began in 2007 as a way to say thank you to a community that helps our business thrive. Each year during the Thanksgiving season, Dermody Properties makes a substantial donation to one or more nonprofit organizations to help them continue their good works throughout the holiday season. The donation is aimed at organizations situated in northern Nevada.
Geographic Focus: Nevada
Contact: Maggie Atwood, Foundation Coordinator; (775) 741-8411 or (775) 858-8080; fax (775) 856-0831; matwood@partnerwithdp.com
Internet: www.partnerwithdp.com/Dermody/foundation.cfm
Sponsor: Dermody Properties Foundation
5500 Equity Avenue
Reno, NV 89502

Dermody Properties Foundation Grants   **827**
The Dermody Properties Foundation was founded in 1988, funded by the profits generated by the hard work and dedication of all the employees at Dermody Properties/DP Partners. The foundation supports nonprofits in Dermody Properties operating communities in its areas of interest, including: family and children, education, services for seniors, and the arts. Organizations and projects that have been supported include Community Child Care Services, the Children's Cabinet, Washoe County School District Educator Scholarships and the Food Bank of Northern Nevada. Grants typically range from $500 to $3,000.
Requirements: Nonprofits in Reno and Las Vegas, Nevada; Chicago, Illinois; Atlanta, Georgia; and Harrisburg, Pennsylvania, are eligible.
Geographic Focus: Georgia, Illinois, Nevada, Pennsylvania
Date(s) Application is Due: Aug 15
Amount of Grant: 500 - 3,000 USD
Contact: Maggie Atwood, Foundation Coordinator; (775) 741-8411 or (775) 858-8080; fax (775) 856-0831; matwood@dermody.com
Internet: www.dermody.com/dp_foundation
Sponsor: Dermody Properties Foundation
5500 Equity Avenue
Reno, NV 89502

Deuce McAllister Catch 22 Foundation Grants   **828**
McAllister was born in Lena, Mississippi, who went on to attend the University of Mississippi. As an Ole Miss Rebel, McAllister broke and set many records as a running back. In college, during his down time, McAllister could be found visiting with children in the community establishing himself as a positive role model on and off the field. In 2001, he was drafted in the first round as the 23rd overall selection by the New Orleans Saints. After one year of orientation in the NFL, McAllister decided he wanted to start a foundation to maximize his giving in the communities he knows best; New Orleans area and Jackson area. Today, Deuce McAllister's Catch 22 Foundation is dedicated to enhancing the lives of under-privileged youth and adolescents in the Gulf South Region primarily through the establishment of positive role models in their lives, providing unique opportunities for them to experience, and a financial commitment to making a difference.
Geographic Focus: Louisiana, Mississippi
Contact: De'Shundra McAllister, Director; (601) 665-3147 or (601) 957-5050; info@catch22foundation.com or deucemcallister?@dmcallister26.com
Internet: www.catch22foundation.com/
Sponsor: Deuce McAllister Catch 22 Foundation
6360 I-55 North, Suite 101
Jackson, MS 39211

Dexter Adams Foundation Grants   **829**
The Dexter Adams Foundation was established in Mansfield, Ohio, in 2012. It was founded in the name of "Little Dex," who lost his battle with leukemia in November of 2012, when he was only 3 years old. His father and mother started the Foundation in an effort to help other families while they are fighting pediatric cancer. Each June, the family hosts the Dexter Adams Memorial Baseball Tournament in nearby Shawnee, Ohio, raising funding to assist families in need. There are no annual deadlines for application submission
Requirements: Anyone with a family member fighting leukemia and in need of financial assistance is eligible to apply.
Geographic Focus: All States
Contact: Shane Adams, Trustee; (419) 862-3018
Sponsor: Dexter Adams Foundation
1069 Lexington Ontario Road
Mansfield, OH 44903

Different Needz Foundation Grants   **830**
The Different Needz Foundation was created in 2009 and was inspired by the life of Luke Jordan. Luke was born with developmental disabilities which caused many physical disabilities and medical conditions. Despite his disabilities, Luke was able to bring out the best in those who knew him. The Different Needz Foundation helps individuals with developmental disabilities obtain the necessary equipment and medical services they need to have the best quality of life. Grant applications are made available in January of each year. Grant awards are announced each year in May. The Foundation considers future needs and provides payment for medical services or equipment directly to the provider. The Foundation has approved grants for services and equipment such as; physical therapy, occupational therapy, speech therapy, medical equipment, a toilet chair, a wheelchair, a

wheelchair lift, summer camp and a tandem bike which was featured by Team Myles in the 2011 Cleveland Triathlon. Initially, grant recipients were mostly from northeast Ohio. Currently, the Foundation's reach has grown to include recipients in Ohio, Wyoming, Massachusetts, Florida, Maryland, Indiana, and California
Geographic Focus: All States
Date(s) Application is Due: Mar 31
Contact: Michelle Petrillo-Carr, President; (216) 904-5151; info@differentneedzfoundation.org
Internet: www.differentneedzfoundation.org/grants/
Sponsor: Different Needz Foundation
8440 East Washington Street #122
Chagrin Falls, OH 44023

Dining for Women Grants 831

Dining for Women funding is available for programs and/or projects that contribute to the empowerment of women and girls in less developed countries. Program and/or projects should be grassroots organizations that work with women and girls in the areas of health, education, environmental sustainability, and business development. Grants support one featured program each month that contributes to the mission to impact the lives, health and welfare of women and girls in developing countries. Awards are for one-to-two years, and total between $35,000 and $45,000.
Requirements: To be eligible, an applicant program must: support women and/or girls who face extreme challenges in developing countries; promote self-sufficiency, economic independence and/or good health for women and girls being supported; tie funding to direct impact on individuals' lives; provide evidence of long-term sustainability and program success; manage a DFW grant ranging between $35,000 and $45,000, which may be distributed over a two-year period; direct a minimum of 75% of expenses to programs; be a 501(c)3 U.S. nonprofit organization; operate independent of religious or political affiliation; provide informative organization website in English; and be able to provide educational materials, including a short video, that are relevant to the funded project/program.
Restrictions: Dining for Women does not fund: group trusts, foundations or other consolidated funding activity; governmental, political or religiously affiliated organizations; or major building projects, large capital expenditures, U.S. administrative fees or expenses and office costs.
Geographic Focus: All States
Date(s) Application is Due: Dec 31
Amount of Grant: 35,000 - 45,000 USD
Samples: Girls Empowerment Project, Heshima Kenya, Nairobi, $50,000 (over two years) - identifying and protecting separated and orphaned refugee children and youth living in Nairobi, Kenya; Midwives Save Lives, Haiti, $50,000 - to reduce maternal and neonatal mortality in Haiti by training Haitian women in the skills needed to save lives; One Heart World-Wide, Nepal, $50,000 - to decrease maternal and newborn mortality and morbidity in remote rural areas of the world.
Contact: Dr. Maggie Aziz, Program Director; (864) 335-8401; grants@diningforwomen.org
Internet: www.diningforwomen.org/Programs/grants
Sponsor: Dining for Women
P.O. Box 25633
Greenville, SC 29616

Dolan Children's Foundation Grants 832

The Dolan Children's Foundation was founded in New York in 1886 by Charles F. and Helen A. Dolan. Charles F. Dolan was the founder of the cable network HBO, and is the owner of Cablevision Systems Corporation, a cable television provider in New York City that also owns Madison Square Garden, Radio City Music Hall, the New York Knicks, and the New York Rangers. The Foundation awards community service grants with a focus on Long Island, New York. Areas of interest include: human services, disability services, mental health, schools, rehabilitation, hospitals, health facilities, and Catholic agencies and churches. Types of support include: general operating support, building and renovations; capital campaigns; equipment purchase and rental; land acquisition; program development; research; and matching grants. There are no application deadlines, though an application form is required. Recent awards have ranged from $25,000 to $3,000,000. Guidelines are available upon request.
Requirements: Schools and other nonprofits in New York City and Long Island are eligible. Applicants outside New York should call or write prior to submitting proposals.
Geographic Focus: New York
Amount of Grant: 25,000 - 3,000,000 USD
Samples: Chaminade High School, Mineola, New York, $3,000,000 - general operating support; Lesley University, Cambridge, Massachusetts, $250,000 - general operating support; Rising Sun Youth Foundation, Flushing, New York, $50,000 - general operating support.
Contact: Robert Vizza, President; (516) 803-9200
Sponsor: Dolan Children's Foundation
340 Crossways Park Drive
Woodbury, NY 11797-2050

Dolan Media Foundation Grants 833

The Dolan Media Foundation was established by the Dolan Media Company in 2005. Based in Minneapolis, Minnesota, the Foundation awards relief grants to individuals for domestic abuse, tornado damage, and home foreclosures. An application form is required, which can be secured by contacting the Foundation office directly. There are no specified annual deadlines.
Requirements: Individuals residing in Minnesota, who are in need, are eligible to apply.
Geographic Focus: Minnesota
Amount of Grant: 500 - 5,000 USD
Contact: Scott J. Pollei, Director; (612) 317-9420; fax (612) 321-0563
Sponsor: Dolan Media Foundation
222 South 9th Street, Suite 2300
Minneapolis, MN 55402-3363

Dollar Energy Fund Grants 834

The Dollar Energy Fund provides assistance and tangible aid to families and individuals experiencing difficulty in affording adequate and safe utility supplies in order to maintain basic living standards. Fields of interest include: economically disadvantaged; housing/shelter; and expense aid. Programs include: Hardship Program—provides grants directly to utility accounts; Customer Assistance Program (CAP)—payment is based on income and household size, not usage; and the Job Training and Career Guidance Program; Low Income Home Energy Assistance Program (LIHEAP)—federally funded program that provides assistance for heating bills.
Requirements: Each program has different eligibility guidelines, so individuals may be eligible for one or more programs. Individuals from Louisiana, Maryland, Ohio, Pennsylvania, Tennessee, Texas. Virginia, and West Virginia are eligible to apply.
Geographic Focus: Louisiana, Maryland, Ohio, Pennsylvania, Tennessee, Texas, Virginia, West Virginia
Contact: Mary Sally, Director of Programs; (412) 431-2800 or (800) 683-7036; fax (412) 431-2084; info@dollarenergy.org or pr@dollarenergy.org
Internet: www.dollarenergy.org
Sponsor: Dollar Energy Fund
P.O. Box 42329
Pittsburgh, PA 15203-0329

Dollar General Family Literacy Grants 835

The Dollar General Corporation awards community grants to direct family literacy service providers. Applicants should note that the Dollar General Literacy Foundation uses the federal government's definition of family literacy when reviewing grant applications. Family literacy programs applying for funding must have the following four components: adult education instruction (Adult Basic Education, GED preparation, or English for speakers of other languages; children's education; parent and child together time (PACT); and parenting classes that teach parents to be the primary teacher for their child.
Requirements: U.S. nonprofits in company operating areas in the 35-state market areas are eligible. In addition, to be eligible for consideration, an organization must be located within 20 miles of a Dollar General store, must not have received funding from the Dollar General Literacy Foundation for the past two consecutive years, and must have met all reporting requirements from previous Dollar General Literacy Foundation grants.
Restrictions: The giving program does not support individuals, general fundraising events or celebration functions, attendance at professional/association conferences or seminars, film and video projects, endowments or capital campaigns, private charities or foundations, purchase of vehicles, advertising, or construction or building costs.
Geographic Focus: Alabama, Arizona, Arkansas, Colorado, Delaware, Florida, Georgia, Illinois, Indiana, Iowa, Kansas, Kentucky, Louisiana, Maryland, Michigan, Minnesota, Mississippi, Missouri, Nebraska, New Jersey, New Mexico, New York, North Carolina, Ohio, Oklahoma, Pennsylvania, South Carolina, South Dakota, Tennessee, Texas, Utah, Vermont, Virginia, West Virginia, Wisconsin
Date(s) Application is Due: Feb 20
Amount of Grant: Up to 10,000 USD
Samples: Henagar Town Library, Henagar, Alabama - general operating support (2020); New Life Outreach Church Ministries, East Chicago, Indiana - general operating support (2020); Together with Families, Hagerstown, Maryland - general operating support (2020).
Contact: Family Literacy Program Coordinator; (615) 855-5201
Internet: www.dgliteracy.org/#family-literacy-grants
Sponsor: Dollar General Corporation
100 Mission Ridge
Goodlettsville, TN 37072

Dollar General Summer Reading Grants 836

Dollar General Literacy Foundation Summer Reading Grants provide funding to local nonprofit organizations and libraries to help with the implementation or expansion of summer reading programs. Programs must target Pre-K through 12th grade students who are new readers, below grade level readers or readers with learning disabilities. The annual application submission deadline is February 20. Grants can range as high as $3,000.
Requirements: U.S. nonprofits in company operating areas in the 35-state market areas are eligible. In addition, to be eligible for consideration, an organization must be located within 20 miles of a Dollar General store, must not have received funding from the Dollar General Literacy Foundation for the past two consecutive years, and must have met all reporting requirements from previous Dollar General Literacy Foundation grants.
Restrictions: The giving program does not support individuals, general fundraising events or celebration functions, attendance at professional/association conferences or seminars, film and video projects, endowments or capital campaigns, private charities or foundations, purchase of vehicles, advertising, or construction or building costs.
Geographic Focus: Alabama, Arizona, Arkansas, Colorado, Delaware, Florida, Georgia, Illinois, Indiana, Iowa, Kansas, Kentucky, Louisiana, Maryland, Michigan, Minnesota, Mississippi, Missouri, Nebraska, New Jersey, New Mexico, New York, North Carolina, Ohio, Oklahoma, Pennsylvania, South Carolina, South Dakota, Tennessee, Texas, Utah, Vermont, Virginia, West Virginia, Wisconsin
Date(s) Application is Due: Feb 20
Amount of Grant: Up to 3,000 USD
Contact: General Summer Grant Committee; (615) 855-5201
Internet: www.dgliteracy.org/#summer-reading
Sponsor: Dollar General Corporation
100 Mission Ridge
Goodlettsville, TN 37072

Dollar General Youth Literacy Grants   837

Youth Literacy Grants provide funding to schools and local nonprofit organizations to help with the implementation or expansion of literacy programs for new readers, below grade level readers and readers with learning disabilities. Organizations requesting funds must provide direct services to one of the groups of readers defined above, and instruction must be designed to meet the varying learning preferences and needs of the defined target population. The annual deadline for application submission is May 21. Awards can range as high as $4,000.

Requirements: U.S. nonprofits or schools in company operating areas in the 35-state market areas are eligible. In addition, to be eligible for consideration, an organization must be located within 20 miles of a Dollar General store, must not have received funding from the Dollar General Literacy Foundation for the past two consecutive years, and must have met all reporting requirements from previous Dollar General Literacy Foundation grants.

Restrictions: The giving program does not support individuals, general fundraising events or celebration functions, attendance at professional/association conferences or seminars, film and video projects, endowments or capital campaigns, private charities or foundations, purchase of vehicles, advertising, or construction or building costs.

Geographic Focus: Alabama, Arizona, Arkansas, Colorado, Delaware, Florida, Georgia, Illinois, Indiana, Iowa, Kansas, Kentucky, Louisiana, Maryland, Michigan, Minnesota, Mississippi, Missouri, Nebraska, New Jersey, New Mexico, New York, North Carolina, Ohio, Oklahoma, Pennsylvania, South Carolina, South Dakota, Tennessee, Texas, Utah, Vermont, Virginia, West Virginia, Wisconsin

Date(s) Application is Due: May 21

Amount of Grant: Up to 4,000 USD

Contact: Youth Literacy Grant Committee; (615) 855-5201

Internet: www.dgliteracy.com/grant-program/youth-grants.aspx

Sponsor: Dollar General Corporation

100 Mission Ridge

Goodlettsville, TN 37072

DOL Youthbuild Grants   838

YouthBuild is a community-based alternative education program for youth between the ages of 16 and 24 who are high school dropouts, adjudicated youth, youth aging out of foster care, youth with disabilities, and other at-risk youth populations. The YouthBuild program simultaneously addresses several core issues facing low-income communities: affordable housing, education, employment, crime prevention, and leadership development. DOL will award grants to organizations to oversee the provision of education, occupational skills training, and employment services to disadvantaged youth in their communities while performing meaningful work and service to their communities. Based on the most recent estimate of funding, DOL hopes to serve approximately 5,200 participants during the grant period of performance, with projects operating in approximately 75 communities across the country. The period of performance for these grant awards will be three (3) years and four (4) months from the effective date of the grant. This includes an up to four-month planning period, two years of core program operations (education, occupational skills training, and youth leadership development activities) for one or more cohorts of youth, plus an additional nine-to-twelve months of follow-up support services and tracking of participant outcomes for each cohort of youth. This grant period of performance includes time for all necessary implementation and start-up activities.

Requirements: Eligible applicants for these grants are public or private non-profit agencies or organizations including agencies that have previously served at-risk youth in a YouthBuild or other similar program. These agencies include, but are not limited to: faith-based and community organizations; an entity carrying out activities under Workforce Investment Act (WIA), such as a local workforce investment board, American Job Center (formerly known as One-Stop Career Center), or local school board; community action agency; state or local housing development agency; Indian tribe or other agency primarily serving American Indians; community development corporation; state or local youth service conservation corps; consortium of such agencies or organizations with a designated lead applicant; or, any other public or private non-profit entity that is eligible to provide education or employment training under a Federal program. Applicants must provide new cash or in-kind resources equivalent to exactly 25 percent of the grant award amount as "matching" funds while additional cost sharing above 25 percent may be committed towards the grant as "leveraged" funds. In order to preserve one of the core aspects of the YouthBuild program as a construction skills training program, all grant programs must offer construction skills training. New applicants for DOL funding must demonstrate success with core construction skills training and are not eligible to offer other vocational training as first-time YouthBuild grantees. Construction skills training is central to the overall philosophy of the YouthBuild program and can provide a visible transformational experience for young people who have rarely had opportunities to see tangible and positive results of their efforts.

Geographic Focus: All States

Date(s) Application is Due: Mar 19

Amount of Grant: Up to 1,100,000 USD

Contact: Kia Mason, Grants Management Specialist; (202) 693-2606; mason.kia@dol.gov

Internet: www.doleta.gov/grants/find_grants.cfm

Sponsor: U.S. Department of Labor

200 Constitution Avenue, NW

Washington, D.C. 20210

Dominion Foundation Grants   839

Dominion Foundation grants are made in four focus areas, and they support a variety of programs: food banks, homeless shelters, land and habitat preservation, STEM (science, technology, engineering, math) education, and neighborhood revitalization, to name a few. Special consideration is given to programs with an energy conservation or energy efficiency component. In the area of Human Needs, the Foundation focus is on: providing warmth and cooling; alleviating hunger; ensuring energy-efficient shelter; providing access to medicine and basic health care; supporting communities through the united way; and disaster

assistance. Since the Dominion Foundation supports a wide range of charitable programs, most grants are in the $1,000 to $15,000 range. Higher amounts may be awarded when a program is an exceptional fit with corporate business or giving priorities, or when there is significant employee involvement in the effort. Requests are considered quarterly by the Foundation's Community Investment Boards – statewide and regional committees comprised of Dominion employees representing key geographic, business and functional areas.

Requirements: Foundation grants are limited to organizations defined as tax-exempt under Section 501(c)3 of the IRS code. Additional grants occasionally may be made directly from the corporation to sponsor special events that benefit a non-profit organization.

Restrictions: Awards are throughout a 10-state area to include: Connecticut, Maryland, Massachusetts, North Carolina, Ohio, Pennsylvania, Rhode Island, Texas, Virginia and West Virginia. Information pertaining to the specific counties served in each state is on the website.

Geographic Focus: Connecticut, Illinois, Indiana, Maryland, Massachusetts, North Carolina, Ohio, Pennsylvania, Rhode Island, Texas, Virginia, West Virginia

Amount of Grant: 1,000 - 250,000 USD

Contact: James C. Mesloh, Executive Director; (800) 730-7217 or (412) 237-2973; fax (412) 690-7608; Educational_Grants@dom.com

Internet: www.dom.com/about/education/grants/index.jsp

Sponsor: Dominion Foundation

501 Martindale Street, Suite 400

Pittsburgh, PA 15222-3199

Donald G. Gardner Humanities Trust Youth Grants   840

n 1944, Donald G. Gardner donated a painting by Frederick C. Frieseke, entitled Breakfast In The Garden, to the City of Ely, Minnesota. It was hung in the Ely Public Library in 1945. In 1989, the painting was sold for $510,000 and the Donald G. Gardner Humanities Trust was established for the enhancement, growth and improvement of: the Ely Public Library; the arts and artisans of Ely and surrounding area, to include the performing arts, the visual arts, and literature; the creating and funding of scholarships; educational and artistic grants; and the cultural and aesthetic environment of the City of Ely and its surrounding area. Youth Grants will provide up to $500: for students who demonstrate a high motivation in the fine arts; to help expose these students to a diversity of viewpoints; and help youth artists afford training opportunities through workshops, classes, lessons or mentor programs. Students may apply to study one of the following fine arts disciplines: literary arts; visual or media arts; music; theater; or dance. The annual deadline for applications is April 24.

Requirements: The application and selection process is limited to students who will be attending the Ely schools in grades 9, 10, 11 and 12. Students are eligible to apply for summer opportunities who will be enrolled in 9th grade in the fall. Students in the 12th grade must complete their grant opportunity by April 1 of their graduation year. Students who have received a Youth Grant in the past are eligible to apply in the following year.

Geographic Focus: Minnesota

Date(s) Application is Due: Apr 24

Amount of Grant: Up to 500 USD

Contact: Keiko L. Williams; (218) 365-2639 or (218) 365-6764; info@gardnertrust.org

Internet: www.gardnertrust.org/scholar.htm

Sponsor: Donald G. Gardner Humanities Trust

P.O. Box 720

Ely, MN 55731

Donald W. Reynolds Foundation Children's Discovery Initiative Grants   841

The Foundation's trustees recognize that a growing number of children's discovery museums and science centers have an opportunity to play a special role in supporting the formal education system. The trustees have launched an initiative aimed at improving and expanding the discovery experiences at hands-on museums in Arkansas, Nevada, and Oklahoma. The critical component of the Foundation's initiative has been the establishment of statewide networks of museums working together to strengthen each museum's capacity and provide shared exhibits and new programs to better reach rural children, their teachers, and families. The networks provide new rotating exhibits, a mobile outreach vehicle – or museum-on-wheels, capacity-building programs, and new interactive discovery experiences to impact children even in the most rural areas of Arkansas and Oklahoma. The networks also provide classroom teachers with new hands-on resources. In addition to establishing collaborative networks of museums, the initiative has supported capital projects and awarded capital planning grants for individual museum projects in Arkansas, Oklahoma, and Nevada.

Requirements: Organizations must first contact the Foundation to discuss their project before submitting a proposal.

Geographic Focus: Arkansas, Nevada, Oklahoma

Samples: Science Museum Oklahoma, Oklahoma City, Oklahoma, $10,757,258 - funding for the Donald W. Reynolds Oklahoma Museum Network (2002-2011); Mid-America Science Museum, Hot Springs, Arkansas, $8,168,696 - exhibit and capital funding (2009-2011).

Contact: Courtney Latta Knoblock, Program Director; (702) 804-6000; fax (702) 804-6099; courtney.latta@dwrf.org or GeneralQuestions@dwrf.org

Internet: www.dwreynolds.org/Programs/Regional/Discovery.htm

Sponsor: Donald W. Reynolds Foundation

1701 Village Center Circle

Las Vegas, NV 89134-6303

Don and May Wilkins Charitable Trust Grants   842

The Don and May Wilkins Charitable Trust was established in Colorado in 1999, with giving centered around the Fort Collins and surrounding area. The Foundation's primary fields of interest include: academic improvement; children and youth programs; and enhancing the educational opportunities of K-12 students. Most often, support comes in the form of: capital campaigns; infrastructure; endowments; program development; and seed money. Approximately forty awards are given annually, ranging up to a maximum of $82,000. There are no formal application materials, and interested parties should begin by forwarding a letter of inquiry to the Foundation office. No annual deadlines have been designated.

Requirements: 501(c)3 organizations serving the residents of Fort Collins and the surrounding area are welcome to apply.

Geographic Focus: Colorado

Amount of Grant: Up to 82,000 USD

Samples: City of Fort Collins, Fort Collins, Colorado, $81,399 - donations for staff Christmas party; Catholic Charities, Fort Collins, Colorado, $17,390 - support for the homeless shelter and senior services; Educo Leadership Adventures, Fort Collins, Colorado, $54,970 - support for the Leadership Adventure Summer Camp.

Contact: J. Brad March, Coordinator; (970) 482-4322

Sponsor: Don and May Wilkins Charitable Trust

110 E. Oak, Suite 200

Fort Collins, CO 80524-7127

Doree Taylor Charitable Foundation Grants 843

The mission of the Doree Taylor Charitable Foundation is to support charitable organizations that provide relief to people in need of basic provisions (including food, housing, shelter); promote the humane care of animals; provide health care services for the underserved; and conduct public radio or television. The Foundation makes grants throughout Maine, but has a priority for organizations located in, or serving the areas of Boothbay Harbor, Southport, and Brunswick. From time to time, the Foundation may make grants to organizations with a national scope. Occasional support will also be provided to colleges, universities, and environmental charitable organizations in Maine. The majority of grants from the Taylor Foundation are 1 year in duration. On occasion, multi-year support is awarded. Award amounts typically range from $2,500 to $250,000. Applications will be accepted twice annually.

Requirements: This grant is available to 501(c)3 charitable organizations who serve the specified regions and causes. Grant requests for general operating support or program support are strongly encouraged and preferred, however capital requests will be considered from time to time. Applications will be submitted online through the Bank of America website. A grant report is required within 1 year of the grant application date, regardless of whether all of the funds have been spent.

Restrictions: The foundation will not contribute to endowments or consider grant requests from individuals, organizations attempting to influence policy through direct lobbying, or political campaigns.

Geographic Focus: All States, Maine

Date(s) Application is Due: Mar 1; Sep 1

Amount of Grant: 2,500 - 250,000 USD

Samples: Lincoln County Dental, Damariscotta, Maine, $114,000 - Awarded for Capital support for the purchase of a fully operational dental clinic and salary support for the Executive Director (2018); Brcrc Addiction Outreach Program, Boothbay Harbor, Maine, $103,680 - Awarded for The Community Navigator Program (2018); Maine St Soc to Protect Animals, South Windham, Maine, $100,000 - Awarded for General Operations and Facility Expansion Arena/Education/Barn Building (2018).

Contact: Michealle Larkins, Philanthropic Administrator; (866) 778-6859; ma.grantmaking@bankofamerica.com

Internet: www.bankofamerica.com/philanthropic/foundation/?fnId=83

Sponsor: Doree Taylor Charitable Foundation

225 Franklin Street, 4th Floor, MA1-225-04-02

Boston, MA 02110-2800

Dorothea Haus Ross Foundation Grants 844

The foundation awards grants to eligible nonprofit organizations that work to relieve suffering among children who are sick, handicapped, injured, disfigured, orphaned, or otherwise vulnerable. Types of support include direct services, medical research, equipment and supplies, and small renovation projects. There are no application deadlines. The foundation has a preference for small grassroots projects that it can fully fund or nearly fully fund with the small grants that it makes. The Ross Foundation is less interested in larger projects or capital campaigns that are better left to larger foundations and organizations.

Requirements: U.S. Charities may apply if: they have 501(c)3 status; they are listed in the current edition of the Cumulative List of Charities published by the U.S. Department of the Treasury; they are a Catholic organization listed in the current edition of the Catholic Director; or they are listed in the Free Methodist Yearbook, or other Protestant Denomination Directory that has a group ruling for tax exemption from the IRS. Although grants are made internationally, Foundation by-laws prohibit sending money directly to foreign charities. Applicants from foreign countries (outside the United States) are encouraged to call or email the foundation prior to submitting any applications.

Restrictions: The Foundation does not fund day-to-day operations, individuals, conferences, day care, or public education. Although the Foundation makes international grants, there are restrictions in some countries for the following reasons: war, widespread violence, or breakdown of law and order; or countries where grants are restricted by the U.S. Government due to a boycott or other reason.

Geographic Focus: All States

Contact: Wayne S. Cook, Ph.D., Foundation Executive; (585) 473-6006; fax (585) 473-6007; Rossfoundation@frontiernet.net

Internet: www.dhrossfoundation.org/index.php?option=com_content&view=article&id=3&catid=1

Sponsor: Dorothea Haus Ross Foundation

1036 Monroe Avenue

Rochester, NY 14620

Dorrance Family Foundation Grants 845

The Dorrance Family Foundation was founded by Bennett Dorrance, co-owner of the Campbell Soup Company. The Foundation gives primarily in the states of Arizona, California, and Hawaii, offering support for projects that work to resolve societal,

educational and environmental problems strategically and make communities a better place. Its two primary areas of interest are education and natural resource conservation. In the area of education, the Foundation awards grants for the funding of: academic needs of low income and/or underserved students; first generation graduates; innovation; literacy; primary, secondary, and post-secondary academics; quality teacher training and recruitment; and science and technology programs. In the area of conservation, the Foundations awards grants for the funding of: forests; innovation; marine and coastal areas; rivers, streams, wetlands, and watersheds; sustainable agriculture, land use, and land management; and wildlife habitats. The Foundation also supports arts and culture, children's medical research, science and other community needs.

Requirements: No formal application form is required, 501(c)3 non-profits operating in Arizona, California, and Hawaii are eligible to apply for these grants. Applicants should submit a proposal consisting of a detailed description of project and amount of funding requested.

Restrictions: No funding available to individuals. The Foundation does not accept unsolicited grant applications. If an organization qualifies for a grant based on the Foundation's grantmaking focus and eligibility requirements, a Letter of Inquiry should be submitted as a preliminary approach.

Geographic Focus: Arizona, California, Hawaii

Amount of Grant: Up to 100,000 USD

Samples: Angel Flight West, Santa Monica, California, $36,000 - support of free airfare transportation in response to health care; North Kohala Community Resource Center, Hawi, Hawaii, $50,000 - support for a variety of different programs; Kamuela Philharmonic Orchestra, Kamuela, Hawaii, $25,000 - support of youth participation.

Contact: Carrie Ostroski; (480) 367-7000; carrieo@dfenterprises.com or info@dmbinc.com

Internet: www.dorrancefamilyfoundation.org/

Sponsor: Dorrance Family Foundation

7600 East Doubletree Ranch Road, Suite 300

Scottsdale, AZ 85258-2137

Dorr Foundation Grants 846

Dorr Foundation grants are made primarily for programs designed to develop new science curricula from sixth to 12th grade. Support is also given to special education projects for youth relating to conservation and the environment if such projects involve the school's curriculum, equipment purchase, program development, emergency funding, and seed money. In addition, some grants are made available to promote research and disseminate information on chemical, metallurgical, and sanitation engineering. Grants are awarded on a national basis, with emphasis in the Northeast states. Types of support include equipment, emergency funds, program development, seed money, curriculum development, scholarship funds, and research. Initial contact should be a phone call. There is no deadline for application submission. No response can be expected unless there is interest on the part of the trustees. Applications are accepted at any time. Typical awards range from $5,000 to $30,000.

Requirements: 501(c)3 tax-exempt organizations are eligible.

Restrictions: Grants are not made to individuals or for operation budgets, continuing support, annual campaigns, deficit financing, endowment funds, or conferences and seminars.

Geographic Focus: Connecticut, Maine, Massachusetts, New Hampshire, New York, Vermont

Amount of Grant: 5,000 - 30,000 USD

Samples: Maritime Museum, Norwalk, Connecticut, $20,000 - building STEM Academy for teachers; Maine Natural History Observatory, Gouldsboro, Maine, $15,000 - population counts of nesting Gulls and cormorants along the coast of Maine; Young Men's Leadership Academy, Kennedy, Texas, $5,561 - Ozone North and South project.

Contact: Barbara McMillan, Chairperson; (603) 433-6438

Sponsor: Dorr Foundation

84 Hillside Drive

Portsmouth, NH 03801-5328

Do Something Awards 847

The Do Something Awards honor dynamic young people for service in the areas of community building, health, and the environment. Award winners are leaders who identify and realize solutions to problems facing local communities across America. Five winners will receive a minimum of $10,000 in community grants and scholarships. Of those five winners, one will be selected by a national, online vote as a Golden Award winner. That Golden Award winner receives a total of $100,000 in community grants, which will enable him or her to take their work to the next level. Winners are announced and recognized at an annual gala in New York City. Application and guidelines are available online.

Requirements: Applicants must be 25 years old or younger. Only winners who are age 18 and under are eligible for a scholarship of $5,000 and a $5,000 community grant. Winners age 19 to 25 receive their entire award in the form of a community grant.

Geographic Focus: All States

Date(s) Application is Due: Dec 15

Amount of Grant: 10,000 - 100,000 USD

Contact: Naomi Hirabayashi; (212) 254-2390, ext. 240; nhirabayashi@dosomething.org

Internet: www.dosomething.org/programs/awards

Sponsor: Do Something

19 West 21st Street, 8th Floor

New York, NY 10010

Do Something Back End Developer Intern 848

The Back End Developer Intern is a fall tech intern who loves coding on the server side. If you enjoy writing PHP, Ruby, Python or Node, this internship is for you! Come expand your technology horizons, build products that scale, and get your work in front of millions of young people. The Intern will be working on one of Do Something's major products, which could be: PHP/Drupal based dosomething.org website; PHP/Laravel user API and

API admin application; Node/RabbitMQ messaging systems; Objective-C iPhone app/ Java Android app; or Python/Flask live data dashboard.

Requirements: General requirements include: ability to travel to the New York City office; commitment to working 12 to 15 hours per week for nine to ten weeks; being a self starter – ability to work well alone and with others; passionate about young people making an impact and committed to social change; member of DoSomething.org; love of the DoSomething.org culture and can work with a quirky, close-knit team. Specific requirements include: knowing at least one programming language; having worked with RESTful APIs before; ability to recognize and advocate for clean code; and curiosity and passion for experimenting with new technologies.

Geographic Focus: All States
Date(s) Application is Due: Aug 14
Amount of Grant: 1,000 USD
Contact: Darren "Dee" Lee, Back-End Engineer; (212) 254-2390; internships@ dosomething.org or deezone@dosomething.org
Internet: www.dosomething.org/about/internships
Sponsor: Do Something
19 West 21st Street, 8th Floor
New York, NY 10010

Do Something Business Development Intern   849

The business development team works with awesome companies who care about young people and social change. The Do Something team is responsible for creating, pitching, and maintaining relationships with corporate sponsors to support the national cause campaigns that activate young people nationwide around social change. Responsibilities include: researching companies and brands that care about young people; cold outreach to potential new sponsors; brainstorming new youth marketing and youth outreach ideas; assisting in the management of our current campaigns/sponsor relations; assisting in pitch process and deck creation; and some administrative work as necessary. Compensation includes: a $1,000 stipend or school credit; tons of fun; a great reference letter; and a chance to work in a super fun and positive work environment. Fall, winter, and summer semester internships are available.

Requirements: General requirements include: ability to travel to the New York City office; commitment to working 12 to 15 hours per week for nine to ten weeks; being a self starter – ability to work well alone and with others; passionate about young people making an impact and committed to social change; member of DoSomething.org; love of the DoSomething. org culture and can work with a quirky, close-knit team. Specific requirements include: outgoing and enthusiastic personality; knowledge of the teen trends of the moment; comfortable talking with the CMO of any company; ability to brainstorm on the spot; excellent communication skills; solid grammar and ability to write concisely; good on the phone; able to think strategically and not afraid to pitch a big idea; and comfortable making new friends in any setting.

Geographic Focus: All States
Date(s) Application is Due: Aug 14
Amount of Grant: 1,000 USD
Contact: Marissa Ranalli, Marketing Manager; (212) 254-2390, ext. 231; internships@ dosomething.org or bizdevinternship@dosomething.org
Internet: www.dosomething.org/about/internships#business-development-intern
Sponsor: Do Something
19 West 21st Street, 8th Floor
New York, NY 10010

Do Something Campaigns Intern   850

This year DoSomething.org will run 200 cause campaigns around issues teens care about. Each campaign is designed with a simple call to action that gives young people tools to create real impact in their communities. There are three basic rules to any cause campaign: Do Something never requires money, an adult, or a car. As a campaigns intern you will work on specific campaign projects related to cause spaces. Do Something is looking for interns who are interested in these areas: discrimination; education; bullying; sex and relationships; violence; physical and mental health; poverty and homelessness; environment; and animal welfare. Responsibilities include: vital support on major staff pick campaigns, including answering member emails, coordinating outreach, writing content; research specific causes and issues, with a goal of figuring out ways that young people can take action on that issue; create campaign ideas and content; assisting in writing member communications for cause campaigns; and basic project management assistance throughout the semester. Compensation includes: a $1,000 stipend or school credit; tons of fun; a great reference letter; and a chance to work in a super fun and positive work environment. Fall, winter, and summer semester internships are available.

Requirements: General requirements include: ability to travel to the New York City office; commitment to working 12 to 15 hours per week for nine to ten weeks; being a self starter – ability to work well alone and with others; passionate about young people making an impact and committed to social change; a member of DoSomething.org; love of the DoSomething. org culture and can work with a quirky, close-knit team. Specific requirements include: strong organizational and project management skills; outgoing and enthusiastic personality; strong communication skills; solid grammar and ability to write concisely; good telephone manner; excellent research and planning skills; and passion for the causes we focus on.

Geographic Focus: All States
Date(s) Application is Due: Aug 14
Amount of Grant: 1,000 USD
Contact: Dave Deluca, Head of Campaigns; (212) 254-2390; campaignsintern@ dosomething.org or internships@dosomething.org
Internet: www.dosomething.org/about/internships#campaigns-intern
Sponsor: Do Something
19 West 21st Street, 8th Floor
New York, NY 10010

Do Something Digital Content Intern   851

Young people are on the Internet and because we're a brand who cares about young people it's important for U.S. to meet them where they are. The Digital Content internship will be all about engaging our existing fans and creating lasting relationships with new ones through our owned social media, editorial, video, and product channels. You'll have to come up with creative and powerful ways to make new connections and to make Do Something's existing connections stronger. Responsibilities include: working with the rest of the content team to create dynamic strategies and draft content; engaging with fans and followers online; moderating Do Something's owned channels; growing Do Something's owned channels; helping the product team in creating products that embolden the user experience of members on DoSomething.org; and helping the marketing and public relations team court talent (traditional and new media) to ensure as many eyes as possible see the campaigns. Compensation includes: a $1,000 stipend or school credit; tons of fun; a great reference letter; and a chance to work in a super fun and positive work environment. Fall, winter, and summer semester internships are available.

Requirements: General requirements include: ability to travel to the New York City office; commitment to working 12 to 15 hours per week for nine to ten weeks; being a self starter – ability to work well alone and with others; passionate about young people making an impact and committed to social change; member of DoSomething.org; love of the DoSomething. org culture and can work with a quirky, close-knit team. Specific requirements include: current college student (Freshman to Senior); incredibly creative with the ability to pivot; strong communication skills (grammar is a must, but you've also got to be succinct and effective in the space of 140 characters); multi-tasker, self-motivated, ability to work well alone or with others; passionate about young people changing the world; committed to social change; and knowledge of Google Drive and Adobe Creative Suite.

Geographic Focus: All States
Date(s) Application is Due: Aug 14
Amount of Grant: 1,000 USD
Contact: Felicia Fitzpatrick; (212) 254-2390; bmathias@dosomething.org
Internet: www.dosomething.org/about/internships#digital-content-intern
Sponsor: Do Something
19 West 21st Street, 8th Floor
New York, NY 10010

Do Something Digital Member Experience Intern   852

The Member Experience Intern is part of Do Something's growing Mobile team. They are responsible for engaging DoSomething members on a one-to-one basis including: managing volunteer programs and creating systems for improving it and retaining more volunteers; providing exceptional member support to young people trying to do campaigns; helping to figure out creative ways to surprise and delight Do Something's 3.6 million members; and helping to create engaging digital experiences via SMS and email for members.

Requirements: General requirements include: ability to travel to the New York City office; commitment to working 12 to 15 hours per week for nine to ten weeks; being a self starter – ability to work well alone and with others; passionate about young people making an impact and committed to social change; member of DoSomething.org; love of the DoSomething. org culture and can work with a quirky, close-knit team. Specific requirements include: strong multi-tasking abilities; impeccable organizational skills and attention to detail; passion for solving problems and putting smiles on people's faces; self-sufficient (the type of person who will search high and low to find an answer yourself before asking someone else); and a positive, upbeat attitude and a seemingly endless supply of patience.

Geographic Focus: All States
Date(s) Application is Due: Aug 14
Amount of Grant: 1,000 USD
Contact: Ariel Scott-Dicker; (212) 254-2390; internships@dosomething.org
Internet: www.dosomething.org/about/internships
Sponsor: Do Something
19 West 21st Street, 8th Floor
New York, NY 10010

Do Something Finance and Human Resources Intern   853

The Do Something Finance and Human Resources internship will give the hands on experience required in this highly demanded and specialized field. Responsibilities include: providing assistance with general bookkeeping duties; helping create and improve financial and human resource systems; performing basic office management and administrative duties; assisting with State solicitations filing; and assisting the Finance team during the annual audit process. Compensation includes: a $1,000 stipend or school credit; tons of fun; a great reference letter; and a chance to work in a super fun and positive work environment. Fall, winter, and summer semester internships are available.

Requirements: General requirements include: ability to travel to the New York City office; commitment to working 12 to 15 hours per week for nine to ten weeks; being a self starter – ability to work well alone and with others; passionate about young people making an impact and committed to social change; member of DoSomething.org; love of the DoSomething. org culture and can work with a quirky, close-knit team. Specific requirements include: outgoing and enthusiastic personality; knowledge of pop culture and the teens trends of the moment; excellent communication skills; solid grammar; ability to convey message clearly; good telephone manner; self-starter; ability to work well alone or with others; passionate about teens changing the world; knowledge of Quickbooks and/or other financial software; and knowledge of Excel.

Geographic Focus: All States
Date(s) Application is Due: Aug 14
Amount of Grant: 1,000 USD
Contact: Ritika Kaushal, Finance and Human Resources Manager; (212) 254-2390; financefallintern@dosomething.org

Internet: www.dosomething.org/about/internships#finance-and-hr-intern
Sponsor: Do Something
19 West 21st Street, 8th Floor
New York, NY 10010

Do Something International Intern 854

The Do Something International Intern will support the International Team and International Affiliate Program. Their focus will be to help build and expand our international affiliate program. This position will report to the Director of International. The Internship pays a $1,000 stipend, up to $175 in travel expenses, and school credit. Responsibilities include: learning the International Affiliate process and phases; helping to develop the wiki and other helpful resources to help international affiliates; keeping the master document up-to-date; assisting affiliates to execute their cause campaigns; helping create strategy to bringing in new affiliates; and helping manage inquires.
Requirements: General requirements include: ability to travel to the New York City office; commitment to working 12 to 15 hours per week for nine to ten weeks; being a self starter – ability to work well alone and with others; passionate about young people making an impact and committed to social change; member of DoSomething.org; love of the DoSomething.org culture and can work with a quirky, close-knit team. Specific requirements include: outgoing and enthusiastic personality; excellent communication skills; solid grammar; ability to convey message clearly; good telephone manner; self-starter; ability to work well alone or with others; passionate about teens changing the world; and knowledge or ability to speak Chinese (or enrollment in a China Studies program a plus).
Geographic Focus: All States
Date(s) Application is Due: Aug 14
Amount of Grant: 1,000 USD
Contact: Micah Nelson, Global Strategist; (212) 254-2390; mnelson@dosomething.org or international@dosomething.org
Internet: www.dosomething.org/about/internships#international-intern
Sponsor: Do Something
19 West 21st Street, 8th Floor
New York, NY 10010

Do Something Intern of Fun 855

The Do Something Intern of Fun will assist the Head of Fun with keeping the org moving. This includes everthing from office management to staff development to planning exciting things and maintaining the Do Something culture. Responsibilities include: office management - using killer problem-solving skills to be a go-to person for anything related to the office and helping keep things organized; hiring - keeping up with current job applications via an online applicant tracking system; staff communication - creating a new version of the Tissue Issue (our office newsletter) each week that makes U.S. smile and think; staff development - helping out with in-office events and intern outings; and other stuff - who knows that other fun might pop up in your time here. Compensation includes: a $1,000 stipend or school credit; tons of fun; a great reference letter; and a chance to work in a super fun and positive work environment. Fall, winter, and summer semester internships are available.
Requirements: General requirements include: ability to travel to the New York City office; commitment to working 12 to 15 hours per week for nine to ten weeks; being a self starter – ability to work well alone and with others; passionate about young people making an impact and committed to social change; member of DoSomething.org; love of the DoSomething.org culture and can work with a quirky, close-knit team. Specific requirements include: obsession with the DoSomething.org office culture; organization skills; an interest in learning about staff development procedures, human resources, and hiring; good phone skills; and ability to write fun, polite emails.
Geographic Focus: All States
Date(s) Application is Due: Aug 14
Amount of Grant: 1,000 USD
Contact: Katie Radford, Head of Fun; (212) 254-2390; funintern@dosomething.org or kradford@dosomething.org
Internet: www.dosomething.org/about/internships#intern-of-fun
Sponsor: Do Something
19 West 21st Street, 8th Floor
New York, NY 10010

Do Something Partnerships and Public Relations Intern 856

Marketing and Public Relations at DoSomething.org is all about creating buzz to support its campaigns. The staff works hard to form mutually beneficial relationships to reach young people and get them involved in taking social action. Primary duties include: helping the marketing and public relations team create strategic and innovative communication and outreach plans; building partnerships; earning press; and engaging celebrity ambassadors to help spread the word, drive conversion, and meet program goals. Strategies to accomplish these duties may include: assisting with the creation and execution of marketing techniques for individual programs; brainstorming how to integrate unique marketing tactics for ongoing campaigns; documenting any relevant press articles that feature DoSomething.org and add to press page of its website; using data to guide strategic marketing campaigns and next steps; and tracking important dates (ex: movie premieres, holidays, upcoming album releases, etc.) that can be used to guide launches and public relations support. Compensation includes: a $1,000 stipend or school credit; tons of fun; a great reference letter; and a chance to work in a super fun and positive work environment. Fall, winter, and summer semester internships are available.
Requirements: General requirements include: ability to travel to the New York City office; commitment to working 12 to 15 hours per week for nine to ten weeks; being a self starter – ability to work well alone and with others; passionate about young people making an impact and committed to social change; member of DoSomething.org; love of the DoSomething.

org culture and can work with a quirky, close-knit team. Specific requirements include: outgoing and enthusiastic personality; knowledge of pop culture and teen trends of the moment; excellent communication skills; solid grammar; ability to convey a message clearly; good telephone manner; self-starter; ability to work well alone or with others; creative; and ability to think outside of the box.
Geographic Focus: All States
Amount of Grant: 1,000 USD
Contact: Colleen Wormsley, Public Relations and Talent Relations Manager; (212) 254-2390; internship@dosomething.org or cwormsley@dosomething.org
Internet: www.dosomething.org/about/internships#partnerships-and-pr-intern
Sponsor: Do Something
19 West 21st Street, 8th Floor
New York, NY 10010

Do Something Scholarships 857

Do Something offers two types of scholarships annually, which include: Campaign Scholarships and Seasonal Scholarships. The amount given varies up to $10,000. The web site offers more than eighty campaign ideas that applicants can become involved in. Those that complete a campaign make themselves eligible to apply for seasonal awards. The annual deadline for each type of scholarship application is June 30, and interested parties should visit the web site often for updates.
Geographic Focus: All States
Date(s) Application is Due: Jun 30
Amount of Grant: Up to 10,000 USD
Contact: Naomi Hirabayashi, CMO; (212) 254-2390, ext. 240; nhirabayashi@dosomething.org
Internet: www.dosomething.org/about/scholarships
Sponsor: Do Something
19 West 21st Street, 8th Floor
New York, NY 10010

Do Something TMI Intern 858

TMI is the agency of DoSomething.org that works with companies, not-for-profits, and governments to help them in the areas of technology, millennials and impact. The TMI Intern works with the agency team on both the business development front (creating and pitching new ideas for potential clients) and on the client services side (research, writing, etc.) supporting existing projects. Primary responsibilities include: research and development for potential Do Something clients - everything from global education to local teen health; researching companies and brands that are relevant to a teen audience; brainstorming new youth marketing and youth outreach ideas; assisting in the management of our current client and sponsor relations; helping create weekly internal reports with teen insights and helpful data; some administrative work as necessary; helping to manage TMI's social media channels (FB, Twitter, LinkedIn); and helping to develop strategies for client campaigns. Compensation includes: a $1,000 stipend or school credit; tons of fun; a great reference letter; and a chance to work in a super fun and positive work environment. Fall, winter, and summer semester internships are available.
Requirements: General requirements include: ability to travel to the New York City office; commitment to working 12 to 15 hours per week for nine to ten weeks; being a self starter – ability to work well alone and with others; passionate about young people making an impact and committed to social change; member of DoSomething.org; love of the DoSomething.org culture and can work with a quirky, close-knit team. Specific requirements include: outgoing and enthusiastic personality; confident working independently and taking ownership of full projects; excellent communication skills; solid grammar; ability to convey message clearly; good telephone manner; passion for social change; interest in CSR, marketing, and everything data; knowledge of pop culture and the teen trends of the moment; and the ability to produce client-facing documents and attend meetings with clients.
Geographic Focus: All States
Date(s) Application is Due: Aug 14
Amount of Grant: 1,000 USD
Contact: Lisa Boyd, (212) 254-2390; lboyd@dosomething.org or intern@tmiagency.org
Internet: www.dosomething.org/about/internships#tmi-intern-the-dosomething.org-agency
Sponsor: Do Something
19 West 21st Street, 8th Floor
New York, NY 10010

Do Something User Experience Research Intern 859

The Do Something User Experience Research Intern will help get the research needed to make a clean, simple, and intuitive user experience. Responsibilities include: fighting for the user - uncovering what is in the best interest of young people who are looking for ways they can create social change; interviews - recruit, screen, and schedule members and other young people for user interviews; research - field feedback from members and review usability videos, and then consolidate learnings in a way that determines if more research is needed or readiness to implement changes; data digging - be an active member of the quantitative and quantitatively driven data team, helping to lead and report on small and large scale surveys; customer service - use of organizational skills and love of efficiency to come up with better systems that give quick responses to users who need help, or clearly communicate to other team members (tech team, campaigns, social media, etc.); innovation - follow the industry wide conversation on UX innovations and research methodologies. Compensation includes: a $1,000 stipend or school credit; tons of fun; a great reference letter; and a chance to work in a super fun and positive work environment. Fall, winter, and summer semester internships are available.
Requirements: General requirements include: ability to travel to the New York City office; commitment to working 12 to 15 hours per week for nine to ten weeks; being a self starter – ability to work well alone and with others; passionate about young people making an impact

and committed to social change; member of DoSomething.org; love of the DoSomething.org culture and can work with a quirky, close-knit team. Specific requirements include: background in a social science (e.g., psychology, sociology, behavioral economics), design (arts), or a related field; curiosity; passion for design or science; and customer service experience.
Geographic Focus: All States
Amount of Grant: 1,000 USD
Contact: Luke Patton, User Experience Designer; (212) 254-2390; internships@dosomething.org or lpatton@dosomething.org
Internet: www.dosomething.org/about/internships#user-experience-research-intern
Sponsor: Do Something
19 West 21st Street, 8th Floor
New York, NY 10010

Do Something Web Developer Intern 860

The Do Something Web Developer Intern will expand his/her technology horizons, build products that scale, and get work in front of millions of young people. Primary responsibilities include: expanding and improving functionality of DoSomething.org, which runs primarily on Drupal 7; contributing to the technical leadership of the tech team by introducing new platforms, tools, and techniques; working closely with product owners and fellow engineers to deliver great experiences across multiple digital channels; picking up platforms and technologies in order to use the right tool for the job (RoR, Flask, shell scripting, Wercker, etc.); continuously build the integration (CI) environment through automation and testing; and working with innovative technologies that increase the ways young people take action (including analytics-driven messaging, Mobile SMS & WAP). Compensation includes: a $1,000 stipend or school credit; tons of fun; a great reference letter; and a chance to work in a super fun and positive work environment. Fall, winter, and summer semester internships are available.
Requirements: General requirements include: ability to travel to the New York City office; commitment to working 12 to 15 hours per week for nine to ten weeks; being a self starter – ability to work well alone and with others; passionate about young people making an impact and committed to social change; member of DoSomething.org; love of the DoSomething.org culture and can work with a quirky, close-knit team. Specific requirements include: experience working with PHP, preferably with Drupal CMS; strong understanding of HTML, CSS, JavaScript; an interest in building things for social good; and familiarity with version control (Do Something uses Github).
Geographic Focus: All States
Amount of Grant: 1,000 USD
Contact: Dave Furnes, Senior Software Engineer; (212) 254-2390; developerintern@dosomething.org or dfurnes@dosomething.org
Internet: www.dosomething.org/about/internships#web-developer-intern
Sponsor: Do Something
19 West 21st Street, 8th Floor
New York, NY 10010

Do Something Writing and Journalism Intern 861

To fill the Writing and Journalism Intern position, the Do Something staff is seeking someone with dynamite writing and research skills, a keen understanding of the DoSomething.org brand and tone, and eagerness to make the world suck less. Responsibilities include: writing and researching new facts pages, and updating existing ones; writing, researching, and editing blog posts about DoSomething.org campaigns for various magazines and sites; maintaining and updating the internal style guide, communications guide, and office glossary; and collaborating with staffers and interns in various departments to create and execute content and marketing strategies. Compensation includes: a $1,000 stipend or school credit; tons of fun; a great reference letter; and a chance to work in a super fun and positive work environment. Fall, winter, and summer semester internships are available.
Requirements: General requirements include: ability to travel to the New York City office; commitment to working 12 to 15 hours per week for nine to ten weeks; being a self starter – ability to work well alone and with others; passionate about young people making an impact and committed to social change; member of DoSomething.org; love of the DoSomething.org culture and can work with a quirky, close-knit team. Specific requirements include: strong writing and research skills; passion for social justice; deep knowledge of pop culture and the latest in the media and social issues; and diligence, and an insanely positive attitude.
Geographic Focus: All States
Amount of Grant: 1,000 USD
Contact: Ben Kassoy, Managing Editor; (212) 254-2390; bkassoy@dosomething.org or internships@dosomething.org
Internet: www.dosomething.org/about/internships#writing-and-journalism-intern
Sponsor: Do Something
19 West 21st Street, 8th Floor
New York, NY 10010

Dr. and Mrs. Paul Pierce Memorial Foundation Grants 862

The Dr. and Mrs. Paul Pierce Memorial Foundation was established in 1963 to support and promote quality education, human services and health care programming for underserved populations. Special consideration is given to charitable organizations that serve the people of Grayson County, Texas. Grants from the Pierce Memorial Foundation are 1 year in duration. Award amounts typically range from $1,000 to $25,000. Applications are accepted twice annually.
Requirements: Applicants must have 501(c)3 tax-exempt status and serve the people of Grayson County, Texas. Applications will be submitted online through the Bank of America website. A grant report is required within 1 year of the grant application date, regardless of whether all of the funds have been spent.

Restrictions: The foundation does not support requests from individuals, organizations attempting to influence policy through direct lobbying, or any political campaigns.
Geographic Focus: Texas
Date(s) Application is Due: Jan 1; Aug 1
Amount of Grant: 1,000 - 25,000 USD
Samples: Grayson County Womens Crisis Line Inc., Sherman, Texas, $10,000 - Awarded for Youth Evolution (2018); House Of Eli Inc., Sherman, Texas, $10,000 - Awarded for general operations of the organization (2018); New Beginning Fellowship Church, Denison, Texas, $19,000 - Awarded to purchase food (2018).
Contact: Kelly Garlock, Philanthropic Client Manager; (800) 357-7094; tx.philanthropic@bankofamerica.com or tx.philanthropic@ustrust.com
Internet: www.bankofamerica.com/philanthropic/foundation/?fnId=91
Sponsor: Dr. and Mrs. Paul Pierce Memorial Foundation
P.O. Box 831041
Dallas, TX 75283-1041

Dr. John T. Macdonald Foundation Grants 863

The Dr. John T. Macdonald Foundation awards grants to eligible Florida nonprofit organizations in Miami-Dade County for medical and health-related programs to community-based programs, with priority given to those serving children, youth, and economically disadvantaged individuals. The foundation supports medical rehabilitation, disease prevention, and health education. Types of support include capital grants, matching/challenge grants, program development grants, seed money grants, and training grants. Deadline listed is for letters of intent; full proposals are by request. Annual deadline dates may vary; contact program staff for exact dates.
Requirements: Florida nonprofit organizations serving the health care needs of people in Miami-Dade County are eligible. Priority will be given to projects in the Coral Gables community.
Restrictions: Grants do not support national projects, multiyear funding requests, for-profit organizations, political candidates or campaigns, religious projects, individuals, or other grantmaking foundations.
Geographic Focus: Florida
Amount of Grant: Up to 550,000 USD
Samples: University of Miami-School of Medicine, Coral Gables, Florida, $526,000 - promotion of healthcare; Biscayne Research Group, Miami Beach, Florida, $12,000 - promotion of healthcare; Open Door Health Center, Homestead, Florida, $37,500 - promotion of healthcare.
Contact: Kim Greene; (305) 667-6017; fax (305) 667-9135; kgreene@jtmacdonaldfdn.org
Internet: jtmacdonaldfdn.org/grants/grants-scholarships/
Sponsor: Dr. John T. Macdonald Foundation
1550 Madruga Avenue, Suite 215
Coral Gables, FL 33146

Draper Richards Kaplan Foundation Grants 864

The Draper Richards Kaplan Foundation awards three-year grants to selected social entrepreneurs to start new nonprofit organizations that are based in the U.S. but national or global in scope with broad social impact. Selected projects will demonstrate innovative ways to solve existing social problems. The Foundation offers financial support as well as strategic and organizational assistance. Proposals are accepted at any time. Examples of previously funded projects are located on the website.
Requirements: Experienced, dedicated social entrepreneurs with a developed idea for a U.S. nonprofit organization are invited to apply. Proposals are accepted for organizations at the beginning of their development. Organizations are usually 0-3 years old and the entrepreneur is prepared to execute an ambitious plan.
Restrictions: The Foundation does not fund local community-based organizations; research; scholarships; think tanks; conferences or one-time events; organizations planning to influence policy through lobbying; or programs promoting religious doctrine.
Geographic Focus: All States
Amount of Grant: 300,000 USD
Contact: Jenny Shilling Stein; (650) 319-7808; fax (650) 323-4060; info@draperrichards.org
Internet: www.drkfoundation.org/what-we-fund.html
Sponsor: Draper Richards Kaplan Foundation
1600 El Camino Road
Menlo Park, CA 94025

Dream Weaver Foundation 865

Established in 2000 in Georgia, the Dream Weaver Foundation offers grant funding primarily in Georgia and Florida. Its major fields of interest include: animals and wildlife; children and youth; the environment; family services; education (all levels); public affairs; religion; and human services. Funding is either directed at general operating costs or specific program development. Target groups include: academics; children and youth; economically disadvantaged; low-income; people with disabilities; and students. There is no formal application required, so interested parties should offer a proposal in the form of a two- or three-page letter. This format should be comprised of a general project description, the needed budgetary allowance, and copies of tax-free status letters. There are no specified annual deadlines. Most recently, grants have ranged from $1,000 to $5,000.
Requirements: 501(c)3 organizations from Georgia and Florida, or these supporting residents of these two states, are eligible to apply.
Restrictions: No grants are given to individuals
Geographic Focus: Florida, Georgia
Amount of Grant: 1,000 - 5,000 USD
Samples: New Horizons Services, Orange City, Florida, $2,000 - general welfare of dogs; The Place of Forsyth County, Cumming, Georgia, $4,000 - general operating costs; Stonecreek Church, Milton, Georgia, $1,000 - general operating costs.

Contact: Charles E. Weaver, President; (770) 781-2823 or (770) 889-2599
Sponsor: Dream Weaver Foundation
6315 Holland Drive
Cumming, GA 30041-4639

DTE Energy Foundation Community Development Grants 866

The foundation supports the principle that locally directed physical and economic development is a uniquely powerful tool for community and neighborhood revitalization. The foundation lends support to nonprofit organizations that spur commercial development or collaborate to develop affordable housing transforming distressed neighborhoods into healthy communities. Examples of projects include: nonprofit commercial development within core utility service areas or in support of DTE Energy Resources development projects; pre-development costs associated with environmental assessment and cleanup; and collaborative funding efforts in support of affordable housing initiatives. Grant amounts generally range from $500 to $150,000, and the application process is distinct for each of the following ranges: $500 to $2,000; $2,001 to $10,000; and any amount greater than $10,000. Applications must be submitted electronically by the stated deadlines.
Requirements: Eligible applicants must meet all of the following criteria: be located in or provide services to a community in which DTE Energy does business; and be a nonprofit (i.e. be exempt for federal income tax under section 501(c)3 of the Internal Revenue Code and not a private foundation, as defined in Section 509(a) of the Code).
Restrictions: The foundation does not provide support to: individuals; political parties; organizations or activities; religious organizations for religious purposes; organizations that are not able to demonstrate commitment to equality and diversity; student group trips; national or international organizations, unless they are providing benefits directly to our service-area residents; projects that may result in undue personal benefit to a member of the DTE Energy Foundation board, or to any DTE Energy employee; conferences unless they are aligned with DTE Energy's business interests; single purpose health organizations; and hospitals, for building or equipment needs.
Geographic Focus: Michigan
Date(s) Application is Due: Apr 13; Jul 13; Oct 12; Dec 28
Amount of Grant: 500 - 150,000 USD
Samples: The Nature Conservancy, Lansing, Michigan, $100,000 - general operating costs; Michigan Thanksgiving Parade Foundation. Detroit, Michigan, $100,000 - general operating costs; City Connect Detroit, Detroit, Michigan, $130,000 - general planning costs.
Contact: Karla D. Hall; (313) 235-9271 or (313) 235-9416; foundation@dteenergy.com
Internet: www.dteenergy.com/dteEnergyCompany/community/foundation/whatWeSupport.html
Sponsor: DTE Energy Foundation
One Energy Plaza, 1046 WBC
Detroit, MI 48226-1279

DTE Energy Foundation Diversity Grants 867

The foundation recognizes that the workplace, the community and the DTE Energy region encompasses a broad mix of individuals with diverse backgrounds, cultures and experiences. Learning to embrace these differences, recognizing their inherent strengths and working together are essential to building strong communities. Diversity grants focus on programs and organizations that promote personal understanding and inclusiveness. The Foundation focus is on programs and organizations that: enhance and promote understanding and inclusiveness by individuals; encourage and advocate for effective, positive change; and celebrate and enhance awareness of different cultures. Grant amounts generally range from $500 to $150,000, and the application process is distinct for each of the following ranges: $500 to $2,000; $2,001 to $10,000; and any amount greater than $10,000. Applications must be submitted electronically by the stated deadlines.
Requirements: Eligible applicants must meet all of the following criteria: be located in or provide services to a community in which DTE Energy does business; and be a nonprofit (i.e. be exempt for federal income tax under section 501(c)3 of the Internal Revenue Code and not a private foundation, as defined in Section 509(a) of the Code).
Restrictions: The foundation does not support: individuals; political parties, organizations or activities; religious organizations for religious purposes; organizations that are not able to demonstrate commitment to equality and diversity; student group trips; national or international organizations, unless they are providing benefits directly to our service-area residents; projects that may result in undue personal benefit to a member of the DTE Energy Foundation board, or to any DTE Energy employee; conferences unless they are aligned with DTE Energy's business interests; single purpose health organizations; and hospitals, for building or equipment needs.
Geographic Focus: Michigan
Date(s) Application is Due: Apr 13; Jul 13; Oct 12; Dec 28
Amount of Grant: 500 - 150,000 USD
Contact: Karla D. Hall; (313) 235-9271 or (313) 235-9416; foundation@dteenergy.com
Internet: www.dteenergy.com/dteEnergyCompany/community/foundation/whatWeSupport.html
Sponsor: DTE Energy Foundation
One Energy Plaza, 1046 WBC
Detroit, MI 48226-1279

DTE Energy Foundation Environmental Grants 868

The DTE Energy Foundation believes economic development and environmental protection are not mutually exclusive. Environmental grants focus on organizations and programs that: protect and restore the environment and enhance the quality of life in the communities that we serve or are home to our facilities; and build understanding of the environment and promote an understanding of the links between environmental stewardship and sustainable development, including education about renewable energy and energy efficiency, that reaches a broad audience. Grant amounts range from $500 to $100,000, and the application process is distinct for each of the following ranges: $500 to

$2,000; $2,001 to $10,000; and any amount greater than $10,000. Applications must be submitted electronically by the stated deadlines.
Requirements: Eligible applicants must meet all of the following criteria: be located in or provide services to a community in which DTE Energy does business; and be a nonprofit (i.e. be exempt for federal income tax under section 501(c)3 of the Internal Revenue Code and not a private foundation, as defined in Section 509(a) of the Code).
Restrictions: The foundation does not provide support to: individuals; political parties, organizations or activities; religious organizations for religious purposes; organizations that are not able to demonstrate commitment to equality and diversity; student group trips; national or international organizations, unless they are providing benefits directly to our service-area residents; projects that may result in undue personal benefit to a member of the DTE Energy Foundation board, or to any DTE Energy employee; conferences unless they are aligned with DTE Energy's business interests; single purpose health organizations; or hospitals, for building or equipment needs.
Geographic Focus: Michigan
Date(s) Application is Due: Apr 13; Jul 13; Oct 12; Dec 28
Amount of Grant: 500 - 100,000 USD
Contact: Karla D. Hall; (313) 235-9271 or (313) 235-9416; foundation@dteenergy.com
Internet: www.dteenergy.com/dteEnergyCompany/community/foundation/whatWeSupport.html
Sponsor: DTE Energy Foundation
One Energy Plaza, 1046 WBC
Detroit, MI 48226-1279

DTE Energy Foundation Health and Human Services Grants 869

The DTE Energy Foundation is at the core of DTE Energy's commitment to the communities and customers it is privileged to serve. The DTE Energy Foundation is dedicated to strengthening the health and human services sector of these communities. Priority will be given to supporting organizations that are in the forefront of addressing the critical, acute human needs brought on by the economic downturn. Grant amounts generally range from $500 to $100,000, and the application process is distinct for each of the following ranges: $500 to $2,000; $2,001 to $10,000; and any amount greater than $10,000. Applications must be submitted electronically by the stated deadlines.
Requirements: Eligible applicants must meet all of the following criteria: be located in or provide services to a community in which DTE Energy does business; and be a nonprofit (i.e. be exempt for federal income tax under section 501(c)3 of the Internal Revenue Code and not a private foundation, as defined in Section 509(a) of the Code).
Restrictions: The Foundation does not provide support to: individuals; political parties, organizations or activities; religious organizations for religious purposes; organizations that are not able to demonstrate commitment to equality and diversity; student group trips; national or international organizations, unless they are providing benefits directly to our service-area residents; projects that may result in undue personal benefit to a member of the DTE Energy Foundation board, or to any DTE Energy employee; conferences unless they are aligned with DTE Energy's business interests; single purpose health organizations; hospitals, for building or equipment needs.
Geographic Focus: Michigan
Date(s) Application is Due: Apr 13; Jul 13; Oct 12; Dec 28
Amount of Grant: 500 - 100,000 USD
Samples: Center for Autism, Ann Arbor, Michigan, $100,000 - general operating support; Girl Scouts of Southeastern Michigan, Detroit, Michigan, $75,000 - general operating costs; Forgotten Harvest, Oak Park, Michigan, $60,000 - general operating costs.
Contact: Karla D. Hall; (313) 235-9271 or (313) 235-9416; foundation@dteenergy.com
Sponsor: DTE Energy Foundation
One Energy Plaza, 1046 WBC
Detroit, MI 48226-1279

DTE Energy Foundation Leadership Grants 870

The foundation believes that leadership encompasses activity on two planes; personal and institutional. In the interest of building thriving communities, the foundation will place special emphasis on programs that promote and nurture leadership traits in young people. In addition, vibrant communities also benefit from the efforts of a core group of institutions dedicated to improving the community's way of life. Foundation focus is on: programs that provide unique experiences to equip individuals with leadership skills; initiatives that improve the strength, stability, sustainability and leadership of the nonprofit sector; and core institutions important to the quality of life in DTE Energy communities. Grant amounts generally range from $500 to $75,000, and the application process is distinct for each of the following ranges: $500 to $2,000; $2,001 to $10,000; and any amount greater than $10,000. Applications must be submitted electronically by the stated deadlines.
Requirements: Eligible applicants must meet all of the following criteria: be located in or provide services to a community in which DTE Energy does business; and be a nonprofit (i.e. be exempt for federal income tax under section 501(c)3 of the Internal Revenue Code and not a private foundation, as defined in Section 509(a) of the Code).
Restrictions: The foundation does not provide support to: individuals; political parties, organizations or activities; religious organizations for religious purposes; organizations that are not able to demonstrate commitment to equality and diversity; student group trips; national or international organizations, unless they are providing benefits directly to our service-area residents; projects that may result in undue personal benefit to a member of the DTE Energy Foundation board, or to any DTE Energy employee; conferences unless they are aligned with DTE Energy's business interests; single purpose health organizations; and hospitals, for building or equipment needs.
Geographic Focus: Michigan
Date(s) Application is Due: Apr 13; Jul 13; Oct 12; Dec 28
Amount of Grant: 500 - 100,000 USD
Contact: Karla D. Hall; (313) 235-9271 or (313) 235-9416; foundation@dteenergy.com
Internet: www.dteenergy.com/dteEnergyCompany/community/foundation/whatWeSupport.html

Sponsor: DTE Energy Foundation
One Energy Plaza, 1046 WBC
Detroit, MI 48226-1279

Dubois County Community Foundation Grants 871

The central purpose of the community foundation is to serve the needs of Dubois County, Indiana, and the philanthropic aims of donors who wish to better their community. The Foundation's fields of interest are: arts, education, environment, beautification programs, health care, human services, recreation, and youth development. Evaluation is based on the project's feasibility, soundness of its implementation plan, viability of subsequent long-term financing, and fulfillment of community need.

Requirements: Organizations should complete the applicant form, agreement, and certification available at the website. Notification of the Board's decision is made approximately four months after the submission deadline.

Restrictions: Giving is concentrated to Dubois County, Indiana. No support is available for the operational expenses of government units or agencies. No grants for operating expenses of nonprofits, funding after the fact, annual fund raising, sponsorship of events, debt retirement, or loans.

Geographic Focus: Indiana
Date(s) Application is Due: Sep 15
Contact: Brad Ward, Chief Executive Officer; (812) 482-5295; fax (812) 482-7461
Internet: www.dccommunityfoundation.org/funds/
Sponsor: Dubois County Community Foundation
600 McCrillus Street, P.O. Box 269
Jasper, IN 47547-0269

Duke Energy Foundation Local Impact Grants 872

The Duke Energy Foundation, along with employee and retiree volunteers, actively works to improve the quality of life in its communities, lending expertise in the form of leadership and financial support through grants to charitable organizations. The Foundation gives primarily in areas of company operations in Indiana, Kentucky, North Carolina, Ohio, Florida, and South Carolina. These are grants $10,000 and under that address one of our designated strategic initiatives and Power for Students. The application is accepted on a rolling-basis.

Requirements: Organizations must: have current tax-exempt status as a public charity under Section 501(c)3 of the United States Internal Revenue Code, be a governmental entity, including school systems; Serve communities that are also served by Duke Energy; serve communities without discrimination against any individual on the basis of race, creed, gender, gender identity, age, sexual orientation or national origin; and have a method by which to measure, track and report one or more program outcomes and specific results that demonstrate measurable community impact.

Restrictions: Foundation grant support is not available for: churches or evangelical organizations; organizations with a substantial purpose of influencing any political, legislative or regulatory cause; fraternal, veteran or labor membership organizations serving only the members of that organization; organizations offering or providing either Duke Energy Corporation, the Duke Energy Foundation, or their respective officers or employees any benefit from the grant; nonprofit organizations that are opposing or intervening parties (or that fund any such parties) in any proceeding in which Duke Energy is a party, or that fund or produce negative advertisements against Duke Energy; individual schools or organizations that operate within an individual school. We will consider school grants at the district level; sports teams or events, with the exception of Power for Students; religious programs, projects or activities; direct cost reduction for electric or natural gas service provided by Duke Energy; external fundraising campaigns or events; general operating expenses; capital investments and improvements; and endowments or other foundations.

Geographic Focus: Florida, Indiana, Kentucky, North Carolina, Ohio, South Carolina
Amount of Grant: Up to 10,000 USD
Contact: Michelle Abbott; (704) 382-7130 or (704) 382-7200; fax (704) 382-7600
Internet: www.duke-energy.com/community/duke-energy-foundation/local-impact
Sponsor: Duke Energy Foundation
526 S Church Street
Charlotte, NC 28201-1007

Dunspaugh-Dalton Foundation Grants 873

Since 1963, the Dunspaugh-Dalton Foundation, Inc. (DDF) has assisted qualifying, exempt 501(c)3 organizations in achieving charitable goals. The Foundation awards grants to eligible nonprofit organizations in the areas of higher, secondary, and elementary education; cpmmunity development; social services; youth services and programs; health associations and hospitals; cultural programs; and civic affairs. Types of support include capital campaigns, continuing support, endowment funds, matching funds, operating support, professorships, and special projects. There are no annual deadlines. The board meets monthly to consider requests.

Requirements: U.S. nonprofit organizations are eligible. The foundation primarily supports programs in California, Florida, and North Carolina.
Restrictions: Individuals are not eligible.
Geographic Focus: California, Florida, North Carolina
Amount of Grant: 5,000 - 50,000 USD
Contact: Sarah Lane Bonner; (305) 668-4192; fax (305) 668-4247; ddf@dunspaughdalton.org
Internet: www.dunspaughdalton.org/application-process.html
Sponsor: Dunspaugh-Dalton Foundation
1500 San Remo Avenue, Suite 103
Coral Gables, FL 33146

Dyson Foundation Mid-Hudson Valley Project Support Grants 874

In 2009 the Dyson Foundation changed its grantmaking priorities to best support the people and communities in its region most vulnerable to the economic downturn. The Foundation's funding now focuses on organizations and activities that address basic needs such as food, housing, health care, and other human services. In limited circumstances, it will also make grants to faith-based organizations, government entities and libraries. The Foundation will also consider limited funding to arts organizations or projects that provide management support or training to other arts organizations, and to arts organizations or projects that can demonstrate the potential to increase local tourism and employment and/or other local economic development as a result of their efforts. Note that there are separate guidelines for Dutchess County and for the other Mid-Hudson Valley counties.

Requirements: IRS 501(c)3 nonprofits that support Hudson Valley, New York, and are not classified as foundations under section 509(a)of the code are eligible. The region is defined as Columbia, Dutchess, Greene, Orange, Putnam, and Ulster counties. Occasionally the foundation awards grants to fiscal sponsors of non-qualifying organizations.

Restrictions: The Foundation is not currently funding certain areas including: the environment, historic preservation, and capital projects. Grants do not support: individuals for any purpose; dinners, fund raising events, tickets, or benefit advertising; direct mail campaigns; service clubs and similar organizations; debt or deficit reduction; governmental units; or international projects or to organizations outside of the United States.

Geographic Focus: New York
Amount of Grant: 1,000 - 1,000,000 USD
Contact: Diana M. Gurieva, Executive Vice President; (845) 790-6312 or (845) 677-0644; fax (845) 677-0650; dgurieva@dyson.org or info@dyson.org
Jennifer Drake, Grants Program Coordinator; (845) 790-6318 or (845) 677-0644; fax (845) 677-0650; jdrake@dyson.org or info@dyson.org
Internet: www.dysonfoundation.org/grantmaking/project-grants
Sponsor: Dyson Foundation
25 Halcyon Road
Millbrook, NY 12545-9611

E. Clayton and Edith P. Gengras, Jr. Foundation Grants 875

The E. Clayton and Edith P. Gengras, Jr. Foundation was established in Connecticut in 1986, with an interest in supporting arts and culture, Christianity, elementary and secondary education, higher education, and community nonprofits and charities. Types of funding given include general operating support and re-granting programs. Though no annual deadlines have been identified, an application form is required. This application should include: program need, a list of board members, proof of 501(c)3 status, and budgetary needs. Most recent awards have ranged from $100 to $100,000, though the majority are less than $5,000.

Restrictions: No grants are awarded directly to individuals.
Geographic Focus: All States
Amount of Grant: 100 - 100,000 USD
Samples: University of Saint Joseph, West Hartford, Connecticut, $10,000 - general operating support (2019); Connecticut Children's Medical Center, Hartford, Connecticut, $10,000 - general operating support (2019); Boys and Girls Club of Hartford, Hartford, Connecticut, $5,000 - general operating support (2019).
Contact: Edith P. Gengras, President and Director; (860) 289-3461
Sponsor: E. Clayton and Edith P. Gengras, Jr. Foundation
300 Connecticut Boulevard
East Hartford, CT 06108-3065

E.J. Grassmann Trust Grants 876

The E.J. Grassmann Trust awards grants in central Georgia and Union County, New Jersey, in support of higher and secondary education, hospitals and health organizations, historical associations, environmental conservation, and social welfare. Primary fields of interest include: arts; Catholic agencies and churches; elementary and secondary education; the environment; natural resources; health care; higher education; historic preservation; historical societies; hospitals; and human services. Types of support include capital campaigns, building construction and/or renovation, equipment acquisition, and endowment funds. Groups with low administrative costs, that have outside funding, and that encourage self-help are preferred. Grants are awarded in May and November. Written proposals should not be longer than four pages.

Restrictions: Grants are not awarded to individuals or for operating expenses, current scholarship funds, conferences, or workshops.
Geographic Focus: Georgia, New Jersey
Date(s) Application is Due: Apr 20; Oct 15
Amount of Grant: 5,000 - 20,000 USD
Samples: Action Ministries, Atlanta, Georgia, $5,900 - capital fund support; Benedictine Academy, Elizabeth, New Jersey, $11,250 - capital fund support; Greater Newark Conservancy, Newark, New Jersey, $7,500 - capital fund support.
Contact: William V. Engel, Executive Director; (908) 753-2440
Sponsor: E.J. Grassmann Trust
P.O. Box 4470
Warren, NJ 07059-0470

E.L. Wiegand Foundation Grants 877

Established in Nevada in 1982, the Foundation provides grants to develop and strengthen programs and projects in Arizona, California, the District of Columbia, Idaho, Nevada, New York, Oregon, Utah, and Washington. Funding is given to educational institutions in the academic areas of science, business, fine arts, and law; and medicine and health organizations in the areas of heart, eye, and cancer surgery, treatment, and research. The Foundation also considers requests for projects that enrich children, communities, public policy, and the arts. Its primary fields of interest include: arts; biology and life sciences; business education; cancer research; chemistry; elementary education; eye research; heart and circulatory diseases and research; higher education; law school education; medical research and institutes; medical school education; museums; performing arts (music and theater); physics; public affairs; secondary education; and visual arts. Grants for educational equipment, including computers and scientific supplies, are also awarded. The board of trustees meets in February, June, and October to choose recipients, but applications may be submitted at any time. Application guidelines are available upon request.

Requirements: Nonprofit organizations in Arizona, California, District of Columbia, Idaho, Nevada, New York, Oregon, Utah, and Washington State are eligible.

Restrictions: Institutions are to be in existence a minimum of five years. Proposals for endowment, debt reduction, ordinary operations, general fund raising, emergency funding, multi-year funding, productions of documentaries, films or media presentations, direct or indirect loans, or for the benefit of specific individuals are excluded from consideration. The Foundation does not award grants to government agencies or to charitable institutions which derive significant support from public tax-funds or United Way.

Geographic Focus: Arizona, California, District of Columbia, Idaho, Nevada, New York, Oregon, Utah, Washington

Amount of Grant: 10,000 - 200,000 USD

Samples: Nevada Museum of Art, Reno, Nevada, $89,000 - exhibit development and support; American Enterprise Institute, Washington, D.C., $500,829 - capital campaign in support of a communications center; Saint Albert the Great School, Reno, Nevada, $500,000 - expansion project.

Contact: Kristen A. Avansino, Executive Director; (775) 333-0310; fax (775) 333-0314

Sponsor: E.L. Wiegand Foundation

165 W Liberty Street, Suite 200

Reno, NV 89501-2902

Earl and Maxine Claussen Trust Grants 878

The Earl and Maxine Claussen Trust was established in 1984. In 1943 Earl Claussen entered the U.S. Navy and served on the Aircraft Carrier Natoma Bay until 1945. In 1947, Earl joined his father and brothers in their successful contracting business, John Claussen Sons General Contractors. The youngest brother of four children, Earl was shortly named president of the company. Earl passed away in 1984, and by 1986, his legacy was beginning to take shape. Always civic-minded, Earl and Maxine had directed their attorney to set up a trust with the assets of their estate which would continue to give back to the community beyond their lifetimes. The Earl and Maxine Claussen Trust began with $780,000 from the estate. Since 1986, the Claussen Trust has given more than $700,000 in grants to numerous non-profit organizations in Grand Island and Hall County. Some of the projects and institutions that the Trust has awarded grants to are Stuhr Museum, Senior High's Best Seats in the House Bleacher Campaign, Crane Meadows Nature Center, the YMCA, College Park, the City of Grand Island for purchase of park land, Grand Island Soccer Club for constructing soccer fields at Fonner Park, and the Edith Abbott Memorial Library for busts of the Abbott Sisters. Though there are no geographic limitations, it was the Claussen's desire to assist the residents of the Grand Island, Nebraska, metropolitan area, which includes Hall, Merrick and Howard counties. Today, the Trust's primary areas of interest include: religion; public and society benefit; human services; health; the environment; animal care; elementary and secondary education; and arts, culture and humanities. The average range of funding is $1,000 to $5,000, with approximately eight awards given each year. The annual deadline for application submission is November 30.

Requirements: Grantees must be qualified as public charities under IRS section 501(c)3. Applications must be submitted through the online grant application form or alternative accessible application designed for assistive technology users.

Geographic Focus: Nebraska

Date(s) Application is Due: Nov 30

Amount of Grant: 1,000 - 5,000 USD

Contact: George Weaver, Special Trustee; (888) 234-1999; fax (877) 746-5889; grantadministration@wellsfargo.com

Internet: www.wellsfargo.com/private-foundations/claussen-trust

Sponsor: Earl and Maxine Claussen Trust

1740 Broadway

Denver, CO 80274

Earth Island Institute Brower Youth Awards 879

Earth Island Institute established The Brower Youth Award for Environmental Leadership in 2000 to honor renowned environmental advocate David Brower. David Brower was quoted as saying, "I love to see what young people can do, before someone old tells them it's impossible." It is with this spirit that the Earth Island Institute recognizes the outstanding leadership efforts of young people who are working for the protection of our shared planet. The Institute elevates the accomplishments of these new leaders and invests in their continued success by providing ongoing access to resources, mentors, and opportunities to develop leadership skills. Completed applications must be submitted online by May 13.

Requirements: Eligibility includes anyone aged 13-22 who is a resident of the United States or Puerto Rico and has shown leadership and produced results in at least one of the following areas: conservation—reducing the negative impacts of the use of natural resources; preservation—saving places, plants, animals, cultures, and Earth-friendly traditions that cannot be replaced if they are destroyed; and restoration—repairing damaged land and water so that it can function ecologically and support the health of human communities and/or native wildlife populations.

Geographic Focus: All States

Date(s) Application is Due: May 13

Amount of Grant: 3,000 USD

Contact: Sanjay Gupta; (510) 859-9100; fax (510) 859-9091; sanjay@earthisland.org

Internet: www.broweryouthawards.org/article.php?list=type&type=54

Sponsor: Earth Island Institute

2150 Allston Way, Suite 460

Berkley, CA 94704-1375

Eastern Bank Charitable Foundation Neighborhood Support Grants 880

The primary mission of the Eastern Bank Charitable Foundation is to contribute, in a meaningful way, to the health and vitality of the various eastern Massachusetts and southern and coastal New Hampshire communities. In the area of Neighborhood Support grants, funding supports organizations within any community served by the bank that does not have 501(c)3 designation. Typically this includes fundraisers, local youth-related activities, chamber of commerce events and other efforts that improve the fabric of our neighborhoods. There is no minimum or maximum dollar value for support in this category, but the average gift is $500. Requests are reviewed on a monthly basis, with notification coming with sixty days of the online submission.

Requirements: Organizations without a 501(c)3 designation operating in northeastern Massachusetts communities served by Eastern Bank are eligible for funding.

Restrictions: The Foundation will not make multi-year commitments regardless of the grant category.

Geographic Focus: Massachusetts

Amount of Grant: Up to 2,500 USD

Samples: Angel Fund, Wakefield, Massachusetts, $1,000 - general program support; Brockton Neighborhood Health Center, Brockton, Massachusetts, $2,500 - general program support; Building Impact, Boston, Massachusetts, $1,000 - neighborhood improvement.

Contact: Laura Kurzrok, Executive Director; (781) 598-7530 or (781)-598-7888; lkurzrok@easternbank.com or foundation@easternbank.com

Internet: www.easternbank.com/site/about_us/community_involvement/Pages/charitable_foundation.aspx

Sponsor: Eastern Bank Charitable Foundation

195 Market Street, EP5-01

Lynn, MA 01901

Eastern Bank Charitable Foundation Partnerships Grants 881

The primary mission of the Eastern Bank Charitable Foundation is to contribute, in a meaningful way, to the health and vitality of the various eastern Massachusetts and southern and coastal New Hampshire communities. In the area of Partnership grants, funding may be used for program or operating support. The Committee gives preference to requests that fund new projects, initiatives, collaborations or capital expenditures. Primary fields of interest include: violence prevention; human services; healthy families; youth programs; K-12 education; heath care; economic revitalization; workforce development; affordable housing; social justice; and the environment. Online requests must be submitted by April 30, with notification of the Committee's decision being received by the end of November. These grants range from $10,000 to $25,000, with the majority of awarded grants in the $10,000 to $15,000 range.

Requirements: Nonprofit 501(c)3 organizations operating in northeastern Massachusetts communities served by Eastern Bank are eligible for funding.

Restrictions: The Foundation will not make multi-year commitments regardless of the grant category. Recipients of major gifts generally will be considered ineligible to reapply for a major gift for a period of three years. Applicants cannot: have an IRS sub-classification of 509(a)3; or be a private foundation.

Geographic Focus: Massachusetts

Date(s) Application is Due: Apr 30

Amount of Grant: 10,000 - 25,000 USD

Contact: Laura Kurzrok, Executive Director; (781) 598-7530 or (781)-598-7888; lkurzrok@easternbank.com or foundation@easternbank.com

Internet: www.easternbank.com/site/about_us/community_involvement/Pages/charitable_foundation.aspx

Sponsor: Eastern Bank Charitable Foundation

195 Market Street, EP5-01

Lynn, MA 01901

Eastern Bank Charitable Foundation Targeted Grants 882

The primary mission of the Eastern Bank Charitable Foundation is to contribute, in a meaningful way, to the health and vitality of the various eastern Massachusetts and southern and coastal New Hampshire communities. In the area of Targeted grants, funding must fall within the Foundation's highlighted, annual mission category. These grants can be used to support an organization in a variety of ways, but the majority are used as program support, support for a specific project or a capital campaign. Primary fields of interest include: violence prevention; human services; healthy families; youth programs; K-12 education; heath care; economic revitalization; workforce development; affordable housing; social justice; and the environment. Online requests must be submitted by March 30, with notification of the Committee's decision being received by the end of May. These grants range up to a maximum of 10,000.

Requirements: Nonprofit 501(c)3 organizations operating in northeastern Massachusetts communities served by Eastern Bank are eligible for funding.

Restrictions: The Foundation will not make multi-year commitments regardless of the grant category. Recipients of major gifts generally will be considered ineligible to reapply for a major gift for a period of three years. Applicants cannot: have an IRS sub-classification of 509(a)3; or be a private foundation. Receiving a Targeted Grant does not impact eligibility for a Partnership or Community Grant.

Geographic Focus: Massachusetts

Date(s) Application is Due: Mar 30

Amount of Grant: Up to 10,000 USD

Contact: Laura Kurzrok, Executive Director; (781) 598-7530 or (781)-598-7888; lkurzrok@easternbank.com or foundation@easternbank.com

Internet: www.easternbank.com/site/about_us/community_involvement/Pages/charitable_foundation.aspx

Sponsor: Eastern Bank Charitable Foundation
195 Market Street, EP5-01
Lynn, MA 01901

Easton Foundations Archery Facility Grants   883

The Easton Foundations support the development of four levels of archery facilities depending on the level of the planned archery programs and the financial commitment of the applicants: Archery Center of Excellence, Archery Center, Community Archery Facility, or Local Club or Recreation Department Facility. The Foundations' plan is to fund facilities at diversified geographic regional locations to create a strong national archery education and training program. The goal is to develop a large national pool of top archers from which to select future Olympic and World Championship teams.
Requirements: Eligible applicants include 501(c)3 organizations, universities, schools, and state/local governments with a proven record of financial stability. The Foundation will favor applicants with an existing base of local archery activities near a major population center (with several universities within one hour drive) with the potential to expand youth, interscholastic, and collegiate archery participation. Applicants must also have strong community support, financial commitments, and in-kind and/or financial contributions to the project. The Foundation does not fix the percentage that it will provide toward project costs, but the range of contribution has been 10-50% of project cost. The amount of support from the Foundation will vary depending on the capabilities of the proposed facility, quality of the planned high performance archery programs, and the local support all focused to achieve the Foundation goal of developing Olympic-style archery.
Geographic Focus: All States
Contact: Doug Engh, Outreach Director; (818) 787-2800; dengh@esdf.org
Internet: www.esdf.org/archery-facilities/
Sponsor: Easton Foundations
7855 Haskell Avenue, Suite 360
Van Nuys, CA 91406

Easton Sports Development Foundation National Archery in the Schools Grants   884

The Easton Sports Development Foundation created a unique program to promote the sport of archery in our schools. The teaching system was developed by world renowned archery coaches having the highest possible level of international experience including coaching on World and Olympic Teams. For a limited time, the program will provide all necessary equipment and professional training to the teachers and school. The Foundations' funding supports archery, youth baseball, softball and cycling, as well as education and medical research.
Requirements: Schools and nonprofit organizations are eligible to apply. Applications must be made through your local state representative (see www.nasparchery.com). Please note that the grant deadlines of September 1 and March 1 only apply to grants that are for $25,000 or more. If your request is for less than $25,000 you can submit it at any time.
Restrictions: In general, for-profit and private sector applicants are not eligible for a grant even though they are doing work that meets the Foundation's objectives.
Geographic Focus: All States
Date(s) Application is Due: Mar 1; Sep 1
Contact: Idida Briones, Programs Administrative Assistant / Grant Administrator; (818) 787-2800 ex. 202; ibriones@esdf.org
Internet: www.esdf.org/apply-for-grant/
Sponsor: Easton Foundations
7855 Haskell Avenue, Suite 360
Van Nuys, CA 91406

Echoing Green Fellowships   885

The program awards full-time fellowships to emerging entrepreneurs to create innovative domestic or international public service projects that seek to catalyze positive social change. The proposed project may be in any public service area, including but not limited to, the environment, arts, education, health, youth service and development, civil and human rights, and community and economic development. The fellowship provides a two-year stipend, health care benefits, online connectivity, access to Echoing Green's network of social entrepreneurs, training, and technical assistance.
Requirements: Applicants must be at least 18 years old and commit to leading the project for at least two years. Partnerships of up to two individuals also are eligible.
Restrictions: Faith-based, research projects, and lobbying activities are not eligible.
Geographic Focus: All States
Date(s) Application is Due: Dec 2
Amount of Grant: 60,000 - 90,000 USD
Contact: Rich Leimsider, Director of Fellow and Alumni Programs; (212) 689-1165; fax (212) 689-9010; Rich@echoinggreen.org or apply@echoinggreen.org
Internet: www.echoinggreen.org/fellowship
Sponsor: Echoing Green Foundation
494 Eighth Avenue, Second Floor
New York, NY 10001

Edna Wardlaw Charitable Trust Grants   886

The Edna Wardlaw Charitable Trust awards general operating grants nationwide to nonprofit organizations in its areas of interest, including: children and youth services; community funds; cultural programs; human services; environmental and natural resources; conservation; health and hospitals; homelessness; international peace; and reproductive health. A formal application is not required, and the annual deadline is June 15. Grants typically range from $1,000 to $20,000.
Geographic Focus: All States
Date(s) Application is Due: Jun 15
Amount of Grant: 1,000 - 20,000 USD

Contact: Gregorie Guthrie, Secretary; (404) 419-3260 or (404) 827-6529
Sponsor: Edna Wardlaw Charitable Trust
One Riverside Building
Atlanta, GA 30327

Edward and Ellen Roche Relief Foundation Grants   887

The Edward and Ellen Roche Relief Foundation was established in 1953 to support organizations serving disadvantaged women and children. Funding will be provided to nonprofits that specifically help ensure the well-being and self-sufficiency of low-income women and their families. Recognizing the diverse array of programs that serve these populations, the Roche Relief Foundation has chosen to focus its limited resources on programs that serve unemployed or underemployed women. Organizations that provide job training and placement will be prioritized. Award amounts range between $5,000 and $30,000.
Requirements: Applicants must have 501(c)3 tax-exempt status and serve the residents of New York City. Applications will be submitted online through the Bank of America website. A grant report is required within 1 year of the grant application date, regardless of whether all of the funds have been spent.
Restrictions: The Roche Relief Foundation generally does not provide funding for projects in the areas of health care or disabilities, to individual schools or child care centers; or to organizations with annual budgets in excess of $10 million. In general, grant requests for endowment campaigns, capital projects, or research will not be considered. The foundation does not support requests from individuals, organizations attempting to influence policy through direct lobbying, or any political campaigns.
Geographic Focus: New York
Date(s) Application is Due: Jun 30
Amount of Grant: 5,000 - 30,000 USD
Samples: New York Women's Foundation, New York City, New York, $30,000 - Awarded for Women's Economic Security and Workforce Development Initiative (2018); Sanctuary of Families, New York City, New York, $30,000 - Awarded for Economic Empowerment Program (EEP) (2018); Community Voices Heard Inc., New York City, New York, $25,000 - Awarded for Advocating and Monitoring Job Creation for NYCHA residents (2018).
Contact: Christine O'Donnell, Philanthropic Client Manager; (646) 855-1011 or (888) 866-3275; ny.grantmaking@bankofamerica.com or christine.l.odonnell@bofa.com
Internet: www.bankofamerica.com/philanthropic/foundation/?fnId=64
Sponsor: Edward and Ellen Roche Relief Foundation
1 Bryant Park, NY1-100-28-05
New York, NY 10036-6715

Edward and Helen Bartlett Foundation Grants   888

Established by a single donor, Edward E, Bartlett, in Oklahoma in 1961, the Foundation primarily offers grant support for: education, particularly public schools; community programs and services; health care; children and youth; and social services. There are no specific application forms or deadlines with which to adhere, and applicants should begin by forwarding a letter of application to the contact listed. In the recent past, grant amounts have ranged between $5,000 to $150,000.
Requirements: Preference id given to non-profit 501(c)3 organizations located in, or serving the residents of, Oklahoma.
Restrictions: No grants are to individuals directly.
Geographic Focus: Oklahoma
Amount of Grant: 5,000 - 150,000 USD
Samples: Clarehouse, Tulsa, Oklahoma, $150,000; Creek County Literacy Program, Sapulpa, Oklahoma, $30,000; Retired Senior Volunteer Program of Tulsa, Tulsa, Oklahoma, $20,000.
Contact: Bruce A. Currie, (918) 586-5273
Sponsor: Edward and Helen Bartlett Foundation
P.O. Box 3038
Milwaukee, WI 53201-3038

Edward and Romell Ackley Foundation Grants   889

The Edward and Romell Ackley Foundation was established in Oregon in 2003 in support of Portland-based programs. The Foundation's primary areas of interest include: adoption; child welfare; diseases and conditions; human services; philanthropy; special hospital care; and youth development. Awards generally are given for operating support. Most recent grants have ranged from $2,500 to $25,000.
Requirements: Oregon-based 501(c)3 organizations serving the residents of Portland are eligible to apply.
Geographic Focus: Oregon
Amount of Grant: 2,500 - 25,000 USD
Samples: Oregon Children's Foundation, Portland, Oregon, $15,000 - general operating support; Dress for Success Oregon, Portland, Oregon, $15,000 - general operating support; CASA for Children, Portland, Oregon, $21,096 - general operating support.
Contact: Robert H. Depew, Trustee; (503) 464-3580 or (503) 275-6564
Sponsor: Edward and Romell Ackley Foundation
P.O. Box 3168
Portland, OR 97208-3168

Edward F. Swinney Trust Grants   890

The Edward F. Swinney Trust was created under will dated January 5, 1944 to be used for the furtherance and development of such public charitable and public educational purposes in the State of Missouri. Grants from the Foundation are 1 year in duration. Award amounts typically range from $5,000 to $250,000.
Requirements: Grant requests for general operating support and program support will be considered. Applications will be submitted online through the Bank of America website.

A grant report is required within 1 year of the grant application date, regardless of whether all of the funds have been spent.

Restrictions: Grant requests for capital support will not be considered. The fund does not support requests from individuals, organizations attempting to influence policy through direct lobbying, or any political campaigns.

Geographic Focus: Missouri

Date(s) Application is Due: Jun 30

Amount of Grant: 5,000 - 250,000 USD

Samples: Union Station Kansas City Inc., Kansas City, Missouri, $200,000 - Awarded for Early Childhood Learning Expansion Project (2018); Curators Of The University Of Missouri Special Tr, Columbia, Missouri, $170,000 - Awarded for Missouri College Advising Corps: Empowering Kansas City Area Students to Go to College and Succeed (2018); Harvesters Community Food Network, Kansas City, Missouri, $150,000 - Awarded for General operations of the organization (2018).

Contact: Tony Twyman, Senior Philanthropic Client Manager; (816) 292-4342; mo.grantmaking@bankofamerica.com or tony.twyman@bofa.com

Internet: www.bankofamerica.com/philanthropic/foundation/?fnId=170

Sponsor: Edward F. Swinney Trust

P.O. Box 831041

Dallas, TX 75283-1041

Edwards Memorial Trust Grants 891

The Edwards Memorial Trust awards grants to eligible Minnesota nonprofit organizations in support of: health care for people without health insurance or who are under-insured; preventive health care for children; and programs for the disabled. Areas of support include health care and hospitals, mental health crisis services, social services, children and youth, and the disabled. Types of support include: building construction and renovation; equipment acquisition; general operating grants; and program development. Types of support include: capital campaigns; sustainability;fundraising; general operating support; program development; and re-granting (endowments). Interested parties should begin by contacting the Foundation with a request to apply. A copy of the tax determination letter and most recent audited financial statements must accompany all applications.

Requirements: Minnesota 501(c)3 tax-exempt organizations in the greater Saint Paul area are eligible.

Geographic Focus: Minnesota

Date(s) Application is Due: May 1; Nov 1

Amount of Grant: 2,000 - 50,000 USD

Samples: Regions Hospital Foundation, St. Paul, Minnesota, $100,000 - general operating support; Children's Health Care Foundation, Roseville, Minnesota, $150,000 - general operating support; 180 Degrees, Minneapolis, Minnesota, $150,000 - general operating support.

Contact: Managing Trustee; (651) 466-8731 or (651) 466-8040

Sponsor: Edwards Memorial Trust

P.O. Box 64713, 101 East Fifth Street

Saint Paul, MN 55164-0713

Edward W. and Stella C. Van Houten Memorial Fund Grants 892

Stella C. Van Houten resided in Bergen County, New Jersey. This foundation, providing funding for health and human services, education, education of medical professionals, and the care of children, was established in 1978 in memory of her husband and herself. The Van Houten's had a particular fondness for the Valley Hospital of Ridgewood, New Jersey and for the Rollins College in Florida. The Foundation continues to honor their preferences with grants to these two organizations in addition to grants to other organizations. The Foundation's mission is to: supports agencies, institutions and services in Passaic and Bergen Counties, New Jersey, having to do with the care or cure of sick or disabled persons or for the care of orphaned children or aged persons; educates students in the medical profession; support for educational purposes; support for the care of children. A target of 10% of the grants each year is for medical scholarships.

Requirements: Passaic and Bergen Counties, New Jersey non-profits are eligible to apply. The application form & guidelines are available online at the Wachovia website. The applications must be submitted by January 31 for a March meeting & August 1 for an October meeting.

Geographic Focus: New Jersey

Date(s) Application is Due: Jan 31; Aug 1

Amount of Grant: 6,000 - 100,000 USD

Samples: Therapeutic Learning Center, Ramsey, NJ, $6,000—speech therapy; William Paterson University Foundation, $20,000—scholarships for undergraduate, minority, and/or graduate nursing students; Christian Health Care Center Foundation, $100,000—to build a Great Room at Heritage Manor East.

Contact: Trustee, c/o Wachovia Bank; grantinquiries2@wachovia.com

Internet: www.wellsfargo.com/private-foundations/van-houten-memorial-fund

Sponsor: Edward W. and Suitella C. Van Houten Memorial Fund

190 River Road, NJ3132

Summit, NJ 07901

Edyth Bush Charitable Foundation Grants 893

The Edyth Bush Charitable Foundation is operated exclusively for charitable, religious, literary, and other exempt purposes. Grants ranging from $5,000 to $50,000 are available for challenge and development purposes, construction and renovation, equipment and expansion of functions, pilot projects and seed start-up of new programs, and study or planning grants. The Foundation has broad interests in human service, education, health care, and the arts. Requests for grants or other funds should be submitted in writing. Grant applications are available via invitation only from the Foundation. If an organization feels that it is eligible after reviewing the Policies and Eligibility section, it should begin by sending the Foundation Grants Manager a letter of inquiry stating the amount sought and purpose of the grant, nature of the organization, and the organization's EIN. Once the Foundation determines an interest

in accepting a grant request from an organization, it will receive instructions from the Grants Manager on how to access the appropriate online application form.

Requirements: The Foundation welcomes grant requests from otherwise eligible tax-exempt organizations under IRS Sections 501(c)3 and Section 509(a) headquartered within the Central Florida region.

Restrictions: The Foundation will ordinarily deny grant requests: from chiefly tax-supported institutions, or their support foundations; for individual scholarships or for individual research grants even if through an exempt or otherwise qualified educational organization; for alcoholism or drug abuse programs or facilities; for routine operating expenses; to pay off deficits or pre-existing debt; for foreign organizations or for foreign expenditure; for travel projects or fellowships; for chiefly church, sacramental, denominational or inter-denominational purposes, except outreach projects for elderly, indigents, needy, youth, or homeless regardless of belief, race, color, creed, or sex; for endowment funds or other purely revenue generating funds; advocacy organizations or advocacy component funding; for cultural or arts organizations unless their collections, exhibits, projects or performances are of demonstrated nationally recognized quality; from organizations having receipts of revenues from memberships and/or contributions of less than $25,000 in the previous year, or from any organization whose IRS Sec. 509(a) publicly supported status will need renewal in the next six (6) months.

Geographic Focus: Florida

Amount of Grant: 5,000 - 50,000 USD

Contact: Heidi Findlay, Grants Manager; (888) 647-4322 or (407) 647-4322; fax (407) 647-7716; hfindlay@edythbush.org

Internet: edythbush.org/grants/

Sponsor: Edyth Bush Charitable Foundation

P.O. Box 1967

Winter Park, FL 32790-1967

Effie Allen Little Foundation Grants 894

The Effie Allen Little Foundation was established in North Carolina in 1954, in honor of Effie Lemuel Allen Little. Effie wanted her legacy to support elementary and secondary education, higher education, social services, and youth organizations. Specifically, the Foundation's fields of interest include: arts and culture; basic and emergency assistance; child care; child development; education at all levels; family services; historic preservation; historical activities; human services; religion; scouting; social services; and youth programs. Giving is limited to the geographical region around Anson County, North Carolina. Support typically takes the form of both general operating funds and program development. Awards generally range up to a maximum of $20,000. There are no annual deadlines for application submission.

Requirements: Any 501(c)3 organization supporting the residents of Anson County, North Carolina, is welcome to apply.

Geographic Focus: North Carolina

Amount of Grant: Up to 20,000 USD

Samples: Anson County Board of Education, Wadesboro, North Carolina, $19,500 - general operating support; Anson County Arts Council, Wadesboro, North Carolina, $10,000 - general operating support; First United Methodist Church, Wadesboro, North Carolina, $10,000 - general operating support.

Contact: Effie Little Richert, President; (704) 694-2213 or (704) 954-1125

Sponsor: Effie Allen Little Foundation

P.O. Box 340

Wadesboro, NC 28170

Effie and Wofford Cain Foundation Grants 895

The Effie and Wofford Cain Foundation gives primarily for higher and secondary education, medical research, and public service organizations. Grants also are awarded to religious organizations (Baptist, Christian, Episcopal, Presbyterian, Salvation Army, and United Methodist), and for aid for the handicapped. Additional fields of interest include elementary and secondary education, early childhood development and education, medical school education, nursing school education, hospitals and general health care and health organizations, religious federated giving programs, government and public administration, African Americans, Latinos, the disabled, the aging, and economically disadvantaged and homeless. Types of support include general operating support, continuing support, annual campaigns, capital campaigns, building/renovations, equipment acquisition, endowment funds, program development, seed money, curriculum development, fellowships, internships, scholarship funds, research, and matching funds. Organizations may reapply for funding every other fiscal year.

Requirements: The foundation only makes grants to 501(c)3 tax-exempt organizations in Texas.

Restrictions: Individuals are ineligible.

Geographic Focus: Texas

Amount of Grant: 1,000 - 150,000 USD

Samples: Vuilding Homes for Heroes, Valley Stream, New York, $150,000 - general operating support; Henderson County Food Pantry, Athens, Texas, $25,000 - general operating support; St. Vincent Citizens Nutrition Program, Los Angeles, California, $62,500 - general operating support.

Contact: Frabklin W. Denius, President and Director; (512) 346-7490; fax (512) 346-7491; info@cainfoundation.org

Sponsor: Effie and Wofford Cain Foundation

4131 Spicewood Springs Road, Suite A-1

Austin, TX 78759-7490

Effie Kuhlman Charitable Trust Grants 896

The Effie Kuhlman Charitable Trust was established in Harrison County, Indiana, in 1989, in honor of the death of ninety-year-old Effie Kuhlman. After moving back to Corydon as a retired Ohio school teacher, Effie became a member of the Corydon Presbyterian Church and held a number of positions in that church. Following her death, Effie's trust supported many local programs, including the Red cross and Harrison County Hospital, as well as the Pyoca youth church camp in Brownstown, Indiana. She was a longtime supporter of youth programs and International mission work. Today, the Trust's primary field of interest for support include: child welfare programs; Christianity; diseases; family services; health and health care; hospital care; human services; Methodism; Protestantism; scouting; social services; and youth development. That support typically comes in the form of general operating funding. Most recent awards have ranged from $5,000 to $10,000. There are no annual deadlines for application submission.

Requirements: Any 501(c)3 that supports the residents of Harrison County, Indiana, or Louisville, Kentucky, are welcome to apply.

Geographic Focus: Indiana, Kentucky

Amount of Grant: 5,000 - 10,000 USD

Samples: Corydon United Methodist Church, Corydon, Indiana, $10,000 - general operating support; Harrison County Hospital, Corydon, Indiana, $5,000 - general operating support; Crusade for Children, Louisville, Kentucky, $5,000 - general operating support.

Contact: Harold E. Dillman, Co-Trustee; (812) 738-2100; fax (812) 738-2108

Sponsor: Effie Kuhlman Charitable Trust

P.O. Box 22, 219 North Capitol Avenue, Suite 200

Corydon, IN 47112-0022

Eide Bailly Resourcefullness Awards 897

Eide Bailly believes that money fuels mission. This hard reality is understood by every nonprofit throughout the country. All understand the push and pull between infinite demand and finite resources. Fortunately for the communities that Eide Bailly serves, nonprofits are very inventive. Nonprofit professionals constantly demonstrate passion and creativity and utilize those qualities to create amazing ways to find and sustain the revenue streams needed to fulfill their missions and continually benefit their communities. The Eide Bailly Resourcefullness Award provides recognition and support to 501(c)3 organizations that have undertaken sustainable, creative, and impactful revenue generation initiatives. Apply by July 13 for the chance to be awarded $10,000 or $2,500.

Requirements: Applications are accepted from IRS 501(c)3 organizations serving the residents of Colorado, Arizona, Minnesota, North Dakota, and Utah. These organizations should serve: racial and ethnic minorities; African Americans or Blacks; Alaskan Natives; Asian Americans or Asians; children and youth; the elderly; Hispanics or Latinos; LGBT groups; men and/or boys; migrant/nomadic; Native Hawaiians; other Pacific Islanders; people with disabilities; the poor or unemployed; or women and/or girls.

Geographic Focus: Arizona, Colorado, Minnesota, Utah

Date(s) Application is Due: Jul 13

Amount of Grant: 2,500 - 10,000 USD

Contact: Lindsay Gasp, Marketing Manager; (303) 586-8520; lgast@eidebailly.com

Internet: www.eidebailly.com/resourcefullness

Sponsor: Eide Bailly

5299 DTC Boulevard, Suite 1000

Greenwood Village, CO 80111

Eileen Fisher Activating Leadership Grants for Women and Girls 898

As a socially conscious company, Eileen Fisher is dedicated to supporting women through social initiatives that address their well-being, to guiding our product and process towards sustaining the environment and to practicing business responsibly with absolute regard for human rights. For the current grant cycle, Eileen Fisher will fund programs that activate leadership qualities in women and girls. We are particularly interested in programs that: bring about self-discovery and personal transformation; help women and/or girls find their inner strength and trust their intuition; address any phase of a woman's and/or girl's life. Each year, grants of $5,000 or more are awarded, including grants for general support and seed funding for grassroots organizations. The application process opens on June 3, and all applications must be received no later than 12:00 noon EST of the deadline date.

Requirements: Applications will be accepted from 501(c)3 nonprofits with preference to organizations that: show an innovative, holistic, effective and direct approach to activating leadership among women and/or girls; form partnerships with other community organizations for deeper impact; demonstrate the long-term sustainability and viability of the organization; show a clear need for the funds and a plan for their use; demonstrate a long-term commitment to their work; establish resonance with the Eileen Fisher company mission and leadership practices; and, are located near the Eileen Fisher offices, retail stores or showrooms or, if outside the United States, via U.S.-based charities only. Grants are open to any applying organization, not just those who have received a grant previously.

Geographic Focus: All States

Date(s) Application is Due: Jul 18

Amount of Grant: 5,000 USD

Contact: Cheryl Campbell, Managing Director; (914) 721-4153; ccampbell@eileenfisher.com

Internet: www.eileenfisher.com/EileenFisherCompany/CompanyGeneralContentPages/SocialConciousness/Self_Image.jsp

Sponsor: Eileen Fisher Community Foundation

2 Bridge Street Suite 230

Irvington, NY 10533

Elizabeth Carse Foundation Grants 899

The Elizabeth Carse Foundation was established in 1970 to promote education and child welfare in Connecticut. Special consideration is given to organizations that provide training to elementary and secondary school teachers in "assisting children to achieve better standards of living." Award amounts typically range from $1,000 from $10,000. Grants from the Carse Foundation are 1 year in duration.

Requirements: Applicants must have 501(c)3 tax-exempt status and serve communities in Connecticut. Applications will be submitted online through the Bank of America website.

A grant report is required within 1 year of the grant application date, regardless of whether all of the funds have been spent.

Restrictions: Applicants will not be awarded a grant for more than 3 consecutive years. Grant requests for general operating support or capital projects will not be considered. The foundation does not support requests from individuals, organizations attempting to influence policy through direct lobbying, or any political campaigns.

Geographic Focus: Connecticut

Date(s) Application is Due: Aug 15

Amount of Grant: 1,000 - 10,000 USD

Samples: Children's Law Center Inc., Hartford, Connecticut, $10,000 - Awarded for Legal Representation (2019); Children's Museum Inc., West Hartford, Connecticut, $10,000 - Awarded for Science Achievement For All (2019); Connecticut 4 H Development Fund Inc., Bloomfield, Connecticut, $10,000 - Awarded for Nature on the Go! (2019).

Contact: Amy R. Lynch, Philanthropic Client Manager; (860) 244-4870; ct.grantmaking@bankofamerica.com or amy.r.lynch@bofa.com

Internet: www.bankofamerica.com/philanthropic/foundation/?fnId=51

Sponsor: Elizabeth Carse Foundation

P.O. Box 1802

Providence, RI 02901-1802

Elizabeth Huth Coates Charitable Foundation Grants 900

Elizabeth Maddux was married to oilman George H. Coates from 1943 until his death in 1973. It was said that George provided the means while Elizabeth provided the philanthropic inspiration which she had learned from her parents growing up in San Antonio. A longtime supporter of the arts and education, she established the Elizabeth Huth Coates Charitable Foundation of 1992 to continue her legacy of support within the San Antonio area. The Foundation's primary fields of interest include: the arts; Catholicism; diseases; education; museums; Protestantism; and zoos. Most recently, awards have ranged from $5,000 to $300,000. The annual deadline for online application submission is December 31.

Requirements: Grants are directed to 501(c)3 organizations which fall within the principal charitable purposes of the foundation.

Geographic Focus: Texas

Date(s) Application is Due: Dec 31

Amount of Grant: 5,000 - 300,000 USD

Samples: Ballet San Antonio, San Antonio, Texas, $20,000 - general operating support; Saint Mary's Hall, San Antonio, Texas, $300,000 - general operating support; San Antonio Museum of Art, San Antonio, Texas, $200,000 - general operating support.

Contact: Brian R. Korb, Senior Vice President; (210) 283-6700 or (210) 283-6500; bkorb@broadwaybank.com

Internet: www.broadwaybank.com/wealthmanagement/FoundationElizabethHuthCoates.html

Sponsor: Elizabeth Huth Coates Charitable Foundation

P.O. Box 17001

San Antonio, TX 78217-0001

Elizabeth Morse Genius Charitable Trust Grants 901

The Elizabeth Morse Genius Charitable Trust, established in 1992, practices values-based grant making. The Trust's values statement includes the following: promoting, instilling, and/or reflecting the values of individual and/or organizational thrift, humility, industry, self-sacrifice, and/or self-sufficiency; relieving human suffering by: performing research and/or promoting education regarding the treatment of disease; assisting youth who are from disadvantaged backgrounds, have troubled childhoods, have physical or mental disabilities, or experience emotional disorders; addressing the concerns of the elderly; and/or providing succor to human kind during time of natural or human-made disasters; Developing Individual Self-Esteem and Dignity: developing within individuals, especially youth from under-served and/or under-resourced communities, a sense of self-esteem and dignity; Encouraging Vigorous Athletic Activity: encouraging vigorous athletic activity, leading to physical health and/or spiritual well-being; and Developing Regional Solutions to Chicago's Regional Challenges: developing regional solutions to Chicago's regional challenges, thereby protecting and/or improving the quality of life for all its citizens. The majority of grants from the Genius Charitable Trust are 1 year in duration. On occasion, multi-year support is awarded. Award amounts typically range from $2,000 to $400,000. The Elizabeth Morse Genius Charitable Trust has a rolling application deadline.

Requirements: Nonprofit organizations serving Chicago and Cook County are eligible to apply. Applying to The Elizabeth Morse Genius Charitable Trust for a grant is a two-step process. Applications will be submitted online through the Bank of America website. A grant report is required within 1 year of the grant application date, regardless of whether all of the funds have been spent.

Restrictions: In general, grant requests for endowment campaigns or capital projects will not be considered. The fund does not support requests from individuals, organizations attempting to influence policy through direct lobbying, or any political campaigns.

Geographic Focus: Illinois

Amount of Grant: 2,000 - 400,000 USD

Samples: Chicago Historical Society, Chicago, Illinois, $416,667 - Awarded for Campaign leadership gift; Lyric Opera Chicago, Chicago, Illinois, $250,000 - Awarded for Continuation of Board diversification efforts and the expansion of personnel diversification; Metropolis Strategies, Chicago, Illinois, $100,000 - Awarded for three years for a part-time fundraiser and the programmatic policy agenda concerning youth.

Contact: Srilatha Lakkaraju, Philanthropic Client Manager; (312) 828-8166; ilgrantmaking@bankofamerica.com

Internet: www.bankofamerica.com/philanthropic/foundation/?fnId=116

Sponsor: Elizabeth Morse Genius Charitable Trust

231 South LaSalle Street, IL1-231-13-32

Chicago, IL 60697-0001

Elkhart County Community Foundation Fund for Elkhart County   902

The Fund for Elkhart County is the county's core grant making program and has the broadest guidelines designed to meet the Foundation's mission to produce a brighter future for all people in Elkhart County in Indiana. Grants are awarded from the fund's earnings on a quarterly basis. More than $550,000 has been awarded from this fund to assist non-profits in Elkhart County.

Requirements: The Fund for Elkhart County grants funding to after-school programs, temporary help for abused women and children, and services for the mentally and physically challenged. Other programs include health and dental care for the underprivileged, services for senior citizens, support of local arts and cultural events, environmental and wildlife services, historical preservations, and capacity building. Applicants should carefully review the website's grant guidelines before applying.

Geographic Focus: Indiana
Date(s) Application is Due: Nov 1
Contact: Fund for Elkhart County Contact; (574) 295-8761
Internet: www.elkhartccf.org/File/static/grant_seekers/FundForElkhartCounty.shtml
Sponsor: Elkhart County Community Foundation
101 S Main Street, P.O. Box 2932
Elkhart, IN 46615

Elkhart County Community Foundation Grants   903

The foundation is looking for innovative programs or projects that address community issues in Indiana's Elkhart County. Community collaboration is encouraged, where organizations work together toward a shared goal with shared responsibility, accountability, and resources. Grants are awarded in the areas of arts and culture, community development, education, youth development, board development and succession planning, and health and human services in addition to continuing support, technical assistance, and matching funds. Most grants are single-year awards, although multi-year grants also will be considered. The staff is available for advice in the preparation of a proposal. Applicants are encouraged to read the Foundation website's "Helpful Tips for Grant Writers." Letters of interest are due to the Foundation by January 1, April 1, June 1, and August 1.

Requirements: Elkhart County non-profit organizations, or those seeking such status, and some governmental agencies, such as the public library or public school system, are eligible.
Restrictions: Support generally will not be given for continuing operating costs of established programs, projects, and agencies. The foundation does not offer support for religious or sectarian purposes. No grants are awarded to individuals (other than scholarships), or for operating budgets or budget deficits, annual funds, conferences, scholarly research, endowments, personal travel, or films.
Geographic Focus: Indiana
Date(s) Application is Due: Mar 1; Jun 1; Sep 1; Nov 1
Contact: Jim Siegmann; (574) 295-8761; fax (574) 389-7497; jim@elkhartccf.org
Internet: www.elkhartccf.org/File/static/grant_seekers/WhatWeFund.shtml
Sponsor: Elkhart County Community Foundation
101 S Main Street, P.O. Box 2932
Elkhart, IN 46615

Ella West Freeman Foundation Grants   904

A.B. Freeman founded the Ella West Freeman Foundation in 1941. Freeman, a successful businessman residing in New Orleans named the Foundation in honor of his wife, the former Ella West. Since its founding, the Foundation has provided the Greater New Orleans community with more than $20,000,000 of support for non-profits in the area. In evaluating requests, the Ella West Freeman Foundation gives special consideration to organizations in the Greater New Orleans area. Within the New Orleans area, the Ella West Freeman Foundation supports a variety of programs in the fields of civic affairs, community development, the arts, education and human resources. Priority is given to funding for specific projects or programs incorporating well-defined objectives and timetables and promising broad public benefits. They are usually given for a period of time not exceeding two years. Longer term projects will usually require evaluation for further funding. Capital projects are considered for organizations with strong records of community service. These applications must demonstrate true need for the proposed facility and they must also provide a credible fund-raising plan as well as demonstrate the capacity to maintain the building and facilities once they are in place. The Foundation uses a two stage application process. Stage 1 submission deadlines for Proposal Summary Sheets are January 20 or September 1 at midnight. If invited to submit a full proposal, the deadlines are March 1 and October 15.

Requirements: 501(c)3 organizations supporting residents of New Orleans are eligible to apply.
Restrictions: Sustaining grants to organizations are given a lower priority. Ordinarily, no operating support is considered for organizations supported by community giving campaigns such as the United Way and the Archbishop's Community Appeal. Decisions regarding grants will be made only at regularly scheduled meetings of the trustees which are usually held twice a year in the spring and fall. Interviews will be conducted only at the initiation of the Foundation.
Geographic Focus: Louisiana
Date(s) Application is Due: Mar 1; Oct 15
Amount of Grant: 2,500 - 50,000 USD
Samples: Bastion Community of Resilience, New Orleans, Louisiana, $50,000 - general program support (2018); New Orleans Police and Justice Foundation, New Orleans, Louisiana, $15,000 - general operating support (2018); Start the Adventure in Reading, New Orleans, Louisiana, $5,000 - literacy program support (2018).
Contact: Toni Myers, Administrator; (504) 207-8541; fax (504) 207-8525; info@EllaWest.org
Internet: www.ellawest.org/application.html
Sponsor: Ella West Freeman Foundation
1100 Poydras Street, Suite 1350
New Orleans, LA 70163

Ellen Abbott Gilman Trust Grants   905

The Ellen Abbott Gilman Trust, established in Massachusetts, has specified a number of fields of interest, including: aging centers and services; multipurpose art centers; children and youth services; education; human and community services; and museums. Support is restricted to the State of Massachusetts, and most often comes in the form of general operations. There are no specified application form or deadlines with which to adhere, and applicants should inquire directly to the Trust for more information.

Requirements: Applicants must be 501(c)3 organizations supporting the residents of Massachusetts.
Geographic Focus: Massachusetts
Amount of Grant: 1,000 - 3,000 USD
Samples: African and American Friendship, Roslindale, Massachusetts, $3,000 - for general operations; Outer Cape Health Services, Wellfleet, Massachusetts, $2,000 - for general operations; Young Achievers Outlook, Mattapan, Massachusetts, $2,000 - for general operations.
Contact: Walter G. Van Dorn, Trustee c/o Kirkpatrick & Lockhart Nicholson Graham; (617) 261-3100; fax (617) 261-3175; walter.vandorn@klgates.com
Sponsor: Ellen Abbott Gilman Trust
KL Gates 1 Lincoln Street
Boston, MA 02111-2905

Elmer Roe Deaver Foundation Grants   906

The Foundation was established by Elmer Roe Deaver in 1947, who served for many years as President of the Quaker City Life Insurance Company in Pennsylvania. The Foundation awards grants to organizations whose programs help relieve poverty to Philadelphia area residents. Applications should be submitted through the online grant application form or alternative accessible application designed for assistive technology users. Applications are accepted year-round. Applications must be submitted by June 1 to be reviewed at the annual grant meeting that occurs in July. Awards typically range from $10,000 to $20,000.

Requirements: To be eligible, organizations must qualify as exempt organizations under Section 501(c)3 of the Internal Revenue Code and serve residents of the Philadelphia, Pennsylvania, area.
Geographic Focus: All States
Amount of Grant: 10,000 - 20,000 USD
Contact: Avery Macon Tucker, Senior Vice President; (888) 234-1999 or (888) 235-4351; grantadministration@wellsfargo.com
Internet: www.wellsfargo.com/private-foundations/deaver-foundation/
Sponsor: Elmer Roe Deaver Foundation
420 Montgomery Street
San Francisco, CA 94163

El Pomar Foundation Anna Keesling Ackerman Fund Grants   907

The El Pomar Foundation is one of the largest and oldest private foundations in the Rocky Mountain West, and it contributes annually through direct grants and community stewardship programs to support Colorado nonprofit organizations. The Anna Keesling Ackerman Fund seeks to continue the charitable intent of Mr. Jasper D. Ackerman, who supported numerous charitable organizations and causes throughout the Pikes Peak Region. The Fund's primary focus is in health, human services, education, arts and humanities, and civic and community initiatives. Grant applications are typically reviewed twice annually in the spring and at the end of the year. If funded, applicants must wait three years (36 months) before submitting a new application. If declined, applicants must wait one year (12 months) before submitting a new application.

Requirements: Nonprofits with 501(c)3 tax status serving the Pikes Peak Region of El Paso and Teller counties are eligible to apply for funding.
Restrictions: The Foundation does not accept grant applications for: other foundations or nonprofits that distribute money to recipients of its own selection; endowments; individuals; organizations that practice discrimination of any kind; organizations that do not have fiscal responsibility for the proposed project; organizations that do not have an active 501(c)3 nonprofit IRS determination letter; camps, camp programs, or other seasonal activities; religious organizations for support of religious programs; cover deficits or debt elimination; cover travel, conferences, conventions, group meetings, or seminars; influence legislation or support candidates for political office; produce videos or other media projects; fund research projects or studies; primary or secondary schools (K-12).
Geographic Focus: Colorado
Amount of Grant: 500 - 500,000 USD
Contact: Nicole Cook, Grants Administrator; (719) 633-7733 or (800) 554-7711; fax (719) 577-5702; grants@elpomar.org
Internet: www.elpomar.org/grant-making/el-pomars-funds/
Sponsor: El Pomar Foundation
10 Lake Circle
Colorado Springs, CO 80906

El Pomar Foundation Grants   908

The El Pomar Foundation's competitive process remains the primary grant making vehicle for organizations throughout Colorado to receive funding. El Pomar is a general purpose foundation, which means the Trustees approve grants across a wide spectrum of focus areas including: arts and culture; civic and community initiatives; education; health; and human services. Under this competitive process the Foundation accepts applications for general operating, programs, and capital support. Grant applications are reviewed three times each year. The board meets May 5, July 19, and October 2.

Requirements: Nonprofits with 501(c)3 tax status serving Colorado are eligible to apply for funding. If funded through the competitive process applicants must wait three years (36 months) before submitting a new application. If declined applicants must wait one year (12 months) before submitting a new application.

Restrictions: The Trustees will not consider any capital grant requests exceeding $100,000, unless initiated by the Foundation. The Foundation does not accept grant applications for: other foundations or nonprofits that distribute money to recipients of its own selection; endowments; individuals; organizations that practice discrimination of any kind; organizations that do not have fiscal responsibility for the proposed project; organizations that do not have an active 501(c)3 nonprofit IRS determination letter; camps, camp programs, or other seasonal activities; religious organizations for support of religious programs; cover deficits or debt elimination; cover travel, conferences, conventions, group meetings, or seminars; influence legislation or support candidates for political office; produce videos or other media projects; fund research projects or studies; primary or secondary schools (K-12).
Geographic Focus: Colorado
Amount of Grant: 500 - 500,000 USD
Samples: Bright Futures, Telluride, Colorado, $55,000 - support of education; Adams State University Foundation, Alamosa, Colorado, $222,000 - general operating support; Community Coalition for Families and Children, Divide, Colorado, $75,000 - human services.
Contact: Nicole Cook, Grants Administrator; (719) 633-7733 or (800) 554-7711; fax (719) 577-5702; grants@elpomar.org
Internet: www.elpomar.org/grant-making/general-information/
Sponsor: El Pomar Foundation
10 Lake Circle
Colorado Springs, CO 80906

Elsie H. Wilcox Foundation Grants   909

Born in 1879 at Grove Farm in Lihue, Kauai, Elsie Hart Wilcox was the daughter of Samuel Whitney and Emma Washburn (Lyman) Wilcox. Elsie lived with her parents and five brothers and sisters at Grove Farm, the plantation established by her prosperous uncle, George Norton Wilcox, in a lifestyle that kept with their missionary heritage of simplicity and few luxuries. Elsie, along with her siblings, was assigned chores at Grove Farm which, along being a sugar plantation, was also a nearly self-sufficient farm. She helped pick fruits and vegetables, tended to the farm animals, and also helped to provide food on the table by hunting and fishing. Elsie died in 1954 at the age of 75. An excerpt from her gravestone reads: "I am among you as one who serves." The Elsie H. Wilcox Foundation was established by Deed of Trust on February 15, 1938, for religious, charitable, scientific, literary, and educational purposes. The Trust provides a flexibility to permit use of income to meet changing requirements or needs. Currently, the Foundation provides partial support to programs and projects of tax-exempt, public charities in Hawaii to improve the quality of life in the state, particularly the island of Kauai. Areas of interest to the Foundation include: education; health organizations; people with disabilities; human services; performing arts; theater; religion; and YM/YMCAs and YM/YWHAs. Types of support include: building and renovation; equipment purchase and rental; and general operating support. Awards typically range from $5,000 to $15,000.
Requirements: 501(c)3 nonprofit organizations in Hawaii are eligible to apply. The Foundation places a special emphasis on the island of Kauai. Contact Paula Boyce to acquire the cover sheet/application forms and any additional guidelines required to begin the application process. Proposals must be submitted by September 1.
Restrictions: No grants to individuals, or for endowments.
Geographic Focus: Hawaii
Date(s) Application is Due: Sep 1
Amount of Grant: 5,000 - 15,000 USD
Contact: Paula Boyce; (808) 538-4945; fax (808) 538-4006; pboyce@boh.com
Elaine Moniz; (808) 694-4944; fax (808) 538-4006; elaine.moniz@boh.com
Internet: www.boh.com/philanthropy/grants/elsie-h-wilcox-foundation
Sponsor: Elsie H. Wilcox Foundation
P.O. Box 3170, Department 758
Honolulu, HI 96802-3170

Elton John AIDS Foundation Grants   910

The Elton John AIDS Foundation (EJAF) was established in the United States in 1992 by Sir Elton John, now headquartered in New York City. In 1993, Sir Elton also established his Foundation as a registered charity in the United Kingdom, headquartered in London. Both organizations pursue the same mission – to reduce the incidence of HIV/AIDS through innovative HIV prevention programs, eliminate stigma and discrimination associated with HIV/AIDS, and support direct HIV-related care for people living with HIV/AIDS. The U.S. organization's grant-making program focuses on the following targeted areas: gay men's mobilization for health; youth mobilization for health; black community mobilization for health; ending injection-related HIV transmission; access to healthcare for ex-offenders; and scaled-up of government HIV programming. EJAF conducts an annual open application grant cycle through a Request for Proposals process launched on or around May 1.
Requirements: Applicants located and conducting work corresponding to EJAF's stated grant-making priorities in the United States, Canada, the Caribbean, and Central and South America are eligible to apply for funding by first submitting an online letter of intent (LOI). After the LOIs have been reviewed, selected applicants will be invited to submit a full online proposal. These proposals are extensively reviewed, and final grant awards are approved by EJAF's Board of Directors.
Geographic Focus: All States, Puerto Rico, U.S. Virgin Islands, Anguilla, Antigua & Barbuda, Argentina, Aruba, Bahamas, Barbados, Belize, Bolivia, Brazil, British Virgin Islands, Canada, Cayman Islands, Chile, Colombia, Costa Rica, Cuba, Dominica, Dominican Republic, Ecuador, El Salvador, Grenada, Guadeloupe, Guatemala, Guyana, Haiti, Honduras, Jamaica, Martinique, Mexico, Montserrat, Nicaragua, Panama, Paraguay, Peru, Saint Kitts And Nevis, Saint Lucia, Saint Vincent and the Grenadines, Suriname, Trinidad and Tobago, Turks and Caicos Islands, Uruguay, Venezuela
Amount of Grant: Up to 100,000 USD
Samples: Association of Nurses in AIDS Care, Reston, Virginia, $50,000 - support of HIV criminalization awareness and advocacy work the Association; The Attic Youth Center,

Philadelphia, Pennsylvania, $50,000 - continued support of the youth development model to engage LGBTQ youth of color who are HIV-positive or at high risk in leadership and career readiness programming; Big Bend Cares, Tallahassee, Florida, $40,000 - continued support for the Black MSM Testing Linkage and Adherence Program started in 2013.
Contact: Anna MacDonald, Grants Support Officer; (212) 219-0670; info@ejaf.org
Internet: www.eltonjohnaidsfoundation.org/what-we-do/what-we-fund/
Sponsor: Elton John AIDS Foundation
584 Broadway, Suite 906
New York, NY 10012

Emerson Kampen Foundation Grants   911

Established in Indiana in 1986, the Emerson Kampen Foundation offers grants primarily in Indiana, though awards have also been given in Illinois and New Jersey. The Foundation's primary fields of interest include: youth groups; Christian agencies and churches; higher education; and YMCAs and YWCAs. Unsolicited applications are not accepted, and interested parties should contact the Foundation in writing prior to forwarding any detailed requests. Grants range from $20,000 to $200,000.
Geographic Focus: Illinois, Indiana, New Jersey
Amount of Grant: 20,000 - 200,000 USD
Samples: YMCA Camp Tecumseh, Lafayette, Indiana, $185,000 - for program development; Indiana University, Bloomington, Indiana, $120,000 - for women's health programs; Kid's Alley, Sewell, New Jersey, $20,000 - for youth program development.
Contact: Joanie Kampen Dunham, Co-Trustee; (856) 223-2872
Sponsor: Emerson Kampen Foundation
101 Cromwell Drive
Mullica Hill, NJ 08062-1807

Emily Hall Tremaine Foundation Learning Disabilities Grants   912

The Emily Hall Tremaine Foundation has been making grants to support children with learning disabilities (LD) and their families since 1992. Left unaddressed, learning disabilities can affect the emotional and physical health and well being of children, in turn preventing a positive experience in the classroom. During the first decade of the foundation's involvement in the field of learning disabilities, support was directed toward public relations campaigns to dispel the stigma often associated with LD. In 2003, the foundation refocused its efforts on the classroom. The foundation identified two key areas where grants can help prepare classrooms to be designed for all types of learners. The foundation's current priorities guiding its grant making are two-fold: early intervention; and technology and teaching. There are no application forms or deadlines. Unsolicited proposals rarely develop into a grant; submit informative letters of inquiry that highlight the organization's mission, goals, history, strategies, and programmatic scope. Awards have recently ranged from $500 to $500,000.
Requirements: Nonprofits educational organizations dealing with learning disabilities may apply for grant support.
Geographic Focus: All States
Date(s) Application is Due: Feb 28
Amount of Grant: 500 - 500,000 USD
Contact: Alexis Bivens, Program Director; (203) 639-5544 or (203) 639-5547; fax (203) 639-5545; bivens@tremainefoundation.org
Internet: www.tremainefoundation.org/learning-differences.html
Sponsor: Emily Hall Tremaine Foundation
171 Orange Street
New Haven, CT 06510

Emily O'Neill Sullivan Foundation Grants   913

The Emily O'Neill Sullivan Foundation was established in Pennsylvania in 1995 with the expressed purpose of supporting a number of causes, including: arts and culture; basic and emergency aid; crime prevention; domesticated animals; local economic development; health and health care; higher education; human services; in-patient medical care; job services; rehabilitation; shelter and residential care; and youth development. The Foundation's target populations include: children and youth; economically disadvantaged people; homeless; low-income; people with disabilities; victims and the oppressed; and victims of crime and abuse. Funding typically comes in the form of individual development, outreach program support, and general programming. There is no specific application format, and letters of application should reach the office prior to December 1. Awards generally range up to a maximum of $1,000, though higher amounts are occasionally approved by the Board.
Geographic Focus: All States
Date(s) Application is Due: Nov 30
Amount of Grant: Up to 1,000 USD
Samples: Rosemont College, Rosemont, Pennsylvania, $5,000 support of undergraduate education programs; Operation Smile, Virginia Beach, Virginia, $800 - support for rehabilitation programming; Philabundance, Philadelphia, Pennsylvania, $700 - support for food aid programs.
Contact: Philip A Sullivan, Trustee; (610) 642-0123
Sponsor: Emily O'Neill Sullivan Foundation
1329 Beaumont Drive
Gladwyne, PA 19035

Emma J. Adams Memorial Fund Grants   914

The Emma J. Adams Memorial Fund was established in New York in 1932, and giving is centered around New York City to aid the indigent elderly through a church-sponsored meals program and ecumenical medical care. Limited giving is also available for nonrecurring grants to elderly individuals who are agency, medically, or professionally-sponsored. Primary fields of interest include adults, aging, and the economically disadvantaged. Grants typically range from $1,500 to $12,000.

Restrictions: No grants are offered for operating budgets, annual campaigns, administrative expenses, building funds, special projects, endowments, or scholarships; no loans. There is no support for programs, or brick and mortar grants.
Geographic Focus: New York
Amount of Grant: 1,500 - 12,000 USD
Contact: Sally Saran, President; (212) 327-0493
Sponsor: Emma J. Adams Memorial Fund
328 Eldert Lane
Brooklyn, NY 11208

Energy by Design Poster Contest 915

Energy by Design is a poster contest developed by Nicor and the National Energy Foundation for children grades K-8 designed to combine a student's artistic talent with the ability to portray how to use energy efficiently. Nicor will provide the materials, the teacher's job is to direct and motivate the students, and the child's job is to produce a beautiful, unique interpretation of what energy efficiency means to them. A grand prize and three finalists are selected in each category, grades K-2, 3-5 and 6-8. Student winners will get a $1,000 savings bond, a pizza party for their class, and a prize pack filled with fun, age-appropriate prizes. Teachers of the grand prize winners will receive a classroom grant of $1,000. Three finalists in each category will receive a $250 savings bond, a pizza party for their class, and a prize pack filled with fun, age-appropriate prizes.
Requirements: Any student K-8 enrolled in a school in Nicor Gas service territory is eligible to participate. (See www.nicor.com/en_us/nicor_inc/nicor_in_the_community/territory_map.htm to determine if you are located in the Nicor service area.) There is no entry fee for participating in the contest. All entries must be original work, either hand drawn or computer generated. Hard copy entry required, electronic files will not be accepted. Because the contest is designed to encourage total class participation, the teacher must submit all of the entries together. Guidelines are available online.
Restrictions: Employees of Nicor and all of its subsidiaries, including Nicor Services, Dykstra, Hawthorn, Trade Winds, Carrier and their immediate families, household members and dependents are not eligible to win prizes. No syndicated, copyrighted or clip art images can be used.
Geographic Focus: Illinois
Date(s) Application is Due: Feb 10
Amount of Grant: 250 - 1,000 USD
Contact: Elissa Richards, Program Director; (800) 616-8326 or (801) 327-9505; fax (801) 908-5400; elissa@nef1.org
Internet: www.energybydesign.org/
Sponsor: National Energy Foundation
4516 South 700 East, Suite 100
Salt Lake City, UT 84107

Ensworth Charitable Foundation Grants 916

The Ensworth Charitable Foundation was established in 1948 to support and promote educational, cultural, human services, religious, and health, art and cultural programs care programming for underserved populations. Grants will be for activities primarily conducted in Hartford and the contiguous neighboring communities. Grants from the Ensworth Charitable Foundation are primarily 1 year in duration. On occasion, multi-year support is awarded. Award amounts typically range from $2,000 to $50,000.
Requirements: Applicants must have 501(c)3 tax-exempt status and serve the people of Hartford, Connecticut, and its surrounding communities. Applications will be submitted online through the Bank of America website. A grant report is required within 1 year of the grant application date, regardless of whether all of the funds have been spent.
Restrictions: Applicants will not be awarded a grant for more than 3 consecutive years. The foundation does not support requests from individuals, organizations attempting to influence policy through direct lobbying, or any political campaigns.
Geographic Focus: Connecticut
Date(s) Application is Due: Jan 15
Amount of Grant: 2,000 - 50,000 USD
Samples: Real Art Ways, Hartford, Connecticut, $40,000 - Awarded for General Operations of Real Art Ways (2018); Immaculate Conception Shelter and Housing Corporation, Hartford, Connecticut, $35,000 - Awarded for General Operations of ImmaCare Inc. (2018); Community Partners in Action, Hartford, Connecticut, $25,000 - Awarded for the Resettlement Program - reentry and basic needs services (2018).
Contact: Amy R. Lynch, Philanthropic Client Manager; (860) 244-4870; ct.grantmaking@bankofamerica.com or amy.r.lynch@bofa.com
Internet: www.bankofamerica.com/philanthropic/foundation/?fnId=53
Sponsor: Ensworth Charitable Foundation
200 Glastonbury Boulevard, Suite # 200
Glastonbury, CT 06033-4458

Entergy Charitable Foundation Education and Literacy Grants 917

The primary goal of the Entergy Charitable Foundation is to support initiatives that help create and sustain thriving communities, with a special focus on education and literacy initiatives. When people are geared with knowledge, they become more effective within their communities. Educated, critically thinking citizens make the community as a whole more powerful. One of the key issues in combating poverty is eliminating illiteracy. Thriving communities depend on self-sufficient, productive citizens. At Entergy, the Foundation believes that an essential element to healthy, thriving communities is creating an environment where every individual has basic reading and writing skills. In considering requests, priority is placed on programs in specific counties or parishes, including areas of: Arkansas, Louisiana, Massachusetts, Michigan, Mississippi, New Hampshire, New York, Texas, and Vermont. Contact the contributions coordinator in your state with any questions regarding your project. Each applicant must complete and submit an online application form. Annual deadlines are February 1, May 1, and July 1.
Requirements: Grants from the Entergy Corporation will only be made to the following types of organizations: non-profit organizations that are tax exempt under section 501(c)3 of the Internal Revenue Code; or schools, hospitals, governmental units and religious institutions that hold nonprofit status similar to that of 501(c)3 organizations.
Restrictions: Entergy will not fund: groups without 501(c)3 or similar non-profit status; administrative expenses (e.g., salaries, office equipment) or recurring expenses that exceed 15% of the requested amount; capital project funding (i.e., building campaigns); political candidates or groups; purchase of uniforms or trips for school-related organizations; amateur sports teams; activities whose sole purpose is promotion or support of a specific religion, denomination, or religious institution; grants to individuals or loans of any type; or any organization owned or operated by an employee of Entergy.
Geographic Focus: Arkansas, Louisiana, Massachusetts, Michigan, Mississippi, New Hampshire, New York, Vermont
Date(s) Application is Due: Feb 1; May 1; Jul 1
Contact: Jennifer Quezergue, (504) 576-2674 or (504) 576-6980; jquezer@entergy.com
Christine Jordan, (504) 576-7705 or (504) 576-6980; cminor@entergy.com
Internet: www.entergy.com/our_community/ECF_grant_guidelines.aspx
Sponsor: Entergy Charitable Foundation
639 Loyola Avenue
New Orleans, LA 70161-1000

Entergy Charitable Foundation Low-Income Initiatives and Solutions Grants 918

The primary goal of the Entergy Charitable Foundation is to support initiatives that help create and sustain thriving communities, with a special focus on low-income initiatives. Such programs may include, but are not limited to: sustaining families and self-sufficiency; technical assistance and training for non-profits; home-ownership preparation; energy management and awareness; and innovative use and promotion of alternative sources of energy. In considering requests, priority is placed on programs in specific counties or parishes, including areas of: Arkansas, Louisiana, Massachusetts, Michigan, Mississippi, New Hampshire, New York, Texas, and Vermont. Contact the contributions coordinator in your state with any questions regarding your project. Each applicant must complete and submit an online application form. Annual deadlines are February 1, May 1, and July 1.
Requirements: Grants from the Entergy Corporation will only be made to the following types of organizations: non-profit organizations that are tax exempt under section 501(c)3 of the Internal Revenue Code; or schools, hospitals, governmental units and religious institutions that hold nonprofit status similar to that of 501(c)3 organizations.
Restrictions: Entergy will not fund: groups without 501(c)3 or similar non-profit status; administrative expenses (e.g., salaries, office equipment) or recurring expenses that exceed 15% of the requested amount; capital project funding (i.e., building campaigns); political candidates or groups; purchase of uniforms or trips for school-related organizations; amateur sports teams; activities whose sole purpose is promotion or support of a specific religion, denomination, or religious institution; grants to individuals or loans of any type; or any organization owned or operated by an employee of Entergy.
Geographic Focus: Arkansas, Louisiana, Massachusetts, Michigan, Mississippi, New Hampshire, New York, Texas
Date(s) Application is Due: Feb 1; May 1; Jul 1
Contact: Jennifer Quezergue, (504) 576-2674 or (504) 576-6980; jquezer@entergy.com
Christine Jordan, (504) 576-7705 or (504) 576-6980; cminor@entergy.com
Internet: www.entergy.com/our_community/ECF_grant_guidelines.aspx
Sponsor: Entergy Charitable Foundation
639 Loyola Avenue
New Orleans, LA 70161-1000

Entergy Corporation Micro Grants 919

The Foundation will bestow a monetary award for projects that effectively impact arts and culture, community improvement and enrichment, education and literacy, and healthy families. Organizations should be located within Entergy's service territory in Arkansas, Louisiana, Mississippi, Massachusetts, Michigan, New Hampshire, New York, Texas, or Vermont. Micro Grant applications are accepted on an ongoing basis. Applicants should allow at least 6 (six) to 8 (eight) weeks for review and notification of the result of a request.
Requirements: 501(c)3 tax-exempt organizations, schools, hospitals, governmental units, and religious institutions are eligible. Each organization may submit only one application per year.
Restrictions: Entergy will not fund: groups without 501(c)3 or similar non-profit status; administrative expenses (e.g., salaries, office equipment) or recurring expenses that exceed 15% of the requested amount; capital project funding (i.e., building campaigns); political candidates or groups; purchase of uniforms or trips for school-related organizations; amateur sports teams; activities whose sole purpose is promotion or support of a specific religion, denomination, or religious institution; grants to individuals or loans of any type; or any organization owned or operated by an employee of Entergy.
Geographic Focus: Arkansas, Louisiana, Massachusetts, Michigan, Mississippi, New Hampshire, New York, Texas, Vermont
Amount of Grant: Up to 1,000 USD
Contact: Jennifer Quezergue, (504) 576-2674 or (504) 576-6980; jquezer@entergy.com
Christine Jordan, (504) 576-7705 or (504) 576-6980; cminor@entergy.com
Internet: www.entergy.com/our_community/micro_grant_guidelines.aspx
Sponsor: Entergy Corporation
639 Loyola Avenue
New Orleans, LA 70161-1000

Entergy Corporation Open Grants for Arts and Culture　920

Entergy's Open Grants Program focuses on improving communities as a whole. The arts are expressions of ourselves heritage, feelings and ideas. To cultivate that, the Corporation supports a diverse range of locally based visual arts, theater, dance and music institutions. The long-term goal is to increase the access to contemporary art for a wider public, including children and the financially disadvantaged. In considering requests for grants, priority is placed on programs in specific counties/parishes, including areas of: Arkansas, Louisiana, Massachusetts, Michigan, Mississippi, New Hampshire, New York, Texas, and Vermont. Applicants should contact the contributions coordinator in their region, which are listed on the web site. Open grant applications are accepted on an ongoing basis. Applications should be submitted at least three months prior to the time the funding is needed.

Requirements: Grants from the Entergy Corporation will only be made to the following types of organizations: non-profit organizations that are tax exempt under section 501(c)3 of the Internal Revenue Code; or schools, hospitals, governmental units and religious institutions that hold nonprofit status similar to that of 501(c)3 organizations.

Restrictions: Entergy will not fund: groups without 501(c)3 or similar non-profit status; administrative expenses (e.g., salaries, office equipment) or recurring expenses that exceed 15% of the requested amount; capital project funding (i.e., building campaigns); political candidates or groups; purchase of uniforms or trips for school-related organizations; amateur sports teams; activities whose sole purpose is promotion or support of a specific religion, denomination, or religious institution; grants to individuals or loans of any type; or any organization owned or operated by an employee of Entergy.

Geographic Focus: Arkansas, Louisiana, Massachusetts, Michigan, Mississippi, New Hampshire, New York, Texas, Vermont

Amount of Grant: Up to 1,000 USD

Contact: Jennifer Quezergue, (504) 576-2674 or (504) 576-6980; jquezer@entergy.com Christine Jordan, (504) 576-7705 or (504) 576-6980; cminor@entergy.com

Internet: www.entergy.com/our_community/Grant_Guidelines.aspx

Sponsor: Entergy Corporation

639 Loyola Avenue

New Orleans, LA 70161-1000

Entergy Corporation Open Grants for Healthy Families　921

Entergy Corporation's Open Grants program focuses on improving communities as a whole. The Corporation believes that children need a good start to grow into healthy, well-adjusted adults. With that in mind, it gives to programs that have a direct impact on children educationally and emotionally. The Corporation is also interested in family programs, like those that better prepare parents to balance the demands of work and home. In considering requests for grants, priority is placed on programs in specific counties/parishes, including areas of: Arkansas, Louisiana, Massachusetts, Michigan, Mississippi, New Hampshire, New York, Texas, and Vermont. Applicants should contact the contributions coordinator in their region, which are listed on the web site. Open grant applications are accepted on an ongoing basis. Applications should be submitted at least three months prior to the time the funding is needed.

Requirements: Grants from the Entergy Corporation will only be made to the following types of organizations: non-profit organizations that are tax exempt under section 501(c)3 of the Internal Revenue Code; or schools, hospitals, governmental units and religious institutions that hold nonprofit status similar to that of 501(c)3 organizations.

Restrictions: Entergy will not fund: groups without 501(c)3 or similar non-profit status; administrative expenses (e.g., salaries, office equipment) or recurring expenses that exceed 15% of the requested amount; capital project funding (i.e., building campaigns); political candidates or groups; purchase of uniforms or trips for school-related organizations; amateur sports teams; activities whose sole purpose is promotion or support of a specific religion, denomination, or religious institution; grants to individuals or loans of any type; or any organization owned or operated by an employee of Entergy.

Geographic Focus: Arkansas, Louisiana, Massachusetts, Michigan, Mississippi, New Hampshire, New York, Texas, Vermont

Amount of Grant: Up to 1,000 USD

Contact: Jennifer Quezergue, (504) 576-2674 or (504) 576-6980; jquezer@entergy.com Christine Jordan, (504) 576-7705 or (504) 576-6980; cminor@entergy.com

Internet: www.entergy.com/our_community/Grant_Guidelines.aspx

Sponsor: Entergy Corporation

639 Loyola Avenue

New Orleans, LA 70161-1000

Environmental Excellence Awards　922

The Environmental Excellence Awards recognize the outstanding efforts of teachers and students across the country who are working at the grassroots level to protect and preserve the environment. Each winning school will receive: all-expenses-paid trip for three students and one chaperon/teacher to one of the SeaWorld or Busch Gardens parks for a special awards event; 100 t-shirts to share with school and community partners; and award trophy for the school and certificates for every student/teacher participant. From the projects, one outstanding environmental educator will be recognized. That educator will receive: all-expenses-paid trip for him/herself and one guest to one of the SeaWorld or Busch Gardens parks for a special awards event in April; all-expenses-paid trip to the National Science Teachers Association (NSTA) national conference; and award trophy and certificate. Previous award-winning projects have been in the areas of habitat restoration, school yard beautification, energy and waste reduction, environmental education and community outreach, wildlife protection, and natural resource conservation.

Requirements: Public and private elementary, secondary, and home schools in the United States and Canada are eligible to apply. Community-based projects, such as those managed and operated by community service organizations, public recreation centers, 4-H clubs and other public, nonprofit groups working to protect the environment at the grassroots level, also are eligible.

Restrictions: Individual students and previous award-winning schools are ineligible.

Geographic Focus: All States

Date(s) Application is Due: Nov 30

Amount of Grant: 5,000 - 10,000 USD

Contact: Program Officer; (877) 792-4332 or (407) 363-2389

Internet: seaworldparks.com/en/seaworld_teachers/environmental-excellence-awards/

Sponsor: Anheuser-Busch Adventure Parks

7007 Sea World Drive

Orlando, FL 32821

EPA Children's Health Protection Grants　923

The objectives of this program are to catalyze community-based and regional projects and other actions that enhance public outreach and communication; assist families in evaluating risks to children and in making informed consumer choices; build partnerships that increase a community's long-term capacity to advance the protection of children's environmental health and safety; leverage private and public investments to enhance environmental quality by enabling community efforts to continue past EPA's ability to provide assistance to communities; and promote protection of children from environmental threats through lessons learned. There are no deadline dates.

Requirements: Eligible applicants include community groups, public nonprofit institutions/organizations, tribal governments, specialized groups, profit organizations, private nonprofit institutions/organizations, and municipal and local governments. Potential applicants are strongly encouraged to discuss proposed projects with or submit preapplications to program staff prior to the completion of a full proposal.

Geographic Focus: All States

Amount of Grant: 5,000 - 250,000 USD

Contact: Office of Children's Health Protection; (202) 564-2188; fax (202) 564-2733; fletcher.bettina@epa.gov

Internet: yosemite.epa.gov/ochp/ochpweb.nsf/content/grants.htm

Sponsor: Environmental Protection Agency

1200 Pennsylvania Avenue, NW

Washington, D.C. 20460

Epilepsy Foundation SUDEP Challenge Initiative Prizes　924

Three million people in the U.S. and 65 million people worldwide have epilepsy, a neurological condition that affects the nervous system and causes seizures. Sudden unexpected death in epilepsy (SUDEP) is the leading cause of death in young adults with uncontrolled seizures. One way the Epilepsy Foundation SUDEP Institute is meeting these needs is with a series of four multidisciplinary prize challenges. The first challenge sought creative and viral advocacy campaign(s) to inform and educate people with epilepsy, families, and the health care community about SUDEP. The second challenge asked solvers to develop an intervention to help people with epilepsy comply with treatment plans and decrease their risk of seizures. In the third challenge, solvers proposed a predictive biomarker or panel of biomarkers to identify people at risk for SUDEP. Identifying biomarkers to predict SUDEP represents a major unmet medical need. Although there are several theories about the causes of SUDEP, who is at risk of dying from epilepsy and how to prevent it remains a mystery. Hence, the fourth and final challenge requires a detailed project plan for the proposed solution for finding a predictive biomarker or panel of biomarkers to identify people at risk for SUDEP or seizures that compromise cardiac or respiratory function. Anyone can be a part of the $1 million SUDEP solution. The Epilepsy Foundation is accepting submissions of solution up through October of 2020. An Award up to $800,000 for the first submission that satisfies all criteria will be granted.

Geographic Focus: All States

Amount of Grant: Up to 800,000 USD

Contact: Sonya B. Dumanis, Senior Director of Innovation; (301) 459-3700; fax (301) 577-2684; sdumanis@efa.org or contactus@efa.org

Internet: www.epilepsy.com/living-epilepsy/our-programs/sudep-institute/sudep-challenge-initiative

Sponsor: Epilepsy Foundation

8301 Professional Place West, Suite 230

Landover, MD 20785-2353

Episcopal Actors' Guild Actors Florence James Children's Holiday Fund Grant　925

The mission of the Episcopal Actors' Guild is to provide emergency aid and support to professional performers of all faiths who are undergoing financial crisis. They are also dedicated to helping emerging artists advance their careers through scholarships, awards, and performance opportunities. Each December, EARP recipients with children are eligible to apply for an additional grant to address holiday needs.

Requirements: To be eligible for this program, you must have been a previous recipient of our Emergency Aid & Relief Program. Qualified applicants live in one of the five boroughs and have an established career working as a performer for at least five consecutive years. To be eligible for EAG Programs and Services, applicants must present the following: proof of status as a professional performing artist; proof of an ongoing and sustained professional career; if ill, a state of economic need because of extenuating circumstances such as debilitating illness; efforts to secure supplementary income by employment outside the performing arts professions; documented proof of financial need; proven lack of other resources; and proof of residency in the New York City area.

Geographic Focus: New York

Contact: Karen Lehman Foster; (212) 685-2927; karen@actorsguild.org

Internet: www.actorsguild.org/services-for-performers.html

Sponsor: Episcopal Church Foundation

815 Second Avenue, Room 400

New York, NY 10017

EQT Foundation Community Enrichment Grants 926

The Foundation focuses its resources on areas that have a direct effect on the stability of communities and in turn, contribute to the success of its business operations in those areas. Through its Community Grants program, the Foundation encourages the development of safe, healthy, diverse, livable communities and bordering regions that can attract and retain residential, commercial and industrial growth and sustain a healthy local economy. Recent examples include: the Main Street programs for commercial business districts; community fairs, festivals and other local traditions; programs that promote awareness, acceptance, empowerment and inclusion of diverse populations, including women, seniors, minorities, veterans and the disabled; and volunteerism and community service programs. The application deadlines are February 1st, May 1st, August 1st, and November 1st.

Requirements: Nonprofit 501(c)3 organizations in southwestern Pennsylvania (Allegheny, Greene and Washington Counties), northern West Virginia (Doddridge, Harrison, Marion, Tyler and Wetzel Counties) and western Ohio (Belmont County).

Restrictions: The EQT Foundation does not consider proposals for: institutions, organizations or groups that are not tax exempt under IRS Section 501(c)3; capital campaigns or costs, including endowments, new construction, building renovations, mortgages/rents, etc; churches or other organizations whose purpose promotes a particular religion or creed; political parties, candidates or public policy advocates; for-profit activities, businesses, associations or organizations; tax-supported entities, including public schools; fraternal, social, union or hobby/recreational clubs or organizations; personnel costs; sporting events, including charity golf outings; scholarship programs (other than those historically supported by EQT); organizations located outside of the United States; and organizations whose mission, operating philosophy or activities are in direct conflict with EQT company policy and could potentially damage the company's reputation or could result in negative publicity for the company.

Geographic Focus: Ohio, Pennsylvania, West Virginia

Date(s) Application is Due: Feb 1; May 1; Aug 1; Nov 1

Amount of Grant: Up to 20,000 USD

Contact: Ellen Rossi, President of EQT Foundation; (412) 553-7703; erossi@eqt.com

Internet: www.eqt.com/community/eqt-foundation/

Sponsor: EQT Foundation

625 Liberty Avenue Suite 1700

Pittsburgh, PA 15222

EQT Foundation Education and Workforce Grants 927

The EQT Foundation focuses its resources on areas that have a direct effect on the stability of communities and in turn, contribute to the success of its business operations in those areas. The Foundation's Education Grants provide economically disadvantaged students with greater access to programs that promote proficiency in core academic skills, including reading, writing, math, science, communications and technology. This includes programming that helps these students effectively prepare to compete in the workforce, and have greater choices regarding the routes available to actively support themselves and make positive social and economic contributions to their communities. Examples include: adult literacy programming; computer camps: science fairs; writing competitions; tutors; scholarships; libraries; career planning and preparation; internships; and mentoring. The annual deadlines are February 1st, May 1st, August 1st, and November 1st.

Requirements: Nonprofit 501(c)3 organizations in southwestern Pennsylvania (Allegheny, Greene and Washington Counties), northern West Virginia (Doddridge, Harrison, Marion, Tyler and Wetzel Counties) and western Ohio (Belmont County).

Restrictions: The EQT Foundation does not consider proposals for: institutions, organizations or groups that are not tax exempt under IRS Section 501(c)3; capital campaigns or costs, including endowments, new construction, building renovations, mortgages/rents, etc; churches or other organizations whose purpose promotes a particular religion or creed; political parties, candidates or public policy advocates; for-profit activities, businesses, associations or organizations; tax-supported entities, including public schools; fraternal, social, union or hobby/recreational clubs or organizations; personnel costs; sporting events, including charity golf outings; scholarship programs (other than those historically supported by EQT); organizations located outside of the United States; and organizations whose mission, operating philosophy or activities are in direct conflict with EQT company policy and could potentially damage the company's reputation or could result in negative publicity for the company.

Geographic Focus: Ohio, Pennsylvania, West Virginia

Date(s) Application is Due: Feb 1; May 1; Aug 1; Nov 1

Amount of Grant: Up to 20,000 USD

Contact: Ellen Rossi, President of EQT Foundation; (412) 553-7703; erossi@eqt.com

Internet: www.eqt.com/community/eqt-foundation/

Sponsor: EQT Foundation

625 Liberty Avenue Suite 1700

Pittsburgh, PA 15222

Erie Chapman Foundation Grants 928

Established in 2007 by Erie D. Chapman III, the former CEO of Baptist Hospital System in Nashville, Tennessee. Giving primarily in Tennessee and Florida, the Foundation's mission is to support the arts and radical loving care in health care. The Foundation also provides funding for the arts in general, as well as to Christian agencies and churches. There are no specific application forms or deadlines with which to adhere, and applicants should begin the process by forwarding a letter in inquiry to Erie D. Chapman III.

Geographic Focus: Florida, Tennessee

Amount of Grant: Up to 20,000 USD

Contact: Erie D. Chapman III, Chief Executive Officer and President; erie.chapman@live.com or erie_chapman@hotmail

Internet: www.eriechapmanfoundation.org

Sponsor: Erie Chapman Foundation

500 Madison Avenue

Nashville, TN 37208

Essex County Community Foundation Dee and King Webster 929
Fund for Greater Lawrence Grants

The Essex County Community Foundation Dee and King Webster Fund for Greater Lawrence (formerly the Webster Family Fund) works to address the opportunity and achievement gaps faced by thousands of youth across Greater Lawrence. The fund was created in honor of R. Kingman "King" Webster, a Lawrence businessman and philanthropist who passed away in 2015 and who believed in the power of access, opportunity, and education for all youth, especially those living in poverty, and how it can provide them with new paths to success and opportunities to reach their full potential. Currently, the fund supports educational and out-of-school time opportunities for youth (with a priority on youth aged 14-18). The Fund seeks to support organizations that: respond to community needs with high quality programs for youth in Greater Lawrence; offer innovative, effective, and measurable solutions to impact youth in positive, sustainable, and empowering ways; and provide young people with engaging and enriching opportunities inside and outside of school that promote skill development, social-emotional health, personal growth, and exposure to new experiences. In addition, the Fund seeks to support collaborative programming with public and private schools that focus on closing the opportunity and achievement gaps faced by Greater Lawrence youth. In addition, the Fund seeks to support collaborative programming with public and private schools that focus on closing the opportunity and achievement gaps faced by Greater Lawrence youth.

Requirements: Only nonprofit organizations, recognized as tax exempt under section 501(c)3 of the Internal Revenue Code, as well as schools, are eligible for consideration. Grants should benefit the residents of Lawrence, Methuen, and/or Andover.

Restrictions: Grants are not made to individuals, for political purposes, or for sectarian or religious purposes.

Geographic Focus: Massachusetts

Date(s) Application is Due: May 1

Amount of Grant: 3,000 - 20,000 USD

Contact: Carol Lavoie Schuster, Vice President of Grants and Nonprofit Services; (978) 777-8876, ext. 133; fax (978) 777-9454; c.lavoieschuster@eccf.org or info@eccf.org

Internet: eccf.org/webster-memorial-fund

Sponsor: Essex County Community Foundation

175 Andover Street, Suite 101

Danvers, MA 01923

Essex County Community Foundation F1rst Jobs Fund Grants 930

Established in 2005, the FirstJobs program provides "first jobs" for teens ages 14-21 on the North Shore. The program benefits teens by providing valuable job training, experience and income, and nonprofit organizations by covering the salary of an additional employee for the summer months. The MassHire-North Shore Workforce Board recruits and trains teens for their first summer job. The WB conducts a series of workshops throughout the year at local high schools on how to interview for jobs, how to dress and act at a job site, etc. First Jobs connects both local businesses and nonprofit organizations needing summer help with teens looking for employment. The First Jobs Fund raises money to support nonprofits who apply for summer teens. Nonprofits can apply for funding to support employment of teens at their agency for four to eight weeks. Potential employers then interview applicants and select the candidate best suited for the stated position. For-profit businesses can support the program by hiring teens or donating to the Fund. Applications are accepted on a rolling basis April 1 through May 15, with no proposals accepted after 12pm, May 15.

Requirements: First Jobs serves teens from the communities of: Beverly, Danvers, Essex, Ipswich, Gloucester, Hamilton, Lynn, Lynnfield, Manchester-by-the-Sea, Marblehead, Middleton, Nahant, Peabody, Rockport, Salem, Saugus, Swampscott, Topsfield, and Wenham.

Geographic Focus: Massachusetts

Date(s) Application is Due: May 15

Contact: Hehershe Busuego, Senior Program Officer; (978) 777-8876, ext. 128; fax (978) 777-9454; h.busuego@eccf.org or info@eccf.org

Internet: eccf.org/f1rst-jobs

Sponsor: Essex County Community Foundation

175 Andover Street, Suite 101

Danvers, MA 01923

Essex County Community Foundation Greater Lawrence Community 931
Fund Grants

The Greater Lawrence Community Fund (formerly Merrimack Valley General Fund) provides program support for nonprofit organizations serving four communities in the Greater Lawrence community of Massachusetts. The Fund Advisory Committee will set annual priorities for funding. Support will be directed at essential needs in four communities in Greater Lawrence: Lawrence, Methuen, Andover and North Andover. These needs include: hunger, clothing, shelter and education. Shelter is defined as affordable housing or shelter programs, but not actual construction projects. The committee will look favorably on collaborative projects. When reviewing proposals, the GLCF Grants Committee considers: programs that meet a documented need, are well planned and include evaluation procedures; organizations that have the capacity to support the proposed project and have a sound financial plan; projects that offer the most significant impact for the contribution dollar; the project's potential impact on the participants; the needs of the target population; and potential for continuation or impact beyond the grant period. Proposals should demonstrate how the requested funds will be used directly in the program itself or in the building of the organization's physical or governing capacity. Usually grants are made for specific programs or activities with objectives that can be assessed within a one-year grant period. General operating support is sometimes provided to

small organizations. One-year grants ranging from $1,000 to $5,000 are awarded. Proposals must be submitted online no later than October 1 each year.
Requirements: Only nonprofit organizations recognized as tax exempt under section 501(c)3 of the Internal Revenue Code are eligible for consideration. Grants should benefit the residents of Lawrence, Andover, North Andover, and/or Methuen.
Restrictions: Funds are not available for: individuals; costs associated with programs or services provided to citizens outside of Essex County; sectarian or religious purposes; political purposes; debt or deficit reduction; capital campaigns for buildings, land acquisition or endowment; or to support academic research. Funding for equipment is limited to purchases that resolve a specific problem, are part of an overall capacity building project and will strengthen the operation of the organization. Equipment for programmatic purposes will not be granted. In general, staff salaries will not be eligible for funding unless the salary is directly tied to developing the capacity of the organization.
Geographic Focus: Massachusetts
Date(s) Application is Due: Oct 1
Amount of Grant: 1,000 - 5,000 USD
Contact: Hehershe Busueg; (978) 777-8876, ext. 128; fax (978) 777-9454; h.busuego@eccf.org or info@eccf.org
Internet: eccf.org/glcf
Sponsor: Essex County Community Foundation
175 Andover Street, Suite 101
Danvers, MA 01923

Essex County Community Foundation Greater Lawrence Summer Fund Grants 932
This Essex County Community Foundation Greater Lawrence Summer Fund connects donors seeking to support enriching summer opportunities for inner-city youth with agencies in need of funds for their programs. The following describe the desired impact of the funds: to respond to community needs for quality summer programs for as many school age youth as possible; to provide youth with opportunities for skill development, personal growth and exposure to new experiences; to promote and encourage interaction and communication among youth and staff from different ethnic and racial backgrounds and from different neighborhoods; and to gain maximum impact of philanthropic dollars for summer programs. Proposals must be submitted and in electronic format no later than March 1. Awards will range from $1,000 to $15,000.
Requirements: The private non-profit agency serving as the fiscal agent for the program must have been determined to be tax exempt under section 501(c)3 of the Internal Revenue Code, and not a private foundation under Section 509(a). This fund is limited to non-sectarian programming for youth of all religious and ethnic backgrounds. Programs sponsored by religious organizations are eligible, provided the enrollment is open to all youth and the program is free of mandatory religious instruction, worship, or other sectarian activities. Grants should benefit the residents of Lawrence, Methuen, North Andover, and/or Andover.
Restrictions: This fund is intended for summer programs serving inner-city school-age youth from Greater Lawrence (Lawrence, Methuen, Andover, and North Andover). Programs serving youth from a diverse geographic area should reserve the funds received through the Summer Fund for youth from these cities.
Geographic Focus: Massachusetts
Date(s) Application is Due: Mar 1
Amount of Grant: 1,000 - 15,000 USD
Contact: Carol Lavoie Schuster, Vice President of Grants and Services; (978) 777-8876, ext. 133; fax (978) 777-9454; c.lavoieschuster@eccf.org or info@eccf.org
Hehershe Busuego, Senior Program Officer; (978) 777-8876, ext. 128; fax (978) 777-9454; h.busuego@eccf.org or info@eccf.org
Internet: eccf.org/glsf
Sponsor: Essex County Community Foundation
175 Andover Street, Suite 101
Danvers, MA 01923

Essex County Community Foundation Merrimack Valley Municipal 933
Business Development and Recovery Fund Grants
The Merrimack Valley Municipal Business Development and Recovery Fund has been made possible by a donation from Columbia Gas. The purpose of the program is to provide direct support to the municipalities and their business communities (not businesses directly) impacted by the recent gas disaster in Andover, North Andover, and Lawrence. It is designed to provide flexible funding and is intended to empower the municipalities to use these grants in a manner that in their view best assists with business and economic recovery in the impacted areas. It is envisioned that this program will: strengthen businesses within the communities impacted by the gas crisis; generate additional opportunities for their growth and long-term success; expand support services and technical assistance for businesses; and contribute to the long-term resiliency of individual businesses and the overall business community. Funding requests should align with overall local and regional economic development and business development plans and priorities within the town/city whenever appropriate. Applications are accepted on a rolling basis.
Requirements: Only non-profit organizations, recognized as tax exempt under section 501(c)3 are eligible for consideration. The MVGF provides grants to the communities of: Lawrence, Methuen, Haverhill, Andover, North Andover, Boxford, Georgetown, Groveland, W. Newbury, Merrimac, Amesbury, Newburyport, Newbury and Salisbury.
Restrictions: Funds are not available for: individuals; state or local government agencies; political purposes; and sectarian or religious purposes. Generally grants are not awarded for: debt or deficit reduction; replacing public funding, or for purposes which are generally a public sector responsibility; supporting academic research; and traveling outside the region.
Geographic Focus: Massachusetts
Amount of Grant: 1,000 - 5,000 USD
Contact: Stratton Lloyd, COO and VP For Community Leadership; (978) 777-8876, ext. 126; fax (978) 777-9454; s.lloyd@eccf.org or info@eccf.org

Internet: eccf.org/MVMBDR
Sponsor: Essex County Community Foundation
175 Andover Street, Suite 101
Danvers, MA 01923

Essex County Community Foundation Women's Fund Grants 934
The Essex County Community Foundation Women's Fund seeks to identify existing programs or projects which offer the most significant impact for the grant dollar. The focus will be to identify programs or projects that serve women and girls in the following fields of funding interest: leadership and empowerment; economic self-sufficiency and security; and health and well being. Priority will be given to organizations that involve women and/or girls in program development and organizational leadership. The Women's Fund Advisory Board will select one field of funding interest per year. By April 1st of each year, the Women's Fund will make grants with a 1 to 3 year commitment to agencies within that year's Field of Funding Interest. Grants will range from $7,000 to $10,000, with a maximum of $21,000 over three years. Agencies which receive a multiple year grant under one Field of Funding Interest may apply for other grants in subsequent years under other Field of Funding Interests. The application window is from September 16 through the deadline of December 2.
Requirements: Non profit organizations located in Essex County which serve women and girls are eligible. Programs sponsored by religious organizations are eligible provided the enrollment is open to all qualified women and girls and the program is free of mandatory sectarian religious instruction.
Restrictions: Generally, funds will not be awarded: to individuals; for debt or deficit reduction; to individuals; for political purposes; for sectarian or religious purposes; to state and local government agencies; for endowment or capital campaigns; for research; for feasibility studies; or to agencies with pending 501(c)3 status or using fiscal sponsors.
Geographic Focus: Massachusetts
Date(s) Application is Due: Dec 2
Amount of Grant: 7,000 - 10,000 USD
Contact: Hehershe Busuego, Senior Program Officer; (978) 777-8876, ext. 128; fax (978) 777-9454; h.busuego@eccf.org or info@eccf.org
Internet: eccf.org/womens-fund
Sponsor: Essex County Community Foundation
175 Andover Street, Suite 101
Danvers, MA 01923

Ethel Sergeant Clark Smith Foundation Grants 935
The activities of the Ethel Sergeant Clark Smith (ESCS) Memorial Fund focuses on grants to organizations located in Southeastern Pennsylvania, with primary emphasis on those serving community needs in Delaware County. Grants will be made for capital projects, operating expenses and special programs in amounts that are meaningful to the success of the individual endeavors of the organizations. However, operating expense grants are typically awarded for charities without capital requirement and under circumstances where continuing funding is not expected. Grants will be made in areas of medical, educational, cultural, arts, health and welfare, and such other areas as the trustee shall identify and determine from time to time, to be responsive to changes in community needs. Application forms are available online and must be submitted by March 1 or September 1 annually.
Requirements: Southeastern Pennsylvania 501(c)3 non-profit organizations with primary emphasis on those serving community needs in Delaware County, Pennsylvania are eligible to apply. Complete applications should include the following: one original copy of the Proposal which includes the purpose and general activities of the organization should be included as well as a description of the proposed project and its justification, a budget and timetable for the project are also required; one copy of audited financial statements for the last fiscal year (or if not audited, Internal Revenue Service form 990) plus an operating budget for the current period and budgets for future period if appropriate; copy of the Internal Revenue Service tax determination letter which shows the organization is tax-exempt under Section 501(c)3 and that it is not a private foundation under section 509 (a) of the Internal Revenue Code. Any organization that is awarded a grant will be required to sign a Grant Agreement Form prior to the distribution of funds. Approximately one year after a grant has been awarded, a Progress Report should be completed by the organization. This information must be submitted prior to the consideration of any new proposals.
Restrictions: Grants will not be considered for the following: deficit financing; construction or renovations to real estate not owned by the charitable entity; salaries; professional fund raiser fees; multi-year grants over three years; to any organization more than once in a given year; to any organization more than three years in succession; any organization receiving a grant over a three year period or in three successive years will not be eligible for a future grant until two years transpire after the three year period.
Geographic Focus: Pennsylvania
Date(s) Application is Due: Mar 1; Sep 1
Contact: Wachovia Bank, N.A., Trustee; grantinquiries4@wachovia.com
Internet: www.wellsfargo.com/private-foundations/smith-memorial-fund-ethel-sergeant-clark
Sponsor: Frank and Lydia Bergen Foundation
620 Brandywine Parkway, Mail Code PA 5042
West Chester, PA 19380

Eulalie Bloedel Schneider Foundation Grants 936
The Eulalie Bloedel Schneider Foundation's mission is to support secular grassroots programs that enhance individual and family self-sufficiency and economic stability. Areas of interest are skill-building and training programs that empower at-risk youth, women and families to develop skills that would bring them towards economic self-sufficiency. The Foundation supports programs that provide job-related educational and skill building opportunities, and those seeking to build character and develop self-reliance and accountability. Artistic and cultural skill-building programs for youth and families that

enhance educational and future career opportunities are also of interest. Types of support include: general operating costs; technical assistance requests for board and staff training (up to $600); and program support for groups that are rooted in a community, member-controlled, continue to attract new members, and have an ongoing method for developing new leadership. Grants typically range from $2,000 to $5,000. A two-page letter describing the project (pre application) is required, and should be received by the third Monday of May; the full proposal deadline is the second Monday of September.

Requirements: Washington 501(c)3 groups in the Puget Sound area are eligible to apply.

Restrictions: The Foundation will not support: groups outside the Puget Sound area; national organizations, even those with projects in the Pacific Northwest; human services or low-income services projects or organizations that are not specifically providing skill-building or training opportunities; programs with a religious or proselytizing approach or mission; educational and outreach programs of large artistic or cultural institutions; museum exhibits or related outreach programs for schools or communities; traditional academic-oriented literacy, tutoring, and mentorship programs; individual requests for research or scholarships; childcare centers, schools, or classroom projects; book, video, film, or home-page productions, unless the expenses occur within the context of a project that fits the foundation's major areas of interest; computer, software, or office equipment purchases unless clearly a component of a project that fits foundation areas of interest; and capital campaigns for building construction or renovations.

Geographic Focus: Washington
Date(s) Application is Due: Sep 11
Amount of Grant: 2,000 - 5,000 USD
Samples: Cocoon House, Everett, Washington, $2,500 - support for the Education and Life Skills Program for homeless youth residents; Pacific Northwest Ballet, Seattle, Washington, $2,000 - support for the Dance Chance program for talented, under served youth; Mason County Literacy, Shelton, Washington, $2,500 - general operating support for a program providing skills and services for non-English speaking residents, school drop-outs, and other adults with low literacy skills.
Contact: Therese Ogle; (206) 781-3472; fax (206) 784-5987; oglefounds@aol.com
Internet: fdncenter.org/grantmaker/schneider
Sponsor: Eulalie Bloedel Schneider Foundation
6723 Sycamore Avenue NW
Seattle, WA 98117

Eva Gunther Foundation Fellowships 937

The Eva Gunther Foundation's work is inspired by the life of Eva Gunther, who was killed by a drunk driver at the age of twelve-and-one-half. Eva was an avid reader, an athlete, a loving daughter, cousin and especially sister, a true friend and a good student. She had a Black Belt in Tae Kwon Do, studied piano, was committed to Judaism and to education–her own and teaching others. She enjoyed baseball, bicycling, skiing, science fiction, mathematics and history. The Foundation has been operating since 1999. Currently, Foundation grant making is limited to the Fellowship Program. Between 1999 and 2008, in addition to the Fellowship program, the Eva Foundation gave one million dollars in program grants to nearly thirty-eight different Bay Area Girls Service organizations. The grants primarily funded scholarships or other resources that allowed more girls to participate in an agency's programming. These agencies worked in a vast array of fields from the arts to on-the-street social work. A Fellowship worth up to $2,000 is granted to successful nominees between the ages of 11 and 18 to do something they really want to do but can't afford. Girls have gone to camp, to arts classes, on college trips, made music, studied dance, attended basketball tournaments, and done just about anything they can imagine. In the simplest terms, an Eva Fellowship is a need-based grant which will allow a girl to have an experience similar to those that Eva had.

Requirements: Applicants must be: 11 to 18 years of age; live in the San Francisco Bay area; prove financial need; have a particular project or program in mind; and be nominated and seconded.
Geographic Focus: California
Amount of Grant: Up to 2,000 USD
Contact: Jennifer Perez Lara; (415) 561-6540, ext. 255; fax (415) 561-5477; jperezlara@pfs-llc.net
Internet: www.evafoundation.org/fellowship/
Sponsor: Eva Gunther Foundation
1660 Bush Street, Suite 300
San Francisco, CA 94109

Evan Frankel Foundation Grants 938

Although it was incorporated in 1978, the Evan Frankel Foundation became an active philanthropic entity according to Evan's wishes upon his death in 1991. The Foundation awards grants in its areas of interest, including higher education, the arts, humanities, health and science, social services, and the environment. Giving is primarily in Manhattan and Suffolk County, New York and Los Angeles, California. Most recent grants have ranged from as little as $500 up to $500,000. Applicants should submit a letter to request, outlining their program and budgetary needs.

Restrictions: Individuals are not eligible.
Geographic Focus: All States
Amount of Grant: 500 - 500,000 USD
Samples: A Place Called Home, Los Angeles, California, $117,000 - social services general operating costs; Harlem Educational Activities Fund, New York, New York, $49,000 - general operating support; East Hampton Library, East Hampton, New York, $204,750 - general operating support.
Contact: Ernest Frankel; (631) 329-0010; fax (631) 329-7102; asff@hamptons.com
Internet: www.evanfrankelfoundation.org/
Sponsor: Evan Frankel Foundation
P.O. Box 5026
East Hampton, NY 11937

Evelyn and Walter Haas, Jr. Fund Education Opportunities Grants 939

When Evelyn and Walter Haas, Jr. created this foundation in 1953, they were motivated by a set of values that still guide the organization today. With their vision of a just and caring society as its touchstone, the Fund supports initiatives and organizations that advance and protect fundamental rights and opportunities for all. Since its founding, the Fund has been an active supporter of programs that provide young people with important life skills. The Fund has played a major role in the growth of the youth development field in the Bay Area. Currently, the Fund is building on a body of educational research and exploring new ways to level the playing field and expand educational opportunities for children and young adults. It is focused on an emerging public-private partnership in San Francisco aimed at closing the achievement gap by grade three. The partnership is developing a community school approach that integrates high quality preschool and elementary school learning. Applicants should begin by contacting the Fund with a two- to three-page letter of inquiry, outlining the proposal and an overall project budget.

Requirements: IRS 501(c)3 organizations in California not classified as private foundations under section 509(a) are eligible. Matching funds are required.

Restrictions: The fund generally does not make grants for capital campaigns, major equipment, basic research, conferences, publications, films or videos, deficit or emergency funding, scholarships, direct mail campaigns, fundraising events, annual appeals, or endowment contributions. Exceptions may be made for requests that form part of a larger effort in which the fund is engaged or for requests from organizations with which the fund has a long-term funding relationship. No exceptions will be made for aid to individuals.

Geographic Focus: California
Amount of Grant: Up to 40,000 USD
Samples: New America Foundation, Washington, D.C., $35,000; California Budget Project, Sacramento, California, $30,000; Pivot Learning Partners, San Francisco, California, $36,000.
Contact: Clayton Juan; (415) 856-1400; fax (415) 856-1500; siteinfo@haasjr.org
Internet: www.haasjr.org/programs-and-initiatives/closing-achievement-gap
Sponsor: Evelyn and Walter Haas, Jr. Fund
114 Sansome Street, Suite 600
San Francisco, CA 94104

Evelyn and Walter Haas, Jr. Fund Gay and Lesbian Rights Grants 940

When Evelyn and Walter Haas, Jr. created this foundation in 1953, they were motivated by a set of values that still guide the organization today. With their vision of a just and caring society as its touchstone, the Fund supports initiatives and organizations that advance and protect fundamental rights and opportunities for all. The Fund is a leading supporter of gay and lesbian equality, based on our founders' vision of a just and caring society where all people are able to live, work and raise their families with dignity. There are three funding priorities in this area: achieving marriage equality in more states; advancing nondiscrimination protections at all levels of government; and building support for gay equality in communities of faith. Applicants should begin by contacting the fund with a two- to three-page letter of inquiry, outlining the proposal and an overall project budget.

Requirements: IRS 501(c)3 organizations in California not classified as private foundations under section 509(a) are eligible. Matching funds are required.

Restrictions: The fund generally does not make grants for capital campaigns, major equipment, basic research, conferences, publications, films or videos, deficit or emergency funding, scholarships, direct mail campaigns, fundraising events, annual appeals, or endowment contributions. Exceptions may be made for requests that form part of a larger effort in which the fund is engaged or for requests from organizations with which the fund has a long-term funding relationship. No exceptions will be made for aid to individuals.

Geographic Focus: All States
Amount of Grant: Up to 1,000,000 USD
Samples: Gay and Lesbian Advocates and Defenders, Boston, Massachusetts, $75,000; Horizons Foundation, San Francisco, California, $61,000; Proteus Fund, Amherst, Massachusetts, $1,000,000.
Contact: Clayton Juan; (415) 856-1400; fax (415) 856-1500; siteinfo@haasjr.org
Internet: www.haasjr.org/programs-and-initiatives/gays-and-lesbians
Sponsor: Evelyn and Walter Haas, Jr. Fund
114 Sansome Street, Suite 600
San Francisco, CA 94104

Evelyn and Walter Haas, Jr. Fund Immigrant Rights Grants 941

When Evelyn and Walter Haas, Jr. created this foundation in 1953, they were motivated by a set of values that still guide the organization today. With their vision of a just and caring society as its touchstone, the Fund supports initiatives and organizations that advance and protect fundamental rights and opportunities for all. The Fund has a long history of working to lift up the voice, leadership, and civic and political participation of immigrant communities. Building on this commitment, the Fund is joining with an array of partners to help build a diverse and powerful movement for immigrant rights and integration. There are three funding priorities in this area: strengthening public understanding about the need for comprehensive immigration reform at the national level; increasing civic participation among immigrants in California; and supporting public education about the need for immigrant-friendly state and local policies in California. Applicants should begin by contacting the fund with a two- to three-page letter of inquiry, outlining the proposal and an overall project budget.

Requirements: IRS 501(c)3 organizations in California not classified as private foundations under section 509(a) are eligible. Matching funds are required.

Restrictions: The fund generally does not make grants for capital campaigns, major equipment, basic research, conferences, publications, films or videos, deficit or emergency funding, scholarships, direct mail campaigns, fundraising events, annual appeals, or endowment contributions. Exceptions may be made for requests that form part of a larger

effort in which the fund is engaged or for requests from organizations with which the fund has a long-term funding relationship. No exceptions will be made for aid to individuals.
Geographic Focus: California
Samples: ACLU Foundation of Southern California, Los Angeles, California, $120,000; Four Freedoms Fund, San Francisco, California, $200,000; Grantmakers Concerned with Immigrants and Refugees, Sebastopol, California, $200,000.
Contact: Clayton Juan; (415) 856-1400; fax (415) 856-1500; siteinfo@haasjr.org
Internet: www.haasjr.org/programs-and-initiatives/immigrants
Sponsor: Evelyn and Walter Haas, Jr. Fund
114 Sansome Street, Suite 600
San Francisco, CA 94104

Evelyn and Walter Haas, Jr. Fund Nonprofit Leadership Grants   942
When Evelyn and Walter Haas, Jr. created this foundation in 1953, they were motivated by a set of values that still guide the organization today. With their vision of a just and caring society as its touchstone, the Fund supports initiatives and organizations that advance and protect fundamental rights and opportunities for all. Strengthening nonprofit leadership is a key grantmaking priority for the Fund. There are two funding priorities in this area: investing in the leadership of grantees so they can more effectively achieve their social change goals; and advancing knowledge and learning about nonprofit leadership. Applicants should begin by contacting the Fund with a two- to three-page letter of inquiry, outlining the proposal and an overall project budget.
Requirements: IRS 501(c)3 organizations in California not classified as private foundations under section 509(a) are eligible. Matching funds are required.
Restrictions: The fund generally does not make grants for capital campaigns, major equipment, basic research, conferences, publications, films or videos, deficit or emergency funding, scholarships, direct mail campaigns, fundraising events, annual appeals, or endowment contributions. Exceptions may be made for requests that form part of a larger effort in which the fund is engaged or for requests from organizations with which the fund has a long-term funding relationship. No exceptions will be made for aid to individuals.
Geographic Focus: California
Amount of Grant: Up to 40,000 USD
Samples: Asian Pacific Environmental Network, Oakland, California, $37,000; Clergy & Laity United for Economic Justice, Los Angeles, California, $35,000; Coleman Advocates for Children and Youth, San Francisco, California, $25,000.
Contact: Clayton Juan; (415) 856-1400; fax (415) 856-1500; siteinfo@haasjr.org
Internet: www.haasjr.org/programs-and-initiatives/helping-nonprofit-leaders-and-their-organizations-succeed
Sponsor: Evelyn and Walter Haas, Jr. Fund
114 Sansome Street, Suite 600
San Francisco, CA 94104

Ewing Marion Kauffman Foundation Grants   943
The vision of the Foundation is to foster a society of economically independent individuals who are engaged citizens, contributing to the improvement of their communities. The Foundation focuses its grant making and operations on two areas: advancing entrepreneurship and improving the education of children and youth. In entrepreneurship, the Foundation works nationwide to catalyze an entrepreneurial society in which job creation, innovation, and the economy flourish. In education, the Foundation works to improve the academic achievement of disadvantaged children and works with partners to support programs that directly impact a child's academic achievement, with a concentrated focus on math, science, and technology skills. The Foundation does not use a grant application form or formal application process. There are no proposal deadlines or established funding limits. Information regarding submission of a letter of inquiry is available online.
Requirements: The foundation only funds programs within the United States. The majority of education grants go to organizations within the Kansas City metropolitan area. The foundation's entrepreneurship efforts fund programs and activities nationally and within the Kansas City area.
Restrictions: The Foundation does not fund: requests from individuals, political, social, or fraternal organizations; endowments, special events, arts, or international programs; provide loans, start-up expenses or seed capital funding for private businesses or scholarships requested by individuals; proposals submitted via audiotape or videotape; institutions that discriminate on the basis of race, creed, gender, national origin, age, disability or sexual orientation in policy or in practice; programs in furtherance of sectarian religious activities, impermissible lobbying, legislative or political activities; programs targeted for people with a specific physical, medical or psychological condition; or medical research or profit-making enterprises.
Geographic Focus: All States
Amount of Grant: Up to 300,000 USD
Samples: AARP Foundation, Washington, D.C., $481,000 - to support to expand the capacity of the Work For Yourself After 50 entrepreneurship education program to accommodate more entrepreneurs across the country (2019); Academy for the Integrated Arts, Kansas City, Missouri, $193,625 - to provide teacher professional development and individualized intervention for struggling students during the 2019-20 and 2020-21 school years (2019); Academy of Management, Inc., Briarcliff Manor, New York, $13,800 - to support for the 2020, 2021, and 2022 annual conferences for the Managerial and Organizational Cognition Division, to encourage research on entrepreneurial cognition (2019).
Contact: Wendy Guillies, President; (816) 932-1000; fax (816) 932-1100; info@emkf.org
Internet: www.kauffman.org/grants
Sponsor: Ewing Marion Kauffman Foundation
4801 Rockhill Road
Kansas City, MO 64110-2046

Ezra Jack Keats Foundation Mini-Grants   944
The Ezra Jack Keats Foundation offers annual mini-grants to school and public libraries for programs that encourage literacy and creativity in children. Programs that will be considered include: innovative workshops; lectures and festivals; and programs targeted at parents and preschool children. Priority will be given to programs relating to the work of Ezra Jack Keats. Guidelines and an application form are available online in the Fall of each year. The annual deadline for application submission is March 31.
Requirements: Public schools, libraries located, and public preschool programs located anywhere in the United States, including Puerto Rico and Guam, are invited to apply for mini-grants.
Restrictions: Grants are not awarded for the purchase of books, tapes, software, and equipment unrelated to the specific project described; or for general operations, administrative costs, or transportation of the audience.
Geographic Focus: All States
Date(s) Application is Due: Mar 31
Contact: Dr. Deborah Pope, Executive Director; foundation@ezra-jack-keats.org
Internet: www.ezra-jack-keats.org/section/ezra-jack-keats-mini-grant-program-for-public-libraries-public-schools/
Sponsor: Ezra Jack Keats Foundation
450 14th Street
Brooklyn, NY 11215-5702

Ezra M. Cutting Trust Grants   945
The Ezra M. Cutting Trust was established in 1965 under the will of Ezra Cutting, who was born in Marlborough, Massachusetts. The Trust supports charitable organizations serving residents of Marlborough. Areas of special interest include agencies serving youth as well as those with programs fostering economic growth and the general quality of life in the City of Marlborough. Award amounts go up to $15,000.
Requirements: Applicants must have 501(c)3 tax-exempt status. Grants are restricted to organizations located in Marlborough, Massachusetts (and to other organizations which serve Marlborough residents) and are generally made for special projects and programs, with a limited number of capital gifts made each year. Applications will be submitted online through the Bank of America website. A grant report is required within 1 year of the grant application date, regardless of whether all of the funds have been spent.
Restrictions: The trust does not support requests from individuals, organizations attempting to influence policy through direct lobbying, or any political campaigns.
Geographic Focus: Massachusetts
Date(s) Application is Due: Jan 15
Samples: United Way of Tri-County Inc., Framingham, Massachusetts, $15,000 - Awarded for Marlborough Community Cupboard (MCC) Food Security and Fuel Assistance (2018); Boys and Girls Clubs of Metrowest Inc., Marlborough, Massachusetts, $12,000 - Awarded for Out-Of-School Programming - Marlborough Clubhouse (2018); Employment Options, Marlborough, Massachusetts, $10,000 - Awarded for Catering Options Social Enterprise (2018).
Contact: Michealle Larkins, Philanthropic Administrator; (866) 778-6859; ma.grantmaking@bankofamerica.com or ma.grantmaking@ustrust.com
Internet: www.bankofamerica.com/philanthropic/foundation/?fnId=80
Sponsor: Ezra M. Cutting Trust
P.O. Box 1802
Providence, RI 02901-1802

F.M. Kirby Foundation Grants   946
Fred Morgan Kirby, a five-and-dime-merchant, opened his first store in Wilkes-Barre, PA in 1887. He merged with the Woolworths in 1912, bringing 94 stores to the merger, and becoming one of the founders of the F.W. Woolworth Company. The F.M. Kirby Foundation was endowed by Fred Morgan Kirby in 1931 and designed to continue in perpetuity through generations of the family. The Foundation was initially funded with approximately $9 million. Fred Morgan Kirby served as president of the Foundation until 1940. His son, Allan P. Kirby, who had well established himself in the business world through the Alleghany Corporation, succeeded his father as president of the Foundation. Today, the F.M. Kirby Foundation aims effectively to manage and utilize that which has been entrusted to it over multiple generations of the Kirby family. It strives to make thoughtful and prudent philanthropic commitments to highly selective grantee partners. The goal is to invest in opportunities that foster self-reliance or otherwise create strong, healthy communities. Foundation grants are made to a wide range of nonprofit organizations in education, health and medicine, the arts and humanities, civic and public affairs, as well as religious, welfare and youth organizations. Grantees are largely in geographic areas of particular interest to the Kirby family. The Foundation has no required application format and applications will be accepted throughout the year. No solicitations by fax or email are accepted.
Requirements: North Carolina, New Jersey, New York, and Pennsylvania tax-exempt organizations are eligible.
Restrictions: Grants are not made to individuals, public foundations or to underwrite fund-raising activities such as benefits, dinners, theater or sporting events.
Geographic Focus: New Jersey, New York, North Carolina, Pennsylvania
Date(s) Application is Due: Oct 31
Amount of Grant: Up to 500,000 USD
Samples: Adirondack Experience, Blue Mountain Lake, New York, $35,000 - support of the 50th Anniversary of the Adirondack Park Agency project (2020); Drew University, Madison, New Jersey, $125,000 - support of the Launch Program (2020); Dolgeville Forward, Dolgeville, New York, $50,000 - support to renovate and rebuild the Center Park (2020).
Contact: S. Dillard Kirby; (973) 538-4800; fax (973) 538-4801; fmkf@fmkirby.com
Internet: fmkirbyfoundation.org/apply/
Sponsor: F.M. Kirby Foundation
17 DeHart Street, P.O. Box 151
Morristown, NJ 07963-0151

F.R. Bigelow Foundation Grants 947

The F.R. Bigelow Foundation supports the civic, educational, religious, and other needs of the community. The Foundation funds program and helps shape initiatives that strengthen and enhance the quality of life in the Saint Paul area. The Foundation will consider grant applications in the following areas of interest: human services; community and economic development; education; health care; and the arts. The Foundation's primary geographic focus is the greater St. Paul metropolitan area, which includes Ramsey, Washington, and Dakota counties with a particular emphasis on serving people who live or work in St. Paul. The Foundation will consider applications for: capital projects, program expansion, or special projects of a time-limited nature; start-up costs for promising new programs that demonstrate sound management and clear goals relevant to community needs; support for established agencies which have temporary or transitional needs; and funds to match contributions received from other sources or to provide a challenge to help raise new contributions. Grant application packets and informational videos are available online. Applicants may wish to submit a letter of inquiry describing the proposed project prior to the preparation of a full proposal.

Requirements: Nonprofit 501(c)3 organizations in the greater St. Paul, Minnesota, metropolitan area are eligible, including Ramsey, Wahington, and Dakota counties.

Restrictions: The Foundation will not consider grant applications for: annual operating expenses; sectarian religious programs; grants to individuals; medical research; and ongoing, open-ended needs.

Geographic Focus: Minnesota

Date(s) Application is Due: May 1; Aug 1; Dec 31

Amount of Grant: 10,000 - 125,000 USD

Contact: Lisa Hansen, Grants Administration Manager; (651) 325-4261 or (800) 875-6167; fax (651) 224-8123; lisa.hansen@mnpartners.org or info@frbigelow.org

Internet: www.frbigelow.org

Sponsor: F.R. Bigelow Foundation

55 Fifth Street, Suite 600

St. Paul, MN 55101-1797

Farmers Insurance Corporate Giving Grants 948

The corporate community relations program awards grants in the areas of education, public safety, arts and culture, civic improvement, and health and human services. Education giving focuses on literacy programs, mentoring programs, adopt-a-school programs, employee matching grants, and aid-to-education undergraduate scholarships. Public safety awards support tougher laws against drunk driving, drug- and alcohol-free graduation night parties, neighborhood crime prevention, highway safety, and earthquake relief. Arts and culture funding supports children's programs and public television. Civic improvement focuses on recognizing exemplary youth, voter registration drives, adopt-a-highway programs, and community paint-a-thons. Health and human services giving supports March of Dimes, United Way, aid for families with cancer, and to migrant farmworkers, and feeding the hungry. There are no application deadlines. Requests for contributions should be in the form of a letter outlining the purpose of the organization or program. The letter also should include the amount requested, its intended use, and a description of how Farmers' support will be recognized. Additional information should include a budget, annual report, proof of tax-exempt status, and a roster of the board of directors.

Requirements: 501(c)3 tax-exempt organizations are eligible.

Restrictions: Farmers does not make charitable contributions to individuals, political candidates, or religious groups or for sports events, advertising or raffle tickets, construction projects, or international programs.

Geographic Focus: All States

Contact: Doris Dunn, Director of Community Relations; (888) 327-6335

Internet: www.farmers.com/corporate_giving.html

Sponsor: Farmers Insurance Group of Companies

4680 Wilshire Boulevard

Los Angeles, CA 90010

Fassino Foundation Grants 949

Established in 1992, the foundation awards grants to community-based organizations in the greater Boston area for programs intended to make a measurable difference in the lives of homeless, abused, and disabled children and women. Fields of interest include: children and youth services, education, family services, and hospitals. Funding comes in the form of general operating support. Preference is given to programs that have defined and measurable goals and can demonstrate a history of success in dealing with family issues. Grant ranges fall in two brackets, and require using the Associated Grant Makers application form.

Requirements: Massachusetts nonprofit organizations serving the greater Boston area are eligible.

Geographic Focus: Massachusetts

Amount of Grant: 10,000 - 50,000 USD

Samples: Lovelane, Lincoln, Massachusetts, $35,000 - special needs horseback riding program; Women's Lunch Place, Boston, Massachusetts, $20,000 - operating support.

Contact: Edward G. Fassino, President; (508) 653-4554; efassino@attbi.com

Sponsor: Fassino Foundation

42 Eliot Hill Road

Natick, MA 01760

Faye L. and William L. Cowden Charitable Foundation Grants 950

William L. Cowden was born in 1910 in Midland County to a prominent ranching family specializing in fine stock and beef cattle. The family also owned extensive mineral interests that were the source of much of the Cowden wealth. Faye L. Cowden was born in 1913 in Charlotte, Texas. One of the Cowden's closest friends was the renowned artist Korczak Ziolkowski (1908-1982), the sculptor of the Crazy Horse Mountain monument in the Black Hills of South Dakota. The Cowdens established the Charitable Foundation in 1988, to help as many people as possible, with an emphasis on children. Its primary purposes are to support: the health, medical care and treatment and rehabilitation of children, including related medical research; the education of children and young adults, and the provision of special educational opportunities for young persons otherwise unable to afford them; the prevention of cruelty to children or animals; and the protection and preservation of wildlife and natural areas. Awards range from $2,500 to $15,000. The annual deadline for online application submission is March 31.

Requirements: Grants are directed to 501(c)3 organizations which fall within the principal charitable purposes of the foundation.

Geographic Focus: Texas

Date(s) Application is Due: Mar 31

Amount of Grant: 2,500 - 15,000 USD

Samples: Brighton School, San Antonio, Texas, $2,500 - general fund contribution; Children's Shelter, San Antonio, Texas, $15,000 - general fund contribution; Cibolo Nature Center, San Antonio, Texas, $15,000 - general fund contribution.

Contact: Tammy Ashby, Trustee; (210) 283-6700 or (210) 283-6500; tashby@broadwaybank.com

Internet: www.broadwaybank.com/wealthmanagement/FoundationFayeLWilliamLCowden.html

Sponsor: Faye L. and William L. Cowden Charitable Foundation

P.O. Box 17001

San Antonio, TX 78217-0001

Fayette County Foundation Grants 951

The Fayette County Foundation is the community's resource for charitable giving. The Foundation serves the entire Fayette County by assisting donors and meeting community needs. To be eligible to receive funding from the Fayette County Foundation a letter of intent must be submitted by March 1, July 1 or October 1 and followed by a completed grant application by the appropriate grant deadline. All grant seekers must have prior governing board approval for the project seeking funding. The approval of signed minutes and a signed letter from governing board must be available to the Fayette County Foundation. Faith-based organizations may apply as long as the project does not mandate participation in a religious activity as a condition for receiving services. Samples of previously funded projects are available at the website.

Requirements: Projects must have public access for all Fayette County citizens. Completed grant application (original plus eight copies) must be received by the Foundation by the last Friday in March, the last Friday in July or the last Friday in October at Noon to be considered for funding.

Restrictions: Legal requirements forbid staff, trustees, directors, committee members and their families from profiting financially from any philanthropic grant. All persons actively connected with the Foundation will consistently strive to avoid self-interest in the processing and disposition of grant request. Only one successful application per 12 months will be considered. Repeat funding for the same project may be considered five years after the initial project on a case by case basis.

Geographic Focus: Indiana

Date(s) Application is Due: Mar 1; Jul 1; Oct 1

Contact: Loree Crowe; (765) 827-9966; fax (765) 827-5836; info@fayettefoundation.com

Internet: www.fayettefoundation.com/default.asp?Page=Grant+Policy&PageIndex=128

Sponsor: Fayette County Foundation

521 N Central Avenue, Suite A, P.O. Box 844

Connersville, IN 47331

FCD New American Children Grants 952

The foundation awards grants to support programs for children, particularly the disadvantaged, and promote their well-being through basic and policy-relevant research about the factors that promote optimal development of children and adolescents; policy analysis, advocacy, services, and public education to enhance the discussion and adoption of social policies that support families in their important child-raising responsibilities; and leadership development activities linked to the programmatic focus of the foundation. Grants focus on the integration of research, policy, and advocacy in two areas: the availability of and access to early childhood education programs and health care for children. Most grants support research, but a small number of direct service grants are made for New York City-based projects that advance the foundation's research and policy analysis efforts. There are no application deadlines; submit a brief letter of inquiry. Full proposals are by invitation only, following a strict pre-proposal process.

Requirements: Nonprofit organizations are eligible.

Restrictions: The foundation does not consider requests for scholarships or support for individuals, capital campaigns, building purchase or renovation, or equipment purchase. The foundation does not make grants outside the United States.

Geographic Focus: All States

Amount of Grant: Up to 800,000 USD

Samples: New America Foundation, Washington, D.C., $770,000 - continued support of the PreK-3rd Education Reform Initiative and the Federal Education Budget Project; Rutgers University Foundation, New Brunswick, New Jersey, $30,000 - support of the Burns Family Endowment for Teacher Leadership in Early Childhood Education; University of Texas at Austin, Austin, Texas, $349,561 - continued support of the Dual-Generation Strategy Initiative Project.

Contact: Dorothy Pflager, Grants Manager; (212) 867-5777; fax (212) 867-5844; dorothy@fcd-us.org or info@fcd-us.org

Internet: fcd-us.org/grants

Sponsor: Foundation for Child Development

295 Madison Avenue, 40th Floor

New York, NY 10017

FCD Young Scholars Program Grants 953

The Foundation for Child Development has endured for over 100 years as a result of the constancy of its commitment to promoting the well-being of children and the flexibility with which it evolves with the times, embracing new strategies as children's needs, our society, and research knowledge have changed. The Foundation's Young Scholars Program (YSP) is no exception to this process of renewal. The Foundation remains steadfastly committed to this flagship program aimed at developing the next generation of developmental scientists who are equipped to advance policy and practice on behalf of the nation's children. FCD is committed to the following issues in developing the next generation of the YSP: empirical and professional mentoring; recruiting scholars from underrepresented groups, notably scholars of color; creating a community of interdisciplinary scholars and supporting collaboration among them; ensuring that pressing policy and practice challenges inform the work of the scholars; fostering the scholars' capacity to translate their work for policy and practice audiences; and expanding opportunities for the young scholars to engage with other FCD grantees by, in part, creating greater thematic coherence across all of FCD's strategic initiatives. Letters of Intent (LOIs) must be received by June 1, and final applications by October 19.
Requirements: Eligible researchers must have received their doctoral degrees (e.g., Ph.D., Ed.D., Psy.D., M.D., J.D., etc) within one to seven years of application submission (ten years for physician applicants). Applicants must hold this degree or its equivalent in one of the behavior or social sciences, or in an allied professional field (i.e., public policy, public health, education, social work, nursing). Applicants must hold a position as a full-time, tenure-track faculty member of a U.S. college or university. The affiliated private non-profit organization must have a minimum operating budget of $2.5 million and a minimum three-year track record in conducting multi-year research projects.
Restrictions: The Foundation does not consider requests for: capital campaigns, the purchase, construction or renovation of buildings, grants for projects outside the United States, the direct provision of preschool education or child care, or health care; or under the foundation's health focus, research, policy, or direct-service projects concerned with specific illnesses.
Geographic Focus: All States
Date(s) Application is Due: Oct 19
Contact: Grants Officer; (212) 867-5777; fax (212) 867-5844; ysp@fcd-us.org
Internet: fcd-us.org/our-work/young-scholars-program
Sponsor: Foundation for Child Development
295 Madison Avenue, 40th Floor
New York, NY 10017

FCYO Youth Organizing Grants 954

Since its inception, FCYO has been focused on increasing philanthropic, intellectual and social capital necessary to strengthen, grow and sustain the field of youth organizing. To strategically resource, build and sustain youth organizing efforts, FCYO aims to: regrant nationally through pooled funds and a fully supported, cost-effective, collaborative learning process; promote networking and infrastructure development to connect and strengthen youth organizing efforts, and support peer exchange and relationship-building; build the capacity of youth organizing groups through convenings, research and documentation, and the development of materials and resources; and strategically partner with key youth organizing intermediaries and youth-serving professionals to strengthen and support grassroots groups at all stages of development. Interested applicants are advised to contact the organization prior to submitting application.
Requirements: Eligible applicants include independent organizations, networks, projects within adult-led organizations, intergenerational organizations, and coalitions. Preference is given to organizations with a significant history of youth organizing and budgets under $1 million. A limited percentage of funds have been set aside for emerging groups.
Geographic Focus: All States
Amount of Grant: 15,000 - 30,000 USD
Contact: Lorraine Marasigan, Program Officer; (212) 725-3386; info@fcyo.org
Internet: www.fcyo.org/grantmaking
Sponsor: Funders Collaborative on Youth Organizing
20 Jay Street, 210B
Brooklyn, NY 11201

Fichtenbaum Charitable Trust Grants 955

The Fichtenbaum Charitable Trust was established in 2017 by Dorace and Morton Fichtenbaum, who lived in Dallas, to provide financial support for charitable, religious, scientific, literary or educational purposes to qualified Texas charitable organizations. Dorace and Morton were both very supportive of the local community throughout their lives. Areas of interest include Medical Research (specifically cancer, heart, vision and Myasthenia Gravis), Education and research for children with mental or physical disabilities, and Children's education and exposure to fine arts. Grants may include capital and program support, research, scholarships and grants to meet challenges or matching funds. The majority of grants from the Foundation are 1 year in duration. Grant amounts will average from $10,000 to $100,000. Larger multi-year commitments can be awarded. The average grant size is $35,000.
Requirements: Successful proposals are unique, necessary and of high priority for the charitable organizations, and do not duplicate other services which are available. Successful proposals seek funding that may not be readily available from other sources for essential projects that are sufficiently described as worthwhile, important and of a substantive nature. Applications will be submitted online through the Bank of America website. A grant report is required within 1 year of the grant application date, regardless of whether all of the funds have been spent.
Restrictions: The fund does not support requests from individuals, organizations attempting to influence policy through direct lobbying, or any political campaigns.
Geographic Focus: Texas
Date(s) Application is Due: May 1

Amount of Grant: 10,000 - 100,000 USD
Contact: Debra Goldstein Phares, Philanthropic Client Director; (800) 357-7094; tx.philanthropic@bankofamerica.com or tx.philanthropic@ustrust.com
Internet: www.bankofamerica.com/philanthropic/foundation/?fnId=302
Sponsor: Fichtenbaum Charitable Trust
P.O. Box 831041
Dallas, TX 75283-1041

Fidelity Charitable Gift Fund Grants 956

Fidelity Charitable is a 501(c)3 public charity established in Massachusetts in 1991, with the expressed purpose of making it easy for donors to leave a lasting impact through philanthropy — in particular, through the Fund's donor-advised giving program, called the Giving Account. Fidelity has streamlined the process of strategic giving for a broad range of donors, allowing them to contribute many types of assets, and plan their giving more systematically, maximizing their generosity. The program offers support for: emergency aid; Christianity; diseases and conditions; elementary and secondary education; higher education; human services; international development; literacy; natural resource conservation; performing arts; and philanthropy. Primary populations served include children and youth, economically disadvantaged, and low-income and poor. Support is typically given in the form of general operations and program development. The Board meets three times annually, in February, June, and October. Contributions are made to pre-selected organizations, and interested parties should begin by writing a letter of introduction.
Requirements: Any 501(c)3 organization in the United States is eligible for support.
Geographic Focus: All States, American Samoa, District of Columbia, Guam, Marshall Islands, Northern Mariana Islands, Puerto Rico, U.S. Virgin Islands
Amount of Grant: Up to 100,000,000 USD
Samples: Maui Food Bank, Wailuku, Hawaii, $32,100 - general operating support; Youth Renewal Fund, New York, New York, $3,287,525 - general operating support; Grand Teton National Park Foundation, Jackson, Wyoming, $325,268 - general operating support.
Contact: Pamela Norley, Fidelity Charitable President; (617) 563-6806 or (800) 952-4438; fax (877) 665-4274
Internet: www.fidelitycharitable.org/
Sponsor: Fidelity Charitable Gift Fund
P.O. Box 770001
Cincinnati, OH 45277-0053

Fidelity Foundation Grants 957

Fidelity Investments Chairman Edward C. Johnson 3rd and his father, the founder of the company, established the Fidelity Foundation in 1965 with several operating principles in mind. These principles, still current today, guide the Foundation's decisions and grantmaking. The Foundation grant program was designed to strengthen the long-term effectiveness of nonprofit institutions. The types of projects it funds, and the way in which it funds them, are specifically intended to help nonprofits build the organizational capabilities they need to better fulfill their missions and serve their constituencies. The Fidelity Foundation considers Letters of Inquiry from organizations with current IRS 501(c)3 public charity status only. Grants are made to fund only significant, transformative projects usually budgeted at $100,000 or more. The Foundation's primary philanthropic investments are allocated to the following sectors: community and social services including youth development, providing access to basic human needs such as food, health care, and housing; museums, historical, and other cultural organizations; financial literacy for youth including financial education and capability; and educational institutions. The Foundation considers influential community projects from organizations in regions around Fidelity Investments' employee sites in the listed metropolitan areas. Organizations of national importance and high-impact projects with potential to inform the nonprofit sector are also of interest. The Foundation seeks to work with organizations on strategic, transformative projects that have the potential to substantially increase the grantee's impact, efficiency, or long-term sustainability. These capacity-building projects fall into three areas: capital investments; planning initiatives; and technology projects. Typically the initial Letter of Inquiry (LOI) review process will take between four and six weeks.
Requirements: Grants are generally made only to organizations with operating budgets of $1,000,000 or more. The Fidelity Foundation considers projects from organizations of regional or national importance throughout the United States. Proposed projects must be budgeted at $100,000 or more.
Restrictions: Grants are not awarded to support sectarian organizations, disease-specific associations, or public school systems. Support does not go to individuals or for scholarships, civic or start-up organizations, corporate memberships, operating support, or participation in benefit events, film, or video projects.
Geographic Focus: All States
Amount of Grant: 100,000 - 1,000,000 USD
Contact: Genie Healy McGowan; (617) 563-6806; info@FidelityFoundation.org
Internet: www.fidelityfoundation.org/grantmaking-guidelines/
Sponsor: Fidelity Foundation
82 Devonshire Street, S2
Boston, MA 02109

Fifth Third Bank Corporate Giving 958

The concept of corporate social responsibility (CSR) is growing in visibility and importance in today's business environment. Fifth Third Bank has a long-standing desire to be a positive, contributing member of the communities it serves. It's a commitment that grew out of the Bank's history—Jacob G. Schmidlapp, one of the Bank's early leaders, was a well-known philanthropist. In 1948, the Bank was the first financial institution in the United States to establish a charitable foundation. In 2010, the Bank framed all of its community support into a Corporate Social Responsibility Report titled, "Responsibility

Begins Here." The report, which is viewable as an interactive web presentation, details the Bank's commitment to being a good corporate citizen. The Bank's approach to CSR originated from its belief that the Company is only as strong as the community it serves. The report outlines the Bank's focus on five key initiatives: financial literacy; youth education; community development; diversity and inclusion; and environmental stewardship.
Requirements: Giving is limited in to communities in which Fifth Third Bank has a presence.
Geographic Focus: Florida, Illinois, Indiana, Kentucky, Michigan, Ohio, Tennessee, West Virginia
Contact: Mark Walton, CRA Manager; (513) 534-7037
Internet: www.53.com/site/about/in-the-community/corporate-social-responsibility.html?
Sponsor: Fifth Third Bank Corporation
38 Fountain Square Plaza, MD 10906E
Cincinnati, OH 45263

Fifth Third Foundation Grants **959**
The Fifth Third Foundation awards grants to eligible nonprofit organizations in its areas of interest, including community development, education, health and human services, and arts and culture. Proposals are favored that are likely to make a substantial difference in the quality of community life; strengthen families and communities; expand meaningful civic engagement and build social capital; use volunteers; help nonprofit organizations build capacity and become more effective; include financial and other strategic commitments from other funding organizations; and leverage change in the capacity of community-wide systems rather than individual organizations. Interested applicants should initially contact the Foundation via a brief letter detailing the organization, its mission, the project it seeks funding for, and an approximate grant amount to be requested.
Requirements: 501(c)3 nonprofit, tax-exempt organizations operating in Fifth Third's geographic regions of Ohio, Kentucky, Indiana, Michigan, Illinois, Tennessee, West Virginia, and Florida are eligible to apply.
Restrictions: The following types of support are ineligible: capital campaigns for individual churches; publicly supported entities, such as public schools or government agencies; elementary schools; and individuals.
Geographic Focus: Florida, Illinois, Indiana, Kentucky, Michigan, Ohio, Tennessee, West Virginia
Contact: Heidi B. Jark, Managing Director; (513) 534-7001 or (513) 534-4397; fax (513) 534-0960; heidi.jark@@53.com
Internet: www.53.com/site/about/in-the-community/foundation-office-at-fifth-third-bank.html?
Sponsor: Fifth Third Foundation
38 Fountain Square Plaza, MD 1090CA
Cincinnati, OH 45263

Finish Line Youth Foundation Founder's Grants **960**
Finish Line Youth Foundation focuses funding on organizations that provide opportunities for youth participation in the following areas: Youth athletic programs - Community-based programs addressing active lifestyle and team building skills; Camps - Established camps with an emphasis on sports and active lifestyle, especially programs serving disadvantaged and special needs kids. These emergency funds grants would be awarded to qualifying organizations that have an emergency need that would somehow be keeping the organization from providing current services. Examples would be natural disasters or other unforeseen circumstances that require special funding to help build or develop facilities or equipment needs.
Requirements: Organizations operating near a Finish Line store with 501(c)3 tax-exempt status that provide opportunities for participation for children and young adults age 18 and under are eligible to apply. Preference is given to organizations whose activities provide direct services to individuals and produce tangible results, rather than those that are policy oriented. The foundation has a particular interest in the potential impact of the program/project and the number of people who will benefit; the organization's fiscal responsibility and management qualifications; and, the ability of an organization to obtain the necessary additional funding to implement a program or project and to provide ongoing funding after the term of the grant has expired.
Restrictions: The Foundation will not make grants to: Organizations not currently exempt from federal taxation under section 501(c)3 of the Internal Revenue Code or created for eligible public purposes (such as public and private schools and state-funded universities and colleges); Political campaigns, or attempts to influence public officials; Organizations that unlawfully discriminate as to race, religion, income, gender, disability or national origin; Projects or programs aimed at promoting the teachings of a particular church or religious denomination, or construction projects of churches and other religious institutions; Fraternal, veterans or labor organizations; Foundations affiliated with a for-profit entity; Endowments; Organizations for on-going operating support; Start up organizations or programs; Reduce debt; Beauty or talent contests; Individuals; Sponsor teams, special events or fundraising activities; Medical, scientific or academic research; Pay for travel or trips.
Geographic Focus: All States
Amount of Grant: 5,000 - 25,000 USD
Contact: Roger Underwood, President; (317) 899-1022 x6741; Youthfoundation@finishline.com
Internet: www.finishline.com/store/youthfoundation/special-grants.jsp
Sponsor: Finish Line Youth Foundation
3308 N Mitthoeffer Road
Indianapolis, IN 46235

Finish Line Youth Foundation Grants **961**
Finish Line Youth Foundation focuses funding on organizations that provide opportunities for youth participation in the following areas: Youth athletic programs - Community-based programs addressing active lifestyle and team building skills; Camps - Established camps with an emphasis on sports and active lifestyle, especially programs serving disadvantaged and special needs kids. The foundation may provide financial support for Programs and Projects (direct costs of youth programming for requests in their areas of interest) or Scholarships (full or partial scholarship funding for camps or youth athletic programs). In general grants range from $1,000 - $5,000.
Requirements: The foundation is particularly interested in: Organizations providing opportunities for participation for children and young adults age 18 and under; Organizations whose activities provide direct services to individuals and produce tangible results, rather than those that are policy oriented; The potential impact of the program/project and the number of people who will benefit; The organization's fiscal responsibility and management qualifications; The ability of an organization to obtain the necessary additional funding to implement a program or project and to provide ongoing funding after the term of the grant has expired; Programs operating near Finish Line stores.
Restrictions: The Foundation will not make grants to: Organizations not currently exempt from federal taxation under section 501(c)3 of the Internal Revenue Code or created for eligible public purposes (such as public and private schools and state-funded universities and colleges); Political campaigns, or attempts to influence public officials; Organizations that unlawfully discriminate as to race, religion, income, gender, disability or national origin; Projects or programs aimed at promoting the teachings of a particular church or religious denomination, or construction projects of churches and other religious institutions; Fraternal, veterans or labor organizations; Foundations affiliated with a for-profit entity; Endowments; Organizations for on-going operating support; Start up organizations or programs; Reduce debt; Beauty or talent contests; Individuals; Sponsor teams, special events or fundraising activities; Medical, scientific or academic research; Pay for travel or trips.
Geographic Focus: All States
Amount of Grant: 1,000 - 5,000 USD
Contact: Roger Underwood, President; (317) 899-1022 x6741; Youthfoundation@finishline.com
Internet: www.finishline.com/store/youthfoundation/guidelines.jsp
Sponsor: Finish Line Youth Foundation
3308 N Mitthoeffer Road
Indianapolis, IN 46235

Finish Line Youth Foundation Legacy Grants **962**
Finish Line Youth Foundation focuses funding on organizations that provide opportunities for youth participation in the following areas: Youth athletic programs - Community-based programs addressing active lifestyle and team building skills; Camps - Established camps with an emphasis on sports and active lifestyle, especially programs serving disadvantaged and special needs kids. The Legacy Grants will be awarded to qualifying organizations in need of improvements and/or renovations to existing buildings, grounds, and property or for new facilities and/or grounds.
Requirements: Organizations operating near a Finish Line store with 501(c)3 tax-exempt status that provide opportunities for participation for children and young adults age 18 and under are eligible to apply. Preference is given to organizations whose activities provide direct services to individuals and produce tangible results, rather than those that are policy oriented. The foundation has a particular interest in the potential impact of the program/project and the number of people who will benefit; the organization's fiscal responsibility and management qualifications; and, the ability of an organization to obtain the necessary additional funding to implement a program or project and to provide ongoing funding after the term of the grant has expired.
Restrictions: The Foundation will not make grants to: Organizations not currently exempt from federal taxation under section 501(c)3 of the Internal Revenue Code or created for eligible public purposes (such as public and private schools and state-funded universities and colleges); Political campaigns, or attempts to influence public officials; Organizations that unlawfully discriminate as to race, religion, income, gender, disability or national origin; Projects or programs aimed at promoting the teachings of a particular church or religious denomination, or construction projects of churches and other religious institutions; Fraternal, veterans or labor organizations; Foundations affiliated with a for-profit entity; Endowments; Organizations for on-going operating support; Start up organizations or programs; Reduce debt; Beauty or talent contests; Individuals; Sponsor teams, special events or fundraising activities; Medical, scientific or academic research; Pay for travel or trips.
Geographic Focus: All States
Amount of Grant: 10,000 - 75,000 USD
Contact: Roger Underwood, President; (317) 899-1022 x6741; Youthfoundation@finishline.com
Internet: www.finishline.com/store/youthfoundation/special-grants.jsp
Sponsor: Finish Line Youth Foundation
3308 N Mitthoeffer Road
Indianapolis, IN 46235

FINRA Smart Investing@Your Library Grants **963**
The Smart Investing@Your Library Grant program is administered jointly by the FINRA Investor Education Foundation and the American Library Association. This special grant program funds public library efforts to provide library patrons with access to effective, unbiased financial education resources. Grant recipients—public libraries and public library networks across the country—use a variety of technologies and outreach strategies to bring quality financial and investor education opportunities within easy reach of diverse groups of library patrons at no cost to them. The grantees partner with an array of organizations, including schools, universities and local agencies, to expand the impact of the services and resources enabled by the grants. Through the program, library patrons are empowered to make smart financial decisions, both for long-term investing and day-to-day money matters. The program is especially concerned with helping those who might otherwise have limited access to important information relevant to their financial well-being.
Requirements: Public libraries and library networks throughout the United States are eligible to apply.
Restrictions: The foundation will not award grants to individuals; organizations affiliated with a current member of the foundation board of directors or FINRA board of governors; securities firms regulated by FINRA; organizations affiliated with a securities firm or individual regulated by FINRA, such as a foundation established by a securities firm;

securities regulators, self-regulatory organizations, or securities industry trade associations; organizations that are termed disqualified persons pursuant to Article III, Section 3(d) of the FINRA by-laws; foreign organizations; or entities that discriminate on the basis of age, color, disability, marital status, national origin, race, religion, sex, sexual orientation, or veteran status. The Foundation will generally not consider proposals to fund: international programs or projects; expenses that are not directly related to the project for which funding is sought; salaries of permanent staff (for example, prorated salaries of administrative and executive personnel, or oversight and coordination activities of a project principal); capital costs, such as building and construction or equipment such as computer hardware and office furniture; pass-through funding (for example, if the 501(c)3 organization plans to turn over the funding to a proprietary organization or consultant); projects with a potential conflict of interest (for example where funded technical support or expertise might be provided by a board member of the 501(c)3 organization); conferences and similar activities that fail to provide a long-term solution or sufficiently broad outreach; distribution methodologies that require ongoing maintenance when the ability to perform upkeep without continued funding is questionable (for example, materials with a short "shelf life" that would require ongoing funding for frequent updating); projects with proprietary elements, such as for-profit activities, use or purchase of copyrighted or trademarked materials, and proprietary research; lobbying, political contributions, fund-raising events, or other similar activities designed to influence legislation or intervene in political campaigns; donations, endowments, challenge grants, matching funds, and other similar programs; or direct or matching payments to members of the public, such as scholarships, assistance with personal and family financial difficulties, registration fees for conferences and training, or similar activities.

Geographic Focus: All States

Amount of Grant: Up to 100,000 USD

Samples: Apache Junction Public Library, Apache Junction, Arizona, $70,200 - partner with the University of Arizona to offer financial literacy classes at the library and other community locations, emphasizing the small steps residents can take to lead a healthy lifestyle, both physically and financially; Florence County Library System, Florence, South Carolina, $47,949 - pursue a multigenerational financial literacy strategy in partnership with the South Carolina Department of Consumer Affairs and others; Monroe County Public Library, Bloomington, Indiana, $79,582 - will target teens and 20-somethings, including Spanish speakers, through 15 workshops and 15 "talk-to-an-expert" sessions on five high-priority topics: budgeting, saving, spending, managing credit and debt, and investing.

Contact: Robert Ganem, (202) 728-8362; robert.ganem@finra.com

Internet: www.finrafoundation.org/grants/library/

Sponsor: FINRA Investor Education Foundation

1735 K Street, NW

Washington, D.C. 20006-1506

Firelight Foundation Grants 964

Firelight provides small grants to community-based organizations selected for their vision and resourcefulness. The Foundation is often the first funder to an organization. Its grantmaking model is framed by a seven-year partnership model, which is divided into three phases. Firelight grantee-partners develop programs unique to the needs of their community. By working across multiple focus areas, our partners are able to address the needs of traumatized or vulnerable children and families effected by poverty, HIV and AIDS. Its primary goals include: providing basic necessities, including clothing, bedding, personal hygiene and shelter; supporting food production, feeding programs and household food assistance for vulnerable children and families; providing materials, skills and knowledge to caregivers to help them generate income and strengthen household resiliency; enhancing the caring relationships that meet the emotional, social, and recreational needs of children and help build life and coping skills; building a supportive and protective environment that prevents and responds to violence, abuse, and the exploitation of children; offering huilding a supportive and protective environment that prevents and responds to violence, abuse, and the exploitation of children; and extending primary health care, preventive care and HIV and AIDS-related preventive and palliative care.

Requirements: The Foundation accepts unsolicited proposals from seven countries in sub-Saharan Africa: Lesotho, Malawi, Rwanda, South Africa, Tanzania, Zambia, and Zimbabwe. In addition, Firelight awards grants to CBOs in Ethiopia, Kenya, and Uganda through solicited proposals.

Restrictions: The foundation does not fund: individuals; organizations or programs designed to influence legislation or elect public officials; programs that limit participation based on race, creed, or nationality; academic or medical research; or fundraising drives or endowments.

Geographic Focus: Ethiopia, Kenya, Lesotho, Malawi, Rwanda, South Africa, Tanzania, Uganda, Zambia, Zimbabwe

Amount of Grant: 500 - 10,000 USD

Contact: Evelyn Brown, Grants Administrator; (831) 429-8750; fax (831) 429-2036; evelyn@firelightfoundation.org

Internet: www.firelightfoundation.org/programs/grantmaking/

Sponsor: Firelight Foundation

740 Front Street, Suite 380

Santa Cruz, CA 95060

FirstEnergy Foundation Community Grants 965

The FirstEnergy Foundation's contributions to local nonprofit organizations help strengthen the social and economic fabric of our communities. Funded solely by FirstEnergy, the Foundation extends the corporate philosophy of providing community support. The Foundation traditionally funds these priorities: help improve the vitality of our communities and support key safety initiatives; promotion of local and regional economic development and revitalization efforts; and support of FirstEnergy employee community leadership and volunteer interests. Application must be mailed in.

Requirements: 501(c)3 organizations within the FirstEnergy Corporation operating companies' service areas - Ohio Edison Company, the Cleveland Electric Illuminating Company, the Toledo Edison Company, Pennsylvania Power Company, Metropolitan Edison Company, Pennsylvania Electric Company, Jersey Central Power and Light Company, Monongahela Power Company, the Potomac Edison Company, West Penn Power Company, FirstEnergy Solutions Corporation, FirstEnergy Generation, and FirstEnergy Nuclear Operations - are eligible to apply.

Restrictions: Funding is not considered for: direct grants to individuals, political or legislative activities; organizations that receive sizable public tax funding; fraternal, religious, labor, athletic, social or veterans organizations - unless the contribution is earmarked for an eligible program or campaign open to all beneficiaries, including those not affiliated with the host organization; national or international organizations; organizations supported by federated campaigns, such as United Way; research; equipment purchases; loans or second party giving, such as endowments, debt retirement, or foundations; or public or private schools.

Geographic Focus: Maryland, New Jersey, Ohio, Pennsylvania, West Virginia

Contact: Lorna Wisham, President; (330) 384-5752; fax (330) 436-8031; FE_Comm_Involve@firstenergycorp.com

Internet: www.firstenergycorp.com/community/firstenergy_foundation.html

Sponsor: FirstEnergy Foundation

76 South Main Street

Akron, OH 44308-1890

FirstEnergy Foundation Science, Technology, Engineering, and 966 Mathematics Grants

The FirstEnergy Foundation supports classroom projects and teacher professional-development initiatives focusing on science, technology, engineering and mathematics (STEM). One of the ways the Foundation supports these activities is by offering science, technology, engineering and mathematics (STEM) education grants of up to $500 to educators at schools and youth groups in communities served by our electric operating companies, other areas where we have facilities, and where we do business. Grants may be used to compensate experts who come to work with students, but not to pay teachers or staff. Resources requested should be integral components of a well-planned classroom project/lesson plan, and important to its success. Grants amount to $1,000.

Requirements: Pre-K-12 educators and youth group leaders in Ohio, Pennsylvania, New Jersey, Maryland, and West Virginia communities served by FirstEnergy are eligible.

Restrictions: Funding is generally not made to individuals, political, or legislative activities. Grants cannot be used to support: school laboratory supplies or equipment for general school use; purchase of equipment like computers, digital cameras, DVD players, display cases, etc; continuation of projects previously funded; routine responsibilities of the educator submitting the proposal; stipends for attending teacher development events; or funding for student participation in the project.

Geographic Focus: Maryland, New Jersey, Ohio, Pennsylvania, West Virginia

Amount of Grant: Up to 1,000 USD

Contact: Lorna Wisham, President; (330) 384-5752; fax (330) 436-8031; FE_Comm_Involve@firstenergycorp.com

Internet: www.firstenergycorp.com/community/education/educational_grants.html

Sponsor: FirstEnergy Foundation

76 South Main Street

Akron, OH 44308-1890

First Hawaiian Bank Foundation Corporate Giving Grants 967

The First Hawaiian Bank Foundation, the charitable arm of First Hawaiian Bank, was established in 1975. It is also the largest corporate foundation contributing to charity in Hawaii, Guam, and the Commonwealth of the Northern Mariana Islands (CNMI). Each year, First Hawaiian Bank, its employees, and the First Hawaiian Bank Foundation donate several million dollars to more than four hundred non-profit organizations in these regions. The Foundation's primary focus remains enriching education opportunities for youth, improving the lives of others, building healthier communities, and invigorating diverse cultural life. The Foundation continues to invest in programs and services that are dedicated to solving community challenges, extending opportunities for young and old, and enriching lives throughout the Hawaiian islands, Guam and CNMI. Currently, the Foundation supports programs that strengthen communities by making grants to non-profit organizations that: meet human services needs; provide educational opportunities; serve children and youth; improve access to healthcare; and enrich lives through culture and the arts.

Requirements: All prospective grant applicants must submit an online application, which is the first step in requesting funds from the Foundation.

Restrictions: The Foundation typically does not fund requests for ongoing operational expenses, endowments, sponsorships, conferences or special events.

Geographic Focus: Hawaii

Date(s) Application is Due: Jan 1; Apr 1; Jul 1; Oct 1

Samples: Kuakini Foundation, Honolulu, Hawaii, $40,000 - funding to purchase two emergency generators on the medical center's Liliha campus; Diamond Head Theater, Honolulu, Hawaii, $66,666 - capital campaign to construct a new Diamond Head Theater; Punahou School, Honolulu, Hawaii, $50,000 - construction support of the Sidney and Minnie Kosasa Community.

Contact: Robert Harrison; (808) 525-7777; fax (808) 525-8708; fhbfoundation@fhb.com

Internet: www.fhb.com/en/caring-for-our-community/corporate-giving/

Sponsor: First Hawaiian Bank Foundation

999 Bishop Street

Honolulu, HI 96813

First Lady's Family Literacy Initiative for Texas Family Literacy Trailblazer Grants 968

The First Lady's Family Literacy Initiative for Texas is a program of the Barbara Bush Texas Fund for Family Literacy. Launched at the Governor's Mansion in Austin in 1996 by Honorary Chair Laura Bush, The First Lady's Family Literacy Initiative for Texas supports family literacy programs that: increase literacy skills and educational levels of under-educated parents; implement a management and accountability system to measure program effectiveness and outcomes on a regular basis; provide a path to post-secondary education (beyond the GED) and employment; improve the quality of parent/child interaction, and adults' parenting skills in support of their children's learning; employ well-trained and dedicated staff who establish learning environments that positively affect recruitment and retention of adult learners; and encourage families to develop a love for books and reading, and prepare children for the school experience Introduce parents to the services of the library. The new Trailblazer Grant of up to $50,000 per year for three consecutive years will be awarded to no more than three organizations. Their term of funding will extend for a total of three years, pending an annual review by leadership of The First Lady's Family Literacy Initiative for Texas.

Requirements: Eligible applicants for both Planning Grants must: be a local educational agency; non-profit 501(c)3 organization; community-based organization; public institution; correctional agency; or a consortium of these agencies. Further, applicants must be based with an established organization that has maintained current non-profit or public status for at least two years as of the date of the application be prepared to document fiscal accountability if requested by The Barbara Bush Texas Fund (i.e., provide copy of most recent annual audit report or IRS return).

Geographic Focus: Texas

Date(s) Application is Due: Mar 5

Amount of Grant: Up to 50,000 USD

Contact: Ken Appelt; (979) 845-6615; fax (979) 845-0952; kappelt@tamu.edu

Internet: www-tcall.tamu.edu/bbush/firstladyAnnounce.html

Sponsor: Barbara Bush Texas Fund for Family Literacy
Riverside Campus, Texas A&M University
College Station, TX 77843-4477

First Lady's Family Literacy Initiative for Texas Implementation Grants 969

The First Lady's Family Literacy Initiative for Texas is a program of the Barbara Bush Texas Fund for Family Literacy. Launched at the Governor's Mansion in Austin in 1996 by Honorary Chair Laura Bush, The First Lady's Family Literacy Initiative for Texas supports family literacy programs that: increase literacy skills and educational levels of under-educated parents; implement a management and accountability system to measure program effectiveness and outcomes on a regular basis; provide a path to post-secondary education (beyond the GED) and employment; improve the quality of parent/child interaction, and adults' parenting skills in support of their children's learning; employ well-trained and dedicated staff who establish learning environments that positively affect recruitment and retention of adult learners; and encourage families to develop a love for books and reading, and prepare children for the school experience Introduce parents to the services of the library. Up to ten Implementation Grants of up to $50,000 will be awarded to Texas organizations. They are intended to: help create a family literacy program that offers three integrated components of adult literacy education (basic literacy, GED Test preparation, or English as a Second Language), pre-literacy or literacy instruction for young children (ages birth through grade 3) of those adults, and interactive literacy activities for the young children together with their parents or primary caregivers; expand an existing literacy program that works with only one generation so that a complete family literacy program (including the required components named above) can be created; allow for an innovative project within an existing family literacy program; or replicate a successful family literacy program with a new population or in a new location.

Requirements: Eligible applicants for both Planning Grants must: be a local educational agency; non-profit 501(c)3 organization; community-based organization; public institution; correctional agency; or a consortium of these agencies. Further, applicants must be based with an established organization that has maintained current non-profit or public status for at least two years as of the date of the application be prepared to document fiscal accountability if requested by The Barbara Bush Texas Fund (i.e., provide copy of most recent annual audit report or IRS return).

Geographic Focus: Texas

Date(s) Application is Due: Mar 5

Amount of Grant: Up to 50,000 USD

Contact: Ken Appelt; (979) 845-6615; fax (979) 845-0952; kappelt@tamu.edu

Internet: www-tcall.tamu.edu/bbush/firstladyAnnounce.html

Sponsor: Barbara Bush Texas Fund for Family Literacy
Riverside Campus, Texas A&M University
College Station, TX 77843-4477

First Lady's Family Literacy Initiative for Texas Planning Grants 970

The First Lady's Family Literacy Initiative for Texas is a program of the Barbara Bush Texas Fund for Family Literacy. Launched at the Governor's Mansion in Austin in 1996 by Honorary Chair Laura Bush, The First Lady's Family Literacy Initiative for Texas supports family literacy programs that: increase literacy skills and educational levels of under-educated parents; implement a management and accountability system to measure program effectiveness and outcomes on a regular basis; provide a path to post-secondary education (beyond the GED) and employment; improve the quality of parent/child interaction, and adults' parenting skills in support of their children's learning; employ well-trained and dedicated staff who establish learning environments that positively affect recruitment and retention of adult learners; and encourage families to develop a love for books and reading, and prepare children for the school experience Introduce parents to the services of the library. Up to five Planning Grants of $5,000 will be awarded to Texas organizations to support a 9-month planning and development process (from June through February), intended to enable an organization to more effectively compete in the next annual First Lady's Family Literacy Initiative for Texas Program Implementation Grant of up to $50,000.

Requirements: Eligible applicants for both Planning Grants must: be a local educational agency; non-profit 501(c)3 organization; community-based organization; public institution; correctional agency; or a consortium of these agencies. Further, applicants must be based with an established organization that has maintained current non-profit or public status for at least two years as of the date of the application be prepared to document fiscal accountability if requested by The Barbara Bush Texas Fund (i.e., provide copy of most recent annual audit report or IRS return).

Geographic Focus: Texas

Date(s) Application is Due: Mar 5

Amount of Grant: Up to 5,000 USD

Contact: Ken Appelt; (979) 845-6615; fax (979) 845-0952; kappelt@tamu.edu

Internet: www-tcall.tamu.edu/bbush/firstladyAnnounce.html

Sponsor: Barbara Bush Texas Fund for Family Literacy
Riverside Campus, Texas A&M University
College Station, TX 77843-4477

First Nations Development Institute Native Agriculture and Food Systems Initiative Scholarships 971

The purpose of the Native Agriculture and Food Systems Scholarship program is to encourage more Native American college students to enter these fields so that they can better assist their communities with these efforts. In an attempt to increase the number of students entering these fields, First Nations will award six $1,000 scholarships annually to Native American college students majoring in agriculture and agriculture-related fields, including but not limited to: agribusiness management, agriscience technologies, agronomy, animal husbandry, aquaponics, fisheries and wildlife, food production and safety, food-related policy and legislation, horticulture, irrigation science, plant-based nutrition, and sustainable agriculture or food systems. The completed application, along with all required attachments, must be received by September 28.

Requirements: Applicants must: be full-time undergraduate or graduate student majoring in agriculture or an agricultural-related field, including food systems; be Native American (enrolled member of a current or terminated federal/state tribe) and able to provide documentation; have at least a 3.0 GPA; and demonstrate a commitment to helping his/her community reclaim local food-system control.

Geographic Focus: All States, American Samoa, Guam, Marshall Islands, Northern Mariana Islands, Puerto Rico, U.S. Virgin Islands

Date(s) Application is Due: Sep 28

Amount of Grant: 1,000 USD

Contact: Kendall Tallmadge, Lead Grants Officer; (303) 774-7836; fax (303) 774-7841; info@firstnations.org or grantmaking@firstnations.org

Internet: firstnations.org/node/517

Sponsor: First Nations Development Institute
2432 Main Street, 2nd Floor
Longmont, CO 80501

First Nations Development Institute Native Arts Initiative Grants 972

First Nations Development Institute (First Nations) works to build healthy economies in Indian Country based on strategies that emphasize Native communities controlling their assets, including cultural assets, institutional assets, natural resource assets and political assets among others. As a cultural asset for Native communities, art has been an integral part of sustaining Native nations, culture, language and traditional beliefs, shaping community and family ties and cultural pride. Yet, the process of colonization has stripped many Native communities of artistic forms and individuals with the capacity to carry on traditional art forms that are integral to their cultures. Factors such as western and religious education systems as well as urbanization and incorporation into the modern economy, among others, have all directly impacted Native American artists and the field of Native American arts, placing continued pathways of cultural traditions in jeopardy. To this end, First Nations established the Native Arts Capacity Building Initiative (NACBI) in 2014 – changing its name to the Native Arts Initiative (NAI) in 2016 – with the goal of stimulating long-term perpetuation, proliferation, and revitalization of traditional artistic and cultural assets in Native communities. The NAI is working to achieve this by creating and strengthening the enabling environments in which Native-led nonprofit organizations and tribal programs are operating to support emerging and established Native artists and sustain traditional Native arts. Under the NAI, these entities receive organizational and programmatic resources, including direct grants and technical assistance and training, to support their efforts to increase control of assets across five asset groups – institutional assets, arts and cultural assets, human capital, social assets, and economic assets – ultimately facilitating the steady inter-generational transference of traditional artistic knowledge in their communities. There are two annual deadlines for application submission: March 9 and October 19.

Requirements: Eligible entities must be Native-controlled intuitions and organizations.

Restrictions: Ineligible organizations include those with programs serving urban Native communities exclusively; programs serving Native people, but not controlled by a majority of Native people; for-profit Native consulting firms, although they may work with grant recipients; for-profit Native businesses, except for income-generating arms of nonprofits; or church or religious organizations, except for traditional Native American spiritual programs.

Geographic Focus: All States, American Samoa, District of Columbia, Guam, Marshall Islands, Northern Mariana Islands, Puerto Rico, U.S. Virgin Islands

Date(s) Application is Due: Mar 9; Oct 19

Amount of Grant: Up to 32,000 USD

Samples: Bois Forte Heritage Museum, Tower, Minnesota, $32,000 - local artists will design and teach traditional arts workshops to community members to address and ensure intergenerational transfer of knowledge of important Bois Forte art forms; Muckleshoot

Indian Tribe, Auburn, Washington, $32,000 - continue to build on the arts inherent to the Muckleshoot people who have for centuries implemented art into their daily lives; Utah Diné Bikéyah, Salt Lake City, Utah, $32,000 - project will work with Native artists in the Four Corners area (New Mexico, Utah, Colorado, and Arizona) to conduct an Arts Assessment and Arts Infrastructure Plan.
Contact: Kendall Tallmadge, Lead Grants Officer; (303) 774-7836; fax (303) 774-7841; info@firstnations.org or grantmaking@firstnations.org
Internet: www.firstnations.org/projects/native-arts-initiative-nai/
Sponsor: First Nations Development Institute
2432 Main Street, 2nd Floor
Longmont, CO 80501

First Nations Development Institute Native Language Immersion Initiative Grants
973

During each funding cycle, First Nations will distribute approximately twelve grant awards of up to $90,000 each to build the capacity of and directly support Native-controlled nonprofit organizations and tribal government programs actively supporting Native language-immersion and culture-retention programs. The Native Language Immersion Initiative seeks to build a dialogue and community of practice around Native language immersion programs and consensus on and momentum for Native language programs. The target age is children to college-age students. Programs should be actively growing new speakers and have plans for assessment and evaluation in place to identify progression in student Native language acquisition. Priority will be given to programs with a long-term, community-based immersion plan. Funding can support curriculum development, technology access, instructional courses and materials, teacher training and other kinds of organizational infrastructure, all aimed toward achieving Native American fluency and academic proficiency. The annual deadline for application submission is March 23.
Requirements: Eligible entities must be Native-controlled intuitions and organizations with an existing language-immersion program providing at least twenty hours per week per school year of Native American language instruction with at least ten students.
Restrictions: Ineligible organizations include those with programs serving urban Native communities exclusively; programs serving Native people, but not controlled by a majority of Native people; for-profit Native consulting firms, although they may work with grant recipients; for-profit Native businesses, except for income-generating arms of nonprofits; or church or religious organizations, except for traditional Native American spiritual programs.
Geographic Focus: All States, American Samoa, District of Columbia, Guam, Marshall Islands, Northern Mariana Islands, Puerto Rico, U.S. Virgin Islands
Date(s) Application is Due: Mar 23
Amount of Grant: Up to 90,000 USD
Samples: Chickaloon Native Village, Chickaloon, Alaska. $90,000 - the preservation of cultural lifeways through the implementation of a curriculum and testing assessment standards developed over the past three years for Ahtna culture and language immersion instruction (2018); Oneida Nation, Oneida, Wisconsin, $90,000 - tribal language department expanded the Oneida immersion program to include the 10-16 students in the Oneida Head Start (2018); Sitting Bull College, Fort Yates, North Dakota, $90,000 - created a comprehensive, coherent Pre-K immersion curriculum based on Dakota/Lakota immersion activities and materials developed since 2012 (2018).
Contact: Kendall Tallmadge, Lead Grants Officer; (303) 774-7836; fax (303) 774-7841; info@firstnations.org or grantmaking@firstnations.org
Internet: www.firstnations.org/projects/native-language-immersion-initiative/
Sponsor: First Nations Development Institute
2432 Main Street, 2nd Floor
Longmont, CO 80501

First Nations Development Institute Native Youth and Culture Fund Grants
974

First Nations launched the Native Youth and Culture Fund in 2002 with generous support from Kalliopeia Foundation and other foundations and tribal, corporate and individual supporters. The NYCF is designed to enhance culture and language awareness, and promote youth empowerment, leadership and community building. This year's funding is provided by Kalliopeia Foundation and an anonymous donor. Including awards made in 2017, First Nations has awarded more 378 grants to Native youth programs throughout the U.S., totaling $6.33 million. In 2018, First Nations awarded 21 grants totaling $400,000. In 2017, First Nations awarded grants to 22 Native organizations across the U.S. totaling $410,000. In 2016, grants were awarded to 24 programs totaling $432,000, and, in 2015, 26 grants were made to American Indian and Native Hawaiian organizations. Thousands of tribal youth have been and are being served through those innovative efforts, which ranged from culture camps and language nests, to business classes and financial education workshops, to agriculture and other food-based activities. Specifically, the Institute is seeking projects that focus on one or more of these four priority areas: preserving, strengthening or renewing cultural and/or spiritual practices, beliefs and values; engaging both youth and elders in activities that demonstrate methods for documenting traditional knowledge, practices and/or beliefs, where culturally appropriate; increasing youth leadership and their capacity to lead through integrated educational or mentoring programs; and increasing access to and sharing of cultural customs and beliefs through the use of appropriate technologies (traditional and/or modern), as a means of reviving or preserving tribal language, arts, history or other culturally relevant topics. First Nations expects to award approximately 20 grants of between $5,000 and $20,000 for projects of no longer than one year in length. There are two stages: stage one is March 8, and those ideas earning the highest scores will be invited to submit proposals by the stage two deadline of May 1.
Requirements: Native American organizations are eligible. Native American includes members of federal, state, and nonrecognized Indian tribes; Alaska Native tribes, villages, or groups; and Native Hawaiians.

Restrictions: Ineligible organizations include those with programs serving urban Native communities exclusively; programs serving Native people, but not controlled by a majority of Native people; for-profit Native consulting firms, although they may work with grant recipients; for-profit Native businesses, except for income-generating arms of nonprofits; or church or religious organizations, except for traditional Native American spiritual programs.
Geographic Focus: All States, American Samoa, District of Columbia, Guam, Marshall Islands, Northern Mariana Islands, Puerto Rico, U.S. Virgin Islands
Date(s) Application is Due: Mar 8; May 1
Amount of Grant: 5,000 - 20,000 USD
Samples: California Indian Basketweavers' Association, Woodland, California, $14,550 - engaged Native American youth ages 12 to 22 in learning about traditional basket-weaving practices including gathering, preparation and storage of basket-weaving materials (2018); Confederated Tribes of Warm Springs, Warm Springs, Oregon, $19,550 - served 160 youth ages 6-17 and will be guided by local artists and elders with support from the Boys and Girls Club of Warm Springs staff (2018); Ohkay Owingeh, Ohkay Owingeh, New Mexico, $19,550 - tribal youth ages 5 to 18 will be provided with greater cultural exposure through a variety of traditional regalia-making classes that will educate, challenge and inspire youth to form lasting linkages to their Native culture and to participate in their cultural ceremonies (2018).
Contact: Kendall Tallmadge, Lead Grants Officer; (303) 774-7836; fax (303) 774-7841; info@firstnations.org or grantmaking@firstnations.org
Internet: www.firstnations.org/projects/native-youth-and-culture-fund/
Sponsor: First Nations Development Institute
2432 Main Street, 2nd Floor
Longmont, CO 80501

First Nations Development Institute Nourishing Native Children: Feeding Our Future Project Grants
975

First Nations Development Institute (First Nations) recently announced its new grantees under its Nourishing Native Children: Feeding Our Future Project that is supported by funding from the Walmart Foundation. The effort provides grants to Native American communities to continue or expand nutrition resources for existing programs that serve American Indian children ages six to fourteen. For many Native children, meals provided by their school, nonprofit service provider, or through a take-home food program (often called backpack programs), may be the most consistent and/or nutritionally-balanced food they receive. The project's two-fold goal is to support Native American community-based feeding programs, and to learn from these programs and other model programs about best practices, challenges, barriers to success, and systemic and policy issues affecting Native children's hunger, and to foster partnerships among programs. Each year the program offers ten grants of $15,000 each, totaling $150,000. The annual deadline for application submission is May 5.
Requirements: Eligible entities must be Native-controlled intuitions and organizations supporting nutrition for Native American children, ages six through fourteen.
Geographic Focus: All States, American Samoa, District of Columbia, Guam, Marshall Islands, Northern Mariana Islands, Puerto Rico, U.S. Virgin Islands
Date(s) Application is Due: May 5
Amount of Grant: 15,000 USD
Contact: Kendall Tallmadge, Lead Grants Officer; (303) 774-7836; fax (303) 774-7841; info@firstnations.org or grantmaking@firstnations.org
Internet: indiangiver.firstnations.org/nl170910-05/
Sponsor: First Nations Development Institute
2432 Main Street, 2nd Floor
Longmont, CO 80501

Fitzpatrick, Cella, Harper & Scinto Pro Bono Services
976

Recognizing the ever-growing need in the community for the provision of legal services to those of limited means, Fitzpatrick has instituted a firm-wide pro bono program that encourages each lawyer in the firm to devote time to pro bono service. The firm's Pro Bono Committee has a representative from each of our three offices: Donald Curry (New York), Brian Klock (Washington, D.C.) and Edward Kmett (Costa Mesa). The firm's pro bono practice has been structured around several "practice areas" focused on particular substantive areas of law. These practice areas include branches of intellectual property law, as well as areas outside intellectual property where there is a particular need for the provision of legal services to people lacking the means to afford them.
Requirements: Pro bono services are provided to needy residents of New York City, Washington, D.C., and Costa Mesa, California, and the surrounding regions where the firm provides legal services.
Geographic Focus: California, District of Columbia, New York
Contact: Donald J. Curry, Pro Bono Coordinator; (212) 218-2100; fax (212) 218-2200
Internet: www.fitzpatrickcella.com/?p=2534
Sponsor: Fitzpatrick, Cella, Harper & Scinto
1290 Avenue of the Americas
New York, NY 10104-3800

Flinn Foundation Scholarships
977

The Flinn Foundation scholarships, in partnership with Arizona's three state universities, provide enriched educational offerings that expand a recipient's life and career options. Students receive a financial package for their entire undergraduate study that includes free tuition, room, and board, funding for study abroad, mentorship from faculty, exposure to world leaders, and fellowship in a community of current and alumni Scholars. Total dollar value exceeds $50,000, in addition to the cash value of tuition provided by the universities. Scholars begin as a group, with a three-week seminar in Central Europe. Each Scholar also receives a stipend for at least one international summer seminar, or a semester or year at a foreign university.
Requirements: Recipients must rank in the top 5 percent of their high school graduating class with at least a 3.5 grade point average; score a minimum of 29 on the ACT or 1300

on the SAT (critical reading and math sections only); demonstrate leadership in a variety of extracurricular activities; and hold U.S. citizenship and residency in Arizona for the two years prior to application. All majors may apply.
Restrictions: Applicants must apply to one of three Arizona universities: Arizona State University, Northern Arizona University, or University of Arizona.
Geographic Focus: Arizona
Date(s) Application is Due: Oct 21
Amount of Grant: 50,000 USD
Contact: Flinn Scholarship Contact; (602) 744-6800; fscholars@flinn.org
Internet: www.flinnscholars.org/news/977
Sponsor: Flinn Foundation
1802 N Central Avenue
Phoenix, AZ 85004-1506

Florence Foundation Grants   978
The Florence Foundation is a public charitable trust for exclusively educational, scientific, literary, religious or charitable purposes. The Foundation was established by Fred F. Florence and Helen Lefkowitz Florence in 1956 to be used for the benefit of humanity. From the little acorn comes the mighty oak: From the original small investment of $5,000, the Florence Foundation has bestowed an excess of $3 million during the past 50 years. The Florence Foundation Board of Governors distribute funds for any of the following uses and purposes: For assisting public charitable, religious or educational institutions, whether supported wholly or in part by private endowment, donation or public taxation; For promoting and aiding scientific research for the advancement of human knowledge, for increasing the productivity of the soil and animal life, for the elimination of disease and the alleviation of human suffering; For providing scholarships or otherwise assisting worthy young men and women, of limited means, in obtaining an education; For the care of the sick, the aged, the needy and the helpless; For providing facilities for public recreation; and for research into the cause of ignorance, poverty, crime and vice, preventing the operation of such causes and remedying or eliminating the conditions resulting therefrom. Grant amounts will range from $5,000 to $50,000. Most grants will be one year in duration.
Requirements: Grants are awarded to qualified 501(c)3 charitable organizations in the state of Texas, with preference given to organizations located in Dallas County and contiguous counties. Trustees may occasionally make discretionary grants outside of the stated geographic area for which unsolicited applications are not accepted. The Florence Foundation will review grant requests for the following types of grants: capital campaigns, programs and special projects, financial aid, and endowment campaigns. Applications will be submitted online through the Bank of America website. A grant report is required within 1 year of the grant application date, regardless of whether all of the funds have been spent.
Restrictions: Due to the limited amount of grant dollars available to distribute each year, applications will only be accepted from organizations with annual operating budgets of less than $20 million. Contributions are not made to or for debt retirement, media productions or publications loans. The foundation does not support requests from individuals, organizations attempting to influence policy through direct lobbying, or any political campaigns.
Geographic Focus: Texas
Date(s) Application is Due: Aug 1
Amount of Grant: 5,000 - 50,000 USD
Contact: Debra Goldstein Phares, Philanthropic Client Director; (214) 209-1830 or (800) 357-7094; tx.philanthropic@bankofamerica.com or tx.philanthropic@ustrust.com
Internet: www.bankofamerica.com/philanthropic/foundation/?fnId=314
Sponsor: Florence Foundation
P.O. Box 831041
Dallas, TX 75283-1041

Florence Hunt Maxwell Foundation Grants   979
The mission of the Florence Hunt Maxwell Foundation is to support charitable organizations that provide for the underserved and indigent community. Grants from the Florence Hunt Maxwell Foundation are primarily one year in duration; on occasion, multi-year support is awarded. Applicants must apply online at the grant website. Applicants are strongly encouraged to do the following before applying: review the downloadable state application procedures for additional helpful information and clarifications; review the downloadable online-application guidelines at the grant website; review the foundation's funding history (link is available from the grant website); review the online application questions in advance; and review the list of required attachments. These will generally include: a list of board members, financial statements (audited, reviewed, or compiled by independent auditor); an organization summary; a list of other funding sources; an IRS Determination letter; and other required documents. All attachments must be uploaded in the online application as PDF, Word, or Excel files. The Florence Hunt Maxwell Foundation application deadline is 11:59 p.m. on April 1. Applicants will be notified of grant decisions by letter within one to two months after the deadline.
Requirements: Applicants must have 501(c)3 tax-exempt status and serve residents of the Metro Atlanta area.
Restrictions: The foundation does not support requests from individuals, organizations attempting to influence policy through direct lobbying, or any political campaigns.
Geographic Focus: Georgia
Date(s) Application is Due: Mar 1
Amount of Grant: Up to 6,500 USD
Samples: Center for the Visually Impaired, Atlanta, Georgia, $6.500 - support of the Low Vision Clinic; Our House, Decatur, Georgia, $3,000 - support of the Interrelated Programs for Homeless Children and Families; Buckhead Christian Ministry, Atlanta, Georgia, $2,500 - general operating support.
Contact: Mark S. Drake, Vice President; (404) 264-1377; mark.s.drake@ustrust.com
Internet: www.bankofamerica.com/philanthropic/foundation.go?fnId=101

Sponsor: Florence Hunt Maxwell Foundation
3414 Peachtree Road, N.E., Suite 1475, GA7-813-14-04
Atlanta, GA 30326-1113

Ford Family Foundation Grants - Access to Health and Dental Services   980
The Health and Dental Services grants increase the health of underserved children through improve access to health and dental services, preventative services, and education. Priority is given to organizations that can demonstrate how grant funding will create clear results and increased capacity; those that show integration of "promising" or "evidence-based" best practice; efforts to increase access for very young children, ages 0-10; and those efforts with evidence of strong regional collaboration and coordination. Lower priority is given to capital funding for large hospitals and medical facilities.
Requirements: Grant requests must meet all of the following requirements before consideration will be given; applicant organizations must have current 501(c)3 public charity status from the IRS, or be a governmental entity, or be an IRS-recognized tribe. It may not be a private foundation as defined in Section 509(a) of the Internal Revenue Code; geographical focus of project must be predominately (60% or more) for the benefit of residents of rural Oregon and Siskiyou County, California. Rural is defined as communities with populations of 30,000 or less and not adjacent to or part of an urban or metropolitan area; must include significant collaboration and community buy-in (as evidenced by in-kind and cash contributions from local and regional sources); must have at least 50% of funding (may include in-kind) for the total project budget committed before applying; organization must not be delinquent in filing final reports for previous grants from the Foundation; organization may not be currently receiving other responsive grant funds from the Foundation. If the organization has received prior funding from the Foundation, they must wait 12 months after the completion of the prior grant before applying again for support.
Restrictions: Funds requested may not exceed one third of the project's total budget. The Foundation will usually not consider funding requests for: projects or programs that are indirectly funded through a fiscal agent; endowments or reserve funds; general fund drives, such as United Way; debt retirement or operating deficits; indirect expenses unrelated to the project or program being funded; sponsorship of fundraising events; or propagandizing or influencing elections or legislation.
Geographic Focus: California, Oregon
Amount of Grant: 50,000 - 100,000 USD
Contact: Grant Contact; (541) 957-5574; fax (541) 957-5720; info@tfff.org
Internet: www.tfff.org/Grants/GeneralInformation/tabid/81/Default.aspx
Sponsor: Ford Family Foundation
1600 NW Stewart Parkway
Roseburg, OR 97401

Ford Family Foundation Grants - Child Abuse Prevention and Intervention   981
The Child Abuse Prevention and Intervention Grants strive to lessen the instances of physical, sexual, and emotional abuse of children in the community through increased access to programs and services. Priority is given to evidence-based programs that show a clear connection between the types of programming and the reduction in child abuse incidence; programs that emphasize screening, intervention and case management to reduce drivers of child abuse and work towards family preservation when best; prevention efforts and efforts targeted at the youngest and most vulnerable children; and efforts with evidence of strong regional collaboration and coordination. The Foundation usually considers funding requests up to 30% of the total project cost. The application is available at the Foundation website.
Requirements: Grant requests must meet all of the following requirements before consideration will be given; applicant organizations must have current 501(c)3 public charity status from the IRS, or be a governmental entity, or be an IRS-recognized tribe. It may not be a private foundation as defined in Section 509(a) of the Internal Revenue Code; geographical focus of project must be predominately (60% or more) for the benefit of residents of rural Oregon and Siskiyou County, California. Rural is defined as communities with populations of 30,000 or less and not adjacent to or part of an urban or metropolitan area; must include significant collaboration and community buy-in (as evidenced by in-kind and cash contributions from local and regional sources); and must have at least 50% of funding (may include in-kind) for the total project budget committed before applying. Organizations must not be delinquent in filing final reports for previous grants from the Foundation. They must also not be currently receiving other responsive grant funds from the Foundation. If the organization has received prior funding from the Foundation, they must wait 12 months after the completion of the prior grant before applying again for support.
Restrictions: The Foundation generally will not consider funding requests for projects or programs that are indirectly funded through a fiscal agent; endowments or reserve funds; general fund drives, such as United Way; debt retirement or operating deficits; indirect expenses unrelated to the project or program being funded; sponsorship of fundraising events; or propagandizing or influencing elections or legislation.
Geographic Focus: California, Oregon
Amount of Grant: 50,000 - 100,000 USD
Contact: Grants Contact; (541) 957-5574; fax (541) 957-5720; info@tfff.org
Internet: www.tfff.org/Grants/GeneralInformation/tabid/81/Default.aspx
Sponsor: Ford Family Foundation
1600 NW Stewart Parkway
Roseburg, OR 97401

Ford Family Foundation Grants - Positive Youth Development   982
Positive Youth Development Grants support programs and facilities that encourage the development of skills, instill values of a successful citizen, and create structure for kids in their free time. Priority is given to structured "out-of-school" programs including youth leadership programs, mentorship programs, and evidence-based programs that show a clear connection between the types of programming and the development of successful citizen

values and behaviors. Types of funding include programmatic, operational, and capital. Funds will be released in less than 60 days, but may take six months to a year, depending on the project scope and review process. The application is available at the Foundation website.
Requirements: Grant requests must meet all of the following *Requirements:* applicant organizations must have current 501(c)3 public charity status from the IRS, or be a governmental entity, or be an IRS-recognized tribe. It may not be a private foundation as defined in Section 509(a) of the Internal Revenue Code; geographical focus of project must be predominately (60% or more) for the benefit of residents of rural Oregon and Siskiyou County, California. Rural is defined as communities with populations of 30,000 or less and not adjacent to or part of an urban or metropolitan area; must include significant collaboration and community buy-in (as evidenced by in-kind and cash contributions from local and regional sources); must have at least 50% of funding (may include in-kind) for the total project budget committed before applying; and the organization must not be delinquent in filing final reports for previous grants from the Foundation. The organization may not be currently receiving other responsive grants funds from the Foundation. If the organization has received prior funding from the Foundation, they must wait 12 months after the completion of the prior grant before applying again for support.
Restrictions: The Foundation will not consider stand-alone, unsupervised athletics facilities. In the case of positive youth development through organized sports and related facilities, the Foundation will only consider under-served communities where there is evidence of strong local support and project prioritization. The Foundation will usually not consider requests for projects or programs that are indirectly funded through a fiscal agent; endowments or reserve funds; general fund drives, such as United Way; debt retirement or operating deficits; indirect expenses unrelated to the project or program being funded; sponsorship of fundraising events; or propagandizing or influencing elections or legislation.
Geographic Focus: California, Oregon
Amount of Grant: 25,000 - 150,000 USD
Contact: Grant Contact; (541) 957-5574; fax (541) 957-5720; info@tfff.org
Internet: www.tfff.org/Grants/GeneralInformation/tabid/81/Default.aspx
Sponsor: Ford Family Foundation
1600 NW Stewart Parkway
Roseburg, OR 97401

Ford Family Foundation Grants - Technical Assistance 983
The Ford Family Foundation Technical Assistance Grants help develop community leaders, effective organizations, and collaborations. Funding categories include: leadership development - supports leadership training for community groups,particularly youth groups; effective organizations - support technical assistance for non-profits to improve their performance; and community collaborations - supports collaborations by organizations or communities in addressing shares issues or opportunities. Priority is given to requests clearly linked to a broad, compelling community need; established organizations with evidence of past success; built on existing investments of the Ford Institute which provide a more advanced level of training; and assistance to a network or cluster of people, organizations, or communities. Funds requested may not exceed 80% of the total project budget, and a minimum of 20% cash match toward the project is required. The application is available at the Foundation website.
Requirements: Grant requests must meet all of the following requirements for consideration: applicant organizations must have current 501(c)3 public charity status from the IRS, or be a governmental entity, or be an IRS-recognized tribe. It may not be a private foundation as defined in Section 509(a) of the Internal Revenue Code; geographical focus of project must be predominately (60% or more) for the benefit of residents of rural Oregon and Siskiyou County, California. Rural is defined as communities with populations of 30,000 or less and not adjacent to or part of an urban or metropolitan area; must include significant collaboration and community buy-in (as evidenced by in-kind and cash contributions from local and regional sources); must have at least 50% of funding (may include in-kind) for the total project budget committed before applying; and the organization must not be delinquent in filing final reports for previous grants from the Foundation.
Restrictions: The Foundation usually will not consider funding for projects or programs that are indirectly funded through a fiscal agent; endowments or reserve funds; general fund drives, such as United Way; debt retirement or operating deficits; indirect expenses unrelated to the project or program being funded; sponsorship of fundraising events; or propagandizing or influencing elections or legislation. Organizations may not be currently receiving other responsive grants funds from the Foundation. If the organization has received prior funding from the Foundation, they must wait 12 months after the completion of the prior grant before applying again for support.
Geographic Focus: California, Oregon
Amount of Grant: 1,000 - 5,000 USD
Contact: Grant Contact; (541) 957-5574; fax (541) 957-5720; info@tfff.org
Internet: www.tfff.org/Grants/GeneralInformation/tabid/81/Default.aspx
Sponsor: Ford Family Foundation
1600 NW Stewart Parkway
Roseburg, OR 97401

Ford Foundation BUILD Grants 984
Over the past 80 years, the Ford Foundation has invested in innovative ideas, visionary individuals, and front-line institutions advancing human dignity around the world. Its social justice mission and vision have guided it through transformations in the foundation, the communities it serves, and the world at large. Inequality is a global reality, and the countries of the Middle East and North Africa are no exception. Widespread social and economic inequality has only deepened in recent decades, with many people living in intolerable conditions and in fragmented or polarized societies. The Foundation works to build strong and resilient institutions across the Middle East and North Africa to help advance social inclusion and reduce inequality in all its forms. It provides multiyear

BUILD grants to a subset of its grantees in the MENA region so that they can invest in core organizational strengthening.
Requirements: The letter of inquiry should include the purpose of the project, problems and issues addressed, information about the applicant organization, estimated overall budget, time period for which funds are requested, and qualifications of those engaged in the project.
Restrictions: Support is not normally given for routine operating costs of institutions or for religious activities. Except in rare cases, funding is not available for the construction or maintenance of buildings. The foundation does not award undergraduate scholarships or make grants for purely personal or local needs.
Geographic Focus: All States, American Samoa, District of Columbia, Guam, Marshall Islands, Northern Mariana Islands, Puerto Rico, U.S. Virgin Islands
Amount of Grant: 75,000 - 250,000 USD
Contact: Rosalie Mistades, Grants Manager; (212) 573-5000; fax (212) 351-3677
Internet: www.fordfound.org/our-work-around-the-world/middle-east-and-north-africa/build-grants/
Sponsor: Ford Foundation
320 East 43rd Street
New York, NY 10017

Forest Foundation Grants 985
The Foundation awards grants to eligible Washington nonprofit organizations in its areas of interest, including community and economic development; environment; and youth development. The Foundation gives primarily to southwestern Washington counties, with emphasis on Pierce, Clallum, Cowlitz; Clark, Grays Harbor, Jefferson, Kitsap, Lewis, Mason, Pacific, Skamania; Thurston; and Wahkiakum. The Foundation Board meets six times per year. Organizations receive notification of funding in within 90 days.
Requirements: The Foundation should be initially approached with an email request for guidelines and instructions. Full proposals are by invitation only. Organizations should submit the following: copy of IRS Determination Letter; a brief history of organization and description of its mission; a listing of board of directors, trustees, officers and other key people and their affiliations; detailed description of project and amount of funding requested; a copy of the organization's current budget and/or project budget.
Restrictions: Grants do not funding for buildings or renovation projects.
Geographic Focus: Washington
Amount of Grant: 15,000 - 150,000 USD
Samples: Tacoma Rescue Mission, Tacoma, WA, $150,000 payable over one year; Tacoma Community College Foundation, Tacoma, WA, $100,000 payable over one year; Helping Hand House, Puyallup, WA, $20,000 payable over one year; Exodus Housing, Sumner, WA, $15,000 payable over one year.
Contact: Angela Baptiste, Grants Administrator; (253) 627-1634; fax (253) 627-6249
Sponsor: Forest Foundation
820 A Street, Suite 345
Tacoma, WA 98402

Foundation Beyond Belief Compassionate Impact Grants 986
Foundation Beyond Belief typically chooses four beneficiaries to receive grants each quarter, but one quarter per year the Foundation features a single, game-changing grant for one innovative organization. This grant is called the Compassionate Impact Grant (CIG). The CIG program supports organizations with social initiatives that are: innovative; transformative; evidence-based; and solving community problems. Targeted populations include: racial and ethnic minorities; African Americans or Blacks; Alaskan Natives; Asian Americans or Asians; children and youth; Hispanics or Latinos; LGBT; men and/or boys; migrants and/or nomadic; people with disabilities; poor and/or unemployed; and women and girls. The Letter of Intent application period is open for about seven weeks annually, and full applications are then by invitation only. Awards typically range from $30,000 to $40,000. The deadline to apply is January 19th.
Requirements: Any 501(c)3 organization is eligible to apply.
Restrictions: Types of programs that are not eligible to apply include: advocacy; after-school programs; juvenile justice; and faith-based organizations.
Geographic Focus: All States, All Countries
Date(s) Application is Due: Jan 19
Contact: Wendy Webber; (248) 229-5274; humanistgiving@foundationbeyondbelief.org
Internet: foundationbeyondbelief.org/grants/
Sponsor: Foundation Beyond Belief
1940 Fountain View Dr #1126
Houston, TX 77057

Foundation Beyond Belief Humanist Grants 987
The Foundation Beyond Belief Humanist Grant program collectively demonstrates humanist generosity and compassion in the nonprofit and philanthropic world. Each quarter the Foundation staff selects four charitable organizations within low-income communities as quarterly beneficiaries, one in each of the following categories: poverty and health; human rights; education; and natural world. At the end of each quarter, all donations designated for the Foundation's featured charities are forwarded, with no percentage retained, and a new slate of beneficiaries selected. Targeted populations include: racial and ethnic minorities; African Americans or Blacks; Alaskan Natives; Asian Americans or Asians; children and youth; Hispanics or Latinos; LGBT; men and/or boys; migrants and/or nomadic; people with disabilities; poor and/or unemployed; and women and girls.
Requirements: Any 501(c)3 organization is eligible to apply.
Restrictions: Types of programs that are not eligible to apply include: advocacy; after-school programs; juvenile justice; and faith-based organizations.
Geographic Focus: All States, All Countries
Amount of Grant: 20,000 - 40,000 USD

Contact: Wendy Webber, Humanist Grants Coordinator; (248) 229-5274; humanistgiving@foundationbeyondbelief.org
Internet: foundationbeyondbelief.org/humanist-giving/about
Sponsor: Foundation Beyond Belief
1940 Fountain View Dr #1126
Houston, TX 77057

Foundation for a Healthy Kentucky Grants   988

The Foundation seeks to address the unmet health care needs of the people of Kentucky through strategic grants designed to improve health status and access to care. Funding is concentrated in the following areas: fitness and nutrition for children and families; youth smoking prevention; and youth substance abuse prevention. The Foundation also hopes to enhance access to health care for low-income and uninsured populations; health care for rural populations; and integrated mental health and medical services.
Requirements: The Foundation accepts proposals for funding only in direct response to a specific Request for Proposals (RFP) or Request for Quotes (RFQ) or grant solicitation issued by the Foundation. Organizations should familiarize themselves with the Foundation's What We Fund page, and the Grant Guidelines to determine whether they are eligible to receive funding. They should sign up for the Foundation's mail/email list to receive grant opportunities and free educational forums. Once the organization receives an RFP announcement, they should review it carefully to see that the goals of the RFP fit with their particular project. If it is acceptable, applicants should submit their proposal according to the guidelines and RFP due dates.
Restrictions: The Foundation will not review unsolicited grant requests except for requests for Matching Grant and Conference Support funds. Grants do not support direct patient care, except as part of demonstration or replication projects; capital campaigns or requests for bricks and mortar (although project related equipment may be included in requests); overhead expenses except in limited amounts for specific projects; organizations that discriminate on the basis of race, gender, age, religion, national origin, sexual orientation, disability, military, or marital status in hiring; multi-year commitments; expenses related to registered legislative agents for the purpose of lobbying; endowment funds; individuals; private, for-profit entities; religious organizations for religious purposes; political causes; or retroactive expenses, deficit reduction, or forgiveness.
Geographic Focus: Kentucky
Samples: Home of the Innocents, Louisville, KY, establish a dental clinic for children in state care, children with special health care needs and other children served by the Home, $250,000; St. Joseph Health System, Lexington, KY, establish primary care clinics in two low-income rural communities, $250,000.
Contact: Susan Zepeda, President/Chief Executive Officer; (502) 326-2583 or (877) 326-2583; fax (502) 326-5748; szepeda@healthyky.org or info@healthy-ky.org
Internet: www.healthyky.org
Sponsor: Foundation for a Healthy Kentucky
9300 Shelbyville Road, Suite 1305
Louisville, KY 40222

Foundation for Appalachian Ohio Access to Environmental Education Mini-Grant   989

The Foundation for Appalachian Ohio Access to Environmental Education Mini-Grants encourage and support creative, local environmental education and stewardship activities for youth that build on the unique assets and strengths of the region's individual communities. Grants ranging from $250 to $1,500 are available to public schools and 501(c)3 community youth organizations. Those who might find interest in applying include public school science and vocational agriculture classes, and youth service clubs such as 4-H, Future Farmers of America, Girl Scouts, Boy Scouts, Big Brothers Big Sisters or Key Clubs. As appropriate, applications to support youth-focused efforts of local government, civic clubs and nonprofits working with youth, including county farm bureaus, city parks and recreation departments, soil and water conservation districts, community colleges, rotary international, and others, may also wish to apply.
Requirements: Applications are available online. The following counties serving Ohio nonprofits are eligible to apply: Adams, Ashtabula, Athens, Belmont, Brown, Carroll, Clermont, Columbiana, Coshocton, Gallia, Guernsey, Harrison, Highland, Hocking, Holmes, Jackson, Jefferson, Lawrence, Mahoning, Meigs, Monroe, Morgan, Muskingum, Noble, Perry, Pike, Ross, Scioto, Trumbull, Tuscarawas, Vinton, and Washington.
Restrictions: Only certain Ohio counties are eligible to apply.
Geographic Focus: Ohio
Date(s) Application is Due: Oct 14
Amount of Grant: 250 - 1,500 USD
Contact: Cara Dingus Brook; (740) 753-1111; fax (740) 753-3333; cbrook@ffao.org
Internet: www.appalachianohio.org/grantees/index.php?page=248
Sponsor: Foundation for Appalachian Ohio
36 Public Square, P.O. Box 456
Nelsonville, OH 45764

Foundation for Health Enhancement Grants   990

The purpose of the Foundation for Health Enhancement is to improve care in the United States by the development of the science of delivery of all kinds of health care, including medical, surgical, dental, nursing, health education, and other curative and preventive health services. The majority of grants from the Foundation for Health Enhancement are one year in duration. Applicants must apply online at the grant website. Applicants are strongly encouraged to do the following before applying: review the downloadable state application procedures for additional helpful information and clarifications; review the downloadable online-application guidelines at the grant website; review the foundation's funding history (link is available from the grant website); review the online application questions in advance; and review the list of required attachments. These will generally include: a list of board members, financial statements (audited, reviewed, or compiled by independent auditor); an organization summary; a list of other funding sources; an IRS Determination letter; and other required documents. All attachments must be uploaded in the online application as PDF, Word, or Excel files. The Foundation for Health Enhancement has biannual deadlines of April 1 and September 1. Applications should be submitted by 11:59 p.m. on the deadline dates. In general, applicants will be notified of grant decisions 3 to 4 months after proposal submission.
Requirements: The Foundation places special emphasis on: preventive health services; smaller qualifying applicants in an area geographically proximate to Chicago and/or the Midwest; and service organizations as opposed to research organizations.
Geographic Focus: Illinois
Date(s) Application is Due: Apr 1; Sep 1
Samples: I-PLUS: Independent Positive Living Under Supervision, North Chicago, Illinois, $10,000; Saint Anthony Hospital Foundation, Chicago, Illinois, $10,000; SOS Children's Villages Illinois, Chicago, Illinois, $10,000.
Contact: George Thorn, Vice President; (312) 828-4154; ilgrantmaking@bankofamerica.com
Internet: www.bankofamerica.com/philanthropic/fn_search.action
Sponsor: Foundation for Health Enhancement
231 South LaSalle Street, IL1-231-13-32
Chicago, IL 60604

Foundation for Rural Service Education Grants   991

As part of its ongoing commitment to rural communities across the country, the Foundation for Rural Service provides annual grants for rural communities served by National Telecommunications Cooperative Association (NTCA) members. The goal of this program is to support local efforts to build and sustain a high quality of life in rural America. Each spring, the Foundation begins accepting applications for the current year's grant process. The application window closes in mid-September and awardees are announced in early December. Grant projects vary but are concentrated in four major areas including: business; community and economic development; education; and telecommunications. Specifically, in the area of education, the Foundation supports technology in the classroom (computers, smart boards, etc.), curriculum development, extracurricular activities, and distance learning programs. Awards typically range from $250 to a maximum of $5,000.
Requirements: Any 501(c)3 organization or K through 12 grade school serving residents that are served by the National Telecommunications Cooperative Association are eligible to apply.
Geographic Focus: All States
Date(s) Application is Due: Sep 10
Amount of Grant: 250 - 5,000 USD
Samples: Gervais High School, Gervais, Oregon, $4,944 - funding for the purchase of 12 Google Chromebooks, carrying cases and wall- mounted screens to enhance and further educational programming (2018); Oakhurst Community College Outreach Center, Oakhurst, California, $5,000 - funding to improve the center's distance learning opportunities by installing distance learning equipment for high school enrichment and dual enrollment classes (2018).
Contact: Brock Streauslin, Program Specialist; (703) 351-2000; fax (703) 351-2001; bstreauslin@frs.org or foundation@frs.org
Internet: www.frs.org/programs/grant-program
Sponsor: Foundation for Rural Service
4121 Wilson Boulevard, Suite 1000
Arlington, VA 22203

Foundation for the Mid South Communities Grants   992

The Foundation for the Mid South was established to bring together the public and private sectors and focus their resources on increasing social and economic opportunity. The foundation's community development work includes five key focuses that, together, enable communities to grow and prosper: Community Enrichment, Economic Development, Leadership Development, Education, and Health and Wellness. Each focus area addresses an essential community element.
Requirements: Contact a program officer to discuss your project prior to submitting a proposal To be eligible for a grant, the applying organization must possess tax-exempt status under section 501(c)3 of the Internal Revenue Code and a certificate from the Mississippi Secretary of State that designates it as a public charity or exempt for the state of Mississippi. Mississippi organizations must register and receive a certificate that designates it as a public charity or exempt for the state of Mississippi when submitting a full proposal. The application, Form URS, and instructions are available at the sponsor's website. All other organizations must apply and receive a notice of exemption, Form CE, from the Mississippi Secretary of State's office, also available from the website. If the proposed work aligns with the Foundation's priorities and goals, eligible organizations may submit the Grant Inquiry Form found on the website.
Restrictions: The Foundation does not award grants to individuals or make grants for personal needs or business assistance. Additionally, funds are not awarded for lobbying activities; ongoing general operating expenses or existing deficits; endowments; capital costs including construction, renovation, or equipment; or international programs.
Geographic Focus: Arkansas, Louisiana, Mississippi
Contact: Denise Ellis; (601) 355-8167; fax (601) 355-6499; bdellis@fndmidsouth.org
Internet: www.fndmidsouth.org/priorities/communities/
Sponsor: Foundation for the Mid South
134 East Amite Street
Jackson, MS 39201

Foundation for the Mid South Education Grants   993

The Foundation for the Mid South was established to bring together the public and private sectors and focus their resources on increasing social and economic opportunity. The Foundation Education Grant program supports efforts that strengthen education systems, by building the capacity of teachers and administrators to better serve student needs and advance learning. It also focuses on enrichment opportunities that provide effective and innovative ways to help students learn.

Requirements: Contact a program officer to discuss your project prior to submitting a proposal To be eligible for a grant, the applying organization must possess tax-exempt status under section 501(c)3 of the Internal Revenue Code and a certificate from the Mississippi Secretary of State that designates it as a public charity or exempt for the state of Mississippi. Mississippi organizations must register and receive a certificate that designates it as a public charity or exempt for the state of Mississippi when submitting a full proposal. The application, Form URS, and instructions are available at the sponsor's website. All other organizations must apply and receive a notice of exemption, Form CE, from the Mississippi Secretary of State's office, also available from the website. If the proposed work aligns with the Foundation's priorities and goals, eligible organizations may submit the Grant Inquiry Form found on the website.

Restrictions: The Foundation does not award grants to individuals or make grants for personal needs or business assistance. Additionally, funds are not awarded for lobbying activities; ongoing general operating expenses or existing deficits; endowments; capital costs including construction, renovation, or equipment; or international programs.

Geographic Focus: Arkansas, Louisiana, Mississippi
Contact: Denise Ellis; (601) 355-8167; fax (601) 355-6499; bdellis@fndmidsouth.org
Internet: www.fndmidsouth.org/priorities/education/
Sponsor: Foundation for the Mid South
134 East Amite Street
Jackson, MS 39201

Foundation of Herkimer and Oneida Counties Youth   **994**
    Sports, Wellness and Recreation Mini-Grants
The Community Foundation serves Oneida and Herkimer Counties, New York, and awards grants for programs that align with community indicators to make long-lasting social impact. Preference is given to requests for support of particular programs or projects that are expected to benefit the community and to requests for capital expenditures and seed money. Additional types of support include: general operating support; endowment funds; fellowships; scholarship funds; consulting services; demonstration grants; matching funds; and technical assistance. In the areas of youth sports, wellness, and recreation, the Foundation offers mini-grants in amounts up to $10,000, to be used to encourage and support community health and wellness through youth programs. There are two annual deadlines for application submission: January 13 and July 14. Applications from organizations not previously known to the Foundation are given the same consideration as requests from those it knows well. The Foundation may cut off acceptance of applications at any time if it is deemed that its current grant agenda is full.

Requirements: The Foundation supports only nonprofit organizations in Oneida and Herkimer counties of New York.

Restrictions: Grants will not normally be made for deficit financing, religious purposes, or financial assistance or scholarships to individuals. The Foundation will consider proposals from faith-based organizations for programs, projects or community spaces that address non-religious needs or issues, and that serve diverse constituencies unrestricted by religious affiliation.

Geographic Focus: New York
Date(s) Application is Due: Mar 31
Amount of Grant: Up to 10,000 USD
Contact: Jan Squadrito, Senior Community Investment Manager; (315) 731-3728 or (315) 735-8212; fax (315) 735-9363; jsquadrito@foundationhoc.org or info@foundationhoc.org
Internet: foundationhoc.org/grant-seeker/
Sponsor: Foundation of Herkimer and Oneida Counties
2608 Genesee Street
Utica, NY 13502

Foundations of East Chicago Education Grants   **995**
The Foundations of East Chicago, Indiana, is funded by the Resorts East Chicago Casino and Hotel. The Foundations is committed to funding programs and initiatives which support the education of its citizens – mind, body and spirit – at every age. Such programs or projects are focused on addressing improvement of the quality of educational achievement of East Chicago students.

Requirements: Applicants must be registered 501(c)3 organizations or schools located in East Chicago, Indiana. If an applicant is not located in East Chicago, it may still qualify if it complies with at least one of the following *Requirements:* the program that an applicant is applying for operates in East Chicago; the funding that an applicant is applying for will go toward assisting East Chicago residents.

Restrictions: All applications must be submitted via Foundations of East Chicago website. The Foundations will not accept any applications in person.

Geographic Focus: Indiana
Amount of Grant: Up to 15,000 USD
Contact: Russell G. Taylor, Executive Director; (219) 392-4225; fax (219) 392-4245; grantinfo@foundationsofeastchicago.org
Internet: foundationsofeastchicago.org/apply-now
Sponsor: Foundations of East Chicago
100 W Chicago Avenue
East Chicago, IN 46312

Foundations of East Chicago Family Support Grants   **996**
The Foundations of East Chicago are committed to improving the lives of every resident of its city. Conceived by the citizens of East Chicago to be independent, citizen-run, private foundations, it derives funding from East Chicago's local casino, and uses this money to support local churches, schools, and nonprofit organizations who know the community best and put in the money in action where it can do the most good. Family Support grants are specifically focused on programs or projects designed to help strengthen the East Chicago Family unit.

Requirements: Applicants must be registered 501(c)3 organizations located in East Chicago, Indiana. If an applicant is not located in East Chicago, it may still qualify if it complies with at least one of the following *Requirements:* the program that an applicant is applying for operates in East Chicago; the funding that an applicant is applying for will go toward assisting East Chicago residents.

Restrictions: All applications must be submitted via Foundations of East Chicago website. The Foundations will not accept any applications in person.

Geographic Focus: Indiana
Amount of Grant: Up to 15,000 USD
Contact: Russell G. Taylor, Executive Director; (219) 392-4225; fax (219) 392-4245; grantinfo@foundationsofeastchicago.org
Internet: foundationsofeastchicago.org/apply-now
Sponsor: Foundations of East Chicago
100 W Chicago Avenue
East Chicago, IN 46312

Foundations of East Chicago Health Grants   **997**
The Foundations of East Chicago are committed to improving the lives of every resident of its city. Conceived by the citizens of East Chicago to be independent, citizen-run, private foundations, it derives funding from East Chicago's local casino, and uses this money to support local churches, schools, and nonprofit organizations who know the community best and put in the money in action where it can do the most good. Health grants are specifically focused on programs or projects which improve the quality of health education, practices and/or services for East Chicagoans.

Requirements: Applicants must be registered 501(c)3 organizations located in East Chicago, Indiana. If an applicant is not located in East Chicago, it may still qualify if it complies with at least one of the following *Requirements:* the program that an applicant is applying for operates in East Chicago; the funding that an applicant is applying for will go toward assisting East Chicago residents.

Restrictions: All applications must be submitted via Foundations of East Chicago website. The Foundations will not accept any applications in person.

Geographic Focus: Indiana
Amount of Grant: Up to 15,000 USD
Contact: Russell G. Taylor, Executive Director; (219) 392-4225; fax (219) 392-4245; grantinfo@foundationsofeastchicago.org
Internet: foundationsofeastchicago.org/apply-now
Sponsor: Foundations of East Chicago
100 W Chicago Avenue
East Chicago, IN 46312

Foundations of East Chicago Youth Development Grants   **998**
The Foundations of East Chicago are committed to improving the lives of every resident of its city. Conceived by the citizens of East Chicago to be independent, citizen-run, private foundations, it derives funding from East Chicago's local casino, and uses this money to support local churches, schools, and nonprofit organizations who know the community best and put in the money in action where it can do the most good. Youth Development grants are specifically focused on programs or projects whose purpose is to improve the social, physical and emotional skills of East Chicago's youth.

Requirements: Applicants must be registered 501(c)3 organizations or schools located in East Chicago, Indiana. If an applicant is not located in East Chicago, it may still qualify if it complies with at least one of the following *Requirements:* the program that an applicant is applying for operates in East Chicago; the funding that an applicant is applying for will go toward assisting East Chicago residents.

Restrictions: All applications must be submitted via Foundations of East Chicago website. The Foundations will not accept any applications in person.

Geographic Focus: Indiana
Amount of Grant: Up to 15,000 USD
Contact: Russell G. Taylor, Executive Director; (219) 392-4225; fax (219) 392-4245; grantinfo@foundationsofeastchicago.org
Internet: foundationsofeastchicago.org/apply-now
Sponsor: Foundations of East Chicago
100 W Chicago Avenue
East Chicago, IN 46312

Four County Community Foundation 21st Century Education Fund Grants   **999**
The Four County Community Foundation is committed to serving the current and emerging needs of the local communities, which includes the villages and cities of Almont, Armada, Capac, Dryden, Imlay City, Metamora and Romeo, Michigan. The 21st Century Education Fund program offers applicants up to $500 for classroom teachers to improve or modify the delivery of the curriculum. These awards are intended to fund specific projects in their entirety. The four annual deadlines for application submission are January 1, April 1, July 1, and October 1.

Requirements: Classroom teachers in both private and public schools located in the Michigan cities and villages of Almont, Armada, Capac, Dryden, Imlay City, Metamora and Romeo are eligible to apply.

Geographic Focus: Michigan
Date(s) Application is Due: Jan 1; Apr 1; Jul 1; Oct 1
Amount of Grant: Up to 500 USD
Contact: Micaela Boomer; (810) 798-0909; fax (810) 798-0908; program@4ccf.org
Internet: 4ccf.org/community/
Sponsor: Four County Community Foundation
231 East St. Clair, P.O. Box 539
Almont, MI 48003

Four County Community Foundation General Grants   1000

The Four County Community Foundation is committed to serving the current and emerging needs of the local communities, which includes the villages and cities of Almont, Armada, Capac, Dryden, Imlay City, Metamora and Romeo, Michigan. General grants are intended to support a variety of charitable purposes, providing grants for non-profits, public schools, and governmental agencies. Major areas of interest include: arts and culture; health care; children and youth programs, athletics; community development and outreach; the environment; higher education; human services; and elementary and secondary education. Support is given for: general operations; capital campaigns; and program development. The four annual deadlines for application submission are January 1, April 1, July 1, and October 1.

Requirements: 501(c)3 organizations, public schools, and governmental agencies in the Michigan cities and villages of Almont, Armada, Capac, Dryden, Imlay City, Metamora and Romeo are eligible to apply.

Geographic Focus: Michigan

Date(s) Application is Due: Jan 1; Apr 1; Jul 1; Oct 1

Amount of Grant: 500 - 50,000 USD

Contact: Micaela Boomer; (810) 798-0909; fax (810) 798-0908; program@4ccf.org

Internet: 4ccf.org/community/

Sponsor: Four County Community Foundation

231 East St. Clair, P.O. Box 539

Almont, MI 48003

Four County Community Foundation Healthy Senior/Healthy Youth Fund Grants   1001

The Four County Community Foundation is committed to serving the current and emerging needs of the local communities, which includes the villages and cities of Almont, Armada, Capac, Dryden, Imlay City, Metamora and Romeo, Michigan. Healthy Senior/Healthy Youth Fund grants are intended to support projects to promote health or provide treatment for health care for senior citizens and youth. Major priorities for seniors include: health and nutrition; pharmaceuticals (e.g., access, costs, medication interactions, etc.); preventing and managing chronic disease; smoking prevention and cessation; long term care alternatives (e.g., community-based long-term care options, assisted living, day care, respite care, and family caregiver support); mental health and aging (suicide, substance abuse, depression); family counseling; and workforce and aging. Major priorities for youth include: violence and conflict resolution; health and nutrition; behavioral risk factors (e.g., substance abuse, alcohol/binge drinking, smoking prevention and cessation, and depression); community alternatives for recreation; day care, preschool, and after school care; early childhood development; access to dental care; and family counseling. Support is typically given for: general operations; capital campaigns; and program development. The four annual deadlines for application submission are January 1, April 1, July 1, and October 1.

Requirements: 501(c)3 organizations, public schools, and governmental agencies in the Michigan cities and villages of Almont, Armada, Capac, Dryden, Imlay City, Metamora and Romeo are eligible to apply.

Geographic Focus: Michigan

Date(s) Application is Due: Jan 1; Apr 1; Jul 1; Oct 1

Amount of Grant: 500 - 50,000 USD

Contact: Micaela Boomer; (810) 798-0909; fax (810) 798-0908; program@4ccf.org

Internet: 4ccf.org/community/

Sponsor: Four County Community Foundation

231 East St. Clair, P.O. Box 539

Almont, MI 48003

Four County Community Foundation Kellogg Group Grants   1002

The Four County Community Foundation is committed to serving the current and emerging needs of the local communities, which includes the villages and cities of Almont, Armada, Capac, Dryden, Imlay City, Metamora and Romeo, Michigan. The Kellogg Group Grant program is intended to fund group grants which provide services to youth. Priority will be given to projects which address the challenges identified in an applicant's recent needs assessment survey. Top priorities include: texting while driving; reckless driving; peer pressure; lack of technology resources; and binge drinking. Support is typically given in the area of program development. The four annual deadlines for application submission are January 1, April 1, July 1, and October 1.

Requirements: 501(c)3 organizations, public schools, and governmental agencies in the Michigan cities and villages of Almont, Armada, Capac, Dryden, Imlay City, Metamora and Romeo are eligible to apply.

Geographic Focus: Michigan

Date(s) Application is Due: Jan 1; Apr 1; Jul 1; Oct 1

Amount of Grant: Up to 10,000 USD

Contact: Micaela Boomer; (810) 798-0909; fax (810) 798-0908; program@4ccf.org

Internet: 4ccf.org/community/

Sponsor: Four County Community Foundation

231 East St. Clair, P.O. Box 539

Almont, MI 48003

Fourjay Foundation Grants   1003

The Fourjay Foundation, established in 1988, supports only those organizations whose chief purpose is to improve health and/or promote education, within Philadelphia, Montgomery, and Bucks counties in southeastern Pennsylvania. The Foundation requires no specific application form. It will consider proposals that address a well-defined need, offer a concrete plan of action, and request a specific amount, from organizations whose staff has the ingenuity, commitment, and motivation to carry out the proposal's objectives. Requests may be for operating support, project specific funds, or capital funds.

Requirements: Organizations serving Philadelphia, Montgomery, and Bucks Counties in southeastern Pennsylvania are eligible.

Restrictions: Funding is not available for: charities operating outside Montgomery, Bucks, or Philadelphia counties; individuals; elementary or secondary educational institutions; museums, musical groups, theaters, or cultural organizations; religious organizations in support of their sacramental or theological functions; political groups or related think tanks; athletic organizations or alumni associations; libraries; public radio or television; United Way or the YMCA; civic organizations; organizations that have applied or been funded within the last 12 month period.

Geographic Focus: Pennsylvania

Date(s) Application is Due: Mar 1; Jun 1; Sep 1; Dec 1

Amount of Grant: 1,000 - 10,000 USD

Contact: Ann T. Bucci; (215) 830-1437; fax (215) 830-0157; abucci@fourjay.org

Sponsor: Fourjay Foundation

2300 Computer Avenue, Building G, Suite 1

Willow Grove, PA 19090-1753

Four J Foundation Grants   1004

The Four J Foundation was founded in Idaho in 1997, with the major fields of interest including: arts and culture; education; children and youth; health and health access; hospital care; and in-patient medical care. The Foundation caters primarily to academics, economically disadvantaged; low-income families; and students. Funding typically takes the form of: ensuring financial stability; fund raising projects; program development; and support of re-granting charitable organizations. Applicants should begin the process of forwarding a letter to the Foundation, along with a detailed description of the project, amount of funding requested, and overall program budget. There are no annual deadlines for submission. An average of forty organizations receive grant awards annually, ranging from $1,000 to $50,000. The vast majority of awards are equal to $10,000 or less.

Requirements: Any 501(c)3 that provides services to communities where Four J operates in Idaho is eligible to apply.

Geographic Focus: Idaho

Amount of Grant: 1,000 - 50,000 USD

Samples: Camp Rainbow Gold, Boise, Idaho, $5,000 support of educational programs; St. Luke's Children's Playground, Boise, Idaho, $50,000 - support of children's medical programming; University of Idaho, Moscow, Idaho, $2,500 - athletic scholarship fund support.

Contact: Anne M. Goss, Director; (208) 344-7150 or (208) 344-6778

Sponsor: Four J Foundation

877 W. Main Street, Suite 800

Boise, ID 83702

Four Lanes Trust Grants   1005

The Four Lanes Trust was established in Washington, D.C., to offer funding support in the metro D.C. area. The Trust's primary fields of interest have been identified as: agriculture; education; and employment programs. The Trust is intended to assist: elementary and secondary school academic achievement; children and youth programs; the economically disadvantaged and disenfranchised; ethnic and racial minorities; and low-income families. Typically, funding comes in the form of general operating support and program development. Interested applicants should forward a letter of application, including: the population served; a statement of the problem that the project will address; a copy of the current year's organizational budget; the project budget; a copy of most recent annual report/audited financial statement or 990; and the amount of funding requested. There are no annual deadlines for submission. Grants typically range from $250 to $2,000, with approximately ten to twelve awards annually.

Requirements: 501(c)3 organizations in Washington, D.C., Maryland, Massachusetts, Virginia, and Maine are eligible to apply.

Geographic Focus: District of Columbia, Maine, Maryland, Massachusetts, Virginia

Amount of Grant: 250 - 2,000 USD

Samples: Apprentice Shop, Rockland, Maine, $250 - general operating support for a boat-building school; D.C. Central Kitchen, Washington, D.C., $2,000 - culinary job training and food distribution; Food Project, Lincoln, Massachusetts, $500 - general operating support.

Contact: Wendy Makins, Director and Treasurer; (202) 965-1204

Sponsor: Four Lanes Trust

3034 P Street, NW

Washington, D.C. 20007-3052

Four Times Foundation Grants   1006

The Four Times Foundation awards grants and capital to eligible Native American nonprofit organizations in the areas of social and economic development. Grants are awarded to individuals pursuing a business venture or starting a nonprofit organization in one of four tribal reservations. Preference will be given to projects benefiting children. Grantees should provide a return to their tribe that is four times the original investment.

Requirements: Individuals pursuing business ventures or starting nonprofit organizations in the following reservations are eligible: Blackfeet Nation in Montana, Rosebud Lakota in South Dakota, White Earth Ojibewa in Minnesota, and the Zuni Pueblo in New Mexico.

Geographic Focus: Minnesota, Montana, New Mexico, South Dakota

Amount of Grant: 500 - 10,000 USD

Contact: Jael Kampfe, Owner; (406) 446-1870; fax (406) 446-1013; jael@fourtimes.org or info@fourtimes.org

Sponsor: Four Times Foundation

16 1/2 North Broadway, P.O. Box 309

Red Lodge, MT 59068

Francis Beidler Foundation Grants 1007

Established in Illinois in 1997, the Francis Beidler Foundation offers support for human service programs in Chicago, Illinois. Its primary fields of interest include: children and youth services; education; health organizations; higher education; children's museums; public affairs; and public safety. There are no established deadlines or application formats. Applicants should begin the process by submitting a letter describing the organization, a detailed overview of the project, and amount of funding requested. Organizational literature should accompany the application letter. Grants range up to $60,000.
Requirements: Organizations serving the Chicago area are eligible to apply.
Geographic Focus: Illinois
Amount of Grant: Up to 60,000 USD
Samples: Better Government Association, Chicago, Illinois, $46,000 - general operations; Catholics for Free Choice, Chicago, Illinois, $13,000 - general operations; Chapin Hall Center for Children, Chicago, Illinois, $34,000 - general operations.
Contact: Thomas B. Dorris, Trustee; (312) 922-3792
Sponsor: Francis Beidler Foundation
53 W. Jackson Boulevard, Suite 530
Chicago, IL 60604-3422

Francis L. Abreu Charitable Trust Grants 1008

The Francis L. Abreu Charitable Trust was established under the will of May Patterson Abreu in honor of her husband, Francis, who died in 1969. The trust supports Atlanta-area nonprofit organizations in its areas of interest, including arts and cultural programs, secondary education, higher education, health associations, human services, and children and youth services. Types of support include capital campaigns, seed money, program development, and matching funds. Requests are reviewed at April and October trustee meetings. Application forms are available online.
Requirements: Georgia nonprofit organizations serving the greater Atlanta area are eligible to apply.
Restrictions: The foundation does not approve requests for operating costs or grants to individuals.
Geographic Focus: Georgia
Date(s) Application is Due: Mar 31; Sep 30
Contact: Peter Abreu, Chairman; (404) 549-6743; fax (404) 549-6752
Internet: www.abreufoundation.org
Sponsor: Francis L. Abreu Charitable Trust
P.O. Box 502407
Atlanta, GA 31150

Frankel Brothers Foundation Grants 1009

Based in Brooklyn, New York, the Frankel Brothers Foundation offers local support in the areas of community and economic development, human services, and Jewish religion. Most recent grants have ranged from $25 to $4,300, with the average being $100 to $1,000. There is no specific application format required, and no identified annual deadlines. Interested parties should forward their entire proposal in two- to three-page letter form, detailing their program, the population served, and budgetary needs.
Requirements: Jewish religious groups and non-profits serving residents of Brooklyn, New York, are eligible to apply.
Geographic Focus: New York
Amount of Grant: 25 - 4,300 USD
Samples: Ohel Children's Home and Family Services, Brooklyn, New York, $100 - general operating support; Edith's Dry Goods, Brooklyn, New York, $20 - general operating support; Bnos Zion of Bobov, Brooklyn, New York, $4,000 - general operating support.
Contact: Naftavi Frankel, Trustee; (718) 855-0751
Sponsor: Frankel Brothers Foundation
32 Court Street
Brooklyn, NY 11201

Franklin County Community Foundation Grants 1010

The Franklin County Foundation's mission is simple - build substantial endowment of funds for a community through contributions large and small. These contributions are endowed, permanently invested to produce income, and never spent. The income earned is used to help meet the community's charitable needs - from social work to art and culture. The FCCF Grant Cycle begins late summer when Letters of Intent are due in the office. After these letters are reviewed, the Grants Selection Committee will send applications to the groups or organizations who meet our grant guidelines.
Requirements: To be eligible to receive funding from the Foundation, a letter of intent must be submitted followed by a completed grant application by the appropriate grant deadline. All grant seekers must have prior governing board approval for the project seeking funding. The approval of signed minutes and a signed letter from governing board must be available to the Franklin County Community Foundation.
Restrictions: Funding will not be considered for the following: operating deficits; operation budgets (salaries); annual fund campaigns: religious or sectarian purposes; propaganda, political or otherwise, attempting to influence litigation or intervene in any political affairs or campaigns on behalf of any candidate for public office so as to endanger the charitable nature of the community trust; public school services required by state law; standard instructional or regular operation costs of non-public schools; repeat funding of projects previously supported by the Foundation; individuals; travel purposes; any purpose that is not in conformity with the constraints placed upon the Foundation by the IRS.
Geographic Focus: Indiana
Date(s) Application is Due: Oct 2
Contact: Shelly Lunsford; (765) 647-6810 or (765) 265-1427; fcfoundation@yahoo.com
Internet: www.franklincountyindiana.com/Grants%20page.htm
Sponsor: Franklin County Community Foundation
527 Main Street
Brookville, IN 47012-1284

Franklin H. Wells and Ruth L. Wells Foundation Grants 1011

The Foundation awards grants to support the arts, community and economic development, education, health care, and human services. Funding is also available for emergency funds, equipment, program development, and seed money. The Foundation board meets in April and October, with funding notification in May and November.
Requirements: Applications are not required. Organizations should initially submit a letter of inquiry, and if accepted, one copy of their proposal.
Restrictions: The Foundation gives primarily to Dauphin, Cumberland, and Perry counties in Pennsylvania. Funding is not available for religious activities, individuals, endowments, debts, and capital campaigns.
Geographic Focus: Pennsylvania
Date(s) Application is Due: Mar 15; Sep 15
Contact: Miles Gibbons Jr., Executive Director; (866) 398-9023; mgibbons989@earthlink.net
Sponsor: Franklin H. Wells and Ruth L. Wells Foundation
One M and T Plaza, 8th Floor
Buffalo, NY 14203-2309

Frank M. Tait Foundation Grants 1012

The Foundation makes grants to nonprofit organizations operating in Montgomery County, OH, for projects focusing on youth activities and culture. Fields of interest include the arts, child development services, education, historical activities, science, YW/YMCAs and YW/YMHAs. Types of support include annual campaigns, building renovation, equipment, matching and challenge support, program development, and seed money. Grants are usually for one year with possible renewal.
Requirements: An application form is not required. After contacting the foundation for a current deadline, organizations should mail a letter of inquiry along with the following: copy of IRS determination letter; copy of most current annual report/audited financial statement/990; and a copy of the current organizational budget and/or project budget. The Foundation Board meets quarterly and notifies organizations of possible funding within two months of submission.
Restrictions: Faxed or emailed proposals are not accepted. Giving is limited to Montgomery County, Ohio. Funding is not available for religious purposes; individuals; endowment funds; operating budgets; continuing support; emergency funds; deficit financing; research; publications; conferences; scholarships; fellowships; selective capital campaigns; or loans.
Geographic Focus: Ohio
Amount of Grant: 5,000 - 100,000 USD
Contact: Jennifer A. Roer, Executive Director; (937) 222-2401; fax (937) 224-6015
Sponsor: Frank M. Tait Foundation
40 North Main Street
Dayton, OH 45423

Frank Reed and Margaret Jane Peters Memorial Fund Grants 1013

The Frank Reed and Margaret Jane Peters Memorial Fund was established in 1934 and 1935 to support and promote quality educational, human services and health care programming for underserved populations. Special consideration is given to charitable organizations that serve youth and children. The Peters Memorial Fund is a generous supporter of the Summer Fund, established by Philanthropy Massachusetts. The Summer Fund is a donor collaborative that provides operating support for summer camps serving low-income urban youth from Boston, Cambridge, Chelsea and Somerville. Excluding the grant made to the Summer Fund, the typical grant range is $10,000 to $40,000. The majority of grants from the Peters Memorial Fund are 1 year in duration. On occasion, multi-year support is awarded.
Requirements: Applicants must have 501(c)3 tax-exempt status. Grant requests for general operating support are strongly encouraged. Program support will also be considered. Small program-related capital expenses may be included in general operating or program requests. Applications will be submitted online through the Bank of America website. A grant report is required within 1 year of the grant application date, regardless of whether all of the funds have been spent.
Restrictions: The fund does not support requests from individuals, organizations attempting to influence policy through direct lobbying, or any political campaigns.
Geographic Focus: Massachusetts
Date(s) Application is Due: Mar 1
Amount of Grant: 10,000 - 40,000 USD
Samples: Philanthropy Massachusetts Inc., Boston, Massachusetts, $150,000 - Awarded for The Summer Fund (2018); Boys and Girls Club of Lawrence, Lawrence, Massachusetts, $20,000 - Awarded for General Operations of the Organization (2018); Boys and Girls Clubs of Metrowest Inc., Marlboro, Massachusetts, $20,000 - Awarded for General Operations of the Organization (2018).
Contact: Michealle Larkins, Philanthropic Administrator; (866) 778-6859; ma.grantmaking@bankofamerica.com or ma.grantmaking@ustrust.com
Internet: www.bankofamerica.com/philanthropic/foundation/?fnId=42
Sponsor: Frank Reed and Margaret Jane Peters Memorial Fund I
225 Franklin Street, MA1-225-04-02
Boston, MA 02110-2801

Frank Reed and Margaret Jane Peters Memorial Fund II Grants 1014

The Frank Reed and Margaret Jane Peters Memorial Fund II was established in 1935 to support and promote quality educational, human-services, and health-care programming for underserved populations. In the area of education, the fund supports academic access, enrichment, and remedial programming for children, youth, adults, and senior citizens that focuses on preparing individuals to achieve while in school and beyond. In the area of health care, the fund supports programming that improves access to primary care for traditionally underserved individuals, health education initiatives and programming that impact at-risk populations, and medical research. In the area of human services the fund tries to meet evolving needs of communities. Currently the fund's focus is on (but is not limited to) youth development, violence prevention, employment, life-skills attainment, and food programs. Grant requests for general operating support are strongly encouraged. Program support will also be considered. Small, program-related capital expenses may be included in general operating or program requests. The majority of grants from the Peters Memorial Fund II are one year in duration; on occasion, multi-year support is awarded. Applicants must apply online at the grant website. Applicants are strongly encouraged to do the following before applying: review the downloadable state application procedures for additional helpful information and clarifications; review the downloadable online-application guidelines at the grant website; review the foundation's funding history (link is available from the grant website); review the online application questions in advance; and review the list of required attachments. These will generally include: a list of board members, financial statements (audited, reviewed, or compiled by independent auditor); an organization summary; a list of other funding sources; an IRS Determination letter; and other required documents. All attachments must be uploaded in the online application as PDF, Word, or Excel files. The application deadline for the Frank Reed and Margaret Jane Peters Memorial Fund II is March 1.

Requirements: Applicants must have 501(c)3 tax-exempt status.

Restrictions: In general, capital requests are not advised. The fund does not support endowment campaigns, events such as galas or award ceremonies, and costs of fundraising events. The fund does not support requests from individuals, organizations attempting to influence policy through direct lobbying, or any political campaigns.

Geographic Focus: Massachusetts

Date(s) Application is Due: Mar 1

Amount of Grant: 10,000 - 40,000 USD

Contact: Michealle Larkins, Vice President; (866) 778-6859; ma.grantmaking@ustrust.com

Internet: www.bankofamerica.com/philanthropic/foundation.go?fnId=42

Sponsor: Frank Reed and Margaret Jane Peters Memorial Fund II

225 Franklin Street, 4th Floor, MA1-225-04-02

Boston, MA 02110

Frank S. Flowers Foundation Grants 1015

The Frank S. Flowers Foundation primarily serves the Gloucester County, New Jersey area. The Foundation's area of interest include: Education—supporting public high schools of Gloucester County, New Jersey, to provide scholarships for college or graduate study, vocational or technical training; Youth—supporting chapters or councils or branches of Y.M.C.A. and Boys Scouts of America located in Gloucester and/or Salem Counties, grants are also considered for organizations having branches or offices in Gloucester County, New Jersey which treat and educate children with special needs; Health-Related—support to non-profit Gloucester County hospitals; Religious organizations—support to churches in the boroughs of Paulsboro and Wenonah, New Jersey. The Foundation also has a specific interest in The Shriner's Hospital for Crippled Children in Philadelphia, Pennsylvania and the Masonic Home Charity Foundation of New Jersey. Grants range from $1,000 - $8,000. Application deadline date is February 15th, application available online. Requestors will receive a letter acknowledging the receipt of their request.

Requirements: Qualifying tax-exempt 501(c)3 organizations are eligible for grants if they meet the purpose of the foundation. Proposals should be submitted in the following format: completed Common Grant Application Form; an original Proposal Statement*; an audited financial report and a current year operating budget; a copy of your official IRS Letter with your tax determination; a listing of your Board of Directors. *Proposal Statement should answer these questions: what are the objectives and expected outcomes of this program/project/request; what strategies will be used to accomplish your objective; what is the timeline for completion; if this is part of an on-going program, how long has it been in operation; what criteria will you use to determine your success; if the request is not fully funded, what other sources can you engage. A Proposal budget should be included if this is for a specific program within your annual budget. Please describe any collaborative ventures.

Restrictions: Grants are not made for political purpose, nor to organizations which discriminate on the basis of race, ethnic origin, sexual or religious preference, age or gender.

Geographic Focus: New Jersey, Pennsylvania

Date(s) Application is Due: Feb 15

Amount of Grant: 1,000 - 8,000 USD

Samples: Holy Trinity Episcopal Church, Parking Lot Rehabilitation—$8,000; Deptford Township High School, $3,000—scholarships; Ronald McDonald House of Southern New Jersey, $5,000—general operations support.

Contact: Gale Y. Sykes; (908) 598-3576; grantinquiries2@wachovia.com

Internet: www.wellsfargo.com/private-foundations/flowers-charitable-trust

Sponsor: Frank S. Flowers Foundation

190 River Road

Summit, NJ 07901

Fred and Gretel Biel Charitable Trust Grants 1016

The Fred and Gretel Biel Charitable Trust was established in 2004 to support and promote quality educational, human-services, and health-care programming for underserved populations. Special consideration is given to organizations that provide food and clothing to low-income individuals and families. Consideration is also given to organizations that serve the economically disadvantaged through the provision of housing, legal assistance, or day-care services. Grant requests for general operating and capital support are encouraged. Grants from the Biel Charitable Trust are one year in duration. Application materials are available for download at the grant website. Applicants are strongly encouraged to review the state application guidelines for additional helpful information and clarifications before applying. Applicants are also encouraged to review the trust's funding history. Between fifty and sixty awards are given annually, ranging from $2,500 to $15,000. The application deadline for the Trust is May 1, and applicants will be notified of grant decisions by June 30.

Requirements: The Biel Charitable Trust typically supports organizations serving the people of King and Snohomish Counties in the Puget Sound region of Washington. Occasionally grants will be made outside of the Puget Sound area. Applicant organizations must have 501(c)3 tax-exempt status.

Restrictions: Requests to assist with debt retirement or to correct an operating deficit will not be considered. Applicants who have received a grant for three consecutive years must wait two years before reapplying to the trust. The trust does not support requests from individuals, organizations attempting to influence policy through direct lobbying, or any political campaigns.

Geographic Focus: Washington

Date(s) Application is Due: May 1

Samples: Haller Lake Christian Health Clinic, Seattle, Washington, $15,000 - general operating support; Caroline Kline Galland Home, Seattle, Washington, $5,649 - Senior Nutrition Program for those clients in need; Cocoon House, Everett, Washington, $5,000 - support of the Street Outreach program.

Contact: Nancy L. Atkinson, Vice President; (206) 358-0912; nancy.l.atkinson@ustrust.com

Internet: www.bankofamerica.com/philanthropic/foundation.go?fnId=120

Sponsor: Fred and Gretel Biel Charitable Trust

800 5th Avenue

Seattle, WA 98104

Frederick McDonald Trust Grants 1017

The Frederick McDonald Trust was established in 1950 to support and promote quality educational, human services, and health care programming for underserved populations. The McDonald Trust specifically serves the people of Albany, New York. The majority of grants from the McDonald Trust are 1 year in duration. On occasion, multi-year support is awarded. Award amounts go up to $20,000.

Requirements: Applicants must have 501(c)3 tax-exempt status. Grant requests for general operating support, program, project and capital support will be considered. Grants are made only to those organizations located in, or serving the people of Albany City. Applications will be submitted online through the Bank of America website. A grant report is required within 1 year of the grant application date, regardless of whether all of the funds have been spent.

Restrictions: The trust does not support requests from individuals, organizations attempting to influence policy through direct lobbying, or any political campaigns.

Geographic Focus: New York

Date(s) Application is Due: Jun 30

Amount of Grant: Up to 20,000 USD

Samples: Senior Services of Albany, Albany, New York, $11,000 - Awarded for General Operations of Senior Services of Albany; Whitney M. Young Jr. Health Center Inc., Albany, New York, $11,000 - Awarded for Campaign for Smiles; American Red Cross, Albany, New York, $10,000 - Awarded for Sound the Alarm.

Contact: Regina Collins, Philanthropic Client Manager; (860) 244-4877; ct.grantmaking@bankofamerica.com or regina.j.collins@bofa.com

Internet: www.bankofamerica.com/philanthropic/foundation/?fnId=63

Sponsor: Frederick McDonald Trust

P.O. Box 1802

Providence, RI 02901-1802

Frederick W. Marzahl Memorial Fund Grants 1018

The Frederick W. Marzahl Memorial Fund was established in 1974 to support and promote quality educational, human-services, and health-care programming for underserved populations in Woodbury, Connecticut. Grants from the Marzahl Memorial Fund are one year in duration. Application materials are available from the Trust. Applicants are strongly encouraged to review the state application guidelines for additional helpful information and clarifications before applying. Applicants are also encouraged. Applicants will be notified of grant decisions by letter within two to three months after the proposal deadline.

Requirements: Applicants must have 501(c)3 tax-exempt status.

Restrictions: Applicants will not be awarded a grant for more than three consecutive years. The fund does not support requests from individuals, organizations attempting to influence policy through direct lobbying, or any political campaigns.

Geographic Focus: Connecticut

Samples: Connecticut Junior Republic Association, Litchfield, Connecticut, $8,000; Flanders Nature Center, Woodbury, Connecticut, $10,000; North Congregational Church, Woodbury, Connecticut, $10,000.

Contact: Senior Trust Officer; (888) 866-3275

Internet: www.bankofamerica.com/philanthropic/fn_search.action

Sponsor: Frederick W. Marzahl Memorial Fund

P.O. Box 1802

Providence, RI 02901-1802

Fremont Area Community Foundation Amazing X Grants 1019

The Amazing X Charitable Trust, a supporting organization of the Fremont Area Community Foundation, was established in the late 1970s by members of the Gerber family to benefit people with disabilities and to address general charitable needs in Newaygo County, Michigan. Grant requests are accepted for: projects or programs that serve people with disabilities; and projects or programs that address general charitable needs. Preferred programs are innovative, collaborative, and have a significant impact on the residents of Newaygo County. Applications are due each year by July 15.

Requirements: Michigan 501(c)3 organizations located in or supporting Newaygo County are eligible for funding. When submitting your proposal, include your organizations: mission, history, description of current programs, activities, and accomplishments; purpose of the grant (describe in detail and include supporting evidence); grant proposal budget form/narrative (form available at the Foundation's website). The following list of attachments must also be included: a copy of the current IRS 501(c)3 determination letter; roster of current governing

board, including addresses and affiliations; finances: organization's current annual operating budget, including all expenses and revenues, audited financial statement (most recently completed), IRS Form 990 (most recently filed), annual report, if available; resumes and job descriptions of the key project personnel; organizational chart; letters of support (up to five).
Restrictions: In order to make the best use of available funds, the Foundation usually will not award grants for the following: grants to individuals; to pay off existing debts; religious programs that require religious affiliation and/or religious instruction to receive services; to further political campaigns; projects that begin prior to notification of Foundation funding; capital improvements on rental or individual private property; or programs or projects that subsidize or supplant funding for services considered general government obligations.
Geographic Focus: Michigan
Date(s) Application is Due: Jul 15
Samples: Ronald McDonald House of Western Michigan, Grand Rapids, Michigan, $15,000 - Family support program (2019); Baldwin Family Health Care, Baldwin, Michigan, $39,000 - In-home respite care (2019); Randy's House, Greenville, Michigan, $10,000 - general operating support (2019).
Contact: Vonda Carr, Grants Manager; (231) 924-5350; fax (231) 924-5391; vcarr@facommunityfoundation.org
Internet: facommunityfoundation.org/grants/types-of-grants/amazing-x-charitable-trust/
Sponsor: Fremont Area Community Foundation
4424 West 48th Street
Fremont, MI 49412

Fremont Area Community Foundation Community Grants   1020
The Fremont Area Community Foundation is focusing its grantmaking resources that enhance the well being of children, youth and families in Newaygo County, Michigan. The Foundation's areas of interest include: arts and culture; community development; education; the environment; and human services. Types of support offered include: building and renovation; capital campaigns; conferences and seminars; consulting services; continuing support; curriculum development; emergency funds; employee matching gifts; endowments; equipment; general operating support; management development; capacity building; matching or challenge support; program-related investments and loans; program development; program evaluation; scholarship funds; seed money; and technical assistance.
Requirements: Michigan 501(c)3 organizations located in or supporting Newaygo County are eligible for funding. When submitting your proposal, include your organizations: mission, history, description of current programs, activities, and accomplishments; purpose of the grant (describe in detail and include supporting evidence); grant proposal budget form/narrative (form available at the Foundation's website). The following list of attachments must also be included: a copy of the current IRS 501(c)3 determination letter; roster of current governing board, including addresses and affiliations; finances: organization's current annual operating budget, including all expenses and revenues, audited financial statement (most recently completed), IRS Form 990 (most recently filed), annual report, if available; resumes and job descriptions of the key project personnel; organizational chart; letters of support (up to five).
Restrictions: In order to make the best use of available funds, the Foundation usually will not award grants for the following: grants to individuals; to pay off existing debts; religious programs that require religious affiliation and/or religious instruction to receive services; to further political campaigns; projects that begin prior to notification of Foundation funding; capital improvements on rental or individual private property; or programs or projects that subsidize or supplant funding for services considered general government obligations.
Geographic Focus: Michigan
Date(s) Application is Due: Mar 1; Sep 1
Amount of Grant: Up to 500,000 USD
Samples: Insight Pregnancy Services, Fremont, Michigan, $6,000 - Educational training for medical staff (2020); Arts Center for Newaygo County, Fremont, Michigan, $10,000 - general operating support (2020); Ashland-Grant Fire District, Grant, Michigan, $14,000 - SAMRC Farmworker Appreciation Day 2020 (2020).
Contact: Vonda Carr, Grants Manager; (231) 924-5350; fax (231) 924-5391; vcarr@facommunityfoundation.org
Internet: facommunityfoundation.org/grants/types-of-grants/community/
Sponsor: Fremont Area Community Foundation
4424 West 48th Street
Fremont, MI 49412

Fremont Area Community Foundation Education Mini-Grants   1021
Fremont Area Community Foundation Education Mini-Grants are available to Newaygo County educators teaching preschool (ages 3-5 years) through 12th grade and are designed to assist the Community Foundation in reaching Goal 2025. That primary goal is to increase the proportion of Newaygo County residents who hold high quality degrees, certifications, or other credentials to 60% by the year 2025. Mini-grants must meet one of the five education grantmaking guidelines, including: kindergarten readiness; STEAM (science, technology, engineering, arts, math); literacy; remediation; and the creation of a positive college and career-oriented culture. The annual deadline is May 31.
Restrictions: In order to make the best use of available funds, the Foundation usually will not award grants for the following: grants to individuals; to pay off existing debts; religious programs that require religious affiliation and/or religious instruction to receive services; to further political campaigns; projects that begin prior to notification of Foundation funding; capital improvements on rental or individual private property; or programs or projects that subsidize or supplant funding for services considered general government obligations.
Geographic Focus: Michigan
Date(s) Application is Due: May 31
Contact: Vonda Carr, Grants Manager; (231) 924-5350; fax (231) 924-5391; vcarr@facommunityfoundation.org
Internet: www.tfacf.org/grants/minigrants.html

Sponsor: Fremont Area Community Foundation
4424 West 48th Street
Fremont, MI 49412

Fremont Area Community Foundation Youth Advisory Committee Grants   1022
The Summer Youth Initiative is a special grantmaking program of the Fremont Area Community Foundation which awards grants of up to $8,000 to provide summer programs for Michigan youth residing in Newaygo County. Priority will be given to programs that: involve a minimum of ten youth; last for a minimum of one week; provide education and recreation; be open and accessible to all interested youth; enhance participants' self-esteem; challenge participants' creativity; and involve participants in some physical exercise and teach healthy lifestyle. Grant applications and proper materials are due by February 1 each year.
Requirements: Organizations applying for a Summer Youth Initiative grant must: be designated as a 501(c)3 non-profit organization or utilize a 501(c)3 organization as a fiscal sponsor; conduct programs to benefit Newaygo County residents; be experienced youth program providers; have oversight of the program by personnel with appropriate credentials; have appropriate youth/staff ratio; provide a positive and safe environment; provide nutritious snack/meal if time warrants; not discriminate on the basis of race, sex, or religious preference; include a plan for evaluation with clearly stated goals and objectives; partner with colleagues and collaborate with other organizations when possible to avoid duplication of services and overlapping of projects.
Restrictions: Fremont Area Community Foundation will not fund: t-shirts; vacation bible schools; camps whose purpose is primarily athletics; and traditional or mandated summer school.
Geographic Focus: Michigan
Date(s) Application is Due: Mar 1
Amount of Grant: Up to 8,000 USD
Samples: City of Newaygo, Newaygo, Michigan, $11,700 - for TrueBlue Academy (2020); Grant Public Schools, Grant, Michigan, $6926 - for Rally Cap Summer Outreach (2020); Harmonized Healing Counseling Services, Inc., White Cloud, Michigan, $2,350 - for LGBTQ+ support (2020).
Contact: Vonda Carr; (231) 924-5350; fax (231) 924-5391; vcarr@facommunityfoundation.org
Internet: facommunityfoundation.org/grants/types-of-grants/yac-grants/
Sponsor: Fremont Area Community Foundation
4424 West 48th Street
Fremont, MI 49412

Friedman Family Foundation Grants   1023
The purpose of this small family foundation is to fund programs that attempt to end the cycle of poverty. To this end, programs are sought that provide tools, support, and opportunity to people in need to overcome the root causes of their poverty, and in which the people to be helped are part of the design and decision making of the organization or project. Priority is given to organizations in the nine counties of the San Francisco Bay area of California. Occasionally projects are considered beyond this region if they offer lessons or benefits for the Bay area. The Foundation provides funding for both general operating support and project support. Typically, awards range from $5,000 to $10,000. Annual application deadlines are February 23, June 15, and November 9.
Requirements: California 501(c)3 nonprofit organizations or public entities with a board or advisory group that is reflective of the population or community being served are eligible.
Restrictions: The foundation generally does not fund films, videos, conferences, seminars, capital, scholarships, individuals, research, or special or fund-raising events.
Geographic Focus: California
Date(s) Application is Due: Feb 23; Jun 15; Nov 9
Amount of Grant: 5,000 - 10,000 USD
Samples: Association for Enterprise Opportunity, Alexandria, Virginia, $10,000 - general operating support; California Association for Microenterprise Opportunity, San Francisco, California, $10,000 - general operating support; Center on Assets, Education and Inclusion, Lawrence, Kansas, $10,000 - general operating support,
Contact: Lisa M. Kawahara, Grants Administrator; (650) 342-8750; fax (866) 223-1078; info@friedmanfamilyfoundation.org
Internet: friedmanfamilyfoundation.org/apply/
Sponsor: Friedman Family Foundation
353 Folsom Street, 2nd Floor
San Francisco, CA 94105-2300

Friends of Hawaii Charities Grants   1024
Friends of Hawaii Charities, Inc. is a tax-exempt Federal 501(c)3 public charity organization that was founded in 1998. Its primary purpose is to generate funding for programs administered by Hawaii's not-for-profit organizations that benefit women, children, youth, and community groups with basic life needs. The application process includes completion of the online grant summary and hard copy grant application accompanied by designated required documents. Friends funds programs that benefit Hawaii's children, youth, women, elderly, and the impoverished in the following areas: arts and education; healthcare and basic needs; and social services. The annual deadline for application submission is December 27.
Requirements: To be considered for funding, an organization must be a public agency or a not-for-profit organization certified under the Section 501(c)3 of the Internal Revenue Service Code. Friends funds programs that benefit Hawaii's children, youth, women, elderly, and the impoverished in the following areas: culture, arts and educations programs; healthcare and basic needs.
Geographic Focus: Hawaii
Date(s) Application is Due: Dec 28
Contact: Corbett Kalama; (808) 792-9339; fax (808) 523-7098; friend@friendsofhawaii.org
Internet: www.friendsofhawaii.org/community/grants-application-and-faqs
Sponsor: Friends of Hawaii Charities
735 Bishop Street, Suite 330
Honolulu, HI 96813

From the Top Alumni Leadership Grants 1025

The From the Top Alumni Leadership Grant program offers two to three grants each year of up to $5,000 each. These awards are given to From the Top alumni ages 18 through 26 for projects that: reflect concern for civic responsibility as artists; expand the professional skills and capacity of the arts leader; include a highly collaborative community outreach and engagement component, particularly with a community or group in need of assistance; and incorporate a plan for a continuing relationship and/or remote follow-up with the community being served. A few potential areas of focus for projects include: video or multimedia that shares music with new audiences; media that explores themes of social/civic change; media that bridges genres with interdisciplinary collaboration; a concert, or concert series, with measurable community impact and/or educational outreach aspects; or work in classrooms, alternative programming, or other types of workshops, seminars, etc. Applicants should submit all required materials by the annual deadline of January 8. Applicants will be notified of their status after March 15.
Requirements: These awards are available to From the Top alumni.
Geographic Focus: All States, American Samoa, District of Columbia, Guam, Marshall Islands, Northern Mariana Islands, Puerto Rico, U.S. Virgin Islands
Date(s) Application is Due: Jan 8
Contact: Javier Caballero, Scholarship and Recruitment Manager; (617) 437-0707, ext. 123; fax (857) 233-4317; jcaballero@fromthetop.org
Internet: www.fromthetop.org/apply/apply-alumni-leadership-grant/
Sponsor: From the Top
140 Clarendon Street, Suite 301
Boston, MA 02116

From the Top Jack Kent Cooke Young Artist Scholarships 1026

In addition to performing on National Public Radio's (NPR's) From the Top with Host Christopher O'Riley, recipients Jack Kent Cooke Young Artist Scholarship receive up to $10,000 to help offset the costs of studying classical music at a high level. Each year, the program chooses approximately twenty exceptional pre-collegiate musicians ages 8 through 18 to receive the award. Applicants should demonstrate: a strong musical ability and a willingness to perform on our NPR show; evidence of a family income insufficient to meet the costs of his/her musical pursuits (new instruments, music lessons, summer festival tuition, and travel, etc.); strong scholastic achievement indicated by good grades, academic awards, and strong test scores; and drive, initiative, maturity, leadership, and a commitment to giving back to one's community. The annual application deadlines are January 7, March 4, and October 1.
Requirements: Classical instrumentalists, vocalists, and composers (ages 8 to 18) who have not yet entered college are eligible to apply. 90% of past recipients come from families with an annual household Adjusted Gross Income of under $60,000. Other factors may apply (cost of living, medical expenses, dependents).
Geographic Focus: All States, American Samoa, District of Columbia, Guam, Marshall Islands, Northern Mariana Islands, Puerto Rico, U.S. Virgin Islands
Date(s) Application is Due: Jan 7; Mar 4; Oct 1
Amount of Grant: 10,000 USD
Contact: Javier Caballero, Scholarship and Recruitment Manager; (617) 437-0707, ext. 123; fax (857) 233-4317; jcaballero@fromthetop.org or scholarship@fromthetop.org
Internet: www.fromthetop.org/apply/scholarship-opportunity-jack-kent-cooke-young-artist-award/
Sponsor: From the Top
140 Clarendon Street, Suite 301
Boston, MA 02116

Fuller E. Callaway Foundation Grants 1027

The Fuller E. Callaway Foundation was founded by the late Fuller E. Callaway, Sr., as a Relief Association chartered by the Superior Court of Troup County, Georgia on December 1, 1917. On his death in 1928, Callaway left a substantial bequest to the Association under his will. The operation of the Association continued under the management of remaining members of Callaway's family. Today, the Foundation awards grants to nonprofit organizations and individuals in LaGrange and Troup County, Georgia. Grants are awarded in the areas of religion, higher and other education, social services, youth, and health. Types of support include: general operating budgets; annual campaigns; building funds; equipment; matching funds; and student aid. Another primary focus of the Foundation is the operation of the historic Callaway home and garden, Hills and Dales Estate, for the education and enrichment of the interested public. Letters of application from organizations are accepted and have deadlines at the end of December, March, June, and September.
Requirements: Nonprofit organizations and individuals in LaGrange and Troup County, Georgia, are eligible for support.
Geographic Focus: Georgia
Amount of Grant: 25,000 - 200,000 USD
Samples: Auburn University Foundation, Auburn, Alabama, $74,585 - scholarship fund contribution; Troup County Baptist Association, LaGrange, Georgia, $5,000 - general operations; Georgia Tech Alumni Association, Atlanta, Georgia, $250 - scholarship fund contribution.
Contact: H. Speer Burdette III, President; (706) 884-7348; fax (706) 884-0201; hsburdette@callaway-foundation.org
Internet: www.callawayfoundation.org/history.php
Sponsor: Fuller E. Callaway Foundation
209 Broome Street, P.O. Box 790
LaGrange, GA 30241-0014

Fuller Foundation Youth At Risk Grants 1028

The Fuller Foundation is a family foundation, inspired by its forward-thinking founder, Alvan T. Fuller. It's purpose is to support non-profit agencies which improve the quality of life for people, animals and the environment. The Foundation also funds the Fuller Foundation of New Hampshire which supports horticultural and educational programs

for the public at Fuller Gardens. In funding Youth at Risk, the Foundation seeks proposals from qualified agencies that involve a minimum of 25 youth, between the ages of 12 and 18, predominately at or below the poverty line, in programs that will: help prevent youth from experiencing the detrimental effects caused by the use of alcohol, tobacco and drugs through the early education of youth and parents; and challenge and empower youth at risk through peer leadership, outdoor adventure education programs, and alternative educational experiences. The Foundation funds programs which help youth reach their potential and lead productive lives. The Foundation favors programs that are year-round, or summer programs which re-enforce values and skills that are learned during the school year. The minimum number of participants is twenty-five. The geographic focus area is predominately the Boston area and the immediate seacoast area of New Hampshire. Through these grants the Foundation strives to effect change, make an impact on the community, and inspire good deeds. The two annual application submission deadlines are January 15 and June 15.
Requirements: Nonprofits in the Boston, Massachusetts, area and the immediate seacoast region of New Hampshire are eligible.
Restrictions: Funding is not available for: capital projects (unless in the opinion of the Trustees, the Foundation gift will have significant impact); individuals; or multi-year grants. Incomplete grants are not considered. Faxed or emailed grant requests will not be accepted.
Geographic Focus: Massachusetts, New Hampshire
Date(s) Application is Due: Jan 15; Jun 15
Amount of Grant: 2,500 - 7,500 USD
Contact: John T. Bottomley; (603) 964-6998; fax (603) 964-8901; atfuller@aol.com
Internet: fullerfoundation.org/focus-areas/youth/
Sponsor: Fuller Foundation
P.O. Box 479
Rye Beach, NH 03871

Fund for the City of New York Grants 1029

The Fund is dedicated to improving the quality of life in the city by supporting efforts to increase the efficiency and effectiveness of government agencies and the nonprofit organizations that are instrumental in promoting a healthy civic environment. The fund's programs concentrate on children and youth and community development and the urban environment. The grants provide project or general support for nonprofit organizations, including a number of watchdog and advocacy organizations. Short-term consultancy grants also are awarded to enable organizations to hire an additional person to help projects through difficult periods. Proposals must be received by April 15 to be considered for the spring cycle and August 15 to be considered for the fall cycle.
Requirements: Applicants are encouraged to contact the Foundation before submitting a letter of inquiry. Unsolicited proposals are not accepted.
Restrictions: Individuals, endowments, and capital campaigns are not eligible to apply.
Geographic Focus: New York
Date(s) Application is Due: Apr 15; Aug 15
Contact: Barbara Cohn Berman; (212) 925-6675; fax (212) 925-5675; bcohn@fcny.org
Internet: www.fcny.org/fcny/core/grants/
Sponsor: Fund for the City of New York
121 Avenue of the Americas, 6th Floor
New York, NY 10013

Furth Family Foundation Grants 1030

The foundation supports children's charity programs in San Francisco and Sonoma County, California. The Foundation gives to the the following fields of interest: arts, education, human services; and public affairs. There are no application deadlines. Applicants should submit a letter describing the organization, proposed budget, and amount requested.
Restrictions: Grants are not made to individuals.
Geographic Focus: California
Amount of Grant: 1,000 - 25,000 USD
Contact: Frederick Furth, Manager; (415) 433-2070; fax (415) 982-1409
Sponsor: Furth Family Foundation
10300 Chalk Hill Road
Healdsburg, CA 95448

G.N. Wilcox Trust Grants 1031

George Norton Wilcox, the son of missionaries Abner and Lucy E. (Hart) Wilcox, was born in Hilo, Hawaii, on August 15, 1839. He was educated at Punahou School on Oahu and graduated from Sheffield Scientific School (Yale) in New Haven, Connecticut. A progressive sugar planter and industrial builder, Wilcox began his career growing sugar at Hanalei, Kauai, in 1863. A year later he went to Grove Farm plantation, of which he eventually became owner. His scientific training made him a leader in improving living condition and developing natural resources on Kauai. He was instrumental in planning water systems for irrigation and household purposes, and bringing electricity, telephone service, and ice to the island. A philanthropist, Wilcox's interests centered largely around religious and educational work. In 1916, he created a trust to build the Salvation Army Home for Boys. Before he died in 1933, he amended the trust to serve a broader scope of purposes. Today, the Trust provides partial support to programs and projects of tax-exempt, public charities in Hawaii to improve the quality of life in the state, particularly the island of Kauai. Grants of one year's duration are awarded in categories of interest to the trust, including education, literacy programs and adult basic education, health, Protestant religion, delinquency and crime prevention, social services, youth services, and culture and the performing arts. Types of support include general operating grants, capital grants, equipment acquisition, seed grants, scholarship funds, and challenge/matching grants. Deadlines dates for general grants are: April 1; July 1; October 1. The deadline date for scholarships is February 15th.
Requirements: Giving is limited to Hawaii, with emphasis on the island of Kauai. To begin application process, contact Paula Boyce for additional guidelines.

Restrictions: Grants are not awarded to support government agencies (or organizations substantially supported by government funds), individuals, or for endowment funds, research, deficit financing, or student aid in scholarships or loans.
Geographic Focus: Hawaii
Date(s) Application is Due: Apr 1; Jul 1; Oct 1
Amount of Grant: Up to 20,000 USD
Samples: Save our Seas Foundation, Honolulu, Hawaii, $2,954 - support for a scholarship fund for youth to participate in the Annual Clean Oceans Conference; Church of the Crossroads, Honolulu, Hawaii, $10,000 - to support the capital campaigns for renovations; Hawaii Public Radio, Honolulu, Hawaii, $3,000 - to support the membership challenge grant.
Contact: Paula Boyce, c/o Bank of Hawaii; (808) 538-4944; fax (808) 538-4647; pboyce@boh.com or emoniz@boh.com
Internet: www.boh.com/philanthropy/grants/g-n-wilcox-trust
Sponsor: G.N. Wilcox Trust
P.O. Box 3170, Department 758
Honolulu, HI 96802-3170

Gamble Foundation Grants   1032

Founded in 1968, the Gamble Foundation is primarily interested in supporting organizations that serve disadvantaged children and youth in San Francisco, Marin and Napa counties. Within the field of youth development, the Foundation focuses on literacy, educational and personal enrichment programs designed to open doors of opportunity for at-risk youth in order to help them succeed in school and become productive, self-sufficient members of society. The Foundation is particularly interested in: agricultural and environmental education; financial and computer literacy; vocational training; and programs that prevent substance abuse and teen violence. To a lesser degree, the Foundation supports environmental organizations that focus on land preservation and sustainability, animal welfare and management, and pollution control. The Foundation is interested in promoting green concepts that increase awareness of science based solutions that help reduce consumption of finite resources. The Foundation prefers to fund specific projects rather than annual appeals. Grants range from $5,000 to $20,000.
Requirements: Northern California 501(c)3 nonprofit organizations, with an emphasis on San Francisco, Marin, and Napa Counties, are eligible to apply. The Board meets in the spring each year and makes grants in late summer.
Restrictions: In general, the Foundation does not support medical research, individuals, endowments, or capital improvements.
Geographic Focus: California
Amount of Grant: 5,000 - 20,000 USD
Contact: Julia Callahan; (415) 561-6540, ext. 250; fax (415) 561-6477; jcallahan@pfs-llc.net
Internet: www.gamblefoundation.org/for-grantseekers/
Sponsor: Gamble Foundation
1660 Bush Street, Suite 300
San Francisco, CA 94109

Gannett Foundation Community Action Grants   1033

The Gannett Foundation is a corporate foundation sponsored by Gannett Co., Inc. The Foundation awards grants to organizations in the communities in which Gannett owns a daily newspaper or television station. These communities include: Montgomery, Alabama; Phoenix and Flagstaff, Arizona; Little Rock and Mountain Home, Arkansas; Palm Springs, Sacramento, Salinas and Visalia, California; Denver and Fort Collins, Colorado; Wilmington, Delaware; Montgomery, Salisbury and PG County, Maryland; Alexandria, Falls Church, Arlington and Fairfax County, Prince William County, Loudoun County, Virginia; Brevard County, Fort Myers, Jacksonville, Pensacola, St. Petersburg, and Tallahassee, Florida; Atlanta and Macon, Georgia; Guam; Hawaii; Indianapolis, Lafayette, Muncie and Richmond, Indiana; Des Moines and Iowa City, Iowa; Louisville, Kentucky; Alexandria, Lafayette, Monroe, Opelousas and Shreveport, Louisiana; Bangor and Portland, Maine; Battle Creek, Detroit, Grand Rapids, Howell, Lansing and Port Huron, Michigan; Minneapolis and St. Cloud, Minnesota; Hattiesburg and Jackson, Mississippi; St. Louis and Springfield, Missouri; Great Falls, Montana; Reno, Nevada; Asbury Park, Bridgewater, Cherry Hill, East Brunswick, Parsippany/Morristown and Vineland, New Jersey; Binghamton, Buffalo, Elmira, Ithaca, Poughkeepsie, Rochester, White Plains and New York City, New York; Asheville and Greensboro, North Carolina; Bucyrus, Chillicothe, Cincinnati, Coshocton, Cleveland, Fremont, Lancaster, Mansfield, Marion, Newark, Port Clinton, and Zanesville, Ohio; Salem, Oregon; Columbia and Greenville, South Carolina; Sioux Falls, South Dakota; Clarksville, Jackson, Knoxville, Murfreesboro and Nashville, Tennessee; St. George, Utah; Burlington, Vermont; Staunton, Virginia; Appleton, Fond du Lac, Green Bay, Manitowoc, Marshfield, Oshkosh, Sheboygan, Stevens Point, Wausau and Wisconsin Rapids, Wisconsin; and the United Kingdom. The community action grant priorities include: education; neighborhood improvement; economic development; youth development; community problem-solving; assistance to disadvantaged people; environmental conservation and; cultural enrichment. The typical grant amount is in the range of $1,000 to $5,000. Grant applications are accepted twice a year.
Requirements: 501(c)3 nonprofit organizations in Gannett-operating areas are eligible. Each local Gannett operation establishes its own priorities, depending upon local needs, and may have additional guidelines and restrictions. Contact the local Gannett organization to learn about its priorities, restrictions, and deadlines. If unsure about an organization's eligibility, an email (or one-page letter) of inquiry to the local community contact is welcome. Send one copy of the application form and your proposal of no more than five pages (plus attachments) to the local newspaper publisher. Do not send a proposal to the foundation offices in McLean, VA, unless it addresses local needs in the Washington, D.C. metropolitan area. Applications should be postmarked no later than February 28th or August 29th. Some locations have earlier deadlines, and they are listed in the Grant Contact list.

Restrictions: Grants will not be considered for the following purposes: individuals; private foundations; organizations not determined by the IRS to be a tax-exempt public charity under 501(c)3; organizations classified by the IRS as 509(a)3; national or regional organizations unless their programs address specific local community needs; programs or initiatives where the primary purpose is the promotion of religious doctrine or tenets; elementary or secondary schools (except to provide special initiatives or programs not provided by regular school budgets); political action or legislative advocacy groups; endowment funds; multiple-year pledge campaigns; medical or research organizations, including organizations funding single disease research; organizations located in or benefiting nations other than the U.S. and its territories; fraternal groups, athletic teams, bands, volunteer firefighters or similar groups.
Geographic Focus: Alabama, Arizona, Arkansas, California, Colorado, Delaware, District of Columbia, Florida, Georgia, Guam, Hawaii, Indiana, Iowa, Kentucky, Louisiana, Maine, Maryland, Michigan, Minnesota, Mississippi, Missouri, Montana, Nevada, New Jersey, New York, North Carolina, Ohio, Oregon, South Carolina, South Dakota, Tennessee, Utah, Vermont, Virginia, Wisconsin, United Kingdom
Date(s) Application is Due: Feb 28; Aug 29
Amount of Grant: 1,000 - 5,000 USD
Contact: Pat Lyle, Exceutiave Director; (703) 854-6000; foundation@gannett.com
Internet: www.gannettfoundation.org/index.htm
Sponsor: Gannett Foundation
7950 Jones Branch Drive
McLean, VA 22107

Gardner Foundation Grants   1034

The Gardner Foundation was established in the State of New York in 1947, with a giving emphasis on Milwaukee, Wisconsin. The Foundation's major mission is to provide grant funding for a wide range of organizations supporting arts and culture, education, and youth services. Its primary fields of interest include: child welfare; community and economic development; elementary and secondary education; employment; homeless services; hospice care; human services; mental health care; museums; performing arts; and reproductive health care. That support typically comes in a variety of forms, which include: annual campaigns; capital and infrastructure; capital campaigns; continuing support; emergency funding; and general operating support. Most recent awards have ranged from $1,000 to $6,000. Application forms and application guidelines are provided. Annual deadlines are at minimum one month prior to Board meetings, which are generally scheduled in April, September, and December. April, September, and December
Requirements: 501(c)3 organizations and schools serving the Milwaukee, Wisconsin, area are eligible to apply.
Geographic Focus: Wisconsin
Date(s) Application is Due: Mar 1; Aug 1; Nov 1
Amount of Grant: 1,000 - 6,000 USD
Samples: 88 Nine Radio, Milwaukee, Wisconsin, $6,000 - general operating funds; Beyond Vision, Milwaukee, Wisconsin, $4,000 - general operating funds; Hunger Task Force, Milwaukee, Wisconsin, $4,000 - general operating funds.
Contact: Theodore Friedlander III, President; (414) 273-0308
Sponsor: Gardner Foundation of Milwaukee
322 E. Michigan Street, Suite 250
Milwaukee, WI 53202-5010

Gardner Foundation Grants   1035

The Gardner Foundation was established in Louisville, Kentucky, in 1979, and giving is primarily centered around the city in which it began. The Foundation's major fields of interest include: the environment; religion; and youth development. Typical forms of support are for infrastructure and general operations. Awards have recently averaged between $250 and $10,000. A formal application can be secured from the Foundation office, and the annual deadline for its submission is May 1.
Requirements: 501(c)3 organizations either based in, or serving the residents of, Louisville, Kentucky, are eligible to apply.
Geographic Focus: Kentucky
Date(s) Application is Due: May 1
Amount of Grant: 250 - 10,000 USD
Samples: Cabbage Patch Settlement House, Louisville, Kentucky, $10,000 - general operations; Nativity Academy of St. Bonaventure Church, Louisville, Kentucky, $10,000 - general operations; Maryhurst School, Louisville, Kentucky, $5,000 - general operations.
Contact: William A. Gardner, Jr., Vice President; (502) 894-4440
Sponsor: Gardner Foundation of Louisville
2301 River Road, Suite 301
Louisville, KY 40206-3040

Gardner W. and Joan G. Heidrick, Jr. Foundation Grants   1036

The Gardner W. and Joan G. Heidrick, Jr. Foundation was established in the State of Texas in 1998, with the expressed purpose of providing support for nonprofit organizations in Texas. North Carolina, and Illinois. The Foundation's primary fields of interest include: higher education programs; human services; and recreation and sports. Typically, support is given in the form of general operating funds. Most recent grants have ranged from $20 to $1,000, with an average of ten awards given each year. A formal application is required, and can be secured directly from the Foundation office. There are no specified annual deadlines.
Requirements: 501(c)3 organizations serving residents of Texas, North Carolina, or Illinois are eligible to apply.
Geographic Focus: Illinois, North Carolina, Texas
Amount of Grant: 20 - 1,000 USD

Samples: American Diabetes, Charlotte, North Carolina, $100 - general operating funds; University of Chicago, Chicago, Illinois, $1,000 - general operations; University of Texas, Austin, Texas, $1,000 - general operations.
Contact: Gardner W. Heidrick, President; (704) 366-7880
Sponsor: Gardner W. and Joan G. Heidrick, Jr. Foundation
8919 Park Road, Suite 4019
Charlotte, NC 28210-2242

GCI Corporate Contributions Grants   1037

GCI's corporate contribution program awards grants to qualified, not-for-profit organizations and charities in Alaska that contribute to the quality of life in the state. Awards are given for proposals that encourage individual growth and positive decision-making. Of special interest are opportunities afforded to Alaska's youth. Emphasis is given to programs where GCI employees have chosen to invest their time and energies. Proposals can be submitted throughout the year, but will only be reviewed the first week of every month. Notification will be mailed within 10 days following award determinations.
Requirements: Proposals should include a cover sheet and no more than two typed pages of narrative. Attachments should be limited to three pages. Only written proposals in the following format will be considered: a cover sheet to include a 50-word abstract of the proposal and appropriate contact information; a description of the proposed project; amount and type of contribution requested (specify exact dollar amount and whether the request is for cash or for in-kind services such as cellular, local, long-distance, cable television or Internet); how the funds will be used; how the proposal aligns with CGI's criteria; mission and history of the program/organization; names of CGI employees involved in the proposed project/program and to what extent; and whether CGI has awarded grants to the organization in the past.
Restrictions: Support is not generally given for travel or travel-related expenses; to individuals; to religious or political organizations; to organizations based outside of Alaska; or, to organizations that discriminate on the basis of age, sex, race, color, national origin, religion, creed, marital status, sexual preference, veteran status, or disability.
Geographic Focus: Alaska
Amount of Grant: Up to 500 USD
Contact: Pebbles Harris, Grant Contact; (907) 868-5553; fax (907) 265-5676
Internet: www.gci.com/about/corporate-giving
Sponsor: GCI Corporation
2550 Denali Street, Suite 1000
Anchorage, AK 99503

Gene Haas Foundation   1038

The Gene Haas Foundation was formed in 1999 to fund the needs of the local community and other deserving charities, at the discretion of its founder, Gene Haas. Of special importance to the Foundation are children's charities and organizations that feed the poor, especially within the local community of Ventura County. In addition, the Foundation provides scholarship funds to community colleges and vocational schools for students entering technical training programs, especially machinist-based certificate and degree programs. Giving is primarily in California.
Requirements: The Gene Haas Foundation provides grants to organizations that are exempt under Internal Revenue Code Section 501(c)3 and currently are classified as a public charity pursuant to Internal Revenue Code Section 509(a)1, 2 or 3 (an "Exempt Public Charity"). Funds from the Gene Haas Foundation must be fully utilized within 2 years of date of grant. Funds that are not expended must be returned unless other arrangements are approved by the Gene Haas Foundation.
Restrictions: Grants provided by the Gene Haas Foundation, or the interest generated from those grants, may not be used to influence any legislation or the outcome of any election, to conduct a voter registration drive or to satisfy a charitable pledge or obligation of any person or organization.
Geographic Focus: California
Amount of Grant: Up to 100,000 USD
Samples: Ventura College Foundation, Ventura, California, $50,000 - matching funds for operating costs; ABS-CBN Foundation, Redwood City, California, $10,000 - operating costs; New West Symphony Association, Thousand Oaks, Cali., $10,000 - operating costs.
Contact: Gene F. Haas, President; (805) 278-1800; info@ghaasfoundation.org
Internet: ghaasfoundation.org/
Sponsor: Gene Haas Foundation
2800 Sturgis Road
Oxnard, CA 93030-8901

General Motors Foundation Grants   1039

With a strong commitment to diversity in all areas, the targeted areas of focus for the Foundation are: driving safety; education; health and human services; civic and community; public policy; arts and culture; and environment and energy. Primary consideration is given to requests that meet the following criteria: exhibit a clear purpose and defined need in one of the foundation's areas of focus; recognize innovative approaches in addressing the defined need; demonstrate an efficient organization and detail the organization's ability to follow through on the proposal; and, explain clearly the benefits to the foundation and the plant city communities. Paper applications are no longer accepted. Completion of an online eligibility quiz is the first step in the application process.
Requirements: Nonprofit, tax-exempt organizations and institutions are eligible to apply. Applications must be made online.
Restrictions: The Foundation not not support organizations that discriminate on the basis of race, religion, creed, gender, age, veteran status, physical challenge or national origin. Contributions are generally not provided for: individuals; religious organizations; political parties or candidates; U.S. hospitals and health care institutions (general operating support); capital campaigns; endowment funds; conferences, workshops or seminars not directly related to GM's business interests.
Geographic Focus: All States
Amount of Grant: Up to 100,000 USD
Contact: Grant Coordinator; (313) 556-5000
Internet: www.gm.com/our-company/social-investment.html
Sponsor: General Motors Foundation
300 Renaissance Center, P.O. Box 300
Detroit, MI 48265-3000

General Service Foundation Human Rights and Economic Justice Grants   1040

The goal of the General Service Foundation's Human Rights and Economic Justice program is to support efforts that protect, promote and create good jobs with living wages for workers, including low-wage workers in the United States and Mexico. The Foundation seeks to: strengthen worker voices; promote public policies that protect labor rights; and democratize corporate power and promote corporate accountability. In assessing potential grantees, the Foundation will apply the following criteria: supporting organizations that work to address needs identified by the underrepresented and low-income communities that area directly impacted, connecting at the local and national level; and concentrating on organizations that take risks and try new ideas to enhance their skills, and reflect the diversity of their constituency. Samples of previously funded projects are posted on the Foundation website.
Requirements: All applicants, regardless of their prior grant history with the Foundation, start their application process by submitting a letter of inquiry in the spring and fall. Organizations should determine if their project is an appropriate fit for the Foundation, then send a letter of inquiry via the Foundation's online application. Letters of inquiry should include: a political and situational analysis, statement of the issues to be addressed under the proposed project, the history and goals of the organization, and an explanation of why the organization or coalition is the entity that is most likely to achieve success; a brief summary of the project, short and long term goals and anticipated outcomes; the approximate starting date and duration of the proposed activities; the total amount of funding needed, the amount requested from the Foundation, a budget, and information about other sources of support; and a copy of IRS tax exempt 501(c)3 letter. If the project is judged appropriate, the organization will be offered an application to submit to the Foundation.
Restrictions: The Foundation does not fund: organizations based outside the United States or Mexico; projects without significant promise of impact beyond a local or state level; research and publications not directly linked to policy outcomes; direct service delivery; and development or relief projects.
Geographic Focus: All States, Mexico
Date(s) Application is Due: Feb 1; Sep 1
Amount of Grant: 5,000 - 35,000 USD
Contact: Holly Bartling, Program Contact-Mexico grants; (202) 232-1005 or (970) 920-6834, ext 4; fax (970) 920-4578; holly@generalservice.org
Mary Estrin, Program Contact-U.S. grants; (970) 920-6834; fax (970) 920-4578; maryestrin@gmail.com
Internet: www.generalservice.org/International%20Peace.htm
Sponsor: General Service Foundation
557 North Mill Street, Suite 201
Aspen, CO 81611

George A. and Grace L. Long Foundation Grants   1041

The George A. and Grace L. Long Foundation was established in 1960 to support and promote quality educational, cultural, human services and health care programming for underserved populations in Connecticut. Bank of America serves as co trustee of the Long Foundation. Grants from the Long Foundation are one year in duration. Award amounts typically range from $2,000 to $13,000.
Requirements: Applicant organizations must have 501(c)3 tax-exempt status and serve the people of Connecticut, as well as have a principal office in Connecticut. The Trustees normally give preference to proposals for specific programs or projects, and normally do not make grants for deficit financing, annual giving or capital projects. An applicant must demonstrate financial responsibility, indicate the qualification of its staff leadership and should indicate why the organization requesting a grant is the logical one to carry out the project. Applications will be submitted online through the Bank of America website. A grant report is required within 1 year of the grant application date, regardless of whether all of the funds have been spent.
Restrictions: Applicants will not be awarded a grant for more than three consecutive years. The fund does not support requests from individuals, organizations attempting to influence policy through direct lobbying, or any political campaigns.
Geographic Focus: Connecticut
Date(s) Application is Due: Apr 1
Amount of Grant: 2,000 - 13,000 USD
Samples: Camp Courant Inc., Hartford, Connecticut, $13,000 - Awarded for 2017 and 2018 Heath and Wellness Services (2018); Almada Lodge-Times Farm Camp Corporation, Andover, Connecticut, $12,000 - Awarded for Inclusive Overnight Summer Camp (2018); Trinity College, Hartford, Connecticut, $10,000 - Awarded for Dream Camp at Trinity College (2018).
Contact: Amy R. Lynch, Philanthropic Client Manager; (860) 244-4870; ct.grantmaking@bankofamerica.com or amy.r.lynch@bofa.com
Internet: www.bankofamerica.com/philanthropic/foundation/?fnId=93
Sponsor: George A. And Grace L. Long Foundation
99 Founders Plaza
East Hartford, CT 06108

George and Ruth Bradford Foundation Grants   1042

The George and Ruth Bradford Foundation awards grants to local nonprofit organizations in the San Francisco Bay Area and Mendocino, California region. Areas of interest include: basic and emergency aid; biodiversity; summer camps; children and youth; community development; economic development; elementary and secondary education; family services; food security; health care; higher education; human services; museums; natural resources; nursing care; performing arts; public affairs; shelter and residential care; special population support; and temporary accommodations. Types of support include general operating support, program development, and scholarship funds. Though giving is centered in the State of California, funding has also gone to Oregon, New Mexico, Michigan, and Kentucky. Most recently, this funding has ranged up to as much as $22,000. There are no specified deadlines, though the Board meets once each month to make award decisions.
Requirements: Primarily, California nonprofit organizations in the San Francisco peninsula and Mendocino, California region are eligible to apply, as well as organizations from Oregon, New Mexico, Michigan, and Kentucky. Letters of inquiry may be submitted throughout the year for review.
Restrictions: No grants to are given directly to individuals.
Geographic Focus: California, Kentucky, Michigan, New Mexico, Oregon
Samples: Community Foundation of Mendo County, Ukiah, California, $22,000 - general operating costs (2018); University of California at Davis Foundation, Davis, California, $10,000 - general university education programs (2018); Anderson Valley Elementary School, Boonville, California, $5,000 - general operating support (2018).
Contact: Myrna L. Oglesby, Secretary; (707) 462-0141; fax (707) 462-0160
Sponsor: George and Ruth Bradford Foundation
P.O. Box 720
Ukiah, CA 95482-0720

George A Ohl Jr. Foundation Grants   1043

The purpose of the George A Ohl Jr. Foundation is to improve the well-being of the citizens of the State of New Jersey through science, health, recreation, education and increased good citizenship. Grants are made to organizations engaged in such work whether through research, publications, health, school or college activities. The Foundation's mission is the relief of the poor; the improvement of living conditions; the care of the sick, the young, the aged, the homeless, the incompetent and the helpless. The foundation will target: 35% of its grants to Community Redevelopment; 35% to Health and Human Services organizations; 15% for Arts and culture; 15% for Educational requests. Application deadlines are: January 22 for a March meeting and, June 15 for an August meeting. Application forms are available online. Applicants will receive notice acknowledging receipt of the grant request, and subsequently be notified of the grant declination or approval.
Requirements: New Jersey 501(c)3 nonprofit organizations are eligible to apply. Proposals should be submitted in the following format: completed Common Grant Application Form; an original Proposal Statement; an audited financial report and a current year operating budget; a copy of your official IRS Letter with your tax determination; a listing of your Board of Directors. Proposal Statements (second item in the above Format) should answer these questions: what are the objectives and expected outcomes of this program/project/request; what strategies will be used to accomplish your objective; what is the timeline for completion; if this is part of an on-going program, how long has it been in operation; what criteria will you use to measure success; if the request is not fully funded, what other sources can you engage; an Itemized budget should be included; please describe any collaborative ventures. Prior to the distribution of funds, all approved grantees must sign and return a Grant Agreement Form, stating that the funds will be used for the purpose intended. Progress reports and Completion reports must also be filed as required for your specific grant. All current grantees must be in good standing with required documentation prior to submitting new proposals to any foundation.
Restrictions: Grants are not made for political purposes, nor to organizations which discriminate on the basis of race, ethnic origin, sexual or religious preference, age or gender
Geographic Focus: New Jersey
Date(s) Application is Due: Jan 22; Jun 15
Amount of Grant: 3,000 - 35,000 USD
Samples: Mountainside Hospital Foundation, $35,000—Modernization of Internal Medicine Residents' Learning Center; Bloomfield College, $10,000—Improving Academic Success Through Technological Support Project; Medical Missions for Children, $5,000—Giggles Theater Programming Support (12 performances).
Contact: Wachovia Bank, N.A., Trustee; grantinquiries2@wachovia.com
Internet: www.wellsfargo.com/private-foundations/ohl-trust
Sponsor: George A Ohl Jr. Foundation
190 River Road, NJ3132
Summit, NJ 07901

George B. Page Foundation Grants   1044

The foundation awards grants to Santa Barbara, CA, nonprofit organizations in support of programs for children and youth, youth development, clubs, and centers; athletics/sports, Special Olympics; community and economic development; education; human services; YM/YWCAs and YM/YWHAs. Types of support include annual campaigns; continuing support; debt reduction; emergency funds; general/operating support; program development; and seed money.
Requirements: Application forms are required, but organizations should initially call or write the Foundation to discuss the project, and request an application.
Restrictions: Funding is not available for individuals, endowment funds, or matching gifts.
Geographic Focus: California
Date(s) Application is Due: Oct 1
Amount of Grant: 2,000 - 50,000 USD
Contact: Sara Sorensen, Trustee; (805) 730-3634

Sponsor: George B. Page Foundation
P.O. Box 1299
Santa Barbara, CA 93102-1299

George E. Hatcher, Jr. and Ann Williams Hatcher Foundation Grants   1045

The George E. Hatcher and Ann Williams Hatcher Foundation was created to support charitable organizations that provide for the relief of diseased people and the relief of human suffering which is due to disease, ill health, physical weakness, physical disability and/or physical injury. In addition, the foundation supports organizations that aid in the promotion and prolongation of life and that support the principle of dying with dignity. Grants from George E. Hatcher and Ann Williams Hatcher Foundation are primarily one year in duration; on occasion, multi-year support is awarded. Applicants must apply online at the grant website. Applicants are strongly encouraged to do the following before applying: review the downloadable state application procedures for additional helpful information and clarifications; review the downloadable online-application guidelines at the grant website; review the foundation's funding history (link is available from the grant website); review the online application questions in advance; and review the list of required attachments. These will generally include: a list of board members; financial statements (audited, reviewed, or compiled by independent auditor); an organization summary; a list of other funding sources; an IRS Determination letter; and other required documents. All attachments must be uploaded in the online application as PDF, Word, or Excel files. The George E. Hatcher and Ann Williams Hatcher Foundation application deadline is 11:59 p.m. on May 31. Applicants will be notified of grant decisions by letter within one to two months after the deadline.
Requirements: Disbursements are authorized to institutions or organizations located in the Middle Georgia area (Bibb County & surrounding communities) which provide health care and/or shelter for individuals (especially children) who cannot otherwise obtain such services due to circumstances beyond their control. A breakdown of number/percentage of people served by specific counties is required on the online application.
Restrictions: The foundation does not support requests from individuals, organizations attempting to influence policy through direct lobbying, or any political campaigns.
Geographic Focus: Georgia
Date(s) Application is Due: May 31
Samples: Macon Volunteer Clinic, Macon, Georgia, $25,000; Rebuilding Macon, Macon, Georgia, $25,000; Methodist Home of the South Georgia Conference, Macon, Georgia, $10,000.
Contact: Quanda Allen, Vice President; (404) 264-1377; quanda.allen@baml.com
Internet: www.bankofamerica.com/philanthropic/fn_search.action
Sponsor: George E. Hatcher, Jr. and Ann Williams Hatcher Foundation
3414 Peachtree Road, N.E., Suite 1475, GA7-813-14-04
Atlanta, GA 30326-1113

George F. Baker Trust Grants   1046

Grants are awarded nationwide, with preference given to nonprofits in the eastern United States, primarily for K-12, higher, and secondary education; hospitals; social services; private foundations; and zoos/zoological societies. Types of support include general operating support and matching funds. There are no application forms or deadlines. The board meets in June and November to consider requests.
Requirements: An application form is not required. Along with a letter of inquiry and brief outline of a proposal, applicants should submit the following: signature and title of chief executive officer; a copy of the organization's IRS determination letter; a detailed description of the project and amount of funding requested; and a listing of additional sources and amount of support. As a result of the enormous number of applications received and limited number of grants, only those applicants who receive a grant will be notified.
Restrictions: Funding is given primarily in Connecticut, Florida, Massachusetts, and New York. Grants are not made to individuals for scholarships or loans.
Geographic Focus: Connecticut, Florida, Massachusetts, New York
Amount of Grant: 1,000 - 50,000 USD
Contact: Rocio Suarez, Executive Director; (212) 755-1890; fax (212) 319-6316; rocio@bakernye.com
Sponsor: George F. Baker Trust
477 Madison Avenue, Suite 1650
New York, NY 10022

George Graham and Elizabeth Galloway Smith Foundation Grants   1047

The George Graham and Elizabeth Galloway Smith Foundation was established in 1960 to serve residents of Buffalo and Orchard Park, New York, although funding is also given throughout the United States. The Foundation's primary mission to support: art and music programs; elementary and secondary education; higher education; science museums; and human services. Awards typically take the form of capital and infrastructure, equipment purchase, program development, and re-granting. A formal application is required, and initial contact should be made by letter to the Foundation office. For requests of $1,000 or more, July 15 is the annual deadline; there is no deadline for requests of less than $1,000. Most recent awards have ranged from $5,000 to $150,000.
Requirements: 501(c)3 organizations serving western New York, primarily Buffalo and Orchard Park, are welcome to apply, as well as organizations throughout the U.S.
Geographic Focus: All States
Date(s) Application is Due: Jul 15
Amount of Grant: 5,000 - 150,000 USD
Samples: Camphill Soltane, Glenmoore, Pennsylvania, $100,000 - unrestricted support for young adults and adults with developmental disabilities; Center Stage Theatrical School and Company, Kingwood, Texas, $5,000 - program development; Morven Museum and Graden, Princeton, New Jersey, $150,000 - capital campaign.

Contact: Ellen S. Morehouse, President; (609) 466-2210
Sponsor: George Graham and Elizabeth Galloway Smith Foundation
1 East Prospect Street, P.O. Box 202
Hopewell, NJ 08525

George H. and Jane A. Mifflin Memorial Fund Grants 1048

The George H. and Jane A. Mifflin Memorial Fund awards grants to Massachusetts nonprofit organizations in its areas of interest, including crime and law enforcement, disadvantaged (economically), education, environment, legal services, and social services. Types of support include capital campaigns, land acquisition, and scholarship funds. Trustees accept grant applications between October 1st and April 15th of each year, as most of the funds for new grants are allocated at the May Trustees meeting. The final grant making decisions and distributions are made at the September meeting. The annual deadline for applications is April 15.
Requirements: Massachusetts 501(c)3 nonprofit organizations are eligible to apply.
Geographic Focus: Massachusetts
Date(s) Application is Due: Apr 15
Contact: Lucy Martins-Jackson, Trustee Assistant; (617) 523-6531; bcarr@lwcotrust.com or mifflinmemorialfund@lwcotrust.com
Internet: www.mifflinmemorialfund.org/
Sponsor: George H. and Jane A. Mifflin Memorial Fund
230 Congress Street
Boston, MA 02110

George H.C. Ensworth Memorial Fund Grants 1049

The George H. C. Ensworth Memorial Fund was established in 1949 to support charitable organizations that focus on health and human services, youth services, enjoyment of the natural environment, education, religion, and the arts. The George H. C. Ensworth Memorial Fund specifically serves the people of Glastonbury, Connecticut. Grants from the Ensworth Memorial Fund are 1 year in duration. Award amounts go up to $11,000.
Requirements: Applicants must have 501(c)3 status and serve the people of Glastonbury, Connecticut. Applications will be submitted online through the Bank of America website. A grant report is required within 1 year of the grant application date, regardless of whether all of the funds have been spent.
Restrictions: Grant requests for capital projects will not be considered. Applicants will not be awarded a grant for more than 3 consecutive years. The fund does not support requests from individuals, organizations attempting to influence policy through direct lobbying, or any political campaigns.
Geographic Focus: Connecticut
Date(s) Application is Due: May 15
Amount of Grant: Up to 11,000 USD
Samples: Nami of Connecticut Inc., Hartford, Connecticut, $10,000 - Awarded for Glastonbury opioid Support Groups (2019); Rushford Center Inc., Meriden, Connecticut, $5,000 - Awarded for Alternative Therapies to Support Recovery (2019); Cuatro Puntos Inc., Salem, Connecticut, $5,000 - Awarded for 2018-2019 Cuatro Puntos Concert Series: United in Diversity (2019).
Contact: Amy R. Lynch, Philanthropic Client Manager; (860) 244-4870; ct.grantmaking@bankofamerica.com or amy.r.lynch@bofa.com
Internet: www.bankofamerica.com/philanthropic/foundation/?fnId=52
Sponsor: George H.C. Ensworth Memorial Fund
P.O. Box 1802
Providence, RI 02901-1802

George H. Sandy Foundation Grants 1050

The George H. Sandy Foundation was established in California with the death of George Howard Sandy on September 9, 1960, a lifelong merchant in the San Meteo, California, area. Sandy worked as a young man for Hale Brothers of San Francisco. Then, in partnership with Siegfried Bestandig, he operated the Sandy and Bestandig Women's apparel shop on Mission Street. In 1912, he opened his own business, known as the National Cloak and Suit House. Eventually, Sandy sold bis interests and devoted himself to real estate and volunteerism throughout the region. Today, the Foundation offers support in the area of human services and education, with emphasis on aid to the handicapped and underprivileged in the San Francisco Bay area. Types of funding include: continuing support; general operating support; and program development. The maximum amount of most recent grants is $50,000.
Requirements: Any 501(c)3 organization serving the residents of the San Francisco Bay area of California are eligible to apply.
Geographic Focus: California
Amount of Grant: Up to 50,000 USD
Samples: Alameda County Community Food Bank, Oakland, California, $50,000 - general operating support (2018); Central City Hospitality House, San Francisco, California, $35,000 - general operating support (2018); Curry Senior Center, San Francisco, California, $60,000 - general operating support (2018).
Contact: Thomas J. Feeney, Trustee; (415) 705-7173
Sponsor: George H. Sandy Foundation
P.O. Box 591717
San Francisco, CA 94159-1717

George I. Alden Trust Grants 1051

The Alden Trust supports independent colleges and universities in New Jersey, New York, Pennsylvania and the six New England states having fulltime traditional undergraduate enrollments of at least 1,000 students and with a total undergraduate and graduate student population (full time equivalents) of under 5,000. Furthermore, the Trust supports YMCAs in Massachusetts and educationally related organizations in the Worcester, Massachusetts area. In addition, it supports independent secondary schools in the immediate Worcester area. With respect to institutions of higher education, the Trust typically supports capital projects for academic purposes and less frequently supports restricted endowment initiatives for need-based scholarship aid, faculty development, or technology enhancement. The Trust currently favors capital projects related to teaching and learning technology in general and to the sciences in particular. Support given to YMCAs is usually for capital projects. Grants provided for educationally related organizations in the Worcester area focus on occasional capital project support.
Requirements: The Trust supports only tax-exempt IRS 501(c)3 non-profit organizations in New Jersey, New York, Pennsylvania, Connecticut, Maine, Massachusetts, New Hampshire, Rhode Island and Vermont. Application guidelines are available at the Foundation's website. Colleges and universities that are first time applicants should not expect grants in excess of $100,000. Applications may be submitted prior to the first day of each of the following months: February, May, August, October, and December. It is advisable to submit applications well in advance of the deadline, in case the Trustees desire additional information.
Restrictions: Grants are not made to individuals.
Geographic Focus: Connecticut, Maine, Massachusetts, New Hampshire, New Jersey, New York, Pennsylvania, Rhode Island, Vermont
Date(s) Application is Due: Feb 15; May 15; Aug 15; Nov 15
Contact: Warner S. Fletcher, Chair; (508) 459-8005; fax (508) 459-8305; trustees@aldentrust.org
Internet: www.aldentrust.org/applicationguidelines.html
Sponsor: George I. Alden Trust
370 Main Street, 11th Floor
Worcester, MA 01608

George J. and Effie L. Seay Foundation Grants 1052

The George J. and Effie L. Seay Foundation was established in 1957 to support and promote programs and services provided by qualifying charitable organizations in the Commonwealth of Virginia. Grants from the Seay Foundation are 1 year in duration. Award amounts typically range from $5,000 to $30,000. Because requests for support usually exceed available resources, organizations are advised to apply to either the Morgan Trust or the Seay Foundation.
Requirements: Applicants must be classified by the Internal Revenue Service (IRS) as a 501(c)3 public charity. The Seay Foundation makes grants primarily for programs and projects designed to provide specific services or training. Requests for general operating grants will not be considered. Applications will be submitted online through the Bank of America website. A grant report is required within 1 year of the grant application date, regardless of whether all of the funds have been spent.
Restrictions: While receipt of a grant does not preclude later support, an organization normally will not be considered for another grant from either the Morgan Trust or the Seay Foundation until at least 3 years after the date of the last grant payment. The foundation does not support requests from individuals, organizations attempting to influence policy through direct lobbying, or any political campaigns.
Geographic Focus: Virginia
Date(s) Application is Due: Apr 1
Amount of Grant: 5,000 - 30,000 USD
Samples: Elk Hill Farm Inc., Goochland, Virginia, $20,000- Awarded for Elk Hill's School-Based Mental Health (2019); Virginia Mentoring Partnership, Richmond, Virginia, $15,000- Awarded for Elevating the Quality and Capacity of Youth Mentoring Programs in Richmond (2019); Art 180 Inc., Richmond, Virginia, $14,000- Awarded for ART 180 Fall Community Programs (2019).
Contact: Lee Parker, Philanthropic Client Manager; (877) 446-1410; D.C.grantmaking@bankofamerica.com or D.C.grantmaking@ustrust.com
Internet: www.bankofamerica.com/philanthropic/foundation/?fnId=126
Sponsor: George J. and Effie L. Seay Foundation
1111 E. Main Street, VA2-300-12-92
Richmond, VA 23219-3531

George Kress Foundation Grants 1053

Incorporated in Wisconsin in 1953, the George Kress Foundation awards grants to eligible Wisconsin nonprofit organizations in its areas of interest, including: arts and culture; boys and girls clubs; children and youth services; Christian agencies and churches; community and economic development; education; family services; health organizations; higher education; historic preservation; historical societies; hospitals; human services; libraries; recreation; United Ways and Federated Giving Programs; and YM/YWCAs and YM/YWHAs. Types of support include: annual campaigns; building and renovation; capital campaigns; continuing support; professorships; program development; and research. Preference is given to nonprofit organizations that benefit the communities of Green Bay and Madison. Most recent awards have ranged from $200 to $50,000. There are no specified annual deadlines for submission.
Requirements: Interested applicants should submit a letter of inquiry describing their proposed project.
Geographic Focus: Wisconsin
Amount of Grant: 200 - 50,000 USD
Contact: John F. Kress, President; (920) 433-5113 or (920) 433-3109
Sponsor: George Kress Foundation
1700 North Webster Avenue, P.O. Box 19017
Green Bay, WI 54307-9017

George P. Davenport Trust Fund Grants   1054

Established in Maine in 1927, the Trust awards grants for education, religion, temperance and needy children. The focus of the Trust is on the economically disadvantaged. Types of support include: building and renovation, emergency funding, general operating funds, capacity building, matching/challenge funds, and seed money. It is recommended that applicants contact the Trust office to make an initial inquiry regarding projects before beginning the application process. Interested applicants should use the standard Maine Philanthropy Center common grant application which is available at mainephilanthropy. org. Grant applications are accepted all year, with no deadlines.

Requirements: Only nonprofit organizations serving the residents of Bath, Maine, and its surrounding area are eligible to apply.
Geographic Focus: Maine
Amount of Grant: 125 - 10,000 USD
Samples: Bath Elementary PTA, Bath, Maine, $6,550 - camp scholarships for youth; Brunswick Area Respite Care, Topsham, Maine, $10,000 - adult disabilities of aging support; Good Shepherd Food Bank, Auburn, Maine, $5,000 - food for the needy.
Contact: Barry M. Sturgeon, Trustee; (270) 443-3431; fax (800) 665-5510; davenporttrust@verizon.net
Sponsor: George P. Davenport Trust Fund
65 Front Street
Bath, ME 04530-2508

George W. Codrington Charitable Foundation Grants   1055

The George W. Codrington Charitable Foundation gives primarily to nonprofit organizations in Ohio, but may consider other areas. The Foundation funds higher education, hospitals, museums, arts groups and performing arts, and youth programs. Types of support include annual and capital campaigns, continuing support, equipment, general/operating support, program development, and research.

Requirements: Application forms are not required. Applicants should submit three copies of the following: their IRS determination letter; a brief history of the organization and description of its mission; the geographic area to be served; a list of the board of directors, trustees, officers, and other key individuals with their affiliations; and a detailed description of the project and amount of funding requested. Proposals should be submitted one month before the board meets in April, June, September, and December. Organizations are notified of funding promptly after the board meeting.
Restrictions: Funding is not available for individuals, endowment funds, or loans.
Geographic Focus: Ohio
Amount of Grant: 1,000 - 50,000 USD
Contact: Craig Martahus, Chair; (216) 566-8674; tommie.robertston@thomasonhine.com
Sponsor: George W. Codrington Charitable Foundation
127 Public Square, 39th Floor
Cleveland, OH 44114-1216

George W.P. Magee Trust Grants   1056

The George W.P. Magee Trust will consider several major capital projects each year specifically benefitting Boy Scouts Councils in Massachusetts. The Trustees shall distribute the net income of the said Trust to such of the councils of the Boy Scouts as are located in the Commonwealth of Massachusetts and as, in the opinion of said Trustees, are performing the most efficient service. The said net income to be used, so far as possible, for the purchase and maintenance of summer camps or training camps in New England for the use of Boy Scouts. These payments shall be made by said Trustees after consultation with the officials of the Boy Scouts of America. Award amounts typically range from $10,000 to $80,000.

Requirements: An architect's rendering and 3 estimates will be requested as part of the application process. Such projects will be considered on the basis of demonstrated ability to improve use of the facilities, ability to maintain the facility once completed, comparative need, and collaborative capability with neighboring councils or camps. One-time maintenance or replacement projects will be considered, both those of an emergency nature, and those which will increase utilization and/or reduce ongoing maintenance or other operating costs. Funding decisions are based on the merits of the projects in the proposal submitted. The level of funding in prior years is not a factor in the decision. If more than one project is identified, there should be an indication of priority. Applications will be submitted online through the Bank of America website. A grant report is required within 1 year of the grant application date, regardless of whether all of the funds have been spent.
Restrictions: New requests will not be considered if projects for previous grants are not completed, unless there are extenuating circumstances. The fund does not support requests from individuals, organizations attempting to influence policy through direct lobbying, or any political campaigns.
Geographic Focus: Massachusetts
Date(s) Application is Due: Sep 15
Amount of Grant: 10,000 - 80,000 USD
Samples: Boy Scouts of America Knox Trail Council, Marlborough, Massachusetts, $70,000 - Awarded for Facility and Infrastructure Improvements at Camp Resolute (2019); Boy Scouts of America, Swansea, Massachusetts, $70,000 - Awarded for Program and Safety Enhancement (2019); Boy Scouts of America-Mohegan Council, Worcester, Massachusetts, $54,000 - Awarded for Main Camp road renewal and update (2018).
Contact: Michealle Larkins, Philanthropic Administrator; (866) 778-6859; ma.grantmaking@bankofamerica.com
Internet: www.bankofamerica.com/philanthropic/foundation/?fnId=134
Sponsor: George W.P. Magee Memorial Trust
P.O. Box 1802
Providence, RI 02901-1802

George W. Wells Foundation Grants   1057

The George W. Wells Foundation was established in 1934 to support and promote quality educational, human services and health care programming for underserved populations. Special consideration is given to charitable organizations that serve the people of Southbridge, Massachusetts and its surrounding communities. Grant requests for general operating support or program support are encouraged. Small, program-related capital expenses may be included in general operating or program requests. The majority of grants from the Wells Foundation are 1 year in duration. On occasion, multi-year support is awarded. Award amounts typically range from $4,000 to $40,000.

Requirements: Applicants must have 501(c)3 tax-exempt status and serve the people of Southbridge, Massachusetts and its surrounding communities. A grant report is required within 1 year of the grant application date, regardless of whether all of the funds have been spent.
Restrictions: The foundation does not support requests from individuals, organizations attempting to influence policy through direct lobbying, or any political campaigns.
Geographic Focus: Massachusetts
Date(s) Application is Due: Jun 1
Amount of Grant: 4,000 - 40,000 USD
Samples: Tri-Valley Inc., Dudley, Massachusetts, $30,000- Awarded for Nutrition Program Services (2018); CASA Project Inc., Worcester, Massachusetts, $25,000-Awarded for Child Court Advocacy Program (2018); Family Health Center Of Worcester Inc., Worcester, Massachusetts, $25,000- Awarded for General Operations of FHC-Southbridge Family Dental Care (2018).
Contact: Michealle Larkins, Philanthropic Administrator; (866) 778-6859; ma.grantmaking@bankofamerica.com or ma.grantmaking@ustrust.com
Internet: www.bankofamerica.com/philanthropic/foundation/?fnId=48
Sponsor: George W. Wells Foundation
225 Franklin Street, 4th Floor
Boston, MA 02110

Georgia-Pacific Foundation Education Grants   1058

Since its inception, the Georgia-Pacific Foundation has recognized the value of education as one of the most important and essential building blocks of a strong, thriving community. It believes that creating, supporting and nurturing worthy educational projects are paramount to achieving its philosophical goals. The Foundation continually seeks to invest in innovative and results-driven educational initiatives that it feels will make a measurable difference in communities. The Foundation is an integral part of a wide array of community-based educational programs around the world. It helps youth transition from school to the workforce, as well as provide employees with job readiness training. The scholarships and technical programs that it funds give students and workers the skills necessary to succeed in today's workplace.

Requirements: Nonprofit organizations in Georgia-Pacific communities are eligible to apply for funding. To find out whether a program qualifies for consideration for a Georgia-Pacific Foundation grant, applicants should complete the Eligibility Survey available online. The Georgia-Pacific Foundation will accept proposals for grants and in-kind donations from January 1 through October 31. It is recommended that applicants submit proposals early in the grant cycle.
Restrictions: No support is given for discriminatory organizations, political candidates, churches or religious denominations, religious or theological schools, social, labor, veteran, alumni, or fraternal organizations not of direct benefit to the entire community, athletic associations, national organizations with local chapters already receiving support, medical or nursing schools, or pass-through organizations. No grants to individuals (except for scholarships), or for emergency needs for general operating support, political causes, legislative lobbying, or advocacy efforts, goodwill advertising, sporting events, general operating support for United Way member agencies, tickets or tables for testimonials or similar benefit events, named academic chairs, social sciences or health science programs, fundraising events, or trips or tours.
Geographic Focus: Alabama, Arkansas, California, Florida, Georgia, Illinois, Indiana, Iowa, Kentucky, Louisiana, Massachusetts, Michigan, Mississippi, New Jersey, New York, North Carolina, Ohio, Oklahoma, Oregon, Pennsylvania, South Carolina, Tennessee, Texas, Virginia, Washington, West Virginia, Wisconsin
Date(s) Application is Due: Oct 31
Contact: Curley M. Dossman, Jr., President; (404) 652-4182; fax (404) 749-2754; cmdossma@gapac.com
Internet: gp.com/gpfoundation/education.html
Sponsor: Georgia-Pacific Foundation
133 Peachtree Street, NE, 39th Floor
Atlanta, GA 30303

Georgia-Pacific Foundation Entrepreneurship Grants   1059

Georgia-Pacific believes that self-sufficiency and economic empowerment are two indispensable elements of every strong community. Entrepreneurs are often the catalysts of these essential components. That is why the Foundation believes that to create long-term value in GP communities, it must identify and nurture the entrepreneurial spirit, especially among youth. The Foundation partners with local elementary schools, high schools and universities that encourage and inspire a student's entrepreneurial spirit and offer incentives such as accreditation and/or certificate programs. It is particularly interested in programs that help a student transition from a classroom environment to a real working business model. The Foundation has supported programs that teach practical economic principles, the benefits of a free enterprise system, and real-world business skills to workers of any age. It realizes that student entrepreneurs, when nurtured and developed, become adult entrepreneurs, creating value and free markets. So, in addition to supporting educational programs for youth, it also supports organizations that help build capacity in small, minority or women owned businesses. There is no specific dollar amount for a request for grants. The dollar amount varies based on the budget requested, program value and Georgia-Pacific funds available. Types of support available include: annual campaigns; building and renovation; capital campaigns; conferences and seminars; continuing support; employee-related scholarships; employee volunteer services; equipment; general operating support; in-kind gifts; program development; scholarship funds; sponsorships; scholarships for individuals.

Requirements: Nonprofit organizations in Georgia-Pacific communities are eligible to apply for funding. To find out whether a program qualifies for consideration for a Georgia-Pacific Foundation grant, applicants should complete the Eligibility Survey available online. The Georgia-Pacific Foundation will accept proposals for grants and in-kind donations from January 1 through October 31. It is recommended that applicants submit proposals early in the grant cycle.

Restrictions: No support is given for discriminatory organizations, political candidates, churches or religious denominations, religious or theological schools, social, labor, veterans', alumni, or fraternal organizations not of direct benefit to the entire community, athletic associations, national organizations with local chapters already receiving support, medical or nursing schools, or pass-through organizations. No grants to individuals (except for scholarships), or for emergency needs for general operating support, political causes, legislative lobbying, or advocacy efforts, goodwill advertising, sporting events, general operating support for United Way member agencies, tickets or tables for testimonials or similar benefit events, named academic chairs, social sciences or health science programs, fundraising events, or trips or tours.

Geographic Focus: Alabama, Arkansas, California, Florida, Georgia, Illinois, Indiana, Iowa, Kentucky, Louisiana, Massachusetts, Michigan, Mississippi, New Jersey, New York, North Carolina, Ohio, Oklahoma, Oregon, Pennsylvania, South Carolina, Tennessee, Texas, Virginia, Washington, West Virginia, Wisconsin

Date(s) Application is Due: Oct 31
Contact: Curley M. Dossman, Jr., President; (404) 652-4182; fax (404) 749-2754; cmdossma@gapac.com
Internet: gp.com/gpfoundation/entrepreneurship.html
Sponsor: Georgia-Pacific Foundation
133 Peachtree Street, NE, 39th Floor
Atlanta, GA 30303

Georgia Council for the Arts Education Program Grants 1060

The mission of Georgia Council for the Arts is to cultivate the growth of vibrant, thriving Georgia communities through the arts. In an effort to place greater emphasis on arts education in Georgia and to align GCA's arts education funding with the Governor's Arts Learning Task Force Recommendations, in fiscal year 2017 GCA launched the Arts Education Program Grant. These grants are for $1,500 to $5,000 and require a one-to-one cash match. The annual deadline for application submission is March 6 at 11:59 p.m.

Requirements: Arts education programs eligible for funding include: arts programs delivered to K-12 students in a variety of disciplines, including visual art, music, theatre, dance, media arts, and creative writing; in-school, after-school, or summer arts programs delivered to K-12 grade students; arts integration or STEAM programs in K-12 grade classrooms; teaching artist residencies in K-12 grade classrooms; and arts assembly programs at K-12 grade schools. All eligible applicants must be located in Georgia, registered with the Georgia Secretary of State, and must have completed all requirements of any previous GCA or state of Georgia grant. Performing arts groups organized as non-profits will be eligible to apply if a majority of the group's members live in Georgia.

Geographic Focus: Georgia
Date(s) Application is Due: Mar 6
Amount of Grant: 1,500 - 5,000 USD
Contact: Allen Bell, Arts in Education Program Mgr; (404) 962-4839; abell@gaarts.org
Internet: gaarts.org/grant-funding/apply-for-a-grant/available-funding
Sponsor: Georgia Council for the Arts
75 Fifth Street, NW, Suite 1200
Atlanta, GA 30308

Geraldine R. Dodge Foundation Education Grants 1061

The Geraldine R. Dodge Foundation's funding in Education is focused on providing transformational experiences for New Jersey's pre-K through 12th grade children who face conditions that limit opportunities for, and access to, educational excellence. Foundation support will be further focused on: experiential learning opportunities that connect educators and students to the arts, to the natural world, and to the local and global community; schools in their efforts to reinvent themselves by exploring alternatives to the traditional public school model. Special consideration will be given to alternatives that emerge from intentional collaborations, between schools and outside agencies, dedicated to fostering the emotional, physical, intellectual, and social development of the entire community; high quality pre-school and primary grade programs and initiatives that provide a foundation for success in communities where children face conditions that limit opportunities for and access to educational excellence; and programs, initiatives, people, and organizations that are connected across disciplines, build on either previous or current Foundation initiatives, and demonstrate clear potential to be maintained without, or with only modest, Foundation funding after an appropriate, and agreed upon period of time.

Requirements: In order to be eligible for funding, an applicant must: be a 501(c)3 organization that makes its home in or has a significant impact on New Jersey; demonstrate that it has the administrative and financial capacity to achieve and assess the stated goals of the proposal; be led by an effective and professional, paid staff; have a high-functioning board, with an expectation of 100% of its trustees making an annual personal contribution; and strive to make connections with other organizations, especially Dodge grantees, working in the same community or on the same issues.

Restrictions: Funding is not provided for: higher education; health; religion; capital programs; equipment purchases; indirect costs; endowment funds; and deficit reduction. The Foundation does not make direct awards to individuals or support lobbying efforts.

Geographic Focus: New Jersey
Date(s) Application is Due: Mar 8; Sep 13; Dec 16
Amount of Grant: 10,000 - 500,000 USD
Samples: Appel Farm arts and Music Center, Elmer, New Jersey, $25,000 - general operating support (2020); Institute of Music for Children, Elizabeth, New Jersey, $35,000 - general operating support (2020); Wharton Institute for the Performing Arts, Berkeley Heights, New Jersey, $45,000 - general operating support (2020).
Contact: Marisa N. Benson, Grants Manager; (973) 695-1187 or (973) 540-8442; fax (973) 540-1211; mbenson@grdodge.org or info@grdodge.org
Internet: www.grdodge.org/what-we-fund/education/
Sponsor: Geraldine R. Dodge Foundation
14 Maple Avenue, Suite 400
Morristown, NJ 07960

Gerber Foundation Environmental Hazards Research Grants 1062

The Environmental Hazards Research Grants fund projects that evaluate the effects of environmental hazards on infants and young children. Applied research projects that document the impact of, or ameliorate effects of, environmental hazards on the growth and development of infants and young children are the focus of this area of interest. Typical projects funded in this area of interest may include projects aimed at exposures and their effects on infants and toddlers, and methods to lessen the effects of exposures. Grants of up to $350,000 can be awarded for research projects that are no longer than 3 years in length. Novice researchers (physicians, PhD candidates, PharmD candidates, and other similar degree candidates) can also receive this grant, but they will only be granted up to $20,000. Awards and time periods vary depending upon the specific project. Applications are accepted in two grant rounds annually.

Requirements: Selection of projects is based upon the overall quality of the research and a determination of best fit with the Foundation's goals. With few exceptions, only organizations with principal operations in the United States and its territories are eligible for funding. Interested applicants will submit a concept paper providing a brief summary of the project, and if the concept paper is accepted, they will then be required to submit a full proposal. The in-direct costs of the project must be limited to no more than 10% (included in the total amount). In-directs applied to a subcontract may not be duplicated on the full grant. Laboratory studies are funded occasionally. However, the Foundation expects that the basic science is a preliminary step required to support a clinical trial and that a clinical study will follow shortly after the funded project is completed.

Restrictions: No grants are made to individuals.
Geographic Focus: All States
Date(s) Application is Due: Feb 15; Aug 15
Amount of Grant: Up to 350,000 USD
Samples: Christina Chambers, San Diego, California, $350,000 - Awarded to study the detection of marijuana metabolites in human milk (2019); Angelica Meinhofer, New York City, New York, $250,000 - Awarded to study mortality, morbidity, and healthcare utilization among newborns with neonatal opioid withdrawal syndrome (2019).
Contact: Barbara J. Ivens, President; 231-924-3175; tgf@gerberfoundation.org
Internet: www.gerberfoundation.org/environmental-hazards/
Sponsor: Gerber Foundation
4747 W 48th Street, Suite 153
Fremont, MI 49412-8119

Gerber Foundation Pediatric Health Research Grants 1063

The Pediatric Health Research Grants focus on promoting health and preventing or treating disease in infants and young children. Of particular interest are applied research projects focused on reducing the incidence of serious neonatal and early childhood illnesses, or improving cognitive, social and emotional aspects of development. Typical projects funded in this area of interest may include projects aimed at better diagnostic techniques (more rapid, specific, sensitive, or less invasive); better treatment (improved, less stressful or painful, optimal dosing, fewer side effects); symptom relief; and preventive measures. Grants of up to $350,000 can be awarded for research projects that are no longer than 3 years in length. Novice researchers (physicians, PhD candidates, PharmD candidates, and other similar degree candidates) can also receive this grant, but they will only be granted up to $20,000. Awards and time periods vary depending upon the specific project. Applications are accepted in two grant rounds annually.

Requirements: Selection of concept papers are based upon the overall quality of the research and a determination of best fit with the Foundation's goals. With few exceptions, only organizations with principal operations in the United States and its territories are eligible for funding. Interested applicants will submit a concept paper providing a brief summary of the project, and if the concept paper is accepted, they will then be required to submit a full proposal. The in-direct costs of the project must be limited to no more than 10% (included in the total amount). In-directs applied to a subcontract may not be duplicated on the full grant. Laboratory studies are funded occasionally. However, the Foundation expects that the basic science is a preliminary step required to support a clinical trial and that a clinical study will follow shortly after the funded project is completed.

Restrictions: No grants are made to individuals.
Geographic Focus: All States
Date(s) Application is Due: Feb 15; Aug 15
Amount of Grant: Up to 350,000 USD
Samples: Leon Hatch III, Nashville, Tennessee, $317,864 - Awarded to to develop and test a ventilator weaning protocol for critically ill neonates (2019); Christopher Russell, Los Angeles, California, $350,000 - Awarded to study the diagnosis and antibiotic management

of pediatric tracheostomy-associated infections (2019); Holly Frost, Denver, Colorado, $349,380 - Awarded for the NO TEARS study: Using Nasopharyngeal Organism Testing to determine outcomes of children with EAR infections (2019).
Contact: Barbara J. Ivens, President; 231-924-3175; tgf@gerberfoundation.org
Internet: www.gerberfoundation.org/pediatric-health/
Sponsor: Gerber Foundation
4747 W 48th Street, Suite 153
Fremont, MI 49412-8119

Gerber Foundation Pediatric Nutrition Research Grants   1064
The Pediatric Nutrition Research Grants respond to a long-time interest of the Foundation in assuring adequate nutrition for infants and young children. Projects include applied research that evaluates the provision of specific nutrients and their related outcomes in infants and young children. Typical projects funded in this area of interest may include projects aimed at benefits or side effects of supplementation of a specific nutrient, effects of deficiencies or excesses of a specific nutrient, timing and dosing of supplementation, and issues related to general growth and feeding. Grants of up to $350,000 can be awarded for research projects that are no longer than 3 years in length. Novice researchers (physicians, PhD candidates, PharmD candidates, and other similar degree candidates) can also receive this grant, but they will only be granted up to $20,000. Awards and time periods vary depending upon the specific project. Applications are accepted in two grant rounds annually.
Requirements: Selection of concept papers are based upon the overall quality of the research and a determination of best fit with the Foundation's goals. With few exceptions, only organizations with principal operations in the United States and its territories are eligible for funding. Interested applicants will submit a concept paper providing a brief summary of the project, and if the concept paper is accepted, they will then be required to submit a full proposal. The in-direct costs of the project must be limited to no more than 10% (included in the total amount). In-directs applied to a subcontract may not be duplicated on the full grant. Laboratory studies are funded occasionally. However, the Foundation expects that the basic science is a preliminary step required to support a clinical trial and that a clinical study will follow shortly after the funded project is completed.
Restrictions: No grants are made to individuals.
Geographic Focus: All States
Date(s) Application is Due: Feb 15; Aug 15
Amount of Grant: Up to 350,000 USD
Samples: Julia Hurwitz, Carmel, Indiana, $247,500 - Awarded to study influence of vitamin A and D supplements on pneumococcus vaccine activity (2019); Joyce Koenig, St. Louis, Missouri, $349,668 - Awarded for a study of Calgranulins and Vitamin D status in preterm infants born after chorioamnionitis (2019); Xunjun Xiao, St. Louis, Missouri, $284,426 - Awarded to study genetic polymorphisms as a risk factor for Failure to Thrive (2019).
Contact: Barbara J. Ivens, President; 231-924-3175; tgf@gerberfoundation.org
Internet: www.gerberfoundation.org/pediatric-nutrition/
Sponsor: Gerber Foundation
4747 W 48th Street, Suite 153
Fremont, MI 49412-8119

Gerber Foundation West Michigan Youth Grants   1065
As the birthplace of the Gerber Foundation, the foundation supports a variety of youth programming within a 4-county area that includes Lake, Muskegon, Newaygo, and Oceana Counties in West Michigan. Grants are geared towards projects serving youth from 0-18 years of age. A special emphasis is placed on projects focused on Health, Nutrition and Dental issues; Early childhood services and Literacy; Parenting Education; Education (including Science, Technology, Engineering, Arts/Agriculture, and Math); and Life Experiences (camp scholarships, Ag Science Education, 4-H and FFA). Although typically under $10,000, grants may range from $100 to $20,000. Grants are generally limited to one-year commitments. Applicants may contact the Foundation office to discuss their project with Foundation staff at any time throughout the year.
Requirements: Agencies must be located in or directly serving youth from one of the 4 counties indicated. Grantees must be a public non-profit (with a 501c3 determination letter from the IRS) or governmental entity in order to apply. Programs that are collaborative and that have support from the broader community are encouraged. Applications must include a project description, information on the organization, and budget information (more detailed requirements can be found on the Gerber Foundation website). Grants under $2,000 will have a shortened application process based on the amount entered. Applications will be submitted online through the Gerber Foundation's online application portal.
Geographic Focus: Michigan
Date(s) Application is Due: Mar 15; Sep 15
Amount of Grant: 100 - 20,000 USD
Samples: Newaygo Area District Library, Newaygo, Michigan - Awarded in the Early Childhood/Literacy category for their STEM Resource Collection (2019); Catholic Charities of West Michigan, Grand Rapids, Michigan - Awarded in the Parenting category for their Healthy Families and Teen Parent programs (2019); Camp Newaygo, Newaygo, Michigan - Awarded in the Education (STEM) category for their Hands on Science program (2019).
Contact: Barbara J. Ivens, President; 231-924-3175; tgf@gerberfoundation.org
Internet: www.gerberfoundation.org/west-michigan-grants-youth-services/
Sponsor: Gerber Foundation
4747 W 48th Street, Suite 153
Fremont, MI 49412-8119

German Protestant Orphan Asylum Foundation Grants   1066
The German Protestant Orphan Asylum (GPOA) Foundation Grants funding to support programs that serve children in Louisiana. The majority of those funded offer programs in the areas of education (tutoring, literacy, LEAP remediation, after school and summer programs, GED prep, early childhood education, child abuse prevention); enrichment (arts/music, mentoring, summer camps); life skills/pre-vocational training (parenting skills, work skills); and school-based health (mental health, vision screenings, immunizations, speech pathology). The Foundation makes grant decisions in May, August, November, and February. The Foundation's average grant award is $10,000 within a range of $1,000 to $40,000.
Requirements: A concept paper is required before submitting a proposal. Applicants should download, complete, then mail one original plus 12 copies of the one-page concept paper at least four months prior to their need for funds. The concept paper will be reviewed, and the organization will be notified whether a full proposal is invited. If a full proposal is invited, the organization should then download and fill out the GPOA Grant Proposal Form, and mail one original plus 12 copies to the Foundation by the deadline.
Restrictions: The Foundation does not fund building or renovation expenses, sponsorship of special events, individual scholarships, or programs which do not serve children in Louisiana. Equipment is rarely funded.
Geographic Focus: Louisiana
Amount of Grant: 4,000 - 40,000 USD
Contact: Lisa Kaichen, Foundation Manager; (985) 674-5328 or (504) 895-2361; fax (504) 674-0490; gpoafoundation@aol.com
Internet: www.gpoafoundation.org/amenities.html
Sponsor: German Protestant Orphan Asylum Association
P.O. Box 158
Mandeville, LA 70470

Gertrude and William C. Wardlaw Fund Grants   1067
Established in 1936 in Georgia, the Gertrude and William C. Wardlaw Fund awards general operating grants to Georgia nonprofit organizations in its areas of interest, including: cultural activities; the arts; community development; education and higher education; and health care and hospitals. Specific application forms are not required, and there are no specified annual deadlines. Grants typically range from $2,500 to $50,000.
Requirements: Georgia nonprofit organizations are eligible to apply.
Geographic Focus: Georgia
Amount of Grant: 2,500 - 50,000 USD
Samples: Metro Atlant Task Force, Atlanta, Georgia, $50,000 - operating costs; Wardlaw School, Atlanta, Georgia, $20,000 - general operating costs; Viola White Water Foundation, Atlanta, Georgia, $2,500 - general operations.
Contact: Gregorie Guthrie, Secretary; (404) 419-3260 or (404) 827-6529
Sponsor: Gertrude and William C. Wardlaw Fund
One Riverside Building
Atlanta, GA 30327

Giant Food Charitable Grants   1068
The Giant Food Charitable Grants provide funding and in-kind assistance to hundreds of charitable events and causes in schools, churches, synagogues, and civic community groups. Giant's focus is hunger relief programs, education, and wellness initiatives. Grant amounts vary, and there are no application deadlines. Submit requests by mail only.
Requirements: Organizations must send requests in writing on their letterhead, along with proof of their 501(c)3 status, and a description of the project.
Restrictions: Funding is available only in areas where Giant Food operates: District of Columbia, Maryland, Virginia, and Delaware.
Geographic Focus: Delaware, District of Columbia, Maryland, Virginia
Contact: Jamie Miller, Grant Administrator; (301) 341-8776; jmiller@giantofmaryland.com
Internet: www.giantfood.com/about_us/community/index.htm
Sponsor: Giant Food Corporation
8301 Professional Place, Suite 115
Landover, MD 20785

Gibson County Community Foundation Recreation Grants   1069
The Gibson County Community Foundation considers proposals for grants on a yearly cycle, which begins each May. At the start of each cycle, a notice is mailed to nonprofit organizations that have applied for grants in the past, have received grants in the past, or have otherwise requested notification of the start of each cycle. Grants in the area of Recreation include projects aimed at improving and promoting recreational and leisure activities, parks, and community sporting events and activities. Samples of previously funded projects are available at the website.
Requirements: The letter of inquiry is the required first step in submitting funding requests. Nonprofits that have submitted a letter of inquiry and been invited to submit a full proposal must attend one of the orientation sessions. The Foundation welcomes proposals from nonprofit organizations that are deemed tax-exempt under sections 501(c)3 and 509(a) of the Internal Revenue Code and from governmental agencies serving the County of Gibson, Indiana. Proposals from nonprofit organizations not classified as a 501(c)3 public charity may be considered provided the project is charitable and supports a community need.
Restrictions: Funding is not available for the following: religious organizations for strictly religious purposes; political parties or campaigns; endowment creation or debt reduction; operating costs (not directly related to the proposed project or program); capital campaigns; annual appeals or membership contributions; travel requests for groups or individuals such as bands, sports teams, or classes. Not more than 20% of any grant request may be for personnel costs, office supplies, or other operating costs. Operating costs for any organization must be directly related to the project or program for which funding is being requested.
Geographic Focus: Indiana

Contact: Sarah Wagner, Regional Director of Development; (812) 386-8082; swagner@ communityfoundationalliance.org
Internet: www.communityfoundationalliance.org/gibson/program-areas/
Sponsor: Gibson County Community Foundation
127 North Hart Street, P.O. Box 180
Princeton, IN 47670

Gibson County Community Foundation Youth Development Grants   1070
The Gibson County Community Foundation considers proposals for grants on a yearly cycle, which begins each May. At the start of each cycle, a notice is mailed to nonprofit organizations that have applied for grants in the past, have received grants in the past, or have otherwise requested notification of the start of each cycle. Grants in the area of Youth Development include activities that strengthen the family unit, help children grow and develop, foster youth sports and athletics, support the YMCA, and support daycare-related issues. Samples of previously funded projects are available at the website.
Requirements: The letter of inquiry is the required first step in submitting funding requests. Nonprofits that have submitted a letter of inquiry and been invited to submit a full proposal must attend one of the orientation sessions. The Foundation welcomes proposals from nonprofit organizations that are deemed tax-exempt under sections 501(c)3 and 509(a) of the Internal Revenue Code and from governmental agencies serving the County of Gibson, Indiana. Proposals from nonprofit organizations not classified as a 501(c)3 public charity may be considered provided the project is charitable and supports a community need.
Restrictions: Funding is not available for the following: religious organizations for strictly religious purposes; political parties or campaigns; endowment creation or debt reduction; operating costs (not directly related to the proposed project or program); capital campaigns; annual appeals or membership contributions; travel requests for groups or individuals such as bands, sports teams, or classes. Not more than 20% of any grant request may be for personnel costs, office supplies, or other operating costs. Operating costs for any organization must be directly related to the project or program for which funding is being requested.
Geographic Focus: Indiana
Contact: Sarah Wagner, Regional Director of Development; (812) 386-8082; swagner@ communityfoundationalliance.org
Internet: www.communityfoundationalliance.org/gibson/program-areas/
Sponsor: Gibson County Community Foundation
127 North Hart Street, P.O. Box 180
Princeton, IN 47670

Gil and Dody Weaver Foundation Grants   1071
Established in Texas in 1980, the Gil and Dody Weaver Foundation offers support throughout the States of Texas, Oklahoma, and Louisiana, with some emphasis on the Dallas-Fort worth area. The Foundation's primary fields of interest include: cancer; children and youth services; education; health organizations; human services; social services; and recreational camps. Major types of support come in the form of: annual campaigns; general operating/continual support; and scholarship funds. Although no formal application is required, the Foundation does provide specific application guidelines. These guidelines require a history of the organization, detailed information about the proposed project, and budgetary needs. The annual deadline is May 31, with final notifications by September 30. Recent grants have ranged from $1,000 to $20,000, with occasional higher amounts for special circumstances.
Requirements: 501(c)3 organization serving the residents of Texas, Oklahoma, and Louisiana, are welcome to apply.
Restrictions: No grants are given to individuals. No applications are accepted from organizations located in states other than Texas, Oklahoma, or Louisiana.
Geographic Focus: California, Colorado, Louisiana, Mississippi, New Mexico, Oklahoma, Texas
Date(s) Application is Due: May 31
Amount of Grant: 1,000 - 20,000 USD
Samples: Cook Children's Health Foundation, Fort Worth, Texas, $12,500 - construction of an urgent care facility; Camp McFadden, Ponca City, Oklahoma, $5,000 - general operation support; Bookspring, Austin, Texas, $2,000 - support of the Reach Out and Read program.
Contact: William R. Weaver, (214) 999-9497 or (214) 999-9494; fax (214) 999-9496
Sponsor: Gil and Dody Weaver Foundation
1845 Woodall Rodgers Freeway, Suite 1275
Dallas, TX 75201-2299

Giving Gardens Challenge Grants   1072
SeedMoney is the new name for what was formerly called Kitchen Gardeners International (KGI), a nonprofit founded in 2003. Each fall, SeedMoney awards one hundred grants ranging in size from $200 to $600 to U.S.-based and global food garden projects. The nonprofit will be doing this through its annual Giving Gardens Challenge, a four-week online giving campaign running from November 15 through December 15. SeedMoney offer two types of grants: challenge grants; and merit grants. Challenge Grants, offering funding of up to $400, are awarded to the fifty projects that raise $600 or more the fastest using the program's crowdfunding tools. Merit grants, offering funding of up to $200, will be awarded to projects that don't win Challenge Grants, but which SeedMoney deems worthy of support. The program will also award an additional $600 bonus grant to the project that raises the most funding.
Requirements: The program offers full and partial grants. A full grant has an approximate value of $400 to $600. There are no geographic limitations on what types of food garden projects will be considered. Past grantees included projects from Portland, Oregon to

Pakistan and many places in between. Applications must be submitted by 5:00 pm Eastern Time of the published deadline date.
Geographic Focus: All States, All Countries
Date(s) Application is Due: Nov 12
Amount of Grant: 400 - 600 USD
Contact: Roger Doiron, Founding Director; (207) 956-0606; info@seedmoney.org or roger@kgi.org
Internet: seedmoney.org/apply/
Sponsor: SeedMoney
3 Powderhorn Drive
Scarborough, ME 04074

Global Fund for Women Grants   1073
The Global Fund for Women supports women's groups that advance the human rights of women and girls. Grants support women's groups based outside the United States by providing small, flexible, and timely grants for operating and project expenses. Grantees address issues that include but are not limited to building peace and ending gender-based violence; advancing health and sexual and reproductive rights; expanding civic and political participation; ensuring economic and environmental justice; increasing access to education; and fostering social change philanthropy. In addition urgent requests for support to organize or participate in local, regional, or international meetings and conferences will be considered outside of the normal grant cycle. These types of requests must come from organizations, not individuals, and must be received at least eight weeks before the event. Funds for these types of grants are limited. Applications and guidelines are available online. Organizations should refer to the staff website for specific contacts according to their applicant origin.
Requirements: The applicant group must be based in a country outside the United States; demonstrate a strong commitment to women's equality and human rights that is clearly reflected in its activities; be a group of women working together; and be governed, directed, and led by women.
Restrictions: Grants do not support individuals; scholarships; academic research; groups based and working primarily or only in the United States; international organizations proposing projects with local partners; groups without a strong women's rights focus; groups headed and managed by men, or without women in the majority of leadership positions; groups whose sole purpose is to generate income or to provide charity to individuals; or political parties or election campaigns.
Geographic Focus: All Countries
Amount of Grant: 5,000 - 50,000 USD
Contact: Program Assistant; (415) 248-4800; fax (415) 202-4801
Internet: www.globalfundforwomen.org/apply-for-a-grant/types-of-grant
Sponsor: Global Fund for Women
222 Sutter Street, Suite 500
San Francisco, CA 94108

Gloria Barron Prize for Young Heroes   1074
The Gloria Barron Prize for Young Heroes honors 25 outstanding young leaders who have made a significant positive difference to people and the planet. Candidates have focused on helping their communities and fellow human beings, in addition to protecting the health and sustainability of the environment. Nominees, who may range in age from 8 to 18 years old, must have been the prime mover of a service activity, and demonstrated positive spirit and high moral purpose in accomplishing their goals. Each winner of the Barron Prize receives: $2,500 to be applied to their higher education or to their service project; a recognition plaque; a certificate of recognition; a signed copy of The Hero's Trail, by Barron Prize founder T.A. Barron; a copy of Dream Big, a documentary film featuring several Barron Prize winners; a heroes study guide, curriculum, and bibliography; the opportunity to be paired with an adult mentor who is passionate about working in the winner's area of interest; the opportunity to connect with other Barron Prize winners through the Young Heroes Listserv; and numerous media opportunities – print, television, and radio. By submitting an entry in the Gloria Barron Prize for Young Heroes, each entrant acknowledges reading and understanding all the eligibility requirements and selection criteria published on the Prize's website and agrees to observe them. Further, each entrant acknowledges and agrees that as a condition of receiving the Prize, the selected individuals will cooperate in publicizing the Barron Prize and will grant rights of the entrant's nomination materials to the Barron Prize.
Requirements: Candidates must be nominated by responsible adults who have solid knowledge of the young person's heroic activities, and who are not related to the nominee. To nominate a young person, the adult nominator must submit a fully-completed nomination packet and reference form located at the prize website. Nominees must have organized and led a service activity which has clearly benefited other people, animals, or the planet. The nominee's service activity must have been initiated and motivated primarily by the nominee. While outside help may have been obtained, the activity must be primarily the nominee's own creation. Nominees must have done more than survive a difficult personal challenge. Their heroism must have made an impact on the world beyond themselves. Nominees must have clearly demonstrated positive spirit, courage, intelligence, generosity, and high moral purpose. Nominees must have shown initiative, tenacity, and unselfishness in pursuit of their goals.
Restrictions: The Prize committee cannot accept nominations for groups of young people, or nominations for projects done solely to complete an assignment for school or work.
Geographic Focus: All States, Canada
Date(s) Application is Due: Apr 30
Amount of Grant: 2,500 USD
Contact: Barbara Ann Richman, Executive Director; (970) 875-1448; ba_richman@ barronprize.org
Internet: www.barronprize.org/about-prize

Sponsor: Barron Prize
545 Pearl Street
Boulder, CO 80302

GMFUS Balkan Trust for Democracy Grants   1075

The Balkan Trust for Democracy (BTD) awards grants to support projects addressing themes of democracy and good governance, policy dialogue and networking, and regional cooperation and European integration. BTD's grant making activities focus primarily on six countries: Albania, Bosnia and Herzegovina, Kosovo, Macedonia, Montenegro, and Serbia. BTD also supports relevant regional initiatives that promote benefits of pan-Balkan network, including civil society stakeholders from Western and Eastern Europe, and in particular those based in Bulgaria, Croatia and Romania. Priority areas within these themes include: civic engagement; youth leadership and empowerment; government accountability and transparency; culture of giving; Euro-Atlantic integration; and dialogue and reconciliation. Supported projects typically achieve their goals through: public debate; leadership development; policy work; civic education; new mechanisms; advocacy; monitoring; implementation and enforcement; shared objectives; best practices; networks; re-granting; and reconciliation. Preference will be given to those proposals designed to increase citizen engagement with government; measurably impact public policy; strengthen leadership skills of individuals and organizations; facilitate cross-border and/or cross-sector cooperation; and encourage the transfer of experiences and innovative ideas through clear communication and dissemination plans. Organizations that are interested in receiving BTD funding are welcome to send a brief concept note in English (no more than 1 page), outlining the project idea and approximate budget amount.
Requirements: Applicants must be civic groups, NGOs, media organizations, think tanks, governments, and education institutions indigenous to BTD program countries. Grants must serve at least one of the following: Albania, Bosnia and Herzegovina, Bulgaria, Croatia, Kosovo, Macedonia, Montenegro, Romania, Serbia and Slovenia.
Restrictions: Individuals and political parties may not apply. International organizations may not apply for direct funding; however cooperative projects between indigenous and non-indigenous organizations will be considered. BTD will also support relevant regional initiatives that include civil society stakeholders from Western and Eastern Europe, and in particular those based in Bulgaria, Croatia and Romania.
Geographic Focus: All States, Albania, Bosnia & Herzegovina, Bulgaria, Croatia, Kosovo, Montenegro, North Macedonia, Romania, Serbia
Contact: Gordana Deli?, Director, Balkan Trust for Democracy; +381 11 3036 454; fax +381 11 3036 455; gdelic@gmfus.org or balkantrust@gmfus.org
Internet: www.gmfus.org/btd-grantmaking
Sponsor: German Marshall Fund of the United States
1744 R Street NW
Washington, D.C. 20009

GNOF Albert N. & Hattie M. McClure Grants   1076

The Albert N. & Hattie M. McClure Fund was established in 1963 and is a donor-advised fund of the Greater New Orleans Foundation (GNOF). The fund supports the emergency bricks and mortar projects (e.g. repairs, replacements, and additions to facilities) of eligible United Way partner agencies. The intent of the McClure Fund is to fill the funding gap between major capital expenses requiring a capital fund drive and minor capital needs which can be planned for and included in an agency's operating budget. Priority consideration will be given to those requests of a capital nature that stem from a crisis and/or emergency. GNOF will consider requests up to $15,000. The application process has no deadline date. Organizations will be notified of funding decisions within sixty days. Organizations can find a downloadable application form at the website and should contact GNOF for mailing instructions.
Requirements: Applicants must be partner agencies of United Way and should contact GNOF for further eligibility requirements.
Geographic Focus: Louisiana
Amount of Grant: Up to 15,000 USD
Contact: Ellen M. Lee, Sr. Vice President, Programs, Community Revitalization Program Director; (504) 598-4663; fax (504) 598-4676; ellen@gnof.org
Internet: www.gnof.org/albert-n-hattie-m-mcclure-fund/
Sponsor: Greater New Orleans Foundation
1055 St. Charles Avenue, Suite 100
New Orleans, LA 70130

GNOF Bayou Communities Grants   1077

In 2012 the Greater New Orleans Foundation (GNOF) established the Bayou Communities Foundation (BCF) that has, as its initial focus, the mission to improve life in the Louisiana parishes of Terrebonne and Lafourche, and that will work to strengthen local nonprofit capacity in compassionate and sustainable coastal communities in Louisiana for generations to come. The impetus to form BCF came from parish residents, who first organized among themselves and then approached GNOF, who had set up similar and successful foundations in St. Bernard, Plaquemines, and Jefferson Parishes after Hurricanes Katrina and Rita and the Gulf Oil Spill. BCF is set up as a GNOF donor-advised fund, an affiliate under GNOF's nonprofit umbrella. The new foundation will receive $500,000 in seed money for the next five years from the Gheens Foundation in Lafourche and has committed to raising $1 million in matching dollars. BCF has also commited to putting at least 90% of its first $100,000 from the Gheens Foundation back into the community through grants. As an affiliate foundation, BCF has access to the expertise of GNOF but makes independent decisions about BCF projects. Organizations interested in obtaining grants through BCF can contact GNOF for more information.
Geographic Focus: Louisiana

Contact: Josephine Everly, Senior Development Officer; (504) 598-4663; fax (504) 598-4676; josephine@gnof.org
Internet: www.gnof.org/
Sponsor: Greater New Orleans Foundation
1055 St. Charles Avenue, Suite 100
New Orleans, LA 70130

GNOF Coastal 5 + 1 Grants   1078

The need for a coordinated strategy to protect and to strengthen Louisiana's coastal communities became painfully obvious to all those who survived Hurricane Katrina, the Gulf Oil Spill and other recent disasters in the Greater New Orleans metropolitan area. Coastal citizens long marginalized by or oblivious to the environmental impacts stemming from decades of poor planning and environmental degradation have been awakened to new realities and possibilities, including a newly-found voice with which to address common challenges in the region's environment, economy, and community leadership. In response to this new physical, political, and economic landscape, the Greater New Orleans Foundation launched the Coastal 5+1 Initiative in 2011. The initiative benefits the five coastal parishes of Jefferson, Lafourche, Plaquemines, St. Bernard, and Terrebonne, along with the coastal-dependent parish of New Orleans. The initiative's goal is to empower local communities to confront pressing coastal issues such as failing ecosystems and global climate change and to connect emerging leaders with immediate, concrete solutions to long-term problems. The initiative will make grants in three program areas: civic engagement and leadership; environment and sustainable communities; and sustainable economic development. The goal of the civic engagement and leadership program is to join Orleans Parish with its southern neighbors in advocating for the coast at the state and federal levels. The goal of the environment and sustainable communities program is to encourage resilience, adaptation, sustainability, and ecological, economic, and cultural vitality through support for equitable, environmentally-focused policies and programs. The sustainable economic development program will support economic opportunities that are unique to the region's resources, such as traditionally viable industries in agriculture, fisheries, and energy production. Workforce development programs specifically tailored to emerging careers in such fields as wetlands restoration and innovative surface-water management, planning, and engineering will also be supported, as well as non-traditional youth outreach and training (including after-school education efforts geared toward empowerment, self-esteem and self-discipline, wealth creation, and asset-building). GNOF accepts Coastal 5+1 applications only through its Request for Proposal (RFP) process. Interested organizations are encouraged to subscribe to GNOF's email newsletter for announcements of future funding opportunities. The subscription link is available from GNOF's Apply-for-a-Grant web page which contains a comprehensive listing of GNOF's current and past funding opportunities. Interested organizations are also encouraged to visit the GNOF website to obtain detailed background information on the initiative, an explanation of its major goals and strategies, and examples of the types of programs it will fund.
Geographic Focus: All States
Amount of Grant: 90,000 - 200,000 USD
Samples: Environmental Defense Fund, New York, New York, $100,000—to bring various stakeholders together to build a shared vision for the Louisiana coast; Coalition to Restore Coastal Louisiana, Baton Rouge, Louisiana, $205,000—to fund the Next Gen Public Outreach program to promote stakeholder engagement in order to build consensus around specific projects within the master plan; Bruno Steiner, Category 5 Wetlands Watch, New Orleans, Louisiana, $90,000—to fund a documentary that will broaden awareness of coastal issues and the way GNOF grantees are working to fix and mitigate the problem.
Contact: Dr. Marco Cocito-Monoc, Director for Regional Initiatives; (504) 598-4663; fax (504) 598-4676; marco@gnof.org
Internet: www.gnof.org/coastal-51-initiative/
Sponsor: Greater New Orleans Foundation
1055 St. Charles Avenue, Suite 100
New Orleans, LA 70130

GNOF Cox Charities of New Orleans Grants   1079

Cox Cable, a grant-making partner of the Greater New Orleans Foundation (GNOF), has established the Cox Charities of New Orleans Fund to improve the quality of life for people in Orleans, Jefferson, St. Charles, and St. Bernard parishes. The fund provides grants from $500 - $2,500 for new, creative, or beneficial programs in the area of youth (target ages, seven through eighteen) and education. Additionally Cox Cable will showcase projects and programs of its grantees on cable television. Grant requests and supporting materials must be emailed to the address provided on this page and must be received by 5:00 p.m. on the annual deadline date which usually occurs in May. Successful applicants are then notified in July. Requests are reviewed by an advisory committee of business and civic leaders. Exact deadlines may vary from year to year. Prospective applicants should verify the current deadline at the GNOF website where they can also obtain complete guidelines and requirements as well as a downloadable application form. Prospective applicants can also subscribe to GNOF's email newsletter for announcements of future funding opportunities. The subscription link is available from GNOF's Apply-for-a-Grant web page which contains a comprehensive listing of GNOF's current and past funding opportunities.
Requirements: Nonprofits in the parishes of Orleans, Jefferson, St. Charles, and St. Bernard are eligible to apply. Applicants must have 501(c)3 status or apply through a fiscal agent who has 501(c)3 status.
Restrictions: Only one application per organization will be accepted.
Geographic Focus: Louisiana
Date(s) Application is Due: May 16
Amount of Grant: 500 - 2,500 USD
Samples: Jefferson Chamber Foundation, Metairie, Louisiana, $1,000—Youth Leadership Program.

Contact: Ellen M. Lee, Sr. Vice President, Programs, Community Revitalization Program Director; (504) 598-4663; fax (504) 598-4676; grants@gnof.org or ellen@gnof.org
Internet: www.gnof.org/cox-charities-of-new-orleans/
Sponsor: Greater New Orleans Foundation
1055 St. Charles Avenue, Suite 100
New Orleans, LA 70130

GNOF Exxon-Mobil Grants 1080

Exxon-Mobil, a grant-making partner of the Greater New Orleans Foundation (GNOF) has established the Exxon-Mobil fund to improve the quality of lives for people in the St. Bernard parish and a portion of Algiers. The fund provides the following types of grants: capital-fund grants for new construction or major renovation; seed-money grants to help start new organizations that respond to an important opportunity in the community; bridge grants to sustain organizations experiencing financial hardships; and grants that support new, creative, or beneficial programs. Amounts up to $4,000 are given in Algiers; amounts up to $10,000 are given in St. Bernard Parish and in extraordinary circumstances may exceed this maximum. Grant requests are reviewed by an advisory committee of business and civic leaders that meets annually. Application materials must be emailed to the address provided on this page and received by the foundation by 5:00 p.m. on August 15. Exact deadlines may vary from year to year. Prospective applicants should verify the current deadline at the GNOF website where they can also obtain complete guidelines and requirements as well as a downloadable application form. Prospective applicants can also subscribe to GNOF's email newsletter for announcements of future funding opportunities. The subscription link is available from GNOF's Apply-for-a-Grant web page which contains a comprehensive listing of GNOF's current and past funding opportunities.
Requirements: While priority is given to nonprofit organizations based in St. Bernard Parish or Algiers, nonprofit organizations servicing these areas will be given consideration. Applicants must have 501(c)3 status or apply through a fiscal agent who has such status.
Geographic Focus: Louisiana
Date(s) Application is Due: Aug 15
Amount of Grant: Up to 10,000 USD
Samples: Los Islenos Heritage and Cultural Society, St. Bernard, Louisiana—install a sewerage system as part of the restoration of the cultural building; Louisiana Philharmonic Orchestra, New Orleans, Louisiana—put on two young-people's concerts in the St. Bernard parish Cultural Arts Center; St. Bernard Wetlands Foundation, Meraux, Louisiana—coordinate and educate student and adult volunteers to maintain and replenish the tree nursery as well as out-planting mature container-grown trees into selected wetland locations.
Contact: Dr. Marco Cocito-Monoc, Sr. Vice President, Programs, Community Revitalization Program Director; (504) 598-4663; fax (504) 598-4676; marco@gnof.org
Internet: www.gnof.org/exxon-mobile-fund/
Sponsor: Greater New Orleans Foundation
1055 St. Charles Avenue, Suite 100
New Orleans, LA 70130

GNOF Freeman Challenge Grants 1081

The Freeman Challenge, a donor-advised fund of the Greater New Orleans Foundation (GNOF), is a memorial tribute to one of New Orleans' leading citizens and philanthropists Richard West Freeman who will be remembered as one of the founders of The United Fund in 1952 (now The United Way). The purpose of The Freeman Challenge is to create long-term financial stability for nonprofit organizations serving the Greater New Orleans thirteen-parish region; the Challenge will match one dollar for every two dollars raised by nonprofits to build their own endowments. Nonprofits can elect to receive one of three matching amounts: $5,000, $10,000, or $15,000. Freeman Challenge grant applications are reviewed by a selection committee of volunteers and GNOF staff that meets annually. The committee looks for nonprofits that represent varying areas of service, e.g. education, the arts, human services, etc. Application materials are due no later 5 p.m. on September 14 and must be emailed to the email address given under the Contact Information section. Exact deadlines may vary from year to year. Prospective applicants should verify the current deadline at the GNOF website where they can also obtain a downloadable brochure about the the program as well as a downloadable application form with guidelines and requirements. Prospective applicants can also subscribe to GNOF's email newsletter for announcements of future funding opportunities. The subscription link is available from GNOF's Apply-for-a-Grant web page which contains a comprehensive listing of GNOF's current and past funding opportunities.
Requirements: To be eligible nonprofit organizations must meet the following *Requirements:* have 501(c)3 status; have been in operation for a minimum of five years; be headquartered in one of Greater New Orleans' thirteen parishes (Assumption, Jefferson, Lafourche, Orleans, Plaquemines, St. Bernard, St. Charles, St. James, St. Johns, St. Tammany, Tangipahoa, Terrebonne, or Washington); presently have no endowment with a market value that exceeds $500,000; show evidence of previous fund-raising success; conduct an annual independent audit; have a volunteer board; and have their board's approval to take part in the Freeman Challenge.
Geographic Focus: Louisiana
Date(s) Application is Due: Jun 25
Amount of Grant: 5,000 - 15,000 USD
Contact: Ellen M. Lee, Sr. Vice President, Programs, Community Revitalization Program Director; (504) 598-4663; fax (504) 598-4676; grants@gnof.org
Internet: www.gnof.org/the-freeman-challenge/
Sponsor: Greater New Orleans Foundation
1055 St. Charles Avenue, Suite 100
New Orleans, LA 70130

GNOF Gert Community Fund Grants 1082

The Gert Community Fund, a donor-advised fund of the Greater New Orleans Foundation (GNOF), was established to enhance the quality of life for people in the Gert Town Community. Program areas include education, housing, generational services, and economic development. In addition, the committee is interested in community-beautification projects (e.g. tree planting, green-space maintenance, and neighborhood cleanup). Requests are reviewed annually by an advisory committee of business and civic leaders; grants for up to $50,000 per year will be considered. Requests must be received via mail by 5:00 p.m. on August 31. Prospective applicants should verify whether the grant is currently open for submission at the GNOF website where they can also obtain complete guidelines and requirements as well as a downloadable application form. Interested organizations can also subscribe to GNOF's email newsletter for announcements of future funding opportunities. The subscription link is available from GNOF's Apply-for-a-Grant web page which contains a comprehensive listing of GNOF's current and past funding opportunities.
Requirements: Nonprofit organizations that serve the Gert Town Community are eligible to apply but are requested to first contact GNOF for more details on the geographical boundaries for the fund. Applicants must have 501(c)3 status or apply through a fiscal agent who has such status.
Restrictions: Only one application per organization will be accepted.
Geographic Focus: All States
Date(s) Application is Due: Aug 31
Amount of Grant: Up to 50,000 USD
Samples: Armstrong Family Services, New Orleans, Louisiana, $5,000—transitional housing program; Audubon Nature Institute, New Orleans, Louisiana, $30,000—scholarships for Gert Town residents to its Zoo Camp; Gert Town Community Center, New Orleans, Louisiana, $34,917—for tutorial and enrichment programs and quarterly community clean-up initiatives.
Contact: Amy Forsyth, Grant Coordinator; (504) 598-4663; fax (504) 598-4676
Internet: www.gnof.org/the-gert-town-community-fund/
Sponsor: Greater New Orleans Foundation
1055 St. Charles Avenue, Suite 100
New Orleans, LA 70130

GNOF IMPACT Grants for Arts and Culture 1083

Through the IMPACT Program, the Greater New Orleans Foundation (GNOF) makes grants to organizations serving the Greater New Orleans region. The ultimate goal of the IMPACT Program is to create a resilient, sustainable, vibrant, and equitable region in which individuals and families flourish and in which the special character of the New Orleans region and its people is preserved, celebrated, and given the means to develop. Specifically GNOF hopes to accomplish the following objectives through its IMPACT grants: provide a much needed source of financial and other support to nonprofit organizations that are struggling in the current financial environment and that are important to the health and vibrancy of the region; develop a better sense of the nonprofit organizations serving the region so GNOF can more effectively match donor desires with effective charitable work; identify and nurture promising new leaders and initiatives, especially in those communities that are in greatest need; and gain knowledge that will help nonprofit leaders and GNOF staff develop better long-term strategies for addressing regional needs and taking best advantage of important opportunities. IMPACT grants are awarded in four categories: Arts and Culture, Youth Development, Education, and Health and Human Services. In the category of Arts and Culture GNOF supports organizations and programs that help preserve and grow the rich cultural heritage of the Greater New Orleans region and ensure that the originators and producers of creative goods and services can continue to enhance community life. Priority will be given to work that has the following goals: to improve the quality of life for artists and performers in the region; to demonstrate the importance of the arts and make the case for increased public support for the arts; and to form alliances and connections between grassroots-based organizations and the business community to expand income-producing opportunities for artists. Interested organizations must submit a letter of intent along with all attachments via one email by 5 p.m. on July 30. GNOF program staff will review all letters of intent and will contact those organizations that are invited to submit a full application for funding. Awards are announced in November. Deadlines may vary from year to year. Interested organizations should verify the current deadline at the GNOF website where they can also obtain complete guidelines and requirements as well as a downloadable application form and cover sheet. Prospective applicants can also subscribe to GNOF's email newsletter for announcements of future funding opportunities. The subscription link is available from GNOF's Apply-for-a-Grant web page which contains a comprehensive listing of GNOF's current and past funding opportunities.
Requirements: Nonprofit, tax-exempt organizations that serve the Greater New Orleans region are eligible to apply for funding. Organizations that are not tax-exempt but have a fiscal agent relationship with a 501(c)3 organization are also eligible.
Restrictions: Through its IMPACT program, the Greater New Orleans Foundation is unable to fund the following types of requests: requests for individual support, either through scholarships or other forms of financial assistance; special events or conferences; programs that promote religious doctrine; endowments; and scientific or medical research.
Geographic Focus: All States
Date(s) Application is Due: Jul 30
Amount of Grant: Up to 20,000 USD
Samples: Arts Council of New Orleans, New Orleans, Louisiana, $20,000—for general operating support; Sweet Home New Orleans, New Orleans, Louisiana, $20,000—for general operating support; Louisiana Cultural Economy Foundation, New Orleans, Louisiana, $25,000—for general operating support.
Contact: Roy Williams, Program Assistant; (504) 598-4663; fax (504) 598-4676; grants@gnof.org or roy@gnof.org
Internet: www.gnof.org/programs/impact/

Sponsor: Greater New Orleans Foundation
1055 St. Charles Avenue, Suite 100
New Orleans, LA 70130

GNOF IMPACT Grants for Youth Development   1084

Through the IMPACT Program, the Greater New Orleans Foundation (GNOF) makes grants to organizations serving the Greater New Orleans region. The ultimate goal of the IMPACT Program is to create a resilient, sustainable, vibrant, and equitable region in which individuals and families flourish and in which the special character of the New Orleans region and its people is preserved, celebrated, and given the means to develop. Specifically GNOF hopes to accomplish the following objectives through its IMPACT grants: provide a much needed source of financial and other support to nonprofit organizations that are struggling in the current financial environment and that are important to the health and vibrancy of the region; develop a better sense of the nonprofit organizations serving the region so GNOF can more effectively match donor desires with effective charitable work; identify and nurture promising new leaders and initiatives, especially in those communities that are in greatest need; and gain knowledge that will help nonprofit leaders and GNOF staff develop better long-term strategies for addressing regional needs and taking best advantage of important opportunities. IMPACT grants are awarded in four categories: Arts and Culture, Youth Development, Education, and Health and Human Services. In the category of Youth Development GNOF supports organizations that undertake the following types of projects: they facilitate access to high quality programs, activities, opportunities, and services for Greater New Orleans youth that will enhance their formal education, providing the cognitive, social, and emotional skills and abilities they need to become productive members of society; they provide professional development in the form of training, education, or tools to youth-development workers that will improve their knowledge, skills, and attitudes in the areas of case management, mentoring services, tutoring, and other remediation services or programs; they provide technical assistance and training to multiple youth-serving organizations to help them define and measure program outcomes and collect and track outcome and other data on participants and participation; they organize and/or increase the advocacy power of youth-serving organizations; and they develop a coordinated, comprehensive plan and strategies to address youth needs by engaging key stakeholders, promoting partnerships and strategic alliances, and identifying a diversified funding base. Interested organizations must submit a letter of intent along with all attachments via one email by 5 p.m. on July 30. GNOF program staff will review all letters of intent and will contact those organizations that are invited to submit a full application for funding. Awards are announced in November. Deadlines may vary from year to year. Interested organizations should verify the current deadline at the GNOF website where they can also obtain complete guidelines and requirements as well as a downloadable application form and cover sheet. Prospective applicants can also subscribe to GNOF's email newsletter for announcements of future funding opportunities. The subscription link is available from GNOF's Apply-for-a-Grant web page which contains a comprehensive listing of GNOF's current and past funding opportunities.
Requirements: Nonprofit, tax-exempt organizations that serve the thirteen parishes of Greater New Orleans are eligible to apply for funding. Organizations that are not tax-exempt but have a fiscal agent relationship with a 501(c)3 organization are also eligible.
Restrictions: Through its IMPACT program, the Greater New Orleans Foundation is unable to fund the following types of requests: requests for individual support, either through scholarships or other forms of financial assistance; special events or conferences; programs that promote religious doctrine; endowments; and scientific or medical research.
Geographic Focus: All States
Date(s) Application is Due: Jul 30
Amount of Grant: Up to 20,000 USD
Samples: BreakOUT!, New Orleans, Louisiana, $15,000—to provide general operating support; Up2Us, New York, New York, $25,000—to support the launch of the Train the Trainer initiative for sports-based youth development providers in New Orleans; New Orleans Kids Partnership, New Orleans, Louisiana, $20,000—to support the Generation K project.
Contact: Roy Williams, Program Assistant; (504) 598-4663; fax (504) 598-4676; grants@gnof.org or roy@gnof.org
Internet: www.gnof.org/programs/impact/
Sponsor: Greater New Orleans Foundation
1055 St. Charles Avenue, Suite 100
New Orleans, LA 70130

GNOF IMPACT Gulf States Eye Surgery Fund   1085

Through the IMPACT Program, the Greater New Orleans Foundation (GNOF) makes grants to organizations serving the Greater New Orleans region. The ultimate goal of the IMPACT program is to create a resilient, sustainable, vibrant, and equitable region in which individuals and families flourish and in which the special character of the New Orleans region and its people is preserved, celebrated, and given the means to develop. Specifically GNOF hopes to accomplish the following objectives through its IMPACT grants: provide a much needed source of financial and other support to nonprofit organizations that are struggling in the current financial environment and that are important to the health and vibrancy of the region; develop a better sense of the nonprofit organizations serving the region so GNOF can more effectively match donor desires with effective charitable work; identify and nurture promising new leaders and initiatives, especially in those communities that are in greatest need; and gain knowledge that will help nonprofit leaders and GNOF staff develop better long-term strategies for addressing regional needs and taking best advantage of important opportunities. IMPACT grants are awarded in four categories: Arts and Culture, Youth Development, Education, and Health and Human Services. In the category of Health and Human Services, special funding is available for organizations that defray the expenses of poor or indigent patients requiring or receiving eye surgery, care, or

treatment. Interested organizations must submit a letter of intent along with all attachments via one email by 5 p.m. on July 30 and should indicate on the IMPACT application cover sheet that they are applying for funding from the Gulf States Eye Surgery Fund. GNOF program staff will review all letters of intent and will contact those organizations that are invited to submit a full application for funding. Awards are announced in November. Deadlines may vary from year to year. Interested organizations should verify the current deadline at the GNOF website where they can also obtain complete guidelines and requirements as well as a downloadable application form and cover sheet. Prospective applicants can also subscribe to GNOF's email newsletter for announcements of future funding opportunities. The subscription link is available from GNOF's Apply-for-a-Grant web page which contains a comprehensive listing of GNOF's current and past funding opportunities.
Requirements: Nonprofit, tax-exempt organizations that serve the thirteen parishes of Greater New Orleans are eligible to apply for funding. Organizations that are not tax-exempt but have a fiscal agent relationship with a 501(c)3 organization are also eligible.
Restrictions: Through its IMPACT program, the Greater New Orleans Foundation is unable to fund the following types of requests: requests for support from individuals, either through scholarships or other forms of financial assistance; special events or conferences; programs that promote religious doctrine; endowments; and scientific or medical research.
Geographic Focus: All States
Date(s) Application is Due: Jul 30
Amount of Grant: Up to 20,000 USD
Samples: Children's Hospital, New Orleans, $60,000—to support vision care for low-income children.
Contact: Roy Williams, Program Assistant; (504) 598-4663; fax (504) 598-4676; grants@gnof.org or roy@gnof.org
Internet: www.gnof.org/programs/impact/
Sponsor: Greater New Orleans Foundation
1055 St. Charles Avenue, Suite 100
New Orleans, LA 70130

GNOF IMPACT Harold W. Newman, Jr. Charitable Trust Grants   1086

Through the IMPACT Program, the Greater New Orleans Foundation (GNOF) makes grants to organizations serving the Greater New Orleans region. The ultimate goal of the IMPACT program is to create a resilient, sustainable, vibrant, and equitable region in which individuals and families flourish and in which the special character of the New Orleans region and its people is preserved, celebrated, and given the means to develop. Specifically GNOF hopes to accomplish the following objectives through its IMPACT grants: provide a much needed source of financial and other support to nonprofit organizations that are struggling in the current financial environment and that are important to the health and vibrancy of the region; develop a better sense of the nonprofit organizations serving the region so GNOF can more effectively match donor desires with effective charitable work; identify and nurture promising new leaders and initiatives, especially in those communities that are in greatest need; and gain knowledge that will help nonprofit leaders and GNOF staff develop better long-term strategies for addressing regional needs and taking best advantage of important opportunities. IMPACT grants are awarded in four categories: Arts and Culture, Youth Development, Education, and Health and Human Services. In the category of Health and Human Services, special funding is available for organizations that provide health-care assistance to residents of New Orleans whose U.S. adjusted gross income for the preceding tax year, when added to any tax-exempt income and income from a spouse for that same year, is at least $75,000 but not more than $200,000. The health-care assistance must be for cancer, heart disease, or Alzheimer's. Interested organizations must submit a letter of intent along with all attachments via one email by 5 p.m. on July 30 and should indicate on the IMPACT application cover sheet that they are applying for funding from the Harold W. Newman, Jr. Charitable Trust. GNOF program staff will review all letters of intent and will contact those organizations that are invited to submit a full application for funding. Awards are announced in November. Deadlines may vary from year to year. Interested organizations should verify the current deadline at the GNOF website where they can also obtain complete guidelines and requirements as well as a downloadable application form and cover sheet. Prospective applicants can also subscribe to GNOF's email newsletter for announcements of future funding opportunities. The subscription link is available from GNOF's Apply-for-a-Grant web page which contains a comprehensive listing of GNOF's current and past funding opportunities.
Requirements: Nonprofit, tax-exempt organizations that serve the thirteen parishes of Greater New Orleans are eligible to apply for funding. Organizations that are not tax-exempt but have a fiscal agent relationship with a 501(c)3 organization are also eligible.
Restrictions: Through its IMPACT program, the Greater New Orleans Foundation is unable to fund the following types of requests: requests for support from individuals, either through scholarships or other forms of financial assistance; special events or conferences; programs that promote religious doctrine; endowments; and scientific or medical research.
Geographic Focus: All States
Date(s) Application is Due: Jul 30
Amount of Grant: Up to 20,000 USD
Contact: Roy Williams, Program Assistant; (504) 598-4663; fax (504) 598-4676; grants@gnof.org or roy@gnof.org
Internet: www.gnof.org/programs/impact/
Sponsor: Greater New Orleans Foundation
1055 St. Charles Avenue, Suite 100
New Orleans, LA 70130

GNOF IMPACT Kahn-Oppenheim Trust Grants   1087

Through the IMPACT Program, the Greater New Orleans Foundation (GNOF) makes grants to organizations serving the Greater New Orleans region. The ultimate goal of the

IMPACT program is to create a resilient, sustainable, vibrant, and equitable region in which individuals and families flourish and in which the special character of the New Orleans region and its people is preserved, celebrated, and given the means to develop. Specifically GNOF hopes to accomplish the following objectives through its IMPACT grants: provide a much needed source of financial and other support to nonprofit organizations that are struggling in the current financial environment and that are important to the health and vibrancy of the region; develop a better sense of the nonprofit organizations serving the region so GNOF can more effectively match donor desires with effective charitable work; identify and nurture promising new leaders and initiatives, especially in those communities that are in greatest need; and gain knowledge that will help nonprofit leaders and GNOF staff develop better long-term strategies for addressing regional needs and taking best advantage of important opportunities. IMPACT grants are awarded in four categories: Arts and Culture, Youth Development, Education, and Health and Human Services. In the category of Health and Human Services, special funding is available for the development and/or improvement of public-health outreach and education programs to inform people about ways to prevent diseases like asthma, diabetes, heart disease, obesity, HIV/AIDS, and others, insofar as these programs involve physical, nutritional, or dietary regimens. Interested organizations must submit a letter of intent along with all attachments via one email by 5 p.m. on July 30 and should indicate on the IMPACT application cover sheet that they are applying for funding from the Kahn-Oppenheim Trust. GNOF program staff will review all letters of intent and will contact those organizations that are invited to submit a full application for funding. Awards are announced in November. Deadlines may vary from year to year. Interested organizations should verify the current deadline at the GNOF website where they can also obtain complete guidelines and requirements as well as a downloadable application form and cover sheet. Prospective applicants can also subscribe to GNOF's email newsletter for announcements of future funding opportunities. The subscription link is available from GNOF's Apply-for-a-Grant web page which contains a comprehensive listing of GNOF's current and past funding opportunities.
Requirements: Nonprofit, tax-exempt organizations that serve the thirteen parishes of Greater New Orleans are eligible to apply for funding. Organizations that are not tax-exempt but have a fiscal agent relationship with a 501(c)3 organization are also eligible.
Restrictions: Through its IMPACT program, the Greater New Orleans Foundation is unable to fund the following types of requests: requests for support from individuals, either through scholarships or other forms of financial assistance; special events or conferences; programs that promote religious doctrine; endowments; and scientific or medical research.
Geographic Focus: All States
Date(s) Application is Due: Jul 30
Amount of Grant: Up to 20,000 USD
Contact: Roy Williams, Program Assistant; (504) 598-4663; fax (504) 598-4676; grants@gnof.org or roy@gnof.org
Internet: www.gnof.org/programs/impact/
Sponsor: Greater New Orleans Foundation
1055 St. Charles Avenue, Suite 100
New Orleans, LA 70130

GNOF New Orleans Works Grants 1088

New Orleans Works (NOW) is a public-private partnership initiative housed at the Greater New Orleans Foundation (GNOF) and funded by a grant from the National Fund for Workforce Solutions (NFWS), a $31-million, five-year effort to fuel high-impact workforce partnerships and to advance 30,000 workers in 32 regions in the U.S., including the Greater New Orleans area. Led by foundations and regional public workforce systems, NOW pools funding, develops strategy, supports economic-sector-based programs and develops workforce partnerships that meet both the career-advancement needs of workers and the workforce needs of employers. Although the people of the Greater New Orleans area are creative, hardworking, and dedicated, the region's economic performance has persistently fallen below its potential. Too often residents are held back by failures in public education, the legacy of racism, and underinvestment in workforce development. Devastating hurricanes in recent years have battered the economy, inflicting costly damage to businesses and infrastructure and spurring the relocation of major corporations and large employers. Furthermore, the economic turmoil caused by the 2010 oil disaster in the Gulf of Mexico demonstrated the perils of the region's over-reliance on too few industries. To attract jobs that provide sustainable family incomes to the area, NOW takes a two-tiered approach, working both with employers and with education and training providers to create a skilled workforce that is aligned with employers' needs, sector by sector. NOW promotes individual, institutional, and system-wide change in order to achieve the following goals: connecting residents with existing and emerging career opportunities; building long-term relationships between employees, employers, and training providers; expanding the minority middle class; creating an enhanced public workforce system; providing a larger pool of skilled workers; and transforming the many lessons learned in community and environmental resilience into economic opportunities and new industries that can bring the region to the forefront of innovation. GNOF accepts NOW applications through its Request for Proposal (RFP) process. Interested organizations are encouraged to subscribe to GNOF's email newsletter for announcements of future funding opportunities. The subscription link is available from GNOF's Apply-for-a-Grant web page which contains a comprehensive listing of GNOF's current and past funding opportunities. NOW's RFP deadlines and economic-sector focus may vary from offering to offering. Interested organizations are encouraged to visit the GNOF website to obtain more detailed and up todate information on the initiative and its RFP process and to contact the NOW Site Director with any questions.
Requirements: Non-profit, not-for-profit, and for-profit organizations are eligible to apply. Job providers should select a training partner that has the sector knowledge and capacity to execute a training intervention that addresses their workforce-development needs. The

funding must be awarded to an entity with the financial management system capability to accept federal funding.
Restrictions: Programs and partnerships funded by the NOW initiative must benefit the Greater New Orleans area.
Geographic Focus: All States
Date(s) Application is Due: Oct 12
Amount of Grant: Up to 250,000 USD
Contact: Bonita Robertson, New Orleans Works Interim Site Director; (504) 598-4663 ext. 40; fax (504) 598-4676; bonita@gnof.org
Danny Murphy, (504) 598-4663; fax (504) 598-4676; danny@gnof.org
Internet: www.gnof.org/new-orleans-works/
Sponsor: Greater New Orleans Foundation
1055 St. Charles Avenue, Suite 100
New Orleans, LA 70130

GNOF Norco Community Grants 1089

Shell Chemicals and Motiva Enterprises, grant-making partners of the Greater New Orleans Foundation (GNOF), have established the Norco Community fund to improve the quality of lives for people in Norco, Louisiana. The fund provides the following types of grants: capital-fund grants for new construction or major renovation; seed-money grants to help start new organizations which respond to an important opportunity in the community; bridge grants to sustain organizations experiencing financial hardships; program grants that support new, creative, or beneficial programs; and grants to organizations with a positive track record. Areas of interest include arts and humanities, community development, education, environment, human services, health care, community building, and youth development. Grant requests are reviewed by an advisory committee of business and civic leaders that meets annually. Application materials must be postmarked no later than September 14 and mailed to the Norco address given under the Contact Information section. If the deadline falls on a weekend or holiday, then the materials must be postmarked by the weekday immediately following; grant requests received after the deadline will be reviewed in the next year's grant cycle. Exact deadlines may vary from year to year. Prospective applicants should verify the current deadline at the GNOF website where they can also obtain complete guidelines and requirements as well as a downloadable application form. Prospective applicants can also subscribe to GNOF's email newsletter for announcements of future funding opportunities. The subscription link is available from GNOF's Apply-for-a-Grant web page which contains a comprehensive listing of GNOF's current and past funding opportunities.
Requirements: Applicants must have 501(c)3 status or apply through a fiscal agent who has such status.
Restrictions: The fund will only consider support for programs that serve the Norco community and its residents.
Geographic Focus: Louisiana
Date(s) Application is Due: Sep 14
Contact: Program Coordinator
Ellen M. Lee, Sr. Vice President, Programs, Community Revitalization Program Director; (504) 598-4663; fax (504) 598-4676; ellen@gnof.org
Internet: www.gnof.org/norco-community-fund/
Sponsor: Greater New Orleans Foundation
1055 St. Charles Avenue, Suite 100
New Orleans, LA 70130

GNOF Organizational Effectiveness Grants and Workshops 1090

In the wake of Hurricane Katrina and the levee failures, many new organizations have sprung up in the greater New Orleans region to address the immediate and pressing needs of recovery at the neighborhood level and up. This surge in activism and engagement holds great promise for the region, but significant issues must be addressed to give this work the greatest impact. Often, dedicated nonprofit leaders and professionals struggle with inexperienced boards, overwhelming fundraising responsibilities, and a lack of resources to develop their own infrastructure and talent. In response, the Greater New Orleans Foundation (GNOF) supports emerging leaders and organizations, empowers organizations in the region to be more competitive in their bids for state and federal funding, and serves as a convener to build connections and relationships within the greater New Orleans nonprofit sector. In partnership with the Marguerite Casey Foundation, GNOF provides training programs for staff and board members of nonprofits in the region to learn new ways of conducting fundraising, working with boards, and managing communications. In partnership with the Kellogg Foundation, GNOF provides technical-assistance grants of up to $4,000 to help nonprofit staff and/or board members increase their capacity to lead, manage, and govern their organizations. Following are examples of ways in which these technical-assistance grants can be used: working with a consultant to assist staff and board in development of fundraising or strategic plans for the organization; hiring a facilitator for a board retreat to grow governance abilities; covering expenses for attendance at a workshop or training session on a specific topic, such as evaluation, strategic communications, financial management, or fundraising; or completing an organizational assessment. All of these forms of technical assistance share the outcome that the grantee organizaqtion's staff and/or board members will be actively involved and will acquire new skills or information that will help the organization to grow and improve. GNOF accepts technical-assistance grant requests on a first-come, first-serve basis until the funding runs out. Priority will be given to requests pertaining to GNOF's current area of focus (advocacy, board governance, evaluation, financial management, fundraising, succession planning, partnering and collaboration, or fundraising). To apply for a GNOF technical-assistance grant, applicants should submit a two-page request along with required supporting documents via email to GNOF's Program Officer for Organizational Effectiveness. A decision will be made on the request approximately four weeks from the date that the request letter is received. Complete guidelines for submission are available at the GNOF website as well as links to capacity-building resources. Prospective applicants are welcome to contact the GNOF Program Officer with any additional questions. To receive further information about GNOF's workshops for nonprofits, interested organizations in the region should check the GNOF website or contact GNOF's Vice-President of Organizational Effectiveness.

Requirements: To be eligible to apply for GNOF's technical-assistance grants, organizations must be current or former (within the last two years) recipients of GNOF discretionary grants and have a primary office located within GNOF's 13-parish service area (Assumption, Jefferson, Lafourche, Orleans, Plaquemines, St. Bernard, St. Charles, St. James, St. John the Baptist, St. Tammany, Tangipahoa, Terrebonne, and Washington). Organizations that have previously received a GNOF technical-assistance grant may apply for additional grants in subsequent years (given funding availability); successful recurring requests will show that the applicant has built upon previous strategies.

Restrictions: Technical-assistance grants may not be used to pay a board member or any party whose direct affiliation with the applicant organization could be construed as or would create a conflict of interest. While prospective applicants may have highly competent professional resources on their boards, GNOF would expect these resources to be provided as an in-kind donation. Technical-assistance grants will not be made for activities that have already occurred or are underway at the time the grant is awarded.

Geographic Focus: Louisiana

Amount of Grant: Up to 4,000 USD

Contact: Kellie Chavez Greene, Program Officer, Organizational Effectiveness; (504) 598-4663; fax (504) 598-4676; kellie@gnof.org
Joann Ricci, Vice-President of Organizational Effectiveness; (504) 598-4663 ext. 23; fax (504) 598-4676; joann@gnof.org

Internet: www.gnof.org/organizational-effectiveness-technical-assistance-grants/

Sponsor: Greater New Orleans Foundation
1055 St. Charles Avenue, Suite 100
New Orleans, LA 70130

GNOF Plaquemines Community Grants 1091

Plaquemines Parish is the "big toe of Louisiana's boot" protruding into the Gulf of Mexico. On August 29, 2005, Hurricane Katrina struck on the west bank of Plaquemines Parish. The 20-foot storm surge hit the southern coastline and gradually inundated the entire parish as it moved northward. A month later, Hurricane Rita's three-foot storm surge caused more damage to the already weakened parish levees, resulting in more flooding. In 2006 the Greater New Orleans Foundation (GNOF) established an affiliate community foundation in Plaquemines Parish, because GNOF believed that the rebuilding process in devastated areas should be led by those who live and work in them. GNOF seeded the Plaquemines Community Foundation (PCF) with $500,000, distributed over a period of five years, with the agreement that PCF would set aside 10% of the seed money as an endowment. The mission of PCF is to improve the quality of life for all citizens of the Plaquemine parish. PCF's board identifies current and emerging needs and addresses those needs through grants, and also fosters relationships with donors to build permanent endowments. Since its inception, the PCF has awarded grants to support education programs and agricultural initiatives. It has also partnered with the Saint Bernard Community Foundation to create the Southeast Louisiana Fisheries Assistance Center, which currently serves as a clearing house for local fishermen to receive free business planning, financial assistance (in the form of grants and low-interest loans), fishing licenses, and industry-specific training services. Plaquemine organizations interested in obtaining grants through PCF can contact GNOF for more information.

Geographic Focus: Louisiana

Samples: The Plaquemines Parish Economic Development and Tourism Department, Belle Chasse, Louisiana, $9,000— to fund an alternative crop project by the Lousiana State University Agricultural Center to increase crop diversity and profitability; The Plaquemines Community CARE Center, Belle Chasse, Louisiana, $50,000—to help support human services programs in the aftermath of the Gulf Oil Spill; Woodlands Trail and Park, Belle Chasse, Louisiana—for the organization's Ecosystem Restoration Project.

Contact: Dr. Marco Cocito-Monoc, Director for Regional Initiatives; (504) 598-4663; fax (504) 598-4676; marco@gnof.org
Perry A. Triche, Chair, Plaquemines Community Foundation Board; (504) 598-4663; fax (504) 598-4676

Internet: www.gnof.org/overview-6/

Sponsor: Greater New Orleans Foundation
1055 St. Charles Avenue, Suite 100
New Orleans, LA 70130

GNOF Stand Up For Our Children Grants 1092

In New Orleans almost one in two children under the age of five lives at or below the federal poverty level. The Greater New Orleans Foundation (GNOF) believes that parental involvement is the best change agent for improving conditions for children. To help address the issue, GNOF, in partnership and with assistance from the W.K. Kellogg Foundation, formed an initiative called Stand Up for Our Children. It identifies and invests in nonprofit organizations that train parents to develop leadership skills that enable them to become more effective advocates, essentially helping their voices to be heard. In 2012 a total of $575,366 was awarded to ten organizations for their success working with parents and advocating for families. In addition to receiving grants, all grantees participated in a learning community designed to share knowledge, foster coalitions and alliances, and document lessons learned. The second round of grants from the Stand Up for Our Children Initiative will take place in 2013. These grants are by invitation only. Interested organizations should contact the GNOF Program Officer (see Contact Information Section) and check the GNOF website for updates. Prospective applicants can also subscribe to GNOF's email newsletter for announcements of future funding opportunities. The subscription link is available from GNOF's Apply-for-a-Grant web page which contains a comprehensive listing of GNOF's current and past funding opportunities.

Geographic Focus: Louisiana

Amount of Grant: 40,000 - 130,000 USD

Samples: Birthing Project of New Orleans, New Orleans, Louisiana, $46,996—to support the Healthy Parents, Healthy Communities program which pairs mentors with parents-to-be to promote healthy birth outcomes; Orleans Public Education Network, New Orleans, Louisiana, $130,500—to implement the national Parent Leadership Training Institute model and to support its neighborhood engagement strategy; Puentes, New Orleans, Louisiana, $50,000—to support its partnership with Families in Schools to increase the school-readiness of Latino children.

Contact: Flint D. Mitchell, Ph.D., Program Officer; (504) 598-4663; fax (504) 598-4676; flint@gnof.org

Internet: www.gnof.org/stand-up-for-our-children-initiative/

Sponsor: Greater New Orleans Foundation
1055 St. Charles Avenue, Suite 100
New Orleans, LA 70130

Go Daddy Cares Charitable Contributions 1093

Go Daddy has a long history of philanthropic work in support of a variety of charitable, community-wide and global organizations. Go Daddy Cares has dedicated manpower and dollars to raise awareness toward the causes of domestic violence, child abuse, and animal shelters. The corporate philanthropy program contributes to nonprofit organizations that focus on causes which are meaningful to its business, customers, employees and the communities in which it operates. In addition to making monetary contributions, Go Daddy encourages its employees to become involved in community organizations.

Requirements: Go Daddy focuses support on the communities where it resides. This includes: Greater Phoenix area; Hiawatha, IA; Denver, CO & Silicon Valley, CA. Nonprofit charitable organizations classified as a 501(c)3 public charity by the Internal Revenue Service and with a current Form 990 are eligible to apply. Charities relating to children, women's causes, animal welfare or technology related initiatives are given priority for financial allocations. All submissions for support must be made online through the Go Daddy Cares Charity Application Form. There are no deadlines, however, advance notice of 3-6 months is required for all sponsorship requests. Only one application per cause, per year will be considered.

Restrictions: Go Daddy does not consider requests for golf tournaments or walks.

Geographic Focus: Arizona, California, Colorado, Iowa

Contact: Nick Fuller, (623) 203-7744; Nick@GoDaddy.com

Internet: godaddycares.com/

Sponsor: Go Daddy
14455 N. Hayden Road, Suite 226
Scottsdale, AZ 85260

Golden Heart Community Foundation Grants 1094

The Golden Heart Community Foundation's grantmaking priorities are still in development, but it will support projects that strengthen the Fairbanks community. The Foundation will include organizations and programs that serve youth, the elderly, recreation, safety, vulnerable populations, and arts and culture. Preference will be given to applications which have the potential to impact a broad range of area residents. Applications should describe measurable outcomes and other sources of support, collaboration and/or cooperation. Applications should also address the sustainability of the proposed program or project for which funding is desired. Currently, no annual deadlines have been established.

Requirements: The Foundation seeks applications from qualified tax-exempt 501(c)3 organizations (or equivalent organizations) in the greater Fairbanks area. Equivalent organizations may include tribes, local or state governments, schools, or Regional Educational Attendance Areas.

Restrictions: Individuals, for profit, and 501(c)4 and (c)6 organizations, non-Alaska based organizations and state or federal government agencies are not eligible for competitive grants. Applications for religious indoctrination or other religious activities, endowment building, deficit financing, fundraising, lobbying, electioneering and activities of a political nature will not be considered, nor will proposals for ads, sponsorships, or special events.

Geographic Focus: Alaska

Contact: Ricardo Lopez, Affiliate Program Officer; (907) 249-6707; fax (907) 334-5780; rlopez@alaskacf.org

Internet: goldenheartcf.org/grants-community-projects/

Sponsor: Golden Heart Community Foundation
P.O. Box 73183
Fairbanks, AK 99707-3183

Goldseker Foundation Non-Profit Management Assistance Grants 1095

Management assistance grants are intended to help smaller, well-established nonprofits make investments in timely organizational development activities that would not otherwise be possible because of limited budget resources. Most management assistance grant recipients have operating budgets of less than $2 million. These grants principally fund the engagement of qualified consulting expertise to conduct the following: strategic planning; fund development and sustainability; financial management systems; improvement; program evaluation; IT assessment and planning (not hardware or software purchases); board development, executive coaching, and succession planning; improving systems of service delivery; mergers, strategic alliances, and partnerships. Applications are accepted throughout the year. The board makes funding decisions approximately once per quarter.

Requirements: Non-profit 501(c)3 organizations that carry out their work principally in metropolitan Baltimore, primarily Baltimore City, are eligible to apply. Preference will be given to those organizations whose programs fit within the Foundation's published areas of interest (community development, education, and human services) but will be considered from any organization that does not conflict with the foundation's grant making policies. Organizations must call the Foundation's Program Officer to review the proposal concept before submitting an application. Applications that arrive without prior approval to submit will not be considered. Organizations with a budget of $250,000 or greater are must pledge a cash match equal to at least 50% of the requested grant amount. Organizations with budgets under $250,000 must pledge a cash match equal to at least 25% of the requested grant amount.

Restrictions: Management Assistance Grants are not intended to be a form of start-up support for new nonprofits. Organizations need to be able to demonstrate program outcomes already achieved and have completed at least two full budget years.

Geographic Focus: Maryland

Contact: Laurie Latuda Kinkel, Program Officer; (410) 837-6115; fax (410) 837-7927; lmlatuda@goldsekerfoundation.org

Internet: www.goldsekerfoundation.org/_grants?program_area_id=2

Sponsor: Morris Goldseker Foundation

1040 Park Avenue, Suite 310

Baltimore, MD 21201

Good+Foundation Grants 1096

Founded in 2001 by Jerry Seinfeld and his wife, Jessica, Good+Foundation is a leading national nonprofit that works to dismantle multi-generational poverty by pairing tangible goods with innovative services for low-income fathers, mothers and caregivers, creating an upward trajectory for the whole family. Jerry and Jessica Seinfeld proactively seek out sponsorships from appropriate companies. Corporate sponsorships include brands like Ergo Baby, Weil, Seventh Generation, and Children's Place. The idea is to create lasting partnerships with companies open to helping with in-store promotions, hosting events, or sponsoring essentials needed for babies and children. With warehouses in New York City and Los Angeles, Good+Foundation partners with approximately 75 innovative anti-poverty programs across the country. Its primary goal is to incentivize parental enrollment and participation in programs like job training, GED attainment, anger management and healthy relationship counseling. In 2010, Good+Foundation expanded programming to intentionally include fathers. Stronger fathers build stronger, more resilient families, which are the backbone of thriving communities. The more we invest in fathers in their capacity to be engaged co-parents, the greater impact we see on children and families as a whole.

Geographic Focus: All States, American Samoa, District of Columbia, Guam, Marshall Islands, Northern Mariana Islands, Puerto Rico, U.S. Virgin Islands

Contact: Alan-Michael Graves, National Program Director; (212) 736-1777 or (310) 439-5463; info@goodplusfoundation.org or alanmichael@goodplusfoundation.org

Internet: goodplusfoundation.org/

Sponsor: Good+Foundation

306 West 37th Street, 8th Floor

New York, NY 10018

Grace Bersted Foundation Grants 1097

The Grace Bersted Foundation was established in 1986 to support and promote quality educational, human services and health care programming for underserved populations. Special consideration is given to charitable organizations that serve the needs of children or the disabled. The Grace Bersted Foundation specifically serves the people of DuPage, Kane, Lake and McHenry counties in Illinois. The majority of grants from the Grace Bersted Foundation are 1 year in duration. Award amounts typically go up to $50,000.

Requirements: Applicant organizations must have 501(c)3 tax-exempt status and an office located in one of the following counties: DuPage, Kane, Lake, or McHenry. Applications will be submitted online through the Bank of America website. A grant report is required within 1 year of the grant application date, regardless of whether all of the funds have been spent.

Restrictions: The foundation does not support requests from individuals, organizations attempting to influence policy through direct lobbying, or any political campaigns.

Geographic Focus: Illinois

Date(s) Application is Due: Aug 1

Amount of Grant: Up to 50,000 USD

Samples: Lambs Residence Number Two, Libertyville, Illinois, $25,000 - Awarded for general operations (2018); Alexian Brothers Bonaventure House, Chicago, Illinois, $20,000 - Awarded for Supportive Housing Programs for Homeless Adults: The Harbor in Waukegan, Illinois, and Scattered-Site Community Housing in Lake County (2018); Ywca Of Lake County, Gurnee, Illinois, $20,000 - Awarded for YWCA Lake County – Youth Leadership and Development Program (2018).

Contact: Srilatha Lakkaraju, Philanthropic Client Manager; (312) 828-8166; ilgrantmaking@bankofamerica.com or ilgrantmaking@ustrust.com

Internet: www.bankofamerica.com/philanthropic/foundation/?fnId=58

Sponsor: Grace Bersted Foundation

P.O. Box 1802

Providence, RI 02901-1802

Graham and Carolyn Holloway Family Foundation Grants 1098

In 1995 the Graham and Carolyn Holloway Family Foundation was formed, providing a formal vehicle for a legacy of charitable giving that began on November 26, 1955 when Graham and Carolyn were first married. From a background of humble beginnings, the couple lived and taught the principles of generosity even before they knew what the word philanthropy meant. The Holloway Family Foundation has awarded over $2,000,000 in grants since its inception, seeking out agencies that are providing the most good in support of the most needy. The Foundation maintains a personal connection to its grantees, choosing carefully to respect the integrity of the donors' intent. The mission of the Foundation is to enhance the quality of life for those people in its communities who are least likely to be able to do that on their own; aiding primarily, but not exclusively: the elderly, individuals with developmental and/or physical disabilities, the chronically or terminally ill, and disadvantaged children. Awards typically range from $2,500 to $10,000. The deadline for consideration of a June distribution is March 15 and the deadline for consideration of a December distribution is October 15.

Requirements: Applicants must have a 501(c)3 status and serve residents of: the Stae of Texas; Colleyville, Texas; Nashville, Tennessee; or Salisbury, North Carolina. population. Recipients are limited to one grant per calendar year.

Geographic Focus: North Carolina, Tennessee, Texas

Date(s) Application is Due: Mar 15; Oct 15

Amount of Grant: 2,500 - 10,000 USD

Samples: Aberg Center for Literacy, Dallas, Texas, $2,500 - general operating support; Helping Restore Ability, Arlington, Texas, $10,000 - general operating support; Saddle Up!, Nashville, Tennessee, $5,000 - general operating support.

Contact: Valerie Holloway Skinner, Vice President; (817) 313-9379; valerie@hollowayfamilyfoundation.org

Internet: www.hollowayfamilyfoundation.org/about.htm

Sponsor: Graham and Carolyn Holloway Family Foundation

P.O. Box 989

Colleyville, TX 76034-0989

Graham Family Charitable Foundation Grants 1099

The Graham Family Charitable Foundation was established in New York in 1999 with the expressed purpose of offering support in its primary fields of interest. These include: Catholicism; child welfare; education; and human services. Awards have been given to organizations in California, Connecticut, Illinois, Massachusetts, and New Mexico, although the Foundation's major geographical focus is the State of New York. Most recent grant amounts have ranged from $500 to $65,000. There are no specified annual deadlines.

Requirements: 501(c)3 organizations throughout the United States are eligible to apply, although the Foundation has a stated purpose of support in New York.

Geographic Focus: All States

Amount of Grant: 400 - 65,000 USD

Samples: Cornell Cooperative, New York, New York, $18,000 - helping families and communities to thrive in a rapidly changing world; East Hampton Day Care, East Hampton, New York, $25,000 - support of affordable daycare; Windward School 13, White Plains, New York, $64,378 - general operating support.

Contact: Monica A. Graham, Graham Partners Trustee; (212) 808-7430 or (917) 327-1700

Sponsor: Graham Family Charitable Foundation

21 Inkberry Street

East Hampton, NY 11937-2243

Graham Foundation Grants 1100

The Graham Foundation was established in York, Pennsylvania, in 1986, and was primarily funded by support from both the Graham Architectural Products Corporation and Graham Engineering. Giving is centered throughout the State of Pennsylvania, though grants are sometimes approved for national organizations. The Foundation's primary fields of interest include: arts and culture; education; and human services. Awards are typically given in support of: annual campaigns; capital campaigns; infrastructure; general operations; program development; sponsorships; and scholarships. There are no annual deadlines specified, and most recent awards have ranged from $200 to $140,000.

Requirements: 501(c)3 organizations serving the residents of York County, Pennsylvania, are eligible to apply.

Geographic Focus: Pennsylvania

Amount of Grant: 200 - 140,000 USD

Samples: Leg Up Farm, Mount Wolf, Pennsylvania, $20,000 - support of the annual capital campaign; Cultural Alliances of York County, York, Pennsylvania, $15,000 - general operating support; Squam Lakes Natural Science Center, Holderness, New Hampshire, $50,000 - general operating support.

Contact: William H. Kerlin, Jr., Trustee; (717) 849-4001 or (717) 849-4045

Sponsor: Graham Foundation

1420 Sixth Avenue, P.O. Box 1104

York, PA 17405-1104

Graham Foundation Grants 1101

The Graham Foundation is a private family foundation located in Greenville, South Carolina. It was established in 1985, and has been funded by the late Allen J. Graham and his daughter, the late Frances G. MacIlwinen. Currently, the foundation focuses primarily on awarding grants in Greenville County and, to a lesser extent, Upstate South Carolina. The Foundation prefers to make grants focused on needs which are specific and contained, such as capital or endowment campaigns, and temporary or restricted supplemental support to an operating budget. Grants are targeted to organizations which can make a significant difference for the betterment of Greenville. Its focus areas include: arts, culture and inspiring spaces; livable communities, strengthening local communities and providing access to affordable housing, reliable and efficient transportation, affordable, healthy food, and other quality-of-life essentials; strong starts, giving young children the critical support they need for a strong start in life; pathways to economic success, empowering people to achieve and sustain long-term economic independence; and community capacity and leadership, fostering leadership and building local capacity to solve problems and improve communities. Recent awards have ranged from $6,000 to $150,000. Annual deadlines for submission of completed applications are April 6 and October 9, with Letters of Intent required by March 2 and September 1, respectively.

Requirements: 501(c)3 organizations serving Greenville County and upstate South Carolina are eligible to apply.

Restrictions: The Foundation does not generally support: unrestricted grants for operating support; political support; national campaigns, issues, or needs; medical facilities or medically oriented requests; fund raising events; or individuals.

Geographic Focus: South Carolina

Date(s) Application is Due: Apr 6; Oct 9

Amount of Grant: 6,000 - 150,000 USD

Samples: Foothills Family Resources, Greenville, South Carolina, $30,000 - general operating support for services to individuals and families; Warehouse Theatre, Greenville, South Carolina, $52,954 - to support its executive leadership transition plan and establish a more permanent housing option for artists in residence; Greenville Tech Foundation, Greenville, South Carolina, $25,000 - stipends for students experiencing a crisis that may lead to drop-out.

Contact: William A. Bridges, Managing Trustee; (864) 233-3688; fax (864) 233-3667; bill@thegrahamfoundation.org

Internet: thegrahamfoundation.org/

Sponsor: Graham Foundation

531 South Main Street, Suite ML-7

Greenville, SC 29601-2500

Grand Circle Foundation Associates Grants 1102

The Grand Circle Foundation Associates Grants fund youth education and discovery by supporting organizations that work with Boston youth. The Foundation invites projects dedicated to improving the future for at-risk children and youth. The Foundation is interested in projects that expand horizons for young people and build confidence in their abilities and future. Projects that improve global literacy and promote global citizenship will be given strong consideration.

Requirements: Funds requested must be for a specific project. Organizations must hold an active 501(c)3 status and their operating budgets must not exceed $3 million. Applicants should submit proposals of no more than two pages to the Project Manager with the following information: detailed description of the organization, and the proposed project; how the project would help others, how much it will cost, its timeline, and how it will be evaluated; and the organization's contact person with phone number and email. Organizations should also attach the following information: a board of directors list; total agency budget; annual report, if available; and evidence of their tax-exempt status.

Restrictions: Grants are awarded only to nonprofit organizations that focus on youth in the Boston neighborhoods of Roxbury, Dorchester, Mattapan, and Allston. The Foundation does not fund individuals, political organizations, advertising, dinner-table sponsorship, religious organizations, general operating expenses, or administrative costs, which includes salaries.

Geographic Focus: Massachusetts

Date(s) Application is Due: Oct 14

Amount of Grant: 500 - 5,000 USD

Contact: Jan Byrnes, Project Manager; (617) 346-6398; fax (617) 346-6030; GCFProjectsandGrants@grandcirclefoundation.org

Internet: www.grandcirclefoundation.org/get-involved/2010-grand-circle-associates-fund.aspx

Sponsor: Grand Circle Foundation

347 Congress Street

Boston, MA 02210

Granger Foundation Grants 1103

The primary purpose of the foundation is to enhance the quality of life within the Greater Lansing Area. The foundation's primary mission is to support Christ-centered activities. It also supports efforts that enhance the lives of community youth. The foundation trustees consider organizations and funding areas that are significant and have far-reaching value. Grants are awarded generally in Michigan's tri-county area (Ingham, Eaton, and Clinton Counties). The application is available online.

Restrictions: Grants do not support endowments, fund raising, social events, conferences, exhibits, church capital funds or improvements, public schools capital funds or improvements, individual clubs (PTO, PTA, etc.), or individuals.

Geographic Focus: Michigan

Date(s) Application is Due: Apr 15; Oct 15

Contact: Alton Granger, Foundation Contact; (517) 393-1670; elee@grangerconstruction.com

Internet: www.grangerfoundation.org/Guidelines.htm

Sponsor: Granger Foundation

P.O. Box 22187

Lansing, MI 48909

Gray Family Foundation Camp Maintenance Grants 1104

John Gray identified the ongoing maintenance of Outdoor School camp facilities as a critical factor in preserving a full range of options for kids to get outside. Beginning in 2014, a grant program established by the Gray Family Foundation has annually invested $455,000 directly into the improvement of existing facilities at Oregon's outdoor residential camps throughout the state. The Foundation works directly with Outdoor School organizations and their network of camps to identify those facilities that have maintenance and improvement needs, serve outdoor school, are geographically dispersed, and reflect the Gray Family Foundation's values regarding inclusion and multi-cultural diversity.

Geographic Focus: Oregon

Date(s) Application is Due: Jun 15

Amount of Grant: Up to 35,000 USD

Samples: Camp Adams, Molalla, Oregon, $35,000 - to fix or upgrade existing camp facilities; Drift Creek Camp, Lincoln City, Oregon, $35,000 - to fix or upgrade existing camp facilities; Twin Rocks Friends Camp, Beach, Oregon, $35,000 - to fix or upgrade existing camp facilities.

Contact: Rana DeBey, Program Associate; (503) 552-3500; grants@grayff.org or rdebey@grayff.org

Internet: grayff.org/funding_category_cpt/camp-maintenance/

Sponsor: Gray Family Foundation

1221 SW Yamhill Street, Suite 100

Portland, OR 97205

Gray Family Foundation Community Field Trips Grants 1105

The Gray Family Foundation is founded on the belief that fostering an understanding and appreciation of our natural world is a crucial part of a child's education. The Foundation directly supports the following programs: outdoor school for 5th and 6th grade students; field trips for 5th–8th graders studying food systems, waste management, watersheds, and land use; and environmental literacy professional development opportunities for teachers. Additionally, the Foundation backs initiatives promoting: maintenance for outdoor school camp facilities; Latino leadership learning and support opportunities; geography education in schools; and statewide environmental literacy programs. In support of Community Field Trips, the Foundation will give preference to: programs providing student field trips to sites featuring civil infrastructure projects designed to protect our communities and ecosystems; organizations that create and maintain shared natural areas located in public transportation districts or within biking and walking range of schools; projects encouraging students, families and communities to learn about and become involved in community gardens, local farms and regional food systems; projects supporting student involvement and hands-on experience with local environmental stewardship activities; and initiatives to improve school curriculum around land use planning and the history and geography of Oregon. Awards can range up to a maximum of $40,000. Annual application submission deadlines are January 15 and July 15.

Requirements: Applicants must involve students in grades five through eight.

Restrictions: The Foundation will not fund: field trips which are overnight in nature (day-trips only; overnight trips must be submitted in our ODS category and be competitive); or costs for students outside of 5th to 8th grade.

Geographic Focus: Oregon

Date(s) Application is Due: Jan 15; Jul 15

Amount of Grant: Up to 40,000 USD

Samples: Cascade Pacific Resource Conservation and Development, Tangent, Oregon, $8,000 - for 200 seventh grade students to take three field trips during the school year to visit a demonstration farm; Gladstone School District No. 115, Gladstone, Oregon, $12,750 - to send fifth through eighth grade students on field trips to wastewater treatment plants and landfills, renewable energy sites and other places focused on environmental issues; White Oak Farm and Education Center, Williams, Oregon, $3,500 - to provide hands-on outdoor learning experiences for children, teachers and parents in Josephine and Jackson counties.

Contact: Nancy Bales, Executive Director; (503) 552-3500; grants@grayff.org or nbales@grayff.org

Internet: grayff.org/funding_category_cpt/community-field-trips/

Sponsor: Gray Family Foundation

1221 SW Yamhill Street, Suite 100

Portland, OR 97205

Gray Family Foundation Geography Education Grants 1106

The goal of the Gray Family Foundation Geography Education program is to promote and support the teaching of geography in K-12 schools throughout Oregon. This program is administered in coordination with a geography education fund from the Oregon Community Foundation and grants a total of $420,000 annually. Currently, the Foundation's efforts in geography education are focused on its partnership with the Portland State University-based Center for Geography Education in Oregon (C-GEO). C-GEO administers annual Geography Teaching Institutes, summer excursions to re-inspire Oregon's geography educators, the Oregon Atlas program, and teacher training activities. The Foundation is also seeking informal proposals from groups interested in exploring new ideas for improving and expanding geography education throughout the state.

Requirements: Funds can only be distributed to 501(c)3 charitable non-profit organizations.

Geographic Focus: Oregon

Contact: Rachael Bashor, Program Officer; (503) 552-3500; grants@grayff.org or rbashor@grayff.org

Internet: grayff.org/funding_category_cpt/geography-education/

Sponsor: Gray Family Foundation

1221 SW Yamhill Street, Suite 100

Portland, OR 97205

Gray Family Foundation Outdoor School Grants 1107

The Gray Family Foundation is founded on the belief that fostering an understanding and appreciation of our natural world is a crucial part of a child's education. The Foundation directly supports the following programs: outdoor school for 5th and 6th grade students; field trips for 5th–8th graders studying food systems, waste management, watersheds, and land use; and environmental literacy professional development opportunities for teachers. Additionally, the Foundation backs initiatives promoting: maintenance for outdoor school camp facilities; Latino leadership learning and support opportunities; geography education in schools; and statewide environmental literacy programs. In support of Outdoor School grants, the Foundation will give preference to programs that: are five days in length; give scholarships to participating students in need as well as programs based at schools exhibiting a high level of need (as measured by the number of students receiving free or reduced lunch); engage college or high school students as mentors; that are well supported by their communities and other partnerships; that incorporate additional curriculum both before and after the trip; and measure students' learning and long-term retention of the material covered. Most recent awards have ranged from $2,000 to $40,000. The annual application submission date is listed as June 15.

Restrictions: The Foundation will not fund: programs which are for one night only (with very few exceptions for pilot programs or very new ODS programs); programs which do not have a financial safety net which allows all students to participate; programs that ask for more than 40% of the total project cost (unless this is your first outdoor school program in which case we will consider your request); or grants over $40,000. Until all Oregon students have a chance to attend outdoor school at least once, we will not fund programs that are designed to send kids a second time (i.e. in 5th and 6th grade).

Geographic Focus: Oregon
Date(s) Application is Due: Jun 15
Amount of Grant: 2,000 - 40,000 USD
Samples: Canby School District, Canby, Oregon, $15,000 - to send sixth grade students to Northwest Regional Educational Service District (NWRESD) at Camp Cedar Ridge or Magruder for three nights; Knappa School District, Astoria, Oregon, $3,000 - to send sixth grade students from Hilda Lahti School to NWRESD at Camp Magruder for three nights; Community Roots School, Silverton, Oregon, $2,000 - to send fifth grade and sixth grade students to the group's first Outdoor School at Camp Namanu for four nights.
Contact: Nancy Bales, Executive Director; (503) 552-3500; grants@grayff.org or nbales@grayff.org
Internet: grayff.org/funding_category_cpt/outdoor-school/
Sponsor: Gray Family Foundation
1221 SW Yamhill Street, Suite 100
Portland, OR 97205

Great Clips Corporate Giving 1108

Each month, Great Clips selects one independent charity and rewards their dedication to greatness in their community with a $1,500 donation. Charities entered will also have the chance to get even more funds at the end of the year. Each charity will receive an additional donation from Great Clips based on the number of votes they receive on EverythingGreat.com.

Requirements: Nonprofit organizations in the United States and Canada may enter the monthly contests. Organizations must include their 501(c)3 number or registration document with the Charities Directorate of the Canada Revenue Agency (in Canada) within the application. The program nominated must align with Great Clips' mission of supporting organizations that inspire U.S. with their creativity, passion and greatness and must positively impact communities where Great Clips salons are located.
Restrictions: The Great Clips Great Giving Program does not provide funding for: political organizations, fraternal groups or social clubs that engage in any kind of political activity; religious organizations, unless they serve the general public in a significant non-denominational way; individuals or individual families; organizations located outside Great Clips markets; capital campaigns; private foundations; sponsorships for music, film and art festivals; support for business expositions/conferences; scholarships; charities that are already supported from government organizations or national charities (e.g. Red Cross, United Way, Children's Miracle Network, etc.); organizations that discriminate on the basis of race, color, gender, sexual orientation, age, religion, physical disability, or national or ethnic origin; or, 501(c)3 organizations or programs/projects that have been in place for less than one year.
Geographic Focus: All States
Amount of Grant: 1,500 USD
Contact: Corporate Giving Manager; (800) 999-5959; fax (952) 844-3444
Internet: everythinggreat.greatclips.com/great-giving/
Sponsor: Great Clips, Inc.
4400 West 78th Street, Suite 700
Minneapolis, MN 55435

Greater Milwaukee Foundation Grants 1109

The Foundation places its highest funding priority on supporting creative efforts to address issues of poverty in the community, particularly grants focused on education, employment, and strengthening children, youth and families. Lower priority is given to projects that do not meet the above criteria and/or do not address issues of persistent poverty. In addition, the Foundation places special emphasis on programs that accomplish the following: improving understanding among people of different backgrounds through support of efforts addressing issues of racial, cultural and economic diversity; and strengthening the voluntary sector by supporting efforts to enhance the management capacities of nonprofit organizations, promote philanthropy, and encourage civic involvement and community service. Additional application information is available online.

Requirements: Grants are made only to 501(c)3 nonprofit organizations and, on occasion, to governmental agencies. Geographically, funding for the discretionary grantmaking program is limited to projects that will significantly improve the lives of people living in Milwaukee, Waukesha, Ozaukee and Washington counties.
Restrictions: Grants for ongoing operational costs or to individuals are not eligible for support from the Foundation's discretionary funds. The Foundation does not provide support for debt reduction, sectarian religious purposes, medical or scientific research, fund drives for sustaining support or organizations that are discriminatory in their practices.
Geographic Focus: Wisconsin
Samples: Milwaukee Chamber Orchestra, Milwaukee, Wisconsin, $25,000 - to support staff and programming expenses as part of its rebuilding efforts; Layton Boulevard West Neighbors, Milwaukee, Wisconsin, $25,000 - to partially fund three staff positions

that help support the agency's work as part of the Foundation's Milwaukee Healthy Neighborhoods Initiative.
Contact: Fran Kowalkiewicz, Grants Manager; (414) 272-5805; fax (414) 272-6235; fkowalkiewicz@greatermilwaukeefoundation.org or info@greatermilwaukeefoundation.org
Internet: www.greatermilwaukeefoundation.org/grant_seekers/
Sponsor: Greater Milwaukee Foundation
101 West Pleasant Street, Suite 210
Milwaukee, WI 53212

Greater Saint Louis Community Foundation Grants 1110

The Greater Saint Louis Community Foundation (GSLCF) was founded in 1915, one year after the first community foundation was established in Cleveland, Ohio. Currently GSLCF administers over 400 individual charitable funds that total $170 million in assets. These funds annually make over $17 million in grants that shape the greater Saint Louis region, touch communities across the nation, and reach across the globe. Historically, the mission of GSLCF has been two-fold: to serve donors and ensure that their dollars work in line with the goals that are important to them; and to promote charitable giving through community investment in nonprofit organizations capable of addressing community issues in measurable ways. To this end GSLCF maintains an online database YOURGivingLink to help donors find deserving nonprofit organizations that match their giving interests. Nonprofits are encouraged to register their organizations with the database; the link is available at the GSLCF website.

Requirements: While the Foundation predominately supports St. Louis area nonprofits, grants are also made to national and international charities.
Geographic Focus: Illinois, Missouri
Contact: Amy Basore Murphy, Director of Scholarships and Donor Services; (314) 588-8200, ext. 139 or (314) 880-4965; fax (314) 588-8088; amurphy@stlouisgives.org
Internet: www.stlouisgives.org/charities/
Sponsor: Greater Saint Louis Community Foundation
319 North Fourth Street, Suite 300
Saint Louis, MO 63102-1906

Greater Sitka Legacy Fund Grants 1111

As an organization, the Greater Sitka Legacy Fund's goal is to support projects of importance to the Sitka community that will help its residents become better stewards of the land. The Fund is continually listening and learning to its residents in order to understand important to them. Grant making priorities are still in development, though the Fund will support projects that strengthen the community. Among others, they will include organizations and programs that serve youth, the elderly, recreation, safety, vulnerable populations, and arts and culture. There are no annual deadlines for applications.

Requirements: The Fund board members seek applications from qualified tax-exempt 501(c)3 organizations that support the organizations and programs in the Sitka area and serve the people's needs in such areas as health, education, community heritage, the arts, vulnerable populations, recreation, safety, and community and economic development.
Restrictions: Individuals, for-profit, and 501(c)4 or 501(c)6 organizations, non-Alaska based organizations and state or federal government agencies are not eligible for competitive grants. Applications for religious indoctrination or other religious activities, endowment building, deficit financing, fundraising, lobbying, electioneering and activities of political nature will not be considered, nor will proposals for ads, sponsorships, or special event and any proposals which discriminate as to race, gender, marital status, sexual orientation, age, disability, creed or ethnicity.
Geographic Focus: Alaska
Contact: Ricardo Lopez, Affiliate Program Officer; (907) 274-6707; fax (907) 334-5780, rlopez@alaskacf.org or greatersitka@alaskacf.org
Internet: greatersitkalegacyfund.org/
Sponsor: Greater Sitka Legacy Fund
700 Katlian Street, Suite B
Sitka, AK 99835

Greater Tacoma Community Foundation Fund for Women and Girls Grants 1112

The overall mission of the Greater Tacoma Community Foundation Fund for Women and Girls program is to promote the power of generosity among women and fund opportunities for women and girls throughout Pierce County, Washington. Distributions from the Fund shall provide assistance to programs that promote intellectual, physical, emotional, social, economic, and cultural growth of women and girls of all ages. Grants will be considered for general operations, equipment, and project support. Application information is available online.

Requirements: Grants will be made to organizations, located primarily in, and serving women and girls of, the greater Tacoma-Pierce County area.
Restrictions: Grants will not be made for annual campaigns, fund raising events, travel expenses, political or lobbying activities, religious organizations for sacramental/theological purposes, endowments, or publications except those that grow out of research and experiments underwritten by the Foundation. Grants will not be awarded for deficit reduction. Grant requests from agencies that are discriminatory to race, sex, age, national origin, religion, physical or mental handicap, veteran status or sexual orientation will not be considered.
Geographic Focus: Washington
Date(s) Application is Due: Jun 15
Amount of Grant: Up to 3,000 USD
Contact: Gina Anstey, Vice President of Programs and Initiatives; (253) 383-5622; fax (253) 272-8099; gina@gtcf.org or info@gtcf.org
Internet: www.gtcf.org/funding/fund-women-girls/

Sponsor: Greater Tacoma Community Foundation
950 Pacific Avenue, Suite 1100, P.O. Box 1995
Tacoma, WA 98402

Greater Tacoma Community Foundation General Operating Grants 1113

The Greater Tacoma Community Foundation General Operating Grants program is designed to strengthen smaller Pierce County nonprofit organizations. These strengthening grants are general typically operating support funds designed to bolster smaller nonprofits who are addressing critical issues to sustain and build a stronger Pierce County. The goal is to support organizations with clear mission and programmatic alignment, who learn from their constituents, participate in field building activities, assess their impact, and share Greater Tacoma Community Foundation's values. Organizations that have never received a grant from the Community Foundation before or that haven't applied for a grant in the past three years are highly encouraged. The annual deadline for grant submissions is January 18
Requirements: Applicants must meet the following qualifications to be eligible for an operating grant: organizations must be aligned with the Greater Tacoma Community Foundation's values; programming must serve residents of Pierce County, Washington; annual operating budget for Pierce County programming must be $1M or less; organizations must not discriminate on the basis of age, race, color, religion, sexual orientation, physical or mental disabilities, gender or national origin; organizations must be inclusive with clients, volunteers, and staff; nonprofit applicants must have applied to be listed in the Greater Tacoma Community Foundation's nonprofit directory; and applicants must be current on all final reports for grants previously funded from Greater Tacoma Community Foundation.
Restrictions: These grants are designed to support nonprofit organizations and do not support individuals, school-based clubs, or capital projects. However, schools and government agencies may apply.
Geographic Focus: Washington
Date(s) Application is Due: Jan 18
Contact: Gina Anstey, Vice President of Programs and Initiatives; (253) 383-5622; fax (253) 272-8099; gina@gtcf.org or info@gtcf.org
Internet: www.gtcf.org/funding/general-operating-grants/
Sponsor: Greater Tacoma Community Foundation
950 Pacific Avenue, Suite 1100, P.O. Box 1995
Tacoma, WA 98402

Greater Tacoma Community Foundation Spark Grants 1114

Spark grants are micro-grants to individuals designed to bring people-powered ideas and dreams to life in Pierce County, sparking positive social and neighborhood change through the efforts of grass-roots leadership. These awards are a maximum of $1,500 and are intended to create community through projects that bring diverse people together. Spark Grants will be awarded twice each year, though the application period is continuous. The cutoff for each grant review cycle is: the second Friday in March; and the second Friday in October.
Requirements: Individual residents in the Greater Tacoma area are eligible to apply.
Geographic Focus: Washington
Date(s) Application is Due: Mar 9; Oct 12
Amount of Grant: Up to 1,500 USD
Contact: Gina Anstey, Vice President of Programs and Initiatives; (253) 383-5622; fax (253) 272-8099; gina@gtcf.org or info@gtrcf.org
Internet: www.gtcf.org/funding/spark-grants/
Sponsor: Greater Tacoma Community Foundation
950 Pacific Avenue, Suite 1100, P.O. Box 1995
Tacoma, WA 98402

Greater Tacoma Community Foundation Youth Program Grants 1115

The Tacoma area Youth Philanthropy Board (YPB) of the Greater Tacoma Community Foundation funds quality out-of-school time programs throughout Pierce County, Washington, that provide youth opportunities to engage, learn and lead. Through this, the YPB members help support their peers as they map out pathways to success in school and life. The YPB believes that self-esteem, empowerment, and healthy choices are vital elements for youth because these are critical in helping youth navigate complex transitions to adulthood, career and life success. The YPB will support programs that reflect these elements, create opportunities for youth to have leadership roles within programming, and value youth voice and youth feedback by developing a platform where program structure and activities are influenced by youth. The average grant request is $7,500, with the annual application deadline being March 2.
Requirements: Organizations must meet the following qualifications to be eligible for a Youth Philanthropy Board grant: serve Pierce County youth ages 11 to 24 with programming outside of school time; provide opportunities for youth to engage, learn, and lead; be aligned with the Greater Tacoma Community Foundation's values; and not discriminate on the basis of age, race, color, religion, sexual orientation, physical or mental disabilities, gender or national origin and be inclusive with clients, volunteers, and staff
Geographic Focus: Washington
Amount of Grant: Up to 10,000 USD
Contact: Gina Anstey, Vice President of Programs and Initiatives; (253) 383-5622; fax (253) 272-8099; gina@gtcf.org or info@gtrcf.org
Internet: www.gtcf.org/funding/youth-program-grants/
Sponsor: Greater Tacoma Community Foundation
950 Pacific Avenue, Suite 1100, P.O. Box 1995
Tacoma, WA 98402

Green Foundation Human Services Grants 1116

The Foundation's mission is to uncover new opportunities, encourage growth and ultimately effect positive change within those institutions that best reflect the core focus areas and the communities it serves. Within the human services area, the Foundation focuses on institutions that provide hope and support to those least able to help themselves as well as the general community; including children, adolescents, the elderly, the homeless, and families who struggle with domestic abuse.
Requirements: 501(c)3 nonprofits (as per the IRS Service Code of 1986) are eligible. Most grant making is limited to institutions that serve the Los Angeles community; however the Foundation will consider requests beyond this geographic boundary for those institutions with the potential to impact communities statewide or nationally.
Restrictions: The Foundation does not provide funds for: those with net assets or fund balances of less than $100,000; multi-year commitments; annual meetings, conferences, and/or seminars; religious programs; capital campaigns; direct mail campaigns; conduit institutions, unified funds, fiscal agents, or institutions using grant funds from donors to support other institutions or individuals; private foundations; or individuals.
Geographic Focus: All States
Amount of Grant: 1,000 - 150,000 USD
Samples: Esperanza Community Housing, Los Angeles, California, $25,000; Foothill Family Service, Pasadena, California, $25,000; Interfaith Community Services, Escondido, California, $25,000.
Contact: Kylie Wright, Program Director; (626) 793-6200, ext. 1; fax (626) 793-6201; kylies@ligf.org
Elena Hermanson, Program Director; (626) 793-6200, ext. 2; fax (626) 793-6201; elenah@ligf.org
Internet: www.ligf.org/humanservices.php
Sponsor: Green Foundation
225 South Lake Avenue, Suite 1410
Pasadena, CA 91101

Green River Area Community Foundation Grants 1117

The Green River Area Community Foundation (GRAF) was organized in 1993 with a mission of advancing philanthropy by serving the charitable interests of donors, enabling increased charitable giving and improving communities by being a permanent philanthropic resource for current and future needs. Presently, the Foundation is dedicated to enriching the quality of life for all citizens in the counties of Daviess, Hancock, McLean, Ohio, Union and Webster, Kentucky. GRACF serves the charitable interests of donors who have established charitable funds as part of a permanent, collective, philanthropic resource for the current and future needs of the region. Two primary funds are used: the Owensboro-Daviess County Community Fund, established in 1995, and the James D. Ryan Memorial Fund, founded the same year. The Foundation is an affiliate of the Community Foundation of Louisville, a tax-exempt public charity that administers charitable funds created by individuals, businesses and organizations for the betterment of their communities.
Requirements: 501(c)3 organizations serving the Kentucky county residents of Daviess, Hancock, McLean, Ohio, Union and Webster are eligible to apply.
Geographic Focus: Kentucky
Contact: Amy Silvert, Executive Director; (270) 926-1860; amy@greenrivercf.org
Internet: www.cflouisville.org/about/green-river-area-community-foundation/
Sponsor: Green River Area Community Foundation
325 W. Main Street, Suite 1110
Louisville, KY 40202

Greenspun Family Foundation Grants 1118

The Greenspun Family Foundation supports many causes with an emphasis on education, health, children, Jewish issues, and the greater Las Vegas community. Preference is given to requests from the Las Vegas area. There are no application forms or deadlines. Applicants should submit a letter of inquiry. Information about current programs supported is available at the Foundation website.
Geographic Focus: Nevada
Amount of Grant: 50,000 - 2,000,000 USD
Samples: University of Nevada at Las Vegas, Las Vegas, Nevada, $2.2 million, payable over one year; Nevada Cancer Institute, Las Vegas, Nevada, $1,000,000, payable over one year; Clark County Public Education, Las Vegas, Nevada, $50,000, payable over one year.
Contact: Dr. Brian Cram, Director; (702) 259-2323 or (702) 259-4023; fax (702) 259-4019; brian.cram@lasvegassun.com
Internet: www.thegreenspuncorp.com/philanthropy.php
Sponsor: Greenspun Family Foundation
901 North Green Valley Parkway, Suite 210
Henderson, NV 89074

Gregory and Helayne Brown Charitable Foundation Grants 1119

The Gregory and Helayne Brown Charitable Foundation, established in 2000, supports scholarship funds, youth programs, and families. The Foundation's primary fields of interest include: human services; philanthropy and volunteerism; and safety/disaster prevention. For general grants, there are no required application forms or annual deadlines for submission, and initial approach to the Foundation should take the form of a letter describing your overall need and budget. Most recent funding awards have ranged from $1,000 on the low end to a maximum of $30,000.
Requirements: 501(c)3 organizations and institutions of higher education in Michigan are eligible to apply.
Geographic Focus: Michigan
Amount of Grant: 1,000 - 30,000 USD

Samples: University of Michigan Foundation, Ann Arbor, Michigan, $30,000 - for the enhancement of educational opportunities; Saginaw Valley State University Foundation, University Center, Michigan, $10,000 - for the enhancement of educational opportunities; Hidden Harvest, Saginaw, Michigan, $1,000 - to provide food for indigent people.
Contact: Gregory S. Brown, President; (989) 792-6200
Sponsor: Gregory and Helayne Brown Charitable Foundation
3716 White Trillium Drive E
Saginaw, MI 48603-1948

Greygates Foundation Grants   1120

The Greygates Foundation was created in 2001 by J. Ronald Gibbs to provide grants to organizations that serve the needs of children, the elderly, the disabled, or the disadvantaged, and to organizations that promote animal welfare or wildlife preservation. The grant award limit is $3,000, and grants are paid in Canadian dollars. The foundation funds the following types of requests: general operating support, capacity building, program support, equipment, and tuition assistance. Proposals are accepted on a rolling basis. Organizations are asked to take an online eligibility quiz before they apply. Application must be made by email. Guidelines are available for download from the trust's website. Applicants are notified promptly when their proposals are received but should expect to wait three to six months for notification of a decision. Questions may be directed to the foundation's administrator.
Requirements: Though funding may be provided for projects in any country, recipient organizations must be Canadian-registered charities. If an organization does not have such status, the foundation will consider making a grant to a Canadian-registered charity acting as a sponsor for the non-recognized organization. The Greygates Foundation grants are generally awarded to smaller nonprofit organizations, but are not limited to such organizations.
Restrictions: The Foundation does not provide funding to individuals or to organizations operated by or receiving significant support from government sources.
Geographic Focus: All States, All Countries
Amount of Grant: Up to 3,000 CAD
Samples: Orphaned Wildlife Rehabilitation Society, Delta, British Columbia, Canada, $2,000 - general operating support for public education and the rehabilitation and release of injured and orphaned birds; Get Bear Smart Society, Whistler, British Columbia, Canada, $3,000 - general operating support to create an environment in which people and bears can safely and respectfully coexist; The Canadian Committee for the Haifa Foundation, Toronto, Ontario, Canada, $2,000 - for the Netzer Association's music therapy for autistic children programme in Haifa, Israel.
Contact: J. Ronald Gibbs, Administrator; (604) 896-1619; beron@telus.net
Janet Ferriaolo, Grants Manager; (415) 332-0166; jferraiolo@adminitrustllc.com
Internet: www.adminitrustllc.com/the-greygates-foundation/
Sponsor: Greygates Foundation
c/o Adminitrust LLC
Sausalito, CA 94965

Griffin Family Foundation Grants   1121

The Griffin Family Foundation was established in 1998 with the intent of granting gifts to promote education and medical causes, and to honor Anna Margaret Griffin's family members, including her father, Fred, who was a respected physician in the Mexico area. Anna Margaret grew up to become a teacher in Mexico Public Schools for many years. She taught Home Economics to include cooking, sewing, cleaning, household maintenance, and managing a household budget, valuable lessons for any individual. Her father, Fred Griffin, did not come from a wealthy family and, in fact, his early life had been marred by tragedy. When he was two years old, a tornado hit the family farm house killing his entire family. Young Fred was found a half mile away lying in a field and was then raised in Audrain County by his aunt and uncle. Dr. Griffin worked sixty hour weeks, 52 weeks a year tending to the medical needs of the residents of Audrain and Montgomery Counties. Anna Griffin preserved her father's legacy by founding the Griffin Family Foundation to provide funding grants for religious, charitable, scientific and literary purposes for Audrain and Montgomery counties. Since its inception in 1998, the Foundation has awarded grants and scholarships totaling over $1.4 million. Typical awards range up to $10,000, and the application can be found at the website. The annual deadlines for submission are March 15 and August 30.
Requirements: Applicant organizations must be 501(c)3 approved and serve the community of Audrain and Montgomery County, Missouri (although the Foundation sometimes gives outside of its primary geographical region).
Geographic Focus: Missouri
Date(s) Application is Due: Mar 15; Aug 30
Amount of Grant: Up to 10,000 USD
Samples: Agape House of Vandalia, Farber, Missouri - for the purchase of a holding tank, $2,300 (2018); Hannibal Lagrange University, Hannibal, Missouri - support of the scholarship fund, $6,600 (2018); Mexico Area Chamber of Commerce, Mexico, Missouri - for municipal projects, $8,380 (2018).
Contact: Dan K. Erdel, Foundation Manager; (573) 581-5280 or (573) 581-1353; dkerdel@brettanderdel.com
Internet: www.griffinfamilyfoundation.com/
Sponsor: Griffin Family Foundation
100 North Jefferson Street
Mexico, MO 65265-3786

Grifols Community Outreach Grants   1122

At Grifols, the primary mission is to enhance and enrich lives, which extends well beyond the patient communities it serves. Through a robust community outreach program, Grifols helps foster strong, vibrant communities in regions where its employees live and work. Each year, Grifols employees spend countless hours volunteering their time to improve the lives of people in need. Grifols encourages employee participation in community outreach activities by supporting a range of local and national causes through donations, corporate sponsorships and company-wide volunteer initiatives. The Grifols Community Relations program focuses on the following service areas: programs that improve the health of neighbors; science education and workforce development; and civic and community.
Requirements: 501(c)3 tax-exempt organizations in Grifols communities (San Francisco East Bay Area, including Alameda, Contra Costa, and Solano Counties; Los Angeles; Seattle; and Philadelphia) are eligible.
Restrictions: In general, Grifols does not support organizations that do not have 501(c)3 tax status; religious, fraternal, service, or veterans' organizations; civic or cultural organizations that do not serve the areas in which Grifols is located; alumni drives and teacher organizations; memorials; municipal and for-profit hospitals; labor unions; city, municipal, or federal government departments; organizations or causes that do not support the company's commitment to non-discrimination and diversity; projects of national scope or from national organizations not related to health care; matching gifts; individuals, including scholarships (other than those awarded as part of the company-sponsored college scholarship program); travel support; fund-raising activities related to individual sponsorship; and fund-raising dinners other than those for health care or medical research organizations aligned with company research and product interests.
Geographic Focus: California, Pennsylvania, Washington
Amount of Grant: 5,000 - 75,000 USD
Contact: Rebecca Barnes, Community Relations; (919) 316-6590; rebecca.barnes@grifols.com
Internet: www.grifols.com/web/eeuu/community_outreach
Sponsor: Grifols
2410 Lillyvale Avenue
Los Angeles, CA 90032-3514

Grotto Foundation Project Grants   1123

The Grotto Foundation works to improve the education and economic, physical and social well-being of citizens, with a special focus on families and culturally diverse groups. The Foundation funds support agencies and institutions dedicated to improving the quality of parenting and well-being of infants and children from birth to six years of age. The Foundation is further interested in increasing public understanding of American cultural heritage, the cultures of nations and the individual's responsibility to fellow human beings.
Requirements: Detailed applications for Native American grants are available online. Applicants are encouraged to contact the Foundation and discuss their early childhood development to be certain it is appropriate for funding.
Restrictions: Policy precludes grants being awarded for capital fund projects, travel, publication of books or manuscripts, undergraduate research projects, or grants to individuals.
Geographic Focus: Minnesota
Date(s) Application is Due: Jan 15; Mar 15; Jul 15; Nov 15
Amount of Grant: Up to 10,000 USD
Contact: Jennifer Kolde, Grants Manager; (651) 209-8010; fax (651) 209-8014; jkolde@grottofoundation.org
Internet: www.grottofoundation.org
Sponsor: Grotto Foundation
1315 Red Fox Road, Suite 100
Arden Hills, MN 55112

Grundy Foundation Grants   1124

The Grundy Foundation's endowment, which sustains the operations of both the museum and library, also provides grantmaking. Grant support is given to projects that benefit the people and institutions of Pennsylvania. Upon availability, the Board of Trustees generally restricts grantmaking to Bucks County public charities, with special consideration to those of Bristol Borough. Grant applications are awarded primarily for capital projects to serve a wide area rather than a single neighborhood. Grantmaking activities include community development, arts and culture, education, environment, health, and human services. The average grant is $2,500.
Requirements: There are no applications or specific deadlines. The Foundation accepts and reviews written requests for funding throughout the year. In general, organizations having other support for core operating expenses and long-term costs of new projects are given priority. Organizations are encouraged to contact the Foundation prior to submission of a grant application. Prospective grantees may use the forms developed by the Delaware Valley Grant makers, if preferred. At a minimum, each proposal must include: One-page summary with contact name, executive director's name, organization name, address, telephone, email, and fax; project summary; amount requested; and total project budget amount; detailed proposal with mission and history of the organization; complete description of the proposed project; project budget, including other sources of support, with indication of whether support is in hand, pledged, requested, or to be requested; expected sources of support for this project in the future; and expected arrangements for future maintenance and repairs; the organization's financial report of IRS 990 filing for the most recent fiscal year (audited reports are preferred); copy of IRS 501(c)3 letter of determination or proof that the organization is a government agency; a list of officers and directors; a copy of report of the organization's activities over the most recent fiscal year. Proposals can be mailed, faxed or sent electronically (faxes and email versions require prior Foundation approval). Videotaped proposals will not be accepted.
Restrictions: The Foundation does not make grants to nonpublic schools, individuals, religious organizations, or for endowments, loans, research, or political activities.
Geographic Focus: Pennsylvania

Contact: Eugene Williams, Executive Director; (215) 788-5460; fax (215) 788-0915; info@grundyfoundation.com
Internet: www.grundymuseum.org/
Sponsor: Grundy Foundation
680 Radcliffe Street, P.O. Box 701
Bristol, PA 19007

GTECH After School Advantage Grants 1125

The GTECH After School Advantage Program is a national community investment program, which provides non-profit community agencies and public schools with state-of-the-art computer labs. These computer centers are designed to provide inner-city children aged five to 15 with a meaningful, yet fun, learning experience during the critical after-school hours, in a safe environment. This initiative is meant to provide an otherwise unavailable educational experience and bridge the digital divide among at-risk children. By applying its knowledge and expertise to this type of program GTECH hopes to increase children's interest in careers in computers and provide them with the necessary tools to help them become more competitive in school and in today's job market.
Requirements: GTECH donates up to $15,000 in state-of-the-art computers, on-line technology, computer software and volunteer hours to each after-school program in inner-city communities where the Company's offices are located nationwide (see states listed below). Applicants must be a non-profit 501(c)3 community agency or public school. Organizations must serve disadvantaged youth aged five to 15, of diverse backgrounds; must have an existing after-school program in need of a computer lab; and must have staffing and monetary support systems in place to sustain the lab.
Geographic Focus: All States
Amount of Grant: Up to 15,000 USD
Samples: Boys and Girls Club of Lynchburg, Lynchburg, VA; SAFE BASE, Iola, KS; Rochambeau Community Library, Providence, RI.
Contact: Elena Chiaradio, (401) 392-7705; Elena.Chiaradio@gtech.com
Internet: gtechlottery.com/our-commitment/community-involvement/
Sponsor: GTECH Corporation
10 Memorial Boulevard
Providence, RI 02903

GTRCF Boys and Girls Club of Grand Traverse Endowment Grants 1126

The Grand Traverse Regional Community Foundation's Boys and Girls Club of Grand Traverse Endowment provides support for programs and services that are consistent with the mission of the Boys and Girls Clubs of enable all young people, especially those who need U.S. most, to reach their full potential as productive, caring, responsible citizens. This can be achieved by providing a safe place for children to learn and grow; supporting ongoing relationships with caring, adult professionals; providing life-enriching programs and character development experiences; and providing hope and opportunity. Grant applications are accepted on an ongoing basis and reviewed three times each year. The annual deadline for review of applications is October 1.
Requirements: Michigan 501(c)3 tax-exempt organizations in Antrim, Benzie, Grand Traverse, Kalkaska, and Leelanau Counties are eligible to apply.
Geographic Focus: Michigan
Date(s) Application is Due: Oct 1
Amount of Grant: Up to 5,000 USD
Samples: Child and Family Services of Northwest Michigan, Traverse City, Michigan, $1,000 - support for recreational therapy and activities; Eagle Village, Hersey, Michigan, $400 - purchase of weighted blankets for residential homes; Michael's Place, Traverse City, Michigan, $1,000 - general operating support of Robin's Nest.
Contact: Gina Thornbury, Grantmaking and Program Officer; (231) 935-4066; fax (231) 941-0021; gthornbury@gtrcf.org or info@gtrcf.org
Internet: www.gtrcf.org/give/our-funds.html/16/
Sponsor: Grand Traverse Regional Community Foundation
250 East Front Street, Suite 310
Traverse City, MI 49684

GTRCF Elk Rapids Area Community Endowment Grants 1127

The Elk Rapids Area Community Endowment was established in 1996 by an anonymous Elk rapids woman who enjoyed the quality of life in the area. She wished to support, activities, facilities and programs in the Elk Rapids area so that others may enjoy the area as much as she did. Grants awards may support projects that enhance the beauty of the Elk Rapids community, such as landscaping improvements for parks and open spaces; transportation to healthcare for the area residents; or other programs and services that provide public benefit. Grant applications are accepted on an ongoing basis and reviewed three times each year. The annual deadline for review of applications is October 1.
Requirements: Michigan 501(c)3 tax-exempt organizations in Antrim County are eligible to apply.
Geographic Focus: Michigan
Date(s) Application is Due: Oct 1
Amount of Grant: Up to 5,000 USD
Samples: Acme Christian Thrift Store and Food Pantry, Williamsburg, Michigan, $2,000 - support of the personal hygiene program; Elk Rapids Area Historical Society, Elk Rapids, Michigan, $1,500 - support of the student kitchen; Elk Rapids High School, Elk Rapids, Michigan, $2,000 - support of the drama educational program.
Contact: Gina Thornbury, Grantmaking and Program Officer; (231) 935-4066; fax (231) 941-0021; gthornbury@gtrcf.org or info@gtrcf.org
Internet: www.gtrcf.org/give/our-funds.html/40/

Sponsor: Grand Traverse Regional Community Foundation
250 East Front Street, Suite 310
Traverse City, MI 49684

GTRCF Genuine Leelanau Charitable Endowment Grants 1128

Established in 2006 by Genuine Leelanau, many donors have joined together to give to a shared interest of supporting children and families in Leelanau County. Grant awards support integrated arts and other projects that benefit Leelanau County children and families in need. Grant applications are accepted on an ongoing basis and reviewed three times each year. The annual deadline for review of applications is October 1.
Requirements: Michigan 501(c)3 tax-exempt organizations in Leelanau County are eligible to apply.
Geographic Focus: Michigan
Date(s) Application is Due: Oct 1
Amount of Grant: Up to 5,000 USD
Samples: Child and Family Services of Northwest Michigan, Traverse City, Michigan, $1,000 - support of youth services programs; Friendship Community Center, Suttons Bay, Michigan, $1,000 - support of the Project LIFT Teen program.
Contact: Gina Thornbury, Grantmaking and Program Officer; (231) 935-4066; fax (231) 941-0021; gthornbury@gtrcf.org or info@gtrcf.org
Internet: www.gtrcf.org/give/our-funds.html/50/
Sponsor: Grand Traverse Regional Community Foundation
250 East Front Street, Suite 310
Traverse City, MI 49684

GTRCF Grand Traverse Families in Action for Youth Endowment Grants 1129

The Grand Traverse Families in Action, an organization that was committed to serving youth and helping young people avoid substance abuse and violence, made a gift to establish the endowment in 2000. Though no longer an organization, the mission and vision of the organization continues through Grand Traverse Families in Action for Youth Endowment. Grant awards support assisting Traverse City youth in avoiding substance abuse and violence. Grant applications are accepted on an ongoing basis and reviewed three times each year. The annual deadline for review of applications is October 1.
Requirements: Michigan 501(c)3 tax-exempt organizations in Antrim, Benzie, Grand Traverse, Kalkaska, and Leelanau Counties are eligible to apply.
Geographic Focus: Michigan
Date(s) Application is Due: Oct 1
Amount of Grant: Up to 5,000 USD
Samples: Catholic Human Services, Traverse City, Michigan, $4,418 - support of the Grand Traverse County Substance Free Task Force.
Contact: Gina Thornbury, Grantmaking and Program Officer; (231) 935-4066; fax (231) 941-0021; gthornbury@gtrcf.org or info@gtrcf.org
Internet: www.gtrcf.org/give/our-funds.html/63/
Sponsor: Grand Traverse Regional Community Foundation
250 East Front Street, Suite 310
Traverse City, MI 49684

GTRCF Healthy Youth and Healthy Seniors Endowment Grants 1130

The Healthy Youth and Healthy Seniors Endowment was established in compliance with an award from the State of Michigan Tobacco Settlement Partnership. Grant awards support programs that improve the health of youth (birth - 18) and/or seniors (age 55 and older). These opportunities may include, but are not limited to, programs that focus on health and nutrition; family counseling; early childhood development; smoking prevention and cessation; daycare, preschool, and after school care. Programs for healthy youth could include: smoking prevention and cessation and substance abuse; violence and conflict resolution; access to dental care; community alternatives for recreation; and child care. Programs for healthy seniors could include: pharmaceuticals (i.e. access, cost, medication interaction); preventing and managing chronic disease (i.e. cancer, heart, lung, stroke); long term care alternatives (i.e. assisted living, respite care, family caregiver support); mental health and aging (i.e. substance abuse, depression); and workforce and aging (i.e. age discrimination, continuing career opportunities). Grant applications are accepted on an ongoing basis and reviewed three times each year. The annual deadline for review of applications is October 1.
Requirements: Michigan 501(c)3 tax-exempt organizations in Antrim, Benzie, Grand Traverse, Kalkaska, and Leelanau Counties are eligible to apply.
Geographic Focus: Michigan
Date(s) Application is Due: Oct 1
Amount of Grant: Up to 5,000 USD
Samples: Hospice of Michigan, Traverse City, Michigan, $2,530 - support of the Open Access program; Leelanau Children's Center, Leelanau, Michigan, $500 - support for the Children Matter Scholarship program.
Contact: Gina Thornbury, Grantmaking and Program Officer; (231) 935-4066; fax (231) 941-0021; gthornbury@gtrcf.org or info@gtrcf.org
Internet: www.gtrcf.org/give/our-funds.html/73/
Sponsor: Grand Traverse Regional Community Foundation
250 East Front Street, Suite 310
Traverse City, MI 49684

GTRCF Joan Rajkovich McGarry Family Education Endowment Grants 1131

Joan Rajkovich McGarry served the Grand Traverse community - her home - throughout her lifetime, both professionally and as a volunteer. The focus of her service was always to make things better for families. She did that through teaching, advocacy and developing opportunities, both economic and educational. The Joan Rajkovich McGarry Family

Education Endowment supports the continutation and further development of programs and services to support Grand Traverse and Leelanau Counties, related to family consumer science. Grant applications are accepted annually each Fall. Applications for programs and activities focused on nutrition and, in particular, school aged children and obesity issues, will be considered. Priority will be given to proposals that are creative, evidence-based, and linked with MSUE Resources. A Fund Advisory Committee of local residents, familiar with the programs of MSUE and the needs of local families reviews the grant proposals and makes funding recommendations to the Community Foundation Board. Grant applications are accepted on an ongoing basis and reviewed three times each year. The annual deadline for review of applications is October 1.
Requirements: Michigan 501(c)3 tax-exempt organizations in Grand Traverse and Leelanau Counties are eligible to apply.
Geographic Focus: Michigan
Date(s) Application is Due: Oct 1
Amount of Grant: Up to 5,000 USD
Samples: Suttons Bay Public Schools, Suttons Bay, Michigan, $1,200 - support of water bottle refilling station and healthy snacks project.
Contact: Gina Thornbury, Grantmaking and Program Officer; (231) 935-4066; fax (231) 941-0021; gthornbury@gtrcf.org or info@gtrcf.org
Internet: www.gtrcf.org/give/our-funds.html/80/
Sponsor: Grand Traverse Regional Community Foundation
250 East Front Street, Suite 310
Traverse City, MI 49684

GTRCF Traverse City Track Club Endowment Grants 1132
The Traverse City Track Club Endowment was established in 2010 by the Board of the Traverse City Track Club who had a vision for and commitment to the long term ability to support the charitable giving efforts of the Club. Grant awards support programs that promote, support, and encourage running, race-walking and walking as a means to promote health, enhanced fitness, family recreation and competition for all individuals. Activities eligible for funding include: cross country programs, track and field programs, summer camp activities, running and/or walking programs, and charitable giving related to running. The annual deadlines for review of applications are March 1 and October 1.
Requirements: Michigan 501(c)3 tax-exempt organizations in Antrim, Benzie, Grand Traverse, Kalkaska, and Leelanau Counties are eligible to apply.
Geographic Focus: Michigan
Date(s) Application is Due: Mar 1; Oct 1
Amount of Grant: Up to 5,000 USD
Samples: Traverse City Central High School, Traverse City, Michigan, $2,821 - purchase of a new tent for cross country and track teams.
Contact: Gina Thornbury, Grantmaking and Program Officer; (231) 935-4066; fax (231) 941-0021; gthornbury@gtrcf.org or info@gtrcf.org
Internet: www.gtrcf.org/give/our-funds.html/175/
Sponsor: Grand Traverse Regional Community Foundation
250 East Front Street, Suite 310
Traverse City, MI 49684

GTRCF Youth Endowment Grants 1133
The Youth Endowment was one of the first in GTRCFs history, and is part of the story of the beginning of the Community Foundation. It was established through a matching grant opportunity from the W.K. Kellogg Foundation. For every $2 that was raised for other endowments, $1 was matched for the Youth Endowment. Donors came together, contributing $4 million to the brand new Community Foundation, allowing for the creation of a $2 million Youth Endowment. High school students from across the region participate in a Youth Advisory Council Program, learning about philanthropy and recommending grants from the Youth Endowment. The annual deadline for review of applications is October 1.
Requirements: Michigan 501(c)3 tax-exempt organizations in Antrim, Benzie, Grand Traverse, Kalkaska, and Leelanau Counties are eligible to apply.
Geographic Focus: Michigan
Date(s) Application is Due: Oct 1
Amount of Grant: Up to 5,000 USD
Samples: Child and Family Services of Northwest Michigan, Benzonia, Michigan, $1,000 - Crisis Intervention and Suicide Prevention program; Communities in Schools of Northwest Michigan, Kalkasca, Michigan, $750 - support of college campus visits for the Forest area; Father Fred Foundation, Traverse City, Michigan, $2,000 - support of Blessings in a Backpack program.
Contact: Gina Thornbury, Grantmaking and Program Officer; (231) 935-4066; fax (231) 941-0021; gthornbury@gtrcf.org or info@gtrcf.org
Internet: www.gtrcf.org/give/our-funds.html/184/
Sponsor: Grand Traverse Regional Community Foundation
250 East Front Street, Suite 310
Traverse City, MI 49684

Gulf Coast Foundation of Community Operating Grants 1134
Through grants and strategic community initiatives, Gulf Coast invests in the work of effective nonprofit organizations that improve quality of life in our region. The Foundation will award operating grants over $10,000, with grant funds to be expended within one year of approval. Currently, the Foundation has four grant cycles for operating grants, which fund the core operating needs of nonprofits and help make them stronger. This includes staff and training, database and accounting systems, marketing and fundraising operations. Organizations that want to diversify income streams and generate new revenue sources may apply for an operating – earned revenue grant. Examples of successful proposals in this

category include using existing facilities to generate rental income or marketing and selling a packaged program/service to other organizations. Groups that want to reduce operating costs may apply for an operating – efficiency grant. Examples of successful proposals in this category include consolidating services with other nonprofits, implementing new or improved technologies such as databases or financial systems, or "greening" offices.
Requirements: The Foundation will make grants to qualified organizations classified as 501(c)3 tax-exempt public charities by the Internal Revenue Service in the counties of Brevard, Charlotte, Citrus, Collier, DeSoto, Glades, Hardee, Hendry, Hernando, Highlands, Hillsborough, Indian River, Lake, Lee, Manatee, Okeechobee, Orange, Osceola, Pasco, Pinellas, Polk, Sarasota, Seminole, Sumter, and St. Lucie. All operating – earned revenue grant applications must provide realistic revenue estimates that result in a return on investment that exceeds the grant amount. Operating – efficiency grant applications must provide a cost?benefit analysis showing how proposed funding approaches will produce cost savings.
Geographic Focus: Florida
Samples: Special Operations Warrior Foundation, $500,000 - immediate financial assistance for special operations personnel, who have been severely wounded, to have his/her family travel and be bedside; Charlotte Behavioral Health Care, $200,000 - addressing mental health, substance abuse, and related psychosocial needs of veterans and their families.
Contact: Kirstin Fulkerson, Philanthropic Advisor; (941) 486-4600; fax (941) 486-4699; info@gulfcoastcf.org
Internet: www.gulfcoastcf.org/resources.php
Sponsor: Gulf Coast Foundation of Community
601 Tamiami Trail South
Venice, FL 34285

Gulf Coast Foundation of Community Program Grants 1135
Gulf Coast Foundation of Community Program Grants address regional priorities identified through its Environmental Scan. The environmental scanning process looked broadly at trends and conditions in its region through interviews with community leaders and analysis of available data. The findings help Gulf Coast identify the best ways to lift the regional economy and sustain community through our grantmaking. Successful program grant applicants will clearly target important regional challenges or opportunities, provide measurable data that will be the basis for assessing their impact, and share stories of transformation through a variety of social and traditional media. Organizations must have strong leadership and competent staff to execute their program and will significantly leverage their own program dollars so that they have "skin in the game" to maximize their program's impact.
Requirements: The Foundation will make grants to qualified organizations classified as 501(c)3 tax-exempt public charities by the Internal Revenue Service in the counties of Brevard, Charlotte, Citrus, Collier, DeSoto, Glades, Hardee, Hendry, Hernando, Highlands, Hillsborough, Indian River, Lake, Lee, Manatee, Okeechobee, Orange, Osceola, Pasco, Pinellas, Polk, Sarasota, Seminole, Sumter, and St. Lucie.
Geographic Focus: Florida
Contact: Kirstin Fulkerson, Philanthropic Advisor; (941) 486-4600; fax (941) 486-4699; info@gulfcoastcf.org
Internet: www.gulfcoastcf.org/resources.php
Sponsor: Gulf Coast Foundation of Community
601 Tamiami Trail South
Venice, FL 34285

Guy I. Bromley Trust Grants 1136
The Guy I. Bromley Trust was established in 1964 to support and promote quality educational, cultural, human services and health care programming. The Bromley Trust supports organizations that serve the residents of Atchison, Kansas and the Greater Kansas City Metropolitan area. Grants from the Foundation are 1 year in duration. Award amounts typically go up to $70,000.
Requirements: Grant requests for general operating support and program support will be considered. Applicants must have 501(c)3 tax-exempt status and serve the residents of Atchison, Kansas and the Greater Kansas City Metropolitan area. Applications will be submitted online through the Bank of America website. A grant report is required within 1 year of the grant application date, regardless of whether all of the funds have been spent.
Restrictions: Grant requests for capital support will not be considered. The trust does not support requests from individuals, organizations attempting to influence policy through direct lobbying, or any political campaigns.
Geographic Focus: Kansas, Missouri
Date(s) Application is Due: May 31
Amount of Grant: Up to 70,000 USD
Samples: Atchison Hospital Association, Atchison, Kansas, $50,000 - Awarded for CT Scanner (2018); YMCA of Greater Kansas City, North Kansas City, Missouri, $50,000 - Awarded in support of Atchison YMCA's construction of an $8.4 million expansion project (2018); Benedictine College, Atchison, Kansas, $20,000 - Awarded for Benedictine College Engineering, Fuse 1 3-D Printing System (2018).
Contact: Tony Twyman, Senior Philanthropic Client Manager; (816) 292-4342; mo.grantmaking@bankofamerica.com or tony.twyman@bofa.com
Internet: www.bankofamerica.com/philanthropic/foundation/?fnId=132
Sponsor: Guy I. Bromley Trust
Bank of America Na Po Box 831
Dallas, TX 75283-1041

H.A. and Mary K. Chapman Charitable Trust Grants 1137
H. Allen Chapman was born in Colorado in 1919. In 1976, he established the H.A. and Mary K. Chapman Charitable Trust, a perpetual charitable private foundation that

maintains endowments to fund charitable grants to public charities. The trustees and staff that administer the foundation also provide public stewardship through service to charitable organizations and causes. A major charitable focus of H. A. Chapman during his life, and the lives of his philanthropic parents, James A. and Leta Chapman, was education and medical research. Though not limited geographically, most grants and public service are within Oklahoma. Grants to human services and civic and community programs and projects are primarily focused in the area of Tulsa. There are two steps in the process of applying for a grant. The first is a Letter of Inquiry from the applicant. This letter is used to determine if the applicant will be invited to take the second step of submitting a formal Grant Proposal.

Requirements: IRS 501(c)3 non-profits are eligible to apply.

Restrictions: Grant requests for the following purposes are not favored: endowments, except as a limited part of a capital project reserved for maintenance of the facility being constructed; deficit financing and debt retirement; projects or programs for which the Chapman Trusts would be the sole source of financial support; travel, conferences, conventions, group meetings, or seminars; camp programs and other seasonal activities; religious programs of religious organizations; project or program planning; start-up ventures are not excluded, but organizations with a proven strategy and results are preferred; purposes normally funded by taxation or governmental agencies; requests made less than nine months from the declination of a previous request by an applicant, or within nine months of the last payment made on a grant made to an applicant; requests for more than one project.

Geographic Focus: Oklahoma

Amount of Grant: Up to 300,000 USD

Samples: Gilcrease Museum Management, Tulsa, Oklahoma, $250,000 - general operating funds; Tulsa Air and Space Museum, Tulsa, Oklahoma, $35,000 - general operating support; Friends of the Fairgrounds Foundation, Tulsa, Oklahoma, $15,000 - general operating funds.

Contact: Andrea Doyle, Program Officer; (918) 496-7882; fax (918) 496-7887; andie@chapmantrusts.com

Internet: www.chapmantrusts.org/grants_programs.html

Sponsor: H.A. and Mary K. Chapman Charitable Trust

6100 South Yale, Suite 1816

Tulsa, OK 74136

H.B. Fuller Foundation Grants   1138

The Foundation makes grants within the corporate headquarters community, and other key H.B. Fuller communities throughout the world. Within Minnesota, the Foundation recently served as a catalyst in drawing attention to and support for early family literacy programs, and now focuses on science, technology, engineering, and math education. In other communities and cultures, the foundation provides critical grants in education, arts/culture, and health/human services. As an international company, the foundation's commitments extend well beyond the Minnesota state borders. Making significant community grants to schools and non-governmental agencies (NGOs) in locations across Latin America, as well as key community investments in six North American cities where the H.B. Fuller Company has manufacturing operations. Most recently, expanding philanthropic giving into Asia. Minnesota STEM/Youth Leadership grants are reviewed twice a year with proposals accepted March 1 through March 31 and August 1 through August 31. All other North American grants are accepted March 1 through October 1. Individual grants typically range from $5,000 to $15,000.

Requirements: 501(c)3 organizations serving the communities where the company has operations are eligible. Available funding is directed from Fuller's headquarters in St. Paul, Minnesota, and the following North American locations where the company operates: Aurora, Illinois; Grand Rapids, Michigan; Greater Atlanta, Georgia; Paducah, Kentucky; and Vancouver, Washington. Organizations incorporated in countries other than the United States must qualify for tax-exempt status according to U.S. tax regulations and comply with national and/or state charity laws.

Restrictions: Funding is not available for: individuals, including scholarships for individuals; fraternal or veterans' organizations except for programs which are of direct benefit to the broader community; religious groups for religious purposes; political/lobbying organizations; travel; basic or applied research; disease specific organizations; courtesy, goodwill or public service advertisements; fundraiser events or sponsorships; general support of education institutions; capital campaigns; or endowments.

Geographic Focus: Georgia, Illinois, Kentucky, Michigan, Minnesota, Washington, Abkhazia, Afghanistan, Armenia, Azerbaijan, Bahrain, Bangladesh, Bhutan, British Indian Ocean Territory, Brunei, Cambodia, China, Christmas Island, Cocos, Cyprus, Hong Kong, India, Indonesia, Iran, Iraq, Israel, Japan, Jordan, Kazakhstan, Kuwait, Kyrgyz Republic (Kyrgystan), Laos, Lebanon, Macau, Malaysia, Maldives, Mongolia, Myanmar (Burma), Nagorno-Karabakh, Nepal, North Korea, Northern Cyprus, Oman, Pakistan, Palestinian Authority, Philippines, Qatar, Russia, Saudi Arabia, Singapore, South Korea, South Ossetia, Sri Lanka, Syrian Arab Republic, Taiwan, Tajikistan, Thailand, Timor-Lester, Turkey, Turkmenistan, United Arab Emirates, Uzbekistan, Vietnam, Yemen

Date(s) Application is Due: Mar 31; Aug 31; Oct 1

Amount of Grant: 5,000 - 15,000 USD

Contact: Jim Owens, President; (651) 236-5104 or (651) 236-5900

Internet: www.hbfuller.com/About_Us/Community/000110.shtml#P0_0

Sponsor: H.B. Fuller Foundation

1200 Willow Lake Boulevard, P.O. Box 64683

Saint Paul, MN 55164-0683

Haddad Foundation Grants   1139

The Haddad Foundation, established in West Virginia in 2003, offers grant support primarily in Boone and Kanawha counties of West Virginia. Its identified fields of interest include: children and youth services; higher education; and human services. Funding

comes in the form of general operations support. There are no specific application forms or deadlines with which to adhere, and initial approach should be with a letter of application. Amounts range up to $10,000.

Requirements: Applicants must be a 501(c)3 organization that serves the residents of either Boone or Kanawha counties, West Virginia.

Geographic Focus: West Virginia

Amount of Grant: Up to 10,000 USD

Samples: Smile Train, New York, New York, $10,000 - general operating support; University of South Florida, Tampa, Florida, $6,400 - general operating support.

Contact: Susan L. Haddad, Director; (304) 925-5418

Sponsor: Haddad Foundation

707 Virginia Street East, Suite 900

Charleston, WV 25301-2716

HAF Barry F. Phelps Leukemia Fund Grants   1140

Barry Phelps was a lifelong resident of Fortuna, California. After suffering with cancer for four years, he died in 1983 at the age of nine. To assist the family with the tremendous cost of an anticipated bone marrow transplant, the community organized a large fundraiser. Barry died before the event, but encouraged family and friends to continue with children with cancer. The Barry F. Phelps Fund was established by the Phelps family after their son passed away. The fund is intended for young survivors of leukemia residing in the Eel River Valley, and assists families with the tremendous cost of an anticipated bone marrow transplant. Applications are available at the website, and may be submitted at any time.

Requirements: Applications must be made through a qualified sponsor, such as a recognized social service agency, school counselor, or medical provider, who will help administer the funds which are granted.

Geographic Focus: California

Amount of Grant: Up to 2,000 USD

Contact: Amy Jester, Program Manager, Health and Nonprofit Resources; (707) 442-2993; fax (707) 442-9072; amyj@hafoundation.org

Internet: www.hafoundation.org/Health-Grants

Sponsor: Humboldt Area Foundation

373 Indianola Road

Bayside, CA 95524

HAF Community Grants   1141

The Humboldt Area Foundation's Community Grants support a broad spectrum of projects that help build strong communities and foster prosperity in the Redwood, Trinity, and Wild Rivers regions. The Community Grant Program accepts submissions from non-profit charitable or public benefit (federal tax-exempt) organizations, public schools, government agencies, and Native American tribal governments. Applicants whose proposals meet the following criteria will be given funding priority: addresses a pressing community issue; supports a project or issue that is clearly important to the community; involves those who are directly impacted by the effort; and makes use of collaborative relationships and partnerships. If the proposal meets one or more of the following criteria, it is considered even stronger: it includes and supports the interests of historically excluded people and groups; makes a lasting impact; develops a plan for sustainability; integrates and promotes youth leadership skills; and develops the leadership skills and abilities of residents to address issues of importance to them. Applications are accepted on a quarterly basis, and must arrive by the given deadline to be considered for the current grant round. Applicants are notified of their status within ten weeks. The application and a list of previously funded projects are available at the website. Though the maximum award is $20,000, typical grants range from $5,000 to $10,000. The annual deadlines for submission of applications are February 1 and August 1.

Requirements: Applicants must be nonprofit charitable or public benefit organizations, public schools, government agencies, Indian tribal governments or have a qualified fiscal sponsor. Applicants must be located within Humboldt, Del Norte or Trinity counties.

Restrictions: Funding is not available for expenses outside the service area such as travel expenses or schools or groups for trips out of the area, cultural groups going on tour, good will ambassadors, or scholarships and fellowships to other countries. Grants cannot be made for the deferred maintenance or annual operating costs of public institutions, churches, services of special tax districts, government or cemeteries. Grants cannot be made for religious activities or projects that exclusively benefit the members of sectarian or religious organizations. Grants cannot pay for expenses that have already been incurred.

Geographic Focus: California

Date(s) Application is Due: Feb 1; Aug 1

Amount of Grant: Up to 20,000 USD

Contact: Craig Woods, Manager; (707) 442-2993; fax (707) 442-3811; craigw@hafoundation.org

Internet: www.hafoundation.org/Grants-Scholarships/Grants/Apply-for-a-Grant/Nonprofits-Agencies

Sponsor: Humboldt Area Foundation

373 Indianola Road

Bayside, CA 95524

HAF Don and Bettie Albright Endowment Fund Grants   1142

Don Albright grew up in Fresno, California. He enlisted in the Marines, serving as flight engineer on a PBY Catalina, an American flying boat and later an amphibious aircraft. Upon his discharge he worked for the Pacific Gas and Electric Company for more than four decades. Don was a mover and a shaker of the community, serving as past presidents of Eureka Chamber of Commerce, United Way, Humboldt Economic Development and West Coast Alliance, serving on the boards of Humboldt Area Foundation, Humboldt Taxpayers League, City of Eureka Visitors and Convention Bureau, Eureka Historical

Society, Boy Scouts, Ingomar Club, and as a member of Eureka Downtown Rotary, North Coast Vintage Aviation and Marine Corps League. Don and Bettie served together on the first Jazz Festival Committee of Eureka. Don loved woodworking as a hobby. He was a devoted husband, father, grandfather and great-grandfather. Don passed away on March 5, 2008. He and Bettie had a wonderful life together and wanted to share this discretionary fund with others in support of a variety of programs.
Requirements: Applicants must be nonprofit charitable or public benefit organizations, public schools, government agencies, Indian tribal governments or have a qualified fiscal sponsor. Applicants must be located within Humboldt, Del Norte or Trinity counties.
Restrictions: Funding is not available for expenses outside the service area such as travel expenses or schools or groups for trips out of the area, cultural groups going on tour, good will ambassadors, or scholarships and fellowships to other countries. Grants cannot be made for the deferred maintenance or annual operating costs of public institutions, churches, services of special tax districts, government or cemeteries. Grants cannot be made for religious activities or projects that exclusively benefit the members of sectarian or religious organizations. Grants cannot pay for expenses that have already been incurred.
Geographic Focus: California
Contact: Cassandra Wagner, Program Manager; (707) 267-9912 or (707) 442-2993; cassandraw@hafoundation.org
Internet: www.hafoundation.org/Giving/Our-Funds
Sponsor: Humboldt Area Foundation
373 Indianola Road
Bayside, CA 95524

HAF Ian Christopher Mackey Newman Fund Grants   1143
The Ian Christopher Mackey Newman Fund was established by Jennifer Mackey to honor her son, Ian Christopher. The Fund is designed to assist minors who are severely physically handicapped and mentally gifted by helping expose these children to educational and worldly activities that they might not otherwise be able to experience. The Fund provides small grants to assist children under the age of 18 with educationally related travel and adventures, preferably outside Humboldt County. The application and additional information are available at the website.
Requirements: Applicants must be located in Humboldt County, under the age of 18, and physically handicapped.
Geographic Focus: California
Date(s) Application is Due: Dec 15
Amount of Grant: 1,350 USD
Contact: Cassandra Wagner, Grants Program Coordinator; (707) 442-2993, ext. 323; fax (707) 442-3811; cassandraw@hafoundation.org
Internet: www.hafoundation.org/haf/grants/affiliated-grants.html
Sponsor: Humboldt Area Foundation
373 Indianola Road
Bayside, CA 95524

HAF JoAllen K. Twiddy-Wood Memorial Fund Grants   1144
The JoAllen K. Twiddy-Wood Memorial Fund provides dental and vision care for children of low and medium income families in Humboldt, Del Norte, Trinity and Shasta Counties who do not qualify for insurance or who are under-insured. Applications are available at the website and are reviewed at any time.
Requirements: Service providers complete a request form for each child in need of assistance. Checks are payable to the business rendering service. Dental requests for uninsured children or those in pain can be submitted for up to $500. Applicants should submit a pretreatment plan with all dental related applications.
Restrictions: Checks cannot be made payable to the family of the child in need, or the entity sponsoring the application. This fund does not assist with medical or dental travel costs.
Geographic Focus: California
Amount of Grant: Up to 500 USD
Contact: Amy Jester, Program Manager, Health and Nonprofit Resources; (707) 442-2993, ext. 374; fax (707) 442-9072; amyj@hafoundation.org
Internet: www.hafoundation.org/haf/grants/affiliated-grants.html
Sponsor: Humboldt Area Foundation
373 Indianola Road
Bayside, CA 95524

HAF Joe Alexandre Memorial Family Fund Grants   1145
The Alexandre family established the Joe Alexandre Memorial Family Fund to support a variety of charitable purposes in honor and memory of Joe Alexandre. Born on the Azores Island of Terceira on May 14, 1937, Joe came to America with his mother, Eva Rocha, as a twelve year-old boy without knowing a word of English. In 1960 he married Loretta Trutalli. They established and operated the Alexandre Dairy in Ferndale while raising three children, Renae, Blake and Kristina. A progressive dairyman, Joe enjoyed improving his business. He served as a director on the Humboldt Creamery Board and as president of the local Portuguese Association. After he retired, he and three partners purchased a restaurant and card room in Ferndale, "Poppa Joe's." He loved to entertain and have a party and he never met a stranger. "You may be gone from this earth, but you will always be remembered by the friends and family who loved and respected you."
Requirements: Applicants must be nonprofit charitable or public benefit organizations, public schools, government agencies, Indian tribal governments or have a qualified fiscal sponsor. Applicants must be located within Humboldt, Del Norte or Trinity counties.
Restrictions: Funding is not available for expenses outside the service area such as travel expenses or schools or groups for trips out of the area, cultural groups going on tour, good will ambassadors, or scholarships and fellowships to other countries. Grants cannot be made for the deferred maintenance or annual operating costs of public institutions, churches,

services of special tax districts, government or cemeteries. Grants cannot be made for religious activities or projects that exclusively benefit the members of sectarian or religious organizations. Grants cannot pay for expenses that have already been incurred.
Geographic Focus: California
Contact: Cassandra Wagner, Program Manager; (707) 267-9912 or (707) 442-2993; cassandraw@hafoundation.org
Internet: www.hafoundation.org/Grants-Scholarships/Grants/Apply-for-a-Grant/Nonprofits-Agencies
Sponsor: Humboldt Area Foundation
373 Indianola Road
Bayside, CA 95524

HAF Laurence and Elaine Allen Memorial Fund Grants   1146
Laurence N. Allen, a native of Nova Scotia, Canada, moved to Arcata at age six and died in 1992 at the age of 87. He was a member of the Arcata City Council and a long-time Arcata businessman. He was a member of the Arcata Lodge No. 106, Free and Accepted Masons, the Oakland Scottish Rite of Eureka, the Aahmes Redwood Shrine of Eureka, the Arcata Kiwanis Club, the Ingomar Club and the Baywood Country Club. Elaine Allen, born in Arcata, died in 1997, at the age of 92. She attended Arcata schools and graduated from Arcata High School. She was a member of Eastern Star and the First Presbyterian Church of Arcata. This was established as an unrestricted gift to the Foundation, and is used to support a variety of programs.
Requirements: Applicants must be nonprofit charitable or public benefit organizations, public schools, government agencies, Indian tribal governments or have a qualified fiscal sponsor. Applicants must be located within Humboldt, Del Norte or Trinity counties.
Restrictions: Funding is not available for expenses outside the service area such as travel expenses or schools or groups for trips out of the area, cultural groups going on tour, good will ambassadors, or scholarships and fellowships to other countries. Grants cannot be made for the deferred maintenance or annual operating costs of public institutions, churches, services of special tax districts, government or cemeteries. Grants cannot be made for religious activities or projects that exclusively benefit the members of sectarian or religious organizations. Grants cannot pay for expenses that have already been incurred.
Geographic Focus: California
Contact: Cassandra Wagner, Program Manager; (707) 267-9912 or (707) 442-2993; cassandraw@hafoundation.org
Internet: www.hafoundation.org/Grants-Scholarships/Grants/Apply-for-a-Grant/Nonprofits-Agencies
Sponsor: Humboldt Area Foundation
373 Indianola Road
Bayside, CA 95524

HAF Mada Huggins Caldwell Fund Grants   1147
The Mada Huggins Caldwell Fund Grants were established to assist youth between the ages of 10 and 18 who have been affected by violent crime. The Fund is to be used to help youth attend Christian activities, including summer camps and other healing activities. The Fund was created by JoAnn Caldwell Sapper for her mother, Mada Huggins Caldwell. The application and additional information are available at the website.
Requirements: Applicants must be nonprofit charitable or public benefit (federal tax exempt) organizations, public schools, government agencies, Indian tribal governments in Humboldt County, or have a qualified fiscal sponsor.
Restrictions: Grants are not made for the deferred maintenance or annual operating costs of public institutions, churches, and services of special tax districts, government or cemeteries. Funding is not available for expenses that have already been incurred.
Geographic Focus: California
Date(s) Application is Due: Apr 13
Amount of Grant: 400 USD
Contact: Cassandra Wagner, Grants Program Coordinator; (707) 442-2993, ext. 323; fax (707) 442-3811; cassandraw@hafoundation.org
Internet: www.hafoundation.org/haf/grants/affiliated-grants.html
Sponsor: Humboldt Area Foundation
373 Indianola Road
Bayside, CA 95524

HAF Native Cultures Fund Grants   1148
Initiated and led by Native Peoples, the Native Culture Fund supports Native arts, cultural revitalization and cultural transmission between generations. The Fund has awarded nearly $1 million to California Native American artists and cultural stewards in support of over 190 community projects. Grants and regional gatherings focus on methods of building greater cultural participation in communities. The service area includes northern and central California. Eligible counties with specific areas are located on a map at the website. Applicants may contact the Foundation for additional information.
Requirements: Eligible areas include urban and rural communities of California from the Tolowa peoples near the Oregon border, inland to the western Nevada border, and south to the Chumash peoples of the Santa Barbara area.
Geographic Focus: California
Contact: Chag Lowry, Program Manager for Native Cultures Fund; (707) 442-2993, ext. 321; fax (707) 442-9072; chagl@hafoundation.org
Internet: www.hafoundation.org/haf/grants/haf-grants.html
Sponsor: Humboldt Area Foundation
373 Indianola Road
Bayside, CA 95524

HAF Phyllis Nilsen Leal Memorial Fund Grants 1149

Louis Leal established this fund in honor of his wife, Phyllis Nilsen Leal. In a letter from 1987, Louis stated: "Having endured many forms of cancer treatments, she (Phyllis) was quite concerned to see the many younger people-children from teens and much younger, undergoing treatment for cancer. I am sure that she would be pleased to have the income from this fund go to helping these youngsters while they are undergoing treatment. Something to help ease their trauma during this period. Maybe buy a piece of equipment for their use. A wheelchair? Possibly to pay for a tutor while at home convalescing." The Memorial Fund provides items to lift the spirits of children receiving cancer treatment or other illnesses. Items may be a piece of equipment, a tutor, books, or toys. Funding ranges up to a maximum of $2,000 per person per fiscal year. There are no annual deadlines. Applications may be submitted at any time and are available at the website.

Requirements: Applications must be made through a qualifying sponsor, such as a recognized service agency, school counselor, or medical provider. This sponsor will help administer whatever funds are granted.

Geographic Focus: California

Amount of Grant: Up to 2,000 USD

Contact: Elena Ketz, Grants & Scholarships Coordinator; (707) 267-9920; fax (707) 422-9072; elenak@hafoundation.org

Internet: www.hafoundation.org/Health-Grants

Sponsor: Humboldt Area Foundation

373 Indianola Road

Bayside, CA 95524

HAF Southern Humboldt Grants 1150

Humboldt Area Foundation's Field of Interest Grant Program was created to connect donors with community projects in their specific areas of interest. The program brings together a collection of funds that focus on specific populations, geographical areas and/or causes. Field of Interest grants are available September 1 through November 1, with notification by December 17. Southern Humboldt Grants may be used for charitable purposes in the Southern Humboldt area. This area is defined as the area that spans from the confluence of the South Fork and Main Fork of the Eel River, to the Mendocino county line at the south, to the Trinity county line on the east, and to the ocean, including Honeydew and Pretolia to the west. Funding varies by the particular source. Applicants should apply specifically to the source that best meets their project needs, and may apply individually to each fund. The application and a list of previously funded projects are available at the website.

Requirements: Applicants to all funds must be nonprofit charitable or public benefit (federal tax exempt) organizations, public schools, government agencies, Indian tribal governments, or have a qualified fiscal sponsor.

Restrictions: Funding is not available for deferred maintenance or annual operating costs of public institutions, churches, or services of special tax districts, government, or cemeteries. Grant will not be made for religious activities or projects that exclusively benefit the members of sectarian or religious organizations. Expenses already incurred are not eligible.

Geographic Focus: California

Date(s) Application is Due: Nov 1

Amount of Grant: 1,000 - 15,000 USD

Contact: Cassandra Wagner, Grants Program Coordinator; (707) 442-2993, ext. 323; fax (707) 442-3811; cassandraw@hafoundation.org

Internet: www.hafoundation.org/haf/grants/haf-grants.html

Sponsor: Humboldt Area Foundation

373 Indianola Road

Bayside, CA 95524

Hahl Proctor Charitable Trust Grants 1151

Before moving to Midland, Hahl Proctor studied voice in a Chicago school of music. Although very active in the ranching industry, she continued to pursue her music interests through her church and other civic organizations. She was an attractive, popular, generous woman who loved to entertain. This trust was established under her will to provide a continuous source of financial assistance to worthwhile charities. The Hahl Proctor Charitable Trust focuses on charitable organizations dedicated to children and families, arts and education. Award amounts typically range between $2,000 and $70,000.

Requirements: Applicants must have 501(c)3 tax-exempt status and serve residents of the Permian Basin Area. Applications will be submitted online through the Bank of America website. A grant report is required within 1 year of the grant application date, regardless of whether all of the funds have been spent.

Restrictions: The trust does not support requests from individuals, organizations attempting to influence policy through direct lobbying, or any political campaigns.

Geographic Focus: Texas

Date(s) Application is Due: May 15

Amount of Grant: 2,000 - 70,000 USD

Samples: Midland Children's Rehabilitation Center, Midland, Texas, $40,000 - Awarded for Equine Therapy (Hippotherapy/Therapeutic Riding) Program Support (2019); Casa de Amigos of Midland Texas Inc., Midland, Texas, $35,000 - Awarded for General Operations of the Organization (2019); West Texas Food Bank, Odessa, Texas, $20,000 - Awarded for Food Pantries in MISD junior high schools (2019).

Contact: Kelly Garlock, Philanthropic Client Manager; (800) 357-7094; tx.philanthropic@bankofamerica.com or tx.philanthropic@ustrust.com

Internet: www.bankofamerica.com/philanthropic/foundation/?fnId=21

Sponsor: Hahl Proctor Charitable Trust

500 West 7th Street, 15th Floor, TX1-497-15-08

Fort Worth, TX 76102-4700

Hall-Perrine Foundation Grants 1152

The Hall-Perrine Foundation Grants funds charitable projects for nonprofit tax-exempt organizations that benefit the Linn County, Iowa community. The Foundation screens grant applications, and those meeting the established criteria are presented to the Board of Directors. The Board reviews proposals approximately four times a year. After a decision has been reached, the organization is notified in writing of whether they have been approved for funding.

Requirements: Potential grantees should first make a preliminary inquiry to determine the Foundation's interest in their request. This communication should briefly describe the background and purposes of the organization and outline the proposed project and its goals. If the Foundation is interested, a grant application will be given to the applicant to be completed in order that the proposal may be properly evaluated. Information requested includes: a description of the organization, including its legal name, history, purposes, and activities; a list of members of the governing board; a clear and detailed description of the purpose for which the grant is requested and the goals to be achieved; the total cost of the project and amount requested with a detailed budget; a list of current and potential sources of financial support; a copy of the organization's most recent audited financial statement or the last IRS Form 990 (income tax return of organization exempt from income tax); and a copy of the IRS determination letter indicating 501(x)3 tax-exempt status.

Geographic Focus: Iowa

Contact: Kristin Novak, Program Officer; (319) 362-9079; fax (319) 362-7220; kristin@hallperrine.org

Internet: www.hallperrine.org/

Sponsor: Hall-Perrine Foundation

115 Third Street SE, Suite 803

Cedar Rapids, IA 52401-1222

Hampton Roads Community Foundation Abused People Grants 1153

The Foundation's mission is to inspire philanthropy and transform the quality of life in southeastern Virginia. Abused People Grants support organizations providing services to abused children and spouses with a special interest in residential facilities for children. Funding is provided by the Sue Cook Winfrey Memorial Fund. The annual deadline for online applications is October 1. Applicants from the Eastern Shore of Virginia should speak with a Program Officer before submitting a proposal. Grants typically range from $5,000 to $200,000.

Requirements: Nonprofit organizations serving residents of south Hampton Roads (Chesapeake, Franklin, Norfolk, Portsmouth, Suffolk, Virginia Beach and Isle of Wight County) and the Eastern Shore of Virginia are eligible.

Geographic Focus: Virginia

Date(s) Application is Due: Oct 1

Amount of Grant: 5,000 - 200,000 USD

Contact: Linda M. Rice, Vice President of Grantmaking; (757) 622-7951; fax (757) 622-1751; lrice@hamptonroadscf.org or grants@hamptonroadscf.org

Internet: www.hamptonroadscf.org/nonprofits/specialInterestGrants.html

Sponsor: Hampton Roads Community Foundation

101 W. Main Street, Suite 4500

Norfolk, VA 23510

Hampton Roads Community Foundation Arts and Culture Grants 1154

The Foundation's mission is to inspire philanthropy and transform the quality of life in southeastern Virginia. Arts and Culture grants support programs offering hands-on arts and cultural experiences for area children. The goal is to help the educational, social or emotional well-being of youth through arts and culture. Programs should be available to all area youth regardless of ability to pay. They should strive to increase participation of youth from economically disadvantaged backgrounds. Applicants should offer meaningful arts and cultural experiences that engage area youth in hands-on activities such as: learning to play a musical instrument; gaining skills in painting, photography or another art medium; writing poetry or other literature; or participating in visual or performing arts. Proposals for program funding must be able to articulate: the program's fit with the Foundation's stated priorities; the program's desired outcomes; and the organization's plan for measuring program effectiveness in reaching outcomes. The annual deadline for online submissions is April 1. Typical awards range from $25,000 to $200,000.

Requirements: Nonprofit organizations serving residents of south Hampton Roads (Chesapeake, Franklin, Norfolk, Portsmouth, Suffolk, Virginia Beach and Isle of Wight County) and the Eastern Shore of Virginia are eligible. Funding is expected to support arts experiences that are encouraged and accessible for all youth. Proposals must be able to articulate the program's fit with the Foundation's stated priorities; the program's desired outcomes; and the plan for measuring the program's effectiveness in reaching outcomes.

Restrictions: Funding is generally not available for: individuals; fundraising events (such as tickets, raffles, auctions or tournaments), annual fundraising appeals or agency celebrations; ongoing operating support; capital projects and facilities and equipment upgrades that can be considered routine maintenance or replacements; houses of worship unless applying for the Nightingale Fund for faith community nursing or the E.K. Sloane Piano Fund; religious activities (organizations and activities that require religious participation); political or fraternal organizations; endowment building; existing obligations, debts/liabilities or costs that the agency has already incurred; scholarly research; scholarships, camper fees, fellowships or travel; passenger vans for transporting youth; national or international organizations or purposes; hospitals and similar health-care facilities unless applying for a Special Interest Grant; projects or services normally considered the responsibility of government; private primary or secondary schools, daycare facilities or academies other than those whose primary purpose is for students with special needs; and capital campaign requests exceeding 5% of campaigns valued at $1 million or more.

Geographic Focus: Virginia

Date(s) Application is Due: Apr 1
Amount of Grant: 25,000 - 200,000 USD
Samples: Mosaic Steel Orchestra, Norfolk, Virginia, $100,000 - over three years to expand a steel drum program that provides musical training to low-income youth in area cities.
Contact: Linda M. Rice, Vice President of Grantmaking; (757) 622-7951; fax (757) 622-1751; lrice@hamptonroadscf.org or grants@hamptonroadscf.org
Internet: www.hamptonroadscf.org/nonprofits/communityGrants-Arts.html
Sponsor: Hampton Roads Community Foundation
101 W. Main Street, Suite 4500
Norfolk, VA 23510

Hampton Roads Community Foundation Community Leadership   **1155**
   Partners Grants
The Hampton Roads Community Foundation's mission is to inspire philanthropy and transform the quality of life in southeastern Virginia. Community Leadership Partners are a group of regional community leaders who pool their resources and set grant priorities each year. Currently, the focus is positively impacting the academic achievement of children from birth through middle-school ages living in low- or moderate-income families in South Hampton Roads. The focus of the grants varies each year. The annual deadline for application submission is May 20. Grant awards typically range from $5,000 to $20,000.
Requirements: Nonprofit organizations serving residents of south Hampton Roads (Chesapeake, Franklin, Norfolk, Portsmouth, Suffolk, Virginia Beach and Isle of Wight County) and the Eastern Shore of Virginia are eligible.
Geographic Focus: Virginia
Date(s) Application is Due: May 20
Amount of Grant: 5,000 - 20,000 USD
Samples: Academy of Music, Norfolk, Virginia, $5,000 - to develop a strings program for third, fourth and fifth graders at Park Place School; Joy Ministries, Virginia Beach, Virginia, $15,000 - to support a reading camp and after-school tutoring and mentoring program for children from low-income neighborhoods in Chesapeake, Norfolk and Virginia Beach; More 2 Give, Norfolk, Virginia, $15,000 - for the Young Ladies, Young Men after-school leadership program for middle-school students living in low- to mid-income neighborhoods.
Contact: Linda M. Rice, Vice President of Grantmaking; (757) 622-7951; fax (757) 622-1751; lrice@hamptonroadscf.org or grants@hamptonroadscf.org
Internet: www.hamptonroadscf.org/donors/communityleadershippartners.html
Sponsor: Hampton Roads Community Foundation
101 W. Main Street, Suite 4500
Norfolk, VA 23510

Hampton Roads Community Foundation Developmental Disabilities Grants   **1156**
The Foundation's mission is to inspire philanthropy and transform the quality of life in southeastern Virginia. Developmental Disabilities Grants are funded by the Laura Turner Fund and the Jennifer Lynn Gray Fund to support organizations and programs that help people with disabilities live better lives. The annual deadline for online applications is October 1. Applicants from the Eastern Shore of Virginia should speak with a Program Officer before submitting a proposal. Awards typically range from $1,000 to $2,000.
Requirements: Nonprofit organizations serving residents of south Hampton Roads (Chesapeake, Franklin, Norfolk, Portsmouth, Suffolk, Virginia Beach and Isle of Wight County) and the Eastern Shore of Virginia are eligible.
Geographic Focus: Virginia
Date(s) Application is Due: Oct 1
Amount of Grant: 1,000 - 2,000 USD
Contact: Linda M. Rice, Vice President of Grantmaking; (757) 622-7951; fax (757) 622-1751; lrice@hamptonroadscf.org or grants@hamptonroadscf.org
Internet: www.hamptonroadscf.org/nonprofits/specialInterestGrants.html
Sponsor: Hampton Roads Community Foundation
101 W. Main Street, Suite 4500
Norfolk, VA 23510

Hampton Roads Community Foundation Education Grants   **1157**
The Foundation's mission is to inspire philanthropy and transform the quality of life in southeastern Virginia. Education Grants seek to improve educational achievement of underperforming students and to promote economic growth by providing opportunities for all students to excel and meet current and future regional workforce demands. Support is provided in the following areas: projects that are proven successful at increasing the likelihood that students from economically disadvantaged backgrounds earn advanced or standard diplomas within four years of entering high school; programs that are proven successful in helping students transition from high school into post-secondary education; and projects that improve kindergarten readiness. The annual deadline for online applications is April 1. Applicants from the Eastern Shore of Virginia should speak with a Program Officer before submitting a proposal.
Requirements: Nonprofit organizations serving residents of south Hampton Roads (Chesapeake, Franklin, Norfolk, Portsmouth, Suffolk, Virginia Beach and Isle of Wight County) and the Eastern Shore of Virginia are eligible. Grants are awarded to nonprofit organizations working in support of or in partnership with the public school system. The Foundation is unable to consider requests to support public school activities directly even if through an education foundation associated with the school system.
Restrictions: Funding is generally not available for: individuals; fundraising events (such as tickets, raffles, auctions or tournaments), annual fundraising appeals or agency celebrations; ongoing operating support; capital projects and facilities and equipment upgrades that can be considered routine maintenance or replacements; houses of worship unless applying for

the Nightingale Fund for faith community nursing or the E.K. Sloane Piano Fund; religious activities (organizations/activities that require religious participation); political or fraternal organizations; endowment building; existing obligations, debts/liabilities or costs that the agency has already incurred; scholarly research; scholarships, camper fees, fellowships or travel; passenger vans for transporting youth; national or international organizations or purposes; hospitals and similar health-care facilities unless applying for a Special Interest Grant; projects or services normally considered the responsibility of government; private primary or secondary schools, daycare facilities or academies other than those whose primary purpose is for students with special needs; and capital campaign requests exceeding 5% of campaigns valued at $1 million or more.
Geographic Focus: Virginia
Date(s) Application is Due: Apr 1
Amount of Grant: 100,000 - 300,000 USD
Samples: ACCESS College Foundation, Norfolk, Virginia, $500,000 - over five years to expand three programs in South Hampton Roads that prepare public school students to succeed in college; ForKids, Norfolk, Virginia, $200,000 - over three years for a pilot program to help homeless children in two South Hampton Roads public elementary schools; Suffolk Educational Foundation, Suffolk, Virginia, $148,000 - over three years to bring the Book Buddies program to elementary schools in Suffolk.
Contact: Linda M. Rice, Vice President of Grantmaking; (757) 622-7951; fax (757) 622-1751; lrice@hamptonroadscf.org or grants@hamptonroadscf.org
Internet: www.hamptonroadscf.org/nonprofits/communityGrants-Education.html
Sponsor: Hampton Roads Community Foundation
101 W. Main Street, Suite 4500
Norfolk, VA 23510

Hampton Roads Community Foundation Environment Grants   **1158**
The Foundation's mission is to inspire philanthropy and transform the quality of life in southeastern Virginia. The Foundation believes training youth to be good environmental stewards is critical to improving the region's natural environment now and in the future. Community Grants for the Environment focus on supporting innovative, sustained programs for middle and high school-aged students. The Foundation believes training youth to be good environmental stewards is critical to improving the region's natural environment now and in the future. It supports programs that provide: hands-on outdoor experiences; education on environmental issues; and opportunities for a group to develop and implement an action plan around a specific environmental issue. Proposals for program funding must be able to measure the program's impact on the pro-environmental behaviors of the youth it serves. Such proposals must be able to articulate: the program fit with the Foundation's stated priorities; the program's desired outcomes; and the organization's plan for measuring program effectiveness in reaching outcomes. Applicants from the Eastern Shore of Virginia should speak with a Program Officer before submitting a proposal. The annual deadline for submission of online applications is January 15.
Requirements: Nonprofit organizations serving residents of south Hampton Roads (Chesapeake, Franklin, Norfolk, Portsmouth, Suffolk, Virginia Beach and Isle of Wight County) and the Eastern Shore of Virginia are eligible. Proposals for program funding must be able to measure the program's impact on the pro-environmental behaviors of the youth it serves.
Restrictions: Funding is generally not available for: individuals; fundraising events (such as tickets, raffles, auctions or tournaments), annual fundraising appeals or agency celebrations; ongoing operating support; capital projects and facilities and equipment upgrades that can be considered routine maintenance or replacements; houses of worship unless applying for the Nightingale Fund for faith community nursing or the E.K. Sloane Piano Fund; religious activities (organizations and activities that require religious participation); political or fraternal organizations; endowment building; existing obligations, debts/liabilities or costs that the agency has already incurred; scholarly research; scholarships, camper fees, fellowships or travel; passenger vans for transporting youth; national or international organizations or purposes; hospitals and similar health-care facilities unless applying for a Special Interest Grant; projects or services normally considered the responsibility of government; private primary or secondary schools, daycare facilities or academies other than those whose primary purpose is for students with special needs; and capital campaign requests exceeding 5% of campaigns valued at $1 million or more.
Geographic Focus: Virginia
Date(s) Application is Due: Jan 15
Amount of Grant: 25,000 - 500,000 USD
Samples: Elizabeth River Project, Portsmouth, Virginia, $100,000 - support for adding a classroom, outdoor wetland learning lab, handicap-accessible canoe and kayak launch, a natural playground and expanded parking; Virginia Gentlemen Foundation, Virginia Beach, Virginia, $250,000 - over two years to help build the 20-acre JT Camp Grom.
Contact: Linda M. Rice, Vice President of Grantmaking; (757) 622-7951; fax (757) 622-1751; lrice@hamptonroadscf.org or grants@hamptonroadscf.org
Internet: www.hamptonroadscf.org/nonprofits/communityGrants-Environment.html
Sponsor: Hampton Roads Community Foundation
101 W. Main Street, Suite 4500
Norfolk, VA 23510

Hampton Roads Community Foundation Nonprofit Facilities   **1159**
   Improvement Grants
The Foundation's mission is to inspire philanthropy and transform the quality of life in southeastern Virginia. Nonprofit Facilities Improvement Grants focus on supporting major capital projects and capital campaigns that are transformative for the organization and the communities served. The Foundation seeks projects that will reduce building operating costs over the long term and minimize the negative environmental impacts associated with construction and operation. "Green" building practices that can reduce heating and

cooling costs, save water, and reduce pollution are encouraged. Strong preference is given to proposals that incorporate these building practices. The annual deadline for applications is January 15. Applicants from the Eastern Shore of Virginia should speak with a Program Officer before submitting a proposal.

Requirements: Nonprofit organizations serving residents of south Hampton Roads (Chesapeake, Franklin, Norfolk, Portsmouth, Suffolk, Virginia Beach and Isle of Wight County) and the Eastern Shore of Virginia are eligible. Applicant organizations should support one of the areas of Foundation work: arts and culture; education; environment; and health and human services.

Restrictions: Funding is generally not available for: individuals; fundraising events (such as tickets, raffles, auctions or tournaments), annual fundraising appeals or agency celebrations; ongoing operating support; capital projects and facilities and equipment upgrades that can be considered routine maintenance or replacements; houses of worship unless applying for the Nightingale Fund for faith community nursing or the E.K. Sloane Piano Fund; religious activities (organizations and activities that require religious participation); political or fraternal organizations; endowment building; existing obligations, debts/liabilities or costs that the agency has already incurred; scholarly research; scholarships, camper fees, fellowships or travel; passenger vans for transporting youth; national or international organizations or purposes; hospitals and similar health-care facilities unless applying for a Special Interest Grant; projects or services normally considered the responsibility of government; private primary or secondary schools, daycare facilities or academies other than those whose primary purpose is for students with special needs; and capital campaign requests exceeding 5% of campaigns valued at $1 million or more.

Geographic Focus: Virginia
Date(s) Application is Due: Jan 15
Amount of Grant: 100,000 - 500,000 USD
Samples: Virginia Arts Festival, Norfolk, Virginia, $500,000 - over five years to add a production and storage facility and outdoor lighting for the regional performing arts festival; Virginia Wesleyan College, Norfolk, Virginia, $350,000 - over three years to help build Goode Hall, an academic building focused on the arts.
Contact: Linda M. Rice, Vice President of Grantmaking; (757) 622-7951; fax (757) 622-1751; lrice@hamptonroadscf.org or grants@hamptonroadscf.org
Internet: www.hamptonroadscf.org/nonprofits/communityGrants-NonprofitFac.html
Sponsor: Hampton Roads Community Foundation
101 W. Main Street, Suite 4500
Norfolk, VA 23510

Hampton Roads Community Foundation Youth Baseball and Softball Grants 1160

The Hampton Roads Community Foundation's mission is to inspire philanthropy and transform the quality of life in southeastern Virginia. The Dal Paull Fund was created in 2005 to provide grants for youth baseball and softball programs in Hampton Roads. Funding is provided for equipment, uniforms, and capital improvements. The annual deadline for receiving applications is February 15. All applicants will be notified by April 1 of the results of their requests. Grants ranging from $500 to $2,500 are awarded.

Requirements: Nonprofit organizations serving residents of south Hampton Roads (Chesapeake, Franklin, Norfolk, Portsmouth, Suffolk, Virginia Beach and Isle of Wight County) and the Eastern Shore of Virginia are eligible.
Geographic Focus: Virginia
Date(s) Application is Due: Feb 15
Amount of Grant: 500 - 2,500 USD
Contact: Linda M. Rice, Vice President of Grantmaking; (757) 627-9686; fax (757) 622-1751; lrice@hamptonroadscf.org or yourpaldal@cox.net
Internet: www.hamptonroadscf.org/nonprofits/dalPaullGrants.html
Sponsor: Hampton Roads Community Foundation
101 W. Main Street, Suite 4500
Norfolk, VA 23510

Hancock County Community Foundation - Field of Interest Grants 1161

Field of Interest Grants are offered to organizations in Hancock County that present programs in one of the following areas: addictions and/or substance abuse education and treatment; arts and culture; Hanson Family Endowment Fund; Kingery Friends of Domestic Animals; Lifelong Learning; and Prevent Child Abuse. Successful applications will: document the program's relevance to the organization's mission, as well as the need in Hancock County for the program; show that the organization has a past record of being financially stable, viable, and able to sustain past the grant's time frame; operate effective programs that benefit Hancock County and its residents; show strong management by organization's Board of Directors and executive staff. Detailed guidelines and the application are available at the website.

Requirements: Organizations must be a certified nonprofit with a physical location in Hancock County in order to apply for any grants. Organizations may apply for funding up to the amount available, but must be in good standing with HCCF.
Restrictions: Organizations are only eligible to receive one Field of Interest Grant. Religious organizations may apply, but only for general community programs. No grants will be made specifically for religious purposes.
Geographic Focus: Indiana
Date(s) Application is Due: Aug 3
Amount of Grant: Up to 25,000 USD
Contact: Alyse Vail, Program Director; (317) 462-8870, ext. 226; fax (317) 467-3330; avail@hccf.cc
Internet: www.hccf.cc/GrantTypes.aspx
Sponsor: Hancock County Community Foundation
312 Main Street
Greenfield, IN 46140

Hank Aaron Chasing the Dream Foundation Grants 1162

Hank Aaron Chasing The Dream Foundation, Inc. (the Foundation) is a nonprofit charitable organization incorporated in February 1995 to provide financial assistance to under-privileged children and children of low-income families to encourage excellence and to help selected children reach otherwise unattainable goals. Generally, financial assistance is provided for educational and self-improvement activities. The Foundation's principal means of support is from corporate and individual donations. There are no specific deadlines with which to adhere, and applicants should contact the office directly.

Geographic Focus: All States
Amount of Grant: Up to 60,000 USD
Samples: Aviation Career Enrichment, Atlanta, Georgia, $18,000; Ballethnic Dance Company, East Point, Georgia, $6,000; Women in Golf Foundation, Stone Mountain, Georgia, $57,935.
Contact: Linda Gulley, Director; (404) 614-2388; lwgulley@bellsouth.net
Sponsor: Hank Aaron Chasing the Dream Foundation
Turner Field, 755 Hank Aaron Drive
Atlanta, GA 30315-1120

Hannaford Charitable Foundation Grants 1163

The Foundation awards grants to nonprofit organizations in its areas of interest, including health and welfare, educational institutions, civic and cultural organizations, and other local charitable organizations. Types of support include capital campaigns, scholarship funds, and exchange programs. There are no application forms or deadlines. Preference for funding is given to organizations or programs that involve Hannaford associates, are located in Hannaford's marketing area, and have the potential to provide ongoing services for their customers. Small to medium requests are reviewed monthly. Allow three to four months for a response to larger requests ($50,00 or more), as these are reviewed quarterly. Large grants are usually reserved for capital drives by organizations with strong community-impact potential.

Requirements: To apply, the organization or program must: have an active and responsible board of trustees; exhibit ethical publicity methods and solicitation of funds; provide for an appropriate audit to reveal income and disbursements in reasonable detail; demonstrate long-term financial viability; be tax-exempt as described in both sections 501(c)3 and 509(a)1, 509(a)3, or 509(a)3 of the Internal Revenue Code. In addition to a letter of inquiry sent to the Foundation, organizations should also send ten copies of the following information: name, address and telephone number of your organization; contact person and title; amount requested; population and geographic area served; a two- or three-sentence mission statement of your organization, with a brief description of its history; a two- or three-page description of the specific project or program for which you are seeking funding; a list of current and potential funding sources; and a recent statement of revenues and expenses. They should also send one set of the following information: a copy of the organization's tax exemption letter, indicating both sections 501(c)3 and 509(1) status; most recent Form 990 return; and a letter attesting that the organization's tax-exempt status is current.
Restrictions: The Foundation does not offer support for the following: individuals; tax-supported institutions; institutions that, by virtue of their charters, programs or policies, are open to a relatively small or restricted segment of the public; operations of veterans, fraternal or religious organizations, except those that make their services fully available to the community on a nonsectarian basis; program advertising; operating expenses; scholarship programs outside of the Foundation's own; and organizations or events outside of the Foundation's marketing area.
Geographic Focus: Maine, Massachusetts, New Hampshire, New York, Vermont
Contact: Grants Administrator; (507) 931-1682
Internet: www.hannaford.com/content.
jsp?pageName=charitableFoundation&leftNavArea=AboutLeftNav
Sponsor: Hannaford Charitable Foundation
P.O. Box 1000
Portland, ME 04104

Hannaford Supermarkets Community Giving 1164

Hannaford Supermarkets plays an active role in improving the quality of life in the communities it serves throughout the states of Maine, New Hampshire, Massachusetts, Vermont, and New York. The corporation provides financial and other forms of support at the local, regional and corporate levels, to eligible not for profit organizations. All requests for local support that are under $100 should be addressed to the Store Manager at the local Hannaford. Requests for support greater than $100 should be entered via the web application. Priority giving areas include: health and wellness; child development; families; and hunger relief.

Requirements: Hannaford requires that requests be submitted at least eight (8) weeks prior to the event.
Restrictions: Hannaford's focus on specific charitable efforts prevent the corporation from supporting: solicitation on our premises; individuals; requests from faith-based agencies for religious purposes; educational scholarships; third party donations; professional development seminars and conferences; political organizations or lobbying groups; travel expenses; adult non-professional sports teams; pageants; private clubs; any organization or event outside our marketing areas, national or international; or any organization that discriminates on the basis of gender, race, ethnicity, religion, and/or sexual orientation.
Geographic Focus: Maine, Massachusetts, New Hampshire, New York, Vermont
Contact: Lori Hamilton, Marketing Director; (207) 883-2911 or (800) 213-9040; lori.hamilton@hannaford.com
Internet: www.hannaford.com/content.
jsp?pageName=Community&leftNavArea=AboutLeftNav

Sponsor: Hannaford Supermarkets
145 Pleasant Hill Road
Scarborough, ME 04074

Hannah's Helping Hands Grants 1165

Hannah and Friends is a 501(c)3 nonprofit organization dedicated to improving the quality of life for children and adults with special needs. The program provides support for Hannah's Helping Hands, which funds quality of life grants for Florida, Indiana (including the greater Michiana area), New York, New Jersey, and Rhode Island families that care for children and adults with special needs. The grants provide low and moderate-income families with stipends that may be used for a wide variety of supports related to their family member. The annual deadline for applications is June 1; the deadline for summer camp applications, however, is April 15.

Geographic Focus: Florida, Indiana, New Jersey, New York, Rhode Island
Date(s) Application is Due: Apr 15; Jun 1
Contact: Kayle Sexton, Grants Coordinator; (574) 217-7860, ext. 1; fax kayle@hannahandfriends.org; grants@hannahandfriends.org or grants@hannahandfriends.org
Internet: www.hannahandfriends.org/resources/hannahs-helping-hands-grants/
Sponsor: Hannah and Friends
51250 Hollyhock Road
South Bend, IN 46637

Harden Foundation Grants 1166

The Harden Foundation considers grants in the following focus areas: children, youth, and families; senior citizens; general health; agricultural education; animal welfare; environment; and arts and culture. The goals of the Foundation are to improve the well-being of youth; strengthen families; develop individual self-reliance and health; prevent inappropriate institutionalization of individuals; improve the quality of life through the cultural activities; encourage more humane treatment of animals; and eliminate duplication and improve coordination of social and community services in Monterey County areas, with emphasis on the Salinas Valley. Organizations may refer to the Foundation website for examples of funded projects in the Monterey area.

Requirements: Organizations should download the Common Grant application from the Foundation's website. Applicants must also include the following attachments: the completed grant application checklist; a completed and signed grant application form, with signature of an authorized representative; a detailed list of Board of Directors and staff roster; organizational chart, if available; current annual budget; a recent financial statement; year-to-date organizational financial statements; a detailed project budget; a list of the ten largest financial gifts received in the most recent fiscal year; a letter from the board chairperson or board member indicating approval for this application; and, if applicable, a completed grant report for a previous grant. The organization must also submit a 3-5 page narrative briefly describing the organization's history, major accomplishments, and their current programs and activities. They should also include a description of their constituency, how they are involved in their work, and how they benefit from the program. The Common Impact Evaluation Plan is not required for Harden Foundation applicants, but applicants must also include the following: a problem statement describing what problems, needs or issues are addressed, how this was determined, and how the project addresses and/or changes the underlying or root cause of the problem. If the funding requested is not for operating support, describe the project, why it is being pursued, and whether it is new or an expansion of an existing program. Include a list of all other grant requests, pending and approved, for this project, showing funding source and amount requested. Please refer to the Common Grant Guidelines for specific instructions on submitting the application. Applications may be mailed, dropped off, or emailed to the Foundation's office. Faxed applications are not accepted.

Restrictions: The Harden Foundation does not make grants to organizations headquartered outside of Monterey County unless they demonstrate service to the Monterey area. The Foundation does not fund: organizations that do not have a current 501(c)3 status; organizations that support sectarian religious programs; creation or addition to endowments; annual events, conferences, or fundraising events; academic or medical research or scholarships to individuals; foundations or associations established for the benefit of an organization which receives substantial tax support; individuals; political parties, candidates or partisan political organizations or activities.

Geographic Focus: California
Date(s) Application is Due: Mar 1; Sep 1
Amount of Grant: 5,000 - 100,000 USD
Contact: Joseph Grainger, Executive Director; (831) 442-3005; fax (831) 443-1429; joe@hardenfoundation.org
Internet: www.hardenfoundation.org/grant-information-introduction.html
Sponsor: Harden Foundation
P.O. Box 779
Salinas, CA 93902

Hardin County Community Foundation Grants 1167

The Hardin County Community Foundation was established to be the vehicle for those interested in fostering the present and future needs of the people of all ages in Hardin County, Ohio. The Foundation's primary fields of interest include: arts; health; education; recreation; and beautification. Most recently, awards have ranged from $400 to $5,000. Applications are accepted annually between February 1 and February 28.

Requirements: Any 501(c)3 organization serving the residents of Hardin County, Ohio, is eligible to apply.
Geographic Focus: Ohio
Date(s) Application is Due: Feb 28
Amount of Grant: 400 - 5,000 USD

Samples: Ada Food Pantry, Ada, Ohio, $500 - support food assistance for the needy; Alger First United Methodist Church- Home Missions, Alger, Ohio, $1,813 - support of mission work; Dolly Parton Imagination Library of Hardin County, Kenton, Ohio, $1,500 - support of children between the ages of birth through 5 to have access to books.
Contact: Saundra Neely, Trustee; hardinfoundation@gmail.com
Internet: hardinfoundation.org/grant-info
Sponsor: Hardin County Community Foundation
P.O. Box 343
Kenton, OH 43326

Harmony Foundation for Children Grants 1168

The Harmony Foundation for Children was established in California as a means of supporting programs and services for children of Sonoma Valley, California. The Foundation's primary fields of interest, therefore, are: sports and recreation; and youth development. An application form is required, which provides a detailed description of the program or project, along with the amount of funding requested. Applicants should begin by approached the Foundation in writing. Typical awards range from $1,000 to $3,000. There are no annual deadlines for submission.

Requirements: Any 501(c)3 organization serving the needs of children and youth in the Sonoma Valley, California, region are eligible to apply.
Geographic Focus: California
Amount of Grant: 1,000 - 3,000 USD
Samples: Sonoma Valley Mentoring Alliance, Sonoma, California, $3000 - support of community mentoring program for children; Sonoma Valley Girls Softball Association, Vineburg, California, $1,000 - support of a community sports program; Boys and Girls Clubs of Sonoma, Sonoma, California, $2,500 - after school program support.
Contact: Amy Ledson, Secretary; (707) 537-3810 or (707) 344-1316; amy@ledson.com
Sponsor: Harmony Foundation for Children
P.O. Box 653
Kenwood, CA 95452

Harmony Grove Foundation Grants 1169

The Harmony Grove Foundation was established in Georgia with the specific mission to support community development, economic development, libraries, human services, and other worthwhile programs in the Jackson County, Georgia, region. Past project support has included: expansion of the Commerce Public Library; the Hardman Preservation Microfilming Project; and the Community Gardens of Commerce. Most recently, awards have ranged from $25,000 to $100,000. There is no official application format, so interested parties should begin by contacting the Foundation office directly. No application deadlines for submission have been identified.

Requirements: Any 501(c)3 serving residents of the Commerce, Georgia, metro area is eligible to apply.
Restrictions: No grants are provided directly to individuals.
Geographic Focus: Georgia
Amount of Grant: 25,000 - 100,000 USD
Contact: Charles W. Blair, Jr., Treasurer; (706) 335-7195 or (706) 335-8205
Sponsor: Harmony Grove Foundation
86 Forest Hills Court
Commerce, GA 30529

Harmony Project Grants 1170

The Harmony Project is an innovative, creative nonprofit foundation established in Ohio in 2001 by Judith Harmony to promote the training of doctors and scientists, as well as research at Children's Hospital in Cincinnati. Currently, its primary mission is to enhance the education and personal development of girls, including self-efficacy, leadership and mother-daughter relationships, and to enrich their cultural and artistic lives. Funding is given for: curriculum development; program development; evaluation; research; and scholarship endowments. That support is provided within the greater Cincinnati area, as well as in northern Kentucky. An application form is required, though an initial approach should be by letter to the Foundation office. There are no specific annual submission deadlines.

Requirements: The Foundation accepts written applications from 509(a)1, 509(a)2, and 509(a)3 organizations supporting the residents of greater Cincinnati and northern Kentucky.
Geographic Focus: Kentucky, Ohio
Contact: Judith Harmony, President; (513) 861-8490; fax (513) 281-4326; jharmony@fuse.net
Internet: www.harmonyproject.org/
Sponsor: Harmony Project
3950 Rose Hill Avenue
Cincinnati, OH 45229-1448

Harold and Rebecca H. Gross Foundation Grants 1171

The Harold and Rebecca H. Gross Foundation was established in 2006 to support and promote charitable organizations with the primary purpose of assisting persons with physical disabilities to become better adjusted to their environments. Grants from the Gross Foundation are primarily 1 year in duration. Multi-year grants may be considered on a case-by-case basis. Award amounts typically range from $10,000 to $70,000.

Requirements: Applicants must have 501(c)3 tax-exempt status. Preference is given to organizations that provide direct services to physically disabled people. Applications will be submitted online through the Bank of America website. A grant report is required within 1 year of the grant application date, regardless of whether all of the funds have been spent.

Restrictions: Grant requests for research or capital projects will not be considered. The foundation does not support requests from individuals, organizations attempting to influence policy through direct lobbying, or any political campaigns.
Geographic Focus: All States
Date(s) Application is Due: Jul 1
Amount of Grant: 10,000 - 70,000 USD
Samples: Connecticut Institute for the Blind DBA Oak Hill, Hartford, Connecticut, $60,000 - Awarded for New England Assistive Technology (NEAT), an Oak Hill Center (2019); Joslin Diabetes Center, Boston, Massachusetts, $60,000 - Awarded for Center for Innovation in Diabetes Education: 2019 Request for Program Support (2019); National Jewish Health, Denver, Colorado, $60,000 - Awarded for Morgridge Academy (2019).
Contact: Amy R. Lynch, Philanthropic Client Manager; (860) 244-4870; ct.grantmaking@bankofamerica.com or amy.r.lynch@bofa.com
Internet: www.bankofamerica.com/philanthropic/foundation/?fnId=115
Sponsor: Harold and Rebecca H. Gross Foundation
200 Glastonbury Boulevard, Suite 200, CT2-545-02-05
Glastonbury, CT 06033

Harold Brooks Foundation Grants 1172

The Harold Brooks Foundation provides assistance to causes and organizations that help the largest possible number of residents of Massachusetts' South Shore communities, especially those that support the basic human needs of South Shore, Massachusetts residents. The Foundation supports nonprofit organizations that have the greatest impact on improving the human condition and/or that provide the neediest South Shore residents with "tools" to help them restore their lives. The Foundation focuses on 5 key areas: education; food, agriculture and nutrition; health; housing and shelter; and mental health. Harold Brooks, of Braintree, Massachusetts, was a successful business executive and entrepreneur who manufactured and sold prefabricated structures and underground bomb shelters during the Cold War. Mr. Brooks died in 1963 and the Foundation that bears his name was established in 1984. The trustee may also consider Harold Brooks Foundation applicants for funding before the Grace E. Brooks Trust. There is no separate application process for this trust. The Grace E. Brooks Trust is a smaller foundation that was established in 1963 to support and promote quality educational, human services and health care programming for underserved populations. Typically, no single organization will receive grants from both the Harold Brooks Foundation and the Grace E. Brooks Trust. Grants are made to support program and project expenses and/or general operating support. Multi-year (2-3 years maximum) requests are welcome. Award amounts typically range from $5,000 to $75,000.
Requirements: The Harold Brooks Foundation seeks to leverage its funding by supporting programs and projects that impact large numbers of residents or that positively affect the lives of the traditionally underserved within South Shore communities. As discussed in its Mission Statement, the Brooks Foundation funds in 5 primary areas— education; food, agriculture and nutrition; health; housing and shelter; and mental health— which are explained in greater detail on the Bank of America website. Grants are made to organizations that serve residents of the following South Shore, Massachusetts areas: Abington, Braintree, Bridgewater, Brockton, Carver, Cohasset, Duxbury, Hanover, Hanson, Hingham, Holbrook, Hull, Marshfield, Norwell, Pembroke, Plymouth, Quincy, Randolph, Rockland, Scituate, Weymouth and Whitman. Applications will be submitted online through the Bank of America website. A grant report is required within 1 year of the grant application date, regardless of whether all of the funds have been spent.
Restrictions: Support for endowment campaigns is not provided. Only 1 request will be accepted from an organization during a 12-month period. The foundation does not support requests from individuals, organizations attempting to influence policy through direct lobbying, or any political campaigns.
Geographic Focus: Massachusetts
Date(s) Application is Due: Apr 1
Amount of Grant: 5,000 - 75,000 USD
Samples: Interfaith Social Services, Quincy, Massachusetts, $40,000 - Awarded for Interfaith Social Services' emergency food program, mental health counseling center and homelessness prevention program (2018); DOVE, Quincy, Massachusetts, $35,000 - Awarded for General Operating Support of the Organization (2018); South Shore Community Action Council, Plymouth, Massachusetts, $30,000- Awarded for Food Resources Program - Senior Access Services (2018).
Contact: Michealle Larkins, Philanthropic Administrator; (866) 778-6859; ma.grantmaking@bankofamerica.com or ma.grantmaking@ustrust.com
Internet: www.bankofamerica.com/philanthropic/foundation/?fnId=34
Sponsor: Harold Brooks Foundation
P.O. Box 1802
Providence, RI 02901-1802

Harold K.L. Castle Foundation Public Education Redesign and Enhancement Grants 1173

The Harold K.L. Castle Foundation has shifted its public education strategy and will now focus more directly on helping students to attain college degrees or industry certificates and transition to jobs that enable a comfortable life. Its priority remains to close the gap in collegiate success between low-income students and their peers. This new direction draws upon the accumulated wisdom of dozens of stakeholders to help map the complex dynamics across Hawaii's K-12 education, post-secondary education and workforce systems. Note that due to the COVID-19 pandemic's economic impact, capital grant requests will not be considered in calendar years 2020 and 2021.
Requirements: Nonprofit organizations serving the people of Hawaii are eligible to apply. Interested applicants must submit an Online Inquiry Form, which is the first step in requesting funds from the foundation. Online Inquiry Forms will be reviewed by foundation staff on a rolling basis, so they may be submitted at any time during the year. Within one

month of receipt of your Online Inquiry Form, the foundation will contact you to request more information, invite you to submit a full proposal, or to inform you that the Foundation will be unable to consider a full proposal due to limited resources and/or a mismatch with Foundation priorities. If you are invited to submit a full proposal, the 2021 deadlines are: January 19th, March 16th, May 18th, August 17th or November 10th. The Foundation generally prefers not to be the only funder of a given project.
Restrictions: Proposals are not considered for: individuals or businesses; ongoing operating expenses (unless it is a new project or organization needing start-up funding); vehicles; computers; endowments; annual fund drives; sponsorships, special events, dinners, galas; organizations based outside of Hawaii; projects taking place outside Hawaii that do not benefit Hawaii. Each organization is limited to one active grant at a time.
Geographic Focus: Hawaii
Date(s) Application is Due: Jan 19; Mar 16; May 18; Aug 17; Nov 10
Amount of Grant: 1,200 - 1,000,000 USD
Samples: Adult Friends for Youth, Honolulu, Hawaii, $57,000 - Mobile Relief and Student Learning Center Hub (2020); Hawaii Technology Academy, Waipahu, Hawaii, $75,000 - expand HTA's Career-Based Education Model (CBEM) (2020); Teach Like a Champion, $19,000 - Enhancing Remote Learning for Hawaii's Students: A Hawaii DOE-Teach Like a Champion Partnership (2020).
Contact: Ann Matsukado, Grants Manager; (808) 263-8920 or (808) 263-7073; fax (808) 261-6918; amatsukado@castlefoundation.org
Internet: castlefoundation.org/investments/education/
Sponsor: Harold K.L. Castle Foundation
1197 Auloa Road
Kailua, HI 96734

Harold K.L. Castle Foundation Strengthening Windward Oahu Communities Grants 1174

The Harold K.L. Castle Foundation builds on the strengths of vibrant Windward Oahu communities through investments that support the region's rich cultural legacy, its youth and families, and its natural resources. Like many Hawai'i-based organizations, the Foundation is rooted in a strong sense of community and place. Prior to creating a family foundation in 1962, Harold K.L. Castle gave generously of his time, energy, and financial resources to the Windward Oahu community in which he lived and worked. With an eye toward the future and a vision of building civic and cultural resources, Castle in his lifetime made substantial gifts of land for Windward churches and schools, and for institutions such as Castle Medical Center and the Windward YMCA. Over its 44-year history, the Foundation has maintained a deep connection to its roots in Windward Oahu and a commitment to contributing to the vitality of communities from Kahuku to Waimanalo. Most recent awards have ranged from $5,000 to $200,000.
Requirements: Nonprofit organizations serving Hawaii are eligible to apply. Interested applicants must submit an Online Inquiry Form, which is the first step in requesting funds from the foundation. Online Inquiry Forms will be reviewed by foundation staff on a rolling basis, so they may be submitted at any time during the year. Within one month of receipt of your Online Inquiry Form, the foundation will contact you to request more information, invite you to submit a full proposal, or to inform you that the Foundation will be unable to consider a full proposal due to limited resources and/or a mismatch with Foundation priorities. The Foundation generally prefers not to be the only funder of a given project.
Restrictions: Proposals are not considered for: individuals or businesses; ongoing operating expenses (unless it is a new project or organization needing start-up funding); vehicles; computers; endowments; annual fund drives; sponsorships, special events, dinners, galas; organizations based outside of Hawaii; projects taking place outside Hawaii that do not benefit Hawaii. Each organization is limited to one active grant at a time.
Geographic Focus: Hawaii
Amount of Grant: 5,000 - 200,000 USD
Contact: Ann Matsukado, Grants Manager; (808) 263-8920 or (808) 263-7073; fax (808) 261-6918; amatsukado@castlefoundation.org
Internet: castlefoundation.org/investments/windward/
Sponsor: Harold K.L. Castle Foundation
1197 Auloa Road
Kailua, HI 96734

Harold K.L. Castle Foundation Windward Youth Leadership Fund Grants 1175

The Windward Youth Leadership Fund (WYLF) is a way for youth to apply for and "earn" up to $5,000 for their club or group activities by doing something positive for Windward Oahu. In addition to engaging youth in community service, one of the primary goals of this small grants program is to help youth build their leadership skills. Although parents, coaches and teachers may provide guidance, the projects must be youth-driven. In the time of COVID-19, The Foundation is looking for service projects that prioritize the following: Support for vulnerable community members, like kupuna or houseless individuals; 'Aina restoration and protection; Food distribution; or, Socio-emotional and academic support for younger students.
Requirements: Groups with at least three participants up to age 18 may apply including, but not limited to: school classes, teams, clubs, etc; youth activity groups, hula halau, music groups, scouts, etc; programs that serve youth; church youth groups; youth sports teams. Applicant groups must have a base in Windward Oahu, a majority of youth participants must be Windward Oahu residents and service projects should serve communities along the Windward coast from Kahuku to Waimanalo. Applicants must be a public school or a nonprofit 501(c)3 organization or have a sponsoring agency that is a 501(c)3 organization that can receive the funds. Youth groups can not use the Windward Youth Leadership Fund to raise funds for their own group by doing a service project that also benefits their own group. Youth groups are also encouraged to undertake projects that broaden their horizons beyond the scope of their everyday activities.

Restrictions: Applications that do not clearly demonstrate participation of youth in the project planning and writing of the proposal will most likely be denied.
Geographic Focus: Hawaii
Amount of Grant: 500 - 5,000 USD
Samples: Puohala Elementary School, Kaneohe, Hawaii, $1,950 - F.O.G. at Puohala (2020); Friends of Kailua High School, Kailua, Hawaii, $5,000 - Protecting our Past: The Cultural Legacy of Ulupo Heiau, Kailua, Koolaupoko, Oahu (2020); Hawaii Education of the Arts, Inc., Kailua, Hawaii, $5,000 - Project "Kupuna Mahalo" (2020); Parent Teacher Community Organization–Laie Elementary, Laie, Hawaii, $4,195 - Hauula Community Clean Up and Heiau Restoration (2020).
Contact: Ann Matsukado, Grants Manager; (808) 263-8920 or (808) 263-7073; fax (808) 261-6918; amatsukado@castlefoundation.org
Internet: castlefoundation.org/investments/youth/
Sponsor: Harold K.L. Castle Foundation
1197 Auloa Road
Kailua, HI 96734

Harris and Eliza Kempner Fund Education Grants   1176
The Harris and Eliza Kempner Fund provides grants primarily in the Galveston, Texas, area to qualifying organizations in the broad areas of the arts and humanities, community development, education, the environment, health, human services, and preservation. In the area of education, the Fund supports: adult and continuing education programs; literacy for all ages; pre-schools, and both public and private elementary and secondary schools. The Fund gives preference to requests for seed money, general operating funds, small capital needs support, and special projects partnering with other funding sources. Applicants should submit proposals through the Kempner Fund's online grant application. The Fund accepts proposals twice a year: March 15 for the program areas of health or human services; and October 15 for the program areas of arts and humanities, community development, the environment, education, and preservation. Directors will consider one proposal per program area per year.
Requirements: The Kempner Fund primarily supports U.S.-based 501(c)3 organizations and non-profit, governmental, and faith-based proposals from Galveston-based or Galveston-serving organizations.
Restrictions: Funding is not available for: fund-raising benefits; direct mail solicitations; grants to individuals; and grants to non-U.S. based organizations. Emailed or printed copies will not be accepted.
Geographic Focus: Texas
Date(s) Application is Due: Oct 15
Amount of Grant: Up to 50,000 USD
Samples: Ambassador Preparatory Academy, Galveston, Texas, $7,000 - in support of field trips to Galveston Opera House (2018); Galveston Bay, Galveston, Texas, $30,000 - general operating support; Moody Early Childhood Center, Galveston, Texas, $40,000 - general operating support.
Contact: Harrette N. Howard, Grants Administrator; (409) 762-1603; fax (409) 762-5435; hnhoward@kempnerfund.org or information@kempnerfund.org
Internet: www.kempnerfund.org/program-areas/
Sponsor: Harris and Eliza Kempner Fund
2201 Market Street, Suite 1250
Galveston, TX 77550-1529

Harris Foundation Grants   1177
Vernon V. Harris came from Kentucky to Oklahoma Territory where he began to fulfill his vision that all Americans should be responsible public citizens. In 1938 he founded the Harris Foundation, a philanthropic foundation that provides grants to religious, charitable, educational, benevolent, or scientific institutions and organizations. The imprint of V.V. Harris still can be seen throughout Oklahoma and today his legacy is continued by members of his family who serve on the Foundation's board. The purpose of this family-directed corporation exists, as is stated in its charter "to establish and promote, encourage, strengthen, assist and maintain religious, charitable, education, benevolent, or scientific institutions and organizations." Today, the Foundation's primary areas of giving include: human services; health and wellness; elementary and secondary education; higher education; community development; religious institutions; animal welfare; and arts and culture. Typically, awards are given for general operating support and program development. The Directors invite proposals from 501(c)3 organizations located in Oklahoma. An online grant application summarizing the need for funding must be submitted. Preference is given to organizations in Central Oklahoma and Enid. The Directors will meet and review all grant applications received by the deadline and will notify each applicant of their granting decisions. Letters of Inquiry are due by March 15, with final grant applications due by August 30.
Requirements: Any 501(c)3 organization serving the residents of Oklahoma are eligible to apply, though preference is given to organizations in Central Oklahoma and Enid.
Geographic Focus: Oklahoma
Date(s) Application is Due: Aug 30
Contact: Will Merrick, Grants Manager; (405) 755-5571 or (405) 820-3817; fax (405) 755-0938; wmerrick@fmiokc.com
Internet: fmiokc.com/clients/harris/
Sponsor: Harris Foundation
2932 NW 122nd Street, Suite D, P.O. 21210
Oklahoma City, OK 73120

Harrison County Community Foundation Grants   1178
The Harrison County Community Foundation (HCCF) awards grants to eligible Indiana nonprofit organizations in its areas of interest, including arts and culture; human services; recreation; government; historical preservation; community projects; education; health and

safety; and environment. The HCCF staff will provide training to all eligible not-for-profits serving the community on the proper completion of our grant application. All applicants are strongly encouraged to attend formal training sessions as announced, typically in May and November.
Requirements: Nonprofit agencies providing services to residents of Harrison County, Indiana, are eligible to apply. Tax-exempt 501(c)3 organizations and schools, religious organizations, and local governmental units are eligible.
Restrictions: The Foundation does not award grants to purchase real estate that has not been identified and an offer accepted; political activities or those designed to influence legislation; individuals; travel associated with a school-sponsored event; or religious organizations for projects that do not serve the general public. Traditional equipment, routine maintenance, or facility improvements will not be funded. Unused funding cannot be carried over into the following year.
Geographic Focus: Indiana
Date(s) Application is Due: Jan 15; Jul 15
Contact: Anna Curts, Grants Manager; (812) 738-6668; fax (812) 738-6864; annac@hccfindiana.org
Internet: www.hccfindiana.org/grants/
Sponsor: Harrison County Community Foundation
1523 Foundation Way, P.O. Box 279
Corydon, IN 47112

Harrison County Community Foundation Signature Grants   1179
Grant requests from the Harrison County Community Foundation (HCCF) in the amount of $200,000 and over are considered Signature Grants. These applications will be reviewed by all members of the Grants Committee. Decisions for Signature Grants may be announced anytime during the year. A vast majority of grant applications should be planned ahead and submitted during our Spring or Fall Grant Cycles, however, the HCCF is aware that some state or federal grants requiring local matching funds are announced on short notice. To support Harrison County serving not-for-profits with local matching funds, we will consider certain grant requests anytime. Emergency grants are awarded to respond to true emergency needs of our community or those that prevent an agency or program from carrying out primary functions or services.
Requirements: Nonprofit agencies providing services to residents of Harrison County, Indiana, are eligible to apply. Tax-exempt 501(c)3 organizations and schools, religious organizations, and local governmental units are eligible.
Restrictions: The Foundation does not award grants to purchase real estate that has not been identified and an offer accepted; political activities or those designed to influence legislation; individuals; travel associated with a school-sponsored event; or religious organizations for projects that do not serve the general public. Traditional equipment, routine maintenance, or facility improvements will not be funded. Unused funding cannot be carried over into the following year.
Geographic Focus: Indiana
Amount of Grant: 200,000 - 500,000 USD
Contact: Anna Curts, Grants Manager; (812) 738-6668; fax (812) 738-6864; annac@hccfindiana.org
Internet: www.hccfindiana.org/grants/
Sponsor: Harrison County Community Foundation
1523 Foundation Way, P.O. Box 279
Corydon, IN 47112

Harry A. and Margaret D. Towsley Foundation Grants   1180
In 1959, Margaret Towsley created the Harry A. and Margaret D. Towsley Foundation with an initial gift of $4 Million in Dow Chemical Company stock. While the Foundation's initial goals were typical of general family foundations, its mission later became focused on programs promoting education, health care, shelter, and nutrition for children. As its assets grew, its areas of concentration expanded into college and university education, medical education, planned parenthood, and interdisciplinary programs with the schools of law and social work. These areas reflected Dr. and Mrs. Towsley's common interest in teaching. The foundation currently awards grants to Michigan organizations in its areas of interest, including environment, medical and preschool education, social services, continuing education, and research in the health sciences. Types of support include annual campaigns, building construction and renovation, capital campaigns, continuing support, employee matching gifts, endowments, general operating support, matching/challenge support, professorships, program development, research, and seed grants. There are no application forms; submit a letter of inquiry between January and the listed deadline.
Restrictions: Not awarded to individuals or for travel, scholarships, fellowships, conferences, books, publications, films, tapes, audio-visual or communication media, or loans.
Geographic Focus: Michigan
Date(s) Application is Due: Mar 31
Contact: Lynn Towsley White, President; (989) 837-1100; fax (989) 837-3240
Sponsor: Harry A. and Margaret D. Towsley Foundation
140 Ashman Street, P.O. Box 349
Midland, MI 48640

Harry and Helen Sands Charitable Trust Grants   1181
Established in Milwaukee, Wisconsin, in 2007, the Harry and Helen Sands Charitable Trust offers its support primarily in West Virginia. Its primary field of interest is to assist in the funding of Christian churches and agencies through general operations money. Giving will also support: abuse prevention; arts and culture; child welfare; community recreation; family services; human services; parks; philanthropy' public safety; religion; scouting programs; shelter and residential care; sports and recreation; youth development; and youth

services. Applicants should adhere to the Foundation guidelines by first requesting a formal application and submitting the completed request by the annual November 1 deadline.
Requirements: Applicants must be 501(c)3 or Christian organizations either located in, or serving the residents of, Wheeling, West Virginia.
Geographic Focus: West Virginia
Date(s) Application is Due: Nov 1
Amount of Grant: Up to 5,000 USD
Contact: Trust Administrator; (304) 234-9400
Sponsor: Harry and Helen Sands Charitable Trust
10 South Dearborn, IL1-0117
Chicago, IL 60603

Harry and Jeanette Weinberg Foundation Grants 1182
The Harry and Jeanette Weinberg Foundation, one of the largest private charitable foundations in the United States, is dedicated to meeting the basic needs of vulnerable people and families experiencing poverty. In the coming year, the Foundation will provide approximately $125 million in grants to nonprofits, primarily in the United States and Israel, that provide direct services in the areas of: housing; health; jobs; elementary and secondary education; and community services. Grants focus on supporting organizations that serve specific populations, including older adults, women and children at risk, people with disabilities, and veterans, as well as the Jewish community. The foundation awards grants to support organizations in the areas of aging and gerontology, disabled, disadvantaged (economically), food distribution, and social services. Types of support include: building construction and renovation; capital campaigns; challenge/matching funds; endowments; general operating support; and material acquisition. Interested parties may submit a letter of inquiry at any time.
Requirements: The Foundation administers the majority of its funding in its priority communities: Baltimore, Chicago, Hawaii, Israel, New York City, Northeastern Pennsylvania, San Francisco, and Rural Communities (primarily surrounding other priority communities). These areas are hometowns representing personal ties to the life and legacy of Harry Weinberg, as well as cities where Weinberg Foundation trustees reside and provide leadership.
Restrictions: Grants are not awarded to institutions of higher education or museums.
Geographic Focus: All States
Amount of Grant: 10,000 - 1,000,000 USD
Contact: Aaron Merki, Managing Director, Programs and Grants; (410) 654-8500; amerki@hjweinberg.org or grantsintake@hjweinberg.org
Corbett A.K. Kalama, Hawaii Offive; (808) 924-1000; ckalama@hjweinberg.org or grantsintake@hjweinberg.org
Internet: www.hjweinbergfoundation.org
Sponsor: Harry and Jeanette Weinberg Foundation
7 Park Center Court
Owings Mills, MD 21117

Harry B. and Jane H. Brock Foundation Grants 1183
The Harry B. and Jane H. Brock Foundation honors a former Fort Payne, Alabama, native who changed the structure of the banking industry in Alabama. Harry Blackwell Brock, Jr., first worked as a truck driver for the Brook-Martin Oil Company, and later worked as a car salesman with John Thomas Motors of Gadsden. In 1964, he co-founded the Central Bank and Trust Company (later known as Compass Bank, now as BBVA Compass). In 1968, together with other investors, he gained voting control of the State National Bank of Alabama and, in 1981, he merged the two banks. By 1987, Central Bancshares of the South was the first bank in Alabama to own a bank in another state. Though Brock retired from the Board of Directors in 1991, he went on to serve on the Board of Directors of: Marathon Industries; the Daniel International Corporation; and Alabama Alliance of Business and Industry. He was inducted into the Alabama Academy of Honor in 1983 and the Alabama Business Hall of Fame in 1993. Brock died on July 29, 2015, at the age of 89. Today, the Foundation named in his honor awards grants to eligible Alabama organizations to support community development and higher education. Primary areas of interest include community service, community funds, education, the environment, higher education, volunteerism, women's services, social services, and cancer treatment and research. Types of support include: annual campaigns, capital campaigns, endowments, general operating support, program development, and research. Written proposals should describe the project and organization and include a copy of the IRS tax-determination letter. The annual deadline is November 1.
Requirements: 501(c)3 tax-exempt organizations serving the residents of Alabama.
Restrictions: No grants to individuals are awarded. Giving primarily in Birmingham and Huntsville, Alabama.
Geographic Focus: Alabama
Date(s) Application is Due: Nov 1
Amount of Grant: 1,000 - 25,000 USD
Contact: Harry B. Brock, Jr., President; (205) 939-0236 or (205) 918-0833; fax (205) 939-0806
Sponsor: Harry B. and Jane H. Brock Foundation
2101 Highland Avenue, Suite 250, P.O. Box 11643
Birmingham, AL 35202-1643

Harry Frank Guggenheim Foundation Research Grants 1184
The Foundation invites proposals in any of the natural sciences, social sciences or humanities that promise to increase understanding of the causes, manifestations, and control of human violence and aggression. Highest priority is given to research that can increase understanding and improve urgent problems of violence and aggression in the modern world. Questions that interest the foundation concern violence and aggression in relation

to social change, intergroup conflict, war, terrorism, crime, and family relationships, among other subjects. Priority will also be given to areas and methodologies not receiving adequate attention and support from other funding sources. Applicants may be citizens of any country. Most awards fall within the range of $15,000 to $40,000 per year for periods of one or two years. Applications for larger amounts and longer durations must be very strongly justified. Applications must be received by August 1, with a decision given in December.
Requirements: Applicants must mail two copies of the typed application in English to the Foundation. Applications may not be faxed or emailed. Along with two copies of the application, applicants must include the following: title page; abstract and survey; budget and its justification; personnel; research plan; other support; protection of subjects; and referee comments. Applicants should refer to the Foundation website for specific instructions on how to submit each of the attachments, and contact the Foundation if they have any questions.
Restrictions: Research with no relevance to understanding human problems will not be supported, nor will proposals to investigate urgent social problems where the Foundation cannot be assured that useful, sound research can be done.While almost all recipients of the Foundation grants possess a Ph.D., M.D., or equivalent degree, there are no formal degree requirements for the grant. The grant, however, may not be used to support research undertaken as part of the requirements for a graduate degree. Applicants need not be affiliated with an institution of higher learning, although most are college or university professors. The foundation awards research grants to individuals (or a few principal investigators at most) for individual projects, but does not award grants to institutions for institutional programs. Individuals who receive research grants may be subject to taxation.
Geographic Focus: All States, All Countries
Date(s) Application is Due: Aug 1
Amount of Grant: 15,000 - 40,000 USD
Contact: Program Officer; (646) 428-0971; fax (646) 428-0981; info@hfg.org
Internet: www.hfg.org/rg/guidelines.htm
Sponsor: Harry Frank Guggenheim Foundation
25 West 53rd Street
New York, NY 10019-5401

Hartford Foundation Regular Grants 1185
The Regular Grants program supports a variety of broad-based areas that reflect the diverse needs and interests of our region, such as: Arts and culture; Education; Family and social services; Health; and, Housing and economic development. An organization may be eligible to apply for one regular grant every three years, selecting its highest priority from one of the following grant types: Program/Project - Grants that support new programs, demonstration projects, studies, or surveys that do not commit the Foundation to recurring costs. May also be used to enhance, expand or strengthen existing programs, services and organizational capacity; Continuation - Additional funding provided at the end of a grant to help an organization reach project outcomes that were not met within the original schedule; Capital Grants - Supporting capital improvements, such as building purchase, construction or renovation, or capital equipment purchase; or, General Operating Support - Grants that support an organization's ongoing activities and stability, as outlined in its strategic plan.
Requirements: 501(c)3 nonprofit organizations serving residents in the following Connecticut towns are eligible to apply: Andover, Avon, Bloomfield, Bolton, Canton, East Granby, East Hartford, East Windsor, Ellington, Enfield, Farmington, Glastonbury, Granby, Hartford, Hebron, Manchester, Marlborough, Newington, Rocky Hill, Simsbury, Somers, South Windsor, Suffield, Tolland, Vernon, West Hartford, Wethersfield, Windsor, and Windsor Locks. Additionally, the board and staff must be representative of the racial/ethnic diversity of the region served.
Restrictions: The Foundation does not make grants from its unrestricted funds for: sectarian or religious activities; grants directly to individuals; grants to private foundations; endowments or memorials; direct or grass-roots lobbying efforts; conferences; research; or informational activities on topics that are primarily national or international in perspective. In addition, the Foundation generally does not make grants for: federal, state, or municipal agencies or departments supported by taxation; sponsorship of or support for one-time events; liquidation of obligations incurred at a previous date; or sustaining support for recurring operating expenses.
Geographic Focus: Connecticut
Amount of Grant: Up to 500,000 USD
Contact: Erika Frank, Program Manager; (860) 548-1888; fax (860) 524-8346; arivera@hfpg.org
Internet: www.hfpg.org/for-nonprofits/types-of-grants/
Sponsor: Hartford Foundation for Public Giving
10 Columbus Boulevard, 8th Floor
Hartford, CT 06106

Hartley Foundation Grants 1186
The Hartley Foundation was established by Michael J. Hartley, founder of Cheap Tickets, in Honolulu in 2001. The company began in 1986 when inter-island carrier Mid Pacific Air gave 3,000 tickets to Hartley's employer at the time, advertising firm Regency Media, as payment for its services at the time Regency closed its Honolulu branch. The tickets were advertised via newspaper classified ads and sold out in two weeks. The company grew into an airline ticket consolidator, acquiring seats from airlines at rates low enough to allow the company to resell them at fares lower than the airline's normal published airfares. Today, it focuses on the leisure market, offering airline tickets, hotel and vacation rentals, rental cars, customized vacation packages, and cruises. Historically, the Foundation, established in 1991, has given primarily in the Honolulu County region. The Foundation's major areas of interest include: agriculture; basic and emergency aid; diseases and conditions; educational services; elementary and secondary education; food aid; food banks; human services; literacy; mentoring; philanthropy; youth development; and youth organizing.

Its target populations are: academics; at-risk youth; children and youth; economically disadvantaged people; ethnic and racial groups; ow-income and poor people; and students. Generally, funding comes in the form of financial sustainability, fund raising contributions, program development, and re-granting. An application form is not required, and interested parties should begin by contacting the Foundation by submitting: descriptive literature about organization; detailed description of project and amount of funding requested; brief history of organization and description of its mission; statement of problem project will address; and results expected from proposed grant. The annual application submission deadline is October 31.
Requirements: 501(c)3 organizations serving residents of the Honolulu area.
Geographic Focus: Hawaii
Date(s) Application is Due: Oct 31
Amount of Grant: Up to 10,000 USD
Samples: Mid-Pacific Institute, Honolulu, Hawaii, $10,000 - support of education, classroom equipment, and professional development.
Contact: Michael J. Hartley, Director; (808) 394-8120 or (808) 735-1305
Sponsor: Hartley Foundation
1003 Bishop Street, Suite 1200
Honolulu, HI 96813

Harvey E. Najim Family Foundation Grants   1187
Established in 2006, the Harvey E. Najim Family Foundation provides grants that support children with food and shelter, clothing, children's education, the medical treatment of children, and other children's charitable purposes in the Greater San Antonio area. Interested applicants should begin by forwarding a Letter of Inquiry (LOI). If the project is recommended, an invitation to submit a full application will be sent by the Foundation. Annual deadlines for LOIs are: February 9, April 27, and August 10. Annual application deadlines are March 16, June 8, and September 14.
Requirements: Only Section 501(c)3 organizations may apply for grants from the Foundation. In addition, the organization must be qualified as 509(a)1 or 509(a)2 and such designation must appear on the IRS Determination letter. If the organization is a 509(a)3, a legal opinion must be attached.
Restrictions: The Najim Family Foundation does not provide funding to higher education organizations or toward higher education, for capital campaigns/expenditures, and multi-year requests.
Geographic Focus: Texas
Date(s) Application is Due: Mar 16; Jun 8; Sep 14
Contact: Lia Payne, Grants Administrator; (210) 255-8435, ext. 18002; lia.payne@najimfoundation.org
Internet: www.najimfoundation.org/index.php?option=com_content&task=view&id=13&Itemid=74
Sponsor: Harvey E. Najim Family Foundation
613 NW Loop 410, Suite 875
San Antonio, TX 78216

Harvey Randall Wickes Foundation Grants   1188
The Foundation awards grants to eligible Michigan nonprofit organizations in its areas of interest, including the arts; children/youth services; education; hospitals; human services; libraries; and recreation. Types of support include annual campaigns, building/renovation, equipment, and seed money. There are no application deadline dates. Applications must be received two weeks prior to board meetings in March, June, September, and December. Award notification is given within two weeks of the board meeting.
Requirements: Michigan 501(c)3 tax-exempt organizations in Saginaw County are eligible.
Restrictions: Funding is not available for government where support is forthcoming from tax dollars, individuals, endowments, travel, conferences, loans, or film or video projects.
Geographic Focus: Michigan
Amount of Grant: 2,500 - 30,000 USD
Samples: $13,000, Saginaw, Michigan Junior Achievement, payable over one year; $20,000, Saginaw, Michigan Holy Cross Children's Services, payable over one year.
Contact: Hugo Braun, Jr., President; (989) 799-1850; fax (989) 799-3327; hrwickes@att.net
Sponsor: Harvey Randall Wickes Foundation
4800 Fashion Square Boulevard, Plaza N., Suite 472
Saginaw, MI 48604-2677

Hasbro Children's Fund Grants   1189
The Hasbro Children's Fund focuses on three core principles: programs which provide hope to children who need it most; play for children who otherwise would not be able to experience that joy; and the empowerment of youth through service. The mission of the Fund is to assist children triumphing over critical life obstacles as well as bringing the joy of play into their lives. Through the Fund's initiatives, the mission is achieved by supporting programs which provide terminal and seriously ill children respite and access to play, educational programs for children at risk, and basics for children in need. The Fund annually provides local community grants which support programs that deliver; stability for children in crisis; pediatric physical and mental health services; hunger security; educational programs; quality out of school time programming and programs that empower youth through service. Interested applicants are asked to submit a letter of inquiry through the online system.
Requirements: Any 501(c)3 serving residents in the locations where Hasbro has operating facilities are eligible to apply. This includes: Rhode Island; Springfield, Massachusetts; Renton, Washington; and Los Angeles, California.
Restrictions: Funding is not available for: religious organizations; individuals; research; political organizations; scholarships; travel stipends; loans; endowments; goodwill advertising; sponsorship of recreational activities; fundraisers; auctions; and schools.

Geographic Focus: California, Massachusetts, Rhode Island, Washington
Amount of Grant: 1,000 - 10,000 USD
Contact: Karen Davis, Vice President of Community Relations; (401) 431-8151; fax (401) 431-8455; hcfinfo@hasbro.com
Internet: www.hasbro.com/corporate/en_US/community-relations/childrens-fund.cfm
Sponsor: Hasbro Children's Fund
1027 Newport Avenue, P.O. Box 200
Pawtucket, RI 02862-1059

Hasbro Corporation Gift of Play Holiday Giving   1190
Hasbro Corporation's Gift of Play Holiday Giving program is designed to empower parents in need with the ability to give their children, who may otherwise go without, a gift on the morning of their holiday. We have specific holiday giving programs in place where Hasbro has a U.S. operating facility. Outside of its operating areas, Hasbro also distributes its holiday giving through its non-profit partner organizations, such as the Marine Corps Toys for Tots Foundation. Last year, Hasbro donated more than $3 million worth of toys and games during the holiday season.
Requirements: 501(c)3 nonprofit organizations in corporate operating areas are eligible. This includes: Rhode Island; Springfield, Massachusetts; Renton, Washington; and Los Angeles, California.
Restrictions: Funding is not available for: religious organizations; individuals; research; political organizations; scholarships; travel stipends; loans; endowments; goodwill advertising; sponsorship of recreational activities; fundraisers; auctions; and schools.
Geographic Focus: California, Massachusetts, Rhode Island, Washington
Amount of Grant: Up to 2,500 USD
Contact: Karen Davis, Vice President of Community Relations; (401) 431-8151; fax (401) 431-8455
Internet: www.hasbro.com/corporate/en_US/community-relations/holiday-giving.cfm
Sponsor: Hasbro Corporation Gift of Play
1027 Newport Avenue, P.O. Box 200
Pawtucket, RI 02862-1059

Hasbro Corporation Gift of Play Hospital and Pediatric Health Giving   1191
A hospital stay can be a scary and stressful situation. The Hasbro Corporation Gift of Play program works closely with staff and child life members of the children's hospitals located where Hasbro has an operating facility, to provide a sense of comfort and normalcy to the young patients while trying to lift their spirits and bring a smile to their face with a toy or game. The following are local hospitals Hasbro supports: Hasbro's Children's Hospital in Providence, Rhode Island; Bradley Hospital in East Providence, Rhode Island; Bay State Children's Hospital in Springfield, Massachusetts; Seattle Children's Hospital in Seattle, Washington; and Children's Hospital Los Angeles in Los Angeles, California. Since 2007, Hasbro and the Garth Brooks Teammates for Kids Foundation have teamed up to open nine Child Life Zones throughout the United States. Teammates for Kids opens Child Life Zones in hospitals to ensure the patients and families have a therapeutic play area where they can learn, play and relax.
Requirements: Children's hospital patients in corporate operating areas are eligible. This includes: Rhode Island; Springfield, Massachusetts; Renton, Washington; and Los Angeles, California.
Geographic Focus: California, Massachusetts, Rhode Island, Washington
Contact: Karen Davis, Vice President of Community Relations; (401) 431-8151; fax (401) 431-8455
Internet: www.hasbro.com/corporate/en_US/community-relations/hospital-support.cfm
Sponsor: Hasbro Corporation Gift of Play
1027 Newport Avenue, P.O. Box 200
Pawtucket, RI 02862-1059

Hasbro Corporation Gift of Play Shelter Support Giving   1192
The Hasbro Corporation Gift of Play Shelter Support Giving program recognizes the plight of homeless children around the world who are living in very difficult situations. In some small way the program hopes to bring a sparkle of hope to these children through donations of Hasbro toys. In addition, the program helps to supply play areas to shelters located where Hasbro has an operating facility> This includes: Rhode Island; Springfield, Massachusetts; Renton, Washington; and Los Angeles, California. It is designed to equip shelter playrooms with toys and games so children will have something to help pass the time and bring a smile to their face. Finally, the program partners with the non-profit organization, Birthday Wishes, to bring birthday parties to homeless children.
Requirements: 501(c)3 nonprofit organizations in corporate operating areas are eligible. This includes: Rhode Island; Springfield, Massachusetts; Renton, Washington; and Los Angeles, California.
Restrictions: Funding is not available for: religious organizations; individuals; research; political organizations; scholarships; travel stipends; loans; endowments; goodwill advertising; sponsorship of recreational activities; fundraisers; auctions; and schools.
Geographic Focus: California, Massachusetts, Rhode Island, Washington
Contact: Karen Davis, Vice President of Community Relations; (401) 431-8151; fax (401) 431-8455
Internet: www.hasbro.com/corporate/en_US/community-relations/shelter-support.cfm
Sponsor: Hasbro Corporation Gift of Play
1027 Newport Avenue, P.O. Box 200
Pawtucket, RI 02862-1059

Hasbro Corporation Gift of Play Summer Camp Support   1193
Through the Hasbro Corporation Gift of Play Summer Camp program, Hasbro supports a number of summer camps serving sick or needy children by donating toys and games.

Summer camps are not only a way for children to create lifelong memories, but to also continue to develop their social skills. The toys are not meant for the children to take home but for their use at the camps. In addition to the program's strategic partnership with the SeriousFun Children's Network, Hasbro supports the Sibling Connections Camp to Belong. This special week-long camp is held specifically for brothers and sisters who have been separated by foster care, in some cases giving them their only opportunity to connect during the year.

Requirements: Summer camps in corporate operating areas are eligible. This includes: Rhode Island; Springfield, Massachusetts; Renton, Washington; and Los Angeles, California.

Restrictions: Funding is not available for: religious organizations; individuals; research; political organizations; scholarships; travel stipends; loans; endowments; goodwill advertising; sponsorship of recreational activities; fundraisers; auctions; and schools.

Geographic Focus: California, Massachusetts, Rhode Island, Washington

Amount of Grant: Up to 2,500 USD

Contact: Karen Davis, Vice President of Community Relations; (401) 431-8151; fax (401) 431-8455

Internet: www.hasbro.com/corporate/en_US/community-relations/summer-camps.cfm

Sponsor: Hasbro Corporation Gift of Play

1027 Newport Avenue, P.O. Box 200

Pawtucket, RI 02862-1059

Hattie M. Strong Foundation Grants 1194

The Hattie M. Strong Foundation makes charitable grants to 501(c)3 charities serving at-risk school-aged children enrolled in public or public charter schools in the city of Washington, D.C. Occasional grants are also made to organizations serving at-risk children in surrounding jurisdictions. The Strong Foundation's current priority is to assist organizations that provide out-of-school-time (OST) programming during the after-school hours, Saturdays, and summer. Preference is given to programs that support, reinforce, and enrich the core academic objectives of the District of Columbia Public Schools, as well as character development, community service, good citizenship, and appreciation of the performing and visual arts. Grants range from $5,000 to $25,000 and are made throughout the Foundation's fiscal year which runs September 1 to August 31. Organizations under consideration for potential grants may be contacted for additional information by the Foundation. In some cases, the Foundation may ask to schedule a site visit.

Requirements: The Strong Foundation no longer accepts unsolicited requests for grants. This decision makes it possible for the Foundation to direct more money to the community while reducing the burden on local charities. That said, the Foundation is always happy to receive information, such as newsletters and other materials, describing the work of local charities that provide OST programming. This may, in fact, inform the direction of its giving.

Restrictions: Funding is not available for building or endowment funds, requests for equipment, research, conferences, special events or benefits, projects designed to educate the general public, or programs of national or international scope.

Geographic Focus: District of Columbia

Date(s) Application is Due: Aug 31

Amount of Grant: 5,000 - 25,000 USD

Contact: Janet Kerr-Tener, Grant Advisor; (703) 313-6791; fax (703) 313-6793; jkerrtener@hattie.org

Jessica Trevelyan, Program Contact; (703) 313-6791; fax (703) 313-6793; jtrevelyan@hattie.org

Internet: www.hmstrongfoundation.org

Sponsor: Hattie M. Strong Foundation

6551 Loisdale Court, Suite 160

Springfield, VA 22150

Hattie Mae Lesley Foundation Grants 1195

The Hattie Mae Lesley Foundation was established in Texas in 2001, with giving centered primarily in the region of the Dallas-Fort Worth metropolitan area. Some awards are also given in the Santa Fe, New Mexico, region. Currently, the Foundation's primary fields of support include: basic and emergency aid; Christianity; elementary and secondary education; family services; human services; legal services; mental health care; opera; orchestral music; out-patient medical care; performing arts; science museums; shelter and residential care; special population support; youth development; and youth services. That support generally takes the form of either capital campaign funding or program development. Most recently, awards have ranged as high as $100,000. There are no specified annual deadlines for application submission.

Requirements: 501(c)3 organizations in the Dallas-Forth Worth region of Texas are welcome to apply, as well as those serving residents of Santa Fe, New Mexico.

Geographic Focus: New Mexico, Texas

Amount of Grant: Up to 100,000 USD

Samples: Fort Worth Opera Association, Fort Worth, Texas, $100,000 - support for the expansion of the Fort Worth Opera studio; Santa Fe Opera Foundation, Santa Fe, New Mexico, $12,500 - support of an apprenticeship program for singers; Battered Women's Foundation, Richland Hills, Texas, $5,000 - support of services for the children of battered women.

Contact: Debra Goldstein Phares, Philanthropic Client Director; (214) 209-1830 or (800) 357-7094; debra.g.phares@ustrust.com or tx.philanthropic@ustrust.com

Internet: www.bankofamerica.com/philanthropic/fn_search.action

Sponsor: Hattie Mae Lesley Foundation

901 Main Street, 19th Floor

Dallas, TX 75202-3714

Hatton W. Sumners Foundation for the Study and Teaching of 1196
Self Government Grants

The Foundation's purpose is to encourage the study, teaching and research in the science and art of self-government so that citizens understand the fundamental principles of democracy in shaping governmental policies. Working through qualified, tax-exempt organizations, the Foundation seeks to reach, educate, and motivate the general public and the current and future leaders of American society. The Foundation gives to youth organizations and higher education. Types of support include: conferences and seminars; continuing support; curriculum development; endowments; fellowships; general operating support; internship funds; matching and challenge support; and research. Application information is available at the Foundation website. Grant applications will be accepted from January 1st through August 1st of each year. Final decisions on grant proposals are made by the Trustees in October of each year.

Requirements: Grants are made only to 501(c)3 tax-exempt organizations in Texas, New Mexico, Oklahoma, Louisiana, Arkansas, Kansas, Nebraska and Missouri.

Restrictions: The Foundation does not fund religious organizations or individual grants.

Geographic Focus: Arkansas, Kansas, Louisiana, Missouri, Nebraska, New Mexico, Oklahoma, Texas

Date(s) Application is Due: Aug 1

Samples: Bill of Rights Institute, Arlington, Virginia: Constitutional seminars in Oklahoma and New Mexico, $23,000; National Center for Policy Analysis, Dallas, Texas: Sumners Distinguished Lecture Series, $250,000; Big Brothers Big Sisters of North Texas, Irving, Texas: character education and civic mentoring programs, $116,400; YMCA Youth and Government Programs in Texas, Oklahoma, and New Mexico: general operating support, $236,200.

Contact: Hugh Akin, Executive Director; (214) 220-2128; fax (214) 953-0737; hugh@hattonsumners.org or info@hattonsumners.org

Internet: www.hattonsumners.org

Sponsor: Hatton W. Sumners Foundation for the Study and Teaching of Self Government

325 North St. Paul Street, Suite 3920

Dallas, TX 75201

Hawai'i Community Foundation Bernice and Conrad von Hamm Fund Grants 1197

The Bernice and Conrad von Hamm Fund supports business education and entrepreneurship projects that focus on business skills, economics, finance and banking, travel industry management, and business internship programs. The committee is particularly interested in projects that promote financial literacy or entrepreneurship among youth, low-income or immigrant populations. Preference will be given to proposals that demonstrate that: focus is consistent with the purposes of the fund-business education; project is targeted to youth, low-income or immigrant populations; project is appropriate for the target population; outcome and evaluation methods are realistic; foundation resources will be leveraged; future funding or sustainability of the project is realistically addressed; organization's board is representative of the community it serves; final reports for any previous awards have been submitted. The Bernice and Conrad von Hamm Fund is now a part of the new FLEX Grants program at the Hawai'i Community Foundation.

Requirements: Grant requests will be considered from organizations that are classified by the IRS as 501(c)3 organizations and not private foundations. Government entities, such as public schools, are also eligible.

Restrictions: Funds are not generally available for: purchase of computers or other equipment without a business education program; general computer training or skills; job training or readiness programs that are not focused on business entrepreneurship.

Geographic Focus: Hawaii

Amount of Grant: 2,000 - 10,000 USD

Contact: Susan Maltezo, Senior Grants Manager; (808) 537-6333 or (888) 731-3863; fax (808) 521-6286; smaltezo@hcf-hawaii.org

Internet: www.hawaiicommunityfoundation.org/grants/flex-grants

Sponsor: Hawaii Community Foundation

827 Fort Street Mall

Honolulu, HI 96813-4317

Hawai'i Community Foundation Children's Trust Fund Community Awareness: 1198
Child Abuse and Neglect Prevention Grants

The Hawaii Children's Trust Fund was established in 1993 to ensure that Hawaii's keiki (children) reach their full potential, developing into healthy, productive, and caring individuals through the advancement of community-based family strengthening programs. By promoting healthy relationships and environments, thriving and safe communities can be created for Hawaii's children, and their children to follow. This funding opportunity supports young parents with young children to prevent child abuse and neglect in Hawaii. Funding is available for direct service programs that address at least one of three protective factors of child abuse and neglect suggested by the Center for the Study of Social Policy (CSSP), specifically: Nurturing and Attachment; Knowledge of Parenting and Child Development; and Social Connections. Specifically, HCTF is interested in programs that include all of the following four elements: a focus on young parents, age 29 or younger, with children age 0 to 5 years old; the provision of innovative direct service to children and families, incorporating or developing knowledge of parenting and child development, increased nurturing and attachment, and/or social support structures; activities that are evidence-based, evidence-informed, or a promising practice, provided within an appropriate cultural context; and a commitment to participating in program evaluation, including a pre/post assessment of clients served utilizing a common assessment tool to be identified by the Hawai'i Community Foundation. Three-year proposals, for approximately $40,000 to $50,000 per year. On-line applications are due by January 18.

Requirements: To be eligible for funding, the applicant must be: a non-profit organization with a 501(c)3 tax-exempt status; providing services in the State of Hawaii, and have done

so for the last two years; and current on all grant reporting requirements with the Hawai'i Community Foundation.
Restrictions: Fiscal sponsorships will not be considered through this funding.
Geographic Focus: Hawaii
Date(s) Application is Due: Jan 18
Amount of Grant: 120,000 - 150,000 USD
Contact: Susan Maltezo, Senior Grants Manager; (808) 537-6333 or (888) 731-3863; fax (808) 521-6286; smaltezo@hcf-hawaii.org
Internet: www.hawaiicommunityfoundation.org/file/HCTF-2017-RFP-website.pdf
Sponsor: Hawaii Community Foundation
827 Fort Street Mall
Honolulu, HI 96813-4317

Hawai'i Community Foundation East Hawaii Fund Grants   **1199**
With the help of KTA Superstores, the estate of Frederick Yokoyama and a committed group of residents, the East Hawaii Fund was established to provide a stronger link between charitable donors and the specific needs of the east side of Hawaii Island. The Fund does not conduct annual fundraising, but instead relies on the generosity of people who want to benefit the region or a specific focus area within, including: education; health; human services; children and youth; or arts and culture. The Fund is now a part of the new FLEX Grants program at the Foundation.
Requirements: Hawai'i organizations that are tax exempt, including nonprofits, 501(c)3 organizations, religious groups that are exempt from taxation, or units of government are eligible to apply.
Restrictions: Projects not likely to be funded: projects that do not benefit the residents of East Hawaii; funds for endowments or for the benefit of specific individuals; out-of-state travel expenses; start-up costs of a new organization.
Geographic Focus: Hawaii
Amount of Grant: 2,000 - 10,000 USD
Contact: Susan Maltezo, Senior Grants Manager; (808) 537-6333 or (888) 731-3863; fax (808) 521-6286; smaltezo@hcf-hawaii.org
Internet: www.hawaiicommunityfoundation.org/strengthening/east-hawaii-fund
Sponsor: Hawaii Community Foundation
827 Fort Street Mall
Honolulu, HI 96813-4317

Hawai'i Community Foundation Ewa Beach Community Trust Fund Grants   **1200**
The Ewa Beach Community Trust Fund was created to support activities and projects of charitable agencies that work to improve the quality of life of the residents of the Ewa area. Preference will be given to: organizations that are based in the Ewa area; have a history of involvement in the community; are partnering with an Ewa organization; projects that involve or serve youth or the elderly; projects that promote positive community identity and relationships; projects that show the ability to obtain other sources of financial support (including donations); projects that result in a measurable or tangible outcome; projects that benefit a greater number of people; and projects that have not been funded within the year. The Fund is now a part of the new FLEX Grants program at the Hawaii Community Foundation. Awards typically range from $1,000 to $2,000.
Requirements: Any nonprofit, tax exempt 501(c)3 organization, neighborhood group or project is eligible if the goal is to improve the quality of life in the Ewa area, and is not political, commercial or self-serving.
Geographic Focus: Hawaii
Date(s) Application is Due: Apr 16
Amount of Grant: 1,000 - 2,000 USD
Contact: Susan Maltezo, Senior Grants Manager; (808) 537-6333 or (888) 731-3863; fax (808) 521-6286; smaltezo@hcf-hawaii.org
Internet: www.hawaiicommunityfoundation.org/grants/flex-grants
Sponsor: Hawaii Community Foundation
827 Fort Street Mall
Honolulu, HI 96813-4317

Hawai'i Community Foundation Family Literacy and   **1201**
   Hawaii Pizza Hut Literacy Grants
The purpose of the Family Literacy and Hawaii Pizza Hut Literacy fund is to increase the literacy of Hawaii residents. English literacy is the primary focus of these funds. Preference will be given to projects that: improve access to programs for low-income, immigrant/ refugee and rural communities by utilizing community-based partnerships, adapting programs to be responsive to diverse cultures, and utilizing technology to increase access; improve quality of programs by utilizing research documented best practices, including nationally documented programs adapted to reflect Hawaii's diverse cultures, including an evaluation component, and/or providing teacher training through workshops or conferences to implement quality literacy programs; for family literacy programs, focus on families with young children (ages 0-8). The annual application deadline is June 22,
Requirements: Hawaii organizations that are tax-exempt, including nonprofit organizations, 501(c)3, and units of government, such as Hawaii's public schools and libraries, are eligible to apply.
Restrictions: Projects are not likely to be funded for: programs that take place as part of a school curriculum; programs that replace DOE funding; major capital projects, although some small facility improvements to improve the ability to deliver a literacy program may be considered.
Geographic Focus: Hawaii
Date(s) Application is Due: Jun 22
Amount of Grant: 5,000 - 20,000 USD
Contact: Susan Maltezo, Senior Grants Manager; (808) 537-6333 or (888) 731-3863;

fax (808) 521-6286; smaltezo@hcf-hawaii.org or give@hawaiicommunityfoundation.org
Internet: www.hawaiicommunityfoundation.org/grants/family_ literacy-hawaii-pizza-hut-literacy
Sponsor: Hawaii Community Foundation
827 Fort Street Mall
Honolulu, HI 96813-4317

Hawai'i Community Foundation Kuki'o Community Fund Grants   **1202**
The Kuki'o Community Fund is interested in supporting programs that offer out-of-school activities for children, youth and families that contribute to increasing positive social development and reducing risk-taking behaviors by providing: attention from caring adults who can serve as healthy role models; opportunities for exploration of new interests; academic support; a sense of belonging to a group and new friendships; opportunities to take on leadership roles; a sense of self-esteem. Preferences will be given to projects that benefit the residents of West Hawai'i. Application information is available online. The Kuki'o Community Fund is now a part of the new FLEX Grants program at the Hawaii Community Foundation.
Requirements: Grants will be made to nonprofit, tax exempt 501(c)3 organizations. Community groups without a 501(c)3 will need to apply through a fiscal sponsor.
Geographic Focus: Hawaii
Date(s) Application is Due: Feb 19
Amount of Grant: Up to 5,000 USD
Contact: Susan Maltezo, Senior Grants Manager; (808) 537-6333 or (888) 731-3863; fax (808) 521-6286; smaltezo@hcf-hawaii.org
Internet: www.hawaiicommunityfoundation.org/strengthening/kukiofund
Sponsor: Hawaii Community Foundation
827 Fort Street Mall
Honolulu, HI 96813-4317

Hawai'i Community Foundation Lana'i Community Benefit Fund   **1203**
The purpose of the Lana'i Community Benefit Fund is to promote and enrich the lifestyle of the residents of Lanai through the support of educational, cultural and recreational activities for the Lanai community with special emphasis on youth, young adults and senior citizens. Priority will be given to proposals that provide clear objectives and reasonable timelines. The Benefit Fund is now a part of the new FLEX Grants program at the Hawaii Community Foundation. Awards typically range from $500 to $5,000,
Requirements: Grants may be made to organizations which are not described as 501(c)3 provided the activities to be supported are charitable and do not involve political lobbying or other non-charitable activities.
Restrictions: Funding for travel and personal expenses or hiring shall be discouraged except to bring speakers, instructors, and other individuals with special talents and abilities from outside of Lanai for activities consistent with the purposes of the Fund.
Geographic Focus: Hawaii
Amount of Grant: 500 - 5,000 USD
Contact: Susan Maltezo, Senior Grants Manager; (808) 537-6333 or (888) 731-3863; fax (808) 521-6286; smaltezo@hcf-hawaii.org
Internet: www.hawaiicommunityfoundation.org/grants/flex-grants
Sponsor: Hawaii Community Foundation
827 Fort Street Mall
Honolulu, HI 96813-4317

Hawai'i Community Foundation Richard Smart Fund Grants   **1204**
The Hawai'i Community Foundation announced in 2012 that grants benefiting the Waimea community on Hawai'i Island would become available through the Richard Smart Fund (also known as the Ho'ohui 'O Waimea Fund) grant program. The award was established in honor of Richard Smart, a philanthropist who gave generously to support education, healthcare, culture and the arts and other charitable activities for the Waimea community. Smart's legacy continues to support the community and lifestyle that he loved, a community where people know each other and care about maintaining the special qualities of Waimea. The Foundation encourages residents and community organizations to submit grant proposals that help to make Waimea a better place to live. Proposals may include (but are not limited to): community volunteerism and/or the scope of volunteer opportunities; raising awareness of local civic issues affecting the residents; collaboration between nonprofit organizations; participation in community-building activities; and increasing communication between long-time and newer residents. Grants range up to a maximum of $10,000. The annual deadline for submitting applications is on August 13. The Fund is now a part of the new FLEX Grants program at the Foundation.
Requirements: A group must be a tax-exempt 501(c)3 organization – such as schools, units of government or neighborhood groups– or have a 501(c)3 fiscal sponsor. Community organizations without 501(c)3 status are eligible to apply for a grant up to $2,000, provided the activities to be supported are charitable. Grants proposals must benefit the Waimea community and can include ongoing or one-time events. Grants awarded will be for a 12 month project.
Geographic Focus: Hawaii
Date(s) Application is Due: Aug 13
Amount of Grant: Up to 10,000 USD
Contact: Susan Maltezo, Senior Grants Manager; (808) 537-6333 or (888) 731-3863; fax (808) 521-6286; smaltezo@hcf-hawaii.org
Internet: www.hawaiicommunityfoundation.org/grants/flex-grants
Sponsor: Hawaii Community Foundation
827 Fort Street Mall
Honolulu, HI 96813-4317

Hawai'i Community Foundation Robert E. Black Fund Grants　　1205

Local businessman and philanthropist Robert E. Black played a major role in the transformation of the Hawai'i Community Foundation from a small community trust to one of the largest public foundations in the country. Black was born and raised in Hawai'i in the 1920s. After attending college on the mainland and serving his country in World War II, he returned to the islands to work in the family business founded by his father. As chairman of the board and president of E.E. Black Construction, Black turned it into one of Hawaii's largest firms, extending its operations throughout the Pacific. He also set aside time and money to give to a number of charities. Organizations in which Black was most active were Hawaii Pacific University, Punahou School, and Bishop Museum. When Black died in 1987, he bequeathed the largest discretionary endowment in Hawaii's history, with more than $60 million dedicated to the Foundation. His desire was for the income from the fund to support five areas of charity, including: health; residential treatment; culture; the arts; and private education. The Fund is now a part of the new FLEX Grants program at the Foundation.

Requirements: Hawai'i organizations that are tax exempt, including nonprofits, 501(c)3 organizations, religious groups that are exempt from taxation, or units of government are eligible to apply.

Restrictions: Funding is not available for: major capitol projects; endowments; or on-going or general operating costs.

Geographic Focus: Hawaii

Amount of Grant: 5,000 - 20,000 USD

Contact: Susan Maltezo, Senior Grants Manager; (808) 537-6333 or (888) 731-3863; fax (808) 521-6286; smaltezo@hcf-hawaii.org

Internet: www.hawaiicommunityfoundation.org/grants/flex-grants

Sponsor: Hawaii Community Foundation

827 Fort Street Mall

Honolulu, HI 96813-4317

Hawai'i Community Foundation Victoria S. and Bradley L. Geist Foundation:　　1206
Capacity Building Grants

The support of projects to increase the capacity of organizations and programs to deliver and grow quality services to foster children and their families is one area of particular interest to the Hawai'i Community Foundation. The Foundation offers this Request for Proposals to provide meaningful support that enables nonprofit organizations and programs to strengthen and grow their capacity to serve foster children, their caregivers and transitioning foster youth. The Foundation seeks to support projects that will increase the capacity of the organization, the program, or the system in the community to deliver quality services to the clientele described under Eligibility Requirements. Capacity building efforts may address: governance and leadership; strategic relationships; evaluation and impact; resource development; internal operations and management; program design, delivery and evaluation; executive and key staff transitions; and staff training. Grants generally range from $5,000 to $40,000 and may be multi-year commitments. For applications to be considered they must be submitted online. Annual deadlines have been specified as: January 17; May 15; and September 15.

Requirements: Tax-exempt Hawaii organizations are eligible to apply. Organizations may be either 501(c)3 or religious organizations. The majority percentage of the organization's or program's clientele or project beneficiaries must be: children in the foster custody of a Hawaii state government agency; or children placed by a Hawaii state government agency in therapeutic foster placement or in kinship, foster, respite, guardianship, permanent custody, adoptive families; or their caregivers, or current foster youth or young adults between the ages of 16 and 24 who have aged out of the state child welfare or mental health systems.

Restrictions: Units of government and public schools are not eligible under this Request for Proposals. Fiscal sponsorships are not permissible.

Geographic Focus: Hawaii

Date(s) Application is Due: May 15; Sep 15

Amount of Grant: 10,000 - 40,000 USD

Contact: Pam Funai, Program Officer; (808) 566-5537 or (888) 731-3863, ext. 537; fax (808) 521-6286; pfunai@hcf-hawaii.org

Internet: www.hawaiicommunityfoundation.org/grants/victoria-s-and-bradley-l-geist-foundation-capacity-building

Sponsor: Hawaii Community Foundation

827 Fort Street Mall

Honolulu, HI 96813-4317

Hawai'i Community Foundation Victoria S. and Bradley L. Geist　　1207
Foundation: Enhancement Grants

The purpose of the Foundation's Enhancements for Foster Children program is to enhance the lives of foster children by providing items and services that allow them to enjoy a quality of life similar to that of their peers. The funds are offered in the belief that every child is special and that their growth should be nurtured and celebrated. The Foundation seeks to make grants to organizations to purchase enhancement items and services for the benefit of eligible children. Grants range from $5,000 to $50,000. Grantees may propose an administrative fee for administering these funds. The annual deadline for online applications is September 15. The grant period is from January 1 through December 31.

Requirements: Tax-exempt Hawaii organizations are eligible to apply. This includes: nonprofit organizations; 501(c)3 organizations; religious organizations that are exempt from taxation; and units of government. Each expenditure must respond to a specific request made by an eligible child's foster caregiver, social worker, therapist, school counselor, guardian ad litem, or similar professional service provider for a specific item or service that will enhance the child's quality of life. Payments must be made to vendors for the benefit of eligible children.

Restrictions: Payments must not be made directly to children or their foster caregivers. Grantees may provide vendor gift cards to children or foster caregivers only in cases where a vendor declines to accept a grantee's check. Enhancements funds are not intended for basic living expenses such as housing, groceries, medical and dental care, and ordinary tuition expenses.

Geographic Focus: Hawaii

Date(s) Application is Due: Sep 15

Amount of Grant: 5,000 - 50,000 USD

Contact: Pam Funai, Program Coordinator; (808) 566-5537 or (888) 731-3863, ext. 537; fax (808) 521-6286; pfunai@hcf-hawaii.org

Internet: www.hawaiicommunityfoundation.org/grants/victoria-s-and-bradley-l-geist-foundation-enhancements

Sponsor: Hawaii Community Foundation

827 Fort Street Mall

Honolulu, HI 96813-4317

Hawai'i Community Foundation Victoria S. and Bradley L. Geist　　1208
Foundation: Supporting Foster Children and Their Caregivers

The support of foster children and their families is one area of particular interest to the Hawai'i Community Foundation. Focus is on happy and healthy foster children and their families sustained through a variety of resources. The Foundation will provide meaningful support for projects that result in the best quality homes and social environments for Hawaii's foster children. Priority is given to projects that will: support the recruitment, training and retention of quality foster parents; support the continued connectivity of foster children to their siblings; allow foster children to enjoy activities similar to those enjoyed by their naturally parented peers; and empower foster children to have as much control as is possible and appropriate over their destinies. Annual deadlines for submission are: January 17; May 15; and September 15.

Requirements: Organizations must be Hawaii based, either units of government (including public schools), a religious organization, or a 501(c)3 organization recognized as such by the I.R.S. Projects must serve a majority percentage of either legally recognized foster children ages birth through 18 and/or prospective or current foster parents.

Restrictions: Capital requests and endowments will not be funded.

Geographic Focus: Hawaii

Date(s) Application is Due: Jan 17; May 15; Sep 15

Amount of Grant: 10,000 - 100,000 USD

Contact: Pam Funai, Program Officer; (808) 566-5537 or (888) 731-3863, ext. 537; fax (808) 521-6286; pfunai@hcf-hawaii.org or foundations@hcf-hawaii.org

Internet: www.hawaiicommunityfoundation.org/grants/victoria-s-and-bradley-l-geist-foundation-supporting-foster-children-and-their-caregivers

Sponsor: Hawaii Community Foundation

827 Fort Street Mall

Honolulu, HI 96813-4317

Hawai'i Community Foundation Victoria S. and Bradley L. Geist　　1209
Foundation: Supporting Transitioning Foster Youth Grants

The Foundation supports the Hawaii Youth Opportunities Initiative, a Co-Investment site with the Jim Casey Youth Opportunities Initiative. In concert with this initiative, the Foundation is offering a Request for Proposals to provide support to Hawaii's transitioning foster youth through projects that are aligned with the Jim Casey Youth Opportunities Initiative and the Hawaii Youth Opportunities Initiative. Successful projects and programs will demonstrate youth engagement in development and be designed to result in improved youth outcomes. Grant seekers are encouraged to align their proposals with the goals of the initiatives and to visit the Jim Casey website for more information. Grants usually range from $10,000 to $75,000 per year. Requests are considered in relationship to the size of the organization's operating. Requests for up to three years will be considered. Annual deadlines for online application submission have been identified as: January 17; May 15; and September 15. budget.

Requirements: Tax-exempt Hawaii organizations are eligible to apply. This includes: nonprofit organizations; 501(c)3 organizations; religious organizations that are exempt from taxation; and units of government. Programs must preferentially and primarily (more than 50%) serve current or former foster youth, age 14 to 24, who were in state child welfare or mental health systems after their 14th birthday, even if they were adopted or legally reunited with their birth families prior to the age of majority.

Restrictions: Capital requests and endowments will not be funded.

Geographic Focus: Hawaii

Date(s) Application is Due: Jan 17; May 15; Sep 15

Amount of Grant: 10,000 - 75,000 USD

Contact: Pam Funai, Program Coordinator; (808) 566-5537 or (888) 731-3863, ext. 537; fax (808) 521-6286; pfunai@hcf-hawaii.org

Internet: www.hawaiicommunityfoundation.org/grants/victoria-s-and-bradley-l-geist-foundation-supporting-transitioning-foster-youth

Sponsor: Hawaii Community Foundation

827 Fort Street Mall

Honolulu, HI 96813-4317

Hawai'i SFCA Art Bento Program @ HiSAM Grants　　1210

The Hawai'i State Foundation on Culture and the Arts offers a museum education program known as the Art Bento Program at HiSAM. This four-part standards-based program is multi-disciplinary, and serves Oahu Department of Education elementary students and their teachers. This unique educational opportunity emphasizes arts and verbal literacy. All four segments of the program actively engage learners and connect to current arts standards and ELA Common Core Standards. Program activities begin in the classroom

with a professional development session for teachers. A teaching artist from the HSFCA's Artistic Teaching Partners (ATP) Roster leads the session. Using reproductions, the ATP models techniques and strategies to elicit student responses to artworks currently on view in the museum. The learning experience continues with a pre-visit to the classroom with the ATP again facilitating a question and response conversation with students and beginning a standards-based lesson.There is no cost to schools to participate in the program and funds for bus transportation are also provided. The annual deadline for application is March 10.
Requirements: Oahu Department of Education school grades two through six are eligible to apply.
Geographic Focus: Hawaii
Date(s) Application is Due: Mar 10
Contact: Susan Hogan, Museum Educator; (808) 586-9958 or (808) 586-0300; fax (808) 586-0308; susan.m.hogan@hawaii.gov
Internet: sfca.hawaii.gov/grants-programs/art-bento/
Sponsor: Hawai'i State Foundation on Culture and the Arts
250 South Hotel Street, 2nd Floor
Honolulu, HI 96813

Hawaiian Electric Industries Charitable Foundation Grants   1211
Named one of the most charitable companies in the state, HEI Charitable Foundation is focused on community programs aimed at promoting educational excellence, economic growth and environmental sustainability. To fulfill its mission of good corporate citizenship, the Foundation funds programs in the categories of: community development; education; the environment; and family services. Particular consideration will be given to organizations or programs which: demonstrate cost-effectiveness; has or will have a significant presence in company communities; provide recognition and goodwill for the company and further the well-being of the company's employees and their interests. Annual deadlines for application submission are January 1, April 1, July 1, and October 1.
Requirements: Hawaii 501(c)3 tax-exempt organizations may apply.
Restrictions: Funds are not available for: activities to replace government support; programs outside the areas served by HEI companies; religious activities of a particular denomination; veterans, fraternal or labor organizations, unless the purpose benefits all the people in the community; political funds; program advertising; special events, e.g., golf tournaments, dinners or functions; direct support for specific individuals.
Geographic Focus: Hawaii
Date(s) Application is Due: Jan 1; Apr 1; Jul 1; Oct 1
Contact: A.J. Halagao, Director of Corporate and Community Advancement; (808) 543-5889 or (808) 543-7960; fax (808) 203-1390; heicf@hei.com
Internet: www.hei.com/CustomPage/Index?keyGenPage=1073751884
Sponsor: Hawaiian Electric Industries Charitable Foundation
P.O. Box 730
Honolulu, HI 96808-0730

Hawaii Children's Cancer Foundation Contributions   1212
The Hawaii Children's Cancer Foundation provides a wide range of services and programs to our families, including financial assistance, support groups, social events, education and advocacy. All HCCF services and programs are entirely free to our families. Among other types of support, this includes Kukua baskets, financial assistance, and book reimbursement. Kukua baskets are "survival kits" that contain everything from gift cards to stuffed animals and blankets to help them have a better hospital stay. The basket is accompanied by a book that tells parents about their child's type of cancer and treatment in easy-to-understand language. The Foundation's most widely used program is financial assistance, which helps families pay expenses not covered by insurance, including housing, utilities, and transportation. And the book reimbursement program provides childhood cancer survivors who are attending college or a vocational training program with funds for the purchase of books, supplies, or equipment. There are no specified annual application deadlines or funding limits.
Geographic Focus: Hawaii
Contact: Donna Witsell, Executive Director; (808) 528-5161; fax (808) 521-4689; info@hccf.org
Internet: hccf.org/family-support/
Sponsor: Hawaii Children's Cancer Foundation
1814 Liliha Street
Honolulu, HI 96817

Hawaii Community Foundation Omidyar Ohana Fund Grants   1213
In 2009, the Honolulu-based Hawaii Community Foundation announced a $50 million commitment from eBay founder Pierre Omidyar and his wife, Pam, to support a number of community initiatives and establish the Omidyar Ohana Fund, which will support the Omidyars' ongoing philanthropic interests in the state. Initially, $16 million of the $50 million was allocated to various initiatives, including a $6 million matching grant to the Punahou School to construct and operate the Omidyar Kindergarten-First Grade Neighborhood complex. Omidyar attended the school as an eighth- and ninth-grader before leaving the state. In addition, $6 million was used to support the launch of the Omidyar Innovation Fund, a competitive grant program designed to spur innovation in Hawaii's social sector, while $4 million in matching funds from the Ohana Fund was used to launch the Community Stabilization Initiative, an $8 million effort to help families in the state weather the recession. Since returning to Hawaii several years ago, the Omidyars have supported many local causes and organizations. Most recently, the couple launched the Ulupono Initiative, a social investment organization that makes nonprofit grants and for-profit investments in organizations working to address issues critical to Hawaii's sustainable future. The Fund is now a part of the new FLEX Grants program at the Foundation, which supports a number of local programs annually.

Requirements: To be eligible for consideration an organization must be a 501(c)3 organization, an educational program, or a unit of government.
Restrictions: Funding is not available for: major capitol projects; endowments; or on-going or general operating costs.
Geographic Focus: Hawaii
Amount of Grant: 10,000 - 50,000 USD
Contact: Susan Maltezo, Senior Grants Manager; (808) 537-6333 or (888) 731-3863; fax (808) 521-6286; smaltezo@hcf-hawaii.org
Internet: www.hawaiicommunityfoundation.org/grants/flex-grants
Sponsor: Hawaii Community Foundation
827 Fort Street Mall
Honolulu, HI 96813-4317

Hawaii Community Foundation Oscar and Rosetta Fish Fund Grants   1214
The Hawaii Community Foundation's competitive grant making is defined around a variety of program areas. Some are targeted to population groups, such as children and youth, the aged, and lower income; some to areas of interest, such as culture and arts, family literacy, and natural resources; and some focus on a specific geographic area, such as Kauai or West Hawaii. The funding priorities reflect those of the many generous and community-spirited individuals, families, and companies that have established funds with the Foundation. The Fish fund was established by Oscar and Rosetta Fish. Rosetta Ramsey moved to Hawaii in the early 1940's from Ohio; she was a Speech Pathologist, and taught speech at the University of Hawaii at Manoa. She then met and later married Oscar Fish, a successful self-made businessman, who also moved to Hawaii from the mainland. He was a member of the University of Hawaii's College of Business Administration's first graduating class in 1959. Before Oscar's death in 1988, the Fish's set up a scholarship fund to help students who are majoring in business. Before Rosetta's death in 1994, she also started a fund with the Hawaii Community Foundation to provide assistance to families who have children needing speech therapy; she cared much about children with speech disorders. The annual application submission deadline is November 30.
Requirements: In most cases, only Hawaii organizations, either as a unit of government or one classified by the Internal Revenue Service as a 501(c)3 may apply.
Geographic Focus: Hawaii
Date(s) Application is Due: Nov 30
Contact: Lisha Kimura, Grants Administrator; (808) 537-6333 or (888) 731-3863; fax (808) 521-6286; lkimura@hcf-hawaii.org or give@hawaiicommunityfoundation.org
Larissa Kick, Program Director; (808) 566-5565 or (888) 731-3863; fax (808) 521-6286; lkick@hcf-hawaii.org or give@hawaiicommunityfoundation.org
Internet: www.hawaiicommunityfoundation.org/strengthening/oscar-rosetta-fish
Sponsor: Hawaii Community Foundation
827 Fort Street Mall
Honolulu, HI 96813

Hawaii Community Foundation Promising Minds Grants   1215
The Hawaii Community Foundation's competitive grant making is defined around a variety of program areas. Some are targeted to population groups, such as children and youth, the aged, and lower income; some to areas of interest, such as culture and arts, family literacy, and natural resources; and some focus on a specific geographic area, such as Kauai or West Hawaii. The funding priorities reflect those of the many generous and community-spirited individuals, families, and companies that have established funds with the Foundation. When the brain is developing at its most rapid rate and babies are forming important social connections, it is easier to lay the foundations for a lifetime of positive behavioral health and wellbeing. The Promising Minds Initiative exists to increase the healthy development of vulnerable children ages 0-5 and build resilience in those who have already experienced the negative effects of trauma in their short lives. Through the Promising Minds Initiative, the Foundation hopes to set the foundations for positive early childhood behavioral health resulting in long-term benefits to individual children and families, as well as more children on-track for Kindergarten with social, emotional and academic readiness. The Initiative is funded by Samuel and Mary Castle Foundation, Harold K. Caste Foundation, Robert Wood Johnson Foundation, Stupski Foundation, the Gwenfread Elaine Allen Fund, the Kʻaniani Fund, and the Omidyar Ohana Fund of the Hawaii Community Foundation. The annual application submission deadline is May 7. An award may not exceed $3,000.
Requirements: Organizations that currently serve children ages 0 to 5 in any of the following early childhood settings are eligible to apply: child care centers; family child interaction learning centers; licensed family child care; or home-based programs (such as home visiting). Organizations can be public, private, or non-profit entities.
Geographic Focus: Hawaii
Date(s) Application is Due: May 7
Amount of Grant: Up to 3,000 USD
Contact: Lisha Kimura, Grants Administrator; (808) 537-6333 or (888) 731-3863; fax (808) 521-6286; lkimura@hcf-hawaii.org
Larissa Kick, Program Director; (808) 537-6333 or (888) 731-3863; fax (808) 521-6286; lkick@hcf-hawaii.org
Internet: www.hawaiicommunityfoundation.org/grants/promising-minds
Sponsor: Hawaii Community Foundation
827 Fort Street Mall
Honolulu, HI 96813

Hawaii Community Foundation Reverend Takie Okumura Family Grants   1216
Takie Okumura came to Honolulu more than 100 years ago, but his contributions to the community are still vital today. He founded Makiki Christian Church with twenty-four members. He started the first Japanese-language school. He was instrumental in founding Mid Pacific Institute. He started the first AJA baseball league. He published newspapers

and wrote eleven books. The Reverend Takie Okumura Family was established by members of the Okumura family to continue the charitable work of Reverend Okumura, focusing on the healthy development of Hawaii's young children and youth. The Fund is now a part of the new FLEX Grants program at the Hawaii Community Foundation. Proposals will be accepted in the following areas: youth (ages 6-20 years old) and young children (ages birth to 5 years old). Priorities will be given to programs which: develop the ability to think critically; understand and appreciate one's own culture and those of others; develop the ability to settle differences peacefully; and strengthen the early care and education community system.

Requirements: Hawai'i organizations that are tax exempt, including nonprofit organizations, 501(c)3 organizations, religious organizations that are exempt from taxation, or units of government are eligible to apply.

Restrictions: Funding is not available for: major capitol projects; endowments; or on-going or general operating costs.

Geographic Focus: Hawaii

Amount of Grant: 5,000 - 15,000 USD

Contact: Susan Maltezo, Senior Grants Manager; (808) 537-6333 or (888) 731-3863; fax (808) 521-6286; smaltezo@hcf-hawaii.org

Internet: www.hawaiicommunityfoundation.org/grants/flex-grants

Sponsor: Hawaii Community Foundation

827 Fort Street Mall

Honolulu, HI 96813-4317

Hawaii Community Foundation Sanford Harmony Pillars of Peace Grants   1217

The Sanford Harmony program is part of the Hawaii Community Foundation's (HCF) Pillars of Peace Hawaii (PoPH) initiative, which began with visits of global peace leaders to Hawaii, including His Holiness the Dalai Lama and Aung San Suu Kyi. While the global peace leader visits will continue to be a part of PoPH, the primary goal of the program is to have a more direct and sustainable impact on Hawaii's youth, to encourage compassionate behavior and acts of aloha, and to grow ethical leaders for Hawaii's future. PoPH strives to reach student audiences with messages and training that reinforces positive behaviors, discourages risky and negative actions, and encourages healthy and successful futures. Through the support of T. Dennis Sanford and the National University Systems, the program includes: enough teacher tool kits to support whole school implementation; professional development, technical assistance, and action planning for goal setting; $1,000 to support professional development, staff time, substitute teacher support, curriculum integration, supplies, and miscellaneous fees; and partner gathering to learn and improve, and to network with fellow Sanford Harmony participants. Up to 15 schools will be considered each year.

Requirements: Applicants must be: a private or public school in the State of Hawaii; a Hawaii-based non-profit organization with 501(c)3 IRS status; and organizations serving 6th grade or younger programs.

Restrictions: Organizations with overdue HCF reports are not eligible. Grants may not be used for: business or organization start-up plans; fund raising events; the benefit of individuals; re-granting; or major capital improvements.

Geographic Focus: Hawaii

Contact: Robbie Ann Kane, Program Contact; (808) 537-6333 or (808) 566-5544; fax (808) 521-6286; rkane@hcf-hawaii.org

Natalie Millon, Program Contact; (808) 537-6333 or (808) 566-5568; fax (808) 521-6286; nmillon@hcf-hawaii.org

Internet: www.hawaiicommunityfoundation.org/grants/open-applications

Sponsor: Hawaii Community Foundation

827 Fort Street Mall

Honolulu, HI 96813-4317

Hawaii Electric Industries Charitable Foundation Grants   1218

The Hawaii Electric Industries (HEI) Charitable Foundation is focused on community programs aimed at promoting environmental sustainability, educational excellence, economic growth, and community development. The Foundation takes pride in serving and giving back to the community through volunteerism, grants, donations, scholarships, and the employee matching gift program. Since 2010, the HEI Charitable Foundation has contributed more than $10 million to local charities and other nonprofit organizations. Moreover, its employees have donated or fund raised over $4 million, and volunteered more than 80,000 hours. While the Foundation supports a diverse range of non-profit organizations, its philanthropic efforts are focused on supporting community programs across Hawaii in the following areas: educational excellence; environmental sustainability; economic growth; and community development. Particular consideration will be given to organizations or programs: which demonstrate cost-effectiveness by maximizing the achievement of goals while utilizing a minimum of resources; in communities where the company has or will have a significant presence; which provide recognition and goodwill for the company; which further the well-being of the company's employees and their interests; which enhance business development opportunities for HEI companies; and which are actively supported by volunteers from the company and/or foster camaraderie within. The application period is open ended, and applicants may apply at any time.

Requirements: Generally, only one donation will be given in a calendar year to any non-profit organization. Multi-year and capital pledges are very limited. In addition, support from the United Way will be a factor in the consideration process. Only 501(c)3 organizations to which contributions are deductible for tax purposes under Section 170 of the Internal Revenue Code (1954) as amended will be eligible for assistance.

Restrictions: Contributions will not normally be provided for: activities to replace government support; programs outside the areas served by HEI companies; religious activities of a particular denomination; veterans, fraternal or labor organizations, unless

the purpose benefits all the people in the community; political funds; program advertising; or direct support for specific individuals.

Geographic Focus: Hawaii

Amount of Grant: Up to 100,000 USD

Samples: After School All-Stars, Honolulu, Hawaii, $15,000 - support of an after school program; Hawaii First Robotics, Honolulu, Hawaii, $16,000 - support for an innovative robotics program; Hawaii Island Community Development Corporation, Honolulu, Hawaii, $25,000 - general operating support.

Contact: Alan M. Oshima, President; (808) 543-7960; fax (808) 203-1390; heicf@hei.com

A.J. Halagao, Director of Corporate and Community Advancement; (808) 543-5889 or (808) 543-7960; fax (808) 203-1390; heicf@hei.com

Internet: www.hei.com/CustomPage/Index?keyGenPage=1073751886

Sponsor: Hawaii Electric Industries Charitable Foundation

P.O. Box 730

Honolulu, HI 96808-0730

Hawaii State Legislature Grant-In-Aid   1219

Each year, the Hawaii State Legislature offers awards in the form of Grant-In-Aid to Hawaii-based organizations meeting the requirements of Section 42F-103, Hawaii Revised Statutes, that are seeking operating support for vital programs serving residents of the State. For each request applicants should submit two (2) complete original applications: one to the House Committee on Finance and one to the Senate Committee on Ways and Means. The deadline for receipt of a hard copy of this application is 4:30 pm on the date determined by the legislative calendar, January 18.

Requirements: All organizations and individuals meeting the requirements of Section 42F-103, Hawaii Revised Statutes, may apply.

Geographic Focus: Hawaii

Date(s) Application is Due: Jan 18

Amount of Grant: Up to 500,000 USD

Samples: Hawaii Literacy, Honolulu, Hawaii, $92,000 - general operating support (2018); Palama Settlement, Honolulu, Hawaii, $365,000 - general operating support (2018).

Contact: Staff Coordinator; (808) 586-6200 or (808) 586-6800

Internet: www.capitol.hawaii.gov/GIA/GIA.aspx

Sponsor: Hawaii State Legislature

State Capitol, Room 208

Honolulu, HI 96813

Hazel and Walter T. Bales Foundation Grants   1220

Established in Indiana in 1989, the Hazel and Walter T. Bales Foundation provides funding for programs in Clark and Floyd counties, Indiana, as well as Jefferson County, Kentucky. The Foundations primary fields of interest include: children and youth services; hospitals; human services; Protestant agencies and churches; and the Salvation Army. Types of funding include: building construction and renovation; continuing support; curriculum development; and matching grants. There are no specific deadlines, and applicants should send a letter of application directly to the Foundation office. Most recent grant awards have ranged from $350 to $13,500.

Geographic Focus: Indiana, Kentucky

Amount of Grant: 350 - 13,500 USD

Samples: Clark County Museum, Jeffersonville, Indiana, $10,000 - general fund contribution; Operation Outreach, Holliston, Massachusetts, $12,000 - books for children; Family and Children Place, Louisville, Kentucky, $10,000 - general fund contribution.

Contact: Lori Lewis, President; (812) 282-2586

Sponsor: Hazel and Walter T. Bales Foundation

630 Broadway

Jeffersonville, IN 47130-8203

Hazen Foundation Public Education Grants   1221

The foundation seeks to assist young people, particularly minorities and those disadvantaged by poverty, to achieve their full potential as individuals and as active participants in a democratic society. The goal of the Foundation's public education program is to foster effective schools for all children, and full partnership for parents and communities in school reform. Hazen will no longer accept unsolicited letters of inquiry but rather will periodically issue Requests for Proposals and Calls for Letters of Inquiry. Organizations that wish to receive a RFP should call the Foundation and leave a message on voicemail extension #7 or submit a request with organizational contact information at the contact U.S. page of the website or send email to hazen@hazenfoundation.org.

Requirements: Grants are awarded only to federally tax-exempt 501(c)3 organizations. The Foundation favors requests from community-based and grassroots organizations in four (4) geographic sites: Los Angeles, Miami/Dade County, the Delta of Mississippi and New York City. Organizations are invited to apply for funding through the RFP process at the discretion of the Foundation. All inquiries will be reviewed by staff, although not all inquiries will receive a response. The Foundation will endeavor to determine whether each inquiring organization meets the criteria for each program area.

Restrictions: The Foundation does not make grants to individuals, schools or school districts, or government agencies. The Foundation does not fund scholarships or fellowships; nor provides funds toward ongoing operational expenses, deficit funding, building construction or maintenance. The Foundation does not make grants to individuals, schools or school districts. In addition, the Foundation does not support organizations in U.S. territories.

Geographic Focus: California, Florida, Louisiana, Mississippi, New York

Amount of Grant: Up to 30,000 USD

Contact: Phillip E. Giles, Program Officer; (212) 889-3034; fax (212) 889-3039; hazen@hazenfoundation.org

Internet: www.hazenfoundation.org/public-education

Sponsor: Edward R. Hazen Foundation
333 Seventh Avenue, 14th Floor
New York, NY 10001

HBF Pathways Out of Poverty Grants 1222

The Pathways Out of Poverty Program focuses on helping needy young people and adults gain a quality education. Proposals are sought that focus on improving student achievement and healthy development of young people of middle school age and above. Projects may include in-school and community-based educational programs, after-school activities, and mentoring programs. Programs designed to increase high school graduation rates are encouraged to apply. For projects serving adults, the Foundation seeks proposals to provide literacy education and GED preparation, and to offer vocational training and job placement. Most grants will be approved for one year, but a small number will receive up to three years of funding, depending on demonstrated need.

Requirements: Non-profit 501(c)3 tax-exempt organizations located in and/or provide services in the greater Washington, D.C., region (defined as the District of Columbia, the counties of Arlington, Fairfax, and the city of Alexandria in Virginia, and Montgomery, and Prince George's counties in Maryland) are eligible. The Foundation uses a two-step, proposal-evaluation process. Applicant organizations are required to submit a letter of inquiry that briefly describes the proposed project's purpose, operation, target audience, timeline, costs, and anticipated impacts. Full proposals are by invitation.

Restrictions: Grants will not be made for capital or endowment programs, nor for sectarian religious purposes. Grants cannot be used for lobbying or other partisan purposes.

Geographic Focus: District of Columbia, Maryland, Virginia

Date(s) Application is Due: Feb 8

Amount of Grant: 5,000 - 25,000 USD

Contact: Marcela Brane, President; (202) 223-8801; fax (202) 223-8804; info@herbblock.org

Sarah Alex, Executive Director; (202) 223-8801; fax (202) 223-8804; info@herbblock.org

Internet: www.herbblockfoundation.org/programs/pathways-poverty

Sponsor: Herb Block Foundation
1730 M Street NW, Suite 901
Washington, D.C. 20036

Hearst Foundations Culture Grants 1223

The Hearst Foundations fund non-profit organizations working in the fields of culture, education, health, and social services. The Foundations have two offices, one in New York which manages funding for non-profits headquartered east of the Mississippi River and one in San Francisco which manages funding for non-profits to the west. About 80% of the Foundations' total funding goes to prior grantees; the Foundations receive approximately 1,200 grant requests annually. The Foundations' cultural funding comprises 25% of their total giving; 60% of the Foundations' cultural funding goes to organizations having budgets over ten-million dollars. In the area of culture, the Foundations look for institutions that offer meaningful programs in the arts and sciences. Preference is given to artist development and training, arts-education programs that address the lack of arts programming in K-12 curricula, and science-education programs that focus on developing academic pathways in science, technology, engineering, and math. Requests which enable engagement by young people and which create a lasting impression are given higher priority. The Foundations provide program, capital, and, on a limited basis, general and endowment support. Requests are accepted year round. These must be submitted via the Foundations' online application portal. Each request goes through an evaluation process that generally spans four to six weeks. The Foundations conduct a site visit of semi-finalists and may also consult with experts in a given field. Applicants will receive an email confirmation of receipt of submission and can follow the status of their request through the online system. Instructions for using the system, guidelines (in the form of an FAQ), and the link to the Foundations' online portal are at the Foundations' website.

Requirements: Grants are made only to 501(c)3 organizations. Well-established nonprofits that primarily serve large demographic and/or geographic constituencies are preferred. Within those, the Foundations identify organizations which achieve truly differentiated results relative to other organizations making similar efforts for similar populations. The Foundations also look for evidence of sustainability beyond their support.

Restrictions: Organizations must wait one year from the date of their notice of decline before the Foundations will consider another request. Grantees must wait a minimum of three years from their grant award date before the Foundations will consider another request. The Foundations do not fund individuals or the following types of requests: those from organizations operating outside the United States; those from organizations with operating budgets under one million dollars; those from organizations involved in publishing, radio, film, or television; those from local chapters of organizations; those from organizations lacking demonstrable long-term impact on populations served; requests to fund tours, conferences, workshops, or seminars; requests to fund advocacy or public-policy research; requests to fund special events, tickets, tables, or advertising for fundraising events; requests for seed money or to fund start-up projects; and request to fund program-related investments.

Geographic Focus: All States

Amount of Grant: Up to 1,000,000 USD

Samples: Arab Community Center for Economic & Social Services Access, Dearborn, Michigan, $50,000—toward the SURA Arts Academy educational programs at the Arab-American National Museum; Cambria Library, Cambria, California, $70,000—towards the capital campaign for a new library; Center of Creative Arts, St. Louis, Missouri, $100,000—to support the Urban Arts Outreach programs.

Contact: Mason Granger, Director of Grants; (212) 649-3750; fax (212) 586-1917; hearst.ny@hearstfdn.org

Annette Hepler, Grants Manager; (415) 908-4500; fax (415) 348-0887;

hearst.sf@hearstfdn.org

Internet: www.hearstfdn.org/funding-priorities/

Sponsor: Hearst Foundations
300 West 57th Street, 26th Floor
New York, NY 10019-3741

Hearst Foundations Social Service Grants 1224

The Hearst Foundations fund non-profit organizations working in the fields of culture, education, health, and social service. The Foundations have two offices, one in New York which manages funding for non-profits headquartered east of the Mississippi River and one in San Francisco which manages funding for non-profits to the west. About 80% of the Foundations' total funding goes to prior grantees; the Foundations receive approximately 1,200 grant requests annually. The Foundations' social-service funding comprises 15% of their total giving; 60% of the Foundations' social-service giving goes to organizations having budgets over five-million dollars. In the area of social service, the Foundations fund direct-service organizations that tackle the roots of chronic poverty by applying effective solutions to the most challenging social and economic problems. Preference is given to affordable-housing, job-creation and job-training, literacy, and youth-development programs. In limited cases, the Foundations fund organizations focusing on domestic abuse, food delivery and food banks, sexual abuse, and substance abuse. The Foundations fund requests for program, capital, and general support. Requests are accepted year round. These must be submitted via the Foundations' online application portal. Each request goes through an evaluation process that generally spans four to six weeks. The Foundations conduct a site visit of semi-finalists and may also consult with experts in a given field. Applicants will receive an email confirmation of receipt of submission and can follow the status of their request through the online system. Instructions for using the system, guidelines (in the form of an FAQ), and the link to the Foundations' online portal are at the Foundations' website.

Requirements: Grants are made only to 501(c)3 organizations. Initiatives of an organization's national headquarters are preferred over those of local chapters. The Foundations give high priority to programs that have proven successful in facilitating economic independence and in strengthening families and that have the potential to scale productive practices in order to reach more people in need.

Restrictions: Organizations must wait one year from the date of their notice of decline before the Foundations will consider another request. Grantees must wait a minimum of three years from their grant award date before the Foundations will consider another request. The Foundations do not fund individuals or the following types of requests: those from organizations operating outside the United States; those from organizations with operating budgets under one million dollars; those from organizations involved in publishing, radio, film, or television; those from organizations lacking demonstrable long-term impact on populations served; requests to fund tours, conferences, workshops, or seminars; requests to fund advocacy or public-policy research; requests to fund special events, tickets, tables, or advertising for fundraising events; requests for seed money or to fund start-up projects; and request to fund program-related investments.

Geographic Focus: All States

Amount of Grant: Up to 100,000 USD

Samples: Arab-American Family Support Center, Brooklyn, New York, $50,000—general support; Alliance House Inc., Salt Lake City, Utah, $35,000—to provide housing for people who are homeless or at risk of homelessness because of mental illness; Alt Consulting, Memphis, Tennessee, $50,000—toward rural and minority economic and business development programs in the Delta.

Contact: Mason Granger, Director of Grants; (212) 649-3750; fax (212) 586-1917; hearst.ny@hearstfdn.org

Annette Hepler, Grants Manager; (415) 908-4500; fax (415) 348-0887; hearst.sf@hearstfdn.org

Internet: www.hearstfdn.org/funding-priorities/

Sponsor: Hearst Foundations
300 West 57th Street, 26th Floor
New York, NY 10019-3741

Hearst Foundations United States Senate Youth Grants 1225

The United States Senate unanimously passed a resolution in 1962 creating the United States Senate Youth Program (USSYP), a national initiative to provide a yearly opportunity for talented young people with demonstrated leadership abilities to deepen their understanding of America's political processes and strengthen their resolve to pursue careers in public service. Two high-school juniors or seniors are selected each year from each state, the District of Columbia, and the Department of Defense Education Activity to serve as delegates to Washington Week which generally takes place the first or second week of March; a first and second alternate is also chosen from each of the entities listed above in the event that a delegate cannot attend. In addition to transportation, accommodations, and meals, each delegate also receives a $5000 undergraduate college scholarship to the college or university of his or her choice with encouragement to continue coursework in history and political science. The selection process is highly competitive; in addition to demonstrating strong leadership capabilities, most participants rank in the top one percent of their state academically. Applications must be obtained and processed through high school principals, guidance counselors, or the state-level selection contact. Selection contacts and deadlines for every state are listed on the USSYP website along with more detailed information and a downloadable brochure about the program and application process. Application procedures and deadlines vary by state; however final selections are due to the Hearst Foundation by December 1. The program has been fully funded since inception by The Hearst Foundations as part of their continuing commitment to preparing young people for citizenship and leadership in participatory democracy.

Requirements: Any high school junior or senior currently serving in any of the following elected or appointed capacities in student government, civic, or educational organizations is eligible to apply: student body president, vice-president, secretary, and/or treasurer; class president, vice-president, secretary, and/or treasurer; student council representative; or representative of any district, regional, or state-level civic and/or educational organization approved by the state selection administrator.
Restrictions: Each applicant must be a permanent resident of the United States and be currently enrolled in a public or private secondary school located in the state in which either one of his or her parents or guardians legally resides. Previous USSYO delegates and scholarship recipients are not eligible to apply.
Geographic Focus: All States
Amount of Grant: 5,000 USD
Contact: Rayne Guilford, Program Director; (415) 908-4540 or (800) 841-7048, ext. 4540; fax (415) 243-0760; USSYP@hearstfdn.org
Internet: www.ussenateyouth.org/index.php
Sponsor: Hearst Foundations
300 West 57th Street, 26th Floor
New York, NY 10019-3741

HEI Charitable Foundation Grants **1226**

Hawaiian Electric Industries (HEI), with its family of companies—Hawaiian Electric Company (HECO), Maui Electric Company (MECO), Hawaii Electric Light Company (HELCO), and American Savings Bank (ASB)—strives to be a trusted and valued leader in improving the economic well-being of the state, promoting the environmental sustainability of the Hawaiian islands, and benefiting the communities in which it serves. Through the HEI Charitable Foundation (HEICF), the HEI companies give back to the community through volunteerism, grants, donations, scholarships, and our employee matching gift program. Giving efforts are focused on supporting community programs across Hawaii in Educational Excellence, Environmental Sustainability, and Economic Growth.
Requirements: Nonprofit 501(c)3 organizations are eligible to apply. Funds can also be donated to governmental entities provided that such funds are used for a public purpose in accordance with IRS rules governing 501(c)3 charitable foundations. Particular consideration will be given to organizations or programs: which demonstrate cost-effectiveness by maximizing the achievement of goals while utilizing a minimum of resources; in communities where the company has or will have a significant presence; which provide recognition and goodwill for the company; which further the well-being of the company's employees and their interests; which enhance business development opportunities for HEI companies; and which are actively supported by volunteers from the company and/or foster camaraderie within.
Restrictions: Generally only one donation will be given in a calendar year to any nonprofit organization. Multi-year and capital pledges are very limited. In additional, support from the United Way will be a factor in the consideration process. Contributions will not normally be provided for: activities to replace government support; programs outside the areas served by HEI companies; religious activities of a particular denomination; Veterans, fraternal or labor organizations, unless the purpose benefits all the people in the community; political funds; program advertising; and, direct support for specific individuals.
Geographic Focus: Hawaii
Date(s) Application is Due: Jan 1; Apr 1; Jul 1; Oct 1
Contact: AJ Halagao, HEI Director of Corporate and Community Advancement; (808) 543-7960 or (808) 543-5889; fax (808) 203-1390; heicf@hei.com
Internet: www.hei.com/phoenix.zhtml?c=101675&p=charitable-foundation
Sponsor: HEI Charitable Foundation
P.O. Box 730
Honolulu, HI 96808-0730

Helen Bader Foundation Grants **1227**

Throughout her life, Helen Bader sought to help others. She played many roles - student, mother, businesswoman, and social worker - believing that everyone should have the opportunity to reach their fullest potential. Growing up in the railroad town of Aberdeen, South Dakota, Helen learned the value of hard work and self-reliance. The Great Depression and the sacrifices of World War II also taught her the importance of reaching out to those in need. Helen attended Downer College in Milwaukee, earning a degree in botany. She married Alfred Bader, a chemist from Austria, and together they started a family and created a business, the Aldrich Chemical Company. From the 1950s to the 1970s, their hard work helped build one of Wisconsin's most successful start-up enterprises of the era. The Baders' eventual divorce led Helen to again become self-reliant. She subsequently finished her Master of Social Work at the University of Wisconsin-Milwaukee. While doing her field work with the Legal Aid Society of Milwaukee, Helen met and helped many people in need, including single mothers and adults with mental illness. In the process, she gained a deeper appreciation for their everyday struggles. After graduation, she worked at the Milwaukee Jewish Home, where working with older adults brought home the many issues of aging. At a time when Alzheimer's disease was almost a complete mystery, she helped open the resident' minds and hearts through dance and music. Helen felt that the residents' quality of life depended upon the small details, so she was happy to run errands or escort them to the symphony. She found herself touched by the arts and studied the violin and guitar at the Wisconsin Conservatory of Music. Helen eventually faced cancer. As the illness began to sap her physical strength, she shared a wish with her family: to continue to aid those in need. She died in 1989. After her death, patterns of Helen's quiet style of philanthropy became more apparent. When she had come across an organization that impressed her, she would just pull out her checkbook without a lot of fanfare. In her name, the Helen Bader Foundation (HBF) supports worthy organizations working in key areas affecting the quality of life in Milwaukee, the state of Wisconsin, and Israel. The foundation also seeks to inspire the generosity in others, as every individual can make a difference through gifts of time, talent, and resources. The foundation will consider multiple-year requests with 24 or 36 month terms. Multi-year grants are subject to annual review before funds for subsequent years are released. The application deadline for the online preliminary proposal is January 5. The application deadline for organizations invited to complete a full proposal is February 2. The link to the online application system is available at the grant website. Application deadlines may vary from year to year. Prospective applicants are encouraged to visit the grant website to verify current deadline dates.
Requirements: Grants are awarded for projects consistent with one or more of the Helen Bader Foundation's program areas: Alzheimer's and aging (national in scope, with priority given to Wisconsin); economic development (restricted to the city of Milwaukee); community partnerships for youth (restricted to the city of Milwaukee); community initiatives (restricted to greater Milwaukee); arts (restricted to the city of Milwaukee); and directed grants and initiatives such as aid and support to Israel (for which proposals must be staff-solicited). Grants are given only to U.S. organizations which are tax exempt under Section 501(c)3 of the Internal Revenue Code or to government entities; grants will only be approved for foreign entities which meet specific charitable status requirements.
Restrictions: The Foundation does not provide direct support for individuals, such as individual scholarships.
Geographic Focus: All States, All Countries
Date(s) Application is Due: Jan 5; Feb 25
Amount of Grant: 10,000 - 100,000 USD
Samples: Aging & Disabiity Resource Center of Portage County, Stevens Point, Wisconsin, $12,000, creation of an Early Memory Loss Program to serve central Wisconsin; Arts at Large, Inc., Milwaukee, Wisconsin, $412,000, inclusive arts programming for low-income children attending six Milwaukee Public Schools in grades K-8 and their affiliated Community Learning Centers; Ben-Gurion University of the Negev, Beer Sheva, Israel, $10,000, Summer School Science Camp for 50 seventh grade Bedouin students from Abu Basma schools.
Contact: Tamara Hogans, Grants Manager; (414) 224-6464; fax (414) 224-1441; tammy@hbf.org or info@hbf.org
Internet: www.hbf.org/apply.htm
Sponsor: Helen Bader Foundation
233 North Water Street, Fourth Floor
Milwaukee, WI 53202

Helen E. Ellis Charitable Trust Grants **1228**

The Helen E. Ellis Charitable Trust was established to carry on the life work of Miss Ellis. A noted sculptor and artist, Miss Ellis was known throughout the community as a strong supporter of artistic talent and endeavored to enrich her community in the arts. As assistant curator of the Old Dartmouth Historical Society, she organized and promoted exhibitions that would foster public participation in the museum. The Helen E. Ellis Charitable Trust strives to continue Miss Ellis' work through grants that support cultural experiences for children and adults in the Westport, Dartmouth and New Bedford, MA areas. The Helen E. Ellis Charitable Trust provides grants to organizations that create programs relating to arts, music, crafts, conservation, wildlife and history preservation. The Trustee will make decisions to award grants consistent with the general objectives of the Helen E. Ellis Charitable Trust, "... with primary consideration to those programs which will confer a benefit upon the citizens of the towns of Westport and Dartmouth and the city of New Bedford, MA. With respect to proposals of equal merit, preference shall be accorded to those submitted by organizations located within the Town of Westport, MA." Award amounts typically go up to $35,000.
Requirements: Requests may be submitted for programs that provide educational or cultural experiences to children and/or adults in the towns of Westport and Dartmouth and the city of New Bedford. The Foundation will consider applications for programs that provide educational or cultural experiences to children and/or adults in the towns of Westport and Dartmouth and the city of New Bedford. Proposed programs must also relate to conservation, wildlife, history of the area, and/or the promotion of music, the arts, and crafts. Project/program requests are preferred. Applications will be submitted online through the Bank of America website. A grant report is required within 1 year of the grant application date, regardless of whether all of the funds have been spent.
Restrictions: The Foundation does not consider requests for the following: multi-year support, endowments, capital campaigns, academic or medical research religious or sectarian purposes, operating budget items (except for limited support of critical programming) or direct grants to individuals or other private foundations. The foundation does not support requests from individuals, organizations attempting to influence policy through direct lobbying, or any political campaigns.
Geographic Focus: Massachusetts
Date(s) Application is Due: Sep 15
Amount of Grant: Up to 35,000 USD
Samples: Town of Westport, Westport, Massachusetts, $34,200 - Awarded for Sustaining our Creative Community through Effective Engagement with Cultural Partners (2018); Old Dartmouth Historical Society, New Bedford, Massachusetts, $5,000 - Awarded for School Programs for Westport, Dartmouth, and New Bedford Youth (2018); Young Mens Christian Association Southcoast Incorporated, New Bedford, Massachusetts, $5,000 - Awarded for New Bedford YMCA Dance Program (2018).
Contact: Michealle Larkins, Philanthropic Administrator; (866) 778-6859; ma.grantmaking@bankofamerica.com or ma.ri.grantmaking@ustrust.com
Internet: www.bankofamerica.com/philanthropic/foundation/?fnId=26
Sponsor: Helen E. Ellis Charitable Trust
P.O. Box 1802
Providence, RI 02901-1802

Helen G., Henry F., & Louise Tuechter Dornette Foundation Grants   1229

The Foundation Office at Fifth Third Bank is committed to making a significant impact on programs and initiatives that create strong, vibrant communities and provide pathways to opportunity. Through the Foundation Office, the visions of individuals, families and institutions are realized, and legacies are attained by allocating the resources of their respective foundations in support of innovative programs and organizations in our communities. The Helen G., Henry F., & Louise Tuechter Dornette Foundation supports nature and the conservation of nature's beauty, as well as organizations that are beneficial to children, with a preference to organizations that Miss Dornette identified during her lifetime. Grants are given for the relief of sickness, suffering, distress, and for the care of young children, the aged, or the helpless and afflicted. Funding is also available for the promotion of education, to improve living conditions, and/or the good and welfare of the state/nation in emergencies. An organization interested in submitting a grant proposal should first submit a Letter of Inquiry (LOI) using the link at the website. LOIs are accepted from October 1 through December 31 each year. The Foundation Office will review each LOI and may contact the applying organization about further discussion of the proposal, which may include a site visit. Each organization will receive either an email declining the inquiry or an invitation to submit a full application online. An invitation to apply will include the foundation funding source, recommended request amount, and a deadline for receipt of the application. The Fifth Third Bank Foundation Office will submit completed applications to the respective Foundation Board or Committee for final review and approval or declination. Grant seekers should allow six to twelve months for the grant making process. In general, the Foundation prefers awarding grants for one year. Most recent awards have ranged from $5,000 to $250,000.

Requirements: Nonprofit organizations that operate in the Greater Cincinnati region and are designated under section 501(c)3 and subsections 509(a)1 or 509(a)2 by the Internal Revenue Service are eligible to apply for a grant.

Restrictions: Nonprofits may apply only once within any 12-month period. The following are ineligible to apply: individuals; individual churches (except for proposals regarding an affiliated school); publicly supported entities such as public schools, government or government agencies; supporting organizations designated 509(a)3 by the IRS; walks, runs, dinners, galas, luncheons and other event sponsorship requests; athletic, band, and other school booster clubs; or startup funding for new programs or organizations (usually not a funding priority). A waiting period of three years is required for prior grant recipients receiving $10,000 or more from any funding source administered by the Fifth Third Bank Foundation Office. This period will begin as of the first payment on the grant.

Geographic Focus: Ohio

Amount of Grant: 5,000 - 250,000 USD

Contact: Heidi B. Jark, Managing Director; (513) 534-7001 or (513) 636-4200

Internet: www.53.com/content/fifth-third/en/personal-banking/about/in-the-community/foundation-office-at-fifth-third-bank.html

Sponsor: Helen G., Henry F., & Louise Tuechter Dornette Foundation

38 Fountain Square Plaza, MD 1090CA

Cincinnati, OH 45202

Helen Gertrude Sparks Charitable Trust Grants   1230

Helen Sparks was born in Fort Worth, Texas, but went to college in the east. After graduation she returned to Fort Worth where she worked with the Fort Worth Little Theater. A cultured woman, she was interested in local artists and supported them by commissioning works. She also enjoyed literature and needlepoint. The Helen Gertrude Sparks Charitable Trust, which made its first distributions in 1971, was created to benefit charitable organizations focused on the elderly who are disabled in any way; children who are disabled, orphaned or disadvantaged; the arts, including performing and nonperforming arts; and education. The Trustee shall always show preference for those organizations which do not receive the predominate portion of their funds from government sources. Preference is given to organizations, operating in, or serving Tarrant County, Texas. This foundation makes approximately 2-3 awards each year and grants are typically between $5,000 and $15,000.

Requirements: Applicants must have 501(c)3 tax-exempt status. The Trust considers requests from charitable organizations that focus on the program areas noted above. Applications will be submitted online through the Bank of America website. A grant report is required within 1 year of the grant application date, regardless of whether all of the funds have been spent.

Restrictions: Eligibility to re-apply for a grant award from the Helen Gertrude Sparks Charitable Trust requires organizations to skip 1 grant cycle (1 year) before submitting a subsequent application. The trust does not support requests from individuals, organizations attempting to influence policy through direct lobbying, or any political campaigns.

Geographic Focus: Texas

Date(s) Application is Due: Aug 1

Amount of Grant: 5,000 - 15,000 USD

Samples: CASA of Tarrant County Inc., Fort Worth, Texas, $10,000 - Awarded for General Operations of the Organization (2018); Wings of Hope Equitherapy, Burleson, Texas, $10,000 - Awarded for Support for Equestrians with disabilities program (2018); Kids Who Care Inc., Fort Worth, Texas, $5,000 - Awarded for General Operations of the Organization.

Contact: Kelly Garlock, Philanthropic Client Manager; (800) 357-7094; tx.philanthropic@bankofamerica.com or tx.philanthropic@ustrust.com

Internet: www.bankofamerica.com/philanthropic/foundation/?fnId=10

Sponsor: Helen Gertrude Sparks Charitable Trust

500 West 7th Street, 15th Floor, TX1-497-15-08

Fort Worth, TX 76102-4700

Helen Irwin Littauer Educational Trust Grants   1231

Mrs. Littauer was born in Fort Worth, Texas, and was a descendant of the Cetti family, a prominent Fort Worth family. She earned a degree in journalism and worked in New York as an editor. In 1952, she moved to Connecticut and became an active community volunteer and was involved in city government. As a result of her passion for teaching, she also worked with troubled youth and was honored with numerous awards for her civic endeavors. Mrs. Littauer established the Educational Trust in 1969 and remained involved in grant decisions until her death in 1989. The Trust considers requests primarily from charitable organizations that provide services to Tarrant County and is particularly interested in, but not limited to, charitable organizations that focus on: scholarships that enable needy, but worthy boys and girls and young adults to attend school, college or university, with a particular emphasis on making scholarships available for attending schools of journalism; promotion of art, education and good citizenship; alleviating human suffering; medical care and treatment for all needy persons, including hospitals and clinics; providing care, education, recreation and/or physical training for needy, orphaned or disabled children; care of needy persons who are sick, aged or disabled; and improvement of living and working conditions of all persons. Grants are typically between $1,000 and $75,000.

Requirements: Applicants must have 501(c)3 tax-exempt status and provide services to Tarrant County, Texas. Applications will be submitted online through the Bank of America website. A grant report is required within 1 year of the grant application date, regardless of whether all of the funds have been spent.

Restrictions: Eligibility to re-apply for a grant award from the Helen Irwin Littauer Educational Trust requires organizations to skip 1 grant cycle (1 year) before submitting a subsequent application. The trust does not support requests from individuals, organizations attempting to influence policy through direct lobbying, or any political campaigns.

Geographic Focus: Texas

Date(s) Application is Due: Mar 1

Amount of Grant: 1,000 - 75,000 USD

Samples: The Arlington Life Shelter, Arlington, Texas, $75,000 - Awarded for Hearts to Homes Capital Campaign (2019); CASA of Tarrant County Inc., Fort Worth, Texas, $40,000 - Awarded for General Operations of the Organization (2019); Communities Foundation of Texas, Dallas, Texas, $25,000 - Awarded for North Texas Giving Day - For use in Tarrant County (2019).

Contact: Kelly Garlock, Philanthropic Client Manager; (800) 357-7094; tx.philanthropic@bankofamerica.com or tx.philanthropic@ustrust.com

Internet: www.bankofamerica.com/philanthropic/foundation/?fnId=18

Sponsor: Helen Irwin Littauer Educational Trust

Bank of America, N.A . P.O. Box 83141

Dallas, TX 75283-1041

Helen V. Brach Foundation Grants   1232

Established in 1974 in Illinois by the wife of Frank Brach, principal owner of the E.J. Brach and Sons Candy Company of Chicago, the foundation operates to prevent cruelty to animals or to children; for religious, charitable, scientific, literary, and education purposes; and for public safety testing through support of Midwest 501(c)3 tax-exempt organizations carrying out programs and activities in these areas. Brach provides grants nationally and has wide-ranging interests. For example, it supports homeless and women's emergency shelters, teen pregnancy prevention programs, parenting education, summer school for disadvantaged children, job training for welfare mothers, orphanages, and scholarships for economically disadvantaged students. Types of support include annual campaigns, building construction and renovation, equipment, general operating support, publications, research, and special projects. The foundation ordinarily does not make multi-year grants or commitments. Applicants are required to complete in full a brief application form, which may be obtained from the office. The board of directors gives final consideration to all applications received in a given year at the board's meeting, which is usually held in March.

Requirements: Although 501(c)3 nonprofits from across the nation are eligible, giving is primarily made in the Midwest, as well as California, Massachusetts, Ohio, Pennsylvania, and South Carolina.

Restrictions: Grants are not made to individuals or to organizations outside the United States. Typically grants are not made in excess of 10 percent of a group's operating budget, which automatically excludes start-up grants.

Geographic Focus: All States

Date(s) Application is Due: Dec 31

Amount of Grant: 5,000 - 25,000 USD

Samples: After School Matters, Chicago, Illinois, $20,000 - for sports and technology program; Brookfield Zoo, Brookfield, Illinois, $50,000 - research program on animal behavior; Hospice of Tuscarawas County, Dover, Ohio, $50,000 - support for Hospice House end-of-life health care facility.

Contact: John P. Hagnell, Associate Director; (312) 372-4417; fax (312) 372-0290

Sponsor: Helen V. Brach Foundation

55 W Wacker Drive, Suite 701

Chicago, IL 60601-1609

Help America Foundation Grants   1233

The Foundation provides volunteers and financial aid to organizations that support the poor and underpriviledged, needy and/or homeless Americans including men, women, children, and veterans of war. The Foundation also supports the families of active military personnel called to duty. The application is available at the Foundation website.

Requirements: To qualify for funds, the organization must be a Section 501(c)3 charitable organization, and complete the online general purpose application with detailed information, including, but not limited to: organizational business detail including contact information; description of plans for fund usage; amount requested; geographic area to be served; potential beneficiaries; organization purpose; tax-exempt status; and applicable financial information.

Geographic Focus: All States

Contact: Linda Curry, Foundation Coordinator; (708) 597-1085; fax (708) 597-1435; D.C.curry@athome.com

Internet: www.helpamericafoundation.org/howtoapply/index.htm

Sponsor: Help America Foundation

5625 West 115th Street

Alsip, IL 60803

Hendricks County Community Foundation Grants 1234

The Hendricks County Community Foundation Grants provide funding for organizations or charitable projects that serve in the following program areas: arts and culture; community development; education; environment; health and human services; and youth. These grants enable organizations to provide effective programs and respond to needs of people in the Hendricks County community.

Requirements: A letter of intent should be submitted to the organization between December 1 and January 11. The Foundation uses the following criteria when reviewing applications: sustainability; effective operations; proven success; strong leadership; innovation and creativity; accessibility; collaboration; and engagement.

Restrictions: The Foundation will not fund: bands, sports teams, or other groups without a philanthropic project; annual appeals, galas or membership contributions; fundraising events such as golf tournaments, walk-a-thons, and fashion shows; grants to individuals; projects aimed at promoting a particular religion or construction projects for religious institutions; operating, program and construction costs at schools, universities and private academies unless there is a significant opportunity for community use or collaboration; organizations or projects that discriminate based upon race, ethnicity, age, gender, sexual orientation; political campaigns or direct lobbying efforts by 501(c)3 organizations; post-event, after-the-fact situations or debt retirement; medical, scientific or academic research; publications, films, audiovisual and media materials, programs produced for artistic purposes or produced for resale.

Geographic Focus: Indiana

Amount of Grant: 500 - 17,500 USD

Samples: Farmers and Hunters Feeding the Hungry, general operating expenses, $3,000; Hendricks County Senior Services, transportation for the elderly and disabled, $5,000; Kingsway Community Care Center, general operating expenses, $2,500.

Contact: Susan Rozzi, Associate Director; (317) 718-1200; fax (317) 718-1033; janet@hendrickscountycf.org

Internet: www.hendrickscountycf.org/grants/oppfund_grants/index.shtml

Sponsor: Hendricks County Community Foundation

5055 East Main Street, Suite A

Avon, IN 46123

Henrietta Lange Burk Fund Grants 1235

The Henrietta Lange Burk Fund was established in 1994 to support and promote quality arts, cultural, educational, health care and human services programming for underserved populations. Special consideration is given to charitable organizations that address the health concerns of older adults through either direct programming or research. The Lange Burk Fund is a private foundation created by Mrs. Henrietta Lange Burk. Mrs. Burk created the Fund as a memorial to her parents, Mr. and Mrs. Henry G. Lange, as well as to her husband, William Burk, and herself. Mrs. Burk was particularly interested in the performing and cultural arts, age-related health problems, research and care and human services organizations, especially those connected to her Protestant background. Award amounts typically range from $2,500 to $35,000, and are given out twice annually.

Requirements: Applicants must have 501(c)3 tax-exempt status and serve residents of the Chicago Metropolitan area. Applications will be submitted online through the Bank of America website. A grant report is required within 1 year of the grant application date, regardless of whether all of the funds have been spent.

Restrictions: The foundation will consider requests for general operating support only if the organization's operating budget is less than $1 million. In general, grant requests for individuals, endowment campaigns or capital projects will not be considered. The foundation does not support requests from individuals, organizations attempting to influence policy through direct lobbying, or any political campaigns.

Geographic Focus: Illinois

Date(s) Application is Due: Jun 1; Nov 1

Amount of Grant: 2,500 - 35,000 USD

Samples: Chicago Fund on Aging and Disability, Chicago, Illinois, $25,000 - Awarded for Holiday Meals Program (2018); Great Chicago Food Depository, Chicago, Illinois, $25,000 - Awarded for Older Adults Programs (2018); Northern Illinois Food Bank, Geneva, Illinois, $25,000 - Awarded for Senior Grocery Program (2018).

Contact: Srilatha Lakkaraju, Philanthropic Client Manager; (312) 828-8166; ilgrantmaking@bankofamerica.com or ilgrantmaking@ustrust.com

Internet: www.bankofamerica.com/philanthropic/foundation/?fnId=61

Sponsor: Henrietta Lange Burk Fund

231 South LaSalle Street, IL1-231-13-32

Chicago, IL 60604

Henry and Ruth Blaustein Rosenberg Foundation Education Grants 1236

The Henry and Ruth Blaustein Rosenberg Foundation provides support primarily in the Baltimore, Maryland region. In the area of Education, the Foundation's primary goals are to promote literacy; provide support for children and youth programs; improve programs that provide services for children with disabilities; and support school readiness for preschool children. Typically, awards range from $10,000 to $70,000, and the majority of grants are multi-year in nature. There are nor specified annual deadlines or application forms.

Requirements: 501(c)3 tax-exempt charitable organizations located in or primarily serving the metropolitan Baltimore area are eligible to apply. An initial application should include the following: information about the program(s) for which funding is requested; need, purpose, activities, and evaluation plan of the proposed program(s); program budget (including sources of anticipated income as well as expenditures) and timeline; dollar amount of funding requested; history, mission, and key accomplishments of your organization; information on Board members and key staff; current institutional operating budget (including major sources of revenue as well as expenditures); copy of an IRS tax status determination letter or information about your fiscal agent.

Restrictions: The foundation does not: make grants or scholarships to individuals; accept unsolicited proposals for academic, scientific, or medical research; or support direct mail, annual giving, membership campaigns, fundraising and commemorative events. The foundations rarely make capital grants unless there is a prior relationship.

Geographic Focus: All States

Amount of Grant: 10,000 - 70,000 USD

Samples: Dyslexia Tutoring Program, Baltimore, Maryland, $60,000 - two year program providing general operating support; Family Tree, Baltimore, Maryland, $70,000 - general operating support; Enoch Pratt Free Library, Baltimore, Maryland, $20,000 - support for the Emergent Literacy Program.

Contact: Henry A. Rosenberg, Jr., President; (410) 347-7201; fax (410) 347-7210; info@blaufund.org

Internet: www.blaufund.org/foundations/henryandruth_f.html

Sponsor: Henry and Ruth Blaustein Rosenberg Foundation

One South Street, Suite 2900

Baltimore, MD 21202

Henry and Ruth Blaustein Rosenberg Foundation Youth Development Grants 1237

The Henry and Ruth Blaustein Rosenberg Foundation provides support primarily in the Baltimore, Maryland region. In the area of Youth Development, the goals are to promote recreation, learning, and leadership development through after-school programs; prevent teen pregnancy; and advocate for policies and practices that improve outcomes for youth. Typically, awards range from $10,000 to $75,000, and the majority of grants are multi-year in nature. There are nor specified annual deadlines or application forms.

Requirements: 501(c)3 tax-exempt charitable organizations located in or primarily serving the metropolitan Baltimore area are eligible to apply. An initial application should include the following: information about the program(s) for which funding is requested; need, purpose, activities, and evaluation plan of the proposed program(s); program budget (including sources of anticipated income as well as expenditures) and timeline; dollar amount of funding requested; history, mission, and key accomplishments of your organization; information on Board members and key staff; current institutional operating budget (including major sources of revenue as well as expenditures); copy of an IRS tax status determination letter or information about your fiscal agent.

Restrictions: The foundation does not: make grants or scholarships to individuals; accept unsolicited proposals for academic, scientific, or medical research; or support direct mail, annual giving, membership campaigns, fundraising and commemorative events. The foundations rarely make capital grants unless there is a prior relationship.

Geographic Focus: Maryland

Amount of Grant: 10,000 - 75,000 USD

Samples: Digital Harbor Foundation, Baltimore, Maryland, $25,000 - support for Maker Foundations, a STEM after school program for middle and high school students; Next One Up Foundation, Baltimore, Maryland, $30,000 - two-year award to support mentoring and coaching of Baltimore City athletes; U.S. Lacrosse Foundation, Sparks, Maryland, $100,000 - three-year grant to support the National Campaign for Lacrosse.

Contact: Henry A. Rosenberg, Jr., President; (410) 347-7201; fax (410) 347-7210; info@blaufund.org

Internet: www.blaufund.org/foundations/henryandruth_f.html

Sponsor: Henry and Ruth Blaustein Rosenberg Foundation

One South Street, Suite 2900

Baltimore, MD 21202

Henry County Community Foundation - TASC Youth Grants 1238

The TASC (Teens About Serving the County) Youth Grants Committee meets four times each school year. The TASC Committee includes one 8th grader, one freshman, one sophomore, one junior, and one senior from each of the five school districts in Henry County. The TASC Committee assignment is to evaluate grant submissions relating to youth and educational programs. These students critically evaluate each grant submission for purpose, scope, need, and viability. They then determine whether each grant will be accepted as is, partially funded, denied, or accepted with conditions. The TASC Committee grant recommendations are then taken to the Henry County Community Foundation Board of Directors for final approval. Guidelines and the application are available at the website.

Requirements: Eligibility for Youth Grants include the following categories: youth organization or club; not for profit 501(c)3; community organization; school (public or private). Grant preferences must directly relate to the foundation's mission statement; address a need for youth of Henry County; provide a time line for completion of project; and benefit the most people. Grants under $2,500 are preferred.

Restrictions: Grant money may not be used for overhead costs, salaries or wages, or direct donations to other organizations.

Geographic Focus: Indiana

Date(s) Application is Due: Feb 24; May 4; Oct 7; Dec 2

Amount of Grant: Up to 2,500 USD

Contact: Beverly Matthews, Executive Director; (765) 529-2235; fax (765) 529-2284; beverly@henrycountycf.org or info@henrycountycf.org
Internet: www.henrycountycf.org/index.
php?submenu=TASC&src=gendocs&ref=Grant%20Guidelines&category=TASC
Sponsor: Henry County Community Foundation
700 S Memorial Drive, P.O. Box 6006
New Castle, IN 47362

Henry County Community Foundation Grants   1239

As a community foundation, the Henry County Community Foundation addresses the broad needs in Henry County, Indiana which include, but are not limited to, the following five categories: health and medical; social services; education; cultural affairs and civic affairs. All requests for grants are reviewed by the Foundation's Grants Committee, which is made up of members of the Board of Directors and several outside advisers. Reviews and recommendations are then presented to the full Board of Directors at its regularly scheduled meetings in April and October. However, the Board reserves the right to consider individual requests at any regularly scheduled meeting, if deemed necessary. The Foundation's grant program emphasizes change-oriented and focused types of grants to achieve certain objectives such as becoming more efficient, increasing fundraising capabilities, delivering better products, etc. The guidelines and application are available at the website.
Requirements: Applications from organizations whose programs benefit the residents of Henry County are accepted only from organizations who attend the spring or fall grant workshops held at the Foundation office. Organizations must be a 501(c)3 tax-exempt or be sponsored by a 501(c) tax-exempt organization. Grants will also be accepted from school and government entities.
Restrictions: The following are not eligible for funding: operating cost; individuals; individuals or groups of individuals to attend seminars or take trips except where there are special circumstances which will benefit the community; sectarian religious purposes. No grants will be made exclusively for endowment purposes of recipient organizations; individuals or organizations that are not charitable organizations; and programs and/or equipment which were committed to prior to the submission of grant application.
Geographic Focus: Indiana
Date(s) Application is Due: Mar 30; Aug 31
Contact: Beverly Matthews, Executive Director; (765) 529-2235; fax (765) 529-2284; beverly@henrycountycf.org or info@henrycountycf.org
Internet: www.henrycountycf.org/index.
php?submenu=Grants&src=gendocs&ref=Grants&category=Grants
Sponsor: Henry County Community Foundation
700 S Memorial Drive, P.O. Box 6006
New Castle, IN 47362

Henry E. Niles Foundation Grants   1240

The mission of the Henry E. Niles Foundation is to help in the nurturing and uplifting of people in need. The Foundation strives to support humanitarian efforts, including faith-based endeavors, that: strengthen education including special education, literacy and others; fight economic hardships through self-help opportunities; enhance public health and sanitation on a global basis. The Foundation has a particular interest in organizations that promote collaborative efforts among groups and organizations. The Board is currently highlighting the following areas: Education – Included in this interest area are primary, secondary and higher education for those motivated individuals who are unable to obtain the benefits of quality education without assistance; Economic Self-Sufficiency – This program area includes but is not limited to: job training, the encouragement and support of entrepreneurialism, mentoring, and micro-credit initiatives; Health & Independence – Special interests here include medical and public health assistance for the elderly, the poor, the disadvantaged and the disabled. Additionally, the Foundation encourages pilot initiatives that test new program models. There are no deadlines; applications are accepted throughout the year.
Requirements: The majority of the Foundation's grantmaking is focused in the northeastern United States and abroad, although, occasionally, grants may be made in other regions of the country as well. All applicants must have tax-exempt 501(c)3 status as a non-profit organization as defined by the Internal Revenue Service. Grants may range from a few thousand dollars up to $100,000. In unique circumstances, the Foundation does consider a more significant grant for a program having a major impact in one or more of its areas of interest.
Restrictions: The Foundation will generally not provide grants to the following: organizations not determined to be tax-exempt under section 501(c)3 of the Internal Revenue Code; general fundraising drives; individuals; government agencies; or organizations that subsist mainly on third party funding and have demonstrated no ability or expended little effort to attract private funding.
Geographic Focus: All States
Amount of Grant: Up to 100,000 USD
Contact: Ashley C. Lantz, (203) 661-1000; fax (203) 629-7300; alantz@fcsn.com
Internet: www.heniles.org/Guidlines.htm
Sponsor: Henry E. Niles Foundation
c/o Fogarty, Cohen, Selby & Nemiroff
Greenwich, CT 06830

Henry F. Koch Residual Trust Grants   1241

When steel proprietor George L. Mesker died in Evansville, Indiana, in 1936, he left $500,000 to buy property to expand Mesker Park. He also set aside $250,000 to provide music in other city parks. The terms of his will were ambiguous, and one of Mesker's trustees and close ally had his own ideas. Henry F. Koch was bent on building an amphitheater and disregarded ideas for anything else. Koch went so far as to sue the city to stop it from

expanding the park, waited for a new administration, then built the amphitheater with the approval of new city leaders. From idea to fruition, it took more than a decade. It cost a little more than $500,000 to build the venue — about $4.6 million in today's dollars. Its construction was a way to keep pace with other cities building entertainment venues for its residents. It opened in June 1952. Of the season's first 19 performances, 'The Waltz King' Wayne King broke in the new venue. Henry F. Koch died at the age of 72 in early October of 1953, and a Residual Trust was established in his honor. The Fund supports general operating costs for a variety of community foundations and nonprofits. There are no annual deadlines.
Requirements: Grants are currently awarded to Indiana 501(c)3 organizations that support Indiana residents.
Geographic Focus: Indiana
Amount of Grant: Up to 10,000 USD
Samples: Evansville Arc, Evansville, Indiana, $5,000 - general operating support (2018); Patchwork Central, Evansville, Indiana, $3,000 - general operating support (2018); Dream Center, Evansville, Indiana, $5,000 - general operating support (2018).
Contact: Trustee; (812) 456-4663 or (513) 534-7001
Sponsor: Henry F. Koch Residual Trust
38 Fountain Square Plaza
Cincinnati, OH 45263-0858

Henry L. Guenther Foundation Grants   1242

The Henry L. Guenther Foundation, established in 1956, awards grants to California nonprofit organizations in its areas of interest, including: creating opportunities for youth; disease research; education; human services; and community services. Grants support hospitals, medical research, and social services. There are two annual deadlines: May 31 and October 31. Application forms and guidelines are available upon request. The board meets in January and July to consider all proposals. Most recent grants have ranged from $5,000 to $500,000.
Requirements: California nonprofit 501(c)3 organizations are eligible to apply. Grants are awarded primarily in southern California.
Restrictions: Grants do not support government agencies, religious organizations for religious purposes, individuals, or debt-reduction requests.
Geographic Focus: California
Date(s) Application is Due: May 31; Oct 31
Amount of Grant: 5,000 - 500,000 USD
Samples: Loma Linda University, Loma Linda, California, $400,000 - for the purchase of a Siemens cyclotron for a new Research Imaging Center to further develop Proton Therapy capabilities in the treatment of neurological diseases; PIH Health Foundation, Whittier, California, $100,000 - to purchase tomosynthesis digital mammography equipment; Sharp Healthcare Foundation, San Diego, California, $250,000 - to build the seventh floor of the Stephen Birch Healthcare Center.
Contact: Sarah C. Milliken, President; (310) 785-0658
Sponsor: Henry L. Guenther Foundation
2029 Century Park D, Suite 4392
Los Angeles, CA 90067-3029

Herbert A. and Adrian W. Woods Foundation Grants   1243

The Herbert A. and Adrian W. Woods Foundation was established on June 9, 1999 upon the death of Mrs. Adrian W. Woods. Mrs. Woods had a long history of charitable giving in the St. Louis community and wanted to establish this foundation to continue that legacy of giving. The Foundation supports charitable organizations primarily in the greater St. Louis, Missouri area. The Herbert A. and Adrian W. Woods Foundation is dedicated to the founders' interests in charitable organizations that serve abused, neglected or troubled children; the poor; the Episcopal Church and affiliates, including outreach program; art and culture in the Metropolitan St. Louis area; animal welfare (in Missouri); and victims of illness or disability, including research in this area. Award amounts typically range from $2,500 to $35,000.
Requirements: Applicants must have 501(c)3 tax-exempt status. The Trustees will consider the donor's past giving history and any special needs of any of the charities she has given to in the past. The Trustees will also consider requests from charitable organizations that fall into one or more of the categories defined above. The following types of requests may be submitted: special projects, capital campaign requests (however, capital grants are awarded only as a source of support among a broad community of funders), challenge or matching grants, and general operation funding. Applications will be submitted online through the Bank of America website. A grant report is required within 1 year of the grant application date, regardless of whether all of the funds have been spent.
Restrictions: The following types of requests will not be considered: multi-year grants (pledges) and endowment creation and funding. The fund does not support requests from individuals, organizations attempting to influence policy through direct lobbying, or any political campaigns.
Geographic Focus: Missouri
Date(s) Application is Due: Sep 1
Amount of Grant: 2,500 - 35,000 USD
Samples: Association on Aging With Developmental Disabilities, St. Louis, Missouri, $20,000 - Awarded for Retirement Support - Individual (2018); Foster Care Coalition of Greater St. Louis, St. Louis, Missouri, $20,000 - Awarded for Foster Care and Adoption Programs (2018); Animal Protective Association of Missouri, St. Louis, Missouri, $20,000 - Awarded for Pet Partners (2018).
Contact: Srilatha Lakkaraju, Philanthropic Client Manager; (312) 828-8166; ilgrantmaking@bankofamerica.com or ilgrantmaking@ustrust.com
Internet: www.bankofamerica.com/philanthropic/foundation/?fnId=7

Sponsor: Herbert A. and Adrian W. Woods Foundation
100 North Broadway, MO2-100-07-15
St. Louis, MO 63102-2728

Herbert Hoover Presidential Library Association Bus Travel Grants   1244
The purpose of the Herbert Hoover Library Association Bus Travel Grant Program is to help schools in covering costs to travel to the Herbert Hoover Presidential Library in West Branch, Iowa. The Herbert Hoover Presidential Library Association is a nonprofit support group for the Hoover Presidential Library-Museum and Hoover National Historic Site in West Branch. The program, funded entirely through contributions from private individuals, corporations, and foundations, is specifically intended to promote public education about and appreciation for Herbert Hoover. The funds will be used strictly for bus transportation cost (gas and bus driver). The formula used to determine the grant amount is $3.00/mile (distance calculated from school to Hoover Complex) with a minimum of $20.00 and a maximum of $300.00 per bus. Annual deadlines for applications are September 28 and February 22.
Requirements: All schools are eligible to apply for the Bus Travel Grant.
Geographic Focus: All States
Date(s) Application is Due: Sep 28
Amount of Grant: 20 - 300 USD
Contact: Delene McConnaha, Manager of Academic Programs; (800) 828-0475 or (319) 643-5327; fax (319) 643-2391; delene.mcconnaha@hooverassociation.org or info@hooverassoc.org
Internet: www.hooverassociation.org/grantsawards/travel_bus_grant_program.php
Sponsor: Herbert Hoover Presidential Library Association
302 Parkside Drive
West Branch, IA 52358

Herman Goldman Foundation Grants   1245
The Herman Goldman Foundation strives to enhance the quality of life through innovative grants in four main areas: health - to achieve effective delivery of physical and mental health care services; social justice - to develop organizational, social, and legal approaches to those who are aid deprived or handicapped; education - for new or improved counseling for effective preschool, vocational and paraprofessional training; and the arts - to increase opportunities for talented youth to receive training and for less affluent individuals to attend quality presentations. Grant making is primarily to 501(c)3 organizations in the metropolitan New York area. Types of support include: annual campaigns; building and renovation; capital campaigns; continuing support; endowments; general operating support; program development; internship funds; research; and seed money. Most recent awards have ranged from $4,000 to $30,000.
Requirements: Applicants should submit a proposal along with a copy of the organization's IRS determination letter. There are no deadlines. The board meets monthly, with grants considered in April, July, and November. Organizations are notified within two to three months of submission.
Restrictions: The Foundation does not fund religious organizations, individuals, or emergency funds.
Geographic Focus: New York
Samples: American Museum of Natural History, New York, New York, $30,000 - general operating support; Brooklyn Youth Chorus Academy, Brooklyn, New York, $5,000 - general operating support; New York Shakespeare Festival, New York, New York, $26,000 - general operating support.
Contact: Richard K. Baron, Executive Director; (212) 461-2132; goldfound@aol.com
Sponsor: Herman Goldman Foundation
44 Wall Street, Suite 1212
New York, NY 10005-2401

Herman H. Nettelroth Fund Grants   1246
The Herman H. Nettelroth Fund has a geographic focus of Jefferson County, Kentucky, where Nettelroth practiced as an attorney for several years. The Trust's primary fields of interest focus on: equipping children's playgrounds; creating and maintaining day nurseries for working mothers; providing children's books for public libraries; providing scholarships for students attending the University of Louisville; creating and maintaining bird sanctuaries; promoting animal rescue work; and providing support for United Way and American Red Cross Disaster Relief Work. PNC meets annually with the Nettelroth Fund's Advisory Committee to review applications. The application deadline for submission is October 15.
Requirements: Any 501(c)3 organization either located in, or supporting the residents of, Jefferson County, Kentucky, are eligible to apply.
Geographic Focus: Kentucky
Date(s) Application is Due: Oct 15
Contact: Jennifer Reitzell, Trustee; (412) 768-5248; jennifer.reitzell@pnc.com
Internet: www1.pnc.com/pncfoundation/charitable_trusts.html
Sponsor: Herman H. Nettelroth Fund
One PNC Plaza, 249 Fifth Avenue, 20th Floor
Pittsburgh, PA 15222

Herman P. and Sophia Taubman Foundation Grants   1247
Herman P. Taubman was a member of the National Campaign Cabinet of the United Jewish Appeal, Southwest chairman of the Israel bond campaign, and a vice-president of the American Committee for the Weizmann Institute. Taubman, who resided in Tulsa, Oklahoma, was also an honorary life member of the Tulsa Jewish Community Council. The Herman P. and Sophia Taubman Foundation was established in Oklahoma in 1955, with giving centered in the states of California, Hawaii, New York, Texas, and Washington. The

Foundation's primary fields of interest include: arts and culture; child welfare; children's museums; research of diseases and conditions; elementary and secondary education; higher education; family services; hospital care; human services; Judaism; orphanages; the performing arts; general philanthropy; shelter and residential care; special population support; supportive housing; universities and colleges; and women's services. Types of support offered include: capital campaigns; infrastructure; endowments; financial stability; general operating support; program development; and research. Though there are no annual deadlines for application submission, interested parties should submit a formal request including a detailed description of the project or program need, and a detailed budget.
Requirements: 501(c)3 organizations and non-profits in the States of California, Hawaii, New York, Texas, and Washington are eligible to apply.
Restrictions: Grants are never given directly to individuals.
Geographic Focus: California, Hawaii, New York, Texas, Washington
Amount of Grant: Up to 250,000 USD
Samples: University of California San Diego, La Jolla, California, $220,000 - general operating; New Seed Foundation, Palo Alto, California, $50,000 - general operating; Jewish Federation of Greater Dallas, Dallas, Texas, $10,000 - general operating.
Contact: H. Perry Taubman, Trustee; (918) 588-6407
Sponsor: Herman P. and Sophia Taubman Foundation
P.O. Box 1620
Tulsa, OK 74101-1620

Highmark Corporate Giving Grants   1248
The Corporation awards grants in the following categories: health; human services; community; education; and arts and culture. The Corporation will consider applications from: programs and services that tie to its mission and have a compelling potential impact to the health and well-being of individuals; national organizations seeking support for local programs; and grassroots and faith-based organizations. Support is expressed in cash grants, sponsorships, and in-kind gifts to non-profit organizations. There are no maximum or minimum awards; however, awards to programs and services are granted based on importance to the Corporation's business, social mission and corporate citizen objectives, as well as the initiative's proposed impact. Interested applicants should submit a brief proposal. For additional information or proposal submission, applicants should contact the Community Affairs department in their county of residence. Contact information by county is available online.
Requirements: The Foundation awards grants within its service area to nonprofit organizations that are defined as tax exempt under section 501(c)3 of the Internal Revenue Code and as public charities under section 509(a) of that code. Eligible counties in Pennsylvania include: Adams, Allegheny, Armstrong, Beaver, Bedford, Berks, Blair, Butler, Cambria, Cameron, Centre, Clarion, Clearfield, Columbia, Crawford, Cumberland, Dauphin, Erie, Elk, Fayette, Forest, Franklin, Fulton, Greene, Huntingdon, Indiana, Jefferson, Juniata, Lancaster, Lawrence, Lebanon, Lehigh, McKean, Mercer, Mifflin, Montour, Northampton, Northumberland, Perry, Potter, Schuylkill, Snyder, Somerset, Union, Venango, Warren, Westmoreland, Washington, and York. All counties in West Virginia and Delaware are eligible to apply.
Restrictions: Proposals are not accepted for: multiple-year grants; capital campaigns; individual causes; seed money or start-up organizations; endowment funds; political causes or campaigns; fraternal or civic groups; religious programming; or organizations that discriminate on the basis of race, religion, sex, disability or national origin.
Geographic Focus: Delaware, Pennsylvania, West Virginia
Contact: Mary Ann Papale, (412) 544-4032; mary.papale@highmark.com or GrantsSWPAApply@highmark.com
Internet: www.highmark.com/hmk2/responsibility/giving/index.shtml
Sponsor: Highmark
120 5th Avenue, Suite 2112
Pittsburgh, PA 15222-3099

Hill Crest Foundation Grants   1249
The Hill Crest Foundation awards grants to Alabama nonprofits, primarily health associations and human services and education, with some funding for the arts. Types of support include: building and renovation; capital campaigns; endowments; equipment; matching and challenge support; professorships; program development; publication; research; scholarship funds; seed money; and technical assistance. There are no deadlines or applications. The Board of Directors meets quarterly.
Requirements: Application forms are not required. Before submitting a proposal, organizations should submit a letter, detailing the project and the amount requested, along with descriptive literature about their organization.
Restrictions: Grantmaking is limited to Alabama. The Foundation does not fund individuals.
Geographic Focus: Alabama
Amount of Grant: 20,000 - 150,000 USD
Samples: Methodist Homes for the Aging, Birmingham, Alabama, $100,000 payable over one year; Alabama Symphonic Association, Birmingham, Alabama, $30,000 payable over one year; Bell Center for Early Intervention Programs, Birmingham, Alabama, $50,000 payable over one year.
Contact: Charles Terry, Chairperson; (205) 425-5800
Sponsor: Hill Crest Foundation
P.O. Box 530507
Mountain Brook, AL 35253-0507

Hillsdale County Community Foundation General Grants   1250
General grants are made from the Hillsdale County Community Foundation named unrestricted endowment funds. General Foundation grants focus on improving the quality of life for the citizens of Hillsdale County. Eligible projects generally fall within

these categories: education; fine arts; social services; community development; recreation; environmental issues; health and wellness; and improvement in the physical, mental, and moral conditions of County residents. There are two annual deadlines for application submissions: May 1 and November 1.
Requirements: The Foundation welcomes applications from the Hillsdale County area or outside Hillsdale County, Michigan, if a significant number of the people to be served reside within Hillsdale County. Applicants shall be tax exempt according to Section 501(c)3 of the Internal Revenue Code.
Geographic Focus: Michigan
Date(s) Application is Due: May 1; Nov 1
Contact: Sharon Bisher, President/CEO; (517) 439-5101; fax (517) 439-5109; s.bisher@abouthccf.org or info@abouthccf.org
Internet: abouthccf.org/grants/
Sponsor: Hillsdale County Community Foundation
2 South Howell Street, P.O. Box 276
Hillsdale, MI 49242

Hillsdale County Community Foundation Love Your Community Grants   1251
The Love Your Community initiative was formed to support projects and programs aimed at enhancing and engaging communities. The strongest proposals demonstrate creativity and innovation, and do not duplicate services or programs already in place. Each grant award will not exceed $2,000. The annual deadline for applications is May 1. Awards are announced each spring.
Requirements: The Foundation requires applicants to call and discuss their project with the President/CEO prior to submitting the application. Applications from the Hillsdale County area or outside Hillsdale County, Michigan are welcome, if a significant number of the people to be served reside within Hillsdale County. Applicants shall be tax exempt according to Section 501(c)3 of the Internal Revenue Code.
Restrictions: The current objectives of the Foundation do not allow grants for: religious or sectarian purposes; individuals; legislative or political purposes; loans; capital campaigns; routine maintenance, including office equipment; administrative costs for maintaining the present operation of an organization, including, but not limited to, staff salaries, wages, and benefits; basic education materials including state mandated/benchmark core curriculum supplies and resources.
Geographic Focus: Michigan
Date(s) Application is Due: May 1
Contact: Sharon Bisher, President/CEO; (517) 439-5101; fax (517) 439-5109; s.bisher@abouthccf.org or info@abouthccf.org
Internet: abouthccf.org/grants/
Sponsor: Hillsdale County Community Foundation
2 South Howell Street, P.O. Box 276
Hillsdale, MI 49242

Hillsdale County Community Foundation Y.O.U.T.H. Grants   1252
Comprised of young adults, the Y.O.U.T.H. (Youth Opportunities Unlimited Throughout Hillsdale) has a mission to meet the needs of young people in Hillsdale County, Michigan, by enhancing the awareness of youth opportunities and offering information and resources through cooperative leadership, while providing financial support for projects to improve the youth communities of Hillsdale County. They make a difference by making responsible decisions with their grant making; awarding money for projects and programs targeted to solve youth issues in a creative and positive manner. Projects support awareness, community service, volunteerism, and fund development.
Requirements: The Foundation welcomes applications from the Hillsdale County area or outside Hillsdale County, Michigan, if a significant number of the people to be served reside within Hillsdale County. Applicants shall be tax exempt according to Section 501(c)3 of the Internal Revenue Code, or public or private schools situated in Hillsdale County, Michigan.
Geographic Focus: Michigan
Date(s) Application is Due: May 1; Nov 1
Contact: Sharon Bisher, President/CEO; (517) 439-5101; fax (517) 439-5109; s.bisher@abouthccf.org or info@abouthccf.org
Internet: abouthccf.org/y-o-u-t-h/
Sponsor: Hillsdale County Community Foundation
2 South Howell Street, P.O. Box 276
Hillsdale, MI 49242

Hispanic Heritage Foundation Youth Awards   1253
The Hispanic Heritage Foundation recognizes outstanding achievements of Hispanic youth in designated cities who are high-school seniors. Recipients are selected for their accomplishments in one of six areas, including: business and entrepreneurship; community service; education; engineering; healthcare and science; and mathematical science. Three awards for each student category and one parent Award are given in each of the regions across the country. One Regional Award winning student from each category and parent will be selected as the National Youth Award recipient in his or her respective category. Applications are available online or from high-school guidance counselors. The annual deadline is April 4.
Requirements: Hispanic high-school seniors from the following cities are eligible: Chicago, Dallas, Houston, Los Angeles, Miami, New York City, Philadelphia, Phoenix, San Antonio, San Diego, San Jose, and the District of Columbia. Winners must demonstrate strength of character and that their Hispanic heritage plays a significant role in their lives.
Geographic Focus: Arizona, California, District of Columbia, Florida, Illinois, New York, Pennsylvania, Texas
Date(s) Application is Due: Apr 4
Amount of Grant: 1,000 - 3,000 USD

Contact: Franklin Sorto, Youth Awards Program Coordinator; (202) 558-9473 or (202) 861-9797; fax (202) 861-9799; contact@hispanicheritageawards.org or info@hispanicheritage.org
Internet: www.hispanicheritage.org/programs/youth-awards/
Sponsor: Hispanic Heritage Foundation
1001 Pennsylvania Avenue, NW
Washington, D.C. 20004

HLTA Visitor Industry Charity Walk Grant   1254
Each year, the Hawaii Lodging and Tourism Association (HLTA) Visitor Industry Charity Walk supports hundreds of local non-profits statewide. All money raised for the Charity Walk on each island stays on that island to support its local charities. Grants will be considered on the basis of an organization's community impact and may vary widely in scope and size. Grants range in size up to a total of $10,000 per organization (not per program); however, grants of more than $10,000 per organization will be considered on special and rare occasions. Preference is giving to organizations that provide the following services: homelessness (social/welfare); children and education; the elderly; crime prevention; veterans; health? and physical fitness; the environment; and arts and cultural events. The application deadline for each island varies, but all are due sometime in late April or early May each year.
Requirements: 501(c)3 non-profit organizations in the state of Hawaii are eligible to apply for Visitor Industry Charity Walk Grants. All grant funding must be used to fund programs in the County in which the funds were raised and utilized to benefit that community. An organization must apply separately to each county for funding to be used in that county.
Restrictions: Funds will not be granted for: capital fund drives; purchase of tangible real property or personal property; or interest or reduction of deficits or loans.
Geographic Focus: Hawaii
Amount of Grant: Up to 10,000 USD
Contact: Jared Higashi, Oahu Contact; (808) 923-0407; jhigashi@hawaiilodging.org or charitywalk@hawaiilodging.org
Bambi Lau, Hawaii Island Contact; (808) 886-8100, ext. 8128
Jolene Ogle, Kauai Contact; (808) 652-8924; hlta.kauai@gmail.com
Lisa H. Paulson, Maui, Molokai, and Lanai Contact; (808) 244-8625 or (808) 244-3094; fax (808) 244-3094; info@mauihla.org
Internet: www.charitywalkhawaii.org/for-non-profits.html
Sponsor: Hawaii Lodging and Tourism Association
2270 Kalakaua Avenue, Suite 1702
Honolulu, HI 96815

Honeywell Corporation Family Safety and Security Grants   1255
Safety and security are top concerns for families everywhere. When it comes to safety and security, Honeywell believes that nothing is more important than protecting our most precious and vulnerable asset - children. The Honeywell Corporation has decades of experience developing and applying technologies that keep families safe and secure where they live, work and travel. Giving in this area is on a national basis within areas of company operations, with emphasis on New Jersey and New York. Applications are required, and potential applicants should begin by contacting the office by email.
Geographic Focus: All States
Contact: Michael Holland, Hometown Solutions Media Contact; (973) 455-2728 or (973) 727-6891; michael.holland@honeywell.com
Internet: honeywell.com/Citizenship/Pages/family-safety-security.aspx
Sponsor: Honeywell Corporation
101 Columbia Road
Morristown, NJ 07962

Honeywell Corporation Got 2B Safe Contest   1256
Honeywell has partnered with the National Center for Missing and Exploited Children (NCMEC) to create the Got 2B Safe! contest, one of the most comprehensive school-based programs designed to teach abduction prevention directly to young children. Since its beginning, Got 2B Safe! has reached over 72,000 schools, and more than 5 million children across the U.S. Teachers enter the contest by submitting lesson plans which highlight four core rules of safety: Check First; Go With a Friend; It's My Body; Tell a Trusted Adult. Each year, 100 first prize winners receive gift certificates of up to $500 for school supplies and five grand-prize winners are awarded a complete classroom makeover worth $10,000.
Requirements: Teachers complete the online registration form and submit a one-page lesson plan demonstrating how they teach the Got 2B Safe personal safety rules to their students.
Geographic Focus: All States
Amount of Grant: Up to 10,000 USD
Contact: Got 2B Safe Coordinator; (877) 841-2840
Michael Holland, Hometown Solutions Media Contact; (973) 455-2728 or (973) 727-6891; michael.holland@honeywell.com
Internet: honeywell.com/Citizenship/Pages/family-safety-security.aspx
Sponsor: Honeywell Corporation
101 Columbia Road
Morristown, NJ 07962

Honeywell Corporation Humanitarian Relief Grants   1257
Do the right work and do it right now, are the principles that guide the actions of the Honeywell Humanitarian Relief Fund (HHRF). Since the fund's creation, Honeywell has been on the forefront of relief efforts worldwide, working in partnership with key organizations like Operation USA and Rebuilding Together. Funded in part by donations from Honeywell employees, the HHRF strives to address both the immediate and long-term needs of those communities affected by natural disasters around the world. Recently,

the Honeywell Corporation has been involved in a wide array of relief efforts including: the Indonesian tsunami, Hurricanes Rita and Katrina, the Sichuan earthquake, Hurricanes Ike and Gustav, and the Haiti earthquake.
Geographic Focus: All States, All Countries
Contact: Michael Holland, Hometown Solutions Media Contact; (973) 455-2728 or (973) 727-6891; michael.holland@honeywell.com
Internet: honeywell.com/Citizenship/Pages/our-values-and-work.aspx
Sponsor: Honeywell Corporation
101 Columbia Road
Morristown, NJ 07962

Honeywell Corporation Leadership Challenge Academy 1258

The Honeywell Leadership Challenge Academy (HCLA) is a week-long, experiential learning program exclusive to children ages 15-18 of full-time Honeywell employees around the world. Financial contributions from Honeywell Hometown Solutions and Honeywell employees help fund the scholarships, which include tuition, meals, accommodation and all materials for the program. Working in small groups, the students are presented with "Challenges" and are encouraged to explore problem-solving scenarios using hands-on science, mathematics, and engineering skills. Many of the activities require students to present their findings or opinions to a panel of experts in the field. Participants learn teamwork and communication in ways that are not easily replicated in the formal classroom. By participating in HCLA, students learn how to work through scientific problems through incremental tests and experiments.
Requirements: Students must have above average grades and an interest in math, science and technology. Participants for the program are selected through a rigorous process based on academic achievement and community involvement. No other special preparation is necessary for the program.
Geographic Focus: All States
Contact: Leadership Challenge Academy Coordinator; (800) 637-7223 or (256) 721-7150 Michael Holland, Hometown Solutions Media Contact; (973) 455-2728 or (973) 727-6891; michael.holland@honeywell.com
Internet: leadership.honeywell.com/
Sponsor: Honeywell Corporation
101 Columbia Road
Morristown, NJ 07962

Honor the Earth Grants 1259

As a unique national Native initiative, Honor the Earth works to raise public awareness, and raise and direct funds to grassroots Native environmental groups. Honor the Earth's Board encourages proposals on Native environmental justice, sustainable development, and cultural preservation, with a grant limit of $5,000. The organization's focus will remain on sustainable Indigenous communities support. Their work also focuses on opposition to fossil fuels extraction and destructive mining practices. Additional information, guidelines, and information on previously funded projects is available at the website. Applicants are encouraged to check back periodically for grant funding through the Building Resilience program. Proposals may be submitted in hard copy or by email. Faxed proposals cannot be accepted.
Requirements: Grants are awarded solely to organizations that are led and managed by Native peoples. Priority is given to grassroots, community-based organizations and groups with a lack of access to federal and/or tribal funding resources.
Restrictions: Funding is not available for individuals.
Geographic Focus: All States, Canada
Date(s) Application is Due: Nov 9
Amount of Grant: 1,000 - 5,000 USD
Contact: Winona LaDuke, Executive Director; (218) 375-3200; HonorGrants@honorearth.org or info@honortheearth.org
Internet: www.honorearth.org/grantmaking
Sponsor: Honor the Earth
607 Main Avenue
Callaway, MN 56521

Horace A. Kimball and S. Ella Kimball Foundation Grants 1260

Although the Horace A Kimball and S. Ella Kimball Foundation was not legally established until July of 1956, its roots along with those of its sister organization, the Phyllis Kimball Johnstone and H. Earle Kimball foundation, go back to the early 1900s. It was then that Horace A. Kimball of Providence, Rhode Island, a retired woolen manufacturer, acquired controlling interest of the Clicquot Club Beverage Company of Millis, Massachusetts. Today, the Kimball Foundation makes grants almost exclusively to Rhode Island operatives (charities) or those benefitting Rhode Island residents and causes. Although, the Foundation considers gifts to all areas in the state, greater emphasis is placed on South County. Areas of interest for the Foundation are: human services; the environment; and health care. Most recent awards have ranged from $2,500 to $25,000. Interested parties can apply either with a mailed hard copy or by using the online application format.
Requirements: The Foundation will consider any organization which has proper 501(c)3 and 509(a) IRS tax classification status. Three main things are needed to apply for funds from the Foundation: a letter of intent or purpose; a financial statement; and verification of 501(c)3 and 509(a) status.
Restrictions: No support for religious organizations. No grants to individuals, or for feasibility studies, capital projects or multi-year commitments.
Geographic Focus: Rhode Island
Date(s) Application is Due: Jul 15
Amount of Grant: 1,000 - 50,000 USD

Samples: Westerly Adult Day Services, Westerly, Rhode Island, $14,000 - general operating support; Pawcatuck Neighborhood Center, Pawtucket, Rhode Island, $2,675 - general operating support; Education Exchange, Westerly, Rhode Island, $25,000 - general operating support.
Contact: Olympia Graeve, Bank Fund Manager; (401) 348-1238 or (401) 348-1234; fax (401) 364-3565
Internet: www.hkimballfoundation.org/Process.php
Sponsor: Horace A. Kimball and S. Ella Kimball Foundation
130 Woodville Road
Hope Valley, RI 02832

Horace A. Moses Charitable Trust Grants 1261

The Horace A. Moses Charitable Trust was established in 1923 to support and promote quality educational, human services, and health care programming for underserved populations. Special consideration is given to charitable organizations that serve the community of Springfield and its surrounding communities. The majority of grants from the Horace A. Moses Charitable Trust are one year in duration. Multi-year support is awarded on occasion. Award amounts typically range from $2,000 to $10,000.
Requirements: Applicants must have 501(c)3 tax-exempt status. Grant requests for general operating support are strongly encouraged. Program support will also be considered. Small program-related capital expenses may be included in general operating or program requests. Applications will be submitted online through the Bank of America website. A grant report is required within 1 year of the grant application date, regardless of whether all of the funds have been spent.
Restrictions: The foundation does not support requests from individuals, organizations attempting to influence policy through direct lobbying, or any political campaigns.
Geographic Focus: Massachusetts
Date(s) Application is Due: Mar 1
Amount of Grant: 2,000 - 10,000 USD
Samples: Homework House Inc., Holyoke, Massachusetts, $5,000 - Awarded for General operations of the organization (2018); Boy Scouts of America, Chicopee, Maryland, $2,000 - Awarded for general operations of the organization (2018); Center for Human Development, Springfield, Massachusetts, $2,000 - Awarded for Support for CHD's Disability Resources Program (2018).
Contact: Caitlin Arnold, Philanthropic Client Manager; (860) 244-4872; ct.grantmaking@bankofamerica.com or caitlin.arnold@bofa.com
Internet: www.bankofamerica.com/philanthropic/foundation/?fnId=37
Sponsor: Horace A. Moses Charitable Trust
P.O. Box 1802
Providence, RI 02901-1802

HRAMF Charles H. Hood Foundation Child Health Research Awards 1262

The Charles H. Hood Foundation was incorporated in 1942 to improve the health and quality of life for children through grant support of New England-based pediatric researchers. The intent of the Child Health Research Awards Program is to support newly independent faculty, provide the opportunity to demonstrate creativity, and assist in the transition to other sources of research funding. Two-year grants of $165,000 ($82,500 per year inclusive of 10% indirect costs) are awarded to researchers who are within five years of their first faculty appointment by the funding start date. Application deadlines occur in the fall of each year on October 7.
Requirements: Applicants must be working in nonprofit academic, medical or research institutions within the six New England states. Grants support hypothesis-driven clinical, basic science, public health, health services research, and epidemiology projects focused on child health. Applicants must hold a doctoral degree with a demonstrated level of independence confirmed by the Department or Division Chair. The Applicant's potential for a lifetime career as an investigator in pediatric research is also critical in the review process. Applicants are required to devote at least 20% effort to the proposed Hood research project. Applicants who have pending R01s or other large applications to the NIH and other agencies are encouraged to submit proposals to the Hood Foundation. Online submissions must be received by April 8, 12:00 Noon, U.S. Eastern time. Printed copies must be received by April 14, 5:00 pm, U.S. Eastern time.
Restrictions: Applicants are ineligible if they have combined federal and non-federal funding totaling $450,000 or more in direct costs at any time during the two years of the Award. This figure refers to external funding only and not an Applicant's start-up package, other intramural support or the Hood Award. Applicants are ineligible if they are currently or have previously been designated as Principal Investigator or Co-P.I. on an R01, P01, Pioneer Award, New Innovator Award or equivalents from federal agencies such as the National Science Foundation (NSF) or Department of Defense (DOD). Applicants who have completed the R00 phase of a K99/R00 are also ineligible for a Hood Award.
Geographic Focus: Connecticut, Maine, Massachusetts, New Hampshire, Rhode Island, Vermont
Date(s) Application is Due: Oct 7
Amount of Grant: 82,500 - 165,000 USD
Contact: Charlene Mancusi, Program Officer; (617) 279-2230 or (617) 451-0049; fax (617) 423-4619; cmancusi@hria.org
Internet: hria.org/tmf/hood/
Sponsor: Health Resources in Action Medical Foundation
2 Boylston Street, 4th Floor
Boston, MA 02116

HRAMF Community Health Improvement Project Grants in Bowdoin Geneva 1263

Funds have been made available to support innovative, small scale Community Health Improvement (CHI) projects in the Bowdoin Geneva community. Funding for this

opportunity comes from Beth Israel Deaconess Medical Center Community Benefits Program and Determination of Need Community Health Initiatives, which are overseen by the Massachusetts Department of Public Health. This RFP is designed to support 2 to 3 CHI pilot projects in the Bowdoin Geneva, community totaling $22,000 in grants. CHI projects address root causes and systemic issues in the community and have outcomes focused on health. We are looking to support community initiatives and projects focusing on: developing capacity for economic growth and power (i.e. urban farming, cultural entrepreneurship); building a community gathering space (i.e. green space, garden, greenhouse); and community and youth of color engagement that supports capacity building (i.e. canvasing, neighborhood planning process, forming a democratic neighborhood association) Through these projects the Bowdoin Geneva Community Advisory Board is seeking to support the lives of people of color throughout Bowdoin Geneva that desire to make this neighborhood a better place. Bowdoin Geneva CAB seeks to find applicants who are interested in creating community spaces that can build stronger relationships between the residents of Bowdoin Geneva. The funding will be for a period of 12 months, starting August 1 through July 31. Proposals must be submitted by August 23.
Requirements: Funds must support innovative, small scale Community Health Improvement (CHI) projects in the Bowdoin Geneva community.
Geographic Focus: Massachusetts
Date(s) Application is Due: Aug 23
Amount of Grant: Up to 10,000 USD
Contact: Jamaih Tappan, Manager, Community Organizing & Communications; (617) 279-2268 or (617) 451-0049; jtappin@hria.org
Internet: hria.org/projects/bowdoingeneva/
Sponsor: Health Resources in Action Medical Foundation
2 Boylston Street, 4th Floor
Boston, MA 02116

HRK Foundation Health Grants
1264
The HRK Foundation is defined by quiet leadership and philanthropy. The Board seeks to improve the fabric of society by promoting healthy families and healthy communities. In the area of Health, the Foundation funds programs that strengthen families and promote healthy lives for children, as well as programs that provide access to health and human services. Within the Saint Croix Valley and Ashland and Bayfield Counties in Wisconsin, the board will consider local community-specific health projects. Types of support include: general operating support; seed funding; community development; matching/challenge grants; equipment acquisition; and annual campaigns. Requests are considered two times each year, with deadlines on March 31 and September 15. Most recent awards in this area have ranged from $20,000 to $25,000.
Requirements: The foundation makes grants only to qualified IRS 501(c)3 organizations that specifically benefit people in the area surrounding Bayport and Saint Paul, Minnesota, and Ashland and Bayfield counties in Wisconsin. The Foundation supports all families, both traditional and non-traditional.
Restrictions: The foundation does not make loans or provide grants to individuals.
Geographic Focus: Minnesota, Wisconsin
Date(s) Application is Due: Sep 15
Amount of Grant: 20,000 - 25,000 USD
Samples: University of Minnesota, Minneapolis, Minnesota, $20,000 - support of the Stem Cell Institute; International Institute of Minnesota, Saint Paul, Minnesota, $25,000 - support for the Mental Health Initiative for New Americans; Medical College of Wisconsin, Milwaukee, Wisconsin, $25,000 - general operating support.
Contact: Kathleen Fluegel, Foundation Director; (651) 298-0550 or (866) 342-5475; fax (651) 298-0551; info@HRKFoundation.org
Internet: www.hrkfoundation.org/purpose.html
Sponsor: HRK Foundation
345 Saint Peter Street, Suite 1200
Saint Paul, MN 55102-1639

HRSA Ryan White HIV AIDS Drug Assistance Grants
1265
The Health Resources and Services Administration, HIV/AIDS Bureau is accepting applications for the Ryan White HIV/AIDS Program (RWHAP) Part B and ADAP Training and Technical Assistance. The purpose of this grant program is to provide technical assistance to Ryan White HIV/AIDS Program Part B grantees on developing and maintaining comprehensive systems of care, integrated planning, monitoring subgrantees, and Affordable Care Act (ACA) implementation and to provide technical assistance to ADAPs on the implementation of cost-containment strategies, financial modeling, wait list management, and ACA implementation. The annual deadline is february 26, and the award ceiling is $427,500.
Requirements: Eligible applicants include: nonprofits having a 501(c)3 status with the IRS, other than institutions of higher education; small businesses; for profit organizations other than small businesses; and nonprofits that do not have a 501(c)3 status with the IRS, other than institutions of higher education.
Geographic Focus: All States
Date(s) Application is Due: Feb 26
Amount of Grant: Up to 427,500 USD
Contact: Laura Cheever, Associate Administrator; (301) 443-1993 or (888) 275-4772; fax (301) 443-8586; lcheever@hrsa.gov
Internet: www.grants.gov/web/grants/view-opportunity.html?oppId=249577
Sponsor: Health Resources and Services Administration
5600 Fishers Lane
Rockville, MD 20857

HSBC Corporate Giving Grants
1266
HSBC believes that banks play a positive role in the economy and society by providing individuals and businesses with the financial services they need to meet their ambitions. Focusing on education and the environment, HSBC builds strong, enduring relationships with a wide range of organizations, providing resources and tools to sustain long-term results. HSBC combines grants, participation, community reinvestment, and employee engagement to support the communities where HSBC personnel live and work. HSBC funds programs in three distinct categories: Education, Environment, and Community.
Requirements: HSBC initiates the majority of its grant relationships. Eligible nonprofits will be invited to submit their proposal for fund to HSBC via the online HSBC Contribution Application. Proposals must be received by November 1 of each year; all organizations will receive a response in writing.
Restrictions: The corporation generally does not support the following: organizations outside of the United States and/or organizations that do not hold 501(c)3 tax deductible status under the Internal Revenue Code; fraternal, veteran, labor, or athletic organizations; for-profit student aid or scholarship programs, aside from those already established by the company; political, lobbying or voter registration programs, or those supporting the candidacy of a particular individual; funds to support travel - group or individual; organizations that might in any way pose a conflict with our corporate values, products, customers or employees; advertising; or individuals.
Geographic Focus: All States
Date(s) Application is Due: Nov 1
Contact: Jan Garner, Program Coordinator; (224) 880-7128; janice.e.garner@us.hsbc.com
Internet: www.us.hsbc.com/1/2/home/about/corporate-sustainability/community-partners
Sponsor: HSBC Bank USA, Inc.
451800 Tysons Boulevard
McLean, VA 22102

HSFCA Biennium Grants
1267
The HSFCA Biennium Grants Program is conducted on a biennial basis in accordance with the State budgetary process. Grant applications supporting projects and services throughout the state are received and reviewed during this process. All grant awards are subject to available funding. The minimum level of funding will be $1,000.
Requirements: An applicant must be a not-for-profit, or nonprofit organization, designated as exempt from federal income tax by the Internal Revenue Service (IRS); or a for-profit organization incorporated under the laws of the State of Hawai'i. Each organization must have at least one year's experience with the type of project proposed or in the project category in which the request is being made. First-time applicants seeking HSFCA funding should contact the HSFCA Contracts Officer prior to applying for grant funds, in order to assess eligibility. Organizations are encouraged to allow sufficient time to make any necessary changes to bylaws or adopt any policy statements that will allow the organization to be eligible for HSFCA funding prior to the deadline for proposals. All grants awarded by HSFCA must be matched on a one-to-one basis from other sources, which may include State funds not from the HSFCA. Up to 40% of the match may be in-kind, and the in-kind used for matching may include volunteer time.
Restrictions: The following are ineligible for HSFCA funding: Building, renovation, maintenance of facilities, or other capital expenditures; Activities completed prior to the project period; Fellowships, scholarships, theses, or dissertations; Fund raising; Grant management fees or indirect cost rates; Commissioning visual artists to execute professional works of art; Costs for food and/or refreshments; Perquisites; Equipment purchases and/or long-term rentals for more than one year of any two year biennium; Foreign travel; Subgrants or regrants; Interest payments, insurance, or similar finance costs; Utilities costs (water, electricity, or telephone); Unitemized miscellaneous; Audits; Maintenance costs of any kind; or, Technology-related expenses, including but not limited to computer hardware or software, Internet, website, or Email, or contracted assistance to design or maintain such services.
Geographic Focus: Hawaii
Date(s) Application is Due: Nov 30
Contact: Charles Medeiros, Contracts Officer; (808) 586-0309; charles.medeiros@hawaii.gov
Internet: sfca.hawaii.gov/grants-programs/biennium-grants/grant-guidelines/
Sponsor: Hawaii State Foundation on Culture and the Arts
250 South Hotel Street, 2nd Floor
Honolulu, HI 96813

HSFCA Folk and Traditional Arts Grants - Culture Learning
1268
The Hawai'i State Foundation on Culture and the Arts (HSFCA) provides limited public funding subsidies to support the preservation of living cultures in the State of Hawai'i through Culture Grants administered by its Folk & Traditional Arts Program. Culture Learning Grants are for inter-generational learning with a focus on children and youth. The primary purpose is to strengthen cultural knowledge, skills and pride within underserved cultural communities.
Requirements: Eligible applicants: are organizations determined to be non-profit by the U.S. Internal Revenue Service and incorporated in the U.S; are based in the State of Hawai'i; meet eligibility requirements per the Hawai'i Revised Statutes; and, have at least one year of relevant project experience. The grant project implementation is for one state Fiscal Biennium of two years, beginning on July 1 of the first year and ending June 30 in the second year. Projects must be implemented entirely in the State of Hawai'i and must be for folk and traditional arts and practices of the living traditions that are relevant to cultural communities in the State of Hawai'i.
Restrictions: Only one application per applicant (teacher, apprentice or organization).
Geographic Focus: Hawaii
Date(s) Application is Due: Mar 1

Contact: Denise Miyahana, Arts Program Specialist; (808) 586-0771;
denise.miyahana@hawaii.gov
Internet: sfca.hawaii.gov/grants-programs/folk-traditional-arts/
Sponsor: Hawaii State Foundation on Culture and the Arts
250 South Hotel Street, 2nd Floor
Honolulu, HI 96813

Hubbard Broadcasting Foundation Grants   1269

The Hubbard Broadcasting Foundation (formerly the Hubbard Foundation) was
established in Minnesota in 1958 by Stanley S. Hubbard, the Chairman and CEO of
Hubbard Broadcasting. In addition to overseeing the operations of the company's radio
and television stations in Minnesota and across the country, he helped develop Conus
Communications, the world's first satellite news gathering organization, and United
States Satellite Broadcasting, a pioneer in Direct Broadcast Satellite television. In 2001,
Hubbard was the charter inductee of the Museum of Broadcasting Hall of Fame. Today,
the Foundation supports Minnesota zoos and organizations involved with arts and culture,
education, health, skin disorders, hockey, human services, and leadership development. Its
primary fields of interest are widespread, and include: arts and culture; child welfare; early
childhood education; elementary and secondary education; health; health care access; higher
education; hospital care; human services; the sport of ice hockey; leadership development;
museums; orchestral music; publishing; school-based health care; skin conditions; theater;
and zoos. Typically, support comes in the form of capital campaign money and general
operating funds. Hundreds of grants are given each year, ranging from $500 to $50,000.
Requirements: Any 501(c)3 organization serving residents Minnesota are eligible.
Occasionally, the Foundation also gives to national organizations.
Geographic Focus: All States, Minnesota
Amount of Grant: 500 - 50,000 USD
Samples: Albuquerque Museum Foundation, Albuquerque, New Mexico, $16,667 - general
operating support; Museum of the Moving Image, Altoona, New York, $25,000 - general
operating support; Augsburg College, Minneapolis, Minnesota, $10,000 - - general
operating support.
Contact: Kathryn Hubbard Rominski, Executive Director; (651) 642-4305 or
(651) 642-4300
Sponsor: Hubbard Broadcasting Foundation
3415 University Avenue
Saint Paul, MN 55114-1019

Hubbard Family Foundation Grants   1270

The Hubbard Family Foundation was established in 1983 to enhance the quality of life for
the citizens of the City of Edmonds and South Snohomish County. The Edmonds School
District #15 is used as the specific geographical boundary in qualifying grant requests. The
majority of grants range between $1,000 and $8,000 and are 1 year in duration. The grants
committee meets quarterly in February, May, September and November. Online grant
applications should be received no later than the 20th of January, April, August or October
in order to be considered at the next grants meeting.
Requirements: The Hubbard Family Foundation primarily supports California-based
organizations that are tax-exempt under Section 501(c)3 of the Internal Revenue Service
Code. Although general operating support requests are considered, the committee does not
typically consider grant support for staff salaries. Specific program/event support and small
capital projects are preferred. Online requests must clearly demonstrate how the proposed
funds will be spent to directly benefit people living within the Edmonds School District
#15. Applications will be submitted online through the Bank of America website. A grant
report is required within 1 year of the grant application date, regardless of whether all of
the funds have been spent.
Restrictions: The foundation does not support requests from individuals, organizations
attempting to influence policy through direct lobbying, or any political campaigns.
Geographic Focus: Washington
Date(s) Application is Due: Jan 20; Apr 20; Aug 20; Oct 20
Amount of Grant: 1,000 - 8,000 USD
Samples: Council on Finance and Administration of the United Methodist Church,
Edmonds, Washington, $7,200 - Awarded for general operations (2019); Lynnwood Food
Bank, Lynnwood, Washington, $7,200 - Awarded for general operations (2019); Edmonds
S Snohomish Historical Society, Edmonds, Washington, $5,000 - Awarded for Museum
Archive Large Format Digitization (2019).
Contact: Jan Aldrich Jacobs, (206) 358-0912; wa.grantmaking@bankofamerica.com or
janet.jacobs@bofa.com
Internet: www.bankofamerica.com/philanthropic/foundation/?fnId=135
Sponsor: Hubbard Family Foundation
Bank of America NA P.O. Box 831
Dallas, TX 75283-1041

Hubbard Family Foundation Grants   1271

The Hubbard Family Foundation was established in 1983 to enhance the quality of life
for the citizens of the City of Edmonds and South Snohomish County, Washington. The
Edmonds School District #15 is used as the specific geographical boundary in qualifying
grant requests. The Foundation's primary interests include: arts, culture, and humanities;
community improvement; capacity building; education; the environment; health; and
human services. The majority of grants range between $1,000 and $5,000 and are one year
in duration. Although operating support requests are considered, specific program and event
support, as well as small capital projects, are encouraged. Proposals should be received no
later than the 20th of January, April, August, or October in order to be considered in the
next grants meeting. The grants committee meets quarterly, in February, May, September
and November.

Requirements: 501(c)3 organizations serving residents of Edmonds and South Snohomish
County, Washington, are eligible to apply.
Geographic Focus: Washington
Date(s) Application is Due: Jan 20; Apr 20; Aug 20; Oct 20
Amount of Grant: 1,000 - 5,000 USD
Samples: Edmonds Center for the Arts, Edmonds, Washington, $5,000 - support of the
accessible bathrooms remodel; Edmonds Daybreakers Foundation, Edmonds, Washington,
$4,000 - support of the Edmonds Jazz Connection including venue retails, instruments,
etc.; Edmonds Driftwood Players, Edmonds, Washington, $2,500 - support of replacing
worn carpet in theater.
Contact: Cindy S. Keyser, Philanthropic Officer; (206) 358-3079;
cindy.s.keyser@ustrust.com
Internet: www.bankofamerica.com/philanthropic/foundation.go?fnId=135
Sponsor: Hubbard Family Foundation
800 5th Avenue, WA1-501-33-23
Seattle, WA 98104

Hubbard Farms Charitable Foundation Grants   1272

Over the course of nearly one hundred years, Hubbard Farms became internationally
recognized for their research and development into chicken breeding and hatching. In
1791, Levi Hubbard settled in the newly founded Walpole area and began working with
poultry in addition to his general farming enterprise. Hubbard Farms was founded in
1921 when Ira's son, Oliver, graduated from the University of New Hampshire with one
of the first majors in poultry and opened the company's doors. Oliver began the poultry
breeding and hatching operations which made his company successful in the international
poultry industry. In the 1930's, he even helped develop a new chicken breed called the New
Hampshire. The Hubbard Farms Charitable Foundation, established in 1996, supports
organizations involved with education, health, recreation, youth development, human
services, minorities, and economically disadvantaged people. The Foundation also awards
scholarships to financially needy students in the fields of poultry science, genetics, and
other life sciences. Its geographic focus is Arkansas, New Hampshire, North Carolina,
Tennessee, and Vermont. Typically, grants are given for general operating support, program
development, and student aid. Applicants should forward a letter to the Foundation office
including: the organizational goals; proposed donation; proof of tax-exempt status; and
prior year's financial statements. Most recent awards have ranged from $150 to $3,500. The
annual submission deadlines are April 1 and October 1.
Requirements: 501(c)3 organizations supporting residents of Arkansas, New Hampshire,
North Carolina, Tennessee, and Vermont are eligible to apply.
Restrictions: Major national or broad area drives to raise funds for popular causes are
normally not appropriate for Foundation contributions.
Geographic Focus: Arkansas, New Hampshire, North Carolina, Tennessee, Vermont
Date(s) Application is Due: Apr 1; Oct 1
Amount of Grant: 150 - 3,500 USD
Samples: Life Span, Charlotte, North Carolina, $3,000 - general operating support;
Pikeville Volunteer Fire Department, Pikeville, Tennessee, $1,000 - general operating
support; Fall Mountain Emergency Food Shelf, Charlestown, New Hampshire, $1,500 -
general operating support.
Contact: Jane F. Kelly, Secretary; (603) 756-3311
Sponsor: Hubbard Farms Charitable Foundation
P.O. Box 505, 195 Main Street
Walpole, NH 03608-0505

Huffy Foundation Grants   1273

The Huffy Foundation gives primarily to areas where the company has operations: California,
Ohio, Pennsylvania, and Wisconsin. These areas include the visual arts; museums;
performing arts; theater; arts/cultural programs; all levels of education; hospitals (general);
health care and associations; recreation; children and youth services; and federated giving
(United Way). Types of support include general and operating support; continuing support;
annual campaigns; capital campaigns; building/renovation programs; emergency funds;
program development; seed money; consulting services; employee matching gifts; and
matching funds. Requests should include a description of the organization, its history and
purpose, a description of the people it serves, and a summary of total budget and funding.
Requirements: The Foundation provides a brochure which delineates the application and
grant guidelines. The Foundation recommends that the initial approach be in the form of
a letter or a proposal. One copy of the letter/proposal should be submitted. There are no
deadlines. The Board meets in February, May, August and November.
Restrictions: Grants are not made to individuals, in support of political activities or of
religious organizations for religious purposes, or organizations that are not tax exempt.
Grants are seldom made for medical research; to endowments; or for operating funds for
organizations located outside the corporation communities.
Geographic Focus: California, Ohio, Pennsylvania, Wisconsin
Contact: Pam Booher, Secretary; (937) 866-6251
Sponsor: Huffy Foundation
225 Byers Road
Miamisburg, OH 45342

Huisking Foundation Grants   1274

In the defense of freedom, Francis Robert Huisking paid the ultimate sacrifice during War
II. As co-captain of a B-24 bomber, he and his crew were lost when the bomber went down
over Italy in 1944. To honor his sacrifice and to perpetuate and preserve as a living memory
the sweet nature, the sterling qualities, the grand character, and the noble attributes he
displayed during the short time he was with us, his parents Charles and Catherine Huisking
founded the Frank R. Huisking Foundation on October 24, 1946. In addition to Charles

and Catherine, the original founding Directors and Officers included five of Francis' seven brothers and sisters; Charles Jr., Evelyn, William, Edward, and Richard. These individuals managed the growth, investments, contributions, and distributions of the Foundation for the next twenty plus years. In 1971, the name of the Foundation was officially changed to the Huisking Foundation. Today, the Foundation's primary fields of interest include: animal welfare; Catholicism; communication media; elementary and secondary education; higher education; historic preservation; hospital care; human services; museums; natural resources; nonprofits; and performing arts. The Foundation is small, and dedicated to the areas outlined above. To assure that funds distributed meet these principles, projects are reviewed and recommended by specific Directors who have knowledge of the project or program and thus supports its goals. This process results in the Board having a greater degree of confidence and assurance that the support being provided clearly meets the principles and intent as set out to honor Frank R. Huisking and his family.
Geographic Focus: All States
Amount of Grant: 200 - 60,000 USD
Contact: Frank Huisking, Treasurer; (203) 426-8618; wwh@huiskingfoundation.org
Internet: www.huiskingfoundation.org/
Sponsor: Huisking Foundation
291 Peddlers Road
Guilford, CT 06437-2324

Humana Foundation Grants   1275
The Humana Foundation was established to promote worthwhile organizations that improve the health and welfare of communities in its headquarters region of Louisville, Kentucky. It supports nonprofit institutions primarily in the areas of domestic and international health, education, and civic and cultural development. Religious organizations are eligible for project-specific support (e.g., social services outreach) or funds for an accredited, church-affiliated educational institution. Grants also are awarded in Humana market areas outside of the headquarters region. Detailed pplication information is available online.
Requirements: Applicant organizations must be 501(c)3 tax-exempt located in communities where Humana has a meaningful presence.
Restrictions: Grants are not given to organizations for seed money. The foundation does not contribute to social, labor, political, veterans, or fraternal organizations. Funds cannot be used solely to support an organization's salary expenses or other administrative costs. The foundation does not support lobbying efforts or political action committees.
Geographic Focus: Arizona, Colorado, Florida, Georgia, Illinois, Indiana, Kansas, Kentucky, Louisiana, Michigan, Ohio, Tennessee, Texas, Utah, Wisconsin
Date(s) Application is Due: Jan 31
Contact: Virginia K. Judd, Executive Director; (502) 580-4140; fax (502) 580-1256; HumanaFoundation@humana.com
Internet: www.humanafoundation.org/
Sponsor: Humana Foundation
500 West Main Street, Suite 208
Louisville, KY 40202-2946

Human Source Foundation Grants   1276
The Human Source Foundation is organized to support charitable and educational initiatives that improve the human condition. The Foundation provides assistance and financial support for programs involved with education, human services, and youth development. Giving is restricted to the state of Texas, primarily in Denton and Fort Worth counties. There are no specific deadlines or application forms, and applicants should begin by forwarding a letter of request.
Requirements: Tax-exempt 501(c)3 organizations serving Texas, primarily Denton and Fort Worth counties, are eligible to apply.
Geographic Focus: Texas
Samples: Botanical Resource of Texas, Fort Worth, Texas, $4,500; Meals on Wheels, Fort Worth, Texas, $7,700.
Contact: Mary G. Palko, President; (817) 926-2799; fax (817) 926-5202; mary@ftw.com
Sponsor: Human Source Foundation
2409 Winton Terrace West, P.O. Box 100423
Fort Worth, TX 76185-0423

Hungry for Music Instrument Gifts   1277
Hungry for Music (HFM) supports music education and cultural enrichment, both in the United States and abroad, by acquiring and distributing quality musical instruments to underserved children with willing instructors and a hunger to play. HFM supports parents who cannot afford to rent or purchase an instrument for their child and music teachers/directors who have identified a child who could use support. The program also supports after-school music programs such as Roots of Music in New Orleans, Junior Appalachian Musicians (JAM) in Southern Virginia, Rhode Island Fiddle Project, Intonation Music Workshop in Chicago, Little Five Points Music Center in Atlanta.
Requirements: Individuals must complete the brief online form at the sponsor's website. Applications are accepted through the end of March; May 15 through June 15; August 15 through September 15; and October 15 through November 15.
Geographic Focus: All States
Date(s) Application is Due: Mar 31; Jun 15; Sep 15; Nov 15
Contact: Jeff Campbell, Director; 202-674-3000; hungryformusic@att.net
Internet: hungryformusic.com/need-an-instrument/
Sponsor: Hungry for Music
2020 Pennsylvania Avenue, NW, No. 384
Washington, D.C. 20006

Huntington Clinical Foundation Grants   1278
The Foundation, established in 1986, supports health care programs and access, higher education, and medical research. Grant amounts range from approximately $1,500 to $8,000, with some larger amounts available. There are no specific applications or deadlines with which to adhere. The Board meets quarterly, and applicants should forward a detailed description of the project and amount of funding requested.
Requirements: Giving is limited to the Huntington, West Virginia, region.
Geographic Focus: West Virginia
Amount of Grant: 1,500 - 8,000 USD
Samples: Cabell County Substance Abuse Prevention Partnership, Huntington, West Virginia, $5,000 - funding for Cabell County REACH; Children's Place, Huntington, West Virginia, $3,000 - purchase of cribs; Marshall University Joan C Edwards School of Medicine, Huntington, West Virginia, $20,000 - scholarship endowment.
Contact: Don Ray, President; (304) 697-4780 or (304 523-6120; fax (304) 523-6051
Sponsor: Huntington Clinical Foundation
P.O. Box 117
Huntington, WV 25706-0117

Huntington County Community Foundation Classroom Education Grants   1279
The Huntington County Community Foundation Classroom Education Grants helps teachers fund new classroom projects or programs that are innovative and designed to stimulate learning. Any classroom teacher in the Huntington County, Indiana, area is eligible to apply, with the maximum amount of funding set at $250.
Requirements: Applicants are required to submit the online proposal form to the Foundation to include the following information: their name, school, their grade level, subject taught, and number of students. They should also include a full description of the project with proposed budget and timeline, along with a list of itemized expenses.
Restrictions: Teachers must be classroom teachers in the Huntington County Community Schools or the Huntington Catholic School districts. Grants are not awarded to existing programs or equipment/supplies for an existing program, personnel development, or travel. Proposals for projects that appear to have already begun or are funded elsewhere will not be considered.
Geographic Focus: Indiana
Date(s) Application is Due: Oct 15
Amount of Grant: 50 - 250 USD
Contact: Michael Howell, Executive Director; (260) 356-8878; fax (260) 356-0921; michael@huntingtonccf.org
Internet: www.huntingtonccf.org/hccf_grant_opportunities.html
Sponsor: Huntington County Community Foundation
356 West Park Drive
Huntington, IN 46750

Huntington County Community Foundation Make a Difference Grants   1280
The Huntington County Community Foundation Make a Difference Grants fund charitable projects that make a positive impact on the residents of Huntington County. Grant areas to be considered include: arts and culture; community development; health and human services; education; and other charitable services. These grants are awarded in spring and fall cycles. Grant decisions on based on the following criteria: the project's beneficial impact on Huntington County, immediate and ongoing; known and anticipated community needs; number of persons that benefit from and/or are affected by the project; and a clear, complete, and comprehensible statement of particulars.
Requirements: Applicants should submit one original and five additional paper clipped sets of the online application packet to include the following: grant proposal form; detailed project and organizational budget; current year-end financial statement; strategic or long-range plan; roster of board members; IRS tax exempt status; and articles of incorporation.
Restrictions: Grants will not be awarded to fund: operational or ongoing recurring (within 60 months) cost of the program; political projects or campaigns; or projects of applicants, or project owners, with taxing authority (e.g. school corporations; units of government).
Geographic Focus: Indiana
Date(s) Application is Due: Apr 15; Oct 15
Contact: Michael Howell, Executive Director; (260) 356-8878; fax (260) 356-0921; michael@huntingtonccf.org
Internet: www.huntingtonccf.org/hccf_grant_opportunities.html
Sponsor: Huntington County Community Foundation
356 West Park Drive
Huntington, IN 46750

IBCAT Nancy Jaynes Memorial Scholarship   1281
The Nancy Jaynes Memorial Scholarship Award is named in honor of the founder of the Indiana Breast Cancer Awareness Trust (IBCAT). Nancy lost her battle with breast cancer in March 2008. Nancy was a Plymouth, Indiana, High School Family and Consumer Sciences teacher. She envisioned the breast cancer license plate to be a traveling billboard and reminder about the importance of early detection and prevention of breast cancer. The mission of the Indiana Breast Cancer Awareness Trust is to increase access to breast cancer screening and diagnosis throughout Indiana. To date, IBCAT has funded over $5 million in grants supporting our mission. The scholarship of up to $2,500 for college or post-secondary technical schooling is awarded to an Indiana High School senior(s) whose parent is currently battling breast cancer or who has lost a parent to breast cancer. The Scholarship Application is available in December/January of each year with a deadline in late January to early February.
Geographic Focus: Indiana
Amount of Grant: Up to 2,500 USD
Contact: Jalana Eash, Grant Committee Chair; (866) 724-2228; fax (812) 868-7773;

ibcat@insightbb.com
Internet: www.breastcancerplate.org/scholarships/
Sponsor: Indiana Breast Awareness Trust
P.O. Box 8212
Evansville, IN

ICCF Youth Advisory Council Grants 1282

Iosco County Community Foundation Youth Advisory Council grants are awarded to non-profits through the Iosco County YAC, a group of students from across the county working to better the lives of other youth in their communities. All parochial and public schools should apply for grants through YAC. Projects and programs should benefit the youth of Iosco County under the age of 18. Applicants may submit requests up to a maximum of $2,500 per application cycle unless otherwise indicated. Mini-grants are also available to a maximum amount of $300. The annual deadline for application submission is a postmark of February 28.

Requirements: IRS 501(c)3 nonprofit organizations, schools, churches (for non-sectarian purposes), cities, townships, and other governmental units serving Iosco County are eligible to apply. An organization may apply each year for a grant.

Restrictions: No program may be funded for more than two (2) consecutive grant cycles or two (2) years, whichever is longer. The Community Foundation will not support the sustained funding of any program. Grants are not given to individuals, except for awards or scholarships from designated donor funds.

Geographic Focus: Michigan
Date(s) Application is Due: Feb 28
Amount of Grant: Up to 2,500 USD
Samples: FISH, Inc. of Oscoda/Tawas Bay Center for the Arts, Oscoda, Michigan, $2,400 - An Exploration of Green Technology; Hale Area Schools, Hale, Michigan, $1,800 - Red Ribbon Week Activities; Huron Hockey and Skating Association, Tawas City, Michigan, $1,600 - Hockey Nets.
Contact: Julie Wiesen, Program Director; (989) 354-6881 or (877) 354-6881; fax (989) 356-3319; wiesenj@cfnem.org
Internet: www.cfnem.org/iccf/grants/yac-grants.html
Sponsor: Iosco County Community Foundation
100 N. Ripley, Suite F, P.O. Box 495
Alpena, MI 49707

Iddings Foundation Capital Project Grants 1283

The Iddings Foundation began as the Iddings Benevolent Trust under the Wills of Roscoe C. and Andrew S. Iddings. The bachelor brothers shared a strong commitment to the Dayton area and created the Foundation as a philanthropic device to serve the needs of all citizens. The brothers' wills specified that their assets should be used for the following purposes: to assist public, charitable, benevolent or educational institutions supported wholly or in part by private donations or public taxes; promote scientific research to advance human knowledge, alleviate human suffering and cure mental illness; care for the sick, aged, blind and helpless, as well as needy men, women and children; and provide treatment and relief of crippled children. Capital Project Grants provide a maximum of $50,000 for building campaigns, special equipment or renovation. All proposals should be in the office of the Iddings Foundation by 9:00 am on the day of the deadline, which includes: March 1, June 1, September 1 and November 1.

Requirements: Applicants must be Ohio-based, tax-exempt organizations whose purpose is to improve the community environment and lives of the citizens, and whose primary focus is on the greater Dayton area. Interested parties must speak with the Administrator before applying for a grant.

Restrictions: Grants are not made to individuals or to organizations outside Ohio. Additionally, there will be no endowment support.

Geographic Focus: Ohio
Date(s) Application is Due: Mar 1; Jun 1; Sep 1; Nov 1
Amount of Grant: 500 - 50,000 USD
Contact: Becky Coughlin, Administrator; (937) 224-1773; fax (937) 224-1871; bcoughlin@iddingsfoundation.org
Internet: iddingsfoundation.org/apply.htm
Sponsor: Iddings Foundation
Ketting Tower, 40 N. Main Street, Suite 1620
Dayton, OH 45423

Iddings Foundation Major Project Grants 1284

The Iddings Foundation began as the Iddings Benevolent Trust under the Wills of Roscoe C. and Andrew S. Iddings. The bachelor brothers shared a strong commitment to the Dayton area and created the Foundation as a philanthropic device to serve the needs of all citizens. The brothers' wills specified that their assets should be used for the following purposes: to assist public, charitable, benevolent or educational institutions supported wholly or in part by private donations or public taxes; promote scientific research to advance human knowledge, alleviate human suffering and cure mental illness; care for the sick, aged, blind and helpless, as well as needy men, women and children; and provide treatment and relief of crippled children. Major Project Grants reflect the Foundation's desire to make an impact on at-risk youth in a long-lasting, meaningful way. All proposals should be in the office of the Iddings Foundation by 9:00 am on the day of the deadline, which includes: March 1, June 1, September 1 and November 1.

Requirements: Applicants must be Ohio-based, tax-exempt organizations whose purpose is to improve the community environment and lives of the citizens, and whose primary focus is on the greater Dayton area. Interested parties must speak with the Administrator before applying for a grant.

Restrictions: Grants are not made to individuals or to organizations outside Ohio. Additionally, there will be no endowment support.

Geographic Focus: Ohio
Date(s) Application is Due: Mar 1; Jun 1; Sep 1; Nov 1
Amount of Grant: 500 - 50,000 USD
Contact: Becky Coughlin, Administrator; (937) 224-1773; fax (937) 224-1871; bcoughlin@iddingsfoundation.org
Internet: iddingsfoundation.org/apply.htm
Sponsor: Iddings Foundation
Ketting Tower, 40 N. Main Street, Suite 1620
Dayton, OH 45423

Iddings Foundation Medium Project Grants 1285

The Iddings Foundation began as the Iddings Benevolent Trust under the Wills of Roscoe C. and Andrew S. Iddings. The bachelor brothers shared a strong commitment to the Dayton area and created the Foundation as a philanthropic device to serve the needs of all citizens. The brothers' wills specified that their assets should be used for the following purposes: to assist public, charitable, benevolent or educational institutions supported wholly or in part by private donations or public taxes; promote scientific research to advance human knowledge, alleviate human suffering and cure mental illness; care for the sick, aged, blind and helpless, as well as needy men, women and children; and provide treatment and relief of crippled children. Medium Project grants fund one-time awards for programs of organizations that are usually past recipients of Foundation funding. All proposals should be in the office of the Iddings Foundation by 9:00 am on the day of the deadline, which includes: March 1, June 1, September 1 and November 1.

Requirements: Applicants must be Ohio-based, tax-exempt organizations whose purpose is to improve the community environment and lives of the citizens, and whose primary focus is on the greater Dayton area. Interested parties must speak with the Administrator before applying for a grant.

Restrictions: Grants are not made to individuals or to organizations outside Ohio. Additionally, there will be no endowment support.

Geographic Focus: Ohio
Date(s) Application is Due: Mar 1; Jun 1; Sep 1; Nov 1
Amount of Grant: 500 - 20,000 USD
Contact: Becky Coughlin, Administrator; (937) 224-1773; fax (937) 224-1871; bcoughlin@iddingsfoundation.org
Internet: iddingsfoundation.org/apply.htm
Sponsor: Iddings Foundation
Ketting Tower, 40 N. Main Street, Suite 1620
Dayton, OH 45423

Iddings Foundation Small Project Grants 1286

The Iddings Foundation began as the Iddings Benevolent Trust under the Wills of Roscoe C. and Andrew S. Iddings. The bachelor brothers shared a strong commitment to the Dayton area and created the Foundation as a philanthropic device to serve the needs of all citizens. The brothers' wills specified that their assets should be used for the following purposes: to assist public, charitable, benevolent or educational institutions supported wholly or in part by private donations or public taxes; promote scientific research to advance human knowledge, alleviate human suffering and cure mental illness; care for the sick, aged, blind and helpless, as well as needy men, women and children; and provide treatment and relief of crippled children. Small Project grants provide up to $2,000 for projects or programs that satisfy community needs. All proposals should be in the office of the Iddings Foundation by 9:00 am on the day of the deadline, which includes: March 1, June 1, September 1 and November 1.

Requirements: Applicants must be Ohio-based, tax-exempt organizations whose purpose is to improve the community environment and lives of the citizens, and whose primary focus is on the greater Dayton area. Interested parties must speak with the Administrator before applying for a grant.

Restrictions: Grants are not made to individuals or to organizations outside Ohio. Additionally, there will be no endowment support.

Geographic Focus: Ohio
Date(s) Application is Due: Mar 1; Jun 1; Sep 1; Nov 1
Amount of Grant: Up to 2,000 USD
Contact: Becky Coughlin, Administrator; (937) 224-1773; fax (937) 224-1871; bcoughlin@iddingsfoundation.org
Internet: iddingsfoundation.org/apply.htm
Sponsor: Iddings Foundation
Ketting Tower, 40 N. Main Street, Suite 1620
Dayton, OH 45423

Ifuku Family Foundation Grants 1287

The Ifuku Family Foundation was established in 2000 by Seiju and Ayako Ifuku, the founders of the Rainbow Drive-In in Honolulu, Hawaii. It is a small, board-run foundation that awards annual grants to Hawaii-based non-profit organizations and schools. The philosophy of the Foundation is to support small, discrete programs that have a direct impact on those in need and to award scholarships in the culinary arts to students who need assistance in paying for tuition, school supplies, or books to complete their two-year programs. It also awards post high school scholarships to qualifying employees and their children. All scholarships are awarded based on the student's need and perseverance — while they have to be the best academically, they also need to convince the board that their choice to continue school will improve or change their lives. There are no specific annual deadlines for submission of applications.

Requirements: any 501(c)3 serving the residents of Oahu are eligible to apply.

Geographic Focus: Hawaii
Contact: Foundation Director; (808) 737-0177
Internet: rainbowdrivein.com/about/ifuku-family-foundation/
Sponsor: Ifuku Family Foundation
P.O. Box 160907
Honolulu, HI 96816

IIE 911 Armed Forces Scholarships 1288
The 911 Armed Forces Scholarships, managed by the Institute of International Education, provide scholarships for the dependent children of active duty U.S. military personnel who were killed in the September 11, 2001, terrorist attacks. Scholarships are one-time awards for study leading to a certificate, associate's or bachelor's degree in the United States or its equivalent at an accredited post-secondary institution in any country.
Requirements: Applicant must be a dependent child of active duty U.S. military personnel killed in the Sept. 11, 2001 terrorist attacks and pursue a certificate or undergraduate degree programs in a college or university in the U.S. or abroad.
Restrictions: Awards will not be provided for study leading to degrees higher than a bachelor's degree.
Geographic Focus: All States
Contact: Council for International Exchange of Scholars (CIES); (202) 898-0600 or (202) 686-4000; fax (202) 326-7754; scholars@iie.org
Internet: www.iie.org/Programs/911-Armed-Forces-Scholarship-Fund
Sponsor: Institute of International Education
1400 K Street NW, 7th Floor
Washington, D.C. 20005-2403

Ike and Roz Friedman Foundation Grants 1289
Established in Nebraska in 1989, the Ike and Roz Friedman Foundation has a mission of supporting Jewish agencies and federated giving programs, health care, the arts, education, and human and children's services. Its primary fields of interest include: arts and culture; child welfare; disease control and cures; higher education; human services; Judaism; museums; and community nonprofits. Interested applicants should submit a letter, which includes: name, address and phone number of organization; a statement of problem the project will address; and a detailed description of project and amount of funding requested. Though are no specified annual deadlines. Most recent awards have ranged from $250 to $130,000, though the majority average between $250 and $5,000.
Requirements: Any 501(c)3 supporting the residents of Nebraska is eligible to apply.
Geographic Focus: Nebraska
Amount of Grant: 250 - 130,000 USD
Samples: Omaha Children's Museum, Omaha, Nebraska, $5,000 - general operating support; Nebraska Jewish Historical Society, Omaha, Nebraska, $1,000 - general operating support; Klutznick Symposium, Omaha, Nebraska, $7,500 - general operating support.
Contact: Susan Cohn, President; (402) 697-1111
Sponsor: Ike and Roz Friedman Foundation
22804 Hansen Avenue
Elkhorn, NE 68022

ILA Arbuthnot Award 1290
The International Literacy Association Arbuthnot Award is given to honor an outstanding college or university proponent of children's and young adults' literature. The awardee, announced annually at the ALA Midwinter Meeting, may be an author, critic, librarian, historian, or teacher of children's literature, who shall prepare a paper considered to be a significant contribution to the field of children's literature. Once the name is made public, institutions wishing to host the lecture may apply. A library school, department of education in college or university, or a children's library system may be considered.
Requirements: Nominees must be IRA members, affiliated with a college or university, and engaged in teacher and/or librarian preparation at the undergraduate and/or graduate level. A current application is available at the IRA website.
Geographic Focus: All States, All Countries
Date(s) Application is Due: Nov 15
Amount of Grant: 800 USD
Contact: Marcie Craig Post, Executive Director; (302) 731-1600 or (800) 336-7323; fax (302) 731-1057; mpost@reading.org
Internet: www.literacyworldwide.org/about-us/awards-grants
Sponsor: International Literacy Association
800 Barksdale Road, P.O. Box 8139
Newark, DE 19714-8139

ILA Children's and Young Adults' Book Awards 1291
The International Literacy Association (ILA) Children's and Young Adults' Book Awards are intended for newly published authors who show unusual promise in the children's and young adults' book field. Awards are given for fiction and nonfiction in each of three categories: primary, intermediate, and young adult. Books from all countries and published in English for the first time during the previous calendar year will be considered. The award is intended for newly published authors who show unusual promise in the children's and young adults' book field. The annual deadline for application submission is March 15.
Requirements: The entry shall be the author's/authors' first or second book (ages preschool to 17).
Geographic Focus: All States, All Countries
Date(s) Application is Due: Mar 15
Contact: Marcie Craig Post, Executive Director; (302) 731-1600 or (800) 336-7323; fax (302) 731-1057; mpost@reading.org

Internet: www.literacyworldwide.org/about-us/awards-grants/ila-children's-and-young-adults'-book-awards
Sponsor: International Literacy Association
800 Barksdale Road, P.O. Box 8139
Newark, DE 19714-8139

ILA Grants for Literacy Projects in Countries with Developing Economies 1292
The Grants for Literacy Projects in Countries with Developing Economies funds literacy projects and the professional development of literacy educators outside the United States. This fund, made possible by voluntary contributions of International Reading Association members, offers annual one-time grants to International Reading Association members from developing countries (using the World Bank definition) who seek support for a literacy project in their own countries. The number of grants (each up to $2,500) will be determined by the amount of donations made to this fund as of June 30 (the annual deadline for application submission) each year.
Requirements: Applicants must meet the following criteria for consideration: reside in the developing country for which the grant is sought; hold International Literacy Association (ILA) membership; submit a specific project plan identifying how the funds will be used to promote literacy, such as the plan will help children/adults/females learn to read; agree to promote the goals of the ILA and indicate how this support will help gain additional members; provide a letter of support from an IRA affiliate council or member that demonstrates an understanding of the applicant's project and proposed use of the funds; and agree to submit a written report to ILA describing how the funds were used, how they benefited their community, and how the funds might have been more appropriately used.
Geographic Focus: All States, All Countries
Date(s) Application is Due: Jun 30
Amount of Grant: Up to 2,500 USD
Contact: Marcie Craig Post, (800) 336-7323 or (302) 731-1600; fax (302) 731-1057; research@reading.org or mpost@reading.org
Internet: www.literacyworldwide.org/about-us/awards-grants/developing-economy-grants
Sponsor: International Literacy Association
800 Barksdale Road, P.O. Box 8139
Newark, DE 19714-8139

Illinois Arts Council Theater Program Grants 1293
Program Grant funds provide artistic and operational support to established organizations that make a significant local, regional, or statewide impact on the quality of life in Illinois. Theatre Program grants are designed to support professional, regional, and community companies, including experimental, street, and children's theater. This includes experimental, musical theatre, street performance, and theatre for young audiences. Available funding ranges from $500 to $30,000, depending upon the applicant organization's overall past operating budget.
Requirements: Nonprofit organizations applying for funding must be chartered in the state of Illinois.
Geographic Focus: Illinois
Date(s) Application is Due: Mar 15
Amount of Grant: 500 - 30,000 USD
Contact: Walter Buford, Director; (312) 814-4992; fax (312) 814-1471; walter.buford@illinois.gov
Internet: www.arts.illinois.gov/Program%20Grant%3A%20Theater
Sponsor: Illinois Arts Council
100 W Randolph Street, Suite 10-500
Chicago, IL 60601-3230

Illinois Arts Council Youth Employment in the Arts Grants 1294
Through the Youth Employment in the Arts (YEA) Program, the IAC will support direct funding to Illinois not-for-profit organizations to offer high quality employment initiatives (internships) for high school students. These projects will provide youth with positive cultural experiences and paid on-the-job training in the arts to enhance their personal development. Applicants may request support for up to four high school interns per IAC program year. Recent high school graduates that have not yet entered college may be considered. The IAC program year is from September 1 through August 31 annually. The IAC will support 16 weeks of an individual internship, up to 20 hours per week. The stipend offered must be no less than the Illinois minimum wage, currently $6.50 an hour. Interns may only participate in one IAC supported internship per year. Internships may be staggered throughout the year, clearly indicate the start and end date of each intern on the budget page.
Requirements: Any Illinois not-for-profit organization that is currently in good standing with the Illinois Secretary of State is eligible to apply.
Restrictions: Individual Illinois schools and school districts are not eligible for this program.
Geographic Focus: Illinois
Date(s) Application is Due: Jul 1
Amount of Grant: Up to 4,000 USD
Contact: Tatiana Gant, Program Director; (312) 814-6765; fax (312) 814-1471; tatiana.gant@illinois.gov
Internet: www.arts.illinois.gov./grants-programs/iac-grants/youth-employment
Sponsor: Illinois Arts Council
100 W Randolph Street, Suite 10-500
Chicago, IL 60601-3230

Illinois Children's Healthcare Foundation Grants 1295
The Illinois Children's Healthcare Foundation works to ensure that all children in Illinois have access to affordable and quality health care. The Foundation focuses its giving on

three specific areas: improving the oral health of underserved children; addressing the mental health needs of children; and increasing the incidence of developmental screening in young children. Types of support include: building/renovation; conferences and seminars; curriculum development; emergency funds; equipment; program development and evaluation; and research. There are no specific deadlines or applications. The Board meets six times per year.

Requirements: Applicants must first contact the Foundation by phone or submit a letter of inquiry to discuss their proposed project.

Restrictions: Giving is limited to Illinois. The following are not eligible for funding: intermediary funding agencies; partisan, lobbying, political or denominational organizations; organizations not determined to be public charities; grants to individuals, endowments general medical research.

Geographic Focus: Illinois

Contact: Tammy Lemke, President; (630) 571-2555; fax (630) 571-2566; tammylemke@ilchf.org or info@ilchf.org

Internet: www.ilchf.org/

Sponsor: Illinois Children's Healthcare Foundation

1200 Jorie Boulevard, Suite 301

Oak Brook, IL 60523-2269

Illinois DNR Schoolyard Habitat Action Grants 1296

The program is a means of funding for teachers and students who are interested in creating or enhancing schoolyard habitat areas. Projects should emphasize student/youth involvement with planning, development, and maintenance, as well as increase the educational and wildlife values of the site. Project examples include: trail development; vegetation planting; designing, establishing and maintaining a schoolyard prairie plot; butterfly garden; watering station; designing and building a bird feeder or feeding station. Guidelines are available online.

Requirements: Teachers, youth group leaders and non-formal educators in Illinois are eligible to apply.

Restrictions: Funding cannot be used for consultant fees, bird seed, fuel, equipment (shovels, rakes, trowels), labor, books, web site development, or land acquisition.

Geographic Focus: Illinois

Date(s) Application is Due: Nov 30

Amount of Grant: Up to 600 USD

Contact: Valerie Keener, Administrator; (217) 524-4126 or (217) 782-7481; fax (217) 782-9552; valerie.keener@illinois.gov or dnr.teachkids@illinois.gov

Internet: www.dnr.illinois.gov/grants/Pages/default.aspx

Sponsor: Illinois Department of Natural Resources

One Natural Resources Way

Springfield, IL 62702-1271

Illinois DNR Youth Recreation Corps Grants 1297

The Illinois Youth Recreation Corps was established for making grants to local sponsors to provide wages to youth operating and instructing in recreational and conservation programs for the benefit of other youth. Such programs shall provide recreational opportunities for children of all age levels and shall include, but not be limited to, the coordination and teaching of physical activities, arts and handicrafts, and learning activities.

Requirements: Potential applicants include local sponsors who can provide necessary facilities, materials and management for summer recreational and conservation activities for youth within the community and who desire a grant for hiring eligible youth as supervisors, instructors, instructional aides or maintenance personnel. Local sponsors must be units of local government or not?for?profit entities. Enrollment (hiring) is limited to citizens of the State of Illinois who, at the time of hiring, are 16, 17, 18 or 19 years of age, and who have skills that can be used in the summer recreation or conservation program.

Restrictions: Youth currently employed in any manner by the local sponsor are not eligible for inclusion in the program.

Geographic Focus: Illinois

Date(s) Application is Due: Jun 30

Contact: Valerie Keener, Administrator; (217) 524-4126 or (217) 782-7481; fax (217) 782-9599; valerie.keener@illinois.gov or dnr.grants@illinois.gov

Internet: www.dnr.illinois.gov/grants/Pages/default.aspx

Sponsor: Illinois Department of Natural Resources

One Natural Resources Way

Springfield, IL 62702-1271

IMLS Grants to State Library Administrative Agencies 1298

Through the IMLS Grants to State Library Administrative Agencies program, the Institute of Museum and Library Services provides funds to State Library Administrative Agencies (SLAAs) using a population-based formula. State libraries may use the appropriation to support statewide initiatives and services. They also may distribute the funds through subgrant competitions or cooperative agreements to public, academic, research, school, and special libraries in their state. Grants to States funds have been used to meet the needs of children, parents, teenagers, adult learners, senior citizens, the unemployed, and the business community. One of the program's statutory priorities is to address underserved communities and persons having difficulty using a library, and approximately ten percent of grant funds in recent years have supported library services for the blind and physically handicapped. The program also meets the needs of the current and future library workforce.

Requirements: State library administrative agencies located in one of the 50 states of the United States, the District of Columbia, the Commonwealth of Puerto Rico, Guam, American Samoa, the U.S. Virgin Islands, the Commonwealth of the Northern Mariana Islands, the Republic of the Marshall Islands, the Federated States of Micronesia, and the Republic of Palau are eligible to submit five-year plans.

Geographic Focus: All States, American Samoa, District of Columbia, Guam, Marshall Islands, Northern Mariana Islands, Puerto Rico, U.S. Virgin Islands

Date(s) Application is Due: Apr 1

Amount of Grant: Up to 2,000,000 USD

Contact: Anthony Smith, Associate Deputy Director; (202) 653-4716 or (202) 653-4657; stateprograms@imls.gov or asmith@imls.gov

Internet: www.imls.gov/grants/grant-programs/grants-states

Sponsor: Institute of Museum and Library Services

955 L'Enfant Plaza North, SW, Suite 4000

Washington, D.C. 20024-2135

IMLS National Leadership Grants for Libraries 1299

National Leadership Grants enable libraries to help people gain the knowledge, skills, attitudes, behaviors, and resources that enhance their engagement in community, work, family, and society. Projects should enable libraries to address current problems in creative ways, develop and test innovative solutions, and expand the boundaries within which cultural heritage institutions operate. The results of these projects will help equip tomorrow's libraries to better meet the needs of a Nation of Learners. Successful proposals will show evidence that they will have national impact and generate results - new tools, research, models, services, practices, or alliances - that can be widely adapted or replicated to extend the benefit of federal support. Proposals will reflect an understanding of current issues and needs, showing the potential for far-reaching impact throughout the library community. Projects will provide creative solutions to issues of national importance and provide leadership for other organizations. Award amounts vary according to type of application: planning grants can range up to $100,000; national forum grants can range up to $150,000; project grants can range up to $1,000,000; and research in service to practice grants can range up to $750,000. All applications should designate one of the following project categories: lifelong learning; community catalysts; or national digital infrastructures and initiatives.

Requirements: All types of libraries, except federal and for-profit libraries, may apply. Eligible libraries include public, school, academic, special, private (not-for-profit), archives, library agencies, library consortia, and library associations. Research libraries and archives that give the public access to services and materials suitable for scholarly research not otherwise available and that are not part of a university or college also are eligible. Digital libraries that make library materials publicly available and provide services including selection, organization, description, reference, and preservation under the supervision of at least one permanent professional staff librarian are eligible to apply. Institutions of higher education, including public and not-for-profit universities and colleges, also are eligible. An academic unit, such as a graduate school of library and information science, may apply as part of an institution of higher education. Library applicants may apply individually or as partners.

Geographic Focus: All States, American Samoa, District of Columbia, Guam, Marshall Islands, Northern Mariana Islands, Puerto Rico, U.S. Virgin Islands

Date(s) Application is Due: Mar 26

Amount of Grant: Up to 1,000,000 USD

Samples: Society of American Archivists, Chicago, Illinois, $249,499 - support for a second cycle of its Archival Census and Education Needs Survey in the United States (2020); South Asian American Digital Archive, Philadelphia, Pennsylvania, $100,000 - support to explore methods, processes, and models for community-based archives (CBAs) to develop accessible educational materials based on their archival collections (2020); Institute for the Study of Knowledge Management in Education, Half Moon Bay, California, $499,624 - to develop, pilot test, and release a beta version of a network service where libraries can share Open Educational Resources (OER) alongside local evaluation and course alignment data for each resource (2020).

Contact: Sarah Boonie, Program Specialist, Libraries; (202) 653-4761 or (202) 653-4657; sboonie@imls.gov or imlsinfo@imls.gov

Internet: www.imls.gov/grants/available/national-leadership-grants-libraries

Sponsor: Institute of Museum and Library Services

955 L'Enfant Plaza North, SW, Suite 4000

Washington, D.C. 20024-2135

Indiana OCRA Quick Impact Placebased (QuIP) Grants 1300

The Quick Impact Placebased (QuIP) Grant program is designed to fund the type of space enhancement and community transformation that sparks community wide conversation and creativity. It is OCRA's belief that these types of social and built environments should occur at the local level and be community driven. It is the people, places and spaces that make Indiana a great place to live. Placemaking involves a working partnership with local governments, residents, community groups, and organizations as well as business and community agencies. OCRA encourages these projects to be community unique and locally inspired. Eligible projects examples might include: alley activation; creative projects to showcase community identity; enhancement of existing or underutilized public assets into a new or usable space; interactive life-size games or game sheds for public use; pop-up public gathering spots; transforming vacant store fronts; and unique signage or identifiers. There are many eligible projects. These dollars should be used to create a small change that spurs conversation and community engagement. The space should in some way be transformed for the better. Existing and underutilized assets should include a new or additional use. Art should be an overall component of your community transformation and used as an agent of change. Grant requests must be btween $2,500 and $5,000, and a local match of 1 to 0.5 is required. Completed applications must be received by June 1.

Requirements: Eligible applicants include: community groups or organizations; local units of government; and elementary through high school, colleges, universities, trade schools, and vocational schools.

Restrictions: Ineligible projects include: administration fees, including grant writing or administration; demolition; events; food, drink or alcohol; gaming and/or gambling activities; illegal or unsanctioned activities; one-time use activities or products; plants, greenery, shrubs or anything of that nature; public restrooms; salaries; small funding portion of a much larger project; spaces that are not open to the public; taxes; or WiFi. The grant amount cannot be less than 10% of total project cost.

Geographic Focus: Indiana
Date(s) Application is Due: Jun 1
Amount of Grant: 2,500 - 5,000 USD
Contact: Tammy Butts, Director of Grant Services; (317) 232-8335 or (317) 233-3762; fax (317) 233-3597; tabutts@lg.in.gov or info@ocra.in.gov
Internet: www.in.gov/ocra/quipgrant.htm
Sponsor: Indiana Office of Community and Rural Affairs
One North Capitol, Suite 600
Indianapolis, IN 46204-2027

Indiana OCRA Rural Capacity Grants (RCG) 1301

The Rural Capacity Grant program was developed to assist rural Indiana communities in their efforts to expand local capacity by means of grassroots community-development efforts, partnership building, and leveraging regional resources. There are two types of Rural Capacity Grants: Rural Entrepreneurial Support, and Workforce and Educational Development. Projects should seek to build the capacity to support local workforce and educational systems. A competitive project will demonstrate innovative approaches to address workforce development and lifelong learning. Examples of projects include, but are not limited to: training programs designed to meet the job market of the area being served; educational projects intended to increase basic skills, such as literacy and math, of the workforce; projects that seek to increase problem-solving, conflict resolution or other workplace-related soft skills, and other projects which address critical education and workforce-development issues. At the time of this writing, the Office of Community and Rural Affairs (OCRA) is not accepting applications due to funding restraints. Interested organizations are encouraged to contact the Project Manager for information on future funding availability.

Requirements: Not-for-profit organizations properly registered with the Secretary of State, educational or governmental entities, local economic-development organizations, Chambers of Commerce, workforce boards, Small Business Development Centers, community foundations, and other non-profit organizations are eligible to apply.

Restrictions: Grant funds and local match cannot be used for: the purchase of equipment over $5,000; administrative expenses in excess of 10% of the grant amount; operational expenses such as rent, utilities, insurance, non-program-related salaries; funding to purchase, improve, or remodel a facility; costs to supplant existing funds (the funding opportunity must be used for expansion of existing services or implementation of new services); or direct financial support to provide start up or operational capital to businesses.

Geographic Focus: Indiana
Amount of Grant: Up to 150,000 USD
Contact: Tammy Butts, Director of Grant Services; (317) 232-8335 or (317) 233-3762; fax (317) 233-3597; tabutts@lg.in.gov
Internet: www.in.gov/ocra/2357.htm
Sponsor: Indiana Office of Community and Rural Affairs
One North Capitol, Suite 600
Indianapolis, IN 46204-2027

ING Foundation Grants 1302

The ING Foundation is the charitable giving arm of ING U.S. The Foundation awards grants to non-profit organizations addressing a variety of community needs and resources. The Foundation focuses on four primary areas: financial literacy (especially programming that empowers individuals to take control of their financial futures through education, financial literacy, and financial planning, with special attention to the needs of young people and minorities); children's education (committed to supporting and improving education for youth in grades K-12, especially children in underserved areas or facing economic disadvantages; diversity); support equity and fairness in societies around the world, funding selected diversity initiatives; and environmental sustainability.

Requirements: Note that the Foundation cannot consider funding for organizations that do not have tax-exempt status under Section 501(c)3 of the U.S. Internal Revenue Code.

Restrictions: The Foundation does not grant awards to individuals; private foundations; religious or fraternal organizations and activities; political, legislative, and/or lobbying causes; capital and/or endowment campaigns or building funds; general or administrative operating costs; or organizations that discriminate on the basis of race, color, creed, gender or national origin. Nor does it support fashion shows, pageants, golf tournaments, sports teams, athletic events, or other funding opportunities that do not align with its strategic areas of giving. Grant requests are reviewed once per quarter by the ING Foundation Advisory Committee.

Geographic Focus: All States
Amount of Grant: 2,500 - 200,000 USD
Contact: Grants Administrator; (770) 980-5417; fax (770) 980-6580; ingfoundation@us.ing.com
Internet: ing.us/about-ing/responsibility/ing-foundation-grants
Sponsor: ING Foundation
5780 Powers Ferry Road NW
Atlanta, GA 30327-4349

Initiaive Foundation Inside-Out Connections Grants 1303

Initiaive Foundation Inside-Out Connections Grants are designed to increase the capacity of local communities to address the needs of children of incarcerated parents in central Minnesota. Children with incarcerated parents are among the most vulnerable populations of children, at high risk for neglect, abuse, behavioral health problems, delinquency and substance abuse. These issues, if left unattended, can produce intergenerational patterns of crime and violence. Initial grants of $5,000 are available, and future challenge grants (requiring matching dollars) may be available for projects that are directly related to coalition plans.

Requirements: The Foundation services communities in the following Minnesota counties: Benton, Cass, Chisago, Crow Wing, Isanti, Kanabec, Mille Lacs, Morrison, Pine, Sherburne, Stearns, Todd, Wadena, and Wright. Initial Grant goals are to: create and support multi-sector coalition teams to determine the needs of children with incarcerated parents; increase the capacity of coalition teams to develop and carry out an action plan around issues such as parent education, family support, child mentoring and community engagement; and increase community awareness and support for children who have a parent in jail or prison. Communities interested in participating on an existing team or starting one may contact the Children, Youth and Families Specialist.

Geographic Focus: Minnesota
Contact: Sara Dahlquist, Children, Youth and Families Specialist; (877) 632-9255; sdahlquist@ifound.org
Internet: www.ifound.org/grants_program.php
Sponsor: Initiative Foundation
405 First Street SE
Little Falls, MN 56345

Initiative Foundation Innovation Fund Grants 1304

The Initiative Foundation exists to improve the quality of life in central Minnesota. The Foundation's highest priorities are: to strengthen children, youth and families; promote economic stability; preserve space, place and natural resources; build capacity of nonprofit organizations; embrace diversity and reduce prejudice; and increase utilization of technology. Average awards are $5,000 and the maximum is generally $10,000. On occasion higher awards are made for multi-community projects or special initiatives. Requests for funding over $10,000 are accepted on an invitation-only basis.

Requirements: Eligible applicants must be 501(c)3 nonprofits or local units of government that serve the communities of Benton, Cass, Chisago, Crow Wing, Isanti, Kanabec, Mille Lacs, Morrison, Pine, Sherburne, Stearns, Todd, Wadena, and/or Wright Counties in Minnesota. Eligible projects must address at least one of the following areas: help communities address opportunities or barriers to business growth and employment with active participation by private, public and not-for-profit sectors; advance economic self-sufficiency for vulnerable children and families by supporting nonprofits that work in these areas; support training programs for future, displaced or underemployed workers that lead to employment or advancement in growing industries; help small businesses survive and grow through access to consulting services, mentorship and education efforts provided by not-for-profit entities; and help communities improve efficiencies through shared services with other units of government or public-private partnerships resulting in faster, higher quality, or more cost-effective services. Qualified organizations are asked to complete a letter of inquiry, which is found at the website. Inquiries are accepted on an ongoing basis and reviewed quarterly. Organizations with proposed projects which fit priority funding areas and meet funding criteria will be invited to submit a full proposal. The application materials will be provided.

Restrictions: The following are ineligible: grants to individuals; expenses incurred prior to the award; capital expenses; any programs or projects that do not directly benefit residents in the fourteen-county service area; replacement of government funding; religious activities; lobbying or campaigning for a candidate, issue or referendum vote; development or purchase of school curriculum or support for school athletic programs; and arts, health-related and media production applications, unless they are part of a strategic plan developed through a Foundation partnership program.

Geographic Focus: Minnesota
Contact: Grants Director; (877) 632-9255; fax (320) 632-9258; grants@ifound.org
Internet: www.ifound.org/grants_index.php
Sponsor: Initiative Foundation
405 First Street SE
Little Falls, MN 56345

Initiative Foundation Minnesota Early Childhood Initiative Grants 1305

Initiative Foundation Minnesota Early Childhood Initiative Grants are a local, regional and statewide partnership with local leaders to ensure that the quality care and education of young children is a top priority. The goal are to: educate citizens about the first five years of rapid brain development that forms lifetime personalities, social skills and learning capacity; promote parents and families as the primary and most important caregivers of young children, and foster the concept that nurturing and educating young children should be also embraced by entire communities; help community coalitions create a shared vision and plan of action around the care and education of young children and their families; provide training, financial and technical assistance and resource/referral services in order to implement quality community-based opportunities for young children; connect with other early childhood-focused communities statewide; promote and advance local, state and national public policy which supports quality care and education for the youngest citizens; and to create and promote "one voice" around the issue of early care and to speak for those who cannot. Selected communities receive an initial grant of $10,000; leadership and planning training; technical assistance; and referrals to resources.

Requirements: The Foundation services communities in the following Minnesota counties: Benton, Cass, Chisago, Crow Wing, Isanti, Kanabec, Mille Lacs, Morrison, Pine, Sherburne, Stearns, Todd, Wadena, and Wright. Selected communities will: build a diverse coalition; survey their community regarding perceptions and awareness around early childhood issues; and create and carry out projects and programs to help children

birth to five-years-old. Coalition are community-based teams made up of parents, childcare providers, kindergarten teachers, school administrators, city officials, business owners and other community members. These teams developed a local vision and plan of action to support young children and their families. Selection is a competitive process. The Foundation selects two communities per round. Contact the Children, Youth and Families Specialist for information.
Geographic Focus: Minnesota
Contact: Sara Dahlquist, Children, Youth and Families Specialist; (877) 632-9255; sdahlquist@ifound.org
Internet: www.ifound.org/grants_program.php
Sponsor: Initiative Foundation
405 First Street SE
Little Falls, MN 56345

Inland Empire Community Foundation Capacity Building for   1306
IE Nonprofits Grants
The Inland Empire Community Foundation invests in the region's nonprofits because they are vital to a healthy and stronger community. Since 2013, IECF has funded nonprofits with capacity grants to help them improve their ability to manage change and respond to opportunities. Capacity building funds provide an opportunity for nonprofits to reflect, learn, and take action in developing short and long-term, sustainable solutions to challenges they face in addressing crucial community needs.
Requirements: The Foundation accepts competitive grant proposals from nonprofit organizations who work to make a difference in the lives of Riverside and San Bernardino County residents throughout the year. Nonprofits wishing to apply need to demonstrate a commitment to building organizational capacity. This includes having developed short and long-term strategies for addressing identified organizational needs based on board and staff assessments or strategic planning. Strong candidates in the competitive grant process should show potential for how the award will make a difference in how the organization is governed, managed, financed, or operated in the future.
Geographic Focus: California
Contact: Celia Cudiamat, Executive Vice President of Grant Programs; (951) 241-7777; fax (951) 684-1911; ccudiamat@iegives.org
Internet: www.iegives.org/impact/overview/#initiatives
Sponsor: Inland Empire Community Foundation
3700 Sixth Street, Suite 200
Riverside, CA 92501

Inland Empire Community Foundation Coachella Valley Youth Grants   1307
The Coachella Valley Youth Grantmakers Fund was established in 2014 by the Community Foundation. High schools students ages 15 to 18, called Youth Grant makers, address issues important to them by participating in grant making, a formal practice of philanthropy. The Coachella Valley Youth Grant makers survey their peers, conduct nonprofit site visits, review grant proposals, and make grant recommendations based on local youth needs. Grant proposals will be accepted that address issues important to youth. Program interest areas are broad based and may include areas of academic preparation, cultural inclusion, awareness and prevention, as well as indirect and direct services that will help youth develop positive assets for strong social, mental and academic growth. Approximately six awards are given each year.
Requirements: Students ages 15 to 18 are eligible to apply to the Youth Grantmakers through their high school administrative or counseling offices. Nonprofit, public benefit corporations with evidence of tax-exempt status under Section 501(c)3 of the Internal Revenue Code and not classified as a private foundation are eligible, as well as educational institutions. These nonprofit agencies should serve youth residing in the Coachella Valley area.
Geographic Focus: California
Contact: Denisha Shackelford, Youth Initiatives Manager; (951) 241-7777; fax (951) 684-1911; dshackelford@iegives.org
Internet: www.iegives.org/impact/overview/#initiatives
Sponsor: Inland Empire Community Foundation
3700 Sixth Street, Suite 200
Riverside, CA 92501

Inland Empire Community Foundation Native Youth Grants   1308
The Native Youth Grantmakers Fund was established by the Community Foundation in February of 2012. The committee consists of local middle schools students who review proposals, conduct site-visits and recommend grants for funding as part of a comprehensive multi-session after school philanthropy program. All grant awards have final approval from he Idyllwild Community Fund Advisors and he Community Foundation Board of Directors. Programs and/or activities should: involve youth in the development and implementation of the project; increase community involvement and volunteerism among youth; promote values of personal responsibility and self-sufficiency in youth; provide an avenue for internal exploration and personal empowerment in youth; respect diversity; and support early intervention and prevention of social problems. Preference will be given to the following types of activities that address issues that are relevant to teens in the Southwest Riverside County: arts, culture, dance, drama, music, and writing; programs led by youth instead of adults; advocacy programs; real life learning experiences; educational classes; service learning; mentoring or tutorial programs; teen hot lines; outdoor experiences, camps, etc; and therapy. Applicants may request amounts up to $1,000.
Requirements: Nonprofit, public benefit corporations with evidence of tax-exempt status under Section 501(c)3 of the Internal Revenue Code and not classified as a private foundation are eligible, as well as educational institutions. These nonprofit agencies should serve youth residing in the Southwest Riverside County community.
Geographic Focus: California

Amount of Grant: Up to 1,000 USD
Contact: Denisha Shackelford, Youth Initiatives Manager; (951) 241-7777; fax (951) 684-1911; dshackelford@iegives.org
Internet: www.iegives.org/impact/overview/#initiatives
Sponsor: Inland Empire Community Foundation
3700 Sixth Street, Suite 200
Riverside, CA 92501

Inland Empire Community Foundation Riverside Youth Grants   1309
The Riverside Youth Grantmakers Fund was established by the Community Foundation in 2009. Riverside high schools students ages 15 to 18, called Youth Grant makers, address issues important to them by participating in grant making, a formal practice of philanthropy. The Youth Grant makers survey their peers, conduct site visits, review grant proposals, and make grant recommendations based on local youth needs. The Fund provides financial support for projects, programs and/or activities that serve youth in such areas as health and human services, arts and culture, and education. Programs and/or activities should: involve youth in the development and implementation of the project; increase community involvement and volunteerism among youth; promote values of personal responsibility and self-sufficiency in youth; provide an avenue for internal exploration and personal empowerment in youth; respect and promote diversity; support early intervention and prevention of social problems; support and encourage youth creativity; and develop civic and public pride in youth. Applicants may request amounts ranging from $1,000 to $2,500.
Requirements: Students ages 15 to 18 are eligible to apply to the Youth Grantmakers through their high school administrative or counseling offices. Nonprofit, public benefit corporations with evidence of tax-exempt status under Section 501(c)3 of the Internal Revenue Code and not classified as a private foundation are eligible, as well as educational institutions. These nonprofit agencies should serve youth residing in the western and southwest Riverside County region.
Restrictions: Agencies that have received Youth Grantmaker funds consecutively for the past two years are not eligible to apply.
Geographic Focus: California
Amount of Grant: 1,000 - 2,500 USD
Contact: Denisha Shackelford, Youth Initiatives Manager; (951) 241-7777; fax (951) 684-1911; dshackelford@iegives.org
Internet: www.iegives.org/impact/overview/#initiatives
Sponsor: Inland Empire Community Foundation
3700 Sixth Street, Suite 200
Riverside, CA 92501

Inland Empire Community Foundation San Bernardino Youth Grants   1310
The San Bernardino Youth Grantmakers Fund was established in 2014 by the Community Foundation. High school students ages 15 to 18, called Youth Grant makers, address issues important to them by participating in grant making, a formal practice of philanthropy. The San Bernardino Youth Grant makers survey their peers, conduct nonprofit site visits, review grant proposals, and make grant recommendations based on local youth needs. The Fund provides financial support for projects, programs and/or activities that serve youth in such areas as health and human services, arts and culture, and education. Programs and/or activities should: involve youth in the development and implementation of the project; increase community involvement and volunteerism among youth; promote values of personal responsibility and self-sufficiency in youth; provide an avenue for internal exploration and personal empowerment in youth; respect and promote diversity; support early intervention and prevention of social problems; support and encourage youth creativity; and develop civic and public pride in youth. Applicants may request amounts ranging from $1,000 to $2,500.
Requirements: Students ages 15 to 18 are eligible to apply to the Youth Grantmakers through their high school administrative or counseling offices. Nonprofit, public benefit corporations with evidence of 501(c)3 tax-exempt status and not classified as a private foundation are eligible, as well as educational institutions. These nonprofit agencies should serve youth residing in the City of San Bernardino and neighboring communities (Colton, Grand Terrace, Highland, Loma Linda, Redlands, Yucaipa).
Geographic Focus: California
Amount of Grant: 1,000 - 2,500 USD
Contact: Denisha Shackelford, Youth Initiatives Manager; (951) 241-7777; fax (212) 889-4959; dshackelford@iegives.org
Internet: www.iegives.org/impact/overview/#initiatives
Sponsor: Inland Empire Community Foundation
3700 Sixth Street, Suite 200
Riverside, CA 92501

Intel Corporation Community Grants   1311
The Intel Corporation is committed to maintaining and enhancing the quality of life in the communities where the company has a major presence. The primary giving focus is education and vigorous support is given to education programs that advance science, math and technology education, particularly for women and underserved populations. The corporation is also committed to the responsible use of natural resources and funding for environmental programs will be considered.
Requirements: 501(c)3 nonprofit organizations in Arizona, California, Colorado, Massachusetts, New Mexico, Oregon, Texas, Utah, and Washington are eligible to apply.
Restrictions: Funds are not available for: programs outside the site community; endowment or capital-improvement campaigns; unrestricted gifts to national or international organizations; sectarian or denominational religious organizations; foundations that are strictly grant-making bodies; private schools; organizations that practice discrimination; sporting events or teams; health care organizations; arts organizations; special occasion

goodwill advertising; scholarship award in the name of another organization; fund raising activities or events, raffles or giveaways; funds for individuals; travel or tours; school extra-curricular activities/clubs; general operating expenses or debt-retirement for organizations.
Geographic Focus: Arizona, California, Colorado, Massachusetts, New Mexico, Oregon, Texas, Utah, Washington
Contact: Gary Niekerk, Director of Corporate Responsibilty; (408) 765-8080 or (916) 356-6861; fax (408) 765-9904; gary.niekerk@intel.com
Internet: www.intel.com/content/www/us/en/corporate-responsibility/intel-invests-in-our-communities.html
Sponsor: Intel Corporation
2200 Mission College Boulevard
Santa Clara, CA 95054-1549

Intel Corporation International Community Grants 1312

The Intel Corporation is committed to maintaining and enhancing the quality of life in the communities where the company has a major presence. Primary focus is on education with a strong interest in support of K-12/higher education and community programs that deliver the kind of educational opportunities that all students will need to prepare themselves to succeed in the 21st century. Intel will support additional programs that improve the quality of life in its site communities. These requests will be evaluated on the basis of the services offered and the program's impact on the community; its impact on the youth of our community; the cost-effectiveness of the program and its ability to be effectively measured and replicated; and the potential for Intel employee involvement. Current international community giving includes: Costa Rica, China, Ireland, India, Israel, Malaysia, Philippines, and Russia.
Requirements: Grants are made for local programs located in Intel communities in Costa Rica, China, Ireland, India, Israel, Malaysia, Philippines, and Russia.
Restrictions: Requests are denied for: programs outside the site community; endowment or capital-improvement campaigns; unrestricted gifts to national or international organizations; sectarian or denominational religious organizations; foundations that are strictly grant-making bodies; private schools; organizations that practice discrimination; sporting events or teams; health care organizations; arts organizations; special occasion goodwill advertising; scholarship awards in the name of another organization; fund raising activities or events, raffles or giveaways; individuals; travel or tours.
Geographic Focus: China, Costa Rica, India, Ireland, Israel, Malaysia, Philippines, Russia
Contact: Gary Niekerk, Director of Corporate Responsibilty; (408) 765-8080 or (916) 356-6861; fax (408) 765-9904; gary.niekerk@intel.com
Internet: www.intel.com/community/international.htm
Sponsor: Intel Corporation
2200 Mission College Boulevard
Santa Clara, CA 95054-1549

IRC Community Collaboratives for Refugee Women and Youth Grants 1313

With support from the Office of Refugee Resettlement through the Community and Family Strengthening Initiative, the International Rescue Committee (IRC) offers funding, technical assistance, and training to refugee service providers nationwide to: provide refugee women and youth with the tools they need to become self-reliant and integrated into their communities; develop model programs that address the unique needs of refugee women and youth; advance awareness of the valuable social and economic contributions refugee women and youth bring to their communities. Applicants should contact the IRC for current applications and deadlines.
Geographic Focus: All States
Contact: Robert Carey, Vice President, Resettlement and Migration Policy; (212) 551-3000; info@theirc.org
Internet: www.theirc.org/community
Sponsor: International Rescue Committee
122 East 42nd Street
New York, NY 10168

Irving S. Gilmore Foundation Grants 1314

The Irving S. Gilmore Foundation endeavors to develop and to enrich the Greater Kalamazoo community of Michigan and its residents by supporting the work of nonprofit organizations. The Foundation's funding priorities are: health and well-being; arts, culture, and humanities; human services; education; and community development. There are six annual deadlines for application submission: January 9, March 1, May 1, July 5, September 1, and November 5. Requests for $7,500 or less may be submitted at any time.
Requirements: The Foundation supports Kalamazoo County projects, programs, and purposes carried out by charitable institutions, primarily public charities and governmental entities.
Restrictions: Grants are not made to individuals. The Foundation does not accept applications via email.
Geographic Focus: Michigan
Date(s) Application is Due: Jan 9; Mar 1; May 1; Jul 5; Sep 1; Nov 1
Amount of Grant: Up to 150,000 USD
Contact: Janice C. Elliott, Vice President of Administration; (269) 342-6411; fax (269) 342-6465
Internet: www.isgilmore.org/application/
Sponsor: Irving S. Gilmore Foundation
136 East Michigan Avenue, Suite 900
Kalamazoo, MI 49007-3915

Isabel Allende Foundation Esperanza Grants 1315

The Isabel Allende Foundation was established in 1996, and is guided by a vision of a world in which women have achieved social and economic justice. The vision includes empowerment of women and girls and protection of women and children. The Foundation feels that the way to achieve empowerment is: reproductive self-determination; health care; and education. Grants typically range from $1,000 to $10,000 and are made to support programs for vulnerable women and children in Chile and California.
Requirements: 501(c)3 organizations (and equivalent international organizations) are eligible to apply. Priority is given to programs in the San Francisco Bay Area and Chile.
Restrictions: The foundation does not fund capital campaigns, individual trips or tours, conferences, or events; and projects that benefit political, religious, and/or military organizations. Individuals are not eligible to receive grants and should not apply.
Geographic Focus: California, Chile
Date(s) Application is Due: Jan 1; Apr 1; Jul 1; Oct 1
Amount of Grant: 1,000 - 5,000 USD
Contact: Lori Barra, Executive Director; (415) 332-1313 or (415) 289-0992; fax (415) 289-1154; lori@isabelallendefoundation.org
Sarah Kessler, Associate; (415) 331-0261; fax (415) 289-1154; sarah@isabelallendefoundation.org
Internet: www.isabelallendefoundation.org/iaf.php?l=en&p=application
Sponsor: Isabel Allende Foundation
116 Caledonia Street
Sausalito, CA 94965

Island Insurance Foundation Grants 1316

The Island Insurance Foundation was established in 2002 in Hawaii, and was classified as a company-sponsored operating foundation in 2003. Today, the Foundation supports: arts and culture; basic and emergency aid; communication media; cultural awareness; disaster relief; diseases and conditions; elementary and secondary education; family services; health and health care; higher education; historical activities; human services; in-patient medical care; performing arts; radio; shelter and residential care; sports; and youth development programs. Its primary geographic focus is Hawaii, though the Foundation also gives to national programs. During the past five years, the Foundation has supported nearly funded 200 grants for 113 organizations totaling more than $1.35 million. Most recently, awards have ranged up to $50,000, though the average grant is less than $10,000. There are no annual deadlines or application formats, and interested parties should submit a letter of application.
Geographic Focus: All States, Hawaii
Amount of Grant: Up to 50,000 USD
Samples: Child and Family Services, Honolulu, Hawaii, $18,040 - general operating support; Filipino Community Center, Honolulu, Hawaii, $2,000 - general operating support; Straub Foundation, Honolulu, Hawaii, $30,000 - general operating support for medical facility.
Contact: Tyler M. Tokioka, President; (808) 564-8309 or (808) 564-8111; info@islandinsurance.com
Internet: www.islandinsurance.com/about/community/
Sponsor: Island Insurance Foundation
1022 Bethel Street
Honolulu, HI 96813-4302

IYI Professional Development Grants 1317

The Professional Development Grant program provides up to $750 to support attendance at continuing education programs identified by youth workers that meet their individual needs and fit their schedules. Grants may be used for conferences, trainings, or workshops that focus on nonprofit management or healthy youth development. Conferences, trainings, or workshops must be significantly related to the applicant's position and agency's mission, and improve the applicant's ability to do his or her job and the agency's ability to foster the healthy development of children and youth. Examples of eligible conference and courses: the National Childcare Conference hosted by the Child Welfare League of America; Search Institute's Healthy Communities Healthy Youth Conference; a social work or nonprofit management course at your local college or university
Requirements: Applicants must be a staff member, board member, or active volunteer of a 501(c)3 organization that provides services to youth. Schools and faith-based youth ministries must submit a not-for-profit tax registration certificate or determination letter in lieu of 501(c)3 status. Organizations must be Indiana-based, serve Indiana youth, and have an Indiana address.
Restrictions: Grants may not be used for: airfare; rental cars; IYI trainings; gas; parking; past events; meals; or books or supplies.
Geographic Focus: Indiana
Date(s) Application is Due: Jan 10; Feb 10; Mar 10; Apr 10; May 10; Jun 10; Jul 10; Aug 10; Sep 10; Oct 10; Nov 10; Dec 10
Amount of Grant: Up to 750 USD
Contact: Nicole Brock, Program Manager; (317) 396-2700 or (800) 343-7060; fax (317) 396-2701; iyi@iyi.org
Internet: 208.106.252.33/fundraising-grants/development-grants.aspx
Sponsor: Indiana Youth Institute
603 E Washington Street, Suite 800
Indianapolis, IN 46204-2692

IYI Responsible Fatherhood Grants 1318

The Institute promotes the healthy development of children and youth by serving the institutions and people of Indiana who work on their behalf. It is IYI's intention to help build the capacity of grassroots coalitions made up of both community and faith-based organizations to provide services that promote responsible fatherhood in their local community or region. The program provides technical assistance and financial awards to five community collaborations that have implemented practical strategies for helping dads become more involved with their children.

Requirements: With federal funding provided by the Promoting Responsible Fatherhood Community Access Grant, IYI seeks to identify and provide grants to five community coalitions of small faith-based and community partnering organizations that will deliver direct services with IYI's coordination. Coalitions must have from six to eight partnering faith-based or community organizations (micro-partners), each having a total annual operating budget of no more than $300,000 OR six or fewer full-time equivalent employees.

Geographic Focus: Indiana
Amount of Grant: Up to 150,000 USD
Contact: Nicole Brock, Program Manager; (317) 396-2700 or (800) 343-7060; fax (317) 396-2701; iyi@iyi.org
Internet: www.iyi.org/parent-involvement/responsible-fatherhood.aspx
Sponsor: Indiana Youth Institute
603 E Washington Street, Suite 800
Indianapolis, IN 46204-2692

J. Bulow Campbell Foundation Grants 1319

The J. Bulow Campbell Foundation supports nonprofit organizations in Alabama, Florida, Georgia, North or South Carolina, and Tennessee in its areas of interest, including: communities; the arts; education; youth; and religious concerns of the Church. Highest priority is given to capital funding rather than providing support for current operating expenses or recurring programs. The board meets quarterly in January, April, July and October. The Foundation does not provide an application form. A formal proposal to the Campbell Foundation is initiated by submitting a letter of request limited to one page.

Requirements: Grants are awarded almost exclusively in Atlanta and Georgia. While organizations in Alabama, Florida, North Carolina, South Carolina and Tennessee are technically eligible to receive grants, the Foundation has provided only limited support outside Georgia, and it does not award grants outside the six-state region.

Restrictions: No grants or loans are made to individuals.
Geographic Focus: Alabama, Florida, Georgia, North Carolina, South Carolina, Tennessee
Date(s) Application is Due: Jan 1; Apr 1; Jul 1; Oct 1
Contact: Anne Greene, Associate Director; (404) 658-9066
Internet: jbcf.org/grantmaking/policy/
Sponsor: J. Bulow Campbell Foundation
3050 Peachtree Road NW, Suite 270
Atlanta, GA 30305

J. Edwin Treakle Foundation Grants 1320

Incorporated in 1963 in Virginia, the J. Edwin Treakle Foundation awards funding to a number of educational, civic, and community organizations in mostly the Gloucester/Hampton Roads/Norfolk region. Some organizations from other areas in Virginia are also funded. The Foundation's primary fields of interest include: animal welfare, arts, children and youth services, community and economic development, disaster assistance (fire prevention and control), education, health care, human services, public libraries, and Protestant agencies and churches. Types of support include annual campaigns, building and renovation, capital campaigns, continuing support, equipment purchase, general operating support, and scholarship funding. Applicants should begin by contacting the Foundation via telephone or by letter to request an application. Requests should be submitted between January 1 and April 30.

Restrictions: No grant funding is offered to individuals.
Geographic Focus: Virginia
Date(s) Application is Due: Apr 30
Amount of Grant: 500 - 50,000 USD
Samples: Gloucester Volunteer Fire and Rescue Squad, Gloucester, Virginia, $50,000 - to purchase ten breathing apparatus and 36 backup filters; Gloucester Library, Gloucester, Virginia, $23,000 - to purchase books and library materials; Matthews Land Conservancy, Matthews, Virginia, $6,000 - to complete the Williams Wharf Project.
Contact: John Warren Cooke, President; (804) 693-0881
Sponsor: J. Edwin Treakle Foundation, Inc.
P.O. Box 1157
Gloucester, VA 23061-1157

J. Knox Gholston Foundation Grants 1321

The J. Knox Gholston Foundation's mission is to support charitable organizations that provide for the education of children within the City of Comer in Madison County, Georgia. The Foundation is interested in capital and instructional projects that advance academic achievement. The Foundation may also consider at times other charitable organizations serving Comer, Georgia. Grants from the J. Knox Gholston Foundation are primarily 1 year in duration. On occasion, multi-year support is awarded. Award amounts typically go up to $250,000.

Requirements: Applicants must have 501(c)3 tax-exempt status and serve residents in Madison County, Georgia. Applications will be submitted online through the Bank of America website. A grant report is required within 1 year of the grant application date, regardless of whether all of the funds have been spent.

Restrictions: The foundation does not support requests from individuals, organizations attempting to influence policy through direct lobbying, or any political campaigns.
Geographic Focus: Georgia
Date(s) Application is Due: Jun 1
Amount of Grant: Up to 250,000 USD

Samples: Madison County Schools, Comer, Georgia, $225,590 - Awarded for general operations of the organizations (2019); Comer Elementary School, Comer, Georgia-$83,000 - Awarded for general operations of the organization (2019); YMCA Endowment Fund of Athens, Athens, Georgia, $4,100 - Awarded for Summer Day Camp Scholarships for Children from Comer, Georgia.
Contact: Mark S. Drake, Vice President; (404) 264-1377; ga.grantmaking@bankofamerica.com or mark.s.drake@bofa.com
Internet: www.bankofamerica.com/philanthropic/foundation/?fnId=98
Sponsor: J. Knox Gholston Foundation
3414 Peachtree Road, N.E., GA7-813-14-04
Atlanta, GA 30326-1113

J. Marion Sims Foundation Teachers' Pet Grant 1322

The J. Marion Sims Foundation Teachers' Pet Grant program was designed to assist educators in meeting the evolving needs of students. The program's aim is to inspire and encourage creative concepts that have the potential for enhancing community life through the education of local youth. Awards will be based on merit, innovation, completeness, the enhancement of existing instruction, and the availability of funding. Recipients are limited to one grant per school year. Grant requests must be submitted via email. Application information is available online.

Requirements: Classroom teachers, media specialists, guidance counselors and other certified support staff (exclusive of after-school programs) serving K-12 students in Lancaster County, Fort Lawn and Great Falls, South Carolina, are invited to apply. Requests will not be considered via fax, postal mail, or hand-delivery.

Restrictions: Digital cameras, DVD or VCR equipment, library books, school beautification projects, and transportation will not be funded.
Geographic Focus: South Carolina
Amount of Grant: Up to 500 USD
Contact: Grants Officer; (803) 286-8772; fax (803) 286-8774; teacherspet@jmsims.org
Internet: www.jmsims.org/grants/teacherspet.html
Sponsor: J. Marion Sims Foundation
800 North White Street, P.O. Box 818
Lancaster, SC 29721

J.W. Gardner II Foundation Grants 1323

The J.W. Gardner II Foundation was established in Illinois in 2002, with an aim to support nonprofit residents of Quincy, Illinois. The Foundation's primary fields of interest include: adult and child mentor programs; animal welfare; child welfare; education; housing development; human services; museums; and scouting programs. Most recent awards have ranged from $1,500 to $50,000, with an average of ten to twelve grants given each year. Most often, these awards are in the form of general operating support. A formal application is required, and should reach the Foundation office by the annual June 30 deadline.

Requirements: 501(c)3 organizations serving Quincy, Illinois are eligible to apply.
Geographic Focus: Illinois
Date(s) Application is Due: Jun 30
Amount of Grant: 1,500 - 50,000 USD
Samples: Quincy Symphony Orchestra, Quincy, Illinois, $1,500 - general operating expense; Cheerful Home Association, Quincy, Illinois, $50,000 - general operating expense; Horizons Social Service, Quincy, Illinois, $20,000 - general operating expense.
Contact: John G. Stevenson, Jr., Director; (217) 277-2526 or (217) 224-0401
Sponsor: J.W. Gardner II Foundation
510 Maine Street, 9th Floor, P.O. Box 140
Quincy, IL 62306-3941

J.W. Kieckhefer Foundation Grants 1324

The Kieckhefer Foundation awards grants to nation-wide 501(c)3 organizations in support of medical research, hospices, and health agencies; family planning services; social services; higher education; youth and child welfare agencies; ecology and conservation; community funds; and cultural programs. Types of support include the following: annual campaigns; building renovation; conferences and seminars; continuing support; emergency funds; endowments; equipment; general operating support; land acquisition; matching and challenge support; program development; publication; and research.

Requirements: Applications are not accepted. Organizations should submit a letter of inquiry to the Foundation, with a description of their project and amount requested.

Restrictions: Grants are not awarded to individuals.
Geographic Focus: All States
Contact: John I. Kieckhefer, Trustee; (928) 445-4010
Sponsor: J.W. Kieckhefer Foundation
116 East Gurley Street
Prescott, AZ 86301-3821

J. Walton Bissell Foundation Grants 1325

The J. Walton Bissell Foundation Grants support 501(c)3 organizations in Connecticut, with emphasis on Hartford. The Foundation gives primarily to the arts and social services, including child welfare and programs for the blind. Funding requests should be submitted four months before funding is needed. Types of support include general operating support, program development, and seed money.

Requirements: Applicants should submit a letter of inquiry, along with a copy of their IRS determination letter, and a copy of their annual report, audited financial statement, or 990.

Restrictions: The Foundation does not grant funding to individuals or endowments.
Geographic Focus: Connecticut
Contact: J. Danford Anthony, Jr., President; (860) 586-8201

Sponsor: J. Walton Bissell Foundation
P.O. Box 370067
West Hartford, CT 06137

J. Watumull Fund Grants 1326

The J. Watumull Fund was established in Honolulu in 1980, with the expressed purpose of: arts and culture; basic and emergency aid; diseases and conditions; elementary and secondary education; family services; health and health care; higher education; human services; mental health care; out-patient medical care; performing arts; shelter and residential care; and university education. Support strategies include: capital and infrastructure; endowments; fellowships; general operating support; program development; re-granting; scholarships; and student aid. There are no specified application deadlines.

Requirements: Any 501(c)3 supporting the residents of Hawaii and India are eligible to apply.
Geographic Focus: Hawaii, India
Amount of Grant: Up to 5,000 USD
Contact: Gulab Watumull, President; (808) 525-5881
Sponsor: J. Watumull Fund
Watumull Building, 307 Lewers Street, 6th Floor, P.O. Box 3708
Honolulu, HI 96811

J. Willard and Alice S. Marriott Foundation Grants 1327

The J. Willard and Alice S. Marriott Foundation is a private family foundation dedicated to helping youth secure a promising future, especially through education on the secondary and higher education levels, mentoring and youth leadership programs. Equally important are organizations that help provide relief from hunger and disasters; support people with disabilities; and create gainful employment opportunities for vulnerable youth and adults. The Foundation awards grants to nonprofit organizations in its areas of interest: scholarship programs; inner city work and; youth programs, with special interest in employment opportunities for young people with disabilities. Interested applicants should prepare a written request which should include a project narrative and attachments. The Board of Trustees meets two times each year, usually in the Spring and Fall.

Requirements: Nonprofit organizations in Maryland, Virginia and the District of Columbia are eligible to apply.
Restrictions: Individuals are ineligible.
Geographic Focus: District of Columbia, Maryland, Virginia
Contact: Arne Sorenson, President; (301) 380-2246; fax (301) 380-8957;
kimberly.howes@marriott.com
Sponsor: J. Willard and Alice S. Marriott Foundation
10400 Fernwood Road
Bethesda, MD 20917

J. William Gholston Foundation Grants 1328

The J. William Gholston Foundation's mission is to support charitable organizations that provide for the education of children within the City of Comer in Madison County, GA. The Foundation was also established to support capital and instructional projects that advance academic achievement. Grants from the J. William Gholston Foundation are primarily 1 year in duration. On occasion, multi-year support is awarded. Award amounts typically go up to $160,000.

Requirements: Applicants must have 501(c)3 tax-exempt status and serve residents in Madison County, Georgia. Applications will be submitted online through the Bank of America website. A grant report is required within 1 year of the grant application date, regardless of whether all of the funds have been spent.
Restrictions: The foundation does not support requests from individuals, organizations attempting to influence policy through direct lobbying, or any political campaigns.
Geographic Focus: Georgia
Date(s) Application is Due: Jun 1
Amount of Grant: Up to 160,000 USD
Samples: Madison County Schools, Comer, Georgia, $145,275 - Awarded for General Operations of the Organization.
Contact: Mark S. Drake, Vice President; (404) 264-1377;
ga.grantmaking@bankofamerica.com or mark.s.drake@bofa.com
Internet: www.bankofamerica.com/philanthropic/foundation/?fnId=99
Sponsor: J. William Gholston Foundation
P.O. Box 40200 F19-300-01-16
Jacksonville, FL 32203-0200

Jack and Dorothy Byrne Foundation Grants 1329

The Foundation was established in 1999 in Etna, New Hampshire, by residents Dorothy Byrne and her husband, the late insurance industry titan John J. (Jack) Byrne, to focus on making financial bequests for cancer research, the Dartmouth College community and "general philanthropy" in the Upper Valley region. It has since expanded those boundaries. The Foundation's origins began with Jack Byrne, the son of an insurance agency owner who became an actuary and later an insurance industry executive and entrepreneur. Jack Byrne's wealth was created by his turnaround of struggling low-cost insurer Geico in the 1970s, when he ruthlessly cut costs, dropped high-risk drivers from coverage and raised rates. The moves attracted the attention of legendary investor Warren Buffett, who began accumulating stock in Geico and whose Berkshire Hathaway company eventually bought the entire insurance company. Later, Jack Byrne accomplished a similar turnaround feat at American Express' Fireman's Fund unit, which was then sold to the German financial services Allianz for $1.1 billion. Byrne transferred some of the Fireman's Fund assets that weren't included in the Allianz deal to White Mountains Insurance, a Hanover-based insurance holding company, in 1991. Today, at the center of the Jack and Dorothy Byrne Foundation is Dorothy Byrne, a woman who tightly guards her privacy and shuns publicity despite the prominence of her family's name throughout the region. The list of Byrne Foundation beneficiaries is lengthy. They include Alice Peck Day Memorial Hospital in Lebanon and the Aloha Foundation summer camps in Fairlee to Windsor High School and the Woodstock Area Job Bank; the Claremont Soup Kitchen and David's House in Lebanon to the Lebanon Opera House and the New London Police Department; the Bugbee Senior Center in White River Junction to the Charlestown Foursquare Church to the Royalton Memorial Library and the Mascoma Wrestling Boosters, there are few people in the Upper Valley whose lives have not been touched by the foundation's financial largesse. The private foundation's grants each year help literally hundreds of community organizations across the Upper Valley, making the two sides of the Connecticut River a fortunate landscape in the realm of private charity. Grant awards range up to a maximum of approximately $100,000, though occasionally have reached as high as $1.5 million.

Requirements: The Foundation predominantly supports communities situated in the "Upper Valley," a distinctive region that at its heart includes towns twinned on opposite banks along a roughly 40-mile stretch of the Connecticut River. Any nonprofit or municipality in the New England region is eligible to apply.
Geographic Focus: Connecticut, Florida, Maine, Massachusetts, New Hampshire, New York, Vermont
Samples: Alice Peck Day Memorial Hospital, Lebanon, New Hampshire, $70,000 - Support of non-profit purpose of organization - Annual Fund and Community Impact Fund (2019); Aloha Foundation, Fairlee, Vermont, $35,000 - general operating support (2019); Artists for Soup, Millbrook, New York, $1,000 - general operating support (2019).
Contact: Robert E. Snyder, Director; (603) 643-7799
Sponsor: Jack and Dorothy Byrne Foundation
80 South Main Street, #102
Hanover, NH 03755

Jack H. and William M. Light Charitable Trust Grants 1330

The Jack H. and William M. Light Charitable Trust was established in Texas in 1998, and makes grant distributions to San Antonio area non-profits on a semiannual basis. Its primary field of interest is human services, particularly the welfare of children in the broadest sense, with an effort to support organizations involved in the health, mental health, and education of children. Types of support include: annual campaigns; capital and infrastructure; capital campaigns; curriculum development; emergency funding; endowment contributions; equipment purchase; general operations; program development; and research. Most recently, awards have ranged from $2,500 to $30,000. The annual deadlines for online application submission are April 30 and October 31.

Requirements: Grants are directed to 501(c)3 organizations which fall within the principal charitable purposes of the foundation, and which have a direct impact on the residents of Bexar, Denton and Harris counties in Texas.
Geographic Focus: Texas
Date(s) Application is Due: Apr 30; Oct 31
Amount of Grant: 2,500 - 30,000 USD
Samples: Houston Pi Beta Phi Foundation, Houston, Texas, $20,000 - general operating support; Camp Allen Conference and Retreat Center, Navasota, Texas, $25,000 - general operating support; Texas Children's Hospital, Houston, Texas, $30,000 - support of the Care Survival Portal.
Contact: Brian R. Korb, Senior Vice President; (210) 283-6700 or (210) 283-6500;
bkorb@broadwaybank.com
Internet: www.broadwaybank.com/wealthmanagement/FoundationWilliamMLight.html
Sponsor: Jack H. and William M. Light Charitable Trust
P.O. Box 17001
San Antonio, TX 78217-0001

Jack Kent Cooke Foundation Good Neighbor Grants 1331

The Good Neighbor Grants program was established in 2012 to identify and strengthen ties with youth-serving nonprofit organizations in the Northern Virginia, metropolitan Washington, D.C., and Maryland areas that are helping students with significant financial need reach their full potential through education. The Jack Kent Cooke Foundation's grant can support the establishment of new programs or the enhancement of existing initiatives that support high potential low-income students. We are most interested in programs that promote engagement, enrichment, creativity, talent development, and intellectual curiosity. Examples of eligible programs include after-school academic and summer enrichment opportunities, college access advising programs, arts, service learning, and STEM programs, innovative approaches that bridge education and technology, and internship programs. Funds may also be used for the development of education-related products that will directly benefit students: handbooks, training guides, and other written and digital media. Selected grantees will receive a one-time grant of between $10,000 and $35,000 that may be used over a one-year period. Funding is intended for application towards specific project or program based costs.

Requirements: 501(c)3 organizations, public and private K-12 school districts, four-year colleges and universities, and two-year community colleges are eligible to apply.
Restrictions: Note that this grant does not fund general operating support, capital improvements, endowments, lobbying, or activities that exclusively benefit the members of sectarian or religious organizations.
Geographic Focus: District of Columbia, Maryland, Virginia
Date(s) Application is Due: Nov 15
Amount of Grant: 10,000 - 35,000 USD
Samples: Traveling Players Ensemble, Leesburg, Virginia, $10,000 - to support full and partial scholarships to financially challenged students from Loudoun County, Virginia (2018); Thurgood Marshall Academy Public Charter School, Washington, D.C., $30,000 - to support efforts that help students apply, enroll, and succeed in college by providing in-school and after-school activities (2018); RESET, Washington, D.C., $10,000 - to

provide inquiry-based STEM programs for kids in schools with a high number of low-income students (2018).
Contact: Astrik Tenney, Grants Program Manager; (703) 723-8000 or (800) 941-3300; fax (703) 723-8030; grants@jkcf.org
Internet: www.jkcf.org/our-grants/good-neighbor-grants/
Sponsor: Jack Kent Cooke Foundation
44325 Woodridge Parkway
Lansdowne, VA 20176

Jack Kent Cooke Foundation Summer Enrichment Grants   **1332**
The Jack Kent Cooke Foundation identifies and invests a portion of its funding in strategic grant initiatives to expand educational opportunities throughout the United States. The Foundation partners with educational leaders that share our commitment to advance the education of exceptionally promising students who have financial need. High-quality summer learning programs can spark student curiosity and passion, augment academic achievement, nurture intellectual peer support, and influence educational and career trajectories. In focus groups conducted by the Jack Kent Cooke Foundation, high-achieving students have consistently identified rigorous summer enrichment programs as among the most important and valuable experiences during their middle and high school years. Research is clear on summer programs' ability to stave off summer learning loss, and evidence is growing to delineate the specific benefits of summer programs for academically talented students. Unfortunately, high-quality summer enrichment programs remain out of reach for many low-income, high-achieving youth who cannot afford the tuition and related costs of residential programs or whose local community does not offer a program specifically geared toward such students. Through the Summer Enrichment program, the Foundation awards grants up to $250,000 per year to nonprofit organizations or universities who provide access to high-quality summer enrichment programs for high-achieving low-income students entering grades 6 through 12.
Requirements: 501(c)3 organizations, four-year colleges and universities, and two-year community colleges are eligible to apply.
Geographic Focus: All States
Amount of Grant: Up to 250,000 USD
Contact: Astrik Tenney, Grants Program Manager; (703) 723-8000 or (800) 941-3300; fax (703) 723-8030; grants@jkcf.org
Internet: www.jkcf.org/our-grants/academic-achievement/
Sponsor: Jack Kent Cooke Foundation
44325 Woodridge Parkway
Lansdowne, VA 20176

Jack Kent Cooke Foundation Young Artist Awards   **1333**
The Jack Kent Cooke Foundation supports talented musicians from limited financial backgrounds through its scholarship programs and sponsorship of the Jack Kent Cooke Young Artist Award. The Foundation recognizes that musically talented youth from low-income families often lack the funding for private lessons, master classes, quality instruments, summer programs, and performance experiences. These musicians miss out on the creativity and stimulation that comes from being surrounded by an ensemble of talented peers sharing high music aspirations and being led by inspiring faculty. From the Top and the Jack Kent Cooke Foundation share a passion for helping exceptional young people reach their potential in all areas of their lives. From the Top is a nonprofit organization that encourages and celebrates the commitment of young people to music and the arts through a variety of media, including nationally broadcast television and radio shows, education programs, and its website. Each year From the Top's Jack Kent Cooke Young Artist Award Program provides 20 outstanding young musicians who demonstrate financial need with a $10,000 scholarship to advance their artistic development and education. In addition, Jack Kent Cooke Young Artists perform on the hit NPR and PBS program, From the Top, and participate in arts leadership training to spread the power of classical music. Since 2005, From the Top has awarded over $1.8M in scholarships to more than 180 talented young people who have used their awards for new instruments, music lessons, summer music program tuition, competition fees, travel costs, computers, recording devices, and more. Jack Kent Cooke Young Artists range from age 8 to 18 and hail from all across the United States and abroad. Young Artists are classically trained instrumentalists, vocalists and/or composers that are also active in community-service projects and academic pursuits. Common to all is a passion for music and a love for sharing it. There are three annual deadlines for application submission: October 1; January 7; and March 4.
Requirements: Classical instrumentalists, vocalists, and composers (ages 8–18) who have not yet entered college are eligible to apply.
Geographic Focus: All States, American Samoa, District of Columbia, Guam, Marshall Islands, Northern Mariana Islands, Puerto Rico, U.S. Virgin Islands
Date(s) Application is Due: Jan 7; Mar 4; Oct 1
Amount of Grant: Up to 10,000 USD
Contact: Astrik Tenney, Grants Program Manager; (703) 723-8000 or (800) 941-3300; fax (703) 723-8030; grants@jkcf.org
Internet: www.jkcf.org/our-grants/artistic-advancement/
Sponsor: Jack Kent Cooke Foundation
44325 Woodridge Parkway
Lansdowne, VA 20176

Jack Satter Foundation Grants   **1334**
The Jack Satter Foundation is a private foundation established by Jack Satter during his lifetime. Born and raised in Boston, Massachusetts, Satter attended Frank V. Thompson Junior High School and then English High School. He served as a sergeant in the Medical Corps while fighting in the European Theatre of World War II. In 1970, he became owner of Colonial Provision Company, a company that sold hot dogs in the New England area,

including to the New York Yankees and Boston Red Sox. In 1978, he became a owner-partner of the Yankees, a position he held for nearly three decades, and in 1983, he sold the Colonial Provision Company. In 1990, he considered selling his share of the team to Daiei founder Isao Nakauchi, though the transaction did not go through. Through 1996, he was worth about $14 million. His philanthropic activities included donating to synagogues in Newton, Massachusetts, an assisted living residence, and the Massachusetts General Hospital. The Jack Satter Cardiac Intensive Care Floor and the Jack Satter Mezzanine and Conference Center are named in his honor. He died at age 92 in Dedham, Massachusetts, on April 7, 2014. Today the Jack Satter Foundation continues his commitment to helping the elderly, particularly Jewish seniors, and emotionally or physically challenged youth. The Foundation makes single and multi-year grants for programs in the broad areas of health care, education, the elderly and the disabled. It funds high-impact programs that primarily serve Massachusetts communities. The Foundation looks for organizations that: align their programs with their mission, goals, and financial resources; have a stable governance structure; emphasize accountability, results, service quality and program excellence; and are sustainable and have a strong financial foundation. Awards range in size from $25,000 to $1 million, depending on the program's size, duration, and/or complexity. Deadlines for Letters of Interest are February 28 and August 31, respectively, with full invited applications due April 30 and October 31.
Restrictions: Funding is not available for: political organizations or campaigns; fundraising activities; unrestricted endowments, deficit reduction, or general operating expenses; or individuals.
Geographic Focus: Massachusetts
Date(s) Application is Due: Apr 30; Oct 31
Amount of Grant: 25,000 - 1,000,000 USD
Contact: Rita Goldberg, Grants Manager; (617) 227-7940, ext. 775 or (617) 557-9766; rgoldberg@hembar.com
Gioia C. Perugini, Program Officer; (617) 557-9777 or (617) 557-9766; gperugini@hembar.com
Internet: hembar.com/jack-satter-foundation
Sponsor: Jack Satter Foundation
75 State Street, 16th Floor
Boston, MA 02109

Jacob and Hilda Blaustein Foundation Israel Program Grants   **1335**
Inspired by Jewish values of tzedakah (the obligation to give to the community), social justice and human rights, the Jacob and Hilda Blaustein Foundation promotes social justice and human rights through its five program areas: Jewish life; Israeli democracy; health and mental health; educational opportunity; and human rights. In the area of Israel Programs, the goal is to strengthen Israel as a democratic, equitable, and pluralistic society. There is a geographic focus on the Negev, a historically disadvantaged area of the country. The Foundation seeks to: address fundamental social, economic, and ethnic inequalities; empower Israel's most vulnerable and disadvantaged populations; and promote liberal and pluralistic approaches to Judaism. The Foundation supports policy research, advocacy, education, community organizing, innovative service provision, and leadership development. There are no annual deadlines, and most recent awards have been multi-year grants ranging from $40,000 to $1,000,000.
Requirements: 501(c)3 organizations in New York City, as well as nonprofits in Israel, are eligible to apply.
Restrictions: Support is unavailable for the following: individuals; scholarships to individuals; unsolicited proposals for academic, scientific, or medical research; direct mail; annual giving; membership campaigns; fundraising; commemorative events.
Geographic Focus: New York, Israel
Amount of Grant: 40,000 - 1,000,000 USD
Samples: Ben-Gurion University of the Negev, New York, New York, $1,000,000 - support for new young faculty members at the Jacob Blaustein Institutes for Desert Research; Association for Civil Rights in Israel, Jerusalem, Israel, $50,000 - support for activities in the Negev ($2017); Hotline for Refugees and Migrants, Tel Aviv, Israel, $60,000 - support for the Hotline's work with asylum seekers and refugees.
Contact: Brenda Bodenheimer Zlatin, Senior Program Manager; (410) 347-7107 or (410) 347-7201; fax (410) 347-7210; info@blaufund.org
Internet: www.blaufund.org/foundations/jacobandhilda_f.html#2
Sponsor: Jacob and Hilda Blaustein Foundation
One South Street, Suite 2900
Baltimore, MD 21202

Jacob G. Schmidlapp Trusts Grants   **1336**
The Foundation Office at Fifth Third Bank is committed to making a significant impact on programs and initiatives that create strong, vibrant communities and provide pathways to opportunity. Through the Foundation Office, the visions of individuals, families and institutions are realized, and legacies are attained by allocating the resources of their respective foundations in support of innovative programs and organizations in our communities. The Jacob G. Schmidlapp Trusts support charitable or educational purposes; for relief in sickness, suffering, and distress; for the care of young children, the aged, or the helpless; and for the promotion of education to improve living conditions. Support is offered in the form of: endowments; equipment; land acquisition; program development; technical assistance; and seed money grants. An organization interested in submitting a grant proposal should first submit a Letter of Inquiry (LOI) using the link at the website. LOIs are accepted from October 1 through December 31 each year. The Foundation Office will review each LOI and may contact the applying organization about further discussion of the proposal, which may include a site visit. Each organization will receive either an email declining the inquiry or an invitation to submit a full application online. An invitation to apply will include the foundation funding source, recommended request amount, and

a deadline for receipt of the application. The Fifth Third Bank Foundation Office will submit completed applications to the respective Foundation Board or Committee for final review and approval or declination. Grant seekers should allow six to twelve months for the grant making process. In general, the Foundation prefers awarding grants for one year. Most recent awards have ranged from $5,000 to $250,000.

Requirements: Nonprofit organizations that operate in the Greater Cincinnati region and are designated under section 501(c)3 and subsections 509(a)1 or 509(a)2 by the Internal Revenue Service are eligible to apply for a grant.

Restrictions: Nonprofits may apply only once within any 12-month period. The following are ineligible to apply: individuals; individual churches (except for proposals regarding an affiliated school); publicly supported entities such as public schools, government or government agencies; supporting organizations designated 509(a)3 by the IRS; walks, runs, dinners, galas, luncheons and other event sponsorship requests; athletic, band, and other school booster clubs; or startup funding for new programs or organizations (usually not a funding priority). A waiting period of three years is required for prior grant recipients receiving $10,000 or more from any funding source administered by the Fifth Third Bank Foundation Office. This period will begin as of the first payment on the grant.

Geographic Focus: Indiana, Kentucky, Michigan, Ohio

Amount of Grant: 5,000 - 250,000 USD

Contact: Heidi B. Jark, Managing Director; (513) 534-7001 or (513) 636-4200

Internet: www.53.com/content/fifth-third/en/personal-banking/about/in-the-community/foundation-office-at-fifth-third-bank.html

Sponsor: Jacob G. Schmidlapp Trust

38 Fountain Square Plaza, MD 1090CA

Cincinnati, OH 45263-0001

James and Abigail Campbell Family Foundation Grants 1337

Established in 1980, the James and Abigail Campbell Family Foundation embraces the values and beliefs of James and Abigail Campbell by investing in Hawaii's people and the communities that nurture them. The Foundation supports projects in the following areas: youth programs that address the challenges of young people; education support for public schools, early childhood education and environmental stewardship; and Hawaiian support for programs that promote values and the health and welfare of Hawaiians. Priority is given to programs located in or serving communities in the following areas of West Oahu: Ewa and Ewa Beach, Kapolei, Makakilo and the Wai'anae Coast. The following types of requests are eligible for consideration: support for special projects that are not part of an organization's ongoing operations; program support when unforeseen circumstances have affected the financial base of an organization; financial assistance to purchase items such as office equipment and to fund minor repairs and renovations. Awards typically range from $5,000 to $200,000, and applications must be postmarked by February 1 for the April/May meeting and August 1 for the October/November meeting.

Requirements: The Foundation will only consider requests from organizations which qualify as non-profit, tax-exempt public charities under Section 501(c)3 and 170(b) of the Internal Revenue Code. To apply for a grant, summarize the following information in a two - three page proposal letter: the nature and purpose of your organization; the objectives of your program, include the grant amount requested and the proposed use of funds; a brief outline on how you plan to accomplish your objectives; a statement of a community problem, need or opportunity that this project will address; the duration for which Foundation funds are needed; other sources of funding currently being sought and future funding sources; methods used to measure the program's effectiveness. In addition to the proposal letter, submit a copy of the following: Internal Revenue Service notification of tax-exempt status; most recent annual financial statement; list of the current Board of Directors; the project's proposed budget; one (1) copy of your complete grant proposal package.

Restrictions: The Foundation will not consider funding for: individuals, endowments, sectarian or religious programs, loans, political activities or highly technical research projects. Only one request per organization will ordinarily be considered in a calendar year. Funds are usually not committed for more than one year at a time.

Geographic Focus: Hawaii

Date(s) Application is Due: Feb 1; Aug 1

Amount of Grant: 5,000 - 200,000 USD

Contact: D. Keola Lloyd, Grants Manager; (808) 674-3167; fax (808) 674-3349; keolal@jamescampbell.com

Internet: www.campbellfamilyfoundation.org/

Sponsor: James and Abigail Campbell Family Foundation

James Campbell Building, Suite 200, 1001 Kamokila Boulevard

Kapolei, HI 96707

James F. and Marion L. Miller Foundation Grants 1338

The James F. and Marion L. Miller Foundation awards single or multiyear grants for projects that advance the arts or education in communities throughout the State of Oregon. The Foundation has also recently adopted several initiatives in the areas of nursing, community college scholarships, new teachers, and sustainability. Requests from the same organization will normally be considered by the trustees only once in a 12-month period and will not be considered until payment of a prior multiyear grant has been completed. Proposals are accepted from eligible applicants throughout the year. The board meets approximately four times annually to review proposals, and applications are reviewed as they are received. Application and guidelines are available online.

Requirements: Oregon 501(c)3 tax-exempt organizations that are not 509(a) private foundations, educational institutions, and governmental entities are eligible.

Restrictions: The foundation generally will not favor proposals seeking funds for direct grants, scholarships, or loans to individuals; endowments; general fund drives or annual appeals; debt retirement or operation deficits; emergency needs; propagandizing or influencing elections or legislation; or projects of religious organizations that principally benefit their own members.

Geographic Focus: Oregon

Amount of Grant: Up to 200,000 USD

Samples: Linn-Benton Council for the Arts, Corvallis, Oregon, $20,000 - capacity-building to create an online Arts Resources Directory; Classroom Law Project, Portland, Oregon, $50,000 - capacity support to hire a Senior Program Manager; Gilbert House Children's Museum, Salem, Oregon, $8,250 - support to purchase classroom technology.

Contact: Gretchen Schackel, Grants Manager; (503) 546-3191; info@millerfnd.org

Internet: www.millerfound.org/about/

Sponsor: James F. and Marion L. Miller Foundation

520 SW Yamhill Street, Suite 520

Portland, OR 97204

James Ford Bell Foundation Grants 1339

The James Ford Bell Foundation supports organizations primarily in Minnesota. Emphasis is on cultural programs, though support is also available for wildlife preservation and conservation, youth agencies, elementary and secondary education, and health and human services. A high priority is given to projects with historical connections to the Bell Family. The Trustees meet in the Spring and Fall. Contact the Foundation prior to sending in a proposal. Unsolicited requests for funds are not accepted.

Requirements: Nonprofit organizations in Minnesota are eligible to apply.

Restrictions: No grants are made directly to individuals, nor for scholarships, fellowships, or political campaigns. No funding is available to units of local government. The Foundation does not respond to requests for memberships, annual appeals, or special events and fundraisers.

Geographic Focus: Minnesota

Contact: Ellen George, Chief of Operations; (612) 377-8400; fax (612) 605-1984; ellen@fpadvisors.com or info@fpadvisors.com

Internet: www.fpadvisors.com/

Sponsor: James Ford Bell Foundation

1818 Oliver Avenue South

Minneapolis, MN 55405-2208

James Graham Brown Foundation Grants 1340

The James Graham Brown Foundation fosters quality of life of Louisville in particular, and the State of Kentucky in general, by helping to make improvements for families and businesses. The Foundation gives priority to projects that: strengthen the impact of core human services and cultural organizations and agencies; support efforts to improve and sustain quality neighborhoods and a thriving downtown area; and support initiatives that strengthen the relationship between business and education to increase growth in human capital and jobs in higher wage, higher knowledge, and high technical areas. It actively supports and funds projects in the fields of education, economic development, health and social services, culture and humanities (excluding performing arts) with an emphasis on community-wide capital campaigns. The Board meets six times annually and determinations are made at the meetings. Funds are dispersed semi-annually.

Requirements: Formal applications must be submitted by the following deadline dates: March 2, Education requests; May 4 and July 6, Quality of life requests. Only organizations that have obtained a tax-exempt designation under Section 501(c)3 of the IRS code may apply. The Foundation grants are limited to the Louisville metropolitan area and the state of Kentucky. Campaigns outside the Jefferson County and Louisville metropolitan area must show evidence of significant local community support before being considered by the foundation for funding.

Restrictions: The Foundation does not support the following: organizations outside of the state of Kentucky; those related either directly or indirectly to the performing arts; requests from religious organizations for religious purposes (including theological seminaries); requests from individuals; requests from political entities; requests from national organizations, even if for local projects.

Geographic Focus: Kentucky

Date(s) Application is Due: May 6; Jul 1

Contact: Tina Walters, Grants Director; (502) 896-2440 or (866) 896-5423; fax (502) 896-1774; grants@jgbf.org or info@jgbf.org

Internet: www.jgbf.org/funding-areas/

Sponsor: James Graham Brown Foundation

4350 Brownsboro Road, Suite 200

Louisville, KY 40207

James K. and Arlene L. Adams Foundation Scholarships 1341

The James K. and Arlene L. Adams Foundation concentrates its giving program primarily in the Cumberland County region of Pennsylvania. The Foundation's primary field of interest is education, providing funding for scholarships and student educational loans. There is no formal application required, and interested individuals should contact the Foundation via a letter of application. The annual deadline is December 31.

Geographic Focus: Pennsylvania

Contact: David H. Radcliff, Trustee; (717) 236-9318

Sponsor: James K. and Arlene L. Adams Foundation

1011 Mumma Road, Suite 201

Lemoyne, PA 17043-1143

James Lee Sorenson Family Impact Foundation Grants 1342

The son of late billionaire James LeVoy Sorenson, James Lee Sorenson graduated from the University of Utah. In 1995, he founded Sorenson Media, a leader in video encoding and streaming tools. Sorenson Media has been instrumental in bringing internet video to

Quicktime and Sorenson Media's encoding technology has been used for website trailers for Disney, Lucasfilm, MGM, and Paramount. Sorenson also co-founded Sorenson Capital. James, his wife Krista, and their family move philanthropy through the Sorenson Impact Foundation, which takes an investment approach in its giving. In its primary grant making areas, the Foundation supports projects that have measurable impact, are sustainable, and create positive change. Grant making involves anti-poverty, education, entrepreneurship, healthcare, and more. The foundation also makes investments in for-profit social enterprises.
Geographic Focus: All States
Date(s) Application is Due: Mar 1; Jun 1; Sep 1; Dec 1
Contact: James Lee Sorenson, Trustee; (801) 490-1000 or (801) 490-1012; ann@sorensoncompanies.com
Internet: sorensonimpactfoundation.org/apply/
Sponsor: James Lee Sorenson Family Impact Foundation
299 South Main Street
Salt Lake City, UT 84111

James LeVoy Sorenson Foundation Grants 1343
James LeVoy Sorenson was an American businessman who founded the Sorenson Companies, a parent company of thirty-two distinct corporations. Born in Rexburg, Idaho, the son of Joseph LeVoy and Emma Blaser Sorenson, he made a fortune in local real estate before expanding in other directions such as innovative technology. Sorenson holds roughly sixty patents, and is credited with a number of medical inventions including the disposable surgical mask and the disposable venous catheter. He was the wealthiest man in Utah with an estimated net worth of $4.5 billion at the time of his death in 2008. The Foundation priorities include funding for: arts and culture; Christian agencies; churches; recreation programs; youth development; and community service initiatives. Application forms are not required, and there is no annual deadline for submissions. However, applications submitted early in the year have a better chance of being awarded funding.
Geographic Focus: Utah
Contact: James Lee Sorenson, Trustee; (801) 461-9700; fax (801) 461-9722
Sponsor: James LeVoy Sorenson Foundation
2511 South West Temple Street
Salt Lake City, UT 84115

James M. Collins Foundation Grants 1344
Established in Texas in 1964 by the late James M. Collins, a Republican who represented the Third Congressional District of Texas from 1968-1983, the Foundation awards grants to Texas nonprofit organizations in its areas of interest, including: the arts; performing arts centers; economic development; health organizations and association; higher education; human services; museums; the Salvation Army; and secondary school. Types of support include: research; program support; and social services. There are no application deadlines or formal applications, and interested partied should begin by contacting the Foundation through an inquiry letter. Most recent funding awards have ranged from $500 up to $50,000.
Requirements: Texas nonprofit organizations are eligible to apply.
Restrictions: Individuals are not eligible.
Geographic Focus: Texas
Amount of Grant: 500 - 50,000 USD
Samples: Baylor University, Waco, Texas, $50,000 - biomedical research; Crystal Charity Ball, Dallas, Texas, $10,000 - general operating expenses; Our Friends Place, Dallas, Texas, $1,000 - general program support.
Contact: Dorothy Dann Collins Torbert, President; (214) 691-2032
Sponsor: James M. Collins Foundation
8115 Preston Road, Suite 680
Dallas, TX 75225

James S. Copley Foundation Grants 1345
Incorporated in California in 1953, the Foundation serves as the philanthropic arm of the Copley Press, Inc., publishers of the Copley newspapers. The foundation offers support in the form of: scholarship funds; capital campaigns; equipment; employee matching gifts; endowments; equipment; building and; renovation grants. Funding organizations involved with arts and culture, education, animals and wildlife, health, recreation, and human services should apply. Giving is restricted primarily in areas of company operations in California, Illinois and Ohio.
Requirements: 501(c)3 tax-exempt organizations in the circulation areas of company newspapers/operations are eligible to apply. These areas include: California, Illinois and Ohio.
Restrictions: Ineligible funding opportunities include: religious, fraternal, or athletic organizations, government agencies, local chapters of national organizations, public elementary, secondary schools, public broadcasting systems, individuals, research, publications, conferences, general operating support, large campaigns and loans.
Geographic Focus: California, Illinois, Ohio
Date(s) Application is Due: Jan 2
Contact: Kim Koch, Secretary; (858) 454-0411, ext. 7671
Sponsor: James S. Copley Foundation
P.O. Box 1530
La Jolla, CA 92038-1530

Jane's Trust Grants 1346
Jane's Trust was created through the beneficence of Jane Bancroft Cook, who died at her home in Cohasset, Massachusetts, in July of 2002. Jane was an heir to her family company, Dow Jones and Company, and a member of its board for 36 years, serving from 1949 through 1985. During that time, the firm's flagship newspaper, the Wall Street Journal, grew to wield international influence and the company evolved from a small private enterprise to become a publicly traded, $4 billion media empire. She was vitally interested in the company and its success, as well as its maintaining journalistic independence and standard of accuracy in its news reporting. Throughout her life, Jane gave large sums to institutions throughout New England, from Massachusetts General Hospital and Harvard University to animal shelters. She also helped create New College in Sarasota, Florida, where she had a second home, a residence that she bequeathed to the college. Jane was known in the communities where she lived as a down-to-earth woman who was generous to the core, and she was an active philanthropist, though she preferred to give anonymously. Today, Jane's Trust aims to continue the legacy of generosity that she established during her lifetime. The amount of funding available from Jane's Trust will vary from year to year. Multiple year grants will be considered on a case-by-case basis. Grants will generally range in size from $50,000 to $150,000, although the Trustees in their discretion may from time to time make awards outside of that range. The Trust's primary fields of interest include: arts and culture; education; the environment; and health and welfare. It will primarily make project, operating, and capital campaign grants. The Trust will consider endowment requests on a case-by-case basis. The Trust may make challenge grants where appropriate. Trustees are interested primarily in applicant organizational projects which benefit underserved populations and disadvantaged communities. The Trust supports collaborations among nonprofit organizations and welcomes joint applications. It encourages grant requests and collaborations that bridge two or more areas of interest. The application is a two step process involving first the submission of an initial inquiry and then, only upon request from the Trustees, the submission of a full proposal. The Trustees meet several times each year to consider requests, although payment of all grants approved by the Trustees is made once a annually, in December. Objectives and goals will be established by the applicant and the Trustees at the time of the initial award. Applicants should complete an online concept paper application, which may be submitted at any time, but must be received by the following dates in order to be considered by the Trustees at their next regular meeting: January 25 for consideration in March and July 15 for consideration in September.
Requirements: Generally, the Trust will make grants to qualifying nonprofit organizations in Maine, New Hampshire, and Vermont, as well as in southwest and central Florida, and in the greater Boston area of Massachusetts. An applicant must be exempt from federal tax under section 501(c)3, or as provided in section 4945 of the Internal Revenue Code, and not a private foundation within the meanings of section 509(a) of the Code. If this is not the case, an applicant may partner with a fiscal sponsor, an organization meeting these requirements that is prepared to certify that the project is a worthwhile endeavor, undertake responsibility to ensure that the grant terms are carried out, and that the funds are properly expended. Fiscal sponsorship must be in place at the time of application.
Restrictions: The Trust does not allocate specific dollar amounts to its areas of interest or to particular geographical areas. Multiple year awards will be rare, and generally will not exceed two years in length. Jane's Trust will not support: direct loans to charitable organizations; attempts to influence legislation; or requests from individuals. The Trust will normally not support public entities, such as municipalities, municipal departments, or public schools directly, but will entertain applications from tax-exempt fiscal sponsors or partners for collaborative projects with municipalities or schools. This limitation does not apply to public colleges and universities.
Geographic Focus: All States
Amount of Grant: 50,000 - 150,000 USD
Samples: Children's Museum and Theatre of Maine, Portland, Maine, $125,000 - or a new museum and theatre on Thompson's Point in Portland (2018); North Country Education Services, Gorham, New Hampshire, $100,000 - for professional development in computer science education for educators in northern New Hampshire (2018); Fair Food Network, Ann Arbor, Michigan, $60,000 - or the Double Up Food Bucks program in New Hampshire (2018).
Contact: Rita Goldberg, Grants Manager; (617) 227-7940, ext. 775 or (617) 557-9766; rgoldberg@hembar.com
Gioia C. Perugini, Program Officer; (617) 557-9777 or (617) 557-9766; gperugini@hembar.com
Internet: hembar.com/janestrust
Sponsor: Jane's Trust
75 State Street, 16th Floor
Boston, MA 02109

Jane Bradley Pettit Foundation Community and Social Development Grants 1347
The Jane Bradley Pettit Foundation awards grants to initiate and sustain projects in the Greater Milwaukee community, with a focus on programs and projects that serve low-income and disadvantaged individuals, women, children, and the elderly. The Foundation has designated two areas for special consideration in the area of Community and Social Development Grants: early childhood development and assistance to women and children in poverty. The Foundation also supports programs which enable youth to develop leadership skills, character and self-esteem. An initial application should be in the form of a letter of intent.
Requirements: Milwaukee-area charitable organizations are eligible.
Geographic Focus: Wisconsin
Date(s) Application is Due: Jan 15; May 15; Sep 15
Amount of Grant: 5,000 - 100,000 USD
Samples: Vision Forward Association, Milwaukee, Wisconsin, $150,000 - for general operations (2019); Urban Ecology Center, Milwaukee, Wisconsin, $15,000 - for general operations (2019); Family Service Agency of Waukesha County, Waukesha, Wisconsin, $5,000 - for general operations (2019).
Contact: Kara Nehring, Director of Administration; (414) 982-2875 or (414) 982-2874; fax (414) 982-2889; knehring@staffordlaw.com
Internet: www.jbpf.org/guidelines/index.html

Sponsor: Jane Bradley Pettit Foundation
1200 N. Mayfair Road, Suite 430
Wauwatosa, WI 53226-3282

Janet Spencer Weekes Foundation Grants 1348

The Janet Spencer Weekes Foundation for children and youth was established in Portland, Oregon, in 1998 by John M. Weekes in honor of his wife, Janet. John is a founding principal of the Portland, Oregon, firm of Dull Olson Weekes Architects (DOWA). Prior to forming DOWA, John was with Skidmore Owings and Merrill. He studied at the University of Copenhagen and graduated from Washington State University where he received the American Institue of Architects (AIA) Gold Medal for Educational Excellence. John has been recognized nationally and internationally as a leader in contemporary educational facility design. His projects have been published extensively, including Architectural Record's 2005 and 2008 Review of Educational Facilities, Architectural Record's 2007 and 2010 Building Case Studies on Education, and the recently released books "Designing the Sustainable School", "Third Teacher" and "Evidence Based Design of Elementary and Secondary Schools." The Foundation has the expressed purpose of serving community nonprofits in the State of Oregon. Its primary areas of interest include: children and youth services; recreation and leisure programs; maritime interests; and elementary and secondary education. There are no specified annual deadlines, and interested parties should submit a letter of application that includes a project description and the amount of funding requested.
Requirements: Any 501(c)3 in the State of Oregon is eligible to apply.
Geographic Focus: Oregon
Amount of Grant: Up to 5,000 USD
Contact: John M. Weekes, Director; (503) 796-2950 or (503) 866-2195
Sponsor: Janet Spencer Weekes Foundation
2235 NE 31st Avenue
Portland, OR 97212-5102

Janson Foundation Grants 1349

The Janson Foundation's primary mission is twofold: to maintain and improve Janson Park for the benefit of the citizens of Columbia, Pennsylvania; and to assist families in financial need by providing food or other supplies. Though there are no identified annual deadlines, a formal application is required. Interested parties should begin by contacting the Foundation.
Requirements: 501(c)3 organizations serving residents of the Columbia, Pennsylvania, area are eligible, as well as individual families in need.
Geographic Focus: Pennsylvania
Amount of Grant: Up to 1,000 USD
Contact: Michael Grab, Vice President; (717) 684-4422 or (717) 684-7444
Sponsor: Janson Foundation
327 Locust Street
Columbia, PA 17512-1120

Janson Foundation Grants 1350

The Janson Foundation was established in 1983 to provide capital grants to deserving charitable organizations located in Skagit County, Washington. Edward W. Janson had a longtime career as a public servant in Skagit County and was committed to the citizens of the county. He established his Foundation to assist the ongoing capital needs of deserving charitable organizations. Mr. Janson was particularly interested in supporting the capital needs of Christian organizations/missions and programs that benefit youth. The Janson Foundation provides support to charitable organizations for the purchase of equipment, the construction of facilities or the acquisition of land. In addition, the Foundation funds the repair of existing facilities and the replacement of aging equipment. The majority of grants from the Janson Foundation are 1 year in duration. On occasion, multi-year support is awarded. Award amounts typically go up to $15,000.
Requirements: Applicants must have 501(c)3 tax-exempt status and support communities in Skagit County, Washington. Applications will be submitted online through the Bank of America website. A grant report is required within 1 year of the grant application date, regardless of whether all of the funds have been spent.
Restrictions: Grant requests for general operating or program support will not be considered. There is a 3-year limit for receiving grants. After an organization receives 3 consecutive years of grant funding from the Janson Foundation, the organization will not be eligible to receive funding for a fourth consecutive year. The organization may apply to the Janson Foundation again after a 1-year hiatus. The foundation does not support requests from individuals, organizations attempting to influence policy through direct lobbying, or any political campaigns.
Geographic Focus: Washington
Date(s) Application is Due: Feb 28
Amount of Grant: Up to 15,000 USD
Samples: Skagit Gleaner, Mount Vernon, Washington, $12,500 - awarded for new vehicle for picking up foods/goods and delivering foods/goods (2018); Brigid Collins Family Support Center, Bellingham, Washington, $9,947 - awarded for Mount Vernon Facility Sidewalk Safety and Accessibility program (2018); Page Ahead Children's Literacy Program, Seattle, Washington, $5,000 - awarded for Book Up Summer program in Skagit County (2018).
Contact: Jan Aldrich Jacobs, (206) 358-0912; wa.grantmaking@bankofamerica.com or janet.jacobs@bofa.com
Internet: www.bankofamerica.com/philanthropic/foundation/?fnId=113
Sponsor: Janson Foundation
P.O. Box 831041
Dallas, TX 75283-1041

Japan Foundation Los Angeles Contests Designed for 1351
Japanese-Language Learners Grants

The Japan Foundation Los Angeles (JFLA) offers grant programs to support K-16 education all over the United States. The JFLA Contests grants provide educational institutions/organizations in the U.S. with financial support (up to $600) for Japanese-language education-related activities (speech contests, quiz contests, and presentations, etc.) that are intended to motivate Japanese-language learners and promote Japanese-language education in the region. Funds may be used to pay for the following expenses: honoraria, transportation, and accommodation for contest judges; venue-related expenses such as rental fees for venue and equipment, etc; prize expenses for contestants (no monetary prizes); and production costs for handouts/programs. Applications will be evaluated on the following criteria: the applicant's role and influence in the region; specific benefits of the project to Japanese-language learners; specific results in the region from the success of the project; project scale (number of contestants and participating schools); and the applicant's previous grant history and need for financial support. Guidelines and a downloadable application form are available at the website. JFLA contest grants have two deadlines: March 20 (for projects held between April 1 and March 31), and September 1 (for projects held between October 1 and March 31). Applicants must inform JFLA of their intention to apply before submitting their application. The application form (original) must arrive at the JFLA by the respective deadlines. Deadlines may vary from year to year. Prospective applicants are advised to verify current deadline dates at the website or by contacting the JFLA. The Japan Foundation was established in 1972 by the Japanese legislature and became one of Japan's "Independent Administrative Institutions" in October 2003. The foundation maintains its headquarters in Tokyo and operates through a network of 21 overseas offices in 20 countries worldwide including offices in New York and Los Angeles, and a Center for Global Partnership, also in New York. The foundation's mission is to promote international cultural exchange and mutual understanding between Japan and other countries. To do so it offers three major categories of programming: Arts & Culture; Japanese Studies; and Japanese-Language Education.
Requirements: Non-profit educational institutions and organizations involved in Japanese-language education are eligible to apply.
Restrictions: The following types of activities and costs are not eligible for support: food and drink; receptions and banquets; rental fee for halls owned by the applicant; applicant's indirect costs and administrative costs; applicant's regular board meetings (and other general meetings); projects for religious or political purposes; and commercial activities. In principle, the Japan Foundation does not provide grants for foreign governments (excluding academic, cultural, or research institutes such as universities and museums) or international organizations to which the Japanese government makes a financial contribution. Organizations whose laws restrict them from receiving aid from foreign governments and their affiliates are not eligible.
Geographic Focus: All States
Date(s) Application is Due: Mar 20; Sep 1
Amount of Grant: Up to 600 USD
Contact: Masayo Matsudaira, Acting Program Officer (Language); (213) 621-2267, ext. 110; fax (213) 621-2590; language@jflalc.org
Internet: www.jflalc.org/grants-jle-contest.html
Sponsor: Japan Foundation Los Angeles
333 South Grand Avenue, Suite 2250
Los Angeles, CA 90071

Japan Foundation Los Angeles Grants for Japanese-Language Courses 1352

The Japan Foundation Los Angeles (JFLA) offers grant programs to support K-16 education all over the United States. JFLA's Grants for Japanese-Language Courses support Japanese-language programs in the U.S. that are facing severe financial difficulties in initiating/expanding/maintaining(surviving) due to budget cuts. The Japan Foundation provides financial support to educational institutions or school districts to supplement the instructor's salary for up to two years. The grant amount can be up to $30,000.00 for the instructor's annual salary including fringe benefits. Applicants may request funding for only one instructor (school districts may request one instructor per school). Instructors may be either full- or part-time. The grant is given on the premise that the Japanese-language program and the instructor's position at the applying institution will become self-sustaining. It is recommended that the applying educational institution submit a commitment letter (supporting letter) from the person who is authorized to make a decision on whether to continue the Japanese-language program at the institute/school district (examples: Dean, Dept. Chair, District Superintendent, Head of the Board of Education, Principal, etc.) at the time of application. Applications will be evaluated on the following criteria: contents of the commitment letter and the applicant's ability to maintain the program and teaching position after completion of the grant; level of the applicant's financial need; applicant's potential to raise funds from other sources; amount of the applicant's own funds being committed to the program; the applicant's role and influence in the region; specific benefits to Japanese-language education in the region; proposed teaching hours of the instructor; expected number of students; feasibility of the applicant's proposal; and the applicant's grant history (applicants who have never received Japan Foundation grant support in the past will receive priority). Guidelines and a downloadable application form are available at the website. Applicants must inform JFLA of their intention to apply before submitting their application. The application form (original) must arrive at the JFLA by the deadline date. The deadline may vary from year to year. Prospective applicants are advised to verify the current deadline date at the website or by contacting the JFLA. The Japan Foundation was established in 1972 by the Japanese legislature and became one of Japan's "Independent Administrative Institutions" in October 2003. The foundation maintains its headquarters in Tokyo and operates through a network of 21 overseas offices in 20 countries worldwide including offices in New York and Los Angeles, and a Center for Global Partnership, also in New York. The foundation's mission is to promote international cultural exchange

and mutual understanding between Japan and other countries. Thus it offers three major categories of programming: Arts & Culture; Japanese Studies; and Japanese-Language Education.
Requirements: Non-profit educational institutions and organizations involved in Japanese-language education are eligible to apply.
Restrictions: The following types of activities and costs are not eligible for support: applicant's indirect costs, administrative costs, and overhead costs other than instructor's salary and fringe benefits; projects for religious or political purposes; and commercial activities. In principle, the Japan Foundation does not provide grants for foreign governments (excluding academic, cultural, or research institutes such as universities and museums) or international organizations to which the Japanese government makes a financial contribution. Organizations whose laws restrict them from receiving aid from foreign governments and their affiliates are not eligible.
Geographic Focus: All States
Date(s) Application is Due: May 2
Amount of Grant: Up to 60,000 USD
Contact: Masayo Matsudaira, Acting Program Officer (Language); (213) 621-2267, ext. 110; fax (213) 621-2590; language@jflalc.org
Internet: www.jflalc.org/grants-jle-courses.html
Sponsor: Japan Foundation Los Angeles
333 South Grand Avenue, Suite 2250
Los Angeles, CA 90071

Japan Foundation Los Angeles Japanese-Language Teaching Materials Purchase Grants 1353

The Japan Foundation Los Angeles (JFLA) offers grant programs to support K-16 education all over the United States. JFLA's Japanese-Language Teaching-Materials Purchase-Program provides up to $1,000 to educational institutions in the U.S. for purchasing textbooks, audio-visual materials, dictionaries, teachers' reference books, etc. for their Japanese-language courses. Applications will be evaluated on the following criteria: the applicant's role and influence in the region; specific benefits of the project to Japanese-language learners; applicant's ability to sustain the Japanese-language program; total number of students enrolled in the applicant's Japanese-language courses; and the applicant's previous grant history and need for financial support. Guidelines and a downloadable application form are available at the website. Teaching-Materials Purchase Grants have two deadlines: April 2 and September 1. The application form (original) must arrive at the JFLA by the respective deadline. Deadlines may vary from year to year. Prospective applicants are advised to verify current deadline dates at the website or by contacting the JFLA. The Japan Foundation was established in 1972 by the Japanese legislature and became one of Japan's "Independent Administrative Institutions" in October 2003. The foundation maintains its headquarters in Tokyo and operates through a network of 21 overseas offices in 20 countries worldwide including offices in New York and Los Angeles, and a Center for Global Partnership, also in New York. The foundation's mission is to promote international cultural exchange and mutual understanding between Japan and other countries. To do so it offers three major categories of programming: Arts & Culture; Japanese Studies; and Japanese-Language Education.
Requirements: Non-profit educational institutions and organizations involved in Japanese-language education are eligible to apply.
Restrictions: Items eligible for support are Japanese-language textbooks, audio-visual materials, dictionaries, teacher's reference books, etc. JFLA will not cover hardware items (e.g. laptop computers, camcorders, digital cameras, projectors, screens) and consumable supplies (papers, pens, etc.). Teaching materials purchased with this grant should become the property of the institutions and are not to be privately owned by instructors or students. Projects for religious or political purposes and commercial activities are not eligible for support. In principle, the Japan Foundation does not provide grants to foreign governments (excluding academic, cultural, or research institutes such as universities and museums) or international organizations to which the Japanese government makes a financial contribution. Organizations whose laws restrict them from receiving aid from foreign governments and their affiliates are not eligible to apply.
Geographic Focus: All States
Date(s) Application is Due: Apr 2; Sep 1
Amount of Grant: Up to 1,000 USD
Contact: Masayo Matsudaira, Acting Program Officer (Language); (213) 621-2267 ext. 110; fax (213) 621-2590; language@jflalc.org
Internet: www.jflalc.org/grants-jle-materials.html
Sponsor: Japan Foundation Los Angeles
333 South Grand Avenue, Suite 2250
Los Angeles, CA 90071

Japan Foundation Los Angeles Mini-Grants for Japanese Arts & Culture 1354

The Japan Foundation Los Angeles (JFLA) supports projects that will enhance further understanding of Japanese arts and culture, or that produce U.S.-Japan collaborative projects in the following areas: the performing arts, exhibitions, film screenings, lectures, and/or symposia and other cultural events. Successful candidates may be granted up to $1,000. Projects will be evaluated on their artistic quality, their expected impact on the audience and the U.S. arts scene, the strength of the project / organization's educational and community activities, and the organization's ability to carry through with the project and capacity to provide future continuity. Priority will be given to those projects that have secured additional funding from sources other than the Japan Foundation. Downloadable application guidelines and an application form are available at the website. Applications must be received by JFLA at least two months prior to the beginning date of the project. JFNY will contact applicants regarding the result two weeks prior to the project starting date. The Japan Foundation was established in 1972 by the Japanese legislature and became one of Japan's "Independent Administrative Institutions" in October 2003. The foundation maintains its headquarters in Tokyo and operates through a network of 21 overseas offices in 20 countries worldwide including offices in New York and Los Angeles, and a Center for Global Partnership, also in New York. The foundation's mission is to promote international cultural exchange and mutual understanding between Japan and other countries. To do so it offers three major categories of programming: Arts & Culture; Japanese Studies; and Japanese-Language Education.
Requirements: Grants will be made to non-profit U.S.-based organizations for projects that take place in states west of the Rocky Mountains (Alaska, Arizona, California, Colorado, Hawaii, Idaho, Montana, Nevada, New Mexico, Oregon, Utah, Washington, and Wyoming.) Grants may be used to cover the following costs: publicity; printing costs of programs, leaflets, or catalogs; honoraria for artists and lecturers; travel expenses for artists and lecturers, including per diem and accommodation expenses; and shipping cost of films, exhibits, and/or other materials related to the proposed event. The applicant should cover theater or space-rental fees, and/or the cost of a reception, if applicable.
Restrictions: Projects must take place in states west of the Rocky Mountains (see list in requirements section). The following entities or activities are not eligible to be funded: individuals and for-profit entities; projects that have already received funding through other Japan Foundation grants; organizations which have received a JFLA grant in the previous fiscal year; language-education programs through Japanese-language workshops and conferences; medical, technical, or scientific projects; and political, religious, social-welfare, fundraising, charitable, and commercial activities. JFLA generally does not fund an organization for more than three consecutive fiscal years.
Geographic Focus: All States
Amount of Grant: Up to 1,000 USD
Contact: Yoshihiro Nihei, Arts & Culture, PR; (213) 621-2267, ext. 109; fax (213) 621-2590; culture@jflalc.org or yoshihiro_nihei@jflalc.org
Internet: www.jflalc.org/grants-ac.html
Sponsor: Japan Foundation Los Angeles
333 South Grand Avenue, Suite 2250
Los Angeles, CA 90071

Japan Foundation New York Small Grants for Arts and Culture 1355

The Japan Foundation New York Office (JFNY) Small Grants for Arts and Culture support projects that nurture further understanding of Japanese arts and culture or that produce U.S.-Japan collaborative projects through the performing arts, exhibitions, film screenings, lectures, and/or symposia and other cultural events. Successful candidates may be granted up to $5,000. Projects will be evaluated on their artistic quality, expected impact on the audience and the U.S. arts scene, strength of educational and community activities, and the organization's ability to carry through with the project and capacity to provide future continuity. Priority will be given to those projects that have secured additional funding from sources other than the Japan Foundation. Application guidelines, supporting-documentation requirements, and a downloadable application form are available at the website. Applications must be received by JFNY at least three months prior to the beginning date of the project. JFNY will contact applicants regarding the result two months prior to the project starting date. The Japan Foundation was established in 1972 by the Japanese legislature and became one of Japan's "Independent Administrative Institutions" in October 2003. The foundation maintains its headquarters in Tokyo and operates through a network of 21 overseas offices in 20 countries worldwide including offices in New York and Los Angeles, and a Center for Global Partnership, also in New York. The foundation's mission is to promote international cultural exchange and mutual understanding between Japan and other countries. To do so it offers three major categories of programming: Arts & Culture; Japanese Studies; and Japanese-Language Education.
Requirements: Grants will be made to non-profit U.S.-based organizations for projects that take place in states east of the Rocky Mountains (these include Alabama, Arkansas, Connecticut, District of Columbia, Delaware, Florida, Georgia, Illinois, Indiana, Iowa, Kansas, Kentucky, Louisiana, Massachusetts, Maryland, Maine, Michigan, Minnesota, Missouri, Mississippi, North Carolina, North Dakota, Nebraska, New Hampshire, New Jersey, New York, Ohio, Oklahoma, Pennsylvania, Rhode Island, South Carolina, South Dakota, Tennessee, Texas, Virginia, Vermont, Wisconsin, and West Virginia). Grants may be used to cover the following costs: publicity; printing costs of programs, leaflets, or catalogs; honoraria for artists and lecturers; travel expenses for artists and lecturers, including per diem and accommodation expenses; and shipping cost of films, exhibits, and/or other materials related to the proposed event. The applicant should cover theater or space-rental fees, and/or the cost of a reception, if applicable.
Restrictions: Projects must take place in states east of the Rocky Mountains (see list in requirements section). Individuals and for-profit entities cannot apply. Projects that have already received funding through other Japan Foundation grants cannot apply. Organizations which have received the JFNY Small Grants for Arts and Culture in the previous fiscal year cannot apply. Japanese-language education programs are excluded, along with martial arts- and medical, technical, or scientific projects. (Applicants should contact the Japan Foundation, Los Angeles for Japanese-language education programs.) The following types of requests are not considered: political; religious; social-welfare; and commercial.
Geographic Focus: All States
Amount of Grant: Up to 5,000 USD
Contact: Yukihiro Ohira, Program Director, Arts & Cultural Exchange; (212) 489-0299; fax (212) 489-0409; info@jfny.org
Internet: www.jfny.org/arts_and_culture/smallgrant.html
Sponsor: Japan Foundation in New York
1700 Broadway, 15th Floor
New York, NY 10019

Japan Foundation New York World Heritage Photo Panel Exhibition   1356

The World Heritage Convention is a document adopted in 1972 by a general session of UNESCO (United Nations Educational, Scientific, and Cultural Organization) and signed by 185 countries to date, including Japan. The document's aims are to preserve for future generations the cultural and natural legacies of the world. By signing, these countries pledged to the world that they would preserve legacies of conspicuous and universal value that were within their borders, and that they accepted the obligation and responsibility to cooperate with other countries in protecting common World-Heritage legacies of mankind. The Japan Foundation, New York (JFNY) is proud to offer the opportunity to host a World-Heritage Photo-Panel Exhibition to cultural and educational institutions throughout the United States, free of charge. This exhibition set consists of 67 spectacular photos of World-Heritage sites in Japan. In appreciation for U.S. support in the wake of the disaster in the Tohoku region, the foundation will bear the expenses for shipping the exhibit. Up to $2000 for exhibition-related expenses is also available to exhibitors. Terms and conditions and a downloadable reservation form are available at the website. A catalog of pictures is also available on request. The Japan Foundation was established in 1972 by the Japanese legislature and became one of Japan's "Independent Administrative Institutions" in October 2003. The foundation maintains its headquarters in Tokyo and operates through a network of 21 overseas offices in 20 countries worldwide. The foundation's mission is to promote international cultural exchange and mutual understanding between Japan and other countries. To do so it offers three major categories of programming: Arts & Culture; Japanese Studies; and Japanese-Language Education. The Japan Foundation New York's focus is to bring Japanese arts and culture to areas in the United States with little previous exposure to Japan.

Requirements: Cultural and educational institutions in the United States are eligible to request this exhibit. Upon the institution's request, JFNY may support up to $2,000 for costs directly related to the exhibition, for instance: costs for hiring art handlers, security guards, receptionists, etc; costs for producing wall text panels; and costs for producing and distributing promotional materials.

Restrictions: JFNY does not support the costs of holding a reception. The photo panels are to be used only for educational and/or non-commercial purposes. JFNY will insure the works during their transit to and from the institution. The institution is responsible for any damages that occur during the period between arrival and pick-up. In accordance with the agreement between the Japan Foundation and the photographer, the institution shall not collect any kind of entrance fee or audience donation. Duplication of the photo panels is strictly prohibited. Television broadcasting of the panels is strictly prohibited without prior consent of JFNY. Exhibiting institutions must credit the loan from JFNY in the program and/or other printed materials as "panels courtesy of The Japan Foundation."

Geographic Focus: All States
Amount of Grant: Up to 2,000 USD
Contact: Yukihiro Ohira, Program Director; (212) 489-0299; fax (212) 489-0409; info@jfny.org
Internet: www.jfny.org/arts_and_culture/worldheritage.html
Sponsor: Japan Foundation in New York
1700 Broadway, 15th Floor
New York, NY 10019

Jaquelin Hume Foundation Grants   1357

The Jacquelin Hume Foundation Grants primarily support K-12 education reform efforts that are national in scope. Grants will be made for general operations, project development, and research. Special projects are generally preferred. One request per organization per year will be considered.

Requirements: An application form is not required. Applicants should submit a one-page letter of inquiry along with the following: the qualifications of key personnel; a copy of the IRS determination letter; a copy of the most recent annual report, audited financial statement, or 990; a detailed description of the project and amount of funding requested; a listing of the board of directors, trustees, officers and other key people, with their affiliations; and a list of past and present donors.

Restrictions: The Foundation does not support organizations outside the U.S. or grants to individuals.

Geographic Focus: All States
Date(s) Application is Due: Mar 15; Sep 15
Contact: Gisele Huff, Executive Director; (415) 705-5115
Sponsor: Jaquelin Hume Foundation
600 Montgomery Street, Suite 2800
San Francisco, CA 94111-2803

Jayne and Leonard Abess Foundation Grants   1358

The Jayne and Leonard Abess Foundation was established in Miami, Florida, in 2004, by the son of City National Bank co-founder, Leonard L. Abess, Sr. The Foundation supports a variety of causes both locally and nationally. Areas of interest include: design arts education, writer's, employment training, human services programs, Jewish agencies and temples, children with special needs, and higher education. The primary type of support is general operating funds. There are no specific applications or deadlines with which to adhere, and applicants should contact the Foundation office directly in writing. This initial contact should include a detailed description of the program, and a budget narrative. Most recently, awards have ranged from $1,000 to $100,000.

Geographic Focus: All States
Amount of Grant: 1,000 - 100,000 USD
Samples: The Gunnery, Washington, Connecticut, $100 - general operating support; American Diabetes Association, Miami, Florida, $1,000 - general operating support; Our Pride Academy, Miami, Florida, $5,000 - general operating support.

Contact: Leonard L. Abess, President; (212) 632-3000 or (212) 632-3200; informed@ftci.com
Sponsor: Jayne and Leonard Abess Foundation
600 Fifth Avenue
New York, NY 10020-2302

Jeffris Wood Foundation Grants   1359

The Jeffris Wood Foundation funds grants to community-based organizations working to provide opportunities for urban youth and economically disadvantaged. The Foundation supports programs that: help urban youth improve their futures, explore their creativity and avoid unwanted pregnancies; help Native American youth connect with their cultural traditions; connect low-income urban youth to nature; and provide services for domestic violence survivors. Current deadlines are posted on the website.

Requirements: Organizations must first submit a one-page letter of inquiry that includes a description of the organization and the project. They should also attach a brief budget describing income and expenses, plus complete contact information. If the request is screened for further consideration, the organization will be asked to submit a full proposal. All materials must be sent by U.S. mail.

Restrictions: Grants are not made to: individuals; scholarships; schools; capital expenses or renovation projects; food or shelter programs (except domestic violence); research or publications; video & web productions; religious programs that are not all inclusive; or athletic events and sponsorships.

Geographic Focus: Washington
Amount of Grant: 1,000 - 3,000 USD
Samples: Broadview Emergency Shelter, Seattle, Washington, serving 400 homeless women with children, $3,000; Neighborcare Health Homeless Youth Clinic, Seattle, Washington, outreach program that meets youth where they live or congregate, $3,000.
Contact: Therese Ogle, Grants Consultant; (206) 781-3472; OgleFounds@aol.com
Internet: foundationcenter.org/grantmaker/jeffriswood/guide.html
Sponsor: Jeffris Wood Foundation
6723 Sycamore Avenue NW
Seattle, WA 98117

Jennings County Community Foundation Grants   1360

The Foundation seeks to serve philanthropic and charitable needs in Jennings County, Indiana, by offering endowment services, grant making, scholarships, donor estate and planned gift services to individuals and qualified organizations serving the community of Jennings County, Indiana. The Foundation's fields of interest for all ages include the following: community service; social service; education; health; environment; and the arts. The Foundation reviews proposals in the spring and fall. Applications will be made available at the spring and fall cycle grant explanation meeting as announced in the local media. At this mandatory meeting the grant guidelines and process will be explained. The grant proposal form is available at the website.

Requirements: Nonprofit 501(c)3 organizations, coalitions, community associations, and other civic groups may apply if providing services in Jennings County. Applicants must also attend an explanation meeting of the guidelines for grants.

Restrictions: The Foundation does not fund political activity; sectarian religious activity; endowment purposed except for limited experimental or demonstration periods; operating budgets except for limited experimental or demonstration periods; and salaries.

Geographic Focus: Indiana
Contact: Barb Shaw, Executive Director; (812) 346-5553; jcffdirector@comcast.net
Internet: www.jenningsfoundation.net/index.html
Sponsor: Jennings County Community Foundation
111 North State Street
North Vernon, IN 47265-1510

Jennings County Community Foundation Women's Giving Circle Grant   1361

The Women's Giving Circle was established to make a lasting impact in the lives of women and children in Jennings County. Grants are available to nonprofit organizations that have a need for assistance on a community project. Grants are for organizations that meet the needs of women and children in the fields of community service, social service, education, health, environment and the arts. The application is available at the website.

Geographic Focus: Indiana
Contact: Barb Shaw, Executive Director; (812) 523-4483 or (812) 346-5553; jccf@jenningsfoundation.net
Sandy Vance, Grant Contact; (812) 592-1280
Darlene Bradshaw, Grant Contact; (812) 346-1742
Linda Erler, Grant Contact; (812) 873-7421
Internet: www.jenningsfoundation.net/php/wgc.php
Sponsor: Jennings County Community Foundation
111 North State Street
North Vernon, IN 47265-1510

Jerry L. and Barbara J. Burris Foundation Grants   1362

The Jerry L. and Barbara J. Burris Foundation was established in Indiana in 1994. Its primary fields of interest include: the arts; cancer research; children and youth services; education; hospitals; human services; museums; Protestant agencies and churches; and zoological societies. Funding typically comes in the form of general operating support and scholarship funding. There are no specific applications or annual deadlines, so applicants should begin by contacting the Foundation directly.

Geographic Focus: Florida, Indiana
Amount of Grant: 1,000 - 10,000 USD

Samples: Shelter for Abused Women and Children, Naples, Florida, $9,000 - general operating fund; Butler University, Indianapolis, Indiana, $10,000 - scholarship fund; Indianapolis Zoological Society, Indianapolis, Indiana, $6,500 - general operating fund.
Contact: Barbara J. Burris, President; (317) 843-5678
Sponsor: Jerry L. and Barbara J. Burris Foundation
P.O. Box 80238
Indianapolis, IN 46280-0238

Jessica Stevens Community Foundation Grants 1363
The Jessica Stevens Community Foundation (JSCF) is taking a different approach in encouraging philanthropy. They are offering up to $12,000 in challenge grants ranging from $500 to $3,000 to nonprofits located in or serving the Northern Susitna Valley, which includes the Trapper Creek, Talkeetna, Sunshine, and Caswell areas. JSCF's primary goal is to support organizations and programs in its community that serve the needs of people in areas such as health, education, human services, arts and culture, and the preservation and enjoyment of the natural environment. The Foundation is also striving to encourage continued growth of grantees with the challenge to match grant awards by seeking new donors or increased contributions. If the challenge is met, JSCF will match the donations dollar for dollar for the amount of the grant. Grant applications are accepted from May 11 to the annual deadline date of July 10.
Requirements: Applications are accepted from 501(c)3 nonprofit organizations, or equivalent organizations located in the state of Alaska. Equivalent organizations may include tribes, local or state governments, schools, or Regional Educational Attendance Areas.
Geographic Focus: Alaska
Date(s) Application is Due: Jul 10
Amount of Grant: 500 - 3,000 USD
Contact: Mariko Sarafin, Senior Program Associate; (907) 249-6609 or (907) 334-6700; fax (907) 334-5780; msarafin@alaskacf.org or info@jessicasfoundation.org
Ricardo Lopez, Affiliate Program Officer; (907) 274-6707 or (907) 334-6700; fax (907) 334-5780; rlopez@alaskacf.org or info@jessicasfoundation.org
Internet: alaskacf.org/blog/grants/jessica-stevens-community-foundation-grant
Sponsor: Jessica Stevens Community Foundation
P.O. Box 436
Talkeetna, AK 99676

Jewish Fund Grants 1364
The Fund awards grants to sustain, enrich, and address the overall health care needs of both the Jewish community and general community in the metropolitan Detroit area. The Fund is particularly interested in supporting projects that: address health care and social welfare needs of vulnerable/at-risk populations within the Jewish community; respond to priority capital and equipment needs of the Detroit Medical Center/Sinai Hospital; improve the health and well-being of vulnerable/at risk populations in the general community; support inclusion of people with special needs into the general activities of the community; enhance positive relationships between the Jewish community and the Detroit community. Highest priority is given to requests for programs that: address a critical need; impact the lives of residents of the Wayne, Oakland and Macomb counties; have a defined plan for sustaining the program beyond the grant period; include a financial or in-kind contribution from the organization; involve collaboration with others; have an outcomes-based evaluation plan; and can be funded and replicated by others. Samples of previously funded grants are available on the Fund website.
Requirements: The Jewish Fund will make grants to 501(c)3 organizations and other non-profits qualified as tax exempt under the Internal Revenue Code. Applicant organizations must provide a current audited financial statement. Applicants are encouraged to contact the Fund and discuss their proposed project with the executive director before applying for funding.
Restrictions: The Fund will usually not support: grants made directly to individuals; loans; grants to support religious activities or sectarian education; overseas projects; capital projects or equipment purchases (except equipment at the DMC/Sinai); endowments; annual fund drives, and fundraising events; and past operating deficits.
Geographic Focus: Michigan
Contact: Margo Pernick, Executive Director; (248) 203-1487; fax (248) 645-7879
Internet: thejewishfund.org/grant-request-guidelines.html
Sponsor: Jewish Fund
6735 Telegraph Road
Bloomfield Hills, MI 48301-2030

Jim Blevins Foundation Grants 1365
The purpose of the Jim Blevins Foundation grant program is to support education, Christian, and Presbyterian organizations within the State of Tennessee. Its primary fields of interest include: Christian agencies and churches; health organizations; higher education; human services; Protestant agencies and churches, and youth services. There are no specific deadlines or applications with which to adhere, and applicants should contact the Foundation directly. Giving is limited to Tennessee.
Geographic Focus: Tennessee
Contact: James V. Blevins, Trustee; (615) 298-5000; jwblev@aol.com
Sponsor: Jim Blevins Foundation
P.O. Box 150056
Nashville, TN 37215

Jim Moran Foundation Grants 1366
The Jim Moran Foundation Grants award funding to 501(c)3 organizations in Florida. The Foundation seeks to improve the quality of life for youth and families through the support of innovative programs and opportunities that meet the ever-changing needs of

the community. The Foundation's funding focuses include: education; elder care programs; family strengthening programs; meaningful after school programs; and youth transitional living programs. Proposals for programs that improve the quality of life for those who are at-risk and economically disadvantaged (without extenuating medical or developmental disabilities) will receive priority consideration. Grants are primarily awarded to the Florida counties of Broward, Palm Beach, and Duval. Applicants submit an online letter of inquiry, and will be notified within 90 days if they qualify to submit the online application.
Requirements: The Foundation will consider only organizations that have received 501(c)3 tax-exempt status under the IRS code. Additionally, the organization must be appropriately recognized by state statutes, laws and regulations that govern tax exempt organizations.
Restrictions: The Foundation will consider requests for operating dollars, but only if they do not exceed 50% of the grant request. The Foundation will not consider requests for capital campaigns, capacity building, healthcare or medical research, or event sponsorships.
Geographic Focus: Florida
Amount of Grant: Up to 1,500,000 USD
Samples: Camelot Community Care, Fort Lauderdale, Florida, $72,165 - support of the Life Transitions Program, which provides extended independent living services and support for at-risk young adults in Broward County (2018); Delray Students First, Delray Beach, Florida, $20,000 - support of the SAT/ACT Tutoring Program (2018); Florida State University Foundation, Tallahassee, Florida, $1,500,000 - support of the Jim Moran School of Entrepreneurship at Florida State University (2018).
Contact: Melanie Burgess, Executive Director; (954) 429-2122; fax (954) 363-6801; information@jimmoranfoundation.org
Internet: www.jimmoranfoundation.org/grants/guidelines
Sponsor: Jim Moran Foundation
100 Jim Moran Boulevard
Deerfield Beach, FL 33442

Joan Bentinck-Smith Charitable Foundation Grants 1367
Established in 1994, the Joan Bentinck-Smith Charitable Foundation offers funding support primarily within its home state of Massachusetts. Its major fields of interest include: children and youth services; education; housing and shelter; human services; and the support of local YMCAs and YWCAs. There are no specified application forms or annual deadlines, so applicants should begin by contacting the Foundation directly. Recent grants have ranged from $500 to $15,000.
Requirements: The Foundation offers funding to 501(c)3 organizations located within, or supporting the residents of, Massachusetts
Geographic Focus: Massachusetts
Amount of Grant: 500 - 15,000 USD
Samples: Cape Cod Council of Churches, Hyannis, Massachusetts, $1,000 - in support of the Visiting Nurse Association; Greater Boston Food Bank, Boston, Massachusetts, $15,000 - in support of the Cape Cod Island Food Bank program; One Youth World Project, Boston, Massachusetts, $2,000 - for operating support.
Contact: Joan Bentinck-Smith, Trustee; (508) 420-4250
Sponsor: Joan Bentinck-Smith Charitable Foundation
1340 Main Street
Osterville, MA 02655-0430

John and Marcia Goldman Foundation Youth Development Grants 1368
The John and Marcia Goldman Foundation Youth Development program seeks to improve young people's life trajectories. Grants provide opportunities for under-served children, youth and their families to participate in a broad range of services and activities to inspire, inform and enhance their lives. The goal of this program is to help engage a harder-to-reach segment of the youth population and address critical service gaps. In order to have a focused impact, the Foundation has chosen to concentrate its resources geographically in the Mid-Peninsula region of the San Francisco Bay Area. Youth Development is the foundation's only open application program area. A Letter of Inquiry (LOI) and coversheet are required to apply for support from the Foundation's Youth Development program. Full proposals are accepted only after submission of an LOI and subsequent invitation to proceed to the proposal stage.
Requirements: Nonprofit organizations serving primarily the San Francisco Bay area of California are eligible to apply.
Restrictions: The fund does not accept applications for research or award grants or scholarships for individuals, conferences, documentary films, or fund-raisers. Unsolicited proposals for support of arts organizations or institutions of primary, secondary, or higher education will not be accepted.
Geographic Focus: California
Amount of Grant: 5,000 - 150,000 USD
Samples: Aim High For High School, San Francisco, California, $150,000 - general program support for the Redwood City Campus Launch; Beyond Barriers Athletic Foundation, Redwood City, California, $20,000 - general operating support; Eastside College Preparatory School, East Palo Alto, California, $10,000 - general operating support.
Contact: Amy Lyons, Executive Director; (415) 744-8787; info@jmgoldmanfoundation.org
Internet: jmgoldmanfoundation.org/youth-development/
Sponsor: John and Marcia Goldman Foundation
101 Second Street, Suite 1625
San Francisco, CA 94105

John Clarke Trust Grants 1369
Dating from April 20, 1676, this historic trust was created under the will of Dr. John Clarke, a Baptist clergyman and physician and one of the co-founders of the first European settlement on Aquidneck Island in 1638. He was born in 1609 and arrived in Boston in 1637

and was one of some 300 persons that founded the colony on Aquidneck Island. He was the author of the Royal Charter of 1663 that maintained Rhode Island as a colony. Dr. Clarke had no surviving children. He practiced medicine, was a minister and held public office, although his chief interest was that of the Christian ministry. He was also very interested in education and is thought to have been involved in establishing a free school for Newport in 1640. Dr. Clarke is buried in a small cemetery on West Broadway in Newport. In his will, written on the date of his death, John Clarke established a perpetual charitable trust. He directed that the income from the trust be used "for the relief of the poor or bringing up of children unto learning from time to time forever." He further instructed the trustees "to have a special regard and care to provide for those that fear the Lord." Award amounts typically go up to $20,000.

Requirements: The trustees of the John Clarke Trust have established a policy of giving preference to organizations located on Aquidneck Island, Rhode Island, and within the East Bay area. However, applications from any Rhode Island 501(c)3 charitable organizations are acceptable. Applications will be submitted online through the Bank of America website. A grant report is required within 1 year of the grant application date, regardless of whether all of the funds have been spent.

Restrictions: The trustees will consider capital grant requests ONLY from Aquidneck Island. The trust does not support requests from individuals, organizations attempting to influence policy through direct lobbying, or any political campaigns.

Geographic Focus: Rhode Island
Date(s) Application is Due: Apr 1; Nov 1
Amount of Grant: Up to 20,000 USD
Samples: Newport Hospital, Newport, Rhode Island, $10,000 - Awarded for Beyond the Building – The Campaign for Newport Hospital Expansion and transformation of the Emergency Department and Intensive Care Unit (2018); Trinity Church, Newport, Rhode Island, $10,000 - Awarded for construction of a replacement building adjacent to Queen Anne Square to be used to house a community meal program, music education program and a job training program for at risk youth (2018); Community Preparatory School, Providence, Rhode Island, $8,400 - Awarded for scholarship aid (2018).
Contact: Perpetua Campbell, Market Philanthropic Administrator; (866) 778-6859; ma.ri.grantmaking@bankofamerica.com or ma.ri.grantmaking@ustrust.com
Internet: www.bankofamerica.com/philanthropic/foundation/?fnId=20
Sponsor: John Clarke Trust
225 Franklin Street, MA1-225-04-02
Boston, MA 02110-2804

John D. and Katherine A. Johnston Foundation Grants 1370

The John D. and Katherine A. Johnston Foundation was established in 1928 to support charitable organizations that work to improve the lives of physically disabled children and adults. Special consideration is given to organizations that serve low-income individuals. Preference is given to charitable organizations that serve children in Newport, Rhode Island. Mr. Johnston stated in his will: "…it is my desire that each child be given the opportunity of acquiring at least a good grammar school education as well as to receive, if desired, the instruction usually afforded by a business or commercial school, and when practicable, that such child be taught some trade or useful employment…" As such, educational, vocational, and job training programs will be a funding priority although healthcare, recreational programs, and access to religious services will be considered. The majority of grants from the Johnston Foundation are 1 year in duration. Award amounts typically range from $1,000 to $10,000.

Requirements: Applicants must have 501(c)3 tax-exempt status. The Johnston Foundation supports charitable organizations in Rhode Island that work to improve the lives of physically disabled low-income children and adults. Preference is given to charitable organizations that serve children in Newport, Rhode Island. Applications will be submitted online through the Bank of America website. A grant report is required within 1 year of the grant application date, regardless of whether all of the funds have been spent.

Restrictions: The foundation does not support requests from individuals, organizations attempting to influence policy through direct lobbying, or any political campaigns.

Geographic Focus: Rhode Island
Date(s) Application is Due: Jul 1
Amount of Grant: 1,000 - 10,000 USD
Samples: Boys and Girls Clubs of Newport, Newport, Rhode Island, $5,000 - awarded for Enhancing Physical Activity for Children with Special Health Needs program (2018); Childrens Friend and Service, Providence, Rhode Island, $5,000 - awarded for supporting the needs of low-income infants and toddlers with speech/oral/motor disabilities (2018); Meeting Street Center, Providence, Rhode Island, $5,000 - awarded for the Carter School's Vocational Skills Center (2018).
Contact: Perpetua Campbell, Market Philanthropic Administrator; (866) 778-6859; ma.grantmaking@bankofamerica.com or ma.ri.grantmaking@ustrust.com
Internet: www.bankofamerica.com/philanthropic/foundation/?fnId=66
Sponsor: John D. and Katherine A. Johnston Foundation
P.O. Box 1802
Providence, RI 02901-1802

John F. Kennedy Center for the Performing Arts National 1371
Rosemary Kennedy Internship

Through the National Rosemary Kennedy Internship Initiative, the VSA and Accessibility Department provides internship opportunities at arts and arts service organizations across the U.S. These programs service youth with disabilities between the ages of 15 and 21 who are seeking careers in the arts, arts administration, and arts education. Existing, new, or innovative programs are encouraged to apply. Proposals are submitted by January 7, with notification on a rolling basis by January 14. Additional submission guidelines are available at the website.

Requirements: Nonprofit contractors must meet the following *Requirements:* at least three years of successful experience operating an internship, apprenticeship, or youth-training program; experience delivering quality internship and/or training opportunities for youth with disabilities between the ages of 15 and 21; identify qualified youth with disabilities to participate in the program; be fiscally sound and have the capacity to manage and execute the proposed program within the designated timeline; comply with any state, local, and, if applicable, school district requirements regarding criminal background checks for program employees, contractors, and volunteers; conduct the program in spaces that are ADA-accessible and be knowledgeable about appropriate accommodations and effective communication for youth with disabilities who choose to participate. Programs must accomplish the following: provide experiential internship, apprenticeship or training opportunities that facilitate the entry and advancement of youth with disabilities into competitive employment in the arts, arts administration or arts education; reflect recognized youth development principles that emphasize the cognitive, social, and behavioral competencies that help youth with disabilities succeed as adults; successfully identify the aptitudes, talents, gifts, competencies, skills necessary to pursue their career or trade pathway of choice in arts-based employment. Programs must have immediate and significant impact with measurable and sustainable outcomes.

Restrictions: The Center will accept only one proposal per contractor. Commercial, for-profit or individual entities, and non-U.S. entities are not eligible.

Geographic Focus: All States
Date(s) Application is Due: Jan 7
Amount of Grant: 5,000 - 25,000 USD
Contact: Sonja Cendak, Artist Services Assistant Manager; (202) 416-8823 or (202) 416-8898; fax (202) 416-4840; scendak@kennedy-center.org
Internet: www.kennedy-center.org/accessibility/career.cfm#Rosemary
Sponsor: John F. Kennedy Center for the Performing Arts
2700 F Street NW
Washington, D.C. 20566

John G. Duncan Charitable Trust Grants 1372

John G. Duncan was born in Sacramento, California, in 1866, and lived a substantial portion of his life in Henderson, Kentucky, where he was actively involved in the philanthropic community. He later relocated to Denver, Colorado, where he also supported a number of different non-profit organizations. Duncan died in 1955 at the age of 89. The John G. Duncan Charitable Trust was established to award grants in the following areas of interest: arts; education; health care; human services; religion; building and renovation; capital campaigns; emergency funds; equipment; program development; seed money; and research. Applications should be submitted through the online grant application form or alternative accessible application designed for assistive technology users. The average award ranges from $5,000 to $10,000. Applications may be submitted year-round, but must be submitted by the following deadlines to be reviewed at the grant meeting held after each date: January 31, April 30, July 31, and October 31.

Requirements: Organizations must have 501(c)3 designation, and serve and operate in Colorado. Organizations are eligible to apply once per calendar year. If a grant is awarded, the organization will be ineligible to apply in the following calendar year.

Restrictions: The foundation does not fund requests to support: general operating expenses; endowments; organizations located outside of Colorado; other grantmaking organizations; or organizations recognized by the IRS as non-functionally integrated supporting organizations per Section 509(a)3 of the Internal Revenue Code.

Geographic Focus: Colorado
Date(s) Application is Due: Jan 31; Apr 30; Jul 31; Oct 31
Amount of Grant: 5,000 - 10,000 USD
Contact: Jason Craig, Trustee; (888) 234-1999; fax (877) 746-5889; grantadministration@ wellsfargo.com
Internet: www.wellsfargo.com/privatefoundationgrants/duncan
Sponsor: John G. Duncan Charitable Trust
1740 Broadway, MAC C7300-483
Denver, CO 80274-0001

John Gogian Family Foundation Grants 1373

The Gogian Foundation supports nonprofit organizations in Los Angeles County that provide services and solutions for developmentally disabled adults and children, concentrating on life skills and vocational training, residential group homes, employment, day services, after school programs, and therapeutic services. The Foundation also supports organizations that provides services for abused or neglected youth including: residential group homes; emancipating foster youth; therapeutic, social, and educational services; institutionalized or incarcerated youth; domestic violence; and family preservation. The Foundation makes grants for new, expanding, or sustaining core programming. It also supports improvements, equipment, and vehicle capital expenditures.

Requirements: Applicants must submit the online Letter of Inquiry to request funding, but submit the filled out form by U.S. mail. Organizations will be notified of the outcome of their LOI within 45 of submittal deadline.

Restrictions: The Foundation does not fund the following: national organizations or their affiliates; individuals; care of animals; arts; culture; research; reduction of existing debt; funding of endowments; lending of funds; fundraising events; or political campaigns or projects designed to influence legislation.

Geographic Focus: California
Date(s) Application is Due: Jan 20; Jun 22
Amount of Grant: 5,000 - 20,000 USD
Contact: Lindsey Stammerjohn, Executive Director; (310) 325-0954; jgff@gogianfoundation.org
Internet: www.gogianfoundation.org/grant/index.html

Sponsor: John Gogian Family Foundation
3305 Fujita Street
Torrance, CA 90505

John H. and Wilhelmina D. Harland Charitable Foundation 1374
Children and Youth Grants

The John H. and Wilhelmina D. Harland Charitable Foundation offers support for: children and youth programs; community services; and arts, culture, and the environment. In the area of children and youth, support is offered for early childhood education, after school and summer programs for Elementary and Middle School Students, and programs that enhance success in public schools. The focus is local rather than regional or national, and priority is given to institutions in metropolitan Atlanta, Georgia. Grants awards support: building and renovation; capital campaigns; equipment; general operating support; challenge support; and scholarship funds. The Foundation prefers a telephone call as opposed to a letter of inquiry for the initial approach. January 10 is the deadline for the spring grant cycle and August 8 is the deadline for the fall grant cycle.

Requirements: Grant support is available to nonprofit organizations in Georgia, with emphasis on the metropolitan Atlanta area.

Restrictions: Grants are not awarded to individuals.

Geographic Focus: Georgia

Date(s) Application is Due: Jan 10; Aug 8

Amount of Grant: 4,000 - 25,000 USD

Samples: Adaptive Learning Center, Atlanta, Georgia, $20,000 - Inclusion Education Program in partnership with Our House; Moving in the Spirit, Atlanta, Georgia, $12,500 - in support of the Girls Leadership Track; Scottdale Child Development Center and Family Resource Center, Atlanta, Georgia, $20,000 - tuition assistance for early childhood education program.

Contact: Jane Hardesty, Executive Director; (404) 264-9912; info@harlandfoundation.org

Internet: harlandfoundation.org/index.php?option=com_content&view=article&id=48&Itemid=55

Sponsor: John H. and Wilhelmina D. Harland Charitable Foundation
Two Piedmont Court, Suite 710
Atlanta, GA 30305-1567

John H. and Wilhelmina D. Harland Charitable Foundation 1375
Community Services Grants

The John H. and Wilhelmina D. Harland Charitable Foundation offers support for: children and youth programs; community services; and arts, culture, and the environment. In the area of community services, support is offered for those specific community services that provide a safety net for those in greatest need, including people with special needs. The focus is local rather than regional or national, and priority is given to institutions in metropolitan Atlanta, Georgia. Grants awards support: building and renovation; capital campaigns; equipment; general operating support; challenge support; and scholarship funds. The Foundation prefers a telephone call as opposed to a letter of inquiry for the initial approach. January 10 is the deadline for the spring grant cycle and August 8 is the deadline for the fall grant cycle.

Requirements: Grant support is available to nonprofit organizations in Georgia, with emphasis on the metropolitan Atlanta area.

Geographic Focus: Georgia

Date(s) Application is Due: Jan 10; Aug 8

Amount of Grant: 5,000 - 30,000 USD

Samples: Atlanta Community Food Bank, Atlanta, Georgia, $25,000 - support of the Mobile Food Pantry Program; Furniture Bank of Metro Atlanta, Atlanta, Georgia, $20,000 - general operating costs; Literacy Action, Atlanta, Georgia, $15,000 - general operating costs.

Contact: Jane Hardesty, Executive Director; (404) 264-9912; info@harlandfoundation.org

Internet: harlandfoundation.org/index.php?option=com_content&view=article&id=48&Itemid=55

Sponsor: John H. and Wilhelmina D. Harland Charitable Foundation
Two Piedmont Court, Suite 710
Atlanta, GA 30305-1567

John M. Weaver Foundation Grants 1376

Established in California in 1997, the John M. Weaver Foundation offers funding support for animals and wildlife, education, human services, school athletics, amateur sports, and recreation activities throughout the State. Population groups targeted include academics, children and youth, and K-12 students. There is no specified application form, and no annual deadlines. Interested parties should contact the Foundation directly with a two- or three-page query letter, describing their project, budgetary needs, and overall timeline. Recent grants have been funded in the amount of $100 to $1,500.

Requirements: Any 501(c)3 located in, or serving the residents of, California are eligible to apply.

Geographic Focus: California

Amount of Grant: 100 - 1,500 USD

Samples: Hanna Boys Center, Sonoma, California, $1,500 - care and education of children; Christian Valley High School, San Jose, California, $200 - enhancement of the athletic program; Bill Wilson Center, Santa Clare, California, $100 - care of children and youth.

Contact: John M. Weaver, President; (408) 268-6471

Sponsor: John M. Weaver Foundation
4760 Sherbourne Drive
San Jose, CA 95124-4845

John P. Ellbogen Foundation Community Grants 1377

John P. "Jack" Ellbogen is the benefactor of the Foundation. He was a Wyoming native, born and raised in Worland. He had a great love for and commitment to his home State. His actions spoke loudly. He attended the University of Wyoming earning a bachelor's degree in History, a Law Degree, and an Honorary Doctorate from the College of Business. He started his career as a land man for Carter Oil Company (Exxon) and went on to become an Independent Oil Producer, forming several oil and gas companies. He attributed his success in business to his education and the outstanding teachers who encouraged him to work to his fullest potential. Throughout his adult life, Jack believed in the importance of a quality education for all Americans. He believed that the classroom teacher was the single most important factor to enhanced student learning. Jack established programs at the University of Wyoming and in Natrona County to emphasize the importance of quality teaching and to recognize and reward teachers for excellence as seen through the eyes of their students. During the later years of his life, he felt an obligation to get involved in the public school system. His research led him to the National Board for Professional Teaching Standards, and the National Board Certification process. A pilot program to test the reception of this process was jointly funded by Jack and Ruth Ellbogen. Jack was actively working on the expansion of the program in the final months of his life. In 2004, the John P. Ellbogen Foundation Board approved the Wyoming National Board Certification Initiative to serve teachers throughout the State of Wyoming. It has become the hallmark of the Foundation. The Foundation requires a Letter of Inquiry (LOI) as the first step in the grant request process. A period of time is set out before each fall Board meeting when the Foundation will receive and review letters that are input into the form online. Formal grant proposals will be invited after letters are reviewed.

Requirements: Grant reports from entities who have been awarded dollars are due one year after the grant has been awarded.

Geographic Focus: Wyoming

Date(s) Application is Due: Mar 30

Amount of Grant: Up to 350,000 USD

Samples: Natrona County School District, Casper, Wyoming, $11,440 - general operating support (2018); Natrona County Public Library, Casper, Wyoming, $5,000 - general operating support (2018); Wyoming Community Foundation, Laramie, Wyoming, $105,000 - general operating support (2018).

Contact: Becca Steinhoff, Executive Director; (307) 761-1898 or (307) 575-2443; fax (307) 742-0703; ellbogenfoundation.wy@gmail.com

Internet: www.ellbogenfoundation.org/index.php/grants/

Sponsor: John P. Ellbogen Foundation
P.O. Box 1670
Laramie, WY 82073

Johnson Controls Foundation Arts and Culture Grants 1378

The Johnson Controls Foundation provides financial gifts to select U.S.-based organizations located in the communities in which the company has a presence. In the area of arts and culture, the Foundation supports organizations in the areas of visual, performing and literary arts, public radio and television, libraries, museums, and related cultural activities.

Requirements: In evaluating requests for funds, the Advisory Board has developed policies and guidelines for giving in Culture and the Arts. Contributions will be given to visual, performing, and literary arts, public radio and television, libraries, museums, and other related cultural activities. Priority will be extended to those serving communities in which Johnson Controls employees live and work, and to those in which these employees are involved with their time and/or funds.

Restrictions: In general, no grants will be made to any political campaign or organization; any municipal, state, federal agency, or department, or to any organization established to influence legislation; any private individual for support of personal needs; any sectarian institutions or programs whose services are limited to members of any one religious group or whose funds are used primarily for the propagation of a religion; for testimonial dinners, fund raising events, tickets to benefits, shows, or advertising; to provide monies for travel or tours, seminars and conferences or for publication of books and magazines or media productions; for specific medical or scientific research projects; foreign-based institutions nor to institutions or organizations for use outside of the United States; fraternal orders or veteran groups; private foundations or to endowment funds. The foundation does not donate equipment, products or labor.

Geographic Focus: All States

Amount of Grant: 500 - 40,000 USD

Contact: Charles A. Harvey, President; (414) 524-1200 or (414) 524-2296

Internet: www.johnsoncontrols.com/publish/us/en/about/our_community_focus/johnson_controls_foundation.html

Sponsor: Johnson Controls Foundation
5757 North Green Bay Avenue, P.O. Box 591
Milwaukee, WI 53201

Johnson County Community Foundation Grants 1379

The Community Foundation seeks to meet the challenges of the Johnson County, Indiana community as a whole. Special attention is given to requests that increase the capacity of not-for-profit organizations to serve the community and requests that demonstrate community support and in-kind investment. The Foundation generally supports three kinds of requests: projects of service to the general community and pilot projects; seed money to enable projects to demonstrate their potential or enhance services; and emergency funding for community needs. Examples of previously funded projects are available at the website.

Requirements: Applicants must submit a letter of inquiry (2-3 pages), also include a copy of their 501(c)3 Letter of Determination. Letters of inquiry should include: a brief statement of the organization's purpose and goals; a brief description of the project, the need and the target population it addresses; short- and long-term outcomes anticipated and plans for

assessing achievements; grant amount needed; a statement about the total agency budget and the project budget; a statement about other funding sources for the agency and/or project, specifying both committed and projected sources of support. Letters of inquiry will be reviewed to determine if the proposed effort fits within the community foundation's grant program. If so, the applicant will be contacted by the Foundation, requesting additional information or a full proposal. The Foundation supports organizations that are tax exempt under Section 501(c)3 of the Internal Revenue Service Code and are not classified as private foundations under Section 509(a) of the Code. In selected cases, it may consider support for projects sponsored by governmental entities.
Restrictions: The Community Foundation does not: take multi-year commitments; support services commonly regarded as the responsibility of government; provide support for political or partisan purposes or for programs in which religious teachings are an integral part; consider more than one proposal from the same organization within a 12-month period; provide discretionary grant support to an organization's ongoing operating budget, building funds, capital campaigns, or endowments; fund raising events and functions; make grants to individuals except for scholarship or special award funds; fund existing obligations or to replenish resources (deficit funding) for such purposes.
Geographic Focus: Indiana
Contact: Kim Minton, Programs Director; (317) 738-2213; fax (317) 738-9113; kimm@jccf.org
Internet: www.jccf.org/index.asp?p=37
Sponsor: Johnson County Community Foundation
398 S Main, P.O. Box 217
Franklin, IN 46131-2311

Johnson County Community Foundation Youth Philanthropy Initiative Grants   1380
The Youth Philanthropy Initiative of Johnson County (YPIJC) is the first countywide youth leadership program focused on inspiring excellence in young people. The program equips young people with opportunities, resources, mentors and tools to solve serious community issues while developing a lifelong commitment to philanthropy. The application and samples of previously funded projects are available at the website.
Requirements: Grants are awarded to 501(c)3 nonprofit organizations and other groups including community organizations, schools, classrooms, religious organizations and youth groups for projects that: are youth-led from writing the proposal to implementation of the project; address a serious community need in Johnson County; bring together diverse people and organization; have a learning component on philanthropy; and increase the development assets of young people.
Geographic Focus: Indiana
Amount of Grant: 50 - 500 USD
Contact: Kim Minton, Director of Grants and Scholarships; (317) 738-2213; fax (317) 738-9113; kimm@jccf.org
Internet: www.jccf.org/Home/GrantsScholarships/YouthGrants/tabid/113/Default.aspx
Sponsor: Johnson County Community Foundation
398 S Main, P.O. Box 217
Franklin, IN 46131-2311

Johnson Foundation Wingspread Conference Support   1381
The Johnson Foundation at Wingspread sponsors grants to partially fund conferences focusing on subjects in the public interest, primarily health issues and the environment. Meeting facilities include Wingspread, the home designed by Frank Lloyd Wright, and formerly owned by Herbert Fisk Johnson of the Johnson and Johnson family. Conferences are intensive, one- to four-day meetings of small groups convened in partnership with nonprofit organizations, public agencies, universities, and other foundations. Strategic interests of the Foundation are education, sustainable development and environment, democracy and community, and family. The Foundation's usual contribution to a conference sponsored by one or more other organizations consists of the provision of the full conference facilities of Wingspread, planning and logistical support by the staff, meals and other amenities for the period of the meeting.
Requirements: To be invited to submit a full proposal, applicants first must submit a brief concept letter, consisting of: a clear statement of purpose; a draft agenda; the identification of key participants; and an estimated budget and schedule. The letter should describe how the conference will enhance collaboration and community, include diverse opinions and perspectives, identify solutions, and result in action.
Geographic Focus: All States
Contact: Conference Coordinator; (262) 639-3211; fax (262) 681-3327; info@johnsonfdn.org
Internet: www.johnsonfdn.org/guidelines.html
Sponsor: Johnson Foundation
33 East Four Mile Road
Racine, WI 53402

Johnson Scholarship Foundation Grants   1382
Theodore Johnson and his wife of 52 years, Vivian M. Johnson, placed great faith in education as a means to help people improve their lives. This was based, in part, on personal experience. Mr. Johnson worked his way through college, and after joining United Parcel Service (UPS) in the early 1920s, obtained an MBA at night school. He rose to the position of Vice President of Labor Relations at UPS. He also bought UPS stocks at every opportunity and these appreciated over his lifetime. Mr. Johnson felt that he had been lucky in life and wanted to help deserving people who had been less fortunate. He and his wife created their foundation to fund scholarship and other educational programs which serve people who demonstrate financial need. The foundation's programming is particularly focused on American Indians, people with disabilities, and people who are socially and economically disadvantaged. The foundation's grants committee meets three times/year

and considers grant proposals at each of its meetings. Interested applicants should submit a letter of inquiry. Interested applicants may contact the foundation for further information.
Requirements: Educational institutions and organizations whose mission is to serve disadvantaged or disabled people are eligible to apply.
Restrictions: The foundation does not fund the following types of requests: requests from individuals; travel projects or fellowships; capital improvement projects; routine operating expenses; pre-existing debts; political advocacy; and programs outside of the United States or Canada.
Geographic Focus: All States, Canada
Samples: Florida School for the Deaf and the Blind, St. Augustine, Florida, $574,000 - Education for Life Transition Program; Project Eye-to-Eye, New York, New York, $180,000 - to build the capacity of a young, innovative non-profit organization designed to provide mentors to middle and high school students with learning disabilities; Enterprise Development International, Bethesda, Maryland, $25,000 - to deliver financial literacy training (in partnership with the Emmanuel Gospel Center) to low-to-moderate-income adults living in inner-city Boston.
Contact: Sharon Wood, Office Manager/Program Officer/Grants Administrator; (561) 659-2005; fax (561) 659-1054; wood@jsf.bz
Internet: www.johnsonscholarships.org/index_new.asp?page=/site/grant_inquiries/index.htm
Sponsor: Johnson Scholarship Foundation
505 South Flagler Drive Suite 1460
West Palm Beach, FL 33401

John W. Anderson Foundation Grants   1383
The John W. Anderson Foundation is an independent foundation established in 1967, in Indiana. The trust was established by John W. Anderson, a manufacturing executive and inventor. Mr. Anderson was president of the Anderson Company. Grants support education; organizations serving youth; higher educational institutions; community funds; scientific or medical research for the purpose of alleviating suffering; care of needy, crippled or orphaned children; care of needy persons who are sick, aged or helpless; improving the health, and quality of life of all persons; human services; and the arts and humanities. The Foundation gives primarily in Lake and Porter counties in northwest Indiana.
Requirements: Nonprofit organizations which are not classified as private foundations under Section 509(a) are eligible to apply. Organizations must serve Lake and Porter counties of Northwest Indiana. Application form not required. Applications for grants should include, but not necessarily be limited to, the following information: purpose of organization and proposed use of grant; An organization may submit a request once in a 12-month period. There are no submission deadlines. Each application is reviewed on a timely basis.
Restrictions: Applications sent by fax will not be considered. No support for elementary and secondary schools, or for business or any for-profit organization, or for supporting organizations classified 509(a)3. No grants to individuals, or for endowment funds, multi-year grants, fund raising events, advertising, seed money, deficit financing; no loans.
Geographic Focus: Indiana
Amount of Grant: 5,000 - 50,000 USD
Samples: Brothers' Keeper, Inc., $75,000. Family and Youth Services Bureau of Porter County, $50,000. South Shore Arts, $15,000. The Nazareth Home, $15,000.
Contact: William N. Vinovich, Vice-Chair; (219) 462-4611
Sponsor: John W. Anderson Foundation
402 Wall Street
Valparaiso, IN 46383-2562

Joni Elaine Templeton Foundation Grants   1384
Ms. Templeton was known to all as having a generous heart and a beautiful soul. She was passionate about helping others. She created the Joni Elaine Templeton Foundation to be operated exclusively for religious, charitable, scientific, literary or education purposes or for the prevention of cruelty to children or animals. The average grant award for a grant cycle has been $5,000, but award amounts can range from $2,000 to $10,000.
Requirements: Preference is given to organizations, operating in, or serving the community of Austin, Texas. Grants are awarded to qualified 501(c)3 charitable organizations. Applications will be submitted online through the Bank of America website. A grant report is required within 1 year of the grant application date, regardless of whether all of the funds have been spent.
Restrictions: The foundation does not support requests from individuals, organizations attempting to influence policy through direct lobbying, or any political campaigns.
Geographic Focus: Texas
Date(s) Application is Due: May 1
Amount of Grant: 2,000 - 10,000 USD
Samples: Juvenile Diabetes Research Foundation International, Austin, Texas, $10,000 - Awarded for educational outreach program related for newly diagnosed T1D familieis (2018); Arc of the Capital Area, Austin, Texas, $10,000 - awarded for a capital pledge donation (2018); Hospice Austin, Austin, Texas, $10,000 - awarded for Hospice Austin Charity and unreimbursed care (2018).
Contact: Kelly Garlock, Philanthropic Client Manager; (800) 357-7094; tx.philanthropic@bankofamerica.com or tx.philanthropic@ustrust.com
Internet: www.bankofamerica.com/philanthropic/foundation/?fnId=161
Sponsor: Joni Elaine Templeton Foundation
Bank of America NA, P.O. Box 831
Dallas, TX 75283-1041

Joseph H. and Florence A. Roblee Foundation Children and Youth Grants   1385
The Joseph H. and Florence A. Roblee Foundation is dedicated to promoting change by supporting organizations that improve quality of life and help individuals to fulfill their

potential. The Foundation arises out of a Judeo-Christian framework and values ecumenical endeavors, and particularly supports programs that work to break down cultural, racial, ethnic, religious, gender, and identity barriers. awards grants to enable organizations to promote change by addressing significant social issues in order to improve the quality of life and help fulfill the potential of individuals. Organizations and churches are encouraged to collaborate in achieving positive change through advocacy, prevention, and systemic improvements. In the area of children and youth, the Foundation supports programs that: provide early childhood services; prevent and address teen pregnancy; prevent and address substance abuse; prevent and address violence and abuse; improve the foster care system; protect and support LGBTQ youth; and provide professional development for child care providers. Types of support include: capacity building; technical assistance; startup funds; planning grants; policy development; advocacy; scholarships; capital support; and endowments. There is a two-part application process: first, organizations should submit the Roblee Foundation Proposal Summary and one page budget; second, invited applicants should submit a full proposal and all required attachments. This entire process should be completed via the Missouri Common Grant Application format. Currently, the Foundation has two funding cycles, with application submission deadlines of January 5 and June 15. The majority of grant awards range from $3,000 to $20,000.
Requirements: The Roblee Foundation, established in 1971, is based in St. Louis, and accepts applications for grants in metropolitan St. Louis, Missouri and Miami-Dade in Florida. First time applicants to the Foundation are required to call foundation staff to explore a project's funding potential.
Restrictions: The Foundation does not award grants to individuals. Unsolicited proposals for support of the arts, medical research, environmental concerns, or other projects outside the stated program areas or geographic regions will not be considered.
Geographic Focus: Florida, Missouri
Date(s) Application is Due: Jan 5; Jun 15
Amount of Grant: 1,000 - 30,000 USD
Samples: Aim High, St. Louis, Missouri, $10,000 - operating funds for academic enhancement program for youth in under served schools; Joe's Place, St. Louis, Missouri, $10,000 - operating expenses for group living home for homeless youth in Maplewood Richmond Heights school district; Pridelines Youth Service, Miami, Florida, $18,000 - operating support for LGBTQ youth programs and services.
Contact: Jane Callahan, Executive Director; (314) 963-7713 or (888) 522-6074; grantapplication@robleefoundation.org
Internet: www.robleefoundation.org/applying.php
Sponsor: Joseph H. and Florence A. Roblee Foundation
8816 Manchester Road, #296
Saint Louis, MO 63144

Joseph H. and Florence A. Roblee Foundation Education Grants   1386

The Joseph H. and Florence A. Roblee Foundation is dedicated to promoting change by supporting organizations that improve quality of life and help individuals to fulfill their potential. The Foundation arises out of a Judeo-Christian framework and values ecumenical endeavors, and particularly supports programs that work to break down cultural, racial, ethnic, religious, gender, and identity barriers. awards grants to enable organizations to promote change by addressing significant social issues in order to improve the quality of life and help fulfill the potential of individuals. Organizations and churches are encouraged to collaborate in achieving positive change through advocacy, prevention, and systemic improvements. In the area of education, the Foundation hopes to improve learning through: supporting systemic change; teacher training and recruitment; elevating the status of teaching; addressing the achievement gap; assuring children enter elementary school ready to learn; and developing the love of learning. Types of support include: capacity building; technical assistance; startup funds; planning grants; policy development; advocacy; scholarships; capital support; and endowments. There is a two-part application process: first, organizations should submit the Roblee Foundation Proposal Summary and one page budget; second, invited applicants should submit a full proposal and all required attachments. This entire process should be completed via the Missouri Common Grant Application format. Currently, the Foundation has two funding cycles, with application submission deadlines of January 5 and June 15. The majority of grant awards range from $3,000 to $20,000.
Requirements: The Roblee Foundation, established in 1971, is based in St. Louis, and accepts applications for grants in metropolitan St. Louis, Missouri and Miami-Dade in Florida. First time applicants to the Foundation are required to call foundation staff to explore a project's funding potential.
Restrictions: The Foundation does not award grants to individuals. Unsolicited proposals for support of the arts, medical research, environmental concerns, or other projects outside the stated program areas or geographic regions will not be considered.
Geographic Focus: Florida, Missouri
Date(s) Application is Due: Jan 5; Jun 15
Amount of Grant: 1,000 - 30,000 USD
Samples: City Academy, St. Louis, Missouri, $8,300 - support of partial costs of salary for Early Childhood Education Specialists; Cornerstone Center for Early Learning, St. Louis, Missouri, $6,610 - support of n-site therapy program for children with developmental delays; Mindful Kids Miami. Miami, Florida, $10,000 - support of Ongoing Mindfulness Training for Miami-Dade County Public Schools.
Contact: Jane Callahan, Executive Director; (314) 963-7713 or (888) 522-6074; grantapplication@robleefoundation.org
Internet: www.robleefoundation.org/applying.php
Sponsor: Joseph H. and Florence A. Roblee Foundation
8816 Manchester Road, #296
Saint Louis, MO 63144

Joseph H. and Florence A. Roblee Foundation Family Grants   1387

The Joseph H. and Florence A. Roblee Foundation is dedicated to promoting change by supporting organizations that improve quality of life and help individuals to fulfill their potential. The Foundation arises out of a Judeo-Christian framework and values ecumenical endeavors, and particularly supports programs that work to break down cultural, racial, ethnic, religious, gender, and identity barriers. awards grants to enable organizations to promote change by addressing significant social issues in order to improve the quality of life and help fulfill the potential of individuals. Organizations and churches are encouraged to collaborate in achieving positive change through advocacy, prevention, and systemic improvements. In the area of families, the Foundation funds: parenting education; family support programs; and advancing the rights of and encourage services for alternative-model families. Types of support include: capacity building; technical assistance; startup funds; planning grants; policy development; advocacy; scholarships; capital support; and endowments. There is a two-part application process: first, organizations should submit the Roblee Foundation Proposal Summary and one page budget; second, invited applicants should submit a full proposal and all required attachments. This entire process should be completed via the Missouri Common Grant Application format. Currently, the Foundation has two funding cycles, with application submission deadlines of January 5 and June 15. The majority of grant awards range from $3,000 to $20,000.
Requirements: The Roblee Foundation, established in 1971, is based in St. Louis, and accepts applications for grants in metropolitan St. Louis, Missouri and Miami-Dade in Florida. Occasionally, funding is provided in this area of support outside of these primary areas. First time applicants to the Foundation are required to call foundation staff to explore a project's funding potential.
Restrictions: The Foundation does not award grants to individuals. Unsolicited proposals for support of the arts, medical research, environmental concerns, or other projects outside the stated program areas or geographic regions will not be considered.
Geographic Focus: All States, Florida, Missouri
Date(s) Application is Due: Jan 5; Jun 15
Amount of Grant: 1,000 - 30,000 USD
Samples: Foster and Adoptive Care Coalition, St. Louis, Missouri, $15,000 - support of the 30 Days to Family program; Grace Hill Settlement House, St. Louis, Missouri, $10,000 - operating support for the Family Support Program at Clay Elementary School; Hoyleton Youth and Family Services, Fairview Heights, Illinois, $12,695 - support for Network of Voices Against Trafficking and Exploitation.
Contact: Jane Callahan, Executive Director; (314) 963-7713 or (888) 522-6074; grantapplication@robleefoundation.org
Internet: www.robleefoundation.org/applying.php
Sponsor: Joseph H. and Florence A. Roblee Foundation
8816 Manchester Road, #296
Saint Louis, MO 63144

Joseph Henry Edmondson Foundation Grants   1388

The Joseph Henry Edmondson Foundation serves the Pikes Peak Region. While grants have been awarded outside this geographic area under unique circumstances, most funding is confined to supporting those nonprofits in this region. The Foundation's primary interests include: welfare of children, the incapacitated, homeless, families, and the elderly; preservation and improvement of the environment and natural resources; the arts; education; health care; community improvements; and charitable outreach. It will consider grant requests for general operations, specific projects, programs, capital needs, and capacity building. The Board of Directors reviews grant proposals at quarterly meetings held in January, April, July, and October. Deadlines for submission are December 1, March 1, June 1, and September 1. Grants range in size from $500 to $100,000 with an average of $10,000.
Requirements: All organizations applying to the Foundation must be a nonprofit, tax-exempt 501(c)3 organization; or be a project or organization under the fiscal agency of a 501(c)3 organization. The Foundation transitioned to an on-line grant application process.
Restrictions: The Foundation does not support the following: organizations that have not secured their legal 501(c)3 designation from the IRS or are not under the fiscal agency of a nonprofit; individuals; special and/or fundraising events; debt reduction; and organizations with an evangelical mission.
Geographic Focus: Colorado
Date(s) Application is Due: Mar 1; Jun 1; Sep 1; Dec 1
Amount of Grant: 500 - 100,000 USD
Contact: Heather L, Carroll, Executive Director; (719) 471-1241
Internet: www.jhedmondson.org/grants-seekers
Sponsor: Joseph Henry Edmondson Foundation
10 Lake Circle
Colorado Springs, CO 80906

Josephine Schell Russell Charitable Trust Grants   1389

The Josephine Schell Russell Charitable Trust was established in Ohio in 1976, with giving limited to supporting the economically disadvantaged in the greater Cincinnati area. The Trust's primary fields of interest include: the arts; children and youth services; health care and health care access; and human services. Types of support include: building and renovation; capital campaigns; equipment purchase or rental; program development; and seed money. Interested applicants should submit one copy of either the Ohio Common Grant Form or the Greater Cincinnati Common Grant Form to the Trust office. Initial approach can also be via telephone contact. The annual quarterly deadlines are February 1, May 1, August 1, and October 1. Most recent awards have ranged from $5,500 to $100,000.
Requirements: 501(c)3 organizations either located in, or serving residents of, the greater Cincinnati area are eligible to apply.
Restrictions: No support is offered for private foundations, or for political, fraternal, labor or advocacy groups. Furthermore, no grants are awarded to individuals, or for endowment

funds, operating budgets, continuing support, annual campaigns, deficit financing, scholarships, or conferences.
Geographic Focus: Kentucky, Ohio
Date(s) Application is Due: Feb 1; May 1; Aug 1; Oct 1
Amount of Grant: 5,500 - 100,000 USD
Samples: Lighthouse Youth Services, Cincinnati, Ohio, $100,000 - support of the Sheakley Center; Humanitarian League, Union, Kentucky, $10,000 - support of a bully prevention program; Cancer Support Community, Cincinnati, Ohio, $60,000 - support for the Heart of Wellness program.
Contact: Mary Alice Koch, Trustee; (513) 651-8463 or (412) 768-5898; mary.koch@pnc.com
Internet: www1.pnc.com/pncfoundation/charitable_trusts.html
Sponsor: Josephine Schell Russell Charitable Trust
One PNC Plaza, 249 Fifth Avenue, 20th Floor
Pittsburgh, PA 15222

Joseph S. Stackpole Charitable Trust Grants   1390
The Joseph S. Stackpole Charitable Trust was established in 1957 to support and promote quality educational and human-services programming for underserved populations. Preference is given to charitable organizations that serve the people of Hartford County, Connecticut. The Stackpole Charitable Trust makes approximately ten to fifteen grants each year. The grant range is $1,000 to $1,500 and grants are one year in duration. Applicants are strongly encouraged to do the following before applying: review the downloadable state application procedures for additional helpful information and clarifications; review the downloadable online-application guidelines at the grant website; review the trust's funding history; review the online application questions in advance; and review the list of required attachments. These will generally include: a list of board members, financial statements (audited, reviewed, or compiled by independent auditor); an organization summary; a list of other funding sources; an IRS Determination letter; and other required documents. All attachments must be uploaded in the online application as PDF, Word, or Excel files.
Requirements: First time applicants are asked to contact the Executive Director before applying to the Stackpole Charitable Trust. Applicants must be classified by the Internal Revenue Service (IRS) as a 501(c)3 public charity.
Restrictions: Grant requests for capital projects will not be considered. Applicants will not be awarded a grant for more than 3 consecutive years. The trust does not support requests from individuals, organizations attempting to influence policy through direct lobbying, or any political campaigns.
Geographic Focus: Connecticut
Amount of Grant: 1,000 - 1,500 USD
Contact: Carol Hauss, Executive Director; (860) 233-3853; fax (860) 838-6442; cj.hauss@lvgh.org
Internet: lvgh.org/Donor/stackpole-charitable-trust/
Sponsor: Joseph S. Stackpole Charitable Trust
30 Arbor Street
Hartford, CT 06106

Journal Gazette Foundation Grants   1391
The Journal Gazette Foundation awards grants to northeastern Indiana nonprofit organizations in its areas of interest, including community funds, education, higher education, health organizations and hospitals, social services, Christian agencies and churches, and youth. Types of support include general operations and capital campaigns. There are no application deadlines; the board meets quarterly to make award decisions. Most recent grants have ranged from $1,000 to $10,000.
Requirements: Indiana nonprofit organizations are eligible to apply. Preference is given to requests from northeastern Indiana.
Restrictions: Grants are not made to individuals.
Geographic Focus: Indiana
Amount of Grant: 1,000 - 10,000 USD
Samples: Audiences Unlimited, Fort Wayne, Indiana, $4,000 - transportation expenses to local fine arts programs for the elderly and disabled; Euell A. Wilson Center, Fort Wayne, Indiana, $5,000 - program assistance; Indiana University School of Journalism, Bloomington, Indiana, $10,000 - support for scholarship fund.
Contact: Customer Service; (260) 424-5257 or (260) 461-8519
Internet: www.journalgazette.net/
Sponsor: Journal Gazette Foundation
600 W. Main Street, P.O. Box 88
Fort Wayne, IN 46802-1498

Jovid Foundation Employment Training Grants   1392
The Jovid Foundation is a philanthropic foundation incorporated in 1990 in the District of Columbia. The Foundation's primary interest is in supporting District of Columbia nonprofit organizations that help District residents in or at risk of long-term poverty to become more self-sufficient. Because the Foundation is small and seeks to make a positive difference, it is particularly interested in funding neighborhood-based efforts that provide employment training programs and services to low-income D.C. adults that help them obtain and retain permanent jobs. In addition, a small number of grants may be made from a discretionary fund. Because the Foundation does not have the staff to review lengthy submissions, it does not accept unsolicited proposals that are already fully developed. The Foundation requests a letter of inquiry (LOI) describing the proposed project. Even if your organization has received funding from Jovid in the past, a new letter of inquiry must first be submitted. Annual deadlines for Letters of Inquiry are January 7, April 8, and August 12. If a full proposal is requested, annual application deadlines are February 11, May 6, and September 9.

Requirements: Washington, D.C., nonprofits are eligible to apply.
Geographic Focus: District of Columbia
Date(s) Application is Due: Feb 11; May 6; Sep 9
Amount of Grant: Up to 20,000 USD
Samples: Byte Back, Washington, D.C., $20,000 - support for computer training; Concerned Black Men, Washington, D.C., $10,000 - support for the Family Services Center; Employment Justice Center, Washington, D.C., $7,500 - support of the Legal Services Program.
Contact: Bob Wittig, Executive Director; (202) 686-2616; fax (202) 686-2621; jovidfoundation@gmail.com
Internet: fdnweb.org/jovid/employment-training-program/
Sponsor: Jovid Foundation
5335 Wisconsin Avenue NW, Suite 440
Washington, D.C. 20015-2003

Joyce and Randy Seckman Charitable Foundation Grants   1393
The Joyce and Randy Seckman Charitable Foundation was established in Georgia in 2000, with the primary purpose of supporting arts and culture, elementary and secondary education, and religious groups. With a geographic focus of the South, and an emphasis on Georgia and North Carolina, most recent awards have ranged from $500 to $22,000. There are no specific annual deadlines, and applications are accepted on a rolling basis. Interested organizations should forward a letter of application directly to the Foundation office, outlining the organization history, the project details, and the amount requested.
Requirements: Any 501(c)3 serving the residents of the Southern states of Alabama, Georgia, Florida, Kentucky, Ohio, North Carolina, or South Carolina are eligible to apply.
Geographic Focus: Alabama, Florida, Georgia, Kentucky, North Carolina, Ohio, South Carolina
Amount of Grant: 500 - 22,000 USD
Samples: St. Francis School, Roswell, Georgia, $1,000 - general operating support; Cincinnati Children's Hospital, Cincinnati, Ohio, $21,534 - general operating support; Chattahoochee Nature Center, Roswell, Georgia, $1,000 - general operating support.
Contact: Joyce Seckman, President; (404) 564-2460 or (850) 916-1548
Sponsor: Joyce and Randy Seckman Charitable Foundation
1454 Waterford Green Court
Marietta, GA 30068

JP Morgan Chase Foundation Arts and Culture Grants   1394
The foundation supports programs in the New York tri-state region, across the nation, and around the world that strengthen communities where JP Morgan Chase employees live and work. In its Arts and Culture grantmaking, the Foundation looks for opportunities to integrate the arts into children's educational opportunities and position arts organizations and artists as key drivers of local economic renewal. The Foundation supports: arts programs in schools and after school; building the capacity of community-based arts institutions; initiatives that stimulate the creation and growth of local cultural economies; broadening of access to artistic excellence and diversity by partnering with major arts and culture groups.
Requirements: Only charitable, not-for-profit organizations are eligible to apply. Refer to the website in order to identify the region in which your program will be administered.
Restrictions: The following types of organizations, activities or purposes are not funded: programs outside the geographic markets we serve; individuals; fraternal organizations; athletic teams or social groups; public agencies; private schools; public schools (K-12), unless in partnership with a qualified not-for-profit organization; parent-teacher associations; scholarships or tuition assistance; higher education, unless program is specifically within guidelines; fundraising events (e.g. golf outings, school events); advertising, including ads in event, performance or athletic programs; volunteer-operated organizations; funds to pay down operating deficits; programs designed to promote religious or political doctrines; endowments or capital campaigns (exceptions are made by invitation only); organizations that discriminate on the basis of race, sex, sexual orientation, age or religion; health or medical-related organizations, unless program fits within stated giving guidelines.
Geographic Focus: Arizona, California, Colorado, Connecticut, Delaware, Florida, Illinois, Indiana, Kentucky, Louisiana, Michigan, New Jersey, New York, Ohio, Oklahoma, Texas, Utah, West Virginia, Wisconsin
Contact: Kimberly B. Davis, President; (212) 270-6000
Internet: www.jpmorganchase.com/corporate/Corporate-Responsibility/global-philanthropy.htm
Sponsor: JP Morgan Chase Foundation
270 Park Avenue
New York, NY 10017

Judith Clark-Morrill Foundation Grants   1395
Established in Indiana, the Judith Clark-Morrill Foundation has specified its primary fields of interest as: the arts; community and economic development; education; and youth development. An application form is required, and there are two annual deadlines: June 1 and December 1. Amount of awards range from $1,000 to $30,000.
Restrictions: No grants are given to individuals, or for student groups, scholarships, annual campaigns, general operating support, travel, or advertising. There are no loans or multi-year grants.
Geographic Focus: Indiana
Date(s) Application is Due: Jun 1; Dec 1
Amount of Grant: 1,000 - 30,000 USD
Samples: St. Martin's Health Care Services, Garrett, Indiana, $25,000 - purchase of medical supplies; Purdue Foundation, West Lafayette, Indiana, $1,000 - donation; Catholic Charities of Fort Wayne, Fort Wayne, Indiana, $3,659 - purchase vehicle to transport food.
Contact: Judith Morrill, President; (260) 357-4141

Sponsor: Judith Clark-Morrill Foundation
P.O. Box 180
Garrett, IN 46738-1350

Judy and Peter Blum Kovler Foundation Grants 1396

The chairman of the board of the Judy and Peter Blum Kovler Foundation and the founder of the Marjorie Kovler Center for Survivors of Torture, Peter Kovler describes his life in philanthropy as the result of a series of accidents, starting with being born into a family that started a foundation. So when he was in his late 20s, he left his career as a journalist and transitioned to giving all his attention to the Kovler Foundation. This stance is an extension of, rather than a break from, his time as a reporter, during which he penned op-eds for The New York Times about the need for humanitarian policy in Southeast Asia and produced three documentaries about world events. One of those documentaries, Hotel Terminus: The Life and Times of Klaus Barbie, won an Academy Award in 1988 for its portrayal of a Nazi criminal who oversaw the occupation in Lyon, France. On the philanthropy side, he still works on projects that aren't the best "dinner table conversation," such as the foundation's work supporting research into pancreatic cancer—which both his mother and grandfather died from—and helping survivors of torture. Other projects are easier to discuss, he says, pointing to their steadfast support of culturally important civic spaces like the Franklin Delano Roosevelt Memorial, an exhibition about Emmett Till at the Smithsonian's National Museum of African American History and Culture, the United States Holocaust Memorial Museum, the Barack Obama Presidential Center, and the new Statue of Liberty Museum that opened on Liberty Island in May 2019. Today, the Judy and Peter Blum Kovler Foundation Grants was founded in Washington, D.C., in 1957, supports arts and culture, children and youth programs, families in crisis, civic affairs, health and health care access, research, and social services. There are no annual deadlines or application formats, and interested organizations should contact the Foundation directly.

Geographic Focus: All States, American Samoa, District of Columbia, Guam, Marshall Islands, Northern Mariana Islands, Puerto Rico, U.S. Virgin Islands

Amount of Grant: Up to 50,000 USD

Samples: After School All-Stars, Los Angeles, California, $5,000 - general operating support (2018); Alliance for Justice, Washington, D.C., $30,000 - general operating support (2018); Clifton Foundation, Little Rock, Arkansas, $50,000 - general operating support (2018).

Contact: Peter Kovler, Director; (312) 664-5050 or (202) 466-0581

Sponsor: Judy and Peter Blum Kovler Foundation
2101 L Street NW, Suite 400
Washington, D.C. 20037

Julia and Tunnicliff Fox Charitable Trust Grants 1397

The Julia and Tunnicliff Fox Charitable Trust was established to provide funding to organizations in the Commonwealth of Virginia primarily for cultural purposes, such as music, art and education. A secondary mission of the Charitable Trust is to benefit disabled and handicapped children and adults through programs and projects, rather than for scientific or medical purposes. The annual application deadline is April 1. Applicants will be notified of funding decisions by July 31.

Requirements: Any 501(c)3 organization supporting the residents of the central Virginia region is eligible to apply. Preference will be given to specific, well-defined project requests for which the results can be evaluated.

Restrictions: In general, requests for general operating support, capital support, and endowments are rarely awarded. Contributions are not made to periodic campaigns for funds by national or community organizations. Requests for support from an organization which has received a grant from the trust will be considered no sooner than three years from the previous grant.

Geographic Focus: Virginia

Contact: Sarah Kay, Vice President; (804) 887-8773; sarah.kay@ustrust.com

Internet: www.bankofamerica.com/philanthropic/foundation.go?fnId=171

Sponsor: Julia and Tunnicliff Fox Charitable Trust
1111 E. Main Street, VA2-300-12-92
Richmond, VA 23219

Julia Richardson Brown Foundation Grants 1398

Established in California in 1997, the Julia Richardson Brown Foundation offers support in its primary fields of interest, which include: the arts, education, and youth development. A specific application form is not required, and there are no specified annual deadlines for submission requests. Most recently, grant awards have ranged from $250 up to $60,000, and were given to non-profit organizations in California, Massachusetts, and Utah. Most awards, however, are given in the San Diego area.

Geographic Focus: California, Massachusetts, Utah

Amount of Grant: 250 - 60,000 USD

Samples: San Diego Symphony, San Diego, CA, $29,250 - opening night sponsor; Brigham Young University, Provo, UT, $7,500 - training awards for Ballroom Dance program; Museum of Photographic Arts, San Diego, CA, $3,000 - education programs.

Contact: Julia Richardson Brown, President; (858) 566-9325

Sponsor: Julia Richardson Brown Foundation
11480 Forestview Lane
San Diego, CA 92131-2318

Julia Temple Davis Brown Foundation Grants 1399

The Foundation, established in 1969, is interested in supporting children and youth programs. Because of the limited size of the trust fund, and limited income available for distribution, the general policy has been to give fewer, but more meaningful grants, rather than spreading the income in smaller amounts to more organizations. The priority has been

to the education of youth, from pre-school through high school, with emphasis on the lower age youngsters. Most recently, the Distribution Committee revised the grant emphasis to continue the focus on youth, but to stress youth programs relating to culture and arts, and the environment. Applications, which can be downloaded, should be postmarked by April 1.

Requirements: Only 501(c)3 organizations serving Hawaii are eligible to apply. Applicants will be notified in writing of the action taken on their requests. The recipient of a grant will be required to submit a narrative report specific to the Foundation's Reporting Guidelines on what has been accomplished as a result of the grant, and a fiscal accounting of the grant expenditures.

Geographic Focus: Hawaii

Date(s) Application is Due: Apr 1

Contact: Paula Boyce, Grants Administration Officer; (808) 538-4945 or (808) 538-4540; fax (808) 538-4006; paula.boyce@boh.com

Elaine Moniz, Administrative Assistant; (808) 694-4944 or (808) 538-4540; fax (808) 538-4006; elaine.moniz@boh.com

Internet: www.boh.com/apps/foundations/FoundationDetails.
aspx?foundation=6&show=0#

Sponsor: Julia Temple Davis Brown Foundation
Charitable Foundation Services #758, P.O. Box 3170
Honolulu, HI 96802-3170

Julius N. Frankel Foundation Grants 1400

The Julius N. Frankel Foundation supports Chicago-area nonprofits in the areas of: arts and performing arts; children and youth service; higher education; hospitals; human services; and medical school education. Recipients have included hospitals, universities, cultural organizations, and social service providers, with an emphasis on large, established organizations. There are no specified application formats or deadlines, though the Board meets at least five times annually. Most recent grant awards have ranged from $25,000 to $200,000. The initial approach should be by letter, detailing the program and budget.

Requirements: Chicago-area nonprofits are eligible to apply.

Restrictions: Individuals are not eligible.

Geographic Focus: Illinois

Amount of Grant: 25,000 - 200,000 USD

Samples: Chicago Opera Theater, Chicago, Illinois, $45,000 - general operations; Chicago Symphony Orchestra, Chicago, Illinois, $150,000 - general support; Lawrence Hall Youth Services, Chicago, Illinois, $50,000 - general operating support.

Contact: Hector Ahumada, Trustee; (312) 461-5154

Sponsor: Julius N. Frankel Foundation
111 W. Monroe Street, Tax Division 10C
Chicago, IL 60603-4096

KaBOOM! Adventure Courses Grant 1401

This new type of playspace was developed in response to the demands of kids and communities looking to engage older kids and teenagers. Through our signature community-build model and with the leadership of our Project Managers, communities will design and build an amazing playspace aimed at kids and teens, aged 10 and older. Adventure course playspaces provide a fun, challenging option for physical activity.

Requirements: To qualify, applicants must: serve youth from low-income population and demonstrate the need for engaging space for older kids; engage older kids and teenagers, 13-years and older, in the planning process; work with the community, with guidance from a dedicated KABOOM! Project Manager, to fundraise toward the cost of equipment; own the land on which you wish to build, or have a long-term lease and get permission from the landowner to construct an adventure course; demonstrate ability to recruit a team of parents, neighbors, teenagers and community members who are excited about serving on the planning committee for a six to eight week period, plus recruit approximately 100-200 community members to participate on Build Day; complete any needed site preparation on at least 3,500 to 4,000 square feet in order to create a flat, dirt surface (e.g., removing old equipment or asphalt, etc.); secure soil tests, utility checks, and build permits in a timely manner; identify community resources to secure additional in-kind contributions such as breakfast and lunch for Build Week, tools, restroom facilities and a dumpster; and accept ownership and maintenance responsibilities for the playspace upon completion of project.

Geographic Focus: All States

Contact: Lindsay Adeyiga, Director; (202) 659-0215; info@kaboom.org

Internet: kaboom.org/grants/adventure-courses

Sponsor: KaBOOM!
4301 Connecticut Avenue NW, Suite ML-1
Washington, D.C. 20008

KaBOOM! Build it Grant 1402

Build it with KABOOM! pairs one of KaBOOM's dedicated funding partners with a community partner who then come together to plan and build a brand-new playground. KaBOOM's community-built playgrounds generate a tangible, achievable win for your community, transforming your space into a great place to play for kids and families.

Requirements: To qualify, projects must: serve a low-income and/or special needs community; have no playground or need to replace an existing unsafe or outdated one; work with the community, with guidance from a dedicated KABOOM! Project Manager, to fundraise toward the cost of equipment; own the land on which you wish to build, or have a long-term lease and get permission from the landowner to construct a playground; demonstrate ability to recruit a team of parents, neighbors, and community members who are excited about serving on the planning committee for an eight to ten week period, plus recruit approximately 100 community members to participate on Build Day; complete any needed site preparation on at least 2,500 square feet in order to create a flat, dirt surface (e.g., removing old equipment or asphalt, etc.); secure soil tests, utility checks, and build

permits in a timely manner; identify community resources to secure additional in-kind contributions such as breakfast and lunch for Build Week, tools, restroom facilities, and a dumpster; and accept ownership and maintenance responsibilities for the playspace upon completion of project.
Geographic Focus: Arizona, California, Colorado, District of Columbia, Florida, Georgia, Illinois, Indiana, Louisiana, Maryland, Michigan, Minnesota, Nebraska, New York, North Carolina, Ohio, Oregon, Tennessee, Texas, Utah, Virginia, Washington, Canada
Contact: Lindsay Adeyiga, Director; (202) 659-0215; grants@kaboom.org
Internet: kaboom.org/grants/build-it-with-kaboom
Sponsor: KaBOOM!
4301 Connecticut Avenue NW, Suite ML-1
Washington, D.C. 20008

KaBOOM! Creative Play Grant   1403
Imagination Playground™ is an innovative design in play equipment that encourages creativity, communication, and collaboration in play. With a collection of custom-designed, oversized blue foam parts, Imagination Playground™ provides a changing array of elements that allow children to turn their playground into a space constantly built and re-built by their imagination. Applications are accepted on a rolling-basis.
Requirements: Municipalities, schools, and child-serving nonprofit organizations are eligible for this opportunity. Applications must: demonstrate need for a Creative Play grant; give evidence of available space and the ability to maintain the Imagination Playground™ in a Cart or Rigamajig®; give anticipated impact that the grant will have on the community and increased play opportunities; and show how demonstrated impact on low income areas and the number of children the grant will serve.
Geographic Focus: All States
Contact: Lindsay Adeyiga, Director; (202) 659-0215; info@kaboom.org
Internet: kaboom.org/grants/creative-play
Sponsor: KaBOOM!
4301 Connecticut Avenue NW, Suite ML-1
Washington, D.C. 20008

KaBOOM! Multi-Sport Courts Grant   1404
Developed in response to the demands of kids, KABOOM! is introducing our newest playspace innovation: Multi-Sport Courts! Sports courts help communities address a lack of play opportunities for older youth that no longer play on playgrounds. The interlocking tiles are easy to install and maintain. Sports courts provide communities with a wide variety of different sports using the same space— such as basketball, hockey, volleyball and many other games.
Requirements: To qualify, applicants must: serve youth from low-income population and demonstrate the need for an engaging space for kids and older youth to play sports; work with the community, with guidance from a dedicated KABOOM! Project Manager, to fundraise toward the cost of equipment; own the land on which you wish to build, or have a long-term lease and get permission from the landowner to construct a sports court; demonstrate ability to recruit a team of parents, neighbors, and community members who are excited about serving on the planning committee for an eight to ten week period, plus recruit approximately 125-200 community members to participate on Build Day; complete any needed site preparation to create a flat asphalt or concrete slab with dimensions from 3,000 sq.ft. to 3,500 sq.ft; secure soil tests, utility checks, and build permits in a timely manner; identify community resources to secure additional in-kind contributions such as breakfast and lunch for Build Week, tools, restroom facilities and a dumpster; and accept ownership and maintenance responsibilities for the sports court upon completion of project.
Geographic Focus: All States
Contact: Lindsay Adeyiga, Director; (202) 659-0215; apply@kaboom.org
Internet: kaboom.org/grants/multi-sport-courts
Sponsor: KaBOOM!
4301 Connecticut Avenue NW, Suite ML-1
Washington, D.C. 20008

KaBOOM! Play Everywhere Design Challenge   1405
The Play Everywhere Design Challenge, supported by the Ralph C. Wilson Jr. Foundation, will award $1 million to communities in Southeast Michigan and Western New York. KABOOM! and the Built to Play initiative, supported by the Ralph C. Wilson, Jr. Foundation, proudly present the Play Everywhere Design Challenge. This design challenge will award $1 million to communities building landmark playspaces that provide kids with equitable opportunities to play. The deadline to apply is October 30th with an early bird and ideal form deadline on August 7th and September 11th, respectively. The award amounts to $1,000,000.
Requirements: To be eligible for a grant, the project must be within the following regions: Southeast Michigan counties: Livingston, Macomb, Monroe, Oakland, St. Clair, Washtenaw and Wayne; Western New York counties: Allegany, Cattaraugus, Chautauqua, Erie, Genesee, Niagara, Orleans, Monroe and Wyoming. In addition, the applicant must be either a registered 501(c)3 nonprofit; a federal, state, or local governmental body or agency; or an entity or individual partnering with a registered 501(c)3 nonprofit acting as a fiscal sponsor. Finally, all applicants must agree to and comply with the Play Everywhere Design Challenge Official Rules.
Geographic Focus: Michigan, New York
Date(s) Application is Due: Oct 30
Amount of Grant: 1,000,000 USD
Contact: Lindsay Adeyiga, Director; (202) 659-0215; fax (202) 659-0210; info@kaboom.org
Internet: kaboom.org/grants/play-everywhere-design-challenge

Sponsor: KaBOOM!
4301 Connecticut Avenue NW, Suite ML-1
Washington, D.C. 20008

Kaiser Permanente Hawaii Region Community Grants   1406
The Kaiser Permanente Hawaii Region Community Grants Program responds to requests from organizations that provide health service regionally throughout Hawaii. From year to year, grant funding priorities can include: community health initiatives, safety net partnerships, care and coverage, and developing and disseminating knowledge. Kaiser Permanente considers funding requests for both sponsorships and grants.
Requirements: Kaiser Permanente considers funding for nonprofit organizations, local government-sponsored projects and educational institutions, with some exceptions. Organizations applying for funding should be prepared to demonstrate that they do not discriminate on the basis of race, color, religious creed, national origin, age, sex, marital status, sexual orientation, gender identity, handicap, disability, medical condition or veteran status, either in their employment or their service policies and practices.
Restrictions: KP Community Grants will not fund: non-charity golf tournament; sports teams; individuals; religious purposes; partisan political activity; events or activities sponsored by alcohol or tobacco corporations; or organizations that promotes the use of alcohol or tobacco.
Geographic Focus: Hawaii
Contact: Nina Y. Miyata, (808) 432-5673; nina.y.miyata@kp.org
Internet: share.kaiserpermanente.org/article/hawaii-grants/
Sponsor: Kaiser Permanente-Hawaii Region
2828 Pa'a Street, Suite 3080
Honolulu, HI 96819

Kalamazoo Community Foundation Early Childhood Learning   1407
and School Readiness Grants
The Kalamazoo Community Foundation envisions a community where all children have an equal chance for learning, growth and development; where children get what they need to begin their education fully prepared in mind, body and spirit; where literacy is nurtured and reinforced at home; and where students are prepared with the skills and competencies they need to succeed in school. Therefore, we invest in quality programs that are informed by best practices and: support literacy-rich home environments that support education and learning; provide parents with resources to help them prepare their children for school; develop pre-literacy skills for children ages 0 to 3, and reinforce literacy and language skills for children ages 3 through 10; break down social, physical, emotional and other barriers to teaching and learning; and facilitate collaboration and continuity among local agencies that address early childhood learning and school readiness. Applications for Early Childhood Learning and School Readiness grants are accepted in April and October.
Requirements: Kalamazoo, Michigan, organizations recognized (or in the process of applying for recognition) under IRS code 501(c)3 are encouraged to contact foundation staff before submitting a request to determine eligibility.
Restrictions: Generally, the foundation does not provide funding for debt retirement, endowments, individuals, travel, religious organizations for religious purposes, meetings, conferences, publications, films, or television and radio programming.
Geographic Focus: Michigan
Date(s) Application is Due: Apr 1; Oct 1
Contact: Jessica Aguilera, Community Investment Manager; (269) 381-4416; fax (269) 381-3146; jaguilera@kalfound.org or info@kalfound.org
Internet: www.kalfound.org/page8490.cfm
Sponsor: Kalamazoo Community Foundation
151 South Rose Street, Suite 332
Kalamazoo, MI 49007-4775

Kalamazoo Community Foundation Good Neighbor Grants   1408
The Good Neighbor Grant program reaches out to individuals and small, grassroots groups to support their efforts in turning their ideas into projects to benefit the Kalamazoo community. These grants place resources for change in the hands of those closest to the issues that need to be addressed, which enables and empowers them to be good neighbors. Grants provide up to $1,000 of support to projects that: enhance bridges between people who are different from each other in some significant way (e.g. race, religion, economic status); engage people—especially those who haven't participated in community activities before—in projects that make a difference in the lives of all those involved; and embrace youths by involving them in project planning and/or providing leadership opportunities.
Requirements: Kalamazoo, Michigan, organizations are encouraged to contact foundation staff before submitting a request to determine eligibility.
Restrictions: Generally, the foundation does not provide funding for debt retirement, endowments, individuals, travel, religious organizations for religious purposes, meetings, conferences, publications, films, or television and radio programming.
Geographic Focus: Michigan
Amount of Grant: Up to 1,000 USD
Contact: Jessica Aguilera, Community Investment Manager; (269) 381-4416; fax (269) 381-3146; jaguilera@kalfound.org or info@kalfound.org
Internet: www.kalfound.org/Grants/GoodNeighborGrants/tabid/291/Default.aspx
Sponsor: Kalamazoo Community Foundation
151 South Rose Street, Suite 332
Kalamazoo, MI 49007-4775

Kalamazoo Community Foundation Individuals and Families Grants   **1409**

The Kalamazoo Community Foundation envisions a community where individuals and families are fully equipped to meet their basic needs, become self-sufficient, maintain their dignity and thrive. Therefore, we invest in quality programs that are informed by best practices and support basic needs, such as: emergency shelter and transitional housing; safety, food, clothing, transportation and quality child care; access to medical, mental, dental and preventative health care; and skill building to help individuals and families maintain or move toward self-sufficiency. Applications deadlines for Individuals and Families grants are January 2 and July 1.

Requirements: Kalamazoo, Michigan, organizations recognized (or in the process of applying for recognition) under IRS code 501(c)3 are encouraged to contact foundation staff before submitting a request to determine eligibility.

Restrictions: Generally, the foundation does not provide funding for debt retirement, endowments, individuals, travel for individuals or groups, religious organizations for religious purposes, meetings, conferences, publications, films, or television and radio programming.

Geographic Focus: Michigan

Date(s) Application is Due: Jan 2; Jul 1

Contact: Jessica Aguilera, Community Investment Manager; (269) 381-4416; fax (269) 381-3146; jaguilera@kalfound.org or info@kalfound.org

Internet: www.kalfound.org/Grants/OurCommunityInvestmentPriorities/tabid/223/Default.aspx

Sponsor: Kalamazoo Community Foundation
151 South Rose Street, Suite 332
Kalamazoo, MI 49007-4775

Kalamazoo Community Foundation John E. Fetzer Institute Fund Grants   **1410**

The John E. Fetzer Institute Fund is an Advised Fund of the Kalamazoo Community Foundation aimed at enriching the lives of community members. Funding requests of up to $5,000 are considered. A committee of five Fetzer Institute staff members makes recommendations to the Kalamazoo Community Foundation board of trustees for grants based on submitted proposals. Before submitting your grant proposal, you must schedule a pre-application conversation with a member of the Community Investment team. This conversation must be scheduled at least two weeks before the grant application deadline. Grant decisions are made about two months after submission annual deadlines, which are January 2, April 1, July 1, and October 1. To learn more or schedule a pre-application conversation, contact the Foundation directly.

Requirements: Kalamazoo, Michigan, organizations recognized (or in the process of applying for recognition) under IRS code 501(c)3 are encouraged to contact foundation staff before submitting a request to determine eligibility.

Restrictions: Generally, the foundation does not provide funding for debt retirement, endowments, individuals, travel, religious organizations for religious purposes, meetings, conferences, publications, films, or television and radio programming.

Geographic Focus: Michigan

Date(s) Application is Due: Jan 2; Apr 1; Jul 1; Oct 1

Amount of Grant: Up to 5,000 USD

Contact: Jessica Aguilera, Community Investment Manager; (269) 381-4416; fax (269) 381-3146; jaguilera@kalfound.org or info@kalfound.org

Internet: www.kalfound.org/Grants/OtherGrantOpportunities/tabid/226/Default.aspx

Sponsor: Kalamazoo Community Foundation
151 South Rose Street, Suite 332
Kalamazoo, MI 49007-4775

Kalamazoo Community Foundation LBGT Equality Fund Grants   **1411**

Grants awarded from the LGBT Equality Fund support greater Kalamazoo area nonprofits that promote equality and celebrate appreciation for the lesbian, gay, bisexual, transgender and questioning community members who live, work and raise their families here. The LGBT Equality Fund has four goals: advocate for human rights and equality to positively impact Kalamazoo County's LGBT community; promote social justice and unity; support activities that celebrate the rich social and cultural contributions of the LGBT community; and strengthen organizations that serve the physical, health and social or emotional needs of the gay and transgender community. The Fund's priority areas are people of color, youths, families, transgender, cross-generational, and leadership development. There are no specified deadlines, and applicants should begin by contacting the Foundation.

Requirements: Kalamazoo, Michigan, organizations recognized (or in the process of applying for recognition) under IRS code 501(c)3 are encouraged to contact foundation staff before submitting a request to determine eligibility.

Restrictions: Generally, the foundation does not provide funding for debt retirement, endowments, individuals, travel, religious organizations for religious purposes, meetings, conferences, publications, films, or television and radio programming.

Geographic Focus: Michigan

Contact: Jessica Aguilera, Community Investment Manager; (269) 381-4416; fax (269) 381-3146; jaguilera@kalfound.org or info@kalfound.org

Internet: www.kalfound.org/Grants/OtherGrantOpportunities/tabid/226/Default.aspx

Sponsor: Kalamazoo Community Foundation
151 South Rose Street, Suite 332
Kalamazoo, MI 49007-4775

Kalamazoo Community Foundation Youth Development Grants   **1412**

The Kalamazoo Community Foundation envisions a community where young people are nurtured and have their developmental needs met; are productive contributors to the community; and are prepared for life beyond high school, whether they choose to pursue higher education or enter our community's workforce. We invest in quality programs that

use effective youth development principles, are informed by best practices and provide youths with: safe access to caring adults through youth/adult partnerships; age-appropriate strategies for growth and development; and opportunities to build social and emotional learning competencies and a positive self identity. Applications deadlines for Youth Development Grants are April 1 and October 1.

Requirements: Kalamazoo, Michigan, organizations recognized (or in the process of applying for recognition) under IRS code 501(c)3 are encouraged to contact foundation staff before submitting a request to determine eligibility.

Restrictions: Generally, the foundation does not provide funding for debt retirement, endowments, individuals, travel, religious organizations for religious purposes, meetings, conferences, publications, films, or television and radio programming.

Geographic Focus: Michigan

Date(s) Application is Due: Apr 1; Oct 1

Contact: Jessica Aguilera, Community Investment Manager; (269) 381-4416; fax (269) 381-3146; jaguilera@kalfound.org or info@kalfound.org

Internet: www.kalfound.org/Grants/OurCommunityInvestmentPriorities/tabid/223/Default.aspx

Sponsor: Kalamazoo Community Foundation
151 South Rose Street, Suite 332
Kalamazoo, MI 49007-4775

K and F Baxter Family Foundation Grants   **1413**

The foundation focuses on the special educational challenges encountered by multiracial children; policy recommendations in support of revised school curricula that will be more supportive of multiracial children without sacrificing either basic skills training or appropriate performance standards; and developing, by means of policy studies and analysis, a realistic template for education reform focused on the student rather than the school. In addition, the foundation will consider funding worthwhile projects in the arts, health care, and other areas related to education. The foundation encourages requests from schools desiring to enhance learning and/or increase number of students served through the use of blended learning. A preliminary email describing your project or program is required before proposals are accepted. The initial inquiry must be made at least 3 weeks before proposals are due on March 1 each year.

Requirements: Biracial children grants are awarded to nonprofit organizations nationwide. Educational grants are now made exclusively to schools, and applicant schools must be fully enrolled and at least 50% of students must qualify for free or reduced lunches or be otherwise identified as low-income.

Restrictions: Education grants are limited to schools in California Unified School Districts, including Berkeley, Los Angeles, Oakland, West Contra Costa Counties. Programs must take place during regular school hours. A site visit is required before an award can be granted.

Geographic Focus: All States

Date(s) Application is Due: Mar 1

Amount of Grant: Up to 150,000 USD

Contact: Stacey Bell, Executive Director; (510) 524-8145; fax (510) 524-4101; staceybell@kfbaxterfoundation.com

Internet: www.kfbaxterfoundation.com/home.html

Sponsor: K and F Baxter Family Foundation
1563 Solano Avenue, #404
Berkeley, CA 94707

Kansas Health Foundation Major Initiatives Grants   **1414**

The Kansas Health Foundation is committed to supporting strategies that will make Kansas a healthier place. The Foundation's focus areas are: promoting the healthy behaviors of Kansans; strengthening the public health system; improving access to health care for Kansas children; growing community philanthropy; providing health data and information to policymakers; and building civic leadership.

Requirements: The Foundation accepts one-page letters of inquiry from organizations that believe they have innovative work that meets the Foundation's mission. The letter of inquiry form is located at the Foundation's website. Organizations may also review samples of previously funded major initiatives on the website.

Geographic Focus: Kansas

Samples: University of Kansas School of Medicine, Wichita, Kansas, supporting the Department of Preventative Medicine and Public Health in its efforts to enhance the public health components of its physicians' education curriculum, $400,000; Worksite Wellness Evaluation, to engage local leaders and organizations in communities throughout Kansas to complete the training necessary to develop worksite wellness plans and to fund a final report of the results, $800,000.

Contact: Nancy Claassen, Grants Manager; (316) 262-676; fax (316) 262-2044; nclaassen@khf.org

Internet: www.kansashealth.org/grant_type/major_initiatives

Sponsor: Kansas Health Foundation
309 East Douglas
Wichita, KS 67202-3405

Kansas Health Foundation Recognition Grants   **1415**

The Kansas Health Foundation Recognition Grants expand the Foundation's support to a broad range of health-related organizations throughout the state. The Foundation defines health broadly, and looks at all the aspects that affect health, including the social factors that contribute to a healthy population (a state of complete physical, mental, and social well-being and not merely the absence of disease or infirmity). While the majority of the Foundation's funding is through invited proposals, the Recognition Grants program is designed to fund unsolicited requests. It is targeted for organizations and agencies proposing meaningful and charitable projects that fit within the Foundation's mission of improving the health of all Kansans.

Requirements: Kansas 501(c)3 nonprofit health organizations are eligible. The application is at the Foundation website and must be submitted online.

Restrictions: The Foundation does not support: medical research; capital campaigns; operating deficits or retirement of debt; endowment programs not initiated by the Foundation; political advocacy of any kind; vehicles, such as vans or buses; medical equipment; construction projects or real estate acquisitions; direct mental health services; or direct medical services.

Geographic Focus: Kansas

Date(s) Application is Due: Mar 15; Sep 15

Amount of Grant: Up to 25,000 USD

Contact: Nancy Claassen, Grants Manager; (800) 373-7681 or (316) 262-7676; fax (316) 262-2044; info@khf.org

Gina Hess, Grant Assistant; (316) 262-7676 or (800) 373-7681; rinfo@khf.org

Internet: www.kansashealth.org/grantmaking/recognitiongrants

Sponsor: Kansas Health Foundation

309 East Douglas

Wichita, KS 67202-3405

Kate B. Reynolds Charitable Trust Health Care Grants 1416

The Kate B. Reynolds Charitable Trust responds to health care and wellness needs and invests in solutions that improve the quality of health for financially needy residents throughout North Carolina. The Health Care Division seeks impact through four program areas: access to primary medical care; behavioral health; community-centered prevention; and diabetes. The Trust funds grants that benefit the financially needy, which may include individuals living at or below 200% of the federal poverty level, the uninsured, and those eligible for Medicaid and/or the free and reduced school lunch program. Grants generally fall into two categories: general operating support; and capital project support. Funded operating program proposals may include both direct services to people in need and support for the organizations, groups, and ideas that can lead to grassroots changes and systemic improvements. In general, the Trust funds: capacity building; direct services; grassroots changes or systemic change efforts; program planning; and technical assistance. The Trust requires advanced consultation by phone or in writing. Online applications deadlines are the second Tuesday in February and the second Tuesday in August.

Requirements: Nonprofit 501(c)3 organizations in North Carolina are eligible to apply.

Restrictions: The Trust generally does not fund: general organizational expenses; mandated community health assessments; medical research; processes for organizational accreditation; programs or projects ordinarily supported by government funds; or support for grantee staff to pursue a degree or other intensive education and training.

Geographic Focus: North Carolina

Date(s) Application is Due: Feb 14; Aug 8

Amount of Grant: 20,000 - 150,000 USD

Contact: Debra Hall, Grants Manager; (336) 397-5513 or (336) 397-5500; debra@kbr.org

Erin Yates, Program Coordinator; (336) 397-5521 or (336) 397-5500; erin@kbr.org

Internet: www.kbr.org/content/health-care-division-grantseekers

Sponsor: Kate B. Reynolds Charitable Trust

128 Reynolda Village

Winston-Salem, NC 27106-5123

Kate B. Reynolds Charitable Trust Poor and Needy Grants 1417

Through the Poor and Needy Division, the Kate B. Reynolds Charitable Trust responds to basic life needs and invests in solutions that improve the quality of life for financially needy residents of Forsyth County. The Poor and Needy division seeks impact through two program areas by providing operating funds: providing basic needs and increasing self reliance. Core issue areas of interest include: community assets; education; health care (both behavioral and oral); and providing a safety net through emergency assistance and supportive housing. The Trust will consider a limited number of capital requests up to $350,000 per request in these four core areas. The Grant Application Process is a two-step process involving consultation with a staff Program Officer, followed by formal submission of a grant application. The consultation can be scheduled by calling the Winston-Salem offices.

Requirements: Nonprofit 501(c)3 organizations in Forsyth County, North Carolina, are eligible to apply.

Restrictions: The Trust generally does not fund: general organizational expenses; mandated community health assessments; medical research; processes for organizational accreditation; programs or projects ordinarily supported by government funds; or support for grantee staff to pursue a degree or other intensive education and training.

Geographic Focus: North Carolina

Date(s) Application is Due: Feb 14; Aug 8

Amount of Grant: 20,000 - 350,000 USD

Contact: Debra Hall, Grants Manager; (336) 397-5513 or (336) 397-5500; debra@kbr.org

Erin Yates, Program Coordinator; (336) 397-5521 or (336) 397-5500; erin@kbr.org

Internet: www.kbr.org/content/poor-and-needy-division-grantseekers

Sponsor: Kate B. Reynolds Charitable Trust

128 Reynolda Village

Winston-Salem, NC 27106-5123

Katharine Matthies Foundation Grants 1418

The Katharine Matthies Foundation was established in 1987 to support and promote quality educational, human services, and health care programming for underserved populations. Special consideration is given to organizations that work to prevent cruelty to children and animals. The Matthies Foundation specifically serves the people of the Lower Naugatuck

Valley. The majority of grants from the Matthies Foundation are 1 year in duration. On occasion, multi-year support is awarded. Award amounts typically go up to $50,000.

Requirements: Applicant organizations must have 501(c)3 tax-exempt status and serve the people of the following Connecticut towns: Seymour, Ansonia, Derby, Oxford, Shelton, or Beacon Falls. Special consideration will be given to organizations that serve the people of Seymour, Connecticut. Applications will be submitted online through the Bank of America website. A grant report is required within 1 year of the grant application date, regardless of whether all of the funds have been spent.

Restrictions: The foundation does not support requests from individuals, organizations attempting to influence policy through direct lobbying, or any political campaigns.

Geographic Focus: Connecticut

Date(s) Application is Due: May 1

Amount of Grant: Up to 50,000 USD

Samples: Boys and Girls Club of the Lower Naugatuck Valley, Shelton, Connecticut, $50,000 - awarded for general operations of the organization (2018); Area Congregations Together Inc., Shelton, Connecticut, $40,000 - awarded for general operations of the organization (2018); BHCare, Ansonia, Connecticut, $40,000 - awarded for general operations of the organization (2018).

Contact: Amy R. Lynch, Philanthropic Client Manager; (860) 244-4870; ct.grantmaking@bankofamerica.com or amy.r.lynch@bofa.com

Internet: www.bankofamerica.com/philanthropic/foundation/?fnId=55

Sponsor: Katharine Matthies Foundation

200 Glastonbury Boulevard, Suite #200

Glastonbury, CT 06033-4056

Katherine John Murphy Foundation Grants 1419

The Katherine John Murphy Foundation was established in 1954 in Atlanta, Georgia by Katherine Murphy Riley. The foundation awards grants to Georgia tax-exempt organizations in its areas of interest, including services for children, education, the environment, and human services. Types of support include annual campaigns, building construction and/or renovation, capital campaigns, continuing support, general operating support, seed grants, and project development. Grants are awarded primarily in Atlanta, Georgia, and select areas of Latin America. Submit a letter of request.

Requirements: Organizations in Atlanta, Georgia, are eligible to apply, as well as select areas of Latin America.

Restrictions: No grants to individuals, or for research, or matching gifts.

Geographic Focus: Georgia, Argentina, Bolivia, Brazil, Chile, Colombia, Costa Rica, Cuba, Dominican Republic, Ecuador, El Salvador, Guatemala, Haiti, Honduras, Mexico, Nicaragua, Panama, Paraguay, Peru, Uruguay, Venezuela

Amount of Grant: 250 - 50,000 USD

Contact: Brenda Rambeau, (404) 589-8090; fdnsvcs.ga@suntrust.com

Internet: www.kjmurphyfoundation.org

Sponsor: Katherine John Murphy Foundation

50 Hurt Plaza, Suite 1210

Atlanta, GA 30303

Kathryne Beynon Foundation Grants 1420

Founded in California in 1967, the Kathryne Beynon Foundation provides support primarily for: hospitals (with a special interest in Asthma); youth agencies; child welfare; Roman Catholic church; higher education, Types of support include: general operating support; building construction/renovation; endowment funds; and scholarship funds. The Board meets quarterly to review grant requests. Applicants should contact the office in writing, outlining their proposal. Application is by invitation only, and there is no deadline date when submitting grant proposals. Contact the Foundation directly for additional guidelines before submitting a full proposal.

Requirements: 501(c)3 southern California tax-exempt organizations are eligible. Preference is given to requests from Pasadena. There are no: deadline dates; formal application form required to submit proposal.

Restrictions: No support to individuals.

Geographic Focus: California

Amount of Grant: 500 - 50,000 USD

Samples: Artists of America, San Pedro, CA, $17,800—Laurel Elementary School, Prep art classes; Assistance League of Southern California, Hollywood, CA, $4,000—children's club/ day nursery; Scripps College, Claremont, CA, $20,000—science scholarship program.

Contact: Robert D. Bannon, Trustee; (626) 584-8800

Sponsor: Kathryne Beynon Foundation

1111 South Arroyo Parkway, Suite 470

Pasadena, CA 91105-3239

Katie's Krops Grants 1421

This grant opportunity will fund projects for kids ages 9 to 16 to start a vegetable garden to feed people in need in their communities. The winner will be awarded a gift card to a garden center in their area (up to $400), support from Katie's Krops, and a digital camera to document the garden and the harvest. Applications for all types of vegetable gardens, such as a container garden if you live in a city or a vegetable garden located in your neighborhood or at your school, will be considered.

Requirements: Applicants must be between the ages of 9 and 16 as of October 1 and must be residents of the United States. No garden experience is necessary, however a good support system of volunteers and a willingness to give back to the community is. All applications must be filled out completely and signed by a parent or legal guardian. Winners will be notified in January, and the garden must be started in the spring.

Restrictions: Only applications that are mailed will be accepted; Emailed or faxed applications will not be accepted.

Geographic Focus: All States
Amount of Grant: 400 - 600 USD
Contact: Katie Stagliano, Founder; (843) 327-3366; katie@katieskrops.com
Internet: katieskrops.com/
Sponsor: Katie's Krops
P.O. Box 1841
Summerville, SC 29484-1841

Katrine Menzing Deakins Charitable Trust Grants   1422

Katrine Deakins was executive secretary to Amon G. Carter and helped found the Amon G. Carter Foundation. She was the Foundation's executive director and was very active in numerous professional, social and charitable organizations throughout her life. Katrine established her own trust in 1987, the Katrine Menzing Deakins Charitable Trust to benefit several favored charities in addition to other charitable organization requests selected each year by the trustees. Preference is given to organizations, operating in, or serving Tarrant County, Texas. Grants are typically between $1,000 and $25,000.
Requirements: Applicants must have 501(c)3 tax-exempt status and serve communities in Tarrant County, Texas. Applications will be submitted online through the Bank of America website. A grant report is required within 1 year of the grant application date, regardless of whether all of the funds have been spent.
Restrictions: Eligibility to re-apply for a grant award from the Katrine Menzing Deakins Charitable Trust requires organizations to skip 1 grant cycle (1 year) before submitting a subsequent application. The trust does not support requests from individuals, organizations attempting to influence policy through direct lobbying, or any political campaigns.
Geographic Focus: Texas
Date(s) Application is Due: Aug 1
Amount of Grant: 1,000 - 25,000 USD
Samples: The Women's Center of Tarrant County Inc., Fort Worth, Texas, $20,000 - awarded for General Counseling Continuum of Care program (2019); Botanical Research Institute of Texas, Fort Worth, Texas, $20,000 - awarded for general operations of the organization (2019); Meals-on-Wheels of Tarrant County, Fort Worth, Texas, $20,000 - awarded for Home-Delivered Meals program (2019).
Contact: Kelly Garlock, Philanthropic Client Manager; (800) 357-7094; tx.philanthropic@bankofamerica.com or tx.philanthropic@ustrust.com
Internet: www.bankofamerica.com/philanthropic/foundation/?fnId=16
Sponsor: Katrine Menzing Deakins Charitable Trust
500 West 7th Street, 15th Floor, TX1-497-15-08
Fort Worth, TX 76102-4700

Kawabe Memorial Fund Grants   1423

The Kawabe Memorial Fund was established in 1971 to support and promote general operations and programs of nonprofit agencies devoted to the care of low-income children, families and seniors. The Fund also provides a few capital grants to churches as well as scholarships to support teachers and the clergy. The Kawabe Memorial Fund typically supports organizations serving the people of the Puget Sound, Washington area. Grants from the Kawabe Memorial Fund are 1 year in duration. Award amounts typically go up to $20,000. Applications to the Kawabe Memorial Fund are due the second Friday in March, June or September.
Requirements: Applicants must have 501(c)3 tax-exempt status and serve communities in Puget Sound, Washington. Grant requests for specific programs are encouraged but requests for general operating support will be considered. Prior to committee consideration of proposals, applicants may be asked to provide additional information by phone. Applications will be submitted online through the Bank of America website. Applicants will be notified by mail of the Committee's funding decisions. A grant report is required within 1 year of the grant application date, regardless of whether all of the funds have been spent.
Restrictions: The fund does not support requests from individuals, organizations attempting to influence policy through direct lobbying, or any political campaigns.
Geographic Focus: Washington
Date(s) Application is Due: Mar 12; Jun 11; Sep 10
Amount of Grant: Up to 20,000 USD
Samples: Asian Counseling and Referral Service, Seattle, WA, $10,000 - awarded for Food Bank, Nutrition and Emergency Feeding program; New Beginnings, Seattle, WA, $7,000 - awarded for Home Safe program; Peace for the Streets By Kids From the Streets, Seattle, WA, $5,000 - awarded for general operations of the organization.
Contact: Natalie Lecher, Grants Consultant; (206) 406-6124; wa.grantmaking@bankofamerica.com or natalie.grantwork@gmail.com
Internet: www.bankofamerica.com/philanthropic/foundation/?fnId=122
Sponsor: Kawabe Memorial Fund
P.O. Box 3977, WA1-501-33-23
Seattle, WA 98124-2477

Kelvin and Eleanor Smith Foundation Grants   1424

The foundation awards grants to northeast Ohio nonprofits in its areas of interest, including nonsectarian education, the performing and visual arts, health care, and environmental conservation and protection. Types of support include general operating support, continuing support, annual campaigns, capital campaigns, building construction/renovation, and equipment acquisition. Since there are no required application forms, each proposal include a cover letter that outlines the reason for the request and the dollar amount. Organizations who have previously received funding from this Foundation may submit a proposal annually. There are no specified annual deadlines.
Requirements: Nonprofit organizations in the greater Cleveland, OH, area are eligible.

Restrictions: Grants are not made in support of individuals or for endowment funds, scholarships, fellowships, matching gifts, or loans.
Geographic Focus: Ohio
Amount of Grant: 3,000 - 150,000 USD
Contact: Carol W. Zett, Grants Manager; (216) 591-9111; fax (216) 591-9557; cwzett@kesmithfoundation.org
Internet: www.kesmithfoundation.org/grantguidelines.html
Sponsor: Kelvin and Eleanor Smith Foundation
30195 Chagrin Boulevard, Suite 275
Cleveland, OH 44124

Kenai Peninsula Foundation Grants   1425

The Kenai Peninsula Foundation offers a competitive grant award process for unrestricted grants to qualified nonprofits offering programs and services in the central Kenai Peninsula area. The Foundation, an affiliate of the Alaska Community Foundation, seeks applications from qualified tax-exempt 501(c)3 nonprofits that support organizations and programs in the central Kenai Peninsula and serve the people's needs in such areas as health, education, community heritage, the arts, vulnerable populations, recreation, safety, and community development. The maximum award is $500, and the annual deadline for submissions is May 15. Awarded grant proposals must be completed within one year.
Requirements: Applications are accepted from qualified 501(c)3 nonprofit organizations, or equivalent organizations located in the state of Alaska. Equivalent organizations may include tribes, local or state governments, schools, or Regional Educational Attendance Areas.
Restrictions: Individuals, for-profit, and 501(c)(4) or (c)(6) organizations, non-Alaska based organizations and state or federal government agencies are not eligible for competitive grants. Applications for religious indoctrination or other religious activities, endowment building, deficit financing, fundraising, lobbying, electioneering and activities of political nature will not be considered, nor will proposals for ads, sponsorships, or special event and any proposals which discriminate as to race, gender, marital status, sexual orientation, age, disability, creed or ethnicity.
Geographic Focus: All States
Date(s) Application is Due: May 15
Amount of Grant: Up to 500 USD
Samples: Hope Community Resources, Anchorage, AK, $300 - purchase of adaptive fishing gear for people with disabilities; Sterling Area Senior Citizens, Sterling, AK, $500 - support for the Moose River Hustle for Meals on Wheels program; Bridges Community Resource Network, Soldotna, AK, $500 - support for PPWCA Youth Outreach.
Contact: Ricardo Lopez, Affiliate Program Officer; (907) 274-6707; fax (907) 334-5780; rlopez@alaskacf.org
Internet: kenaipeninsulafoundation.org/projects/
Sponsor: Kenai Peninsula Foundation
P.O. Box 1612
Soldotna, AK 99669

Kennedy Center National Symphony Orchestra Youth Fellowships   1426

The National Symphony Orchestra (NSO) Youth Fellowship Program is an orchestral training program for students in grades 9 through 12. Past NSO Youth Fellowship participants have gone on to achieve great success with orchestras throughout the country including Philadelphia, Atlanta, Cleveland, Houston, in addition to the National Symphony Orchestra. The program is intended for serious music students interested in pursuing orchestral music as a career. Open by audition only, this full-scholarship program provides students in the Washington, D.C. metropolitan area with the following opportunities: study with a National Symphony Orchestra musician; chamber music coaching by a member of the National Symphony Orchestra; observe rehearsals and attend concerts; and participate in master classes and discussions with musicians, conductors, guest artists, and NSO/Kennedy Center management. This is a monitored, performance-oriented program, designed to encourage students to become professional orchestral musicians. Participation by ethnic minorities is encouraged. Priority is given to students entering 9th and 10th grades in order to provide as sustained a training as possible. The application is available at the website.
Requirements: The Fellowships are open, by audition, to students entering grades 9 through 12 in the following locations: metropolitan Washington Council of Governments (COG): D.C.; Charles, Frederick, Montgomery, Prince George's counties in Maryland; and Arlington, Fairfax, Loudoun, and Prince William counties in Virginia. Fellowships may be awarded to students who play any of the following instruments: violin, viola, cello, bass, flute, oboe, clarinet, bassoon, horn, trumpet, trombone tuba, harp, and percussion. Additional guidelines for submission are posted at the website.
Restrictions: Students in higher grades will be considered only when positions cannot be filled by younger students. Those who play piano, organ, or saxophone are not eligible for the fellowship. Applicants in grades 6 through 8 may be considered on a case by case basis.
Geographic Focus: District of Columbia, Maryland, Virginia
Date(s) Application is Due: May 7
Contact: Syrah Gunning, NSO Youth Fellowships Coordinator; (202) 416-8820; fax (202) 416-4845
Internet: www.kennedy-center.org/nso/nsoed/youthfellowship.cfm
Sponsor: John F. Kennedy Center for the Performing Arts
2700 F Street NW
Washington, D.C. 20566

Kenneth T. and Eileen L. Norris Foundation Grants 1427

The foundation supports Los Angeles County nonprofits in the areas of: medicine—to improve access to health care, increase knowledge through research, and provide facilities for those activities to take place; youth—to provide constructive activities, positive role models, and opportunities for disadvantaged, disabled, and misguided children; community—to support law enforcement agencies, good citizenship, and environmental conservation; culture—to support museums, symphony orchestras, and dance and theater companies; and education and science—to focus on private education, especially secondary and college levels. Types of support include general operating support, continuing support, building construction and/or renovation, equipment acquisition, endowment funds, program development, professorships, scholarship funds, research, and matching funds. Education/science and medicine projects are accepted between May 1 and June 30; youth requests are accepted between February 15 and March 31; cultural (the arts) and community requests are accepted between December 1 and January 31; and medicine proposals are due between May 1 and June 30.

Requirements: Grants are awarded to organizations in southern California.
Geographic Focus: California
Date(s) Application is Due: Jan 31; Mar 31; Jun 30
Amount of Grant: 5,000 - 25,000 USD
Contact: Lisa D. Hansen, Chairperson; (562) 435-8444; fax (562) 436-0584; grants@ktn.org
Internet: www.norrisfoundation.org/grant.html
Sponsor: Kenneth T. and Eileen L. Norris Foundation
11 Golden Shore, Suite 450
Long Beach, CA 90802

Kentucky Arts Council Access Assistance Grants 1428

The Kentucky Arts Access Assistance support arts programs that serve populations whose opportunities to experience the arts may be limited by age, geographic location, ethnicity, economic status, disability, or other factors. A different population is chosen each grant cycle to benefit from these arts programs. Grants are available for up to $10,000, with a 25 percent cash match. The deadline is January 15, with program guidelines and application instructions available at the website. Applicants are encouraged to contact the Arts Council if they are unsure about their organization's eligibility.

Requirements: This grant supports quality arts programming in environments where arts are not the primary emphasis. Public libraries, co-operative extension offices, nursing homes, social service agencies, health departments, state agencies, correctional facilities, college and university programs, and other community-based organizations serving Kentuckians may apply
Restrictions: Organizations receiving general operating support from the Kentucky Arts Council are not eligible.
Geographic Focus: Kentucky
Date(s) Application is Due: Jan 15
Amount of Grant: Up to 10,000 USD
Samples: Norton Center for the Arts, Boyle County, Kentucky, $10,000; Kentucky Center for the Performing Arts, Jefferson County, Kentucky, $7,880; The Jewish Community Center of Louisville, Jefferson County, Kentucky, $10,000.
Contact: Sarah Schmitt, Arts Access Director; (502) 564-8110, ext. 492 or (888) 833-2787; fax (502) 564-2839; sarah.schmitt@ky.gov
Internet: artscouncil.ky.gov/Grants/AAA.htm
Sponsor: Kentucky Arts Council
500 Mero Street, 21st Floor, Capital Plaza Tower
Frankfort, KY 40601-1987

Ketchikan Community Foundation Grants 1429

The Foundation's vision for the Ketchikan community includes a diversified local economy that provides family-supported employment, access to affordable housing and healthcare, a vibrant arts community, and multiple recreational and quality educational opportunities. The community it envisions will attract and retain multi-generations of citizens, while honoring and recognizing cultural diversity. The primary goal, therefore, is to support projects of importance to the community that will help its residents become better stewards of the land. Grant making priorities are still in development, though the Foundation will support projects that strengthen the community. Among others, they will include organizations and programs that serve youth, the elderly, recreation, safety, vulnerable populations, and arts and culture. No annual deadlines for applications have been identified.

Requirements: The Foundation seeks applications from qualified tax-exempt 501(c)3 organizations that support the organizations and programs in the Ketchikan region that serve the people's needs in such areas as health, education, community heritage, the arts, vulnerable populations, recreation, safety, and community and economic development.
Restrictions: ndividuals, for-profit, and 501(c)4 or 501(c)6 organizations, non-Alaska based organizations and state or federal government agencies are not eligible for competitive grants. Applications for religious indoctrination or other religious activities, endowment building, deficit financing, fundraising, lobbying, electioneering and activities of political nature will not be considered, nor will proposals for ads, sponsorships, or special event and any proposals which discriminate as to race, gender, marital status, sexual orientation, age, disability, creed or ethnicity.
Geographic Focus: Alaska
Contact: Ricardo Lopez, Affiliate Program Officer; (907) 274-6707; fax (907) 334-5780; rlopez@alaskacf.org or ketchikan@alaskacf.org
Internet: ketchikancf.org/grants/
Sponsor: Ketchikan Community Foundation
P.O. Box 5256
Ketchikan, AK 99901

Kettering Family Foundation Grants 1430

The Kettering Family Foundation was founded by Eugene W. Kettering, son of Charles F. Kettering, and his wife Virginia W. Kettering in 1956. Today, the Foundation supports a broad range of charitable activities of interest to the Board of Trustees, which is composed of members of the Kettering Family. Because funding decisions are driven by the interests of the trustees, Request Summaries endorsed by a trustee at the time of submission are considered a priority. Primary areas of interest include: arts, culture and humanities; education; environment; health and medical needs; human services; and public and societal benefit. The Foundation strongly recommended that you contact the office to discuss your proposed program before you start the application process

Requirements: 501(c)3 tax-exempt organizations are eligible to apply.
Restrictions: A Request Summary will not be accepted for any of the following purposes: religious organizations for religious purposes; individual public elementary or secondary schools or public school districts; multi-year grants; grants or loans to individuals; tickets; advertising or sponsorships of fundraising events; efforts to carry on propaganda or otherwise attempt to influence legislation; or activities of 509(a)3 Type III Supporting Organizations.
Geographic Focus: All States
Date(s) Application is Due: Mar 15; Jun 15; Sep 15; Dec 15
Contact: Judith M. Thompson, Executive Director; (303) 756-7664 or (937) 228-1021; fax (888) 719-1185; info@ketteringfamilyphilanthropies.org
Internet: www.ketteringfamilyfoundation.org/main.html
Sponsor: Kettering Family Foundation
40 North Main Street, #1480
Dayton, OH 45423

Kevin J Major Youth Sports Scholarships 1431

The Kevin J Major Youth Sports Foundation, created in memory of Kevin J. Major, was established to make a difference in the lives of youths by providing financial, motivational and educational opportunities to those who don't otherwise have the necessary means to participate in structured sports. The scholarships provide funds to young athletes of their families in financial need, to enable them to participate in structured sports programs.

Requirements: Applicants must be: 19 years old or younger; participate in a structured sports program (Youth Sports Association, organization, athletic camp or comparable); demonstrate financial need; a resident of Western Massachusetts (Hampden, Hampshire, Franklin, Worcester or Berkshire Counties) though others may be considered. There are no specific deadlines. Applicants will be required to include proof of financial need.
Geographic Focus: Massachusetts
Contact: Scholarship Officer; (413) 429-6168; seakevry@gmail.com
Internet: www.kevinmajorfoundation.com/scholarship-application
Sponsor: Kevin J Major Youth Sports Foundation, Inc.
P.O. Box 655
Westfield, MA 01086

Kimball Foundation Grants 1432

The Kimball Foundation was established by William R. Kimball and Sara H. Kimball in California in 1997. The Foundation supports programs focusing on one or more of the following areas: college access and persistence, helping disadvantaged youth build academic skills and prepare for, apply to, and succeed in college; cultural enrichment, providing youth with equal access to participatory arts education fostering an appreciation of the arts while promoting community engagement through cultural experiences; environmental education, particularly high engagement programs that provide outdoor experiential, wilderness, and environmental science education; and vocational development, providing disadvantaged youth with work-readiness, in-demand skills training, set in workplace-like environments, including internships and paid employment opportunities. Applicants should submit requests, file reports, and review their grant history online, in order to streamline the application process. Deadlines vary, so applicants should check the website often.

Requirements: The foundation supports: public charities operating under an IRS 501(c)3 status or fiscally sponsored by a 501(c)3 organization; and organizations serving the residents of San Francisco, Marin, San Mateo, and Sonoma counties, and limited to Palo Alto in Santa Clara County.
Restrictions: No grants are awarded to individuals, or for endowment drives, events, annual appeals, videos, medical research, religious organizations, or the environment.
Geographic Focus: California
Amount of Grant: 1,000 - 60,000 USD
Contact: Jonny Moy, Grants Manager; (415) 561-6540, ext. 216; fax (415) 561-5477; jmoy@pfs-llc.net
Internet: www.kimballfoundation.org/for-grantseekers/
Sponsor: Kimball Foundation
1660 Bush Street, Suite 300
San Francisco, CA 94109-5308

Kimball International-Habig Foundation Education Grants 1433

The Kimball-Habig Foundation was established by company founder, Arnold F. Habig, in 1951 for the purpose of supporting charitable causes within the communities in which Kimball operates, or from which it draws employees. The Foundation is funded by a percentage of profit earnings by the company. In keeping with the corporate philosophy and guiding principles, the Foundation is committed to helping the communities in which they operate to become even better places to live. Supporting that goal, the foundation focuses its funding and resources on grants to organizations and programs that most directly benefit those U.S. communities in which Kimball has operations or facilities, or from which it draws employees. To improve education for children, from preschool through high school, and for adults via continuing education and development, Kimball supports programs that foster: critical thinking skills; reading and comprehension; and technology and business interests. Awards are typically for general operating support. Though there are no specific deadlines, the Board meets quarterly, during the last week in March, June, September, and December, to award grants applied for during the previous 90 days.

Requirements: All requests for funding made to the Kimball Foundation must be made using the online request form. All requests must be in writing (via this online form), and absolutely no verbal or phone call requests will be processed or acknowledged. Major requests (those over $2,000) are reviewed, assessed and approved quarterly. Standard requests (those under $2,000) are reviewed and approved monthly. Standard requests are reviewed by the foundation board on or about the 25th of each month.

Geographic Focus: California, Florida, Idaho, Indiana, Kentucky, China, Mexico, Poland

Contact: R Gregory Kincer, Vice President Corporate Development; (812) 482-8255 or (812) 482-8701; habigfoundation@kimball.com

Internet: www.kimballinternational.com/giving-spirit

Sponsor: Kimball International-Habig Foundation

1600 Royal Street

Jasper, IN 47549-1001

Kimball International-Habig Foundation Health and Human Services Grants   1434

The Kimball-Habig Foundation was established by company founder, Arnold F. Habig, in 1951 for the purpose of supporting charitable causes within the communities in which Kimball operates, or from which it draws employees. The Foundation is funded by a percentage of profit earnings by the company. In keeping with the corporate philosophy and guiding principles, the Foundation is committed to helping the communities in which they operate to become even better places to live. Supporting that goal, the foundation focuses its funding and resources on grants to organizations and programs that most directly benefit those U.S. communities in which Kimball has operations or facilities, or from which it draws employees. In the area of health and human services, the Foundation's main focus is to improve the human condition and help to alleviate suffering by assisting local community organizations, charities, faith-based initiatives, and social services, in their efforts by considering the following types of requests: care and protection of children and infants; care and protection of at-risk women and families; care and protection of the elderly and infirmed; provision of healthcare, medical, and counseling services; and provision of basic social and support services. Awards are typically for general operating support. Though there are no specific deadlines, the Board meets quarterly, during the last week in March, June, September, and December, to award grants applied for during the previous 90 days.

Requirements: All requests for funding made to the Kimball Foundation must be made using the online request form. All requests must be in writing (via this online form), and absolutely no verbal or phone call requests will be processed or acknowledged. Major requests (those over $2,000) are reviewed, assessed and approved quarterly. Standard requests (those under $2,000) are reviewed and approved monthly. Standard requests are reviewed by the foundation board on or about the 25th of each month.

Geographic Focus: California, Florida, Idaho, Indiana, Kentucky, China, Mexico, Poland

Contact: R Gregory Kincer, Vice President Corporate Development; (812) 482-8255 or (812) 482-8701; habigfoundation@kimball.com

Internet: www.kimball.com/foundation.aspx

Sponsor: Kimball International-Habig Foundation

1600 Royal Street

Jasper, IN 47549-1001

KIND Causes Monthly Grants   1435

The KIND Foundation aims to deepen what has been the KIND brand's mission since day one: do the kind thing for your body, your taste buds and your world. KIND Causes was established in 2013 by KIND Snacks to provide a platform for socially impactful ideas to come to life. As of October 2016, the KIND Foundation began running this program as a grant giving vehicle to further the work of people and organizations who are dedicated to improving their communities. Each month, KIND Causes supports both individuals and organizations working to make the world a little kinder with $10,000 grants. Applicants should submit a socially impactful cause that helps people in need, and the KIND Causes community will determine which to fund by voting on their favorite cause.

Requirements: To be eligible, grantees must be at least eighteen years of age and legal residents of the U.S. or Canada (excluding the Province of Quebec). To be eligible, your cause proposal must be designed to be completed within six months of winning and within a $10,000 budget.

Restrictions: Applicants do not have to be a 501(c)3 to submit; KIND Causes is open to anyone with a socially-impactful idea that impact people in need.

Geographic Focus: All States, Canada

Amount of Grant: 10,000 USD

Contact: Dana Rosenberg, KIND Movement Director; (212) 616-3006, ext. 205 or (855) 884-5463; fax (212) 616-3005; contact@thekindfoundation.org or causes@thekindfoundation.org

Internet: www.kindsnacks.com/foundation/causes/how-it-works/

Sponsor: KIND Foundation

55 West 21st Street

New York, NY 10010-6809

Kinder Morgan Foundation Grants   1436

The Kinder Morgan Foundation focuses exclusively on academic education and the arts. It supports programs that benefit traditionally underserved youth, including minorities and girls, with a majority of contributions directed to STEM programs. The organization supporting the program and the program itself must have clearly defined objectives and demonstrate strong community ties. Programs must be located in Kinder Morgan's selected areas of operations or benefit youth in these areas. Typical grants are between $5,000 and

$20,000, and nonprofits, public schools and private schools may apply. Applications need to be submitted for review by the 1st of February, May, August, and November.

Requirements: Nonprofits, public schools and private schools may apply. In the United States, nonprofits and private schools must have 501(c)3 designation from the Internal Revenue Service (not applicable to public schools). An organization is eligible to apply if it is located within 30 miles of the following areas of Kinder Morgan's operations: Birmingham, Alabama, Phoenix, Arizona, Tucson, Arizona, Concord, California, Carson, California, Colorado Springs, Colorado, Lakewood, Colorado, Tampa, Florida, Alpharetta, Georgia, Downers Grove, Illinois, Chicago, Illinois, Shreveport, Louisiana, Port Sulphur, Louisiana, Harvey, Louisiana, Williston, North Dakota, Port Newark, New Jersey, Tulsa, Oklahoma, Midland, Texas, Pasadena, Texas, Houston, Texas, El Paso, Texas, Norfolk, Virginia, and Vancouver, Washington. The program must serve more than 500 underserved youth in grades K-12 and have a proven track record of success.

Restrictions: The following are not eligible for grants: individual applicants or individual pursuits; political causes, candidates or lobbying efforts; programs or organizations outside the United States; operating expenses; capital projects (except libraries); projects of religious denominations; advertising; sponsorships; service clubs, fraternal organizations or third-party fundraisers; travel for individuals or groups; conventions, conferences, seminars or other special events; mentoring, leadership, stewardship or other social development programs; or programs that include age groups outside our K-12 criteria. The Foundation will not provide support more than once per calendar year to the same organization and we do not make multi-year commitments.

Geographic Focus: Alabama, Arizona, California, Colorado, Florida, Georgia, Illinois, Louisiana, New Jersey, North Dakota, Oklahoma, Texas, Virginia, Washington

Date(s) Application is Due: Feb 1; May 1; Aug 1; Nov 1

Amount of Grant: 1,000 - 5,000 USD

Contact: Maureen Bulkley, Community Relations Coordinator; (713) 420-4792 or (713) 369-9000; km_foundation@kindermorgan.com

Internet: www.kindermorgan.com/pages/community/

Sponsor: Kinder Morgan Foundation

1001 Louisiana Street

Houston, TX 77002

Kindle Project SpiderWeave Flow Fund Grants   1437

Operating as an experimental philanthropy organization the Kindle Project experiments with programming and lets it evolve over time. Some programs are part of its annual work and some are pilots and experiments. Through grant making, innovative programming and dynamic collaborations, Kindle Project fosters a nexus of extraordinary, creative ideas and cultivators to imagine and inspire change. The SpiderWeave Flow Fund has been created with a spirit of curiosity, openness and an attitude of joy for the unexpected. The 2017 cohort decided to expand the circle and each nominate one new Flow Funder to join the SpiderWeave mix. The Kindle Project's SpiderWeaving crew has doubled in size and remains a cohort of all women. SpiderWeave is about deep collaboration and relationship building. It's the basics of what makes Kindle what it is.

Geographic Focus: All States

Samples: Green River Doula Network, Northampton, Massachusetts - support to facilitate access to doulas for families in the childbearing year (2018); Embrace Race, Amherst, Massachusetts - funding for community of parents and caregivers – of all colors – supporting each other to raise children who are informed, thoughtful, and brave about race (2018); Tehahonkohta Scott Martin, San Clemente, California - support for an educational promoter at the Akwesasne Freedom School, a Kanien'kéha (mohawk) language immersion school (2018).

Contact: Arianne Shaffer, Program Facilitator; (505) 983-7463; connect@kindleproject.org

Internet: kindleproject.org/programs/

Sponsor: Kindle Project

1000 Cordova Place, #351

Santa Fe, NM 87505

Kind World Foundation Grants   1438

The Kind World Foundation was established in South Dakota in 1991, with the expressed purpose to encourage and support charitable programs and activities that enhance the quality of life and best serve the public good. Funding priorities are environmental concerns, animal welfare, human services, education, and the arts. Types of support include general operating support, continuing support, annual campaigns, capital campaigns, building construction/renovation, equipment acquisition, endowment funds, seed grants, research, consulting services, and matching funds. Although the foundation supports regional and national programs, major grants are usually limited to the greater Siouxland area, including northwest Iowa, southeast South Dakota, and northeast Nebraska. Challenge grants and matching gift proposals receive special consideration. Proposals may be submitted at any time and are reviewed by the board of directors on a revolving basis. The board meets in January, April, July, October, and as needed. It is suggested that applicants contact the office prior to submitting a formal application. Most recent awards have ranged from $500 to as much as $1,200,000.

Geographic Focus: California, Iowa

Amount of Grant: 500 - 1,250,000 USD

Samples: Briar Cliff University, Sioux City, Iowa, $2,500 - general operating support; Greater Santa Barbara Ice Skating Association, Santa Barbara, California, $125,000 - general operating support; Morningside College, Sioux City, Iowa, $1,200,000 - general operating support.

Contact: Lee L. Lysne, Executive Director; (402) 697-8000

Sponsor: Kind World Foundation

1125 South 103rd Street, Suite 425

Omaha, NE 68124-6025

Kirby Laing Foundation Grants 1439

The first of the Trusts was established by Sir John Laing in 1952. A builder by trade, Sir John was responsible for moving the family firm from Carlisle to London, where it grew into a global construction company, John Laing. Sir John was a devout Christian and member of the Brethren Movement; his Christian faith was the motivation for the Company's pioneering concern for the welfare of its staff and the establishment of the first of his grant-making trusts, the J W Laing Trust, which is now administered by the Stewards Company in Bath. Successive generations of the Laing family have built on this example of Christian philanthropy, establishing their own charitable trusts and foundations. The Kirby Laing Foundation was established in 1972 by Sir Kirby Laing, with the intention that both income and capital should be applied, at the Trustees' discretion, for general charitable purposes. The Trustees' primary areas of giving are: the promotion of the evangelical Christian faith; education and youth development, focused particularly on STEM education and vocational training in traditional crafts; medical welfare and research, with a particular emphasis on dementia, stroke and neuro-degenerative diseases; culture and the environment, focused on improving access for young people and the disabled, particularly to projects with a national focus/impact, and on encouraging young talent in opera and the performing arts; and overseas development projects, with a special interest in projects benefiting women and girls in low income countries in Asia. Grants typically range between £2,000 and £10,000, but the trustees have the capacity to make a number of larger grants each year. There is no pro-forma application form but the Trust does ask applicants to download and complete an application cover sheet, which is available on completion of an eligibility quiz.
Requirements: The application cover sheet should be accompanied by a covering letter and concise project proposal, about 3 to 4 pages in length, which should include the following information: description of the project/activity for which funding is sought (this should identify the need the project addresses and the difference it will make); anticipated start and end date of the project; a detailed budget breakdown; fundraising plan, to include anticipated sources of funding, funds already secured and plans for securing the shortfall (including any loan arrangements, sale of assets); and arrangements for monitoring and evaluating the project.
Geographic Focus: All States, All Countries
Contact: Elizabeth Harley, Trust Director; 020 8238 8890; fax 020 8238 8897
Internet: www.laingfamilytrusts.org.uk/about-us/kirby-laing-foundation/
Sponsor: Laing Family Trusts
33 Bunns Lane
London, NW7 2DX

Kirkpatrick Foundation Grants 1440

The Kirkpatrick Foundation lends support to organizations with projects and programs that compliment the vision and mission of the Foundation, within the primary fields of interest of arts and culture, education, natural and built environments, animal research, and conservation. The Foundation encourages preliminary discussion to explore potential project proposals. Grant proposals are considered only from not-for-profit organizations qualified as public charities under Section 501(c)3 of the IRS. Organizations should have at least a three-year track record of programming and have maintained current financial records, a working board of directors and management, governance and accountability structures in place. The Foundation also considers requests from public and private educational institutions and faith-based educational programs. Priority is given to organizations serving Oklahoma with particular emphasis placed on programs and services directly benefiting citizens of the Oklahoma City metropolitan area.
Requirements: Organizations are encouraged to contact the Foundation before beginning the grant application process to determine if the project idea is compatible with Foundation interest areas. First time applicants must complete an on-line eligibility quiz to access the Small Grant Application or Letter of Inquiry. A small proposal of $5,000 or less may be submitted by completing the electronic Small Grant Application. These requests may be submitted throughout the year for future projects not already funded by the Foundation. Small grant requests will typically receive notification of a funding decision within 30 days of submitting the application. The Large Grant application procedure is a two-step electronic process beginning with a Letter of Inquiry. There is no set upper limit on the amount requested, but organizations should seek advice from Foundation staff on an appropriate range, and see the website for further instructions for submission.
Restrictions: Capital campaigns and endowments are not regularly funded. Grants may not be used to fund indirect costs or foundation fees. Grants are also not awarded to: individuals; lobbying organizations; medical and health related causes; social welfare; school trips including for marching bands; and athletic programs.
Geographic Focus: Oklahoma
Date(s) Application is Due: Jan 15; Jul 15
Amount of Grant: 1,000 - 130,000 USD
Contact: Meaghan Hunt Wilson, Program Associate; (405) 608-0934; fax (405) 608-0942; mhuntwilson@kirkpatrickfoundation.com
Internet: www.kirkpatrickfoundation.com/Grants/tabid/58/Default.aspx
Sponsor: Kirkpatrick Foundation
1001 West Wilshire Boulevard, Suite 201
Oklahoma City, OK 73116

Klingenstein-Simons Fellowship Awards in the Neurosciences 1441

The Klingenstein-Simons Fellowship Awards in the Neurosciences support, in the early stages of their careers, young investigators engaged in basic or clinical research that may lead to a better understanding of epilepsy. The fund recognizes that to accomplish this goal it is necessary to encourage a variety of new approaches. Several areas within the neurosciences are of particular interest to the fund: cellular and molecular neuroscience studies of the mechanisms of neuronal excitability and development, and of the genetic basis of seizure disorders; neural systems studies of the integrative function of the nervous system; and

clinical research studies designed to improve the prevention, diagnosis, treatment and the understanding of the causes of epilepsy. The annual deadline for application submission is February 15.
Requirements: Applicants must hold the PhD and/or MD degrees, and have completed all research training, including post-doctoral training. U.S. citizenship is not a requirement, but it is expected that candidates will be permanent residents of the U.S. and that their research will be carried out in U.S. institutions.
Restrictions: The fund does not contribute to endowments and rarely contributes to buildings or other kinds of capital projects.
Geographic Focus: All States
Date(s) Application is Due: Feb 15
Contact: Kathleen Pomerantz, Vice President; (212) 492-6193 or (212) 492-6181; kathleen.pomerantz@klingenstein.com
Internet: www.klingfund.org
Sponsor: Esther A. and Joseph Klingenstein Fund
125 Park Avenue, Suite 1700
New York, NY 10017

Knox County Community Foundation Recreation Grants 1442

The Knox County Community Foundation is a nonprofit, public charity created by and for the people of Knox County, Indiana. The Foundation helps nonprofits fulfill their missions by strengthening their ability to meet community needs through grants that assist charitable programs, address community issues, support community agencies, launch community initiatives, and support leadership development. Grant proposals are accepted once each year according to the grant cycle. Proposal requirements may change from year to year; therefore, grant seekers are advised to contact the foundation or see the foundations website, prior to beginning the grant application process. Grants are normally given as one-time support of a project but may be considered for additional support for expansions or outgrowths of an initial project. At the start of each cycle, a notice is mailed to nonprofit organizations that have applied for grants in the past, have received grants in the past, or have otherwise requested notification of the start of each cycle. Grants in the area of Recreation include projects aimed at improving and promoting recreational and leisure activities, parks, and community sporting events and activities. Samples of previously funded projects are available at the website.
Requirements: The Foundation welcomes proposals from nonprofit organizations that are deemed tax-exempt under sections 501(c)3 and 509(a) of the Internal Revenue Code and from governmental agencies serving the County of Knox, Indiana. Proposals from nonprofit organizations not classified as a 501(c)3 may be considered provided the project is charitable and supports a community need. Proposals submitted by an entity under the auspices of another agency must include a written statement signed by the agency's board president on behalf of the board of directors agreeing to act as the entity's fiscal sponsor, to receive grant monies if awarded, and to oversee the proposed project.
Restrictions: Project areas not considered for funding are: religious organizations for strictly religious purposes; political parties or campaigns; endowment creation or debt reduction; operating costs; capital campaigns; annual appeals or membership contributions; travel requests for groups or individuals such as bands, sports teams, or classes. Not more than 20% of any grant request may be for personnel costs, office supplies, or other operating costs. Operating costs for any organization must be directly related to the project or program for which funding is being requested.
Geographic Focus: Indiana
Contact: Annette Nowaskie, Development and Program Assistant; (812) 886-0093; fax (812) 886-0133; annette@knoxcountyfoundation.org
Internet: www.communityfoundationalliance.org/knox/program-areas/
Sponsor: Knox County Community Foundation
20 North Third Street, Suite 301, P.O. Box 273
Vincennes, IN 47591

Knox County Community Foundation Youth Development Grants 1443

The Knox County Community Foundation is a nonprofit, public charity created by and for the people of Knox County, Indiana. The Foundation helps nonprofits fulfill their missions by strengthening their ability to meet community needs through grants that assist charitable programs, address community issues, support community agencies, launch community initiatives, and support leadership development. Grant proposals are accepted once each year according to the grant cycle. Proposal requirements may change from year to year; therefore, grant seekers are advised to contact the foundation or see the foundations website, prior to beginning the grant application process. Grants are normally given as one-time support of a project but may be considered for additional support for expansions or outgrowths of an initial project. At the start of each cycle, a notice is mailed to nonprofit organizations that have applied for grants in the past, have received grants in the past, or have otherwise requested notification of the start of each cycle. Grants in the area of Youth Development include activities that strengthen the family unit, help children grow and develop, foster youth sports and athletics, support the YMCA, and support daycare-related issues. Samples of previously funded projects are available at the website.
Requirements: The Foundation welcomes proposals from nonprofit organizations that are deemed tax-exempt under sections 501(c)3 and 509(a) of the Internal Revenue Code and from governmental agencies serving the County of Knox, Indiana. Proposals from nonprofit organizations not classified as a 501(c)3 may be considered provided the project is charitable and supports a community need. Proposals submitted by an entity under the auspices of another agency must include a written statement signed by the agency's board president on behalf of the board of directors agreeing to act as the entity's fiscal sponsor, to receive grant monies if awarded, and to oversee the proposed project.
Restrictions: Project areas not considered for funding are: religious organizations for strictly religious purposes; political parties or campaigns; endowment creation or debt reduction;

operating costs; capital campaigns; annual appeals or membership contributions; travel requests for groups or individuals such as bands, sports teams, or classes. Not more than 20% of any grant request may be for personnel costs, office supplies, or other operating costs. Operating costs for any organization must be directly related to the project or program for which funding is being requested.

Geographic Focus: Indiana
Contact: Annette Nowaskie, Development and Program Assistant; (812) 886-0093; fax (812) 886-0133; annette@knoxcountyfoundation.org
Internet: www.communityfoundationalliance.org/knox/program-areas/
Sponsor: Knox County Community Foundation
20 North Third Street, Suite 301, P.O. Box 273
Vincennes, IN 47591

Koch Family Foundation (Annapolis) Grants   1444

The Koch Family Foundation was established in 1993 by Gary W. Koch, founder and owner of Koch Homes, an Annapolis-based home construction firm. Its primary areas of giving include: arts and culture; disease treatment and research; elementary and secondary education; fire prevention and control; health care and health care access; higher education; housing development; in-patient medical care; mental health care; nursing care; rehabilitation; and youth development and youth programs. The Foundation's primary geographical focus is the State of Maryland, although some giving also occurs in Michigan, Tennessee, Virginia, Pennsylvania, New York, and Massachusetts. Support most often is awarded for financial sustainability, fundraising events, program development, re-granting, and research. Awards range as high as $10,000, although the average is $1,000. There are no specified annual deadlines, and interested parties should forward a letter of application.
Requirements: Any 501(c)3 supporting residents of Maryland, Michigan, Tennessee, Virginia, Pennsylvania, New York, and Massachusetts is eligible to apply.
Geographic Focus: All States
Amount of Grant: Up to 10,000 USD
Samples: Severn School, Severne, Maryland, $2,500 - support for elementary and secondary education program development; Anne Arundel Community College Foundation, Arnold, Maryland, $1,000 - support for community college education program development; Maryland Therapeutic Riding, Crownsville, Maryland, $1,000 - support for animal therapy.
Contact: Gary W. Koch, President; (410) 573-5720; fax (410) 573-5257; gkoch@kochhomes.com
Sponsor: Koch Family Foundation (Annapolis)
2661 Riva Road, Suite 220
Annapolis, MD 21401-7364

Kodak Community Relations Grants   1445

Kodak has always been a brand known for community outreach and the support of causes – from the funding of parks and universities to the inception of the United Way. This culture of giving dates back to the company's founder, George Eastman (1854-1932), inventor, entrepreneur and philanthropist. In the early 1900s, Eastman was one of the richest men in the world and one of the four largest donors in history to that point. By his death, he would give away approximately $2 billion of his wealth to charitable causes (as measured in today's dollars). Today, the people of Kodak remain true to Eastman's foundational values through volunteerism, community support, and a focus on giving. Much of Kodak's focus today remains on education and literacy, as well as healthcare. The application process is open-ended, with Letters of Inquiry accepted at any time.
Requirements: Nonprofit organizations in company-operating areas nationwide are eligible to apply.
Restrictions: Kodak does not support individuals; a commitment beyond three to five years; endowed chairs; university capital campaigns; event sponsorships; operating costs of organizations that receive funds from a Kodak supported United Way; legislators, political organizations, or campaigns; or sectarian organizations whose programs are limited to members of one religious group.
Geographic Focus: All States
Date(s) Application is Due: Apr 30
Amount of Grant: Up to 20,000 USD
Contact: Community Relations Manager; (716) 724-3041; fax (716) 724-1376
Internet: www.kodak.com/gb/en/corp/Blog/Blog_Post/?contentId=4295013807
Sponsor: Eastman Kodak Corporation
343 State Street
Rochester, NY 14650-0517

Kodiak Community Foundation Grants   1446

As an organization, the Kodiak Community Foundation's goal is to support projects of importance to Kodiak residents that will help them become better stewards of the land. As in a maritime community, these residents have strong ties to the natural elements. Many depend on Kodiak's local fish and wildlife for subsistence and livelihoods. Despite the changing landscape of funding in the state of Alaska, Kodiak is aware of the importance of self-reliance. Its citizens have come together to produce local initiatives for a vision-oriented legacy. This is how the Kodiak Community Foundation began; with a dream of providing the means for improvement in the quality of life within the town. Grant making priorities are still in development, though the Foundation will support programs and projects that serve youth, the elderly, recreation, safety, vulnerable populations, and arts and culture. There are no established annual deadlines for applications.
Requirements: The Foundation seeks applications from qualified tax-exempt 501(c)3 organizations that support the organizations and programs in the Kodiak region and serve the people's needs in such areas as health, education, community heritage, the arts, vulnerable populations, recreation, safety, and community and economic development.

Restrictions: Individuals, for-profit, and 501(c)4 or 501(c)6 organizations, non-Alaska based organizations and state or federal government agencies are not eligible for competitive grants. Applications for religious indoctrination or other religious activities, endowment building, deficit financing, fundraising, lobbying, electioneering and activities of political nature will not be considered, nor will proposals for ads, sponsorships, or special event and any proposals which discriminate as to race, gender, marital status, sexual orientation, age, disability, creed or ethnicity.
Geographic Focus: Alaska
Contact: Ricardo Lopez, Affiliate Program Officer; (907) 274-6707; fax (907) 334-5780; rlopez@alaskacf.org or kodiak@alaskacf.org
Internet: kodiakcf.org/projects/
Sponsor: Kodiak Community Foundation
P.O. Box 400
Kodiak, AK 99615

Kohl's Cares Scholarships   1447

The program honors young people between the ages of 6 and 18 who have made a difference in their communities. Scholarships are awarded to winners toward their postsecondary education. Awards are made on the store, regional, and national levels. This year, more than 2,200 kids will be recognized with over $440,000 in scholarships and prizes: store winners will receive a $50 Kohl's Gift Card; regional winners will each be awarded a $1,000 scholarship for post-secondary education; and national winners will each be awarded a total of $10,000 in scholarships for post-secondary education. In addition, Kohl's will contribute $1,000 to a nonprofit organization on behalf of each national winner.
Requirements: Nominations may be made online or by visiting a local Kohl's store for a program brochure. To be eligible, the student must meet the following criteria as of March 15: must be between the ages of 6 and 18 and not yet a high school graduate; actions must be described in detail and should document efforts above and beyond what is expected of a child his or her age; and volunteer efforts must have occurred in the last year.
Geographic Focus: All States
Date(s) Application is Due: Mar 15
Amount of Grant: 50 - 10,000 USD
Contact: Program Coordinator; (319) 341-2932; kohls@act.org
Internet: www.kohlscorporation.com/CommunityRelations/scholarship/program-information.asp
Sponsor: Kohl's Department Stores
N56 W 17000 Ridgewood Drive
Menomonee Falls, WI 53051

Kopp Family Foundation Grants   1448

The Kopp Family Foundation supports programs in Minnesota that impact youth, women, the elderly, and emergency human services; elementary and secondary education; and Roman Catholic churches and organizations. There are no specific deadlines and the Foundation board meets six times a year.
Requirements: The Foundation accepts the Minnesota Common Grant application form. Organizations should initially submit a letter of inquiry, then wait for approval to submit a proposal application. Applicants should receive funding notification within two months of submission.
Geographic Focus: Minnesota
Amount of Grant: 2,000 - 50,000 USD
Samples: St. Stephens Human Services, Minneapolis, MN, $10,000, payable over one year; Project for Pride in Living, Minneapolis, MN, $50,000, payable over one year; Minneapolis Community and Technical College Foundation, $50,000.
Contact: Lindsey Lang, Administrator; (952) 841-0438; fax (952) 841-0411; foundation@koppinvestments.com
Sponsor: Kopp Family Foundation
8400 Normandale Lake Boulevard
Bloomington, MN 55437-3837

Koret Foundation Grants   1449

The Koret Foundation supports projects in the San Francisco Bay Area (Alameda, Contra Costa, Marin, San Francisco, San Mateo, and Santa Clara Counties) related to the following: arts and culture; community development; higher education; Jewish life and culture; primary and secondary education; and youth development. It also supports projects in Israel related to economic development, higher education, and security.
Requirements: Applicants should review grant guidelines, then submit the following: a letter of inquiry; timetable for implementation and evaluation of project; population and geographic area to be served; copy of IRS determination letter; copy of most recent annual report/audited financial statement/990; how project's results will be evaluated or measured; descriptive literature about organization; listing of board of directors, trustees, officers and other key people and their affiliations; detailed description of project and amount of funding requested; and a copy of he current year's organizational budget and/or project budget.
Restrictions: Giving is limited to the Bay Area counties of San Francisco, Alameda, Contra Costa, Marin, Santa Clara, and San Mateo, California. Giving also in Israel and on a national basis for Jewish funding requests. No support for private foundations, or veterans, fraternal, military, religious, or sectarian organizations whose principal activity is for the benefit of their own membership. Funding is not available for individuals, endowment funds, or deficit financing.
Geographic Focus: All States, Israel
Contact: Marina Lum, Grants Manager; (415) 882-7740; fax (415) 882-7775; info@KoretFoundation.org
Internet: www.koretfoundation.org/apply/application.shtml

Sponsor: Koret Foundation
33 New Montgomery Street, Suite 1090
San Francisco, CA 94105-4526

Kosasa Foundation Grants 1450
The Kosasa Foundation was established in Honolulu in 1994 by Paul J. Kosasa, President and Chief Executive Officer of MNS Ltd. He is also on the board of Central Pacific Financial Corp., Central Pacific Bank (Honolulu, Hawaii) and Hawaii Community Foundation. The Foundations primary fields of interest include: arts and culture; basic and emergency aid; child welfare; elementary and secondary education; health and health care; higher education; human services; natural resources; performing arts; shelter and residential care; special population support; and youth development. Most often, support is given in the form of general operating support and program development. Typical awards range up to a maximum of $50,000, with a geographic focus on the State of Hawaii. Over the past five years, the Foundation has funded 235 grants to 89 organizations totaling $3,477,500, with the vast majority of funding supporting human service programs.
Requirements: Any 501(c)3 organization supporting program areas of focus in Hawaii are eligible to apply.
Geographic Focus: Hawaii
Amount of Grant: Up to 50,000 USD
Samples: Hawaiian Humane Society, Honolulu, Hawaii, $50,000 - general operating support for animal population control; Child and Family Services, Honolulu, Hawaii, $25,000 - fight against elder abuse; Hui Malama O Ke Kai Foundation, Honolulu, Hawaii, $25,000 - general operating support for human services programs.
Contact: Thomas S. Kosasa, Director; (808) 591-2550
Sponsor: Kosasa Foundation
766 Pohukaina Street
Honolul, HI 96813-5307

Kosciusko County Community Foundation Endowment 1451
Youth Services (KEYS) Grants
Kosciusko Endowment Youth Services (KEYS) grants are available for educational projects serving Kosciusko County. Grant amounts typically range from $100 to $1,000, and are reviewed by KEYS members. Grant applications are due February 1 and October 1, with notifications made six weeks after each deadline.
Requirements: Applicants should submit the online application form, along with the following: an explanation of the purpose and importance of the project; the number and age groups this project will affect; an itemized list of materials and/or project items requested and their costs; other funding sources the organization has asked for or received for this project; whether project is achievable with partial funding; and a copy of the organization's 501(c)3 IRS letter.
Geographic Focus: Indiana
Date(s) Application is Due: Feb 1; Oct 1
Amount of Grant: 100 - 1,000 USD
Samples: Akron Elementary School, karaoke machines to practice speaking skills, $200; Edgewood Middle School, microscopes to study freshwater environment, $667; Whitko High School, summer enrichment art classes, $500.
Contact: Kosciusko Endowment Youth Services Contact; (574) 267-1901; fax (574) 268-9780
Internet: www.kcfoundation.org/seekingfunds/educationgrants.php
Sponsor: Kosciusko County Community Foundation
102 East Market Street
Warsaw, IN 46580

Kosciusko County Community Foundation Grants 1452
The Kosciusko County Community Foundation serves Kosciusko County, Indiana. Nonprofit organizations serving Kosciusko County are eligible to apply in seven areas of interest: arts and culture, human services, civic projects, recreation, environment, health, and education. Grant applications and guidelines can be obtained at the Foundations office or website. Grant awards are announced nine weeks after each deadline.
Requirements: Grant seekers are strongly encouraged to call the Foundation's program staff to discuss a grant proposal before submitting a formal application. Once the proposal has been discussed, complete and submit a grant application with the required attachments: 6 copies of the original application; 1 copy of the IRS determination letter; 7 copies of the board of directors listing with names and addresses for all; 7 copies of staff listing with names and addresses for all; 7 copies of current internal financial statements; and 7 copies of program/project budget. Do not provide copies of news articles, brochures or other miscellaneous supporting information.
Restrictions: The Foundation will not consider grants for: individuals; political activities or those designated to influence legislation; national organizations (unless the monies are to be used solely to benefit citizens of Kosciusko County); fundraising projects;the direct benefit of the donor or the donor's family; religious organizations for the sole purpose of furthering that religion (this prohibition does not apply to funds created by donors who have specifically designated religious organizations as beneficiaries of the funds); contributions to endowments.
Geographic Focus: Indiana
Date(s) Application is Due: Jan 15; May 15; Sep 15
Contact: Stephanie Overbey, Communication & Program Director; (574) 267-1901; fax (574) 268-9780; stephanie@kcfoundation.org
Internet: www.kcfoundation.org/grants.html
Sponsor: Kosciusko County Community Foundation
102 E Market Street
Warsaw, IN 46580

Kosciusko County Community Foundation REMC Operation Round Up Grants 1453
The Kosciusko County Community Foundation serves the residents of Kosciusko County, Indiana. Kosciusko Rural Electric Membership Corporation (REMC) encourages its members to round up their electric bills to the nearest whole dollar. The extra funds are deposited into the Kosciusko REMC Operation Round Up Grants, which supports a variety of charitable causes in communities served by Kosciusko REMC. Applications are due the 15th of the following months: February, April, June, August, October, and December. Grant notifications take place within six weeks after the deadline.
Requirements: Applicants must submit the online application, along with a list of the organization's board of directors, officers, or trustees, and their phone numbers; a one page cover letter that specifies the amount requested and details about how the funds will be used locally; a copy of the organization's 501(c)3 letter; and a copy of the organization's most current financial statements.
Geographic Focus: Indiana
Date(s) Application is Due: Feb 15; Apr 15; Jun 15; Aug 15; Oct 15; Dec 15
Amount of Grant: 500 - 5,000 USD
Samples: Boys and Girls Club of Kosciusko County; provide meals to children, $2,500: Fort Wayne Philharmonic, Inc; support of three concerts, $1,000: College Mentors for Kids; launch a College Mentors for Kids at Grace College, $5,000.
Contact: Stephanie Overbey, Communication and Program Director; (574) 946-0906; fax (574) 946-0971; Stephanie@kcfoundation.org
Internet: www.kcfoundation.org/seekingfunds/remc.php
Sponsor: Kosciusko County Community Foundation
102 East Market Street
Warsaw, IN 46580

Kovler Family Foundation Grants 1454
The Blum-Kovler Foundation was established in 1985 after Everett Kovler retired from his position as President of James Beam Distilling Company. The Foundation awards general operating grants to eligible nonprofit organizations in its areas of interest, including social services, Jewish welfare funds, higher education, health services and medical research, and cultural programs. The foundation also supports youth- and child-welfare agencies and public-interest and civic-affairs groups. Grants are awarded primarily in the Chicago metropolitan area and in the Washington, D.C. area, though funding is also provided nationally. There are no application forms. Applicants should submit a one to two page written proposal with a copy of their IRS determination letter by mid-November to considered for the current year. Typical grant awarded is between $1,000 and $5,000, though a few are as much as $100,000.
Requirements: Illinois and District of Columbia nonprofit organizations are eligible.
Geographic Focus: All States, District of Columbia, Illinois
Samples: After School Matters, Chicago, IL, $1,000 - for child welfare programs (2018); Boys and Girls Club of Chicago, Chicago, IL, $1,000 - for child welfare programs (2018); Camp of Dreams, Chicago, IL, $2,500 - for child welfare programs (2018).
Contact: Johnathan Kolver, President; (312) 664-5050
Sponsor: Kovler Family Foundation
875 North Michigan Avenue, Suite 3400
Chicago, IL 60611-1958

Kovler Family Foundation Grants 1455
The Kovler Family Foundation awards grants in the areas of the arts, children/youth services, medical research (particularly diabetes), education, human services, higher education, human services, and Jewish federated giving programs. General operating or research grants are awarded primarily in the Chicago metropolitan area. There are no application forms. Applicants should submit a one to two page written proposal letter with a copy of their IRS determination letter by mid-November. Typical grant awarded is between $1,000-$5,000.
Requirements: Illinois nonprofit organizations are eligible to apply.
Restrictions: The Foundation does not award grants to individuals.
Geographic Focus: Illinois
Samples: Columbia College, Chicago, Illinois, $5,000, payable over one year; School of the Art Institute of Chicago, Chicago, Illinois, $1,500, payable over one year; University of Chicago, Chicago, Illinois, $1,000, payable over one year.
Contact: Jonathan Kovler, President and Treasurer; (312) 664-5050
Sponsor: Kovler Family Foundation
875 North Michigan Avenue
Chicago, IL 60611-1958

Kroger Company Donations 1456
Kroger has a long history of bringing help to the communities they serve. They contribute annually in funds, food, and products to support local communities. Support is limited to: Hunger Relief; Women's Health; Children's Health and Wellbeing; K-12 Education; Advancing Diversity; Sustaining the Environment; and, Grassroots Community Programs.
Requirements: Only organizations with a 501(c)3 charitable determination are eligible for donations. Organizations may contact their locally owned Kroger store (Kroger, Dillon's, Fred Meyer, Fry's, QFC, Ralph's, Smith's, Baker's, City Market, Food4Less, Foods Co., Gerbes, JayC, King Soopers, Owen's, Pay Less, Kwik Shop, Littman Jewelers, Loaf'n Jug, QuikStop, The Little Clinic, Tom Thumb, Turkey Hill, and Fred Meyer Jewelers) or the Fiscal Administrator at Kroger's corporate office for addition information about requesting a donation. An organization may receive support once per calendar year.
Restrictions: The Foundation does not make donations toward the following: Individuals; Capital campaigns; Travel expenses; Political campaigns; Sectarian or religious organizations, for projects that serve only its own members or adherents; or Organizations that discriminate on the basis of gender, race, religion, sexual orientation or nationality.

Geographic Focus: All States
Contact: Fiscal Administraor; (513) 762-4449; fax (513) 762-1295
Internet: www.communitygifts.com/Default.aspx?Zip-Code-
Locator=Enabled&ReturnTo=/Default.aspx
Sponsor: Kroger Foundation
1014 Vine Street
Cincinnati, OH 45202-1100

Laclede Gas Charitable Trust Grants 1457
The Trust represents Laclede Gas Company's recognition of its civic responsibility to those in its service area. Areas of interest include human needs and services; education and educational institutions; arts and culture; and civic and community projects. The Trust funds operating support, special projects and annual support. Application forms are available on the website. There are no deadlines. The Trustees of the Charitable Trust meet at least semi-annually.
Requirements: Eligible applicants must be 501(c)3 organizations. Only organizations in the Laclede Gas Company's service area are eligible. The service area includes the city of St. Louis and ten other counties in Eastern Missouri. See the website for a map specifying the service area.
Restrictions: The following is not eligible: individuals, family support or family reunions; advertising; political, labor, fraternal or religious organizations or civic clubs; individual K-8 schools or school-affiliated clubs or events (public or private); sports, athletic events or athletic programs; travel related events, including student trips or tours; development or production of books, films, videos or television programs; and endowment or memorial campaigns. No contribution will be made to an organization if the contribution may impair the independence of a member of Laclede's Board of Directors.
Geographic Focus: Missouri
Samples: Academy of Science, St. Louis, Missouri, $3,000 - operating support; Barnes Jewish Foundation, St. Louis, Missouri, $40,000 - operating support; and YMCA of reater St. Louis, $60,000 - operating support.
Contact: Grants Administrator; (314) 421-1979
Internet: www.lacledegas.com/service/trust.php
Sponsor: Laclede Gas Charitable Trust
720 Olive Street, Room 1517
Saint Louis, MO 63101

LaGrange County Community Foundation Grants 1458
The mission of the LaGrange County Community Foundation (LCCF) is to inspire and sustain leadership, generosity and service. Its purpose is to help community service organizations sponsor plans to meet critically important needs. The Foundation funds grants for innovative and creative projects and programs that are responsive to changing community needs in the areas of, but not restricted to: health and human services, environment, arts and culture, and recreation.
Requirements: Non-profit organizations, schools and qualifying government agencies serving the citizens of LaGrange County are invited to apply for a grant through the foundation's application process. In addition to the online application, applicants should submit a complete list of their organization's board of directors and their occupations; a copy of their specific line item budget with projected income and expenses, a copy of the organization's most recent operating budget; documentation to prove the organization's non-profit status.
Restrictions: The foundation does not make grants to individuals, except in the form of academic scholarships. Grants are generally given one-time only for specific purposes and will typically not be awarded to provide annual operating expenses or support. A grant will not be awarded to replenish funds previously expended. Grants are made with the understanding that the foundation has no obligation or commitment to provide additional support to the grantee. Grants may not be used for any political campaign, or to influence legislature of any government body other than through making available the results of nonpartisan analysis, study, and research.
Geographic Focus: Indiana
Date(s) Application is Due: Aug 1
Contact: Laura Lemings, Program Officer; (260) 463-4363; fax (260) 463-4856; llemings@lccf.net
Internet: www.lccf.net/grants.html
Sponsor: LaGrange County Community Foundation
109 E Central Avenue, Suite 3
LaGrange, IN 46761

LaGrange Independent Foundation for Endowments (L.I.F.E.) 1459
LaGrange Independent Foundation for Endowments, or L.I.F.E., is a philanthropic group of young people in LaGrange County. Representatives from four county schools are selected when they enter grade 8 and serve throughout their high school career as the advisory committee for the donor advised non-permanent fund held by the foundation. Grant applications submitted to the LCCF office are evaluated by the L.I.F.E Youth Pod in order to select recommended recipients.
Requirements: Nonprofit organizations including schools in LaGrange county are eligible to apply. Grants are awarded during the school year. The application is available at the foundation's website.
Geographic Focus: Indiana
Samples: LaGrange Communities Youth Centers, after school programming for youth: Lakeland High School, Protective suits for use in Sheriff's Dept. Rape Agression Defense (RAD) training for women: Prairie Heights Leo Club: Boomerang Backpack program for young people in elementary schools.

Contact: Laura Lemings, Executive Director; (260) 463-4363; fax (260) 463-4856; llemings@lccf.net
Internet: www.lccf.net/life.html
Sponsor: LaGrange County Community Foundation
109 E Central Avenue, Suite 3
LaGrange, IN 46761

Laidlaw Foundation Multi-Year Grants 1460
Laidlaw Foundation promotes positive youth development through inclusive youth engagement in the arts, environment and in community. The Foundation offers funding and other support to youth-led groups that have ideas and strategies for tackling issues that affect communities and the broader society. Multi-Year Grants support core operating and capacity strengthening within youth-led groups. Generally, 2-3 Multi-Year Grants are made each year.
Requirements: In order for a group to be eligible for multi-year funding there must be a history of partnering with the Foundation and the group must have received a previous grant. Groups of young people aged 14–25 are eligible to apply. They must be located within the greater Toronto area, specifically in the Greater Golden Horseshoe area. Applicants must have charitable status or partner with an organization with charitable status whose purposes are consistent with the work of the applicant group. Regardless of the type of group applying, young people must write the application, plan the project and make the project happen. Applicants should contact the Foundation about application.
Restrictions: The following is not eligible: projects outside of Canada; local projects outside of Ontario; fundraising campaigns, dinners, benefits, endowments, sponsorships, emergency funding or other special events; one-time or annual conferences, events or workshops; building or capital campaigns, renovations, furnishings, vehicles or other acquisitions; deficit reduction programs; non-secular and faith-based activities; scholarships or bursaries (other than those initiated by the Foundation); personal appeals for financial support; retroactive requests for projects already completed; campus-based or school-based groups and/or in-school programming; youth advisory committees to non-youth-led organizations; and summer camps or youth programs of organizations.
Geographic Focus: Canada
Date(s) Application is Due: Sep 7
Amount of Grant: 50,000 CAD
Contact: Ana Skinner, Youth Organizing Administrator; (416) 964-3614, ext. 307; fax (416) 975-1428; askinner@laidlawfdn.org
Internet: www.laidlawfdn.org/youth-organizing-program
Sponsor: Laidlaw Foundation
365 Bloor Street E, Suite 2000
Toronto, ON M4W 3L4 Canada

Laidlaw Foundation Youh Organizing Catalyst Grants 1461
Laidlaw Foundation promotes positive youth development through inclusive youth engagement in the arts, environment and in community. The Foundation offers funding and other support to youth-led groups that have ideas and strategies for tackling issues that affect communities and the broader society. Catalyst Grants are small 'seed' grants for a group of young people to test out an idea; do community research around issues that concern them; to develop partnerships, networks and collaborations; and to respond to a time sensitive situation. Generally four to six Catalyst Grants are funded each year. There are no deadlines. Contact the Foundation to discuss the project. The process generally takes six to eight weeks.
Requirements: Groups of young people aged 14–25 are eligible to apply. They must be located within the greater Toronto area, specifically in the Greater Golden Horseshoe area. Applicants must have charitable status or partner with an organization with charitable status whose purposes are consistent with the work of the applicant group. Regardless of the type of group applying, young people must write the application, plan the project and make the project happen.
Restrictions: The following is not eligible: projects outside of Canada; local projects outside of Ontario; fundraising campaigns, dinners, benefits, endowments, sponsorships, emergency funding or other special events; one-time or annual conferences, events or workshops; building or capital campaigns, renovations, furnishings, vehicles or other acquisitions; deficit reduction programs; non-secular and faith-based activities; scholarships or bursaries (other than those initiated by the Foundation); personal appeals for financial support; retroactive requests for projects already completed; campus-based or school-based groups and/or in-school programming; youth advisory committees to non-youth-led organizations; and summer camps or youth programs of organizations.
Geographic Focus: Canada
Amount of Grant: 5,000 CAD
Contact: Ana Skinner, Youth Organizing Administrator; (416) 964-3614, ext. 307; fax (416) 975-1428; askinner@laidlawfdn.org
Internet: www.laidlawfdn.org/youth-organizing-program
Sponsor: Laidlaw Foundation
365 Bloor Street E, Suite 2000
Toronto, ON M4W 3L4 Canada

Laidlaw Foundation Youth Organizaing Initiatives Grants 1462
Laidlaw Foundation promotes positive youth development through inclusive youth engagement in the arts, environment and in community. The Foundation offers funding and other support to youth-led groups that have ideas and strategies for tackling issues that affect communities and the broader society. Initiative Grants support youth-led groups to implement a specific project they have developed; to focus on strengthening their group or organizational capacity; and to develop collaborations, partnerships and networks. Generally 12-20 initiative are funded per year.

Requirements: Groups of young people aged 14–25 are eligible to apply. They must be located within the greater Toronto area, specifically in the Greater Golden Horseshoe area. Applicants must have charitable status or partner with an organization with charitable status whose purposes are consistent with the work of the applicant group. Regardless of the type of group applying, young people must write the application, plan the project and make the project happen. Before developing a full proposal, applicants should contact the Foundation to determine project eligibility. Applications are available on the website.
Restrictions: The following is not eligible: projects outside of Canada; local projects outside of Ontario; fundraising campaigns, dinners, benefits, endowments, sponsorships, emergency funding or other special events; one-time or annual conferences, events or workshops; building or capital campaigns, renovations, furnishings, vehicles or other acquisitions; deficit reduction programs; non-secular and faith-based activities; scholarships or bursaries (other than those initiated by the Foundation); personal appeals for financial support; retroactive requests for projects already completed; campus-based or school-based groups and/or in-school programming; youth advisory committees to non-youth-led organizations; and summer camps or youth programs of organizations.
Geographic Focus: Canada
Date(s) Application is Due: Mar 9; Sep 7
Amount of Grant: 10,000 - 5,000 CAD
Samples: Amadeusz/Albion Neighbourhood Services, Toronto, Ontario, Canada, $50,000 - project support; Bright Future Alliance, Toronto, Ontario, Canada, $35,960 - project support; and Youth Arts and Entertainment Council/Elora Centre for the Arts, Elora, Ontario, Canada, $11,825 - project support.
Contact: Ana Skinner, Youth Organizing Administrator; (416) 964-3614, ext. 307; fax (416) 975-1428; askinner@laidlawfdn.org
Internet: www.laidlawfdn.org/youth-organizing-program
Sponsor: Laidlaw Foundation
365 Bloor Street E, Suite 2000
Toronto, ON M4W 3L4 Canada

Lake County Community Fund Grants 1463
The Lake County Community Grant was established to be responsive to community projects throughout Lake County in the areas of arts and culture, civic affairs, community development, education, the environment, health, human services, and youth services. The Foundation will make grants to non-profit organizations implementing projects with the most potential to improve the quality of life of a substantial number of residents of Lake County. Geographic distribution may be considered in awarding grants. Grants typically range from $1,000 to $25,000.
Requirements: Funding priorities include projects that: develop or test new solutions to community problems; address prevention as well as remediation; assist underserved community resources; provide a sustained effect for a substantial number of residents; improve the efficiency of non-profit groups; provide a favorable ratio between the amount of money requested and number of people served; facilitate collaboration among organizations without duplicating services; encourage volunteerism, civic engagement, and development. Applicants must submit the online detailed application, along with the grant narrative, project budget, a list of applicant's board of directors, summary of the organization's current fiscal year operating budget as well as financial audit or review; evidence of Board approval for this application, copy of tax exempt status, and organization's profile on GuideStar (www.guidestar).
Restrictions: The Legacy Foundation does not support: general operating expenses; endowment campaigns, annual campaigns, or fundraising events; travel grants; grants for individual schools or sponsorship of sports teams; previously incurred debt or retroactive funding for current projects; individuals and independent scholarly research projects; and religious or sectarian programs, political parties, or campaigns.
Geographic Focus: Indiana
Date(s) Application is Due: Mar 1; May 1; Sep 1; Nov 1
Amount of Grant: 1,000 - 25,000 USD
Contact: Barry Tyler, Jr., Community Initiatives Officer; (219) 736-1880; fax (219) 736-1940; legacy@legacyfoundationlakeco.org or btyler@legacyfdn.org
Internet: www.legacyfoundationlakeco.org/grantsfundingopps.html
Sponsor: Legacy Foundation
1000 East 80th Place, 302 South
Merrillville, IN 46410

Lalor Foundation Postdoctoral Fellowships 1464
The Lalor Foundation postdoctoral fellowship program supports promising new researchers in establishing scientific and teaching careers. The mission of the program is to support these researchers early in their work so that they can become independently funded in the field of mammalian reproductive biology as related to the regulation of fertility. The individual nominated by the applicant institution for the postdoctoral fellowship for conduct of the work may be a citizen of any country. Fellowships will be $42,000 per year for coverage of fellowship stipend, fringes and institutional overhead.
Requirements: U.S. institutions must be exempt from federal income taxes under Section 501(c)3 of the U.S. Internal Revenue Code and must submit a determination letter from the Internal Revenue Service stating that it is not a private foundation. The individual nominated should have training and experience at least equal to the Ph.D. or M.D. level and should not have a faculty appointment (i.e., instructor, lecturer or higher). Potential fellows should not have held the doctoral degree more than two years from receipt of the degree.
Restrictions: Institutional overhead may not exceed 10 percent of the total fellowship award.
Geographic Focus: All States
Date(s) Application is Due: Jan 15
Amount of Grant: 42,000 USD

Contact: Susan Haff, (617) 426-7080, ext. 323; fax (617) 426-5441; shaff@gmafoundationst.com or fellowshipmanager@gmafoundations.com
Internet: www.lalorfound.org/?page_id=13
Sponsor: Lalor Foundation
77 Summer Street, 8th Floor
Boston, MA 02110-1006

Land O'Lakes Foundation California Region Grants 1465
The California Regions Grants were developed specifically for selected Land O'Lakes dairy communities in the Orland, Tulare, Kings, Bakersfield, and Ontario regions. The program works to improve quality of life through donations to valuable projects and charitable endeavors recommended by the Foundation's California dairy member-leaders. Community organizations may be eligible for funding of $500 to $5,000 for local projects and programs. Funds could be used to support such worthwhile projects as: backing local food pantries or emergency feeding efforts; aiding 4-H or FFA programs; building a new park pavilion for the community; or purchasing books for the community library.
Requirements: To be considered, grant proposals must demonstrate how the donation will be used to help improve community quality of life. Grants are restricted to organizations that have been granted tax-exempt status under Section 501(c)3 of the Internal Revenue Code. Foundation awards grants to projects that address the following focus areas: hunger relief; youth and education; civic improvements; and arts and culture. Applicants may refer to the online application for further information about the application process.
Restrictions: Grants will not be awarded for the following purposes: scholarship funds; gifts or fundraisers for individuals; non-public church use; or projects that do not demonstrate a broad application of the principles established in the Foundation's mission statement.
Geographic Focus: California
Contact: Martha Atkins-Sakry, Executive Assistant; (651) 481-2470; fax (651) 481-2212; MLAtkins-Sakry@landolakes.com
Internet: www.landolakesinc.com/company/corporateresponsibility/foundation/californiagrants/default.aspx
Sponsor: Land O'Lakes Foundation
P.O. Box 64101
St. Paul, MN 55164-0150

Land O'Lakes Foundation Community Grants 1466
Land O'Lakes Foundation Community Grants provide support to nonprofit organizations that are working to improve communities where Land O'Lakes has a large concentration of members or employees. These include organizations that: provide funding to human services; work to alleviate hunger; build knowledge and leadership skills of rural youth; address and solve regional problems; and promote artistic endeavors, especially in underserved rural areas, touring or outreach programs. Special emphasis is directed toward programs that address issues of hunger and are statewide, regional, or national in scope. Requests for more than $5,000 are reviewed in February, June, August, and December. There is no deadline for requests for less than $5,000, but it may take up to three months to fully consider the request. Arts and culture requests are due on May 1. The application is available online.
Requirements: Grants are restricted to organizations that have tax-exempt status under Section 501(c)3 of the Internal Revenue Code. Grants are limited to one per organization per calendar year.
Restrictions: Applications for the following year will only be accepted on or after January 1. Funding generally will not be used for the following categories: lobbying, political and religious organizations; veteran, fraternal and labor organizations; individuals; fundraising events, dinners or benefits; advertising; college/university capital/endowment funds; scholarships; travel expenses for individuals/groups; racing/sports sponsorships; or disease/medical related, including research or treatment.
Geographic Focus: Arkansas, California, Idaho, Illinois, Indiana, Iowa, Kansas, Michigan, Minnesota, Mississippi, Missouri, Nebraska, North Dakota, Ohio, Oregon, Pennsylvania, South Dakota, Texas, Washington, Wisconsin
Amount of Grant: 500 - 10,000 USD
Contact: Martha Atkins-Sakry, Executive Assistant; (651) 481-2470; fax (651) 481-2212; MLAtkins-Sakry@landolakes.com
Internet: www.landolakesinc.com/company/corporateresponsibility/foundation/communitygrants/description/default.aspx
Sponsor: Land O'Lakes Foundation
P.O. Box 64101
St. Paul, MN 55164-0150

Land O'Lakes Foundation Mid-Atlantic Grants 1467
The Land O'Lakes Foundation Mid-Atlantic Grants were developed specifically for the company's dairy communities in Maryland, New Jersey, New York, Pennsylvania, and Virginia. The program works to improve quality of life by supporting worthy projects and charitable endeavors initiated by our Mid-Atlantic dairy-member leaders. Community organizations applying for grants may be eligible for donations of $500 to $5,000 for local projects and programs. Funds could be used to support such worthwhile projects as: backing local food pantries or emergency feeding efforts; aiding 4-H or FFA programs; building a new park pavilion for the community; establishing a local wetland preserve; or purchasing books for the community library. Application procedures are available online.
Requirements: Applications are initiated by Land O'Lakes farmer-members. An Area Procurement Specialist (APS) review is also part of this process. To be considered, grant proposals must demonstrate how the donation will be used to help improve community quality of life. Mid-Atlantic grants are generally restricted to organizations that have been granted tax-exempt status under Section 501(c)3 of the Internal Revenue Code. The Foundation awards grants to projects that best address the following areas: hunger relief;

youth and education; rural leadership; civic improvements; soil and water preservation; and art and culture.

Restrictions: Grants will not be awarded for the following purposes: scholarship funds, gifts or fund raisers for individuals, or non-public religious use.

Geographic Focus: Maryland, New Jersey, New York, Pennsylvania, Virginia

Amount of Grant: 500 - 5,000 USD

Contact: Martha Atkins-Sakry, Executive Assistant; (651) 481-2470 or (651) 481-2212; MLAtkins-Sakry@landolakes.com

Internet: www.landolakesinc.com/company/corporateresponsibility/foundation/midatlanticgrants/default.aspx

Sponsor: Land O'Lakes Foundation

P.O. Box 64101

St. Paul, MN 55164-0150

Lands' End Corporate Giving Program   1468

The Corporation awards grants to nonprofits for youth and family services programs in their area of company operations in Wisconsin. Areas of interest include education, community development, environment, and health and human services.

Requirements: Wisconsin nonprofits are eligible. Organizations should submit the following: a timetable for implementation and evaluation of the project; statement of the problem that the project will address; population and geographic area to be served; name, address and phone number of organization; copy of IRS determination letter; copy of most recent annual report/audited financial statement/990; how the project's results will be evaluated or measured; list of company employees involved with the organization; detailed description of project and amount of funding requested; contact person; copy of current year's organizational budget and/or project budget; and listing of additional sources and amount of support. Applicants should also include a description of their past involvement with Lands' End, if any.

Restrictions: The Foundation does not consider grants for organizations without nonprofit status; individuals; political organizations, campaigns, or candidates for public office; lobbying groups; advertising in programs, bulletins, yearbooks, or brochures; testimonial/awards dinners; endowments; loans; religious groups for religious purposes; pageants; purchasing of land; salaries; administrative costs; international programs; research programs; or general operating expenses.

Geographic Focus: Wisconsin

Date(s) Application is Due: Mar 31; Jun 30; Sep 30; Dec 31

Contact: Jessica Winzenried, Corporate Giving Manager; (608) 935-6776 or (608) 935-6728; fax (608) 935-6432; donate@landsend.com

Sponsor: Lands' End

2 Lands' End Lane

Dodgeville, WI 53595

Latkin Charitable Foundation Grants   1469

The Latkin Charitable Foundation awards grants to eligible California nonprofit organizations to: assist and promote the welfare and health of the elderly; prevent cruelty to animals; provide educational scholarships for deserving students enrolled in institutions of higher learning; provide medical assistance, supplies, and equipment for persons suffering as a result of calamity or disaster; prevent child abuse; and provide assistance to the needy. Areas of interest include human services, aging centers and services, and family services. Types of support include general operating funds, emergency funds, equipment acquisition, and scholarship endowments. Annual deadlines are April 1 and October 1.

Requirements: California 501(c)3 nonprofit organizations serving Santa Barbara County are eligible to apply.

Geographic Focus: California

Date(s) Application is Due: Apr 1; Oct 1

Amount of Grant: 2,000 - 5,000 USD

Samples: Academy of Healing Arts for Teens, Santa Barbara, California, $3,000 - funding for after-school programs for teens; Community Partners in Caring, Santa Maria, California, $3,000 - fund a portion of the Volunteer Manager and Volunteer Coordinator's salaries; Friendship Adult Day Care Center, Santa Barbara, California, $4,000 - funding toward the H.E.A.R.T. (Help Elders At Risk Today) program, which provides services for low income individuals.

Contact: Janice Gibbons, c/o Union Bank; (805) 564-6211 or (805) 564-6200

Sponsor: Latkin Charitable Foundation

P.O. Box 45174

San Francisco, CA 94145-0174

Laura B. Vogler Foundation Grants   1470

The Vogler Foundation supports innovative programs and projects in New York City and Long Island in the areas of education, health care, and social services. The Foundation is particularly interested in organizations that serve and support children, the elderly, and the disadvantaged. Types of support include general operating support, program development, research grants, and seed money grants. Grants provide one-time, nonrenewable support. Most recent grant awards have ranged from $2,500 to $5,000. The annual deadlines for applications are March 1, July 1, and November 1.

Requirements: Nonprofit 501(c)3 organizations in New York City and Long Island, New York, may submit proposals.

Restrictions: Grants are not awarded to support building or endowment funds, annual fund-raising campaigns, or matching gifts. Requests for funds for conferences, seminars, or loans are not accepted.

Geographic Focus: New York

Date(s) Application is Due: Mar 1; Jul 1; Nov 1

Amount of Grant: 2,500 - 5,000 USD

Samples: Brooklyn Public Library, Brooklyn, New York, $3,000 - support of a creative aging program for adults 55-years-old and older; Cathedral Church of St. John the Divine, New York, New York, $3,500 - fighting poverty; Jewish Guild for the Blind, New York, New York, $5,000 - rehabilitation services to visually impaired/blind children.

Contact: Lawrence L. D'Amato, President; (718) 423-3000; fax (631) 251-7162; voglerfound@gmail.com

Internet: sites.google.com/site/voglerfoundation/

Sponsor: Laura B. Vogler Foundation

51 Division Street, P.O. Box 501

Sag Harbor, NY 11963

Laura Bush Foundation for America's Libraries Grants   1471

The Laura Bush Foundation supports the education of children by awarding grants to school libraries to update, extend, and diversify the book collections of America's school libraries. In order to promote a love of reading, the goal of the Laura Bush Foundation (LBF) is to provide books and reading materials to the school libraries and students that most need them. Consequently, grants are available only for library books and magazine/serial copies and subscriptions. The Foundation makes grants of up to $6,000 to update, extend, and diversify the book collections of the libraries that receive them.

Requirements: Any school may apply, but priority for grants will be given to those schools in which a high percentage of the school population receives free or reduced lunches, and are unlikely to have books and reading materials at home. All applications must be made online through the Foundation website. Applicants are encouraged to read Frequently Asked Questions and the Scoring Rubric sections on the website before filling out the application and to use Explorer to complete the form.

Restrictions: The Foundation is unable to honor requests for staffing, shelving, furniture, equipment, software, videos, classroom book sets or any kind of book guides, tests or exams.

Geographic Focus: All States, Puerto Rico, U.S. Virgin Islands

Date(s) Application is Due: Dec 31

Amount of Grant: Up to 6,000 USD

Contact: Alicia Reid, Grants Manager; (202) 955-5890 or (202) 263-4774; laurabushfoundation@cfncr.org

Internet: www.laurabushfoundation.org/foundation.html

Sponsor: Laura Bush Foundation for America's Libraries

1201 15th Street NW, Suite 420

Washington, D.C. 20005

Laura Jane Musser Intercultural Harmony Grants   1472

The Laura Jane Musser Grants seek to promote mutual understanding and cooperation between groups and citizens of different cultural backgrounds within defined geographical areas through collaborative, cross-cultural exchange projects. Priority is given to projects that: include members of various cultural communities working together on projects with common goals; build positive relationships across cultural lines; engender intercultural harmony, tolerance, understanding, and respect; enhance intercultural communication, rather than cultural isolation, while at the same time celebrating and honoring the unique qualities of each culture. To be eligible for funding, projects must demonstrate: need in the community for the intercultural exchange project; grassroots endorsement by participants across cultural lines, as well as their active participation in planning and implementation of the project; the ability of the organization to address the challenges of working across the cultural barriers identified by the project; and tangible benefits in the larger community. Projects can be carried out in a number of areas, including, but not limited to the arts, community service, and youth activities. Detailed guidelines for the proposal are available at the Musser website. The deadline to apply is October 15th, and awards vary from $5,000 to $25,000.

Requirements: Organizations eligible for support include 501(c)3 nonprofits; organizations that are forming if they have a documented fiscal agent relationship; and organizations located within one of the eligible states. Funding will cover new programs or projects within their first three years or the planning and implementation phase of a project.

Restrictions: Capital expenses, general operating expenses, and ongoing program support are not eligible for funding.

Geographic Focus: Colorado, Hawaii, Michigan, Minnesota, New York, Texas, Wyoming

Date(s) Application is Due: Oct 15

Amount of Grant: 5,000 - 25,000 USD

Samples: Conexiones, Morris, Minnesota, $5,500 - to fund Conexiones Day 2020 (2020); Project FINE, Winona, Minnesota, $25,000 - to fund welcoming table (2020); The Yes Network, St. Cloud, Minnesota, $25,000 - to fund the art of community building (2020).

Contact: Mary Karen Lynn-Klimenko, Grants Program Manager; (612) 825-2024; ljmusserfund@earthlink.net

Internet: musserfund.org/intercultural-harmony/

Sponsor: Laura Jane Musser Fund

318 West 48th Street

Minneapolis, MN 55419

Laura L. Adams Foundation Grants   1473

Established in New York in 2001 with a donation on behalf of Laura L. Adams, offers grants primarily in New York. The Foundation's major field of interest include education, health care, and recreation. Types of support include general operating funds and scholarship funding. Most recent grants have ranged from $875 to $12,500. A formal application is required, and the annual deadline for submission is October 31.

Requirements: 501(c)3 organizations either in, or serving the residents of, New York state are eligible to apply.

Geographic Focus: New York

Date(s) Application is Due: Oct 31

Amount of Grant: 875 - 12,500 USD
Samples: Buffalo Storm Basketball Club, Buffalo, New York, $10,000 - amateur sports organization; Immaculate Academy, Hamburg, New york, $12,500 - general operating support for education; Amanda Hanson Foundation, Orchard Park, New York, $875 - scholarship fund.
Contact: Harold Summar, Director; (716) 854-8000 or (716) 854-2899
Sponsor: Laura L. Adams Foundation
P.O. Box 466
Hamburg, NY 14075-0466

Laura Moore Cunningham Foundation Grants 1474

The Laura Moore Cunningham Foundation is dedicated to advancing the State of Idaho. Priorities include rural healthcare, educational programs for children, programs in underserved communities, and programs for underserved populations. Each year the Foundation accepts applications from throughout the State, allowing organizations of all types to express their need. The Foundation is interested in organizations that run in a cost-effective manner, serving large numbers of people who are truly in need.
Requirements: Eligible applicants must be 501(c)3 Idaho organizations. The Foundation does not limit giving to a certain type of program or need; however administrative costs are not preferred.
Restrictions: Individuals are ineligible.
Geographic Focus: Idaho
Date(s) Application is Due: May 15
Samples: The Peregrine Fund, Boise, Idaho, $100,000 - education programs; Teton Valley Health Care Foundation, Driggs, Idaho, $30,000 - boiler upgrade; and Jerome Public Library, Jerome, Idaho, $4,000 - new library books.
Contact: Harry L. Bettis, President and Treasurer; (208) 472-4066; lmcf_idaho@msn.com
Internet: lauramoorecunningham.org/Applying_for_Grants.html
Sponsor: Laura Moore Cunningham Foundation
P.O. Box 1157
Boise, ID 83701

Laurel Foundation Grants 1475

Laurel Foundation Grants focus on programs in Pittsburgh and southwestern Pennsylvania that offer long-term benefits for participants and the community. The Foundation favors programs from nonprofit organizations that foster individual responsibility and self-sufficiency; exhibit a commitment to sound fiscal and program management; implement collaborative efforts; and demonstrate measurable outcomes. Types of funding include those that concentrate in the fields of arts and culture; education; environment; and public/society benefit. Organizations are advised to carefully review the Foundation website to gauge its possible interest prior to submitting a full proposal. If there is uncertainty, a brief, one-page letter of inquiry may be sent to the President, including a summary of the project and related costs.
Requirements: Nonprofit organizations in Pittsburgh and southwestern Pennsylvania may submit applications. The Board meets in June and December. Proposals submitted for consideration at these meetings must be received by April 1 and October 1. Proposals may follow the format of the Common Grant Application, which can be accessed at the Grantmakers of Western Pennsylvania website.
Restrictions: Individuals are not eligible for funding, nor are grants made for scholarships or fellowships. Social and cultural organizations whose services fall outside the Greater Pittsburgh area are not encouraged to submit a request. Laurel Foundation does not ordinarily approve multi-year grants, preferring instead to monitor the status of a program prior to additional funding approval.
Geographic Focus: Pennsylvania
Date(s) Application is Due: Apr 1; Oct 1
Amount of Grant: 5,000 - 55,000 USD
Samples: Grist Mill Productions, Jennerstown, PA, general operating support for the theater season of the Mountain Playhouse, $35,000; Ohio Valley General Hospital, McKees Rocks, PA, School of Nursing Simulation Laboratory to provide world-class vocational nursing medical training using state-of-the-art simulation facilities, $35,000; Animal Rescue League of Western Pennsylvania, Pittsburgh, PA, help replace the existing roof of the Wildlife Center to benefit the animals in their care, $40,000; Allegheny Institute for Public Policy, Pittsburgh, PA, general operating support for the institute's research efforts in the areas of mass transit, education, and economic development and to publish the finding in its weekly Policy Briefs, $10,000.
Contact: Elizabeth Tata, President and Secretary; (412) 765-2400; laurelcontact@laurelfdn.org
Internet: www.laurelfdn.org/grants_program.html
Sponsor: Laurel Foundation
2 Gateway Center, Suite 1800
Pittsburgh, PA 15222

Laurie H. Wollmuth Charitable Trust Grants 1476

The Laurie H. Wollmuth Charitable Trust was established in New York in 2000, following the sudden and tragic death of an executive of Goldman Sachs. with the expressed purpose to support religious organizations, youth programs, and education. Its primary region of giving is centered in the State of New Jersey. Since there are no formal application materials required, interested parties should forward a proposal letter, which includes a detailed description of project and amount of funding requested. There are no annual deadlines. Most recently, awards have ranged from $500 to $15,000.
Geographic Focus: New Jersey
Amount of Grant: 500 - 15,000 USD

Samples: New Jersey Rockets Youth Hockey association, Berkeley Heights, New Jersey, $500 - general operating support; Pingry School, Martinsville, New Jersey, $15,000 - general operating support.
Contact: Rory Deutsch, Trustee; (212) 382-3300
Sponsor: Laurie H. Wollmutch Charitable Trust
500 Fifth Avenue, Suite 1200
New York, NY 10110

Lavina Parker Trust Grants 1477

The Lavina Parker Trust was established in 1992 to provide support for mentally disabled children living in Kay County, Oklahoma. The Lavina Parker Trust accepts applications from charitable organizations for the purpose of "aiding, maintaining, educating, helping, assisting and providing medical and psychiatric care for mentally disabled children under 19 years of age in Kay County, Oklahoma." This foundation makes three to four awards each year and grants are typically between $20,000 and $44,000.
Requirements: Applicants must have 501(c)3 tax-exempt status and serve communities in Kay County, Oklahoma. Applications will be submitted online through the Bank of America website.
Restrictions: The trust does not support requests from individuals, organizations attempting to influence policy through direct lobbying, or any political campaigns.
Geographic Focus: Oklahoma
Date(s) Application is Due: Jun 15
Amount of Grant: 20,000 - 44,000 USD
Samples: Blackwell Public School Foundation, Blackwell, OK, $44,000 - awarded for general operations of the organization (2018); Newkirk Public Schools, Newkirk, OK, $22,000 - awarded to add a part-time special education paraprofessional and a full-time teacher (2018).
Contact: Kelly Garlock, Philanthropic Client Manager; (800) 357-7094; tx.philanthropic@bankofamerica.com or tx.philanthropic@ustrust.com
Internet: www.bankofamerica.com/philanthropic/foundation/?fnId=156
Sponsor: Lavina Parker Trust
P.O. Box 831041
Dallas, TX 75283-1041

Lee and Ramona Bass Foundation Grants 1478

The Foundation was established in 1993 to support nonprofit organizations that provide important services for people, primarily within the state of Texas. Funding is provided in the following categories: schools, colleges and universities within Texas, with emphasis placed upon faculty development and liberal arts programs; community programs and projects, particularly related to the arts and the environment, such as museums, zoos, and educational/research institutions; and national and regional conservation programs. Preliminary inquiries are requested, in the form of a letter briefly describing the organization and the program or project. Formal proposals are accepted only after the Foundation has responded to the preliminary inquiry.
Requirements: Eligible applicants must have 501(c)3 organizations.
Restrictions: No grants are made to individuals.
Geographic Focus: All States
Samples: Intercollegiate Studies Institute, Wilmington, Delaware, $700,000 (over 2 years) - support for the Western Civilization Program and the website marketing program; and The Peregrine Fund, Inc., Boise, Idaho, $1,500,000 (over 3 years) - recovery of the Northern Aplomado Falcon.
Contact: Valleau Wilkie Jr., Executive Director; (817) 336-0494; fax (817) 332-2176; cjohns@sidrichardson.org
Internet: www.leeandramonabass.org/grantguidlines.html
Sponsor: Lee and Ramona Bass Foundation
309 Main Street
Fort Worth, TX 76102

Legler Benbough Foundation Grants 1479

The mission of the Foundation is to improve the quality of life of the people in the City of San Diego. To accomplish that mission, the Foundation focuses on three target areas: providing economic opportunity; enhancing cultural opportunity; and providing a focus for health, education and welfare funding. Interested applicants may submit an initial letter requesting funds. When the Foundation wishes to pursue the request, it will provide an application form to the applicant. Initial letters preceding applications are due by February 15 and August 15. Applications (for invited applicants) are due by March 15 and September 15.
Requirements: Awards are made only in the Foundation's focus areas. Funding focuses on activities in support of San Diego city arts and cultural institutions, scientific or research organizations, and health, education and welfare programs.
Restrictions: The following are not funded: capital projects unless there is a special situation where capital expenditure is the best way to achieve a stated objective; awards to individuals; awards for special events, fundraising or recognition events; and projects in the area of the homeless, AIDS, alcohol or drug rehabilitation or treatment and seniors.
Geographic Focus: California
Contact: Peter Ellsworth, President; (619) 235-8099; fax (619) 235-8077; peter@benboughfoundation.org
Thomas E. Cisco, Treasurer; (619) 235-8099; fax (619) 235-8077; thomas@benboughfoundation.org
Internet: www.benboughfoundation.org/criteria.php
Sponsor: Legler Benbough Foundation
2550 5th Avenue, Suite 132
San Diego, CA 92103-6622

LEGO Children's Fund Grants   1480

The LEGO Group is committed to helping children develop their creativity and learning skills through constructive play. The LEGO Children's Fund extends this commitment to local and national organizations that support innovative projects and programming to cultivate and celebrate a child's exploration of personal creativity and creative problem-solving in all forms. The Fund will provide quarterly grants for programs, either in part or in total, with a special interest paid to collaborative efforts and in providing matching funds to leverage new dollars into the receiving organization. Priority consideration will be given to programs that both meet the Fund's goals and are supported in volunteer time and effort by LEGO employees.

Requirements: Nonprofit organizations organizations and groups who cater to children ages birth - 14 with 501(c)3 status located anywhere in the United States are eligible to apply. Also eligible are educational organizations as defined in USC 26 § 170 (C) with specific, identifiable needs primarily in these areas of support: (1) Early childhood education and development that is directly related to creativity; (2) Technology and communication projects that advance learning opportunities. Special consideration will be given to applications from the Connecticut and Western Massachusetts area; groups that support disadvantaged children; groups that are supported by LEGO employee volunteers; and, special projects or programs designed to elevate a child's opportunities for exploring creativity. There are no restrictions on grant amounts up to the quarterly allocation. Typical awards, however are between USD $500 and USD $5,000.

Restrictions: The Foundation does not support: Individuals, scholarships, tuition, research, etc; Sectarian or religious oriented activities; Political activities including direct or grass roots lobbying; Offset the costs of tuition for undergraduate, graduate, or post-graduate education; Direct humanitarian and/or disaster relief; Capital campaigns; Debt retirement programs; Debt that has been incurred including mortgages, lines of credit, etc; Ongoing operating costs including completed projects, existing staff costs, existing organizational overhead, etc; Support general or annual fund raising drives; Support institutional benefits; Honorary functions; General endowments, annual appeals or similar appeals; Support overhead costs, operating budgets or staff salaries; Capital projects including, but not limited to, buildings, furniture or renovation projects; Deficit financing; Operating budgets; Efforts routinely supported by government agencies or the general public; Expansion or continuation funding of existing programs.

Geographic Focus: All States
Date(s) Application is Due: Jan 15; Apr 15; Jul 15; Oct 15
Amount of Grant: 500 - 5,000 USD
Contact: Grant Administrator; 860-763-6670; LEGOChildrensFund@lego.com
Internet: www.legochildrensfund.org/Guidelines.html
Sponsor: LEGO Children's Fund
P.O. Box 916
Enfield, CT 06083-0916

Lemelson-MIT InvenTeam Grants   1481

The Lemelson-MIT Awards honor both established and rising inventors for their ingenuity, creativity and contribution to invention and innovation. Lemelson-MIT InvenTeams are teams of high school students, teachers, and mentors that receive grants up to $10,000 each to invent technological solutions to real-world problems. InvenTeam grants support a non-competitive, team-based approach to foster inventiveness among high school students. The initiative evolved from the High School Invention Apprenticeship (1998-2002). InvenTeam students rely on inquiry and hands-on problem solving as they apply lessons from science, technology, engineering, and math (STEM) to develop invention prototypes. Interactive, self-directed learning coupled with STEM curricula are essential for experiencing invention. Students learn to work in teams, while collaborating with intended users of their inventions. They partner with professionals in their communities to enrich their experiences.

Requirements: Grants are awarded to teams under the supervision of teacher applicants, who are expected to work collaboratively with their teams in the spirit of self-directed learning. Teams may be formed in class or as extracurricular activities.

Geographic Focus: All States
Date(s) Application is Due: Sep 6
Amount of Grant: Up to 10,000 USD
Contact: Ian A. Waitz, Dean of Engineering; (617) 253-0218 or (617) 253-3291; fax (617) 258-8276; invent@mit.edu or iaw@mit.edu
Joshua Schuler, Executive Director; (617) 452-2147; fax (617) 258-8276
Internet: web.mit.edu/inventeams/
Sponsor: Massachusetts Institute of Technology
77 Massachusetts Avenue, Room 1-206
Cambridge, MA 02139-4307

Leo Goodwin Foundation Grants   1482

The Leo Goodwin Foundation offers grants in the areas of arts, culture, humanities; education; health; human services; and public benefit. Types of support include: capital campaigns for museums and performing arts centers; literacy programs and educational foundations; community college scholarships; cancer research institutes; boys and girls clubs; and child care organizations. There are no deadlines, and organizations may apply at any time. The trustees meet once a month to assess requests for funding.

Requirements: Applicants must be 501(c)3 nonprofit organizations in the state of Florida. All requests must be submitted with the following information: cover letter stating purpose of program and amount requested; objectives, demographics - social and economic status, age, gender, etc; how funds will be used; operating budget, current audited statement and tax return; IRS 501(c)3 status letter; non-recovation statement; funding sources with amounts received; names and information of governing board members; outcome measures and results; and strategic partners or alliances in delivery of services.

Restrictions: Individuals are not eligible.
Geographic Focus: Florida
Amount of Grant: 1,000 - 25,000 USD
Contact: Helen Furia, Trustee; (954) 772-6863; fax (954) 491-2051; hfurialgj@bellsouth.net
Internet: leogoodwinfoundation.org/
Sponsor: Leo Goodwin Foundation
800 Corporate Drive, Suite 500
Fort Lauderdale, FL 33334-3621

Leola Osborn Trust Grants   1483

The Leola Osborn Trust accepts applications from charitable organizations for the purpose of "aiding maintaining, helping, educating and providing medical care and treatment for mentally disabled and underprivileged children, under the age of 22 years and residing in Tonkawa, Oklahoma, or within a distance of 10 miles of the city limits of Tonkawa, Oklahoma." This foundation makes up to two awards each year and grants are typically between $1,000 and $6,000.

Requirements: Applicants must have 501(c)3 tax-exempt status and serve communities in Tonkawa, Oklahoma. Applications will be submitted online through the Bank of America website. A grant report is required within 1 year of the grant application date, regardless of whether all of the funds have been spent.

Restrictions: The trust does not support requests from individuals, organizations attempting to influence policy through direct lobbying, or any political campaigns.

Geographic Focus: Connecticut
Date(s) Application is Due: Jun 15
Amount of Grant: 1,000 - 6,000 USD
Samples: Tonkawa Public Schools, Tonkawa, Oklahoma, $6,000 - awarded to purchase equipment, assessment materials, therapy materials, and curriculum to serve special education students (2018); Tonkawa Public Library, Tonkawa, Oklahoma, $4,000 - awarded for program support (2018).
Contact: Kelly Garlock, Philanthropic Client Manager; (800) 357-7094; tx.philanthropic@bankofamerica.com or tx.philanthropic@ustrust.com
Internet: www.bankofamerica.com/philanthropic/foundation/?fnId=157
Sponsor: Leola Osborn Trust
Bank of America NA P.O. Box 831
Dallas, TX 75283-1041

Leo Niessen Jr., Charitable Trust Grants   1484

Leo Niessen lived in Abington Township, Montgomery County, Pennsylvania. In 1993, his Foundation was funded from a testamentary bequest. He was a charitable man, who also made substantial philanthropic gifts to Holy Redeemer Hospital during his lifetime. He had a special affinity for Red Cloud Indian School of Pine Ridge, South Dakota. To this day, the Co-trustees of his Foundation continue to support this school, as well as the Hospital and The Society for the Propagation of the Faith. All grants are made in the memory of Leo Niessen and his family. The Foundation also supports organizations: that provide health services for all ages; which educate the needy and educable at all academic levels, without regard to age; working for and on behalf of youth and the elderly, and which provide assistance to the homeless and economically disadvantaged; which provide spiritual and emotional guidance. Application Deadlines are, January 31 and July 31. Application forms are available online. Applicants will receive notice acknowledging receipt of the grant request, and subsequently be notified of the grant declination or approval.

Requirements: Pennsylvania 501(c)3 nonprofit organizations are eligible to apply. Proposals should be submitted in the following format: completed Common Grant Application Form; an original Proposal Statement; an audited financial report and a current year operating budget; a copy of your official IRS Letter with your tax determination; a listing of your Board of Directors. Proposal Statements (second item in the above Format) should answer these questions: what are the objectives and expected outcomes of this program/project/request; what strategies will be used to accomplish your objective; what is the timeline for completion; if this is part of an on-going program, how long has it been in operation; what criteria will you use to measure success; if the request is not fully funded, what other sources can you engage; an Itemized budget should be included; please describe any collaborative ventures. Prior to the distribution of funds, all approved grantees must sign and return a Grant Agreement Form, stating that the funds will be used for the purpose intended. Progress reports and Completion reports must also be filed as required for your specific grant. All current grantees must be in good standing with required documentation prior to submitting new proposals to any foundation.

Restrictions: Grants are not made for political purposes, nor to organizations which discriminate on the basis of race, ethnic origin, sexual or religious preference, age or gender. The Niessen Foundation normally does not consider grants for endowment.

Geographic Focus: Pennsylvania
Date(s) Application is Due: Jan 31; Jul 31
Amount of Grant: 10,000 - 60,000 USD
Contact: Wachovia Bank, N.A., Trustee; grantinquiries3@wachovia.com
Internet: www.wellsfargo.com/private-foundations/niessen-charitable-trust
Sponsor: Leo Niessen Jr., Charitable Trust
Wachovia Bank, N A. PA 1279, 1234 East Broad Street
Philadelphia, PA 19109-1199

Leonsis Foundation Grants   1485

The Leonsis Foundation primarily focuses on innovative programs that create opportunities for children under the age of 18. The Foundation is particularly interested in educational and mentoring programs which incorporate Internet technology. Types of support include continuing support; general operating support; scholarship funds; and program development

Requirements: Organizations submit a letter of inquiry about their program before a proposal is accepted. There are no deadline dates.

Restrictions: Funding is not available for individuals.

Geographic Focus: District of Columbia, Maryland, Virginia

Contact: Ellen Kennedy Folts, Grants Administrator; (202) 266-2294; fax (202) 347-5580; leonsisfdn@aol.com

Internet: www.leonsisfoundation.org

Sponsor: Leonsis Foundation

627 North Glebe Road, Suite 850

Arlington, VA 22203-2110

Lewis H. Humphreys Charitable Trust Grants 1486

The Lewis H. Humphreys Charitable Trust was established in 2004 to support and promote quality educational, cultural, human services and health care programming for underserved and disadvantaged populations. The Humphreys Trust supports organizations that serve the residents of East Central Kansas. Grants from the Trust are 1 year in duration. Award amounts go up to $100,000.

Requirements: Applicants must have 501(c)3 tax-exempt status and serve the residents of Kansas. Grant requests for general operating support, program support and capital support will be considered. Grant requests for capital support such as for buildings, land and major equipment should meet a compelling community need and offer a broad social benefit. Applications will be submitted online through the Bank of America website. A grant report is required within 1 year of the grant application date, regardless of whether all of the funds have been spent.

Restrictions: The trust does not support requests from individuals, organizations attempting to influence policy through direct lobbying, or any political campaigns.

Geographic Focus: Kansas

Date(s) Application is Due: Mar 31

Amount of Grant: Up to 100,000 USD

Samples: Harvesters Community Food Network, Kansas City, Missouri, $75,000 - awarded for Harvesters Community Food Network; United Methodist Homes, Topeka, Kansas, $57,929 - awarded for unrestricted contribution for the use at Aldersgate Village; Stormont-Vail Foundation, Topeka, Kansas, $55,723 - awarded in support of the Learning Lab for Nursing Students: Training our Future Health Care Professionals.

Contact: Tony Twyman, Senior Philanthropic Client Manager; (816) 292-4342; mo.grantmaking@bankofamerica.com or tony.twyman@bofa.com

Internet: www.bankofamerica.com/philanthropic/foundation/?fnId=114

Sponsor: Lewis H. Humphreys Charitable Trust

1200 Main Street, 14th Floor

Kansas City, MO 64121-9119

LGA Family Foundation Grants 1487

The LGA Family Foundation was established in Honolulu in 1997, with a primary objective to support nonprofit organizations in California and Hawaii. It major areas of interest include: arts and culture; basic and emergency aid; communication media; domesticated animals; elementary and secondary education; family services; health and health care; higher education; historic preservation; human services; museums; natural resources; and nursing care. Its target populations are: academics; Children and youth; economically disadvantaged; low-income and poor people; and students. The Foundation's primary support strategies include: financial sustainability; general operating support; program development; and research. Generally, grant awards range from $1,000 to $50,000, with an average of eighteen awards each year. There are no annual deadlines for application submission.

Requirements: Any 501(c)3 organization supporting residents of Hawaii or California are eligible to apply.

Geographic Focus: California, Hawaii

Amount of Grant: 1,000 - 50,000 USD

Samples: University of Colorado Foundation, Denver, Colorado, $325,000 - disease research; Parker School, Waimea, Hawaii, $100,000 - general operating support for elementary and secondary schools; Hawaii Mission Children's Society, Honolulu, Hawaii, $25,000 - historic preservation.

Contact: Frank C. Atherton II, President; (808) 694-4540

Sponsor: LGA Family Foundation

111 South King Street, P.O. Box 3170, Deptartment 715

Honolulu, HI 96802-3170

Liberty Bank Foundation Grants 1488

The foundation's charitable giving is focused primarily on organizations that provide meaningful programs and activities that benefit people within Liberty Bank's market area. Of particular interest are programs and activities that provide assistance and opportunities to improve the quality of life for people of low income, especially families in crisis or at-risk. Top priorities for funding include community and economic development—affordable housing for low/moderate-income individuals and families, community and neighborhood capacity-building, and community services targeted to low/moderate-income individuals; education—programs that address the needs of low/moderate-income individuals; health care and human services—outreach and educational programs on health issues, quality child care, homeless shelters and services, services for victims of domestic violence, and transitional housing assistance; and arts and culture—programs that increase access to arts and culture for people of low income who might not otherwise be able to participate in them. Grants generally support specific programs rather than capital projects, equipment, or general operating expenses. Organizations that have received funding in two consecutive calendar years should refrain from reapplying for one calendar year. Contact the office to discuss the project prior to applying. Guideline and application are available online.

Requirements: 501(c)3 tax-exempt organizations are eligible.

Restrictions: Individuals, fraternal groups, and organizations that are not open to the general public are ineligible. Grants do not support annual funds of colleges, universities or hospitals; trips, tours, or conferences; scientific or medical research; deficit spending or debt liquidation; lobbying or otherwise influencing the outcome of the legislative or electoral process; religious groups, except for nonsectarian programs; or endowments or other foundations.

Geographic Focus: Connecticut

Date(s) Application is Due: Mar 31; Jun 30; Sep 30; Dec 31

Contact: Grants Administrator; (860) 704-2181; smurphy@liberty-bank.com

Internet: www.liberty-bank.com/liberty_foundation.asp

Sponsor: Liberty Bank Foundation

P.O. Box 1212

Middletown, CT 06457

Libra Foundation Grants 1489

The Libra Foundation awards grants to Maine nonprofits in its areas of interest, including art, culture, and humanities; education; health; human services; environment; justice; public/society benefit; and religion. The Foundation makes grants to organizations that it expects to develop innovative and sustainable Maine-based business initiatives and programs that provide for the welfare and betterment of children. The aforementioned activities comprise the majority of the Foundation's charitable giving.

Requirements: Organizations must be in Maine and 501(c)3 nonprofits to apply.

Restrictions: Individuals are ineligible. The Foundation does not provide funding to supplement annual campaigns, regular operating needs, multi-year projects, individuals, scholarships, or travel.

Geographic Focus: Maine

Date(s) Application is Due: Feb 15; May 15; Aug 15; Nov 15

Samples: Farnsworth Art Museum, Rockland, Maine, general operating support, $10,000; Portland Museum of Art, Portland, Maine, general operating support, $20,000; MaineHealth, Portland, Maine, start-up of a leading center for childhood health, $100,000; Pineland Farms, New Gloucester, Maine, develop, operate and staff Pineland Farms, Inc., for agricultural promotion, education, and research in Maine, $2,895,000.

Contact: Elizabeth Flaherty, Executive Assistant; (207) 879-6280

Internet: librafoundation.org/application-procedures

Sponsor: Libra Foundation

Three Canal Plaza, Suite 500

Portland, ME 04112-8516

Lied Foundation Trust Grants 1490

The foundation awards grants primarily to Nebraska and Nevada nonprofits in its areas of youth organizations, higher education, and arts and culture. The foundation favors programs that have some educational aspect to them. Types of support include building construction/renovation, equipment acquisition, program development, endowment funds, and scholarship funds.

Requirements: Nonprofit organizations in Nevada, Nebraska, Kansas and Iowa may apply. There is no specific form to complete.

Geographic Focus: Iowa, Kansas, Nebraska, Nevada

Contact: Christina Hixson, Trustee; (702) 878-1559

Sponsor: Lied Foundation Trust

3907 West Charleston Boulevard

Las Vegas, NV 89102

Lil and Julie Rosenberg Foundation Grants 1491

The Lil and Julie Rosenberg Foundation was established in Connecticut in 1963. It was founded in memory of Julius Rosenberg, founder of Hartley and Parker in 1941, which grew to become one of the premier wholesalers of fine wines and spirits in the State of Connecticut. Julius started his venture in the alcoholic beverage industry in his late teens at Star Liquor Distributors in New York. Owned by his brother, Abraham, Star Liquor Distributors was the first company to be issued a liquor license in New York State after Prohibition. After several years with Star, Julius and his wife, Lil, moved to Bridgeport, Connecticut, to open what would be called Hartley and Parker, situated on Crescent Avenue. In the mid-1950s, Hartley and Parker moved to a larger warehouse on Front Street and, in 1966, Julius built an even larger warehouse facility located in Stratford. Today, the Foundation has a mission of supporting Jewish organizations and public charities in Connecticut and sometimes nationally. Its primary fields of interest include: human services; Judaism; community nonprofits; education; science; literary works; testing for public safety; fostering national or international amateur sports competition (as long as it doesn't provide athletic facilities or equipment); and the prevention of cruelty to children and animals. There are no annual deadlines for application, and interested parties should submit a detailed description of project and amount of funding requested. Typical awards range from $500 to $5,000.

Requirements: 501(c)3 organizations serving the residents of Connecticut are eligible.

Geographic Focus: Connecticut

Amount of Grant: 500 - 5,000 USD

Samples: American Cancer Society, Norwalk, Connecticut, $500 - medical research; Anti Defamation League, New Haven Connecticut, $2,000 - social services support; Fairfield County Community Foundation, general operating support.

Contact: Jerry Rosenberg, President; (203) 375-5671; fax (203) 378-1463

Sponsor: Lil and Julie Rosenberg Foundation

100 Browning Street

Stratford, CT 06615-7130

Lilly Endowment Summer Youth Grants   1492

The Summer Youth Grants focus on providing safe and positive experiences for children and teens ages 4 to 19 years old at little or no cost. Grants are given to programs in residential and daily care, enhancement and youth employment. Grant recipients represent organizations ranging from churches and area community centers to theaters and parks, offering sports, overnight camping, arts, community service and tutoring.

Requirements: Organizations should write a preliminary letter of no more than two pages, explaining their organization, project, and amount of support they are requesting. The Endowment will respond to all preliminary inquiries, and if the project warrants further consideration, the organization may be asked to submit a full proposal.

Restrictions: Inquiry letters must be sent through the mail. Emailed or faxed requests will not be considered. The Endowment does not usually support loans or cash grants to private individuals; requests to discharge preexisting debts; health care projects; mass media projects; endowment or endowed chairs; libraries; or projects outside of Indianapolis.

Geographic Focus: Indiana

Contact: Willis K. Bright, Jr., Director, Youth Programs; (317) 916-7358 or (317) 924-5471; fax (317) 926-4431

Barbara S. DeHart, Youth Program Contact; (317) 916-7345

Internet: www.lillyendowment.org/ed_syp.html

Sponsor: Lilly Endowment

2801 N Meridian Street, P.O. Box 88068

Indianapolis, IN 46208-0068

Lily Palmer Fry Memorial Trust Grants   1493

The Lily Palmer Fry Memorial Trust was established in 1954 to support and promote summer camp opportunities for underserved children. Special consideration is given to traditional camp programs that take urban children out of the city to experience the natural environment. Bank of America serves as co-trustee of the Fry Memorial Trust, in conjunction with 2 relatives of Lily Palmer Fry. Grants from the Fry Memorial Trust are 1 year in duration. Award amounts typically range from $1,000 to $12,000.

Requirements: Organizations must serve residents of New York City and Westchester County, New York, and Fairfield and Hartford Counties, Connecticut. Applications will be submitted online through the Bank of America website. A grant report is required within 1 year of the grant application date, regardless of whether all of the funds have been spent.

Restrictions: The Fry Memorial Trust prefers to fund "camperships" for children and not other expenses of the camp such as supplies, salaries, etc. The trust does not support requests from individuals, organizations attempting to influence policy through direct lobbying, or any political campaigns.

Geographic Focus: Connecticut, New York

Date(s) Application is Due: Feb 1

Amount of Grant: 1,000 - 12,000 USD

Samples: Friends of Green Chimneys, Brewster, New York, $7,000 - awarded for Summer Camp Scholarship program (2018); American School for the Deaf, West Hartford, Connecticut, $5,000 - awarded for support of Camp Isola Bella (2018); Artists Collective, Hartford, Connecticut, $5,000 - awarded for Rite of Passage Summer program (2018).

Contact: Amy R. Lynch, Philanthropic Client Manager; (860) 244-4870; ct.grantmaking@bankofamerica.com or amy.r.lynch@bofa.com

Internet: www.bankofamerica.com/philanthropic/foundation/?fnId=71

Sponsor: Lily Palmer Fry Memorial Trust

200 Glastonbury Boulevard, Suite # 200, CT2-545-02-05

Glastonbury, CT 06033-4056

Linden Foundation Grants   1494

The Linden Foundation funds direct program support, general operating support, and occasionally very modest capital needs associated with a particular program. Existing programs, expansion of successful pilot programs, and new programs may all be considered for funding. The Foundation generally makes initial grants for amounts up to $10,000. The Foundation prefers to fund partial support for a project and welcomes the opportunity to join with other philanthropic funders in underwriting an endeavor. Please note that the Linden Foundation is not currently accepting any new inquiries or applications.

Requirements: The Linden Foundation will invite selected organizations to submit proposals. No unsolicited Full Proposals will be considered. Please note that most of the Foundation's grants budget is allocated to renewed funding since much of the Foundation's funding is multi-year. All grant applicants must be non-profit, 501(c)3 organizations, generally serving disadvantaged, low-income communities in the following areas: the northern side of the greater Boston area, with emphasis on communities inside Route 128 and the North Shore to the Gloucester area; and, the counties of the Lakes Region and northern New Hampshire.

Restrictions: No grants will be made to individuals, public schools, charter schools, colleges, or universities. No grants will be made to support community organizing, political lobbying efforts, or stand-alone enrichment activities, such as tickets to artistic and musical performances. Due to limited funding, no grants will be made for computer centers or general operating support for community centers.

Geographic Focus: Massachusetts, New Hampshire

Date(s) Application is Due: Jun 1; Dec 1

Contact: Ruth Victorin, Foundation Assistant; (617) 426-7080 ext. 288; fax (617) 426-7087; rvictorin@gmafoundations.com

Internet: www.lindenfoundation.org/grants.html

Sponsor: Linden Foundation

77 Summer Street, 8th Floor

Boston, MA 02110-1006

Linford and Mildred White Charitable Fund Grants   1495

The Linford and Mildred White Charitable Fund was established in 1956 to support and promote quality educational, human services, and health care programming for underserved populations within the city of Waterbury, Connecticut, and its surrounding communities. Grants from the White Charitable Fund are 1 year in duration. Award amounts typically range from $1,000 to $5,000.

Requirements: Applicant organizations must have 501(c)3 status and serve the people of Waterbury, Connecticut, and its vicinity. Applications will be submitted online through the Bank of America website. A grant report is required within 1 year of the grant application date, regardless of whether all of the funds have been spent.

Restrictions: Grant requests for capital projects will not be considered. Applicants will not be awarded a grant for more than 3 consecutive years. The fund does not support requests from individuals, organizations attempting to influence policy through direct lobbying, or any political campaigns.

Geographic Focus: Connecticut

Date(s) Application is Due: Jun 15

Amount of Grant: 1,000 - 5,000 USD

Samples: Children's Law Center Inc., Hartford, Connecticut, $5,000 - awarded for legal representation - Waterbury and surrounding areas (2018); Shakesperience Productions Inc., Waterbury, Connecticut, $5,000 - awarded for Waterbury Interactive: Our City, Our Neighborhoods (2018); Palace Theater Group, Waterbury, Connecticut, $5,000 - awarded for open captioning for Broadway Series performances (2018).

Contact: Amy R. Lynch, Philanthropic Client Manager; (860) 244-4870; ct.grantmaking@bankofamerica.com or amy.r.lynch@bofa.com

Internet: www.bankofamerica.com/philanthropic/foundation/?fnId=74

Sponsor: Linford and Mildred White Charitable Fund

P.O. Box 1802

Providence, RI 02901-1802

Lisa and Douglas Goldman Fund Grants   1496

Established in 1992 the Lisa and Douglas Goldman Fund is a private foundation committed to providing support for charitable organizations that enhance society. As natives of San Francisco, the Goldmans place a high priority on projects that have a positive impact on San Francisco and the Bay Area. Interests and priorities include: children and youth; civic affairs; civil and human rights; education; environmental affairs; health; Jewish affairs; literacy; organizational development; population; social and human services; and sports and recreation.

Requirements: After reviewing the Fund's interests and priorities interested applicants may submit an initial letter of inquiry. Applicants who receive a favorable response will be invited to submit a formal proposal with supporting materials. Applicants are encouraged to contact the Fund directly with questions regarding the appropriateness of a project. There are no deadlines.

Restrictions: The following are ineligible: grants to individuals; documentaries and films; events/conferences; books and periodicals; research; and deficit budgets. Applications for annual support are not accepted. Organizations may submit only one request per year.

Geographic Focus: All States

Amount of Grant: 10,000 - 100,000 USD

Samples: MapLight, Berkeley, California, $35,000 - to create a website to help identify the sources of secret money in politics and to support more in-depth media coverage of the topic; MomsRising Education Fund, Bellevue, Washington, $50,000 - to increase outreach to women and mothers about gun safety issues and educate candidates, the media, and the public about gun safety policies; Women's Community Clinic, San Francisco, California, $75,000 - to provide medication abortion to its clients.

Contact: Nancy S. Kami, Executive Director; (415) 771-1717; fax (415) 771-1797; nkami@ldgfund.org

Internet: fdncenter.org/grantmaker/goldman

Sponsor: Lisa and Douglas Goldman Fund

120 Kearny Street

San Francisco, CA 94104-4505

LISC Affordable Housing Grants   1497

Local Initiatives Support Corporation (LISC) helps local organization become strong and stable neighborhood institutions characterized by effective and responsible fiscal management and capable of carrying out a range of community revitalization activities. Overall, LISC helps community development organizations transform distressed communities and neighborhoods into healthy and sustainable communities that are good places to live, do business, work, and raise families. Through LISC local program offices, the organization provides grant funding to assist organizations to develop affordable housing, educational opportunities, economic development, financial stability, health, safety, and community leadership. In the area of affordable housing, LISC helps make quality, affordable housing available to low-income and vulnerable residents - from seniors to veterans to the formerly homeless - in under-served communities. Grants are designed and provided consistent with local program office strategies and local community development needs, and have typically come in the form of: organizational development grants that assist community organizations to improve its administrative structures, management and financial systems, and real estate development and management capacities; strategic planning grants to cover costs associated with the creation of new programs that are important to an organization's overall mission and needs of the community's residents; and project grants to help cover costs associated with real estate development that further neighborhood revitalization goals. Applicants should check the website for contacts in various parts of the LISC service area.

Requirements: Affordable housing initiatives are carried out in all 31 LISC local offices and in rural counties across the country. These include neighborhoods where soaring prices in hot real estate markets threaten to edge out longtime residents, as well as in legacy markets, where the flight of industry and jobs has left a vacuum of disinvestment and poverty and where housing can stimulate economic growth.

Geographic Focus: All States
Amount of Grant: 10,000 - 100,000 USD
Contact: Beth Marcus, Senior Vice President, Corporate and Foundation Relations; (212) 455-9800; fax (212) 682-5929; info@lisc.org
Internet: www.lisc.org/our-initiatives/affordable-housing/
Sponsor: Local Initiatives Support Corporation
501 Seventh Avenue, 7th Floor
New York, NY 10018-5903

LISC Capacity Building Grants   1498

LISC believes that it takes local partners on the ground to make any real, lasting change in a community. Local organizations know their neighborhoods the best and any solution must come from the ground up. LISC was founded on that belief with the mission to help these local organizations become strong and stable neighborhood institutions characterized by effective and responsible fiscal management and capable of carrying out a range of community revitalization activities. Today, its local partners are tasked with addressing a staggering range of community needs and demands. Organizations that formed to tackle a deficit of affordable housing may now take on everything from workforce development, small business development, community safety, and disaster relief. LISC's job is to make this happen through grants, technical assistance, and training delivered through its on-the-ground staff in 33 local offices and experts in its national programs who focus on important components of community revitalization such as housing, economic development, safety, education, and sports and recreation. This capacity building support is designed and provided consistent with local community development needs.

Requirements: Any 501(c)3 organization across the U.S. is eligible to apply.
Geographic Focus: All States
Amount of Grant: 10,000 - 1,000,000 USD
Contact: Beth Marcus, Senior Vice President, Corporate and Foundation Relations; (212) 455-9800; fax (212) 682-5929; info@lisc.org
Internet: www.lisc.org/our-model/capacity-building/
Sponsor: Local Initiatives Support Corporation
501 Seventh Avenue, 7th Floor
New York, NY 10018-5903

LISC Community Leadership Operating Grants   1499

LISC's work hinges on the insight, experience and expertise of hundreds of community development groups rebuilding neighborhoods across the country. The better they do their job, the better LISC can do its job, and the more communities it supports. LISC helps them to become more effective change-makers, and accomplishes this through financing, in the form of operating grants and working capital. And it happens via training programs and learning opportunities for staff and leadership at the community development corporations (CDCs) and many other local groups with whom we partner. LISC likes to share its resources: it makes these resources available to colleagues in the field within and beyond the LISC footprint — to social service organizations, arts groups, child care providers, local business associations and youth and recreation groups, to name a few.

Requirements: In order to be eligible, projects must be sponsored by community-based nonprofit 501(c)3 organizations or middle or high schools.
Geographic Focus: All States
Amount of Grant: Up to 250,000 USD
Contact: Beth Marcus, Senior Vice President, Corporate and Foundation Relations; (212) 455-9800; fax (212) 682-5929; info@lisc.org
Internet: www.lisc.org/our-initiatives/community-leadership/
Sponsor: Local Initiatives Support Corporation
501 Seventh Avenue, 7th Floor
New York, NY 10018-5903

LISC Education Grants   1500

Local Initiatives Support Corporation (LISC) helps local organization become strong and stable neighborhood institutions characterized by effective and responsible fiscal management and capable of carrying out a range of community revitalization activities. Overall, LISC helps community development organizations transform distressed communities and neighborhoods into healthy and sustainable communities that are good places to live, do business, work, and raise families. Through LISC local program offices, the organization provides grant funding to assist organizations to develop affordable housing, educational opportunities, economic development, financial stability, health, safety, and community leadership. In the area of Education, LISC understands that communities can flourish when families have access to quality early childhood education, high-performing schools and enrichment activities for their children, and when adults can get the skills training and continuing education they need to land and advance in living wage jobs. to increase educational choice and access to good schools, Charter School Financing at LISC supports public charter schools that put their all into preparing students for college, career and life. And because early childhood education is well-documented as the single most effective means for closing the achievement gap, LISCs Early Childhood Facilities program (also known as the Community Investment Collaborative for Kids or CICK) has invested $56.5 million to help plan, build or refurbish nearly 223 early childhood facilities in under-served places. LISC also supports learning beyond the traditional classroom, and that extends well past childhood. LICS funds hundreds of community partners who bring college-readiness, high-school equivalency and professional development programs, and an extraordinary range of after school and summer enrichment options, to the neighborhoods where they work. Its Bridges to Career Opportunities programs offer intensive literacy

and math classes for job-seekers who need to master basic skills in order to train for solid employment. Grants are designed and provided consistent with local program office strategies and local community development needs, and have typically come in the form of: organizational development grants that assist community organizations to improve its administrative structures, management and financial systems, and real estate development and management capacities; strategic planning grants to cover costs associated with the creation of new programs that are important to an organization's overall mission and needs of the community's residents; and project grants to help cover costs associated with real estate development that further neighborhood revitalization goals. Applicants should check the website for contacts in various parts of the LISC service area.

Requirements: Education initiatives are carried out in all of 31 LISC local offices and in rural counties across the country.
Geographic Focus: All States
Amount of Grant: 10,000 - 100,000 USD
Contact: Beth Marcus, Senior Vice President, Corporate and Foundation Relations; (212) 455-9800; fax (212) 682-5929; info@lisc.org
Internet: www.lisc.org/our-initiatives/education/
Sponsor: Local Initiatives Support Corporation
501 Seventh Avenue, 7th Floor
New York, NY 10018-5903

LISC Financial Stability Grants   1501

With support from the Social Innovation Fund, this LISC program awards funds to be used to support an integrated service model that focuses on improving the financial situation for low- to moderate-income families by helping people boost earnings, reduce expenses, and make appropriate financial decisions that lead to asset-building. These centers provide individuals and families with services across three critical and interconnected areas: employment placement, job retention, and skill improvement; financial coaching and counseling; and accessing income support and public benefits. Grants of at least $100,000 will be awarded; applicants must demonstrate a 1:1 cash match of non-federal funding.

Requirements: Eligible organizations must have 501(c)3 status and be located in the following cities: Chicago; greater Cincinnati (including northern Kentucky); metropolitan Detroit; Duluth, Minnesota; Houston; Indianapolis; Minneapolis/St. Paul; Providence/Woonsocket, Rhode Island; San Diego; and the San Francisco Bay Area (including Oakland, Richmond, San Francisco, and San Jose).
Geographic Focus: California, Illinois, Indiana, Kentucky, Michigan, Minnesota, Ohio, Rhode Island, Texas
Contact: Beth Marcus, Senior Vice President; (212) 455-9800; fax (212) 682-5929; infgor@lisc.org
Internet: www.lisc.org/our-initiatives/financial-stability/
Sponsor: Local Initiatives Support Corporation
501 Seventh Avenue, 7th Floor
New York, NY 10018-5903

Lloyd G. Balfour Foundation Attleboro-Specific Charities Grants   1502

The Lloyd G. Balfour Foundation was established in 1973. The Foundation's 3 primary focus areas reflect Mr. Balfour's strong affinity for the employees of the Balfour Company, his commitment to the city of Attleboro, Massachusetts, and his lifelong interest in education. Specifically, the Lloyd G. Balfour Foundation Attleboro-Specific Charities Grant supports organizations that serve the people of Attleboro, Massachusetts with special consideration given to organizations that provide educational, human services and health care programming for underserved populations. Award amounts can range from $5,000 to $125,000.

Requirements: 501(c)3 organizations serving the residents of Attleboro, Massachusetts are eligible to apply. To better support the capacity of nonprofit organizations, multi-year funding requests are encouraged. Applications will be submitted online through the Bank of America website. A grant report is required within 1 year of the grant application date, regardless of whether all of the funds have been spent.
Restrictions: The foundation does not support requests from individuals, organizations attempting to influence policy through direct lobbying, or any political campaigns.
Geographic Focus: Massachusetts
Date(s) Application is Due: Mar 1
Amount of Grant: 5,000 - 125,000 USD
Samples: Sturdy Memorial Foundation Inc., Attleboro, Massachusetts, $125,000 - awarded for campaign to modernize and enhance Sturdy Memorial Hospital's over all aesthetic and name new 20-bed private unit (2019); Attleboro Public Schools, Attleboro, Massachusetts, $100,000 - awarded for Balfour Academic Support activities (2019).
Contact: Michelle Larkins, Philanthropic Administrator; (866) 778-6859; ma.grantmaking@bankofamerica.com or ma.grantmaking@ustrust.com
Internet: www.bankofamerica.com/philanthropic/foundation/?fnId=31
Sponsor: Lloyd G. Balfour Foundation
225 Franklin Street, 4th Floor
Boston, MA 02110-2801

Lloyd G. Balfour Foundation Scholarships   1503

The Lloyd G. Balfour Foundation was established in 1973. The Foundation's 3 primary focus areas reflect Mr. Balfour's strong affinity for the employees of the Balfour Company, his commitment to the city of Attleboro, Massachusetts, and his lifelong interest in education. Specifically, the Lloyd G. Balfour Foundation Scholarships provide support to employees of the Balfour Company, as well as to their children, grandchildren and other deserving Attleboro High School students. Balfour scholarships are administered through the Attleboro Scholarship Foundation. Award amounts typically range from $300,000 to $450,000.

Requirements: To better support the capacity of nonprofit organizations, multi-year funding requests are encouraged. Applications will be submitted online through the Bank of America website. A grant report is required within 1 year of the grant application date, regardless of whether all of the funds have been spent.
Restrictions: The foundation does not support requests from individuals, organizations attempting to influence policy through direct lobbying, or any political campaigns.
Geographic Focus: Massachusetts
Date(s) Application is Due: Mar 1; Jun 1; Nov 1
Amount of Grant: 300,000 - 450,000 USD
Samples: Attleboro Scholarship Foundation Inc., Attleboro, Massachusetts, $450,000 - awarded for L.G. Balfour Foundation Scholarship program (2019).
Contact: Michelle Larkins, Philanthropic Administrator; (866) 778-6859; ma.grantmaking@bankofamerica.com or ma.grantmaking@ustrust.com
Wendy Holt, Executive Director; (508) 226-4414; fax (508) 226-5647; asf10@verizon.net
Internet: www.bankofamerica.com/philanthropic/foundation/?fnId=31
Sponsor: Lloyd G. Balfour Foundation
225 Franklin Street, 4th Floor
Boston, MA 02110-2801

Locations Foundation Legacy Grants   1504

The Locations Foundation was established in Honolulu in 1988, with the expressed purpose of offering support to organizations involved with: health; diabetes; youth; and human services. Its primary fields of interest include: adult and child mentoring; basic and emergency aid; cancer treatment; child welfare; Christianity; communication media; diabetes; domesticated animals; elementary and secondary education; family services; health care access; housing; human services; literacy; nonprofit operations; reading promotion; special populations; sports; and youth development. Major target populations are: academics; children and youth; the economically disadvantaged; females; low-income; and students. In most cases, the Foundation offers funding in the form of general operating support; program development; re-granting; and scholarship funds. Typically, awards range $10,000 up to a maximum of $25,000. There are no specified application forms or deadlines, and interested parties should submit a letter of application.
Requirements: Locations Foundation Legacy Grants are awarded to schools or organizations that are not private foundations.
Geographic Focus: Hawaii
Amount of Grant: Up to 25,000 USD
Samples: After-School All-Stars, Honolulu, Hawaii, $5,000 - support of the youth development program; Center for Tomorrow's Leaders, Honolulu, Hawaii, $1,500 - general operating support for youth development; Child and Family Services, Honolulu, Hawaii, $5,000 - general operating support.
Contact: Renee Dona, Director of Human Resources; (808) 735-4200; renee.dona@locationshawaii.com or thefoundation@locationshawaii.com
Ashley Lee, Employee Relations Manager; (808) 738-3239 or (808) 735-4200; fax (808) 738-8732; ashley.lee@locationshawaii.com or thefoundation@locationshawaii.com
Internet: www.locationshawaii.com/about-us/locations-foundation/legacy-grant-for-educators/
Sponsor: Locations Foundation
614 Kapahulu Avenue, 3rd Floor
Honolulu, HI 96815-3846

Lockheed Martin Corporation Foundation Grants   1505

The Lockheed Martin Corporation Foundation funds grants that enhance the communities where Lockheed Martin employees work and live. Lockheed Martin will consider grant requests that best support the Corporation's strategic focus areas and reflect effective leadership, fiscal responsibility, and program success. Those focus areas include: education—K-16 science, technology, engineering and math (STEM) education; customer and constituent relations—causes of importance to customers and constituents, including the U.S. military and other government agencies; community relations—building partnerships between employee volunteers and the civic, cultural, environmental, and health and human services initiatives that strengthen the communities where employees work. Applications are accepted year-round. Evaluations are typically performed quarterly.
Requirements: To be considered for grant funding, organizations must meet all of the following criteria: apply through Lockheed Martin's online CyberGrants system; have a non-profit tax exempt classification under Section 501(c)3 of the Internal Revenue Service Code, or equivalent international non-profit classification, or be a public elementary/secondary school, or be a qualifying US-based institute of higher education; align with one or more of Lockheed Martin's three strategic focus areas: delivering standards-based science, technology, engineering and math (STEM) education to students in K-16; investing in programs that support the long term success of the military and their families; and supporting the vitality of the communities where employees live and work; agree to act in accordance with Lockheed Martin's contribution acknowledgement *Requirements:* organization/grantee will comply with all applicable requirements of the Patriot Act and the Voluntary Anti-Terrorist Guidelines and will not use any portion of the grant funds for the support, direct or indirect, of acts of violence or terrorism or for any organization engaged in or supporting such acts; be located or operate in a community in which Lockheed Martin has employees or business interests; demonstrate fiscal and administrative responsibility and have an active, diverse board, effective leadership, continuity and efficiency of administration; be limited to one grant per year, except in unusual circumstances.
Restrictions: Some grant applications may not be able to be considered until the next year's budget cycle, particularly those received in the second half of the year. Grants are generally not made to: organizations that unlawfully discriminate on the basis of race, ethnicity, religion, national origin, age, military veteran's status, ancestry, sexual orientation, gender

identity or expression, marital status, family structure, genetic information, or mental or physical disability; private K-12 schools, unless the contribution is in acknowledgement of employee volunteer service provided to the school; home-based child care/educational services; individuals; professional associations, labor organizations, fraternal organizations or social clubs; social events sponsored by social clubs; athletic groups, clubs and teams, unless the contribution is in acknowledgement of employee volunteer service provided to the school; religious organizations for religious purposes; or advertising in souvenir booklets, yearbooks or journals unrelated to Lockheed Martin's business interests.
Geographic Focus: California, Colorado, Florida, Georgia, Louisiana, Maryland, Minnesota, Mississippi, New Jersey, New Mexico, New York, Ohio, Pennsylvania, South Carolina, Texas, Virginia, Canada
Contact: Emily Simone, Corporate Community Relations; (301) 897-6000 or (301) 897-6866; fax (301) 897-6485; david.e.phillips@lmco.com
Internet: www.lockheedmartin.com/us/who-we-are/community.html
Sponsor: Lockheed Martin Corporation Foundation
6801 Rockledge Drive
Bethesda, MD 20817-1836

Lois and Richard England Family Foundation Out-of-School-Time Grants 1506

The Lois and Richard England Family Foundation is a private family foundation founded in 1990. The Foundation is committed to the improvement of the lives of children in underserved communities in Washington, D.C. Its current focus is Out-of-School-Time Grants that provide academic support and/or enrichment during after-school and summer hours. Recognizing middle school is a critical time in a young person's life, programs that serve youth as they transition from elementary though middle school to high school is a priority. There are no deadlines. The Foundation considers Grants in the spring. Organizations typically will be notified in writing of funding decisions no later than June 30.
Requirements: Applicants must be 501(c)3 organizations serving Washington, D.C. The Foundation supports general operations and will conider funding specific programs, capacity building, strategic planning, evaluation, program development, matching grants and endowment/reserve funds. Interested organizations should email the Foundation indicating the organization's mission, budget, website and contact information. A representative from the Foundation will reply via email or phone within 30 days.
Restrictions: Unsolicited proposals are not accepted.
Geographic Focus: District of Columbia
Amount of Grant: 5,000 - 50,000 USD
Samples: Boys and Girls Club of Greater Washington, Washington, D.C., $25,000 - to support after school programs for middle school children; Latin American Youth Center, Washington, D.C., $25,000 - to support after school programs for middle school children; and Building Bridges Across the River, Washington, D.C., $10,000 - general operations support.
Contact: Julia Baer-Cooper, Program Advisor; (301) 657-7737; fax (301) 657-7738; englandfamilyfdn@verizon.net
Internet: foundationcenter.org/grantmaker/england/interests.html
Sponsor: Lois and Richard England Family Foundation
P.O. Box 34-1077
Bethesda, MD 20827

Long Island Community Foundation Grants   1507

The Foundation awards grants to eligible New York nonprofit organizations in the following program areas: arts; community development; education; environment; health; mental health; hunger; technical assistance; and youth violence prevention. Projects are preferred that accomplish specific tasks, solve problems, address needs of the disadvantaged, help a large number of people, and use community resources. Specific guidelines for each category and the application are available on the Foundation website. Applicants are encouraged to view recent grants on the website in order to judge if their project is appropriate for the Foundation.
Requirements: New York nonprofit organizations are eligible.
Restrictions: Grants are not made for the following: individuals; building or capital campaigns; medical or scientific research; equipment purchases; budget deficits; endowments; event sponsorships; re-granting purposes; or religious or political purposes.
Geographic Focus: New York
Date(s) Application is Due: Aug 24
Samples: Long Island Arts Alliance, Long Island, New York, strengthen the Long Island arts infrastructure through arts education advocacy forums, and a study about the economic significance of the nonprofit arts community, $30,000; Citizens Campaign Fund for the Environment, Long Island, New York, to analyze and grade 16 sewage treatment plants on Long Island, $25,000; Mental Health Association of Nassau County, Long Island, New York, to support a geriatric mental health training program that will increase access to quality mental health for the elderly, $15,000.
Contact: Nancy Arnold, Grants Administrator; (516) 348-0575; fax (516) 348-0570; narnold@licf.org
Internet: www.licf.org/grants
Sponsor: Long Island Community Foundation
1864 Muttontown Road
Syosset, NY 11791

Lotus 88 Foundation for Women and Children Grants   1508

The foundation's mission is to promote the empowerment of women and children through supporting their economic, emotional, and spiritual development. The foundation's focus area is American Indian Country. Grants are awarded in Indian Country for two strategic purposes: revitalizing the council tipis as spiritual, cultural, and service centers; and

providing the basic needs through community building. Community building grants are intended to promote and support community building in Indian Country to improve basic living conditions and to encourage a more positive future. Tipi project grants are made to help tribal women living on reservation or off reservation in building community. Grants support cultural and social services, tribal gatherings, educational programs, healing and purification ceremonies, and retreats. Each proposal should identify the specific needs and uses for the tipi and should identify a nonprofit program partner working in the tribal area who will work with the foundation on the project. Contact the Foundation directly for application and additional guideline information.
Requirements: Projects in American Indian communities are eligible.
Geographic Focus: All States
Contact: Patricia Stout, President; (510) 841-4123; fax (510) 841-4093; benita@lotus88.org
Internet: lotus88.net/
Sponsor: Lotus 88 Foundation for Women and Children
127 University Avenue, P.O. Box 10728
Berkeley, CA 94710

Louie M. and Betty M. Phillips Foundation Grants   1509
The Foundation supports a variety of organizations in the fields of health, human services, civic affairs, education, and the arts. Types of support include annual operating grants for selected organizations contributing significantly to the Nashville area; one-year project and program grants for specific projects or equipment; and capital support (five-years maximum) for major capital projects of organizations with strong records of community service. The application and a list of previously funded projects are available at the Foundation website.
Requirements: Nonprofit organizations are eligible. With rare exceptions, grants are limited to organizations in the greater Nashville area.
Restrictions: The Foundation does not support individuals or their projects, private foundations, political activities, advertising, or sponsorships. In general, the Foundation does not support projects, programs, or organizations that serve a limited audience; disease-specific organizations; biomedical or clinical research; organizations whose principal impact is outside the Nashville area; or tax-supported institutions.
Geographic Focus: Tennessee
Date(s) Application is Due: Jun 1; Nov 1
Amount of Grant: 500 - 35,000 USD
Samples: Walden's Puddle Wildlife Rehabilitation Center, Nashville, Tennessee, operating support, $10,000; Safe Haven Family Shelter, Nashville, Tennessee, operating support, $5,000; Men of Valor, Nashville, Tennessee, capital and operating support, $35,000; Boys and Girls Club of Davidson County, Nashville, Tennessee, capital and operating support, $12,500.
Contact: Louie Buntin, Grant Coordinator; (615) 385-5949; fax (615) 385-2507; louie@phillipsfoundation.org
Internet: www.phillipsfoundation.org
Sponsor: Louie M. and Betty M. Phillips Foundation
3334 Powell Avenue, P.O. Box 40788
Nashville, TN 37204

Louis and Sandra Berkman Foundation Grants   1510
The Louis and Sandra Berkman Foundation was established in Steubenville, Ohio, in 1952, with giving centered in the States of Ohio and Pennsylvania. The Foundation honors the memory of Louis Berkman, who started in business in the late 1920s in the scrap iron and steel industry. In 1931, he incorporated The Louis Berkman Company in Steubenville. He died in 2013 at the age of 104. The Foundation, which has operated for more than sixty years, has been instrumental in establishing he H.L. Berkman Faculty and Staff Dining Room and the Sandra Weiss Berkman Studio for Ceramic Arts at Bethany College in Bethany, West Virginia. The Foundation also made possible the Learning Resource Center, the Louis Berkman Fireside Lounge in the J.C. Williams Center, and the Science and Technology Building at Franciscan University of Steubenville. The Foundation also played a significant roll in the construction of the Louis and Sandra Berkman Amphitheater at the Old Forth Steuben Project in downtown Steubenville. Over the course of the past several years, the Foundation has contributed extensively to Catholic Central High School in Steubenville, and to the creation of the Berkman Theater at Lanman Hall, which was completed in the Spring of 2012. Today, the foundation's primary interests include support for: art museums; arts and culture; biodiversity; elementary and secondary education; the environment; health and health care; higher education; plant biology; and religion. Typically, funding is provided for: general operating support; program development; research; and research evaluation. The annual deadline for application submission is July 1.
Requirements: Any 501(c)3 organization is eligible to apply.
Geographic Focus: All States
Date(s) Application is Due: Jul 1
Amount of Grant: Up to 200,000 USD
Samples: Agnes Irwin School, Bryn Mawr, Pennsylvania, $35,000 - general operating support; Cornell University, Ithaca, New York, $180,000 - research; Philadelphia Museum of Art, Philadelphia, Pennsylvania, $10,000 - general operating support.
Contact: Robert A. Paul, President; (740) 283-3722
Linda Pirkle, Trustee; (412) 652-9480
Sponsor: Louis and Sandra Berkman Foundation
330 North 7th Street, P.O. Box 820
Steubenville, OH 43952-5576

Louis Calder Foundation Grants   1511
The Louis Calder Foundation seeks to promote the educational and scholastic development of children and youth by improving academic content at charter and parochial schools and at community based organizations. The Foundation's grant making will focus on opportunities for schools and community based organizations in communities within the Northeast Corridor with populations no greater than 500,000 to undertake such efforts during the regular school hours as well as the out-of-school or extended-day hours. New and existing charter schools, parochial schools and community based organizations are invited to submit a letter of inquiry with a summary of their plans to improve or initiate programs and projects designed to deliver classical education in areas of literacy, history, ethics, mathematics and the sciences. The Foundation has no formal application form and requests that organizations use the Philanthropy New York Common Application Form (available at the Foundation's website).
Requirements: New and existing charter schools, parochial schools and community based organizations are invited to submit a letter of inquiry with a summary of their plans to improve or initiate programs and projects designed to deliver classical education in areas of literacy, history, ethics, mathematics and the sciences. There is no application deadline when applying for funding.
Restrictions: The Foundation does not provide long term continuing program support and requests for renewed support are considered on the basis of reports received, site visits and Foundation priorities.
Geographic Focus: All States
Amount of Grant: 5,000 - 600,000 USD
Samples: Achievement First, Inc., New Haven, Connecticut, $300,000 - program expansion; Friends of Catholic Urban Schools, St. Paul, Minnesota, $229,000 - curriculum development in three consortium schools; Core Knowledge Foundation, Charlottesville, Virginia, $600,000 - Core Knowledge Language Arts K-2 curriculum.
Contact: Holly Nuechterlein, Grant Program Director; (203) 966-8925; fax (203) 966-5785; proposals@calderfdn.org
Internet: www.louiscalderfdn.org/gguide.html
Sponsor: Louis Calder Foundation
175 Elm Street
New Canaan, CT 06840

Lubrizol Corporation Community Grants   1512
The Lubrizol Corporation has a long-standing commitment to the local communities in which it operates. The Corporation believes that enhancing the quality of life and building and maintaining positive relationships is the right thing to do. It all began with its founders' corporate philosophy, whose legacy is a culture of active community support. Today, the Corporation continues their model by providing dollars and people to support a wide variety of educational, cultural and charitable organizations. One of the ways that Lubrizol and its employees provide support to its local communities is through various charitable outreach efforts. Employees volunteer their time to offer assistance to local organizations, making use of their individual skills. An annual event in Northeast Ohio that exemplifies this type of charitable outreach is the Building Bonds event. Applicants should contact the Corporate Community Involvement office for further guidelines.
Requirements: IRS 501(c)3 organizations in or serving the following regions may apply: Wickliffe, Ohio; Cleveland, Ohio; Brussels, Belgium; and Hong Kong.
Geographic Focus: Ohio, Belgium, Hong Kong
Contact: Karen Lerchbacher, Administrator; (440) 347-1797; fax (440) 347-1858; karen.lerchbacher@lubrizol.com
Internet: www.lubrizol.com/CorporateResponsibility/Community.html
Sponsor: Lubrizol Corporation
29400 Lakeland Boulevard
Wickliffe, OH 44092-2298

Lubrizol Foundation Grants   1513
The Lubrizol Foundation makes grants in support of education, health care, human services, civic, cultural, youth and environmental activities of a tax-exempt, charitable nature. Scholarships, fellowships, and awards are generally made in the fields of chemistry and chemical and mechanical engineering at colleges and universities. Types of support include the following: annual campaigns; building/renovation; capital campaigns; continuing support; employee matching gifts; employee volunteer services; equipment; fellowships; general/operating support; scholarship funds. Priority is given to the greater Cleveland, Ohio and Houston, Texas areas. The Lubrizol Foundation typically reviews and decides upon requests quarterly. There are no deadlines by which you need to submit your proposal. Proposals may be submitted via postal mail or email, but not by fax. Applicants will receive written notification of the decision on their proposal.
Requirements: Written applications of established Ohio and Texas nonprofit charitable organizations will be considered on a case by case basis. Grant proposals should include the following: a cover letter that summarizes the purpose of the request, signed by the executive officer of the organization or development office; a narrative of specific information related to the subject of the request; current audited financial statements and a specific project budget, if applicable; documentation of the organization's Federal tax-exempt status, e.g., a copy of the 501(c)3 determination letter. Additional descriptive literature (e.g., an annual report, brochures, etc.) that accurately characterizes the overall activities of the organization is appreciated. Upon review, further information may be requested including an interview and site visit.
Restrictions: Grants are not made for religious or political purposes, to individuals nor, generally, to endowments.
Geographic Focus: Ohio, Texas
Amount of Grant: 2,000 - 250,000 USD
Samples: Big Brothers Big Sisters of Greater Cleveland, Cleveland, OH, $2,500 - for operating support; American Red Cross, Houston, Texas, $25,000 - for Hurricane Ike Disaster Relief Fund; Hospice of the Western Reserve, Cleveland, OH, $250,000 - toward construction of new faculty.

Contact: Karen Lerchbacher, Administrator; (440) 347-1797; fax (440) 347-1858; karen.lerchbacher@lubrizol.com
Internet: www.lubrizol.com/CorporateResponsibility/Lubrizol-Foundation.html
Sponsor: Lubrizol Foundation
29400 Lakeland Boulevard, 053A
Wickliffe, OH 44092-2298

Lucile Packard Foundation for Children's Health Grants   1514

The vision of the Foundation is that all children in the communities the Foundation serves are able to reach their maximum health potential. The Foundation invests in programs and projects that have the potential to improve California's systems of care for children with special health care needs and their families. Funding is provided for programs that address improving care for children with special needs in the following areas: system reform; care coordination/enhanced medical home; pediatric education; quality measures focused on children with special health care needs; data collection and/or analysis; and advocacy.
Requirements: Generally the Foundation invites applications for grant proposals. However, organizations that have not been invited may submit a letter of inquiry if the organization meets the organizational criteria and if their proposed program falls within the Foundation's focus area. Applicants should review program and organizational criteria first. Eligible organizations: are classified as tax exempt under 501(c)3 or are a public or educational entity, or collaborations of nonprofit and public agencies with a designated fiscal sponsor, or entities that have a charitable purpose; have demonstrated capacity to implement effective, culturally competent programs, reach intended populations, and achieve clear, reasonable and measureable goals and objectives; and promote and maintain nondiscriminatory policies in programs and the workplace. Eligible programs or projects are those that hold promise of improving the systems of care for Children with Special Health Care Needs (CSHCN). Eligible programs should: be focused primarily on California; have potential for national applicability; have the potential to improve the system of care for children with special needs; demonstrate an understanding of the complex system of care for CSHCN and builds on existing knowledge and systems; have potential to affect a large number of CSHCN; have potential for impact within five years; have reasonable evidence of sustainability; have reasonable evidence of replicability; and present opportunities for collaboration.
Restrictions: Unsolicited full proposals should not be submitted. The following are not funded: disease-specific projects; individuals; scholarships; support for candidates for political office; private foundations; religious organizations for religious purposes; fundraising sponsorships; annual fund appeals; capital campaigns; and basic scientific research.
Geographic Focus: California
Contact: Amanda Frederickson, Annual Giving Program Manager; (650) 736-0676; amanda.frederickson@lpfch.org
Internet: www.lpfch.org/programs/cshcn/process.html
Sponsor: Lucile Packard Foundation for Children's Health
400 Hamilton Avenue, Suite 340
Palo Alto, CA 94301

Lucy Downing Nisbet Charitable Fund Grants   1515

The Lucy Downing Nisbet Charitable Fund was established in 2002 to support and promote educational, health and human services, and arts programming for underserved populations. The Foundation specifically serves organizations located in and serving the people of Vermont. Special consideration is given to organizations in the area of healthcare/nursing, domestic violence awareness, heart disease, or endangered species, and organizations located in and serving the people of Morrisville, Vermont. Grant size generally ranges from $5,000 to $50,000 and grants are 1 year in duration. Bank of America, N.A. serves as co-trustee of the Nisbet Fund along with Ward F. Cleary, Esq.
Requirements: The foundation specifically serves organizations located in and serving the people of Vermont. Applicants must have 501(c)3 tax-exempt status. Applications will be submitted online through the Bank of America website. A grant report is required within 1 year of the grant application date, regardless of whether all of the funds have been spent.
Restrictions: The trustees do not make grants for deficit financing, annual giving, endowments or capital projects. The fund does not support requests from individuals, organizations attempting to influence policy through direct lobbying, or any political campaigns.
Geographic Focus: Vermont
Date(s) Application is Due: Jan 15
Amount of Grant: 5,000 - 50,000 USD
Samples: Copley Hospital Inc., Morrisville, Vermont, $50,000 - Awarded for capital campaign for the surgical center (2018); Central Vermont Adult Basic Education Inc., Barre, Vermont, $10,000 - Awarded for CVABE's Functional Literacy program: a human service program serving Morrisville, Vermont area residents with low literacy who need education to become employed and/or function more successfully in life (2018); Howardcenter Inc., Burlington, Vermont, $10,000 - Awarded for street outreach (2018).
Contact: Amy R. Lynch, Philanthropic Client Manager; (860) 244-4870; ct.grantmaking@bankofamerica.com or amy.r.lynch@bofa.com
Internet: www.bankofamerica.com/philanthropic/foundation/?fnId=78
Sponsor: Lucy Downing Nisbet Charitable Fund
P.O. Box 1802
Providence, RI 1802

Ludwick Family Foundation Grants   1516

Founded in 1990 by Arthur and Sarah Ludwick, the Ludwick Family Foundation is a California-based philanthropic organization established exclusively for charitable, scientific, literary, and educational purposes. Grants are awarded to United States or U.S. based international organizations in adherence to the mission of Ludwick Family Foundation and its founding documents. The foundation tends to fund tangible types of items that will remain with and can be used repeatedly by the organization. Since the Foundation only considers invited applications, interested parties should begin by contacting the office with a concept before submitting anything in writing.
Requirements: Eligible applicants include U.S. or U.S.-based international organizations, 501(c)3 nonprofit public charities, and government agencies (any level). All grants are to be used exclusively for charitable, public benefit purposes.
Restrictions: The foundation does not grant requests for salaries, general operating expenses, scholarships, endowment funds, fundraising events or capital campaigns, feasibility studies, consulting fees, or advertising. The foundation will no longer accept any unsolicited requests for research or from public/private schools (K-12), universities/colleges, child daycare/development centers, hospitals, or libraries. Grant consideration will be given only to those organizations that have been invited to submit formal proposals and that have completed the application process.
Geographic Focus: All States
Amount of Grant: 5,000 - 50,000 USD
Contact: Trista Campbell, Program Officer; (626) 852-0092; fax (626) 852-0776; ludwickfndn@ludwick.org
Internet: www.ludwick.org
Sponsor: Ludwick Family Foundation
203 South Glendora Avenue, Suite B, P.O. Box 1796
Glendora, CA 91740

Luella Kemper Trust Grants   1517

The Luella Kemper Trust was established in 1986 to support and promote quality education and human services programming for underserved populations. Special consideration is given to charitable organizations that serve the people of Grayson County, Texas. Grants from the Kemper Trust are 1 year in duration. Award amounts typically range from $2,500 to $15,000. Applications are accepted twice annually.
Requirements: Applicants must have 501(c)3 tax-exempt status and serve communities in Grayson County, Texas. Applications will be submitted online through the Bank of America website. A grant report is required within 1 year of the grant application date, regardless of whether all of the funds have been spent.
Restrictions: The trust does not support requests from individuals, organizations attempting to influence policy through direct lobbying, or any political campaigns.
Geographic Focus: Texas
Date(s) Application is Due: Jan 1; Aug 1
Amount of Grant: 2,500 - 15,000 USD
Samples: Grayson County College Foundation, Denison, Texas, $10,000 - awarded for support of the Grayson College Center of Excellence for Veteran Student Success (2018); Grayson Grand Central Station, Sherman, Texas, $10,000 - awarded for Grand Central Station roof replacement (2018); Girl Scouts of Northeast Texas, Dallas, Texas, $5,000 - awarded for the Girl Scout Leadership Experience for Girls in Grayson County (2018).
Contact: Kelly Garlock, Philanthropic Client Manager; (800) 357-7094; tx.philanthropic@bankofamerica.com or tx.philanthropic@ustrust.com
Internet: www.bankofamerica.com/philanthropic/foundation/?fnId=90
Sponsor: Luella Kemper Trust
901 Main Street, 19th Floor, TX1-492-19-11
Dallas, TX 75202-3714

Lumpkin Family Foundation Healthy People Grants   1518

Historically, the Lumpkin Family Foundation has supported entities that provide services that help keep people in its geographic area healthy. Requests will be evaluated on how well they accomplish one or more of the following: support the creativity of nonprofit organizations by seeding new projects and encouraging experimentation and innovation; support organizations demonstrating outstanding leadership in their field or community; promote the effectiveness of organizations and the nonprofit sector by supporting planning, learning and the professional development of staff and board leaders; facilitate collaboration across traditional organization or sector boundaries for community benefit; and develop public understanding of issues and promote philanthropic support necessary to address issues of community importance.
Requirements: Grants are awarded to nonprofit organizations that serve the community without discrimination on the basis of race, sex, or religion. Special consideration will be given to organizations and programs in East Central Illinois.
Restrictions: Proposals will not be considered from organizations that are not 501(c)3 tax-exempt; organizations whose primary purpose is to influence legislation; political causes, candidates, organizations or campaigns; individuals; or religious organizations, unless the particular program will benefit a large portion of the community and does not duplicate the work of other agencies in the community.
Geographic Focus: All States
Amount of Grant: 1,000 - 50,000 USD
Contact: Bruce Karmazin, (217) 234-5915 or (217) 235-3361; fax (217) 258-8444; Bruce@lumpkinfoundation.org
Internet: www.lumpkinfoundation.org/bWHATbwefund/HealthyPeople.aspx
Sponsor: Lumpkin Family Foundation
121 South 17th Street
Mattoon, IL 61938

Lumpkin Family Foundation Strong Community Leadership Grants   1519

The Lumpkin Family Foundation believes that well managed, mission-driven nonprofit organizations produce more effective and sustainable programs. When organizations work collaboratively on matters of common concern they accomplish more, give greater voice to their concerns, have a deeper impact on their clients and, ultimately, create stronger, more vibrant communities. The Foundation is committed to making grants to support nonprofits in building their leadership and working together on issues impacting the communities it cares about. It accepts applications that address organizational capacity or encourage civic engagement and community leadership. Requests will be evaluated on how well they accomplish one or more of the following: support the creativity of nonprofit organizations by seeding new projects and encouraging experimentation and innovation; support organizations demonstrating outstanding leadership in their field or community; promote the effectiveness of organizations and the nonprofit sector by supporting planning, learning and the professional development of staff and board leaders; facilitate collaboration across traditional organization or sector boundaries for community benefit; and develop public understanding of issues and promote philanthropic support necessary to address issues of community importance.

Requirements: Grants are awarded to nonprofit organizations that serve the community without discrimination on the basis of race, sex, or religion. Special consideration will be given to organizations and programs in East Central Illinois. Other communities receiving consideration for grant funding include: San Francisco, California; Albuquerque, New Mexico; St. Louis, Missouri; Terre Haute, Indiana; Chicago, Illinois; Madison, Wisconsin; Chautauqua County, New York; Silver Creek, New York; Philadelphia, Pennsylvania; and Norwalk, Connecticut.

Restrictions: Proposals will not be considered from organizations that are not 501(c)3 tax-exempt; organizations whose primary purpose is to influence legislation; political causes, candidates, organizations or campaigns; individuals; or religious organizations, unless the particular program will benefit a large portion of the community and does not duplicate the work of other agencies in the community.

Geographic Focus: California, Connecticut, Illinois, Indiana, Missouri, New Mexico, New York, Wisconsin

Amount of Grant: 1,000 - 10,000 USD

Contact: Annie Hernandez, Program Officer; (217) 234-5702 or (217) 235-3361; fax (217) 258-8444; Annie@lumpkinfoundation.org

Internet: www.lumpkinfoundation.org/bWHATbwefund/StrongCommunityLeadership.aspx

Sponsor: Lumpkin Family Foundation
121 South 17th Street
Mattoon, IL 61938

Lynn and Foster Friess Family Foundation Grants 1520

Established in 1981, the Lynn and Foster Friess Family Foundation primarily offers support to faith-based inner-city programs, particularly those that provide one-to-one mentoring services. Aside from its religious focus, other major areas of interest include disaster and emergency management, elementary and secondary education, philanthropy, and youth development. Its primary geographic focus is on the states of Wyoming, Georgia, Arizona, and the District of Columbia. Funding strategies include: building and renovations, capital and infrastructure, equipment purchase, general operating support, land acquisition, and rent. Awards have recently ranged as high as $2.5 million. Since there are no formal applications, applicants should submit a detailed project description, along with a budgeted amount requested. There are no specified deadlines.

Requirements: 501(c)3 organizations aligned with the Foundation's funding aims and supporting the residents of Wyoming, Washington, D.C., Georgia, and Arizona are welcome to apply.

Geographic Focus: Arizona, District of Columbia, Georgia, Wyoming

Amount of Grant: Up to 2,500,000 USD

Contact: Foster S. Friess, President; (307) 733-9587

Sponsor: Lynn and Foster Friess Family Foundation
P.O. Box 9790
Jackson, WY 83002-9790

M.A. Rikard Charitable Trust Grants 1521

The M.A. Rikard Charitable Trust was founded in Alabama in 2001 with the expressed purpose of supporting nonprofit organizations in Alabama, Florida, Georgia, Hawaii, Tennessee, and Washington. Currently, the Trust's primary areas of interest include: adult education; biodiversity; Christianity; diseases and conditions; elementary and secondary education; health care access; higher education; historical activities; housing development; human services; in-patient medical care; literacy programs; mentoring; nonprofit organizations; and reading promotion. Generally, its target populations have been academics, children and youth; economically disadvantaged; low-income; and students. Most often, funding comes in the form of program development, re-granting, research, and evaluation. Recent awards have ranged up to a maximum of $75,000. The initial approach is a letter of inquiry, and there are no specified annual deadlines for application submission.

Geographic Focus: Alabama, Florida, Georgia, Hawaii, Tennessee, Washington

Amount of Grant: Up to 25,000 USD

Samples: Kula Aupuni Niihau KahelelanI Aloha, Kehaha, HI, $17,500 - general operating support; Mount Baker School District, Deming, WA, $1,500 - general operating support; Oglethorpe University, Atlanta, GA, $65,000 - general operating support.

Contact: Frank A. Rikard, Trustee; (205) 868-6156

Sponsor: M.A. Rikard Charitable Trust
800 Shades Creek Parkway, Suite 125
Birmingham, AL 35209

M. Bastian Family Foundation Grants 1522

Established in 1993, the M. Bastian Family Foundation supports nonprofit organizations in its areas of interest, including music, the arts, higher education, health care and health organizations, religion (Christian and Latter-day Saints), social services, and wildlife conservation. Types of support include general operating support and scholarship funds.

Contact the office for application forms. There are no application deadlines. Awards range as high as $400,000.

Requirements: Funding focus is primarily in Utah.

Restrictions: Grants are not made to individuals.

Geographic Focus: All States

Amount of Grant: 2,000 - 400,000 USD

Samples: Utah Valley University Foundation, Orem, Utah, $400,000 - to assist the university with their fine arts and performing arts programs (2018); Alpine Foundation, American Fork, Utah, $10,000 - general scholarship funding (2018); Academy for Child Advocacy and Family Support, Provo, Utah, $40,000 - general operating support (2018).

Contact: McKay S. Matthews, Program Contact; (801) 225-2455

Sponsor: M. Bastian Family Foundation
51 West Center Street, Suite 305
Orem, UT 84057

M.D. Anderson Foundation Grants 1523

The Anderson Foundation funds projects for the improvement of working class conditions among workers, and for the establishment, support and maintenance of hospitals, homes and institutions for the care of the young, sick, the aged, and the helpless. The Foundation also gives for the improvement of general living conditions and for the promotion of health, science, education, and the advancement of knowledge. Funding is given for aging center and services; education; employment; government/public administration; health care; human services; medical specialties public policy and research; and youth services. Types of support include building and/or renovation, equipment, matching/challenge support, research, and seed money.

Requirements: Organizations should submit a letter of inquiry with the following information: a copy of their IRS determination letter; a detailed description of their project and amount of funding requested; a copy of the current year's organizational budget and/or project budget; and a listing of additional sources and amount of support. Applicants should submit five copies of the proposal. There are no deadlines. The Board meets once a month, with organizations contacted within four weeks.

Restrictions: Funding is given primarily in Texas, with emphasis on the Houston area. Grants are not available to individuals, operating funds, or endowments.

Geographic Focus: Texas

Amount of Grant: 25,000 - 200,000 USD

Samples: Methodist Hospital Foundation, San Antonio, Texas, molecular imaging initiative at the hospital research institute, $200,000 payable over one year; YMCA capital campaign, Houston, Texas, $100,000 payable over one year; Scott and White Memorial Hospital, Temple, Texas, toward support of indigent care program through the development and implementation of the Family Medicine Community Clinic, $25,00 payable over one year.

Contact: Karen Jenkins, Grant Contact; (713) 216-1095

Sponsor: M.D. Anderson Foundation
P.O. Box 2558
Houston, TX 77252-8037

M.J. Murdock Charitable Trust General Grants 1524

The M.J. Murdock Charitable Trust General Grants provides support for education, arts and culture, and health and human services. The Trust considers educational projects in formal and informal settings, emphasizing enhancement or expansion, as well as new educational approaches. Of special interest to the Trust are the following: performance and visual arts projects which enrich the cultural environment of the region and educational outreach efforts; and programs that emphasize preventative efforts which address physical, spiritual, social, and psychological needs, with a focus on youth. Grants are awarded for capital projects, program initiation, expansion, or for increased organizational capacity. Organizations are encouraged to view the grants awarded link for examples of previously funded grants.

Requirements: Before proceeding, interested parties should review the General Grant Application Guidelines to see if their organization is eligible or their project is appropriate for application to the Trust. After determining eligibility and appropriateness, organizations must submit a letter of inquiry before proceeding with the application. Upon approval, the organization will use the Trust's General Grant Application form and procedures.

Restrictions: The Trust only funds programs in the Pacific Northwest region: Alaska, Idaho, Montana, Oregon, and Washington. The following requests for funding are not considered: specific individuals and/or their personal benefit; individuals unauthorized to act on behalf of a qualified tax-exempt organization; funds that will ultimately be passed through to other organizations; propagandizing or for influencing legislation and elections; institutions that in policy or practice unfairly discriminate against race, ethnic, origin, sex, creed, or religion; sectarian or religious organizations whose principal activity is for the primary benefit of their own members; or for long-term loans, debt retirement, or operational deficits. The following funding requests are rarely considered: normal ongoing operations or the continuation of existing projects; endowments or revolving funds that act as such; continuation of programs previously financed from other external sources; urgent needs, emergency, or gap funding; organizations organized or operating outside any state or territory of the United States.

Geographic Focus: Alaska, Idaho, Montana, Oregon, Washington

Samples: Blachet House of Hospitality, Portland, Oregon, $450,000, to serve Portland homeless; Billings District Council of the Society of St. Vincent de Paul, Billings, Montana, to expand client services, $100,000; Whidbey Institute, Clinton, Washington, for program expansion to enhance civic engagement, $150,000.

Contact: Marybeth Stewart Goon, Senior Program Assistant; (360) 694-8415; fax (360) 694-1819

Internet: www.murdock-trust.org/grants/general-grants.php

Sponsor: M.J. Murdock Charitable Trust
703 Broadway, Suite 710
Vancouver, WA 98660

Mabel A. Horne Fund Grants   1525
The Mabel A. Horne Fund was established in 1957 to support and promote quality educational, human services and health care programming for underserved populations in Massachusetts. The majority of grants from the Mabel A. Horne Fund are one year in duration. On occasion, multi-year support is awarded. Award amounts typically go up to $25,000.
Requirements: Applicants must have 501(c)3 tax-exempt status and serve communities in Massachusetts. Grant requests for general operating support or program support are encouraged. Small, program-related capital expenses may be included in general operating or program requests. Applications will be submitted online through the Bank of America website. A grant report is required within 1 year of the grant application date, regardless of whether all of the funds have been spent.
Restrictions: The fund does not support requests from individuals, organizations attempting to influence policy through direct lobbying, or any political campaigns.
Geographic Focus: Massachusetts
Date(s) Application is Due: Jan 15
Amount of Grant: Up to 25,000 USD
Samples: Justice Resource Institute Inc. dba YouthHarbors, Jamaica Plain, Massachusetts, $15,000 - Awarded for general operations of YouthHarbors (2018); More Than Words, Boston, Massachusetts, $15,000 - Awarded for general operations of the organization (2018); School on Wheels of Massachusetts, East Bridgewater, Massachusetts, $15,000 - Awarded for general operations of the organization (2018).
Contact: Michealle Larkins, Philanthropic Administrator; (866) 778-6859; ma.grantmaking@bankofamerica.com or ma.grantmaking@ustrust.com
Internet: www.bankofamerica.com/philanthropic/foundation/?fnId=29
Sponsor: Mabel A. Horne Fund
P.O. Box 831041
Dallas, TX 75283-1041

Mabel F. Hoffman Charitable Trust Grants   1526
The Mabel F. Hoffman Charitable Trust was established in 1969 to support and promote quality educational, human services and health care programming for underserved populations. Special consideration is given to charitable organizations that serve the people of Hartford, Connecticut. Grants from the Hoffman Charitable Trust are 1 year in duration. The Hoffman Trust makes approximately 12 modest size grants per year. Award amounts typically range from $1,000 to $5,000.
Requirements: Applicants must have 501(c)3 tax-exempt status. Applications will be submitted online through the Bank of America website. A grant report is required within 1 year of the grant application date, regardless of whether all of the funds have been spent.
Restrictions: Grant requests for capital projects will not be considered. Applicants will not be awarded a grant for more than three consecutive years. The trust does not support requests from individuals, organizations attempting to influence policy through direct lobbying, or any political campaigns.
Geographic Focus: Connecticut
Date(s) Application is Due: Jun 23
Amount of Grant: 1,000 - 5,000 USD
Samples: Hands on Hartford, Hartford, Connecticut, $2,500 - awarded for Healthy Food for Kids programming (2018); Malta House of Care Inc., Hartford, Connecticut, $2,500 - awarded for Free Primary Health Care for Uninsured Adults programming (2018); Four-H Development Fund, Bloomfield, Connecticut, $5,000 - awarded for the Auerfarm Explorers program.
Contact: Amy R. Lynch, Philanthropic Client Manager; (860) 244-4870; ct.grantmaking@bankofamerica.com or amy.r.lynch@bofa.com
Internet: www.bankofamerica.com/philanthropic/foundation/?fnId=3
Sponsor: Mabel F. Hoffman Charitable Trust
99 Founders Plaza
East Hartford, CT 06108

Mabel H. Flory Charitable Trust Grants   1527
The Mabel H. Flory Charitable Trust was established in Virginia in 1979, and it currently funds organizations in Washington, D.C. metro area and Baltimore, Maryland. Support is available for research designed to develop new cures and methods of treatment for: children with hearing and sight problems; arthritis in both children and adults; and aphasia related problems. Most recent grant awards have ranged from $4,000 to $10,000.
Requirements: Initial approach should be in the form of a letter, prior to the deadline date.
Restrictions: No grants are given to individuals.
Geographic Focus: District of Columbia, Maryland
Date(s) Application is Due: Aug 31
Amount of Grant: 4,000 - 10,000 USD
Samples: Georgetown University, Washington, D.C., $10,000 - research purposes; Arthritis Foundation, Washington, D.C., $10,000 - research purposes; Foundation Fighting Blindness, Columbia, Maryland, $10,000 - research purposes.
Contact: BB&T Trustee; (703) 531-2053 or (888) 575-4586
Sponsor: Mabel H. Flory Charitable Trust
P.O. Box 2907
Wilson, NC 27894-2907

Mabel Louise Riley Foundation Family Strengthening Small Grants   1528
Mabel Louise Riley Foundation Family Strengthening Grants fund activities and projects in the greater Dudley area of Roxbury and Dorchester, Massachusetts, that build, strengthen, and support families. The Foundation will give priority to projects and activities which focus on: mending the social fabric of the neighborhood; building, strengthening, and supporting personal and family development; broadening the horizons of individuals and families; removing barriers to employment; increasing parental involvement; beautifying outdoor spaces; and community engagement. Examples include: out-of-school activities for youth or inter-generational activities; parenting seminars; life skills workshops (cooking, sewing, etc.); support groups and services for single parents; community support for reintegrating residents from situations such as recovery, incarceration, etc; or neighborhood cleanups. In addition to resident volunteers, volunteer-run neighborhood groups and associations are eligible. Nonprofit 501(c)3 status is not required, but the organization must be organized for charitable activities for the benefit of the families and neighborhoods. Anticipated funding will be in the range of $500 to $5,000 per grant. The average grant size is $1,200 to $2,500.
Requirements: The application is available at the website and must include detailed information about the organization, its proposed project, and budget.
Restrictions: Large social service agencies, community-based organizations, and for-profit entities are not eligible. Grant funds may not be used to pay salaries.
Geographic Focus: Massachusetts
Date(s) Application is Due: Apr 25
Amount of Grant: 500 - 5,000 USD
Contact: Nancy A. Saunders, Administrative Manager; (617) 399-1850; fax (617) 399-1851; nsaunders@rileyfoundation.com or info@rileyfoundation.com
Internet: www.rileyfoundation.com/sginfo.htm
Sponsor: Mabel Louise Riley Foundation
77 Summer Street, 8th Floor
Boston, MA 02110

Mabel Louise Riley Foundation Grants   1529
Mabel Louise Riley Foundation Grants are made to charities incorporated in Massachusetts, with preference for the city of Boston. The Foundation's current priorities include: collaboration with other funders; education and social services for disadvantaged children and adolescents; preschool reading programs; community development that will benefit low-income and minority neighborhoods, including job development and training, and housing; citywide efforts in Boston and vicinity that promote cultural improvements and the arts; grants that, despite some risk, offer high impact or significant benefits for a community; and improvement of race relations and neighborhood safety issues. The Foundation is especially interested in leveraging its grants by funding new programs that can become self-sufficient or which may serve as a model in other geographic areas. Grants from the Foundation normally range from $50,000 to $100,000. Occasionally, when the Foundation decides to pursue a special initiative, the Trustees will consider smaller or larger funding commitments. Multiple year funding may be available, if necessary to fulfill the funding objectives.
Requirements: Applicants are required to submit a proposal of no more than two pages without a cover letter before submitting a formal grant request. This summary should briefly describe the purposes and objectives of the proposal, the history of the applicant, and the amount requested from the Foundation. In addition to the two-page summary, a copy of the IRS 501(c)3 Determination Letter and a program budget should be included. If the filing of a formal grant request is authorized, it must be made using the Common Proposal Form of the Associated Grant Makers (AGM). The narrative portion of the request should not exceed five pages and the attachments required by the Common Proposal Form must be included: AGM Cover Summary;; executive summary (one page snapshot of proposal narrative); current financial statements (balance sheet and P/L); most recent audited financial statement; IRS Form 990, Form 990EZ, or Form 990-N (if applicable); program budget (multi-year, if applicable); organizational budget (multi-year, if applicable); board of trustees/directors (with affiliations); resumes of key project personnel; and sources of funding with amounts (secured and pending). Each formal grant request must contain a clear statement of how the success or failure of the program will be evaluated, including an outcome chart, if applicable. There are no deadlines for these proposal summaries; it is an ongoing process. The Foundation will notify the applicant if the submission of a formal grant request is authorized.
Restrictions: Applicants whose formal grant requests have been denied must wait one full year before reapplying. Grant recipients should expect to wait two full years before submitting a new request. Funding is usually not granted for: grants to defray annual deficits, for regular operating budgets, or as the sole source of support for an agency; grants to governmental agencies or on behalf of individuals for personal needs, travel, research, loans or scholarships, and political purposes.
Geographic Focus: Massachusetts
Amount of Grant: 50,000 - 100,000 USD
Contact: Nancy A. Saunders, Grants Administrator; (617) 399-1850; fax (617) 399-1851; nsaunders@rileyfoundation.com or info@rileyfoundation.com
Internet: www.rileyfoundation.com
Sponsor: Mabel Louise Riley Foundation
77 Summer Street, 8th Floor
Boston, MA 02110

Mabel Y. Hughes Charitable Trust Grants   1530
The Mabel Y. Hughes Charitable Trust was established under the last will and testament of Mabel Y. Hughes, a resident of Denver, Colorado, who died on April 9, 1969. Her legacy of giving continues through grants to charitable organizations in the state of Colorado. The Trust awards funding to nonprofit organizations in its areas of interest, including: children and youth services; education; family services; health care; higher education; human

services; children's and art museums; performing arts centers; performing arts, opera; and reproductive health and family planning. Types of support include: annual campaigns; continuing support; emergency funds; endowments; equipment; general/operating support; program development; research; and seed money. Approximately fifty awards are given each year, with the average grant size ranging from $5,000 to $25,000. Applications must be submitted by March 1, July 1 or November 1 to be reviewed at the grant meeting that occurs after each deadline.

Requirements: Organizations should submit a letter of inquiry to the Trust, and if their project is appropriate for funding, they will be asked to submit a proposal.

Restrictions: The Trust does not support funding for individuals, deficit financing, scholarships, fellowships, or loans.

Geographic Focus: Colorado
Date(s) Application is Due: Mar 1; Jul 1; Nov 1
Amount of Grant: 5,000 - 30,000 USD
Contact: Peggy Toal, Private Client Services; (720) 947-6725 or (888) 234-1999; fax (877) 746-5889; grantadministration@ wellsfargo.com
Sponsor: Mabel Y. Hughes Charitable Trust
1740 Broadway
Denver, CO 80274

MacLellan Foundation Grants 1531

MacLellan Foundation Grants support Christian causes in the U.S. and around the world. The MacLellan Foundation partners with many ministries worldwide. Inquiry letters and applications are accepted throughout the year and only online.

Requirements: Nonprofit 501(c)3 organizations and public charities are eligible. A letter of inquiry is required before submitting an application. Guidelines and local, national, or international letters of inquiry are available on the website.

Geographic Focus: All States, All Countries
Contact: Jenny Petersen, Grants Manager; (423) 755-1366; fax (423) 755-1640; info@maclellan.net or support@maclellan.net
Internet: maclellan.net/application
Sponsor: MacLellan Foundation
820 Broad Street, Suite 300
Chattanooga, TN 37402

Macquarie Bank Foundation Grants 1532

The Foundation is one of Australia's oldest and largest corporate foundations contributing more than $150 million to more than 1500 community organizations world-wide since 1985. The Foundation focuses its resources in five core areas - the arts, education, environment, health, and welfare. The Foundation is also committed to projects specifically aimed at supporting indigenous communities. The Foundation's funding criteria is flexible and open. It welcomes applications from a diverse range of community organizations that are working in innovative ways to provide long-term benefits. Funding levels are flexible and are dictated by the needs of the organization and funding availability. Each application is assessed on its individual merit, with priority given to programs which support a broad section of the community at a regional, state or national level; have the involvement or potential for involvement of Macquarie Bank staff through volunteering, fundraising, pro bono work and board and/or management committee involvement; are located in cities/countries where Macquarie Bank staff are located; and deliver long-term benefits and build community sustainability. Prospective applicants are encouraged to check the Foundation website or contact Foundation Staff for more information on how to apply.

Geographic Focus: All States, All Countries
Amount of Grant: 100 - 500,000 USD
Samples: Po Leung Kuk, Hong Kong, $HK190,000 - a charitable organization supporting disadvantaged children; Oxfam Trailwalker, Melbourne, Australia, $A325,000 (2009-2010); Princess Margaret Hospital Foundation, Toronto, Ontario, Canada, $C350,000 - Ride to Conquer Cancer (2009-2010).
Contact: Heather Matwejev, Macquarie Bank Foundation, Asia; +61 2 8232 6951; fax +61 2 8232 0019; heather.matwejev@macquarie.com or foundation@macquarie.com
Lisa George, Macquarie Bank Foundation, Australia; +61 2 8232 6951; fax +61 2 8232 0019; foundation@macquarie.com or lisa.george@macquarie.com
Gail Cunningham, Macquarie Bank Foundation, Canada; +61 2 8232 6951; fax +61 2 8232 0019; foundation@macquarie.com or gail.cunningham@macquarie.com
Rachel Engel, Macquarie Bank Foundation, Europe/Middle East/Africa; +61 2 8232 6951; fax +61 2 8232 0019; foundation@macquarie.com or rachel.engel@macquarie.com
Kathryn O'Neal-Dunham, Macquarie Bank Foundation, United States; +61 2 8232 6951; fax +61 2 8232 0019; foundation@macquarie.com or kathryn.dunham@macquarie.com
Internet: www.macquarie.com/mgl/com/foundation/about/application-guidelines
Sponsor: Macquarie Bank Foundation
GPO Box 4294
Sydney, NSW 1164 Australia

Madison Community Foundation Altrusa International of Madison Grants 1533

Altrusa International of Madison, Inc. is a women's service club that has provided direct service and funding for community organizations since 1923. Altrusa established a donor advised fund with the Foundation in 1986 to further its aim of providing service to the community. Grants from the Altrusa Fund are made in the area of literacy and education broadly defined including: projects to help children and youth meet their full educational potential; projects designed to expand opportunities for people returning to school or the workforce or for retraining; projects for people who need assistance to succeed in school so that they are able to be self-supporting; projects that foster parental involvement with their

children's schooling; and projects that focus on lifelong learning. Grant applications and guideline are available at the website.

Geographic Focus: Wisconsin
Date(s) Application is Due: Feb 1
Amount of Grant: 1,000 - 10,000 USD
Contact: Tom Linfield, Vice President; (608) 232-1768 or (888) 400-7643; fax (608) 232-1772; tlinfield@madisoncommunityfoundation.org
Internet: www.madisoncommunityfoundation.org/Page.aspx?pid=274
Sponsor: Madison Community Foundation
2 Science Court, P.O. Box 5010
Madison, WI 53705

Madison Community Foundation Fund for Children Grants 1534

The Fund for Children is a component fund of the Madison Community Foundation, advised by executives of American Girl, LLC, a subsidiary of Mattel, Inc. Grants support innovative programming for children ages 0-18 in Dane County. Grants support programs that: expose children to excellence in arts, culture, entertainment, or hands-on education related to the arts or the environment; illustrate collaboration with other local organizations and/or schools in Dane County; support or complement classroom curriculum; foster cooperation between children, parents and teachers; serve children in Dane County; and where funding can be leveraged to secure matching grants from other funding sources. The Fund entertains request for a minimum of $10,00.

Requirements: Eligible non-profit 501(c)3 organizations or governmental bodies, including schools and municipalities, must serve the people of Dane County and conduct business without discrimination on the basis of race, religion, gender, sexual preference, age, marital status, disability or national origin. Eligible projects will: have a long-term impact on Dane County residents and/or the physical environments in Dane County; include meaningful, reasonable, and measurable outcomes; use innovative approaches to address community issues; strengthen and enhance community assets; build the self-sufficiency of individuals and/or organizations; attract additional funding; and use partnerships and/or collaboration.

Restrictions: The Fund does not support the following: annual operations; endowments, individuals or scholarships; travel funds, benefit tickets, or courtesy advertising; organizations that might in any way pose a conflict with the Fund's goals, programs, products or employees; health and human services programs; and capital projects or equipment.

Geographic Focus: Wisconsin
Date(s) Application is Due: Aug 1
Contact: Tom Linfield, Vice President; (608) 232-1768 or (888) 400-7643; fax (608) 232-1772; tlinfield@madisoncommunityfoundation.org
Internet: www.madisoncommunityfoundation.org/Page.aspx?pid=273
Sponsor: Madison Community Foundation
2 Science Court, P.O. Box 5010
Madison, WI 53705

Madison Community Foundation Grants 1535

Madison Community Foundation Grants are designed to gather ideas and advance initiatives that impact lives and the community for the long term. Focus areas include arts, children, community development, elderly, environment, learning, and youth. Capital and program grants are offered. Capital grants support the construction, purchase and renovation of facilities, land acquisition, and occasionally the purchase of vehicles or equipment. Program grants support new programs or expansion of existing programs that have a track record of success. Capital grants average $55,000, and program grants average $35,000. Approximately 25 percent of the applications received are funded at some level. The Foundation is rarely the sole financial supporter of projects. Applicants must submit a letter of inquiry. Selected applicants will then be invited to complete a full grant application. Letters of inquiry are due January 18 and July 15. A letter of inquiry form and additional guidelines may be found at the website.

Requirements: Eligible non-profit 501(c)3 organizations or governmental bodies, including schools and municipalities, must serve the people of Dane County and conduct business without discrimination on the basis of race, religion, gender, sexual preference, age, marital status, disability or national origin. Eligible projects will: have a long-term impact on Dane County residents and/or the physical environments in Dane County; include meaningful, reasonable, and measurable outcomes; use innovative approaches to address community issues; strengthen and enhance community assets; build the self-sufficiency of individuals and/or organizations; attract additional funding; and use partnerships and/or collaboration.

Restrictions: The Foundation does not fund: individuals; endowments not held by the Foundation; debt retirement; lobbying; annual campaigns; scholarships; religious organizations for religious purposes; short-term events such as conferences, festivals, fund raising functions and celebrations; substance abuse treatment; health care services, including mental health; and capital grants to support ongoing maintenance.

Geographic Focus: Wisconsin
Samples: Alzheimer's and Dementia Alliance of Wisconsin, Madison, Wisconsin, $32,421 - for a neighborhood-based program to increase counseling and screening in the African American community; Boys and Girls Club of Dane County, Madison, Wisconsin, $100,000 - to provide tutoring, mentorship, college field trips, summer internships, and other support; and Center for Resilient Cities, Madison, Wisconsin, $100,000 - to help fund the Community Center portion of the Resilience Research Center.
Contact: Tom Linfield, Vice President; (608) 232-1763 or (888) 400-7643; fax (608) 232-1772; tlinfield@madisoncommunityfoundation.org
Internet: www.madisoncommunityfoundation.org/Page.aspx?pid=264
Sponsor: Madison Community Foundation
2 Science Court, P.O. Box 5010
Madison, WI 53705

Madison County Community Foundation - City of Anderson Quality of Life Grant 1536

The Madison County Community Foundation - Quality of Life Grant is used as economic development quality of life assistance to non-profits. Generated through the City of Anderson's food and beverage tax, the grant is dispersed to those non-profits who have no voting representation on the committee; are not solely supporting non-secular activities with these funds; carry proof of 501(c)3 status; and are requesting funding for projects with outcomes rather than operational expenses. The grants must be used to increase quality of life for all rather than limited access.

Requirements: Application forms and guidelines are available from the Foundation office or may be downloaded from the Foundation website at www.madisoncf.org. The application is available at the City of Anderson website at www.cityofanderson.com.

Restrictions: Funding is limited to the city of Anderson, Indiana. Funding is not available for: annual fund campaigns; individuals; capital debt reduction; sectarian religious purposes; gifts to endowments; political campaigns; medical, scientific, or health research; student loans, scholarship/fellowship programs, or travel grants; programs and/or equipment which were committed prior to the grant application being submitted; organizations without responsible fiscal agents and adequate accounting procedures; schools and government agencies; normal operational expenses of the organization. Funding is limited to grants for one year.

Geographic Focus: Indiana

Date(s) Application is Due: Sep 15

Amount of Grant: 1,000 - 10,000 USD

Contact: Tammy Bowman, Program Director; (765) 644-0002; fax (765) 662-1438; tbowman@madisoncf.org

Internet: www.madisoncf.org/index.
php?submenu=grantNO&src=gendocs&ref=GrantProcess&category=Non_Profits

Sponsor: Madison County Community Foundation
33 West 10th Street, Suite 600
Anderson, IN 46015-1056

Madison County Community Foundation General Grants 1537

The Madison County Community Foundation General Grants are made to support projects and programs of non-profit agencies located in or serving residents of Madison County. Grants are typically made in the spring and fall and range from $500 to $10,000 with rare exceptions. Proposals are reviewed by a Grants Committee and those chosen are then approved by the Foundation Board. The priorities of the foundation are arts and culture, education, economic development, civic affairs, and health and human services.

Requirements: Organizations should complete the online application and include the following detailed information: their project and cost; organization information; a project narrative that includes the objective, financial need, justification; constituency; evaluation plan and community impact; additional and/or future funding; professional references and collaborative value. They should also include a list of project expenses and project income. Eight copies of the complete application package should be sent to the Program Director, along with one copy for each of the board of directors, IRS tax exempt letter, and financial statement.

Geographic Focus: Indiana

Amount of Grant: 500 - 10,000 USD

Contact: Tammy Bowman, Program Director; (765) 644-0002; fax (765) 644-3392; tbowman@madisoncf.org

Internet: www.madisoncf.org/index.
php?submenu=Grants&src=gendocs&ref=Grants&category=Non_Profits

Sponsor: Madison County Community Foundation
33 West 10th Street, Suite 600
Anderson, IN 46015-1056

Maggie Welby Foundation Grants 1538

Inspired by the life and memory of Maggie Welby, the Maggie Welby Foundation seeks to aid students (grades K-12) and families in financial need, in order to help fulfill the dreams and hopes that Maggie realized in every person she touched during her life. The Foundation offers grants for children and families that have a financial need for a particular purpose. Grants may extend to children and families in need of help with bills, athletic opportunities, medical needs, or an opportunity that a child would not otherwise have. All grants are awarded to the family, but are paid directly to the specific purpose for which the grant was applied. Organizations that directly benefit children can also receive grants on an annual need. Foundation awards grants twice per year in the months of July and December. The annual deadlines are June 30 and November 30.

Requirements: Applicants must utilize the on-line grant application process.

Restrictions: The Maggie Welby Foundation does not accept applications for Ipads.

Geographic Focus: All States

Date(s) Application is Due: Nov 30

Contact: Jamie Welby, President; (314) 330-6947; jamie.welby@maggiewelby.org or info@maggiewelby.org

Internet: maggiewelby.org/Grants.html

Sponsor: Maggie Welby Foundation
7 Needle Court
Dardenne Prairie, MO 63368

Maggie Welby Foundation Scholarships 1539

The Maggie Welby Foundation offers scholarships for children grades Kindergarten through twelfth grade. The scholarships are awarded annually to children who demonstrate a financial need, and complete the online Foundation Scholarship Application. Helping people in need was a very important part of Maggie's life. These scholarships are an extension of Maggie's love to help kids in need. The Foundation awards scholarships twice per year in the months of July and December. The annual deadlines are June 30 and November 30.

Requirements: Only applications received online will be accepted.

Geographic Focus: All States

Date(s) Application is Due: Jun 30; Nov 30

Contact: Jamie Welby, President; (314) 330-6947; jamie.welby@maggiewelby.org or info@maggiewelby.org

Internet: maggiewelby.org/Scholarships.html

Sponsor: Maggie Welby Foundation
7 Needle Court
Dardenne Prairie, MO 63368

Maine Community Foundation Edward H. Daveis Benevolent Fund Grants 1540

The Maine Community Foundation's Edward H. Daveis Benevolent Fund Grants program was established by the will of his daughter, Mabel Stewart Daveis. Grants are awarded for projects that benefit the communities of the greater Portland area. Grants focus on Portland organizations that work with young children, their families, and teachers, in addition to youth leadership program for students through high school. Programs that demonstrate their success may be eligible for funding for up to three years. Collaboration among nonprofits is encouraged. The application is available at the Foundation website. Collaboration among nonprofits is encouraged. A letter from the executive director of each collaborating organization is required, clearly explaining the level of involvement and responsibility. The maximum award is $10,000, and the online application annual deadline is October 15.

Requirements: Applicants must be 501(c)3 organizations eligible to accept tax-deductible donations as outlined in Section 170(c) of the Internal Revenue Code.

Restrictions: Religious groups are eligible but funding will not be provided for religious purposes. Funding is not provided for the following: political campaigns, or to support attempts to influence legislation of any governmental body other than through making available the results of non-partisan analysis, study and research; ongoing operating support; endowments or capital campaigns; camperships; or capital equipment over $250.

Geographic Focus: Maine

Date(s) Application is Due: Oct 15

Amount of Grant: Up to 10,000 USD

Samples: Breakwater School, Portland, Maine, $6,000 - for an early childhood play area in Phase II of Nason's Corner Park and Playscape Project; Northeast Hearing and Speech Center, Portland, Maine, $5,000 - to screen preschoolers for lifelong success; Telling Room, Portland, Maine, $5,000 - to support the Young Writers and Leaders program.

Contact: Stephanie Eglinton, Senior Program Officer; (877) 7000-6800, ext. 2205 or (207) 667-9735; fax (207) 667-0447; seglington@mainecf.org or info@mainecf.org

Internet: www.mainecf.org/Grants/AvailableGrantsDeadlines/
EdwardHDaveisBenevolentFund.aspx

Sponsor: Maine Community Foundation
245 East Main Street
Ellsworth, ME 04605

Maine Community Foundation Equity Grants 1541

The mission of the Maine Community Foundation Equity Grants is to strengthen lesbian, gay, bisexual, transgender, and queer (LGBTQ) organizations and community-based initiatives in Maine that address LGBTQ issues and needs. The vision driving the grants is one of inclusive, diverse, prejudice-free communities for the LGBTQ population and for all people in Maine. Two types of proposals encouraged are project grants and capacity building grants. Project grants support a wide variety of projects, particularly those serving people living in rural and underserved communities in Maine. Priority areas are access to health care and reduction of health disparities; support for LGBTQ elders; education to promote respect and understanding of LGBTQ people; equality for LGBTQ families and individuals; reduction of anti-LGBTQ violence; social and cultural community-building activities; and support for LGBTQ youth. Capacity building grants support organizations whose primary mission is to serve Maine's LGBTQ community. Successful applicants will be able to describe how enhancing their organizational capacity will ultimately benefit the communities they serve. A list of previously funded projects are posted on the Foundation website. Applications are available at the Foundation's website.

Requirements: Applicants must be 501(c)3 organizations eligible to accept tax-deductible donations as outlined in Section 170(c) of the Internal Revenue Code.

Restrictions: Religious groups are eligible but funding will not be provided for religious purposes. Funding is not provided for the following: political campaigns, or to support attempts to influence legislation of any governmental body other than through making available the results of non-partisan analysis, study and research; ongoing operating support; endowments or capital campaigns; camperships; or capital equipment over $250.

Geographic Focus: Maine

Date(s) Application is Due: Sep 15

Amount of Grant: 7,500 USD

Samples: Gay Lesbian and Straight Education Network, Southern Maine Chapter, Portland, Maine, $7,500, for board self-assessment and training; Out As I Want To Be, Rockland, Maine, $5,000, to fund a capacity-building coordinator; and Youth MOVE Maine, Portland, Maine, $3,470, to create a training video for health care providers.

Contact: Ken Town, Grant Contact; (207) 685-4715; ktown@hotmail.com

Internet: www.mainecf.org/equityfund.aspx

Sponsor: Maine Community Foundation
245 East Main Street
Ellsworth, ME 04605

Maine Community Foundation Peaks Island Grants 1542

The Foundation's Peaks Island Grants benefit the community of Peaks Island and its residents by supporting the work of local nonprofits and responding to the emerging needs of the island and its residents. A high priority is funding projects that focus on bringing Peaks Island residents together. The intent is that the relationships formed will provide the context for long-term conversations to enhance life on Peaks. Applications are available on the Foundation's website.
Requirements: Applicants must be 501(c)3 organizations eligible to accept tax-deductible donations as outlined in Section 170(c) of the Internal Revenue Code.
Geographic Focus: Maine
Date(s) Application is Due: Jun 21
Amount of Grant: 300 - 10,000 USD
Samples: Brackett Memorial Church, Peaks Island, ME, $7,000, to expand the Tween Program; Fifth Maine Regiment Museum, Peaks Island, ME, $5,000, to underwrite the costs of constructing a handicap accessible restroom; and Peaks Island Children's Workshop, Peaks Island, ME, $9,563, to assist in the transition to a Small Child Care Facility.
Contact: Pam Cleghorn, Grants Administrator; (877) 700-6800; fax (207) 667-0447; pcleghorn@mainecf.org
Internet: www.mainecf.org/peaksfund.aspx
Sponsor: Maine Community Foundation
245 East Main Street
Ellsworth, ME 04605

Maine Community Foundation Penobscot Valley Health Association Grants 1543

The Penobscot Valley Health Association supports projects that propose innovative ways to strengthen the health and welfare of the greater Bangor community. Priority is given to proposals that involve the targeted population in the design, implementation and evaluation of the project, draw upon the strengths of the community, and foster collaboration between community groups. Applications are available at the Foundation's website, along with a list of previously funded projects.
Requirements: Applicants must be 501(c)3 organizations eligible to accept tax-deductible donations as outlined in Section 170(c) of the Internal Revenue Code.
Geographic Focus: Maine
Date(s) Application is Due: Feb 15
Amount of Grant: Up to 10,000 USD
Samples: 32nd Degree Masonic Learning Centers for Children, Bangor, Maine, $5,000, for tutoring services for children with dyslexia in the greater Bangor area; Evaluation Practice Group, Newburgh, Maine, $9,560, to support the Hooves of Hope equine therapy program for children with disabilities; and Hammond Street Senior Center, Bangor, Maine, $18,828, to support programs for healthy aging in the Bangor region.
Contact: Amy Pollien, Grants Administrator; (877) 700-6800, ext 1109; fax (207) 667-0447; grants@mainecf.org or apollien@mainecf.org
Internet: www.mainecf.org/PVHAFund.aspx
Sponsor: Maine Community Foundation
245 East Main Street
Ellsworth, ME 04605

Maine Community Foundation People of Color Fund Grants 1544

The objective of the People of Color Grants is to help communities of color achieve greater racial equity in Maine. The People of Color Grants support communities seeking to develop their leadership, knowledge, tools, and skills. The targeted beneficiaries of the funding are self-identified people of color. Both project grants (for initiatives that advance racial equity) and organizational development grants (to increase the efficiency and effectiveness of organizations that serve communities of color) are awarded. Priority is given to funding three areas of interest: leadership development, civic engagement, and youth. Applicants can be found at the Foundation's website, along with a list of previously funded projects.
Requirements: Applicants must be 501(c)3 organizations eligible to accept tax-deductible donations as outlined in Section 170(c) of the Internal Revenue Code. Applicants also must provide services or support to an identifiable community of color in Maine and have people of color in leadership positions with significant responsibilities. Only projects in which a majority of the participants or intended recipients are people of color are supported.
Restrictions: General operating support is not funded. Funding is also not available for lobbying or religious activities, program expenses already incurred, annual appeals, or endowment campaigns.
Geographic Focus: Maine
Date(s) Application is Due: Mar 15
Amount of Grant: Up to 7,500 USD
Samples: Penobscot Nation Boys and Girls Club, Indiana Island, Maine, $4,500, for a prevention program for Native American youth; Trinity Episcopal Church - Urban Ministry Center, Lewiston, Maine, $7,000, for the "street leader" project that will provide paid internships for students who will act as mentors to elementary age youth while receiving leadership/job training; and Daniel Hanley Center For Health Leadership, Portland, Maine, $2,500, to support planning for a new Health Ambassadors program to address health disparities in underserved populations in Maine.
Contact: Leila DeAndrade, Grants Administrator; (877) 700-6800; fax (207) 667-0447; ldeandrade@mainecf.org
Internet: www.mainecf.org/peopleofcolorfund.aspx
Sponsor: Maine Community Foundation
245 East Main Street
Ellsworth, ME 04605

Maine Community Foundation Vincent B. and Barbara G. Welch Grants 1545

The Welch grants are made to institutions primarily in the greater Portland area. Projects and programs in the following areas are given preference: youth, education, health care, alcoholic rehabilitation, and arts and culture. Applications are available at the Community Foundation's website, in addition to an extensive list of previously funded projects and programs.
Requirements: Applicants must be 501(c)3 organizations eligible to accept tax-deductible donations as outlined in Section 170(c) of the Internal Revenue Code.
Restrictions: Funding is not available for program expenses that have already been accumulated.
Geographic Focus: Maine
Date(s) Application is Due: Aug 1
Amount of Grant: Up to 75,000 USD
Contact: Pam Cleghorn, Senior Program Officer; (877) 700-6800, ext 2205; fax (207) 667-0447; pcleghorn@mainecf.org or info@mainecf.org
Internet: www.mainecf.org/welch.aspx
Sponsor: Maine Community Foundation
245 East Main Street
Ellsworth, ME 04605

Maine Women's Fund Economic Security Grants 1546

Recognizing that women's ability to take care of themselves and their families and to contribute to their communities depend upon their ability to obtain financial security, the Maine Women's Fund provides grants to support projects and organizations that build economic security for Maine women and girls. Specifically, the fund invests in organizations that focus in four strategic areas to create systemic change: education and youth development; entrepreneurship and better jobs and wages; financial literacy and asset building; and policy and leadership. Applicants may request general operating support or program/project support. Downloadable guidelines are available from the grant web page. The fund makes the application available to applicants in early December. Completed applications will be reviewed by a group of women selected from the community for their expertise and commitment to social change. Reviewers will evaluate proposals on several factors including alignment with the Maine Women's Fund values, the likelihood of systemic change occurring, the quality of the project implementation and evaluation plan, and the capacity of the organization or group.
Requirements: Nonprofit organizations or groups that demonstrate tax-exempt status under the Internal Revenue Service Code 501(c)3 or groups that submit an application through a fiscal agent with tax-exempt status that agrees to accept funds on its behalf are eligible to apply. Organizations must serve women and girls who reside in Maine. The fund invests in programs and organizations that are focused on creating tangible social change, and not simply service delivery. The fund prefers to support organizations that have limited access to other donors.
Restrictions: Organizations are limited to receiving one grant per year. The fund will not provide over 10% of an organization's annual budget. The fund will not support the following types of entities or activities: projects that discriminate on the basis of ethnicity, race, color, creed, religion, gender or gender identity, national origin, age, disability, marital status, sexual orientation, or veteran's status; individuals; scholarships; capital or endowment; biomedical research; debt reduction; fundraising events; campaigns for political office; organizations that limit or oppose women's right to self determination; or agencies of state or federal government (unless they are part of an eligible community collaborative). Faith-based organizations are eligible to apply; however, projects and services provided by these must not present or incorporate religion in any manner.
Geographic Focus: Maine
Amount of Grant: Up to 15,000 USD
Samples: The Community Schools, Camden, Maine, Passages - a home-based high school degree program for young parents; A Company of Girls, Portland, Maine - an award-winning, nationally recognized after school theater & arts prevention program for low income, high-risk and special needs girls ages 7-18; Maine Centers for Women, Work, and Community, Ellsworth, Maine - entrepreneurship training and technical assistance.
Contact: Sonya Tomlinson, Office & Grants Manager; (207) 774-5513; fax (207) 774-5533; grants@mainewomensfund.org or thewomen@mainewomensfund.org
Internet: www.mainewomensfund.org/grants/economic_security_initiative/
Sponsor: Maine Women's Fund
565 A Congress Street, Suite 306, P.O. Box 5135
Portland, ME 04101

Maine Women's Fund Girls' Grantmaking Initiative 1547

The Girls' Grantmaking Initiative is an opportunity for young women, in grades 8-12, to get hands on with decision-making and philanthropy. In addition to making grants to projects or organizations supporting girls, program participants gain a deeper understanding of philanthropy, practical experience working together to make decisions, and the opportunity to work with other girls who are passionate about social issues. Interested applicants are encouraged to contact the Office and Grants Manager for more information. The Maine Women's Fund is a public grant-making foundation dedicated to creating lasting change by investing in the power of women and the dreams of girls.
Requirements: Nonprofit organizations or groups that demonstrate tax-exempt status under the Internal Revenue Service Code 501(c)3 or groups that submit an application through a fiscal agent with tax-exempt status that agrees to accept funds on its behalf are eligible to apply.
Restrictions: Organizations must serve women and girls who reside in Maine.
Geographic Focus: Maine
Contact: Sonya Tomlinson, Office & Grants Manager; (207) 774-5513; fax (207) 774-5533; grants@mainewomensfund.org or thewomen@mainewomensfund.org

Internet: www.mainewomensfund.org/grants/economic_security_initiative/
Sponsor: Maine Women's Fund
565 A Congress Street, Suite 306, P.O. Box 5135
Portland, ME 04101

Make Sense Foundation Grants 1548

The Make Sense Foundation is a non-profit organization created in 2002 by Joni Rogers-Kante, founder and CEO of SeneGence International. The foundation thrives on donating to deserving non-profit organizations throughout the country that are also committed to making a real difference in the lives of women and children. The Foundation funds agencies in its communities that: fight hunger and poverty; support victims of domestic violence and abuse; serve the homeless; provide training and educational opportunities; invest in at-risk youth; promote health, wellness, and healing; rescue victims of sex trafficking; and help victims of natural disasters. There are no specific deadlines for the online application.
Requirements: Any non-profit agency serving the needs of women and children may apply for support from the Make Sense Foundation.
Geographic Focus: All States
Contact: Vickie Beyer, Executive Director; (918) 248-1278
Internet: senegencemsf.wufoo.com/forms/z1f2b9fh0hparw7/
Sponsor: Make Sense Foundation
301 South Main Street
Sapulpa, OK 74066

Malone Family Foundation Atypical Development Initiative Grants 1549

The Malone Family Foundation wishes to announce a new initiative to fund education and service centers for developmentally atypical children. Two grant programs will be initiated. The first will fund developmentally based educational and service delivery centers for children with developmental challenges. The second will fund curriculum development for this population, primarily within the context of these centers. The grant for the establishment of centers will be competitive and awarded to one organization per year. This is a seed grant with some matching grant characteristics and the opportunity to apply for further funding after five years of documented compliance. The application process is extensive, specific, and designed to assist the organization in solidifying mission and building capacity. Previous foundation grants are not required. Applications must be received by April 1.
Requirements: Applicants must have public nonprofit status with the IRS. Potential applicants may include groups of support professionals (speech, occupational, music, art therapists, teachers) or institutions such as universities wishing to establish centers to meet the merged educational, pre-vocational and therapeutic needs of children with traits associated with developmental syndromes such as Autism Spectrum Disorder. Joint venture applications will be considered if they are robust and specific.
Geographic Focus: All States
Date(s) Application is Due: Apr 1
Contact: Tracy Lee Amonette, Director; (720) 875-5201; tracy.malonefdn@gmail.com
Internet: www.malonefamilyfoundation.org/atypical-development.html
Sponsor: Malone Family Foundation
12300 Liberty Boulevard
Englewood, CO 80112

Manuel D. and Rhoda Mayerson Foundation Grants 1550

The Manuel and Rhoda Mayerson Foundation Grants supports organizations in its areas of interest, including children and youth, people with disabilities, health and well-being, arts and culture, housing and homelessness, and Jewish life and culture. Types of support include building construction/renovation, conferences and seminars, matching/challenge grants, seed grants, and technical assistance. The board meets quarterly.
Requirements: Grants are only awarded to nonprofit, tax-exempt organizations as defined by Section 501(c)3 of the Internal Revenue Code, to organizations that are public charities under Section 509(a)(1),(2), or (3) of the Internal Revenue Code, and to those that comply with the requirement of Section 4945(d)(3) or (4) of the Code. In making funding decisions, the Foundation is responsive to sound strategic planning, organizational stability, leadership, creativity, entrepreneurial visioning, leveraging of resources, collaboration and empowerment of people. Additionally, there is a focus on providing funding to worthy efforts that otherwise struggle to find vital support. The application is located on the Foundation website.
Restrictions: The Foundation funds projects in Israel, in addition to Cincinnati, Ohio; Berkeley, California; and Boca Raton, Florida. The Foundation does not make grants in support of any non-charitable purpose or to organizations that promote racial, ethnic or religious disharmony, hatred or violence.
Geographic Focus: California, Florida, Ohio, Israel
Amount of Grant: 1,000 - 30,000 USD
Contact: Manuel Mayerson, Foundation President; (513) 621-7500; fax (513) 621-2864; info@mayersonfoundation.org
Internet: mayersonfoundation.org/GrantMaking/HowtoApply/tabid/609/Default.aspx
Sponsor: Manuel D. and Rhoda Mayerson Foundation
312 Walnut Street, Suite 3600
Cincinnati, OH 45202

Marathon Petroleum Corporation Grants 1551

The Marathon Petroleum Corporation offers grant support within its home-base of Ohio, as well as throughout the states of Illinois, Indiana, Kentucky, Louisiana, Michigan, Texas, and West Virginia. Occasionally, it also gives to national organizations, Its primary purposes are aligned with its core values of health and safety, diversity and inclusion, environmental stewardship and honesty and integrity. With that in mind, special emphasis is also directed toward programs that empower the socially or economically disadvantaged, and provide opportunities for students to reach their full potential. Fields of interest include: the arts, children and youth services, community and economic development, education, the environment, health care, human services, and public affairs. Types of support include: annual campaigns, cause-related marketing, employee matching gifts, general operating support, in-kind donations, and scholarships to individuals.
Geographic Focus: Illinois, Indiana, Kentucky, Louisiana, Michigan, Ohio, Texas, West Virginia
Contact: Bill Conlisk, 419-422-2121; whconlisk@marathonpetroleum.com
Internet: www.marathonpetroleum.com/Corporate_Citizenship/
Sponsor: Marathon Petroleum Corporation
539 South Main Street
Findlay, OH 45840-3229

March of Dimes Program Grants 1552

Every year the March of Dimes provides millions of dollars in grants and scholarships. The program supports community programs and education for professionals, with a primary aim to prevent birth defects, premature birth, and infant mortality. The March of Dimes Program Grants fund a number of maternal-child health community programs each year in collaboration with MDs local chapters. External organizations can apply for funding to support programs working to improve the health of mothers and babies. For more information, applicants should contact their nearest local March of Dimes chapter.
Requirements: 501(c)3 organizations throughout the country are eligible to apply.
Geographic Focus: All States
Amount of Grant: Up to 25,000 USD
Contact: Grants Administrator; (914) 997-4781 or (914) 997-4609; fax (914) 997-4560; researchgrants@marchofdimes.com
Internet: www.marchofdimes.org/professionals/scholarships-and-grants.aspx
Sponsor: March of Dimes
1275 Mamaroneck Avenue
White Plains, NY 10605

Marcia and Otto Koehler Foundation Grants 1553

The Marcia and Otto Koehler Foundation supports charitable organizations with a focus that includes, but is not limited to, the support of Medical Research and medical care facilities; programs that encourage the fine arts in the City of San Antonio, including the display, production or performance of artistic works; and the promotion of the physical, mental and moral well-being of boys and girls in the San Antonio, Texas area by providing education, recreation, guidance and medical care. At the age of 15, due to the death his father, Otto A. Koehler traveled to San Antonio, Texas, as a ward of his uncle. After serving in World War I, he became a Graduate Brewmaster and was later named Chairman of the Board and President of what became Pearl Brewing Company until his death in 1969. Mr. and Mrs. Koehler were active philanthropists during their lifetime. Marcia Koehler established the Marcia and Otto Koehler Foundation prior to her death in 1981. Grants typically range between $5,000 and $20,000.
Requirements: Preference is given to organizations operating within (or providing service to) residents of San Antonio, Texas. Eligibility to re-apply for a grant award from the Marcia and Otto Koehler Foundation requires organizations to skip 1 grant cycle (1 year) before submitting a subsequent application. Applications will be submitted online through the Bank of America website. A grant report is required within 1 year of the grant application date, regardless of whether all of the funds have been spent.
Restrictions: The foundation does not support requests from individuals, organizations attempting to influence policy through direct lobbying, or any political campaigns.
Geographic Focus: Texas
Date(s) Application is Due: Feb 1
Amount of Grant: 5,000 - 20,000 USD
Samples: St Jude's Center for Young Children Inc., Bulverde, Texas, $17,500 - awarded for general operating support for all 3 locations - SJRC Texas (2018); San Antonio Metropolitan Ministries, San Antonio, Texas, $17,500 - awarded for program administration/oversight, transportation and education supplies (2018); Special Olympics of Texas, Austin, Texas, $17,500 - awarded for Greater San Antonio Area Special Olympics Texas program (for children and youth) (2018).
Contact: Debra Goldstein Phares, Philanthropic Client Manager; (210) 270-5422; fax (800) 357-7094; tx.philanthropic@bankofamerica.com
Internet: www.bankofamerica.com/philanthropic/foundation/?fnId=145
Sponsor: Marcia and Otto Koehler Foundation
P.O. Box 831041
Dallas, TX 75283-1041

Mardag Foundation Grants 1554

The Mardag Foundation is committed to making grants to qualified nonprofit organizations in Minnesota that help enhance and improve the quality of life, inspire learning, revitalize communities, and promote access to the arts. The Foundation focuses their grantmaking in these priority areas: improving the lives of at-risk families, children, youth, and young adults; supporting seniors to live independently; building the capacity of arts and humanities organizations to benefit their communities; and supporting community development throughout the St. Paul area. Grants normally support; capital projects, program expansion and special projects of a time-limited nature; start-up costs for promising new programs that demonstrate sound management and clear goals relevant to community needs; support for established agencies that have temporary or transitional needs; funds to match contributions received from other sources or to provide a challenge to raise new contributions. Applicants are encouraged to submit a brief summary of their project prior to preparation of a full proposal to see if the project fits the guidelines and interests of the foundation. The

Foundation's grantmaking meetings are in April, August, and November. Generally, full proposals must be received three months prior to a meeting date.
Requirements: Nonprofit 501(c)3 organizations are eligible to apply. Organizations must be in the East Metro area of Dakota, Ramsey, or Washington counties.
Restrictions: The Foundation does not fund: programs exclusively serving Minneapolis and the surrounding West Metro area; scholarships and grants to individuals; ongoing annual operating expenses; sectarian religious programs; medical research; federated campaigns; conservation or environmental programs; events and conferences; programs serving the physically, developmentally or mentally disabled; capital campaigns of private secondary schools; and capital and endowment campaigns of private colleges and universities. The Foundation will review, on their own merits, grant applications received from private secondary schools and private colleges and universities for purposes not excluded in the information above.
Geographic Focus: Minnesota
Date(s) Application is Due: May 1; Aug 1; Dec 31
Amount of Grant: 5,000 - 50,000 USD
Samples: American Composers Forum, St. Paul, Minnesota, $15,000 - teaching artist training for composers; Bridges of Hope, St. Paul, Minnesota, $20,000 - family support services program.
Contact: Lisa Hansen, Grants Administration Manager; (651) 224-5463 or (800) 875-6167; lisa.hansen@mnpartners.org
Internet: www.mardag.org/apply_for_a_grant/
Sponsor: Mardag Foundation
55 Fifth Street East, Suite 600
St. Paul, MN 55101

Margaret and James A. Elkins Jr. Foundation Grants　　1555
The Elkins Foundation Grants support nonprofit programs and organizations in the metropolitan Houston, Texas area. Grants are given primarily for charitable, religious, scientific, or educational and literacy programs, including public safety testing, and the prevention of cruelty to children and animals. Fields of interest include: biology/life sciences; child development, education; child development, services; children and youth services; Christian agencies and churches; elementary and secondary education; engineering and technology; health organizations, association; higher education; hospitals (general); medical research, institute; medical education; religion; science; and safety/disasters. The Foundation also supports: building renovation; capital campaigns; emergency funds; endowments; equipment; program development; and research.
Requirements: Applications are not required. Applicants should submit a letter of inquiry, along with a copy of their most recent annual report, audited financial statement, or 990 form. Board meetings vary, and there is no deadline.
Restrictions: Grants are not made to individuals, or to support annual fundraising campaigns or operating deficits.
Geographic Focus: Texas
Amount of Grant: 5,000 - 400,000 USD
Samples: Saint Thomas Episcopal Church, Houston, Texas, for renovation support, $10,000; Sam Houston State University, Huntsville, Texas, for restoration support, $20,000; University of Texas at Austin, Austin, Texas, for educational fellowship fund, $100,000; Spark School Park Program, Houston, Texas, for program support, $5,000.
Contact: Larry Medford, Secretary-Treasurer; (713) 652-2052
Sponsor: Margaret and James A. Elkins Jr. Foundation
1001 Fannin Street, 1166 First City Tower
Houston, TX 77002

Margaret M. Walker Charitable Foundation Grants　　1556
Margaret M. Walker Charitable Foundation was established in Pennsylvania in order to offer support for Christian ministries, relief services organizations, children, women and family services, and food services. Specific fields of interest include: Christian agencies and churches; family services; food distribution; human services; minorities and immigrants; and women's shelters. Types of support include: building and renovation; capital campaigns; equipment; general operating support; and program development. Most recent awards have ranged from $2,000 to $60,000. There are no specific application forms, so interested parties should submit a letter outlining the project and amount of funding requested.
Requirements: 501(c)3 organizations either located in, or serving residents of, Pennsylvania are eligible to apply.
Geographic Focus: Pennsylvania
Amount of Grant: 2,000 - 60,000 USD
Samples: Community Food Warehouse of Shenango Valley, Farrell, Pennsylvania, $5,000 - general operating support; Buhl Park Corporation, Sharon, Pennsylvania, $50,000 - general operating support; Pennsylvania Great Lakes Region, Sharon, Pennsylvania, $60,000 - general operating support.
Contact: Foundation Administrator; (330) 743-7000
Sponsor: Margaret M. Walker Charitable Foundation
42 McClurg Road
Youngstown, OH 44512

Margaret T. Morris Foundation Grants　　1557
The Margaret T. Morris Foundation awards grants, primarily in Arizona, in its areas of interest, including: animal welfare; arts; children and youth, services; education; environment; higher education; homeless service; human services; marine science; medical research and education; mental health and crisis services; museums; performing arts; reproductive health and family planning; and hospices. The Foundation's types of support include: building renovation; capital campaigns; debt reduction; endowments;

general operating support; land acquisition; matching and challenge support; and program development. The Board of Directors meets in August, December, and as needed.
Requirements: Applications are not accepted. Applicants should submit a letter of inquiry with their request for funding and a description of the project.
Geographic Focus: Arizona
Contact: Thomas Polk, Trustee; (928) 445-4010
Sponsor: Margaret T. Morris Foundation
P.O. Box 592
Prescott, AZ 86302-0592

Margaret Wiegand Trust Grants　　1558
Established in Wisconsin, the Margaret Wiegand Trust provides grant funding for individuals who are legally blind and need assistance, care, maintenance, and educational needs. The primary fields of interest, therefore, is human services aimed people with visual disabilities. Grants are given directly to individuals or via a scholarship funding program.
Requirements: Applicants should be residents of Waukesha County, Wisconsin, and referred from the Waukesha Rehabilitation Office or other community service organizations.
Geographic Focus: Wisconsin
Contact: Anne McCullough, (214) 965-2908 or (866) 888-5157
Sponsor: Margaret Wiegand Trust
10 S. Dearborn, IL1-0117
Chicago, IL 60603

Marie C. and Joseph C. Wilson Foundation Rochester Small Grants　　1559
The Marie and Joseph Wilson Foundation strives to improve the quality of life through initiating and supporting projects that measurably demonstrate a means of creating a sense of belonging within the family and community. The Foundation considers 501(c)3 organization requests ranging from $1,000 to $25,000. Grant applications are accepted on an ongoing basis. Foundation board members review applications as they are received. The review committee meets once a month except for July and August. Because the Foundation receives a large number of applications, responses may take up to four months. Prior to the receiving funding, grant recipients are required to sign a grant agreement contract. Written progress reports are required at six months and one year following the date of the grant.
Requirements: The Foundation review committee looks for one or more of the following conditions in a proposal: the proposal is a well-planned approach to delivering services; Foundation support would be catalytic to the project's success; the proposal is efficient in its use of funds and expenses are reduced by sharing resources with other agencies or groups; and a collaborative network exists that multiplies the impact of the grant. Applicants may contact the Foundation for a current application form.
Restrictions: Grants are limited to 501(c)3 organizations serving the Rochester, New York area. Grants will not be made to individuals, partisan political organizations, or to support lobbying efforts. Requests for capital projects also will not be considered.
Geographic Focus: New York
Amount of Grant: 1,000 - 25,000 USD
Samples: Association for the Blind and Visually Impaired, Rochester, New York, for a full-time children's programming and recreational coordinator, $25,000; Charles Settlement House, Rochester, New York, Teen Clubs, a neighborhood-based program for teens that reduces violent behavior and teen pregnancy while encouraging community service, $10,000; Horizons at Harley, Rochester, New York, a summer enrichment program that offers academic, cultural, wellness, and recreational activities for children from inner-city Rochester, $24,000.
Contact: Megan Bell, Executive Director; (585) 461-4696; fax (585) 473-5206
Internet: www.mcjcwilsonfoundation.org/funding.cfm
Sponsor: Marie C. and Joseph C. Wilson Foundation
160 Allens Creek Road
Rochester, NY 14618-3309

Marietta McNeill Morgan and Samuel Tate Morgan Jr. Trust Grants　　1560
The Marietta McNeill Morgan and Samuel Tate Morgan, Jr. Trust was established in 1962 to support and promote quality educational and human services programming in the Commonwealth of Virginia. Grants from the Morgan Trust are 1 year in duration. Award amounts typically range from $5,000 to $80,000.
Requirements: Applicants must have 501(c)3 tax-exempt status and serve the State of Virginia. Applications will be submitted online through the Bank of America website. A grant report is required within 1 year of the grant application date, regardless of whether all of the funds have been spent.
Restrictions: The Morgan Trust only makes grants for specific capital expenditures and not for general capital campaign expenditures. The Morgan Trust only makes grants for specific capital expenditures and not for general capital campaign expenditures. While receipt of a grant does not preclude later support, an organization normally will not be considered for another grant from either the Morgan Trust until at least 3 years after the date of the last grant payment. The trust does not support requests from individuals, organizations attempting to influence policy through direct lobbying, or any political campaigns.
Geographic Focus: Virginia
Date(s) Application is Due: Apr 1
Amount of Grant: 5,000 - 80,000 USD
Samples: Patrick Henry Memorial Foundation, Brookneal, Virginia, $81,807 - awarded for Eugene B. Casey Education and Event Center HVAC construction costs (2019); Apple Ridge Farm Incorporated, Roanoke, Virginia, $55,000 - awarded for All Aboard: Next Stop the Apple Ridge Station! (2018); Bradley Free Clinic of Roanoke Valley Inc., Roanoke, Virginia, $50,000 - awarded for A Fresh Look for Free Care: Capital Improvements and Building Repairs Project (2018).
Contact: Lee Parker, Philanthropic Client Manager; (877) 446-1410;

D.C.grantmaking@bankofamerica.com or D.C.grantmaking@ustrust.com
Internet: www.bankofamerica.com/philanthropic/foundation/?fnId=125
Sponsor: Marietta McNeill Morgan and Samuel Tate Morgan Jr. Trust
1111 E. Main Street, VA2-300-12-92
Richmond, VA 23219-3531

Marin Community Foundation Affordable Housing Grants   1561
Marin Community Foundation (MCF) is dedicated to creating housing opportunities in Marin that are affordable and accessible to families and individuals with lower incomes. To support this goal, the Affordable Housing grants fund three strategic areas: increase public support for affordable housing and influence zoning changes that support affordable housing; make investments in affordable housing, both rental properties and owned housing that take advantage of specific market opportunities; and help people at risk of homelessness to remain housed. The grant program manager may be emailed through the grant website.
Requirements: There will not be an open competitive process for these grants. RFPs will be issued to community organizations that are being invited to apply for support under all three strategies. Nonprofit organizations will be invited to submit a Letter of Intent (LOI) in response to a Request for Proposal issued for each of the Strategic Initiatives on the Foundation website. After MCF staff reviews the LOIs, selected applicants will be invited to complete and submit a full proposal. If invited to submit an LOI, nonprofit groups should first register with the Grant Application Center, MCF's online grants application system.
Geographic Focus: California
Contact: Kathleen Harris, Program Director; (415) 464-2549
Internet: www.marincf.org/grants-and-loans/grants/strategic-initiatives/increasing-affordable-housing
Sponsor: Marin Community Foundation
5 Hamilton Landing, Suite 200
Novato, CA 94949

Marin Community Foundation Arts Education Grants   1562
Arts education advocates firmly believe that understanding and appreciating the arts and cultural experiences are vital components of every young person's education and development. The goal of this Community Grant area is to support efforts to provide standards-based arts education for all Marin public school students. The Foundation also recognizes that a full education in the arts also takes place in various out-of-school settings, through community arts activities and organizations. With Strategy 1, an organization would conduct a demonstration project that meets state arts education standards. Information about the project is available at the website. Strategy 2 involves supporting innovative arts programs for underserved students in Marin County. For current information about each strategy, organizations may call or contact the program director directly through the Foundation website.
Geographic Focus: California
Date(s) Application is Due: Apr 13
Contact: Shirin Vakharia, Program Director; (415) 464-2523
Internet: www.marincf.org/grants-and-loans/grants/community-grants/arts-education
Sponsor: Marin Community Foundation
5 Hamilton Landing, Suite 200
Novato, CA 94949

Marin Community Foundation Arts in the Community Grants   1563
The Arts in the Community Grants strive to promote a vibrant and accessible arts community for all Marin County residents by increasing public engagement in the arts. The Foundation focuses its support on arts and cultural programming for underserved populations, including low-income residents; people of color; lesbian, gay, bisexual, transgender, and questioning (LGBTQ); immigrants; individuals living in rural settings; and youth whose many challenges include not experiencing the benefits of the arts. The Foundation is looking to support an array of arts and cultural programming and activities that engage underserved residents. The most competitive projects will satisfy one or more of the following criteria: respond to a clearly demonstrated community need; demonstrate organizational capacity to meet those needs; offer programming that is culturally relevant to the constituency served; present a program budget that includes a variety of funding sources; and articulate measurable outcomes.
Requirements: Grants are limited to qualified nonprofit organizations directly serving residents of Marin County. All applicants are encouraged to contact the program director before beginning the application. Organizations must submit applications using MCF's grant application center located on the website, so they may submit all information online.
Restrictions: The Foundation does not provide support for: individuals artists; special event sponsorship; scholarship programs; innovative or standards-based arts education in school programs; underwriting support to provide free tickets to performances or events as a stand alone project; expressive arts therapies; or capital projects.
Geographic Focus: California
Date(s) Application is Due: Sep 23
Contact: Shirin Vakharia, Program Director; (415) 464-2523
Internet: www.marincf.org/grants-and-loans/grants/community-grants/arts-in-the-community
Sponsor: Marin Community Foundation
5 Hamilton Landing, Suite 200
Novato, CA 94949

Marin Community Foundation Closing the Education Achievement Gap Grants   1564
The goal of the Closing the Education Achievement Gap grant is to close the achievement gap between high-achieving students and those who are falling behind. The Marin Community Foundation believes that taking action to address this gap across Marin County will result in students of all ages ready to learn; increase proficiency in English and

math; attend high-quality schools; and graduate from high school prepared to apply to, enroll in, and complete college or other post-secondary education options. Under Strategy 2, the Foundation's goal is to increase college readiness for low-income students and students of color from San Rafael City Schools, Novato Unified, Sausalito Marin City, and Shoreline Unified. The Foundation aims to do this through project grants to organizations providing academic and personal support to middle and high school students, as well as to those that provide college navigation and scholarship support. The Foundation strives to develop a grants portfolio that includes effective stand-alone programs, collaborative and innovative partnerships, and networking and referral activities aimed at filling in that gap. The grant program director may be emailed through the Foundation website.
Requirements: Organizations should review the guidelines to determine if their program fits the parameters of the project. All applicants are required to have a preliminary phone call with the program officer before beginning the application, and should contact the associate program officer to schedule a phone appointment. Organizations applying for support under this approach should register with the Grant Application Center link located on the Foundation website. This system enables submission and completion of all application materials online. Once registered, organizations may submit a full proposal (note: this process will not use a Letter of Intent). Current guidelines, deadlines, and applications are available on the Foundation website.
Geographic Focus: California
Contact: Marcia Quinones, Program Director; (415) 464-2537; fax (415) 464-2555
Internet: www.marincf.org/grants-and-loans/grants/strategic-initiatives/education
Sponsor: Marin Community Foundation
5 Hamilton Landing, Suite 200
Novato, CA 94949

Marin Community Foundation Ending the Cycle of Poverty Grants   1565
The goal of the Marin Community Foundation Cycle of Poverty Grant is to end the cycle of poverty experienced by poor and low-income individuals and families. The Foundation believes that low-wage earners can escape the cycle of poverty if they have the tools and resources traditionally available to middle- and high-income earners. This initiative shifts the focus of the Foundation's investment from providing short-term services to people in poverty to creating lasting solutions to poverty and engaging individuals and families, institutions, and the community in efforts to build assets.
Requirements: Nonprofits interested in potential participation for Strategy 1 should contact the program director listed in the contact area for further information.
Geographic Focus: California
Contact: Kathleen Harris, Program Director; (415) 464-2549
Internet: www.marincf.org/grants-and-loans/grants/strategic-initiatives/ending-cycle-of-poverty
Sponsor: Marin Community Foundation
5 Hamilton Landing, Suite 200
Novato, CA 94949

Marin Community Foundation Improving Community Health Grants   1566
The Improving Community Health Grants is interested in funding two complimentary priorities: strengthening the delivery of health services with direct health services or community clinics; and addressing the social determinants of health so that everyone has the opportunity to live a long, healthy life regardless of income, education, or racial/ethnic background. Community, neighborhood, or geographically-focused research projects that assess the role of poverty, housing, education, transportation, healthy food, physical activity, and/or other community factors are strongly encouraged to apply. Proposed research projects should contribute to the development and/or implementation of public and/or school policies aimed at addressing social, economic, and/or political factors that contribute to the community's health. The proposed assessments should include leadership, input, and direction from the community. In addition to thorough community/neighborhood assessments, the Foundation is interested in supporting the development, advocacy, and implementation of policies and/or practices that impact the health of a low-income community or community of color. Projects that propose building infrastructure to improve the social conditions, economic opportunities, and/or physical environments in which people live, work, learn, and play will also be considered (e.g., infrastructure and technology for farmers to accept food stamps at the farmers market).
Requirements: To be eligible for funding, organizations must have a nonprofit tax-exempt status or a fiscal sponsor with a nonprofit tax-exempt status. Applicants must serve Marin County. The program director can be emailed directly through the Foundation website.
Geographic Focus: California
Contact: Wendy Todd, Program Director; (415) 464-2541
Internet: www.marincf.org/grants-and-loans/grants/community-grants/improving-community-health
Sponsor: Marin Community Foundation
5 Hamilton Landing, Suite 200
Novato, CA 94949

Marin Community Foundation Social Justice and Interfaith   1567
  Understanding Grants
The Marin Community Foundation Social Justice and Interfaith Understanding Grants are committed to supporting efforts that increase awareness, mobilize communities, and catalyze social change to address social inequities in Marin County. The Foundation defines social justice as equal access to social, political, and economic opportunities and resources. It defines interfaith understanding as communication between and among faith communities that crosses religious lines with an aim to explore common ground in beliefs and values. The Foundation funds two strategies depending on the particular program: 1) to increase community engagement to identify and address social justice issues, and 2) to increase collaboration and dialogue among religious institutions, faith-based communities, and community members. The funding varies by strategy (from $10,000 to $70,000 for

strategy 1, and from $10,000 to $50,000 for strategy 2), but both strategies have the same deadline and application process. Each strategy funds staff support and operational costs, with strategy one also funding tech assistance. Organizations should refer to the website for specific information about each strategy.

Requirements: Organizations may apply online for either strategy with the same application process. They are also encouraged to contact the program officer by phone or to email directly through the website.

Restrictions: Strategy 1 does not fund the following: direct social or health services; religious programs that are strictly sectarian; and emergency or capital expenditures, such as computer hardware or software. Strategy 2 does not fund the following: individuals; coalitions that do not have a lead organization; endowments or private foundations; religious organizations that are strictly sectarian; federal, state, or municipal agencies; and political campaigns.

Geographic Focus: California
Date(s) Application is Due: Nov 18
Amount of Grant: 10,000 - 70,000 USD
Contact: Shirin Vakharia, Program Director; (415) 464-2523
Internet: www.marincf.org/grants-and-loans/grants/community-grants/social-justice-and-interfaith-understanding
Sponsor: Marin Community Foundation
5 Hamilton Landing, Suite 200
Novato, CA 94949

Marin Community Foundation Stinson Bolinas Community Grants 1568

The Stinson/Bolinas Community Grants were created and are supported by a group of local donors. The founders act as advisors, recommending which projects should be supported by this community effort. The maximum grant is $3,000 per grant cycle, and there is no minimum amount. The Foundation assumes that all proposed projects will be completed within twelve months from the beginning of grant support. Although matching funds, donated materials, equipment and services are not required, they are strongly encouraged and will make an application more competitive. If a grant includes a funding request for labor or services, utilizing local resources is encouraged. Priority will be given to applicants who: have received, or expect to receive, funds from other sources that match, or will match, the funds requested in this application (expected receipts need to be based on documented information provided to applicants by other prospective funding sources); and have received significant levels of gifts-in-kind (services, equipment, etc.) for the project to be supported by this application. Application materials are available at the Bolinas and Stinson Beach libraries and from the grant's website. Materials should be mailed to the Stinson Beach contact location.

Requirements: To be eligible, an applicant must be an organization or individual whose project benefits the Stinson Beach and/or Bolinas communities. Organizations are encouraged to contact the grants consultant to discuss their project before submitting an application.

Geographic Focus: California
Date(s) Application is Due: Apr 30; Oct 31
Amount of Grant: Up to 3,000 USD
Samples: The Bolinas Museum, Bolinas, California, to fund the museum's Arts and Issues series which offers free public lectures, concerts and film screenings, $600; Marin Literacy Program, Marin, California, $2000; West Marin Senior Services, West Marin, California, to support elders in Stinson Beach and Bolinas, $2000; Stinson Beach Preschool, Stinson Beach, California, to fund tuition assistance, $3000.
Contact: Kristen Turek, Senior Philanthropic Advisor; (415) 464-2531; fax (415) 464-4555
Belle Wood, Grant Consultant; (415) 868-2043; belle_wood@att.net
Internet: www.marincf.org/grants-and-loans/grants/stinson-bolinas-community-fund
Sponsor: Marin Community Foundation
5 Hamilton Landing, Suite 200
Novato, CA 94949

Marion and Miriam Rose Fund Grants 1569

The Marion and Miriam Rose Fund was established to support childcare facilities serving dependent, neglected, indigent and emotionally disturbed children and children in foster care in Little Rock, Arkansas. The Marion and Miriam Rose Fund was created under the wills of Mr. George B. Rose and Mrs. Marion Rose. The majority of grants from the Rose Fund are one year in duration. Award amounts typically range from $5,000 to $30,000.

Requirements: Organizations must be located in, or serve the children of Little Rock, Arkansas. Applications will be submitted online through the Bank of America website.

Restrictions: The Fund will consider requests for general operating support only if the organization's operating budget is less than $1 million. In general, grant requests for individuals, endowment campaigns or capital projects will not be considered. The fund does not support requests from individuals, organizations attempting to influence policy through direct lobbying, or any political campaigns.

Geographic Focus: Arkansas
Date(s) Application is Due: Mar 1
Amount of Grant: 5,000 - 30,000 USD
Samples: Our House, Little Rock, Arkansas, $30,000 - awarded for Our Families: Improving Outcomes for Children and Families with High Barriers to Success (2018); The First Tee, Little Rock, Arkansas, $25,000 - awarded for the national school program initiative (2018); Access Group Inc., Little Rock, Arkansas, $25,000 - awarded for Star Institute Feeding Clinic support (2018).
Contact: Debra Goldstein Phares, Philanthropic Client Director; (800) 357-7094; tx.philanthropic@bankofamerica.com or tx.philanthropic@ustrust.com
Internet: www.bankofamerica.com/philanthropic/foundation/?fnId=15
Sponsor: Marion and Miriam Rose Fund
P.O. Box 831041
Dallas, TX 75283-1041

Marion Gardner Jackson Charitable Trust Grants 1570

The Marion Gardner Jackson Charitable Trust was established by Marion Gardner Jackson, the granddaughter of local industrialist, Robert W. Gardner, founder of the Gardner-Denver Company. Before her death in 1976, Mrs. Jackson set up a perpetual trust to aid religious, charitable, scientific, literary and educational organizations. Preference is given to organizations in Quincy, Illinois and surrounding communities in Adams County. For capital grants, applicants may apply for a grant of up to $50,000 to support capital projects. The project must support the mission of the organization and/or the stated outcome of a program or project. For program/operating support grants, applicants with organizational budgets of $10 million or less may apply for grants of $10,000 up to $50,000 for operating or program support. For program support grants, the yearly request may not be more than 30% of the program's budget. The majority of grants from the Marion Gardner Jackson Charitable trust are 1 year in duration.

Requirements: Organizations can submit 1 application per year and will not receive more than 1 award from the Trust in any given year. Applications will be submitted online through the Bank of America website. A grant report is required within 1 year of the grant application date, regardless of whether all of the funds have been spent.

Restrictions: Any organizations receiving a multi-year award from the Trust that continues into the next grant year are not eligible to apply for an additional grant until the end of the grant cycle. The trust does not support requests from individuals, organizations attempting to influence policy through direct lobbying, or any political campaigns.

Geographic Focus: All States, Illinois
Date(s) Application is Due: Aug 31
Amount of Grant: Up to 50,000 USD
Samples: Culver-Stockton College, Canton, Missouri, $50,000 - awarded for dining hall renovation (2018); John Wood Community College Foundation, Quincy, Illinois, $47,600 - awarded for Interactive Classrooms in JWCC Buildings B and C (2018); Good Samaritan Home, Quincy, Illinois, $45,551 - for the purchase of Power Shower chairs for seniors (2018).
Contact: Srilatha Lakkaraju, Philanthropic Client Manager; (312) 828-8166; ilgrantmaking@bankofamerica.com or ilgrantmaking@ustrust.com
Internet: www.bankofamerica.com/philanthropic/foundation/?fnId=60
Sponsor: Marion Gardner Jackson Charitable Trust
135 South LaSalle Street, IL4-135-14-19
Chicago, IL 60603

Marion I. and Henry J. Knott Foundation Discretionary Grants 1571

Founded in 1977, the Marion I. and Henry J. Knott Foundation is a Catholic family foundation committed to honoring its founders' legacy of generosity to strengthen the community within the Archdiocese of Baltimore. Henry J. Knott, the eldest of six boys, grew up in a lively household in the Baltimore area. His father was a hard-working carpenter. Marion Isabel Burk, who was orphaned at the age of eleven, grew up cooking and looking after the children in a small boarding house and received little formal education as a result. Henry and Marion met on a blind date arranged by a good friend in 1926, while Henry was taking classes at Loyola College, and were married in 1928. They went on to build a large family (thirteen children, one lost to cancer) and a thriving construction business. Henry was the first developer in Baltimore to employ the practice of prefabricating wall panels in a factory and then sending them out to construction sites. Projects moved at a blistering pace and eventually led Henry to become the President of Arundel Corporation. Henry and Marion who knew firsthand the challenge of raising a large family always practiced philanthropy. The foundation makes awards in five Program categories: Arts and Humanities; Catholic Activities; Education (Catholic schools, nonsectarian private schools specifically catering to special needs, and private colleges and universities); Health Care; and Human Services. Within the five program categories, the foundation funds within five project categories, including capital expenses, development, new and/or ongoing programs, operating expenses, and technology. In addition to its standard granting program, the Knott Foundation provides a limited number of Discretionary Grants (20-30) throughout the year. These grants, ranging between $500 to $2,500, are designed to increase the Foundation's grant-making options as well as its responsiveness to community needs. Grants are awarded based on the proposed project, the availability of funds, and other current requests for funding. To apply for a discretionary grant, applicants should submit a brief (one page) Letter of Inquiry (LOI) on their organization's letterhead. The LOI should describe the applicant's project or program, detail the applicant's needs, and provide a time frame for use of the award if granted. In addition to the LOI, the applicant should also submit a 501(c)3 status letter, a project budget if applicable, and a list of the board of directors. Discretionary requests are accepted and awarded on a rolling basis throughout the year. Although not guaranteed, approved funds are usually disbursed within one to two weeks of the discretionary grant's approval date. Interested applicants should visit the website for further details and guidelines.

Requirements: Discretionary grant requests must be in alignment with the foundation's areas of geographic and programmatic giving. Funding is limited to 501(c)3 organizations serving Baltimore City and the following counties in Maryland: Allegheny, Anne Arundel, Baltimore, Carroll, Frederick, Garrett, Harford, Howard, and Washington. Applicants may apply through a fiscal sponsor. The fiscal sponsor must be a 501(c)3 nonprofit organization that has a formal relationship and Memorandum of Understanding (MOU) with the applicant. Selected applicants will need to submit a copy of their most recent IRS 990 and/or audited financials.

Restrictions: The following will not be funded: organizations that have not been in operation for at least one year, scholarships, public education/public sector agencies, pro-choice or reproductive health programs, individuals, annual giving, political activities, one-time only events/seminars/workshops, legal services, environmental activities, medical research, day care centers, endowment funds for arts/humanities, national/local chapters for specific diseases, agencies that redistribute grant funds to other nonprofits, reimbursables or any prior expenses, or government agencies that form 501(c)3 nonprofits to fund public sector projects.

Geographic Focus: Maryland
Amount of Grant: 500 - 10,000 USD

Samples: Archbishop Curley High School, Baltimore, Maryland, $500 - support renovation of the track; Baltimore Chesapeake Bay Outward Bound School, Baltimore, Maryland, $2,500 - support life skill and character education for Baltimore youth; Loyola Blakefield High School, Towson, Maryland, $5,000 - support the purchasing of equipment and other resources.
Contact: Kathleen McCarthy, Grants Manager; (410) 235-7068; fax (410) 889-2577; knott@knottfoundation.org or info@knottfoundation.org
Internet: www.knottfoundation.org/grants/how_to_apply/for_a_discretionary_grant
Sponsor: Marion I. and Henry J. Knott Foundation
3904 Hickory Avenue
Baltimore, MD 21211-1834

Marion I. and Henry J. Knott Foundation Standard Grants   1572

Founded in 1977, the Marion I. and Henry J. Knott Foundation is a Catholic family foundation committed to honoring its founders' legacy of generosity to strengthen the community within the Archdiocese of Baltimore. Henry J. Knott, the eldest of six boys, grew up in a lively household in the Baltimore area. His father was a hard-working carpenter. Marion Isabel Burk, who was orphaned at the age of eleven, grew up cooking and looking after the children in a small boarding house and received little formal education as a result. Henry and Marion met on a blind date arranged by a good friend in 1926, while Henry was taking classes at Loyola College, and were married in 1928. They went on to build a large family (thirteen children, one lost to cancer) and a thriving construction business. Henry was the first developer in Baltimore to employ the practice of prefabricating wall panels in a factory and then sending them out to construction sites. Projects moved at a blistering pace and eventually led Henry to become the President of Arundel Corporation. Henry and Marion who knew firsthand the challenge of raising a large family always practiced philanthropy. The foundation makes both standard and discretionary awards in five Program categories: Arts and Humanities; Catholic Activities; Education (Catholic Schools, Nonsectarian private schools specifically catering to special needs, and private colleges and universities); Health Care; and Human Services. Within the five program categories, the foundation funds within five project categories, including capital expenses, development, new and/or ongoing programs, operating expenses, and technology. The Knott Foundation uses a two-step online application process for its standard-grants program. Step one requires the submission of an online Letter of Inquiry (LOI) along with a Financial Analysis Form. Applicants whose LOIs are approved will move on to step two which requires online submission of a full proposal. Applicants are given the opportunity to submit a draft of their proposal for comments and feedback prior to their final submission. The review process for the foundation's standard grants program takes approximately four months from the date of the LOI submission until a final funding decision is made. The Knott Foundation accepts standard-grant applications three times per year - February, June and October. LOIs and proposals must be received by 5 p.m. on the applicable deadline date. Complete details, guidelines, and links to the online submission system are available at the grant website.
Requirements: Funding is limited to 501(c)3 organizations serving Baltimore City and the following counties in Maryland: Allegheny, Anne Arundel, Baltimore, Carroll, Frederick, Garrett, Harford, Howard, and Washington. Applicants may apply through a fiscal sponsor. The fiscal sponsor must be a 501(c)3 nonprofit organization that has a formal relationship and Memorandum of Understanding (MOU) with the applicant.
Restrictions: Organizations that are denied funding at the LOI stage of the grant process are eligible to apply again during the next grant cycle; organizations that are denied funding after submitting a full grant proposal must wait one year before reapplying; organizations that receive a grant award must wait two years before reapplying. The following will not be funded: organizations that have not been in operation for at least one year, scholarships, public education/public sector agencies, pro-choice or reproductive health programs, individuals, annual giving, political activities, one-time only events/seminars/workshops, legal services, environmental activities, medical research, day care centers, endowment funds for arts/humanities, national/local chapters for specific diseases, agencies that redistribute grant funds to other nonprofits, reimbursables or any prior expenses, or government agencies that form 501(c)3 nonprofits to fund public sector projects.
Geographic Focus: Maryland
Date(s) Application is Due: Mar 7; Jul 9; Nov 12
Amount of Grant: Up to 100,000 USD
Samples: Adoptions Together, Calverton, Maryland, $49,463 - support digital enhancements to the Heart Gallery, a physical display featuring adoptable children in foster care; Baltimore Center Stage, Baltimore, Maryland, $50,000 - support for accessibility for blind, deaf, and autistic populations; Mount St. Mary's University, Emmitsburg, Maryland, $40,000 - upport equipment acquisition in the Division of Chemistry.
Contact: Kathleen McCarthy, Grants Manager; (410) 235-7068; fax (410) 889-2577; knott@knottfoundation.org or info@knottfoundation.org
Internet: www.knottfoundation.org/grants
Sponsor: Marion I. and Henry J. Knott Foundation
3904 Hickory Avenue
Baltimore, MD 21211-1834

Marisla Foundation Human Services Grants   1573

Marisla Foundation was established in 1986 and currently operates with three full-time program directors and one half-time assistant administrator. Of the hundreds of proposals received each year only a small number are funded. In the area of Human Services, applications should address the needs of women, primarily focusing on physical, emotional and mental health, and financial well being. Grants support activities and integrated approaches to homelessness, substance abuse, domestic violence, and vocational training. The Foundation strongly discourages the submission of multiple applications from one organization. This includes chapters or field offices. The Foundation Board of Directors makes funding decisions on a quarterly basis. Applications may be completed online at any time within the two-month windows. Applications should be submitted by midnight

Eastern Standard Time (U.S.) or 9:00 pm Pacific Standard Time (U.S.) on January 15, April 15, July 15, and October 15.
Requirements: The Foundation is able to support only those organizations that have received tax-exempt status under section 501(c)3 of the Internal Revenue Code or that are governmental entities. Marisla funds its Human Services grants in Orange County and Los Angeles through the Orange County Community Foundation.
Restrictions: Grants are not made to individuals or for activities that support candidates for political office. The Foundation also will not review more than one application per year (any twelve-month period) from any organization, with the exception of organizations that are fiscal sponsors of nonprofits.
Geographic Focus: California
Date(s) Application is Due: Jan 15; Apr 15; Jul 15; Oct 15
Amount of Grant: Up to 1,000,000 USD
Samples: Hawaii Community Foundation, Honolulu, Hawaii, $816,000 - general operating support; Hills for Everyone, Brea, California, $40,000 - general operating support; Food and Water Watch, Los Angeles, California, $25,000 - campaign to ban fracking in California.
Contact: Peggy Lauer, Administrator; (800) 839-5316 or (949) 494-0365; peggy@marisla.org or premiersupport@foundationsource.com
Internet: online.foundationsource.com/public/home/marisla
Sponsor: Marisla Foundation
668 North Coast Highway, PMB 1400
Laguna Beach, HI 92651-1513

Marjorie Moore Charitable Foundation Grants   1574

The Marjorie Moore Charitable Foundation was established in 1957 to support and promote quality educational, cultural, human services, environmental, and health care programming for underserved populations. The Moore Charitable Foundation specifically serves the people of Kensington and Berlin, Connecticut. Grants from the Moore Foundation made in support of operations or programming are 1 year in duration. Multi-year grants for long-term capital projects will be considered on a case-by-case basis. Award amounts go up to $75,000.
Requirements: Applicant organizations must have 501(c)3 tax-exempt status and serve the people of Kensington or Berlin, Connecticut. Preference is given to organizations that provide human services or health care programming. Applications will be submitted online through the Bank of America website. A grant report is required within 1 year of the grant application date, regardless of whether all of the funds have been spent.
Restrictions: The foundation does not support requests from individuals, organizations attempting to influence policy through direct lobbying, or any political campaigns.
Geographic Focus: Connecticut
Date(s) Application is Due: Dec 1
Amount of Grant: Up to 75,000 USD
Samples: Kensington Congregational Church, Kensington, Connecticut, $75,000 - awarded for Expanding on God's Grace: Renovation and Expansion of the Parish Hall (2018); Kensington Volunteer Firemans Association, Kensington, Connecticut, $10,000 - awarded for parking lot paving project (2018); Mooreland Hill School, Kensington, Connecticut, $10,000 - awarded for subsidized funding of facilities rental for Berlin YMCA, Berlin Basketball, Berlin Cheer, and other Kensington/Berlin organizations and individuals (2018).
Contact: Amy R. Lynch, Philanthropic Client Manager; (860) 244-4870; ct.grantmaking@bankofamerica.com or amy.r.lynch@bofa.com
Internet: www.bankofamerica.com/philanthropic/foundation/?fnId=56
Sponsor: Marjorie Moore Charitable Foundation
P.O. Box 1802
Providence, RI 02901-1802

Mark W. Coy Foundation Grants   1575

The Mark W. Coy Foundation (formerly the Beverly Aronson Richey Foundation) was established in Indiana in 2003 with the expressed purpose of providing financial support for education, human services, and religious programs. Typically, awards are given directly to individuals in the State of Indiana. Most recently, funding has ranged from $1,000 to $10,000. There is no formal application required, and interested parties should begin by contacting the Foundation directly. No annual deadlines for application submission have been identified.
Requirements: Individuals and religious organizations in the State of Indiana are eligible to apply.
Geographic Focus: Indiana
Amount of Grant: 1,000 - 10,000 USD
Samples: Jon and Cynthia Martens, Indianapolis, Indiana, $2,000 - social improvement; Tim and Whitney Gray, Noblesville, Indiana, $1,000 - social improvement; Saint Matthew Parish, Indianapolis, Indiana, $10,000 - foreign mission work.
Contact: Beverly A. Richey, President; (317) 623-3372 or (317) 835-7709
Sponsor: Mark W. Coy Foundation
7863 North 700 West
Fairland, IN 46126-9544

Mark Wahlberg Youth Foundation Grants   1576

The Mark Wahlberg Youth Foundation was established in May of 2001 by Mark Wahlberg, a lifelong member and advocate of the Boys and Girls Clubs of America, for the purpose of raising and distributing funds to youth service and enrichment programs. Its mission is to assist youth in order to ensure that no child is limited or prevented from attaining their lifetime goal or dream due to financial circumstances. The pregrant application qualifies programs to send a full application if approved. Proposals are accepted year-round, and there are no annual deadlines.
Requirements: Nonprofit organizations serving youth in inner city areas across the U.S. are eligible.
Geographic Focus: All States
Contact: Rose Cortina, Cortina Business Management Contact; (617) 454-1125
Internet: www.markwahlbergyouthfoundation.org/grant-app/

Sponsor: Mark Wahlberg Youth Foundation
P.O. Box 610287
Newton, MA 02461

Marquette Bank Neighborhood Commitment Grants 1577

Marquette Bank opened its doors for business May 12, 1945, with a philosophy and commitment to provide financial services to meet the savings and borrowing needs of the southwest Chicagoland area communities. Each quarter, the Bank focuses efforts on giving back in a different area of need: shelter, hunger, education and health/wellness. From fundraising to food drives, volunteer activities to scholarship opportunities, Marquette Bank is committed to making neighborhoods a better place to live and work. Through these efforts, it hopes to create an even closer relationship with its neighbors and continue to strengthen the neighborhoods it cares about so much.

Requirements: Any 501(c)3 organization serving the southwest Chicago area is eligible to apply.
Geographic Focus: Illinois
Amount of Grant: Up to 100,000 USD
Contact: Grants Director; (888) 254-9500
Internet: www.emarquettebank.com/neighborhood/marquette-neighborhood-commitment/
Sponsor: Marquette Bank
143rd 9533 West 143rd Street
Orland Park, IL 60462

Marriott International Corporate Giving Grants 1578

The Marriott International Corporate Giving program is primarily interested in supporting areas of company operations, with emphasis on global and national organizations. The corporations major aim is to make charitable contributions to nonprofit organizations involved with: food and shelter; environmental stewardship; readiness for hotel careers; children, almost exclusively through a partnership with Children's Miracle Network; and organizations that embrace diversity and disabilities. Primary fields of interest mentioned are: agriculture and food; civil and human rights; disabled; minorities; employment and training; the environment; and housing and shelter. Only proposals submitted via email will be accepted. Application forms are not required, so applicants should begin by forwarding a letter. Though there are no specified deadlines, applicants should request funding a minimum of six weeks prior to the need.

Geographic Focus: All States
Contact: Steven J. McNeil, (301) 380-3000; community.engagement@marriott.com
Internet: www.marriott.com/corporate-social-responsibility/corporate-responsibility.mi
Sponsor: Marriott International Corporate Giving Grants
10400 Fernwood Road
Bethesda, MD 20817-1102

Marshall County Community Foundation Grants 1579

The Marshall County Community Foundation (MCCF) was established as a 501(c)3 not-for-profit organization with the defined purpose of serving the citizens of Marshall County, Indiana. The Foundation uses the following criteria when reviewing proposals: is there an established need and will the project achieve the desired result; is it appropriate for Marshall County to fund or is it too large; does it fit the County's areas of interest and geography; is it new or innovative; and does it foster collaboration with multiple impacts. Fund decisions are made within 90 days of each submission deadline. The application is available at the Foundation website.

Requirements: Only charitable organizations with a verifiable 501(c)3 status or equivalent will be considered. If 501(c)3 status is not available, organizations must find another organization to host the project or program.
Restrictions: Funding is not available for individuals; sectarian or religious purposes; long term funding; or for events that have already taken place.
Geographic Focus: Indiana
Date(s) Application is Due: Feb 1; Aug 1
Amount of Grant: Up to 10,000 USD
Contact: Linda Yoder, Executive Director; (574) 935-5159; fax (574) 936-8040
Internet: www.marshallcountycf.org/grants.htm
Sponsor: Marshall County Community Foundation
2701 North Michigan Street, P.O. Box 716
Plymouth, IN 46563

Marsh Corporate Grants 1580

The corporate giving program targets nonprofit organizations in corporate communities. Support goes to food banks - financial support and in-kind product donations, and nutrition programs that provide free hot meals for underprivileged children; education and youth programs - operating grants or project support to human service agencies that provide services to people, particularly children, in need in Marsh communities, and projects that directly benefit children, promote the education of children, or encourage the positive development of children; community development - support for operations or projects to community and civic organizations that focus on civic involvement, citizen participation, or positive improvements that benefit the community; arts - cultural and arts organizations that serve broad audiences with programming of the highest quality, and one-time capital grants for arts and cultural facilities; and hometown or neighborhood activities - grass-roots organizations that focus their efforts on improving their immediate community through activities that benefit families in their hometowns or neighborhoods.

Restrictions: Marsh is unable to provide support to for-profit organizations (employee recognition programs, company events, etc.) and third-party organizations.
Geographic Focus: Indiana, Ohio
Contact: Community Relations Manager; (317) 594-2100 or (800) 845-7686; fax (317) 594-2705
Internet: www.marsh.net/about/community/marsh-giving/

Sponsor: Marsh Supermarkets
9800 Crosspoint Boulevard
Indianapolis, IN 46256

Martha Holden Jennings Foundation Grants-to-Educators 1581

The program supports the foundation's basic objective of recognizing and encouraging outstanding classroom or school programs for public schools or non-religious private schools working with public schools in Ohio. The Distribution Committee meets ten months of the year (not in July or December). This program enables educators to submit proposals for grants up to $3,000. Applications should be submitted by the 20th of the preceding month to be considered.

Requirements: Ohio public and private classroom teachers are eligible to apply.
Restrictions: Funding for bus transportation, conferences, teacher stipends, field trips/ admission fees, substitutes, technology equipment, capital assets, refreshments, storage units, incentives, school supplies, rewards and T-shirts are not Foundation budget priorities. Funding is considered for equipment, only when there is a direct connection to the project.
Geographic Focus: Ohio
Amount of Grant: Up to 3,000 USD
Contact: Kathy L. Kooyman, Grants Manager; (216) 589-5700; fax (216) 589-5730
Internet: www.mhjf.org/grants_educators.html
Sponsor: Martha Holden Jennings Foundation
1228 Euclid Avenue, Suite 710
Cleveland, OH 44115

Martin C. Kauffman 100 Club of Alameda County Scholarships 1582

The mission of the Martin C. Kauffman 100 Club of Alameda County is to provide immediate financial assistance to the families of police officers and firefighters killed in the line of duty in Alameda County, California. To that end, it is a priority of the club to provide college scholarships for the children of fallen heroes, as well as an annual Christmas savings bond. A maximum of $14,500 can be awarded annually for these purposes.

Requirements: Recipients must be widows, widowers, and/or dependents of police officers and firefighters who have lost their lives in the line of duty in Alameda County, California.
Geographic Focus: California
Amount of Grant: Up to 14,500 USD
Contact: Christine Maderos; (510) 818-0337; fax (925) 566-8590; MK100Club@astound.net
Internet: www.100clubalamedacounty.org/
Sponsor: Martin C. Kauffman 100 Club of Alameda County
767 Brannan Place
Concord, CA 94518

Martin Family Foundation Grants 1583

The Martin Family Foundation is a private foundation based in Casper, Wyoming, that was founded in 2001. As of 2019 they had $2.5 million in revenue and $24 million in assets. The Martin Family Foundation makes grants to other organizations, such as $250,000 to The Vine Foundation for "Program Support Grants"; $250,000 to Seed of Hope for "Tuition Assistance"; $184,750 to Bella Natural Women's Care for "General Operation, Community Expansion Grant"; $175,000 to Alliance for Choice in Education (ACE) for "Foundation Grants"; and $135,000 to Capuchin Province of Mid-America for "Vocation Support." The Foundation's primary fields of interest, therefore, include: primary and secondary education; higher education; health care; religious organizations; family services; and general community nonprofits. Awards typically range up to $200,000, though the vast majority fall into the $100,000 range or less. There are no specified annual deadlines for application submission.

Geographic Focus: All States
Amount of Grant: Up to 200,000 USD
Samples: Alliance for Choice in Education, Denver, Colorado, $175,000 - general operating support funding (2018); Bella Natural Women's Care, Englewood, Colorado, $184,750 - general operating support funding (2018); Boys and Girls Club of Yellowstone County, Billings, Montana, $55,000 - support for a scholarship fund (2018); Casper Youth for Christ, Casper, Wyoming, $30,000 - - general operating support funding (2018).
Contact: Larry G. Bean, Director; (307) 268-7128
Sponsor: Martin Family Foundation
441 Landmark Drive, P.O. Box 50190
Casper, WY 82609-0190

Mary A. Crocker Trust Grants 1584

The trust supports nonprofit organizations in northern California in the areas of education and the environment. The trust gives priority to programs that aid elementary and secondary schools in the Bay area, encourage academic excellence, enhance student involvement in the community, and provide alternative approaches to traditional education. Grants in the environment category are awarded in the areas of sustainable agriculture and forestry, waste management and recycling, population, water quality, and land-use management. Funding will be provided for seed money, program development, and matching grants. The board meets in the spring and fall to consider requests.

Requirements: Interested organizations must first submit a one-page letter of interest by the corresponding deadline date. Approximately eight to twelve organizations will be invited to submit a full proposal. Preference will be given to organizations founded and based in the Bay Area (as opposed to national organizations). Nonprofits in the following counties are eligible to apply: San Francisco, San Mateo, Santa Clara, Alameda, Contra Costa, Marin, Sonoma, Solano and Napa.
Restrictions: Grants are not awarded to individuals or for deficit financing, religious purposes, scholarships, equipment, operating funds, continuing support, annual campaigns, or building funds.

Geographic Focus: California
Date(s) Application is Due: Mar 25; Oct 28
Samples: Adopt a Watershed (CA)—for curriculum development and teacher training for an environmental education project, $20,000; California Academy of Sciences (CA)—to support a science summer camp for Bay area youth, $10,000; American Farmland Trust (CA)—for a population-growth project in the central valley aimed at educating the public on consequences of urban sprawl and the loss of agricultural lands, $25,000.
Contact: Abby Wilder, Executive Director; (650) 576-3384; staff@mactrust.org
Internet: www.mactrust.org/historyandguidelines.html
Sponsor: Mary A. Crocker Trust
57 Post Street, Suite 610
San Francisco, CA 94104

Mary Black Foundation Active Living Grants   **1585**
The Mary Black Foundation makes grants to nonprofit organizations in Spartanburg County, South Carolina, region. The Foundation has three applications for active living grants: Programs and Services assist people in becoming more physically active, either for recreation or for transportation; Policies and Places have a direct impact on whether people have the opportunity to be active; and Planning and Capacity Building for organizations that have as part of their core mission to increase active living. Each area of Active Living has different goals and grant submission procedures. The Foundation accepts applications quarterly: March 1, June 1, September 1, and December 1.
Requirements: Nonprofit organizations in South Carolina's Spartanburg County are eligible. Before submitting an application for a grant in Active Living, potential applicants must meet with the Foundation's program staff.
Restrictions: The Foundation does not accept applications from individuals or general fundraising solicitations.
Geographic Focus: South Carolina
Date(s) Application is Due: Mar 1; Jun 1; Sep 1; Dec 1
Amount of Grant: 2,000 - 200,000 USD
Samples: City of Woodruff, Woodruff, South Carolina, $150,000 - to support the Woodruff Greenway Trail; Partners for Active Living, Spartanburg, South Carolina, $75,900 - for the last year of a three-year grant to support a community initiative to increase usage of the 1.9-mile Mary Black Foundation Rail Trail; Spartanburg County School District One, Spartanburg, South Carolina, $198,000 - to support the Inman Trail.
Contact: Amy Page; (864) 573-9500; fax (864) 573-5805; apage@maryblackfoundation.org
Internet: www.maryblackfoundation.org/active-living/targeted-results
Sponsor: Mary Black Foundation
349 East Main Street, Suite 100
Spartanburg, SC 29302

Mary Black Foundation Early Childhood Development Grants   **1586**
The Mary Black Foundation makes grants to nonprofit organizations in Spartanburg County, South Carolina, region. The goals of its investment in early childhood development are: more children in Spartanburg County will enter school ready to learn; and fewer adolescents in Spartanburg County will experience an unintended pregnancy. The Foundation has three applications for early childhood development grants: Programs and Services provide direct assistance, social support, resources, and information to children and teens and their families or to those who work with them; Policies and Places refer to the environmental conditions that affect early childhood development and adolescent pregnancy; and Planning and Capacity Building for organizations that have as part of their core missions the improvement of early childhood development or the reduction of adolescent pregnancy. The Foundation accepts applications quarterly: March 1, June 1, September 1, and December 1.
Requirements: Nonprofit organizations in South Carolina's Spartanburg County are eligible. Before submitting an application for a grant in Early Childhood Development, potential applicants must meet with the Foundation's program staff.
Restrictions: The Foundation does not accept applications from individuals or general fundraising solicitations.
Geographic Focus: South Carolina
Date(s) Application is Due: Mar 1; Jun 1; Sep 1; Dec 1
Amount of Grant: 2,500 - 300,000 USD
Samples: Woodruff Primary School, Spartanburg, South Carolina, $2,500 - to support the NAEYC programs for three- and four-year olds; Spartanburg County School District Seven, Spartanburg, South Carolina, $300,000 - for the second year of a three-year grant to support a high quality child development center program for children ages birth to five; Middle Tyger Community Center, Spartanburg, South Carolina, $91,000 - to support the Adolescent Family Life Program.
Contact: Amy Page; (864) 573-9500; fax (864) 573-5805; apage@maryblackfoundation.org
Internet: www.maryblackfoundation.org/early-childhood-development/targeted-results
Sponsor: Mary Black Foundation
349 East Main Street, Suite 100
Spartanburg, SC 29302

Mary Cofer Trigg Trust Fund Grants   **1587**
The Mary Cofer Trigg Trust Fund has a geographic focus of Hardin County, Kentucky. Its benefactor, Mary Cofer Trigg, passed away in 1973, yet she lives on through the the good works made possible by the Fund. Currently, the Fund has been designated to assist in supporting: children and youth programs; families; at-risk youth; housing the poor; and providing food for those in need. PNC meets annually with the Fund's Advisory Committee to review and approve applications. The deadline for submission of those applications is October 15.
Requirements: Non-profit agencies that serve Hardin County, Kentucky, residents are eligible to apply each year.

Geographic Focus: Kentucky
Date(s) Application is Due: Oct 15
Amount of Grant: Up to 50,000 USD
Contact: Jennifer Reitzell, Trustee; (412) 768-5248; jennifer.reitzell@pnc.com
Internet: www1.pnc.com/pncfoundation/charitable_trusts.html
Sponsor: Mary Cofer Trigg Trust Fund
One PNC Plaza, 249 Fifth Avenue, 20th Floor
Pittsburgh, PA 15222

Mary D. and Walter F. Frear Eleemosynary Trust Grants   **1588**
Walter Francis Frear was a lawyer and judge in the Kingdom of Hawaii and Republic of Hawaii, and the third Territorial Governor of Hawaii from 1907 to 1913. The Mary D. and Walter F. Frear Eleemosynary Trust was established to sponsor educational projects. Grants are awarded to Hawaii nonprofit organizations in the areas of child welfare and youth, education, social services, music, and the arts. Types of support include building construction and renovation, capital campaigns, conferences and seminars, equipment acquisition, general operating support, matching/challenge grants, program development, and seed grants. There are three annual deadlines specified, and applicants should begin by contacting the Trust administrative office.
Requirements: Grant applications are accepted from qualified tax-exempt charitable organizations in Hawaii.
Restrictions: Grants are not made to individuals, nor for endowments, reserve purposes, deficit financing, or travel.
Geographic Focus: Hawaii
Date(s) Application is Due: Jan 1; Jul 1; Oct 1
Amount of Grant: 5,000 - 25,000 USD
Contact: Paula Boyce, Grants Administrator, c/o Bank of Hawaii; (808) 537-8822; fax (808) 538-4007; pboyce@boh.com
Sponsor: Mary D. and Walter F. Frear Eleemosynary Trust
130 Merchant Street, P.O. Box 3170
Honolulu, HI 96802-3170

Mary E. Babcock Foundation   **1589**
The Mary E. Babcock Foundation was established in Ohio with the specific purposes of supporting community development, economic development, and education within the Johnstown, Ohio, region. An application form is required, and applicants should begin by submitting a detailed description of the project and a detailed budget as part of that application. There are no specified annual deadlines, and recent grant funding has ranged up to $8,000.
Requirements: Nonprofit 501(c)3 organizations serving residents of the Johnstown, Ohio, area are eligible to apply.
Geographic Focus: Ohio
Amount of Grant: Up to 8,000 USD
Samples: Mary E. Babcock Library, Johnstown, Ohio, $7,832 - a newspaper project; Apple Blossom Flowers Landscaping, Johnstown, Ohio, $5,140 - flowers and landscaping of the town square; St. Albans Township Fire Department, Alexandria, Ohio, purchase of a thermal imaging camera.
Contact: Stuart Parsons, Treasurer; (740) 366-6561
Sponsor: Mary E. Babcock Foundation
1436 Estates Drive
Newark, OH 43055-1772

Mary K. Chapman Foundation Grants   **1590**
Mary K. Chapman was born in Oklahoma in 1920. She graduated from the University of Tulsa and worked as a nurse before her marriage to Allen Chapman in 1960. After the death of her husband in 1979, Mary Chapman maintained her own personal charitable giving program. Before her death in 2002, she established The Mary K. Chapman Foundation, a charitable trust founded to perpetuate her own charitable giving program. This foundation was fully funded with a bequest from her estate in 2005. Mary K. Chapman was very interested in supporting education, but as a former nurse and a very compassionate person, much of her charity was directed to health, medical research, and educating and caring for the less fortunate and disadvantaged. There are two steps in the process of applying for a grant. The first is a Letter of Inquiry from the applicant. This letter is used to determine if the applicant will be invited to take the second step of submitting a formal Grant Proposal.
Requirements: IRS 501(c)3 non-profits are eligible to apply.
Restrictions: Grant requests for the following purposes are not favored: endowments, except as a limited part of a capital project reserved for maintenance of the facility being constructed; deficit financing and debt retirement; projects or programs for which the Chapman Trusts would be the sole source of financial support; travel, conferences, conventions, group meetings, or seminars; camp programs and other seasonal activities; religious programs of religious organizations; project or program planning; start-up ventures are not excluded, but organizations with a proven strategy and results are preferred; purposes normally funded by taxation or governmental agencies; requests made less than nine months from the declination of a previous request by an applicant, or within nine months of the last payment made on a grant made to an applicant; requests for more than one project.
Geographic Focus: Oklahoma
Amount of Grant: Up to 300,000 USD
Samples: Arts and Humanities Council of Tulsa, Tulsa, Oklahoma, $200,000 - Brady District Visual Arts Center capital campaign; Tulsa Zoo Management, Tulsa, Oklahoma, $300,000 - general operating fund; Northeastern Oklahoma A&M College, Miami, Oklahoma, $197,000 - equipment and furnishings for NEO athletic training facility.
Contact: Andie Doyle; (918) 496-7882; fax (918) 496-7887; andie@chapmantrusts.com
Internet: www.chapmantrusts.org/grants_programs.php

Sponsor: Mary K. Chapman Foundation
6100 South Yale, Suite 1816
Tulsa, OK 74136

Mary Kay Foundation Domestic Violence Shelter Grants 1591

Every October, The Mary Kay Foundation observes National Domestic Violence Awareness Month by awarding grants to deserving women's domestic violence shelters across the United States. During the past year, the Foundation awarded $20,000 grants to more than 150 women's domestic violence shelters across the nation for a total of $3 million. Each year, the Foundation awards a grant to at least one domestic violence shelter in every state. Any remaining funds are distributed based on state population. Grant applications are reviewed by the Domestic Violence Shelter Grant Committee, which makes recommendations to the TMKF Board of Directors. After reviewing these recommendations, the Foundation's Board of Directors selects the final grant recipients. Domestic violence shelter grant applications are available from this Web site or from The Mary Kay Foundation from January to June 30 each year. We announce grant recipients in the fall to coincide with National Domestic Violence Awareness Month in October.
Geographic Focus: All States
Amount of Grant: 20,000 USD
Samples: Abused Women's Aid in Crisis, Inc., Anchorage, Alaska, $20,000; Domestic Violence Services of Greater New Haven (DVS), New Haven, Connecticut, $20,000; Crisis Intervention Service Shelter, Mason City, Iowa, $20,000.
Contact: Lana Rowe, (972) 687-4822 or (877) 652-2737; Lana.Rowe@mkcorp.com
Jennifer Cook, (972) 687-5889 or (972) 687-4822; Jennifer.cook@mkcorp.com or MKCares@marykayfoundation.org
Internet: www.marykayfoundation.org/Pages/ShelterGrantProgram.aspx
Sponsor: Mary Kay Foundation
P.O. Box 799044
Dallas, TX 75379-9044

Maryland State Arts Council Arts in Communities Grants 1592

The Arts in Communities Program was created to extend the Maryland State Arts Council (MSAC) funding to a broader range of organizations than are presently served, and to better reach underserved audiences. The program serves two kinds of organizations: those for which Arts in Communities Grants provide an introduction to MSAC grants programs; and/or community organizations planning specific arts events or projects. Eligible organizations include arts organizations, after-school programs, civic groups, libraries, museums, religious organizations, schools, social clubs, or other community-based groups that present arts programs and projects.
Requirements: Not-for-profit Maryland organizations may apply for support of arts activities that will take place in Maryland. Eligibility is limited to organizations that have not already been awarded MSAC funding for activities taking place in the same fiscal year. An organization may submit only one application per deadline and may receive only one Grant per fiscal year. Applicants must apply through the eGRANT system located on the website.
Geographic Focus: Maryland
Date(s) Application is Due: Apr 28; Aug 4; Oct 6
Contact: Pamela Dunne, Program Director; (410) 767-6484; pdunne@msac.org
Internet: www.msac.org/aic
Sponsor: Maryland State Arts Council
175 West Ostend Street, Suite E
Baltimore, MD 21230

Maryland State Department of Education 21st Century Community 1593
Learning Centers Grants

The U.S. Department of Education provides funds to states in support of 21st Century Community Learning Centers. The Maryland State Department of Education's CCLC sponsors a competitive grant program designed to support implementation of out of school time and/or expanded learning time programming. The purpose of the 21st Century Community Learning Centers (21st CCLC) is to create community learning centers that provide students with academic enrichment opportunities as well as additional services designed to complement their regular academic program. Community learning centers must offer families of participating students literacy instruction and related educational development programs. Proposed activities target students and families of students who attend schools eligible for Title I schoolwide programs or schools that serve a high percentage of students from low-income families. Grantees are expected to attend bi-monthly networking meetings. These meetings offer technical assistance from the Maryland State Department of Education personnel, peer to peer technical assistance, and other outside resources selected by the coordinator based on expressed needs of the grantees.
Requirements: Grantees consist of schools, local school systems, faith-based organizations, and community-based organizations.
Geographic Focus: Maryland
Date(s) Application is Due: Apr 13
Contact: Michial A. Gill, Director of Grants Administration; (410) 767-3170 or (410) 371-6955; fax (410) 333-0810; michial.gill@maryland.gov
Internet: www.marylandpublicschools.org/about/Pages/Grants/index.aspx
Sponsor: Maryland State Department of Education
200 West Baltimore Street
Baltimore, MD 21201-2595

Maryland State Department of Education Coordinating Entity Services for 1594
the Maryland Child Care Resource Centers Network Grants

The purpose of the Coordinating Entity Services for the Maryland Child Care Resource Centers Network grant is to retain services from a non-profit organization with significant experience managing child care information and referral services for parents, providing professional development services for child care professionals, and providing technical assistance to improve the quality of child care services. The grantee shall act as the Statewide Coordinating Entity overseeing operations of the regional Child Care Resource Centers. Together, these Centers make up the Maryland Child Care Resource Center Network to assure that required components are addressed. Total funding available for a one-year period is $3,466,524. The annual deadline for completed application submission is April 13.
Requirements: Any not for profit community-based agency or organization which has the capacity to provide a child care information and referral system, as well as professional development, technical assistance, and training services is eligible to apply.
Geographic Focus: Maryland
Date(s) Application is Due: Apr 13
Amount of Grant: 3,466,524 USD
Contact: Michial A. Gill, Director of Grants Administration; (410) 767-3170 or (410) 371-6955; fax (410) 333-6033; michial.gill@maryland.gov
Equity Assurance and Compliance Office; (410) 767-0426; fax (410) 767-0431
Internet: www.marylandpublicschools.org/about/Pages/Grants/index.aspx
Sponsor: Maryland State Department of Education
200 West Baltimore Street
Baltimore, MD 21201-2595

Maryland State Department of Education Judith P. Hoyer Early Care and 1595
Education Center Grants

The Judith P. Hoyer Early Care and Education Center Grant will provide funds for the continuation of Judith P. Hoyer Early Child Care and Education Center Partnerships (Judy Centers) in Maryland, serving children birth through 5 years. Judy Centers will provide comprehensive early care and education services for young children and their families to promote continuous improvement toward school readiness. The estimated annual grant award is $175,000 to $330,000. The annual deadline for completed application submission is April 20.
Requirements: Local Boards of Education that operated a Judy Center during the past fiscal years are eligible to apply. Proposals must contain the following to be considered for funding: Judy Center Partnerships that include public prekindergarten, kindergarten, Early Intervention and preschool special education, and licensed/registered and accredited child care providers. The Judy Center must also include at least five of the following participating partners and services: Head Start programs; regional child care resource centers; community health programs; local public libraries; family literacy programs; Family Support Network; early childhood programs associated with institutions of higher education; local colleges and universities for higher education; job training programs; and Healthy Families and/or other home visiting programs.
Geographic Focus: Maryland
Date(s) Application is Due: Apr 20
Amount of Grant: 175,000 - 330,000 USD
Contact: Michial A. Gill, Director of Grants Administration; (410) 767-3170 or (410) 371-6955; fax (410) 333-6033; michial.gill@maryland.gov
Internet: www.marylandpublicschools.org/about/Pages/Grants/index.aspx
Sponsor: Maryland State Department of Education
200 West Baltimore Street
Baltimore, MD 21201-2595

Maryland State Department of Education Striving Readers Comprehensive 1596
Literacy Grants

The purpose of the Striving Readers Comprehensive Literacy grant is to increase student achievement in literacy. Through the use of local needs assessments and evidence-based strategies, the grant will advance literacy for all children from birth through grade 12 and align literacy plans in Local Education Agencies across the state. Priority will be given to applications that incorporate one or more of the following: emphasis on disadvantaged children, including children living in poverty, English learners, and children with disabilities; alignment from birth to grade 5; use of strategies, programs, and interventions with strong or moderate evidence; partnerships in early literacy with nonprofit providers of early childhood education, with a demonstrated record of effectiveness in improving language and early literacy development of children from birth to age five; and a strategic professional learning plan. The estimated range of each award is $300,000 to $1,000,000 per year or $900,000 to $3,000,000 over the three-year term of the grant. The annual application deadline is April 26.
Requirements: Applications must contain the following to be considered for funding: a draft comprehensive literacy plan driven by a needs assessment and aligned to Maryland's State Comprehensive Literacy Plan, Maryland's Keys to Comprehensive Literacy; use of evidence-based strategies and interventions; a plan for each age span based upon the needs assessment (birth to age 5, Kindergarten to grade five, grades six to eight, and grades nine to twelve); a budget and budget narrative that includes a breakdown by grade spans for 15% of funding supporting birth to age five; 40% of funding supporting kindergarten to grade five; 20% of funding supporting grade six to grade 8; and 20% of funding supporting grade nine to grade 12; and a detailed evaluation and accountability plan that shows how the activities are expected to produce discernible outcomes in literacy related to educator practices and student outcomes.
Geographic Focus: Maryland
Date(s) Application is Due: Apr 26
Amount of Grant: 900,000 - 3,000,000 USD
Contact: Michial A. Gill, Director of Grants Administration; (410) 767-3170 or (410) 371-6955; fax (410) 333-6033; michial.gill@maryland.gov
Internet: www.marylandpublicschools.org/about/Pages/Grants/index.aspx
Sponsor: Maryland State Department of Education
200 West Baltimore Street
Baltimore, MD 21201-2595

Mary Owen Borden Foundation Grants 1597

The Mary Owen Borden Foundation Grants support programs that address the needs of economically disadvantaged youth and their families. This includes needs such as health, family planning, education, counseling, childcare, substance abuse, and delinquency. Other areas of interest for the foundation include affordable housing, conservation, environment, and the arts. Grants average $10,000, and the maximum grant is $15,000. In unique circumstances, the Foundation considers a more significant grant for a program having a major impact in their areas of interests.

Requirements: New Jersey nonprofits in Monmouth and Mercer Counties are eligible. Most of the Foundation's grant go to nonprofit entities in Trenton, Asbury Park, and Long Branch.

Geographic Focus: New Jersey

Date(s) Application is Due: Mar 15; Sep 15

Amount of Grant: Up to 15,000 USD

Contact: Quinn McKean; (732) 741-4645; fax (732) 741-2542; qmckean@aol.com

Internet: fdncenter.org/grantmaker/borden/guide.html

Sponsor: Mary Owen Borden Foundation

4 Blackpoint Horseshoe

Rumson, NJ 07760

Mary S. and David C. Corbin Foundation Grants 1598

The Corbin Foundation gives primary consideration to charitable organizations and/or local chapters of national charities located in Akron and Summit County, Ohio, although extremely worthy causes outside of this preferred area may be considered. Areas of interest include arts and culture; civic and community; education; health care; housing; social services; medical research; and youth. The Foundation meets in May and November to consider requests. Grant requests must be received no later than March 1 for consideration in May and September 1 for consideration in November. The application and guidelines are available at the Foundation website.

Requirements: The Foundation has a general application cover sheet which applicants must complete. Organizations should also send a brief letter on their letterhead, submitting one original and one copy of all application materials.

Restrictions: Only written applications will be considered. Telephone and personal interviews are discouraged unless requested by the Foundation. The Foundation does not fund individuals; annual fundraising campaigns; ongoing requests for general operating support (although some repeat grants are made); operating deficits; or organizations which in turn make grants to others.

Geographic Focus: Ohio

Date(s) Application is Due: Mar 1; Sep 1

Contact: Erika J. May; (330) 762-6427; fax (330) 762-6428; corbin@nls.net

Internet: foundationcenter.org/grantmaker/corbin/guide.html

Sponsor: Mary S. and David C. Corbin Foundation

Akron Central Plaza

Akron, OH 44308-1830

Mary W.B. Curtis Trust Grants 1599

The terms of the Mary W.B. Curtis Trust require funding to be made to programs devoted to training boys and young men in good citizenship. Programs which include girls and young women are eligible to apply, but the funds requested must be allocated to benefit only the boys and young men participating in the program. The geographical focus of the Trust's funding is the greater Boston area. The Trustees will consider requests for a single year of funding. Organizations may be funded for up to three consecutive years, but are then asked to take the following year off. After a one year break, organizations are welcome to apply to the Trust again. Grant awards are typically $5,000 to $10,000. The Trustees will occasionally consider a request outside of this range. The deadline for submitting a proposal is December 31. Proposals must be received by 5 p.m. in order to be reviewed by the Trustees. Requests will be considered by the Trustees at the annual meeting the following spring, and notice of Trustees' decisions will be sent in April. There is no formal application to the Mary W.B. Curtis Trust or annual report to distribute. The Trustees will accept the Philanthropy Massachusetts Common Proposal Form. Grant awards typically range from $5,000 to $10,000.

Requirements: To apply, a proposal should including the following: detailed proposal, including a description of the organization's mission, description of the program, and the number of persons to be served; financial information, including an organizational and program budget, expense and revenue sources, and the most recent audited financial statement and IRS Form 990; determination letter from the Internal Revenue Service (IRS) confirming federal tax-exempt status under Section 501(c)3 and classification as not a private foundation within the meanings of Section 509(a) of the Internal Revenue Code; and Philanthropy Massachusetts Common Proposal Cover Sheet.

Geographic Focus: Massachusetts

Date(s) Application is Due: Dec 31

Amount of Grant: 5,000 - 10,000 USD

Samples: Blessed Stephen Bellesini, O.S.A. Academy, Inc., Boston, Massachusetts, $7,500 - to support the boys participating in the Alumni Support program (2018); Raw Art Works, Boston, Massachusetts, $5,000 - to support the boys participating in mentor-based youth development programming (2018); Camp Starfish, Boston, Massachusetts, $5,000 - to support boys benefiting from the Mary W. B. Curtis Campership Fund (2018).

Contact: Rita Goldberg; (617) 227-7940, ext. 775 or (617) 557-9766; rgoldberg@hembar.com

Gioia C. Perugini; (617) 557-9777 or (617) 557-9766; gperugini@hembar.com

Internet: hembar.com/client_services/mary-wb-curtis-trust

Sponsor: Mary W.B. Curtis Trust

75 State Street, 16th Floor

Boston, MA 02109

Mary Wilmer Covey Charitable Trust Grants 1600

The Mary Wilmer Covey Charitable Trust was created to support charitable organizations that promote education including instruction and training that help to build human capabilities. It also supports organizations that focus on relieving human suffering due to disease, ill health, physical weakness, disability, or injury; and supports organizations that work to prolong life and improve the quality of life, especially for children. Grants from the Mary Wilmer Covey Charitable Trust are primarily one year in duration; on occasion, multi-year support is awarded. Applicants must apply online at the grant website. The annual application deadline is September 1 at 11:59 p.m. Applicants will be notified of grant decisions by letter within one to two months after the deadline. Applicants are strongly encouraged to do the following before applying: review the downloadable state-specific application procedures at the grant website; review the downloadable online-application guidelines at the grant website; review the trust's funding history (link is available from the grant website); review the online application questions in advance; and review the list of required attachments. These will generally include: a list of board members, financial statements (audited, reviewed, or compiled by independent auditor); an organization summary; a list of other funding sources; an IRS Determination letter; and other required documents. All attachments must be uploaded in the online application as PDF, Word, or Excel files.

Requirements: Applicants must have 501(c)3 tax-exempt status. Preference is given to charitable organizations located in Macon, Georgia; Richmond, Virginia; and Chatham Hall, Virginia.

Restrictions: The trust does not support requests from individuals, organizations attempting to influence policy through direct lobbying, or any political campaigns.

Geographic Focus: Georgia, Virginia

Date(s) Application is Due: Sep 1

Amount of Grant: Up to 9,000 USD

Samples: Chatham Hall, Chatham, Virginia, $9,000 - support of the Chatham Hall Scholarship program; Childrens Hospital Foundation, Richmond, Virginia, $9,000 - general operating support; Georgia Council on Economic Education, Atlanta, Georgia, $5,000 - support of increasing economic and personal finance literacy.

Contact: Mark S. Drake, Vice President; (404) 264-1377; mark.s.drake@ustrust.com

Internet: www.bankofamerica.com/philanthropic/foundation.go?fnId=96

Sponsor: Mary Wilmer Covey Charitable Trust

3414 Peachtree Road, N.E., Suite 1475, GA7-813-14-04

Atlanta, GA 30326-1113

Massachusetts Cultural Council Local Cultural Council (LCC) Grants 1601

The Local Cultural Council (LCC) Program is the largest grassroots cultural funding network in the nation supporting thousands of community-based projects in the arts, humanities, and sciences annually. The program promotes the availability of rich cultural experiences for every Massachusetts citizen. Each year, local councils award more than $2 million in grants to more than 5,000 cultural programs statewide. These include school field trips, afterschool programs, concerts, festivals, lectures, theater, dance, music, and film. LCC projects take place in schools, community centers, libraries, elder care facilities, town halls, parks, and wherever communities come together. Applicants may apply to the LCC Program for projects, operating support, ticket subsidy programs, artist residencies, fellowships or other activities, based on local priorities and needs. Local councils may also choose to fund cultural field trips for children, grades pre-K through 12, by subsidizing the cost for children to attend programs in the arts, humanities and interpretive sciences (including performances, educational tours and exhibits).

Requirements: Individuals, schools, and cultural organizations are eligible to apply for project support from their local council. Funding for cultural field trips is also available. Applicants should contact their LCC before completing an application.

Geographic Focus: Massachusetts

Date(s) Application is Due: Oct 15

Contact: Jenifer Lawless, Program Manager for Local Cultural Councils; (617) 727-3668, ext. 325 or (800) 232-0960; fax (617) 727-0044; jenifer.lawless@art.state.ma.us

Internet: www.massculturalcouncil.org/programs/lccgrants.asp

Sponsor: Massachusetts Cultural Council

10 St. James Avenue, 3rd Floor

Boston, MA 02116-3803

Massachusetts Cultural Council YouthReach Grants 1602

Across Massachusetts, nonprofit cultural organizations and human service agencies are providing at-risk youth with in-depth experiences in arts and culture. Whether it's linking a high school dropout to a teaching artist, or introducing an incarcerated teen to Shakespeare, these programs find innovative ways to inspire positive growth. Activities take place outside of the school, after regular school hours, in the summer, or on weekends – in times and places where kids most need constructive activities. The MCC's YouthReach Initiative promotes out-of-school arts, humanities and science opportunities that nurture the spirit of creative inquiry in young people by: providing young people with in-depth arts, humanities, or interpretive science experiences that create opportunities to interact directly with practicing artists, humanists and scientists, and to develop techniques or skills for creative inquiry; demonstrating a clear understanding of young people in need; demonstrating a clear ability to infuse arts, humanities, or science learning programs with the principles of youth development; and marshaling the resources of the community and fostering substantive collaboration between cultural organizations and other community institutions addressing young people in need. Successful YouthReach programs typically work with young people somewhere between 12 and 20 years of age. Applicants should request grants of up to $10,000 per year. Actual grant amounts will be determined by the money available and the number of projects recommended for funding. The annual application deadlines include: January 12 for new YouthReach funding; and May 3 for continued YouthReach funding.

Requirements: The primary applicant for a YouthReach project must be: a cultural organization or an organization with a strong programming history in the proposed project's primary discipline (arts, humanities, or interpretive sciences); incorporated in Massachusetts as a non-profit organization; and current in its tax-exempt status under IRS Section 501(c)3. All YouthReach grants must be matched. First-cycle grants can be matched with cash and in-kind support. However, in-kind goods and services may not exceed 50 percent of the match.

Restrictions: YouthReach funds cannot be used for in-school programs during the typical school day. Capital expenses will not be considered as part of the budget of a YouthReach project and should not be included in the funding request.

Geographic Focus: Massachusetts
Date(s) Application is Due: Jan 12; May 3
Contact: H. Mark Smith, YouthReach Program Manager; (617) 727-3668, ext. 253 or (800) 232-0960; fax (617) 727-0044; mark.smith@art.state.ma.us
Sponsor: Massachusetts Cultural Council
10 St. James Avenue, 3rd Floor
Boston, MA 02116-3803

MassMutual Foundation Edonomic Development Grants 1603

The MassMutual Foundation invites local-focused nonprofit organizations expanding economic opportunity to apply for an Economic Development grant. The Foundation strives to improve the economic and social well-being of the city of Springfield, Massachusetts, with a primary focus on the State Street Corridor and downtown. Its support of cultural vitality extends to Enfield, and will invest in programs that: support the growing entrepreneurial sector; stimulate and support economic growth; expedite the revitalization process; strengthen community infrastructure; and enrich cultural vitality. The Foundation strongly prioritizes funding for organizations that demonstrate excellence in the following areas: innovation; collaboration; strong leadership; sustainable funding; clear goals; data-driven problem-solving and results; and root causes of a challenge. The annual deadlines for application are January 15, July 15, and September 15.

Requirements: Eligible recipient organizations must be certified as tax-exempt entities under Section 501(c)3 of the Internal Revenue Code.
Restrictions: Ineligible recipients include: religious organizations, except when providing services to the community at large; individuals, through direct grants or scholarships; or events such as golf tournaments or walkathons.
Geographic Focus: Connecticut, Massachusetts
Amount of Grant: 1,000 - 50,000 USD
Contact: Program Officer; (413) 744-4973 or (413) 744-5811; massmutualfoundation@massmutual.com
Internet: www.massmutual.com/about-us/corporate-responsibility
Sponsor: MassMutual Foundation
1277 State Street
Springfield, MA 01103

Mathile Family Foundation Grants 1604

The Mathile Foundation awards grants to eligible Ohio nonprofit organizations in its areas of interest, including Catholic schools, low income and at-risk children to focus on academic excellence; leadership and professional development; faith formation; finance and governance; and student support. With these initiatives, the Foundation hopes to increase the number of low income post secondary graduates. The Foundation also strives to help nonprofit organizations accomplish meaningful change in the lives of those most vulnerable by investing in opportunities for educational, social-emotional, and physical development for children and their families. The Foundation also considers funding for capital and operating expenses. The Foundation considers proposals for grant amounts of $1,000 and higher. Multi-year funding requests may be considered for up to three years. The size of the request should be 10% of the project's budget. Proposal are accepted four times a year, with funding decisions made within 100 days of submission. Proposal forms with a list of additional information required are available at the Foundation website. For first time applicants, a letter of inquiry is recommended. All letters or applications must be submitted online.

Requirements: Organizations who request funds must be tax-exempt under the IRS Code Section 501(c)3. Ohio nonprofit organizations are eligible. Giving primarily is limited to the Dayton area. Organizations outside this area will only be considered under special circumstances.
Restrictions: Funding is not considered for endowment funds; mass funding appeals; sponsorships; advertising for fundraising events tickets; grants or loans to individuals; or political campaigns or activities.
Geographic Focus: Ohio
Date(s) Application is Due: Feb 1; May 1; Aug 1; Nov 1
Amount of Grant: 1,000 - 250,000 USD
Contact: Mary Walsh, Trustee; (937) 264-4600; fax (937) 264-4805; mffinfo@mathilefamilyfoundation.org
Internet: mathilefamilyfoundation.org/grantmaking/guidelines
Sponsor: Mathile Family Foundation
P.O Box 13615
Dayton, OH 45413-0615

Matilda R. Wilson Fund Grants 1605

Matilda Rausch Dodge Wilson died on September 19, 1967, leaving most of her wealth to the Matilda R. Wilson Fund, a charitable trust she had established in Detroit in 1944. Today, the Matilda R. Wilson Fund awards grants, primarily in southeast Michigan, in support of the arts, youth agencies, higher education, hospitals, and social services. Types of support include building construction/renovation, endowments, equipment acquisition, general operating support, matching/challenge grants, program development, research, and scholarship funds. There are no application forms; initial approach should be a letter of request. The board considers requests at board meetings in January, April, and September.

Requirements: Michigan tax-exempt organizations are eligible.
Restrictions: Grants or loans are not made to individuals.

Geographic Focus: Michigan
Amount of Grant: 10,000 - 100,000 USD
Contact: David P. Larsen, Grants Administrator; (313) 259-7777; fax (313) 393-7579; roosterveen@bodmanllp.com
Sponsor: Matilda R. Wilson Fund
1901 Saint Antoine Street, 6th Floor
Detroit, MI 48226-2310

Matson Adahi I Tano' Grants 1606

Matson has taken a leadership role in promoting "green"" initiatives in its business and community service activities. Exclusive to Guam is Matson's environmental and community relations program, Adahi I Tano' — which means "taking care of the land." Through this program, Matson donates the use of container equipment on Guam for environmental cleanup projects arranged by non-profit organizations and pays for the trucking expenses incurred in the delivery and pickup of the containers. Then, the non-profit organizations that successfully complete a cleanup receives a $500 cash contribution from Matson.

Requirements: Groups must be a non-profit organization recognized by the Government of Guam. Project must be for a specific cleanup location as designated by Matson (in coordination with the Islandwide Beautification Task Force). Festival trash collection or community trash drops off will not be considered. Groups must use the Matson Adahi I Tano' container for their project. Adahi I Tano' program applications are reviewed by an advisory committee. The committee meets on the last Wednesday of each month. Applications must be received by Matson by the close of business on the Friday before the committee meeting date if it is to be considered.
Restrictions: Participation is limited to one project per group per calendar year.
Geographic Focus: Guam
Amount of Grant: Up to 500 USD
Contact: Gloria Perez, (671) 475-5961; adahiitano@matson.com
Internet: www.matson.com/community/guam/index.html
Sponsor: Matson, Inc.
1411 Sand Island Parkway
Honolulu, HI 96819

Matson Community Giving Grants 1607

Matson, Inc. is a U.S. transportation services company headquartered in Honolulu, Hawaii. Matson established its charitable giving program to administer all of the company's community support activities. It contributes funds, material goods and services to assist in the development and operation of not-for-profit, charitable and community organizations in the geographic locations in which Matson has business operations. Areas of interest include maritime environment and ocean resource conservation, energy; education, including transportation careers training and development; human services, such as community health and safety needs; culture and arts, libraries and learning centers, cultural identity, historic presence; and civic and community programs.

Requirements: IRS-designated charities or non-profit community organizations are eligible to apply. Priority is given to to organizations or programs which serve the communities in which Matson has, or anticipates having, a significant presence or which enhance business development opportunities for the company; are actively supported by Matson employees; are cost-effective and likely to be sustainable; have plans for measurable results. Generally, only one donation will be given in a calendar year to any non-profit organization.
Restrictions: Donations will not be made to or on behalf of individuals, to endowments, or to support political or lobbying activities. With rare exception, Matson does not wish to be the sole funder.
Geographic Focus: Alaska, California, Guam, Hawaii
Contact: Linda Howe, (800) 462-8766; giving@matson.com
Internet: www.matson.com/community/index.html
Sponsor: Matson, Inc.
1411 Sand Island Parkway
Honolulu, HI 96819

Matson Ka Ipu 'Aina Grants 1608

Matson's longstanding environmental community partnership in Hawaii is called Ka Ipu 'Aina, a Hawaiian expression which translates to "container for the land." The trash removal program was established in 2001 and, in the generation since, has been successful in partnering with non-profit groups to clean up both the inland and coastal areas throughout the state of Hawaii. With this program, which is available on Oahu, Maui, Kauai and Hawaii Island, Matson donates the use of container equipment for cleanup projects arranged by non-profit organizations. Matson also pays for the trucking expenses incurred in the delivery and pickup of the containers and bears the expense of properly disposing of the debris. Finally, Matson makes a $1,000 cash contribution to each of the non-profits that successfully complete a cleanup initiative. A Ka Ipu 'Aina project must be a specific area clean up; the collection of trash from a fair/festival or from a neighborhood/community is not an eligible project. A group may use the container for as long as three days.

Requirements: Applicant groups must be a IRS designated 501(c)3 non-profit organization with federal charitable tax-exempt status. Participation is limited to one project per charity per calendar year. Priority will be given to groups which have not participated before or which have not participated in the last three years. Oahu applications are accepted four times a year, during one-month open application periods for cleanups in the following quarter (see deadline notes below). Neighbor Island applications are accepted continuously during the year.
Geographic Focus: Hawaii
Date(s) Application is Due: Jan 31; Apr 30; Jul 31; Oct 31
Amount of Grant: Up to 1,000 USD
Contact: Keahi Birch, (808) 848-1252; kbirch@matson.com
Buzz Fernandez, (808) 871-7351; bfernandez@matson.com

Patrick Ono, (808) 245-6724; pono@matson.com
Russell Chin, (808) 961-5286; rchin@matson.com
Internet: www.matson.com/community/hawaii/index.html
Sponsor: Matson, Inc.
1411 Sand Island Parkway
Honolulu, HI 96819

Maurice Amado Foundation Grants 1609

For several decades the Foundation primarily supported organizations that served members of the Sephardic Jewish community, promoted knowledge of Sephardic Jewish culture and heritage, and expanded knowledge of the contributions of Sephardic Jews to Jewish life. More recently, the Foundation has awarded grants to a wide array of charitable organizations that reflect the philanthropic interests of the Foundation's directors and advisors.
Requirements: Prospective grantees may call the Foundation's Executive Director to determine if the grant seeker's organizational need fit the Foundation's current grantmaking interests. They may email the Executive Director with the name of the organization, its mission, and for what purpose funding is requested. The letter of inquiry should be no more than one page.
Geographic Focus: All States
Contact: Pam Kaizer; (818) 980-9190; pkaizer@mauriceamadofoundation.org
Internet: www.mauriceamadofdn.org
Sponsor: Maurice Amado Foundation
12400 Ventura Boulevard, #809
Studio City, CA 91604

Maurice J. Masserini Charitable Trust Grants 1610

The trust awards one-year grants to eligible San Diego County, California nonprofit organizations in its areas of interest, including children and youth, aging, music, higher education, and marine sciences. Types of support include building construction/renovation, equipment acquisition, program development, research grants, matching grants, development grants, internships, and scholarships.
Requirements: San Diego County, California, 501(c)3 tax-exempt organizations are eligible. Interested organizations should contact the trust with a letter of inquiry prior to submitting a formal proposal.
Geographic Focus: California
Amount of Grant: Up to 25,000 USD
Contact: Robert Roszkos, (213) 253-3235
Sponsor: Maurice J. Masserini Charitable Trust
c/o Wells Fargo Bank N.A.
Philadelphia, PA 19106-2112

Maurice R. Robinson Fund Grants 1611

Established in New York City in 1960, the Maurice R. Robinson Fund offers support primarily along the east coast region, with emphasis in the New York metropolitan area. The Foundation's primary fields of interest include: arts and culture; education; higher education; museums; natural history; planetariums; and children and youth programs. Strategies include advocacy, curriculum development, general operating support, internships, program development, scholarship funding, and seed money. There are no specified annual deadlines, and awards can range up to $500,000.
Requirements: Any 501(c)3 organization in New York and surrounding states are eligible to apply.
Geographic Focus: Connecticut, District of Columbia, Maryland, Massachusetts, New York, Rhode Island, Virginia
Amount of Grant: Up to 500,000 USD
Samples: Trinity Washington University, Washington, D.C., $10,000 - general operating support; Alliance for Young Artists and Writers, New York, New York, $510,000 - general operating support.
Contact: Ernie Fleishman, President; (866) 888-5157
Sponsor: Maurice R. Robinson Fund
10 South Dearborn Street, IL1-0117
Chicago, IL 60603-2300

Max and Anna Levinson Foundation Grants 1612

The Levinson Foundation makes grants to nonprofit organizations committed to developing a more just, caring, ecological, and sustainable world. They seek people and organizations that combine idealism, dedication, and genuine concern with rigorous analysis and strategic plans, and that foster a sense of social connection, mutual recognition, and solidarity. Their funding is distributed among three categories: environment, including ecosystem protection and biological diversity, alternative energy and conversion into the oil economy, alternative agriculture and local green development, climate change, and the development of environmental movements; social, including the promotion of a more democratic, equitable, just and rewarding society, world peace, protection of civil and human rights, alternative media, arts and education, community-based economic development, youth leadership, and violence prevention and response; Jewish/Israel—including Jewish culture, religion, and spirituality, Yiddish, building Jewish community in the Diaspora, Jewish organizations for social change, and peace, social, and environmental issues in Israel. There are no deadlines. Grants are awarded in the $15,000 to $25,000 range. Applicants may refer to the website for types of previous support given to organizations.
Requirements: Applicants within the giving criteria may apply, but grantees must submit the online letter of inquiry to see if they are eligible for funding.
Geographic Focus: All States
Amount of Grant: 15,000 - 25,000 USD
Contact: Charlotte Levinson; (505) 995-8802; info@levinsonfoundation.org
Internet: www.levinsonfoundation.org

Sponsor: Max and Anna Levinson Foundation
P.O. Box 6309
Santa Fe, NM 87502-6309

May and Stanley Smith Charitable Trust Grants 1613

Created in 1989, the May and Stanley Smith Charitable Trust supports organizations serving people in the United States, Canada, the United Kingdom, Australia, the Bahamas, and Hong Kong – places that May and Stanley Smith lived in or spent time in during their lifetimes. The trust supports organizations that offer opportunities to children and youth, elders, the disabled and critically ill, and disadvantaged adults and families which enrich the quality of life, promote self-sufficiency, and assist individuals in achieving their highest potential. The trust will fund requests for general-operating, capacity-building, and program support. All grant seekers (including previously-funded organizations) should follow the step-by-step application process laid out at the website to determine eligibility and fit with the trust's funding goals. Eligible organizations whose projects fall within the trust's areas of interest must submit an online Letter of Inquiry (LOI) from the grant website. The trust's staff will review these and invite selected applicants to submit a full proposal. LOIs may be submitted at any time during the year. Processing a grant application from receipt of the LOI to funding notification generally takes between four and six months.
Requirements: The May and Stanley Smith Charitable Trust has a two-stage application process: an online letter of inquiry (LOI) submission followed by an invited proposal submission. Processing a grant application from receipt of the LOI to funding notification generally takes between four and six months. Please note that proposals are accepted by invitation only. Applications are accepted from organizations meeting the Trust's program area priorities and serving individuals living in British Columbia, Canada and the Western United States: Alaska, Arizona, California, Colorado, Hawaii, Idaho, Montana, Nevada, New Mexico, Oregon, Texas, Utah, Washington, and Wyoming. The Trust makes grants to nonprofit organizations that are tax exempt under Section 501(c)3 of the IRS Code and not classified as a private foundation under Section 509(a) of the Code, and to non-U.S. organizations that can demonstrate that they would meet the requirements for such status. Organizations can also submit applications through a sponsoring organization if the sponsor has 501(c)3 status, is not a private foundation under 509(a), and provides written authorization confirming its willingness to act as the fiscal sponsor. The Trust will only accept proposals sent by regular or express mail services that do not require a signature upon delivery.
Restrictions: The trust rarely supports 100% of a project budget, or more than 25 percent of an organization budget, and takes into account award sizes from other foundations. The trust prefers to fund organizations receiving less than 30% of total revenue from government sources. The trust does not fund the following types of organizations or requests: organizations which are not, or would not qualify as, a 501(c)3 public charity; hospitals or hospital foundations; medical clinics or services; scientific or medical research; building funds or capital projects; schools and universities (except those receiving less than 25% of their operating funds from families and those serving a 100% disabled population); endowment funds; individuals; organizations or programs operated by governments; film or media projects; start-up programs or organizations; proselytizing or religious activities that promote specific religious doctrine or that are exclusive and discriminatory; public policy, research, or advocacy; public awareness, education, or information campaigns/programs; debt reduction; conferences or benefit events; projects which carry on propaganda or otherwise attempt to influence legislation; projects which participate or intervene in any political campaign on behalf of or in opposition to any candidate for public office; projects which conduct, directly or indirectly, any voter registration drive; and organizations that pass through funding to an organization or project that would not be eligible for direct funding as described above.
Geographic Focus: All States, Australia, Bahamas, Canada, Hong Kong, United Kingdom
Amount of Grant: 10,000 - 200,000 USD
Samples: Adoption Exchange, Aurora, Colorado, $150,000 - two years of support for the adoption of hard to place foster youth; Covenant House Alaska, Anchorage, Alaska, $200,000 - two years of support for Alaska's youth who are homeless or at risk of homelessness; Just In Time for Foster Youth, San Diego, California, $120,000 - two years of support for foster youth to achieve self-sufficiency.
Contact: Dan Gaff, Grants Manager; (415) 332-0166; grantsmanager@adminitrustllc.com or dgaff@adminitrustllc.com
Internet: www.adminitrustllc.com/may-and-stanley-smith-charitable-trust/grant-program-areas/
Sponsor: May and Stanley Smith Charitable Trust
770 Tamalpais Drive, Suite 309
Corte Madera, CA 94925

McCarthy Family Foundation Charity Fund Grants 1614

The McCarthy Family Foundation Charity Fund was established in 1956. The trustees have a preference for organizations and programs focusing in the areas of education, food, health and housing and shelter programs. Preference will be given to agencies operating North of Boston, Massachusetts, east of Route 93 to the ocean and South of the New Hampshire border. Focus may be emphasized, but not limited to, the communities of Lynn, Salem, Beverly, Peabody, Gloucester, Ipswich, Newburyport and Salisbury. Award amounts typically range from $2,500 to $15,000. Bank of America acts as co-trustee for the McCarthy Family Foundation Charity Fund in conjunction with Elton McCausland, Claudia Luck, David Moran, Esq. and Kevin Stiles, Esq. Grants are given out twice annually.
Requirements: Requests for general operating and program support will be considered, as will requests for specific program-enabling capital improvements. Grants may be subject to matching obligations and payable over multiple years. On very rare occasions, the trustees will consider needs for emergency grants. Site visits may be conducted prior to decision making meetings. Prior grantees must submit a 1 page expenditure report prior to any subsequent grant being considered. Applications will be submitted online through the Bank of America website. A grant report is required within 1 year of the grant application date, regardless of whether all of the funds have been spent.

Restrictions: The fund does not support requests from individuals, organizations attempting to influence policy through direct lobbying, or any political campaigns.
Geographic Focus: Massachusetts
Date(s) Application is Due: Mar 31; Sep 30
Amount of Grant: 2,500 - 15,000 USD
Samples: Express Yourself, Beverly, Massachusetts, $10,000 - awarded for Express Yourself: Celebrating 25th Year of Youth Performances (2018); Girls Inc. of Lynn, Lynn, Massachusetts, $10,000 - awarded for Odyssey After School program for middle school girls (2018); Pingree School, South Hamilton, Massachusetts, $10,000 - awarded for Prep at Pingree program (2018).
Contact: Michealle Larkins, Philanthropic Administrator; (866) 778-6859; ma.grantmaking@bankofamerica.com or ma.grantmaking@ustrust.com
Internet: www.bankofamerica.com/philanthropic/foundation/?fnId=139
Sponsor: McCarthy Family Foundation Charity Fund
P.O. Box 1802
Providence, RI 02901-1802

McCombs Foundation Grants 1615

The McCombs Foundation, established in 1981, makes grants to Texas nonprofit charitable, philanthropic, educational, and benevolent organizations. Areas of interest include arts, athletics, education and higher education, historic preservation, medical research, philanthropy, recreation and sports, youth services, and voluntarism. There are no application deadlines or forms. Applicants should submit a letter of application stating a brief history of the organization, any available printed support materials, and a budget detail. Final notification takes approximately two weeks.
Requirements: Texas nonprofit organizations are eligible. Application form not required.
Restrictions: No grants are given to individuals.
Geographic Focus: Texas
Amount of Grant: 1,000 - 6,000,000 USD
Samples: University of Texas, Houston, Texas, $5,000,000 - Anderson Cancer Center; Saint Mary's Hall, San Antonio, Texas, $300,000 - general operations.
Contact: Gary Woods, Treasurer; (210) 821-6523
Sponsor: McCombs Foundation
755 East Mulberry, Suite 600
San Antonio, TX 78212

McConnell Foundation Grants 1616

The McConnell Foundation awards grants to California nonprofit organizations in its areas of interest, including arts and culture, community development, recreation, social services, children, youth and education, sustainable/livable communities, and the environment. Grants primarily fund the purchase of equipment or building related projects for small and large projects in each county. Requests of up to $50,000 are accepted for projects of benefit to the giving area. Grants are made at three levels, according to the applicant's location. Each county may apply for $1,000 to $10,000. Grants are made to Modoc and Trinity county for $10,000 to $30,000, and grants are made to Shasta, Siskiyou, and Tehama counties for $10,000 to $50,000. Application forms and materials are available at the website for the Shasta Community Foundation who administers the grants.
Requirements: California nonprofit organizations serving Shasta, Siskiyou, Trinity, Tehama, and Modoc counties are eligible.
Restrictions: Grants do not support individuals, religious organizations, research institutions, endowment funds, annual fund drives, budget deficits, or building purchase/construction.
Geographic Focus: California
Date(s) Application is Due: Sep 5
Amount of Grant: Up to 50,000 USD
Contact: Kerry Caranci, Senior Program and Operations Officer; (530) 244-1219 or (530) 926-5486; kerry@shastarcf.org or info@shastarcf.org
Internet: www.mcconnellfoundation.org
Sponsor: McConnell Foundation
800 Shasta View Drive
Redding, CA 96003

McCune Charitable Foundation Grants 1617

The Marshall L. and Perrine D. McCune Charitable Foundation is dedicated to enriching the health, education, environment, and cultural and spiritual life of New Mexicans. The Foundation engages in proactive grantmaking that seeks to foster positive social change. Specifically, the Foundation funds projects that benefit New Mexico in the areas of arts, economic development, education, environment, health, and social services. It is working to stimulate economic diversity, nurture sustainability, and bridge the economic gaps that exist in our communities with the aim of creating wealth for all New Mexicans.
Requirements: Grants can be awarded to qualified 501(c)3 nonprofit organizations, federally recognized Indian tribes, public schools, and governmental agencies. Applications are available online via the Foundation's website.
Restrictions: Grants are not awarded to individuals or to support endowments.
Geographic Focus: New Mexico
Date(s) Application is Due: Sep 30
Amount of Grant: Up to 150,000 USD
Contact: Norty Kalishman, M.D.; (505) 983-8300; mccune@nmmccune.org
Internet: www.nmmccune.org/
Sponsor: McCune Charitable Foundation
345 East Alameda Street
Santa Fe, NM 87501

McCune Foundation Education Grants 1618

The McCune Foundation's grants are assigned to one of four program areas, including: education, human services, humanities, and civic. In the area of education, the Foundation promotes excellence in the institutions of higher education, independent elementary and secondary schools, and ancillary education programs (general education). The education program supports capital projects, research and development, financial aid, programming, and endowment to accomplish the following strategic priorities: leverage university research capacity to enhance the region's competitive advantage in economic development; use universities as anchors for community revitalization strategies; increase access to independent schools and higher education; recruit and retain exceptional faculty; and develop and deliver quality enrichment programs for school aged children, particularly with a focus on math, science and reading.
Requirements: The foundation supports 501(c)3 organizations in southwestern Pennsylvania and throughout the country, with emphasis on the Pittsburgh area. This area includes the following counties: Allegheny, Beaver, Butler, Armstrong, Westmoreland, and Washington. To apply, an organization should send a brief (2 to 3 page) initial inquiry, preferably using the Foundation's website. The letter should contain: project overview - describe what the proposed efforts are intended to achieve for the region as well as for the organization; what activities/actions are planned to meet the stated goals; project timeline; resources required - total cost of the project; anticipated income, including private and public funders; amount of funding requested; IRS 501(c)3 determination letter - attach a copy (either scanned via email or hard copy via regular mail); and a copy of the organization's latest audit (either scanned via email or hard copy via regular mail).
Restrictions: Grants are not awarded to individuals or for general operating purposes or loans. Unsolicited proposals from outside the funding area are not accepted.
Geographic Focus: All States
Amount of Grant: 1,000 - 1,000,000 USD
Samples: A Wilson Center for African American Culture, Pittsburgh, Pennsylvania, $10,000 - access and services for artists' programs; Airlift Research Foundation, Sharpsburg, Pennsylvania, $10,000 - leadership excellence program; Pennsylvania Institute for Conservation Education, Elysburg, Pennsylvania, $10,000 - wildlife leadership academy.
Contact: Henry S. Beukema; (412) 644-8779; fax (412) 644-8059; info@mccune.org
Internet: www.mccune.org/foundation:Website,mccune,grants
Sponsor: McCune Foundation
750 Sixth PPG Place
Pittsburgh, PA 15222

McCune Foundation Humanities Grants 1619

The McCune Foundation's grants are assigned to one of four program areas, including: education, human services, humanities, and civic. In the area of humanities, the Foundation focuses on culture, preservation, and religion and values. Cultural investments are made from the vantage point of regional economic development and the perspective that a city is more livable with a strong arts and culture sector, and a performance epicenter downtown that attracts patrons and out-of-town visitors. The humanities area supports capital projects, endowment grants, technology, marketing, planning, and programming for the following strategic priorities: promote regional historic and cultural assets; attract new audiences and future generations of residents who appreciate the humanities; contribute to the economic development of the downtown corridor; guard the region's history and religious legacy; and support Christian education through academic institutions.
Requirements: The foundation supports 501(c)3 organizations in southwestern Pennsylvania and throughout the country, with emphasis on the Pittsburgh area. This area includes the following counties: Allegheny, Beaver, Butler, Armstrong, Westmoreland, and Washington. To apply, an organization should send a brief (2 to 3 page) initial inquiry, preferably using the Foundation's website. The letter should contain: project overview - describe what the proposed efforts are intended to achieve for the region as well as for the organization; what activities/actions are planned to meet the stated goals; project timeline; resources required - total cost of the project; anticipated income, including private and public funders; amount of funding requested; IRS 501(c)3 determination letter - attach a copy (either scanned via email or hard copy via regular mail); and a copy of the organization's latest audit (either scanned via email or hard copy via regular mail).
Restrictions: Grants are not awarded to individuals or for general operating purposes or loans. Unsolicited proposals from outside the funding area are not accepted.
Geographic Focus: All States
Amount of Grant: 1,000 - 1,000,000 USD
Samples: National Dance Institute of New Mexico, Albuquerque, New Mexico, $100,000 - general support; Historical Society of Western Pennsylvanie, Pittsburgh, Pennsylvania, $400,000 - operating support; Pittsburgh Arts and Lectures, Pittsburgh, Pennsylvania, $9,665 - lecture on art and life.
Contact: Henry S. Beukema, (412) 644-8779; fax (412) 644-8059; info@mccune.org
Internet: www.mccune.org/foundation:Website,mccune,grants
Sponsor: McCune Foundation
750 Sixth PPG Place
Pittsburgh, PA 15222

McGraw-Hill Companies Community Grants 1620

McGraw-Hill focuses its charitable efforts on its goal of financial capability for all. The Corporation partners with nonprofit organizations to help individuals gain the necessary knowledge to make smart savings, credit and spending decisions. McGraw-Hill also extends its support to organizations that share the Corporation's dedication to the arts and culture, education and health and human services. The company gives priority consideration to organizations and projects that: promote and support excellence in education and learning, with a primary emphasis on financial literacy; further financial literacy in the communities and markets where the many diverse businesses of The McGraw-Hill Companies operate; utilize unique applications of innovative and developing technologies; extend their reach globally; can be evaluated and can serve as models elsewhere; are staffed and administered by people with demonstrated competence and experience in their fields; have been determined tax-exempt 501(c)3 organizations and qualify as public charities under IRS rules, or are the local country-specific equivalent of a charitable nonprofit organization.

Requirements: Proposals must include the following: a program narrative (no more than three pages); a detailed organization overview; a concise description of the grant's purpose; and all required attachments. If the request is considered eligible, a meeting may be arranged with the Corporate Responsibility and Sustainability staff. On-site visits may also be made. Proposals are accepted at any time, with funding decisions made quarterly.

Restrictions: McGraw-Hill does not support courtesy advertising, pledges for a walk-a-thon, or similar activities. Funding is also not available for the following: institutions and agencies clearly outside the company's primary geographic concerns and interests; libraries and schools of higher education and K-12; political activities or organizations established to influence legislation; sectarian or religious organizations; member-based organizations, i.e., fraternities, labor, veterans, athletic, social clubs; individuals; endowment funds; or loans. Grants are not renewed automatically. Requests for renewed support must be submitted each year.

Geographic Focus: All States

Contact: Susan Wallman, Manager, Corporate Contributions; (212) 512-6480; fax (212) 512-3611; susan_wallman@mcgraw-hill.com

Internet: www.mcgraw-hill.com/site/cr/community/giving#section_2

Sponsor: McGraw-Hill Companies

1221 Avenue of the Americas, 20th Floor

New York, NY 10020-1095

McGregor Fund Human Services Grants   1621

In keeping with its mission, the McGregor Fund emphasizes support for activities in the city of Detroit and Wayne, Oakland and Macomb counties that address emergency needs for housing, food, clothing and other direct aid. In addition, support may be provided for activities that address the root causes of poverty, homelessness and hunger, and help individuals and families achieve personal and financial stability and other life-changing outcomes. After reviewing the Fund's grant making guidelines and application procedures, applicants can submit the online General Inquiry Form. Applicants can also email or call Heidi Alcock to explore the organization's eligibility for grant consideration, the purpose of the prospective grant proposal, and the plans and budget for both implementation and evaluation. Trustee meetings are scheduled four times per year, generally in March, June, September and December. Grant requests may be submitted at any time, but requests typically take up to three months for staff review. Awards in this area have recently ranged from $32,000 to $300,000.

Requirements: Organizations in the metropolitan Detroit, Michigan, area, are eligible. Requests will be considered from organizations located elsewhere for programs or projects that significantly benefit the metropolitan Detroit area (city of Detroit and Wayne, Oakland, and Macomb counties).

Restrictions: The fund discourages proposals for student scholarships, travel, seminars, conferences, workshops, film or video projects, as well as disease-specific organizations and their local affiliates.

Geographic Focus: Michigan

Amount of Grant: 30,000 - 300,000 USD

Samples: Coalition for Temporary Shelter, Detroit, Michigan, $300,000 - general operating support; Crossroads of Michigan, Detroit, Michigan, $100,000 - support general operations of the Crossroads emergency assistance program; Lighthouse of Oakland County, Pontiac, Michigan, $100,000 - support general operations for emergency services.

Contact: Heidi A. Alcock, Director of Grant Development and Communications; (313) 963-3495; fax (313) 963-3512; heidi@mcgregorfund.org

Internet: www.mcgregorfund.org/programs-priorities/human-services/

Sponsor: McGregor Fund

333 West Fort Street, Suite 2090

Detroit, MI 48226-3134

McInerny Foundation Grants   1622

The McInerny Foundation is one of the largest charitable foundations in the State of Hawaii. Its funds originated from the estates of twin brothers, William and James McInerny, and their older sister, Ella McInerny, whose wealth was generated in large part by a distinguished clothing establishment in the city of Honolulu. Today, the Foundation awards grants to Hawaii nonprofit organizations in its areas of interest, including: arts and culture; community; education; environment; health; and, human services. Types of support include: general operating funding; continuing support; building construction and renovation; equipment acquisition; program development; seed money; scholarship funds; and matching funds. The July 1 deadline is for capital funds; the November 15 deadline date is for scholarship funds. All other requests are accepted at any time year-round.

Requirements: Organizations must be exempt from federal taxes under Section 501(c)3 of the Internal Revenue Code and be classified as a public charity. Eligibility also requires 100% Board of Director financial participation and commitment of school principal (if applicable). The Foundation will also accept the use of a fiscal sponsor.

Restrictions: Grants are not awarded in support of religious institutions, individuals, endowment funds, deficit financing, or research.

Geographic Focus: Hawaii

Date(s) Application is Due: Jul 1; Nov 15

Amount of Grant: 3,000 - 250,000 USD

Contact: Paula Boyce, (808) 538-4945; fax (808) 538-4006; paula.boyce@boh.com

Claire Tarumoto, AVP & Grants Admin.; (808) 694-4945; Claire.Tarumoto@boh.com

Internet: www.boh.com/apps/foundations/FoundationDetails.aspx?foundation=7&show=0

Sponsor: McInerny Foundation

P.O. Box 3170, Department 758

Honolulu, HI 96802-3170

McLean Contributionship Grants   1623

Originally established in 1951 as The Bulletin Contributionship for charitable, educational and scientific purposes, the Contributionship became The McLean Contributionship on May 1, 1980 when the association of the McLean family with the Bulletin ended. Independent Publications, also owned by the McLean family, continues as the main financial supporter of the Contributionship. The Contributionship favors projects that stimulate a better understanding of the natural environment and encourage the preservation of its important features; encourage more compassionate and cost-effective care for the ill and aging in an atmosphere of dignity and self-respect; or promote education, medical, scientific, or on occasion, cultural developments that enhance quality of life. In addition, the Trustees from time to time support projects which motivate promising young people to assess and develop their talents despite social and economic obstacles or encourage those in newspaper and related fields to become more effective and responsible in helping people better understand how events in their communities and around the world affect them. The Trustees meet several times a year. The Contribution accepts and processes applications for grants throughout the year. Applications must be received at least six weeks before a meeting date. Interested organizations may view the annual-meeting schedule on the Application Procedure page at the grant website. The Contributionship accepts the common-grant-application form of Delaware Valley Grantmakers Association. Application may also be made by letter (guidelines are included on the Application Procedure web page).

Requirements: Applicants must show evidence of tax-exempt status.

Restrictions: Geographic area is limited to the following locations: Greater Philadelphia area; Nashua, New Hampshire; Dubois Pennsylvania; and Central Florida. The Contributionship does not fund the costs or expenses of existing staff allocated to a project it is asked to support.

Geographic Focus: Florida, New Hampshire, Pennsylvania

Amount of Grant: 2,000 - 100,000 USD

Samples: A Little Taste of Everything, Philadelphia, Pennsylvania, $1,400 - towards maintaining and enhancing their living roof; Visiting Nurse Association of Greater Philadelphia, Philadelphia, Pennsylvania, $50,000 - toward the installation of the Horizon Enterprise Content Management System; National Constitution Center, Philadelphia, Pennsylvania - towards the upgrade of eight poorly-functioning exhibit cases housing artifacts uncovered during the Center's groundbreaking.

Contact: Sandra McLean, Executive Director; (610) 527-6330; fax (610) 527-9733

Internet: fdncenter.org/grantmaker/mclean

Sponsor: McLean Contributionship

945 Haverford Road, Suite A

Bryn Mawr, PA 19010-3814

McLean Foundation Grants   1624

The sole purpose of the McLean Foundation is to enhance the quality of life for the people of Humboldt county through grantmaking to qualified organizations. The Foundation directs a significant portion of its efforts toward projects that support children and youth, the elderly, social welfare, health and medical needs, as well as supporting the capacity of the local nonprofit sector. Applicants are encouraged to contact the Foundation for further information.

Requirements: Nonprofit organizations in Humboldt county are eligible to apply. Community organizations that meet the needs of the children and youth, the elderly, social welfare, and health and medical needs are also eligible to apply.

Geographic Focus: California

Contact: Leigh Pierre-Oetker, Executive Director; (707) 725-1722; fax (707) 725-1959; leigh@mcleanfoundation.org

Internet: www.northerncalifornianonprofits.org/content/view/102/92/

Sponsor: Mel and Grace McLean Foundation

1336 Main Street

Fortuna, CA 95540

Mead Family Foundation Grants   1625

Jaylee Mead and her husband, Gilbert, came, in some ways, from different universes. Gilbert was an heir to the riches of Consolidated Papers in Wisconsin — one of the largest papermakers in North America — while Jaylee was the daughter of a general store owner in rural North Carolina. They worked together for years at the Goddard Space Flight Center in Greenbelt, he as a geophysicist and she as an astronomer, one of the few women of her generation to pursue a career in astrophysics. Besides their love of the stars, the Meads shared a love of the performing arts. Beginning in the late 1980s, after years of quiet patronage of local playhouses, they established themselves as two of the most generous arts philanthropists in the capital. Together, they helped transform Washington's cultural scene by donating more than $50 million to local theaters, including Studio Theatre and Arena Stage. The Mead Family Foundation (formerly the Gilbert and Jaylee Mead Family Foundation) was officially established in Maryland in 1989, with giving centered in Maryland, Washington D.C., and North Carolina. Currently, its primary fields of interest include: arts education; elementary and secondary education; family services; and youth organizations. The annual deadline for application submission is March 15, with awards ranging from $5,000 to $30,000.

Requirements: Any 501(c)3 organization supporting the residents of Maryland, North Carolina, and Washington, D.C., are eligible to apply.

Geographic Focus: District of Columbia, Maryland, North Carolina

Amount of Grant: 5,000 - 30,000 USD

Samples: Alice Aycock Poe Center for Health Education, Raleigh, North Carolina, $5,000 - general operating support; American University School of Communication, Washington, D.C., $5,000 - general operating support; Bethesda Chevy Chase High School Education Foundation, Bethesda, Maryland, $30,000 - general operating support.

Contact: Elizabeth Mead, President; (301) 761-4433

Sponsor: Mead Family Foundation

3 Bethesda Metro Center, Suite 350

Bethesda, MD 20814

Meadows Foundation Grants 1626

The Meadows Foundation seeks to assist people and institutions of Texas improve the quality and circumstances of life for themselves and future generations. Grants are made in five areas of interest: arts and culture, human services, health, education, and civic and public affairs. Within those three areas, the Foundation seeks to fund programs that: improve educational outcomes of Texas students; preserve and enhance the natural environment; and address the detection and treatment of mental illness.Projects should show the ability to continue and expand after the grant period.

Requirements: Grants are made to qualified organizations in Texas or programs benefiting Texas residents. Applicants must prove one or more of the following conditions in their proposal: Foundation support would be vital or catalytic to a proposed project's success; the project is well planned and the agency has the capacity to execute the plan; and financial support from other sources exists to ensure that the project will be implemented and continue after the grant period. Applications can be found at the website and should be submitted online.

Restrictions: Grants are not made to: individuals; for church or seminary construction; annual fund-raising events or drives; biomedical research; out-of-state performances or competition expenses; single artistic events or performances; or professional conferences and symposia.

Geographic Focus: Texas

Amount of Grant: 10,000 - 600,000 USD

Samples: Dallas Summer Musicals, Dallas, Texas, $600,000 - emergency working capital to complete the 2011 through 2013 seasons; Faith and Philanthropy Institute, Euless, Texas, $25,000 - for expanding training programs to faith and community-based organizations to improve service delivery; Breakthrough, Austin, Texas, $100,000 - expanding an education-support program that prepares low-income, minority students to graduate from high school and succeed in college.

Contact: Cynthia Cass, Grants Administrator; (214) 826-9431 or (800) 826-9431; fax (214) 827-7042; grants@mfi.org

Bruce H. Esterline, Vice President for Grants; (214) 826-9431

Internet: www.mfi.org

Sponsor: Meadows Foundation of Texas

3003 Swiss Avenue

Dallas, TX 75204-6090

MeadWestvaco Foundation Sustainable Communities Grants 1627

The Foundation began as the Mead Corporation Foundation in 1957 and the Westvaco Foundation in 1953, anchored in shared values for community and environmental enrichment. Since merging in 2003, it has offered more than $36 million in support to targeted programs. Adding to this, company employee volunteers have donated over 572,000 hours to more than 3,000 qualified organizations. Across its diverse efforts, the Foundation focuses on three key areas for strategic grants and volunteer initiatives. In the area of Sustainable Communities, it partners with organizations that help people and families rely on themselves, and offers support to their neighbors. The Foundation's support of central business districts gives communities a strong center around which to grow. And its work with youth programs nurtures tomorrow's community leaders. The Foundation's primary focus is to address important community needs and improve the quality of life in communities where MeadWestvaco operates.

Requirements: Nonprofit 501(c)3 organizations in or serving the following U.S. areas are eligible to apply: Cottonton and Lanett, Alabama; Bentonville, Arkansas; Chino, Corona, and Tecate, California; District of Columbia; Miami and St. Petersburg, Florida; Atlanta, Roswell, Smyrna, and Waynesboro, Georgia; Bartlett, Chicago, Itasca, Lake in the Hills, Schaumburg, and West Chicago, Illinois; Winfield, Kansas; Wickliffe, Kentucky; DeRidder, Louisiana; Minneapolis, Minnesota; Grandview, Missouri; Reno, Nevada; North Brunswick, Rumson, and Tinton Falls, New Jersey; New York, New York; Mebane, North Carolina; Cincinnati and Powell, Ohio; North Charleston and Summerville, South Carolina; Coppell, Evadale, and Silsbee, Texas; Appomattox, Covington, Low Moor, Raphine, and Richmond, Virginia; and Elkins and Rupert, West Virginia. Most areas worldwide are also eligible.

Geographic Focus: Alabama, Arkansas, California, District of Columbia, Florida, Georgia, Illinois, Kansas, Louisiana, Minnesota, Nevada, New Jersey, New York, North Carolina, Ohio, South Carolina, Texas, Virginia, West Virginia, All Countries

Amount of Grant: 250 - 1,500,000 USD

Samples: Chicago Horticultural Society, Chicago, Illinois, $2,500 - environmental support; Downtown Dayton Partnership, Dayton, Ohio, $$25,000 - civic betterment; Richmond Ballet, Richmond, Virginia, $15,000 - arts and culture.

Contact: Christine W. Hale, Manager, Contributions Programs; (804) 444-2531; fax (804) 444-1971; foundation@mwv.com

Kathryn A. Strawn, Vice President and Executive Director; (804) 327-6402; fax (804) 444-1971; foundation@mwv.com

Internet: www.meadwestvaco.com/corporate.nsf/mwvfoundation/applicationsGuidelines

Sponsor: MeadWestvaco Foundation

501 South 5th Street

Richmond, VA 23219-0501

Mead Witter Foundation Grants 1628

Incorporated in Wisconsin in 1951, the Foundation awards grants to nonprofits in company operating locations, primarily in central and northern Wisconsin. Local community programs are funded, focusing on education, including scholarships in higher education and direct contributions to colleges and universities. Grants are made to support the arts, health care, human services, youth organizations, environmental programs, and Christian and Roman Catholic organizations for nonreligious purposes. Types of support include general operating support, continuing support, annual campaigns, capital campaigns, building construction and renovation, equipment acquisition, endowment funds, professorships, seed grants, scholarship funds, and employee-matching gifts. The board meets twice annually to consider requests. Full proposal is by invitation only.

Requirements: Wisconsin 501(c)3 organizations may apply.

Restrictions: The foundation does not support religious, athletic, or fraternal groups, except when these groups provide needed special services to the community at large; direct grants or scholarships to individuals; community foundations; or flow-through organizations that redispense funds to other charitable causes.

Geographic Focus: Wisconsin

Amount of Grant: 25,000 - 18,000,000 USD

Samples: Carroll University, Waukesha, Wisconsin, $1,030,000; Medical College of Wisconsin, Milwaukee, $512,000; Beloit College, Beloit, $300,000.

Contact: Cynthia Henke, President; (715) 424-3004; fax (715) 424-1314

Sponsor: Mead Witter Foundation

P.O. Box 39

Wisconsin Rapids, WI 54495-0039

Medtronic Foundation Community Link Arts, Civic, and Culture Grants 1629

At Medtronic, the Foundation makes it a priority to enhance the vitality of the communities where its employees live and work. The CommunityLink program helps the Foundation accomplish this by supporting health, education and community programs throughout the world. The Medtronic Foundation CommunityLink Arts, Civic, and Culture Grants supports programs in the U.S. that celebrate the arts and encourage access to the arts in communities where Medtronic employees live and work. The Foundation looks for opportunities to contribute to programs that increase access to the arts, especially for lower-income families. The Foundation aids cultural organizations making a significant contribution to the life of the community and supports civic organizations addressing the needs of disadvantaged people. The application and current guidelines are available at the website.

Requirements: Only U.S. 501(c)3 nonprofit organizations and equivalent international organizations may apply. Organizations must be located in areas where Medtronic has employees.

Restrictions: The Foundation does not fund the following: Continuing Medical Education (CME) grants; 501(c)3 type 509(a)3 supporting organizations; capital or capital projects; fiscal agents; fundraising events/activities, social events or goodwill advertising; general operating support; general support of educational institutions; greater Twin Cities United Way supported programs; individuals, including scholarships for individuals; lobbying, political or fraternal activities; long-term counseling or personal development; program endowments; purchases of automatic external defibrillators (AEDs); religious groups for religious purposes; private foundations; or research.

Geographic Focus: Arizona, California, Colorado, Florida, Indiana, Massachusetts, Minnesota, Tennessee, Texas, Washington

Date(s) Application is Due: Nov 16

Contact: Deb Anderson, Grants Administrator; (763) 514-4000 or (800) 633-8766; fax (763) 505-2648; deb.anderson@medtronic.com

Internet: www.medtronic.com/foundation/programs_cl_us.html

Sponsor: Medtronic Foundation

710 Medtronic Parkway

Minneapolis, MN 55432-5604

Medtronic Foundation CommunityLink Health Grants 1630

At Medtronic, the Foundation makes it a priority to enhance the vitality of the communities where its employees live and work. The CommunityLink program helps the Foundation accomplish this by supporting health, education and community programs throughout the world. The CommunityLink Health Grants support programs that improve the health and welfare of people, with a focus on Medtronic's areas of expertise. The Foundation gives priority to programs that help people develop and maintain health lifestyles, with particular interest in programs that reduces differences in health care and that support healthy lifestyles, such as nutrition and fitness. The application and guidelines are located on the Foundation website. Guidelines and funding varies depending on location.

Requirements: Only U.S. 501(c)3 nonprofit organizations and equivalent international organizations may apply.

Restrictions: The Foundation does not fund the following: Continuing Medical Education (CME) grants; 501(c)3 type 509(a)3 supporting organizations; capital or capital projects; fiscal agents; fundraising events/activities, social events or goodwill advertising; general operating support; general support of educational institutions; greater Twin Cities United Way supported programs; individuals, including scholarships for individuals; lobbying, political or fraternal activities; long-term counseling or personal development; program endowments; purchases of automatic external defibrillators (AEDs); religious groups for religious purposes; private foundations; or research.

Geographic Focus: Arizona, California, Colorado, Florida, Indiana, Massachusetts, Minnesota, Puerto Rico, Tennessee, Texas, Washington, Canada, Ireland, Japan, Netherlands, Switzerland

Date(s) Application is Due: Nov 16

Contact: Deb Anderson, Grants Administrator; (763) 514-4000 or (800) 633-8766; fax (763) 505-2648; deb.anderson@medtronic.com

Internet: www.medtronic.com/foundation/programs_cl.html

Sponsor: Medtronic Foundation

304 Landmark Center, 75 West Fifth Street

St. Paul, MN 55102

Medtronic Foundation Community Link Human Services Grants 1631

At Medtronic, the Foundation makes it a priority to enhance the vitality of the communities where its employees live and work. The CommunityLink program helps the Foundation accomplish this by supporting health, education and community programs throughout the world. The CommunityLink Human Services Grants support human services in the U.S. that

help individuals become more self-sufficient. Programs reach out to a wide range of people, such as: economic literacy programs to help low-income women gain economic stability; peer counseling for teens in crisis situations; homeless shelters; and subsidized childcare programs for low-income parents. The application and current guidelines are available at the website.
Requirements: Only U.S. 501(c)3 nonprofit organizations and equivalent international organizations may apply. Applicants must be located in U.S. areas where Medtronic has employees.
Restrictions: The Foundation does not fund the following: Continuing Medical Education (CME) grants; 501(c)3 type 509(a)3 supporting organizations; capital or capital projects; fiscal agents; fundraising events/activities, social events or goodwill advertising; general operating support; general support of educational institutions; greater Twin Cities United Way supported programs; individuals, including scholarships for individuals; lobbying, political or fraternal activities; long-term counseling or personal development; program endowments; purchases of automatic external defibrillators (AEDs); religious groups for religious purposes; private foundations; or research.
Geographic Focus: Arizona, California, Colorado, Florida, Indiana, Massachusetts, Minnesota, Tennessee, Texas, Washington
Date(s) Application is Due: Nov 16
Contact: Deb Anderson, Grants Administrator; (763) 514-4000 or (800) 633-8766; fax (763) 505-2648; deb.anderson@medtronic.com
Internet: www.medtronic.com/foundation/programs_cl.html
Sponsor: Medtronic Foundation
710 Medtronic Parkway
Minneapolis, MN 55432-5604

Medtronic Foundation Strengthening Health Systems Grants   1632
Non-communicable diseases (NCDs), including cardiovascular disease, diabetes, cancer, and chronic respiratory disease, are the leading cause of death and disability in the world. But while prevention initiatives and lifesaving treatments have been developed for NCDs, they are not widely available in many low- and middle-income countries. The Strengthening Health Systems Grants expand access to quality healthcare by strengthening health systems and integrating NCDs into primary care in developing countries. The Medtronic Foundation will work with a limited number of chronic disease centers and experts on a global level, and in our priority countries, to address the prevention and management of NCDs. Our emphasis will be on integrating NCDs into primary healthcare, and on improving global understanding of best practices in diabetes and cardiovascular disease. Grants are awarded for specific projects and programs. Being preselected as a potential grantee does not guarantee that a grant will be awarded, as projects are evaluated on their individual merits. Organizations should also consult the website for a detailed list of proposal criteria. Applications are accepted throughout the year, but review of an application usually takes four to five months.
Requirements: Organizations should be located in the countries served by this grant. After reviewing the general guidelines, applicants should send a two- or three-page letter of inquiry. After reviewing the letter, a Foundation representative may recommend that a full proposal is submitted.
Restrictions: Grants for endowment, equipment, or for capital projects are not considered. The Foundation does not support individuals, religious groups for religious purposes, fundraising events or activities, social events or goodwill advertising, reimbursable medical treatment, scientific research, lobbying, or political or fraternal activities.
Geographic Focus: Austria, Belarus, Brazil, Bulgaria, China, Croatia, Czech Republic (Czechia), Germany, Hungary, India, Liechtenstein, Moldova, Poland, Romania, Russia, Serbia, Slovakia, Slovenia, South Africa, Switzerland, Ukraine
Amount of Grant: 50,000 - 250,000 USD
Contact: Deb Anderson, Grants Administrator; (763) 514-4000 or (800) 633-8766; fax (763) 505-2648; deb.anderson@medtronic.com
Internet: www.medtronic.com/foundation/programs_shs_guidelines.html
Sponsor: Medtronic Foundation
710 Medtronic Parkway
Minneapolis, MN 55432-5604

Memorial Foundation for Children Grants   1633
Memorial Foundation for Children Grants are made solely to programs with nonprofit organizations that benefit the care and education of children in the Richmond, Virginia, metropolitan area.
Requirements: Giving is limited to the Richmond, Virginia area, including Chesterfield, Goochland, Hanover, and Henrico counties. Organizations should submit the following: a copy of the IRS determination letter; a brief history of their organization and description of its mission; copy of their most recent annual report, audited financial statement, or 990 form; a detailed description of the project and amount of funding requested; and a copy of the current year's organizational budget and/or project budget.
Geographic Focus: Virginia
Date(s) Application is Due: May 31
Samples: Association for the Support of Children with Cancer, Richmond, Virginia, $30,000 payable over one year; Richmond, Virginia, Boys Choir, $21,000 payable over one year.
Contact: Karl McTaggart, Grants Administrator; (804) 782-7114
Sponsor: Memorial Foundation for Children
P.O. Box 26665
Richmond, VA 23261-6665

Mercedes-Benz USA Corporate Contributions Grants   1634
The company has committed to conducting programs with the concentration of funds geared toward educational causes and organizations, in particular those that help to empower the next generation and underserved groups; diversity programs; and women's initiatives. Specific programs in the categories of health and human services, and civic

and community also are supported. There are no application forms or annual deadlines. Applicants should begin by submitting a proposal idea to the nearest company facility.
Requirements: IRS 501(c)3, 4, 6, or 9 organizations whose primary influences and business operations are in the United States and who enhance the quality of life in Mercedes-Benz communities are eligible. These company communities include: Tuscaloosa, Alabama; Carson, California; Irvine, California; Rancho Cucamonga, California; Jacksonville, Florida; Carol Stream, Illinois; Itasca, Illinois; Rosemont, Illinois; Belcamp, Maryland; Baltimore, Maryland; Montvale, New Jersey; Parsippany, New Jersey; Robinsville, New Jersey; and Fort Worth, Texas.
Geographic Focus: Alabama, California, Florida, Illinois, Maryland, New Jersey, Texas
Amount of Grant: 2,500 - 5,000 USD
Contact: Robert Moran, Director of Communications; (201) 573-2245 or (201) 573-0600; fax (201) 573-4787; robert.moran@mbusa.com
Internet: www.mbusa.com/mercedes/about_us/mbcommunity
Sponsor: Mercedes-Benz USA
One Mercedes Drive
Montvale, NJ 07645

Merck Family Fund Urban Farming and Youth Leadership Grants   1635
The primary goals of the Merck Family Fund are to restore and protect the natural environment and ensure a healthy planet for generations to come; and to strengthen the social fabric and the physical landscape of the urban community. In the area of Urban Farming and Youth Leadership, the Fund will support programs in low-income urban areas in the Northeast that are harnessing the power of young people to create urban farms and local markets. Specifically, the Fund welcomes proposals that: provide high quality leadership development and employment for youth; support highly productive urban farming projects and increase local access to fresh food; and engage residents in food access and food security issues in the community. Upon submitting a letter of inquiry, applicants will be notified of a decision, by email, typically within one week. If invited, full proposals must be submitted through this online application system no later than August 1, at 5:00pm EST for the November decision, and February 1, at 5:00pm for Spring decision.
Requirements: United States tax-exempt organizations are eligible. Priority will be given to projects that originate in the six New England states, New York, New Jersey and the Delaware Valley region including Philadelphia, Pennsylvania, and Wilmington, Delaware. New and returning requests for support must use the online application system to submit a letter of inquiry prior to a formal application.
Restrictions: The Fund does not support individuals, for-profit organizations, or candidates for political office. The Fund does not generally support: governmental organizations, academic research or books; endowments, debt reduction, annual fund-raising campaigns, capital construction, purchase of equipment, the acquisition of land, or film or video projects.
Geographic Focus: Delaware, Maine, Maryland, Massachusetts, New Hampshire, New Jersey, New York, Pennsylvania, Rhode Island, Vermont
Date(s) Application is Due: Feb 1; Aug 1
Amount of Grant: 3,000 - 50,000 USD
Samples: Capital District Community Gardens, Troy, New York, $26,000 - to increase food access and economic opportunities by providing entrepreneurial training and employment to teens on urban farms; Nuestras Raices, Holyoke, Massachusetts, $50,000 - to convert a vacant lot into an urban garden and train and employ youth in farming, organizing, and entrepreneurship; St. Mary's Nutrition Center, Lewiston, Maine, $40,000 - to increase the sustainability of the Nutrition Center to train and employ young people and grow and distribute food from urban farms.
Contact: Jenny Russell; (617) 696-3580; fax (617) 696-7262; merck@merckff.org
Internet: www.merckff.org/programs.html
Sponsor: Merck Family Fund
303 Adams Street, P.O. Box 870245
Milton Village, MA 02187

Merck Family Fund Youth Transforming Urban Communities Grants   1636
The primary goals of the Merck Family Fund are to restore and protect the natural environment and ensure a healthy planet for generations to come; and to strengthen the social fabric and the physical landscape of the urban community. In the area of Youth Transforming Urban Communities, the goals have been to support a cadre of young social justice leaders across the country; to link local campaigns with national movements; and to document the impact of their work on communities and themselves. Upon submitting a letter of inquiry, applicants will be notified of a decision, by email, typically within one week. If invited, full proposals must be submitted through this online application system no later than August 1, at 5:00pm EST for the November decision, and February 1, at 5:00pm for Spring decision.
Requirements: United States tax-exempt organizations are eligible. New and returning requests for support must use the online application system to submit a letter of inquiry prior to a formal application.
Restrictions: The Fund does not support individuals, for-profit organizations, or political candidates. The Fund does not generally support: governmental organizations, academic research or books; endowments, debt reduction, annual fund-raising campaigns, capital construction, purchase of equipment, the acquisition of land, or film or video projects.
Geographic Focus: All States
Date(s) Application is Due: Feb 1; Aug 1
Amount of Grant: 10,000 - 45,000 USD
Samples: Campaign for Quality Education, Long Beach, California, $15,000 - to support a youth-led statewide alliance of grassroots, civil rights, policy and research organizations committed to educational equity for all communities served by California's public schools; Hyde Square Task Force, Jamaica Plain, Massachusetts, $45,000 - to empower youth to examine the social, economic, and political forces affecting their lives and act as agents of change in their communities and schools; Padres y Jovenes Unidos, Denver, Colorado, $45,000 - to equip youth members with the tools they need to organize for social, racial, economic, and educational justice.
Contact: Jenny Russell; (617) 696-3580; fax (617) 696-7262; merck@merckff.org

Internet: www.merckff.org/programs.html
Sponsor: Merck Family Fund
303 Adams Street, P.O. Box 870245
Milton Village, MA 02187

Mericos Foundation Grants 1637

The Mericos Foundation primarily awards grants to organizations based in California with emphasis on Santa Barbara. Fields of interest include aging; animals/wildlife; environment; arts and arts education; child development; children and youth; elementary and secondary education; higher education; hospitals; medical care; medical research; libraries; and museums (art and natural history). Types of support include building/renovation, equipment, fellowships, general/operating support, matching/challenge support, and program development. Grants are usually initiated by the foundation. Interested organizations should contact the Vice-President to discuss their project.
Requirements: Nonprofit organizations in California are eligible to apply.
Restrictions: Grants are not made to individuals.
Geographic Focus: California
Amount of Grant: 15,000 - 200,000 USD
Samples: Music Academy of the West, Santa Barbara, California, $125,000; Friends of Independent Schools and Better Education, Tacoma, Washington, $25,000; Los Angeles Children's Chorus, Pasadena, California, $25,000.
Contact: Linda Blinkenberg, Vice President; (626) 441-5188; fax (626) 441-3672
Sponsor: Mericos Foundation
625 South Fair Oaks Avenue, Suite 360
South Pasadena, CA 91030-2630

Meriden Foundation Grants 1638

The foundation awards grants to eligible Connecticut nonprofit organizations in its areas of interest, including arts, children and youth, civic affairs, Christian organizations and churches, health organizations and hospitals, higher education, public libraries, and social services. Types of support include annual campaigns, general operating support, scholarships, and social services delivery. There are no application deadlines. A formal application is required, and the initial approach should be a letter, on organizational letterhead, describing the project and requesting an application.
Requirements: Connecticut nonprofit organizations in the Meriden-Wallingford area are eligible.
Geographic Focus: Connecticut
Amount of Grant: 175 - 10,000 USD
Samples: Best Friends Animal Sanctuary, Kanab, Utah, $3,500 - general operations; Church of the Holy Angels, Meriden, Connecticut, $3,296 - general operations; Franciscan Home Care and Hospice, Meriden, Connecticut, $5,000 - to purchase laptop computers.
Contact: Jeffrey F. Otis, Director; (203) 782-4531; fax (203) 782-4530
Sponsor: Meriden Foundation
123 Bank Street
Waterbury, CT 06702-2205

Merrick Foundation Grants 1639

The goal of Merrick Foundation is to improve the quality of life in the Merrick County area of Nebraska by supporting needs that are not being met in the areas of civic, cultural, health, education and social service. Grants are awarded on the condition that grantees attend Merrick Foundation's Annual Meeting on the 4th Monday of November and provide a poster board display demonstrating the goal, progress or completion of their grant project. Proposals from organizations demonstrating broad community support for their proposed programs are given priority consideration. Most recent awards have ranged from $5,800 to $45,000. Grant requests over $10,000 may be required to attend a regular meeting for explanations and/or clarifications. Grants over $15,000 shall be reviewed in January and June. Deadline dates for submitting applications are due the 10th of each month or the following Monday if the 10th falls on a weekend. Grants are approved every month except December.
Requirements: Only organizations in Merrick County or organizations serving Merrick County residents are eligible to apply.
Restrictions: The Foundation does not make grants to individuals, for religious purposes, or organizations that operate for profit. he Foundation as a general policy gives less consideration to applications from tax-supported institutions, veterans and labor organizations, social clubs and fraternal organizations. A grant cannot be used for political purposes.
Geographic Focus: Nebraska
Date(s) Application is Due: Jan 1; Feb 1; Mar 1; Apr 1; May 1; Jun 1; Jul 1; Aug 1; Sep 1; Oct 1; Nov 1
Amount of Grant: 5,800 - 45,000 USD
Samples: St. Paul's Lutheran Church, Grand Island, Nebraska, $12,000 - community help programs; Merrick County Child Development Center, Central City, Nebraska, $15,000 - general operating costs; Platte Peer Group, Chapman, Nebraska, $45,000 - park development project support.
Contact: Chuck Griffith, Executive Director; (308) 946-3707; merrickfoundation@gmail.com
Internet: www.merrick-foundation.org/grants.htm
Sponsor: Merrick Foundation
1532 17th Avenue, P.O. Box 206
Central City, NE 68826

Merrick Foundation Grants 1640

The Merrick Foundation was established in 1948 by Ward S. Merrick, Sr., as a memorial to his father F.W. Merrick and at the request of F.W.'s wife, Elizabeth B. Merrick. The mission of the Foundation is to enhance the quality of life and the improvement of health for Oklahoma residents and their communities, with a primary emphasis on south central Oklahoma. With this goal in mind, the Foundation trustees are committed to furthering the philanthropic vision of Ward S. Merrick, Sr., by awarding grants to charitable organizations that foster independence and achievement, and that stimulate educational, economic, and cultural growth. Primary fields of interest include: the arts; higher education; human services; medical research; and youth services. The majority of awards are given for general operations. Most recent grants have ranged from $500 to $25,000. The grants committee will review all request letters received through the online grant application process and will email instructions on how to complete an application to qualifying charities. Grant applications will be due October 1 each year.
Requirements: The trustees invite proposals from 501(c)3 organizations located in Oklahoma. A letter of request is due by the August 15 deadline, summarizing the project for funding must be submitted through the online grant application process.
Geographic Focus: Oklahoma
Date(s) Application is Due: Oct 1
Amount of Grant: 500 - 25,000 USD
Samples: Arbuckle Life Solutions, Ardmore, Oklahoma, $5,000 - general operation support; CASA of Southern Oklahoma, Oklahoma City, Oklahoma, $10,000 - general operating support; Delta Upsilon Fraternity, Oklahoma City, Oklahoma, $5,000 - general operating support.
Contact: Randy Macon, Executive Director; 405-755-5571; fax (405) 755-0938; fwmerrick@foundationmanagementinc.com
Internet: www.foundationmanagementinc.com/foundations/merrick-foundation/
Sponsor: Merrick Foundation
2932 NW 122nd Street, Suite D
Oklahoma City, OK 73120-1955

Mertz Gilmore Foundation NYC Communities Grants 1641

In 1959, Joyce Mertz and her parents, LuEsther and Harold, established a family foundation called the Mertz Foundation. Joyce married Robert Wallace Gilmore in June of 1964, and the couple began managing the Foundation's operations. Their strong personal convictions influenced both their approach to grant making and their funding interests. Together with their colleague and friend, Bayard Rustin, they became strong advocates for peace and civil rights issues for a number of years. Their grant making was a logical extension of that work. They also were committed passionately to the quality of life in New York City where they lived and made grants to performing arts institutions and to groups working to protect the city's environment. Their interest in the environment led them to support programs reaching beyond the city to include state, national and global issues as well. Through its NYC Communities Grant program, the Foundation supports work in low-income neighborhoods that emerges from, and actively engages, local efforts while looking for opportunities to support collaborative campaigns. The Program's grants fall into three categories: support to community-based organizations working on multiple fronts; support to technical assistance providers that help community-based organizations address organizational needs; and, support to collaborative campaigns.
Requirements: Submit a letter of inquiry (not a full proposal) of no more than three pages describing the mission of the organization and the purpose of the request. Staff will respond to all communications, and, if appropriate, invite a full proposal. Do not submit videos, DVDs/CDs, press clippings, books, or other materials unless they are requested. Across all funding categories, the Foundation will evaluate the ability of organizations to work in partnership and raise additional funds for proposed work.
Restrictions: The Foundation does not accept proposals for: individuals; endowments, annual fund appeals or fundraising events; conferences, workshops; sectarian religious concerns; scholarships, fellowships, research, loans, or travel; film or media projects; or publications.
Geographic Focus: New York
Date(s) Application is Due: Jan 17
Amount of Grant: Up to 150,000 USD
Samples: Voices of Women Organizing Project, New York, New York, $90,000 to provide general support for the Battered Women's Justice, Rights of Children, and Housing campaigns; Brandworkers International, Long Island City, New York, $100,000 - to provide general support for organizing workers in the local food production industry; MinKwon Center for Community Action, Flushing, New York, $100,000 - to provide general support for organizing, education, and advocacy initiatives that address the needs of the Korean American community.
Contact: Rachael Young, (212) 475-5581; fax (212) 777-5226; ryoung@mertzgilmore.org
Internet: www.mertzgilmore.org/program-areas/nyc-communities/
Sponsor: Mertz Gilmore Foundation
218 East 18th Street
New York, NY 10003-3694

Mertz Gilmore Foundation NYC Dance Grants 1642

In 1959, Joyce Mertz and her parents, LuEsther and Harold, established a family foundation called the Mertz Foundation. Joyce married Robert Wallace Gilmore in June of 1964, and the couple began managing the Foundation's operations. Their strong personal convictions influenced both their approach to grant making and their funding interests. Together with their colleague and friend, Bayard Rustin, they became strong advocates for peace and civil rights issues for a number of years. Their grant making was a logical extension of that work. They also were committed passionately to the quality of life in New York City where they lived and made grants to performing arts institutions and to groups working to protect the city's environment. Their interest in the environment led them to support programs reaching beyond the city to include state, national and global issues as well. The Foundation has an extensive history of supporting dance in New York City, reflecting Joyce Mertz Gilmore's passion for dance. The Foundation continues to fund contemporary dance presenters located throughout the city's five boroughs. Its objective remains to support and invigorate the presenting field to serve New York City's artists and audiences. The Program's grants fall into two categories: support for presenters; and funding for advocacy and support services.
Requirements: The Foundation will accept proposals from organizations based in New York City. Submit a letter of inquiry (not a full proposal) of no more than three pages describing

the mission of the organization and the purpose of the request. Staff will respond to all communications, and, if appropriate, invite a full proposal. Do not submit videos, DVDs/CDs, press clippings, books, or other materials unless they are requested. Across all funding categories, the Foundation will evaluate the ability of organizations to work in partnership and raise additional funds for proposed work.

Restrictions: The Foundation will not make grants for individual artists or companies, or organizations based outside of New York City. Additionally, the Foundation does not accept proposals for: individuals; endowments; annual fund appeals or fundraising events; conferences, workshops; sectarian religious concerns; scholarships, fellowships, research, loans, or travel; film or media projects; or publications.

Geographic Focus: New York
Date(s) Application is Due: Jan 17
Amount of Grant: Up to 100,000 USD
Samples: Baryshnikov Arts Center, New York, $60,000 - support the development and presentation of dance; Bronx Museum of the Arts, Bronx, New York, $50,000 - to expand the Bronx Museum's role as a presenting institution for dance; Fiorello H. LaGuardia Community College Foundation, LaGuardia Performing Arts Center, Long Island City, New York, $20,000 - to support dance presentations.
Contact: Leah Krauss, (646) 723-2225; fax (212) 777-5226; lkrauss@mertzgilmore.org
Internet: www.mertzgilmore.org/index.php/programs/nyc-dance
Sponsor: Mertz Gilmore Foundation
218 East 18th Street
New York, NY 10003-3694

Mervin Bovaird Foundation Grants 1643

The foundation awards grants, with a focus on Tulsa, OK, to nonprofit organizations such as churches, homeless shelters, medical centers, nursing homes, parochial schools, religious welfare organizations, the Salvation Army, and youth organizations. Areas of interest include arts, community development, education, environment, health care and health organizations, and social services. Types of support include general operating support, matching, project, and research grants.

Requirements: Nonprofit organizations in and serving the population of Tulsa, Oklahoma, are eligible. Applicants should submit a brief letter of inquiry, including program and organization descriptions.
Geographic Focus: Oklahoma
Date(s) Application is Due: Nov 15
Amount of Grant: Up to 250,000 USD
Contact: R. Casey Cooper, (918) 592-3300; casey.cooper@cmw-law.com
Sponsor: Mervin Bovaird Foundation
401 South Boston Avenue, Suite 3300
Tulsa, OK 74103

Meta and George Rosenberg Foundation Grants 1644

The Meta and George Rosenberg Foundation was established in California in 1991 in honor of Meta and George Rosenberg. Meta, who would become an Emmy-winning executive producer of the durable television series "The Rockford Files," married talent agent George "Rosey" Rosenberg in 1947, and the two of them soon began representing writers and actors. They also sold innovative series to television networks, including "Julia," starring Diahann Carroll as an African American nurse and single mother; "Hogan's Heroes," a comedy set in a World War II German prison camp; and "Ben Casey," among the first series showcasing medicine as drama. Throughout her career, Meta pursued an interest in photography, collecting the works of internationally known photographers such as Henri Cartier-Bresson, Ansel Adams, and Irving Penn, and aiming her own Leica camera at street scenes from Los Angeles to Paris. Currently, the Foundation's primary fields of interest include: arts and culture; children's diseases; elementary and secondary education; AIDS; and human services. Funding is concentrated in southern California, with some grants being awarded in the State of Iowa. The annual deadline for application submission is August 31. Most recent awards have ranged from $10,000 to $140,000.

Geographic Focus: California, Iowa
Date(s) Application is Due: Aug 31
Amount of Grant: 10,000 - 140,000 USD
Samples: Project Grad Los Angeles, North Hollywood, California, $8,400 - general operating support; University of Iowa Foundation, Iowa City, Iowa, $70,000 - general fund contribution; Engage the Art of Aging, Burbank, California, $30,000 - general operating support.
Contact: Wallace D. Franson, President and Director; (323) 634-2400
Sponsor: Meta and George Rosenberg Foundation
5900 Wilshire Boulevard, Suite 2300
Los Angeles, CA 90036-5050

MetLife Foundation Preparing Young People Grants 1645

MetLife Foundation partners with local, national and global nonprofit organizations to address issues impacting communities worldwide within the following thematic programs. The Foundation's Preparing Young People program helps young people navigate opportunities and obstacles by supporting initiatives focusing on student achievement and youth development. In deciding the amount of support, the factors considered include availability of funds, relative priorities and funding patterns. On occasion, the Foundation establishes particular areas of interest for emphasis within a program area. When this is done, the Foundation actively searches out promising opportunities for grants and may issue requests for proposals.

Requirements: To be considered for a MetLife Foundation grant, an organization must be a qualified 501(c)3 organization with a valid IRS Tax ID based in the United States. In the evaluation of the organization, the factors considered include the organization's general structure, objectives, history and management capability; its relationship to the community

and the population to be served; its position relative to organizations performing similar functions; and its financial position and sources of income. In the evaluation of a project, the factors considered include the project's goals and implementation plans; length of time for the project to be complete; the ultimate disposition of the project; benefits of the projects; and the sources of financial and other support.

Restrictions: The Metlife Foundation is not seeking applications for any of the following: private foundations; religious, fraternal, political, athletic or social organizations; hospitals; individuals; local chapters of national organizations; disease-specific organizations; labor groups; organizations primarily engaged in patient care or direct treatment, drug treatment centers and community health clinics; direct contributions to elementary and secondary schools (including charter, parochial and private schools); endowments; courtesy advertising or festival participation; or sponsorships (golf tournaments, dinners, etc.). Grant renewals are not automatic and cannot be guaranteed from year to year.

Geographic Focus: All States
Contact: A. Dennis White, C.E.O. and President; (212) 578-6272; fax (212) 578-0617; metlifefoundation@metlife.com
Internet: www.metlife.com/metlife-foundation/about/index.html?WT.ac=GN_metlife-foundation_about
Sponsor: MetLife Foundation
1095 Avenue of the Americas
New York, NY 10036-6797

MetroWest Health Foundation Grants to Reduce the Incidence of High 1646
Risk Behaviors Among Adolescents

Since 1999, the MetroWest Health Foundation has provided over funds to non-profit and government organizations to improve health services within its 25-town service area. The Foundation describes its grantmaking efforts as both reactive and proactive. Its reactive grantmaking includes two annual requests for proposals (spring and fall) where grant applications are solicited from area organizations. These requests for proposals target specific needs or areas of interest, such as access to health care, disease prevention and health promotion. Its proactive grantmaking targets community needs identified by the Foundation. Here the Foundation develops more comprehensive strategies for addressing community health needs. To date, the Foundation's proactive grantmaking has targeted such issues as child obesity, racial and ethnic health disparities, and adolescent substance abuse.

Requirements: The Foundation supports programs that directly benefit the health of those who live and work in one of the 25 communities served by the Foundation: Ashland, Bellingham, Dover, Framingham, Franklin, Holliston, Hopedale, Hopkinton, Hudson, Marlborough, Medfield, Medway, Mendon, Milford, Millis, Natick, Needham, Norfolk, Northborough Sherborn, Southborough, Sudbury, Wayland, Wellesley and Westborough. Such support is limited to organizations that qualify as tax-exempt under Section 501(c)3 of the IRS Code, or organizations that are recognized as instrumentalities of state or local government. The Foundation requires applicants to submit concept papers prior to a full proposal. Concept papers help the Foundation assess whether or not the proposed project is aligned with its funding priorities. Only a limited number of proposals will be funded with a maximum grant amount of $25,000; applications may be for one, two or three years in duration, and funds cannot be used to supplant ongoing government operations or support. Applications involving schools must submit a letter signed by the Superintendent indicating support for the request. The Foundation will provide grants to municipalities and nonprofit organizations to implement programs that address youth risk behaviors as reported by the MetroWest Adolescent Health Survey. For this grant round, the focus will only be on: (a) efforts to reduce the rate of marijuana use among adolescents; (b) efforts to reduce the incidence of teenage pregnancy. Preference will be given to interventions that are evidence-based or, if no programs meet this criteria, are research-based or recognized as promising practices. In addition, communities with similar risk behavior data and demographics may consider applying for regional approaches in order to maximize impact, although funding will still be subject to the individual grant maximum.

Restrictions: The Foundation does not provide grants to individuals, nor does it provide funds for endowments, fundraising drives and events, retirement of debt, operating deficits, projects that directly influence legislation, political activities or candidates for public office, or programs that are customarily operated by hospitals in Massachusetts. The Foundation does not award grants to organizations that discriminate in the provision of services on the basis of race, color, religion, gender, age, ethnicity, marital status, disability, sexual orientation or veteran status.

Geographic Focus: Massachusetts
Date(s) Application is Due: Apr 12
Amount of Grant: Up to 25,000 USD
Samples: Pelham Apts. Recreation and Computer Network Center, $4,500 to support teen pregnancy prevention programs.
Contact: Cathy Glover, Grants Managment Director; (508) 879-7625; fax (508) 879-7628; cglover@mwhealth.org or cglover@mchcf.org
Internet: www.mwhealth.org/GrantsampScholarships/Overview/tabid/180/Default.aspx
Sponsor: MetroWest Health Foundation
161 Worcester Road, Suite 202
Framingham, MA 01701

Metzger-Price Fund Grants 1647

The Metzger-Price Fund, established in New York in 1970, is an independent foundation trust which offers support to the handicapped, health services, child welfare, social service agencies, recreation, and the elderly. Its primary fields of interest include: services and centers for the aged, child and youth services, community and economic development, education, family support services, health care services and health care access, and human services. The Fund's target groups include the elderly, disabled, economically disadvantaged, homeless, women, and other minorities. Funding is directed toward continuing support, general operations, and program development. There are no specific application forms or deadlines, though the board meets to discuss proposals four times each year (January, April, July, and October). An applicant's initial approach should be in the form of an application letter submitted two months prior to each board meeting.

Requirements: 501(c)3 organizations serving the residents of New York, New York, are encouraged to apply.

Restrictions: No grants to individuals, or for capital campaigns or building funds; no multiple grants in single calendar year to same organization.

Geographic Focus: New York

Amount of Grant: 1,000 - 5,000 USD

Contact: Isaac A. Saufer; (212) 867-9501 or (212) 867-9500; fax (212) 599-1759

Sponsor: Metzger-Price Fund, Inc.

230 Park Avenue, Suite 2300

New York, NY 10169-0005

Meyer Foundation Benevon Grants   1648

Eugene Meyer was an investment banker, public servant under seven U.S. presidents, and owner and publisher of the Washington Post. His wife Agnes Ernst Meyer was an accomplished journalist, author, lecturer, and citizen activist. Eugene and Agnes created the Meyer Foundation in 1944. For more than sixty-five years the Meyer Foundation has identified, listened to, and invested in visionary leaders and effective community-based nonprofit organizations that work to create lasting improvements in the lives of low-income people in the Washington, D.C. metropolitan region. The foundation offers program, operating, and capital support to eligible organizations in four priority program areas: education, healthy communities, economic security, and a strong nonprofit sector. Additionally Meyer has developed a partnership with Benevon, a firm that provides training and coaching to help nonprofits implement its proprietary model for raising money from individual donors. Meyer will make a limited number of grants each year to current Meyer grantees who are planning to implement the Benevon fundraising model. These grants offset the cost of attending either of Benevon's two-day training programs—$15,000 for Benevon 101 and $22,000 for its follow-up Sustainable Funding Program—plus travel and lodging for a seven-member team. Moreover Meyer will consider up to three years of additional grant support to organizations who demonstrate success with the model so that they may continue to participate in Benevon's Sustainable Funding Program, which provides ongoing training and coaching for five years. The deadlines for submitting Benevon applications occur in January and June; exact dates may vary from year to year. Interested organizations should visit the Meyer website to obtain detailed guidelines, downloadable application forms, and current deadline dates. Applications, along with any required attachments, must be submitted electronically via Meyer's online submission system.

Requirements: 501(c)3 organizations who are current Meyer grantees are eligible to apply. Meyer grantees are usually located within and primarily serve the Washington, D.C. region. The foundation defines the Washington, D.C. region to include the following counties and cities: Washington, D.C; Montgomery and Prince George's counties in Maryland; Arlington, Fairfax, and Prince William counties in Virginia; and the cities of Alexandria, Falls Church, and Manassas Park, Virginia.

Restrictions: Only current Meyer grantees are eligible for Benevon grants. Eligibility extends for two years from the date of an organization's last Meyer grant awarded through the foundation's regular grant-making program.

Geographic Focus: District of Columbia, Maryland, Virginia

Date(s) Application is Due: Jan 10; Jun 6

Amount of Grant: 15,000 - 22,000 USD

Contact: Maegan Scott; (202) 534-1860; mscott@meyerfdn.org

Internet: www.meyerfoundation.org/our-programs/Benevon

Sponsor: Meyer Foundation

1250 Connecticut Avenue, Northwest, Suite 800

Washington, D.C. 20036

Meyer Foundation Education Grants   1649

Eugene Meyer was an investment banker, public servant under seven U.S. presidents, and owner and publisher of the Washington Post. His wife Agnes Ernst Meyer was an accomplished journalist, author, lecturer, and citizen activist. Eugene and Agnes created the Meyer Foundation in 1944. For more than sixty-five years the Meyer Foundation has identified, listened to, and invested in visionary leaders and effective community-based nonprofit organizations that work to create lasting improvements in the lives of low-income people in the Washington, D.C. metropolitan region. The foundation offers program, operating, and capital support in four priority program areas: education, healthy communities, economic security, and a strong nonprofit sector. In the area of education, the foundation supports a broad range of work, all designed to ensure that young people graduate from high school, go on to earn post-secondary credentials, and enter the skilled work force. This work includes programming that facilitates the following outcomes: successful transitions for children of low-income families throughout their entire education; multiple pathways for children and youth to enter the skilled work force; and education reform in K-12 public education in the D.C. area. Letters of Intent (LOIs) may be submitted through the foundation's online application system twice a year, in January and June; exact deadline dates may vary from year to year. Applicants will receive an email confirming receipt of their LOI within two to three weeks of submission and will be notified two months after the LOI deadline whether or not they will be invited to submit a full proposal for the board meetings in April and October. Prospective applicants should visit the foundation's website for detailed funding guidelines and current deadline dates before submitting an LOI.

Requirements: Eligible applicants must be 501(c)3 organizations that are located within and primarily serve the Washington, D.C. region defined by the foundation to include the following geographic areas: Washington, D.C; Montgomery and Prince George's counties in Maryland; Arlington, Fairfax, and Prince William counties in Virginia; and

the cities of Alexandria, Falls Church, and Manassas Park, Virginia. The foundation looks for organizations that demonstrate visionary and talented leadership, effectiveness, sustainability, and long-term impact.

Restrictions: The foundation does not fund short-term or seasonal programs, individual public or private schools, PTAs, organizations that provide out-of-school programs solely for elementary-school children, government agencies, for-profit businesses, individuals (including scholarships or other forms of financial assistance), scientific or medial research, special events or conferences, or endowments.

Geographic Focus: District of Columbia, Maryland, Virginia

Amount of Grant: 1,500 - 50,000 USD

Samples: Advocates for Justice and Education, Washington, D.C., $50,000—general operating support; Beacon House, Washington, D.C., $25,000—general operating support; DanceMakers, Lanham, Maryland, $20,000—to support the One Step Forward program.

Contact: Julie Rogers; (202) 483-8294; fax (202) 328-6850; jrogers@meyerfdn.org

Internet: www.meyerfoundation.org/our-programs/grantmaking/education

Sponsor: Meyer Foundation

1250 Connecticut Avenue, Northwest, Suite 800

Washington, D.C. 20036

Meyer Foundation Healthy Communities Grants   1650

Eugene Meyer was an investment banker, public servant under seven U.S. presidents, and owner and publisher of the Washington Post. His wife Agnes Ernst Meyer was an accomplished journalist, author, lecturer, and citizen activist. Eugene and Agnes created the Meyer Foundation in 1944. For more than sixty-five years the Meyer Foundation has identified, listened to, and invested in visionary leaders and effective community-based nonprofit organizations that work to create lasting improvements in the lives of low-income people in the Washington, D.C. metropolitan region. The foundation offers program, operating, and capital support in four priority program areas: education, healthy communities, economic security, and a strong nonprofit sector. In the area of health, the foundation funds programming that facilitates the following outcomes for low-income people in the Washington, D.C. metropolitan area: access to high-quality primary care that integrates mental and behavioral health care and eliminates health disparities; access to affordable places to live, healthful food to eat, and services that promote health and personal safety; public policies at the state and local level that are aimed at strengthening the safety net, reducing poverty, and improving lives. The foundation funds clinics, social-service organizations, community-organizing groups, and multi-issue research and advocacy groups and gives priority to issues such as homelessness, child abuse, domestic violence, and rape. In the case of service organizations, the foundations gives priority to those who track participant outcomes with quantitative and qualitative measures. Letters of Intent (LOIs) may be submitted through the foundation's online application system twice a year, in January and June; exact deadline dates may vary from year to year. Applicants will receive an email confirming receipt of their LOI within two to three weeks of submission and will be notified two months after the LOI deadline whether or not they will be invited to submit a full proposal for the board meetings in April and October. Prospective applicants should visit the foundation's website for detailed funding guidelines and current deadline dates before submitting an LOI.

Requirements: Eligible applicants must be 501(c)3 organizations that are located within and primarily serve the Washington, D.C. region defined by the foundation to include the following geographic areas: Washington, D.C; Montgomery and Prince George's counties in Maryland; Arlington, Fairfax, and Prince William counties in Virginia; and the cities of Alexandria, Falls Church, and Manassas Park, Virginia. The foundation looks for organizations that demonstrate visionary and talented leadership, effectiveness, sustainability, and long-term impact.

Restrictions: The foundation does not fund medical or scientific research, organizations or programs focused on a single disease or medical condition, capital for construction or development of housing, start-up housing developers, operating support for housing developers, AIDS-related programs (the foundation supports these exclusively through the Washington AIDS Partnership), government agencies, for-profit businesses, individuals (including scholarships or other forms of financial assistance), special events or conferences, or endowments.

Geographic Focus: All States

Amount of Grant: 1,500 - 50,000 USD

Samples: Calvary Women's Services, Washington, D.C., $25,000—general operating support; Anacostia Watershed Society, Bladensburg, Maryland, $30,000—to support general operations over two years; Arlington Free Clinic, Arlington, Virginia, $35,000—to support general operations.

Contact: Julie Rogers; (202) 483-8294; fax (202) 328-6850; jrogers@meyerfdn.org

Internet: www.meyerfoundation.org/our-programs/grantmaking/healthy-communities

Sponsor: Meyer Foundation

1250 Connecticut Avenue, Northwest, Suite 800

Washington, D.C. 20036

Meyer Foundation Management Assistance Grants   1651

Eugene Meyer was an investment banker, public servant under seven U.S. presidents, and owner and publisher of the Washington Post. His wife Agnes Ernst Meyer was an accomplished journalist, author, lecturer, and citizen activist. Eugene and Agnes created the Meyer Foundation in 1944. For more than sixty-five years the Meyer Foundation has identified, listened to, and invested in visionary leaders and effective community-based nonprofit organizations that work to create lasting improvements in the lives of low-income people in the Washington, D.C. metropolitan region. The foundation offers program, operating, and capital support to eligible organizations in four priority program areas: education, healthy communities, economic security, and a strong nonprofit sector. Additionally the foundation has a Management Assistance Program (MAP) available to current grantees only. MAP provides grants of up to $25,000 to help Meyer grantees strengthen their management and leadership so they can serve the community more effectively. Organizations generally use MAP grants to hire consultants to help board and staff accomplish work that requires time, energy, expertise, and innovative thinking beyond everyday operations. Examples of such work include strengthening executive and board leadership, conducting organizational planning and assessment, and improving financial management and sustainability. MAP grants have proven especially beneficial to groups experiencing significant organization transitions such as shifts in funding sources, the departure of a founder, or rapid growth. MAP application deadlines coincide with those of the foundation's regular grant-making cycle; however, for time-sensitive or out-of-cycle requests (e.g. executive transition, mergers, and financial planning), organizations should use the MAP email address to get in touch with the foundation. The foundation's regular grant-making cycles start in January and in June when Letters of Intent (LOIs) are accepted through the foundation's online application system; exact deadline dates may vary from year to year. The foundation reviews MAP LOIs within one month of receiving the request. If the proposed project meets the criteria for funding and if sufficient funds remain in the budget, foundation staff will schedule a site visit or meeting to discuss the project with the applicant's executive director and key board members and staff. On the basis of the site visit, applicants will be invited to submit a full proposal. If the foundation approves the grant, the program officer will notify the executive director, usually within three months after the LOI was submitted. Prospective applicants should visit the foundation's website for detailed funding guidelines and current deadline dates before submitting an LOI.

Requirements: 501(c)3 organizations who are current Meyer grantees are eligible to apply. Meyer grantees are usually located within and primarily serve the Washington, D.C. region. The foundation defines the Washington, D.C. region to include the following counties and cities: Washington, D.C; Montgomery and Prince George's counties in Maryland; Arlington, Fairfax, and Prince William counties in Virginia; and the cities of Alexandria, Falls Church, and Manassas Park, Virginia. Grantees are responsible for paying a percentage of the total cost of their MAP project based on their annual budget; matches are as follows: 5% for an annual budget less than $250,000; 10% for an annual budget of $250,000 to $500,000; 15% for an annual budget of $500,000 to $1 million; 20% for an annual budget of $1 million to $2 million; 25% for an annual budget of $2 million to $3 million; 30% for an annual budget of $3 million to $4 million; 40% for an annual budget of $4 million to $5 million; and 50% for an annual budget of over $5 million.

Restrictions: Only current Meyer grantees are eligible for management assistance. Eligibility extends for two years from the date of an organization's last Meyer grant awarded through the foundation's regular grant-making program.

Geographic Focus: District of Columbia, Maryland, Virginia

Amount of Grant: 5,000 - 25,000 USD

Samples: Maryland Association of Nonprofit Organizations, Baltimore, Maryland, $15,000—to support the executive search.

Contact: Jane Robinson Ward, Grants Manager; (202) 483-8294; fax (202) 328-6850; map@meyerfdn.org or jward@meyerfdn.org

Internet: www.meyerfoundation.org/our-programs/management-assistance/

Sponsor: Meyer Foundation

1250 Connecticut Avenue, Northwest, Suite 800

Washington, D.C. 20036

Meyer Memorial Trust Emergency Grants   **1652**

Meyer Memorial Trust Emergency Grants are intended for sudden, unanticipated and unavoidable challenges that, if not addressed immediately, could threaten an organization's stability and/or ability to achieve its mission. Examples of emergencies would include: natural disaster; theft or damage to equipment required to operate core programs; or an accident or unexpected occurrence that causes facilities to be inaccessible or programs unable to be operated until the situation is resolved. Emergency proposals can be considered at any program meeting. The application and frequently asked questions are available at the Trust's website.

Requirements: Any 501(c)3 organization supporting the residents of Oregon are welcome to apply. Applicants must fall into one of these categories: a nonprofit agency recognized as tax-exempt by the Internal Revenue Service; a public educational institution; a government or recognized Tribal agency; or an organization that is requesting funding for a project that has a charitable, tax-exempt purpose. Further requirements include that the applicant must: be seeking funding for work that takes place within the state of Oregon; provide equal opportunity in leadership, staffing in service regardless of age, gender, race, ethnicity, sexual orientation, disability, national origin, political affiliation or religious belief; and not require attendance at or participation in religious/faith activities as a condition of service delivery nor require adherence to religious/faith beliefs as a condition of service or employment.

Restrictions: Processing grant requests may take up to 45 days. MMT's Emergency Grants are not intended to address an organization's failure to comply with legal requirements or problems that can be attributed to organizational neglect; failure to plan for likely contingencies, such as the breakdown of aging equipment; or to replace a gradual loss of organizational funding. In addition, the Emergency Grant program cannot be used solely to expedite the standard processing time for a Responsive or Grassroots Grants application.

Geographic Focus: Oregon

Amount of Grant: 7,500 - 100,000 USD

Samples: Wheeler County, Fossil, Oregon, $10,000 - for an emergency roof repair for Isobel Edwards Hall, which houses the senior meals program and other community programs; Northwest Professional Dance Project, Portland, Oregon, $25,000 - to help this Portland-based dance company weather a challenging disruption of operations; Corvallis Community Children's Centers, Corvallis, Oregon, $53,000 - to help this community childcare provider address a sudden, unanticipated financial emergency.

Contact: Chanta Chhay, Grants Manager; (503) 228-5512; chanta@mmt.org

Internet: mmt.org/our-portfolios/

Sponsor: Meyer Memorial Trust

425 NW 10th Avenue, Suite 400

Portland, OR 97209

Meyer Memorial Trust Responsive Grants   **1653**

Responsive Grants are awarded in the areas of human services; health; affordable housing; community development; conservation and environment; public affairs; arts and culture; and education. Funding ranges from $40,000 to $300,000, with grants periods from one to three years in length. Responsive grants help support many kinds of projects, including core operating support, building and renovating facilities, and strengthening organizations. There are two stages of consideration before Responsive Grants are awarded. Initial Inquiries are accepted at any time through MMT's online grants application. Applicants that pass initial approval are invited to submit full proposals. The full two-step proposal investigation usually takes five to seven months. Final decisions on Responsive Grants are made by trustees monthly, except in January, April and August. Additional information about the application process, along with the online application, is available at the website.

Requirements: Any 501(c)3 organization supporting the residents of Oregon are welcome to apply. Applicants must fall into one of these categories: a nonprofit agency recognized as tax-exempt by the Internal Revenue Service; a public educational institution; a government or recognized Tribal agency; or an organization that is requesting funding for a project that has a charitable, tax-exempt purpose. Further requirements include that the applicant must: be seeking funding for work that takes place within the state of Oregon; provide equal opportunity in leadership, staffing in service regardless of age, gender, race, ethnicity, sexual orientation, disability, national origin, political affiliation or religious belief; and not require attendance at or participation in religious/faith activities as a condition of service delivery nor require adherence to religious/faith beliefs as a condition of service or employment.

Restrictions: The Trust does not fund: work that does not have a significant impact in Oregon; direct grants, scholarships or loans to individuals; endowments; general fund drives, annual appeals, special events or, except in rare cases, conference sponsorships; Program Related Investments (loans and guarantees) to a specific project; elimination of operating deficits; medical research; animal welfare; hospital capital construction; projects/organizations that do not meet the Trust's nondiscrimination policy; earmarks for purposes of influencing legislation; or any expenditures that would violate Meyer's, or a grantee's, tax-exempt status.

Geographic Focus: Oregon

Amount of Grant: 40,000 - 300,000 USD

Samples: Crow's Shadow Institute, Pendleton, Oregon, $165,000 - for organizational support to help boost the programming capacity of this arts organization serving members of the Confederated Tribes of the Umatilla Indian Reservation; Immigration Counseling Service, Portland, Oregon, $66,500 - for outreach, education and legal services to support immigrant integration across Oregon; College Possible, Gresham, Oregon, $135,000 - to support college access and a success program for low-income Portland students.

Contact: Chanta Chhay, Grants Manager; (503) 228-5512; chanta@mmt.org

Internet: mmt.org/our-portfolios/

Sponsor: Meyer Memorial Trust

425 NW 10th Avenue, Suite 400

Portland, OR 97209

MFRI Community Mobilization Grants   **1654**

One of the primary missions of the Military Family Research Institute is to assist communities in supporting local members of the military and their families. To that end, MFRI offers competitive small monetary grants of up to $2,500 to community organizations and family support groups that strive to improve the quality of life for military families. MFRI designed the competitive Community Mobilization Grant program to support, grow and influence programs and practices that assist and support military families and veterans in local Indiana communities. Grants that include a component related to homelessness, education, employment and/or mental wellness will receive a higher priority in the competitive grant scoring. The grants may be used to: increase availability and resources to innovative programming designed to support and assist military families and veterans across Indiana; increase access to resources available to military families; increase community awareness and understanding of the military family experience; and decrease the unmet needs of military families in Indiana communities. Two annual deadlines have been identified as April 15 and August 15.

Requirements: This program is open only to Family Readiness Groups in the state of Indiana.

Restrictions: No grant funds can be used for the purchase or consumption of alcoholic beverages. Purdue policy does not allow the use of university funds to purchase gift cards (gas cards, visa or MC gift cards, etc) though gift certificates are an allowable use. Also, no grant funds will be issued to an individual; all checks will be made out to organizations.

Geographic Focus: Indiana

Date(s) Application is Due: Apr 15; Aug 15

Amount of Grant: Up to 2,500 USD

Contact: Martina Sternberg, Assistant Director; (765) 496-3469; msternbe@purdue.edu

Internet: www.mfri.purdue.edu/programs/community-mobilization.aspx

Sponsor: Military Family Research Institute at Purdue University

Purdue West Down Under, 1402 W State Street

West Lafayette, IN 47907-2062

MGM Resorts Foundation Community Grants   **1655**

The MGM Resorts Foundation invites proposals from nonprofit agencies providing direct services to people living in its communities. All of the funds allocated through the Foundation come from employee contributions and their desire to make a difference in the communities where they live and work. Foundation grant allocations are 100% employee-driven. The Foundation empowers MGM Resorts employees to choose to make direct contributions to the agency of their choice, or to contribute to the Community Grant Funds, which provides grants to nonprofits through an annual Request for Proposal (RFP) process. MGM Resorts Foundation grants are for a one-year period and do not automatically renew. Continued or expanded projects and programs (your organization is currently providing these services) can request a per year maximum grant of $65,000 in Southern Nevada;

$10,000 in Northern Nevada, Mississippi and the Detroit, Michigan area. New projects and programs (your organization is not currently providing these services) can request a per year maximum grant of $35,000 in Southern Nevada; $5,000 in Northern Nevada, Mississippi and the Detroit, Michigan area.

Requirements: To receive a grant from the Foundation, your agency must meet the following *Requirements:* Operate as an IRS 501(c)3 organization and have been doing so for a minimum of 36 months; provide service within the regions MGM Resorts employees live, work and care for their families (Nevada, Mississippi, and the greater Detroit, Michigan area); your organization's administrative costs must be 25% or under; provide a human service; and, meet the MGM Resorts diversity policy: open to all people, without regard to race, color, creed, sex, sexual orientation, religion, disability, or national origin. Agencies must request funding for projects/programs that provide services in the following focus areas: Strengthening Neighborhoods (self-sufficiency, revitalization of communities); Strengthening Children (early childhood development, success in school, prevention / intervention); and, Strength in Difficult Times (recovery and counseling services). Proposals must be received by the Foundation by 5:00 pm of the deadline date.

Restrictions: The program does not support the following types of organizations or activities: projects/programs that are exclusively for medical research; public schools or privately funded / tuition-based schools; governmental entities; religious organizations that do not have 501(c)3 status; pass-through agencies (organizations whose staff does not provide direct client services but who allocate funding to subsequent organizations to provide projects/programs and services); sponsorship of special events and/or fundraising activities; capital campaigns or endowment funds; political issues, such as, election campaigns, issue endorsements, bill drafts or legislation reform; organizations that require clients to embrace specific beliefs or traditions; projects/programs that are exclusively recreational or athletic sponsorships; membership-based organizations without a sliding fee scale and scholarship system already in place.

Geographic Focus: Michigan, Mississippi, Nevada
Date(s) Application is Due: May 2
Amount of Grant: 5,000 - 65,000 USD
Contact: Shelley Gitomer, Vice President of Philanthropy & Community Engagement; (702) 692-9643; foundation@mgmresorts.com
Internet: www.mgmresortsfoundation.org/grants/
Sponsor: MGM Resorts Foundation
3260 Industrial Road
Las Vegas, NV 89109

MGN Family Foundation Grants   1656

The MGN Family Foundation makes grants to qualified 501(c)3 organizations specializing in the following areas: education; health care and medical research; children in need; armed service personnel. Areas of particular interest include: colleges, universities and private schools, examples would be: to fund a chair to provide lecturers in literature, philosophy or the arts, and provide scholarships; hospitals and clinics that specialize in excellent patient care and continuing medical research such as Memorial Sloan-Kettering Cancer Center and the Mayo and Cleveland Clinics are other examples, also under consideration would be hospice organizations that provide palliative care to the dying; organizations that support children in need whether due to emotional, physical abuse, neglect or disadvantaged circumstances. Support can be for basic necessities such as food, shelter, education, medical as well as, spiritual and emotional counseling; in light of recent events, this Foundation would like to offer assistance to our servicemen/ servicewomen and their families through those charities which give support to their unique needs. The examples provided above reflect the true mission and goals of the MGN Foundation. There should be no exclusions due to race or creed, provided all applicants have a strong moral base and core values in the areas of education, health care, welfare of children and service personnel and their families. The Foundation Board meets semi-annually in May and November. Applications are due by April 1st and October 1st. Application form is available online.

Requirements: Qualified 501(c)3 organizations specializing in the following areas: education; health care and medical research; children in need; armed service personnel. To apply, submit seven (7) sets of the following items: Grant application form completed, dated, and signed by the Chief Executive Officer or Chairman of the Board of the organization; list of Board of Directors; Financial Statement (audited if available), for the most recent complete fiscal year; copy of IRS 501(c)3 Determination Letter. If you wish, you may submit your proposal in a narrative format of not more than two pages in addition to the completed application form. Optional materials may be submitted but are not required (such as brochures discussing or depicting the activities of the organization).

Restrictions: Do not staple materials or place them in a bound notebook.
Geographic Focus: All States
Date(s) Application is Due: Apr 1; Oct 1
Amount of Grant: 1,000 - 10,000 USD
Samples: Agnes Scott College, $3,000—scholarship; Vermont National Guard Charitable Foundation, Inc., $3,000—wounded veteran program; Center for Molecular Medicine and Immunology/Garden State, $5,000—foster research for new technologies in the diagnosis, detection and treatment of cancer.
Contact: Pamela Nothstein, Grants Manager; (843) 937-4614; grantinquiries7@wachovia.com
Internet: www.mgnfamilyfoundation.org/
Sponsor: MGN Family Foundation
16 Broad Street (SC1000)
Charleston, SC 29401

Michael and Susan Dell Foundation Grants   1657

The Michael and Susan Dell Foundation's primary goal is to support and initiate programs that directly serve the needs of children living in urban poverty. The Foundation focuses on education, health, and family economic stability to help ensure that underprivileged

children escape poverty to become healthy, productive adults. Priority is given to initiatives addressing children's health, education and microfinance, as well as initiatives in India and Central Texas that specifically address the needs of children. Grant amounts vary, but generally the Foundation does not fund more than 25% of a project's budget or more than 10% of an organization's total annual operating expenses.

Requirements: Before beginning a formal grant application, organizations must meet basic eligibility requirements for funding, then submit an online grant proposal via the Foundation website. The proposal will be reviewed, then the organization will receive an emailed response to the proposal within six weeks. Organizations are encouraged to review the Foundation's priorities before beginning the proposal. They are also encouraged to review the master grant list page for more in-depth explanations, including specific instructions for the online grant proposal.

Restrictions: Proposals must be submitted through the Foundation's online form. Proposals by mail are not accepted. In general, the Foundation does not support programs or organizations that fall outside of their key focus areas, nor does it accept proposals to support individuals, medical research projects, event fundraisers or sponsorships, endowments, or lobbying of any kind.

Geographic Focus: Texas, India, South Africa
Contact: Janet Mountain; (512) 732-2765; fax (512) 600-5501; info@msdf.org
Internet: www.msdf.org/grants/Grant_Application
Sponsor: Michael and Susan Dell Foundation
P.O. Box 163867
Austin, TX 78716-3867

Michael Reese Health Trust Core Grants   1658

The primary focus of the Michael Reese Health Trust is to improve the health status and well-being of vulnerable populations in the Chicago metropolitan area. The Health Trust is committed to supporting community-based health-related services and education that are effective, accessible, affordable, and culturally competent. It is especially interested in efforts to address the barriers that prevent vulnerable groups from accessing quality health care, and in programs that deliver comprehensive, coordinated services. Each year, the Health Trust awards a small number of Core grants. Core grants are larger, multi-year grants designed to strengthen both program quality and organizational capacity. Organizations approved by Health Trust staff may request up to $100,000 a year for each of three years for a total of up to $300,000.

Requirements: Nonprofit organizations operating in the Chicago metropolitan area are eligible to apply, but preference is given to organizations within the City of Chicago. The applicant must have a 501(c)3 and non-private foundation determination letter from the Internal Revenue Service and be designated as a public charity under section 509(a)1 or 509(a)2, of the Internal Revenue Code. Generally, the Health Trust does not provide grants to 509(a)3 "supporting organizations." Organizations must be non-discriminatory in the hiring of staff and in providing services on the basis of race, religion, gender, sexual orientation, age, national origin or disability. Qualified applicants must have prior approval from Health Trust staff to submit a Core grant request. Contact the Program Officer by phone or by email to discuss how your organization would use a Core grant. Once staff approval has been obtained, the sponsor will send an invitation to submit a Letter of Inquiry for a Core grant through its online application process. The Health Trust awards grants twice a year. The submission deadlines for Letters of Inquiry are June 15 (for grants to run January 1 through December 31) and December 15 (for grants to run July 1 through June 30). If the due date falls on a weekend, they will accept submissions until 5:00pm the following business day. Core grants should focus on the following: quality of services; planning for and supporting staff, volunteers and activities fundamental to the organization's health-related mission; mission-related infrastructure needs; and/or sustainability of the agency and its health services. Use of evidence-based practices or using the Core grant to systematically learn about and implement evidence-based practices is encouraged. Participation in this program requires a willingness to share findings and lessons learned in order to assist other Health Trust grantees and others in the field.

Restrictions: Grants do not support: lobbying, propaganda, or other attempts to influence legislation; sectarian purposes (programs that promote or require a religious doctrine); capital needs, such as buildings, renovations, vehicles, and major equipment; durable medical equipment; fundraising events, including sponsorship, tickets, and advertising; or, debt reduction; individual and scholarship support. In general, the Health Trust does not provide endowment support.

Geographic Focus: Illinois
Date(s) Application is Due: Jun 15; Dec 15
Amount of Grant: Up to 300,000 USD
Contact: Jennifer M. Rosenkranz, (312) 726-1008; jrosenkranz@healthtrust.net
Internet: www.healthtrust.net/content/how-apply/new-applicants/application-procedures
Sponsor: Michael Reese Health Trust
150 North Wacker Drive, Suite 2320
Chicago, IL 60606

Michael Reese Health Trust Responsive Grants   1659

The primary focus of the Michael Reese Health Trust is to improve the health status and well-being of vulnerable populations in the Chicago metropolitan area. The Health Trust is committed to supporting community-based health-related services and education that are effective, accessible, affordable, and culturally competent. It is especially interested in efforts to address the barriers that prevent vulnerable groups from accessing quality health care, and in programs that deliver comprehensive, coordinated services. Responsive grants generally range from $25,000-$60,000. The Health Trust will entertain requests for program support and general operating and for both one-year and multi-year projects. However, multi-year grants are generally considered for organizations that have received significant prior Health Trust support. Requests may be for continuation or expansion of a current program, or a new program.

Requirements: Nonprofit organizations operating in the Chicago metropolitan area are eligible to apply, but preference is given to organizations within the City of Chicago. The applicant must have a 501(c)3 and non-private foundation determination letter from the Internal Revenue Service and be designated as a public charity under section 509(a)1 or 509(a)2, of the Internal Revenue Code. Generally, the Health Trust does not provide grants to 509(a)3 "supporting organizations." Organizations must be non-discriminatory in the hiring of staff and in providing services on the basis of race, religion, gender, sexual orientation, age, national origin or disability. The Health Trust awards grants twice a year. The submission deadlines for Letters of Inquiry are June 15 (for grants to run January 1 through December 31) and December 15 (for grants to run July 1 through June 30). If the due date falls on a weekend, they will accept submissions until 5:00pm the following business day.
Restrictions: Grants do not support: lobbying, propaganda, or other attempts to influence legislation; sectarian purposes (programs that promote or require a religious doctrine); capital needs, such as buildings, renovations, vehicles, and major equipment; durable medical equipment; fundraising events, including sponsorship, tickets, and advertising; or, debt reduction; individual and scholarship support. In general, the Health Trust does not provide endowment support.
Geographic Focus: Illinois
Date(s) Application is Due: Jun 15; Dec 15
Amount of Grant: 25,000 - 60,000 USD
Contact: Jennifer M. Rosenkranz, Senior Program Officer for Responsive Grants; (312) 726-1008; fax (312) 726-2797; jrosenkranz@healthtrust.net
Internet: www.healthtrust.net/content/how-apply/new-applicants/grantmaking-guidelines
Sponsor: Michael Reese Health Trust
150 North Wacker Drive, Suite 2320
Chicago, IL 60606

Michelin North America Challenge Education 1660

The Michelin Challenge Education program provides support to public Title 1 schools in the form of tutors, mentors, lunch buddies and financial contributions. Michelin's goal for the program is to provide human capital to positively impact the lives of disadvantaged children. With emphasis on reading, science and math, the program has spread throughout all Michelin locations in the U.S. and is being introduced in Canada. Improved test scores validate that the involvement of Michelin employees is making a difference. Michelin also makes charitable contributions to nonprofit organizations involved with STEM (science, technology, engineering, and math) education, the environment, and automotive safety.
Requirements: Support is given on a national basis in areas of company operations in Alabama, Indiana, Kentucky, North Carolina, Oklahoma, and South Carolina, and in Canada.
Restrictions: No support is provided for religious organizations not of direct benefit to the entire community, political candidates or lobbying organizations, fraternal, labor, veterans', or similar organizations with a limited constituency, or anti-business organizations. No grants are awarded to individuals, or for travel, national conferences, sports events, or other one-time, short-term events, advertising, or team sponsorships or athletic scholarships.
Geographic Focus: Alabama, Indiana, Kentucky, North Carolina, Oklahoma, South Carolina, Canada
Contact: Stephanie Tarbet; (864) 458-4548; Stephanie.Tarbet@us.michelin.com
Internet: michelinmedia.com/community-relations/
Sponsor: Michelin North America Corporate Giving
P.O. Box 19001, 1 Parkway South
Greenville, SC 29602-9001

Michelle O'Neill Foundation Grants 1661

The Michelle O'Neill Foundation is a not-for-profit organization (exempt from Federal Income tax under Section 501(c)3 of the Internal Revenue Code) to benefit children with cancer and special needs. The Foundation was established in 1997 in memory of a courageous young woman whose love of life and incredible courage have inspired U.S. to carry out her wish of helping others and letting people know that we care. The Foundation hosts an annual volleyball tournament fundraiser the first Saturday after Labor Day on Grand Avenue in Long Beach, New York, when people gather to play or just watch the competitive and recreational games, enjoy music, raffles, food and merchandise. It raised approximately $17,000 in 1997 at its 1st Annual Michelle O'Neill volleyball tournament. The Foundation's mission is to provide financial assistance and relief to families who are facing the economic and emotional stresses associated with caring for a child with a catastrophic illness and to support oncology organizations that serve them.
Geographic Focus: All States
Contact: Carol O'Neill, President; info@monfoundation.org
Internet: www.monfoundation.org/
Sponsor: Michelle O'Neill Foundation
P.O. Box 478
Long Beach, NY 11561

Michigan Women Forward Grants 1662

In 1986, Mary Jo Pulte gathered a group of 30 Michigan women to discuss philanthropy and the imbalance in donations to women's programs. At that time, only 3% of philanthropic dollars went to programs for women and girls in the United States. Empowered to change that statistic, the women founded Michigan Women Forward, formerly known as Michigan Women's Foundation: the only public, statewide foundation devoted to the economic and personal well-being of Michigan women and girls. Michigan Women Forward (MWF) is committed to creating positive change for Michigan's women and girls. As a statewide foundation, MWF seeks to transform Michigan to achieve equality and empowerment for its women and girls. The Foundation does this by raising funds to support and collaborate with individuals and organizations to address and eliminate barriers to economic and social

equality for Michigan women and girls. The range for mini-grants is $1,000 to $5,000; the range for social impact grants is $10,000 to $50,000.
Requirements: All funding requests must be from Michigan based organizations that: are non-profits and tax exempt under IRS code, section 501(c)3; serve Michigan women and girls, with emphasis on low-income, marginalized and diverse populations; and address at least one of the MWF's funding priorities and create social change.
Restrictions: The foundation does not fund: organizations outside of the state of Michigan; endowments or tickets/tables for special events; capital campaigns or building projects; individual requests for scholarships, tuition reimbursements, grants, or loans; political campaigns, political organizations, Political Action Committees (PACs), or lobbying.
Geographic Focus: Michigan
Date(s) Application is Due: Jul 31
Amount of Grant: 1,000 - 50,000 USD
Contact: Joyce L. Suber, Executive Director; (313) 771-3514 or (313) 962-1920; fax (313) 962-1926; grants@miwf.org or jsuber@miwf.org
Internet: www.miwf.org/
Sponsor: Michigan Women Forward
1155 Brewery Park Boulevard, Suite 350
Detroit, MI 48207

Michigan Youth Livestock Scholarship and State-Wide Scholarship 1663

Since 2000, the Michigan Youth Livestock Scholarship Fund (MYLSF) has been awarding scholarships annually to outstanding youth who exhibit at the Michigan State Fair, Michigan livestock Expo and Michigan Dairy Expo. Applications will be judged on fair participation, leadership, citizenship, and scholastic standing. The MYLSF Scholarship will award up to $1,500 to a single recipient; the State-Wide Scholarship will award up to $1,000 to a single recipient.
Requirements: Applicants must be graduating high school seniors or high school graduates continuing their education at accredited institutions in the year in which they are applying. For the MYLSF Scholarship they must be a youth exhibitor at the Michigan State Fair, the Michigan Livestock Expo or the Michigan Dairy Expo for a minimum of three (3) calendar years prior to the year of application. For the Statewide Scholarship they must be a youth exhibitor at a local, county, state-wide exhibition or state fair for a minimum of three (3) years prior to the year of application. Preference will be given to applicants pursuing agricultural or related fields. Applicants may apply for and receive a scholarship more than once, preference given to new applicants and past nonrecipients. Scholarship winners will be announced at the Michigan Livestock Sale-Abration.
Geographic Focus: Michigan
Date(s) Application is Due: May 31
Amount of Grant: 1,000 - 1,500 USD
Contact: Ernie Birchmeier, (517) 323-7000 x2024; ebirchm@michfb.com
Mary Kelpinski, (517) 853-3782; Kelpinski@mipork.org
Internet: www.michigan.gov/mdard/0,4610,7-125-1571_40997—-,00.html
Sponsor: Michigan Department of Agriculture and Rural Development
P.O. Box 30017
Lansing, MI 48909

Micron Technology Foundation Community Grants 1664

The Micron Foundation funds educational and community grants in specific program areas in communities where Micron has manufacturing facilities. These sites are: Boise, Idaho; Manassas, Virginia; Singapore; Avezzano, Italy; and Nishiwaki, Japan. The Foundation's goals are to fund high-impact programs that drive advancements in education, with emphasis on science, math and engineering. Specifically, the Foundation seeks to: provide opportunities for hands-on experiences; improve teacher content knowledge; support extracurricular science and math opportunities; provide advanced learning opportunities with advanced placement classes; and fund charitable programs that address the priorities and concerns of Micron communities.
Requirements: Applicants must be 501(c)3 organizations or a publicly funded academic group in an area where Micron has a presence. Applications can be downloaded at the website but must be submitted by mail.
Restrictions: Funding is not provided for: general operating costs; individuals; religious, fraternal, veteran or political organizations; luncheons, dinners, auctions, or events; travel and related expenses; courtesy advertisement; endowment campaigns; organizations which promote or practice discrimination; organizations outside of Micron communities; Annual Fund drives; "pass-through" organizations or private foundations; or projects seeking to influence elections or legislation.
Geographic Focus: Idaho, Virginia, Italy, Japan, Singapore
Contact: Kami Faylor, Program Contact; (208) 363-3675; mtf@micron.com
Internet: www.micron.com/about/giving/foundation/comgrants.html
Sponsor: Micron Technology Foundation
8000 South Federal Way, P.O. Box 6
Boise, ID 83707-0006

Microsoft Software Donations 1665

Microsoft awards software product donations to a variety of nonprofit organizations in both the Puget Sound area, where its headquarters are located, and around the country. For this program, grants will be awarded to large nonprofit organizations with multiple locations to help enhance communications, boost organizational efficiency, make use of the Internet, and improve services to clients. Applicants may request a limited number of full-packaged products and up to 1000 licenses per product. Donations are demand-driven, based on the requests of individual nonprofits to meet their organizational needs. The process for requesting a software donations depends on the location of your organization.

Requirements: Eligible are 501(c)3 nonprofit organizations. Applicants must have the hardware capable of running the software requested and must have the IT staff or a technology assistance provider, for both the national and field offices, to implement and maintain the software offered with this award.
Restrictions: Applicants may not be hospitals or medical clinics; political, labor, religious, or fraternal organizations; educational institutions, public or private; or government organizations.
Geographic Focus: All States
Contact: Lori Forte Harnick, General Manager, Citizenship and Public Affairs; (425) 882-8080; fax (425) 936-7329; cause@microsoft.com or giving@microsoft.com
Internet: www.microsoft.com/about/philanthropies/
Sponsor: Microsoft Corporation
One Microsoft Way
Redmond, WA 98052-6399

Microsoft YouthSpark Grants   **1666**
Through the YouthSpark initiative, Microsoft pledges to create opportunities for 300 million youth. The company partners with youth-serving nonprofits to encourage youth to change their lives and make a real impact in their local communities and on the global stage. YouthSpark grants are awarded to nonprofit organizations designed to support youth development. Through the global initiative, scores of nonprofit organizations around the world will receive cash donations and other resources to provide computer science education to diverse populations of young people in their communities and prepare them with the computational-thinking and problem-solving skills necessary for success in an increasingly digital world.
Geographic Focus: All States, All Countries
Contact: Lori Forte Harnick, General Manager, Citizenship and Public Affairs; (425) 882-8080; fax (425) 936-7329; cause@microsoft.com or giving@microsoft.com
Internet: www.microsoft.com/about/philanthropies/youthspark/
Sponsor: Microsoft Corporation
One Microsoft Way
Redmond, WA 98052-6399

Mid-Iowa Health Foundation Community Response Grants   **1667**
Mid-Iowa Health Foundation awards grants to organizations working towards improving the health of people in greater Des Moines, Iowa. The Foundation is interested in work that affects specific health results and aligns with community-identified priorities. The focus for Community Response grants is the Greater Des Moines Health Safety Net System. The health care safety net provides appropriate, timely and affordable health services to people who experience barriers to accessing services from other providers due to financial, cultural, linguistic, or other issues. These core safety net providers offer care to patients in Greater Des Moines, Iowa regardless of their ability to pay for services, and primarily serve vulnerable, low-income patients who are uninsured, publicly insured or underinsured. Community Response grants average $10,000 to $30,000. The Foundation may consider partially funding a proposal, if acceptable to the grantee.
Requirements: Applicant organizations must: be tax-exempt, 501(c)3 and/or 509(a) status; serve the greater Des Moines, Iowa area (Polk, Warren, and/or Dallas Counties); and, offer health programs and services aligned with the Foundation's mission. The Foundation will consider proposals from core safety net providers for: preventive and primary safety net health services, including behavioral and oral health; critical elements of the safety net system such as coordinated outreach, system navigation, and culturally competent services; meeting increased demands on a safety net system with capacity, financial and workforce stressors. Mid-Iowa Health Foundation reviews Community Response proposals once annually. Proposals are due by noon on October 1; if the 1st falls on a weekend, proposals are due by noon on the preceding Friday.
Restrictions: The Mid-Iowa Health Foundation does not consider proposals for: individuals; scholarships; conference registration fees; programs that promote religious activities; general operations or special camps of disease- or condition-specific organizations; capital campaigns; endowment campaigns; debt reduction; or, fund raising events.
Geographic Focus: Iowa
Date(s) Application is Due: Oct 1
Amount of Grant: Up to 30,000 USD
Contact: Denise Swartz, Sr. Program Officer; (515) 277-6411; dswartz@midiowahealth.org
Internet: www.midiowahealth.org/grants.html
Sponsor: Mid-Iowa Health Foundation
3900 Ingersoll Avenue, Suite 104
Des Moines, IA 50312

Middlesex Savings Charitable Foundation Basic Human Needs Grants   **1668**
Since June of 2000, the Middlesex Savings Charitable Foundation has provided more than $2 million in grants to over 200 non-profit organizations providing critical community services throughout Eastern and Central Massachusetts. Established as a nonprofit, private charitable foundation, the Foundation carries out the philanthropic mission of Middlesex Savings Bank, supporting nonprofit organizations, services and programs in a wide variety of fields, including education, public health and welfare, the arts, and community development. The Basic Human Needs Program funds projects and programs whose primary focus is on food, shelter, and clothing for low-and moderate-income and vulnerable populations. Food pantries may apply, but the request must be for a program or other initiative, with no more than 25% of grant proceeds used towards the purchase of food related to the broader initiative. Grant requests of up to $20,000 will be considered. Applicants may apply online. The annual deadlines are April 1 and August 1.
Requirements: Eastern Massachusetts 501(c)3 tax-exempt organizations serving one or more communities served by Middlesex Savings Bank, including Acton, Ashland, Ayer, Bedford, Bellingham, Berlin, Bolton, Boxborough, Carlisle, Chelmsford, Concord, Dover, Dunstable, Framingham, Franklin, Groton, Harvard, Holliston, Hopedale, Hopkinton,

Hudson, Lexington, Lincoln, Littleton, Marlborough, Maynard, Medfield, Medway, Mendon, Milford, Millis, Natick, Needham, Newton, Norfolk, Northborough, Pepperell, Sherborn, Shirley, Southborough, Stow, Sudbury, Townsend, Tyngsborough, Upton, Walpole, Waltham, Wayland, Wellesley, Westborough, Westford, and Weston, are eligible. Projects for which support is requested should benefit people who live or work in the region.
Restrictions: The foundation will not fund political or sectarian activities.
Geographic Focus: Massachusetts
Date(s) Application is Due: Apr 1; Aug 1
Amount of Grant: Up to 20,000 USD
Contact: Mike Kuza, (508) 315-5361 or (508) 315-5360; mkuza@middlesexbank.com
Internet: www.middlesexbank.com/community-and-us/community-support/Pages/charitable-foundation.aspx
Sponsor: Middlesex Savings Charitable Foundation
P.O. Box 5210
Westborough, MA 01581-5210

Middlesex Savings Charitable Foundation Capacity Building Grants   **1669**
Since June of 2000, the Middlesex Savings Charitable Foundation has provided more than $2 million in grants to over 200 non-profit organizations providing critical community services throughout Eastern and Central Massachusetts. Established as a nonprofit, private charitable foundation, the Foundation carries out the philanthropic mission of Middlesex Savings Bank, supporting nonprofit organizations, services and programs in a wide variety of fields, including education, public health and welfare, the arts, and community development. The Capacity Building Program funds initiatives designed to strengthen and increase the impact of local non-profits by improving their organizational capacity. Desired outcomes for non-profits selected to receive grants through this program include one or more of the following: improved governance and leadership; improved staff skills; improved management systems and practices; completed strategic plans; improved, expanded, or additional services; and expanded strategic assets, including financial and human resources. Successful applicants will be able to describe how their enhanced capacity will ultimately benefit the communities that they serve. Grant requests of up to $20,000 will be considered. Applicants may apply online. The annual deadlines are April 1 and August 1.
Requirements: Eastern Massachusetts 501(c)3 tax-exempt organizations serving one or more communities served by Middlesex Savings Bank, including Acton, Ashland, Ayer, Bedford, Bellingham, Berlin, Bolton, Boxborough, Carlisle, Chelmsford, Concord, Dover, Dunstable, Framingham, Franklin, Groton, Harvard, Holliston, Hopedale, Hopkinton, Hudson, Lexington, Lincoln, Littleton, Marlborough, Maynard, Medfield, Medway, Mendon, Milford, Millis, Natick, Needham, Newton, Norfolk, Northborough, Pepperell, Sherborn, Shirley, Southborough, Stow, Sudbury, Townsend, Tyngsborough, Upton, Walpole, Waltham, Wayland, Wellesley, Westborough, Westford, and Weston, are eligible. Projects for which support is requested should benefit people who live or work in the region. Given the continuing economic challenges faced by MSCF communities, the Board will be focusing upon, and giving preference to, grant submissions from organizations providing basic human services such as food and shelter.
Restrictions: The Foundation will not fund political or sectarian activities.
Geographic Focus: Massachusetts
Date(s) Application is Due: Apr 1; Aug 1
Amount of Grant: Up to 20,000 USD
Contact: Mike Kuza, (508) 315-5361 or (508) 315-5360; mkuza@middlesexbank.com
Internet: www.middlesexbank.com/community-and-us/community-support/Pages/charitable-foundation.aspx
Sponsor: Middlesex Savings Charitable Foundation
P.O. Box 5210
Westborough, MA 01581-5210

Middlesex Savings Charitable Foundation Educational Opportunities Grants   **1670**
Since June of 2000, the Middlesex Savings Charitable Foundation (MSCF) has provided more than $2 million in grants to over 200 non-profit organizations providing critical community services throughout Eastern and Central Massachusetts. Established as a nonprofit, private charitable foundation, the Foundation carries out the philanthropic mission of Middlesex Savings Bank, supporting nonprofit organizations, services and programs in a wide variety of fields, including education, public health and welfare, the arts, and community development. The Educational Opportunities Program is designed to encourage organizations to provide unique and meaningful educational opportunities to youths and adults. Programs include, but are not limited to: job training and job readiness programs; adult education and English as a Second Language; credit education and home buying seminars; and youth enrichment programs. Grant requests of up to $20,000 will be considered. Applicants may apply online. The annual deadlines are April 1 and August 1.
Requirements: Eastern Massachusetts 501(c)3 tax-exempt organizations serving one or more communities served by Middlesex Savings Bank, including Acton, Ashland, Ayer, Bedford, Bellingham, Berlin, Bolton, Boxborough, Carlisle, Chelmsford, Concord, Dover, Dunstable, Framingham, Franklin, Groton, Harvard, Holliston, Hopedale, Hopkinton, Hudson, Lexington, Lincoln, Littleton, Marlborough, Maynard, Medfield, Medway, Mendon, Milford, Millis, Natick, Needham, Newton, Norfolk, Northborough, Pepperell, Sherborn, Shirley, Southborough, Stow, Sudbury, Townsend, Tyngsborough, Upton, Walpole, Waltham, Wayland, Wellesley, Westborough, Westford, and Weston, are eligible. Projects for which support is requested should benefit people who live or work in the region.
Restrictions: The foundation will not fund political or sectarian activities.
Geographic Focus: Massachusetts
Date(s) Application is Due: Apr 1; Aug 1
Amount of Grant: Up to 20,000 USD
Contact: Mike Kuza, (508) 315-5361 or (508) 315-5360; mkuza@middlesexbank.com

Internet: www.middlesexbank.com/community-and-us/community-support/Pages/charitable-foundation.aspx
Sponsor: Middlesex Savings Charitable Foundation
P.O. Box 5210
Westborough, MA 01581-5210

Mile High United Way Strategic Investment Grants 1671

Through the Strategic Investment Grant program, Mile High United Way invests in proven programs that work to achieve lasting, measurable results focused on ensuring that: children enter school ready to succeed; children are reading at or above grade level by the end of third grade; youth graduate from high school ready for post-secondary education and entry into the workforce; and individuals and families have their basic needs met and are afforded every opportunity to move toward economic success. Grant proposals will be accepted from October 12 through the annual deadline of November 20. All applications should be submitted online.
Restrictions: Paper or email submissions will not be considered.
Geographic Focus: All States
Date(s) Application is Due: Nov 20
Contact: Gayle Walker; (303) 561-2361; gayle.walker@unitedwaydenver.org
Internet: unitedwaydenver.org/strategic-investment-grants
Sponsor: Mile High United Way
711 Park Avenue West
Denver, CO 80205

Milken Family Foundation Grants 1672

The purpose of the Milken Family Foundation is to discover and advance inventive and effective ways of helping people help themselves and those around them lead productive and satisfying lives. The Foundation advances this mission primarily through its work in education and medical research. In education, the Foundation is committed to: strengthening the profession by recognizing and rewarding outstanding educators, and by expanding their professional leadership and policy influence attracting, developing, motivating and retaining the best talent to the teaching profession by means of comprehensive, whole school reform; stimulating creativity and productivity among young people and adults through programs that encourage learning as a lifelong process; and building vibrant communities by involving people of all ages in programs that contribute to the revitalization of their community and to the well-being of its residents. In medical research, the Foundation is committed to: advancing and supporting basic and applied medical research, especially in the areas of prostate cancer and epilepsy, and recognizing and rewarding outstanding scientists in these areas; and supporting basic health care programs to assure the well-being of community members of all ages. Applicants may request funding at any time.
Requirements: Grants are made to 501(c)3 tax-exempt organizations. Grant recipients must have the financial potential to sustain the program for which funding is sought following the period of Foundation support. Preventive programs with long-range goals receive the closest consideration. Applicants should submit a brief written statement that includes: description of project, goals, procedure and personnel; brief background of organization, including number of years in operation, other areas of activity, applicant's qualifications for support, annual operating budget, and previous and current sources of funding; and a letter of exemption from the Internal Revenue Service.
Restrictions: Grants are not made directly to individuals.
Geographic Focus: All States
Samples: Brentwood School, Los Angeles, California, $12,500, educational programs; AIDS Project Los Angeles, Los Angeles, California, $250, medical research; and Center for Jewish Community Studies, Balitomore, Maryland, $70,000, educational programs.
Contact: Richard Sandler; (310) 570-4800; fax (310) 570-4801; admin@mff.org
Internet: www.mff.org/about/about.taf?page=funding
Sponsor: Milken Family Foundation
1250 Fourth Street, 6th Floor
Santa Monica, CA 90401-1353

Miller Foundation Grants 1673

The Miller Foundation focuses on assisting local nonprofit, charitable organizations and governmental agencies with projects that provide the following for the Battle Creek, Michigan, area: economic development; education; health service; human service; neighborhood improvement; arts and culture; recreation and tourism; and leadership. The Miller Foundation Board of Trustees meets every other month to consider grant applications: January, March, May, July, September, and November. Applicants should submit grant applications by the 1st of the month for it to be considered at that month's Board meeting.
Requirements: Nonprofit 501(c)3 organizations located in and working to improve the Battle Creek community are eligible. Organizations should submit a preliminary letter of request, briefly describing their project, its estimated cost, amount requested, and funding from other sources. After reviewing the initial letter, the Foundation staff, if appropriate, will send a formal grant application to the requesting organization.
Restrictions: The Foundation seldom funds an entire project but rather joins with others as they work to improve the quality of life in the Battle Creek community. The Foundation does not make grants to individuals or for continuing operating funds of nonprofit organizations.
Geographic Focus: Michigan
Date(s) Application is Due: Jan 1; Mar 1; May 1; Jul 1; Sep 1; Nov 1
Contact: Sara Wallace, Executive Director; (269) 964-3542; fax (269) 964-8455
Internet: themillerfoundation.com/grants.htm
Sponsor: Miller Foundation
310 WahWahTaySee Way
Battle Creek, MI 49015

Mill Spring Foundation Grants 1674

The Houghton-Carpenter Foundation, more recently renamed the Mill Spring Foundation, was established in Pennsylvania in 1951. Currently, the Foundation's primary fields of interest include: arts and culture; child welfare; communication media; elementary and secondary education; human services; youth development; and zoos. In all cases, these interest areas should serve children and youth, low-income and the poor, people with physical or psycho-social disabilities, visually impaired, or young adults. Funding typically comes in the form of: annual campaigns; capital campaigns; continuing support; emergency funds; equipment purchase; general operations; or program development. Application guidelines are available upon request. Most recent grants have ranged from $500 to $10,000
Requirements: Applicants should submit the following: a copy of the most recent annual report, audited financial statement, or 990; and a copy of the IRS Determination Letter.
Geographic Focus: Pennsylvania
Amount of Grant: 500 - 10,000 USD
Samples: Bethesda Project, Philadelphia, Pennsylvania, $10,000 - care for abandoned poor; National Liberty Museum, Philadelphia, Pennsylvania, $10,000 - life skills program support for inner city youth; Philadelphia Zoo, Philadelphia, Pennsylvania, $10,000 - support of the Corporate Partners program.
Contact: William F. MacDonald Jr., Trustee; (215) 643-9916; wfmacdjr@gmail.com
Sponsor: Mill Spring Foundation
P.O. Box 270
Ambler, PA 19002-0270

Milton and Sally Avery Arts Foundation Grants 1675

Established in 1983 with a donation from Sally M. Avery, the Foundation supports organizations in New York. Awards are restricted to art education, with emphasis on the visual arts, and to further the development of artists through nonprofit institutions, and to artists' communities and residency programs. Current fields of interest include: arts; arts education; elementary and secondary education; higher education; visual arts (painting and sculpture). There are no particular application forms or deadlines. Initial approach should be by letter. The Board meets once per year on January 9th.
Restrictions: No support is offered for religious or political organizations, and no grants are given to individuals.
Geographic Focus: New York
Samples: American Federation of Arts, New York, New York, $4,000 - general operating support; Artist's Space, New York, New York, $5,000 - general operating support; Brooklyn Museum, Brooklyn, New York, $5,000 - general operating support.
Contact: March Avery Cavanaugh; (212) 420-9160 or (212) 595-7338; fax (212) 595-2840
Sponsor: Milton and Sally Avery Arts Foundation
300 Central Park West, Suite 16J
New York, NY 10024

Milton Hicks Wood and Helen Gibbs Wood Charitable Trust Grants 1676

Milton and Helen Wood were modest people who valued hard work. Milton worked as a chemist for Proctor and Gamble, ultimately funding a charitable trust with money made from company stock. Family was important to Helen, and she spent her time and focus supporting her husband in his work. The Milton Hicks Wood and Helen Gibbs Wood Charitable Trust awards approximately 2-3 grants per year to human services organizations in Texas. Grants are typically between $5,000 and $15,000.
Requirements: Applicants must have 501(c)3 tax-exempt status and serve communities in Texas. Applications will be submitted online through the Bank of America website. A grant report is required within 1 year of the grant application date, regardless of whether all of the funds have been spent.
Restrictions: The trust does not support requests from individuals, organizations attempting to influence policy through direct lobbying, or any political campaigns.
Geographic Focus: Texas
Date(s) Application is Due: Aug 1
Amount of Grant: 5,000 - 15,000 USD
Samples: Community Enrichment Center, North Richland Hills, Texas, $5,000 - awarded for Homeless Employment Services; Special Olympics Texas, Fort Worth, Texas, $5,000 - awarded for Greater Ft. Worth Special Olympics Texas program (Youth); Salvation Army Dallas-Fort Worth Metroplex Command, Fort Worth, Texas, $5,000 - awarded to be used solely for social services in Tarrant County, Texas.
Contact: Kelly Garlock, Philanthropic Client Manager; (800) 357-7094; tx.philanthropic@bankofamerica.com or tx.philanthropic@ustrust.com
Internet: www.bankofamerica.com/philanthropic/foundation/?fnId=13
Sponsor: Milton Hicks Wood and Helen Gibbs Wood Charitable Trust
Bank of America NA P.O. Box 831
Dallas, TX 75283-1041

Mimi and Peter Haas Fund Grants 1677

The Mimi and Peter Haas Fund supports early childhood development. Their primary focus is for activities that provide San Francisco's young (ages 2-5), low-income children and their families with access to high-quality early childhood programs that are part of a comprehensive, coordinated system. The Fund recognizes the importance of connecting the work of its direct service grants to the ongoing discussions of public policy and seek specific opportunities to collaborate with organizations to improve early childhood settings. The Fund will also continue trustee-initiated grantmaking to arts, education, public affairs, and health and human services organizations. Applicants should contact the trustee office to begin the application process. There are no particular application forms or deadlines with which to adhere.
Geographic Focus: California
Amount of Grant: Up to USD
Contact: Lynn Merz; (415) 296-9249; fax (415) 296-8842; mphf@mphf.org

Sponsor: Mimi and Peter Haas Fund
201 Filbert Street, 5th Floor
San Francisco, CA 94133-3238

Minnie M. Jones Trust Grants 1678

The Minnie M. Jones Trust was established in 1953 to support and promote quality education programming for underserved children. Special consideration is given to charitable organizations that serve the youth of Denison, Texas and Grayson County, Texas. Grants from the Jones Trust are 1 year in duration. Award amounts go up to $30,000. Grants are awarded twice annually.

Requirements: Applicants must have 501(c)3 tax-exempt status and serve communities in Texas. Applications will be submitted online through the Bank of America website. A grant report is required within 1 year of the grant application date, regardless of whether all of the funds have been spent.

Restrictions: The trust does not support requests from individuals, organizations attempting to influence policy through direct lobbying, or any political campaigns.

Geographic Focus: Texas

Date(s) Application is Due: Jan 1; Aug 1

Amount of Grant: Up to 30,000 USD

Samples: Salvation Army, Sherman, Texas, $10,000 - awarded for Life Skill Classes (2018); Grayson County College Foundation, Denison, Texas, $20,000 - awarded for The Clara Blackford and W. Aubrey Smith Foundation-Grayson College Career and Education Scholarship Fund; Boys and Girls Club of Denison Inc., Denison, Texas, $18,000 - awarded for Moving Great Futures Into the Next Generation Project.

Contact: Kelly Garlock, Philanthropic Client Manager; (800) 357-7094; tx.philanthropic@bankofamerica.com or tx.philanthropic@ustrust.com

Internet: www.bankofamerica.com/philanthropic/foundation/?fnId=92

Sponsor: Minnie M. Jones Trust
P.O. Box 831041
Dallas, TX 75283-1041

MLB Tomorrow Fund Grants 1679

The Baseball Tomorrow Grant funds programs, fields, and equipment purchases for youth baseball in the United States and around the world. Grants enable applicants to address needs unique to their communities. The funds may be used to finance a new program, expand or improve an existing program, undertake a new collaborative effort, or obtain facilities or equipment necessary for youth baseball or softball programs. Organizations seeking to implement or improve a youth baseball and/or softball program for youth ages 10 to 16 are encouraged to apply. Grants are awarded on a quarterly basis after a thorough and selective application process which can last from three to six months. The selection process consists of the following steps: letter of inquiry review; application review and evaluation; site visit; and final selection by the Board of Directors. Organizations are encouraged to apply for the grant to fund grant writing for their project, if needed, with information available at the website. The application or letter of inquiry and all supporting materials must be mailed to the MLB New York address.

Requirements: Organizations are encouraged to carefully review the application process before applying. Evaluation criteria are specific to the individual organization's needs, including field lights, travel and and specific instructions and contacts for international applicants. Applicants should also review the frequently asked questions section, application help guide, budget template, and samples of previous grant recipients on the website.

Restrictions: Grants are not a substitute for existing funding or fundraising activities. Grants do not support routine or recurring operating costs or funding for construction or maintenance of buildings.

Geographic Focus: All States, Canada

Date(s) Application is Due: Jan 1; Apr 1; Jul 1; Oct 1

Amount of Grant: 40,000 USD

Contact: Baseball Tomorrow Grant Contact; (212) 931-7800; fax (212) 949-5654; btf@mlb.com

Internet: mlb.mlb.com/NASApp/mlb/mlb/official_info/community/btf.jsp

Sponsor: Major League Baseball
245 Park Avenue, 31st floor
New York, NY 10167

Mockingbird Foundation Grants 1680

The Mockingbird Foundation (Mockingbird) is a non-profit organization founded by Phish (the rock band) fans in 1996. Since then Mockingbird has distributed over $750,000 to support music-education programs for children. The foundation provides funding through its competitive grants, emergency-related grants, and tour-related grants. Emergency-related grants and tour-related grants are unsolicited grants. Emergency grants come from an Emergency Fund in which 3% of Mockingbird's gross revenues are designated for music-education programs affected by disasters (e.g., hurricanes and tornadoes). Tour-related grants support music-education programs in communities touched by Phish tours and are intended to inspire support for music and arts education and to generate positive press coverage. Competitive grants are awarded to schools and nonprofit organizations through a two-tiered grant-application process. Applicants must first complete an initial inquiry form at Mockingbird's website. If an applicant's project is selected for further consideration, the applicant will then be invited to submit a full and formal proposal. Initial inquiries may be submitted at any time. Mockingbird typically reviews inquiries in August and September, invites full proposals by Halloween, and announces new grants sometime between Christmas and the end of January. Mockingbird encourages projects with diverse or unusual musical styles, genres, forms, and philosophies; projects with unconventional outlets and forms of instruction as well as instruction in unconventional forms; projects that foster creative expression in any musical form (including composition, instrumentation, vocalization, or improvisation); and projects in which skills, as outcomes, are less assessable or even irrelevant. Projects should be experiential and directly engage students with creating and expressing

music. Preference is given to programs that benefit disenfranchised groups, including those with low skill levels, income, education, disabilities, or terminal illness, and/or those in foster-care homes, hospitals, and prisons. Prospective applicants should review the instructions and guidelines given at the website for complete details before making application.

Requirements: Schools and 501(c)3 nonprofit organizations in the United States are eligible. Applicants may apply through a sponsor who meets these qualifications. Mockingbird is particularly interested in organizations with low overhead, innovative approaches, and/or collaborative elements to their work. The foundation encourages geographic diversity and has funded forty-three states to date. Mockingbird is interested in targeting children 18 years or younger, but will consider projects that benefit college students, teachers/instructors, or adult students.

Restrictions: Grants are made on a one-time basis and are non-renewable and non-transferable. Mockingbird does not normally support individuals, fund-raising organizations or events, research, and programs that promote or engage in religious or political doctrine. It is hoped that applicants for Mockingbird grants hire staff and provide services without discriminating on the basis of race, religion, gender, sexual orientation, age, national origin, or disability. Mockingbird supports the provision of instruments, texts, and office materials, and the acquisition of learning space, practice space, performance space, and instructors/instruction. Mockingbird is particularly interested in projects that foster self-esteem and free expression, but does not fund music therapy which is neither education nor music appreciation which does not include participation.

Geographic Focus: All States

Amount of Grant: 100 - 5,000 USD

Samples: Arcola Elementary School, Silver Spring, Maryland, $5,000 - for the purchase of instruments; Tuscano Elementary School, Phoenix, Arizona $2,650 - for the purchase of instruments; Center For World Music, San Diego, California, $5,000 - for the purchase of instruments; Douglas Anderson School of the Arts, Jacksonville, Florida, $2,000 - support of a city tour.

Contact: Ellis Godard, Executive Director; ellis@mbird.org

Internet: mbird.org/funding/guidelines/

Sponsor: Mockingbird Foundation
6948 Luther Circle
Moorpark, CA 93021-2569

Monsanto Access to the Arts Grants 1681

The Monsanto Fund works to substantially and meaningfully improve people's lives around the world. In the St. Louis area, the Fund is designed to help arts organizations broaden opportunities for underserved children and adults in the performing, visual or literary arts. Grants help organizations reach underserved groups and communities, identify the barriers, real or perceived, that keep them from participating in the arts, and implement strategies to reduce barriers and engage them in arts education experiences. Most grants range from $25,000 to $50,000.

Requirements: Eligible applicants must be not-for-profit organizations focused on the arts or offering arts education programming located in one of the 16 eligible St. Louis counties. Preference will be given to organizations that have been in operation for 3 or more years. Preference will be given to arts experiences that are ongoing, rather than one-time events, and can demonstrate a change over time in awareness and interest in arts among young people and/or adults. For school-aged students, preference will be given to programming that is tied to and integrated with educational goals.

Restrictions: Schools are not eligible to apply, however programming can take place in a school. Funding is not intended to cover the purchase or creation of new artwork. Up to 20% of the requested grant amount can be utilized for overhead costs. Only one grant per organization per year will be awarded.

Geographic Focus: Missouri

Date(s) Application is Due: Feb 28; Aug 31

Amount of Grant: 150,000 USD

Contact: Deborah J. Patterson, President; (314) 694-1000; fax (314) 694-6572; monsantofund@monsanto.com

Internet: www.monsantofund.org/grants/st-louis/#access-to-arts

Sponsor: Monsanto Fund
800 North Lindbergh Boulevard
Saint Louis, MO 63167

Monsanto Kids Garden Fresh Grants 1682

In partnership with Gateway Greening, the Monsanto Fund is a proud supporter of youth-centered gardens throughout the world. Gardens are invaluable tools in teaching children how to grow food, showing them the important role food plays in health, and an opportunity to integrate hands-on lessons in not only math and science but all subjects. When the fruits and vegetables grown in youth gardens are integrated into home and school meals, they are a source of vitamins and nutrients children need for cognitive development as well as a source of pride for the kids who helped grow them. There is no cash award. Grantees receive the following: assistance with project planning, coordination, and installation; plant materials, seeds, seedlings, plant beds, soil, compost, mulch, garden tools, season extension items such as materials for hoop houses and cold frames, a produce scale, and a garden sign; curricula to use with young people/students; ongoing technical assistance including training for staff, volunteers, and educators, access to Gateway Greening's education library, garden visits, and workshops; and additional volunteers if needed.

Requirements: To be eligible organizations must be located in St. Louis or St. Louis County and be serving children or youth, 60% of whom qualify for free or reduced lunch. K–12 public schools or school districts, K–12 private, charter, or independent schools, licensed child care facilities, or youth-focused nonprofit organizations serving ages 5–21 that meet this criteria are eligible. Preference will be given to organizations that have been in operation for 3 or more years.

Restrictions: Prior grantees may apply every year for an extension or expansion provided all evaluation paperwork has been submitted and all award expectations have been fulfilled.
Geographic Focus: Missouri
Date(s) Application is Due: May 1
Contact: Deborah J. Patterson, President; (314) 694-1000; fax (314) 694-6572; monsantofund@monsanto.com
Internet: www.monsantofund.org/grants/st-louis/#kids-garden-fresh
Sponsor: Monsanto Fund
800 North Lindbergh Boulevard
Saint Louis, MO 63167

Monsanto Science and Math K-12 Grants   **1683**
The Monsanto Fund works to substantially and meaningfully improve people's lives around the world. In the St. Louis area, the Fund supports programs that inspire and nurture students' interest in science and/or math, offer innovative approaches to teaching or learning in science and math, and foster student achievement in science and/or math. Priority will be given to programs using evidenced-based methodology. Most grants range from $25,000 to $50,000.
Requirements: Eligible applicants must be: a K-12 public school district; part of the Archdiocese School System, a charter school, a K–12 independent or private school with a substantial student population who are economically disadvantaged; or a nonprofit organization that offers student educational enrichment programming or teacher professional development in science and/or math; and located in one of the 16 eligible St. Louis counties. Preference will be given to organizations that have been in operation for 3 or more years.
Restrictions: Private or independent schools are eligible if over 50% of the students served are economically disadvantaged. Up to 20% of the requested grant amount can be utilized for overhead costs. Only one grant per organization per year will be awarded.
Geographic Focus: Missouri
Date(s) Application is Due: Feb 28; Aug 31
Amount of Grant: 150,000 USD
Contact: Deborah J. Patterson; (314) 694-1000; fax (314) 694-6572; monsanto.fund@monsanto.com
Internet: www.monsantofund.org/grants/st-louis/#science-math
Sponsor: Monsanto Fund
800 North Lindbergh Boulevard
Saint Louis, MO 63167

Monsanto United States Grants   **1684**
The Monsanto Fund works to substantially and meaningfully improve people's lives around the world. To encourage the growth of farming communities across the United States, as well as support the communities in which Monsanto employees live and work, the Monsanto Fund invests in various programs across rural America. One area of support is providing basic educational support designed to improve education in farming communities around the world, including supporting schools, libraries, science centers, farmer training programs and academic programs that enrich or supplement school programs. A second area of support is meeting critical needs in communities by supporting nonprofit organizations that help with things such as food security, sanitation, access to clean water, public safety and various other local needs.
Requirements: Applicant must be a tax-exempt public charity with proof of a current 501(c)3 tax letter. Exceptions include government instrumentalities such as public hospitals, public schools, libraries, villages and municipalities. The proposed project must fit within the focus areas of education K-12 or human needs/services. The nonprofit must be experienced and reputable.
Restrictions: Up to 20% of the requested grant amount can be utilized for overhead costs. Funding will not be provided for the following: individual aid or personal support; underwriting deficits; fraternal, labor or veterans organizations, unless the project benefits the general public; benefits, dinners, advertisements; religious, politically partisan or similar groups; endowments; activities that directly support Monsanto marketing programs; projects in which the Monsanto Company has a financial interest or could derive a financial benefit through cash or rights to intellectual property; and organizations that discriminate based on race, creed, ethnicity, religion, sex, age or national origin. United States Grants are restricted to locations outside of the St. Louis region, as that region is funded by other grant programs. The Fund does not work with start-up organizations. The nonprofit must be financially sound. Proof of most current audit is necessary for requests for $10,000 or more.
Geographic Focus: All States
Date(s) Application is Due: Feb 28
Amount of Grant: 20,000 USD
Contact: Deborah J. Patterson; (314) 694-1000; monsantofund@monsanto.com
Internet: www.monsantofund.org/grants/usa/
Sponsor: Monsanto Fund
800 North Lindbergh Boulevard
Saint Louis, MO 63167

Montana Arts Council Cultural and Aesthetic Project Grants   **1685**
In 1975, the Montana Legislature set aside a percentage of the Coal Tax to restore murals in the Capitol and support other cultural and aesthetic projects. This unique funding source is a Cultural Trust, with grant money allocated every two years. Grant funds are derived from the interest earned on the Cultural Trust. In 1983, the Legislature established a Cultural and Aesthetic Projects Advisory Committee with 16 members, half appointed by the Montana Arts Council and half by the Montana Historical Society. The committee reviews all grant proposals and makes funding recommendations to the Legislature, which determines who will receive grant funds. Applications must be for cultural and aesthetic projects including, but not limited to, the visual, performing, literary and media arts, history, archaeology, folklore, archives, collections, research, historic preservation and the construction or renovation of cultural facilities. Applications are encouraged for

applicants serving rural communities, racial and ethnic groups, people with disabilities, institutionalized populations, youth and the aging.
Requirements: Any person, association, group, or a governmental agency may submit an application for funding. Individuals may apply to special projects using a fiscal agent, which is a 501(c)3 incorporated nonprofit tax-exempt organization that is eligible to apply for Cultural Trust grants. You must contact the Montana Arts Council prior to submitting a grant application if you intend to use a fiscal agent. Proposals must be submitted in one of four categories: (1) Special Projects Requesting $4,500 or Less - organizations that are all-volunteer or employ no more than one half-time person; (2) Special Projects - for the expansion of ongoing programs, adding staff or increasing staff time and for specific cultural and aesthetic activities, services or events of limited duration; (3) Operational Support - for cultural institutions that have been formally organized for at least two years with an ongoing program and with paid professional staff and whose budgets reflect only the cost of continuing their program; (4) Capital Expenditures - for additions to a collection or for acquisition of works of art, artifacts or historical documents, historic preservation, purchase of equipment over $5,000, or the construction or renovation of cultural facilities. For Special Projects $4,500 and Under, Special Projects and Operational Support, each grant dollar is matched with one dollar in cash or in-kind goods and services. For Capital Expenditures, each grant dollar is matched with three dollars in cash or in-kind goods and services. Applications must be received by 5:00 pm of the deadline date.
Restrictions: Hard-copy applications will not be accepted. Applications must be completed online. Funds will not be awarded to support projects created to meet school accreditation standards or other mandated requirements or supplant other funds for current or ongoing programs operated by schools, colleges or universities.
Geographic Focus: Montana
Date(s) Application is Due: Aug 1
Amount of Grant: 2,000 - 15,000 USD
Contact: Kristin Han Burgoyne, (406) 444-6449; kburgoyne@mt.gov
Internet: art.mt.gov/orgs/orgs_ca.asp
Sponsor: Montana Arts Council
830 North Warren, First Floor
Helena, MT 59620-2201

Montana Community Foundation Big Sky LIFT Grants   **1686**
The Foundation is committed to improving the lives of Montanans by helping individuals and families achieve their philanthropic goals and by supporting Montana nonprofit organizations. The Foundation administers Big Sky LIFT (Lifting Individuals and Families with Financial Troubles), an emergency relief fund providing grants to families and individuals who are struggling financially due to the economic downturn in Big Sky. Grants will be available in amounts up to $1,000 for individuals and $2,500 for families.
Requirements: Eligible applicants must live or work in the Big Sky area and demonstrate financial hardship. Verify eligibility and application deadlines from the website or by contacting the Foundation.
Geographic Focus: Montana
Date(s) Application is Due: Dec 15
Contact: Cathy Cooney, Program Director; (406) 443-8313, ext. 108; fax (406) 442-0482; ccooney@mtcf.org or info@mtcf.org
Internet: www.mtcf.org/lift.html
Sponsor: Montana Community Foundation
101 North Last Chance Gulch, Suite 211
Helena, MT 59601

Montana Community Foundation Grants   **1687**
The Foundation is committed to improving the lives of Montanans by helping individuals and families achieve their philanthropic goals and by supporting Montana nonprofit organizations. The Foundation has discretionary control over a small number of funds for which the organization maintains competitive grantmaking opportunities for community leaders. Grants range from $5,000 to $50,000.
Restrictions: Unsolicited general grant applications are not accepted, but when there is a competitive grant opportunity the application information is posted on the website.
Geographic Focus: Montana
Samples: Acts of Kindness, Stevensville, Montana, $8,500 - support for Northwest Area Foundation/MCF Horizons Program; American Legion Post 14, Bozeman, Montana, $10,000 - support for new building; and Big Sky Institute for the Advancement of Nonprofits, Helena, Montana, $50,175 - school computers expansion project.
Contact: Cathy Cooney, Program Director; (406) 443-8313, ext. 108; fax (406) 442-0482; ccooney@mtcf.org or info@mtcf.org
Internet: www.mtcf.org/receive.html
Sponsor: Montana Community Foundation
101 North Last Chance Gulch, Suite 211
Helena, MT 59601

Montana Community Foundation Women's Grants   **1688**
The Women's Foundation of Montana is an endowed fund of the Montana Community Foundation. The Women's Foundation of Montana is the leading funder of change for women and girls in Montana. The goals of the Women's Foundation Grants are: to fund programs to build economic self-sufficiency for women and help girls to be economically self-sufficient in adulthood; to provide operating support to organizations creating a systemic change that will increase opportunities for economic self-sufficiency for women and girls; and to promote awareness of the issues affecting economic self-sufficiency for women and girls and build support for systemic change to enhance the economic status of women.
Requirements: Grant funds may support current programs, test new ideas and methods, improve organizational efficiency, or support advocacy efforts. Contact the Program Director for funding information.

Geographic Focus: Montana
Amount of Grant: 1,000 - 10,000 USD
Samples: homeWORD, Missoula, Montana, $5,000 - to support a financial literacy education course for low income women and families; Montana Credit Unions for Community Development, Statewide, Montana, $10,000 - to support current financial education programs; and Montana Women Vote, Billings, Missoula, Bozeman, Helena, and Great Falls, Montana, $10,000 - to support voter education and mobilization, leadership development, and policy advocacy efforts.
Contact: Jen Euell; (406) 443-8313; fax (406) 442-0482; jeuell@mtcf.org or info@mtcf.org
Internet: www.mtcf.org/wfmt.html
Sponsor: Montana Community Foundation
101 North Last Chance Gulch, Suite 211
Helena, MT 59601

Montgomery County Community Foundation Health and Human Services Fund Grants   **1689**
The Montgomery County Community Foundation Grants help fund non-profit organizations and agencies in Montgomery County, Indiana. Significant grants have been awarded to organizations such as the Crawfordsville District Public Library, Boys and Girls Club, and the Family Crisis Shelter. Grants in the area of health and human services include activities that: improve and promote health outcomes; provide general and rehabilitative health services; offer mental health services; provide crisis intervention programs; strengthen associations or services associated with specific diseases, disorders, and medical disciplines; and support medical research. There are three annual deadlines, including: February 12; July 16; and October 8.
Requirements: Grant applications will be accepted from any new or existing nonprofit organization in Montgomery County. These organizations must be a tax-exempt organization whose purposes are described in Section 501(c)3 of the Internal Revenue Service Code. Grant applications will also be accepted from local governmental entities, such as the three Montgomery County school corporations, for charitable purposes. A strong proposal will have several or all of the following characteristics: an estimate of who and how many will benefit; show long term potential; address a community problem of some significance for which funding is not covered by the regular budget; present an innovative and practical approach to solve a community problem or project; identify possible future funding, if needed; give evidence of the stability and qualifications of the organization applying; show cooperation within the organization and avoid duplication effort.
Restrictions: The Foundation will usually not fund any of the following: grants to individuals; programs which are religious or sectarian in nature, except when the program is open to the entire community; operating expenses such as salaries and utilities; parades, festivals and sporting events; endowment funds; any propaganda, political or otherwise, attempting to influence legislation or intervene in any political affairs or campaigns; an organization's past debts or existing obligations; or post-event or after-the-fact situations.
Geographic Focus: Indiana
Date(s) Application is Due: Feb 12; Jul 16; Oct 8
Amount of Grant: Up to 50,000 USD
Samples: Servants at Work, Indianapolis, Indiana, $2,500 - to build ramps for local individuals who are wheelchair-bound; Sunshine Vans, Crawfordsville, Indiana, $10,500 - to purchase 10 digital radios and related equipment for the vans; Women's Resource Center, Crawfordsville, Indiana, $4,000 - to purchase baby items for the Great Expectations program, pregnancy tests and ultrasound supplies.
Contact: Cheryl Keim, Grants and Community Relations Coordinator; (765) 362-1267; fax (765) 361-0562; cheryl@mccf-in.org
Internet: www.mccf-in.org/health-and-human-services-funds
Sponsor: Montgomery County Community Foundation
119 East Main Street
Crawfordsville, IN 47933

Montgomery County Community Foundation Libby Whitecotton Fund Grants   **1690**
The Montgomery County Community Foundation grants help fund non-profit organizations and agencies in Montgomery County, Indiana. Created in memory of Libby Whitecotton, this fund is intended to assist Montgomery County families who have children with physical disabilities. It could provide items related to accessibility, such as a ramp for a wheelchair bound child or a fence for an autistic child. Respite care for the parents will be considered. To be considered are the financial circumstances of the family, the degree of handicap, the urgency for treatment or therapy, the need for improved or additional facilities or equipment, and the potential for alleviating the severity of the handicap. For the Libby Whitecotton Fund, an applicant should prepare a one page proposal which: describes the child's physical or mental disability; explains how the funds will be used; and describes how this will benefit the child and his or her family. Proposals are accepted at any time throughout the year, as funds remain available.
Requirements: Grant applications will be accepted from any new or existing nonprofit organization in Montgomery County. These organizations must be a tax-exempt organization whose purposes are described in Section 501(c)3 of the Internal Revenue Service Code. Grant applications will also be accepted from local governmental entities, such as the three Montgomery County school corporations, for charitable purposes. A strong proposal will have several or all of the following characteristics: an estimate of who and how many will benefit; show long term potential; address a community problem of some significance for which funding is not covered by the regular budget; present an innovative and practical approach to solve a community problem or project; identify possible future funding, if needed; give evidence of the stability and qualifications of the organization applying; show cooperation within the organization and avoid duplication effort.
Restrictions: The Foundation will usually not fund any of the following: grants to individuals; programs which are religious or sectarian in nature, except when the program is open to the

entire community; operating expenses such as salaries and utilities; parades, festivals and sporting events; endowment funds; any propaganda, political or otherwise, attempting to influence legislation or intervene in any political affairs or campaigns; an organization's past debts or existing obligations; or post-event or after-the-fact situations.
Geographic Focus: Indiana
Contact: Cheryl Keim, Grants and Community Relations Coordinator; (765) 362-1267; fax (765) 361-0562; cheryl@mccf-in.org
Internet: www.mccf-in.org/unrestricted-grant-cycle
Sponsor: Montgomery County Community Foundation
119 East Main Street
Crawfordsville, IN 47933

Montgomery County Community Foundation Youth Services Grants   **1691**
The Montgomery County Community Foundation Grants help fund non-profit organizations and agencies in Montgomery County, Indiana. Significant grants have been awarded to organizations such as the Crawfordsville District Public Library, Boys and Girls Club, and the Family Crisis Shelter. Grants in the area of Youth Services include activities that strengthen the family unit, help children grow and develop, foster youth sports and athletics, support the YMCA, and support daycare-related issues. There are three annual deadlines, including: February 12; July 16; and October 8.
Requirements: Grant applications will be accepted from any new or existing nonprofit organization in Montgomery County. These organizations must be a tax-exempt organization whose purposes are described in Section 501(c)3 of the Internal Revenue Service Code. Grant applications will also be accepted from local governmental entities, such as the three Montgomery County school corporations, for charitable purposes. A strong proposal will have several or all of the following characteristics: an estimate of who and how many will benefit; show long term potential; address a community problem of some significance for which funding is not covered by the regular budget; present an innovative and practical approach to solve a community problem or project; identify possible future funding, if needed; give evidence of the stability and qualifications of the organization applying; show cooperation within the organization and avoid duplication effort.
Restrictions: The Foundation will usually not fund any of the following: grants to individuals; programs which are religious or sectarian in nature, except when the program is open to the entire community; operating expenses such as salaries and utilities; parades, festivals and sporting events; endowment funds; any propaganda, political or otherwise, attempting to influence legislation or intervene in any political affairs or campaigns; an organization's past debts or existing obligations; or post-event or after-the-fact situations.
Geographic Focus: Indiana
Date(s) Application is Due: Feb 12; Jul 16; Oct 8
Amount of Grant: Up to 50,000 USD
Samples: Boys and Girls Club of Montgomery County, Crawfordsville, Indiana, $45,000 - to repair, pave, and stripe half the parking lot; Mountie Mission, Crawfordsville, Indiana, $5,000 - to support its annual Back to School Backpack project; Youth Camps, Camp Rotary, Crawfordsville, Indiana, $3,000 - to replace windows in the Bunkhouse at Camp Rotary.
Contact: Cheryl Keim, Grants and Community Relations Coordinator; (765) 362-1267; fax (765) 361-0562; cheryl@mccf-in.org
Internet: www.mccf-in.org/youth-funds
Sponsor: Montgomery County Community Foundation
119 East Main Street
Crawfordsville, IN 47933

Moody Foundation Grants   **1692**
The Moody Foundation awards grants in the areas of education; social services; children; and community development. Inquiry letters are accepted at any time. Because the Foundation trustees meet four times a year to consider grant awards, the application process may take up to six months. Up to three projects may be submitted in order of highest priority. The inquiry form is available at the Foundation website.
Requirements: Grants are limited to Texas nonprofit 501(c)3 organizations.
Geographic Focus: Texas
Amount of Grant: 5,000 - 6,000,000 USD
Samples: Alley's House, Dallas, Texas, assistance in providing services to teen mothers and their children, $10,000; Austin Independent School District, Austin, Texas, planning and implementation of the School for Young Men, a school for boys in grades 6-12 designed to address the academic, social, emotional, and behavioral needs specific to boys and young men, $4.6 million; Christus Foundation for Healthcare/Our Daily Bread, Houston/Galveston, Texas, rehabilitating homeless men and women who are addicted to drugs or alcohol through the New Beginnings program, $20,000.
Contact: Colleen Trammell, Assistant to Grants Director; (409) 763-5333; fax (409) 763-5564; colleent@moodyf.org
Internet: www.moodyf.org/HTMLversion/grantappset.htm
Sponsor: Moody Foundation
2302 Post Office Street, Suite 704
Galveston, TX 77550

Moran Family Foundation Grants   **1693**
The Moran Family Foundation supports innovative programs that promote healthy development of at-risk children and at-risk families whose lives are impacted by the challenges of poverty. The foundation is pursuing opportunities to partner with and support organizations focusing on strengthening its surrounding communities by promoting and preserving Catholic values.
Requirements: The Moran Family Foundation supports 501(c)3 tax-exempt organizations in the Greater Washington D.C. area as well as the Greater Cleveland, Ohio region and does not accept unsolicited requests for funding. Eligible organizations should query

the foundation prior to submitting a formal proposal. Invited organizations may use the "Common Grant Letter of Intent" and the "Common Grant Application" designed by the Washington Regional Association of Grantmakers. These forms can be found on their web site at www.washingtongrantmakers.org.
Restrictions: The foundation does not make grants to individuals.
Geographic Focus: District of Columbia, Ohio, Virginia
Contact: Grants Administrator; moranfamfdn@aol.com
Internet: fdnweb.org/moran/
Sponsor: Moran Family Foundation
1489 Chain Bridge Road, Suite 200
McLean, VA 22101

Morgan Adams Foundation Research Grants   1694
The Morgan Adams Foundation supports laboratory and clinical research in the area of pediatric cancer, with an emphasis on cancers of the brain and spine. The Foundation's particular interest is to provide seed and bridge grants for viable investigations not yet ripe enough for total funding by larger organizations. Additionally, the Foundation is able to partially fund translational studies, experimental therapeutics studies and/or Phase I and II clinical trials on a case by case basis. The Foundation is seeking out projects that are highly collaborative and/or multi-institutional in nature, hoping to facilitate through the strategic placement of funding, more rapid trials development in order to get the best possible treatment options into circulation with the greatest expediency possible. Through careful consideration and placement of its funding, the Foundation encourages and supports research intended to improve treatment effectiveness, improve treatment outcomes and improve the quality of life for children battling cancer.
Geographic Focus: All States
Contact: Joan Slaughter, Executive Director; (303) 758-2130; fax (303) 758-2134; joan@morganadamsfoundation.org or info@morganadamsfoundation.org
Internet: morganadamsfoundation.hotpressplatform.com/funding-research/how-funds-become-hope
Sponsor: Morgan Adams Foundation
5303 East Evans Avenue, Suite 200
Denver, CO 80222

Morris K. Udall and Stewart L. Udall Foundation Parks in Focus Program   1695
The program mission is to connect underserved youth to nature through photography during action-packed outdoor excursions to local natural areas and immersion trips to National Parks. The program combines photography and environmental education with active, hands-on outdoor adventures guided by passionate and knowledgeable leaders and mentors.
Requirements: The program is intended for middle-school youth who rarely venture beyond their neighborhoods.
Restrictions: The original program was a partnership with the Boys and Girls Clubs of Tucson, Arizona. There have been expansion initiative in Tucson, Arizona, East Palo Alto, California, Big Rapids, Michigan, and Missoula, Montana. Future expansion is anticipated. Contact the Foundation for additional information.
Geographic Focus: Arizona, California, Michigan, Montana
Contact: Melissa Milage, (520) 670-5609; millage@udall.gov
Internet: pif.udall.gov/
Sponsor: Morris K. Udall and Stewart L. Udall Foundation
130 S Scott Avenue
Tucson, AZ 85701-1922

Morris Stulsaft Foundation Early Childhood Education Grants   1696
The Morris Stulsaft Foundation values strong and effective leadership and innovative programs that support low-income children and youth. The foundation will consider requests for professional development and for programs that encourage parental engagement. Strong applicants will be infant, toddler, and pre-school centers that demonstrate a commitment to quality early childhood development through program design, excellent facilities, family engagement, and qualified staff. They must serve some combination of children ages 0 to 5, a majority of whom are from low-income families. The foundation is also open to requests from external organizations that provide high quality professional development to the type of centers outlined above, and/or develop the early childhood expertise of Transitional Kindergarten teachers. The Foundation will consider capital requests, but an organization must be invited to apply.
Requirements: Organizations headquartered in and serving the five San Francisco Bay Area counties of Alameda, Marin, northern San Mateo (extending south to Redwood City), San Francisco, and west Contra Costa are eligible to apply. Only one request from an organization will be considered in a 12-month period.
Restrictions: The foundation does not award grants to individuals or independent schools; also does not support conferences, events, endowments, fund development, or deficit reduction.
Geographic Focus: California
Date(s) Application is Due: Dec 1
Contact: Jessica Sutton; (415) 561-6540, ext. 238; fax (415) 561-6477; jsutton@pfs-llc.net
Internet: www.stulsaft.org/early-childhood-education/
Sponsor: Morris Stulsaft Foundation
1660 Bush Street, Suite 300
San Francisco, CA 94109

Morris Stulsaft Foundation Educational Support for Children Grants   1697
The Morris Stulsaft Foundation values programs that bring stability into the lives of young persons by: helping children succeed in school, fostering the development of healthy and trusting relationships, and supporting social and emotional development. Strong applicants provide services that are informed by current trauma theory and practice, consider community and personal risk factors, and provide a foundation for lifelong learning.

The Foundation considers programs that provide services such as tutoring, mentoring, community engagement, or leadership development.
Requirements: Programs do not need to be located in specific neighborhoods, but must serve a high percentage (over 85%) of children that come from families that live below the poverty level, live in single-mother households, receive public assistance, or live with adults who are unemployed. Additional consideration may be given to programs that serve foster youth and/or homeless youth, and children of color. Organizations headquartered in and serving the five San Francisco Bay Area counties of Alameda, Marin, northern San Mateo (extending south to Redwood City), San Francisco, and west Contra Costa are eligible to apply. Only one request from an organization will be considered in a 12-month period.
Restrictions: The foundation does not award grants to individuals or independent schools; also does not support conferences, events, endowments, fund development, or deficit reduction.
Geographic Focus: California
Date(s) Application is Due: Jun 29
Contact: Jessica Sutton; (415) 561-6540, ext. 238; fax (415) 561-6477; jsutton@pfs-llc.net
Internet: www.stulsaft.org/educational-support-for-children/
Sponsor: Morris Stulsaft Foundation
1660 Bush Street, Suite 300
San Francisco, CA 94109

Morris Stulsaft Foundation Participation in the the Arts Grants   1698
The Morris Stulsaft Foundation values strong and effective leadership and innovative programs that support low-income children and youth. Strong applicants will offer opportunities for under-served young people to actively participate in the arts. Programs should be connected to a school or school district, either by providing classes during the school-day or after-school. Programs must also offer participants a minimum of fifteen hours of hands-on art-making experience in any one summer or semester. Participants in this program should be between the ages of five and eighteen.
Requirements: Organizations headquartered in and serving the five San Francisco Bay Area counties of Alameda, Marin, northern San Mateo (extending south to Redwood City), San Francisco, and west Contra Costa are eligible to apply. Only one request from an organization will be considered in a 12-month period. Programs should align with the California State Board of Education Standards for Visual and Performing Arts.
Restrictions: The foundation does not award grants to individuals or independent schools; also does not support conferences, events, endowments, fund development, or deficit reduction.
Geographic Focus: California
Date(s) Application is Due: Mar 2
Contact: Jessica Sutton; (415) 561-6540, ext. 238; fax (415) 561-6477; jsutton@pfs-llc.net
Internet: www.stulsaft.org/participation-in-the-arts/
Sponsor: Morris Stulsaft Foundation
1660 Bush Street, Suite 300
San Francisco, CA 94109

Morris Stulsaft Foundation Pathways to Work Grants   1699
The Morris Stulsaft Foundation believes that early work experience is a predictor of long-term employment as an adult and is achieved by: providing hands-on job experiences; fostering the understanding of work as an integral and satisfying aspect of life; and, connecting youth to fields in which there are current job opportunities and career ladders, such as construction, healthcare, and technology. Strong applicants will serve low-income young people. Priority will be given to programs serving foster and homeless youth and youth from neighborhoods of concentrated disadvantage (see definition above).
Requirements: Programs must provide or connect youth to paid work experience, teach soft skills, and encourage high school completion. The foundation is particularly interested in programs leading to careers in which there are current and emerging job sectors in the Bay Area. Partnerships with high schools and community colleges that provide work-based learning and/or apprenticeships will be considered. Organizations headquartered in and serving the five San Francisco Bay Area counties of Alameda, Marin, northern San Mateo (extending south to Redwood City), San Francisco, and west Contra Costa are eligible to apply. Only one request from an organization will be considered in a 12-month period.
Restrictions: The foundation does not award grants to individuals or independent schools; also does not support conferences, events, endowments, fund development, or deficit reduction.
Geographic Focus: California
Date(s) Application is Due: Aug 24
Contact: Jessica Sutton; (415) 561-6540, ext. 238; fax (415) 561-6477; jsutton@pfs-llc.net
Internet: www.stulsaft.org/pathways-to-work/
Sponsor: Morris Stulsaft Foundation
1660 Bush Street, Suite 300
San Francisco, CA 94109

Morton K. and Jane Blaustein Foundation Educational Opportunity Grants   1700
The Morton K. and Jane Blaustein Foundation makes grants in the United States and abroad. Support is provided in the program areas of educational opportunity, health, and human rights and social justice. Preference is given to programs in Baltimore, Maryland, New York City, and Washington, D.C. The goal of the Educational Opportunity program is to improve educational opportunities and outcomes for disadvantaged and vulnerable youth, particularly through quality teaching, summer learning and promoting policies and practices that make schools more fair and inclusive. There are no annual deadlines, and the Foundation accepts applications on a rolling basis. Most recent awards have ranged from $25,000 to $500,000.
Requirements: 501(c)3 organizations in Maryland, Washington, D.C., and New York are eligible to apply.
Restrictions: No support is given for fundraising events, or direct mail solicitations. Grants are not made to individuals.
Geographic Focus: District of Columbia, Maryland, New York
Amount of Grant: 25,000 - 500,000 USD

Samples: Center for Inspired Teaching, Washington, D.C., $50,000 - renewed support for teacher training and residencies in D.C. public schools based on progressive educational practices; Baltimore Youth Arts, Baltimore, Maryland, $20,000 - support for summer arts programming for youth in the juvenile justice system; Soccer Without Borders Baltimore, Baltimore, Maryland, $15,000 - support for the International Summer Academy, where new refugee and immigrant youth participate in sports, the arts and language classes.
Contact: Tanya C. Herbick; (410) 347-7206; fax (410) 347-7210; info@blaufund.org
Internet: www.blaufund.org/foundations/mortonandjane_f.html#1
Sponsor: Morton K. and Jane Blaustein Foundation
One South Street, Suite 2900
Baltimore, MD 21202

Moses Kimball Fund Grants   1701

The Moses Kimball Fund was established in Massachusetts, in 1925, founded by Helen Kimball, former president of the New England Hospital for Women and Children, in honor of her father. Trustees emphasize grants to organizations which either provide jobs to minorities and disadvantaged members of the Greater Boston community, or links between educational organizations and the needy members of the adjacent communities. Their primary fields of interest include: education; employment services; families; human services; and youth development. Populations served include: children and youth; families; minorities; and the economically disadvantaged. Most recent awards have ranged from $2,000 to $14,000. The annual application deadline for submission is March 1.
Requirements: Fund Trustees accept grant applications between June 1 and March 1 each year. Grant making decisions and distributions are made at the Trustees meeting in April. Any 501(c)3 serving the residents of Massachusetts is eligible to apply.
Geographic Focus: Massachusetts
Date(s) Application is Due: Mar 1
Amount of Grant: 2,000 - 14,000 USD
Contact: Susan Harrington; (617) 523-6531; moseskimballfund@lwcotrust.com
Internet: www.moseskimballfund.org/
Sponsor: Moses Kimball Fund
230 Congress Street
Boston, MA 02110-2409

Motiv8 Foundation Grants   1702

Tennessee Titans starting quarterback Marcus Mariota grew up seeing the positive power of sport first-hand, which fueled his personal mission to use his platform as a professional athlete to create change. Driven by this mission, he established the Motiv8 Foundation during his rookie year to promote and support a healthy mind and body among youth in Hawaii, Oregon, and Tennessee. The Foundation aims to create and support economic and educational programs and athletic activities to provide an alternative outlet for youth of troubled neighborhoods and backgrounds. The Foundation's programming centers around the tools for success that will allow more children to fully matriculate through grade-school and eventually attend college. Since its launch, the Motiv8 Foundation has awarded hundreds of thousands of dollars towards healthy lifestyle programming, and will continue to fulfill its mission through signature programs, strategic partnerships, and fundraising initiatives. Symbolic of not only the Foundation's mission, the Motiv8 name also honors Mariota's connection to his lifelong jersey number, and the "808" area code of his hometown, Honolulu, Hawaii. As President of the Foundation, he oversees all programming decisions and drives fundraising efforts. Interested applicants should include a letter requesting donation on company/entity letterhead (letter should include Federal ID number). Preference is given to non-profits with current 501(c)3 status.
Requirements: 501(c)3 organizations supporting children in Hawaii, Tennessee, and Oregon are eligible to apply.
Geographic Focus: Hawaii, Oregon, Tennessee
Contact: Ed Nishioka, Director; ed@nishiokamedia.com or info@motiv8foundation.com
Internet: motiv8foundation.com/
Sponsor: Motiv8 Foundation
P.O. Box 256651
Honolulu, HI 96825

Mr. Holland's Opus Foundation Melody Grants   1703

The Mr. Holland's Opus Foundation donates both new and refurbished instruments to school and after-school music programs that lack the resources to keep up with equipment loss due to attrition, depreciation and wear over time, and to accommodate students on waiting lists or who have to share instruments. The Foundation committee selects music programs that: demonstrate financial need and whose students are from low-income families; have an established music program and strong participation; show administrative support of the program; have knowledgeable and professional teachers; present a compelling case for how the grant will benefit their students.
Requirements: Public, private and charter schools may apply, however, schools must be Title 1 or or serve a population of at least 40% that qualify for the National Lunch Program. Schools must have an established instrumental music program (i.e. concert band, marching band, jazz band and/or orchestra) that is at least three years old. Schools must have an existing inventory of instruments. Teachers that teach at more than one school within the school district can only apply for one school per grant cycle. Full or partial requests may be awarded consisting of new and/or refurbished instruments. Current guidelines and pre-applications are available at the website.
Restrictions: The Foundation does not award cash grants. Other exclusions are programs outside the United States; teacher salaries or music lessons; programs or individuals outside of the foundation's three programs; or events, concerts, and festivals.
Geographic Focus: All States
Contact: Tricia Steel; (818) 762-4328; fax (818) 762-4329; tricia@mhopus.org

Internet: www.mhopus.org/Apply
Sponsor: Mr. Holland's Opus Foundation
4370 Tujunga Avenue, Suite 330
Studio City, CA 91604

Mr. Holland's Opus Foundation Michael Kamen Solo Award   1704

The Mr. Holland's Opus Foundation donates both new and refurbished instruments to school and after-school music programs that lack the resources to keep up with equipment loss due to attrition, depreciation and wear over time, and to accommodate students on waiting lists or who have to share instruments. The Foundation's Michael Kamen Solo Award helps outstanding student musicians who cannot obtain an appropriate instrument. Students must have completed at least five years of study on their instrument to apply. Instruments with a retail value of up to $20,000 are awarded. Only students who are still in high school may apply.
Requirements: Current guidelines and pre-applications are available online.
Restrictions: Students who have already received an instrument from the Foundation may not re-apply.
Geographic Focus: All States
Amount of Grant: Up to 20,000 USD
Contact: Tricia Steel; (818) 762-4328; fax (818) 762-4329; tricia@mhopus.org
Internet: www.mhopus.org/Apply
Sponsor: Mr. Holland's Opus Foundation
4370 Tujunga Avenue, Suite 330
Studio City, CA 91604

Mr. Holland's Opus Foundation Special Projects Grants   1705

Mr. Holland's Opus Foundation donates both new and refurbished instruments to school and after-school music programs that lack the resources to keep up with equipment loss due to attrition, depreciation, and wear over time, and to accommodate students on waiting lists or who have to share instruments. The Foundation strives to enable more students to participate and to experience a quality music education. The Foundation's Special Project Grants help before and after-school music programs that are at least three years old, serve primarily school-age youth from low-income families, or students attending Title 1 schools. Programs must have an existing inventory of instruments. The committee selects music programs that: demonstrate financial need and whose students are from low-income families; have an established music program and strong participation; show administrative support of the program; have knowledgeable and professional teachers; present a compelling case for how the grant will benefit their students. Full or partial requests of new and/or refurbished instruments may be awarded. Guidelines and application forms are available on the foundation's Web site.
Requirements: All applicants submit a pre-qualification form, and if the program meets the Foundation's guidelines, they are invited to apply for a grant for new instruments and/or repairs to instruments already in their inventory. Applications are reviewed by the Foundation's grant committee once each year.
Restrictions: Funding is not available for programs outside the United States; teacher salaries or music lessons; programs or individuals outside of the Foundation's three programs; events, concerts, or festivals; or summer camps.
Geographic Focus: All States
Contact: Tricia Steel; (818) 762-4328; fax (818) 762-4329; tricia@mhopus.org
Internet: www.mhopus.org/Apply
Sponsor: Mr. Holland's Opus Foundation
4370 Tujunga Avenue, Suite 330
Studio City, CA 91604

Ms. Foundation for Women Building Democracy Grants   1706

Through their funding, the Ms. Foundation aims to change systems that prevent people from participating fully in government and civil society. It supports groups that advocate for changes to the criminal justice and immigration systems so that all women, families and communities have the opportunity and resources to lead healthy, safe lives and benefit from the democratic principles of equity and justice. The Foundation promotes the voices of those who have been excluded from decision making, especially low-income women, women of color, youth, LGBTQ individuals, and immigrants. The Foundation strives to invest in long-term civic engagement and support strategies that bring in new constituencies and expand social movements.
Requirements: Applicants must be nonprofit tax exempt organizations.
Geographic Focus: All States
Contact: Grants Administrator; (212) 742-2300; info@ms.foundation.org
Internet: ms.foundation.org/our_work/broad-change-areas/building-democracy
Sponsor: Ms. Foundation for Women
12 MetroTech Center, 26th Floor
Brooklyn, NY 11201

Ms. Foundation for Women Economic Justice Grants   1707

With Ms. Foundation funding support, organizations are advancing the solutions of those most affected by economic injustice to address a range of issues including worker rights and access to quality, living-wage jobs, affordable child care, paid sick leave, job training and other critical policies and programs necessary for women to achieve economic security and strengthen our national economy overall. The Ms. Foundation delivers grant support for the implementation of economic recovery legislation in areas such as unemployment insurance and child care subsidies. The Foundation also works to promote women's access to higher wages and greater economic security in emerging industries such as green jobs.
Requirements: Applicants must be tax exempt nonprofit organizations.
Geographic Focus: All States
Contact: Grants Administrator; (212) 742-2300; info@ms.foundation.org
Internet: ms.foundation.org/our_work/broad-change-areas/economic-justice

Sponsor: Ms. Foundation for Women
12 MetroTech Center, 26th Floor
Brooklyn, NY 11201

Ms. Foundation for Women Ending Violence Grants   **1708**

The Ms. Foundation works in partnership with grassroots, state, and national organizations to end gender-based violence by transforming policies, beliefs, and behaviors that threaten the well-being of individuals, families and communities nationwide. The Foundation supports a range of community-based strategies to stop violence before it occurs—to prevent violence directed against women, girls, and LGBTQ individuals. The Foundation also supports a movement to advance a community-based, social justice approach to child sexual abuse.
Requirements: Applicants must be tax exempt nonprofits organizations.
Geographic Focus: All States
Contact: Grants Administrator; (212) 742-2300; info@ms.foundation.org
Internet: ms.foundation.org/our_work/broad-change-areas/ending-violence
Sponsor: Ms. Foundation for Women
12 MetroTech Center, 26th Floor
Brooklyn, NY 11201

Mt. Sinai Health Care Foundation Health of the Jewish Community Grants   **1709**

The Mt. Sinai Health Care Foundation seeks to assist Greater Cleveland's organizations and leaders to improve the health and well-being of the Jewish and general communities now and for generations to come. The Foundation will support projects that build organizational capacity in those Jewish organizations that address these needs. The Board of Directors of the Foundation meets on a quarterly basis to review proposals.
Requirements: 501(c)3 nonprofits serving greater Cleveland, Ohio may submit proposals for grant support. The foundation welcomes and encourages an informal conversation with program staff prior to the submission of a grant request.
Restrictions: In general, the foundation does not support general operating expenses, direct provision of health services, building or equipment expenses, fund-raising events, projects outside of greater Cleveland, endowment funds, lobbying, program advertising, grants for individuals, or scholarships.
Geographic Focus: Ohio
Date(s) Application is Due: Jan 1; Apr 1; Jul 1; Oct 1
Contact: Ann Freimuth; (216) 421-5500; fax (216) 421-5633; aks17@case.edu
Internet: www.mtsinaifoundation.org/whatwefund_jewishcommunity.html
Sponsor: Mount Sinai Health Care Foundation
11000 Euclid Avenue
Cleveland, OH 44106-1714

Mt. Sinai Health Care Foundation Health of the Urban Community Grants   **1710**

In the tradition of The Mt. Sinai Medical Center, the Foundation is committed to improving the health of Greater Cleveland's most vulnerable individuals and families. To achieve impact in this area, scale is a significant factor. The Foundation seeks to support especially those projects focusing on health promotion and disease prevention that have the potential to access large populations through existing community infrastructure. To optimize impact in large populations, partnering with both public and private funding sources may be appropriate and necessary. Of particular interest are proposals in the areas of health-related early childhood development and health-related aging.
Requirements: 501(c)3 nonprofits serving greater Cleveland, Ohio may submit proposals for grant support. The foundation welcomes and encourages an informal conversation with program staff prior to the submission of a grant request.
Restrictions: In general, the foundation does not support general operating expenses, direct provision of health services, building or equipment expenses, fund-raising events, projects outside of greater Cleveland, endowment funds, lobbying, program advertising, grants for individuals, or scholarships.
Geographic Focus: Ohio
Date(s) Application is Due: Jan 1; Apr 1; Jul 1; Oct 1
Contact: Ann Freimuth; (216) 421-5500; fax (216) 421-5633; aks17@case.edu
Internet: www.mtsinaifoundation.org/whatwefund_urbancommunity.html
Sponsor: Mount Sinai Health Care Foundation
11000 Euclid Avenue
Cleveland, OH 44106-1714

NAA Foundation High Five Grants   **1711**

The Foundation strives to develop engaged and literate citizens in a diverse society. The Foundation invests in and supports programs designed to enhance student achievement through newspaper readership and appreciation of the First Amendment. In an effort to support 21st century learning, Grants are made to middle schools to help launch or sustain student newspapers. Schools receiving funding must agree to use the "High Five" curriculum in their publication efforts and then report on their usage. Suggested uses for funding include, but are not limited to, adviser training and technology purchases. See the website for application deadline or contact the Director for information.
Requirements: Schools are encouraged to seek a professional newspaper and/or a university or college as partners. Applications from urban, rural or minority-majority schools are welcomed. Projects will be selected based upon: defined level of need; plan for effectively providing the school community with fact-based news, information and opinions; submission of a budget that details projected fund expenditures and targets long-term needs; outlined level of professional newspaper and additional partner commitment (if applicable); and prospects for long-term success beyond the Grant period.
Geographic Focus: All States
Amount of Grant: 2,000 USD
Contact: Sandy Woodcock, Director; (571) 366-1008; fax (571) 366-1195;

sandy.woodcock@naa.org or NAAFoundation@naa.org
Internet: www.naafoundation.org/Grants/Student-Journalism/High-Five.aspx
Sponsor: Newspaper Association of America Foundation
4401 Wilson Boulevard, Suite 900
Arlington, VA 22203

Narragansett Number One Foundation Grants   **1712**

Narragansett Number One Foundation (NNOF) is a Maine nonprofit corporation established by Pat and Erwin Wales on September 7, 2001, thirteen days after winning the national Powerball lottery drawing. The Wales formed the Foundation to share their good fortune with others and to encourage other possible donors to help their community and state. Giving is concentrated first on helping the Foundation's neighbors in Buxton, Maine, and surrounding areas. NNOF provides funds for start-up expenses, new or special projects, and general operating support.
Requirements: Nonprofit 501(c)3 organizations in any state, possession of the United States, or political subdivision (a public school, town, city or government agency) if the proposed grant is to be used exclusively for public purposes are eligible to apply. Priority will be given to public charities in the Town of Buxton, Maine and the surrounding areas with focus on schools, fire departments, police departments, parks, recreational facilities, religious organizations, libraries, shelters for children, the homeless and abused persons, museums and shelters for animals. Once the immediate needs of this geographic area in southern Maine are addressed, it is likely that future grants will be made to charities throughout Maine and in other states. Applications should be received by NNOF no earlier than November 1 and no later than April 1 of the following year. Grants will be awarded on or before June 30.
Restrictions: Grants do not support individuals, campaigns to elect candidates to public office, lobbying or propaganda campaigns, or programs or projects that discriminate.
Geographic Focus: Maine
Date(s) Application is Due: Apr 1
Contact: Pat Wales, President
Internet: www.nnof.org/apply.htm
Sponsor: Narragansett Number One Foundation
P.O. Box 779
Bar Mills, ME 04004

NASE Foundation Future Entrepreneur Scholarship   **1713**

The NASE Foundation Future Entrepreneur Scholarship program provides financial aid to a selected individual to assist them in obtaining an undergraduate college or university degree. One Scholarship of $24,000 will be awarded annually. Consideration is based upon: leadership abilities; academic performance; business aspirations and goals; quality of business plan; quality of essay or video essay; extracurricular activities; teacher recommendations; school and community participation; and financial need. The scholarship can be applied to tuition, fees, books, supplies and equipment required for course load.
Requirements: Applicants must meet all of the following criteria to be eligible for this scholarship: be a high school senior, college freshman, sophomore or junior; have a grade point average of 3.0 or above on a 4.0 scale; and own and operate his or her own business. A student may transfer from one institution to another and retain the award, provided that the student's degree program at their new institution correlates to their business and or their career goals.
Geographic Focus: All States
Date(s) Application is Due: Apr 1
Amount of Grant: Up to 24,000 USD
Contact: Katie Vlietstra, Vice President for Public Affairs; (800) 649-6273 or (800) 232-6273
Internet: www.nase.org/HRA105/Foundation/Programs
Sponsor: National Association for the Self-Employed Foundation
P.O. Box 241
Annapolis Junction, MD 20701-0241

Nash Avery Foundation Grants   **1714**

The Nash Avery Foundation was established in Minnesota in 2005, and named in honor Nash Wicka, who was diagnosed with Duchenne muscular dystrophy in 2002. The Foundation supports research of muscular dystrophy, primarily in both Minnesota and Massachusetts. Most recent grants have ranged up to approximately $50,000, although a limit has not been established. Though there are no specific annual deadlines for submission, a formal application process is required.
Requirements: Any 501(c)3 organization researching Duchenne muscular dystrophy is eligible to apply.
Geographic Focus: All States
Amount of Grant: Up to 100,000 USD
Samples: A.T. Still University of Health Sciences, Kirksville, Missouri - evaluating the utility of anti-inflammatory agents that prevent muscle cell death as potential treatments for DMD; Brown University, Providence, Rhode Island - research of Utrophin, a compensatory protein that can act as a substitute for dystrophin, the missing protein in DMD boys; Children's National Medical Center, Washington, D.C. - investigating four experimental drugs (Celastrol, Resveratrol, Lipoxin A, Cyclosporine A analog) that may prevent muscle degeneaeration and increase muscle function.
Contact: Thomas C Wicka, Director; (612) 325-5700 or (952) 582-2933;
nashaveryfoundation@gmail.com
Sponsor: Nash Avery Foundation
4904 Merilane Avenue
Edina, MN 55436-1359

Natalie W. Furniss Foundation Grants   **1715**

The Mission of the Furniss Foundation is to promote the humane treatment of animals by providing funding to societies for the prevention of cruelty to animals.

Requirements: Qualifying tax-exempt 501(c)3 organizations operating in the state of New Jersey are eligible to apply. Applications are accepted Ocotber 1 - December 1. Complete the Common Grant Application form available at the Wachovi website to apply for funding.
Restrictions: Grants are not made for political purposes, nor to organizations which discriminate on the basis of race, ethnic origin, sexual or religious preference, age or gender.
Geographic Focus: New Jersey
Date(s) Application is Due: Dec 1
Samples: Oasis Animal Sanctuary, Inc., $4,200—animal sterilization program; Woodford Cedar Run Wildlife Refuge, Inc., $4,5000—winter operating support for wildlife rehab; Society for the Prtevention of Cruelty to Animals, $5,000—humane education in Cumberland Co. School system; Greyhound Friends of New Jersey, Inc., $5,000—broken leg program.
Contact: Wachovia Bank, N.A., Trustee; grantinquiries6@wachovia.com
Internet: www.wellsfargo.com/private-foundations/furniss-foundation
Sponsor: Natalie W. Furniss Foundation
100 North Main Street
Winston Salem, NC 27150

Nathalie and Gladys Dalkowitz Charitable Trust Grants 1716

The Dalkowitz family members were prominent merchants and investors in San Antonio, Texas, Mexico and elsewhere. The Dalkowitz family's first store was located across from City Hall in San Antonio. Sisters Nathalie and Gladys Dalkowitz were sophisticated, educated and cultural ladies who were members of the San Antonio Women's Club. They were particularly fond of the artistic, musical and cultural aspects of life in San Antonio. While proud of their Jewish heritage, they were ecumenical in their philanthropic support of other religions. The trust was established under the will of Nathalie Dalkowitz in memory of her sister, Gladys and other members of her family. Nathalie died in 1992 at the age of 102. The Nathalie and Gladys Dalkowitz Charitable Trust serves a broad and diverse field of interests within Bexar County, Texas (San Antonio area). The sisters favored arts and culture, education, Jewish organizations and other ecumenical programs. Grants typically range between $1,000 and $10,000.
Requirements: Grants are limited to or for the use of 501(c)3 charitable organizations in the San Antonio, Texas, area that are organized and operated exclusively for religious, charitable, scientific, literary, artistic or educational purposes. Applications will be submitted online through the Bank of America website. A grant report is required within 1 year of the grant application date, regardless of whether all of the funds have been spent.
Restrictions: Eligibility to re-apply for a grant award from the Nathalie and Gladys Dalkowitz Charitable Trust requires organizations to skip 1 grant cycle (1 year) before submitting a subsequent application. The trust does not support requests from individuals, organizations attempting to influence policy through direct lobbying, or any political campaigns.
Geographic Focus: Texas
Date(s) Application is Due: Feb 1
Amount of Grant: 1,000 - 10,000 USD
Samples: San Antonio Children's Museum, San Antonio, Texas, $8,000 - awarded for DoSeum For All program (2018); American Red Cross - San Antonio Chapter, San Antonio, Texas, $8,000 - awarded for Home Fire Campaign program (2018); Barshop Jewish Community Center of San Antonio, San Antonio, Texas, $8,000 - awarded for An Ethical Start, Sheva and Discover CATCH (2018).
Contact: Debra Goldstein Phares, Philanthropic Client Manager; (800) 357-7094; tx.philanthropic@bankofamerica.com or tx.philanthropic@ustrust.com
Internet: www.bankofamerica.com/philanthropic/foundation/?fnId=142
Sponsor: Nathalie and Gladys Dalkowitz Charitable Trust
P.O. Box 831041
Dallas, TX 75283-1041

Nathan B. and Florence R. Burt Foundation Grants 1717

The Nathan B. and Florence R. Burt Foundation is a non-profit corporation incorporated on December 13, 1984. The Foundation was established by the late Nathan and Florence Burt, the founder of the widely formerly known Burt Chevrolet, and other auto retailing businesses. The Foundation generally restricts its grants to organizations dealing with and affecting the needs of children and senior citizens, primarily in, but not limited to, the Denver metropolitan area of Colorado. It prefers a grant application for specific purposes, programs, or needs rather than general administrative or operational costs. The deadline for submitting a grant application is April 27.
Requirements: Grants are awarded primarily to Colorado 501(c)3 charitable and educational organizations. Applicants should emphasis a specific purpose, program, or need with the online application.
Restrictions: The Foundation does not make grant for general operating or capital construction costs, individuals, or political causes, organizations, or candidates.
Geographic Focus: Colorado
Date(s) Application is Due: Apr 27
Contact: Gregory Dickson; (303) 393-0615 or (303) 863-8400; fax (303) 832-4703
Internet: www.burtfoundation.org/grantapp.htm
Sponsor: Nathan B. and Florence R. Burt Foundation
4155 East Jewell Avenue, Suite 814
Denver, CO 80222

Nathan Cummings Foundation Grants 1718

The Nathan Cummings Foundation is rooted in the Jewish tradition and committed to democratic values and social justice, including fairness, diversity, and community. It seeks to build a socially and economically just society that values nature and protects the ecological balance for future generations; promotes humane health care; and fosters arts and culture that enriches communities. The Foundation's core programs include arts and culture; the environment; health; interprogram initiatives for social and economic justice; and the Jewish life and values/contemplative practice programs. Basic themes informing the Foundation's

approach to grantmaking are: concern for the poor, disadvantaged, and underserved; respect for diversity; promotion of understanding across cultures; and empowerment of communities in need. The Board meets twice a year. Applicants should apply by January 15 to be considered for the spring Board meeting and by August 15 to be considered for the fall Board meeting.
Requirements: Eligible applicants must be 501(c)3 organizations. A two or three page letter of inquiry may be submitted with the following information: basic organizational information; contact person; grant purpose; key personnel; project budget and total organizational budget; amount requested and the length of time for which funds are being requested; and other funding sources. Projects that most closely fit with the Foundation's goals will be invited to submit a complete application.
Restrictions: The following is not funded: individuals; scholarships; sponsorships; capital or endowment campaigns; foreign-based organizations; specific diseases; local synagogues or institutions with local projects; Holocaust related projects; projects with no plans for replication; and general support for Jewish education.
Geographic Focus: All States
Samples: Alliance for Justice, Washington, D.C., $10,000 - general support; American Friends of the Heschel Center, Inc., Jersey City, New Jersey, $150,000 - envisioning a political agenda for 21st century Israel; and American Jewish World Service, Inc., New York, New York, $100,000 - group leadership training program.
Contact: Armanda Famiglietti, Director of Grants Management; (212) 787-7300; fax (212) 787-7377; info@nathancummings.org
Internet: www.nathancummings.org/programs/index.html
Sponsor: Nathan Cummings Foundation
475 10th Avenue, 14th Floor
New York, NY 10018

Nathaniel and Elizabeth P. Stevens Foundation Grants 1719

The Foundation awards funding to eligible Massachusetts nonprofit organizations to improve the quality of life in the greater area comprising Lawrence and Merrimack Valley. Funding includes operating support, program support, special projects, renovations, capital and equipment. The Foundation Trustees generally meet monthly, with the exceptions of July and August. Applicants are encouraged to seek other sources of funding while waiting for funding decisions. Awards range from $250 to $30,000.
Requirements: Eligible applicants must be 501(c)3 Massachusetts charitable organizations. Applications will be considered for experimental and demonstration projects, program expansion, evaluation, renovations, new construction projects and capital funding. Grants may be made to a 501(c)3 organization for the benefit of another organization awaiting its own tax-exempt status. A complete proposal should include: most recent annual financial statement (preferably audited); institutional income and expense budget for current fiscal year; detailed program budget for which support is being requested; and starting and completion dates of proposed program and planned cash flow. If an organization's proposal is complete and fits within the guidelines of the Foundation, the applicant organization may be contacted to provide further information. Contact information should be included with the application.
Restrictions: Awards are not made to the following: individuals; national organizations; annual giving campaigns; and state or federal agencies. The Foundation will not consider a proposal from an organization previously funded until a full report of the expenditures of the previous grant has been submitted. The Trustees will not consider more than one application from an agency in the same calendar year except for summer youth programs.
Geographic Focus: Massachusetts
Samples: ABC Masconomet, Topsfield, Massachusetts, $7,500 - operating support; Lazarus House, Lawrence, Massachusetts, $14,000 - food preparation program and renovation; and Youth Development Organization, Lawrence, Massachusetts, $30,000 - operating support.
Contact: Joshua Miner, Executive Director; (978) 688-7211; fax (978) 686-1620; grantprocess@stevensfoundation.com
Sponsor: Nathaniel and Elizabeth P. Stevens Foundation
P.O. Box 111
North Andover, MA 01845

National 4-H Council Grants 1720

National 4-H Council grants give young people and adults the opportunity to take on issues critical to their lives, families, and communities. Youth and adults work together to design the project, write the proposal, and evaluate funded projects. The grants are offered to 4-H programs in local communities, counties, and states. Grant deadlines are determined in conjunction with our funding partners. Once a particular grant is announced, grant proposals are normally solicited for a four- to eight-week period.
Requirements: Grants are awarded to 4-H Extension groups. Organizations must log on the online grants portal and created a user ID and password to access funding opportunities.
Restrictions: Grants are not available to individuals.
Geographic Focus: All States
Contact: Jill Bramble, Senior Vice President for Development; (301) 961-2800
Internet: 4-h.org/professionals/grants/
Sponsor: National 4-H Council
7100 Connecticut Avenue
Chevy Chase, MD 20815

National 4-H Youth in Action Awards 1721

The 4-H Youth in Action program recognizes four confident young leaders in the 4-H core pillar areas: agriculture, civic engagement, healthy living, and STEM. Each Pillar Winner will experience an exciting year of telling their 4-H story and celebrating their leadership. Winners receive: $5,000 higher education scholarship; a promotional video showcasing their 4-H impact story; an all-expenses paid trip to Washington, D.C. for National 4-H Council's Legacy Awards; networking opportunities with 4-H celebrities and other prominent alumni; and recognition as the official 4-H youth spokesperson for

their pillar. One Pillar Winner will be selected as the 4-H Youth in Action National Award Winner and will receive an additional higher education scholarship.
Restrictions: Only 4-H members may apply.
Geographic Focus: All States
Amount of Grant: 5,000 USD
Contact: Jill Bramble, Senior Vice President for Development; (301) 961-2800
Internet: 4-h.org/parents/4-h-youth-in-action-awards/#!how-to-apply
Sponsor: National 4-H Council
7100 Connecticut Avenue
Chevy Chase, MD 20815

National Cowboy and Western Heritage Museum Awards 1722
Through its three Halls of Fame, the National Cowboy and Western Heritage Museum honors and memorializes the men and women who have through their exemplary lives, careers, and achievements embodied and perpetuated the heritage of the American West. Every inductee, whether a real cowboy in the Hall of Great Westerners, a "reel" cowboy in the Hall of Great Western Performers, or a rodeo cowboy in the Rodeo Hall of Fame, perpetuates and enriches facets of this Western heritage. By honoring them, the Museum, in a sense, provides a generational continuity with the past, present and future and bears witness to an evolving American West. Currently, the following awards are given annually: Western Heritage Awards; the Chester A. Reynolds Award; the Ben Johnson Memorial Award; and the Tad Lucas Award.
Geographic Focus: All States
Contact: Catherine Page-Creppon, Director of PR & Museum Events; (405) 478-2250, ext. 221 or (405) 478-4714; cpage@nationalcowboymuseum.org
Internet: www.nationalcowboymuseum.org/info/awards-hof/default.aspx
Sponsor: National Cowboy and Western Heritage Museum
1700 NE 63rd Street
Oklahoma City, OK 73111

National Schools of Character Awards Program 1723
The annual awards program recognizes K-12 schools and districts demonstrating outstanding character education initiatives that yield positive results in student behavior, school climate, and academic performance. Although winners may differ in method, content, and scope, all emphasize core ethical values such as honesty, respect, responsibility, and caring. Selected schools and districts receive a cash award, national recognition, and a featured position in CEP's National Schools of Character publication. Application and guidelines are available online.
Requirements: To be eligible, a school needs to have been engaged in character education for at least three full school years A district needs to have been engaged in character education for a minimum of four full school years.
Restrictions: Previous winners are not eligible to apply.
Geographic Focus: All States
Date(s) Application is Due: Dec 5
Contact: Character Awards Contact; (800) 988-8081 or (202) 296-7743; fax (202) 296-7779; geninfo@character.org
Internet: www.character.org/site/c.gwKUJhNYJrF/b.993295/k.4970/National_Schools_of_Character_Awards.htm
Sponsor: Character Education Partnership
1025 Connecticut Avenue NW, Suite 1011
Washington, D.C. 20036

National Wildlife Federation Craig Tufts Educational Scholarship 1724
The Craig Tufts Educational Scholarship was established in memory of Craig Tufts, chief naturalist of National Wildlife Federation. Each year the Federation grants an award for one youth to attend a Family Nature Summit. The scholarship funds travel, room and board and program fees for the award winner and an accompanying parent or guardian. The application with additional instructions is located at the Federation website.
Requirements: Anyone between the ages of 8 and 18 may apply. The applicants will submit an original essay that addresses the following questions: what are your favorite outdoor or nature-related activities; describe a memorable outdoor or nature-related experience and the impact it had on you; what aspects of the Family Summit program are you most interested in and why; describe why attending a week-long adventure camp would be important to you; and describe how you would share your experience with others. Each essay must be accompanied by the online application form. The essay must be written by the applicant, no more than three pages, double spaced, typed in 12-point font or legibly handwritten; and include all contact information for the applicant.
Geographic Focus: All States
Date(s) Application is Due: Mar 30
Contact: Tufts Award Coordinator; (800) 822-9919; fax (703) 438-6468; tuftsaward@nwf.org
Internet: www.nwf.org/Get-Outside/What-We-Do/Craig-Tufts-Scholarship.aspx
Sponsor: National Wildlife Federation
11100 Wildlife Center Drive
Reston, VA 20190

National YoungArts Foundation Awards 1725
Dedicated to inspiring young artists for America's future, the National YoungArts Foundation's mission is to identify emerging artists and assist them at critical junctures in their educational and professional development. The Foundation's core program, YoungArts, contributes to the cultural vitality of the nation by investing in the artistic development of thousands of gifted artists in cinematic arts, dance, jazz, music, photography, theater, visual arts, voice and writing. YoungArts is open to high school seniors and other 17 and 18-year-old artists in the performing, literary and visual arts. Finalists share in an awards package valued up to $900,000, including more than $500,000 in cash awards, $3 million in scholarship opportunities and the chance to be named a Presidential Scholar in the Arts. Each year, approximately 6,000 to 8,000 students register for the YoungArts program and approximately ten percent receive cash awards.
Geographic Focus: All States
Date(s) Application is Due: Oct 17
Amount of Grant: Up to 10,000 USD
Contact: Letty Bassart, Director of Artistic Programs; (305) 377-1140, ext. 1705; fax (305) 377-1149; lbassart@youngarts.org or info@youngarts.org
Internet: www.youngarts.org/apply
Sponsor: National YoungArts Foundation
2100 Biscayne Boulevard
Miami, FL 33137

Nationwide Insurance Foundation Grants 1726
The Nationwide Insurance Foundation's mission is to improve the quality of life in communities in which a large number of Nationwide members, associates, agents and their families live and work. The foundation's grants fall into three categories: General Operating Support, Program and/or Project Support, and Capital Support. Funding priorities are then placed into one of four tiers. Tier 1-Emergency and basic needs: the foundation partners with organizations that provide life's necessities. Tier 2-Crisis stabilization: the foundation partners with organizations that provide resources to prevent crises or help pick up the pieces after one occurs. Tier 3-Personal and family empowerment: Nationwide helps at-risk youth and families in poverty situations who need tools and resources to advance their lives by partnering with organizations that assist individuals in becoming productive members of society. Tier 4-Community enrichment: the foundation partners with organizations that contribute to the overall quality of life in a community.
Requirements: In the following communities, the Nationwide Insurance Foundation will consider funding 501(c)3 organizations from all four tiers of funding priorities: Columbus, Ohio; Des Moines, Iowa; Scottsdale, Arizona. In the following communities, only Tiers 1 and 2 of the foundation's funding priorities will be considered: Sacramento, California; Denver, Colorado; Gainesville, Florida; Atlanta (Metro), Georgia; Baltimore, Maryland; Lincoln, Nebraska; Raleigh/Durham, North Carolina; Syracuse, New York; Canton, Ohio; Cleveland, Ohio; Harrisburg, Pennsylvania; Philadelphia (Metro), Pennsylvania; Nashville, Tennessee; Dallas (Metro), Texas; San Antonio, Texas; Lynchburg, Virginia; Richmond, Virginia; Wausau, Wisconsin.
Restrictions: The Nationwide Insurance Foundation generally does not fund national organizations (unless the applicant is a local branch or chapter providing direct services) or organizations located in areas with less than 100 Nationwide associates. Also, the foundation does not fund the following: Organizations that are not tax-exempt under paragraph 501(c)3 of the U.S. Internal Revenue Code; Fund-raising events such as walk-a-thons, telethons or sponsorships; Individuals for any purpose; Athletic events or teams, bands and choirs (including equipment and uniforms); Debt-reduction or retirement campaigns; Research; Public or private primary or secondary schools; Requests to support travel; Groups or organizations that will re-grant the foundation's gifts to other organizations or individuals (except United Way); Endowment campaigns; Veterans, labor, religious or fraternal groups (except when these groups provide needed services to the community at-large); Lobbying activities.
Geographic Focus: Arizona, California, Colorado, Florida, Georgia, Iowa, Maryland, Nebraska, New York, North Carolina, Ohio, Pennsylvania, Tennessee, Texas, Virginia, Wisconsin
Date(s) Application is Due: Sep 1
Amount of Grant: 5,000 - 50,000 USD
Contact: Chad Jester, (614) 249-4310 or (877) 669-6877; corpcit@nationwide.com
Internet: www.nationwide.com/about-us/nationwide-foundation.jsp
Sponsor: Nationwide Insurance Foundation
1 Nationwide Plaza, MD 1-22-05
Columbus, OH 43215-2220

NCMCF Youth Advisory Council Grants 1727
The North Central Michigan Community Foundation Youth Advisory Council is a group of students from Crawford, Ogemaw, and Oscoda counties. Working with adult advisors, the members learn about philanthropy and how to improve their communities through the grant-making process. Using funds from the W.K. Kellogg Foundation, the students award grants to local non-profit organizations that are supporting projects and programs that benefit youth under the age of 18 in the three-county area. Applicants may submit requests up to a maximum of $2,500 per application cycle unless otherwise indicated. Applicants may submit maximum requests as follows: $2,500 for programs in Ogemaw County; $1,000 for programs in Crawford or Oscoda Counties. Mini-grants up to $300 are also available. The annual deadline for application submission is a postmark of January 4.
Requirements: Regular grant requests require the applicant to make a three-minute presentation about their project. IRS 501(c)3 nonprofit organizations, schools, churches (for non-sectarian purposes), cities, townships, and other governmental units serving the three-county area of Crawford, Ogemaw, and Oscoda counties may apply
Restrictions: Grants are not given to individuals, except for awards or scholarships from designated donor funds.
Geographic Focus: Michigan
Date(s) Application is Due: Jan 4
Amount of Grant: Up to 2,500 USD
Contact: Julie Wiesen, Program Director; (989) 354-6881 or (877) 354-6881; fax (989) 356-3319; wiesenj@cfnem.org
Internet: www.cfnem.org/ncmcf/grants/yac-grants.html
Sponsor: North Central Michigan Community Foundation
100 N. Ripley, Suite F, P.O. Box 495
Alpena, MI 49707

NCSS Award for Global Understanding 1728

Each year the National Council for the Social Studies honors the outstanding performance of teachers, researchers, and other worthy individuals and programs by encouraging unique and innovative social studies education projects through its award and grant programs. The purpose of this Award is to recognize a social studies educator (or a team of educators) who has made notable contributions in helping social studies students increase their understanding of the world. The award, granted at the NCSS Annual Conference, consists of a $2,000 cash award; commemorative gift; a session to present at the NCSS annual conference; complimentary NCSS conference registration; and up to $700 in transportation/lodging reimbursement.

Requirements: NCSS membership is required. Nominees must be social studies educators who are affecting the global understanding of Pre-K through 12 students; and address several elements of global education as outlined at the web site.

Geographic Focus: All States
Date(s) Application is Due: Jun 30
Amount of Grant: 2,700 USD
Contact: Jordan Grote, (301) 588-1800, ext. 107; fax (301) 588-2049; jgrote@ncss.org
Internet: www.socialstudies.org/awards/globalunderstanding
Sponsor: National Council for the Social Studies
8555 Sixteenth Street, Suite 500
Silver Spring, MD 20910

NCSS Carter G. Woodson Book Awards 1729

Carter G. Woodson was a distinguished African American historian and educator who wrote books for adults and young people. The award is given for the most distinguished social science books appropriate for young readers that depict ethnicity in the United States. The purpose of these awards is to encourage the writing, publishing, and dissemination of outstanding social science books for young readers that treat topics related to ethnic minorities and relations sensitively and accurately. Authors are invited to the conference to receive the award and have an opportunity to talk about their work during a special panel discussion session at the conference. They are also provided a book signing opportunity. Evaluation guidelines for each book level are available at the website.

Requirements: Books nominated for the award should deal with the experience of one or more racial/ethnic minority groups in the United States. To be eligible, the book must meet the following criteria: accurately reflect the perspectives, cultures, and values of the particular ethnic group or groups; informational or nonfiction (i.e., primarily a trade or supplementary book as opposed to a book that is primarily a text book); written for children or young people; well written and reflect originality in presentation and theme; published in the year preceding the year in which the award is presented; and published in the United States, although the author of the book need not be a U.S. citizen.

Geographic Focus: All States
Contact: Prema Cordeiro, Program Manager; (301) 588-1800, ext. 106; fax (301) 588-2049; pcordeiro@ncss.org or excellence@ncss.org
Internet: www.socialstudies.org/awards/woodson
Sponsor: National Council for the Social Studies
8555 Sixteenth Street, Suite 500
Silver Spring, MD 20910

NCSS Christa McAuliffe Reach for the Stars Award 1730

The Reach for the Stars award honors Christa McAuliffe and teachers with dreams. Proposals should provide a plan for reporting to NCSS members the realization of the applicant's dream to improve social studies education. The purpose of the $2,500 award is to help a social studies educator make his or her dream of innovative social studies a reality. Grants will be given to help classroom teachers in developing and implementing imaginative, innovative, and illustrative social studies teaching strategies; and supporting student implementation of innovative social studies, citizenship projects, field experiences, and community connections. Selection criteria is posted on the website.

Requirements: To be eligible applicants must be members of NCSS; full-time social studies teachers or social studies teacher educators currently engaged with K-12 students; and involved with "Reach for the Stars" projects that represent excellence and innovation in social studies education, and have the potential of serving as a model for other teachers.

Geographic Focus: All States
Date(s) Application is Due: Jun 30
Amount of Grant: 2,500 USD
Contact: Prema Cordeiro, Program Manager; (301) 588-1800, ext. 106; fax (301) 588-2049; pcordeira@ncss.org or excellence@ncss.org
Internet: www.socialstudies.org/awards/fasse/fasse-mcauliffe
Sponsor: National Council for the Social Studies
8555 Sixteenth Street, Suite 500
Silver Spring, MD 20910

NEA Foundation Read Across America Event Grants 1731

NEA State Affiliates may apply for a Read Across America Event Grant to enhance state affiliate-coordinated Read Across America events and/or activities. Affiliates may apply for any amount up to a maximum of $20,000. Ideally, event(s) or activities should occur on or about NEA's Read Across America Day, which is typically held in early March each year. Examples of appropriate events and/or activities include: statewide cat-a-van type tours that make school visits to conduct reading events and celebrate NEA's Read Across America, to be coordinated with the Local Association; multiple school events on or about early March; using the RAA Resource Calendar as a guide, events/activities that emphasis diverse books and authors for diverse audiences; larger reading event(s) with members and students, held at public venues such as children's museums, sports or entertainment facilities, libraries, or other public venue that will

accommodate several classes of students (possibly from multiple schools); and other Association-recommended event or activity. The annual deadline for application submission is December 2.

Geographic Focus: All States
Date(s) Application is Due: Dec 2
Amount of Grant: Up to 20,000 USD
Contact: Jesse Graytock, Grants Manager; (202) 822-7839 or (202) 822-7708; fax (202) 822-7779; jgraytock@nea.org or neafoundation@nea.org
Steven Grant, (202) 822-7272 or (202) 822-7708; fax (202) 822-7779; sgrant@nea.org
Internet: www.nea.org/grants/58935.htm
Sponsor: National Education Association Foundation
1201 Sixteenth Street NW, Suite 416
Washington, D.C. 20036

NEA Foundation Read Across America Library Books Awards 1732

The National Education Association Foundation Read Across America awards help public schools serving economically disadvantaged students purchase books for school libraries. One hundred approved awards will be payable to the applicant's school in the amount of $1,000. Only one eligible applicant per school may submit an application. Applications should be submitted as an email attachment. The annual deadline for application submissions is January 25.

Requirements: The applicant must be a practicing pre-K througg 12th grade teacher or education-support professional in a U.S. public school; be a member of the National Education Association; and agree to serve as the contact person for the award and all related public-relations activities. At least 40 percent of the students in the applicant's school must be eligible for the free or reduced-price lunch program.

Restrictions: Funds may not be used for lobbying or religious purposes or to pay stipends, salaries, or administrative fees. Employees, members of the board of directors, and immediate family members of the staff and board of the foundation or the National Education Association are not eligible. Funds are not transferable and will paid only to the school identified in the application form.

Geographic Focus: All States
Date(s) Application is Due: Jan 25
Amount of Grant: 1,000 USD
Contact: Jesse Graytock, Grants Manager; (202) 822-7839 or (202) 822-7708; fax (202) 822-7779; jgraytock@nea.org or neafoundation@nea.org
Internet: www.nea.org/grants/886.htm
Sponsor: National Education Association Foundation
1201 Sixteenth Street NW, Suite 416
Washington, D.C. 20036

NEA Student Program Communities Redefining Education Advocacy 1733
Through Empowerment (CREATE) Grants

The NEAs Communities Redefining Education Advocacy Through Empowerment (CREATE) Grants are chapter and/or statewide community service projects that positively promote the NEA Student Program through strategies designed to enhance public education, increase advocacy and outreach to communities; support younger educators involvement in the Association; and supports the development of innovative approaches to engagement. CREATE grants will be awarded for projects that align with one or more of the core values of the NEA Student Program: Teacher Quality (up to $3,000), Community Outreach (up to $3,000), and Political Action (up to $2,000). Annual deadlines for application submission are February 16 and October 30.

Requirements: All applications must be submitted electronically. All applications requesting amounts over $1,000 or more must include a one- to three-minute video presentation describing the project. Applications that require a video submission will be narrowed down and featured online for public voting. The top three videos in each category will be awarded their requested grant amount.

Geographic Focus: All States, American Samoa, District of Columbia, Guam, Marshall Islands, Northern Mariana Islands, Puerto Rico, U.S. Virgin Islands
Date(s) Application is Due: Feb 16; Oct 30
Amount of Grant: Up to 3,000 USD
Contact: Evette Brown, NEA Student Program; (202) 822-7176 or (202) 822-7708; fax (202) 822-7974; ebrown@nea.org
Internet: www.nea.org/grants/61972.htm
Sponsor: National Education Association
1201 16th Street NW, Suite 712
Washington, D.C. 20036-3290

NEH Family and Youth Programs in American History Grants 1734

As part of the We the People initiative, NEH invites proposals for public programs that encourage intergenerational learning about and reflection on significant topics in U.S. history and culture. Grants will support programming tailored to youth and/or family audiences at museums, libraries, historical societies and sites, parks, and other places in the community. The projects should: strengthen knowledge and appreciation of American history among young people through activities outside the classroom; or encourage families to explore themes and ideas from American history together. NEH encourages projects that: highlight documents and artifacts significant to American history; make humanities content central to the project; and collaborate with other organizations to extend the reach of the project.

Requirements: Any U.S. nonprofit organization with 501(c)3 tax exempt status is eligible, as are state and local governmental agencies and tribal governments.

Restrictions: Activities that take place at schools during regular school hours or as part of the school curriculum are not eligible. Individuals are not eligible to apply.

Geographic Focus: All States
Date(s) Application is Due: Jan 11
Amount of Grant: 40,000 - 400,000 USD

Contact: Kathy Toavs, Program Analyst; (202) 606-8474 or (202) 606-8463; ktoavs@neh.gov
Patti Van Tuyl, Senior Program Officer; (202) 606-8299 or (202) 606-8463; pvantuyl@neh.gov
Internet: www.neh.gov/grants/guidelines/familyyouthprograms.html
Sponsor: National Endowment for the Humanities - 1
1100 Pennsylvania Avenue NW, Room 511
Washington, D.C. 20506

NEH Picturing America Awards   1735
The National Endowment for the Humanities believes that engaging, masterful works of art can bring the story of America to life. When displayed on the walls of your classroom or library, Picturing America's noteworthy, high-quality images offer an innovative way to teach American history and culture. These images, and the accompanying Teachers Resource Book, help students better understand America's diverse people and places and connect them to our nation's travails and triumphs. Visual stimulation enhances learning and makes it more enjoyable. Art can introduce social studies, literature, civics, and even science and math in an immediate, tangible way. With Picturing America, students develop a deeper understanding of history and our shared human—and American—experience. Picturing America benefits include: an innovative, free resource that provides educators with an engaging way to teach American history, culture, and other subjects through the use of artistic images; public, private, parochial, and charter and home school consortia (K-12), as well as public libraries in the United States and its territories, may receive a total of 40 high-quality, laminated reproductions (approximately 24" x 36"); an illustrated Teachers Resource Book, with activities organized by elementary, middle and high school levels; and access to the Picturing America Web site, which contains additional information and resources, including innovative lesson plans.
Requirements: Public, private, parochial, and charter and home school consortia (K-12) may apply.
Geographic Focus: All States
Contact: Kathy Toavs, Program Analyst; (202) 606-8474 or (202) 606-8463; ktoavs@neh.gov or wethepeople@neh.gov
Patti Van Tuyl, Senior Program Officer; (202) 606-8299 or (202) 606-8463; pvantuyl@neh.gov or wethepeople@neh.gov
Internet: picturingamerica.neh.gov/educators.php
Sponsor: National Endowment for the Humanities - 1
1100 Pennsylvania Avenue NW, Room 511
Washington, D.C. 20506

Nellie Mae Education Foundation District-Level Change Grants   1736
The Nellie Mae Education Foundation District-Level Systems Change Grants support the shift in high school-level education in New England to prepare students to thrive in a global, complex, fast changing society. Grant programs promote student centered models of schooling that offer a path away from a one size fits all approach to a more customized approach to maximize learning for all students. The initiative focuses on three priority areas: developing school and district designs and practices that enable all learners to achieve high standards; creating sustainable policy change to support these new approaches; and generating public will and increasing demand for changes in practice. Examples of allowable activities for funding include: engaging central office, school administrators, and teachers in identifying current initiatives and how they compete with or support a student centered learning frame; surveying student needs and challenges and what motivates them to achieve academically and personally; creating greater building level autonomy and funding streams based on student needs rather than programs; researching feasibility, designing and planning for the appropriate blended learning model including visits to blended learning schools; using technology as an essential tool in learning environments and professional development; or administrator visits from student centered schools. The Foundation will support self-assessment activities, efforts to build, forge or nurture a common vision and mission for the work, and integration of this work with other school/district initiatives. Funds can support purchasing online and hardcopy literacy materials to support complex Common Core State Standards (CCSS) text demands; engaging a team of district stakeholders to conduct an analysis of culture of the system's various dimensions; or administrative visits from student centered schools. Proposal information, including the request for proposal, a list of supplemental materials and instructions, questions to address in the proposal, a list of frequently asked questions and previously funded projects, and an instructional webinar, is located at the Foundation website.
Requirements: The Foundation's activities include both making grants to the public charities it supports and providing services to those organizations. The Foundation operates exclusively to promote the charitable and educational purposes of nonprofit educational organizations, including universities, colleges, secondary schools, elementary schools and other educational organizations that are described in the IRS Code Section 501(c)3.
Restrictions: Funding for this project is concentrated on urban school districts and learning centers in Connecticut, Massachusetts, and Rhode Island. The Foundation does not fund capital campaigns, endowments, scholarships or fellowships, debt reduction or cash reserves, building construction or renovation, and certain indirect costs.
Geographic Focus: Connecticut, Massachusetts, Rhode Island
Date(s) Application is Due: Oct 18
Amount of Grant: 25,000 - 1,000,000 USD
Samples: New England Resource Center for Higher Education, Boston, Massachusetts, Project Compass: a multi-year initiative that supports institutions seeking to systematize changes essential to expanding, sustaining, and integrating rigorous, evidence-based efforts to retain larger numbers of underserved students, $375,000; Sanford School Department, Sanford, Maine, based on the Reinventing Schools Coalition (RISC) model, a model that focuses on a research based approach to student-centered, proficiency based learning where students demonstrate proficiency at commonly understood and meaningful standards, $1.1 million; Hyde Park Task Force, Youth Organizing Project, Jamaica Plain, Massachusetts, project that focuses on developing 50 urban youth leaders who successfully advocate for

themselves and their peers in their communities and schools by engaging in community organizing campaigns, $25,000.
Contact: Stephanie Cheney, Senior Manager, Grants and Special Programs; (781) 348-4240; fax (781) 348-4299; scheney@nmefdn.org
Internet: www.nmefoundation.org/grants/district-level-systems-change
Sponsor: Nellie Mae Education Foundation
1250 Hancock Street, Suite 205N
Quincy, MA 02169

Nell J. Redfield Foundation Grants   1737
The foundation awards grants to eligible Nevada organizations in its areas of interest, including biomedical research, health care and health organizations, elderly, children with disabilities, education, human services, and religion. Types of support include building construction/renovation, capital campaigns, equipment acquisition, program development, and scholarship funds. Deadlines are at least ten days before a regularly scheduled quarterly meeting of the Board (March, June, September and December). Contact the office to request the application form and guidelines.
Requirements: Nevada nonprofit organizations are eligible with preferences for organizations in northern Nevada.
Geographic Focus: Nevada
Amount of Grant: Up to 100,000 USD
Contact: Gerald C. Smith; (775) 323-1373; redfieldfoundation@yahoo.com
Sponsor: Nell J. Redfield Foundation
P.O. Box 61
Reno, NV 89502

Nestle Purina PetCare Educational Grants   1738
Nestlé Purina PetCare has a rich history of community involvement in greater St. Louis, Missouri, their world headquarters for pet food, and in the cities with manufacturing facilities. The company supports established organizations with diverse boards, effective leadership, clear objectives, sound financial practices and multiple sources of support. Educational Grants are generally given for programs that focus on educational opportunities for disadvantaged youth. Programs might include college readiness, character education, after school programs and field trips.
Requirements: Organizations located in the greater St. Louis area or in a city where the company has manufacturing facilities are eligible. The St. Louis area includes an area within a 100-mile radius of downtown St. Louis. Cities with manufacturing facilities include: Allentown, Pennsylvania; Atlanta, Georgia; Bloomfield, Missouri; Cape Girardeau, Missouri; Clinton, Iowa; Crete, Nebraska; Davenport, Iowa; Denver, Colorado; Dunkirk, New York; Flagstaff, Arizona; Fort Dodge, Iowa; Hager City, Wisconsin; Jefferson, Wisconsin; King William, Virginia; Maricopa, California; Mechanicsburg, Pennsylvania; Oklahoma City, Oklahoma; Springfield, Missouri; St. Joseph, Missouri; Weirton, West Virginia; and Zanesville, Ohio. Application can be made at the website.
Geographic Focus: Arizona, California, Colorado, Georgia, Iowa, Missouri, Nebraska, New York, Ohio, Oklahoma, Pennsylvania, Virginia, West Virginia, Wisconsin
Contact: Public Relations Manager; (314) 982-1000
Internet: www.nestlepurina.com/CharitableGiving.aspx
Sponsor: Nestle Purina PetCare Company
Checkerboard Square
Saint Louis, MO 63164

Nestle Purina PetCare Youth Grants   1739
Nestlé Purina PetCare has a rich history of community involvement in greater St. Louis, Missouri, their world headquarters for pet food, and in the cities with manufacturing facilities. The company supports established organizations with diverse boards, effective leadership, clear objectives, sound financial practices and multiple sources of support. Youth Grants are generally given for programs that focus on the education and well being of disadvantaged youth. These might include youth camps or youth employment programs.
Requirements: Organizations located in the greater St. Louis area or in a city where the company has manufacturing facilities are eligible. The St. Louis area includes an area within a 100-mile radius of downtown St. Louis. Cities with manufacturing facilities include: Allentown, Pennsylvania; Atlanta, Georgia; Bloomfield, Missouri; Cape Girardeau, Missouri; Clinton, Iowa; Crete, Nebraska; Davenport, Iowa; Denver, Colorado; Dunkirk, New York; Flagstaff, Arizona; Fort Dodge, Iowa; Hager City, Wisconsin; Jefferson, Wisconsin; King William, Virginia; Maricopa, California; Mechanicsburg, Pennsylvania; Oklahoma City, Oklahoma; Springfield, Missouri; St. Joseph, Missouri; Weirton, West Virginia; and Zanesville, Ohio. Application can be made at the website.
Geographic Focus: Arizona, California, Colorado, Georgia, Iowa, Missouri, Nebraska, New York, Ohio, Oklahoma, Pennsylvania, Virginia, West Virginia, Wisconsin
Contact: Public Relations Manager; (314) 982-1000
Internet: www.nestlepurina.com/CharitableGiving.aspx
Sponsor: Nestle Purina PetCare Company
Checkerboard Square
Saint Louis, MO 63164

Nestle Very Best in Youth Competition   1740
Nestlé sponsors the biennial Nestlé Very Best In Youth competition which was created to spotlight the best in youth leadership. The competition identifies teens whose efforts are making a profound impact in lives other than their own. Nestlé donates $1,000 in the name of each winner to the charity of his or her choice. Nestlé also awards trips for winners and a parent or guardian to Los Angeles, California for the Nestlé Very Best In Youth awards ceremony. The trip includes round trip coach air travel, hotel accommodations for three

nights, and spending money. Each contestant receives a certificate of achievement from Nestlé and samples of Nestlé products.

Requirements: Contestants must be between thirteen and eighteen and have parental or legal guardian permission to submit an entry form. Contestants must demonstrate good citizenship, a strong academic record, and show how they have made a special contribution to their school, church or community. Application include two letters of recommendation, a transcript or current report card, and a consent form signed by a parent or legal guardian. The website provides an-line application and deadline information.

Geographic Focus: All States

Contact: Community Affairs Director; (818) 549-6677; NestleVeryBestInYouth@us.nestle.com

Internet: verybestinyouth.nestleusa.com/Public/

Sponsor: Nestle USA

800 North Brand Boulevard

Glendale, CA 91203

Nevada Community Foundation Grants 1741

The Foundation is committed to improving the lives of southern Nevadans today and for future generations by matching acts of caring to the many needs in the community. The Foundation has committed its discretionary dollars to multi-year funding of programs that are aligned with Ready for Life®, a statewide collaborative movement to ensure that all Nevada youth are "ready for life" and supported by a community ethic that values education, links youth to workforce opportunities, and creates a safe learning environment for students. There are also corporate granting programs from time to time. Applicants are encouraged to check updates on the website frequently for upcoming grant programs and deadlines.

Geographic Focus: Nevada

Samples: Boys Hope Girls Hope of Nevada, Las Vegas, Nevada, $20,021 - program support; Meadows School, Las Vegas, Nevada, $39,563 - program support; and Boys and Girls Club of Henderson, Las Vegas, Nevada, $58,897 - program support.

Contact: Gian F. Brosco, Esq.; (702) 892-2326; fax (702) 892-8580; gian.brosco@nevadacf.org

Internet: www.nevadacf.org/nonprofits/

Sponsor: Nevada Community Foundation

1635 Village Center Circle, Suite 160

Las Vegas, NV 89134

New Covenant Farms Grants 1742

The New Covenant Farms program, established in Idaho in 2000 by the L.M. Davenport Warehouse, provides funding and goods for children and families in both Texas and Mexico. Types of support include: cash; housing; clothing; food; education; and other necessities. There are no specific deadlines, though written applications are required. Applicants should include: name and location; exemption status; what food products and distribution needs are required; and budget.

Geographic Focus: Texas, Mexico

Samples: Rick Caywood Ministries, Crawford, Texas, $3,500—food distribution to the poor; Rio Bravo Ministries, Mission, Texas,—home to 65 children in Reynosa Tam, Mexico; Instituto De Magdiel, Matamoros Tam, Mexico—training students for Christian Ministry.

Contact: Lewis M. Davenport III, President; (208) 934-5600 or (208) 934-5609

Sponsor: New Covenant Farms

1737 East 1800 South

Gooding, ID 83330-5095

New Earth Foundation Grants 1743

New Earth Foundation seeks to fund innovative projects that enhance life on our planet and brighten the future, furthering peace. Smaller, newer 501(c)3 organizations are the focus of grants given, so that the foundation's gift can make a more significant contribution to the work of the recipient organization. The grants given by NEF support a wide variety of projects in many fields of endeavor, including but not limited to environmental initiatives that are working to help eliminate pollution and to save the planet's ecosystems, community efforts that create models of social sustainability, educational innovations that prepare youth to become the socially responsible leaders of the future, and strategies that offer economic improvement and opportunities. NEF particularly appreciates projects that are replicable so that excellent ideas and work can multiply and benefit many.

Requirements: 501(c)3 nonprofit organizations are eligible to apply. To begin the application process submit (electronically) a Letter of Inquiry to the foundation, providing basic information about your organization and about your program/project. After reviewing the Letter of Inquiry, you may be invited to submit a complete application.

Restrictions: NEF does not fund organizations that: offer mainstream social services or are local organizations that are affiliated with a national organization such as Boys & Girls Clubs, Big Brothers/Big Sisters, Habitat for Humanity, the Cancer Society and other such organizations; are good candidates for governmental funding; are involved in community housing and renovation; have standard forms of after-school programs, outdoor summer camps/expeditions, or gardening programs; are land and building preservation programs; are capital improvement/building projects; are involved in land purchases. However, NEF may consider community housing, after school programs, children, youth, summer camps or garden programs that are significantly innovative, transformative and effective.

Geographic Focus: All States

Amount of Grant: 5,000 - 7,500 USD

Contact: Dr. Bara Loveland, President; newearthfoundation@foundationsource.com

Internet: www.newearthfoundation.org/apply.html

Sponsor: New Earth Foundation

P.O. Box 100

Sedona, AZ 86339

Newfoundland and Labrador Arts Council ArtSmarts Grants 1744

The objectives of the Newfoundland and Labrador Arts Council (NLAC) ArtSmarts Grants are to build long-term, self sufficient local partnerships that link young people, artists or arts organizations, schools, and the broader community; to enable schools to integrate arts activities in a variety of subject areas that align with the provincial curriculum; to provide opportunities for young people to actively participate in the arts, thereby encouraging them to develop their intellectual and communication skills; and to enhance appreciation of the importance of culture and the arts, thereby encouraging long-term support for artists and arts organizations.

Requirements: Only schools and school boards in the provincial K-12 system may apply. Projects must incorporate artistic disciplines served by the NLAC. These are dance (contemporary and traditional styles), film and video, new media arts (computer animation, online art creation), multidiscipline (exploring two or more art forms), music (classical, modern, traditional), theatre (including storytelling and circus), visual arts (including traditional crafts, photography, pottery) and creative writing. Questions regarding eligibility should be directed to the Program Manager before applying.

Restrictions: Funding is up to 80% of the overall cost of a project, to a maximum grant of $5,500. The remaining 20% of the project costs (cash or in kind) must be confirmed at the time of application.

Geographic Focus: Canada

Date(s) Application is Due: May 31

Amount of Grant: 5,500 CAD

Samples: Bishop Abraham School, St. John's, Newfoundland and Labrador, Canada, $4,800 - funding for communities coming together project; Ecole des Grands-Vents, St. John's, Newfoundland and Labrador, Canada, $1,704 - funding for the art of shadow puppetry project; and Goulds Elementary, St. John's, Newfoundland and Labrador, Canada, $5,344 - funding for oral traditions project.

Contact: Ken Murphy, Program Manager; (709) 726-2212 or (866) 726-2212; fax (709) 726-0619; kmurphyl@nlac.ca

Internet: www.nlac.ca/grants/artsmarts.htm

Sponsor: Newfoundland and Labrador Arts Council

Newman Building, 1 Springdale Street, P.O. Box 98

St Johns, NL A1C 5H5 Canada

Newfoundland and Labrador Arts Council School Touring Grants 1745

The Newfoundland and Labrador Arts Council (NLAC) School Touring Grants are available to professional artists, groups and not-for-profit arts organizations to support significant touring productions to schools throughout the province. Offered in partnership with the Department of Education through its Cultural Connections Strategy, Grants provide students with direct access to high quality artistic experiences. Grants cover touring costs only (i.e. travel, accommodation, per diem, artist and technician fees, tour administration, royalties, and limited rehearsal).

Requirements: Grants are open to all artistic disciplines served by the NLAC (dance, film, multi-discipline, music, theatre, visual arts, writing). Professional individual applicants: must be Canadian citizens or have Permanent Resident Status; must be current residents of Newfoundland and Labrador for a minimum of twelve consecutive months immediately prior to the time of application; and must be at least eighteen years of age or hold post-secondary standing. Professional groups and not-for-profit organizations: must have the development of the arts as its primary mandate; must have been active in Newfoundland and Labrador for a minimum of twelve consecutive months at the time of application; must have at least half its members (for groups) or board members (for organizations) residing in Newfoundland and Labrador; must have the majority of members be at least eighteen years of age or hold post-secondary standing; and must pay artist fees of an acceptable national standard. Applicants with concerns regarding eligibility are encouraged to contact the Program Manager before applying.

Restrictions: A professional artist, group, or not-for-profit arts organization can apply for one Grant per school year.

Geographic Focus: Canada

Date(s) Application is Due: Jun 15

Amount of Grant: 20,000 CAD

Samples: Nickel Independent Film Festival, St. John's, Newfoundland and Labrador, Canada, $11,043 - Nickel Festival/Reel Youth Rural High School Film Tour; Opera Roadshow, St. John's, Newfoundland and Labrador, Canada, $17,772 - New Opera Tour: Le Nez de la Sorciere/The Witch's Nose; and Soundbone Traditional Arts Foundation Inc., Ladle Cove, Newfoundland and Labrador, Canada, $17,980 - Traditional Music and Dance Tour 2012.

Contact: Ken Murphy, Program Manager; (709) 726-2212 or (866) 726-2212; fax (709) 726-0619; kmurphy@nlac.ca

Internet: www.nlac.ca/grants/school.htm

Sponsor: Newfoundland and Labrador Arts Council

Newman Building, 1 Springdale Street, P.O. Box 98

St Johns, NL A1C 5H5 Canada

Newfoundland and Labrador Arts Council Visiting Artists Grants 1746

The Newfoundland and Labrador Arts Council Visiting Artists Grants are for schools to bring individual artists, groups of artists, or arts organizations into the school to provide students with direct personal contact with practicing professional artists. Grants cover artist fees, materials, and travel costs. Grants are offered in partnership with the Cultural Connections Strategy of the Newfoundland and Labrador Department of Education, the Newfoundland and Labrador Teachers' Association, and the Newfoundland and Labrador Arts Council. Funding is up to $500 to cover artist fees and up to $200 for art supplies or equipment rental required for a project. Travel subsidies for schools on the island are up to $200 and for schools in Labrador up to $500. There is no deadline, but schools must submit an application at least two weeks before the artist or group is due to come to the school.

Requirements: Eligible applicants include teachers at any school in the provincial K-12 system. Each grade configuration (K-3, 4-6, 7-9, 10-12) in a school is eligible to receive one

Grant per school year, or a school can receive one Grant for every 150 students enrolled, to a maximum of four Grants per school year. Each visit must involve at least 10 students.
Restrictions: Teachers or classes with current ArtsSmarts or Learning Through the Arts Grants are not eligible.
Geographic Focus: Canada
Samples: Bishop Feild Elementary, St. John's, Newfoundland and Labrador, Canada, $700 - printmaker; Bishop's College, St. John's, Newfoundland and Labrador, Canada, $900 - visual artist; and Mary Queen of Peace, St. John's, Newfoundland and Labrador, Canada, $700 - visual artist.
Contact: Ken Murphy, Program Manager; (709) 726-2212 or (866) 726-2212; fax (709) 726-0619; kmurphy@nlac.ca
Internet: www.nlac.ca/grants/vap.htm
Sponsor: Newfoundland and Labrador Arts Council
Newman Building, 1 Springdale Street, P.O. Box 98
St Johns, NL A1C 5H5 Canada

New Hampshire Charitable Foundation Community Unrestricted Grants   1747

The New Hampshire Charitable Foundation seeks to improve the quality of life for New Hampshire citizens by distributing funding to qualifying organizations and scholarship assistance to the state's residents. Areas of support include arts, humanities, environment and conservation, health, and social and community services. Types of support include seed grants, scholarships and scholarship funds, program development, technical assistance, demonstration grants, development grants, endowments, and training grants. Eight regional divisions of the Foundation exist to benefit particular areas of the state: Capital, Lakes, Manchester, Monadnock, Nashua, North Country, Piscataqua, and Upper Valley. Although a limited number of multi-year grants are made, awards are not usually repeated or renewed. This competitive grants program awards unrestricted grants to support an organization's general operations (rather than a particular project or capacity-building effort). This program was formerly called 'Operating Grants.'
Requirements: Organizations serving New Hampshire and selected communities in Maine and Vermont within the Foundation's eight regions are eligible. Applicants must be recognized as tax-exempt under Section 501(c)3 of the Internal Revenue Code. In general, organizations are eligible for one grant per calendar year from the Foundation's Community Grants Program (including Unrestricted and Express grants).
Restrictions: Through the Community Grants program, the Foundation does not make unrestricted grants to: Municipal, County or State Government; Public and Private schools; Religious organizations, unless all services being funded are non-discriminatory, non-sectarian and benefit the larger community; Hospitals; or Colleges and Universities.
Geographic Focus: New Hampshire
Date(s) Application is Due: Oct 2
Amount of Grant: Up to 20,000 USD
Contact: Anne Phillips, (603) 225-6641, ext. 232 or (800) 464-6641, ext. 232; fax (603) 225-1700; Anne.Phillips@nhcf.org
Wendy Cahill, Senior Community Grants Associate; (603) 225-6641, ext. 21249 or (800) 464-6641, ext. 21249; fax (603) 225-1700; Wendy.Cahill@nhcf.org
Internet: www.nhcf.org/how-can-we-help-you/apply-for-a-grant/unrestricted-grant-program/
Sponsor: New Hampshire Charitable Foundation
37 Pleasant Street
Concord, NH 03301-4005

New Hampshire Charitable Foundation Neil and Louise Tillotson Fund -   1748
Empower Coös Youth Grants

The New Hampshire Charitable Foundation seeks to improve the quality of life for New Hampshire citizens by distributing funding to qualifying organizations and scholarship assistance to the state's residents. Areas of support include arts, humanities, environment and conservation, health, and social and community services. Types of support include seed grants, scholarships and scholarship funds, program development, technical assistance, demonstration grants, development grants, endowments, and training grants. Eight regional divisions of the Foundation exist to benefit particular areas of the state: Capital, Lakes, Manchester, Monadnock, Nashua, North Country, Piscataqua, and Upper Valley. Although a limited number of multi-year grants are made, awards are not usually repeated or renewed. Neil and Louise Tillotson Fund - Empower Coös Youth Grants support programs in Coos County, New Hampshire and Essex County, Vermont and surrounding communities in both states that focus on: reducing carbon emissions; increasing extracurricular activities for youth; and strengthening community engagement. This grant program awards support of up to $10,000 to eligible organizations. The application submission deadline is January 16.
Requirements: Organizations recognized as tax-exempt by the IRS are eligible, including U.S. nonprofit organizations with 501(c)3 status, tax-exempt public agencies, schools, municipalities, and places of worship for non-religious, non-denominational, and inclusive programming.
Geographic Focus: New Hampshire, Vermont
Date(s) Application is Due: Jan 16
Amount of Grant: Up to 10,000 USD
Contact: Anne Phillips, (603) 225-6641, ext. 232 or (800) 464-6641, ext. 232; fax (603) 225-1700; Anne.Phillips@nhcf.org
Internet: www.nhcf.org/how-can-we-help-you/apply-for-a-grant/empower-coos-youth-grants-program/
Sponsor: New Hampshire Charitable Foundation
37 Pleasant Street
Concord, NH 03301-4005

New Hampshire Department of Justice Children's Justice Act Coronavirus   1749
Emergency Grants

Recognizing the impact of the coronavirus on public and non-profit agencies involved in the handling of child abuse and neglect cases, the New Hampshire Department of Justice announces the availability of federal funding through the Children's Justice Act Grant (CJA). This emergency funding is targeted at agencies that have immediate needs as a direct result of this current public health crisis. The total amount of federal funding available is $30,000. Funds awarded under this sub-grant must be used by September 30. Examples of permissible activities include: equipment or supplies (including technology needed to work remotely as a result of the coronavirus); training (costs relative to providing training, creating training materials, registration fees for training etc.); new or increased operating expenses (new cell phone service agreements, upgraded Internet services, or virtual meeting software etc.); or other vital operating expenses (utility bills, rent, insurance) that were impacted as a result of the coronavirus.
Requirements: Eligible applicants for CJA funding are public or non-profit organizations that are involved in either the assessment, investigative or judicial handling of cases of child abuse and neglect.
Restrictions: Funds may not be used to supplant state or local funds but must be used to increase the amounts of such funds that would, in the absence of federal funds, be made available.
Geographic Focus: New Hampshire
Amount of Grant: Up to 30,000 USD
Contact: Thomas Kaempfer, Program Agency Contact; (603) 271-8090 or (603) 271-3658; thomas.kaempfer@doj.nh.gov or grants.apps@doj.nh.gov
Internet: www.doj.nh.gov/grants-management/funding-availability.htm
Sponsor: New Hampshire Department of Justice
33 Capitol Street
Concord, NH 03301

New Jersey Center for Hispanic Policy, Research and Development   1750
Innovative Initiatives Grants

The Center for Hispanic Policy, Research and Development (CHPRD) was established in 1975 to address the needs of the Hispanic community, recognizing that it was imperative to pay particular attention to this segment of the population, which may have been historically neglected. The CHPRD seeks to empower, provide financial support and technical assistance to primarily Hispanic community-based organizations throughout New Jersey and also ensures the executive and legislative branches are informed of legislative initiatives with potential impact on the Hispanic community. CHPRD seeks to aggressively promote a new model of community development that is focused on making REAL impacts in people's lives while helping community based organizations achieve greater self-sufficiency. In the area of Innovative Initiatives, funding is available to promote and encourage innovative community service programs that are culturally competent, and whose effective services address specific target areas. The CHPRD will fund nonprofit organizations for start-up monies for innovative initiatives and services that contribute to one of the following target areas: children at risk; prevention of health risks and diseases; Senior Citizen Information and Referral Services; or Mental Health Support Services responsive to cultural needs.
Requirements: Funding for this program is available to public/private non-profit and community-based-organizations whose primary focus is the implementation of programs that address the needs of the Hispanic community of the State of New Jersey. All non-profit, private organizations must have: 501(c)3 Federal non-profit status for at least one year prior to submission of application; a clearly articulated Hispanic mission and focus for the organization and its programs; valid Articles of Incorporation filed prior to July 1, 2008; and, at the time of application, have been in existence and actively providing public programs or services for at least the past three years. Primary consideration for CHPRD funding will be provided to Hispanic community based organizations (HCBOs) that provide direct services and whose staff, board and clientele mirrors the community it will serve.
Restrictions: Ineligible applicants include organizations that are unincorporated, incorporated in another state, or incorporated as profit-making entities. Organizations, agencies, institutions, or projects that do not have organizational goals related to the Hispanic community or a specific Hispanic project to propose will not be considered.
Geographic Focus: New Jersey
Contact: Administrator; (609) 984-3223; fax (609) 633-7141
Internet: www.nj.gov/state/programs/dos_program_chprd_grants.html
Sponsor: New Jersey Department of State
225 West State Street, P.O. Box 301
Trenton, NJ 08625-0301

New Jersey Office of Faith Based Initiatives English as a Second   1751
Language Grants

The mission of the Office of Faith-based Initiatives is to eliminate all barriers to funding and other resource opportunities, create greater access for partnership and enhance the capacity of faith and community-based organizations to effectively design, implement successful programming and efficiently manage the day-to-day operations of their organizations. The English as a Second Language program will assist and instruct non-English speaking individuals to learn the Basic English Language with lessons designed around everyday scenarios and circumstances. Applications are submitted to the OFBI on the System for Administering Grants Electronically (SAGE) and reviewed by an outside independent panel. Final determinations will be made by the Director. The maximum request is $20,000, and the annual application deadline is July 30.
Requirements: To be eligible to receive a grant under this program, an applicant must submit a joint application as the lead agency in conjunction with a minimum of three collaborating organizations. Teachers in the program must be certified and have the necessary ESL credentials. The lead agency must: be a faith-based non-profit and/or community-based organization; be incorporated in the State of New Jersey as a non-profit corporation or a foreign non-profit corporation; be tax-exempt by determination of the Internal Revenue Service in accordance with Section 501(c)3; be in good standing with the Department of Treasury, Business Service Center; be registered with the New Jersey Division of Consumer

Affairs, Charitable Registration and Investigation Section; submit a formal Memorandum of Understanding (MOU) with collaborative partners within 180 days of contract execution; and provide letters of support from all collaborating partners with the application.
Restrictions: Collaborating organizations may not partner with the lead organization's sister organization and/or for profit and non-profit organizations led by the same person or governing entity. Houses of Worship are eligible to partner as a collaborating organization, but cannot receive state funds that are granted to lead organizations.
Geographic Focus: New Jersey
Date(s) Application is Due: Jul 30
Amount of Grant: Up to 20,000 USD
Contact: Administrator; (609) 292-8286 or (609) 984-6952; fax (609) 633-7141
Internet: www.nj.gov/state/programs/dos_program_faith_based_funding.html
Sponsor: New Jersey Department of State
225 W. State Street, P.O. Box 456
Trenton, NJ 08625

New Jersey Office of Faith Based Initiatives Services to At Risk Youth Grants   1752
The mission of the Office of Faith-based Initiatives is to eliminate all barriers to funding and other resource opportunities, create greater access for partnership and enhance the capacity of faith and community-based organizations to effectively design, implement successful programming and efficiently manage the day-to-day operations of their organizations. The Services to At Risk Youth program should include, but is not limited to: promoting self esteem; promoting entrepreneurial initiatives; preventing gang participation; preventing substance abuse; developing effective study habits; promoting public speaking; and providing after school homework assistance and tutorial services. Applications are submitted to the OFBI on the System for Administering Grants Electronically (SAGE) and reviewed by an outside independent panel. Final determinations will be made by the Director. The maximum request is $25,000, and the annual application deadline is July 30.
Requirements: To be eligible to receive a grant under this program, an applicant must submit a joint application as the lead agency in conjunction with a minimum of three collaborating organizations. At least one of the collaborating agencies within this category must be a school. The lead agency must: be a faith-based non-profit and/or community-based organization; be incorporated in the State of New Jersey as a non-profit corporation or a foreign non-profit corporation; be tax-exempt by determination of the Internal Revenue Service in accordance with Section 501(c)3; be in good standing with the Department of Treasury, Business Service Center; be registered with the New Jersey Division of Consumer Affairs, Charitable Registration and Investigation Section; submit a formal Memorandum of Understanding (MOU) with collaborative partners within 180 days of contract execution; and provide letters of support from all collaborating partners with the application.
Restrictions: Collaborating organizations may not partner with the lead organization's sister organization and/or for profit and non-profit organizations led by the same person or governing entity. Houses of Worship are eligible to partner as a collaborating organization, but cannot receive state funds that are granted to lead organizations.
Geographic Focus: New Jersey
Date(s) Application is Due: Jul 30
Amount of Grant: Up to 25,000 USD
Contact: Administrator; (609) 292-8286 or (609) 984-6952; fax (609) 633-7141
Internet: www.nj.gov/state/programs/dos_program_faith_based_funding.html
Sponsor: New Jersey Department of State
225 W. State Street, P.O. Box 456
Trenton, NJ 08625

New York Foundation Grants   1753
The Foundation supports groups in New York City that are working on problems of urgent concern to residents of disadvantaged communities and neighborhoods. Support is provided to organizations that work in ways that inspire New Yorkers to become more educated and active participants in the overall life of the city. The Foundation places a priority on supporting community organizing and advocacy strategies. While support is given to groups that utilize multiple strategies, including direct service, preference is given to those moving toward incorporating advocacy and organizing. Of particular interest is start-up grants to new, untested programs that have few other sources of support. Interested applicants should send a letter of inquiry outlining the project and the budget.
Requirements: Eligible projects must: involve New York City or a particular neighborhood of the city; address a critical or emerging need, particularly involving youth or the elderly; and articulate how a grant from the Foundation would advance the applicant's work.
Restrictions: The following is not eligible: grants to individuals or to capital campaigns; support of research studies, films, conferences, or publications; requests from outside New York City except from organizations working on statewide issues of concern to youth, the elderly, or the poor; and grants outside of the United States. Letters of inquiry are accepted by mail only, not fax or email.
Geographic Focus: New York
Date(s) Application is Due: Mar 1; Jul 1; Nov 1
Amount of Grant: 40,000 - 50,000 USD
Samples: Battered Women's Resource Center, New York, New York, $45,000 - community organizing support; Brotherhood/Sister Sol, New York, New York, $42,500 - for a social change training program for youth activists and organizers aged 14-18; and Cidadao Global, New York, New York, $45,000 - to promote the human rights of immigrants and strengthen citizen participation.
Contact: Maria Mottola, Executive Director; (212) 594-8009
Internet: www.nyf.org/how/guidelines
Sponsor: New York Foundation
350 Fifth Avenue, Room 2901
New York, NY 10118

NFL Charities NFL Player Foundation Grants   1754
NFL Charities supports the charitable and community service activities of both current and former NFL players by making grants that support the charitable efforts and missions of non-profit organizations of current and former NFL players.
Requirements: This grant is available to current and former NFL Players with non-profit organizations designated as a 501(c)3 or 509 of the IRS code. The organization must be established by the player, or the player must be a full-time, salaried employee of the non-profit organization (former player only). The applying organization must be located within the area of the player's current or former NFL team or in his hometown. Furthermore, the player must demonstrate active involvement with the organization. Former player applicants must be vested in the Bert Bell/Pete Rozelle NFL Retirement Plan in order to apply. Additionally, administrative costs must be less than 35% of the total budget, and the player's foundation must be recognized by the Council on Foundations and practicing under National Standards for U.S. Community Foundations. Grants applications must be completed online through the Grant Application Management System (G.A.M.S.).
Restrictions: Grants cannot be made to memorial foundations that were established on behalf of deceased NFL players. This grant will NOT provide support to organizations that seek funding solely to support a youth football camp.
Geographic Focus: All States
Date(s) Application is Due: Oct 29
Contact: Clare Graff, (212) 450-2435 or (917) 816-2885; clare.graff@nfl.com
Internet: www.nflcharities.org/grants/player_foundation
Sponsor: NFL Charities
280 Park Avenue, 17th Floor
New York, NY 10017

NFL Charities Pro Bowl Community Grants in Hawaii   1755
NFL Charities annually allocates $100,000 in grants to Hawaiian non-profit organizations in support of youth health and education programs. Organizations may provide: Educational and youth literacy services, assistance with study towards college or other post-secondary pursuits, and/or motivation and incentive programs that encourage youth to learn, to stay in school and to complete one's education; mentorship, psychological, therapeutic and/or necessary remedial services to support recovery, individual support or some kind of leadership empowerment; substance and/or physical/emotional abuse prevention and assistance programs; programs that promote good health, nutrition, hygiene, participation in athletics and physical fitness; and medical care, hospice and/or long-term health support services for youth and their families. Applications must be submitted through the online NFL Charities Grant Application Management System (G.A.M.S.) will be accepted.
Requirements: Organizations must be a 501(c)3 located in Hawaii and serve Hawaiian youth.
Restrictions: Only non-profit organization that are defined as tax-exempt under Section 501(c)3 of the IRS Code and are located and dedicated to serving youth in the state of Hawaii are eligible to apply. Grants cannot be made to individuals.
Geographic Focus: Hawaii
Date(s) Application is Due: Dec 23
Amount of Grant: 1,000 - 8,000 USD
Contact: Clare Graff, (212) 450-2435 or (917) 816-2885; clare.graff@nfl.com
Internet: www.nflcharities.org/grants/pro_bowl
Sponsor: NFL Charities
280 Park Avenue, 17th Floor
New York, NY 10017

NHSCA Artist Residence Grants   1756
Grants from the New Hampshire State Council on the Arts are a public investment in the cultural life of the state. Each competitive grant category is designed to meet an important purpose and need, and aligns with the Council's current strategic plan. Artist Residence Grants provide partial funding to bring juried teaching artists into classrooms and public schools to support creative learning and skills development in the arts. AIR grants support partial costs for artist residencies in a variety of arts disciplines, including all forms of visual arts (ceramics, drawing, painting, printmaking, weaving, etc.), dance, film/video, music, theater, traditional arts and creative writing. Artist Residencies in Schools projects funded by the State Arts Council are intended to set a model for this work. Therefore, the criteria are extensive and multi-faceted. We encourage schools who have never applied for a State Arts Council funded artist residency to contact the grants coordinator who can help you plan for this exciting opportunity. Participation in the arts increase students' abilities to problem solve, collaborate, use critical thinking skills and make decisions. Research studies show that an education in the arts has broad academic value, enables students to reach high levels of academic achievement, improves overall school performance and supports an environment that is most conducive to overall learning. Teaching artists reach students who may not excel or achieve well in other curriculum areas. Requests may be made for $1,000 to $7,500. The annual deadline for application submission is April 2.
Requirements: At a minimum, grants must be matched on a one-to-one basis. Any public school (pre-Kindergarten to Grade 12), or nonprofit organizations serving as alternative education sites for special needs students (pre-K to age 21) in New Hampshire, that are publicly funded or have 501(c)3 status from the Internal Revenue Service and are incorporated in the State of New Hampshire may apply.
Restrictions: A school may not receive more than one AIR grant during a school year per school or school level (elementary, middle and high school within a greater school complex). Schools that have been awarded AIR grants of $3,000 or more for three consecutive years must wait one year before applying for an AIR grant again. (This is an effort to encourage new school applicants to apply.) Private or parochial schools are not eligible for AIR grants, due to limited funds.
Geographic Focus: New Hampshire
Date(s) Application is Due: Apr 2
Amount of Grant: 1,000 - 7,500 USD

Contact: Cassandra Erickson Mason, Chief Grants Officer; (603) 271-7926 or
(603) 271-2789; fax (603) 271-3584; cassandra.mason@dncr.nh.gov
Internet: www.nh.gov/nharts/grants/partners/artistresidencies.htm
Sponsor: New Hampshire State Council on the Arts
19 Pillsbury Street, 1st Floor
Concord, NH 03301

NHSCA Conservation License Plate Grants   1757
Grants from the New Hampshire State Council on the Arts are a public investment
in the cultural life of the state. Each competitive grant category is designed to meet an
important purpose and need, and aligns with the Council's current strategic plan. Since
2001, the Conservation License Plate program has contributed to the ongoing success of
more than 150 projects around New Hampshire. All funds raised through the purchase
of Conservation License Plates are used for the promotion, protection and investment in
New Hampshire's natural, cultural and historic resources. The NH Division of Historical
Resources Conservation License Plate Grant Program awards grants through this program
for a maximum of $10,000 for the preservation and restoration of publicly owned historic
resources. Requests may be made for $2,000 to $20,000. Eligible projects include: projects
that conserve publicly owned artwork or arts documents that contribute to New Hampshire's
cultural heritage; projects that maintain or preserve artistic elements and function of cultural
facilities (e.g. murals, ornamental plaster work, theater curtains, stained glass windows,
weather vanes, etc.) while make those facilities and the arts programming that takes place
in them, more accessible to the public, including people with disabilities; and projects that
improve public access to historic artwork or arts documents while protecting and preserving
the originals. The annual Letter of Intent to apply must be received by the May 8 deadline,
with final application submission due by June 19.
Requirements: New Hampshire municipalities and towns, county agencies, state agencies
(other than the Department of Cultural Resources and its Divisions), federal agencies,
or nonprofit organizations that manage publicly owned historic cultural facilities, arts
documents or artworks that contribute to the state's cultural heritage that: have submitted
all required reports on past State Arts Council grants; and are in good standing with the
State Arts Council and the NH Attorney General's Office.
Restrictions: This grant does not support: projects that are receiving other State Arts Council
funds; or more than one application per applicant during the grant period (July 1 to June 30).
Geographic Focus: New Hampshire
Date(s) Application is Due: Jun 19
Amount of Grant: 2,000 - 20,000 USD
Contact: Cassandra Erickson Mason, Chief Grants Officer; (603) 271-7926 or
(603) 271-2789; fax (603) 271-3584; cassandra.mason@dcr.nh.gov
Kayla Schweitzer, Grants Coordinator; (603) 271-0795 or (603) 271-2789;
fax (603) 271-3584; kayla.schweitzer@dncr.nh.gov
Internet: www.nh.gov/nharts/grants/culturalconservation.htm
Sponsor: New Hampshire State Council on the Arts
19 Pillsbury Street, 1st Floor
Concord, NH 03301

NHSCA Youth Arts Project Grants: For Extended Arts Learning   1758
Grants from the New Hampshire State Council on the Arts are a public investment in the
cultural life of the state. Each competitive grant category is designed to meet an important
purpose and need, and aligns with the Council's current strategic plan. Youth Project
Grants fund high-quality arts and cultural education programs that encourage creativity,
develop new arts skills and foster academic success for young people (K-12). The overall
goal of this grant category is to provide young people opportunities to engage in the arts
beyond the normal school day so that they can develop creative problem solving skills
and become more engaged in their communities. Activities may take place after regular
school hours, in the summer or on weekends, in or outside of the school. Partnerships
between schools, arts organizations and community organizations that provide high quality
arts learning experiences for youth in under-served communities around the state are
encouraged. Grants fund programs in all arts disciplines, including dance, theater, media,
music, visual arts, craft, and creative writing. Requests may range from $1,000 to $7,500.
The annual application submission deadline is March 27.
Requirements: For this purpose, an under-served community is considered one in which individuals
lack access to arts programs due to economic conditions, cultural or ethnic background, disability
or geographic isolation. At a minimum, grants must be matched on a one-to-one basis. Not-for-
profit organizations with incorporation in New Hampshire and a 501(c)3 tax-exempt status from
the Internal Revenue Service, schools, school districts or SAUs may apply, who also meet the
following conditions: make all their programs and facilities accessible to people with disabilities;
have submitted all required reports on past State Arts Council grants; and are in good standing
with the NH Secretary of State's Office and the NH Attorney General's Office.
Restrictions: State Arts Council funds may not be matched by other State Arts Council
or National Endowment for the Arts funds. This grant does not support: projects already
receiving funding from any other State Arts Council grant category; general operating
expenses not directly related to the project; or any cost item listed in the glossary under
ineligible expenses (see website).
Geographic Focus: New Hampshire
Date(s) Application is Due: Mar 26
Amount of Grant: 1,000 - 7,500 USD
Contact: Cassandra Erickson Mason, Chief Grants Officer; (603) 271-7926 or
(603) 271-2789; fax (603) 271-3584; cassandra.mason@dncr.nh.gov
Internet: www.nh.gov/nharts/grants/youtharts.htm
Sponsor: New Hampshire State Council on the Arts
19 Pillsbury Street, 1st Floor
Concord, NH 03301

Nick Traina Foundation Grants   1759
The Foundation supports organizations involved in the diagnosis, research, treatment, and/
or family support of manic-depression, and other forms of mental illness, suicide prevention,
child abuse and children in jeopardy, and provides assistance to struggling musicians in the
areas of mental illness. The Foundation may give special consideration to proposals that
address manic-depression in children and young adults. There are no deadlines and there is
no formal application form. The Board meets four times a year to review proposals.
Requirements: Applicants must be 501(c)3 organizations. Proposals should be kept to three
pages in addition to attachments and should include: the organization's purpose, including
a description of its history and mission and the population served; the reason for the grant
request, including the amount requested and how the funds will be used; whether the
request is for general organizational support or for a specific project (including the duration
of a specific project); a copy of the IRS determination letter; and a copy of the most recent
annual report and the last two years' financial statements.
Restrictions: Organizations may apply for one grant each calendar year. Requests from
individuals are ineligible. Grant funding focuses on the San Francisco Bay area.
Geographic Focus: California
Samples: At the Crossroads, San Francisco, California, $11,000; Homeless Youth Alliance,
San Francisco, California, $27,000; and The Caduceus Society, Abilene, Texas, $1,000.
Contact: Danielle Steel, President; (415) 771-4224; info@nicktrainafoundation.org
Internet: nicktrainafoundation.com/grants.htm
Sponsor: Nick Traina Foundation
P.O. Box 470427
San Francisco, CA 94147-0427

Nicole Brown Foundation Grants   1760
Grants will be considered for organizations whose primary purpose is to teach the public
about the extent, dangers, and causes of domestic violence, including spousal and child
abuse; intervene in the cycle of violence by providing alternative housing for victims of
abuse; treat victims of domestic violence through medical care and counseling; and seek
to end the abusive actions of abusers by appropriate treatment and intervention programs.
Contact program staff for availability and deadlines.
Requirements: 501(c)3 public charities designated as shelters are eligible. Shelters must have
been in existence for one full year.
Restrictions: Individuals are ineligible.
Geographic Focus: All States
Contact: Denise Brown, President; (949) 283-5330; info@nbcf.org
Internet: www.nicolebrown.org/
Sponsor: Nicole Brown Foundation
P.O. Box 3777
Dana Point, CA 92629

NIMH Early Identification and Treatment of Mental Disorders in Children   1761
and Adolescents Grants
This program supports research on early identification and treatment of mental disorders in
children and adolescents. In particular, this announcement intends to encourage research
on disorders such as schizophrenia, schizoaffective disorder, bipolar disorder, major
depression, obsessive-compulsive disorder, and anorexia nervosa, alone or comorbid with
other common mental or substance abuse disorders. PA: PA-00-094
Requirements: Applications may be submitted by domestic for-profit and nonprofit
organizations, both public and private; units of state or local governments; and eligible
agencies of the federal government.
Geographic Focus: All States
Amount of Grant: 125,000 - 250,000 USD
Contact: Shelli Avenevoli, (301) 443-5944; avenevos@mail.nih.gov
Internet: grants.nih.gov/grants/guide/notice-files/NOT-MH-08-006.html
Sponsor: National Institute of Mental Health
6001 Executive Boulevard
Bethesda, MD 20892

Nissan Neighbors Grants   1762
Nissan Neighbors is an affiliate-wide, community-focused initiative dedicated to touching
lives and improving communities through charitable contributions and in-kind donations
to organizations that reflect the diverse interests of employees and also support Nissan's
focus areas. which are education, the environment, and humanitarian aid. Through its
philanthropic efforts, Nissan seeks to reinforce its commitment to corporate citizenship by
making a positive and visible contribution to American neighborhoods. Nissan works closely
with select groups to determine the best way to advance their efforts and carefully tailor our
assistance to meet each organization's needs. On-line applications are accepted year round.
Requirements: Eligible applicants must: be 501(c)3 organizations; support projects
compatible with one of their focus areas (education, the environment, and humanitarian
aid); and serve communities surrounding Nissan's affiliate locations (southern California;
middle Tennessee; south central Mississippi; Dallas/Ft. Worth; and metro Detroit).
Geographic Focus: California, Michigan, Mississippi, Tennessee, Texas
Samples: Nashville Public Television, Nashville, Tennessee, $60,000; Museum of African
American History, Detroit, Michigan, $15,000; and Community Nashville, Nashville,
Tennessee, $50,000.
Contact: Grants Administrator; (615) 725-1501; nissanfoundation@nissan-usa.com
Internet: www.nissanusa.com/about/corporate-info/community-relations.html
Sponsor: Nissan Foundation
P.O. Box 685001, mailstop B5B
Franklin, TN 37076-5001

NJSCA Artists in Education Residencies   **1763**

The Artists-in-Education (AIE) grants are provided by the New Jersey Artists in Education Consortium (NJAIE) whose mission is to make the arts a basic part of a sound, quality education for all students Pre-K through 12, and to provide quality professional development for teachers through long-term residencies with professional teaching artists. The focus for the residency may be class work with students and/or professional development for school staff. AIE residencies focus on direct learning about the arts and the processes of creating art, including the skills, techniques, and concepts of the art form. The program places professional artists in one year, two year or mini residencies in dozens of New Jersey schools each year. Residencies are offered in several different arts disciplines (Dance, Music, Theatre, Opera/Music Theatre, Visual Arts, Design Arts, Crafts, Photography, Media Art, Creative Writing, Interdisciplinary and Folk Arts) and are applied for by the school or other sponsoring agency. An AIE grant covers artist fees, an on-site evaluation, and a partial scholarship for one faculty member to attend the Artist/Teacher Institute (aTi). NJAIE also has an application / certification process for artists to become eligible for residencies. Residency artists are paid $275 per residency day (a residency day is based on four 45-minute class periods). All applicants are encouraged to attend an AIE Technical Assistance Workshop, which includes an introduction and overview of the AIE Program, a step-by-step "walk through" of the current guidelines and application, and a question-and-answer period. Attendees receive NJDOE professional development hours that can be used towards the New Jersey Department of Education requirements. For answers to questions on one-year, two-year and mini AIE grants, interested schools and artists are encouraged to contact the Arts Education Administrator.
Requirements: Any New Jersey public, private, or parochial school, pre-K-12, is eligible to apply for an artist in residence grant. Professional practicing artists or artist companies or teams in all disciplines are eligible to apply to be considered for artist in residence positions. The school/district must provide a 1:1 dollar match at least equal to the total grant request. School matching funds should adequately support the proposed residency in all aspects, including supplies, equipment, teacher-release time, administrative time, etc. Matching funds can be made in cash and/or resources that already exist in the school budget (mini grants are designed to give a taste of the benefits of an AIE long-term residency in a three-day mini- model and do not require a school match). Schools must fill out an online application at the New Jersey State Council on the Arts website (www.njartscouncil.org/grant_afag.cfm) as well as mail ONE signed, complete hard copy of the grant application form with all required supporting materials. Artists must mail completed applications to AIE Artists 2012, New Jersey State Council on the Arts, P.O. Box 306, Trenton, New Jersey 08625-306. AIE artists must reapply every three years to renew their eligibility. Schools applying for one and two year residencies are required to do the following: appoint an Administrative Coordinator, On-Site Coordinator and a Teacher Liaison (if applicable) to lead the project; form a Steering Committee to establish goals for the residency and provide support, assistance and resources for the artist; enroll at least one faculty member in the Artist/Teacher Institute (aTi) and the Administrative Coordinator in Administrators' Day at aTi; hold a planning meeting with Steering Committee members, classroom teachers, residency artist and AIE partner to develop the residency plan and schedule; host a residency for no less than twenty (20) school days each year; work collaboratively with the residency artist to provide appropriate time, space and materials to conduct the residency; introduce the residency artist and the project to the school and community at a presentation to the school board; arrange at least one professional development workshop that the residency artist will lead for all teachers before the residency starts; identify the core students who will meet with the residency artist every day of the residency; identify the participating students who will work with the residency artist on a less regular basis, but will benefit from workshops, lectures, demonstrations, etc; ensure that a teacher is in the classroom with the residency artist at all times to maintain a productive working environment and to enable successful follow-up activities; arrange at least one field trip and/or schedule a visiting artist/company that will enhance the residency; arrange a culminating event or activity to share the residency with the community; provide publicity to the local press regarding the artist and the AIE residency; develop a plan for and carry out the documentation/evaluation of the residency; prepare a final report and evaluation, which is due within 30 days of completion of the residency. Two-year grantees must prepare and submit a Plan for the 2nd-Year Full Residency. The Plan must be approved prior to the release of second-year grant funds.
Restrictions: Although creative writing is one of the many disciplines supported, only proposals to sponsor long-term writing residencies are covered by this program. Short-term writing residencies (5 days) are coordinated through the New Jersey Writers Project, and administered by Playwrights Theatre of New Jersey. Schools interested in interdisciplinary or folk arts residencies must first consult with AIE staff. Only schools that have successfully completed a one-year AIE grant may apply for the two-year AIE grant.
Geographic Focus: New Jersey
Date(s) Application is Due: Feb 4; Mar 4
Amount of Grant: 825 - 12,000 USD
Samples: Poetry & Puppetry Residency, Normandy Park School, Morristown, New Jersey; Jazz Music Residency, Clinton Elementary School, Maplewood, New Jersey; Sculpture Residency, Maple Shade High School, Maple Shade, New Jersey; Folk Arts/Basketry Residency, Bells School, Bellmawr, New Jersey.
Contact: Shelley Benaroya, Arts Education Administrator; (609) 243-9000 or (877) 652-7833; fax (609) 989-1440; shelley@arts.sos.state.nj.us or sbenaroya@yanj.org
Internet: www.njaie.org/
Sponsor: New Jersey State Council on the Arts
225 West State Street, P.O. Box 306
Trenton, NJ 08625-0306

NJSCA Arts Education Special Initiative Grants   **1764**

Arts Education Special Initiative (AESI) grants are awarded to recipients of New Jersey State Council on the Arts General Operating Support (GOS) grants or General Program Support (GPS) grants to support development or expansion of programs that make substantial contributions to quality arts education in schools. This grant category intends to aid arts organizations in developing their full potential as community resources to educational systems throughout New Jersey and create a stronger infrastructure for arts education statewide.
Requirements: Applicants must be incorporated in the State of New Jersey as a 501(c)3 organization or be a unit of government; be registered with the New Jersey Charities Registration Bureau; have a clearly articulated mission relating to the arts; have been in existence and actively providing public programs or services for at least the past two years at time of application; have a board of directors empowered to formulate policies and be responsible for the governance and administration of the organization, its programs and finances; and be a GOS or GPS applicant/grantee. Matching funds are required and must be cash, not in-kind. For each dollar received from the Council, the grantee must show three additional dollars raised and spent, based on operating income. Applicants must apply online and should be advised that the prerequisite pre-registraton process requires up to 72 hours for completion by the system administrator before they can access the system.
Restrictions: Applicants may apply either to the Council or to their County Arts Agency, not both, in a given year. Prospective NJSCA applicants that have been receiving support through their County Arts Agency up to now should attend a scheduled NJSCA grant workshop, work closely with Council staff and their County Arts Agency in filing their Notice of Intent to Apply, and may also want to schedule a meeting early in the process with Council staff. Because the funding periods for the County Arts Agency grants and the State Council grants overlap by six months, applicants should discuss their situation in advance of the Notice of Intent to Apply with the State Council to determine eligibility. K-12 schools and school districts are not eligible to apply, but may be a partner or collaborator on a project with an eligible applicant.
Geographic Focus: New Jersey
Date(s) Application is Due: Feb 23
Samples: Appel Farm Arts & Music Center, Salem, New Jersey, $13,757; Barnegat Bay Decoy & Baymen's Museum, Ocean, New Jersey, $6,720; McCarter Theatre Center/Performing Arts, Mercer, New Jersey, $9,188; Montclair Art Museum, Essex, New Jersey, $5,432; Rutgers-Camden Center for the Arts, Camden, New Jersey, $11,025
Contact: Steve Runk; (609) 292-6130; fax (609) 989-1440; steve.runk@sos.state.nj.us
Internet: www.njartscouncil.org/grant.cfm
Sponsor: New Jersey State Council on the Arts
225 West State Street, P.O. Box 306
Trenton, NJ 08625-0306

Noble County Community Foundation Grants   **1765**

The Noble County Community Foundation makes grants for innovative, creative projects and programs responsive to changing community needs in the areas of health and human services, education, arts and culture, and civic affairs. The funding is not limited to these areas and grant seekers are encouraged to respond to emerging community needs. The Foundation considers only not-for-profit projects that: promote cooperation among organizations without duplicating services; promote volunteer involvement; demonstrate practical approaches to current community issues; enhance or improve an organization's self-sufficiency and effectiveness; emphasize prevention. In addition, the Foundation considers projects that: affect a broad segment of the population; are pilot programs clearly replicable in their design and have reasonable prospects for future support; serve people whose needs are not being met by existing services and which encourage independence; move the community to a higher cultural awareness. The Foundation offers grants in April, June, August, and December, with decisions made 60 days after each deadline. Applicants are encouraged to contact the Foundation before submitting a proposal to find out if the project is appropriate for funding. Applicants should refer to the website for further information.
Requirements: In applying for grants, the following points must be addressed (with explanation if information is not available): the specific purpose and the need for the funds requested; the need for the program/project in the community; the amount requested; a detailed description of how the money would be spent; a statement of how the project will improve life in Noble County and how the outcomes will be measured; recent grants received and applications pending for this program/project; a listing of the current board and/or project organizers and their contact information; a copy of the organization's IRS tax-exempt letter stating 501(c)3 status; and for schools applying, a letter of support from the organization's superintendent/principal. After the organization's request has been received, it may be contacted by a Foundation representative requesting a site visit or additional information.
Restrictions: Discretionary funds will not be used under any circumstances to support: deficit spending; political purposes; annual fund campaigns; lobbying; organizations whose primary function is to allocate funds to other charitable organizations or projects; projects that do not serve residents of Noble County; travel; augmenting endowments; underwriting for fundraising events; loans.
Geographic Focus: Indiana
Date(s) Application is Due: Mar 2; May 2; Jul 2; Nov 2
Amount of Grant: 500 - 5,000 USD
Samples: Mad Anthonys Children's Hope House, Fort Wayne, Indiana, $2,000 - to subsidize the $95 per day cost of housing Noble County families in need of a place to stay while their child is hospitalized in a Fort Wayne hospital; Fort Wayne Women's Bureau, Fort Wayne, Indiana, $1,500 - to subsidize the implementation of the REACT Program, Assault Prevention for Teens, in Noble County; Town of Albion Parks Department, Albion, Indiana, $1,800 - to subsidize the cost of purchasing playground equipment.
Contact: Linda Speakman-Yerick, Executive Director; (260) 894-3335; fax (260) 894-9020; linda@noblecountycf.org or info@noblecountrycf.org
Margarita White, Program Officer; (260) 894-3335; fax (260) 894-9020; margarita@noblecountycf.org or info@noblecountrycf.org
Internet: noblecountycf.org/noble-county-community-foundation-inc-grants/
Sponsor: Noble County Community Foundation
1599 Lincolnway South
Ligonier, IN 46767

Norcliffe Foundation Grants 1766

The Norcliffe Foundation is a private nonprofit family foundation established in 1952 by Paul Pigott for the purpose of improving the quality of life for all people in the Puget Sound region. The foundation provides grants in the areas of health, education, social services, civic improvement, religion, culture and the arts, the environment, historic preservation and youth programs. Foundation funding types include capital campaigns for building and equipment, certain operating budgets, endowments, challenge/matching grants, land acquisition, new projects, start-up funds, renovation, and research. Requests for publication, videos/films, and website production may be considered as may scholarships, fellowships / chairs, conferences / seminars, social enterprise development, and technical assistance. Multi-year and renewable funding may be considered. Applications are accepted year-round. One copy of a letter proposal and/or common grant application form should be directed to the President in care of the Foundation Manager at the contact information given. An initial phone call is optional. Guidelines, instructions, and a copy of the common grant proposal form are provided at the website. Funding decisions and notification generally occur three to six months after receipt of request.

Requirements: 501(c)3 organizations in the Puget Sound region in and around Seattle, Washington are eligible to apply.

Restrictions: The Norcliffe Foundation does not provide the following types of assistance: deficit financing, emergency funds, grants to individuals, matches to employee-giving, Program-Related Investments / Loans (PRIs), in-kind services, volunteer / loaned executive, and internships. Applicants may only submit one request per year from date of funding or denial. Applicants who have previously received grants of $50,000 or more from the Foundation must wait two years from final payment before submitting a new application.

Geographic Focus: Washington

Amount of Grant: 1,000 - 25,000 USD

Contact: Arline Hefferline, Foundation Manager; (206) 682-4820; fax (206) 682-4821; arline@thenorcliffefoundation.com

Internet: www.thenorcliffefoundation.com/

Sponsor: Norcliffe Foundation

999 Third Avenue, Suite 1006

Seattle, WA 98104-4001

Norman Foundation Grants 1767

The Norman Foundation supports efforts that strengthen the ability of communities to determine their own economic, environmental and social well-being, and that help people control those forces that affect their lives. These efforts may: promote economic justice and development through community organizing, coalition building and policy reform efforts; work to prevent the disposal of toxics in communities, and to link environmental issues with economic and social justice; link community-based economic and environmental justice organizing to national and international reform efforts. The following is considered when evaluating grant proposals: does the project arise from the hopes and efforts of those whose survival, well-being and liberation are directly at stake; does it further ethnic, gender and other forms of equity; is it rooted in organized, practical undertakings; and is it likely to achieve systemic change. In pursuing systemic change, the Foundation would hope that: the proposed action may serve as a model; the spread of the model may create institutions that can survive on their own; their establishment and success may generate beneficial adaptations by other political, social and economic institutions and structures. The Foundation provides grants for general support, projects, and collaborative efforts. We also welcome innovative proposals designed to build the capacity of social change organizations working in our areas of interest. Priority is given to organizations with annual budgets of under $1 million.

Requirements: Programs must be 501(c)3 tax-exempt organizations that focused on domestic United States issues. Prospective grantees should initiate the application process by sending a short two or three page letter of inquiry to the Program Director (fax, email or regular mail). There are no set deadlines, and letters of inquiry are reviewed throughout the year. The Foundation only accepts full proposals upon positive response to the letter of inquiry. The letter of inquiry should briefly explain: the scope and significance of the problem to be addressed; the organization's proposed response and (if appropriate) how this strategy builds upon the organization's past work; the specific demonstrable effects the project would have if successful, especially its potential to effect systemic (fundamental, institutional and significant) change; how the project promotes change on a national level and is otherwise related to the foundation's guidelines; the size of the organization's budget. All inquiries will be acknowledged and, if deemed promising, the Foundation will request a full proposal.

Restrictions: The Foundation does not make grants to individuals or universities; or to support conferences, scholarships, research, films, media and arts projects; or to capital funding projects, fundraising drives or direct social service programs, such as shelters or community health programs. The Foundation's grant making is restricted to U.S.-based organizations.

Geographic Focus: All States

Amount of Grant: 5,000 - 30,000 USD

Samples: Direct Action Welfare Group, Charleston, West Virginia, $20,000 - renewed support of statewide organizing and empowerment of people living in poverty in West Virginia; Interfaith Action of Southwest Florida, Immokalee, Florida, $20,000 - renewed support for joint work with Coalition of Immokalee Workers in support of low-wage farmworkers in Florida; Alaska Community Action on Toxics, Anchorage, Alaska, $30,000 - renewed support for work with tribal villages and other communities to eliminate environmental contaminants.

Contact: June Makela; (212) 230-9830; fax (212) 230-9849; norman@normanfdn.org

Internet: www.normanfdn.org/

Sponsor: Norman Foundation

147 East 48th Street

New York, NY 10017

North Dakota Community Foundation Grants 1768

The Foundation serves North Dakota communities statewide with the goal of improving the quality of life for the state's citizens. The Foundation does not have a narrow area of focus. Each project is reviewed on its own merits with an emphasis on helping applicants who have limited access to other sources of funding. Applicants may submit a concise letter of request not to exceed two pages describing the organization, the project, the approximate project cost, and the amount requested from the Foundation. If the Board is interested in additional information, formal application materials will be sent.

Requirements: Eligible applicants must be 501(c)3 organizations in North Dakota.

Restrictions: The Foundation accepts applications by mail but not by fax or email. Only one request per agency per year may be submitted. The following is not funded: grants to organizations and projects that exist to influence legislation, carry on propaganda, participate in political campaigns, or which threaten to cause significant controversy or divisiveness; grants to individuals; and multi-year grant commitments. Low priority is given to the following: projects already substantially supported by government, or which in the opinion of the Board, can and should be provided for by taxes; grants for sectarian projects; grants to national organizations; and organizations which field substantial fund-raising each year with paid and volunteer staff.

Geographic Focus: North Dakota

Date(s) Application is Due: Aug 15

Samples: Save the Hens Foundation, Inc., Sheldon, North Dakota, $8,500 - community programming; Park River Volunteer Fire Department, Park River, North Dakota, $7,500 - health promotion; and Kiddie Korner Preschool and Day Care, Park River, North Dakota, $5,500 - children's programming.

Contact: Kevin Dvorak, President and CEO; (701) 222-8349; kdvorak@ndcf.net

Internet: www.ndcf.net/Information/GrantGuidelines.asp

Sponsor: North Dakota Community Foundation

309 North Mandan Street, Suite 2, P.O. Box 387

Bismarck, ND 58502-0387

Northern Chautauqua Community Foundation Community Grants 1769

The foundation awards grants to nonprofit, tax-exempt organizations located in Northern Chautauqua County, New York. Priority will be given to programs representing innovative and efficient approaches to serving community needs and opportunities, projects that assist citizens whose needs are not met by existing services, projects that expect to test or demonstrate new approaches and techniques in the solutions of community problems, and projects that promote volunteer participation and citizen involvement in the community. Consideration will be given to the potential impact of the request and the number of people who will benefit. Seed grants will be awarded to initiate promising new programs in the foundation's field of interest as well as challenge grants to encourage matching gifts. Except in unusual circumstances, grants are approved for one year at a time. Contact the foundation office for an application.

Requirements: IRS 501(c)3 organizations in Northern Chautauqua County, New York, are eligible.

Restrictions: Areas generally not funded are capital campaigns to establish or add to endowment funds, general operating budgets for existing organizations, publication of books, conferences, or annual fund-raising campaigns.

Geographic Focus: New York

Date(s) Application is Due: Mar 23; Sep 21

Amount of Grant: 12,500 USD

Contact: Diane E. Hannum, Executive Director; (716) 366-4892; fax (716) 366-3905; dhannum@nncfoundation.org or info@nccfoundation.org

Internet: www.nccfoundation.org/Grantseekers/ApplyforaGrant/tabid/256/Default.aspx

Sponsor: Northern Chautauqua Community Foundation

212 Lake Shore Drive West

Dunkirk, NY 14048

North Face Explore Fund 1770

The North Face Explore Fund is a grant-giving program committed to supporting nonprofit, community organizations that break down the barriers to getting youth outdoors. The goal of the Explore Fund is to inspire the next generation of young explorers and conservationists by funding groups that help kids discover nature's playground. Grants will be given up to $2,500 (only one Explore Fund Grant will be given to an organization in each calendar year).

Requirements: The Explore Fund will support organizations that encourage youth outdoor participation, focusing primarily on creating more connections of children to nature, increasing access to both front & backcountry recreation, as well as providing education for both personal & environmental health. Organizations must have clearly defined goals and objectives, target a specific issue/youth community, are action-oriented and quantifiable, and are committed to long-term change; have 501(c)3 status, or are seeking this designation; and, build community and encourage public involvement. As The Explore Fund is intended to function as complementary support, the sponsor strongly encourages applicants to seek additional, concurrent funding from other funding sources. Applications that come with matching dollars will be viewed favorably and this will be taken into consideration during the granting process. To determine eligibility, applicants can take the eligibility quiz available at the sponsor's website.

Restrictions: The following will not be funded: Organizations without 501(c)3 status; general education efforts that do not include an experiential component that involves getting youth outdoors; research; conferences; endowment funds; or, political campaigns. The Explore Fund grants may not be used for indirect costs, overhead, and other expenses not directly related to the project or program. Fringe benefits are also excluded, as are salaries.

Geographic Focus: All States

Date(s) Application is Due: Oct 5

Amount of Grant: Up to 2,500 USD

Contact: Fund Manager

Internet: www.explorefund.org

Sponsor: North Face
14450 Doolittle Drive
San Leandro, CA 94577

Northland Foundation Grants 1771
The Northland Foundation provides resources to programs that value children and families and help the next generation develop into responsible, caring adults; provide individuals and families with the tools to become self-reliant through economic and social justice; and encourage older adults to share their vitality and wisdom. Eligible projects must address one of the following three priority areas: Connecting Kids and Communities/Strengthening Families; Opportunities for Self-Reliance; Aging with Independence.
Requirements: Non-profit 501(c)3 organizations in the seven-county area of Aitkin, Carlton, Cook, Itasca, Koochiching, Lake, and Saint Louis Counties of Minnesota are eligible. Interested applicants should contact Grants Program staff to determine if the project is a promising candidate. A pre-application form (available online) may be submitted for review. The Foundation's Board reviews pre-applications monthly. Pre-applications received by the 15th of the month are reviewed the following month. After review applicants are notified by letter if a full proposal is requested and when it is due. On average, consideration of a full proposal takes sixty to ninety days.
Restrictions: Grants do not support individuals, religious programs, endowments, fundraising campaigns, buildings or major equipment, festivals, traditional government services, or programs for which public support has been cut.
Geographic Focus: Minnesota
Contact: Erik Torch, Grant Program Manager; (800) 433-4045 or (218) 723-4040; fax (218) 723-4048; erik@northlandfdn.org
Internet: www.northlandfdn.org/Grants/
Sponsor: Northland Foundation
202 West Superior Street, Suite 610
Duluth, MN 55802

Northrop Grumman Corporation Grants 1772
Northrop Grumman is committed to supporting communities throughout the U.S., especially those where its employees live and work. The Contributions Program seeks to address critical issues and needs by providing financial assistance to accredited schools and 501(c)3 nonprofit organizations. The majority of these contributions address education, services for veterans and the military, health and human services, and the environment.
Requirements: The following information must be included in the grant request: Tax Exempt Number; non-profit contact name, title, address, phone number, fax number; brief history of the organization, mission statement, goals and objectives; type and scope of services offered, and the geographical area served; specific details as to how requested funds would be used; project budget and amount requested; demographic impact; current operating budget including latest financial statement; list of other corporate funders; list of directors and/or officers, and their affiliations; Northrop Grumman employee sponsor, if applicable (name and phone number); and contact information.
Restrictions: Grants are not awarded to: religious organizations; political groups; fraternal organizations; individuals; athletic groups or activities, including charity-benefit sporting events; charter schools, unless they have open enrollment and hold the same standards as public schools; bands or choirs; capital campaigns; organizations providing services primarily to animals; communities outside of the United States; or organizations whose programs discriminate based on race, color, age, sex, religion, national origin, sexual orientation, disability, veteran status or any other characteristic protected by law.
Geographic Focus: All States
Date(s) Application is Due: Apr 30; Sep 30
Contact: Cheryl Horn, cheryl.horn@ngc.com
Internet: www.northropgrumman.com/corporate-responsibility/corporate-citizenship/contribution-guidelines.html
Sponsor: Northrop Grumman Corporation
1840 Century Park East
Los Angeles, CA 90067

Northrop Grumman Foundation Grants 1773
Northrop Grumman's priority is to provide opportunities related to science, technology, engineering and mathematics (STEM) for students and teachers. The foundation supports diverse and sustainable NATIONAL-LEVEL programs that enhance the education experience for students and provide teachers with the training and tools they need to be successful in the classroom.
Requirements: Grant requests must be submitted online via the Foundation's website. Grant requests must include: tax exempt number; non-profit or institution contact name, title, address, phone number, fax number; brief history of the organization, mission statement, goals and objectives; type and scope of services offered, and the geographical area serviced; specific details as to how requested funds would be used; project budget and amount requested; demographic impacted; current operating budget including latest financial statement; list of other corporate funders; list of directors and/or officers, and their affiliations; Northrop Grumman employee sponsor, if applicable (name and phone number); and contact information.
Restrictions: The Foundation will not consider the following requests: individuals; fundraising events such as raffles, walk-a-thons, banquets or dinners; campus student organizations, fraternities, sororities, and honor societies; religious schools or colleges whose primary focus is to promote religious beliefs; athletic teams, support organizations; advertising or underwriting expenses; capital campaigns; endowments; tuition; choirs, bands, or drill teams.
Geographic Focus: All States
Amount of Grant: 500 - 200,000 USD
Samples: University of Nevada, Las Vegas, Nevada, $30,000 - to purchase computer equipment and software for the Transportation Research Center; California State

University at Long Beach, Long Beach, Caliornia, $10,000 - for curriculum development in software engineering.
Contact: Carleen Beste, (888) 478-5478; carleen.beste@ngc.com
Internet: www.northropgrumman.com/corporate-responsibility/corporate-citizenship/foundation-grant-guidelines.html
Sponsor: Northrop Grumman Foundation
1840 Century Park E, MS 131/CC
Los Angeles, CA 90067

NRA Foundation Grants 1774
Grant requests must conform to, and foster the purposes set forth in The NRA Foundation's Articles of Incorporation. These purposes are as follows: to promote, advance and encourage firearms and hunting safety; to educate individuals, including the youth of the United States, with respect to firearms and firearms history and hunting safety and marksmanship, as well as with respect to other subjects that are of importance to the well-being of the general public; to conduct research in furtherance of improved firearms safety and marksmanship facilities and techniques; to support activities of the National Rifle Association of America, but only to the extent that such activities are in furtherance of charitable, educational or scientific purposes within the meaning of section 501(c)3 of the Internal Revenue Code; to engage in any other activity that is incidental to, connected with, or in advancement of the foregoing purposes and that is within the scope of allowable purposes under 26 U.S.C. 501(c)3.
Requirements: Any organization, association or other entity, whether formally incorporated or not, that has, as a minimum, a unique federal employer identification number (EIN) issued by the Internal Revenue Service. Eligible organizations may apply for an NRA Foundation grant for a qualifying project. Additionally, allowable projects must qualify under IRS 501(c)3 regulations in one of the following categories: charitable; scientific; testing for public safety; literary; educational; fostering national/international amateur sports competition (cannot include the provision of athletic facilities or equipment.)
Restrictions: The following organizations are not eligible for grants: political candidates or organizations; labor organizations; state fund committees; friends of NRA committees; private business/private enterprise; other organizations or groups that have not been assigned a federal employer identification number by the Internal Revenue Service. The following activities are not eligible for funding: projects which confer private benefit upon the applying organization/group; deficit financing; projects for commercial ventures; projects which require membership in the NRA or in the applying organization/group; applications from organizations or groups that have not submitted a final report for a previously awarded grant. In addition, the following limitations/restrictions apply to grants which are otherwise eligible for funding: no funding will be awarded to an applicant for payment of administrative fees, office overhead, or other similar charges; the Foundation does not approve multi-year funding of projects; requests must be submitted for consideration each year. Funding cannot be given for competitions requiring NRA or other club or association membership. In addition, although grants may be sought for the purpose of fostering national or international amateur sports competition, grant awards cannot be made for the purpose of providing facilities or equipment to be used in such competitions.
Geographic Focus: All States
Amount of Grant: 5,000 - 9,000,000 USD
Contact: Wayne Sheets, Executive Director; (800) 423-6894; nraf@nrahq.org
Internet: www.friendsofnra.org/National.aspx?cid=9
Sponsor: National Rifle association Foundation
11250 Waples Mill Road
Fairfax, VA 22030

NSF Perception, Action and Cognition (PAC) Research Grants 1775
The PAC program funds theoretically motivated research on a wide-range of topic areas related to typical human behavior with particular focus on perceptual, motor, and cognitive processes and their interactions. Central research topics for consideration by the program include (but are not limited to) vision, audition, haptics, attention, memory, written and spoken language, spatial cognition, motor control, categorization, reasoning, and concept formation. Of particular interest are emerging areas, such as the interaction of sleep or emotion with cognitive or perceptual processes, epigenetics of cognition, computational models of cognition, and cross-modal and multimodal processing. The program welcomes a wide range of perspectives, such as individual differences, symbolic and neural-inspired computation, ecological approaches, genetics and epigenetics, nonlinear dynamics and complex systems, and a variety of methodologies spanning the range of experimentation and modeling. The PAC program is open to co-review of proposals submitted to other programs both within the Social, Behavioral, and Economic Sciences Directorate and across other directorates. The proposal window for conference applications is May 15 through June 15; and the proposal windows for research applications are July 15 through August 1 and January 15 through February 1.
Requirements: Proposals may be returned without review if the major focus is 1) the organization of neural activity or brain networks; 2) understanding clinical populations; or 3) non-human animals without a clear and direct impact on our understanding of human perception, action, or cognition. Investigators are encouraged to send the program director a one-page summary of the proposed research before submitting a proposal, in order to determine its appropriateness for the PAC program. Note that a single-copy document that accompanies the proposal but technically is not part of the proposal must be submitted to provide information about the collaborators and other affiliations of all individuals serving as a PI, co-PI, or senior personnel. This information should be prepared in accordance with the PAPPG Chapter II.C.1.
Geographic Focus: All States, American Samoa, District of Columbia, Guam, Marshall Islands, Northern Mariana Islands, Puerto Rico, U.S. Virgin Islands
Date(s) Application is Due: Feb 1; Jun 15; Aug 1
Amount of Grant: 1,100 - 5,000,000 USD

Contact: Betty K. Tuller, Program Director; (703) 292-7238; btuller@nsf.gov
Larry Gottlob, Program Director; (703) 292-4383 or (703) 292-5111; lgottlob@nsf.gov
Internet: www.nsf.gov/funding/pgm_summ.jsp?pims_id=5686
Sponsor: National Science Foundation
2415 Eisenhower Avenue
Alexandria, VA 22314

NSF Social Psychology Grants   1776
The Social Psychology program at NSF supports basic research on human social behavior, including cultural differences and development over the life span. Among the many research topics supported are: attitude formation and change, social cognition, personality processes, interpersonal relations and group processes, the self, emotion, social comparison and social influence, and the psycho-physiological and neurophysiological bases of social behavior. The scientific merit of a proposal depends on four important factors: the problems investigated must be theoretically grounded; the research should be based on empirical observation or be subject to empirical validation; the research design must be appropriate to the questions asked; and the proposed research must advance basic understanding of social behavior. Annual full proposal target dates are July 16 and January 16.
Requirements: Except where a program solicitation establishes more restrictive eligibility criteria, individuals and organizations in the following categories may submit proposals: universities and colleges; non-profit, non-academic organizations; for-profit organizations; state and local governments; unaffiliated individuals; foreign organizations; and other Federal agencies.
Geographic Focus: All States, All Countries
Date(s) Application is Due: Jan 16; Jul 16
Contact: Steven Breckler, Program Director; (703) 292-7369 or (703) 292-5111; fax (703) 292-9068; sbreckle@nsf.gov
Internet: www.nsf.gov/funding/pgm_summ.jsp?pims_id=5712
Sponsor: National Science Foundation
2415 Eisenhower Avenue
Alexandria, VA 22314

NSTA Distinguished Informal Science Education Award   1777
The Distinguished Informal Science Education Award honors one NSTA member who has made extraordinary contributions to the advancement of science education in an informal or nontraditional school setting, such as a science-technology center, museum, or community science center. The award consists of three nights' hotel accommodation and $500 toward expenses to attend the NSTA National Conference on Science Education. Awardees will be honored at the Awards Banquet held during the NSTA conference. The application is available for download at the website. Completed applications must be received by December 18.
Requirements: This award is open to NSTA members who are not classroom teachers and who have demonstrated their dedication to informal science education.
Restrictions: Applicants may apply for more than one award but are eligible to win only one NSTA award per year. Each application must be based on a unique program and process. Submission of the same idea and materials to different NSTA award programs will result in the disqualification of all applications. If an applicant's idea or project has received an NSTA award in the past, that idea or project is not eligible to receive an additional award.
Geographic Focus: All States
Date(s) Application is Due: Dec 18
Amount of Grant: 500 USD
Contact: Amanda Upton, Manager, NSTA Nominations and Teacher Awards Programs; (703) 312-9217; fax (703) 243-7177; nominations@nsta.org or awards@nsta.org
Internet: www.nsta.org/about/awards.aspx#distinformal
Sponsor: National Science Teachers Association
1840 Wilson Boulevard
Arlington, VA 22201

NSTA Faraday Science Communicator Award   1778
The Faraday Science Communicator Award is named in honor of Michael Faraday (1791–1867), the English chemist and physicist who is known for his pioneering experiments in electricity and magnetism. Through lectures and letters, Faraday led people of all ages to a greater understanding of the natural scientific laws that govern U.S. all. The Faraday Science Communicator Award will recognize and reward an individual or organization that has inspired and elevated the public's interest in and appreciation of science. The awardee receives an all-expense-paid trip (up to $2,500) to attend the NSTA National Conference; all awardees will receive recognition in NSTA publications and will be given an opportunity to participate in a poster session during the conference. The application is available for download at the website. Completed applications must be received by December 17.
Requirements: Individual—The individual will not be a classroom teacher, but will work in, or have developed a compatible setting for science communication: i.e., museum, nature center, zoo, state park, aquarium, radio, television, internet, or other science-rich institutions or media. The individual may also be connected to a science setting through his or her involvement with civic organizations and child-education facilities: e.g., preK child-development centers, 4-H clubs, Girl and Boy Scouts, Girls and Boys Clubs of America, and so on. Organizational—The organization will facilitate and provide exemplary opportunities for science communication to the public. The organization will desire to instill in the public an appreciation for science through communication efforts at the local, state, and national levels.
Restrictions: Applicants may apply for more than one award but are eligible to win only one NSTA award per year. Each application must be based on a unique program and process. Submission of the same idea and materials to different NSTA award programs will result in the disqualification of all applications. If an applicant's idea or project has received an NSTA award in the past, that idea or project is not eligible to receive an additional award.

Geographic Focus: All States
Date(s) Application is Due: Dec 17
Amount of Grant: Up to 2,500 USD
Contact: Amanda Upton, Manager, NSTA Nominations and Teacher Awards Programs; (703) 312-9217; fax (703) 243-7177; awards@nsta.org or nominations@nsta.org
Internet: www.nsta.org/about/awards.aspx#faraday
Sponsor: National Science Teachers Association
1840 Wilson Boulevard
Arlington, VA 22201

NYFA Artists in the School Community Planning Grants   1779
Planning grants emphasize collaborations between schools, teaching artists, and/or cultural organizations to prepare for first-time Implementation projects or to further develop existing Implementation projects. Planning Grants offer schools the opportunity to assess needs, identify resources, and explore pilot program ideas. Applicants may apply for one year of planning support with the intent to apply for an Implementation grant in the same fiscal year. Funding of Planning grants does not guarantee funding of Implementation grants. The award is not designed to support artist-student contact, though pilot activities are acceptable. Awards are matching grants and range from $500 to $2,000. NYFA contributes up to 50% of total project costs.
Requirements: Schools, school districts, BOCES, Teacher Centers, colleges and universities or on Indian nation land in New York State are eligible to apply. Applicants must provide, through in-kind resources and cash, matching support for artist fees, materials and supplies, teacher release time, teacher compensation and all other project costs. In-kind contributions cannot exceed 1/3 of the applicant's match.
Restrictions: Nonprofit cultural organizations are not eligible to apply. New York State non-profit organizations may work collaboratively with schools and artists; however the school must be the lead organization. Planning Grants can only be used for artist fees and/or artist materials and supplies.
Geographic Focus: New York
Date(s) Application is Due: Nov 5
Amount of Grant: 500 - 2,000 USD
Contact: Susan Ball, Interim Director of Programs; (212) 366-6900, ext. 321; fax (212) 366-1778; sball@nyfa.org or ASC_Plannning@nyfa.org
Internet: www.nyfa.org/level3.asp?id=35&fid=2&sid=22
Sponsor: New York Foundation for the Arts
20 Jay Street, 7th Floor
Brooklyn, NY 11201

NYSCA Arts Education: Community-based Learning Grants   1780
Community-based Learning grants support a range of projects that provide in-depth and sustained experiences to learners of all ages for the creation and understanding of art through ongoing arts learning activities in community settings. Participants may include children, adults, families, and life- long learners in community and/or inter-generational settings. Grants are particularly focused on rural and under-served communities who have limited access to arts programming. Activities may include workshops, classes, and training in the arts. Eligible projects may be offered by arts organizations or community-based organizations with established arts activities, in partnership with artists and arts groups. Funds may be used for art materials, documentation of the project, transportation of art materials or instruments necessary for the project, and a percentage of the applicant organization's administrative staff time.
Requirements: All participating artists must be guaranteed a fee, which applicants are expected to indicate in the project budget. Projects must be in-depth, sequential learning projects. First-time applicants are required to call the program staff before the registration deadline.
Restrictions: Workshops and training programs for professional artists, as well as programs that are primarily therapeutic in nature are ineligible for support. This grant does not support one-time workshops, single performances, or one-time visits to cultural institutions. Professional training of artists is not supported with this grant. The grant may not exceed 50% of the total project cost.
Geographic Focus: New York
Date(s) Application is Due: Apr 1
Contact: Kathleen Masterson, Sr. Program Officer; (212) 741-2622; kmasterson@nysca.org
Internet: www.nysca.org/public/guidelines/arts_education/community.htm
Sponsor: New York State Council on the Arts
300 Park Ave South, 10th Floor
New York, NY 10010

NYSCA Arts Education: General Operating Support Grants   1781
General Operating Support grants fund an organization's ongoing work, rather than a specific project or program in order to help organizations become more effective in fulfilling their mission, especially in arts education. The Council examines the nature, scope, and quality of an organization's programs and activities, its managerial and fiscal competence, and its public service when considering the provision and level of support.
Requirements: Applicants must register before February 22 to be considered for funding that fiscal year. In addition, applicant's must meet the following conditions: have a primary focus in arts education; have an organizational mission primarily devoted to arts and culture with a prior record of accomplishment in producing or presenting cultural activities; demonstrate fiscal stability as indicated by such factors as a positive Fund Balance, have an absence of substantial and recurring organizational deficits, a realistic and balanced organizational budget, have diverse revenue sources, and strong internal controls; one or more qualified staff; a viable board of directors and officers that exercises oversight and accountability for governance, operations, programming and finances; and must have ongoing programs, exhibitions, productions, or other art and cultural activities that are open to the general

public. Applications can be found at the website and must be completed online. First time applicants must contact program staff before registration deadline.

Restrictions: Applicants cannot apply for both General Operating Support and General Program Support. Grants will be no less than $5,000 and shall not exceed 25% of an organization's budget.

Geographic Focus: New York

Date(s) Application is Due: Apr 1

Contact: Kathleen Masterson, Sr. Program Officer; (212) 741-2622; kmasterson@nysca.org

Internet: www.nysca.org/public/guidelines/arts_education/general_operating.htm

Sponsor: New York State Council on the Arts

300 Park Ave South, 10th Floor

New York, NY 10010

NYSCA Arts Education: General Program Support Grants 1782

The purpose of General Program Support (GPS) is to offer unrestricted support for ongoing activities of arts and cultural programs that are operated as independent entities within their own organization or for significant arts programming within a non-profit whose mission is not art-based (for example, a performing arts center that is operated as a separate entity within a college). The Council examines the nature, scope, and quality of an organization's programs and activities, its managerial and fiscal competence, and its public service when considering the provision and level of GPS support.

Requirements: To be eligible to apply, an organization must meet each of the following conditions: significant ongoing activities that address the focus in the discipline in which the organization is seeking General Program Support; organization makes evident a substantial commitment to arts and culture, with a prior record of accomplishment in producing or presenting cultural activities; demonstrate fiscal stability as indicated by such factors as a positive fund balance, an absence of substantial and/or recurring organizational deficits, a realistic and balanced organizational budget, diverse revenue sources, a significant ongoing financial commitment by the applicant to its arts and cultural program, and strong internal controls; at least one qualified, salaried administrative staff responsible for the program; a viable board of directors, advisory board, or other governance structure specifically responsible for oversight and accountability for operations, programming and finances of this program; and must have ongoing programs, exhibitions, productions or other arts and cultural activities that are open to the general public. In addition, applicants must register with the Council before February 22 to be considered for funding that fiscal year. Applications are available at the website and must be submitted online. First time applicants must contact the Council before the registration deadline.

Restrictions: Organizations receiving General Program Support from the Arts in Education Program are not eligible for General Operating Support. Grants will be no less than $5,000 and shall not exceed 25% of the arts or cultural program's budget.

Geographic Focus: New York

Date(s) Application is Due: Apr 1

Contact: Kathleen Masterson, Sr. Program Officer; (212) 741-2622; kmasterson@nysca.org

Internet: www.nysca.org/public/guidelines/arts_education/general_program.htm

Sponsor: New York State Council on the Arts

300 Park Ave South, 10th Floor

New York, NY 10010

NYSCA Arts Education: Local Capacity Building Grants (Regrants) 1783

Local Capacity Building grants offer support to organizations to administer regrant programs that support arts partnerships between schools and cultural organizations or individual artists. Local Capacity Building programs generally support projects that are small and represent first-time or new forays into arts in education on the part of the school applicants. Each Local Capacity Building program site serves a specific region of the state and is expected to promote the regrant program, coordinate application and panel review processes, and provide ongoing technical assistance and professional development.

Requirements: Applicants must have: a full-time, paid executive director; a designated, qualified staff member (preferably not the executive director) to serve as coordinator of the program; and resources to provide appropriate technical assistance, outreach, and professional development opportunities for constituent schools, artists, and cultural organizations in the service area. First time applicants are required to call program staff before the registration deadline. Applications are at the website and must be submitted online.

Restrictions: NYSCA does not fund: operating expenses of privately owned facilities, such as homes or studios; components of an organization's budget that are not directed toward programs in New York State; and competitions or contests.

Geographic Focus: New York

Date(s) Application is Due: Apr 1

Contact: Kathleen Masterson, Sr. Program Officer; (212) 741-2622; kmasterson@nysca.org

Internet: www.nysca.org/public/guidelines/arts_education/local_capacity.htm

Sponsor: New York State Council on the Arts

300 Park Ave South, 10th Floor

New York, NY 10010

NYSCA Arts Education: Services to the Field Grants 1784

The Services to the Field grant is designed to support innovative projects of statewide or regional scope, and statewide significance, which support the development of the arts education field. Projects supported through this category must provide tangible services to multiple organizations statewide, or within a specific region(s). Funding may be requested to support professional development for field-specific capacity-building within multiple organizations. Research projects are ineligible for support.

Requirements: New and returning applicants are required to consult with NYSCA staff in advance of the registration deadline to discuss eligibility. Eligible projects must focus on: 1) building the capacity of cultural organizations and the field in general to engage in arts

education and lifelong learning partnerships; or 2) improving the practice and knowledge base of the field at large. Applications can be found at the website and must be submitted online.

Restrictions: The requested amount should not exceed 50% of the total project budget. NYSCA does not fund: operating expenses of privately owned facilities, such as homes or studios; components of an organization's budget that are not directed toward programs in New York State; and competitions or contests. Research projects are also ineligible for support.

Geographic Focus: New York

Date(s) Application is Due: May 1

Contact: Kathleen Masterson, Sr. Program Officer; (212) 741-2622; kmasterson@nysca.org

Internet: www.nysca.org/public/guidelines/arts_education/services.htm

Sponsor: New York State Council on the Arts

300 Park Ave South, 10th Floor

New York, NY 10010

NYSCA Electronic Media and Film: Film Festivals Grants 1785

Film Festivals grants are available for the public presentation of film, video and new media offered in cinemas, community centers, galleries, libraries and museums. The presentation of work by New York State artists is strongly encouraged. Programming including youth media is also welcome. Touring exhibitions that circulate to three or more sites throughout New York State are also encouraged.

Requirements: Applicants must register with the Council by February 22 to be considered for funding. In addition, applicants must have completed three years of festival programming to a public audience. First-time applicants are required to call program staff before the registration deadline. All grants are also two year, multiyear awards.

Restrictions: Projects will not be considered for support when screenings and the use of technology is in the service of another discipline or objective other than film and electronic media as an art form. Also, requests should not exceed 50% of the total project budget.

Geographic Focus: New York

Date(s) Application is Due: Apr 1

Contact: Karen Helmerson, Sr. Program Officer; (212) 741-3003; khelmerson@nysca.org

Internet: www.nysca.org/public/guidelines/electronic_media/festivals.htm

Sponsor: New York State Council on the Arts

300 Park Ave South, 10th Floor

New York, NY 10010

NYSCA Electronic Media and Film: General Operating Support 1786

General Operating Support sponsors an organization's ongoing work, rather than a specific project or program. The Council examines the nature, scope, and quality of an organization's programs and activities, its managerial and fiscal competence, and its public service when considering the provision and level of support. Support is awarded on multi-year basis.

Requirements: Applicants must register with the Council before February 22 to be considered for funding. In addition, applicants must have: a primary focus in Electronic Media and Film; an organizational mission that is primarily devoted to arts and culture with a prior record of accomplishment in producing or presenting cultural activities; demonstrated fiscal stability as indicated by such factors as a positive Fund Balance, an absence of substantial and/or recurring organizational deficits, a realistic and balanced organizational budget, diverse revenue sources, and strong internal controls; one or more qualified, salaried administrative staff; a viable board of directors and officers that exercises oversight and accountability for governance, operations, programming and finances; and ongoing programs, exhibitions, productions or other art and cultural activities that are open to the general public. First-time applicants are required to call staff before the registration deadline.

Restrictions: General Operating Support grants will be no less than $5,000 and shall not exceed 25% of the applicant organization's budget. Also, applicants cannot apply for both General Operating Support and General Program Support.

Geographic Focus: New York

Date(s) Application is Due: Apr 1

Contact: Karen Helmerson; (212) 741-3003 or (212) 741-7847; khelmerson@nysca.org

Internet: www.nysca.org/public/guidelines/electronic_media/general_operating.htm

Sponsor: New York State Council on the Arts

300 Park Ave South, 10th Floor

New York, NY 10010

NYSCA Electronic Media and Film: General Program Support 1787

General Program Support grants fund activities of arts and cultural programs that are operated as independent entities within their own organization, or for significant arts programming within a nonprofit whose mission is not art-based. The Council examines the nature, scope, and quality of an organization's programs and activities, its managerial and fiscal competence, and its public service when considering the provision and level of support.

Requirements: Applicants must register with NYSCA before February 22 to be eligible for funding the following fiscal year. An applicant for General Program Support must also meet the following conditions: have significant ongoing activities that address a focus in Electronic Media and Film; substantial commitment to arts and culture, with a prior record of accomplishment in producing or presenting cultural activities; demonstrate fiscal stability as indicated by such factors as a positive fund balance, an absence of substantial, recurring organizational deficits, a realistic and balanced organizational budget, diverse revenue sources, and strong controls; one or more qualified, salaried administrative staff; a viable board of directors and officers that exercises oversight and accountability for governance, operations, programming and finances; and must have ongoing programs, exhibitions, productions or other art and cultural activities that are open to the general public. First time applicants are required to call program staff before the registration deadline. Applications are available at the website and should be submitted online.

Restrictions: General Program Support grants will be no less than $5,000 and shall not exceed 25% of the program's budget, based on the income and expense statement for the organization's most recently completed fiscal year. In addition, applicants cannot apply for both General Operating Support and General Program Support. NYSCA does not fund: major expenditures for the establishment of new organizations; accumulate deficits; debt reductions; programs of public universities or New York state agencies or departments; programs of public school districts or their affiliates; activities restricted to an organization's membership; operating expenses or fellowships at professional training schools that are not ope to the general public; programs that are essentially recreational, rehabilitation, or therapeutic; operating expenses of privately owned facilities, such as homes or studios; components of an organization's budget that are not directed toward programs in New York State; competitions or contests; out-of-state travel expenses; or hospitality or entertainment costs of receptions, performance or museum openings, or fundraising benefits.

Geographic Focus: New York
Date(s) Application is Due: Apr 1
Contact: Karen Helmerson, Senior Program Officer; (212) 741-3003 or (212) 741-7847; khelmerson@nysca.org or fchiu@nysca.org
Internet: www.nysca.org/public/guidelines/electronic_media/general_program.htm
Sponsor: New York State Council on the Arts
300 Park Ave South, 10th Floor
New York, NY 10010

NYSCA Electronic Media and Film: Screenings Grants   1788

Screenings grants are available for the public presentation of film, video and new media offered in cinemas, community centers, galleries, libraries and museums. Funding is available to a variety of screenings, including series and year-round programming. The presentation of work by New York State artists is strongly encouraged. Programming including youth media is also welcome. Touring exhibitions that circulate to three or more sites throughout New York State are also encouraged.
Requirements: Applicants must register with the Council by February 22 to be considered for funding. Film Screenings grants only support moving image media, film, or video programs and series in a cinematic setting for public audiences, including outdoor venues. All applicants are encouraged to contact the Council before submitting a proposal, but first-time applicants MUST contact the program staff. Applications are at the website and should be submitted online.
Restrictions: Film screenings on DVD or through the Internet are rarely supported. Projects will not be considered for support when screenings and the use of technology are in the service of another discipline or objective other than film and electronic media as an art form. Also, the request amount should NOT exceed 50% of the total project budget.
Geographic Focus: New York
Date(s) Application is Due: Apr 1
Contact: Karen Helmerson, Senior Program Officer; (212) 741-3003 or (212) 741-7847; khelmerson@nysca.org or fchiu@nysca.org
Internet: www.nysca.org/public/guidelines/electronic_media/screenings.htm
Sponsor: New York State Council on the Arts
300 Park Ave South, 10th Floor
New York, NY 10010

NYSCA Electronic Media and Film: Workspace Grants   1789

The Workspace grants fund public workshops, production facilities, artists' residencies and workspace (virtual as well as physical), and technical assistance at low cost. This category also supports equipment purchase. Workspace proposals with an emphasis on reaching under-served populations are encouraged. The Workspace grant also encourages the participation of media artists as educators and mentors in the development of programs and in facilities design. Electronic Media and Film welcomes proposals that help professional and mature media artists advance their knowledge and use of new technologies. Support for facilities, residencies and workshops may be incorporated into a single request.
Requirements: Applicants must register with the Council by February 22 to be eligible for funding. Requests should demonstrate an integrated view of technology planning, management and program design, and demonstrate capacity for salaried administrative staff, technical support and the ability to maintain regular business hours. Proposals must also show strong evidence of film and electronic media as an art form in production standards and training curriculum. Training and workshops at the Workspace must address the art as well as the craft of teaching film, new media, sound art, and video. In addition, if this grant serves youth, participants must be at least 15 years old in after-school, pre-professional training programs for young artists and/or independent youth media summer workshops. If applying for a Residency Request, applicants should facilitate networking and professional development opportunities through interaction with other artists, arts professionals and the local community, as well as allow maximum flexibility for artists to do their work. First-time applicants are required to call program staff before the registration deadline.
Restrictions: This grant does not support youth media projects in K-12 schools. Also, request amounts should not exceed 50% of the total project budget.
Geographic Focus: New York
Date(s) Application is Due: Apr 1
Contact: Karen Helmerson, Senior Program Officer; (212) 741-3003 or (212) 741-7847; khelmerson@nysca.org or fchiu@nysca.org
Internet: www.nysca.org/public/guidelines/electronic_media/workspace.htm
Sponsor: New York State Council on the Arts
300 Park Ave South, 10th Floor
New York, NY 10010

NYSCA Music: Community Music Schools Grants   1790

Community Music Schools grants support the multiple core activities of community music schools. Although the school may have a single or multidisciplinary focus, for the purpose of this category, the school's principal focus should be music instruction. In addition, residencies, performances, and presentations by professional artists should serve the instructional components of the school and provide additional opportunities for the broader community to engage in arts activities.
Requirements: Applicants must register with the Council by February 22 to be considered for funding. To be eligible, a community music school must be a permanent, non-degree granting nonprofit institution that has been in operation for a minimum of two years. Also, the institution must own or operate an accessible cultural facility, have a cumulative enrollment of at least 100 students, offer year-round instruction and programming, have professional artists on staff, have sequential curriculum to serve a multifaceted enrollment, and articulate standards of mastery to allow beginning and advanced students. First-time applicants must contact Music staff before registration deadline. Applications are available at the website and should be submitted online.
Restrictions: Requested support will not exceed 25% of the project budget. PreK-12 classes during school hours are not eligible for support.
Geographic Focus: New York
Date(s) Application is Due: Apr 1
Contact: Beverly D'Anne, Senior Program Officer; (212) 741-3232; bdanne@nysca.org
Internet: www.nysca.org/public/guidelines/music/community_schools.htm
Sponsor: New York State Council on the Arts
300 Park Ave South, 10th Floor
New York, NY 10010

NYSCA Music: General Operating Support Grants   1791

General Operating Support grants represent an investment by NYSCA in an organization's ongoing work, rather than a specific project or program, in order to help organizations become more effective in fulfilling their mission. The Council examines the nature, scope, and quality of an organization's programs and activities when considering the provision and level of support. Support for this grant is awarded on a multi-year basis.
Requirements: Applicants must register with NYSCA before February 22 to be eligible for funding. An applicant for general operating support must also meet the following conditions: have a primary focus in Music; have an organizational mission that is primarily devoted to arts and culture with a prior record of accomplishment in producing or presenting cultural activities; demonstrate fiscal stability as indicated by such factors as a positive fund balance, an absence of substantial, recurring organizational deficits, a realistic and balanced organizational budget, diverse revenue sources, and strong controls; one or more qualified, salaried administrative staff; a viable board of directors and officers that exercises oversight and accountability for governance, operations, programming and finances; and must have ongoing programs, exhibitions, productions or other art and cultural activities that are open to the general public. First time applicants are required to call program staff before the registration deadline. Applications are available at the website and should be submitted online.
Restrictions: Applicants cannot apply for both General Operating Support and General Program Support. Grants will be no less than $5,000 and shall not exceed 25% of an organization's budget.
Geographic Focus: New York
Date(s) Application is Due: Apr 1
Contact: Beverly D'Anne, Senior Program Officer; (212) 741-3232; bdanne@nysca.org
Internet: www.nysca.org/public/guidelines/music/general_operating.htm
Sponsor: New York State Council on the Arts
300 Park Ave South, 10th Floor
New York, NY 10010

NYSCA Music: General Program Support Grants   1792

The purpose of General Program Support (GPS) is to offer unrestricted support for ongoing activities of arts and cultural programs that are operated as independent entities within their own organization or for significant arts programming within a non-profit whose mission is not art-based (for example, a performing arts center that is operated as a separate entity within a college). The Council examines the nature, scope, and quality of an organization's programs and activities, its managerial and fiscal competence, and its public service when considering the provision and level of GPS support.
Requirements: Applicants must register with NYSCA before February 22 to be eligible for funding the following fiscal year. An applicant for General Program Support must also meet the following conditions: have significant ongoing activities that address a focus in Music; substantial commitment to arts and culture, with a prior record of accomplishment in producing or presenting cultural activities; demonstrate fiscal stability as indicated by such factors as a positive fund balance, an absence of substantial, recurring organizational deficits, a realistic and balanced organizational budget, diverse revenue sources, and strong controls; one or more qualified, salaried administrative staff; a viable board of directors and officers that exercises oversight and accountability for governance, operations, programming and finances; and must have ongoing programs, exhibitions, productions or other art and cultural activities that are open to the general public. First-time applicants are required to call program staff before the registration deadline. Applications are available at the website and should be submitted online.
Restrictions: General Program Support grants will be no less than $5,000 and shall not exceed 25% of the program's budget, based on the income and expense statement for the organization's most recently completed fiscal year. In addition, applicants cannot apply for both General Operating Support and General Program Support.
Geographic Focus: New York
Date(s) Application is Due: Apr 1
Contact: Beverly D'Anne, Senior Program Officer; (212) 741-3232; bdanne@nysca.org
Internet: www.nysca.org/public/guidelines/music/general_program.htm
Sponsor: New York State Council on the Arts
300 Park Ave South, 10th Floor
New York, NY 10010

NYSCA Special Arts Services: General Program Support Grants 1793

General Program Support grants sponsor an organization's ongoing activities of arts and cultural programs that are operated as independent entities within their own organization or for significant arts programming within a non-profit whose mission is not art based. The Council examines the nature, scope, and quality of an organization's programs and activities, its managerial and fiscal competence, and its public service when considering the provision and level of support.

Requirements: Applicants must register with the Council by February 22 to be considered for funding. Also, organizations must: have significant ongoing activities that address a focus in Special Arts Services; make evident a substantial commitment to arts and culture, with a prior record of accomplishment in producing or presenting cultural activities; demonstrate fiscal stability as indicated by such factors as a positive fund balance, an absence of substantial, recurring organizational deficits, a realistic and balanced organizational budget, diverse revenue sources, and strong controls; one or more qualified, salaried administrative staff; a viable board of directors and officers that exercises oversight and accountability for governance, operations, programming and finances; and must have ongoing programs, exhibitions, productions or other art and cultural activities that are open to the general public. Organizations applying to Special Arts Services should have appropriate representation at the staff and board level reflecting the communities served. First-time applicants are required to call program staff before the registration deadline. Applications are available at the website and should be submitted online.

Restrictions: Total requested amounts may not exceed 25% of the total project budget and must be more than $5,000. Applicants may not apply for both General Operating Support and General Program Support grants. Also, organizations whose projects are directed toward general audiences or organizations in which artists do not represent those communities previously mentioned are not eligible for support and should consult the guidelines of other areas of support.

Geographic Focus: New York

Date(s) Application is Due: Apr 1

Contact: Robert Baron, Senior Program Officer; (212) 741-7755; rbaron@nysca.org

Internet: www.nysca.org/public/guidelines/special_arts_services/general_program.htm

Sponsor: New York State Council on the Arts

300 Park Ave South, 10th Floor

New York, NY 10010

NYSCA Special Arts Services: Instruction and Training Grants 1794

Instruction and Training grants offer an opportunity for study aimed toward professional careers in the arts and/or instruction in the traditional art of an ethnic community for members of that community. The goal of this category is to foster professional development in a variety of arts disciplines and techniques, including those with a particular interest in preserving the traditions of specific cultures. Support is offered in three distinct courses of study of professionally-directed instruction and training in any art discipline. These are, in order of priority: Professional Development, Traditional Arts Study, and Pre-Professional Development.

Requirements: Applicants must register with the Council by February 22 to be eligible for funding. Also, organizational priorities must serve African/Caribbean, Asian/Pacific Islander, Latino/Hispanic, and Native American/Indian populations, as well as organizations serving the disabled community whose members seek career development opportunities. Applicant organizations must state which course of study they are providing. Classes must be ongoing and taught by accomplished artists in community-based venues. Application organizations must also provide guidance through all levels of artistic development. In all cases, organizations are required to provide documentation of the results of their programs. First-time applicants are required to call Special Arts Services staff before the registration deadline.

Restrictions: Total requested amounts should not exceed 50% of the total project budget. In addition, the following programs are not eligible for support: single-instructor programs; programs offered in cooperation with schools, school districts, or BOCES, and offered during school hours, or which take place immediately after school hours in school facilities; programs that are essentially recreational, rehabilitative or therapeutic; one-time workshops or programs of very short duration; summer camp activities that are not an integral part of year-round instruction and training programs.

Geographic Focus: New York

Date(s) Application is Due: Apr 1

Contact: Robert Baron, Senior Program Officer; (212) 741-7755; rbaron@nysca.org

Internet: www.nysca.org/public/guidelines/special_arts_services/instruction_training.htm

Sponsor: New York State Council on the Arts

300 Park Ave South, 10th Floor

New York, NY 10010

NYSCA Theatre: Professional Performances Grants 1795

Professional Performances grants offers support to professional theatre companies with ongoing production and development programs, and to service organizations that build and reinforce administrative and institutional skills, provide resources and information, assist in the professional development of artists, and enhance education about and access to theatre for all audiences. NYSCA also encourages and supports the development of emerging theatre companies that demonstrate artistic potential and/or accomplishment. Funding can be directed toward artists' fees, salaries and production expenses.

Requirements: Applicants must register with the Council by February 22 to be considered for funding. In addition, theatre companies: must have produced for two seasons before applying for support; must stage at least one public production per year; must have an artistic director; and must be able to document payment to artistic personnel in their budgets. First-time applicants are required to call Theatre staff before the registration deadline. Applications are available at the website and should be submitted online.

Restrictions: Request funds should not exceed 50% of the total proposed project budget. Also, Theatre support will not be available for community theatre, commercial or student productions, carnivals, sideshows, parades, variety shows, or drama therapy programs.

Geographic Focus: New York

Date(s) Application is Due: Apr 1

Contact: Robert Zukerman, Senior Program Officer; (212) 741-7077; rzukerman@nysca.org

Internet: www.nysca.org/public/guidelines/theatre/performances.htm

Sponsor: New York State Council on the Arts

300 Park Ave South, 10th Floor

New York, NY 10010

NZDIA Community Organization Grants Scheme 1796

The Community Organization Grants Scheme, or COGS, provides grants to non-profit organizations delivering community-based social services that contribute to achieving locally-determined outcomes. Locally elected volunteers on 37 COGS committees make decisions based on the likelihood that the organizations receiving grants will deliver the community benefits and outcomes described in their grant requests. Organizations requesting COGS grants need to show how their community-based services or projects will contribute to: encouraging participation in communities; promoting community leadership; developing community capability; promoting social, economic and cultural equity; or reducing the downstream social and economic costs to communities and government. Grants are contributions for: the running or operational costs of organizations that provide community-based social services; community development costs, such as hui, training, planning, evaluation and facilitator fees; and community projects or event costs that encourage participation in communities, promote community leadership, and promote social, economic and cultural equity. COGS committees deliver services to one or more of these priority sectors: M?ori; women; Pacific communities; other ethnic communities; older people; rural isolated people; people with disabilities; families; youth and children; unemployed people; and community-based organizations with limited access to other government funding. The annual funding round opportunity begins on April 11, with an application deadline of May 23. Decisions will be announced by July 27.

Requirements: Citizens or organizations from these places in the Pacific may put in a request for funding: American Samoa; Australia; Cook Islands; Federated States of Micronesia (Chuuk, Kosrae, Pohnpei and Yap); Fiji; French Polynesia; Guam; Kiribati; Marshall Islands; Nauru; New Caledonia; New Zealand; Niue; Northern Mariana Islands; Palau; Papua New Guinea; Pitcairn; Samoa; Solomon Islands; Tokelau; Tonga; Tuvalu; Vanuatu; and Wallis and Futuna.

Restrictions: COGS does not fund: individuals;fundraisers, including professional or commercial fundraisers whose purpose is to distribute money to others; services that duplicate existing services, unless the request demonstrates there is a good reason for both services to exist; services or activities that have already been delivered or have taken place prior to the closing date; debt repayment or debt servicing; reimbursement of past transactions or for completed work; social functions, except if, for cultural reasons, the event brings people together in order to achieve other significant community benefits or outcomes; alcohol and similar substances, such as kava; requests where there is evidence of a conflict of interest, which has not been disclosed or managed appropriately; publishing any material of a technical nature, unless it is consistent with the applicable policies and guidelines produced by the relevant government or government-approved authorities; capital items purchases such as land, buildings, renovations, machinery, vehicles and/or furniture; services or activities that promote commercial, political or religious activities, including political advocacy projects, employment and/or business initiatives and commercial enterprises; activities or projects specifically intended to generate a profit, though profits are allowed if the purpose is to achieve ongoing sustainability for the project; or services, activities or programs to be delivered overseas.

Geographic Focus: American Samoa, Guam, Marshall Islands, Northern Mariana Islands, Australia, Cook Islands, Fiji, French Polynesia, Kiribati, Micronesia, Nauru, New Caledonia, New Zealand, Niue, Palau, Papua New Guinea, Pitcairn, Solomon Islands, Tokelau, Tonga, Tuvalu, Vanuatu, Wallis and Furuna Islands

Date(s) Application is Due: May 23

Contact: Robyn Nicholas, General Manager Community Operations; 0800 824 824 or (03) 546 0904; robyn.nicholas@dia.govt.nz or community.matters@dia.govt.nz

Internet: www.communitymatters.govt.nz/community-organisations-grants-scheme/

Sponsor: New Zealand Department of Internal Affairs

P.O. Box 805, 147 Lambton Quay

Wellington, 6140 New Zealand

NZDIA Lottery Minister's Discretionary Fund Grants 1797

The Lottery Minister's Discretionary Fund provides grants to not-for-profit organizations and individuals for community projects that fall outside the scope of the other Lottery committees that distribute grants. The Fund may provide grants for: overseas travel to help towards airfares, accommodation and travel costs for a representative to attend an event or conference overseas; volunteer fire-fighting services for small contributions towards one-off projects. Organizations need to show how the grant will benefit the community and show evidence that funding is not available from Fire and Emergency New Zealand; animal welfare projects. Organizations need to show how the community will benefit from their animal welfare project; and training in financial planning and/or good governance. It supports representatives from community groups to attend a training course, or community groups hosting in-house training using an external training provider. Grants are made to organizations and individuals whose requests show how they will achieve and measure the outcomes and benefits for New Zealand communities of their projects or overseas travel.

Requirements: Training must be provided by a recognized professional training establishment or an individual with suitable qualifications and experience in financial planning and/or good governance. Trainer fees and assistance towards reasonable related venue costs, travel and accommodation will be considered.

Restrictions: Lottery grants may not be used for any of the following: repaying or servicing debt; refinancing loans, deposits or underwriting projects; commercial, political and/or religious objectives, including employment and/or business initiatives, commercial enterprises, political advocacy or projects which seek to change legislation; fundraisers and projects which seek to raise funds in or for a specific sector, or are involved with the training or employment of fundraisers; projects which seek to redistribute funding to others; overseas aid or disaster relief; alcohol and drug treatment, education and support services; medical expenses, operations, treatments or the purchase of major items of health equipment; capital investment or trust funds; or projects or activities completed (retrospective funding) or items bought before the request. In addition. the Fund does not support: conferences or forums, unless the primary reason for attendance is training in financial planning and/or good governance; registration or training that maintains an individual's registration with a professional organization; permanent residential housing services or community housing; gambling education/prevention/treatment services; or a second request for the same project in the same funding year (1 July to 30 June).
Geographic Focus: New Zealand
Contact: Robyn Nicholas, General Manager Community Operations; 0800 824 824 or (03) 546 0904; robyn.nicholas@dia.govt.nz or community.matters@dia.govt.nz
Internet: www.communitymatters.govt.nz/lottery-ministers-discretionary-fund/
Sponsor: New Zealand Department of Internal Affairs
P.O. Box 805, 147 Lambton Quay
Wellington, 6140 New Zealand

O. Max Gardner Foundation Grants   1798
The O. Max Gardner Foundation was established in North Carolina in 1946, in honor of Oliver Maxwell Gardner. Born in Shelby, North Carolina, Gardner was orphaned as a young child, but went on to to attend North Carolina State University (then known as North Carolina A&M) on a scholarship, where he majored in chemical engineering, was involved in ROTC, played on the football team, managed the baseball team, served as the senior class president, and maintained active membership in the Sigma Nu Fraternity. Gardner returned to Shelby to practice law and married Fay Webb, daughter of prominent politician James L. Webb and niece of Congressman E. Yates Webb. He was elected governor in 1928 and, later, Gardner-Webb University was named for he and his wife. The O. Max Gardner Foundation awards grants in its primary fields of interest, which include: community development; education; human services; and religion. Its geographic area is in and around the community of Shelby, although some grants are given statewide. There is no formal application and no identified annual deadlines. Most recent awards have ranged from $500 to $21,000, with twenty to twenty-five grants approved each year.
Requirements: Although applications are preferred from 501(c)3 organizations serving the residents of Shelby, North Carolina, area, including all of Cleveland County. Some giving is open to other non-profits across the State.
Geographic Focus: North Carolina
Amount of Grant: 500 - 21,000 USD
Samples: Cleveland County Arts, Shelby, North Carolina, $1,500 - general operations; Cleveland County Library System, Shelby, North Carolina, $6,202 - general donation for operations; University of North Carolina, Chapel Hill, North Carolina, $18,000 - general operations.
Contact: John Mull Gardner, President; (704) 487-0755
Sponsor: O. Max Gardner Foundation
P.O. Box 2286
Shelby, NC 28151-0277

Oak Foundation Child Abuse Grants   1799
The foundation awards grants worldwide to address international social and environmental issues, particularly those that have a major impact on the lives of the disadvantaged. In the Child Abuse Program, the Foundation envisions a world in which all children are protected from sexual abuse and sexual exploitation. Recognising that for many children these forms of abuse do not exist in isolation from other forms of abuse and violence, Oak supports initiatives that: directly address sexual abuse and sexual exploitation; and/or diminish other forms of abuse and violence that are related to or impact upon sexual abuse and sexual exploitation. Oak has a particular interest in promoting and supporting learning from the work of partners. This is done through the identification of learning opportunities within its existing partnerships, as well as through new partnerships specifically designed to drive learning forward across the sector.
Requirements: Within this program, Oak funds organizations in the United States, Canada, Brazil, Bulgaria, Ethiopia, Latvia, Mexico, Moldova, Netherlands, South Africa, Switzerland, Tanzania, and Uganda.
Restrictions: Oak does not provide support to individuals, and does not provide funding for scholarships or tuition assistance for undergraduate or postgraduate studies. The Foundation also does not fund religious organizations for religious purposes, election campaigns, or general fund-raising drives.
Geographic Focus: All States, Brazil, Bulgaria, Canada, Ethiopia, Latvia, Mexico, Moldova, Netherlands, South Africa, Switzerland, Tanzania, Uganda, United Kingdom
Amount of Grant: 25,000 - 2,000,000 USD
Samples: Anti-Slavery International, London, England, $137,008 - safe house for victims of domestic violence; Firelight Foundation, Santa Cruz, California, $844,955 - generating learning to enhance community-based child protection mechanisms; Ethiopian Sociology Social Anthropology and Social Work Association, Addis Ababa, Ethiopia, $167,023 - enhancing competences of professionals to prevent child sexual abuse and exploitation.
Contact: Florence Bruce, Director, Child Abuse Programs; cap@oakfnd.ch
Internet: www.oakfnd.org/node/1296
Sponsor: Oak Foundation
Case Postale 115 58, Avenue Louis Casai
Geneva, Cointrin 1216 Switzerland

Oak Foundation Housing and Homelessness Grants   1800
The foundation awards grants worldwide to address international social and environmental issues, particularly those that have a major impact on the lives of the disadvantaged. In the Housing and Homelessness Program, the Foundation aims to promote economic self-sufficiency, increase the availabilty and supply of affordable housing, and prevent homelessness.
Requirements: Within this program, Oak's geographic focus is currently on: Boston, New York and Philadelphia in the United States; London, Belfast, South Wales and Glasgow in the United Kingdom; and Ranchi and Kolkata in India. Projects which have national impact in the U.S. and the United Kingdom are also funded.
Restrictions: Oak does not provide support to individuals, and does not provide funding for scholarships or tuition assistance for undergraduate or postgraduate studies. The Foundation also does not fund religious organizations for religious purposes, election campaigns, or general fund-raising drives.
Geographic Focus: All States, India, United Kingdom
Amount of Grant: 25,000 - 2,000,000 USD
Samples: New Philanthropy Capital, London, England, $56,000 - to provide access to youth offending data by homelessness charities; Picture the Homeless, Bronx, New York, $228,300 - in support of the Housing Not Warehousing program.
Contact: Amanda Beswick, Director, Housing and Homelessness Program; hhp@oakfnd.org
Internet: www.oakfnd.org/node/1298
Sponsor: Oak Foundation
Case Postale 115 58, Avenue Louis Casai
Geneva, Cointrin 1216 Switzerland

Ober Kaler Community Grants   1801
The Ober Kaler Community Grants aid nonprofit organizations dedicated to addressing the education and welfare needs of at-risk children and youth in Washington, D.C. and Baltimore. The Grants are administered by a group of employees within the firm who then review and award the three annual grants. Applications and a list of previous recipients are available online.
Requirements: Tax-exempt 501(c)3 nonprofit organizations are eligible. Churches, synagogues, parochial, and public schools also may apply if their umbrella organizations have tax-exempt status.
Restrictions: Individuals, government agencies and religious organizations requesting funds for sectarian activities are not eligible for funding. The following are also not eligible for grant consideration: start-up funding; capital campaigns; fund raising; galas; advertising; political campaigns and supporting events/tournaments; and scholarships.
Geographic Focus: District of Columbia, Maryland
Date(s) Application is Due: Aug 1
Contact: Grants Coordinator; (410) 230-7185; oberkalergrants@ober.com or info@ober.com
Internet: www.ober.com/our_firm/community-grants
Sponsor: Ober Kaler Grimes and Shriver
100 Light Street
Baltimore, MD 21202

OceanFirst Foundation Home Runs for Heroes Grants   1802
The OceanFirst Foundation concentrates its grantmaking around four core priority areas: health and wellness; housing; improving quality of life; and youth development and education. In addition, grants are made to support emerging community needs and special initiatives consistent with the priorities of the Foundation. The Foundation has teamed up with the Lakewood BlueClaws, a minor league team of the Philadelphia Phillies organization, to honor and provide support to the brave men and women who protect our country. Specifically, the Home Runs for Heroes program provides financial support to select military-based charities that meet the emergency needs of local service men and women – active and retired - and their families. For each home run hit at FirstEnergy Park during the season by the Lakewood BlueClaws, the Foundation provides a $1,000 donation.
Requirements: Home Runs for Heroes grants are open to nonprofits that support military men and women who live within the Foundation's service communities.
Restrictions: The Foundation, in general, does not fund outside these specific strategic areas or provide support to organizations that cannot demonstrate a significant level of service within the OceanFirst market area. The Foundation cannot provide funding for the following: individuals; research; organizations not exempt under Section 501(c)3 of the Internal Revenue Code; religious congregations; political causes, candidates, organizations or campaigns; organizations whose primary purpose is to influence legislation; or sports leagues and teams.
Geographic Focus: New Jersey
Contact: Katherine Durante, Executive Director; (732) 240-4500, ext. 1742 or (732) 341-4676; fax (732) 473-9641; kdurante@oceanfirstfdn.org or info@oceanfirstfdn.org
Internet: www.oceanfirstfdn.org/home-runs-for-heroes-grants/
Sponsor: OceanFirst Foundation
975 Hooper Avenue
Toms River, NJ 08753

OceanFirst Foundation Major Grants   1803
The OceanFirst Foundation concentrates its grantmaking around four core priority areas: health and wellness; housing; improving quality of life; and youth development and education. In addition, grants are made to support emerging community needs and special initiatives consistent with the priorities of the Foundation. Requests for Major Grants are defined as those that are more than $5,000 for program or project support. Such requests must address one of the Foundation's priorities, and applicants must be able to demonstrate a significant impact within the OceanFirst market area. Potential applicants are strongly encouraged to review the application and requirement checklist prior to completing a request to ensure that all qualifications can be met. The application deadline is April 1.

Requirements: Organizations may request one major grant per year and if the request is declined, the organization must wait one year before reapplying to the Foundation.
Restrictions: The Foundation, in general, does not fund outside these specific strategic areas or provide support to organizations that cannot demonstrate a significant level of service within the OceanFirst market area. The Foundation cannot provide funding for the following: individuals; research; organizations not exempt under Section 501(c)3 of the Internal Revenue Code; religious congregations; political causes, candidates, organizations or campaigns; organizations whose primary purpose is to influence legislation; or sports leagues and teams.
Geographic Focus: New Jersey
Date(s) Application is Due: Apr 1
Amount of Grant: 5,000 - 100,000 USD
Contact: Katherine Durante, Executive Director; (732) 240-4500, ext. 1742 or (732) 341-4676; fax (732) 473-9641; kdurante@oceanfirstfdn.org or info@oceanfirstfdn.org
Internet: www.oceanfirstfdn.org/major-grants/
Sponsor: OceanFirst Foundation
975 Hooper Avenue
Toms River, NJ 08753

OceanFirst Foundation Summer Camp Grants 1804
The OceanFirst Foundation concentrates its grantmaking around four core priority areas: health and wellness; housing; improving quality of life; and youth development and education. In addition, grants are made to support emerging community needs and special initiatives consistent with the priorities of the Foundation. Past recipients of Summer Camp Grants have offered all kinds of interesting, safe and engaging activities, both in-person and virtual, including Scouting, STEAM education, farming, theater, and youth empowerment. Organizations selected to receive Summer Camp Grants must agree to use funds awarded to provide camp scholarships of up to $250 per child to cover the cost of a camp experience. The deadline to apply for a Summer Camp Grant is February 15.
Requirements: Summer Camp grants are open to nonprofits, youth organizations, and education foundations with tax-exempt status.
Restrictions: The Foundation, in general, does not fund outside these specific strategic areas or provide support to organizations that cannot demonstrate a significant level of service within the OceanFirst market area. The Foundation cannot provide funding for the following: individuals; research; organizations not exempt under Section 501(c)3 of the Internal Revenue Code; religious congregations; political causes, candidates, organizations or campaigns; organizations whose primary purpose is to influence legislation; or sports leagues and teams.
Geographic Focus: New Jersey
Date(s) Application is Due: Feb 15
Amount of Grant: Up to 10,000 USD
Contact: Katherine Durante, Executive Director; (732) 341-4676 or (732) 341-4676; fax (732) 473-9641; kdurante@oceanfirstfdn.org or info@oceanfirstfdn.org
Internet: www.oceanfirstfdn.org/summer-camp-grants/
Sponsor: OceanFirst Foundation
975 Hooper Avenue
Toms River, NJ 08753

Office Depot Corporation Community Relations Grants 1805
The corporate giving program awards grants to nonprofit organizations aligned with Office Depot's mission to directly impact the health, education, and welfare of children. Office Depot supports nonprofit organizations at the local level with donations of products, contributions of funds, and efforts to encourage employees and customers to become involved. To request a monetary donation, provide a brief description of the organization, the federal tax-ID number, an explanation of what is being requested, and the rationale based on Office Depot's charitable giving guidelines. The request should be submitted on organization letterhead and sent to the office.
Requirements: 501(c)3 nonprofit organizations are eligible.
Restrictions: Grants do not support individuals, advertising, athletic teams or events, fashion shows; project graduation, capital campaigns, individual or group travel, political causes, film/video projects, or nonprofit organizations that spend more than 25 percent of their revenue on management overhead and fundraising expenses.
Geographic Focus: All States
Contact: Melissa Perlman, Public Relations; (561) 438-0704; Melissa.Perlman@officedepot.com
Internet: www.community.officedepot.com/local.asp
Sponsor: Office Depot Corporation
2200 Old Germantown Road
Delray Beach, FL 33445

Office Depot Foundation Education Grants 1806
Everywhere Office Depot conducts business, its belief in the fundamental importance of corporate citizenship is readily apparent. The Office Depot Foundation's commitment to education is longstanding and broad-based. Through far-reaching programs, it attempts to impact students from preschools and kindergartens to university classrooms and laboratories. As part of its commitment to the Foundation mission - Listen Learn Care - the Foundation recognizes the importance of supporting children, parents and teachers through initiatives that are designed to make a difference around the world. An online eligibility survey and grant application can be found on the Grant Making Guidelines page. Applications are retrieved on a monthly basis and are reviewed by a committee. Applicants should allow at least twelve weeks for a response. Grant amounts will be a minimum of $50 and a maximum of $3,000 (very limited). The majority of grants issued are in the vicinity of $1,000 and are supported by in-kind donations when inventory allows.
Requirements: 501(c)3 nonprofit organizations are eligible to apply.

Restrictions: Office Depot does not contribute to individuals and does not make donations in return for advertising. In addition, grants do not support athletic teams or events; fashion shows; project graduation; capital campaigns; individual or group travel; political causes; film/video projects; or nonprofit organizations that spend more than 25 percent of their revenue on management overhead and fundraising expenses.
Geographic Focus: All States
Amount of Grant: 50 - 3,000 USD
Contact: Mary Wong, President; (561) 438-2895 or (561) 438-4276; mwong@jkggroup.com
Sabrina Conte, (561) 438-8752; Sabrina.conte@officedepot.com
Internet: devel.jkggroup.com/od/foundation/education.asp
Sponsor: Office Depot Foundation
6600 North Military Trail
Boca Raton, FL 33496

OHA 'Ahahui Grants 1807
The Office of Hawaiian Affairs is a public agency with a high degree of autonomy. OHA is responsible for improving the well-being of Native Hawaiians. OHA enhances Hawaiian well-being by collaborating with various organizations to strengthen Hawaiian community's resources. The 'Ahahui Grants program provides funding support to eligible organizations hosting that align with at least one of OHA's Strategic Results, provide significant benefits to the Native Hawaiian community, and offer OHA valuable public relations, recognition benefits and community engagement opportunities to fulfill its vision to raise a beloved nation.
Requirements: To be eligible for consideration, applicant organizations must: have IRS tax-exempt non-profit status; be registered with Hawaii Compliance Express (HCE) with "compliant" status, current and dated within three months of the application deadline; and be in compliance and in good standing with OHA. Events eligible for an 'Ahahui Grant must be a community event benefiting Native Hawaiians. All applicants must provide matching funds in the amount of at least 10% of the total event cost. Matching funds can be in the form of cash and/or in-kind contributions.
Restrictions: This grant program is not intended to support fundraisers; award and recognition events; individuals and groups seeking financial assistance to participate in an event; building dedications or groundbreaking ceremonies; events occurring outside the State of Hawaii; church or religious events; music concerts; events occurring as part of an ongoing programmatic service; sponsorship of individuals or teams; or travel subsidies to attend an event.
Geographic Focus: Hawaii
Date(s) Application is Due: Apr 27; Sep 21
Amount of Grant: Up to 100,000 USD
Contact: Karlen Oneha, Grants Specialist; (808) 594-1809 or (808) 594-1835; karleno@oha.org or grantsinfo@oha.org
Jason Paloma, Grants Specialist; (808) 594-1835; jasonp@oha.org or grantsinfo@oha.org
Internet: www.oha.org/grants
Sponsor: Office of Hawaiian Affairs
560 N. Nimitz Highway, Suite 200
Honolulu, HI 96817

OHA Community Grants for Culture 1808
The Office of Hawaiian Affairs is a public agency with a high degree of autonomy. OHA is responsible for improving the well-being of Native Hawaiians. OHA enhances Hawaiian well-being by collaborating with various organizations to strengthen Hawaiian community's resources. The Community Grants program supports non-profit organizations whose projects and programs serve the Native Hawaiian community and align with OHA's Strategic Results. There are seven categories under which organizations can submit applications for these two-year awards: culture; health (substance abuse); health (Kupuna); education; housing; income; and land. Each category offers different optional orientation sessions. In the area of Culture, the primary purpose is to strengthen identity of Native Hawaiians, which will enable them to preserve, practice and perpetuate their culture. Cultural activities were once an integral part of traditional Hawaiian society and practiced by all within the community as part of daily life. Western influences have diminished traditional Hawaiian society and cultural practices. Diseases drastically reduced the Native Hawaiian population. Foreign beliefs replaced traditional values and changed the way Native Hawaiians learned and disseminated knowledge. As a result, many Native Hawaiians have become disconnected from cultural practices and knowledge. It is hoped that, through this grant program, these cultural practices will be reinforced, thus supporting the Native Hawaiian identity, strengthening the family, and connecting all members of the community. These cultural practices will also help to provide a link to past and future generations. The annual deadline for online application submission is January 4.
Requirements: To be eligible for funding consideration, an applicant must: have IRS tax-exempt non-profit status, or be a government agency; be registered to do business in the State of Hawaii; be compliant with all laws governing entities doing business in the State of Hawaii; demonstrate to OHA that they are in compliance and in good standing with the State of Hawaii; provide services to the Hawaiian community in the State of Hawaii; provide a 20 percent match in costs from other funding sources; and be in compliance and in good standing with OHA.
Geographic Focus: Hawaii
Date(s) Application is Due: Jan 4
Contact: Karlen Oneha, Grants Specialist; (808) 594-1809 or (808) 594-1835; karleno@oha.org or grantsinfo@oha.org
Jason Paloma, Grants Specialist; (808) 594-1835; jasonp@oha.org or grantsinfo@oha.org
Internet: www.oha.org/grants
Sponsor: Office of Hawaiian Affairs
560 N. Nimitz Highway, Suite 200
Honolulu, HI 96817

OHA Community Grants for Education 1809

The Office of Hawaiian Affairs is a public agency with a high degree of autonomy. OHA is responsible for improving the well-being of Native Hawaiians. OHA enhances Hawaiian well-being by collaborating with various organizations to strengthen Hawaiian community's resources. The Community Grants program supports non-profit organizations whose projects and programs serve the Native Hawaiian community and align with OHA's Strategic Results. There are seven categories under which organizations can submit applications for these two-year awards: culture; health (substance abuse); health (Kupuna); education; housing; income; and land. Each category offers different optional orientation sessions. In the area of Education, the primary goal is to improve Native Hawaiian conditions of learning such that Native Hawaiian students achieve academic success, cultural connection, and strengthened sense of well-being. In essence, OHA seeks to provide Native Hawaiian students with learning opportunities that are culturally relevant, and provide specific strategies to help them understand the math and reading concepts with which they are struggling. The annual deadline for online application submission is January 4.
Requirements: To be eligible for funding consideration, an applicant must: have IRS tax-exempt non-profit status, or be a government agency; be registered to do business in the State of Hawaii; be compliant with all laws governing entities doing business in the State of Hawaii; demonstrate to OHA that they are in compliance and in good standing with the State of Hawaii; provide services to the Hawaiian community in the State of Hawaii; provide a 20 percent match in costs from other funding sources; and be in compliance and in good standing with OHA.
Geographic Focus: Hawaii
Date(s) Application is Due: Jan 4
Contact: Karlen Oneha, Grants Specialist; (808) 594-1809 or (808) 594-1835; karleno@oha.org or grantsinfo@oha.org
Jason Paloma, Grants Specialist; (808) 594-1835; jasonp@oha.org or grantsinfo@oha.org
Internet: www.oha.org/grants
Sponsor: Office of Hawaiian Affairs
560 N. Nimitz Highway, Suite 200
Honolulu, HI 96817

Ohio Arts Council Artist in Residence Grants for Sponsors 1810

The Artist in Residence program brings schools and community organizations together with artists to share in-depth, engaging, personal and sustained arts learning experiences. Using experienced artists listed in the Arts Learning Artist Directory, the Artist in Residence program offers opportunities for learners of all ages to participate in the creative process, bridge cultural differences and cultivate fresh ways of seeing, responding to and learning through the arts. Applicants should demonstrate that they value collaborative learning and show that they are prepared to host an artist in residence by providing evidence of broad-based planning efforts, flexibility, appropriate evaluation strategies and strong organizational support. The OAC also recognizes the hard work of established residency sponsors by allowing them to apply for two-year grants, reducing their administrative burden. By bringing together artists and members of the public to cultivate creativity, the Artist in Residence program transforms lives and contributes to the growth of individuals, communities and society as a whole. The Artist in Residence program (AIR) provides one- or two-year grants to place accomplished professional artists in a variety of educational and community settings to facilitate learning in, through and about the arts.
Requirements: Applicant organizations must have nonprofit status. They include, but are not limited to, public, charter or parochial schools (prekindergarten through university level) and other community organizations such as neighborhood centers, senior centers, arts organizations, faith-based organizations, libraries and social service agencies. Sponsors must provide one-third of the artist's fee, daily lunch and supplies. Budgets for supplies typically range from $25 to $300 per week, depending on the discipline and the length of the residency. Sponsors should find free or reduced-rate housing for the artist(s). All applications to the OAC must be submitted via the online application system, OLGA. Notify the OAC about your organization's intention to apply. You are also strongly encouraged to submit a draft application to the Arts Learning Office at least 30 days before the final deadline date. To submit a draft, simply follow the instructions at the beginning of the application form through OLGA.
Restrictions: Residency-related activities designed in preparation for or in conjunction with competitions or residencies that typically are part of the ongoing program responsibilities of an organization or institution (usually higher education) are ineligible. Residencies may be planned for a minimum of two weeks to a maximum of eight weeks in length. A maximum of four classes or contact sessions per day may be scheduled with the artist in residence.
Geographic Focus: Ohio
Date(s) Application is Due: Mar 1
Amount of Grant: Up to 6,400 USD
Contact: Dia Foley, Grants Office Director; (614) 728-4429 or (614) 466-2613; fax (614) 466-4494; dia.foley@oac.state.oh.us
Internet: www.oac.state.oh.us/grantsprogs/guidelines/ArtistinResidence.asp
Sponsor: Ohio Arts Council
30 E. Broad Street, 33rd Floor
Columbus, OH 43215-3414

Ohio County Community Foundation Board of Directors Grants 1811

The Ohio County Community Foundation may, on occasion, find it necessary to issue discretionary small grants from the unrestricted funds outside the Grants Committee recommendations and full Board approval. These grants are on a first come, first serve basis until allotted funding for the current calendar year has been exhausted. Each grant application will be reviewed after submission to ensure the application is complete and the organization is eligible to make application. Specifically, Board of Directors Grants are given in an amount not to exceed $300 per application with a maximum of $600 per year per organization and a maximum of four Board Grants per year.

Requirements: Grants will only be awarded for projects and programs that benefit the residents of Ohio County. Applicants must qualify as an exempt organization under the IRS Code 501(c), or be sponsored by such organizations, or qualify as a governmental or educational entity or possess similar attributes per IRS Code Section 509(a). Grants applied for brick and mortar projects must be only for charitable purposes, to further the mission of a public charity.
Restrictions: No grants will be made solely to individuals but can be made for the benefit of certain individuals for such purposes as scholarships and special programs through educational institutions and other sponsoring recipient organizations. In addition, no grants will be made specifically for sectarian religious purposes but can be made to religious organizations for general community programs.
Geographic Focus: Indiana
Amount of Grant: Up to 300 USD
Contact: Stephanie Scott, Program Coordinator; (812) 438-9401; fax (812) 438-9488; sscott@occfrisingsun.com
Internet: www.occfrisingsun.com/CombineApplicationSmallGrants.htm
Sponsor: Ohio County Community Foundation
591 Smart Drive, P.O. Box 170
Rising Sun, IN 47040

Ohio County Community Foundation Grants 1812

The Ohio County Community Foundation is charged with assisting donors in building, managing, and distributing a lasting source of charitable funds for the good of Ohio County. The Foundation funds projects and programs for economic development, education, human services, cultural affairs, and health. The Foundation will: offer grant awards that strive to anticipate the changing needs of the community and be flexible in responding to them; focus on those types of grants which will have the greatest benefit per dollar granted; encourage the participation of other contributions by using matching, challenge and other grant techniques; offer funding that closely relates and coordinates with the programs of other sources for funding, such as the government, other foundations, and associations; induces grant recipients to achieve certain objectives such as becoming more efficient, increasing fundraising capabilities, and delivering better products; and consider grants in the form of technical assistance and staff assisted special projects which are intended to respond to a variety of needs in the county.
Requirements: Grants will be made only to organizations whose programs benefit the residents of Ohio County. The Foundation uses the following criteria when evaluating proposals: is there an established need for the program or project; are there other more compatible sources for potential funding; does the Foundation have adequate sources to respond: and does the grant support a charitable purpose.
Restrictions: Funding is not available to individuals. Grants are not made to enable individuals or groups to take trips except where there are special circumstances which will benefit the larger community.
Geographic Focus: Indiana
Date(s) Application is Due: Apr 15; Oct 15
Amount of Grant: Up to 3,000 USD
Contact: Stephanie Scott, Program Coordinator; (812) 438-9401; fax (812) 438-9488; sscott@occfrisingsun.com
Internet: www.occfrisingsun.com/GrantApplicationNew.htm
Sponsor: Ohio County Community Foundation
591 Smart Drive, P.O. Box 170
Rising Sun, IN 47040

Ohio County Community Foundation Mini-Grants 1813

The Ohio County Community Foundation assists donors in building, managing and distributing a lasting source of charitable funds for the good of Ohio County. The Foundation Mini-Grants fund projects and programs for economic development, education, human services, cultural affairs, and health. Amounts do not exceed $100 per application with a maximum of $200 per year per organization and a maximum of four mini-grants per year. These grants are on a first come, first serve basis until allotted funding for the current calendar year has been exhausted.
Requirements: Grants will be made only to organizations whose programs benefit the residents of Ohio County. The Foundation uses the following criteria when evaluating proposals: is there an established need for the program or project; are there other more compatible sources for potential funding; does the Foundation have adequate sources to respond; and does the grant support a charitable purpose.
Restrictions: Funding is not available to individuals. Grants are not made to enable individuals or groups to take trips except where there are special circumstances which will benefit the larger community.
Geographic Focus: Indiana
Amount of Grant: Up to 100 USD
Contact: Stephanie Scott, Program Coordinator; (812) 438-9401; fax (812) 438-9488; sscott@occfrisingsun.com
Internet: www.occfrisingsun.com/CombineApplicationSmallGrants.htm
Sponsor: Ohio County Community Foundation
591 Smart Drive, P.O. Box 170
Rising Sun, IN 47040

Ohio Valley Foundation Grants 1814

The Foundation Office at Fifth Third Bank is committed to making a significant impact on programs and initiatives that create strong, vibrant communities and provide pathways to opportunity. Through the Foundation Office, the visions of individuals, families and institutions are realized, and legacies are attained by allocating the resources of their respective foundations in support of innovative programs and organizations in our communities. The Ohio Valley Foundation specifically supports small equipment and capital improvement projects in the Ohio Valley. An organization interested in submitting a grant proposal should first submit a Letter of Inquiry (LOI) using the link at the website.

LOIs are accepted from October 1 through December 31 each year. The Foundation Office will review each LOI and may contact the applying organization about further discussion of the proposal, which may include a site visit. Each organization will receive either an email declining the inquiry or an invitation to submit a full application online. An invitation to apply will include the foundation funding source, recommended request amount, and a deadline for receipt of the application. The Fifth Third Bank Foundation Office will submit completed applications to the respective Foundation Board or Committee for final review and approval or declination. Grant seekers should allow six to twelve months for the grant making process. In general, the Foundation prefers awarding grants for one year. Most recent awards have ranged from $5,000 to $250,000.

Requirements: Nonprofit organizations that operate in the Greater Cincinnati region and are designated under section 501(c)3 and subsections 509(a)1 or 509(a)2 by the Internal Revenue Service are eligible to apply for a grant.

Restrictions: Nonprofits may apply only once within any 12-month period. The following are ineligible to apply: individuals; individual churches (except for proposals regarding an affiliated school); publicly supported entities such as public schools, government or government agencies; supporting organizations designated 509(a)3 by the IRS; walks, runs, dinners, galas, luncheons and other event sponsorship requests; athletic, band, and other school booster clubs; or startup funding for new programs or organizations (usually not a funding priority). A waiting period of three years is required for prior grant recipients receiving $10,000 or more from any funding source administered by the Fifth Third Bank Foundation Office. This period will begin as of the first payment on the grant.

Geographic Focus: Ohio
Amount of Grant: 5,000 - 250,000 USD
Contact: Heidi B. Jark, Managing Director; (513) 534-7001 or (513) 636-4200
Internet: www.53.com/content/fifth-third/en/personal-banking/about/in-the-community/foundation-office-at-fifth-third-bank.html
Sponsor: Ohio Valley Foundation
38 Fountain Square Plaza, MD 1090CA
Cincinnati, OH 45202

Olga Sipolin Children's Fund Grants   1815

The Olga Sipolin Children's Fund was established in 1998 to provide for the basic needs of underserved children in Connecticut. Preference is given to charitable organizations that have a direct impact on the social welfare of children through the provision of housing, clothing, food and medical care. Grants from the Sipolin Children's Fund are 1 year in duration. Award amounts go up to $5,000. Bank of America serves as co-trustee of the Sipolin Children's Fund.

Requirements: Applicants must have 501(c)3 tax-exempt status that serve communities in Connecticut. Applications will be submitted online through the Bank of America website. A grant report is required within 1 year of the grant application date, regardless of whether all of the funds have been spent.

Restrictions: Grant requests for capital projects are generally not considered. Applicants will not be awarded a grant for more than 3 consecutive years. The fund does not support requests from individuals, organizations attempting to influence policy through direct lobbying, or any political campaigns.

Geographic Focus: Connecticut
Date(s) Application is Due: Nov 1
Amount of Grant: Up to 5,000 USD
Samples: Klingberg Family Centers, New Britain, Connecticut, $5,000 - awarded for Positive Parenting program (Triple P); Catholic Charities Archdiocese of Hartford, Hartford, Connecticut, $5,000 - awarded for Waterbury Diaper Bank; Mercy Housing and Shelter Corporation, Hartford, Connecticut, $5,000 - awarded for the St. Elizabeth House Friendship Center.
Contact: Amy R. Lynch, Philanthropic Client Manager; (860) 244-4870; ct.grantmaking@bankofamerica.com or amy.r.lynch@bofa.com
Internet: www.bankofamerica.com/philanthropic/foundation/?fnId=1
Sponsor: Olga Sipolin Children's Fund
P.O. Box 1802
Providence, RI 02901-1802

Olive B. Cole Foundation Grants   1816

The Olive B. Cole Foundation provides funding to organizations located within or serving residents of DeKalb, LaGrange, Noble and Steuben counties in Indiana. Job creation, entrepreneurship, arts and culture, hospital care, human services, youth services, and education are areas of interest. Applicants may submit a one-page preliminary letter which includes a description of the organization, the proposed project, and the funding needed. Some applicants may be asked to submit a full proposal. All applicants will receive a written response to their funding request.

Requirements: Indiana nonprofit organizations or government entities are eligible.

Restrictions: Faxed requests will not be considered. Loans or cash grants are not made to individuals. Normally the Foundation does not make grants to religious organizations, to endowments, or to national fund drives. The Foundation does not encourage grants where the Foundation is asked to fund the entire project.

Geographic Focus: Indiana
Amount of Grant: 100 - 120,000 USD
Samples: Auburn Cord Duesenberg Museum, Auburn, Indiana, $105,000 - general operating costs; Audiances Unlimited, Fort Wayne, Indiana, $6,250 - general operating costs; Auburn Police Department, Auburn, Indiana, $5,000 - general operating costs.
Contact: Maclyn T. Parker, President; (260) 436-2182
Sponsor: Olive B. Cole Foundation
6207 Constitution Drive
Fort Wayne, IN 46804

Olive Higgins Prouty Foundation Grants   1817

The Olive Higgins Prouty Foundation was established in Massachusetts in 1952, in honor of an American novelist and poet, best known for her 1922 novel Stella Dallas and her pioneering consideration of psychotherapy in her 1941 novel Now, Voyager. The Foundation's primary fields of interest continue to be: arts and culture; child welfare; higher education; hospital care; music; and secondary education. Giving is generally centered around New Bedford and Worcester, Massachusetts, although it sometimes is given out-of-state. Support is typically given for annual campaigns, capital campaigns, and general operations. Amounts range from $1,000 to $50,000, with approximately forty awards given annually. Applications should be submitted in letter form, along with details of the proposal and budgetary needs. The annual deadline for submission is September 30.

Requirements: Any 501(c)3 serving the residents of New Bedford and Worcester, Massachusetts, are eligible to apply, along with a selection of out-of-state organizations.
Geographic Focus: All States
Amount of Grant: 1,000 - 50,000 USD
Samples: Prospect Hill Academy Charter School, Cambridge, Massachusetts, $5,000 - general operating support; Children's Hospital Corporation, $46,000 - general operating support; Mattapoisett Public Library, Mattapoisett, Massachusetts, $2,000 - general operating support.
Contact: Charlene Teja, Philanthropic Administrator; (617) 434-6565 or (401) 278-6058
Sponsor: Olive Higgins Prouty Foundation
P.O. Box 1802, One Financial Plaza
Providence, RI 02901-1802

Olive Smith Browning Charitable Trust Grants   1818

Established in 1978, the Olive Smith Browning Charitable Trust offers funding to organizations located in the Twin Falls, Idaho, region. Its primary fields of interest include: arts, culture, and humanities; education; the environment; animal welfare; human services; religion; community development; and health care. The annual deadline for application submission is May 31. There are no specified application formats, so applicants should begin by sending their proposal overview directly to the trustee in charge of managing the trust. Most recent grants have ranged from $2,000 to $10,000, with an average of ten awards each year and a total annual giving of $35,000. Grant decisions are generally communicated by July 31 for applications received by the deadline.

Requirements: Applicants should be 501(c)3 organizations either located in, or serving the residents of, Twin Falls, Idaho.
Restrictions: No grants are given to individuals.
Geographic Focus: Idaho
Date(s) Application is Due: May 31
Amount of Grant: 2,000 - 10,000 USD
Samples: Twin Falls Baseball Tomorrow, Twin Falls, Idaho, $2,000 - general operating support; Lee Pesky Learning Center, Boise, Idaho, $5, 000 - general operating support; Magic Valley Symphony Orchestra, Twin Falls, Idaho, $4,000 - general operating support.
Contact: Carla Colfack, Trust Officer; (208) 736-1217 or (888) 730-4933
Internet: www.wellsfargo.com/privatefoundationgrants/browning
Sponsor: Olive Smith Browning Charitable Trust
P.O. Box 53456, MAC S4101-22G
Phoenix, AZ 85072-3456

Olivia R. Gardner Foundation Grants   1819

The Olivia R. Gardner Foundation was established in Georgia in 2003 as a means of awarding grants in Georgia, Florida, and in some areas of North Carolina. The Foundation's primary fields of interest include: elementary and secondary education; higher education; the arts; and human services. Most recent awards have ranged from $1,000 to $15,000, although much higher amounts are sometimes given to higher education institutions. Between twenty and twenty-five grants are awarded each year. A formal application is required, and can be secured by contacting the Foundation office. There are no identified annual deadlines for submission.

Requirements: Any 501(c)3 organization serving residents of Georgia, Florida, or North Carolina are eligible to apply.
Geographic Focus: Florida, Georgia, North Carolina
Amount of Grant: 1,000 - 65,000 USD
Samples: Vero Beach Museum of Art, Vero Beach, Florida, $2,500 - general operations; Safe Space, Louisburg, North Carolina, $2,500 - general operations; Atlanta Speech School, Atlanta, Georgia, $5,000 - educational support.
Contact: Olivia R. Gardner, President; (404) 355-4747
Sponsor: Olivia R. Gardner Foundation
402 Indies Drive
Vero Beach, FL 32963

OMNOVA Solutions Foundation Education Grants   1820

The OMNOVA Solutions Foundation strives to be a strengthening thread in the fabric of society through donations to OMNOVA Solutions communities in the areas of education, civic enhancement, health and welfare, and arts and culture. Preference is given to community projects that involve OMNOVA employees and requests that are recommended by the Foundation coordinators at OMNOVA facilities. In the area of Education, the Foundation funds: K thru 12 schools, to address specific improvements and opportunities in reading and economic literacy, and math and science; school-to-work readiness; initiatives that encourage professional development for teachers; parental involvement; and adult literacy. While some unrestricted funding is provided, the Foundation prefers to fund specific projects. There are no annual submission deadlines specified, and applicants should allow about six weeks for a response.

Requirements: The Foundation supports non-profit, tax-exempt organizations, established for public use, which hold an active 501(c)3 status under the Internal Revenue Service Code. While the Foundation funds a limited number of national projects, priority emphasis is

placed on organizations in those communities where OMNOVA conducts business and where the Company's employees live and work. These communities include: Calhoun, Georgia; Fitchburg, Massachusetts; Columbus, Mississippi; Salem, New Hampshire; Pine Brook, New Jersey; New York, New York; Charlotte, Greensboro, and Monroe, North Carolina; Akron, Beachwood, Fairlawn, Maumee, and Mogadore, Ohio; Auburn and Jeannette, Pennsylvania; Chester, South Carolina; Houston and Stafford, Texas; and Green Bay, Wisconsin.
Restrictions: The Foundation does not support: individuals, private foundations, fraternal, social, labor or veterans organizations; organizations that discriminate because of race, color, creed or national origin; organizations that benefit only a few people; political parties, candidates or lobbying activities; organizations and programs that might pose a potential conflict of interest for OMNOVA; local athletic or sports programs and purchase of sports equipment; travel funds for tours, expeditions or trips by individuals or groups; courtesy advertising, benefits, raffle tickets and other fund raising events involving purchases of tables, tickets or advertisements; churches or religious organizations; organizations that offer a direct benefit to the trustees of the Foundation, to employees or to directors of the corporation; or research grants and conferences.
Geographic Focus: Georgia, Massachusetts, Mississippi, New Hampshire, New Jersey, New York, North Carolina, Ohio, Pennsylvania, South Carolina, Texas, Wisconsin
Contact: S. Theresa Carter; (216) 682-7067 or (330) 869-4291; teresa.carter@omnova.com
Internet: www.omnova.com/en/corporate/community/grant-categories
Sponsor: OMNOVA Solutions Foundation
25435 Harvard Road
Beachwood, OH 44122-6201

Onan Family Foundation Grants **1821**
The Onan Family Foundation is a private philanthropy located in Minneapolis, Minnesota making grants in the near by community. The foundation makes grants to tax-exempt organizations in the areas of education, social welfare, cultural and civic affairs, and religion. Special interest is given to programs that are centered in Minneapolis and Saint Paul, Minnesota. Grant requests should be sent to the foundation well in advance of the semi-annual board of trustees meetings in May and October. Grant requests should be made using the Minnesota Common Grant.
Requirements: The Onan Family Foundation makes grants only to pre-selected organizations located in Minneapolis and Saint Paul, Minnesota, and does not accept unsolicited grant requests. The purpose of this statement is twofold: 1) Information to those from whom we have requested a grant proposal; 2) A reminder to our ongoing recipients that we want a request from them each year.
Restrictions: Grants are not made to individuals or to organizations that attempt to influence legislation, carry on propaganda, or participate or intervene in a New York political campaign. Grants for endowment purposes, to capital funds, or for trips or tours are generally not supported.
Geographic Focus: Minnesota
Amount of Grant: 2,000 - 15,000 USD
Samples: Agriculture and Energy Resource Center, Minneapolis, Minnesota, $8,000; People Responding in Social Ministry, Saint Paul, Minnesota, $12,000; Orme School, Orme, Arizona, $1,500.
Contact: Patricia Onan, Executive Director; (612) 544-4702; office@onanfamily.org
Internet: www.onanfamily.org/~onanfami/index.php?id=9
Sponsor: Onan Family Foundation
P.O. Box 50667
Minneapolis, MN 55405

OneFamily Foundation Grants **1822**
The foundation awards grants to eligible Washington nonprofit organizations working to improve the lives of women living in poverty and at-risk youth, for support services for abused women, and for efforts to end sexual abuse against women and children. Consideration is given to programs that provide training and skills development to low-income women and services providing basic needs such as shelter, counseling, food, and childcare; educational and mentoring projects to help prevent teen pregnancy; job-training programs for youth and school/community-based programs to help low-income youth complete their education; parenting, training, and education programs to help break the cycle of family violence; shelters and services to support abused and neglected children and women; and hands-on programs to encourage philanthropy among children and youth. Grants will support operating expenses, special projects, and minor capital costs necessary to assure the success of a funded project. For general grants, two-page preapplication letters are due on the third Friday in March, July, and November and final proposals are due the second Friday in January, May, and September. Annual deadlines may vary; contact program staff for exact dates.
Requirements: Nonprofit 501(c)3 organizations based in King County, Snohomish County, or the Olympic Peninsula of Washington State are eligible to apply for funding.
Restrictions: Grants are not made to: individuals, scholarships, schools, research, summer camps, athletic events, video or film projects, website development, book publications. No multi-year requests are considered. Groups who have been declined three times are ineligible to reapply.
Geographic Focus: Washington
Amount of Grant: 5,000 - 12,000 USD
Samples: Amara Parenting and Adoption, Seattle, Washington, $12,000 - to foster-adoption the program, training for foster parents, and support for hard-to-place children; First Step Family Support Center, Port Angeles, Washington, $11,154 - Parent-Child Interaction Therapy; Indian Law Resource Center, Helena, Washington. $8,000 - Safe Women/Strong Nations, breaking the cycle of violence against Native women.
Contact: Therese Ogle, Foundation Advisor; (206) 781-3472; fax (206) 784-5987; Oglefounds@aol.com
Internet: fdncenter.org/grantmaker/onefamily
Sponsor: OneFamily Foundation
6723 Sycamore Avenue NW
Seattle, WA 98117

Ontario Arts Council Artists in Communities and Schools Project Grants **1823**
The Artists in Communities and Schools Project Grant program supports the research, development and realization of community-engaged arts projects. Activities involve professional Ontario artists and community members working together to develop and design a creative experience. These experiences may include co-creation. Skill building is a core component of projects. There are three categories: planning to help cover the costs of co-planning and co-design of the project between artists and communities; projects to help cover the costs of realizing a community-engaged arts project; and two-year projects to help cover the costs of continuous multi-phased community-engaged arts project for two years. Essentially, the program provides grants to allow professional artists from all artistic expressions and cultures to provide in-depth learning experiences for Ontario educators and learners. The program's priorities are to support projects that: work with sectors beyond the arts, such as health, education, justice and the environment; provide a sense of community, social connection, civic engagement and contribute to building a more just society; reduce barriers to arts participation; increase access to the arts for under served or marginalized communities; and employ Ontario artists in Ontario communities. Generally, the program funds: artists' fees; support specialist fees (including translators, Elders, therapists, etc.); honoraria for project participants; snack and beverage expenses for participants; travel expenses; venue or studio rental; equipment and materials costs; administrative costs associated with the artists or arts ad hoc group, collective, or organization; and marketing, outreach, and promotion expenses. The annual deadlines for applications are March 15, June 20, September 13, and December 18. The maximum awards are: $10,000 for planning; $15,000 for projects; and $25,000 for two year projects. Up to $5,000 in additional funds are available in any category for mentorship costs of both mentees and mentors.
Requirements: Eligible applicants include: individuals and co-applicants who are Ontario residents with a permanent physical address in Ontario; ad hoc groups/collectives, based in Ontario, made up of at least 50 per cent professional artists; Ontario-based not-for-profit arts organizations and non-arts organizations; school boards not partnered in OAC's Artists in Residence (education) program (for artist fees and travel expenses only); and schools run by First Nations or Indigenous education authorities.
Restrictions: Ineligible applicants include: municipalities, colleges and/or universities; individuals employed by a school involved in the project on a full- or part-time basis during the project; school boards who are partnered with the Ontario Arts Council in the Artists in Residence (education) program; organizations that receive a grant in the Arts Organizations in Communities and Schools – Operating program; or organizations that receive an operating grant in other OAC programs, with the exception of organizations mandated to serve one or more of OAC's priority groups. The following are not eligible to apply to the Two-Year Project category: organizations receiving OAC operating funding; or those seeking support for seasonal camps, festivals, or events. The program does not fund; events or activities that take place outside of Ontario; tours; professional productions for young audiences; capital expenses, including purchase of equipment; art therapy; faculty or student projects associated with their research, course work or studies; non-arts partner administrative activities; or school board costs beyond artists' fees and travel.
Geographic Focus: Canada
Date(s) Application is Due: Feb 15; Jun 20; Sep 13; Dec 18
Amount of Grant: Up to 30,000 CAD
Contact: Philippe Mesly, Program Administrator; (416) 961-1660, ext. 5144 or (800) 387-0058, ext. 5144; pmesly@arts.on.ca
Internet: www.arts.on.ca/grants/artists-in-communities-and-schools-projects
Sponsor: Ontario Arts Council
121 Bloor Street East, 7th Floor
Toronto, ON M4W 3M5 Canada

Ontario Arts Council Arts Organizations in Communities and Schools Operating Grants **1824**
The Arts Organizations in Communities and Schools Operating Gran program provides operating funding to Ontario-based, not-for-profit, multidisciplinary, community-engaged arts organizations working in Ontario communities or schools. The program's priorities are to support organizations that: generate and host high-quality, innovative work that cultivates a rich engagement between artists and participants or communities; implement strategies to reduce or eliminate barriers to public engagement in the arts; and engage Ontario artists to work with communities and schools. The annual deadline for application submissions is April 4, with awards announced in August.
Requirements: Ontario-based, not-for-profit corporations, or national not-for-profit corporations with the head office in Ontario are eligible to apply. Organizations must have: at least $75,000 in total revenues for the last fiscal year, and in projected revenues for the current and requested years (for applicants not currently receiving funding from this program); at least two years of sustained, regular, ongoing programming, as of the application date; a range of revenue sources; and an active board of directors or governing body.
Restrictions: Organizations that are not currently receiving operating funding may only apply in the first year of a multi-year cycle. Ineligible applicants include; non-arts organizations; municipalities; and colleges and universities.
Geographic Focus: Canada
Date(s) Application is Due: Apr 4
Contact: Nas Khan, Officer; (416) 969-7428 or (800) 387-0058, ext. 7428; nkhan@arts.on.ca
Philippe Mesly; (416) 961-1660, ext. 5144 or (800) 387-0058, ext. 5144; pmesly@arts.on.ca
Internet: www.arts.on.ca/grants/arts-organizations-in-communities-and-schools-ope

Sponsor: Ontario Arts Council
121 Bloor Street East, 7th Floor
Toronto, ON M4W 3M5 Canada

Ontario Arts Council Indigenous Culture Fund Indigenous Artists in   1825
Communities and Schools Project Grants
The Ontario Arts Council Indigenous Culture Fund Indigenous Artists in Communities and Schools Project Grants program supports projects that bring together Ontario-based Indigenous artists or elders to: work with individuals or groups of people from a community on collaborative activities that create a meaningful arts experience and transmit artistic skills and knowledge; and teach arts workshops in schools during the upcoming school year, engaging children and youth in creative, active, hands-on and in-depth arts experiences. There are five categories: community arts projects to help cover the costs of participatory activities that promote learning, collaboration and/or engagement in the arts; Indigenous languages through the arts to help cover the costs of artistic and community-engaged projects in which the primary purpose is the transmission of Indigenous languages through the arts; training for community artists and animators to help cover the costs of Indigenous artists and animators working in community and non-arts settings to seek training and mentorship opportunities that will strengthen their community arts, arts training or arts education practice; Indigenous artists in schools projects to help cover the costs of activities that promote learning, collaboration and/or engagement in the arts; and Indigenous artists in northern fly-in communities to support applicants from fly-in communities working anywhere in Ontario and applicants from anywhere in Ontario working in fly-in communities. Depending on the category, awards can range as high as $17,000. There are two annual deadlines for application submission: February 22 and August 29.
Requirements: Eligible applicants include: professional artists and elders who self-identify as First Nations, Metis, or Inuit, and are Ontario residents; ad hoc group or collectives comprised of individuals, of whom at least 50 per cent identify as Indigenous; not-for-profit Indigenous organizations, centers, and councils; elders and language or knowledge keepers, who are engaged in an artistic practice; helpers who are co-applicants or named in the project and included in the budget; Ontario schools run by First Nations or Indigenous education authorities, applying to bring in Indigenous artists; and part-time teachers. All applicants must have a permanent physical address in Ontario.
Restrictions: Ineligible applicants include: students; municipalities; colleges and/or universities; or teachers employed full-time by a school board, private school, or a school run by a First Nation or First Nation education authority during the during the period of time the project will take place. Overall, the program will not fund: events or activities that take place outside of Ontario; fundraising activities; capital expenses; talent shows; school board costs beyond artists fees and travel; non-arts partner staff or administrative activities; or faculty or student projects associated with their research, course work, or studies.
Geographic Focus: Canada
Date(s) Application is Due: Feb 22; Aug 29
Amount of Grant: Up to 17,000 USD
Contact: Kateri Gauthier, Program Administrator; (416) 969-7424 or (800) 387-0058, ext. 7424; kgauthier@arts.on.ca
Internet: www.arts.on.ca/grants/indigenous-artists-in-communities-and-schools-proj-en
Sponsor: Ontario Arts Council
121 Bloor Street East, 7th Floor
Toronto, ON M4W 3M5 Canada

Ontario Arts Foundation Ruth and Sylvia Schwartz Children's Book Awards   1826
Toronto-based photographer Sylvia Schwartz set up the literary prize in 1976 in memory of her sister Ruth, a respected Toronto bookseller. In 2004, the Schwartz family decided to rename the prize to honor Sylvia as well. The annual prize recognizes Canadian writers and illustrators who demonstrate excellence in English language children's literature. Each year, the Ontario Arts Council selects the school and the juries, while the Ontario Arts Foundation, the Ruth Schwartz Foundation and the Canadian Booksellers Association select the short list of books. The annual prize is $6,000.
Requirements: To be eligible, a candidate must be: a Canadian citizen; studying in Ontario or a resident of Ontario studying outside Ontario; and between the ages of 20 and 35 (as of January 1 of the award year).
Restrictions: Previous recipients of the award are not eligible.
Geographic Focus: Canada
Amount of Grant: 6,000 CAD
Contact: Alan F. Walker; (416) 969-7413; fax (416) 961-7796; awalker@arts.on.ca
Internet: www.arts.on.ca/awards/ontario-arts-foundation-awards-and-funds
Sponsor: Ontario Arts Foundation
121 Bloor Street East, 7th Floor
Toronto, ON M4W 3M5 Canada

Oppenstein Brothers Foundation Grants   1827
Grants are awarded in the metropolitan area of Kansas, City, Missouri, primarily for social services and early childhood, elementary, secondary, adult-basic, vocational, and higher education; family planning and services; social services and welfare agencies; Jewish welfare organizations; and programs for youth, the handicapped, disadvantaged, mentally ill, homeless, minorities, and elderly. Additional areas of interest include arts/cultural programs, the performing arts, museums, health care and health organizations, and AIDS research. The foundation considers requests for building and renovation, capital campaigns, curriculum development, emergency funds, equipment, general operating support, program development, seed money, technical support, conferences and seminars, consulting services, and matching funds. Application guidelines are available on request. The board meets every

other month. Deadlines are generally three weeks prior to board meetings. Notification of award will take place within two to four months.
Requirements: Nonprofit organizations serving the metropolitan area of Kansas City, Missouri are eligible to apply.
Restrictions: The foundation primarily supports 501(c)3 nonprofit organizations serving the metropolitan area of Kansas City, Missouri. Grants are not awarded to support individuals or for annual campaigns.
Geographic Focus: Missouri
Amount of Grant: 5,000 - 15,000 USD
Samples: Associated Youth Services, Kansas City, Kansas, $10,000; Child Advocacy Services Center, Kansas City, Missouri, $25,000; Spay and Neuter Kansas City, Kansas City, Missouri, $5,000.
Contact: Beth Radtke, Program Officer; (816) 234-2577
Sponsor: Oppenstein Brothers Foundation
922 Walnut Street, Suite 200
Kansas City, MO 64106-1809

Orange County Community Foundation Grants   1828
The Orange County Community Foundation makes grants for a variety of purposes, including education, the arts, youth and recreation, health and human services, and the environment. Grants that receive the highest priority include programs or projects that reach the highest percentage of Orange County as a whole; are preventative rather than remedial; increase individual access to community resources and promote independence; examine and address the underlying causes of local problems and issues; attract volunteer resources and support; strengthen the non-profit sector; encourage collaboration among organizations; build the capacity of the organization; and offer services not already available in the community. Applications and specific guidelines for individual grants are available at the website.
Requirements: Grants must meet legal and tax requirements as to purpose and may be made only to non-profit organizations and government agencies. However, for-profit entities which apply will be considered if their project or program serves a charitable purpose.
Restrictions: Funding is not available for the following: political parties or political campaigns; sectarian religious purposes (but can be made to religious organizations for general community programs); endowment creation or debt reduction; programs or equipment that were committed to prior to the grant application being submitted; new or routine maintenance construction projects (except renovations of existing facilities that enable the organization to provide a better quality of service to Orange County); annual giving or capital campaigns; or normal operating expenses (except start-up expenses).
Geographic Focus: Indiana
Date(s) Application is Due: Jul 7
Contact: Imojean Dedrick, Executive Director; (812) 723-4150; fax (812) 723-7304; imodedrick@orangecountycommunityfoundation.org
Internet: 184.172.138.191/~orange/services/grants/
Sponsor: Orange County Community Foundation - Indiana
112 West Water Street
Paoli, IN 47454

Orange County Community Foundation Grants   1829
The Foundation's mission is to encourage, support and facilitate philanthropy in Orange County, California. One of our most important strategic priorities is strengthening the capacity of Orange County's nonprofit sector. Foundation Grants are made possible by the income earned from unrestricted, field-of-interest endowment funds and legacy funds. Grants funding is determined through research of community needs and approved by the Board. In addition, Grants are periodically administered in partnership with statewide and national foundations as well as Foundation donors to advance special projects and initiatives in Orange County. Fields of interest include arts and culture, environment, education, health, an human services.
Requirements: Nonprofits agencies in Orange County, California, are eligible. Unsolicited grant proposals are not accepted. Nonprofit agencies wishing to apply should pay special attention to the website for requests for proposal and deadlines. Every grant has a formal application and its own annual cycle.
Geographic Focus: California
Samples: A Community of Friends, Los Angeles, California, $25,000 - human services support; Acacia Adult Day Services, Garden Grove, California, $5,325 - health and wellness support; and Acres of Love, Laguna Niguel, California, $90,000 - human services support.
Contact: Patricia Benevenia; (949) 553-4202, ext. 37; fax (949) 553-4211; penevenia@oc-cf.org
Internet: www.oc-cf.org/Page.aspx?pid=496
Sponsor: Orange County Community Foundation
4041 MacArthur Boulevard, Suite 510
Newport Beach, CA 92660

Ordean Foundation Catalyst Grants   1830
The Ordean Foundation makes gifts to the community through grants to non-profit organizations. The Foundation's focus on poverty is the core principle for the organization. It approaches its mission both by supporting basic needs (food, shelter, clothing, health care, and personal safety) and strategies to break generational cycles of poverty (social justice, youth development, education, and job training). The Catalyst Grant Program is designed to quickly respond to emerging and unmet community needs. These one-time grants of up to $20,000 provide support for pilot projects, events, initiatives, capacity-building, program development, or capital needs. Catalyst grants are highly competitive and there are limited funds available annually. Ordean accepts unsolicited Letters of Inquiry (LOI) on an ongoing basis through its Catalyst Grant Program. After reviewing LOIs and determining

if the request falls within our funding priorities, Ordean may invite an organization to submit a Full Proposal for funding consideration. LOIs are accepted on a rolling basis and reviewed quarterly. Ordean typically funds 2-4 projects each quarter.

Requirements: To be eligible for funding, proposals must be compatible with Ordean's mission and must be submitted by organizations that are classified as a public charity with valid tax-exempt status under section 501(c)3 of the Internal Revenue Code (organizations without legal tax-exempt status may apply through a fiscal sponsor). The Ordean Foundation awards grants to qualified organizations located in, serving, or directly impacting residents of the City of Duluth and/or adjacent communities in St. Louis County.

Restrictions: No support for direct religious purposes, or for political campaigns or lobbying activities. No grants to individuals (directly), or for endowment funds, travel, conferences, seminars or workshops, telephone solicitations, benefits, dinners, research, including biomedical research, deficit financing, national fund raising campaigns, or to supplant government funding. Ordean grants may not be used for election campaigns, lobbying activities, or direct religious purposes. The Ordean Foundation does not make grants to private foundations or individuals.

Geographic Focus: Minnesota
Amount of Grant: 1,000 - 20,000 USD
Contact: Don Ness, Executive Director; (218) 726-4785; fax (218) 726-4848; dness@ordean.org or admin@ordean.org
Internet: ordean.org/what-we-fund/
Sponsor: Ordean Foundation
424 West Superior Street, Suite #501
Duluth, MN 55802

Ordean Foundation Partnership Grants 1831

The Ordean Foundation makes gifts to the community through grants to non-profit organizations. The Foundation's focus on poverty is the core principle for the organization. It approaches its mission both by supporting basic needs (food, shelter, clothing, health care, and personal safety) and strategies to break generational cycles of poverty (social justice, youth development, education, and job training). The Ordean Foundation believes in the importance of relationships in philanthropy. By making long-term connections, we deepen our understanding of critical community challenges and the organizations that we fund. Ordean's Partnership Grant Program supports this key value. Partnership Grants provide financial support to local programs that address poverty by providing food, shelter, medical and dental care, mental health services, youth programming, and/or education and employment services. Partnership Grant proposals are available to existing Ordean Foundation grantees by invitation only.

Requirements: To be eligible for funding, proposals must be compatible with Ordean's mission and must be submitted by organizations that are classified as a public charity with valid tax-exempt status under section 501(c)3 of the Internal Revenue Code (organizations without legal tax-exempt status may apply through a fiscal sponsor). The Ordean Foundation awards grants to qualified organizations located in, serving, or directly impacting residents of the City of Duluth and/or adjacent communities in St. Louis County.

Restrictions: No support for direct religious purposes, or for political campaigns or lobbying activities. No grants to individuals (directly), or for endowment funds, travel, conferences, seminars or workshops, telephone solicitations, benefits, dinners, research, including biomedical research, deficit financing, national fund raising campaigns, or to supplant government funding. Ordean grants may not be used for election campaigns, lobbying activities, or direct religious purposes. The Ordean Foundation does not make grants to private foundations or individuals.

Geographic Focus: Minnesota
Contact: Don Ness, Executive Director; (218) 726-4785; fax (218) 726-4848; dness@ordean.org or admin@ordean.org
Internet: ordean.org/what-we-fund/
Sponsor: Ordean Foundation
424 West Superior Street, Suite #501
Duluth, MN 55802

Oregon Community Foundation Black Student Success Community 1832
Network Grants

The educational challenges that face marginalized Black children and their families in Oregon are too great for one organization or group to tackle alone. Success requires strategic ongoing collaboration. The Oregon BSS Network will facilitate meaningful partnerships and coalitions to tackle root causes of educational inequity. The Network brings together community organizations rooted in the Black community to strategize and provide direction on best practices for advancing Black Student Success. The annual deadline for applications is March 6, with awards of $20,000 distributed to twenty organizations each year.

Requirements: Organizations/coalitions eligible for this grant opportunity must: have 501(c)3 status as a public charity (not a private foundation), be a public entity, or have a qualified fiscal sponsor; have staff and leadership reflective of the African/Black community (or communities) that is served; and serve a significant number of clients/children/families from African/Black communities.

Geographic Focus: Oregon
Date(s) Application is Due: Mar 6
Amount of Grant: 20,000 USD
Contact: Marcy Bradley, Program Officer; (503) 227-6846; mbradley@oregoncf.org
Internet: oregoncf.org/grants-and-scholarships/grants/black-student-success-grants/
Sponsor: Oregon Community Foundation
1221 SW Yamhill Street, Suite 100
Portland, OR 97205

Oregon Community Foundation Community Grants 1833

The Oregon Community Foundation's Community Grant program addresses community needs and fosters civic leadership and engagement throughout the state. The program awards about 220 to 240 grants each year, mostly to small- and moderate-size nonprofits. The average grant award is $20,000. OCF typically receives 300 to 350 proposals per grant cycle and funds 110 to 120 of these. Concerns central to OCF's evaluation of proposed projects include: the strength of local support for the project; the strength of the applicant organization; and whether the project addresses a significant community need. Four different application areas are considered: health and well being of vulnerable populations (30 to 40 percent of grants); educational opportunities and achievement (30 to 40 percent of grants); arts and cultural organizations (15 to 25 percent of grants); and community livability, environment and citizen engagement (10 to 20 percent of grants). The two annual deadlines for application submission are January 15 and July 15.

Requirements: Applicants must: have 501(c)3 tax-exempt status and be classified as a public entity rather than a private foundation as defined by section 509(a) of the Internal Revenue Code (alternatively, they must have a qualified fiscal sponsor (i.e., a sponsoring tax-exempt organization that is tax-exempt); and have submitted required evaluation reports for all prior grants from the Foundation.

Restrictions: Organizations are not eligible to apply who either currently have an active Community Grant, or who are requesting funding for a program or project that has been previously funded by a Community Grant. Generally speaking, applicants may submit only one Community Grant application per 12-month period. Activities typically not eligible for funding include: annual fund appeals or endowment funds; sponsorship of one-time events or performances; sponsorship of regular events or performances (e.g., a season); projects in individual schools; grants to scholarship or regranting programs; subsidies to allow individuals to participate in conferences; capital projects that will not clearly benefit the community; purchases or activities that occur prior to grant decisions; deficit funding; replacement of government funding; lobbying to influence legislation; scientific research; religious activities; or operating support (except where a grant may have strategic impact on the long-term viability of programs of high priority).

Geographic Focus: Oregon
Date(s) Application is Due: Jan 15; Jul 15
Amount of Grant: Up to 40,000 USD
Contact: Joel Harmon, Administrative Assistant; (503) 227-6846; fax (503) 274-7771; jharmon@oregoncf.org or grants@oregoncf.org
Internet: oregoncf.org/grants-and-scholarships/grants/community-grant-program/
Sponsor: Oregon Community Foundation
1221 SW Yamhill Street, Suite 100
Portland, OR 97205

Oregon Community Foundation Community Recovery Grants 1834

Given the health, economic and racial crises our nation is grappling with, we are intensifying a focused response to address gaps in opportunity among communities facing the greatest risk and the most disproportionate impacts. These include quality education, good jobs, stable housing, access to health care, a web of community connections. Grant making priority will be given to organizations working to address disproportionate impact on Black, Indigenous, and people of color in Oregon. We continue to have a statewide reach, and strongly encourage applications from organizations who target these historically marginalized populations living in rural communities. The deadline for applications is July 17. Awards will range up to a maximum of $100,000.

Requirements: 501(c)3 organizations and government entities are eligible to apply.
Geographic Focus: Oregon
Date(s) Application is Due: Jul 17
Amount of Grant: Up to 100,000 USD
Contact: Melissa Adelman, Director of Grants Management; (503) 944-2121; madelman@oregoncf.org or grants@oregoncf.org
Internet: oregoncf.org/grants-and-scholarships/grants/oregon-community-recovery-grants/
Sponsor: Oregon Community Foundation
1221 SW Yamhill Street, Suite 100
Portland, OR 97205

Oregon Community Foundation Edna E. Harrell Community Children's 1835
Fund Grants

The Edna E. Harrell Community Children's Fund of Oregon Community Foundation was established in 2014 to support programs for youth whose families do not have the financial resources for children's programs and activities. This fund should help broaden life experience for children by supporting programs that provide enrichment activities such as summer camps, after-school programs, arts programs, church programs, athletic programs, and activities provided by schools to residents of Baker County and North Powder. The annual application deadline is January 15. Proposals are reviewed by a committee and grants are awarded in the spring.

Requirements: The Fund supports organizations and programs that improve the lives of underserved youth in Baker County and the North Powder area.
Geographic Focus: Oregon
Date(s) Application is Due: Jan 15
Contact: Belle Cantor, Program Officer; (503) 227-6846; fax (503) 274-7771; bcantor@oregoncf.org or grants@oregoncf.org
Internet: oregoncf.org/grants-and-scholarships/grants/edna-e-harrell-community-childrens-fund/
Sponsor: Oregon Community Foundation
1221 SW Yamhill Street, Suite 100
Portland, OR 97205

Oregon Community Foundation K-12 Student Success: Out-of-School Grants 1836
The K-12 Student Success: Out-of-School Time program will invest more than $5 million to bolster student attendance and academic success among Oregon's middle school students of color, rural and low-income students. It provides funding to community-based programs that offer best practice after-school and summer academic support, positive adult role models and parent engagement programming. Best practice programs increase student attendance and academic achievement, and decrease risky behaviors, particularly for our target population. This initiative expands OCF's longstanding support for mentoring, community schools, and youth services. Grant awards range from $25,000 to $60,000 per year. Applications are accepted from June 1 through the annual deadline of June 30.
Geographic Focus: Oregon
Date(s) Application is Due: Jun 30
Amount of Grant: 25,000 - 60,000 USD
Contact: Comet James, Program Associate for Scholarships and Grants; (503) 227-6846; fax (503) 274-7771; cjames@oregoncf.org
Belle Cantor, Program Officer; (503) 227-6846; fax (503) 274-7771; bcantor@oregoncf.org
Internet: oregoncf.org/grants-and-scholarships/grants/k-12-student-success-out-of-school-initiative/
Sponsor: Oregon Community Foundation
1221 SW Yamhill Street, Suite 100
Portland, OR 97205

Oren Campbell McCleary Charitable Trust Grants 1837
The Oren Campbell McCleary Charitable Trust provides funding to Massachusetts-based nonprofits in a number of fields of interest, which include: agriculture; fishing; forestry; art and music therapy; arts and culture; food security; health; health care; human services; music; performing arts; performing arts education; rehabilitation; visual arts; youth development; youth mentoring; and youth organizing. Typically, awards have ranged from $20,000 to $50,000, and are given in the form of general operating support. There are no specified annual deadlines, and interested organizations should contact the Trust with an overview of the program, its financial needs, and a list of officers.
Requirements: Any 501(c)3 supporting residents of Massachusetts are welcome to apply.
Geographic Focus: Massachusetts
Amount of Grant: 20,000 - 50,000 USD
Samples: Community Music Center of Boston, Boston, Massachusetts, $45,000 - general operating support (2019); Food Project, Lincoln, Massachusetts, $25,000 - general operating support (2019); Raw Arts Works, Lynn, Massachusetts, $35,000 - general operating support (2019).
Contact: Miki Akimoto, Trustee; (888) 866-3275 or (617) 434-4652
Sponsor: Oren Campbell McCleary Charitable Trust
225 Franklin Street
Providence, RI 02901-1802

OSF Baltimore Community Fellowships 1838
Each year, up to 10 individuals are awarded a Baltimore Community Fellowship to implement innovative projects that seek to improve the circumstances and capacity of an underserved community in Baltimore City. The goals of these fellowships are to encourage public and community service careers, expand the number of mentors and role models available to youth in inner-city neighborhoods, and promote entrepreneurial initiatives that empower communities to increase opportunities and improve the quality of life for their residents. Beginning in 2020, up to two fellows with a demonstrated interest in addressing issues related to substance use and addiction will be designated as Addiction and Health Equity (AHE) Fellows. Preference will be given to applicants with lived experience of drug use and addiction and those whose proposed work intersects multiple marginalized groups (e.g., substance use policy impacting LGBTQ+ communities, or homeless individuals or people with disabilities). Fellowship awards are in the amount of $60,000 for a term of 18 months.
Requirements: Applicants may come from all walks of life, including but not limited to business management, the arts, law, public health, education, architecture, and engineering. Individuals from underserved communities and people of color are strongly encouraged to apply. Applicants may apply for a fellowship to work under the auspices of a nonprofit organization in Baltimore City, or to work independently. Applications will be submitted online through the Open Society Foundations Baltimore website.
Geographic Focus: All States
Amount of Grant: 60,000 USD
Samples: Elyshia Aseltine, Townson, Maryland, $60,000 - Awarded to establish Fair Chance Higher Education as a Center that supports criminal justice system-impacted people in their pursuit of higher education (2019); Janet Glover-Kerkvliet, Baltimore, Maryland, $60,000 - Awarded to establish the Baltimore Job Hunters Support Group (BJHSG) to support the long-term unemployed and under-employed (2019); Damien A. Haussling, Baltimore, Maryland, $60,000 - Awarded to develop the Baltimore Furniture Bank to connect low-income individuals and families to much needed gently used furniture and other household items (2019).
Contact: Katy Caldwell, Program Associate of Community Fellowships Program; (443) 909-7381 or (410) 234-1091; fax (410) 234-2816; katy.caldwell@opensocietyfoundations.org or osi.baltimore@opensocietyfoundations.org
Internet: www.osibaltimore.org/fellowship-application/
Sponsor: Open Society Foundations
201 North Charles Street, Suite 1300
Baltimore, MD 21201

OSF Baltimore Criminal and Juvenile Justice Grants 1839
The Open Society Institute-Baltimore's Criminal and Juvenile Justice Program seeks to reduce the use of incarceration and its social and economic costs without compromising public

safety, and promote justice systems that are fair, are used as a last resort, and offer second chances. It supports advocacy, public education, research, grassroots organizing, litigation and demonstration projects that focus on reforming racial and social inequities at critical stages of the criminal and juvenile justice systems-from arrest to reentry into the community. The program prioritizes initiatives that look to reform arrests and pre-trial detention policies to reduce Baltimore City's pre-trial detention population, reform parole and probation policies to reduce Maryland's prison population, and ensure the successful re-entry and reintegration of people with criminal records. Applications are accepted at any time.
Requirements: The Criminal and Juvenile Justice Program will support only organizations that focus on Baltimore or, if state-wide, will significantly benefit Baltimore City residents. Applications must include a Letter of Inquiry that will be submitted through the OSF Baltimore website. However, OSI solicits the majority of the proposals that it ultimately supports.
Restrictions: Open Society Institute-Baltimore does not support capital campaigns, events, endowments, scholarship, travel, and grants to individuals.
Geographic Focus: Maryland
Contact: Tara Huffman, Director, Criminal and Juvenile Justice Program; (410) 234-1091; fax (410) 234-2816; tara.huffman@opensocietyfoundations.org
Internet: www.osibaltimore.org/programs-and-impact/criminal-and-juvenile-justice/
Sponsor: Open Society Foundations
201 North Charles Street, Suite 1300
Baltimore, MD 21201

OSF Baltimore Education and Youth Development Grants 1840
Youth in Baltimore City Public Schools (City Schools) overwhelmingly experience the effects of concentrated and, most often, generational poverty, coupled with limited exposure to opportunities, which is compounded by discriminatory treatment in and out of school. Approximately 85% of City Schools' students live in poverty and over 90% are students of color (81% African American, 10% Latino). Equitable education provides the most accessible egress out of the crippling cycle of poverty which is most readily achieved by removing prohibitive barriers and nullifying inequitable practices that push children out of school and into the school to prison pipeline. The Education Program seeks to ensure that all student groups are fully included in schooling and other opportunities that prepare them for success in adulthood. To accomplish these goals, OSI's Education Program will advance four strategies: to implement and scale restorative and other complementary practices that improve school climate and address bullying; to assist City Schools in institutionalizing the High Value High Schools model initiated by OSI/OSF; to advocate for long-term, adequate school funding for Baltimore City Schools; and to advocate for policies and practices that include and protect marginalized student populations, including African American students, immigrant students, LGBTQ students, and students with disabilities. Applications are accepted at any time.
Requirements: The Education and Youth Development Program will support only organizations that focus on Baltimore or, if state-wide, will significantly benefit Baltimore City residents. Applications must include a Letter of Inquiry that will be submitted through the OSF Baltimore website. However, OSI solicits the majority of the proposals that it ultimately supports.
Restrictions: Open Society Institute-Baltimore does not support capital campaigns, events, endowments, scholarship, travel, and grants to individuals.
Geographic Focus: Maryland
Contact: Karen E. Webber, Director of Educaton and Youth Development; (410) 234-1091; fax (410) 234-2816; karen.webber@opensocietyfoundations.org or osi.baltimore@opensocietyfoundations.org
Internet: www.osibaltimore.org/programs-and-impact/education-and-youth-development/
Sponsor: Open Society Foundations
201 North Charles Street, Suite 1300
Baltimore, MD 21201

OSF Early Childhood Program Grants 1841
The Early Childhood Program promotes the well-being of young children through a rights-based approach and a commitment to social justice, emphasizing parent and community engagement, professional development, and government accountability. The program grew from the successful Step by Step initiative, which introduced a child-centered and community approach into previously rigid, teacher-centered education systems in Central and Eastern Europe during the 1990s. Step by Step continues to shape early childhood teaching in 25 countries, supported by NGO members of the International Step by Step Association. The Early Childhood Program's current objectives are promoting equity and social inclusion and building the field of early childhood education. The program promotes equity and inclusion by focusing on the rights of three groups of children who are especially at risk of systemic exclusion: refugees and migrants, children with disabilities and developmental delays, and Roma children.
Requirements: The Early Childhood Program aims to strengthen early childhood education at the global, regional, and country levels. We promote innovation and evidence building, and we use our convening power to improve collaboration and boost political interest in, and funding for, the field. The program is primarily active in Central and Eastern Europe, Central Asia, the Middle East, Southeast Asia, and Southern and Western Africa, with growing engagement in Latin America.
Geographic Focus: All States, All Countries
Contact: Tina Hyder, Deputy Director of Early Childhood Program; +44-207-031-0200; fax +44-207-031-0201; tina.hyder@opensocietyfoundations.org
Internet: www.opensocietyfoundations.org/who-we-are/programs/early-childhood-program
Sponsor: Open Society Foundations
4th Floor Herbal House
London, EC1R 5EN United Kingdom

OSF Education Program Grants in Kyrgyzstan 1842

The Education Program will continue supporting initiatives aimed at creating conditions for improved access to education for children with special educational needs and those from socially vulnerable groups. The Program will also promote the standards and tools for managing a multicultural and multiethnic educational environment in order to strengthen the role of the school as a center of social consolidation. In addition, the Program will once again hold an annual competition to support initiatives of civil society and educational organizations working to improve access to education for children with special educational needs, and providing direct services to such children and their parents. The areas of support will include providing access to education for children at risk; supporting the efforts of schools and local communities to address the challenges related to the creation of an inclusive school environment in a multinational and multilingual setting; supporting the integration of children with disabilities in general education schools; consolidating the principles of an inclusive approach in educational policies and practices; raising the level of public awareness about inclusion-related problem, and specifically, the awareness of parents about the opportunities for receiving timely and quality support for children at risk. The Program will also provide assistance to the Ministry of Education in the development and piloting of curricula and materials within the framework of the new generation. As part of this, the Program will supports initiatives of civil society and state bodies aimed at promoting a multilingual education in the Kyrgyz Republic as a means of integrating and uniting society, and supporting linguistic diversity in the education system of the country. The main objective of this support is to facilitate the development, testing and implementation of educational materials for multilingual (bilingual) education in the Kyrgyz Republic.

Requirements: The Education Program looks to support initiatives aimed at improving educational services for children with disabilities. In this regards, the Program efforts will be focused on building synergies of state bodies, the civil sector and educational organizations in order to develop and implement a holistic model of inclusive education in the Kyrgyz Republic.

Geographic Focus: Kyrgyz Republic (Kyrgystan)
Contact: Valentin Deichman, Educational Program Director; +996 (312) 66-34-75; fax +996 (312) 66-34-48; valentin@soros.kg or office@soros.kg
Internet: soros.kg/srs/en/home_en/who-we-are/programs/education-program/
Sponsor: Open Society Foundations
55-a Logvinenko Street
Bishkek, 720040 Kyrgyzstan

OSF Education Support Program Grants 1843

The Education Support Program advances the right to education through grant making and advocacy. For two decades, the program has supported efforts that seek to ensure that states meet their obligations to this fundamental right and make tangible progress in advancing inclusivity and equity. They support good practice in inclusive education for groups of children that are typically marginalized and excluded based on ability, geography, ethnicity, or socioeconomic status. They also strengthen democratic participation through the involvement of social movements of those most affected by education policy—students, parents, and teachers—to achieve durable systemic change in national education systems.

Requirements: The Education Support Program is based in London, New York, and Berlin. They work with Open Society's regional and national foundations, civil society partners, social movements, and governments.

Geographic Focus: All Countries
Contact: Hugh McLean, Senior Program Advisor; +44-207-031-0200; fax +44-20-7031-0201; hugh.mclean@opensocietyfoundations.org
Internet: www.opensocietyfoundations.org/who-we-are/programs/education-support-program
Sponsor: Open Society Foundations
4th Floor Herbal House
London, EC1R 5EN United Kingdom

OSF Soros Justice Youth Activist Fellowships 1844

The Soros Justice Fellowships fund outstanding individuals to undertake projects that advance reform, spur debate, and catalyze change on a range of issues facing the U.S. criminal justice system. The fellowships are part of a larger effort within the Open Society Foundations to reduce the destructive impact of current criminal justice policies on the lives of individuals, families, and communities in the United States by challenging the overreliance on incarceration and extreme punishment, and ensuring a fair and accountable system of justice. The Youth Activist Fellowship, in partnership with the Open Society Youth Exchange, specifically supports outstanding individuals aged 18 to 25 to take on projects of their own design that address some aspect of the U.S. criminal justice system. Projects can range from public education and training to grassroots organizing and policy advocacy to social media campaigns and other forms of creative communications. Youth Activist Fellowships come with an award of $57,500 for full-time, 18-month projects (the award is pro-rated for part-time or 12-month projects).

Requirements: Youth Activist Fellowships must be undertaken in partnership with a host organization. Projects can be full-time or part-time, 12 or 18 months, and can begin anytime between July and November. All projects must, at a minimum, relate to one or more of the following U.S. criminal justice reform goals: reducing the number of people who are incarcerated or under correctional control, challenging extreme punishment, and promoting fairness and accountability in our systems of justice. We strongly encourage applications for projects that demonstrate a clear understanding of the intersection of criminal justice issues with the particular needs of low-income communities, communities of color, immigrants, LGBTQ people, women and children, and those otherwise disproportionately affected by harsh criminal justice policies, as well as applications for projects that cut across various criminal justice fields and related sectors, such as education, health and mental health, housing, and employment. We especially welcome applications from individuals directly affected by, or with significant direct personal experience with, the policies, practices,

and systems their projects seek to address (e.g., applicants who have themselves been incarcerated, applicants who have a family member or loved one who has been incarcerated and whose fellowship project emerges from that experience, or applicants who are survivors of violence or crime). Applications will be submitted online through the OSF website.

Restrictions: Funding is not available for enrollment for degree or non-degree study at academic institutions, including dissertation research. Projects that address criminal justice issues outside the U.S. are not eligible, but applicants can be based outside the U.S., if their work pertains to a U.S. issue. Funding is also not available for past recipients of the Social Justice Fellowship, or lobbying activities.

Geographic Focus: All States
Date(s) Application is Due: Nov 20
Amount of Grant: 57,500 USD
Samples: Bobby Tsow, Portland, Oregon - Awarded to challenge the state of Oregon's harsh treatment of young people who come into conflict with the law (2019); Christine Minhee, Seattle, Washington - Awarded to track opioid litigation efforts nationally and develop ways to ensure accountability in the administration of opioid settlements (2019); Kris Henderson, Philadelphia, Pennsylvania - Awarded to develop a transformative justice training program focused on trauma and healing (2019).
Contact: Adam Culbreath, Project Manager; (212) 548-0600; adam.culbreath@opensocietyfoundation
Internet: www.opensocietyfoundations.org/grants/soros-justice-fellowships
Sponsor: Open Society Foundations
224 West 57th Street
New York, NY 10019

OSF Young Feminist Leaders Fellowships 1845

With the goal of supporting the next generation of feminist activists in Latin America, the Open Society Foundations' Youth Exchange and Women's Rights Program are joining together to create the Young Feminist Leaders Fellowship. The Young Feminist Leaders Fellowships will support dynamic youth activists, aged 22 to 30 and based in Latin America, who want to launch a project of their own design to foster a more just, inclusive, accessible, democratic, and feminist future for Latin America. Successful projects will reflect on the upcoming 25th anniversary of the Beijing Declaration and Platform for Action, address current realities, and propose a specific and detailed idea for advancing women's rights and gender justice. This 12-month fellowship program explicitly recognizes the threats of discrimination to an open society and seeks to create a leadership pipeline to promote young people who have personal, direct experiences with interpersonal and institutional prejudice.

Requirements: Applicants must be between 22 and 30 years of age at the start of the fellowship. Applicants must also be based in Latin America and demonstrate proficiency in English, Spanish, and/or Portuguese. Furthermore, applicants should also be at the early stages of their careers and want to learn more about how to increase their effectiveness as an activist and organizer around issues of gender justice and equality across movements. Applicants should have demonstrated experience in community organizing or activism on a local, national, or regional level. Applicants who are directly affected by or have direct lived experience of the challenges, policies, practices, acute forms of discrimination, and systems that perpetuate dominant narratives or identity-based stereotypes are strongly encouraged to apply. We are looking for candidates who have not had easy access to existing leadership pipelines but are eager to seize an opportunity for growth and development. Successful candidates will be required to partner with a host organization for the 12-month duration of the fellowship. Fellowship projects can be full-time (minimum of 35 hours/week) or part-time (20 hours/week). Applications must include a resume/CV and a full written proposal, and they must be submitted by email to the Youth Exchange Program.

Restrictions: Young Feminist Leaders Fellowships do not fund enrollment in an academic institution for degree or non-degree study, including dissertation research. However, candidates who apply for a part-time fellowship may continue their academic studies on their personal time. The Fellowship also do not fund lobbying. Please carefully review our Tax Law Lobbying Rules before submitting an application. If awarded a fellowship, applicants must agree to refrain from engaging in restricted lobbying activities during the term of the fellowship. Current employees of Open Society Foundations, the Association for Women's Rights in Development, El Instituto de Liderazgo Simone de Beauvoir (The Leadership Institute of Simone de Beauvoir), and the Equipo Latinoamericano de Justicia y Género (The Latin American Team of Justice and Gender) are not eligible to apply. Applicants can only submit a single written proposal for a single proposed project. Those who make multiple submissions or propose several project ideas in a single submission will not be considered.

Geographic Focus: Puerto Rico, Argentina, Bolivia, Brazil, Chile, Colombia, Costa Rica, Cuba, Dominican Republic, Ecuador, El Salvador, French Guiana, Guadeloupe, Guatemala, Haiti, Honduras, Martinique, Mexico, Nicaragua, Panama, Paraguay, Peru, Uruguay, Venezuela
Date(s) Application is Due: May 3
Contact: Kavita Ramdas, Director; (212) 548-0600; fax (212) 548-4662; kavita.ramdas@opensocietyfoundations.org
Internet: www.opensocietyfoundations.org/grants/fostering-latin-americas-next-generation-of-feminist-leaders
Sponsor: Open Society Foundations
224 West 57th Street
New York, NY 10019

OSF Youth Action Fund Grants in Kyrgyzstan 1846

The Youth Action Fund is a mini-grant program that focuses on identifying, inspiring and supporting dedicated young people to mobilize and influence their peers to promote, protect and support human rights. In a world of acute problems requiring immediate actions, human rights issues take a leading role, attracting the attention of the general population to the obstacles of the full implementation of rights under the Universal Declaration of

Human Rights and other international and national laws. In Kyrgyzstan, human rights abuses worth highlighting include: a lack of access to legal services for population in more remote regions of the country; bride kidnapping and domestic violence; and the fact that the UN Convention on the Rights of Person with Disabilities has not been ratified, leaving disabled people with limited opportunities. Through YAF more than 250 young activists have contributed to the development of the country through projects using innovative methods to address issues affecting youth, their families, and their communities. Annually, through an open and competitive call for proposals, YAF focuses on supporting projects designed by and implemented by young Kyrgyz citizens between the ages of 16 and 28. These young people receive grants between $600 and $2,000 USD. YAF supports proposals in six categories: the promotion of rights of youth and persons with disabilities; women's rights; youth and the justice system; arts and culture to promote human rights; the right to adequate housing; and the right to equal access to medical care.
Requirements: Interested applicants should contact the YAF coordinator for more information.
Geographic Focus: Kyrgyz Republic (Kyrgystan)
Amount of Grant: 600 - 2,000 USD
Contact: Chorobekova Zhanyl-Myrza; +996-312-66-34-75, ext 133 or +996-550-94-73-94; fax +996-312-66-34-48; chorobekovaz@gmail.com or yaf.kyrgyzstan@gmail.com
Internet: soros.kg/en/programs/youth-program/youth-action-fund-kyrgyzstan
Sponsor: Open Society Foundations
55-a Logvinenko Street
Bishkek, 720040 Kyrgyzstan

Oticon Focus on People Awards 1847
Oticon Focus on People Awards, a national awards program now past its 14th year, honors hearing-impaired students, adults, and advocacy volunteers who have demonstrated through their accomplishments that hearing loss does not limit a person's ability to make a difference in their families, communities and the world. By spotlighting people with hearing loss and their contributions, Oticon aims to change outdated stereotypes that discourage people from seeking professional help for their hearing loss. Focus on People Awards are offered in four categories: Student (for young people with hearing loss, ages 6-21, who are full-time students); Adults (for people with hearing loss, ages 21 and above); Advocacy (for adults with hearing loss, ages 21 and above who actively volunteer their time in advocacy or support efforts for the hearing-impaired and deaf community); and Practitioner (a special award for hearing-care professionals who go "above and beyond"). First-place category winners will receive a $1,000 award and a $1,000 donation by Oticon to a not-for-profit cause of their choice. First-place winners in the Student, Adult, and Advocacy categories will also receive a set of advanced-technology Oticon hearing solutions. Second place winners in each category will receive a $500 award and third-place winners will receive a $250 award. Guidelines and a nomination form are available online during the annual nomination period. The deadline for nomination may vary from year to year. Applicants are encouraged to visit the grant website to verify the current deadline date.
Requirements: Anyone may nominate themselves or another individual with a hearing loss. Nominees in the Practitioner category are not required to have a hearing loss. Full-time students who volunteer their time in advocacy should apply for the Student category.
Geographic Focus: All States
Date(s) Application is Due: Jul 27
Amount of Grant: 250 - 2,000 USD
Contact: Peer Lauritsen; (732) 560-1220; fax (732) 560-0029; peoplefirst@oticonusa.com
Internet: www.oticonusa.com/Oticon/Professionals/FocusOnPeople.html
Sponsor: Oticon Corporation
29 Schoolhouse Road
Somerset, NJ 08873

OtterCares Champion Fund Grants 1848
The OtterCares Foundation champions innovative education that inspires youth to become entrepreneurs and philanthropists who create lasting and impactful change in their communities. The Champion Fund was created to provide funding for youth athletics in Larimer and Weld counties of Colorado. Quarterly deadlines are January 15, April 15, July 15 and October 15.
Requirements: In order to be considered for a grant through the Armor Fund, your request should meet the following criteria: Funding supports an athletic league, not an individual team; the organization is recognized by the IRS as a 501(c)3 public charity; the organization is located in Larimer or Weld County; funding supports program costs for scholarships for students who cannot otherwise afford to play or equipment for the league; if funding request is to support scholarships, a formal scholarship program/process must be in place for the league's youth participants.
Restrictions: The Armor Fund does not provide support for: political campaigns and/or legislative lobbying efforts; reproductive choice advocacy groups; direct support for individuals; building/construction projects; general operating support/unrestricted funds; travel expenses; tournament fees; general team sponsorship.
Geographic Focus: Colorado
Date(s) Application is Due: Jan 15; Apr 15; Jul 15; Oct 15
Amount of Grant: Up to 2,000 USD
Contact: Gary Rogers, Executive Director; (970) 490-8990
Internet: www.ottercares.org/grants/champion-fund/
Sponsor: OtterCares Foundation
401 W. Oak Street
Fort Collins, CO 80521

OtterCares Impact Fund Grants 1849
The OtterCares Foundation champions innovative education that inspires youth to become entrepreneurs and philanthropists who create lasting and impactful change in

their communities. The Impact Fund was designed to assist with programs that advance the foundation's purpose of championing innovative education that inspires youth to become entrepreneurs and philanthropists and provides program-specific grants to charitable organizations located in either Larimer or Weld counties of Colorado.
Requirements: Applicants must be 501(c)3 public charities for a program that directly serves youth in either Larimer or Weld Counties, Colorado. The request must be for a singular, specific program that is both innovative and educational. The proposed program must contribute to OtterCares purpose of championing innovative education that inspires youth to become entrepreneurs and philanthropists. The results of funding and the end impacts of the youth activities benefit the Larimer or Weld County communities. Applications for the Impact Fund are accepted on an ongoing basis with adherence to quarterly deadlines of March 1, June 1, September 1, and December 1.
Restrictions: The Impact Fund does not provide support for the following: political campaigns and/or legislative lobbying efforts; reproductive choice advocacy groups; direct support for individuals; building/construction projects; general operating support/unrestricted funds; travel expenses; organizations redirecting funding outside of Larimer or Weld counties.
Geographic Focus: Colorado
Date(s) Application is Due: Mar 1; Jun 1; Sep 1; Dec 1
Contact: Gary Rogers, Executive Director; (970) 490-8990
Internet: www.ottercares.org/grants/impact-fund/
Sponsor: OtterCares Foundation
401 W. Oak Street
Fort Collins, CO 80521

OtterCares Inspiration Fund Grants 1850
The OtterCares Foundation champions innovative education that inspires youth to become entrepreneurs and philanthropists who create lasting and impactful change in their communities. The Inspiration Fund (formerly known as the Pursuit Fund) provides program-specific grants to charitable organizations located in either Boston or San Diego. Applications for the Inspiration Fund are accepted on an ongoing basis with adherence to quarterly deadlines of March 1, June 1, September 1, and December 1. The typical grant award from the Inspiration Fund could be from $500 to $3,500.
Requirements: Applicants must be 501(c)3 public charities for a program that directly serves youth in either Boston or San Diego. The request must be for a singular, specific program that is both innovative and educational. The proposed program must contribute to OtterCares' purpose of championing innovative education that inspires youth to become entrepreneurs and philanthropists. The results of funding and the end impacts of the youth activities must benefit either the Boston or San Diego communities.
Restrictions: The Impact Fund does not provide support for the following: political campaigns and/or legislative lobbying efforts; reproductive choice advocacy groups; direct support for individuals; building/construction projects; general operating support/unrestricted funds; travel expenses; organizations redirecting funding outside of the Boston or San Diego communities.
Geographic Focus: California, Massachusetts
Date(s) Application is Due: Mar 1; Jun 1; Sep 1; Dec 1
Amount of Grant: 500 - 3,500 USD
Contact: Gary Rogers, Executive Director; (970) 490-8990
Internet: www.ottercares.org/grants/inspiration-fund/
Sponsor: OtterCares Foundation
401 W. Oak Street
Fort Collins, CO 80521

OtterCares NoCO Fund Grants 1851
The OtterCares Foundation champions innovative education that inspires youth to become entrepreneurs and philanthropists who create lasting and impactful change in their communities. The NoCO Fund (formerly known as the Commuter Fund) was created to provide sponsorship for single-day charitable events in either Larimer or Weld counties of Colorado. Amounts up to $2,000 will be considered.
Requirements: The event must be hosted by and benefit an organization that is recognized by the IRS as a 501(c)3 public charity. The event must take place in Larimer or Weld County (Colorado) and must benefit citizens of one or both counties. Grant requests should submitted at least 45 days prior to the event's sponsorship deadline and must include information about all available sponsorship levels. OtterCares gives special consideration to requests for events that contribute to the foundation's purpose of championing innovative education that inspires youth to become entrepreneurs and philanthropists and include an educational component that teaches attendees about services an organization provides and/or community need(s) that it meets. Applications for the Commuter Fund are accepted on an ongoing basis and evaluated monthly.
Restrictions: The Commuter Fund does not provide support for the following: political campaigns and/or legislative lobbying efforts; reproductive choice advocacy groups; direct support for individuals; school trips.
Geographic Focus: Colorado
Amount of Grant: Up to 2,000 USD
Contact: Gary Rogers, Executive Director; (970) 490-8990
Internet: www.ottercares.org/grants/noco-fund/
Sponsor: OtterCares Foundation
401 W. Oak Street
Fort Collins, CO 80521

Outrigger Duke Kahanamoku Foundation Athletic Event Grants 1852
The purpose of the Outrigger Duke Kahanamoku Foundation Athletic Event Grant program is to sponsor, promote and encourage participation in state, national and international competitions in the sports of canoeing, surfing, kayaking, swimming, water

polo and volleyball. Applicant events should: provide personal history in the event; describe the applicant's training program; describe up to three years of previous competition; provide documented results of competition with records and times; provide a grant budget; and describe other forms of fundraising being pursued. Note that the Foundation awards only one grant per person, event or group per fiscal year. Applications are accepted from July 1 through the annual deadline of September 15.

Requirements: To qualify an applicant must: be a resident of Hawai'i and an American citizen; demonstrate financial need; have participated in competitive sports and can produce a record of accomplishments; and be applying for a specific upcoming event.

Geographic Focus: Hawaii

Contact: Kate Growney; (808) 545-4880; fax (808) 532-0560; info@dukefoundation.org

Internet: dukefoundation.org/scholarships-and-grants/

Sponsor: Outrigger Duke Kahanamoku Foundation

P.O. Box 160924, 4354 Pahoa Avenue

Honolulu, HI 96816

Outrigger Duke Kahanamoku Foundation Athletic Team Grants 1853

The purpose of the Outrigger Duke Kahanamoku Foundation Athletic Team Grant program is to sponsor, promote and encourage participation in state, national and international competitions in the sports of canoeing, surfing, kayaking, swimming, water polo and volleyball. Applicant teams should: provide personal history in the event; describe the applicant's training program; describe up to three years of previous competition; provide documented results of competition with records and times; provide a grant budget; and describe other forms of fundraising being pursued. Note that the Foundation awards only one grant per person, event or group per fiscal year. Applications are accepted from July 1 through the annual deadline of September 15.

Requirements: To qualify an applicant must: be a resident of Hawai'i and an American citizen; demonstrate financial need; have participated in competitive sports and can produce a record of accomplishments; and be applying for a specific upcoming event.

Geographic Focus: Hawaii

Date(s) Application is Due: Sep 15

Contact: Kate Growney; (808) 545-4880; fax (808) 532-0560; info@dukefoundation.org

Internet: dukefoundation.org/scholarships-and-grants/

Sponsor: Outrigger Duke Kahanamoku Foundation

P.O. Box 160924, 4354 Pahoa Avenue

Honolulu, HI 96816

P. Buckley Moss Foundation for Children's Education Endowed Scholarships 1854

Through the P. Buckley Moss Foundation for Children's Education Endowed Scholarship program, up to $1,000.00 will be awarded to one or more high school seniors with financial need, a certified language-related learning difference, and artistic talent who plan a career in visual arts. Scholarships are potentially renewable for up to three additional years for a 4-year college. Students should be taking art classes during each semester. In keeping with the goals of renowned artist Pat Buckley Moss, who struggled with dyslexia during her school years, this scholarship represents her dedication to young people who have learning disabilities and are aspiring towards a career in the visual arts. Pat attended Cooper Union for the Advancement of Science and Art in New York City. Established in 1859, Cooper Union is the only private, full-scholarship college in the United States dedicated exclusively to preparing students for the professions of art, architecture, and engineering. The annual deadline for application submission is March 31.

Requirements: Criteria for eligibility for the P. Buckley Moss Endowed Scholarship include: graduating high school senior; verified specific language-related learning disability; verified financial need; visual arts talent; acceptance to accredited four-year college or university or two-year community college; and intent to pursue a career in a visual arts.

Geographic Focus: All States

Date(s) Application is Due: Mar 31

Amount of Grant: 1,000 USD

Contact: Robert "Bob" Almond, Executive Director; (800) 430-1320 or (804) 725-7378; foundation@mossfoundation.org

Internet: mossfoundation.org/current_scholarships.html

Sponsor: P. Buckley Moss Foundation for Children's Education

74 Poplar Grove Lane

Mathews, VA 23109

P. Buckley Moss Foundation for Children's Education Teacher Grants 1855

The P. Buckley Moss Foundation for Children's Education Teacher Grant awards of up to $1,000 recognize outstanding teachers who consistently integrate the arts into their teaching of children, especially those with learning disabilities and other special needs. The teacher awards are to recognize the creative, innovative and original work prepared by the nominee(s). These awards are to show awareness and appreciation of outstanding work of teachers who are helping their students be successful. The awards are dual focused: the teacher(s) receives a cash award and the teacher's art education program receives a cash award for further continuation and expansion. The awards also encourage and reward instructional collaboration among teachers whenever arts are included in the classroom learning experience as an essential component in the education of all children. The annual deadline for application submission is September 30.

Requirements: Programs eligible for an award must be established and have shown a progression of success. Teachers may nominate themselves for this award.

Geographic Focus: All States

Date(s) Application is Due: Sep 30

Amount of Grant: Up to 1,000 USD

Samples: Oneco Elementary, Bradenton, Florida, $530 - for the purchase of art supplies (acrylic and watercolor paints, and markers (2020); Ashville Middle School, Ashville,

Alabama, $982 - for the purchase of art supplies (poster board, markers, colored pencils, paint) for Ashville Middle Puzzle Piece Art Mural (2020); R.M. Miano Elementary, Los Baños, California, $585 - for the purchase of art supplies (paints, pencils and markers) for the Renaissance program (2020).

Contact: Robert "Bob" Almond, Executive Director; (800) 430-1320 or (804) 725-7378; foundation@mossfoundation.org

Internet: mossfoundation.org/grants.html

Sponsor: P. Buckley Moss Foundation for Children's Education

74 Poplar Grove Lane

Mathews, VA 23109

Pacers Foundation Be Drug-Free Grants 1856

The foremost priority of the Pacers Foundation is to help Indiana's youth through the nonprofit organizations that serve them. The foundation's areas of interest are youth programs that address childhood obesity, keep kids in school, prevent and treat adolescent and teenage alcohol/drug abuse, encourage tolerance and prevent bullying, and that help girls build self-esteem during the crucial preteen and teenage years. The foundation's Be Drug-Free grants support the efforts of Indiana groups that help young substance abusers to achieve and maintain their sobriety, help youth who are at serious risk of substance abuse to stay drug and alcohol free, and that educate high-risk youth about the potential consequences of drug and/or alcohol abuse (chronic dependence and links to criminal behavior, high-risk sexual activity, etc.). Substance abuse treatment programs, substance abuse education programs, counseling programs, after-school programs that focus on creating positive alternatives to "the streets," and other similarly focused groups should consider applying. Other types of organizations focused on youth substance abuse may also apply. Grants are one year in length and range from $5,000 to $20,000. Organizations that achieve the results set forth in their applications may apply for continued support in subsequent years. A link to application guidelines and forms is provided at the grant website.

Requirements: 501(c)3 tax-exempt organizations are eligible.

Restrictions: Pacers Foundation does not provide support for: individuals, emergency funds, political candidates or parties, fundraisers, or corporate memberships. Requests to support fundraisers are reviewed by Pacers Sports & Entertainment, not Pacers Foundation. These requests should be directed to Marilynn Wernke, Pacers Sports & Entertainment, at the sponsor address given. Although the foundation will occasionally support efforts of national significance or efforts outside of the state, it remains primarily committed to its hometown of Indianapolis and its home state of Indiana.

Geographic Focus: All States

Date(s) Application is Due: Sep 30

Amount of Grant: 5,000 - 20,000 USD

Contact: Dan Gaines, Foundation Coordinator; (317) 917-2864; fax (317) 917-2599; dgaines@pacers.com or foundation@pacers.com

Internet: www.pacersfoundation.org/grants/

Sponsor: Pacers Foundation

125 South Pennsylvania Street

Indianapolis, IN 46204

Pacers Foundation Be Educated Grants 1857

The foremost priority of the Pacers Foundation is to help Indiana's youth through the nonprofit organizations that serve them. The foundation's areas of interest are youth programs that address childhood obesity, keep kids in school, prevent and treat adolescent and teenage alcohol/drug abuse, encourage tolerance and prevent bullying, and that help girls build self-esteem during the crucial preteen and teenage years. The foundation's Be Educated grants support the efforts of Indiana groups that help struggling students to stay in school and out-of-school youth to re-engage in learning. Mentoring and/or tutoring programs, alternative schools, and after-school programs with an emphasis on learning should consider applying. Other types of organizations with a focus on youth education may also apply. Grants are one year in length and range from $5,000 - $20,000. Organizations that achieve the results set forth in their applications may apply for continued support in subsequent years. A link to application guidelines and forms is provided at the grant website.

Requirements: 501(c)3 tax-exempt organizations are eligible.

Restrictions: Pacers Foundation does not provide support for: individuals, emergency funds, political candidates or parties, fundraisers, or corporate memberships. Requests to support fundraisers are reviewed by Pacers Sports & Entertainment, not Pacers Foundation. These requests should be directed to Marilynn Wernke, Pacers Sports & Entertainment, at the sponsor address given. Although the foundation will occasionally support efforts of national significance or efforts outside of the state, it remains primarily committed to its hometown of Indianapolis and its home state of Indiana.

Geographic Focus: All States

Date(s) Application is Due: Sep 30

Amount of Grant: 5,000 - 20,000 USD

Contact: Dan Gaines, Foundation Coordinator; (317) 917-2864; fax (317) 917-2599; dgaines@pacers.com or foundation@pacers.com

Roberta Courtright, Community Relations and Special Projects Manager; (317) 917-2757; fax (317) 917-2599; rcourtright@pacers.com or foundation@pacers.com

Internet: www.pacersfoundation.org/grants/

Sponsor: Pacers Foundation

125 South Pennsylvania Street

Indianapolis, IN 46204

Pacers Foundation Be Healthy and Fit Grants 1858

The foremost priority of the Pacers Foundation is to help Indiana's youth through the nonprofit organizations that serve them. The foundation's areas of interest are youth programs that address childhood obesity, keep kids in school, prevent and treat adolescent and teenage

alcohol/drug abuse, encourage tolerance and prevent bullying, and that help girls build self-esteem during the crucial preteen and teenage years. The foundation's Be Healthy and Fit grants support the efforts of Indiana groups that help overweight and obese youth and/or those who are at serious risk of becoming overweight to make healthier choices with respect to diet and exercise and to cope with the psychosocial effects of, and the stigma associated with, being overweight or obese; and that help educate schools and families about the root causes of obesity and the importance of nutrition and exercise in preventing and fighting obesity. School-based programs, health centers (including mental health programs focused on the psychosocial effects of childhood obesity), organizations focused on fighting and/or treating obesity, and groups focused on educating others about obesity should consider applying. Grants are one year in length and range from $5,000 to $20,000. Organizations that achieve the results set forth in their applications may apply for continued support in subsequent years. A link to application guidelines and forms is provided at the grant website.
Requirements: 501(c)3 tax-exempt organizations are eligible.
Restrictions: Pacers Foundation does not provide support for: individuals, emergency funds, political candidates or parties, fundraisers, or corporate memberships. Requests to support fundraisers are reviewed by Pacers Sports and Entertainment, not Pacers Foundation. These requests should be directed to Marilynn Wernke, Pacers Sports and Entertainment, at the sponsor address given. Although the foundation will occasionally support efforts of national significance or efforts outside of the state, it remains primarily committed to its hometown of Indianapolis and its home state of Indiana.
Geographic Focus: All States
Date(s) Application is Due: Jun 30
Amount of Grant: 5,000 - 20,000 USD
Contact: Dan Gaines, Foundation Coordinator; (317) 917-2864; fax (317) 917-2599; dgaines@pacers.com or foundation@pacers.com
Roberta Courtright, Community Relations and Special Projects Manager; (317) 917-2757; fax (317) 917-2599; rcourtright@pacers.com or foundation@pacers.com
Internet: www.pacersfoundation.org/grants/
Sponsor: Pacers Foundation
125 South Pennsylvania Street
Indianapolis, IN 46204

Pacers Foundation Be Tolerant Grants **1859**
The foremost priority of the Pacers Foundation is to help Indiana's youth through the nonprofit organizations that serve them. The foundation's areas of interest are youth programs that address childhood obesity, keep kids in school, prevent and treat adolescent and teenage alcohol/drug abuse, encourage tolerance and prevent bullying, and that help girls build self-esteem during the crucial preteen and teenage years. The foundation's Be Tolerant grants support the efforts of Indiana groups that teach tolerance and respect for diversity; that focus on breaking down racial, ethnic, religious and other barriers by bringing youth from "all walks of life" together and exposing youth to cultures and "ways of life" other than their own; and that carry out anti-bullying and anti-stigma programs. School-based programs, faith-based programs, and other non-profit organizations focused on teaching tolerance should consider applying. Grants are one year in length and range from $5,000 to $20,000. Organizations that achieve the results set forth in their applications may apply for continued support in subsequent years. A link to application guidelines and forms is provided at the grant website.
Requirements: 501(c)3 tax-exempt organizations are eligible.
Restrictions: Pacers Foundation does not provide support for: individuals, emergency funds, political candidates or parties, fundraisers, or corporate memberships. Requests to support fundraisers are reviewed by Pacers Sports & Entertainment, not Pacers Foundation. These requests should be directed to Marilynn Wernke, Pacers Sports & Entertainment, at the sponsor address given. Although the foundation will occasionally support efforts of national significance or efforts outside of the state, it remains primarily committed to its hometown of Indianapolis and its home state of Indiana.
Geographic Focus: All States
Date(s) Application is Due: Mar 30
Amount of Grant: 5,000 - 20,000 USD
Contact: Dan Gaines, Foundation Coordinator; (317) 917-2864; fax (317) 917-2599; dgaines@pacers.com or foundation@pacers.com
Internet: www.pacersfoundation.org/grants/
Sponsor: Pacers Foundation
125 South Pennsylvania Street
Indianapolis, IN 46204

Pacers Foundation Indiana Fever's Be YOUnique Fund Grants **1860**
The priority of the Pacers Foundation is to help Indiana's youth through the nonprofit organizations that serve them. The foundation's areas of interest are youth programs that address childhood obesity, keep kids in school, prevent and treat adolescent and teenage alcohol/drug abuse, encourage tolerance and prevent bullying, and that help girls build self-esteem during the crucial preteen and teenage years. The Indiana Fever's Be Younique Fund grants support the efforts of Indiana groups that help girls build self-esteem; that promote positive body imagery; and that educate girls about dating violence and/or provide services to those who have experienced such violence. School-based programs and other non-profit organizations focused on empowering girls should consider applying. Grants are one year in length and range from $5,000 to $20,000. Organizations that achieve the results set forth in their applications may apply for continued support in subsequent years.
Requirements: 501(c)3 tax-exempt organizations are eligible.
Restrictions: Pacers Foundation does not provide support for: individuals, emergency funds, political candidates or parties, fundraisers, or corporate memberships. Requests to support fundraisers are reviewed by Pacers Sports & Entertainment, not Pacers Foundation. These requests should be directed to Marilynn Wernke, Pacers Sports & Entertainment, at the sponsor address given. Although the foundation will occasionally support efforts of national significance or efforts outside of the state, it remains primarily committed to its hometown of Indianapolis and its home state of Indiana.
Geographic Focus: All States
Date(s) Application is Due: Mar 30
Amount of Grant: 5,000 - 20,000 USD
Contact: Dan Gaines, Foundation Coordinator; (317) 917-2864; fax (317) 917-2599; dgaines@pacers.com or foundation@pacers.com
Roberta Courtright, Community Relations and Special Projects Manager; (317) 917-2757; fax (317) 917-2599; rcourtright@pacers.com or foundation@pacers.com
Internet: www.wnba.com/archive/wnba/fever/community/community_beyouniquefund.html
Sponsor: Pacers Foundation
125 South Pennsylvania Street
Indianapolis, IN 46204

PacifiCare Foundation Grants **1861**
The foundation's mission is to improve the quality of life for residents of areas where PacifiCare Health Systems does business. The foundation's focus areas are: child/youth, including child care, youth activity programs, at-risk youth, and counseling programs; education, including school programs that promote self-esteem, encourage academic achievement and the development of specific skills, literacy programs, training programs, and programs that improve the effectiveness of the educational system; health, including prevention, health education, access to health care, and improved quality of health care of targeted populations; human/social services, including housing, shelters, education, protection, community development, crime prevention, food, transportation, and other social services for targeted populations; and senior, including social services, nutrition, education, volunteer, and and adult day care. Preference will be given to proposals for specific projects. Requests for operating costs will be considered if the request is very specific and clearly defined. Seed grant requests also receive consideration. Organizations funded by the foundation are welcome to reapply annually. Application forms are available on the foundation's website.
Requirements: IRS 501(c)3 nonprofit organizations serving residents of PacifiCare regions in Arizona, California, Colorado, Nevada, Oklahoma, Oregon, Texas, and Washington are eligible. The proposal must include two copies of the following: application form; checklist form; cover letter accompanying the proposal, signed by either the CEO or appointee of the organization, summarizing the proposed project, the problem addressed, the amount requested, and the name and phone number of the contact person; the written proposal, which should not exceed 2-5 pages in length and should include background information, description of the problem, need or issue being addressed, and a complete description of the proposed project; most recent audited financial statement and 990; current operating budget and line item budget for the specific project; list of major funders and amounts; list of board of directors; and one paragraph summary of previous support from the PacifiCare Foundation.
Restrictions: The foundation will not consider grants for arts/cultural programs, associations, annual campaigns, associations (professional/technical), capital campaigns, challenge/matching grants, hosting/supporting conferences, individual support, private foundations, programs that promote religious doctrine, research, scholarships, or sponsorship of special events.
Geographic Focus: Arizona, California, Colorado, Nevada, Oklahoma, Oregon, Texas, Washington
Date(s) Application is Due: Jan 1; Jul 1
Amount of Grant: 2,000 - 10,000 USD
Samples: Casa de Esperanza, Green Valley, Arizona, $10,000 - to provide inter-generational community programming for children and the elderly; Escape Family Resource Center, Houston, Texas, $10,000 - for a school-based child abuse prevention and family support program.
Contact: Riva Gebel, Director; (714) 825-5233
Internet: www.pacificare.com/vgn/images/portal/cit_60701/127503Guidelines_for_Charitable_Giving.pdf
Sponsor: PacifiCare Foundation
P.O. Box 25186, MS LC03-159
Santa Ana, CA 92799

Packard Foundation Children, Families, and Communities Grants **1862**
The Foundation's Children, Families, and Communities Grants strive to ensure that all children have the opportunity to reach their full potential. Strategies address two interrelated and fundamental needs that must be met for children to thrive: health and education. The Foundation's grants have three goals. The central goal is to create publicly supported, high-quality preschool opportunities for all three- and four-year-olds. This is funded through Preschool for California's Children Grants. A second goal is to ensure that all children receive appropriate health care by creating nationwide systems that provide access to health insurance for all children. Work is done in over a dozen states and at the federal level through Children's Health Insurance Grants. A third goal is to strengthen California's public commitment to school-based, after-school programs, while also spurring the expansion of these programs into summer. Such expanded learning opportunities that are aligned with the school day promote positive youth development for elementary and middle school children. The Foundation emphasizes literacy, good nutrition, and out-of-door experiences in these expanded learning settings. Work is supported at the federal level through After School and Summer Enrichment Grants. Samples of previously funded projects are discussed on the Foundation website.
Requirements: The Foundation provides grants for charitable, educational, or scientific purposes, primarily from tax-exempt, charitable organizations. See the Foundation's website for current opportunities.
Geographic Focus: All States
Contact: Meera Mani, Director; (650) 948-7658; cfc@packard.org
Internet: www.packard.org/what-we-fund/children-families-and-communities/
Sponsor: David and Lucile Packard Foundation
343 Second Street
Los Altos, CA 94022

Packard Foundation Local Grants
1863

The Foundation supports an array of nonprofit organizations in geographic areas that are significant to the Packard family. These include the five California counties that surround the Foundation's headquarters in Los Altos, California (San Mateo, Santa Clara, Santa Cruz, Monterey, and San Benito) as well as Pueblo, Colorado, the birthplace of David Packard. The goal in supporting these communities is to help make them stronger and more vibrant places where all families can thrive and reach their potential. To achieve this goal, Local Grants focus resources on addressing five fundamental issue areas: arts; children and youth; conservation and science; food and shelter; and population and reproductive health. There are no deadlines. Samples of previously funded projects are discussed at the Foundation website.

Requirements: The Foundation accepts grant proposals only for charitable, educational, or scientific purposes, primarily from tax-exempt, charitable organizations. An online letter of inquiry form is available at the Foundation's website. Applicants typically receive a response within three to six weeks. If accepted, further details about completing a full proposal will be provided.

Restrictions: The following is not funded: public policy work, capital campaigns, specific performances or productions, one-time events, event sponsorships, religious or business organizations, and individuals. Requests should generally not exceed 25% of the organization's operating budget.

Geographic Focus: California, Colorado

Amount of Grant: 15,000 - 150,000 USD

Samples: TC Hoffman and Associates LLC, Oakland, California, $149,900 - conservation and science; The Legal Aid Society, Employment Law Center, San Francisco, California $10,000 - children, families and communities; and Silicon Valley Community Foundation, Mountain View, California, $25,000 - special opportunities for children, conservation and population.

Contact: Linda Schuurmann Baker, Program Officer, Santa Cruz and Monterey Counties; (650) 917-7238; fax (650) 948-1361; local@packard.org

Curt Riffle, Program Officer, Conservation and Science; (650) 948-7658; fax (650) 948-1361

Internet: www.packard.org/what-we-fund/local-grantmaking/

Sponsor: David and Lucile Packard Foundation

343 Second Street

Los Altos, CA 94022

Pajaro Valley Community Health Health Trust Insurance/Coverage & Education on Using the System Grants
1864

The Trust provides grants for projects that advance our mission to improve the health and quality of life for all people of the greater Pajaro Valley. The primary goals of the Health Insurance/Coverage & Education on Using the System Initiative are to increase the number of Pajaro Valley residents with health insurance, increase residents understanding and appropriate use of a medical home (family practitioner), and decrease inappropriate use of the emergency department. The Trust will support programs that increase the number of Pajaro Valley residents that have health insurance, as well as programs that improve access to health care for our community's more vulnerable populations. Additionally, the Trust will look at community-wide solutions to these issues.

Requirements: Applicant organizations must provide or plan to provide programs/services benefiting the health of residents in the Trust's primary geographic service area. Communities within this service area include Watsonville, Pajaro, Freedom, and Aromas. The home office of the applicant organization need not be located in the Pajaro Valley, but the applicant organization must demonstrate that it provides or plans to provide services that directly benefit residents of the Pajaro Valley. The applicant organization must be a nonprofit, 501(c)3 tax-exempt organization; a school-based health program; or have a 501(c)3, tax-exempt organization as a fiscal sponsor.

Restrictions: In general, the Trust's Board of Directors prefers not to fund programs or projects administered by a city, county, state, or federal government with the exception of school-based health programs. In general, the Trust does not give grants to: projects that do not substantially benefit residents of the Pajaro Valley; projects and proposals unrelated to the Trust's mission, eligibility requirements, and current strategic plan funding priorities and objectives; individuals, with the exception of the Trust's scholarship programs; religious organizations for secular purposes; endowments, building campaigns, annual fund appeals, fundraising events, or celebrations; or commercial ventures.

Geographic Focus: California

Contact: Raquel Ramirez Ruiz, Director of Programs; (831) 763-6456 or (831) 761-5639; fax (831) 763-6084; info@pvhealthtrust.org or raquel_dhc@pvhealthtrust.org

Internet: www.pvhealthtrust.org/grants_core.html

Sponsor: Pajaro Valley Community Health Trust

85 Nielson Street

Watsonville, CA 95076

Pajaro Valley Community Health Trust Diabetes and Contributing Factors Grants
1865

The Trust provides grants for projects that advance our mission to improve the health and quality of life for all people of the greater Pajaro Valley. The primary goals of the Diabetes and Contributing Factors Initiative are to reduce the risk factors associated with diabetes, reduce complications related to diabetes, and decrease the prevalence of childhood and adult obesity in the Pajaro Valley. The Trust will mobilize communities in the tri-county area to prevent the increase of type-2 diabetes in youth and young adult populations; teach diabetes self-management, and provide medical nutrition therapy to people living with diabetes thereby preventing the life-threatening complications associated with diabetes. Further, the Trust will promote "best practices" in clinical management of diabetes throughout the region. The Trust will seek to minimize factors that contribute to diabetes, including obesity, poor nutrition, and lack of physical activity.

Requirements: Applicant organizations must provide or plan to provide programs/services benefiting the health of residents in the Trust's primary geographic service area. Communities within this service area include Watsonville, Pajaro, Freedom, and Aromas.

The home office of the applicant organization need not be located in the Pajaro Valley, but the applicant organization must demonstrate that it provides or plans to provide services that directly benefit residents of the Pajaro Valley. The applicant organization must be a nonprofit, 501(c)3 tax-exempt organization; a school-based health program; or have a 501(c)3, tax-exempt organization as a fiscal sponsor.

Restrictions: In general, the Trust's Board of Directors prefers not to fund programs or projects administered by a city, county, state, or federal government with the exception of school-based health programs. In general, the Trust does not give grants to: projects that do not substantially benefit residents of the Pajaro Valley; projects and proposals unrelated to the Trust's mission, eligibility requirements, and current strategic plan funding priorities and objectives; individuals, with the exception of the Trust's scholarship programs; religious organizations for secular purposes; endowments, building campaigns, annual fund appeals, fundraising events, or celebrations; or commercial ventures.

Geographic Focus: California

Amount of Grant: 5,000 - 30,000 USD

Samples: Community Action Board of Santa Cruz County, Santa Cruz, California, $10,000 - to support the REAL for Diabetes Prevention project; Ecology Action, Willits, California, $9,000 - to support the Boltage program, a daily student biking and walking tracking program; Mesa Verde Gardens, Mesa Verde, California, $15,000 - to support the start-up of a second Community Garden.

Contact: Raquel Ramirez Ruiz, Director of Programs; (831) 763-6456 or (831) 761-5639; fax (831) 763-6084; info@pvhealthtrust.org or raquel_dhc@pvhealthtrust.org

Internet: www.pvhealthtrust.org/grants_core.html

Sponsor: Pajaro Valley Community Health Trust

85 Nielson Street

Watsonville, CA 95076

Pajaro Valley Community Health Trust Oral Health: Prevention & Access Grants
1866

The Trust provides grants for projects that advance our mission to improve the health and quality of life for all people of the greater Pajaro Valley. The primary goals of the Oral Health Initiative are to reduce the risk factors associated with oral health disease, increase the number of Pajaro Valley residents with ready access to comprehensive dental care, and decrease the prevalence of dental disease among residents of the Pajaro Valley. The Trust's goals include improving access to dental treatment and preventing dental disease. Through this initiative, the Trust will look at systematic issues facing oral health care, particularly in the areas of prevention and access to care, and work with others in the community to remove these barriers.

Requirements: Applicant organizations must provide or plan to provide programs/services benefiting the health of residents in the Trust's primary geographic service area. Communities within this service area include Watsonville, Pajaro, Freedom, and Aromas. The home office of the applicant organization need not be located in the Pajaro Valley, but the applicant organization must demonstrate that it provides or plans to provide services that directly benefit residents of the Pajaro Valley. The applicant organization must be a nonprofit, 501(c)3 tax-exempt organization; a school-based health program; or have a 501(c)3, tax-exempt organization as a fiscal sponsor.

Restrictions: In general, the Trust's Board of Directors prefers not to fund programs or projects administered by a city, county, state, or federal government with the exception of school-based health programs. In general, the Trust does not give grants to: projects that do not substantially benefit residents of the Pajaro Valley; projects and proposals unrelated to the Trust's mission, eligibility requirements, and current strategic plan funding priorities and objectives; individuals, with the exception of the Trust's scholarship programs; religious organizations for secular purposes; endowments, building campaigns, annual fund appeals, fundraising events, or celebrations; or commercial ventures.

Geographic Focus: California

Amount of Grant: 5,000 - 30,000 USD

Samples: Dientes Community Dental Care, Santa Cruz, California, $10,000 - to support the delivery of dental services to low-income, uninsured adults from the Pajaro Valley; Salud Para La Gente, Watsonville, California, $10,000 - to support the delivery of dental services to low-income, uninsured adults from the Pajaro Valley.

Contact: Raquel Ramirez Ruiz, Director of Programs; (831) 763-6456 or (831) 761-5639; fax (831) 763-6084; info@pvhealthtrust.org or raquel_dhc@pvhealthtrust.org

Internet: www.pvhealthtrust.org/grants_core.html

Sponsor: Pajaro Valley Community Health Trust

85 Nielson Street

Watsonville, CA 95076

Palmer Foundation Grants
1867

The Palmer Foundation was founded by Rogers Palmer and his wife, Mary, in 1990. Today, the Foundation considers proposals that empower young people up to the age of 25. General categories include arts and culture, education, health, and human services. In making awards, the foundation places the highest priority on proposals that demonstrate a level of cooperation with other organizations, including leveraging financial and in-kind support from other groups; clearly avoids duplication of existing services; where applicable, demonstrates potential for continued funding from internal or other sources after the grant period; and offer challenge grants in order to stimulate support of the project by other organizations or individuals. The board will review Letters of Intent each month through the listed deadlines; full proposals are by invitation. Letters of intent may be submitted online. After review, applicants should wait for an invitation to apply.

Requirements: 501(c)3 tax-exempt organizations are eligible. The foundation's geographical region is usually limited to the Mid West states, the Mid Atlantic states, Guatemala, and El Salvador.

Restrictions: The foundation does not usually support the following types of activities: grants to individuals or scholarships; endowment drives or capital campaigns; general operating expenses for an existing project, except to support an innovative program during the initial years of operation; grants for political activities, sectarian religious purposes, or

individual medical or scientific research projects; or repeated funding to the same program or organization for the same purposes on an annual or ongoing basis.
Geographic Focus: All States
Contact: Charlly Enroth, Director; (202) 595-1020; fax (202) 833-5540; admin@thepalmerfoundation.org
Internet: www.thepalmerfoundation.org
Sponsor: Palmer Foundation
1201 Connecticut Avenue, NW, Suite 300
Washington, D.C. 20036

Parke County Community Foundation Grants 1868
The Parke County Community Foundation Grants fund fields of interest which are community-enhancing such as agricultural interests, family support, fine arts/culture, handicapped persons, historic preservation, individual township interests, religion, scholarship/education, and youth/recreation. The Foundation accepts grant applications year-round.
Requirements: Applications for grants are accepted from any new or existing charitable organization or community agency with a charitable purpose in Parke County. Organizations should fill out the online application with the following information: a detailed description of their organization, project, and budget required; other organizations who might partner with them with a similar project. For requests of $1,000 or less, a one-page letter or email is acceptable. This letter should describe the project, sharing the organization's perception of need. It should also describe who and how many are likely to benefit and the factors the organization will use to evaluate its success. Applicants are encouraged to contact the Foundation to discuss if their project is appropriate for funding before submitting the application.
Restrictions: The Foundation usually funds only to nonprofit organizations, but may fund other organizations if the project is designed to assist the needy and promote well-being in Parke County.
Geographic Focus: Indiana
Contact: Brad Bumgardner, Executive Director; (765) 569-7223; fax (765) 569-5383; bradbum@yahoo.com or parkeccf@yahoo.com
Internet: www.parkeccf.org/Grants.html
Sponsor: Parke County Community Foundation
115 North Market Street
Rockville, IN 47872

Parker Foundation (California) Grants 1869
The Parker Foundation was founded for charitable purposes leading to the betterment of life for all people of San Diego County, California. Areas of grant support include culture (visual arts, performing arts, museums/zoos), adult and youth services, medical, education, community activities, and environmental. Initial grant proposals must be submitted in writing. The format can be found on the website. Generally proposals are considered at the next Board meeting, which is generally monthly. Meeting dates can be found on the website under Board Schedule.
Requirements: Applicants must be 501(c)3 organizations.
Restrictions: While occasional grant support is given to religious organizations, those grants are only made for direct support to nonsectarian educational or service projects.
Geographic Focus: California
Samples: San Diego Opera Association, San Diego, California, $75,000 - to purchase pARTicipate software to enhance social networking capabilities; San Diego Air & Space Museum, San Diego, California, $35,000 - for high density shelving for film archives; and Escondido Children's Museum, Escondido, California, $20,000 - for operating expenses to support programs and exhibitions.
Contact: Program Contact; (760) 720-0630; fax (760) 420-1239
Internet: www.TheParkerFoundation.org
Sponsor: Parker Foundation: California
2604-B El Camino Real, Suite 244
Carlsbad, CA 92008

Parker Foundation (Virginia) Grants to Support Christian Evangelism 1870
The foundation awards grants nationwide to Christian agencies and churches that are working for redemptive purposes in accordance with Biblical truth, morality, and mission. Grants support specific projects that aim to make successful organizations more effective or for the start up of a new project. Areas of interest include world evangelism, evangelical leadership development, and Christian social relief and public persuasion. Contact the Foundation for application materials. There are no deadlines.
Requirements: 501(c)3 organizations are eligible.
Geographic Focus: All States
Samples: Fellowship of Christians in Universities & Schools, Charlottesville, Virginia, $10,000 - support ministry to high school and college students.
Contact: Brian Broadway, Program Contact; (804) 285-5416
Sponsor: Parker Foundation: Virginia
701 East Byrd Street, 17th Floor
Richmond, VA 23219

Parkersburg Area Community Foundation Action Grants 1871
Community Action Grants help organizations by supporting vital projects in the fields of arts and culture, education, health and human services, community and economic development, youth and family services, and recreation. The Foundation accepts applications for the spring deadline on March 1 and for the fall deadlines on September 1. Applicants are encouraged to contact the Foundation with any questions about the grants or the application process.
Requirements: Grants are awarded to 501(c)3 tax-exempt nonprofit organizations in specific counties of West Virginia (Calhoun; Doddridge; Gilmer; Jackson; Pleasants; Mason; Ritchie; Roane; Wirt; and Wood) and Washington County, Ohio.
Restrictions: Grants do not support religious purposes, travel, meetings, seminars, student exchange programs, annual campaigns, endowment funds, operating budgets, or debt reduction.
Geographic Focus: Ohio, West Virginia

Date(s) Application is Due: Mar 1; Sep 1
Amount of Grant: 1,000 - 10,000 USD
Contact: Marian Clowes; (866) 428-4438 or (304) 428-4438; info@pacfwv.com
Internet: www.pacfwv.com
Sponsor: Parkersburg Area Community Foundation
501 Avenuery Street, P.O. Box 1762
Parkersburg, WV 26102-1762

PAS Freddie Gruber Scholarship 1872
Freddie Gruber began his drumming career in New York in the late 1940s. He played in the only big band to feature bebop sax innovator Charlie Parker, and he became close friends with Buddy Rich, a relationship that continued until Buddy's passing in 1987. In the early '60s Gruber played his way through Chicago and Las Vegas, eventually arriving in Los Angeles, where he became a key player in that city's jazz scene. But Gruber soon discovered his true calling—teaching others how to play drums. Over the next forty years, Freddie's students included a cross-section of drummers whose playing profoundly influenced the music of the times, among them John Guerin, Ian Wallace, Steve Smith, Dave Weckl, Mike Baird, Johnny "Vatos" Hernandez, David Bronson, Peter Erskine, Burleigh Drummond, and Neil Peart. One early student, Don Lombardi, founded the Drum Workshop company. Freddie had an unparalleled understanding of the physical "dance" involved in playing the instrument—the ergonomic relationship of the drummer to the drums. Without ever trying to disrupt a particular drummer's "character," he helped each student discover, express, and refine his own voice. This annual, one year scholarship, is to assist an incoming college freshman or current college student with tuition to an established, accredited institution of higher education, for the purpose of advanced study in the area of percussion, including but not limited to drumset. Scholarship is for one academic year, students may apply in subsequent years (no more than three years total). All materials must be postmarked by April 30. Winners will be announced no later than July 1.
Requirements: An applicant must be a current subscriber to PAS at the VIP Pass level or higher. The scholarship monies will be paid directly to such institution. An expert panel will evaluate the student's skills in the area of drumset performance. All applicants must submit a completed application, a letter of recommendation verifying age and school attendance, and a video that is no longer than ten minutes in length.
Geographic Focus: All States
Date(s) Application is Due: Apr 30
Contact: Amber Fox, Program Manager; (317) 974-4488; fax (317) 974-4499; afox@pas.org
Internet: www.pas.org/get-involved/scholarships-grants
Sponsor: Percussive Arts Society
110 West Washington Street, Suite A
Indianapolis, IN 46204

PAS John E. Grimes Timpani Scholarship 1873
John Grimes, former Vice President of the Boston Musicians' Association for over a decade, was an advocate for musicians' intellectual property, economic rights, and social justice. As a Professor at Boston Conservatory he was one of the world's expert early music timpanists, performing regularly with the Boston Baroque and Handel & Haydn Society Orchestras. He also performed with Boston Ballet, Boston Lyric Opera, Cantata Singers, and other Boston-based organizations. In December of 2012 John received a Certificate of Recognition from the United States Senate stating that he was a guiding light for musicians in the labor movement in New England...a champion for all musicians, working tirelessly as an advocate for students, immigrants, and those in need. John earned a Bachelor of Music degree from the University of Miami, a Master of Music from the New England Conservatory. He also pursued doctoral studies at the University of California, San Diego. This $1,000 scholarship is open to timpani students (ages 18–26) interested in pursuing the study of period timpani playing. Scholarship may be applied to lessons, travel to study, etc., as long as the focus is baroque/classical period timpani playing. All materials must be submitted by April 30. Winners will be announced no later than July 1.
Requirements: The scholarship is open to any full-time student registered in an accredited college or university school of music during the current academic year. Applicant must be a current member of the Percussive Arts Society.
Geographic Focus: All States
Date(s) Application is Due: Apr 30
Amount of Grant: 1,000 USD
Contact: Amber Fox, Programs Manager; (317) 974-4488; fax (317) 974-4499; afox@pas.org
Internet: www.pas.org/get-involved/scholarships-grants
Sponsor: Percussive Arts Society
110 West Washington Street, Suite A
Indianapolis, IN 46204

Paso del Norte Health Foundation Grants 1874
The Paso del Norte Health Foundation (PdNHF) is one of the largest private foundations on the U.S. - Mexico border. It was established in 1995 from the sale of Providence Memorial Hospital to Tenet Healthcare Corporation for $130 million. The purpose of the Foundation is to improve the health and promote the wellness of the people living in West Texas, Southern New Mexico, and Ciudad Juárez, Mexico through education and prevention. The foundation currently issues RFPs for the following initiatives: physical activity and balanced nutrition; tobacco, alcohol, and illicit drug use; health care and mental health services; healthy families and social environments; and leadership. Interested organizations can sign up for the foundation's RFP mailing list at the grant website. The foundation does not accept unsolicited proposals but offers workshops when new RFPs are issued and also encourages organizations to contact the Program Officer with suggestions and ideas for new programs, especially as they relate to the foundation's initiatives.
Requirements: Proposals must be solicited, and must be linked to an established initiative. Applicants must be 501(c)3 or equivalent organizations operated for charitable, educational,

or religious purposes. Funding is principally for in-field intervention projects. Research, studies, or planning activities may be considered only if they directly assist in the implementation of a project. Ineligible expenses include general operating and overhead expenses, capital acquisition or construction (such as property or buildings), purchase of motorized vehicles, and the direct provision of medical services and medicines for acute care. *Restrictions:* Funding is not provided to individuals. Proposals are only considered from the Paso del Norte region which encompasses El Paso and Hudspeth Counties in West Texas; Doña Ana, Luna, and Otero Counties in Southern New Mexico; and Ciudad Juárez and Chihuahua in Northern Mexico.
Geographic Focus: Texas, Mexico
Contact: Enrique Mata, Senior Program Officer; (915) 544-7636, ext. 1918; fax (915) 544-7713; emata@pdnhf.org or health@pdnhf.org
Internet: www.pdnhf.org/index.php?option=com_content&view=article&id=91&Itemid=68&lang=us
Sponsor: Paso del Norte Health Foundation
221 N. Kansas, Suite 1900
El Paso, TX 79901

PAS PASIC International Scholarships 1875
The Percussive Arts Society (PAS) is a music service organization promoting percussion education, research, performance and appreciation throughout the world. PAS provides several scholarships assisting students to attend the annual Percussive Arts Society International Convention (PASIC), which features over 120 concerts, clinics, master classes, labs, workshops, panels and presentations. Each scholarship recipient will receive a PASIC registration, a PASIC souvenir t-shirt, and $500 toward the cost of transportation/lodging. A downloadable application is available at the grant website.
Requirements: Applicants must be active PAS members at time of application and during the convention.
Geographic Focus: All States
Date(s) Application is Due: Jun 29
Amount of Grant: 535 USD
Contact: Amber Fox, Programs Manager; (317) 974-4488; fax (317) 974-4499; afox@pas.org
Internet: www.pas.org/get-involved/scholarships-grants
Sponsor: Percussive Arts Society
110 West Washington Street, Suite A
Indianapolis, IN 46204

PAS SABIAN/PASIC Scholarship 1876
Sabian Ltd. works in conjunction with PAS to offer a PASIC scholarship to residents of Canada. The scholarship recipient will receive transportation to the convention city, four nights hotel accommodation, PASIC Registration, PASIC souvenir T-Shirt and, a one year PAS Membership. Scholarship will not exceed $1,500 CDN. The application period closes June 29.
Requirements: To be eligible, an applicant must be a Canadian, full-time university undergraduate (Percussion Major).
Geographic Focus: All States
Date(s) Application is Due: Jun 29
Amount of Grant: Up to 1,500 USD
Contact: Amber Fox, Programs Manager; (317) 974-4488; fax (317) 974-4499; afox@pas.org
Internet: www.pas.org/get-involved/scholarships-grants
Sponsor: Percussive Arts Society
110 West Washington Street, Suite A
Indianapolis, IN 46204

PAS Sabian Larrie London Memorial Scholarship 1877
The late great session drummer Larrie Londin was a man who liked to share with others. That sharing continues through the PAS/SABIAN Larrie Londin Memorial Scholarship. Created to support promising young drummers with their drumset studies, the scholarship awards $1,000 to a selected drummer between the ages of 18 and 24 and awards $500 to a selected drummer who is age 17 or under. Awardees will also receive a one-year membership to the Percussive Arts Society. A downloadable application form is made available at the grant website during the application period.
Requirements: Students aged 18-24 must be enrolled in, or apply funds to an accredited, structured music education program.
Geographic Focus: All States
Date(s) Application is Due: Apr 30
Amount of Grant: 500 - 1,000 USD
Contact: Amber Fox, Programs Manager; (317) 974-4488; fax (317) 974-4499; afox@pas.org
Internet: www.pas.org/get-involved/scholarships-grants
Sponsor: Percussive Arts Society
110 West Washington Street, Suite A
Indianapolis, IN 46204

PAS Zildjian Family Opportunity Fund Grants 1878
The Percussive Arts Society (PAS) is a music service organization promoting percussion education, research, performance and appreciation throughout the world. The Zildjian fund provides funding for percussion-based presentations directed to underserved youth, ages pre-school through high school. All services funded are free of charge to participants and take place in local community settings. Downloadable guidelines and application are available online. All application materials must be received by July 1. Awards will be announced no later than September 15.
Requirements: Applicant/Artist must be a current member of the Percussive Arts Society. All funded activities must be complete by September 15 of the following year.
Geographic Focus: All States
Date(s) Application is Due: Jul 1
Amount of Grant: 500 - 3,000 USD

Contact: Amber Fox, Programs Manager; (317) 974-4488; fax (317) 974-4499; afox@pas.org
Internet: www.pas.org/get-involved/scholarships-grants
Sponsor: Percussive Arts Society
110 West Washington Street, Suite A
Indianapolis, IN 46204

Patricia Kisker Foundation Grants 1879
The Foundation Office at Fifth Third Bank is committed to making a significant impact on programs and initiatives that create strong, vibrant communities and provide pathways to opportunity. Through the Foundation Office, the visions of individuals, families and institutions are realized, and legacies are attained by allocating the resources of their respective foundations in support of innovative programs and organizations in our communities. The Patricia Kisker Foundation supports organizations that benefit or serve children, and educational, musical or arts organizations, as well as organizations which Patricia Kisker supported during her lifetime. An organization interested in submitting a grant proposal should first submit a Letter of Inquiry (LOI) using the link at the website. LOIs are accepted from October 1 through December 31 each year. The Foundation Office will review each LOI and may contact the applying organization about further discussion of the proposal, which may include a site visit. Each organization will receive either an email declining the inquiry or an invitation to submit a full application online. An invitation to apply will include the foundation funding source, recommended request amount, and a deadline for receipt of the application. The Fifth Third Bank Foundation Office will submit completed applications to the respective Foundation Board or Committee for final review and approval or declination. Grant seekers should allow six to twelve months for the grant making process. In general, the Foundation prefers awarding grants for one year. Most recent awards have ranged from $5,000 to $250,000.
Requirements: Nonprofit organizations that operate in the Greater Cincinnati region and are designated under section 501(c)3 and subsections 509(a)1 or 509(a)2 by the Internal Revenue Service are eligible to apply for a grant.
Restrictions: Nonprofits may apply only once within any 12-month period. The following are ineligible to apply: individuals; individual churches (except for proposals regarding an affiliated school); publicly supported entities such as public schools, government or government agencies; supporting organizations designated 509(a)3 by the IRS; walks, runs, dinners, galas, luncheons and other event sponsorship requests; athletic, band, and other school booster clubs; or startup funding for new programs or organizations (usually not a funding priority). A waiting period of three years is required for prior grant recipients receiving $10,000 or more from any funding source administered by the Fifth Third Bank Foundation Office. This period will begin as of the first payment on the grant.
Geographic Focus: All States
Amount of Grant: 5,000 - 250,000 USD
Contact: Heidi B. Jark, Managing Director; (513) 534-7001 or (513) 636-4200
Internet: www.53.com/content/fifth-third/en/personal-banking/about/in-the-community/foundation-office-at-fifth-third-bank.html
Sponsor: Patricia Kisker Foundation
38 Fountain Square Plaza, MD 1090CA
Cincinnati, OH 45202

Patrick and Aimee Butler Family Foundation Community Human Services Grants 1880
The Butler Family Foundation makes grants through Community Grants, the Foundation Initiative Fund, and Special Projects programs. Community Grants are competitive and primarily support the Twin Cities metropolitan area of St. Paul and Minneapolis. The Foundation has a special concern for the condition of women and children in society, particularly those living in poverty. The Foundation seeks to foster a supportive environment for all families to ensure children's healthy development. Priority will be given to enhance the ability of individuals and families to break dependencies and achieve self-reliance in the following areas: Abuse - including domestic and family violence, pornography, and prostitution; Chemical dependency; Affordable housing - including housing and services for homeless youth; Children and Families - with an emphasis on early childhood development and parenting education. Strategies that offer both practical help to those in need and advocate for systems change will be favored. The Foundation is most likely to make general operating or program support grants.
Requirements: Minnesota 501(c)3 nonprofits are eligible to apply.
Restrictions: The Butler Family Foundation does not make grants to organizations through fiscal agents. The Foundation does not make loans or grants to individuals. No grants are made outside of the United States. The Foundation does not fund criminal justice, economic development or education, work or vocational programs, films or videos, health care, hospitals, medical research, elementary or secondary education, and music or dance.
Geographic Focus: Minnesota
Date(s) Application is Due: Feb 7; Jun 6
Amount of Grant: 5,000 - 30,000 USD
Contact: Kerrie Blevins, Foundation Director; (651) 222-2565; fax (651) 222-2566; kerrieb@butlerfamilyfoundation.org
Internet: www.butlerfamilyfoundation.org/guidelines2011.html
Sponsor: Patrick and Aimee Butler Family Foundation
332 Minnesota Street, Suite E-1420
Saint Paul, MN 55101-1369

Paul and Edith Babson Foundation Grants 1881
The focus of the Foundation is to provide opportunities for the people of Greater Boston. Grants are awarded for specific types of activities in the following areas: entrepreneurship and economic development (programs focused on providing and encouraging youth and community entrepreneurship education, community economic development, job training for youth, and urban youth business and enterprise initiatives); culture, education and

leadership development (programs focused on education and leadership development opportunities for young people through team sports, art, dance, music and theater); and environment and community building (programs focused on community building through urban community gardens and urban greenspace initiatives).
Requirements: IRS 501(c)3 tax-exempt organizations in the Greater Boston, Massachusetts, area are eligible. Applicants must telephone or email prior to applying, and then a preliminary letter may be sent. After review the Board may request a full proposal.
Restrictions: Only one preliminary letter may be submitted in a 12-month period. The following is ineligible: support for specific individuals, scholarships, films, videos, conferences, fundraising or donor cultivation events.
Geographic Focus: Massachusetts
Date(s) Application is Due: Feb 6; Sep 9
Amount of Grant: 5,000 - 40,000 USD
Samples: Bird Street Community Center, Boston, Massachusetts, $10,000 - boy's glass arts entrepreneurship program; Boston Schoolyard Funders, Boston, Massachusetts, $10,000 - outdoor classroom programs; and Boston Natural Areas Network, Boston, Massachusetts, $10,000 - operating support.
Contact: Elizabeth Nichols, Program Officer; (617) 523-8368; fax (617) 523-8949; pebabsonfdn@babsonfoundations.org
Internet: www.babsonfoundations.org/peguidelines.htm
Sponsor: Paul and Edith Babson Foundation
50 Congress Street
Boston, MA 02109-4017

PCA-PCD Organizational Short-Term Professional Development and Consulting Grants 1882
The Pennsylvania Council on the Arts (PCA) is a state agency whose mission is to foster the arts in Pennsylvania and broaden the availability and appreciation of those arts throughout the state. Through its Preserving Cultural Diversity (PCD) Division, PCA supports development of organizations from the African-American, Asian-American, Hispanic/Latino, and Native-American communities. Eligible organizations may submit requests up to $2,000 to engage consultants to address specific artistic, programmatic, administrative, or technical needs. PCD's Organizational Short-Term Professional Development and Consulting program does not have its own section on the PCD webpage at the time of this writing but is discussed in the downloadable guide for PCD's Strategies for Success grants and may share the application used for PCA's general professional development grants. Both documents are available from the download section of the website. Applicants are encouraged to contact the Program Director or Program Associate for more information on eligibility and how to apply.
Requirements: PCD's Organizational Short-Term grants are intended to extend organizational development opportunities to African-American, Asian-American, Latino/Hispanic, and Native-American organizations that may be ineligible to participate in PCD's Strategies for Success Program. Requests must be postmarked at least 8 weeks before the assistance is needed.
Geographic Focus: Pennsylvania
Amount of Grant: Up to 2,000 USD
Contact: Charon Battles, Preserving Diverse Cultures Program Director; (717) 787-6883 or (717) 787-1521; fax (717) 783-2538; cbattles@pa.gov
Jewel Jones-Fulp, Preserving Diverse Cultures Program Associate; (717) 787-6883 or (717) 787-1521; jjonesfulp@pa.gov
Internet: pacouncilonthearts.org/pca.cfm?id=47&level=Third&sid=48
Sponsor: Pennsylvania Council on the Arts
216 Finance Building
Harrisburg, PA 17120

PCA-PCD Professional Development for Individual Artists Grants 1883
The Pennsylvania Council on the Arts (PCA) is a state agency whose mission is to foster the arts in Pennsylvania and broaden the availability and appreciation of those arts throughout the state. Through its Preserving Cultural Diversity (PCD) Division, PCA supports development of individual artists from the African-American, Asian-American, Hispanic/Latino, and Native-American communities. Individual artists may request up to $200 for conferences and other professional development opportunities. In the past funds have have been used to cover conference fees, non-credit career advancement, and promotional materials. Priority is given to artists who were not funded by PCD's program in the prior year. PCD's Professional Development for Individual Artists program does not have its own section on the PCD webpage at the time of this writing but is discussed in the downloadable guide for PCD's Strategies for Success grants and may share the application used for PCA's general professional development grants. Both documents are available from the download section of the website. Applicants are encouraged to contact the Program Director or Program Associate for more information.
Requirements: Individual artists working within the communities targeted by PCD's Strategies for Success program and African Americans, Asian Americans, Hispanic/Latinos, and Native Americans in Pennsylvania are eligible to apply.
Geographic Focus: Pennsylvania
Amount of Grant: Up to 200 USD
Contact: Charon Battles, Preserving Diverse Cultures Program Director; (717) 787-6883 or (717) 787-1521; fax (717) 783-2538; cbattles@pa.gov
Jewel Jones-Fulp, Preserving Diverse Cultures Program Associate; (717) 787-6883 or (717) 525-5544; fax (717) 783-2538; jjonesfulp@pa.gov
Internet: pacouncilonthearts.org/pca.cfm?id=47&level=Third&sid=48
Sponsor: Pennsylvania Council on the Arts
216 Finance Building
Harrisburg, PA 17120

PCA Art Organizations and Art Programs Grants for Presenting Organizations 1884
The Pennsylvania Council on the Arts (PCA) is a state agency in the Office of the Governor. The mission of PCA is to foster the excellence, diversity, and vitality of the arts in Pennsylvania and to broaden the availability and appreciation of those arts throughout the state. Funding for the Council on the Arts comes through the General Assembly and from the National Endowment for the Arts. PCA offers various funding tracks for organizations that offer arts programming. The Arts Organizations and Arts Programs (AOAP) funding track has been created to provide continuous support for established organizations who have offered arts programming for a year or longer. Organizations must be invited by the PCA to apply for AOAP grants. The invitation usually is extended to organizations in PCA's Entry Track or Strategies for Success programs who have consistently received positive reviews by PCA advisory panels. Organizations on the AOAP track receive annual funding in renewable three-year blocks (subject to past performance); applicants submit full applications every three years and interim applications in intervening years. Organizations may also be removed from the AOAP track for various reasons. The AOAP track is divided into thirteen categories: art museums; arts in education organizations; arts service organizations; crafts; dance; folk and traditional arts; literature; theatre; film and electronic media; local arts; music; presenting organizations; and visual arts. In the presenting organizations category, the PCA supports organizations that present professional performing artists. These presentations may occur in a variety of settings. A performing arts presenter has the following responsibilities: engaging professional touring artists; paying their fees; handling the local presentation, promotion, and ticket sales; and arranging for the facilities and technical support for the event(s). Presenters work with artists, managers, educators, and community groups to bring artists into a community in concerts and less formal arrangements. The presenting field includes the following types of organizations: cultural centers; theatres; galleries and museums; arts centers; libraries; college and university artist series; festivals; concert, music, dance and theatre associations; and civic or cultural groups and programs that promote cooperative programming and activity between Pennsylvania presenting organizations. Both interim and full applications for AOAP grants for Presenting Organizations must be completed using various online systems (available from the grant website), then printed, assembled, and mailed by the postmark date. The PCA encourages applicants to upload any required work samples and attachments through their online system. DVDs must be mailed. The application process is explained in the complete guide (PDF document) which may be accessed from the download section of the website. Application deadlines may vary from year to year. Applicants should visit the calendar section of the website to verify current deadline dates.
Requirements: The AOAP Grants for Presenting Organizations support organizations that present professional performing artists. Organizations and programs that exclusively present local artists should apply for AOAP Grants in the Local Arts category. Pennsylvania artists or ensembles who self-produce their home seasons or local performances should apply for AOAP Grants in one of the arts genre categories (Dance, Music, Theatre, etc.). In general, the PCA supports the following types of organizations: 501(c)3 corporations; units of government; or school districts providing arts programming and/or arts services in Pennsylvania. Organizations are required to provide proof of incorporation and activity in Pennsylvania before applications are reviewed or funds awarded. Unincorporated groups (and in some instances, individuals) may apply to the PCA through a nonprofit organization that acts as a fiscal sponsor. Applicants applying through a fiscal sponsor organization must meet the same requirements as other applicants except for nonprofit status. Unless otherwise specified in the guidelines, PCA awards must be matched on a dollar-for-dollar basis in cash. In-kind goods and services may not be used to match PCA funds. The PCA generally will support no more than 25% of an organizational budget, and usually considerably less.
Restrictions: The AOAP Grants for Presenting Organizations do not fund presenters who present nonprofessional, avocational, student, or school-related artists or ensembles (faculty) seasons. In general, the PCA does not fund nor can the match for PCA funds be used for the following expenses or activities: capital expenditures, including equipment costing $500 per item or more; activities for which academic credit is given; activities that have already been completed; activities that have a religious purpose; performances and exhibitions not available to the general public; performances and exhibitions outside Pennsylvania; cash prizes and awards; benefit activities; hospitality expenses (e.g. receptions, parties, gallery openings); lobbyists' payments; and competitions.
Geographic Focus: Pennsylvania
Date(s) Application is Due: Jan 13
Contact: Philip Horn, Executive Director and Presenting Organizations Program Director; (717) 787-6883 or (717) 787-1530; fax (717) 783-2538; phorn@pa.gov
Internet: www.pacouncilonthearts.org/pca.cfm?id=1&level=Third&sid=48
Sponsor: Pennsylvania Council on the Arts
216 Finance Building
Harrisburg, PA 17120

PCA Arts in Education Residencies 1885
The Pennsylvania Council on the Arts (PCA) is a state agency whose mission is to foster the arts in Pennsylvania and broaden the availability and appreciation of those arts throughout the state. PCA develops and supports quality arts-education programs in schools and community settings for all Pennsylvanians by providing artist-in-residency grants. Schools and community organizations interested in hiring a resident artist may submit applications for either a single-residency or a multi-residency. Multi-residencies are more complex than single-residencies in that they are conducted at multiple sites with multiple artists under the management of a single organization. Multi-residencies may include residencies within individual schools, in-service workshops, other professional development for artists and/or educators, and other arts-education programming and are intended to leverage arts-in-education programs in rural and other areas where access to the arts has been limited. PCA's artists-in-residency program is administered regionally by eleven Arts in Education (AIE) partners throughout the state. Organizations interested in obtaining the services of an artist in residence are encouraged to apply through their AIE partner organization (contact

information is available at the grant website in the form of a regional map). Organizations may apply directly to PCA as well (organizations in regions of Pennsylvania that still remain to be covered by an AIE Partner must apply to the PCA directly). The direct application process is explained in the complete guide (PDF document) which may be accessed from the download section of the website. Applicants applying through an AIE partner should also download the guide but should contact the partner or visit the partner's website as well. (Applicants should note that details of the application process may vary not only among partners but from the central PCA as well). Annual deadlines for artists-in-education residencies may vary; applicants should contact their AIE partner or visit the calendar section of the PCA website to verify current deadline dates. PCA maintains an annual Directory of Artists in Education from which applicants may select artists. Applicants may access the Directory online or contact PCA or their AIE Partner for a printed copy. Artists who would like to be included in the Directory should contact the AIE Partner in their region for guidelines and application materials. AIE Partners recruit, select, train, place and evaluate the artists in their regions. Interested artists are also encouraged to visit PCA's Arts-in-Education website for more information on the Directory and PCA's residency grants.
Requirements: Pennsylvania schools, institutions, arts organizations, government agencies, local arts agencies, institutions of higher education and other 501(c)3 nonprofit organizations are eligible for Arts In Education funding. Organizations receiving support through other funding areas of the PCA are eligible to apply for AIE funding. Resident and visiting artists must be paid at a minimum rate of $175 per day for the residency. Grant awards from the PCA under the Arts In Education Division are matching grants. A twenty-day minimum residency is required for a 1:1 PCA match. Residencies under 20 days in length require the applicant to fund up to 70% of the total project. The focus of residency activities should be on developing students' creative capabilities and technical skills (as opposed to producing a finished product, performance, or exhibition, although these activities may be included in the residency). Residency projects must be developed collaboratively by both the host organization and the artist(s) who take part. The application must be signed by both the host organization and the artist(s) who will take part in the residency. Organizations coordinating their residency through their AIE Partner should also coordinate their artist selection with their AIE Partner. Artists not listed in the annual Directory of Artists in Education must submit five samples of their work and a resume with the application. Applicants must list a host coordinator on the application. Host-coordinators serve as a liaison between artist(s), site(s), and the groups involved and are responsible for the management of all elements of the residency including consulting with the artist to schedule the overall residency, residency activities, and appropriate groups for workshops and performances. In the instance of a multi-residency application, a host-coordinator must be designated to serve as a central contact for participating schools and the AIE Division. It is helpful if this person is the one responsible for coordinating with local schools/sites in developing and writing the multi-residency application. In a multi-residency application, each school/site must identify an on-site coordinator to assist the host coordinator and artist(s) with scheduling, identification of core groups, requisition of supplies, equipment or custodial services, and publicity for staff, students and the community.
Restrictions: Artists outside of Pennsylvania may participate. The work of the teaching artist in a residency or project is seen as an enhancement of the work of the professional educator in the educational setting; therefore residency artists may NOT be used to replace staff or faculty or to substitute teach. The PCA will not fund residencies less than ten days. Expenses for residencies are limited to: artists' fees, including those of visiting artists; artist travel expenses; and multi-residency host-coordinator administrative expenses of up to twenty five percent (25%) of the residency funding. Funds may be used only for eligible expenses.
Geographic Focus: Pennsylvania
Date(s) Application is Due: Apr 2
Amount of Grant: 600 - 4,400 USD
Contact: Jamie Dunlap; (717) 787-6883 or (717) 525-5542; jadunlap@pa.gov
Internet: www.pacouncilonthearts.org/aie/educators.cfm
Sponsor: Pennsylvania Council on the Arts
216 Finance Building
Harrisburg, PA 17120

PCA Arts Management Internship 1886
The Pennsylvania Council on the Arts (PCA) is a state agency whose mission is to foster the arts in Pennsylvania and broaden the availability and appreciation of those arts throughout the state. Through its Arts Management Internships, PCA's Preserving Cultural Diversity Division enables novice and intermediate arts administrators in culturally specific organizations to sharpen their management skills. Participation includes a four-phase instructional program that provides classroom, laboratory, and field experience. The program begins in the month of June with a three-day certification workshop (six hours per day) in the fundamentals of management. University faculty will supervise each participant's progress. In phase two (four to six weeks in duration), participants will view firsthand the operations of the PCA. During this phase, participants will assist PCA program directors in the review and processing of grant applications. Participants will gain further knowledge during this phase through supervised site visits to the field. PCA will award a $5,000 stipend and up to $500 housing stipend for the PCA residency. Phase three will place participants in a four-month internship with a regional host organization that has an annual budget of $100,000 or more and two independent PCA-approved readings in arts management. During this phase interns will focus on multi-cultural funding, programming, marketing, and audience outreach as a part of the host organization's management team. The skills and confidence learned in the prior phases will enable the intern to make valuable contributions to the host-site program. The final phase is participation in an online course in Arts Management administered by the Arts Extension Service, a national, nonprofit arts service organization. Prospective applicants should visit the grant website and also contact the Program Director or the Program Associate for information on how to apply. Organizations interested in hosting an intern should visit the grant website and contact

the Program Director or Program Associate for an AMI Site Manual. Host organizations receive a four-month intern and a $750 stipend.
Requirements: Prospective interns should contact the Program Director or Program Associate for eligibility criteria. Prospective host organizations should be deeply rooted in and reflective of the African-American, Asian-American, Hispanic/Latino, and Native-American perspectives and have programs and staff that are representative of those communities. Generally, these organizations should have current or proposed multi-cultural programming, annual operating budgets of $100,000 or more, 501(c)3 status, and a minimum of two administrative staff with a minimum of twenty (20) hours per week per staff position.
Geographic Focus: Pennsylvania
Amount of Grant: 750 - 5,500 USD
Contact: Charon Battles, Preserving Diverse Cultures Program Director; (717) 787-6883 or (717) 787-1521; fax (717) 783-2538; cbattles@pa.gov
Internet: pacouncilonthearts.org/pca.cfm?id=47&level=Third&sid=48
Sponsor: Pennsylvania Council on the Arts
216 Finance Building
Harrisburg, PA 17120

PCA Arts Organizations and Arts Program Grants for Music 1887
The Pennsylvania Council on the Arts (PCA) is a state agency in the Office of the Governor. The mission of PCA is to foster the excellence, diversity, and vitality of the arts in Pennsylvania and to broaden the availability and appreciation of those arts throughout the state. Funding for the Council on the Arts comes through the General Assembly and from the National Endowment for the Arts. PCA offers various funding tracks for organizations that offer arts programming. The Arts Organizations and Arts Programs (AOAP) funding track has been created to provide continuous support for established organizations who have offered arts programming for a year or longer. Organizations must be invited by the PCA to apply for AOAP grants. The invitation usually is extended to organizations in PCA's Entry Track or Strategies for Success programs who have consistently received positive reviews by PCA advisory panels. Organizations on the AOAP track receive annual funding in renewable three-year blocks (subject to past performance); applicants submit full applications every three years and interim applications in intervening years. Organizations may also be removed from the AOAP track for various reasons. The AOAP track is divided into thirteen categories: art museums; arts in education organizations; arts service organizations; crafts; dance; folk and traditional arts; literature; theatre; film and electronic media; local arts; music; presenting organizations; and visual arts. In the music category, the PCA supports music organizations and programs the primary purpose of which includes public performances. Both interim and full applications for AOAP grants for music must be completed using various online systems (available from the grant website), then printed, assembled, and mailed by the postmark date. The PCA encourages applicants to upload any required work samples and attachments through their online system. DVDs must be mailed. The application process is explained in the complete guide (PDF document) which may be accessed from the download section of the website. Application deadlines may vary from year to year. Applicants should visit the calendar section of the website to verify current deadline dates.
Requirements: In general, the PCA supports the following types of organizations: 501(c)3 corporations; units of government; or school districts providing arts programming and/or arts services in Pennsylvania. Organizations are required to provide proof of incorporation and activity in Pennsylvania before applications are reviewed or funds awarded. Unincorporated groups (and in some instances, individuals) may apply to the PCA through a nonprofit organization that acts as a fiscal sponsor. Applicants applying through a fiscal sponsor organization must meet the same requirements as other applicants except for nonprofit status. Unless otherwise specified in the guidelines, PCA awards must be matched on a dollar-for-dollar basis in cash. In-kind goods and services may not be used to match PCA funds. The PCA generally will support no more than 25% of an organizational budget, and usually considerably less.
Restrictions: In general, the PCA does not fund nor can the match for PCA funds be used for the following expenses or activities: capital expenditures, including equipment costing $500 per item or more; activities for which academic credit is given; activities that have already been completed; activities that have a religious purpose; performances and exhibitions not available to the general public; performances and exhibitions outside Pennsylvania; cash prizes and awards; benefit activities; hospitality expenses (e.g., receptions, parties, gallery openings); lobbyists' payments; and competitions.
Geographic Focus: Pennsylvania
Date(s) Application is Due: Jan 13
Contact: Lori Frush Schmelz, Music Program Director; (717) 787-6883 or (717) 787-1523; fax (717) 783-2538; lschmelz@pa.gov
Internet: www.pacouncilonthearts.org/pca.cfm?id=1&level=Third&sid=48
Sponsor: Pennsylvania Council on the Arts
216 Finance Building
Harrisburg, PA 17120

PCA Arts Organizations and Arts Programs Grants for Art Museums 1888
The Pennsylvania Council on the Arts (PCA) is a state agency in the Office of the Governor. The mission of PCA is to foster the excellence, diversity, and vitality of the arts in Pennsylvania and to broaden the availability and appreciation of those arts throughout the state. Funding for the Council on the Arts comes through the General Assembly and from the National Endowment for the Arts. PCA offers various funding tracks for organizations that offer arts programming. The Arts Organizations and Arts Programs (AOAP) funding track has been created to provide continuous support for established organizations who have offered arts programming for a year or longer. Organizations must be invited by the PCA to apply for AOAP grants. The invitation usually is extended to organizations in PCA's Entry Track or Strategies for Success programs who have consistently received positive reviews by PCA advisory panels. Organizations on the AOAP track receive annual funding in renewable three-year blocks (subject to past performance); applicants

submit full applications every three years and interim applications in intervening years. Organizations may also be removed from the AOAP track for various reasons. The AOAP track is divided into thirteen categories: art museums; arts in education organizations; arts service organizations; crafts; dance; folk and traditional arts; literature; theatre; film and electronic media; local arts; music; presenting organizations; and visual arts. In the art museums category, PCA supports organizations whose primary mission is to present, interpret, and preserve fine art objects of outstanding aesthetic quality. The PCA seeks to ensure the enlightened interpretation and care of the state's artistic heritage and to foster the relationships between museums and their communities through support for exhibitions, educational programs, collections care programs, and institutional operations. Both interim and full applications for AOAP grants for Art Museums must be completed using various online systems (available from the grant website), then printed, assembled, and mailed by the postmark date. The PCA encourages applicants to upload any required work samples and attachments through their online system. DVDs must be mailed. The application process is explained in the complete guide (PDF document) which may be accessed from the download section of the website. Application deadlines may vary from year to year. Applicants should visit the calendar section of the website to verify current deadline dates.

Requirements: In general, the PCA supports the following types of organizations: 501(c)3 corporations; units of government; or school districts providing arts programming and/or arts services in Pennsylvania. Organizations are required to provide proof of incorporation and activity in Pennsylvania before applications are reviewed or funds awarded. Unincorporated groups (and in some instances, individuals) may apply to the PCA through a nonprofit organization that acts as a fiscal sponsor. Applicants applying through a fiscal sponsor organization must meet the same requirements as other applicants except for nonprofit status. Unless otherwise specified in the guidelines, PCA awards must be matched on a dollar-for-dollar basis in cash. In-kind goods and services may not be used to match PCA funds. The PCA generally will support no more than 25% of an organizational budget, and usually considerably less.

Restrictions: The AOAP Grants for Art Museums do not fund organizations that provide only ongoing exhibition programs. Those organizations may be able to apply for AOAP Craft or Visual Arts Grants, depending on the focus of the exhibition series. In general, the PCA does not fund nor can the match for PCA funds be used for the following expenses or activities: capital expenditures, including equipment costing $500 per item or more; activities for which academic credit is given; activities that have already been completed; activities that have a religious purpose; performances and exhibitions not available to the general public; performances and exhibitions outside Pennsylvania; cash prizes and awards; benefit activities; hospitality expenses (e.g., receptions, parties, gallery openings); lobbyists' payments; and competitions.

Geographic Focus: Pennsylvania

Date(s) Application is Due: Jan 13

Contact: Bryan Holtzapple, Art Museums Program Director; (717) 787-6883 or (717) 787-1520; fax (717) 783-2538; bholtzappl@pa.gov
Marcella Shoffner; (717) 787-6883 or (717) 525-5545; mshoffner@pa.gov

Internet: www.pacouncilonthearts.org/pca.cfm?id=1&level=Third&sid=48

Sponsor: Pennsylvania Council on the Arts
216 Finance Building
Harrisburg, PA 17120

PCA Arts Organizations and Arts Programs Grants for Arts Education Organizations
1889

The Pennsylvania Council on the Arts (PCA) is a state agency in the Office of the Governor. The mission of PCA is to foster the excellence, diversity, and vitality of the arts in Pennsylvania and to broaden the availability and appreciation of those arts throughout the state. Funding for the Council on the Arts comes from the citizens of Pennsylvania and from the National Endowment for the Arts. PCA offers various funding tracks for organizations that offer arts programming. The Arts Organizations and Arts Programs (AOAP) funding track has been created to provide continuous support for established organizations that have offered arts programming for a year or longer. Organizations must be invited by the PCA to apply for AOAP grants. The invitation usually is extended to organizations in PCA's Entry Track or Strategies for Success programs who have consistently received positive reviews by PCA advisory panels. Organizations on the AOAP track receive annual funding in renewable three-year blocks (subject to past performance); applicants submit full applications every three years and interim applications in intervening years. Organizations may also be removed from the AOAP track for various reasons. The AOAP track is divided into thirteen categories: art museums; arts in education organizations; arts service organizations; crafts; dance; folk and traditional arts; literature; theatre; film and electronic media; local arts; music; presenting organizations; and visual arts. In the arts education organizations category, the PCA supports organizations or departments whose primary mission and activities include arts education or arts-in-education programs with a significant public participation component. Arts-education programming can consist of arts workshops, classes, and/or programs. Both interim and full applications for AOAP grants for arts education organizations must be completed using various online systems (accessible from the grant website), then printed, assembled, and mailed by the postmark date. The PCA encourages applicants to upload any required work samples and attachments through the online system. DVDs must be mailed. The application process is explained in the complete guide (PDF document) which may be accessed from the download section of the website. Application deadlines may vary from year to year. Applicants should visit the calendar section of the website to verify current deadline dates.

Requirements: Single-discipline arts organizations or organizations providing art-education programming and activities are eligible to apply for these grants. In general, the PCA supports the following types of organizations: 501(c)3 corporations; units of government; or school districts providing arts programming and/or arts services in Pennsylvania. Organizations are required to provide proof of incorporation and activity in Pennsylvania before applications are reviewed or funds awarded. Unincorporated groups (and in some instances, individuals) may apply to the PCA through a nonprofit organization that acts

as a fiscal sponsor. Applicants applying through a fiscal sponsor organization must meet the same requirements as other applicants except for nonprofit status. Unless otherwise specified in the guidelines, PCA awards must be matched on a dollar-for-dollar basis in cash. In-kind goods and services may not be used for match. The PCA generally will support no more than 25% of an organizational budget, and usually considerably less.

Restrictions: AOAP Grants for Arts Education Organizations do not fund public schools, school districts, intermediate units, other local educational agencies, or private and parochial schools (however, these organizations may apply to PCA's Arts-In-Education Division for artist residencies). In general, the PCA does not fund nor can the match for PCA funds be used for the following expenses or activities: capital expenditures, including equipment costing $500 per item or more; activities for which academic credit is given; activities that have already been completed; activities that have a religious purpose; performances and exhibitions not available to the general public; performances and exhibitions outside Pennsylvania; cash prizes and awards; benefit activities; hospitality expenses (e.g., receptions, parties, gallery openings); lobbyists' payments; and competitions.

Geographic Focus: Pennsylvania

Date(s) Application is Due: Jan 13

Contact: Jamie Dunlap, Arts Education Organization Program Director; (717) 787-6883 or (717) 525-5542; fax (717) 783-2538; jadunlap@pa.gov

Internet: www.pacouncilonthearts.org/pca.cfm?id=1&level=Third&sid=48

Sponsor: Pennsylvania Council on the Arts
216 Finance Building
Harrisburg, PA 17120

PCA Arts Organizations and Arts Programs Grants for Arts Service Organizations
1890

The Pennsylvania Council on the Arts (PCA) is a state agency in the Office of the Governor. The mission of PCA is to foster the excellence, diversity, and vitality of the arts in Pennsylvania and to broaden the availability and appreciation of those arts throughout the state. Funding for the Council on the Arts comes through the General Assembly and from the National Endowment for the Arts. PCA offers various funding tracks for organizations that offer arts programming. The Arts Organizations and Arts Programs (AOAP) funding track has been created to provide continuous support for established organizations who have offered arts programming for a year or longer. Organizations must be invited by the PCA to apply for AOAP grants. The invitation usually is extended to organizations in PCA's Entry Track or Strategies for Success programs who have consistently received positive reviews by PCA advisory panels. Organizations on the AOAP track receive annual funding in renewable three-year blocks (subject to past performance); applicants submit full applications every three years and interim applications in intervening years. Organizations may also be removed from the AOAP track for various reasons. The AOAP track is divided into thirteen categories: art museums; arts in education organizations; arts service organizations; crafts; dance; folk and traditional arts; literature; theatre; film and electronic media; local arts; music; presenting organizations; and visual arts. In the arts service organizations category, the PCA supports organizations whose primary mission is to provide services to Pennsylvania arts organizations and artists (national service organizations can only be funded for arts services provided in Pennsylvania). Both interim and full applications for AOAP Arts Service Organization grants must be completed using various online systems (available from the grant website), then printed, assembled, and mailed by the postmark date. The PCA encourages applicants to upload any required work samples and attachments through their online system. DVDs must be mailed. The application process is explained in the complete guide (PDF document) which may be accessed from the download section of the website. Application deadlines may vary from year to year. Applicants should visit the calendar section of the website to verify current deadline dates.

Requirements: In general, the PCA supports the following types of organizations: 501(c)3 corporations; units of government; or school districts providing arts programming and/or arts services in Pennsylvania. Organizations are required to provide proof of incorporation and activity in Pennsylvania before applications are reviewed or funds awarded. Unincorporated groups (and in some instances, individuals) may apply to the PCA through a nonprofit organization that acts as a fiscal sponsor. Applicants applying through a fiscal sponsor organization must meet the same requirements as other applicants except for nonprofit status. National service organizations may occasionally be supported if they provide services in Pennsylvania. Unless otherwise specified in the guidelines, PCA awards must be matched on a dollar-for-dollar basis in cash. In-kind goods and services may not be used to match PCA funds. The PCA generally will support no more than 25% of an organizational budget, and usually considerably less.

Restrictions: In general, the PCA does not fund nor can the match for PCA funds be used for the following expenses or activities: capital expenditures, including equipment costing $500 per item or more; activities for which academic credit is given; activities that have already been completed; activities that have a religious purpose; performances and exhibitions not available to the general public; performances and exhibitions outside Pennsylvania; cash prizes and awards; benefit activities; hospitality expenses (e.g. receptions, parties, gallery openings); lobbyists' payments; and competitions.

Geographic Focus: Pennsylvania

Date(s) Application is Due: Jan 13

Contact: Jamie Dunlap, Arts Service Program Director; (717) 787-6883 or (717-525-5542; fax (717) 783-2538; jadunlap@pa.gov

Internet: www.pacouncilonthearts.org/pca.cfm?id=1&level=Third&sid=48

Sponsor: Pennsylvania Council on the Arts
216 Finance Building
Harrisburg, PA 17120

PCA Arts Organizations and Arts Programs Grants for Crafts 1891

The Pennsylvania Council on the Arts (PCA) is a state agency in the Office of the Governor. The mission of PCA is to foster the excellence, diversity, and vitality of the arts in Pennsylvania and to broaden the availability and appreciation of those arts throughout the state. Funding for the Council on the Arts comes through the General Assembly and from the National Endowment for the Arts. PCA offers various funding tracks for organizations that offer arts programming. The Arts Organizations and Arts Programs (AOAP) funding track has been created to provide continuous support for established organizations who have offered arts programming for a year or longer. Organizations must be invited by the PCA to apply for AOAP grants. The invitation usually is extended to organizations in PCA's Entry Track or Strategies for Success programs who have consistently received positive reviews by PCA advisory panels. Organizations on the AOAP track receive annual funding in renewable three-year blocks (subject to past performance); applicants submit full applications every three years and interim applications in intervening years. Organizations may also be removed from the AOAP track for various reasons. The AOAP track is divided into thirteen categories: art museums; arts in education organizations; arts service organizations; crafts; dance; folk and traditional arts; literature; theatre; film and electronic media; local arts; music; presenting organizations; and visual arts. In the crafts category, the PCA supports a wide range of organizations who have a mission to present exhibitions and provide instruction, criticism, long-term residencies, and other professional development to craft artists. Both interim and full applications for AOAP grants for crafts must be completed using various online systems (accessible from the grant website), then printed, assembled, and mailed by the postmark date. The PCA encourages applicants to upload any required work samples and attachments through the online system. DVDs must be mailed. The application process is explained in the complete guide (PDF document) which may be accessed from the download section of the website. Application deadlines may vary from year to year. Applicants should visit the calendar section of the website to verify current deadline dates.

Requirements: In general, the PCA supports the following types of organizations: 501(c)3 corporations; units of government; or school districts providing arts programming and/or arts services in Pennsylvania. Organizations are required to provide proof of incorporation and activity in Pennsylvania before applications are reviewed or funds awarded. Unincorporated groups (and in some instances, individuals) may apply to the PCA through a nonprofit organization that acts as a fiscal sponsor. Applicants applying through a fiscal sponsor organization must meet the same requirements as other applicants except for nonprofit status. Unless otherwise specified in the guidelines, PCA awards must be matched on a dollar-for-dollar basis in cash. In-kind goods and services may not be used for match. The PCA generally will support no more than 25% of an organizational budget, and usually considerably less.

Restrictions: In general, the PCA does not fund nor can the match for PCA funds be used for the following expenses and activities: capital expenditures, including equipment costing $500 per item or more; activities for which academic credit is given; activities that have already been completed; activities that have a religious purpose; performances and exhibitions not available to the general public; performances and exhibitions outside Pennsylvania; cash prizes and awards; benefit activities; hospitality expenses, i.e. receptions, parties, gallery openings; lobbyists' payments; and competitions.

Geographic Focus: Pennsylvania
Date(s) Application is Due: Jan 13
Contact: Bryan Holtzapple, Crafts Program Director; (717) 787-6883 or (717) 787-1520; fax (717) 783-2538; bholtzappl@pa.gov
Internet: www.pacouncilonthearts.org/pca.cfm?id=1&level=Third&sid=48
Sponsor: Pennsylvania Council on the Arts
216 Finance Building
Harrisburg, PA 17120

PCA Arts Organizations and Arts Programs Grants for Dance 1892

The Pennsylvania Council on the Arts (PCA) is a state agency in the Office of the Governor. The mission of PCA is to foster the excellence, diversity, and vitality of the arts in Pennsylvania and to broaden the availability and appreciation of those arts throughout the state. Funding for the Council on the Arts comes through an annual state appropriation by the General Assembly and from the National Endowment for the Arts. PCA offers various funding tracks for organizations that offer arts programming. The Arts Organizations and Arts Programs (AOAP) funding track has been created to provide continuous support for established organizations who have offered arts programming for a year or longer. Organizations must be invited by the PCA to apply for AOAP grants. The invitation usually is extended to organizations in PCA's Entry Track or Strategies for Success programs who have consistently received positive reviews by PCA advisory panels. Organizations on the AOAP track receive annual funding in renewable three-year blocks (subject to past performance); applicants submit full applications every three years and interim applications in intervening years. Organizations may also be removed from the AOAP track for various reasons. The AOAP track is divided into thirteen categories: art museums; arts in education organizations; arts service organizations; crafts; dance; folk and traditional arts; literature; theatre; film and electronic media; local arts; music; presenting organizations; and visual arts. In the dance category, the PCA supports nonprofit dance organizations whose primary purpose includes public performances. The PCA supports ethnic, modern, classical, jazz, tap, and vernacular dance projects. Both interim and full applications for AOAP grants for Dance must be completed using various online systems (available from the grant website), then printed, assembled, and mailed by the postmark date. The PCA encourages applicants to upload any required work samples and attachments through their online system. DVDs must be mailed. The application process is explained in the complete guide (PDF document) which may be accessed from the download section of the website. Application deadlines may vary from year to year. Applicants should visit the calendar section of the website to verify current deadline dates.

Requirements: In general, the PCA supports the following types of organizations: 501(c)3 corporations; units of government; or school districts providing arts programming and/or arts services in Pennsylvania. Organizations are required to provide proof of incorporation and activity in Pennsylvania before applications are reviewed or funds awarded. Unincorporated groups (and in some instances, individuals) must apply to the PCA through a nonprofit organization that acts as a fiscal sponsor. Applicants applying through a fiscal sponsor organization must meet the same requirements as other applicants except for nonprofit status. Unless otherwise specified in the guidelines, PCA awards must be matched on a dollar-for-dollar basis in cash. In-kind goods and services may not be used to match PCA funds. The PCA generally will support no more than 25% of an organizational budget, and usually considerably less.

Restrictions: The AOAP dance program does not fund dance schools, civic ballets, training institutions, or nonprofessional dance companies, except for those activities which engage professional guest teachers and choreographers; nor does it fund programs in which a professional performing organization is contracted by another organization to perform. (In the latter case, the presenting organization should apply under the Presenting Organizations category.) In general, the PCA does not fund nor can the match for PCA funds be used for the following expenses or activities: capital expenditures, including equipment costing $500 per item or more; activities for which academic credit is given; activities that have already been completed; activities that have a religious purpose; performances and exhibitions not available to the general public; performances and exhibitions outside Pennsylvania; cash prizes and awards; benefit activities; hospitality expenses (e.g. receptions, parties, gallery openings); lobbyists' payments; and competitions.

Geographic Focus: Pennsylvania
Date(s) Application is Due: Jan 13
Contact: Charon Battles; (717) 787-1521 or (717) 787-6883; cbattles@pa.gov
Jewel Jones-Fulp; (717) 787-6883 or (717) 525-5544; jjonesfulp@pa.gov
Internet: www.pacouncilonthearts.org/pca.cfm?id=1&level=Third&sid=13
Sponsor: Pennsylvania Council on the Arts
216 Finance Building
Harrisburg, PA 17120

PCA Arts Organizations and Arts Programs Grants for Film and Electronic Media 1893

The Pennsylvania Council on the Arts (PCA) is a state agency in the Office of the Governor. The mission of PCA is to foster the excellence, diversity, and vitality of the arts in Pennsylvania and to broaden the availability and appreciation of those arts throughout the state. Funding for the Council on the Arts comes from the citizens of Pennsylvania (through an annual state appropriation by the General Assembly) and from the National Endowment for the Arts. PCA offers various funding tracks for organizations that offer arts programming. The Arts Organizations and Arts Programs (AOAP) funding track has been created to provide continuous support for established organizations who have offered arts programming for a year or longer. Organizations must be invited by the PCA to apply for AOAP grants. (Applicants to PCA's Entry Track or Strategies for Success programs may be invited to apply to the AOAP Track; transition to the AOAP Track begins with constant positive reviews by PCA advisory panels.) Organizations on the AOAP track receive annual funding in three-year blocks, subject to past performance; organizations may also be removed from the AOAP Track for various reasons. Applicants must submit full applications every three years and interim applications in intervening years. The AOAP track grants are divided into thirteen categories: art museums; arts in education organizations; arts service organizations; crafts; dance; folk and traditional arts; literature; theatre; film and electronic media; local arts; music; presenting organizations; and visual arts. In the Film and Electronic Media category, the PCA supports organizations or programs that create, produce, exhibit or distribute media arts and have a commitment to advancing the field through an emphasis on the creative use of the medium. (NOTE: past applicants to the Broadcast of the Arts Project category must contact the Film and Electronic Media Program Director for guidance.) Both interim and full applications for AOAP grants for Film and Electronic Media must be completed using various online systems (available from the grant website), then printed, assembled, and mailed by the postmark date. The PCA encourages applicants to upload any required work samples and attachments through their online system. DVDs must be mailed. The application process is explained in the complete guide (PDF document) which may be accessed from the download section of the website. Application deadlines may vary from year to year. Applicants should visit the calendar section of the website to verify current deadline dates.

Requirements: In general, the PCA supports the following types of organizations: 501(c)3 corporations; units of government; or school districts providing arts programming and/or arts services in Pennsylvania. Organizations are required to provide proof of incorporation and activity in Pennsylvania before applications are reviewed or funds awarded. Unincorporated groups (and in some instances, individuals) may apply to the PCA through a nonprofit organization that acts as a fiscal sponsor. Applicants applying through a fiscal sponsor organization must meet the same requirements as other applicants except for nonprofit status. Unless otherwise specified in the guidelines, PCA awards must be matched on a dollar-for-dollar basis in cash. In-kind goods and services may not be used to match PCA funds. The PCA generally will support no more than 25% of an organizational budget, and usually considerably less.

Restrictions: AOAP Grants for Film and Electronic Media do not support commercial, strictly instructional, promotional, or archival projects; profit-making theatres/exhibitors; student organizations; or public TV or radio. In general, the PCA does not fund nor can the match for PCA funds be used for the following expenses and activities: capital expenditures, including equipment costing $500 per item or more; activities for which academic credit is given; activities that have already been completed; activities that have a religious purpose; performances and exhibitions not available to the general public; performances and exhibitions outside Pennsylvania; cash prizes and awards; benefit activities; hospitality expenses, i.e. receptions, parties, gallery openings; lobbyists' payments; and competitions.

Geographic Focus: Pennsylvania
Date(s) Application is Due: Jan 13
Contact: Lori Frush Schmelz, Film and Electronic Media Program Director; (717) 787-6883 or (717) 787-1523; fax (717) 783-2538; lschmelz@pa.gov
Philip Horn; (717) 787-6883 or (717) 787-1530; fax (717) 783-2538; phorn@pa.gov
Charlotte Flynn Michalski, Executive Assistant to the Council and the Executive Director; (717) 787-6883 or (717) 787-1524; fax (717) 783-2538; cmichalski@pa.gov
Internet: www.pacouncilonthearts.org/pca.cfm?id=1&level=Third&sid=48
Sponsor: Pennsylvania Council on the Arts
216 Finance Building
Harrisburg, PA 17120

PCA Arts Organizations and Arts Programs Grants for Literature 1894

The Pennsylvania Council on the Arts (PCA) is a state agency in the Office of the Governor. The mission of PCA is to foster the excellence, diversity, and vitality of the arts in Pennsylvania and to broaden the availability and appreciation of those arts throughout the state. Funding for the Council on the Arts comes through an annual state appropriation by the General Assembly and from the National Endowment for the Arts. PCA offers various funding tracks for organizations that offer arts programming. The Arts Organizations and Arts Programs (AOAP) funding track has been created to provide continuous support for established organizations who have offered arts programming for a year or longer. Organizations must be invited by the PCA to apply for AOAP grants. The invitation usually is extended to organizations in PCA's Entry Track or Strategies for Success programs who have consistently received positive reviews by PCA advisory panels. Organizations on the AOAP track receive annual funding in renewable three-year blocks (subject to past performance); applicants submit full applications every three years and interim applications in intervening years. Organizations may also be removed from the AOAP track for various reasons. The AOAP track is divided into thirteen categories: art museums; arts in education organizations; arts service organizations; crafts; dance; folk and traditional arts; literature; theatre; film and electronic media; local arts; music; presenting organizations; and visual arts. In the literature category, the PCA supports publications, readings, and other activities that deliver programs and services. Funds are awarded to publishers of fiction and poetry, creative nonfiction, children's literature, and for public readings that make the work of contemporary writers more available in the state. College-based literature programs and publications will be considered if the activity is not for academic credit and if the applicant can demonstrate broad community participation. Applicants should provide a clear editorial vision and the literary impact of the publication(s), the diversity of authors, and clear evidence that writers are paid fees generally accepted as fair and in cash. Circulation and marketing strategies, production quality and quality-cost ratio, and design are considered. PCA Panelists consider the diversity and excellence of the writers that have been presented, the applicant's demonstrated ability to expand or develop new and diverse audiences, the quality of previous programming, and the effectiveness of promotional strategies. Both interim and full applications for AOAP grants for Literature must be completed using various online systems (available from the grant website), then printed, assembled, and mailed by the postmark date. The PCA encourages applicants to upload any required work samples and attachments through their online system. DVDs must be mailed. The application process is explained in the complete guide (PDF document) which may be accessed from the download section of the website. Application deadlines may vary from year to year. Applicants should visit the calendar section of the website to verify current deadline dates.
Requirements: In general, the PCA supports the following types of organizations: 501(c)3 corporations; units of government; or school districts providing arts programming and/or arts services in Pennsylvania. Organizations are required to provide proof of incorporation and activity in Pennsylvania before applications are reviewed or funds awarded. Unincorporated groups (and in some instances, individuals) may apply to the PCA through a nonprofit organization that acts as a fiscal sponsor. Applicants applying through a fiscal sponsor organization must meet the same requirements as other applicants except for nonprofit status. Unless otherwise specified in the guidelines, PCA awards must be matched on a dollar-for-dollar basis in cash. In-kind goods and services may not be used to match PCA funds. The PCA generally will support no more than 25% of an organizational budget, and usually considerably less.
Restrictions: AOAP Grants for Literature do not fund nor may the match for PCA funds be used for the following expenses or activities: scholarly writing; publications printing primarily student work; student-run publications; vanity press or self publications; literary projects for which academic credit is given; writing competitions, prizes or awards; capital expenditures, including equipment costing $500 per item or more; activities that have already been completed; activities that have a religious purpose; performances and exhibitions not available to the general public; performances and exhibitions outside Pennsylvania; benefit activities; hospitality expenses (e.g. receptions, parties, gallery openings); and lobbyists' payments.
Geographic Focus: Pennsylvania
Date(s) Application is Due: Jan 13
Contact: Philip Horn, Executive Director and Literature Program Director; (717) 787-6883 or (717) 787-1530; fax (717) 783-2538; phorn@pa.gov
Charlotte Flynn Michalski, Executive Assistant to the Council and the Executive Director; (717) 787-6883 or (717) 787-1524; fax (717) 783-2538; cmichalski@pa.gov
Jewel Jones-Fulp; (717) 787-6883 or (717) 525-5544; jjonesfulp@pa.gov
Internet: www.pacouncilonthearts.org/pca.cfm?id=1&level=Third&sid=48
Sponsor: Pennsylvania Council on the Arts
216 Finance Building
Harrisburg, PA 17120

PCA Arts Organizations and Arts Programs Grants for Local Arts 1895

The Pennsylvania Council on the Arts (PCA) is a state agency in the Office of the Governor. The mission of PCA is to foster the excellence, diversity, and vitality of the arts in Pennsylvania and to broaden the availability and appreciation of those arts throughout the state. Funding for the Council on the Arts comes through the General Assembly and from the National Endowment for the Arts. PCA offers various funding tracks for organizations that offer arts programming. The Arts Organizations and Arts Programs (AOAP) funding track has been created to provide continuous support for established organizations who have offered arts programming for a year or longer. Organizations must be invited by the PCA to apply for AOAP grants. The invitation usually is extended to organizations in PCA's Entry Track or Strategies for Success programs who have consistently received positive reviews by PCA advisory panels. Organizations on the AOAP track receive annual funding in renewable three-year blocks (subject to past performance); applicants submit full applications every three years and interim applications in intervening years. Organizations may also be removed from the AOAP track for various reasons. The AOAP track is divided into thirteen categories: art museums; arts in education organizations; arts service organizations; crafts; dance; folk and traditional arts; literature; theatre; film and electronic media; local arts; music; presenting organizations; and visual arts. In the local arts category, the PCA supports organizations and programs that provide a wide range of arts activities and significant public participation in the arts in a specified community or region. These agencies support, coordinate, and provide a broad range of arts programs and administrative services based on the needs and resources of the designated community. Both interim and full applications for AOAP grants for local arts must be completed using various online systems (accessible from the grant website), then printed, assembled, and mailed by the postmark date. The PCA encourages applicants to upload any required work samples and attachments through the online system. DVDs must be mailed. The application process is explained in the complete guide (PDF document) which may be accessed from the download section of the website. Application deadlines may vary from year to year. Applicants should visit the calendar section of the website to verify current deadline dates.
Requirements: Applicants to the local arts program must be a multi-discipline arts center, multi-discipline arts council, multi-discipline arts festival, and/or a multi-discipline arts program in a social service center or other nonprofit organization or a government agency. In general, the PCA supports the following types of organizations: 501(c)3 corporations; units of government; or school districts providing arts programming and/or arts services in Pennsylvania. Organizations are required to provide proof of incorporation and activity in Pennsylvania before applications are reviewed or funds awarded. Unincorporated groups (and in some instances, individuals) may apply to the PCA through a nonprofit organization that acts as a fiscal sponsor. Applicants applying through a fiscal sponsor organization must meet the same requirements as other applicants except for nonprofit status. Unless otherwise specified in the guidelines, PCA awards must be matched on a dollar-for-dollar basis in cash. In-kind goods and services may not be used to match PCA funds. The PCA generally will support no more than 25% of an organizational budget, and usually considerably less.
Restrictions: The AOAP Grants for Local Arts do not fund single-discipline arts organizations or programs. In general, the PCA does not fund nor can the match for PCA funds be used for the following expenses or activities: capital expenditures, including equipment costing $500 per item or more; activities for which academic credit is given; activities that have already been completed; activities that have a religious purpose; performances and exhibitions not available to the general public; performances and exhibitions outside Pennsylvania; cash prizes and awards; benefit activities; hospitality expenses (e.g., receptions, parties, gallery openings); lobbyists' payments; and competitions.
Geographic Focus: Pennsylvania
Date(s) Application is Due: Jan 13
Contact: Lori Frush Schmelz, Local Arts Program Director; (717) 787-6883 or (717) 787-1523; fax (717) 783-2538; lschmelz@pa.gov
Jewel Jones-Fulp, Local Arts Program Associate; (717) 525-5544 or (717) 787-6883; fax (717) 783-2538; jjonesfulp@pa.gov
Internet: www.pacouncilonthearts.org/pca.cfm?id=1&level=Third&sid=48
Sponsor: Pennsylvania Council on the Arts
216 Finance Building
Harrisburg, PA 17120

PCA Arts Organizations and Arts Programs Grants for Theatre 1896

The Pennsylvania Council on the Arts (PCA) is a state agency in the Office of the Governor. The mission of PCA is to foster the excellence, diversity, and vitality of the arts in Pennsylvania and to broaden the availability and appreciation of those arts throughout the state. Funding for the Council on the Arts through the General Assembly and from the National Endowment for the Arts. PCA offers various funding tracks for organizations that offer arts programming. The Arts Organizations and Arts Programs (AOAP) funding track has been created to provide continuous support for established organizations that have offered arts programming for a year or longer. Organizations must be invited by the PCA to apply for AOAP grants. The invitation usually is extended to organizations in PCA's Entry Track or Strategies for Success programs who have consistently received positive reviews by PCA advisory panels. Organizations on the AOAP track receive annual funding in renewable three-year blocks (subject to past performance); applicants submit full applications every three years and interim applications in intervening years. Organizations may also be removed from the AOAP track for various reasons. The AOAP track is divided into thirteen categories: art museums; arts in education organizations; arts service organizations; crafts; dance; folk and traditional arts; literature; theatre; film and electronic media; local arts; music; presenting organizations; and visual arts. In the theatre category, the PCA supports production and presentation of plays, the writing and production of new plays, the exploration of new theatre forms, touring, ticket subsidy, and other programs that make theatre more available to Pennsylvania citizens of all ages. Both interim and full applications for AOAP grants for Theatre must be completed using various online systems (available from the grant website), then printed, assembled, and mailed by the postmark date. The PCA encourages applicants to upload any required work samples and attachments through their online system. DVDs must be mailed. The application process is explained in the complete guide (PDF document) which may be accessed from the download section of the website. Application deadlines may vary from year to year. Applicants should visit the calendar section of the website to verify current deadline dates.

Requirements: In general, the PCA supports the following types of organizations: 501(c)3 corporations; units of government; or school districts providing arts programming and/or arts services in Pennsylvania. Organizations are required to provide proof of incorporation and activity in Pennsylvania before applications are reviewed or funds awarded. Unincorporated groups (and in some instances, individuals) may apply to the PCA through a nonprofit organization that acts as a fiscal sponsor. Applicants applying through a fiscal sponsor organization must meet the same requirements as other applicants except for nonprofit status. Unless otherwise specified in the guidelines, PCA awards must be matched on a dollar-for-dollar basis in cash. In-kind goods and services may not be used to match PCA funds. The PCA generally will support no more than 25% of an organizational budget, and usually considerably less.

Restrictions: In general, the PCA does not fund nor can the match for PCA funds be used for the following expenses or activities: capital expenditures, including equipment costing $500 per item or more; activities for which academic credit is given; activities that have already been completed; activities that have a religious purpose; performances and exhibitions not available to the general public; performances and exhibitions outside Pennsylvania; cash prizes and awards; benefit activities; hospitality expenses (e.g. receptions, parties, gallery openings); lobbyists' payments; and competitions.

Geographic Focus: Pennsylvania
Date(s) Application is Due: Jan 13
Contact: Philip Horn, Executive Director and Theatre Program Director; (717) 787-6883 or (717) 787-1530; fax (717) 783-2538; phorn@pa.gov
Charlotte Flynn Michalski, Executive Assistant to the Council and the Executive Director; (717) 787-6883 or (717) 787-1524; fax (717) 783-2538; cmichalski@pa.gov
Marcella Shoffner, Theatre Program Associate; (717) 787-6883 or (717) 525-5545; fax (717) 783-2538; mshoffner@pa.gov
Internet: www.pacouncilonthearts.org/pca.cfm?id=1&level=Third&sid=48
Sponsor: Pennsylvania Council on the Arts
216 Finance Building
Harrisburg, PA 17120

PCA Arts Organizations and Arts Programs Grants for Traditional and Folk Arts 1897
The Pennsylvania Council on the Arts (PCA) is a state agency in the Office of the Governor. The mission of PCA is to foster the excellence, diversity, and vitality of the arts in Pennsylvania and to broaden the availability and appreciation of those arts throughout the state. Funding for the Council on the Arts comes through an annual state appropriation by the General Assembly and from the National Endowment for the Arts. PCA offers various funding tracks for organizations that offer arts programming. The Arts Organizations and Arts Programs (AOAP) funding track has been created to provide continuous support for established organizations who have offered arts programming for a year or longer. Organizations must be invited by the PCA to apply for AOAP grants. The invitation usually is extended to organizations in PCA's Entry Track or Strategies for Success programs who have consistently received positive reviews by PCA advisory panels. Organizations on the AOAP track receive annual funding in renewable three-year blocks (subject to past performance); applicants submit full applications every three years and interim applications in intervening years. Organizations may also be removed from the AOAP track for various reasons. The AOAP track is divided into thirteen categories: art museums; arts in education organizations; arts service organizations; crafts; dance; folk and traditional arts; literature; theatre; film and electronic media; local arts; music; presenting organizations; and visual arts. In the folk and traditional arts category, the PCA supports traditional arts programming, services to artists and communities practicing traditional arts and customs, and the conservation of the traditional arts and customs found in the Commonwealth. Both interim and full applications for AOAP grants for Traditional and Folk Arts must be completed using various online systems (available from the grant website), then printed, assembled, and mailed by the postmark date. The PCA encourages applicants to upload any required work samples and attachments through their online system. DVDs must be mailed. The application process is explained in the complete guide (PDF document) which may be accessed from the download section of the website. Applicants are strongly encouraged to contact the PCA or the Institute for Cultural Partnerships for technical support, if needed. Application deadlines may vary from year to year. Applicants should visit the calendar section of the website to verify current deadline dates.

Requirements: In general, the PCA supports the following types of organizations: 501(c)3 corporations; units of government; and school districts providing arts programming and/or arts services in Pennsylvania. Organizations are required to provide proof of incorporation and activity in Pennsylvania before applications are reviewed or funds awarded. Unincorporated groups (and in some instances, individuals) may apply to the PCA through a nonprofit organization that acts as a fiscal sponsor. Applicants applying through a fiscal sponsor organization must meet the same requirements as other applicants except for nonprofit status. Unless otherwise specified in the guidelines, PCA awards must be matched on a dollar-for-dollar basis in cash. In-kind goods and services may not be used to match PCA funds. The PCA generally will support no more than 25% of an organizational budget, and usually considerably less.

Restrictions: This program does not fund oral history programs that do not include contemporary traditions, nor does it fund the production or marketing of historical crafts, or other traditions that are not part of the living heritage of particular communities. In general, the PCA does not fund nor can the match for PCA funds be used for the following expenses or activities: capital expenditures, including equipment costing $500 per item or more; activities for which academic credit is given; activities that have already been completed; activities that have a religious purpose; performances and exhibitions not

available to the general public; performances and exhibitions outside Pennsylvania; cash prizes and awards; benefit activities; hospitality expenses (e.g. receptions, parties, gallery openings); lobbyists' payments; and competitions.
Geographic Focus: Pennsylvania
Date(s) Application is Due: Jan 13
Contact: Philip Horn; (717) 787-6883 or (717) 787-1530; fax (717) 783-2538; phorn@pa.gov
Charlotte Flynn Michalski, Executive Assistant to the Council and the Executive Director; (717) 787-6883 or (717) 787-1524; fax (717) 783-2538; cmichalski@pa.gov
Amy E. Skillman, Director; 717-238-1770; fax (717) 238-3336
Marcella Shoffner, Folk and Traditional Arts Program Associate; (717) 787-6883 or (717) 525-5545; mshoffner@pa.gov
Internet: www.pacouncilonthearts.org/pca.cfm?id=1&level=Third&sid=48
Sponsor: Pennsylvania Council on the Arts
216 Finance Building
Harrisburg, PA 17120

PCA Arts Organizations and Arts Programs Grants for Visual Arts 1898
The Pennsylvania Council on the Arts (PCA) is a state agency in the Office of the Governor. The mission of PCA is to foster the excellence, diversity, and vitality of the arts in Pennsylvania and to broaden the availability and appreciation of those arts throughout the state. Funding for the Council on the Arts comes through the General Assembly and from the National Endowment for the Arts. PCA offers various funding tracks for organizations that offer arts programming. The Arts Organizations and Arts Programs (AOAP) funding track has been created to provide continuous support for established organizations who have offered arts programming for a year or longer. Organizations must be invited by the PCA to apply for AOAP grants. The invitation usually is extended to organizations in PCA's Entry Track or Strategies for Success programs who have consistently received positive reviews by PCA advisory panels. Organizations on the AOAP track receive annual funding in renewable three-year blocks (subject to past performance); applicants submit full applications every three years and interim applications in intervening years. Organizations may also be removed from the AOAP track for various reasons. The AOAP track is divided into thirteen categories: art museums; arts in education organizations; arts service organizations; crafts; dance; folk and traditional arts; literature; theatre; film and electronic media; local arts; music; presenting organizations; and visual arts. In the visual arts category, the PCA supports contemporary visual arts organizations and programs that have a primary mission to provide high-quality exhibitions, programs, and activities such as publications and education/instruction. The PCA defines visual arts as including (but not limited to) painting, sculpture, graphic art, photography, architecture, interdisciplinary arts, and electronic and digital art. Both interim and full applications for AOAP grants for visual arts must be completed using various online systems (accessible from the grant website), then printed, assembled, and mailed by the postmark date. The PCA encourages applicants to upload any required work samples and attachments through the online system. DVDs must be mailed. The application process is explained in the complete guide (PDF document) which may be accessed from the download section of the website. Application deadlines may vary from year to year. Applicants should visit the calendar section of the website to verify current deadline dates.

Requirements: In general, the PCA supports the following types of organizations: 501(c)3 corporations; units of government; or school districts providing arts programming and/or arts services in Pennsylvania. Organizations are required to provide proof of incorporation and activity in Pennsylvania before applications are reviewed or funds awarded. Unincorporated groups (and in some instances, individuals) may apply to the PCA through a nonprofit organization that acts as a fiscal sponsor. Applicants applying through a fiscal sponsor organization must meet the same requirements as other applicants except for nonprofit status. Unless otherwise specified in the guidelines, PCA awards must be matched on a dollar-for-dollar basis in cash. In-kind goods and services may not be used for match. The PCA generally will support no more than 25% of an organizational budget, and usually considerably less.

Restrictions: In general, the PCA does not fund nor can the match for PCA funds be used for the following expenses and activities: capital expenditures, including equipment costing $500 per item or more; activities for which academic credit is given; activities that have already been completed; activities that have a religious purpose; performances and exhibitions not available to the general public; performances and exhibitions outside Pennsylvania; cash prizes and awards; benefit activities; hospitality expenses (e.g., receptions, parties, and gallery openings); lobbyists' payments; and competitions.
Geographic Focus: Pennsylvania
Date(s) Application is Due: Jan 13
Contact: Bryan Holtzapple, Visual Arts Program Director; (717) 787-6883 or (717) 787-1520; bholtzappl@pa.gov
Marcella Shoffner, Visual Arts Program Director; (717) 787-6883 or (717) 525-5545; fax (717) 783-2538; mshoffner@pa.gov
Internet: www.pacouncilonthearts.org/pca.cfm?id=1&level=Third&sid=48
Sponsor: Pennsylvania Council on the Arts
216 Finance Building
Harrisburg, PA 17120

PCA Busing Grants 1899
The Pennsylvania Council on the Arts (PCA) is a state agency in the Office of the Governor. The mission of PCA is to foster the excellence, diversity, and vitality of the arts in Pennsylvania and to broaden the availability and appreciation of those arts throughout the state. Funding for the Council on the Arts comes from the citizens of Pennsylvania (through an annual state appropriation by the General Assembly) and from the National Endowment for the Arts. The PCA's Busing Program provides grants of up to $250 to assist groups attending arts events of artistic merit that might otherwise be inaccessible because

of transportation problems. The program primarily serves groups living a distance from major cities, inner-city audiences for whom public transportation is inadequate, and special groups (i.e. people with disabilities or the elderly) for whom transportation is a problem. Requests may be submitted at any time, but must be postmarked at least 30 days prior to the beginning of the event for which funding is requested.

Requirements: The group must make its own provisions for the purchase of tickets to the events. In most cases, the group attending the arts event and not the arts organization attended should apply. If the group attending is not incorporated, the organization producing the event may apply on their behalf, if a letter of intent from the attending group is enclosed. This is a non-matching award.

Restrictions: Trips to events outside of Pennsylvania will not be supported.

Geographic Focus: Pennsylvania

Amount of Grant: Up to 250 USD

Contact: Charon Battles, Preserving Diverse Cultures Program Director; (717) 787-6883 or (717) 787-1521; cbattles@pa.gov

Jewel Jones-Fulp, Preserving Diverse Cultures Program Associate; (717) 787-6883 or (717) 525-5544; fax (717) 783-2538; jjonesfulp@pa.gov

Jamie Dunlap, Accessibility Program Director; (717) 525-5542; jadunlap@pa.gov

Marcella Shoffner, Accessibility Program Assistant; (717) 525-5545; mshoffner@pa.gov

Internet: pacouncilonthearts.org/pca.cfm?id=48&level=Third&sid=48

Sponsor: Pennsylvania Council on the Arts

216 Finance Building

Harrisburg, PA 17120

PCA Entry Track Arts Organizations and Arts Programs Grants for Art Museums 1900

The Pennsylvania Council on the Arts (PCA) is a state agency in the Office of the Governor. The mission of PCA is to foster the excellence, diversity, and vitality of the arts in Pennsylvania and to broaden the availability and appreciation of those arts throughout the state. Funding for the Council on the Arts comes from the citizens of Pennsylvania (through an annual state appropriation by the General Assembly) and from the National Endowment for the Arts. PCA offers various funding tracks for organizations that offer arts programming. The Entry Track for Arts Organizations and Arts Programs is the point of entry for organizations wishing to eventually receive on-going support from PCA's multi-year/renewable Arts Organizations and Arts Programs Grants. Entry-Track grants support eligible organizations that generally have a history of at least one-year consistent arts/cultural programming. Entry-Track grants fall into three categories: Community Arts, Performance and Presenting, and Visual Arts and Electronic Media. The Community Arts category includes arts-education, arts-service, folk and traditional arts, local multi-discipline arts center, arts-council, and arts-festival programs. The Performance and Presenting category includes dance, literature, music, presenting-organization, and theatre programs. The Visual Arts and Electronic Media category includes art-museum, crafts, film and electronic media, interdisciplinary-arts, and visual-arts programs. Within the Visual Arts and Electronic Media/art-museums category, PCA supports organizations whose primary mission is to present, interpret, and preserve fine art objects of outstanding aesthetic quality. The PCA seeks to ensure the enlightened interpretation and care of the state's artistic heritage and to foster the relationships between museums and their communities through support for exhibitions, educational programs, collections care programs, and institutional operations. The application for an Entry-Track grant for art museums must be completed using various online systems (available from the grant website), then printed, assembled, and mailed by the postmark date. The PCA encourages applicants to upload any required work samples and attachments through their online system. DVDs must be mailed. The application process is explained in the complete guide (PDF document) which may be accessed from the download section of the website. Application deadlines may vary from year to year. Applicants should visit the calendar section of the website to verify current deadline dates.

Requirements: All applicants must contact PCA's Entry Track Coordinator prior to applying for the first time to discuss eligibility. Generally, organizations are eligible to apply to the Entry Track if they meet the folowing criteria: their average operating budget is over $200,000; they have at least one year of ongoing stable arts programming; and they are a nonprofit, tax-exempt corporation, unit of government, or school district providing arts programming and/or arts services in Pennsylvania. Organizations are required to provide proof of incorporation and activity in Pennsylvania before applications are reviewed or funds awarded. Non-arts organizations must clearly define an ongoing arts program that has been in existence for at least one year and submit with their application a board resolution demonstrating clear commitment to the applicant's art program. Unincorporated groups (and in some instances, individuals) may apply to the PCA through a nonprofit organization that acts as a fiscal sponsor. Applicants applying through a fiscal sponsor organization must meet the same requirements as other applicants except for nonprofit status. Unless otherwise specified in the guidelines, PCA awards must be matched on a dollar-for-dollar basis in cash. In-kind goods and services may not be used to match PCA funds. The PCA generally will support no more than 25% of an organizational budget, and usually considerably less. Interested organizations who may not meet the eligibility requirements of the Entry Track may be eligible to apply for grants from PCA's Pennsylvania Partners in the Arts (PPA), a decentralized funding program which offers both ongoing support and arts projects funding opportunities.

Restrictions: PCA's Entry-Track grants for Art Museums do not fund organizations that provide only ongoing exhibition programs. Those organizations may be able to apply for AOAP Craft or Visual Arts Grants, depending on the focus of the exhibition series. Ensembles and/or organizations from the African-American, Asian- American, Hispanic/Latino, and Native-American communities may apply for either a PCA Strategies-for-Success grant or an Entry-Track grant, but not for both. Organizations planning a one-time-only arts project should apply for PCA's Pennsylvania Partners in the Arts grants.

In general, the PCA does not fund nor can the match for PCA funds be used for the following expenses and activities: capital expenditures, including equipment costing $500 per item or more; activities for which academic credit is given; activities that have already been completed; activities that have a religious purpose; performances and exhibitions not available to the general public; performances and exhibitions outside Pennsylvania; cash prizes and awards; benefit activities; hospitality expenses, i.e. receptions, parties, gallery openings; lobbyists' payments; and competitions.

Geographic Focus: Pennsylvania

Date(s) Application is Due: Jan 13

Contact: Jamie Dunlap, Entry Track Program Director; (717) 787-6883 or (717) 525-5542; fax (717) 783-2538; jadunlap@pa.gov

Jewel Jones-Fulp, Entry Track Program Associate; (717) 787-6883 or (717) 525-5544; fax (717) 783-2538; jjonesfulp@pa.gov

Internet: www.pacouncilonthearts.org/pca.cfm?id=2&level=Third&sid=48

Sponsor: Pennsylvania Council on the Arts

216 Finance Building

Harrisburg, PA 17120

PCA Entry Track Arts Organizations and Arts Programs Grants for Arts Education Organizations 1901

The Pennsylvania Council on the Arts (PCA) is a state agency in the Office of the Governor. The mission of PCA is to foster the excellence, diversity, and vitality of the arts in Pennsylvania and to broaden the availability and appreciation of those arts throughout the state. Funding for the Council on the Arts comes from the citizens of Pennsylvania (through an annual state appropriation by the General Assembly) and from the National Endowment for the Arts. PCA offers various funding tracks for organizations that offer arts programming. The Entry Track for Arts Organizations and Arts Programs is the point of entry for organizations wishing to eventually receive on-going support from PCA's multi-year/renewable Arts Organizations and Arts Programs Grants. Entry-Track grants support eligible organizations that generally have a history of at least one-year consistent arts/cultural programming. Entry-Track grants fall into three categories: Community Arts, Performance and Presenting, and Visual Arts and Electronic Media. The Community Arts category includes arts-education, arts-service, folk and traditional arts, local multi-discipline arts center, arts-council, and arts-festival programs. The Performance and Presenting category includes dance, literature, music, presenting-organization, and theatre programs. The Visual Arts and Electronic Media category includes art-museum, crafts, film and electronic media, interdisciplinary-arts, and visual-arts programs. Within the Community Arts/arts-education organizations category, the PCA supports organizations or departments whose primary mission and activities are arts education or arts-in-education that include a significant public participation component. Arts-education programming can be arts workshops, classes, and/or programs. The application for an Entry-Track grant for arts-education organizations must be completed using various online systems (available from the grant website), then printed, assembled, and mailed by the postmark date. The PCA encourages applicants to upload any required work samples and attachments through their online system. DVDs must be mailed. The application process is explained in the complete guide (PDF document) which may be accessed from the download section of the website. Application deadlines may vary from year to year. Applicants should visit the calendar section of the website to verify current deadline dates.

Requirements: Single-discipline arts organizations or organizations providing programs whose primary mission is to provide art-education programming and activities can apply for these grants. All applicants must contact PCA's Entry Track Coordinator prior to applying for the first time to discuss eligibility. Generally, organizations are eligible to apply to the Entry Track if they meet the folowing criteria: their average operating budget is over $200,000; they have at least one year of ongoing stable arts programming; and they are a nonprofit, tax-exempt corporation, unit of government, or school district providing arts programming and/or arts services in Pennsylvania. Organizations are required to provide proof of incorporation and activity in Pennsylvania before applications are reviewed or funds awarded. Non-arts organizations must clearly define an ongoing arts program that has been in existence for at least one year and submit with their application a board resolution demonstrating clear commitment to the applicant's art program. Unincorporated groups (and in some instances, individuals) may apply to the PCA through a nonprofit organization that acts as a fiscal sponsor. Applicants applying through a fiscal sponsor organization must meet the same requirements as other applicants except for nonprofit status. Unless otherwise specified in the guidelines, PCA awards must be matched on a dollar-for-dollar basis in cash. In-kind goods and services may not be used to match PCA funds. The PCA generally will support no more than 25% of an organizational budget, and usually considerably less. Interested organizations who may not meet the eligibility requirements of the Entry Track may be eligible to apply for grants from PCA's Pennsylvania Partners in the Arts (PPA), a decentralized funding program which offers both ongoing support and arts projects funding opportunities.

Restrictions: Ensembles and/or organizations from the African-American, Asian-American, Hispanic/Latino, and Native-American communities may apply for either a PCA Strategies-for-Success grant or an Entry-Track grant, but not for both. Organizations planning a one-time-only arts project should apply for PCA's Pennsylvania-Partners-in-the-Arts grants. Entry-Track grants for arts-education organizations do not fund public schools, school districts, intermediate units, other local educational agencies, or private and parochial schools (however, these organizations may apply to PCA's Arts-In-Education Division for artist residencies). In general, the PCA does not fund nor can the match for PCA funds be used for the following expenses and activities: capital expenditures, including equipment costing $500 per item or more; activities for which academic credit is given; activities that have already been completed; activities that have a religious purpose; performances and exhibitions not available to the general public; performances and exhibitions outside

Pennsylvania; cash prizes and awards; benefit activities; hospitality expenses, i.e. receptions, parties, gallery openings; lobbyists' payments; and competitions.
Geographic Focus: Pennsylvania
Date(s) Application is Due: Jan 13
Contact: Jamie Dunlap, Entry Track Program Director; (717) 787-6883 or (717) 525-5542; fax (717) 783-2538; jadunlap@pa.gov
Jewel Jones-Fulp, Entry Track Program Associate; (717) 787-6883 or (717) 525-5544; fax (717) 783-2538; jjonesfulp@pa.gov
Internet: www.pacouncilonthearts.org/pca.cfm?id=2&level=Third
Sponsor: Pennsylvania Council on the Arts
216 Finance Building
Harrisburg, PA 17120

PCA Entry Track Arts Organizations and Arts Programs Grants for Arts Service Organizations **1902**

The Pennsylvania Council on the Arts (PCA) is a state agency in the Office of the Governor. The mission of PCA is to foster the excellence, diversity, and vitality of the arts in Pennsylvania and to broaden the availability and appreciation of those arts throughout the state. Funding for the Council on the Arts comes from the citizens of Pennsylvania (through an annual state appropriation by the General Assembly) and from the National Endowment for the Arts. PCA offers various funding tracks for organizations that offer arts programming. The Entry Track for Arts Organizations and Arts Programs is the point of entry for organizations wishing to eventually receive on-going support from PCA's multi-year/renewable Arts Organizations and Arts Programs Grants. Entry-Track grants support eligible organizations that generally have a history of at least one-year consistent arts/cultural programming. Entry-Track grants fall into three categories: Community Arts, Performance and Presenting, and Visual Arts and Electronic Media. The Community Arts category includes arts-education, arts-service, folk and traditional arts, local multi-discipline arts center, arts-council, and arts-festival programs. The Performance and Presenting category includes dance, literature, music, presenting-organization, and theatre programs. The Visual Arts and Electronic Media category includes art-museum, crafts, film and electronic media, interdisciplinary-arts, and visual-arts programs. Within the Community Arts/arts-service category, the PCA supports organizations whose primary mission is to provide services to Pennsylvania arts organizations and artists (national service organizations can only be funded for arts services provided in Pennsylvania). The application for an Entry-Track grant for arts service organizations must be completed using various online systems (available from the grant website), then printed, assembled, and mailed by the postmark date. The PCA encourages applicants to upload any required work samples and attachments through their online system. DVDs must be mailed. The application process is explained in the complete guide (PDF document) which may be accessed from the download section of the website. Application deadlines may vary from year to year. Applicants should visit the calendar section of the website to verify current deadline dates.
Requirements: All applicants must contact PCA's Entry Track Coordinator prior to applying for the first time to discuss eligibility. Generally, organizations are eligible to apply to the Entry Track if they meet the folowing criteria: their average operating budget is over $200,000; they have at least one year of ongoing stable arts programming; and they are a nonprofit, tax-exempt corporation, unit of government, or school district providing arts programming and/or arts services in Pennsylvania. Organizations are required to provide proof of incorporation and activity in Pennsylvania before applications are reviewed or funds awarded. Non-arts organizations must clearly define an ongoing arts program that has been in existence for at least one year and submit with their application a board resolution demonstrating clear commitment to the applicant's art program. Unincorporated groups (and in some instances, individuals) may apply to the PCA through a nonprofit organization that acts as a fiscal sponsor. Applicants applying through a fiscal sponsor organization must meet the same requirements as other applicants except for nonprofit status. Unless otherwise specified in the guidelines, PCA awards must be matched on a dollar-for-dollar basis in cash. In-kind goods and services may not be used to match PCA funds. The PCA generally will support no more than 25% of an organizational budget, and usually considerably less. Interested organizations who may not meet the eligibility requirements of the Entry Track may be eligible to apply for grants from PCA's Pennsylvania Partners in the Arts (PPA), a decentralized funding program which offers both ongoing support and arts projects funding opportunities.
Restrictions: Ensembles and/or organizations from the African-American, Asian-American, Hispanic/Latino, and Native-American communities may apply for either a PCA Strategies-for-Success grant or an Entry-Track grant, but not for both. Organizations planning a one-time-only arts project should apply for PCA's Pennsylvania Partners in the Arts grants. In general, the PCA does not fund nor can the match for PCA funds be used for the following expenses or activities: capital expenditures, including equipment costing $500 per item or more; activities for which academic credit is given; activities that have already been completed; activities that have a religious purpose; performances and exhibitions not available to the general public; performances and exhibitions outside Pennsylvania; cash prizes and awards; benefit activities; hospitality expenses, i.e. receptions, parties, gallery openings; lobbyists' payments; and competitions.
Geographic Focus: Pennsylvania
Date(s) Application is Due: Jan 13
Contact: Jamie Dunlap, Entry Track Program Director, Accessibility Programs Director; (717) 787-6883 or (717) 525-5542; fax (717) 783-2538; jadunlap@pa.gov
Jewel Jones-Fulp, Entry Track Program Associate; (717) 787-6883 or (717) 525-5544; fax (717) 783-2538; jjonesfulp@pa.gov
Internet: www.pacouncilonthearts.org/pca.cfm?id=2&level=Third
Sponsor: Pennsylvania Council on the Arts
216 Finance Building
Harrisburg, PA 17120

PCA Entry Track Arts Organizations and Arts Programs Grants for Crafts **1903**

The Pennsylvania Council on the Arts (PCA) is a state agency in the Office of the Governor. The mission of PCA is to foster the excellence, diversity, and vitality of the arts in Pennsylvania and to broaden the availability and appreciation of those arts throughout the state. Funding for the Council on the Arts comes from the citizens of Pennsylvania (through an annual state appropriation by the General Assembly) and from the National Endowment for the Arts. PCA offers various funding tracks for organizations that offer arts programming. The Entry Track for Arts Organizations and Arts Programs is the point of entry for organizations wishing to eventually receive on-going support from PCA's multi-year/renewable Arts Organizations and Arts Programs Grants. Entry-Track grants support eligible organizations that generally have a history of at least one-year consistent arts/cultural programming. Entry-Track grants fall into three categories: Community Arts, Performance and Presenting, and Visual Arts and Electronic Media. The Community Arts category includes arts-education, arts-service, folk and traditional arts, local multi-discipline arts center, arts-council, and arts-festival programs. The Performance and Presenting category includes dance, literature, music, presenting-organization, and theatre programs. The Visual Arts and Electronic Media category includes art-museum, crafts, film and electronic media, interdisciplinary-arts, and visual-arts programs. Within the Visual Arts and Electronic Media/crafts category, the PCA supports a wide range of organizations who have a mission to present exhibitions and provide instruction, criticism, long-term residencies, and other professional development to craft artists. The application for an Entry-Track grant for crafts must be completed using various online systems (available from the grant website), then printed, assembled, and mailed by the postmark date. The PCA encourages applicants to upload any required work samples and attachments through their online system. DVDs must be mailed. The application process is explained in the complete guide (PDF document) which may be accessed from the download section of the website. Application deadlines may vary from year to year. Applicants should visit the calendar section of the website to verify current deadline dates.
Requirements: All applicants must contact PCA's Entry Track Coordinator prior to applying for the first time to discuss eligibility. Generally, organizations are eligible to apply to the Entry Track if they meet the folowing criteria: their average operating budget is over $200,000; they have at least one year of ongoing stable arts programming; and they are a nonprofit, tax-exempt corporation, unit of government, or school district providing arts programming and/or arts services in Pennsylvania. Organizations are required to provide proof of incorporation and activity in Pennsylvania before applications are reviewed or funds awarded. Non-arts organizations must clearly define an ongoing arts program that has been in existence for at least one year and submit with their application a board resolution demonstrating clear commitment to the applicant's art program. Unincorporated groups (and in some instances, individuals) may apply to the PCA through a nonprofit organization that acts as a fiscal sponsor. Applicants applying through a fiscal sponsor organization must meet the same requirements as other applicants except for nonprofit status. Unless otherwise specified in the guidelines, PCA awards must be matched on a dollar-for-dollar basis in cash. In-kind goods and services may not be used to match PCA funds. The PCA generally will support no more than 25% of an organizational budget, and usually considerably less. Interested organizations who may not meet the eligibility requirements of the Entry Track may be eligible to apply for grants from PCA's Pennsylvania Partners in the Arts (PPA), a decentralized funding program which offers both ongoing support and arts projects funding opportunities.
Restrictions: Ensembles and/or organizations from the African-American, Asian-American, Hispanic/Latino, and Native-American communities may apply for either a PCA Strategies-for-Success grant or an Entry-Track grant, but not for both. Organizations planning a one-time-only arts project should apply for PCA's Pennsylvania Partners in the Arts grants. In general, the PCA does not fund nor can the match for PCA funds be used for the following expenses and activities: capital expenditures, including equipment costing $500 per item or more; activities for which academic credit is given; activities that have already been completed; activities that have a religious purpose; performances and exhibitions not available to the general public; performances and exhibitions outside Pennsylvania; cash prizes and awards; benefit activities; hospitality expenses, i.e. receptions, parties, gallery openings; lobbyists' payments; and competitions.
Geographic Focus: Pennsylvania
Date(s) Application is Due: Jan 13
Contact: Bryan Holtzapple, Crafts Program Director; (717) 787-6883 or (717) 787-1520; fax (717) 783-2538; bholtzappl@pa.gov
Marcella Shoffner, Crafts Program Associate, Accessibility Programs Associate; (717) 787-6883 or (717) 525-5545; fax (717) 783-2538; mshoffner@pa.gov
Jamie Dunlap, Entry Track Program Director, Accessibility Programs Director; (717) 787-6883 or (717) 525-5545; fax (717) 783-2538; mshoffner@pa.gov
Jewel Jones-Fulp; (717) 787-6883 or (717) 525-5544; fax (717) 783-2538; jjonesfulp@pa.gov
Internet: www.pacouncilonthearts.org/pca.cfm?id=2&level=Third
Sponsor: Pennsylvania Council on the Arts
216 Finance Building
Harrisburg, PA 17120

PCA Entry Track Arts Organizations and Arts Programs Grants for Dance **1904**

The Pennsylvania Council on the Arts (PCA) is a state agency in the Office of the Governor. The mission of PCA is to foster the excellence, diversity, and vitality of the arts in Pennsylvania and to broaden the availability and appreciation of those arts throughout the state. Funding for the Council on the Arts comes from the citizens of Pennsylvania (through an annual state appropriation by the General Assembly) and from the National Endowment for the Arts. PCA offers various funding tracks for organizations that offer arts programming. The Entry Track for Arts Organizations and Arts Programs is the point of entry for organizations wishing to eventually receive on-going support from PCA's multi-year/renewable Arts Organizations and Arts Programs Grants. Entry-Track grants

support eligible organizations that generally have a history of at least one-year consistent arts/cultural programming. Entry-Track grants fall into three categories: the Community Arts category includes arts-education organizations, arts-service organizations, folk and traditional arts, local arts (multi-discipline arts centers), arts councils, and arts festivals; the Performance and Presenting category includes dance, literature, music, presenting organizations, and theatre; and the Visual Arts and Electronic Media category includes art museums, crafts, film and electronic media, interdisciplinary arts, and visual arts. In the dance sub-category, the PCA supports nonprofit dance organizations whose primary purpose includes public performances. The PCA supports ethnic, modern, classical, jazz, tap, and vernacular dance projects. The application for an Entry-Track grant for dance must be completed using various online systems (available from the grant website), then printed, assembled, and mailed by the postmark date. The PCA encourages applicants to upload any required work samples and attachments through their online system. DVDs must be mailed. Applicants are strongly encouraged to visit the grant website for complete information, guidelines, and deadlines and to contact the PCA for technical support, if needed.
Requirements: All applicants must contact PCA's Entry Track Coordinator prior to applying for the first time to discuss eligibility. Generally, organizations are eligible to apply to the Entry Track if: their average operating budget is over $200,000; they have at least one year of ongoing stable arts programming; and if they are a nonprofit, tax-exempt corporation, unit of government, or school district providing arts programming and/or arts services in Pennsylvania. Organizations are required to provide proof of incorporation and activity in Pennsylvania before applications are reviewed or funds awarded. Non-arts organizations must clearly define an ongoing arts program that has been in existence for at least one year and submit with their application a board resolution demonstrating clear commitment to the applicant's art program. Unincorporated groups (and in some instances, individuals) may apply to the PCA through a nonprofit organization that acts as a fiscal sponsor. Applicants applying through a fiscal sponsor organization must meet the same requirements as other applicants except for nonprofit status. Unless otherwise specified in the guidelines, PCA awards must be matched on a dollar-for-dollar basis in cash. In-kind goods and services may not be used to match PCA funds. The PCA generally will support no more than 25% of an organizational budget, and usually considerably less. Interested organizations who may not meet the eligibility requirements of the Entry Track may be eligible to apply for grants from PCA's Pennsylvania Partners in the Arts (PPA), a decentralized funding program which offers both ongoing support and arts projects funding opportunities.
Restrictions: The Entry-Track dance sub-category does not fund dance schools, civic ballets, training institutions, or nonprofessional dance companies, except for those activities which engage professional guest teachers and choreographers; or programs in which a professional performing organization is contracted by another organization to perform. In the last instance, the presenting organization should apply under the Entry-Track presenting organizations sub-category. Ensembles and/or organizations from the African-American, Asian- American, Hispanic/Latino, and Native-American communities may apply for either a PCA Strategies-for-Success grant or an Entry-Track grant, but not for both. Organizations planning a one-time-only arts project should apply for PCA's Pennsylvania Partners in the Arts grants. In general, the PCA does not fund the following nor can the match for PCA funds be used for these expenses: capital expenditures, including equipment costing $500 per item or more; activities for which academic credit is given; activities that have already been completed; activities that have a religious purpose; performances and exhibitions not available to the general public; performances and exhibitions outside Pennsylvania; cash prizes and awards; benefit activities; hospitality expenses, i.e. receptions, parties, gallery openings; lobbyists' payments; and competitions.
Geographic Focus: Pennsylvania
Date(s) Application is Due: Jan 13
Contact: Jamie Dunlap, Entry Track Program Director, Accessibility Programs Director; (717) 787-6883 or (717) 525-5542; fax (717) 783-2538; jadunlap@pa.gov
Jewel Jones-Fulp, Entry Track Program Associate; (717) 787-6883 or (717) 525-5544; fax (717) 783-2538; jjonesfulp@pa.gov
Internet: www.pacouncilonthearts.org/pca.cfm?id=2&level=Third
Sponsor: Pennsylvania Council on the Arts
216 Finance Building
Harrisburg, PA 17120

PCA Entry Track Arts Organizations and Arts Programs Grants for Film and Electronic Media   1905
The Pennsylvania Council on the Arts (PCA) is a state agency in the Office of the Governor. The mission of PCA is to foster the excellence, diversity, and vitality of the arts in Pennsylvania and to broaden the availability and appreciation of those arts throughout the state. Funding for the Council on the Arts comes from the citizens of Pennsylvania (through an annual state appropriation by the General Assembly) and from the National Endowment for the Arts. PCA offers various funding tracks for organizations that offer arts programming. The Entry Track for Arts Organizations and Arts Programs is the point of entry for organizations wishing to eventually receive on-going support from PCA's multi-year/renewable Arts Organizations and Arts Programs Grants. Entry-Track grants support eligible organizations that generally have a history of at least one-year consistent arts/cultural programming. Entry-Track grants fall into three categories: Community Arts, Performance and Presenting, and Visual Arts and Electronic Media. The Community Arts category includes arts-education, arts-service, folk and traditional arts, local multi-discipline arts center, arts-council, and arts-festival programs. The Performance and Presenting category includes dance, literature, music, presenting-organization, and theatre programs. The Visual Arts and Electronic Media category includes art-museum, crafts, film and electronic media, interdisciplinary-arts, and visual-arts programs. Within the Visual Arts and Electronic Media/film and electronic media category, the PCA supports organizations or programs that create, produce, exhibit or distribute media arts and have a commitment to advancing the field through an emphasis on the creative use of the medium.

The application for an Entry-Track grant for film and electronic media must be completed using various online systems (available from the grant website), then printed, assembled, and mailed by the postmark date. The PCA encourages applicants to upload any required work samples and attachments through their online system. DVDs must be mailed. The application process is explained in the complete guide (PDF document) which may be accessed from the download section of the website. Application deadlines may vary from year to year. Applicants should visit the calendar section of the website to verify current deadline dates.
Requirements: All applicants must contact PCA's Entry Track Coordinator prior to applying for the first time to discuss eligibility. Generally, organizations are eligible to apply to the Entry Track if they meet the folowing criteria: their average operating budget is over $200,000; they have at least one year of ongoing stable arts programming; and they are a nonprofit, tax-exempt corporation, unit of government, or school district providing arts programming and/or arts services in Pennsylvania. Organizations are required to provide proof of incorporation and activity in Pennsylvania before applications are reviewed or funds awarded. Non-arts organizations must clearly define an ongoing arts program that has been in existence for at least one year and submit with their application a board resolution demonstrating clear commitment to the applicant's art program. Unincorporated groups (and in some instances, individuals) may apply to the PCA through a nonprofit organization that acts as a fiscal sponsor. Applicants applying through a fiscal sponsor organization must meet the same requirements as other applicants except for nonprofit status. Unless otherwise specified in the guidelines, PCA awards must be matched on a dollar-for-dollar basis in cash. In-kind goods and services may not be used to match PCA funds. The PCA generally will support no more than 25% of an organizational budget, and usually considerably less. Interested organizations who may not meet the eligibility requirements of the Entry Track may be eligible to apply for grants from PCA's Pennsylvania Partners in the Arts (PPA), a decentralized funding program which offers both ongoing support and arts projects funding opportunities.
Restrictions: Ensembles and/or organizations from the African-American, Asian-American, Hispanic/Latino, and Native-American communities may apply for either a PCA Strategies-for-Success grant or an Entry-Track grant, but not for both. Organizations planning a one-time-only arts project should apply for PCA's Pennsylvania Partners in the Arts grants. In general, the PCA does not fund nor can the match for PCA funds be used for the following expenses and activities: capital expenditures, including equipment costing $500 per item or more; activities for which academic credit is given; activities that have already been completed; activities that have a religious purpose; performances and exhibitions not available to the general public; performances and exhibitions outside Pennsylvania; cash prizes and awards; benefit activities; hospitality expenses, i.e. receptions, parties, gallery openings; lobbyists' payments; and competitions.
Geographic Focus: Pennsylvania
Date(s) Application is Due: Jan 13
Contact: Jamie Dunlap, Entry Track Program Director, Accessibility Programs Director; (717) 787-6883 or (717) 525-5542; fax (717) 783-2538; jadunlap@pa.gov
Jewel Jones-Fulp, Entry Track Program Associate; (717) 787-6883 or (717) 525-5544; fax (717) 783-2538; jjonesfulp@pa.gov
Internet: www.pacouncilonthearts.org/pca.cfm?id=2&level=Third
Sponsor: Pennsylvania Council on the Arts
216 Finance Building
Harrisburg, PA 17120

PCA Entry Track Arts Organizations and Arts Programs Grants for Literature   1906
The Pennsylvania Council on the Arts (PCA) is a state agency in the Office of the Governor. The mission of PCA is to foster the excellence, diversity, and vitality of the arts in Pennsylvania and to broaden the availability and appreciation of those arts throughout the state. Funding for the Council on the Arts comes from the citizens of Pennsylvania (through an annual state appropriation by the General Assembly) and from the National Endowment for the Arts. PCA offers various funding tracks for organizations that offer arts programming. The Entry Track for Arts Organizations and Arts Programs is the point of entry for organizations wishing to eventually receive on-going support from PCA's multi-year/renewable Arts Organizations and Arts Programs Grants. Entry-Track grants support eligible organizations that generally have a history of at least one-year consistent arts/cultural programming. Entry-Track grants fall into three categories: Community Arts, Performance and Presenting, and Visual Arts and Electronic Media. The Community Arts category includes arts-education, arts-service, folk and traditional arts, local multi-discipline arts center, arts-council, and arts-festival programs. The Performance and Presenting category includes dance, literature, music, presenting-organization, and theatre programs. The Visual Arts and Electronic Media category includes art-museum, crafts, film and electronic media, interdisciplinary-arts, and visual-arts programs. Within the Performance and Presenting/literature category, the PCA supports publications, readings and other activities that deliver programs and services. Funds are awarded to publishers of fiction, poetry, creative nonfiction, and children's literature as well as for public readings that make the work of contemporary writers more available in the state. College-based literature programs and publications will be considered if the activity is not for academic credit and if the applicant can demonstrate broad community participation. Applicants should provide a clear editorial vision, make a case for the literary impact of the publication(s, show the diversity of authors, and demonstrate clear evidence that writers are paid fees generally accepted as fair and in cash. Circulation and marketing strategies, production quality and quality-cost ratio, and design are considered. PCA Panelists consider the diversity and excellence of the writers that have been presented, the organization's demonstrated ability to expand or develop new and diverse audiences, the quality of previous programming, and the effectiveness of promotional strategies. The application for an Entry-Track grant for literature must be completed using various online systems (available from the grant website), then printed, assembled, and mailed by the postmark date. The PCA encourages applicants

to upload any required work samples and attachments through their online system. DVDs must be mailed. The application process is explained in the complete guide (PDF document) which may be accessed from the download section of the website. Application deadlines may vary from year to year. Applicants should visit the calendar section of the website to verify current deadline dates.
Requirements: All applicants must contact PCA's Entry Track Coordinator prior to applying for the first time to discuss eligibility. Generally, organizations are eligible to apply to the Entry Track if they meet the folowing criteria: their average operating budget is over $200,000; they have at least one year of ongoing stable arts programming; and they are a nonprofit, tax-exempt corporation, unit of government, or school district providing arts programming and/or arts services in Pennsylvania. Organizations are required to provide proof of incorporation and activity in Pennsylvania before applications are reviewed or funds awarded. Non-arts organizations must clearly define an ongoing arts program that has been in existence for at least one year and submit with their application a board resolution demonstrating clear commitment to the applicant's art program. Unincorporated groups (and in some instances, individuals) may apply to the PCA through a nonprofit organization that acts as a fiscal sponsor. Applicants applying through a fiscal sponsor organization must meet the same requirements as other applicants except for nonprofit status. Unless otherwise specified in the guidelines, PCA awards must be matched on a dollar-for-dollar basis in cash. In-kind goods and services may not be used to match PCA funds. The PCA generally will support no more than 25% of an organizational budget, and usually considerably less. Interested organizations who may not meet the eligibility requirements of the Entry Track may be eligible to apply for grants from PCA's Pennsylvania Partners in the Arts (PPA), a decentralized funding program which offers both ongoing support and arts projects funding opportunities.
Restrictions: Entry-Track grants for literature do not fund nor may the match for PCA funds be used for the following expenses or activities: scholarly writing; publications printing primarily student work; student-run publications; vanity press or self publications; literary projects for which academic credit is given; writing competitions, prizes or awards; activities that have already been completed; activities that have a religious purpose; performances and exhibitions not available to the general public; performances and exhibitions outside Pennsylvania; benefit activities; capital expenditures, including equipment costing $500 per item or more; hospitality expenses (eg., receptions, parties, and gallery openings); and lobbyists' payments. Ensembles and/or organizations from the African-American, Asian- American, Hispanic/Latino, and Native-American communities may apply for either a PCA Strategies-for-Success grant or an Entry-Track grant, but not for both. Organizations planning a one-time-only arts project should apply for PCA's Pennsylvania Partners in the Arts grants.
Geographic Focus: Pennsylvania
Date(s) Application is Due: Jan 13
Contact: Jamie Dunlap, Entry Track Program Director, Accessibility Programs Director; (717) 787-6883 or (717) 525-5542; fax (717) 783-2538; jadunlap@pa.gov
Jewel Jones-Fulp, Entry Track Program Associate; (717) 787-6883 or (717) 525-5544; fax (717) 783-2538; jjonesfulp@pa.gov
Sponsor: Pennsylvania Council on the Arts
216 Finance Building
Harrisburg, PA 17120

PCA Entry Track Arts Organizations and Arts Programs Grants for Local Arts 1907
The Pennsylvania Council on the Arts (PCA) is a state agency in the Office of the Governor. The mission of PCA is to foster the excellence, diversity, and vitality of the arts in Pennsylvania and to broaden the availability and appreciation of those arts throughout the state. Funding for the Council on the Arts comes from the citizens of Pennsylvania (through an annual state appropriation by the General Assembly) and from the National Endowment for the Arts. PCA offers various funding tracks for organizations that offer arts programming. The Entry Track for Arts Organizations and Arts Programs is the point of entry for organizations wishing to eventually receive on-going support from PCA's multi-year/renewable Arts Organizations and Arts Programs Grants. Entry-Track grants support eligible organizations that generally have a history of at least one-year consistent arts/cultural programming. Entry-Track grants fall into three categories: Community Arts, Performance and Presenting, and Visual Arts and Electronic Media. The Community Arts category includes arts-education, arts-service, folk and traditional arts, local multi-discipline arts center, arts-council, and arts-festival programs. The Performance and Presenting category includes dance, literature, music, presenting-organization, and theatre programs. The Visual Arts and Electronic Media category includes art-museum, crafts, film and electronic media, interdisciplinary-arts, and visual-arts programs. In the Community Arts/local, multi-discipline arts-center category, the PCA supports organizations and programs that provide a wide range of arts activities and significant public participation in the arts in a specified community or region. These agencies support, coordinate, and provide a broad range of arts programs and administrative services based on the needs and resources of the designated community. The application for an Entry-Track grant for local arts must be completed using various online systems (available from the grant website), then printed, assembled, and mailed by the postmark date. The PCA encourages applicants to upload any required work samples and attachments through their online system. DVDs must be mailed. The application process is explained in the complete guide (PDF document) which may be accessed from the download section of the website. Application deadlines may vary from year to year. Applicants should visit the calendar section of the website to verify current deadline dates.
Requirements: Applicants for this category must be a multi-discipline arts center, multi-discipline arts council, multi-discipline arts festival, and/or a multi-discipline arts program in a social service center or other nonprofit organization or a government agency. All applicants must contact PCA's Entry Track Coordinator prior to applying for the first time to discuss eligibility. Generally, organizations are eligible to apply to the Entry Track if they meet the folowing criteria: their average operating budget is over $200,000; they have at least one year of ongoing stable arts programming; and they are a nonprofit, tax-exempt corporation, unit of government, or school district providing arts programming and/or arts services in Pennsylvania. Organizations are required to provide proof of incorporation and activity in Pennsylvania before applications are reviewed or funds awarded. Non-arts organizations must clearly define an ongoing arts program that has been in existence for at least one year and submit with their application a board resolution demonstrating clear commitment to the applicant's art program. Unincorporated groups (and in some instances, individuals) may apply to the PCA through a nonprofit organization that acts as a fiscal sponsor. Applicants applying through a fiscal sponsor organization must meet the same requirements as other applicants except for nonprofit status. Unless otherwise specified in the guidelines, PCA awards must be matched on a dollar-for-dollar basis in cash. In-kind goods and services may not be used to match PCA funds. The PCA generally will support no more than 25% of an organizational budget, and usually considerably less. Interested organizations who may not meet the eligibility requirements of the Entry Track may be eligible to apply for grants from PCA's Pennsylvania Partners in the Arts (PPA), a decentralized funding program which offers both ongoing support and arts projects funding opportunities.
Restrictions: Entry-Track grants for local arts do not fund single-discipline arts organizations or programs. Ensembles and/or organizations from the African-American, Asian-American, Hispanic/Latino, and Native-American communities may apply for either a PCA Strategies-for-Success grant or an Entry-Track grant, but not for both. Organizations planning a one-time-only arts project should apply for PCA's Pennsylvania Partners in the Arts Projects grants. In general, the PCA does not fund the following nor can the match for PCA funds be used for the following expenses or activities: capital expenditures, including equipment costing $500 per item or more; activities for which academic credit is given; activities that have already been completed; activities that have a religious purpose; performances and exhibitions not available to the general public; performances and exhibitions outside Pennsylvania; cash prizes and awards; benefit activities; hospitality expenses, i.e. receptions, parties, gallery openings; lobbyists' payments; and competitions.
Geographic Focus: Pennsylvania
Date(s) Application is Due: Jan 13
Contact: Jamie Dunlap, Entry Track Program Director, Accessibility Programs Director; (717) 787-6883 or (717) 525-5542; fax (717) 783-2538; jadunlap@pa.gov
Internet: www.pacouncilonthearts.org/pca.cfm?id=2&level=Third
Sponsor: Pennsylvania Council on the Arts
216 Finance Building
Harrisburg, PA 17120

PCA Entry Track Arts Organizations and Arts Programs Grants for Music 1908
The Pennsylvania Council on the Arts (PCA) is a state agency in the Office of the Governor. The mission of PCA is to foster the excellence, diversity, and vitality of the arts in Pennsylvania and to broaden the availability and appreciation of those arts throughout the state. Funding for the Council on the Arts comes from the citizens of Pennsylvania (through an annual state appropriation by the General Assembly) and from the National Endowment for the Arts. PCA offers various funding tracks for organizations that offer arts programming. The Entry Track for Arts Organizations and Arts Programs is the point of entry for organizations wishing to eventually receive on-going support from PCA's multi-year/renewable Arts Organizations and Arts Programs Grants. Entry-Track grants support eligible organizations that generally have a history of at least one-year consistent arts/cultural programming. Entry-Track grants fall into three categories: Community Arts, Performance and Presenting, and Visual Arts and Electronic Media. The Community Arts category includes arts-education, arts-service, folk and traditional arts, local multi-discipline arts center, arts-council, and arts-festival programs. The Performance and Presenting category includes dance, literature, music, presenting-organization, and theatre programs. The Visual Arts and Electronic Media category includes art-museum, crafts, film and electronic media, interdisciplinary-arts, and visual-arts programs. Within the Performance and Presenting/music category, the PCA supports music organizations and programs whose primary purpose includes public performances. The application for an Entry-Track grant for music must be completed using various online systems (available from the grant website), then printed, assembled, and mailed by the postmark date. The PCA encourages applicants to upload any required work samples and attachments through their online system. DVDs must be mailed. The application process is explained in the complete guide (PDF document) which may be accessed from the download section of the website. Application deadlines may vary from year to year. Applicants should visit the calendar section of the website to verify current deadline dates.
Requirements: All applicants must contact PCA's Entry Track Coordinator prior to applying for the first time to discuss eligibility. Generally, organizations are eligible to apply to the Entry Track if they meet the folowing criteria: their average operating budget is over $200,000; they have at least one year of ongoing stable arts programming; and they are a nonprofit, tax-exempt corporation, unit of government, or school district providing arts programming and/or arts services in Pennsylvania. Organizations are required to provide proof of incorporation and activity in Pennsylvania before applications are reviewed or funds awarded. Non-arts organizations must clearly define an ongoing arts program that has been in existence for at least one year and submit with their application a board resolution demonstrating clear commitment to the applicant's art program. Unincorporated groups (and in some instances, individuals) may apply to the PCA through a nonprofit organization that acts as a fiscal sponsor. Applicants applying through a fiscal sponsor organization must meet the same requirements as other applicants except for nonprofit status. Unless otherwise specified in the guidelines, PCA awards must be matched on a dollar-for-dollar basis in cash. In-kind goods and services may not be used to match PCA funds. The PCA generally will support no more than 25% of an organizational budget, and usually considerably less. Interested organizations who may not meet the eligibility requirements of the Entry Track

may be eligible to apply for grants from PCA's Pennsylvania Partners in the Arts (PPA), a decentralized funding program which offers both ongoing support and arts projects funding opportunities.
Restrictions: Ensembles and/or organizations from the African-American, Asian-American, Hispanic/Latino, and Native-American communities may apply for either a PCA Strategies-for-Success grant or an Entry-Track grant, but not for both. Organizations planning a one-time-only arts project should apply for PCA's Pennsylvania Partners in the Arts grants. In general, the PCA does not fund nor can the match for PCA funds be used for the following expenses and activities: capital expenditures, including equipment costing $500 per item or more; activities for which academic credit is given; activities that have already been completed; activities that have a religious purpose; performances and exhibitions not available to the general public; performances and exhibitions outside Pennsylvania; cash prizes and awards; benefit activities; hospitality expenses, i.e. receptions, parties, gallery openings; lobbyists' payments; and competitions.
Geographic Focus: Pennsylvania
Date(s) Application is Due: Jan 13
Contact: Jamie Dunlap, Entry-Track Program Director, Accessibility Programs Director; (717) 787-6883 or (717) 525-5542; fax (717) 783-2538; jadunlap@pa.gov
Internet: www.pacouncilonthearts.org/pca.cfm?id=2&level=Third
Sponsor: Pennsylvania Council on the Arts
216 Finance Building
Harrisburg, PA 17120

PCA Entry Track Arts Organizations and Arts Programs Grants for Presenting Organizations 1909
The Pennsylvania Council on the Arts (PCA) is a state agency in the Office of the Governor. The mission of PCA is to foster the excellence, diversity, and vitality of the arts in Pennsylvania and to broaden the availability and appreciation of those arts throughout the state. Funding for the Council on the Arts comes from the citizens of Pennsylvania (through an annual state appropriation by the General Assembly) and from the National Endowment for the Arts. PCA offers various funding tracks for organizations that offer arts programming. The Entry Track for Arts Organizations and Arts Programs is the point of entry for organizations wishing to eventually receive on-going support from PCA's multi-year/renewable Arts Organizations and Arts Programs Grants. Entry-Track grants support eligible organizations that generally have a history of at least one-year consistent arts/cultural programming. Entry-Track grants fall into three categories: Community Arts, Performance and Presenting, and Visual Arts and Electronic Media. The Community Arts category includes arts-education, arts-service, folk and traditional arts, local multi-discipline arts center, arts-council, and arts-festival programs. The Performance and Presenting category includes dance, literature, music, presenting-organization, and theatre programs. The Visual Arts and Electronic Media category includes art-museum, crafts, film and electronic media, interdisciplinary-arts, and visual-arts programs. Within the Performance and Presenting/presenting-organizations category, the PCA supports organizations that present professional performing artists. These presentations may occur in a variety of settings. A performing arts presenter organization engages professional touring artists, pays their fees, handles the local presentation, promotion and ticket sales, and arranges for the facilities and technical support for the event(s). Presenters work with artists, managers, educators, and community groups to bring artists into a community in concerts and less formal arrangements. The presenting field includes cultural centers, theatres, galleries and museums, arts centers, libraries, college and university artist series, festivals, concert, music, dance or theatre associations, and civic or cultural organizations and programs that promote cooperative programming and activity between Pennsylvania presenting organizations. The application for an Entry-Track grant for presenting organizations must be completed using various online systems (available from the grant website), then printed, assembled, and mailed by the postmark date. The PCA encourages applicants to upload any required work samples and attachments through their online system. DVDs must be mailed. Applicants are strongly encouraged to visit the grant website for complete information, guidelines, and deadlines and to contact the PCA for technical support, if needed.
Requirements: Entry-Track grants in the presenting organizations sub-category support organizations that present professional performing artists. Organizations and programs that exclusively present local artists should apply for Entry-Track grants in the local arts sub-category. Pennsylvania artists or ensembles who self-produce their home seasons or local performances should apply in one of the Entry-Track arts genre sub-categories (Dance, Music, Theatre, etc.). All applicants must contact PCA's Entry Track Coordinator prior to applying for the first time to discuss eligibility. Generally, organizations are eligible to apply to the Entry Track if they meet the folowing criteria: their average operating budget is over $200,000; they have at least one year of ongoing stable arts programming; and they are a nonprofit, tax-exempt corporation, unit of government, or school district providing arts programming and/or arts services in Pennsylvania. Organizations are required to provide proof of incorporation and activity in Pennsylvania before applications are reviewed or funds awarded. Non-arts organizations must clearly define an ongoing arts program that has been in existence for at least one year and submit with their application a board resolution demonstrating clear commitment to the applicant's art program. Unincorporated groups (and in some instances, individuals) may apply to the PCA through a nonprofit organization that acts as a fiscal sponsor. Applicants applying through a fiscal sponsor organization must meet the same requirements as other applicants except for nonprofit status. Unless otherwise specified in the guidelines, PCA awards must be matched on a dollar-for-dollar basis in cash. In-kind goods and services may not be used to match PCA funds. The PCA generally will support no more than 25% of an organizational budget, and usually considerably less. Interested organizations who may not meet the eligibility requirements of the Entry Track may be eligible to apply for grants from PCA's Pennsylvania Partners in the Arts (PPA), a decentralized funding program which offers both ongoing support and arts projects funding opportunities.
Restrictions: Entry-Track grants in the presenting organizations sub-category do not fund presenters who present nonprofessional, avocational, student, or school-related artists or ensembles (faculty) seasons. Ensembles and/or organizations from the African-American, Asian- American, Hispanic/Latino, and Native-American communities may apply for either a PCA Strategies-for-Success grant or an Entry-Track grant, but not for both. Organizations planning a one-time-only arts project should apply for PCA's Pennsylvania Partners in the Arts grants. In general, the PCA does not fund nor can the match for PCA funds be used for the following expenses and activities: capital expenditures, including equipment costing $500 per item or more; activities for which academic credit is given; activities that have already been completed; activities that have a religious purpose; performances and exhibitions not available to the general public; performances and exhibitions outside Pennsylvania; cash prizes and awards; benefit activities; hospitality expenses, i.e. receptions, parties, gallery openings; lobbyists' payments; and competitions.
Geographic Focus: Pennsylvania
Date(s) Application is Due: Jan 13
Contact: Jamie Dunlap, Entry Track Program Director, Accessibility Programs Director; (717) 787-6883 or (717) 525-5542; fax (717) 783-2538; jadunlap@pa.gov
Jewel Jones-Fulp, Entry Track Program Associate; (717) 787-6883 or (717) 525-5544; fax (717) 783-2538; jjonesfulp@pa.gov
Sponsor: Pennsylvania Council on the Arts
216 Finance Building
Harrisburg, PA 17120

PCA Entry Track Arts Organizations and Arts Programs Grants for Theatre 1910
The Pennsylvania Council on the Arts (PCA) is a state agency in the Office of the Governor. The mission of PCA is to foster the excellence, diversity, and vitality of the arts in Pennsylvania and to broaden the availability and appreciation of those arts throughout the state. Funding for the Council on the Arts comes from the citizens of Pennsylvania (through an annual state appropriation by the General Assembly) and from the National Endowment for the Arts. PCA offers various funding tracks for organizations that offer arts programming. The Entry Track for Arts Organizations and Arts Programs is the point of entry for organizations wishing to eventually receive on-going support from PCA's multi-year/renewable Arts Organizations and Arts Programs Grants. Entry-Track grants support eligible organizations that generally have a history of at least one-year consistent arts/cultural programming. Entry-Track grants fall into three categories: Community Arts, Performance and Presenting, and Visual Arts and Electronic Media. The Community Arts category includes arts-education, arts-service, folk and traditional arts, local multi-discipline arts center, arts-council, and arts-festival programs. The Performance and Presenting category includes dance, literature, music, presenting-organization, and theatre programs. The Visual Arts and Electronic Media category includes art-museum, crafts, film and electronic media, interdisciplinary-arts, and visual-arts programs. Within the Performance and Presenting/theater category, the PCA supports production and presentation of plays, the writing and production of new plays, the exploration of new theatre forms, touring, ticket subsidy, and other programs that make theatre more available to Pennsylvania citizens of all ages. The application for an Entry-Track grant for theatre must be completed using various online systems (available from the grant website), then printed, assembled, and mailed by the postmark date. The PCA encourages applicants to upload any required work samples and attachments through their online system. DVDs must be mailed. The application process is explained in the complete guide (PDF document) which may be accessed from the download section of the website. Application deadlines may vary from year to year. Applicants should visit the calendar section of the website to verify current deadline dates.
Requirements: All applicants must contact PCA's Entry Track Coordinator prior to applying for the first time to discuss eligibility. Generally, organizations are eligible to apply to the Entry Track if they meet the folowing criteria: their average operating budget is over $200,000; they have at least one year of ongoing stable arts programming; and they are a nonprofit, tax-exempt corporation, unit of government, or school district providing arts programming and/or arts services in Pennsylvania. Organizations are required to provide proof of incorporation and activity in Pennsylvania before applications are reviewed or funds awarded. Non-arts organizations must clearly define an ongoing arts program that has been in existence for at least one year and submit with their application a board resolution demonstrating clear commitment to the applicant's art program. Unincorporated groups (and in some instances, individuals) may apply to the PCA through a nonprofit organization that acts as a fiscal sponsor. Applicants applying through a fiscal sponsor organization must meet the same requirements as other applicants except for nonprofit status. Unless otherwise specified in the guidelines, PCA awards must be matched on a dollar-for-dollar basis in cash. In-kind goods and services may not be used to match PCA funds. The PCA generally will support no more than 25% of an organizational budget, and usually considerably less. Interested organizations who may not meet the eligibility requirements of the Entry Track may be eligible to apply for grants from PCA's Pennsylvania Partners in the Arts (PPA), a decentralized funding program which offers both ongoing support and arts projects funding opportunities.
Restrictions: Ensembles and/or organizations from the African-American, Asian-American, Hispanic/Latino, and Native-American communities may apply for either a PCA Strategies-for-Success grant or an Entry-Track grant, but not for both. Organizations planning a one-time-only arts project should apply for PCA's Pennsylvania Partners in the Arts grants. In general, the PCA does not fund nor can the match for PCA funds be used for the following expenses and activities: capital expenditures, including equipment costing $500 per item or more; activities for which academic credit is given; activities that have already been completed; activities that have a religious purpose; performances and exhibitions not available to the general public; performances and exhibitions outside Pennsylvania; cash prizes and awards; benefit activities; hospitality expenses, i.e. receptions, parties, gallery openings; lobbyists' payments; and competitions.

Geographic Focus: Pennsylvania
Date(s) Application is Due: Jan 13
Contact: Jamie Dunlap, Entry Track Program Director, Accessibility Programs Director; (717) 787-6883 or (717) 525-5542; fax (717) 783-2538; jadunlap@pa.gov
Jewel Jones-Fulp, Entry Track Program Associate; (717) 787-6883 or (717) 525-5544; fax (717) 783-2538; jjonesfulp@pa.gov
Internet: www.pacouncilonthearts.org/pca.cfm?id=2&level=Third
Sponsor: Pennsylvania Council on the Arts
216 Finance Building
Harrisburg, PA 17120

PCA Entry Track Arts Organizations and Arts Programs Grants for Traditional and Folk Arts 1911

The Pennsylvania Council on the Arts (PCA) is a state agency in the Office of the Governor. The mission of PCA is to foster the excellence, diversity, and vitality of the arts in Pennsylvania and to broaden the availability and appreciation of those arts throughout the state. Funding for the Council on the Arts comes from the citizens of Pennsylvania (through an annual state appropriation by the General Assembly) and from the National Endowment for the Arts. PCA offers various funding tracks for organizations that offer arts programming. The Entry Track for Arts Organizations and Arts Programs is the point of entry for organizations wishing to eventually receive on-going support from PCA's multi-year/renewable Arts Organizations and Arts Programs Grants. Entry-Track grants support eligible organizations that generally have a history of at least one-year consistent arts/cultural programming. Entry-Track grants fall into three categories: Community Arts, Performance and Presenting, and Visual Arts and Electronic Media. The Community Arts category includes arts-education, arts-service, folk and traditional arts, local multi-discipline arts center, arts-council, and arts-festival programs. The Performance and Presenting category includes dance, literature, music, presenting-organization, and theatre programs. The Visual Arts and Electronic Media category includes art-museum, crafts, film and electronic media, interdisciplinary-arts, and visual-arts programs. Within the Community-Arts/folk and traditional arts category, the PCA supports traditional arts programming, services to artists and communities practicing traditional arts and customs, and the conservation of the traditional arts and customs found in the Commonwealth. The application for an Entry-Track grant for traditional and folk arts must be completed using various online systems (available from the grant website), then printed, assembled, and mailed by the postmark date. The PCA encourages applicants to upload any required work samples and attachments through their online system. DVDs must be mailed. The application process is explained in the complete guide (PDF document) which may be accessed from the download section of the website. Application deadlines may vary from year to year. Applicants should visit the calendar section of the website to verify current deadline dates.
Requirements: All applicants must contact PCA's Entry Track Coordinator prior to applying for the first time to discuss eligibility. Generally, organizations are eligible to apply to the Entry Track if they meet the folowing criteria: their average operating budget is over $200,000; they have at least one year of ongoing stable arts programming; and they are a nonprofit, tax-exempt corporation, unit of government, or school district providing arts programming and/or arts services in Pennsylvania. Organizations are required to provide proof of incorporation and activity in Pennsylvania before applications are reviewed or funds awarded. Non-arts organizations must clearly define an ongoing arts program that has been in existence for at least one year and submit with their application a board resolution demonstrating clear commitment to the applicant's art program. Unincorporated groups (and in some instances, individuals) may apply to the PCA through a nonprofit organization that acts as a fiscal sponsor. Applicants applying through a fiscal sponsor organization must meet the same requirements as other applicants except for nonprofit status. Unless otherwise specified in the guidelines, PCA awards must be matched on a dollar-for-dollar basis in cash. In-kind goods and services may not be used to match PCA funds. The PCA generally will support no more than 25% of an organizational budget, and usually considerably less. Interested organizations who may not meet the eligibility requirements of the Entry Track may be eligible to apply for grants from PCA's Pennsylvania Partners in the Arts (PPA), a decentralized funding program which offers both ongoing support and arts projects funding opportunities.
Restrictions: Entry-Track grants do not support oral history programs that do not include contemporary traditions, or the production or marketing of historical crafts, or other traditions that are not part of the living heritage of particular communities. Ensembles and/or organizations from the African-American, Asian- American, Hispanic/Latino, and Native-American communities may apply for either a PCA Strategies-for-Success grant or an Entry-Track grant, but not for both. Organizations planning a one-time-only arts project should apply for PCA's Pennsylvania Partners in the Arts grants. In general, the PCA does not fund nor can the match for PCA funds be used for the following expenses and activities: capital expenditures, including equipment costing $500 per item or more; activities for which academic credit is given; activities that have already been completed; activities that have a religious purpose; performances and exhibitions not available to the general public; performances and exhibitions outside Pennsylvania; cash prizes and awards; benefit activities; hospitality expenses, i.e. receptions, parties, gallery openings; lobbyists' payments; and competitions.
Geographic Focus: Pennsylvania
Date(s) Application is Due: Jan 13
Contact: Jamie Dunlap, Entry Track Program Director, Accessibility Programs Director; (717) 787-6883 or (717) 525-5542; fax (717) 783-2538; jadunlap@pa.gov
Jewel Jones-Fulp, Entry Track Program Associate; (717) 787-6883 or (717) 525-5544; fax (717) 783-2538; jjonesfulp@pa.gov

Internet: www.pacouncilonthearts.org/pca.cfm?id=2&level=Third
Sponsor: Pennsylvania Council on the Arts
216 Finance Building
Harrisburg, PA 17120

PCA Entry Track Arts Organizations and Arts Programs Grants for Visual Arts 1912

The Pennsylvania Council on the Arts (PCA) is a state agency in the Office of the Governor. The mission of PCA is to foster the excellence, diversity, and vitality of the arts in Pennsylvania and to broaden the availability and appreciation of those arts throughout the state. Funding for the Council on the Arts comes from the citizens of Pennsylvania (through an annual state appropriation by the General Assembly) and from the National Endowment for the Arts. PCA offers various funding tracks for organizations that offer arts programming. The Entry Track for Arts Organizations and Arts Programs is the point of entry for organizations wishing to eventually receive on-going support from PCA's multi-year/renewable Arts Organizations and Arts Programs Grants. Entry-Track grants support eligible organizations that generally have a history of at least one-year consistent arts/cultural programming. Entry-Track grants fall into three categories: Community Arts, Performance and Presenting, and Visual Arts and Electronic Media. The Community Arts category includes arts-education, arts-service, folk and traditional arts, local multi-discipline arts center, arts-council, and arts-festival programs. The Performance and Presenting category includes dance, literature, music, presenting-organization, and theatre programs. The Visual Arts and Electronic Media category includes art-museum, crafts, film and electronic media, interdisciplinary-arts, and visual-arts programs. Within the Visual Arts and Electronic Media/visual-arts category, the PCA supports contemporary visual arts organizations and ongoing programs whose primary mission is to provide high-quality exhibitions and other programs and activities such as publications and education/instruction. The PCA defines visual arts as including, but not limited to, painting, sculpture, graphic art, photography, architecture, interdisciplinary arts, electronic and digital art. The application for an Entry-Track grant for visual arts must be completed using various online systems (available from the grant website), then printed, assembled, and mailed by the postmark date. The PCA encourages applicants to upload any required work samples and attachments through their online system. DVDs must be mailed.
Requirements: All applicants must contact PCA's Entry Track Coordinator prior to applying for the first time to discuss eligibility. Generally, organizations are eligible to apply to the Entry Track if they meet the folowing criteria: their average operating budget is over $200,000; they have at least one year of ongoing stable arts programming; and they are a nonprofit, tax-exempt corporation, unit of government, or school district providing arts programming and/or arts services in Pennsylvania. Organizations are required to provide proof of incorporation and activity in Pennsylvania before applications are reviewed or funds awarded. Non-arts organizations must clearly define an ongoing arts program that has been in existence for at least one year and submit with their application a board resolution demonstrating clear commitment to the applicant's art program. Unincorporated groups (and in some instances, individuals) may apply to the PCA through a nonprofit organization that acts as a fiscal sponsor. Applicants applying through a fiscal sponsor organization must meet the same requirements as other applicants except for nonprofit status. Unless otherwise specified in the guidelines, PCA awards must be matched on a dollar-for-dollar basis in cash. In-kind goods and services may not be used to match PCA funds. The PCA generally will support no more than 25% of an organizational budget, and usually considerably less. Interested organizations who may not meet the eligibility requirements of the Entry Track may be eligible to apply for grants from PCA's Pennsylvania Partners in the Arts (PPA), a decentralized funding program which offers both ongoing support and arts projects funding opportunities.
Restrictions: Ensembles and/or organizations from the African-American, Asian-American, Hispanic/Latino, and Native-American communities may apply for either a PCA Strategies-for-Success grant or an Entry-Track grant, but not for both. Organizations planning a one-time-only arts project should apply for PCA's Pennsylvania Partners in the Arts grants. In general, the PCA does not fund nor can the match for PCA funds be used for the following expenses and activities: capital expenditures, including equipment costing $500 per item or more; activities for which academic credit is given; activities that have already been completed; activities that have a religious purpose; performances and exhibitions not available to the general public; performances and exhibitions outside Pennsylvania; cash prizes and awards; benefit activities; hospitality expenses, i.e. receptions, parties, gallery openings; lobbyists' payments; and competitions.
Geographic Focus: Pennsylvania
Date(s) Application is Due: Jan 13
Contact: Bryan Holtzapple, Visual Arts Program Director; (717) 787-6883 or (717) 787-1520; fax (717) 783-2538; bholtzappl@pa.gov
Marcella Shoffner, Visual Arts Program Associate, Accessibility Programs Associate; (717) 787-6883 or (717) 525-5544; fax (717) 783-2538; mshoffner@pa.gov
Jamie Dunlap, Entry Track Program Director, Accessibility Programs Director; (717) 787-6883 or (717) 525-5542; fax (717) 783-2538; jadunlap@pa.gov
Internet: www.pacouncilonthearts.org/pca.cfm?id=2&level=Third
Sponsor: Pennsylvania Council on the Arts
216 Finance Building
Harrisburg, PA 17120

PCA Management/Technical Assistance Grants 1913

The Pennsylvania Council on the Arts (PCA) is a state agency in the Office of the Governor. The mission of PCA is to foster the excellence, diversity, and vitality of the arts in Pennsylvania and to broaden the availability and appreciation of those arts throughout the state. Funding for the Council on the Arts comes from the citizens of Pennsylvania (through an annual state appropriation by the General Assembly) and from the National Endowment for the Arts. The PCA's Management/Technical Assistance Grants are available to organizations to address specific artistic, programmatic, administrative, or technical needs throughout the year. Up to $2,000 in funding may be requested to engage consultants to address specific issues and recommend action in the following areas: cultural, financial, or strategic planning; creating and improving the artistic quality of the documentation for an organization (i.e. slides, tapes, etc.); mission, board, staff, or program development; audience development or marketing; fundraising; and evaluating and planning to make facilities, programs, and staff accessible to individuals with disabilities. Requests of $2,000 or less may be submitted at any time, but must be postmarked at least 30 days prior to the beginning of the project for which funding is requested. Applications are available from the downloads section of the website.

Requirements: Most awards are non-matching. Organizations are encouraged to contact the Program Director or Program Assistant to clarify any eligibility questions.

Restrictions: Generally, the PCA will only fund to a maximum of $4,000 per year.

Geographic Focus: Pennsylvania

Amount of Grant: Up to 2,000 USD

Contact: Charon Battles, Preserving Diverse Cultures Program Director; (717) 787-6883 or (717) 787-1521; fax (717) 783-2538; cbattles@pa.gov

Jewel Jones-Fulp, Preserving Diverse Cultures Program Associate; (717) 787-6883 or (717) 525-5544; fax (717) 783-2538; jjonesfulp@pa.gov

Internet: pacouncilonthearts.org/pca.cfm?id=48&level=Third&sid=48

Sponsor: Pennsylvania Council on the Arts

216 Finance Building

Harrisburg, PA 17120

PCA Pennsylvania Partners in the Arts Program Stream Grants 1914

Pennsylvania Partners in the Arts (PPA) is a partnership between local organizations and the Pennsylvania Council on the Arts (PCA) that has the aim of making arts programs available to communities that may have been underserved by state arts funding. Administered by thirteen regional partners across the state, the PPA re-grants funds to support a wide variety of local and community arts activities in every county in Pennsylvania. The PPA offers two streams of funding opportunities, the Project Stream and the Program Stream. The Project Stream provides grants of up to $3,000 to eligible organizations or individuals to conduct arts projects. The Program Stream provides ongoing support to eligible organizations with an established history of PCA support. Applications for PPA Program Stream grants must be completed using various online systems (available from the grant website), then printed, assembled, and mailed along with any required attachments/work samples by the postmark date to the applicant's regional PPA Partner (contact information is available at the grant website in the form of a regional map). The application process is explained in the complete guide (PDF document) which may be accessed from the download section of the website. Application deadlines may vary from year to year. Applicants should visit the calendar section of the website to verify current deadline dates.

Requirements: Organizations must have been notified by the PCA or a PPA Partner that they have met the eligibility requirements and have been invited to apply to the PPA Program Stream. In general, the PCA supports the following types of organizations: nonprofit, 501(c)3, tax-exempt corporations; units of government; or school districts providing arts programming and/or arts services in Pennsylvania. Organizations are required to provide proof of incorporation and activity in Pennsylvania before applications are reviewed or funds awarded. Unincorporated groups (and in some instances, individuals) may apply to the PCA through a nonprofit organization that acts as a fiscal sponsor, but they must satisfy all requirements except for nonprofit status. The PCA may also accept applications from national service organizations based outside of Pennsylvania that have a strong presence in Pennsylvania. Unless otherwise specified in the guidelines, PCA awards must be matched on a dollar-for-dollar basis in cash. The PCA generally will support no more than 25% of an organizational budget, and usually considerably less. Organizations or individuals who do not meet the eligibility criteria for Entry Track or PPA Program Stream, may be eligible for PPA Project Stream funding.

Restrictions: Applicants are permitted to submit one application per year to Program Stream. Applicants for PPA Program Stream funding may not also apply for PPA Project funding or the PCA's Arts Organizations and Arts Programs (AOAP) Track, or Entry Track for the same time period. In general, the PCA does not fund the following nor can the match for PCA funds be used for these expenses: capital expenditures, including equipment costing $500 per item or more; activities for which academic credit is given; activities that have already been completed; activities that have a religious purpose; performances and exhibitions not available to the general public; performances and exhibitions outside Pennsylvania; cash prizes and awards; benefit activities; hospitality expenses, i.e. receptions, parties, gallery openings; lobbyists' payments; and competitions. In-kind goods and services may not be used to match PCA funds. PPA Program Stream funds cannot be used to match other PCA grants.

Geographic Focus: Pennsylvania

Date(s) Application is Due: Mar 5

Contact: Lori Frush Schmelz, Pennsylvania Partners in the Arts Program Director; (717) 787-6883 or (717) 787-1523; fax (717) 783-2538; lschmelz@pa.gov

Internet: pacouncilonthearts.org/pca.cfm?id=36&level=Third&sid=48

Sponsor: Pennsylvania Council on the Arts

216 Finance Building

Harrisburg, PA 17120

PCA Pennsylvania Partners in the Arts Project Stream Grants 1915

Pennsylvania Partners in the Arts (PPA) is a partnership between local organizations and the Pennsylvania Council on the Arts (PCA) that has the aim of making arts programs available to communities that may have been underserved by state arts funding. Administered by thirteen regional partners across the state, the PPA re-grants funds to support a wide variety of local and community arts activities in every county in Pennsylvania. The PPA offers two streams of funding opportunities, the Program Stream and the Project Stream. The Program Stream offers ongoing support to arts organizations and arts programs with an established history of PPA support while the Project Stream provides grants of up to

$3,000 to eligible organizations or individuals to conduct one-time arts projects. Preference is weighted (75% of available funding vs. 25% of available funding) to art projects not conducted with or in venues already supported by the PCA. A list of arts organizations and programs the PCA already supports is available at the grant website or from the PPA Partner Organizations. Applications for PPA Project Stream grants must be completed using various online systems (available from the grant website), then printed, assembled, and mailed along with any required attachments/work samples by the postmark date to the applicant's regional PPA Partner (contact information is available at the grant website in the form of a regional map). The application process is explained in the complete guide (PDF document) which may be accessed from the download section of the website. Application deadlines may vary from year to year. Applicants should visit the calendar section of the website to verify current deadline dates.

Requirements: In general, the PCA supports the following types of organizations: 501(c)3 corporations; units of government; or school districts providing arts programming and/or arts services in Pennsylvania. Organizations are required to provide proof of incorporation and activity in Pennsylvania before applications are reviewed or funds awarded. Unincorporated groups and individuals may apply to the PCA through a nonprofit organization that acts as a fiscal sponsor, but they must satisfy all requirements except for nonprofit status. Organizations or individuals who do not meet the eligibility criteria for PCA Entry Track or PPA Program Stream may be eligible for PPA Project Stream funding. (Alternatively, organizations who have received Project Stream funding for multiple years may qualify to transition to the PPA Program Stream if they have consistent arts programming and good assessments from the Project Stream review panels.) Proposed projects for Project Stream must be arts activities conducted for the benefit of the public (for-profit organizations are ineligible) and take place in the applicant's PPA service region. First- and second-time PPA Project Stream recipients are not required to match the requested amount; however third-time recipients must show a 1:1 cash match of funds requested for their third and any subsequent projects.

Restrictions: Applicants may submit one Project Stream application per PPA service region per grant period. PPA Project Stream applicants may not apply to the following grant programs for the same period: PPA Program Stream, PCA Arts Organizations Arts Programs (AOAP) track; or PCA Entry Track. PPA Project Stream applicants may apply to the following PCA grant programs during the same period: Arts in Education Residencies; Preserving Diverse Cultures; and Professional Development and Consulting. Applicants, if individuals, must be at least eighteen years old. In general, the PCA does not fund nor can the match for PCA funds be used for the following expenses: capital expenditures, including equipment costing $500 per item or more; activities for which academic credit is given; activities that have already been completed; activities that have a religious purpose; performances and exhibitions not available to the general public; performances and exhibitions outside Pennsylvania; cash prizes and awards; benefit activities; hospitality expenses, i.e. receptions, parties, gallery openings; lobbyists' payments; and competitions. In-kind goods and services may not be used to match PCA funds. PCA funds may not be used as match for other PCA funds.

Geographic Focus: Pennsylvania

Date(s) Application is Due: Jun 15

Amount of Grant: Up to 3,000 USD

Contact: Lori Frush Schmelz, Pennsylvania Partners in the Arts Program Director; (717) 787-6883 or (717) 787-1523; fax (717) 783-2538; lschmelz@pa.gov

Jamie Dunlap; (717) 787-6883 or (717) 525-5542; fax (717) 783-2538; jadunlap@pa.gov

Internet: pacouncilonthearts.org/pca.cfm?id=42&level=Third&sid=48

Sponsor: Pennsylvania Council on the Arts

216 Finance Building

Harrisburg, PA 17120

PCA Professional Development Grants 1916

The Pennsylvania Council on the Arts (PCA) is a state agency in the Office of the Governor. The mission of PCA is to foster the excellence, diversity, and vitality of the arts in Pennsylvania and to broaden the availability and appreciation of those arts throughout the state. Funding for the Council on the Arts comes from the citizens of Pennsylvania (through an annual state appropriation by the General Assembly) and from the National Endowment for the Arts. The PCA's Professional Growth Opportunities Grants are available to individual artists for peer to peer consultations and for registration and travel fees for arts conferences, seminars and workshops. More than one person may be included on the application. Requests may be submitted at any time, but must be postmarked at least 30 days prior to the beginning of the project for which funding is requested. Applications are available from the downloads section of the website.

Requirements: Individuals are encouraged to contact the PCA with any questions.

Geographic Focus: Pennsylvania

Amount of Grant: Up to 500 USD

Contact: Charon Battles, Preserving Diverse Cultures Program Director; (717) 787-6883 or (717) 787-1521; fax (717) 783-2538; cbattles@pa.gov

Jewel Jones-Fulp, Preserving Diverse Cultures Program Associate; (717) 787-6883 or (717) 525-5544; jjonesfulp@pa.gov

Internet: pacouncilonthearts.org/pca.cfm?id=48&level=Third&sid=48

Sponsor: Pennsylvania Council on the Arts

216 Finance Building

Harrisburg, PA 17120

PCA Strategies for Success Grants - Advanced Level 1917

The Pennsylvania Council on the Arts (PCA) is a state agency whose mission is to foster the arts in Pennsylvania and broaden the availability and appreciation of those arts throughout the state. Through its Strategies for Success grants, PCA's Preserving Cultural Diversity Division supports development of organizations from the African-

American, Asian-American, Hispanic/Latino, and Native-American communities. PCA offers its Strategies for Success grants at three different levels: Basic, Intermediate, and Advanced. Funding at each level depends on an annual evaluation. The Advanced Level focuses on arts organizations that have consistent arts and cultural programming and are viewed as institutions within their communities. This level recognizes an organization's preparedness for institutional status. Such organizations must document a track record of quality presentations and commitment to and from their community. The PCA awards up to $20,000 to support the following types of projects: fundraising, long-range planning, program development, facility development, board development, and expansion. Recipients must present a budget that shows $40,000 ($20,000 PCA and $20,000 match) of activity for a combination of staffing and/or program activity. Prospective applicants may download a detailed guide (PDF document) and grant application (Microsoft Excel) from the downloads section of the grant website. Application deadlines may vary from year to year. Applicants are encouraged to view the calendar at the grant website to verify current deadline dates.

Requirements: To be eligible to apply at the advanced level, organizations must have been in operation for a minimum of ten consecutive years and have all the following: an average fiscal budget of approximately $125,000; a Federal I.D. Number and 501(c)3 status; a formal, structured board of directors; a salaried staff with at least two full-time staff members; a demonstrated use of volunteers; a formal bookkeeping system; a yearly audit; regular office hours and an accessible place of business; an established long-range plan (for at least three years); a demonstrated marketing program; evidence of structured annual fund-raising activities; and an established community support and awareness program.

Restrictions: Eligibility for Strategies for Success Grants is restricted to organizations and artists from the African-American, Asian-American, Latino/Hispanic and Native-American communities. Generally, the combined length of an organization's participation in the Strategies for Success program at the Basic and Intermediate Levels may not exceed 6 years with no more than three years spent at the same level. Generally, the maximum length of an organizations' participation in the Advanced level is 2 years. However, graduates of the Program or organizations experiencing difficulty in advancing to the next level may request an extension.

Geographic Focus: Pennsylvania
Date(s) Application is Due: Mar 3
Amount of Grant: Up to 20,000 USD
Contact: Charon Battles, Preserving Diverse Cultures Program Director; (717) 787-6883 or (717) 787-1521; fax (717) 783-2538; cbattles@pa.gov
Jewel Jones-Fulp, Preserving Diverse Cultures Program Associate; (717) 787-6883 or (717) 525-5544; fax (717) 783-2538; jjonesfulp@pa.gov
Internet: pacouncilonthearts.org/pca.cfm?id=47&level=Third&sid=48
Sponsor: Pennsylvania Council on the Arts
216 Finance Building
Harrisburg, PA 17120

PCA Strategies for Success Grants - Basic Level 1918

The Pennsylvania Council on the Arts (PCA) is a state agency whose mission is to foster the arts in Pennsylvania and broaden the availability and appreciation of those arts throughout the state. Through its Strategies for Success grants, PCA's Preserving Cultural Diversity Division supports development of organizations from the African-American, Asian-American, Hispanic/Latino, and Native-American communities. PCA offers its Strategies for Success grants at three different levels: Basic, Intermediate, and Advanced. Funding at each level depends on an annual evaluation. Basic-Level grants support organizations seeking assistance in the development of a formal board structure, more consistent arts programming, and establishment of 501(c)3 status. The PCA awards up to $2,500 in non-matching funds for consultants (as assigned by agreement/consent of the PCA), and up to $2,500 in non-matching funds for programs for a maximum total of $5,000.

Requirements: Applicants must have at least a two-year history of arts/cultural programming; be an unincorporated ensemble or arts program or organization interested in organization/program development; and have a 2-3 year average arts/cultural fiscal budget of less than $24,000. Basic-Level applicants may also submit an application for a Pennsylvania Partners in the Arts grant or to the Arts Organizations Arts Programs track (provided the applicant meets eligibility requirements for those programs). First-time applicants are encouraged to contact the Preserving Diverse Cultures Division Director prior to completing an application.

Restrictions: Eligibility is restricted to organizations and artists from the African American, Asian American, Latino/Hispanic and Native American communities. Generally, the combined length of an organization's participation in the Strategies for Success program at the Basic and Intermediate Levels may not exceed 6 years with no more than three years spent at the same level. Generally, the maximum length of an organizations' participation in the Advanced level is 2 years. However, graduates of the Program or organizations experiencing difficulty in advancing to the next level may request an extension.

Geographic Focus: Pennsylvania
Date(s) Application is Due: Mar 5
Amount of Grant: Up to 5,000 USD
Contact: Charon Battles, Preserving Diverse Cultures Program Director; (717) 787-6883 or (717) 787-1521; fax (717) 783-2538; cbattles@pa.gov
Internet: pacouncilonthearts.org/pca.cfm?id=47&level=Third&sid=48
Sponsor: Pennsylvania Council on the Arts
216 Finance Building
Harrisburg, PA 17120

PCA Strategies for Success Grants - Intermediate Level 1919

The Pennsylvania Council on the Arts (PCA) is a state agency whose mission is to foster the arts in Pennsylvania and broaden the availability and appreciation of those arts throughout

the state. Through its Strategies for Success grants, PCA's Preserving Cultural Diversity Division supports development of organizations from the African-American, Asian-American, Hispanic/Latino, and Native-American communities. PCA offers its Strategies for Success grants at three different levels: Basic, Intermediate, and Advanced. Funding at each level depends on an annual evaluation. The Intermediate level is designed for arts organizations or programs within social service, community, and non-arts organizations interested in developing professionally-staffed arts programs (with active boards of directors and professional staff). The primary focus of the Intermediate level is capacity building and assisting in administrative and programmatic stabilization. To that end PCA awards up to $2,500 in non-matching funds for consultants (as assigned by agreement/consent of the PCA), up to $2,500 in non-matching funds for program assistance; and up to $5,000 in matching funds for the implementation or augmentation of one administrative staff position or long-term contracted service. The intent of the funded staff position is to assist the organization in developing professional staff who are committed to the growth of the organization. Allowable programmatic expenses include printing, staff training, conference expenses (fees, lodging, and transportation not to exceed $500), and artists' fees. Prospective applicants may download a detailed guide (PDF document) and grant application (Microsoft Excel) from the downloads section of the grant website. Application deadlines may vary from year to year. Applicants are encouraged to view the calendar at the grant website to verify current deadline dates.

Requirements: To be eligible for Intermediate Level Strategies for Success grants, organizations must meet the following criteria: have an average fiscal budget of $24,000 to $100,000; have a Federal I.D. Number and pending 501(c)3 status; have a formal board of directors with committee structure and regular meetings; use a formal bookkeeping system; keep regular office hours and an accessible place of business; show evidence of fund-raising; demonstrate consistent community and audience support; provide annual programming that is artistically significant and that effectively presents cultural activities; have been in operation for three consecutive years; and have at least one staff position (20 hours per week or more).

Restrictions: Eligibility for Strategies for Success Grants is restricted to organizations and artists from the African American, Asian American, Latino/Hispanic and Native American communities. Generally, the combined length of an organization's participation in the Strategies for Success program at the Basic and Intermediate Levels may not exceed 6 years with no more than three years spent at the same level. Generally, the maximum length of an organizations' participation in the Advanced level is 2 years. However, graduates of the Program or organizations experiencing difficulty in advancing to the next level may request an extension.

Geographic Focus: Pennsylvania
Date(s) Application is Due: Mar 5
Amount of Grant: Up to 10,000 USD
Contact: Charon Battles, Preserving Diverse Cultures Program Director; (717) 787-6883 or (717) 787-1521; fax (717) 783-2538; cbattles@pa.gov
Jewel Jones-Fulp, Preserving Diverse Cultures Program Associate; (717) 787-6883 or (717) 525-5544; fax (717) 783-2538; jjonesfulp@pa.gov
Internet: pacouncilonthearts.org/pca.cfm?id=47&level=Third&sid=48
Sponsor: Pennsylvania Council on the Arts
216 Finance Building
Harrisburg, PA 17120

PDF Community Organizing Grants 1920

Peace Development Fund awards Community Organizing Grants to any organization in the United States, Haiti and/or Mexico that fit into PDF's guidelines. Specifically, this award sponsors organizations that focus on social justice, organizing to shift powers, working to build a movement, dismantling oppression, and creating new structures in these geographical areas. The average award is $5,000, and the annual deadline for submission of applications is December 30.

Requirements: Applications are available at PDF's website and must be emailed to grants@peacefund.org by 5:00 pm Pacific Standard Time on the due date. This grant is highly competitive and the Fund will only award grants to organizations that align with PDF's guidelines.

Restrictions: PDF will not fund programs outside the U.S., Mexico or Haiti unless specified for a special initiative or Donor Advised fund. Also, PDF will not fund: individuals and/or organizations with strong leadership from only one person; conferences and other one-time events; audio-visual productions and distribution, including TV, radio, publications, films, etc; research that is not directly linked to an organizing strategy; academic institutions or scholarships; other grant-making organizations; or organizations with large budgets ($250,000 or more) or who have access to other sources of funding.

Geographic Focus: All States, Puerto Rico, Haiti, Mexico
Date(s) Application is Due: Dec 30
Amount of Grant: 2,000 - 6,000 USD
Contact: Emily Serafy Cox, Foundation Officer; (415) 642-0900 or (413) 256-8306, ext. 100; fax (415) 642-8200; emily@peacefund.org or grants@peacefund.org
Internet: www.peacedevelopmentfund.org/grants-and-programs/community-organizing-grants-program/
Sponsor: Peace Development Fund
44 North Prospect Street, P.O. Box 1280
Amhert, MA 01004-1280

PDF Fiscal Sponsorship Grant 1921

The Peace Development Fund's Fiscal Sponsorship grant seeks to support programs that are dedicated to equality and social justice. Specifically, this award supports organizations that focus on social justice, organizing to shift powers, working to build a movement, dismantling oppression, and creating new structures in these geographical areas. Overall, it provides administrative infrastructure and extends the legal framework of fiscal sponsorship to grassroots groups and projects so they can carry out their work without the burden of managing donations and other tax-exempt requirements. Applications are accepted on a rolling basis and only through the online application portal.

Requirements: Applications will only be accepted in English. In addition, projects must involve public education and/or other charitable 501(c)3 organizations.

Restrictions: PDF does not fund: programs whose primary geographic focus is outside of the United States, U.S. Territories, Latin America and the Caribbean Basin; individuals and/or organizations with strong leadership from only one person; conferences and other one-time events; audio-visual productions and distribution, including TV, radio, publications, films, etc; research that is not directly linked to an organizing strategy; academic institutions or scholarships; other grant-making organizations; and projects with a primary focus on "conflict resolution."

Geographic Focus: All States, Puerto Rico, U.S. Virgin Islands, Haiti, Mexico

Contact: Paul Haible; (415) 642-0900 or (413) 256-8306; paul@peacefund.org Emily Serafy-Cox; (413) 256-8306, ext. 100 or (415) 642-0900; emily@peacefund.org

Internet: www.peacedevelopmentfund.org/grants-and-programs/fiscal-sponsorship-program/

Sponsor: Peace Development Fund

44 North Prospect Street, P.O. Box 1280

Amhert, MA 01004-1280

Peabody Foundation Grants   1922

The Peabody Foundation was established in 1894 in Massachusetts. Grants provide care, treatment, rehabilitation, education, and assistance to children with physical disabilities as well as encouraging and supporting medical research in the causes of crippling disease, particularly in children. The majority of recipient organizations will be located in the Boston, Massachusetts area. Proposals may be submitted at any time and are reviewed in the spring. Funding ranges from $20,000 to $200,000. Interested organizations should contact the Administrative Director for application procedures and eligibility information.

Restrictions: Grants are not made to individuals. Giving is limited to Massachusetts, with emphasis on the Boston area.

Geographic Focus: Massachusetts

Date(s) Application is Due: Feb 1

Amount of Grant: 20,000 - 200,000 USD

Samples: Agassiz Village, Lexington, Massachusetts, $35,000 - to benefit disabled children and/or related research; Brigham and Women's Hospital, Boston, Massachusetts, $75,000 - to benefit disabled children and/or related research; Cotting School for Handicapped Children, Lexington, Massachusetts, $41,000.

Contact: Judi Mullen, Administrative Director; (508) 728-8780; jemullen12@comcast.net Jonathan Bashein, Office Administrator; (617) 345-1000 or (617) 310-4100; fax (617) 345-1300; jbashein@nixonpeabody.com

Sponsor: Peabody Foundation

100 Summer Street

Boston, MA 02110-2131

Pediatric Brain Tumor Foundation Early Career Development Grants   1923

The Pediatric Brain Tumor Foundation (PBTF) is a 501(c)3 nonprofit charitable organization whose mission is as follows: to find the cause of and cure for childhood brain tumors by supporting medical research; to increase public awareness about the severity and prevalence of childhood brain tumors; to aid in the early detection and treatment of childhood brain tumors; to support a national database on all primary brain tumors; and to provide educational and emotional support for children and families affected by this life-threatening disease. The goal of the PBTF's Early Career Development grants program is to support talented researchers in the field of pediatric brain tumors who are in the first five years of their first faculty position. The expectation is that this funding will facilitate awardees' transition to becoming fully independent investigators.

Requirements: Applicant organizations must be 501(c)3 institutions located in the U.S., Canada, and Australia.

Geographic Focus: All States

Amount of Grant: Up to 400,000 USD

Samples: Dana-Farber Cancer Institute, Boston, Massachusetts, $300,000 - resistance to BET-bromodomain inhibitors in MYC-amplified medulloblastoma; Heinrich-Heine University, Dusseldorf, Germany, $300,000 - unraveling medulloblastoma biology by proteomics; University of California, San Francisco, California, $300,000 - genetic susceptibility to ependymoma and interaction with perinatal risk factors.

Contact: Robin Boettcher, President and CEO; (800) 253-6530 or (828) 665-6891; fax (828) 665-6894; rboettcher@curethekids.org or pbtfus@pbtfus.org

Internet: www.curethekids.org/research/what-we-fund/research-funding/#.WMAQXYVExWa

Sponsor: Pediatric Brain Tumor Foundation

302 Ridgefield Court

Asheville, NC 28806

Pediatric Brain Tumor Foundation Early Career Development Grants   1924

The Pediatric Brain Tumor Foundation (PBTF) is a 501(c)3 nonprofit charitable organization whose mission is as follows: to find the cause of and cure for childhood brain tumors by supporting medical research; to increase public awareness about the severity and prevalence of childhood brain tumors; to aid in the early detection and treatment of childhood brain tumors; to support a national database on all primary brain tumors; and to provide educational and emotional support for children and families affected by this life-threatening disease. The goal of the PBTF's Early Career Development grants program is to support talented researchers in the field of pediatric brain tumors who are in the first five years of their first faculty position. The expectation is that this funding will facilitate awardees' transition to becoming fully independent investigators.

Requirements: Applicant organizations must be 501(c)3 institutions located in the U.S., Canada, Germany, and Australia.

Geographic Focus: All States, Australia, Canada, Germany

Amount of Grant: Up to 400,000 USD

Samples: Dana-Farber Cancer Institute, Boston, Massachusetts, $300,000 - resistance to BET-bromodomain inhibitors in MYC-amplified medulloblastoma; Heinrich-Heine University, Dusseldorf, Germany, $300,000 - unraveling medulloblastoma biology by proteomics; University of California, San Francisco, California, $300,000 - genetic susceptibility to ependymoma and interaction with perinatal risk factors.

Contact: Robin Boettcher, President and CEO; (800) 253-6530 or (828) 665-6891; fax (828) 665-6894; rboettcher@curethekids.org or pbtfus@pbtfus.org

Internet: www.curethekids.org/research/what-we-fund/research-funding/#.WMAQXYVExWa

Sponsor: Pediatric Brain Tumor Foundation

302 Ridgefield Court

Asheville, NC 28806

Pediatric Brain Tumor Foundation Institute Grants   1925

The Pediatric Brain Tumor Foundation (PBTF) is a 501(c)3 nonprofit charitable organization whose mission is as follows: to find the cause of and cure for childhood brain tumors by supporting medical research; to increase public awareness about the severity and prevalence of childhood brain tumors; to aid in the early detection and treatment of childhood brain tumors; to support a national database on all primary brain tumors; and to provide educational and emotional support for children and families affected by this life-threatening disease. PBTF Institute grants concentrate investment in centers with well-recognized expertise in pediatric brain tumor research. This enables the Foundation to be flexible with project selection and to reprioritize during the funding period based on project performance. Other advantages of the Institute model include: enhanced coordination of discovery and translational research efforts; greater sharing and leveraging of core resources between recipient centers; and enhanced exchange of experimental findings and approaches between principal investigators.

Requirements: Institute projects must be hypothesis-driven basic or translational scientific research on pediatric brain tumors. Applicant organizations must be 501(c)3 institutions located in the U.S., Canada, and Australia.

Geographic Focus: All States, Australia, Canada

Amount of Grant: Up to 1,000,000 USD

Samples: Hospital for Sick Children, Toronto, Canada, $1,000,000 - epigenetic alterations define lethal CMP-positive ependymomas of infancy; Duke University, Durham, North Carolina, $400,000 - development of a peptide vaccine for DIPG; University of California, San Francisco, California, $300,000 - oligodendrocyte developmental methylome to characterize progenitors for pediatric glioma.

Contact: Robin Boettcher, President and CEO; (800) 253-6530 or (828) 665-6891; fax (828) 665-6894; rboettcher@curethekids.org or pbtfus@pbtfus.org

Internet: www.curethekids.org/research/what-we-fund/research-funding/#.WMANToVExWY

Sponsor: Pediatric Brain Tumor Foundation

302 Ridgefield Court

Asheville, NC 28806

Pediatric Brain Tumor Foundation Opportunity Grants   1926

The Pediatric Brain Tumor Foundation (PBTF) is a 501(c)3 nonprofit charitable organization whose mission is as follows: to find the cause of and cure for childhood brain tumors by supporting medical research; to increase public awareness about the severity and prevalence of childhood brain tumors; to aid in the early detection and treatment of childhood brain tumors; to support a national database on all primary brain tumors; and to provide educational and emotional support for children and families affected by this life-threatening disease. Research initiatives that the Foundation judges to be critical to filling in the gaps and enhancing the pediatric brain tumor research landscape are eligible for opportunity grants. Discussions with the Research Advisory Network and the broader scientific community helps to identify candidates for funding. Applications are accepted by invitation only. However, the Foundation welcomes discussion of research ideas that fit with its strategic priorities, particularly if the ideas involve multi-institutional efforts.

Requirements: Institute projects must be hypothesis-driven basic or translational scientific research on pediatric brain tumors. Applicant organizations must be 501(c)3 institutions located in the U.S., Canada, and Australia.

Geographic Focus: All States, Australia, Canada

Amount of Grant: Up to 500,000 USD

Samples: University of California, San Francisco, California, $500,000 - support for the Pacific Pediatric Neuro-Oncology Consortium, Operations Center; University of California, San Diego, California, $234,000 - Immunosignature Strategy for Development of Clinical Biomarkers and Identification of New Drug Target Candidates for Pediatric Brain Cancer; Children's Oncology Group, Philadelphia, Pennsylvania, $100,000 - support for Project: Every Child.

Contact: Robin Boettcher, President and CEO; (800) 253-6530 or (828) 665-6891; fax (828) 665-6894; rboettcher@curethekids.org or pbtfus@pbtfus.org

Internet: www.curethekids.org/research/what-we-fund/research-funding/#.WMApJ4VExWb

Sponsor: Pediatric Brain Tumor Foundation

302 Ridgefield Court

Asheville, NC 28806

Pediatric Cancer Research Foundation Grants   1927

Since its establishment in 1982 as a grass-roots organization, the Pediatric Cancer Research Foundation (PCRF) has focused its efforts upon improving the care, quality of life, and survival rate of children with malignant diseases. With these ends in mind, PCRF concentrates on laboratory research that will translate into immediate treatment for children with cancer. PCRF primarily funds research that brings innovative new drugs and treatment regimens to children. Proposals should be based on molecular, cellular, or integrated systems; be conceptually innovative; and have a clear plan for study and future clinical use of the factual data obtained. Current areas of foundation funding include stem-cell transplantation, stem-cell biology, molecular oncology, and molecular and cellular genetics. Awards will generally be made for a one- to three-year period at the Board's discretion. Renewals for additional years may be made for promising projects as recognized by the Scientific Review Committee. Prospective applicants can download the application form at the PCRF website. Completed applications must be received at the PCRF office by 5:00 PM on May 1st. If a deadline falls on a Saturday or Sunday, the applications are due the next business day.

Requirements: Applications may be submitted by individuals holding a M.D., Ph.D., or equivalent degree and working in domestic non-profit organizations such as universities, colleges, hospitals, or laboratories (the "sponsoring institution"). Applications may be multi-institutional in nature. Applicants currently holding a grant may re-apply for extension of similar research by submitting a Renewal Application.

Restrictions: No overhead or indirect costs to institutions will be funded.

Geographic Focus: All States

Date(s) Application is Due: May 1

Samples: Columbia University, New York, NY, $740,548; Children's Hospital of Los Angeles, Los Angeles, CA, $64,250; MD Anderson, Houston, TX, $37,500.

Contact: Joseph M. Galosic, Director of Scientific Affairs; (949) 859-6312; fax (949) 859-6323; admin@pcrf-kids.org

Internet: www.pcrf-kids.org/

Sponsor: Pediatric Cancer Research Foundation

9272 Jeronimo Road, Suite 122

Irvine, CA 92618

PEN America Phyllis Naylor Grant for Children's and Young Adult Novelists 1928

The Grant is made possible by a substantial contribution from PEN America Member Phyllis Reynolds Naylor, the prolific author of more than 140 books, including Now I'll Tell You Everything, the 28th and final book in the acclaimed Alice series, as well as Faith, Hope, and Ivy June and Shiloh, the first novel in a quartet, which won the 1992 Newbery Medal. On establishing the grant, Mrs. Naylor said: "We truly work 'blind,' with no assurance whatsoever that anyone will be interested in our final product. It takes enormous stamina and resolve and optimism to live with our characters for a year or more—and it's my hope that the grant, modest as it is, will let the author know that an expert panel of PEN judges has faith in the writer, admires his work, and trusts that he will be able to bring to paper what he sees in his head." The PEN America Phyllis Naylor Grant for Children's and Young Adult Novelists is offered annually to an author of children's or young adult fiction for a novel-in-progress. Previously called the PEN/Phyllis Naylor Working Writer Fellowship, the award was developed to help writers whose work is of high literary caliber and assist a writer at a crucial moment in their career to complete their novel. The author of the winning manuscript, selected blindly by judges unaware of nominees' names, will receive an award of $5,000. A list of previous award winners is available at the PEN website. The annual submission cycle opens on April 1, with the deadline being August 1.

Requirements: A candidate is a writer of children or young-adult fiction in financial need, who has published at least two books, but no more than five, during the past 10 years that have been warmly received by literary critics but have not generated sufficient income to support the author. Writers must be nominated by an editor or fellow writer. The nominator should write a letter of support, describing in some detail how the candidate meets the criteria for the Fellowship. The nominator should also provide: a list of the candidate's published work, accompanied by copies of reviews, where possible; three copies of the outline of the current novel in progress, together with 50–75 pages of the text; and on a separate piece of paper, a brief description of the candidate's recent earnings and a statement about why monetary support will make a particular difference in the applicant's writing life at this time. If the candidate is married or living with a domestic partner, please include a brief description of total family income and expenses.

Restrictions: Picture books are not eligible.

Geographic Focus: All States

Date(s) Application is Due: Aug 1

Amount of Grant: 5,000 USD

Contact: Jane Marchant, Manager, Literary Awards; (646) 779-4813 or (212) 334-1660; fax (212) 334-2181; jmarchant@pen.org or awards@pen.org

Internet: pen.org/pen-phyllis-naylor-grant/

Sponsor: PEN America

588 Broadway, Suite 303

New York, NY 10012

PennPAT Artist Technical Assistance Grants 1929

Created as a unique public/private partnership and administered by the Mid Atlantic Arts Foundation, Pennsylvania Performing Arts on Tour (PennPAT) increases opportunities for professional Pennsylvania-based performing artists to obtain successful touring engagements in Pennsylvania and other states. Artists may apply directly for two types of grants: Artist Technical Assistance Grants and Strategic Opportunity Grants. Artist Technical Assistance Grants support projects that advance tour readiness and improve marketing and other tour-management capabilities. Projects may include the following types of expense: hiring a consultant on a short-term basis to assist or advise on various artistic, management, and marketing-related aspects of touring; costs to attend or participate in workshops or conferences that address issues and practices of touring; development of newly designed marketing materials (video, audio, web, press pack, brochure, etc.) that raise the level of quality, communication, and professionalism in the artist's presentation to presenters; registration, travel, and showcase fees for artists adjudicated into a major showcase; travel and registration costs for an artist to exhibit at a regional booking conference for the first time; and expanding the artist's ability to tour by

making the artist more affordable or more attractive to presenters. Prospective applicants must first contact the PennPAT Director to discuss the project. If the project is deemed eligible, PennPAT will email or mail the guidelines and application to the applicant. Artists may submit applications on an ongoing basis, at least six weeks prior to the start of the proposed project. Grants will generally be awarded for up to 50% of project costs, up to a maximum of $5,000 per calendar year. Applicants may include documented in-kind contributions as part of their match.

Requirements: Applicants must be included in the PennPAT artist roster for the time in which the project will take place. Information on how to be included in the artist roster is available at the PennPAT website. In addition, the applicant must have submitted all final reports on previous projects by the report due date.

Restrictions: Technical Assistance Grants will NOT support the following expenses: purchase of equipment, supplies or other costs related to normal business activities; compensation for staff; travel, lodging, or fees related to a touring engagement; and projects related to artistic development. Artists may apply for and receive multiple grants in each category (Artist Technical Assistance and Strategic Opportunity), but may not receive more than $5,000 in each category during a calendar year (maximum $10,000 per year, per artist).

Geographic Focus: Pennsylvania

Amount of Grant: Up to 5,000 USD

Contact: Katie West; (215) 496-9424 ext. 4; katie@pennpat.org or info@pennpat.org Jenny Filer, Program Assistant; (215) 496-9424 ext. 3; jenny@pennpat.org

Internet: www.pennpat.org/Grants.aspx?id=124&ekmensel=216_submenu_284_btnlink

Sponsor: Pennsylvania Performing Arts on Tour

230 South Broad Street, Suite 1003

Philadelphia, PA 19102

PennPAT Fee-Support Grants for Presenters 1930

Created as a unique public/private partnership and administered by the Mid Atlantic Arts Foundation, Pennsylvania Performing Arts on Tour (PennPAT) increases opportunities for professional Pennsylvania-based performing artists to obtain successful touring engagements in Pennsylvania and other states. To this end, PennPAT provides grants and marketing support to both presenters and artists, as well as training for artists. PennPat offers three types of grants to presenting organizations: Fee-Support Grants, New Directions Grants, and Presenter Travel Grants. Fee-Support Grants provide funding to presenters in support of touring engagements with artists listed on the PennPAT Artist Roster. Fee-Support Grants have two application deadlines: February 15 for projects that fall within a two year period beginning the following June; and October 15 for projects that fall within a two-year and three-month period beginning the following February. Applications must be submitted through the Mid Atlantic Arts Foundation eGrant system (link is available from the PennPAT website) by the deadline date. Applications must also be mailed to PennPAT and postmarked by the deadline date. Fee-Support Grants will fund up to 50% of the contracted artist fees, travel, and lodging. This amount is often capped at $20,000 per grant. Complete application guidelines (PDF) can be downloaded from the grant website. Applicants are also encouraged to read the FAQ section of the website.

Requirements: To be eligible for Fee-Support grants, applicants must meet PennPat's definition of a presenting organization; be a 501(c)3 organization or a unit of government; and be located in Delaware, the District of Columbia, Maryland, New Jersey, New York, Ohio, Pennsylvania, the U.S. Virgin Islands, Virginia, or West Virginia. Eligible projects must include a tentative contract for an engagement with a PennPAT roster artist (who lives or is based outside the community where the presentation will take place); and include at least one public performance at a venue within the eligible states/jurisdictions listed above. Complementary activities (e.g. master classes, workshops, lecture/demonstrations, school performances) are also strongly encouraged and should be included in the artist's contract. A presenting organization is defined as an organization that selects, engages and pays touring performing artists to perform works created elsewhere by those or other artists, which will be performed in many locations. Presenters manage all local arrangements for the performance (e.g. providing space, local technical support, advertising/promotion) and facilitate the interaction between artists and audiences.

Restrictions: Presenters may apply at more than one deadline for Fee-Support and New Directions grants. Presenters may request funds for more than one artist, however, they must submit a separate application for each separately contracted engagement. Applicants must not have any overdue outstanding reports from previous PennPAT or Mid Atlantic Foundation grants. PennPAT will not fund the following activities: programs or events that primarily serve a confined audience (e.g. K-12 schools, university classes, summer camps, nursing homes); arts-in-education projects; programs or events in which the roster artist is not the primary focus of the performance; fundraising events; programs or events that are commercial in nature or in which the arts are not the primary focus (e.g. sidewalk sales, food festivals, fireworks displays); or home-season engagements. Applications for engagements that are less than 50 miles from the artist's home community must explain why the project should be considered a touring engagement. K-12, college, and university projects must include substantive participation and attendance from outside the school population.

Geographic Focus: Delaware, District of Columbia, Maryland, New Jersey, New York, Ohio, Pennsylvania, U.S. Virgin Islands, Virginia, West Virginia

Date(s) Application is Due: Feb 15; Oct 15

Amount of Grant: Up to 20,000 USD

Contact: Katie West; (215) 496-9424 ext. 4; katie@pennpat.org or info@pennpat.org Jenny Filer; (215) 496-9424 ext. 3; jenny@pennpat.org or info@pennpat.org

Internet: www.pennpat.org/Grants.aspx?id=114&ekmensel=216_submenu_228_btnlink

Sponsor: Pennsylvania Performing Arts on Tour

230 South Broad Street, Suite 1003

Philadelphia, PA 19102

PennPAT New Directions Grants for Presenters 1931

Created as a unique public/private partnership and administered by the Mid Atlantic Arts Foundation, Pennsylvania Performing Arts on Tour (PennPAT) increases opportunities for professional Pennsylvania-based performing artists to obtain successful touring engagements in Pennsylvania and other states. To this end, PennPAT provides grants and marketing support to both presenters and artists, as well as training for artists. PennPat offers three types of grants to presenting organizations: Fee-Support Grants, New Directions Grants, and Presenter Travel Grants. New Directions Grants provide funding to presenters in support of touring engagements with artists listed on the PennPAT Artist Roster. Unlike the Fee-Support Grants, New Directions Grants provide support for more complex projects that fall outside the scope of traditional presenting models. These longer-term projects should offer an opportunity for both creative and audience development for the roster artist involved and should build relationships among artists, presenters and community members through collaborative activities while presenting at least one public performance. New Directions have two application deadlines: February 15 for projects that fall within a two year period beginning the following June; and October 15 for projects that fall within a two-year and three-month period beginning the following February. Applications must be submitted through the Mid Atlantic Arts Foundation eGrant system (link is available from the PennPAT website) by the deadline date. Applications must also be mailed to PennPAT and postmarked by the deadline date. New Directions Grants will fund up to to 50% of the total project costs. Eligible project costs may include the following expenses for planning and implementing the project: artist fees and travel expenses, marketing and publicity, printing, space rental, technical costs, and reasonable administrative costs. Project costs are often capped at $30,000 per grant. Complete application guidelines (PDF) can be downloaded from the grant website. Applicants are also encouraged to read the FAQ section of the website.

Requirements: Presenters applying for New Directions grants must contact the PennPAT Director in advance. To be eligible for New Directions grants, applicants must meet PennPat's definition of a presenting organization; be a 501(c)3 organization or a unit of government; and be located in Delaware, the District of Columbia, Maryland, New Jersey, New York, Ohio, Pennsylvania, the U.S. Virgin Islands, Virginia, or West Virginia. Eligible projects must be jointly submitted and include a tentative contract for an engagement with a PennPAT roster artist (who lives or is based outside the community where the presentation will take place); include at least one public performance at a venue within the eligible states/jurisdictions listed above; provide the PennPAT roster artist with an extended residency (at least seven days) that will allow time and conditions conducive to the artist's personal creative development; and include activities that will promote greater understanding of the roster artist's work and/or increase or broaden audiences for the roster artist's public performance. A presenting organization is defined as an organization that selects, engages and pays touring performing artists to perform works created elsewhere by those or other artists, which will be performed in many locations. Presenters manage all local arrangements for the performance (e.g. providing space, local technical support, advertising/promotion) and facilitate the interaction between artists and audiences.

Restrictions: Generally, a roster artist will not be funded for more than one New Directions project per year. Presenters may apply at more than one deadline for Fee-Support and New Directions grants. Presenters may request funds for more than one artist, however, they must submit a separate application for each separately contracted engagement. Applicants must not have any overdue outstanding reports from previous PennPAT or Mid Atlantic Foundation grants. PennPAT will not fund the following activities: programs or events that primarily serve a confined audience (e.g. K-12 schools, university classes, summer camps, nursing homes); arts-in-education projects; programs or events in which the roster artist is not the primary focus of the performance; fundraising events; programs or events that are commercial in nature or in which the arts are not the primary focus (e.g. sidewalk sales, food festivals, fireworks displays); or home-season engagements. Applications for engagements that are less than 50 miles from the artist's home community must explain why the project should be considered a touring engagement. K-12, college, and university projects must include substantive participation and attendance from outside the school population.

Geographic Focus: Delaware, District of Columbia, Maryland, New Jersey, New York, Ohio, Pennsylvania, U.S. Virgin Islands, Virginia, West Virginia

Date(s) Application is Due: Feb 15; Oct 15

Amount of Grant: Up to 30,000 USD

Contact: Katie West; (215) 496-9424 ext. 4; katie@pennpat.org or info@pennpat.org
Jenny Filer; (215) 496-9424 ext. 3; jenny@pennpat.org or info@pennpat.org

Internet: www.pennpat.org/Grants.aspx?id=114&ekmensel=216_submenu_228_btnlink

Sponsor: Pennsylvania Performing Arts on Tour
230 South Broad Street, Suite 1003
Philadelphia, PA 19102

PennPAT Presenter Travel Grants 1932

Created as a unique public/private partnership and administered by the Mid Atlantic Arts Foundation, Pennsylvania Performing Arts on Tour (PennPAT) increases opportunities for professional Pennsylvania-based performing artists to obtain successful touring engagements in Pennsylvania and other states. To this end, PennPAT provides grants and marketing support to both presenters and artists, as well as training for artists. PennPat offers three types of grants to presenting organizations: Presenter Travel Grants, Fee-Support Grants, and New Directions Grants. Presenter Travel Grants are provided to U.S. presenters who are interested in booking a PennPAT roster artist and would like to first see a live performance by that artist. Funds may be used to attend a full public performance by a PennPAT roster artist, either at home or on tour (presenter may be based anywhere in the U.S.). Grants are available for up to $500 and may cover, on a reimbursement basis, up to 100% of reasonable travel/lodging cash expenses related to this project. Applications must be received at the PennPAT office at least six weeks prior to the performance date. Applicants will be notified on the status of their proposal within

four weeks of the application receipt date. The grant application may be downloaded from the grant website.

Requirements: Applicants must be 501(c)3 organizations or units of governments based within the United States that present touring performing artists and groups.

Restrictions: Conference registration fees are NOT eligible. Organizations may receive up to two Presenter Travel Grants per year. Applicants must not have any overdue outstanding reports from previous PennPAT or Mid Atlantic Foundation grants.

Geographic Focus: All States

Amount of Grant: Up to 500 USD

Contact: Katie West; (215) 496-9424 ext. 3; katie@pennpat.org or info@pennpat.org
Jenny Filer; (215) 496-9424 ext. 3; jenny@pennpat.org or info@pennpat.org

Internet: www.pennpat.org/Grants.aspx?id=114&ekmensel=216_submenu_228_btnlink

Sponsor: Pennsylvania Performing Arts on Tour
230 South Broad Street, Suite 1003
Philadelphia, PA 19102

PennPAT Strategic Opportunity Grants 1933

Created as a unique public/private partnership and administered by the Mid Atlantic Arts Foundation, Pennsylvania Performing Arts on Tour (PennPAT) increases opportunities for professional Pennsylvania-based performing artists to obtain successful touring engagements in Pennsylvania and other states. Artists may apply directly for two types of grants: Artist Technical Assistance Grants and Strategic Opportunity Grants. Strategic Opportunity Grants support artists' overseas travel costs for international touring engagements that represent a strategic opportunity for the artist to expand his/her future touring ability. Prospective applicants must first contact the PennPAT Director to discuss the project. If the project is deemed eligible, PennPAT will email or mail the guidelines and application to the applicant. Artists may submit applications on an ongoing basis, at least six weeks prior to the start of the proposed project. Grants will generally be awarded for up to 50% of reasonable cash expenses for travel and lodging, up to a maximum of $5,000 per calendar year.

Requirements: Projects must include at least one performance that is open to and marketed to the general public. Applicants must be included in the PennPAT artist roster for the time in which the project will take place. Information on how to be included in the artist roster is available at the PennPAT website. In addition, the applicant must have submitted all final reports on previous PennPAT and Mid Atlantic Foundation projects by the report due date.

Restrictions: Mid Atlantic Arts Foundation also provides grants for international touring engagements through the USArtists International (USAI) program. PennPAT roster artists must explore PennPAT Strategic Opportunity Grants as a first option for support of international touring engagements. If a PennPAT roster artist also chooses to apply to USAI, the maximum amount of support for a single project through both programs combined will not exceed $15,000. Grants will NOT support the following activities and expenses: engagements that consist primarily of workshops, training or conference sessions; engagements in which the artist must produce their own performances (e.g. artists who are self-selected, have no established venue, or receive no artistic fee other than percentage of box office receipts); events that are academic in nature, are competitions, or for which ensembles must pay a participation, registration, or tuition fee; and purchase of equipment, supplies, or other costs related to normal business activities.

Geographic Focus: Pennsylvania

Contact: Katie West; (215) 496-9424 ext. 4; katie@pennpat.org or info@pennpat.org
Jenny Filer; (215) 496-9424 ext. 3; jenny@pennpat.org

Internet: www.pennpat.org/Grants.aspx?id=126&ekmensel=216_submenu_286_btnlink

Sponsor: Pennsylvania Performing Arts on Tour
230 South Broad Street, Suite 1003
Philadelphia, PA 19102

Pentair Foundation Education and Community Grants 1934

The Pentair Foundation focuses awards in two focus areas: education and community projects. Educational projects should focus on: supporting science and math education; providing "school-to-work" initiatives that prepare a student for the professional world; projects that offer alternative education; and programs that support art education. Community programs should focus on: water quality education, conservation and action; assistance to individuals in achieving self-sufficiency; entrepreneurial opportunities; opportunities for youth to gain life skills; services for youth in crisis; access to health care services; and assistance, education and rehabilitation services for those suffering from mental and/or physical disabilities and life-threatening illness.

Requirements: Nonprofit organizations, including schools and school districts, in communities where Pentair has a presence may apply. Application must be completed online and is located at the Foundation's website.

Restrictions: The foundation does not support individuals; political, lobbying, or fraternal activities; religious groups for religious purposes; medical research by individuals; scholarships to individuals; fundraising events, sponsorships, or advertising support; travel or tour expenses; conferences, seminars, workshops, or symposiums; athletic or sports-related organizations; non 501(c)3 organizations or those operating under a fiscal agent.

Geographic Focus: Wisconsin

Date(s) Application is Due: Mar 1; Jun 1; Oct 1

Amount of Grant: 2,000 - 50,000 USD

Samples: Casa Pacifica Centers for Children and Families, Camarillo, California, $15,654- project support; Center for Excellence in Education, McLean, Virginia, $2,268- general operating support

Contact: Susan Carter, Grants Administrator; (763) 656-5237; susan.carter@pentair.com

Internet: www.pentair.com/About_pentair_foundation.aspx

Sponsor: Pentair Foundation
5500 Wayzata Boulevard, Suite 800
Minneapolis, MN 55416

PepsiCo Foundation Grants   1935

The foundation's three focus areas include health (food security, improved and optimum nutrition, and energy balance), environment (water security, sustainable agriculture, and adaptive approaches to climate change), and education (access to education, dropout prevention, women's empowerment, and skills training for the under-served). Additionally the foundation provides financial assistance, in-kind product donations, and human-resource contributions to help respond to people and communities affected by major disasters. The foundation divides its grants into two categories: major requests (over $100,000) and other requests ($100,000 and under). Foundation staff must solicit proposals for all major grants. All other requests must be submitted as a Letter of Interest (LOI) to the email address given. Specific guidelines for LOI contents are available at the website. LOIs are reviewed on a rolling basis. Consideration regularly takes several months, especially during peak periods. PepsiCo Foundation was established in 1962 for charitable and educational purposes. In the 1970s, the Foundation began to support fitness research, and by the 1980s had established a focus on preventive medicine. Later, the Foundation's focus was expanded to funding fitness education for youth. Today the foundation has evolved its goals to reflect the needs of under-served populations and has extended its grant-making to the global community.
Requirements: Eligible organizations must have official tax-exempt status under Section 501(c)3 of the Internal Revenue Code (or the equivalent of such status) and have a primary focus in the areas of health, environment, or education. In evaluating requests, the foundation will consider the following criteria: the extent to which the request addresses specific goals, methodologies, and approaches; the degree to which the request advances or fulfills PepsiCo Foundation's stated goals and priorities; evidence of proven success in the field or scope of work specific to the request; and a method by which to measure and track impact and progress.
Restrictions: PepsiCo Foundation does not fund the following entities (or causes): individuals; private charities or foundations; organizations not exempt under Section 501(c)3 of the Internal Revenue Code and not eligible for tax-deductible support; religious organizations; political causes, candidates, organizations, or campaigns; organizations that discriminate on the basis of age, race, citizenship or national origin, disability or disabled-veteran status, gender, religion, marital status, sexual orientation, military service or status, or Vietnam-era veteran status; organizations whose primary purpose is to influence legislation; endowments or capital campaigns; playgrounds, sports fields, or equipment; film, music, TV, video, and media production companies; sports sponsorships; performing arts tours; and association memberships.
Geographic Focus: All States, All Countries
Amount of Grant: Up to 100,000 USD
Samples: Save the Children, Westport Connecticut, $3 million - to help promote the survival and well-being of children living in rural India and Bangladesh; Safe Water Network, Westport, Connecticut, $3.35 million - to implement safe water initiatives for village water systems in Ghana, India, and Kenya, as well as rainwater-harvesting systems in India; Diplomas Now, Baltimore, Maryland, $6 million - to invest in a proven approach to helping the toughest schools in America's largest cities succeed in helping every student graduate, ready for college or a career.
Contact: Maura Smith, President; (914) 253-3153 or (914) 253-2000; fax (914) 253-2788; pepsico.foundation@pepsico.com
Internet: www.pepsico.com/Purpose/PepsiCo-Foundation/Grants.html
Sponsor: PepsiCo Foundation
700 Anderson Hill Road
Purchase, NY 10577

Percy B. Ferebee Endowment Grants   1936

Grants from the Percy B. Ferebee Endowment are awarded to support charitable, scientific and literary projects, and in particular, governmental and civic projects designed to further the cultural, social, economic and physical well-being of residents of Cherokee, Clay, Graham, Jackson, Macon and Swain Counties of North Carolina and the Cherokee Indian Reservation. Grants are also awarded in the form of scholarships to assist worthy and talented young men and women who reside in said counties in pursuing their college/university degree education within the state of North Carolina. The deadline for the submission of a grant application is September 30. The deadline for scholarship applications is January 31. Application forms are available online. Applicants will receive notice acknowledging receipt of the grant request, and subsequently be notified of the grant declination or approval.
Requirements: 501(c)3 non-profits in the Cherokee, Clay, Graham, Jackson, Macon and Swain Counties of North Carolina are eligible to apply for grants. Proposals should be submitted in the following format: completed Common Grant Application Form; an original Proposal Statement; an audited financial report and a current year operating budget; a copy of your official IRS Letter with your tax determination; a listing of your Board of Directors. Proposal Statements (second item in the above Format) should answer these questions: what are the objectives and expected outcomes of this program/project/request; what strategies will be used to accomplish your objective; what is the timeline for completion; if this is part of an on-going program, how long has it been in operation; what criteria will you use to measure success; if the request is not fully funded, what other sources can you engage; an Itemized budget should be included; please describe any collaborative ventures. Prior to the distribution of funds, all approved grantees must sign and return a Grant Agreement Form, stating that the funds will be used for the purpose intended. Progress reports and Completion reports must also be filed as required for your specific grant. All current grantees must be in good standing with required documentation prior to submitting new proposals to any foundation. Scholarship recipients must be a resident of these areas and must attend a college or university in the state of North Carolina. Contact the Foundation for additional application requirements.
Restrictions: Grants are not made for political purposes, nor to organizations which discriminate on the basis of race, ethnic origin, sexual or religious preference, age or gender.
Geographic Focus: North Carolina
Date(s) Application is Due: Jan 31; Sep 30

Amount of Grant: 3,000 - 15,000 USD
Samples: Nantahala Regional Library, $15,000—general operating support; Macon County Historical Society, $7,500—general operating expenses; Reach, Inc. Resources Education Assistance Counseling & Housing, $4,000—general operating support.
Contact: Wachovia Bank, N.A., Trustee; grantinquiries6@wachovia.com
Internet: www.wellsfargo.com/private-foundations/ferebee-endowment
Sponsor: Percy B. Ferebee Endowment
Wachovia Bank, NC6732, 100 North Main Street
Winston Salem, NC 27150

Perkin Fund Grants   1937

Established in 1967 in New York, the Perkin Fund is a charitable family foundation that provides grants to established institutions in the fields of astronomy, medicine and scientific research. In recent years, the Fund has also supported leading institutions in the arts, education and social services. The Fund reflects the broad interests of the founders, Richard S. and Gladys T. Perkin, and their family. Prior to his death in 1969, Mr. Perkin had been a founder and Chairman of the Board of the Perkin-Elmer Corporation, a leading manufacturer of scientific instruments and optical systems. Following Perkin's death, and until her death in 2001, Mrs. Perkin served as Chairman of the Board of Trustees of the Perkin Fund, lending her support to the advancement of scientific endeavors. Today, the Perkin Fund continues to be led by members of the Perkin family who, along with non-family Trustees, serve the Perkin Fund without compensation. The Fund continues to be primarily interested in scientific research, education, medicine and related disciplines. However, over the past twenty years, the Fund has grown in size and broadened its mandate. This has enabled the Trustees to consider a limited number of requests in the areas of human services and the arts. The Fund bases its grants on written requests from qualified institutions for support of worthwhile projects and programs. The Trustees evaluate these proposals to determine which are deemed especially important and fall within the Fund's guidelines. Types of support have included: annual campaigns; capital and infrastructure; continuing support; endowments; equipment purchase and rental; fellowships; general operating support; program development; and research and research evaluation. Recent award amounts have ranged up to a maximum of $50,000.
Requirements: Giving is primarily limited to 501(c)3 organizations that support the residents in Connecticut, Massachusetts, and New York.
Geographic Focus: Connecticut, Massachusetts, New York
Date(s) Application is Due: Mar 15; Sep 15
Amount of Grant: Up to 50,000 USD
Samples: Blue Ocean Society for Marine Conservation, Portsmouth, New Hampshire, $25,000 - general operating support; Columbia Business School, New York, New York, $20,000 - general operating support; Harvard Fencing Team, Cambridge, Massachusetts, $50,000 - general operating support.
Contact: Winifred P. Gray, Program Contact; (978) 468-2266; theperkinfund@verizon.net
Sponsor: Perkin Fund
176 Bay Road, P.O. Box 2220
South Hamilton, MA 01982-2232

Perkins-Ponder Foundation Grants   1938

The mission of the Perkins-Ponder Foundation is to assist charitable organizations that provide for the aid and assistance of dependent and economically disadvantaged, aged females and under-privileged children of Bibb County. Grants from the Perkins-Ponder Foundation are primarily 1 year in duration. On occasion, multi-year support is awarded. Award amounts typically range from $2,000 to $45,000.
Requirements: Applicants must have 501(c)3 tax-exempt status. Applicants must serve the residents of Bibb County, Georgia. Applications will be submitted online through the Bank of America website. A grant report is required within 1 year of the grant application date, regardless of whether all of the funds have been spent.
Restrictions: The foundation does not support requests from individuals, organizations attempting to influence policy through direct lobbying, or any political campaigns.
Geographic Focus: Georgia
Date(s) Application is Due: Feb 1
Amount of Grant: 2,000 - 45,000 USD
Samples: Boys and Girls Clubs of Central Georgia Inc., Macon, Georgia, $7,500 - awarded for Project Learn (2019); The Mentors Project of Bibb County Inc., Macon, Georgia, $7,500 - awarded for general operations of the organization (2019); Twin Cedars Youth and Family Services Inc., La Grange, Georgia, $6,000 - awarded for general operations of the organization (2019).
Contact: Mark S. Drake, Vice President; (404) 264-1377; ga.grantmaking@bankofamerica.com or mark.s.drake@bofa.com
Internet: www.bankofamerica.com/philanthropic/foundation/?fnId=102
Sponsor: Perkins-Ponder Foundation
P.O. Box 40200, FL9-100-10-19
Jacksonville, FL 32203-0200

Perkins Charitable Foundation Grants   1939

In 1835, Akron was just a village. The Perkins family was determined to help it become something greater. Surveyor General Simon Perkins influenced Ohio politicians to ensure that the Ohio and Erie Canal ran through Akron. That decision helped the village become a major transportation and business hub. And although General Simon Perkins remained in Warren, he sent his son, Colonel Simon Perkins, to Akron to oversee the family's business interests here. The Perkins Charitable Foundation Trust was established in 1950, by members of the Perkins family. The Foundation gives primarily for elementary and secondary education, higher education, the arts, environmental conservation, animals, wildlife, health and medical care, and children, youth and social services. The Foundation

offers funding on a national basis, with some emphasis on Ohio and Vermont. Typically takes the form of general operating funding, program development, and re-granting.
Requirements: Contact the Foundation's office by letter or phone prior to your proposal. No Application form is required, and there are no specific annual deadlines for submission.
Restrictions: No grants are given to individuals.
Geographic Focus: All States, California, Connecticut, Florida, Massachusetts, Ohio, Rhode Island, Vermont, Virginia
Amount of Grant: Up to 62,000 USD
Samples: Madeira School, McLean, Virginia, $62,000 - general operating support; Nature Conservancy, Idaho Falls, Idaho, $10,000 - general operating support; Thomas County Humane Society, Thomasville, Georgia, $7,000 - general operating support.
Contact: Marilyn Best, Secretary; (216) 621-0465
Sponsor: Perkins Charitable Foundation
1030 Hanna Building, 1422 Euclid Avenue
Cleveland, OH 44115-2001

Perpetual Benevolent Fund   1940
Established in 1932, the Perpetual Benevolent Fund assists residents of Newton, Waltham and Watertown, Massachusetts who are experiencing financial hardship. The Fund makes grants to public charities working to relieve the financial burden of local individuals and families in crisis. Award amounts typically range from $5,000 to $45,000. Grants are awarded twice annually.
Requirements: Grants are made to public charities that serve individuals and families in Newton, Waltham and Watertown. Applications will be submitted online through the Bank of America website. A grant report is required within 1 year of the grant application date, regardless of whether all of the funds have been spent.
Restrictions: Applications for general operating support, endowment, capital projects or multi-year funding are not accepted. Only one application will be accepted from an organization during a twelve-month period. The fund does not support requests from individuals, organizations attempting to influence policy through direct lobbying, or any political campaigns.
Geographic Focus: Massachusetts
Date(s) Application is Due: Mar 1; Sep 1
Amount of Grant: 5,000 - 45,000 USD
Samples: Springwell Inc., Watertown, Massachusetts, $15,000 - Awarded for Nutrition Program for Vulnerable Seniors (2018); Boys and Girls Club of Newton, Newton, Massachusetts, $15,000 - Awarded for Summer Day Camp Tuition Financial Aid for Teens and Youth from Families in Need (2018); Newton Community Service Center, Newton, Massachusetts, $10,000 - Awarded for counseling and consultation services and early literacy program grant (2018).
Contact: Michealle Larkins; (866) 778-6859; ma.grantmaking@bankofamerica.com
Internet: www.bankofamerica.com/philanthropic/foundation/?fnId=141
Sponsor: Perpetual Benevolent Fund
P.O .Box 1802
Providence, RI 02901-1802

Perry and Sandy Massie Foundation Grants   1941
Perry Massie is the other son of Buzzard Massie, founder of the Gold Prospectors Association of America, an organization dedicated to finding and mining gold on a small, recreational scale. The organization was founded in 1968 "to preserve and promote the great heritage of the North American Prospector." Today, Perry and his wife, Sandy, are co-directors of the Perry and Sandy Massie Foundation, with primary fields of interest including: adult and child mentoring; community college education; elementary and secondary education; human services; and youth development. The Foundation's geographic focus is the State of Arizona, particularly the Prescott region, though a few awards are given in other states. Most recent grant awards have ranged from $1,000 to $375,000. There are no annual deadlines with which to adhere, and interested parties should submit a letter of application to the Foundation office.
Requirements: Any 501(c)3 organization serving the residents of Prescott, Arizona, and its surrounding area is eligible to apply.
Geographic Focus: Arizona
Amount of Grant: Up to 375,000 USD
Samples: Boys to Men Mentoring, Prescott, Arizona, $50,000 - general operating support; Yavapai Big Brothers and Big Sisters, Prescott, Arizona, $371,337 - general operating support; Yavapai College Foundation, Prescott, Arizona, $270,000 - general operating support.
Contact: Perry Massie, Director; (800) 551-9707 or (928) 717-1480
Sponsor: Perry and Sandy Massie Foundation
2004 Promontory
Prescott, AZ 86305-2520

Perry County Community Foundation Recreation Grants   1942
The Perry County Community Foundation is a nonprofit, public charity created for the people of Perry County, Indiana. The Foundation connects donors with the causes they care about. The Foundation will accept grant proposals from all charitable organizations seeking funding; however, special attention will be given to projects that promote healthy living and that offer training and/or support to potential small business entrepreneurship. The Foundation considers proposals for grants on a yearly cycle which begins each July 7 and runs through the annual deadline of September 14. At the start of each cycle, a notice is mailed to nonprofit organizations that have applied for or received grants in the past, or have otherwise requested notification of the start of each cycle. The grant committee makes its recommendations on funding to the Foundation's Board of Trustees, which will make final funding recommendations to the board of directors of the Community Foundation Alliance. All organizations who submit proposals are notified of committee's decision no later than December 1. Grants in the area of Recreation include projects aimed at improving

and promoting recreational and leisure activities, parks, and community sporting events and activities. Samples of previously funded projects are available at the website.
Requirements: The Foundation welcomes proposals from nonprofit organizations that are 501(c)3 and 509(a) tax-exempt under the IRS code and from governmental agencies serving the County of Perry, Indiana. Proposals from nonprofit organizations not classified as a 501(c)3 public charity may be considered if the project is charitable and supports a community need. Proposals submitted by an entity under the auspices of another agency must include a written statement signed by the agency's board president on behalf of the board of directors agreeing to act as the entity's fiscal sponsor, to receive grant monies if awarded, and to oversee the proposed project.
Restrictions: Project areas not considered for funding: religious organizations for religious purposes; political parties or campaigns; endowment creation or debt reduction; operating costs; capital campaigns; annual appeals or membership contributions; travel requests for groups or individuals such as bands, sports teams, or classes.
Geographic Focus: Indiana
Date(s) Application is Due: Sep 14
Contact: Renate Warner, Regional Director of Community Engagement and Impact; (812) 547-3176; rwarner@communityfoundationalliance.org or research@newberry.org
Internet: www.communityfoundationalliance.org/perry/program-areas/
Sponsor: Perry County Community Foundation
817 12th Street, P.O. Box 13
Tell City, IN 47586-1785

Perry County Community Foundation Youth Development Grants   1943
The Perry County Community Foundation is a nonprofit, public charity created for the people of Perry County, Indiana. The Foundation connects donors with the causes they care about. The Foundation will accept grant proposals from all charitable organizations seeking funding; however, special attention will be given to projects that promote healthy living and that offer training and/or support to potential small business entrepreneurship. The Foundation considers proposals for grants on a yearly cycle which begins each July 7 and runs through the annual deadline of September 14. At the start of each cycle, a notice is mailed to nonprofit organizations that have applied for or received grants in the past, or have otherwise requested notification of the start of each cycle. The grant committee makes its recommendations on funding to the Foundation's Board of Trustees, which will make final funding recommendations to the board of directors of the Community Foundation Alliance. All organizations who submit proposals are notified of committee's decision no later than December 1. Grants in the area of Youth Development include activities that strengthen the family unit, help children grow and develop, foster youth sports and athletics, support the YMCA, and support daycare-related issues. Samples of previously funded projects are available at the website.
Requirements: The Foundation welcomes proposals from nonprofit organizations that are 501(c)3 and 509(a) tax-exempt under the IRS code and from governmental agencies serving the County of Perry, Indiana. Proposals from nonprofit organizations not classified as a 501(c)3 public charity may be considered if the project is charitable and supports a community need. Proposals submitted by an entity under the auspices of another agency must include a written statement signed by the agency's board president on behalf of the board of directors agreeing to act as the entity's fiscal sponsor, to receive grant monies if awarded, and to oversee the proposed project.
Restrictions: Project areas not considered for funding: religious organizations for religious purposes; political parties or campaigns; endowment creation or debt reduction; operating costs; capital campaigns; annual appeals or membership contributions; travel requests for groups or individuals such as bands, sports teams, or classes.
Geographic Focus: Indiana
Date(s) Application is Due: Sep 14
Contact: Renate Warner; (812) 547-3176; rwarner@communityfoundationalliance.org or renate@perrycommunityfoundation.org
Internet: www.communityfoundationalliance.org/perry/program-areas/
Sponsor: Perry County Community Foundation
817 12th Street, P.O. Box 13
Tell City, IN 47586-1785

Peter and Elizabeth C. Tower Foundation Intellectual Disabilities Grants   1944
Elizabeth Nelson Clarke was born in Mt. Vernon, New York, in 1920, and Peter Tower in Niagara Falls, New York, in 1921. They met while attending Cornell University and married in the summer of 1942. Two daughters, Mollie and Cynthia, were born in 1944 and 1947. Peter entered the Army Air Force in January 1943. After service in Texas and Europe, he hoped to find work in the fledgling air transport business which he expected to thrive. Taking a "temporary" clerk job for the family's customhouse broker business C. J. Tower and Sons, he stayed on to see the partnership evolve into a corporation. In 1986 it processed a total of $45 billion worth of merchandise and Peter then sold the business to McGraw-Hill Inc. who later sold it to the Federal Express Company, which utilizes Tower skills and systems worldwide. Meanwhile, Liz, who had studied art at Cornell, had become a notable artist, working mostly in oils. True to other personal philosophies, Peter and Liz knew that with prosperity came responsibility. Their desire was to assure that the resources they had acquired over the years were put to good use and to see the benefits spread among many. Formed December 31, 1990, the Peter and Elizabeth C. Tower Foundation seeks to support community programming that will help children, adolescents, and young adults affected by substance abuse, learning disabilities, mental illness, and intellectual disabilities achieve their full potential. The foundation's funding objective in the intellectual disabilities category is to improve service delivery for children, adolescents, and young adults to age 26 with intellectual disabilities. The foundation defines an intellectual disability as a disability characterized by significant limitations both in intellectual functioning and adaptive behavior, which covers many everyday social and practical skills. This disability

originates before the age of 18. The Foundation will give preference to projects addressing one or more of the following priority areas: reducing obstacles to seeking services/treatment; stigma reduction; transitional services; early identification and linkage to services; effective treatment/programming; co-occurring disorders; and provider workforce shortage and readiness (capacity building). The foundation will also consider other project ideas that have the potential to advance its objective in the category. Typical funding range is $25,000 to $75,000 per year. Multi-year grants are encouraged; projects should be sustainable after grant funding ends. Preference is given to projects where the majority of costs are both new to the organization and directly related to the proposed initiative. Applicants must first call the foundation to clarify the intent, scope, and details of the technology initiative; establish the organization's eligibility for the initiative; and to discuss their capacity and readiness to undertake the technology planning process. Based on this telephone call, the Foundation will determine whether or not it wishes to request a full application from the organization. Arrangements for this pre-screening telephone call must be made prior to January 24 for the first funding cycle, May 16 for the second funding cycle, or August 29 for the third funding cycle. The deadlines for full proposals are February 7 for the first cycle, May 30 for the second cycle, and September 12 for the third cycle. Successful applicants will be notified by April 11, August 1, November 14.

Requirements: Letters of inquiry must be mailed or hand-delivered. Emailed and faxed copies will not be accepted. Signature of organization's Executive Director, Superintendent or Headmaster is required; designee signatures are not acceptable.

Restrictions: The Foundation accepts only one letter of inquiry per applicant. The Foundation makes grants only to: tax-exempt organizations with 501(c)3 tax-exempt status from the Internal Revenue Service that are neither private foundations nor described as 509(a)3 organizations; diocesan and public school districts; charter schools; and to nonprofit public benefit corporations. Organizations must be located in and primarily serve residents of one of the following geographic areas: Barnstable County, Massachusetts; Dukes County, Massachusetts; Essex County, Massachusetts; Nantucket County, Massachusetts; Erie County, New York; or Niagara County, New York. The Foundation does not provide funds that: may be used for the private benefit of any grant recipient or affiliated person; attempt to influence legislation; attempt to influence or intervene in any political campaign; support capital campaigns or improvements; support individual scholarships; provide general operating support; or that subsidize individuals for the cost of care.

Geographic Focus: Massachusetts, New York
Date(s) Application is Due: Feb 7; May 30; Sep 12
Amount of Grant: 25,000 - 75,000 USD
Contact: Tracy A. Sawicki, Executive Director; (716) 689-0370; fax (716) 689-3716; info@thetowerfoundation.org or tas@thetowerfoundation.org
Donald W. Matteson; (716) 689-0370; fax (716) 689-3716; dwm@thetowerfoundation.org
Internet: thetowerfoundation.org/what-we-fund/core-issues/
Sponsor: Peter and Elizabeth C. Tower Foundation
2351 North Forest Road
Getzville, NY 14068-1225

Peter and Elizabeth C. Tower Foundation Learning Disability Grants   1945

Elizabeth Nelson Clarke was born in Mt. Vernon, New York, in 1920, and Peter Tower in Niagara Falls, New York, in 1921. They met while attending Cornell University and married in the summer of 1942. Peter entered the Army Air Force in January 1943. After serving in Texas and Europe, he took a "temporary" clerk job for the family's customhouse broker business C. J. Tower and Sons. Two daughters, Mollie and Cynthia, were born in 1944 and 1947. Although he had hoped to find work in the fledgling air transport business which he expected to thrive, he stayed with Tower and Sons to see the partnership evolve into a corporation. In 1986 it processed a total of $45 billion worth of merchandise and Peter then sold the business to McGraw-Hill Inc. who later sold it to the Federal Express Company, which utilizes Tower skills and systems worldwide. Meanwhile, Liz, who had studied art at Cornell, had become a notable artist, working mostly in oils. True to other personal philosophies, Peter and Liz knew that with prosperity came responsibility. Their desire was to assure that the resources they had acquired over the years were put to good use and that the benefits were spread among many. Formed December 31, 1990, the Peter and Elizabeth C. Tower Foundation supports community programming that helps children, adolescents, and young adults affected by substance abuse, learning disabilities, mental illness, and intellectual disabilities achieve their full potential. Learning disabilities are defined as neurological disorders affecting the brain's ability to receive, process, store, and respond to information. These constitute disorders in one or more of the basic psychological processes involved in understanding or using language, spoken or written, and may manifest themselves in the imperfect ability to listen, think, speak, read, write, spell or do mathematical calculations. These disorders do not include learning problems that are primarily the result of visual, hearing, or motor abilities, of mental retardation, of emotional disturbance, of traumatic brain injury, or of environmental, cultural, or economic disadvantage. Typical funding range is $25,000 to $75,000 per year. Multi-year grants are encouraged; projects should be sustainable after grant funding ends. Preference is given to projects where the majority of costs are both new to the organization and directly related to the proposed initiative. Applicants must first call the foundation to clarify the intent, scope, and details of the technology initiative; establish the organization's eligibility for the initiative; and to discuss their capacity and readiness to undertake the technology planning process. Based on this telephone call, the Foundation will determine whether or not it wishes to request a full application from the organization. Arrangements for this pre-screening telephone call must be made prior to January 24 for the first funding cycle, May 16 for the second funding cycle, or August 29 for the third funding cycle. The deadlines for full proposals are February 7 for the first cycle, May 30 for the second cycle, and September 12 for the third cycle. Successful applicants will be notified by April 11, August 1, November 14.

Requirements: Eligible organizations must focus on providing services and programming that will help children, adolescents, and young adults affected by substance abuse, learning disabilities, mental illness, and intellectual disabilities achieve their full potential.

Restrictions: Certain general restrictions apply to all grant-seeking organizations. The Foundation makes grants only to the following: tax-exempt organizations with 501(c)3 tax-exempt status that are neither private foundations nor described as 509(a)3 organizations; diocesan and public school districts; charter schools; and nonprofit public benefit corporations. Organizations must be located in and primarily serve residents of one of the following geographic areas: Barnstable County, Massachusetts; Dukes County, Massachusetts; Essex County, Massachusetts; Nantucket County, Massachusetts; Erie County, New York; or Niagara County, New York. The Foundation does not provide funds for the following purposes: the private benefit of any grant recipient or affiliated person; attempts to influence legislation; attempts to influence or intervene in any political campaign; capital campaigns or improvements; individual scholarships; general operating support; or subsidy of individuals for the cost of care.

Geographic Focus: Massachusetts, New York
Date(s) Application is Due: Feb 7; May 30; Sep 12
Amount of Grant: 25,000 - 75,000 USD
Contact: Tracy A. Sawicki, Executive Director; (716) 689-0370; fax (716) 689-3716; info@thetowerfoundation.org or tas@thetowerfoundation.org
Donald W. Matteson; (716) 689-0370; fax (716) 689-3716; dwm@thetowerfoundation.org
Internet: thetowerfoundation.org/what-we-fund/core-issues/
Sponsor: Peter and Elizabeth C. Tower Foundation
2351 North Forest Road
Getzville, NY 14068-1225

Peter and Elizabeth C. Tower Foundation Mental Health Grants   1946

Elizabeth Nelson Clarke was born in Mt. Vernon, New York, in 1920, and Peter Tower in Niagara Falls, New York, in 1921. They met while attending Cornell University and married in the summer of 1942. Two daughters, Mollie and Cynthia, were born in 1944 and 1947. Peter entered the Army Air Force in January 1943. After service in Texas and Europe, he hoped to find work in the fledgling air transport business which he expected to thrive. Taking a "temporary" clerk job for the family's customhouse broker business C. J. Tower and Sons, he stayed on to see the partnership evolve into a corporation. In 1986 it processed a total of $45 billion worth of merchandise and Peter then sold the business to McGraw-Hill Inc. who later sold it to the Federal Express Company, which utilizes Tower skills and systems worldwide. Meanwhile, Liz, who had studied art at Cornell, had become a notable artist, working mostly in oils. True to other personal philosophies, Peter and Liz knew that with prosperity came responsibility. Their desire was to assure that the resources they had acquired over the years were put to good use and to see the benefits spread among many. Formed December 31, 1990, the Peter and Elizabeth C. Tower Foundation seeks to support community programming that will help children, adolescents, and young adults affected by substance abuse, learning disabilities, mental illness, and intellectual disabilities achieve their full potential. The foundation has a particular interest in serious mental illnesses, including major depression, schizophrenia, bipolar disorder, obsessive-compulsive disorder (OCD), panic disorder, post-traumatic stress disorder (PTSD) and borderline personality disorder. The foundation's annual mental health grants seek to prevent or alleviate psychological disorders in children, adolescents, and young adults to age 26. The foundation will give preference to projects involving one or more of the following priorities: providing direct benefit to individuals with serious mental illness; reducing barriers to seeking treatment or services; reducing stigma and prejudice often associated with mental illness; fostering social and emotional development; providing early identification and linkage to services; treating co-occurring disorders; offering life-skills programming for persons with serious mental illness; building provider workforce readiness (capacity building); providing indicated or selected prevention programming; and providing effective treatment/programming. The foundation will also consider other project ideas that have the potential to advance its objective in the category. Typical funding range is $25,000 to $75,000 per year. Multi-year grants are encouraged; projects should be sustainable after grant funding ends. Preference is given to projects where the majority of costs are both new to the organization and directly related to the proposed initiative. Applicants must first call the foundation to clarify the intent, scope, and details of the technology initiative; establish the organization's eligibility for the initiative; and to discuss their capacity and readiness to undertake the technology planning process. Based on this telephone call, the Foundation will determine whether or not it wishes to request a full application from the organization. Arrangements for this pre-screening telephone call must be made prior to January 24 for the first funding cycle, May 16 for the second funding cycle, or August 29 for the third funding cycle. The deadlines for full proposals are February 7 for the first cycle, May 30 for the second cycle, and September 12 for the third cycle. Successful applicants will be notified by April 11, August 1, November 14.

Requirements: To be eligible to apply, organizations must operate programs that provide services for children, adolescents, or young adults to age 26 with psychological disorders; and/or offer programming to prevent the onset of psychological disorders in children, adolescents, and young adults to age 26 who, based on a range of socio-economic factors, have a higher-than-average likelihood of developing these conditions. Letters of inquiry must be mailed or hand-delivered. Emailed and faxed copies will not be accepted. Signature of organization's Executive Director, Superintendent or Headmaster is required; designee signatures are not acceptable.

Restrictions: The Foundation accepts only one letter of inquiry per applicant. Universal programs (programs applied to general population groups without reference to or identification of those at particular risk) will not be considered for funding. Certain general restrictions apply to all grant-seeking organizations. The Foundation makes grants only to: tax-exempt organizations with 501(c)3 tax-exempt status from the Internal Revenue Service that are neither private foundations nor described as 509(a)3 organizations; diocesan and public school districts; charter schools; and to nonprofit public benefit corporations.

Organizations must be located in and primarily serve residents of one of the following geographic areas: Barnstable County, Massachusetts; Dukes County, Massachusetts; Essex County, Massachusetts; Nantucket County, Massachusetts; Erie County, New York; or Niagara County, New York. The Foundation does not provide funds that: may be used for the private benefit of any grant recipient or affiliated person; attempt to influence legislation; attempt to influence or intervene in any political campaign; support capital campaigns or improvements; support individual scholarships; provide general operating support; or that subsidize individuals for the cost of care.
Geographic Focus: Massachusetts, New York
Date(s) Application is Due: Feb 7; May 30; Sep 12
Amount of Grant: 25,000 - 75,000 USD
Contact: Tracy A. Sawicki, Executive Director; (716) 689-0370; fax (716) 689-3716; info@thetowerfoundation.com or tas@thetowerfoundation.org
Donald W. Matteson; (716) 689-0370; fax (716) 689-3716; dwm@thetowerfoundation.org
Internet: thetowerfoundation.org/what-we-fund/core-issues/
Sponsor: Peter and Elizabeth C. Tower Foundation
2351 North Forest Road
Getzville, NY 14068-1225

Peter and Elizabeth C. Tower Foundation Small Grants   1947
Elizabeth Nelson Clarke was born in Mt. Vernon, New York, in 1920, and Peter Tower in Niagara Falls, New York, in 1921. They met while attending Cornell University and married in the summer of 1942. Peter entered the Army Air Force in January 1943. After service in Texas and Europe, he hoped to find work in the fledgling air transport business which he expected to thrive. Taking a temporary clerk job for the family's customhouse broker business C. J. Tower and Sons, he stayed on to see the partnership evolve into a corporation. In 1986 it processed a total of $45 billion worth of merchandise and Peter then sold the business to McGraw-Hill Inc. who later sold it to the Federal Express Company, which utilizes Tower skills and systems worldwide. Meanwhile, Liz, who had studied art at Cornell, had become a notable artist, working mostly in oils. True to other personal philosophies, Peter and Liz knew that with prosperity came responsibility. Their desire was to assure that the resources they had acquired over the years were put to good use and to see the benefits spread among many. Formed December 31, 1990, the Peter and Elizabeth C. Tower Foundation seeks to support community programming that will help children, adolescents, and young adults affected by substance abuse, learning disabilities, mental illness, and intellectual disabilities achieve their full potential. The Mental Health Mini-Grant initiative seeks to prevent or alleviate psychological disorders in children, adolescents, and young adults up to age 26, as well as to build mental health providers' capacity. The small grants program provides funding for short-term organizational needs in a simplified and expedited manner. Eligible applicants can apply for a one-year grant of up to $30,000. Activities eligible for the Small Grant program include: capacity development activities (e.g. organizational assessments, strategic planning, leadership development, professional development for staff)' planning and development (distinct from service delivery); and one-time capital projects or equipment purchases. Applicants must first call the foundation to clarify the intent, scope, and details of the technology initiative; establish the organization's eligibility for the initiative; and to discuss their capacity and readiness to undertake the technology planning process. Based on this telephone call, the Foundation will determine whether or not it wishes to request a full application from the organization. Arrangements for this pre-screening telephone call must be made prior to January 24 for the first funding cycle, May 16 for the second funding cycle, or August 29 for the third funding cycle. The deadlines for full proposals are February 7 for the first cycle, May 30 for the second cycle, and September 12 for the third cycle. Successful applicants will be notified by April 11, August 1, November 14.
Requirements: Letters of application from community-based organizations must have the Executive Director/CEO's original signature. Requests from school districts, private schools, or charter schools must have the Superintendent/School Headmaster's original signature.
Restrictions: Only one request per community-based organization, charter school, private school or school district will be accepted. Small grant monies may not be used for: the purchase of office equipment, furniture or supplies; computers or smart boards; non-mental health reference materials or consumable items; screening or assessment tools; subscriptions to journals and/or newsletters; professional development or staff training; staff salaries or other general operating expense; or for capital improvements. Certain general restrictions apply to all grant-seeking organizations. The Foundation makes grants only to: tax-exempt organizations with 501(c)3 tax-exempt status from the Internal Revenue Service that are neither private foundations nor described as 509(a)3 organizations; diocesan and public school districts; charter schools; and to nonprofit public benefit corporations. Organizations must be located in and primarily serve residents of one of the following geographic areas: Barnstable County, Massachusetts; Dukes County, Massachusetts; Essex County, Massachusetts; Nantucket County, Massachusetts; Erie County, New York; or Niagara County, New York. The Foundation does not provide funds that: may be used for the private benefit of any grant recipient or affiliated person; attempt to influence legislation; attempt to influence or intervene in any political campaign; support capital campaigns or improvements; support individual scholarships; provide general operating support; or that subsidize individuals for the cost of care.
Geographic Focus: Massachusetts, New York
Date(s) Application is Due: Feb 7; May 30; Sep 12
Amount of Grant: Up to 30,000 USD
Contact: Tracy A. Sawicki, Executive Director; (716) 689-0370; fax (716) 689-3716; info@thetowerfoundation.org or tas@thetowerfoundation.org
Chuck Colston, Program Officer; (716) 689-0370 x206; cec@thetowerfoundation.org
Internet: thetowerfoundation.org/what-we-fund/grant-opportunities/
Sponsor: Peter and Elizabeth C. Tower Foundation
2351 North Forest Road
Getzville, NY 14068-1225

Peter and Elizabeth C. Tower Foundation Substance Use Disorders Grants   1948
Elizabeth Nelson Clarke was born in Mt. Vernon, New York, in 1920, and Peter Tower in Niagara Falls, New York, in 1921. They met while attending Cornell University and married in the summer of 1942. Peter entered the Army Air Force in January 1943. After serving in Texas and Europe, he took a "temporary" clerk job for the family's customhouse broker business C. J. Tower and Sons. Two daughters, Mollie and Cynthia, were born in 1944 and 1947. Although he had hoped to find work in the fledgling air transport business which he expected to thrive, he stayed with Tower and Sons to see the partnership evolve into a corporation. In 1986 it processed a total of $45 billion worth of merchandise and Peter then sold the business to McGraw-Hill Inc. who later sold it to the Federal Express Company, which utilizes Tower skills and systems worldwide. Meanwhile, Liz, who had studied art at Cornell, had become a notable artist, working mostly in oils. True to other personal philosophies, Peter and Liz knew that with prosperity came responsibility. Their desire was to assure that the resources they had acquired over the years were put to good use and that the benefits were spread among many. Formed December 31, 1990, the Peter and Elizabeth C. Tower Foundation supports community programming that helps children, adolescents, and young adults affected by substance abuse, learning disabilities, mental illness, and intellectual disabilities achieve their full potential. Substance Abuse is defined as the use of illegal drugs or the use of prescription or over-the-counter drugs or alcohol for purposes other than those prescribed, or in excessive amounts. Substance abuse may lead to social, physical, emotional, and job-related problems. The typical funding range is $25,000 to $75,000 per year. Multi-year grants are encouraged; projects should be sustainable after grant funding ends. Preference is given to projects where the majority of costs are both new to the organization and directly related to the proposed initiative. Applicants must first call the foundation to clarify the intent, scope, and details of the technology initiative; establish the organization's eligibility for the initiative; and to discuss their capacity and readiness to undertake the technology planning process. Based on this telephone call, the Foundation will determine whether or not it wishes to request a full application from the organization. Arrangements for this pre-screening telephone call must be made prior to January 24 for the first funding cycle, May 16 for the second funding cycle, or August 29 for the third funding cycle. The deadlines for full proposals are February 7 for the first cycle, May 30 for the second cycle, and September 12 for the third cycle. Successful applicants will be notified by April 11, August 1, November 14.
Requirements: Eligible organizations must focus on providing services and programming that help children, adolescents, and young adults affected by substance abuse, learning disabilities, mental illness, and intellectual disabilities to achieve their full potential.
Restrictions: Certain general restrictions apply to all grant-seeking organizations. The Foundation makes grants only to: tax-exempt organizations with 501(c)3 tax-exempt status that are neither private foundations nor described as 509(a)3 organizations; diocesan and public school districts; charter schools; and to nonprofit public benefit corporations. Organizations must be located in and primarily serve residents of one of the following geographic areas: Barnstable County, Massachusetts; Dukes County, Massachusetts; Essex County, Massachusetts; Nantucket County, Massachusetts; Erie County, New York; or Niagara County, New York. The Foundation does not provide funds for the following purposes: the private benefit of any grant recipient or affiliated person; attempts to influence legislation; attempts to influence or intervene in any political campaign; capital campaigns or improvements; individual scholarships; general operating support; or subsidy of individuals for the cost of care.
Geographic Focus: Massachusetts, New York
Date(s) Application is Due: Feb 7; May 30; Sep 12
Amount of Grant: 25,000 - 75,000 USD
Contact: Tracy A. Sawicki, Executive Director; (716) 689-0370; fax (716) 689-3716; info@thetowerfoundation.org or tas@thetowerfoundation.org
Donald W. Matteson; (716) 689-0370; fax (716) 689-3716; dwm@thetowerfoundation.org
Internet: thetowerfoundation.org/what-we-fund/core-issues/
Sponsor: Peter and Elizabeth C. Tower Foundation
2351 North Forest Road
Getzville, NY 14068-1225

Peter and Elizabeth C. Tower Foundation Technology Initiative Grants   1949
The Peter and Elizabeth C. Tower Technology Initiative program connects not-for-profit organizations to technological expertise in order to develop and execute a strategic technology plan. A strategic technology plan aligns an organization's administrative and business needs (as outlined in the organization's strategic plan) with its technology needs thus allowing it to function more efficiently and effectively. The application process for the technology initiative grants occurs in two phases: in Phase I, the foundation provides funds to hire a technology consultant to conduct a technology inventory and needs assessment and to assist an organization in developing a three-to-five-year technology plan; in Phase II, the foundation provides a dollar-for-dollar match (up to $125,000) to organizations wishing to implement their technology plans. The Tower Foundation anticipates making multiple Phase II awards in each of the geographic areas it serves. Each matching grant will be for a time period of up to three years; funds will be disbursed each year, not as a single lump sum. Grant awards will vary. The foundation does not accept unsolicited proposals. Applicants must first call the foundation to clarify the intent, scope, and details of the technology initiative; establish the organization's eligibility for the initiative; and to discuss their capacity and readiness to undertake the technology planning process. Based on this telephone call, the Foundation will determine whether or not it wishes to request a full application from the organization. Arrangements for this pre-screening telephone call must be made prior to January 24 for the first funding cycle, May 16 for the second funding cycle, or August 29 for the third funding cycle. The deadlines for full proposals are February 7 for the first cycle, May 30 for the second cycle, and September 12 for the third cycle. Successful applicants will be notified by April 11, August 1, November 14.
Requirements: Organizations must be located in and primarily serve residents of one of the following geographic areas: Barnstable County, Massachusetts; Dukes County, Massachusetts;

Essex County, Massachusetts; Nantucket County, Massachusetts; Erie County, New York; or Niagara County, New York. Organizations must focus on the following: providing services for children, adolescents and young adults to age 26 with intellectual disabilities; treating mental illness among children, adolescents and young adults to age 26; or preventing or treating substance abuse among children, adolescents and young adults to age 26. To be eligible for Phase II technology initiative grants, organizations must have already developed a strategic technology plan (based on an up-to-date strategic plan) that recommends specific technologies/policies/practices, identifies their relationship to administrative needs, and provides an estimated implementation budget for each recommendation. Preference will be given to technology plans that also do the following: identify the current state of the organization's technology (including network infrastructure, desktop/server hardware and software, staff skills and training needs, end-user support, periodic systems maintenance, and current practices, policies, procedures, and documentation); place a priority on each recommendation, as well as identify benefits associated with each recommendation and consequences of failing to implement recommendations; and propose an implementation timeline and replacement schedule. Organizations funded through this initiative are expected to provide dollar for dollar matching funds for the Tower Foundation's award. These funds may be obtained through any source of unrestricted funds or awards designated for the technology implementation project specifically.
Restrictions: The foundation makes technology initiative grants only to private and charter schools, nonprofit public benefit corporations, and organizations with 501(c)3 tax-exempt status that are neither private foundations nor described as 509(a)3 organizations. Diocesan and public school districts are not eligible to apply for technology initiative grants. Phase II grant money may not used for the following: the private benefit of any grant recipient or affiliated person; endowments; non-technology capital projects or campaigns; the development of an organization's strategic plan; the development of a strategic technology plan; the development of custom software applications or websites; advanced information technology training or certifications; general operating support; or individual scholarships. Please note that the RFP does not provide funds for hiring new staff nor does it provide funds for existing staff to conduct Phase II technology-initiative-grant activities.
Geographic Focus: Massachusetts, New York
Date(s) Application is Due: Feb 7; May 30; Sep 12
Amount of Grant: Up to 125,000 USD
Contact: Tracy A. Sawicki, Executive Director; (716) 689-0370; fax (716) 689-3716; info@thetowerfoundation.org or tas@thetowerfoundation.org
Donald W. Matteson; (716) 689-0370; fax (716) 689-3716; dwm@thetowerfoundation.org
Internet: thetowerfoundation.org/what-we-fund/grant-opportunities/
Sponsor: Peter and Elizabeth C. Tower Foundation
2351 North Forest Road
Getzville, NY 14068-1225

Peter and Elizabeth C. Tower Foundation Technology Planning Grants   1950
The Peter and Elizabeth C. Tower Technology Planning grants program connects not-for-profit organizations to technological expertise in order to develop and execute a strategic technology plan. A strategic technology plan aligns an organization's administrative and business needs (as outlined in the organization's strategic plan) with its technology needs thus allowing it to function more efficiently and effectively. The application process for the technology planning grants occurs in two phases: in Phase I, the foundation provides funds to hire a technology consultant to conduct a technology inventory and needs assessment and to assist an organization in developing a three-to-five-year technology plan; in Phase II, the foundation provides a dollar-for-dollar match (up to $125,000) to organizations wishing to implement their technology plans. The Tower Foundation anticipates making multiple Phase I awards in each of the geographic areas it serves. Each grant will be for a one-year time period. Grant awards will range from $10,000 to $50,000 depending on the size of the organization and the complexity of its business needs. The Foundation does not accept unsolicited proposals. Applicants must first call the foundation to clarify the intent, scope, and details of the technology initiative; establish the organization's eligibility for the initiative; and to discuss their capacity and readiness to undertake the technology planning process. Based on this telephone call, the Foundation will determine whether or not it wishes to request a full application from the organization. Arrangements for this pre-screening telephone call must be made prior to January 24 for the first funding cycle, May 16 for the second funding cycle, or August 29 for the third funding cycle. The deadlines for full proposals are February 7 for the first cycle, May 30 for the second cycle, and September 12 for the third cycle. Successful applicants will be notified by April 11, August 1, November 14.
Requirements: Organizations must be located in and primarily serve residents of one of the following geographic areas: Barnstable County, Massachusetts; Dukes County, Massachusetts; Essex County, Massachusetts; Nantucket County, Massachusetts; Erie County, New York; or Niagara County, New York. Organizations must focus on the following: providing services for children, adolescents and young adults to age 26 with intellectual disabilities; preventing or treating mental illness among children, adolescents and young adults to age 26; or preventing or treating substance abuse among children, adolescents and young adults to age 26. Additionally, organizations must have completed a strategic planning document within the past 36 months explicitly identifying technology as a focal area.
Restrictions: The foundation makes technology initiative grants only to private and charter schools, nonprofit public benefit corporations, and organizations with 501(c)3 tax-exempt status that are neither private foundations nor described as 509(a)3 organizations. Diocesan and public school districts are not eligible to apply for technology initiative grants. Phase I grant money may not used for the following: the private benefit of any grant recipient or affiliated person; endowments; capital projects or campaigns; staffing costs associated with technology planning or implementation; the development of an agency's strategic plan; general operating support; individual scholarships; or the purchase of computer hardware or software.
Geographic Focus: Massachusetts, New York
Date(s) Application is Due: Feb 7; May 30; Sep 12

Amount of Grant: 10,000 - 50,000 USD
Contact: Tracy A. Sawicki, Executive Director; (716) 689-0370 x206; fax (716) 689-3716; info@thetowerfoundation.org or tas@thetowerfoundation.org
Donald W. Matteson; (716) 689-0370; fax (716) 689-3716; dwm@thetowerfoundation.org
Internet: thetowerfoundation.org/what-we-fund/grant-opportunities/
Sponsor: Peter and Elizabeth C. Tower Foundation
2351 North Forest Road
Getzville, NY 14068-1225

Petersburg Community Foundation Grants   1951
The Petersburg Community Foundation has a competitive award process for unrestricted grants. Applications are available online. Most recently, total grant funds allocated equaled a combined $11,000, with awards ranging from $1,000 to $3,000. Specific areas of interest include: arts and culture; education; literacy; library support; community development; animals; the environment; medical supplies; medical care and access; and service delivery programs. Preference will be given to applications which have the potential to impact a broad range of Petersburg area residents. Applications should detail measurable and achievable outcomes and demonstrate other sources of support, collaboration and/or cooperation. Applications should also address the sustainability of the proposed program or project for which funding is desired. Awarded grant proposals must be completed within one year. The annual deadline for applications is April 17.
Requirements: The Foundation seeks applications from qualified tax-exempt 501(c)3 organizations that support the organizations and programs in the Petersburg area and serve the people's needs in such areas as health, education, community heritage, the arts, vulnerable populations, recreation, safety, and community and economic development.
Restrictions: Individuals, for-profit, and 501(c)4 or 501(c)6 organizations, non-Alaska based organizations and state or federal government agencies are not eligible for competitive grants. Applications for religious indoctrination or other religious activities, endowment building, deficit financing, fundraising, lobbying, electioneering and activities of political nature will not be considered, nor will proposals for ads, sponsorships, or special event and any proposals which discriminate as to race, gender, marital status, sexual orientation, age, disability, creed or ethnicity.
Geographic Focus: Alaska
Date(s) Application is Due: Apr 17
Amount of Grant: 1,000 - 3,000 USD
Samples: Clausen Museum, Petersburg, Alaska, $1,000 - support for the purchase of display drawers; Petersburg Children's Center, Petersburg, Alaska, $1,500 - enhancing early literacy and language through stories, music and movement program support; Petersburg Public Library, Petersburg, Alaska, $2,500 - support for the Learners to Makers: a Youth STEAM program initiative
Contact: Ricardo Lopez, Affiliate Program Officer; (907) 274-6707 or (907) 249-6609; fax (907) 334-5780; rlopez@alaskacf.org or petersburg@alaskacf.org
Internet: petersburgcf.org/projects/
Sponsor: Petersburg Community Foundation
P.O. Box 1024
Petersburg, AK 99833

Pettus Foundation Grants   1952
The Pettus Foundation was established in Missouri in 1960 in honor of James T. Pettus, Jr. Pettus, who died in January of 2012, was a member of Trinity Presbyterian Church, an Army Veteran of WWII, 70th Division, and owner of Weiss-Pettus Printing Company until his retirement. The Foundation currently supports at-risk children, under- and unemployed people, child development, child educational development, domesticated animals, economic development, elementary and secondary education, family services, higher education, human services, natural resources, reproductive health care, shelter and residential care, and special populations. Most often, grants take the form of: continuing support; general operating support; program development; and scholarships. The Foundation's primary geographic program focus is in Missouri and Hawaii, though awards are often given nationwide. These awards typically range up to a maximum of $25,000, with larger grants sometimes considered. There is no formal application formats, and the annual deadline is the 2nd Friday in January.
Requirements: Any 501(c)3 supporting the Foundation's primary focus areas is eligible to apply.
Restrictions: No awards are given for capital campaigns.
Geographic Focus: All States
Date(s) Application is Due: Jan 10
Amount of Grant: Up to 25,000 USD
Samples: Saint Louis Public Schools Foundation, Saint Louis, Missouri, $25,000 - operating support for elementary and secondary education; Hongwanji Mission School, Honolulu, Hawaii, $15,000 - operating support for elementary and secondary education.
Contact: Lisa Hamilton, Trustee; (312) 630-6000; grants@stlgives.org
Sponsor: Pettus Foundation
1175 Mill Crossing Drive, #100
Creve Coeur, MO 63141-6192

PeyBack Foundation Grants   1953
The PeyBack Foundation was established by NFL quarterback Peyton Manning with the purpose of promoting the future success of disadvantaged youth by assisting programs that provide leadership and growth opportunities for children at risk (ages 6-18). The nature of the programs and their immediate long-term benefit shall be guiding considerations in funding grants. Although the foundation does not have a dollar limit on grant requests, most grant amounts range between $1,500 and $10,000. The deadline to submit a PeyBack Foundation Grant Application is February 1 each year. In order to be considered, all applications must be submitted in entirety to the PeyBack Foundation by this date.

Requirements: Due to the close association of Peyton Manning with the Indiana, Tennessee, Denver, and the New Orleans Metropolitan area, programs and projects related to the youth in these areas are of primary concern to the foundation. Proposals will be only considered from organizations that have tax-exempt status under Section 501(c)3 of the Internal Revenue Code. A proposal asking to consider providing a portion of the support for a project will generally receive greater preference than one seeking exclusive funding. Download the required application form at the website.

Restrictions: The following are not areas that the PeyBack Foundation supports: organizations without 501(c)3 tax-exempt status will immediately be eliminated; Fundraising and sponsorship events (e.g., golf tournaments, telethons, banquets); Groups outside of Indiana, Tennessee and New Orleans, LA; Projects/groups benefiting an individual or just a few persons; Building/renovating expenses of any kind; To defray meeting, conferences, workshops or seminars expenses; Payment of travel of individuals or groups; Re-granting organizations; Post-event fundraising; Multi-year gifts.

Geographic Focus: Colorado, Indiana, Louisiana, Tennessee
Date(s) Application is Due: Feb 1
Amount of Grant: 1,500 - 10,000 USD
Contact: Elizabeth Ellis, Executive Director; (877) 873-9225; PeyBack@PeytonManning.com
Internet: www.peytonmanning.com/peyback-foundation/requests/funding-requests
Sponsor: PeyBack Foundation
6325 North Guilford, Suite 201
Indianapolis, IN 46220

Peyton Anderson Foundation Grants 1954

The Peyton Anderson Foundation initiates projects to meet needs in the community and reacts to requests from charitable organizations in Macon, Bibb County, and Middle Georgia.
Requirements: Applicants must serve Macon and/or Bibb County Georgia in order to be considered for funding. Preference is given to organizations that have a substantial presence in Bibb County. Applications can be downloaded from the Foundation's website and must contain the original application plus five (5) copies, including copies of all required application items. In addition, organizations must submit one (1) copy of the organization's current annual operating budget, IRS determination letter, and most recent annual financial statement.
Restrictions: Grants may not be made to private foundations, individuals, private schools, endowments, churches, or for festivals and trips. Grants are also only awarded to organizations with current 501(c)3 status that benefit Macon and Bibb County, Georgia. DO NOT include any forms or information other than what is required above.
Geographic Focus: Georgia
Date(s) Application is Due: Apr 1; Aug 1
Amount of Grant: 1,000 - 500,000 USD
Samples: Meals On Wheels of Macon and Bibb, Macon, Georgia, $1,420 - support for the annual holiday feast for all; Mid-State Children's Challenge Projects, Inc., Macon, Georgia, $60,000 - funding to retire debt and complete renovation; Medcen Community Health Foundation, Inc., Macon, Georgia, $500,000 - for renovation and expansion of all critical care units, and medical/surgical, neuro and surgical trauma.
Contact: Juanita T. Jordan; (478) 743-5359; fax (478) 742-5201; jtjordan@pafdn.org or grants@pafdn.org
Internet: www.peytonanderson.org
Sponsor: Peyton Anderson Foundation
577 Mulberry Street, Suite 830
Macon, GA 31201

Peyton Anderson Scholarships 1955

The Peyton Anderson Scholarship supports students from Bibb County, Georgia in pursuing higher education.
Requirements: To apply for the scholarship, students must: be U.S. citizens and graduating seniors of a public or private high school in Bibb County, Georgia; have attended school and have resided in Bibb County, Georgia for during the previous 2 years; have at least a 2.0 GPA; must be enrolled full-time in a college or university immediately following their high school graduation; must have financial need determined by the FAFSA; and demonstrated active involvement in their communities.
Restrictions: Individuals who do not fall into the above requirements or are family members of the Peyton Anderson Foundation trustees, staff, or scholarship selection may not apply.
Geographic Focus: Georgia
Date(s) Application is Due: Apr 1
Amount of Grant: 5,000 USD
Contact: Jean Fallis; (478) 314-0948; fax (478) 742-5201; scholarships@pafdn.org
Internet: www.peytonandersonscholars.org/
Sponsor: Peyton Anderson Foundation
577 Mulberry Street
Macon, GA 31201

PG&E Bright Ideas Grants 1956

Bright Ideas grants are designed to tap into the expertise and commitment of our teachers and to foster environmental stewardship in our future leaders. This year, PG&E will be awarding more than $400,000 in grants to green school campuses, providing unique environmental learning opportunities for students.
Requirements: Credentialed teachers, professors, instructors, principals, deans, department heads, distinct administrators and facilities managers of K-12 public schools served by PG&E may all apply to receive a $1,000, $2,500, $5,000, or $10,000 grant to promote environmental stewardship in any of the five following categories: educational solar projects; youth energy and environmental programs; renewable energy or science related field trips; green your school projects; and professional development, service learning projects and workforce development programs.
Geographic Focus: California

Date(s) Application is Due: Mar 20; Sep 20
Amount of Grant: 1,000 - 10,000 USD
Contact: Linda Romero; (415) 973-4951 or (800) 743-5000; LMRH@pge.com
Internet: www.pge.com/about/community/education/brightideasgrants/
Sponsor: Pacific Gas and Electric Corporation Foundation
P.O. Box 770000, MC B32
San Francisco, CA 94177-0001

PG&E Community Vitality Grants 1957

With the goal to strengthen the economic development and social vitality of its communities, the company awards grants to eligible nonprofit organizations located in its service area of northern and central California. Grant making is focused in four primary areas: environmental stewardship—including projects to improve or restore habitat, air and water quality projects, solar and other alternative energy development, and energy efficiency projects; aid to schools—including public schools serving pre-school and K-12 students, universities, teacher training, after-school programs, and kids safety training; emergency preparedness—including efforts to improve community and family disaster preparedness, nonprofit emergency planning, and recovery projects; and, economic vitality—including efforts to retain and expand jobs in local communities, workforce development programs, and policy planning activities. The contributions program is funded throughout the calendar year, however, applications are requested in the fall. Multi-year grants are not awarded. Current grantees must submit a new request for annual funding. An application may be downloaded online. Corporate employee associations also sponsor scholarship programs for college-bound high school students and employees of the company, including the Asian Employees Association, Black Employees Association, Filipino Employees Association, and PrideNetwork.
Requirements: Northern and central California 501(c)3 nonprofit organizations and government programs/agencies in the corporation's service area are eligible.
Restrictions: Grants do not support individuals; tickets for contests, raffles, or other activities with prizes; religious organizations (unless the request specifically supports a program offered to the public on a nondiscriminatory basis and without regard to the recipient's religious affiliation); film, television, or video productions; capital campaigns, endowment funds, academic chairs, or fellowships; debt-reduction campaigns; political and partisan organizations or events; sports tournaments; trips or tours for individuals or groups; talent or beauty contests; or conferences.
Geographic Focus: California
Amount of Grant: 1,000 - 200,000 USD
Contact: Charitable Contributions Administrator; (415) 973-4951; charitablecontributions@pge.com
Internet: www.pge.com/about_us/community/charitable/index.html
Sponsor: Pacific Gas and Electric Corporation Foundation
P.O. Box 770000, MC B32
San Francisco, CA 94177-0001

PGE Foundation Grants 1958

The foundation awards grants to Oregon nonprofit organizations in its areas of interest, including preschool through college education, healthy families, arts and cultural events, and the environment. The foundation also supports Community 101, a signature program of the foundation that helps high school youth experience the value of community service learning and philanthropy. The program includes student volunteerism and student grant making and is student-led. A PGE Foundation Grant request consists of two steps, both of which are submitted online: Letter of Inquiry (open to all who qualify); and Full Application (at the invitation of the PGE Foundation). Letters of Inquiry are due on: January 12, April 6, July 13, and November 16. The Foundation considers just one request per year from an organization.
Requirements: Applicant organizations must be a 501(c)3 charitable, nonprofit, tax-exempt organizations; and domiciled in Oregon to serve Oregonians.
Restrictions: The following types of requests are not eligible: bridge grants, debt retirement, or operational deficits; endowment funds; general fund drives or annual appeals; requests to support political entities, ballot-measure campaigns, or candidates for political office; requests from organizations that discriminate against individuals on the basis of creed, color, gender, sexual orientation, age, religion, or national origin; requests from fraternal, sectarian, and religious organizations if the grant is intended for the principal benefit of the organization's own members or adherents; any activities or organizations for which support would violate IRS regulations for private foundations; direct grants to individuals; travel expenses; conferences, symposiums, festivals, events, team sponsorships, or user fees; or salaries of employees, with the exception of costs relating directly to the funded project. The foundation generally does not fund capital requests that include building improvements, equipment purchases, or anything considered an asset of the organization.
Geographic Focus: Oregon
Amount of Grant: 1,000 - 25,000 USD
Samples: BodyVox, Portland, Oregon, $20,000 - to renovate the new BodyVox Dance Center in Portland; Chalkboard Project, Portland, Oregon, $15,000 - for the Creative Leadership Achieves Student Success Project, which works to create new and expanded teaching career paths in Oregon; Broadway Rose Theatre Company, Tigard, Oregon, $5,000 - for the Summer Youth Outreach Program, which provides low-income youth scholarships for drama camps/workshops, and discount performance tickets.
Contact: Carole Morse; (503) 464-8818; fax (503) 464-2929; pgefoundation@pgn.com
Internet: www.pgefoundation.org/eligibility.html
Sponsor: PGE Foundation
One World Trade Center, 3rd Floor, 121 SW Salmon Street
Portland, OR 97204

Philanthrofund Foundation Grants 1959

Founded in 1987 the Philanthrofund Foundation (PFund) is one of only a handful of foundations in the nation created specifically by and for LGBT communities. It provides grants to emerging non-profit organizations and projects that would otherwise not get funded, awards scholarships, develops leaders, and inspires giving. PFund manages more than $1.3 million in assets, enjoying the support of committed donors and dedicated volunteers from LGBT and allied communities. PFund awards over $140,000 annually to LGBT-related individuals and organizations throughout the Upper Midwest — in Minnesota, Iowa, North Dakota, South Dakota and Wisconsin. PFund funds nonprofits that focus their programming or projects within one of the following three pillars of social justice: achieving equal rights through advocacy and civic engagement; ensuring access, safety and security in such areas as housing, schools and healthcare; and creating power through community as a result of organizing, events and the arts. Interested organizations must submit a letter of inquiry through PFund's online inquiry system. Guidelines for content are available to download from the grant web page. Letters of inquiry are accepted from June 1 to August 1. From these applicants are selected to submit a full proposal which is due October 1.

Requirements: Eligible organizations must support PFund's mission and vision and satisfy the following criteria: have a program or service area in Minnesota, Iowa, North Dakota, South Dakota and/or Wisconsin; complete and submit a final report for any past grants from PFund; complete PFund's Certificate of Non-discrimination; and have proof of 501(c)3 or 501(c)4 status or a fiscal agent with 501(c)3 or 501(c)4 status. In the selection process, PFund considers the following criteria: whether an applicant's programs benefit LGBT and allied communities; whether a proposal addresses the depth and complexity of critical issues in LGBT communities; whether a proposed program has a clear vision of social change that address intersections of multiple forms of oppression; whether an applicant offers a wide variety of programs, including those that serve targeted populations, e.g., by gender, race and age; whether organizations and programs represent a broad range of fields, e.g., the arts, social change, advocacy, health and wellness, and education; whether organizations and programs have limited appeal to traditional funding sources; and whether genuine collaboration exists among organizations with similar goals that will, whenever possible, result in uniqueness of efforts.

Restrictions: PFund's grant program does not fund the following activities/entities: religious organizations for religious purposes; political campaigns; individual persons; fundraising events; for-profit organizations; public agencies for mandated services; and projects for the fulfillment of requirements toward a degree-granting program. PFund recognizes the importance of grassroots and direct lobbying efforts for many LGBT organizations and will consider proposals for lobbying efforts on behalf of LGBT issues as a limited part of its annual grant-making cycle, within the limits set by the 501(h) section of the tax code-legislation which allows a certain amount of expenditures by nonprofits to be used for lobbying and advocacy activities. Organizations with an annual budget of less than $500,000 and a mission focus on LGBT people and issues may apply for general operating funds and/or project support. Larger organizations may apply only for project-specific support and are limited to receiving annual support for the same project for no more than three (3) consecutive years. (This is not multi-year project funding; new grant applications must be made annually). In assessing such applications, the foundation is positively influenced by an organization's demonstrated commitment to including LGBT communities and individuals at all levels of the organization and in its activities and programming.

Geographic Focus: Iowa, Minnesota, North Dakota, South Dakota, Wisconsin
Date(s) Application is Due: Oct 1
Amount of Grant: Up to 10,000 USD
Samples: Freedom, Inc., Madison, Wisconsin, $10,000 - building a movement in the Queer Black and Queer Southeast Asia communities of Madison and Milwaukee; Project 515, Minneapolis, Minnesota, $8,000 - to ensure that same-sex couples and their families have equal rights and considerations under Minnesota Law; Shades of Yellow, Saint Paul, Minnesota, $10,000 - emerging projects that address the struggles and complex intersections of Hmong lesbian, gay, bisexual, transgender, queer and ally identities.
Contact: Kayva Yang, Program Officer; (800) 435-1402 or (612) 870-1806; fax (612) 871-6587; kyang@PFundOnline.org or info@PFundOnline.org
Internet: www.pfundonline.org/grants.html
Sponsor: Philanthrofund Foundation
1409 Willow Street, Suite 109
Minneapolis, MN 55403

Phil Hardin Foundation Grants 1960

The Phil Hardin Foundation targets its funding to education in the State of Mississippi. Specific priorities are to strengthen the capacity of communities to nurture and educate young children; the capacity of higher education institutions to renew communities and their economies; the capacity of communities for locally initiated educational improvement and economic development; and state- and local-level policy and leadership initiatives that fit with foundation goals. Types of support include general operating support, continuing support, building construction/renovation, equipment acquisition, endowment funds, program development, conferences and seminars, professorships, publication, seed grants, fellowships, scholarship funds, research, and matching funds. The foundation also operates four K-12 fellowship programs. Deadlines vary between programs; contact program staff for specific fellowship deadlines.

Requirements: Applicants must either be based in Mississippi or the project must benefit Mississippi, depending on the program. Contact program staff for eligibility.
Geographic Focus: Mississippi
Amount of Grant: Up to 1,000,000 USD
Samples: Covington County Vocational Technical Center, Collins, Mississippi, $2,000 - support of the Click, Click, Boom program; Meridian Public School District, Meridian, Mississippi, $100,000 - recruitment, retention and incentive program for highly-effective educators; Trinity Dyslexia Education Center, Meridian, Mississippi, $15,000 - general operating costs.
Contact: Lloyd Gray, (601) 483-4282; fax (601) 483-5665; info@philhardin.org
Internet: www.philhardin.org/application-and-instructions.cfm

Sponsor: Phil Hardin Foundation
2750 North Park Drive
Meridian, MS 39305

Philip Boyle Foundation Grants 1961

Established in 1989 and based in Norman, Oklahoma, the mission of the Philip Boyle Foundation is to carry on the legacy of Philip Boyle's philanthropy. The Foundation's primary fields of interest include: education; human services; and religion. Awards take the form of general operating support funds. The Foundation will support charities that operate in central Oklahoma and that make a difference in the quality of life of all who are served. Most recently, grants have ranged from $2,500 to $10,000. A formal online application is required, and the annual deadline for submission is May 15.

Requirements: The trustees invite proposals from 501(c)3 organizations located in central Oklahoma. An online grant application summarizing the project(s) for funding must be submitted.
Restrictions: No grants are awarded to individuals.
Geographic Focus: Oklahoma
Date(s) Application is Due: May 15
Amount of Grant: 2,500 - 10,000 USD
Samples: Center for Children and Families, Norman, Oklahoma, $15,000 - general operating funds (2018); Sunbeam Family Services, Oklahoma City, Oklahoma, $10,000 - general operating funds (2018); Citizens Caring for Children, Oklahoma City, Oklahoma, $5,000 - general operating funds (2018).
Contact: Jim Cobb, President; 405-755-5571; fax (405) 755-0938
Internet: fmiokc.com/clients/philip-boyle/
Sponsor: Philip Boyle Foundation
2932 NW 122nd Street, Suite D
Oklahoma City, OK 73120

Philip L. Graham Fund Education Grants 1962

The Philip L. Graham Fund awards Education grants to organizations in the Washington, D.C., metropolitan area, including Maryland and Virginia. The Fund is committed to supporting efforts to advance and expand educational offerings for the children of the Washington, D.C., metropolitan area. The Fund gives highest priority to programs that improve public education at the pre-college level for disadvantaged, low-income students and schools that address other special needs segments of the population. In recognition of the role charter schools play in the public education landscape of Washington, D.C., the Fund awards grants each year to three high-quality public charter schools that have demonstrated solid growth in student achievement, strong school and board leadership, significant parental involvement, and prudent financial planning and sustainability. In keeping with the Fund's giving philosophy, requests for one-time special needs receive highest priority. The Fund also recognizes the significant contributions that institutions of higher learning make in the intellectual, economic, and cultural well-being of the community. The Fund awards grants on a solely discretionary basis to area colleges and universities. Interested partied must submit a Letter of Inquiry (LOI) online prior to each submission deadline. The annual LOI deadlines are March 16, June 29, and December 2. Recent awards have ranged from $20,000 to $250,000.

Requirements: Applicants are required to submit a letter of inquiry through the Fund's online application system before one of three deadline dates. Organizations must be a tax-exempt 501(c)3 organization to apply and located within the greater Washington D.C., metropolitan area.
Restrictions: Proposals from newly created public charter schools are not accepted. Proposals for the following purposes are not considered: advocacy or litigation; research; endowments; special events, conferences workshops or seminars; travel expenses; annual giving campaigns, benefits or sponsorships; courtesy advertising; and production of films or publications. Also, independent schools, institutions of post-secondary education, national or international organizations, and hospitals are not eligible to apply. Grants are also not made to: individuals; religious, political or lobbying activities; to membership organizations; or to any organization that has received a grant from the Fund within the previous thirty-six months.
Geographic Focus: District of Columbia, Maryland, Virginia
Date(s) Application is Due: Apr 1; Jul 15; Dec 15
Amount of Grant: 20,000 - 250,000 USD
Samples: Center for Alexandria's Children, Alexandria, Virginia, $25,000 - support curriculum development and for general operating support; Quest Arts for Everyone, Baltimore, Maryland, $25,000 - support arts integration programming in 41 Prince George's County Public Schools; Washington Jesuit Academy, Washington, D.C., $50,000 - purchase two school vans for daily use by teachers, coaches, and alumni mentors to transport students and graduates.
Contact: Eileen F. Daly, President; (202) 334-6640; fax (202) 334-4498; plgfund@ghco.com
Internet: www.plgrahamfund.org/content/interest-areas/education
Sponsor: Philip L. Graham Fund
1300 North 17th Street, Suite 1700
Arlington, VA 22209

Phoenix Coyotes Charities Grants 1963

Coyotes Charities seeks to enhance the quality of life throughout Arizona communities by supporting non-profit organizations that promote healthcare, educational, cultural, arts, and sports-related programs for children. The Charities will fund activities that accomplish the following goals: to focus on the health and well-being of youth through community awareness, information dissemination, and treatment or prevention; to promote the value of quality education through provision of in-school or after-school enrichment programs that equip children for the future; to develop the artistic potential of youth, allow youth to share in the vital cultural currents of the Arizona community, and help youth learn to create with their hands; to encourage physical activities, exercise, teamwork, self-esteem, goal setting, and a healthy lifestyle through community outreach, organized sports, or mentorship programs. Interested organizations may download an application from the grant

website. Mailed applications must be postmarked by the deadline date. Hand-delivered applications must be received by a Coyotes Charities representative in the Phoenix Coyotes offices by 5:00 p.m. on the deadline date. Deadlines may vary from year to year. Applicants are encouraged to verify the current deadline date at the grant website.
Requirements: Organizations must be classified as a public charity and exempt from federal taxes under 501(c)3 of the Internal Revenue Code. Organizations must align with the Coyotes Charities mission statement by being focused on improving the lives of children in Arizona.
Restrictions: Giving is limited to the state of Arizona. The foundation will not support the following entities: individuals; sports teams or leagues; religious, fraternal, or political institutions; schools or their affiliated organizations (booster clubs, PTAs, etc.); governmental municipalities; or environmental groups.
Geographic Focus: Arizona
Date(s) Application is Due: Jun 24
Amount of Grant: Up to 5,000 USD
Contact: Doug Moss; (623) 772-3200; fax (623) 872-2000; coyotes.charities@phoenixcoyotes.com
Internet: coyotes.nhl.com/club/page.htm?id=32747
Sponsor: Phoenix Coyotes Charities
6751 N. Sunset Boulevard #200
Glendale, AZ 85305

Phoenix Suns Charities Grants 1964
Ranging in size from $1,000 to $10,000, Phoenix Suns Charities Program Grants are intended for Arizona non-profit organization whose programs and activities focus on helping children and families maximize their potential. The foundation's largest annual gift, the Playmaker Award, is a one-time $100,000 grant which can be used for capital or programs, or a combination of both. For this grant, Suns Charities looks favorably on collaborative ideas and naming or branding opportunities.
Requirements: Applications and supporting documents must be submitted electronically through ZoomGrants at the Suns website. Organizations must consider the prerequisites, answer all questions and carefully follow directions. Applications are available in November, evaluated by Suns board members in April and May, with funding in June.
Geographic Focus: Arizona
Date(s) Application is Due: Apr 1
Amount of Grant: 1,000 - 10,000 USD
Contact: Kathryn Pidgeon; (602) 379-7948; fax (602) 379-7990; kpidgeon@suns.com
Internet: www.nba.com/suns/charities.html
Sponsor: Phoenix Suns
201 East Jefferson Street
Phoenix, AZ 85004

Piedmont Health Foundation Grants 1965
The Piedmont Health Care Foundation was established in 1985 through the sale of the first HMO in Greenville County, South Carolina. During the past 25 years, the foundation has invested more than $3.4 million in dozens of nonprofit organizations in the Greenville, South Carolina area. The Piedmont Health Care Foundation has played an important role in catalyzing and providing seed funding to critical projects, and it has provided operating and programmatic funds needed by local health-service organizations. In looking ahead, the foundation recognizes that much of what makes a healthy community takes place outside of the health-care system. So for its 25th anniversary, the foundation decided to change its name to the Piedmont Health Foundation. The foundation currently focuses on the area of policy, system, and environmental change to reduce childhood obesity rates. Applications are accepted on a quarterly basis. Downloadable guidelines and editable forms are provided at the foundation website. Applicants should email their completed forms to the address given by midnight of the deadline date.
Requirements: Nonprofit organizations that serve Greenville County are eligible to apply.
Geographic Focus: South Carolina
Date(s) Application is Due: Jan 31; Apr 10; Jul 10; Oct 10
Amount of Grant: 1,000 - 15,000 USD
Samples: Communities in Schools, Greenville, South Carolina, $5,500 - health initiative program in Title I Greenville County schools; Greenville Forward, Greenville, South Carolina, $7,500 - Gardening for Good community gardens and urban farms; Taylors Free Medical Clinic, Taylors, South Carolina, $15,000 - to support clinic's pharmacy operation.
Contact: Katy Smith, Executive Director; (864) 370-0212; fax (864) 370-0212; katypughsmith@bellsouth.net or katysmith@piedmonthealthfoundation.org
Internet: www.phcfdn.org/grantmaking.php
Sponsor: Piedmont Health Foundation
P.O. Box 9303
Greenville, SC 29604

Piedmont Natural Gas Corporate and Charitable Contributions 1966
Piedmont Natural Gas supports local non-profit organizations sponsored by its employees through matching gifts, financial assistance and volunteer support.
Requirements: Piedmont supports 501(c)3 organizations that are sponsored or assisted by its employees. Eligible organizations with employee sponsors are also able to apply for Employee Matching Gifts. Applications are available at Piedmont's website.
Restrictions: As a general rule, grants do not support: individuals or non-501(c)3 organizations; pre-college level private schools except through employee matching gifts; travel and conferences; third-party professional fund-raising organizations; controversial social causes; fraternal and veterans organizations or private clubs; religious organizations with programs limited to or expressly for their membership only; agencies already receiving corporate support through United Way or a united arts drive, with the exception of approved capital campaigns; or athletic events and programs.
Geographic Focus: North Carolina, South Carolina, Tennessee

Contact: George Baldwin, Managing Director; (704) 731-4063; fax (704) 731-4086; george.baldwin@piedmontng.com
Internet: www.piedmontng.com/ourcommunity/communityoutreach.aspx
Sponsor: Piedmont Natural Gas Corporation
4720 Piedmont Row Drive
Charlotte, NC 28210

Piedmont Natural Gas Foundation Environmental Stewardship and Energy Sustainability Grant 1967
Piedmont Natural Gas Foundation awards one grant to organizations in North Carolina, South Carolina and Tennessee that provide one or more of the following objectives: increase access to interaction with nature and the environment; promote local accountability or actions to create cleaner cities, reduce emissions and incorporate conscious environmental decision-making; incorporate energy and/or environmental education in K-12 schools and curriculum; promote a general awareness about environmental and energy-related issues for the public; and/or preserve or restore a community's existing natural resources, including green/open space.
Requirements: Organizations are invited to apply for Environmental Stewardship and Energy Sustainability grants through a Request for Proposal process. Also, organizations must be a 501(c)3 non-profit organization or a qualified government entity. All grant requests must be submitted through Piedmont's online grant application form located at Piedmont's website.
Restrictions: Piedmont Natural Gas Foundation will not fund: religious, fraternal, political or athletic groups; four-year colleges and universities; private foundations; or social or veterans' organizations. In addition to these restrictions, contributions will generally not be made to or for: individuals; pre-college level private schools, except through the Employee Matching Gifts program; travel and conferences; third-party professional fundraising organizations; controversial social causes; religious organizations with programs limited to or expressly for their membership only; athletic events and programs; agencies already receiving Piedmont support through United Way or a united arts drive, with the exception of an approved capital campaign; or any proposal outside of the geographic area where Piedmont Natural Gas does business.
Geographic Focus: North Carolina, South Carolina, Tennessee
Amount of Grant: 500 - 30,000 USD
Contact: George Baldwin; (704) 731-4063; fax (704) 731-4086; george.baldwin@piedmontng.com
Internet: www.piedmontng.com/ourcommunity/ourfoundation.aspx#guidelines
Sponsor: Piedmont Natural Gas Foundation
4720 Piedmont Row Drive
Charlotte, NC 28210

Piedmont Natural Gas Foundation Health and Human Services Grants 1968
Piedmont Natural Gas Foundation's Health and Human Services grant focuses funding toward: organizations providing outreach services to community members with basic needs, including shelter, food and clothing; substance abuse or mental illness; organizations providing services or programs for a range of human service needs including youth engagement and mentoring, special needs and disability assistance, substance abuse or mental illnesses, transitional housing and situational homelessness support, and gang violence prevention; organizations providing emergency/disaster relief; increased access to critical healthcare services and comprehensive medical treatment including preventative care, prescription medication, medical exams, screenings, immunizations and dental care; and increased access to mental health services.
Requirements: Organizations must be a 501(c)3 non-profit organization or a qualified government entity. All grant requests must be submitted through Piedmont's online grant application form located at Piedmont's website.
Restrictions: Piedmont Natural Gas Foundation will not fund: religious, fraternal, political or athletic groups; four-year colleges and universities; private foundations; or social or veterans' organizations. In addition to these restrictions, contributions will generally not be made to or for: individuals; pre-college level private schools, except through the Employee Matching Gifts program; travel and conferences; third-party professional fundraising organizations; controversial social causes; religious organizations with programs limited to or expressly for their membership only; athletic events and programs; agencies already receiving Piedmont support through United Way or a united arts drive, with the exception of an approved capital campaign; or any proposal outside of the geographic area where Piedmont Natural Gas does business.
Geographic Focus: North Carolina, South Carolina, Tennessee
Amount of Grant: 500 - 30,000 USD
Contact: George Baldwin; (704) 731-4063; fax (704) 731-4086; george.baldwin@piedmontng.com
Internet: www.piedmontng.com/ourcommunity/ourfoundation.aspx#guidelines
Sponsor: Piedmont Natural Gas Foundation
4720 Piedmont Row Drive
Charlotte, NC 28210

Piedmont Natural Gas Foundation K-12 Science, Technology, Engineering and Math (STEM) Grant 1969
The Piedmont Natural Gas Foundation K-12 STEM grant focuses funding toward: programs and accountability measures that enhance student performance, grade level readiness, literacy, graduation rates and overall success for students; development of high-quality leadership in schools and classrooms, including recruitment and retention of teachers and principals; programs that incorporate science, technology, math and engineering skills critical to success in a global economy; programs that promote positive behaviors and motivation to stay in school; and incorporation of energy and environmental education in K-12 schools and curriculum.
Requirements: Organizations must be a 501(c)3 non-profit organization or a qualified government entity. All grant requests must be submitted through Piedmont's online grant application form located at Piedmont's website.

Restrictions: Piedmont Natural Gas Foundation will not fund: religious, fraternal, political or athletic groups; four-year colleges and universities; private foundations; or social or veterans' organizations. Contributions will generally not be made to or for: individuals; pre-college level private schools, except through the Employee Matching Gifts program; travel and conferences; third-party professional fundraising organizations; controversial social causes; religious organizations with programs limited to or expressly for their membership only; athletic events and programs; agencies already receiving Piedmont support through United Way or a united arts drive, with the exception of an approved capital campaign; or any proposal outside of the geographic area where Piedmont Natural Gas does business.
Geographic Focus: North Carolina, South Carolina, Tennessee
Amount of Grant: 500 - 30 USD
Contact: George Baldwin; (704) 731-4063; george.baldwin@piedmontng.com
Internet: www.piedmontng.com/ourcommunity/ourfoundation.aspx#governance
Sponsor: Piedmont Natural Gas Foundation
4720 Piedmont Row Drive
Charlotte, NC 28210

Pike County Community Foundation Recreation Grants   1970

The Pike County Community Foundation is a charitable organization formed to strengthen the Pike County, Indiana community by awarding grants to local nonprofits, by bringing individuals together to address community needs, and by offering personalized charitable gift planning services to donors. At the start of each cycle, a notice is mailed to nonprofit organizations that have previously applied for and received grants, or have otherwise requested notification of each cycle. Proposals are accepted from July 6 through the September 8 deadline. The grants committee will make its recommendations on funding to the Foundation's Board of Trustees, which will make final funding recommendations to the board of directors of the Community Foundation Alliance. All organizations that have submitted grant proposals are notified of the final outcome no later than December 1. Grants in the area of Recreation include projects aimed at improving and promoting recreational and leisure activities, parks, and community sporting events and activities. Samples of previously funded projects are available at the website.
Requirements: The Foundation welcomes proposals from nonprofit organizations that are deemed tax-exempt under sections 501(c)3 and 509(a) of the Internal Revenue Code and from governmental agencies serving Pike County. Proposals from nonprofit organizations not classified as a 501(c)3 public charity may be considered provided the project is charitable and supports a community need. Proposals submitted by an entity under the auspices of another agency must include a written statement signed by the agency's board president on behalf of the board of directors agreeing to act as the entity's fiscal sponsor, to receive grant monies if awarded, and to oversee the proposed project.
Restrictions: Project areas not considered for funding include: religious organizations for religious purposes; political parties or campaigns; endowment creation or debt reduction; operating costs; capital campaigns; annual appeals or membership contributions; travel requests for groups or individuals such as bands, sports teams, or classes.
Geographic Focus: Indiana
Date(s) Application is Due: Sep 8
Contact: Cindy Gaskins; (812) 354-6797; director@pikecommunityfoundation.org
Internet: www.communityfoundationalliance.org/pike/program-areas/
Sponsor: Pike County Community Foundation
714 Main Street, P.O. Box 587
Petersburg, IN 47567

Pike County Community Foundation Youth Development Grants   1971

The Pike County Community Foundation is a charitable organization formed to strengthen the Pike County, Indiana community by awarding grants to local nonprofits, by bringing individuals together to address community needs, and by offering personalized charitable gift planning services to donors. At the start of each cycle, a notice is mailed to nonprofit organizations that have previously applied for and received grants, or have otherwise requested notification of each cycle. Proposals are accepted July 6 through the September 8 deadline. The grants committee will make its recommendations on funding to the Foundation's Board of Trustees, which will make final recommendations to the board of directors of the Community Foundation Alliance. All organizations that have submitted grant proposals are notified of the final outcome no later than December 1. Grants in the area of Youth Development include activities that strengthen the family unit, help children grow and develop, foster youth sports and athletics, support the YMCA, and support daycare-related issues.
Requirements: The Foundation welcomes proposals from nonprofit organizations that are deemed tax-exempt under sections 501(c)3 and 509(a) of the Internal Revenue Code and from governmental agencies serving Pike County. Proposals from nonprofit organizations not classified as a 501(c)3 public charity may be considered provided the project is charitable and supports a community need. Proposals submitted by an entity under the auspices of another agency must include a written statement signed by the agency's board president on behalf of the board of directors agreeing to act as the entity's fiscal sponsor, to receive grant monies if awarded, and to oversee the proposed project.
Restrictions: Project areas not considered for funding include: religious organizations for religious purposes; political parties or campaigns; endowment creation or debt reduction; operating costs; capital campaigns; annual appeals or membership contributions; travel requests for groups or individuals such as bands, sports teams, or classes.
Geographic Focus: Indiana
Date(s) Application is Due: Sep 8
Contact: Cindy Gaskins; (812) 354-6797; director@pikecommunityfoundation.org
Internet: www.communityfoundationalliance.org/pike/program-areas/
Sponsor: Pike County Community Foundation
714 Main Street, P.O. Box 587
Petersburg, IN 47567

Pinnacle Entertainment Foundation Grants   1972

The Pinnacle Entertainment Foundation awards grants in its primary fields of interest, including: the arts; children and youth services; food banks; community foundations; health care; patient services; higher education; hospitals; the humanities; performing arts; and recreation programs. Types of support include: general operating funds; program development; scholarship funds; and sponsorships. Applications are limited to two per calendar year, per organization. An online application form is required, and should include: plans for acknowledgement; a detailed description of project and amount of funding requested; a brief history of organization and description of its mission; contact information; and a copy of the IRS Determination Letter.
Requirements: 501(c)3 organizations serving the residents of Louisiana or Nevada are eligible to apply.
Restrictions: The Foundation does not support: organizations that are not 501(c)3 entities; political causes, candidates, organizations or campaigns; organizations whose primary purpose is to influence legislation; organizations that discriminate on the basis of age, color, disability, disabled veteran status, gender, race, religion, national origin, marital status, sexual orientation or military service; administrative expenses or programs with administrative expenses in excess of 15%; capital project funding; purchase of uniforms or trips for school-related organizations and booster clubs, youth athletics or amateur sports teams; activities whose sole purpose is promotion or support of a specific religion, denomination or religious institution; fraternal, alumni, trade, professional or social organizations; individuals; medical fundraisers; political or partisan organizations or candidates; or study or travel grants (scholarships, stipends, writing allowances).
Geographic Focus: Louisiana, Nevada
Amount of Grant: 5,000 - 60,000 USD
Samples: McNeese State University Foundation, Lake Charles, Louisiana, $60,000 - general operating funds; West Jefferson Hospital Foundation, Marrero, Louisiana, $50,000 - general operating funds; University of Nevada Las Vegas Foundation, Las Vegas, Nevada, $12,500 - general operating funds.
Contact: Shelly Peterson, (702) 541-7777 or (818) 710-2719
Internet: www.pnkinc.com/pinnacle-entertainment-foundation/
Sponsor: Pinnacle Entertainment Foundation
8918 Spanish Ridge Avenue
Las Vegas, NV 89148-1302

Pinnacle Foundation Grants   1973

The Pinnacle Foundation was established in the State of Washington with a primary interest in family, military family support, critical housing, and homeless programs. Although there are no specified annual deadlines, a formal application is required. The standard application should include contact information, a description of the charitable function, and an overview of the project.
Geographic Focus: All States
Contact: Stanley J. Harrelson, President; (206) 215-9700 or (206) 215-9747
Sponsor: Pinnacle Foundation
2801 Alaskan Way, Suite 310
Seattle, WA 98121-1136

Piper Jaffray Foundation Communities Giving Grants   1974

The foundation supports organizations and programs that enhance the lives of people living and working in communities in which the company has offices. Of primary interest is support for organizations that increase opportunities for individuals to improve their lives and help themselves. Highest priority is given to family stability programs (including housing, family violence, responsible parenting), early childhood development, job training/career development, youth development, and adult education services. The foundation will also consider requests from organizations that work to increase citizen understanding or involvement in civic affairs or that enhance the artistic and cultural life of the community. Requests for general operating support from proven nonprofit organizations will be considered. Requests for project and capital support will be considered on a very selective basis. Support for higher education and K-12 public and private schools is provided primarily through the company gift-matching program. Contact the foundation for deadline dates.
Requirements: IRS 501(c)3 organizations located in the Minneapolis/Saint Paul metropolitan area should submit requests directly to the foundation. Organizations located outside the Minneapolis/Saint Paul metropolitan area should submit requests to the nearest Piper Jaffray office for forwarding to the foundation. Offices are located in communities in Arizona, California, Colorado, Idaho, Illinois, Iowa, Kansas, Kentucky, Minnesota, Missouri, Montana, Nebraska, Nevada, North Dakota, Ohio, Oregon, South Dakota, Tennessee, Utah, Washington, Wisconsin, and Wyoming.
Restrictions: Requests will not be considered from newly formed nonprofit organizations; individuals; teams; religious, political, veterans, or fraternal organizations; or organizations working to treat or eliminate specific diseases. Support is not available for basic or applied research, travel, event sponsorship, benefits or tickets, or to eliminate an organization's operating deficit.
Geographic Focus: Arizona, Arkansas, California, Colorado, Idaho, Illinois, Iowa, Kansas, Kentucky, Minnesota, Missouri, Montana, Nebraska, Nevada, North Dakota, Ohio, Oregon, South Dakota, Tennessee, Utah, Washington, Wisconsin, Wyoming
Date(s) Application is Due: Mar 18
Amount of Grant: 1,000 - 5,000 USD
Contact: Connie McCuskey; (612) 303-1309; fax (612) 342-6085; communityrelations@pjc.com
Internet: www.piperjaffray.com/2col_largeright.aspx?id=127
Sponsor: Piper Jaffray Foundation
800 Nicollet Mall, Suite 800
Minneapolis, MN 55402

Piper Trust Arts and Culture Grants   1975

The Piper Trust's grantmaking focuses on Virginia Galvin Piper's commitment to improving the quality of life for residents of Maricopa County. Piper Trust's particular interest lies with projects that benefit young children, adolescents and older adults in Maricopa County. The Trust makes grants to faith-based organizations that serve these target populations in a manner consistent with program guidelines. For Arts and Culture grants, the trust is focused on improved business and financial operations; collaborations for greater effectiveness and efficiencies; and, revenue generation, cost reduction, and mergers.
Requirements: Piper Trust makes grants to actively operating Section 501(c)3 organizations in Maricopa County. These organizations must have been in operation for at least three years from the effective date of their IRS ruling. Special rules apply to private foundations and 509(a)3 (Type III) organizations. There are no deadlines on initial proposals, and letters of inquiry throughout the year are reviewed throughout the year. If the Trust asks for a full proposal, its disposition depends on its completeness and the meeting schedule of the Piper trustees. Virginia G. Piper Charitable Trust requires all arts and culture grantees to participate in the Arizona Cultural Data Project (Arizona CDP). The Arizona CDP is a powerful online management tool designed to strengthen arts and cultural organizations by providing an amazing array of reports designed to increase management capacity, inform decision-making, and document the economic value of the arts.
Restrictions: Individuals are not eligible.
Geographic Focus: Arizona
Amount of Grant: Up to 350,000 USD
Contact: Ellen Solowey, Program Officer; (480) 556-7133; esolowey@pipertrust.org
Internet: pipertrust.org/our-grants/arts-culture/
Sponsor: Virginia G. Piper Charitable Trust
1202 East Missouri Avenue
Phoenix, AZ 85014

Piper Trust Children Grants   1976

The Piper Trust's grantmaking focuses on Virginia Galvin Piper's commitment to improving the quality of life for residents of Maricopa County. Piper Trust's particular interest lies with projects that benefit young children, adolescents and older adults in Maricopa County. The Trust makes grants to faith-based organizations that serve these target populations in a manner consistent with program guidelines. For Children grants, the trust is focused on improved parent and caregiver child-rearing know-how; assistance for children without resources or with special needs; enhanced child care practices and after school care; and, integrated early childhood policies and practices.
Requirements: Piper Trust makes grants to actively operating Section 501(c)3 organizations in Maricopa County. These organizations must have been in operation for at least three years from the effective date of their IRS ruling. Special rules apply to private foundations and 509(a)3 (Type III) organizations. There are no deadlines on initial proposals, and letters of inquiry throughout the year are reviewed throughout the year. If the Trust asks for a full proposal, its disposition depends on its completeness and the meeting schedule of the Piper trustees.
Geographic Focus: Arizona
Contact: Terri Leon, Program Officer; (480) 556-7121; tleon@pipertrust.org
Internet: pipertrust.org/our-grants/children/
Sponsor: Virginia G. Piper Charitable Trust
1202 East Missouri Avenue
Phoenix, AZ 85014

Piper Trust Education Grants   1977

The Piper Trust's grantmaking focuses on Virginia Galvin Piper's commitment to improving the quality of life for residents of Maricopa County. Piper Trust's particular interest lies with projects that benefit young children, adolescents and older adults in Maricopa County. The Trust makes grants to faith-based organizations that serve these target populations in a manner consistent with program guidelines. For Education grants, the trust is most interested in proposals that address improved early learning environments, academic enhancements for youth, and engagement of older adults in learning.
Requirements: Piper Trust makes grants to actively operating Section 501(c)3 organizations in Maricopa County. These organizations must have been in operation for at least three years from the effective date of their IRS ruling. Special rules apply to private foundations and 509(a)3 (Type III) organizations. There are no deadlines on initial proposals, and letters of inquiry throughout the year are reviewed throughout the year. If the Trust asks for a full proposal, its disposition depends on its completeness and the meeting schedule of the Piper trustees.
Geographic Focus: Arizona
Contact: Terri Leon, Program Officer; (480) 556-7121; tleon@pipertrust.org
Sponsor: Virginia G. Piper Charitable Trust
1202 East Missouri Avenue
Phoenix, AZ 85014

Piper Trust Healthcare and Medical Research Grants   1978

The Piper Trust's grantmaking focuses on Virginia Galvin Piper's commitment to improving the quality of life for residents of Maricopa County. Piper Trust's particular interest lies with projects that benefit young children, adolescents and older adults in Maricopa County. The Trust makes grants to faith-based organizations that serve these target populations in a manner consistent with program guidelines. For Healthcare and Medical Research grants, the trust is most interested in proposals that address improved facilities for children, adolescents and older adults; better trained healthcare workforce; increased access to basic healthcare; and, centers for advancement in personalized medicine.
Requirements: Piper Trust makes grants to actively operating Section 501(c)3 organizations in Maricopa County. These organizations must have been in operation for at least three years from the effective date of their IRS ruling. Special rules apply to private foundations and 509(a)3 (Type III) organizations. There are no deadlines on initial proposals, and letters of inquiry

throughout the year are reviewed throughout the year. If the Trust asks for a full proposal, its disposition depends on its completeness and the meeting schedule of the Piper trustees.
Geographic Focus: Arizona
Contact: Terri Leon, Program Officer; (480) 556-7121; tleon@pipertrust.org
Internet: pipertrust.org/our-grants/healthcare-medical-research/
Sponsor: Virginia G. Piper Charitable Trust
1202 East Missouri Avenue
Phoenix, AZ 85014

Piper Trust Reglious Organizations Grants   1979

The Piper Trust's grantmaking focuses on Virginia Galvin Piper's commitment to improving the quality of life for residents of Maricopa County. Piper Trust's particular interest lies with projects that benefit young children, adolescents and older adults in Maricopa County. Grantmaking for religious organizations reflects Piper's objectives and strategies in the Children, Older Adults, Education, and Healthcare program areas. For Religious Organizations grants, the trust is most interested in proposals that address assessments of learning environments in faith-based preschools and quality improvement projects and housing alternatives for older adults.
Requirements: Piper Trust makes grants to actively operating Section 501(c)3 organizations in Maricopa County. These organizations must have been in operation for at least three years from the effective date of their IRS ruling. Special rules apply to private foundations and 509(a)3 (Type III) organizations. There are no deadlines on initial proposals, and letters of inquiry throughout the year are reviewed throughout the year. If the Trust asks for a full proposal, its disposition depends on its completeness and the meeting schedule of the Piper trustees.
Geographic Focus: Arizona
Contact: Terri Leon, Program Officer; (480) 556-7121; tleon@pipertrust.org
Internet: pipertrust.org/our-grants/religious-organizations/
Sponsor: Virginia G. Piper Charitable Trust
1202 East Missouri Avenue
Phoenix, AZ 85014

Pittsburgh Foundation Affordable Housing Grants   1980

The Pittsburgh Foundation is a community foundation that works in partnership with nonprofit organizations to meet community needs. In the area of basic needs grants that help to create self-sufficient individuals and families, the Foundation supports projects that address the following focus areas: quality pre-K through 12 education; affordable housing; public transportation; healthy children and adults; and opportunities for meaningful work. Specifically, Affordable Housing grants increase the supply of financial support for housing for low and moderate-income families and seniors, thus reducing the number of people who become homeless. Applicants should first forward a Letter of Inquiry, which will lead to an invited full application for acceptable projects. The annual deadlines for Letters of Inquiry are: December 8, February 23, May 15, and September 1. Annual deadlines for full applications are: January 4, March 10, June 5, and September 25.
Requirements: To be eligible for funding from the Pittsburgh Foundation's discretionary funds, a nonprofit organization must be located within Allegheny County or demonstrate service to Allegheny County residents. The Foundation only makes grants to nonprofits designated by the IRS as 501(c)3 organizations. If an organization does not have 501(c)3 status, it may apply utilizing a fiscal sponsor.
Geographic Focus: Pennsylvania
Date(s) Application is Due: Jan 4; Mar 10; Jun 5; Sep 25
Amount of Grant: Up to 250,000 USD
Samples: Pittsburgh United, Pittsburgh, Pennsylvania, $125,000 - to support a campaign for a city-wide affordable housing strategy; Neighborhood Housing Services, Larimer, Pennsylvania, $100,000 - to provide financial education and counseling to residents in Larimer; Chartiers Community MH/MR Center, Pittsburgh, Pennsylvania, $28,775 - to support the Healthy Housing Outreach Program.
Contact: Michelle McMurray, Senior Program Officer, Health and Human Services; (412) 394-2610 or (412) 391-5122; fax (412) 391-7259; mcmurraym@pghfdn.org
Internet: pittsburghfoundation.org/basic-needs-grants
Sponsor: Pittsburgh Foundation
5 PPG Place, Suite 250
Pittsburgh, PA 15222-5414

Pittsburgh Foundation Healthy Children and Adults Grants   1981

The Pittsburgh Foundation is a community foundation that works in partnership with nonprofit organizations to meet community needs. In the area of basic needs grants that help to create self-sufficient individuals and families, the Foundation supports projects that address the following focus areas: quality pre-K through 12 education; affordable housing; public transportation; healthy children and adults; and opportunities for meaningful work. Specifically, Healthy Children and Adults awards improve community-based systems of care that support the physical and mental health of vulnerable populations in Allegheny County. The annual deadlines for Letters of Inquiry are: December 8, February 23, May 15, and September 1. Annual deadlines for full applications are: January 4, March 10, June 5, and September 25.
Requirements: To be eligible for funding from the Pittsburgh Foundation's discretionary funds, a nonprofit organization must be located within Allegheny County or demonstrate service to Allegheny County residents. The Foundation only makes grants to nonprofits designated by the IRS as 501(c)3 organizations. If an organization does not have 501(c)3 status, it may apply utilizing a fiscal sponsor.
Geographic Focus: Pennsylvania
Date(s) Application is Due: Jan 4; Mar 10; Jun 5; Sep 25
Amount of Grant: Up to 250,000 USD
Samples: Southwest Pennsylvania Environmental Health Project, Pittsburgh, Pennsylvania, $93,000 - to create a community-sourcing site for documenting evidence of health, air

and water impacts from shale gas extraction; Community Human Services Corporation, Pittsburgh, Pennsylvania, $90,000 - to support an integrated in-home services intervention for vulnerable seniors with chronic health conditions; Healthy Village Learning Institute, Pittsburgh, Pennsylvania, $30,000 - to support the Healthy Village Learning Institute program for youth ages 8-16 in McKeesport.
Contact: Michelle McMurray, Senior Program Officer, Health and Human Services; (412) 394-2610 or (412) 391-5122; fax (412) 391-7259; mcmurraym@pghfdn.org
Internet: pittsburghfoundation.org/basic-needs-grants
Sponsor: Pittsburgh Foundation
5 PPG Place, Suite 250
Pittsburgh, PA 15222-5414

PMI Foundation Grants   1982
The PMI Foundation awards grants nationally, with emphasis on California, to a wide range of organizations with the goal of expanding homeownership. The foundation also contributes generously to deserving causes and charities in the areas of arts and culture, health and human services, education, civic organizations, and community development. Application guidelines are available for download from the PMI website. There are no application deadlines. Check with foundation staff to verify whether they are currently accepting applications.
Requirements: 501(c)3 organizations are eligible. Requests must target the disadvantaged, the poor, and distressed populations. Requests must either focus on increasing affordable housing opportunities or directly contribute to the quality of life in under-served communities.
Restrictions: The PMI Foundation does not accept requests for the following purposes: individuals; fraternal, veteran, labor, athletic or religious organizations serving a limited constituency; political or lobbying organizations, or those supporting the candidacy of a particular individual; travel funds; and films, videotapes or audio productions.
Geographic Focus: All States
Amount of Grant: 200 - 200,000 USD
Samples: Habitat for Humanity (East Bay), Oakland, California, $25,000; Animal Rescue Foundation, Walnut Creek, California, $2,500; Consumer Credit Counseling Services, San Francisco, California, $35,000.
Contact: Laura Kinney, Foundation Grant Administrator; (925) 658-6562
Internet: www.pmifoundation.org/index.html
Sponsor: PMI Foundation
3003 Oak Road
Walnut Creek, CA 94597-2098

PNC Foundation Affordable Housing Grants   1983
The PNC Foundation supports a variety of nonprofit organizations with a special emphasis on those that work to achieve sustainability and touch a diverse population. In particular, funding is provided to those that support early childhood education and/or economic development. With this program the Foundation understands the critical need for affordable housing for low-and moderate-income individuals, and is committed to providing support to nonprofit organizations that: give counseling and services to help these individuals maintain their housing stock; offer transitional housing units and programs; and offer credit counseling assistance to individuals, helping them to prepare for home ownership.
Requirements: Organizations receiving support from the PNC Foundation must have a current Internal Revenue Service tax-exempt designation and be eligible to receive charitable contributions. In addition, the proposed activity must occur in a community where PNC has a significant presence. This includes select counties in the following states: Alabama; Arizona; Colorado; Delaware; District of Columbia; Florida; Georgia; Illinois; Indiana; Kansas; Kentucky; Maryland; Massachusetts; Michigan; Minnesota; Missouri; New Jersey; North Carolina; Ohio; Pennsylvania; South Carolina; Tennessee; Texas; Virginia; and Wisconsin.
Restrictions: The Foundation will not provide support for: organizations that discriminate by race, color, creed, gender or national origin; religious organizations, except for non-sectarian activities; advocacy groups; operating funds for agencies that receive funds through PNC United Way allocation; individuals or private foundations; annual funds of hospitals or colleges and universities; conferences and seminars; or tickets and goodwill advertising.
Geographic Focus: Alabama, Arizona, Colorado, Delaware, District of Columbia, Florida, Georgia, Illinois, Indiana, Kansas, Kentucky, Maryland, Massachusetts, Michigan, Minnesota, Missouri, New Jersey, North Carolina, Ohio, Pennsylvania, South Carolina, Tennessee, Texas, Virginia, Wisconsin
Contact: Sally McCrady, Chairwoman; (412) 768-8371; sally.mccrady@pnc.com
Internet: www.pnc.com/en/about-pnc/corporate-responsibility/philanthropy/pnc-foundation.html
Sponsor: PNC Foundation
630 Liberty Avenue, Tenth Floor
Pittsburg, PA 15222-2705

PNC Foundation Community Services Grants   1984
The PNC Foundation supports a variety of nonprofit organizations with a special emphasis on those that work to achieve sustainability and touch a diverse population. In particular, funding is provided to those that support early childhood education and/or economic development. Through this program, support is given to social services organizations that benefit the health, education, quality of life or provide essential services for low-and moderate-income individuals and families. The Foundation supports job training programs and organizations that provide essential services for their families. PNC provides support for early learning and educational enrichment programs for children in low-and moderate-income families as well as for the construction of community facilities that benefit low-and moderate-income communities.
Requirements: Organizations receiving support from the PNC Foundation must have a current Internal Revenue Service tax-exempt designation and be eligible to receive charitable contributions. In addition, the proposed activity must occur in a community where PNC has a significant presence. This includes select counties in the following states: Alabama; Arizona;

Colorado; Delaware; District of Columbia; Florida; Georgia; Illinois; Indiana; Kansas; Kentucky; Maryland; Massachusetts; Michigan; Minnesota; Missouri; New Jersey; North Carolina; Ohio; Pennsylvania; South Carolina; Tennessee; Texas; Virginia; and Wisconsin.
Restrictions: The Foundation will not provide support for: organizations that discriminate by race, color, creed, gender or national origin; religious organizations, except for non-sectarian activities; advocacy groups; operating funds for agencies that receive funds through PNC United Way allocation; individuals or private foundations; annual funds of hospitals or colleges and universities; conferences and seminars; or tickets and goodwill advertising.
Geographic Focus: Alabama, Arizona, Colorado, Delaware, District of Columbia, Florida, Georgia, Illinois, Indiana, Kansas, Kentucky, Maryland, Massachusetts, Michigan, Minnesota, Missouri, New Jersey, North Carolina, Ohio, Pennsylvania, South Carolina, Tennessee, Texas, Virginia, Wisconsin
Contact: Sally McCrady, Chairwoman; (412) 768-8371; sally.mccrady@pnc.com
Internet: www.pnc.com/en/about-pnc/corporate-responsibility/philanthropy/pnc-foundation.html
Sponsor: PNC Foundation
630 Liberty Avenue, Tenth Floor
Pittsburg, PA 15222-2705

PNC Foundation Education Grants   1985
The PNC Foundation's priority is to form partnerships with community-based nonprofit organizations within the markets PNC serves in order to enhance educational opportunities for children. Funding is provided for educational programs for children and youth, particularly early education initiatives that serve low-and moderate-income children (birth through five), their teachers and families. Priority is given to programs that focus in the areas of math, science or the arts and include one or some combination of the following: direct services for children in their classroom or community; professional development for teachers; family engagement of children being served by grants; and volunteer opportunities for PNC employees. See the website for proposal instructions. All philanthropic giving is directed regionally. Inquiries and proposals should be directly addressed to the local PNC representative. Names and contact information are listed on an interactive map on the website.
Requirements: Organizations receiving support from the PNC Foundation must have a current Internal Revenue Service tax-exempt designation and be eligible to receive charitable contributions. In addition, the proposed activity must occur in a community where PNC has a significant presence. This includes select counties in the following states: Alabama; Arizona; Colorado; Delaware; District of Columbia; Florida; Georgia; Illinois; Indiana; Kansas; Kentucky; Maryland; Massachusetts; Michigan; Minnesota; Missouri; New Jersey; North Carolina; Ohio; Pennsylvania; South Carolina; Tennessee; Texas; Virginia; and Wisconsin.
Restrictions: The following is not supported: organizations that discriminate by race, color, creed, gender or national origin; religious organizations, except for non-sectarian activities; advocacy groups; operating funds for agencies that receive funds through PNC United Way allocation; individuals or private foundations; annual funds of hospitals or colleges and universities; conferences and seminars; and tickets and goodwill advertising.
Geographic Focus: Alabama, Arizona, Colorado, Delaware, District of Columbia, Florida, Georgia, Illinois, Indiana, Kansas, Kentucky, Maryland, Massachusetts, Michigan, Minnesota, Missouri, New Jersey, North Carolina, Ohio, Pennsylvania, South Carolina, Tennessee, Texas, Virginia, Wisconsin
Contact: Sally McCrady, Chairwoman; (412) 768-8371; sally.mccrady@pnc.com
Internet: www.pnc.com/en/about-pnc/corporate-responsibility/philanthropy/pnc-foundation.html
Sponsor: PNC Foundation
630 Liberty Avenue, Tenth Floor
Pittsburg, PA 15222-2705

PNC Foundation Grow Up Great Early Childhood Grants   1986
Organizations receiving support from the PNC Foundation must have a current Internal Revenue Service tax-exempt designation and be eligible to receive charitable contributions. In addition, the proposed activity must occur in a community where PNC has a significant presence. With this program the Foundation supports educational programs for children and youth, particularly early education initiatives that serve low-and moderate-income children (birth through age five), their teachers and families. Priority is given to programs that focus in the areas of math, science, the arts or financial education and include one or some combination of the following; Direct services for children in their classroom or community, Professional development for teachers, Family engagement in the early education of children being served by grants and Volunteer opportunities for PNC employees.
Requirements: Organizations receiving support from the PNC Foundation must have a current Internal Revenue Service tax-exempt designation and be eligible to receive charitable contributions. In addition, the proposed activity must occur in a community where PNC has a significant presence. This includes select counties in the following states: Alabama; Arizona; Colorado; Delaware; District of Columbia; Florida; Georgia; Illinois; Indiana; Kansas; Kentucky; Maryland; Massachusetts; Michigan; Minnesota; Missouri; New Jersey; North Carolina; Ohio; Pennsylvania; South Carolina; Tennessee; Texas; Virginia; and Wisconsin.
Restrictions: The Foundation will not provide support for: organizations that discriminate by race, color, creed, gender or national origin; religious organizations, except for non-sectarian activities; advocacy groups; operating funds for agencies that receive funds through PNC United Way allocation; individuals or private foundations; annual funds of hospitals or colleges and universities; conferences and seminars; or tickets and goodwill advertising.
Geographic Focus: Alabama, Arizona, Colorado, Delaware, District of Columbia, Florida, Georgia, Illinois, Indiana, Kansas, Kentucky, Maryland, Massachusetts, Michigan, Minnesota, Missouri, New Jersey, North Carolina, Ohio, Pennsylvania, South Carolina, Tennessee, Texas, Virginia, Wisconsin

Contact: Sally McCrady, Chairwoman; (412) 768-8371 or (888) 762-2265; fax (412) 705-3584; sally.mccrady@pnc.com
Internet: www.pnc.com/en/about-pnc/corporate-responsibility/philanthropy/pnc-foundation.html
Sponsor: PNC Foundation
630 Liberty Avenue, Tenth Floor
Pittsburg, PA 15222-2705

PNC Foundation Revitalization and Stabilization Grants 1987

The PNC Foundation supports a variety of nonprofit organizations with a special emphasis on those that work to achieve sustainability and touch a diverse population. In particular, funding is provided to those that support early childhood education and/or economic development. Through its Revitalization and Stabilization program, the Foundation supports nonprofit organizations that serve low-and moderate-income neighborhoods by improving living and working conditions. Support is given to organizations that help stabilize communities, eliminate blight and attract and retain businesses and residents to the community.
Requirements: Organizations receiving support from the PNC Foundation must have a current Internal Revenue Service tax-exempt designation and be eligible to receive charitable contributions. In addition, the proposed activity must occur in a community where PNC has a significant presence. This includes select counties in the following states: Alabama; Arizona; Colorado; Delaware; District of Columbia; Florida; Georgia; Illinois; Indiana; Kansas; Kentucky; Maryland; Massachusetts; Michigan; Minnesota; Missouri; New Jersey; North Carolina; Ohio; Pennsylvania; South Carolina; Tennessee; Texas; Virginia; and Wisconsin.
Restrictions: The Foundation will not provide support for: organizations that discriminate by race, color, creed, gender or national origin; religious organizations, except for non-sectarian activities; advocacy groups; operating funds for agencies that receive funds through PNC United Way allocation; individuals or private foundations; annual funds of hospitals or colleges and universities; conferences and seminars; or tickets and goodwill advertising.
Geographic Focus: Alabama, Arizona, Colorado, Delaware, District of Columbia, Florida, Georgia, Illinois, Indiana, Kansas, Kentucky, Maryland, Massachusetts, Michigan, Minnesota, Missouri, New Jersey, North Carolina, Ohio, Pennsylvania, South Carolina, Tennessee, Texas, Virginia, Washington, Wisconsin
Contact: Sally McCrady, Chairwoman; (412) 768-8371 or (888) 762-2265; fax (412) 705-3584; sally.mccrady@pnc.com
Internet: www.pnc.com/en/about-pnc/corporate-responsibility/philanthropy/pnc-foundation.html
Sponsor: PNC Foundation
630 Liberty Avenue, Tenth Floor
Pittsburg, PA 15222-2705

PNM Reduce Your Use Grants 1988

Reduce Your Use Grants help nonprofit organizations put their energy-saving ideas into action with grants up to $5,000. Since its inception in 2008, this program has awarded more than $1.5 million to nonprofits around the state of New Mexico to help them decrease their energy use in order to free up funds for their mission-based programs.
Requirements: All Reduce Your Use Grant submissions should include activities designed to educate your employees, clients and community about the importance of energy conservation. Priority will be given to organizations that have PNM employees and retirees actively volunteering with them. 501(c)3 nonprofit organizations are eligible to apply. Applications will be awarded throughout the state in communities PNM serves or where PNM has a significant presence. As the state's largest electricity provider, PNM serves more than 500,000 New Mexico residential and business customers in Greater Albuquerque, Rio Rancho, Los Lunas and Belen, Santa Fe, Las Vegas, Alamogordo, Ruidoso, Silver City, Deming, Bayard, Lordsburg and Clayton. It also serves the New Mexico tribal communities of the Tesuque, Cochiti, Santo Domingo, San Felipe, Santa Ana, Sandia, Isleta and Laguna Pueblos.
Restrictions: Reduce Your Use Grants will not be awarded to any of the following groups, programs or activities: individual teachers, schools or school districts; individuals; organizations without current or active IRS 501(c)3 status; payments of loans, interest, taxes or debt retirement; sectarian or religious programs for religious purposes; special events, annual events, camps or one-time only events; veterans, labor and political organizations or campaigns; municipalities (however, if a municipality uses a 501(c)3 nonprofit organization as a fiscal agent, they may qualify); organizations outside of PNM Resources service territory; organizations that are not registered with the appropriate state registration agency or are not in good standing with the registration body; organizations that limit membership and services based on race, religion, color, creed, sex, sexual orientation, age or national origin.
Geographic Focus: New Mexico
Amount of Grant: Up to 5,000 USD
Contact: Jennifer Scacco, Project Manager; (505) 241-2864; Jennifer.Scacco@pnmresources.com
Internet: www.pnm.com/reduceyouruse
Sponsor: PNM Resources Foundation
414 Silver Avenue SW
Albuquerque, NM 87102

Poetry Foundation Young People's Poet Laureate 1989

Naomi Shihab Nye is the Poetry Foundation's Young People's Poet Laureate, serving from 2019 to 2021. Awarded by the Poetry Foundation for a two-year term, the Young People's Poet Laureate aims to raise awareness that young people have a natural receptivity to poetry and are its most appreciative audience, especially when poems are written specifically for them. Awarded every two years, the $25,000 laureate title is given to a living writer in recognition of a career devoted to writing exceptional poetry for young readers. The laureate advises the Poetry Foundation on matters relating to young people's literature and may engage in a variety of projects to help instill a lifelong love of poetry among the nation's developing readers. This laureateship aims to promote poetry to children and their families, teachers, and librarians over the course of its two-year tenure.
Geographic Focus: All States
Amount of Grant: Up to 25,000 USD
Contact: Caren Yanis, Chair; (312) 787-7070; info@poetryfoundation.org
Internet: www.poetryfoundation.org/learn/young-peoples-poet-laureate
Sponsor: Poetry Foundation
61 West Superior Street
Chicago, IL 60654

Pohlad Family Foundation Large Capital Grants 1990

The Pohlad Family Foundation concentrates their funding on the arts, health and human services, capital grants, and youth programs. The Foundation strives to support programs that: support all types and sizes of art programs of interest to diverse audiences; provide essential and effective human services to disadvantaged children and families; fund a range of services from emergency needs to workforce development; and have a positive multi-year impact. The Foundation carefully selects the large capital grant requests it considers each year. Generally these grants are for significant investments in major building renovation or expansion. Grants awarded are expected to be between $50,000 and $250,000. Large capital building project requests requiring funding from the state of Minnesota will not be considered until a decision on that funding has been made. Full final online proposals are due each year by May 16.
Requirements: Only applications for projects that are in the final phase (75% or more completed) of fundraising and are construction-ready will be considered. Organizations that meet all of the following criteria may apply: be established and operating for at least five consecutive years in the Twin Cities; be located and provide direct services to a large number of people living in the Twin Cities area; have experienced staff and board leadership to implement this grant; have not received a large capital grant from the Pohlad Foundation during the past seven years; demonstrate need for expansion, sufficient start-up working capital, and have a realistic plan for sustainable ongoing operating revenue; have annual operating budgets between $4 million and $25 million; have secured at least 75% of the funds needed for the proposed project; and comply with the Foundation's general grant guidelines.
Restrictions: No grant will exceed 10% of the total capital costs. Funding is not available for: direct funding to individuals; health or housing-related emergency assistance to individuals; benefits, fundraisers, walk-a-thons, telethons, galas, or other revenue generating events; advertising; organizations that discriminate on the basis of race, gender, religion, culture, age, physical ability or disability, sexual orientation, gender identity, status as a military veteran or genetic information; veterans' and fraternal organizations; political or lobbying organizations; replacement of government funding.
Geographic Focus: Minnesota
Date(s) Application is Due: May 16
Amount of Grant: 50,000 - 250,000 USD
Contact: Briana Riley, Program Manager; (612) 661-3954 or (612) 661-3910; fax (612) 661-3715; briley@pohladfoundation.org
Internet: www.pohladfoundation.org/grantmaking/program-descriptions-guidelines/
Sponsor: Pohlad Family Foundation
60 South Sixth Street, Suite 3900
Minneapolis, MN 55402

Pohlad Family Foundation Small Capital Grants 1991

The Pohlad Family Foundation concentrates their funding on the arts, health and human services, capital grants, and youth programs. The Foundation strives to support programs that: support all types and sizes of art programs of interest to diverse audiences; provide essential and effective human services to disadvantaged children and families; fund a range of services from emergency needs to workforce development; and have a positive multi-year impact. The Foundation makes a limited number of capital grants (approximately twenty grants annually in recent years) for smaller infrastructure projects to help organizations serve more people and/or be more effective and efficient in implementing their core strategies. Recent projects include facility renovations and relocations, purchase of new technology (computers, servers), and vehicle upgrades for transport of program participants. Although most awards range from $10,000 to $30,000, grants have ranged from $2,500 to $50,000 depending on the scope of the proposed project. The annual deadline for final online applications is May 16.
Requirements: Applicant organizations must be 501(c)3 non-profit organizations. Priority is given to organizations that demonstrate a commitment to their communities by ensuring that their governing bodies include representatives from within the community and projects that directly benefit communities in need.
Restrictions: Funding is not available for: direct funding to individuals; health or housing-related emergency assistance to individuals; benefits, fundraisers, walk-a-thons, telethons, galas, or other revenue generating events; advertising; organizations that discriminate on the basis of race, gender, religion, culture, age, physical ability or disability, sexual orientation, gender identity, status as a military veteran or genetic information; veterans' and fraternal organizations; political or lobbying organizations; replacement of government funding.
Geographic Focus: Minnesota
Date(s) Application is Due: May 16
Amount of Grant: 2,500 - 50,000 USD
Contact: Briana Riley, Program Manager; (612) 661-3954 or (612) 661-3910; fax (612) 661-3715; briley@pohladfoundation.org
Internet: www.pohladfoundation.org/grantmaking/program-descriptions-guidelines/
Sponsor: Pohlad Family Foundation
60 South Sixth Street, Suite 3900
Minneapolis, MN 55402

Pohlad Family Foundation Summer Camp Scholarships 1992

The Pohlad Family Foundation concentrates their funding on the arts, health and human services, capital grants, and youth programs. The Foundation strives to support programs that: support all types and sizes of art programs of interest to diverse audiences; provide essential and effective human services to disadvantaged children and families; fund a range of services from emergency needs to workforce development; and have a positive multi-year impact. The Foundation's Summer Camp Scholarships program was initiated in 1999 with the expressed purpose of providing families with young people between the ages 7 and 16 financial assistance needed to attend residential camping programs intended to enrich a child's life experience. Such camping programs should provide opportunities for social, emotional, intellectual, moral, and physical development. The program places a high priority on awarding scholarships to youth that have not had a previous residential camping experience. Most grants are made to education, human service, and other nonprofit organizations that work with economically disadvantaged children and families, but that do not operate a summer camp program themselves. Applications must be complete and submitted by January 27.

Requirements: Applications are considered only in response to a request for proposal or an invitation to apply. Organizations must be 501(c)3 non-profit organizations. Priority is given to organizations that demonstrate a commitment to their communities by ensuring that their governing bodies include representatives from within the community and projects that directly benefit communities in need.

Restrictions: This grant does not fund scholarships for youth who have already attended camp twice. Grants and scholarships are focused in Minnesota, primarily St. Paul and Minneapolis. Funding is not available for: direct funding to individuals; health or housing-related emergency assistance to individuals; benefits, fundraisers, walk-a-thons, telethons, galas, or other revenue generating events; advertising; organizations that discriminate on the basis of race, gender, religion, culture, age, physical ability or disability, sexual orientation, gender identity, status as a military veteran or genetic information; veterans' and fraternal organizations; political or lobbying organizations; replacement of government funding.

Geographic Focus: Minnesota
Date(s) Application is Due: Jan 27
Amount of Grant: 5,000 - 18,000 USD
Contact: Briana Riley, Program Manager; (612) 661-3954; briley@pohladfoundation.org
Internet: www.pohladfoundation.org/grantmaking/program-descriptions-guidelines/
Sponsor: Pohlad Family Foundation
60 South Sixth Street, Suite 3900
Minneapolis, MN 55402

Pohlad Family Foundation Youth Advancement Grants 1993

The Pohlad Family Foundation concentrates their funding on the arts, health and human services, capital grants, and youth programs. The Foundation strives to support programs that: support all types and sizes of art programs of interest to diverse audiences; provide essential and effective human services to disadvantaged children and families; fund a range of services from emergency needs to workforce development; and have a positive multi-year impact. The Foundation's Youth Advancement grants provide support to programs that serve low-income youth ages 16 to 24 that are disconnected from education and employment. The Foundation believes that youth are assets, but many do not have access to the opportunity to reach their full potential. It further understands the critical nature of healthy development through young adulthood and that this age is a time of establishing social norms and skills fundamental to lifelong success. Finally, the Foundation realizes that the community's social and economic vitality requires young people to gain skills needed to participate in the workforce.

Requirements: Applications are considered only in response to a request for proposal or an invitation to apply. Organizations must be 501(c)3 non-profit organizations. Priority is given to organizations that demonstrate a commitment to their communities by ensuring that their governing bodies include representatives from within the community and projects that directly benefit communities in need.

Restrictions: Grants and scholarships are focused in Minnesota, primarily St. Paul and Minneapolis. Funding is not available for: direct funding to individuals; health or housing-related emergency assistance to individuals; benefits, fundraisers, walk-a-thons, telethons, galas, or other revenue generating events; advertising; organizations that discriminate on the basis of race, gender, religion, culture, age, physical ability or disability, sexual orientation, gender identity, status as a military veteran or genetic information; veterans' and fraternal organizations; political or lobbying organizations; replacement of government funding.

Geographic Focus: Minnesota
Contact: Briana Riley, Program Manager; (612) 661-3954; briley@pohladfoundation.org
Internet: www.pohladfoundation.org/grantmaking/program-descriptions-guidelines/
Sponsor: Pohlad Family Foundation
60 South Sixth Street, Suite 3900
Minneapolis, MN 55402

Pokagon Fund Grants 1994

The mission of the Pokagon Fund is to enhance the lives of the residents in the New Buffalo region of southwest Michigan through the financial support of local governments, nonprofits, charities and other organizations. Funding supports initiatives in the areas of health and human services, education, arts and culture, recreation, and environment. A number of distinct application forms are available at the website, including: a discretionary application; a band application; a municipal application; and a bus application. Annual deadlines for all application submissions are January 15, April 15, July 15, and October 15.

Requirements: 501(c)3 organizations throughout the Pokagon service area are eligible to apply.
Geographic Focus: Michigan
Date(s) Application is Due: Jan 15; Apr 15; Jul 15; Oct 15
Contact: Janet Cocciarelli, Exec. Director; (269) 469-9322; jcocciarelli@pokagonfund.org
Internet: www.pokagonfund.org/How.asp
Sponsor: Pokagon Fund
821 E. Buffalo Street
New Buffalo, MI 49117

Polk County Community Foundation Bradley Breakthrough Community Benefit Grants 1995

Since 1975, the Polk County Community Foundation has been dedicated to improving the quality of life in the community centered in and around Polk County, North Carolina. Bradley Breakthrough Community Benefit Grants must significantly improve the quality of life of Polk County residents for generations. The Bradley Board seeks grantmaking opportunities which result in long-term impacts for the community as a whole, and which may require a long-range view. Past grants have purchased and protected land for public benefit, including Alexander's Ford at Bradley Nature Preserve and a Bradley Nature Preserve in Saluda. There are two grant cycles annually, with deadlines of February 23 and August 30. Total funding available is $150,000.

Requirements: Grant proposals are accepted from local Polk County, North Carolina, nonprofits and governmental entities who share the Foundation's goal of improving the quality of life for all in the community.

Restrictions: The foundation does not award grants to individuals, except for educational awards. Grants are not allocated anywhere but where they directly benefit local citizens.

Geographic Focus: North Carolina
Date(s) Application is Due: Feb 23; Aug 30
Amount of Grant: 2,000 - 50,000 USD
Contact: Elizabeth Nager; (828) 859-5314; fax (828) 859-6122; foundation@polkccf.org
Internet: www.polkccf.org/index.php/grants/for-organizations/competitive-grants
Sponsor: Polk County Community Foundation
255 South Trade Street
Tryon, NC 28782-3707

Polk County Community Foundation Free Community Events Grants 1996

Since 1975, the Polk County Community Foundation has been dedicated to improving the quality of life in the community centered in and around Polk County, North Carolina. Recently, the Foundation has begun to offer grants for free community events, an initiative of the Foundation's Board of Directors to support face to face social interactions that build community in ways small and large. Gatherings funded by these grants are intended to benefit residents who have chosen to make the community their home, to give people an excuse to strike up a conversation and get to know your neighbors. Past grants have funded free entertainment at the Upstairs Artspace, heart-healthy banquets in Green Creek, programs for children and Shakespeare fans at the Polk County Public Library, and a Play Day for children and families in Saluda. All events are 100% free. The Foundation encourages applicants to consider incorporating one or more of the following into your project (not required): developing or sharing a common interest; healthy living emphasis, such as local and/or healthy food; physical activities; the use of public gathering spots, such as parks, libraries, and schools; or events that bring together local people from diverse demographic backgrounds around a common interest or passion. There are three grant cycles annually, with deadlines of January 26, March 8, and August 16. Awards will range from $3,000 to $8,000.

Requirements: Grant proposals are accepted from local Polk County, North Carolina, nonprofits and governmental entities who share the Foundation's goal of improving the quality of life for all in the community.

Restrictions: The foundation does not award grants to individuals, except for educational awards. Grants are not allocated anywhere but where they directly benefit local citizens.

Geographic Focus: North Carolina
Date(s) Application is Due: Jan 26; Mar 8; Aug 16
Amount of Grant: 3,000 - 8,000 USD
Contact: Elizabeth Nager; (828) 859-5314; fax (828) 859-6122; foundation@polkccf.org
Internet: www.polkccf.org/index.php/grants/for-organizations/competitive-grants
Sponsor: Polk County Community Foundation
255 South Trade Street
Tryon, NC 28782-3707

Polk County Community Foundation Kirby Harmon Field Fund Grants 1997

Since 1975, the Polk County Community Foundation has been dedicated to improving the quality of life in the community centered in and around Polk County, North Carolina. The Kirby Harmon Field Fund grant is to be used in support of sports and recreational activities oriented toward the development of teamwork and good citizenship among the youth in the area. The events should be free to the public. Materials and minor capital improvements may be part of the fund request, if they are part of the activity. This fund has supported a series of free tennis clinics for area youth and the Kirby Cup, a free soccer camp held annually at Harmon Field. The annual deadline for applications is March 8, with awards decisions being announced by May 18. The awards funding can range up to a maximum of $4,600.

Requirements: Grant proposals are accepted from local Polk County, North Carolina, nonprofits and governmental entities who share the Foundation's goal of improving the quality of life for all in the community.

Restrictions: The foundation does not award grants to individuals, except for educational awards. Grants are not allocated anywhere but where they directly benefit local citizens.

Geographic Focus: North Carolina
Date(s) Application is Due: Mar 8
Amount of Grant: Up to 4,600 USD
Contact: Elizabeth Nager; (828) 859-5314; fax (828) 859-6122; foundation@polkccf.org
Internet: www.polkccf.org/index.php/grants/for-organizations/competitive-grants
Sponsor: Polk County Community Foundation
255 South Trade Street
Tryon, NC 28782-3707

Polk County Community Foundation Marjorie M. and Lawrence R. Bradley Endowment Fund Grants 1998

Since 1975, the Polk County Community Foundation has been dedicated to improving the quality of life in the community centered in and around Polk County, North Carolina. The

late Mr. and Mrs. Bradley created the Marjorie M. and Lawrence R. Bradley Endowment Fund of Polk County in 2005, leaving virtually their entire estate for the benefit of the community. This bequest directed the Board of the Polk County Community Foundation to implement the Bradleys' charitable dreams of providing charitable, education, medical and community benefits to their community. There are several Bradley grant programs for the long-term benefit of the Polk County community. In addition to the Bradley Community Benefit Grants, the Bradley Fund contributes to the annual distribution budget for Unrestricted Grants and provides college scholarships through funds named in their honor, such as the Bradley Achievement Awards and the Puddin' Hill Awards.
Requirements: Grant proposals are accepted from local Polk County, North Carolina, nonprofits and governmental entities who share the Foundation's goal of improving the quality of life for all in the community.
Restrictions: The foundation does not award grants to individuals, except for educational awards. Grants are not allocated anywhere but where they directly benefit local citizens.
Geographic Focus: North Carolina
Amount of Grant: 2,000 - 50,000 USD
Contact: Elizabeth Nager; (828) 859-5314; fax (828) 859-6122; foundation@polkccf.org
Internet: www.polkccf.org/index.php/grants/for-organizations/competitive-grants
Sponsor: Polk County Community Foundation
255 South Trade Street
Tryon, NC 28782-3707

Polk County Community Foundation Mary F. Kessler Fund Grants   1999
Since 1975, the Polk County Community Foundation has been dedicated to improving the quality of life in the community centered in and around Polk County, North Carolina. Mary Kessler's fond connection to the Tryon and Landrum communities, along with her desire to have a permanent philanthropic role in them, led her to create this endowment fund. Kessler grants support projects in Tryon and Landrum that result in physical and scenic improvements, development, or beautification, as well as those with cultural, intellectual, and educational benefits. Past Kessler awards have funded the Children's Theater Festival's Super Saturday, planting noble trees at Harmon Field, restoration of the historic Landrum Railroad Depot as a performance venue, and the O.P. Earle Elementary School's Community Arts Evenings, which involved local artists in the arts education of its students and the public.
Requirements: Grant proposals are accepted from local Polk County, North Carolina, nonprofits and governmental entities who share the Foundation's goal of improving the quality of life for all in the community.
Restrictions: The foundation does not award grants to individuals, except for educational awards. Grants are not allocated anywhere but where they directly benefit local citizens.
Geographic Focus: North Carolina
Contact: Elizabeth Nager; (828) 859-5314; fax (828) 859-6122; foundation@polkccf.org
Internet: www.polkccf.org/index.php/grants/for-organizations/competitive-grants
Sponsor: Polk County Community Foundation
255 South Trade Street
Tryon, NC 28782-3707

**Polk County Community Foundation Seasonal Assistance and Cheer   2000
Grants for Charitable Programs**
Since 1975, the Polk County Community Foundation has been dedicated to improving the quality of life in the community centered in and around Polk County, North Carolina. With its Seasonal Assistance and Cheer grant program, the Foundation seeks to support the efforts and good works of the numerous local organizations that run assistance programs during the winter months. To respond to the needs of the community, the Board incorporated unrestricted gifts to the Foundation to create this program. Seasonal Assistance awards are made to charitable groups to help spread holiday cheer to members of the community who find themselves in unfortunate circumstances. Past grants have been used to provide festive gatherings for those who might otherwise not have the opportunity, mittens and other winter clothing for children and adults, emergency heating assistance, and holiday gifts for children.
Requirements: Grant proposals are accepted from local Polk County, North Carolina, nonprofits and governmental entities who share the Foundation's goal of improving the quality of life for all in the community.
Restrictions: The foundation does not award grants to individuals, except for educational awards. Grants are not allocated anywhere but where they directly benefit local citizens.
Geographic Focus: North Carolina
Contact: Elizabeth Nager; (828) 859-5314; fax (828) 859-6122; foundation@polkccf.org
Internet: www.polkccf.org/index.php/grants/for-organizations/competitive-grants
Sponsor: Polk County Community Foundation
255 South Trade Street
Tryon, NC 28782-3707

Polk County Community Foundation Unrestricted Grants   2001
Since 1975, the Polk County Community Foundation has been dedicated to improving the quality of life in the community centered in and around Polk County, North Carolina. The Foundation's Unrestricted grants program serves a particularly important purpose because it allows the Board of Directors the freedom to develop grantmaking programs and award grants to address the needs of the community as they change over time. Unrestricted grants are awarded to fund projects of value to the community such as capital expenses (non-recurring annual budget items), new projects and new programs. Basic operating expenses may be funded in the case of start-up organizations, small nonprofit organizations with operating expenses under $75,000 in the prior fiscal year, and in exceptional circumstances. There are two grant cycles annually, with deadlines of June 21 and November 17.
Requirements: Grant proposals are accepted from local Polk County, North Carolina, nonprofits and governmental entities who share the Foundation's goal of improving the quality of life for all in the community.

Restrictions: The foundation does not award grants to individuals, except for educational awards. Grants are not allocated anywhere but where they directly benefit local citizens.
Geographic Focus: North Carolina
Date(s) Application is Due: Jun 21; Nov 17
Amount of Grant: 2,000 - 50,000 USD
Contact: Elizabeth Nager; (828) 859-5314; fax (828) 859-6122; foundation@polkccf.org
Internet: www.polkccf.org/index.php/grants/for-organizations/competitive-grants
Sponsor: Polk County Community Foundation
255 South Trade Street
Tryon, NC 28782-3707

Porter County Community Foundation Health and Wellness Grant   2002
The Porter County Community Foundation Health and Wellness Fund awards grants to nonprofit organizations that promote, support, and/or advance health care in Porter County. Funding priorities include: increasing health care access for the underserved; improving and promoting healthy lifestyles for youth; and improving the nonprofit's operational capabilities to provide health care services. The maximum award amount is $25,000.
Requirements: In addition to the application, all grant application packets must include the following information: a grant request cover page; a grant narrative; a project budget; a current operating budget and financial statement; the names and principal occupations of the organization's Board of Directors; the organization's grant application approval by their Board of Directors; and a copy of the organization's 501(c)3 tax exemption ruling.
Restrictions: Grants will not be made to: individuals; membership contributions; event sponsorships; programs that are sectarian or religious in nature; political organizations or candidates; contributions to endowment campaigns; campaigns to reduce previously incurred debt; and programs already completed.
Geographic Focus: Indiana
Date(s) Application is Due: Jun 15
Amount of Grant: Up to 25,000 USD
Contact: Brenda Sheetz; (219) 465-0294; fax (219) 464-2733; brenda@pccf.gives
Internet: www.pccf.gives/nonprofits/grant-guidelines.html
Sponsor: Porter County Community Foundation
1401 Calumet Avenue
Valparaiso, IN 46383

Porter County Community Foundation PCgivingproject Grants   2003
Established by a group of passionate young leaders and families, the PCgivingproject brings inspiring young philanthropists together to invest in the future of Porter County by collectively funding grants for charitable initiatives that support innovative education and youth development programs that serve children and youth, birth through age 18. The program or project for which funding is being requested should address the needs and opportunities that support the Fund's purpose of improving the quality of life for our community's children of all ages. Grant proposals should be in the Foundation office by no later than 12:00 p.m. on April 3 each year.
Requirements: Philadelphia nonprofits are eligible.
Geographic Focus: Indiana
Date(s) Application is Due: Apr 3
Contact: Brenda A. Sheetz; (219) 465-0294; fax (219) 464-2733; brenda@pccf.gives
Internet: www.pccf.gives/nonprofits/grant-guidelines.html
Sponsor: Porter County Community Foundation
1401 Calumet Avenue
Valparaiso, IN 46383

Porter County Community Foundation Sparking the Arts Fund Grants   2004
Porter County Community Foundation Sparking the Arts Fund Grants program was created to foster a more visible role for the arts in Porter County which, in turn, can create a richer, more beautiful quality of life for the area's citizens. The program or project for which funding is being requested should support and/or promote the arts within the county in the following ways: promote public performances or displays of art works; enhance the capacity of arts organizations and the arts community; promote artistic quality and growth; foster and support local talent of all ages through art organizations; and inspire community pride. Grant proposals should be in the Foundation office by no later than 12:00 p.m. on May 15 each year.
Requirements: In addition to the online application form, all application packets must include the following information: a grant request cover page; a grant narrative (see application for narrative details); a project budget; a copy of the organization's current year operating budget; the organization's most recent financial statement; names and principal occupations of the Board of Directors; evidence of Board approval for this application; a copy of the organization's 501(c)3 tax exemption.
Restrictions: The grant will not fund the following: projects or programs that do not address issues facing women and/or children; scholarship programs including daycare and program participation fees; annual appeals or membership contributions; event sponsorships; programs that are sectarian or religious in nature; political organizations or candidates; contributions to endowment campaigns; campaigns to reduce previously incurred debt; individuals; programs already completed and/or equipment already contracted for; and travel for bands, sports teams and similar groups.
Geographic Focus: Indiana
Date(s) Application is Due: May 15
Contact: Brenda A. Sheetz; (219) 465-0294; fax (219) 464-2733; brenda@pccf.gives
Internet: www.pccf.gives/nonprofits/grant-guidelines.html
Sponsor: Porter County Community Foundation
1401 Calumet Avenue
Valparaiso, IN 46383

Porter County Community Foundation Women's Fund Grants   2005

The Women's Fund Grant program of Porter County seeks to improve the quality of life for women and children in Porter County by collectively funding high impact grants for charitable initiatives with the same purpose. The group will award a $45,000 grant to a nonprofit organization in support of a project or program that addresses the issues of women and children and is sustainable. Priority will be given to innovative programs that demonstrate positive outcomes in one of the following areas: education and training to promote economic security and self-sufficiency; leadership development and programs designed to build self-esteem; access to women's health services and healthy lifestyles; safe environments and freedom from violence; and access to affordable daycare services that will expand hours of service, increase the number served on a sustainable basis and/or improve quality.

Requirements: In addition to the online application form, all application packets must include the following information: a grant request cover page; a grant narrative (see application for narrative details); a project budget; a copy of the organization's current year operating budget; the organization's most recent financial statement; names and principal occupations of the Board of Directors; evidence of Board approval for this application; a copy of the organization's 501(c)3 tax exemption.

Restrictions: The grant will not fund the following: projects or programs that do not address issues facing women and/or children; scholarship programs including daycare and program participation fees; annual appeals or membership contributions; event sponsorships; programs that are sectarian or religious in nature; political organizations or candidates; contributions to endowment campaigns; campaigns to reduce previously incurred debt; individuals; programs already completed and/or equipment already contracted for; and travel for bands, sports teams and similar groups.

Geographic Focus: Indiana
Date(s) Application is Due: Mar 15
Amount of Grant: Up to 45,000 USD
Contact: Brenda Sheetz; (219) 465-0294; fax (219) 464-2733; brenda@pccf.gives
Internet: www.pccf.gives/nonprofits/grant-guidelines.html
Sponsor: Porter County Community Foundation
1401 Calumet Avenue
Valparaiso, IN 46383

Portland Foundation - Women's Giving Circle Grant   2006

The mission of The Portland Foundation Women's Giving Circle is to build a community of women philanthropists through the pooling of knowledge and resources for the purpose of providing grants to Jay County organizations and initiatives that address mutually-agreeable issues. The Circle awards grants which focus on enhancing the capacity of Jay County's not-for-profit organizations to support programming that addresses needs for youth and families. The Circle strives to fund innovative endeavors to benefit Jay County residents from toddlers to senior citizens.

Requirements: Organizations are encouraged to contact the Foundation to discuss whether their project is appropriate for funding. The application is available at the Foundation site. In addition to the application, proposals should include 10 copies of the following information: a copy of the IRS determination letter confirming tax-exempt status; organization's most recent financial statement, including budget and year-to-date income and expenses; and a detailed list of the Board of Directors.

Restrictions: The following are excluded from funding: organizations for religious or sectarian purposes; make-up of operating deficits, post-event or after-the-fact situations; endowment or capital projects and campaigns; for any propaganda, political or otherwise, attempting to influence legislation or intervene in any political affairs or campaigns; and dinner galas, advertising or other special fundraising events.

Geographic Focus: Indiana
Amount of Grant: 200 - 1,000 USD
Samples: Arts Place, Inc., Arts in the Parks Clay Camp and Family Pottery Nights, $525; Jay County Public Library, 1000 Books Before Kindergarten, $525; State of the Heart Hospice, Camp BEARable, $200.
Contact: Douglas Inman; (260) 726-4260; fax (260) 726-4273; tpf@portlandfoundation.org
Internet: www.portlandfoundation.org/womens-giving-circle-grant
Sponsor: Portland Foundation
112 East Main Street
Portland, IN 47371

Portland General Electric Foundation Grants   2007

Portland General Electric is committed to improving the quality of life for all Oregonians. The Foundation focuses giving in three areas: education, arts and culture, and healthy families. Education funding dedicates awards to scholarships, innovation in classroom instruction, transitional bridges between grade levels, career readiness and at-risk youth programs. Arts and Culture awards support youth programs and adult cultural programs that enhances understanding in communities. Healthy Families funding promotes access and services in areas of health, domestic violence, parenting, foster care, and other services that benefit families.

Requirements: 501(c)3 nonprofits in Oregon that address issues in the three focus areas of the Foundation are eligible for funding. Applicants must first submit a Letter of Inquiry to the Foundation; applicants may then be invited to submit a full application. Both of these steps must be completed online.

Restrictions: The foundation does not fund: bridge grants, debt retirement or operational deficits; endowment funds; general fund drives or annual appeals; political entities, ballot measure campaigns or candidates for political office; organizations that discriminate against individuals on the basis of creed, color, gender, sexual orientation, age, religion or national origin; fraternal, sectarian and religious organizations; individuals; travel expenses; or conferences, symposiums, festivals, events, team sponsorships or user fees. The Foundation also does not directly fund public K-12 education.

Geographic Focus: Oregon

Date(s) Application is Due: Jan 11; Apr 5; Jul 5; Nov 1
Amount of Grant: 2,500 - 10,000 USD
Samples: Artists Repertory Theatre, Oregon, $7,500 - for educational programming; Chess for Success, Oregon, $5,000 - after-school chess programs and tournaments for elementary schools; Lifeworks NW, Oregon, $10,000 - vocational assistance to adults living with severe mental illness.
Contact: Paige Haxton; (503) 464-8818; fax (503) 464-2929; pgefoundation@pgn.com
Internet: www.pgefoundation.org/how_we_fund.html
Sponsor: Portland General Electric Foundation
121 SW Salmon Street, One World Trade Center, 3rd Floor
Portland, OR 97204

Posey Community Foundation Women's Fund Grants   2008

The Posey County Community Foundation is a nonprofit, public charity created by and for the people of Posey County, Indiana. The Posey County's Women's Fund makes yearly grants to support a variety of projects or programs serving women and girls in Posey County, Indiana. These programs include those that prevent domestic violence, secure family-supporting jobs, promote health and education, and develop confidence. Grant proposals are accepted once each year. Grants are normally given as one time support of a project but may be considered for additional support for expansions or outgrowths of an initial project. The annual deadline for application submission is February 20. The application form and examples of previously funded projects available at the website.

Requirements: Projects must address the needs which support the Fund's mission by providing opportunities, encouragement, knowledge, information, and hope for the community's women and girls. The Women's Fund welcomes proposals from non-profit organizations that are tax-exempt under sections 501(c)3 and 509(a) of the Internal Revenue Code and from governmental agencies serving Posey County women and girls. Proposals from other non-profit organizations that address issues facing women and girls in the county may be accepted. Proposals submitted by an entity under the auspices of another agency must include a written statement signed by the agency's board president on behalf of the board of directors agreeing to act as the entity's fiscal sponsor, to receive grant monies if awarded, and to oversee the proposed project.

Geographic Focus: Indiana
Date(s) Application is Due: Feb 20
Amount of Grant: Up to 5,000 USD
Contact: Monica Spencer, Director; (812) 838-0288; fax (812) 838-8009; monica@poseycommunityfoundation.org
Internet: www.communityfoundationalliance.org/grant/womens-fund-grant-program/
Sponsor: Posey County Community Foundation
402 Main Street, P.O. Box 746
Mt. Vernon, IN 47620

Posey County Community Foundation Recreation Grants   2009

The Posey County Community Foundation is a nonprofit, public charity created by and for the people of Posey County, Indiana. Grant proposals are accepted once each year as a one-time project support. At the beginning of each cycle in January, notices are sent to nonprofit organizations that have previously applied for grants, have received grants in the past, or have otherwise requested notification. Applicants are encouraged to schedule a meeting with the Foundation's director to receive an overview of the grant process. Proposals are accepted from January through August 1. The grants committee will make its recommendations on funding to the Foundation's Board of Trustees, which will make final funding recommendations to the board of directors of the Community Foundation Alliance. All organizations that have submitted grant proposals are notified of the final outcome no later than December 1. Grants in the area of Recreation include projects aimed at improving and promoting recreational and leisure activities, parks, and community sporting events and activities. Samples of previously funded projects are available at the website.

Requirements: The Foundation welcomes funding requests from nonprofit organizations that are 501(c)3 or 509(a) tax exempt, and from governmental agencies serving Posey County. For those organizations not tax exempt, requests may be considered if the project is charitable and supports a community need. Proposals submitted by an entity under the auspices of another agency must include a written statement signed by the agency's board president on behalf of the board of directors agreeing to act as the entity's fiscal sponsor, to receive grant monies if awarded, and to oversee the proposed project.

Restrictions: Project areas not considered for funding include: religious organizations for religious purposes; political parties or campaigns; endowment creation or debt reduction; operating costs; capital campaigns; annual appeals or membership contributions; travel requests for groups or individuals such as bands, sports teams, or classes.

Geographic Focus: Indiana
Date(s) Application is Due: Aug 1
Amount of Grant: Up to 5,000 USD
Contact: Monica Spencer, Regional Director; (812) 838-0288; fax (812) 838-8009; monica@poseycommunityfoundation.org
Internet: www.communityfoundationalliance.org/posey/program-areas/
Sponsor: Posey County Community Foundation
402 Main Street, P.O. Box 746
Mt. Vernon, IN 47620

Posey County Community Foundation Youth Development Grants   2010

The Posey County Community Foundation is a nonprofit, public charity created by and for the people of Posey County, Indiana. Grant proposals are accepted once each year as a one-time project support. At the beginning of each cycle in January, notices are sent to nonprofit organizations that have previously applied for grants, have received grants in the past, or have otherwise requested notification. Applicants are encouraged to schedule a meeting with the Foundation's director to receive an overview of the grant process. Proposals are accepted from

January through August 1. The grants committee will make its recommendations on funding to the Foundation's Board of Trustees, which will make final funding recommendations to the board of directors of the Community Foundation Alliance. All organizations that have submitted grant proposals are notified of the final outcome no later than December 1. Grants in the area of Youth Development include activities that strengthen the family unit, help children grow and develop, foster youth sports and athletics, support the YMCA, and support daycare-related issues. Samples of previously funded projects are available at the website.
Requirements: The Foundation welcomes funding requests from nonprofit organizations that are 501(c)3 or 509(a) tax exempt, and from governmental agencies serving Posey County. For those organizations not tax exempt, requests may be considered if the project is charitable and supports a community need. Proposals submitted by an entity under the auspices of another agency must include a written statement signed by the agency's board president on behalf of the board of directors agreeing to act as the entity's fiscal sponsor, to receive grant monies if awarded, and to oversee the proposed project.
Restrictions: Project areas not considered for funding include: religious organizations for religious purposes; political parties or campaigns; endowment creation or debt reduction; operating costs; capital campaigns; annual appeals or membership contributions; travel requests for groups or individuals such as bands, sports teams, or classes.
Geographic Focus: Indiana
Date(s) Application is Due: Aug 1
Amount of Grant: Up to 5,000 USD
Contact: Monica Spencer, Regional Director; (812) 838-0288; fax (812) 838-8009; monica@poseycommunityfoundation.org
Internet: www.communityfoundationalliance.org/posey/program-areas/
Sponsor: Posey County Community Foundation
402 Main Street, P.O. Box 746
Mt. Vernon, IN 47620

Posse Foundation Scholarships **2011**

Founded in 1989, the Posse Foundation started because of one student who said, "I never would have dropped out of college if I had my posse with me." That simple idea of sending a group of students to college together to act as a support system for one another was the impetus for a college-access program that has demonstrated a 90% college graduation rate since its inception. The Posse Scholarship Program identifies, through an alternative evaluation strategy, public high-school students with extraordinary academic and leadership potential who may be overlooked by SAT scores and other traditional college measures. In collaboration with partner colleges, the program places these students in supportive, multicultural teams—posses—of ten students each. The Posse Foundation's partner colleges and universities then award four-year, full-tuition leadership scholarships to these students. By aiding universities in their recruiting process and by helping students make the transition from high-school to college, the Foundation hopes to improve college recruitment, retention, and completion rates for students of different cultural and racial backgrounds. The Posse Foundation has local offices in nine major cities: Atlanta, Georgia; Boston, Massachusetts; Chicago, Illinois; Washington, D.C; Houston, Texas; Los Angeles, California; Miami, Florida; New Orleans, Louisiana; and New York City. These offices accept annual nominations from local high schools and community-based organizations that work with high-school juniors and seniors. Schools and organizations that nominate Posse Scholars should contact their local Posse office for details about the nomination process and timeline at the beginning of each year; lists of local offices with their contact information and email addresses as well as names of their staff are available at the Posse website. Examples of Posse's partner institutions of higher education include Boston University, Brandeis University, Bryn Mawr College, Carleton College, Cornell University, Depauw University, Northwestern University, Texas A&M University, University of Wisconsin-Madison, Vassar College, and Wheaton College. The complete list of partner institutions (currently forty-four of them) along with the Posse cities they serve is available at the Posse website. Posse also partners with graduate programs which provide scholarships and other forms of financiaol assistance to Posse alumni interested in earning advanced degrees. Additionally, Posse partners with exceptional companies and organizations worldwide to place their alumni in internship programs as well as offering other career services to Posse graduates.
Requirements: To be eligible, a high school senior must be nominated by their high school or a community-based organization, be in the first term of their senior year in high school, demonstrate leadership within their high school, community, or family, and demonstrate academic potential. Nominating schools and community-based organizations must be located in Atlanta, Boston, Chicago, Washington D.C., Houston, Los Angeles, Miami, New Orleans, and New York City and must be registered with their local Posse Office. Schools and organizations may register via email. Guidelines for registering, as well as local Posse email addresses, are provided at the Posse website.
Geographic Focus: California, District of Columbia, Florida, Georgia, Illinois, Louisiana, Massachusetts, New York, Texas
Contact: Program Coordinator; (212) 405-1691; info@possefoundation.org
Internet: www.possefoundation.org/about-posse/program-components/recruitment/nomination-process
Sponsor: The Posse Foundation
14 Wall Street, Suite 8A-60
New York, NY 10005

Powell Family Foundation Grants **2012**

The foundation awards grants to nonprofits in the Kansas City area for support of programs in the areas of environment, civic affairs, and youth. Types of support include general operating support, continuing support, annual campaigns, capital campaigns, equipment acquisition, and program/project development. There are no application forms. Letters of intent must be received 30 days preceding board meetings. The foundation prefers written inquiries and will send guidelines if the project meets foundation criteria.
Requirements: Nonprofits in, or serving the residents of, Missouri are eligible.
Restrictions: The foundation does not support welfare or social services programs.
Geographic Focus: Missouri
Amount of Grant: 2,500 - 25,000 USD
Contact: George Powell, Jr., President; (913) 236-0003; fax (913) 262-0058
Sponsor: Powell Family Foundation
4350 Shawnee Mission Parkway, Suite 280
Fairway, KS 66205-2528

Powell Foundation Grants **2013**

The purpose of the Powell Foundation is to distribute funds for public charitable purposes, principally for the support, encouragement and assistance to education, health, conservation, and the arts with a direct impact within the Foundation's geographic zone of interest The Foundation places priority on organizations and programs that serve residents in Harris, Travis and Walker counties, Texas, principally in the fields of education, the arts, health and conservation. The Foundation's current emphasis is in the field of public education in the broadest sense. Other areas of interest continue to be community service projects focused on the needs of children, the disadvantaged, the urban environment, and the visual and performing arts, especially in the Greater Houston, Texas area. The Foundation operates on a calendar year and its Board meets twice a year in the spring and in the fall. Submission of proposals is required at least two months prior to a meeting for consideration at that meeting. To allow for optimum consideration and due diligence, those seeking grants are encouraged to apply to the foundation on an ongoing basis. Grants that do not make the deadline for one meeting will be carried forward to the next meeting. Each request must be in writing and should be accompanied by the proposal summary and the required list of attachments. See the foundation's website for additional guidelines.
Requirements: Texas IRS 501(c)3 tax-exempt organizations serving Harris, Walker, and Travis counties are eligible to apply.
Restrictions: Normally, the Foundation will not support: requests for building funds or grant commitments extending into successive calendar years; grants to religious organizations for religious purposes; fund raising events or advertising; grants to other private foundations; grants to cover past operating deficits or debt retirement; grants for support to individuals; grants that impose the exercise of responsibility upon the Foundation. For example: private operating foundations or certain supporting organizations.
Geographic Focus: Texas
Amount of Grant: 1,000 - 20,000 USD
Samples: Alley Theatre, Houston, Texas - educational outreach support; Travis Audubon Society, Houston, Texas - operational support; Great Expectations Foundation, Tahlequah, Oklahoma - professional development and mentoring for teachers.
Contact: Caroline J. Sabin; (713) 523-7557; fax (713) 523-7553; info@powellfoundation.org
Internet: www.powellfoundation.org/powellguide.htm
Sponsor: Powell Foundation of Houston
2121 San Felipe, Suite 110
Houston, TX 77019-5600

PPCF Community Grants **2014**

The Pikes Peak Community Foundation gives priority to high-impact initiatives that provide maximum benefit for the community. In addition, the Foundation prefers to fund specific programs and projects that demonstrate measurable results. Primary areas of funding include: civic improvement; community development; education; the environment; health; and human services. Interested applicants should first forward an online letter of inquiry (LOI), detailing their proposal. If approved, an email with a link to the online application will be provided. There are three annual deadlines for completed full applications, including: March 1, July 1, and November 1.
Requirements: Any 501(c)3 organization serving the residents of the Pikes Peak region, defined as El Paso County, Teller County, and adjacent communities, is eligible to apply.
Restrictions: The Foundation generally does not fund: organizations that do not have an active 501(c)3 tax status; other foundations or organizations that distribute money to nonprofit recipients of its own selection; debt retirement, endowments or other reserve funds; individuals; medical, scientific, or academic research; political or religious doctrine; sponsorships; camperships; travel; vehicle purchases; conference fees; symposium fees; workshop fees; writing, publications, or distribution of books, articles, newsletters, and electronic media; annual memberships; or dinners.
Geographic Focus: Colorado
Date(s) Application is Due: Mar 1; Jul 1; Nov 1
Contact: Whitney Calhoun; (719) 389-1251, ext. 115; wcalhoun@ppcf.org or info@ppcf.org
Internet: www.ppcf.org/community-grants/
Sponsor: Pikes Peak Community Foundation
730 North Nevada Avenue
Colorado Springs, CO 80903

PPCF Edson Foundation Grants **2015**

The Edson Foundation was formed by Al Edson, and initial funding came upon his death. Al overcame many challenges growing up and became a successful business person and contributing member of the community. The Foundation carries on his legacy in support of youth in the Pikes Peak region by supporting nonprofits that provide educational support, mentoring, and character development. The Foundation provides funding to educational programs that: promote youth empowerment; encourage innovation; help in personal development; provide mentoring; encourage creativity; and develop professionalism. Such programs should include: personal growth and development skills; job skills; pro-social behaviors; skills to mature; exploration of career paths; pursuit of education; life skills training; and personal safety. Generally, grants range in size from $5,000 to $10,000. Board review letters of inquiry (LOIs) twice a year. Letters submitted between November 1 and

May 31 will be considered at the Foundation's July 1 meeting. If approved, an email with a link to the online application will be provided. Applications submitted between June 1 and October 31 will be considered at the Foundation's December 1 meeting.
Requirements: Funding is generally limited to nonprofit 501(c)3 organizations in the Pikes Peak region, defined as El Paso County, Teller County, and adjacent communities.
Restrictions: In general, emergency funding will not be considered and an organization may only apply one time per calendar year. The Foundation generally does not fund: organizations that do not have an active 501(c)3 tax status; other foundations or organizations that distribute money to nonprofit recipients of its own selection; debt retirement, endowments or other reserve funds; individuals; medical, scientific, or academic research; political or religious doctrine; sponsorships; camperships; travel; vehicle purchases; conference fees; symposium fees; workshop fees; writing, publications, or distribution of books, articles, newsletters, and electronic media; annual memberships; or dinners.
Geographic Focus: Colorado
Date(s) Application is Due: Jul 1; Dec 1
Amount of Grant: 5,000 - 10,000 USD
Contact: Whitney Calhoun, Program Manager; (719) 389-1251, ext. 115; wcalhoun@ppcf.org or edsonfoundation@gmail.com
Internet: www.ppcf.org/home/for-community/how-can-we-help/grant-seekers/edson-foundation-grants/
Sponsor: Pikes Peak Community Foundation
730 North Nevada Avenue
Colorado Springs, CO 80903

PPCF Esther M. and Freeman E. Everett Charitable Foundation Grants   2016
Established in Colorado in 2001 and currently managed by the Pikes Peak Community Foundation (PPCF), the Esther M. and Freeman E. Everett Charitable Foundation gives to programs located primarily in Colorado and Wisconsin. Its major fields of interest include: the arts; children and youth services; education; community foundations; and human services. Since there are no specified application forms, applicants should submit a copy of their IRS determination letter, along with a brief overview of the program, need, outcomes, and budget. There are no annual deadlines, and grant amounts typically range between $1,000 and $10,000.
Geographic Focus: Colorado, Wisconsin
Amount of Grant: 1,000 - 10,000 USD
Samples: Project Angel Heart, Denver, Colorado, $5,000 - general operating support; Peak Vista Community Health Centers Foundation, Colorado Springs, Colorado, $4,000 - general operating support; Girls on the Run of the Rockies, Grand Junction, Colorado, $3,000 - general operating support.
Contact: Whitney Calhoun; (719) 389-1251, ext. 115; wcalhoun@ppcf.org
Sponsor: Pikes Peak Community Foundation
730 North Nevada Avenue
Colorado Springs, CO 80903

PPG Industries Foundation Grants   2017
Funding requests for a variety of project proposals that advance the foundation's interests are eligible for consideration. These may include capital projects, operating grants and special projects. In general, the foundation gives priority to applications from organizations dedicated to enhancing the welfare of communities in which PPG is a resident. Historically the foundation has supported nonprofits in the areas of human services, health and safety, civic and community affairs, education, and cultural and arts. Requests for funding are accepted year-round. Determinations are made by the foundation's screening committee and board of directors.
Requirements: Applicants must use PPG's online grant making system to apply. The link is on the website. PPG Industries Foundation will review applications on a regular basis and will contact all grantseekers with proposals of interest. Organizations located in the Pittsburgh area and organizations of national scope should direct any questions to the executive director of the foundation. Organizations serving communities where PPG facilities are located should direct any questions to the local PPG Industries Foundation agent in their area. A list of these may be found at the PPG Foundation website under the Foundation Governance link.
Restrictions: The foundation will not award grants for: advertising or sponsorships; endowments; political or religious purposes; projects which would directly benefit PPG Industries, Inc; or special events and telephone solicitations. Operating grants are not made to United Way agencies.
Geographic Focus: All States, Pennsylvania
Samples: YMCA of Metropolitan Milwaukee, South Shore Center, Milwaukee, Wisconsin, $3,000 - funding supports SPLASH swimming program for second-graders; Carlisle Regional Performing Arts Center, location unspecified, $3,000 - funding supports maintenance, technology upgrade costs; Robert Morris University, Moon Township, Pennsylvania, $350,000 - funding supports renovation of the Career and Leadership Development Center.
Contact: Sue Sloan; (412) 434-2453; fax (412) 434-4666; foundation@ppg.com
Internet: www.ppg.com/en/ppgfoundation/Pages/Grant_Policies.aspx
Sponsor: PPG Industries Foundation
One PPG Place
Pittsburgh, PA 15272

Premera Blue Cross Grants   2018
Premera is committed not only to improving the health of its members, but is also dedicated to making a difference in the communities it serves through its corporate philanthropy and community service program. Premera supports community programs, events and charities each year with financial and in-kind donations as well as volunteer time. The company invites all eligible charitable organizations to submit requests for funding. It focuses giving criteria on key areas that have an impact on the health and well-being of people in its communities. In order to address the common risk factors related to many of the major

diseases and health conditions that have a large impact on the residents in our communities, Premera supports nonprofit organizations and programs that address wellness, with a specific focus on exercise and stress management. Applications are accepted online only.
Requirements: Proposals for donations must: be from organizations that are defined as exempt from taxation under Section 501(a) as organizations described in Section 501(c)3 of the Internal Revenue Code; or a government agency or program, a public school or school district (but only if the contribution or gift is made for exclusively public purposes). Applicants must assist residents in the areas it serves in Washington.
Restrictions: Premera generally does not make contributions to capital campaigns. Premera funds are not used for charitable grants or contributions to: individuals; organizations that are for profit; arts organizations; religious organizations, unless the gift is designated to an ongoing secular community service program sponsored by these organizations and does not propagate a belief in a specific faith; or organizations that discriminate against individuals based on age, gender, race, religion, ethnicity, disability or sexual orientation, or that discriminate against individuals on any impermissible basis, or which advocate a position contrary to established public policy.
Geographic Focus: Washington
Contact: Stefanie Bruno; (509) 252-7431 or (425) 918-5933; stefanie.bruno@premera.com
Internet: www.premera.com/wa/visitor/about-premera/corporate-citizenship/giving-guidelines/
Sponsor: Premera Blue Cross
7001 220th Street SW, Building 1
Mountlake Terrace, WA 98043-2160

Presidio Fencing Club Youth Fencers Assistance Scholarships   2019
Presidio Fencing Club has been offering need-based scholarships since 2006 as part of its Youth Fencers Assistance Program (YFAP). In 2009, the Central Coast Fencing Foundation helped to expand the YFAP program by securing a grant from the Santa Barbara Foundation and the Orfalea Foundation to provide partial funding to four deserving students. Although the Santa Barbara Foundation Scholarships have since expired, the Presidio Fencing Club still tries to offer financial assistance to continuing students through club scholarships.
Requirements: Applications for fencing scholarships will be considered according to the following criteria: Residency–scholarships are to be used only by youth residing in Santa Barbara County for payment of tuition for fencing instruction at Presidio Fencing Club; Financial need–applicants must demonstrate financial need; Achievement in Fencing–applicants need not be experienced fencers, but they must have been taking lessons for a minimum of three continuous months and demonstrate an interest in the sport. Applicants must set goals for competitive achievement in the sport of fencing and work towards the fulfillment of those goals; Good moral and ethical character; Academic Standing–Applicants must maintain a GPA of 2.5 on a 4.0 scale during the academic year.
Geographic Focus: All States, California
Contact: Tim Robinson, Head Coach; (805) 403-6895; tim@presidiofencing.com
Internet: presidiofencing.com/yfap.html
Sponsor: Presidio Fencing Club
216 East Cota Street
Santa Barbara, CA 93101

Price Chopper's Golub Foundation Grants   2020
Price Chopper's Golub Foundation provides financial support to eligible charitable organizations with a current 501(c)3 tax exempt status. Contributions are made through planned, continued giving programs in the areas of health and human services, arts, culture, education, and youth activities, within Price Chopper marketing areas. To be considered for funding, mail a written request, on letterhead for the organization seeking the donation, six to eight weeks prior to needed support or response deadlines. The Foundation reviews capital campaign requests quarterly, so please allow three to four months for a response.
Requirements: The Foundation's six state marketing area includes a specific mile radius around its stores in New York (Albany, Broome, Cayuga, Chenango, Clinton, Columbia, Cortland, Delaware, Dutchess, Essex, Franklin, Fulton, Greene, Hamilton, Herkimer, Jefferson, Lewis, Madison, Montgomery, Oneida, Onondaga, Orange, Oswego, Otsego, Rensselaer, St. Lawrence, Saratoga, Schenectady, Schoharie, Sullivan, Tioga, Tompkins, Ulster, Warren, and Washington counties), Massachusetts (Berkshire, Hampden, Hampshire, Middlesex, and Worcester counties), Vermont (Addison, Bennington, Caledonia, Chittenden, Essex, Franklin, Grand Isle, Lamoille, Orange, Orleans, Rutland, Washington, Windham, and Windsor counties), Pennsylvania (Lackawanna, Luzerne, Pike, Susquehanna, Wayne, and Wyoming counties), Connecticut (Hartford, Litchfield, New Haven, Tolland, and Windham counties) and New Hampshire (Cheshire, Grafton, and Sullivan counties).
Restrictions: The Foundation does not support: individuals; annual meetings; endowments; film and video projects; program advertising; funding for travel; organizations or events outside of its marketing area; events to raise funds for groups outside of its local community; conferences, conventions, or symposiums; publishing; operating expenses; scholarship programs outside of its own; or capital campaigns of national, religious or political organizations.
Geographic Focus: Connecticut, Massachusetts, New Hampshire, New York, Pennsylvania, Vermont
Contact: Deborah Tanski; (518) 356-9450 or (518) 379-1270; fax (518) 374-4259
Internet: www.pricechopper.com/GolubFoundation/GolubFoundation_S.las
Sponsor: Price Chopper's Golub Foundation
P.O. Box 1074
Schenectady, NY 12301

Priddy Foundation Operating Grants   2021
The Priddy Foundation is a general purpose foundation, interested primarily in programs that have the potential for lasting and favorable impact on individuals and organizations. Considerations for funding include the geographic area served by the project, the individuals and groups served, the problem being addressed, the availability of existing resources and the degree of need. Although the Foundation is wary of fostering annual budget dependency on

the part of a grantee agency, its board recognizes that there are circumstances in which a grant for general operating purposes might be critical to an organization's success or viability. Such grants would be for a limited period of time. Among other conditions which might be imposed, based on a specific organization's application, a grantee organization will be required to present a practicable plan to achieve self-sufficiency without additional foundation funding. During the term of the grant the grantee organization might also be required to enter into a formal consulting arrangement with a Center for Non-profit Management, or a similar organization, also with the objective of becoming self-sufficient. Deadlines for preliminary applications are February 1 and August 1, while final applications are due March 1 and September 1.

Requirements: 501(c)3 Texas and Oklahoma nonprofit organizations are eligible. The foundation considers grant applications from organizations in the Wichita Falls, Texas area. In Texas, this includes the following counties: Archer, Baylor, Childress, Clay, Cottle, Foard, Hardeman, Haskell, Jack, King, Knox, Montague, Stonewall, Throckmorton, Wichita, Wilbarger, Wise, and Young. In Oklahoma, it includes the following counties: Comanche, Cotton, Jackson, Jefferson, Stephens, and Tillman.

Restrictions: The Priddy Foundation does not normally make grants for the following purposes: operating deficits; endowments; debt retirement; organizations that make grants to others; charities operated by service clubs; a request for capital funds for a project previously supported; any grant that would tend to obligate the foundation to future funding; fund raising programs and events; grants that impose expenditure responsibility on the foundation; grants to individuals, including individual scholarship awards; start-up funding for new organizations; individual public elementary or secondary schools (K-12); religious institutions except for non-sectarian, human service programs offered on a non-discriminatory basis; basic or applied research; media productions or publications; school trips; conferences or other educational events except through an organizational development grant; or direct grants to volunteer fire departments.

Geographic Focus: Oklahoma, Texas
Date(s) Application is Due: Mar 1; Sep 1
Amount of Grant: 20,000 - 120,000 USD
Samples: Communities In Schools, Wichita Falls, Texas, $120,00 - program operations; Wichita Falls Alliance for the Mentally Ill, Wichita Falls, Texas, $20,000 - operating support; Wichita-Archer-Clay Christian Womens Job Corps, Wichita Falls, Texas, $30,000 - operating support.
Contact: Debbie C. White; (940) 723-8720; fax (940) 723-8656; debbiecw@priddyfdn.org
Internet: priddyfdn.org/policy/
Sponsor: Priddy Foundation
807 Eighth Street, Suite 1010
Wichita Falls, TX 76301-3310

Priddy Foundation Organizational Development Grants   2022

The Priddy Foundation is a general purpose foundation, interested primarily in programs that have the potential for lasting and favorable impact on individuals and organizations. Considerations for funding include the geographic area served by the project, the individuals and groups served, the problem being addressed, the availability of existing resources and the degree of need. In the area of Organizational Development, the Foundation will consider grants to organizations for such things as board and staff development, planning initiatives, technical assistance, technology enhancements, and capital projects. Organizational development grants will be dependent on a comprehensive plan supported by the organization's board, outside professional assistance (e.g., Center for Non-profit Management), if appropriate, and absolute linkage between the development plan and the ability of the organization to achieve its mission more effectively. Deadlines for preliminary applications are February 1 and August 1, while final applications are due March 1 and September 1.

Requirements: 501(c)3 Texas and Oklahoma nonprofit organizations are eligible. The foundation considers grant applications from organizations in the Wichita Falls, Texas area. In Texas, this includes the following counties: Archer, Baylor, Childress, Clay, Cottle, Foard, Hardeman, Haskell, Jack, King, Knox, Montague, Stonewall, Throckmorton, Wichita, Wilbarger, Wise, and Young. In Oklahoma, it includes the following counties: Comanche, Cotton, Jackson, Jefferson, Stephens, and Tillman.

Restrictions: The Priddy Foundation does not normally make grants for the following purposes: operating deficits; endowments; debt retirement; organizations that make grants to others; charities operated by service clubs; a request for capital funds for a project previously supported; any grant that would tend to obligate the foundation to future funding; fund raising programs and events; grants that impose expenditure responsibility on the foundation; grants to individuals, including individual scholarship awards; start-up funding for new organizations; individual public elementary or secondary schools (K-12); religious institutions except for non-sectarian, human service programs offered on a non-discriminatory basis; basic or applied research; media productions or publications; school trips; conferences or other educational events except through an organizational development grant; or direct grants to volunteer fire departments.

Geographic Focus: Oklahoma, Texas
Date(s) Application is Due: Mar 1; Sep 1
Amount of Grant: 1,500 - 120,000 USD
Samples: Association of Small Foundations, Washington, D.C., $1,500 - organizational development and support; Christ Academy, Wichita Falls, Texas, $28,864 - high school scholarship fund development; Clay County Senior Citizens, Henrietta, Texas, $15,000 - mission programming.
Contact: Debbie C. White; (940) 723-8720; fax (940) 723-8656; debbiecw@priddyfdn.org
Internet: priddyfdn.org/policy/
Sponsor: Priddy Foundation
807 Eighth Street, Suite 1010
Wichita Falls, TX 76301-3310

Priddy Foundation Program Grants   2023

The Priddy Foundation is a general purpose foundation, interested primarily in programs that have the potential for lasting and favorable impact on individuals and organizations. Considerations for funding include the geographic area served by the project, the individuals and groups served, the problem being addressed, the availability of existing resources and the degree of need. In the area of Program Grants, the Foundation gives highest priority to organizations seeking funds for service extension or implementation of new services. Projects should make a difference in the lives of people served by dealing effectively with known problems or opportunities. Results should be capable of evaluation against defined standards of measurement. Proposals should be realistic concerning the ability of the organization to conduct the program and to sustain the program beyond the period a grant from the Foundation may cover. Deadlines for preliminary applications are February 1 and August 1, while final applications are due March 1 and September 1.

Requirements: 501(c)3 Texas and Oklahoma nonprofit organizations are eligible. The foundation considers grant applications from organizations in the Wichita Falls, Texas area. In Texas, this includes the following counties: Archer, Baylor, Childress, Clay, Cottle, Foard, Hardeman, Haskell, Jack, King, Knox, Montague, Stonewall, Throckmorton, Wichita, Wilbarger, Wise, and Young. In Oklahoma, it includes the following counties: Comanche, Cotton, Jackson, Jefferson, Stephens, and Tillman.

Restrictions: The Priddy Foundation does not normally make grants for the following purposes: operating deficits; endowments; debt retirement; organizations that make grants to others; charities operated by service clubs; a request for capital funds for a project previously supported; any grant that would tend to obligate the foundation to future funding; fund raising programs and events; grants that impose expenditure responsibility on the foundation; grants to individuals, including individual scholarship awards; start-up funding for new organizations; individual public elementary or secondary schools (K-12); religious institutions except for non-sectarian, human service programs offered on a non-discriminatory basis; basic or applied research; media productions or publications; school trips; conferences or other educational events except through an organizational development grant; or direct grants to volunteer fire departments.

Geographic Focus: Oklahoma, Texas
Date(s) Application is Due: Mar 1; Sep 1
Amount of Grant: 1,500 - 1,500,000 USD
Samples: Wichita Adult Literacy Council, Wichita Falls, Texas, $25,000 - basic program funding; Kairos Prison Ministry International, Winter Park, Florida, $10,000 - Wichita Falls Area Kairos Outside Program; Presbyterian Children's Homes and Services, Wichita Falls, Texas, $90,000 - child and foster care program.
Contact: Debbie C. White; (940) 723-8720; fax (940) 723-8656; debbiecw@priddyfdn.org
Internet: priddyfdn.org/policy/
Sponsor: Priddy Foundation
807 Eighth Street, Suite 1010
Wichita Falls, TX 76301-3310

Pride Foundation Grants   2024

The Pride Foundation works to strengthen the lesbian, gay, transgender, and bisexual community primarily in Washington state and extending to the four neighboring states of Alaska, Idaho, Montana, and Oregon. The Foundation awards grants to projects in arts and recreation; education, advocacy, and outreach; health and community service; HIV/AIDS service delivery and prevention; lesbian health; and youth and family services. Applicants will first submit the letter of inquiry online applications by August 19. If organizations are invited to submit the full application, they will be notified by September 23. Funds will be available in December.

Requirements: IRS 501(c)3 tax-exempt organizations or organizations affiliated with tax-exempt organizations are eligible. Projects or programs must directly benefit the lesbian, gay, bisexual, and transgender community; people affected by HIV/AIDS; and/or their friends and families.
Restrictions: Grants to individuals cannot be considered.
Geographic Focus: Alaska, Idaho, Montana, Oregon, Washington
Date(s) Application is Due: Sep 20
Amount of Grant: Up to 5,000 USD
Contact: Jeff Hedgepeth; (800) 735-7287 or (206) 323-3318; jeff@pridefoundation.org
Internet: www.pridefoundation.org/grants/overview/
Sponsor: Pride Foundation
1122 East Pike, PMB 1001
Seattle, WA 98122

Progress Energy Foundation Energy Education Grants   2025

The foundation partners with nonprofits in Florida, North Carolina, and South Carolina to help customer communities understand and adapt to the new realities posed by the shifting energy landscape. Grants focus on energy education, workforce development and the environment, with priority given to energy-related grants. Energy education grants promote energy literacy in K-12 schools through teacher education, curriculum development and experiential learning opportunities for students. Nonprofit organizations providing services to Progress Energy customers in the focus areas may apply online.

Requirements: Florida, North Carolina, and South Carolina nonprofit organizations serving the residents of the corporation's service area are eligible. Nonprofits applying for a foundation grant must be exempt under Section 501(c)(3) of the IRS code.
Restrictions: Grants are limited to nonprofit organizations that serve Progress Energy customer areas. No support for religious organizations not of direct benefit to the entire community, political candidates or organizations, lobbying organizations, athletic, labor, or fraternal groups, or individual K-12 schools. No grants to individuals, or for political causes or campaigns, endowments, or capital campaigns.
Geographic Focus: Florida, North Carolina, South Carolina
Date(s) Application is Due: Feb 1

Amount of Grant: 10,000 - 100,000 USD
Contact: Grants Manager; (919) 546-6189; fax (919) 546-4338; grants@pgnmail.com
Internet: www.progress-energy.com/commitment/community/grant-programs/index.page?
Sponsor: Progress Energy Foundation
P.O. Box 2591
Raleigh, NC 27602-2591

ProLiteracy National Book Fund Grants   2026
The ProLiteracy National Book Fund makes grants to adult literacy and adult basic education programs. The NBF supports the following initiatives: basic literacy; adult education; English language instruction; GED/HSE preparation; and family literacy. Grants have ranged from $500 to $2,000, although greater or lesser funding amounts are considered. Grant requests significantly over the $2,000 level are not typically funded. The annual deadline for applications is March 15.
Requirements: Programs applying for a grant must agree to provide, from local sources, a cash payment equal to 20% of the total amount being requested in the grant application to defray the costs of NBSF administration.
Restrictions: The NBF does not award grants to individuals, nor does it fund requests to provide books for lending libraries or other resource centers where NBF materials are not directly linked to use with students receiving literacy instruction. Also, programs that request NBF materials to use strictly as free distribution items are not funded.
Geographic Focus: All States
Date(s) Application is Due: Mar 15
Amount of Grant: 500 - 2,000 USD
Contact: Alicia Suskin, Program Director; (888) 528-2224 or (315) 422-9121; fax (315) 422-6369; nbf@proliteracy.org
Internet: proliteracy.org/What-We-Do/Programs-Projects/National-Book-Fund
Sponsor: ProLiteracy
104 Marcellus Street
Syracuse, NY 13204

Proteus Fund Grants   2027
Proteus Fund is a foundation committed to advancing justice through democracy, human rights and peace. Proteus Fund collaborative grant making initiatives work on some of the most cutting edge issues of our time. Each initiative is uniquely structured and focused to achieve the goals of its funding partners and led by experienced program staff. Proteus Fund works to connect this work to other social movements and resources while providing a full compliment of services to support the work, including partnership development, marketing, grants and financial management and administrative support.
Geographic Focus: All States
Contact: Beery Adams Jimenez, Grants Manager; (413) 256-0349; info@proteusfund.org
Internet: www.proteusfund.org/initiatives
Sponsor: Proteus Fund
101 University Drive, Suite A2
Amherst, MA 01002

Prudential Foundation Education Grants   2028
Areas of interest are ready-to-learn programs, ready-to-work programs, and ready-to-live programs. In order to promote sustainable communities and improve social outcomes for community residents, the Foundation focuses on the following areas: education leadership to support reform in public education by increasing the capacity of educators, parents, and community residents to implement public school reform; and youth development to build skills and competencies needed for young people to be productive citizens (this includes expanding arts education opportunities and supporting effective out-of-school-time programs for young people). Finally, the Foundation also funds organizations whose efforts influence policy that adapts promising practices and evidence-based approaches to instruction and learning in schools. Types of support include operating support, continuing support, annual campaigns, seed money, matching funds and employee matching gifts, consulting services, technical assistance, employee-related scholarships, research, capital campaigns, conferences and seminars, and projects/programs. The Foundation is especially interested in proposals that anticipate and address potential major problems. Funds are targeted to areas where Prudential has a strong presence. Applicant should make initial contact with a brief letter to determine whether a more detailed proposal would be acceptable.
Requirements: The Prudential Foundation supports nonprofit, charitable organizations, and programs whose mission and operations are broad and non-discriminatory, and especially focuses its resources to support organizations whose activities address social needs or benefit underserved groups and communities. Priority in order of preference goes to programs in Newark, New Jersey, and surrounding communities; Los Angeles, California; Hartford, Connecticut; New York, New York; Chicago, Illinois; Jacksonville, Florida; Atlanta, Georgia; Minneapolis, Minnesota; Philadelphia and Scranton, Pennsylvania; Houston and Dallas, Texas; Dubuque, Iowa; Phoenix, Arizona; Honolulu, Hawaii; and New Orleans, Louisiana.
Restrictions: The Foundation does not fund: organizations that are not tax-exempt under paragraph 501(c)3 of the U.S. Internal Revenue Code; labor, religious, political, lobbying, or fraternal groups—except when these groups provide needed services to the community at large; direct grants or scholarships to individuals; support for single-disease health groups; or good will advertising.
Geographic Focus: Arizona, California, Connecticut, Florida, Georgia, Hawaii, Illinois, Iowa, Louisiana, Minnesota, New Jersey, New York, Pennsylvania, Texas
Amount of Grant: Up to 1,000,000 USD
Contact: Lata N. Reddy, Vice President and Head of Corporate Social Responsibility; (973) 802-4791; community.resources@prudential.com
Internet: www.prudential.com/links/about/corporate-social-responsibility

Sponsor: Prudential Foundation
751 Broad Street, 15th Floor
Newark, NJ 07102-3777

Prudential Spirit of Community Awards   2029
The Prudential Spirit of Community Awards program is the United States' largest youth recognition program based exclusively on volunteer community service. The program was created in 1995 by Prudential in partnership with the National Association of Secondary School Principals (NASSP) to honor middle level and high school students for outstanding service to others at the local, state, and national level. The program's goals are to applaud young people who already are making a positive difference in their towns and neighborhoods, and to inspire others to think about how they might contribute to their communities. The award recognizes middle- and high-school students for volunteer community service. Honorees will receive a monetary award and a trip to Washington, D.C. Ten national honorees will each receive an additional monetary prize, and a monetary prize will be given to a charitable organization of his or her choice. Applications are available at more than 40,000 public and private middle and high schools throughout the United States. The Prudential Spirit of Community Awards program is also conducted in Japan, South Korea, Taiwan, Ireland, and India, where Prudential has significant business operations.
Requirements: Any student in grades five through 12 as of November 1 who resides in one of the 50 states, the District of Columbia, or Puerto Rico, and has engaged in volunteer activities since September 1 of last year is eligible.
Geographic Focus: All States, India, Ireland, Japan, South Korea, Taiwan
Date(s) Application is Due: Nov 6
Amount of Grant: 1,000 - 5,000 USD
Contact: Spirit of Community Awards Coordinator; (855) 670-4787 or (973) 802-4568; fax (973) 802-4718; spirit@applyists.com or spirit@prudential.com
Internet: spirit.prudential.com/awards/how-to-apply
Sponsor: Prudential Insurance Company
751 Broad Street, 15th Floor
Newark, NJ 07102

PSEG Corporate Contributions Grants   2030
The PSEG family of companies provide support for dinners, events, and targeted sponsorships serving the places the corporation does business in: New Jersey; New Haven and Bridgeport, Connecticut; and Albany and Long Island, New York. Limited funding is available for arts, sports, community fairs, and other community functions. Grant requests may be submitted through the Foundation's online general application format on a rolling basis until October 31 each year. There are four annual deadlines, including: February 15; May 15; August 15; and October 31. Proposals should be received at least eight weeks prior to the event date.
Requirements: Applications will be reviewed using the following criteria: the organization must be an IRS approved 501(c)3 or a 170(B); alignment with one or more of the Foundation's giving focus areas; organization or program resides or benefits in the places where the company does business; program effectiveness, including demonstrated and anticipated outcomes and impacts; and program feasibility based on organization staff and organization budget.
Restrictions: The following types of organizations or programs are not eligible for funding: individuals; organizations not exempt under Section 501(c)3 of the IRS code; sectarian purpose programs that promote religious doctrines or exclude participants based on religion; political causes, candidates, organizations or campaigns; organizations that discriminate on the basis of race, sex, sexual orientation or religion; organizations with a primary purpose of influencing legislation; athletic, labor or fraternal groups; endowments; or programs and organizations for which PSEG is asked to serve as the sole funder.
Geographic Focus: Connecticut, New Jersey, New York
Date(s) Application is Due: Feb 15; May 15; Aug 15; Oct 31
Contact: Ellen Lambert, Corporate Contributions Manager; (973) 430-5074 or (973) 430-7000; ellen.lambert@pseg.com or corporatecitizenship@pseg.com
Internet: www.pseg.com/info/community/new_site/our_giving/guidelines.jsp
Sponsor: Public Service Enterprise Group
80 Park Plaza, 10C
Newark, NJ 07102

PSEG Foundation Safety and Preparedness Grants   2031
The PSEG Foundation is a 501(c)3 entity that provides grants to charitable organizations aligned with the Foundation's focus areas. In the area of Safety and Preparedness, the Foundation seeks to keep people and their homes safe, particularly around electricity and natural gas, and to prepare for and respond to emergencies. Working with Voluntary or Community Organizations Active in Disasters (V/COAD), the Foundation seeks to educate and prepare families, as well as strengthen the capacity of our emergency response organizations and staff. Through its partnerships, the Foundation is pre-investing in disaster relief in order to activate immediately and provide life-saving aid. This includes support for activities in advance of a disaster, including: training volunteers; securing shelter locations; stocking warehouses; and maintaining disaster-relief vehicles. Furthermore, understanding that burn and trauma centers provide critical care when its employees and customers need it most, the Foundation supports these centers throughout its service and operating territories in New Jersey, Connecticut and New York. In partnership with the hospitals, it develops and delivers certified training in burn and trauma safety education and prevention. Grant requests may be submitted through the Foundation's online general application format on a rolling basis until October 31 each year. There are four annual deadlines, including: February 15; May 15; August 15; and October 31.
Requirements: Applications will be reviewed using the following criteria: the organization must be an IRS approved 501(c)3 or a 170(B); alignment with one or more of the Foundation's giving focus areas; organization or program resides or benefits in the places where the company

does business; program effectiveness, including demonstrated and anticipated outcomes and impacts; and program feasibility based on organization staff and organization budget.

Restrictions: The following types of organizations or programs are not eligible for funding: individuals; organizations not exempt under Section 501(c)3 of the IRS code; sectarian purpose programs that promote religious doctrines or exclude participants based on religion; political causes, candidates, organizations or campaigns; organizations that discriminate on the basis of race, sex, sexual orientation or religion; organizations with a primary purpose of influencing legislation; athletic, labor or fraternal groups; endowments; or programs and organizations for which PSEG is asked to serve as the sole funder.

Geographic Focus: Connecticut, New Jersey, New York

Date(s) Application is Due: Feb 15; May 15; Aug 15; Oct 31

Contact: Ellen Lambert, PSEG Foundation President; (973) 430-5074 or (973) 430-7000; ellen.lambert@pseg.com or corporatecitizenship@pseg.com

Internet: www.pseg.com/info/community/new_site/our_giving/safety.jsp

Sponsor: Public Service Enterprise Group Foundation

80 Park Plaza, T-10

Newark, NJ 07102

Public Education Power Grants   2032

Mary and Robert Pew of North Palm Beach, Florida and Grand Rapids, Michigan created the Mary and Robert Pew Public Education Fund in 1998 as a supporting organization to the Community Foundation for Palm Beach and Martin Counties. The Pews' primary philanthropic objective is to positively impact children's lives by providing access to high-quality instruction and educational enhancements. The fund supports initiatives that improve public education for economically-disadvantaged children through professional development for teachers, leadership development, and improving best practices in early childhood development. Most proposals are invited by the Pew Fund staff; however, interested parties wishing to share ideas may submit a brief description of their innovation through an online form at the grant website.

Restrictions: Giving is limited to Martin and Palm Beach counties, Florida.

Geographic Focus: Florida

Samples: Atlantic Community High School, Delray Beach, Florida, $40,000 - classroom libraries and professional development for reading; School District of Palm Beach County, West Palm Beach, Florida, $1,102,874 - for Galvanizing Change in Mathematics and Science Education for schools feeding into Boynton Beach High School and Glades Central High School; South Grade Elementary School, Lake Worth, Florida, $7,500 - to support band instrument lessons.

Contact: Louise Grant, Executive Director; (561) 659-6800 or (561) 691-6044; fax (561) 623-5467; louigrant1@aol.com

Internet: pewfund.org/?q=node/4

Sponsor: Mary and Robert Pew Public Education Fund

601 Heritage Drive Suite 206

Jupiter, FL 33458

Public Welfare Foundation Juvenile Justice Grants   2033

Public Welfare Foundation grants are awarded primarily to grassroots organizations in the United States and abroad, with emphasis on the environment, disadvantaged elderly and youth, population and reproductive health, economic development, welfare reform, health, human rights and global security, criminal justice, and community development. The Foundation's Juvenile Justice Program supports groups working to end the criminalization and reliance on incarceration of youth in the United States. In particular, the Program makes grants to groups that are working to: advance state policies that dramatically restrict juvenile justice systems' use of incarceration and out-of-home placements and prioritize the use of community-based programs for youth; end the practice of trying, sentencing, and incarcerating youth in the adult criminal justice system; and promote the fair and equitable treatment of youth of color who come into contact with the juvenile justice system. Types of support include: matching funds; operating budgets; seed money; continuing support; and special projects. The Foundation has a two-step application process that includes both a letter of inquiry (LOI) and a full proposal. The Foundation invites full proposals only after reviewing letters of inquiry. Proposal with cover letter should be addressed to the Steering Committee. Typical awards range from $15,000 to $500,000.

Requirements: Nonprofit organizations and, in certain cases, organizations without 501(c)3 status, may apply for grant support.

Restrictions: Grants will not be made to individuals or for religious purposes, building funds, capital improvements, endowments, scholarships, graduate work, foreign study, conferences, seminars, publications, research, workshops, consulting services, annual campaigns, or deficit financing.

Geographic Focus: All States

Amount of Grant: 15,000 - 500,000 USD

Samples: Center on Juvenile and Criminal Justice, San Francisco, California, $165,000 - support for the Pacific Juvenile Defender Center to develop and implement litigation strategies for reducing transfer of youth to the adult system in California; Legal Aid Justice Center, Charlottesville, Virginia, $400,000 - support to close two juvenile correctional centers and reinvest the savings into community based services; Southern Coalition for Social Justice, Durham, North Carolina, $100,000 - support for the Youth Justice Project.

Contact: Maria-Veronica Banks, Grants Manager; (202) 965-1800; fax (202) 265-8851; mbanks@publicwelfare.org

Internet: www.publicwelfare.org/grants-process/program-guidelines/

Sponsor: Public Welfare Foundation

1200 U Street, NW

Washington, D.C. 20009-4443

Public Welfare Foundation Special Initiative to Advance Civil Legal Aid Grants   2034

Public Welfare Foundation grants are awarded primarily to grassroots organizations in the United States and abroad, with emphasis on the environment, disadvantaged elderly and youth, population and reproductive health, economic development, welfare reform, health, human rights and global security, criminal justice, and community development. A targeted cluster of grants is awarded through the Foundation's Special Initiative to strengthen core elements of the national legal aid infrastructure, including innovations for better and more effective service delivery. Civil legal aid helps people to overcome the pressing legal problems of everyday life — home foreclosures; evictions and landlord tenant disputes; divorce and child custody cases; domestic violence; unfair employment and wage claims; and denial of government benefits or health insurance. Types of support include: matching funds; operating budgets; seed money; continuing support; and special projects. The Foundation has a two-step application process that includes both a letter of inquiry (LOI) and a full proposal. The Foundation invites full proposals only after reviewing letters of inquiry. Proposal with cover letter should be addressed to the Steering Committee. Typical awards range from $40,000 to $1,250,000.

Requirements: Nonprofit organizations and, in certain cases, organizations without 501(c)3 status, may apply for grant support. Eligible exceptions are listed in the guidelines (available upon request).

Restrictions: Grants will not be made to individuals or for religious purposes, building funds, capital improvements, endowments, scholarships, graduate work, foreign study, conferences, seminars, publications, research, workshops, consulting services, annual campaigns, or deficit financing.

Geographic Focus: All States

Amount of Grant: 40,000 - 1,250,000 USD

Samples: Georgetown University, Washington, D.C., $40,000 - support to the Justice Lab; National Center for State Courts, Williamsburg, Virginia, $1,250,000 - support for advancing the meaningful Access to Justice for All project; New Venture Fund, Washington, D.C., $900,000 - support for Voices for Civil Justice: A Breakthrough Strategic Communications Initiative for Civil Legal Aid.

Contact: Maria-Veronica Banks, Grants Manager; (202) 965-1800; fax (202) 265-8851; mbanks@publicwelfare.org

Internet: www.publicwelfare.org/civil-legal-aid/

Sponsor: Public Welfare Foundation

1200 U Street, NW

Washington, D.C. 20009-4443

Public Welfare Foundation Special Opportunities Grants   2035

Public Welfare Foundation grants are awarded primarily to grassroots organizations in the United States and abroad, with emphasis on the environment, disadvantaged elderly and youth, population and reproductive health, economic development, welfare reform, health, human rights and global security, criminal justice, and community development. The Special Opportunities program supports projects reflecting the Foundation's mission and underlying values, including its longstanding commitment to racial equity and justice. These are one-time only grants that are especially timely and compelling. At times, this kind of grant serves as a laboratory for new ideas. Relatively few of these grants are given. Types of support include: matching funds; operating budgets; seed money; continuing support; and special projects. The Foundation has a two-step application process that includes both a letter of inquiry (LOI) and a full proposal. The Foundation invites full proposals only after reviewing letters of inquiry. Proposal with cover letter should be addressed to the Steering Committee. Typical awards range from $30,000 to $100,000.

Requirements: Nonprofit organizations and, in certain cases, organizations without 501(c)3 status, may apply for grant support. Eligible exceptions are listed in the guidelines (available upon request).

Restrictions: Grants will not be made to individuals or for religious purposes, building funds, capital improvements, endowments, scholarships, graduate work, foreign study, conferences, seminars, publications, research, workshops, consulting services, annual campaigns, or deficit financing.

Geographic Focus: All States

Amount of Grant: 30,000 - 100,000 USD

Samples: Namati, Washington, D.C., $30,000 - support to explore opportunities in the U.S. in order to broaden its global network of community paralegals working to advance justice and legal empowerment; Smithsonian Institution, Washington, D.C., $100,000 - support for exhibition development and construction of the new National Museum of African American History and Culture; National Center for State Courts, Williamsburg, Virginia, $50,000 - support for a national multimedia community engagement project on public trust and confidence in the courts.

Contact: Maria-Veronica Banks, Grants Manager; (202) 965-1800; fax (202) 265-8851; mbanks@publicwelfare.org

Internet: www.publicwelfare.org/grants-process/program-guidelines/

Sponsor: Public Welfare Foundation

1200 U Street, NW

Washington, D.C. 20009-4443

Publix Super Markets Charities Local Grants   2036

Publix Super Markets Charities has long focused on youth and education. The Foundation supports efforts on the areas of youth, education (specifically literacy), and the plight of the homeless and hungry.

Requirements: The Foundation's charitable focus is toward nonprofit agencies and it supports many other efforts in Florida, Georgia, South Carolina, Alabama and Tennessee. Grant requests may be made writing and should include the following: organizational information including a brief history and mission; a copy of the Internal Revenue Service 501(c)3 determination letter; a brief budget; and a list of the Board of Directors. If requesting support for a particular project, include the total cost, the amount committed by the applicant, the amount requested, and the support received from other community

organizations. Any applicable deadlines should be specified. The Foundation Board meets monthly and generally it takes six to eight weeks to process a request.
Restrictions: No grants funding is made to individuals.
Geographic Focus: Alabama, Florida, Georgia, South Carolina, Tennessee
Samples: Florida Southern College, Lakeland, Florida, $400,000, project grant; Community Partnership for Homeless, Miami, Forida, $89,000, project grant; and Childrens Museum of Tampa, Tampa, Florida, $60,000, project grant.
Contact: Sharon Miller, Executive Director; (863) 680-5339
Internet: www.publix.com/about/CommunityInvolvement.do
Sponsor: Publix Super Markets Charities
P.O. Box 407
Lakeland, FL 33802-0407

Puerto Rico Community Foundation Grants 2037
The Foundation wishes to develop the capacities of communities in Puerto Rico so that they may achieve social transformation and economic self-sufficiency, by stimulating investment in communities and maximizing the impact and yield of each contribution. Grants are awarded in the areas of: education; community development; financial development; development of social interest housing; and philanthropy. Types of support include: general operating support; emergency funds; conferences and seminars; professorships; publications; research; technical assistance; consulting services; and matching funds. There are no application deadlines; the board meets in March, June, September, and December to consider requests.
Requirements: Organizations applying for grants must: be duly incorporated and registered as a nonprofit organization, according to the laws of the Commonwealth of Puerto Rico; be located and offer services in Puerto Rico. Additionally, applicants must present a copy of the following documents: certificate of good standing from the State Department; certificate from the Treasury Department; statement of organization's total budget for the year for which funds are solicited; financial statements; list of current members of Board of Directors.
Restrictions: The foundation does not make grants to support individuals, annual campaigns, seed money, endowments, deficit financing, scholarships, or building funds.
Geographic Focus: Puerto Rico
Amount of Grant: 1,000 - 40,000 USD
Contact: Grants Administrator; (787) 721-1037; fax (787) 721-1673; fcpr@fcpr.org
Internet: www.fcpr.org/
Sponsor: Puerto Rico Community Foundation
P.O. Box 70362
San Juan, PR 00936-8362
Puerto Rico

Pulaski County Community Foundation Grants 2038
The Pulaski County Community Foundation was established to serve the citizens of Pulaski County, Indiana. The Foundation welcomes grant requests from any nonprofit organization in Pulaski County. The Foundation also invites applications to help fund new organizations who meet demonstrated needs or benefit the community through creative and innovative projects and programs. Grant seekers may access the online application but are also encouraged to discuss their project with the Foundation office before submitting a grant proposal.
Requirements: The Foundation favors grant requests which: impact a substantial number of people in the Pulaski community; propose practical solutions to current problems or address a current community interest; examine and address underlying causes of local needs; encourage cooperation and elimination of duplicate services; build the capacity of the applying organization; are from established non-profit organizations.
Restrictions: Grants are made only to organizations that serve the Pulaski county area. As a general rule, the Foundation does not make grants from its discretionary funds for the following: ongoing operating expenses or annual fund raising drives; existing obligations, debt reduction or building campaigns; individuals or travel expenses; loans or endowments; political purposes. Grantees are required to complete a Final Report (program and financial) detailing how the grant funds were spent.
Geographic Focus: Indiana
Contact: Wendy Rose; (574) 946-0906; fax (574) 946-0971; wrose@pulaskionline.org
Internet: www.pulaskionline.org/content/view/97/432/
Sponsor: Pulaski County Community Foundation
127 E. Pearl Street, P.O.Box 407
Winamac, IN 46996

Pulido Walker Foundation 2039
Established in 1996, the Pulido Walker Foundation offers grant support throughout California and South Carolina (though awards are occasionally given in other states). Its primary fields of interest include: the arts; general education; health and health care organizations; higher education; and a variety of human services. Typically, awards are given for general operating support. A formal application should be secured from the Foundation office, though no annual application deadlines have been identified. Most recent grants have ranged from $100 to $10,000.
Requirements: 501(c)3 organizations either located in, or serving residents of, California and South Carolina are eligible to apply.
Geographic Focus: California, South Carolina
Amount of Grant: 100 - 10,000 USD
Samples: American Diabetes Association, San Diego, California, $1,000 - general operating support; Classics for Kids Foundation, Holliston, Massachusetts, $10,000 - general operating support; Ranch Santa Fe, California, $1,000 - general operating support.
Contact: Donna J. Walker, President; (858) 756-6150 or (858) 558-9200
Sponsor: Pulido Walker Foundation
P.O. Box 1334
Rancho Santa Fe, CA 92067-1334

Putnam County Community Foundation Grants 2040
The Putnam County Community Foundation is a nonprofit public charity established to administer funds, award grants and provide leadership, enriching the quality of life and strengthening community in Putnam County. The Foundation makes grants to qualified nonprofit organizations seeking to make a different in Putnam County and its residents. Grants are made in the following areas: animal welfare; arts and culture; civic and community; economic development; education; environment; health and human services; recreation; and youth. The application and samples of previously funded grants are available at the website.
Requirements: To be considered for funding, organizations must first submit a preliminary grant application form. The Grants Committee will review all preliminary applications to determine who will be invited to submit a full grant application.
Restrictions: Funding is not allowed for the following: individuals; ongoing operational expenses, i.e. salaries, rent, and utilities; projects that do not serve Putnam County citizens; projects normally fully funded by units of government; programs to build or fund an endowment; religious activities or programs that appear to serve one denomination and not the community at large; political organizations or campaigns; national and state-wide fund raising projects; for-profit companies; or projects requesting retroactive funding.
Geographic Focus: Indiana
Date(s) Application is Due: Feb 1; Mar 9; Aug 1; Sep 9
Contact: M. Elaine Peck, Executive Director; (765) 653-4978; fax (765) 653-6385; epeck@pcfoundation.org or info@pcfoutation.org
Internet: www.pcfoundation.org/grant_what_we_fund.html
Sponsor: Putnam County Community Foundation
2 South Jackson Street, P.O. Box 514
Greencastle, IN 46135

Quaker Oats Company Kids Care Clubs Grants 2041
The Kids Care Clubs supports the organization's mission to raise compassionate, community-minded kids. The program aims to promote youth volunteerism, increase the number of Kids Care Clubs and build a network of moms, teachers, youth leaders and others interested in sharing experiences and insights. In the first year, Quaker awarded more than $25,000 in grants to deserving Kids Care Clubs to bring good moments to more than 10,000 people in need. In addition, more than 575 new facilitators signed up and started new Kids Care Clubs to help young volunteers get involved. Quaker is looking forward to continuing to inspire youth volunteerism through its partnership with Kids Care Clubs. Projects are eligible for mini-grants and in-kind donations from the sponsors.
Geographic Focus: All States
Date(s) Application is Due: Feb 1
Contact: Maureen Byrne, Director, Youth & Family Engagement; (203) 656-8052 or (866) 269-0510; MByrne@generationOn.org or kidscare@generationOn.org
Internet: www.quakeroats.com/about-quaker-oats/content/community-programs/kids-care.aspx
Sponsor: Quaker Oats Company
P.O. Box 049003
Chicago, IL 60604-9003

Qualcomm Grants 2042
The philanthropic endeavors of Qualcomm develop and strengthen communities worldwide. Qualcomm invests human and financial resources in inspirational, innovative programs that serve diverse populations. Specifically their goal is to create educated, healthy, sustainable, culturally vibrant communities and to support employees' commitment to global communities through various programs. The company focuses primarily in geographic regions where they have a business presence. There are three focus areas. First is educated communities. The company is committed to improving science, technology, engineering and math education for students during their primary, secondary, and higher education years, and to expanding educational opportunities for under-represented students. Second is healthy, sustainable communities. The company strives to better the lives of underserved populations by providing basic human needs, with a focus on enhancing the welfare of children. They are also committed to protecting and enhancing our global environment. Third is culturally vibrant communities. Through their support of arts education and outreach programs, they help young people develop innovative minds and expand cultural enrichment opportunities to in-need populations. Applicants may submit a letter of inquiry form online and some organizations will be invited to submit a proposal for funding consideration. The submission deadlines are based on the grantmaking focus areas. The schedule can be found on the website.
Requirements: Eligible applicants must be 501(c)3 organizations.
Restrictions: The following are not eligible: individuals; sporting events without a charitable beneficiary; sectarian or denominational religious groups; faith-based schools unless the school accepts students from all religious and non-religious backgrounds and the students are not required to adhere to or convert to any religious doctrine; faith-based organizations unless the programs are broadly promoted and the program's beneficiaries are not encouraged or required to learn about, adhere, or convert to any religious doctrine; organizations that advocate, support, or practice activities inconsistent with Qualcomm's non-discrimination policies, whether based on race, religion, color, national origin, ancestry, mental or physical disability, age, gender, gender identity and/or expression, sexual orientation, veteran status, pregnancy, medical condition, marital status, or other basis protected by law; primary and secondary schools (note, however, these entities may be eligible for employee matching grants as long as they are not deemed ineligible by other exclusions and restrictions); and political contributions.
Geographic Focus: California, Colorado, Georgia, New Jersey, North Carolina, Texas
Contact: Corporate Giving Administrator; (858) 651-3200; fax (858) 651-3255; giving@qualcomm.com
Internet: www.qualcomm.com/citizenship/global-social-responsibility/philanthropy/guidelines
Sponsor: Qualcomm
5775 Morehouse Drive
San Diego, CA 92121

R.C. Baker Foundation Grants 2043

The R.C. Baker Foundation makes grants to U.S. nonprofit organizations for projects and programs that support social services for youth and the elderly, crime prevention, education, religion (Christian, Episcopal, Friends, Jewish, Methodist, and Presbyterian), scientific research, culture, and health. Support will be provided for fellowships and scholarships, general operating grants, challenge/matching grants, emergency funds, building funds, equipment, continuing support, annual campaigns, capital campaigns, renovation projects, and special projects. A cover letter should be submitted with a one- to two-page proposal. Annual deadlines are May 1 and October 1. The board meets in June and November to consider requests.

Requirements: 501(c)3 nonprofit organizations are eligible to apply.

Geographic Focus: All States

Date(s) Application is Due: May 1; Oct 1

Amount of Grant: 1,000 - 280,000 USD

Samples: A Bridge for Kids, San Diego, California, $2,750 - general operating support; Adventure Cycling Association, Missoula, Montana, $3,000 - general operating support; Friends of the Children's Museum, La Habra, California, $2,500 - general operating support.

Contact: Frank Laurence Scott, Jr., President; (760) 632-3600

Sponsor: R.C. Baker Foundation

330 Encinitas Boulevard, Suite 101

Encinitas, CA 92024-3723

R.D. and Joan Dale Hubbard Foundation Grants 2044

The R.D. and Joan Dale Hubbard Foundation awards grants to nonprofits organizations in California, Kansas, New Mexico, Oklahoma, and Texas. The Foundation's primary interests include: child welfare; hospital care; low income support programs; early childhood development, elementary schools, secondary schools, and higher education; museums; and other cultural programs. Types of support include: annual campaigns, building construction and renovation, endowments, matching support, professorships, scholarship funds, and scholarships to individuals. Proposals are reviewed throughout the year, and there are no specified annual deadlines.

Requirements: Nonprofit organizations in California, Kansas, New Mexico, Oklahoma, and Texas are eligible.

Geographic Focus: California, Kansas, New Mexico, Oklahoma, Texas

Amount of Grant: 10,000 - 60,000 USD

Samples: American Quarter Horse Foundation, Amarillo, Texas. $51,000 - general operating support; Autury National Center, Los Angeles, California, $25,000 - general operating support; Barbara Sinatra Children's Center, Rancho Mirage, California, $10,000 - general operating support.

Contact: Robert Donaldson, Executive Director; (575) 258-5919; fax (575) 258-3749

Sponsor: R.D. and Joan Dale Hubbard Foundation

103 Sierra Blanca Drive, P.O. Box 2498

Ruidoso, NM 88345

R.D. Beirne Trust Grants 2045

The R. D. Beirne Trust was established under the will of Roderick D. Beirne to support and promote quality human services programming for the physically incapacitated, underprivileged and underserved populations. Special consideration is given to charitable organizations that serve the blind, elderly and orphans of Grayson County, Texas. Grants from the R. D. Beirne Trust are 1 year in duration. Award amounts typically range from $3,000 to $13,000. The R.D. Beirne Trust has two deadlines annually.

Requirements: Grants are limited to or for the use of 501(c)3 charitable organizations that serve communities in Grayson County, Texas. Applications will be submitted online through the Bank of America website. A grant report is required within 1 year of the grant application date, regardless of whether all of the funds have been spent.

Restrictions: The trust does not support requests from individuals, organizations attempting to influence policy through direct lobbying, or any political campaigns.

Geographic Focus: Texas

Date(s) Application is Due: Jan 1; Aug 1

Amount of Grant: 3,000 - 13,000 USD

Samples: Your Health Clinic, Sherman, Texas, $10,000 - Awarded for Callie Clinic Emergency Financial Assistance (2018); Special Olympics Texas Inc., Dallas, Texas, $7,000 - Awarded for Greater Dallas Area Special Olympics program (For Grayson County); Denison Helping Hands, Denison, Texas, $7,500 - Awarded for Feeding the Hungry program.

Contact: Kelly Garlock, Philanthropic Client Manager; (800) 357-7094; tx.philanthropic@bankofamerica.com or tx.philanthropic@ustrust.com

Internet: www.bankofamerica.com/philanthropic/foundation/?fnId=150

Sponsor: R.D. Beirne Trust Fund

P.O. Box 831041

Dallas, TX 75283-1041

R.J. McElroy Trust Grants 2046

The R.J. McElroy Trust was founded in 1965. Its benefactor was a pioneer Iowa broadcaster. Grant funding is provided to organizations which provide educational benefits to deserving youth. The Trust gives higher priority to funding programs than it does to funding capital projects. It prefers to provide seed money for new projects with organizations building a firm financial basis including other funding sources after one to three years.

Requirements: Eligible applicants must be 501(c)3 non-profit organizations. Governmental entities are eligible. Organizations must be in the following areas of Iowa: Allamakee, Benton, Black Hawk, Bremer, Buchanan, Butler, Chickasaw, Clayton, Delaware, Dubuque, Fayette, Floyd, Franklin, Grundy, Howard, Hardin, Tama, Winneshiek, and rural Linn county. Before applying applicants are asked contact the Executive Director by phone or email to ensure eligibility. Applications are available on the website.

Restrictions: The Trust does not make grants to individuals or to religious organizations for religious programming.

Geographic Focus: Iowa

Date(s) Application is Due: Mar 1; Jun 1; Sep 1; Dec 1

Amount of Grant: 1,000 - 50,000 USD

Contact: Stacy Van Gorp, Executive Director; (319) 287-9102; fax (319) 287-9105; vangorp@mcelroytrust.org

Internet: mcelroytrust.org/grantProposalGuidlines.html

Sponsor: R.J. McElroy Trust

425 Cedar Street, Suite 312

Waterloo, IA 50701

R.S. Gernon Trust Grants 2047

The R. S. Gernon Trust was established in 1975 to support and promote quality educational, human services, and health care programming for underserved populations. The Gernon Trust specifically serves the people of Norwich, Connecticut. Grants from the R. S. Gernon Trust are primarily 1 year in duration. On occasion, multi-year support is awarded. Award amounts typically go up to $10,000.

Requirements: Applicants must have 501(c)3 tax-exempt status and serve the people of Norwich, Connecticut. Applications will be submitted online through the Bank of America website. A grant report is required within 1 year of the grant application date, regardless of whether all of the funds have been spent.

Restrictions: Grant requests for capital projects are generally not considered. Applicants will not be awarded a grant for more than 3 consecutive years. The trust does not support requests from individuals, organizations attempting to influence policy through direct lobbying, or any political campaigns.

Geographic Focus: Connecticut

Date(s) Application is Due: Aug 15

Amount of Grant: Up to 10,000 USD

Samples: Catholic Charities Diocese of Norwich, Norwich, Connecticut, $5,000 - Awarded for Emergency Basic Needs (2019); Eastern Connecticut Symphony, New London, Connecticut, $5,000 - Awarded for ECSO Music in the Schools (2019); Madonna Place Inc., Norwich, Connecticut, $5,000 - Awarded for the Family Support Center (2019).

Contact: Amy R. Lynch, Philanthropic Client Manager; (860) 244-4870; ct.grantmaking@bankofamerica.com or amy.r.lynch@bofa.com

Internet: www.bankofamerica.com/philanthropic/foundation/?fnId=54

Sponsor: R.S. Gernon Trust

P.O. Box 1802

Providence, RI 02901-1802

Radcliffe Institute Carol K. Pforzheimer Student Fellowships 2048

The Arthur and Elizabeth Schlesinger Library on the History of Women in America invites Harvard undergraduates to make use of the library's collections with competitive awards of amounts up to $2,500 for relevant research projects. Preference will be given to applicants pursuing research in the history of work and the family, community service and volunteerism, the culinary arts, or women's health. The research may be, but is not required to be, in connection with a project for academic credit. Applications will be evaluated on the significance of the research and the project's potential contribution to the advancement of knowledge as well as its creativity in drawing on the library's holdings. The awards may be used to cover photocopying, other incidental research expenses, or living expenses in lieu of term time or summer employment. See website for current deadlines and application.

Requirements: Each application must include: the Schlesinger Library Grants and Fellowships cover page; a project description (no longer than four double-spaced pages in twelve-point font) indicating the purpose of the research, the Schlesinger Library holdings to be consulted, and the significance of these holdings to the project overall; a one-page bibliography of principal secondary sources consulted in designing the research; a résumé no longer than two pages; the name of one reference who has agreed to send a supporting letter; and a proposed budget indicating how the funds requested will be spent.

Restrictions: Only Harvard undergraduates are eligible. Funding does not cover the purchase of durable equipment.

Geographic Focus: All States

Amount of Grant: Up to 2,500 USD

Contact: (617) 496-3048; science@radcliffe.edu

Internet: www.radcliffe.edu/schles/pforzheimer_grant.aspx

Sponsor: Radcliffe Institute for Advanced Study

10 Garden Street

Cambridge, MA 02138

Radcliffe Institute Oral History Grants 2049

The Arthur and Elizabeth Schlesinger Library invites scholars who are conducting oral history interviews relevant to the history of women or gender in the United States to apply for funding support. This grant stipulates that the interviews take place in accordance with guidelines of the Oral History Association, that consent is obtained from interviewees for their words to be viewed by researchers worldwide, and that true copies or transcripts of the original recording of the oral interviews, as well as copies of the consent forms, be deposited in the Schlesinger Library. Applicants may request support to cover travel expenses, living expenses, transcription services, and incidental research materials. Applications will be evaluated on the significance of the research and documentation planned and the project's potential contribution to the advancement of knowledge.

Requirements: Each application must include: the Schlesinger Library Grants and Fellowships cover page; a project description (no longer than four double-spaced pages) indicating the purpose of the research, the persons to be interviewed, and the interview arrangements; a curriculum vitae of no more than two pages; the name of one reference who has agreed to send a supporting letter; and a proposed budget indicating how the requested funds will be spent. A brief report about work accomplished under the grant will be due no later than one year from the date of the award.

Restrictions: The grant does not cover funding for durable equipment. Non-US citizens are eligible but should contact the library regarding visas and other required paperwork prior to applying.
Geographic Focus: All States, All Countries
Amount of Grant: Up to 3,000 USD
Contact: Grants Administrator; (617) 495-8647; fax (617) 496-4640; slgrants@radcliffe.edu
Internet: www.radcliffe.edu/schles/oral_history_grant.aspx
Sponsor: Radcliffe Institute for Advanced Study
10 Garden Street
Cambridge, MA 02138

Ralph C. Wilson, Jr. Foundation Preparing for Success Grant   2050

Strong work ethic, confidence and a desire to learn are attributes that can be instilled at a young age and carried through adulthood. The Preparing for Success focus area is centered on providing the communication, teamwork and critical-thinking skills people need to grow and adapt throughout their life and career. This begins with building a strong foundation of social-emotional skills for young children by supporting the capacity and quality of Early Childhood providers and programs across our two regions. In Afterschool, the Foundation seeks to support activities outside the classroom that play a critical role in allowing children and teens to explore their interests and talents, ultimately preparing them for tomorrow's workforce. For Young Adults & Working Families, the Foundation looks to create pathways for people to achieve greater economic mobility through honing technical and employability skills that are necessary to access good jobs and that fill current and future skills gaps in the economies of the two regions we serve. The application is open on a rolling-basis.
Geographic Focus: Michigan, New York
Amount of Grant: Up to 1,500,000 USD
Samples: Ann Arbor SPARK, Ann Arbor, Michigan, $100,000 - to support plans for the American Center for Mobility at Willow Run (2019); Bing Youth Institute, Detroit, Michigan, $200,000 - to support the Bing Youth Institute's BINGO (Boys Inspired through Nurturing, Growth and Opportunities) Mentoring Program in Detroit to bring together men of color serving as mentors to young high school men of color (2019); Detroit Employment Solutions Corporation, Detroit, Michigan, $1,500,000 - to support the transformation of the A. Philip Randolph Technical Education Center into a state-of-the-art construction and skilled trades training facility for youth and adults in metro Detroit (2019).
Contact: Deb Barney, Grants Manager; (313) 885-1895; info@ralphcwilsonjrfoundation.org
Internet: www.ralphcwilsonjrfoundation.org/our-focus/preparing-for-success/
Sponsor: Ralph C. Wilson, Jr. Foundation
3101 East Grand Boulevard, Suite 200
Detroit, MI 48202

Ralph C. Wilson, Jr. Foundation Youth Sports and Recreation Grant   2051

If kids are active, the outcomes are great – for all of us. Active kids have better cognitive function, better mental health and educational outcomes, and fewer health problems throughout life. And the downstream benefits of avoided lost productivity and future healthcare costs are in the billions-of-dollars for our communities, if we could just get and keep kids moving more. That's exactly what the Foundation's Youth Sports & Recreation focus area hopes to do, by supporting more access for kids to get active through sport regardless of their zip code or ability. The Foundation has teamed up with the Aspen Institute's Sport & Society program and a constellation of local and national partners to do so. Much of the work revolves around Aspen's "8 Plays" listed below that help outline what good looks like in youth sports and helps guide grant making. Overall, the Foundation supports people, places and programs that do this well in some of our most under-resourced communities.
Geographic Focus: Michigan, New York
Samples: Challenger Miracle League of Greater Rochester, Rochester, New York, $488,000 - to support the construction of a barrier-free field and pavilion and build out the organization's capacity to manage and maintain the Miracle Field Complex, located at Ridge Park Athletic Complex in Webster, New York (2019); WNY Girls in Sports, Buffalo, New York, $1,466,200 - to support the expansion of the Western New York Girls in Sports events and better connect young girls to existing sports and recreation programs and opportunities (2019); Downtown Boxing Gym Youth Program, Detroit, Michigan, $500,000 - to support the growth of this after school sports program, including an apprenticeship program to develop the next generation of boxing gym leaders to carry the mission forward (2019).
Contact: Deb Barney, Grants Manager; (313) 885-1895; info@ralphcwilsonjrfoundation.org
Internet: www.ralphcwilsonjrfoundation.org/our-focus/active-lifestyles/youth-sports-and-recreation/
Sponsor: Ralph C. Wilson, Jr. Foundation
3101 East Grand Boulevard, Suite 200
Detroit, MI 48202

Ralph M. Parsons Foundation Grants   2052

The Ralph M. Parsons Foundation strives to support and facilitate the work of the region's best nonprofit organizations, recognizing that many of those in need today will go on to shape the future of Southern California, to define it, redefine it, and help it set and achieve new goals. The Foundation focuses on four areas: social impact, civic and cultural programs, health, and higher education. Applicants may submit a letter of inquiry, and there are no deadlines. If the Foundation decides to explore specifics of the request in more detail, applicants will be asked to submit a full proposal. Guidance will be provided in writing. Approximately 200 awards are made per year ranging from $25,000 to $50,000.
Requirements: Eligible applicants are 501(c)3 organizations located in Los Angeles County. Some occasional exceptions are made in the area of higher education. Excellence, access for disadvantaged populations, and the active participation of volunteers, board and staff are key characteristics the Foundation seeks in its applicants. Funding of direct services is a priority.

Restrictions: The following is ineligible: fundraising events, dinners and mass mailings; direct aid to individuals; conferences, seminars, workshops, etc; sectarian, religious or fraternal purposes; federated fundraising appeals; support of candidates for political office or to influence legislation; for-profit organizations or businesses; organizations outside of Los Angeles County (with occasional exceptions in the area of higher education); animal welfare; environment; documentary filmmaking; and scientific and/or medical research. Scholarship support is provided only to nonprofit institutions; individuals are not eligible to apply.
Geographic Focus: California
Samples: 24th Street Theatre, Los Angeles, California, $50,000, general support; Archdiocese of Los Angeles Education Foundation, Los Angeles, California, $75,000, tuition assistance to disadvantaged, low income children; and Arts in Education Aid Council, Los Angeles, California, $10,000, capacity-building support for this agency which provides arts eduction at public schools in the San Fernando Valley.
Contact: Wendy Garen, President and Chief Executive Officer; (213) 362-7600
Internet: www.rmpf.org
Sponsor: Ralph M. Parsons Foundation
1888 West Sixth Street, Suite 700
Los Angeles, CA 90017

Random Acts of Kindness Foundation Lesson Plan Contest   2053

Through the dissemination of ideas and the development of materials and programs, the Random Acts of Kindness Foundation has helped kindness coordinators - including educators, students, community members, faith groups, service clubs, and others - incorporate kindness into thousands of schools and communities. In supporting the global kindness movement, the foundation collects lesson plans and makes them available to others interested in promoting kindness in their schools. To honor the efforts of these teachers, the foundation will make an award to the teachers who submit the ten best random-acts-of-kindness lesson plans. Complete guidelines and an entry form are available on the Web site.
Requirements: Teachers or past/retired teachers involved in kindness projects and/or activities in their classrooms are eligible.
Geographic Focus: All States
Date(s) Application is Due: Jul 31
Amount of Grant: 100 USD
Contact: Gary Dixon, President; (800) 660-2811 or (303) 297-1964; fax (303) 297-2919; Rakinfo@actsofkindness.org or info@randomactsofkindness.org
Internet: www.actsofkindness.org/classroom/contest/index.asp
Sponsor: Random Acts of Kindness Foundation
1727 Tremont Place
Denver, CO 80202

Raskob Foundation for Catholic Activities Grants   2054

The Raskob Foundation is an independent private Catholic family foundation that makes grants worldwide for projects and programs associated with the Catholic Church. Grants support elementary and secondary education, community action and development, missionary activities, ministries (including youth and parish), health care, social concerns, AIDS victims, finance and development, and relief services. Types of support include operating budgets, seed money, emergency funds, equipment, land acquisition, conferences and seminars, program-related investments, renovation projects, special projects, and matching funds. Deadlines are June 8 and August 8 for the fall meeting; and December 8 and February 8 for the spring meeting.
Requirements: Roman Catholic organizations listed in the Kenedy Directory of Official Catholic Organizations may apply. Organizations should refer to the application guidelines for specific instruction on how to apply and information to submit.
Restrictions: The Foundation does not accept applications for the following purposes: tuition, scholarships or fellowships; reduction of debt; endowment funds; grants made by other grantmaking organizations; individual scholarly research; lobbying or legislation; or projects completed prior to our board meetings (mid-May and late November).
Geographic Focus: All States, All Countries
Amount of Grant: 5,000 - 15,000 USD
Contact: Maureen Horner; (302) 655-4440; fax (302) 655-3223; info@rfca.org
Internet: www.rfca.org/en/Grantmaking/tabid/63/Default.aspx
Sponsor: Raskob Foundation for Catholic Activities
P.O. Box 4019
Wilmington, DE 19807

Rasmuson Foundation Tier One Grants   2055

The Rasmuson Foundation supports non-profit organizations which strive to improve the quality of life for people throughout the state of Alaska. Tier One Grants provide funding of up to $25,000 for capital projects, technology updates, capacity building, program expansion, and creative works. The Foundation encourages applicants to discuss proposals prior to submission. Applications are available on the website and are accepted at any time. The Foundation accepts Tier 1 grant applications year-round, with review and awards handled on a rolling basis throughout the year. Organizations will be notified via email when an application has been received. If an applicant organization is successful, a formal grant agreement and grant check will be sent.
Requirements: Alaskan organizations that have received 501(c)3 status and are classified as not a private foundation under section 509(a) of the Internal Revenue Service Code, units of government, and federally-recognized tribes are eligible.
Restrictions: For religious organizations, only projects with a broad community impact are considered. For units of government and tribes, only projects with a broad community impact beyond traditional government functions are considered. The following is not eligible: general operations, administrative, indirect, or overhead costs; deficits or debt reduction; endowments; scholarships; fundraising events or sponsorships; in general, K-12 education; reimbursement for items already purchased; and electronic health records and other emerging technologies.

Geographic Focus: Alaska
Amount of Grant: Up to 25,000 USD
Samples: Alaska Association for Historic Preservation, Anchorage, Alaska, $20,000 - to restore launch control building on Nike Site Summit in Anchorage; Yakutat Tlingit Tribe, Yakutat, Alaska, $18,837 - to upgrade building infrastructure and purchase equipment for a culture camp in Yakutat; Valley Residential Services, Wasilla, Alaska, $23,845 - for technology upgrades.
Contact: Barbara Bach, Director of Grant Management; (907) 297-2825 or (907) 297-2700; fax (907) 297-2770; bbach@rasmuson.org or rasmusonfdn@rasmuson.org
Internet: www.rasmuson.org/index.php?switch=viewpage&pageid=32
Sponsor: Rasmuson Foundation
301 West Northern Lights Boulevard, Suite 400
Anchorage, AK 99503

Rasmuson Foundation Tier Two Grants   2056

The Rasmuson Foundation supports non-profit organizations which strive to improve the quality of life for people throughout the state of Alaska. Tier Two Grants are available of more than $25,000 for large capital (building) projects, projects of demonstrable strategic importance or innovative nature, or the expansion or start-up of innovative programs that address issues of broad community or statewide significance. Tier 2 grants may also support technology updates and creative works. The project must demonstrate long-term benefits or impacts, and be initiated by an established organization(s) with a history of accomplishment. Applying for a Tier 2 grant is a two-step process. The first step is to prepare and submit a Letter of Inquiry. If the Foundation is interested in the project, then the organization will be invited to submit a full Tier 2 proposal. Tier 2 Letter of Inquiry reviews can take up to 90 days. Tier 2 grants are awarded during the biannual board meetings, which generally take place in early July and early December.
Requirements: Alaskan organizations that have received 501(c)3 status and are classified as not a private foundation under section 509(a) of the Internal Revenue Service Code, units of government, and federally-recognized tribes are eligible.
Restrictions: For religious organizations, only projects with a broad community impact are considered. For units of government and tribes, only projects with a broad community impact beyond traditional government functions are considered. The following is not eligible: general operations, administrative, indirect, or overhead costs; deficits or debt reduction; endowments; scholarships; fundraising events or sponsorships; in general, K-12 education; reimbursement for items already purchased; and electronic health records and other emerging technologies.
Geographic Focus: Alaska
Amount of Grant: 25,000 - 3,000,000 USD
Samples: Southcentral Foundation, Anchorage, Alaska, $2,605,000 - construction of NUKA Institute and start-up operations; Anchorage Museum Association, Anchorage, Alaska, $495,000 - implementation of a Polar Lab; Alaska Pacific University, Anchorage, Alaska, $500,000 - initiatives to enhance sustainability.
Contact: Barbara Bach, Director of Grant Management; (907) 297-2825 or (907) 297-2700; fax (907) 297-2770; bbach@rasmuson.org or rasmusonfdn@rasmuson.org
Sponsor: Rasmuson Foundation
301 West Northern Lights Boulevard, Suite 400
Anchorage, AK 99503

Rathmann Family Foundation Grants   2057

The foundation's main funding areas are education, with priority given to science and math; the arts; children and youth health organizations; and preservation of the environment. Types of support include general operating support, continuing support, capital campaigns, equipment acquisition, endowment funds, program development, conferences and seminars, seed grants, curriculum development, fellowships, internships, scholarship funds, research, and matching funds. There are no specific deadlines or application forms, and interested parties should begin by contacting the Foundation directly.
Requirements: Grants are awarded to organizations in the San Francisco Bay, California area; the Annapolis, Maryland area; the Seattle, Washington area; the Philadelphia, Pennsylvania area: and metropolitan Minneapolis/Saint Paul, Minnesota.
Restrictions: Grants are not awarded to/for private foundations; religious organizations for religious activities; civil rights; social action; advocacy organizations; fraternal groups; political purposes; mental health counseling; individuals; or fundraisers, media events, public relations, annual appeals, or propaganda.
Geographic Focus: California, Maryland, Minnesota, Pennsylvania, Washington
Amount of Grant: 1,000 - 100,000 USD
Contact: Rick Rathmann, (410) 349-2376; fax (410) 349-2377
Sponsor: Rathmann Family Foundation
1290 Bay Dale Drive, P.O. Box 352
Arnold, MD 21012

Ray Charles Foundation Grants   2058

In 1986, the Ray Charles Foundation — a private non-profit organization — was created by Ray Charles. In that same year he founded the Robinson Foundation for Hearing Disorders in Los Angeles, California. This non-profit organization was formed and operated by Ray Charles and operated under this name until the suggestion was made to change its name in 2006 after the death of Ray Charles. So, in 2006, the name of the Foundation was changed to the Ray Charles Foundation in order to bring awareness to his name, his philanthropic generosity and his foundation. Today, the Foundation's mission is to administer grants for scientific, educational and charitable purposes; to encourage, promote and educate, as to the causes and cures for diseases and disabilities of the hearing impaired and to assist organizations and institutions in their social educational and academic advancement of programs for the youth, and carry on other charitable and educational activities associated with these goals as allowed by law. Foundation considers funding for educational programs that provide academic services to disadvantaged and underprivileged youth in the area of arts, sciences, college

preparation, after school tutoring. Funding is favored for educational programs and resources for youth with hearing disorders and/or who are visually impaired or blind. Lastly, funding will be considered to qualifying institutions and museums whose mission it is to provide musical, cultural education and access to the arts to underprivileged and disadvantaged youth. Foundation accepts and reviews applications between May 1 and September 30.
Requirements: The Foundation funds grants to organizations and programs incorporated and delivering services in the United States. An organization that is certified as tax exempt under Section 501(c)3 of the U.S. Internal Revenue Code is eligible for consideration.
Restrictions: The Foundation does not fund organizations and programs outside of the United States.
Geographic Focus: All States, American Samoa, District of Columbia, Guam, Marshall Islands, Northern Mariana Islands, Puerto Rico, U.S. Virgin Islands
Contact: Valerie Ervin, President; (323) 737-8000; fax (323) 737-0148; info@theraycharlesfoundation.org
Internet: www.theraycharlesfoundation.org/RCF_GrantQualifications.html
Sponsor: Ray Charles Foundation
2107 West Washington Boulevard
Los Angeles, CA 90018-1536

Ray Foundation Grants   2059

The Foundation wishes to encourage creativity, responsibility, and self-reliance on the part of the grant recipients. The Foundation has a particular interest in aviation and the development of strategies and programs which address the involvement and education of children and young adults in aviation and flight. There are no submission deadlines.
Requirements: Eligible applicants must be 501(c)3 organizations. Interested applicants should send a letter, not to exceed two pages, summarizing their request and including the following: applicant's name as recognized by the Internal Revenue Service; applicant's address and telephone number; the date of the application; the nature, history and purpose of the organization; the organization's tax exempt status, including a copy of the Internal Revenue Service determination letter; a brief general description of the organization's need or problem to be addressed; a brief preliminary budget for the project, including the amount requested from the Foundation and proposed sources and amounts of other funding; plans for cooperation with other institutions and organizations, if any; the signature and title of the organization's project director and chief administrative officers indicating approval of the request.
Geographic Focus: All States
Samples: The Heritage Foundation, Washington, D.C., $15,000, internships; University of North Dakota Foundation, Grand Forks, North Dakota, $100,000, scholarships; and University of North Dakota, Center for Innovation, Grand Forks, North Dakota, $50,000, internship.
Contact: James C. Ray, President; (239) 649-5733
Sponsor: Ray Foundation, Inc.
100 Aviation Drive South
Naples, FL 34104

Raymond Austin Hagen Family Foundation Grants   2060

The Raymond Austin Hagen Family was established in California in 2005, and its primary purposes include: providing musical instruments to youths to promote arts education; offering access and/or tickets to musical performances to youths; and to provide music lessons to school-age children. To formal applications are required, and recipients are selected by committees comprised from local Huntington Beach, California, school groups.
Geographic Focus: California
Amount of Grant: 1,000 - 1,000 USD
Contact: Helen Hagen, President; (714) 840-4150
Sponsor: Raymond Austin Hagen Family Foundation
3631 Rebel Circle
Huntington Beach, CA 92649-2513

Raytheon Middle School Grants and Scholarships   2061

Raytheon dedicates resources to creating a greater awareness and appreciation of math among young people. Through its MathMovesU program sixth, seventh, and eighth grade students are invited to answer the question, "How does math put the action in your passion?" Students must demonstrate an enthusiasm for math and the ability to illustrate the importance of math in the hobby/sport/subject/activity the student cares about the most. Up to 150 awards of $1,000 each are made to student recipients. Student awards can be used for a campership applied to tuition and fees at a science, technology, engineering, or math-related summer camp or a traditional scholarship applied to freshman year in post secondary school. A matching award of $1,000 is made to the recipient's school to be used for math-related programs.
Requirements: Eligible applicants must: be United States citizens or legal residents; be enrolled in sixth, seventh or eighth grade as of the application deadline date; create a multimedia or paper submission illustrating the importance of math in the hobby/sport/subject/activity the applicant cares about the most, specifically addressing "How does math put the action in your passion?"; and include representations of actual math equations related to the subject. Submissions are evaluated based on creativity, originality, time commitment, the use of math equations to demonstrate how math is important in the student's hobby/sport/subject/activity, and how well the question "How does math put the action in your passion?" is addressed. The application form is on Raytheon's website.
Restrictions: Camperships must be used within the summer of the award or no later than the following summer. Awards are not renewable, however, students may reapply each year they meet eligibility requirements. Home-schooled students are eligible, however, the matching school grant will be forfeited if they become a recipient.
Geographic Focus: All States
Date(s) Application is Due: Jan 18
Contact: Community Relations Officer; (781) 522-3000; corporatecontributions@raytheon.com
Scholarship Management Services; (507) 931-1682

Internet: www.raytheon.com/responsibility/community/mmu/scholar/index.html
Sponsor: Raytheon Company
870 Winter Street
Waltham, MA 02451

RCF General Community Grants 2062

Six times a year, the Richland County Foundation awards General Community Grants to nonprofit organizations through a competitive process. In doing so, the Foundation looks to partner with nonprofit organizations to respond to current community needs in the following areas: education; health services; arts and culture; community services; children, youth and families; human services; environment; and employment and economic development. Application deadlines are 5:00 p.m. on the first Friday of January, March, May, July, September, and November. Applications must be at the Foundation Office by 5:00 p.m. on the due date to meet the deadline. Final decisions on all grant applications are made by the Board of Trustees approximately 6 – 8 weeks following the grant deadline.
Requirements: 501(c)3 public charities, government entities, schools, and nonprofit medical facilities serving residents of Richland County are eligible to apply. The application procedure should begin with a telephone call to the Program Officer to schedule an initial meeting to discuss the project. The Foundation typically looks for several of the following key elements in submitted applications: a one-time grant, especially for a pilot project which can serve as a model or be replicated; a project in which the Foundation is a funding partner, rather than the sole funder; a project or program which promotes volunteer involvement; an organization which can demonstrate the ability to sustain the project in the future when Foundation grant dollars end; projects or programs which are a collaborative effort(s) among nonprofit organizations in the community which eliminate duplication of services; a project which is likely to make a clear difference in the quality of life of a substantial number of people; an organization which is proposing a practical approach to a solution of a current community problem; a project or program which is focusing on prevention; and a worthy community project for which a grant from the Foundation will most likely leverage additional financial support. Applicants who have a program or project that meets these criteria are encouraged to contact the Foundation to discuss submitting an application.
Restrictions: Community grants are awarded from endowed, unrestricted and field of interest funds. Richland County Foundation typically does not provide funding from unrestricted funds for the following: sectarian activities of religious organizations; operating expenses for annual drives or to eliminate debt; medical, scientific or academic research; individuals other than for college scholarships; travel to or in support of conferences, or travel for groups such as bands, sports teams and classes (unless through special grant programs such as Summertime Kids or the Teacher Assistance Program); capital improvements to building and property not owned by the organization or covered by a long term lease; computer systems; projects that taxpayers support or expected to support; and political issues.
Geographic Focus: Ohio
Samples: Ashland University, Ashland, Ohio, $250,000 - this grant is part of a $15.5 million campaign to build a College of Nursing facility in Richland County; Richland Community Development Group, Mansfield, Ohio, $50,000 - this supports phase two of a pilot project to coordinate a county-wide collaborative effort for both economic and community development.
Contact: Bradford Groves; (419) 525-3020; fax (419) 525-1590; bgroves@rcfoundation.org
Rebecca Smith; (419) 525-3020; fax (419) 525-1590; bsmith@rcfoundation.org
Internet: www.richlandcountyfoundation.org/grant-information/types-of-grants/community
Sponsor: Richland County Foundation
24 West Third Street, Suite 100
Mansfield, OH 44902-1209

RCF Individual Assistance Grants 2063

Twice a year, the Richland County Foundation awards Individual Assistance Grants to nonprofit organizations which operate programs that assist the needy. Grant dollars may be used for emergency assistance, basic human needs and sustaining basic health. Application deadlines are 5:00 p.m. on the first Friday of March and September. Applications must be at the Foundation Office by 5:00 p.m. on the due date to meet the deadline. Final decisions on all grant applications are made by the Board of Trustees approximately 6 – 8 weeks following the grant deadline. Community grants are awarded from endowed, unrestricted and field of interest funds.
Requirements: 501(c)3 public charities, government entities, schools, and nonprofit medical facilities providing emergency assistance, basic human needs, and basic health programs for residents of Richland County are eligible to apply. The application procedure should begin with a telephone call to the Program Officer to schedule an initial meeting to discuss the project.
Geographic Focus: Ohio
Samples: Salvation Army, Mansfield, Ohio, $25,000 - provide emergency rent and mortgage assistance for their clients; Mansfield Memorial Homes, Mansfield, Ohio, two grants totaling $35,000 - for programs that assist the elderly; The Homemaker Home Healthcare Program, Mansfield, Ohio, $20,000 - to pay for home health services that include personal care, light housekeeping, and limited errand-runs to assist the elderly (2011)
Contact: Bradford Groves; (419) 525-3020; fax (419) 525-1590; bsmith@rcfoundation.org
Rebecca Smith; (419) 525-3020; fax (419) 525-1590; bsmith@rcfoundation.org
Internet: www.richlandcountyfoundation.org/grant-information/types-of-grants/community
Sponsor: Richland County Foundation
24 West Third Street, Suite 100
Mansfield, OH 44902-1209

RCF Summertime Kids Grants 2064

Richland County Foundation's Summertime Kids Grants provide funding to nonprofit organizations that develop creative, educational and fun-filled activities for Richland County children throughout the summer months. Proposals are due the second Friday in February and must be at the Foundation Office by 5:00 p.m. on the due date to meet the deadline.

The application with original signatures plus 18 copies must be submitted (the Foundation requests that applicants refrain from attachments). Awards will be announced in early April.
Requirements: 501(c)3 organizations, schools, churches, government entities and health service organizations serving residents of Richland County are eligible to apply. Collaborating applicants should submit only one application and note on it the lead agency.
Restrictions: Grant dollars should be used for direct programming expenses rather than operational expenses.
Geographic Focus: Ohio
Amount of Grant: Up to 2,500 USD
Samples: City of Mansfield, Mansfield, Ohio - "Hooked on Fishing"; Ohio Bird Sanctuary, Mansfield, Ohio - Nature Camp; Raemelton Therapeutic Equestrian Center, Mansfield, Ohio - Summer Horse Camp.
Contact: Becky Smith; (419) 525-3020; fax (419) 525-1590; bsmith@rcfoundation.org
Kristina Johnston, Administrative Assistant; (419) 525-3020; fax (419) 525-1590; kjohnston@rcfoundation.org
Internet: richlandcountyfoundation.spirecms.com/grant-information/types-of-grants/summertime-kids
Sponsor: Richland County Foundation
24 West Third Street, Suite 100
Mansfield, OH 44902-1209

RCF The Women's Fund Grants 2065

Richland County Foundation makes grants annually from "The Women's Fund" a permanent endowment established in 1996 to promote the physical, intellectual, emotional, social, economic, and cultural growth of women of all ages. While the current grant cycle is open to any nonprofit organization for programs which benefit women and girls in Richland County, a preference will be given to programs addressing childhood obesity, which exclusively target girls up to the age of (18) eighteen. The Foundation offers a workshop in August for interested applicants. Details are available at the grant website. Grant applications will be available at the workshop and will be made available for download from the website afterwards. Awards will be announced at the annual Women's Fund Luncheon in November.
Requirements: 501(c)3 public charities, government entities, schools, and nonprofit medical facilities serving residents of Richland County are eligible to apply. Deadline dates may vary from year to year. Interested applicants are encouraged to check the website, call the Program Officer with any questions and attend the Foundation's annual workshop for this grant.
Geographic Focus: Ohio
Date(s) Application is Due: Sep 16
Amount of Grant: 250 - 10,000 USD
Samples: Center for Individual and Family Services, Mansfield, Ohio - "Ladies in Recovery"; Emergency Pregnancy Contact, Mansfield, Ohio - "Helping Mom Succeed III"; Eastern Elementary School, Lexington, Ohio - "Women in Science Day"
Contact: Bradford Groves; (419) 525-3020; fax (419) 525-1590; bgroves@rcfoundation.org
Rebecca Smith; (419) 525-3020; fax (419) 525-1590; bsmith@rcfoundation.org
Internet: richlandcountyfoundation.spirecms.com/womens-fund/womens-fund-application-process
Sponsor: Richland County Foundation
24 West Third Street, Suite 100
Mansfield, OH 44902-1209

Reinberger Foundation Grants 2066

Clarence T. Reinberger was born in 1894 on Cleveland's west side, and began his business career in the 1920's as a pioneer in the automobile replacement parts field. Starting as a clerk in the Cleveland retail store of the National Automotive Parts Association's (NAPA) Automotive Parts Company, he became president of that company in 1948. In the 1960's the Automotive Parts Company merged with the Genuine Parts Company of Atlanta. Mr. Reinberger held the position of Chairman of the Board of Genuine Parts Company until his death in 1968. Louise Fischer Reinberger was born in Germany. After graduation from high school in the United States, she was employed by the Halle Brothers Company, a large Cleveland department store. The Reinberger Foundation was established by Mr. and Mrs. Reinberger in 1966. Mr. Reinberger left a substantial bequest to the Foundation at his death in 1968. Upon Mrs. Reinberger's death in 1984, the major portion of her estate was also bequeathed to the Foundation. Although the Reinbergers had no children, the foundation continues to be managed by several generations of Mr. Reinberger's family. Since its inception, the foundation has distributed over $91,000,000 to the non-profit community. The foundation divides its support among the following program areas: Arts, Culture, and Humanities; Education; Human Service - Health; and Human Service - Other. Categories supported under Arts, Culture and Humanities include museums, visual arts, performing arts, media and communication, arts education, zoos, and public recreation. Categories supported under Education include K-12 schools, early childhood education, adult education/literacy, libraries, and workforce development. Categories supported under Human Service - Health include hospitals and clinics, substance abuse prevention/treatment, medical and disease research, disease prevention, and speech and hearing. Categories supported under Human Service - Other include children and youth services, residential and home care, emergency food programs, youth development, domestic violence, and temporary housing/homeless shelters. Letters of Inquiry for grants of any type may be submitted according to the following program-area schedule: Education - March 1; Human Service (Health) - June 1; Human Service (Other) - September 1; and Arts, Culture, and Humanities - December 1. Letters of Inquiry may either be sent by U.S. Mail or emailed and are due in the foundation office by the deadline date. Full proposals are accepted only at the request of the foundation.
Requirements: Applicants must be 501(c)3 organizations. Preferential consideration is given to organizations serving Northeast Ohio, or the greater-Columbus area.

Restrictions: No loans are made, nor are grants given to individuals. The Reinberger Foundation does not make more than one grant to a particular organization during a given calendar year, nor will new proposals be considered until existing multi-year commitments have been paid.
Geographic Focus: Ohio
Date(s) Application is Due: Mar 1; Jun 1; Sep 1; Dec 1
Samples: Cleveland Zoological Society, Cleveland, Ohio, $100,000; Cuyahoga Community College Foundation, Cleveland, Ohio, $37,500; The Free Medical Clinic of Greater Cleveland, Cleveland, Ohio, $50,000; Community Kitchen, Inc., Columbus, Ohio, $5,000.
Contact: Karen R. Hooser, President; (216) 292-2790; fax (216) 292-4466; info@reinbergerfoundation.org
Internet: reinbergerfoundation.org/apply.html
Sponsor: Reinberger Foundation
30000 Chagrin Boulevard #300
Cleveland, OH 44122

Ressler-Gertz Foundation Grants 2067
The Ressler-Gertz Foundation was established in 1997 in California by Jami Gertz and Antony Ressler. Jami Beth Gertz, born October 28, 1965, in Chicago, is an American actress and investor. Gertz is known for her early roles in the films Crossroads, The Lost Boys, Less Than Zero and Quicksilver, the 1980s TV series Square Pegs and 1996's Twister, as well as for her roles as Judy Miller in the CBS sitcom Still Standing and as Debbie Weaver in the ABC sitcom The Neighbors. Along with husband Tony Ressler, she is a part-owner of the Atlanta Hawks of the National Basketball Association. Gertz married executive Antony Ressler in 1989. She and her husband are members of the investment group led by Mark Attanasio which purchased the MLB franchise Milwaukee Brewers. Gertz-Ressler High Academy, a member of The Alliance for College-Ready Public Schools, is named for Gertz and her husband. They also became owners of the NBA team Atlanta Hawks in 2015. The Foundations contributes to organizations that support education, the arts, and other community nonprofits. Awards range as high as $500,000.
Geographic Focus: All States
Amount of Grant: Up to 500,000 USD
Samples: Anderson Ranch Arts Center, Snowmass, Colorado, $25,000 - general operations (2018); Campbell Hall, Studio City, California, $460,000 - general operating support (2018); Peer Health Exchange, San Francisco, California, $100,000 - general operating support (2018).
Contact: Jami Gertz, Trustee; (818) 981-2240
Sponsor: Ressler-Gertz Foundation
16130 Ventura Boulevard, Suite 320
Encino, CA 91436-2531

RGk Foundation Grants 2068
RGK Foundation awards grants in the broad areas of Education, Community, and Medicine/Health. The foundation's primary interests within Education include programs that focus on formal K-12 education (particularly mathematics, science and reading), teacher development, literacy, and higher education. Within Community, the foundation supports a broad range of human services, community improvement, abuse prevention, and youth development programs. Human service programs of particular interest to the foundation include children and family services, early childhood development, and parenting education. The foundation supports a variety of Community Improvement programs including those that enhance non-profit management and promote philanthropy and voluntarism. Youth development programs supported by the foundation typically include after-school educational enrichment programs that supplement and enhance formal education systems to increase the chances for successful outcomes in school and life. The foundation is also interested in programs that attract female and minority students into the fields of mathematics, science, and technology. The foundation's current interests in the area of Medicine/Health include programs that promote the health and well-being of children, programs that promote access to health services, and Foundation-initiated programs focusing on ALS. Annual deadlines for applicants are March 6, June 12, and September 16.
Requirements: Although there are no geographic restrictions to the foundation's grantmaking program, the foundation no longer accepts unsolicited requests for international agencies or programs. All applicants must complete an electronic Letter of Inquiry (LOI) from the website as the first step. RGK Foundation will entertain one electronic LOI per organization in a twelve-month period. While the foundation occasionally awards grants for operating expenses, capital campaigns, endowments, and international projects, such grants are infrequent and usually initiated by the foundation. Grants are made only to nonprofit organizations certified as tax exempt under Sections 501(c)3 or 170(c) of the IRS code. Hospitals, educational institutions, and governmental institutions meeting these requirements are eligible to apply.
Restrictions: The foundation refrains from funding annual funds, galas or other special-event fundraising activities; debt reduction; emergency or disaster relief efforts; dissertations or student research projects; indirect and/or administrative costs; sectarian religious activities, political lobbying, or legislative activities; institutions that discriminate on the basis of race, creed, gender, or sexual orientation in policy or in practice; or loans, scholarships, fellowships, or grants to individuals; unsolicited requests for international organizations or programs or for ALS research projects.
Geographic Focus: All States
Amount of Grant: 1,000 - 200,000 USD
Samples: Chicago Youth Programs, Chicago, Illinois, $15,000 - support to expand early literacy services in four high-need Chicago neighborhoods; Menninger Clinic Foundation, Houston, Texas, $13,860 - support for genetic analysis of adolescent blood samples for the McNair Initiative for Neuroscience Discovery; Colorado Humanities, Greenwood Village, Colorado, $25,000 - support for Motheread/Fatheread Early Childhood and Family Literacy Program.
Contact: Suzanne Haffey; (512) 474-9298; fax (512) 474-7281; shaffey@rgkfoundation.org
Internet: www.rgkfoundation.org/public/guidelines

Sponsor: RGk Foundation
1301 West 25th Street, Suite 300
Austin, TX 78705-4236

Richard and Caroline T. Gwathmey Memorial Trust Grants 2069
The Richard and Caroline T. Gwathmey Memorial Trust was established by Mrs. Elizabeth Gwathmey Jeffress in 1981 in memory of her parents. Mrs. Jeffress was particularly interested in the history, literature, art and architecture of Virginia. The grants award the efforts of nonprofits focused on the following issue areas: Ensuring access to basic services – food, health care, shelter and/or safety; Creating, sustaining and retaining a viable workforce for Virginia; Preserving and protecting the environment; Providing access to arts, culture and/or humanities; Preserving the important history of Virginia; and Improving educational outcomes for disadvantaged children, youth and/or adults. Nonprofit organizations focusing on the first three issues will be awarded after the first annual deadline, and nonprofit organizations focusing on the final three issues will be awarded after the second annual deadline. Visit the Bank of America website for more information on how to determine which deadline best fits your organization. Award amounts typically range from $5,000 to $60,000. The grants commonly support one year of funding for general operating support.
Requirements: Applicants must have 501(c)3 tax-exempt status and serve the residents of the State of Virginia. The Gwathmey Memorial Trust Allocation Committee is keenly focused on making geographically diverse investments across the Commonwealth of Virginia. Applications should be from established non-profit organizations seeking support for its overall operations, or a specific project with well-defined outcomes, clear definition of the return on investment and funding from an array of sources beyond the Gwathmey Memorial Trust. Applications will be submitted online through the Bank of America website. A grant report is required within 1 year of the grant application date, regardless of whether all of the funds have been spent.
Restrictions: No capital or endowment support will be considered. Nonprofits that receive support from the Gwathmey Memorial Trust will not be considered for additional funding sooner than 3 years from the award date of the previous grant. The trust does not support requests from individuals, organizations attempting to influence policy through direct lobbying, or any political campaigns.
Geographic Focus: Virginia
Date(s) Application is Due: Mar 1; Sep 1
Amount of Grant: 5,000 - 60,000 USD
Samples: Eastern Shore Rural Health System Incorporated, Onancock,, Virginia, $55,000 - Awarded for Construction of the Eastville Community Health Center (2019); Blue Sky Fund, Richmond, Virginia, $35,000 - Awarded for Blue Sky Fund Explorers Program for Elementary School Students (2019); Fairfield Foundation TBS, White Marsh, Virginia, $30,000 - Awarded for Expanding Fairfield Foundation's Educational Outreach Using New Technologies in the Field and Classroom (2019).
Contact: Lee Parker, Philanthropic Client Manager; (877) 446-1410; fax (804) 788-2673; D.C.grantmaking@bankofamerica.com or D.C.grantmaking@ustrust.com
Internet: www.bankofamerica.com/philanthropic/foundation/?fnId=123
Sponsor: Richard and Caroline T. Gwathmey Memorial Trust
1111 E. Main Street, VA2-300-12-92
Richmond, VA 23219-3531

Richard Davoud Donchian Foundation Grants 2070
The Richard Davoud Donchian Foundation was founded after Mr. Donchian's death in April of 1993. Extending Mr. Donchian's lifetime passion, its mission is to help others meet their potential and achieve high degrees of personal and professional success. The Foundation's Board of Directors is continuous in its efforts to preserve the Donchian legacy of leadership and integrity, as well as its commitment to learning and personal growth. Consequently, the Foundation concentrates its primary giving activities in the areas of ethical leadership in business and community affairs; education, personal development and literacy; and moral, ethical and spiritual advancement in all areas of life. Applications are accepted throughout the year and are reviewed in the order they are received. The Foundation encourages pilot initiatives that test new program models.
Requirements: The majority of the Foundation's grantmaking is focused in the northeastern United States, although, occasionally, grants may be made in other regions of the country and/or abroad. All applicants must have tax-exempt 501(c)3 status as a non-profit organization as defined by the Internal Revenue Service. The applicant must have an active board of directors with policy-making authority. Grants may range from a few thousand dollars up to $50,000. In unique circumstances, the Foundation does consider a more significant grant for a program having a major impact in one or more of our areas of interest. Of particular interest to the Foundation are organizations that promote partnerships and collaborative efforts among multiple groups and organizations. Priority will be given to requests that show specific plans for funding beyond the present and program innovation and tangible outcomes, with an emphasis on opportunities for significant and lasting social improvement.
Restrictions: The Foundation generally will not provide grants for the following: organizations not determined to be tax-exempt under section 501(c)3 of the Internal Revenue Code; individuals; general fundraising drives; endowments; government agencies; or organizations that subsist mainly on third party funding and have demonstrated no ability or expended little effort to attract private funding.
Geographic Focus: Connecticut, Delaware, District of Columbia, Florida, Maine, Maryland, New Jersey, New York, North Carolina, South Carolina, Vermont, Virginia
Amount of Grant: Up to 50,000 USD
Contact: Donchian Administrator, (203) 629-8552; fax (203) 547-6112; rdd@fsllc.net
Internet: www.foundationservices.cc/RDD2/grantrequests.htm#Guidelines
Sponsor: Richard Davoud Donchian Foundation
640 W. Putnam Avenue, 3rd Floor
Greenwich, CT 06830

Richard J. Stern Foundation for the Arts Grants 2071

The Richard J. Stern Foundation for the Arts offers funding to organizations engaged in supporting the arts in the 5-county, metropolitan Kansas City, Missouri, area, including the performing arts and art education. Primary area of interest include: arts and culture; arts services; communication media; community improvement; elementary and secondary education; higher education; historical activities; human services; humanities; libraries; museums; music; performing arts; and theater. Populations served include academics and children. In the majority of cases, that funding support comes in the form of: capital and infrastructure; capital campaigns; continuing support; emergency funds; equipment purchase and rental;; financial sustainability; general operating support; presentations and productions; and program development. Since a formal application form is not required, interested applicants should forward a letter of interest with a hand-written proposal. There are no application submission deadlines, though the Board meets quarterly to consider funding. Awards range as high as $30,000.
Requirements: Qualifying charitable organizations that are not private foundations and are engaged in supporting the arts in the greater Kansas City are are eligible to apply.
Geographic Focus: Kansas, Missouri
Amount of Grant: Up to 30,000 USD
Samples: Academy for the Integrated Arts, Kansas City, Missouri, $25,000 - purchase of art and music supplies; Coterie, Kansas City, Missouri, $30,000 - general operating support; Heart of America Shakespeare Festival, Kansas City, Missouri, $10,000 - general operating support.
Contact: Beth Ratke, Commerce Bank Trustee; (816) 234-2577 or (816) 234-2568
Sponsor: Richard J. Stern Foundation for the Arts
118 West 47th Street
Kansas City, MO 64112-9969

Richards Foundation Grants 2072

Founded by Roy Richards, Jr. in 1990, the Richards Foundation supports organizations in Carrollton, Georgia, and other communities that are working to break the cycles that create economic disadvantage and social needs. The children of Roy Richards, Sr., continue the tradition of community involvement and caring begun long ago by Mr. and Mrs. Richards.
Requirements: Awards are made to groups and individuals who give service to others. Application should be made in writing with information regarding how funds will be used.
Geographic Focus: All States
Samples: Bluefield Project, San Francisco, California, $100,000, fund charity; Chamber Music Charleston, Charleston, South Carolina, $2,500, fund charity; Charleston Academy Music, Charleston, South Carolina, $45,000, fund charity.
Contact: Judy Windom, (770) 832-4097; fax (770) 832-5265; Judy_Windom@southwire.com
Sponsor: Richards Foundation
P.O. Box 800
Carrollton, GA 30112

Richard W. Goldman Family Foundation Grants 2073

The Richard W. Goldman Family Foundation was established in Delaware with the expressed purposes of supporting higher education and human services throughout California, Connecticut, Washington, D.C., and New York. Its primary focus groups include: academics; economically disadvantaged; and low-income. Typically, that support comes in the form of financial sustainability, fund raising, general operations, re-granting, research, and evaluation programs. There are no specified application deadlines, and interested parties should begin with a letter to the Foundation office. Approximately fifteen to twenty awards are given each year, ranging from $50,000 t0 $600,000.
Requirements: Any 501(c)3 supporting residents of California, Connecticut, and New York are eligible to apply.
Geographic Focus: California, Connecticut, District of Columbia, New York
Amount of Grant: 50,000 - 600,000 USD
Samples: Corporation for Enterprise Development, Washington, D.C., $400,000 - general operating support; National Association for the Education of Young Children, Washington, D.C., $100,000 - general operating support; Parent-Child Home Program, Garden City, New York, $200,000 - general operating support.
Contact: Alice R. Goldman, President; (202) 595-1020
Sponsor: Richard W. Goldman Family Foundation
1201 Connecticut Avenue, NW, Suite 300
Washington, D.C. 20036

Richland County Bank Grants 2074

The Richland County Bank has had a long tradition of community involvement, dedication and volunteerism. The Bank is committed to supporting the community in which it serves. In addition to monetary contributions, the bank encourages its employees to take an active role in our community. As a corporate sponsor, we support various organizations in Richland and surrounding counties, including: Vernon, Crawford, Grant, Iowa, and Sauk counties. Areas of interest include: health care; higher education; agricultural agencies; community development; children and youth programs; and scholarship funds.
Requirements: Applicants must be 501(c)3 organizations serving the Wisconsin counties of Richland, Vernon, Crawford, Grant, Iowa, or Sauk.
Geographic Focus: Wisconsin
Contact: Gail Surrem, Vice President; (608) 647-6306
Internet: www.richlandcountybank.com/aboutInvolvement.cfm
Sponsor: Richland County Bank
195 West Court Street
Richland Center, WI 53581

Ricks Family Charitable Trust Grants 2075

The Ricks Family Charitable Trust (formerly known as the 1104 Foundation) offers support to religious programs, health, education, children and youth, and community service organizations. Most recently, amounts have ranged from $100 to $1,000. There are no application forms or deadlines to which applicants must adhere, and interested parties should contact the Trust prior to submitting a proposal. Though giving is primarily restricted to the Charlotte, North Carolina, region, grants are also awarded to state-wide organizations which are aligned with the foundation's interests.
Geographic Focus: North Carolina
Samples: Sharon United Methodist Church, Charlotte, North Carolina, $250 - general operating support; First Presbyterian Church, Charlotte, North Carolina, $1,000 - general operating support; Alzheimers Association, Charlotte, North Carolina, $500 - general operating support.
Contact: Charles V. Ricks, Trustee; (704) 537-0526
Sponsor: Ricks Family Charitable Trust
6000 Monroe Road, Suite 100
Charlotte, NC 28212-6119

Riedman Foundation Grants 2076

Established in the State of New York in 1980, the Riedman Foundation offers financial support primarily in the Rochester, New York, region. Its primary fields of interest include: abuse prevention; aquatic wildlife protection; arts and culture; biodiversity; child welfare; communication media; community and economic development; elementary and secondary education; family services; higher education; in-patient medical care; public libraries; museums; performing arts; philanthropy; science museums; and zoos. Most often, funding is given in the form of general operating support. Awards range up to as much as $125,000. Grant applications are accepted year round.
Requirements: Any 501(c)3 organization serving the residents of the Rochester, New York, area are eligible to apply.
Geographic Focus: New York
Amount of Grant: Up to 125,000 USD
Samples: Fish Hatchery at Powder Mills Park, Pittsford, New York, $125,000 - general operating support; George Eastman House, Rochester, New York, $2,500 - general operating support; Rochester General Hospital, Rochester, New York, $10,000 - general operating support.
Contact: David Riedman, Principal Manager; (585) 232-4424 or (585) 232-1000
Sponsor: Riedman Foundation
45 East Avenue, 8th Floor
Rochester, NY 14604-2219

Ripley County Community Foundation Grants 2077

The Ripley County Community Foundation (RCCF) was established to improve the quality of life for Ripley County, Indiana residents. The mission of the Ripley County Community Foundation is to assist donors in building an enduring source of charitable assets to benefit the citizens and qualified organizations of Ripley County. The RCCF strives to provide responsible stewardship of the gifts donated; to promote leadership in addressing Ripley County's issues; and to make grants in the fields of community service, social service, education, health, environment, and the arts.
Requirements: Grant applicants must qualify as 501(c)3 or 509(a) tax exempt organizations or hold sponsorship with such organizations. Because the grant guidelines and policies are brief and do not address every aspect of the RCCF granting program, the most effective means of making initial contact with the RCCF is through a letter or phone call of inquiry to the RCCF.
Restrictions: Funding is not available for the following: individuals; travel or lodging expenses to enable individuals or groups to attend seminars or take trips; endowment purposes of recipient organizations; programs funded prior to the RCCF date for grant decisions; to repay acquisition costs for equipment already purchased or paid for; for acquisition of weapons, firearms or destructive devices; sectarian religious purposes; to attempt to influence legislation or to intervene in any political campaign. RCCF reserves the right to refuse any and all grant applications.
Geographic Focus: Indiana
Date(s) Application is Due: Sep 14
Amount of Grant: Up to 2,500 USD
Contact: Jane Deiwert, Program Officer; (877) 234-5220 or (812) 933-1098; fax (812) 933-0096; jdeiwert@rccfonline.org
Internet: www.rccfonline.org/grants.asp
Sponsor: Ripley County Community Foundation
4 South Park, Suite 210
Batesville, IN 47006

Ripley County Community Foundation Small Project Grants 2078

Small Project Grants are available throughout the year (not just during the traditional Fall Granting Cycle) for amounts up to $500. The projects must meet the Foundation's charitable guidelines for traditional grants. Organizations may only apply for one small project grant each year; they may also apply for a grant during the traditional fall granting cycle if they receive a small project grant. Organizations may only apply for one larger grant in the fall. Applications will be accepted anytime during the year but decisions will only be made by the 30th of April, June, August, and October.
Requirements: To be considered, application must be made by the second Friday of each of these months. Applications not received by the second Friday will be held for the next Small Project Grant period.
Geographic Focus: Indiana
Date(s) Application is Due: Apr 30; Jun 30; Aug 30; Oct 30
Amount of Grant: Up to 500 USD
Contact: Jane Deiwert, Program Officer; (877) 234-5220 or (812) 933-1098;

fax (812) 933-0096; jdeiwert@rccfonline.org
Internet: www.rccfonline.org/grants.asp
Sponsor: Ripley County Community Foundation
4 South Park, Suite 210
Batesville, IN 47006

RISCA Project Grants for Individuals   2079
Rhode Island State Council of the Arts (RISCA) Project Grants are competitive funds available to individual artists. These grants provide $500 to $3,000 awards to artist instigated and organized arts projects with a strong public component. Through PGI, RISCA supports highly creative and talented artists who seek to create, produce, perform, teach, or share their work with the public. Projects might include the coordination and/or creation of: community arts events; public performances; arts workshops and classes; public visual art; and creative collaborations. These grants are for individuals creating work outside of nonprofit or other institutional support and structures. There are two annual deadlines for application submission: April 1 (for grant activities between July 1 and June 30); and October 1 (for grant activities between January 1 and June 30).
Requirements: Individual artists must be at least 18 years of age and a current, legal resident of the State of Rhode Island to apply for RISCA Project Grants for Individual Artists. Additionally an individual artist must: have established legal residence in Rhode Island for a minimum of twelve consecutive months prior to the date of application; and be a United States citizen or Green Card holder.
Restrictions: These grants are not for individuals looking to support their studio practice, but for projects that directly engage Rhode Island residents in some way. Students attending high school or students pursuing undergraduate or graduate degrees in an arts discipline or an arts-related subject area at the time of application may not apply. Individuals who are paid staff of a non-profit organization that receives general operating support or project grant support from RISCA cannot apply for funding for projects that are part of that organization's programming. Individuals who are paid staff or proprietors of a for-profit organization cannot apply for funding for projects that are a product or service of that organization. Individuals and organizations cannot apply for funding for the same project at the same deadline. Members of the RISCA staff, Council, and their spouses and immediate relatives are also ineligible to apply.
Geographic Focus: Rhode Island
Date(s) Application is Due: Apr 1; Oct 1
Amount of Grant: 500 - 3,000 USD
Samples: Adam Anderson, Providence, Rhode Island, $1,000 - support for his SUNS Interim Park Project (2018); Alfonso Acevedo, Central Falls, Rhode Island, $2,500 - support for New Millennium Art Factory Central Falls Connecting the Art With Their Neighborhood (2018); Beatrice Mcgeoch, Providence, Rhode Island, $1,500 - support for completion of illustrations and text for four new nature-based coloring pages (2018).
Contact: Mollie Flanagan, Director of Individual Artists Programs; (401) 222-3881; fax (401) 521-1351; dan@arts.ri.gov or info@risca.state.ri.us
Christina Di Chiera, Director of Individual Artists Programs; (401) 222-3881 or (401) 222-3880; fax (202) 222-3018; mollie.flanagan@arts.ri.gov
Internet: risca.online/grants/project-grants-for-individuals/
Sponsor: Rhode Island State Council on the Arts
One Capitol Hill, Third Floor
Providence, RI 02908-1034

Robbins-de Beaumont Foundation Grants   2080
Established in Massachusetts in 1992, the Robbins-de Beaumont Foundation offers funding nationally, and seeks nonprofit organizations whose goals are helping people reach their full potential as contributing members of their family, neighborhoods, and society at large. Limited funds are available for unsolicited grants for new, innovative projects which address identified needs of the community served and have relatively modest operating budgets. The foundation also has an interest in the education of children and adults in the areas of parenting, volunteerism, employment and life skills, preservation of the environment, the performing and visual arts, and substance abuse. A formal proposal is by invitation only, after review of initial concept paper. The concept paper should not exceed two pages. If given a go-ahead, the formal application consists of: program description; population served; budgetary needs; and how project will be sustained once the grant maker support is completed. The annual deadline for the concept paper is March 1, with full proposals due by June 30. Most recent awards have ranged from $5,000 to $30,000.
Restrictions: No support is offered to organizations whose primary focus is mental health, medical training, physical and mental disabilities, special programs, or for organizations whose annual operating budget exceeds $1,000,000, or which have been in existence for over ten years. No grants are given to individuals, or for capital campaigns, debt reduction or cash reserves, endowments, multi-year pledges, seed money, or start up costs.
Geographic Focus: All States
Date(s) Application is Due: Jun 30
Amount of Grant: 5,000 - 30,000 USD
Samples: Berkshire Children and Families, Pittsfield, Massachusetts, $10,000 - general operating support; Bikes Not Bombs, Jamaica Plain, Massachusetts, $20,000 - general operating support; Berkshire South Regional Community Center, Barrington, Massachusetts, $20,000 - general operating support..
Contact: John K. Graham, (617) 338-2445 or (617) 338-2800; jgraham@sandw.com
Sponsor: Robbins-de Beaumont Foundation
1 Post Office Square
Boston, MA 02109-2106

Robbins Charitable Foundation Grants   2081
The Robbins Charitable Foundation, based in Brookline, Massachusetts, provides support throughout the State of Massachusetts in its primary fields of interest. These interest areas include: arts and culture; the environment; health organizations; and religious welfare programs. Typically, awards are given for general operations, and most recent grants have ranged from $50 to $800. There is no formal application required, and no specified annual deadlines for submission. Interested parties should begin by contacting the Foundation office directly.
Requirements: 501(c)3 organizations in the State of Massachusetts are eligible to apply.
Restrictions: No grants are given directly to individuals.
Geographic Focus: Massachusetts
Amount of Grant: 50 - 800 USD
Samples: Dana Farber Jimmy Fund, Brookline, Massachusetts, $320 - general operating support; Perkins Institute for the Blind, Watertown, Massachusetts, $200 - general operating support; Museum of Fine Arts, Boston, Massachusetts, $500 - general operating support.
Contact: Phillis Robbins, Trustee; (617) 566-4919
Sponsor: Robbins Charitable Foundation
77 Marion Street
Brookline, MA 02246

Robbins Family Charitable Foundation Grants   2082
The Robbins Family Charitable Foundation, based in Omaha, Nebraska, provides grant support for local non-profit organizations. The Foundation's primary fields of interest include: children and youth services; community development; families; K-12 education; neighborhood development; religious programs; and emergency services. Funding is typically provided for general operating costs, with most recent awards ranging from $1,500 to $12,500. Though there are no identified annual submission deadlines, a formal application is required. Interested parties should begin by contacting the Foundation office directly.
Requirements: 501(c)3 organizations either located in, or serving residents of, Omaha, Nebraska, are eligible to apply.
Geographic Focus: Nebraska
Amount of Grant: 1,500 - 12,500 USD
Samples: World Herald Goodfellows Charities, Omaha, Nebraska, $10,000 - general operations; Nebraska Lutheran Outdoor Ministries, Omaha, Nebraska, $8,500 - general operations; Abide Network, Omaha, Nebraska, $2,500 - general operations.
Contact: Leslie J. Robbins, Jr.; (402) 333-7058 or (402) 690-6101; lesrobbins@cox.net
Sponsor: Robbins Family Charitable Foundation
18025 Oak Street
Omaha, NE 68130-6037

Robert and Betty Wo Foundation Grants   2083
In 1909, Ching Sing Wo (C.S. Wo.) opened a small general merchandise store on North King Street in downtown Honolulu. As the Hawaiian Islands prospered, so did his store. In 1947, when C.S. Wo's three sons — Robert, James, and William — joined their father, they began an enterprise that has grown to become Hawaii's leading furniture retailer. In the early 1980's, the third generation of the Wo family entered the company and introduced a contemporary perspective and diversity to meet the changing times. The Robert (eldest son) and Betty Wo Foundation was founded in Hawaii in 1990, with the expressed purpose of supporting: health and human services; elementary and secondary education; family service programs; higher education; in-patient medical care; museums; community nonprofits; performing arts; shelter and residential care; and youth development. The vast majority of funding has gone to Hawaii, California, and Iowa. During the past five years, the Foundation has given more than sixty grants to more than thirty nonprofit organizations, totaling nearly $700,000 in awards. This funding has ranged up to a maximum of $75,000. There are no specified annual deadlines, and interested parties should approach the Foundation directly.
Geographic Focus: California, Hawaii, Iowa
Amount of Grant: Up to 75,000 USD
Samples: Queens Medical Center, Honolulu, Hawaii, $25,000, general medical operating support; Hawaii Literacy, Honolulu, Hawaii, $3,000 - general operating support; Assets School, Honolulu, Hawaii, $10,000 - general operating support for special needs student programs.
Contact: Robert C. Wo, President; (808) 545-5966 or (808) 543-5388; fax (808) 543-5366
Sponsor: Robert and Betty Wo Foundation
702 South Beretania Street
Honolulu, HI 96813

Robert and Helen Haddad Foundation Grants   2084
The Robert and Helen Haddad Foundation, established in Indiana in 2002, supports the arts, Christian agencies and churches, education, and health care. There is a specific application form, though no deadlines with which to adhere. Applicants should submit a letter of application, which includes a copy of the IRS determination letter, a brief history of the organization and its mission, and a detailed description of the project and amount of funding requested.
Requirements: 501(c)3 organizations that serve the residents of Indiana are welcome to apply.
Geographic Focus: Indiana
Amount of Grant: 1,000 - 20,000 USD
Samples: Gleaners Food Bank of Indiana, Indianapolis, Indiana, $15,000; Child Abuse Prevention Council of Batholomew County, Columbus, Indiana, $2,000.
Contact: Kevin Alerding, (317) 236-2435 or (317) 236-2415; kevin.alerding@icemiller.com
Sponsor: Robert and Helen Haddad Foundation
3460 Commerce Drive
Columbus, IN 47201-2204

Robert and Helen Harmony Fund for Needy Children Grants 2085

The Robert and Helen Harmony Fund for Needy Children was established at The Dayton Foundation in 1993 by Robert and Helen Harmony for the purpose of providing quality camping opportunities for children in Montgomery, Greene, Clark, Darke, Miami, Preble, Butler or Warren counties in Ohio, who otherwise would not be able to attend camp because of financial need. Grant awards are made annually.

Requirements: In order to receive Harmony campership funds, a camp must be a resident camp and offer a broad range of nature and recreational programs (as opposed to nature camps only) utilizing properly trained staff. Medical/specialty camps offering residential programs for children also are encouraged to apply. To be eligible for a grant, an organization must: be recognized as a 501(c)3 tax-exempt nonprofit organization, according to the Internal Revenue Code, and be established for at least two years and have a track record of sustainability; benefit the citizens in the Greater Dayton Region, (Montgomery, Clark, Miami, Greene, Darke, Preble, Butler, and Warren counties); have a diversity/inclusion policy; demonstrate systemic collaboration; and address needs that are not met fully by existing organizational or community resources. Eligible camps must be accredited for the camping season by the American Camping Association or a comparable accrediting agency.

Restrictions: The Foundation generally does not award discretionary grants for: general organizational operations and ongoing programs, operational deficits or reduced or lost funding; individuals, scholarship, travel; fundraising drives; special events; political activities; public or private schools; endowment funds; hospitals and universities for internal programs; matching grants (unless local dollars are needed to fulfill a condition for a state or federal grant); neighborhood or local jurisdiction projects; newly organized not-for-profit organizations; or publications, scientific, medical or academic research projects.

Geographic Focus: Ohio

Contact: Tania Pending Arseculeratne, Community Engagement Officer; (937) 225-9966 or (937) 222-0410; fax (937) 222-0636; tarseculeratne@daytonfoundation.org

Internet: www.daytonfoundation.org/grntfdns.html#harmony

Sponsor: Robert and Helen Harmony Fund for Needy Children

1401 S. Main Street, Suite 100

Dayton, OH 45409

Robert Bowne Foundaion Edmund A. Stanley, Jr. Research Grants 2086

The foundation provides research grants as part of the Afterschool Matters Initiative to foster high quality cutting-edge research that has a lasting impact on the field. Research should support either original empirical research in or about community-based youth programs during the non-school hours or research syntheses or policy analyses of community-based youth programs.

Requirements: This is a national grant competition, and research may be conducted in any state. Contact foundation for application details.

Geographic Focus: All States

Amount of Grant: 10,000 USD

Contact: Anne Lawrence; (212) 792-6250; anne.lawrence@bownefoundation.org

Internet: www.bownefoundation.org/index.php?option=com_content&view=category &layout=blog&id=74&Itemid=96

Sponsor: Robert Bowne Foundation

6 East 39th Street, 10th Floor

New York, NY 10016

Robert Bowne Foundation Fellowships 2087

Fellowships are dedicated to building capacity in youth program staff to design and conduct research in the areas of youth development and education during the out-of-school hours. The goals of the fellowships include generating and disseminating research in the area of education in community-based organizations serving youth, building a network of scholars, contributing to basic knowledge, improving practice, and informing policy.

Requirements: Robert Bowne Foundation Research Fellows are selected by application and work in youth programs in New York City. They meet twice monthly for six months and monthly for the remainder of the year. Fellows become members of a community of researchers, learn methods of qualitative research, read and discuss research articles, and conduct site-specific research projects. Fellows participate in a writing institute where they write a research article or article for publication and present at a research roundtable. Contact foundation for application.

Geographic Focus: New York

Contact: Anne Lawrence; (212) 792-6250; anne.lawrence@bownefoundation.org

Internet: bownefoundation.org/index.php?option=com_content&view=category&layout=blog&id=74&Itemid=96

Sponsor: Robert Bowne Foundation

6 East 39th Street, 10th Floor

New York, NY 10016

Robert Bowne Foundation Literacy Grants 2088

The foundation awards grants to out-of-school-time programs that support literacy. The foundation defines literacy as engagement in reading, writing, listening, and speaking in order to better understand ourselves, others, and the world around us. The foundation seeks to have a long-term and substantial effect on the field of out-of-school-time education. The priority is supporting individual programs that make literacy education an integral part of their work, provide quality experiences for young people, and seek to evolve as learning opportunities by supporting ongoing development of participants, staff, families and community leaders. The foundation seeks to build program capacity to support literacy development.

Requirements: Grants awarded to 501(c)3 agencies located within one of the five boroughs of New York City or in rare instances to an agency located outside the City if it serves New York City children. Agencies must serve youth (preschool to age 21).

Restrictions: Grants are not awarded to religious organizations, primary or secondary schools, colleges or universities, individuals, to support in-school projects or projects following a traditional remedial model of instruction or to support capital campaigns or endowments.

Geographic Focus: New York

Amount of Grant: 20,000 - 30,000 USD

Samples: Youth Community Center, Inc., New York, New York, $30,000 - general support; Cornerstone Learning Center, New York, New York, $25,000 - general support.

Contact: Anne Lawrence; (212) 792-6250; anne.lawrence@bownefoundation.org

Internet: bownefoundation.org/index.php?option=com_content&view=article&id=54&Itemid=69

Sponsor: Robert Bowne Foundation

6 East 39th Street, 10th Floor

New York, NY 10016

Robert Bowne Foundation Youth-Centered Grants 2089

The foundation awards grants to youth-centered programs with a clear mission that encourage participants to express their emerging identities. The foundation recognizes that learning and development require ongoing feedback and that assessment and program evaluation are integrated throughout programs. Supported programs will include activities, techniques and material tailored to the interests, strengths and needs of the youth being served. Successful programs will have high quality content and instruction and celebrate young people's achievements.

Requirements: Grants awarded to 501(c)3 agencies located within one of the five boroughs of New York City or in rare instances to an agency located outside the City if it serves New York City children. Agencies must serve youth (preschool to age 21).

Restrictions: Grants are not awarded to religious organizations, primary or secondary schools, colleges or universities, individuals, to support in-school projects or projects following a traditional remedial model of instruction or to support capital campaigns or endowments.

Geographic Focus: New York

Amount of Grant: 20,000 - 30,000 USD

Samples: Good Shepherd, New York, New York, $25,000 - youth programming; The After-School Corporation, New York, New York, $25,000 - youth programming; Dorothy Bennett Mercy Center, New York, New York, $25,000 - after school program.

Contact: Anne Lawrence; (212) 792-6250; anne.lawrence@bownefoundation.org

Internet: bownefoundation.org/index.php?option=com_content&view=article&id=54&Itemid=69

Sponsor: Robert Bowne Foundation

6 East 39th Street, 10th Floor

New York, NY 10016

Robert F. Lange Foundation Grants 2090

Robert F. Lange Foundation was established in Honolulu in 1972, with the expressed purpose of supporting art museums, Asian arts and culture, child welfare, cultural awareness, family services, health, and human services. Its geographic focus is the State of Hawaii, with target groups including: children and youth; economically disadvantaged; infants and toddlers; and low-income and poor. Its major support strategies are capital, infrastructure, and program development. There are no annual deadlines or formal applications, and interested organizations should begin by contacting the Foundation directly. Recent awards have ranged from $100,000 to $500,000.

Requirements: 501(c)3 organizations supporting residents of Hawaii are eligible to apply.

Geographic Focus: Hawaii

Amount of Grant: 100,000 - 500,000 USD

Samples: Child and Family Service, Ewa Beach, Hawaii, $236,000 - general operating support; Honolulu Academy of Arts, Honolulu, Hawaii, $235,000 - general operating support.

Contact: John Lockwood, President and Director; (808) 694-4525

Sponsor: Robert F. Lange Foundation

P.O. Box 3170, Deptartment 715

Honolulu, HI 96802-3170

Robert Lee Adams Foundation Grants 2091

Established in 1993, the Robert Lee Adams Foundation offers general operating support funding throughout the State of California, though its region of concentration is the Los Angeles metropolitan area. The Foundation's primary fields of interest have been youth camps and human services. Applications are required and accepted at any time, though interested parties should first contact the office with a one- to two-page letter of interest delineating the need and budgetary desires.

Geographic Focus: California

Contact: Julian Eli Capata, Trustee; (213) 739-2022

Sponsor: Robert Lee Adams Foundation

3580 Wilshire Boulevard, 10th Floor

Los Angeles, CA 90010-2543

Robert Lee Blaffer Foundation Grants 2092

Established in Indiana in 2001, the Robert Lee Blaffer Foundation offers support primarily in the State of Indiana. The Foundations primary fields of interest include: education; operating support for community charities; and human services. There is no specific application form, and organizations interested in applying should contact the office directly. Final submissions should be in the form of a letter which includes: name and description of the requesting organization; and purpose of the grant; budget detail. The annual deadline is March 31.

Geographic Focus: Indiana

Date(s) Application is Due: Mar 31

Amount of Grant: Up to 25,000 USD

Samples: New Harmony Foundation, New Harmony, Indiana, $23,800 - general operating expenses; Ribeyre Gymnasium Restoration, New Harmony, Indiana, $14,000 - general

operating expenses; Evansville Philharmonic Orchestra, Evansville, Indiana, $9,897 - general operating expenses.
Contact: Gary Gerard, Secretary; (812) 682-3631
Sponsor: Robert Lee Blaffer Foundation
P.O. Box 399
New Harmony, IN 47631-0399

Robert R. McCormick Tribune Foundation Community Grants 2093

The Communities Program helps to transform communities by giving under-served people access to programs which improve their lives. The McCormick Foundation partners with media outlets, sports teams and philanthropic organizations to raise money for local needs and provides matching funds to increase the impact of charitable giving. Through the partnership, grants are made to qualified nonprofit organization with programs that help transition low-income children, adults and families to self-sufficiency. To achieve greater impact, the Foundation focuses on programs for children and youth in education, literacy, health & wellness and abuse prevention; hunger & housing; and adult workforce development and literacy. The McCormick Foundation is committed to measurable change with these projects and monitors the impact of all grants made. Community grants are made on the basis of requests received from 501(c)3 organizations in each local community where the Foundation has fundraising partners (Chicago, Denver, Fort Lauderdale, Los Angeles, Orlando, Washington, D.C., and Long Island, New York). Each fund partner has a unique set of guidelines that emphasize the needs of the particular community. Areas of focus include: child abuse prevention and treatment; child and youth education; health and wellness; housing; hunger; literacy; workforce development; and youth sports.
Requirements: Organizations must apply through the individual funding partners listed on the Foundation website. Specific information, including contacts, is included at each website.
Restrictions: Funding is not available for individuals or for-profit organizations.
Geographic Focus: California, Colorado, District of Columbia, Florida, Illinois, New York
Contact: Lesley Kennedy, Communities Program Officer; (312) 445-5000; info@mccormickfoundation.org
Internet: www.mccormickfoundation.org/page.aspx?pid=594
Sponsor: Robert R. McCormick Tribune Foundation
205 North Michigan Avenue, Suite 4300
Chicago, IL 60601

Robert R. Meyer Foundation Grants 2094

The Robert R. Meyer Foundation is a private foundation established in 1949 by Mr. Robert R. Meyer and further funded by bequests from the wills of Robert R. Meyer and John Meyer. Mr. Meyer desired that assets from his foundation be used to address needs in Birmingham and its vicinity. The foundation has made awards in the areas of arts and culture, education, environment, health, human services, and public/society benefit. The foundation meets twice a year in the spring and fall to review proposals. Applicants should contact the Trustee for application forms and guidelines.
Requirements: Giving is limited to 501(c)3 organizations in the metropolitan Birmingham, Alabama area. All applicant organizations are encouraged (but not required) to join the Alabama Association of Nonprofits.
Geographic Focus: Alabama
Date(s) Application is Due: Mar 1; Sep 1
Amount of Grant: 5,000 - 100,000 USD
Samples: A+ College Ready, Birmingham, Alabama, $50,000—to increase participation and performance of high school students in rigorous, college-level advancement placement courses in math, science, and English; Alabama Ballet, Birmingham, Alabama, $25,000— to help fund a new full-length ballet, Alice in Wonderland, in collaboration with the Alabama Symphony; Alabama Ear Institute, Mountain Brook, Alabama, $12,000—to help fund the Auditory-Verbal Mentoring Program.
Contact: Carla B. Gale, Vice President and Trust Officer; (205) 326-5382
Sponsor: Robert R. Meyer Foundation
P.O. Box 11647
Birmingham, AL 35202-1647

Robert W. Knox, Sr. and Pearl Wallis Knox Charitable Foundation 2095

Robert W. Knox, Jr., a resident of Houston, Texas, established the Foundation in 1964 in honor of his parents Robert W. Knox, Sr. and Pearl Wallis Knox. Robert W. Knox, Sr., a well-known physician in Houston, married Pearl Wallis of Galveston in 1892. Dr. Knox was president of the Texas State Medical Association, Chief Surgeon for the Southern Pacific Railway and helped establish several hospitals in the San Antonio, Houston and Louisiana areas. Robert Knox was active in the real estate business in Houston and was a veteran of both world wars. The Foundation is for religious, charitable, scientific, literary or educational purposes or for the prevention of cruelty to children or animals within the United States. Preference is given to charitable organizations serving Harris County, Texas and surrounding counties. The average grant award for a grant cycle is $5,000 - $10,000.
Requirements: Grants are awarded to qualified 501(c)3 charitable organizations within the United States, with preference given to charitable organizations serving Harris County, Texas. Applications will be submitted online through the Bank of America website. A grant report is required within 1 year of the grant application date, regardless of whether all of the funds have been spent.
Restrictions: Eligibility to re-apply for a grant award from the Knox Charitable Foundation requires organizations to skip one grant cycle (one year) before submitting a subsequent application. The foundation does not support requests from individuals, organizations attempting to influence policy through direct lobbying, or any political campaigns.
Geographic Focus: All States, Texas
Date(s) Application is Due: Apr 1
Amount of Grant: 5,000 - 10,000 USD

Contact: Debra Goldstein Phares, Philanthropic Client Director; (800) 357-7094; tx.philanthropic@bankofamerica.com or tx.philanthropic@ustrust.com
Internet: www.bankofamerica.com/philanthropic/foundation/?fnId=164
Sponsor: Robert W. Knox, Sr. and Pearl Wallis Knox Charitable Foundation
P.O. Box 831041
Dallas, TX 75283-1041

Robin Hood Foundation Grants 2096

The foundation's mission is to end poverty in New York City. Robin Hood makes grants to poverty-fighting organizations that are direct service providers operating in the five boroughs of New York City and has a continuing commitment to community-based programs and strong leaders in the city's poorest neighborhoods. First time grant requests are generally in the area of $100,000 to $200,000. Robin Hood will consider requests for a variety of purposes, including specific programs, salaries or start-up costs. Capital, renovation and general operating funds are given only to those groups already receiving Robin Hood support.
Requirements: Robin Hood seeks to fund 501(c)3 tax-exempt nonprofits in New York City with the following characteristics: proven track record; bold idea that is feasible; clear sense of mission and the steps needed to accomplish that mission; strong, committed leadership; existing evaluation procedures or willingness to evaluate programs and measure outcomes; commitment to, and knowledge of, the population served; high quality, dedicated staff; financial stability; and, respect or standing in its community and relationships with other organizations in the community. Applications are accepted year-round, and grant decisions will be made on a quarterly basis although decisions may take up to one year. Contact the Grants Manager before completing an application.
Restrictions: Programs that do not wish to evaluate the outcomes of their efforts should not apply. In general, Robin Hood does not make grants to technical assistance providers, other funders, or individuals. Robin Hood does not give grants to distribute propaganda, or to attempt to influence legislation or the outcome of any public election or to engage in any activity that is not exclusively charitable, scientific or educational. Robin Hood will not support organizations that discriminate against people seeking either services or employment based on race, sex, religion, age, sexual orientation or physical disability.
Geographic Focus: New York
Amount of Grant: Up to 200,000 USD
Contact: Karen Moody; (212) 227-6601; fax (212) 227-6698; grants@robinhood.org
Internet: www.robinhood.org/programs/get-funding
Sponsor: Robin Hood Foundation
826 Broadway, 9th Floor
New York, NY 10003

Robinson Foundation Grants 2097

Established in Oklahoma in 1976, the Robinson Foundation has the expressed mission to support Catholic education and the homeless. Giving is centered around the metro Tulsa, Oklahoma, region. Typically, that support comes in the form of general operations, capital campaigns, infrastructure, emergency funding, and program development. There are no specified annual deadlines, and an initial approach should be in the form of an application letter. Most recent awards have ranged from $5,000 to $100,000, with an average number annually being upwards of thirty awards.
Requirements: Any 501(c)3 organization serving the residents of Tulsa, Oklahoma, are eligible to apply.
Geographic Focus: Oklahoma
Amount of Grant: Up to 100,000 USD
Samples: Catholic Charities, Tulsa, Oklahoma, $50,000 - general operating support; Day Center for the Homeless, Tulsa, Oklahoma, $35,000 general operating support; Community Food Bank of Eastern Oklahoma, Tulsa, Oklahoma, $40,000 - general operating support.
Contact: Anne M. Roberts, Trustee; (918) 877-2200 or (918) 557-5151
Sponsor: Robinson Foundation
1127 East 33rd Place
Tulsa, OK 74105-2501

Rockwell Collins Charitable Corporation Grants 2098

The Rockwell Collins Charitable Corporation has identified two distinct funding priorities, and special consideration will be given to proposals that integrate these issues: education and youth development, with emphasis in math, science and engineering; and culture and the arts, with emphasis on youth educational programs. Rockwell Collins also contributes to health, human services, and civic organizations. Special consideration is given to qualifying organizations where employees volunteer; however, the majority of gifts to these organizations are made through Rockwell Collins United Way corporate contributions or employee campaigns. A list of contacts by region is detailed on the web site.
Requirements: Applying organizations must be tax exempt under the federal code; able to provide current full, certified, audited financial statements; and not be private foundations. Non-US organizations must provide nongovernmental organization (NGO) documentation.
Restrictions: Funding will not be considered for general endowments, deficit reduction, grants to individuals, federated campaigns, religious organizations for religious purposes, or fraternal or social organizations.
Geographic Focus: All States
Amount of Grant: Up to 5,000 USD
Contact: Jenny Becker, Manager Community Relations; (319) 295-7444; fax (319) 295-9374; jlbecker@rockwellcollins.com or communityrelations@rockwellcollins.com
Internet: www.rockwellcollins.com/Our_Company/Corporate_Responsibility/Community_Overview/Charitable_Giving.aspx
Sponsor: Rockwell Collins Corporation
400 Collins Road NE
Cedar Rapids, IA 52498-0001

Roger L. and Agnes C. Dell Charitable Trust I Grants 2099

The Roger L. and Agnes C. Dell Charitable Trust I's major program purpose is given to the arts, youth services, and the Episcopal religion. The trust's fields of interest include: Federated giving programs; Higher education; Protestant agencies and churches; youth programs, and services. Types of support are for general operating and scholarships. Initial approach should be by letter, and there are no specified annual deadlines.

Requirements: 501(c)3 organizations, primarily in the Fergus Falls, Minnesota, and northwest Minnesota area.
Geographic Focus: Minnesota
Amount of Grant: 100 - 50,000 USD
Contact: Stephen F. Rufer, Trust Manager; (651) 466-8040 or (218) 998-9408; fax (218) 736-3950; s.rufer@pemlaw.com
Sponsor: Roger L. and Agnes C. Dell Charitable Trust I
P.O. Box 64713
St. Paul, MN 55164

Roger L. and Agnes C. Dell Charitable Trust II Grants 2100

The Roger L. and Agnes C. Dell Charitable Trust II's major purpose is to assist education, the arts, and human service programs. The trust awards grants to eligible Minnesota nonprofit organizations in its areas of interest, including arts and culture, education, human services, Jewish agencies and temples, YMCAs, YWCAs, youth, and service programs. Types of support include funding for general operations and for specific project proposals. There are two annual deadlines for application submission: June 15 and October 15.

Requirements: Minnesota 501(c)3 tax-exempt organizations in Fergus Falls and the surrounding area are eligible.
Restrictions: Individuals are not eligible for grants.
Geographic Focus: Minnesota
Date(s) Application is Due: Jun 15; Oct 15
Amount of Grant: 100 - 50,000 USD
Contact: Stephen F. Rufer, Trust Manager; (651) 466-8040 or (218) 998-9408; fax (218) 736-3950; s.rufer@pemlaw.com
Sponsor: Roger L. and Agnes C. Dell Charitable Trust II
P.O. Box 64713
St. Paul, MN 55164

Ron and Sanne Higgins Family Foundation Grants 2101

The Ron and Sanne Higgins Family Foundation was established in Hawaii in 2001, with primary interest areas including: arts and culture; community development; economic development; elementary and secondary education; and philanthropy. With grants limited to the State of Hawaii, awards are given in the form of general operating support, program development, and capital campaigns. There are no specific deadlines, though the board meets to make decisions in March and September. Most recent grants have ranged from $25,000 to $100,000, with an average of four to six grants annually.

Requirements: Any 501(c)3 serving the residents of Hawaii are eligible to apply.
Geographic Focus: Hawaii
Amount of Grant: 25,000 - 300,000 USD
Samples: Bishop Museum, Honolulu, Hawaii, $300,000 - support of the Hawaiian Hall restoration campaign; Honolulu Waldorf School, Honolulu, Hawaii, $25,000 - support of the annual fund campaign; Polynesian Voyaging Society, Honolulu, Hawaii, $100,000 - general operating support.
Contact: Ron Higgins, Trustee; (808) 394-5714
Sponsor: Ron and Sanne Higgins Family Foundation
P.O. Box 25040
Honolulu, HI 96825-0040

Roney-Fitzpatrick Foundation Grants 2102

The Roney-Fitzpatrick Foundation was established to offer support in the central region of New Jersey (although grants are sometimes given throughout the United States). Its primary fields of interest include both education and human service programs. Types of funding are limited to general operating costs. There are no specified application formats or annual deadlines, and interested parties should begin by contacting the grant office with a letter describing the program and financial need. Recent funding amounts have ranged from $300 to $6,000.

Requirements: Nonprofit organizations throughout the United States are eligible to apply, although emphasis is on central New Jersey.
Restrictions: Foundation grants are not given to individuals.
Geographic Focus: All States
Amount of Grant: 4,600 - 200,000 USD
Samples: University of Miami, School of Business, Coral Gables, Florida, $6,000 - general operating costs; SPCA of Monterey County, Salinas, California, $2,500 - general operating costs; Madeira School, McLean, Virginia, $500 - general operating costs.
Contact: Edwin J. Fitzpatrick, Trustee; (212) 922-8189
Sponsor: Roney-Fitzpatrick Foundation
P.O. Box 185
Pittsburgh, PA 15230-0185

Rose Community Foundation Child and Family Development Grants 2103

Through its Child and Family Development program, the Rose Community Foundation invests resources in developing and improving early childhood care outside the home, including advocacy initiatives aimed at increasing public awareness of and access to high-quality child care. It also supports parent education programs that help parents raise children who are physically and emotionally healthy, and mentally prepared to learn. Recognizing that economic self-sufficiency is the key to strong families, the Foundation supports employment and training programs that help people find stable jobs, and support services that help them advance up the career ladder. In addition, the Foundation funds organizations that offer family support services, such as child care, health care, affordable housing and other efforts essential to parents who need to work full-time. There are no annual deadlines.

Requirements: Colorado 501(c)3 tax-exempt organizations serving the residents of Adams, Arapahoe, Boulder, Denver, Douglas, and Jefferson Counties are eligible.
Restrictions: The Foundation will generally not support: grants to individuals or endowments, including academic chairs and scholarships; grants to one organization to be passed to another; annual appeals or membership drives; fundraisers and other one-time events; or financial support for political candidates. An application will not be accepted if: reports for a prior grant to the organization/program in question are past due; or the same applicant has other applications pending.
Geographic Focus: Colorado
Contact: Elsa I. Holguin, Senior Program Officer; (303) 398-7414 or (303) 398-7400; fax (303) 398-7430; eholguin@rcfdenver.org
Internet: rcfdenver.org/nonprofits-and-grants/what-we-fund/child-and-family-development/
Sponsor: Rose Community Foundation
600 South Cherry Street, Suite 1200
Denver, CO 80246-1712

Rose Community Foundation Education Grants 2104

The Foundation's grantmaking in education reflects the principle that school programs, policies and practices should ensure the highest possible quality teaching in a community's classrooms. While the Foundation focuses its resources on efforts that lead to improved student achievement, it places greatest emphasis on two priorities in prekindergarten through grade 12. The first is quality teaching. Research consistently shows that more than any other factor in school, the quality of a student's teacher has the greatest impact on his or her performance. As a result, Rose Community Foundation values efforts to recruit, develop and retain great educators. The second priority is systemic change in individual schools and in public education. While the root causes of low student performance are many, schools and school districts do not always have the systems in place to advance learning and close persistent learning gaps between high-achieving and low-achieving students. There are no annual deadlines.

Requirements: Colorado 501(c)3 tax-exempt organizations serving the students of Adams, Arapahoe, Boulder, Denver, Douglas, and Jefferson Counties are eligible.
Restrictions: The Foundation will generally not support: grants to individuals or endowments, including academic chairs and scholarships; grants to one organization to be passed to another; annual appeals or membership drives; fundraisers and other one-time events; or financial support for political candidates. An application will not be accepted if: reports for a prior grant to the organization/program in question are past due; or the same applicant has other applications pending.
Geographic Focus: Colorado
Contact: Janet Lopez, Education Program Officer; (303) 398-7415 or (303) 398-7400; fax (303) 398-7430; jlopez@rcfdenver.org
Internet: rcfdenver.org/nonprofits-and-grants/what-we-fund/education/
Sponsor: Rose Community Foundation
600 South Cherry Street, Suite 1200
Denver, CO 80246-1712

Rose Community Foundation Health Grants 2105

The Rose Community Foundation recognizes that improving access to quality care requires well-informed, visionary leaders. For this reason, the Foundation promotes initiatives that develop health-policy and public-health leadership. While the Foundation invests in health leadership that can improve access to quality care over the long term, it also works to effect more immediate change. Committed to improving access to care for low-income children, youth and families, the Foundation continues to support efforts to enroll them in programs such as Child Health Plan Plus (CHP+), a publicly supported health insurance program. Because at least half of all premature deaths are the result of lifestyle choices that individuals may be able to change, the Foundation also supports health promotion and disease prevention programs that encourage healthy choices and discourage behaviors that lead to illness and injury. In addition, the Foundation funds community organizations that provide information about the steps individuals can take to prevent such conditions as diabetes, teen pregnancy, HIV, heart disease and cancer. There are no annual deadlines.

Requirements: Colorado 501(c)3 tax-exempt organizations serving the residents of Adams, Arapahoe, Boulder, Denver, Douglas, and Jefferson Counties are eligible.
Restrictions: The Foundation will generally not support: grants to individuals or endowments, including academic chairs and scholarships; grants to one organization to be passed to another; annual appeals or membership drives; fundraisers and other one-time events; or financial support for political candidates. An application will not be accepted if: reports for a prior grant to the organization/program in question are past due; or the same applicant has other applications pending.
Geographic Focus: Colorado
Contact: Whitney Gustin Connor, Program Officer; (303) 398-7410 or (303) 398-7400; fax (303) 398-7430; wconnor@rcfdenver.org
Internet: rcfdenver.org/nonprofits-and-grants/what-we-fund/health/
Sponsor: Rose Community Foundation
600 South Cherry Street, Suite 1200
Denver, CO 80246-1712

Rose Hills Foundation Grants 2106

The Rose Hills Foundation supports organizations that promote the welfare of humankind, including but not limited to: arts and culture; civic and community services; education; community-based health programs; youth activities; and the advancement of knowledge. Giving is centered in southern California, with emphasis on the San Gabriel Valley and

East Los Angeles area. The Foundation accepts and processes applications throughout the year with the expectation of grant distributions every six months. Depending on timing, requests are reviewed at six annual Board Meetings. At times, there may be an approximate wait of up to six months prior to a request being reviewed. Grants range from $5,000 to million dollar commitments. Foundation directors may opt to grant less than the amount requested, depending upon resources available, or spread payments over more than one year. *Requirements:* Preferential attention is given to organizations that exhibit the following criteria: a history of achievement, good management, and a stable financial condition; self-sustaining programs that are unlikely to depend on future Foundation funding; significant programs that make a measurable impact; funding that is matched or multiplied by other sources; projects or programs that benefit people of southern California; and programs that reach the greatest number of people at the most reasonable cost. Organizations should send a two page letter of introduction (LOI) addressed to the Foundation's President. Initial correspondence should include the following information: brief purpose and history of organization; brief outline of program/project for which funds are being sought; program/project budget; specific amount being requested from Foundation; geographic area, demographics of population, and the number of individuals served annually; list of Board of Directors; current operating budget and most recent audited financials (if not available, please provide most recent financial statement); copy of IRS determination letter; and a detailed funding history. *Restrictions:* Funding is not available for propagandizing, influencing legislation and/or elections or promoting voter registration; political candidates, political campaigns or organizations engaging in political activities; programs which promote religious doctrine; individuals (except as permitted by the IRS); governmental agencies; or endowments.
Geographic Focus: California
Amount of Grant: 5,000 - 1,000,000 USD
Contact: Victoria B. Rogers; (626) 696-2220; vbrogers@rosehillsfoundation.org
Internet: www.rosehillsfoundation.org/AppProcedures.htm
Sponsor: Rose Hills Foundation
225 South Lake Avenue, Suite 1250
Pasadena, CA 91101

Rosenberg Charity Foundation Grants 2107

The Rosenberg Charity Foundation was established in Brooklyn, New York, in 2001, with its primary founding contribution made by the U.S. Chocolate Corporation. The Foundation's major fields of interest include the support of: basic and emergency aid; communication media; health care; Judaism; mental health care; youth development; assisting indigent people through human services; and religion studies. There are no specific annual deadlines for submission, though an application form is required. Interested parties should begin by forwarding a written query directly to the Foundation. Most recent awards have ranged from $10 to $11,000, with the majority of nearly 250 annual grants being less than $1,000. *Requirements:* 501(c)3 organizations serving residents of the New York metro area, as well as Jewish agencies and schools, are eligible to request funding.
Geographic Focus: All States
Amount of Grant: Up to 11,000 USD
Samples: Bais Rochel School, Brooklyn, New York, $250 - general operating support for an all-girls Jewish school; Yeshiva Aderes Hatorah, Lakewood, New Jersey, $2,000 - general operating support; Central UTA, Brooklyn, New York, $10,600 - general operating support.
Contact: David Rosenberg; (718) 387-9200 or (718) 788-2345; jacob@hbacct.com
Sponsor: Rosenberg Charity Foundation
933 46th Street
Brooklyn, NY 11219-2332

Rosenberg Foundation Immigrant Rights and Integration Grants 2108

In the more than seven decades since making its first grant, the Rosenberg Foundation has distinguished itself as an ally of the state's most vulnerable residents. From its early work supporting efforts on behalf of Japanese American families returning from internment camps to its recent initiative to reduce the incarceration rates for women in California, the Foundation's aim has remained consistent: to achieve significant and lasting improvements in the lives of Californians. In the area of Immigrant Rights and Integration, the Foundation works with its grant partners to ensure that immigrant populations are part of the civic and economic life of California through a multi-pronged strategy that includes supporting grassroots advocacy, uplifting emerging leaders in underserved communities, enforcing voting and language rights, and strengthening the communications capacity of immigrant rights advocates. The Foundation works closely with social justice advocates, policy makers and other thought leaders throughout the state to identify the strategies that will best help achieve positive impact in California within each program. As such, most of its grantee partners are identified and contacted by the Foundation staff first. While the Foundation does accept unsolicited inquiries, its approach to grantmaking means that it can fund only a few of them. Interested applicants should begin by forwarding a one- to two-page letter of inquiry which includes: a description of project and its objectives; a description of sponsoring organization; and the total request amount, project amount, and size of agency budget. Full proposals should be sent upon request.
Requirements: Applicants must meet the following criteria: nonprofit organizations that are tax-exempt under Section 501(c)3 of the Internal Revenue Service Code and not classified as a private foundation under Section 509(a) of the Code (or public agencies); for all program areas, be based in or managing significant activities in California; and work toward missions and project goals that are clearly aligned with the Foundation's grantmaking priorities. *Restrictions:* The Rosenberg Foundation does not provide grants: to individuals or to for-profit entities; for general fundraising benefits and events; or for endowment campaigns.
Geographic Focus: California
Amount of Grant: 1,000 - 100,000 USD
Contact: Linda Moll, Grants Manager; (415) 644-9777; fax (415) 357-5016;

linda@rosenfound.org or info@rosenbergfound.org
Internet: rosenbergfound.org/grantmaking/immigrant-worker-rights/
Sponsor: Rosenberg Foundation
131 Steuart Street, Suite 650
San Francisco, CA 94105

Rosenberg Fund for Children Clinton and Muriel Jencks Memorial Fund Grants 2109

The Rosenberg Fund for Children (RFC) provides for the educational and emotional needs of children of targeted progressive activists, and youth who are targeted activists themselves. In most instances, professionals and institutions directly receive the grants to provide services at no or reduced cost to beneficiaries. In March 2008, Muriel Sobelman-Jencks established an annual grant of $1,000 in memory of her husband, Clinton E. Jencks, El Palomino, organizer for United Mine, Mill and Smelter Workers, Local 890. Clinton played himself in Salt of the Earth, the only American film to be blacklisted. The movie depicted the McCarthy era strike by New Mexico zinc miners and the struggle of women to achieve equality, and became one of 400 motion pictures selected by the Library of Congress for the National Film Registry. This annual grant is designated to assist children of workers who have been penalized, injured, fired, jailed or have died for their organizing efforts to build unions, improve working conditions and elevate living standards for all in the work force. The Fund was renamed the Clinton and Muriel Jencks Fund after Muriel's passing in 2017 to honor her life along with Clinton's. The deadline for applications for spring grants is March 21 and for fall grants is October 13. Typically, grant amounts range up to a maximum of $3,000.
Requirements: Applications may be submitted by parents, custodians, and guardians to benefit children in the United States whose parents' pursuit of progressive values has left them unable to fully provide for that child as a result of being targeted as outlined above. The young adult children 18 years or older of targeted activists may submit applications on their own behalf. Applications may also be submitted by or on behalf of targeted activist youth whose targeting has resulted in a significant adverse life impact. Applicants must meet the RFC's funding criteria. *Restrictions:* The RFC is unable to consider grants for general living expenses, like housing, clothing, and food, or for those who have sufficient alternative sources of support. The RFC does not pay legal expenses. The RFC usually does not make grants directly to activists, custodians, or guardians.
Geographic Focus: All States
Date(s) Application is Due: Mar 21; Oct 13
Amount of Grant: Up to 3,000 USD
Contact: Sophie Chambers; (413) 529-0063; fax (413) 529-0802; granting@rfc.org
Internet: www.rfc.org/namedfunds
Sponsor: Rosenberg Fund for Children
116 Pleasant Street, Suite 348
Easthampton, MA 01027

Rosenberg Fund for Children Edith and George Ziefert Fund Grants 2110

The Rosenberg Fund for Children (RFC) provides for the educational and emotional needs of children of targeted progressive activists, and youth who are targeted activists themselves. In most instances, professionals and institutions directly receive the grants to provide services at no or reduced cost to beneficiaries. In December 2005, Edith Ziefert, the widow of George Ziefert, established the first endowed memorial fund in the RFC's history. This fledgling endowment has been buoyed by two substantial contributions from the Ziefert family and has been supplemented by numerous other donations from family friends. Following Edith's passing in November 2010, her name was added to the Fund as well. The Edith and George Ziefert fund is one family's way of honoring their relatives by continuing their legacy of support for progressive ideals. The deadline for applications for spring grants is March 21 and for fall grants is October 13. Typically, grant amounts range up to a maximum of $3,000. *Requirements:* Applications may be submitted by parents, custodians, and guardians to benefit children in the United States whose parents' pursuit of progressive values has left them unable to fully provide for that child as a result of being targeted as outlined above. The young adult children 18 years or older of targeted activists may submit applications on their own behalf. Applications may also be submitted by or on behalf of targeted activist youth whose targeting has resulted in a significant adverse life impact. Applicants must meet the RFC's funding criteria. *Restrictions:* The RFC is unable to consider grants for general living expenses, like housing, clothing, and food, or for those who have sufficient alternative sources of support. The RFC does not pay legal expenses. The RFC usually does not make grants directly to activists, custodians, or guardians.
Geographic Focus: All States
Date(s) Application is Due: Mar 21; Oct 13
Amount of Grant: Up to 3,000 USD
Contact: Sophie Chambers; (413) 529-0063; fax (413) 529-0802; granting@rfc.org
Internet: www.rfc.org/namedfunds
Sponsor: Rosenberg Fund for Children
116 Pleasant Street, Suite 348
Easthampton, MA 01027

Rosenberg Fund for Children Grants 2111

The Rosenberg Fund for Children (RFC) provides for the educational and emotional needs of children of targeted progressive activists, and youth who are targeted activists themselves. In most instances, professionals and institutions directly receive the grants to provide services at no or reduced cost to beneficiaries. Subject to its financial ability, the program will fund such things as: counseling; school tuition; camp tuition; cultural lessons; after-school programs; prison visits; educational or therapeutic travel; and post high-school books and supplies for college or other educational training. The deadline for applications for spring grants is March 21 and for fall grants is October 13. Typically, grant amounts range up to a maximum of $3,000. *Requirements:* Applications may be submitted by parents, custodians, and guardians to benefit children in the United States whose parents' pursuit of progressive values has left them unable to fully provide for that child as a result of being targeted as outlined above. The young adult children 18 years or older of targeted activists may submit applications on their own behalf. Applications may also be submitted by or on behalf of targeted activist youth whose targeting has resulted in a significant adverse life impact. Applicants must meet the RFC's funding criteria.

Restrictions: The RFC is unable to consider grants for general living expenses, like housing, clothing, and food, or for those who have sufficient alternative sources of support. The RFC does not pay legal expenses. The RFC usually does not make grants directly to activists, custodians, or guardians.
Geographic Focus: All States
Date(s) Application is Due: Mar 21; Oct 13
Amount of Grant: Up to 3,000 USD
Contact: Sophie Chambers; (413) 529-0063; fax (413) 529-0802; granting@rfc.org
Internet: www.rfc.org/granting
Sponsor: Rosenberg Fund for Children
116 Pleasant Street, Suite 348
Easthampton, MA 01027

Rosenberg Fund for Children Herman Warsh Fund Grant 2112
The Rosenberg Fund for Children (RFC) provides for the educational and emotional needs of children of targeted progressive activists, and youth who are targeted activists themselves. In most instances, professionals and institutions directly receive the grants to provide services at no or reduced cost to beneficiaries. The Herman Warsh Memorial Fund was announced in the spring of 2006. Herman was one of Robert Meeropol's initial supporters when Robert was launching the RFC. Herman and his wife, Maryanne Mott, generously helped the RFC in its infancy and remained steadfast supporters. Following Herman's death, Maryanne established this award in his memory. Each fall, one RFC grant will receive support from the Herman Warsh Fund. The deadline for applications for fall grants is October 13. Typically, grant amounts range up to a maximum of $3,000.
Requirements: Applications may be submitted by parents, custodians, and guardians to benefit children in the United States whose parents' pursuit of progressive values has left them unable to fully provide for that child as a result of being targeted as outlined above. The young adult children 18 years or older of targeted activists may submit applications on their own behalf. Applications may also be submitted by or on behalf of targeted activist youth whose targeting has resulted in a significant adverse life impact. Applicants must meet the RFC's funding criteria.
Restrictions: The RFC is unable to consider grants for general living expenses, like housing, clothing, and food, or for those who have sufficient alternative sources of support. The RFC does not pay legal expenses. The RFC usually does not make grants directly to activists, custodians, or guardians.
Geographic Focus: All States
Date(s) Application is Due: Oct 13
Amount of Grant: Up to 3,000 USD
Contact: Sophie Chambers; (413) 529-0063; fax (413) 529-0802; granting@rfc.org
Internet: www.rfc.org/namedfunds
Sponsor: Rosenberg Fund for Children
116 Pleasant Street, Suite 348
Easthampton, MA 01027

Rosenberg Fund for Children Moish and Lillian Antopol Memorial Fund Grants 2113
The Rosenberg Fund for Children (RFC) provides for the educational and emotional needs of children of targeted progressive activists, and youth who are targeted activists themselves. In most instances, professionals and institutions directly receive the grants to provide services at no or reduced cost to beneficiaries. "Our parents, Moish and Lillian Antopol, were hounded by the FBI for labor organizing and Communist Party activities promoting human brotherhood, justice and world peace. All of that was considered subversive during our childhood years from the 1940s through the early 1960s. Our father's imprisonment occurred before we were born (his cell-mate, also a labor organizer during the Depression, was our mother's brother who arranged a blind date at a Communist Youth Organization rally). The memories of our childhood experiences enable U.S. to empathize with the families helped by the RFC. We understand the pressures of living under government scrutiny and illegal surveillance. In our blue-collar family, the blacklist caused constant financial insecurity. Our parents did not intend for U.S. to sense their defiance and fear, to feel isolated in our neighborhood, to get indigestion when FBI agents barged in at dinner times, to learn wariness or to shoulder the terrible burden of keeping dangerous secrets. With gratitude, we remember sharing ongoing support with our family's brave and generous comrades and the freedom of being with their children. We cherish enduring images of our mother leading songs, our father leading discussions, and the fun we had at Party picnics. Our lives have honored our parents' values. With this fund in our parents' memory we carry forward our legacy to another generation of activists who continue the struggle for freedom, justice and peace." The deadline for Moish and Lillian Antopol Memorial Fund Grant applications for spring grants is March 21 and for fall grants is October 13. Typically, grant amounts range up to a maximum of $3,000.
Requirements: Applications may be submitted by parents, custodians, and guardians to benefit children in the United States whose parents' pursuit of progressive values has left them unable to fully provide for that child as a result of being targeted as outlined above. The young adult children 18 years or older of targeted activists may submit applications on their own behalf. Applications may also be submitted by or on behalf of targeted activist youth whose targeting has resulted in a significant adverse life impact. Applicants must meet the RFC's funding criteria.
Restrictions: The RFC is unable to consider grants for general living expenses, like housing, clothing, and food, or for those who have sufficient alternative sources of support. The RFC

does not pay legal expenses. The RFC usually does not make grants directly to activists, custodians, or guardians.
Geographic Focus: All States
Date(s) Application is Due: Mar 21; Oct 13
Amount of Grant: Up to 3,000 USD
Contact: Sophie Chambers; (413) 529-0063; fax (413) 529-0802; granting@rfc.org
Internet: www.rfc.org/namedfunds
Sponsor: Rosenberg Fund for Children
116 Pleasant Street, Suite 348
Easthampton, MA 01027

Rosenberg Fund for Children Ozzy Klate Memorial Fund Grants 2114
The Rosenberg Fund for Children (RFC) provides for the educational and emotional needs of children of targeted progressive activists, and youth who are targeted activists themselves. In most instances, professionals and institutions directly receive the grants to provide services at no or reduced cost to beneficiaries. In the fall of 2007, the RFC announced a named fund established by a couple as a tribute to their son. The Ozzy Klate Memorial Fund of the Community Foundation of Western Massachusetts, provides a minimum of $1,500 annually to support one or more of the RFC's spring grants. The Fund's founders have established the following criteria: the awards will provide for one or more teenagers who have demonstrated motivation, dedication, inspiration and productivity in the creative arts and progressive social thought, action and spiritual liberation. Whenever possible the fund will benefit teenagers or programs in Western Massachusetts. The deadline for applications for spring grants is March 21.
Requirements: Applications may be submitted by parents, custodians, and guardians to benefit children in the United States whose parents' pursuit of progressive values has left them unable to fully provide for that child as a result of being targeted as outlined above. The young adult children 18 years or older of targeted activists may submit applications on their own behalf. Applications may also be submitted by or on behalf of targeted activist youth whose targeting has resulted in a significant adverse life impact. Applicants must meet the RFC's funding criteria.
Restrictions: The RFC is unable to consider grants for general living expenses, like housing, clothing, and food, or for those who have sufficient alternative sources of support. The RFC does not pay legal expenses. The RFC usually does not make grants directly to activists, custodians, or guardians.
Geographic Focus: All States
Date(s) Application is Due: Mar 21
Amount of Grant: Up to 1,500 USD
Contact: Sophie Chambers; (413) 529-0063; fax (413) 529-0802; granting@rfc.org
Internet: www.rfc.org/namedfunds
Sponsor: Rosenberg Fund for Children
116 Pleasant Street, Suite 348
Easthampton, MA 01027

Roy and Christine Sturgis Charitable Trust Grants 2115
The Roy and Christine Sturgis Charitable Trust was established in 1981 to support and promote quality educational, cultural, human services and health care programming for all people. Roy Sturgis was one of ten children of an Arkansas farmer and homemaker. He dropped out of school after the tenth grade to join the Navy during World War I. Mr. Sturgis returned to his family home in southern Arkansas after the war and went to work in the local sawmills. In 1933, Roy Sturgis married Texas native Christine Johns. They became very successful in the timber, lumber and sawmill industries in Arkansas, owned other prosperous business enterprises and had notable success managing their investments. Mr. and Mrs. Sturgis spent most of their lives in Arkansas and Dallas, Texas. They did not have children, but were particularly interested in educational opportunities for young people. In addition, Mr. and Mrs. Sturgis supported organizations working in the areas of health, social services and the arts. The majority of grants from the Sturgis Charitable Trust are 1 year in duration. On occasion, multi-year support is awarded. Grants are awarded to qualified charitable organizations in both Arkansas and Texas. Approximately 65% of the Trust's annual distributions are made within the state of Arkansas. The remaining 35% of grants are distributed within the state of Texas. For grants made within the state of Texas, strong preference is given to organizations located in the Dallas area. Award amounts typically range from $5,000 to $155,000.
Requirements: 501(c)3 nonprofit organizations in Texas and Arkansas are eligible. The Sturgis Charitable Trust encourages requests for the following types of grants: capital, project-related, Medical Research and endowment campaigns. Funding for start-up programs and limited general operating requests will also be considered. Applications will be submitted online through the Bank of America website. A grant report is required within 1 year of the grant application date, regardless of whether all of the funds have been spent.
Restrictions: Organizations that receive a 1-year grant from the Roy and Christine Sturgis Charitable Trust must skip 2 years before submitting a subsequent application. Organizations that receive a multi-year grant from the Roy and Christine Sturgis Charitable Trust are not eligible to re-apply until 2 years after the close of the grant cycle. The trust does not support requests from individuals, organizations attempting to influence policy through direct lobbying, or any political campaigns.
Geographic Focus: Arkansas, Texas
Date(s) Application is Due: Mar 1
Amount of Grant: 5,000 - 155,000 USD
Samples: University of Arkansas Foundation, Fayetteville, Arkansas, $155,000 - Awarded for Undergraduate and Graduate Student Support to Endow the Roy and Christine Sturgis International Honors Scholars Program (2018); Arkansas Children's Hospital Foundation, Little Rock, Arkansas, $100,000 - Awarded for South Wing Expansion (2018); Hendrix

College, Conway, Arkansas, $100,000 - Awarded for Hendrix College Wellness and Athletics Facilities (2018).
Contact: Debra Goldstein Phares, Philanthropic Client Director; (800) 357-7094; tx.philanthropic@bankofamerica.com or tx.philanthropic@ustrust.com
Internet: www.bankofamerica.com/philanthropic/foundation/?fnId=88
Sponsor: Roy and Christine Sturgis Charitable Trust
901 Main Street, 19th Floor
Dallas, TX 75202-3707

Roy J. Carver Charitable Trust Statewide Scholarships   2116
The Roy J. Carver Charitable Trust Statewide Scholarship program centers on providing substantial scholarships to students who struggle to overcome significant social and economic obstacles in the pursuit of their education or who may be living in circumstances that may not normally be taken into account by other financial aid programs. Scholarships are available to full-time (12 hours or more) students who will be starting their junior year in the fall semester of the award year. While amounts may vary, average awards are $5,200 at public universities and $7,600 at the private colleges. Scholarships may be renewed for the senior year, but such renewal is not automatic, and students must re-apply on-line. Potential applicants must apply directly on-line to the participating college or university of their choice by clicking on the application link on the Trust's web-site.
Requirements: Eligible applicants include: sophomore students currently enrolled in one of the three Regents' universities or in one of the 23 participating four-year private institutions; sophomore students currently attending a community college in Iowa, who intend to transfer to one of the participating four-year institutions as a junior in the fall semester of the award year; or junior year Carver Scholar recipients intending to seek renewal for their senior year. Students applying for scholarships must be a United States citizen and have graduated from an accredited high school in the state of Iowa or have been a resident of the state of Iowa for at least five consecutive years immediately prior to application. Students must have a minimum cumulative grade point average of 2.8 on a 4.0 scale.
Geographic Focus: Illinois, Iowa
Date(s) Application is Due: Apr 1
Amount of Grant: 12,800 USD
Contact: Dr. Troy K. Ross; (563) 263-4010; fax (563) 263-1547; info@carvertrust.org
Internet: www.carvertrust.org/scholarships/
Sponsor: Roy J. Carver Charitable Trust
202 Iowa Avenue
Muscatine, IA 52761-3733

Roy J. Carver Charitable Trust Youth Services and Recreation Grants   2117
Projects receiving Trust funding under the Youth Services and Recreatio program designation are typically designed to complement curriculum-based education and encourage individual development and physical well-being. Of the grants awarded within this category, a significant portion has been directed toward the efforts of organizations advocating for disadvantaged and disabled youth and their families. As an example, improving the conditions at adolescent residential facilities in Iowa has represented an important area of Trust charitable giving. In addition, grants to help communities establish safe and affordable recreation opportunities are also part of the youth-directed programming. The Trust offers strategic funding for the development of public recreation facilities and related activities for children.
Requirements: Priority is given to projects in the Iowa counties of Muscatine, Louisa, and Scott, as well as Rock Island and Mercer Counties in Illinois. Overall, grants are made to 501(c)3 tax-exempt organizations in Iowa and western Illinois.
Restrictions: The trust does not support annual campaigns or ongoing operations, direct grants to individuals, religious activities, organizations without 501(c)3 status, fund-raising benefits or program advertising, or political parties or candidates.
Geographic Focus: Illinois, Iowa
Date(s) Application is Due: Feb 15; May 15; Aug 15; Nov 15
Amount of Grant: 10,000 - 25,000 USD
Samples: Children's Therapy Center of the Quad Cities, Rock Island, Illinois, $25,000 - to assist in the acquisition of a facility; Davenport Parks and Recreation, Davenport, Iowa, $25,000 - to support the development of recreational facilities for disabled individuals; Wilton Community School District, Wilton, Iowa, $22,875 - to assist with improvements to the all-weather track.
Contact: Dr. Troy K. Ross; (563) 263-4010; fax (563) 263-1547; info@carvertrust.org
Internet: www.carvertrust.org/program-areas/youth/
Sponsor: Roy J. Carver Charitable Trust
202 Iowa Avenue
Muscatine, IA 52761-3733

RR Donnelley Foundation Grants   2118
The RR Donnelley Foundation believes that a combination of values to strengthen the communities in which the employees of Donnelley and Sons live and work. Drawing on its tradition of supporting youth, education, inclusion and diversity, the Foundation is responsive to the emerging needs that challenge employees and their communities. The Foundation works to enhance the support it provides by acting in collaboratively with other agencies that help U.S. enable their mission. Types of support include: monetary contributions and grants; sponsorship of events; volunteering; memberships; and internship opportunities.
Requirements: Nonprofit organizations working in areas of company operations are eligible.
Restrictions: The Foundation usually does not: contribute printing; make grants to religious organizations; make grants to political organizations; make grants for television, radio, film or video; make grants for hospitals, clinical care, medical research or equipment; or award scholarships, except through the National Merit Scholarship program.

Geographic Focus: All States
Date(s) Application is Due: Nov 1
Contact: Susan M. Levy, Vice-President; (312) 326-8712 or (312) 326-8000; fax (312) 326-7156; susan.levy@rrd.com or communityrelations@rrd.com
Internet: www.rrdonnelley.com/about/diversity-inclusion/community.aspx
Sponsor: RR Donnelley Foundation
77 West Wacker Drive
Chicago, IL 60601-1696

Ruby K. Worner Charitable Trust Grants   2119
The Ruby Worner Charitable Trust was established in Illinois in 1996, and is currently managed by PNC Charitable Trusts. The Trust was named in honor of Ruby K. Worner (1901-1995). She went on to earn three degrees from the University of Chicago, and then began a two-year academic career in a small women's college in Oklahoma. From there she moved to federal service and continued to expand into the international arena, working as a United States representative in the United Nations. An expert on textile chemistry, she also served the Department of Agriculture. Through its FirstGrant program, the Trust offers up to $1,000 awards designed to help classroom teachers accomplish creative and innovative projects they would otherwise be unable to fund because of budget limitations. Annual deadlines for applications are May 1 and October 1.
Requirements: Available to schools and school districts located in the following counties of central Illinois: Peoria, Tazewell, Woodford, Marshall, Fulton, Henry, and Mason.
Geographic Focus: Illinois
Date(s) Application is Due: May 1; Oct 1
Amount of Grant: Up to 1,000 USD
Samples: Willow School, Pekin, Illinois, $778 - to Implement Common Core by means of Math workshops where students work in groups to learn new concepts; Princeville Grade School, Princeville, Illinois, $1,000 - to provide a visual hands-on connection for developing the descriptive vocabulary of young elementary students; Lettie Brown Elementary, Morton, Illinois, $710 - to engage students and increase their understanding of math skills and reading of informational texts through the creative and innovative approach of using fiction and non-fiction texts to introduce math concepts.
Contact: Amanda Creps, Trustee; (412) 762-0873; amanda.creps@pnc.com
Internet: www1.pnc.com/pncfoundation/charitable_trusts.html
Sponsor: Ruby K. Worner Charitable Trust
One PNC Plaza, 249 Fifth Avenue, 20th Floor
Pittsburgh, PA 15222

Ruddie Memorial Youth Foundation Grants   2120
The Foundation's mission is to identify and disseminate innovative and effective programs that help disadvantaged youth reach their full potential. Three types of grants are available. Evaluation grants fund the evaluation of innovative youth programs or services with the purpose of identifying which programs and services are effective. Replication grants fund the replication of methods that a Foundation-funded outcome evaluation demonstrated to be effective in helping disadvantaged youth to reach their full potential. Dissemination grants fund the diffusion of practices that Foundation-funded outcome evaluation has shown to be effective in helping disadvantaged youth reach their full potential.
Requirements: Eligible youth organizations are: 501(c)3 nonprofits; small to medium sized with budgets of less than $5 million; and based in Baltimore, Boston, Madison, Milwaukee, Philadelphia, San Francisco, and Washington, D.C.
Geographic Focus: California, District of Columbia, Maryland, Massachusetts, Pennsylvania, Wisconsin
Date(s) Application is Due: Jul 18
Amount of Grant: 5,000 - 30,000 USD
Samples: Huckleberry Youth Programs, San Francisco, California, $25,000 - for education evaluationl Children's Health Education Center, Milwaukee, Wisconsin, $15,000 - for education replication.
Contact: Grants Administrator; contact@rmyf.org
Internet: www.rmyf.org
Sponsor: Ruddie Memorial Youth Foundation
6479 Forest Hills Court
Frederick, MD 21701-7687

Rush County Community Foundation Grants   2121
The Rush County Community Foundation, is a nonprofit public charity established in 1991 to serve donors, award grants and scholarships, and provide leadership to enrich and enhance the quality of life in Rush County, Indiana. The Rush County Community Foundation now holds over 130 funds, and have permanent endowment assets of over $6.5 million. As a public foundation, it helps donors provide grant making dollars for not-for-profit organizations that serve Rush County citizens. For additional information contact the Foundations office.
Requirements: Funding projects must serve the Rush County citizens.
Geographic Focus: Indiana
Contact: Garry Cooley; (765) 938-1177; fax (765) 938-1719; garryc@rushcountyfoundation.org
Internet: www.rushcountyfoundation.org/funds.php
Sponsor: Rush County Community Foundation
117 North Main Street
Rushville, IN 46173

Ruth Anderson Foundation Grants   2122

The Ruth Anderson Foundation was established in Florida in 1989, and currently awards grants to Florida nonprofit organizations throughout Dade County. The Foundation's funding interests include: AIDS research; children and youth services; homeless/housing shelters; human services; and substance abuse services. There are no application forms or annual deadlines. The initial approach should consist of a brief exploratory letter; full proposals will be by invitation only. The board meets throughout the year to consider requests for funding. Most recent awards have ranged from $1,500 to $10,000, and between ten and fifteen awards are given each year.

Requirements: Miami Dade County 501(c)3 tax-exempt organizations are eligible.
Restrictions: Grants are not awarded to individuals.
Geographic Focus: Florida
Amount of Grant: 1,500 - 10,000 USD
Samples: Sunrise Community, Miami, Florida, $10,000 - services support for the developmentally challenged; Camillus House, Miami, Florida, $10,000 - support for shelter programs for homeless men; Dade Heritage Trust, Miami, Florida, $10,000 - preservation and restoration of historical buildings.
Contact: Ruth Admire, Administrator; (305) 444-6121; fax (305) 444-5508; info@sullivanadmire.com or ruth.admire@sullivanadmire.com
Internet: www.sullivanadmire.com/charitable.html
Sponsor: Ruth Anderson Foundation
255 Ponce de Leon Boulevard, Suite 320
Coral Gables, FL 33134

Ruth and Henry Campbell Foundation Grants   2123

The Ruth and Henry Campbell Foundation was established in 1957 with the expressed purpose of supporting: child welfare programs; elementary and secondary education; and human services. Awards are typically limited to programs in Virginia. Types of support being offered include: annual campaigns; capital campaign projects; infrastructure; general operating funding; and scholarship funds. Most recent grants have ranged up to a maximum of $50,000. Interested applicants should submit a letter to the Foundation office, which includes an overall description of the program and funding needed. There are no specified annual deadlines for submission.

Requirements: Any 501(c)3 organization supporting the residents of the State of Virginia are welcome to apply.
Geographic Focus: Virginia
Amount of Grant: Up to 50,000 USD
Samples: Courtland Youth Athletic Association, Courtland, Virginia, $5,000 - general operating support; City of Franklin, Franklin, Virginia, $20,000 - general operating support; Southampton Economic Development, Franklin, Virginia, $25,000 - general operating support.
Contact: Paul Camp Marks, Director; (919) 881-6497 or (855) 739-2921
Sponsor: Ruth and Henry Campbell Foundation
1525 West W.T. Harris Boulevard, D1114-044
Charlotte, NC 28262-8522

Ruth and Vernon Taylor Foundation Grants   2124

The foundation awards grants to nonprofit organizations in the areas of arts and humanities, civic and public affairs, secondary schools, higher education, environment, hospitals, human services, health, youth services, and social services. Types of support include general operating support, building construction and renovation, endowment funds, and research. The foundation suggests that initial contact be made in writing, since unsolicited requests for funds are not accepted. The Board meets in May and September.

Requirements: Organizations located in Colorado, Illinois, Montana, New Jersey, New York, Pennsylvania, Texas, or Wyoming are eligible.
Restrictions: Grants are not awarded to individuals.
Geographic Focus: Colorado, Illinois, Montana, New Jersey, New York, Pennsylvania, Texas, Wyoming
Amount of Grant: 1,000 - 20,000 USD
Contact: Douglas Taylor, Trustee; (303) 893-5284; fax (303)893-8263
Sponsor: Ruth and Vernon Taylor Foundation
518 17th Street, Suite 1670
Denver, CO 80202

Ruth Camp Campbell Charitable Trust Grants   2125

The Ruth Camp Campbell Charitable Trust, established in Virginia in 1976, was founded in honor of the widow of Henry M. Campbell, daughter of the late Paul Douglas and Ella Cobb Camp, a member of the Franklin Baptist Church, the Women's Missionary Society, and taught Sunday School for a number of years. Being very philanthropic, she gave the land for Paul D. Camp Community College and a gymnasium for Southampton Academy. Currently, the Trust offers grants in support of a variety of areas, including: child welfare; Christianity; diseases; elementary and secondary education; higher education; hospital care; human services; and Protestantism. Its geographic focus is Florida, North Carolina, South Carolina, and Virginia. In the vast majority of cases, grants take the form of general operating support, most recently ranging from $1,000 to $42,000.

Geographic Focus: Virginia
Amount of Grant: 1,000 - 42,000 USD
Samples: Village at Woods Edge, Franklin, Virginia, $11,000 - general operating support; Southeast 4-H Educational Center, Wakefield, Virginia, $30,000 - general operating support; Virginia Military Institute Foundation, Lexington, Virginia, $42,000 - general operating support.
Contact: John M. Camp, III, Director; (212) 493-8000
Sponsor: Ruth Camp Campbell Charitable Trust
717 Clay Street, P.O. Box 813
Franklin, VA 23851

RWJF Childhood Obesity Grants   2126

Through its Childhood Obesity Grant program, RWJF has developed three integrated strategies to reverse the childhood obesity epidemic: funding local organizations to make positive changes at the community level, advocating for healthier policies in the public and private sectors, and providing grants to researchers and evaluators to strengthen the evidence about what works. The Foundation's grant making is centered on advancing these strategies in ways that make it easier for all children to lead healthy lives. The program is intended to improve understanding of school, community, state and national policies and environmental factors affecting youth diet, physical activity, obesity, and tobacco, alcohol and drug use, and to evaluate the effectiveness of interventions to prevent youth obesity.

Requirements: Eligible applicants for research grants are scholars associated with educational institutions, research organizations, health care providers or other public or nonprofit organizations. Preference will be given to public entities or nonprofit organizations tax exempt under Section 501(c)3 of the Internal Revenue Code. Applicants may be independent of or associated with organizations currently receiving grants.
Geographic Focus: All States
Contact: C. Tracy Orleans, Senior Program Officer/Senior Scientist; (609) 627-5962 or (877) 843-7953; cto@rwjf.org
Internet: www.rwjf.org/en/about-rwjf/program-areas/childhood-obesity/programs-and-grants.html
Sponsor: Robert Wood Johnson Foundation
Route 1 and College Road East, P.O. Box 2316
Princeton, NJ 08543-2316

RWJF Healthy Eating Research Grants   2127

Healthy Eating Research is a national program that supports research to identify, analyze, and evaluate environmental and policy strategies that can promote healthy eating among children and prevent childhood obesity. Special emphasis is given to research projects that benefit children in the low-income and racial/ethnic populations at highest risk for obesity. The program funds two types of research grants: studies to identify and/or evaluate promising school food environment and policy changes (12- to 18-month awards up to $100,000 each, and 18- to 36-month awards up to $400,000 each); and analyses of macro-level policy or system determinants of school food environments and policies (12- to 18-month awards up to $75,000 each). Applications must be submitted through the online process in response to future calls for proposals. Calls for Proposals and their guidelines are available online.

Requirements: Preference will be given to those applicants that may be either public entities or nonprofit organizations that are tax-exempt under Section 501(c)3 of the Internal Revenue Code. Applicant organizations must be based in the United States or U.S. Territories. The focus of this program is the United States; studies of policies in other countries will be considered only to the extent that they may directly inform U.S. policy. The experience and qualifications of the research team is one of the primary criteria for proposal review. A doctorate or terminal degree is preferred for the principal investigator.
Restrictions: This program does not fund demonstration projects. The foundation does not award grants to private individuals or applicants from outside the U.S. or U.S. Territories. No faxed, emailed or mailed proposals will be accepted.
Geographic Focus: All States
Amount of Grant: Up to 400,000 USD
Contact: Kathy Kosiak; (800) 578-8636; fax (612) 624-9328; healthyeating@umn.edu
Internet: www.healthyeatingresearch.org/
Sponsor: Robert Wood Johnson Foundation
Route 1 and College Road East, P.O. Box 2316
Princeton, NJ 08543-2316

S. D. Bechtel, Jr. Foundation / Stephen Bechtel Fund Character and   2128
Citizenship Development Grants

The Foundation/Fund believe that all people are capable of making positive choices and ethical decisions, and of becoming active citizens. For young people, it is critical that they are provided with consistent and sound mentoring, and the encouragement to participate in new learning opportunities to realize their full potential and become responsible and active citizens. The directors have a strong interest in programs for young people that build character and programs for the broader public that advance an understanding of, and commitment to, the practice of citizenship. The Foundation/Fund support organizations working to achieve the following objectives: increasing opportunities for youth in the San Francisco Bay Area to interact with exemplary role models and participate in a variety of worthwhile learning opportunities so that they are able to develop a framework for ethical living; and advancing a vibrant and productive national conversation about why active citizenship matters and how Americans can cultivate and sustain these values.

Requirements: The primary geographic focus of the Foundation/Fund is the San Francisco Bay area. The Foundation/Fund support non-profit organizations providing quality programs in science, technology, engineering and math (STEM) education, environment, environmental education, character and citizenship development and preventive healthcare and selected research; provide capital support; provide operational support; and provide project support.
Restrictions: The Foundation/Fund do not provide endowment funding, international grants, or grants for individuals.
Geographic Focus: California
Date(s) Application is Due: Oct 1
Amount of Grant: 5,000 - 25,000 USD
Contact: Program Coordinator; (415) 284-8675; sdbjr@sdbjrfoundation.org
Internet: www.sdbjrfoundation.org/program_areas.htm#Char_citiz
Sponsor: S. D. Bechtel, Jr. Foundation / Stephen Bechtel Fund
P.O. Box 193809
San Francisco, CA 94119-3809

S. Spencer Scott Fund Grants 2129

Samuel Spencer Scott was an American publishing executive. He joined Harcourt, Brace in 1920 and developed the company's educational department into a business generating a million dollars in annual revenue. He became the president of Harcourt, Brace and Company in 1948 and held that position until his retirement in 1954. He died in 1971 while traveling at Pompano Beach, Florida. Established in New York in 1949, the S. Spencer Scott Fund serves the residents of Connecticut, Rhode Island, New York, Vermont, Maine, Maryland, New Hampshire, Pennsylvania, and Massachusetts. Its primary fields of interest include: the arts; museums; education; and religion. There are no particular application forms or annual deadlines, and applicants are advised to contact the Fund directly. Funding general is given for general operations, and amounts range from $250 to $10,000.

Requirements: Any 501(c)3 organization serving the residents of Connecticut, Rhode Island, New York, Vermont, Maryland, Maine, New Hampshire, Pennsylvania, and Massachusetts are eligible to apply.

Geographic Focus: Connecticut, Maine, Maryland, Massachusetts, New Hampshire, New York, Pennsylvania, Rhode Island, Vermont

Amount of Grant: 250 - 10,000 USD

Samples: Connecticut River Museum, Essex, Connecticut, $2,100 - general operating support; Friends of the Wissahickon, Philadelphia, Pennsylvania, $250 - general operating support; Hope 4 Horses, Boxford, Massachusetts, $500 - general operating support; Hurricane Island Foundation, Portland, Maine, $10,000 - general operating support.

Contact: Suzette Hearn, Treasurer; (212) 286-2600

Sponsor: S. Spencer Scott Fund

665 5th Avenue, 6th Floor

New York, NY 10022

Sabina Dolan and Gladys Saulsbury Foundation Grants 2130

The Sabina Dolan and Gladys Saulsbury Foundation was established in New Haven, Connecticut, to support needy children who wish to attend summer camp. Its primary fields of interest are education and human services. Types of grant support include: general operations for human services agencies; and awards given to individuals. Amounts generally range from $100 to $2,500. There are no specified annual application deadlines, though a formal application is required. Interested parties should contact the Foundation directly.

Geographic Focus: Connecticut

Amount of Grant: 100 - 2,500 USD

Contact: Edward J. Dolan, President; (203) 787-3513 or (203) 789-1605

Sponsor: Sabina Dolan and Gladys Saulsbury Foundation

400 Orange Street

New Haven, CT 06511-6405

SACF Youth Advisory Council Grants 2131

The Straits Area Community Foundation Youth Advisory Council is a group of students from Cheboygan County and Mackinaw City. Working with an adult advisor, the members learn about philanthropy and how to improve their communities through the grant-making process. Using funds from the W.K. Kellogg Foundation, the students award grants to local non-profit organizations that are supporting projects and programs that benefit youth under the age of 18 in the Straits Area. All parochial and public schools should apply for grants through SAYAC. Highest priority will be given to projects or programs addressing the following youth needs as determined by the biannual needs assessment survey: drug use; alcohol use; bullying; teen pregnancy; and academic stress. Applicants may submit requests up to a maximum of $1,000 per application cycle unless otherwise indicated. Mini-grants up to $300 are also available. Application submissions should be postmarked by March 15 and December 15 to meet the annual deadlines.

Requirements: IRS 501(c)3 nonprofit organizations, schools, churches (for non-sectarian purposes), cities, townships, and other governmental units serving Cheboygan County or Mackinaw City are eligible to apply. An organization may apply each year for a grant.

Restrictions: No program may be funded for more than two (2) consecutive grant cycles or two (2) years, whichever is longer. The Foundation will not support the sustained funding of any program. Grants are not given to individuals, except for awards or scholarships from designated donor funds.

Geographic Focus: Michigan

Date(s) Application is Due: Mar 15; Dec 15

Amount of Grant: Up to 1,000 USD

Samples: Bishop Baraga Catholic School, Cheboygan, Michigan, $1,000 - Battle of the Books; Cheboygan County Humane Society, Cheboygan, Michigan, $1,000 - Publication of Kind News; Wolverine Community Schools, Wolverine, Michigan, $800 - Personal Narrative Photo Story.

Contact: Julie Wiesen; (989) 354-6881 or (877) 354-6881; wiesenj@cfnem.org

Internet: www.cfnem.org/sacf/grants/yac-grants.html

Sponsor: Straits Area Community Foundation

100 N. Ripley, Suite F, P.O. Box 495

Alpena, MI 49707

Sadler Family Foundation Grants 2132

In 1948, folks drove from miles around to the first Sadler's Smokehouse, located along Highway 79 in Henderson, Texas. At that time, the Sadler family car-hopped their pit-smoked beef brisket and pulled pork sandwiches, which were always served with a hot cherry pepper on the side. In 1961, Harold Sadler opened up his own Sadler's Smokehouse in Lufkin, Texas. Harold had a real passion for making a high quality, premium pit-smoked brisket. With the opening of their first food processing plant, the Sadlers decided to focus entirely on their fast emerging wholesale food service business. It was only a matter of time before this authentic-tasting barbecue expanded onto the shelves of stores across the country. The business eventually grew to the point that, in 1984, Sadler's

Smokehouse expanded to a 40-acre business site housing the company's headquarters and a more than 300,000 square foot state-of-the-art processing plant. As a way to give back to the community, the Sadler Family Foundation was established in 2001. Its primary fields of interest include: Christian organizations; youth sports; elementary and secondary education; higher education; graduate and professional education; and theology. Applicants should submit a detailed description of the program and the amount of funding requested. Most recent awards for general operating support have ranged from $3,500 to as much as $630,000. There are no annual application deadlines for submission.

Requirements: Any 501(c)3 organization adhering to the Foundation's mission in support of the residents of Texas and New Mexico are eligible to apply.

Geographic Focus: New Mexico, Texas

Amount of Grant: 3,500 - 630,000 USD

Samples: Gospel for Muslims, Dallas, Texas, $628,875 - general operating support; Boys and Girls Club of Rusk County, Henderson, Texas, $3,600 - general operating support; Dallas Baptist University, Dallas, Texas, $125,000 - general operating support; Faith Comes by Hearing, Albuquerque, New Mexico, $8,400 - general operating support.

Contact: Harold Sadler, Director; (903) 646-0996 or (903) 787-0788

Sponsor: Sadler Family Foundation

P.O. Box 1746

Henderson, TX 75653-1088

Saeman Family Foundation A Charitable Trust Grants 2133

John V. Saeman, Jr., was born August 29, 1936, in Madison, Wisconsin, and raised in nearby farming community of Cross Plains. His father and brother were involved with the Saeman Lumber Company which had been started by Saeman's grandfather in 1876 and remains a family business today. While his journeys have taken him far from home, Saeman has remained true to the rock-solid American values he learned in his youth. After graduating from Loras College in Dubuque, Iowa, Saeman served in the United States Marine Corps. He then moved to Los Angeles, where he was introduced to the world of telecommunications when he took a sales position with Subscription Television (STV), a joint venture between the Reuben H. Donnelley Corporation and Lear Siegler. STV was the nation's first provider of Pay per View programming over co-axial cable. This 3 channel system featuring movies, sports and cultural programs operated in Southern and Northern California. In 1965, he moved to Denver and began his association with Bill Daniels. In 1972, he was named president of the brokerage division and in 1974, president and CEO of all Daniels companies. In his early years with Daniels & Associates, Saeman worked in all facets of the company with system operating responsibilities in California, Nevada, Oregon and Washington State. Saeman also brokered cable systems to the Times Mirror Company, King Broadcasting, the Seattle Times, the San Francisco Chronicle, The Tribune Corp., and many others. His key merger while in California was his marriage to his wife Carolyn, who for more than 40 years has been his best friend and partner. Today, John and Carol, now joined by their children and their spouses, fund the needs of many religious, non-profit, and community organizations through the Saeman Family Foundation, established in Colorado in 1994. Giving primarily to philanthropic endeavors in support of the Roman Catholic Church, funding is also provided for education, health associations, children, youth, family services, and human services throughout Colorado.

Requirements: Funding is offered to 501(c)3 organizations that support the residents and nonprofits of Colorado.

Geographic Focus: Colorado

Amount of Grant: 500 - 50,000 USD

Samples: Augustine Institute, Greenwood Village, Colorado, $46,997 - general operating fund; Colorado Family Action Foundation, Castle Rock, Colorado, $25,000 - general operating fund; FOCUS, Colorado Springs, Colorado, $50,000 - general operating fund.

Contact: Richard O. Campbell, Director; (720) 642-7300

Sponsor: Saeman Family Foundation A Charitable Trust

270 Saint Paul Street, Suite 300

Denver, CO 80206

Saginaw Community Foundation Discretionary Grants 2134

Saginaw Community Foundation's Discretionary Grants are designed to meet the needs of a wide variety of nonprofit organizations. The Foundation's grants are intended to help residents build a strong community by addressing pressing needs in the County.

Requirements: Applicants must first call the Foundation to discuss the project with the staff. To be eligible for funding, organizations must have a nonprofit status and directly benefit Saginaw County. Grants are ordinarily only made for one year. Applications must be received by mail, or dropped off at the agency.

Restrictions: The Saginaw Community Foundation does not support: operating budgets; basic municipal services; basic educational functions; endowment campaigns; previously incurred debt; or sectarian religious programs.

Geographic Focus: Michigan

Date(s) Application is Due: Feb 1; May 1; Aug 1; Nov 1

Amount of Grant: Up to 10,000 USD

Samples: Temple Theatre Foundation, Saginaw, Michigan, $10,000 - For "Arts Take Stage" program; Saginaw Township Community Schools, Saginaw, Michigan, $8,807 - Teacher grants.

Contact: Kendra Kempf, Program Associate/FORCE Coordinator; (989) 755-0545; fax (989) 755-6524; kendra@saginawfoundation.org

Internet: www.saginawfoundation.org/grants_and_scholarships/grants/

Sponsor: Saginaw Community Foundation

100 South Jefferson, Suite 201

Saginaw, MI 48602

Saginaw Community Foundation YWCA Fund for Women and Girls Grants 2135
YWCA Fund for Women and Girls Grants support projects and programs that benefit
women and girls of Saginaw County. Specifically, its goals are: to support the physical,
intellectual, emotional, social and spiritual needs of women, children and families; and to
foster the elimination of racism and sexism.
Requirements: Applicants must first call the Foundation to discuss the project with the
staff. To be eligible for funding, organizations must have a nonprofit status and directly
benefit Saginaw County. Grants are ordinarily only made for one year. Applications can
be downloaded at the website but must be received by mail or dropped off at the agency.
Restrictions: The Saginaw Community Foundation does not support: operating budgets;
basic municipal services; basic educational functions; endowment campaigns; previously
incurred debt; or sectarian religious programs.
Geographic Focus: Michigan
Date(s) Application is Due: Feb 1; May 1; Aug 1; Nov 1
Amount of Grant: Up to 5,000 USD
Contact: Kendra Kempf, Program Associate/FORCE Coordinator; (989) 755-0545;
fax (989) 755-6524; kendra@saginawfoundation.org
Internet: www.saginawfoundation.org/grants_and_scholarships/grants/
Sponsor: Saginaw Community Foundation
100 South Jefferson, Suite 201
Saginaw, MI 48602

Saginaw County Community Foundation Youth FORCE Grants 2136
Saginaw County Youth FORCE Grants directly benefit young people. Priority of this grant
is placed on projects that: include youth in the planning and implementation; empower
youth and increase their awareness of community issues; and are first-time funding requests.
Requirements: Applicants must contact the Community Foundation before submitting
a grant application to discuss the proposed project. Student organizations applying for
FORCE funds must have an adult supervisor. Also, organizations must be 501(c)3 and the
proposed program must directly benefit Saginaw County. Applications can be downloaded
at the website but must be sent by mail or hand-delivered at the office.
Restrictions: Applicants to FORCE grants must be 20 years of age or younger. In addition,
Saginaw Community Foundation does not fund: operating budgets; basic municipal
services; basic educational functions; endowment campaigns; previously incurred debt; or
sectarian religious programs.
Geographic Focus: Michigan
Date(s) Application is Due: Feb 1; Nov 1
Amount of Grant: Up to 10,000 USD
Contact: Kendra Kempf, Program Associate/FORCE Coordinator; (989) 755-0545;
fax (989) 755-6524; kendra@saginawfoundation.org
Internet: www.saginawfoundation.org/grants_and_scholarships/grants/
Sponsor: Saginaw Community Foundation
100 South Jefferson, Suite 201
Saginaw, MI 48602

Saigh Foundation Grants 2137
Fred M. Saigh was born in Springfield, Illinois on June 27, 1905, the son of Lebanese
immigrants who owned a chain of grocery stores. He passed away in 1999. Although he is
best known as the owner of the St. Louis Cardinals (1948 - 1953), many of his friends and
acquaintances will always remember him as a perceptive and caring benefactor - "a one-
man charity fund," in the words of sportswriter Mike Eisenbath. The Saigh Foundation
continues the important work begun by Mr. Saigh by assisting St. Louis-area organizations
that benefit children and youth, particularly in the areas of education and healthcare. The
foundation is particularly interested in stimulating the development of new ventures, as
well as in supporting organizations that feature innovative approaches or programs. Like
Mr. Saigh, the foundation is especially dedicated to aiding those who might not otherwise
receive assistance. Proposals are requested at least three months before any quarterly
meeting. These are normally held in January, April, July, and October. The foundation uses
a customized version of the Missouri Common Grant Application (CGA). It is available
at the grant website along with guidelines and budget templates and should be submitted
via mail or fax to the address given.
Requirements: Saint Louis-area nonprofit organizations are eligible.
Restrictions: The foundation does not participate in annual appeals, dinner functions, and
fundraising events; capital campaigns; loans and deficits; grants for films and travel; or
nonprofit organizations outside of the metropolitan Saint Louis area.
Geographic Focus: Missouri
Samples: Juvenile Diabetes Research Foundation; Junior Achievement of Mississippi;
Salvation Army.
Contact: JoAnn Hejna; (314) 862-3055; fax (314) 862-9288; saigh@thesaighfoundation.org
Mary Kemp; (314) 862-3055; fax (314) 862-9288; saigh@thesaighfoundation.org
Internet: www.thesaighfoundation.org/grant_guide.html
Sponsor: Saigh Foundation
7777 Bonhomme Avenue, Suite 2007
Saint Louis, MO 63105

Saint Ann Legacy Grants 2138
The Sisters of Charity of St. Augustine formed the Saint Ann Foundation in 1973 with
an endowment from the sale of the Saint Ann Hospital, a maternity hospital that served
Cleveland's women and babies for 100 years. The Saint Ann Legacy Grant program
recognizes the Saint Ann Foundation's vision to be a resource for ministries of women
religious, particularly those that improve the lives of women and children. The Sisters
of Charity Foundation of Cleveland awards grants to support the ministries of women
religious as as they work to meet the needs of God's people. Grants may be awarded to

ministries of women religious in Northeast Ohio, defined as the Dioceses of Cleveland
and Youngstown.
Requirements: Organizations must have a tax-exempt status as nonprofit organizations, as
identified by the Internal Revenue Service Code. Ministries of women religious include
those that are sponsored or led by Catholic Sisters or programs at other organizations where
women religious are significantly involved.
Restrictions: Grants are not made to individuals.
Geographic Focus: Ohio
Date(s) Application is Due: Jun 16
Amount of Grant: 20,000 USD
Contact: Erin McIntyre, Program Officer, Religious Communities;
(216) 241-9300 ext. 232; fax (216) 241-9345; emcintyre@socfcleveland.org
Internet: www.socfcleveland.org/our-focus-areas/religious-communities/saint-ann-
legacy-grants/
Sponsor: Sisters of Charity Foundation of Cleveland
The Halle Building, 1228 Euclid Avenue, Suite 330
Cleveland, OH 44115-1834

Saint Louis Rams Foundation Community Donations 2139
The foundation supports nonprofits that help inspire positive change for youth in the Saint
Louis area. Programs that impact youth in the general fields of education, literacy, health, and
recreation will be considered. Annually, the Rams provide to charitable groups more than 3,500
items, helping recipient organizations raise thousands of dollars through raffles, auctions and
other fundraising endeavors. Other types of financial support include program development
grants and general operating grants. The foundation does not accept unsolicited requests, but
initial information may be sent for the office to keep on file for future opportunities.
Requirements: Nonprofits in the metropolitan Saint Louis, Missouri, area, including
southern Illinois and eastern Missouri, are eligible. Preference is given to organizations
that partner with other local nonprofits and offer creative approaches for more than grants
(i.e., personnel involvement or in-kind support) and ways the Rams can participate.
Restrictions: The Rams do not provide monetary contributions or merchandise donations
for the following: businesses, retail and otherwise; capital campaigns/start-up funding
for new businesses; on-line auctions; chamber of commerce/city/neighborhood festivals
such as homecoming celebrations and carnivals that do not directly benefit a charitable
organization; class reunions; family reunions; pageant contestants (beauty and otherwise);
student ambassador/exchange programs; or non-charity events and organizations such as
company picnics, employee golf tournaments, employee recognition/incentive programs,
card clubs, car shows, "poker runs", and organized adult leisure sports teams.
Geographic Focus: Missouri
Date(s) Application is Due: Jan 1; Jul 1
Contact: Donations Coordinator; (314) 516-8788 or (314) 982-7267; fax (314) 770-0392
Internet: www.stlouisrams.com/community/donations.html
Sponsor: Saint Louis Rams Foundation
1 Rams Way
Saint Louis, MO 63045

Salmon Foundation Grants 2140
Established in New York in 1991, the Salmon Foundation provides funding to nonprofit
organizations for programs providing for children and youth programs, family services,
and education. Grants are awarded for projects, scholarship support, operating support,
and capital funding. Funding ranges from $2,000 to $40,000.
Requirements: Funding provided to nonprofit organizations. Organizations tend to be on
the east coast and include Connecticut, New Hampshire, Vermont, Ohio, Pennsylvania,
Alabama, Tennessee, Virginia, California, Maryland, Colorado and District of Columbia.
Restrictions: No individual scholarships are made.
Geographic Focus: Alabama, California, Colorado, Connecticut, District of Columbia,
Maryland, New Hampshire, Pennsylvania, Tennessee, Virginia
Amount of Grant: 2,000 - 40,000 USD
Samples: Aspen Education Foundation, Aspen, Colorado, $7,500 - elementary math and
literacy program support; Baltimore Symphony Orchestra, Baltimore, Maryland, $15,000
- support for the OrchKids program; The Family Place, Norwich, Vermont, $30,000 - for
the Families Learning Together Program.
Contact: Emily Grand, Administrator; (212) 708-9316 or (212) 812-4362
Sponsor: Salmon Foundation, Inc.
6 West 48th Street, 10th Floor
New York, NY 10036-1802

Saltchuk Corporate Giving 2141
Founded in 1982, Saltchuk is family owned and operated, and has grown to include seven
business units; TOTE, Foss, Interstate, Carlile, Northern Aviation Services, Tropical
Shipping, and Northstar Petroleum which deliver critical transportation and logistics, air
cargo, marine services, trucking and petroleum distribution services to their communities.
The name, Saltchuk, comes from a trading language, Chinook Jargon, that was developed
by the natives of the Pacific Rim in North America. After the period of contact the
language adopted words used by the Europeans that the natives traded with – principally
French and English. The term "Saltchuk" means saltwater. Today, Saltchuk believes in
supporting the communities in which its companies are located and its employees live.
The company strives to be excellent corporate citizens, ever mindful of its commitment
to integrity, job safety, environmental stewardship, and giving back to the communities it
serves. It encourages cross-group collaboration and share information about its charitable
donations and practices throughout its organization, and with its customers and partners.
The corporation's primary interest areas include: arts and culture; community development;

elementary and secondary education; the environment; health care; social services; and youth programs. Its geographic focus is Alaska, Hawaii, Washington, and the Caribbean though the corporation occasionally gives elsewhere.

Requirements: Programs and projects making an impact in the areas of Post-Secondary Education and Youth Development will be considered. When submitting requests directly to Saltchuk, applicants should select the nearest region.

Geographic Focus: Alaska, Florida, Hawaii, Puerto Rico, Washington

Amount of Grant: Up to 20,000 USD

Contact: Emily Reiter, Director of Communications and Marketing; (206) 652-1129 or (206) 652-1111; emilyr@saltchuk.com or cjohnson@nac.aero

Cheryl Johnson, Regional Contact; (907) 249-5127 or (206) 652-1111; cjohnson@nac.aero

Natalia Lagmay, Regional Contact; (808) 543-9441 or (206) 652-1111; nlagmay@htbyb.com

Internet: www.saltchuk.com/about-us/giving

Sponsor: Saltchuk

450 Alaskan Way, Suite 708

Seattle, WA 98104

Salt River Project Health and Human Services Grants   2142

Salt River Project (SRP) is an energy/utilities company serving electric customers and water shareholders in the Phoenix metropolitan area. SRP provides funding to nonprofit organizations that address critical needs within its service communities. SRP is committed to safe and healthy communities. Health and Human Services Grants support programs that reach out to underserved communities to promote the individual's ability to overcome barriers and be self-sufficient; increase the community's ability to care for individuals who are in need of food, shelter, and safety from violent or crisis situations; increase the ability of children to participate in youth programs which promote personal development and positive life choices; support increasing underserved communities' access to hospitals and medical care as an integral part of a thriving community; and sponsor programs that seek to highlight the never ceasing need for water and electric safety.

Requirements: Eligible applicants must be 501(c)3 nonprofit, organizations within SRP's service area. SRP's service area is central Arizona and includes the following cities and towns: Phoenix, Mesa, Tempe, Paradise Valley, Fountain Hills, Scottsdale, Apache Junction, Peoria, Queen Creek, Avondale, Chandler, Gilbert, Glendale, Guadalupe, and Tolleson. There are no specific grant deadlines. Requests are reviewed in an on-going process which typically takes eight weeks.

Restrictions: The following are ineligible: individuals, including support for specific students, researchers, travel expenses, conference fees; organizations that discriminate on the basis of race, creed, color, sex, or national origin; endowment programs; medical research projects or medical procedures for individuals; professional schools of art, academic art programs, individual high school or college performing groups; political or lobbying groups or campaigns; fraternal organizations, veterans' organizations, professional associations, and similar membership groups; public or commercial broadcasting programs; religious activities or church-sponsored programs limited to church membership; and debt-reduction campaigns. SRP does not donate services, including water or electricity, or equipment for which a fee is normally charged.

Geographic Focus: Arizona

Contact: Corporate Contributions Administrator; (602) 236-5900; webmstr@srpnet.com

Internet: www.srpnet.com/community/contributions/guidelines.aspx

Sponsor: Salt River Project

1521 North Project Drive

Tempe, AZ 85281-1298

Samueli Foundation Education Grants   2143

The Samueli Foundation considers grants to agencies, primarily in Orange County, California, that serve the community, and whose programs meet the guidelines listed. Grants are usually approved for a defined period of time, but may be paid over a multi-year period. In the area of Education, its goals are to: promote excellence in the field of engineering in higher education, primarily in Southern California; stimulate interest in U.S. K-12 students in STEM (Science, Technology, Engineering and Mathematics) coursework, research and careers through integration of technology and innovative teaching methods; and provide all students access to quality education. The Foundation has a two-phase application process, the first of which is a Letter of Inquiry. If there is interest upon review of the Letter, the Foundation will contact applicants for further information and may request submission of a formal application for funding consideration.

Requirements: 501(c)3 tax-exempt organizations and K-12th grade schools are eligible.

Restrictions: The foundation does not fund umbrella fund raising organizations, political campaigns, or grants to individuals.

Geographic Focus: All States

Amount of Grant: 1,000 - 50,000 USD

Contact: Gerald R. Solomon; (949) 760-4400; fax (949) 760-4110; Info@samueli.org

Internet: www.samueli.org/funding-priorities/education/

Sponsor: Samueli Foundation

2101 East Coast Highway, 3rd Floor

Corona del Mar, CA 92625

Samueli Foundation Youth Services Grants   2144

The Samueli Foundation considers grants to agencies, primarily in Orange County, California, that serve the community, and whose programs meet the guidelines listed. Grants are usually approved for a defined period of time, but may be paid over a multi-year period. In the area of Youth Services, its goals are to provide: mentoring, educational and enrichment opportunities to at risk youth; and comprehensive services and support for foster care youth. The Foundation has a two-phase application process, the first of which is a Letter of Inquiry. If there is interest upon review of the Letter, the Foundation will contact applicants for further information and may request submission of a formal application for funding consideration.

Requirements: 501(c)3 tax-exempt organizations throughout California are eligible to apply.

Restrictions: The foundation does not fund umbrella fund raising organizations, political campaigns, or grants to individuals.

Geographic Focus: California

Amount of Grant: 1,000 - 50,000 USD

Contact: Gerald R. Solomon; (949) 760-4400; fax (949) 760-4110; Info@samueli.org

Internet: www.samueli.org/funding-priorities/youth-services/

Sponsor: Samueli Foundation

2101 East Coast Highway, 3rd Floor

Corona del Mar, CA 92625

Samuel N. and Mary Castle Foundation Grants   2145

The Samuel N. and Mary Castle Foundation is committed to providing resources to improve the life of Hawaii's children and families by improving the quality and quantity of early education. Efforts are concentrated on creating greater social equality and opportunity through improving access to high quality pre-K education. Secondarily, the Foundation provides limited support for he arts, health, historical and cultural projects, where these projects serve children 0-5. Grants generally range from $5,000 to $25,000. Grants for major capital improvements typically range from $10,000 to $100,000. The deadlines are January 8 for the February trustee meeting, May 14 for the July/August meeting, and September 3 for the December meeting.

Requirements: Eligible organizations must be tax exempt, publicly supported and charitable as determined by the Internal Revenue Service. Grants are primarily awarded to organizations located within the state of Hawaii, for programs and projects benefiting the people of Hawaii. Proposed programs or projects must be in response to a documented community need, and not solely an organizational need. Grants may be awarded for innovative programs, demonstration projects and "start-up" funding. Program and project support does not generally exceed three years, and funding must be applied for on a yearly basis. Applicants must contact the Foundation's Executive Director by letter, email, phone, or a personal visit before making fund application. A site visit may be required if the organization has not applied before or in many years.

Restrictions: The following are ineligible: charter schools; organizations outside of the U.S; endowments; regular operating costs such as salaries, rents, or maintenance; more than 40-50 percent of total project costs; programs not open to all racial and ethnic groups; projects in which parents and the community have not been appropriately involved in planning and funding; publication projects; general student scholarships for tuition, travel, or conferences; video projects; and annual fund drives or sponsorships. The Foundation only rarely funds in the U.S. outside Hawaii. All mainland U.S. applications must be invited by the Trustees to be considered for funding.

Geographic Focus: Hawaii

Date(s) Application is Due: Jan 8; May 14; Sep 3

Amount of Grant: 5,000 - 100,000 USD

Samples: Ae Kamalii Pre-School, Lihue, Hawaii, $25,600 - repairs and supplies, professional development (2020); Catholic Diocese of Honolulu – Hawaii Catholic Schools, Honolulu, Hawaii, $50,000 - tuition assistance for low-income families in Catholic pre-schools; University of Hawaii Foundation, Honolulu, Hawaii, $30,000 - study of compensation for pre-school teachers (2020); Child and Family Service, Ewa, Hawaii, $75,000 - program support for Helping Families and Guardians with Children 0-5 (2020); Hawaii Children's Action Network, Honolulu, Hawaii, $100,000 - operating support (2020).

Contact: Alfred L. Castle, Executive Director; (808) 522-1101; fax (808) 522-1103; snandmarycastle@hawaii.rr.com

Internet: fdnweb.org/castle/grantmaking/

Sponsor: Samuel N. and Mary Castle Foundation

733 Bishop Street, Suite 1275

Honolulu, HI 96813

Samuel S. Johnson Foundation Grants   2146

The Samuel S. Johnson Foundation was incorporated in 1948 and supports organizations primarily in the Oregon and Clark County, Washington, region. The Foundation gives to: formal education programs leading to an R.N. status or baccalaureate or higher college/university degree in nursing; vocational education programs targeting high school drop-outs and high school grads who are not able to pursue junior college or higher formal education and which offer them job-specific technical training, mentoring or coaching; emergency food assistance programs; rural mobile health screening/care projects benefiting the uninsured medically needy; environmental programs, coastal & marine ecosystems, sustainable agriculture and communities. Most recent awards have range from $1,000 to $30,000. Though there are no specified deadlines, the board meets in July and November to make grant making decisions.

Requirements: Grants are awarded to non-profit organizations in Oregon and Clark County, Washington. Contact the Foundation for current focus and guidelines with a phone call before submitting a proposal. No Application form is required, however you must include the following in your proposal: copy of IRS Determination Letter; brief history of organization and description of its mission; copy of most recent annual report/audited financial statement/990; listing of board of directors, trustees, officers and other key people and their affiliations; detailed description of project and amount of funding requested; contact person; copy of current year's organizational budget and/or project budget; listing of additional sources and amount of support. Include one copy of the proposal. The board meets twice a year, in May and October, with no deadline date for the submitting of proposals. If your proposal is accepted, you will receive notification within 2 - 3 weeks after the board meets.

Restrictions: No support for foreign organizations. No grants or scholarships to individuals, or for leadership training or staff development, campaigns to retire debt, annual campaigns, deficit financing, construction, sole underwriting of major proposals or projects, demolition or endowments.
Geographic Focus: Oregon, Washington
Amount of Grant: 500 - 26,000 USD
Samples: Oregon Historical Society, Portland, Oregon, $30,000 - World War II exhibit,; Marion Historical Foundation, Salem, Oregon, $5,000 - general operations; Helping Hands Outreach, Seaside, Oregon, $7,500 - general operations.
Contact: Mary A. Krenowicz, Secretary; (541) 548-8104; mary@tssjf.org
Sponsor: Samuel S. Johnson Foundation
P.O. Box 356
Redmond, OR 97756-0079

San Antonio Area Foundation Annual Responsive Grants   2147
The San Antonio Area Foundation's Annual Responsive Grant program has two annual cycles, each with their own funding categories. During cycle one, with an annual online application deadline of February 10, the funding mechanism has two distinctive categories that: enable children and families to lead safe and productive lives; and promote healthy lifestyles with an emphasis on reducing obesity and diabetes, are preventative in nature or educate the community in prevention, and/or increase access to comprehensive healthcare, including dental, vision and mental services. Cycle two, with an online application deadline of July 14, concentrates on supporting programs that: improve the health and wellness of animals, educate our community about animal care and/or provide spay/neuter and/or adoption services; promote accessibility to the arts, encourage broad participation from all parts of our community and/or provide arts education and outreach; and enhance the quality of life for seniors.
Requirements: The San Antonio Area Foundation makes grants from its funds, with help from its donors, to nonprofit organizations improving the quality of life in Bexar County and the following surrounding counties: Frio, Atascosa, Karnes, Wilson, Guadalupe, Gonzales, Comal, Blanco, Kendall, Gillespie, Kerr, Bandera and Medina.
Geographic Focus: Texas
Date(s) Application is Due: Feb 10; Jul 14
Contact: Lydia R. Saldana, Program Officer; (210) 228-3753 or (210) 225-2243; fax (210) 225-1980; lsaldana@saafdn.org or info@saafdn.org
Internet: www.saafdn.org/Nonprofits/Grants.aspx
Sponsor: San Antonio Area Foundation
303 Pearl Parkway, Suite 114
San Antonio, TX 78215

San Antonio Area Foundation Capital and Naming Rights Grants   2148
The San Antonio Area Foundation's Capital and Naming Rights Grant program provides funding support for local capital projects and significant naming rights opportunities in honor of the late John L. Santikos. Proposals should meet one or more of the following criteria: be new, unique and/or introduce national best practices in the San Antonio area; or demonstrate exceptional, potential impact measured by one or more of the following: number of people served, type and scope of impact it will foster, and opportunities for scalability. Primary interest areas include: people in need (individuals with mental and physical challenges, seniors, victims of child abuse, and victims of disasters); health (healthcare and wellness, and medical research seed funding); youth and education (college and university programs, Pre-K to 12, scholarships, and youth development); and arts and culture (arts education; libraries; museums; public parks, public radio, and public television). Application for funding will follow two steps: interested organizations should submit an online Letter of Inquiry (LOI), available beginning June 13, and due by midnight, July 22. Finalists will be invited to submit an online formal proposal on August 26, with a deadline of September 26.
Requirements: Requests to the John L. Santikos Charitable Foundation, a fund of the San Antonio Area Foundation, for capital support are limited to organizations that are: 501(c)3 charities, academic and public sector institutions; located in Atascosa, Bandera, Bexar, Comal, Guadalupe, Kendall, Medina and Wilson counties; and within the charitable interest areas set forth by Santikos. Proposals must present a significant naming rights opportunity and will be limited to requests for: renovation, restoration, construction, acquisition and expansion projects; or existing programs.
Restrictions: This program does not consider funding for endowments.
Geographic Focus: Texas
Date(s) Application is Due: Sep 26
Amount of Grant: Up to 1,000,000 USD
Samples: Clarity Child Guidance Center, San Antonio, Texas, $672,280 - renovation of a regional inpatient hospital facility treating children diagnosed with significant mental health needs; Haven for Hope, San Antonio, Texas, $1,000,000 - support of a new welcome center that coordinates homeless care services on the Haven for Hope campus; Hondo Public Library, Hondo, Texas, $125,000 - support for the library's Imagination Stations.
Contact: Michelle Lugalia-Hollon, Director, Program Initiatives; (210) 242-4775 or (210) 225-2243; mlugaliahollon@saafdn.org
Internet: www.saafdn.org/Nonprofits/Grants/CapitalNamingRights.aspx
Sponsor: San Antonio Area Foundation
303 Pearl Parkway, Suite 114
San Antonio, TX 78215

San Antonio Area Foundation High School Completion Grants   2149
The San Antonio Area Foundation's High School Completion Grant program supports out-of-school time programs that provide academic, recreational and cultural activities to keep youth in school. The program typically funds: 501(c)3 public charities in Bexar County that provide out-of-school-time (OST) activities for students in third through

ninth grades; organizations that provide evidence that students improve in the areas of school attendance, academic performance, and/or behavior; organizations that provide opportunities for students to engage in leadership activities and/or families to participate in the program; organizations that have a relationship with a public or charter school in Bexar County; and organizations that provide a letter of support signed by a teacher, counselor or administrator that refers to the project described in the application and describe its impact on students' school attendance, behavior in school and/or academic performance. The annual application deadline is March 10.
Requirements: Any 501(c)3 organization or school program that supports K-12 students in Bexar County, Texas, is eligible to apply.
Restrictions: The program does not fund: endowments; debt reduction; operating deficits; indirect costs; scholarships for colleges and universities; individuals; capital campaigns; or political activities, organizations, or lobbying efforts intended to influence legislation. Each organization may submit only one application per deadline.
Geographic Focus: Texas
Date(s) Application is Due: Mar 10
Contact: Gavin Nichols, Director; (210) 242-4720 or (210) 225-2243; gnichols@saafdn.org
Internet: www.saafdn.org/Nonprofits/Grants/HighSchoolCompletion.aspx
Sponsor: San Antonio Area Foundation
303 Pearl Parkway, Suite 114
San Antonio, TX 78215

San Antonio Area Foundation Special and Urgent Needs Funding Grants   2150
The San Antonio Area Foundation's Special and Urgent Needs Funding (SUNF) goal is to help an organization meet its mission while managing an unbudgeted, unforeseen, and time-sensitive emergency or help the organization take advantage of an unexpected opportunity that will enhance its work. The SUNF meets the need for a rapid funding response where the alternative traditional timeline would result in the loss of a critical safety net service or opportunity where other funding sources are not available. The SUN Fund provides one-time grants up to $20,000 to: respond to an urgent need that could not have been anticipated and for which there are no other sources of funding; or take advantage of an unforeseen opportunity. Although not limited to, preference is given to applications where the organization has made its own commitment to the project through an allocation of some of its funds. Applications for the SUNF are accepted and reviewed on an on-going basis. An approval or denial notification will be sent to grant applicant within six business days of submission.
Requirements: Grant funding is available to 501(c)3 nonprofit organizations in Bexar, Atascosa, Bandera, Comal, Guadalupe, Kendall, Medina and Wilson counties.
Restrictions: The Special and Urgent Needs Funding program does not make grants for: endowments; capital campaigns; religious purposes; individuals; debt reduction; indirect costs; scholarships for colleges, universities and trade schools; political activities, organizations, or lobbying efforts intended to influence legislation; non-emergency work that has already been completed; operating deficits or deficits due to gradual loss of funding, loss of government funding, or waiting for government reimbursement; startup program expenses; operating expenses for strategic planning, organizational development needs, or ongoing program work; or expenses that should have been anticipated or result from failure to exercise proper maintenance or duty of care.
Geographic Focus: Texas
Contact: Gavin Nichols; (210) 242-4720 or (210) 225-2243; gnichols@saafdn.org
Internet: www.saafdn.org/Nonprofits/Grants/SpecialandUrgentNeeds.aspx
Sponsor: San Antonio Area Foundation
303 Pearl Parkway, Suite 114
San Antonio, TX 78215

San Antonio Area Foundation Strengthening Nonprofits Grants   2151
The San Antonio Area Foundation's Strengthening Nonprofits Grant program helps to build the organizational capacity of nonprofit agencies and help them better fulfill their missions and serve their clients. Funding is available for: leadership training, coaching, professional/staff development; strategic planning, consulting services, and technology resources; peer learning; and learning communities. Nonprofit agencies should submit a Phase I grant to apply for funding to conduct the Core Capacity Assessment Tool (CCAT), an online assessment to identify the agency's strengths and opportunities for improvement. Phase I applications can be submitted any time throughout the year, with deadlines occurring at midnight Central time on the first business day of each month. Nonprofit agencies that conduct the CCAT from the Phase I grant will convene their Board of Directors and senior staff members to develop a plan for strengthening their agency that aligns with the assessment results, which forms the basis for the Phase II funding request. Phase II applications can be submitted from February 1 through May 8.
Requirements: Grant funding is available to 501(c)3 nonprofit organizations in Bexar, Atascosa, Bandera, Comal, Guadalupe, Kendall, Medina and Wilson counties.
Restrictions: Strengthening Nonprofits grants do not fund: current operating budgets; programs or direct service delivery; computer hardware; capital projects; endowments; debt reduction; operating deficits; indirect costs; programs for individual churches, parishes, or congregations that do not benefit the community-at-large; or political activities, organizations, or lobbying efforts intended to influence legislation.
Geographic Focus: Texas
Date(s) Application is Due: May 8
Contact: Sandie Palomo-Gonzalez, Director, Capacity Building; (210) 242-4730 or (210) 225-2243; spalomogonzalez@saafdn.org
Internet: www.saafdn.org/Nonprofits/Grants/StrengtheningNonprofits.aspx
Sponsor: San Antonio Area Foundation
303 Pearl Parkway, Suite 114
San Antonio, TX 78215

Sand Hill Foundation Environment and Sustainability Grants 2152
The Sand Hill Foundation funds organizations with strong leadership, visionary plans for the future, and cultures of continuous learning. The Foundation seeks to leverage every grant by providing funding at the right time for the greatest impact. In the area of Environment and Sustainability, the Foundation understands that ensuring a robust ecosystem requires a long-term view and sustained commitment to future generations. Its concentration areas include: conservation, with open space preservation and stewardship, as well as environmentally-sustainable business and farming practices; and environmental education, with local programs that offer in-depth learning and promote a lifetime of environmental stewardship, science-based educational opportunities that use environmental experiences or principles to contribute to California teaching standards, and opportunities for low-income students to learn and live outdoors. New organizations generally receive project support. Organizations that have received previous grants from the Sand Hill Foundation may also be eligible for capital, capacity building, and general operating support.
Requirements: The Foundation funding serves San Mateo and northern Santa Clara counties, from the Pacific Coast to the San Francisco Bay, and from Daly City to Mountain View. To be eligible for funding, an organization must be: a 501(c)3 tax-exempt organization and work within the Foundation's geographic and programmatic focus areas.
Geographic Focus: California
Amount of Grant: Up to 100,000 USD
Samples: Alliance for Climate Education, Oakland, California, $20,000 - support for climate science education and youth leadership development; Education Outside, San Francisco, California, $15,000 - support of the Redwood City expansion; Filoli, Woodside, California, $3,000 - general operating support.
Contact: Jamie Heisch; (650) 854-9310; fax (650) 854-8031; jheisch@pfs-llc.net
Internet: www.sandhillfoundation.org/focus_area/environmental-sustainability/
Sponsor: Sand Hill Foundation
3000 Sand Hill Road, 4-120
Menlo Park, CA 94025

Sand Hill Foundation Health and Opportunity Grants 2153
The Sand Hill Foundation funds organizations with strong leadership, visionary plans for the future, and cultures of continuous learning. The Foundation seeks to leverage every grant by providing funding at the right time for the greatest impact. In the area of Health and Opportunity, the Foundation funds organizations offering programs and services that provide pathways for low-income families and youth to stabilize, grow and thrive. Its concentration areas include: health; economic opportunity; and educational opportunity. Proposals in the focus area of Health and Opportunity are accepted at any time and have no proposal deadlines. New organizations generally receive project support. Organizations that have received previous grants from the Sand Hill Foundation may also be eligible for capital, capacity building, and general operating support.
Requirements: The Foundation funding serves San Mateo and northern Santa Clara counties, from the Pacific Coast to the San Francisco Bay, and from Daly City to Mountain View. To be eligible for funding, an organization must be: a 501(c)3 tax-exempt organization and work within the Foundation's geographic and programmatic focus areas.
Geographic Focus: California
Amount of Grant: 5,000 - 300,000 USD
Samples: Adolescent Counseling Services, Redwood, California, $20,000 - support of the on-campus counseling program; Bay Area Cancer Connections, Palo Alto, California, $5,000 - general operating support; Children's Health Council, Palo Alto, California, $300,000 (three years) - support for the Teen Mental Health initiative.
Contact: Jamie Heisch; (650) 854-9310; fax (650) 854-8031; jheisch@pfs-llc.net
Internet: www.sandhillfoundation.org/focus_area/health-opportunity/
Sponsor: Sand Hill Foundation
3000 Sand Hill Road, 4-120
Menlo Park, CA 94025

Sand Hill Foundation Small Capital Needs Grants 2154
The Sand Hill Foundation funds organizations with strong leadership, visionary plans for the future, and cultures of continuous learning. The Foundation understands that there are times when one-time expenditures are necessary that fall outside the annual budget. With that in mind, the Foundation offers grants of up to $35,000 for capital costs that will meet an urgent need or funding to strengthen an organization. Proposals in the focus area of Small Capital Needs have two submission cycles; from March 1 to March 31; and from August 1 to August 31. Organizations that have received previous grants from the Sand Hill Foundation may also be eligible for capacity building and general operating support.
Requirements: The Foundation funding serves San Mateo and northern Santa Clara counties, from the Pacific Coast to the San Francisco Bay, and from Daly City to Mountain View. To be eligible for funding, an organization must be: a 501(c)3 tax-exempt organization and work within the Foundation's geographic and programmatic focus areas.
Geographic Focus: California
Date(s) Application is Due: Mar 31; Aug 31
Amount of Grant: Up to 100,000 USD
Samples: Health Connected, Redwood City, California, $30,000 - support of office infrastructure and capital improvements; JobTrain, Menlo Park, California, $30,000 - support of technology and equipment; Marine Science Institute, Redwood City, California, $35,000 - support of dock reinforcement.
Contact: Jamie Heisch; (650) 854-9310; fax (650) 854-8031; jheisch@pfs-llc.net
Internet: www.sandhillfoundation.org/focus_area/capital-needs/
Sponsor: Sand Hill Foundation
3000 Sand Hill Road, 4-120
Menlo Park, CA 94025

SanDisk Corporation Community Sharing Grants 2155
Since being established in May 2003, the SanDisk Corporate Fund has linked SanDisk's corporate giving program with the Silicon Valley Community Foundation (SVCF), a non-profit organization that specializes in philanthropic and charitable giving programs. This is just one way that SanDisk shares its financial success, and growing resources, with the communities served by their employees. SanDisk is committed to being an asset in the communities where their employees live and work. The Community Sharing Committee acts as a facilitator to carry out this vision by making donations to non-profit organizations, foundations, and community groups. To maximize the results of their efforts, SanDisk focus on programs that support individuals and families, education in engineering and computer science, youth development, and community enrichment through the arts. The above areas are the Community Sharing Committee's primary focus, however, the committee will also consider applications that fall under the following focus areas: environmental; animal rescue needs; disaster recovery efforts.
Geographic Focus: All States
Date(s) Application is Due: Jan 1; Apr 1; Jul 1; Oct 1
Contact: Corporate Office; (408) 801-1000 or (866) 726-3475; fax (408) 801-8657
Internet: www.sandisk.com/about/corp-responsibility/community-engagement
Sponsor: SanDisk Corporation
601 McCarthy Boulevard
Milpitas, CA 95035

Sands Cares Grants 2156
The Venetian Foundation was formed on December 7, 2000, by the Venetian Casino Resort. Today, the Las Vegas Sands Corporation's primary philanthropic initiative is pursued through Sands Corporation. Sands pursues a mission of supporting charitable organizations and endeavors that concentrate on assisting youth, promoting health, and expanding educational opportunities within the local communities. The Corporation also supports causes that empower minority communities and improve underprivileged areas, as well as other valuable charitable and philanthropic activities permitted under relevant tax-exempt laws. Sands pursues a mission of supporting charitable organizations and endeavors that concentrate on assisting youth, promoting health, and expanding educational opportunities within our local communities. The Corporation also supports causes that empower minority communities and improve underprivileged areas, as well as other valuable charitable and philanthropic activities permitted under relevant tax-exempt laws. Charitable requests along with supporting documents may either be faxed or mailed.
Requirements: All charitable requests must be submitted in writing. Written requests should include the following: agency/organization information (brochures, information packet, list of the board of directors, history, background, or other helpful information); 501(c)3 tax identification number; contact person; mailing address and telephone number; overview of project or event at hand; date, time, location for event requests; purpose of request; very specific information about the amount/item(s) requested; and target population which will benefit from support.
Geographic Focus: Nevada, Pennsylvania, Macau, Singapore
Amount of Grant: 5,000 - 100,000 USD
Contact: Corporate Citizenship Department; (702) 607-1677; fax (702) 607-1044; foundation@venetian.com
Internet: www.sands.com/sands-cares/our-commitment.html
Sponsor: Sands Corporation
3355 Las Vegas Boulevard South
Las Vegas, NV 89109-8941

Sandy Hill Foundation Grants 2157
The Sandy Hill Foundation offers grants to eligible nonprofit organizations in the areas of education, health care, and social services. The Foundation gives primarily to the arts and culture, higher education, hospitals, health associations, social services, and federated giving programs. Their areas of interest include: the arts; child and youth services; community and economic development; health organizations and associations; higher education; hospitals; human services; Protestant agencies and churches; recreation camps; and United Way and Federated Giving Programs. It also offers college scholarships for designated local area schools.
Requirements: There is no application or specific deadline for nonprofit giving. See contact information for current scholarship application due April 1.
Restrictions: The foundation gives primarily to the greater Hudson Falls, NY area. No grants are given to individuals.
Geographic Focus: New York
Amount of Grant: Up to USD
Contact: Nancy Juckett Brown, Trustee; (518) 791-3490; administrator@sandyhillfoundation.org or njbrown@sandyhillfoundation.org
Internet: www.sandyhillfoundation.org/
Sponsor: Sandy Hill Foundation
P.O. Box 399
Gilbertsville, PA 19525-0399

San Juan Island Community Foundation Grants 2158
The foundation's mission is to enhance the quality of life on San Juan Island and make a positive difference in the community. The foundation awards grants to tax-exempt organizations in its areas of interest, including arts and culture, health and wellness, local economy, community infrastructure, environment, education, and basic social needs.
Requirements: The Foundation only gives grants to tax-exempt organizations which include 501(c)3's, local non-profit branches of 501(c)1's, government agencies, non-profit schools and religious organizations (but only for non-religious purposes). Faith-based organizations are eligible but only for non-religious and unrestricted public service projects. Foundation

grants, by policy, are targeted to the local community and would usually only be given to an outside nonprofit for work that affected the local community. A meeting with Foundation representatives is required before a grant application is submitted. Call the office to request a "pre-grant application 1-on-1 meeting". Partner funding will be a critical component of each required, pre-submission meeting including careful identification of the resources that will be allocated by the applying organization itself. The required grant application can be downloaded from the website or requested by phone. Applications may be submitted at anytime following the required online registration and the pre-submission 1:1 meeting with Foundation representatives.
Restrictions: Grants do not support religious organizations where the funds would be used to further the organization's religious purposes; individuals; other endowments; political purposes; or any purpose that discriminates as to race, creed, ethnic group, or gender.
Geographic Focus: Washington
Date(s) Application is Due: Apr 28; Jul 22; Oct 27; Dec 30
Amount of Grant: 500 USD
Contact: Jeanne Peihl, Grants & Scholarships Coordinator; (360) 378-1001; info@sjicf.org
Internet: sjicf.org/for-nonprofits/
Sponsor: San Juan Island Community Foundation
P.O. Box 1352
Friday Harbor, WA 98250

Santa Fe Community Foundation Seasonal Grants-Fall Cycle 2159

Through its outreach to nonprofits, donors and community leaders, the Foundation organizes its annual grants cycle into a two-season grants program. Each season (Spring and Fall) focuses on its own specific goals and strategies. The Foundation is devoted to building healthy and vital communities in the region where: racial, cultural or economic differences do not limit access to health, education or employment; diverse audiences enjoy the many arts and cultural heritages of our region; and, all sectors of its community take responsibility for ensuring a healthy environment. The areas of interest for the Fall Cycle are Arts, Animal Welfare, and Health and Human Services. For Arts proposals, projects should: increase public engagement in the arts; and, support public policy, community organizing or public information to strengthen the arts segment of the creative economy locally. For Health and Human Services proposals, projects should: improve the health of underserved residents of the Santa Fe region; improve access to affordable healthy food; strengthen the delivery of homelessness services; improve safety for children, women, families, sexual minorities and the elderly; and/or, support public policy, civic engagement, community organizing or public information to improve the health and well-being of local residents. For Animal Welfare proposals, the Foundation has approximately $25,000 available for animal welfare-related grants, and will include summaries of all animal welfare proposals (that meet basic due diligence) in the 'Giving Together' catalogue that accompanies the Fall Community Grant Cycle. The Giving Together catalogue is then shared with the Foundation's fundholders who are invited to make grants toward any proposal in the catalogue.
Requirements: Applications will be accepted from organizations that: are located in or serve the people of Santa Fe, Rio Arriba, Taos, Los Alamos, San Miguel or Mora Counties; are tax-exempt under Section 501(c)3 of the Internal Revenue Code or are a public or governmental agency or a federally recognized tribe in the state of New Mexico, or that have a fiscal sponsor; employ staff and provide services without discrimination on the basis of race, religion, sex, age, national origin, disability, or sexual orientation; and, are at least three years old. Each nonprofit entity may only apply for funding once per year. All grants will be $5,000, $10,000 or $15,000, depending on your annual budget. For organizations whose annual budget is under $150,000, you may apply for a $5,000 grant; for organizations whose annual budget is between $150,000 and $500,000, you may apply for a $10,000 grant; for organizations with an annual budget over $500,000, you may apply for a $15,000 grant. Grant applications will be accepted online only. Applications must be received by 5:00 pm of the deadline date.
Restrictions: The foundation does not award grants for religious purposes, capital campaigns or endowments, scholarships, or individuals. Organizations that received a community grant from SFCF in the last calendar year are not eligible to apply for a community grant in the current calendar year.
Geographic Focus: New Mexico
Date(s) Application is Due: Aug 26
Amount of Grant: 5,000 - 15,000 USD
Contact: Christa Coggins; (505) 988-9715 x 7002; ccoggins@santafecf.org
Diane Hamamoto, Executive Assistant and Community Philanthropy Associate; (505) 988-9715 x 7008; dhamamoto@santafecf.org
Internet: www.santafecf.org/nonprofits/grantseekers/general-grant-information
Sponsor: Santa Fe Community Foundation
501 Halona Street
Santa Fe, NM 87505

Sapelo Foundation Social Justice Grants 2160

The Sapelo Foundation is a private family foundation focusing its funding within the State of Georgia. The Foundation is particularly interested in projects that involve multiple groups that work cooperatively toward common goals, accomplish systemic reform, and have a statewide impact. In addition, the Foundation gives special attention to low-resource regions in the state and innovative, community-based projects within the Foundation's focus areas. The Foundation believes that the development of sound public policy is crucial to effective government and the empowerment of the citizenry. Therefore, it is the aim of the Foundation to strengthen representative democracy in Georgia through efforts that educate the public about government institutions and policies, promote civic engagement and responsibility, and monitor government performance. Currently, the Foundation's primary focus is a strategic campaign advocating for fairness for children in the state's

justice system. Grants range from $1,000 to $60,000, and the average award is between $5,000 and $25,000.
Requirements: Georgia 501(c)3 nonprofit organizations are eligible.
Restrictions: The Foundation does not give priority to: academic research; local government entities; human services programs; criminal justice programs designed to rehabilitate and/or punish individuals; senior citizen's programs; after-school mentoring/tutoring programs; single-site day care facilities; homeless shelters or programs; affordable housing; or programs serving the physically or developmentally disabled. The Foundation does not support projects operating solely within the Metro Atlanta Area. The Foundation does not fund the following: brick-and-mortar, building projects or renovations, including construction materials and labor costs; endowment funds; fraternal groups or civic clubs; health care initiatives or medical research; individuals; national or regional organizations, unless their programs specifically benefit Georgia and all funds are spent within the state; organizations that are not tax-exempt; or payment of debts.
Geographic Focus: Georgia
Date(s) Application is Due: Mar 1; Sep 1
Amount of Grant: 1,000 - 60,000 USD
Contact: Phyllis Bowen, Executive Director; (912) 265-0520; fax (912) 254-1888; info@sapelofoundation.org or sapelofoundation@mindspring.com
Internet: www.sapelofoundation.org/index.html
Sponsor: Sapelo Foundation
1712 Ellis Street, 2nd Floor
Brunswick, GA 31520

Sara Elizabeth O'Brien Trust Grants 2161

The Sara Elizabeth O'Brien Trust was established in 1981 to support charitable organizations that provide treatment or care to those who are blind or have cancer. The O'Brien Trust also supports Medical Research in the areas of blindness or cancer. The O'Brien Trust funds in 2 primary areas: Direct Service and Medical Research. The proposal process and deadlines differ accordingly. For Direct Service, the O'Brien Trust supports organizations in Massachusetts in the area of health and human services to provide treatment, care, training and/or rehabilitation to individuals living with blindness or who have cancer. Grant requests for general operating support are considered as well as program requests. Program-related capital expenses may be included in general operating or program requests. For Medical Research, the O'Brien Trust's grant review process for Medical Research is administered by The Medical Foundation, a division of Health Resources in Action (HRiA). More information on this section of the grant can be found on the HRiA website. Award amounts typically go up to $80,000.
Requirements: Applicants must have 501(c)3 tax-exempt status and support organizations in Massachusetts. Applications will be submitted online through the Bank of America website. A grant report is required within 1 year of the grant application date, regardless of whether all of the funds have been spent.
Restrictions: The trust does not support requests from individuals, organizations attempting to influence policy through direct lobbying, or any political campaigns.
Geographic Focus: Massachusetts
Date(s) Application is Due: May 1
Amount of Grant: Up to 80,000 USD
Samples: Boston Medical Center, Boston, Massachusetts, $53,200 - Awarded for medical research fellowship (2018); Partners Healthcare System Inc., Somerville, Massachusetts, $51,250 - Awarded for medical research fellowship (2018); Joslin Diabetes Center, Boston, Massachusetts, $51,250 - Awarded for medical research fellowship (2018).
Contact: Michealle Larkins, Philanthropic Administrator; (866) 778-6859; ma.grantmaking@bankofamerica.com or ma.grantmaking@ustrust.com
Internet: www.bankofamerica.com/philanthropic/foundation/?fnId=39
Sponsor: Sara Elizabeth O'Brien Trust
P.O. Box 1802
Providence, RI 02110-1802

Sarah G. McCarthy Memorial Foundation 2162

The Sarah G. McCarthy Memorial Foundation was established in 1948 in memory of the donor's mother. The foundation considers requests from charitable organizations located in Peabody, Massachusetts or whose work directly impacts the residents of Peabody. The trustees are specifically interested in the areas of education, housing and shelter, agriculture, food, health and historical research. Grants are made year to year with a five-year maximum. Exceptions will only be made upon demonstrated need. Grants range from $2,000 to $15,000 based on how well the proposed use meets a given need, collaborative effort is evidenced, and the number of persons impacted is quantifiable. Applications are accepted twice annually, with decisions being made at biannual board meetings.
Requirements: Requests for general operating and program support will be considered, as will requests for specific program-enabling capital improvements. Grants may be subject to matching obligations and payable over multiple years. On very rare occasions, the trustees will consider needs for emergency grants. Site visits may be conducted prior to decision making meetings. Prior grantees must submit a one-page expenditure report prior to any subsequent grant being considered. Applications will be submitted online through the Bank of America website. A grant report is required within 1 year of the grant application date, regardless of whether all of the funds have been spent.
Restrictions: The foundation does not support requests from individuals, organizations attempting to influence policy through direct lobbying, or any political campaigns.
Geographic Focus: Massachusetts
Date(s) Application is Due: Mar 31; Sep 30
Amount of Grant: 2,000 - 15,000 USD
Samples: Citizens Inn, Peabody, Massachusetts, $10,000 - Awarded for No Child Goes Hungry in Peabody/Summer Lunch program (2018); Leap for Education Inc., Salem,

Massachusetts, $5,000 - Awarded for College Success program (CSP) in Peabody (2018); Science from Scientists Inc., Bedford, Massachusetts, $5,000 - Awarded for In-School Module-Based STEM Enrichment program for Thomas Carroll Elementary School (2018).
Contact: Michealle Larkins, Philanthropic Administrator; (866) 778-6859; ma.grantmaking@bankofamerica.com or ma.grantmaking@ustrust.com
Internet: www.bankofamerica.com/philanthropic/foundation/?fnId=140
Sponsor: Sarah G. McCarthy Memorial Foundation
P.O. Box 1802
Providence, RI 02901-1802

Sarkeys Foundation Grants   2163
Governed by a dedicated Board of Trustees, the foundation that bears SJ Sarkeys' name is deeply committed to furthering his vision to improve the quality of life in Oklahoma. The Foundation provides grants to a diverse group of nonprofit organizations and institutions, almost all of which are located in Oklahoma. Major areas of foundation support include education, arts and cultural endeavors, scientific research, animal welfare, social service and human service needs, and cultural and humanitarian programs of regional significance. Grant proposals are considered at the April and October meetings of the board of trustees.
Requirements: Most organizations classified by the IRS as being a 501(c)3 that is not a private foundation and is headquartered and offering services in Oklahoma may apply. Preference is given to organizations that have been in operation at least 3 years. Organizations are required to submit a Letter of Inquiry to determine whether they meet the criteria and priorities for funding. Representatives are encouraged to speak with a program officer for more information and to ask any questions about the process. An organization may submit one request in a twelve month period.
Restrictions: The Sarkeys Foundation will not fund: local programs appropriately financed within the community; direct mail solicitations and annual campaigns; out of state institutions; hospitals; operating expenses; purchase of vehicles; grants to individuals; responsibility for permanent financing of a program; programs whose ultimate intent is to be profit making; start-up funding for new organizations; feasibility studies; grants which trigger expenditure responsibility by Sarkeys Foundation; direct support to government agencies; individual public or private elementary or secondary schools, unless they are serving the needs of a special population which are not being met elsewhere; and religious institutions and their subsidiaries.
Geographic Focus: Oklahoma
Date(s) Application is Due: Feb 3; Aug 1
Amount of Grant: Up to 50,000 USD
Contact: Susan Frantz; (405) 364-3703; susan@sarkeys.org or sarkeys@sarkeys.org
Linda English Weeks; (405) 364-3703; linda@sarkeys.org or sarkeys@sarkeys.org
Internet: www.sarkeys.org/grant_guidelines.html
Sponsor: Sarkeys Foundation
530 East Main Street
Norman, OK 73071

Sartain Lanier Family Foundation Grants   2164
The Sartain Lanier Family Foundation awards grants to Georgia nonprofits in support of education, health and human services, arts, environment, and community development, with the majority of new grantmaking in the area of education. Types of support include building and renovation; capital campaigns; endowments; general operating support; program development; and program-related investments and loans. The foundation's board meets in May and December of each year to consider grant requests, which will be by invitation only. Interested applicants should provide an organizational overview for consideration purposes. Prior to submitting a full proposal, interested parties should submit a letter limited to two pages summarizing the request. The letter should include a brief description of the organization and its purpose, the project for which funding is requested, the total cost of the project, and the amount being requested.
Requirements: Nonprofit organizations in the southeastern United States are eligible to apply if invited to do so; however, the majority of recipients are located in Georgia and specifically the Atlanta metro area.
Restrictions: The foundation does not make grants for individuals; churches or religious organizations for projects that primarily benefit their own members; partisan political purposes; tickets to charitable events or dinners, or to sponsor special events or fundraisers.
Geographic Focus: Georgia
Amount of Grant: 5,000 - 1,000,000 USD
Samples: Emery University, Atlanta, Georgia, $250,000 - general operating support; Vanderbilt University, Nashville, Tennessee, $1,024,250 - general operating support; East Lake Foundation, Atlanta, Georgia, $60,000 - general operating support.
Contact: Patricia E. Lummus, Executive Director; (404) 564-1259; fax (404) 564-1251; plummus@lanierfamilyfoundation.org
Internet: www.lanierfamilyfoundation.org/funding-priorities/
Sponsor: Sartain Lanier Family Foundation
25 Puritan Mill, 950 Lowery Boulevard NW
Atlanta, GA 30318

SAS Institute Community Relations Donations   2165
SAS (pronounced "sass") once stood for "statistical analysis system," and began at North Carolina State University as a project to analyze agricultural research. As demand for such software grew, SAS was founded in 1976 to help all sorts of customers - from pharmaceutical companies and banks to academic and governmental entities. Coming from such beginnings, SAS is committed to corporate citizenship and supports the community through a generous financial program, in-kind giving, and employee volunteerism. SAS's donations program focuses primarily on strategic educational initiatives in the geographic area surrounding SAS world headquarters in Cary, South Carolina, that increase interest

and achievement in the science, technology, engineering, and math (STEM) disciplines. In particular, SAS supports programs that focus on the integration of technology with teaching and learning in ways that will strengthen the education system and increase the number of students entering STEM careers. Programs must also show that their efforts have a long-term impact and affect significant numbers of people, without discrimination. Acting on the philosophy of reduce-reuse-recycle, SAS donates surplus computer hardware, office equipment, and other tangible items to organizations that can benefit from the donation. Priority goes to schools, other educational organizations, and organizations with which SAS employees are personally involved. SAS also offers several products and services at no cost to K-12 schools as well as to colleges and universities. Application guidelines and an interactive application form for SAS's donation program are available at the company website. To apply, applicants must complete and print the form and mail it (along with any required supporting documentation) to the address given.
Requirements: Eligible organizations must meet the following criteria: have 501(3)c status with the IRS; have a responsible board of directors serving without compensation; show financial stability as evidenced by annual financial statements; employ ethical methods of publicity, promotion, and solicitation of funds; raise funds without payment of commissions, street solicitations or mailing of unordered tickets; operate from a detailed annual budget; request funds for programs or operations with a minimal portion applied to overhead; and use SAS in-kind donations to benefit organizational members or constituents.
Restrictions: The following programs and activities are not funded: sponsorship of professional athletic or amateur sports teams or individuals; single events such as walk-a-thons, fundraisers, workshops, seminars, etc; religious causes; political parties, candidates or issues; organizations that are in any way exclusive; trips and tours; independent film/video productions; and requests from individuals.
Geographic Focus: North Carolina
Samples: Wake County Public School System; Triangle High Five Partnership; North Carolina State University.
Contact: George Farthing, (919) 677-8000; CommunityRelations@sas.com
Internet: www.sas.com/company/csr/education.html#s1=4
Sponsor: SAS Institute
100 SAS Campus Drive
Cary, NC 27513-2414

Scheumann Foundation Grants   2166
Established in Indiana in 2002, the Scheumann Foundation offers grants in support of youth services, recreation, camps, and housing development within the State of Indiana. There are no specific application forms or annual deadlines. With that in mind, applicants should forward a two- to three-page letter of application outlining their program and budgetary needs. Most recent awards have ranged from $500 to $400,000.
Requirements: Giving is restricted to non-profit programs serving youth and families within Indiana.
Geographic Focus: Indiana
Amount of Grant: 500 - 400,000 USD
Samples: Ball State University, Muncie, Indiana, $400,000 - for football stadium fund; Purdue University Foundation, West Lafayette, Indiana, $50,000 - youth sports fund; CSPM Tecumseh YMCA, Brookston, Indiana, $25,000 - general operating fund.
Contact: John B. Scheumann, President; (765) 742-0300
Sponsor: Scheumann Foundation
P.O. Box 811
Lafayette, IN 47902-0811

Schlessman Family Foundation Grants   2167
The foundation awards grants to Colorado nonprofits in its areas of interest: education, disadvantaged youth programs and services, elderly/senior programs, special needs groups, and established cultural institutions (such as museums, libraries and zoos). Performing arts grants are available but are very limited.
Requirements: Grants are limited to Colorado charities, primarily greater metro-Denver organizations. The Foundation accepts, but does not require, the Colorado Common Grant Application. All requests must be in writing and discourages lengthy proposals with multiple attachments. If additional information is required, you will be contacted. Proposals are accepted throughout the year, however they must be postmarked on or before the deadline date if they are to be considered in time for the once-a-year distributions on March 31.
Restrictions: The following are ineligible: individuals, start-ups, support for benefits or conferences, public/private/charter schools.
Geographic Focus: Colorado
Date(s) Application is Due: Dec 31
Contact: Patricia Middendorf, (303) 831-5683; contact@schlessmanfoundation.org
Internet: www.schlessmanfoundation.org
Sponsor: Schlessman Family Foundation
1555 Blake Street, Suite 400
Denver, CO 80202

Schramm Foundation Grants   2168
The foundation awards grants to Colorado nonprofit organizations in its areas of interest, including arts and culture, civic affairs, community development, education (elementary, secondary, and higher), health care, housing, humanities, medical research, science, social services delivery, technology, women's issues, and youth. Types of support include building construction/renovation, continuing support, equipment acquisition, general operating support, matching/challenge grants, program development, and scholarship funds. Applications are accepted from July 1 through August 31 (postmarked).

Requirements: Colorado 501(c)3 nonprofit organizations are eligible. Preference is given to requests from the Denver area. Applications must clearly express the reason(s) for the request, attach financial statements and copy of exemption letter.

Restrictions: Grants do not support advertising, advocacy organizations, individuals, international organizations, political organizations, religious organizations, school districts, special events, or veterans organizations.

Geographic Focus: Colorado
Date(s) Application is Due: Aug 31
Amount of Grant: 500 USD
Contact: Gary Kring, President; (303) 861-8291
Sponsor: Schramm Foundation
800 Grant Street, Suite 330
Denver, CO 80203-2944

Scott B. and Annie P. Appleby Charitable Trust Grants 2169

The trust supports programs and projects of nonprofit organizations in the categories of higher education, cultural programs, and child welfare. Types of support include general operating support, continuing support, capital campaigns, building construction and renovation, research, and scholarship funds. An application form is required, although there are no specified deadlines. Most recent awards have ranged from $1,000 to $100,000.

Requirements: The foundation awards grants to nonprofit organizations in the United States. There are no deadlines. Interested applicants are encouraged to submit a letter describing the intent and purpose of the organization with a specific proposal for allocation of funds.

Geographic Focus: All States
Amount of Grant: 1,000 - 100,000 USD
Samples: Asheville Art Museum, Asheville, North Carolina, $100,000 - general operations; Medical Foundation of North Carolina, Chapel Hill, North Carolina, $25,000 - general operations; Regents of the University of California, Oakland, California, $40,000 - general operations.
Contact: Benjamin N. Colby, Co-Trustee; (941) 329-2628; bncolby@uci.edu
Sponsor: Scott B. and Annie P. Appleby Charitable Trust
c/o The Northern Trust Company
Sarasota, FL 34236

Scott County Community Foundation Grants 2170

The purpose of the Scott County Community Foundation is to improve the quality of life of the residents of Scott County, Indiana. Grant funding will focus on the encouragement of programs that enhance cooperating and collaboration among institutions within the Scott County community. Funding focuses on effectiveness of special non-recurring projects which enrich health, education, cultural or recreational situations in Scott County. Specific areas of interest include community service; social service; education; the arts; environment; and entrepreneurship. Special consideration is given to agencies who partner with other organizations to complete a unified project. Funding will seek to offer leverage funds through the use of seed money, match and challenge grants. Applications are typically accepted in the spring and recipients announced during the summer. The application and additional guidelines are available at the Foundation website.

Restrictions: The Foundation does not typically fund: on going operational expenses; existing obligations; services primarily supported by tax dollars or responsibility of a public agency; individuals or travel expenses; multi-year grants or repeat funding; advocacy or political purposes; religious or sectarian purposes; and loans or endowments.

Geographic Focus: Indiana
Contact: Jaime Toppe; (812) 752-2057; fax (812) 752-9257; info@scottcountyfoundation.org
Internet: www.scottcountyfoundation.org/grants.htm
Sponsor: Scott County Community Foundation
60 North Main Street, P.O. Box 25
Scottsburg, IN 47170

Screen Actors Guild Foundation BookPALS Assistance 2171

Founded in 1993 by actress Barbara Bain, the BookPALS (Performing Artists for Literacy in Schools) program does is a signature children's literacy program of the SAG Foundation designed to provide an opportunity for performers, gifted in the art of storytelling, to help develop a love of reading in children and give back to their local communities. Though the program does not award monetary grants, it offers an all-volunteer team consisting exclusively of professional actors - SAG, AFTRA, and EQUITY members - who read aloud to children at public elementary schools in at-risk neighborhoods, helping introduce them to the world of reading and literacy.

Requirements: Public elementary schools in at-risk neighborhoods in the following cities/states are eligible to apply: Arizona, Atlanta, Boston, Coachella Valley, Florida, Las Vegas, Los Angeles, Minnesota, New York, San Francisco, Washington D.C., Baltimore. To request a BookPAL for your school or classroom, submit the online form at the sponsor's website. The form can also be printed and completed offline to be submitted by mail or fax.

Geographic Focus: Arizona, California, District of Columbia, Florida, Georgia, Maryland, Massachusetts, Minnesota, Nevada, New York
Contact: Robin Roy, National Director of Literacy Programs; (323) 684-8606; rroy@bookpals.net
Internet: sagfoundation.org/childrens-literacy/about/
Sponsor: Screen Actors Guild Foundation
5757 Wilshire Boulevard, Suite 124
Los Angeles, CA 90036

Screen Actors Guild Foundation PencilPALS Assistance 2172

PencilPALS (Performing Artists for Literacy in Schools) is a program of the SAG Foundation designed to make reading and writing a first-person experience for children in elementary and middle schools. Students are paired with volunteer adult PencilPALS with whom they share their thoughts and daily experiences by writing letters, cards, notes, poems, and books. PencilPALS write back and before long, inter-generational relationships prosper between the children and their PencilPALS. As a result of the program, writing and spelling skills are greatly improved, and test scores increase markedly in these areas. Reading skills are also strengthened, as children are eager to read letters from their PencilPALS to one another and to the class. Sharing their letters and stories affords each child a sense of pride in his or her own writing.

Requirements: Public elementary schools in at-risk neighborhoods in the following cities/states are eligible to apply: Arizona, Atlanta, Boston, Coachella Valley, Florida, Las Vegas, Los Angeles, Minnesota, New York, San Francisco, Washington D.C., Baltimore. To request a PencilPAL for your school or classroom, submit the online form at the sponsor's website. The form can also be printed and completed offline to be submitted by mail or fax.

Geographic Focus: Arizona, California, District of Columbia, Florida, Georgia, Maryland, Massachusetts, Minnesota, Nevada, New York
Contact: Robin Roy, National Director of Literacy Programs; (323) 684-8606; rroy@bookpals.net
Internet: sagfoundation.org/childrens-literacy/bookpals/pencilpals/
Sponsor: Screen Actors Guild Foundation
5757 Wilshire Boulevard, Suite 124
Los Angeles, CA 90036

Screen Actors Guild Foundation StagePALS Assistance 2173

StagePALS (Performing Artists for Literacy in Schools) is the newest literacy outreach program created by the SAG Foundation. SAG-AFTRA performers share their skills and talent with students in at-risk middle schools that are no longer able to offer arts programs due to budget cuts. Over the course of 10 weeks a professional teaching artist visits each classroom twice each week and provides warm-up exercises, speech instruction, writing practices and prompts, and rehearsal. The teaching artist works with the classroom teacher to choose an appropriate unit of study around which the writing is focused. Not only do the classroom teachers guide the writing, they also actively participate in the theater exercises with their students. Professional actors come in as volunteers for one session to help with the monologue writing and for one session to coach the students' acting.

Requirements: Public elementary schools in at-risk neighborhoods in the following cities/states are eligible to apply: Arizona, Atlanta, Boston, Coachella Valley, Florida, Las Vegas, Los Angeles, Minnesota, New York, San Francisco, Washington D.C., Baltimore. To request a StagePAL for your school or classroom, submit the online form at the sponsor's website. The form can also be printed and completed offline to be submitted by mail or fax.

Geographic Focus: Arizona, California, District of Columbia, Florida, Georgia, Maryland, Massachusetts, Minnesota, New York
Contact: Robin Roy, National Director of Literacy Programs; (323) 684-8606; rroy@bookpals.net
Internet: sagfoundation.org/childrens-literacy/bookpals/stagepals/
Sponsor: Screen Actors Guild Foundation
5757 Wilshire Boulevard, Suite 124
Los Angeles, CA 90036

Seattle Foundation Arts and Culture Grants 2174

The Seattle Foundation believes that the arts play a crucial role in the health of the community. The Foundation awards grants to nonprofits in all fields that improve the quality of life for King County residents, and is currently looking to fund organizations working to make significant progress towards the following three arts and culture strategies: broaden community engagement in the arts; support a continuum of arts education for students; and preserve and fully utilize arts space. The Foundation awards grants to provide general support to organizations. The next deadline for Arts and Culture is February 1.

Requirements: To qualify for a grant from the Foundation's Grantmaking program, an organization must: be a 501(c)3 tax-exempt nonprofit organization; serve residents of King County, Washington; and provide programming in arts and culture that aligns with one of the Foundation's three strategies.

Restrictions: Grants are not made to individuals or to religious organizations for religious purposes. Grants will not be awarded for: endowment; funding of conferences or seminars; operating expenses for public or private elementary and secondary schools, colleges and universities; fundraising events such as walk-a-thons, tournaments, auctions and general fundraising solicitations; or the production of books, films, or videos.

Geographic Focus: Washington
Date(s) Application is Due: Feb 1
Contact: Ceil Erickson, Grantmaking Director; (206) 515-2131 or (206) 515-2109; fax (206) 622-7673; grantmaking@seattlefoundation.org or c.erickson@seattlefoundation.org
Internet: www.seattlefoundation.org/nonprofits/grantmaking/artsandculture/Pages/GrantmakingforArtsCulture.aspx
Sponsor: Seattle Foundation
1200 Fifth Avenue, Suite 1300
Seattle, WA 98101-3151

Seattle Foundation Basic Needs Grants 2175

The Seattle Foundation is committed to providing the most vulnerable people in the region with tools to strengthen their economic resilience. Foundation work focuses on ensuring that no one falls between the cracks by supporting organizations that prevent homelessness, ensure the availability of affordable housing, and make sure that everyone has access to nutritious food. Its goals are to: support efforts to provide nutritious food and increase healthier options for vulnerable populations year-round; provide support services to get people back into housing; and support people who are struggling to stay housed. The next deadline for Basic Needs is September 1.

Requirements: To qualify for a grant from the Foundation's Grantmaking program, an organization must: be a 501(c)3 tax-exempt nonprofit organization; serve residents of King County, Washington; and provide programming in basic needs that aligns with one of the Foundation's three strategies.

Restrictions: Capital campaign funding requests are considered a low priority. Organizations that have less than a three-year operating history after receiving its 501(c)3 classification are considered a low priority. Multi-year grants are not considered.

Geographic Focus: Washington
Date(s) Application is Due: Sep 1
Amount of Grant: 15,000 - 50,000 USD
Contact: Ceil Erickson, Grantmaking Director; (206) 515-2131 or (206) 515-2109; grantmaking@seattlefoundation.org or c.erickson@seattlefoundation.org
Internet: www.seattlefoundation.org/nonprofits/grantmaking/basicneeds/Pages/GrantsforBasicNeeds.aspx
Sponsor: Seattle Foundation
1200 Fifth Avenue, Suite 1300
Seattle, WA 98101-3151

Seattle Foundation Benjamin N. Phillips Memorial Fund Grants   2176
The Benjamin N. Phillips Memorial Fund was established by the estate of Joy Phillips to honor her late husband in 2006 as an area of interest fund of The Seattle Foundation. The goal of the Fund is to make grants to organizations improving the lives of Clallam County, Washington, residents. The Benjamin N. Phillips Memorial Fund is interested in supporting organizations that have: a mission statement that clearly defines the organization's purpose and reflects its understanding of the communities they serve; a clear articulation of why it believed what it is doing is important and that it will be effective and produce desired results; clearly defined priorities, goals and measurable outcomes; experienced and highly qualified staff and volunteer leadership; a skilled governing board whose knowledge includes management, fundraising and the community served; a funding plan appropriate to agency size and developmental state-guiding development efforts; sound financial management practices; support in the community and constituent involvement; and proven ability to mobilize financial and in-kind support, including volunteers. Grants are predominantly made for one year, with no implied renewal funding. However, a two-year grant will be considered if a case is made for why funding is required for a longer period. An example of this exception is a planning or capacity-building process occurring over a two-year period of time. Approximately $250,000 will be distributed annually, with grants ranging in size from $1,000 to $25,000; the average grant size is $11,000.

Requirements: To qualify for a grant from the Foundation, an organization must: be a 501(c)3 tax-exempt nonprofit organization serving residents of Clallam County, Washington.

Geographic Focus: Washington
Date(s) Application is Due: Jul 1
Amount of Grant: 1,000 - 25,000 USD
Samples: Compassion and Choices of Washington, Seattle, Washington, $10,000 - support two years of added outreach, partnership development and fund development activities in Clallam County; First Book of Clallam County, Seattle, Washington, $1,000 - to support the purchase of books for low-income children; Juan de Fuca Festival of the Arts, Port Angeles, Washington, $8,000 - support sponsorship of Baka Beyond workshops and concerts.
Contact: Ceil Erickson, Grantmaking Director; (206) 515-2131 or (206) 515-2109; fax (206) 622-7673; c.erickson@seattlefoundation.org or phillips@seattlefoundation.org
Internet: www.seattlefoundation.org/nonprofits/phillips/Pages benjaminphillipsmemorialfund.aspx
Sponsor: Seattle Foundation
1200 Fifth Avenue, Suite 1300
Seattle, WA 98101-3151

Seattle Foundation C. Keith Birkenfeld Memorial Trust Grants   2177
Keith Birkenfeld was an educator, world traveler and philanthropist who died September 7, 2005. He retired from the Bellevue School District, where he spent 20 years as a high school teacher of international relations and U.S. history, and later as an administrator. He spent his last 25 years living on Bainbridge Island and traveling the world, meeting interesting and famous people. He was raised in Bremerton and was well-known around Kitsap County for his generous spirit. The C. Keith Birkenfeld Memorial Trust was established in 2006 as an Area of Interest Fund of The Seattle Foundation. The goal of the Trust is to make one-time grants to organizations improving the quality of life for Puget Sound residents. Grants are awarded annually, with Kitsap County charitable organizations receiving first consideration. Previous grants made by the Trust range from $3,000 to $400,000, with an average grant size of $96,000.

Requirements: Eligible applicants are organizations: that have current status as a tax-exempt 501(c)3 public charity, as determined by the IRS, or have a fiscal sponsor with this status; and working in the arts, horticulture, wildlife, maritime and human service sectors, particularly agencies serving Kitsap County residents;

Restrictions: Organizations with religious affiliations will be considered for grants only if their activities address the needs of the wider community without regard to religious belief; proposed projects may not contain any content or activity intended to proselytize, even when participation in such activities is voluntary. In general, the entirety of a project's costs will not be awarded and only one grant will be made by the Trust over the course of the project.

Geographic Focus: Washington
Amount of Grant: 3,000 - 400,000 USD
Samples: Bainbridge Community Foundation, Bainbridge Island, Washington, $33,000 - to support the Birkenfeld Humanitarian Award; Central Stage Theatre of County

Kitsap, Silverdale, Washington, $15,000 - to support remodelling projects to improve the community theatre space; Hope in Christ Ministries, Seattle, Washington, $125,000 - support the Oasis Teen Shelter capital project.
Contact: Ceil Erickson, Grantmaking Director; (206) 515-2131 or (206) 515-2109; fax (206) 622-7673; grantmaking@seattlefoundation.org or c.erickson@seattlefoundation.org
Internet: www.seattlefoundation.org/nonprofits/birkenfeld/Pages/CKeithBirkenfeldMemTrust.aspx
Sponsor: Seattle Foundation
1200 Fifth Avenue, Suite 1300
Seattle, WA 98101-3151

Seattle Foundation Education Grants   2178
The Seattle Foundation is committed to providing every child with a high-quality education. Because educational attainment is among the most powerful factors in determining whether children will reach their potential as healthy, productive adults, the Foundation feels that it is critical to provide the region's most vulnerable youth with a robust continuum of support at all stages of their education, from cradle to career. To realize this vision, grantmaking supports strong public schools at the systems level and student success at the individual level. The Foundation's goals are to: prepare young people for college and career success; promote parent and community involvement in helping students succeed in school; and advocate for high-quality public schools through authentic community engagement and effective professional development for teachers and school leaders.

Requirements: An organization must: be a 501(c)3 tax-exempt nonprofit organization or public agency (including educational institutions); serve residents of King County; and provide programming that aligns with one of the Foundation's three education strategies.

Restrictions: Operating expenses for public or private elementary and secondary schools, colleges and universities are not considered. The following are typically considered a low priority: capital campaign funding requests; organizations that have less than a three-year operating history after receiving their 501(c)3 classification; organizations that have an annual operating budget less than $100,000 as reflected in the most recently filed IRS Form 990; and youth-serving organizations that don't target and track outcomes related to education success. Grants are not made to individuals or to religious organizations for religious purposes. Grants will not be awarded for: endowment; funding of conferences or seminars; operating expenses for public or private elementary and secondary schools, colleges and universities; fundraising events such as walk-a-thons, tournaments, auctions and general fundraising solicitations; or the production of books, films, or videos.

Geographic Focus: Washington
Date(s) Application is Due: Nov 1
Amount of Grant: 15,000 - 50,000 USD
Contact: Ceil Erickson, Grantmaking Director; (206) 515-2131 or (206) 515-2109; fax (206) 622-7673; grantmaking@seattlefoundation.org or c.erickson@seattlefoundation.org
Internet: www.seattlefoundation.org/nonprofits/grantmaking/education/Pages/Education.aspx
Sponsor: Seattle Foundation
1200 Fifth Avenue, Suite 1300
Seattle, WA 98101-3151

Seattle Foundation Health and Wellness Grants   2179
The Seattle Foundation is committed to fostering health and wellness for people throughout the King County, Washington, region. The Foundation awards grants to nonprofits in all fields that improve the quality of life for county residents, and is focused on making sure that everyone in the county has access to quality care, including physical and dental health, cognitive, emotional, and mental health. Goals within the Health and Wellness element are to: improve access to: basic healthcare, especially services and treatment for those who are low-income, uninsured and/or underinsured; support efforts designed to reduce and/or eliminate disparities in health status due to poverty and/or race; foster efforts to strengthen the ability and capacity of providers to deliver quality services; and support efforts that protect the safety net for the vulnerable in our community through case management, treatment, and counseling services. The fields of interest and populations captured in this element include: healthcare, dental care, mental health, domestic violence, developmentally disabled, physically disabled, seniors, and birth to three programs, substance abuse programs and child welfare programs. The deadline for Health and Wellness is May 1.

Requirements: An organization must: be a 501(c)3 tax-exempt nonprofit organization; serve residents of King County; and provide programming in Health and Wellness that aligns with one of its three strategies.

Restrictions: The Foundation does not support disease-specific organizations and does not support health research projects. Multi-year grants are not considered.

Geographic Focus: Washington
Date(s) Application is Due: May 1
Amount of Grant: 15,000 - 50,000 USD
Contact: Ceil Erickson, Grantmaking Director; (206) 515-2131 or (206) 515-2109; grantmaking@seattlefoundation.org or c.erickson@seattlefoundation.org
Internet: www.seattlefoundation.org/nonprofits/grantmaking/healthwellness/Pages/HealthWellness.aspx
Sponsor: Seattle Foundation
1200 Fifth Avenue, Suite 1300
Seattle, WA 98101-3151

Sensient Technologies Foundation Grants   2180
The foundation supports organizations involved with arts and culture; children/youth, services; community/economic development; education; education, fund raising/fund distribution; education, research; family services; food services; general charitable giving; health care; higher education; homeless, human services; hospitals (general); human services; medical research, institute; mental health/crisis services; nutrition; performing

arts; residential/custodial care, hospices; United Ways and Federated Giving Programs; Urban/community development; and voluntarism promotion. The foundation's types of support include: annual campaigns; capital campaigns; emergency funds; endowments; general operating support; matching/challenge support; program development; research; and scholarship funds.

Requirements: An application form is not required. Submit a letter of inquiry as an initial approach. The advisory board meets in January and June/July or as needed, with deadline for proposal review one month prior to board meetings.

Restrictions: The foundation gives primarily to its areas of interest in Indianapolis, Indiana; St. Louis, Missouri; and Milwaukee, Wisconsin. It does not support sectarian religious, fraternal, or partisan political organizations. It does not give grants to individuals.

Geographic Focus: Indiana, Missouri, Wisconsin

Contact: Douglas L. Arnold, (414) 271-6755; fax (414) 347-4783

Sponsor: Sensient Technologies Foundation

777 E Wisconsin Avenue

Milwaukee, WI 53202-5304

Serco Foundation Grants   2181

Servco believes in the importance of being a good neighbor and partners with nonprofit organizations in its local communities where they live and work. In addition, hundreds of its employees volunteer for a host of worthy causes, ranging from blood drives to Special Olympics to beach clean-ups. Employees also give their time by serving on the boards of non-profit organizations, schools, parent/teacher associations, and cultural groups, while others participate as coaches and volunteers of all kinds. The Servco Foundation was established in 1986 by Servco Pacific, (Servco) in recognition of its responsibility as a corporate citizen to the communities it serves. The Foundation has been principally funded from past earnings of Servco and its affiliates, which have operations in automotive, consumer products and real estate businesses. The Foundation provides support to various cultural, social, service, and educational agencies and institutions throughout the State of Hawaii and beyond. Over 100 organizations benefit annually, and they, in turn, continue to provide outstanding service to the community. The employees of Servco are the people behind the Foundation's donations.

Requirements: any 501(c)3 serving the residents of Hawaii and Australia are eligible to apply.

Geographic Focus: Hawaii, Australia

Contact: Glenn Inouye, Foundation Director; (808) 564-1300 or (808) 564-2337; glenn.inouye@servco.com or donations@servco.com

Internet: servco.com/philanthropy/servco_foundation.php

Sponsor: Servco Foundation

P.O. Box 2788

Honolulu, HI 96803

Seward Community Foundation Grants   2182

As an organization, the Seward Community Foundation goal is to support projects that enhance the quality of life for Seward and Moose Pass residents, addressing immediate needs while working toward long-term improvements. The Foundation is continually listening and learning about what is important to its residents. Currently, grantmaking supports organizations and programs that serve the needs of people of all ages in such areas as health, education, recreation, social services, arts and culture, the environment, and community development. The Foundation seeks projects that offer maximum impacts for its community and shows collaboration with other organizations. Typically, awards have ranged from $1,000 to $5,000, though larger grants are considered. The annual application cycle begins on January 1 and runs through the deadline of March 1.

Requirements: Applications are accepted from qualified 501(c)3 nonprofit organizations, or equivalent organizations located in the state of Alaska and serving the Seward/Moose Valley region. Equivalent organizations may include tribes, local or state governments, schools, or Regional Educational Attendance Areas.

Geographic Focus: Alaska

Date(s) Application is Due: Mar 1

Amount of Grant: 500 - 25,000 USD

Samples: Qutekcak Native Tribe, Seward, Alaska, $1,000 - support for the Seward Native Youth Olympics (NYO) State Meet; Independent Living Center, Seward, Alaska, $$6,750 - support for the TRAILS program; Seward Little League, Seward, Alaska, $2,500 - purchase of a pitching machine for youth team.

Contact: Mariko Sarafin, Senior Program Associate; (907) 249-6609 or (907) 334-6700; fax (907) 334-5780; msarafin@alaskacf.org

Internet: sewardcf.org/projects/

Sponsor: Seward Community Foundation

P.O. Box 933

Seward, AK 99664

Seward Community Foundation Mini-Grants   2183

The Seward Community Foundation Mini-Grant program is available throughout the year. These are a quick method to assist nonprofit organizations and projects in the Seward/Moose Pass communities. The maximum grant award is up to $1,000 and can be applied for easily with the Foundation's online application. The Foundation's advisory board will review applications after they are submitted, generally at their next scheduled meeting. These meeting are held on the 3rd Wednesday of every month.

Requirements: Applications are accepted from qualified 501(c)3 nonprofit organizations, or equivalent organizations located in the state of Alaska and serving the Seward/Moose Valley region. Equivalent organizations may include tribes, local or state governments, schools, or Regional Educational Attendance Areas.

Geographic Focus: Alaska

Amount of Grant: Up to 1,000 USD

Samples: Seward Nordic Ski Club, Seward, Alaska, $475 - ssupport of the Moose Pass Rendezvous Ski Race; Seward PTSA, Seward, Alaska, $500 - support for the Kenai Peninsula College Jump Start program; SeaView Community Services, Seward, Alaska, $1,000 - matching grant for Special Needs Housing project.

Contact: Mariko Sarafin, Senior Program Associate; (907) 249-6609 or (907) 334-6700; fax (907) 334-5780; msarafin@alaskacf.org

Internet: sewardcf.org/projects/

Sponsor: Seward Community Foundation

P.O. Box 933

Seward, AK 99664

Seybert Foundation Grants   2184

The Seybert Foundation supports nonprofit organizations providing services for disadvantaged youth in Philadelphia. The foundation is interested in projects for abused, deprived children and youth counseling services. The institute also supports special projects that encourage disadvantaged children in Philadelphia public elementary schools to develop leadership and academic skills. Core grants will be in the amount of $20,000 over a 2-year period ($10,000 per year). Recipients must provide a detailed narrative and financial report on how the funds were spent. The deadline for requests for support is May 17, and applicants will receive notification by July.

Requirements: IRS 501(c)3 tax-exempt nonprofit organizations operating to benefit children and youth in Philadelphia, Pennsylvania, are eligible. The applicant organization must have a minimum operating budget of $1.5 million.

Restrictions: The Seybert Foundation discourages applications from schools. While we fund many organizations that operate programming in schools, we do not currently provide operating support for schools themselves.

Geographic Focus: Pennsylvania

Date(s) Application is Due: May 17

Amount of Grant: Up to 10,000 USD

Samples: After School Activities Partnership, Philadelphia, Pennsylvania, $10,000 - general operating support (2020); Wagner Free Institute of Science, Philadelphia, Pennsylvania, $10,000 - children's and family outreach programs (2020); Philadelphia Youth Basketball, Philadelphia, Pennsylvania, $10,000 - general operating support (2020).

Contact: Theresa Jackson; (215) 821-8144; admin@seybertfoundation.org

Internet: www.grants-info.org/seybert/guidelines.htm

Sponsor: Seybert Foundation

P.O. Box 52758

Philadelphia, PA 19115

Share Our Strength Grants   2185

Share Our Strength awards grants to nonprofit organizations, schools, and other eligible organizations who are involved in the following activities: increasing access to after school snack and meal programs, or child care programs, supported through the Child and Adult Care Food Program (CACFP); increasing access to summer meal programs supported through the Summer Food Service Program or the National School Lunch "Seamless Summer" Program; educating and enrolling more eligible families in SNAP/WIC; increasing the availability of Universal School Breakfast through alternative models such as in-classroom breakfast and grab-n-go; and advocacy around any of the above anti-hunger issues. Proposals are typically accepted in the spring and early summer. There are no specific limitations on what type of expenses are allowed.

Requirements: Organizations that have received grants within the past two years will be automatically notified of available grant opportunities. All others should submit a letter of inquiry (no more than 2 pages; one page preferred), describing how the proposed project will help increase access to the programs outlined in the Share Our Strength grants' programs initiatives. Letters of inquiry should be emailed to grants@strength.org, with the subject line "NKH proposal - name of organization - program" (i.e. summer, afterschool, SNAP, etc.). Share Our Strength will notify the organization within two weeks if they will be inviting a full proposal. Applicants should refer to the website for guidelines and frequently asked questions before submitting a proposal.

Geographic Focus: All States

Amount of Grant: 5,000 - 10,000 USD

Contact: Chuck Scofield, Chief Development Officer; (800) 761-4227 or (202) 393-2925; fax (202) 347-5868; info@strength.org

Internet: www.strength.org/grants/

Sponsor: Share Our Strength

1730 M Street NW, Suite 700

Washington, D.C. 20036

Shell Deer Park Grants   2186

The company supports organizations that work to improve the quality of life and the general welfare of its employees and the citizens of their home communities. Contributions are made in the areas of education and workforce development, health and human services, the environment, civic and community betterment, and arts and culture. In addition to local community funds, support may be given to institutions for the handicapped, associations for the blind, or other well-established organizations that enjoy wide community support and receive no support from local United Funds. Financial aid to education is directed primarily to accredited colleges and universities where the company has significant operations, where it recruits, or where research of interest or applicability to its business is being conducted. Approximately one-half of Pennzoil's corporate giving is directed toward educational support. Corporate contributions to hospitals, clinics, rehabilitation centers, and other health-related organizations are restricted to building programs, equipment additions, and unusual research programs. Contributions to campaigns conducted for the more prevalent diseases or disabilities may also be considered. Contributions are made to organizations engaged in the performing or visual arts, museums, zoos, libraries, and other cultural endeavors. Support will be given to selected civic organizations working to improve the quality of life in local Pennzoil communities. There may be causes outside the preceding classifications that are deserving of support and to which consideration will be given on an individual basis.

Requirements: Shell Deer Park will place priority on charitable contributions to eligible nonprofit organizations in nearby Texas communities, including Deer Park, Pasadena, La Porte, and North Channel.

Restrictions: Shell does not generally support: individuals; private foundations; non-profit organizations without a current 501(c)3 exempt status; conferences, workshops, or seminars not directly related to Shell business interests; religious organizations that do not serve the general public on a non-denominational basis; or organizations located in or benefiting nations other than U.S. and its territories.

Geographic Focus: Texas
Contact: Janet Noble; (713) 246-7301 or (713) 246-7137; fax (713) 246-7800
Internet: www.shell.us/about-us/projects-and-locations/deer-park-manufacturing-site/social-investment-and-grants.html
Sponsor: Shell Deer Park
5900 Highway 225, P.O. Box 100
Deer Park, TX 77536

Shelley and Donald Rubin Foundation Grants 2187

The foundation is primarily interested in supporting the inclusion of art from non-Western European cultures into the mainstream of scholarship and display. In addition, the foundation supports research, action, and other projects designed to reveal and understand barriers to the full access of all people to American society and the larger international community. Areas of particular interest include, but are not limited to: access to health care; AIDS and its effects on society's institutions; the celebration of ethnic and cultural diversity that simultaneously encourages intergroup understanding; and cultural and arts programs that encourage individual and community identity. Projects in other areas that are most often funded are those that in themselves serve as catalysts for social change, addressing emerging problems as well as better known, long-standing problems in new ways. On a limited basis, programs eligible for funding may also include evaluation, technical assistance, and demonstration projects leading to the development of innovative models. Most recent awards have ranged from $2,500 to $100,000.

Requirements: Only organizations with tax-exempt status under U.S. Internal Revenue Code, or those with qualifying fiscal sponsors, will be considered. Organizations must be active in the five boroughs of New York City. Potential grantees must be organizations that supply one or more of the following to audiences: arts education; public art; art in community and service centers; artistic activism; community-based museums; art in the service of social justice or change; and promotion of under-recognized artistic practice.

Restrictions: Grants do not support individuals, capital projects, endowments, scholarships, fellowships, or fund raising activities.

Geographic Focus: New York
Amount of Grant: 2,500 - 100,000 USD
Contact: Alexander Gardner, Executive Director; (212) 780-2035; erich@sdrubin.org
Internet: www.sdrubin.org/guidelines.htm
Sponsor: Shelley and Donald Rubin Foundation
17 West 17th Street, 9th Floor
New York, NY 10011

Shell Oil Company Foundation Community Development Grants 2188

The mission of the Shell Oil Company Foundation is to help foster the general well being of communities where Shell Oil Company employees live and work and to provide educational opportunities that prepare students and faculty to succeed while meeting the needs of the ever-changing workplace. Focus areas for funding include: community development; education; and the environment. In the area of community development, the focus is on civic and human needs in the community while promoting healthy lifestyles, major and cultural arts that promote access to under-served students and communities, and disaster relief efforts. The Foundation funds a broad array of community outreach projects, particularly in areas where employees work and live. These projects range from local neighborhood improvement efforts to regional non-profit organizations. The Foundation is especially interested in supporting groups that reflect the diversity and inclusiveness of its communities, which is a Shell core value.

Requirements: Shell will consider charitable contributions to eligible nonprofit organizations with priority consideration given to organizations serving in or near U.S. communities where Shell has a major presence.

Restrictions: Shell Oil Company and the Shell Oil Company Foundation will not consider contributions for the following purposes: individuals; private foundations; non-profit organizations without a current 501(c)3 exempt status; conferences or symposia; endowment funds; fraternal and labor organizations; capital campaigns; conferences, workshops, or seminars not directly related to Shell business interests; religious organizations that do not serve the general public on a non-denominational basis; organizations located in or benefiting nations other than U.S. and its territories; or organizational operating expenses.

Geographic Focus: All States
Amount of Grant: 10,000 - 50,000 USD
Contact: Nancy Tootle, External Relations Social Investment Manager; (832) 337-0635 or (832) 337-2034; nancy.tootle@shell.us
Internet: www.shell.us/sustainability/request-for-a-grant-from-shell.html
Sponsor: Shell Oil Company Foundation
One Shell Plaza 910 Louisiana, Suite 4478A
Houston, TX 77002

Shield-Ayres Foundation Grants 2189

The Shield-Ayres Foundation was established in Texas in 1977 with a primary interest in supporting health, human services, the environment, education, and the arts. The Foundation's focus is to help children and youth, economically disadvantaged, low-income, and students. Types of funding include: advocacy; annual campaigns; capital campaigns; emergency funding; endowments; financial sustainability; fund raising; general operating support; land acquisition; leadership and professional development; outreach; policy and system reform; program development; education; and volunteer development. Interested parties should begin by forwarding a Letter of Inquiry to the Foundation office. It that inquiry results in a favorable response, an invitation to apply will be extended. Online application deadlines are February 15 and August 15.

Requirements: The Foundation funds organizations with programs that focus primarily in Austin, San Antonio, or select other areas where we have special interests. Organizations are eligible to apply once in a twelve-month period, regardless of the approval status of the organization's last application. Organizations are eligible to receive grants from the Shield-Ayres Foundation for up to three consecutive years.

Restrictions: The Foundation does not: lend or grant money to individuals; make grants intended to support candidates for political office; or grant money to private foundations.

Geographic Focus: Texas
Date(s) Application is Due: Feb 15; Aug 15
Amount of Grant: 5,000 - 25,000 USD
Samples: Alamo College Foundation, San Antonio, Texas, $25,000 - support of the Challenge Center; Environmental Defense Fund, New York, New York, $25,000 - support of the Lester Prairie Chicken Habitat Exchange; Greenlights, Austin, Texas, $10,000 - general operating support.
Contact: Cindy Raab, Executive Director; (512) 467-4021; info@shield-ayresfoundation.org
Internet: www.shield-ayresfoundation.org/grant-making/funding-priorities/
Sponsor: Shield-Ayres Foundation
3101 Bee Caves Road, Suite 260
Austin, TX 78746-5574

Shimizu Foundation Scholarships 2190

Established in Hilo, Hawaii, in 2001, the Shimizu provides scholarship awards to students that show enthusiasm to better themselves and their community, have a minimum 2.7 accumulated GPA in high school, maintain a minimum accumulated 3.0 in their 1st year in college, and are majoring in business, primarily accounting, but would consider other business related majors as well. Some giving is also available for pre-determined organizations that assist individuals in the areas of health, shelter, hospice cost, and welfare. The annual deadline for applications is March 31.

Geographic Focus: Hawaii
Date(s) Application is Due: Mar 31
Contact: Keith T. Shimizu, Director; (808) 329-8787; kshimizu@ktscpa.com
Sponsor: Shimizu Foundation
58 Kamana Street
Hilo, HI 96720-4147

Shopko Foundation Community Charitable Grants 2191

The Shopko Foundation is proud of Shopko's roots as a retail health and optical care provider. To maximize its impact, the Foundation has a narrow focus on areas of giving that support the health of Shopko customers, teammates and communities. The Foundation also recognizes that education is fundamental to an individual's health and functionality in society. To achieve its vision, the Shopko Foundation believes in supporting community projects that may be accessed by, and its contribution made well known to, customers and teammates of Shopko. Funds will support established non-profit organizations with a proven record of success in maintaining solid, critical programs or innovative new organizations and programs supported by established non-profits or successful leadership. Grant funding will be $1,000 or less.

Requirements: Nonprofit 501(c)3 organizations located within 25 miles of a Shopko store are eligible to apply. Grants to accredited publicly/privately funded schools, colleges, and universities will be considered. Grant requests must be submitted at least 45 days prior to the date of the scheduled event to ensure sufficient time for review. Requests should be related to a specific program or project, rather than related to general fundraising.

Restrictions: In general, the Shopko Foundation does not support the following: Programs or events that do not support the Foundation's mission; Programs or events outside of Shopko communities; Sponsorship of cultural exhibits; Events which provide assistance to a specific individual; Advertising in event programs or yearbooks; Religious organizations (however gifts designated for, and restricted to, human services or humanitarian purposes may be eligible); Political or fraternal organizations; Events with multiple or competing business sponsors; Organizations that discriminate on the basis of sex, creed, national origin or religion; Charitable requests in support of raffle, auctions, benefits or similar fundraising events. Applications via postal mail will not be accepted.

Geographic Focus: California, Idaho, Illinois, Indiana, Iowa, Kansas, Kentucky, Michigan, Minnesota, Missouri, Montana, Nebraska, North Dakota, Ohio, Oregon, South Dakota, Utah, Washington, Wisconsin, Wyoming
Amount of Grant: Up to 1,000 USD
Contact: Michelle Hansen, Program Director; (920) 429-4054; fax (920) 496-4225; shopkofoundation@shopko.com or michelle.hansen@shopko.com
Internet: www.shopko.com/thumbnail/Company/Community-Giving/Shopko-Foundation/pc/2176/c/2181/2185.uts?&pageSize=
Sponsor: Shopko Foundation
700 Pilgrim Way
Green Bay, WI 54304

Shopko Foundation Green Bay Area Community Grants 2192

The Shopko Foundation is proud of Shopko's roots as a retail health and optical care provider. To maximize its impact, the Foundation has a narrow focus on areas of giving that support the health of Shopko customers, teammates and communities. The Foundation also recognizes that education is fundamental to an individual's health and functionality in society. The Foundation strives to enhance the quality of life in the Green Bay area through charitable causes, events and activities that support healthy lifestyles for residents. Its goal is to make Shopko communities a better place to live by supporting programs and services that improve the health and education of its residents. Grants awarded through this program support larger or long-term community wide projects.

Requirements: Nonprofit 501(c)3 organizations located in the Green Bay area are eligible to apply. Grants to accredited publicly/privately funded schools, colleges, and universities will be considered. Requests should be related to a specific program or project, rather than related to general fundraising.

Restrictions: In general, the Shopko Foundation does not support the following: Programs or events that do not support the Foundation's mission; Programs or events outside of Shopko communities; Sponsorship of cultural exhibits; Events which provide assistance to a specific individual; Advertising in event programs or yearbooks; Religious organizations (however gifts designated for, and restricted to, human services or humanitarian purposes may be eligible); Political or fraternal organizations; Events with multiple or competing business sponsors; Organizations that discriminate on the basis of sex, creed, national origin or religion; Charitable requests in support of raffle, auctions, benefits or similar fundraising events. Applications via postal mail will not be accepted.

Geographic Focus: Wisconsin

Contact: Michelle Hansen, Program Director; (920) 429-4054; fax (920) 496-4225; shopkofoundation@shopko.com or michelle.hansen@shopko.com

Internet: www.shopko.com/thumbnail/Company/Community-Giving/Shopko-Foundation/pc/2176/c/2181/2185.uts?&pageSize=

Sponsor: Shopko Foundation

700 Pilgrim Way

Green Bay, WI 54304

Sick Kids Foundation Community Conference Grants 2193

The Sick Kids Foundation Community Conference Grant program supports events which are organized by or for families with children with health challenges, including but not limited to children with acute illness, chronic illness, and disabilities. Support is offered for conferences, workshops or symposia which are relevant to the health of Canada's children. These events focus on information sharing with families and health professionals and/or community organizations. Funding may be awarded for the following items: expenses associated with keynote speakers, i.e. honoraria, economy travel, budget hotel accommodation and meals; audiovisual equipment rental required for presentations; write up of conference for wider distribution after the event (in newsletter, on website etc.); registration fees for parents, children and community groups; on-site babysitting; and conference facilities. Awards are limited to an annual maximum request of $5,000. There are three deadlines for applications each fiscal year: May 31; September 30; and January 31.

Requirements: Eligible events must: address issues that are relevant to child health in Canada; support the parent-child-professional partnership by having a focus on information sharing between families, health professionals, and community organizations; include knowledgeable and credible presenters; take place in Canada; and be sponsored by a registered Canadian charitable organization.

Restrictions: Academic conferences are not eligible for funding. The following items are not eligible for Foundation funding through this program: salaries; computer rentals; registration fees for speakers or conference planners; planning meetings; or individuals seeking reimbursement for attending or presenting at events. The Foundation will only fund organizations.

Geographic Focus: Canada

Date(s) Application is Due: Jan 31; May 31; Sep 30

Amount of Grant: Up to 5,000 CAD

Contact: Ted Garrard, President; (416) 813-6166 or (800) 661-1083; fax (416) 813-5024; ted.garrard@sickkidsfoundation.com

Internet: www.sickkidsfoundation.com/about-us/grants/community-conference-grants

Sponsor: Sick Kids Foundation

525 University Avenue, 14th Floor

Toronto, ON M5G 2L3 Canada

Sick Kids Foundation New Investigator Research Grants 2194

Sick Kids Foundation New Investigator Research Grants are jointly sponsored by SickKids Foundation and the Canadian Institutes of Health Research Institute of Human Development, Child and Youth Health. Grant recipients may obtain up to three years of support for research in the biomedical, clinical, health systems and services, population and public health sectors. The program provides support to child health researchers early in their careers. It is intended that New Investigator Research Grants will enhance the grant recipient's capacity to compete with more senior investigators for research grants from other funders. The Foundation funds research that has the potential to have a significant impact on child health outcomes. Multi-year grants range up to $300,000.

Requirements: The applicant must be a new investigator as of the application deadline. For the purpose of this award, a new investigator is defined as an individual who as a principal or co-principal investigator has not received combined operating grant funding of $500,000 or more (Canadian dollars) and is within five years of their first academic appointment. Academic appointment is defined as an appointment which allows an individual to apply for research grants as an independent investigator.

Geographic Focus: Canada

Amount of Grant: Up to 300,000 CAD

Samples: Dr. Jacob Jaremko, University of Alberta, Edmonton, Alberta, Canada, $257,245 - 3D Ultrasound in Hip Dysplasia; Dr. Alexander Beristain, University of British Columbia, Vancouver, British Columbia, Canada, $299,385 - Effect of Obesity-Associated Inflammation on the Maternal-Fetal Interface in Early Pregnancy; Dr. Sarah Fraser, University of Montreal, Montreal, Quebec, Canada, $283,288 - Collaborative Mental Health Care from Communities, to Professionals, to Policy Change for Inuit of Canada.

Contact: Ted Garrard, President; (416) 813-6166 or (800) 661-1083; fax (416) 813-5024; ted.garrard@sickkidsfoundation.com

Internet: www.sickkidsfoundation.com/about-us/grants/new-investigator-research-grants

Sponsor: Sick Kids Foundation

525 University Avenue, 14th Floor

Toronto, ON M5G 2L3 Canada

Sidgmore Family Foundation Grants 2195

The Sidgmore Family Foundation honors the legacy of John W. Sidgmore by taking a proactive approach to helping others succeed. The Foundation desires to use its resources to find creative and innovative solutions so that people may achieve their full potential and become responsible, healthy and productive members of society. In recognition that an impoverished environment limits the possibilities for people to develop and thrive, the Sidgmore Family Foundation is particularly interested in funding organizations that: improve the quality of education and teacher training; further the advancement of knowledge in the field of medicine with a special emphasis on hearing and cardiology; utilize entrepreneurial skills to explore and develop creative, scalable, and sustainable solutions to critical social problems; and, provide support and services to those in need in the Washington D.C. area. Grants are awarded to organizations that have a clear, replicable plan for success, measured sustainable results, and high approval ratings from charity evaluator organizations, such as Charity Navigator. The Foundation also awards multi-year grants that can sustain a program or project.

Requirements: Nonprofit 501(c)3 organizations are eligible. Preference is given to organizations that serve residents in the Washington, D.C. metropolitan area, Maryland, and Virginia. Applicants must begin the process with an initial Letter of Inquiry (LOI). LOIs will receive a response if the Foundation wishes to receive a proposal from your organization.

Restrictions: The Sidgmore Family Foundation does not make grants to individuals, national health organizations, government agencies, or political and public policy advocacy groups.

Geographic Focus: All States

Contact: M. Gelbwaks, Director; (516) 541-2713; SidgmoreFound@aol.com

Internet: www.sidgmorefoundation.com/#application_process

Sponsor: Sidgmore Family Foundation

71 Leewater Avenue

Massapequa, NY 11758

Sidney and Sandy Brown Foundation Grants 2196

Sidney and Sandy Brown Foundation was established by Sidney R. Brown and his wife, Sandy, in New Jersey in 2001. Sidney is Chief Executive Officer of National Freight Industries, a premier integrated supply chain solutions company, which is one of the largest privately-held third party logistics companies in the country. Brown joined National Freight in the early 1980's when the company was focused mainly on over-the-road trucking services. Over the next 25 years the company evolved into four affiliated companies providing transportation services (National Freight), warehousing and inventory management (National Distribution Centers), dedicated fleets and transportation management (Interactive Logistics) and real estate development (Real Estate). The Foundation's major fields of interest are the support of: health; elementary and secondary education; higher education; the arts; and religion. Its primary geographic focus is Washington, D.C., New Jersey, and Pennsylvania. An application form is not required, and interested organizations should begin by forwarding a letter of interest outlining their program and/or organization, accompanied by current budgetary request. Most recent awards have ranged from $250 to $50,000. There are no specified annual deadlines for submission.

Requirements: Any 501(c)3 organization serving residents of Pennsylvania, New Jersey, or Washington, D.C. is eligible to apply

Geographic Focus: District of Columbia, New Jersey, Pennsylvania

Amount of Grant: 250 - 50,000 USD

Contact: Sidney Brown, Trustee; (856) 470-5011

Sponsor: Sidney and Sandy Brown Foundation

1650 Market Street, Suite 3200

Philadelphia, PA 19103-7393

Sidney Stern Memorial Trust Grants 2197

The Sidney Stern Memorial Trust, a California-based charity, was established in 1974 through the last will and testament of S. Sidney Stern, and funded entirely from his estate. The Trust provides grants and funding to various non-profit organizations throughout the country. The board of the Trust meets regularly to review applications and make funding decisions. Primary areas of interest for funding include: civil rights; children; community development; disabled causes; education; literacy; health; science; social services; and Native Americans. Recipients of grants have included: local public media outlets; educational programs; literacy programs; archaeological centers; international aid organizations; and performing arts programs for children. There are no specific application forms or deadlines, and interested 501(c)3 organizations should follow the application guidelines.

Requirements: The Trust prefers all correspondence to be sent by mail. No personal or email requests will be entertained. All organizations applying for funding must be recognized by the IRS as 501(c)3 certified, verifiable via GuideStar Charity Check. Folders containing lengthy brochures, pictorial pamphlets or CDs should not be included. Although the foundation supports projects and organizations across the country, most grants are offered to proposals from California.

Restrictions: The Trust does not award grants to individuals, political candidates or campaigns, lobbying projects or programs to directly influence legislation, or for conferences or redistribution.
Geographic Focus: All States
Amount of Grant: 750 USD
Contact: Betty Hoffenberg; (800) 352-3705; info@sidneysternmemorialtrust.org
Internet: sidneysternmemorialtrust.org/
Sponsor: Sidney Stern Memorial Trust
P.O. Box 457
Pacific Palisades, CA 90272

Siebert Lutheran Foundation Grants   2198
The Siebert Lutheran Foundation is an independent, private foundation established by the late Albert F. Siebert, to fund Christian ministries identified with Lutheran churches and organizations in Wisconsin. Specific areas of interest vary from time to time. At present, the Foundation is supportive of the following: clergy and lay education and training; community development and outreach; health ministry; evangelism; and youth programs. Grants are occasionally made to provide seed money or start-up costs for a program or project. In such instances, the participation of other donors is desired. Grants are made only to Lutheran organizations exempt under Section 501(c)3 of the Internal Revenue Code and are generally awarded for a one-year period.
Requirements: The Foundation utilizes an on-line grant application. Potential grant applicants, who represent Wisconsin congregations or Wisconsin recognized service organizations in the Lutheran church, may complete the Foundation's formal, online, letter of inquiry. A telephone call is not necessary prior to completing the letter of inquiry for Lutheran organizations in Wisconsin. If your organization does not meet the above criteria and you would like to discuss possible funding, contact the Foundation office.
Restrictions: The Foundation does not approve grants for the following: endowment funds; fellowships and scholarships; trusts; and other grant-making foundations. Grants are generally not made to churches for capital or operating expenses. No grants are made outside the United States.
Geographic Focus: Wisconsin
Date(s) Application is Due: Mar 1; Jun 1; Sep 1; Dec 1
Contact: Deborah Engel, Operations and Program Officer; (262) 754-9160; fax (262) 754-9162; deb@siebertfoundation.org or contactus@siebertfoundation.org
Internet: www.siebertfoundation.org/Grant-Application.htm
Sponsor: Siebert Lutheran Foundation
300 North Corporate Drive, Suite 200
Brookfield, WI 53045

Sierra Health Foundation Responsive Grants   2199
The Sierra Health Foundation Responsive Grants are designed to promote health and well-being in Northern California communities. Fields of interest include: AIDS; alcoholism; biomedicine; child development, education; child development, services; children/ youth, services; community/economic development; crime/violence/ prevention, youth; family services; health care; health organizations, association; human services; leadership development; medical care, rehabilitation; mental health/crisis services; nutrition; substance abuse, services; and youth development. The Foundation funds employee matching gifts, in-kind gifts, program development, program evaluation; and technical assistance. Examples of Foundation funding include food banks, homeless shelters, senior citizen agencies, youth and family centers, job readiness programs, and faith based organizations.
Requirements: The Foundation funds the following northern California counties: Alpine, Amador, Butte, Calaveras, Colusa, El Dorado, Glenn, Lassen, Modoc, Mono, Nevada, Placer, Plumas, Sacramento, San Joaquin, Shasta, Sierra, Siskiyou, Solano (eastern), Stanislaus, Sutter, Tehama, Trinity, Tuolumne, Yolo and Yuba. Organizations may contact the Foundation for current application procedures and deadlines.
Restrictions: The Foundation does not fund individuals or endowments.
Geographic Focus: California
Amount of Grant: Up to 25,000 USD
Contact: Kathy Mathews, Grants Administrator; (916) 922-4755; fax (916) 922-4024; kmathews@sierrahealth.org or grants@sierrahealth.org
Internet: www.sierrahealth.org/doc.aspx?129
Sponsor: Sierra Health Foundation
1321 Garden Highway
Sacramento, CA 95833-9754

Silicon Valley Community Foundation Education Grants   2200
The Silicon Valley Community Foundation makes strategic grants from its discretionary funds. For the past several years it has prioritized solving grant making strategies to meet the most pressing needs in the region. This funding opportunity targets closing the middle school achievement gap in mathematics through in-school and out-of-school strategies. The Foundation aims to solicit the best thinking of public school districts and other public sector agencies, nonprofit service providers, professional and research institutions and other entities serving San Mateo and Santa Clara counties. Most of the proposals funded will focus on program implementation, while the Foundation also welcomes requests for planning grants as stand-alone endeavors where a compelling case can be made for them. The Foundation expects to award approximately fifteen grants annually in the range of $50,000 to $250,000 for a minimum of one year; multi-year grants may be awarded in certain cases at the discretion of the community foundation. Out-of-school proposals are due on September 23 and in-school proposals are due on December 16.
Requirements: San Mateo and Santa Clara County-serving organizations are eligible. Organizations headquartered outside the two-county region must demonstrate significant service to the area. Organizations with a 501(c)3 designation (such as teacher education

and curriculum support organizations) or those that have a fiscal sponsor with a 501(c)3 designation, public institutions (such as schools or school districts) or other entities that have a designated charitable purpose are also eligible.
Geographic Focus: California
Date(s) Application is Due: Sep 23; Dec 16
Amount of Grant: 50,000 - 250,000 USD
Contact: Manuel Santamaria, Vice President, Strategic Initiatives and Grantmaking; (650) 450-5400 or (650) 450-5487; fax (650) 450-5401; mjsantamaria@siliconvalleycf.org
Internet: www.siliconvalleycf.org/content/education
Sponsor: Silicon Valley Community Foundation
2440 West El Camino Real, Suite 300
Mountain View, CA 94040

Simpson Lumber Charitable Contributions   2201
Simpson has been in the forest products business since 1890 and currently has two operating subsidiaries: Simpson Door Company and Simpson Tacoma Kraft Company, LLC. The mission of Simpson's contributions program is to improve the quality of life in communities where the company has a significant number of employees living and working; and to serve as a catalyst for employees to become involved and to provide leadership in their communities. The company's broad areas of interest include education, health and human services, and efforts to enhance its operating communities. Contributions are generally made where the company has operations. To the extent possible, contributions will support organizations of interest to, or recommended by, Simpson employees. Simpson prefers to make capital contributions that will benefit the operating communities for the long term as opposed to contributing operating funds. Generally, support is committed for one year at a time and in amounts less than $5,000. Interested applicants should write to Simpson's Public Affairs department to request application materials. Simpson's review committees meet once per year to consider funding applications. The application deadline is May 15. For requests less than $1,000, applicants should contact Simpson's Public Affairs department.
Requirements: 501(c)3 organizations that serve Pierce, Thurston, Lewis, Mason, Grays Harbor, and Cowlitz counties in Washington are eligible to apply. Criteria taken into account in determining the amount of any contributions are as follows: degree of support from company employees; relative size and importance of company operations in the community (balance among Simpson communities); needs of organization or program for which funding is requested; amount of previous company contributions to the organization; amount committed by other companies, foundations, and/or governments (projects should demonstrate broad-based community support); and proximity of the requesting organization to Simpson operations or administrative offices.
Geographic Focus: Washington
Date(s) Application is Due: May 15
Amount of Grant: Up to 5,000 USD
Contact: Raymond P. Tennison, President; (253) 779-6400
Beverly Holland, Public Affairs Manager; (253) 779-6400
Internet: www.simpson.com/communitycontribute.cfm
Sponsor: Simpson Lumber Company, LLC
917 East 11th Street
Tacoma, WA 98421

Singing for Change Foundation Grants   2202
The Singing for Change Foundation offers annual competitive grants to progressive U.S. nonprofit organizations that address the root causes of social or environmental problems. SFC is interested in funding projects that improve the quality of life for people and that empower individuals to effect positive change in their communities. Most likely to be considered are organizations that keep their overhead low and collaborate with other groups in their community to find innovative ways of solving common problems. Areas of interest include children and youth—health, education, and protection of children and their families; disenfranchised groups—projects that help people overcome social or economic barriers to education or employment, promote the empowerment of individuals toward self-sufficiency and provide opportunities for personal growth, and demonstrate human equality and encourage people to cross boundary lines to help others and the environment; and the environment—programs that promote environmental awareness and teach people methods of conservation, protection and the responsible use of natural resources. Submit a one-page letter of interest describing the organization and project; full proposals are by invitation.
Requirements: U.S. nonprofit organizations are eligible.
Restrictions: The Singing for Change Foundation does not consider grants to: individuals; government agencies; public or private schools; art, music, or recreational programs, even if offered to disenfranchised groups; political organizations; religious organizations; medical research or disease treatment organizations; basic-needs programs (that exist to supply food or clothing); single service programs such as individual counseling.
Geographic Focus: All States
Amount of Grant: 1,000 - 10,000 USD
Samples: America's Second Harvest of Coastal Georgia, Savannah, Georgia, $5,000 - support for the Kids' Cafe, a unique program dealing with poverty; Bahama Village Music Program, Key West, Florida, $4,009 - support for free music education to the children of Bahama Village residents; Boys Hope Girls Hope of New Orleans, New Orleans, Louisiana, $1,000 - general operations.
Contact: Judith Ranger Smith, Executive Director; (843) 388-7730; judithrangersmith@gmail.com or info@singingforchange.com
Internet: www.singingforchange.org/grant_information.html
Sponsor: Singing for Change Foundation
P.O. Box 729
Sullivan's Island, SC 29482

Sioux Falls Area Community Foundation Community Fund Grants 2203

The purpose of the Sioux Falls Area Foundation (SFACF)'s grant making program is to provide support across a wide spectrum of charitable needs and interests. Grant making categories include arts and humanities (e.g., theatre, music, arts, dance, cultural development, historic preservation, library programs, and museums); community affairs and development (e.g., citizen participation, public use of parks and recreation, administration of justice, economic development, employment, and training); education (e.g., lifelong-learning activities in formal educational settings, support of educational facilities and systems, and scholarships); environment (e.g., protection of natural areas, conservation of energy, prevention and elimination of pollution or hazardous waste, wildlife protection, and water quality); health (e.g., improvement of healthcare, prevention of substance abuse; support of mental-health needs, and medical research); human services (e.g., assistance to families, youth, the elderly, disabled, special groups, social service providers, and those who stand in need); and religion (e.g., support for churches, religious institutions, and religion programs). SFACF offers two grant programs from its unrestricted funds: Spot Grants for projects up to $3,000 and Community Fund Grants for projects over $3,000. The majority of Community Fund Grants are made in the range of $5,000 to $10,000. Proposals for Community Fund Grants must be submitted using a standard application form (available from the SFACF office or downloadable from the website). Applications are accepted anytime and will be reviewed by the Grants Committee at their next scheduled meeting. Meetings take place six times a year: January, March, May, July, September, and November (a schedule is posted at the SFACF website).

Requirements: Nonprofit organizations serving residents in the Sioux Falls, South Dakota area (Minnehaha, Lincoln, McCook, and Turner counties) are eligible to apply. SFACF considers grant requests for programs that require start-up funds to address important community needs or opportunities, expansion of programs that meet important community needs or opportunities, assistance to organizations weathering unforeseen or unusual financial crises; programs that increase an organization's capacity to advance its mission more efficiently or effectively; and programs or studies that inform the community's understanding of needs or opportunities. Requests are evaluated by the following criteria: comparative benefit to the community; the organization's capacity to achieve the stated objectives; the amount of support requested versus the number of people benefited; a well-planned approach to achieving stated objectives; a reasonable expectation that the program can be sustained over time (where applicable); the organization's history of working collaboratively to address community needs and opportunities; and when applicable, the organization's past SFACF grant performance.

Restrictions: SFACF does not consider grant requests for individuals, national fundraising efforts, political advocacy, and sectarian religious programs. The following types of requests are discouraged: large capital improvements or construction drives; ongoing operational support; reduction or elimination of organizational deficits; reimbursement of expenses undertaken prior to submission of a grant application; computer hardware and software, unless these are the focus of a new or enhanced program; public art for which approval and placement has not yet been secured; and multi-year requests.

Geographic Focus: South Dakota

Date(s) Application is Due: Jan 1; Mar 1; May 1; Jul 1; Sep 1; Nov 1

Contact: Andy Patterson; (605) 336-7055, ext. 15; fax (605) 336-0038; apatterson@sfacf.org
Patrick Gale, Program Officer; (605) 336-7055, ext. 20; fax (605) 336-0038; pgale@sfacf.org

Internet: www.sfacf.org/applying-for-grants/

Sponsor: Sioux Falls Area Community Foundation
200 North Cherapa Place
Sioux Falls, SD 57103-2205

Sioux Falls Area Community Foundation Spot Grants 2204

The purpose of the Sioux Falls Area Foundation (SFACF)'s grant making program is to provide support across a wide spectrum of charitable needs and interests. Grant making categories include arts and humanities (e.g., theatre, music, arts, dance, cultural development, historic preservation, library programs, and museums); community affairs and development (e.g., citizen participation, public use of parks and recreation, administration of justice, economic development, employment, and training); education (e.g., lifelong-learning activities in formal educational settings, support of educational facilities and systems, and scholarships); environment (e.g., protection of natural areas, conservation of energy, prevention and elimination of pollution or hazardous waste, wildlife protection, and water quality); health (e.g., improvement of healthcare, prevention of substance abuse; support of mental-health needs, and medical research); human services (e.g., assistance to families, youth, the elderly, disabled, special groups, social service providers, and those who stand in need); and religion (e.g., support for churches, religious institutions, and religion programs). SFACF offers two grant programs from its unrestricted funds: Community Fund Grants for projects over $3,000 and Spot Grants for projects up to $3,000. Spot Grant proposals may be submitted at any time and do not require SFACF's standard application form. Applicants should include the following components in their requests: a typed summary of their program in two pages or fewer; signatures of the organization's executive director and board chair; a board of directors roster; a copy of the organization's IRS tax determination letter; and a project budget. In most cases, SFACF will review and respond to Spot Grant requests within two weeks of receipt. SFACF has provided complete guidelines and an informative FAQ at their website.

Requirements: Nonprofit organizations serving residents in the Sioux Falls, South Dakota area (Minnehaha, Lincoln, McCook, and Turner counties) are eligible to apply. SFACF considers grant requests for programs that require start-up funds to address important community needs or opportunities, expansion of programs that meet important community needs or opportunities, assistance to organizations weathering unforeseen or unusual financial crises; programs that increase an organization's capacity to advance its mission more efficiently or effectively; and programs or studies that inform the community's understanding of needs or opportunities. Requests are evaluated by the following criteria: comparative benefit to the community; the organization's capacity to achieve the stated objectives; the amount of support requested versus the number of people benefited; a well-planned approach to achieving stated objectives; a reasonable expectation that the program can be sustained over time (where applicable); the organization's history of working collaboratively to address community needs and opportunities; and when applicable, the organization's past SFACF grant performance.

Restrictions: SFACF does not consider grant requests for individuals, national fundraising efforts, political advocacy, and sectarian religious programs. The following types of requests are discouraged: large capital improvements or construction drives; ongoing operational support; reduction or elimination of organizational deficits; reimbursement of expenses undertaken prior to submission of a grant application; computer hardware and software, unless these are the focus of a new or enhanced program; public art for which approval and placement has not yet been secured; and multi-year requests.

Geographic Focus: South Dakota

Amount of Grant: Up to 3,000 USD

Contact: Andy Patterson; (605) 336-7055, ext. 15; fax (605) 336-0038; apatterson@sfacf.org
Patrick Gale; (605) 336-7055, ext. 20; fax (605) 336-0038; pgale@sfacf.org

Internet: www.sfacf.org/applying-for-grants/

Sponsor: Sioux Falls Area Community Foundation
200 North Cherapa Place
Sioux Falls, SD 57103-2205

Skaggs Family Foundation Grants 2205

The Skaggs Family Foundation has a philanthropic vision that is predicated on the unshakable conviction that empowered people can shape a better society for everyone. The Foundation awards highly targeted grants that are focused on making a meaningful, enduring difference, both incremental and transformational changes for individuals and communities. The Foundation supports human rights and equality; essential human needs; and community development. Basic human rights and equal opportunity drives the Foundation's focus on aggressively fighting injustice, defending the most vulnerable, and enhancing opportunities for all. Open access to the essentials of life drive the Foundation's focus on maintaining a vital safety net: critical health care, feeding and support, and education and job training opportunities. Giving back drives the Foundation's focus on bettering the areas that we call home, where it is working to create and sustain long-term health and economic opportunities for those in acute need.

Requirements: Any 501(c)3 organization supporting the Skaggs Family Foundation priority areas is eligible to apply.

Geographic Focus: All States

Amount of Grant: Up to 100,000 USD

Contact: Robert Skaggs, President; info@theskaggsfamilyfoundation.org

Internet: www.theskaggsfamilyfoundation.org/about/

Sponsor: Skaggs Family Foundation
1985 Riviera Drive, Suite 103-140
Mount Pleasant, SC 29464

Skaggs Family Foundation Grants 2206

The Skaggs Family Foundation has a philanthropic vision that is predicated on the unshakable conviction that empowered people can shape a better society for everyone. The Foundation awards highly targeted grants that are focused on making a meaningful, enduring difference, both incremental and transformational changes for individuals and communities. The Foundation supports human rights and equality; essential human needs; and community development. Basic human rights and equal opportunity drives the Foundation's focus on aggressively fighting injustice, defending the most vulnerable, and enhancing opportunities for all. Open access to the essentials of life drive the Foundation's focus on maintaining a vital safety net: critical health care, feeding and support, and education and job training opportunities. Giving back drives the Foundation's focus on bettering the areas that we call home, where it is working to create and sustain long-term health and economic opportunities for those in acute need.

Requirements: Any 501(c)3 organization supporting the Skaggs Family Foundation priority areas is eligible to apply.

Geographic Focus: All States

Amount of Grant: Up to 100,000 USD

Contact: Robert Skaggs, President; info@theskaggsfamilyfoundation.org

Internet: www.theskaggsfamilyfoundation.org/about/

Sponsor: Skaggs Family Foundation
1985 Riviera Drive, Suite 103-140
Mount Pleasant, SC 29464

Skaggs Foundation Grants 2207

The Skaggs Foundation, supported by the Samuel D. Skaggs Investment firm, was established in 1962 in California, and currently provides funding throughout Alaska. The Foundation's primary areas of interest include: arts and culture; animals and wildlife; preservation; the environmental protection; children's services; special education; environmental education; natural resources; and marine science. Types of support available with these funds include: continuing support; endowments; equipment; general operating support; internship funds; land acquisition; matching or challenge funding; program evaluation; research; and technical assistance. Typical awards range up to a maximum of $15,000.

Requirements: Nonprofit organizations are eligible, preference is given to requests from Alaska. The initial approach should be a one or two page letter of inquiry. There is no formal application form. Applicants should submit the following: copy of IRS Determination Letter; copy of current year's organizational budget and/or project budget; one copy of the proposal.

Restrictions: No grants are given directly to individuals.

Geographic Focus: Alaska
Date(s) Application is Due: May 1
Amount of Grant: Up to 15,000 USD
Samples: Alaska Arts Southeast, Sitka, Alaska, $15,000 - general operating support; Sitka Sound Science Center, Sitka, Alaska, $8,000 - support of the annual fellowship program; Preservation Theater, Douglas, Alaska, $2,500 - support of the Theater in the Wild program; Rivers Without Borders, Clinton, Alaska, $5,000 - general operating support.
Contact: Samuel D. Skaggs Jr., President; (907) 463-4843 or (907) 463-5511
Sponsor: Skaggs Foundation
119 Seward Street, Suite 7
Juneau, AK 99801

Skatepark Project Built to Play Skatepark Grants   2208
The Tony Hawk Foundation believes encouraging free play and providing youth with opportunities to develop active, healthy lifestyles are key to ensuring their well being. With childhood obesity rates more than tripling since 1980, access to parks is no longer a luxury—it's essential to the health of our children. Children in low-income families are particularly at risk, in part because they have fewer opportunities to participate in organized sports leagues and activities. Fighting obesity has become a critical national priority, with long-term health risks including—but not limited to—heart disease, high cholesterol, depression, and even cancer. More importantly, healthier kids are happier. Two of the nation's most prominent advocates for youth have joined together to address this issue. The Tony Hawk Foundation has partnered with the Ralph C. Wilson, Jr. Foundation to promote the creation of free, public skateparks in the 16 counties of Southeast Michigan and Western New York served by RCWJRF. The deadlines to apply are January 27 and September 1.
Requirements: The Built to Play Skatepark Program primarily considers skatepark projects that: are designed and built from durable, low-maintenance materials by qualified and experienced skatepark contractors; include local skaters in leadership and volunteer roles throughout the planning, fundraising, and design process; will serve low- to middle-income areas and/or areas with a high population of "at-risk" youth; can demonstrate a strong grassroots commitment to the project, particularly in the form of fundraising by local skateboarders and other community groups; encourage skaters to look after their own safety and the safety of others without restricting their access to the park or over-regulating their use of it; are open during daylight hours, 365 days a year; don't charge an entrance fee or require registration; are in areas that currently have no accessible skateboarding facilities; and are committed to a process that minimizes the environmental impact of the skatepark. Only organizations seeking to build free, public skateparks in the 16 counties listed below are eligible to apply for the Built to Play Skatepark Grant: Michigan- Livingston, Macomb, Monroe, Oakland, St. Clair, Washtenaw and Wayne counties; New York- Allegany, Chautauqua, Cattaraugus, Erie, Genesee, Monroe, Niagara, Orleans and Wyoming counties.
Geographic Focus: Michigan, New York
Date(s) Application is Due: Jan 27; Sep 1
Amount of Grant: Up to 250,000 USD
Contact: Alec Beck, Program Manager; (760) 477-2479; play@tonyhawkfoundation.org
Internet: tonyhawkfoundation.org/builttoplay/
Sponsor: Skatepark Project
1611-A S Melrose Drive, Suite 360
Vista, CA 92081

SME Education Foundation Youth Program Grants   2209
The strategy of the program is to expose students to math, science, engineering and technology in order to make an informed decision about pursuing a career in these areas. The foundation's goal is to create a pathway that will offer students information and awareness in middle school leading to education in high school that will matriculate to a college or university degree in manufacturing engineering or a closely related field. Particular emphasis is placed on involving women and minority students.
Requirements: Project directors working at a middle or high school, two or four year degree granting institution or a non-profit organization located in North America may submit a proposal. Matching funds are highly recommended. Applicants are encouraged to secure matching funds in order to make their proposal more competitive. It is highly unlikely that the foundation will fund a youth grant that has no matching funds.
Restrictions: Prospective applicants are encouraged to contact the program staff prior to submitting an application. The foundation will accept one time applications requesting up to $25,000 for project support, up to three years. Multiple requests for a single project will not be considered.
Geographic Focus: All States, Antigua & Barbuda, Bahamas, Barbados, Belize, Costa Rica, Cuba, Dominica, Dominican Republic, El Salvador, Grenada, Guatemala, Haiti, Honduras, Jamaica, Mexico, Nicaragua
Amount of Grant: Up to 25,000 USD
Contact: Bart A. Aslin, Chief Executive Officer; (313) 425-3302 or (313) 425-3300; fax (313) 425-3411; baslin@sme.org or foundation@sme.org
Internet: www.smeef.org/grants/index.php
Sponsor: Society of Manufacturing Engineers Education Foundation
One SME Drive, P.O. Box 930
Dearborn, MI 48121-0930

Smith Richardson Foundation Direct Service Grants   2210
The Smith Richardson Foundation makes a small number of direct service grants to organizations in North Carolina and Connecticut that provide innovative services for disadvantaged children and families. Applicants seeking direct service grants should prepare a short letter describing the mission of the organization, the population it serves, and the nature of the services it delivers. Applicants should also indicate the size of their

organization's budget and the costs of the program for which they are seeking support from the Foundation.
Requirements: Direct service organizations located outside of North Carolina or Connecticut, as well as national direct service charities, will not be considered.
Restrictions: The Foundation does not provide support for: deficit funding or previously established projects; building or construction projects; arts and humanities projects; historic restoration projects; research projects in the physical sciences; evaluations of direct service organizations conducted internally; or educational or other support to individuals.
Geographic Focus: Connecticut, North Carolina
Contact: Marin J. Strmecki; (203) 222-6222; fax (203) 222-6282; jhollings@srf.org
Sponsor: Smith Richardson Foundation
60 Jesup Road
Westport, CT 06880-4311

Sobrato Family Foundation Grants   2211
Foundation Grants are targeted toward strong community-based organizations that promote self-reliance and economic independence, and positively contribute to the quality of life for economically, physically and/or emotionally challenged individuals in Santa Clara, Southern San Mateo and Southern Alameda Counties. The Foundation's interests include, but are not limited to, the areas of: education; health; human services including crime and legal related services, employment training, housing and shelter, human services and food programs, and youth development; and public/societal benefit organizations, specifically nonprofit capacity building agencies. The Foundation generally awards operating support in the range of one to eight percent of an agency's three-year average renewable private cash contributed income (excluding unique one-time gifts, bequests, capital campaign and endowment contributions). Grants range from $20,000 to over $400,000. To apply potential applicants must take an eligibility questionnaire on line at the Foundation's website. Eligible applicants will then be instructed on how and when to apply.
Requirements: Eligible applicants must: be a 501(c)3 organization; have locally raised renewable private cash contributed income of at least $300,000 per year over a three-year average; serve at least 50% of their primary clients in the California counties of Santa Clara, Southern San Mateo and Southern Alameda; serve clients who are economically, emotionally and/or physically challenged; and have a primary mission that is aligned with the Foundation's priorities of education, health, human services and public/societal benefit.
Restrictions: The following are ineligible: agencies whose largest program expense supports mental health, the environment or the arts; fiscally-sponsored programs or organizations; fundraising events or endowment campaigns; school-managed clubs or individual schools, unless an invitation is extended; medical research or specific diseases; projects created or operated by public government agencies or departments; and public libraries or their foundations.
Geographic Focus: California
Samples: Sacred Heart Nativity School, San Jose, California, $102,500, education funding; JobTrain, Menlo Park, California, $205,000, employment preparation and training; and Second Harvest Food Bank of Santa Clara and San Mateo Counties, San Jose, California, food bank funding, $438,250.
Contact: Mara Williams Low, Manager; (408) 996-9500; fax (408) 996-9516; MLow@Sobrato.org or grants@Sobrato.org
Internet: www.sobrato.com/foundation
Sponsor: Sobrato Family Foundation
10600 N De Anza Boulevard, Suite 225
Cupertino, CA 95014

Sobrato Family Foundation Meeting Space Grants   2212
The Sobrato Family Foundation is dedicated to helping create and sustain a vibrant and healthy community, where all Silicon Valley residents have equal opportunity to live, work and be enriched. To accomplish this purpose, the Foundation invests in strong community-based nonprofits that promote self-reliance and economic independence, and positively contribute to the quality of life for economically, physically and/or emotionally challenged individuals in Santa Clara, Southern San Mateo and Southern Alameda Counties. There are three Conference Center locations. The Redwood Shores Center is located at 330-350 Twin Dolphin Drive in Redwood City; the San Jose Center is located at 1400 Parkmoor Avenue in San Jose; and the Milpitas Center is located at 600 Valley Way in Milpitas.
Requirements: All Bay Area 501(c)3 organizations and local public agencies are eligible to use the Foundation's nonprofit conference facilities at no charge, on a first-come, first-served reservation basis. All activities must be related to and support the charitable mission of their agency. A $1 million General Liability Certificate of Insurance naming the Sobrato Foundation, Silicon Valley Community Foundation, the Sobrato Family Foundation and the Sobrato Organization and their related entities as additionally insured is required for every meeting use. Reservation can be made by sending an email request which includes: contact name, phone and email address; the nonprofit's legal name and employer identification number; the date and start and end time of the meeting (including set up & take down); the number of expected meeting attendees; and the preferred Conference Center.
Restrictions: Commercial, religious, and partisan political activities are prohibited. The rooms are not available for use by individuals, groups without 501(c)3 status, or those that cannot produce the required certificate of insurance.
Geographic Focus: California
Contact: Community Conference Coordinator; (408) 466-0700; fax (408) 996-9516; Meetings@Sobrato.org
Internet: www.sobrato.org/what-we-do/meeting-space-grants-eligibility
Sponsor: Sobrato Family Foundation
10600 N De Anza Boulevard, Suite 225
Cupertino, CA 95014

Sobrato Family Foundation Office Space Grants **2213**
The Sobrato Family Foundation is dedicated to helping create and sustain a vibrant and healthy community, where all Silicon Valley residents have equal opportunity to live, work and be enriched. To accomplish this purpose, the Foundation invests in strong community-based nonprofits that promote self-reliance and economic independence, and positively contribute to the quality of life for economically, physically and/or emotionally challenged individuals in Santa Clara, Southern San Mateo and Southern Alameda Counties. The Foundation has two office business parks available for multi-tenant nonprofit centers: Sobrato Center for Nonprofits Milpitas, and Sobrato Center for Nonprofits San Jose. A third center in Redwood Shores is scheduled for future opening.
Requirements: There is a competitive review process for Office Space Grants. Awards are based on the following: alignment with the Foundation's mission and client service priorities; the organization's capacity to support its mission, including program quality and effectiveness, staff and board leadership, and the organization's reputation and experience; the organization's capital structure to support its mission; and the organization's effective use of space relative to the available unit(s) open. Application can be made on-line from the Foundation's website.
Geographic Focus: California
Contact: Mara Williams Low, Manager; (408) 466-0700; fax (408) 996-9516;
MLow@Sobrato.org or grants@Sobrato.org
Internet: www.sobrato.org/what-we-do/office-space-grants
Sponsor: Sobrato Family Foundation
10600 N De Anza Boulevard, Suite 225
Cupertino, CA 95014

Social Justice Fund Northwest Criminal Justice Giving Project Grants **2214**
Social Justice Fund Northwest is a public membership foundation that supports organizations working for structural change, to improve the lives of people most affected by political, economic and social inequities. The Criminal Justice Giving Project is a diverse group of people who have committed to building community together, learning about intersections of race and class in the systems that criminalize poor people of people of color and about the movement for social justice, and working together to fund strategic, inspiring, and under-resourced community organizing. Criminal Justice Giving Project grants are one-year awards of up to $15,000 each to support social change in Idaho, Montana, Oregon, Washington and Wyoming, specifically focused on criminal justice issues. Such issues are defined broadly to include all of the systems which criminalize the lives of people of color and poor people. Examples include, but are not limited to, immigration, school discipline, child protective services and foster care, in addition to issues which directly involve the criminal justice system.
Requirements: To be eligible for any Social Justice Fund grant program, an organization must: be a nonprofit organization with 501(c)3 or 501(c)4 status as determined by the IRS, or be a federally recognized American Indian tribal government or agency; be led by people who are most directly affected by the problems that the organization or project is addressing; carry out most of its work in Idaho, Montana, Oregon, Washington, and/or Wyoming; and satisfy evaluation requirements for all previous Social Justice Fund grants. The committee welcomes applications from people with all levels of English fluency and formal education; therefore, grammatical and spelling errors will not negatively impact scores. In addition, small and/or new organizations are encouraged to apply. If your organization does not have tax-exempt status or sponsorship, but might otherwise be a good fit for this grant, contact Social Justice Fund staff so that they can assist you with your eligibility.
Geographic Focus: Idaho, Montana, Oregon, Washington, Wyoming
Date(s) Application is Due: May 11
Amount of Grant: Up to 15,000 USD
Contact: Mijo Lee; (206) 624-4081; fax (206) 382-2640; mijo@socialjusticefund.org
Karen Toering, (206) 624-4081; fax (206) 382-2640; karen@socialjusticefund.org
Internet: www.socialjusticefund.org/apply-grant
Sponsor: Social Justice Fund Northwest
1904 Third Avenue, Suite 806
Seattle, WA 98101

Social Justice Fund Northwest Economic Justice Giving Project Grants **2215**
Social Justice Fund Northwest is a public membership foundation that supports organizations working for structural change, to improve the lives of people most affected by political, economic and social inequities. Economic Justice Giving Project grants are one-year awards of up to $10,000 each to support social change in Idaho, Montana, Oregon, Washington and Wyoming, specifically focused on economic justice issues. Such issues are defined broadly to include work that addresses the root causes of economic inequity using community led solutions to build power among its members (ie. workers, families, faith communities etc.) to advocate for and create thriving communities. Examples of this activity include, but are not limited to: worker and consumer protections, transportation access, healthcare solutions, affordable housing, tax policy, and impacts of the wealth divide on low income, people of color, immigrants, disability and LGBTQ populations.
Requirements: To be eligible for any Social Justice Fund grant program, an organization must: be a nonprofit organization with 501(c)3 or 501(c)4 status as determined by the IRS, or be a federally recognized American Indian tribal government or agency; be led by people who are most directly affected by the problems that the organization or project is addressing; carry out most of its work in Idaho, Montana, Oregon, Washington, and/or Wyoming; and satisfy evaluation requirements for all previous Social Justice Fund grants.
Geographic Focus: Idaho, Montana, Oregon, Washington, Wyoming
Date(s) Application is Due: Jun 8
Amount of Grant: 10,000 USD
Contact: Kylie Gursky; (206) 624-4081; fax (206) 382-2640; kylie@socialjusticefund.org
Karen Toering; (206) 624-4081; fax (206) 382-2640; karen@socialjusticefund.org
Internet: www.socialjusticefund.org/apply-grant
Sponsor: Social Justice Fund Northwest
1904 Third Avenue, Suite 806
Seattle, WA 98101

Sony Corporation of America Grants **2216**
Sony Corporation of America consists of three operating companies as well as the corporate headquarters, which is based in New York City: Sony Electronics, Inc. (headquarters in San Diego, California); Sony Pictures Entertainment, Inc. (headquarters in Culver City, California); and Sony Music Entertainment, Inc. (headquarters in New York City). Each company, as well as the overall corporation, has its own philanthropic priorities and resources (e.g. grants, product donations, and recordings and screenings) that benefit a multitude of causes. Taken together the corporation's areas of interest cover arts and culture; health and human services; civic and community outreach, education; the environment; disaster response; and volunteerism. The core of Sony's various corporate philanthropy programs are their contributions to the communities in which Sony employees work and live; however, the corporation and subsidiaries contribute to national nonprofits as well. In the past, types of support have included general operating budgets, continuing support, annual campaigns, seed grants, building construction, equipment acquisition, endowment funds, employee matching gifts, internships, and employee-related scholarships. Sony Corporation of America and its subsidiaries welcome requests for support throughout the year. There is no grant application form. Requests must be submitted in writing to the corporation or its operating companies. Contact information is given on this page and at the website. Guidelines for what to include in the application as well as more information on types of programs the corporation and/or its subsidiaries have supported are available at the grant website. Notification of grant-request approval or rejection will be made in writing within one month of receipt of all proposed materials.
Requirements: U.S. nonprofits, including schools and school districts, are eligible.
Restrictions: The corporation does not consider multi-year requests for support. The following types of organizations will not be funded: organizations that discriminate on the basis of race, color, creed, gender, religion, age, national origin, or sexual orientation; partisan political organizations, committees, or candidates and public office holders; religious organizations in support of their sacramental or theological functions; labor unions; endowment or capital campaigns of national origin; organizations whose prime purpose is to influence legislation; testimonial dinners in general; for-profit publications or organizations seeking advertisements or promotional support; individuals seeking self-advancement; foreign or non-U.S.-based organizations; and organizations whose mission is outside of the U.S.
Geographic Focus: All States
Amount of Grant: 1,000 - 100,000 USD
Contact: Janice Pober, Senior Vice President, Corporate Social Responsibility;
(310) 244-7737; SPE_CSR@spe.sony.com
Karen E. Kelso, Vice-President; (212) 833-8000; SCA_CSR@sonyusa.com
Julie Wenzel, Senior Manager, Community Relations; (858) 942-2400;
SELCommunityAffairs@am.sony.com
Internet: www.sony.com/SCA/philanthropy/guidelines.shtml
Sponsor: Sony Corporation of America
550 Madison Avenue, 33rd Floor
New York, NY 10022-3211

Sorenson Legacy Foundation Grants **2217**
The Sorenson Legacy Foundation has a broad spectrum of philanthropic interests and supports endeavors that: encourage and support the long-term preservation and enhancement of the quality of life of all humankind, especially of families and children; assist the disenfranchised of society, such as but not limited to, abused spouses and children, in order that they receive the full benefits of membership in society and fulfill their potential as human beings; promote medical research and the development of innovative medical technologies for saving lives and alleviating pain and suffering; promote the development of the arts, including art education in schools, assistance of promising young artists, and support of performing arts organizations; promote community development and security, adequate and affordable housing, and education and job training; promote law and order generally and provide youth with alternatives to gangs, crime and socially nonproductive behavior; protect and enhance the environment, preserve wild and open spaces, and promote development of parks and green spaces; promote the development of science, culture and recreation; promote world peace and unity through a greater understanding, tolerance and harmony among religious, national and ethnic groups; advance the programs at private and state universities and colleges that are consistent with the foundation's charter; and, advance the mission of the Church of Jesus Christ of Latter-day Saints in all its places. Grant applications are reviewed by the foundation's board of directors on a quarterly basis. There are four identified deadline for submission: March 1; June 1; September 1; and December 1.
Requirements: All Sorenson Legacy Foundation applications will be reviewed and screened to ensure that applications are appropriate within the foundation's charter and are approved and in good standing with IRS 501(c)3 requirements. All grant submissions must use the downloadable grant application.
Geographic Focus: All States
Date(s) Application is Due: Mar 1; Jun 1; Sep 1; Dec 1
Contact: Lisa Meiling, Executive Director; (801) 461-9797 or (801) 461-9700;
lisa@sorensonlegacyfoundation.org
Internet: www.sorensonlegacyfoundation.org/grant_seekers/application_guidelines
Sponsor: Sorenson Foundation
6900 S. 900 E., Suite 230
Midvale, UT 84047

Southern California Edison Education Grants 2218

Southern California Edison (SCE) is one of the nation's largest electric utilities, delivering power to 15 million people in 50,000 square-miles across central, coastal and Southern California, excluding the City of Los Angeles and some other cities. Edison invests significant resources in developing and nurturing partnerships with community-based organizations in SCE's service territory through targeted philanthropic giving in four areas of priority: education; the environment; the under served; and public safety and emergency preparedness. In the area of education, Edison views 21st century workforce preparation as a key business imperative. Many of Edison's educational initiatives focus on increasing math, science and technology-literacy skills. In-kind gifts of laptop and desktop computers are provided to public and private schools serving K-12 student populations and to nonprofit organizations located in and adjacent to the Edison service territory. Applications for grants are accepted during the following funding cycles: March 1 to March 31; May 1 to May 31; August 1 to August 31; and October 1 to October 31 The majority of funding requests generally take between six and eight weeks for review. Organizations are eligible to receive one grant per calendar year.

Requirements: To be eligible for donations of laptop and desktop computers, schools must be state-accredited and not-for-profit.

Restrictions: Edison's grant programs do not support: individuals; private charities or foundations not aligned with our principle areas of charitable giving; religious organizations, unless the particular program will benefit a large portion of a community without regard to religious affiliation; political causes, candidates, organizations or campaigns; organizations whose primary purpose is to influence legislation; fraternities or sororities; endowments or capital campaigns; research studies or video projects, including student films and documentaries, unless related to initiatives Edison International is already supporting; local, regional or national sports teams or activities; medical research and disease-specific initiatives; medical procedures for individuals; tickets for contests, raffles or other activities with prizes; promotional merchandise; any group whose activities are not in the best interest of Edison International, its affiliates, employees, shareholders, customers or the communities it serves; or donations to charities in lieu of compensation to an individual for services rendered to the company (or any of its affiliates).

Geographic Focus: California

Date(s) Application is Due: Mar 31; May 31; Aug 31; Oct 31

Amount of Grant: Up to 25,000 USD

Contact: Alex Garibay, Customer Experience; (626) 302-9706 or (866) 840-6438; alejandro.garibay@SCE.com or edison.gifts@sce.com

Internet: www.edison.com/home/community/our-funding-priorities.html

Sponsor: Southern California Edison

P.O. Box 800

Rosemead, CA 91770

Southern Minnesota Initiative Foundation AmeriCorps Leap Grants 2219

Southern Minnesota Initiative Foundation has been a catalyst for economic growth in twenty Minnesota counties since 1986. The Foundation works to build a prosperous region with vibrant communities and innovative businesses. To accomplish this, the Foundation invests in strategic efforts in early childhood education and economic development. There are Grant opportunities for individuals and organizations/groups that focus on the social and emotional development of young children. Programs may engage an AmeriCorps member in service for eleven months. Members are recruited, connected, and matched to site service partner positions. Placements are made as members are engaged in the program. Members begin the LEAP service term the the last week in August and serve through the following July.

Requirements: Southern Minnesota 501(c)3 nonprofit organizations in existence for at least one year, local units of government, or public school districts serving the residents of the following counties are eligible: Blue Earth, Brown, Dodge, Faribault, Fillmore, Freeborn, Goodhue, Houston, Le Sueur, Martin, Mower, Nicollet, Olmsted, Rice, Sibley, Steele, Wabasha, Waseca, Watonwan, and Winona.

Geographic Focus: Minnesota

Contact: Teri Steckelberg; (507) 455-3215, ext. 132; teris@smifoundation.org

Internet: smifoundation.org/childed.php?sec=3#leap

Sponsor: Southern Minnesota Initiative Foundation

525 Florence Avenue, P.O. Box 695

Owatonna, MN 55060-0695

Southern Minnesota Initiative Foundation BookStart Grants 2220

Southern Minnesota Initiative Foundation has been a catalyst for economic growth in twenty Minnesota counties since 1986. The Foundation works to build a prosperous region with vibrant communities and innovative businesses. To accomplish this, the Foundation invests in strategic efforts in early childhood education and economic development. The Foundation's BookStart Grants provide books to organizations committed to distributing books and literacy programming directly to young people.

Requirements: Southern Minnesota 501(c)3 nonprofit organizations in existence for at least one year, local units of government, or public school districts serving the residents of the following counties are eligible: Blue Earth, Brown, Dodge, Faribault, Fillmore, Freeborn, Goodhue, Houston, Le Sueur, Martin, Mower, Nicollet, Olmsted, Rice, Sibley, Steele, Wabasha, Waseca, Watonwan, and Winona. Applications are available in March of each year. For more information about the Grants and the application process, contact the Early Childhood Coordinator.

Geographic Focus: Minnesota

Contact: Teri Steckelberg; (507) 455-3215, ext. 132; teris@smifoundation.org

Internet: smifoundation.org/childed.php?sec=3#bookstart

Sponsor: Southern Minnesota Initiative Foundation

525 Florence Avenue, P.O. Box 695

Owatonna, MN 55060-0695

Southern Minnesota Initiative Foundation Community Growth Grants 2221

Southern Minnesota Initiative Foundation has been a catalyst for economic growth in twenty Minnesota counties since 1986. The Foundation works to build a prosperous region with vibrant communities and innovative businesses. To accomplish this, the Foundation invests in strategic efforts in early childhood education and economic development. The Foundation's Community Growth Initiative Grants bring community members together to evaluate the assets of the community, set goals, and accomplish a project of choice. The Foundation provides facilitation, technical assistance, and up to $15,000 to assist asset based community development efforts that lead to economic growth and prosperity.

Requirements: Southern Minnesota 501(c)3 nonprofit organizations in existence for at least one year, local units of government, or public school districts serving the residents of the following counties are eligible: Blue Earth, Brown, Dodge, Faribault, Fillmore, Freeborn, Goodhue, Houston, Le Sueur, Martin, Mower, Nicollet, Olmsted, Rice, Sibley, Steele, Wabasha, Waseca, Watonwan, and Winona. Communities are selected through a request for proposal process.

Geographic Focus: Minnesota

Amount of Grant: 15,000 USD

Contact: Jennifer Heien, Grants Associate; (507) 455-3215; fax (507) 455-3215, ext. 133; jenniferh@smifoundation.org

Internet: smifoundation.org/applications.php

Sponsor: Southern Minnesota Initiative Foundation

525 Florence Avenue, P.O. Box 695

Owatonna, MN 55060-0695

Southern Minnesota Initiative Foundation Home Visiting Grants 2222

The Southern Minnesota Initiative Foundation has been a catalyst for economic growth in twenty Minnesota counties since 1986. The Foundation works to build a prosperous region with vibrant communities and innovative businesses. To accomplish this, the Foundation invests in early childhood education and economic development. The Foundation's Home Visiting Grants enhance and increase visitation services. The Foundation is committed to ensuring that all young children thrive and have a healthy life of learning, achieving, and succeeding. Through home visiting programs, families expecting a child or having an infant voluntarily meet with a trained professional who provides information about the child's development, parenting support, and community resources. Measurable results of effective home visitation programs include increased immunization rates, increased enrollment in early learning classes and fewer incidences of abuse and neglect.

Requirements: Tax-exempt nonprofit organizations or units or agencies of local, state, or federal government located in or serving residents of the Foundation's twenty-county service area (Blue Earth, Brown, Dodge, Faribault, Fillmore, Freeborn, Goodhue, Houston, Le Sueur, Martin, Mower, Nicollet, Olmsted, Rice, Sibley, Steele, Wabasha, Waseca, Watonwan, and Winona counties) are eligible.

Geographic Focus: Minnesota

Contact: Teri Steckelberg, Early Childhood Coordinator; (507) 455-3215, ext. 132; teris@smifoundation.org

Internet: smifoundation.org/childed.php?sec=3#homevisitation

Sponsor: Southern Minnesota Initiative Foundation

525 Florence Avenue, P.O. Box 695

Owatonna, MN 55060-0695

Southern Minnesota Initiative Foundation Incentive Grants 2223

Southern Minnesota Initiative Foundation has been a catalyst for economic growth in twenty Minnesota counties since 1986. The Foundation works to build a prosperous region with vibrant communities and innovative businesses. To accomplish this, the Foundation invests in strategic efforts in early childhood education and economic development. The Foundation's Incentive Grants support new asset-based approaches to current opportunities. Support for early childhood development projects prepare young children for a life of learning, achieving and succeeding. This may include early literacy projects, health promotion, kindergarten transition programs, programs that support social and emotional development, programs that support skilled and knowledgeable child care providers, or similar projects. Support for economic development projects help communities grow local business while building on the assets of the region. In particular, support is provided for partnerships which help increase the capacity of community/organizational efforts to support entrepreneurs and advance the development of bio science initiatives. Projects may include training, collaboration development and technical assistance programs, or similar projects.

Requirements: Tax-exempt nonprofit organizations or units or agencies of local, state, or federal government located in or serving residents of the Foundation's twenty-county service area (Blue Earth, Brown, Dodge, Faribault, Fillmore, Freeborn, Goodhue, Houston, Le Sueur, Martin, Mower, Nicollet, Olmsted, Rice, Sibley, Steele, Wabasha, Waseca, Watonwan, and Winona counties) are eligible. Priority consideration is given to applications which best demonstrate: asset-based approaches (projects that maximize the strengths, talents, and resources of the local community); collaboration and partnership (projects that work with other organizations in unique and effective ways); measurable results (projects that can show quantitative results in the Foundation's focus areas); sustainability of local or other funding streams (projects that have solid plans for continuation outside of Foundation funding); and leveraged funding (projects that access all available resources and maximize the Foundation's investment). All Grants require dollar-for-dollar match. At least twenty-five percent of the match must be cash in hand at the time of the award. No more than seventy-five percent of the match can be in-kind support. In-kind support is defined as goods or services (rather than cash) that are used to directly benefit the project. Grant applications are reviewed twice annually, with submission deadlines in February and August.

Restrictions: The following are excluded: individuals, businesses, or other for-profit organizations; general operating expenses; capital campaigns or endowments; existing deficits or projects already in progress or completed; organizations that have not satisfied a past grant obligation; replacement of discontinued government funding; and funds for re-granting or to establish loan pools.
Geographic Focus: Minnesota
Amount of Grant: 20,000 USD
Contact: Jennifer Heien; (507) 455-3215, ext. 133; jenniferh@smifoundation.org
Internet: smifoundation.org/entre.php?sec=2#incgrants
Sponsor: Southern Minnesota Initiative Foundation
525 Florence Avenue, P.O. Box 695
Owatonna, MN 55060-0695

Southern New England Folk and Traditional Arts Apprenticeship Grants 2224

Folk or traditional arts are those artistic practices that have an occupational, geographic, ethnic, community or family base, and are shared and understood by all as part of that community's aesthetic heritage. The apprenticeship grants are designed to foster the sharing of traditional artistic skills through the apprenticeship learning model of regular, intensive, one-on-one teaching by a master artist to a student/apprentice, both of whom share a common base, as defined above. Sponsored by the Institute for Community Research (Connecticut Cultural Heritage Arts Program), Rhode Island State Council on the Arts (Folk Arts Program) and Massachusetts Cultural Council (Folk and Traditional Arts Program), the apprenticeship grants enable masters and apprentices to travel and teach across state lines. Master artists may also apply to share their skills or repertoires with an equally accomplished master artist from the same community in another of the three states. Only one application is allowed per person. This year six to nine master/apprentice pairs will be selected to receive teaching contracts. The amount each pair will receive will depend on the number of contracts awarded. Previous amounts have been around $2000. Applicants are encouraged to contact the sponsor to verify current proposal deadline and submission requirements.
Requirements: Massachusetts, Rhode Island, and Connecticut residents may apply as master artists or apprentices. Master and apprentice artists must share an occupational, geographic, ethnic, community or family base. Most of the funding should go towards the master artist's fee. Modest materials and/or travel costs may be allowable. The Institute for Community Research generates and carefully monitors all contract work.
Geographic Focus: Connecticut, Massachusetts, Rhode Island
Date(s) Application is Due: Oct 13
Amount of Grant: 2,000 USD
Samples: Chue Yang, Massachusetts with Mai See Her and Mai Xion, Connecticut - Hmong needlework; Daniel Boucher, Rhode Island with Nate Ouellette, Connecticut - Franco American fiddling repertoire; Angel Sanches, Massachusetts with Lydia Perez, Rhode Island - Puerto Rican veijigante masks
Contact: Lynne Williamson, M.Litt., Director, Connecticut Cultural Heritage Arts Program; (860) 278-2044 ext. 251; fax (860) 278-2141; lynne.williamson@icrweb.org
Maggie Holtzberg, Ph.D., Folk and Traditional Arts Coordinator; (617) 727-3668; fax (617) 727-0044; maggie.holtzberg@art.state.ma.us
Internet: www.arts.ri.gov/folkarts/FolkandTraditionalArtsGrantInfo.php
Sponsor: Rhode Island State Council on the Arts
One Capitol Hill, Third Floor
Providence, RI 02908-1034

South Madison Community Foundation - Teacher Creativity Mini Grants 2225

The South Madison Community Foundation - Teacher Creativity Mini Grants offer Lapel Elementary School teachers the opportunity to receive grants to help cover learning experiences that they feel are important to their students' education, but are outside the budget of their school. These grants are to be used for classroom supplies, class projects, programs, music or art instruction, educational materials, and other uses that would enhance classroom instruction. The Foundation encourages creativity and is reluctant to fund on-going projects that have been funded through this program in the past. Applications can be found at the Foundation's website.
Requirements: Teachers must fill out the online application and discuss the purpose of their project, what they hope their class will learn, whether funded materials can be used or shared with future classes, and how they plan to fund the project if it exceeds $100.
Restrictions: Applicants must be teachers at Lapel Elementary School. The Foundation is reluctant to provide funding for on-going projects and projects that have been funded through this program in the past. Once a grant is received, the Foundation anticipates that the funds shall be expended during the school year awarded.
Geographic Focus: Indiana
Date(s) Application is Due: Sep 1
Amount of Grant: Up to 100 USD
Contact: Barbara Switzer; (765) 778-8444; barbara@southmadisonfoundation.org
Internet: www.southmadisonfoundation.org/lapel-elementary-mini-grants-south-madison-indiana-community-foundation.html
Sponsor: South Madison Community Foundation
233 South Main Street
Pendleton, IN 46064

Southwest Initiative Foundation Grants 2226

The Southwest Initiative Foundation is a regional community foundation dedicated to advancing southwest Minnesota through leadership, relationship building, program development, and philanthropy. The Foundation works to ensure that southwest Minnesota is a highly productive and engaged region where growing numbers of people choose to live. Most Grants awarded have a strong connection to their current initiatives including: renewable energy; entrepreneurship; connected communities; early childhood; the Paul &

Alma Schwan Aging Trust Fund; and the Student Enrichment Fund. Grants generally range from $1,000 to $20,000 and require a fifty percent match through in-kind and other cash contributions.
Requirements: Proposals must demonstrate a benefit within the following eighteen counties in southwest Minnesota: Big Stone, Chippewa, Cottonwood, Jackson, Kandiyohi, Lac qui Parle, Lincoln, Lyon, McLeod, Meeker, Murray, Nobles, Pipestone, Redwood, Renville, Rock, Swift, and Yellow Medicine. The Foundation prefers applicants located within the eighteen-county area it serves and that ideas and visions are generated locally. Applicants must be a 501(c)3 organization, a unit of government, or a public agency. Successful proposals should: include involvement early in the proposed project and throughout implementation by targeted and diverse populations; incorporate an innovative approach and avoid duplication of efforts; have clearly stated goals and measurable outcomes; and exhibit evidence of appropriate partnerships. Applicants complete an online pre-application questionnaire and after submission are either invited to make a full application or declined..
Restrictions: Funding for the following is generally ineligible: capital expenditures; religious purposes or activities; lobbying or political activities; for-profit businesses; debt retirement; ongoing, open ended grant funding; administrative budgets for existing organizations; arts; programs or services mandated by law or to replace government funding; and national fundraising campaigns, ticket sales, fundraising dinners, endowment drives, or other similar activities. Churches and religious organizations may apply for support for activities that benefit the larger community but not for activities that have a sectarian religious purpose.
Geographic Focus: Minnesota
Contact: Nancy Fasching, Senior Administration and Grants Officer; (320) 587-5858 or (800) 594-9480; fax (320) 587-3838; nancyf@swifoundation.org
Internet: www.swifoundation.org/grants.html
Sponsor: Southwest Initiative Foundation
15 3rd Avenue NW
Hutchinson, MN 55350

Special Olympics Eunice Kennedy Shriver (EKS) Fellowships 2227

The Eunice Kennedy Shriver (EKS) Program aims to develop leadership on the field of intellectual disability through development of cross-sector bonds among professionals working in the field of intellectual disability in developing countries. Fellowships will be granted to candidates with a commitment to NGO or governmental efforts that support people with intellectual disabilities. Participants will receive an intense, hands-on learning experience that will benefit them both professionally and personally. Fellows will receive Mentors in their Host Programs that will support their learning. Likewise, the Special Olympics Program in their home country will provide aid in their six-month volunteer project upon their return. Fellows will also receive programmatic support from a dedicated team of professionals based in the Washington, D.C Special Olympics headquarters office. All housing, food, transportation to and from the host country and other travel as directed by Special Olympics, Inc. will be covered at the U.S. government per diem rate. In addition, a stipend for other living expenses will be awarded to each Fellow in the Program.
Requirements: Fellows will be financially responsible for obtaining their passports and visas.
Geographic Focus: All States
Contact: Lisa Dietz; (202) 824-0228; fax (202) 824-0200; ldietz@specialolympics.org
Internet: www.specialolympics.org/EKS_fellowship.aspx
Sponsor: Special Olympics
1133 19th Street, NW
Washington, D.C. 20036-3604

Special Olympics Project UNIFY Grants 2228

Following the groundswell of enthusiasm and interest from the 2009 Global Youth Activation Summit, Special Olympics Project UNIFY has announced funding opportunities for youth advocates across North America. Special Olympics' Project UNIFY is a U.S. national program, funded by the U.S. Department of Education. The goal of Project UNIFY is to activate youth around the country in an effort to develop school communities where all young people are agents of change - fostering respect, dignity and advocacy for people with intellectual disabilities by utilizing the programs and initiatives of Special Olympics. The Program's intent is to provide Sub Award (Grant) opportunities of up to $5,000 for youth to implement projects that demonstrate the principles of Project UNIFY and the eight motions of the Global Youth Activation Summit Assembly.
Requirements: To be eligible for consideration for this sub award (grant), you must be at least 12 years of age up to 20 years, or a current undergraduate student in college. A Special Olympics North America Program is required to be your main partner organization.
Geographic Focus: All States
Date(s) Application is Due: Dec 31
Contact: Oscar J. Harrell, Grants Manager; (202) 824-0269; oharrell@specialolympics.org
Internet: www.specialolympics.org/project_unify_grants.aspx
Sponsor: Special Olympics
1133 19th Street, NW
Washington, D.C. 20036-3604

Special Olympics Youth Fan Grants 2229

Special Olympics is the leader in cutting-edge research and evaluation to better understand the many challenges faced by people with intellectual disabilities and the significant impact of Special Olympics on their lives. The program's independent research is also a driving force for realizing improved policies, laws and rights for people with intellectual disabilities around the world. Projects may be research-based or programmatic (conferences, health promotion programs, etc), but if they are programmatic they must still contain an evaluation component.
Geographic Focus: All States

Contact: Kathleen Palermo, Grants Coordinator – Healthy Athletes; (202) 628-3630 or (202) 824-0238; fax (202) 628-3926; kpalermo@specialolympics.org
Internet: www.specialolympics.org/research_studies.aspx
Sponsor: Special Olympics
1133 19th Street, NW
Washington, D.C. 20036-3604

Speer Trust Grants   2230
The purpose of the Trust is to assist organizations in Delaware or the Eastern Shore of Maryland addressing poverty by encouraging the poor to gain responsibility and control over their lives. Projects or programs should provide an opportunity to partner with members of the Presbyterian Church. An online application is available at the website.
Requirements: Eligible applicants must be a 501(c)3 organization with a Board of Directors; provide services in Delaware or the Eastern Shore of Maryland; and work in partnership with a Presbyterian church on the proposed project.
Restrictions: Organizations are funded only once a year. A second year of funding is provided only if there is an expansion or new component of the previous project. Organizations that are not 501(c)3 tax-exempt or that do not have a Board of Directors are not necessarily denied but may not qualify for the amount requested.
Geographic Focus: Delaware, Maryland
Date(s) Application is Due: Apr 1; Oct 15
Samples: Habitat for Humanity, Wilmington, Delaware, $10,000 - A Brush of Kindness, a program serving low income homeowners who struggle to maintain the exterior of their homes; Connections CSP, Inc., Wilmington, Delaware, $20,000 - Connect to Work, a program providing employment and economic development services for the residents of Sparrow Run; and YWCA Delaware, Georgetown, Delaware, $15,000 - ESTEEM, a program targeting low income middle and high school youth 11 to 17.
Contact: Jacqueline Taylor, Executive Director; (302) 366-0595; fax (302) 366-0714; SpeerOffice@ncpresbytery.org
Internet: www.speertrust.org/Apply.asp
Sponsor: Speer Trust
256 Chapman Road, Suite 205
Newark, DE 19702

Spencer County Community Foundation Recreation Grants   2231
The Spencer County Community Foundation is a nonprofit, public charity created for the people of Spencer County, Indiana. The Foundation helps nonprofits fulfill their missions by strengthening their ability to meet community needs through grants that assist charitable programs, address community issues, support community agencies, launch community initiatives, and support leadership development. Grant proposals are accepted year round, and encompasses three different request levels: level one requests of $2,500 and below, with an online grant application required to apply); level two requests of $2,501 to $10,000, with an online grant application also required to apply; and level three requests over $10,000, with an online letter of inquiry and face-to-face meeting with the grants committee required to apply). Grants are typically given as one time support of a project, but may be considered for additional support for expansions or outgrowths of an initial project. Funding requests will be reviewed throughout the year as follows: level one on September 15, December 15, March 15, and June 15; level two on December 15 and June 15; and level three is open-ended. Grants in the area of Recreation include projects aimed at improving and promoting recreational and leisure activities, parks, and community sporting events and activities. Samples of previously funded projects are available at the website.
Requirements: The Spencer County Community Foundation welcomes proposals from nonprofit organizations that are tax exempt under sections 501(c)3 and 509(a) and from governmental agencies serving the County of Spencer, Indiana. Proposals from nonprofit organizations not classified as a 501(c)3 public charity may be considered if the project is charitable and supports a community need. Proposals submitted by an entity under the auspices of another agency must include a written statement signed by the agency's board president on behalf of the board of directors agreeing to act as the entity's fiscal sponsor, to receive grant monies if awarded, and to oversee the proposed project. School administrators and teachers planning to apply for a grant must contact the Foundation prior to beginning the application process to discuss guidelines pertaining to funding requests from school personnel and school corporation oversight of the application process.
Restrictions: Project areas not considered for funding: religious organizations for religious purposes; political parties or campaigns; endowment creation or debt reduction; or annual appeals or membership contributions.
Geographic Focus: Indiana
Date(s) Application is Due: Mar 15; Jun 15; Sep 15; Dec 15
Amount of Grant: Up to 20,000 USD
Contact: Laura Harmon, Regional Director; (812) 649-5724; laura@spencercommunityfoundation.org or lharmon@communityfoundationalliance.org
Internet: www.communityfoundationalliance.org/spencer/program-areas/
Sponsor: Spencer County Community Foundation
Lincoln Commerce Center
Rockport, IN 47635

Spencer County Community Foundation Women's Fund Grants   2232
The Spencer County Women's Fund is about strong, caring, and focused women determined to make a difference. Throughout history, women have shaped the world as national leaders, advocates for social justice, scientists, authors, teachers, and healers. Every day, women make positive contributions to the world, and when visionary women work together around a common cause, they have an even greater impact – like the Women's Fund. In 2006, a group of visionary women started the Women's Fund as a permanent resource to support local programs that give opportunities, encouragement, knowledge, and hope to

our community's women and girls. As the endowment grows, it will be used to make yearly grants supporting a variety of resources serving women of all ages, such as programs that prevent domestic violence, secure family-supporting jobs, promote health and education and, perhaps most importantly, develop confidence. Grant proposals are accepted once each year. Grants are normally given as one time support of a project but may be considered for additional support for expansions or outgrowths of an initial project. The annual deadline for application submission is February 20. The application form and examples of previously funded projects available at the website.
Requirements: Projects must address the needs which support the Fund's mission by providing opportunities, encouragement, knowledge, information, and hope for the community's women and girls. The Women's Fund welcomes proposals from non-profit organizations that are tax-exempt under sections 501(c)3 and 509(a) of the Internal Revenue Code and from governmental agencies serving Spencer County, Indiana, women and girls. Proposals from other non-profit organizations that address issues facing women and girls in the county may be accepted. Proposals submitted by an entity under the auspices of another agency must include a written statement signed by the agency's board president on behalf of the board of directors agreeing to act as the entity's fiscal sponsor, to receive grant monies if awarded, and to oversee the proposed project.
Geographic Focus: Indiana
Date(s) Application is Due: Feb 20
Amount of Grant: Up to 10,000 USD
Contact: Laura Harmon, Regional Director; (812) 649-5724; laura@spencercommunityfoundation.org or lharmon@communityfoundationalliance.org
Sponsor: Spencer County Community Foundation
Lincoln Commerce Center
Rockport, IN 47635

Spencer County Community Foundation Youth Development Grants   2233
The Spencer County Community Foundation is a nonprofit, public charity created for the people of Spencer County, Indiana. The Foundation helps nonprofits fulfill their missions by strengthening their ability to meet community needs through grants that assist charitable programs, address community issues, support community agencies, launch community initiatives, and support leadership development. Grant proposals are accepted year round, and encompass three different request levels: level one requests of $2,500 and below, with an online grant application required to apply; level two requests of $2,501 to $10,000, with an online grant application also required to apply; and level three requests over $10,000, with an online letter of inquiry and face-to-face meeting with the grants committee required to apply. Grants are typically given as one time support of a project, but may be considered for additional support for expansions or outgrowths of an initial project. Funding requests will be reviewed throughout the year as follows: level one on September 15, December 15, March 15, and June 15; level two on December 15 and June 15; and level three is open-ended. Grants in the area of Youth Development include activities that strengthen the family unit, help children grow and develop, foster youth sports and athletics, support the YMCA, and support daycare-related issues.
Requirements: The Spencer County Community Foundation welcomes proposals from nonprofit organizations that are tax exempt under sections 501(c)3 and 509(a) and from governmental agencies serving the County of Spencer, Indiana. Proposals from nonprofit organizations not classified as a 501(c)3 public charity may be considered if the project is charitable and supports a community need. Proposals submitted by an entity under the auspices of another agency must include a written statement signed by the agency's board president on behalf of the board of directors agreeing to act as the entity's fiscal sponsor, to receive grant monies if awarded, and to oversee the proposed project. School administrators and teachers planning to apply for a grant must contact the Foundation prior to beginning the application process to discuss guidelines pertaining to funding requests from school personnel and school corporation oversight of the application process.
Restrictions: Project areas not considered for funding: religious organizations for religious purposes; political parties or campaigns; endowment creation or debt reduction; or annual appeals or membership contributions.
Geographic Focus: Indiana
Date(s) Application is Due: Mar 15; Jun 15; Sep 15; Dec 15
Amount of Grant: Up to 20,000 USD
Contact: Laura Harmon, Regional Director; (812) 649-5724; laura@spencercommunityfoundation.org or lharmon@communityfoundationalliance.org
Internet: www.communityfoundationalliance.org/spencer/program-areas/
Sponsor: Spencer County Community Foundation
Lincoln Commerce Center
Rockport, IN 47635

Sphinx Competition Awards   2234
The Sphinx Competition is held every year in Detroit, Michigan, and offers young Black and Latino classical-string players a chance to compete under the guidance of an internationally renowned panel of judges. The competition is divided into two age divisions, junior (age 18 and under) and senior (ages 18 - 26). To enter the contest, contestants must upload a current biography, repertoire list, high-resolution headshot, and video audition using the repertoire list supplied by the Sphinx organization. The upload link is available at the competition website, along with complete submission guidelines. Contestants must pay a $35 registration fee to enter the contest. 18 semi-finalists (nine from each age division) will be selected from the initial entries to compete in the live semi-final and final rounds of the competition which takes place in February. Senior Division Prizes will be awarded as follows: 1st Place - $10,000 cash prize, solo appearances with major orchestras, performance with the Sphinx Symphony Orchestra at the Finals Concert, and professional CD through White Pine Music; 2nd Place - $5,000 cash prize and performance with the Sphinx Symphony Orchestra at the Finals Concert; 3rd Place - $3,500 cash prize and performance

with the Sphinx Symphony Orchestra at the Finals Concert. Junior Division prizes will be awarded as follows: 1st Place - $5,000 cash prize, solo appearances with major orchestras, performances with the Sphinx Symphony Orchestra and at Finals Concert, and nationally-broadcast radio appearance on "From the Top"; 2nd Place - $3,500 cash prize, performance with the Sphinx Symphony Orchestra; and 3rd Place - $2,000 cash prize, performance with the Sphinx Symphony Orchestra. All semi-finalists will have invaluable educational and professional development opportunities during the competition and throughout the ensuing year. Deadlines may vary from year to year; applicants are encouraged to verify current deadline and competition dates.
Requirements: Black and Latino string players (violin, viola, cello, and double bass) under 18 (junior division) and 18-26 (senior division) residing in the U.S. are eligible to apply.
Restrictions: Participants in the Junior Division must not have reached their 18th birthday by February 15. Participants in the Senior Division must be at least 18 years old but not have reached their 27th birthday by February 17. Contestants must not have been a 1st Place Winner in their division in any previous Sphinx Competition.
Geographic Focus: All States
Date(s) Application is Due: Nov 13
Amount of Grant: Up to 10,000 USD
Contact: Andre Dowell, Artistic Administrator and Competition Director; (313) 877-9100 ext. 712; competition@sphinxmusic.org or andre@sphinxmusic.org
Internet: www.sphinxmusic.org/application-process.html
Sponsor: Sphinx Organization
400 Renaissance Center, Suite 2550
Detroit, MI 48243

Stan and Sandy Checketts Foundation Grants 2235
Stan Checketts, a member of The Church of Jesus Christ of Latter-day Saints from Cache Valley, Utah, has been inventing thrill rides and attractions for 40 years. According to a press release from Soaring Eagle, Checketts has more of his rides in amusement parks than any other person in the entertainment industry. In 1997, he was named National Entrepreneur of the Year by USA Today. His thrill rides have been featured in the Guinness Book of World Records, and he was highlighted in Rolling Stone Magazine in August of 2002. Established by Stan and Sandy Checketts in Utah in 1998, the Foundation's primary focus is on human services and helping individuals defray medical expenses. Primary fields of interest include: children and youth programs, health care, housing and shelter programs, human services, and recreation. Types of support are general operating funds and grants to individuals. Applicants should submit a detailed description of the project, along with the amount of funding requested. There are no annual deadlines for submission, and the primary geographic focus is the State of Utah.
Requirements: Any 501(c)3 organization adhering to the Foundation mission and supporting the residents of Utah are welcome to apply.
Geographic Focus: Utah
Amount of Grant: Up to 2,000 USD
Samples: Logan Regional Hospital, Logan, Utah, $1,500 - support for an interventional cardiology center; Cache Valley SCTB Local, Logan, Utah, $1,000 - general operating support.
Contact: Stan Checketts, President; (435) 752-1987; fax (435) 752-1948
Sponsor: Stan and Sandy Checketts Foundation
15 South Main, #400
Logan, UT 84341-1734

Starke County Community Foundation Grants 2236
The Starke Community Foundation offers grants to schools and teachers with the maximum amount of $500 per school. The following school systems are eligible to apply: Knox, North Judson-San Pierre and Oregon-Davis. Areas of interest include: community development; education; health and human services; youth; environment and recreation; and arts and culture. Applicants may fill out the online application, but are advised to contact the program coordinator to discuss their project before applying.
Requirements: The Foundation favors activities that: reach a broad segment of the community, especially those citizens whose needs are not being met by existing services that are normally expected to be provided by private rather than government sources; request seed money to realize innovative opportunities to meet needs in the community; stimulate and encourage additional funding; promote cooperation and avoid duplication of effort; help make a charitable organization more effective and efficient and better able to be self-sustaining; and one time projects or needs.
Restrictions: The Foundation will not consider grants for: religious organizations for the sole purpose of furthering that religion (this prohibition does not apply to funds created by donors who have specifically designated religious organizations as beneficiaries of the funds); political or lobbying activities; national organizations (unless the monies are to be used solely to benefit citizens of Starke County); grants that directly benefit the donor or the donor's family; fundraising projects; and contributions to endowments.
Geographic Focus: Indiana
Date(s) Application is Due: Sep 30
Amount of Grant: 500 USD
Contact: Grants Coordinator; (574) 223-2227 or (877) 432-6423
Internet: www.nicf.org/starke/grants.html
Sponsor: Starke County Community Foundation
1512 South Heaton Street
Knox, IN 46534

Starr Foundation Grants 2237
The Starr Foundation was established in Arkansas in 1991, with the expressed purpose of providing support to various fields of interest. These included: art museums; arts and culture; child welfare; education; equal opportunity; family services; housing development;

and human services. Targeted groups are comprised of: children and youth; economically disadvantaged; ethnic and racial minorities; low-income; and people with disabilities. Most recent awards have ranged from $500 to $5,000. There are no annual deadlines or formal applications, and interested parties should begin by sending a letter of application.
Requirements: Any 501(c)3 organization serving residents of Little Rock, Arkansas, may apply.
Geographic Focus: Arkansas
Amount of Grant: Up to 5,000 USD
Samples: 20th Century Club Lodge, Little Rock, Arkansas, $1,500 - general operating funds; Alzheimer's Arkansas, Little Rock, Arkansas, $1,000 - general operating support; Arkansans for the Arts (formerly known as Arts Advocates), Little Rock, Arkansas, $5,000 - general operating support.
Contact: Wilma Jo Ann Starr, President; (501) 521-9990; florence.davis@starrfdn.org or grants@starrfoundation.org
Sponsor: Starr Foundation
210 Raven Woods Lane
Fayetteville, AR 72701

State Farm Good Neighbor Citizenship Company Grants 2238
State Farm values the importance of keeping its neighbors safe, with funding directed toward: improving driver, vehicle, and roadway safety; shielding homes from fires, criminals, and natural disasters; supporting disaster preparedness programs and recovery services; and enhancing personal financial security. In general, grants are awarded for specific programs in the giving categories described, rather than for one-time events or capital campaigns. Grant requests must be submitted in writing on the requesting organization's letterhead. One proposal per organization per year will be considered if it meets the guidelines. Guidelines are available online.
Requirements: U.S. and Canadian 501(c)3 tax-exempt educational organizations are eligible.
Restrictions: The foundation does not fund individuals seeking personal; politically partisan programs; religious programs; or organizations outside the United States and Canada.
Geographic Focus: All States
Amount of Grant: 5,000 - 100,000 USD
Contact: Good Neighbors Grants Coordinator; (309) 766-2161; fax (309) 766-2314; home.sf-foundation.494b00@statefarm.co
Internet: www.statefarm.com/about-us/corporate-responsibility/community-grants/good-neighbor-citizenship-grants
Sponsor: State Farm Insurance Company
1 State Farm Plaza, B-4
Bloomington, IL 61710-0001

Staunton Farm Foundation Grants 2239
The Staunton Farm Foundation is a family foundation established in 1937 in accordance with the wishes of Matilda Staunton Craig, who wanted her estate to be used to benefit people with mental illness. The Foundation awards grants in the field of mental health in southwestern Pennsylvania. Projects that represent new and different approaches for organizations and ultimately affect patient care are encouraged. Support may be for more than one year, but the project must become self-sustaining following the grant period. Applicants should submit a letter of intent; full proposals are by invitation.
Requirements: Nonprofit organizations in the 10-county area in southwestern Pennsylvania including Washington, Greene, Fayette, Westmoreland, Armstrong, Butler, Lawrence, Beaver, Indiana, and Allegheny are eligible.
Geographic Focus: Pennsylvania
Date(s) Application is Due: Jun 1; Dec 1
Contact: Joni S. Schwager, Executive Director; (412) 281-8020; fax (412) 232-3115; jschwager@stauntonfarm.org
Internet: www.stauntonfarm.org
Sponsor: Staunton Farm Foundation
650 Smithfield Street, Suite 210
Pittsburgh, PA 15222

Stein Family Charitable Trust Grants 2240
Katie, Harriet, Lillie and Laura Stein grew up in New York and retired in Fort Worth, Texas where their brother owned and operated Stein's Jewelry. The sisters were dedicated to the education and welfare of young people. Out of this concern, they created a trust to help Tarrant County charitable organizations that serve children with physical or mental disabilities. The Stein Family Charitable Trust accepts applications from charitable organizations that provide "relief, treatment and aid of children who are residents of Tarrant County, Texas, suffering from physical or mental infirmity...who, in the judgment of the trustee, are in need of such relief, treatment or aid." Preference is given to organizations, operating in, or serving Tarrant County. This foundation makes approximately 5 to 7 awards each year and grants are typically between $1,000 and $15,000.
Requirements: Charitable organizations must have 501(c)3 tax-exempt status and serve children with disabilities in Tarrant County. Applications will be submitted online through the Bank of America website. A grant report is required within 1 year of the grant application date, regardless of whether all of the funds have been spent.
Restrictions: Eligibility to re-apply for a grant award from the Stein Family Charitable Trust requires organizations to skip 1 grant cycle (1 year) before submitting a subsequent application. The trust does not support requests from individuals, organizations attempting to influence policy through direct lobbying, or any political campaigns.
Geographic Focus: Texas
Date(s) Application is Due: Aug 1
Amount of Grant: 1,000 - 15,000 USD
Samples: Camp Fire First Texas, Fort Worth, Texas, $10,000 - Awarded for amp El Tesoro inclusion program (2019); Gill Children's Services Inc., Fort Worth, Texas, $10,000 -

Awarded for general operations of the organization (2019); MHMR Visions, Fort Worth, Texas, $10,000 - Awarded for HealthySteps program(2019).
Contact: Debra Goldstein Phares, Philanthropic Client Director; (800) 357-7094; tx.philanthropic@bankofamerica.com or tx.philanthropic@ustrust.com
Internet: www.bankofamerica.com/philanthropic/foundation/?fnId=11
Sponsor: Stein Family Charitable Trust
P.O. Box 831041
Dallas, TX 75283-1041

Stella and Charles Guttman Foundation Grants   **2241**
The majority of grants are made to organizations providing services to people in the New York City metropolitan area. Beginning in 2014, the Stella and Charles Guttman Foundation intends to direct a substantial portion of its grantmaking to programs that serve low income infants, toddlers and preschoolers as they transition to kindergarten. Special emphasis will be placed on programs that improve quality, expand services and create a strong continuum of care for children ages 0 to 3 in high-need neighborhoods. Systemic investments in early childhood programs may include the expansion of evidence-based home visiting programs, infant health and mental health programs and professional development for center-based teachers, as well as home-based caregivers. The Foundation is also committed to fund programs in neighborhoods with high levels of poverty and a large concentration of public housing. In addition to early childhood programs, the Foundation will support programs that work to build a network of education, health and social services for children from birth through college graduation.
Requirements: Charitable 501(c)3 or 170(b)1 organizations are eligible with a strong emphasis on New York City and Israel.
Restrictions: The foundation does not make grants directly to individuals or to organizations not qualified as charitable, for foreign travel or study, to initiate or defend public interest litigation, to support anti-vivisectionist causes, or to religious organizations for religious observances.
Geographic Focus: New York
Amount of Grant: 25,000 - 100,000 USD
Samples: Citizens' Committee for Children of New York, New York, New York, $50,000 - support of educational, policy and advocacy initiatives focused on early childhood education; Good Shepherd Services, Brooklyn, New York, $50,000 - support of the Bronx Opportunity Network, a collaboration of seven community-based organizations; Henry Street Settlement, New York, New York, $100,000 - support of the Henry Street capital campaign and the renovation of the Charles and Stella Guttman Building.
Contact: Elizabeth Olofson, Executive Director; (212) 371-7082; fax (212) 371-8936; eolofson@guttmanfoundation.org
Internet: www.guttmanfoundation.org
Sponsor: Stella and Charles Guttman Foundation
122 East 42nd Street, Suite 2010
New York, NY 10168

Sterling-Turner Charitable Foundation Grants   **2242**
The charitable foundation awards grants to Texas organizations, primarily for higher and secondary education, adult basic education and literacy, social services, youth, the elderly, fine and performing arts groups and other cultural programs, church support and religious programs (Catholic, Jewish, and Protestant), hospitals and health services, hospices, research, conservation, and civic and urban affairs. Grants are awarded for general operating support, annual campaigns, capital campaigns, continuing support, building construction/renovation, equipment acquisition, endowment funds, program and project development, conferences and seminars, curriculum development, fellowships, scholarship funds, research, and matching funds. The board meets in April.
Requirements: Nonprofit Texas organizations in the following counties are eligible to apply: Fort Bend, Harris, Kerr, Tom Green, and Travis. Only those 501(c)3 organizations with offices located within the counties being considered within the State of Texas may submit and all funds must be managed, used and services provided within those counties in the State of Texas. All funds must be used within the requesting county. If the organization is a 509(a)3, there is a template for a required letter of explanation as to why your organization falls under the category that must be submitted for consideration. All documents must be received by 5:00 pm of the deadline date.
Restrictions: Individuals are ineligible.
Geographic Focus: Texas
Date(s) Application is Due: Mar 1
Amount of Grant: 5,000 - 25,000 USD
Contact: Patricia Stilley, Executive Director; (713) 237-1117; fax (713) 223-4638; pstilley@stfdn.org or jarnold@sterlingturnerfoundation.org
Internet: sterlingturnerfoundation.org/information_and_instructions.htm
Sponsor: Sterling-Turner Charitable Foundation
5850 San Felipe Street, Suite 125
Houston, TX 77057-3292

Sterling and Shelli Gardner Foundation Grants   **2243**
The Sterling and Shelli Gardner Foundation was established by co-founders and operators of "Stampin' Up!", a multi-million dollar catalog-based business, in Utah in 2002. The Foundation's major fields of interest include: community and economic development; education; and human services. With a geographic focus throughout the State of Utah, applicants should request a formal application from the Foundation office. The Foundation awards between thirty and forty grants each year, and amounts have recently ranged from $500 to $40,000. Most often, these awards are unrestricted contributions applied toward general operating costs. There are no specified annual deadlines, and applications are taken on a rolling basis.
Requirements: Any 501(c)3 organization serving residents of Utah are eligible to apply.
Geographic Focus: Utah
Amount of Grant: 500 - 40,000 USD
Samples: Ability Found, Salt Lake City, Utah, $5,000 - general operating support for disabled individuals; Friday's Kids Respite, Orem, Utah, $2,500 - general operations; Courage Reins, Highland, Utah, $35,000 - general operations.
Contact: Megan White, Administrator; (801) 717-6789
Sponsor: Sterling and Shelli Gardner Foundation
610 W. Westfield Road
Alpine, UT 84004-1501

Steven B. Achelis Foundation Grants   **2244**
Steven B. Achelis is the founder, owner, and president of EQUIS International. His company is a leading provider of investment analysis, portfolio management, and stock market data collection software. Established in 1990 in Utah, the Steve B. Achelis Foundation is a small private foundation with limited resources. Typical grants range between $500 and $6,000 with an average grant of $2,000. Total annual grants are approximately $50,000. Applicants should include: a description of the services provided; a copy of the applicant's 501(c)3 IRS ruling letter; and a breakdown of revenue sources and expenditures. Though giving is aimed primarily in Salt Lake City, the foundation also offers awards nationwide. There are no specified annual deadlines.
Geographic Focus: All States
Amount of Grant: 500 - 6,000 USD
Contact: Steven B. Achelis, Trustee; (801) 560-5733 or (801) 972-4800; fax (801) 272-1148; info@eMedic.com or steve@rescuerigger.com
Internet: stevesfoundation.org/guidelines.htm
Sponsor: Steven B. Achelis Foundation
6154 Oak Canyon Drive, P.O. Box 71342
Salt Lake City, UT 84121-6344

Stillson Foundation Grants   **2245**
The Foundation Office at Fifth Third Bank is committed to making a significant impact on programs and initiatives that create strong, vibrant communities and provide pathways to opportunity. Through the Foundation Office, the visions of individuals, families and institutions are realized, and legacies are attained by allocating the resources of their respective foundations in support of innovative programs and organizations in our communities. The Stillson Foundation supports organizations that benefit or serve children, and provides assistance to those charities the Stillsons supported during their lifetime. An organization interested in submitting a grant proposal should first submit a Letter of Inquiry (LOI) using the link at the website. LOIs are accepted from October 1 through December 31 each year. The Foundation Office will review each LOI and may contact the applying organization about further discussion of the proposal, which may include a site visit. Each organization will receive either an email declining the inquiry or an invitation to submit a full application online. An invitation to apply will include the foundation funding source, recommended request amount, and a deadline for receipt of the application. The Fifth Third Bank Foundation Office will submit completed applications to the respective Foundation Board or Committee for final review and approval or declination. Grant seekers should allow six to twelve months for the grant making process. In general, the Foundation prefers awarding grants for one year. Most recent awards have ranged from $5,000 to $250,000.
Requirements: Nonprofit organizations that operate in the Greater Cincinnati region and are designated under section 501(c)3 and subsections 509(a)1 or 509(a)2 by the Internal Revenue Service are eligible to apply for a grant.
Restrictions: Nonprofits may apply only once within any 12-month period. The following are ineligible to apply: individuals; individual churches (except for proposals regarding an affiliated school); publicly supported entities such as public schools, government or government agencies; supporting organizations designated 509(a)3 by the IRS; walks, runs, dinners, galas, luncheons and other event sponsorship requests; athletic, band, and other school booster clubs; or startup funding for new programs or organizations (usually not a funding priority). A waiting period of three years is required for prior grant recipients receiving $10,000 or more from any funding source administered by the Fifth Third Bank Foundation Office. This period will begin as of the first payment on the grant.
Geographic Focus: Ohio
Amount of Grant: 5,000 - 250,000 USD
Contact: Heidi B. Jark, Managing Director; (513) 534-7001 or (513) 636-4200
Internet: https://www.53.com/content/fifth-third/en/personal-banking/about/in-the-community/foundation-office-at-fifth-third-bank.html
Sponsor: Stillson Foundation Fifth Third Bank
38 Fountain Square Plaza, MD 1090CA
Cincinnati, OH 45202

Stinson Foundation Grants   **2246**
The Stinson Foundation focuses on charitable organizations dedicated to children and families, arts and education in the Permian Basin Area in Texas. Sue Stinson's life was guided by a philosophy of optimism and cheerfulness. Before moving from her native Virginia to Midland in the mid-1930s, she taught in a one-room school in a Virginia Mennonite farming community and lived in a tent in the Arizona desert. She found humor and beauty in adverse situations, and the good in her life always took precedence and kept her going. This foundation makes approximately 10 awards each year and grants are typically between $2,000 and $10,000.
Requirements: Applicants must have 501(c)3 tax-exempt status and serve residents of the Permian Basin, Texas area. Applications will be submitted online through the Bank of America website. A grant report is required within 1 year of the grant application date, regardless of whether all of the funds have been spent.

Restrictions: The foundation does not support requests from individuals, organizations attempting to influence policy through direct lobbying, or any political campaigns.
Geographic Focus: Texas
Date(s) Application is Due: May 15
Amount of Grant: 2,000 - 10,000 USD
Samples: Casa of West Texas, Midland, TX, $10,000 - for general operations of the organization (2018); High Sky Children's Ranch Inc., Midland, TX, $10,000 - for High Sky Children's Ranch Equine Therapy program (2018); West Texas Jazz Society, Midland, TX, $10,000 - for general operations of the organization (2018).
Contact: Kelly Garlock, Philanthropic Client Manager; (800) 357-7094; tx.philanthropic@bankofamerica.com or tx.philanthropic@ustrust.com
Internet: bankofamerica.com/philanthropic/foundation/?fnId=22
Sponsor: Stinson Foundation
Bank of America NA P.O. Box 831
Dallas, TX 75283-1041

Stocker Foundation Grants 2247
The Stocker Foundation aims to lessen the achievement-gap for under-resourced prekindergarten through third grade public school students by investing in programs that strengthen reading literacy. The foundation remains an all-family board, headquartered in Lorain, Ohio. Annual grant distributions focus first on Lorain County, Ohio, the place where assets were generated. Then, in communities where other trustees reside (see below).
Requirements: The Stocker Foundation provides grants to 501(c)3 nonprofit organizations and to selected public sector activities. Grants are considered and decided upon one time annually in the area of improved reading literacy outcomes for under-resourced prekindergarten through fifth grade public school students. Funds are made to organizations in Lorain and Cuyahoga counties, Ohio; Pima County, Arizona; Alameda and San Francisco counties, California; Bernalillo and Dona Ana counties, New Mexico; King County, Washington; and Hartford County, Connecticut. Areas of interest include: supplemental programs that move students toward grade-level reading mastery; comprehensive intervention strategies that increase overall literacy achievement by fourth grade; book distribution programs that increase students' access to print materials, encourage students' reading outside of the classroom, and develops students' life-long love of reading; and, programs that support emerging literacy and reading skills among prekindergarten (children enter kindergarten ready to read). Some limited funding is available for services that can help remove barriers toward reading success. All organizations seeking funding must first submit a Letter of Inquiry (LOI). The specific guidelines for the LOI can be downloaded from the sponsor's website. LOIs are due no later than July 1. For those LOIs moving forward, a full proposal is due by October 1 for a spring decision.
Restrictions: In general, the foundation does not award grants toward: debt reduction, research projects, tickets or advertising for fundraising events, individuals, religious exclusivism, or capital campaigns.
Geographic Focus: Arizona, California, Connecticut, New Mexico, Ohio, Washington
Date(s) Application is Due: Oct 1
Amount of Grant: Up to 100,000 USD
Contact: Patricia O'Brien, Executive Director; (440) 366-4884; fax (440) 366-4656; pobrien@stockerfoundation.org
Internet: www.stockerfoundation.org/grants.aspx
Sponsor: Stocker Foundation
201 Burns Road
Elyria, OH 44035

Storm Castle Foundation Grants 2248
The Storm Castle Foundation offers grants primarily in California, with its major fields of interest including: arts and culture; diseases and conditions; education; and human services. An application form is required, and should include: a listing of board of directors, trustees, officers and other key people and their affiliations; a detailed description of project and amount of funding requested; and descriptive literature about organization. Most recent awards have ranged from $500 to $10,000. There are no identified annual deadlines, and interested parties should begin by contacting the Foundation by mail.
Requirements: U.S. 501(c)3 organizations serving the residents of California, Montana, and Massachusetts are eligible to apply.
Geographic Focus: All States, California, Georgia, Pennsylvania
Amount of Grant: 500 - 50,000 USD
Samples: Back On My Feet, Philadelphia, Pennsylvania, $1,000 - general operating support; Bishop's Ranch, Healdsburg, California, $2,500 - educational support; Crystal Springs Uplands School, Hillsborough, California, $47,500 - general operating support for education.
Contact: Julia Loewy Davidson, President; (650) 233-8120 or (415) 362-5990
Sponsor: Storm Castle Foundation
2775 Sand Hill Road, Suite 100
Menlo Park, CA 94025-7085

Strake Foundation Grants 2249
The Foundation supports hospitals, schools, colleges, and Catholic charities, as well as projects focusing in adult basic education and literacy, museums, and arts and culture. Support is considered for operating budgets, capital campaigns, special projects, research, matching funds and general purposes.
Requirements: Awards are made to 501(c)3 organizations located only in the United States, primarily in Texas. Organizations may submit only one request per calendar year. There are no set amounts for requests, however awards generally range between $2,000 and $20,000 with a few exceptions as high as $50,000.
Restrictions: Awards are not made to support individuals, nor for deficit financing, consulting services, technical assistance, publications, or loans.

Geographic Focus: All States
Samples: Corporation for Educational Radio and Television, New York, NY, $2,500–to support the 'Black American Conservatism' companion website; El Centro de Corazon, Houston, TX, $$7,500–operating support; Fund for American Studies, Washington, D.C., $5,000–scholarship support.
Contact: George Strake, Jr., President; (713) 216-2400; foundation@strake.org
Sponsor: Strake Foundation
712 Main Street, Suite 3300
Houston, TX 77002

Stranahan Foundation Grants 2250
The Stranahan Foundation was created in 1944 by brothers Frank D. and Robert A. Stranahan, founders of the Champion Spark Plug Company in Toledo, Ohio. The purpose of the foundation is to assist individuals and groups in their efforts to become more self-sufficient and contribute to the improvement of society and the environment. The foundation supports a multitude of important programs that fit within five priority areas of interest: Human Services, Ecological Well-Being, Arts & Culture, Education, and Mental & Physical Health. Grant funds may be used for start up support for a new program, operating support, expansion or capacity building, or capital support.
Requirements: Nonprofit organizations with 501(c)3 tax-exempt status are eligible to apply. While the foundation awards funds nationwide, its focus is on the Toledo, Ohio area. All applicants must, as a first step, submit a letter of inquiry to the Stranahan Foundation. Full proposals are by invitation only and may only be submitted by organizations that are invited to apply after their letter of inquiry has been accepted and reviewed. The Foundation will contact those organizations invited to submit a full proposal and notify those that are not eligible to apply. Instructions and forms for letters of inquiry and full grant proposals can be found on the website.
Restrictions: The Stranahan Foundation does not normally consider proposals for funding in the following areas: personal businesses; reduction or elimination of deficits; projects that are located outside of the United States; endowment fund campaigns; government sponsored or controlled projects; or individuals. Additionally, the foundation will not support organizations that discriminate in the leadership, staffing or service provision on the basis of age, gender, race, ethnicity, sexual orientation, disability, national origin, political affiliation or religious beliefs.
Geographic Focus: All States
Date(s) Application is Due: Jul 1
Amount of Grant: 1,000 USD
Contact: Pam Roberts; (419) 882-5575; proberts@stranahanfoundation.org
Internet: www.stranahanfoundation.org/index.php?src=gendocs&ref=Grantmaking Priorities&category=Main
Sponsor: Stranahan Foundation
4169 Holland-Sylvania Road, #201
Toledo, OH 43623

Streisand Foundation Grants 2251
Established in 1986 in New York, the Foundation was founded by Barbra Streisand, singer-songwriter and actress. Streisand has won two Academy Awards, eight Grammy Awards, five Emmy Awards, a Special Tony Award, and is one of very few entertainers to have won all of these honors. In 2001, Streisand received the AFI Life Achievement Award, as well as she is the highest ranking female artist on the Recording Industry Association of America's (RIAA) Top Selling Artists list. Today, the Foundation awards grants for national programs affecting women and at-risk youth. Areas of support include programs for children and youth, with a focus on the economically disadvantaged; civil rights, with emphasis on race relations between African Americans and Jews; AIDS research, advocacy, service, and litigation; nuclear disarmament; and environmental preservation. Types of support include general operating grants, technical assistance, and project-specific support. Applicants are asked to submit one- to two-page letters of inquiry. Invited applications are accepted between September 1 and the December 1 deadline.
Requirements: National 501(c)3 nonprofits and California projects in the Los Angeles area are eligible.
Restrictions: Grants are not made to individuals nor do they support start-up organizations, endowments, or capital campaigns.
Geographic Focus: All States
Date(s) Application is Due: Dec 1
Amount of Grant: Up to 30,000 USD
Samples: Union of Concerned Scientists, Cambridge, Massachusetts - general operating support; Brennan Center for Justice, New York, New York - general operating support; Iraq And Afghanistan Veterans Of America (IAVA), New York, New York - general operating support; Mother Jones, San Francisco, California - general operating support.
Contact: Margery Tabankin, Executive Director; fax (310) 314-8396; stfnd@aol.com
Internet: www.barbrastreisand.com/streisand-foundation/
Sponsor: Streisand Foundation
1327 Ocean Avenue, Suite H
Santa Monica, CA 90401

Strong Foundation Grants 2252
The Strong Foundation traces its history to the establishment of a free dental clinic at Palama Settlement in 1914, of which George R. Carter became a trustee in 1915. Subsequently, his wife, Helen Strong Carter, established the Honolulu Dental Infirmary in 1920 in memory of her father and mother, Henry A. Strong and Helen P. Strong of Rochester, New York. Its purpose was to train dental hygienists and to improve the teeth of the school children of Honolulu. She established the Strong Foundation to finance the Honolulu Dental Infirmary. The annual deadline for application submission is March 1.

Requirements: Grants will be made to Hawaii 501(c)3 charities only; grants are predominantly for capital needs and of a major nature; and grants are primarily to be youth oriented. You must obtain a trustee sponsor in order to apply for a grant. Proposals that don't have a trustee sponsor will be declined. Sponsorship generally includes trustee involvement with the charity or the program; the trustee should be sufficiently knowledgeable about the charity and its request to be its champion at the foundation's annual meeting.
Restrictions: There are no multi-year grants or grants to endowments, and each organization will be limited to a maximum of one grant every three years. The Strong Foundation requests that no public acknowledgment be made of grant awards.
Geographic Focus: Hawaii
Date(s) Application is Due: Mar 1
Contact: Carol Tom; (808) 694-4525 or (800) 272-7262; carol.tom@boh.com
Internet: www.boh.com/apps/foundations/foundationdetails.aspx?foundation=12&show=1
Sponsor: Strong Foundation
P.O. Box 3170
Honolulu, HI 96802-3170

Subaru of America Foundation Grants　　　　2253
The Subaru of America Foundation was established in 1984 to support the communities where facilities are located. The Foundation seeks partnerships and awards grants in the area of education to nonprofit organizations that: engage youth and encourage their active participation in the learning experience, including (but not limited to) professional development for educators, programs that enhance math and science education, and literacy improvement and education; promote environmental stewardship and education for youth, including (but not limited to) school gardens and science exploration as it pertains to the environment; and benefit youth through grade 12. Listed application deadline dates are for letters of inquiry; full proposals are by invitation. Application and guidelines are available online.
Requirements: 501(c)3 nonprofits in the following regions are eligible to apply: southern New Jersey (mainly Camden and Burlington counties); Philadelphia, Pennsylvania; Westhampton, New Jersey; Orlando, Florida; Atlanta, Georgia; Washington, D.C.; Itasca and Chicago, Illinois; Minneapolis, Minnesota; Columbus, Ohio; Dallas, Texas; Denver, Colorado; Phoenix, Arizona; San Diego, California; Los Angeles, California; San Francisco, California; Portland, Oregon and Seattle, Washington.
Restrictions: Consideration will not be given to organizations whose fund balances exceed $5 million. The trustees prefer not to fund individuals; veterans, fraternal, and labor organizations; government agencies; direct support of churches, religious, or sectarian groups; social, membership, or other groups that serve the special interests of their constituency; advertising; sponsorships of special events, purchase of tables, and athletic campaigns; capital campaigns; political organizations, campaigns, or candidates running for public office; organizations that benefit individuals outside the United States; or organizations that, in policy or practice, discriminate against a person or group on the basis of age, political affiliation, race, national origin, ethnicity, gender, religious belief, disability, or sexual orientation. Vehicle donations will not be considered. As a general rule, national organizations are not eligible.
Geographic Focus: Colorado, Georgia, Illinois, New Jersey
Date(s) Application is Due: Jan 30; Aug 31
Amount of Grant: 1,000 - 10,000 USD
Contact: Foundation Manager; (856) 488-8500; fax (956) 488-3274; foundation@subaru.com
Internet: www.subaru.com/company/soa-foundation/index.html
Sponsor: Subaru of America Foundation
P.O. Box 6000, Subaru Plaza
Cherry Hill, NJ 08034-6000

Subaru of Indiana Automotive Foundation Grants　　　　2254
The Subaru of Indiana Automotive Foundation is committed to making gifts to qualifying organizations, institutions, or entities within Indiana that will improve the quality of life and help meet the needs of the residents of the state. The foundation awards cash grants that are used to support the funding of specific capital projects in the areas of: arts and culture, education, and health and welfare. Grants must be used for investments in facilities, equipment, or real estate made by qualifying organizations. Grant requests must be for $1,000 or more, with a maximum requested amount of $10,000. Funding can be used for investments in facilities, equipment, or real estate (non-operation funding). Applications for grants will be accepted from January 1 through March 31 to be considered for a grant to be dispersed by June 15. Applications will be accepted from July 1 through September 30 to be considered for a grant to be dispersed by December 15.
Requirements: Applying organizations must be 501(c)3 tax-exempt, with a chapter or office in Indiana; an education institution located in Indiana; or an Indiana governmental or quasi-governmental entity.
Restrictions: Support will not be provided for operating costs, routine expenses, or deficit reduction; endowments or memorials; fundraising events, conferences, meals, or travel; or annual fund drives. Support will not be provided to individuals; organizations located outside of Indiana or organizations that are not tax-exempt; for-profit businesses; organizations whose primary purpose is to influence legislation or support political candidates; religious institutions for religious purposes or fraternal organizations; or organizations that discriminate in the provision of services on the basis of race, sex, color, national origin, disability, age, religious affiliation, or any other unlawful basis.
Geographic Focus: Indiana
Date(s) Application is Due: Mar 31; Sep 30
Amount of Grant: 1,000 - 10,000 USD
Contact: Shannon Walker, Grants Administrator; (765) 449-6565; fax (765) 449-6952; shannon.walker@subaru-sia.com
Internet: www.siafoundation.org

Sponsor: Subaru of Indiana Automotive Foundation
P.O. Box 6479
Lafayette, IN 47903

Summit Foundation Grants　　　　2255
The Summit Foundation supports charitable organizations that enhance the quality of life in Summit County, Colorado, and neighboring communities. Grants are awarded twice each year, in June and in December, to agencies providing programs or services in the areas of health and human service, art and culture, education, environment and sports. The Foundation funds specific projects and programs which have measurable results.
Requirements: Applicants for funding must be tax exempt under the provisions of section 501(c)3 and 170(b)1(a)(i.V.I.) of the Internal Revenue Code.
Restrictions: The Foundation will not fund any political campaign on behalf of any issue or candidate. Additionally, The Foundation does not fund religious programs. Organizations requesting funding support will only be considered for funding once in a calendar year. Requests for programs or projects already completed are not eligible for funding.
Geographic Focus: Colorado
Date(s) Application is Due: Apr 20; Oct 15
Contact: Megan Nuttelman, Program Officer; (970) 453-5970; fax (970) 453-1423; sumfound@colorado.net or megan@summitfoundation.org
Internet: www.summitfoundation.org/?page_id=65#landhere
Sponsor: Summit Foundation
103 S Harris Street, Suites 201 and 204, P.O. Box 4000
Breckenridge, CO 80424

Sunoco Foundation Grants　　　　2256
The Sunoco Foundation invests in projects that promote local education and workforce development or that make communities great places to live and work. Grants are primarily awarded to nonprofits located where Sunoco has a major presence. The foundation considers all types of efforts, including homelessness, housing, community development, seniors and education. The Sunoco Foundation aligns giving and business strategy with focus on three key areas—Fueling Minds: Educate and Develop Skills for the Workforce; Fueling the Planet: Promote Environmental Stewardship and Responsibility; and, Fueling Communities: Make them great places to live and work.
Requirements: Applicants must successfully complete an eligibility quiz before submitting an online letter of inquiry. If the letter of inquiry matches the foundation's priorities, the applicant will be invited to submit a full proposal. The Foundation prefers to fund specific projects rather than operating budgets.
Restrictions: Requests for deficit funding, individuals, benefit fundraisers, endowments, surveys, studies, religious groups, fraternal organizations, athletic groups, schools, single diseases, and non-tax exempt organizations are generally not considered.
Geographic Focus: Alabama, Connecticut, Delaware, District of Columbia, Florida, Georgia, Indiana, Kentucky, Maine, Maryland, Massachusetts, Michigan, New Hampshire, New Jersey, New York, North Carolina, Ohio, Pennsylvania, Rhode Island, South Carolina, Tennessee, Vermont, Virginia, West Virginia
Contact: Ruth Clauser; (215) 977-3000; fax (215) 977-3409; raclauser@sunocoinc.com
Internet: online.foundationsource.com/public/home/sunoco
Sponsor: Sunoco Foundation
1735 Market Street, Suite Ll
Philadelphia, PA 19103

SunTrust Bank Trusteed Foundations Greene-Sawtell Grants　　　　2257
The Greene-Sawtell Foundation was established by Forest Greene and Alice Greene Sawtell, who served as the first Advisory Committee. Under the terms of the document which established the Foundation, the advisory committee was created to select the charitable organizations which the Foundation would support. SunTrust Bank, as Trustee, now determines which charitable, religious and educational organizations will receive support from the Foundation. The Bank's Foundation Trustees consider organizations which the Foundation has supported in the past, those in which Alice Sawtell had a personal interest, and those which are of a similar nature to the organizations in which she had an interest. The geographic focus of the Trust is metropolitan Atlanta. The Trustees will consider requests for capital improvements such as buildings, furniture and equipment, and alterations to existing structures. Applications also will be considered for special projects of a community nature, special studies, surveys, research and pilot programs which do not commit the funds to recurring expenditures. Community benefit and return on investment are primary considerations in distribution decisions. Other Distribution Committee considerations include: emphasis on metropolitan Atlanta; organization/community coordination and support; timeliness and precedence; organization management and governance; grant multiplier effect; human value and self-help emphasis; ultimate benefit to the community; financial management; and implementation of a strategic plan. The three annual deadlines for submission have been identified as March 31, August 31, and November 30.
Requirements: Nonprofit organizations in areas where SunTrust Bank has a major presence are eligible.
Restrictions: These foundations do not accept unsolicited grant applications from outside metropolitan Atlanta unless an organization has been specifically named by the donor as an eligible recipient.
Geographic Focus: Georgia
Date(s) Application is Due: Mar 31; Aug 31; Nov 30
Amount of Grant: 1,000 - 20,000 USD
Contact: Kay Miller, Secretary of the Distribution Committee; (404) 588-8250
Internet: www.suntrust.com/Microsites/foundation/funds.htm
Sponsor: SunTrust Bank Trusteed Foundations
P.O. Box 4418, Mail Code 041
Atlanta, VA 30302

SunTrust Bank Trusteed Foundations Nell Warren Elkin and William Simpson Elkin Grants
2258

The Nell Warren Elkin and William Simpson Elkin Foundation was created as a memorial by Miss Margaret R. Warren, Miss Charlotte L. Warren and Mrs. Josephine Warren Asbury, sisters of Nell Warren Elkin. The following charitable institutions were suggested by the Foundation's founders as worthy and valuable organizations. However, the Foundation's trustee is not required to make grants to these organizations and will entertain proposals from other organizations: Robert Winship Cancer Clinic of Atlanta; A.G. Rhodes of Atlanta; Georgia Heart Association of Atlanta; Bible Study Hour of Philadelphia; American Bible Society of New York City; and Emory University of Atlanta. The Trustees will consider requests for capital improvements such as buildings, furniture and equipment, and alterations to existing structures. Applications also will be considered for special projects of a community nature, special studies, surveys, research and pilot programs which do not commit the funds to recurring expenditures. Community benefit and return on investment are primary considerations in distribution decisions. Other Distribution Committee considerations include: emphasis on metropolitan Atlanta; organization/community coordination and support; timeliness and precedence; organization management and governance; grant multiplier effect; human value and self-help emphasis; ultimate benefit to the community; financial management; and implementation of a strategic plan. The three annual deadlines for submission have been identified as March 31, August 31, and November 30.
Requirements: Nonprofit organizations in areas where SunTrust Bank has a major presence are eligible.
Restrictions: These foundations do not accept unsolicited grant applications from outside metropolitan Atlanta unless an organization has been specifically named by the donor as an eligible recipient.
Geographic Focus: All States, Georgia, New York, Pennsylvania
Date(s) Application is Due: Mar 31; Aug 31; Nov 30
Amount of Grant: 1,000 - 20,000 USD
Contact: Kay Miller, Secretary of the Distribution Committee; (404) 588-8250
Internet: www.suntrust.com/Microsites/foundation/funds.htm
Sponsor: SunTrust Bank Trusteed Foundations
P.O. Box 4418, Mail Code 041
Atlanta, VA 30302

Susan A. and Donald P. Babson Charitable Foundation Grants
2259

The Foundation's focus is the enrichment and empowerment of people of all ages around the world, so as to prevent exploitation, poverty, and injustice. Applicants may submit a two-page concept letter by the deadline. Selected applicants will be asked to provide additional information. Grants range was $1,000 to $10,000, and the average size is $3,121.
Requirements: Applicants must be 501(c)3 organizations.
Restrictions: The Foundation does not make capital grants. A limited number of multi-year grants might be considered in each grant cycle.
Geographic Focus: All States
Date(s) Application is Due: Feb 28
Amount of Grant: 1,000 - 10,000 USD
Samples: University of Virginia, Serpentine Society, Charlottesville, Virginia, $10,000 – operating support; Massachusetts Peace Action, Cambridge, Massachusetts, $5,000 - new development initiative; and Sharon Arts Center, Peterborough, New Hampshire,
Contact: Michelle Jenney; (617) 391-3087; mjenney@gmafoundations.com
Internet: www.babsonfoundation.org/?page_id=5
Sponsor: Susan A. and Donald P. Babson Charitable Foundation
77 Summer Street, 8th Floor
Boston, MA 02110

Suspened: Community Foundation for Greater Atlanta State Farm Education Assist Fund Grants
2260

The State Farm Education Assist Fund is being launched in 2018 to build safer, stronger and better educated communities in South DeKalb. The fund provides mini-grants (grants of $1,500 or less) to South DeKalb community groups and nonprofit organizations taking an active role in strengthening and improving their communities. The fund is administered by a select group of promising young State Farm Scholars from the South DeKalb area who are currently attending Georgia State University's Perimeter College and have a passion for giving back to their home community. State Farm, well known for being a "good neighbor" by "being there" for its customers, was founded in 1922 by retired farmer and insurance salesman George Jacob "G.J." Mecherle. Originally a single-line auto insurance company, State Farm now offers 100 products and services in five different lines of business, including property and life insurance, banking products and mutual funds. As a mutual company, State Farm is focused on its policyholders. Its mission is to help people manage the risks of everyday life, recover from the unexpected and realize their dreams. It insures more cars and homes than any other insurer in the U.S., handling nearly 39,000 claims per day. State Farm is currently ranked number 33 on the Fortune 500 list of largest companies. Grants are awarded based on a number of factors, including those outlined on page 3 and 4 of these guidelines. Grants will range from $500-$1,500for a6-to-12month grant period. Each grantee will be asked to complete a report on its progress and challenges at the end of the grant period. The fund is particularly interested in supporting community-led projects and efforts in the following issue areas: youth development and leadership; college access and completion; community development; and workforce development. The annual grant application deadline is June 14.
Requirements: To apply for a grant organizations must: be located and providing services within the Foundation's 23-county service area; spend funds within the 23-county service area; be classified by the U.S. Internal Revenue Service under Section 501(c)3 of the I.R.S. code as a nonprofit, tax-exempt organization, donations to which are deductible

as charitable contributions under Section 170(c)2 and the I.R.S. determination must be current; be registered with the Georgia Secretary of State as a nonprofit; have a minimum two-year operating history after the date of receipt of its 501(c)3 classification; have annual operating expenses greater than $100,000 as reflected in the most recently filed IRS form 990; have at least one full-time paid employee (paid minimum wage or more, working 2,080 hours or more) for the 12 months prior to submitting a Letter of Intent; and have a current written strategic or business plan for the whole organization that covers at least 24 months which includes the organization's entire current fiscal year.
Restrictions: The following entities are not eligible to apply for funding: individual persons; private for-profit businesses; organizations that require participation in religious services and/or religious education as a condition of receiving services; or organizations that have discriminatory policies and/or practices on the basis of race, color, national origin, age, disability, sex/gender, marital status, familial status, parental status, religion, sexual orientation, genetic information or political beliefs.
Geographic Focus: Georgia
Date(s) Application is Due: Jun 14
Contact: Mindy Kao, Volunteer Manager; (404) 588-3215 or (404) 688-5525; fax (404) 688-3060; mkao@cfgreateratlanta.org
Internet: cfgreateratlanta.org/nonprofits/available-grants/
Sponsor: Community Foundation for Greater Atlanta
191 Peachtree Street NE, Suite 1000
Atlanta, GA 30303

Swindells Charitable Foundation Grants
2261

The Swindells Charitable Foundation was established in 1993 to support "the relief of sick, suffering and indigent; aged men and women; and/or for the support of public and charitable hospitals." Preference is given to organizations in Connecticut that serve sick and economically disadvantaged children or older adults. The Swindells Charitable Foundation also makes grants to public and charitable hospitals. Grants from the Swindells Charitable Foundation are one year in duration. Award amounts typically go up to $10,000.
Requirements: Applicants must have 501(c)3 tax-exempt status and serve communities in Connecticut. Applications will be submitted online through the Bank of America website. A grant report is required within 1 year of the grant application date, regardless of whether all of the funds have been spent.
Restrictions: Applicants will not be awarded a grant for more than three consecutive years. The Foundation does not support requests from individuals, organizations attempting to influence policy through direct lobbying, or any political campaigns. Capital requests will not be considered.
Geographic Focus: Connecticut
Date(s) Application is Due: Aug 1
Amount of Grant: Up to 10,000 USD
Samples: Martin House Inc., Norwich, Connecticut, $5,000 - Awarded for basic needs - Food Security Program (2019); Life Bridge Community Services, Bridgeport, Connecticut, $5,000 - Awarded for LifeBridge Basic Needs Services (2019); Family and Children's Aid, Danbury, Connecticut, $5,000 - Awarded for Waterbury Child Guidance Center (2019).
Contact: Amy R. Lynch, Philanthropic Client Manager; (860) 244-4870; ct.grantmaking@bankofamerica.com or amy.r.lynch@bofa.com
Internet: www.bankofamerica.com/philanthropic/foundation/?fnId=73
Sponsor: Swindells Charitable Foundation
P.O. Box 1802
Providence, RI 02901-1802

Sylvia Adams Charitable Trust Grants
2262

The Sylvia Adams Charitable Trust supports organizations that work with: children and young people; those with a disability; and those living in poverty or who are disadvantaged. In the area of children and young people, the Trust is particularly interested in: work which addresses the needs of children at risk of neglect and who are affected by lack of appropriate parenting; and work with young people that will give them the chance to acquire essential life skills such as communication, self discipline, motivation and empathy (this includes projects that focus on challenging activities, sport, the arts and access to the natural environment). For those with disability, the Trust has a particular emphasis on: innovations that have the potential to bring about significant improvements (excluding medical research); sporting and cultural activities, and access to the natural environment; and conditions that are less publicized or generally known and therefore attract less public support. For those experiencing poverty or social exclusion, the Trust includes: work which addresses homelessness; and particular problems facing some rural communities. Primary fields of interest include: education; water and sanitation; high impact health initiatives; and projects to help small scale farmers. Grants will normally be in the range of 5,000 pounds to 30,000 pounds. Occasionally the Trustees may make a grant up to 50,000 pounds. Most grants will be for one or two years, though in certain circumstances a grant may be made over three years.
Requirements: The Trust supports residents of Hertfordshire (local projects), the United Kingdom (rural poverty), and overseas (far reaching poverty). For work in Hertfordshire and the United Kingdom, most of the organizations that the Trust will make grants to will be registered charities. However it will also consider applications from organizations that are delivering work which is legally charitable. For overseas work, the Trust will only make grants to United Kingdom registered charities, but seek those whose activities are strengthening the capacity of local NGO's.
Restrictions: The Trust will not consider localized United Kingdom projects outside Hertfordshire. It will only consider United Kingdom work which has a wider impact. The Trust does not fund: individuals; overseas countries other than those specified in Current Specific Areas of Concern; work that solely benefits elderly people; or support to organizations helping animals, medical research or environmental causes.
Geographic Focus: United Kingdom

Amount of Grant: 5,000 - 50,000 EUR
Contact: Jane Young, Director; 01707 259259; fax 01707 259268; info@sylvia-adams.org.uk
Internet: www.sylvia-adams.org.uk/what_we_will_fund/index.php
Sponsor: Sylvia Adams Charitable Trust
24 The Common, Sylvia Adams House
Hatfield, HERTS AL10 0NB United Kingdom

Sylvia Perkin Perpetual Charitable Trust Grants 2263

The Sylvia Perkin Perpetual Charitable Trust was established in 1986 in Lehigh Valley, Pennsylvania, by the wife of Morris Perkin. Morris was born and raised in Allentown and practiced law there until his death in August, 1976. He was graduated from Allentown High School, Pennsylvania State University and the Harvard University School of Law. He stepped into the local Dorney printing shop in 1952 and ordered a desk diary that he had been using to keep track of the time he spent with clients. The idea expanded into "Lawyer's Day Planner" and eventually the "Day-Timers Planner" products. The Sylvia Perkin Perpetual Charitable Trust was established in 1985 with a goal to support museums, educational television stations, private colleges and universities, medical facilities and research, public health and welfare, community support, the arts, historical societies, and Jewish organizations, and institutions. Specifically, the Foundation funds: adult education; arts and culture; arts services; basic and emergency aid; child welfare programs; communication media; elementary and secondary education; family services; higher education;p historic preservation; historical activities; human services; Judaism; community nonprofits; performing arts; and youth development. Typically, this funding is given in the form of general operating support, individual development, program development, re-granting, and scholarship funds. Most recent grants have ranged up to a maximum of $52,000. The annual deadline for application submission is February 1.
Requirements: Any 501(c)3 nonprofit organization supporting the residents of Allentown, Pennsylvania, is eligible to apply.
Geographic Focus: Pennsylvania
Date(s) Application is Due: Feb 1
Amount of Grant: Up to 52,000 USD
Samples: Jewish Family Services, Allentown, Pennsylvania, $51,900 - general operating support; Cedar Crest College, Allentown, Pennsylvania, $20,000 - general operating support; Lehigh Valley Children's Center, Allentown, Pennsylvania, $7,000 - general operating support.
Contact: Jed Rapoport, Co-Trustee; (704) 590-2828
Internet: www.wellsfargo.com/private-foundations/perkin-charitable-trust
Sponsor: Sylvia Perkin Perpetual Charitable Trust
One West 4th Street, 4th Floor
Winston-Salem, NC 27101

T.L.L. Temple Foundation Grants 2264

The T.L.L. Temple Foundation was established in 1962 by Georgie Temple Munz in honor of her father, Thomas Lewis Latané Temple, an East Texas lumberman and founder of Southern Pine Lumber Company, which later became Temple Industries. It was her wish to create a charitable foundation that would operate primarily to improve the quality of life for the inhabitants of Deep East Texas. The foundation supports organizations devoted to programs in the areas in education, public health, public affairs, human services, arts and culture, and the environment. Since its inception, the T.L.L. Temple Foundation has been committed to supporting environmental initiatives devoted to the conservation of forest lands and river systems, and the preservation of native plant and wildlife species—to protect and ensure the perpetuity of these significant natural resources.
Requirements: The foundation primarily makes grants to projects located and/or to be operated in the area constituting the East Texas pine timber belt and Miller County, Arkansas in which T.L.L. Temple founded and operated his timber production and manufacturing enterprises. Governmental units exempt under the IRS code and 501(c)3 nonprofit organizations (not classified as a private foundation) are eligible to apply. There are no specific deadlines.
Restrictions: Grants do not support private foundations. Grants are not made to individuals for scholarships, research or other purposes.
Geographic Focus: Arkansas, Texas
Contact: Millard F. Zeagler, Executive Director; (936) 634-3900; fax (936) 639-5199
Sponsor: T.L.L. Temple Foundation
204 Champions Drive
Lufkin, TX 75901-7321

TAC Arts Access Grant 2265

The Arts Access (AA) grants are made possible through the National Endowment for the Arts. AA grants offer direct support for projects to arts organizations of color and to non-arts organizations whose programs and services primarily benefit persons of color. Award amounts range from $500 to $9,000 for arts organizations of color and from $500 to $7,000 for non-arts organizations whose programs and services primarily benefit persons of color. Arts Access grants must be matched one-to-one (1:1). Applications must contain a clear, single-project focus and must be limited to only one expense category on the budget. A project may start no earlier than July 1 and must end no later than June 15 of the applicable fiscal year. Most applicants will be asked to participate in an on-site review conducted by a member of the TAC's staff and/or an independent consultant. New applicants may not submit an application without prior consultation with TAC's Director of Arts Access. The consultation deadline is January 14 at 4:30pm (CST). Deadline dates may vary from year to year; applicants are encouraged to call the Director of Arts Access or check the TAC website for current deadlines.
Requirements: Any applicant is eligible for support of its arts activities if it is a nonprofit arts organization of color or if it is a nonprofit organization whose programs and services

primarily benefit persons of color. In either case, the applicant must be legally chartered in Tennessee and in possession of a determination letter from the Internal Revenue Service declaring the organization exempt from federal income tax under section 501(c)3 of the Internal Revenue Code. At least 51% of the organization's Board must reflect the culture of the target population. Before or at the time of application, all first-time 501(c)3 grant applicants must provide the TAC with copies of their non-profit status documentation including a copy of the organization's: Tennessee State Charter; IRS 501(c)3 Determination Letter; and a recent copy of the organization's by-laws. All applicants must provide a valid IRS Employer Identification Number that is issued in the name of the applicant organization. Three deadlines exist for the Arts Access Grants: first, new applicants must consult with TAC staff members (in person) before 4:30 p.m. (CST), January 14; second, the application must be completed and submitted via TAC's eGRANT system by January 18, 4:30 p.m. (CST); third, the required number of hard copies mentioned in the application guidelines (available at the grant website) including all supplemental materials must be postmarked or hand-delivered to the TAC by January 18th, 4:30 p.m. (CST). Proposed art projects must involve one or more TAC recognized classical art forms including: visual art, craft, media, music, theater, dance, folk and ethnic, or literary arts.
Restrictions: K-12 schools are not eligible to apply for Arts Access grants. Applicants eligible to apply in more than one TAC grant category in a single fiscal year must apply for unrelated projects each time. It is the responsibility of all applicants to read the legal requirements section at the TAC website (under the Grants tab) for further restrictions and requirements before making application.
Geographic Focus: Tennessee
Date(s) Application is Due: Jan 18
Amount of Grant: 500 - 9,000 USD
Contact: Rod Reiner, Deputy Director and Director of Arts Access; (615) 741-2093; fax (615) 741-8559; rod.reiner@tn.gov
Internet: www.tn.gov/arts/grant_categories.htm
Sponsor: Tennessee Arts Commission
401 Charlotte Avenue, Citizens Plaza Building
Nashville, TN 37243-0780

TAC Arts Education Funds for At-Risk Youth 2266

Funds for At-Risk Youth (FAY) grants support arts-based after-school or summer-camp programs designed specifically for elementary and secondary-school at-risk children by providing hands-on, immersion-based arts activities (applications for projects that are primarily performance or demonstration-based with minimal hands-on participation will not be considered). Projects must have professional artists at the core and may involve any art discipline including performing, visual, literary and folk and ethnic arts, and film. FAY grants do not require a dollar for dollar match; however, applicants are strongly encouraged to match the grant as much as possible to strengthen the competitiveness of the application. In-kind contributions cannot be used for matching purposes, but will strengthen the application. Applications must have a single project focus. Organizations with expansive education programs should narrow their focus to one component of their overall educational programming. Funds may be requested for only one of the following: professional artist fees, in-state travel and/or lodging for artists, space rental (for locations in which the applicant must pay to use), marketing and consumable supplies related to the project. The applications that are most competitive are often those that request funding for professional artist fees.
Requirements: The U.S. Department of Education includes in its definition of at-risk status any "primary or secondary grade student who is at risk as a result of substance abuse, teen pregnancy, recent migration, disability, ESL (limited English proficiency), juvenile delinquency, illiteracy, extreme poverty, or dropping out of school." Proposed projects must be tailored to one or more of these underserved groups. Organizations applying for a FAY grant must submit proof that 100% of the students participating are classified "at-risk" in the following ways: applicants who are Title I Schools or organizations partnering with Title I schools should submit documentation from an appropriate school official authenticating that 100% of participating students attend a Title I school and qualify for free/reduced lunch status; applicants partnering with a non-Title 1 school should submit a letter from a school guidance counselor, principal, or other appropriate school official involved in selecting participants that details the selection criteria and process used to verify that 100% of participants are at-risk based on one or more of the established indicators; applicants not partnering with a school and who by mission only serve at-risk youth should submit a brief letter (maximum one page) from the executive director of the organization which includes the organization's mission and lists the criteria and process used in selecting students for participation in the project. In no case is it necessary to provide names of participating students. Three deadlines exist for FAY grant applications: first, all applicants must notify the Director of Arts Education via email of their intent to apply no later than one week prior to the application deadline; second, the application must be submitted via TAC's eGRANT system by January 10th at 4:30pm CST (the eGRANT link is available at the grant website); third, the required number of printed copies of the eGRANT application and any required attachments must be postmarked or hand-delivered to the TAC by January 10 at 4:30pm CST. Because deadlines vary from year to year, applicants should contact the Director of Arts Education or check the TAC website for current deadlines. Projects may not begin until July 1 and must conclude by June 15. In order to be eligible for FAY grants, applicants must be one of the following: a non-profit organization, government agency or social service organization whose primary mission is to serve at-risk youth; a library; a non-profit arts organization; an arts council; or a K-12 school or school system. All non-profit applicants must possess 501(c)3 status and be chartered in the state of Tennessee. Private educational institutions must be non-profit and meet the same tax-exemption criteria. Arts organizations located within five miles of the Tennessee border in neighboring states may apply if there is clear demonstration that the projects and activities for which funds are being requested significantly serve Tennesseans. These out-of-state organizations must meet all

eligibility requirements of Tennessee-based organizations including being chartered in the state. Additionally, residents of Tennessee must be appropriately represented on the organization's governing board. It is the responsibility of all applicants to read the legal section at the TAC website (under the Grants tab) for further requirements before making application. In order to be eligible for FAY grants, projects must: serve a population defined by the organization's mission; directly involve participants in a hands-on learning experience; demonstrate a clear and beneficial educational focus which reflects thorough planning and implementation; clearly define instructional goals, objectives, hands-on activities, problem-solving or critical-thinking components, and evaluation methods; explain how any state or national standards, if listed, relate to outcomes being evaluated; provide learners with historical and/or social context; demonstrate and/or reinforce the skill sets needed for the artistic medium being used; and include an "end-of-project" sharing event (e.g.: a performance, exhibition, reading, or presentation that demonstrates for parents, school and community what the students learned during the project; a participatory family night that involves adults and students in joint hands-on art activities as they relate to the project; a related arts field trip to an in-state museum gallery, concert, or performance for the participants which includes a guided lesson). Applicants are encouraged (but not required) to link content to state and/or national curriculum standards (state standards may be accessed from the Tennessee Department of Education's website). Applicants should include an appropriate evaluation component that measures the planning, implementation, and successes of the program and addresses improvements or expansion of future projects. Projects funded by the TAC in previous years must include an evaluation summary.

Restrictions: Applicants already receiving funding for the same project through another TAC grant including, but not limited to, arts education, are not eligible. Funds from other TAC grants within this fiscal year may not be used with this project. Funds may NOT be used for: projects in which the artist is to serve as the arts teacher in the absence of any on-going arts education programs; permanent staff of an organization; incentives for participation including cash awards; projects designed primarily as performances, demonstrations, or exhibits with only minimal impact and limited hands-on participation; competitions and/or tours in which students are presenting, performing, and/or exhibiting; out-of-state travel; individual private lesson instruction; payment for apprentices or interns; capital outlay for permanent or non-consumable materials or equipment purchases (such as musical instruments, books, cameras, easels, etc.); planned fundraising activities; after-school clubs; field trips; scholarships or competitions; food; grant writing fees; non-classical art forms including, but not limited to culinary arts, martial arts, healing arts, exercise programs, acrobatics or gymnastics; payments to an employee or official of the State of Tennessee (exceptions exist – contact the TAC for details). FAY funds cannot be used for salary support for full-time employees but a portion of the employee's salary related to the amount of time spent on the FAY project may be used as part of the applicant's cash match. This type of match is called a "soft match." Expenditures for capital improvements (buildings or construction), for equipment purchases including but not limited to musical instruments, cameras, computers, etc., food or refreshments, or for elimination of an accumulated deficit may be used as matching funds up to $2,500 if these are related to the project. Expenditures for field trips may be used as a match. TAC does not allow the use of federally assigned indirect cost ratios in calculating grant requests or matching TAC funds. TAC will not make grants to an organization with a standing deficit unless a plan to reduce that deficit is submitted with the application.

Geographic Focus: Alabama, Arkansas, Georgia, Kentucky, Mississippi, Missouri, North Carolina, Tennessee, Virginia
Date(s) Application is Due: Jan 10
Amount of Grant: 500 - 5,000 USD
Contact: Kim Leavitt; (615) 532-5934; fax (615) 741-8559; kim.leavitt@tn.gov
Internet: www.tn.gov/arts/grant_categories.htm
Sponsor: Tennessee Arts Commission
401 Charlotte Avenue, Citizens Plaza Building
Nashville, TN 37243-0780

TAC Arts Education Mini Grants   **2267**
Tennessee Arts Commission (TAC) Mini Grants are smaller grants designed to introduce new applicants to the grant making process or to provide support to arts education providers who have unanticipated short-term (maximum one week) or one-day arts education projects. Projects may consist of, but are not limited to, community activities for adult learners, after-school programs for at-risk youth, in-school curriculum-based opportunities, arts-based service learning, or teacher training. Funds may only be used for professional teaching artist fees. Applicants may apply for mini grants throughout TAC's fiscal year or until all funds are expended. Funding is on a first-come, first-serve basis. Arts Education Mini Grant applications are reviewed "in-house" by TAC members and staff. Funding notification will take approximately 30 days from the time the application is submitted. Applicants have 30 days from the end of the project to submit receipts and all required close-out paperwork. The earliest start date for a project is July 1. The latest end date for a project is May 15.

Requirements: Applicants must contact the Director of Arts Education before making application. Projects must utilize a Commission-approved Artist-in-Residence. A roster of approved Artists-in-Residence may be found on TAC's website: click "Arts Education" on the Programs tab pop-up menu and then click "Roster" on the Artist Roster button's pop-up menu. Information for artists interested in participating in education residencies may be found here as well. Click "Arts Education" on the Programs tab pop-up menu and then click "Overview" on the Artist Roster button's pop-up menu to get the "Teaching Artist Program" page. Three deadlines exist for the Mini Grants: first, applicants must notify the Director of Arts Education prior to submitting an eGrant; second, the application must be completed and submitted via TAC's eGRANT system at least (30) days prior to the beginning of the project; third, the required number of hard copies including all supplemental materials must be postmarked or hand-delivered to the TAC at least thirty (30) days prior to the beginning of the project. An organization is eligible to apply for

funding of its arts activities if it is legally chartered in Tennessee and has 501(c)3 not-for-profit tax-exemption status, or if it is a public or private educational institution (such as an elementary or secondary school), a school board, a governmental agency or a college or university. Private educational institutions must be not-for-profit and meet the same tax-exemption criteria. Colleges and universities are eligible only for activities that clearly serve the needs of surrounding communities or the State and are designed to involve a broad audience. Activities that are credit-producing or are oriented primarily to students and the academic community are not eligible. Arts organizations located within five miles of the Tennessee border in neighboring states may apply if there is clear demonstration that the projects and activities for which funds are being requested significantly serve Tennesseans. These out-of-state organizations must meet all eligibility requirements of Tennessee-based organizations including being chartered in the state. Additionally, residents of Tennessee must be appropriately represented on the organization's governing board. It is the responsibility of all applicants to read the legal requirements section at the TAC website (under the Grants tab) for further requirements before making application. Before or at the time of application, all first-time 501(c)3 grant applicants must provide the TAC with copies of their non-profit status documentation including a copy of the organization's: Tennessee State Charter; IRS 501(c)3 Determination Letter; and a recent copy of the organization's by-laws. All applicants must provide a valid IRS Employer Identification Number that is issued in the name of the applicant organization. AE Mini Grant, projects must: directly involve participants in a hands-on learning experience (applications that are performance or demonstration based where learners are primarily spectators will not be considered); have a clear and beneficial educational focus; include an instructional component that defines the goals and objectives of the project; explains how any referenced state or national standards are included in the instruction and related to outcomes being evaluated; provides learners with historical and/or social context; and demonstrates and/or reinforces the skill set needed for the artistic medium being used.

Restrictions: Requests may not be made for artists to direct and/or conduct performances or to mount exhibitions. Projects in which the artist is primarily performing, demonstrating or exhibiting work with minimal hands-on instruction and/or impact will not be considered. Funds may only be used for teaching artist fees. Projects must be a minimum of one day (6 hours of instruction) in length up to a maximum of one week. Organizations applying for any other TAC Arts Education grant may not apply for a Mini Grant in the same fiscal year. Organizations may not apply for more than one Mini Grant in any fiscal year. Funds may not be used for permanent staff of an organization.

Geographic Focus: Alabama, Arkansas, Georgia, Kentucky, Mississippi, Missouri, North Carolina, Tennessee, Virginia
Amount of Grant: 500 - 1,000 USD
Contact: Kim Leavitt; (615) 532-5934; fax (615) 741-8559; kim.leavitt@tn.gov
Internet: www.tn.gov/arts/grant_categories.htm
Sponsor: Tennessee Arts Commission
401 Charlotte Avenue, Citizens Plaza Building
Nashville, TN 37243-0780

TAC Arts Education Teacher Incentive Grants   **2268**
The Arts Education Teacher Incentive (AE-TI) grants are designed to help full-time educators and artists on the TAC (Tennessee Arts Commission) approved Teaching Artist Roster and arts education administrators who work directly in or with K-12 schools to take advantage of unique opportunities that will significantly benefit their work or career development in arts integration. Arts integration involves integrating standards-based performing, visual, and literary arts into non-arts subjects such as math, science and reading. Funds may only be requested for professional development opportunities in which arts integration is the primary focus. Membership conferences in which arts integration may be one of many topics or is a secondary focus will not be considered. Applicants may apply for AE-TI grants throughout TAC's fiscal year OR until all AE-TI funds are expended ("first come, first served"). Applicants should verify eligibility of the professional development opportunity and availability of funds with the Director of Arts Education before submitting an application. Requests may range from $300 to $1,000 for specific, documented, TAC-approved training in arts integration that will occur during the applicable fiscal year. AE-TI funds are awarded on a reimbursement basis to individual applicants (organizations, schools or any other groups may not apply). Funds may be requested for registration fees (if paid by the individual applicant) and transportation costs (for the individual applicant only). Transportation costs include airfare (for out-of-state opportunities) and mileage or rental car fees (for both in-state and out-of-state opportunities). Applicants may request a $100 stipend for each full day of training (7 or more hours) and $50 for each half day (less than 7 hours). AE-TI grantees who receive an award of $600 or over will be sent a 1099 form for IRS tax purposes. A cash match is NOT required in this category, but demonstrates the applicant's commitment toward the project. TI grant applications are reviewed "in-house" by TAC members and staff. Funding notification takes place approximately 30 days from the time the application is submitted. Applicants have 30 days from the end of the professional development opportunity to submit receipts and all required close-out paperwork.

Requirements: General full-time classroom teachers, arts specialists, principals, TAC roster teaching artists, and arts education administrators who work directly in or with public or private elementary, middle, or high schools in Tennessee are eligible to apply. Applicants must be at least 18 years of age and be legal residents of Tennessee at the time of application with a permanent Tennessee mailing address. The TAC will accept as evidence of residency a valid Tennessee voter registration card, a State of Tennessee driver's license, or in cases where residency is questioned, a copy of the applicant's most recently filed Federal Income Tax Form 1040. Training must be a minimum of TWO consecutive full days to be eligible for funding and must support a minimum request of $300. If approved, funds are paid to the applicant on a reimbursement basis. Payment will be made only after the applicant has completed the project and has submitted: proof of attendance such as a certificate or letter from a conference administrator verifying the applicant attended the entire opportunity; receipts in the applicant's name that verify expenditures (hotel or travel expenditures in a spouse's name or roommate's name will not be accepted); and an invoice addressed to the TAC for the full amount noted in the grant award email. All receipts must be in the name of the applicant; when applicants share travel and rooming expenses, grant funds will be awarded to the applicant named on the receipt (it is the responsibility of the applicant, NOT the TAC, to sort out shared expenses). Three deadlines exist for the TI grants: first, applicants must notify the Director of Arts Education prior to submitting an eGrant; second, the application must be completed and submitted via TAC's eGRANT system at least (30) days prior to the beginning of the project; third, the required number of hard copies including all supplemental materials must be postmarked or hand-delivered to the TAC at least thirty (30) days prior to the beginning of the project. Applicants are strongly encouraged to submit realistic budget projections in their application by pricing airline tickets, verifying price and taxes per night for hotel stays and using mapquest to estimate mileage. Providing realistic expenses will save time and paperwork during the close-out process and expedite payment.

Restrictions: Those not eligible to apply include: organizations; full-time State of Tennessee employees; members of the TAC, its staff, and members of their families; full-time registered students working toward a degree or diploma in an educational institution; teaching assistants; and artists not on the TAC roster. Only one AE-TI grant will be awarded to an individual in a single fiscal year. A maximum of five may be awarded to individuals employed at any given school or organization in any grant cycle. Applicants who are attending the same opportunity and sharing transportation and/or rooming costs with another applicant may not "double-dip" and ask for reimbursement of expenses that were not incurred. For example, two applicants sharing a room may not both claim the total cost of the room. AE-TI funds do not reimburse for: strictly commercial activities (i.e. projects that are primarily revenue- producing and benefit the applicant financially); opportunities in which a prospective applicant would be compensated in any way for presenting, including waived registration fees; professional development that does not have arts integration as its primary focus; fees for medical, legal, accounting, or insurance; food; the applicant's own artistic or consultant fees; release time or sabbatical from work; purchase of equipment and/or supplies; projects that are currently or could potentially be funded under another TAC Arts Education category; expenses involved in establishing, maintaining, or administering an organization or company; and membership dues.

Geographic Focus: Tennessee

Amount of Grant: 300 - 1,000 USD

Contact: Kim Leavitt; (615) 532-5934; fax (615) 741-8559; kim.leavitt@tn.gov

Internet: www.tn.gov/arts/grant_categories.htm

Sponsor: Tennessee Arts Commission

401 Charlotte Avenue, Citizens Plaza Building

Nashville, TN 37243-0780

TAC Touring Arts and Arts Access Touring Arts Grants 2269

The Tennessee Art Commission (TAC)'s Touring Arts Program bring professional artists (primarily from Tennessee) to communities across the state by providing financial assistance to qualified presenters/sponsors. The Touring Arts Program offers two categories of funding: the Touring Arts (TOUR) grants and the Arts Access Touring Arts (AA-TR) grants. The AA-TR grants are funded in part by the National Endowment for the Arts and are designed to stimulate and encourage the presentation of performing, visual and literary arts by professional Tennessee artists of color or artists with disabilities. One-to-one (1:1) dollar matching may be required from the applicant. TOUR grants support professional Tennessee performing artists and groups; however, TOUR applicants may apply to engage one out-of-state artist or group per fiscal year. Both AA-TR and TOUR funds are used to pay a portion of the artist's fee, which is established by the artist. Prior to submitting an application, the applicant must contact the artist or his/her manager and book the artist with a binding contract containing a clause stating the performance will occur contingent upon Tennessee Arts Commission funding, or a letter of intent to hire (see guidelines at the grant website for further details). AA-TR and TOUR grant requests will be paid by reimbursement after the event. Due to reporting requirements, artist fees funded under these grants must be paid directly to the artist by the grantee (and not to an artist representative or management company). Tennessee presenters who receive National Endowment for the Arts/South Arts Regional Touring funding through South Arts may apply for matching support for one out-of-state artist through the TOUR category. AA-TR grant applicants must contact the Deputy Director before submitting an application. New TOUR grant applicants must contact the Director of Performing Arts before submitting an application. AA-TR and TOUR applications must be submitted electronically through the eGRANT system at the grant website a minimum of thirty (30) days prior to the beginning of the presentation. Also, the printed eGrant application and all required documents and materials must be postmarked or hand-delivered to the TAC office a minimum of thirty (30) days prior to the beginning of the presentation. The earliest starting date for a presentation project is July 1. The latest end date for a presentation project is June 15. This program is open until June 15 or until all funds are expended ("first come, first served").

Requirements: A Tennessee organization is eligible for funding support of its presenting activities if it meets the following criteria: it is legally chartered in Tennessee and has 501(c)3 not-for-profit tax-exemption status; it is an entity of government (such as a park, recreational organization or library); it is a public or private school; it is a college or university. Private educational institutions must be not-for-profit and meet the tax-exemption criteria described above. Arts organizations located within five miles of the Tennessee border in neighboring states may apply if there is clear demonstration that the presentations for which funds are being requested significantly serve Tennesseans. These out-of-state organizations must meet all eligibility requirements of Tennessee-based organizations including being chartered in the State of Tennessee. Additionally, residents of Tennessee must be appropriately represented on an out-of-state organization's governing board. It is the responsibility of all applicants to read the legal requirements section at the

TAC website (under the Grants tab) for further requirements before making application. Before or at the time of application, all first-time 501(c)3 grant applicants must provide the TAC with copies of their non-profit status documentation including a copy of the organization's: Tennessee State Charter; IRS 501(c)3 Determination Letter; and a recent copy of the organization's by-laws. Sponsored artists and performing groups must have a history of being financially compensated for their artistic work. This compensation must be a major source of support for their livelihood. They must also have a history of touring and have high quality promotional materials, e.g. printed information, CD's, DVD's and Web sites. An educational/outreach activity must be included in the proposal. This activity needs to be separate from the live public performance, and include interaction between the artist(s) and an audience (not necessarily the same audience that attended the public performance). Examples of educational/outreach activities are pre- or post-performance talkbacks, lecture/demonstrations, hands-on workshops, or master classes. Criteria (in addition to the availability of funds and eligibility of the applicant) include evidence that the presenter is introducing new or untried performing arts events that will broaden audience appreciation for a variety of art forms; evidence of cooperation with other sponsors/presenters through "block" (group) booking; evidence that the presenter is serving audiences in rural communities or isolated settings and/or other underserved constituencies; evidence of one or more education/outreach activities; evidence of promotion efforts toward filling the house; and evidence of generating substantial percentage of expenses.

Restrictions: A sponsored artist or group (two or more persons) may receive up to $8000 in combined awards from both AA-TR and TOUR grants in the applicable fiscal year. Presenters may not apply for both AA-TR and TOUR grants for the same project. Colleges and universities are eligible only for activities that clearly serve the needs of surrounding communities or the State and that are designed to involve a broad audience. Activities that are credit-producing or are oriented primarily to students and the academic community are not eligible. Schools, colleges, and universities must schedule public performances outside of school hours, and demonstrate that they are open and marketed to the public. The following activities are not eligible for funding under the Touring Arts Program: any activity used as a planned fundraising event; projects that do not include a public performance component and an additional education/outreach component; and guest artist appearances that are part of a producing arts organization (e.g. orchestra, theater company, dance company or opera company)'s own performance, concert or production. Only one public performance and outreach activity by an artist or group residing within the presenter's county will be allowed per organization in both the AA-TR and TOUR categories.

Geographic Focus: Alabama, Arkansas, Georgia, Kentucky, Mississippi, Missouri, North Carolina, Tennessee, Virginia

Amount of Grant: 350 - 4,000 USD

Contact: Hal Partlow; (615) 741-2093; fax (615) 741-8559; hal.partlow@tn.gov

Rod Reiner, Deputy Director; (615) 741-2093; fax (615) 741-8559; rod.reiner@tn.gov

Internet: www.tn.gov/arts/grant_categories.htm

Sponsor: Tennessee Arts Commission

401 Charlotte Avenue, Citizens Plaza Building

Nashville, TN 37243-0780

Target Corporation Community Engagement Fund Grants 2270

Target Corporation Community Engagement Funds (CEF) allow its stores and distribution center leaders across the country to support local programs and organizations that bring joy to families and address critical needs in their communities. Grants focus on arts, reading, and family violence prevention. In the area of arts, the company's goal is to make the arts more accessible and affordable for the entire family. Grants support programs that provide art exhibits, classes, or performances. Programs that bring arts to schools or kids to the arts are encouraged. In the area of reading, the company funds programs that promote a love of reading or encourage children to read together with their families. Preference is given to programs that focus on programs that inspire young readers (birth through third grade). The corporation also awards All-Around Scholarships—including four national scholarships and two smaller scholarships for each Target store—to high school seniors and college students age 24 or younger. The scholarships recognize volunteer work as well as academic achievement. In the area of family violence prevention, the company funds programs that help prevent family violence, such as parent education, family counseling, support groups, and shelters. Organizations making efforts to reduce domestic violence or prevent child abuse and neglect receive preference.

Requirements: IRS 501(c)3 tax-exempt organizations in company-operating areas are eligible.

Restrictions: Grants do not support capital drives, religious organizations, medical or health-related causes, housing or rehabilitation programs, treatment programs (i.e., substance abuse), athletic teams or events, or fundraisers/benefits. Organizations in Alaska, Hawaii, and Vermont are not eligible.

Geographic Focus: All States

Amount of Grant: 1,000 - 3,000 USD

Contact: Tracey Burton; (612) 761-9219; fax (612) 696-5088; guidelines@target.com

Internet: corporate.target.com/corporate-responsibility/philanthropy/corporate-giving/youth-soccer-grants

Sponsor: Target Corporation

1000 Nicollet Mall, TPS-3080

Minneapolis, MN 55403

Target Corporation Soccer Grants 2271

The Target Corporation youth soccer grants program provides support for player registration fees, player and field equipment, and training and professional development for volunteer coaches. Any eligible school, government agency, non-profit organization or non-profit regional/local soccer organization within the U.S., serving youth 5 to 18 years old, can apply. A preference will be given to programs serving in-need communities. As part of the program, Target will provide annual $1,000 grants on behalf of each Target store and distribution center in the U.S. to federally tax-exempt section 501(c)3 charitable organizations, accredited schools, or public agencies located in the U.S. or one of its protectorates that have soccer programs serving youth. Applications are accepted from August 1 through September 1 each year.

Requirements: Public and private kindergarten through 12th grade schools are eligible to apply, as well as 501(c)3 organizations supporting youth soccer.

Geographic Focus: All States, American Samoa, District of Columbia, Guam, Marshall Islands, Northern Mariana Islands, Puerto Rico, U.S. Virgin Islands

Date(s) Application is Due: Sep 1

Amount of Grant: 1,000 USD

Contact: Tracey Burton; (612) 761-9219; fax (612) 696-5088; guidelines@target.com

Internet: corporate.target.com/corporate-responsibility/philanthropy/corporate-giving/youth-soccer-grants

Sponsor: Target Corporation

1000 Nicollet Mall, TPS-3080

Minneapolis, MN 55403

Target Foundation Global Grants   2272

As a global organization with a multinational supply chain the Target Foundation is committed to improving economic opportunities for families around the world, helping them to sustain themselves and their communities long-term. Through its Global Grant program, the Target Foundation will invest in organizations that are building the capacity of people and communities to create livelihood opportunities that sustain long-term prosperity for families in emerging economies. Its primary focuses include: to equip organizations and systems with the capacity to create sustainable economic opportunity for families; to enable access to financial solutions that help families maintain and grow their assets to promote economic resilience; and to equip people and communities with the tools and knowledge needed to solve their problems and shape the institutions touching their lives.

Requirements: Investments through this program are made by invitation only. However, the Foundation recognizes there is great work being done by organizations that may be unfamiliar to its team. If you believe your work aligns and would like U.S. to know, please share more about your organization and programs via a National General Information Form.

Restrictions: Self-nominations are not accepted.

Geographic Focus: All States, All Countries

Amount of Grant: 10,000 - 50,000 USD

Contact: Tracey Burton; (612) 761-9219; fax (612) 696-5088; guidelines@target.com

Internet: corporate.target.com/corporate-responsibility/philanthropy/Target-Foundation/global

Sponsor: Target Foundation

1000 Nicollet Mall, TPS-3080

Minneapolis, MN 55403

Tata Trust Grant for Certificate Course in Holistic inclusion of   2273
Learners with Diversities

The Tata Trust offers several educational grants for higher education. Many of these Tata scholars are not only carrying out path-breaking research and teaching at reputed institutions but are also manning and leading national and international banking, commercial and financial institutions, multinational corporations, providing quality health care and legal services and entering sunrise industries such as IT, Biotechnology, Computing, including areas such as machine learning, artificial intelligence, robotics and so on. The Grant for Certificate Course in Holistic inclusion of Learners with Diversities, a course on inclusive education specially designed for in-service educators (teachers) and individuals of the community supporting children's educational needs. This course has been implemented by Aatman Academy for Research and Training under the guidance of the Institute on Community Integration of the University of Minnesota.

Geographic Focus: Minnesota

Contact: R Pavithra Kumar, Chief Program Director; 91 22 6665 8282; fax 91 22 6135 8369; talktous@tatatrusts.org or igpedu@tatatrusts.org

Internet: www.tatatrusts.org/our-work/individual-grants-programme/education-grants

Sponsor: Tata Trust

Bombay House, 24 Homi Mody Street

Mumbai, 400 001 India

Tauck Family Foundation Grants   2274

The Tauck Family Foundation Grants focus on organizations and programs that are committed to Bridgeport's elementary school children, and to strengthening their capacity to help these children build the social and emotional skills they need to succeed throughout their educations. The desire is to help create better outcomes for children from low‑income families and to focus the foundation's efforts in a way that would strengthen its nonprofit investees over time.

Requirements: The Tauck Family Foundation has selected its first portfolio of investees and has made a multi-year commitment to those organizations. As a result the foundation is not accepting proposals at this time. However, the Tauck Family Founation continues to be interested in learning about organizations developing the essential life skills of Bridgeport children. Nonprofit 501(c)3 organizations that meet the eligibility guidelines are free to submit an inquiry (via the foundation's website). Eligibility guidelines are as follows: be a non-profit, 501(c)3 organization; work (or have a specific strategy to work) with elementary (kindergarten through fifth grade) students in Bridgeport, Connecticut (organizations may be based in other cities/towns as long as they work with a significant number - more than 100 - of Bridgeport children in grades K-5); have an operating budget of $300,000 or more; consider the development of life skills of youth from low-income families to be core to the organization's mission; be interested in developing organizationally and receiving capacity building support, as needed and including: (a) going through an intensive Theory of Change process with the Tauck Family Foundation's consultants, and (b) implementing

performance management systems to measure and monitor the development of children's self-control, persistence, mastery orientation, and academic self-efficacy.

Geographic Focus: Connecticut

Contact: Mirellise Vazquez, Program Officer; (203) 899-6824; fax (203) 286-1340; mirellise@tauckfoundation.org

Internet: www.tauckfamilyfoundation.org/how-to-apply

Sponsor: Tauck Family Foundation

P.O. Box 5020

Norwalk, CT 06856

Teaching Tolerance Diverse Democracy Grants   2275

K-12 educators know it's critical their students develop the civic competencies to fully engage in the democratic process, whether at the community, local, state or national level. Diverse Democracy Grants are available to teachers wishing to promote student civic engagement or participation in the democratic process. Grants awards range from $500 to $5,000 for classroom or school projects and up to $10,000 for projects on the district level. Applications will be accepted on a rolling basis.

Requirements: Educators nationwide in public or private K-12 spaces, as well as in alternative schools, therapeutic schools and juvenile justice facilities are eligible to apply. Preference will be for projects that will help students become empowered voting advocates in their communities or one that encourages older high school students to register and vote.

Restrictions: Educators working outside of the U.S., or at community-based, informal learning sites are not eligible to apply at this time.

Geographic Focus: All States

Date(s) Application is Due: Aug 31

Amount of Grant: 500 - 10,000 USD

Contact: Jey Ehrenhalt; (334) 264-0286; fax (334) 264-3121

Internet: www.tolerance.org/about/educator-grant-guidelines

Sponsor: Teaching Tolerance

400 Washington Avenue

Montgomery, AL 36104

Teaching Tolerance Social Justice Educator Grants   2276

The program supports educators who embrace and embed anti-bias principles throughout their schools. These grants, ranging from $500-$10,000, will support projects that promote affirming school climates and educate youth to thrive in a diverse democracy. Teaching Tolerance grants will fund three different types of projects: school-level, classroom-level and district-level. At the school and district levels, leadership teams will use the grants to improve school climate, reduce hate, support culturally responsive practices and implement anti-bias curricula. At the classroom level, teachers will use the grants to fund programming that promotes empathy and kindness, positive identity development, perspective taking, critical thinking about injustice and collective action.

Requirements: Educators nationwide in public or private K-12 spaces, as well as in alternative schools, therapeutic schools and juvenile justice facilities are eligible to apply.

Restrictions: Educators working outside of the U.S., or at community-based, informal learning sites are not eligible to apply at this time.

Geographic Focus: All States

Amount of Grant: 500 - 10,000 USD

Contact: Jey Ehrenhalt; (334) 264-0286; fax (334) 264-3121

Internet: www.tolerance.org/about/educator-grant-guidelines#educator-grant-guidelines

Sponsor: Teaching Tolerance

400 Washington Avenue

Montgomery, AL 36104

Teagle Foundation Grants   2277

The Teagle Foundation's commitment to promoting and strengthening liberal education grounds their grant funding. Awards generally encourage collaboration among institutions, seeking to generate new knowledge on issues of importance to higher education. The Foundation is committed to widely disseminating this knowledge. The Foundation's signature Outcomes and Assessment initiative grows from their conviction that nothing has as much potential to affect students' educational experience as a sustained and systematic assessment of what and how they learn. The College-Community Connections program provides grants to community-based organizations in New York City that help disadvantaged young people prepare for and succeed in college, and works to build closer ties between these organizations and area colleges and universities. Requests for grant support will be considered following a two-stage application process. First, the Foundation asks that prospective grantees share brief concept papers. After review of the concept papers, a limited number of applicants will then be invited to submit full proposals. Concept papers are considered on a rolling basis. The Teagle Board of Directors reviews all grant requests when it meets in February, May, and November. If a proposal is invited, program staff will confer with the applicant to determine the appropriate timeline for submitting a full proposal in time for potential review by the Board.

Requirements: The Teagle Foundation invites proposals from two- and four-year colleges, universities, higher education consortia, and non-profit entities that share its commitment to the liberal arts and aim to pursue programs under one of its current initiatives.

Restrictions: The Foundation does not accept unsolicited proposals.

Geographic Focus: All States

Amount of Grant: 10,000 - 100,000 USD

Contact: Loni Bordoloi Pazich, Pgm. Director; (212) 373-1972; info@teaglefoundation.org

Internet: www.teaglefoundation.org/Grants-Initiatives/How-We-Grant

Sponsor: Teagle Foundation

570 Lexington Avenue, 38th Floor

New York, NY 10022

TechKnowledgey Community Impact Grants 2278

TechKnowledgey, Inc. is a midwest IT company offering hybrid cloud solutions, integrated IT services, and managed print services. TechKnowledgey services a wide reach from its headquarters in Goshen, Indiana. The Community Impact Grants are offered to not for profit, startup, faith-based, and community organizations. Funding varies from year to year and depends on the grant committee's evaluation of potential impact. Grants can be awarded in the form of IT equipment, hours of tech time, free/discounted services, or cash (up to $10,000). Requests are reviewed on a monthly basis.

Requirements: Nonprofit, startup, faith-based and community organizations in northern Indiana are eligible to apply. Organizations in and around Goshen, Elkhart and South Bend are of greater interest.

Geographic Focus: Indiana
Amount of Grant: Up to 10,000 USD
Contact: Boyd Smith, Founder; (574) 971-4267
Internet: www.techknowledgeyinc.com/engage/community-grant-application-form/
Sponsor: TechKnowledgey, Inc.
1840 W. Lincoln Avenue
Goshen, IN 46526

TE Foundation Grants 2279

The foundation provides grants to nonprofit organizations in areas where Tyco Electronics has a significant employee population and for specific projects or programs in broad categories, including education (with an emphasis on math and science), community impact, and arts and culture. In addition to a matching gifts program for employee contributions to accredited high schools, colleges, and universities, the foundation makes direct grants for programs that address a business or community concern of Tyco Electronics. Organizations that support pre-college math and science education receive special attention. Agencies that promote personal growth, career opportunities, and economic self-sufficiency are encouraged to apply, as are local chapters of health- and civic-related organizations. Special attention is given to community-wide arts organizations that solicit and allocate funds for a number of arts groups and institutions. Local public television and radio stations are encouraged to apply for funding of specific education initiatives. Capital campaigns of significant arts and cultural organizations serving communities in which the corporation has a major presence also will receive consideration. Grants also are awarded to support general operations, program development, and employee matching gifts. Applications are accepted throughout the year but are considered on the listed application deadlines.

Requirements: The TE Foundation limits grants to U.S. organizations that qualify as nonprofit under Section 501(c)3 of the Internal Revenue Code. Requests receive preferential review if the organization is supported by TE employees as volunteers.

Restrictions: The foundation generally will not support organizations in geographic areas where Tyco Electronics has few or no employees; individuals, private foundations, national organizations, or service clubs; fraternal, social, labor or trade organizations; organizations that discriminate on the basis of race, religion, color, national origin, physical or mental conditions, veteran or marital status, age, or sex; churches or religious organizations, with the exception of nondenominational programs sponsored by a church or religious group such as a food bank, youth center or non-sectarian education programs; political campaigns; loans or investments; or programs that pose a potential conflict of interest.

Geographic Focus: California, Massachusetts, Michigan, North Carolina, Pennsylvania, South Carolina, Texas, Virginia
Date(s) Application is Due: Mar 15; Jun 15; Sep 15; Dec 15
Amount of Grant: 250 - 25,000 USD
Contact: Mary Rakoczy, (717) 592-4869; fax (717) 592-4022; TEfoundation@te.com
Internet: www.te.com/en/about-te/responsibility/community.html
Sponsor: Tyco Electronics Foundation
c/o TE Corporation
Harrisburg, PA 17105-3608

Tellabs Foundation Grants 2280

The Tellabs Foundation awards grants to eligible nonprofits in the following areas: educational programs with a particular focus on local and national programs and curricula for engineering, science, mathematics and technology; health and human services programs for projects involving health and wellness-related, research, education and treatment in the United States (The primary focus is on projects involving hospitals and health care facilities); and environmental programs that encourage the understanding and protection of the environment. Generally, grants are awarded for specific programs rather than for general operating funds or capital projects. The primary focus of the foundation is to support programs in areas in which Tellabs employees live and work. Tellabs Inc and its affiliates also have direct giving programs, including an employee matching gift program, giving to the United Way, and limited direct corporate grants. The board meets quarterly (January, April, July and October); submit proposals at least four weeks before scheduled meetings.

Requirements: Tellabs operates in five primary locations: Petaluma, San Jose, and Santa Clara, California; Naperville, Illinois; and Dallas, Texas. Unless invited by the Foundation board to submit a full grant proposal, all applicants or programs must first submit a letter of inquiry. There is no set format, but it should be 1-2 pages in length. All grant recipients must be recognized by the IRS as tax exempt, not-for-profit organizations under Section 501(c)3 of the Internal Revenue Code. Contact program staff for company locations.

Restrictions: The foundation generally will not consider requests from: organizations that do not have a 501(c)3 status; political organizations or parties, candidates for political office, and lobbying organizations; labor unions or organizations; local athletic or sports programs; service organizations raising money for community purposes; individuals; travel funds for tours, expeditions, or trips by individuals or groups; dues or gifts to national or local alumni groups, clubs or fraternities; institutional memberships or subscription fees for publications; gifts to individual churches, synagogues or other entities organized exclusively for religious

purposes; donations for benefit events, raffle tickets or fundraising efforts that involve value returned to the donor; organizations not operating for the benefit of the general public or that have discriminatory practices; any grantee who receives funds of $50,000 or more shall not be entitled to submit another grant proposal for three years from the date of grant.

Geographic Focus: California, Illinois, Texas
Amount of Grant: 10,000 - 100,000 USD
Samples: Playsmart Literacy, Chicago, Illinois, $25,000 - general operating support (2018); Victory Ranch, Ottumwa, Iowa, $75,000 - general operating support (2018); Naperville Heritage Society, Naperville, Illinois, $10,000 - general operating support (2018); Dupage Children's Museum, Naperville, Illinois, $500,000 - general operating support (2018).
Contact: Carol Gavin; (630) 939-2923; fax (630) 798-4778; carol.gavin@tellabs.com
Sponsor: Tellabs Foundation
1415 West Diehl Road, Mail Stop 10
Naperville, IL 60563-2349

Telluride Foundation Community Grants 2281

The foundation offers an annual granting cycle for nonprofit organizations that serve people living and/or working in Colorado's San Miguel County. The foundation awards grants to local nonprofit organizations involved in the arts, education, athletics, childcare, land conservation, environmental, minority programs, and other community-based efforts. Additionally, the foundation provides local nonprofits with technical assistance, such as training seminars, grant writing and consulting and capacity building services. Foundation grants are awarded once a year, at the end of December, with grant awards being distributed the following year. Grants will fall generally in the range of $500 and above, depending on the amount available for distribution.

Requirements: The Telluride Foundation will consider grant applications from 501(c)3 organizations meeting the following eligibility *Requirements:* conduct activities and programs consistent with the Foundation's mission; serve people living or working in San Miguel County (primary emphasis of grant making is to organizations based in San Miguel, Ouray and west Montrose counties—all other organizations must document a strong case to meet "serving people that live and/or work in San Miguel County."). Applicants without 501(c)3 status, but which have applied to the IRS for such status, may apply. Applicants without 501(c)3 status, but which are operating under an organization qualified as a 501(c)3 organization, may apply separately if they have their own advisory board and have the written consent of the qualified organization.

Restrictions: Grants will not be awarded for building/renovation; equipment that could be capitalized on a financial statement; capital campaigns; debt reduction or retiring past operating deficits; fellowships or other grants to individuals; loans; non-educational publications; litigation; political campaigns; operating support for organizations that conduct lobbying or political action campaigns, economic development, endowment funds, religious organizations for religious purposes, graduate and post-graduate research, or candidates for political office.

Geographic Focus: Colorado
Date(s) Application is Due: Oct 28
Amount of Grant: 500 USD
Contact: April Montgomery; (970) 728-8717; fax (970) 728-9007; april@telluridefoundation.org
Internet: www.telluridefoundation.org/index.php?page=community-grants
Sponsor: Telluride Foundation
220 E. Colorado Avenue, Suite 106
Telluride, CO 81435

Telluride Foundation Emergency/Out of Cycle Grants 2282

The Telluride Foundation Board of Directors recognizes that there will be times when its annual grant cycle does not work for all organizations and their needs. Out-of-cycle grants are requests that fall out of the Foundation's annual cycle of granting. Because of timing issues or emergencies that arise, not all organizations can fit their request into the regular October to December cycle. Out-of-cycle grants are not intended to be a catch-all for organizations that fail to anticipate the October-December cycle or to meet a budget crises, which occur from poor financial planning. The grants are intended to address needs that arise through external or uncontrollable emergencies and that present a compelling story of an unmet and necessary need.

Requirements: The Telluride Foundation will consider grant applications from 501(c)3 organizations meeting the following eligibility *Requirements:* conduct activities and programs consistent with the Foundation's mission; serve people living or working in San Miguel County (primary emphasis of grant making is to organizations based in San Miguel, Ouray and west Montrose counties—all other organizations must document a strong case to meet "serving people that live and/or work in San Miguel County."). Only two types of needs will be considered: Timing-needs which arise because of timing issues on the part of the organization; and, Human Emergencies. Needs which do not fall into one of these two narrow categories will be considered and the request must be for a project or program described under "Types of Support" in the regular grant guidelines.

Restrictions: Grants will not be awarded for building/renovation; equipment that could be capitalized on a financial statement; capital campaigns; debt reduction or retiring past operating deficits; fellowships or other grants to individuals; loans; non-educational publications; litigation; political campaigns; operating support for organizations that conduct lobbying or political action campaigns, economic development, endowment funds, religious organizations for religious purposes, graduate and post-graduate research, or candidates for political office.

Geographic Focus: Colorado
Contact: April Montgomery; (970) 728-8717; fax (970) 728-9007; april@telluridefoundation.org
Internet: www.telluridefoundation.org/index.php?page=emergency-out-of-cycle-grants
Sponsor: Telluride Foundation
220 E. Colorado Avenue, Suite 106
Telluride, CO 81435

Telluride Foundation Technical Assistance Grants   **2283**

The Telluride Foundation offers local nonprofits with the option of applying for a Technical Assistance Grant. The grants provide an easy, effective way for nonprofit organizations to improve their operational efficiency through a proven, turnkey program for assessing and addressing individual organization's needs. The objective is to provide the nonprofit a professional third part assessment of their current needs then a professional nonprofit consultant to assist through the solution process. The assessment may identify the need for an updated business plan, strategic plan, marketing plan, Board of Directors development, etc. The consultant will assist the organizations staff and Board through the development of the plan. The Assessment will be conducted by the Community Resource Center or a consultant choosen by the nonprofit, if approved by the Telluride Foundation, and will be shared with the Telluride Foundation. The Telluride Foundation will pay for the assessment and will fund part or the entire consultant fees. If selected for a TA, the non-profit will not be eligible for future funding from the Telluride Foundation until they have completed the TA process.

Requirements: The Telluride Foundation will consider grant applications from 501(c)3 organizations meeting the following eligibility *Requirements:* conduct activities and programs consistent with the Foundation's mission; serve people living or working in San Miguel County (primary emphasis of grant making is to organizations based in San Miguel, Ouray and west Montrose counties—all other organizations must document a strong case to meet "serving people that live and/or work in San Miguel County."). Applicants without 501(c)3 status, but which have applied to the IRS for such status, may apply. Applicants without 501(c)3 status, but which are operating under an organization qualified as a 501(c)3 organization, may apply separately if they have their own advisory board and have the written consent of the qualified organization. A request for a Technical Assistance Grant may be included in a Community Grant application requesting project or general operating funds or a nonprofit may only request Technical Assitance Funds using the Community Grant application.

Restrictions: Grants will not be awarded for building/renovation; equipment that could be capitalized on a financial statement; capital campaigns; debt reduction or retiring past operating deficits; fellowships or other grants to individuals; loans; non-educational publications; litigation; political campaigns; operating support for organizations that conduct lobbying or political action campaigns, economic development, endowment funds, religious organizations for religious purposes, graduate and post-graduate research, or candidates for political office.

Geographic Focus: Colorado

Date(s) Application is Due: Oct 28

Contact: April Montogomery; (970) 728-8717; fax (970) 728-9007; april@telluridefoundation.org

Internet: www.telluridefoundation.org/index.php?page=technical-assistance-grants

Sponsor: Telluride Foundation

220 E. Colorado Avenue, Suite 106

Telluride, CO 81435

Tension Envelope Foundation Grants   **2284**

Incorporated in 1954 in Missouri, the Tension Envelope Foundation supports nonprofits in company-operating areas, with an emphasis on Jewish welfare funds, community funds, higher education, health, civic affairs, culture and the arts, and youth. Funding typically is provided for general operating costs. There are no annual deadlines or guidelines, and the foundation does not distribute an annual report. To apply for a grant, send proposal with an overview of the project, budget, and proof of 501(c)3 status, requesting an application form in the process. The board meets several times each year.

Requirements: 501(c)3 nonprofits in California, Iowa, Kansas, Minnesota, Missouri, North Carolina, Tennessee, and Texas are eligible. Primary consideration is in the Kansas City metro area.

Geographic Focus: California, Iowa, Kansas, Minnesota, Missouri, North Carolina, Tennessee, Texas

Amount of Grant: 100 - 70,000 USD

Contact: William L. Berkley, Director; (816) 471-3800

Sponsor: Tension Envelope Foundation

819 E 19th Street, 5th Floor

Kansas City, MO 64108-1781

Terra Foundation Chicago K–12 Education Grants   **2285**

The Terra Foundation supports activities that bring American art into Chicago's classrooms, with the aim of helping teachers enrich curricula and enhance learning. To achieve these goals, the foundation funds projects that strengthen Chicago teachers' knowledge of historical American art (circa 1500–1980) and the ability to teach with it effectively. Grant funding is available for: professional-development programs; the development and dissemination of instructional resources about the history of American art, with training designed to help teachers use those resources effectively. Professional-development programs should be designed to accomplish the following: deepen teachers' knowledge of American art history and visual culture; enhance teachers' ability to use American art in meaningful and innovative ways as part of the curriculum; and advance teachers' skills in guiding students to think critically about American art, make personal connections and responses to it, and understand its relationships to American history and culture. Letters of Inquiry (LOIs) are required, and should be followed by a full proposal after an invitation is extended. There are two funding cycles each year: fall cycle LOIs are due by May 15, followed by a July 15 deadline for full applications; and spring cycle LOIs are due by September 16, followed by a November 15 deadline for full applications.

Requirements: The foundation only accepts proposals from institutions with United States 501(c)3 status or governmental organizations. Applicants must be based in the city of Chicago and their project must be directed primarily toward teachers in Chicago schools. An exception may be made only when projects for which funding is requested take place in the Chicago area and teachers from schools in the city of Chicago make up the majority of the audience served.

Geographic Focus: Illinois

Date(s) Application is Due: Jul 15; Nov 15

Contact: Amy Gunderson, Grants Manager; (312) 654-2275 or (312) 664-3939; gunderson@terraamericanart.org or grants@terraamericanart.org

Jenny Siegenthaler, Program Director for Education Grants and Initiatives; (312) 654-2253 or (312) 664-3939; siegenthaler@terraamericanart.org or grants@terraamericanart.org

Internet: www.terraamericanart.org/what-we-offer/grant-fellowship-opportunities/chicago-k-12-education-grants/

Sponsor: Terra Foundation

120 East Erie Street

Chicago, IL 60611

Textron Corporate Contributions Grants   **2286**

Textron Inc. was founded in 1923 as a small textile company and has since become one of the world's best known multi-industry companies. Textron focuses philanthropic giving in the following areas: workforce development and education; healthy families/vibrant communities; and sponsorships. In the area of workforce development and education, the company focuses on job-training and employment development (eg., school-to-work, welfare-to-work, job-training for underserved-audiences, literacy, and English-as a-Second-Language programs). In the area of healthy families/vibrant communities, the company focuses on arts and culture (with emphasis on outreach programs that enhance learning and target low- and moderate-income individuals), community revitalization (eg., affordable housing and economic development in low-income areas), and health and human-service organizations (eg., food pantries, homeless shelters, and services for low-income residents). In the area of sponsorships, the company encourages volunteerism and sponsors worthwhile events that benefit the communities where employees live and work. Textron's grant history has included funding of general-operating costs, capital campaigns, building construction/renovation, equipment acquisition, program development, conferences and seminars, publication, seed money, fellowships, scholarship funds, research, technical assistance, consulting services, and matching funds. Downloadable guidelines (PDF) and application (Word document) are available online. The completed application and required accompanying documentation must be received via mail by the deadline date.

Requirements: Textron targets its giving to nonprofit agencies located in its headquarters state of Rhode Island and those locations where the company has divisional operations. Organizations outside of Rhode Island should contact the Textron company in their area; a listing of Textron businesses along with their contact information can be accessed by clicking the "Contact Us" link at the Textron website.

Restrictions: Textron will review only one request per organization during a 12-month period. Contributions will not be made to the following types of organizations: organizations without 501(c)3 status as defined by the Internal Revenue Service; individuals; political, fraternal or veterans organizations; religious institutions when the grant would support sectarian activities; and organizations that discriminate by race, creed, gender, ethnicity, sexual orientation, disability, age or any other basis prohibited by law.

Geographic Focus: Georgia, Illinois, Kansas, Louisiana, Maryland, Massachusetts, New York, North Carolina, Pennsylvania, Rhode Island, Texas, Germany, United Kingdom

Date(s) Application is Due: Mar 1; Sep 1

Contact: Director of Community Affairs; (401) 421-2800; fax (401) 457-2225

Internet: www.textron.com/CorpResponsibility/Charitable-Giving

Sponsor: Textron Charitable Trust

40 Westminster Street

Providence, RI 02903

Thelma Braun and Bocklett Family Foundation Grants   **2287**

The Thelma Braun and Bocklett Family Foundation was established in 1980 to support and promote quality education, cultural, human services and health care programming for underserved populations. Miss Braun was a gifted musician who spent many years playing the organ and piano for area organizations and churches. She never married and had no children of her own, but she truly loved the young people in the area. Special consideration is given to charitable organizations that serve the people of Grayson County, Texas, especially in the area of arts and education. The majority of grants from the Braun and Bocklett Family Foundation are 1 year in duration. Award amounts typically go up to $30,000. Applications are accepted twice annually.

Requirements: Applicants must have 501(c)3 tax-exempt status and serve communities in Grayson County, Texas. Applications will be submitted online through the Bank of America website. A grant report is required within 1 year of the grant application date, regardless of whether all of the funds have been spent.

Restrictions: The foundation does not support requests from individuals, organizations attempting to influence policy through direct lobbying, or any political campaigns.

Geographic Focus: Texas

Date(s) Application is Due: Jan 1; Aug 1

Amount of Grant: Up to 30,000 USD

Samples: Denison Isd, Denison, Isd, $30,000 - Awarded for Denison High School's Thelma Braun Center for Performing Arts (2019); Pottsboro Independent School District, Pottsboro, Texas, $20,000 - Awarded for Pottsboro High School Theatre Department (2019); Salvation Army, Sherman, Texas, $10,000 - Awarded for the Salvation Army Band, Music and Arts program (2019).

Contact: Kelly Garlock; (800) 357-7094; tx.philanthropic@bankofamerica.com

Internet: www.bankofamerica.com/philanthropic/foundation/?fnId=86

Sponsor: Thelma Braun and Bocklett Family Foundation

P.O. Box 831041

Dallas, TX 75283-1041

Thelma Doelger Charitable Trust Grants   **2288**

Established in California in 1995, the Thelma Doelger Charitable Trust awards grants in the San Francisco Bay. Giving is primarily aimed at animal welfare, social services, medical centers, and children and youth services. The Trust's major fields of interest include: aging centers and services; animal welfare; boys and girls clubs; children and youth services; higher education; hospitals; human services; museums; and zoos. Grants typically take the form of general purposes and support of operating budgets. Most recently, awards have ranged from $3,000 to $50,000. Though a formal application is required, there are no annual submission deadlines. The initial approach should be by letter or telephone, requesting the application.

Requirements: Nonprofit organizations in the San Francisco Bay area of northern California may submit grant requests.

Restrictions: Individuals are not eligible.

Geographic Focus: California

Amount of Grant: 3,000 - 50,000 USD

Samples: Seton Medical Center, Daly City, California, $35,000 - general operating costs; Marin Humane Society, Novato, California, $50,000 - general operating costs; Curi Odyssey (formerly Coyote Point Museum), San Mateo, California, $50,000 - general operating costs.

Contact: D. Eugene Richard, Trustee; (650) 755-2333

Sponsor: Thelma Doelger Charitable Trust

950 Daly Boulevard, Suite 300

Daly City, CA 94015-3004

Thomas and Agnes Carvel Foundation Grants   **2289**

Just hearing the name "Carvel" brings to mind soft ice cream, chocolate or vanilla, swirling into a cone. Or an ice cream cake, gaily decorated for the holidays. Or maybe you recall the late founder of the business, Tom Carvel himself, with his deliberately unpolished voice, starring in his own homespun television commercials. But there is more to the Carvel empire than frozen desserts. The Carvel Foundation, with headquarters on East Grassy Sprain Road in Yonkers, New York, has been granting money to nonprofit agencies, organizations and institutions for more than 40 years. The fFoundation, begun by Thomas Carvel and his wife, Agnes, as a grass-roots operation with a mom-and-pop style of giving, moved into a contemporary mode of philanthropy in 1992. Thomas Carvel, who died in 1990 at the age of 85, lived in Ardsley and liked to help his neighbors. However, in the early 1990s, a new board of directors decided "to make the foundation more visible in the community," to make its presence felt on a larger scale. The directors felt they should limit the number of gifts but "make each one more significant." Today, the Thomas and Agnes Carvel Foundation awards support for general charitable purposes as well as for nutrition research and youth programs to nonprofit organizations in the tri-state area comprising New York, New Jersey, and Connecticut. Types of support include general operations grants, capital grants, grants in aid, program and project grants, matching gifts, and research grants. Application should be by letter and should outline the project, budget, and staffing of the project for which funding is being requested. Typical awards range up to a maximum of $30,000, though occasionally are much higher. The Foundation offers between 150 and 175 awards each year. There are no specific deadlines, and applicants should forward a letter of application to the Foundation office.

Requirements: IRS 501(c)3 organizations serving residents of New York, New Jersey, and Connecticut are eligible to apply.

Restrictions: Grants are not made to individuals.

Geographic Focus: Connecticut, New Jersey, New York

Amount of Grant: 1,000 - 150,000 USD

Samples: Elizabeth Seton Children's Foundation, Yonkers, New York, $25,000 - unrestricted funding support; Fraxa Foundation, LaGrangeville, New York, $60,000 - unrestricted funding support; Freehold Borough Educational Fund, Freehold, New Jersey, $1,000 - unrestricted funding support,

Contact: Peter Smith, President; (914) 793-7300

Sponsor: Thomas and Agnes Carvel Foundation

35 East Grassy Sprain Road

Yonkers, NY 10710-4620

Thomas J. Atkins Memorial Trust Fund Grants   **2290**

The Thomas J. Atkins Memorial Trust Fund was established in 1946 to support and promote quality educational, human services, and health care programming for underserved populations. The Atkins Memorial Trust Fund specifically serves the people of Middlesex County, Connecticut. Preference is given to organizations and programs that provide for the relief of human distress and suffering. Grants from the Atkins Memorial Trust Fund are 1 year in duration. Award amounts typically go up to $10,000.

Requirements: 501(c)3 organizations are eligible to apply. Preference is also given to organizations serving the people of Middletown, Connecticut. Organizations serving the people of Middlesex County will also be considered. Applications will be submitted online through the Bank of America website. A grant report is required within 1 year of the grant application date, regardless of whether all of the funds have been spent.

Restrictions: The fund does not support requests from individuals, organizations attempting to influence policy through direct lobbying, or any political campaigns.

Geographic Focus: Connecticut

Date(s) Application is Due: Oct 1

Amount of Grant: Up to 10,000 USD

Samples: The Connection, Middletown, Connecticut, $10,000 - Awarded for general program support for Eddy Shelter of Middlesex County; St. Vincent De Paul Place Middletown Inc., Middletown, Connecticut, $10,000 - Awarded for Meals and Community Assistance program; High Hopes Theraputic Riding Inc., Old Lyme, Connecticut, $5,000 - Awarded for financial aid program.

Contact: Amy R. Lynch, Philanthropic Client Manager; (860) 244-4870; ct.grantmaking@bankofamerica.com or amy.r.lynch@bofa.com

Internet: www.bankofamerica.com/philanthropic/foundation/?fnId=49

Sponsor: Thomas J. Atkins Memorial Trust Fund

P.O. Box 1802

Providence, RI 02901-1802

Thomas J. Long Foundation Community Grants   **2291**

Through its Community Grants program, the Foundation awards grants to charitable organizations in the San Francisco East Bay and in five selected fields of interest: Arts & Culture, Conservation, Education, Health, and Human Services. The Foundation gives preference to proposals received from organizations that provide direct benefit to low income children and youth, the elderly and disabled persons. Safety net services, and programs focused on economic self-sufficiency are also favored.

Requirements: The Foundation awards grants to selected tax-exempt charitable organizations that have been recognized by the IRS as being described in Section 501(c)3 and 509(a)1 or 509(a)2 of the Internal Revenue Code. The Foundation primarily funds charitable programs and services which are of particular benefit to residents of the East Bay counties of Alameda and Contra Costa. Organizations that are considering a proposal for grant support should have an established presence in these communities including an office and/or dedicated staff permanently assigned to the East Bay. Proposals which do not focus on the East Bay are unlikely to be funded and it is rarely worthwhile to submit a proposal. The Thomas J. Long Foundation uses a formal grant process to administer its grant making program. All forms used in the grant process are available only through the Foundation's on-line grants management system. Requests for funding or reports submitted in any other manner will not be accepted. Grant proposals are accepted on a continuous basis throughout the year.

Restrictions: The Foundation does not ordinarily award grants for the following: 509(a)3 supporting organizations; government entities; individuals; advocacy or influencing public policy; endowments; international grants; loan repayments; research or studies; capital campaigns (invitation only); projects or programs that have already taken place; or, national organizations headquartered outside of the San Francisco Bay Area.

Geographic Focus: California

Contact: Nancy Shillis, Program Officer; (925) 944-3800; fax (925) 944-3573

Internet: www.thomasjlongfdn.org/?q=grants

Sponsor: Thomas J. Long Foundation

2950 Buskirk Avenue, Suite 160

Walnut Creek, CA 94597

Thomas Sill Foundation Grants   **2292**

Mr. Sill lived his entire life in Winnipeg and practiced as a chartered accountant for many years. He was an astute investor who built a fortune which became the basis for the Thomas Sill Foundation. The foundation provides encouragement and financial support to qualifying Manitoba organizations that strive to improve the quality of life in the province. The foundation awards grants in the following areas of interest: Responses to Community (agencies addressing poverty, women's shelters, qualifying daycares, mentally and physically challenged people, and community well-being); Health (eye care, palliative care, mental illness); Education (students at risk, including adults); Arts and Culture; Heritage (museums, architecture, projects); and, Environment (water issues). Grants awarded may be capital, operating or project in nature.

Requirements: Registered charities may obtain an application form by phoning the foundation office, at which time a preliminary discussion will determine eligibility. There are no deadlines by which applications must be submitted. Applicants should allow four months, from the submission of a request, to receive a response.

Restrictions: Successful applicants must wait two years before submitting another request.

Geographic Focus: Canada

Amount of Grant: 1,000 - 50,000 CAD

Contact: Hugh Arklie; (204) 947-3782; fax (204) 956-4702; hugha@tomsill.ca

Internet: thomassillfoundation.com/guidelines/

Sponsor: Thomas Sill Foundation

206-1661 Portage Avenue

Winnipeg, MB R3J 3T7 Canada

Thomas W. Bradley Foundation Grants   **2293**

Established in 1976 in Maryland, the Thomas W. Bradley Foundation offer grants in the greater metropolitan Baltimore, Maryland, area. Funding is limited to organizations which work with or benefit mentally or physically handicapped children. Primary fields of interest include: children, children's services, and the developmentally disabled. Funding comes in the form of general operating support. Application forms are required, and applicants should submit the following: name, address and phone number of organization; copy of IRS Determination Letter; a brief history of the organization and description of its mission; a listing of board of directors, trustees, officers and other key people and their affiliations; a detailed description of project and amount of funding requested; and a copy of the current year's organizational budget and project budget. There are no specific deadlines.

Requirements: Only 501(c)3 organizations that serve the residents of Maryland should apply, and the Foundation gives preference in the Baltimore metropolitan area.

Restrictions: No grants, scholarships, fellowships, prizes, or similar benefits are made to individuals.

Geographic Focus: Maryland

Amount of Grant: 5,000 - 10,000 USD

Samples: Muscular Dystrophy Association, Baltimore, Maryland, $10,000 - general operating support (2019); Arts Every Day, Baltimore, Maryland, $10,000 - for general operations (2019); YMCA for Central Maryland, Towson, Maryland, $10,000 - general operating support (2019).

Contact: Robert L. Pierson, Trustee; (410) 821-3006; fax (410) 821-3007

Sponsor: Thomas W. Bradley Foundation

305 W. Chesapeake Avenue, Suite 308

Towson, MD 21204-4440

Thomas W. Briggs Foundation Grants 2294

In 1928, Thomas Winston Briggs, a Memphian, founded the Welcome Wagon Company. From its modest beginnings in the Mid-South, the company grew to become Welcome Wagon International with its corporate headquarters in Memphis and offices in New York, San Francisco, Toronto, Canada and London, England. Welcome Wagon became a household word throughout the world and its 8,000 Hostesses were a familiar symbol of community service and friendship. Throughout his life, the interests of the community were always foremost in the mind of Briggs, with the needs of the community helping to guide his business. Those ideals were also the basis of the Thomas W. Briggs Foundation which was chartered by Briggs in New York in 1957. Today, the Foundation provides gifts that help serve the needs of thousands in the Memphis, Tennessee, area. The focus of the funding includes: youth projects and programs; education; social services; arts and cultural organizations; and civic organizations that promote quality of life. The Foundation will consider funding for seed money, capital support, multi-year gifts, entrepreneurial/innovative efforts and for annual operating activities that will help take an existing effort to scale. Awards a total of about $750,000 a year in two funding cycles. Although some grants are multi-year pledges, many fall in the one-year $5,000 to $25,000 range.
Requirements: Applicants are asked to submit an electronic application, giving a brief history of the organization, stating goals and services provided and a list of present sources of funding. Shelby County, Tennessee, nonprofit organizations are eligible to apply.
Restrictions: The Foundation does not support public and private schools, churches and synagogues, nationally affiliated organizations and seminars, as well as special events. The Foundation does not accept requests from any organization in two successive application cycles unless specifically deferred by Briggs to the next cycle and does not accept applications from organizations with an existing pledge.
Geographic Focus: Tennessee
Date(s) Application is Due: Feb 1; Aug 1
Amount of Grant: 5,000 - 25,000 USD
Contact: Margaret Craddock; (901) 680-0276; fax (901) 767-1135; twbriggs@aol.com
Internet: www.thomaswbriggsfoundation.com/funding.html
Sponsor: Thomas W. Briggs Foundation
119 South Main Street, Suite 500
Memphis, TN 38103

Thorman Boyle Foundation Grants 2295

The Thorman Boyle Foundation was established in California in 2000, with its primary fields of interest designated as: anti-discrimination; arts and culture; basic and emergency aid; economic development; environmental justice; human services; individual liberties; and youth development. There are no formal application materials required, and interested parties should forward a letter of application stating their organization's purpose, as well as overall budgetary needs. Most recently, grant awards have ranged from $100 to a maximum of $2,000. No annual deadlines for submission have been identified.
Requirements: Though giving is primarily limited to 501(c)3 organizations either located in, or serving the residents of, California, the Foundation has, on occasion, awarded grants outside of this region.
Geographic Focus: All States
Amount of Grant: 100 - 2,000 USD
Contact: Mary E. Boyle, President; (650) 856-7445 or (510) 552-5068
Sponsor: Thorman Boyle Foundation
P.O. Box 2757
Cupertino, CA 95015

Thrasher Research Fund Grants 2296

The Thrasher Research Fund provides grants for pediatric medical research. Because significant solutions for many children's health problems remain undiscovered, the Fund invites a broad array of applications. The Thrasher Research Fund seeks to foster an environment of creativity and discovery aimed at finding solutions to children's health problems. The Fund awards grants for research that offers substantial promise for meaningful advances in prevention and treatment of children's diseases, particularly research that offers broad-based applications.
Requirements: Principal Investigators must be qualified in terms of education and experience to conduct research. A doctoral-level degree is required. There are no citizenship or residency requirements. The Fund is open to applications from institutions both inside and outside the United States.
Restrictions: The fund does not award grants for educational programs; general operating expenses; general bridge funding for incomplete projects; construction or renovation of buildings or facilities; loans, student aid, scholarships, tuition; or, support of other funding organizations. Grants generally are not awarded for conferences, workshops, or symposia. Proposals in the areas of research on human fetal tissue or behavioral science research will not be considered.
Geographic Focus: All States, All Countries
Amount of Grant: 100,000 - 350,000 USD
Contact: Megan Duncan, MSPH, Research Manager; (801) 240-4720; fax (801) 240-1625; DuncanME@thrasherresearch.org
Aaron V. Pontsler, M.S., MBA, Research Manager; (801) 240-6385; fax (801) 240-1625; PontslerAV@thrasherresearch.org
Internet: www.thrasherresearch.org/sites/www_thrasherresearch_org/Default.aspx?page=28
Sponsor: Thrasher Research Fund
68 S. Main Street, Suite 400
Salt Lake City, UT 84101

Three Guineas Fund Grants 2297

In 2009, Three Guineas Fund restructured as a private foundation. The fund makes grants in education and the environment consistent with the foundation's bylaws, while keeping its core commitment to women and girls. Currently, the fund welcomes projects that create access to opportunity for women and girls, especially in education and the economy. Grantmaking includes projects that advance and support girls and women in the areas of entrepreneurship; science, math, and technology; leadership; sports; access to education and the economy; and dissemination and distribution of strategies, research, or documentation of women's and girls' issues. Types of support include start-up projects and general operating grants for established programs. The fund is open to multi-year grants. Submit a letter of inquiry; full proposals are by request only.
Requirements: 501(c)3 tax-exempt organizations and organizations with a fiscal agent with that status are eligible.
Restrictions: The fund does not make grants to support direct service projects, unless they are of strategic interest as potentially scalable models; scholarship programs; film production; fundraising events; conferences; or individuals.
Geographic Focus: All States
Date(s) Application is Due: Jun 15
Contact: Grants Administrator; (415) 348-1581; fax (415) 348-1584; info@3gf.org
Internet: www.3gf.org/index.html
Sponsor: Three Guineas Fund
153 Upper Terrace
San Francisco, CA 94117

Threshold Foundation Justice and Democracy Grants 2298

The Threshold Foundation Justice and Democracy grants support organizations working for human rights for youth impacted by the criminal justice and drug policy systems. Grants fund organizations or programs aimed at reforming criminal justice systems and drug policy, with a focus on youth, either directly through civic action and legislative initiatives or through the development and implementation of specific rehabilitation programs or alternatives to incarceration. This focus includes but is not limited to policies that negatively impact youth (the "school-to-prison" pipeline), sentencing reform, substituting treatment for incarceration, and decriminalization of specific currently illegal drugs. Grants also support organizations working on civic participation, aimed at expanding political rights for those who live in historically disenfranchised communities. Focus will be on organizations incorporating a sustainable, bottom-up model of electoral power-building led by and for historically under-represented constituencies. Core strategies could include leadership development, community organizing, civic engagement and coalition building. Up to four $100,000 grants are made, payable over three to four years. Organizations should contact the Foundation for current dates and guidelines for letter of inquiry submission.
Requirements: Funding is made to 501(c)3 organizations and programs, as well as programs and organizations with a 501(c)3 fiscal sponsor. The applicant's actual budget for the last completed fiscal year, as well as projected budgets for the three fiscal years in which the first, second, and third annual grant payments would be used, must be below $800,000. If the organization has both a 501(c)3 and a 501(c)4, their combined organizational budgets must be below $800,000. Requested amount for year one should be between $25,000 and $40,000. Funding in the second and succeeding years is conditional on the grantee's compliance with reporting requirements, continued progress toward the stated goals and outcomes, and demonstrated impact of activities.
Geographic Focus: All States
Amount of Grant: 100,000 USD
Contact: Craig Harwood; (415) 561-6400; fax (415) 561-6401; tholdgrants@tides.org
Internet: www.thresholdfoundation.org/?id=268
Sponsor: Threshold Foundation
P.O. Box 29903
San Francisco, CA 94129-0903

Threshold Foundation Queer Youth Grants 2299

Through a funding collaborative, the Threshold Foundation and Liberty Hill Foundation makes multi-year grants to grassroots, local, state, or national nonprofit organizations located in the U.S., working to improve the quality of life among gay, lesbian, bisexual, transgender, queer, and questioning (GLBTQQ) youth. The Queer Youth grants award funding to innovative and effective leadership development programs or organizing projects that empower GLBTQQ youth to improve societal conditions that affect them and make a long-term difference to their movement. At least four $100,000 grants, payable over three to five years, will be made to groups with specific work that matches the grant guidelines. Letters of intent are due October 3, with full proposals by invitation only.
Requirements: Eligible groups must have an organizational budget of $5 million or less (only applies to the group applying for the grant, not the fiscal sponsor) and a total budget for their youth work of $750,000 or less.
Geographic Focus: All States
Date(s) Application is Due: Feb 1
Amount of Grant: 100,000 USD
Contact: Margarita Ramirez, Deputy Director of Grantmaking; (323) 556-7200, ext 215 or (323) 556-7200; fax (323) 556-7240; mramirez@libertyhill.org
Internet: www.thresholdfoundation.org/?id=319
Sponsor: Threshold Foundation
P.O. Box 29903
San Francisco, CA 94129-0903

Tides Foundation Friends of the IGF Fund Grants 2300

The California-based activist Drummond Pike established the Tides Foundation in 1976, naming it after a Sausalito bookstore that catered to a leftist readership. Today, the Foundation is a signatory to Philanthropy's Promise, and consequently commits a significant percentage of its grant making dollars to meeting the needs of underserved communities, including the financial support of advocacy and civic engagement. Tides Foundation has established a fund to support the United Nations to advance the mission of the Internet Governance Forum (IGF). The IGF is a forum for multi-stakeholder policy dialogue, to support the United Nations Secretary-General in carrying out the mandate from the World Summit on the Information Society (WSIS). Tides Foundation has established the Friends of the IGF Fund to raise voluntary financial contributions from individuals, corporations, non-profit organizations and other nongovernmental entities to provide financial support to the United Nations for the IGF Project. The Friends of the IGF Fund is committed to: independent fund management; transparency in the fundraising and grant-making process; broad support of the IGF mission, which includes funding the IGF Secretariat and its related initiatives for the advancement of the goals of the IGF, through the United Nations IGF Trust Fund; and minimal fund maintenance charge (3% of all contributions).
Requirements: Applications are accepted from all fifty states, its territories, and United Nations countries throughout the world.
Geographic Focus: All States, All Countries
Amount of Grant: Up to 50,000 USD
Contact: Edward Wang, Program Associate; (415) 561-6387 or (415) 561-6400; fax (415) 561-6401; info@tides.org or ewang@tides.org
Internet: www.tides.org/impact/funds-initiatives/friends-of-the-igf-fund/
Sponsor: Tides Foundation
P.O. Box 29198
San Francisco, CA 94129-0198

Tides Foundation Girl Rising Fund Grants 2301

The California-based activist Drummond Pike established the Tides Foundation in 1976, naming it after a Sausalito bookstore that catered to a leftist readership. Today, the Foundation is a signatory to Philanthropy's Promise, and consequently commits a significant percentage of its grant making dollars to meeting the needs of underserved communities, including the financial support of advocacy and civic engagement. The Girl Rising Fund was established in 2012 to drive resources to established girl-focused programs in the developing world. Girl Rising is a groundbreaking feature film and a global social action campaign for girls' education. Areas of support include: scholarships; health care services; and critical life skills training.
Requirements: Nonprofits supporting programs for young girls and women throughout the world are eligible to apply.
Restrictions: Tides does not accept requests from universities, schools, individuals, or corporations; nor for capital campaigns, endowments, or film production.
Geographic Focus: All Countries
Amount of Grant: Up to 1,000,000 USD
Samples: Foundation to Educate Girls Globally, Mumbai, India, $5,000 - general operating support; G(irls)20 Summit, Toronto, Canada, $75,000 - general operating support; Girls Not Brides, London, England, $664,000 - general operating support.
Contact: Edward Wang, Program Associate; (212) 456-5857 or (415) 561-6400; fax (415) 561-6401; info@tides.org or info@girlrising.com
Internet: www.tides.org/impact/funds-initiatives/girl-rising-fund/
Sponsor: Tides Foundation
P.O. Box 29198
San Francisco, CA 94129-0198

Tides Foundation Grants 2302

The California-based activist Drummond Pike established the Tides Foundation in 1976, naming it after a Sausalito bookstore that catered to a leftist readership. Today, the Foundation is a signatory to Philanthropy's Promise, and consequently commits a significant percentage of its grant making dollars to meeting the needs of underserved communities, including the financial support of advocacy and civic engagement. Hence, the Foundation actively promotes change toward a healthy society and channels its grant making to the following issue areas: arts, culture and alternative media; civic participation; death penalty abolishment; drug policy reform; economic development; economic and racial justice; environmental justice; gay, lesbian, bisexual, and transgender issues; HIV/AIDS; Native communities; peace strategies; women's empowerment and reproductive health; youth development and organizing; and violence prevention. The foundation prefers to fund creative, effective solutions to problems. Hundreds of awards are given annually, with no specified deadlines. Grant awards have most recently ranged from as little as $500 to as much as $7 million.
Requirements: Nonprofit organizations are eligible to apply. Preference is given to those nonprofits engaged in grassroots organizing.
Restrictions: Tides does not accept requests from universities, schools, individuals, or corporations; nor for capital campaigns, endowments, or film production.
Geographic Focus: All States, All Countries
Amount of Grant: 1,000 - 7,000,000 USD
Samples: Academy for the Love of Learning, Santa Fe, New Mexico, $2,300,000 - general operating support; National Association of Child Care Workers, Cape Town, South Africa, $100,000 - general operating support; Penobscot East Resource Center, Stonington, Maine, $150,000 - general operating support.
Contact: Edward Wang; (415) 561-6400 or (415) 561-6300; fax (415) 561-6401; info@tides.org
Internet: www.tides.org/impact/funds-initiatives/
Sponsor: Tides Foundation
P.O. Box 29198
San Francisco, CA 94129-0198

TJX Foundation Grants 2303

The primary mission of the foundation is to support programs that provide basic-need services to disadvantaged children, women, and families in communities in which TJX does business. The TJX Foundation is currently focused on supporting 501(c)3 charities that conform to the following giving guidelines: Civic/Community - Emphasis is on programs that teach disadvantaged persons independent living skills and that work to improve race/cultural relations; Domestic Violence Prevention - Support will target immediate emergency services and shelter accommodations for victims and family members affected by abusive situations as well as programming that works to break the cycle of violence; Education - Support will target programs that provide academic and vocational opportunities for the disadvantaged, including early intervention, mentoring, tutoring, GED and college coursework, as well as programs that teach English; Health - Support will target programs that provide early and comprehensive prenatal services and healthy-baby education and, in some cases, research; Social Services - support for programs for disadvantaged children and families, including those that provide food and other basic needs, counseling and family support, adoption services, and youth development—also programs that provide direct services to those with mental or physical impairments. Emergency assistance programs, such as disaster relief intervention projects, are also supported through the Foundation.
Requirements: IRS 501(c)3 tax-exempt organizations are eligible. Support is focused on organizations in communities where one or more of TJX's divisions operates a home office, a store or distribution facility, and whose programs help to: promote strong families, provide emergency shelter, enhance education/job readiness, and build community ties. A required Eligibility Questionnaire can be found at the sponsor's website.
Restrictions: The foundation will not fund international organizations, other giving organizations, prison populations/offenders and ex-offenders, capital campaign requests, cash reserves, computer purchases, conferences/seminars, consultant fees/salaries, conventions, education loans, endowments, fellowships, films/photography, individual requests, new construction, political organizations, programs in operation for less than 12 months, publications, public policy research/advocacy, renovations, building expansions, salary-only requests, seed money/start-up costs, training money/stipend, travel grants/transportation, and unrestricted grants.
Geographic Focus: All States
Date(s) Application is Due: Mar 3; Jul 7
Contact: Christine Strickland; (774) 308-3199 or (774) 308-5722; tjx_foundation@tjx.com
Internet: www.tjx.com/corporate_community_foundation.asp
Sponsor: TJX Foundation
770 Cochituate Road, Route 300-1BN
Framingham, MA 01701

Toby Wells Foundation Grants 2304

The Toby Wells Foundation welcomes funding requests from recognized 501(c)3 non-profit organizations operating programs within San Diego County for initiatives that support the Foundation's work in enhancing the lives of youth, people with disabilities, and animals. Specific areas of interest include programs that: assist youth in developing a positive self-image; bring youth and animals together for mutual benefit; enhance the lives of individuals with spinal cord injuries; and support the "No Kill" philosophy of animals by providing animals with a second chance.
Requirements: Proposals must be submitted in hard-copy format by mail only. If an organization is uncertain whether the program for which they are requesting funding qualifies, they may submit an online letter of inquiry. The Foundation will respond to the submission and help the organization determine whether to submit a full proposal.
Restrictions: Letters of inquiry and proposals are accepted throughout the year, but funding decisions are not determined until December. The Foundation does not provide funding to individual or endowments. All of its funding is limited to programs or organizations in San Diego County.
Geographic Focus: California
Date(s) Application is Due: Sep 5
Contact: Adrienne Wells Castaneda, Executive Director; (858) 391-2973; fax (858) 391-2979; adrienne@tobywells.org
Internet: www.tobywells.org/funding-guidelines
Sponsor: Toby Wells Foundation
P.O. Box 519
Poway, CA 92074

Todd Brock Family Foundation Grants 2305

Established in Texas in 2007, the Todd Brock Family Foundation offers support for educational programs, children, athletics, research, and community projects, as well Protestant agencies and churches. A formal application is required, and applicants should forward the entire proposal to the office. The Foundation rarely offers funding outside of Texas. There are no deadlines for submitting a completed proposal, and grants have most recently ranged from $300 to $250,000.
Geographic Focus: Texas
Samples: Memorial High School Boosters, Houston, Texas. $1,000 - funding for annual gold tournament; Legacy Christian Academy, Beaumont, Texas, $250,000 - for general operations; Yellowstone Academy, Houston, Texas, $25,000 - support for low-income children and families.
Contact: Todd O. Brock, President; (409) 833-6226; fax (409) 832-3019
Sponsor: Todd Brock Family Foundation
1670 E Cardinal Drive, P.O. Box 306
Beaumont, TX 77704-0306

Tom C. Barnsley Foundation Grants   2306

The Tom C. Barnsley Foundation was founded in Dallas, Texas, in 1977, and named for Thomas C. Barnsley, a Mexia, Texas, rancher who was murdered in 1932. The Foundation's primary fields of interest include: elementary and secondary education; boys clubs; human services; youth programs; and religion. Most often, awards are given in the form of general operating support. Generally, grants range from $4,000 to $6,000. There are no specified annual application deadlines, and interested organizations should begin by contacted the Foundation trustee directly.

Requirements: Grants awards are given to 501(c)3 organizations in Crane County, Texas, and its surrounding counties.

Geographic Focus: Texas

Amount of Grant: 4,000 - 6,000 USD

Samples: Rankin Senior 4-H Club, Rankin, Texas, $4,300 - general operating support; West Texas Boys Ranch, San Angelo, Texas, $4,300 - general operating support; Crane Cowboy Church, Crane, Texas, $4,300 - general operating support.

Contact: Trustee; (214) 209-2396 or (214) 209-1067

Sponsor: Tom C. Barnsley Foundation

901 Main Street, P.O. Box 831041

Dallas, TX 75283-1041

Toshiba America Foundation Grades 7-12 Science and Math Grants   2307

Toshiba America Foundation (TAF) funds projects with potential for improving classroom teaching and learning in science and mathematics classrooms for grades 7-12. In particular TAF is interested in projects designed by teachers or small teams of teachers that engage students in positive and challenging learning experiences in their own schools. Many successful grantees have designed projects that tap into the natural curiosity of their students, enable students to frame their own scientific questions, and incorporate the expertise of community partners. Proposals for projects $5,000 and under are reviewed on a rolling basis and may be submitted anytime. Proposals for projects over $5,000 are reviewed twice a year and must be submitted by February 1st or August 1st each year. Before submitting a completed proposal, teachers are encouraged to call the Toshiba America Foundation team to discuss their project ideas and to learn more about the application process and the Foundation's grant-making guidelines. The foundation has also made a special commitment to support projects in regions where Toshiba America Group companies have offices.

Requirements: Any 7-12 teacher in a public or private (not-for-profit) school may apply. Proposals from private school teachers must include the school's IRS 501(c)3 tax exemption letter or qualifying state tax exemption notice. Proposals from public school teachers must include a copy of the school's state tax exempt certificate (or other evidence of public school status as recognized by an appropriate local or state government agency). The Foundation strongly encourages projects planned and led by individual teachers or teams of teachers for their own classrooms.

Restrictions: Toshiba America Foundation will not contribute to general operations, capital projects, endowments, conferences, independent study, fund raising events, or similar activities. Religious or political causes will not be supported. Organizations that discriminate on the basis of sex, race, age, disability or religion are not eligible for funding. No grants will be made to individuals. Summer projects or after school programs cannot be considered. Salaries, facility maintenance, textbooks, video production, audio-visual equipment (e.g. electronic white boards, document projectors, student response systems) and education research will not be funded. No grants are available for computer hardware. No single school may receive more than one grant at a time. No new applications will be considered from grantees until final reports are approved. TAF funding is usually directed to K-12 schools. Educational nonprofits and universities working with K-12 teachers are occasionally considered, but must call the foundation first.

Geographic Focus: All States

Date(s) Application is Due: Feb 1; Aug 1

Samples: Sue McIninch, New Kent High School, New Kent, Virginia, amount unspecified - Sue McIninch's students have successfully built two hives, added bees and are monitoring them closely with plans to add two additional hives in the spring; instructors' names unspecified, North Penn High School, Lansdale, Pennsylvania, $4,930 - students from the school's Engineering Academy participated in a new nanotechnology research project and shared their findings with the public via the internet; instructors' names unspecified, Greater Hartford Academy of Mathematics and Science (GHAMS), West Hartford, Connecticut, $18,650 - students participate in a hands-on elective course "The Algal BioDiesel Project" to study, evaluate, produce and test alternative (non-petroleum) fuel sources (this project began with a TAF grant in 2006).

Contact: Laura Cronin, Foundation Manager; (212) 596-0620; fax (212) 221-1108; foundation@tai.toshiba.com or 6to12Applications@tai.toshiba.com

Internet: www.toshiba.com/taf/612.jsp

Sponsor: Toshiba America Foundation

1251 Avenue of the Americas, 41st Floor

New York, NY 10020

Toshiba America Foundation K-6 Science and Math Grants   2308

Toshiba America Foundation (TAF) funds projects with potential for improving classroom teaching and learning in science and mathematics classrooms for grades K-6. In particular TAF is interested in projects designed by teachers or small teams of teachers that engage students in positive and challenging learning experiences in their own schools. Many successful grantees have designed projects that tap into the natural curiosity of their students, enable students to frame their own scientific questions, and incorporate the expertise of community partners. Before submitting a completed proposal, teachers are encouraged to call the Toshiba America Foundation team to discuss their project ideas and to learn more about the application process and the Foundation's grant-making guidelines.

The foundation has also made a special commitment to support projects in regions where Toshiba America Group companies have offices.

Requirements: Any K-5 teacher in a public or private (not-for-profit) school is eligible for a grant to support science or math education up to $1,000. Private school teachers must attach an IRS 501(c)3 tax exemption letter or qualifying state tax exemption notice to the application. The Foundation strongly encourages projects planned and led by individual teachers or teams of teachers for their own classrooms.

Restrictions: Toshiba America Foundation will not contribute to general operations, capital projects, endowments, conferences, independent study, fund raising events, or similar activities. Religious or political causes will not be supported. Organizations that discriminate on the basis of sex, race, age, disability or religion are not eligible for funding. No grants will be made to individuals. Summer projects or after school programs cannot be considered. Salaries, facility maintenance, textbooks, video production, audio-visual equipment (e.g. electronic white boards, document projectors, student response systems) and education research will not be funded. No grants are available for computer hardware. No single school may receive more than one grant at a time. No new applications will be considered from grantees until final reports are approved. TAF funding is usually directed to K-12 schools. Educational nonprofits and universities working with K-12 teachers are occasionally considered, but must call the foundation first.

Geographic Focus: All States

Date(s) Application is Due: Oct 1

Amount of Grant: Up to 1,000 USD

Samples: "Anaheim Inventors," Anaheim, California - Southern California students will work in small groups to conduct the research necessary to develop new inventions that will be useful to their fellow students and will present their results at a school-wide convention; "Crazy Catapults," New Brunswick, New Jersey - fourth and fifth graders will apply their knowledge of simple machines, force, motion and energy to the design and construction of model catapults, trebuchets and super zany machines in the spirit of cartoonist and engineer of the elaborate, Rube Goldberg, using mostly recycled materials; "Maple Syrup and Climate Change," Vermont - students will visit a sugar bush operation to learn how trees are chosen for tapping, study the mechanics of the tree tapping, assist with the process of transforming sap to syrup and evaluate the role of syrup in the local economy as well as learn about the threats to maple trees posed by climate change.

Contact: Laura Cronin, Foundation Manager; (212) 596-0620; fax (212) 221-1108; foundation@tai.toshiba.com or Kto5Applications@tai.toshiba.com

Internet: www.toshiba.com/taf/k5.jsp

Sponsor: Toshiba America Foundation

1251 Avenue of the Americas, 41st Floor

New York, NY 10020

Toyota Motor Manufacturing of Alabama Grants   2309

Established in 2001, Toyota Motor Manufacturing of Alabama manufactures V6 and V8 engines for light trucks, with operations include machining and assembly. TMMAL believes in becoming an integral part of the community by improving the quality of life where its team members live and work. TMMAL provides funding to education, health and human services, civic affairs, arts and culture, and environmental organizations. TMMAL prefers to support programs that are sustainable, diverse, and have an educational focus. Grants are provided to support the development and implementation of programs that generally range from $50,000 to $200,000. Applications are reviewed quarterly, in May, August, November, and February. Submission deadlines for applications are April 15, July 15, October 15, and January 15. The review process can take up to six months.

Requirements: Applicant organizations must have 501(c)3 tax-exempt status, be located within or serve population(s) of Madison County, Alabama, and present a proposal that satisfies the mission, guidelines and limitations of the corporation.

Restrictions: The Toyota Motor Manufacturing of Alabama does not make grants for publications, lobbying activities, advertising, capital campaigns or endowments. Individuals are ineligible to apply. Toyota will not make grants to the following types of organizations: those not recognized as 501(c)3 by the Internal Revenue Service; those that practice discrimination by race, creed, color, sex, age or national origin; those that serve only their own memberships, such as fraternal organizations, labor organizations or religious groups; or political parties or candidates.

Geographic Focus: Alabama

Date(s) Application is Due: Jan 15; Apr 15; Jul 15; Oct 15

Amount of Grant: 50,000 - 200,000 USD

Contact: Grants Administrator; (256) 746-5000; fax (256) 746-5906

Internet: www.toyota.com/usa/community/grant-guidelines-applications/

Sponsor: Toyota Motor Manufacturing of Alabama

1 Cottonvalley Drive

Huntsville, AL 35810

Toyota Motor Manufacturing of Indiana Grants   2310

Toyota Motor Manufacturing of Indiana offers funding in support of residents from the Indiana counties of Daviess, Dubois, Gibson, Knox, Pike, Posey, Spencer, Warrick, and Vanderburgh. Counties in Illinois include Wabash and White, as well as the Kentucky counties of Daviess and Henderson. TMMI supports a variety of programs, including youth and education, health and human services, civic and community, the environment, and arts and culture. Grants are provided to support the development and implementation of programs that generally range from $50,000 to $200,000. Submission deadlines for applications are February 15, May 15, August 15, and November 15, with notification of results by the end of the month following the deadline.

Requirements: Applicant organizations must have 501(c)3 tax-exempt status, and be located within or serve population(s) of: Indiana, specifically Daviess, Dubois, Gibson, Knox, Pike, Posey, Spencer, Warrick, and Vanderburgh counties; Illinois, specifically Wabash and

White counties; or Kentucky, specifically Daviess and Henderson ountiesdoes not make grants for publications, lobbying activities, advertising, capital campaigns or endowments. Individuals are ineligible to apply. Toyota will not make grants to the following types of organizations: those not recognized as 501(c)3 by the Internal Revenue Service; those that practice discrimination by race, creed, color, sex, age or national origin; those that serve only their own memberships, such as fraternal organizations, labor organizations or religious groups; or political parties or candidates. Applicants must present a proposal that satisfies the mission, guidelines and limitations of the corporation.

Restrictions: Toyota Motor Manufacturing of Indiana does not make grants for publications, lobbying activities, advertising, capital campaigns or endowments. Individuals are ineligible to apply. Toyota will not make grants to the following types of organizations: those not recognized as 501(c)3 by the Internal Revenue Service; those that practice discrimination by race, creed, color, sex, age or national origin; those that serve only their own memberships, such as fraternal organizations, labor organizations or religious groups; or political parties or candidates.

Geographic Focus: Illinois, Indiana, Kentucky
Date(s) Application is Due: Feb 15; May 15; Aug 15; Nov 15
Amount of Grant: 50,000 - 200,000 USD
Contact: Grants Administrator; (812) 387-2000 or (812) 387-2266; fax (812) 387-2002
Internet: www.toyota.com/usa/community/grant-guidelines-applications/
Sponsor: Toyota Motor Manufacturing of Indiana
4000 Tulip Tree Drive
Princeton, IN 47670

Toyota Motor Manufacturing of Kentucky Grants 2311

Toyota Motor Manufacturing of Kentucky proves its commitment to the community, as well as to the state, through both monetary contributions and personal involvement of TMMK team members. Besides being a major contributor to United Way of the Bluegrass, which serves eight central Kentucky counties, many employees are members of and serve on community organization boards. Its funding priorities include: the committed to the education of people of all ages - in particular, TMMK participates in educational programs that will help ensure the success of Kentucky's reform related programs; health and human services, by supporting the advancement of physical and mental health for people of all ages; arts and culture, by preservation and advancement of the arts and culture, particularly for our children; the environment, by supporting a variety of efforts to provide for the education, sustainability and preservation of our environment; civic and community progress, by helping make a difference by supporting groups that address local and state issues as well as provide leadership programs for developing human capital; and minorities and diversity, by supporting the advancement and growth of opportunity, inclusion, respect, equality and justice for all people. Grants are provided to support the development and implementation of programs that generally range from $50,000 to $200,000. Submission deadlines for applications are February 1, May 1, August 1, and November 1.

Requirements: Applicant organizations must have 501(c)3 tax-exempt status, and be located within or serve population(s) of any county in Kentucky, with the exception of Boone, Kenton and Campbell. Applicants must also present a proposal that satisfies the mission, guidelines and limitations of the corporation.

Restrictions: Toyota Motor Manufacturing of Kentucky does not make grants for publications, lobbying activities, advertising, capital campaigns or endowments. Individuals are ineligible to apply. Toyota will not make grants to the following types of organizations: those not recognized as 501(c)3 by the Internal Revenue Service; those that practice discrimination by race, creed, color, sex, age or national origin; those that serve only their own memberships, such as fraternal organizations, labor organizations or religious groups; or political parties or candidates.

Geographic Focus: Kentucky
Date(s) Application is Due: Feb 1; May 1; Aug 1; Nov 1
Amount of Grant: 50,000 - 200,000 USD
Contact: Grants Administrator; (502) 868-2000; fax (502) 868-3060
Internet: www.toyotageorgetown.com/comm2.asp
Sponsor: Toyota Motor Manufacturing of Kentucky
1001 Cherry Blossom Way
Georgetown, KY 40324

Toyota Motor Manufacturing of Mississippi Grants 2312

Toyota Motor Manufacturing of Mississippi supports sustainable and diverse programs and organizations focusing on youth and education, health and human services, civic and community, the environment, and arts and culture. TMMMS prefers to support program specific grants rather than event sponsorships. Grants are provided to support the development and implementation of programs that generally range from $50,000 to $200,000. Submission deadlines for applications are February 1, May 15, August 15, and November 15. Grant request status notification will be provided to applicants within 45 days of the application deadline.

Requirements: The geographic scope of funding is centered around Pontotoc County, Union County, and Lee County, all in West Virginia.

Restrictions: Toyota Motor Manufacturing of Mississippi does not make grants for publications, lobbying activities, advertising, capital campaigns or endowments. Individuals are ineligible to apply. Toyota will not make grants to the following types of organizations: those not recognized as 501(c)3 by the Internal Revenue Service; those that practice discrimination by race, creed, color, sex, age or national origin; those that serve only their own memberships, such as fraternal organizations, labor organizations or religious groups; or political parties or candidates.

Geographic Focus: All States
Date(s) Application is Due: Feb 1; May 15; Aug 15; Nov 15
Amount of Grant: 50,000 - 200,000 USD

Contact: Grants Administrator; (662) 317-3281 or (662) 538-5902
Internet: www.toyota.com/usa/community/grant-guidelines-applications/#limitations
Sponsor: Toyota Motor Manufacturing of Mississippi
1200 Magnolia Drive
Blue Springs, MS 38828

Toyota Motor Manufacturing of Texas Grants 2313

As a good corporate citizen, Toyota Motor Manufacturing of Texas contributes to economic and social development in local communities. Giving back to the communities where its team members live and work is a priority. The corporation believes in helping people improve the quality of life in their communities through educational and family literacy programs. It also partners with leading organizations that educate children and their families about creating a cleaner, greener and healthier world. TMMTX makes grants to support programs and events benefiting the following categories: youth and education, health and human services, arts and culture, civic and community, and the environment. Requests are reviewed quarterly. Grants are provided to support the development and implementation of programs that generally range from $50,000 to $200,000. Submission deadlines for applications are January 31, April 30, September 30, and October 31 of every calendar year.

Requirements: Applicant organizations must have 501(c)3 tax-exempt status and be located within or serve population(s) of Bear County, Texas, and its adjacent counties.

Restrictions: TMMTX does not donate vehicles. Nor does it make grants for publications, lobbying activities, advertising, capital campaigns or endowments. Individuals are ineligible to apply. Toyota will not make grants to the following types of organizations: those not recognized as 501(c)3 by the Internal Revenue Service; those that practice discrimination by race, creed, color, sex, age or national origin; those that serve only their own memberships, such as fraternal organizations, labor organizations or religious groups; or political parties or candidates.

Geographic Focus: Texas
Date(s) Application is Due: Jan 31; Apr 30; Sep 30; Oct 31
Amount of Grant: 50,000 - 200,000 USD
Contact: Grants Administrator; (210) 263-4000
Internet: www.toyota.com/usa/community/grant-guidelines-applications/#limitations
Sponsor: Toyota Motor Manufacturing of Texas
1 Lone Star Pass
San Antonio, TX 78264

Toyota Motor Manufacturing of West Virginia Grants 2314

Toyota Motor Manufacturing of West Virginia is committed to continuing the worldwide Toyota tradition of community involvement and support. In response to the needs and interests of its team members and the community, Toyota has designed a corporate donations program focusing on specific issues and geographic areas with its first priority of improving the quality of life in the community in which it operates. TMMWV provides funding to education, health and human services, civic and community, arts and culture, and environmental organizations. TMMWV's education donations focus primarily on projects that serve K-12 students in the public setting. Community development activities must improve the economy or the quality of life for the people in the region. Health and human services projects must be aimed at significantly improving health or health care, or providing assistance to families in need. Environmental activities must be designed to preserve, restore, or improve the quality of air, natural or wildlife resources. Grants are provided to support the development and implementation of programs that generally range from $50,000 to $200,000. Grants are reviewed quarterly, in March, June, September, and December. Submission deadlines for applications are March 1, June 1, October 1, and January 1.

Requirements: Top priority is given to Putnam County; second priority is given to Cabell, Jackson, Kanawha, Lincoln and Mason counties; and there is a limited participation in important statewide projects.

Restrictions: Toyota Motor Manufacturing of West Virginia does not make grants for publications, lobbying activities, advertising, capital campaigns or endowments. Individuals are ineligible to apply. Toyota will not make grants to the following types of organizations: those not recognized as 501(c)3 by the Internal Revenue Service; those that practice discrimination by race, creed, color, sex, age or national origin; those that serve only their own memberships, such as fraternal organizations, labor organizations or religious groups; or political parties or candidates.

Geographic Focus: West Virginia
Date(s) Application is Due: Jan 1; Mar 1; Jun 1; Oct 1
Amount of Grant: 50,000 - 200,000 USD
Contact: Grants Administrator; (304) 937-7000
Internet: www.toyota.com/usa/community/grant-guidelines-applications/#limitations
Sponsor: Toyota Motor Manufacturing of West Virginia
1 Sugar Maple Lane
Buffalo, WV 25033

Toyota Motor North America of New York Grants 2315

Toyota Motor North America offers grant funding nationally, focusing on three primary areas: the environment, safety, and education. National programs in these areas must have a broad reach by impacting several major U.S. cities, communities or groups. In the local New York City area, Toyota also focuses on those three major areas, and provides other local assistance as well, including arts and culture, civic and community, health and human services and leadership development. Toyota prefers to support programs, rather than sponsor events. Organizations must apply for each new grant requested, and subsequent funding is contingent upon evaluation of previous activities. The geographic scope is the continental U.S. for programs national in scope and the New York City area for community-based programs. Only online applications are accepted.

Requirements: Applicant organizations must have 501(c)3 tax-exempt status, be located within or serve population(s) either on a national scope or specifically in the New York City area, and present a proposal that satisfies the mission, guidelines and limitations of the corporation.

Restrictions: Toyota Motor North America of New York does not make grants for publications, lobbying activities, advertising, capital campaigns or endowments. Individuals are ineligible to apply. Toyota will not make grants to the following types of organizations: those not recognized as 501(c)3 by the Internal Revenue Service; those that practice discrimination by race, creed, color, sex, age or national origin; those that serve only their own memberships, such as fraternal organizations, labor organizations or religious groups; or political parties or candidates.

Geographic Focus: All States
Amount of Grant: 50,000 - 200,000 USD
Contact: Grants Administrator; (212) 223-0303; fax (212) 759-7670
Internet: www.toyota.com/usa/community/grant-guidelines-applications/
Sponsor: Toyota Motor North America
601 Lexington Avenue, 49th Floor
New York, NY 10022

Toyota Motor Sales, USA Grants   2316
Toyota Motor Sales, USA, offers grant funding within the Torrance, California for community‐based programs. The program's funding scope primarily supports education, environment and safety, but also funds civic groups, arts and culture, health and human services. Toyota Motor Sales prefers to support programs, rather than sponsor events. Organizations must apply for each new grant requested, and subsequent funding is contingent upon evaluation of previous activities. Only online applications are accepted.

Requirements: Applicant organizations must have 501(c)3 tax-exempt status, be located within or serve population(s) in the Torrance, California, region, and present a proposal that satisfies the mission, guidelines and limitations of the corporation.

Restrictions: Toyota Motor Sales, USA does not make grants for publications, lobbying activities, advertising, capital campaigns or endowments. Individuals are ineligible to apply. Toyota will not make grants to the following types of organizations: those not recognized as 501(c)3 by the Internal Revenue Service; those that practice discrimination by race, creed, color, sex, age or national origin; those that serve only their own memberships, such as fraternal organizations, labor organizations or religious groups; or political parties or candidates.

Geographic Focus: California
Amount of Grant: 50,000 - 200,000 JPY
Contact: Grants Administrator; (310) 468-5249 or (310) 468-4216; fax (310) 468-7840
Internet: www.toyota.com/usa/community/grant-guidelines-applications/
Sponsor: Toyota Motor Sales, USA
19001 S. Western Avenue
Torrance, 90501

Toyota Technical Center Grants   2317
For more than 35 years, Toyota Technical Center, a division of Toyota Motor Engineering and Manufacturing, has been the driving force behind Toyota's North American engineering and research and development activities. Established in 1977 and headquartered in Michigan, TTC has Research and Development facilities in Ann Arbor, Saline, Plymouth and Livonia. TTC focuses on education (specifically math and science), environment, and safety, as well as programs that enrich the lives of children, families and the communities within the specified locations listed. Grants are provided to support the development and implementation of programs that generally range from $50,000 to $200,000. Submission deadlines for applications are March 1, June 1, September 1, and December 1. The review process can take up to six months.

Requirements: Applicant organizations must have 501(c)3 tax-exempt status, and be located within or serve population(s) of: Michigan, specifically Washtenaw County; Arizona, specifically Maricopa County; or California, specifically Los Angeles County. Applicants must present a proposal that satisfies the mission, guidelines and limitations of the corporation.

Restrictions: The Toyota Technical Center does not make grants for publications, lobbying activities, advertising, capital campaigns or endowments. Individuals are ineligible to apply. Toyota will not make grants to the following types of organizations: those not recognized as 501(c)3 by the Internal Revenue Service; those that practice discrimination by race, creed, color, sex, age or national origin; those that serve only their own memberships, such as fraternal organizations, labor organizations or religious groups; or political parties or candidates.

Geographic Focus: Arizona, California, Michigan
Date(s) Application is Due: Mar 1; Jun 1; Sep 1; Dec 1
Amount of Grant: 50,000 - 200,000 USD
Contact: Grants Administrator; (734) 695-2600
Internet: www.toyota.com/usa/community/grant-guidelines-applications/
Sponsor: Toyota Technical Center
8777 Platt Road
Saline, MI 48176

Toyota USA Foundation Education Grants   2318
The Toyota USA Foundation is committed to enhancing the quality of K-12 education by supporting innovative programs and building partnerships with organizations dedicated to improving the teaching and learning of mathematics, science and environmental science. A high priority is placed on the following: creative and innovative programs which develop the potential of students and/or teachers; programs which are broad in scope and incorporate

systemic approach; and cost-effective programs that possess a high potential for success with relatively low duplication of effort. Grants are provided to support the development and implementation of programs that generally range from $50,000 to $200,000. Foundation reviews applications continually and does not have deadlines. The review process can take up to six months.

Requirements: Applicant organizations must have 501(c)3 tax-exempt status, be located within and serve population(s) in the United States, and present a proposal that satisfies the guidelines and limitations of the foundation.

Restrictions: The foundation does not support routine institutional expenses, general operating costs, annual fund drives, or deficit reductions; endowments, capital campaigns, or any building and/or construction costs; fund-raising events, dinners or lunches, advertising, mass mailings; travel; lobbying organizations, fraternal groups, veteran organizations, religious groups, or labor organizations; equipment (unless a small component of an otherwise eligible program); conferences; or publication subsidies. The Foundation will only fund a program one time; however, a grant recipient may present a new program for consideration after three years.

Geographic Focus: All States
Amount of Grant: 50,000 - 200,000 USD
Contact: Patricia Salas Pineda, Foundation Administrator; (212) 715-7486
Internet: www.toyota.com/usa/community/grant-guidelines-applications/overview.html
Sponsor: Toyota USA Foundation
9 West 57th Street, Suite 4900
New York, NY 10019

Toyota USA Foundation Environmental Grants   2319
The Toyota USA Foundation is committed to environmental causes. It supports nonprofit organizations that promote environmental stewardship, education and research. Its Environmental programs also reflect our commitment to representing and engaging diverse populations and communities. In 2008, the Foundation launched TogetherGreen, a $20 million, five-year alliance with Audubon to fund conservation projects, train environmental leaders, and offer volunteer opportunities to significantly benefit the environment. Grants are provided to support the development and implementation of programs that generally range from $50,000 to $200,000. Foundation reviews applications continually and does not have deadlines. The review process can take up to six months.

Requirements: Applicant organizations must have 501(c)3 tax-exempt status, be located within and serve population(s) in the United States, and present a proposal that satisfies the guidelines and limitations of the foundation.

Restrictions: The foundation does not support routine institutional expenses, general operating costs, annual fund drives, or deficit reductions; endowments, capital campaigns, or any building and/or construction costs; fund-raising events, dinners or lunches, advertising, mass mailings; travel; lobbying organizations, fraternal groups, veteran organizations, religious groups, or labor organizations; equipment (unless a small component of an otherwise eligible program); conferences; or publication subsidies. The Foundation will only fund a program one time; however, a grant recipient may present a new program for consideration after three years.

Geographic Focus: All States
Amount of Grant: 50,000 - 200,000 USD
Contact: Patricia Salas Pineda, Foundation Administrator; (212) 715-7486
Internet: www.toyota.com/usa/community/grant-guidelines-applications/overview.html
Sponsor: Toyota USA Foundation
9 West 57th Street, Suite 4900
New York, NY 10019

Toyota USA Foundation Safety Grants   2320
At the Toyota USA Foundation, safety is a priority from the vehicles the Corporation puts on the road to the people who drive them. Since 2004, the Foundation has sponsored and created programs that educate drivers and passengers of all ages across the U.S. on critical safety behaviors. Its signature program is Toyota Driving Expectations (TDE), a free program for teen drivers and their parents. The goal of TDE is to proactively take America's driving youth through a safe driving experience. Grants are provided to support the development and implementation of programs that generally range from $50,000 to $200,000. Foundation reviews applications continually and does not have deadlines. The review process can take up to six months.

Requirements: Applicant organizations must have 501(c)3 tax-exempt status, be located within and serve population(s) in the United States, and present a proposal that satisfies the guidelines and limitations of the foundation.

Restrictions: The foundation does not support routine institutional expenses, general operating costs, annual fund drives, or deficit reductions; endowments, capital campaigns, or any building and/or construction costs; fund-raising events, dinners or lunches, advertising, mass mailings; travel; lobbying organizations, fraternal groups, veteran organizations, religious groups, or labor organizations; equipment (unless a small component of an otherwise eligible program); conferences; or publication subsidies. The Foundation will only fund a program one time; however, a grant recipient may present a new program for consideration after three years.

Geographic Focus: All States
Amount of Grant: 50,000 - 200,000 USD
Contact: Patricia Salas Pineda, Foundation Administrator; (212) 715-7486
Internet: www.toyota.com/usa/community/grant-guidelines-applications/overview.html
Sponsor: Toyota USA Foundation
9 West 57th Street, Suite 4900
New York, NY 10019

Trinity Trust Summer Youth Mini Grants   2321

The Trinity Trust is committed to supporting children and youth, and values programs that offer opportunities for them to learn, play and develop in a safe, productive setting while school is not in session. The Trust recognizes that organizations offering summer programs for children and youth are integral to providing those opportunities. Small grants are awarded so that agencies may expand and enrich summer recreation programs serving Trinity County children operating between June and September. Funding is based on the following criteria: a high number of low-income, disabled or other disadvantaged youth are served; youth in outlying areas would have few summer alternatives for productive activities; operating hours are extensive throughout the summer; and high numbers of at-risk youth are served. Additional funding may be considered for the following organization: a large number of scholarships to the organization's summer program are provided; the program requires no fee; good use is made of available resources and/or collaborations; programs provide developmental as well as well recreational opportunities; and organizations request items to help ensure the safety of program participants. Grants are normally provided to support expenses such as sports and recreational equipment, arts and craft supplies, special events, and field trips and camperships for low-income participants. The average grant is $400, but may increase with some circumstances. The application and additional information is available at the website.

Requirements: Nonprofit organizations serving Trinity County youth programs offered between June 1 and September 1 are eligible to apply.
Geographic Focus: California
Date(s) Application is Due: Mar 15
Amount of Grant: 400 USD
Contact: Duane Heryford, Trinity Trust Administrator; (530) 623-0320
Christine Witt, Director of Donor and Grantmaking Services; (707) 442-2993, ext. 302; fax (707) 442-3811; chrisw@hafoundation.org
Internet: www.trinity-trust.org/content/view/92/83/
Sponsor: Trinity Trust
P.O. Box 3216
Weaverville, CA 96093

TSYSF Individual Scholarships   2322

Teemu Selänne, nicknamed "The Finnish Flash," is a Finnish professional ice hockey winger. An offensive player known for his skill and speed, Selänne has led the NHL in goal-scoring three times and has been named to the league's First All-Star Team on two occasions. He has won the Stanley Cup once with the Ducks in 2007. The Teemu Selänne Youth Sports Foundation (TSYSF) provides financial, educational and inspirational opportunities for children and their families through structured sports programs. Individual scholarships are available for youth (and their families) who want to play in organized sports but lack the financial means to do so.

Requirements: The required scholarship application must be filled out (available at website) and submitted with copies of: current Federal tax return; proof of current income status (copies of last 3 months' paycheck stubs, etc.); and a return envelope for the foundation's decision. Families submitting for more than one child need to submit only one copy of the requested supporting documents. There are no specific deadlines. Scholarship applications take a minimum of eight weeks before the Board makes a decision.
Geographic Focus: All States
Contact: Scholarship Coordinator, (949) 544-3110; fax (949) 309-3845; info@tsysf.org
Internet: tsysf.org/tsysf-grant-scholarship-application/
Sponsor: Teemu Selänne Youth Sports Foundation
22431 Antonio Parkway, Suite B160-800
Rancho Santa Margarita, CA 92688

TSYSF Team Grants   2323

Teemu Selänne, nicknamed "The Finnish Flash," is a Finnish professional ice hockey winger. An offensive player known for his skill and speed, Selänne has led the NHL in goal-scoring three times and has been named to the league's First All-Star Team on two occasions. He has won the Stanley Cup once with the Ducks in 2007. The Teemu Selänne Youth Sports Foundation (TSYSF) provides financial, educational and inspirational opportunities for children and their families through structured sports programs. Team grants are available for youth athletic teams.

Requirements: The required grant application form must be filled out (available at website) and submitted with copies of: documentation of any scholarships, grants or fundraising revenues received by team and/or players and/or projected revenue if not yet received; confirmed team travel schedule; and a return envelope for the foundation's decision. Organizations with multiple teams may submit just one application instead of one for each team within the organization. There are no specific deadlines. Scholarship applications take a minimum of eight weeks before the Board makes a decision.
Geographic Focus: All States
Contact: Grants Administrator, (949) 544-3110; fax (949) 309-3845; info@tsysf.org
Internet: tsysf.org/tsysf-grant-scholarship-application/
Sponsor: Teemu Selänne Youth Sports Foundation
22431 Antonio Parkway, Suite B160-800
Rancho Santa Margarita, CA 92688

Tull Charitable Foundation Grants   2324

Priority interest areas for awarding grants, in Georgia, are education, health and human services, youth development, and the arts. Requests for major capital projects are eligible for consideration. Requests for endowments and for the start-up of new initiatives are sometimes considered.

Requirements: The Foundation's Trustees limit grant awards to 501(c)3 organizations based in the State of Georgia. Requests from organizations located outside of Georgia are not considered. It is preferred that an applicant organization be able to demonstrate a broad base of financial support for a proposed project from its own community and constituency prior to asking for support of that project from the Foundation. Prior to submitting a full proposal, it is recommended (but not required) that an applicant organization contact the Foundation via a concise letter-of-intent in order to determine the potential eligibility of the request.
Restrictions: Grants are not available for operating support, research, conferences and seminars, legislative lobbying or other political purposes, special events, or individuals; nor to churches, sports booster clubs, to sponsor events or to retire accumulated debt. The Foundation does not utilize fiscal agents to handle funds for organizations that do not have an IRS certification letter.
Geographic Focus: Georgia
Date(s) Application is Due: Mar 3; Jun 2; Sep 2; Dec 2
Contact: Carol D. Aiken, Assistant to the Director; (404) 659-7079; carol@tullfoundation.org
Internet: www.tullfoundation.org/app_procedures.asp
Sponsor: Tull Charitable Foundation
50 Hurt Plaza, Suite 1245
Atlanta, GA 30303

Turner B. Bunn, Jr. and Catherine E. Bunn Foundation Grants   2325

The Foundation, established in North Carolina in 2000, gives primarily to children and youth services, Christian agencies and churches, educational programs, and human services supporting residents of North Carolina. An application form is not required, and applicants should submit the following: brief history of organization and description of its mission; copy of IRS Determination Letter; and a detailed description of project and amount of funding requested. There are no annual deadlines, and applicants should submit the entire proposal via mail.
Geographic Focus: North Carolina
Samples: Barton College Scholarship Fund, Wilson, North Carolina, $8,600; Boys and Girls Club of Coastal Carolina, Morehead City, North Carolina, $3,800; Hope Station Renovation, Wilson, North Carolina
Contact: Turner B. Bunn III, Director; (252) 243-3136; fax (252) 243-8293; tbb3@nc.rr.com
Sponsor: Turner B. Bunn, Jr. and Catherine E. Bunn Foundation
P.O. Box 3299
Wilson, NC 27895-3299

Turner Foundation Grants   2326

The Turner Foundation believes each organization to be important and that the best person to convey the passion for your organization is you. The Foundation supports initiatives that enhance the quality of life in the greater Springfield/Clark County community through artistic, educational, environmental, recreational, family, healthcare, historic preservation, community beautification and revitalization programs. In most cases, discretionary grants fall in the range of $5,000 to $15,000.
Requirements: To be considered for a discretionary grant, each organization must serve the people of Clark County Ohio, be a tax-exempt non-profit with a 501(c)3 classification from the IRS, and have a governing board.
Restrictions: The Turner Foundation does not fund individuals, churches, legislative action groups, annual fundraising campaigns, scholarships, fraternal groups or political groups and issues.
Geographic Focus: Ohio
Date(s) Application is Due: Sep 14
Amount of Grant: 5,000 - 30,000 USD
Contact: Grants Director; (937) 325-1300; fax (937) 325-0100; email@hmturnerfoundation.org
Internet: www.hmturnerfoundation.org/grants.html
Sponsor: Turner Foundation
4 West Main Street, Suite 800
Springfield, OH 45502

Turtle Bay Foundation Grants   2327

The Turtle Bay Foundation was established in 2012 to enrich Oahu's North Shore through environmental, educational, recreational, and cultural opportunities. The Foundation oversees the numerous charitable contributions of Turtle Bay Resort, acting as a partner in the community and supporting the resort's mission of making one of the world's last greatest places even better. Foundation (TBF) funds programs that make a significant impact in its communities and directly improves the lives of their people. The primary purpose of the funding is to directly support program needs and minimize overhead and administration. The grant selection is a thoughtful process that draws upon the mana'o of the community and calls for partners with comparable and complementary goals. Turtle Bay Foundation supports programs that strengthen its values. The organizations may include those pertaining to: educational and cultural sites; educational organizations; environmental stewardship; health care; housing and job training; preservation of historic and cultural sites; and sports and recreational teams and organizations. The Foundation's preference is to fund programs and events, as opposed to providing general revenues for applicants. Examples of funding purposes that are generally considered secondary to the Turtle Bay Foundation grants guidelines include: endowment campaigns; salaries for staff and professionals; and general overhead and operating costs, such as rent, travel expenses, equipment maintenance, and administrative expenses. The Foundation will provide a limited number of grants, ranging in value from $500 to $2,000, in accordance with its criteria as applied at its sole discretion. In addition to cash funding, the Foundation also supports gift-in-kind donations - goods or services rendered from the Turtle Bay Resort. This includes, but is not limited to, hotel rooms, restaurant meals, golf, spa treatments, etc. Such gifts-in-kind can often be converted to cash by organizations that are conducting silent auctions and other fund-raising efforts. The annual deadline for application submission is the second Friday in October.

Requirements: Any 501(c)3 organization supporting residents of O'ahu, particularly the north shore region, are eligible to apply.
Geographic Focus: Hawaii
Date(s) Application is Due: Oct 11
Amount of Grant: 500 - 2,000 USD
Samples: Waialua Robotics Program, Waialua, Hawaii, $1,000 - program development; Friends of Kahuku Library, Kahuku, Hawaii, $750 - general program support; Clover 4-H Livestock Club, Haleiwa, Hawaii, $1,000 - general program support.
Contact: Kiele Muraco; (808) 447-6953 or (808) 232-2285
Internet: www.turtlebayresort.com/About/The-Resort/Turtle-Bay-Foundation
Sponsor: Turtle Bay Foundation
57-091 Kamehameha Highway
Kahuku, HI 96731

Twenty-First Century Foundation Grants 2328

Founded in 1971, the Twenty-First Century Foundation's mission is to lead, innovate, and influence black community change through strategic philanthropy. As one of the few African American endowed public foundations in the U.S., the Foundation works to advance the welfare of the black community by providing small grants to organizations committed to racial and social justice. Today, the Foundation continues to be a leader and philanthropic champion in support of efforts to improve the life outcomes of black men and boys, both through its own initiatives and as the incubator of the 2025 Campaign for Black Men and Boys.
Requirements: 501(c)3 status or 509(a) organizations are eligible.
Geographic Focus: All States
Amount of Grant: Up to 10,000 USD
Contact: Executive Director; (212) 662-3700; fax (212) 662-6690
Internet: www.opensocietyfoundations.org/about/us-programs/grantees/twenty-first-century-foundation
Sponsor: Twenty-First Century Foundation
271 W 125th Street, Suite 303
New York, NY 10027-4424

Tyler Aaron Bookman Memorial Foundation Trust Grants 2329

The Tyler Aaron Bookman Memorial Foundation was established by Neil and Jill Bookman in memory of their eleven-year-old son, Tyler, who died of a brain tumor. His parents, based on Tyler's love of learning, started the Foundation with the money they had saved for his college education. To them, education is key to breaking the cycle of poverty. With funding centered in Camden, New Jersey, and adjoining states, the Foundation's primary fields of interest is support of health care and research, Catholic churches and agencies, and children and youth education. There are no specific deadlines with which to adhere, and applicants should initially approach the Foundation by way of letter requesting an application form.
Restrictions: No grants are given to individuals.
Geographic Focus: New Jersey, North Carolina, Pennsylvania
Amount of Grant: Up to 30,000 USD
Samples: La Salle University, Philadelphia, Pennsylvania, $12,699; Pediatric Brain Tumor Foundation, Asheville, North Carolina, $27,000; Children's Hospital of Philadelphia, Philadelphia, Pennsylvania, $15,000.
Contact: Neil S. Bookman, Trustee; (215) 646-2192 or (267) 216-7718; fax (215) 654-6060
Sponsor: Tyler Aaron Bookman Memorial Foundation
426 Newbold Road
Jenkintown, PA 19046-2851

U.S. Bank Foundation Grants 2330

The Foundation contributes to the strength and vitality of communities through charitable contributions. They seek to build strong partnerships and lasting value in communities by supporting organizations that improve the educational and economic opportunities of low- and moderate-income individuals and families and enhance the cultural and artistic life of communities. Funding priorities include: economic opportunity (including affordable housing, self-sufficiency and economic development); education; culture and artistic enrichment; and human services. Support is provided for unrestricted general operating support, program support, capital support, contributions of equipment and property. Application deadlines vary by state. See website for states deadlines and state contacts.
Requirements: Applicants must be 501(c)3 not for profit organizations and located in a community with a U.S. Bank office.
Restrictions: The Foundation will not provide funding for: organizations that are 501(c)3 not for profits; fraternal organizations, merchant associations, chamber memberships or programs, or 501(c)4 or 6 organizations; section 509(a)3 supporting organizations; fundraising events or sponsorships; "pass through" organizations or private foundations; organizations outside U.S. Bancorp communities; programs operated by religious organizations for religious purposes; political organizations or organizations designed primarily to lobby; individuals; travel and related expenses; endowment campaigns; deficit reduction; organizations receiving primary funding from United Way; and organizations whose practices are not in keeping with the company's equal opportunity policy.
Geographic Focus: Arizona, Arkansas, California, Colorado, Idaho, Illinois, Iowa, Kansas, Kentucky, Minnesota, Missouri, Montana, Nebraska, Nevada, New Mexico, North Dakota, Ohio, Oregon, South Dakota, Tennessee, Utah, Washington, Wisconsin, Wyoming
Contact: Grants Administrator; 612-659-2000
Internet: www.usbank.com/cgi_w/cfm/about/community_relations/grant_guidelines.cfm
Sponsor: U.S. Bank Foundation
800 Nicollet Mall, 23rd Floor
Minneapolis, MN 55402

U.S. Cellular Corporation Grants 2331

The U.S. Cellular Corporation strives to build a connection with communities that extend beyond its business by supporting causes that strengthens every neighborhood where it's customers live, work and play. The Corporation awards grants to projects or programs that have significant relevance within its operating communities and that relate to the following strategic areas of concern: civic and community, education, health and human service, environment, and arts and culture. Furthermore, through its Associate Matching program, it matches associates' charitable donations to nonprofit organizations dollar-for-dollar, up to $2,500 per year, with an annual cap of $250,000.
Requirements: 501(c)3 tax-exempt organizations within the Corporation's areas of operation are eligible to apply. This includes parts of: Iowa; Missouri; Oklahoma; northern Texas; Nebraska; southern Wisconsin; northwestern Illinois; north central Indiana; Oregon; northern California; southern Washington; eastern Tennessee; North Carlina; western Virginia; western Maryland; and eastern West Virginia.
Restrictions: The corporation will not make charitable contributions to the following entities: individuals; agencies that discriminate on the basis of race, color, creed, or national origin; political causes, candidates, legislative lobbying, or advocacy groups; endowments or memorials; construction or renovation projects (except Habitat for Humanity); religious organizations seeking to further a denominational or sectarian purpose; social, labor, alumni, or fraternal organizations serving a limited constituency; primary, secondary, or charter schools; special occasion, good-will, and single-interest magazines; local athletic or sports programs, walk-a-thons, and little leagues; or travel funds for tours, expeditions, or trips.
Geographic Focus: California, Illinois, Indiana, Iowa, Maryland, Missouri, Nebraska, North Carolina, Oklahoma, Oregon, Tennessee, Texas, Virginia, Washington, West Virginia, Wisconsin
Contact: External Communications Department; (773) 399-8900; fax (773) 399-8937; communityprograms@uscellular.com
Internet: www.uscellular.com/about/community-outreach/index.html
Sponsor: U.S. Cellular Corporation
8410 W Bryn Mawr, Suite 700
Chicago, IL 60634

U.S. Department of Education Promise Neighborhoods Grants 2332

The Promise Neighborhoods program is authorized under the Elementary and Secondary Education Act of 1965 (ESEA), as amended by the Every Student Succeeds Act (ESSA). The vision of the program is that all children and youth growing up in Promise Neighborhoods have access to great schools and strong systems of family and community support that will prepare them to attain an excellent education and successfully transition to college and a career. The purpose of Promise Neighborhoods is to significantly improve the educational and developmental outcomes of children and youth in our most distressed communities, and to transform those communities by: identifying and increasing the capacity of eligible entities that are focused on achieving results for children and youth throughout an entire neighborhood; building a complete continuum of cradle-to-career solutions of both educational programs and family and community supports, with great schools at the center; integrating programs and breaking down agency silos so that solutions are implemented effectively and efficiently across agencies; developing the local infrastructure of systems and resources needed to sustain and scale up proven, effective solutions across the broader region beyond the initial neighborhood; and learning about the overall impact of the Promise Neighborhoods program and about the relationship between particular strategies in Promise Neighborhoods and student outcomes, including through a rigorous evaluation of the program. The estimated average size of each award will be $5,000,000, with approximately five to seven grants being approved annually. Depending upon Congressional funding, the annual application submission date has typically fallen during the first week of September.
Requirements: Eligible entities include: nonprofit organizations, which may include faith-based nonprofit organizations; institutions of higher education; and Indian tribes in partnership with their local schools and local education agencies.
Geographic Focus: All States, American Samoa, District of Columbia, Guam, Marshall Islands, Northern Mariana Islands, Puerto Rico, U.S. Virgin Islands
Amount of Grant: Up to 7,000,000 USD
Samples: Association of Alaska School Boards, Southeast Alaska, $4,191,225 - Supporting Transitions and Educational Promise Southeast (STEPS) Alaska; Berea College, Hazard, Kentucky, $6,000,000 - support of the Perry Promise Neighborhood program; California State University, East Bay Foundation, Hayward, California, $5,921,282 - support of the South Hayward Promise Neighborhood.
Contact: Adrienne Hawkins; (202) 453-5638 or (202) 453-7200; adrienne.hawkins@ed.gov Elson Nash, Program Contact; (202) 453-6615 or (202) 453-7200; elson.nash@ed.gov
Internet: innovation.ed.gov/what-we-do/parental-options/promise-neighborhoods-pn/
Sponsor: U.S. Department of Education
400 Maryland Avenue, SW
Washington, D.C. 20202-5960

Union Bank, N.A. Corporate Sponsorships and Donations 2333

As part of its ten-year community committment, Union Bank has pledged to annually distribute at least two percent of its annual after-tax net profit to help meet the needs of the communities it serves, a commitment that has resulted in donations exceeding $72 million dollars during the first six years. This two-percent charitable commitment is achieved through contributions and sponsorships made directly by the bank (through the corporate contribution program) and through grants and investments made by the bank's foundation (Union Bank Foundation). The bank's corporate contributions program is intended to enhance the bank's reputation and visibility by supporting the charitable work of its employees and clients. The bank funds donations and sponsorships supporting a broad range of charitable categories, including community economic development, affordable housing, education, health and human services, culture and arts, emergency services, and the environment. The bank is particularly interested in donations and sponsorships that support low-income populations and promote and enhance diversity in all its forms. The bank's local-area contribution committees consider applications at their monthly meetings. Applications are accepted via an online application system accessible from the bank website. Please note that event-sponsorship applications should be submitted at least ninety days in advance of the event date.

Requirements: 501(c)3 nonprofits in company-operating areas in California and the Pacific Northwest are eligible (e.g., San Diego, San Francisco, Los Angeles, Anaheim, Berkeley, Del Mar, Fresno, Irvine, Mission Grove, Pasadena, Sacramento, Salinas, San Jose, Santa Ana, and Torrance, California). A branch locator is available at the bank's website.

Restrictions: The bank does not support the following requests from the following entities or for the following items: individuals; veterans, military, fraternal, or professional organizations; political organizations or programs; service club activities; other intermediary foundations (i.e., foundations which, in turn, make grants to other charities); churches or religious groups (except separately incorporated community development corporations); educational institution operating funds; and individual elementary or secondary schools.

Geographic Focus: California, Oregon, Washington

Samples: Oaks Christian School, Westlake Village, California; Mayfield Junior College, Cathedral City, California; Latino Theater Company, Los Angeles, California.

Contact: J.R. Raines, Assistant Vice President; (619) 230-3105; CSRGroup@unionbank. com or charitablegiving@unionbank.com

Karen Murakami, Assistant Vice President; (415) 765-3890; CSRGroup@unionbank.com or charitablegiving@unionbank.com

Internet: www.unionbank.com/global/about/corporate-social-responsibility/foundation/foundation-grants.jsp#products-tab-item-2

Sponsor: Union Bank, N.A.
350 California Street
San Francisco, CA 94104

Union Bank, N.A. Foundation Grants   2334

As part of its ten-year community committment, Union Bank has pledged to annually distribute at least two percent of its annual after-tax net profit to help meet the needs of the communities it serves, a commitment that has resulted in donations exceeding $72 million dollars during the first six years. The two-percent charitable commitment is achieved through contributions and sponsorships made directly by the bank and through grants and investments made by the Union Bank Foundation, a nonprofit public-benefit corporation which serves as an agent for the bank. Because of its belief that the long-term success of the Union Bank business-model is dependent upon the existence of healthy communities, Union Bank Foundation focuses its philanthropy on building innovative initiatives and partnerships to cultivate healthy communities, which it identifies as possessing the following characteristics: stable families with high rates of home ownership; availability of affordable housing; livable-wage job opportunities; accessible public transportation; convenient access to professional services (e.g., doctors, lawyers, and accountants); adequate public services (e.g., police, fire, and sanitation); safe public places to relax and recreate (e.g., parks, libraries, theaters); clean air and water supplies; a high level of civic engagement; a community constituency possessing diverse income levels; well-funded public schools; successful small business owners who live in the community; a variety of retail shops and restaurants; and traditional financial institutions providing access to capital in or adjacent to the community. With an eye toward being an agent of positive change in Union Bank communities, the foundation focuses on the following strategic program areas (targeting resources especially to benefit low- to moderate-income populations): Affordable Housing; Community Economic Development; Education; and Environment. In the area of Affordable Housing, the foundation focuses on for-sale housing, rental housing, special-needs housing, senior housing, transitional-living facilities, emergency/homeless shelters, youth housing, self-help housing, farm-worker housing, pre-development funding to nonprofit developers, and capacity building for nonprofit housing organizations. In the area of Community Economic Development area, the foundation focuses on small business development, individual development, and neighborhood development. Small business development includes micro-enterprise development and support, technical assistance/entrepreneurial training, organizations that promote access to capital for business or farms meeting Small Business Administration criteria, and job creation. Individual development includes job training/apprenticeship, welfare-to-work programs, wealth-accumulation/asset-building programs, life-skills training, financial-literacy/credit-counseling programs, mortgage credit counseling, business education, and intervention/prevention programs for at-risk youth. Neighborhood Development includes gang prevention/gang intervention programs, crime prevention, dispute resolution/mediation/violence prevention, reduction of liquor outlets, improved quality of food in local markets, childcare and daycare programs, drug- and alcohol-rehabilitation programs, independent living programs, organizational capacity building and funding for operating/administrative expenses, and community organizing to engage, inform and empower citizenry. In the area of Education, the foundation focuses on scholarship programs, tutoring programs, general education degree (GED) preparation, English as a second language (ESL) programs, computer education, support for the teaching profession, teacher training, literacy programs, parent education, visual- and performing-arts-organizations outreach programs, enrichment programs, and capacity-building. In the area of Environment the foundation focuses on brown-field remediation, science and education relevant to green building, energy upgrade and conservation, rehabilitation and cleanup, coastal/creek- and reserve-cleanup and preservation, urban green-space projects, environmental education, aquariums and museums, ecology and recycling centers, and state parks, nature centers, conservancy centers, botanical gardens, and wildlife centers. The Union Bank Foundation prefers program grants, but will consider requests for core operating support and/or capacity-building grants to support exceptional work within

its strategic funding categories. The foundation considers applications at its bimonthly board meetings. Applications are accepted via an online application system accessible from the foundation website. Applicants must choose from three categories when they apply. These are requests for $1,000 or less, requests for $1001 to $25,000, and requests for over $25,000. Prospective applicants should review the foundation's application guidelines and instructions, which are available at the foundation website. Questions may be directed to the foundation officers listed on this page.

Requirements: 501(c)3 nonprofits in company-operating areas in California and the Pacific Northwest are eligible (e.g., San Diego, San Francisco, Los Angeles, Anaheim, Berkeley, Del Mar, Fresno, Irvine, Mission Grove, Pasadena, Sacramento, Salinas, San Jose, Santa Ana, and Torrance, California). A branch locator is available at the sponsor website.

Restrictions: The foundation does not support the following requests from the following entities or for the following items: individuals; veterans, military, fraternal, or professional organizations; political organizations or programs; service club activities; other intermediary foundations (i.e., foundations which, in turn, make grants to other charities); churches or religious groups (except separately incorporated community development corporations); educational institution operating funds; and individual elementary or secondary schools.

Geographic Focus: California, Oregon, Washington

Amount of Grant: 5,000 - 25,000 USD

Samples: Asian Business Center, Los Angeles, California; Catholic Charities of San Diego, San Diego, California; Audubon California, Sacramento, California.

Contact: J.R. Raines; (619) 230-3105; charitablegiving@unionbank.com

Karen Murakami; (415) 765-3890; charitablegiving@unionbank.com

Internet: www.unionbank.com/global/about/corporate-social-responsibility/foundation/foundation-grants.jsp

Sponsor: Union Bank Foundation
P.O. Box 45174
San Francisco, CA 94145-0174

Union Labor Health Foundation Angel Fund Grants   2335

The Union Labor Health Foundation Angel Fund provides small grants to meet immediate medical or health related needs of individuals living in Humboldt County. The Fund serves the needs of children and adults. Decisions about grant requests are contingent upon funding criteria and the availability of current funds. Most grants are approved in the $25-$250 range. Grants in excess of $500 are seldom approved. The following items are typically funded: medically related examinations, procedures and equipment; eye exams and eyeglasses ($130 maximum, requires a copy of the perscription if exam has been completed); medically related travel ($200 maximum) (non-emergency requires a form completed by a physician); prescriptions (emergency, short-term); items to improve accessibility/independence for disabled or elderly individuals; orthopedic needs ($180 maximum); compression stockings ($160 maximum); dental procedures for youth through age 19. Other items that are occasionally funded include the following: local bus tickets (for transportation to medical appointments); wheelchair accessibility items; pool therapy; therapy equipment; minor home repairs (if related to a medical, safety, accessibility or independence need); camps for kids with special needs, when other sources of funding (i.e. scholarships) have been researched and are not available; psychological counseling/evaluation, only on an emergency basis and with a long term management plan; and children's bike helmets (distributed through the Eureka Police Department). Applications are accepted at any time and are reviewed every Wednesday. There is generally a two week turn-around time on application review and check processing..

Requirements: Applications must be made through a qualified sponsor, such as a recognized social service agency, school counselor, or medical provider. The sponsor will then help to administer the funds which are granted. Applications should be filled out as specifically as possible, including the medical condition of the applicant and whether they can pay a portion of the cost of the item or service. Applications should also include any comparison shopping for the item, and whether additional sources have been sought. If the applicant is a cancer survivor, the application should indicate if they are in contact with the American Cancer Society, and if they have been approved for financial assistance. For children with medical needs, the application should indicate if the California Children's Services is involved.

Restrictions: The following items are usually not funded: adult dental care; dentures; hearing aids; lift chair; acupuncture/massage; care providers; weight loss programs; CPAP machines; counseling (long term); aerochamber; burial/cremation/funeral expenses; tattoo removal; iPad/iPod; cell phone; vision therapy; rent/deposits/utility bills; car payments/vehicle maintenance; birth certificates; green cards; driver's license or driver education courses; waste removal; smoke alarms; wood for stove; baby items; child care; parenting classes; woodstove barriers/fireplace gates; summer camp; or dog training.

Geographic Focus: California

Amount of Grant: 25 - 250 USD

Contact: Jill Moore, Program Coordinator, Community Strategies; (707) 442-2993, ext. 314; fax (707) 442-9072; jillm@hafoundation.org

Internet: www.ulhf.org/content/view/91/82/

Sponsor: Union Labor Health Foundation
363 Indianola Road
Bayside, CA 95524

Union Labor Health Foundation Dental Angel Fund Grants   2336

The Union Labor Health Foundation (ULHF), a supporting organization of the Humboldt Area Foundation, provides funds for the Dental Angel Fund. The Dental Angel Fund was created to meet dental-related needs of individual youth and youth groups in Humboldt County in situations where emergency funds are required. The Fund is designed to meet the needs of children up to the age of 19 who are residents of Humboldt County. Applications are accepted at any time and reviewed periodically, with a two week turn-around time. The application is available at the website.

Requirements: The application should include a pre-treatment plan from the treating dentist. *Restrictions:* A third party must apply for the individual. Funding is not available for orthodontia or cosmetic dental needs. Service providers may not make requests for their own reimbursement and individuals may not apply on their own behalf.
Geographic Focus: California
Contact: Jill Moore, Program Coordinator, Community Strategies; (707) 442-2993, ext. 314; fax (707) 442-9072; jillm@hafoundation.org
Internet: www.ulhf.org/content/view/91/82/
Sponsor: Union Labor Health Foundation
363 Indianola Road
Bayside, CA 95524

Union Pacific Foundation Community and Civic Grants 2337
The Foundation has a strong interest in promoting organizational effectiveness among nonprofits. To that end, this Foundation dedicates the majority of their grants to help nonprofit organizations build their capacity, increase their impact, and operate more efficiently and effectively. Grants are made primarily to proposals in the areas of community and civic, and health and human services. The community and civic grants category focuses on assisting community-based organizations and related activities that improve and enrich the general quality of life in the community. This category includes organizations such as aquariums, botanical gardens, children's museums, history/science museums, public libraries, public television and radio, and zoos.
Requirements: The Foundation will accept only online applications; printed copies of the application are not available and will not be accepted. Grants are made to institutions located in communities served by Union Pacific Corporation and its operating company Union Pacific Railroad Company.
Restrictions: The Foundation will not consider a request from or for: individuals; organizations/projects/programs that do not fit within the Foundation's funding priorities; organizations without a Section 501(c)3 public charity determination letter from the Internal Revenue Service; organizations that channel grant funds to third parties; organizations whose dominant purpose is to influence legislation or participate/intervene in political campaigns on behalf of or against any candidate for public office; organization/projects/programs for which the Foundation is asked to serve as the sole funder; organizations that already have an active multi-year Union Pacific Foundation grant; religious organizations for non-secular programs (i.e. programs which promote religious doctrine); organizational deficits; local affiliates of national health/disease-specific organizations; non-U.S.-based charities; organizations whose program activities are mainly international; elementary or secondary schools; athletic programs or events; donations of railroad equipment; conventions, conferences or seminars; fellowships or research; loans; labor organizations; or organizations whose programs have a national scope.
Geographic Focus: Arizona, Arkansas, California, Colorado, Idaho, Illinois, Iowa, Kansas, Louisiana, Minnesota, Missouri, Montana, Nebraska, Nevada, New Mexico, Oklahoma, Oregon, Tennessee, Texas, Utah, Washington, Wisconsin, Wyoming
Date(s) Application is Due: Aug 15
Contact: Darlynn Myers, Director; (402) 271-5600; fax (402) 501-2291; upf@up.com
Internet: www.up.com/found/grants.shtml
Sponsor: Union Pacific Foundation
1400 Douglas Street, Stop 1560
Omaha, NE 68179

Union Pacific Foundation Health and Human Services Grants 2338
The Foundation has a strong interest in promoting organizational effectiveness among nonprofits. To that end, this foundation dedicates the majority of their grants to help nonprofit organizations build their capacity, increase their impact, and operate more efficiently and effectively. Grants are made primarily to proposals in the areas of community and civic, and health and human services. The health and human services category assists organizations dedicated to improving the level of health care or providing human services in the community. Types of support include general operating support, continuing support, capital campaigns, building construction and renovation, curriculum development, equipment acquisition, program development, and matching funds.
Requirements: The Foundation will accept only online applications; printed copies of the application are not available and will not be accepted. Grants are made to institutions located in communities served by Union Pacific Corporation and its operating company Union Pacific Railroad Company.
Restrictions: The Foundation generally will not consider a request from or for: individuals; organizations/projects/programs that do not fit within the Foundation's funding priorities; organizations without a Section 501(c)3 public charity determination letter from the Internal Revenue Service; organizations that channel grant funds to third parties; organizations whose dominant purpose is to influence legislation or participate/intervene in political campaigns on behalf of or against any candidate for public office; organization/projects/programs for which the Foundation is asked to serve as the sole funder; organizations that already have an active multi-year Union Pacific Foundation grant; religious organizations for non-secular programs; organizational deficits; local affiliates of national health/disease-specific organizations; non U.S.-based charities; organizations whose program activities are mainly international; elementary or secondary schools; athletic programs or events; donations of railroad equipment; conventions, conferences or seminars; fellowships or research; loans; labor organizations; or organizations whose programs have a national scope.
Geographic Focus: Arizona, Arkansas, California, Colorado, Idaho, Iowa, Kansas, Louisiana, Minnesota, Missouri, Montana, Nebraska, Nevada, New Mexico, Oklahoma, Oregon, Tennessee, Texas, Utah, Washington, Wisconsin, Wyoming
Date(s) Application is Due: Aug 15
Contact: Darlynn Myers, Director; (402) 271-5600; fax (402) 501-2291; upf@up.com

Internet: www.up.com/found/grants.shtml
Sponsor: Union Pacific Foundation
1400 Douglas Street, Stop 1560
Omaha, NE 68179

Union Square Arts Award 2339
The Union Square Arts Award recognizes the central leadership role played by arts and culture in providing educational opportunities for young people, building collaborations and promoting social change. The Arts Award supports organizations working with youth and families in low-income communities across New York City in all artistic disciplines: creative writing, dance, music, theater, visual and media arts. Each Arts Award consists of a grant of up to $35,000, comprehensive technical assistance, and the opportunity to apply for re-grants to help build long-term organizational sustainability and community engagement.
Requirements: Candidates for Union Square Arts Award are identified through a nomination process. Nominations are reviewed throughout the year and may be submitted by anyone familiar with the organization's contributions and accomplishments. Submissions must describe the nominee's work and outline why the organization should be considered for an Award. Nominations may be made online, by mail, or fax.
Restrictions: Recipient organizations are less than ten-years-old with annual operating budgets under $1 million.
Geographic Focus: New York
Amount of Grant: Up to 35,000 USD
Contact: Denise Beek, Program Associate; (212) 213-6140; fax (212) 213-6372
Internet: www.unionsquareawards.org/arts-program
Sponsor: Union Square Awards
9 East 38th Street, 2nd floor
New York, NY 10016

Union Square Award for Social Justice 2340
Recipients of the the Union Square Award have changed public policies, litigated landmark cases, created innovative models of service, and built important community institutions. Award recipients address concerns and build organizations that bring diverse communities into public discourse. Specifically, the Union Square Award supports work in the following areas: homelessness and hunger; HIV/AIDS prevention, education, and treatment; family and community development; youth leadership and organizing; economic self-sufficiency; and conflict resolution. The Award identifies organizations that have not yet received substantial funding and public recognition. It consists of a general operating support grant of $50,000, comprehensive technical assistance, and the opportunity to apply for re-grants to help build long-term organizational sustainability and community engagement.
Requirements: Candidates for the Award are identified through a nominations process. Nominations are reviewed throughout the year and may be submitted by anyone familiar with the organization's contributions and accomplishments. Submissions must describe the nominee's work and outline why the organization should be considered for an Award. Nominations may be made through the online form and are accepted online, by mail, or fax.
Restrictions: Only organizations in the New York City area are eligible for nomination.
Geographic Focus: New York
Amount of Grant: 50,000 USD
Contact: Denise Beek, Program Associate; (212) 213 6140; fax (212) 213-6372
Internet: www.unionsquareawards.org/awards-program
Sponsor: Union Square Awards
9 East 38th Street, 2nd floor
New York, NY 10016

United Friends of the Children Scholarships 2341
Established in California in 1980 by Nancy MacNeil Daly Riordan, longtime philanthropist, children's advocate, director of the W.M. Keck Foundation, and wife of former Los Angeles Mayor Richard Riordan. Nancy Daly spent her life advocating for children and ensuring that our future generations are not forgotten. Her commitment to children - especially foster children - across the country led to the establishment of countless organizations, committees and even legislation for increased funding for children's rights. She established United Friends of the Children in Los Angeles, California, in 1980 as a mechanism of addressing the unmet needs of the County's foster youth by providing support services to help them finish high school, find housing, attend college, and build the skills necessary to support themselves. Currently, the program works to ensure that current and former foster youth have access to a high-quality education and the opportunity to pursue their goals, by offering eligible students $3,000 a year for up to five years for college-related expenses, as well as ongoing support to promote graduation from college.
Requirements: Eligible applicants must be Los Angeles County foster or probation youth currently in their senior year of high school with a cumulative 2.7 GPA or above who plan on attending a four-year college or university.
Geographic Focus: California
Contact: Polly Williams, (213) 580-1812 or (213) 580-1850; info@unitedfriends.org
Internet: www.unitedfriends.org/programs/
Sponsor: United Friends of the Children
1055 Wilshire Boulevard, Suite 1955
Los Angeles, CA 90017-5602

UnitedHealthcare Children's Foundation Grants 2342
UnitedHealthcare Children's Foundation grants provide financial help and assistance for families with children that have medical needs not covered or not fully covered by their commercial health insurance plan. The Foundation aims to fill the gap between what medical services and items a child needs and what their commercial health benefit plan will pay for. The amount awarded to an individual within a 12-month period is limited to either

$5,000 or 85% of the fund balance, whichever amount is less. Awards to any one individual are limited to a lifetime maximum of $10,000.

Requirements: The applicant must be: 16 years old or younger and live in the United States and receive and pay for care/items in the United States; and be covered by a commercial health insurance plan and limits for the requested service are either exceeded, or no coverage is available and/or the costs are a serious financial burden on the family. An application must be submitted prior to the child's 17th birthday.

Restrictions: The following set of items are excluded from grant consideration: alternative treatments, including listening, vision, cognitive, neuro-feedback and social skills therapy; dental or orthodontic treatment, unless related to a serious medical condition (such as cleft palate); drugs not licensed by the FDA; educational and tutoring programs; camps; home improvements and modifications; vehicles (cars, vans, trucks, etc.); service dogs or other animals, unless to support the visually impaired; biofeedback; biomedical consultations; chelation therapy, unless for proven medical indication of lead or copper or iron; heavy metal toxicity testing; hyperbaric oxygen treatment; herbal testing; Relationship Development Intervention (RDI); infertility, pregnancy, and birthing; autopsy; burial costs; funeral costs; clinical trials; or tablets (such as iPads,etc.), computers, mobile devices and other recreational electronics not specifically designed for medical or clinical treatment purposes.

Geographic Focus: All States

Amount of Grant: Up to 5,000 USD

Contact: Customer Servive Representative; (855) 698-4223; customerservice@uhccf.org

Internet: www.uhccf.org/apply/

Sponsor: UnitedHealthcare Children's Foundation

P.O. Box 41, 9700 Health Care Lane

Minneapolis, MN 55440-0041

United Healthcare Community Grants in Michigan 2343

United Healthcare is dedicated to helping people nationwide live healthier lives by simplifying the health care experience, meeting consumer health and wellness needs, and sustaining trusted relationships with care providers. United Healthcare Community grants offer funds for specific proposals from community organizations to improve nutrition and physical activity resources for Michigan's youth. Initial grants will range from $20,000 to $30,000. Proposals are due May 1, and successful awardees will be notified September 30.

Requirements: 501(c)3 organizations either located in, or serving the residents of, Michigan are eligible to apply.

Geographic Focus: All States

Date(s) Application is Due: May 1

Amount of Grant: 20,000 - 30,000 USD

Contact: Molly McMillen, (952) 931-6029 or (866) 633-2446; molly.mcmillen@uhc.com or communitygrants@uhc.com

Internet: www.businesswire.com/news/home/20150420006768/en/UnitedHealthcare-Award-120000-Grants-Michigan-Organizations-Dedicated#.VUKOS2bfit8

Sponsor: United Healthcare Services

5901 Lincoln Drive

Minneapolis, MN 55436

United Methodist Committee on Relief Hunger and Poverty Grants 2344

The United Methodist Committee on Relief provides grants to organizations that work to eradicate the root causes of hunger and poverty. The Committee supports these initiatives both in the United States and around the world, and has provided grants to partners such as Agricultural Missions, Grassroots International, the United Methodist Church of Sierra Leone, and Abraham's Table. At this time, grant applications are by invitation only, so interested parties should begin by contacted the Committee to discuss their proposal.

Geographic Focus: All States, All Countries

Contact: Shannon Trilli, Director of Global Health Initiatives; (212) 870-3870 or (212) 870-3951; strilli@umcor.org or umcor@umcor.org

Internet: www.umcor.org/UMCOR/Programs/Global-Development/Hunger-and-Poverty-Grants/Hunger-and-Poverty-Grants

Sponsor: United Methodist Committee on Relief

475 Riverside Drive, Room 1520

New York, NY 10115

United Methodist Health Ministry Fund Grants 2345

Grantmaking is the Health Fund's primary means of achieving its mission, and we see each grant as an opportunity to move toward the goal of healthy Kansans. To maximize impact with available resources, the Health Fund is targeting the following three areas for funding: access; fit kids; ready for life. In addition to these general focus areas, the Health Fund seeks to support Kansas United Methodist churches in health ministry work through the Healthy Congregations Covenant program. Grants are awarded to health care projects proposed by eligible organizations to respond to needs and build on assets of local, regional, and state situations. These grants generally have one or more of the following purposes: develop new or expanded, sustainable program resources to provide quality services; change the delivery system to meet new demands, improve access/quality, or reduce cost; test innovative ideas for improved service delivery; offer public education for improvement of individual and community health care; provide group opportunities for health care providers to improve critical skills; and develop technical expertise, collaborations, and similar supports for improvement and change in health care service delivery and education.

Geographic Focus: Kansas

Contact: Virginia Elliott; (620) 662-8586; fax (620) 662-8597; velliott@healthfund.org

Kim Moore, President; (620) 662-8586; fax (620) 662-8597; kmoore@healthfund.org

Internet: www.healthfund.org/funding.php

Sponsor: United Methodist Health Ministry Fund

100 East First Avenue, P.O. Box 1384

Hutchinson, KS 67504-1384

United Methodist Women Brighter Future for Children and Youth Grants 2346

United Methodist Women offers grants of up to $4,000 for projects that address the needs of young people five to eighteen years of age in the areas of violence and/or abuse prevention and/or treatment. Preference will be given to organizations that have significant involvement of women and youth at the grassroots level; demonstrate the ability to raise additional funds from other sources; provide direct, comprehensive services to young people; promote respect for and appreciation of racial/ethnic diversity; and cultivate spiritual life and values. Funding proposals in Spanish are accepted. Interested parties should contact the Foundation to first discuss their proposal, and full grant applications are by invitation only.

Requirements: The Women's Division funds small-scale, community and church-based programs and projects. New or existing projects are eligible to apply. Projects should demonstrate the ability to raise additional funds from other sources.

Restrictions: Groups affiliated with national organizations, hospitals, organizations with budgets totaling more than $3,000,000 are not normally within the realm of funding. Building improvements, computer hardware, one-time only events, or summer events and activities are not eligible for funding.

Geographic Focus: All States

Amount of Grant: Up to 4,000 USD

Contact: Marva Usher-Kerr, Executive Secretary; (212) 870-3738; fax (212) 870-3736; MUsherke@unitedmethodistwomen.org

Internet: new.gbgm-umc.org/umw/give/brighterfuture/

Sponsor: United Methodist Women

475 Riverside Drive, Room 1503

New York, NY 10115

United Technologies Corporation Grants 2347

United Technologies Corporation (UTC) grant-making is centered on the geographic regions where its employees live and work. Additionally the corporation focuses its grants on the following four areas of interest: supporting vibrant communities, building sustainable cities, advancing STEM education, and investing in emerging markets. A more detailed description of each area follows. UTC supports vibrant communities by supporting community revitalization initiatives, health and human service programs, and arts and culture. UTC defines sustainable cities as those that are safe and energy efficient to protect people, assets, and natural resources. In support of sustainable cities, UTC focuses on sustainable building practices, urban green space, and preservation of natural habitats to offset green-house gas emissions. To advance science, technology, engineering, and mathematics (STEM) education and to develop the next generation of engineers and scientists, UTC targets programs that include employee volunteerism to spark students' interest and inspire innovation, especially in minorities and women. As it invests in emerging markets, UTC seeks to lay a foundation for responsible citizenship from the inception of business expansion by supporting communities through employee engagement in China and India. Grant seekers have the option of applying either to UTC corporate headquarters or to a UTC business unit (Pratt & Whitney, Otis, Carrier, Sikorsky, UTC Fire & Security, and Hamilton Sundstrand). Either way, application is made online at the grant website given. Grant applications are accepted between January 1 and June 30 each year. Awardees will receive notification within one quarter of their application submission (or in the case of a UTC-business-unit application, in the first quarter of the calendar year in which funding will occur).

Requirements: 501(c)3 organizations in the U.S. and equivalent nonprofit organizations in the corporation's emerging markets are eligible.

Restrictions: Non-profit organizations may apply only once a year and to only one UTC business - either Corporate Headquarters or one of the UTC business units (see description section). UTC will not fund individuals, religious activities or organizations, municipalities, alumni groups (unless the award is distributed to the eligible higher education institution), booster clubs, sororities or fraternities, political groups, organizations engaged in or advocating illegal action, or any organization determined by UTC to have a conflict of interest. Additionally the corporation will not support fees for publication or merchandise.

Geographic Focus: All States, All Countries

Date(s) Application is Due: Jun 30

Contact: Andrew Olivastro, Manager, Community Affairs; (860) 728-7000; fax (860) 728-7041; contribu@corphq.utc.com

Internet: www.utc.com/Corporate+Responsibility/Community/Apply+for+a+grant

Sponsor: United Technologies Corporation

United Technologies Building

Hartford, CT 06101

University of Chicago Chapin Hall Doris Duke Fellowships 2348

Chapin Hall at the University of Chicago offers the Doris Duke Fellowships for the Promotion of Child Well-Being. These fellowships are designed to identify and develop a new generation of leaders interested in and capable of creating practice and policy initiatives that will enhance child development and improve the nation's ability to prevent all forms of child maltreatment. The fellows receive an annual stipend of $30,000 for up to two years to support the completion of their dissertation and related research at their academic institution. Up to 15 fellowships are awarded annually. Fellows are guided by an academic mentor whom they select; fellows also identify a policy or practice mentor to assist them in better understanding how to frame their research questions with an eye toward maximizing policy and practice relevance. Applicants may be enrolled in any discipline. The formal application period will run from August 1 through December 1.

Requirements: Applicants must be enrolled in an accredited U.S. doctoral program and have substantially completed the coursework required to be advanced to candidacy. They are expected to complete or make significant progress on their dissertation within the two-year fellowship period. Applicants must be U.S. citizens or permanent residents in the U.S.

Geographic Focus: All States

Date(s) Application is Due: Dec 1
Amount of Grant: 30,000 USD
Contact: Emily Siegel, Fellowship Administrator; (773) 256-5227; fax (773) 256-5351;
ddfellowship@chapinhall.org or esiegel@chapinhall.org
Internet: www.chapinhall.org/fellowships/doris-duke-fellowships
Sponsor: University of Chicago
1313 East 60th Street
Chicago, IL 60637

UPS Corporate Giving Grants   2349
As a complement to its foundation, UPS also makes charitable contributions to nonprofit
organizations directly. UPS is focused on creating opportunities for its customers and
supporting communities around the world. As part of this commitment, the Corporation
sponsors numerous sports teams, as well as community and cultural events in the
neighborhoods where it does business. Current sponsorships include: motorsports; the
Chinese women's volleyball team; golf; and a wide variety of community programs around
the globe.
Requirements: Due to the high volume of requests that the Corporation receives, all
opportunities must be submitted via the website for consideration. UPS does not accept
hard copy sponsorship proposals.
Geographic Focus: All States
Contact: Ken Sternad, President; (404) 828-6374; fax (404) 828-7435
Internet: www.upssponsorships.com/#
Sponsor: United Parcel Service (UPS) Foundation
55 Glenlake Parkway NE
Atlanta, GA 30328

UPS Foundation Community Safety Grants   2350
The work of the UPS Foundation brings together UPS expertise and philanthropic dollars
to address areas of critical importance to improving the safety of communities and the
effectiveness of organizations committed to assisting them in times of need. UPS has a long-
standing reputation as a leading provider of transportation and logistics services in times of
disaster. The Foundation is supporting organizations that are injecting new thinking and
innovative solutions to further leverage UPS's skills in this area.
Requirements: IRS 501(c)3 tax-exempt organizations are eligible to apply.
Restrictions: The foundation does not award grants to individuals, religious organizations or
theological functions, or church-sponsored programs limited to church members. Grants
supporting capital campaigns, endowments, or operating expenses are seldom approved.
Geographic Focus: All States
Amount of Grant: 1,000 - 200,000 USD
Contact: Ken Sternad, President; (404) 828-6374; fax (404) 828-7435
Internet: responsibility.ups.com/UPS+Foundation/Focus+On+Giving/Community+Safety
Sponsor: United Parcel Service (UPS) Foundation
55 Glenlake Parkway NE
Atlanta, GA 30328

UPS Foundation Economic and Global Literacy Grants   2351
Since 1989, the UPS Foundation has committed more than $26.4 million addressing
the variety of challenges presented by illiteracy. Initially focused on adult literacy and
later on workforce and family literacy, today the foundation builds on UPS's knowledge
to enable global commerce by teaching people how to effectively compete by enhancing
their economic and global literacy. The goal of the Foundation's current grant making is
enhancing the economic literacy in communities through programming that teaches the
fundamentals of free enterprise and the foundations of economic education. In addition to
helping people around the world learn the basics of entrepreneurship and self-sufficiency,
the UPS Foundation will also support emerging entrepreneurs through grants to innovative
micro enterprise organizations who teach the business skills necessary for success in today's
global economy.
Requirements: IRS 501(c)3 tax-exempt organizations are eligible to apply.
Restrictions: The foundation does not award grants to individuals, religious organizations or
theological functions, or church-sponsored programs limited to church members. Grants
supporting capital campaigns, endowments, or operating expenses are seldom approved.
Geographic Focus: All States
Amount of Grant: 1,000 - 200,000 USD
Contact: Ken Sternad, President; (404) 828-6374; fax (404) 828-7435
Internet: responsibility.ups.com/UPS+Foundation/Focus+On+Giving/
Economic+and+Global+Literacy
Sponsor: United Parcel Service (UPS) Foundation
55 Glenlake Parkway NE
Atlanta, GA 30328

USAID Community Livelihoods Project in Yemen Grant   2352
The Community Livelihoods Project in Yemen will be expected to build on and complement
ongoing activities during the transition phase between the existing portfolio of USAID/
Yemen projects and this flagship initiative. Very close coordination and collaboration with
the Mission's future National Governance Project (NGP) will be extremely important
during the implementation of the CLP. The implementer also will partner with and make
extensive use of local, Yemeni organizations during the implementation of the project. The
implementer also will coordinate with USAID's future Monitoring and Evaluation Project
to help ensure that program results are tracked against stability measures. The strategy will
be released when this solicitation is released for bid. USAID anticipates an award for a base
period of three years with the potential for follow-on activities dependent on performance
and availability of funding. Subject to the availability of funds, the estimated budget for

the three year base period is approximately $65 million. A single award is expected in the
amount of $65,000,000 and, at the present, there is no designated application deadline.
Requirements: Eligibility to apply includes: U.S. or non-U.S. non-governmental
organizations; for profit or non-profit U.S. or Non-U.S. organizations; and non-profit
university educational institutions.
Geographic Focus: All States, American Samoa, District of Columbia, Guam, Marshall
Islands, Northern Mariana Islands, Puerto Rico, U.S. Virgin Islands, All Countries
Amount of Grant: 65,000,000 USD
Contact: Botros Wilson, Acquisitions Specialist; +20-2-516-6921 or +20-2-522-7000;
fax +20-2-522-7197; YemenNGPRFA1@usaid.gov or bwilson@usaid.gov
Internet: www.grants.gov/web/grants/view-opportunity.html?oppId=50471
Sponsor: U.S. Agency for International Development
Ronald Reagan Building, 1300 Pennsylvania Avenue, NW
Washington, D.C. 20523-1000

USAID Family Planning and Reproductive Health Methods Grants   2353
The United States Agency for International Development (USAID) is seeking concept
papers from qualified U.S. nonprofit non-Governmental Organizations (NGOs) for a
program titled Family Planning and Reproductive Health Methods to Address Unmet
Need, for funding of Cooperative Agreements. The purpose of this APS is to support the
research, development, and introduction of technologies and approaches that better meet
the needs of women and girls as their sexual and reproductive health concerns change over
time. The General Objectives of the APS are to: refine existing FP methods to address
method-related reasons for non-use; respond to product-related issues about currently
available FP methods that arise at purchase and/or from the field, and that may affect
provider/user perceptions and/or the supply chain; develop new FP methods that address
method-related reasons for non-use, and/or fill gaps in the existing method mix; conduct
research to foster the introduction and uptake of new and/or underutilized woman-initiated
methods, particularly non-hormonal barriers, contraceptive vaginal rings, and fertility
awareness methods based on knowledge and monitoring of the menstrual cycle; and develop
multipurpose prevention technologies (MPTs) that address the simultaneous risks of
unintended pregnancy, HIV, and other sexually transmitted infections (STIs) – particularly
Herpes Simplex Virus (HSV) and Human Papillomavirus (HPV). The funding range of
awards is $500,000 to $80,000,000.
Requirements: Eligible organizations include registered U.S. and non-U.S. private non-
governmental organizations, non-profit organizations, and for-profit organizations willing
to forego profit.
Geographic Focus: All States, American Samoa, District of Columbia, Guam, Marshall
Islands, Northern Mariana Islands, Puerto Rico, U.S. Virgin Islands, All Countries
Date(s) Application is Due: Jan 14
Amount of Grant: 500,000 - 80,000,000 USD
Contact: Marcus Moon; (202) 567-4406 or (202) 712-4810; fax (202) 216-3524;
mmoon@usaid.gov
Internet: www.grants.gov/web/grants/view-opportunity.html?oppId=215873
Sponsor: U.S. Agency for International Development
Ronald Reagan Building, 1300 Pennsylvania Avenue, NW
Washington, D.C. 20523-1000

USAID Global Development Alliance Grants   2354
The U.S. Agency for International Development (USAID) is committed to increasing the
sustainable impact of its development assistance programs through strategic alliances with
the private sector. Such alliances enable the Agency to leverage private sector markets,
expertise, interests, and assets in a manner that solves critical development problems and
promotes effective market led development. They also enable the private sector to leverage
USAID's expertise, assets and working relationships in a manner that advances business
success and fosters the broader economic growth and poverty reduction that is vital to
sustaining such success. Through strategic and ongoing collaboration, the private sector
and USAID are better able to increase the impact, reach, efficiency, and effectiveness of
our respective investments in developing countries worldwide. This Global Development
Alliance (GDA) Annual Program Statement (APS) is designed to catalyze, facilitate and
support such collaboration.
Requirements: USAID seeks to develop new and innovative alliances with the private
sector, including local and multinational corporations, foundations, non-governmental
organizations, and academia.
Restrictions: Proposals that do not leverage resources by at least matching the amount
requested will not be considered.
Geographic Focus: All States, American Samoa, District of Columbia, Guam, Marshall
Islands, Northern Mariana Islands, Puerto Rico, U.S. Virgin Islands, All Countries
Date(s) Application is Due: Nov 18
Contact: Ken Lee, Senior Partnerships Advisor; (202) 712-4810 or (202) 712-0000;
fax (202) 216-3524; kenlee@usaid.gov or gda@usaid.gov
Internet: www.usaid.gov/gda
Sponsor: U.S. Agency for International Development
Ronald Reagan Building, 1300 Pennsylvania Avenue, NW
Washington, D.C. 20523-1000

USAID Innovations in Feed the Future Monitoring and Evaluation Grants   2355
The United States Agency for International Development invites applications for funding
from qualified U.S. and non-U.S., non-profit or for-profit non-governmental organizations
(NGOs) and international organizations to carry out activities that develop, test or apply
innovative methods for monitoring or evaluating Feed the Future/Global Food Security
Strategy activities or programs. There is no award floor or award ceiling that has been
identified. The current closing date for application submission is October 12.

Requirements: All qualified entities are eligible to apply, including U.S. and non-U.S., non-profit or for-profit NGOs, Institutes of Higher Education, and Public International Organizations or international organizations (PIO or IO). Further, USAID strongly encourages submissions from new and varied partners.
Restrictions: Individuals are not eligible to apply. Applicants from organizations based in, or applications with an operational focus in, the following countries are not eligible: Cuba, Iran, North Korea and Syria.
Geographic Focus: All States, All Countries
Date(s) Application is Due: Oct 12
Contact: Paul Burford, Agreement Officer; (202) 567-5303; pburford@usaid.gov
Internet: www.grants.gov/web/grants/view-opportunity.html?oppId=297972
Sponsor: U.S. Agency for International Development
Ronald Reagan Building, 1300 Pennsylvania Avenue, NW
Washington, D.C. 20523-1000

USAID Integrated Youth Development Activity Grants **2356**
The United States Agency for International Development's Mission in the Democratic Republic of the Congo (USAID/DRC) is seeking applications from qualified and eligible organizations for a three-year, approximately $22.15 million activity that will increase youth resilience to conflict and violence in eastern DRC. This activity will include approximately $17 million in Basic Education funding, $2.8 million in Higher Education funding, $1 million in Economic Growth funding, $600,000 in Family Planning funding, and $750,000 in Democracy, Human Rights and Governance (DRG) funding for civic education, citizen participation and public accountability. In addition, USAID/DRC is currently negotiating a Global Development Alliance (GDA) with a third party entity to provide a household cash transfer component to this activity. If this partnership is realized, USAID will require the Applicant to collaborate with USAID and the third party entity on beneficiary selection, as well as an external evaluation of the Integrated Youth Development Activity. Through this Notice of Funding Opportunity (NOFO), USAID intends to fund the successful Applicant whose activity provides youth in eastern DRC with access to basic education combined with opportunities to develop and exercise skills that allow them to positively engage in economic, social and political life in their communities. It is anticipated that a single award will be approved, ranging from $20,000,000 to $22,150,000. The current closing date for application submission is January 4.
Requirements: Qualified U.S. and non-U.S. Non-Governmental Organizations (NGOs), U.S. Private Voluntary Organizations (PVOs), and U.S. and non-U.S. for profit firms (provided they forgo profit) may participate in this funding opportunity.
Geographic Focus: All States, All Countries
Date(s) Application is Due: Jan 4
Amount of Grant: 20,000,000 - 22,150,000 USD
Contact: Patrick Kollars, Supervisory Agreement Officer; +243 81 700 5701; pkollars@usaid.gov or KinshasaProposals@usaid.gov
Malu Boyenge, Acquisition and Assistance Specialist; +243 81 700 5701; mboyenge@usaid.gov or KinshasaProposals@usaid.gov
Internet: www.grants.gov/web/grants/view-opportunity.html?oppId=298025
Sponsor: U.S. Agency for International Development
Ronald Reagan Building, 1300 Pennsylvania Avenue, NW
Washington, 20523-1000

USAID National Governance Project in Yemen Grant **2357**
USAID-Yemen intends to announce a full and open competition to implement a National Governance Project (NGP) Grant. The announcement is subject to the availability of funds. The NGP is intended to facilitate more equitable socio-economic development by strengthening public policies and institutions that will contribute to mitigating the drivers of instability in Yemen. A more equitable, representative, transparent, responsive, and reliable Yemeni government that meets the needs of its most vulnerable citizens is one way to help achieve USAID's objectives. As the needs in Yemen are great, the implementer will focus on initiatives that directly satisfy the needs identified in USAID's strategy, that are supported by the Republic of Yemen Government's or that would require relatively little effort to garner support, and that will have the biggest strategic impact for the resources expended. Activities will quickly and effectively mitigate critical threats to stability in Yemen by reestablishing trust, respect, and, in some communities, legitimacy for the Government of Yemen. Youth will be a particularly important demographic group throughout implementation. The implementer will partner with and make extensive use of local, Yemeni organizations during the implementation of the project. The estimated budget for the three year base period is approximately $20 million. Staff are unable to entertain meetings or respond to queries with prospective implementers at this stage. Please check the website for updated information including the application date. One award of $20,000,000 will be funded.
Requirements: Eligibility to apply includes: U.S. or non-U.S. non-governmental organizations; for profit or non-profit U.S. or Non-U.S. organizations; and non-profit university educational institutions.
Geographic Focus: All States, American Samoa, District of Columbia, Guam, Marshall Islands, Northern Mariana Islands, Puerto Rico, U.S. Virgin Islands, All Countries
Amount of Grant: 20,000,000 USD
Contact: Botros Wilson, Acquisitions Specialist; +20-2-516-6921 or +20-2-522-7000; fax +20-2-522-7197; bwilson@usaid.gov or YemenNGPRFA1@usaid.gov
Internet: www.grants.gov/web/grants/view-opportunity.html?oppId=50473
Sponsor: U.S. Agency for International Development
Ronald Reagan Building, 1300 Pennsylvania Avenue, NW
Washington, D.C. 20523-1000

USAID Nigeria Education Crisis Response Grants **2358**
The purpose of this notice is to announce an Annual Program Statement (APS) for the USAID/Nigeria Education Crisis Response. The overarching goal of the program is to expand enrollment in appropriate, protective and relevant educational options for the girls, boys, and youth that are affected by violence in Northeastern Nigeria. Activities will provide targeted assistance for the girls, boys, and youth that are affected by violence in the region, and ensure that children and youth have continued access to an instructional routine in Adamawa and the buffer States of Bauchi and Gombe (with other States to be determined as needs require and conditions permit). Within this goal, the Education Crisis Response will address the following problems: expected large increase in drop-out rates in affected States; over-crowding of classrooms and learning spaces due to influx of displaced populations; limited access for displaced children; shortage of qualified teachers and instructional materials for formal and non-formal education; children traumatized by violence and abductions, and families fear of sending their children to school; marginalization of girls and children with disabilities; and rising tensions between host communities and displaced populations. Programs may have a maximum duration of 36 months. Priority will be given to applications that can be launched rapidly. USAID anticipates awarding approximately two to six awards ranging anywhere from minimum grant size of $300,000 and a maximum grant size of $15,000,000 made available either to one grantee, multiple grantees, or no grantees depending on the quality of the applications. Subject to the availability of funds, USAID intends to provide the funding in the total range of approximately $30,000,000. Currently, applications may be submitted at any time.
Requirements: The application eligibility is unrestricted. Applicants must have established financial management, monitoring and evaluation, internal control systems, and policies and procedures that comply with established U.S. Government standards, laws, and regulations. All potential awardees will be subject to a responsibility determination (this may include a pre-award survey) issued by a warranted Agreements Officer in USAID.
Geographic Focus: All States, Nigeria
Amount of Grant: 300,000 - 15,000,000 USD
Contact: Abdullahi Sadiq, Acquisitions and Assistance Specialist; +234 9 461 9300; abujaeduprocurements@usaid.gov
Internet: www.grants.gov/web/grants/view-opportunity.html?oppId=259510
Sponsor: U.S. Agency for International Development
Ronald Reagan Building, 1300 Pennsylvania Avenue, NW
Washington, D.C. 20523-1000

USAID Office of Foreign Disaster Assistance and Food for Peace Grants **2359**
The USAID office in Accra, Cameroon, supports humanitarian interventions for conflict-affected populations through its Office of Foreign Disaster Assistance and Food for Peace program, in partnership with the World Food Program. It assists refugees and internally displaced persons due to regional conflicts. Its programs address acute malnutrition, provide free quality health care for children, and improve livelihoods through unconditional cash transfers to vulnerable households to assist them to meet basic needs. It also provides cash-for-work activities to support households while restoring community infrastructure damaged by the conflict. It establishes safe spaces for women and girls to receive psycho-social support, learn ways to mitigate gender based violence, and gain practical skills to foster independence and self-sufficiency.
Geographic Focus: All States, American Samoa, District of Columbia, Guam, Northern Mariana Islands, Puerto Rico, U.S. Virgin Islands
Contact: Carell Laurent, Principal Officer; +233-302-741-200; fax +233-21-741-365
Haider Haider, Program Contact; (202) 712-5422; hahaider@usaid.gov
Internet: www.usaid.gov/cameroon/our-work/working-in-crisis-and-conflict
Sponsor: U.S. Agency for International Development
Ronald Reagan Building, 1300 Pennsylvania Avenue, NW
Washington, D.C. 20523-1000

USAID School Improvement Program Grants **2360**
Marginalized Palestinian areas suffer from a multitude of political, security and socioeconomic problems that hinder development work and put the population at serious risk. The Palestinian Authority (PA) has limited authority and capability to reach all Palestinian areas to provide meaningful support to its residents. The School Improvement Program will implement interventions to improve the educational environment and quality of education in the most disadvantaged Palestinian areas. This program will provide support to public and private schools in the most disadvantaged Palestinian areas. The primary goal of the program is to improve access to quality education and mitigate challenges to youth development in marginalized areas. The sub-goals include: improved educational facilities through renovation; improved teaching and learning through teacher training as appropriate, provision of educational resources, and collaboration with local communities; and expanded opportunities for youth development through extracurricular activities, career counseling and training in schools after hours. Illustrative outcomes include: improved human and physical educational resources that contribute to narrowing the achievement gap between students in underserved and better served Palestinian areas; organized and sustained extracurricular activities and youth programs; established networks between teachers, administrators, counselors, officials and community representatives in the targeted schools aiming at improving the quality of education and youth programming; enhanced community involvement in school decision-making; and strengthened educational institutions that provide services to learners. One award is anticipated, ranging from $4,000,000 to $20,000,000.
Requirements: U.S. Non-Governmental Organizations (NGOs), U.S. Private Voluntary Organizations (PVOs), Public International Organizations (PIOs), and U.S. for profit firms (provided they forgo profit) are eligible to apply.
Geographic Focus: All States, American Samoa, District of Columbia, Guam, Marshall Islands, Northern Mariana Islands, Puerto Rico, U.S. Virgin Islands, All Countries

Amount of Grant: 4,000,000 - 20,000,000 USD
Contact: Sandy Sakran, Acquisition and Assistance Specialist; +972-3-511-4870 or +972-3-511-4848; fax +972-3-511-4888; ssakran@usaid.gov or wbg@usaid.gov
Internet: www.grants.gov/web/grants/view-opportunity.html?oppId=175614
Sponsor: U.S. Agency for International Development
Ronald Reagan Building, 1300 Pennsylvania Avenue, NW
Washington, D.C. 20523-1000

USAID U.S.-Egypt Learning Grants **2361**
The purpose of the USAID U.S.-Egypt Learning Program is to provide targeted technical assistance and training support to the Government of Egypt to enable it to effectively implement a sustainable, nation-wide early grade learning (reading and mathematics) as well as develop an approach for improving the instruction of English in primary school. Over the last three years, the Ministry of Education has demonstrated strong commitment to design and scale up an Early Grade Reading Program (EGRP) that was developed in 2010 under a USAID-funded program (GILO – Girls for Improved Learning Outcomes). Most recently the Ministry of Education (MOE) has decided to incorporate a mathematics component in the early grade reading program. At the same time, the Ministry would like to improve the instruction of English. Given the Ministry's strong commitment and experience, it is expected to take the lead in the US-Egypt Learning Program. The role of the grantee will be a supportive one. The grantee will solidify and build on the EGRP strategies and approaches introduced by GILO, and expand them to be fully institutionalized. Specifically the grantee will collaborate with the MOE to: strengthen early grade reading instruction, and improve mathematics and English language teaching and learning materials and instructional approaches; develop cost-effective national assessments for reading and mathematics as well and monitoring and reporting systems; institutionalize pre-service and in-service professional development systems for early grade teachers and supervisors; and improve the education delivery system and build the capacity of Governorate and Idara (district) teams to develop and implement education plans that include budgets for early grade learning, incentives, and needed human resources. The maximum grant award will be $20,000, and there is no current closing date identified.
Requirements: Eligibility to apply includes: U.S. or non-U.S. non-governmental organizations; for profit or non-profit U.S. or Non-U.S. organizations; and non-profit university educational institutions.
Geographic Focus: All States, American Samoa, District of Columbia, Guam, Marshall Islands, Northern Mariana Islands, Puerto Rico, U.S. Virgin Islands, All Countries
Amount of Grant: Up to 20,000 USD
Contact: Sherine Gerguis, Grantor; +20-2-522-6925 or +20-2-522-7000; fax +20-2-522-7197; sgerguis@usaid.gov
Internet: www.grants.gov/web/grants/view-opportunity.html?oppId=252969
Sponsor: U.S. Agency for International Development
Ronald Reagan Building, 1300 Pennsylvania Avenue, NW
Washington, D.C. 20523-1000

USDA Child and Adult Care Food Program **2362**
The Child and Adult Care Food Program approves the quality of day care by making it more affordable for many low income families. Each day millions of children receive nutritious meals and snacks through the program. The program also provides meals and snacks to over 100,000 adults who receive care in nonresidential adult day care centers. The program alo provides meals to children residing in emergency shelters, and snacks and suppers to youths participating in eligible after school care programs. Disbursement is made on the basis of the number of lunches, suppers, breakfasts, and snacks served, using annually adjusted reimbursement rates specified by law. Program institutions may receive reimbursement for not more than three meals per day per participant. Specific guidelines and current applications are available at the website.
Requirements: City, local or county governments; other public entities; or private nonprofit organizations are eligible to apply. Each site operated must meet applicable state and local health, safety, and sanitation standards. Meals must meet minimum requirements of the United States Department of Agriculture (USDA). Organizations desiring to participate must agree to operate a nonprofit food service that is available to all eligible children.
Geographic Focus: All States
Contact: Tim O'Connor, Associate Administator; (703) 305-2054
Internet: www.fns.usda.gov/cnd/care/CACFP/aboutcacfp.htm
Sponsor: U.S. Department of Agriculture
1400 Independence Avenue SW
Washington, D.C. 20250

USDA WIC Nutrition Education Innovations Grants **2363**
The USDA Food and Nutrition Service announces the availability of funds to establish a USDA Center for WIC Nutrition Education Innovations, involving researcher-initiated projects to demonstrate creative approaches to evaluate or develop aspects of the Special Supplemental Nutrition Program for Women, Infants and Children (WIC), coordinate activities among researchers, and widely disseminate findings. The WIC Program was established to counteract the negative effects of poverty and nutritional risk on prenatal and pediatric health. The Program provides a combination of direct nutritional supplementation; nutrition education and counseling; and increased access to health care and social service providers for pregnant, breastfeeding, and postpartum women, infants, and children up to the age of five years. States, U.S. territories, and tribal organizations receive federal grants which are used to cover the cost of foods purchased with WIC benefits, along with specified nutrition services and administrative costs. Grant recipients shall work cooperatively with FNS to: support researcher-initiated projects that use a common approach in reporting findings to ensure transparency, and facilitate a meta-analysis of all projects; coordinate activities among researchers; effectively use technology and digital media to achieve desired outcomes; and advance communication and coordination to improve target behaviors. Specific guidelines are available at the website, including OMB and USDA forms needed for the application packet. The application is located at grants.gov.
Requirements: Private institutions of higher education eligible to apply for funding.
Geographic Focus: All States
Date(s) Application is Due: May 25
Amount of Grant: Up to 2,000,000 USD
Contact: Leslie Byrd, Grant Contact; (703) 305–2383; leslie.byrd@fns.usda.gov
Internet: www.fns.usda.gov/ora/menu/DemoProjects/WICResearch/WICResearchGrant.htm
Sponsor: U.S. Department of Agriculture
1400 Independence Avenue SW
Washington, D.C. 20250

USDEd Gaining Early Awareness and Readiness for Undergraduate Programs (GEAR UP) Grants **2364**
This discretionary grant program is designed to increase the number of low-income students who are prepared to enter and succeed in postsecondary education. GEAR UP provides six- or seven-year grants to states and partnerships to provide services at high-poverty middle and high schools. GEAR UP grantees serve an entire cohort of students beginning no later than the seventh grade and follow the cohort through high school. GEAR UP funds are also used to provide college scholarships to low-income students. State grants are competitive six-year matching grants that must include both an early intervention component designed to increase college attendance and success and raise the expectations of low-income students and a scholarship component. Partnership grants are competitive six-year matching grants that must support an early intervention component and may support a scholarship component designed to increase college attendance and success and raise the expectations of low-income students.
Requirements: For state grants, applicants must consist of one or more local educational agencies and one or more degree granting institutions of higher education; and not less than two other community organizations or entities, such as businesses, professional organizations, State agencies, institutions or agencies sponsoring programs authorized under subpart 4, or other public or private agencies or organizations. For partnership grants, applicants must consist of one or more local educational agencies; and one or more degree granting institutions of higher education; and not less than two other community organizations or entities, such as businesses, professional organizations, State agencies, institutions or agencies sponsoring programs authorized under subpart 4, or other public or private agencies or organizations. An applicant can only implement a 7-year grant if the project is designed to provide services through the students' first year of attending an institution of higher education (IHE).
Geographic Focus: All States, District of Columbia
Contact: Craig Pooler; (202) 453-6195; Craig.Pooler@ed.gov
Internet: www2.ed.gov/programs/gearup/index.html
Sponsor: U.S. Department of Education
400 Maryland Avenue, SW
Washington, D.C. 20202

UUA Actions of Public Witness Grants **2365**
The Fund for Unitarian Universalist Social Responsibility has matching grants available of up to $1,500 to congregations participating in actions of public witness. These matching grants support congregations mobilizing at critical times to take action in a broad range of arenas of social and environmental justice. These awards are available on a rolling basis, and are for projects where the urgency of the action required is outside the ordinary time constraints of the Association's regular grants.
Requirements: Challenge or matching grants are commonly granted to encourage Unitarian Universalist generosity, and to increase support for social action. Grants are typically made for one year. Second-year funding is possible after submitting a new proposal and a final (or interim) report. Third-year funding for the same project is unusual.
Restrictions: Grants are not made to individuals. Generally, grants are not given for equipment, capital campaigns, or endowments. Grants are not made for activities that are part of the ongoing work of Unitarian Universalist institutions. Grants may not be used as a pass-through from a congregation to a local non-profit organization, but may go towards enhancing Unitarian Universalist involvement in a project.
Geographic Focus: All States, Canada, Mexico
Amount of Grant: Up to 1,500 USD
Contact: Michelle A. Rediker, Grants Administrator; (617) 971-9600 or (617) 742-2100; fax (617) 742-0321; mrediker@uua.org or uufunding@gmail.com
Internet: www.uufunding.org/actions-of-public-witness.html
Sponsor: Unitarian Universalist Association
24 Farnsworth Street
Boston, MA 02210-1409

UUA Congregation-Based Community Organizing Grants **2366**
The Congregation-Based Community Organizing program provides matching Grants for congregations to participate in a CBCO organization, either for membership or for training. Applications are no longer accepted on a rolling deadline, but should be submitted by the regular Fund for Unitarian Universalist Social Responsibility annual postmark deadlines of March 15 for the Spring granting cycle and September 15 for the Fall granting cycle. Decisions are announced in June and December, respectively. The maximum grant amount is $20,000, while the average grant is $8,000.
Requirements: Challenge or matching grants are commonly granted to encourage Unitarian Universalist generosity, and to increase support for social action. Grants are typically made for one year. Second-year funding is possible after submitting a new proposal and a final (or interim) report. Third-year funding for the same project is unusual.

Restrictions: Grants are not made to individuals. Generally, grants are not given for equipment, capital campaigns, or endowments. Grants are not made for activities that are part of the ongoing work of Unitarian Universalist institutions. Grants may not be used as a pass-through from a congregation to a local non-profit organization, but may go towards enhancing Unitarian Universalist involvement in a project.
Geographic Focus: All States, Canada, Mexico
Date(s) Application is Due: Mar 15; Sep 15
Amount of Grant: Up to 20,000 USD
Contact: Michelle A. Rediker, Grants Administrator; (617) 971-9600 or (617) 742-2100; fax (617) 742-0321; mrediker@uua.org or uufunding@gmail.com
Internet: www.uufunding.org/congregation-based-community-organizing.html
Sponsor: Unitarian Universalist Association
24 Farnsworth Street
Boston, MA 02210-1409

UUA Fund Grants 2367

Grants are made to Unitarian Universalist organizations in the U.S., Mexico, and Canada that: grow and strengthen Unitarian Universalist institutions and community life; nurture and celebrate our liberal religious heritage; and encourage a generosity of spirit among Unitarian Universalists that is reflected in commitments of time, money and energy. Priority is given to innovative, challenging or experimental programs that will have wide denominational impact or that address needs unmet by the institutional structure of the denomination. The Association rarely makes grants for projects where the impact is limited to the applicant organization. Applications for conferences or meetings must detail measurable outcomes, products or services that will result from the event. Applications are not accepted on a rolling deadline basis, but should be submitted by the annual postmark deadlines of March 15 for the Spring granting cycle and September 15 for the Fall granting cycle. Decisions are announced in June and December, respectively. The maximum grant amount is $20,000, while the average grant is $8,000.
Requirements: Challenge or matching grants are commonly granted to encourage Unitarian Universalist generosity, and to increase support for social action. Grants are for one year. Second-year funding is possible after submitting a new proposal and a final (or interim) report. Third-year funding for the same project is unusual.
Restrictions: Grants are not made to individuals. Generally, grants are not awarded for equipment, building renovations or improvements, capital campaigns, endowments, or feasibility studies. Grants are not made for activities that are considered to be part of the ongoing work of Unitarian Universalist organizations or congregations.
Geographic Focus: All States, Canada, Mexico
Date(s) Application is Due: Mar 15; Sep 15
Amount of Grant: Up to 20,000 USD
Samples: Arlington Street Church, Boston, Massachusetts, $6,500 - to translate the new Visitors' Guide for Arlington Street Church's Tiffany Stained Glass Memorial Windows into five languages; Hungarian Unitarian Church/ Archives in Kolosva, Kolosvar, Romania, $5,000 - for a collaborative research project between the Unitarian Archivist in Kolozsv ar and an American Unitari an minister to document the story of Anna Eddy Richmond; Sacred Fire Unitarian Universalist, Carrboro, North Carolina, $9,000 - to continue to create and grow more convenanted communities across the country.
Contact: Michelle A. Rediker, Grants Administrator; (617) 971-9600 or (617) 742-2100; fax (617) 742-0321; mrediker@uua.org
Internet: www.uufunding.org/fund-for-unitarian-universalism.html
Sponsor: Unitarian Universalist Association
24 Farnsworth Street
Boston, MA 02210-1409

UUA International Fund Grants 2368

The Fund for International Unitarian Universalism makes grants to strengthen Unitarian Universalist organizations or projects working internationally. Awards are made to Unitarian Universalist organizations or projects working internationally to: promote the growth of Unitarian Universalist ideals and values; strengthen Unitarian Universalist institutions and community life; nurture and celebrate the free faith; and encourage a generosity among Unitarian Universalists that is reflected in commitments of time, money and energy. Priority is given to innovative, challenging or experimental programs or projects that address needs unmet by institutional structures. The Association prefers projects with plans for generating income from diverse sources, including contributions from members of the group applying. Challenge or matching grants are commonly granted to encourage Unitarian Universalist generosity, and to increase support for social action. Grants are typically made for one year. Second-year funding is possible after submitting a new proposal and a final (or interim) report. Third-year funding for the same project is unusual. The Fund accepts applications once a year, postmarked by March 15.
Requirements: Challenge or matching grants are commonly granted to encourage Unitarian Universalist generosity, and to increase support for social action. Grants are typically made for one year. Second-year funding is possible after submitting a new proposal and a final (or interim) report. Third-year funding for the same project is unusual.
Restrictions: Grants are not made to individuals. Generally, grants are not given for equipment, capital campaigns, or endowments. Grants are not made for activities that are part of the ongoing work of Unitarian Universalist institutions. Grants may not be used as a pass-through from a congregation to a local non-profit organization, but may go towards enhancing Unitarian Universalist involvement in a project.
Geographic Focus: All States, Canada, Mexico
Date(s) Application is Due: Mar 15; Sep 15
Amount of Grant: Up to 20,000 USD
Samples: David Ferenc Unitarian Youth Association, Kolosvar, Romania, $7,000 - to strengthen and celebrate the ties between young and old, the past and the future;

International Women's Convocation, Houston, Texas, $3,000 - to support the transition of the micro-finance project in Uganda to a community-based group with local leadership and to seek consultative status with the United Nations Economic and Social Council; Unitarian Union of North East India, Shillong, Meghalaya, India, $6,000 - for workshops, social gatherings, special worship services and discussions to develop a strong connection to Unitarian Universalist faith and beliefs.
Contact: Michelle A. Rediker, Grants Administrator; (617) 971-9600 or (617) 742-2100; fax (617) 742-0321; mrediker@uua.org
Internet: www.uufunding.org/fund-for-international-unitarian-universalism.html
Sponsor: Unitarian Universalist Association
24 Farnsworth Street
Boston, MA 02210-1409

UUA Just Society Fund Grants 2369

Just Society Fund grants are made to non-Unitarian Universalist groups in the U.S. and Canada that meet all three of the following criteria: uses community organizing to bring about systemic change leading to a more just society; mobilizes those who have been disenfranchised and excluded from resources, power and the right to self-determination; and has an active focused campaign to create systemic change. Priority is given to active, specific campaigns to create change in the economic, social, and political structures that affect their lives. The Association expects the organization's infrastructure, including leadership, membership and systems of accountability to be developed by the time of the application, and welcomes projects that are less likely to receive conventional funding because of the innovative or challenging nature of the work or the economic and social status of the constituency. The maximum grant is $15,000, though most awards are between $6,000 and $8,000. Applications are not accepted on a rolling deadline basis, but should be submitted by the annual postmark deadlines of March 15 for the Spring granting cycle and September 15 for the Fall granting cycle. Decisions are announced in June and December, respectively.
Requirements: Challenge or matching grants are commonly granted to encourage Unitarian Universalist generosity, and to increase support for social action. Grants are typically made for one year. Second-year funding is possible after submitting a new proposal and a final (or interim) report. Third-year funding for the same project is unusual.
Restrictions: The Association does not fund: social services; educational programs; advocacy projects; training of individuals; re-granting; equipment; capital campaigns; politically partisan efforts; educational institutions; medical or scientific research; or cultural programs. Grants are not made to individuals. The Association will consider funding films, publications, or curricula only if they are an integral part of a strategy of collective action for social change.
Geographic Focus: All States, Canada
Date(s) Application is Due: Mar 15; Sep 15
Amount of Grant: Up to 15,000 USD
Samples: Southern Center for Human Rights, Atlanta,Georgia, $12,500 - for a campaign organized by women prisoners to shut down the dilapidated prison, replace it with and improved facilities that include a nursery for babies born to incarcerated women and advocate for a system that promotes restorative justice; Alliance for Appalachia, Knoxville, Tennessee, $5,000 - for organizing to build local and regional power to link the issues of mountaintop removal, toxic pollution left by mining, safe water and the need for a healthy environment as a foundation for a healthy economy; Arab American Action Network, Chicago, Illinois, $10,000 - to organizing to end the use of Suspicious Activity Reports, which enable law enforcement to racially profile Arabs and Muslims.
Contact: Michelle A. Rediker, Grants Administrator; (617) 971-9600 or (617) 742-2100; fax (617) 742-0321; mrediker@uua.org
Internet: www.uufunding.org/fund-for-a-just-society.html
Sponsor: Unitarian Universalist Association
24 Farnsworth Street
Boston, MA 02210-1409

UUA Social Responsibility Grants 2370

Grants are made to Unitarian Universalist organizations in the U.S., Canada, and Mexico that: increase the direct involvement of Unitarian Universalists in service, advocacy and/or community organizing to create justice in the larger community; link Unitarian Universalists with the larger community; and foster a generosity of spirit and action in all aspects of Unitarian Universalist communities. Priority is given to: new programs and those at a point of significant growth; and work creating social and economic justice. The Association prefers projects with income from diverse sources and expect contributions from the members of the applicant organization. Applications are not accepted on a rolling deadline basis, but should be submitted by the annual postmark deadlines of March 15 for the Spring granting cycle and September 15 for the Fall granting cycle. Decisions are announced in June and December, respectively. The maximum grant amount is $20,000, while the average grant is $8,000.
Requirements: Challenge or matching grants are commonly granted to encourage Unitarian Universalist generosity, and to increase support for social action. Grants are typically made for one year. Second-year funding is possible after submitting a new proposal and a final (or interim) report. Third-year funding for the same project is unusual.
Restrictions: Grants are not made to individuals. Generally, grants are not given for equipment, capital campaigns, or endowments. Grants are not made for activities that are part of the ongoing work of Unitarian Universalist institutions. Grants may not be used as a pass-through from a congregation to a local non-profit organization, but may go towards enhancing Unitarian Universalist involvement in a project.
Geographic Focus: All States, Canada, Mexico
Date(s) Application is Due: Mar 15; Sep 15
Amount of Grant: Up to 20,000 USD

Samples: Church of Belfast, Belfast, Maine, $16,270 - for a program to lower crime and recidivism, foster the rehabilitation of offenders and support systemic change in the schools and criminal/juvenile justice systems; Black Lives Matter to Wisconsin, Brookfield, Wisconsin, $2,000 - in support of Beyond the Banner III, Walking the Walk workshop on taking action for racial justice; Michigan Unitarian Universalist Social Justice Network, Royal Oak, Michigan, $12,000 - to support Michigan Unitarian Universalist congregation's implementation of the Black Lives Matter Action of Immediate Witness program.
Contact: Michelle A. Rediker, Grants Administrator; (617) 971-9600 or (617) 742-2100; fax (617) 742-0321; mrediker@uua.org
Internet: www.uufunding.org/fund-for-uu-social-responsibility.html
Sponsor: Unitarian Universalist Association
24 Farnsworth Street
Boston, MA 02210-1409

V.V. Cooke Foundation Grants   2371

The V.V. Cooke Foundation awards grants to nonprofits throughout the State of Kentucky, with an emphasis on support of the Baptist Church and religious organizations, schools and higher education institutions, and medical education. Children and youth organizations also receive support. Types of funding include: general operating support; continuing support; annual campaigns; capital campaigns; building construction and renovation; equipment acquisition; program development; and professorships. Application deadlines are specified as January 15, April 15, July 15, and October 15.
Requirements: Grants are awarded to nonprofit 501(c)3 organizations in Kentucky.
Restrictions: Grants are not awarded to individuals or for general endowment funds, scholarships, fellowships, or loans.
Geographic Focus: Kentucky
Date(s) Application is Due: Jan 15; Apr 15; Jul 15; Oct 15
Amount of Grant: 100 - 50,000 USD
Contact: Carl Thomas, Executive Director; (502) 901-3179; carl.vvcooke@gmail.com
Sponsor: V.V. Cooke Foundation
P.O. Box 7664, 220 Mount Mercy Drive
Pewee Valley, KY 40056-0202

Valley-Wide Health Systems Nurse Family Partnerships   2372

Valley-Wide Health Systems offers several special programs that complement its various service lines. These programs are designed to enhance the overall patient experience offered by its health centers. The Systems work to assist every member of the family. Its Nurse Family Partnership funding program is a nationwide, free, voluntary program for low-income, first-time mothers. Nurse Home Visitors offer program services to mothers and their children throughout all six counties of the San Luis Valley, plus Fremont and Custer counties, and serve clients who are currently seeing area providers. Program services begin in pregnancy and proceed until the child's second birthday. NFP provides mothers and their families (as desired or appropriate) with important education by nurse home visitors. The program has three primary goals: improve pregnancy outcomes by helping women improve behavior related to substance use, nutrition and prenatal care; improve child health and development by promoting responsible and competent care of children; and improve parent's life course by promoting prevention of subsequent unintended pregnancy, completion of education, finding employment, and strengthening support systems. Nurse home visitors work with families on personal health; environmental health and safety; quality of care giving for infant and toddler; maternal life course development; and formal and informal support systems.
Requirements: Available to residents living within the San Luis Valley, plus Fremont and Custer counties.
Geographic Focus: Colorado
Contact: Jeanne Darricades; (719) 587-1001 or (719) 589-5161; info@vwhs.org
Internet: vwhs.org/special-programs/nurse-family-partnership/
Sponsor: Valley-Wide Health Systems
128 Market Street
Alamosa, CO 81101

Vanderburgh Community Foundation Men's Fund Grants   2373

The Men's Fund of Vanderburgh County focuses the efforts of men philanthropists to create positive social change by funding projects that address current needs in our community. Its primary purpose is to improve the quality of life in Vanderburgh County by collectively funding significant grants to charitable initiatives. Grant proposals are accepted once each year. Grants are normally given as one time support of a project but may be considered for additional support for expansions or outgrowths of an initial project. The annual deadline for application submission is February 20.
Requirements: Projects must address the needs which support the Fund's mission by providing opportunities, encouragement, knowledge, information, and hope for the community's men and boys. The Men's Fund welcomes proposals from non-profit organizations that are tax-exempt under sections 501(c)3 and 509(a) of the Internal Revenue Code and from governmental agencies serving Vanderburgh County, Indiana, men and boys. Proposals from other non-profit organizations that address issues facing men and boys in the county may be accepted. Proposals submitted by an entity under the auspices of another agency must include a written statement signed by the agency's board president on behalf of the board of directors agreeing to act as the entity's fiscal sponsor, to receive grant monies if awarded, and to oversee the proposed project.
Restrictions: Project areas not considered for funding include the following: projects or programs of organizations that are not committed to gender equity; funding to reduce or retire debt; projects that focus solely on the spiritual needs and growth of a church congregation or members of other religious organizations; political parties or campaigns; operating costs not directly related to the proposed project (the organization's general

operating expenses including equipment, staff salary, rent, and utilities); event sponsorships, annual appeals, and membership contributions; travel expenses for groups or individuals such as bands, sports teams, or classes; scholarships or other grants to individuals.
Geographic Focus: Indiana
Date(s) Application is Due: Feb 20
Amount of Grant: 1,000 - 10,000 USD
Contact: Sarah Wagner, Regional Director of Development; (812) 422-1245; fax (812) 429-0840; swagner@communityfoundationalliance.org
Internet: www.communityfoundationalliance.org/vanderburgh/mens-fund/
Sponsor: Vanderburgh County Community Foundation
401 South East 6th Street, Suite 203
Evansville, IN 47713

Vanderburgh Community Foundation Recreation Grants   2374

The Vanderburgh Community Foundation is a nonprofit, public charity created for the people of Vanderburgh County, Indiana. The Foundation allows nonprofits to fulfill their missions by strengthening their ability to meet community needs through grants that assist charitable programs, address community issues, support community agencies, launch community initiatives, and support leadership development. The grant cycle is open year-round, and funding requests will be reviewed throughout the year with quarterly deadlines as follows: March 1; June 1; September 1; and December 1. Grants in the area of Recreation include projects aimed at improving and promoting recreational and leisure activities, parks, and community sporting events and activities. Samples of previously funded projects are available at the website.
Requirements: The Foundation gives primarily to 501(c)3 tax-exempt organizations in Vanderburgh County, Indiana. Organizations must first submit a preliminary proposal to determine their eligibility. Proposals will be reviewed within thirty days, then select applicants will receive a formal invitation to submit a full proposal.
Restrictions: The following project areas are not considered for funding: religious organizations for religious purposes; political parties or campaigns; endowment creation or debt reduction; capital campaign; operating costs not directly related to the proposed project; annual appeals or membership contributions; and travel requests for groups or individuals such as bands, sports teams, or classes.
Geographic Focus: Indiana
Date(s) Application is Due: Mar 1; Jun 1; Sep 1; Dec 1
Amount of Grant: 1,000 - 10,000 USD
Contact: Sarah Wagner, Regional Director of Development; (812) 422-1245; fax (812) 429-0840; swagner@communityfoundationalliance.org
Internet: www.communityfoundationalliance.org/vanderburgh/program-areas/
Sponsor: Vanderburgh County Community Foundation
401 South East 6th Street, Suite 203
Evansville, IN 47713

Vanderburgh Community Foundation Youth Development Grants   2375

The Vanderburgh Community Foundation is a nonprofit, public charity created for the people of Vanderburgh County, Indiana. The Foundation allows nonprofits to fulfill their missions by strengthening their ability to meet community needs through grants that assist charitable programs, address community issues, support community agencies, launch community initiatives, and support leadership development. The grant cycle is open year-round, and funding requests will be reviewed throughout the year with quarterly deadlines as follows: March 1; June 1; September 1; and December 1. Grants in the area of Youth Development include activities that strengthen the family unit, help children grow and develop, foster youth sports and athletics, support the YMCA, and support daycare-related issues. Samples of previously funded projects are available at the website.
Requirements: The Foundation gives primarily to 501(c)3 tax-exempt organizations in Vanderburgh County, Indiana. Organizations must first submit a preliminary proposal to determine their eligibility. Proposals will be reviewed within thirty days, then select applicants will receive a formal invitation to submit a full proposal.
Restrictions: The following project areas are not considered for funding: religious organizations for religious purposes; political parties or campaigns; endowment creation or debt reduction; capital campaign; operating costs not directly related to the proposed project; annual appeals or membership contributions; and travel requests for groups or individuals such as bands, sports teams, or classes.
Geographic Focus: Indiana
Date(s) Application is Due: Mar 1; Jun 1; Sep 1; Dec 1
Amount of Grant: 1,000 - 10,000 USD
Contact: Sarah Wagner, Regional Director of Development; (812) 422-1245; fax (812) 429-0840; swagner@communityfoundationalliance.org
Internet: www.communityfoundationalliance.org/vanderburgh/program-areas/
Sponsor: Vanderburgh County Community Foundation
401 South East 6th Street, Suite 203
Evansville, IN 47713

Vanderburgh County Community Foundation Women's Fund Grants   2376

The Vanderburgh Community Foundation Women's Fund is about strong, caring, and focused women determined to make a difference. Throughout history, women have shaped the world as national leaders, advocates for social justice, scientists, authors, teachers, and healers. Every day, women make positive contributions to the world, and when visionary women work together around a common cause, they have an even greater impact – like the Women's Fund. In 2006, a group of visionary women started the Women's Fund as a permanent resource to support local programs that give opportunities, encouragement, knowledge and hope to our community's women and girls. As the endowment grows, it will be used to make yearly grants supporting a variety of resources serving women of all ages, such as programs that prevent domestic violence, secure family-supporting jobs, promote health and education and, perhaps most importantly, develop confidence. Grant proposals are accepted once each year. Grants are normally given as one time support of a project but may be considered for additional support for expansions or outgrowths of an initial project. The annual deadline for application submission is February 20.

Requirements: Projects must address the needs which support the Fund's mission by providing opportunities, encouragement, knowledge, information, and hope for the community's women and girls. The Women's Fund welcomes proposals from non-profit organizations that are tax-exempt under sections 501(c)3 and 509(a) of the Internal Revenue Code and from governmental agencies serving Vanderburgh County, Indiana, women and girls. Proposals from other non-profit organizations that address issues facing women and girls in the county may be accepted. Proposals submitted by an entity under the auspices of another agency must include a written statement signed by the agency's board president on behalf of the board of directors agreeing to act as the entity's fiscal sponsor, to receive grant monies if awarded, and to oversee the proposed project.

Restrictions: Project areas not considered for funding include the following: projects or programs of organizations that are not committed to gender equity; funding to reduce or retire debt; projects that focus solely on the spiritual needs and growth of a church congregation or members of other religious organizations; political parties or campaigns; operating costs not directly related to the proposed project (the organization's general operating expenses including equipment, staff salary, rent, and utilities); event sponsorships, annual appeals, and membership contributions; travel expenses for groups or individuals such as bands, sports teams, or classes; scholarships or other grants to individuals.

Geographic Focus: Indiana
Amount of Grant: 1,000 - 10,000 USD
Contact: Sarah Wagner, Regional Director of Development; (812) 422-1245; fax (812) 429-0840; swagner@communityfoundationalliance.org
Internet: www.communityfoundationalliance.org/vanderburgh/vanderburgh-womens-fund/
Sponsor: Vanderburgh County Community Foundation
401 South East 6th Street, Suite 203
Evansville, IN 47713

Van Kampen Boyer Molinari Charitable Foundation Grants   2377

The Van Kampen Boyer Molinari Charitable Foundation primarily provides grants in the states of Illinois, Michigan, California, New Jersey, and New York (although support is sometimes given outside of these states). The Foundation's primary fields of interest include: the arts; athletics and sports (primarily equestrianism); cancer research; children and youth services; education; health organizations; specialty hospitals; and human services. Target populations include children and youth, and awards range from $5,000 to $70,000. There is no specific application form, so applicants should provide a letter detailing their program and budgetary needs. There are no deadlines with which to adhere.

Geographic Focus: All States
Amount of Grant: 5,000 - 75,000 USD
Samples: Dressage Kids, Cheshire, Connecticut, $61,521 - youth development programs; Every Women's Place, Muskegon, Michigan, $29,135 - community development program; Horse Sports by the Bay, Traverse City, Michigan - horse show operations and promotions.
Contact: Joan M. Mack, President; (616) 402-2238 or (561) 707-2337
Sponsor: Van Kampen Boyer Molinari Charitable Foundation
5440 East Farr Road
Fruitport, MI 49415-9751

Vermillion County Community Foundation Grants   2378

The role of the Vermillion County Community Foundation is to offer financial assistance to projects that preserve the area's history, enrich lives, and provide for the future of Vermillion County. Grant proposal information is available at the Foundation's office.

Geographic Focus: Indiana
Samples: Kappa Delta Phi Sorority, eyeglasses for needy children; Little Italy Festival, entertainment; Central Elementary School, bully program materials; Cayuga Christian Church, Thanksgiving food baskets.
Contact: Larry Lynn, Board President; (765) 832-8665; lecrly72@hughes.net
Internet: www.thevccf.org/communit.htm
Sponsor: Vermillion County Community Foundation
407 South Main Street
Clinton, IN 47842

Vernon K. Krieble Foundation Grants   2379

The Foundation was established in 1984 by the family of Professor Vernon K. Krieble, scientist, educator, inventor, and entrepreneur. Recognizing that the Foundation's assets are the product of a free and democratic society, the founders considered it fitting that those assets be used "to further democratic capitalism and the preserve and promote a society of free, educated, healthy and creative individuals." The Foundation offers support to non-profit charitable and educational organizations that demonstrate leadership in furthering the original objectives, so that future generations can aspire to and achieve their full potential in a free society. Awards range from $2,500 to $50,000. There are no deadlines.

Requirements: Nonprofit 501(c)3 organizations are eligible. Funding is provided only for those organizations and projects which involve public policy research and education on issues supporting the preservation, and in some cases the restoration, or freedom and democracy in the United States, according to the principles of the Founding Fathers. Written proposals should include a summary of the project, the project budget, the amount requested, the qualifications of individuals involved, and a copy of the organization's Internal Revenue Service determination letter.

Geographic Focus: All States

Samples: Foundation for West Hartford Schools, West Hartford, CT, $2,500 - general support; Leadership Program of the Rockies, Denver, CO, $50,000 - general support; and Atlas Economic Research Foundation, Arlington, VA, $25,000 - general support.
Contact: Helen E. Krieble, President; (303) 758-3956; fax (303) 488-0068
Internet: www.krieble.org/grants
Sponsor: Vernon K. Krieble Foundation
1777 S Harrison Street, Suite 807
Denver, CO 80210

Victor E. Speas Foundation Grants   2380

The Victor E. Speas Foundation was established in 1947 to provide medical care for the needy, to further Medical Research and to support and promote quality educational, cultural, human services and health care programming. The Speas Foundation supports organizations that serve the residents of Kansas City, Missouri. Grants from the Trust are 1 year in duration. Award amounts typically range from $5,000 to $250,000.

Requirements: Applicants must have 501(c)3 tax-exempt status and serve the residents of Kansas City, Missouri. Grant requests for general operating support and program support will be considered. Applications will be submitted online through the Bank of America website. A grant report is required within 1 year of the grant application date, regardless of whether all of the funds have been spent.

Restrictions: Grant requests for capital support will not be considered. The foundation does not support requests from individuals, organizations attempting to influence policy through direct lobbying, or any political campaigns.

Geographic Focus: Missouri
Date(s) Application is Due: Jul 31
Amount of Grant: 5,000 - 250,000 USD
Samples: YMCA of Greater Kansas City, North Kansas City, Missouri, $250,000 - Awarded for Downtown YMCA/Kirk Family Community Center - Coordinated Clinical Community Care (2018); Kansas City University of Medicine and Biosciences, Kansas City, Missouri, $250,000 - Awarded for Center for Medical and Surgical Simulation (2018); Mattie Rhodes Center, Kansas City, Missouri, $200,000 - Awarded for Mattie Rhodes Cultural Arts Community Center (2018).
Contact: Tony Twyman, Senior Philanthropic Client Manager; (816) 292-4342; mo.grantmaking@bankofamerica.com or tony.twyman@bofa.com
Internet: www.bankofamerica.com/philanthropic/foundation/?fnId=130
Sponsor: Victor E. Speas Foundation
1200 Main Street, 14th Floor
Kansas City, MO 64121-9119

Victoria S. and Bradley L. Geist Foundation Enhancement Grants   2381

The purpose of the Victoria S. and Bradley L. Geist Foundation's Enhancements for Foster Children program is to enhance the lives of foster children by providing items and services that allow them to enjoy a quality of life similar to that of their peers. The funds are offered in the belief that every child is special and that their growth should be nurtured and celebrated. Grants range from $5,000 to $50,000. Grantees may propose an administrative fee for administering these funds.

Requirements: Tax-exempt Hawaii organizations are eligible to apply. This includes nonprofit organizations, 501(c)3 organizations, religious organizations that are exempt from taxation, and units of government.

Restrictions: Enhancements funds are not intended for basic living expenses such as housing, groceries, medical and dental care, and ordinary tuition expenses.

Geographic Focus: Hawaii
Date(s) Application is Due: Sep 15
Amount of Grant: 5,000 - 50,000 USD
Contact: Michelle Kauhane; (808) 566-5545 or (888) 731-3863; mkauhane@hcf-hawaii.org
Lisha Kimura, Grants Administrator; (808) 566-5537 or (888) 731-3863, ext. 537; fax (808) 521-6286; lkimura@hcf-hawaii.org
Internet: www.hawaiicommunityfoundation.org/grants/victoria-s-and-bradley-l-geist-foundation-enhancements
Sponsor: Victoria S. and Bradley L. Geist Foundation
827 Fort Street Mall
Honolulu, HI 96813-4317

Victoria S. and Bradley L. Geist Foundation Grants Supporting Foster Care   2382
and Their Caregivers

Victoria and Bradley Geist were single children who grew up in non-traditional families. They created their successes in life through their own personal efforts. The Geists were quiet philanthropists who gave anonymously and generously. During their lives, they planned to use the wealth they had accumulated to establish the Victoria S. and Bradley L. Geist Foundation. The Foundation wishes to support foster children and their caregivers. The Foundation recognizes that the appropriate resources and support for foster children and their caregivers contribute to healthier and happier lives. The Foundation offers this Request for Proposals to provide meaningful support for efforts that will result in supportive homes and experiences for Hawaii's foster children.

Requirements: Tax-exempt Hawaii organizations are eligible to apply. This includes nonprofit organizations, 501(c)3 organizations, religious organizations that are exempt from taxation, and units of government.

Restrictions: Requests are considered in relationship to the size of the organization's operating budget. Capital requests and endowments will not be funded.

Geographic Focus: Hawaii
Date(s) Application is Due: Jan 15; May 14; Sep 15
Amount of Grant: 10,000 - 100,000 USD

Contact: Michelle Kauhane, Senior Vice President; (808) 566-5545 or (888) 731-3863; mkauhane@hcf-hawaii.org

Lisha Kimura, Grants Administrator; (808) 566-5537 or (888) 731-3863, ext. 537; fax (808) 521-6286; lkimura@hcf-hawaii.org

Internet: www.hawaiicommunityfoundation.org/grants/victoria-s-and-bradley-l-geist-foundation-supporting-foster-children-and-their-caregivers

Sponsor: Victoria S. and Bradley L. Geist Foundation

827 Fort Street Mall

Honolulu, HI 96813-4317

Victoria S. and Bradley L. Geist Foundation Grants Supporting Transitioning Foster Youth   2383

The Victoria S. and Bradley L. Geist Foundation recognizes that transitioning foster youth will succeed and give back to the community when they have positive and supportive peer and adult networks, opportunities to pursue employment and post-secondary education and training, and basic supports available in the community when needed. Preference will be given to efforts that seek youth input and engagement in initial and ongoing program development and work in one or more of the following areas: effectively connect youth with opportunities and community resources for employment and post-secondary education and training; support positive, lifelong adult connections; support positive peer networks; support youth efforts in community service and in advocacy efforts to improve the child welfare system; and support youth in meeting basic needs. Grants usually range from $10,000 to $100,000 per year.

Requirements: Tax-exempt Hawaii organizations are eligible to apply. This includes nonprofit organizations, 501(c)3 organizations, religious organizations that are exempt from taxation, and units of government.

Restrictions: Requests are considered in relationship to the size of the organization's operating budget. Capital requests and endowments will not be funded.

Geographic Focus: Hawaii

Date(s) Application is Due: Jan 15; May 14; Sep 15

Amount of Grant: 10,000 - 100,000 USD

Contact: Michelle Kauhane, Senior Vice President; (808) 566-5545 or (888) 731-3863; mkauhane@hcf-hawaii.org

Lisha Kimura, Grants Administrator; (808) 566-5537 or (888) 731-3863, ext. 537; fax (808) 521-6286; lkimura@hcf-hawaii.org

Internet: www.hawaiicommunityfoundation.org/grants/victoria-s-and-bradley-l-geist-foundation-supporting-transitioning-foster-youth

Sponsor: Victoria S. and Bradley L. Geist Foundation

827 Fort Street Mall

Honolulu, HI 96813-4317

Vigneron Memorial Fund Grants   2384

The Vigneron Memorial Fund was established in 1959 to support charitable organizations that work to improve the lives of physically disabled children and adults. Preference is given to charitable organizations that serve children in the city of Providence or the town of Narragansett, Rhode Island. The majority of grants from the Vigneron Memorial Fund are 1 year in duration. Award amounts typically go up to $15,000.

Requirements: Applicants must have 501(c)3 tax-exempt status and serve communities in either Providence or Narragansett, Rhode Island. Applications will be submitted online through the Bank of America website. A grant report is required within 1 year of the grant application date, regardless of whether all of the funds have been spent.

Restrictions: The fund does not support requests from individuals, organizations attempting to influence policy through direct lobbying, or any political campaigns.

Geographic Focus: Rhode Island

Date(s) Application is Due: Jul 1

Amount of Grant: Up to 15,000 USD

Samples: Ronald McDonald House of Providence, Providence, Rhode Island, $12,000 - Awarded for Adopt a Room program (2018); Rhode Island Hospital Foundation, Providence, Rhode Island, $12,000 - Awarded for Expanding Pediatric Ophthalmology Clinic Assessment and Treatment Capabilities (2018); United Methodist Health Care Center, East Providence, Rhode Island, $10,000 - Awarded for purchase of Rehab/Comfort chairs for skilled nursing care residents (2018).

Contact: Perpetua Campbell, Market Philanthropic Administrator; (866) 778-6859; ma.ri.grantmaking@bankofamerica.com or ma.ri.grantmaking@ustrust.com

Internet: www.bankofamerica.com/philanthropic/foundation/?fnId=67

Sponsor: Vigneron Memorial Fund

P.O. Box 1802

Providence, RI 02901-1802

Virginia Commission for the Arts Artists in Education Residency Grants   2385

The primary purpose of Virginia Commission for the Arts Artists in Education Residency Grants is to place professional artists of various artistic disciplines in residencies for elementary and secondary students and their teachers. Residencies must be designed to reinforce the arts instruction provided by the school/school division. This program provides elementary and secondary students, teachers, and the community at large opportunities to work with professional artists. The residencies enhance arts instruction in the school curriculum and highlight the importance of the arts as essential components of a complete education and a valued part of community life. Each residency must include workshops for a core group of students, at least one formal teacher workshop conducted by the artist, and community performances/exhibitions and activities/workshops. Residencies of ten days or more must also include studio time for the artists. If any residency activities take place outside of the regular school day, transportation should be available so that all students can participate. Generally, the Commission will award no more than 50 percent of the total cash

cost of the residency program. First-time applicants, however, may request up to two-thirds (2/3) of the total eligible cash cost of the residency. Only the following residency expenses are eligible for funding: salary for the resident artist(s); consumable materials for the artist's workshops; consumable materials for the workshop participants; travel (standard rate per mile) for the residency artist(s); program documentation (audio or video tapes, slides); and honorarium and travel expenses for the artist(s) for one on-site pre-residency planning day (to take place during the fiscal year of the grant award and prior to the residency).

Requirements: Virginia elementary and secondary schools which meet the Basic Eligibility criteria are eligible to apply for funding through this program. Private, federally tax-exempt schools that are in compliance with the Civil Rights Act and the Rehabilitation Act may also submit applications. School divisions may also apply on behalf of several schools; however, they must comply with all Commission requirements regarding the minimum length of each residency, residency components, on-site coordinator, etc. Tax-exempt arts, service, and civic organizations may work in partnership with the local school(s) in planning and implementing the residency program.

Restrictions: Grant funds may not be used for teachers presently working within the school/ school division or the organization/institution. Funds from other Commission programs may not be used to match any portion of residency income. Generally the Commission will not fund the same type of residency and/or the same artist(s) in the same school or school division for more than three years. Applications which involve the same discipline in the same school division with many of the same artists must include an explanation as to how this program differs substantially from past programs and why the same discipline or artist was selected.

Geographic Focus: Virginia

Contact: Cathy Welborn, Program Coordinator; (804) 225-3132; fax (804) 225-4327; catherine.welborn@arts.virginia.gov

Internet: www.arts.virginia.gov/grants/strengthening/residency_grants.html

Sponsor: Virginia Commission for the Arts

223 Governor Street, 2nd Floor

Richmond, VA 23219-2010

Virginia Foundation for the Humanities Folklife Apprenticeships   2386

The Virginia Folklife Program was established in 1989 as part of the Virginia Foundation for the Humanities (VFH) in order to sustain, preserve, and pass forward the diverse folk traditions of Virginia. The Folklife Apprenticeship Program annually awards eight nine-month apprenticeships each year. Applications will be judged on the following criteria: traditional nature of the proposed art or skill; expertise of the master artist; demonstrated level of commitment by the master artist and the apprentice to the apprenticeship; potential impact of the apprenticeship on the continued vitality of the tradition; relevance and importance of the tradition to the cultural history of Virginia; and the feasibility of the work plan and the coherence of the overall apprenticeship. More detailed information is available at the foundation website along with a downloadable application form and guidelines (Word). The application must be completed by both the master and apprentice and mailed to the contact information given. The packet must be postmarked on or prior to the deadline date. Deadlines may vary from year to year. Prospective applicants are encouraged to verify current deadline dates at the website or by contacting the foundation.

Requirements: The Virginia Folklife Apprenticeship Program welcomes applications for apprenticeships in all forms of Virginia's traditional, expressive culture. The master artist and apprentice should both be residents of Virginia. If one or both of the participants reside outside of Virginia, a compelling case must be made regarding the connection of the applicants to Virginia, and the importance of their proposed traditional skill to Virginia culture. It is also preferred, though not required, that masters and apprentices belong to the same cultural community.

Geographic Focus: Virginia

Date(s) Application is Due: Jun 30

Amount of Grant: Up to 2,300 USD

Samples: Sammy Shelor (master) and Ashley Nale (apprentice), Meadows of Dan, Virginia - bluegrass banjo; Dave Young (master) and Yvonne V. Young (apprentice), Waynesboro, Virginia - cobbling; Dudley Biddlecomb (master) and Peter Hedlund (apprentice), Fairport, Virginia - oyster aquaculture.

Contact: Jon Lohman, Director, Virginia Folklife Program; (434) 243-7030 or (434) 924-3296; fax (434) 296-4714; folklife@virginia.edu

Internet: virginiafolklife.org/apprentice-program/about-the-program/

Sponsor: Virginia Foundation for the Humanities

145 Ednam Drive

Charlottesville, VA 22903-4629

Virginia Foundation for the Humanities Open Grants   2387

The Virginia Foundation for the Humanities (VFH) was established in 1974 as a nonprofit organization dedicated to promoting the humanities, and to using the humanities to address issues of broad public concern. Since 1974, the VFH has awarded more than 3,000 grants, supporting tens of thousands of separate activities, and serving audiences in every city and county in Virginia. Goals of the VFH grant program are as follows: to encourage the development of high-quality educational programs in the humanities; to support accessible programs that reach the broadest possible audience in Virginia; to support the work of humanities institutions - museums, libraries, historical societies, colleges, and universities - as well as other non-profit organizations working within the humanities; to explore the stories that define Virginia and its people; and to address the issues that are most important to communities in Virginia. Projects supported include exhibits, public forums and discussions, media programs (film, video, radio, and digital media), publications, research, teachers' institutes and seminars, oral history projects, lectures and conferences, and other kinds of programs that draw on the resources of the humanities, address important issues, and enrich the cultural life of the state. The program names six key-priority areas of interest:

Books, Reading, and Literacy; Rights and Responsibilities; Media and Culture; Violence and Community; Science, Technology, and Society; and Virginia History. Other identified areas of interest are teacher-education programs (especially those related to Virginia's Standards of Learning); African-American history and culture; Native-American history and culture; history and culture of minority communities in Virginia; Virginia's folklife and traditional culture(s); and the future of rural Virginia. The foundation's interest is not confined to only these topics. Open Grant applications are usually considered in three annual grant cycles with deadlines of October 15, February 1, and May 1. Applications should be submitted via the VFH online system (available at the foundation's website) which requires as a first step, creation of an account and password. Grant guidelines are available at the website in downloadable Word format. All applicants are urged to contact the staff prior to submission of their proposals. Draft proposals are strongly encouraged and are recommended to be submitted at least three weeks prior to the deadline to allow time for a thorough staff review.

Requirements: Any incorporated non-profit organization in Virginia is eligible to apply. Incorporated non-profit organizations based outside of Virginia are also eligible if their project deals with a subject directly related to Virgina and a significant audience within the state is anticipated. All VFH grants must be matched with at least an equal amount of cost share, which can be in the form of cash or in-kind contributions from non-Federal sources. Sources and amounts of anticipated cost share should be indicated at the time of the proposal.

Restrictions: VFH Grants may not be used to support the following: advocacy or political action programs that promote a particular solution or point of view; creative or performing arts, unless they are used in a supporting role to enhance discussion of issues or interpretation; research or writing unless these are integral to programs having a direct public audience; subvention of publications; courses for credit, except those designed especially for teachers; acquisition of equipment; building construction, restoration, or preservation; meals, other than necessary travel expenses for program personnel; international travel; indirect costs; and projects whose primary audience is children or youth.

Geographic Focus: All States, Canada
Date(s) Application is Due: Feb 1; May 1; Oct 15
Amount of Grant: Up to 10,000 USD
Samples: Southern Memorial Association, Lynchburg, Virginia - Remembering Tinbridge Hill publication project; Living Archives, New York, New York - The Loving Story film documentary project; Eastern Shore of Virginia Historical Society, Onancock, Virginia - Stories from the Shore oral history project.
Contact: David Bearinger, Director of Grants and Public Programs; (434) 924-3296; fax (434) 296-4714; dab@virginia.edu
Jeanne Nicholson Siler, (434) 924-3296; fax (434) 296-4714; vhfgrants@virginia.edu
Internet: virginiahumanities.org/grants/
Sponsor: Virginia Foundation for the Humanities
145 Ednam Drive
Charlottesville, VA 22903-4629

Virginia W. Kettering Foundation Grants   2388

The Virginia W. Kettering Foundation, a private family foundation in Dayton, Ohio, was activated in 2003 when Virginia Kettering passed away at the age of 95. To continue her legacy of confident determination and passionate commitment to the Dayton area, Virginia Kettering directed the stewards of her foundation to support charitable organizations for charitable purposes within Montgomery, Greene, Clark, Miami, Darke, Preble, Butler and Warren Counties. The Foundation's Distribution Committee meets biannually (April and October) to make funding decisions. Primary areas of support include: arts, culture and humanities; education; environment; health and medical needs; human services; and public and societal benefit. There are two annual deadlines for invited applicants: March 15 and September 15.

Requirements: 501(c)3 organizations located in, or that serve, the counties of Montgomery, Greene, Clark, Miami, Darke, Preble, Butler and Warren in Ohio.

Restrictions: A Request Summary will not be accepted for any of the following purposes: religious organizations for religious purposes; public elementary or secondary schools or public school districts; multi-year grants; grants or loans to individuals; tickets, advertising or sponsorships of fundraising events; efforts to carry on propaganda or otherwise attempt to influence legislation; or activities of 509(a)3 Type III Supporting Organizations.
Geographic Focus: Ohio
Date(s) Application is Due: Mar 15; Sep 15
Amount of Grant: 5,000 - 50,000 USD
Contact: Judith M. Thompson, Executive Director; (973) 228-1021; fax (888) 719-1185; info@ketteringfamilyphilanthropies.org
Internet: www.cfketteringfamilies.com/vwk/application-process
Sponsor: Virginia W. Kettering Foundation
40 North Main Street, #1480
Dayton, OH 45423

Volkswagen Group of America Corporate Contributions Grants   2389

The Volkswagen Group of America Corporate Contributions Grant program accepts proposals broadly from programs servicing needs in healthcare, wellness, children, medical research, education and diversity. Support is primarily available to areas of company operations in Washington, D.C., Tennessee, and Virginia. The Corporation's primary areas of interest at the current time include: arts and culture; health and health care; human service programs; vocational education; and youth programs and development. These awards typically take the form of sponsorships and general operating support. There are no specific deadlines for application submission, so interested organizations should begin by forwarding a letter of application providing a program overview, current request details, and budgetary needs.

Requirements: The review committee does meet quarterly to go over proposals received, and considers the type of organization, its mission, and the intended use of the funds.
Restrictions: Grants are available to 501(c)3 organizations only.
Geographic Focus: District of Columbia, Tennessee, Virginia
Amount of Grant: 1,000 - 2,500 USD
Contact: Community Giving Administrator; (248) 754-5000; philanthropy@vw.com
Internet: www.volkswagengroupofamerica.com/community
Sponsor: Volkswagen Group of America
2200 Ferdinand Porsche Drive
Herndon, VA 20171

Volvo Adventure Environmental Awards   2390

The Volvo Adventure Environmental Award is for teams of between two and five young people working on a practical action project that will improve their school or community environment. The young people aged 13 to 16 should be devising action plans to help their environment under the following five headings: biodiversity - helping animals and plants in the community or school; waste - reduction, reuse, and recycle; water - conserve or improve water quality in the community or school; transport - travel (environmental impact); and energy - reduce energy use or make it more sustainable. The best entry from each country will be asked to join an international conference to present their ideas in Sweden, and where they can win: 1st place = $10,000, 2nd = $6,000, and 3rd = $4,000. All of the ideas and action plans will be published and presented to the United Nations Environment Program.

Requirements: Applicant groups must meet the following criteria: have (or have plans to start) an environmental project in the team's school or local community; team is writing and implementing a practical action plan that will improve the team's school or community environment; and team has at least one adult who can act as a referee for the group.
Restrictions: Projects must be submitted in English.
Geographic Focus: All States, All Countries
Date(s) Application is Due: Jan 31
Amount of Grant: 4,000 - 10,000 USD
Contact: Geno Effler; (949) 341-6715 or (949) 351-1495; geffler@volvocars.com
Internet: www.volvoadventure.org/guidelines.aspx
Sponsor: Volvo Cars of North America
One Premier Place
Irvine, CA 92618

Volvo Bob the Bunny's Cartoon Competition   2391

Bob the Bunny's competition is aimed at younger adventurers aged between 10 to 12 years old at the time that the competition opens on July 1. To enter, applicants first form a team of one to three members, identify a local environmental issue, and create an A4 cartoon or storyboard illustrating the issue and actions that you might take to solve it. The submissions should be sent to Volvo before the competition deadline of February 28 each year. Before entering, students and teachers are advised to review the Environmental Journey, a web-based resource that introduces basic environmental knowledge in a colourful and interactive way. The main purpose of the training is to raise students' awareness about environmental issues, and their motivation to care for our environment. The Environmental Journey can be used as part of your environmental studies, or as support for a Volvo Adventure project.
Geographic Focus: All States
Date(s) Application is Due: Feb 28
Contact: Geno Effler; (949) 341-6715 or (949) 351-1495; geffler@volvocars.com
Internet: www.volvoadventure.org/home.aspx
Sponsor: Volvo Cars of North America
One Premier Place
Irvine, CA 92618

VSA/Metlife Connect All Grants   2392

VSA and MetLife Foundation have designed the Arts Connect All funding opportunity to encourage arts organizations to create or enhance multi-session, inclusive education programs by strengthening partnerships with local public schools. The goals of Arts Connect All are the following: enable more students with disabilities to experience social, cognitive, and cultural development through arts learning alongside their peers without disabilities; create educational access and inclusion in the arts for students with disabilities; and document the contributions that arts organizations make to inclusive education in public schools. VSA and MetLife Foundation invite proposals from arts organizations creating or enhancing inclusive educational programs that undertake all of the following: incorporate inclusive teaching practices; provide access to students with all types of disabilities; develop social, cognitive, and artistic skills; involve people with disabilities in planning and implementation; build staff, teacher, and/or artist knowledge and skill of inclusive practices; and collaborate with public schools, actively engaging students, parents, and school administrators. A maximum of 10 awards of up to $15,000 will be given to selected organizations. Examples of appropriate use of funds may include, but are not limited to: expanding existing accessibility programs into educational efforts, program development support, knowledge and skill building of inclusive practices, and promotional/outreach efforts to expand audience. Grants will be awarded based on their ability to address the following: identify, assess, and address constituent and community need; collaborate at a high level with public schools; model innovative and multi-modal approaches for inclusion of people with disabilities; involve people with disabilities in the planning and implementation of educational programming; increase access to program activities, content, and materials by everyone, including students with or without disabilities; implement evaluation strategies that investigate the relationship between program goals, program activities, and the development of participant social, cognitive, and artistic skills; and; and deliver the program as articulated in the application packet. The application and additional guidelines for the proposal are available at the website.

Requirements: Nonprofit 501(c)3 performing and/or exhibiting arts organizations, including museums, theaters, and multidisciplinary arts presenters that are creating or have an established educational program are eligible to apply. Organizations must have as their primary mission the goal of advancing the arts and/or a specific art form. All eligible programs must: have students with disabilities and without disabilities learning together at the same time and place; involve kindergarten through grade 12 public school students in the target audience; be ongoing or have multiple sessions; take place during or after school hours; receive awards in a maximum of three grant cycles (second or third year grants must expand or enhance programs funded in a previous cycle). Only certain arts organizations located in and partnering with public schools in specific metropolitan areas are eligible. A full list of specific locations is posted on the website.

Restrictions: The following entities are not eligible to apply: individuals; schools, universities, performing or visual arts departments of universities, and foundations raising funds for schools or universities; arts and/or arts education programs of disability organizations and of non-presenting/non-exhibiting arts educations organizations; programs that have received Arts Connect All grants in three consecutive grant cycles; and VSA affiliates.

Geographic Focus: Arizona, California, Colorado, Connecticut, Florida, Georgia, Maryland, Massachusetts, Michigan, Minnesota, Missouri, North Carolina, Oklahoma, Oregon, Pennsylvania, Rhode Island, Tennessee, Texas, Washington
Date(s) Application is Due: Nov 19
Amount of Grant: Up to 15,000 USD
Contact: Stephanie Litvak, Coordinator for Arts Connect All; (202) 416-8898; fax (202) 416-4840; vsainfo@kennedy-center.org or support@artsapp.com
Internet: www.kennedy-center.org/education/vsa/programs/arts_connect_all.cfm
Sponsor: John F. Kennedy Center for the Performing Arts
2700 F Street NW
Washington, D.C. 20566

VSA/Volkswagen Group of America Exhibition Awards   2393

VSA and Volkswagen Group of America team up to recognize and showcase emerging artists with disabilities, ages 16-25, who are living in the U.S. This collaboration supports these artists at a critical time when many are deciding whether to pursue the arts as a career. The award validates, and helps finance, that life-defining choice. Every year, fifteen artists are selected for the exhibition and share cash awards generously provided by Volkswagen Group of America: a $20,000 grand prize, a $10,000 first award, a $6,000 second award, and 12 awards of excellence of $2,000 each. The awards are available each year, but programs, themes, and requirements vary.

Geographic Focus: All States
Amount of Grant: Up to 60,000 USD
Contact: Betty Siegel, VSA Director; (202) 416-8898; fax (202) 416-4840; vsainfo@kennedy-center.org or support@artsapp.com
Internet: www.kennedy-center.org/education/vsa/programs/momentum.cfm
Sponsor: John F. Kennedy Center for the Performing Arts
2700 F Street NW
Washington, D.C. 20566

VSA International Art Program for Children with Disabilities Grants   2394

An affiliate of the Kennedy Center for the Performing Arts, VSA was founded by Ambassador Jean Kennedy Smith. With a national and international network, it provides arts and education opportunities for youth and adults with disabilities and increases access to the arts for all. VSA presents a unique opportunity for student-artists with disabilities from around the world to display their artwork side-by-side in an online exhibition. A selection of artwork from the online entries will be chosen for a live exhibition at the U.S. Department of Education in Washington D.C. Children with disabilities are encouraged to create a family portrait that illustrates themselves among the people that provide love, support, and encouragement in their lives - their families. Portraying themselves with some of the most important people in their lives gives testament to the idea that family - no matter how big or how small - help shape who we are and provide the foundation for who we will be. Additional information about how to submit artwork is available at the website.

Requirements: Any children with a disability, ages 5-18, may submit their work. Each entry requires full information about the artist, their disability, and the work submitted.
Restrictions: Work submitted must be two dimensional, and no larger than 18x24 inches.
Geographic Focus: All States, All Countries
Date(s) Application is Due: Jul 1
Contact: Betty Siegel, VSA Director; (202) 416-8898; fax (202) 416-4840; vsainfo@kennedy-center.org or support@artsapp.com
Internet: www.kennedy-center.org/education/vsa/programs/vsa_iap.cfm
Sponsor: John F. Kennedy Center for the Performing Arts
2700 F Street NW
Washington, D.C. 20566

VSA International Young Soloists Award   2395

The VSA International Young Soloists Competition annually selects up to four outstanding musicians, ages 14-25, to supports and encourage them in their pursuit of a career. These emerging musicians (two U.S. and two international) each receive $2,500, professional development opportunities, and a performance at the John F. Kennedy Center for the Performing Arts in Washington, D.C.

Requirements: Any musician who has a disability, ages 14-25, is eligible to apply as either a domestic applicant (U.S. citizen or legal resident) or an international applicant (from outside the U.S., including citizens of other countries living in the U.S. such as those on student visas). The competition is open to both individual musicians and ensembles of two to five members. In order for ensembles to be eligible, at least one member must have a disability, all members must be ages 14-25, and all members must meet the criteria for either

domestic or international applicants (for example, an ensemble applying as an international applicant must be comprised of all international members). All genres of music are accepted, including, but not limited to the following: classical; jazz; hip-hop/rap; rock/alt rock; pop; indie; bluegrass; folk; country; R&B/blues; Latin; and World.

Geographic Focus: All States, All Countries
Date(s) Application is Due: Jan 29
Amount of Grant: 2,500 USD
Contact: Betty Siegel, VSA Director; (202) 416-8898; fax (202) 416-4840; vsainfo@kennedy-center.org or support@artsapp.com
Internet: www.kennedy-center.org/education/vsa/programs/young_soloists.cfm
Sponsor: John F. Kennedy Center for the Performing Arts
2700 F Street NW
Washington, D.C. 20566

VSA Playwright Discovery Award   2396

The Playwright Discovery Award invites middle- and high-school students to take a closer look at the world around them, examine how disability affects their lives and the lives of others, and express their views through the art of playwriting. Playwrights may write from their own experience or about an experience in the life of another person or fictional character. The Division 1 winner (grades 6 through 8) receives $375 for his/her school and will have their script published in the award year's VSA Playwright Discovery Program booklet. The Division 2 winner (grades 9 through 12) receives a $750 scholarship, $375 for his/her school, and the winning script published in the award year's VSA Playwright Discovery Program booklet. Candidates may apply at the website.

Requirements: Authors must be U.S. citizens or permanent U.S. residents. Any student with or without a disability is eligible to apply. Co-authorships of up to five students is allowed, but all authors must fulfill eligibility requirements. The application must include information for all authors. The first page of all script submissions must be a cover sheet, which includes the title of the play, cast list, and numbers of scenes. All scripts must incorporate the subject of disability. A disability is defined in the Americans with Disabilities Act as a physical or mental impairment that substantially limits one or more of the major life activities of an individual. An impairment is a physiological disorder affecting one or more of a number of body systems, or a mental or psychological disorder. The disability may be visible, such as a blind character who uses a wheelchair, or invisible, such as a character with a learning or developmental disability. All entries must be one-act scripts of fewer than 40 pages in length. Acceptable entries include traditional theater, film, or TV scripts, non-linear scripts, scripts that do not rely on spoken language, and/or scripts that emphasize the use of multimedia, non-traditional technologies/techniques, puppetry and audience participation. Entries will be accepted preferably in traditional text format, but may also be submitted as video or audio files. Entries must be original, unproduced, and unpublished at the time of submission. Additional requirements are posted at the website.

Restrictions: Scripts that do not address disability are not eligible. Entries should not show identifying information about the author(s).
Geographic Focus: All States
Date(s) Application is Due: Jun 1
Amount of Grant: 375 - 750 USD
Contact: Betty R. Siegel, VSA Director; (202) 416-8898; fax (202) 416-4840; support@artsapp.com or vsainfo@kennedy-center.org
Internet: www.kennedy-center.org/education/vsa/programs/playwright_discovery.cfm
Sponsor: John F. Kennedy Center for the Performing Arts
2700 F Street NW
Washington, D.C. 20566

W.H. and Mary Ellen Cobb Charitable Trust Grants   2397

The Cobbs were originally from Kentucky, but moved to the Texas Panhandle where they owned and operated several clothing stores. Although they did not have children of their own, they were interested in the well-being of children and therefore established their charitable trust to benefit local charities in the Panhandle whose mission has a strong "emphasis on helping children." The W.H. and Mary Ellen Cobb Charitable Trust considers requests from charitable organizations whose primary focus is the provision of services that benefit children. This foundation makes approximately 5-7 awards each year and grants are typically between $1,000 and $25,000.

Requirements: Organizations must be geographically located within the Texas Panhandle; serve residents of the Panhandle, Amarillo, and vicinity; and have 501(c)3 tax-exempt status. Applications will be submitted online through the Bank of America website. A grant report is required within 1 year of the grant application date, regardless of whether all of the funds have been spent.

Restrictions: The trust does not support requests from individuals, organizations attempting to influence policy through direct lobbying, or any political campaigns.
Geographic Focus: Texas
Date(s) Application is Due: Aug 1
Amount of Grant: 1,000 - 25,000 USD
Samples: Wesley Community Center, Amarillo, Texas, $15,000 - Awarded for general operations for the Amarillo Wesley Community Center (2018); Saint Andrews Episcopal Church, Amarillo, Texas, $15,000 - Awarded for renovation of concrete entrance to the local school (2018); Buckner Children and Family Services of North Texas, Dallas, Texas, $10,000 - Awarded for Buckner FYi Center support (2018).
Contact: Kelly Garlock, Philanthropic Client Manager; (800) 357-7094; tx.philanthropic@bankofamerica.com or tx.philanthropic@ustrust.com
Internet: www.bankofamerica.com/philanthropic/foundation/?fnId=5
Sponsor: W.H. and Mary Ellen Cobb Charitable Trust
P.O. Box 831041
Dallas, TX 75283-1041

W.M. Keck Foundation Southern California Grants 2398

The Southern California program seeks to promote the education and healthy development of children and youth, strengthening families and enhancing the lives of people in the Greater Los Angeles area through its support of organizations that provide arts and cultural enrichment, civic and community services, early childhood and pre-college education, and health care. A special emphasis is placed on projects that focus on children and youth from low-income families, special needs populations, and safety-net services. Collaborative initiatives, as well as projects arising from the vision of one organization's strong leadership, are supported. Historically, grants range from $100,000 to $1 million, and typically are under $500,000. Applicants are strongly urged to contact Foundation staff well in advance of submitting a Phase I Application. The best times for these contacts are between January 1 and February 15 leading up to a May 1 submittal, or between July 1 and August 15 leading up to a November 1 submittal.

Requirements: Nonprofit organizations, including colleges and universities, pursuing relevant projects in Los Angeles County are eligible to apply.

Restrictions: Grants are not considered for: general operating expenses, endowments or deficit reduction; general and federated campaigns, including fundraising events, dinners or mass mailings; individuals; conference or seminar sponsorship; book publication and film or theater productions; public policy research; institutions that are located outside the United States; institutions that do not have at least three consecutive full, certified, audited financial statements; conduit organizations, unified funds or organizations that use grant funds from donors to support other organizations or individuals; or institutions that are subsidiaries or affiliates of larger entities that do not have a separate board of directors and independent audited financial statements.

Geographic Focus: California

Date(s) Application is Due: May 1; Nov 1

Amount of Grant: 100,000 - 1,000,000 USD

Samples: Alliance for a Better Community, Los Angeles, California, $200,000 - to build the capacity of parents to participate in various forms of civic learning and engagement in order to support their student's achievement; Alliance for Children's Rights, Los Angeles, California, $250,000 - o ensure that implementation of the California Fostering Connections to Success Act.

Contact: Margie Antonetti, Grants and Database Specialist; (213) 680-3833; fax (213) 614-0934; mantonetti@wmkeck.org or SoCal@wmkeck.org

Internet: www.wmkeck.org/grant-programs/southern-california-program.html

Sponsor: W.M. Keck Foundation

550 S Hope Street, Suite 2500

Los Angeles, CA 90071

W.P. and Bulah Luse Foundation Grants 2399

The W.P. and Bulah Luse Foundation was established in 1947. Mr. Luse, a self-made wildcatter in the early Texas oilfields, and his wife Bulah created this foundation to support and promote quality education, human services and health care programming for underserved populations. Special consideration is given to charitable organizations that serve the people of Dallas, Texas, and its surrounding communities. The majority of grants from the Luse Foundation are 1 year in duration. Award amounts typically range from $2,000 to $20,000. Applications are accepted twice annually.

Requirements: Applicants must have 501(c)3 tax-exempt status and serve communities in Dallas, Texas. Applications will be submitted online through the Bank of America website. A grant report is required within 1 year of the grant application date, regardless of whether all of the funds have been spent.

Restrictions: Organizations that receive a 1-year grant from the W.P. and Bulah Luse Foundation must skip 2 years before submitting a subsequent application. The foundation does not support requests from individuals, organizations attempting to influence policy through direct lobbying, or any political campaigns.

Geographic Focus: Texas

Date(s) Application is Due: Jun 1; Dec 1

Amount of Grant: 2,000 - 20,000 USD

Samples: Wesley-Rankin Community Center, Dallas, Texas, $15,000 - Awarded for Peak, Ascend, and Summit Afterschool programs (2018); St. Bernard of Clairvaux Catholic School, Dallas, Texas, $12,000 - Awarded for tuition assistance (2018); Dallas Center for the Performing Arts Foundation, Dallas, Texas, $10,000 - Awarded for AT&T Performing Arts Center Education Expansion Initiative (2018).

Contact: Kelly Garlock, Philanthropic Client Manager; (800) 357-7094; tx.philanthropic@bankofamerica.com or tx.philanthropic@ustrust.com

Internet: www.bankofamerica.com/philanthropic/foundation/?fnId=87

Sponsor: W.P. and Bulah Luse Foundation

901 Main Street, 19th Floor, TX1-492-19-11

Dallas, TX 75202-3714

W.W. Smith Charitable Trust Basic Needs Grants 2400

The W.W. Smith Charitable Trust awards Basic Needs grants regionally in its areas of interest, including proposals that address specifically food, clothing, and shelter for children and the aged. Resources are concentrated in areas where the most need can be discerned and where government or private assistance has not been available. Types of support include capital projects, challenge/matching grants, general operating grants, program grants, and research grants. Requests for grants for food, clothing, and shelter for children and the aged are considered throughout the year. Grants applications are accepted in this category twice annually: June 15 and December 15. Awards may be for more than one year but not for more than three years.

Requirements: Grant recipients are limited to organizations within the five-county area of Pennsylvania including Buck, Chester, Delaware, Montgomery, and Philadelphia Counties. Organizations must be tax-exempt and not classified as private foundations or private operating foundations.

Restrictions: After three consecutive years of funding, at least two years must elapse before further applications from the organization may be considered.

Geographic Focus: Pennsylvania

Date(s) Application is Due: Jun 15; Dec 15

Amount of Grant: 15,000 - 100,000 USD

Contact: Brian Jones, Food, Clothing, and Shelter Administrator; (610) 397-1844; fax (610) 397-1680; info@wwsmithcharitabletrust.org

Internet: www.wwsmithcharitabletrust.org/basicneeds.html

Sponsor: W.W. Smith Charitable Trust

200 Four Falls Corporate Center, Suite 300

West Conshohocken, PA 19428

Walker Area Community Foundation Grants 2401

The Walker Area Community Foundation supports nonprofit organizations in specific fields of interest, which include: arts and humanities; children and youth; education; elder care; the environment; health and medicine; recreation; and social services. In order to make the greatest impact with the funds available, the Foundation prefers requests that: address a critical community need; get at the root causes of a problem; do not duplicate existing services unless they serve a population not already being served; are pilot projects which, if successful, can be expanded to serve a wider population or be duplicated by other organizations; involve collaboration and cooperation with other organizations and agencies; and include an effective mechanism for measuring the impact of The Community Foundation's investment.

Requirements: Requests from public school systems must come from the superintendent's office. If the request is for an individual school, it must be for a pilot project that, if successful, would be duplicated in other schools in the system. Requests from large organizations with many branches or departments (e.g. colleges, universities, the YMCA and public libraries) must come through the development or president's office and have the approval of the head of that office. Ordinarily, the Foundation does not make grants for: operating expenses unless they are for the initial stages of a pilot project; program expenses that occur on a regular basis; or regularly supported activities of fundraising organizations.

Restrictions: No grants are made to or for: individuals; religious organizations for religious purposes; dinners, balls or other ticketed events; political purposes; lobbying activities; replacement of government grants or funding; endowments; or other discretionary pools.

Geographic Focus: Alabama

Contact: Mimi Hudson; (205) 302-0001; fax (205) 302-0424; mhudson@wacf.org

Alaina Hallmark; (205) 302-0001; fax (205) 302-0424; ahallmark@wacf.org

Internet: www.wacf.org/how-to-apply-for-a-grant.html

Sponsor: Walker Area Community Foundation

611 8th Avenue

Jasper, AL 35501

Wallace Foundation Grants 2402

The mission of The Wallace Foundation is to expand learning and enrichment for disadvantaged children and the vitality of the arts for everyone. The Foundation rarely funds unsolicited proposals but instead determines which nonprofits or governmental bodies (such as school districts) might have the interest in and ability to work with them to carry out efforts aimed at answering important field questions. The Wallace Foundation considers proposals by invitation only. An introductory letter is strongly encouraged prior to any work on a proposal.

Requirements: U.S. nonprofit organizations are eligible. Grantees general fall into one of three categories: (1) organizations funded to develop and test possible solutions to important public problems; (2) commissioned researchers who to contribute to the field's knowledge and help evaluate what is and is not working; and (3) organizations that help the Foundation get both issues and solutions before policymakers, field leaders and those who can otherwise influence policy and practice.

Restrictions: Grants do not support religious or fraternal organizations; international programs; conferences; historical restoration; health, medical, or social service programs; environmental/conservation programs; capital campaigns; emergency funds or deficit financing; private foundations; or individuals.

Geographic Focus: All States

Amount of Grant: 75,000 - 4,000,000 USD

Contact: Holly Dodge, Grants Administration Manager; (212) 251-9700; fax (212) 679-6990

Internet: www.wallacefoundation.org/about-wallace/pages/funding-guidelines.aspx

Sponsor: Wallace Foundation

140 Broadway, 49th Floor

New York, NY 10005

Walmart Foundation Inclusive Communities Grants 2403

Walmart's founder, Sam Walton, introduced the charitable philosophy, operate globally, give back locally. With that in mind, the Walmart Foundation supports local programs in an effort to impact neighborhoods where its employees live and work. Areas of focus include education, workforce development/economic opportunity, health and wellness, and environmental sustainability. Awards range from $250 to $2,500. The annual grant cycle begins February 1 and the application deadline is December 31. Organizations are encouraged to limit the number of pending applications to 25.

Requirements: Applicants must fit within one of the Foundation's four focus areas and be one of the following: hold a current tax-exempt status under Section 501(c)3, 4, 6 or 19 of the Internal Revenue Code; be a recognized government entity that is requesting funds exclusively for public purposes; be a K-12 public/private school, charter school, community/junior college, state/private college or university; or be a church or other

faith based organization with proposed projects that address and benefit the needs of the community at large.
Restrictions: Applicants must offer programs that benefit the local community. Applicants receiving sponsorship at the national level are excluded from applying..
Geographic Focus: All States
Amount of Grant: 250 - 2,500 USD
Contact: Julie Gehrki; (479) 273-4000 or (800) 530-9925; fax (479) 273-6850
Internet: walmart.org/what-we-do/strengthening-community/local-community-support
Sponsor: Walmart Foundation
702 SW 8th Street, Department 8687, No. 0555
Bentonville, AR 72716-0555

Walmart Foundation National Local Giving Grants   **2404**
The Walmart Foundation's mission is to create opportunities so people can live better. The National Local Giving program allows the Foundation to work strategically with organizations working across one or more states to address social issues strongly aligned with its focus areas. The Foundation often provides funds to organizations that have local affiliates around the country, and the majority of grants from this program include re-grants to implement programs in local communities. These grants support initiatives focused on: hunger relief and healthy eating; sustainable food production and supply; women's economic empowerment; and career opportunities. The Program awards grants of $250,000 and above. Applicants should submit program ideas using the letter of inquiry (LOI) format.
Requirements: Applicants must be 501(c)3 organizations; recognized by the Internal Revenue Service as a public charity within the meaning of either Section 509(a)1 or 509(a)2 of the Internal Revenue Code; and must operate on a national scope through the existence of chapters or affiliates in a large number of states around the country; or possess a regional/local focus, but seek funding to replicate program activities nationally. In the case of proposals seeking funding for replication, organizations must demonstrate the capacity to support national expansion and be ready to begin the replication process.
Restrictions: The Foundation does not accept unsolicited proposals but does accept letters of inquiry providing a general understanding of the problem or issue, the need for the proposed solution and the applicant's capacity to carry out the work. If the applicant is selected to submit a full proposal, guidelines and additional information will be provided. The letter of intent is submitted online. Funding exclusions include: association and chamber memberships; athletic sponsorships (teams/events); capital campaigns and endowments (defined as any plans to raise funds for a significant purchase or expense, such as new construction, major renovations or to help fund normal budgetary items); faith-based organizations when the proposed grant will only benefit the organization or its members; general operating expenses; political causes, candidates, organizations or campaigns; research projects; scholarships (tuition, room and board or any other expense related to college, university, or vocational school attendance); and sponsorship of fundraising events (galas, walks, races, tournaments).
Geographic Focus: All States
Contact: Julie Gehrki; (479) 273-4000 or (800) 530-9925; fax (479) 273-6850
Internet: walmart.org/what-we-do/strengthening-community/local-community-support
Sponsor: Walmart Foundation
702 SW 8th Street, Department 8687, No. 0555
Bentonville, AR 72716-0555

Walmart Foundation State Giving Grants   **2405**
The Walmart Foundation's mission is to create opportunities so people can live better. State Giving Grants support initiatives aligned with their mission and having a long-lasting, positive impact within a state or region. Interest areas include: hunger relief and healthy eating; sustainable food production and supply; women's economic empowerment; and career opportunities. The Foundation has a particular interest in supporting the following populations: veterans and military families, traditionally under-served groups, individuals with disabilities, and people impacted by natural disasters. Awards range between $25,000 and $250,000. There are four distinct application cycles (each open for about five days) focused on different giving areas and geographical areas. See the web site for specifics.
Requirements: Applicants must be 501(c)3 organizations. Applications accepted online only.
Restrictions: Funding awarded in a particular state must be fully allocated within that state. Applications accepted online only.
Geographic Focus: All States
Date(s) Application is Due: Jan 30; May 1; Jul 17; Sep 18
Amount of Grant: 25,000 - 250,000 USD
Contact: Julie Gehrki; (479) 273-4000 or (800) 530-9925; fax (479) 273-6850
Internet: walmart.org/what-we-do/strengthening-community/local-community-support
Sponsor: Walmart Foundation
702 SW 8th Street, Department 8687, No. 0555
Bentonville, AR 72716-0555

Walter J. and Betty C. Zable Foundation Grants   **2406**
The Walter J. and Betty C. Zable Foundation was established in San Diego, California, in 2007. Its bylaws do not restrict awards to specific areas, though the Foundation has historically funded medical and science activities, programs that benefit youth and underprivileged individuals, active and retired military personnel, and sports related activities. Requests from other areas will be considered. Support generally comes in the form of operating funding, program development, re-granting, and support of scholarships funds. The average award in recent years has been $20,000. The Foundation grants generally benefit San Diego County organizations. The Board meets four times per year to review grant requests. Currently the board meets the first Wednesday of the month in February, May, August and November. Grant requests are accepted throughout the year.

Requirements: The Foundation requires all applicants to be 501(c)3 organizations. Applications must be submitted at least one month prior to the scheduled board meetings to be considered at the next meeting. Applications received by mail or personal delivery will be returned with a request to apply online.
Restrictions: No grant funds can be used for offshore organizations or activities without specific foundation approval. Multiple requests in the same year will not be reviewed.
Geographic Focus: California
Amount of Grant: Up to 100,000 USD
Samples: Alzheimer's Association, San Diego, California, $100,674 - support of family services programs; Aseltine School, San Diego, California, $20,000 - general operating support; Community Resource Center, Encinitas, California, $20,000 - general operating support.
Contact: Warren Magill, President; (619) 294-7005; info@zablefoundation.org
Internet: www.zablefoundation.org/grant-process/
Sponsor: Walter J. and Betty C. Zable Foundation
1660 Hotel Circle North, Suite 710
San Diego, CA 92108

Walter S. and Evan C. Jones Testamentary Trust   **2407**
The Walter S. and Evan C. Jones Testamentary Trust was established in 1961 to provide educational and medical support to those residing in Lyon, Coffey and Osage counties in Kansas. Over time the trust been allowed to take on additional charitable support such as human services and community development projects. Walter and Evan were successful farmers and cattlemen, which was the source of wealth for this very generous gift bestowed upon these communities. The original trust was established to help develop a cure for polio. In the early 1960s when a vaccine was licensed, it was at the judgment of the courts to administer the trust as it is today. Award amounts go up to $1,000,000. Application are accepted four times annually.
Requirements: Applicants must have 501(c)3 tax-exempt status and serve communities in Lyon, Coffey and Osage counties in Kansas. Grant requests for general operating support, program support and capital support will be considered. Grant requests for capital support such as for buildings, land and major equipment should meet a compelling community need and offer a broad social benefit. Applications will be submitted online through the Bank of America website. A grant report is required within 1 year of the grant application date, regardless of whether all of the funds have been spent.
Restrictions: The trust does not support requests from individuals, organizations attempting to influence policy through direct lobbying, or any political campaigns.
Geographic Focus: Kansas
Date(s) Application is Due: Mar 20; Jun 20; Sep 20; Dec 20
Amount of Grant: Up to 1,000,000 USD
Samples: Walter S and Evan C Jones Foundation, Emporia, Kansas, $541,213 - Awarded in support of the further mission of the Jones Trust by providing medical and educational assistance (2019); SOS Inc., Emporia, Kansas, $345,000 - Awarded for SOS, Inc. comprehensive campaign (2019); KVC Hospitals Inc., Olathe, Kansas, $200,000 - Awarded for KVC Children's Psychiatric Hospital - Wichita (2019).
Contact: Tony Twyman, Senior Philanthropic Client Manager; (816) 292-4342; mo.grantmaking@bankofamerica.com or tony.twyman@bofa.com
Internet: www.bankofamerica.com/philanthropic/foundation/?fnId=166
Sponsor: Walter S. and Evan C. Jones Testamentary Trust
P.O. Box 831041
Dallas, TX 75283-1041

Walton Family Foundation Education Grants   **2408**
The Walton Family Foundation is committed to improving K-12 student achievement in the United States. The Foundation's core strategy is to infuse competitive pressure into America's K-12 education system by increasing the quantity and quality of school choices available, especially in low-income communities. Their three distinct initiatives are shaping public policy, creating quality schools, and improving existing schools.
Requirements: An organization interested in applying for a grant must send a brief letter of inquiry succinctly describing the organization and the proposed project, specifying and briefly explaining its relevance to a particular Foundation funding area and initiative, and providing an estimate of the funds that would be requested. If, based on the letter of inquiry, the project appears to match the Foundation's funding criteria and priorities, the applicant may be invited to submit a formal grant proposal and budget.
Restrictions: An applicant should not submit a formal grant proposal until receiving an invitation following submission of a letter of inquiry. An invitation to submit a formal grant proposal does not mean that funding will be approved.
Geographic Focus: All States
Samples: Agudath Israel of Illinois, Chicago, Illinois, $500,000 - shaping public policy; Academy for Global Citizenship Charter School, Chicago, Illinois, $250,000 - creating quality schools; Achievement Network, LTD, Chicago, Illinois, $62,500 - improving existing schools.
Contact: Brenda Dean; (479) 464-1570; fax (479) 464-1580; bdean@wffmail.com
Internet: www.waltonfamilyfoundation.org/educationreform
Sponsor: Walton Family Foundation
P.O. Box 2030
Bentonville, AR 72712

Walton Family Foundation Public Charter Startup Grants   **2409**
The Walton Family Foundation is committed to improving K-12 student achievement in the United States. The Foundation's core strategy is to infuse competitive pressure into America's K-12 education system by increasing the quantity and quality of school choices available, especially in low-income communities. The Grants support the creation of public charters by providing grants to school developers as they launch new schools. Grantees are

school developers who primarily serve low-income children in targeted geographies, and can demonstrate the capacity to dramatically raise student achievement.

Requirements: Applicants must demonstrate strong potential for delivering excellent academic results for K through 12 students, as measured by standardized achievement tests; serve significant low-income student populations; not represent a for-profit entity; have an endorsement from a Foundation program officer or one of the Foundation's state-based grant partners; and draw a majority of its students from a targeted districts.

Restrictions: Only public charter schools drawing a majority of their students from these districts may apply: any district in Arkansas; Phoenix Metro in Arizona; Los Angeles Unified Districts 4-7 in California; Denver Public Schools in Colorado; Tampa/Hillsborough County in Florida; Atlanta Public Schools in Georgia; Chicago Public Schools in Illinois; Indianapolis Public Schools in Indiana; Orleans Parish in Louisiana; Detroit Public Schools in Michigan; Minneapolis Public Schools in Minnesota; St. Louis Public Schools in Missouri; Albany Public Schools and Harlem Districts 4 and 5 in New York; Columbus Public Schools in Ohio; District of Columbia Public Schools in Washington, D.C; and Milwaukee Public Schools in Wisconsin. For other public charter schools opening in Arizona, California, Colorado, Florida, Georgia, Illinois, Missouri, New York, Ohio, or Washington, D.C., see the website's Local and National Partners page. For affiliates of a charter management organization (CMO) or school leader fellowship program, see the website's Local and National Partners page. For verify whether or not an organization qualifies for a grant, email questions before beginning the process. See website for details.

Geographic Focus: Arizona, Arkansas, California, Colorado, District of Columbia, Florida, Georgia, Illinois, Indiana, Louisiana, Michigan, Minnesota, Missouri, New York, Ohio, Wisconsin
Contact: Brenda Dean; (479) 464-1570; fax (479) 464-1580; bdean@wffmail.com
Internet: www.waltonfamilyfoundation.org/grantees/public-charter-startup-grant-program
Sponsor: Walton Family Foundation
P.O. Box 2030
Bentonville, AR 72712

Warrick County Community Foundation Recreation Grants 2410
The Warrick County Community Foundation is a nonprofit, public charity created for the people of Warrick County, Indiana. The Foundation helps nonprofits fulfill their missions by strengthening their ability to meet community needs through grants that assist charitable programs, address community issues, support community agencies, launch community initiatives, and support leadership development. Funding requests are accepted once each year according to the Foundation's grant cycle. Application requirements may change from year to year; therefore, grant seekers are advised to revisit the web page prior to beginning the grant application process. Grants are normally given as one-time support of a project, but may be considered for additional support and for expansions or outgrowths of an initial project. Applications are accepted from December 1 through the February 1 deadline. Grants in the area of Recreation include projects aimed at improving and promoting recreational and leisure activities, parks, and community sporting events and activities. Samples of previously funded projects are available at the website.

Requirements: The Foundation welcomes proposals from nonprofit organizations that are deemed tax-exempt under sections 501(c)3 and 509(a) of the IRS code and from governmental agencies serving Warrick County, Indiana. Proposals from nonprofit organizations not classified as a 501(c)3 public charity may be considered if the project is charitable and supports a community need.

Restrictions: Project areas not considered for funding include: religious organizations for religious purposes; political parties or campaigns; endowment creation or debt reduction; operating costs; capital campaigns; annual appeals or membership contributions; or travel requests for groups or individuals such as bands, sports teams, or classes.
Geographic Focus: Indiana
Date(s) Application is Due: Feb 1
Amount of Grant: Up to 10,000 USD
Contact: Melinda Waldroup, Director of Programs and Strategic Engagement; (812) 429-1191, Ext. 3 or (812) 455-8220; mwaldroup@communityfoundationalliance.org
Internet: www.communityfoundationalliance.org/warrick/program-areas/
Sponsor: Warrick County Community Foundation
224 West Main Street, P.O. Box 215
Boonville, IN 47601

Warrick County Community Foundation Women's Fund 2411
The Warrick County Community Foundation Women's Fund distributes grants supporting a variety of resources serving women of all ages that will improve self-esteem and self-image among women and girls; promote health and improve accessibility and affordability of health care; help mothers improve parenting skills; provide avenues for career advancement through education and training; and create positive change for Warrick County's women and girls. Its primary mission is to improve the quality of life in Warrick County by collectively funding significant grants to support local programs that give opportunities, encouragement, knowledge, and hope to the Warrick County community. The annual deadline for Letters of Inquiry is February 5.

Requirements: A letter of inquiry of no more than two typed papers is required to apply for a Women's Fund grant. Funding requests will be considered from nonprofit, charitable organizations serving Warrick County women and girls. The letter should describe the project and funding requested, the need or issue the project will address, what will be accomplished, and the project's timetable. Organizations should also include contact information and an IRS determination letter (or an explanation of why no IRS letter is included). Projects must address the needs which support the Fund's mission by providing opportunities, encouragement, knowledge, information, and hope for the community's women and girls. The Women's Fund welcomes proposals from non-profit organizations that are tax-exempt under sections 501(c)3 and 509(a) of the Internal Revenue Code and

from governmental agencies serving Warrick County, Indiana, women and girls. Proposals from other non-profit organizations that address issues facing women and girls in the county may be accepted. Proposals submitted by an entity under the auspices of another agency must include a written statement signed by the agency's board president on behalf of the board of directors agreeing to act as the entity's fiscal sponsor, to receive grant monies if awarded, and to oversee the proposed project.

Restrictions: Project areas not considered for funding include: projects or programs of organizations that are not committed to gender equity; funding to reduce or retire debt of the organization; projects that focus solely on the spiritual needs and growth of a church congregation or members of other religious organizations; political parties or campaigns; operating costs not directly related to the proposed project (the organization's general operating expenses including equipment, staff salary, rent, and utilities); event sponsorships, annual appeals, and membership contributions; travel expenses for groups or individuals such as bands, sports teams, or classes; scholarships or other grants to individuals.
Geographic Focus: Indiana
Amount of Grant: 1,000 - 10,000 USD
Contact: Susan Gess Sublett, Regional Director of Annual Giving; (812) 897-2030 or 812-429-1191; ssublett@communityfoundationalliance.org or susan@communityfoundation.org
Internet: www.communityfoundationalliance.org/warrick/about-us/warrick-womens-fund/
Sponsor: Warrick County Community Foundation
224 West Main Street, P.O. Box 215
Boonville, IN 47601

Warrick County Community Foundation Youth Development Grants 2412
The Warrick County Community Foundation is a nonprofit, public charity created for the people of Warrick County, Indiana. The Foundation helps nonprofits fulfill their missions by strengthening their ability to meet community needs through grants that assist charitable programs, address community issues, support community agencies, launch community initiatives, and support leadership development. Funding requests are accepted once each year according to the Foundation's grant cycle. Application requirements may change from year to year; therefore, grant seekers are advised to revisit the web page prior to beginning the grant application process. Grants are normally given as one-time support of a project, but may be considered for additional support and for expansions or outgrowths of an initial project. Applications are accepted from December 1 through the February 1 deadline. Grants in the area of Youth Development include activities that strengthen the family unit, help children grow and develop, foster youth sports and athletics, support the YMCA, and support daycare-related issues. Samples of previously funded projects are available at the website.

Requirements: The Foundation welcomes proposals from nonprofit organizations that are deemed tax-exempt under sections 501(c)3 and 509(a) of the IRS code and from governmental agencies serving Warrick County, Indiana. Proposals from nonprofit organizations not classified as a 501(c)3 public charity may be considered if the project is charitable and supports a community need.

Restrictions: Project areas not considered for funding include: religious organizations for religious purposes; political parties or campaigns; endowment creation or debt reduction; operating costs; capital campaigns; annual appeals or membership contributions; or travel requests for groups or individuals such as bands, sports teams, or classes.
Geographic Focus: Indiana
Date(s) Application is Due: Feb 1
Amount of Grant: Up to 5,000 USD
Contact: Melinda Waldroup, Director of Programs and Strategic Engagement; (812) 429-1191, Ext. 3 or (812) 455-8220; mwaldroup@communityfoundationalliance.org
Internet: www.communityfoundationalliance.org/warrick/program-areas/
Sponsor: Warrick County Community Foundation
224 West Main Street, P.O. Box 215
Boonville, IN 47601

Washington Area Fuel Fund Grants 2413
For more than 160 years, Washington Gas has been an integral part of the growing metropolitan region of Washington D.C. Chartered by the 30th Congress and signed into law by President James Polk in 1848, the company has developed a Charitable Giving Program that is designed to make a meaningful and lasting impact on the communities it serves. The company's signature philanthropic program is the Washington Area Fuel Fund (WAFF). An unforeseen financial crisis brought on by an accident, medical problem, or loss of income can force a family or a senior citizen to choose between food and warmth. When all other government assistance has run out or simply is not available, WAFF has paid for all types of fuel to heat homes of families in need. The Salvation Army disburses WAFF assistance through its 11 offices located throughout the Washington metropolitan area from January 1 through May 31. Once eligibility for WAFF assistance is established, The Salvation Army will issue a check for the appropriate amount and mail it directly to the applicant's utility company or supplier. A list of Salvation Army Offices with their addresses and phone numbers is available at the web site.

Requirements: Eligible applicants must be in an emergency situation and be no longer eligible for any government energy-assistance programs. Applicants must also meet WAFF income guidelines and live in one of the following geographic areas: the District of Columbia; Calvert, Charles, Montgomery, Prince George's, or St. Mary's Counties in Maryland; and Arlington, Fairfax, Loudoun, and Prince William Counties (or in the Cities of Alexandria, Fairfax, and Falls Church) in Virginia. Applicants must apply to The Salvation Army office in the city or county in which they live.

Restrictions: Funds should be used principally for the payment of heating bills, but may also be used for the purchase and installation of low-cost energy-conservation measures.
Geographic Focus: District of Columbia, Maryland, Virginia

Contact: Ernest R. Holz, Director of Divisional Development and Planning; (202) 756-2692; fax (202) 464-7208; Ernie_Holz@uss.salvationarmy.org
Kelly Gibson, Senior Specialist, Community Involvement; (202) 624-6335; fax (202) 624-6010; kgibson@washgas.com
Internet: www.washingtonareafuelfund.org/get-assistance/
Sponsor: Washington Gas Company
101 Constitution Avenue, North West, 3rd Floor
Washington, D.C. 20080

Washington Area Women's Foundation African American Women's Giving   2414
  Circle Grants
Founded in 2004, the African American Women's Giving Circle (AAWGC) is a charitable fund established out of The Women's Foundation. The circle includes 15-25 women who have each made a financial commitment of $5,000 over a two-year period and agreed to work together as part of a shared grantmaking and learning experience. The AAWGC makes grants that support African American women-led organizations that improve the lives of African American women and girls in the Washington metropolitan region.
Requirements: Nonprofit organizations in the Washington metropolitan area are eligible to apply.
Geographic Focus: District of Columbia
Contact: Nicole Cozier, Chief of Strategic Operations; (202) 347-7737, ext. 203; fax (202) 347-7739; ncozier@wawf.org
Internet: community.thewomensfoundation.org/page.aspx?pid=223
Sponsor: Washington Area Women's Foundation
1331 H Street, NW, Suite 1000
Washington, D.C. 20005

Washington Area Women's Foundation Rainmakers Giving Circle Grants   2415
Launched in 2003, The Women's Foundation's Rainmakers Giving Circle's mission is to improve the lives of young women in the Washington metropolitan area by supporting programs that foster their empowerment, self-esteem and ability to achieve their full potential. The Rainmakers Giving Circle supports programs for young women and girls (10-21) that encourage the healthy development of and prevention of risk factors among young women and girls. The Rainmakers focus on programs that empower and increase competence among young women and girls in the areas of employment, education, health, and life skills. The Rainmakers contribute to programs where the grants make a significant impact in the continuation, expansion or enhancement of the program. Rainmakers Giving Circle members commit to give $5,000 each to the giving circle over two years.
Requirements: Nonprofit organizations in the Washington metropolitan area are eligible to apply.
Geographic Focus: District of Columbia
Date(s) Application is Due: Dec 5
Contact: Nicole Cozier; (202) 347-7737, ext. 203; fax (202) 347-7739; ncozier@wawf.org
Internet: community.thewomensfoundation.org/page.aspx?pid=222
Sponsor: Washington Area Women's Foundation
1331 H Street, NW, Suite 1000
Washington, D.C. 20005

Washington County Community Foundation Grants   2416
The Washington County Community Foundation offers grants to nonprofit organizations in Washington County. Organizations may sign up to be notified of current grant cycles and criteria.
Requirements: Funding will be made to nonprofit organizations whose programs benefit Washington County residents. Grant recipients must show that their financial affairs are being properly administered and may be required to submit audited balance sheets and operating statements.
Restrictions: Applicants are required to attend an orientation meeting before beginning the grant writing process. Funding is not available for the following: political parties or campaigns; sectarian religious purposes that do not serve the general public; programs or equipment that was committed to prior to the grant application submission; or endowment creation or debt reduction.
Geographic Focus: Indiana
Contact: Judy Johnson, Executive Director; (812) 883-7334; info@wccf.biz
Internet: wccf.biz/grants/grant-criteria.html
Sponsor: Washington County Community Foundation
1707 North Shelby Street, P.O. Box 50
Salem, IN 47167

Washington Gas Charitable Giving Contributions   2417
For more than 160 years, Washington Gas has been an integral part of the growing metropolitan region of Washington D.C. Chartered by the 30th Congress and signed into law by President James Polk in 1848, the company has developed a Charitable Giving Program that is designed to make a meaningful and lasting impact on the communities it serves. Washington Gas focuses on three primary areas: education, the environment, and health. Types of support offered are grants, in-kind contributions, and volunteer resources. In the area of education, emphasis is placed on the development of math, science, technology, and business skills in K-12 youth. Consideration is also given to arts-related programs. In the area of the environment, emphasis is placed on programs that promote cleaner air and water programs that protect and preserve the ecological system of the metropolitan area. In the area of health, consideration is given to health organizations that strive to improve the health and well-being of individuals within the community. Emphasis is also placed on energy assistance programs for low-income residents to heat and cool their homes, reducing ilness and casualties resulting from exposure to extreme

temperatures. The company accepts applications on a rolling basis. Basic guidelines are listed at the website and provided in a downloadable PDF file. Applications must be mailed to the contact information given. Notification of acceptance or rejection generally takes fifteen business days or longer.
Requirements: 501(c)3 organizations are eligible to apply. Support is provided primarily in Washington, D.C., Maryland, and Virginia. The company prefers to support specific programs over general funding.
Restrictions: Support is not provided to religious organizations for sectarian purposes, political associations, organizations with strictly a sports focus, individuals, and requests for capital or endowment campaigns.
Geographic Focus: District of Columbia, Maryland, Virginia
Contact: Tracye Funn, (703) 750-1000; tfunn@washgas.com
Internet: www.washgas.com/pages/CharitableGiving
Sponsor: Washington Gas Company
101 Constitution Avenue, North West, 3rd Floor
Washington, D.C. 20080

Watson-Brown Foundation Grants   2418
The Watson-Brown Foundation awards grants to qualifying organizations that have an abiding interest in the history and culture of the south and southeast. Grants take many forms, including: book subventions; museum and archive support; preservation awards; educational programming; and research support. Typical recipients include: colleges and universities; scholarly societies; and other public charities that collect or advance knowledge of the region. The Foundation supports historic preservation in part through its Junior Board of Trustees, a talented group of high school students that makes grant awards to worthy preservation projects in east central Georgia. The majority of grants awarded support southern studies and related programming at the college level. Academic disciplines and areas of interest also include: history; English; literature; law; agricultural education; and historic preservation. Types of support the Foundation will consider to advance its mission include: operating support; publication subventions; research grants; and program grants. The annual deadline for a particular year is April 15 of that year.
Requirements: 501(c)3, 509(a)1, 509(a)2, and 509(a)3 nonprofit organizations are eligible. Generally, the foundation supports only organizations, institutions, or programs located in the southeastern region of the United States.
Restrictions: Grants do not support individuals (except for scholarships awarded through the foundation's internal scholarship program); religious programs, or political/lobbying activities; debt reduction; advertising or marketing efforts; social events such as sports tournaments or galas; or individual projects for more than one year.
Geographic Focus: Alabama, Arkansas, Florida, Georgia, Kentucky, Louisiana, Mississippi, Missouri, North Carolina, South Carolina, Tennessee, Virginia, West Virginia
Date(s) Application is Due: Apr 15
Contact: Tad Brown; (706) 595-8886; fax (706) 595-3948; tbrown@watson-brown.org
Internet: www.watson-brown.org/grants/index.html
Sponsor: Watson-Brown Foundation
310 Tom Watson Way
Thomson, GA 30824

Wayne County Foundation Grants   2419
The Foundation seeks to serve the charitable, cultural, educational, and community needs of the citizens in Wayne County, Indiana. Areas of interest include animal welfare; agriculture; the performing arts; cancer and glaucoma research/ child abuse prevention; delinquency prevention; the environment; historic preservation; homelessness; human service needs; literacy; mental health; special needs therapy; and senior citizens. Grants will be made primarily to established organizations that serve the county. The programs of such organizations will reflect the concerns of community leadership. Types of support include equipment, program development, conferences and seminars, publication, seed money, and scholarship funds. Normally, grant commitments are for one year. Deadlines vary according to program.
Requirements: The following information must be submitted to apply: the completed application cover; a statement of need; project description and anticipated community impact; a brief description of the applicant's history, purpose, and population served; a plan to evaluate the success or effectiveness of the proposed project; the project budget and narrative budget; the 501(c)3 determination letter; a list of Board members with contact information; evidence of the Board's approval for application; statement of financial position and operating statement; and current Form 990.
Restrictions: The Foundation will not support annual fund campaigns; operating or capital debt reduction; religious purposes; grants to individuals or for travel purposes; services commonly regarded as the responsibility of government such as fire and police protection; public school services required by state law; standard instructional or regular operating costs of nonpublic schools; or repeat funding of projects previously supported in recent grant periods.
Geographic Focus: Indiana
Date(s) Application is Due: Apr 1; Jul 30; Oct 1
Contact: Stephen C. Borchers, Executive Director; (765) 962-1638; fax (765) 966-0882; steve@waynecountyfoundation.org
Internet: www.waynecountyfoundation.org/index.html
Sponsor: Wayne County Foundation
33 South 7th Street, Suite 1
Richmond, IN 47374

Weaver Foundation Grants   2420
The mission of the Weaver Foundation is to help the Greater Greensboro community enhance and improve the quality of life and the economic environment for its citizens while developing a sense of philanthropy, civic education, and commitment in current and

future generations of the founders' families. The focus areas include support for education; programs for children and youth; protection of the environment; efforts to reduce poverty and improve the lives of the disadvantaged and the needy; advancement of human and civil rights, racial tolerance, and diversity; enhancement of parks, recreation, and the quality of life; and economic development. Inquiries are welcomed via letter, telephone, or email; full proposals are by invitation. Grants are generally made quarterly.

Requirements: 501(c)3 nonprofits serving the greater Greensboro, North Carolina, community are eligible.

Restrictions: The foundation does not support political programs or voter registration efforts, conferences, travel, video production, fraternal groups, individuals, or religious organizations.

Geographic Focus: North Carolina

Amount of Grant: 500 - 50,000 USD

Samples: North Carolina Zoological Society, Greensboro, North Carolina, $5,000 - general operating support; Barnabas Network, Greensboro, North Carolina, $40,000 - self-sufficiency through capacity building support; Family Service of the Piedmont, Piedmont, North Carolina, $45,000 - Greensboro Children's Advocacy Center support.

Contact: Lee McAllister; (336) 378-7910; fax (336) 275-9602; info@weaverfoundation.com

Internet: weaverfoundation.com/guidelines/

Sponsor: Weaver Foundation

324 West Wendover Avenue, Suite 300, P.O. Box 26040

Greensboro, NC 27408-8440

Weaver Popcorn Foundation Grants 2421

Established in Indiana in 1997, the Weaver Popcorn Foundation offers funding throughout the State of Indiana. Its primary fields of interest include: boy scouts; children and youth services; education; family services; domestic violence; health care; higher education; human services; and secondary school programs. The primary type of funding is general operating support. A formal application is not required, and interested parties should submit a brief overview/history of the organization, its mission, and an outline of budgetary needs. There are no annual deadlines specified. Typical awards range from $250 to $20,000, though some grants have reached as much as $125,000.

Requirements: Any Indiana non-profit is eligible to apply.

Geographic Focus: Indiana

Amount of Grant: 250 - 125,000 USD

Samples: Bishop Chatard High School, Indianapolis, Indiana, $5,000 - general operations; Heritage Pointe, Warren, Indiana, $1,000 - general operations; Marian University, Indianapolis, Indiana, $550,000 - general operations.

Contact: Brian Hamilton, Chief Financial Officer; (317) 688-1308

Sponsor: Weaver Popcorn Foundation

4485 South Perry Worth Road

Whitestown, IN 46075-8804

Wege Foundation Grants 2422

The Wege Foundation awards grants in Michigan in five specific categories: education, environment, arts and culture, health care, and human services. Areas of interest include children and youth services; Christian agencies and churches; community development; elementary and secondary education; environmental resources; higher education; hospitals (general); human services; museums; and performing arts. The Foundation strives to be an inspiration for other communities. According to the Foundation's vision, "Grand Rapids inspires others to create communities that forge a balance in the environment, health, education, and arts to encourage healthier lives in mind, body, and spirit."

Requirements: Grants are awarded to nonprofit organizations in the greater Kent County, MI, area, with emphasis on the Grand Rapids area. The applicant may access the application after an online quiz.

Restrictions: The Foundation only funds organizations classified as tax-exempt under section 501(c)3 of the Internal Revenue Code. Grants are not awarded for operating budgets.

Geographic Focus: Michigan

Date(s) Application is Due: Feb 15; Sep 15

Contact: Jody Price, Corporate Financial Officer; (616) 957-0480; fax (616) 957-0616; jprice@wegefoundation.org

Internet: www.wegefoundation.com/seekingagrant/seekingagrant.html

Sponsor: Wege Foundation

P.O. Box 6388

Grand Rapids, MI 49516-6388

Welborn Baptist Foundation Promotion of Early Childhood Development Grants 2423

The Welborn Baptist Foundation is seeking to fund lasting change in the communities it serves. Towards that end, the Foundation will assess grant proposals based on: demonstrated long-term results, or exceptional potential for such results based on well-established research; addressing root causes rather than symptoms; fit with the Foundation's target areas of emphasis; deep, established collaborations with (not just referrals from) other like-minded organizations; excellent prospects for long-term sustainability without Foundation resources; and a clear implementation plan that enables successes to be replicated elsewhere. Ultimate success in the Promotion of Early Childhood Development target area would be reflected in every child entering kindergarten at grade level reading readiness, as well as physically, socially, and emotionally ready to learn. As such, the Foundation's historical support has focused on key determinants of this success such as high-quality child care, parent engagement, and school readiness programs. These areas will continue to be paramount; the Foundation is also interested in considering: research-based initiatives which improve outcomes for high-risk children in child care with family, friends, and/or

neighbors; and not-for-profit child care programs embedding best practices on increasing physical activity and healthier eating.

Requirements: Giving is limited to: Gallatin, Saline, Wabash, Wayne and White counties in Illinous; Dubois, Gibson, Perry, Pike, Posey, Spencer, Vanderburgh, and Warrick counties in Indiana; and Henderson County, Kentucky. Applicants must submit a Letter of Interest (LOI). All secular, church and other faith-based not-for-profit organizations that are tax exempt under section 501(c)3 of the IRS Code are eligible. Participation beyond the Letter of Interest stage is by invitation only.

Restrictions: The following program and project areas will not be considered for funding: scholarships, loans, grants or fellowship support directly to or for the benefit of specific and known individuals; establishment of, or contributions to, a permanent endowment, foundation, trust or permanent interest-bearing account; carrying on of propaganda or attempt to influence legislation or public elections; restricting the services, facilities or employment provided by the grant to individuals based on race, creed, color, sex, or national origin; any governmental agencies reporting to an elected or appointed official (except for schools governed by citizens boards); any requests for funding for deficits or retirement of debt; fundraising events; annual fund drives; venture capital for competitive profit making ventures; or basic scientific research. Additionally, it should be noted that the Foundation does not fund applications seeking replacement dollars (i.e., funding to substitute for dollars lost from another grantor).

Geographic Focus: Illinois, Indiana, Kentucky

Contact: Kevin Bain, Executive Director; (812) 437-8260 or (877) 437-8260; fax (812) 437-8269; info@welbornfdn.org

Internet: www.welbornfdn.org/grant-process/funding-targets

Sponsor: Welborn Baptist Foundation

Twenty-One Southeast Third Street, Suite 610

Evansville, IN 47708

Welborn Baptist Foundation School Based Health Grants 2424

The Welborn Baptist Foundation is seeking to fund lasting change in the communities it serves. Towards that end, the Foundation will assess grant proposals based on: demonstrated long-term results, or exceptional potential for such results based on well-established research; addressing root causes rather than symptoms; fit with the Foundation's target areas of emphasis; deep, established collaborations with (not just referrals from) other like-minded organizations; excellent prospects for long-term sustainability without Foundation resources; and a clear implementation plan that enables successes to be replicated elsewhere. The School Based Health target area, known as HEROES, is a three-year commitment, during which a school will focus on implementing the Centers for Disease Control's Coordinated School Health Model (CSH) into their school environment and begin to change their school's culture. The funding from WBF is geared towards the Physical Education/Physical Activity and Nutrition components of CSH, but the schools are also expected to begin making changes in the other six components as well.

Requirements: Giving is limited to: Gallatin, Saline, Wabash, Wayne and White counties in Illinous; Dubois, Gibson, Perry, Pike, Posey, Spencer, Vanderburgh, and Warrick counties in Indiana; and Henderson County, Kentucky. Applicants must submit a Letter of Interest (LOI). All secular, church and other faith-based not-for-profit organizations that are tax exempt under section 501(c)3 of the IRS Code are eligible. Participation beyond the Letter of Interest stage is by invitation only.

Restrictions: The following program and project areas will not be considered for funding: scholarships, loans, grants or fellowship support directly to or for the benefit of specific and known individuals; establishment of, or contributions to, a permanent endowment, foundation, trust or permanent interest-bearing account; carrying on of propaganda or attempt to influence legislation or public elections; restricting the services, facilities or employment provided by the grant to individuals based on race, creed, color, sex, or national origin; any governmental agencies reporting to an elected or appointed official (except for schools governed by citizens boards); any requests for funding for deficits or retirement of debt; fundraising events; annual fund drives; venture capital for competitive profit making ventures; or basic scientific research. Additionally, it should be noted that the Foundation does not fund applications seeking replacement dollars (i.e., funding to substitute for dollars lost from another grantor).

Geographic Focus: Illinois, Indiana, Kentucky

Contact: Kevin Bain, Executive Director; (812) 437-8260 or (877) 437-8260; fax (812) 437-8269; info@welbornfdn.org

Internet: www.welbornfdn.org/grant-process/funding-targets

Sponsor: Welborn Baptist Foundation

Twenty-One Southeast Third Street, Suite 610

Evansville, IN 47708

Welborn Foundation Promotion of Healthy Adolescent Development Grants 2425

The Welborn Baptist Foundation is seeking to fund lasting change in the communities it serves. Towards that end, the Foundation will assess grant proposals based on: demonstrated long-term results, or exceptional potential for such results based on well-established research; addressing root causes rather than symptoms; fit with the Foundation's target areas of emphasis; deep, established collaborations with (not just referrals from) other like-minded organizations; excellent prospects for long-term sustainability without Foundation resources; and a clear implementation plan that enables successes to be replicated elsewhere. The Foundation's ultimate objective in funding proposals in the Healthy Adolescent Development target area is for every adolescent in the community to have the coping skills and access to positive influences that will maximize their personal development and health. Consequently, the Foundation's primary focus is on: programs that result in fewer adolescents indulging in high-risk behaviors (with a particular emphasis on substance abuse); and programs that result in more adolescents having the self image, educational attainment, and coping skills that are associated with consistent and significant adult involvement in their lives (with a particular emphasis on mentoring and enhanced family relationships).

Requirements: Giving is limited to: Gallatin, Saline, Wabash, Wayne and White counties in Illinous; Dubois, Gibson, Perry, Pike, Posey, Spencer, Vanderburgh, and Warrick counties in Indiana; and Henderson County, Kentucky. Applicants must submit a Letter of Interest (LOI). All secular, church and other faith-based not-for-profit organizations that are tax exempt under section 501(c)3 of the IRS Code are eligible. Participation beyond the Letter of Interest stage is by invitation only.

Restrictions: The following program and project areas will not be considered for funding: scholarships, loans, grants or fellowship support directly to or for the benefit of specific and known individuals; establishment of, or contributions to, a permanent endowment, foundation, trust or permanent interest-bearing account; carrying on of propaganda or attempt to influence legislation or public elections; restricting the services, facilities or employment provided by the grant to individuals based on race, creed, color, sex, or national origin; any governmental agencies reporting to an elected or appointed official (except for schools governed by citizens boards); any requests for funding for deficits or retirement of debt; fundraising events; annual fund drives; venture capital for competitive profit making ventures; or basic scientific research. Additionally, it should be noted that the Foundation does not fund applications seeking replacement dollars (i.e., funding to substitute for dollars lost from another grantor).

Geographic Focus: Illinois, Indiana, Kentucky

Contact: Kevin Bain, Executive Director; (812) 437-8260 or (877) 437-8260; fax (812) 437-8269; info@welbornfdn.org

Internet: www.welbornfdn.org/grant-process/funding-targets

Sponsor: Welborn Baptist Foundation

Twenty-One Southeast Third Street, Suite 610

Evansville, IN 47708

Wells County Foundation Grants   **2426**

The Wells County Foundation Grants give priority to programs having a positive effect on the Wells County community. Grant making fields of interest include arts and culture, education, civic affairs, youth, environment, community development, animal welfare, recreation, and health and human services. In reviewing grant proposals, the Foundation gives careful consideration to: the potential impact of the request and the number of people benefited; an innovative approach; the degree to which the applicant works with or complements the services of other community organizations; the extent of local involvement and support for the project; the organization's demonstrated fiscal responsibility and management qualification; and the organization's ability to obtain necessary additional and future funding.

Requirements: Applicants are encouraged to contact the Foundation to discuss their project. They should be prepared to give a brief discussion to enable the Foundation to determine whether the request falls within the grant-making guidelines. In addition, the staff will inform the applicant of the deadline for the most current grant cycle. Grant proposals for projects should include the following: a title page with the organization's contact information, the project's title and amount requested; a proposal narrative, summarizing what issues the project will address, its expectations, how many will benefit, the role of volunteers, its planned evaluation, and a signed endorsement by the Board of Directors; financial information, with the project budget, two pricing quotes for equipment requested, a list of other funding sources, and the project's funding for the future; and organizational information, including a brief history with mission and purpose, list of officers, financial statement or audit, and a copy of the tax exemption the IRS.

Restrictions: No grants will be made to any political organization or to support attempts to influence the legislation of any governing body than through making available to the community at large the results of non-partisan analysis, study and/or research.

Geographic Focus: Indiana

Date(s) Application is Due: Feb 15; Jun 15; Oct 17

Samples: Bluffton Parks & Recreation Department, purchase of an ADA compliant pool lift chair for the Wells Community swimming pool so that patrons can enter and exit the pool independently, $7,000; Community Action of Northeast Indiana (CANI), provide emergency assistance to Wells County families through CANI's Homeles Prevention Rapid Re-housing Program so that families can work toward self-sufficiency, $3,000; Family Centered Services, Inc, to provide administrative funding for the Youth As Resources program so that young people can design and carry out service projects that address specific community needs, $7,000.

Contact: Tammy Slater, Chief Executive Officer; (260) 824-8620; fax (260) 824-3981; wellscountyfound@wellscountyfound.org

Internet: www.wellscountyfound.org/Grants.html

Sponsor: Wells County Foundation

360 North Main Street, Suite C

Bluffton, IN 46714

Westerman Foundation Grants   **2427**

The mission of the Westerman Foundation is to provide financial support to educational institutions with emphasis on Catholic education; Christian based organizations, which promote family unity and values; and programs, which provide assistance to the poor and the abused. Founded by Laura "Jane" Westerman in June of 2000, the Foundation has provided over $5.4 million in grant funding to over 240 organizations across the United States. Most recently, the Covid-19 pandemic has prompted the Foundation to be nimble and responsive to the changing needs of nonprofit organizations and the families and communities that they serve. Small grants of $5,000 or less are given, as well as larger grants up to $50,000 maximum. The annual application submission deadline is August 1.

Requirements: Any 501(c)3 organization whose purpose is aligned with Foundation priorities is eligible to apply.

Geographic Focus: All States

Date(s) Application is Due: Aug 1

Amount of Grant: Up to 50,000 USD

Samples: Bishop John Carroll School, Oklahoma City, Oklahoma - general operating support for Catholic education (2020); Dallas Area Rape Crisis Center, Dallas, Texas - general operating support for rape and domestic abuse victims (2020); Wesley-Rankin Community Center, Dallas, Texas - general operating support of community programs for the poor (2020).

Contact: Valerie H. Goddard, Executive Director; (813) 257-9477; v.goddard@thewestermanfoundation.org or info@thewestermanfoundation.org

Internet: www.thewestermanfoundation.org/copy-of-grants

Sponsor: Westerman Foundation

3225 South MacDill Avenue, Suite 129

Tampa, FL 33629

Western Indiana Community Foundation Grants   **2428**

The Western Indiana Community Foundation focuses its attention on local needs within the geographical boundaries as set by the Board of Directors. Primary fields of interest include: health, charitable service, education, cultural affairs, and community improvement. The Foundation is especially interested in learning of plans for: start-up costs for new programs; one-time projects or needs; and capital needs beyond an applicant's capabilities and needs. Grant applications may be submitted throughout the year. Applicants will be notified immediately following the Board of Directors decision.

Requirements: Organizations must fill out the online application and include the following information: their full contact information, description of the project, and grant request amount; other funding sources for the project, an itemized expenses list and project timeline; the organization's IRS tax exempt status, how they plan to evaluate the project, and a description of public relations plans/foundation funding. The application packet should then be mailed to the Foundation,

Restrictions: The Foundation will not consider: grants for individuals; organizations for political or religious purposes; support for regular operating budgets; contributions to endowments; providing for long term funding; post-event situations; or apparel such as school/sport uniforms.

Geographic Focus: Indiana

Amount of Grant: Up to 10,000 USD

Samples: City of Covington - $1,600 for mobile life guard chairs at the city swimming pool; Friendship Circle Center - $3,373 annual payout for operations and parking lot resurfacing; Fountain County Mentoring - $2,605 for youth field trip to Chicago's Shedd Aquarium and Museum of Science and Industry; Covington High School - $500 - for SAFE-TALK training session for faculty and staff to help identify students who are high risk for suicide or other self-destructive behaviors.

Contact: Dale White, Executive Director; (765)-793-0702; fax (765)-793-0703; dwhite@wicf-inc.org or info@wicf-inc.org

Internet: www.wicf-inc.org/grant_guidelines.asp

Sponsor: Western Indiana Community Foundation

135 South Stringtown Road

Covington, IN 47932-0175

Western New York Foundation Grants   **2429**

The Foundation supports sustainable organizations that improve the quality of life in Western New York. The Foundation makes investments that build on nonprofits' proven strengths in order to improve their effectiveness and their ability to fulfill their missions. Funding is provided in these categories: human services; education; urban and rural development; arts, culture, and humanities; and housing, park and land use. Deadline dates for the Alignment Determination Application (Letter of Inquiry) submissions are June 30 and November 30. If approved, a formal go-ahead will be given to submit an Organizational Assessment Application, with a deadline three weeks after receiving the go-ahead.

Requirements: Western New York State 501(c)3 organizations located within one of the following counties are eligible: Allegany, Cattaraugus, Chautauqua, Erie, Genesee, Niagara, and Wyoming. All applicants must have three years of 990 filings in order to be eligible to apply for a grant.

Restrictions: Only one application may be submitted at a time. Funded organizations may reapply two years following the final payment of an award. The following are ineligible: religious organizations for religious purposes; political organizations, campaigns, and candidates; municipal and government entities; grants or loans to individuals; fundraising events, i.e. sponsorships, tables, dinners, and telethons; endowments; scholarships; operating expenses; hospital capital campaigns; and general capital campaigns.

Geographic Focus: New York

Contact: Beth Kinsman Gosch, Executive Director; (716) 839-4225; fax (716) 883-1107; bgosch@wnyfoundation.org

Internet: www.wnyfoundation.org

Sponsor: Western New York Foundation

11 Summer Street, Fourth Floor

Buffalo, NY 14209

West Virginia Commission on the Arts Challenge America Partnership Grants   **2430**

The primary purpose of the West Virginia Commission on the Arts Challenge America Partnership Grants is to strengthen America's communities through the unique power of the arts. The focus of the program is on arts education and outreach documentation and evaluation, with funds available for projects in the areas of arts education, access to the arts, positive alternatives for youth, cultural heritage/preservation, and community arts development. All applicants must submit a letter of intent by December 1.

Requirements: Nonprofit West Virginia arts organizations with current West Virginia Division of Culture and History or West Virginia Commission on the Arts grants or past successful grant administration track records with proven success of incorporating artists and arts projects in community development, health or social improvement, and economic development programs are eligible. College and university arts faculty and departments that present community outreach and arts in education opportunities to the region surrounding their institution are also eligible. Applicants must provide 50% cash match.

Geographic Focus: West Virginia
Date(s) Application is Due: Feb 1
Amount of Grant: 15,000 USD
Contact: Barbara Anderson, Grants Administrator; (304) 558-0240; fax (304) 558-2779; Barbie.J.Anderson@wv.gov
Internet: www.wvculture.org/arts/grantbook/tech.htm#challenge
Sponsor: West Virginia Commission on the Arts
1900 Kanawha Boulevard E
Charleston, WV 25305-0300

West Virginia Commission on the Arts Long-Term Artist Residencies   2431

The primary purpose of the Long-Term Artist Residencies is to provide funding for curriculum-based, hands-on projects that involve an identified group of students and teachers in the creative process and integrate the arts into daily instruction. Projects must provide teachers with the tools that will enable them to continue to utilize the arts after the residency is completed and the artist leaves. Residency projects (5 weeks or longer, up to one year) present an artist in a series of programs that demonstrate his/her artistry and skills. Residencies are a partnership between the sponsor, whether a school or community, and the artist. The residency should be organized to meet specific goals developed by a residency committee and should stress the creative aspects of the artist's work including interpretation of the training and skills required to be an artist. A residency committee comprising community leaders, artists, educators, and other appropriate persons must be organized and must select an artist who meets the commission's criteria and who will also best suit the structure of the project in terms of talent, personality, working methods, medium, etc. Applications should include a description of program sites, equipment, curriculum objectives, artist selection procedure, schedule, budget, evaluation procedures, housing and travel arrangements for the artist, and plans for professional development workshops for teachers and administrators. Financial assistance for the long-term residency is limited to two years unless the sponsor can justify the need to continue the support because of the rural or underserved audience involved in the project. Sponsors of long-term residencies may request 50 percent artist contract fee as well as expenses, and supplies needed for the residency, up to a maximum request of $12,000. A letter of intent is requested by December 1; full application is due by March 1.

Requirements: Residency sponsors may be West Virginia schools, community arts organizations, arts institutions, or libraries. The eligibility of other types of organizations will be considered case by case.
Geographic Focus: West Virginia
Date(s) Application is Due: Mar 1
Amount of Grant: Up to 12,000 USD
Contact: Barbara Anderson, Arts in Education Coordinator; (304) 558-0240; fax (304) 558-2779; Barbie.J.Anderson@wv.gov
Internet: www.wvculture.org/arts/grantbook/artsined.htm#long
Sponsor: West Virginia Commission on the Arts
1900 Kanawha Boulevard E
Charleston, WV 25305-0300

West Virginia Commission on the Arts Short-Term Artist Residencies   2432

The Short-Term Artist Residencies primary purpose is to provide funding for curriculum-based, hands-on projects that involve an identified group of students and teachers in the creative process and integrate the arts into daily instruction. Projects must provide teachers with the tools that will enable them to continue to utilize the arts after the residency is completed. Residency projects (1 - 4 weeks or total of 5 - 20 days over a longer period of time) present an artist in a series of programs that demonstrate his/her artistry and skills. Residencies are a partnership between the sponsor, whether a school or community, and the artist. The residency should be organized to meet specific goals developed by a residency committee and should stress the creative aspects of the artist's work including interpretation of the training and skills required to be an artist. All residencies should be developed using the West Virginia Department of Education Fine Arts Content Standards and Objectives.

Requirements: Residency sponsors may be West Virginia schools, community arts organizations, arts institutions, or libraries. The eligibility of other types of organizations will be considered case-by-case. Applicant must provide a 50% cash match.
Geographic Focus: West Virginia
Date(s) Application is Due: Mar 1
Contact: Barbara Anderson, Grants Coordinator; (304) 558-0240; fax (304) 558-2779; Barbie.J.Anderson@wv.gov
Internet: www.wvculture.org/arts/grantbook/artsined.htm#short
Sponsor: West Virginia Commission on the Arts
1900 Kanawha Boulevard E
Charleston, WV 25305-0300

West Virginia Commission on the Arts Special Projects Grants   2433

The purpose of the West Virginia Commission on the Arts Special Projects Grants is to provide funding for new and ongoing projects that establish, expand or advance both school curriculum and arts education programming. Funding supports projects that actively engage students or educators beyond arts "exposure" experiences. These projects typically occur in classroom or school settings but support is also available for projects benefiting students, teachers, or artists occurring outside of school. Proposals might include, but are not limited to: teacher or student hands-on arts workshops, development of education

programs by artists or arts organizations that will tour the schools; summer or after-school programs; creation of educational materials in conjunction with arts programs; projects that strengthen a current school arts program by adding unavailable components; and innovative partnerships between schools and community arts organizations. Funding is limited to 50% of the fees for artists, specialists, consultants; equipment/materials required to develop the project is limited to $150.

Requirements: West Virginia schools, non-profit arts organizations or other community organizations incorporating the arts into their mission. Projects should be developed using the West Virginia Department of Education Fine Arts Content Standards and Objectives. A 50% cash match is required.
Geographic Focus: West Virginia
Date(s) Application is Due: Mar 1
Contact: Barbara Anderson, Grants Manager; (304) 558-0240; fax (304) 558-2779; Barbie.J.Anderson@wv.gov
Internet: www.wvculture.org/arts/grantbook/artsined.htm#special
Sponsor: West Virginia Commission on the Arts
1900 Kanawha Boulevard E
Charleston, WV 25305-0300

WestWind Foundation Reproductive Health and Rights Grants   2434

Concerned with an exploding population in the Latin American and Caribbean region caused by inadequate access to reproductive health services, the Trustees of the WestWind Foundation decided to create a program that would support NGOs that work to provide services and improve access both in the region and in other parts of the globe. The goals of the Reproductive Health and Rights program are to support NGOs that seek to: improve access to reproductive health services, particularly in the LAC region; promote reproductive health and rights, both domestically and abroad; and promote adolescent sexual and reproductive health, both domestically and in the LAC region. he foundation supports organizations that seek to advance a range of reproductive health issues, including, but not limited to: supporting emergency contraception; promoting adolescent sexuality education and empowerment; preventing maternal mortality; and providing post-abortion care. Applicants should submit an online Letter of Inquiry (LOI) prior to the annual deadline. Typically, WestWind will respond to LOIs between four to six weeks after the letter has been received.

Requirements: The RHR Program currently supports non-governmental organizations (NGOs) that work both domestically and abroad to improve women's access to reproductive health services. Grants in the RHRP area are made primarily to U.S. based organizations for: international projects in the Latin America and Caribbean region; and projects that have national significance. There is also a small portion of funds that are available for global, opportunistic projects.
Geographic Focus: All States
Date(s) Application is Due: Mar 1
Amount of Grant: 5,000 - 225,000 USD
Samples: Advocates for Youth, Washington, D.C., $100,000 - in support of international advocacy and programs; Catholics for Choice, Washington, D.C., $45,000 - general operating support; Public Health Institute/International Health Programs, Santa Cruz, California, $100,000 - project support for the Adolescent Girls Advocacy and Leadership Initiative (AGALI).
Contact: Kristen Miller, Program Consultant; (434) 977-5762, ext. 24; fax (434) 977-3176; bonnell@westwindfoundation.org or info@westwindfoundation.org
Internet: www.westwindfoundation.org/program-areas/reproductive-health-rights/
Sponsor: WestWind Foundation
204 East High Street
Charlottesville, VA 22902

Weyerhaeuser Family Foundation Health Grants   2435

The Weyerhaeuser Family Foundation supports programs of national and international significance that promote the welfare of human and natural resources. These efforts will enhance the creativity, strengths and skills already possessed by those in need and reinforce the sustaining processes inherent in nature. The Foundation supports multi-site, national or international projects dealing with mental health, chemical dependency and population and family planning. Multi-site, national and international educational projects will also be considered. The Letter of Intent is the first step in the application process and should be no more than two pages, to which you must attach a one-page budget summary and an Application Cover Sheet-General program. The average grant can range up to $25,000.

Requirements: U.S. nonprofit, tax-exempt organizations are eligible.
Restrictions: The General Program does not fund projects serving only local or regional domestic areas; to be eligible, projects must be multi-site, national or international. In addition, the Foundation will not consider proposals in the following areas: books or media projects, unless the project is connected to other areas of Foundation interest; capital projects; individuals, scholarships or fellowships; land acquisitions or trades; lobbying activity; ongoing projects or general operating support for an organization; organizations located outside the United States; or research projects.
Geographic Focus: All States
Date(s) Application is Due: Apr 1; Aug 1
Amount of Grant: Up to 25,000 USD
Contact: Peter A. Konrad; (303) 993-5385; pkonrad@konradconsulting.com
Internet: www.wfamilyfoundation.org/general_program.html
Sponsor: Weyerhaeuser Family Foundation
2000 Wells Fargo Place, 30 East Seventh Street
St. Paul, MN 55101-4930

Whatcom Community Foundation Grants   2436

Whatcom Community Foundation is a nonprofit, publicly-supported philanthropic institution that manages a pool of charitable funds whose income is used to meet the changing needs of the greater Whatcom County community. The Foundation serves as a funding partner to area nonprofits that engage in community-building projects in Whatcom County. Funding is provided in the following fields: arts and culture; children with special healthcare needs; environment; mental health; and youth and family. Through the South Fork Community Fund, awards are also made to support effective educational, social and recreational programs, and services for children, youth and families to help build community in the South Fork Valley area. Additional information regarding funding available and deadlines is posted to the website as it becomes available.

Requirements: Washington tax-exempt nonprofit organizations serving Whatcom County are eligible. The Foundation is primarily interested in working with organizations and individuals to build community capacity, which is defined as the combined influence of the community's commitment, resources, and skills which can be utilized to build on community strengths and address community challenges.

Restrictions: The Foundation will not: review incomplete grant applications or those out of the requested format; make grants when the activities are not clearly described; make grants when the outcomes are not specific or realistic; make grants when the income and expense statements are incomplete or unclear; make grants for capital requests (bricks and mortar), endowment funds, debt retirement, political campaigns, religious activities, memberships in civic organizations or trade associations, courtesy advertising, tickets for benefits, and fundraising events; make grants to individuals or for-profit organizations; or make grants to organizations that discriminate on the basis of gender, religion, sexual orientation, ethnicity, national origin or physical ability. The Foundation is less likely to: fund organizational or operating support; make grants for more than one year; support one-time events; make grants that provide direct service without building community; make grants over $10,000; make grants directly or indirectly to governmental organizations; or make grants for capital equipment over $500.

Geographic Focus: Washington
Date(s) Application is Due: Jan 31
Amount of Grant: 1,000 - 10,000 USD
Samples: Alzheimer Society of Washington, Bellingham, Washington, $3,000 - program support; Futurewise Whatcom, Bellingham, Washington, $10,000 - program support; and Northwest Indian College, Bellingham, Washington, $10,000 - program support.
Contact: Pamela Jons, Director of Advancement and Programs; (360) 671-6463; fax (360) 671-6437; pjons@whatcomcf.org
Internet: www.whatcomcf.org/apply_for_grant.html
Sponsor: Whatcom Community Foundation
119 Grand Avenue, Suite A
Bellingham, WA 98225

White County Community Foundation - Landis Memorial Scholarship   2437

The White County Community Foundation - Landis Memorial Scholarship is available to Twin Lakes graduating seniors intending to pursue higher education at a college, university, or school of training. Applicants must be well-rounded students who are active in their school, community, or church, with a B average or better. Financial need will be a strong consideration. Any college major is eligible.

Requirements: In addition to the online application, student submit a personal insight essay; an official high school transcript; a copy of their college acceptance letter; and a written recommendation from a teacher. The application packet may be sent to the student's guidance office by February 7 or to the Foundation by February 29.

Geographic Focus: Indiana
Date(s) Application is Due: Feb 7; Feb 29
Amount of Grant: 10,000 USD
Contact: Lesley Wineland Goss; (574) 583-6911; fax (574) 583-8757; director@whitecf.org
Internet: www.whitecf.org/GrantScol.html
Sponsor: White County Community Foundation
1001 South Main Street
Monticello, IN 47960

White County Community Foundation - Women Giving Together Grants   2438

The White County Community Foundation - Women Giving Together Grants address White County's women and families, and inspire women to strengthen White County through charitable giving. Members of Women Giving Together believe that high priority issues should be addressed thoughtfully to inspire social change and improve the quality of life in White County. Grant funding focuses on community enhancement, education, and social/human services. Program priorities: must serve a charitable purpose; serve the needs of the women and families of the greater White County area; demonstrate an innovative and unique approach; and indicate other funding sources.

Requirements: Applicants are encouraged to contact the Foundation to be certain their project meets the Foundation's guidelines. Organizations submit the online application to include the following information: their organization's contact information and organization's mission statement; amount requested for the project with its timeline; a narrative that describes the organization, its need, project description, and how it will benefit the White County area; a list of those responsible, with timeline and funding sources other than the WGT; how the project will be financed in the future and how it will affect the community. Organizations should also submit a detailed budget; financial statements; the IRS determination letter; and a list of board members and their authorization for the project.

Restrictions: Projects not funded include: non-charitable projects and organizations; projects fully funded by local government; projects to fund an endowment, ongoing operating budgets, existing deficit, debt reduction, or multi-year, long-term funding; religious activities that do not serve the community as a whole; special events such as parades, festivals, or sporting activities; political organizations or campaigns; national and state fundraising efforts; project that indicate discrimination.

Geographic Focus: Indiana
Date(s) Application is Due: Oct 1
Contact: Lesley Wineland Goss; (574) 583-6911; fax (574) 583-8757; director@whitecf.org
Internet: www.whitecf.org/WGTGrant.html
Sponsor: White County Community Foundation
1001 South Main Street
Monticello, IN 47960

Whitehorse Foundation Grants   2439

The Whitehorse Foundation was established in 1990 as a supporting organization of The Seattle Foundation. The mission of The Whitehorse Foundation is to fund organizations working to improve the quality of life for residents of Snohomish County, Washington. Each grant application to the Foundation is thoughtfully considered by the Foundation's Board of Trustees. There is a two-step application process. The first step in seeking support is to submit a concise two-page letter of inquiry describing your project and request. The second step is a formal application process for those requests that are determined to meet the Foundation's funding criteria. Letters of inquiry can be submitted at any time and the board meets twice a year to consider funding requests. Grants are made to nonprofit organizations for project support or ongoing operating support. The Foundation is interested in programs in the early stages of development, which convey an achievable funding plan (demonstrating strong community commitment) or a compelling impact. The Foundation is interested in programs that: focus on prevention and root causes of problems rather than intervention; address many problems at once, rather than one problem at a time; strengthen families' capacity to support, nurture and guide their children; promote responsible parenthood to improve children's emotional, economic and social well-being; enable families to acquire the knowledge and skills needed for self-sufficiency; involve families and community residents in program design, development and management; will have a significant and ongoing impact; and offer opportunities for leveraging resources by forming partnerships with other grantmakers, other nonprofits, the government and the private sector.

Requirements: The Whitehorse Foundation supports nonprofit organizations in Snohomish County that work to improve the lives of children, youth and families. All applicant organizations must qualify as tax-exempt under section 501(c)3 of the IRS code.

Geographic Focus: Washington
Amount of Grant: Up to 250,000 USD
Samples: Cocoon House, Everett, Washington, $45,000 - to support the home visiting component of Project S.A.F.E.; Deaconess Children's Services, Everett, Washington, $40,000 - to support the Teen Parent Advocacy Program; Lutheran Community Services Northwest, Sea Tac, Washington, $230,000 - to support the Family Support Centers in Snohomish County.
Contact: Ceil Erickson, Grantmaking Director; (206) 515-2131 or (206) 515-2109; c.erickson@seattlefoundation.org or grantmaking@seattlefoundation.org
Internet: www.seattlefoundation.org/nonprofits/whitehorse/Pages/ WhitehorseFoundation.aspx
Sponsor: Whitehorse Foundation
1200 Fifth Avenue, Suite 1300
Seattle, WA 98101-3151

Whiting Foundation Grants   2440

Whiting Foundation Grants award funds in the Genesee County area, including the city of Flint, Michigan, with emphasis on basic human needs, the needs of the underprivileged, and cultural activities. Awards range from $2,500 to $25,000.

Requirements: There is no application form. Applicants should submit a concise request describing the proposed activity and an explanation of the need. A current and future budget with details of administrative and salary expenses should be included.

Geographic Focus: Michigan
Date(s) Application is Due: Apr 30
Samples: Flint Cultural Center Corp., Flint, Michigan, $25,500 - parking lot and lobby lighting; St. Paul's Episcopal Church, Flint, Michigan, $2,500 - summer concert series; and Flint Cultural Center Corporation, Flint, Michigan, $10,000 - music in the park.
Contact: Donald E. Johnson, Jr., President; (810) 767-3600
Sponsor: Whiting Foundation
718 Harrison Street
Flint, MI 48502

Whitney Foundation Grants   2441

The Foundation awards grants to nonprofit organizations primarily in Minnesota in its areas of interest, including AIDS prevention, arts, children and youth services, education, and human services. Types of support include program development, annual campaigns, and continuing support. Application forms are not required. Awards range from $100 to $5,000.

Requirements: Eligible applicants must be 501(c)3 organizations.

Geographic Focus: Minnesota
Samples: Marjorie McNeely Conservatory, St. Paul, Minnesota, $500 - general support; Lake Forest Hospital Foundation, Lake Forest, Illinois, $250 - general support; and Minnesota Zoo Foundation, Apple Valley, Minnesota, $250 - general support.
Contact: Carol VanOrnum, (952) 835-2577
Sponsor: Whitney Foundation
601 Carlson Parkway
Minnetonka, MN 55305

WHO Foundation Education/Literacy Grants 2442

The WHO Foundation nationally supports grass-roots charities serving the overlooked needs of women and children. Grants are provided to organizations dedicated to education and literacy of children. Up to $5,000 can be requested for after-school programs, libraries, tutoring, mentoring programs, preschool or early education, shelters, child care programs, or other programs benefiting women and children.

Requirements: In order to qualify for funding, an organization must have a 501(c)3 status in their name (no affiliates accepted) and must have been incorporated for a minimum of 3 years prior to application. Funding will be considered, but not guaranteed, to charities which focus on education and meet the following criteria: total organization budget of $3 million or less; all Government funding totaling less than 30% of income; and, United Way funding of less than 30% of income. Funding requests must be made using the WHO Foundation application. Electronic and faxed submissions will not be accepted. Please note that the foundation does not wish to receive phone calls.

Restrictions: Funding will not be given to the following types of organizations, activities, or purposes: personal requests, loans or scholarships to individuals; international programs or projects; government agencies; fiscal agents; religious organizations; foundations that are grant making institutions; advertising in charitable publications; sports organizations; research projects; travel for individuals or groups; conferences, galas, charity balls, sponsorships, seminars, or reunions; capital campaigns; or salaries.

Geographic Focus: All States, American Samoa, Guam, Marshall Islands, Northern Mariana Islands, Puerto Rico, U.S. Virgin Islands

Amount of Grant: Up to 5,000 USD

Contact: Cindy Turek, Executive Director; (800) 946-4663 or (972) 341-3019; fax (972) 341-3080; who@beauticontrol.com

Internet: www.whofoundation.org/WHO_FundingEd.htm

Sponsor: Women Helping Others Foundation

P.O. Box 816029

Dallas, TX 75381-6029

WHO Foundation General Grants 2443

The WHO Foundation nationally supports grass-roots charities serving the overlooked needs of women and children. Grants are provided to organizations serving women and/or children in the United States and Puerto Rico. Specific projects and programs addressing health, education, and social service needs are the priority. The foundation recognizes the value of new programs created to respond to changing needs and will consider funding projects of an original or pioneering nature within an existing organization. Application and guidelines are available for download at the sponsor's website.

Requirements: 501(c)3 nonprofit organizations in the United States and Puerto Rico are eligible. Organizations must have been incorporated for a minimum of three years prior to application. Preference will be given to organizations with an operating budget of $3 million or less, those not dependent upon government grants, and those with greater organizational program costs than personnel costs. Funding requests must be made using the WHO Foundation application. Electronic and faxed submissions will not be accepted.

Restrictions: The following types of organizations, activities or purposes will not be considered: personal requests, loans or scholarships to individuals; educational institutions; endowment campaigns; international programs or projects; government agencies; fiscal agents; religious organizations (including young Men's and Women's Christian Association); political causes, candidates, organizations or campaigns; foundations that are grant making institutions; advertising in charitable publications; sports organizations; labor groups; research projects; travel for individuals or groups; conferences, galas, charity balls, sponsorships, seminars, or reunions; capital campaigns; salaries; or building campaigns (i.e. Habitat for Humanity).

Geographic Focus: All States, Puerto Rico

Amount of Grant: 5,000 - 30,000 USD

Contact: Cindy Turek, Executive Director; (800) 946-4663 or (972) 341-3019; fax (972) 341-3080; who@beauticontrol.com

Internet: www.whofoundation.org/WHO_FundingCriteria.htm

Sponsor: Women Helping Others Foundation

P.O. Box 816029

Dallas, TX 75381-6029

WHO Foundation Volunteer Service Grants 2444

The WHO Foundation nationally supports grass–roots charities serving the overlooked needs of women and children. Grants are provided to organizations serving women and/or children in the United States and Puerto Rico. Specific projects and programs addressing health and social service needs are its priority. The Foundation recognizes the value of new programs created to respond to changing needs and will consider funding projects of an original or pioneering nature within an existing organization. Funding will be considered for: human services, including homelessness, abuse and neglect, hunger, and domestic violence; health services, including the medically uninsured, therapeutic programs, and physical or mental disabilities; and education, including free afterschool programs, adult education, job training, GED programs, and literacy. Applications must be received no later than June 2. Grant requests from $1,000 up to $40,000 will be considered.

Requirements: In order to qualify for funding, an organization must have a 501(c)3 rating in their name (no affiliates or fiscal agents accepted) for a minimum of three (3) years prior to application. All funds must be used in the calendar year in which they are received.

Restrictions: Funding will not be considered for: personal requests, loans or scholarships to individuals; international programs or projects; conferences or seminars; travel for individuals or groups; educational institutions and their foundations; political causes, candidates, organizations or campaigns; religious purposes, including church groups and activities; foundations that are grant making institutions; research projects; annual or capital fund campaigns, underwriting or sponsor events; salaries; endowment funds; sports organizations or athletic activities; or animal welfare.

Geographic Focus: All States, Puerto Rico

Date(s) Application is Due: Jun 2

Contact: Cindy Turek, Executive Director; (800) 946-4663 or (972) 341-3019; fax (972) 341-3080; who@beauticontrol.com

Internet: www.whofoundation.org/Funding/index.asp

Sponsor: Women Helping Others Foundation

P.O. Box 816029

Dallas, TX 75381-6029

Whole Foods Foundation 2445

The Whole Foods Foundation makes various charitable contributions and awards grants in its company locations throughout the United States, Canada, and the United Kingdom. The primary areas of interest include: agricultural programs; elementary and secondary education; environmental programs; gardens; literacy; mentoring; family support; housing; health access; and human services. Typically, awards range up to a maximum of $20,000, and are given in the form of general operating support and sponsorships. An online application is required, though there are no specified deadlines. Final notification typically takes between six and eight weeks.

Requirements: Support is limited to 501(c)3 organizations supporting residents near company operations in Alabama, Arizona, Arkansas, California, Colorado, Connecticut, District of Columbia, Florida, Georgia, Hawaii, Illinois, Indiana, Kansas, Kentucky, Louisiana, Maine, Maryland, Massachusetts, Michigan, Minnesota, Missouri, Nebraska, Nevada, New Jersey, New Mexico, New York, North Carolina, Ohio, Oklahoma, Oregon, Pennsylvania, Rhode Island, South Carolina, Tennessee, Texas, Utah, Virginia, Washington, and Wisconsin, and in Canada and the United Kingdom.

Geographic Focus: Alabama, Arizona, Arkansas, California, Colorado, Connecticut, District of Columbia, Florida, Georgia, Hawaii, Illinois, Indiana, Kansas, Kentucky, Louisiana, Maine, Maryland, Massachusetts, Michigan, Minnesota, Missouri, Nebraska, Nevada, New Jersey, New Mexico, New York, North Carolina, Ohio, Oklahoma, Oregon, Pennsylvania, Rhode Island, South Carolina, Tennessee, Texas, Utah, Virginia, Washington, Wisconsin, Canada, United Kingdom

Amount of Grant: Up to 20,000 USD

Contact: Grants Administrator; (512) 477-4455 or (844) 936-8255; fax (512) 482-7000; info@wholefoodsfoundation.org

Internet: www.wholefoodsmarket.com/donate

Sponsor: Whole Foods Foundation

550 Bowie Street

Austin, TX 78703-4644

Whole Kids Foundation School Garden Grants 2446

Whole Kids Foundation's mission is to improve children's nutrition and wellness with the goal of ending the childhood obesity epidemic. Through partnerships with innovative organizations, schools and educators the Foundation works to provide children access to healthier choices and aims to help children reach their full potential through the strength of a healthy body. School Garden Grants are a collaboration between Whole Kids Foundation, Whole Foods Market and FoodCorps. Learning about the process of growing food helps children develop a deep understanding of the connection between healthy eating and a healthy body. School gardens offer an opportunity to integrate math, science and health curriculum into a dynamic, interactive setting. They also provide a base of knowledge that allows children to take an active role in healthy food choices.

Requirements: Applicants must: be a nonprofit school or school district (public, private or charter, elementary, middle or secondary) or a 501(c)3 nonprofit organization working in partnership with one or more schools; be located in the United States, Canada, or the United Kingdom; have the capacity to manage grant funds responsibly and the skills and experience necessary to undertake a project involving school gardens; demonstrate that the garden project has strong participation from stakeholders, including the school principal, volunteers and a community partner; demonstrate thoughtful consideration is being given to the technical challenges of school garden construction and maintenance: soil testing, water availability, tool storage and municipal regulations; and articulate a compelling plan for integrating the garden into the life of the school and community, including plans to put the garden's produce to good use. Funding priority is given to both limited-resource communities and to projects that demonstrate strong buy-in from stakeholders.

Restrictions: There is a limit of one garden grant per school.

Geographic Focus: All States, Canada, United Kingdom

Date(s) Application is Due: Dec 31

Amount of Grant: 2,000 - 2,000 USD

Contact: Nona Evans, Executive Director; info@gardengrantapplication.org

Internet: www.wholekidsfoundation.org/gardengrants.php

Sponsor: Whole Kids Foundation

550 Bowie Street

Austin, TX 78703

Widgeon Point Charitable Foundation Grants 2447

The foundation supports nonprofits in New York and Connecticut in its areas of interest, including secondary, higher, legal, and medical education; youth; zoos; museums; arts and culture; conservation and environment; historic preservation; family planning; libraries; and religion. Types of support include general operating budgets, capital campaigns, building funds, endowment funds, equipment acquisition, conferences and seminars, publications, and renovation projects. There are no application deadlines. Applicants should submit a two-page letter of application.

Requirements: Nonprofits in New York and Connecticut are eligible. The foundation does not accept unsolicited proposals. Interested and qualified organizations should submit a letter of inquiry prior to preparing a formal proposal. There are no specific deadlines.

Restrictions: Grants are not awarded to individuals or for endowments, capital costs, renovation, equipment, conferences, publications, and media projects.
Geographic Focus: Connecticut, New York
Amount of Grant: 1,000 - 25,000 USD
Contact: Jeffrey Coopersmith, (516) 483-5800 or (516) 483-5815; jcoopersmith@csvpc.com
Sponsor: Widgeon Point Charitable Foundation
50 Charles Lindbergh Boulevard, Suite 605
Uniondale, NY 11553-3650

Wild Rivers Community Foundation Holiday Partnership Grants 2448
The Wild Rivers Community Foundation hosts an annual Holiday Partnership to assist our community with raising resources over the holidays for those in need. Organizations in Del Norte and Curry County, who help provide emergency supplies, food, winter clothing, hygiene products and gifts to children and adults in the region during the upcoming holiday season are encouraged to link with each other during this program. The application and additional information are available at the website.
Requirements: Applicants must be nonprofit organizations serving children and adults in the counties of Del Norte or Curry.
Geographic Focus: California
Date(s) Application is Due: Nov 1
Contact: Geneva Wiki; (707) 465-1238; fax (707) 465-1209; gwiki@wildriverscf.org
Internet: www.wildriverscf.org/content/view/112/108/
Sponsor: Wild Rivers Community Foundation
879 J Street, Suite I
Crescent City, CA 95531

Wild Rivers Community Foundation Summer Youth Mini Grants 2449
The Wild Rivers Community Foundation is committed to supporting children and youth, and values programs that offer opportunities for them to learn, play and develop in a safe, productive setting while school is not in session. The Foundation recognizes that organizations offering summer programs for children and youth are integral to providing those opportunities. Small grants are awarded to agencies to expand and enrich summer recreation programs for Del Norte and Curry County children operating between June and September. Grants are normally made for expenses such as sports and recreational equipment, arts and craft supplies, special events and field trips, and camperships for low-income participants. The Summer Youth Program often provides grants to help defray the costs of transportation, equipment, and scholarships. The application and additional information are available at the website.
Requirements: Applicants must be nonprofit organizations that provide summer youth programs in the counties of Del Norte or Curry.
Geographic Focus: California
Date(s) Application is Due: Apr 1
Amount of Grant: Up to 450 USD
Contact: Gina Zottola; (707) 465-1238; fax (707) 465-1209; gzottola@wildriverscf.org
Internet: www.wildriverscf.org/content/view/106/
Sponsor: Wild Rivers Community Foundation
879 J Street, Suite I
Crescent City, CA 95531

Wilkins Family Foundation Grants 2450
The Wilkins Family Foundation was established in Kansas in 1994 by C. Howard Wilkins, Jr., the former owner of Pizza Hut, and the U.S. Ambassador to the Netherlands from 1989 to 1992. Currently, the Foundation awards grants to U.S. nonprofit organizations in its areas of interest, including: special projects; community service organizations; economic development activities; and cultural organizations involved with education and health issues of children 17 years of age and younger. Letters of interest are accepted at any time; full proposals are by invitation only.
Requirements: 501(c)3 tax-exempt organizations are eligible.
Restrictions: The Foundation does not make multiyear commitments and prefers to fund causes, rather than management expenses.
Geographic Focus: All States
Contact: C. Howard Wilkins, Jr.; (316) 685-8281; proposals@wilkinsfamilyfoundation.org
Sponsor: Wilkins Family Foundation
302 N Rock Road, Suite 200
Wichita, KS 67206-2255

William A. Badger Foundation Grants 2451
The Nabors to Neighbors Foundation was created in 2007 to assist charitable organizations focusing on need based projects for direct programming, capital and operating initiatives. This is a family foundation dedicated to organizations that deliver measurable results, seek partnerships and collaborations, utilize their resources within their respective communities while working to increase equity for those most in need. The Foundation encourages nonprofit organizations to apply who specialize in, though not limited to, improving the lives of children, education and medical initiatives. The Foundation makes no geographic restrictions on distributions. However, it has been the practice of the Trustees to make grants within Whitfield County, specifically Dalton, located in north Georgia. Requests must be postmarked by February 1, July 9 or October 1 in order to be considered.
Requirements: The Nabors to Neighbors Foundation makes grants to qualified 501(c)3 organizations. All requests must include: background information on the organization, including a brief history, the organization's current address and phone number and the name and title or the primary contact; the goals, objectives, and budget for the one project or program for which funds are being requested; the amount of the grant requested; summary of how the funds will be used; supporting financial information on the organization, to

include current financial status and listing of Board of Trustees; copy of organization's tax exemption letter from the Internal Revenue Service. Application form is available online and all requests must be postmarked by February 1, July 9 or October 1.
Restrictions: Grants are not made to: individuals; an organization to be used as pass-through funds for an ineligible organization Faith-based organizations without a 501(c)3 exemption; organizations with political purposes, nor to organizations which discriminate on the basis of race, ethnic origin, sexual or religious preference, age or gender.
Geographic Focus: All States
Date(s) Application is Due: Feb 1; Jul 9; Oct 1
Contact: Trustee, c/o Wachovia Bank; grantinquiries8@wachovia.com
Sponsor: Nabors to Neighbors Foundation
3280 Peachtree Road NE, Suite 400, MC G0141-041
Atlanta, GA 30305

William A. Cooke Foundation Grants 2452
Born in 1903, William A. Cooke served Louisa County for almost a century before his passing in 2001. As an attorney, a real-estate developer, a life-long member of the Louisa Volunteer Fire Department, and a substitute jurist, he was a pillar of the community in every way. The William A. Cooke Foundation provides funding for projects that benefit the residents of Louisa and Orange counties. In the past, the Foundation has been able to support a diverse range of public projects, including the Earthquake Relief Fund, the Cooke-Haley Theatre, renovation of area homes, and adult education programs. The first step in applying to the Foundation is submitting a short letter of inquiry. These letters are reviewed in an ongoing basis, with no annual deadlines for application submission.
Requirements: To be eligible for consideration, projects must be efforts involving a governmental unit or a not for profit tax exempt 501(c)3 organization as described in Section 509(a)1 or 2 of the Internal Revenue Code. Projects must have the support of appropriate organizations and must benefit the inhabitants of Louisa and/or Orange Counties.
Geographic Focus: Virginia
Amount of Grant: Up to 50,000 USD
Samples: Louisa Little League, Louisa, Virginia, $16,000 - improvements to baseball field; Louisa Historical Society, Louisa, Virginia, support of the Sargeant Museum; Louisa County Public Schools, Louisa, Virginia, $31,000 - general operating support.
Contact: Randall L. Tingler; (540) 967-0881; fax (540) 967-0711; rltingler1@gmail.com
Internet: wacookefoundation.com/pages/grant_fund.html
Sponsor: William A. Cooke Foundation
P.O. Box 462, 211 West Main Street
Louisa, VA 23093

William A. Miller Foundation Grants 2453
Established through a donation by Jayne Miller in Indiana in 2000, the William A. Miller Foundation gives support primarily in Hagerstown, Indiana. Its primary focus is on community and economic development, and it will consider support for the arts, community education, and general operating support for community area non-profits. There are no specific application formats or deadlines, and applicants should apply directly to the U.S. Bank office in the form of a two- to three-page letter.
Geographic Focus: Indiana
Amount of Grant: Up to 10,000 USD
Samples: Town of Hagerstown, Hagerstown, Indiana, $7,819 - general operations.
Contact: Trustee; (765) 965-2293
Sponsor: William A. Miller Foundation
P.O. Box 1118
Cincinnati, OH 45201-1118

William and Flora Hewlett Foundation Education Grants 2454
The William and Flora Hewlett Foundation has been making grants since 1967 to solve social and environmental problems at home and around the world. Two types of Education Grants are funded. The first is deeper learning which delivers the skills and knowledge students need to succeed in a world that is changing at an unprecedented pace. Deeper learning prepares students to: master core academic content; think critically and solve complex problems; work collaboratively; communicate effectively; and learn how to learn (e.g., self-directed learning). The second is open educational resources which are high-quality, openly licensed, online educational materials that offer an extraordinary opportunity for people everywhere to share, use, and reuse knowledge. Open educational resources demonstrate great potential as a mechanism for instructional innovation as networks of teachers and learners share best practices.
Requirements: Applicants whose project or organization aligns closely with the Foundation's goals and strategies, may submit a brief on-line letter of inquiry. The Foundation will provide Education Grants supporting deeper learning to organizations that: promote policies or strategies that create incentives for K-12 schools and community colleges to focus on deeper learning; build the capacity of the education system and teaching practices both online and in the classroom to reach large numbers of students with deeper learning; support proof points, including model K-12 schools and community colleges, and fund research that promotes deeper learning as an attainable and necessary goal for all students; and develop new, innovative models to increase access for all students and to improve deeper learning. The Foundation will provide Education Grants supporting open educational resources primarily by supporting the infrastructure needed to sustain a well-functioning open educational ecosystem and demonstration projects that strengthen student access to deeper learning in K-12 and community colleges.
Restrictions: The Foundation does not consider requests to fund student aid, individual scholarships, construction, equipment and computer purchases, health research, or health education programs. Few, if any, letters of inquiry are funded. A full proposal should not be submitted unless expressly requested. The majority of awards are made to organizations

by invitation. Due to the volume of submissions the Foundation does not respond to phone calls or emails regarding letters of inquiry. Submissions via the online letter of inquiry form receive a response within thirty days or as soon thereafter as possible.

Geographic Focus: All States

Samples: National Conference of State Legislatures, Denver, Colorado, $125,000, building awareness and capacity at the state level for college- and career-ready reform; Stanford University, Stanford, California, $150,000, national cost analysis on performance assessment and related outreach to policymakers.

Contact: Barbara Chow; (650) 234-4500; fax (650) 234-4501; info@hewlett.org

Internet: www.hewlett.org/Grantseekers

Sponsor: William and Flora Hewlett Foundation

2121 Sand Hill Road

Menlo Park, CA 94025

William and Flora Hewlett Foundation Environmental Grants 2455

The William and Flora Hewlett Foundation has been making grants since 1967 to solve social and environmental problems at home and around the world. The Foundation's Environmental Grants goals are to: conserve the Western United States and Canada for wildlife and people; slow global climate change by reducing greenhouse gas emissions; ensure that the United States energy supply is clean and consumption is efficient; and address environmental problems that disproportionately affect disadvantaged communities in the San Francisco Bay Area. Support for western conservation support four key strategies: land (protecting large open spaces); water (restoring river flows and conserve areas near rivers and streams); energy (reducing fossil fuel development and increase energy efficiency and renewable energy sources; and broad-based support (building broad-based support for land, water, and energy goals among key stakeholders). Support for energy and climate pursue strategies in three areas: global climate policy; national energy policy; and sustainable transportation. Support for the San Francisco Bay Area is provided to regional organizations partnering with residents of these communities to: improve and expand urban parks; support outdoor recreation programs for youth; and improve public transportation available to these communities.

Requirements: Applicants whose project or organization aligns closely with the Foundation's goals and strategies, may submit a brief on-line letter of inquiry. Western conservation is supported in twelve states and three Canadian provinces: Alaska, Arizona, California, Colorado, Idaho, Montana, Nevada, New Mexico, Oregon, Washington, Wyoming, British Columbia, Alberta, and Yukon.

Restrictions: The Foundation does not consider requests to fund student aid, individual scholarships, construction, equipment and computer purchases, health research, or health education programs. Few, if any, letters of inquiry are funded. A full proposal should not be submitted unless expressly requested. The majority of awards are made to organizations by invitation. Due to the volume of submissions the Foundation does not respond to phone calls or emails regarding letters of inquiry. Submissions via the online letter of inquiry form receive a response within thirty days or as soon thereafter as possible.

Geographic Focus: All States, Canada

Samples: Western Resource Advocates, Denver, Colorado, $25,000, board development; Defenders of Wildlife, Washington, D.C., $42,000, strategic planning.

Contact: Tom Steinbach; (650) 234-4500; fax (650) 234-4501; info@hewlett.org

Internet: www.hewlett.org/programs/environment-program

Sponsor: William and Flora Hewlett Foundation

2121 Sand Hill Road

Menlo Park, CA 94025

William and Flora Hewlett Foundation Quality Education in Developing 2456 Countries Grants

The William and Flora Hewlett Foundation has been making grants since 1967 to solve social and environmental problems at home and around the world. The Foundation's Quality Education in Developing Countries Grants support global advocacy and in-country efforts to improve children's learning. Grant activities are concentrated in three areas: tracking learning outcomes to increase awareness and accountability for student learning; improving instruction by supporting the development of effective instructional approaches that improve student learning in many schools at low cost; and mobilizing resources by advocating for sufficient resources to improve educational quality and for those resources to be used efficiently.

Requirements: Applicants whose project or organization aligns closely with the Foundation's goals and strategies, may submit a brief on-line letter of inquiry.

Restrictions: The Foundation does not support: activities in countries outside of those listed; individual schools; tuition or scholarships; work in secondary schools; work in colleges or universities; private schools; vocational schools; apprenticeship programs; health or school feeding programs; information communication technologies; infrastructure or building projects; conferences, environmental education; and orphanages Few, if any, letters of inquiry are funded. A full proposal should not be submitted unless expressly requested. The majority of awards are made to organizations by invitation. Due to the volume of submissions the Foundation does not respond to phone calls or emails regarding letters of inquiry. Submissions via the online letter of inquiry form receive a response within thirty days or as soon thereafter as possible.

Geographic Focus: Ghana, India, Kenya, Mali, Senegal, Tanzania, Uganda

Samples: New Schools Venture Fund, San Francisco, California, $100,000, education; Yale University, New Haven, Connecticut, $825,000, education.

Contact: Ruth Levine; (650) 234-4500; fax (650) 234-4501; info@hewlett.org

Internet: www.hewlett.org/programs/global-development-and-population-program/quality-education

Sponsor: William and Flora Hewlett Foundation

2121 Sand Hill Road

Menlo Park, CA 94025

William and Sandy Heitz Family Foundation Grants 2457

The William and Sandy Heitz Family Foundation was established in Milwaukee, Wisconsin, in 1994. The Foundation's primary fields of interest include: cancer research; the study of diseases and conditions; graduate and professional education; health and health care; heart and circulatory system diseases; human services; independent living for people with disabilities; medical education; public health; and special population support. Population groups targeted are: academics; children and youth; the economically; people with disabilities; hearing impairments; vision impairments; and students. Types of funding include: equipment purchase; general operating support; program development; and research and evaluation. Applicants should submit a detailed description of project and the amount of funding requested. Most recent awards have ranged from $250 to $75,000. There are no specified annual deadlines for application submission.

Requirements: Any 501(c)3 organization serving the Foundation's primary fields of interest are eligible to apply.

Geographic Focus: All States

Amount of Grant: 250 - 75,000 USD

Samples: Clemson University Foundation, Clemson, South Carolina, $250 - education; Medical College of Wisconsin, Milwaukee, Wisconsin, $75,000 - research support; Lukemia Lymphoma Foundation, Port Chester, New York, $2,000 - research support.

Contact: Sandra Heintz, President; (262) 377-3970

Sponsor: William and Sandy Heitz Family Foundation

10800 N. Haddonstone Place

Mequon, WI 53092

William B. Dietrich Foundation Grants 2458

The Foundation awards funding to nonprofits preferably for local needs. There are no submission deadlines. Areas of interest include children, the elderly, AIDS, museums, and libraries.

Requirements: Applicants may apply in writing, outlining the nature of the organization, the intended use of funds requested. A copy of the Internal Revenue Service determination letter should be submitted.

Restrictions: No grants are provided for individuals.

Geographic Focus: All States

Samples: AIDS Project, Los Angeles, California, $25,000 - general purposes; Fleisher Art Memorial, Philadelphia, Pennsylvania, $50,000 - general purposes; and University of Pennsylvania, Philadelphia, Pennsylvania, $155,750 - Museum of Archeology and Anthropology.

Contact: Frank G. Cooper, President; (215) 979-1919

Sponsor: William B. Dietrich Foundation

P.O. Box 58177

Philadelphia, PA 19102-8177

William B. Stokely Jr. Foundation Grants 2459

The Foundation participates in scholarship funding at various colleges and universities mainly in eastern Tennessee. Grants are made to the educational institutions, which then distribute funds through their scholarship programs. Consideration also is given to requests from the arts, health service, civic organizations, and youth services. The Foundation does not require completion of a formal application, nor are there established deadline dates. All proposals must be submitted in writing.

Geographic Focus: Tennessee

Amount of Grant: 250 - 100,000 USD

Samples: Joni and Friends Knoxville, Knoxville, Tennessee, $10,000 - disability ministry; Mercy Health Partners, Knoxville, Tennessee, $100,000 - medical services; and Friends of he Great Smoky Mountains, Kodak, Tennessee, $10,000 - land conservation.

Contact: William Stokely III, President; (865) 966-4878

Sponsor: William B. Stokely Jr. Foundation

620 Campbell Station Road, Suite 27

Knoxville, TN 37922-1636

William Bingham Foundation Grants 2460

As a family foundation, the William Bingham Foundation furthers the philanthropic intent of its founder, Elizabeth Bingham Blossom, to support organizations in the fields of education, science, health and human services, and the arts. A current area of interest is unsolicited proposals from organizations currently addressing water quality issues related to hydraulic fracturing in the Marcellus Shale drilling areas in New York, West Virginia, Ohio, Maryland, and Virginia. Awards range from $10,000 to $35,000.

Requirements: Grants are made only to public U.S. charities and range in size depending on program budget and goals. Although there are no additional geographic restrictions, grants often reflect the needs of the communities in which Trustees reside. From time to time, the Foundation selects a particular area of interest for requests coming from organizations with which they do not currently have a relationship. Currently proposals are accepted only from organizations that have been invited to apply. Organizations that have been invited to submit a grant proposal may contact the Foundation to obtain application forms.

Restrictions: Capital grants for new construction are limited to projects that seek U.S. Green Building Council LEED (Leadership in Energy and Environmental Design) certification at least at the Silver level. Grants for renovation are limited to projects that seek LEED certification. The Foundation limits higher education grants to Colleges and Universities that have signed the American College and University Presidents Climate Commitment. No grants are made to individuals.

Geographic Focus: All States

Samples: Association of Nature Center Administrators, Logan, Utah, $12,000 - for development of a strategic plan; Bowdoin College, Brunswick, Maine, $35,000 - for purchase of instruments and equipment for the Department of Earth and Oceanographic

Science; and McKee Botanical Garden, Vero Beach, Florida, $35,000 - for suport of the Garden Discovery Backpacks program.

Contact: Laura Gilbertson, Chief Administrator; (440) 331-6350; fax (440) 331-6810; info@WBinghamFoundation.org

Internet: www.wbinghamfoundation.org/procedures.html

Sponsor: William Bingham Foundation

20325 Center Ridge Road, Suite 629

Rocky River, OH 44116-3554

William Blair and Company Foundation Grants 2461

Contributing to the community is an important part of the culture of William Blair and Company. The Foundation was officially established in Illinois in 1980, with giving primarily centered around metropolitan Chicago. All partners of the firm contribute part of their individual share of profits to the Foundation. Donation requests are made to the Foundation by partners and employees. The Foundation supports a broad range of causes including: civic affairs; public safety; arts and culture; higher education; youth-oriented activities; healthcare research; cultural affairs; and civic charities. Types of support include: annual campaigns; building and renovation; capital campaigns; general operating support; endowments; fellowships; internship programs; and scholarship funding. There are no specific deadlines or applications forms. Funding typically ranges from $500 to $25,000.

Requirements: Requests can be made by sending a letter with a general description of the organization and its special purpose. Activities should have a significant impact on the Chicago metropolitan area.

Geographic Focus: Illinois

Samples: Doctors without Borders, Chicago, Illinois, $20,500 - general operating support; Department of Prints & Drawing at the Art Institute of Chicago, Illinois, $5,000 - general operating support.

Contact: E. David Coolidge III, Vice President; (312) 236-1600

Sponsor: William Blair and Company Foundation

222 W Adams Street, 28th Floor

Chicago, IL 60606

William Caspar Graustein Memorial Fund Corinne G. Levin Education Grants 2462

The mission of the William Caspar Graustein Memorial Fund is to improve the effectiveness of education in fostering both personal development and leadership for all children in Connecticut. The Fund has set three goals: engage young children more deeply in their own education; to support Connecticut communities in improving education for their elementary and pre-school children; and to develop both statewide and local leadership, dedicated to improving and advocating for education. The Levin Education Grants were established to honor the memory and continue the work of Corinne G. Levin, educator, civil libertarian, mentor and promoter of the health and welfare of children. The Fund is designed to enhance access and the quality of education for all children in Connecticut. The Fund aims to strengthen mutual trust and respect between parents and educators by supporting opportunities to work together. The Levin Fund believes that successful interactions will deepen relationships, cultivate new ideas, and encourage parents and teachers to build on positive experiences that benefit young children. The Levin Fund welcomes proposals from diverse community and school groups serving children in day care, pre-school, and kindergarten through grade eight. Preference is given to small projects that promote partnerships; build the capacity of parents and teachers regarding educational innovation; provide opportunities for the self-directed continuing education of educators; allow in-school educational resources for parents; support study/discussion groups to create common understanding of educational concerns; and provide workshops that build concepts/skills to improve education for young children. Funding is open to any Connecticut parent, school and community groups, and nonprofit organizations working on behalf of education and children in Connecticut.

Requirements: Organizations should contact the Memorial Fund for an application. Two copies of the application are due by November 1 and May 1 before board of director meetings. Applicants are notified of the Board's decision within one week of the meeting.

Restrictions: Funding is not available for organizations without a 501(c)3 IRS determination letter; individuals; religious organizations for sectarian purposes; capital campaigns; political causes and activities; or scholarships.

Geographic Focus: Connecticut

Date(s) Application is Due: May 1; Nov 1

Amount of Grant: 500 - 1,000 USD

Contact: Elaine Pace, Grants Manager; (203) 230-3330; fax (203) 230-3331; epace@wcgmf.org

Internet: www.wcgmf.org/grants_other_clf.html

Sponsor: William Caspar Graustein Memorial Fund

2319 Whitney Avenue, Suite 2B

Hamden, CT 06518

William E. Barth Foundation Grants 2463

The William E. Barth Foundation was established as a charitable, non-operating, private foundation through a donation by Louise Barth Laffan and Dorothy Barth Jockell. The Foundation was established in honor of Laffan's and Jockell's brother, William E. Barth. Laffan and Jockell each taught in the Jefferson County School System. Throughout their lifetimes, they exemplified a strong interest in the welfare of children. Today, the Foundation awards grants to eligible Kentucky nonprofit organizations to improve the quality of life in the area. Special interest is given to projects that benefit local children. Grants have supported the area's zoological garden, art museum, and rehabilitation facility. The board meets once a year to review requests.

Requirements: Kentucky nonprofit organizations serving Louisville and Jefferson County are eligible to apply.

Restrictions: No support is provided for political organization or individuals.

Geographic Focus: Kentucky

Date(s) Application is Due: May 31

Amount of Grant: Up to 20,000 USD

Samples: University of Louisville, Louisville, Kentucky, $4,000 - general operations; Louisville Zoo, Louisville, Kentucky, $20,000 - construction and renovation; Project Warm, Louisville, Kentucky, $3,000 - operating support.

Contact: Allen Dodd III, (502) 584-1108; information@doddanddodd.com

Internet: www.doddattorneys.com/CM/Custom/William-E-Barth-Foundation.asp

Sponsor: William E. Barth Foundation

325 W Main Street, 2000 Waterfront Plaza

Saint Louisville, KY 40202

William E. Dean III Charitable Foundation Grants 2464

Dr. William Evans Dean III (Bill) attended the University of Texas at Austin and the University of Nevada. He served his country in Vietnam as part of the U.S. Air Force and later graduated with honors from dental school. In addition to all these accomplishments, he was a registered Texas longhorn rancher, recreational pilot and avid animal lover. His passion for helping others continues in perpetuity through the establishment of the William E. Dean III Charitable Foundation, which he created in 2009. The Dean III Foundation was created exclusively for charitable, religious, scientific, literary and educational purposes. In his lifetime, Dr. William Evans Dean favorably considered applications in support of helping canines and soldiers with the transition back into civilian life, or for the prevention of cruelty to animals. William E. Dean III Charitable Foundation grants typically range between $5,000 and $250,000.

Requirements: Charitable grants are awarded to 501(c)3 organizations within the United States and the District of Columbia. Applications will be submitted online through the Bank of America website. A grant report is required within 1 year of the grant application date, regardless of whether all of the funds have been spent.

Restrictions: Eligibility to re-apply for a grant award from the Foundation requires the organization to skip 1 grant cycle (1 year) before submitting a subsequent application. The trust does not support requests from individuals, organizations attempting to influence policy through direct lobbying, or any political campaigns.

Geographic Focus: All States

Date(s) Application is Due: Jul 1

Amount of Grant: 5,000 - 250,000 USD

Samples: Haven for Hope, San Antonio, Texas, $250,000 - Awarded for unrestricted gift - sustainability (2018); American National Red Cross, Austin, Texas, $163,825 - Awarded to support hurricane relief (2018); San Antonio Food Bank Inc., San Antonio, Texas, $163,825 - Awarded to replenish shelves at historic lows (2018).

Contact: Debra Goldstein Phares, Philanthropic Client Director; (800) 357-7094; tx.philanthropic@bankofamerica.com or tx.philanthropic@ustrust.com

Internet: www.bankofamerica.com/philanthropic/foundation/?fnId=163

Sponsor: William E. Dean III Charitable Foundation

P.O. Box 831041

Dallas, TX 75283-1041

William Foulds Family Foundation Grants 2465

The William Foulds Family Foundation was established in 1984 to support and promote quality educational, cultural, and recreational programming for underserved populations. Preference is given to charitable organizations that serve the people of Manchester, Connecticut. Grants from the Foulds Family Foundation are 1 year in duration. Award amounts go up to $8,000. Bank of America acts as co-trustee of the Foulds Family Foundation, in conjunction with Mr. Gerald A. Joseloff.

Requirements: Applicants must have 501(c)3 tax-exempt status and serve communities in Connecticut. The William Foulds Family Foundation does not use the standard grant application, and interested applicants should email the grant's Bank of America contact to receive an application (indicate in the email subject line: Foulds Family Foundation application request). In order to facilitate review of your proposal, please submit 3 copies of your completed grant application.

Restrictions: Grant requests for capital projects will not be considered. Applicants will not be awarded a grant for more than 3 consecutive years. The foundation does not support requests from individuals, organizations attempting to influence policy through direct lobbying, or any political campaigns.

Geographic Focus: Connecticut

Date(s) Application is Due: Apr 30

Amount of Grant: Up to 8,000 USD

Samples: North United Methodist Church, Manchester, Connecticut, $8,055 - annual grant for religious objects, uses, and purposes for the church (2018); Boy Scouts of America, East Hartford, Connecticut, $5,925 - awarded for Scoutreach in Greater Manchester (2018); Hartford Symphony Orchestra Inc., Hartford, Connecticut, $5,370 - annual grant for musical instruments for the symphony (2018).

Contact: Amy R. Lynch, Philanthropic Client Manager; (860) 244-4870; ct.grantmaking@bankofamerica.com or amy.r.lynch@bofa.com

Internet: www.bankofamerica.com/philanthropic/foundation/?fnId=104

Sponsor: William Foulds Family Foundation

200 Glastonbury Boulevard, Suite #200, CT2-545-02-05

Glastonbury, CT 06033-4056

William G. and Helen C. Hoffman Foundation Grants 2466

Helen C. Hoffman resided in the Village of South Orange, New Jersey. Her foundation was established in 1998 in memory of herself and her husband after the death of their daughter Corinne Blair. Her testamentary wish was to establish this foundation for charitable, religious, scientific, literary, and educational purposes. Her preference was to support blindness and its cure. Approximately 90% of the grants will provide support to the blind and, to medical research for the prevention of blindness. The remaining 10% will fund annual grants in the following areas of interest: education, the arts, environment and, social/civic causes. Requests must be received by January 15 for the March meeting and, August 22 for the October meeting. Application forms are available online. Applicants will receive notice acknowledging receipt of the grant request, and subsequently be notified of the grant declination or approval.

Requirements: Any U.S. 501(c)3 non-profit organizations may apply. Proposals should be submitted in the following format: completed Common Grant Application Form; an original Proposal Statement; an audited financial report and a current year operating budget; a copy of your official IRS Letter with your tax determination; a listing of your Board of Directors. Proposal Statements (second item in the above Format) should answer these questions: what are the objectives and expected outcomes of this program/project/request; what strategies will be used to accomplish your objective; what is the timeline for completion; if this is part of an on-going program, how long has it been in operation; what criteria will you use to measure success; if the request is not fully funded, what other sources can you engage; an Itemized budget should be included; please describe any collaborative ventures. Prior to the distribution of funds, all approved grantees must sign and return a Grant Agreement Form, stating that the funds will be used for the purpose intended. Progress reports and Completion reports must also be filed as required for your specific grant. All current grantees must be in good standing with required documentation prior to submitting new proposals to any foundation.

Restrictions: Grants are not made for political purposes, nor to organizations which discriminate on the basis of race, ethnic origin, sexual or religious preference, age or gender.

Geographic Focus: All States

Date(s) Application is Due: Jan 15; Aug 22

Amount of Grant: 5,000 - 15,000 USD

Samples: Tri-County Scholarship Fund, $5,000—scholarships for economically disadvantaged students to receive a private elementary/secondary education; New Eyes for the Needy, Inc., $20,000— eyeglasses for poor Kentuckians; Christian Health Care Center Foundation, $10,000— support senior subsidies for adult day services.

Contact: Wachovia Bank, N.A., Trustee; grantinquiries2@wachovia.com

Internet: www.wellsfargo.com/private-foundations/hoffman-foundation

Sponsor: William G. and Helen C. Hoffman Foundation

190 River Road, NJ3132

Summit, NJ 07901

William G. Gilmore Foundation Grants 2467

The William G. Gilmore Foundation supports nonprofits primarily in the San Francisco Bay Area of California. Some funding is also available in Pueblo, Colorado, and Portland, Oregon. Support is concentrated primarily in: the arts; health services and care; children and youth programs; and social services. The foundation has two submissions windows each year: March 20 through March 30 for grants considered at the June board meeting; and September 20 through September 30 for grants considered at the December board meeting. Awards typically range from $1,000 to $50,000.

Requirements: California, Colorado, and Oregon 501(c)3 nonprofits are eligible to apply. Contact the Foundation for additional application information.

Restrictions: No grants are given directly to individuals.

Geographic Focus: California, Colorado, Oregon

Date(s) Application is Due: Mar 30; Sep 30

Amount of Grant: 1,000 - 50,000 USD

Contact: Jessica Sutton; (415) 561-6540, ext. 238; fax (415) 561-5477; jsutton@pfs-llc.net

Internet: www.williamggilmorefoundation.org/for-grantseekers/application-procedures/

Sponsor: William G. Gilmore Foundation

1660 Bush Street, Suite 300

San Francisco, CA 94109

William J. and Dorothy K. O'Neill Foundation Responsive Grants 2468

The William J. and Dorothy K. O'Neill Foundation's grant making activities include: family; health; arts and culture; community; animals; elementary and secondary education; environment; employment; fatherhood; recreation; religion; law enforcement and crime reduction; literacy; human services; and housing. Types of support include: general operating support; program development; seed grants; and matching funds. The Foundation has no formal application form; requests should be made in writing. Grants are awarded for capacity building activities that develop or improve the effectiveness, impact and strength of: the organization's Board of Trustees and/or its Board leadership; the organization's strategic plan; the organization's staff; and the organization's programs. Grant requests should include the amount; specific project goals, objectives, approach, and methods; project budget and timeline; other sources of funding; evaluation plan; qualifications and experience of key personnel; description of organization; most recent annual report; and copy of IRS classification letter. Requests may be submitted at any time, but will be considered four times each year when the grant making committee meets. Annual deadline dates may vary; contact program staff for exact dates.

Requirements: 501(c)3 organizations in metropolitan areas where O'Neill family members currently live are eligible, including Washington, D.C; Naples, Florida; Big Island, Hawaii; Baltimore/Annapolis, Maryland; New York, New York area; Cincinnati and Cleveland, Ohio; Columbus and Licking County, Ohio; Richmond and Virginia Beach, Virginia; and Houston, Texas.

Restrictions: The Foundation does not make grants to individuals, to organizations that are wholly outside the United States, or in response to form letters for annual appeals.

Geographic Focus: District of Columbia, Florida, Hawaii, Maryland, New York, Ohio, Texas, Virginia

Date(s) Application is Due: Feb 21; Aug 1

Amount of Grant: Up to 50,000 USD

Samples: Cleveland Sight Center, Cleveland, Ohio, $25,000 - support of early intervention for children with visual impairments (2018); Neighborhood Place of Puna, Keaau, Hawaii, $30,000 - support for the Homeless Family Outreach program (2018); Comunilife, New York, New York, $20,000 - support for the Life is Precious Family Strengthening project (2018).

Contact: Marci Lu, Senior Program Officer; (216) 831-4134, ext.105; fax (216) 831-3779; mlu@oneill-foundation.org or oneillfdn@aol.com

Leslie Perkul, President; (216) 831-4134, ext 103; fax (216) 831-3779; lperkul@oneill-foundation.org or oneillfdn@aol.com

Internet: oneill-foundation.org/apply-for-a-grant/

Sponsor: William J. and Dorothy K. O'Neill Foundation

7575 Northcliff Avenue, Suite 205

Cleveland, OH 44144

William J. and Gertrude R. Casper Foundation Grants 2469

William J. Casper was the grandson of the founder of the Leinenkugel Brewing Company, Jacob Leinenkugel. William served as the firm's president from 1964 until he retired in 1971. He also served as chairman of the company's board of directions until 1989. That's when he and his wife, Gertrude, established the William J. and Gertrude R. Casper Foundation. In supporting the residents of Chippewa Falls, the Foundation's primary fields of interest include scholarship awards to students who are residents of Chippewa Falls, as well as grants to organizations that improve the quality of life for its residents. Awards will support: arts and culture; child welfare; higher education; and human services. Types of support include: building and renovations; infrastructure; capital campaigns; exhibitions; general operating support; presentations and productions; program development; re-granting; and student financial aid. There are no annual deadlines specified, and a letter of application is required.

Requirements: Any 501(c)3 organization supporting the residents of Chippewa Falls, Wisconsin, are eligible to apply.

Geographic Focus: Wisconsin

Amount of Grant: Up to 50,000 USD

Samples: Community Foundation of Chippewa County, Chippewa Falls, Wisconsin, $50,000 - general operating funds; Booster Club Spring Extravaganza, Chippewa Falls, Wisconsin, $15,500 - general operating funds; Hallie Girls Softball, Chippewa Falls, Wisconsin, $5,300 - general operating funds.

Contact: Kim King, (715) 723-6618 or (414) 765-5118

Sponsor: William J. and Gertrude R. Casper Foundation

P.O. Box 3194

Milwaukee, WI 53201-3194

William J. and Tina Rosenberg Foundation Grants 2470

The William J. and Tina Rosenberg Foundation was established in Florida in 1970, with giving centered in the Dade County area. Currently, the Foundation's primary fields of interest include: public education; the environment; disadvantaged; social services; cultural programs; museums; and health care. Types of support are: emergency funds; general operating support; and seed money. There are no specific annual deadlines, and interested parties should send a letter of application directly to the Foundation. Most recent awards have ranged from $5,000 to $50,000.

Restrictions: No grant support is given to private schools or individuals.

Geographic Focus: Florida

Amount of Grant: 5,000 - 50,000 USD

Samples: Museum of Science, Miami, FL, $50,000 - general operating support; Historical Association of Southern Florida, Miami, FL, $25,000 - general operating support; Women's Emergency Network, Miami, Florida, $5,000 - promoting access to the Network.

Contact: Pam Admire, Administrator; (305) 444-6121; fax (305) 444-5508; info@sullivanadmire.com or pam.admire@sullivanadmire.com

Internet: www.sullivanadmire.com/charitable.html

Sponsor: William J. and Tina Rosenberg Foundation

255 Ponce de Leon Boulevard, Suite 320

Coral Gables, FL 33134

William J. Brace Charitable Trust 2471

The William J. Brace Charitable Trust was established in 1958 to support and promote quality educational, cultural, human services and health care programming, with a preference for the following 3 areas: Education and health of children, Health and care of older adults, and Hospitals in Kansas City, Missouri. The Brace Charitable Trust generally supports organizations that serve the residents of Kansas City, Missouri. Grants from the Trust are 1 year in duration. Award amounts typically range from $5,000 to $100,000.

Requirements: The Trust generally supports 501(c)3 organizations that serve the residents of Kansas City, Missouri. Applications will be submitted online through the Bank of America website. A grant report is required within 1 year of the grant application date, regardless of whether all of the funds have been spent.

Restrictions: Grant requests for capital support will not be considered. The trust does not support requests from individuals, organizations attempting to influence policy through direct lobbying, or any political campaigns.

Geographic Focus: Missouri

Date(s) Application is Due: Oct 31

Amount of Grant: 5,000 - 100,000 USD

Samples: Kansas City Care Clinic, Kansas City, Missouri, $100,000 - Awarded for Pediatric Primary Care (2019); Partnership for Regional Educational Preparation, Kansas City, Missouri, $50,000 - Awarded for general operating support (2019); Mid America Regional Council, Kansas City, Missouri, $40,000 - Awarded for Sustaining Age-Friendly Efforts in the Kansas City Region (2019).

Contact: Tony Twyman, Senior Philanthropic Client Manager; (816) 292-4342; mo.grantmaking@bankofamerica.com or tony.twyman@bofa.com
Internet: www.bankofamerica.com/philanthropic/foundation/?fnId=127
Sponsor: William J. Brace Charitable Trust
1200 Main Street, 14th Floor
Kansas City, MO 64121-9119

William M. Weaver Foundation Grants 2472

Established in Texas in 2003 by the William M. Weaver Charitable Trust, the Foundation offers funding support primarily in Dawson County, Texas. Its major fields of interest include: community development; economic development; and Protestant agencies and churches. Financial support typically comes in the form of general operating costs. There are no specified application forms required, so interested parties should formulate a proposal in letter form. This two- or three-page approach should include a detailed program overview, budgetary needs, and any goals that the organization has established. There are no annual deadlines listed. Most recent grants have ranged from $1,500 to $175,000.
Requirements: Any 501(c)3 nonprofit or Protestant agency/church serving the residents of Dawson County, Texas, are eligible to apply.
Geographic Focus: Texas
Amount of Grant: 1,500 - 175,000 USD
Samples: Dawson County Senior Citizens Center, Lamesa, Texas, $64,322 - general building renovations; City of Laemesa, Lamesa, Texas, $173,296 - public recreation facilities support; First Presbyterian Church, Lamesa, Texas, $58,257 - general operating support.
Contact: Elwood Freeman, President; (806) 872-5457 or (800) 554-8969
Sponsor: William M. Weaver Foundation
2651 JBS Parkway, Building 4, Suite E
Odessa, TX 79762

William Ray and Ruth E. Collins Foundation Grants 2473

The Collins Foundation was established by William Ray and Ruth E. Collins for charitable, religious and educational purposes of organizations within Boulder County, Colorado. The Collins' were residents of Boulder, and they were co-owners of a clothing and shoe store. The Foundation's primary fields of interest include: the arts; culture; humanities; education; the environment; animals; health; human services; and religion. The average funding range is $1,000 to $5,000, with approximately thirty awards given each year. Applications are accepted year-round, though they must be submitted by November 30 to be reviewed at the annual grant meeting that occurs in January.
Requirements: Giving is limited to charitable organizations operating in or supporting Boulder County, Colorado. Grantees must be qualified as public charities under section 501(c)3. Applications must be submitted through the online grant application form or alternative accessible application designed for assistive technology users.
Geographic Focus: Colorado
Date(s) Application is Due: Nov 30
Amount of Grant: 1,000 - 5,000 USD
Contact: George Weaver, Special Trustee; (888) 234-1999; fax (877) 746-5889; grantadministration@ wellsfargo.com
Internet: www.wellsfargo.com/privatefoundationgrants/collins
Sponsor: William Ray and Ruth E. Collins Foundation
1740 Broadway
Denver, CO 80274

Williams Companies Homegrown Giving Grants 2474

Williams' approach to community involvement – as part of our Core Values & Beliefs – is to serve as an exceptional neighbor in communities where employees live and our businesses operate. Williams and its employees volunteer at local schools, give to United Way and support local non-profits through our giving programs and volunteer activities. Involvement in the communities where we operate is at the heart of Williams. Grants are awarded to 501(c)3 nonprofit organizations in areas with a large company presence in support of civic, arts and culture, education, and health and human services programs and projects. The Homegrown Giving Program provides a resource for employees – involved in local non-profit organizations and schools – to identify ways to positively impact their communities. Because every community has unique needs, Homegrown Giving is geared for operating support, specific projects, sponsorships and education programs that benefit a Williams community. Donations range in dollar amounts from $100 to $5,000. Preferred submission time for contribution requests is February through November. Upon receipt of completed information, applicants should allow a minimum of six weeks for a response. Requests are reviewed on an ongoing basis.
Requirements: Nonprofit organizations located where Williams companies operate are eligible to apply.
Geographic Focus: Alabama, Louisiana, New Jersey, North Carolina, Oklahoma, Pennsylvania, South Carolina, Texas, Virginia
Amount of Grant: 100 - 5,000 USD
Contact: Keith Isbell, Williams Community Relations Office; 918-573-2000 or 800-945-5426; communityrelationstulsa@williams.com or keith.isbell@williams.com
Internet: www.williams.com/community
Sponsor: Williams Companies
One Williams Center, 47th Floor
Tulsa, OK 74172

William T. Grant Foundation Scholars Program 2475

The William T. Grant Scholars Program supports promising early-career researchers from diverse disciplines, who have demonstrated success in conducting high-quality research and are seeking to further develop and broaden their expertise. Candidates are nominated by a supporting institution and must submit five-year research plans that demonstrate creativity, intellectual rigor, and a commitment to continued professional development. Every year, four to six William T. Grant Scholars are selected and each receives $350,000 distributed over a five-year period.
Requirements: To be eligible for consideration, applicants must: be employed at a nonprofit institution, either in the United States or abroad; submit a project that is consistent with the Foundation's Current Research Interests; address issues that have compelling relevance for theory, and policies or practices, affecting the settings of youth ages 8 to 25 in the United States or a vulnerable subpopulation of those youth; and have received their terminal degree within seven years of submitting their application.
Restrictions: The Foundation rarely funds international work. The William T. Grant Scholars award must not replace the institution's current support of the applicant's research nor should it duplicate any other funding, received or pending.
Geographic Focus: All States
Date(s) Application is Due: Jul 6
Amount of Grant: 350,000 USD
Contact: Irene Williams, Grants Coordinator; (212) 752-0071; fax (212) 752-1398; iwilliams@wtgrantfdn.org or info@wtgrantfdn.org
Internet: www.wtgrantfoundation.org/funding_opportunities/fellowships/william_t__grant_scholars/william_t_grant_scholars
Sponsor: William T. Grant Foundation
570 Lexington Avenue, 18th Floor
New York, NY 10022-6837

Wilton and Effie Hebert Foundation Grants 2476

The Wilton and Effie Hebert Foundation was established in Texas in 1992, with funding aimed primarily at supporting programs that serve children and youth, as well as hospitals and health organizations. Funding is also available for elementary and secondary education, higher education, social services of all types, and Catholic organizations and churches. Support typically takes the form of capital and infrastructure, general operating funding, individual development programs, research and evaluation, and scholarship funds. There are no annual deadlines for application submissions, and awards generally range up to a maximum of $40,000.
Requirements: Any 501(c)3 organization serving the residents of Texas is eligible to apply.
Restrictions: Funding is not given directly to individuals.
Geographic Focus: Texas
Amount of Grant: Up to 40,000 USD
Samples: Art Museum of Southeast Texas, Beaumont, Texas, $10,000 - general operating support; Effie and Wilton Herbert Public Library, Port Neches, Texas, $39,000 - general operating support; Marion and Ed Hughes Public Library, Nederland, Texas, $38,000 - general operating support.
Contact: James M. Black, Attorney at Law; (409) 982-9433 or (409) 727-2345
Sponsor: Wilton and Effie Hebert Foundation
P.O. Box 908
Port Neches, TX 77619

Windham Foundation Grants 2477

Since its founding, the Windham Foundation has provided more than $10 million in grants to non-profit organizations to serve its mission of promoting Vermont's rural communities. Particular emphasis is given to projects which enhance the unique qualities of Vermont's small town life, support its natural and working landscape, sustain Vermont's social, cultural and natural resources or preserve its history and traditions while enhancing day-to-day community life. Grants are made to nonprofit organizations (501(c)3 with programs active in Vermont. The Foundation assists organizations in the following areas: agriculture and the food systems; disadvantaged youth; environmental enhancement; education (pre-K through college); public policy issues; promotion of the arts, crafts, and Vermont traditions; human services; and historical preservation. Proposals are evaluated on their fit for the Foundation; likelihood of success; fiscal strength; evidence of community support; capital and historical preservation; land conservation and farm viability. There is no fixed limit on the amount of grant requests although most will be within the $5,000 to $10,000 range. Grants are reviewed on a quarterly basis by the Board of Trustees. The committee recommendations are submitted to the Board for final approval at quarterly meetings. Although applications are reviewed quarterly, grant requests may be submitted at any time of the year.
Requirements: The Foundation does not pre-screen applications although it will respond to letters of inquiry or questions directed to the grants administrator. Personal interviews or site visits are not required but may be requested by the Foundation as part of the process. All applications must be submitted electronically. Applicants will be notified by mail of the Foundation's decision 10 to 12 weeks after the deadline.
Restrictions: Funding is not available for endowment campaigns; sporting activities, outings or events; fraternal or religious organizations, including schools with religious affiliation; individual fellowships or scholarships; summer camps, playgrounds or day care facilities, and skate parks unless part of a comprehensive after school program; specific cultural performances; publications or surveys; or affiliates of national organizations focused on particular diseases or those that provide emergency relief efforts.
Geographic Focus: Vermont
Date(s) Application is Due: Feb 15; May 3; Aug 2; Nov 2
Amount of Grant: 5,000 - 10,000 USD
Contact: Becky Nystrom, Executive Assistant; (802) 843-2211, ext. 10; fax (802) 843-2205; info@windham-foundation.net
Internet: www.windham-foundation.org/programs/grants.html
Sponsor: Windham Foundation
225 Townshend Road
Grafton, VT 05146

Winifred Johnson Clive Foundation Grants 2478

The Winifred Johnson Clive Foundation funds projects within the areas of education, the arts, and wildlife conservation, promoting the welfare of children and animals, responding to the challenges of aging, and supporting victims of domestic violence, abuse, and neglect. The trustees of the Winifred Johnson Clive Foundation live in many places throughout the United States. To be eligible for grant consideration, organizations must receive an invitation from a current trustee in order to submit an application. The annual deadlines for invited application submissions are February 24 and August 24.
Geographic Focus: All States
Date(s) Application is Due: Feb 24; Aug 24
Amount of Grant: 1,000 - 20,000 USD
Contact: Jessica Sutton; (415) 561-6540, ext. 238; fax (415) 561-5477; jsutton@pfs-llc.net
Internet: www.wjclivefoundation.org/for-grantseekers/
Sponsor: Winifred Johnson Clive Foundation
1660 Bush Street, Suite 300
San Francisco, CA 94109

WinnCompanies Charitable Giving 2479

WinnCompanies and its 3,000 team members believe it has an obligation to make positive contributions to the communities in which it does business. The pursuit of its daily mission strengthens communities by developing and managing multifamily housing, creating stable and safe homes, preserving and re-purposing historic structures, increasing the tax base, and generating jobs and economic vitality. At the same time, the company expresses its commitment to and support for the surrounding communities through a wide array of charitable, volunteer, and service-related activities. The social impact of its corporate citizenship efforts is embodied in the WinnCares program, which includes philanthropy and charitable contributions, partnerships with community non-profits, and the volunteering performed by its team members at the more than 580 properties it owns or manages nationwide.
Requirements: Any 501(c)3 organizations supporting residents of Massachusetts, North Carolina, Kentucky, Alaska, New Mexico, Virginia, Texas, Hawaii, or South Carolina are eligible to apply.
Geographic Focus: Alaska, Hawaii, Kentucky, Massachusetts, New Mexico, North Carolina, South Carolina, Texas, Virginia
Amount of Grant: Up to 20,000 USD
Contact: Gilbert J. Winn, President; (617) 742-4500; fax (617) 742-0725
Internet: www.winncompanies.com/winncares/
Sponsor: WinnCompanies
6 Faneuil Hall Market Place
Boston, MA 02109

Wiregrass Foundation Grants 2480

Wiregrass Foundation makes grants to nonprofit community organizations that positively impact the health, education, and quality of life of the Dothan area. The Foundation has three different types of grant applications: project grants, micro-grants, and capital improvement grants. For all grant programs, the Foundation considers applications four times per year at its April, June, August, and October Board of Directors' meetings. Each interested applicant must first register for an account, and then take an eligibility quiz before proceeding to the actual application. Annual grant application submission deadlines are: March 1; May 1; July 1; and September 1.
Requirements: Grants are made to eligible organizations that serve the population residing within a 50 mile radius of Dothan. Preference is given to organizations that are based in one or more of the four counties of Houston, Henry, Dale, and Geneva, Alabama. Organizations that have met one of the following criteria for at least the last 2 years are eligible to apply: a tax-exempt organization described in Section 501(c)3 of the Internal Revenue Code (which includes religious, charitable, educational, scientific and certain other organizations) that is not a private foundation; a private operating foundation described in Section 4940(d) of the Internal Revenue Code; or an organization described in Section 170(c)1 (governmental entities) or Section 511(a)2B (state colleges and universities) of the Internal Revenue Code.
Restrictions: Grants are not made to private foundations, supporting organizations described in Section 509(a)3 of the Internal Revenue Code, private or publicly held corporations, limited liability companies, or partnerships. It is not the Foundation policy to fund: churches, political organizations or causes, grants outside of the defined service area, individuals or fraternal bodies, ongoing general operating expenses, projects of a national or statewide scope, projects of more than 5 years' duration, or fundraisers. In addition, due to its focus on school systems, it is not the Foundation's policy to fund individual schools or school programs (extracurricular, internal, etc.), nor does the Foundation fund individual scholarships for students.
Geographic Focus: Alabama
Date(s) Application is Due: Mar 1; May 1; Jul 1; Sep 1
Contact: Cindy Bedsole; (334) 699-1031 or (334) 793-3122; office@wiregrassfoundation.org
Internet: wiregrassfoundation.org/?page_id=70
Sponsor: Wiregrass Foundation
1532 Whatley Drive
Dothan, AL 36303

Wisconsin Energy Foundation Grants 2481

The mission of the Foundation is to create brighter futures for the communities in which Wisconsin Energy Corporation does business, enhancing the growth and success of the company. The Foundation supports initiatives promoting economic health, arts and culture, education and environment.

Requirements: Applicants must be a 501(c)3 organization located in a community served by Wisconsin Energy Corporation. See the geographical funding area map on the website. Applications must be submitted online from the website.
Geographic Focus: Michigan, Wisconsin
Date(s) Application is Due: Jan 31; Apr 30; Jul 31; Oct 31
Contact: Patricia McNew; (414) 221-2107; patti.mcnew@we-energies.com
Internet: www.wec-foundation.com
Sponsor: Wisconsin Energy Foundation
231 West Michigan Street
Milwaukee, WI 53201

Wold Foundation Grants 2482

The Wold Foundation promotes charitable, scientific and educational programs with preference given to Wyoming citizens and Wyoming youth. It builds healthier societies and economic environments by supporting institutions and programs that preserve western values, promote free enterprise and conservative public policies. The Foundation's primary interest areas include: agriculture; Christianity; elementary and secondary education; family services; health care; higher education; human services; museums; shelter and residential care; sports; visual arts; and youth development. Funding generally comes in the form of general operating support and program support. There is a tremendous demand placed on the Foundation's resources and every effort is made to be as effective as possible in awarding the funds that are available for distribution. There are two grant funding cycles per year, with the application submission deadlines being April 15 and October 15. Awards have recently ranged as high as $500,000, though the vast majority are $5,000 or less.
Requirements: Applicant organizations must be classified as 501(c)3 by the Internal Revenue Service and operate within the continental United States. The Foundation will consider only one request per year from each organization and would generally prefer to consider special projects.
Restrictions: The Foundation will not consider grants to institutions which, in policy, or practice unfairly discriminate on the basis of sex, age or religion. The Foundation will not accept requests for individuals. Though it is impractical to detail all parameters, the Foundation generally will not: make loans or grants to individuals or loans to organizations; engage in conduit funding - i.e., make a grant to an exempt organization which passes the funds on to another organization; grant funds to retire debt; purchase memberships or blocks of tickets; purchase tickets for fund-raising dinner, parties, balls or other social fund- raising events; schedule interviews with the Foundation Trustees unless the Trustees initiate the meeting; fund churches or church projects; grant monies to endowment funds; support projects involving court action; or reconsider previously denied proposals.
Geographic Focus: Arizona, Colorado, Oregon, Wyoming
Date(s) Application is Due: Apr 15; Oct 15
Amount of Grant: Up to 500,000 USD
Samples: Science Zone, Casper, Wyoming, $5,000 - support for a zoo program (2018); St. Mark's Episcopal Church, Casper, Wyoming, $4,000 - support for the vocal music program (2018).
Contact: Glenda Thomas, Executive Director; (307) 265-7252; gthomas@woldfoundation.org
Internet: woldfoundation.org/guidelinesrestrictions
Sponsor: Wold Foundation
139 West 2nd Street, #200
Casper, WY 82601

Wolfe Associates Grants 2483

Wolfe Associates Grants are made in the following fields: health and medicine; religion; education; culture, community service, youth skills development, and business. Awards range from $500 to $25,000.
Requirements: Applicants must be 501(c)3 organizations. Funding is primarily made to, but is not limited to, Ohio organizations. Application is made by sending a cover with a brief summary of the request, the amount requested, a copy of the organization's Internal Revenue Service determination letter and most recent form 990, and financial statements. There are no submission deadlines.
Geographic Focus: Ohio
Samples: Baldwin-Wallace College, Berea, Ohio, $5,000, education funding; Columbus State Community College, Columbus, Ohio, $500, education funding; Columbus Association for Performing Arts, Columbus, Ohio, $25,000, culture and environment funding.
Contact: Rita J. Wolfe, Vice President; (614) 460-3782
Sponsor: Wolfe Associates
34 S Third Street
Columbus, OH 43215

Women's Fund of Hawaii Grants 2484

The mission of Women's Fund of Hawaii is to support innovative, grassroots programs that empower women and girls statewide. The Fund provides information and education on women's and girls' philanthropy, shines a light on women's and girls' issues, and increases the visibility of our grantees. The Fund will make grants to organizations or programs that: help the most vulnerable women and girls realize their potential; promote women's financial security and girls' strengths and leadership; address the factors that stand the way of women's success, including violence, adolescent pregnancy, low self-esteem, physical and mental health problems substance abuse, prostitution, incarceration, immigrant status, homophobia, inadequate childcare, sports inequities, reproductive rights, poverty, disabilities and racism; and/or build on the gifts, strengths and assets of women and girls and promote their well-being. The program has an interest in supporting (but is not limited to): girls' programs; programs serving Native Hawaiian women and girls; and programs in rural areas throughout the state. Awards range up to a maximum of $5,000.
Requirements: Any 501(c)3 organization serving women and girls of Hawaii is eligible to apply.

Restrictions: The program does not fund: scholarships; individuals; organizations that aim to convert people to specific religious beliefs; or organizations not serving girls and/or women in Hawaii.
Geographic Focus: Hawaii
Date(s) Application is Due: Apr 17; Sep 18
Amount of Grant: Up to 5,000 USD
Contact: Leela Bilmes Goldstein; (808) 439-6388; info@womensfundhawaii.org
Internet: womensfundhawaii.org/grants-guidelines/
Sponsor: Women's Fund of Hawaii
P.O. Box 438
Honolulu, HI 96809-0438

Women's Fund of Hawaii Grants   2485
Women's Fund of Hawaii issues Requests for Proposals twice a year, in the spring and in the fall, with awards given in June and December of up to $5,000. WFH supports programs serving women and girls in Hawaii that embody their values and beliefs. They give to a wide range of programs, particularly those that promote women's financial security and dignity, and girls' strengths and leadership and programs that build on the gifts, strengths, and assets of women and girls and promote their well-being.
Requirements: Organizations applying must serve girls and/or women in Hawaii. WFH has a special interest in (but funding is not limited to): funding girls' programs; funding programs serving Native Hawaiian women and girls; funding programs in rural areas throughout the state. The program will fund nonprofit organizations, as well as programs that are sponsored projects of nonprofit organizations serving as fiscal agents.
Restrictions: Women's Fund of Hawaii does not fund: scholarships; individuals; organizations that aim to convert people to specific religious beliefs; or organizations not serving girls and/or women in Hawaii.
Geographic Focus: Hawaii
Amount of Grant: Up to 5,000 USD
Contact: Leela Bilmes Goldstein, PhD; (808) 439-6388; grants@womensfundhawaii.org
Internet: womensfundhawaii.org/our-grants/
Sponsor: Women's Fund of Hawaii
P.O. Box 438
Honolulu, HI 96809-0438

Wood-Claeyssens Foundation Grants   2486
The Foundation awards grants to eligible California nonprofit organizations. Types of support include annual campaigns, capital campaigns, continuing support, and general operating support. An application is available on the website.
Requirements: California 501(c)3 organizations serving Santa Barbara and Ventura Counties are eligible.
Restrictions: Funding is not available to individuals or to organizations that discriminate on the basis of age, gender, race, ethnicity, sexual orientation, disability, national origin, political affiliation or religious belief.
Geographic Focus: California
Date(s) Application is Due: Jun 30
Samples: Senior Concerns, Thousand Oaks, California, $15,000; Many Mansions, Thousand Oaks, California, $30,000; and Dream Foundation, Santa Barbara, California, $30,000.
Contact: Noelle Claeyssens Burkey, President; (805) 966-0543; fax (805) 966-1415; wcf0543@gmail.com
Internet: www.woodclaeyssensfoundation.com/Funding.htm
Sponsor: Wood-Claeyssens Foundation
P.O. Box 30586
Santa Barbara, CA 93130-0586

Wood Family Charitable Trust Grants   2487
The Wood Family Charitable Trust was established in 2007 to support and promote quality educational, human services, and health care programming for underserved populations. The Wood Charitable Trust specifically serves the people of Vale, Oregon and its surrounding communities. The majority of grants from the Wood Charitable Trust are 1 year in duration. On occasion, multi-year support is awarded. Award amounts typically go up to $15,000, with some exceptions.
Requirements: The Wood Charitable Trust specifically serves the people of Vale, Oregon and its surrounding communities. Applicants must have 501(c)3 tax-exempt status. Grant requests for general operating support are strongly encouraged. Program support will also be considered. Small, program-related capital expenses may be included in general operating or program requests. Applications will be submitted online through the Bank of America website. A grant report is required within 1 year of the grant application date, regardless of whether all of the funds have been spent.
Restrictions: The trust does not support requests from individuals, organizations attempting to influence policy through direct lobbying, or any political campaigns.
Geographic Focus: Oregon
Date(s) Application is Due: Mar 1
Amount of Grant: Up to 15,000 USD
Samples: Vale School District, Vale, Oregon, $11,000 - awarded for safety upgrade (2018); Malheur County History Society, Ontario, Oregon, $10,000 - awarded for general operation of the organization (2018); City of Vale, Vale, Oregon, $7,900 - awarded for general operations of the Vale Municipal Pool (2018).
Contact: Jan Aldrich Jacobs, (206) 358-0912; wa.grantmaking@bankofamerica.com or janet.jacobs@bofa.com
Internet: www.bankofamerica.com/philanthropic/foundation/?fnId=107
Sponsor: Wood Family Charitable Trust
Bank of America NA, P.O. Box 831
Dallas, TX 75283-1041

Woods Charitable Fund Education Grants   2488
The Woods Charitable Fund seeks to strengthen the community by improving opportunities and life outcomes for all people in Lincoln, Nebraska. Areas of interest include human services; education; civic and community; and arts and culture. The Fund gives considerations to programs and initiatives related to the following: support to organizations that haven't traditionally served refugees and immigrants but are trying to integrate them into their client bases and work forces; expanding English language education for New Americans; helping develop community acceptance and appreciation for New Americans; and extending research and planning concerning immigrants and refugees in Lincoln. In the area of Education, Woods believes that educational systems face the challenge of preparing individuals for a rapidly changing society. Today, more than ever before, education touches the lives of people of all ages – students at all levels, newcomers learning a second language and culture, adults retraining to handle new job responsibilities. The Fund looks forward to opportunities to review proposals from existing educational institutions and from creative new programs to meet the challenge. Interested applicants are asked to contact the Fund by telephone or by sending a two page letter of intent, including budget information, by mail, facsimile or email. After reviewing the letter of intent, the Fund may request a complete application. Grants range from $1,000 to $200,000 with the average size being $25,000.
Requirements: Generally applicants should be 501(c)3 organizations serving Lincoln, Nebraska.
Restrictions: The following are ineligible: capital projects for health care institutions; environmental programs; funding of endowments; fundraising benefits or program advertising; individual needs; medical and scientific research; programs for individual schools; religious programs; residential care and medical clinics; scholarships and fellowships; and sponsorships. College and university proposals are reviewed only if they directly involve faculty and/or students in applied projects of benefit and concern to the community. Ineligible organizations are those that have had proposals approved or declined in the preceding twelve months or that are recipients of active, multiyear grants. This does not apply when organizations are involved in collaborative proposals.
Geographic Focus: Nebraska
Amount of Grant: 1,000 - 200,000 USD
Samples: Lincoln Public Schools, Lincoln, Nebraska, $220,000 - support of Community LINKS, a collaboration of student services provided by community organizations, teachers and staff members to help Lincoln High School freshmen and sophomores at risk of dropping out; Madonna Foundation, Lincoln, Nebraska, $15,000 - support of Kit's Academy Therapeutic Learning Classroom, which helps children who have had an accident or illness continue their schoolwork during recovery and learn strategies to aid their return to school; Spring Creek Prairie Audubon Center, Denton, Nebraska, $20,000 - continued support of the Center's summer educational programming for Lincoln's youth.
Contact: Kathy Steinauer Smith, Community Investment Director; (402) 436-5971; fax (402) 742-0123; ksteinauersmith@woodscharitable.org
Internet: woodscharitable.org/areas-of-interest/
Sponsor: Woods Charitable Fund
1248 'O' Street, Suite 1130
Lincoln, NE 68508

Woods Fund of Chicago Grants   2489
The goal of Woods Fund of Chicago is to increase opportunities for less advantaged people and communities in the metropolitan area, including the opportunity to shape decisions affecting them. The Foundation supports nonprofits in engaging people in civic life, addressing the causes of poverty and other challenges facing the region, promoting more effective public policies, reducing racism and other barriers to equal opportunity, and building a sense of community and common ground. The Foundation is particularly interested in supporting those organizations and initiatives that focus on enabling work and reducing poverty within Chicago's less-advantaged communities. Grants are concentrated in five program areas: community organizing; the intersection of community organizing and public policy; arts and social justice; capacity building; and spotlight initiatives. Applicants must submit an inquiry form. If the Foundation responds favorably, applicants will be asked to submit a full application. In the Spring round, Letters of Inquiry are accepted through December 5, with go-ahead responses by December 16 and final applications due January 9. In the Fall round, Letters of Inquiry are accepted through May 22, with go-ahead responses by June 9 and final applications due July 7.
Requirements: Applicants must be 501(c)3 organizations in the metropolitan Chicago area.
Restrictions: Areas not eligible include: business or economic development projects; capital campaigns, capital projects, and capital acquisitions; endowments; fundraising benefits or program advertising; health care organizations; housing construction or rehabilitation; individual needs; medical or scientific research; programs in and for individual public and private schools; religious or ecumenical programs; residential care, rehabilitation, counseling, clinics and recreational programs; scholarships and fellowships; and social and welfare services, except special projects with a clear public policy strategy.
Geographic Focus: Illinois
Date(s) Application is Due: Jan 9; Jul 7
Contact: Deborah D. Clark; (312) 782-2698; fax (312) 782-4155; D.C.lark@woodsfund.org
Internet: www.woodsfund.org/grantmaking
Sponsor: Woods Fund of Chicago
35 East Wacker Drive, Suite 1760
Chicago, IL 60601

World of Children Education Award   2490
The World of Children Awards program was created to recognize and elevate those selfless individuals who make a difference in the lives of children here in the USA and across the globe, regardless of political, religious or geographical boundaries. These courageous leaders recognize that our children are the world's most important asset. The Education Award,

in the amount of $50,000, was announced at the 2014 Annual Awards Ceremony in New York City. Beginning in January of the following year, the organization formally began accepting nominations for this new award category. The Award recognizes individuals making extraordinary contributions to the education of children thus providing them the platform from which to become fully productive members of society.
Requirements: Nominations must be submitted in English. Nominees must: be the founder or co-founder of an existing nonprofit in good standing that can receive grant funds if awarded; be under the age of 21 by the submission deadline; be submitted by an organization established for a minimum of 3 years; have been doing this work with their organization for a minimum of 3 years; not support an organization designed to specifically advance any one religion or political position; and be available to attend the Awards Ceremony in New York City.
Geographic Focus: All States
Date(s) Application is Due: Apr 1
Amount of Grant: 50,000 USD
Contact: Lynn Wallace Naylor, Executive Director; (925) 452-8272; fax (925) 452-8229; lynn@worldofchildren.org or contact@worldofchildren.org
Internet: www.worldofchildren.org/theaward/awards-we-give/education-award/
Sponsor: World of Children
11501 Dublin Boulevard, Suite 200
Dublin, CA 94568

World of Children Health Award   2491
The World of Children Awards program was created to recognize and elevate those selfless individuals who make a difference in the lives of children here in the USA and across the globe, regardless of political, religious or geographical boundaries. These courageous leaders recognize that our children are the world's most important asset. The Health Award, in the amount of up to $50,000, recognizes individuals making extraordinary contributions to children through the fields of health, medicine, or the sciences. The Award honors this courageous leader at an annual Awards Ceremony and grants them funds to elevate their work. The annual deadline for nominations is April 1.
Requirements: Nominations must be submitted in English. Nominees for the Award must have; created, managed or otherwise supported a sustainable program which has significantly contributed to the improved health of children; do this work over and above their normal employment, or work for little or no pay; have been doing this for a minimum of 10 years; and have an existing non-profit organization in good standing, which can receive grant funds if awarded.
Restrictions: Organizations are not eligible; however a nominee or group of nominees may be part of an organization.
Geographic Focus: All States
Date(s) Application is Due: Apr 1
Amount of Grant: 50,000 USD
Contact: Lynn Wallace Naylor, Executive Director; (925) 452-8272; fax (925) 452-8229; lynn@worldofchildren.org or contact@worldofchildren.org
Internet: www.worldofchildren.org/theaward/awards-we-give/health-award/
Sponsor: World of Children
11501 Dublin Boulevard, Suite 200
Dublin, CA 94568

World of Children Humanitarian Award   2492
The World of Children Awards program was created to recognize and elevate those selfless individuals who make a difference in the lives of children here in the USA and across the globe, regardless of political, religious or geographical boundaries. These courageous leaders recognize that our children are the world's most important asset. The Humanitarian Award, with a maximum of $50,000, recognizes an individual who has made a significant contribution to children in the areas of social services, education or humanitarian services. The Award honors this humanitarian leader at an annual Awards Ceremony and grants them funds to elevate their work. The annual deadline for nominations is April 1.
Requirements: Nominations must be submitted in English. The nominee must: have created, managed or otherwise supported a sustainable program which has significantly contributed to children's opportunities to be safe, to learn, and to grow; do this work over and above their normal employment, OR work for little or no pay; have been doing this for a minimum of 10 years; and have an existing non-profit organization in good standing, which can receive grant funds if awarded.
Restrictions: Organizations are not eligible; however a nominee or group of nominees may be part of an organization.
Geographic Focus: All States
Date(s) Application is Due: Apr 1
Amount of Grant: 50,000 USD
Contact: Lynn Wallace Naylor, Executive Director; (925) 452-8272; fax (925) 452-8229; lynn@worldofchildren.org or contact@worldofchildren.org
Internet: www.worldofchildren.org/theaward/awards-we-give/humanitarian-award/
Sponsor: World of Children
11501 Dublin Boulevard, Suite 200
Dublin, CA 94568

World of Children Youth Award   2493
The World of Children Awards program was created to recognize and elevate those selfless individuals who make a difference in the lives of children here in the USA and across the globe, regardless of political, religious or geographical boundaries. These courageous leaders recognize that our children are the world's most important asset. The Youth Award, in the amount of $25,000, recognizes youth that are making extraordinary contributions to the

lives of other children. The Award honors this young leader at an annual Awards Ceremony and grants them funds to elevate their work.
Requirements: Nominations must be submitted in English. Nominees must: be the founder or co-founder of an existing nonprofit in good standing that can receive grant funds if awarded; be under the age of 21 by the submission deadline; be submitted by an organization established for a minimum of 3 years; have been doing this work with their organization for a minimum of 3 years; not support an organization designed to specifically advance any one religion or political position; and be available to attend the Awards Ceremony in New York City.
Restrictions: Organizations are not eligible; however a nominee or group of nominees may be part of an organization.
Geographic Focus: All States
Date(s) Application is Due: Apr 1
Amount of Grant: 25,000 USD
Contact: Lynn Wallace Naylor, Executive Director; (925) 452-8272; fax (925) 452-8229; lynn@worldofchildren.org or contact@worldofchildren.org
Internet: www.worldofchildren.org/theaward/awards-we-give/youth-award/
Sponsor: World of Children
11501 Dublin Boulevard, Suite 200
Dublin, CA 94568

WSF GoGirlGo! New York Grants   2494
GoGirlGo! New York City offers grants to support girl-serving organizations that seek to enhance the lives of girls using sports, physical activity and life lessons taught through its GoGirlGo! curriculum, and that are located in New York City's five boroughs. Grants can be used for coaching, athletic equipment, uniforms, transportation, facility rental and league/tournament fees.
Requirements: In general, grants will support New York City girl-serving agencies conducting sport and physical activity programs and using the GoGirlGo! curriculum that serve girls aged 5 to 13. Eligible applicants will be asked to meet criteria such as: be nonprofit organizations with a 501(c)3 designation; have committed and experienced adult leadership; deliver a minimum 12-week sport and physical activity program, with preference given to organizations working consistently with girls throughout the year; commitment to implement the GoGirlGo! educational curriculum (provided free of charge); send a representative(s) to participate in GoGirlGo! Leadership Institutes; participate in program evaluation, reporting and exposure activities. Applications must be made online; applications that are emailed or faxed will not be accepted.
Restrictions: Programs that require compulsory religious participation, requesting funding towards the purchase of land, construction of buildings, event sponsorships, providing scholarships to individuals and/or the purchase/care of animals, or requesting retroactive funding are not eligible to apply.
Geographic Focus: New York
Date(s) Application is Due: May 9
Amount of Grant: 2,500 USD
Contact: Elizabeth Flores-Amaya, (516) 307-3915; EFlores-Amaya@ WomensSportsFoundation.org
Internet: www.womenssportsfoundation.org/wsf_program_categories/girl-serving-programs/#
Sponsor: Women's Sports Foundation
247 West 30th Street
New York, NY 10001

WSF Rusty Kanokogi Fund for the Advancement of U.S. Judo Grants   2495
The Rusty Kanokogi Fund for the Advancement of U.S. Judo was established in 2009 to provide direct financial assistance to afford young female judoka the opportunity to train and compete worldwide in pursuit of Olympic excellence. Established by Richard Ader, the Fund is named in honor of the late Rena "Rusty" Kanokogi who is considered the mother of women's judo. Kanokogi held a seventh-degree black belt in judo, making her the highest-ranking American woman in the sport of judo and she fought for more than two decades to make judo an Olympic sport. Grants can be used for coaching, specialized training, equipment, attire and/or travel. A total of $5,000 in grants will be awarded each calendar year.
Requirements: Individual applicants must be U.S. citizens or legal residents and be eligible to compete for a U.S. national team. Applicants must be in training for national and international competition. An individual may be awarded only one grant from the Women's Sports Foundation per calendar year and a maximum of three grants to an individual in a lifetime.
Geographic Focus: All States, American Samoa, District of Columbia, Guam, Marshall Islands, Northern Mariana Islands, Puerto Rico, U.S. Virgin Islands
Amount of Grant: Up to 5,000 USD
Contact: Anne Peltier, (646) 833-0424; APeltier@WomensSportsFoundation.org
Internet: www.womenssportsfoundation.org/wsf_program_categories/athlete-serving-programs/
Sponsor: Women's Sports Foundation
247 West 30th Street
New York, NY 10001

WSF Sports 4 Life Grants   2496
Sports 4 Life offers community funding and seeks to effect sustainable improvement to the overall health and development of girls in these communities through grant making, leadership training and capacity-building efforts. Sports 4 Life, cofounded by the Women's Sports Foundation and espnW in 2014, was created based on the knowledge that while sports participation offers tremendous life-long benefits – from improved physical health

and self-esteem, to better grades in school and enhanced leadership skills – young girls of color are disproportionately excluded. The program seeks to increase the participation and retention of African-American and Hispanic girls, ages 11-18, in developmental youth sports programs. Together, the Women's Sports Foundation and espnW will award a total program minimum of $175,000 each year. Funding can be used for coaching, curriculum, equipment, uniforms, transportation, facility rental, tournaments and/or team-building activities, all while fostering the Sports 4 Life benefits: leadership, self-esteem, confidence and perseverance.

Requirements: The Women's Sports Foundation has developed a two-step application process that involves an LOI application and a follow-up grant application. In general, applicants should be a non-profit school, parks and recreation department, non-profit organization or an amateur sports league. Eligible applicants must demonstrate that their program meets the following criteria: serves predominately African-American or Hispanic girls (representing more than 70% of the enrolled program participants); has the ability to deliver structured, developmental sports programming to girls ages 11 to 18 through experienced and committed leadership; has the ability to provide ongoing funding to implement sports programming after the life of the funding has expired; and, complies with all of the applicable Federal Civil Rights laws, including the requirements pertaining to developing and submitting an Equal Employment Opportunity Plan (EEOP), reporting Findings of Discrimination, and providing language services to Limited English Proficiency (LEP) persons.

Restrictions: Any application that is late, incomplete or requesting funds for an event or purchase of equipment that will occur before the applicant would receive the grant money will not be accepted. Other conditions under which an application will not be accepted: applications that are emailed or faxed; applications for programs that require compulsory religious participation; applications requesting funding towards the purchase of land, construction of buildings, event sponsorships, providing scholarships to individuals and/or the purchase/care of animals; or applications requesting retroactive funding.

Geographic Focus: All States, American Samoa, District of Columbia, Guam, Marshall Islands, Northern Mariana Islands, Puerto Rico, U.S. Virgin Islands
Contact: Elizabeth Flores-Amaya, (516) 307-3915;
EFlores-Amaya@WomensSportsFoundation.org
Internet: www.womenssportsfoundation.org/wsf_program_categories/girl-serving-programs/#
Sponsor: Women's Sports Foundation
247 West 30th Street
New York, NY 10001

WSF Sports 4 Life Regional Grants   2497
The Regional Sports 4 Life Program, funded by the Ralph C. Wilson, Jr. Foundation, is modeled after the success of the national Sports 4 Life Program. Regionally, WSF seeks to strengthen community organizations within the designated regions of Western New York and Southeast Michigan under a four-year model that supports capacity building and direct service. The goal is to develop and/or expand quality youth developmental sport programs for girls with greater sustainability and stronger outcomes. A signature part of this program is the technical assistance and youth development expertise that WSF will provide to Regional partners. Funding in the first two years of the program will be used for organizational capacity building. Funding in the remaining two years of the program will be used to support direct service and may include coaching, curriculum, equipment, uniforms, transportation, facility rental, tournaments and/or team-building activities, all while fostering the Sports 4 Life benefits: leadership, self-esteem, confidence, and perseverance. The Women's Sports Foundation will award up to $20,000 annually to a total of four programs for up to 4 years.

Requirements: Applicants must be a non-profit school, parks and recreation department, non-profit organization or amateur sports league and possess a 501(c)3 status at the time the application is submitted and be located in the fifty (50) United States, District of Columbia or U.S. Territories. The program must be located in Southeast Michigan or Western New York. Eligible applicants must demonstrate that their program meets the following criteria: serves girls in underserved communities, with an emphasis on girls of color; has the ability to deliver structured, developmental sports programming to girls ages 11 to 18 through experienced and committed leadership; has the ability to provide ongoing funding to implement sports programming after the life of the funding has expired; complies with all of the applicable Federal Civil Rights laws, including the requirements pertaining to developing and submitting an Equal Employment Opportunity Plan (EEOP), reporting Findings of Discrimination, and providing language services to Limited English Proficiency (LEP) persons.

Geographic Focus: All States, American Samoa, District of Columbia, Guam, Marshall Islands, Northern Mariana Islands, Puerto Rico, U.S. Virgin Islands
Amount of Grant: Up to 5,000 USD
Contact: Elizabeth Flores-Amaya, (516) 307-3915;
EFlores-Amaya@WomensSportsFoundation.org
Internet: www.womenssportsfoundation.org/wsf_program_categories/girl-serving-programs/#
Sponsor: Women's Sports Foundation
247 West 30th Street
New York, NY 10001

WSF Travel and Training Fund Grants   2498
The fund provides direct financial assistance to aspiring athletes with successful competitive records who have the potential to achieve even higher performance levels and rankings. The goal of the fund is to relieve women/girl athletes of the financial burden associated with competing at higher levels and to permit them to concentrate on their training. Requests for assistance are considered for coaching, specialized training, equipment, attire, and/or travel. Individual grants will vary between $2,500 and $10,000. Up to $75,000 in grants will be awarded each calendar year.

Requirements: Women's/girls' teams with regional and/or national rankings or successful competitive records who have the potential to achieve higher performance levels and rankings are eligible. Individual applicants and all members of a team must be U.S. citizens or legal residents and eligible to compete for the U.S. National Team. Applicants must have: amateur status; demonstrate financial need; a successful competitive record within their sport and/or age group; and must demonstrate the ability, based on competitive record and years in training, to reach and compete at an elite level. An individual or team may be awarded only one grant per calendar year and a maximum of three grants to an individual or team in a lifetime.

Restrictions: High school and college/university varsity and/or recreation teams are not eligible. Any athlete who is a member of a team already applying for a team grant may not also apply for an individual grant in the same grant period.

Geographic Focus: All States, American Samoa, District of Columbia, Guam, Marshall Islands, Northern Mariana Islands, Puerto Rico, U.S. Virgin Islands
Date(s) Application is Due: Apr 16
Amount of Grant: 2,500 - 10,000 USD
Contact: Anne Peltier, (646) 833-0424 or (800) 227-3988;
APeltier@WomensSportsFoundation.org
Internet: www.womenssportsfoundation.org/wsf_programs/travel-training/
Sponsor: Women's Sports Foundation
247 West 30th Street
New York, NY 10001

WSLBDF Quarterly Grants   2499
The Walter S. and Lucienne B. Driskill Foundation (WSLBDF) is searching for novel and innovative programs that inspire young minds to utilize their innate curiosity and creativity, filling their lives with meaning, passion, purpose, hope, and a thirst for knowledge. High-impact organizations that align with the Foundation's mission are identified and invited to submit a proposal. A significant portion of their grantmaking is geographically focused in Chicago and DuPage metro areas. Unsolicited proposals will not be considered; request a short form application via email.

Requirements: 501(c)3 Nonprofit organizations servicing populations in Chicago and DuPage County are eligible to apply. An organization may only submit one application per fiscal year. Programs must create a positive, measurable impact for K-12 students and support learners to recognize their innate curiosity.

Restrictions: WSLBDF grants are not intended for: individuals, for-profit organizations, or tax-generating entities (municipalities, school districts, etc.); religious groups for religious purposes; programs that exclude participation on the basis of race or religion; production of audio, film or video; capital campaigns or projects; applications to support travel; lobbying, political or fraternal activities; organizations not exempt under Section 501(c)3 of the IRS code or unaccredited public/private schools; funding for academic or scientific research; loans; or programs outside of Chicago or DuPage County.

Geographic Focus: Illinois
Contact: Katelyn M. Moon; (312) 266-2484; kmm@driskillfoundation.org
Internet: www.driskillfoundation.org/what-we-do/grant-application-process/
Sponsor: Walter S. and Lucienne B. Driskill Foundation
P.O. Box 9067
Naperville, IL 60567

Wyoming Community Foundation COVID-19 Response and Recovery Grants   2500
For 30 years the Wyoming Community Foundation (WYCF) has connected people who care with causes that matter to build a better Wyoming. WYCF has granted over $70 million to charitable causes while also providing a variety of supports to our nonprofit agency fund holders. WYCF serves donors and communities by connecting them to causes they care most about. The COVID-19 Response and Recovery Funds. The Wyoming Community Foundation is working with a donor to continue to provide rapid financial support to frontline nonprofits working with vulnerable populations to offset the impacts of the virus in their communities. The COVID-19 Response and Recovery Fund will provide resources to nonprofits and other organizations directly supporting vulnerable residents and families in Wyoming. In this first phase, the Community Foundation are prioritizing organizations that are currently serving communities and individuals who are immediately and disproportionately suffering from this crisis. While all applicants will be considered, those meeting basic needs, addressing education, health (including PPE), and addressing the community and family environment will given highest priority. Typically, not more than $5,000 per application should be requested. The annual deadlines are listed as June 15 and December 15.

Requirements: Generally, Wyoming nonprofit 501(c)3 organizations are eligible. While the COVID-19 fund is not available to individuals or to support a for-profit business, it it will offer flexible funding to organizations that are well experienced in providing for critical needs.

Restrictions: Activities or programs for lobbying are ineligible.
Geographic Focus: Wyoming
Date(s) Application is Due: Jun 15; Dec 15
Amount of Grant: Up to 5,000 USD
Contact: Kevin Rossi; (307) 721-8300; fax (307) 721-8333; kevin@wycf.org or wcf@wycf.org
Micah Richardson, Director of Communications and Programs; (307) 721-8300;
fax (307) 721-8333; micah@wycf.org
Internet: wycf.org/covid19/
Sponsor: Wyoming Community Foundation
1472 North 5th Street, Suite 201
Laramie, WY 82072

Wyoming Community Foundation General Grants 2501

The Wyoming Community Foundation offers a variety of General Grants. WYCF gives priority to nonprofit organizations who: address an identified community need; partner with other nonprofits or programs to enhance services without duplication; and leverage dollars received from WYCF to obtain additional or future funding. Low priority is given to: block grants; capital campaigns; annual campaigns; and debt retirement projects. The majority of general grant amounts awarded are between $1,000 and $5,000, with other amounts considered. The annual deadlines for submission are June 15 and December 15, with notification by September 15 and March 15, respectively.

Requirements: Generally, only nonprofit organizations exempt from federal taxation under Section 501(c)3 of the Internal Revenue Code are eligible to apply. Occasionally, public and/or governmental agencies are also eligible.

Restrictions: Grants are not made to individuals and cannot be made for lobbying purposes. The Community Foundation will accept only one application per organization for any given grant deadline and a final report must be submitted prior to submitting a new grant request.

Geographic Focus: Wyoming

Date(s) Application is Due: Jun 15; Dec 15

Amount of Grant: Up to 5,000 USD

Contact: Kevin Rossi, Grant Coordinator; (307) 721-8300; fax (307) 721-8333; kevin@wycf.org
Micah Richardson, Director of Communications and Programs; (307) 721-8300; fax (307) 721-8333; micah@wycf.org

Internet: wycf.org/available-grants/

Sponsor: Wyoming Community Foundation
1472 North 5th Street, Suite 201
Laramie, WY 82072

Wyoming Community Foundation Hazel Patterson Memorial Grants 2502

The Wyoming Community Foundation offers a variety of funding awards, including the Hazel Patterson Memorial Grant. WYCF gives priority to nonprofit organizations in Johnson County who: address an identified community need; partner with other nonprofits or programs to enhance services without duplication; and leverage dollars received from WYCF to obtain additional or future funding. Low priority is given to: block grants; capital campaigns; annual campaigns; and debt retirement projects. The majority of grant amounts awarded are between $1,000 and $5,000, with other amounts considered. The annual deadline for submission is June 15, with notification by September 15.

Requirements: Generally, only nonprofit organizations exempt from federal taxation under Section 501(c)3 of the Internal Revenue Code are eligible to apply. Occasionally, public and/or governmental agencies are also eligible.

Restrictions: Grants are not made to individuals and cannot be made for lobbying purposes. The Community Foundation will accept only one application per organization for any given grant deadline and a final report must be submitted prior to submitting a new grant request.

Geographic Focus: Wyoming

Date(s) Application is Due: Jun 15

Amount of Grant: Up to 5,000 USD

Contact: Kevin Rossi, Grant Coordinator; (307) 721-8300; fax (307) 721-8333; kevin@wycf.org
Micah Richardson, Director of Communications and Programs; (307) 721-8300; fax (307) 721-8333; micah@wycf.org

Sponsor: Wyoming Community Foundation
1472 North 5th Street, Suite 201
Laramie, WY 82072

Wyoming Department of Education McKinney-Vento Subgrant 2503

The purpose of McKinney-Vento subgrant funding is to facilitate the enrollment, attendance, and success of homeless students in school. Services provided with McKinney-Vento subgrant funds must not replace the regular academic program and must be designated to expand upon or improve services provided to homeless students, as part of the school's regular academic program, including compliance with the McKinney-Vento Act and related statutes. Federal funds are available to each state to support programs that meet the needs of homeless children and youths. The Wyoming Department of Education (WDE) must use the funds to competitively distribute subgrants to Local Education Agencies (LEAs) for the establishment of projects which promote the identification, enrollment, attendance, and success of homeless children and youths in school and preschool. LEAs may apply for federal funds that can be used for establishing and improving the LEAs homeless program. As well as, providing activities for, and services to, homeless children and youths, including preschool age homeless children, that enable such children and youths to enroll in, attend and succeed in school, and in preschool programs. In addition, funds can be used to pay for all or part of the LEA's homeless liaisons salary, and it can be used for professional development related to homelessness for the homeless liaison, school and district staff.

Requirements: All LEAs in Wyoming are eligible to apply for this subgrant through a competitive grant process, regardless of the number of homeless students identified and served. Projects must be in compliance with the McKinney-Vento Act and related statutes which should include facilitation of the identification, enrollment, attendance, and success of homeless students in school; services provided with McKinney-Vento subgrant funds must not replace the regular academic program and must be designated to expand upon or improve services provided to homeless students, as part of the school's regular academic program. Awards will be based on: the quality of the project; availability and awarding of funds; the need of the LEA to ensure compliance with all McKinney-Vento requirements focusing on improvement to or development and implementations of McKinney-Vento policies, procedures and the identification of homeless children and youths, including preschool age children, to ensure that schools are compliant with the law, and identifying students accurately; improvement to or development of coordinated, community-driven connectivity plan to ensure quality services to children and youths experiencing homelessness and unaccompanied homeless youths; and commitment to providing services, support, and education for all homeless children and youths.

Restrictions: The number of proposals funded depends on the number and quality of proposals received by the WDE by the close of the application window. WDE reserves the right to close the application without award if no acceptable applications are submitted during this competition window.

Geographic Focus: Wyoming

Date(s) Application is Due: Jul 1

Amount of Grant: Up to 5,500 USD

Contact: Shannon Cranmore, Homeless Education State Coordinator; (307) 777-3672 or (307) 777-7675; fax (307) 777-6234; shannon.cranmore@wyo.gov

Internet: edu.wyoming.gov/in-the-classroom/federal-programs/homeless-ed/mckinney-vento-subgrant/

Sponsor: Wyoming Department of Education
122 W. 25th St. Suite E200
Cheyenne, WY 82002

Wyomissing Foundation Community Grants 2504

Since 1927, the Wyomissing Foundation has awarded more than 1400 grants in support of diverse projects, ranging from the vital work of local community organizations to major initiatives unfolding on the world stage. The Foundation funds several categories of grants and periodically changes the categories to meet changing community needs. Community grants are directly managed by Foundation staff in order to address issues in Berks County in at least one of the following categories: arts and culture, health and human services, environment, education, or community development. These grants are typically designed to help: establish new programs or projects; expand or enhance effective existing programs or projects; support organizational development and capacity building; support capital campaigns; and provide general operating support for effective organizations, in limited situations. Current initial contact Letter of Intent deadlines include: August 24, November 24, and February 24. Final application deadline submission dates are: September 15; December 15; and March 15, respectively.

Requirements: Giving primarily in Berks County, Pennsylvania, and contiguous counties; limited support also in the mid-Atlantic area. Organizations wishing to apply should prepare an outline of the scope and need of the project on their own letterhead. The application should not exceed two pages and should include total budgeted costs and the funds anticipated from other sources. Organizations must be nonprofit and classified 501(c)3 tax-exempt by the Internal Revenue Service; in limited circumstances, the use of a fiscal agent is permissible.

Restrictions: As a general rule, the Foundation does not fund operating support on a sustained basis. Proposals that are not generally considered include: requests for endowments; operating funds on a sustaining basis; funds for individuals, social or fraternal organizations or profit-making enterprises; purchase of tickets, tables, advertisements or sponsorships; parties, conferences, fairs or festivals; animal rights programs; or those activities that would jeopardize the Foundation's charitable status.

Geographic Focus: Pennsylvania

Date(s) Application is Due: Mar 15; Sep 15; Dec 15

Amount of Grant: 1,000 - 25,000 USD

Contact: Karen Rightmire; (610) 376-7494; fax (610) 372-7626; krightmire@wyofound.org

Internet: wyomissingfoundation.org/grants/

Sponsor: Wyomissing Foundation
960 Old Mill Road
Wyomissing, PA 19610

Wyomissing Foundation Thun Family Organizational Grants 2505

Since 1927, the Wyomissing Foundation has awarded more than 1400 grants in support of diverse projects, ranging from the vital work of local community organizations to major initiatives unfolding on the world stage. The Foundation funds several categories of grants and periodically changes the categories to meet changing community needs. Thun Family Grants are made only through direct descendants of Ferdinand and Anna Thun. Family Grants are awarded by a committee of family members using grant guidelines specific to the Family Grants Program. The program was developed to meet the following goals: to increase family participation in the Wyomissing Foundation; to involve family members in philanthropic activity in order to make an impact on issues in communities with which they identify; and to find and fund innovative projects/programs in other communities that could be replicated by the Wyomissing Foundation. The objective of the FGP's grant making is to fund grants in the following general fields of interest: conservation and environment; arts and culture; human services and health care; education; community and economic development; and social justice. Thun Family Organizational Development Grants will support nonprofits' organizational needs, including operating support, technical assistance, leadership development and organizational capacity building. Current initial contact Letter of Intent deadlines include: August 24, November 24, and February 24. Final application deadline submission dates are: September 15; December 15; and March 15, respectively. Awards typically range as high as $25,000.

Requirements: Giving primarily in Berks County, Pennsylvania, and contiguous counties; limited support also in the mid-Atlantic area. Organizations wishing to apply should prepare an outline of the scope and need of the project on their own letterhead. The application should not exceed two pages and should include total budgeted costs and the funds anticipated from other sources. Organizations must be nonprofit and classified 501(c)3 tax-exempt by the Internal Revenue Service; in limited circumstances, the use of a fiscal agent is permissible.

Geographic Focus: Pennsylvania

Date(s) Application is Due: Mar 15; Sep 15; Dec 15

Amount of Grant: Up to 25,000 USD

Contact: Karen Rightmire; (610) 376-7494; fax (610) 372-7626; krightmire@wyofound.org
Internet: wyomissingfoundation.org/grants/thun-family-grant-program/
Sponsor: Wyomissing Foundation
960 Old Mill Road
Wyomissing, PA 19610

Wyomissing Foundation Thun Family Program Grants 2506

Since 1927, the Wyomissing Foundation has awarded more than 1400 grants in support of diverse projects, ranging from the vital work of local community organizations to major initiatives unfolding on the world stage. The Foundation funds several categories of grants and periodically changes the categories to meet changing community needs. Thun Family Grants are made only through direct descendants of Ferdinand and Anna Thun. Family Grants are awarded by a committee of family members using grant guidelines specific to the Family Grants Program. The program was developed to meet the following goals: to increase family participation in the Wyomissing Foundation; to involve family members in philanthropic activity in order to make an impact on issues in communities with which they identify; and to find and fund innovative projects/programs in other communities that could be replicated by the Wyomissing Foundation. The objective of the FGP's grant making is to fund grants in the following general fields of interest: conservation and environment; arts and culture; human services and health care; education; community and economic development; and social justice. Thun Family Program Grants will support the activities nonprofits undertake, such as direct service, policy advocacy, and education of the public. Current initial contact Letter of Intent deadlines include: August 24, November 24, and February 24. Final application deadline submission dates are: September 15; December 15; and March 15, respectively. Awards typically range as high as $25,000.
Requirements: Giving primarily in Berks County, Pennsylvania, and contiguous counties; limited support also in the mid-Atlantic area. Organizations wishing to apply should prepare an outline of the scope and need of the project on their own letterhead. The application should not exceed two pages and should include total budgeted costs and the funds anticipated from other sources. Organizations must be nonprofit and classified 501(c)3 tax-exempt by the Internal Revenue Service; in limited circumstances, the use of a fiscal agent is permissible.
Geographic Focus: All States
Date(s) Application is Due: Mar 15; Sep 15; Dec 15
Amount of Grant: Up to 25,000 USD
Contact: Karen Rightmire; (610) 376-7494; fax (610) 372-7626; krightmire@wyofound.org
Internet: wyomissingfoundation.org/grants/thun-family-grant-program/
Sponsor: Wyomissing Foundation
960 Old Mill Road
Wyomissing, PA 19610

Xerox Foundation Grants 2507

Xerox Foundation Grants assist a variety of social, civic and cultural organizations that provide broad-based programs and services in cities where our employees work and live. The Foundation also remains committed to a program of grants to colleges and universities to prepare qualified men and women for careers in business, science, government, and general education. The Foundation seeks to further advance knowledge in science and technology, and to enhance learning opportunities for minorities and the disadvantaged. Worldwide, Xerox philanthropy tries to engage national leadership in addressing major social problems and to support programs in education, employability and cultural affairs. Other areas of particular focus include programs responsive to the national concern for the environment and the application of information technology. Large grants may be approved for more than one year (multi-year grants). All organizations that have previously received support on an annual basis from the Foundation, must re-submit a request each year to be evaluated for continued support.
Requirements: Grants are made only to 501(c)3 and 509(a) organizations. No specific application form is used. Requests for grants/funding should be submitted in letter form describing the project or program. This request should contain the legal name of the organization, the official contact person, its tax-exempt status, a brief description of its activities and programs, the purpose for which the grant is being requested, the benefits expected, the plans for evaluation, the projected budget, and the expected sources and amount of needed funds.
Restrictions: The foundation declines requests to support individuals; capital grants (new construction or renovation); endowments or endowed chairs; organizations supported by United Way, unless permission has been granted by United Way to a member agency to conduct a capital fund drive or a special benefit; political organizations or candidates; religious or sectarian groups; or municipal, county, state, federal, or quasi-government agencies.
Geographic Focus: All States
Amount of Grant: 500 - 50,000 USD
Contact: Joseph M. Cahalan, President; (203) 968-2453 or (203) 968-3000
Internet: www.xerox.com/about-xerox/citizenship/xerox-foundation/enus.html
Sponsor: Xerox Foundation
45 Glover Avenue, P.O. Box 4505
Norwalk, CT 06856-4505

Yampa Valley Community Foundation Erickson Business Week Scholarships 2508

The Foundation supports programs benefiting the Yampa Valley community. The purpose of the Erickson Business Week Scholarships is to enable a student to attend the annual Business Week conference sponsored by the Colorado Chapter of Junior Achievement.
Requirements: Applicants should complete the online Junior Acheivement Business Week application and then call the Foundation for further instructions.
Geographic Focus: Colorado

Contact: Jennifer Shea, Program Manager; (907) 879-8632; jennifer@yvcf.org
Internet: www.yvcf.org/scholarship-apply.php
Sponsor: Yampa Valley Community Foundation
465 Anglers Drive, Suite 2-G
Steamboat Springs, CO 80488

Yampa Valley Community Foundation Erickson Christian Heritage Scholarships 2509

The Foundation supports programs benefiting the Yampa Valley community. The purpose of the Erickson Christian Heritage Scholarships is to enable a transfer student from public school to Christian Heritage School.
Requirements: Student must have a financial need and be seeking the educational environment provided by the Christian Heritage School.
Geographic Focus: Colorado
Contact: Jennifer Shea, Program Manager; (907) 879-8632; jennifer@yvcf.org
Internet: www.yvcf.org/scholarship-apply.php
Sponsor: Yampa Valley Community Foundation
465 Anglers Drive, Suite 2-G
Steamboat Springs, CO 80488

Yawkey Foundation Grants 2510

The Yawkey Foundation is committed to continuing the legacy of Tom and Jean Yawkey by making significant and positive impacts on the quality of life of children, families, and the underserved in the areas of New England and Georgetown County, South Carolina. Funding supports the areas of health care, education, human services, youth and amateur athletics, arts and culture, and conservation and wildlife. Request should be limited to $25,000 unless otherwise directed. Applications are currently accepted only from organizations previously funded by the Foundation. Deadlines are: arts and culture, conservation, and health care March 1; human services June 15; education September 1; and youth and amateur athletics November 15.
Requirements: Eligible applicants must be tax-exempt 501(c)3 organizations. Proposals must provide significant benefits to a broad constituency either in New England or Georgetown County, South Carolina. The Foundation has a particular concern for organizations that serve disadvantaged children and families and also considers the following: relevance of the proposed project or program to the Foundation's areas of interest; need outlined in the proposal and how the organization has and will continue to address that need; the organization's fiscal health and ability to manage its resources effectively; ability of the project or program to leverage funding and support from other sources; ability of the organization and its staff to achieve the desired results; adequacy of proposed activities, budget, and timetable to achieve the desired results; and evidence of appropriate cooperation with other organizations.
Restrictions: All final reports for prior funding must be submitted before applying for additional funding. Only one request may be submitted during a twelve-month period. Organizations that have received three or more years of consecutive funding will not be eligible to reapply for funding for a one-year period. The Foundation does not make grants to: organizations that are not tax-exempt under section 501(c)3 of the Internal Revenue Service; individuals; private foundations; 509(a)3 Type III non-functionally integrated organizations; organizations or programs that provide benefits outside of the United States; legislative lobbying; foundations created by political or governmental or for-profit organizations; political campaigns and causes; government agencies, or agencies directly benefiting public entities; public school districts and public schools (including charter schools); community and economic development corporations or programs; advocacy groups; operating deficits or retirement of debt; general endowments; general capital campaigns; events, conferences, seminars, and group travel; awards, prizes, and monuments; fraternal, trade, civic, or labor organizations; music, video, or film production; feasibility or research studies; pass-through, intermediary organizations or foundations; religious organizations for sectarian purposes; and workforce development programs.
Geographic Focus: Connecticut, Maine, Massachusetts, New Hampshire, Rhode Island, South Carolina, Vermont
Contact: Nancy Brodnicki, Grants Program Administrator; (781) 329-7470
Internet: www.yawkeyfoundation.org/grant_guidelines.html
Sponsor: Yawkey Foundation
990 Washington Street
Dedham, MA 02026-6716

Youths' Friends Association Grants 2511

The Youths' Friends Association offers grants nationally, primarily for international relief, higher education, elementary education, and secondary education (sometimes through scholarship support earmarked for high school students). Support is also provided for: adoption; arts and culture; basic and emergency aid; child welfare; Christianity; communication media; diseases and conditions; family services; health care; human services; job services; mental health care; performing arts; shelter and residential care; social services; special population support; and youth development. Types of funding include general operating support, program development, scholarships, and seed money. Typically, most recent awards have ranged up to a maximum of $15,000. Though an application is required, there are no specified annual deadlines.
Geographic Focus: All States
Amount of Grant: Up to 15,000 USD
Contact: Walter J. Graver, Director; (843) 671-5060
Sponsor: Youths' Friends Association
100 Park Avenue
New York, NY 10017-5387

YSA ABC Summer of Service Awards
2512

ABC, in partnership with Youth Service America, is calling on young change-makers to apply for an ABC Summer of Service Award. Winners receive a $1,000 award to help make a lasting, positive change in the world. Young people located in and around ABC-affiliate communities who are creating lasting, positive change through volunteer and community service projects are ideal applicants. YSA is especially interested in ongoing, youth-led projects that highlight the creativity and commitment of young people working to meet the needs of others.

Requirements: Youth ages 5-18 located in and around ABC-affiliate communities are eligible to submit their good work and be considered for an ABC Summer of Service Award. Applications are due by midnight on September 1. Applicants must have already implemented a service project in their community. The ABC Summer of Service Award is recognizing youth that have already served their community. All applicants are required to have a sponsoring organization or school. The award check will be sent to the sponsoring organization or school. The sponsoring organization or school will accept the award funds for the applicant and work with them to utilize the funds. YSA cannot send award funds to an individual. Applicants younger than 13, must have a parent or guardian prepare and submit the application for them.

Geographic Focus: All States
Date(s) Application is Due: Sep 1
Amount of Grant: 1,000 USD
Contact: Amanda McDonald, Senior Grants Manager; (202) 296-2992; fax (202) 296-4030; McDonald@ysa.org or info@ysa.org
Internet: www.ysa.org/ABC
Sponsor: Youth Service America
1101 15th Street NW, Suite 200
Washington, D.C. 20005

YSA Get Ur Good On Grants
2513

The Get Ur Good On Grants, a program started by Miley Cyrus and Youth Service America in 2009, offers young people around the world an opportunity to help make a lasting positive change. Youth, ages 5 to 25, worldwide are eligible to apply for a $500 Get Ur Good On Grant to support youth-led projects. Projects must address a demonstrated community need or issue and must take place during Global Youth Service Day

Geographic Focus: All States
Date(s) Application is Due: Mar 10
Amount of Grant: 500 USD
Contact: Kevin Hollander, (202) 296-2992; fax (202) 296-4030; khollander@ysa.org
Internet: www.gysd.org/gysd_grants
Sponsor: Youth Service America
1101 15th Street NW, Suite 200
Washington, D.C. 20005

YSA Global Youth Service Day Lead Agency Grants
2514

Youth Service America and State Farm will support up to 100 Global Youth Service Day (GYSD) and Semester of Service Lead Agencies for Global Youth Service Day (mid-April). Lead Agencies are local, regional, or statewide organizations across the United States, and the Canadian provinces of Alberta, Ontario, or New Brunswick that increase the scale, visibility, and impact of Global Youth Service Day by taking a lead role in their city, region, or state. These Lead Agencies convene a planning coalition of at least 10 partner organizations that collectively engage at least 600 youth volunteers in service on GYSD, engage local media and elected officials, and plan a high profile signature project or celebration of service. The Agencies receive a $2,000 GYSD planning grant sponsored by State Farm, travel support to attend the Youth Service Institute, and ongoing training and technical assistance from Youth Service America to ensure a successful Global Youth Service Day or Semester of Service. Past Lead Agencies have leveraged their position as a GYSD Lead Agency to strengthen their programs, form new partnerships, expand their volunteer base, garner media attention, gain support from local public officials, and secure additional funding.

Requirements: Lead agencies must be located in one of the 50 states, the District of Columbia, or the Canadian provinces of Alberta, Ontario, or New Brunswick; demonstrate the organizational capacity to fulfill the responsibilities of a lead agency; have the ability to engage a variety of community groups; have the ability to plan to mobilize a citywide, regional, or statewide National Youth Service Day celebration involving more than 500 youth volunteers in service over the weekend of the event; and respond to quick deadline press opportunities.

Geographic Focus: All States, Canada
Date(s) Application is Due: Jul 17
Amount of Grant: 2,000 USD
Contact: Chris Wagner; (202) 296-2992; fax (202) 296-4030; outreach@ysa.org
Internet: www.ysa.org/grants/leadagency
Sponsor: Youth Service America
1101 15th Street NW, Suite 200
Washington, D.C. 20005

YSA GYSD Regional Partner Grants
2515

YSA is accepting applications from organizations around the world to serve as Regional Partners for Global Youth Service Day. YSA will select and support one to two Regional Partners in each of the following regions with a $5,000 planning grant: Latin America and the Caribbean; South America; Western Europe; Eastern Europe; Africa; North Africa and the Middle East; Asia; and Southeast Asia. Regional Partners can be regional offices of international organizations, regional organizations or networks, or national organizations that have partners in neighboring countries. Regional Partners will be responsible for promoting and coordinating GYSD in their region, mobilizing partner organizations and Country Partners in their region, working with media and government officials, tracking projects, and assisting with grant reviews and translations.

Requirements: The GYSD Regional Partner program is only open to organizations outside the United States.
Geographic Focus: All Countries
Date(s) Application is Due: Jul 31
Amount of Grant: 5,000 USD
Contact: Amanda McDonald, Grants Manager; (202) 296-2992; fax (202) 296-4030; McDonald@ysa.org or info@ysa.org
Internet: www.ysa.org/grants/regionalpartners
Sponsor: Youth Service America
1101 15th Street NW, Suite 200
Washington, D.C. 20005

YSA MLK Day Lead Organizer Grants
2516

YSA (Youth Service America) and CNCS (the Corporation for National and Community Service) will provide MLK Day Lead Organizer grants to organizations for Martin Luther King Day of Service activities. MLK Day Lead Organizers will engage youth and adult volunteers on MLK Day (especially families volunteering together), use service as a strategy to meet important community needs, and build partnerships with other organizations in their community to achieve scale, visibility, and impact on MLK Day. Grant amounts are $1,000, $2,000, $3,000 and $4,000. Each grant amount has a different minimum number of volunteers and coalition partners required. YSA will award between 16 and 64 grants, depending on how many grantees are selected for each grant amount. YSA will accept applications in two rounds: from June 6 – July 17 and from September 1 – September 30. Round one applicants will be notified by August 16 and round two applicants will be notified by October 20. Applicants declined from round 1 may edit their application and resubmit during round 2.

Requirements: The program is open to organizations from all 50 states and the District of Columbia. YSA is especially looking for applicants in the following metropolitan areas: New York City, Los Angeles, Chicago, Philadelphia, Dallas-Fort Worth, San Francisco-Oakland-San Jose, Boston, Atlanta, Washington, D.C., Houston, Detroit, Phoenix, Seattle-Tacoma, Tampa-St. Petersburg-Sarasota, Minneapolis-St. Paul, Miami-Fort Lauderdale, Denver, Cleveland-Akron, Orlando-Daytona Beach-Melbourne, and Sacramento. Preference will be given to the following types of organizations: Volunteer centers; K-12 schools or school districts; colleges and universities; youth development organizations; nonprofits and community organizations who address one or more of the priority issue areas.

Geographic Focus: All States
Date(s) Application is Due: Sep 30
Amount of Grant: 1,000 - 4,000 USD
Contact: Chris Wagner; (202) 296-2992; fax (202) 296-4030; outreach@ysa.org
Internet: www.ysa.org/grants/mlkday
Sponsor: Youth Service America
1101 15th Street NW, Suite 200
Washington, D.C. 20005

YSA National Child Awareness Month Youth Ambassador Grants
2517

A project of YSA (Youth Service America) and Festival of Children Foundation, this year-long Ambassadorship will help youth (ages 16-22) combat critical issues facing young people today. National Child Awareness Month (NCAM) Youth Ambassadors will serve as community leaders, raising public awareness and affecting change around their issue area. Fifty-one NCAM Youth Ambassadors will be selected - one per state and District of Columbia - creating a powerful national network of young people who raise their collective voice in service to other youth. Youth Ambassadors will receive an all-expense paid, three-day leadership training on Capitol Hill; $1,000 grant to support the development of a youth-focused service initiative; ongoing networking opportunities with other NCAM Youth Ambassadors across the country; ongoing training and mobilization resources; a platform to grow their service initiatives.

Requirements: Eligible applicants must be between ages 16-22, and reside in the United States; attend the training in Washington, D.C. (mid-September, expenses are covered); participation in Global Youth Service Day (mid-April); and, collaborate with a sponsoring organization or school.

Geographic Focus: All States
Amount of Grant: 1,000 USD
Contact: Amanda Villacorta; (202) 296-2992; fax (202) 296-4030; info@ysa.org
Internet: www.ysa.org/grants/NCAM
Sponsor: Youth Service America
1101 15th Street NW, Suite 200
Washington, D.C. 20005

YSA NEA Youth Leaders for Literacy Grants 2518

Youth Leaders for Literacy will award 30 young people from across the U.S. each with $500 grants. Successful projects will be youth-led and address an established literacy need in the applicant's school or community. The projects will launch on NEA's Read Across America Day on March 2nd and culminate on Global Youth Service Day (mid-April).

Requirements: All 50 states and the District of Columbia are eligible to apply. Youth ages 5-25 are welcome to apply along with an adult ally (an adult ally is a non-controlling mentor who offers support and guidance in the fulfillment of the service project).

Geographic Focus: All States

Amount of Grant: 500 USD

Contact: Amanda McDonald, Senior Grants Manager; (202) 296-2992; fax (202) 296-4030; McDonald@ysa.org or info@ysa.org

Internet: www.ysa.org/grants/nea-youth-leaders-literacy

Sponsor: Youth Service America

1101 15th Street NW, Suite 200

Washington, D.C. 20005

YSA Radio Disney's Hero for Change Award 2519

Radio Disney is offering young change-makers the chance to be a Hero for Change. Heroes for change are young change-makers located in Radio Disney communities who are creating positive change through volunteer and service projects. Continue to be a Hero for Change through protecting the planet, providing meals to those who need them, or giving kids just like you the resources to star in their own play, be an athlete or an artist. Winners receive a $500 award to help make a lasting, positive change in the world, plus a chance to meet other amazing young people at the Radio Disney Music Awards in Los Angeles this April. The annual deadline is March 24.

Requirements: Young heroes, ages 5 to 18, that live near Radio Disney communities and are creating positive change through service are eligible to apply.

Geographic Focus: All States

Date(s) Application is Due: Mar 24

Amount of Grant: 500 USD

Contact: Amy Floryan; (202) 296-2992; afloryan@ysa.org or info@ysa.org

Internet: www.ysa.org/RadioDisney

Sponsor: Youth Service America

1101 15th Street NW, Suite 200

Washington, D.C. 20005

YSA Sodexo Lead Organizer Grants 2520

Sodexo Lead Organizers will work with ten or more partner organizations to engage at least 600 youth volunteers in learning about and addressing the issue of childhood hunger in their communities, beginning during Hunger and Homelessness Awareness Week (November) and continuing through Global Youth Service Day (GYSD). Sodexo Lead Organizers will also build new partnerships in their community and increase public awareness about the issue of hunger and young people's role in solving the problem. Finally, they will report on their efforts to YSA and document effective strategies for engaging youth in addressing childhood hunger. Twelve organizations will receive $2,000 in financial assistance as well as travel and lodging expenses for the Youth Service Institute provided by Sodexo Foundation.

Requirements: The Sodexo Lead Organizer grant program is open to U.S. organizations only.

Geographic Focus: All States

Date(s) Application is Due: Jul 15

Amount of Grant: Up to 2,000 USD

Contact: Amanda McDonald, Grants Manager; (202) 296-2992; fax (202) 296-4030; McDonald@ysa.org or info@ysa.org

Internet: www.ysa.org/grants/sodexoleadorganizer

Sponsor: Youth Service America

1101 15th Street NW, Suite 200

Washington, D.C. 20005

YSA State Farm Good Neighbor YOUth In The Driver Seat Grants 2521

Learning to drive is one of the most exciting milestones in a teen's life. To support teens and their teachers in this rite of passage, YSA and State Farm are offering YOUth in the Driver Seat, a service and learning program that includes training, ongoing support, and a $1,500 grant to implement a fourteen week project that encourages safe driving habits, service to the community, and student achievement. With help from the service-learning experts at YSA, teachers and their students will design their own academic-standards-based project. Past participants have included an English class that created public service announcements about safe driving, a Science class that studied the physics of safe driving, a Civics class that launched a town-wide good driver campaign, and more.

Requirements: Grant applicants must meet the following *Requirements:* be a resident of the 50 states or the District of Columbia, and be a certified teacher or professor who currently teaches in a public, private, faith-based, charter, or higher education institution within the 50 states or the District of Columbia; or be a school-based service-learning coordinator, whose primary role is to coordinate service-learning projects in a school or university as described above, or be a youth between the ages of 5 and 25. Teachers or school-based service-learning coordinators should secure approval from the principal or other relevant leadership before submitting a service-learning project proposal.

Geographic Focus: All States

Date(s) Application is Due: Jun 23

Amount of Grant: Up to 1,500 USD

Contact: Amy Floryan, Grants Manager; (202) 296-2992; fax (202) 296-4030; afloryan@ysa.org or info@ysa.org

Internet: www.ysa.org/grants/YOUthInTheDriverSeat

Sponsor: Youth Service America

1101 15th Street NW, Suite 200

Washington, D.C. 20005

YSA UnitedHealth HEROES Service-Learning Grants 2522

The UnitedHealth HEROES program is a service-learning, health literacy initiative developed by UnitedHealthcare and YSA. The program awards grants to help youth, ages 5-25, create and implement local, hands-on programs to fight childhood obesity through walking, running or hiking programs. Each grant engages participating youth in service-learning, an effective teaching and learning strategy that supports student learning, academic achievement, and workplace readiness. The grants encourage semester-long projects that launch on Martin Luther King, Jr. Day of Service and culminate on Global Youth Service Day.

Requirements: Schools, service-learning coordinators, non-profits, and students in the health professions located in all 50 states and the District of Columbia are eligible to apply for the $500-$1,000 grants.

Geographic Focus: All States

Amount of Grant: 1,000 USD

Contact: Amanda McDonald, Senior Grants Manager; (202) 296-2992; fax (202) 296-4030; McDonald@ysa.org or info@ysa.org

Internet: www.ysa.org/HEROES

Sponsor: Youth Service America

1101 15th Street NW, Suite 200

Washington, D.C. 20005

Z. Smith Reynolds Foundation Small Grants 2523

The Z. Smith Reynolds Foundation now offers a Small Grants Process for grant requests of up to $35,000 per year for up to two years. Small grants are made in the areas of community building and economic development, the environment, governance, public policy and civic engagement, pre-collegiate education, and social justice or equity. In addition to funding projects that achieve the goals of each focus area, the foundation has an interest in building the capacity of organizations and in promoting organizational development. New programs, rather than those that are well-established and well-funded, receive priority consideration. Types of support include operating budgets, continuing support, annual campaigns, seed grants, matching funds, projects/programs, conferences and seminars, and technical assistance. The annual application deadlines for invited applicants are February 1 and August 1.

Requirements: The foundation makes grants only to invited nonprofit, tax-exempt, charitable organizations and institutions in North Carolina.

Restrictions: The foundation does not give priority to: the arts; capital campaigns; computer hardware or software purchases; conferences, seminars, or symposiums; crisis intervention programs; fund raising events; historic preservation; local food banks; or substance abuse treatment programs.

Geographic Focus: North Carolina

Date(s) Application is Due: Feb 1; Aug 1

Amount of Grant: Up to 35,000 USD

Contact: Maurice, Executive Director; (336) 725-7541, ext. 105; fax (336) 725-6069; mgreen@zsr.org or info@zsr.org

Internet: www.zsr.org/grants-programs/grants

Sponsor: Z. Smith Reynolds Foundation

102 West Third Street, Suite 1110

Winston-Salem, NC 27101

Zane's Foundation Grants 2524

Zane's, Inc., situated in northeast Ohio, was established in memory of the Youssef family's youngest son, who had severe disabilities. Funding is aimed at assisting families who have children with special needs. Though there are no specified annual deadlines or amount limits, an online application process is utilized. All types of programs and support will be considered, including equipment, summer camp, medical needs, and family assistance.

Requirements: Applicants must reside in the northeast Ohio region.

Geographic Focus: Ohio

Amount of Grant: Up to 2,500 USD

Contact: Stacy Youssef, President; (330) 677-9263

Internet: zanesfoundation.org/site/?page_id=17

Sponsor: Zane's, Inc.

P.O. Box 1642

Stow, OH 44224

Zellweger Baby Support Network Grants 2525

The Zellweger Baby Support Network was started by a small group of parents whose lives have been affected in some way by a rare disorder. The Network provides support to families dealing with Zellweger syndrome. Its mission is to promote, advance, and improve awareness of Zellweger syndrome and other peroxisomal disorders, to assist, support, and aid, financially or otherwise, individuals and families affected by Zellweger syndrome. Grants are given to individuals. Grant amounts range from $100 to $1,000.

Geographic Focus: All States

Amount of Grant: 100 - 1,000 USD

Contact: Pam Swartzenberg Freeth, President; (605) 645-2983

Internet: www.zbsn.org/

Sponsor: Zellweger Baby Support Network

530 West Jackson Boulevard

Spearfish, SD 57783

Zollner Foundation Grants 2526

Fred Zollner was born on January 22, 1901, in Little Falls, Minnesota, to Theodore and Margaret Zollner. His father, Theodore Zollner, was an inventor and manufacturer of machinery. Zollner Corporation, formed in 1912, manufactured pistons for companies such as Ford, General Motors and John Deere. In 1931, the Zollner Corporation was moved to Fort Wayne, Indiana. Fred Zollner passed away on June 21, 1982 at the age of 81, leaving behind a great legacy in the Fort Wayne area. There are sports facilities named after Mr. Zollner such as the Fred Zollner Memorial Stadium, Fred Zollner Tennis Complex, and the Fred Zollner Athletic Stadium at Trine University. The Foundation's primary purpose is to provide financial support for both education and youth development in Fort Wayne, Indiana, and Golden Beach, Florida. Its major fields of interest include: Boy Scouts; k-12 education; higher education; and youth development programs. Types of support include: annual campaigns; building and renovation; capital campaigns; operating support; and equipment purchase. Recent grant amounts have ranged up to $200,000, though generally from $4,000 to $24,000. The annual deadline is June 1, and a formal application is required.

Geographic Focus: Florida, Indiana
Date(s) Application is Due: Jun 1
Amount of Grant: 4,000 - 200,000 USD
Contact: Grant Administrator; (888) 234-1999 or (877) 214-0762; fax (877) 746-5889; grantadministration@wellsfargo.com
Internet: www.wellsfargo.com/privatefoundationgrants/zollner
Sponsor: Zollner Foundation
1919 Douglas Street, 2nd Floor
Omaha, NE 68102-1310

Zonta International Foundation Young Women in Public Affairs Award 2527

Established in 1990 by past international president, Leneen Forde, the Young Women in Public Affairs Award honors young women of age 16 to 19, who demonstrate a commitment to leadership in public policy, government and volunteer organizations. The program operates at the Zonta club, district/region and international levels. Zonta clubs provide awards for club recipients, and district/region and international awards are funded by the Zonta International Foundation. District recipients receive $1,000, and ten international recipients are selected from the district/region recipients to receive awards of $4,000 each. Desired attributes include: active commitment to volunteerism; experience in local or student government; volunteer leadership achievements; knowledge of Zonta International and its programs; and advocating in Zonta International's mission of advancing the status of women worldwide.

Requirements: Women of any nationality who are students of age 16 to 19 on April 1 each year, studying and living, or working in a Zonta district/region, are eligible to apply. Note that applicants from geographic areas where no clubs are located will be considered and also eligible for the District/Region Award.
Geographic Focus: All States, All Countries
Amount of Grant: 1,000 - 4,000 USD
Contact: Martina Gamboa; (630) 928-1400; fax (630) 928-1559; mgamboa@zonta.org
Internet: foundation.zonta.org/Our-Programs/Educational-Programs/Young-Women-in-Public-Affairs-Award
Sponsor: Zonta International Foundation
1211 West 22nd Street, Suite 900
Oak Brook, IL 60523

ZYTL Foundation Grants 2528

Established in Colorado in 1998, the ZYTL Foundation offers funding primarily in its home state. The Foundation's major fields of interest include: health services; human services; and religious programs. The type of funding given is always general operating support, which typically ranges from $100 up to a maximum of $5,000. A formal application is required, and can be secured by contacting the Foundation directly. There are no specified annual deadlines for the submission of application materials.

Requirements: Any 501(c)3 organization serving the residents of Colorado, as well as national serving groups, are eligible to apply.
Restrictions: Grant awards are nor given directly to individuals.
Geographic Focus: All States
Amount of Grant: 100 - 5,000 USD
Contact: Janice K. Zapapas, President; (303) 770-1974
Sponsor: ZYTL Foundation
7975 South Eudora Circle
Centennial, CO 80122

SUBJECT INDEX

AIDS

Abbott Fund Global AIDS Care Grants, 47
Abbott Fund Science Education Grants, 48
Charles Delmar Foundation Grants, 564
Community Foundation for the Capital Region
    Grants, 687
Community Foundation of Louisville AIDS Project
    Fund Grants, 716
Dyson Foundation Mid-Hudson Valley Project
    Support Grants, 874
Elton John AIDS Foundation Grants, 910
Firelight Foundation Grants, 964
Fund for the City of New York Grants, 1029
Hasbro Children's Fund Grants, 1189
HRSA Ryan White HIV AIDS Drug Assistance
    Grants, 1265
Iddings Foundation Major Project Grants, 1284
Iddings Foundation Medium Project Grants, 1285
Iddings Foundation Small Project Grants, 1286
M. Bastian Family Foundation Grants, 1522
Meta and George Rosenberg Fdn Grants, 1644
Oppenstein Brothers Foundation Grants, 1827
Puerto Rico Community Foundation Grants, 2037
Ruth Anderson Foundation Grants, 2122
Shelley and Donald Rubin Foundation Grants, 2187
Streisand Foundation Grants, 2251
Tides Fdn Friends of the IGF Fund Grants, 2300

AIDS Counseling

Community Fdn for the Capital Region Grants, 687
Community Foundation of Louisville AIDS Project
    Fund Grants, 716
Dyson Foundation Mid-Hudson Valley Project
    Support Grants, 874
Elton John AIDS Foundation Grants, 910
HRSA Ryan White HIV AIDS Drug Assistance
    Grants, 1265
Union Square Award for Social Justice, 2340

AIDS Education

Abbott Fund Science Education Grants, 48
Community Foundation for the Capital Region
    Grants, 687
Community Foundation of Louisville AIDS Project
    Fund Grants, 716
Dyson Foundation Mid-Hudson Valley Project
    Support Grants, 874
Elton John AIDS Foundation Grants, 910
GNOF IMPACT Kahn-Oppenheim Tr Grts, 1087
HRSA Ryan White HIV AIDS Drug Assistance
    Grants, 1265
Iddings Foundation Medium Project Grants, 1285
Iddings Foundation Small Project Grants, 1286
Meta and George Rosenberg Fdn Grants, 1644
Portland Fdn - Women's Giving Circle Grant, 2006
Pride Foundation Grants, 2024
Sierra Health Foundation Responsive Grants, 2199
Tides Fdn Friends of the IGF Fund Grants, 2300
Union Square Award for Social Justice, 2340
USAID Nigeria Ed Crisis Response Grants, 2358

AIDS Prevention

Abbott Fund Global AIDS Care Grants, 47
Abbott Fund Science Education Grants, 48
Community Foundation for the Capital Region
    Grants, 687
Community Foundation of Louisville AIDS Project
    Fund Grants, 716
Dyson Foundation Mid-Hudson Valley Project
    Support Grants, 874
Elton John AIDS Foundation Grants, 910
GNOF IMPACT Kahn-Oppenheim Tr Grts, 1087
HRSA Ryan White HIV AIDS Drug Assistance
    Grants, 1265
Meta and George Rosenberg Fdn Grants, 1644
RCF General Community Grants, 2062
Tides Fdn Friends of the IGF Fund Grants, 2300
Union Square Award for Social Justice, 2340

Aboriginal Studies

Elmer Roe Deaver Foundation Grants, 906
Ontario Arts Council Indigenous Culture Fund
    Indigenous Artists in Communities and Schools
    Project Grants, 1825

Abortion

Lalor Foundation Postdoctoral Fellowships, 1464

Academic Achievement

3M Company Fdn Community Giving Grants, 5
Abell Foundation Education Grants, 53
Albertsons Companies Foundation Nourishing
    Neighbors Grants, 221
Albert W. Rice Charitable Foundation Grants, 223
Alfred E. Chase Charitable Foundation Grants, 233
American Savings Foundation Program Grants, 261
Arthur M. Blank Family Foundation Atlanta Falcons
    Youth Foundation Grants, 307
Best Buy Children's Fdn @15 Scholarship , 415
Cargill Corporate Giving Grants, 503
Carnegie Corporation of New York Grants, 511
Charles H. Pearson Foundation Grants, 566
CICF John Harrison Brown and Rob Burse Grt, 607
Cleo Foundation Grants, 632
CNCS AmeriCorps State and National Grants, 643
Community Foundation Serving Riverside and San
    Bernardino Counties Impact Grants, 742
David Robinson Foundation Grants, 791
Dept of Ed Fund for the Improvement of Education--
    Partnerships in Character Ed Pilot Projects, 825
Don and May Wilkins Charitable Trust Grants, 842
Fdn for the Mid South Communities Grants, 992
Four Lanes Trust Grants, 1005
Frank Reed and Margaret Jane Peters Memorial Fund
    II Grants, 1014
Gamble Foundation Grants, 1032
Greater Milwaukee Foundation Grants, 1109
Harold Brooks Foundation Grants, 1172
Hartley Foundation Grants, 1186
Hattie M. Strong Foundation Grants, 1194
Hawai'i Community Foundation Kuki'o Community
    Fund Grants, 1202
HBF Pathways Out of Poverty Grants, 1222
HEI Charitable Foundation Grants, 1226
Hispanic Heritage Foundation Youth Awards, 1253
Inland Empire Community Foundation Coachella
    Valley Youth Grants, 1307
Inland Empire Community Foundation Native Youth
    Grants, 1308
Inland Empire Community Foundation Riverside
    Youth Grants, 1309
Inland Empire Community Foundation San
    Bernardino Youth Grants, 1310
J. Knox Gholston Foundation Grants, 1321
J. William Gholston Foundation Grants, 1328
Lewis H. Humphreys Charitable Trust Grants, 1486
Lloyd G. Balfour Foundation Attleboro-Specific
    Charities Grants, 1502
Marie C. and Joseph C. Wilson Foundation Rochester
    Small Grants, 1559
Mary A. Crocker Trust Grants, 1584
Meyer Foundation Education Grants, 1649
Monsanto United States Grants, 1684
Nellie Mae Education Foundation District-Level
    Change Grants, 1736
Peyton Anderson Scholarships, 1955
Public Education Power Grants, 2032
RGk Foundation Grants, 2068
Ron and Sanne Higgins Family Fdn Grants, 2101
Roney-Fitzpatrick Foundation Grants, 2102
SACF Youth Advisory Council Grants, 2131
Seybert Foundation Grants, 2184
Speer Trust Grants, 2230
Subaru of America Foundation Grants, 2253
USDEd Gaining Early Awareness and Readiness for
    Undergrad Programs (GEAR UP) Grants, 2364
WSLBDF Quarterly Grants, 2499

Wyoming Department of Education McKinney-Vento
    Subgrant, 2503
Z. Smith Reynolds Foundation Small Grants, 2523

Addictions

Ann Ludington Sullivan Foundation Grants, 279
Daniels Drug and Alcohol Addiction Grants, 780
Four County Community Foundation Kellogg Group
    Grants, 1002
MGM Resorts Foundation Community Grants, 1655
Weyerhaeuser Family Fdn Health Grants, 2435

Adolescent Health

Agnes M. Lindsay Trust Grants, 140
Appalachian Regional Commission Health Care
    Grants, 288
Benton Community Foundation - The Cookie Jar
    Grant, 404
CFFVR Basic Needs Giving Partnership Grants, 537
Cigna Civic Affairs Sponsorships, 610
Collective Brands Foundation Saucony Run for Good
    Grants, 656
Cone Health Foundation Grants, 745
DTE Energy Foundation Health and Human Services
    Grants, 869
Foundations of East Chicago Health Grants, 997
General Service Foundation Human Rights and
    Economic Justice Grants, 1040
Humana Foundation Grants, 1275
Kansas Health Fdn Major Initiatives Grants, 1414
Kroger Company Donations, 1456
Marie C. and Joseph C. Wilson Foundation Rochester
    Small Grants, 1559
Medtronic Foundation Strengthening Health Systems
    Grants, 1632
MetroWest Health Foundation Grants to Reduce
    the Incidence of High Risk Behaviors Among
    Adolescents, 1646
Phoenix Coyotes Charities Grants, 1963
Porter County Community Foundation Health and
    Wellness Grant, 2002
RCF The Women's Fund Grants, 2065
Seattle Foundation Health and Wellness Grants, 2179
United Healthcare Commty Grts in Michigan, 2343
United Methodist Health Ministry Fund Grts, 2345
Women's Fund of Hawaii Grants, 2484

Adolescent Psychiatry

AACAP Educational Outreach Program for Child
    and Adolescent Psychiatry Residents, 23
AACAP Educational Outreach Program for General
    Psychiatry Residents, 24
AACAP George Tarjan Award for Contributions in
    Developmental Disabilities, 25
AACAP Irving Philips Award for Prevention, 26
AACAP Jeanne Spurlock Lecture and Award on
    Diversity and Culture, 27
AACAP Mary Crosby Congressional Fellowships, 31
AACAP Rieger Psychodyn Psychotherapy Award, 33
AACAP Rieger Service Program Award for
    Excellence, 34
AACAP Robert Cancro Academic Leadership
    Award, 35
AACAP Sidney Berman Award for the School-Based
    Study and Intervention for Learning Disorders and
    Mental Ilness, 36
AACAP Simon Wile Leadership in Consultation
    Award, 37
AACAP Systems of Care Special Program
    Scholarships, 39
American Psychiatric Fdn Call for Proposals, 257
American Psychiatric Foundation Typical or Troubled
    School Mental Health Education Grants, 258

Adolescent Psychology

Mill Spring Foundation Grants, 1674
NIMH Early Identification and Treatment of Mental
    Disorders in Children and Adolescents Grts, 1761

Adolescents

ALA Teen's Top Ten Awards, 214
AT&T Fdn Community Support and Safety, 320
Bernard and Audre Rapoport Foundation Democracy and Civic Participation Grants, 409
Best Buy Children's Foundation @15 Community Grants , 414
Best Buy Children's Foundation National Grants, 417
Best Buy Children's Foundation Twin Cities Minnesota Capital Grants, 418
FCD New American Children Grants, 952
Laura B. Vogler Foundation Grants, 1470
MetroWest Health Foundation Grants to Reduce the Incidence of High Risk Behaviors Among Adolescents, 1646
Peyton Anderson Scholarships, 1955
Ralph C. Wilson, Jr. Foundation Preparing for Success Grant, 2050
Robert Bowne Foundaion Edmund A. Stanley, Jr. Research Grants, 2086
Robert Bowne Foundation Fellowships, 2087
Robert Bowne Foundation Literacy Grants, 2088
Robert Bowne Fdn Youth-Centered Grants, 2089
Susan A. and Donald P. Babson Charitable Foundation Grants, 2259
Welborn Foundation Promotion of Healthy Adolescent Development Grants, 2425
Women's Fund of Hawaii Grants, 2484

Adoption

Abell-Hanger Foundation Grants, 52
ACF Abandoned Infants Assistance Grants, 70
ACF Adoption Opportunities Grants, 71
ACF Child Abuse Prevention and Treatment Act Discretionary Funds Grants, 74
ACF Promoting Safe and Stable Families (PSSF) Program Grants, 89
Allan C. and Lelia J. Garden Foundation Grants, 236
Joseph H. and Florence A. Roblee Foundation Family Grants, 1387
Victoria S. and Bradley L. Geist Foundation Enhancement Grants, 2381
Youths' Friends Association Grants, 2511

Adult Basic Education

AEGON Transamerica Foundation Education and Financial Literacy Grants, 132
Akron Community Fdn Education Grants, 151
BBF Florida Family Literacy Initiative Grants, 386
BBF Maryland Family Literacy Initiative Implementation Grants, 389
Bernard and Audre Rapoport Foundation Education Grants, 410
Charles Nelson Robinson Fund Grants, 569
Community Foundation for the Capital Region Grants, 687
Community Foundation of Louisville Education Grants, 724
First Lady's Family Literacy Initiative for Texas Family Literacy Trailblazer Grants, 968
First Lady's Family Literacy Initiative for Texas Implementation Grants, 969
First Lady's Family Literacy Initiative for Texas Planning Grants, 970
Georgia-Pacific Foundation Education Grants, 1058
Harris and Eliza Kempner Fund Ed Grants, 1176
LISC Capacity Building Grants, 1498
Locations Foundation Legacy Grants, 1504
Luella Kemper Trust Grants, 1517
M.A. Rikard Charitable Trust Grants, 1521
May and Stanley Smith Charitable Trust Grants, 1613
McCune Charitable Foundation Grants, 1617
Nationwide Insurance Foundation Grants, 1726
OHA Community Grants for Education, 1809
OMNOVA Solutions Fdn Education Grants, 1820
PacifiCare Foundation Grants, 1861
PepsiCo Foundation Grants, 1935
Philip L. Graham Fund Education Grants, 1962
Polk County Community Foundation Marjorie M. & Lawrence R. Bradley Endowment Grants, 1998

Reinberger Foundation Grants, 2066
Robbins-de Beaumont Foundation Grants, 2080
USAID Nigeria Ed Crisis Response Grants, 2358
WHO Foundation Volunteer Service Grants, 2444
Xerox Foundation Grants, 2507

Adult Development

Bernard and Audre Rapoport Foundation Democracy and Civic Participation Grants, 409
Bernard and Audre Rapoport Foundation Education Grants, 410
Community Foundation for SE Michigan Youth Leadership Grant, 686
Julia and Tunnicliff Fox Chartbl Trust Grants, 1397
NSF Social Psychology Grants, 1776

Adult and Continuing Education

AEGON Transamerica Foundation Education and Financial Literacy Grants, 132
Akron Community Fdn Education Grants, 151
ALA Coretta Scott King Book Donation Grant, 168
Albert W. Cherne Foundation Grants, 222
Appalachian Regional Commission Business Development Revolving Loan Fund Grants, 285
Appalachian Regional Commission Education and Training Grants, 286
Atkinson Foundation Community Grants, 325
Atlanta Foundation Grants, 326
BBF Florida Family Literacy Initiative Grants, 386
BBF Maine Family Literacy Initiative Implementation Grants, 387
BBF Maine Family Literacy Initiative Planning Grants, 388
BBF Maryland Family Literacy Initiative Implementation Grants, 389
BBF Maryland Family Literacy Initiative Planning Grants, 390
BBF National Grants for Family Literacy, 391
Benton Community Foundation Grants, 405
Bernard and Audre Rapoport Foundation Education Grants, 410
Blandin Foundation Invest Early Grants, 438
Blue River Community Foundation Grants, 458
Brown County Community Foundation Grants, 475
Carl B. and Florence E. King Foundation Grants, 506
CFFVR Basic Needs Giving Partnership Grants, 537
CFFVR Schmidt Family G4 Grants, 548
Charles Nelson Robinson Fund Grants, 569
Chicago Board of Trade Foundation Grants, 580
CIGNA Foundation Grants, 611
Cisco Systems Foundation San Jose Community Grants, 615
Community Foundation of Bartholomew County Heritage Fund Grants, 690
Community Foundation of Bartholomew County James A. Henderson Award for Fundraising, 691
Community Foundation of Greater Fort Wayne - Community Endowment and Clarke Endowment Grants, 705
Community Foundation of Louisville Education Grants, 724
Community Foundation of Western Massachusetts Grants, 741
Dayton Power and Light Foundation Grants, 802
Dollar General Family Literacy Grants, 835
Edward F. Swinney Trust Grants, 890
Entergy Charitable Foundation Education and Literacy Grants, 917
Essex County Community Foundation Merrimack Valley Municipal Business Development and Recovery Fund Grants, 933
F.R. Bigelow Foundation Grants, 947
First Lady's Family Literacy Initiative for Texas Family Literacy Trailblazer Grants, 968
First Lady's Family Literacy Initiative for Texas Implementation Grants, 969
First Lady's Family Literacy Initiative for Texas Planning Grants, 970
G.N. Wilcox Trust Grants, 1031
Georgia-Pacific Foundation Education Grants, 1058

Harris and Eliza Kempner Fund Ed Grants, 1176
Hattie M. Strong Foundation Grants, 1194
James Ford Bell Foundation Grants, 1339
John H. and Wilhelmina D. Harland Charitable Foundation Children and Youth Grants, 1374
Joseph H. and Florence A. Roblee Foundation Education Grants, 1386
Julia and Tunnicliff Fox Chartbl Trust Grants, 1397
Kimball International-Habig Foundation Education Grants, 1433
Kirkpatrick Foundation Grants, 1440
Liberty Bank Foundation Grants, 1488
LISC Capacity Building Grants, 1498
Locations Foundation Legacy Grants, 1504
Lubrizol Foundation Grants, 1513
M.A. Rikard Charitable Trust Grants, 1521
Mardag Foundation Grants, 1554
Marie C. and Joseph C. Wilson Foundation Rochester Small Grants, 1559
McCune Charitable Foundation Grants, 1617
McCune Foundation Education Grants, 1618
Middlesex Savings Charitable Foundation Educational Opportunities Grants, 1670
Nationwide Insurance Foundation Grants, 1726
Norcliffe Foundation Grants, 1766
OHA Community Grants for Education, 1809
OMNOVA Solutions Fdn Education Grants, 1820
Oppenstein Brothers Foundation Grants, 1827
PacifiCare Foundation Grants, 1861
Parkersburg Area Community Foundation Action Grants, 1871
Peyton Anderson Foundation Grants, 1954
Philip L. Graham Fund Education Grants, 1962
Piper Jaffray Foundation Communities Giving Grants, 1974
Polk County Community Foundation Marjorie M. and Lawrence R. Bradley Endowment Fund Grants, 1998
Pulaski County Community Foundation Grants, 2038
Robbins-de Beaumont Foundation Grants, 2080
Samuel S. Johnson Foundation Grants, 2146
Schlessman Family Foundation Grants, 2167
Sioux Falls Area Community Foundation Community Fund Grants, 2203
Sioux Falls Area Community Foundation Spot Grants, 2204
Sorenson Legacy Foundation Grants, 2217
Strake Foundation Grants, 2249
Sylvia Perkin Perpetual Charitable Trust Grants, 2263
TAC Arts Education Mini Grants, 2267
Thomas Sill Foundation Grants, 2292
UPS Foundation Economic and Global Literacy Grants, 2351
USAID Nigeria Ed Crisis Response Grants, 2358
WHO Foundation Volunteer Service Grants, 2444
Xerox Foundation Grants, 2507

Adults

Avery-Fuller-Welch Children's Fdn Grants, 336
Bay Area Community Foundation Bay County Healthy Youth/Healthy Seniors Fund Grants, 374
Charles Delmar Foundation Grants, 564
Charles Nelson Robinson Fund Grants, 569
Emma J. Adams Memorial Fund Grants, 914
GNOF Gert Community Fund Grants, 1082
J.W. Gardner II Foundation Grants, 1323
Mabel H. Flory Charitable Trust Grants, 1527
Piper Trust Education Grants, 1977
Piper Trust Reglious Organizations Grants, 1979
Union Labor Health Fdn Angel Fund Grants, 2335
Wild Rivers Community Foundation Holiday Partnership Grants, 2448

Aerospace

Hubbard Family Foundation Grants, 1270

Africa

Aid for Starving Children Emerg Aid Grants, 144
Aid for Starving Children Health and Nutrition Grants, 145

Aid for Starving Children Homes and Education
Grants, 146
Aid for Starving Children Water Projects Grants, 147

Africa, Sub-Saharan
Firelight Foundation Grants, 964

African American Students
ACF Head Start and/or Early Head Start Grantee
- Clay, Randolph, and Talladega Counties,
Alabama, 82
ACF Head Start and/or Early Head Start Grantee -
St. Landry Parish, Louisiana, 83
CFGR SisterFund Grants, 554
CFGR Ujima Legacy Fund Grants, 555
Oregon Community Foundation Black Student
Success Community Network Grants, 1832
OSF Baltimore Education and Youth Development
Grants, 1840

African American Studies
CFGR SisterFund Grants, 554
George J. and Effie L. Seay Foundation Grants, 1052
Virginia Foundation for the Humanities Open
Grants, 2387

African Americans
ACF Head Start and/or Early Head Start Grantee
- Clay, Randolph, and Talladega Counties,
Alabama, 82
ACF Head Start and/or Early Head Start Grantee -
St. Landry Parish, Louisiana, 83
ALA Coretta Scott King-John Steptoe Award for
New Talent, 166
ALA Coretta Scott King-Virginia Hamilton Award
for Lifetime Achievement, 167
ALA Coretta Scott King Book Donation Grant, 168
CFGR SisterFund Grants, 554
CFGR Ujima Legacy Fund Grants, 555
Charles Delmar Foundation Grants, 564
CMS Historically Black Colleges and Universities
(HBCU) Health Services Research Grants, 639
Community Foundation of St. Joseph County African
American Community Grants, 737
Effie and Wofford Cain Foundation Grants, 895
Eide Bailly Resourcefullness Awards, 897
Foundation Beyond Belief Compassionate Impact
Grants, 986
Foundation Beyond Belief Humanist Grants, 987
Oregon Community Foundation Black Student
Success Community Network Grants, 1832
Oregon Community Foundation Community
Recovery Grants, 1834
OSF Baltimore Education and Youth Development
Grants, 1840
Twenty-First Century Foundation Grants, 2328
Virginia Foundation for the Humanities Open
Grants, 2387
Washington Area Women's Foundation African
American Women's Giving Circle Grants, 2414

African Art
Christensen Fund Regional Grants, 600
NYSCA Special Arts Services: General Program
Support Grants, 1793

After-School Programs
ACF Head Start and/or Early Head Start Grantee
- Clay, Randolph, and Talladega Counties,
Alabama, 82
ACF Head Start and/or Early Head Start Grantee -
St. Landry Parish, Louisiana, 83
ALA Coretta Scott King Book Donation Grant, 168
Alaska Community Foundation Afterschool Network
Engineering Mindset Mini-Grant, 196
American Savings Fdn After School Grants, 259
Arthur M. Blank Family Foundation Pathways to
Success Grants, 312
Arthur M. Blank Family Foundation Pipeline Project
Grants, 313

Cal Ripken Sr. Foundation Grants, 497
Carnegie Corporation of New York Grants, 511
CFFVR Basic Needs Giving Partnership Grants, 537
CFFVR Mielke Family Foundation Grants, 544
CICF Summer Youth Grants, 608
CNCS AmeriCorps State and National Grants, 643
Collective Brands Foundation Saucony Run for Good
Grants, 656
Community Foundation of Eastern Connecticut
Norwich Youth Grants, 699
Daviess County Community Foundation Advancing
Out-of-School Learning Grants, 792
DeKalb County Community Foundation VOICE
Grant, 816
Dermody Properties Foundation Grants, 827
Edward W. and Stella C. Van Houten Memorial Fund
Grants, 892
Foundation for the Mid South Education Grants, 993
Frank M. Tait Foundation Grants, 1012
Fremont Area Community Foundation Community
Grants, 1020
German Protestant Orphan Asylum Foundation
Grants, 1066
GNOF Coastal 5 + 1 Grants, 1078
GNOF IMPACT Grants for Youth Dev, 1084
Grand Circle Foundation Associates Grants, 1102
GTECH After School Advantage Grants, 1125
Hawai'i Community Foundation Kuki'o Community
Fund Grants, 1202
HBF Pathways Out of Poverty Grants, 1222
Helen Bader Foundation Grants, 1227
Hillsdale County Community Foundation General
Grants, 1250
Jeffris Wood Foundation Grants, 1359
Jim Moran Foundation Grants, 1366
John Clarke Trust Grants, 1369
LISC Education Grants, 1500
Lois and Richard England Family Foundation Out-
of-School-Time Grants, 1506
Louis Calder Foundation Grants, 1511
Luella Kemper Trust Grants, 1517
Mabel Louise Riley Foundation Family Strengthening
Small Grants, 1528
Marin Community Foundation Arts Education
Grants, 1562
Marin Community Foundation Stinson Bolinas
Community Grants, 1568
Maryland State Arts Council Arts in Communities
Grants, 1592
Maryland State Dept of Education 21st Century
Community Learning Centers Grants, 1593
Meyer Foundation Education Grants, 1649
Milton Hicks Wood and Helen Gibbs Wood
Charitable Trust Grants, 1676
Monsanto United States Grants, 1684
Montana Community Foundation Grants, 1687
Morris Stulsaft Foundation Early Childhood
Education Grants, 1696
Mr. Holland's Opus Foundation Special Projects
Grants, 1705
National 4-H Youth in Action Awards, 1721
Nestle Purina PetCare Educational Grants, 1738
New Jersey Office of Faith Based Initiatives Services
to At Risk Youth Grants, 1752
NFL Charities NFL Player Foundation Grants, 1754
NSTA Faraday Science Communicator Award, 1778
Oregon Community Foundation K-12 Student
Success: Out-of-School Grants, 1836
Pacers Foundation Be Educated Grants, 1857
Packard Foundation Children, Families, and
Communities Grants, 1862
PG&E Community Vitality Grants, 1957
Phoenix Coyotes Charities Grants, 1963
Piper Trust Children Grants, 1976
Piper Trust Education Grants, 1977
Priddy Foundation Program Grants, 2023
RCF Summertime Kids Grants, 2064
Robert Bowne Foundaion Edmund A. Stanley, Jr.
Research Grants, 2086
Robert Bowne Foundation Fellowships, 2087

Robert Bowne Foundation Literacy Grants, 2088
Robert Bowne Fdn Youth-Centered Grants, 2089
Rosenberg Fund for Children Edith and George
Ziefert Fund Grants, 2110
Rosenberg Fund for Children Grants, 2111
Rosenberg Fund for Children Herman Warsh Fund
Grant, 2112
Rosenberg Fund for Children Moish and Lillian
Antopol Memorial Fund Grants, 2113
Samuel S. Johnson Foundation Grants, 2146
Share Our Strength Grants, 2185
Susan A. and Donald P. Babson Charitable
Foundation Grants, 2259
TAC Arts Education Mini Grants, 2267
Tauck Family Foundation Grants, 2274
Terra Fdn Chicago K-12 Education Grants, 2285
VSA/Metlife Connect All Grants, 2392
W.H. and Mary Ellen Cobb Chartbl Trust Grts, 2397
Wallace Foundation Grants, 2402
West Virginia Commission on the Arts Special
Projects Grants, 2433
WHO Foundation Volunteer Service Grants, 2444
William Blair and Company Foundation Grants, 2461
William G. and Helen C. Hoffman Foundation
Grants, 2466
Wisconsin Energy Foundation Grants, 2481

Age Discrimination
ALFJ International Fund Grants, 231
Allstate Corporate Giving Grants, 242
Allstate Foundation Hometown Commitment Grants, 243
Allstate Foundation Safe and Vital Communities
Grants, 244
Allstate Foundation Tolerance, Inclusion, and
Diversity Grants, 245
Thorman Boyle Foundation Grants, 2295

Aging/Gerontology
Abington Foundation Grants, 54
Alpha Natural Resources Corporate Giving, 246
Caesars Foundation Grants, 492
Carl B. and Florence E. King Foundation Grants, 506
Carl W. and Carrie Mae Joslyn Trust Grants, 510
Charles Delmar Foundation Grants, 564
CNCS Foster Grandparent Projects Grants, 646
Community Memorial Foundation Responsive
Grants, 743
Cralle Foundation Grants, 760
Effie and Wofford Cain Foundation Grants, 895
Emma J. Adams Memorial Fund Grants, 914
Harry and Jeanette Weinberg Fdn Grants, 1182
Helen Bader Foundation Grants, 1227
Horace A. Kimball and S. Ella Kimball Foundation
Grants, 1260
Latkin Charitable Foundation Grants, 1469
M.D. Anderson Foundation Grants, 1523
Maurice J. Masserini Charitable Trust Grants, 1610
McLean Contributionship Grants, 1623
Mericos Foundation Grants, 1637
Metzger-Price Fund Grants, 1647
Northland Foundation Grants, 1771
NZDIA Community Org Grants Scheme, 1796
Ordean Foundation Catalyst Grants, 1830
Ordean Foundation Partnership Grants, 1831
Piper Trust Healthcare and Med Rsrch Grants, 1978
Posey Community Foundation Women's Grants, 2008
Powell Foundation Grants, 2013
Southwest Initiative Foundation Grants, 2226
Spencer County Community Foundation Women's
Fund Grants, 2232
Thelma Doelger Charitable Trust Grants, 2288
Vanderburgh Community Foundation Men's Fund
Grants, 2373
Vanderburgh County Community Foundation
Women's Fund Grants, 2376
Vigneron Memorial Fund Grants, 2384
Walker Area Community Foundation Grants, 2401
Warrick County Community Foundation Women's
Fund, 2411
Winifred Johnson Clive Foundation Grants, 2478

Agribusiness
First Nations Development Institute Native Agriculture and Food Systems Initiative Scholarships, 971
McCune Charitable Foundation Grants, 1617
Sand Hill Foundation Environment and Sustainability Grants, 2152

Agricultural Collectives/Cooperatives
Giving Gardens Challenge Grants, 1072

Agricultural Geography
Gray Family Foundation Geography Education Grants, 1106

Agricultural Planning/Policy
GNOF Coastal 5 + 1 Grants, 1078
Max and Anna Levinson Foundation Grants, 1612

Agriculture
Anderson Foundation Grants, 271
Blue Grass Community Foundation Rowan County Fund Grants, 453
Camille Beckman Foundation Grants, 499
CONSOL Youth Program Grants, 747
David Robinson Foundation Grants, 791
First Nations Development Institute Native Agriculture and Food Systems Initiative Scholarships, 971
Flinn Foundation Scholarships, 977
Gamble Foundation Grants, 1032
Giving Gardens Challenge Grants, 1072
GNOF Plaquemines Community Grants, 1091
Marriott Int Corporate Giving Grants, 1578
Max and Anna Levinson Foundation Grants, 1612
McCune Charitable Foundation Grants, 1617
Oren Campbell McCleary Chartbl Trust Grants, 1837
PepsiCo Foundation Grants, 1935
Puerto Rico Community Foundation Grants, 2037
Richland County Bank Grants, 2074
Samuel S. Johnson Foundation Grants, 2146
Sarah G. McCarthy Memorial Foundation, 2162
Tom C. Barnsley Foundation Grants, 2306
Windham Foundation Grants, 2477
Wold Foundation Grants, 2482

Agriculture Education
Camille Beckman Foundation Grants, 499
Charles Nelson Robinson Fund Grants, 569
Dean Foods Community Involvement Grants, 805
First Nations Development Institute Native Agriculture and Food Systems Scholarships, 971
Giving Gardens Challenge Grants, 1072
Gray Family Foundation Community Field Trips Grants, 1105
Harden Foundation Grants, 1166
Marriott Int Corporate Giving Grants, 1578
McCune Charitable Foundation Grants, 1617
Michigan Youth Livestock Scholarship and State-Wide Scholarship, 1663
Richland County Bank Grants, 2074
Tom C. Barnsley Foundation Grants, 2306
Watson-Brown Foundation Grants, 2418

Agriscience
First Nations Development Institute Native Agriculture and Food Systems Initiative Scholarships, 971

Agronomy
First Nations Development Institute Native Agriculture and Food Systems Initiative Scholarships, 971

Alaskan Natives
ACF Community-Based Child Abuse Prevention (CBCAP) Tribal and Migrant DiscretionaryGrants, 77
ACF Native American Social and Economic Development Strategies for Alaska Grants, 87

ACF Native Youth Initiative for Leadership, Empowerment, and Development Grants, 88
ACF Social and Economic Development Strategies Grants, 93
ACF Sustainable Employment and Economic Development Strategies Grants, 95
ACF Tribal Maternal, Infant, and Early Childhood Home Visiting Program: Development and Implementation Grants, 97
ACF Tribal Maternal, Infant, and Early Childhood Home Visiting Program: Implementation and Expansion Grants, 98
Alaska State Council on the Arts Cultural Collaboration Project Grants, 211
Eide Bailly Resourcefullness Awards, 897
Foundation Beyond Belief Compassionate Impact Grants, 986
Foundation Beyond Belief Humanist Grants, 987

Alcohol Education
Daniels Drug and Alcohol Addiction Grants, 780
Four County Community Foundation Kellogg Group Grants, 1002
George P. Davenport Trust Fund Grants, 1054
GTRCF Grand Traverse Families in Action for Youth Endowment Grants, 1129
SACF Youth Advisory Council Grants, 2131
Sierra Health Foundation Responsive Grants, 2199
Weyerhaeuser Family Fdn Health Grants, 2435

Alcohol/Alcoholism
ACF Social and Economic Development Strategies Grants, 93
Achelis and Bodman Foundation Grants, 101
Achelis Foundation Grants, 102
Alex Stern Family Foundation Grants, 229
Atkinson Foundation Community Grants, 325
Cleo Foundation Grants, 632
Daniels Drug and Alcohol Addiction Grants, 780
Farmers Insurance Corporate Giving Grants, 948
First Nations Development Institute Native Youth and Culture Fund Grants, 974
Foundation for a Healthy Kentucky Grants, 988
Fuller Foundation Youth At Risk Grants, 1028
George P. Davenport Trust Fund Grants, 1054
GTRCF Grand Traverse Families in Action for Youth Endowment Grants, 1129
Hasbro Children's Fund Grants, 1189
Hawai'i Community Foundation Kuki'o Community Fund Grants, 1202
Huffy Foundation Grants, 1273
Maine Community Foundation Vincent B. and Barbara G. Welch Grants, 1545
Mary Owen Borden Foundation Grants, 1597
Mid-Iowa Health Foundation Community Response Grants, 1667
NIMH Early Identification and Treatment of Mental Disorders in Children and Adolescents Grts, 1761
Ordean Foundation Catalyst Grants, 1830
Ordean Foundation Partnership Grants, 1831
Pacers Foundation Be Drug-Free Grants, 1856
Pajaro Valley Community Health Health Trust Insurance/Coverage & Education on Using the System Grants, 1864
Peter and Elizabeth C. Tower Foundation Small Grants, 1947
Peter and Elizabeth C. Tower Foundation Substance Use Disorders Grants, 1948
Puerto Rico Community Foundation Grants, 2037
Ruth Anderson Foundation Grants, 2122
Sioux Falls Area Community Foundation Spot Grants, 2204
Union Bank, N.A. Foundation Grants, 2334
Weyerhaeuser Family Fdn Health Grants, 2435
Whitney Foundation Grants, 2441

Allied Health Education
Pajaro Valley Community Health Trust Diabetes and Contributing Factors Grants, 1865

Alternative Education
AEGON Transamerica Foundation Education and Financial Literacy Grants, 132
Akron Community Fdn Education Grants, 151
Baton Rouge Area Foundation Community Coffee Fund Grants, 363
Community Foundation of Louisville Education Grants, 724
Delta Air Lines Foundation Youth Development Grants, 824
Evelyn and Walter Haas, Jr. Fund Education Opportunities Grants, 939
Georgia-Pacific Foundation Education Grants, 1058
Herbert Hoover Presidential Library Association Bus Travel Grants, 1244
Morton K. and Jane Blaustein Foundation Educational Opportunity Grants, 1700
Office Depot Foundation Education Grants, 1806
OMNOVA Solutions Fdn Education Grants, 1820
Pacers Foundation Be Educated Grants, 1857
Philip L. Graham Fund Education Grants, 1962
Polk County Community Foundation Marjorie M. and Lawrence R. Bradley Endowment Fund Grants, 1998
Southern California Edison Education Grants, 2218
William Caspar Graustein Memorial Fund Corinne G. Levin Education Grants, 2462

Alternative Fuels
BMW of North America Charitable Contribs, 460
Entergy Charitable Foundation Low-Income Initiatives and Solutions Grants, 918
Max and Anna Levinson Foundation Grants, 1612
PG&E Community Vitality Grants, 1957

Alternative Modes of Education
Community Foundation of Jackson County Classroom Education Grants, 713
Mary A. Crocker Trust Grants, 1584
Morton K. and Jane Blaustein Foundation Educational Opportunity Grants, 1700
Pentair Foundation Education and Community Grants, 1934
Seattle Foundation Education Grants, 2178

Alzheimer's Disease
ACCF of Indiana Angel Funds Grants, 62
Austin S. Nelson Foundation Grants, 333
Caesars Foundation Grants, 492
CFFVR Robert and Patricia Endries Family Foundation Grants, 547
Dyson Foundation Mid-Hudson Valley Project Support Grants, 874
F.M. Kirby Foundation Grants, 946
Fremont Area Community Foundation Community Grants, 1020
G.N. Wilcox Trust Grants, 1031
GNOF IMPACT Harold W. Newman, Jr. Charitable Trust Grants, 1086
Helen Bader Foundation Grants, 1227
Henrietta Lange Burk Fund Grants, 1235
Peyton Anderson Foundation Grants, 1954

American History
Alabama Humanities Foundation Major Grants, 159
Hearst Foundations United States Senate Youth Grants, 1225
Herbert Hoover Presidential Library Association Bus Travel Grants, 1244
NEH Family and Youth Programs in American History Grants, 1734
OHA Community Grants for Culture, 1808
Radcliffe Institute Carol K. Pforzheimer Student Fellowships, 2048
Richard and Caroline T. Gwathmey Memorial Trust Grants, 2069

American Indian Culture
McCune Charitable Foundation Grants, 1617

American Indian History
McCune Charitable Foundation Grants, 1617
NEH Family and Youth Programs in American
    History Grants, 1734

American Indian Language
McCune Charitable Foundation Grants, 1617
Ontario Arts Council Indigenous Culture Fund
    Indigenous Artists in Communities and Schools
    Project Grants, 1825

American Studies
Herbert Hoover Presidential Library Association Bus
    Travel Grants, 1244
McCune Charitable Foundation Grants, 1617

Animal Behavior/Ethology
McCune Charitable Foundation Grants, 1617

Animal Care
Ann L. and Carol Green Rhodes Charitable Trust
    Grants, 278
Austin Community Foundation Grants, 332
Central Pacific Bank Foundation Grants, 530
Charles H. Hall Foundation, 565
Community Foundation of Madison and Jefferson
    County Grants, 731
Dean Foods Community Involvement Grants, 805
Doree Taylor Charitable Foundation Grants, 843
Earl and Maxine Claussen Trust Grants, 878
Faye L. and William L. Cowden Charitable
    Foundation Grants, 950
Gamble Foundation Grants, 1032
Huisking Foundation Grants, 1274
Kirkpatrick Foundation Grants, 1440
Latkin Charitable Foundation Grants, 1469
Margaret T. Morris Foundation Grants, 1557
Matilda R. Wilson Fund Grants, 1605
McCune Charitable Foundation Grants, 1617
Michigan Youth Livestock Scholarship and State-
    Wide Scholarship, 1663
Narragansett Number One Foundation Grants, 1712
Natalie W. Furniss Foundation Grants, 1715
Perkins Charitable Foundation Grants, 1939
PMI Foundation Grants, 1982
Puerto Rico Community Foundation Grants, 2037
Robert W. Knox, Sr. and Pearl Wallis Knox
    Charitable Foundation, 2095
San Antonio Area Foundation Annual Responsive
    Grants, 2147
SanDisk Corp Community Sharing Grants, 2155
Santa Fe Community Foundation Seasonal Grants-
    Fall Cycle, 2159
Seattle Foundation Benjamin N. Phillips Memorial
    Fund Grants, 2176
Toby Wells Foundation Grants, 2304
William E. Dean III Charitable Fdn Grants, 2464
William J. and Dorothy K. O'Neill Foundation
    Responsive Grants, 2468

Animal Development
McCune Charitable Foundation Grants, 1617

Animal Diseases/Pathology
Jane's Trust Grants, 1346

Animal Rescue
Ann L. and Carol Green Rhodes Trust Grants, 278
David and Betty Sacks Foundation Grants, 788
Go Daddy Cares Charitable Contributions, 1093
Harris Foundation Grants, 1177
Herman H. Nettelroth Fund Grants, 1246
Joni Elaine Templeton Foundation Grants, 1384
Kirkpatrick Foundation Grants, 1440
Lucy Downing Nisbet Charitable Fund Grants, 1515
San Antonio Area Foundation Annual Responsive
    Grants, 2147
Toby Wells Foundation Grants, 2304
William E. Dean III Charitable Fdn Grants, 2464
William Ray and Ruth E. Collins Fdn Grants, 2473

Animal Research Policy
Klingenstein-Simons Fellowship Awards in the
    Neurosciences, 1441

Animal Rights
Ann L. and Carol Green Rhodes Charitable Trust
    Grants, 278
Charles H. Hall Foundation, 565
David and Betty Sacks Foundation Grants, 788
Doree Taylor Charitable Foundation Grants, 843
Harrison County Community Fdn Grants, 1178
Harrison County Community Foundation Signature
    Grants, 1179
Helen V. Brach Foundation Grants, 1232
Horace A. Kimball and S. Ella Kimball Foundation
    Grants, 1260
Joni Elaine Templeton Foundation Grants, 1384
Kind World Foundation Grants, 1438
Natalie W. Furniss Foundation Grants, 1715
Perkins Charitable Foundation Grants, 1939
Thelma Doelger Charitable Trust Grants, 2288

Animal Science
First Nations Development Institute Native
    Agriculture and Food Systems Initiative
    Scholarships, 971

Animal Welfare
Austin S. Nelson Foundation Grants, 333
Avery Family Trust Grants, 338
Back Home Again Foundation Grants, 344
Central Pacific Bank Foundation Grants, 530
Community Foundation of Muncie and Delaware
    County Maxon Grants, 734
Cresap Family Foundation Grants, 766
David and Betty Sacks Foundation Grants, 788
Earl and Maxine Claussen Trust Grants, 878
Faye L. and William L. Cowden Charitable
    Foundation Grants, 950
Go Daddy Cares Charitable Contributions, 1093
Greygates Foundation Grants, 1120
Harden Foundation Grants, 1166
Harris Foundation Grants, 1177
Harrison County Community Foundation Signature
    Grants, 1179
Herbert A. and Adrian W. Woods Foundation
    Grants, 1243
Herman H. Nettelroth Fund Grants, 1246
J. Edwin Treakle Foundation Grants, 1320
J.W. Gardner II Foundation Grants, 1323
John M. Weaver Foundation Grants, 1376
Joni Elaine Templeton Foundation Grants, 1384
Katharine Matthies Foundation Grants, 1418
Lil and Julie Rosenberg Foundation Grants, 1491
Lucy Downing Nisbet Charitable Fund Grants, 1515
Matilda R. Wilson Fund Grants, 1605
McCune Charitable Foundation Grants, 1617
NZDIA Lottery Minister's Discretionary Fund
    Grants, 1797
Olive Smith Browning Charitable Trust Grants, 1818
Pettus Foundation Grants, 1952
PMI Foundation Grants, 1982
Robert R. Meyer Foundation Grants, 2094
Robert W. Knox, Sr. and Pearl Wallis Knox
    Charitable Foundation, 2095
San Antonio Area Foundation Annual Responsive
    Grants, 2147
Santa Fe Community Foundation Seasonal Grants-
    Fall Cycle, 2159
Sarkeys Foundation Grants, 2163
Seattle Foundation Benjamin N. Phillips Memorial
    Fund Grants, 2176
Thelma Doelger Charitable Trust Grants, 2288
Thorman Boyle Foundation Grants, 2295
Wells County Foundation Grants, 2426
William E. Dean III Charitable Fdn Grants, 2464
William Ray and Ruth E. Collins Fdn Grants, 2473
Winifred Johnson Clive Foundation Grants, 2478

Animals as Pets
Ann L. and Carol Green Rhodes Charitable Trust
    Grants, 278
Avery Family Trust Grants, 338
Central Pacific Bank Foundation Grants, 530
Community Foundation of Madison and Jefferson
    County Grants, 731
Curtis Foundation Grants, 771
Emily O'Neill Sullivan Foundation Grants, 913
LGA Family Foundation Grants, 1487
Mericos Foundation Grants, 1637
Pettus Foundation Grants, 1952
Santa Fe Community Foundation Seasonal Grants-
    Fall Cycle, 2159

Animals for Assistance/Therapy
Curtis Foundation Grants, 771
Kovler Family Foundation Grants, 1454
LGA Family Foundation Grants, 1487
Lumpkin Family Fdn Healthy People Grants, 1518
May and Stanley Smith Charitable Trust Grants, 1613
Robert R. Meyer Foundation Grants, 2094

Anorexia Nervosa
NIMH Early Identification and Treatment of Mental
    Disorders in Children and Adolescents Grts, 1761

Appalachia
Appalachian Regional Commission Education and
    Training Grants, 286

Aquaculture/Hydroponics
First Nations Development Institute Native
    Agriculture and Food Systems Initiative
    Scholarships, 971

Aquariums
Riedman Foundation Grants, 2076
Union Bank, N.A. Foundation Grants, 2334

Aquatic Ecology
GNOF Plaquemines Community Grants, 1091
Riedman Foundation Grants, 2076

Archaeology
Montana Arts Council Cultural and Aesthetic Project
    Grants, 1685

Archery
Easton Foundations Archery Facility Grants, 883
Easton Sports Development Foundation National
    Archery in the Schools Grants, 884

Architecture
OSF Baltimore Community Fellowships, 1838
PCA Arts Organizations and Arts Programs Grants
    for Visual Arts, 1898
PCA Entry Track Arts Organizations and Arts
    Programs Grants for Visual Arts, 1912

Archives
ALA Louise Seaman Bechtel Fellowship, 173
Brown Foundation Grants, 476
Montana Arts Council Cultural and Aesthetic Project
    Grants, 1685

Art Appreciation
Akron Community Foundation Arts and Culture
    Grants, 150
Alden and Vada Dow Fund Grants, 225
Alliant Energy Foundation Community Giving for
    Good Sponsorship Grants, 240
Ann L. and Carol Green Rhodes Charitable Trust
    Grants, 278
Arthur M. Blank Family Foundation Art of Change
    Grants, 306
California Arts Cncl Statewide Networks Grants, 493
Carl B. and Florence E. King Foundation Grants, 506
Chicago Neighborhood Arts Program Grants, 582

Community Foundation for SE Michigan Livingston County Grants, 683
Community Foundation of Madison and Jefferson County Grants, 731
CONSOL Youth Program Grants, 747
Hahl Proctor Charitable Trust Grants, 1151
Helen Bader Foundation Grants, 1227
Helen Gertrude Sparks Charitable Trust Grants, 1230
Japan Foundation Los Angeles Mini-Grants for Japanese Arts & Culture, 1354
Japan Foundation New York Small Grants for Arts and Culture, 1355
Massachusetts Cultural Council Local Cultural Council (LCC) Grants, 1601
NYSCA Arts Education: Community-based Learning Grants, 1780
NYSCA Arts Education: General Operating Support Grants, 1781
NYSCA Arts Education: General Program Support Grants, 1782
NYSCA Arts Ed: Services to the Field Grants, 1784
NYSCA Electronic Media and Film: General Operating Support, 1786
NYSCA Electronic Media and Film: General Program Support, 1787
NYSCA Electronic Media and Film: Screenings Grants, 1788
NYSCA Electronic Media and Film: Workspace Grants, 1789
NYSCA Special Arts Services: General Program Support Grants, 1793
NYSCA Special Arts Services: Instruction and Training Grants, 1794
NYSCA Theatre: Prof Performances Grants, 1795
Phoenix Coyotes Charities Grants, 1963
PMI Foundation Grants, 1982
RISCA Project Grants for Individuals, 2079
Sorenson Legacy Foundation Grants, 2217
Stinson Foundation Grants, 2246
TAC Touring Arts and Arts Access Touring Arts Grants, 2269

Art Conservation
Akron Community Foundation Arts and Culture Grants, 150
Christensen Fund Regional Grants, 600
McCune Charitable Foundation Grants, 1617
NYSCA Arts Ed: Services to the Field Grants, 1784
NYSCA Electronic Media and Film: Screenings Grants, 1788
NYSCA Special Arts Services: General Program Support Grants, 1793
NYSCA Special Arts Services: Instruction and Training Grants, 1794
PCA Entry Track Arts Orgs and Arts Programs Grants for Traditional and Folk Arts, 1911
Shelley and Donald Rubin Foundation Grants, 2187

Art Criticism
Akron Community Foundation Arts and Culture Grants, 150
PCA Arts Organizations and Arts Programs Grants for Visual Arts, 1898
PCA Entry Track Arts Organizations and Arts Programs Grants for Visual Arts, 1912

Art Education
2 Depot Square Ipswich Charitable Foundation Grants, 3
3M Company Fdn Community Giving Grants, 5
Abbott Fund Community Engagement Grants, 46
Abell-Hanger Foundation Grants, 52
Adobe Foundation Action Grants, 126
Akron Community Foundation Arts and Culture Grants, 150
Ann L. and Carol Green Rhodes Charitable Trust Grants, 278
Arizona Commission on the Arts Learning Collaboration Grant, 291

Arizona Commission on the Arts Youth Arts Engagement Grant, 292
Arts Council of Greater Lansing Young Creatives Grants, 314
Bank of Hawaii Foundation Grants, 360
Bernard and Audre Rapoport Foundation Arts and Culture Grants, 407
California Arts Cncl Statewide Networks Grants, 493
Camille Beckman Foundation Grants, 499
Charlotte Martin Foundation Youth Grants, 571
Chicago Community Trust Arts and Culture Grants: Improving Access to Arts Learning, 581
Chicago Neighborhood Arts Program Grants, 582
Christensen Fund Regional Grants, 600
Cisco Systems Foundation San Jose Community Grants, 615
City of Oakland Cultural Funding Grants, 618
Community Foundation of Eastern Connecticut Ossen Fund for the Arts Grants, 700
Crescent Porter Hale Foundation Grants, 767
Energy by Design Poster Contest, 915
Faye L. and William L. Cowden Charitable Foundation Grants, 950
George A Ohl Jr. Foundation Grants, 1043
Guy I. Bromley Trust Grants, 1136
Hearst Foundations Culture Grants, 1223
Helen Bader Foundation Grants, 1227
Helen Gertrude Sparks Charitable Trust Grants, 1230
Herman Goldman Foundation Grants, 1245
Horace A. Moses Charitable Trust Grants, 1261
HSFCA Biennium Grants, 1267
Illinois Arts Council Youth Employment in the Arts Program Grants, 1294
Japan Foundation Los Angeles Mini-Grants for Japanese Arts & Culture, 1354
Japan Foundation New York Small Grants for Arts and Culture, 1355
Jayne and Leonard Abess Foundation Grants, 1358
John F. Kennedy Center for the Performing Arts National Rosemary Kennedy Internship, 1371
Joseph S. Stackpole Charitable Trust Grants, 1390
Julia Temple Davis Brown Foundation Grants, 1399
Kathryne Beynon Foundation Grants, 1420
Lied Foundation Trust Grants, 1490
Lubrizol Foundation Grants, 1513
Madison Community Foundation Grants, 1535
Marin Community Foundation Arts Education Grants, 1562
Marin Community Foundation Arts in the Community Grants, 1563
Marion I. and Henry J. Knott Foundation Discretionary Grants, 1571
Marion I. and Henry J. Knott Foundation Standard Grants, 1572
Martha Holden Jennings Foundation Grants-to-Educators, 1581
Massachusetts Cultural Council Local Cultural Council (LCC) Grants, 1601
Massachusetts Cultural Cncl YouthReach Grts, 1602
McCune Charitable Foundation Grants, 1617
Mead Family Foundation Grants, 1625
Mimi and Peter Haas Fund Grants, 1677
Mr. Holland's Opus Foundation Special Projects Grants, 1705
National YoungArts Foundation Awards, 1725
Newfoundland and Labrador Arts Council ArtSmarts Grants, 1744
NHSCA Artist Residence Grants, 1756
NHSCA Youth Arts Project Grants: For Extended Arts Learning, 1758
NJSCA Artists in Education Residencies, 1763
NJSCA Arts Ed Special Initiative Grants, 1764
NYFA Artists in the School Community Planning Grants, 1779
NYSCA Arts Education: Community-based Learning Grants, 1780
NYSCA Arts Education: General Operating Support Grants, 1781
NYSCA Arts Education: General Program Support Grants, 1782

NYSCA Arts Education: Local Capacity Building Grants (Regrants), 1783
NYSCA Arts Ed: Services to the Field Grants, 1784
NYSCA Electronic Media and Film: General Program Support, 1787
NYSCA Electronic Media and Film: Workspace Grants, 1789
NYSCA Special Arts Services: General Program Support Grants, 1793
NYSCA Special Arts Services: Instruction and Training Grants, 1794
NYSCA Theatre: Prof Performances Grants, 1795
Ontario Arts Council Artists in Communities and Schools Project Grants, 1823
Ontario Arts Council Arts Organizations in Communities and Schools Operating Grants, 1824
Ontario Arts Council Indigenous Culture Fund Indigenous Artists in Communities and Schools Project Grants, 1825
P. Buckley Moss Foundation for Children's Education Teacher Grants, 1855
Patricia Kisker Foundation Grants, 1879
PCA Arts in Education Residencies, 1885
PCA Arts Organizations and Arts Programs Grants for Arts Education Organizations, 1889
PCA Arts Organizations and Arts Programs Grants for Crafts, 1891
PCA Arts Organizations and Arts Programs Grants for Visual Arts, 1898
PCA Entry Track Arts Organizations and Arts Programs Grants for Arts Education Organizations, 1901
PCA Entry Track Arts Organizations and Arts Programs Grants for Crafts, 1903
Pentair Foundation Education and Community Grants, 1934
Phoenix Coyotes Charities Grants, 1963
PMI Foundation Grants, 1982
Rasmuson Foundation Tier Two Grants, 2056
RISCA Project Grants for Individuals, 2079
San Antonio Area Foundation Capital and Naming Rights Grants, 2148
Screen Actors Guild PencilPALS Assistance, 2172
Sorenson Legacy Foundation Grants, 2217
Stinson Foundation Grants, 2246
TAC Arts Education Funds for At-Risk Youth, 2266
TAC Arts Education Mini Grants, 2267
TAC Arts Education Teacher Incentive Grants, 2268
TAC Touring Arts and Arts Access Touring Arts Grants, 2269
Target Corporation Community Engagement Fund Grants, 2270
Virginia Commission for the Arts Artists in Education Residency Grants, 2385
Virginia Foundation for the Humanities Folklife Apprenticeships, 2386
VSA/Metlife Connect All Grants, 2392
Washington Gas Charitable Contributions, 2417
West Virginia Commission on the Arts Challenge America Partnership Grants, 2430
West Virginia Commission on the Arts Special Projects Grants, 2433
WSLBDF Quarterly Grants, 2499

Art History
Akron Community Foundation Arts and Culture Grants, 150
Arizona Commission on the Arts Youth Arts Engagement Grant, 292
California Arts Cncl Statewide Networks Grants, 493
Chicago Neighborhood Arts Program Grants, 582
McCune Charitable Foundation Grants, 1617

Art Museums
A.C. and Penney Hubbard Foundation Grants, 19
Arthur M. Blank Family Foundation Art of Change Grants, 306
Bernard and Audre Rapoport Foundation Arts and Culture Grants, 407
Bradley C. Higgins Foundation Grants, 467

California Arts Cncl Statewide Networks Grants, 493
Campbell Foundation Grants, 500
Chapman Family Charitable Trust Grants, 561
Donald W. Reynolds Foundation Children's
    Discovery Initiative Grants, 841
Elizabeth Huth Coates Charitable Foundation
    Grants, 900
Helen E. Ellis Charitable Trust Grants, 1228
Hubbard Broadcasting Foundation Grants, 1269
Jerry L. and Barbara J. Burris Fdn Grants, 1362
Kovler Family Foundation Grants, 1454
Louis and Sandra Berkman Foundation Grants, 1510
Maurice R. Robinson Fund Grants, 1611
McCune Charitable Foundation Grants, 1617
Mericos Foundation Grants, 1637
NJSCA Arts Ed Special Initiative Grants, 1764
NYSCA Arts Education: General Operating Support
    Grants, 1781
NYSCA Arts Education: General Program Support
    Grants, 1782
NYSCA Electronic Media and Film: General
    Operating Support, 1786
NYSCA Electronic Media and Film: General
    Program Support, 1787
NYSCA Electronic Media and Film: Screenings
    Grants, 1788
NYSCA Electronic Media and Film: Workspace
    Grants, 1789
Parker Foundation (California) Grants, 1869
PCA Arts Organizations and Arts Programs Grants
    for Art Museums, 1888
PCA Entry Track Arts Organizations and Arts
    Programs Grants for Art Museums, 1900
Richard J. Stern Foundation for the Arts Grants, 2071
Robert F. Lange Foundation Grants, 2090
Ron and Sanne Higgins Family Fdn Grants, 2101
S. Spencer Scott Fund Grants, 2129
Seattle Foundation C. Keith Birkenfeld Memorial
    Trust Grants, 2177
Starr Foundation Grants, 2237
William A. Cooke Foundation Grants, 2452
William J. and Tina Rosenberg Fdn Grants, 2470
Wilton and Effie Hebert Foundation Grants, 2476

Art Therapy
Bernard and Audre Rapoport Foundation Arts and
    Culture Grants, 407
Community Foundation for the Capital Region
    Grants, 687
Oren Campbell McCleary Chartbl Trust Grants, 1837
Parker Foundation (California) Grants, 1869

Art Works/Artifacts
Akron Community Foundation Arts and Culture
    Grants, 150
California Arts Cncl Statewide Networks Grants, 493
McCune Charitable Foundation Grants, 1617
Ontario Arts Council Indigenous Culture Fund
    Indigenous Artists in Communities and Schools
    Project Grants, 1825
Shelley and Donald Rubin Foundation Grants, 2187

Art in Public Places
Abbott Fund Community Engagement Grants, 46
Akron Community Foundation Arts and Culture
    Grants, 150
Amica Insurance Company Sponsorships, 268
Arthur M. Blank Family Foundation Art of Change
    Grants, 306
California Arts Cncl Statewide Networks Grants, 493
Chicago Neighborhood Arts Program Grants, 582
Ellen Abbott Gilman Trust Grants, 905
Entergy Corporation Open Grants for Arts and
    Culture, 920
Golden Heart Community Foundation Grants, 1094
HSFCA Biennium Grants, 1267
Massachusetts Cultural Council Local Cultural
    Council (LCC) Grants, 1601
NYSCA Arts Education: Community-based
    Learning Grants, 1780

NYSCA Arts Education: General Program Support
    Grants, 1782
NYSCA Electronic Media and Film: Screenings
    Grants, 1788
NYSCA Electronic Media and Film: Workspace
    Grants, 1789
NYSCA Special Arts Services: General Program
    Support Grants, 1793
NYSCA Theatre: Prof Performances Grants, 1795
Ontario Arts Council Indigenous Culture Fund
    Indigenous Artists in Communities and Schools
    Project Grants, 1825
Richard J. Stern Foundation for the Arts Grants, 2071
Shelley and Donald Rubin Foundation Grants, 2187
TAC Arts Access Grant, 2265
VSA International Art Program for Children with
    Disabilities Grants, 2394

Art, Experimental
PCA Arts Organizations and Arts Programs Grants
    for Arts Education Organizations, 1889
PCA Arts Organizations and Arts Programs Grants
    for Film and Electronic Media, 1893
PCA Entry Track Arts Organizations and
    Arts Programs Grants for Arts Education
    Organizations, 1901
PCA Entry Track Arts Orgs and Arts Programs
    Grants for Film and Electronic Media, 1905

Arthritis
ACCF of Indiana Angel Funds Grants, 62
Mabel H. Flory Charitable Trust Grants, 1527

Artificial Reproduction
USAID Family Planning and Reproductive Health
    Methods Grants, 2353

Artist Studios
Chicago Neighborhood Arts Program Grants, 582

Artists in Residence
City of Oakland Cultural Funding Grants, 618
NHSCA Artist Residence Grants, 1756
NHSCA Youth Arts Project Grants: For Extended
    Arts Learning, 1758
NJSCA Artists in Education Residencies, 1763
NYFA Artists in the School Community Planning
    Grants, 1779
NYSCA Arts Education: General Program Support
    Grants, 1782
NYSCA Arts Education: Local Capacity Building
    Grants (Regrants), 1783
NYSCA Arts Ed: Services to the Field Grants, 1784
NYSCA Electronic Media and Film: Workspace
    Grants, 1789
Ohio Arts Council Artist in Residence Grants for
    Sponsors, 1810
PCA Arts in Education Residencies, 1885
PCA Arts Organizations and Arts Programs Grants
    for Crafts, 1891
PCA Arts Organizations and Arts Programs Grants
    for Visual Arts, 1898
PCA Entry Track Arts Organizations and Arts
    Programs Grants for Crafts, 1903
PCA Entry Track Arts Organizations and Arts
    Programs Grants for Visual Arts, 1912
PennPAT New Directions Grants for Presenters, 1931
TAC Arts Access Grant, 2265
TAC Arts Education Mini Grants, 2267
West Virginia Commission on the Arts Long-Term
    Artist Residencies, 2431
West Virginia Commission on the Arts Short-Term
    Artist Residencies, 2432

Arts Administration
Alcatel-Lucent Technologies Foundation Grants, 224
Arizona Commission on the Arts Youth Arts
    Engagement Grant, 292
California Arts Cncl Statewide Networks Grants, 493
California Arts Cncl Technical Assistance Grts, 494

Georgia Council for the Arts Education Grants, 1060
John F. Kennedy Center for the Performing Arts
    National Rosemary Kennedy Internship, 1371
NYSCA Theatre: Prof Performances Grants, 1795
PCA-PCD Organizational Short-Term Professional
    Development and Consulting Grants, 1882
PCA Arts Management Internship, 1886
PCA Arts Organizations and Arts Programs Grants
    for Arts Service Organizations, 1890
PCA Arts Organizations and Arts Programs Grants
    for Local Arts, 1895
PCA Entry Track Arts Organizations and Arts
    Programs Grants for Arts Service Orgs, 1902
PCA Entry Track Arts Organizations and Arts
    Programs Grants for Local Arts, 1907
PCA Management/Techl Assistance Grants, 1913
PCA Pennsylvania Partners in the Arts Program
    Stream Grants, 1914
PCA Pennsylvania Partners in the Arts Project
    Stream Grants, 1915
TAC Arts Access Grant, 2265

Arts Festivals
Amica Insurance Company Sponsorships, 268
California Arts Cncl Statewide Networks Grants, 493
Entergy Corporation Open Grants for Arts and
    Culture, 920
Macquarie Bank Foundation Grants, 1532
Massachusetts Cultural Council Local Cultural
    Council (LCC) Grants, 1601
Newfoundland and Labrador Arts Council School
    Touring Grants, 1745
NYSCA Arts Education: Community-based
    Learning Grants, 1780
NYSCA Arts Education: General Operating Support
    Grants, 1781
NYSCA Arts Education: General Program Support
    Grants, 1782
NYSCA Arts Ed: Services to the Field Grants, 1784
NYSCA Electronic Media and Film: General
    Program Support, 1787
NYSCA Electronic Media and Film: Screenings
    Grants, 1788
NYSCA Special Arts Services: General Program
    Support Grants, 1793
NYSCA Special Arts Services: Instruction and
    Training Grants, 1794
OceanFirst Foundation Major Grants, 1803
OHA 'Ahahui Grants, 1807
PCA Art Organizations and Art Programs Grants for
    Presenting Organizations, 1884
PCA Entry Track Arts Organizations and Arts
    Programs Grants for Presenting Orgs, 1909
PCA Pennsylvania Partners in the Arts Program
    Stream Grants, 1914
PCA Pennsylvania Partners in the Arts Project
    Stream Grants, 1915
TAC Arts Access Grant, 2265

Arts and Culture
1st Source Foundation Community Involvement
    Grants, 1
3M Company Fdn Community Giving Grants, 5
A.C. and Penney Hubbard Foundation Grants, 19
ABS Foundation Grants, 56
Abundance Foundation Local Community Grants, 58
ACCF Dennis and Melanie Bieberich Community
    Enrichment Fund Grants, 59
ACCF John and Kay Boch Fund Grants, 60
ACCF of Indiana Anonymous Community
    Enrichment Fund Grants, 63
ACCF of Indiana Bank of Geneva Heritage Fund
    Grants, 64
ACCF of Indiana First Merchants Bank / Decatur
    Bank and Trust Fund Grants, 66
ACCF of Indiana Michael Basham Community
    Enrichment Fund Grants, 67
ACCF of Indiana Ron and Susie Ballard Community
    Enrichment Fund Grants, 68

ACCF Ralph Biggs Memorial Community Enrichment Fund Grants, 69

ACF Native American Social and Economic Development Strategies for Alaska Grants, 87

ACF Social and Economic Development Strategies Grants, 93

Ackerman Foundation Grants, 103

Adams-Mastrovich Family Foundation Grants, 113

Adams Family Fdn of Nora Springs Grants, 118

Adelaide Breed Bayrd Foundation Grants, 123

Ahearn Family Foundation Grants, 142

Alaska Community Foundation Cordova Community Foundation Grants, 201

Alaska Community Foundation Cordova Community Foundation Mini-Grants, 202

Alaska Community Foundation Kenai Peninsula Foundation Grant, 205

Alaska Community Foundation Petersburg Community Foundation Mini-Grants, 208

Alaska Community Foundation Seward Community Foundation Grant, 209

Alaska State Council on the Arts Youth Cultural Heritage Fast Track Grants, 212

Albert E. and Birdie W. Einstein Fund Grants, 220

Albert W. Cherne Foundation Grants, 222

Allegis Group Foundation Grants, 237

Alvah H. and Wyline P. Chapman Foundation Grants, 248

American Indian Youth Running Strong Grants, 256

Amica Companies Foundation Grants, 266

Amway Corporation Contributions, 269

Anna Fitch Ardenghi Trust Grants, 274

Ann Ludington Sullivan Foundation Grants, 279

Arizona Commission on the Arts Learning Collaboration Grant, 291

Arizona Commission on the Arts Youth Arts Engagement Grant, 292

Arkema Foundation Grants, 298

Arthur M. Blank Family Foundation Art of Change Grants, 306

Arthur M. Blank Family Foundation Molly Blank Fund Grants, 310

Arts Council of Greater Lansing Young Creatives Grants, 314

Assisi Fdn of Memphis Capital Project Grants, 317

Assisi Foundation of Memphis General Grants, 318

Assisi Foundation of Memphis Mini Grants, 319

Atlas Insurance Agency Foundation Grants, 329

Avery Family Trust Grants, 338

Avery Foundation Grants, 339

Back Home Again Foundation Grants, 344

Bank of America Charitable Foundation Matching Gifts, 356

Bank of America Corporation Sponsorships, 359

Bank of Hawaii Foundation Grants, 360

Bay Area Community Fdn Auburn Area Chamber of Commerce Enrichment Fund Grants, 373

Bay Area Community Foundation Community Initiative Fund Grants, 376

Beckman Coulter Foundation Grants, 394

Belvedere Community Foundation Grants, 399

Bernard and Audre Rapoport Foundation Arts and Culture Grants, 407

Bill Graham Memorial Foundation Grants, 429

Blackford County Community Fdn Grants, 434

Blandin Foundation Itasca County Area Vitality Grants, 439

Blue Grass Community Foundation Clark County Fund Grants, 444

Blue Grass Community Foundation Fayette County Fund Grants, 446

Blue Grass Community Foundation Franklin County Fund Grants, 447

Blue Grass Community Foundation Harrison County Fund Grants, 448

Blue Grass Community Foundation Madison County Fund Grants, 450

Blue Grass Community Foundation Magoffin County Fund Grants, 451

Blue Grass Community Foundation Morgan County Fund Grants, 452

Blue Grass Community Foundation Rowan County Fund Grants, 453

Blue Grass Community Foundation Woodford County Fund Grants, 454

Blumenthal Foundation Grants, 459

Bodenwein Public Benevolent Foundation Grants, 461

Boeing Company Contributions Grants, 462

Bradley C. Higgins Foundation Grants, 467

British Columbia Arts Council Youth Engagement Program Grants, 473

Burlington Industries Foundation Grants, 481

Burton D. Morgan Foundation Hudson Community Grants, 482

California Arts Cncl Statewide Networks Grants, 493

Camille Beckman Foundation Grants, 499

Castle Foundation Grants, 518

Castle Foundation Grants, 517

CFF Winter Park Community Grants, 551

CFGR Community Impact Grants, 552

Charles H. Hall Foundation, 565

Chicago Community Trust Arts and Culture Grants: Improving Access to Arts Learning, 581

Chicago Neighborhood Arts Program Grants, 582

Chilkat Valley Community Foundation Grants, 588

Claremont Savings Bank Foundation Grants, 623

Clayton F. and Ruth L. Hawkridge Foundation Grants, 630

Clayton Fund Grants, 631

CNO Financial Group Community Grants, 650

Community Foundation for Greater Atlanta Spark Clayton Grants, 667

Community Foundation for Greater Atlanta Spark Newton Grants, 668

Community Foundation for Greater Atlanta Strategic Restructuring Fund Grants, 669

Community Foundation for Greater Buffalo Niagara Area Foundation Grants, 673

Community Foundation for Kettering Grants, 676

Community Foundation for San Benito County Grants, 677

Community Foundation for SE Michigan Detroit Auto Dealers Association Charitable Foundation Fund Grants, 681

Community Foundation of Boone County Grants, 694

Community Foundation of Crawford County, 695

Community Foundation of Eastern Connecticut Ossen Fund for the Arts Grants, 700

Community Foundation of Greater Chattanooga Grants, 704

Community Fdn Of Greater Lafayette Grants, 710

Community Foundation of Louisville Anna Marble Memorial Fund for Princeton Grants, 717

Community Fdn of Morgan County Grants, 732

Community Foundation of Muncie and Delaware County - Kitselman Grants, 733

Community Foundation of Muncie and Delaware County Maxon Grants, 734

Community Foundation Serving Riverside and San Bernardino Counties Impact Grants, 742

Countess Moira Charitable Foundation Grants, 752

Covenant Educational Foundation Grants, 754

Crane Fund Grants, 763

Cresap Family Foundation Grants, 766

Dana Brown Charitable Trust Grants, 777

Daniel and Nanna Stern Family Fdn Grants, 778

David Alan and Susan Berkman Rahm Foundation Grants, 785

David and Betty Sacks Foundation Grants, 788

Dayton Foundation Huber Heights Grants, 797

Dayton Foundation Vandalia-Butler Grants, 799

Dayton Power and Light Foundation Grants, 802

Decatur County Community Foundation Large Project Grants, 811

Decatur County Community Foundation Small Project Grants, 812

DeKalb County Community Foundation Grants, 815

Del Mar Foundation Community Grants, 820

Dorrance Family Foundation Grants, 845

Dyson Foundation Mid-Hudson Valley Project Support Grants, 874

E. Clayton and Edith P. Gengras, Jr. Foundation Grants, 875

E.J. Grassmann Trust Grants, 876

Earl and Maxine Claussen Trust Grants, 878

Eastern Bank Charitable Foundation Partnerships Grants, 881

Eastern Bank Charitable Foundation Targeted Grants, 882

Effie Allen Little Foundation Grants, 894

Elizabeth Huth Coates Charitable Foundation Grants, 900

Elkhart County Community Foundation Fund for Elkhart County, 902

Ella West Freeman Foundation Grants, 904

Elmer Roe Deaver Foundation Grants, 906

El Pomar Foundation Grants, 908

Emily O'Neill Sullivan Foundation Grants, 913

Ensworth Charitable Foundation Grants, 916

Eulalie Bloedel Schneider Foundation Grants, 936

Evan Frankel Foundation Grants, 938

Faye L. and William L. Cowden Charitable Foundation Grants, 950

Fifth Third Foundation Grants, 959

First Hawaiian Bank Foundation Corporate Giving Grants, 967

First Nations Development Institute Native Arts Initiative Grants, 972

Four County Community Foundation General Grants, 1000

Four J Foundation Grants, 1004

Franklin H. Wells and Ruth L. Wells Foundation Grants, 1011

Frank M. Tait Foundation Grants, 1012

Furth Family Foundation Grants, 1030

George A. & Grace L. Long Fdn Grants, 1041

George H.C. Ensworth Memorial Fund Grants, 1049

George J. and Effie L. Seay Foundation Grants, 1052

George Kress Foundation Grants, 1053

Georgia Council for the Arts Education Grants, 1060

GNOF IMPACT Grants for Arts and Culture, 1083

Golden Heart Community Foundation Grants, 1094

Graham Foundation Grants, 1100

Graham Foundation Grants, 1101

Greater Sitka Legacy Fund Grants, 1111

Green River Area Community Fdn Grants, 1117

Grundy Foundation Grants, 1124

GTRCF Elk Rapids Area Community Endowment Grants, 1127

GTRCF Genuine Leelanau Charitable Endowment Grants, 1128

GTRCF Joan Rajkovich McGarry Family Education Endowment Grants, 1131

Guy I. Bromley Trust Grants, 1136

HAF Don and Bettie Albright Endowment Fund Grants, 1142

HAF Joe Alexandre Mem Family Fund Grants, 1145

HAF Laurence and Elaine Allen Memorial Fund Grants, 1146

Hampton Roads Community Foundation Arts and Culture Grants, 1154

Hampton Roads Community Foundation Nonprofit Facilities Improvement Grants, 1159

Hancock County Community Foundation - Field of Interest Grants, 1161

Harden Foundation Grants, 1166

Hardin County Community Foundation Grants, 1167

Harmony Project Grants, 1170

Harris Foundation Grants, 1177

Harrison County Community Fdn Grants, 1178

Harrison County Community Foundation Signature Grants, 1179

Harry and Helen Sands Charitable Trust Grants, 1181

Harvey Randall Wickes Foundation Grants, 1188

Hawai'i Community Foundation Richard Smart Fund Grants, 1204

Hawai'i Community Foundation Robert E. Black Fund Grants, 1205

Hawaiian Electric Industries Charitable Foundation Grants, 1211
Hawaii Community Foundation Omidyar Ohana Fund Grants, 1213
Hearst Foundations Culture Grants, 1223
Helen Bader Foundation Grants, 1227
Helen E. Ellis Charitable Trust Grants, 1228
Helen Gertrude Sparks Charitable Trust Grants, 1230
Hendricks County Community Fdn Grants, 1234
Herbert A. and Adrian W. Woods Foundation Grants, 1243
Herman P. and Sophia Taubman Fdn Grants, 1247
HSFCA Biennium Grants, 1267
HSFCA Folk and Traditional Arts Grants - Culture Learning, 1268
Hubbard Broadcasting Foundation Grants, 1269
Hubbard Family Foundation Grants, 1271
Hubbard Family Foundation Grants, 1270
Iddings Foundation Capital Project Grants, 1283
Ike and Roz Friedman Foundation Grants, 1289
Inland Empire Community Foundation Capacity Building for IE Nonprofits Grants, 1306
Inland Empire Community Foundation Coachella Valley Youth Grants, 1307
Inland Empire Community Foundation Native Youth Grants, 1308
Inland Empire Community Foundation Riverside Youth Grants, 1309
Inland Empire Community Foundation San Bernardino Youth Grants, 1310
Island Insurance Foundation Grants, 1316
J. Watumull Fund Grants, 1326
James LeVoy Sorenson Foundation Grants, 1343
Jane's Trust Grants, 1346
Jayne and Leonard Abess Foundation Grants, 1358
Jennings County Community Foundation Women's Giving Circle Grant, 1361
Jessica Stevens Community Foundation Grants, 1363
Johnson Controls Foundation Arts and Culture Grants, 1378
Joseph Henry Edmondson Foundation Grants, 1388
Journal Gazette Foundation Grants, 1391
Joyce and Randy Seckman Charitable Foundation Grants, 1393
Judy and Peter Blum Kovler Foundation Grants, 1396
Julia and Tunnicliff Fox Chartbl Trust Grants, 1397
Julia Richardson Brown Foundation Grants, 1398
Julia Temple Davis Brown Foundation Grants, 1399
Kenai Peninsula Foundation Grants, 1425
Ketchikan Community Foundation Grants, 1429
Kettering Family Foundation Grants, 1430
Koch Family Foundation (Annapolis) Grants, 1444
Kodiak Community Foundation Grants, 1446
Kosasa Foundation Grants, 1450
Laclede Gas Charitable Trust Grants, 1457
Laidlaw Foundation Youh Organizing Catalyst Grants, 1461
Laidlaw Foundation Youth Organizaing Initiatives Grants, 1462
Lake County Community Fund Grants, 1463
Land O'Lakes Fdn California Region Grants, 1465
Land O'Lakes Foundation Community Grants, 1466
Laura Musser Intercultural Harmony Grants, 1472
Laurel Foundation Grants, 1475
Legler Benbough Foundation Grants, 1479
Leo Goodwin Foundation Grants, 1482
LGA Family Foundation Grants, 1487
Libra Foundation Grants, 1489
Louis and Sandra Berkman Foundation Grants, 1510
Lucy Downing Nisbet Charitable Fund Grants, 1515
Madison Community Foundation Fund for Children Grants, 1534
Madison County Community Foundation - City of Anderson Quality of Life Grant, 1536
Maine Community Foundation Vincent B. and Barbara G. Welch Grants, 1545
Marietta McNeill Morgan and Samuel Tate Morgan Jr. Trust Grants, 1560
Marin Community Foundation Arts in the Community Grants, 1563

Marion I. and Henry J. Knott Foundation Discretionary Grants, 1571
Marion I. and Henry J. Knott Foundation Standard Grants, 1572
Marjorie Moore Charitable Foundation Grants, 1574
Massachusetts Cultural Council Local Cultural Council (LCC) Grants, 1601
Massachusetts Cultural Cncl YouthReach Grts, 1602
MassMutual Foundation Edonomic Development Grants, 1603
Matson Community Giving Grants, 1607
Maurice J. Masserini Charitable Trust Grants, 1610
Maurice R. Robinson Fund Grants, 1611
McCarthy Family Fdn Charity Fund Grants, 1614
McCune Charitable Foundation Grants, 1617
McCune Foundation Humananities Grants, 1619
McGraw-Hill Companies Community Grants, 1620
MeadWestvaco Foundation Sustainable Communities Grants, 1627
Medtronic Foundation Community Link Arts, Civic, and Culture Grants, 1629
Merrick Foundation Grants, 1640
Merrick Foundation Grants, 1639
Meta and George Rosenberg Fdn Grants, 1644
Meyer Memorial Trust Responsive Grants, 1653
Michelin North America Challenge Education, 1660
Middlesex Savings Charitable Foundation Capacity Building Grants, 1669
Miller Foundation Grants, 1673
Milton and Sally Avery Arts Foundation Grants, 1675
Monsanto Access to the Arts Grants, 1681
Montana Arts Council Cultural and Aesthetic Project Grants, 1685
Montana Community Foundation Grants, 1687
Morris Stulsaft Foundation Participation in the the Arts Grants, 1698
Nathalie and Gladys Dalkowitz Charitable Trust Grants, 1716
Nathaniel and Elizabeth P. Stevens Foundation Grants, 1719
Newfoundland and Labrador Arts Council ArtSmarts Grants, 1744
Newfoundland and Labrador Arts Council School Touring Grants, 1745
Newfoundland and Labrador Arts Council Visiting Artists Grants, 1746
Nissan Neighbors Grants, 1762
Norcliffe Foundation Grants, 1766
North Dakota Community Foundation Grants, 1768
NYSCA Arts Education: Community-based Learning Grants, 1780
NYSCA Arts Education: General Operating Support Grants, 1781
NYSCA Arts Education: General Program Support Grants, 1782
NYSCA Arts Ed: Services to the Field Grants, 1784
NYSCA Electronic Media and Film: General Operating Support, 1786
NYSCA Electronic Media and Film: General Program Support, 1787
NYSCA Electronic Media and Film: Screenings Grants, 1788
NYSCA Electronic Media and Film: Workspace Grants, 1789
NYSCA Special Arts Services: General Program Support Grants, 1793
NYSCA Special Arts Services: Instruction and Training Grants, 1794
NYSCA Theatre: Prof Performances Grants, 1795
O. Max Gardner Foundation Grants, 1798
OceanFirst Foundation Major Grants, 1803
OHA Community Grants for Culture, 1808
Olive Higgins Prouty Foundation Grants, 1817
Olive Smith Browning Charitable Trust Grants, 1818
Olivia R. Gardner Foundation Grants, 1819
Ontario Arts Council Artists in Communities and Schools Project Grants, 1823
Ontario Arts Council Arts Organizations in Communities and Schools Operating Grants, 1824
Orange County Community Foundation Grants, 1829

Orange County Community Foundation Grants, 1828
Oregon Community Fdn Community Grants, 1833
Oren Campbell McCleary Chartbl Trust Grants, 1837
OSF Baltimore Community Fellowships, 1838
OSF Youth Action Fund Grants in Kyrgyzstan, 1846
Packard Foundation Local Grants, 1863
Palmer Foundation Grants, 1867
Parke County Community Foundation Grants, 1868
Patricia Kisker Foundation Grants, 1879
Paul and Edith Babson Foundation Grants, 1881
PCA Pennsylvania Partners in the Arts Program Stream Grants, 1914
PCA Pennsylvania Partners in the Arts Project Stream Grants, 1915
Perkin Fund Grants, 1937
Petersburg Community Foundation Grants, 1951
Peyton Anderson Foundation Grants, 1954
Piedmont Natural Gas Corporate and Charitable Contributions, 1966
Pinnacle Entertainment Foundation Grants, 1972
PMI Foundation Grants, 1982
Pohlad Family Fdn Large Capital Grants, 1990
Pokagon Fund Grants, 1994
Polk County Community Foundation Bradley Breakthrough Community Benefit Grants, 1995
Polk County Community Foundation Marjorie M. and Lawrence R. Bradley Endowment Fund Grants, 1998
Polk County Community Foundation Mary F. Kessler Fund Grants, 1999
Polk County Community Foundation Unrestricted Grants, 2001
Porter County Community Foundation Sparking the Arts Fund Grants, 2004
Portland General Electric Foundation Grants, 2007
PPG Industries Foundation Grants, 2017
Price Chopper's Golub Foundation Grants, 2020
Priddy Foundation Program Grants, 2023
Pulido Walker Foundation, 2039
Rasmuson Foundation Tier Two Grants, 2056
Ray Charles Foundation Grants, 2058
Ressler-Gertz Foundation Grants, 2067
Richard J. Stern Foundation for the Arts Grants, 2071
Riedman Foundation Grants, 2076
Robbins-de Beaumont Foundation Grants, 2080
Robbins Charitable Foundation Grants, 2081
Robert F. Lange Foundation Grants, 2090
Robert Lee Blaffer Foundation Grants, 2092
Ron and Sanne Higgins Family Fdn Grants, 2101
Rose Hills Foundation Grants, 2106
S. Spencer Scott Fund Grants, 2129
Samuel N. and Mary Castle Foundation Grants, 2145
San Antonio Area Foundation Annual Responsive Grants, 2147
Sandy Hill Foundation Grants, 2157
Sarkeys Foundation Grants, 2163
Seattle Foundation Arts and Culture Grants, 2174
Seattle Foundation C. Keith Birkenfeld Memorial Trust Grants, 2177
Serco Foundation Grants, 2181
Seward Community Foundation Grants, 2182
Seward Community Foundation Mini-Grants, 2183
Shell Oil Company Foundation Community Development Grants, 2188
Shield-Ayres Foundation Grants, 2189
Sidney and Sandy Brown Foundation Grants, 2196
Sioux Falls Area Community Foundation Community Fund Grants, 2203
Sioux Falls Area Community Foundation Spot Grants, 2204
Skaggs Foundation Grants, 2207
Sony Corporation of America Grants, 2216
Starke County Community Foundation Grants, 2236
Sterling and Shelli Gardner Foundation Grants, 2243
Steven B. Achelis Foundation Grants, 2244
Stinson Foundation Grants, 2246
Storm Castle Foundation Grants, 2248
SunTrust Bank Trusteed Foundations Greene-Sawtell Grants, 2257

SunTrust Bank Trusteed Foundations Nell Warren Elkin and William Simpson Elkin Grants, 2258
Sylvia Perkin Perpetual Charitable Trust Grants, 2263
Telluride Foundation Community Grants, 2281
Textron Corporate Contributions Grants, 2286
Thelma Braun and Bocklett Family Foundation Grants, 2287
Thomas and Agnes Carvel Foundation Grants, 2289
Thomas J. Long Foundation Community Grants, 2291
Toyota Motor Manuf of Alabama Grants, 2309
Toyota Motor Manufacturing of Indiana Grants, 2310
Toyota Motor Manuf of Mississippi Grants, 2312
Toyota Motor Manufacturing of Texas Grants, 2313
Toyota Motor Manufacturing of West Virginia Grants, 2314
Toyota Motor North America of NY Grants, 2315
Toyota Motor Sales, USA Grants, 2316
U.S. Bank Foundation Grants, 2330
Union Bank, N.A. Corporate Sponsorships and Donations, 2333
United Technologies Corporation Grants, 2347
Virginia Foundation for the Humanities Open Grants, 2387
Virginia W. Kettering Foundation Grants, 2388
Volkswagen Group of America Corporate Contributions Grants, 2389
VSA/Volkswagen Group of America Exhibition Awards, 2393
W.M. Keck Fdn Southern California Grants, 2398
Walker Area Community Foundation Grants, 2401
Washington County Community Fdn Grants, 2416
Wells County Foundation Grants, 2426
Western New York Foundation Grants, 2429
West Virginia Commission on the Arts Special Projects Grants, 2433
Whiting Foundation Grants, 2440
William A. Cooke Foundation Grants, 2452
William B. Stokely Jr. Foundation Grants, 2459
William Bingham Foundation Grants, 2460
William Foulds Family Foundation Grants, 2465
William J. and Gertrude R. Casper Foundation Grants, 2469
William J. and Tina Rosenberg Fdn Grants, 2470
William Ray and Ruth E. Collins Fdn Grants, 2473
Winifred Johnson Clive Foundation Grants, 2478
Wisconsin Energy Foundation Grants, 2481
Woods Fund of Chicago Grants, 2489
Wyoming Community Fdn General Grants, 2501
Wyoming Community Foundation Hazel Patterson Memorial Grants, 2502
Wyomissing Foundation Community Grants, 2504
Wyomissing Foundation Thun Family Organizational Grants, 2505
Wyomissing Foundation Thun Family Program Grants, 2506
Yawkey Foundation Grants, 2510
Youths' Friends Association Grants, 2511

Arts, Fine
Anderson Foundation Grants, 271
Crystelle Waggoner Charitable Trust Grants, 768
David and Betty Sacks Foundation Grants, 788
Fichtenbaum Charitable Trust Grants, 955
GNOF IMPACT Grants for Arts and Culture, 1083
Hearst Foundations Culture Grants, 1223
Helen Bader Foundation Grants, 1227
Helen E. Ellis Charitable Trust Grants, 1228
Helen Gertrude Sparks Charitable Trust Grants, 1230
Hillsdale County Community Foundation General Grants, 1250
J. Edwin Treakle Foundation Grants, 1320
Katrine Menzing Deakins Chartbl Trust Grants, 1422
Lewis H. Humphreys Charitable Trust Grants, 1486
Massachusetts Cultural Council Local Cultural Council (LCC) Grants, 1601
NJSCA Arts Ed Special Initiative Grants, 1764
Patricia Kisker Foundation Grants, 1879
PCA-PCD Professional Development for Individual Artists Grants, 1883

PCA Arts Organizations and Arts Programs Grants for Arts Service Organizations, 1890
PCA Entry Track Arts Organizations and Arts Programs Grants for Arts Service Orgs, 1902
PCA Pennsylvania Partners in the Arts Program Stream Grants, 1914
PCA Pennsylvania Partners in the Arts Project Stream Grants, 1915
PCA Professional Development Grants, 1916
PCA Strategies for Success Grants - Basic Level, 1918
PCA Strategies for Success Grants - Intermediate Level, 1919
PennPAT Artist Technical Assistance Grants, 1929
PennPAT Strategic Opportunity Grants, 1933
RISCA Project Grants for Individuals, 2079
Stinson Foundation Grants, 2246
TAC Arts Access Grant, 2265

Arts, General
1st Source Foundation Community Involvement Grants, 1
2 Depot Square Ipswich Charitable Foundation Grants, 3
A.C. and Penney Hubbard Foundation Grants, 19
Aaron Foundation Grants, 42
Abbott Fund Community Engagement Grants, 46
ABS Foundation Grants, 56
ACCF Dennis and Melanie Bieberich Community Enrichment Fund Grants, 59
ACCF John and Kay Boch Fund Grants, 60
ACCF of Indiana Anonymous Community Enrichment Fund Grants, 63
ACCF of Indiana Bank of Geneva Heritage Fund Grants, 64
ACCF of Indiana First Merchants Bank / Decatur Bank and Trust Fund Grants, 66
ACCF of Indiana Michael Basham Community Enrichment Fund Grants, 67
ACCF of Indiana Ron and Susie Ballard Community Enrichment Fund Grants, 68
ACCF Ralph Biggs Memorial Community Enrichment Fund Grants, 69
Achelis Foundation Grants, 102
Acuity Charitable Foundation Grants, 110
Adams-Mastrovich Family Foundation Grants, 113
Adams County Community Foundation Grants, 115
Adams Family Foundation I Grants, 116
Adams Family Fdn of Nora Springs Grants, 118
Adobe Foundation Action Grants, 126
Adobe Fdn Community Investment Grants, 127
Advance Auto Parts Corporate Giving Grants, 131
A Friends' Foundation Trust Grants, 136
Ahearn Family Foundation Grants, 142
AHS Foundation Grants, 143
Air Products Foundation Grants, 148
Albert W. Cherne Foundation Grants, 222
Alcatel-Lucent Technologies Foundation Grants, 224
Alden and Vada Dow Fund Grants, 225
Alex Stern Family Foundation Grants, 229
Allegis Group Foundation Grants, 237
Alpha Natural Resources Corporate Giving, 246
Alvah H. and Wyline P. Chapman Foundation Grants, 248
Ameren Corporation Community Grants, 251
American Savings Foundation Program Grants, 261
American Schlafhorst Foundation Grants, 262
Amerigroup Foundation Grants, 264
Amway Corporation Contributions, 269
Anderson Foundation Grants, 271
Andrew Family Foundation Grants, 272
Ann L. and Carol Green Rhodes Charitable Trust Grants, 278
Arizona Commission on the Arts Learning Collaboration Grant, 291
Arizona Commission on the Arts Youth Arts Engagement Grant, 292
Arkema Foundation Grants, 298
Arthur Ashley Williams Foundation Grants, 302
Arthur M. Blank Family Foundation Art of Change Grants, 306

Arthur M. Blank Family Foundation Pipeline Project Grants, 313
Atlanta Foundation Grants, 326
Atlas Insurance Agency Foundation Grants, 329
Austin Community Foundation Grants, 332
Back Home Again Foundation Grants, 344
Bank of America Charitable Foundation Matching Gifts, 356
Bank of Hawaii Foundation Grants, 360
Barrasso, Usdin, Kupperman, Freeman, and Sarver Corporate Grants, 362
Baton Rouge Area Foundation Grants, 365
Batts Foundation Grants, 367
Bay Area Community Fdn Auburn Area Chamber of Commerce Enrichment Fund Grants, 373
Bay Area Community Foundation Community Initiative Fund Grants, 376
Bay Area Community Foundation Semiannual Grants, 382
Ben B. Cheney Foundation Grants, 402
Benton Community Foundation Grants, 405
Benwood Foundation Community Grants, 406
Bernard and Audre Rapoport Foundation Arts and Culture Grants, 407
Bill Graham Memorial Foundation Grants, 429
Black Hills Corporation Grants, 435
Blanche and Irving Laurie Foundation Grants, 436
Blue Grass Community Foundation Clark County Fund Grants, 444
Blue Grass Community Foundation Fayette County Fund Grants, 446
Blue Grass Community Foundation Franklin County Fund Grants, 447
Blue Grass Community Foundation Harrison County Fund Grants, 448
Blue Grass Community Foundation Hudson-Ellis Grants, 449
Blue Grass Community Foundation Madison County Fund Grants, 450
Blue Grass Community Foundation Magoffin County Fund Grants, 451
Blue Grass Community Foundation Morgan County Fund Grants, 452
Blue Grass Community Foundation Rowan County Fund Grants, 453
Blue Grass Community Foundation Woodford County Fund Grants, 454
Blue River Community Foundation Grants, 458
Bothin Foundation Grants, 464
Bradley-Turner Foundation Grants, 466
Bradley C. Higgins Foundation Grants, 467
Bridgestone Americas Trust Fund Grants, 469
Brinker Int Corporation Charitable Giving, 471
British Columbia Arts Council Youth Engagement Program Grants, 473
Brown County Community Foundation Grants, 475
Brown Foundation Grants, 476
Burton D. Morgan Foundation Hudson Community Grants, 482
Bush Foundation Event Sponsorships, 485
Cabot Corporation Foundation Grants, 490
California Arts Cncl Statewide Networks Grants, 493
Callaway Foundation Grants, 496
Camille Beckman Foundation Grants, 499
Campbell Soup Foundation Grants, 501
Carl B. and Florence E. King Foundation Grants, 506
Carl M. Freeman Foundation FACES Grants, 507
Castle Foundation Grants, 518
CFFVR Clintonville Area Foundation Grants, 539
CFFVR Frank C. Shattuck Community Grants, 541
CFFVR Project Grants, 546
CFFVR Robert and Patricia Endries Family Foundation Grants, 547
CFFVR Shawano Area Community Foundation Grants, 549
CFFVR Women's Fund for the Fox Valley Region Grants, 550
CFF Winter Park Community Grants, 551
CFGR Community Impact Grants, 552
Charles H. Hall Foundation, 565

Charles Lafitte Foundation Grants, 567
Chicago Board of Trade Foundation Grants, 580
Chicago Neighborhood Arts Program Grants, 582
CIGNA Foundation Grants, 611
Cincinnati Bell Foundation Grants, 612
Cincinnati Milacron Foundation Grants, 613
Citizens Bank Charitable Foundation Grants, 616
City of Oakland Cultural Funding Grants, 618
Claremont Savings Bank Foundation Grants, 623
Clark County Community Foundation Grants, 626
Clayton F. and Ruth L. Hawkridge Foundation
   Grants, 630
Clayton Fund Grants, 631
Cleveland Browns Foundation Grants, 633
Colgate-Palmolive Company Grants, 652
Collins Foundation Grants, 658
Community Foundation for Greater Atlanta Strategic
   Restructuring Fund Grants, 669
Community Foundation for Greater Buffalo
   Competitive Grants, 670
Community Foundation for Greater Buffalo Niagara
   Area Foundation Grants, 673
Community Foundation for Greater Buffalo Ralph C.
   Wilson, Jr. Legacy Fund Grants, 674
Community Foundation for Kettering Grants, 676
Community Foundation for the National Capital
   Region Community Leadership Grants, 688
Community Foundation of Bartholomew County
   Heritage Fund Grants, 690
Community Foundation of Bartholomew County
   James A. Henderson Award for Fundraising, 691
Community Foundation of Crawford County, 695
Community Foundation of Eastern Connecticut
   General Southeast Grants, 696
Community Foundation of Greater Chattanooga
   Grants, 704
Community Foundation of Greater Fort Wayne -
   Community Endowment and Clarke Endowment
   Grants, 705
Community Foundation of Greater Fort Wayne -
   Edna Foundation Grants, 706
Community Foundation of Greater Greensboro
   Community Grants, 708
Community Foundation of Henderson County
   Community Grants, 711
Community Foundation of Louisville Anna Marble
   Memorial Fund for Princeton Grants, 717
Community Fdn of Randolph County Grants, 735
Community Foundation of St. Joseph County African
   American Community Grants, 737
Community Foundation of Switzerland County
   Grants, 739
Community Fdn of Wabash County Grants, 740
Community Foundation of Western Massachusetts
   Grants, 741
Cooke Foundation Grants, 748
Cooper Tire and Rubber Foundation Grants, 749
Corina Higginson Trust Grants, 750
Cralle Foundation Grants, 760
Crane Fund Grants, 763
Crayola Champ Creatively Alive Children Grts, 764
Cudd Foundation Grants, 769
CUNA Mutual Group Fdn Community Grants, 770
Dana Brown Charitable Trust Grants, 777
Daniel and Nanna Stern Family Fdn Grants, 778
David Alan and Susan Berkman Rahm Foundation
   Grants, 785
Dayton Foundation Dayton Youth Enrichment Fund
   Grant, 795
Dayton Foundation Grants, 796
Dayton Foundation Huber Heights Grants, 797
Dayton Power and Light Foundation Grants, 802
Deaconess Community Foundation Grants, 803
Dearborn Community Foundation City of
   Lawrenceburg Community Grants, 809
Delaware Community Foundation Grants, 817
Dermody Properties Foundation Grants, 827
Donald G. Gardner Humanities Tr Youth Grts, 840
Dorrance Family Foundation Grants, 845
Dubois County Community Foundation Grants, 871

Dyson Foundation Mid-Hudson Valley Project
   Support Grants, 874
E. Clayton and Edith P. Gengras, Jr. Foundation
   Grants, 875
E.J. Grassmann Trust Grants, 876
E.L. Wiegand Foundation Grants, 877
Earl and Maxine Claussen Trust Grants, 878
Eastern Bank Charitable Foundation Partnerships
   Grants, 881
Eastern Bank Charitable Foundation Targeted
   Grants, 882
Edward W. and Stella C. Van Houten Memorial Fund
   Grants, 892
Effie Allen Little Foundation Grants, 894
Elizabeth Huth Coates Charitable Foundation
   Grants, 900
Elizabeth Morse Genius Charitable Trust Grants, 901
Elkhart County Community Foundation Grants, 903
Ella West Freeman Foundation Grants, 904
Ellen Abbott Gilman Trust Grants, 905
Elmer Roe Deaver Foundation Grants, 906
El Pomar Foundation Anna Keesling Ackerman Fund
   Grants, 907
El Pomar Foundation Grants, 908
Elsie H. Wilcox Foundation Grants, 909
Emily O'Neill Sullivan Foundation Grants, 913
Energy by Design Poster Contest, 915
Ensworth Charitable Foundation Grants, 916
Entergy Corporation Micro Grants, 919
Entergy Corporation Open Grants for Arts and
   Culture, 920
Erie Chapman Foundation Grants, 928
Essex County Community Foundation Merrimack
   Valley Municipal Business Development and
   Recovery Fund Grants, 933
Ethel Sergeant Clark Smith Foundation Grants, 935
Evan Frankel Foundation Grants, 938
F.M. Kirby Foundation Grants, 946
F.R. Bigelow Foundation Grants, 947
Farmers Insurance Corporate Giving Grants, 948
Fayette County Community Foundation Grants, 951
Fidelity Foundation Grants, 957
First Hawaiian Bank Foundation Corporate Giving
   Grants, 967
First Nations Development Institute Native Arts
   Initiative Grants, 972
Foundations of East Chicago Education Grants, 995
Four County Community Foundation General
   Grants, 1000
Francis L. Abreu Charitable Trust Grants, 1008
Franklin County Community Fdn Grants, 1010
Fremont Area Community Foundation Amazing X
   Grants, 1019
Fremont Area Community Foundation Community
   Grants, 1020
General Motors Foundation Grants, 1039
George A. & Grace L. Long Fdn Grants, 1041
George and Ruth Bradford Foundation Grants, 1042
George A Ohl Jr. Foundation Grants, 1043
George H.C. Ensworth Memorial Fund Grants, 1049
George W. Codrington Charitable Foundation
   Grants, 1055
Georgia Council for the Arts Education Grants, 1060
GNOF Exxon-Mobil Grants, 1080
GNOF Freeman Challenge Grants, 1081
GNOF IMPACT Grants for Arts and Culture, 1083
GNOF Norco Community Grants, 1089
Golden Heart Community Foundation Grants, 1094
Graham Foundation Grants, 1100
Graham Foundation Grants, 1101
Greater Milwaukee Foundation Grants, 1109
Greater Saint Louis Community Fdn Grants, 1110
Greater Sitka Legacy Fund Grants, 1111
Greater Tacoma Community Foundation General
   Operating Grants, 1113
Green River Area Community Fdn Grants, 1117
GTRCF Elk Rapids Area Community Endowment
   Grants, 1127
GTRCF Genuine Leelanau Charitable Endowment
   Grants, 1128

GTRCF Joan Rajkovich McGarry Family Education
   Endowment Grants, 1131
H.A. and Mary K. Chapman Charitable Trust
   Grants, 1137
H.B. Fuller Foundation Grants, 1138
HAF Don and Bettie Albright Endowment Fund
   Grants, 1142
HAF Joe Alexandre Mem Family Fund Grants, 1145
HAF Laurence and Elaine Allen Memorial Fund
   Grants, 1146
Hardin County Community Foundation Grants, 1167
Harris Foundation Grants, 1177
Harrison County Community Foundation Signature
   Grants, 1179
Harry and Helen Sands Charitable Trust Grants, 1181
Hartford Foundation Regular Grants, 1185
Hawai'i Community Foundation East Hawaii Fund
   Grants, 1199
Hawai'i Community Foundation Richard Smart Fund
   Grants, 1204
Hawai'i Community Foundation Robert E. Black
   Fund Grants, 1205
Hawaiian Electric Industries Charitable Foundation
   Grants, 1211
Hawaii Community Foundation Omidyar Ohana
   Fund Grants, 1213
Hearst Foundations Culture Grants, 1223
Helen Bader Foundation Grants, 1227
Helen E. Ellis Charitable Trust Grants, 1228
Helen Gertrude Sparks Charitable Trust Grants, 1230
Herman Goldman Foundation Grants, 1245
Herman P. and Sophia Taubman Fdn Grants, 1247
Hill Crest Foundation Grants, 1249
Hillsdale County Community Foundation Love Your
   Community Grants, 1251
HLTA Visitor Industry Charity Walk Grant, 1254
Horace A. Kimball and S. Ella Kimball Foundation
   Grants, 1260
Hubbard Family Foundation Grants, 1271
Hubbard Family Foundation Grants, 1270
Huffy Foundation Grants, 1273
Humana Foundation Grants, 1275
Huntington County Community Foundation Make a
   Difference Grants, 1280
Iddings Foundation Capital Project Grants, 1283
Ike and Roz Friedman Foundation Grants, 1289
Illinois Arts Council Youth Employment in the Arts
   Program Grants, 1294
Inland Empire Community Foundation Coachella
   Valley Youth Grants, 1307
Inland Empire Community Foundation Native Youth
   Grants, 1308
Inland Empire Community Foundation Riverside
   Youth Grants, 1309
Inland Empire Community Foundation San
   Bernardino Youth Grants, 1310
Irving S. Gilmore Foundation Grants, 1314
Island Insurance Foundation Grants, 1316
J. Bulow Campbell Foundation Grants, 1319
J. Edwin Treakle Foundation Grants, 1320
J. Walton Bissell Foundation Grants, 1325
J. Watumull Fund Grants, 1326
James and Abigail Campbell Family Foundation
   Grants, 1337
James F. and Marion L. Miller Fdn Grants, 1338
James Ford Bell Foundation Grants, 1339
James Graham Brown Foundation Grants, 1340
James LeVoy Sorenson Foundation Grants, 1343
James M. Collins Foundation Grants, 1344
James S. Copley Foundation Grants, 1345
Jane's Trust Grants, 1346
Japan Foundation Los Angeles Mini-Grants for
   Japanese Arts & Culture, 1354
Japan Foundation New York Small Grants for Arts
   and Culture, 1355
Jayne and Leonard Abess Foundation Grants, 1358
Jennings County Community Fdn Grants, 1360
Jerry L. and Barbara J. Burris Fdn Grants, 1362
John F. Kennedy Center for the Performing Arts
   National Rosemary Kennedy Internship, 1371

John G. Duncan Charitable Trust Grants, 1372
Johnson Controls Foundation Arts and Culture Grants, 1378
John W. Anderson Foundation Grants, 1383
Josephine Schell Russell Chartbl Trust Grants, 1389
JP Morgan Chase Fdn Arts and Culture Grants, 1394
Judith Clark-Morrill Foundation Grants, 1395
Judy and Peter Blum Kovler Foundation Grants, 1396
Julia and Tunnicliff Fox Chartbl Trust Grants, 1397
Julia Richardson Brown Foundation Grants, 1398
Julia Temple Davis Brown Foundation Grants, 1399
Julius N. Frankel Foundation Grants, 1400
K and F Baxter Family Foundation Grants, 1413
Katharine Matthies Foundation Grants, 1418
Katherine John Murphy Foundation Grants, 1419
Kathryne Beynon Foundation Grants, 1420
Kenai Peninsula Foundation Grants, 1425
Kenneth T. and Eileen L. Norris Fdn Grants, 1427
Ketchikan Community Foundation Grants, 1429
Kind World Foundation Grants, 1438
Kirkpatrick Foundation Grants, 1440
Kodak Community Relations Grants, 1445
Kodiak Community Foundation Grants, 1446
Kosasa Foundation Grants, 1450
Kosciusko County Community Fdn Grants, 1452
Kovler Family Foundation Grants, 1455
Land O'Lakes Foundation Mid-Atlantic Grants, 1467
Leo Niessen Jr., Charitable Trust Grants, 1484
Lewis H. Humphreys Charitable Trust Grants, 1486
LGA Family Foundation Grants, 1487
Liberty Bank Foundation Grants, 1488
Lied Foundation Trust Grants, 1490
Lotus 88 Foundation for Women and Children Grants, 1508
Louie M. and Betty M. Phillips Fdn Grants, 1509
Louis and Sandra Berkman Foundation Grants, 1510
Louis Calder Foundation Grants, 1511
Lubrizol Foundation Grants, 1513
Lucy Downing Nisbet Charitable Fund Grants, 1515
Ludwick Family Foundation Grants, 1516
M. Bastian Family Foundation Grants, 1522
M.J. Murdock Charitable Trust General Grants, 1524
Macquarie Bank Foundation Grants, 1532
Madison County Community Foundation General Grants, 1537
Manuel D. and Rhoda Mayerson Fdn Grants, 1550
Marathon Petroleum Corporation Grants, 1551
Marcia and Otto Koehler Foundation Grants, 1553
Mardag Foundation Grants, 1554
Margaret T. Morris Foundation Grants, 1557
Marietta McNeill Morgan and Samuel Tate Morgan Jr. Trust Grants, 1560
Marsh Corporate Grants, 1580
Martha Holden Jennings Foundation Grants-to-Educators, 1581
Mary K. Chapman Foundation Grants, 1590
Mary Owen Borden Foundation Grants, 1597
Mary S. and David C. Corbin Fdn Grants, 1598
Massachusetts Cultural Council Local Cultural Council (LCC) Grants, 1601
Massachusetts Cultural Cncl YouthReach Grts, 1602
Matilda R. Wilson Fund Grants, 1605
McCombs Foundation Grants, 1615
McConnell Foundation Grants, 1616
McInerny Foundation Grants, 1622
Mead Family Foundation Grants, 1625
Mead Witter Foundation Grants, 1628
Mericos Foundation Grants, 1637
Meriden Foundation Grants, 1638
Merrick Foundation Grants, 1640
Merrick Foundation Grants, 1643
Mervin Bovaird Foundation Grants, 1643
MGN Family Foundation Grants, 1656
Michelin North America Challenge Education, 1660
Middlesex Savings Charitable Foundation Capacity Building Grants, 1669
Mimi and Peter Haas Fund Grants, 1677
Nathalie and Gladys Dalkowitz Charitable Trust Grants, 1716
Nathan Cummings Foundation Grants, 1718

NEH Family and Youth Programs in American History Grants, 1734
New Earth Foundation Grants, 1743
NHSCA Conservation License Plate Grants, 1757
Noble County Community Foundation Grants, 1765
O. Max Gardner Foundation Grants, 1798
OceanFirst Foundation Major Grants, 1803
Ohio Arts Council Artist in Residence Grants for Sponsors, 1810
Ohio Valley Foundation Grants, 1814
Olive Higgins Prouty Foundation Grants, 1817
Olive Smith Browning Charitable Trust Grants, 1818
Olivia R. Gardner Foundation Grants, 1819
Ontario Arts Council Artists in Communities and Schools Project Grants, 1823
Ontario Arts Council Arts Organizations in Communities and Schools Operating Grants, 1824
Oppenstein Brothers Foundation Grants, 1827
Oregon Community Fdn Community Grants, 1833
P. Buckley Moss Foundation for Children's Education Endowed Scholarships, 1854
P. Buckley Moss Foundation for Children's Education Teacher Grants, 1855
Parkersburg Area Community Foundation Action Grants, 1871
Patricia Kisker Foundation Grants, 1879
PCA-PCD Professional Development for Individual Artists Grants, 1883
PCA Art Organizations and Art Programs Grants for Presenting Organizations, 1884
PCA Arts Organizations and Arts Programs Grants for Arts Service Organizations, 1890
PCA Arts Organizations and Arts Programs Grants for Crafts, 1891
PCA Arts Organizations and Arts Programs Grants for Local Arts, 1895
PCA Entry Track Arts Organizations and Arts Programs Grants for Arts Service Orgs, 1902
PCA Entry Track Arts Organizations and Arts Programs Grants for Crafts, 1903
PCA Entry Track Arts Organizations and Arts Programs Grants for Presenting Orgs, 1909
PCA Entry Track Arts Organizations and Arts Programs Grants for Theatre, 1910
PCA Pennsylvania Partners in the Arts Program Stream Grants, 1914
PCA Pennsylvania Partners in the Arts Project Stream Grants, 1915
PCA Professional Development Grants, 1916
PCA Strategies for Success Grants - Basic Level, 1918
PCA Strategies for Success Grants - Intermediate Level, 1919
PennPAT Artist Technical Assistance Grants, 1929
PennPAT Strategic Opportunity Grants, 1933
Perkin Fund Grants, 1937
Petersburg Community Foundation Grants, 1951
Peyton Anderson Foundation Grants, 1954
PGE Foundation Grants, 1958
Phil Hardin Foundation Grants, 1960
Phoenix Coyotes Charities Grants, 1963
Phoenix Suns Charities Grants, 1964
Pinnacle Entertainment Foundation Grants, 1972
Piper Jaffray Foundation Communities Giving Grants, 1974
Piper Trust Arts and Culture Grants, 1975
PMI Foundation Grants, 1982
Pohlad Family Fdn Large Capital Grants, 1990
Pohlad Family Fdn Small Capital Grants, 1991
Pokagon Fund Grants, 1994
Polk County Community Foundation Bradley Breakthrough Community Benefit Grants, 1995
Polk County Community Foundation Marjorie M. and Lawrence R. Bradley Endowment Fund Grants, 1998
Polk County Community Foundation Mary F. Kessler Fund Grants, 1999
Polk County Community Foundation Unrestricted Grants, 2001
Porter County Community Foundation Sparking the Arts Fund Grants, 2004

Posey Community Foundation Women's Fund Grants, 2008
Powell Family Foundation Grants, 2012
Powell Foundation Grants, 2013
PPCF Esther M. and Freeman E. Everett Charitable Foundation Grants, 2016
Price Chopper's Golub Foundation Grants, 2020
Pride Foundation Grants, 2024
PSEG Corporate Contributions Grants, 2030
Puerto Rico Community Foundation Grants, 2037
Pulaski County Community Foundation Grants, 2038
Putnam County Community Fdn Grants, 2040
R.D. and Joan Dale Hubbard Fdn Grants, 2044
Rasmuson Foundation Tier One Grants, 2055
Rasmuson Foundation Tier Two Grants, 2056
Rathmann Family Foundation Grants, 2057
Ray Charles Foundation Grants, 2058
Ressler-Gertz Foundation Grants, 2067
Richard and Caroline T. Gwathmey Memorial Trust Grants, 2069
Richard J. Stern Foundation for the Arts Grants, 2071
Riedman Foundation Grants, 2076
Ripley County Community Foundation Grants, 2077
Ripley County Community Foundation Small Project Grants, 2078
RISCA Project Grants for Individuals, 2079
Robbins-de Beaumont Foundation Grants, 2080
Robbins Charitable Foundation Grants, 2081
Robert and Helen Haddad Foundation Grants, 2084
Robert Lee Blaffer Foundation Grants, 2092
Robert R. Meyer Foundation Grants, 2094
Roger L. and Agnes C. Dell Charitable Trust II Grants, 2100
Ron and Sanne Higgins Family Fdn Grants, 2101
Rosenberg Fund for Children Ozzy Klate Memorial Fund Grants, 2114
Roy and Christine Sturgis Charitable Tr Grts, 2115
Rush County Community Foundation Grants, 2121
Ruth and Vernon Taylor Foundation Grants, 2124
S. Spencer Scott Fund Grants, 2129
Saint Louis Rams Foundation Community Donations, 2139
Samuel N. and Mary Castle Foundation Grants, 2145
Samuel S. Johnson Foundation Grants, 2146
San Antonio Area Foundation Annual Responsive Grants, 2147
SanDisk Corp Community Sharing Grants, 2155
San Juan Island Community Foundation Grants, 2158
Santa Fe Community Foundation Seasonal Grants-Fall Cycle, 2159
Sartain Lanier Family Foundation Grants, 2164
Schramm Foundation Grants, 2168
Scott County Community Foundation Grants, 2170
Seattle Foundation Arts and Culture Grants, 2174
Seattle Foundation C. Keith Birkenfeld Memorial Trust Grants, 2177
Sensient Technologies Foundation Grants, 2180
Shield-Ayres Foundation Grants, 2189
Shopko Fdn Community Charitable Grants, 2191
Sidney and Sandy Brown Foundation Grants, 2196
Sioux Falls Area Community Foundation Community Fund Grants, 2203
Sioux Falls Area Community Foundation Spot Grants, 2204
Skaggs Foundation Grants, 2207
Sony Corporation of America Grants, 2216
South Madison Community Foundation - Teacher Creativity Mini Grants, 2225
Spencer County Community Foundation Women's Fund Grants, 2232
Stella and Charles Guttman Foundation Grants, 2241
Sterling and Shelli Gardner Foundation Grants, 2243
Stinson Foundation Grants, 2246
Storm Castle Foundation Grants, 2248
Strake Foundation Grants, 2249
Stranahan Foundation Grants, 2250
Subaru of Indiana Automotive Fdn Grants, 2254
Summit Foundation Grants, 2255
Sunoco Foundation Grants, 2256

SunTrust Bank Trusteed Foundations Greene-Sawtell
    Grants, 2257
SunTrust Bank Trusteed Foundations Nell Warren
    Elkin and William Simpson Elkin Grants, 2258
Sylvia Perkin Perpetual Charitable Trust Grants, 2263
TAC Arts Access Grant, 2265
Target Corporation Community Engagement Fund
    Grants, 2270
Tauck Family Foundation Grants, 2274
TE Foundation Grants, 2279
Telluride Foundation Community Grants, 2281
Tension Envelope Foundation Grants, 2284
Thelma Braun and Bocklett Family Foundation
    Grants, 2287
Thomas and Agnes Carvel Foundation Grants, 2289
Thomas W. Briggs Foundation Grants, 2294
Tides Foundation Grants, 2302
Toyota Motor Manuf of Alabama Grants, 2309
Toyota Motor Manufacturing of Indiana Grants, 2310
Toyota Motor Manuf of Mississippi Grants, 2312
Toyota Motor Manufacturing of Texas Grants, 2313
Toyota Motor Manufacturing of West Virginia
    Grants, 2314
Toyota Motor Sales, USA Grants, 2316
Tull Charitable Foundation Grants, 2324
Turner Foundation Grants, 2326
U.S. Cellular Corporation Grants, 2331
United Technologies Corporation Grants, 2347
Vanderburgh Community Foundation Men's Fund
    Grants, 2373
Vanderburgh County Community Foundation
    Women's Fund Grants, 2376
Virginia Commission for the Arts Artists in
    Education Residency Grants, 2385
Volkswagen Group of America Corporate
    Contributions Grants, 2389
VSA/Volkswagen Group of America Exhibition
    Awards, 2393
VSA International Art Program for Children with
    Disabilities Grants, 2394
Walker Area Community Foundation Grants, 2401
Wallace Foundation Grants, 2402
Warrick County Community Foundation Women's
    Fund, 2411
Wayne County Foundation Grants, 2419
Western New York Foundation Grants, 2429
West Virginia Commission on the Arts Challenge
    America Partnership Grants, 2430
Widgeon Point Charitable Foundation Grants, 2447
William A. Cooke Foundation Grants, 2452
William A. Miller Foundation Grants, 2453
William G. and Helen C. Hoffman Foundation
    Grants, 2466
William G. Gilmore Foundation Grants, 2467
William J. and Dorothy K. O'Neill Foundation
    Responsive Grants, 2468
William J. and Gertrude R. Casper Foundation
    Grants, 2469
William Ray and Ruth E. Collins Fdn Grants, 2473
Williams Comps Homegrown Giving Grants, 2474
Winifred Johnson Clive Foundation Grants, 2478
Woods Fund of Chicago Grants, 2489
Wyoming Community Fdn General Grants, 2501
Wyoming Community Foundation Hazel Patterson
    Memorial Grants, 2502
Wyomissing Foundation Community Grants, 2504
Wyomissing Foundation Thun Family Organizational
    Grants, 2505
Wyomissing Foundation Thun Family Program
    Grants, 2506
Xerox Foundation Grants, 2507
Youths' Friends Association Grants, 2511

Asian Americans
Ben B. Cheney Foundation Grants, 402
Eide Bailly Resourcefullness Awards, 897
Foundation Beyond Belief Compassionate Impact
    Grants, 986
Foundation Beyond Belief Humanist Grants, 987

Asian Arts
Bothin Foundation Grants, 464
Christensen Fund Regional Grants, 600

Assisted-Living Programs
Adelaide Breed Bayrd Foundation Grants, 123
California Endowment Innovative Ideas Challenge
    Grants, 495
CFFVR Basic Needs Giving Partnership Grants, 537
CFGR Jenkins Foundation Grants, 553
Christine and Katharina Pauly Charitable Trust
    Grants, 601
Clark and Ruby Baker Foundation Grants, 625
CNCS AmeriCorps State and National Grants, 643
CNCS Senior Corps Retired and Senior Volunteer
    Program Grants, 648
Marjorie Moore Charitable Foundation Grants, 1574
Mary Black Foundation Active Living Grants, 1585
May and Stanley Smith Charitable Trust Grants, 1613
McLean Contributionship Grants, 1623
Perkins-Ponder Foundation Grants, 1938
Priddy Foundation Program Grants, 2023
Reinberger Foundation Grants, 2066
Union Bank, N.A. Corporate Sponsorships and
    Donations, 2333
Union Bank, N.A. Foundation Grants, 2334

Assistive Technology
John D. and Katherine A. Johnston Foundation
    Grants, 1370
May and Stanley Smith Charitable Trust Grants, 1613
Vigneron Memorial Fund Grants, 2384

Asthma
GNOF IMPACT Kahn-Oppenheim Tr Grts, 1087
Kathryne Beynon Foundation Grants, 1420
Medtronic Foundation Strengthening Health Systems
    Grants, 1632

At-Risk Students
AASA Urgent Need Mini-Grants, 43
Advance Auto Parts Corporate Giving Grants, 131
Baystate Financial Charitable Foundation Grants, 385
Bernard and Audre Rapoport Foundation Arts and
    Culture Grants, 407
Bernard and Audre Rapoport Foundation Education
    Grants, 410
Best Buy Children's Foundation @15 Community
    Grants , 414
Charles H. Pearson Foundation Grants, 566
CNCS AmeriCorps State and National Grants, 643
Community Foundation of Louisville Madi and Jim
    Tate Fund Grants, 727
CUNA Mutual Group Fdn Community Grants, 770
DOL Youthbuild Grants, 838
Elizabeth Morse Genius Charitable Trust Grants, 901
Foundation for the Mid South Education Grants, 993
Golden Heart Community Foundation Grants, 1094
Greater Sitka Legacy Fund Grants, 1111
GTECH After School Advantage Grants, 1125
Hartley Foundation Grants, 1186
Henry E. Niles Foundation Grants, 1240
Kenai Peninsula Foundation Grants, 1425
Ketchikan Community Foundation Grants, 1429
Kevin J Major Youth Sports Scholarships, 1431
Kodiak Community Foundation Grants, 1446
LEGO Children's Fund Grants, 1480
Lewis H. Humphreys Charitable Trust Grants, 1486
Mardag Foundation Grants, 1554
Marin Community Foundation Closing the Education
    Achievement Gap Grants, 1564
MetroWest Health Foundation Grants to Reduce
    the Incidence of High Risk Behaviors Among
    Adolescents, 1646
Meyer Foundation Education Grants, 1649
Michael Reese Health Trust Responsive Grants, 1659
Pacers Foundation Be Educated Grants, 1857
Petersburg Community Foundation Grants, 1951
Piper Trust Education Grants, 1977
Portland General Electric Foundation Grants, 2007

Public Education Power Grants, 2032
Screen Actors Guild PencilPALS Assistance, 2172
Screen Actors Guild StagePALS Assistance, 2173
Sidgmore Family Foundation Grants, 2195
Stocker Foundation Grants, 2247
Tauck Family Foundation Grants, 2274
Thomas Sill Foundation Grants, 2292
Union Bank, N.A. Foundation Grants, 2334
USDEd Gaining Early Awareness and Readiness for
    Undergrad Programs (GEAR UP) Grants, 2364
Wyoming Department of Education McKinney-Vento
    Subgrant, 2503

At-Risk Youth
ABC Charities Grants, 50
Abell Foundation Education Grants, 53
Abundance Foundation Local Community Grants, 58
ACF Abandoned Infants Assistance Grants, 70
ACF Adoption Opportunities Grants, 71
ACF Basic Center Program Grants, 73
ACF Child Abuse Prevention and Treatment Act
    Discretionary Funds Grants, 74
ACF Child Welfare Training Grants, 75
ACF Community-Based Child Abuse Prevention
    (CBCAP) Grants, 76
ACF Community-Based Child Abuse
    Prevention (CBCAP) Tribal and Migrant
    DiscretionaryGrants, 77
ACF Ethnic Community Self Help Grants, 80
ACF Infant Adoption Awareness Training Program
    Grants, 84
ACF Promoting Safe and Stable Families (PSSF)
    Program Grants, 89
ACF Runaway and Homeless Youth Training and
    Technical Assistance Center Grants, 92
ACF Street Outreach Program Grants, 94
ACF Transitional Living Program and Maternity
    Group Homes Grants, 96
ACF Tribal Maternal, Infant, and Early Childhood
    Home Visiting Program: Development and
    Implementation Grants, 97
ACF Tribal Maternal, Infant, and Early Childhood
    Home Visiting Program: Implementation and
    Expansion Grants, 98
ACF Unaccompanied Refugee Children Grants, 99
ACF Voluntary Agencies Matching Grants, 100
Adelaide Christian Home For Children Grants, 124
Advance Auto Parts Corporate Giving Grants, 131
Aid for Starving Children Emerg Aid Grants, 144
Aid for Starving Children Health and Nutrition
    Grants, 145
Aid for Starving Children Homes and Education
    Grants, 146
Alaska Community Foundation Children's Trust Tier
    1 Community Based Child Abuse and Neglect
    Prevention Grants, 198
Alaska Community Foundation Children's Trust Tier
    1 Parenting and Child Development Educational
    Grants, 199
Alaska Community Foundation Children's Trust Tier
    2 Innovation Grants, 200
Alaska Community Foundation GCI Suicide
    Prevention Grant, 203
Alaska Community Foundation Ketchikan
    Community Foundation Grant, 206
Albert W. Cherne Foundation Grants, 222
Alfred E. Chase Charitable Foundation Grants, 233
Alliance for Strong Families and Communities
    Grants, 239
Allstate Foundation Tolerance, Inclusion, and
    Diversity Grants, 245
Amelia Sillman Rockwell and Carlos Perry Rockwell
    Charities Fund Grants, 250
American Indian Youth Running Strong Grants, 256
Amway Corporation Contributions, 269
Armstrong McDonald Foundation Children and
    Youth Grants, 300
Arthur M. Blank Family Foundation AMB West
    Community Fund Grants, 304

Arthur M. Blank Family Foundation Molly Blank Fund Grants, 310
ATA Local Community Relations Grants, 324
Avery Dennison Foundation Education Grants, 337
Bank of Hawaii Foundation Grants, 360
Bank of the Orient Community Giving, 361
Baton Rouge Area Foundation Every Kid a King Fund Grants, 364
Batters Up USA Equipment Grants, 366
Bay Area Community Foundation Semiannual Grants, 382
Bayer Fund Community Development Grants, 383
Baystate Financial Charitable Foundation Grants, 385
Ben Cohen StandUp Foundation Grants, 403
Bernard and Audre Rapoport Foundation Arts and Culture Grants, 407
Bernard and Audre Rapoport Foundation Community Building and Social Service Grants, 408
Bernard and Audre Rapoport Foundation Democracy and Civic Participation Grants, 409
Bernard and Audre Rapoport Foundation Education Grants, 410
Bernard and Audre Rapoport Foundation Health Grants, 411
Best Buy Children's Foundation @15 Community Grants, 414
Bright Promises Foundation Grants, 470
Bushrod H. Campbell and Adah F. Hall Charity Fund Grants, 486
Campbell Foundation Grants, 500
CFFVR Basic Needs Giving Partnership Grants, 537
CFFVR Robert and Patricia Endries Family Foundation Grants, 547
CFFVR Schmidt Family G4 Grants, 548
CFGR Community Impact Grants, 552
CFGR SisterFund Grants, 554
CFGR Ujima Legacy Fund Grants, 555
Charles H. Pearson Foundation Grants, 566
Charles Lafitte Foundation Grants, 567
Chicago Community Trust Arts and Culture Grants: Improving Access to Arts Learning, 581
Christine and Katharina Pauly Charitable Trust Grants, 601
Christopher Ludwick Foundation Grants, 602
Citizens Bank Charitable Foundation Grants, 616
Cleveland H. Dodge Foundation Grants, 637
CMS Research and Demonstration Grants, 640
CNCS AmeriCorps State and National Grants, 643
CNCS Foster Grandparent Projects Grants, 646
CNO Financial Group Community Grants, 650
Collective Brands Foundation Payless Gives Shoes 4 Kids Grants, 655
Columbus Foundation Traditional Grants, 663
Community Foundation of Crawford County, 695
Community Foundation of Eastern Connecticut Norwich Youth Grants, 699
Community Foundation of Greater Greensboro Community Grants, 708
Community Foundation of Louisville Boyette and Edna Edwards Fund Grants, 718
Corina Higginson Trust Grants, 750
Countess Moira Charitable Foundation Grants, 752
Covenant to Care for Children Crisis Food Pantry Giving, 756
Covenant to Care for Children Enrichment Fund Grants, 758
CUNA Mutual Group Fdn Community Grants, 770
Deaconess Foundation Advocacy Grants, 804
Delta Air Lines Foundation Youth Development Grants, 824
DOL Youthbuild Grants, 838
Dorrance Family Foundation Grants, 845
Edward and Romell Ackley Foundation Grants, 889
Elizabeth Morse Genius Charitable Trust Grants, 901
EPA Children's Health Protection Grants, 923
Eulalie Bloedel Schneider Foundation Grants, 936
Fidelity Charitable Gift Fund Grants, 956
First Hawaiian Bank Foundation Corporate Giving Grants, 967

First Nations Development Institute Native Youth and Culture Fund Grants, 974
Ford Family Foundation Grants - Child Abuse Prevention and Intervention, 981
Ford Family Foundation Grants - Positive Youth Development, 982
Foundations of East Chicago Youth Development Grants, 998
Four County Community Foundation General Grants, 1000
Four County Community Foundation Healthy Senior/Healthy Youth Fund Grants, 1001
Frank Reed and Margaret Jane Peters Memorial Fund II Grants, 1014
Frederick W. Marzahl Memorial Fund Grants, 1018
Friends of Hawaii Charities Grants, 1024
Fuller Foundation Youth At Risk Grants, 1028
Gannett Foundation Community Action Grants, 1033
German Protestant Orphan Asylum Foundation Grants, 1066
Go Daddy Cares Charitable Contributions, 1093
Golden Heart Community Foundation Grants, 1094
Grand Circle Foundation Associates Grants, 1102
Greater Sitka Legacy Fund Grants, 1111
Greater Tacoma Community Foundation Youth Program Grants, 1115
GTECH After School Advantage Grants, 1125
GTRCF Boys and Girls Club of Grand Traverse Endowment Grants, 1126
Harry and Jeanette Weinberg Fdn Grants, 1182
Hartley Foundation Grants, 1186
Harvey E. Najim Family Foundation Grants, 1187
Hasbro Children's Fund Grants, 1189
Hawai'i Community Foundation Children's Trust Fund Community Awareness: Child Abuse and Neglect Prevention Grants, 1198
Hearst Foundations Social Service Grants, 1224
Helen Irwin Littauer Educational Trust Grants, 1231
Henry and Ruth Blaustein Rosenberg Foundation Youth Development Grants, 1237
Henry E. Niles Foundation Grants, 1240
Herbert A. and Adrian W. Woods Foundation Grants, 1243
Hillsdale County Community Foundation Y.O.U.T.H. Grants, 1252
Horace A. Moses Charitable Trust Grants, 1261
Initiaive Fdn Inside-Out Connections Grants, 1303
IYI Responsible Fatherhood Grants, 1318
Jack H. and William M. Light Charitable Trust Grants, 1330
Jack Kent Cooke Fdn Good Neighbor Grants, 1331
Jim Moran Foundation Grants, 1366
Joseph H. and Florence A. Roblee Foundation Children and Youth Grants, 1385
Josephine Schell Russell Chartbl Trust Grants, 1389
Judy and Peter Blum Kovler Foundation Grants, 1396
Kenai Peninsula Foundation Grants, 1425
Ketchikan Community Foundation Grants, 1429
Kevin J Major Youth Sports Scholarships, 1431
Kodiak Community Foundation Grants, 1446
LEGO Children's Fund Grants, 1480
Leo Goodwin Foundation Grants, 1482
Lilly Endowment Summer Youth Grants, 1492
Lily Palmer Fry Memorial Trust Grants, 1493
Locations Foundation Legacy Grants, 1504
Lois and Richard England Family Foundation Out-of-School-Time Grants, 1506
Lumpkin Family Foundation Strong Community Leadership Grants, 1519
Mabel A. Horne Fund Grants, 1525
Mardag Foundation Grants, 1554
Marin Community Foundation Closing the Education Achievement Gap Grants, 1564
Marion and Miriam Rose Fund Grants, 1569
Mary Black Foundation Early Childhood Development Grants, 1586
Mary Cofer Trigg Trust Fund Grants, 1587
Maryland State Dept of Education Coordinating Entity Services for the Maryland Child Care Res Centers Network Grants, 1594

Mary Owen Borden Foundation Grants, 1597
Mathile Family Foundation Grants, 1604
MetroWest Health Foundation Grants to Reduce the Incidence of High Risk Behaviors Among Adolescents, 1646
Meyer Foundation Education Grants, 1649
MGM Resorts Foundation Community Grants, 1655
Michael Reese Health Trust Responsive Grants, 1659
Michigan Women Forward Grants, 1662
Mid-Iowa Health Foundation Community Response Grants, 1667
Mill Spring Foundation Grants, 1674
Minnie M. Jones Trust Grants, 1678
Monsanto Kids Garden Fresh Grants, 1682
Monsanto United States Grants, 1684
Montgomery County Community Foundation Youth Services Grants, 1691
Moran Family Foundation Grants, 1693
Morris Stulsaft Foundation Early Childhood Education Grants, 1696
Morris Stulsaft Foundation Educational Support for Children Grants, 1697
Morris Stulsaft Foundation Participation in the the Arts Grants, 1698
Morris Stulsaft Foundation Pathways to Work Grants, 1699
National 4-H Youth in Action Awards, 1721
Nationwide Insurance Foundation Grants, 1726
Nestle Purina PetCare Educational Grants, 1738
Nestle Purina PetCare Youth Grants, 1739
New Jersey Center for Hispanic Policy, Research and Development Innovative Initiatives Grants, 1750
New Jersey Office of Faith Based Initiatives Services to At Risk Youth Grants, 1752
NFL Charities NFL Player Foundation Grants, 1754
NYFA Artists in the School Community Planning Grants, 1779
Ober Kaler Community Grants, 1801
OneFamily Foundation Grants, 1822
OSF Early Childhood Program Grants, 1841
OSF Soros Justice Youth Activist Fellowships, 1844
OtterCares Champion Fund Grants, 1848
Pacers Foundation Be Drug-Free Grants, 1856
Pacers Foundation Be Educated Grants, 1857
Perry County Community Foundation Youth Development Grants, 1943
Peter and Elizabeth C. Tower Foundation Intellectual Disabilities Grants, 1944
Peter and Elizabeth C. Tower Foundation Mental Health Grants, 1946
Peter and Elizabeth C. Tower Foundation Small Grants, 1947
Petersburg Community Foundation Grants, 1951
PeyBack Foundation Grants, 1953
Pike County Community Foundation Youth Development Grants, 1971
Piper Trust Children Grants, 1976
Piper Trust Education Grants, 1977
Pohlad Family Foundation Youth Advancement Grants, 1993
Porter County Community Foundation Health and Wellness Grant, 2002
Portland General Electric Foundation Grants, 2007
Posey County Community Foundation Youth Development Grants, 2010
Presidio Fencing Club Youth Fencers Assistance Scholarships, 2019
Public Education Power Grants, 2032
Public Welfare Fdn Juvenile Justice Grants, 2033
Richard Davoud Donchian Foundation Grants, 2070
Robbins Family Charitable Foundation Grants, 2082
Robert F. Lange Foundation Grants, 2090
Rosenberg Fund for Children Clinton and Muriel Jencks Memorial Fund Grants, 2109
SACF Youth Advisory Council Grants, 2131
Saginaw County Community Foundation Youth FORCE Grants, 2136
Saltchuk Corporate Giving, 2141
Samueli Foundation Education Grants, 2143
SAS Institute Community Relations Donations, 2165

Schlessman Family Foundation Grants, 2167
Screen Actors Guild BookPALS Assistance, 2171
Screen Actors Guild PencilPALS Assistance, 2172
Screen Actors Guild StagePALS Assistance, 2173
Sidgmore Family Foundation Grants, 2195
Sobrato Family Foundation Grants, 2211
Sobrato Family Fdn Meeting Space Grants, 2212
Sobrato Family Foundation Office Space Grants, 2213
Spencer County Community Foundation Youth
     Development Grants, 2233
Stella and Charles Guttman Foundation Grants, 2241
Stocker Foundation Grants, 2247
Strong Foundation Grants, 2252
TAC Arts Education Mini Grants, 2267
Tauck Family Foundation Grants, 2274
Thomas Sill Foundation Grants, 2292
Threshold Fdn Justice and Democracy Grants, 2298
Trinity Trust Summer Youth Mini Grants, 2321
TSYSF Individual Scholarships, 2322
TSYSF Team Grants, 2323
Turtle Bay Foundation Grants, 2327
U.S. Bank Foundation Grants, 2330
Union Bank, N.A. Foundation Grants, 2334
United Friends of the Children Scholarships, 2341
Vanderburgh Community Foundation Youth
     Development Grants, 2375
Victor E. Speas Foundation Grants, 2380
Warrick County Community Foundation Youth
     Development Grants, 2412
Whiting Foundation Grants, 2440
Women's Fund of Hawaii Grants, 2484
Wood-Claeyssens Foundation Grants, 2486
YSA National Child Awareness Month Youth
     Ambassador Grants, 2517
Z. Smith Reynolds Foundation Small Grants, 2523

Athletics
Abby's Legendary Pizza Foundation Grants, 49
Adidas Corporation General Grants, 125
Anthony Munoz Foundation Straight A Student
     Campaign Grants, 280
Ar-Hale Family Foundation Grants, 290
Baltimore Community Foundation Mitzvah Fund for
     Good Deeds Grants, 349
Baltimore Ravens Corporate Giving, 350
Bank of America Corporation Sponsorships, 359
Batters Up USA Equipment Grants, 366
Calvin Johnson Jr. Foundation Mini Grants, 498
Charlotte Martin Foundation Youth Grants, 571
Chassé Youth Leaders Fund Grants, 573
Chatham Athletic Foundation Grants, 574
Clark Electric Cooperative Grants, 627
Collective Brands Foundation Saucony Run for Good
     Grants, 656
Community Foundation of Louisville CHAMP Fund
     Grants, 720
CONSOL Energy Academic Grants, 746
CONSOL Youth Program Grants, 747
Easton Sports Development Foundation National
     Archery in the Schools Grants, 884
El Pomar Foundation Grants, 908
Finish Line Youth Foundation Founder's Grants, 960
Finish Line Youth Foundation Grants, 961
Finish Line Youth Foundation Legacy Grants, 962
Foundation of Herkimer and Oneida Counties Youth
     Sports, Wellness and Recreation Mini-Grants, 994
Four County Community Foundation General
     Grants, 1000
George B. Page Foundation Grants, 1044
Gibson County Community Foundation Recreation
     Grants, 1069
GTRCF Traverse City Track Club Endowment
     Grants, 1132
John and Marcia Goldman Foundation Youth
     Development Grants, 1368
John M. Weaver Foundation Grants, 1376
Kevin J Major Youth Sports Scholarships, 1431
Knox County Community Foundation Recreation
     Grants, 1442
NFL Charities NFL Player Foundation Grants, 1754

NFL Charities Pro Bowl Community Grants in
     Hawaii, 1755
Olive Smith Browning Charitable Trust Grants, 1818
OtterCares Champion Fund Grants, 1848
Outrigger Duke Kahanamoku Foundation Athletic
     Event Grants, 1852
Outrigger Duke Kahanamoku Foundation Athletic
     Team Grants, 1853
Perry County Community Foundation Recreation
     Grants, 1942
Polk County Community Foundation Kirby Harmon
     Field Fund Grants, 1997
Presidio Fencing Club Youth Fencers Assistance
     Scholarships, 2019
Stein Family Charitable Trust Grants, 2240
Telluride Foundation Community Grants, 2281
Textron Corporate Contributions Grants, 2286
Todd Brock Family Foundation Grants, 2305
TSYSF Individual Scholarships, 2322
TSYSF Team Grants, 2323
Van Kampen Boyer Molinari Charitable Foundation
     Grants, 2377
WSF Sports 4 Life Grants, 2496
Yawkey Foundation Grants, 2510

Attention Deficit Hyperactivity Disorder
AACAP Pilot Rsrch Awd for Att-Deficit Disorder, 32

Audience Development
Air Products Foundation Grants, 148
PCA Art Organizations and Art Programs Grants for
     Presenting Organizations, 1884
PCA Arts Organizations and Arts Programs Grants
     for Dance, 1892
PCA Arts Organizations and Arts Programs Grants
     for Film and Electronic Media, 1893
PCA Arts Organizations and Arts Programs Grants
     for Literature, 1894
PCA Arts Organizations and Arts Programs Grants
     for Local Arts, 1895
PCA Arts Organizations and Arts Programs Grants
     for Theatre, 1896
PCA Arts Organizations and Arts Programs Grants
     for Traditional and Folk Arts, 1897
PCA Entry Track Arts Organizations and Arts
     Programs Grants for Dance, 1904
PCA Entry Track Arts Orgs and Arts Programs
     Grants for Film and Electronic Media, 1905
PCA Entry Track Arts Organizations and Arts
     Programs Grants for Local Arts, 1907
PCA Entry Track Arts Organizations and Arts
     Programs Grants for Presenting Orgs, 1909
PCA Entry Track Arts Organizations and Arts
     Programs Grants for Theatre, 1910
PCA Entry Track Arts Orgs and Arts Programs
     Grants for Traditional and Folk Arts, 1911
PCA Management/Techl Assistance Grants, 1913
PCA Pennsylvania Partners in the Arts Program
     Stream Grants, 1914
PCA Pennsylvania Partners in the Arts Project
     Stream Grants, 1915
PennPAT Fee-Support Grants for Presenters, 1930
PennPAT New Directions Grants for Presenters, 1931
PennPAT Presenter Travel Grants, 1932
Piper Trust Arts and Culture Grants, 1975
Wallace Foundation Grants, 2402
West Virginia Commission on the Arts Long-Term
     Artist Residencies, 2431

Audio Production
ALA Amazing Audiobks for Young Adults Awd, 155
ALA Notable Children's Recordings Awards, 180
ALA Odyssey Award for Excellence in Audiobook
     Production, 182
NYSCA Electronic Media and Film: Workspace
     Grants, 1789
PCA Arts Organizations and Arts Programs Grants
     for Film and Electronic Media, 1893
PCA Entry Track Arts Orgs and Arts Programs
     Grants for Film and Electronic Media, 1905

Audiovisual Materials
ALA Bookapalooza Grants, 161
ALA BWI Collection Development Grant, 164
ALA Notable Children's Recordings Awards, 180
ALA Notable Children's Videos Awards, 181
ALA Odyssey Award for Excellence in Audiobook
     Production, 182
Cincinnati Bell Foundation Grants, 612
Japan Foundation Los Angeles Japanese-Language
     Teaching Materials Purchase Grants, 1353

Autism
Autism Speaks Norma and Malcolm Baker Recreation
     Grants, 335
Montgomery County Community Foundation Libby
     Whitecotton Fund Grants, 1690

Automotive Engineering
BMW of North America Charitable Contribs, 460

Aviation
Ray Foundation Grants, 2059

Band Music
NYSCA Music: Commty Music Schools Grants, 1790
NYSCA Music: Gen Operating Support Grants, 1791
NYSCA Music: Gen Program Support Grants, 1792
PennPAT Artist Technical Assistance Grants, 1929
PennPAT Strategic Opportunity Grants, 1933

Bankruptcy
Telluride Fdn Emergency Grants, 2282

Baptist Church
AHS Foundation Grants, 143
Alvah H. and Wyline P. Chapman Foundation
     Grants, 248
Bradley-Turner Foundation Grants, 466
Chapman Family Foundation, 562
Effie and Wofford Cain Foundation Grants, 895
Harry and Helen Sands Charitable Trust Grants, 1181
V.V. Cooke Foundation Grants, 2371

Basic Living Expenses
Akron Community Foundation Health and Human
     Services Grants, 152
Amica Companies Foundation Grants, 266
Ben B. Cheney Foundation Grants, 402
Carl R. Hendrickson Family Foundation Grants, 509
Swindells Charitable Foundation Grants, 2261

Basic Skills Education
AEGON Transamerica Foundation Education and
     Financial Literacy Grants, 132
Akron Community Fdn Education Grants, 151
Albert W. Cherne Foundation Grants, 222
Alpha Natural Resources Corporate Giving, 246
Atkinson Foundation Community Grants, 325
Atlanta Foundation Grants, 326
Benton Community Foundation Grants, 405
Bernard and Audre Rapoport Foundation Education
     Grants, 410
Blue River Community Foundation Grants, 458
Brown County Community Foundation Grants, 475
Carl B. and Florence E. King Foundation Grants, 506
CenturyLink Clarke M. Williams Foundation
     Matching Time Grants, 531
Chicago Board of Trade Foundation Grants, 580
CIGNA Foundation Grants, 611
Community Foundation of Bartholomew County
     Heritage Fund Grants, 690
Community Foundation of Bartholomew County
     James A. Henderson Award for Fundraising, 691
Community Foundation of Greater Fort Wayne -
     Community Endowment and Clarke Endowment
     Grants, 705
Community Foundation of Louisville Education
     Grants, 724
Community Foundation of Western Massachusetts
     Grants, 741

Corina Higginson Trust Grants, 750
Dayton Power and Light Foundation Grants, 802
DOL Youthbuild Grants, 838
Entergy Charitable Foundation Education and
    Literacy Grants, 917
Evelyn and Walter Haas, Jr. Fund Education
    Opportunities Grants, 939
F.R. Bigelow Foundation Grants, 947
Fremont Area Community Foundation Education
    Mini-Grants, 1021
G.N. Wilcox Trust Grants, 1031
George W. Wells Foundation Grants, 1057
Georgia-Pacific Foundation Education Grants, 1058
Hattie M. Strong Foundation Grants, 1194
HSBC Corporate Giving Grants, 1266
John H. and Wilhelmina D. Harland Charitable
    Foundation Children and Youth Grants, 1374
Joseph H. and Florence A. Roblee Foundation
    Education Grants, 1386
Kirkpatrick Foundation Grants, 1440
Mardag Foundation Grants, 1554
Mary Wilmer Covey Charitable Trust Grants, 1600
May and Stanley Smith Charitable Trust Grants, 1613
McCune Foundation Education Grants, 1618
Michael and Susan Dell Foundation Grants, 1657
Middlesex Savings Charitable Foundation
    Educational Opportunities Grants, 1670
Norcliffe Foundation Grants, 1766
Office Depot Foundation Education Grants, 1806
OHA Community Grants for Education, 1809
OMNOVA Solutions Fdn Education Grants, 1820
Oppenstein Brothers Foundation Grants, 1827
PacifiCare Foundation Grants, 1861
Parkersburg Area Community Foundation Action
    Grants, 1871
PepsiCo Foundation Grants, 1935
Peyton Anderson Foundation Grants, 1954
Robert Bowne Foundaion Edmund A. Stanley, Jr.
    Research Grants, 2086
Robert Bowne Foundation Fellowships, 2087
Robert Bowne Foundation Literacy Grants, 2088
Robert Bowne Fdn Youth-Centered Grants, 2089
Seattle Foundation Education Grants, 2178
Sony Corporation of America Grants, 2216
Southern California Edison Education Grants, 2218
Sterling-Turner Charitable Foundation Grants, 2242
Strake Foundation Grants, 2249
USAID Integrated Youth Development Activity
    Grants, 2356
USAID Nigeria Ed Crisis Response Grants, 2358

Beautification
Eastern Bank Charitable Foundation Neighborhood
    Support Grants, 880
GNOF Gert Community Fund Grants, 1082
Hardin County Community Foundation Grants, 1167
Matson Ka Ipu 'Aina Grants, 1608
Mertz Gilmore Foundation NYC Communities
    Grants, 1641
Telluride Foundation Community Grants, 2281

Behavioral Medicine
Premera Blue Cross Grants, 2018

Bigotry
Colin Higgins Foundation Courage Awards, 653

Bilingual/Bicultural Education
Kalamazoo Community Foundation Early Childhood
    Learning and School Readiness Grants, 1407
OSF Education Program Grants in Kyrgyzstan, 1842

Biochemistry
AOCS Thomas H. Smouse Memorial Fellowship, 282
Greater Milwaukee Foundation Grants, 1109
Lalor Foundation Postdoctoral Fellowships, 1464

Biodiversity
HSBC Corporate Giving Grants, 1266
Illinois DNR Youth Recreation Corps Grants, 1297

Louis and Sandra Berkman Foundation Grants, 1510
M.A. Rikard Charitable Trust Grants, 1521
Max and Anna Levinson Foundation Grants, 1612
Perkin Fund Grants, 1937
Riedman Foundation Grants, 2076
Volvo Adventure Environmental Awards, 2390

Biographies
ALA Schneider Family Book Awards, 191

Biological Sciences
James Ford Bell Foundation Grants, 1339
Margaret and James A. Elkins Jr. Fdn Grants, 1555

Biology
Collins Foundation Grants, 658
Marion I. and Henry J. Knott Foundation Standard
    Grants, 1572

Biology, Cellular
CFF Research Grants, 534

Biology, Conservation
Christensen Fund Regional Grants, 600

Biology, Reproductive
Lalor Foundation Postdoctoral Fellowships, 1464
USAID Family Planning and Reproductive Health
    Methods Grants, 2353

Biomass Fuels
McCune Charitable Foundation Grants, 1617

Biomedical Education
Piper Trust Healthcare and Med Rsrch Grants, 1978
Sierra Health Foundation Responsive Grants, 2199

Biomedical Research
A.L. Mailman Family Foundation Grants, 20
Achelis and Bodman Foundation Grants, 101
Achelis Foundation Grants, 102
Avery Foundation Grants, 339
Beckman Coulter Foundation Grants, 394
Bushrod H. Campbell and Adah F. Hall Charity
    Fund Grants, 486
Campbell Soup Foundation Grants, 501
Catherine Holmes Wilkins Foundation Charitable
    Grants, 520
Charles Lafitte Foundation Grants, 567
Children's Tumor Foundation Young Investigator
    Awards, 587
CMS Research and Demonstration Grants, 640
Community Foundation of Louisville Dr. W.
    Barnett Owen Memorial Fund for the Children of
    Louisville and Jefferson County Grants, 723
Countess Moira Charitable Foundation Grants, 752
David Alan and Susan Berkman Rahm Foundation
    Grants, 785
Dorothea Haus Ross Foundation Grants, 844
Effie and Wofford Cain Foundation Grants, 895
Fidelity Foundation Grants, 957
Florence Foundation Grants, 978
Gil and Dody Weaver Foundation Grants, 1071
Greenspun Family Foundation Grants, 1118
Grifols Community Outreach Grants, 1122
H.A. and Mary K. Chapman Charitable Trust
    Grants, 1137
Harry A. and Margaret D. Towsley Foundation
    Grants, 1180
J.W. Kieckhefer Foundation Grants, 1324
Jack H. and William M. Light Charitable Trust
    Grants, 1330
Kenneth T. and Eileen L. Norris Fdn Grants, 1427
Kovler Family Foundation Grants, 1454
LGA Family Foundation Grants, 1487
Louis and Sandra Berkman Foundation Grants, 1510
Lumpkin Family Fdn Healthy People Grants, 1518
M.J. Murdock Charitable Trust General Grants, 1524
Margaret T. Morris Foundation Grants, 1557
Mary K. Chapman Foundation Grants, 1590

Mary S. and David C. Corbin Fdn Grants, 1598
McCombs Foundation Grants, 1615
McLean Contributionship Grants, 1623
Mericos Foundation Grants, 1637
Merrick Foundation Grants, 1640
MGN Family Foundation Grants, 1656
Nash Avery Foundation Grants, 1714
Nell J. Redfield Foundation Grants, 1737
Norcliffe Foundation Grants, 1766
NSF Perception, Action and Cognition (PAC)
    Research Grants, 1775
Peabody Foundation Grants, 1922
Pediatric Brain Tumor Foundation Early Career
    Development Grants, 1924
Pediatric Brain Tumor Foundation Early Career
    Development Grants, 1923
Pediatric Brain Tumor Fdn Institute Grants, 1925
Pediatric Brain Tumor Foundation Opportunity
    Grants, 1926
Pediatric Cancer Research Foundation Grants, 1927
Piper Trust Healthcare and Med Rsrch Grants, 1978
Reinberger Foundation Grants, 2066
RGk Foundation Grants, 2068
Sarkeys Foundation Grants, 2163
Sensient Technologies Foundation Grants, 2180
Sick Kids Foundation Community Conference
    Grants, 2193
Sick Kids Foundation New Investigator Research
    Grants, 2194
Sidgmore Family Foundation Grants, 2195
Tellabs Foundation Grants, 2280
University of Chicago Chapin Hall Doris Duke
    Fellowships, 2348
Victor E. Speas Foundation Grants, 2380
William and Sandy Heitz Family Fdn Grants, 2457
William G. and Helen C. Hoffman Foundation
    Grants, 2466

Biomedical Research Training
Harmony Project Grants, 1170
Piper Trust Healthcare and Med Rsrch Grants, 1978

Biomedicine
Lumpkin Family Fdn Healthy People Grants, 1518
Mary K. Chapman Foundation Grants, 1590
Prudential Foundation Education Grants, 2028

Biotechnology
Lumpkin Family Fdn Healthy People Grants, 1518

Bipolar Disorder
Peter and Elizabeth C. Tower Foundation Mental
    Health Grants, 1946

Birth/Congenital Defects
CDI Interdisciplinary Research Intvs Grants, 526
March of Dimes Program Grants, 1552
TJX Foundation Grants, 2303

Bisexuals
ALA Rainbow Project Book List Award, 187
Appalachian Community Fund LGBTQ Fund
    Grants, 284
Kalamazoo Community Foundation LBGT Equality
    Fund Grants, 1411
Ms. Fdn for Women Ending Violence Grants, 1708
New York Foundation Grants, 1753
Philanthrofund Foundation Grants, 1959

Blacks
CFGR SisterFund Grants, 554
CFGR Ujima Legacy Fund Grants, 555
Community Foundation of Louisville Madi and Jim
    Tate Fund Grants, 727
Oregon Community Foundation Black Student
    Success Community Network Grants, 1832
Oregon Community Foundation Community
    Recovery Grants, 1834
Oregon Community Foundation K-12 Student
    Success: Out-of-School Grants, 1836

Public Welfare Foundation Special Opportunities
    Grants, 2035
UUA Actions of Public Witness Grants, 2365
UUA Congregation-Based Community Organizing
    Grants, 2366
UUA Fund Grants, 2367
UUA International Fund Grants, 2368
UUA Just Society Fund Grants, 2369
UUA Social Responsibility Grants, 2370

Bone Marrow
HAF Barry F. Phelps Leukemia Fund Grants, 1140

Book Awards
AAAS/Subaru SB&F Prize for Excl in Sci Books, 22
ALA Alex Awards, 153
ALA Amazing Audiobks for Young Adults Awd, 155
ALA Amelia Bloomer Book List Award, 156
ALA Best Fiction for Young Adults Award, 160
ALA Booklist Editors' Choice Books for Youth
    Awards, 162
ALA Children's Literature Legacy Award, 165
ALA Coretta Scott King-John Steptoe Award for
    New Talent, 166
ALA John Newbery Medal, 172
ALA Margaret A. Edwards Award, 175
ALA Michael L. Printz Award, 177
ALA Mildred L. Batchelder Award, 178
ALA Notable Children's Books Awards, 179
ALA Notable Children's Recordings Awards, 180
ALA Notable Children's Videos Awards, 181
ALA Odyssey Award for Excellence in Audiobook
    Production, 182
ALA Popular Paperbacks for Young Adults Awds, 184
ALA Quick Picks for Reluctant Young Adult Readers
    Award, 186
ALA Rainbow Project Book List Award, 187
ALA Randolph Caldecott Medal, 188
ALA Robert F. Sibert Informational Book Medal
    Award, 189
ALA Schneider Family Book Awards, 191
ALA Teen's Top Ten Awards, 214
ALA Theodor Seuss Geisel Award, 215
ALA William C. Morris Debut YA Award, 217
ChLA Book Award, 590
ChLA Carol Gay Award, 591
ChLA Edited Book Award, 592
ChLA Mentoring Award, 597
ChLA Phoenix Award, 598
ChLA Phoenix Picture Book Award, 599
ILA Children's and Young Adults' Book Awds, 1291
PEN America Phyllis Naylor Grant for Children's and
    Young Adult Novelists, 1928

Books
AAAS/Subaru SB&F Prize for Excl in Sci Books, 22
ALA Alex Awards, 153
ALA Amazing Audiobks for Young Adults Awd, 155
ALA Amelia Bloomer Book List Award, 156
Alabama Humanities Foundation Major Grants, 159
ALA Best Fiction for Young Adults Award, 160
ALA Booklist Editors' Choice Books for Youth
    Awards, 162
ALA Children's Literature Legacy Award, 165
ALA Coretta Scott King-John Steptoe Award for
    New Talent, 166
ALA Coretta Scott King Book Donation Grant, 168
ALA Great Books Giveaway Competition, 170
ALA John Newbery Medal, 172
ALA Margaret A. Edwards Award, 175
ALA Michael L. Printz Award, 177
ALA Mildred L. Batchelder Award, 178
ALA Notable Children's Books Awards, 179
ALA Notable Children's Recordings Awards, 180
ALA Notable Children's Videos Awards, 181
ALA Odyssey Award for Excellence in Audiobook
    Production, 182
ALA Popular Paperbacks for Young Adults Awds, 184
ALA PRIME TIME Family Reading Time Grts, 185

ALA Quick Picks for Reluctant Young Adult Readers
    Award, 186
ALA Rainbow Project Book List Award, 187
ALA Randolph Caldecott Medal, 188
ALA Robert F. Sibert Informational Book Medal
    Award, 189
ALA Schneider Family Book Awards, 191
ALA Teen's Top Ten Awards, 214
ALA Theodor Seuss Geisel Award, 215
ALA William C. Morris Debut YA Award, 217
Arizona State Library LSTA Collections Grants, 295
Armstrong McDonald Foundation Special Needs
    Grants, 301
Covenant to Care for Children Enrichment Fund
    Grants, 758
Greater Sitka Legacy Fund Grants, 1111
Herman H. Nettelroth Fund Grants, 1246
ILA Children's and Young Adults' Book Awds, 1291
Kenai Peninsula Foundation Grants, 1425
Petersburg Community Foundation Grants, 1951
ProLiteracy National Book Fund Grants, 2026
Virginia Foundation for the Humanities Open
    Grants, 2387

Botanical Gardens
Herbert A. and Adrian W. Woods Foundation
    Grants, 1243
Kelvin and Eleanor Smith Foundation Grants, 1424
Louis and Sandra Berkman Foundation Grants, 1510
PMI Foundation Grants, 1982
Union Bank, N.A. Foundation Grants, 2334
Union Pacific Fdn Community & Civic Grants, 2337
Widgeon Point Charitable Foundation Grants, 2447
William Bingham Foundation Grants, 2460

Botany
Claremont Community Foundation Grants, 622

Brain
A-T Children's Project Grants, 16
A-T Children's Project Post Doctoral Fellowships, 17
Stein Family Charitable Trust Grants, 2240

Brain Tumors
Children's Brain Tumor Fdn Research Grants, 584
Children's Tumor Foundation Young Investigator
    Awards, 587
Pediatric Brain Tumor Foundation Early Career
    Development Grants, 1924
Pediatric Brain Tumor Foundation Early Career
    Development Grants, 1923
Pediatric Brain Tumor Fdn Institute Grants, 1925
Pediatric Brain Tumor Foundation Opportunity
    Grants, 1926

Breast Cancer
Acuity Charitable Foundation Grants, 110
Campbell Soup Foundation Grants, 501
CFFVR Women's Fund for the Fox Valley Region
    Grants, 550
GNOF IMPACT Harold W. Newman, Jr. Charitable
    Trust Grants, 1086
IBCAT Nancy Jaynes Memorial Scholarship, 1281
Premera Blue Cross Grants, 2018
William and Sandy Heitz Family Fdn Grants, 2457

Broadcast Media
Akron Community Foundation Arts and Culture
    Grants, 150
NSTA Faraday Science Communicator Award, 1778
Reinberger Foundation Grants, 2066

Building/Construction
Ahearn Family Foundation Grants, 142
Appalachian Regl Commission Housing Grants, 289
Best Buy Children's Foundation Twin Cities
    Minnesota Capital Grants, 418
Central Pacific Bank Foundation Grants, 530
Clark and Ruby Baker Foundation Grants, 625

Community Foundation for SE Michigan Chelsea
    Community Fdn Capacity Building Grants, 679
Courtney S. Turner Charitable Trust Grants, 753
GNOF Albert N. & Hattie M. McClure Grants, 1076
GNOF Coastal 5 + 1 Grants, 1078
GNOF Exxon-Mobil Grants, 1080
GNOF Norco Community Grants, 1089
Hampton Roads Community Foundation Nonprofit
    Facilities Improvement Grants, 1159
Hazel and Walter T. Bales Foundation Grants, 1220
Iddings Foundation Capital Project Grants, 1283
J. William Gholston Foundation Grants, 1328
Janson Foundation Grants, 1350
Jennings County Community Fdn Grants, 1360
Josephine Schell Russell Chartbl Trust Grants, 1389
Katharine Matthies Foundation Grants, 1418
Kosciusko County Community Foundation REMC
    Operation Round Up Grants, 1453
Lotus 88 Foundation for Women and Children
    Grants, 1508
Marietta McNeill Morgan and Samuel Tate Morgan
    Jr. Trust Grants, 1560
Marjorie Moore Charitable Foundation Grants, 1574
Norcliffe Foundation Grants, 1766
Richard and Caroline T. Gwathmey Memorial Trust
    Grants, 2069
Robert R. Meyer Foundation Grants, 2094
UUA Fund Grants, 2367
Vermillion County Community Fdn Grants, 2378
Vigneron Memorial Fund Grants, 2384

Bullying
Bella Vista Fdn GSS Healthy Living Grants, 396
Ben Cohen StandUp Foundation Grants, 403
New Jersey Office of Faith Based Initiatives Services
    to At Risk Youth Grants, 1752
Pacers Foundation Be Tolerant Grants, 1859
SACF Youth Advisory Council Grants, 2131

Burns
Austin S. Nelson Foundation Grants, 333

Business
Appalachian Regional Commission Business
    Development Revolving Loan Fund Grants, 285
Appalachian Regional Commission Entrepreneurship
    and Business Development Grants, 287
AT&T Fdn Community Support and Safety, 320
Burton D. Morgan Foundation Youth
    Entrepreneurship Grants, 483
Chesapeake Bay Trust Mini Grants, 578
Collins C. Diboll Private Foundation Grants, 657
Community Memorial Foundation Responsive
    Grants, 743
E.L. Wiegand Foundation Grants, 877
Hispanic Heritage Foundation Youth Awards, 1253
OSF Baltimore Community Fellowships, 1838
Phoenix Suns Charities Grants, 1964
Prudential Foundation Education Grants, 2028
United Technologies Corporation Grants, 2347
Wolfe Associates Grants, 2483
Xerox Foundation Grants, 2507
Yampa Valley Community Foundation Erickson
    Business Week Scholarships, 2508

Business Administration
Cargill Corporate Giving Grants, 503
Richard Davoud Donchian Foundation Grants, 2070

Business Development
ACF Social and Economic Development Strategies
    Grants, 93
Appalachian Regional Commission Business
    Development Revolving Loan Fund Grants, 285
Appalachian Regional Commission Entrepreneurship
    and Business Development Grants, 287
Do Something Business Development Intern, 849
Draper Richards Kaplan Foundation Grants, 864
Ewing Marion Kauffman Foundation Grants, 943
Foundations of East Chicago Education Grants, 995

Four Times Foundation Grants, 1006
General Motors Foundation Grants, 1039
Helen Bader Foundation Grants, 1227
ING Foundation Grants, 1302
JP Morgan Chase Fdn Arts and Culture Grants, 1394
NASE Fdn Future Entrepreneur Scholarship, 1713
Priddy Fdn Organizational Devel Grants, 2022
Pulaski County Community Foundation Grants, 2038
SunTrust Bank Trusteed Foundations Greene-Sawtell
    Grants, 2257
SunTrust Bank Trusteed Foundations Nell Warren
    Elkin and William Simpson Elkin Grants, 2258
TechKnowledgey Community Impact Grants, 2278

Business Education
3M Company Fdn Community Giving Grants, 5
Abell-Hanger Foundation Grants, 52
Allstate Corporate Giving Grants, 242
Allstate Corp Hometown Commitment Grants, 243
Allstate Foundation Safe and Vital Communities
    Grants, 244
Appalachian Regional Commission Business
    Development Revolving Loan Fund Grants, 285
Appalachian Regional Commission Entrepreneurship
    and Business Development Grants, 287
Benton Community Foundation Grants, 405
Blue River Community Foundation Grants, 458
Brown County Community Foundation Grants, 475
Coleman Foundation Entrepreneurship Education
    Grants, 651
Community Foundation of Bartholomew County
    Heritage Fund Grants, 690
Community Foundation of Bartholomew County
    James A. Henderson Award for Fundraising, 691
Community Foundation of Greater Fort Wayne -
    Community Endowment and Clarke Endowment
    Grants, 705
Essex County Community Foundation Women's
    Fund Grants, 934
F.M. Kirby Foundation Grants, 946
General Motors Foundation Grants, 1039
Hawai'i Community Foundation Bernice and Conrad
    von Hamm Fund Grants, 1197
James M. Collins Foundation Grants, 1344
McCune Charitable Foundation Grants, 1617
Shimizu Foundation Scholarships, 2190
Target Corporation Community Engagement Fund
    Grants, 2270
Union Bank, N.A. Foundation Grants, 2334
Washington Gas Charitable Contributions, 2417
Yampa Valley Community Foundation Erickson
    Business Week Scholarships, 2508

Business Ethics
Richard Davoud Donchian Foundation Grants, 2070

Business and Commerce
GNOF New Orleans Works Grants, 1088
HEI Charitable Foundation Grants, 1226

COVID-19
Community Foundation for Greater Buffalo Ralph
    C. Wilson, Jr. Youth Sports COVID-19 Fund
    Grants, 675
New Hampshire Department of Justice Children's
    Justice Act Coronavirus Emergency Grants, 1749
Wyoming Community Foundation COVID-19
    Response and Recovery Grants, 2500

Canada
British Columbia Arts Council Youth Engagement
    Program Grants, 473
Sick Kids Foundation New Investigator Research
    Grants, 2194

Canadian History
ATA Inclusive Learning Communities Grants, 323

Canadian Studies
ATA Inclusive Learning Communities Grants, 323

Cancer Detection
Austin S. Nelson Foundation Grants, 333
CDI Interdisciplinary Research Intvs Grants, 526
CFFVR Jewelers Mutual Chartbl Giving Grants, 543
General Motors Foundation Grants, 1039
Gil and Dody Weaver Foundation Grants, 1071
GNOF IMPACT Harold W. Newman, Jr. Charitable
    Trust Grants, 1086
Hawaii Children's Cancer Fdn Contributions, 1212
Michelle O'Neill Foundation Grants, 1661
Morgan Adams Foundation Research Grants, 1694
Pediatric Cancer Research Foundation Grants, 1927
William and Sandy Heitz Family Fdn Grants, 2457

Cancer Prevention
Acuity Charitable Foundation Grants, 110
Austin S. Nelson Foundation Grants, 333
Camille Beckman Foundation Grants, 499
Catherine Holmes Wilkins Foundation Grants, 520
CFFVR Jewelers Mutual Chartbl Giving Grants, 543
Fichtenbaum Charitable Trust Grants, 955
Gil and Dody Weaver Foundation Grants, 1071
GNOF IMPACT Harold W. Newman, Jr. Charitable
    Trust Grants, 1086
GNOF IMPACT Kahn-Oppenheim Tr Grts, 1087
Hawaii Children's Cancer Fdn Contributions, 1212
Locations Foundation Legacy Grants, 1504
Medtronic Foundation Strengthening Health Systems
    Grants, 1632
Michelle O'Neill Foundation Grants, 1661
Morgan Adams Foundation Research Grants, 1694
Pediatric Cancer Research Foundation Grants, 1927
RCF General Community Grants, 2062
William and Sandy Heitz Family Fdn Grants, 2457

Cancer/Carcinogenesis
ACCF of Indiana Angel Funds Grants, 62
Alex Stern Family Foundation Grants, 229
CFFVR Robert and Patricia Endries Family
    Foundation Grants, 547
Charles Lafitte Foundation Grants, 567
Chicago Board of Trade Foundation Grants, 580
E.L. Wiegand Foundation Grants, 877
Farmers Insurance Corporate Giving Grants, 948
General Motors Foundation Grants, 1039
GNOF IMPACT Harold W. Newman, Jr. Charitable
    Trust Grants, 1086
Greenspun Family Foundation Grants, 1118
Grifols Community Outreach Grants, 1122
Pediatric Cancer Research Foundation Grants, 1927
Premera Blue Cross Grants, 2018
Robert R. Meyer Foundation Grants, 2094
Sara Elizabeth O'Brien Trust Grants, 2161
Stella and Charles Guttman Foundation Grants, 2241
Union Bank, N.A. Foundation Grants, 2334
Victor E. Speas Foundation Grants, 2380

Canoeing
Outrigger Duke Kahanamoku Foundation Athletic
    Event Grants, 1852
Outrigger Duke Kahanamoku Foundation Athletic
    Team Grants, 1853

Cardiology
Abbott Fund Science Education Grants, 48

Cardiovascular Diseases
Abbott Fund Science Education Grants, 48
E.L. Wiegand Foundation Grants, 877
GNOF IMPACT Harold W. Newman, Jr. Charitable
    Trust Grants, 1086
GNOF IMPACT Kahn-Oppenheim Tr Grts, 1087
Lucy Downing Nisbet Charitable Fund Grants, 1515
Medtronic Foundation Strengthening Health Systems
    Grants, 1632
Premera Blue Cross Grants, 2018

Cardiovascular Health
CDI Interdisciplinary Research Intvs Grants, 526
DTE Energy Health & Human Services Grants, 869

GNOF IMPACT Kahn-Oppenheim Tr Grts, 1087
Lucy Downing Nisbet Charitable Fund Grants, 1515
Medtronic Foundation Strengthening Health Systems
    Grants, 1632
Premera Blue Cross Grants, 2018

Care Givers
CNCS Senior Corps Retired and Senior Volunteer
    Program Grants, 648

Career Education and Planning
Akron Community Fdn Education Grants, 151
Alaska Airlines Corporation Career Connections for
    Youth Grants, 193
Alaska Airlines Foundation LIFT Grants, 194
AT&T Foundation Education Grants, 321
Burton D. Morgan Foundation Youth
    Entrepreneurship Grants, 483
Cisco Systems Foundation San Jose Community
    Grants, 615
Cleveland Browns Foundation Grants, 633
Community Foundation of Boone County - Women's
    Grants, 693
Daniels Fund Youth Development Grants, 784
Duke Energy Foundation Local Impact Grants, 872
Essex County Community Foundation Women's
    Fund Grants, 934
Ewing Marion Kauffman Foundation Grants, 943
Grifols Community Outreach Grants, 1122
Harold K.L. Castle Foundation Public Education
    Redesign and Enhancement Grants, 1173
Highmark Corporate Giving Grants, 1248
Matson Community Giving Grants, 1607
Meyer Foundation Education Grants, 1649
OMNOVA Solutions Fdn Education Grants, 1820
Pentair Foundation Education and Community
    Grants, 1934
Piper Jaffray Foundation Communities Giving
    Grants, 1974
PPCF Edson Foundation Grants, 2015
SME Education Fdn Youth Program Grants, 2209
TE Foundation Grants, 2279
Toyota USA Foundation Education Grants, 2318
USAID Integrated Youth Development Activity
    Grants, 2356
USDEd Gaining Early Awareness and Readiness for
    Undergrad Programs (GEAR UP) Grants, 2364

Catholic Church
Adams-Mastrovich Family Foundation Grants, 113
AHS Foundation Grants, 143
Alvah H. and Wyline P. Chapman Foundation
    Grants, 248
Ar-Hale Family Foundation Grants, 290
Avery Foundation Grants, 339
Better Way Foundation Grants, 419
Chapman Family Foundation, 562
Charles Delmar Foundation Grants, 564
Claude A. and Blanche McCubbin Abbott Charitable
    Trust Grants, 628
Collins C. Diboll Private Foundation Grants, 657
Crescent Porter Hale Foundation Grants, 767
Dolan Children's Foundation Grants, 832
Dorothea Haus Ross Foundation Grants, 844
Elizabeth Huth Coates Charitable Foundation
    Grants, 900
Furth Family Foundation Grants, 1030
Graham Family Charitable Foundation Grants, 1099
Harry and Helen Sands Charitable Trust Grants, 1181
Helen V. Brach Foundation Grants, 1232
Huisking Foundation Grants, 1274
Joyce and Randy Seckman Foundation Grants, 1393
Marion I. and Henry J. Knott Foundation
    Discretionary Grants, 1571
Marion I. and Henry J. Knott Foundation Standard
    Grants, 1572
Moran Family Foundation Grants, 1693
Piper Trust Reglious Organizations Grants, 1979
Raskob Fdn for Catholic Activities Grants, 2054
Robinson Foundation Grants, 2097

Saeman Family Fdn A Charitable Grants, 2133
Saint Ann Legacy Grants, 2138
Strake Foundation Grants, 2249
Tyler Aaron Bookman Memorial Foundation Trust
    Grants, 2329
Westerman Foundation Grants, 2427

Cemeteries
Community Foundation of Louisville Children's
    Memorial Marker Fund Grants, 721

Cerebral Palsy
Austin S. Nelson Foundation Grants, 333
CFFVR Robert and Patricia Endries Family
    Foundation Grants, 547
Circle K Corporation Contributions Grants, 614
F.M. Kirby Foundation Grants, 946
Hampton Roads Community Foundation
    Developmental Disabilities Grants, 1156
Robert R. Meyer Foundation Grants, 2094

Cervical Cancer
GNOF IMPACT Harold W. Newman, Jr. Charitable
    Trust Grants, 1086

Chamber Music
ACMP Foundation Community Music Grants, 108
CFKF Instrument Matching Grants, 556
Jack Kent Cooke Fdn Young Artist Awards, 1333
NYSCA Music: Commty Music Schools Grants, 1790
NYSCA Music: Gen Program Support Grants, 1792
PennPAT Strategic Opportunity Grants, 1933

Charter Schools
Achelis and Bodman Foundation Grants, 101
Achelis Foundation Grants, 102
ALA Coretta Scott King Book Donation Grant, 168
Alaska Community Foundation Anchorage Schools
    Foundation Grant, 197
Meyer Foundation Education Grants, 1649
Mr. Holland's Opus Foundation Melody Grants, 1703
NEH Picturing America Awards, 1735
Terra Fdn Chicago K–12 Education Grants, 2285
VSA/Metlife Connect All Grants, 2392

Chemical Effects
Weyerhaeuser Family Fdn Health Grants, 2435

Chemical Engineering
Dorr Foundation Grants, 846
Lubrizol Foundation Grants, 1513

Chemistry
AOCS Thomas H. Smouse Memorial Fellowship, 282
Lubrizol Foundation Grants, 1513
Marion I. and Henry J. Knott Foundation Standard
    Grants, 1572

Chemistry Education
Delta Air Lines Foundation Youth Development
    Grants, 824
Dorr Foundation Grants, 846
George I. Alden Trust Grants, 1051

Child Abuse
ACF Child Abuse Prevention and Treatment Act
    Discretionary Funds Grants, 74
ACF Community-Based Child Abuse Prevention
    (CBCAP) Grants, 76
ACF National Human Trafficking Hotline Grants, 86
ACF Social and Economic Development Strategies
    Grants, 93
Adidas Corporation General Grants, 125
Alaska Community Foundation Children's Trust Tier
    1 Community Based Child Abuse and Neglect
    Prevention Grants, 198
Alaska Community Foundation Children's Trust Tier
    2 Innovation Grants, 200
Anne Arundel Women Giving Together Regular
    Grants, 275

Austin S. Nelson Foundation Grants, 333
Baxter International Foundation Grants, 369
Carl B. and Florence E. King Foundation Grants, 506
CFFVR Schmidt Family G4 Grants, 548
Charles H. Hall Foundation, 565
Charles Lafitte Foundation Grants, 567
Children's Trust Fund of Oregon Fdn Grants, 585
Children's Trust Fund of Oregon Foundation Small
    Grants, 586
Covenant to Care for Children Enrichment Fund
    Grants, 758
Crane Fund for Widows and Children Grants, 762
Curtis Foundation Grants, 771
Elkhart County Community Foundation Fund for
    Elkhart County, 902
Fassino Foundation Grants, 949
Ford Family Foundation Grants - Child Abuse
    Prevention and Intervention, 981
Hampton Roads Community Foundation Abused
    People Grants, 1153
Harry and Helen Sands Charitable Trust Grants, 1181
Hasbro Children's Fund Grants, 1189
Hattie Mae Lesley Foundation Grants, 1195
Hawai'i Community Foundation Children's Trust
    Fund Community Awareness: Child Abuse and
    Neglect Prevention Grants, 1198
Hearst Foundations Social Service Grants, 1224
Herbert A. and Adrian W. Woods Foundation
    Grants, 1243
Initaive Fdn Inside-Out Connections Grants, 1303
Jane Bradley Pettit Foundation Community and
    Social Development Grants, 1347
Jim Moran Foundation Grants, 1366
Joni Elaine Templeton Foundation Grants, 1384
Joseph H. and Florence A. Roblee Foundation
    Children and Youth Grants, 1385
Katharine Matthies Foundation Grants, 1418
Latkin Charitable Foundation Grants, 1469
Linford & Mildred White Charitable Grants, 1495
Marion and Miriam Rose Fund Grants, 1569
Meyer Fdn Healthy Communities Grants, 1650
New Hampshire Department of Justice Children's
    Justice Act Coronavirus Emergency Grants, 1749
Nicole Brown Foundation Grants, 1760
Oak Foundation Child Abuse Grants, 1799
Olga Sipolin Children's Fund Grants, 1815
Patrick and Aimee Butler Family Foundation
    Community Human Services Grants, 1880
Perkin Fund Grants, 1937
Riedman Foundation Grants, 2076
Robert R. McCormick Tribune Foundation
    Community Grants, 2093
Robert R. Meyer Foundation Grants, 2094
San Antonio Area Foundation Capital and Naming
    Rights Grants, 2148
Seybert Foundation Grants, 2184
Target Corporation Community Engagement Fund
    Grants, 2270
Westerman Foundation Grants, 2427
WHO Foundation Volunteer Service Grants, 2444
Winifred Johnson Clive Foundation Grants, 2478
Women's Fund of Hawaii Grants, 2485

Child Care
ACF Early Care and Education Research Scholars:
    Child Care Research Scholars, 78
Allan C. and Lelia J. Garden Foundation Grants, 236
Bay Area Community Foundation Civic League
    Endowment Fund Grants, 375
Collective Brands Foundation Payless Gives Shoes 4
    Kids Grants, 655
Daniels Fund Early Childhood Education Grants, 781
DeKalb County Community Foundation VOICE
    Grant, 816
Effie Allen Little Foundation Grants, 894
Frank Reed and Margaret Jane Peters Memorial Fund
    Grants, 1013
Gerber Fdn West Michigan Youth Grants, 1065
GNOF Stand Up For Our Children Grants, 1092

GTRCF Boys and Girls Club of Grand Traverse
    Endowment Grants, 1126
Hawaii Community Foundation Promising Minds
    Grants, 1215
Herman H. Nettelroth Fund Grants, 1246
Initiative Foundation Minnesota Early Childhood
    Initiative Grants, 1305
John D. and Katherine A. Johnston Foundation
    Grants, 1370
Joseph H. and Florence A. Roblee Foundation
    Children and Youth Grants, 1385
Leo Goodwin Foundation Grants, 1482
Linden Foundation Grants, 1494
Marion and Miriam Rose Fund Grants, 1569
Medtronic Foundation Community Link Human
    Services Grants, 1631
Ms. Fdn for Women Economic Justice Grants, 1707
Oregon Community Foundation Community
    Recovery Grants, 1834
Perkins-Ponder Foundation Grants, 1938
Piper Trust Children Grants, 1976
Seattle Foundation C. Keith Birkenfeld Memorial
    Trust Grants, 2177
U.S. Bank Foundation Grants, 2330
Union Bank, N.A. Foundation Grants, 2334
Women's Fund of Hawaii Grants, 2484

Child Development
Abby's Legendary Pizza Foundation Grants, 49
Alaska Community Foundation Children's Trust Tier
    1 Parenting and Child Development Educational
    Grants, 199
Bay Area Community Foundation Civic League
    Endowment Fund Grants, 375
Bernard and Audre Rapoport Foundation Health
    Grants, 411
Children's Trust Fund of Oregon Fdn Grants, 585
Children's Trust Fund of Oregon Foundation Small
    Grants, 586
Community Foundation for SE Michigan Head Start
    Innovation Fund, 682
Effie Allen Little Foundation Grants, 894
Frank M. Tait Foundation Grants, 1012
Gerber Foundation Environmental Hazards Research
    Grants, 1062
Gerber Fdn Pediatric Health Research Grants, 1063
Gerber Foundation Pediatric Nutrition Research
    Grants, 1064
Gerber Fdn West Michigan Youth Grants, 1065
GTRCF Boys and Girls Club of Grand Traverse
    Endowment Grants, 1126
Hannaford Supermarkets Community Giving, 1164
Initiative Foundation Minnesota Early Childhood
    Initiative Grants, 1305
KaBOOM! Adventure Courses Grant, 1401
KaBOOM! Build it Grant, 1402
KaBOOM! Creative Play Grant, 1403
KaBOOM! Multi-Sport Courts Grant, 1404
Kalamazoo Community Foundation Youth
    Development Grants, 1412
Malone Family Foundation Atypical Development
    Initiative Grants, 1549
Mericos Foundation Grants, 1637
Minnie M. Jones Trust Grants, 1678
OSF Early Childhood Program Grants, 1841
Pettus Foundation Grants, 1952
Piper Trust Healthcare and Med Rsrch Grants, 1978
Ralph C. Wilson, Jr. Foundation Preparing for
    Success Grant, 2050
Ralph C. Wilson, Jr. Foundation Youth Sports and
    Recreation Grant, 2051
Southern Minnesota Initiative Foundation
    AmeriCorps Leap Grants, 2219
Southern Minnesota Initiative Foundation Incentive
    Grants, 2223
Stinson Foundation Grants, 2246
Welborn Baptist Foundation Promotion of Early
    Childhood Development Grants, 2423
Welborn Foundation Promotion of Healthy
    Adolescent Development Grants, 2425

Child Psychiatry

AACAP Educational Outreach Program for Child and Adolescent Psychiatry Residents, 23

AACAP Educational Outreach Program for General Psychiatry Residents, 24

AACAP George Tarjan Award for Contributions in Developmental Disabilities, 25

AACAP Irving Philips Award for Prevention, 26

AACAP Jeanne Spurlock Lecture and Award on Diversity and Culture, 27

AACAP Junior Investigator Awards, 29

AACAP Mary Crosby Congressional Fellowships, 31

AACAP Pilot Rsrch Awd for Att-Deficit Disorder, 32

AACAP Rieger Psychodyn Psychotherapy Award, 33

AACAP Rieger Service Program Award for Excellence, 34

AACAP Robert Cancro Academic Leadership Award, 35

AACAP Sidney Berman Award for the School-Based Study and Intervention for Learning Disorders and Mental Ilness, 36

AACAP Simon Wile Leadership in Consultation Award, 37

AACAP Systems of Care Special Program Scholarships, 39

American Psychiatric Fdn Call for Proposals, 257

American Psychiatric Foundation Typical or Troubled School Mental Health Education Grants, 258

Lavina Parker Trust Grants, 1477

Child Psychology/Development

Adidas Corporation General Grants, 125

Allen Foundation Educational Nutrition Grants, 238

Carnegie Corporation of New York Grants, 511

Chicago Board of Trade Foundation Grants, 580

Colorado Interstate Gas Grants, 661

Effie and Wofford Cain Foundation Grants, 895

FCD New American Children Grants, 952

Helen Bader Foundation Grants, 1227

Mericos Foundation Grants, 1637

Mimi and Peter Haas Fund Grants, 1677

NIMH Early Identification and Treatment of Mental Disorders in Children and Adolescents Grts, 1761

NSF Perception, Action and Cognition (PAC) Research Grants, 1775

NSF Social Psychology Grants, 1776

OSF Early Childhood Program Grants, 1841

Piper Jaffray Foundation Communities Giving Grants, 1974

Child Sexual Abuse

ACF Child Abuse Prevention and Treatment Act Discretionary Funds Grants, 74

ACF National Human Trafficking Hotline Grants, 86

ACF Street Outreach Program Grants, 94

Alaska Community Foundation Children's Trust Tier 1 Community Based Child Abuse and Neglect Prevention Grants, 198

Alaska Community Foundation Children's Trust Tier 2 Innovation Grants, 200

Austin S. Nelson Foundation Grants, 333

CFFVR Schmidt Family G4 Grants, 548

Hawai'i Community Foundation Children's Trust Fund Community Awareness: Child Abuse and Neglect Prevention Grants, 1198

Hearst Foundations Social Service Grants, 1224

Joseph H. and Florence A. Roblee Foundation Children and Youth Grants, 1385

Ms. Fdn for Women Ending Violence Grants, 1708

New Hampshire Department of Justice Children's Justice Act Coronavirus Emergency Grants, 1749

Oak Foundation Child Abuse Grants, 1799

Patrick and Aimee Butler Family Foundation Community Human Services Grants, 1880

Robert R. Meyer Foundation Grants, 2094

Westerman Foundation Grants, 2427

Women's Fund of Hawaii Grants, 2484

Child Support

ACL Alternatives to Guardianship Youth Resource Center Grants, 104

A Little Hope Grants, 235

Joni Elaine Templeton Foundation Grants, 1384

Marion and Miriam Rose Fund Grants, 1569

Public Welfare Foundation Special Initiative to Advance Civil Legal Aid Grants, 2034

R.D. Beirne Trust Grants, 2045

Child Welfare

Achelis and Bodman Foundation Grants, 101

Agnes M. Lindsay Trust Grants, 140

Alex Stern Family Foundation Grants, 229

A Little Hope Grants, 235

Alliance for Strong Families and Communities Grants, 239

Anne Arundel Women Giving Together Regular Grants, 275

AT&T Foundation Health and Human Services Grants, 322

Baton Rouge Area Foundation Every Kid a King Fund Grants, 364

Bay Area Community Foundation Civic League Endowment Fund Grants, 375

Bernard and Audre Rapoport Foundation Health Grants, 411

Brookdale Fdn Relatives as Parents Grants, 474

C.H. Robinson Worldwide Foundation Grants, 489

Caplow Applied Sci (CappSci) Children's Prize, 502

Carl B. and Florence E. King Foundation Grants, 506

Castle Foundation Grants, 518

Charles Lafitte Foundation Grants, 567

Clara Abbott Foundation Need-Based Grants, 620

Clayton Fund Grants, 631

Collective Brands Foundation Saucony Run for Good Grants, 656

Community Foundation for the Capital Region Grants, 687

Community Foundation of Louisville Dr. W. Barnett Owen Memorial Fund for the Children of Louisville and Jefferson County Grants, 723

Community Foundation of Louisville Human Services Grants, 726

Corina Higginson Trust Grants, 750

D. W. McMillan Foundation Grants, 776

David M. and Marjorie D. Rosenberg Foundation Grants, 790

Dorothea Haus Ross Foundation Grants, 844

Edward and Ellen Roche Relief Fdn Grants, 887

Effie Allen Little Foundation Grants, 894

Effie Kuhlman Charitable Trust Grants, 896

Ezra M. Cutting Trust Grants, 945

Faye L. and William L. Cowden Charitable Foundation Grants, 950

FCD Young Scholars Program Grants, 953

First Hawaiian Bank Foundation Corporate Giving Grants, 967

Gardner Foundation Grants, 1034

Gerber Fdn West Michigan Youth Grants, 1065

Graham Family Charitable Foundation Grants, 1099

Greygates Foundation Grants, 1120

GTRCF Boys and Girls Club of Grand Traverse Endowment Grants, 1126

Harry and Helen Sands Charitable Trust Grants, 1181

Hawaii Community Foundation Promising Minds Grants, 1215

Hawaii Community Foundation Reverend Takie Okumura Family Grants, 1216

Helen V. Brach Foundation Grants, 1232

Hubbard Broadcasting Foundation Grants, 1269

Huffy Foundation Grants, 1273

Ike and Roz Friedman Foundation Grants, 1289

J.W. Gardner II Foundation Grants, 1323

J.W. Kieckhefer Foundation Grants, 1324

Janson Foundation Grants, 1350

John D. and Katherine A. Johnston Foundation Grants, 1370

John H. and Wilhelmina D. Harland Charitable Foundation Children and Youth Grants, 1374

Joseph Henry Edmondson Foundation Grants, 1388

Katherine John Murphy Foundation Grants, 1419

Kathryne Beynon Foundation Grants, 1420

Kosasa Foundation Grants, 1450

Kovler Family Foundation Grants, 1454

Lil and Julie Rosenberg Foundation Grants, 1491

Locations Foundation Legacy Grants, 1504

Maryland State Dept of Education Coordinating Entity Services for the Maryland Child Care Res Centers Network Grants, 1594

McCarthy Family Fdn Charity Fund Grants, 1614

Minnie M. Jones Trust Grants, 1678

Morris Stulsaft Foundation Educational Support for Children Grants, 1697

Oak Foundation Child Abuse Grants, 1799

Ober Kaler Community Grants, 1801

Olga Sipolin Children's Fund Grants, 1815

Olive Higgins Prouty Foundation Grants, 1817

OneFamily Foundation Grants, 1822

Pettus Foundation Grants, 1952

Piper Trust Children Grants, 1976

Public Welfare Foundation Special Initiative to Advance Civil Legal Aid Grants, 2034

R.D. Beirne Trust Grants, 2045

Ricks Family Charitable Trust Grants, 2075

Riedman Foundation Grants, 2076

Robert R. McCormick Tribune Foundation Community Grants, 2093

Robert W. Knox, Sr. and Pearl Wallis Knox Charitable Foundation, 2095

Ruth and Henry Campbell Foundation Grants, 2123

Scott B. and Annie P. Appleby Charitable Trust Grants, 2169

Stein Family Charitable Trust Grants, 2240

Sylvia Perkin Perpetual Charitable Trust Grants, 2263

University of Chicago Chapin Hall Doris Duke Fellowships, 2348

Victoria S. and Bradley L. Geist Foundation Enhancement Grants, 2381

W.H. and Mary Ellen Cobb Chartbl Trust Grts, 2397

William E. Barth Foundation Grants, 2463

William J. and Gertrude R. Casper Foundation Grants, 2469

William J. and Tina Rosenberg Fdn Grants, 2470

Wilton and Effie Hebert Foundation Grants, 2476

Zane's Foundation Grants, 2524

Child/Maternal Health

Abbott Fund Access to Health Care Grants, 45

ADA Foundation Samuel Harris Children's Dental Health Grants, 111

AEGON Transamerica Foundation Health and Wellness Grants, 133

Alcatel-Lucent Technologies Foundation Grants, 224

Bernard and Audre Rapoport Foundation Health Grants, 411

Blackford County Community Foundation - WOW Grants, 433

California Endowment Innovative Ideas Challenge Grants, 495

CFF Research Grants, 534

CFFVR Schmidt Family G4 Grants, 548

Children's Brain Tumor Fdn Research Grants, 584

Cleveland Browns Foundation Grants, 633

Community Foundation of Boone County - Women's Grants, 693

DTE Energy Foundation Health and Human Services Grants, 869

Edwards Memorial Trust Grants, 891

Edward W. and Stella C. Van Houten Memorial Fund Grants, 892

EPA Children's Health Protection Grants, 923

F.M. Kirby Foundation Grants, 946

FCD Young Scholars Program Grants, 953

Gerber Foundation Environmental Hazards Research Grants, 1062

Gerber Fdn Pediatric Health Research Grants, 1063

Gerber Foundation Pediatric Nutrition Research Grants, 1064

GNOF Stand Up For Our Children Grants, 1092

HRAMF Charles H. Hood Foundation Child Health
    Research Awards, 1262
Illinois Children's Healthcare Fdn Grants, 1295
Jewish Fund Grants, 1364
Kansas Health Fdn Major Initiatives Grants, 1414
Kansas Health Foundation Recognition Grants, 1415
Kroger Company Donations, 1456
Long Island Community Foundation Grants, 1507
March of Dimes Program Grants, 1552
Mary Black Foundation Active Living Grants, 1585
Michael Reese Health Trust Responsive Grants, 1659
Mid-Iowa Health Foundation Community Response
    Grants, 1667
Morris Stulsaft Foundation Educational Support for
    Children Grants, 1697
Pajaro Valley Community Health Health Trust
    Insurance/Coverage & Education on Using the
    System Grants, 1864
Pediatric Brain Tumor Foundation Early Career
    Development Grants, 1923
Pediatric Brain Tumor Foundation Early Career
    Development Grants, 1924
Pediatric Brain Tumor Fdn Institute Grants, 1925
Pediatric Brain Tumor Foundation Opportunity
    Grants, 1926
Pediatric Cancer Research Foundation Grants, 1927
Porter County Community Foundation Health and
    Wellness Grant, 2002
Porter County Community Foundation Women's
    Fund Grants, 2005
Premera Blue Cross Grants, 2018
RGk Foundation Grants, 2068
Robert R. Meyer Foundation Grants, 2094
Saigh Foundation Grants, 2137
Seattle Foundation Health and Wellness Grants, 2179
Sidgmore Family Foundation Grants, 2195
Tides Fdn Friends of the IGF Fund Grants, 2300
TJX Foundation Grants, 2303
United Healthcare Commty Grts in Michigan, 2343
University of Chicago Chapin Hall Doris Duke
    Fellowships, 2348
USAID Family Planning and Reproductive Health
    Methods Grants, 2353
USDA WIC Nutrition Ed Innovations Grants, 2363
WHO Foundation General Grants, 2443
Wilkins Family Foundation Grants, 2450
William E. Barth Foundation Grants, 2463

Children (Patients)
1st Touch Foundation Grants, 2
A-T Children's Project Post Doctoral Fellowships, 17
AKF Grants for Children, 149
Bernard and Audre Rapoport Foundation Health
    Grants, 411
Children's Tumor Foundation Young Investigator
    Awards, 587
DeKalb County Community Foundation VOICE
    Grant, 816
Dyson Foundation Mid-Hudson Valley Project
    Support Grants, 874
Ford Family Foundation Grants - Access to Health
    and Dental Services, 980
Gerber Foundation Environmental Hazards Research
    Grants, 1062
Gerber Fdn Pediatric Health Research Grants, 1063
Gerber Foundation Pediatric Nutrition Research
    Grants, 1064
Giant Food Charitable Grants, 1068
HAF Barry F. Phelps Leukemia Fund Grants, 1140
HAF JoAllen K. Twiddy-Wood Memorial Fund
    Grants, 1144
HAF Phyllis Nilsen Leal Mem Fund Grants, 1149
Maggie Welby Foundation Grants, 1538
Moody Foundation Grants, 1692
Portland Fdn - Women's Giving Circle Grant, 2006
Richard Davoud Donchian Foundation Grants, 2070
Salt River Project Health and Human Services
    Grants, 2142
Sara Elizabeth O'Brien Trust Grants, 2161
Swindells Charitable Foundation Grants, 2261

Union Labor Health Fdn Angel Fund Grants, 2335
UnitedHealthcare Children's Fdn Grants, 2342
Zane's Foundation Grants, 2524

Children and Youth
1st Touch Foundation Grants, 2
2 Depot Square Ipswich Charitable Foundation
    Grants, 3
3M Company Fdn Community Giving Grants, 5
3M Company Foundation Health and Human
    Services Grants, 6
520 Charitable Foundation Grants, 14
A-T Children's Project Grants, 16
A-T Children's Project Post Doctoral Fellowships, 17
A.L. Mailman Family Foundation Grants, 20
A.L. Spencer Foundation Grants, 21
AACAP Junior Investigator Awards, 29
AACAP Pilot Rsrch Awd for Att-Deficit Disorder, 32
A and B Family Foundation Grants, 40
Aaron Foundation Grants, 41
Abbott Fund Community Engagement Grants, 46
Abby's Legendary Pizza Foundation Grants, 49
ABC Charities Grants, 50
Abeles Foundation Grants, 51
ABS Foundation Grants, 56
Abundance Foundation Local Community Grants, 58
ACCF Dennis and Melanie Bieberich Community
    Enrichment Fund Grants, 59
ACCF John and Kay Boch Fund Grants, 60
ACCF Marlene Bittner Memorial Community
    Enrichment Fund Grants, 61
ACCF of Indiana Angel Funds Grants, 62
ACCF of Indiana Anonymous Community
    Enrichment Fund Grants, 63
ACCF of Indiana Bank of Geneva Heritage Fund
    Grants, 64
ACCF of Indiana First Merchants Bank / Decatur
    Bank and Trust Fund Grants, 66
ACCF of Indiana Michael Basham Community
    Enrichment Fund Grants, 67
ACCF of Indiana Ron and Susie Ballard Community
    Enrichment Fund Grants, 68
ACCF Ralph Biggs Memorial Community
    Enrichment Fund Grants, 69
ACF Abandoned Infants Assistance Grants, 70
ACF Adoption Opportunities Grants, 71
ACF American Indian and Alaska Native Early Head
    Start Expansion Grants, 72
ACF Basic Center Program Grants, 73
ACF Child Abuse Prevention and Treatment Act
    Discretionary Funds Grants, 74
ACF Child Welfare Training Grants, 75
ACF Community-Based Child Abuse Prevention
    (CBCAP) Grants, 76
ACF Community-Based Child Abuse
    Prevention (CBCAP) Tribal and Migrant
    DiscretionaryGrants, 77
ACF Early Care and Education Research Scholars:
    Child Care Research Scholars, 78
ACF Early Care and Education Research Scholars:
    Head Start Graduate Student Research Grants, 79
ACF Head Start and/or Early Head Start Grantee
    - Clay, Randolph, and Talladega Counties,
    Alabama, 82
ACF Head Start and/or Early Head Start Grantee -
    St. Landry Parish, Louisiana, 83
ACF Infant Adoption Awareness Training Program
    Grants, 84
ACF Marriage Strengthening Research &
    Dissemination Center Grants, 85
ACF National Human Trafficking Hotline Grants, 86
ACF Native Youth Initiative for Leadership,
    Empowerment, and Development Grants, 88
ACF Promoting Safe and Stable Families (PSSF)
    Program Grants, 89
ACF Runaway and Homeless Youth Training and
    Technical Assistance Center Grants, 92
ACF Social and Economic Development Strategies
    Grants, 93
ACF Street Outreach Program Grants, 94

ACF Transitional Living Program and Maternity
    Group Homes Grants, 96
ACF Tribal Maternal, Infant, and Early Childhood
    Home Visiting Program: Development and
    Implementation Grants, 97
ACF Tribal Maternal, Infant, and Early Childhood
    Home Visiting Program: Implementation and
    Expansion Grants, 98
ACF Unaccompanied Refugee Children Grants, 99
ACF Voluntary Agencies Matching Grants, 100
Achelis and Bodman Foundation Grants, 101
Achelis Foundation Grants, 102
ACL Alternatives to Guardianship Youth Resource
    Center Grants, 104
ACL Disability and Rehabilitation Research Projects
    (DRRP) Program: Independent Living Transition
    Services for Youth and Young Adults Grants, 105
ACL Rehabilitation Research and Training Center
    (RRTC) on Employment of Transition-Age Youth
    with Disabilities Grants, 107
Active Living Research Grants, 109
Acuity Charitable Foundation Grants, 110
Adam Don Foundation Grants, 112
Adams and Reese Corporate Giving Grants, 114
Adams Family Foundation I Grants, 116
Adams Family Foundation II Grants, 117
Adams Family Fdn of Nora Springs Grants, 118
Adams Family Foundation of Ohio Grants, 119
Adams Rotary Memorial Fund A Grants, 122
Adelaide Breed Bayrd Foundation Grants, 123
Adelaide Christian Home For Children Grants, 124
Adidas Corporation General Grants, 125
Advance Auto Parts Corporate Giving Grants, 131
AEGON Transamerica Foundation Health and
    Wellness Grants, 133
Aetna Foundation Regional Health Grants, 134
Aetna Foundation Summer Academic Enrichment
    Grants, 135
A Friends' Foundation Trust Grants, 136
AGFT A Gift for Music Grants, 138
AGFT Pencil Boy Express, 139
Agnes M. Lindsay Trust Grants, 140
Ahearn Family Foundation Grants, 142
Aid for Starving Children Emerg Aid Grants, 144
Aid for Starving Children Health and Nutrition
    Grants, 145
Aid for Starving Children Homes and Education
    Grants, 146
Aid for Starving Children Water Projects Grants, 147
AKF Grants for Children, 149
ALA ALSC Distinguished Service Award, 154
ALA Amelia Bloomer Book List Award, 156
ALA Baker and Taylor Summer Reading Program
    Grant, 158
ALA Best Fiction for Young Adults Award, 160
ALA Bookapalooza Grants, 161
ALA Booklist Editors' Choice Books for Youth
    Awards, 162
ALA Bound to Stay Bound Books Scholarships, 163
ALA Children's Literature Legacy Award, 165
ALA Coretta Scott King-John Steptoe Award for
    New Talent, 166
ALA Coretta Scott King-Virginia Hamilton Award
    for Lifetime Achievement, 167
ALA Coretta Scott King Book Donation Grant, 168
ALA Fabulous Films for Young Adults Award, 169
ALA Great Books Giveaway Competition, 170
ALA Innovative Reading Grant, 171
ALA John Newbery Medal, 172
ALA Louise Seaman Bechtel Fellowship, 173
ALA MAE Award for Best Literature Program for
    Teens, 174
ALA Margaret A. Edwards Award, 175
ALA May Hill Arbuthnot Honor Lecture Award, 176
ALA Michael L. Printz Award, 177
ALA Mildred L. Batchelder Award, 178
ALA Notable Children's Books Awards, 179
ALA Notable Children's Recordings Awards, 180
ALA Notable Children's Videos Awards, 181

ALA Odyssey Award for Excellence in Audiobook Production, 182

ALA Penguin Random House Young Readers Group Award, 183

ALA Popular Paperbacks for Young Adults Awds, 184

ALA Quick Picks for Reluctant Young Adult Readers Award, 186

ALA Rainbow Project Book List Award, 187

ALA Randolph Caldecott Medal, 188

ALA Robert F. Sibert Informational Book Medal Award, 189

ALA Sara Jaffarian School Library Award for Exemplary Humanities Programming, 190

ALA Schneider Family Book Awards, 191

ALA Scholastic Library Publishing Award, 192

Alaska Airlines Corporation Career Connections for Youth Grants, 193

Alaska Airlines Foundation LIFT Grants, 194

Alaska Children's Trust Conference/Training Sponsorship, 195

Alaska Community Foundation Afterschool Network Engineering Mindset Mini-Grant, 196

Alaska Community Foundation Children's Trust Tier 1 Community Based Child Abuse and Neglect Prevention Grants, 198

Alaska Community Foundation Children's Trust Tier 1 Parenting and Child Development Educational Grants, 199

Alaska Community Foundation Children's Trust Tier 2 Innovation Grants, 200

Alaska Community Foundation Ketchikan Community Foundation Grant, 206

Alaska Conservation Fdn Youth Mini Grants, 210

Alaska State Council on the Arts Youth Cultural Heritage Fast Track Grants, 212

ALA Sullivan Award for Public Library Admintrs Supporting Services to Children, 213

ALA Teen's Top Ten Awards, 214

ALA Theodor Seuss Geisel Award, 215

ALA William C. Morris Debut YA Award, 217

ALA YALSA Presidential Citation Award, 218

Albert and Ethel Herzstein Charitable Foundation Grants, 219

Albert E. and Birdie W. Einstein Fund Grants, 220

Albert W. Cherne Foundation Grants, 222

Albert W. Rice Charitable Foundation Grants, 223

Alcatel-Lucent Technologies Foundation Grants, 224

ALFJ International Fund Grants, 231

Alfred E. Chase Charitable Foundation Grants, 233

Alfred J Mcallister and Dorothy N Mcallister Foundation Grants, 234

A Little Hope Grants, 235

Allan C. and Lelia J. Garden Foundation Grants, 236

Allegis Group Foundation Grants, 237

Allen Foundation Educational Nutrition Grants, 238

Alliance for Strong Families and Communities Grants, 239

Alloy Family Foundation Grants, 241

Allstate Foundation Tolerance, Inclusion, and Diversity Grants, 245

Alpha Natural Resources Corporate Giving, 246

Altria Group Positive Youth Dev Grants, 247

Alvah H. and Wyline P. Chapman Foundation Grants, 248

Amelia Sillman Rockwell and Carlos Perry Rockwell Charities Fund Grants, 250

Ameren Corporation Community Grants, 251

American Indian Youth Running Strong Grants, 256

American Savings Fdn After School Grants, 259

American Savings Foundation Program Grants, 261

American Schlafhorst Foundation Grants, 262

Amerigroup Foundation Grants, 264

AMERIND Community Service Project Grants, 265

Amway Corporation Contributions, 269

Anderson Foundation Grants, 271

Andrew Family Foundation Grants, 272

Anheuser-Busch Foundation Grants, 273

Anna Fitch Ardenghi Trust Grants, 274

Anne J. Caudal Foundation Grants, 276

Anthony Munoz Foundation Straight A Student Campaign Grants, 280

Antone and Edene Vidinha Charitable Grants, 281

Appalachian Regional Commission Health Care Grants, 288

Arizona Commission on the Arts Learning Collaboration Grant, 291

Arizona State Library LSTA Learning Grants, 297

Armstrong McDonald Foundation Children and Youth Grants, 300

Arthur M. Blank Family Foundation AMB West Community Fund Grants, 304

Arthur M. Blank Family Foundation American Explorers Grants, 305

Arthur M. Blank Family Foundation Art of Change Grants, 306

Arthur M. Blank Family Foundation Atlanta Falcons Youth Foundation Grants, 307

Arthur M. Blank Family Foundation Atlanta United Foundation Grants, 308

Arthur M. Blank Family Foundation Inspiring Spaces Grants, 309

Arthur M. Blank Family Foundation Molly Blank Fund Grants, 310

Arthur M. Blank Family Foundation Pathways to Success Grants, 312

Arthur M. Blank Family Foundation Pipeline Project Grants, 313

Arts Council of Greater Lansing Young Creatives Grants, 314

Aspen Community Foundation Grants, 316

AT&T Fdn Community Support and Safety, 320

ATA Local Community Relations Grants, 324

Atkinson Foundation Community Grants, 325

Atlanta Women's Foundation Sue Wieland Embracing Possibility Grants, 328

Atwood Foundation General Grants, 330

Aunt Kate Foundation Grants, 331

Austin S. Nelson Foundation Grants, 333

Avery-Fuller-Welch Children's Fdn Grants, 336

Avery Dennison Foundation Education Grants, 337

Avery Foundation Grants, 339

Avista Foundation Vulnerable and Limited Income Population Grants, 341

Babcock Charitable Trust Grants, 343

Back Home Again Foundation Grants, 344

Bainum Family Foundation Grants, 345

Baltimore Community Foundation Building Stronger Neighborhoods Regionwide Grants, 347

Baltimore Community Foundation Children's Fresh Air Society Fund Grants, 348

Baltimore Community Foundation Mitzvah Fund for Good Deeds Grants, 349

Baltimore Ravens Corporate Giving, 350

Baltimore Ravens Foundation Play 60 Grants, 351

Baltimore Ravens Fdn Youth Football Grants, 353

Bank of America Charitable Foundation Basic Needs Grants, 354

Bank of America Charitable Foundation Matching Gifts, 356

Bank of America Corporation Sponsorships, 359

Bank of Hawaii Foundation Grants, 360

Bank of the Orient Community Giving, 361

Barrasso, Usdin, Kupperman, Freeman, and Sarver Corporate Grants, 362

Baton Rouge Area Foundation Every Kid a King Fund Grants, 364

Batters Up USA Equipment Grants, 366

Batts Foundation Grants, 367

Baxter International Foundation Grants, 369

Bay and Paul Foundations PreK-12 Transformative Learning Practices Grants, 370

Bay Area Community Foundation Arenac County Healthy Youth/Healthy Seniors Fund Grants, 372

Bay Area Community Fdn Auburn Area Chamber of Commerce Enrichment Fund Grants, 373

Bay Area Community Foundation Bay County Healthy Youth/Healthy Seniors Fund Grants, 374

Bay Area Community Foundation Civic League Endowment Fund Grants, 375

Bay Area Community Foundation Dow CommunityGives Youth Service Prog Grants, 377

Bay Area Community Foundation Elizabeth Husband Fund Grants, 378

Bay Area Community Foundation Nathalie Awrey Memorial Fund Grants, 381

Bayer Fund Community Development Grants, 383

Baystate Financial Charitable Foundation Grants, 385

BBF Florida Family Literacy Initiative Grants, 386

BBF Maryland Family Literacy Initiative Implementation Grants, 389

BBF Maryland Family Literacy Initiative Planning Grants, 390

Bella Vista Foundation Pre-3 Grants, 397

Belvedere Cove Foundation Grants, 400

Ben Cohen StandUp Foundation Grants, 403

Bernard and Audre Rapoport Foundation Arts and Culture Grants, 407

Bernard and Audre Rapoport Foundation Education Grants, 410

Bernard and Audre Rapoport Foundation Health Grants, 411

Bierhaus Foundation Grants, 421

Bikes Belong Foundation Paul David Clark Bicycling Safety Grants, 422

Bikes Belong Foundation REI Grants, 423

Bill and Melinda Gates Foundation Water, Sanitation and Hygiene Grants, 428

Bindley Family Foundation Grants, 430

Blackford County Community Foundation - WOW Grants, 433

Blackford County Community Fdn Grants, 434

Black Hills Corporation Grants, 435

Blanche and Irving Laurie Foundation Grants, 436

Blandin Foundation Invest Early Grants, 438

Blockbuster Corporate Contributions, 440

Blossom Fund Grants, 441

Blue Cross Blue Shield of Minnesota Fdn - Healthy Children: Growing Up Healthy Grants, 442

Blue Mountain Community Foundation Warren Community Action Fund Grants, 457

BMW of North America Charitable Contribs, 460

Bothin Foundation Grants, 464

Bradley-Turner Foundation Grants, 466

Brian G. Dyson Foundation Grants, 468

Bridgestone Americas Trust Fund Grants, 469

Brinker Int Corporation Charitable Giving, 471

British Columbia Arts Council Youth Engagement Program Grants, 473

Brookdale Fdn Relatives as Parents Grants, 474

Brown Foundation Grants, 476

Bryan Adams Foundation Grants, 480

Burlington Industries Foundation Grants, 481

Bushrod H. Campbell and Adah F. Hall Charity Fund Grants, 486

C.F. Adams Charitable Trust Grants, 488

C.H. Robinson Worldwide Foundation Grants, 489

Cadillac Products Packaging Company Foundation Grants, 491

Caesars Foundation Grants, 492

Cal Ripken Sr. Foundation Grants, 497

Campbell Foundation Grants, 500

Campbell Soup Foundation Grants, 501

Caplow Applied Sci (CappSci) Children's Prize, 502

Carl B. and Florence E. King Foundation Grants, 506

Carl W. and Carrie Mae Joslyn Trust Grants, 510

Carroll County Community Foundation Grants, 513

Case Foundation Grants, 514

Castle Foundation Grants, 517

Castle Industries Foundation Grants, 519

Catherine Holmes Wilkins Foundation Charitable Grants, 522

Central Pacific Bank Foundation Grants, 530

CFFVR Appleton Education Foundation Grants, 536

CFFVR Basic Needs Giving Partnership Grants, 537

CFFVR Clintonville Area Foundation Grants, 538

CFFVR Frank C. Shattuck Community Grants, 541

CFFVR Infant Welfare Circle of Kings Daughters Grants, 542

CFFVR Mielke Family Foundation Grants, 544

CFFVR Myra M. and Robert L. Vandehey Foundation Grants, 545
CFFVR Project Grants, 546
CFFVR Robert and Patricia Endries Family Foundation Grants, 547
CFFVR Schmidt Family G4 Grants, 548
CFFVR Shawano Area Community Foundation Grants, 549
CFFVR Women's Fund for the Fox Valley Region Grants, 550
CFF Winter Park Community Grants, 551
CFGR Community Impact Grants, 552
CFGR SisterFund Grants, 554
CFGR Ujima Legacy Fund Grants, 555
CFNEM Youth Advisory Council Grants, 558
Chapman Charitable Foundation Grants, 560
Chapman Family Charitable Trust Grants, 561
Chapman Family Foundation, 562
Charles Crane Family Foundation Grants, 563
Charles Delmar Foundation Grants, 564
Charles H. Hall Foundation, 565
Charles H. Pearson Foundation Grants, 566
Charles Lafitte Foundation Grants, 567
Charles N. and Eleanor Knight Leigh Foundation Grants, 568
Charlotte and Joseph Gardner Fdn Grants, 570
CHC Foundation Grants, 575
Chesapeake Bay Trust Environmental Education Grants, 577
Chicago Board of Trade Foundation Grants, 580
Chick and Sophie Major Memorial Duck Calling Contest Scholarships, 583
Children's Trust Fund of Oregon Fdn Grants, 585
Children's Trust Fund of Oregon Foundation Small Grants, 586
Children's Tumor Foundation Young Investigator Awards, 587
Christine and Katharina Pauly Charitable Trust Grants, 601
Christopher Ludwick Foundation Grants, 602
CICF Howard Intermill and Marion Intermill Fenstermaker Grants, 605
CICF Indianapolis Fdn Community Grants, 606
CICF John Harrison Brown and Rob Burse Grt, 607
CICF Summer Youth Grants, 608
Circle K Corporation Contributions Grants, 614
Citizens Bank Charitable Foundation Grants, 616
Citizens Savings Foundation Grants, 617
Clara Abbott Foundation Need-Based Grants, 620
Claremont Community Foundation Grants, 622
Claremont Savings Bank Foundation Grants, 623
Clayton Baker Trust Grants, 629
Cleo Foundation Grants, 632
Cleveland Browns Foundation Grants, 633
Cleveland Foundation Higley Fund Grants, 634
Cleveland Foundation Legacy Village Lyndhurst Community Fund Grants, 636
Cleveland H. Dodge Foundation Grants, 637
CNCS AmeriCorps State and National Grants, 643
CNCS Foster Grandparent Projects Grants, 646
CNCS Social Innovation Grants, 649
CNO Financial Group Community Grants, 650
Collective Brands Foundation Grants, 654
Collective Brands Foundation Payless Gives Shoes 4 Kids Grants, 655
Collective Brands Foundation Saucony Run for Good Grants, 656
Columbus Foundation Traditional Grants, 663
Community Foundation for Greater Buffalo Competitive Grants, 670
Community Foundation for Greater Buffalo Josephine Goodyear Foundation Grants, 672
Community Foundation for Greater Buffalo Ralph C. Wilson, Jr. Youth Sports COVID-19 Fund Grants, 675
Community Foundation for Kettering Grants, 676
Community Foundation for San Benito County Grants, 677
Community Foundation for San Benito County Martin Rajkovich Children's Fund Grants, 678

Community Foundation for SE Michigan Detroit Auto Dealers Association Charitable Foundation Fund Grants, 681
Community Foundation for SE Michigan Livingston County Grants, 683
Community Foundation for the National Capital Region Community Leadership Grants, 688
Community Foundation of Abilene Future Fund Grants, 689
Community Foundation of Crawford County, 695
Community Foundation of Eastern Connecticut General Southeast Grants, 696
Community Foundation of Eastern Connecticut Norwich Youth Grants, 699
Community Foundation of Grant County Grants, 703
Community Foundation of Greater Chattanooga Grants, 704
Community Foundation of Greater Fort Wayne - Edna Foundation Grants, 706
Community Foundation of Greater Greensboro Teen Grantmaking Council Grants, 709
Community Fdn Of Greater Lafayette Grants, 710
Community Foundation of Jackson County Seymour Noon Lions Club Grant, 714
Community Foundation of Louisville Boyette and Edna Edwards Fund Grants, 718
Community Foundation of Louisville C. E. and S. Endowment for the Parks Fund Grants, 719
Community Foundation of Louisville CHAMP Fund Grants, 720
Community Foundation of Louisville Children's Memorial Marker Fund Grants, 721
Community Foundation of Louisville Dr. W. Barnett Owen Memorial Fund for the Children of Louisville and Jefferson County Grants, 723
Community Foundation of Louisville Human Services Grants, 726
Community Foundation of Louisville Youth Philanthropy Council Grants, 730
Community Foundation of Muncie and Delaware County - Kitselman Grants, 733
Community Foundation of Muncie and Delaware County Maxon Grants, 734
Community Fdn of Randolph County Grants, 735
Community Foundation of Western Massachusetts Grants, 741
Community Foundation Serving Riverside and San Bernardino Counties Impact Grants, 742
Con Edison Corporate Giving Civic Grants, 744
Corina Higginson Trust Grants, 750
Covenant to Care for Children Crisis Food Pantry Giving, 756
Covenant for Children Critical Goods Grants, 757
Covenant to Care for Children Enrichment Fund Grants, 758
Cralle Foundation Grants, 760
Crane Fund for Widows and Children Grants, 762
Crane Fund Grants, 763
Credit Suisse Foundation Education Grants, 765
Cresap Family Foundation Grants, 766
Cudd Foundation Grants, 769
CUNA Mutual Group Fdn Community Grants, 770
Curtis Foundation Grants, 771
D. W. McMillan Foundation Grants, 776
Dana Brown Charitable Trust Grants, 777
Daniels Fund Amateur Sports Grants, 779
Daniels Fund Early Childhood Education Grants, 781
Daniels Fund K-12 Education Reform Grants, 783
Daniels Fund Youth Development Grants, 784
David Alan and Susan Berkman Rahm Foundation Grants, 785
David and Barbara B. Hirschhorn Foundation Education and Literacy Grants, 786
David and Laura Merage Foundation Grants, 789
Daviess County Community Foundation Recreation Grants, 793
Daviess County Community Foundation Youth Development Grants, 794
Dayton Foundation Huber Heights Grants, 797
Dayton Foundation Rike Family Scholarships, 798

Dayton Power and Light Company Foundation Signature Grants, 801
Dayton Power and Light Foundation Grants, 802
Deaconess Community Foundation Grants, 803
Deaconess Foundation Advocacy Grants, 804
Dean Foods Community Involvement Grants, 805
Dean Foundation Grants, 806
Dearborn Community Foundation City of Lawrenceburg Youth Grants, 810
Decatur County Community Foundation Small Project Grants, 812
DeKalb County Community Foundation VOICE Grant, 816
Delaware Community Foundation Grants, 817
Del Mar Foundation Community Grants, 820
Delmarva Power & Light Contributions, 821
Delta Air Lines Foundation Youth Development Grants, 824
Dermody Properties Fdn Capstone Award, 826
Dermody Properties Foundation Grants, 827
Deuce McAllister Catch 22 Foundation Grants, 828
Dollar General Youth Literacy Grants, 837
DOL Youthbuild Grants, 838
Donald G. Gardner Humanities Tr Youth Grts, 840
Donald W. Reynolds Foundation Children's Discovery Initiative Grants, 841
Don and May Wilkins Charitable Trust Grants, 842
Dorothea Haus Ross Foundation Grants, 844
Dorrance Family Foundation Grants, 845
Do Something Scholarships, 857
Dr. John T. Macdonald Foundation Grants, 863
DTE Energy Foundation Leadership Grants, 870
Dyson Foundation Mid-Hudson Valley Project Support Grants, 874
E.L. Wiegand Foundation Grants, 877
Eastern Bank Charitable Foundation Neighborhood Support Grants, 880
Eastern Bank Charitable Foundation Partnerships Grants, 881
Eastern Bank Charitable Foundation Targeted Grants, 882
Edna Wardlaw Charitable Trust Grants, 886
Edward and Ellen Roche Relief Fdn Grants, 887
Edward and Helen Bartlett Foundation Grants, 888
Edward and Romell Ackley Foundation Grants, 889
Edwards Memorial Trust Grants, 891
Edward W. and Stella C. Van Houten Memorial Fund Grants, 892
Edyth Bush Charitable Foundation Grants, 893
Effie Allen Little Foundation Grants, 894
Effie Kuhlman Charitable Trust Grants, 896
Eide Bailly Resourcefullness Awards, 897
Elizabeth Carse Foundation Grants, 899
Elizabeth Morse Genius Charitable Trust Grants, 901
Ellen Abbott Gilman Trust Grants, 905
Elmer Roe Deaver Foundation Grants, 906
Elsie H. Wilcox Foundation Grants, 909
Emerson Kampen Foundation Grants, 911
Emily O'Neill Sullivan Foundation Grants, 913
Entergy Corporation Micro Grants, 919
Entergy Corporation Open Grants for Healthy Families, 921
Epilepsy Foundation SUDEP Challenge Initiative Prizes, 924
Episcopal Actors' Guild Actors Florence James Children's Holiday Fund Grant, 925
EQT Fdn Education and Workforce Grants, 927
Essex County Community Foundation Greater Lawrence Summer Fund Grants, 932
Essex County Community Foundation Merrimack Valley Municipal Business Development and Recovery Fund Grants, 933
Ethel Sergeant Clark Smith Foundation Grants, 935
Eulalie Bloedel Schneider Foundation Grants, 936
Eva Gunther Foundation Fellowships, 937
Ezra M. Cutting Trust Grants, 945
F.R. Bigelow Foundation Grants, 947
Fassino Foundation Grants, 949
Fayette County Foundation Grants, 951
FCD New American Children Grants, 952

FCD Young Scholars Program Grants, 953
Fichtenbaum Charitable Trust Grants, 955
Fidelity Charitable Gift Fund Grants, 956
Fidelity Foundation Grants, 957
Finish Line Youth Foundation Founder's Grants, 960
Finish Line Youth Foundation Grants, 961
Finish Line Youth Foundation Legacy Grants, 962
Firelight Foundation Grants, 964
First Hawaiian Bank Foundation Corporate Giving
  Grants, 967
First Nations Development Institute Native Youth
  and Culture Fund Grants, 974
First Nations Development Institute Nourishing
  Native Children: Feeding Our Future Project
  Grants, 975
Florence Foundation Grants, 978
Florence Hunt Maxwell Foundation Grants, 979
Ford Family Foundation Grants - Access to Health
  and Dental Services, 980
Ford Family Foundation Grants - Child Abuse
  Prevention and Intervention, 981
Ford Family Foundation Grants - Positive Youth
  Development, 982
Ford Family Foundation Grants - Technical
  Assistance , 983
Forest Foundation Grants, 985
Foundation Beyond Belief Compassionate Impact
  Grants, 986
Foundation Beyond Belief Humanist Grants, 987
Foundation for Appalachian Ohio Access to
  Environmental Education Mini-Grants, 989
Fdns of East Chicago Family Support Grants, 996
Foundations of East Chicago Youth Development
  Grants, 998
Four County Community Foundation General
  Grants, 1000
Four County Community Foundation Healthy
  Senior/Healthy Youth Fund Grants, 1001
Fourjay Foundation Grants, 1003
Four Lanes Trust Grants, 1005
Four Times Foundation Grants, 1006
Francis Beidler Foundation Grants, 1007
Francis L. Abreu Charitable Trust Grants, 1008
Frank M. Tait Foundation Grants, 1012
Frank Reed and Margaret Jane Peters Memorial Fund
  Grants, 1013
Frank Reed and Margaret Jane Peters Memorial Fund
  II Grants, 1014
Frank S. Flowers Foundation Grants, 1015
Frederick McDonald Trust Grants, 1017
Frederick W. Marzahl Memorial Fund Grants, 1018
Fremont Area Community Foundation Amazing X
  Grants, 1019
Fremont Area Community Foundation Community
  Grants, 1020
Fremont Area Community Foundation Youth
  Advisory Committee Grants, 1022
Friends of Hawaii Charities Grants, 1024
Fuller Foundation Youth At Risk Grants, 1028
Fund for the City of New York Grants, 1029
Furth Family Foundation Grants, 1030
Gamble Foundation Grants, 1032
Gardner Foundation Grants, 1035
GCI Corporate Contributions Grants, 1037
Gene Haas Foundation, 1038
George A. & Grace L. Long Fdn Grants, 1041
George and Ruth Bradford Foundation Grants, 1042
George A Ohl Jr. Foundation Grants, 1043
George B. Page Foundation Grants, 1044
George H.C. Ensworth Memorial Fund Grants, 1049
George J. and Effie L. Seay Foundation Grants, 1052
George Kress Foundation Grants, 1053
George P. Davenport Trust Fund Grants, 1054
George W. Codrington Charitable Foundation
  Grants, 1055
George W.P. Magee Trust Grants, 1056
George W. Wells Foundation Grants, 1057
Gerber Foundation Environmental Hazards Research
  Grants, 1062
Gerber Fdn Pediatric Health Research Grants, 1063

Gerber Foundation Pediatric Nutrition Research
  Grants, 1064
Gerber Fdn West Michigan Youth Grants, 1065
German Protestant Orphan Asylum Foundation
  Grants, 1066
Giant Food Charitable Grants, 1068
Gibson County Community Foundation Recreation
  Grants, 1069
Gibson County Community Foundation Youth
  Development Grants, 1070
Gil and Dody Weaver Foundation Grants, 1071
Gloria Barron Prize for Young Heroes, 1074
GNOF Coastal 5 + 1 Grants, 1078
GNOF Cox Charities of New Orleans Grants, 1079
GNOF Exxon-Mobil Grants, 1080
GNOF Gert Community Fund Grants, 1082
GNOF IMPACT Grants for Youth Dev, 1084
GNOF Norco Community Grants, 1089
Go Daddy Cares Charitable Contributions, 1093
Golden Heart Community Foundation Grants, 1094
Grace Bersted Foundation Grants, 1097
Graham and Carolyn Holloway Family Foundation
  Grants, 1098
Grand Circle Foundation Associates Grants, 1102
Granger Foundation Grants, 1103
Greater Sitka Legacy Fund Grants, 1111
Greater Tacoma Community Foundation Spark
  Grants, 1114
Greater Tacoma Community Foundation Youth
  Program Grants, 1115
Green River Area Community Fdn Grants, 1117
Greenspun Family Foundation Grants, 1118
Gregory and Helayne Brown Charitable Foundation
  Grants, 1119
Greygates Foundation Grants, 1120
Grotto Foundation Project Grants, 1123
GTRCF Boys and Girls Club of Grand Traverse
  Endowment Grants, 1126
GTRCF Elk Rapids Area Community Endowment
  Grants, 1127
GTRCF Genuine Leelanau Charitable Endowment
  Grants, 1128
GTRCF Grand Traverse Families in Action for Youth
  Endowment Grants, 1129
GTRCF Youth Endowment Grants, 1133
Gulf Coast Foundation of Community Operating
  Grants, 1134
Gulf Coast Foundation of Community Program
  Grants, 1135
H.B. Fuller Foundation Grants, 1138
Haddad Foundation Grants, 1139
HAF Community Grants, 1141
HAF Ian Chris Mackey Newman Fund Grts, 1143
HAF Mada Huggins Caldwell Fund Grants, 1147
Hahl Proctor Charitable Trust Grants, 1151
Hall-Perrine Foundation Grants, 1152
Hampton Roads Community Foundation Abused
  People Grants, 1153
Hampton Roads Community Foundation Arts and
  Culture Grants, 1154
Hampton Roads Community Foundation Community
  Leadership Partners Grants, 1155
Hampton Roads Community Foundation Education
  Grants, 1157
Hampton Roads Community Foundation
  Environment Grants, 1158
Hampton Roads Community Foundation Youth
  Baseball and Softball Program Grants, 1160
Hancock County Community Foundation - Field of
  Interest Grants, 1161
Hank Aaron Chasing the Dream Fdn Grants, 1162
Hannah's Helping Hands Grants, 1165
Harden Foundation Grants, 1166
Harmony Foundation for Children Grants, 1168
Harold Brooks Foundation Grants, 1172
Harold K.L. Castle Foundation Windward Youth
  Leadership Fund Grants, 1175
Harry and Jeanette Weinberg Fdn Grants, 1182
Harry B. and Jane H. Brock Foundation Grants, 1183

Harry Frank Guggenheim Foundation Research
  Grants, 1184
Hartford Foundation Regular Grants, 1185
Hartley Foundation Grants, 1186
Harvey E. Najim Family Foundation Grants, 1187
Harvey Randall Wickes Foundation Grants, 1188
Hasbro Children's Fund Grants, 1189
Hasbro Corp Gift of Play Holiday Giving, 1190
Hasbro Corporation Gift of Play Hospital and
  Pediatric Health Giving, 1191
Hasbro Corporation Gift of Play Shelter Support
  Giving, 1192
Hasbro Corporation Gift of Play Summer Camp
  Support, 1193
Hattie Mae Lesley Foundation Grants, 1195
Hawai'i Community Foundation Children's Trust
  Fund Community Awareness: Child Abuse and
  Neglect Prevention Grants, 1198
Hawai'i Community Foundation Family Literacy and
  Hawaii Pizza Hut Literacy Grants, 1201
Hawai'i Community Foundation Richard Smart Fund
  Grants, 1204
Hawai'i Community Foundation Victoria S. and
  Bradley L. Geist Foundation: Capacity Building
  Grants, 1206
Hawai'i Community Foundation Victoria S. and
  Bradley L. Geist Foundation: Enhancement
  Grants, 1207
Hawai'i Community Foundation Victoria S. and
  Bradley L. Geist Foundation: Supporting Foster
  Children and Their Caregivers, 1208
Hawai'i Community Foundation Victoria S. and
  Bradley L. Geist Foundation: Supporting
  Transitioning Foster Youth Grants, 1209
Hawaii Children's Cancer Fdn Contributions, 1212
Hawaii Community Foundation Omidyar Ohana
  Fund Grants, 1213
Hawaii Community Foundation Oscar and Rosetta
  Fish Fund Grants, 1214
Hawaii Community Foundation Reverend Takie
  Okumura Family Grants, 1216
Hawaii Community Foundation Sanford Harmony
  Pillars of Peace Grants, 1217
HBF Pathways Out of Poverty Grants, 1222
Helen Bader Foundation Grants, 1227
Helen G., Henry F., & Louise Tuechter Dornette
  Foundation Grants, 1229
Helen Gertrude Sparks Charitable Trust Grants, 1230
Helen V. Brach Foundation Grants, 1232
Henry and Ruth Blaustein Rosenberg Foundation
  Education Grants, 1236
Henry and Ruth Blaustein Rosenberg Foundation
  Youth Development Grants, 1237
Henry County Community Foundation - TASC
  Youth Grants, 1238
Henry County Community Foundation Grants, 1239
Henry F. Koch Residual Trust Grants, 1241
Henry L. Guenther Foundation Grants, 1242
Herbert A. and Adrian W. Woods Foundation
  Grants, 1243
Herman Goldman Foundation Grants, 1245
Herman H. Nettelroth Fund Grants, 1246
Hillsdale County Community Foundation General
  Grants, 1250
Hillsdale County Community Foundation
  Y.O.U.T.H. Grants, 1252
HLTA Visitor Industry Charity Walk Grant, 1254
Honeywell Corporation Family Safety and Security
  Grants, 1255
Honeywell Corporation Got 2B Safe Contest, 1256
Horace A. Kimball and S. Ella Kimball Foundation
  Grants, 1260
HSBC Corporate Giving Grants, 1266
Hubbard Farms Charitable Foundation Grants, 1272
Humana Foundation Grants, 1275
Huntington Clinical Foundation Grants, 1278
ICCF Youth Advisory Council Grants, 1282
Iddings Foundation Capital Project Grants, 1283
Iddings Foundation Major Project Grants, 1284
Iddings Foundation Medium Project Grants, 1285

Iddings Foundation Small Project Grants, 1286
ILA Children's and Young Adults' Book Awds, 1291
Illinois Arts Council Youth Employment in the Arts
    Program Grants, 1294
Illinois Children's Healthcare Fdn Grants, 1295
ING Foundation Grants, 1302
Initiaive Fdn Inside-Out Connections Grants, 1303
Initiative Foundation Innovation Fund Grants, 1304
Initiative Foundation Minnesota Early Childhood
    Initiative Grants, 1305
Inland Empire Community Foundation Capacity
    Building for IE Nonprofits Grants, 1306
Inland Empire Community Foundation Coachella
    Valley Youth Grants, 1307
Inland Empire Community Foundation Native Youth
    Grants, 1308
Inland Empire Community Foundation Riverside
    Youth Grants, 1309
Inland Empire Community Foundation San
    Bernardino Youth Grants, 1310
Intel Corporation Int Community Grants, 1312
IRC Community Collaboratives for Refugee Women
    and Youth Grants, 1313
Irving S. Gilmore Foundation Grants, 1314
Isabel Allende Foundation Esperanza Grants, 1315
Island Insurance Foundation Grants, 1316
IYI Responsible Fatherhood Grants, 1318
J. Bulow Campbell Foundation Grants, 1319
J. Edwin Treakle Foundation Grants, 1320
J. Knox Gholston Foundation Grants, 1321
J.W. Gardner II Foundation Grants, 1323
J. Willard and Alice S. Marriott Fdn Grants, 1327
Jack H. and William M. Light Charitable Trust
    Grants, 1330
Jack Kent Cooke Fdn Good Neighbor Grants, 1331
Jack Satter Foundation Grants, 1334
Jacob G. Schmidlapp Trusts Grants, 1336
James and Abigail Campbell Family Foundation
    Grants, 1337
James Ford Bell Foundation Grants, 1339
James M. Collins Foundation Grants, 1344
James S. Copley Foundation Grants, 1345
Jane Bradley Pettit Foundation Community and
    Social Development Grants, 1347
Janet Spencer Weekes Foundation Grants, 1348
Janson Foundation Grants, 1350
Jaquelin Hume Foundation Grants, 1357
Jim Blevins Foundation Grants, 1365
Jim Moran Foundation Grants, 1366
Joan Bentinck-Smith Charitable Fdn Grants, 1367
John and Marcia Goldman Foundation Youth
    Development Grants, 1368
John Clarke Trust Grants, 1369
John D. and Katherine A. Johnston Foundation
    Grants, 1370
John Gogian Family Foundation Grants, 1373
John H. and Wilhelmina D. Harland Charitable
    Foundation Children and Youth Grants, 1374
John P. Ellbogen Fdn Community Grants, 1377
Johnson Controls Foundation Arts and Culture
    Grants, 1378
John W. Anderson Foundation Grants, 1383
Joni Elaine Templeton Foundation Grants, 1384
Joseph H. and Florence A. Roblee Foundation
    Children and Youth Grants, 1385
Joseph H. and Florence A. Roblee Foundation
    Education Grants, 1386
Joseph Henry Edmondson Foundation Grants, 1388
Josephine Schell Russell Chartbl Trust Grants, 1389
Joseph S. Stackpole Charitable Trust Grants, 1390
Journal Gazette Foundation Grants, 1391
Joyce and Randy Seckman Charitable Foundation
    Grants, 1393
JP Morgan Chase Fdn Arts and Culture Grants, 1394
Judith Clark-Morrill Foundation Grants, 1395
Judy and Peter Blum Kovler Foundation Grants, 1396
Julia and Tunnicliff Fox Chartbl Trust Grants, 1397
Julia Richardson Brown Foundation Grants, 1398
Julia Temple Davis Brown Foundation Grants, 1399
Julius N. Frankel Foundation Grants, 1400

Kalamazoo Community Foundation Early Childhood
    Learning and School Readiness Grants, 1407
Kalamazoo Community Foundation Good Neighbor
    Grants, 1408
Kalamazoo Community Foundation Individuals and
    Families Grants, 1409
Kalamazoo Community Foundation Youth
    Development Grants, 1412
K and F Baxter Family Foundation Grants, 1413
Kate B. Reynolds Charitable Trust Poor and Needy
    Grants, 1417
Katharine Matthies Foundation Grants, 1418
Kathryne Beynon Foundation Grants, 1420
Katie's Krops Grants, 1421
Katrine Menzing Deakins Chartbl Trust Grants, 1422
Kawabe Memorial Fund Grants, 1423
Kenai Peninsula Foundation Grants, 1425
Ketchikan Community Foundation Grants, 1429
Kimball Foundation Grants, 1432
Kimball International-Habig Foundation Health and
    Human Services Grants, 1434
Kirkpatrick Foundation Grants, 1440
Knox County Community Foundation Recreation
    Grants, 1442
Knox County Community Foundation Youth
    Development Grants, 1443
Koch Family Foundation (Annapolis) Grants, 1444
Kosasa Foundation Grants, 1450
Kosciusko County Community Foundation
    Endowment Youth Services (KEYS) Grants, 1451
Kosciusko County Community Fdn Grants, 1452
Kovler Family Foundation Grants, 1455
LaGrange Independent Foundation for Endowments
    (L.I.F.E.), 1459
Laidlaw Foundation Youh Organizing Catalyst
    Grants, 1461
Laidlaw Foundation Youth Organizaing Initiatives
    Grants, 1462
Land O'Lakes Foundation Community Grants, 1466
Land O'Lakes Foundation Mid-Atlantic Grants, 1467
Lands' End Corporate Giving Program, 1468
Laura B. Vogler Foundation Grants, 1470
Laura Musser Intercultural Harmony Grants, 1472
Laura Moore Cunningham Foundation Grants, 1474
Laurie H. Wollmuth Charitable Trust Grants, 1476
Lavina Parker Trust Grants, 1477
LEGO Children's Fund Grants, 1480
Leo Goodwin Foundation Grants, 1482
Leo Niessen Jr., Charitable Trust Grants, 1484
Leonsis Foundation Grants, 1485
Lilly Endowment Summer Youth Grants, 1492
Lily Palmer Fry Memorial Trust Grants, 1493
Lisa and Douglas Goldman Fund Grants, 1496
LISC Community Leadership Operating Grts, 1499
Lloyd G. Balfour Foundation Attleboro-Specific
    Charities Grants, 1502
Locations Foundation Legacy Grants, 1504
Lois and Richard England Family Foundation Out-
    of-School-Time Grants, 1506
Long Island Community Foundation Grants, 1507
Lotus 88 Foundation for Women and Children
    Grants, 1508
Louis Calder Foundation Grants, 1511
Lucile Packard Foundation for Children's Health
    Grants, 1514
Ludwick Family Foundation Grants, 1516
Lynn and Foster Friess Family Fdn Grants, 1520
Mabel A. Horne Fund Grants, 1525
Mabel F. Hoffman Charitable Trust Grants, 1526
Mabel H. Flory Charitable Trust Grants, 1527
Mabel Louise Riley Foundation Family Strengthening
    Small Grants, 1528
Mabel Louise Riley Foundation Grants, 1529
MacLellan Foundation Grants, 1531
Madison Community Foundation Fund for Children
    Grants, 1534
Madison Community Foundation Grants, 1535
Maggie Welby Foundation Grants, 1538
Maggie Welby Foundation Scholarships, 1539

Maine Community Foundation Edward H. Daveis
    Benevolent Fund Grants, 1540
Maine Community Fdn Peaks Island Grants, 1542
Maine Community Foundation People of Color Fund
    Grants, 1544
Maine Community Foundation Vincent B. and
    Barbara G. Welch Grants, 1545
Maine Women's Fund Girls' Grantmaking Intv, 1547
Make Sense Foundation Grants, 1548
Malone Family Foundation Atypical Development
    Initiative Grants, 1549
Manuel D. and Rhoda Mayerson Fdn Grants, 1550
Marathon Petroleum Corporation Grants, 1551
Marcia and Otto Koehler Foundation Grants, 1553
Mardag Foundation Grants, 1554
Margaret M. Walker Charitable Fdn Grants, 1556
Margaret T. Morris Foundation Grants, 1557
Marin Community Foundation Arts in the
    Community Grants, 1563
Marion and Miriam Rose Fund Grants, 1569
Mark Wahlberg Youth Foundation Grants, 1576
Marsh Corporate Grants, 1580
Martin C. Kauffman 100 Club of Alameda County
    Scholarships, 1582
Martin Family Foundation Grants, 1583
Mary Black Foundation Early Childhood
    Development Grants, 1586
Mary Cofer Trigg Trust Fund Grants, 1587
Maryland State Arts Council Arts in Communities
    Grants, 1592
Maryland State Dept of Education Coordinating
    Entity Services for the Maryland Child Care Res
    Centers Network Grants, 1594
Mary W.B. Curtis Trust Grants, 1599
Mary Wilmer Covey Charitable Trust Grants, 1600
Massachusetts Cultural Cncl YouthReach Grts, 1602
Mathile Family Foundation Grants, 1604
Maurice J. Masserini Charitable Trust Grants, 1610
Maurice R. Robinson Fund Grants, 1611
May and Stanley Smith Charitable Trust Grants, 1613
McCarthy Family Fdn Charity Fund Grants, 1614
McCombs Foundation Grants, 1615
McConnell Foundation Grants, 1616
McCune Foundation Education Grants, 1618
McLean Contributionship Grants, 1623
McLean Foundation Grants, 1624
Mead Family Foundation Grants, 1625
Medtronic Foundation Community Link Human
    Services Grants, 1631
Memorial Foundation for Children Grants, 1633
Mercedes-Benz USA Corporate Contributions
    Grants, 1634
Merck Family Fund Urban Farming and Youth
    Leadership Grants, 1635
Merck Family Fund Youth Transforming Urban
    Communities Grants, 1636
Mericos Foundation Grants, 1637
Meriden Foundation Grants, 1638
Merrick Foundation Grants, 1640
Meta and George Rosenberg Fdn Grants, 1644
Metzger-Price Fund Grants, 1647
Meyer Foundation Education Grants, 1649
MGM Resorts Foundation Community Grants, 1655
MGN Family Foundation Grants, 1656
Michael and Susan Dell Foundation Grants, 1657
Microsoft YouthSpark Grants, 1666
Mid-Iowa Health Foundation Community Response
    Grants, 1667
Milken Family Foundation Grants, 1672
Mill Spring Foundation Grants, 1674
Milton and Sally Avery Arts Foundation Grants, 1675
Milton Hicks Wood and Helen Gibbs Wood
    Charitable Trust Grants, 1676
Minnie M. Jones Trust Grants, 1678
MLB Tomorrow Fund Grants, 1679
Mockingbird Foundation Grants, 1680
Monsanto Access to the Arts Grants, 1681
Monsanto Kids Garden Fresh Grants, 1682
Monsanto United States Grants, 1684

Montana Arts Council Cultural and Aesthetic Project Grants, 1685
Montgomery County Community Foundation Youth Services Grants, 1691
Moody Foundation Grants, 1692
Morgan Adams Foundation Research Grants, 1694
Morris Stulsaft Foundation Early Childhood Education Grants, 1696
Morris Stulsaft Foundation Educational Support for Children Grants, 1697
Morris Stulsaft Foundation Participation in the the Arts Grants, 1698
Morris Stulsaft Foundation Pathways to Work Grants, 1699
Morton K. and Jane Blaustein Foundation Educational Opportunity Grants, 1700
Moses Kimball Fund Grants, 1701
Motiv8 Foundation Grants, 1702
Narragansett Number One Foundation Grants, 1712
NASE Fdn Future Entrepreneur Scholarship, 1713
Nathan B. and Florence R. Burt Fdn Grants, 1717
Nathan Cummings Foundation Grants, 1718
National 4-H Youth in Action Awards, 1721
National Wildlife Federation Craig Tufts Educational Scholarship, 1724
NCMCF Youth Advisory Council Grants, 1727
Nestle Purina PetCare Educational Grants, 1738
Nestle Purina PetCare Youth Grants, 1739
Nestle Very Best in Youth Competition, 1740
Nevada Community Foundation Grants, 1741
New Covenant Farms Grants, 1742
New Earth Foundation Grants, 1743
Newfoundland and Labrador Arts Council School Touring Grants, 1745
Newfoundland and Labrador Arts Council Visiting Artists Grants, 1746
New Hampshire Charitable Foundation Neil and Louise Tillotson Fund - Empower Coös Youth Grants, 1748
New Hampshire Department of Justice Children's Justice Act Coronavirus Emergency Grants, 1749
New Jersey Center for Hispanic Policy, Research and Development Innovative Initiatives Grants, 1750
New Jersey Office of Faith Based Initiatives Services to At Risk Youth Grants, 1752
NFL Charities NFL Player Foundation Grants, 1754
NFL Charities Pro Bowl Community Grants in Hawaii, 1755
North Dakota Community Foundation Grants, 1768
North Face Explore Fund, 1770
Northland Foundation Grants, 1771
NRA Foundation Grants, 1774
NZDIA Community Org Grants Scheme, 1796
Oak Foundation Child Abuse Grants, 1799
Ober Kaler Community Grants, 1801
OceanFirst Foundation Summer Camp Grants, 1804
Office Depot Corporation Community Relations Grants, 1805
Office Depot Foundation Education Grants, 1806
Ohio County Community Foundation Grants, 1812
Ohio County Community Fdn Mini-Grants, 1813
Ohio Valley Foundation Grants, 1814
Olga Sipolin Children's Fund Grants, 1815
Olive B. Cole Foundation Grants, 1816
Olive Smith Browning Charitable Trust Grants, 1818
OneFamily Foundation Grants, 1822
Ontario Arts Council Indigenous Culture Fund Indigenous Artists in Communities and Schools Project Grants, 1825
Ontario Arts Foundation Ruth and Sylvia Schwartz Children's Book Awards, 1826
Ordean Foundation Catalyst Grants, 1830
Ordean Foundation Partnership Grants, 1831
OSF Baltimore Education and Youth Development Grants, 1840
OSF Early Childhood Program Grants, 1841
OSF Education Program Grants in Kyrgyzstan, 1842
OSF Soros Justice Youth Activist Fellowships, 1844
OSF Young Feminist Leaders Fellowships, 1845
OSF Youth Action Fund Grants in Kyrgyzstan, 1846

OtterCares Champion Fund Grants, 1848
OtterCares Impact Fund Grants, 1849
OtterCares Inspiration Fund Grants, 1850
OtterCares NoCO Fund Grants, 1851
Pacers Foundation Be Drug-Free Grants, 1856
Pacers Foundation Be Educated Grants, 1857
Pacers Foundation Be Healthy and Fit Grants, 1858
Pacers Foundation Be Tolerant Grants, 1859
Pacers Foundation Indiana Fever's Be YOUnique Fund Grants, 1860
Packard Foundation Children, Families, and Communities Grants, 1862
Packard Foundation Local Grants, 1863
Pajaro Valley Community Health Health Trust Insurance/Coverage & Education on Using the System Grants, 1864
Palmer Foundation Grants, 1867
Parker Foundation (California) Grants, 1869
Patricia Kisker Foundation Grants, 1879
Patrick and Aimee Butler Family Foundation Community Human Services Grants, 1880
Paul and Edith Babson Foundation Grants, 1881
Peabody Foundation Grants, 1922
Pediatric Brain Tumor Foundation Early Career Development Grants, 1923
Pediatric Brain Tumor Foundation Early Career Development Grants, 1924
Pediatric Brain Tumor Fdn Institute Grants, 1925
Pediatric Brain Tumor Foundation Opportunity Grants, 1926
Pediatric Cancer Research Foundation Grants, 1927
PEN America Phyllis Naylor Grant for Children's and Young Adult Novelists, 1928
PepsiCo Foundation Grants, 1935
Perkin Fund Grants, 1937
Perkins-Ponder Foundation Grants, 1938
Perkins Charitable Foundation Grants, 1939
Perpetual Benevolent Fund, 1940
Perry County Community Foundation Recreation Grants, 1942
Perry County Community Foundation Youth Development Grants, 1943
Peter and Elizabeth C. Tower Foundation Learning Disability Grants, 1945
Peter and Elizabeth C. Tower Foundation Mental Health Grants, 1946
Peter and Elizabeth C. Tower Foundation Small Grants, 1947
Peter and Elizabeth C. Tower Foundation Substance Use Disorders Grants, 1948
Peter and Elizabeth C. Tower Foundation Technology Initiative Grants, 1949
Peter and Elizabeth C. Tower Foundation Technology Planning Grants, 1950
Petersburg Community Foundation Grants, 1951
Pettus Foundation Grants, 1952
PeyBack Foundation Grants, 1953
Peyton Anderson Foundation Grants, 1954
Phil Hardin Foundation Grants, 1960
Philip Boyle Foundation Grants, 1961
Phoenix Coyotes Charities Grants, 1963
Phoenix Suns Charities Grants, 1964
Piedmont Health Foundation Grants, 1965
Pike County Community Foundation Recreation Grants, 1970
Pike County Community Foundation Youth Development Grants, 1971
Pinnacle Entertainment Foundation Grants, 1972
Pinnacle Foundation Grants, 1973
Piper Trust Arts and Culture Grants, 1975
Piper Trust Children Grants, 1976
Pittsburgh Foundation Healthy Children and Adults Grants, 1981
PNC Foundation Education Grants, 1985
Pohlad Family Foundation Summer Camp Scholarships, 1992
Pohlad Family Foundation Youth Advancement Grants, 1993
Polk County Community Foundation Bradley Breakthrough Community Benefit Grants, 1995

Polk County Community Foundation Kirby Harmon Field Fund Grants, 1997
Polk County Community Foundation Marjorie M. and Lawrence R. Bradley Endowment Fund Grants, 1998
Polk County Community Foundation Seasonal Assistance and Cheer Grants for Charitable Programs, 2000
Porter County Community Foundation Health and Wellness Grant, 2002
Porter County Community Foundation PCgivingproject Grants, 2003
Portland Fdn - Women's Giving Circle Grant, 2006
Posey Community Foundation Women's Fund Grants, 2008
Posey County Community Foundation Recreation Grants, 2009
Posey County Community Foundation Youth Development Grants, 2010
Powell Family Foundation Grants, 2012
Powell Foundation Grants, 2013
PPCF Edson Foundation Grants, 2015
PPCF Esther M. and Freeman E. Everett Charitable Foundation Grants, 2016
Presidio Fencing Club Youth Fencers Assistance Scholarships, 2019
Price Chopper's Golub Foundation Grants, 2020
Prudential Foundation Education Grants, 2028
PSEG Corporate Contributions Grants, 2030
Public Education Power Grants, 2032
Public Welfare Fdn Juvenile Justice Grants, 2033
Pulaski County Community Foundation Grants, 2038
Putnam County Community Fdn Grants, 2040
Quaker Oats Company Kids Care Clubs Grants, 2041
Qualcomm Grants, 2042
R.D. and Joan Dale Hubbard Fdn Grants, 2044
R.D. Beirne Trust Grants, 2045
R.J. McElroy Trust Grants, 2046
Ralph C. Wilson, Jr. Foundation Preparing for Success Grant, 2050
Ralph C. Wilson, Jr. Foundation Youth Sports and Recreation Grant, 2051
Ralph M. Parsons Foundation Grants, 2052
Rathmann Family Foundation Grants, 2057
Ray Charles Foundation Grants, 2058
Raytheon Middle School Grants and Schols, 2061
RCF General Community Grants, 2062
RCF Summertime Kids Grants, 2064
Reinberger Foundation Grants, 2066
RGk Foundation Grants, 2068
Richard and Caroline T. Gwathmey Memorial Trust Grants, 2069
Richard Davoud Donchian Foundation Grants, 2070
Richland County Bank Grants, 2074
Ricks Family Charitable Trust Grants, 2075
Robbins-de Beaumont Foundation Grants, 2080
Robbins Family Charitable Foundation Grants, 2082
Robert and Betty Wo Foundation Grants, 2083
Robert and Helen Harmony Fund for Needy Children Grants, 2085
Robert Bowne Foundaion Edmund A. Stanley, Jr. Research Grants, 2086
Robert Bowne Foundation Fellowships, 2087
Robert Bowne Foundation Literacy Grants, 2088
Robert Bowne Fdn Youth-Centered Grants, 2089
Robert F. Lange Foundation Grants, 2090
Robert R. McCormick Tribune Foundation Community Grants, 2093
Robert R. Meyer Foundation Grants, 2094
Robert W. Knox, Sr. and Pearl Wallis Knox Charitable Foundation, 2095
Rockwell Collins Charitable Corp Grants, 2098
Roger L. and Agnes C. Dell Charitable Trust I Grants, 2099
Roger L. and Agnes C. Dell Charitable Trust II Grants, 2100
Ron and Sanne Higgins Family Fdn Grants, 2101
Roney-Fitzpatrick Foundation Grants, 2102
Rose Community Foundation Child and Family Development Grants, 2103

Rose Community Foundation Education Grants, 2104
Rosenberg Fund for Children Clinton and Muriel
    Jencks Memorial Fund Grants, 2109
Rosenberg Fund for Children Edith and George
    Ziefert Fund Grants, 2110
Rosenberg Fund for Children Grants, 2111
Rosenberg Fund for Children Herman Warsh Fund
    Grant, 2112
Rosenberg Fund for Children Moish and Lillian
    Antopol Memorial Fund Grants, 2113
Rosenberg Fund for Children Ozzy Klate Memorial
    Fund Grants, 2114
Roy and Christine Sturgis Charitable Tr Grts, 2115
Roy J. Carver Charitable Trust Youth Services and
    Recreation Grants, 2117
Ruddie Memorial Youth Foundation Grants, 2120
Rush County Community Foundation Grants, 2121
Ruth Anderson Foundation Grants, 2122
Ruth Camp Campbell Charitable Trust Grants, 2125
RWJF Childhood Obesity Grants, 2126
RWJF Healthy Eating Research Grants, 2127
S. D. Bechtel, Jr. Foundation / Stephen Bechtel Fund
    Character and Citizenship Dev Grants, 2128
Sabina Dolan and Gladys Saulsbury Foundation
    Grants, 2130
SACF Youth Advisory Council Grants, 2131
Sadler Family Foundation Grants, 2132
Saginaw Community Foundation Discretionary
    Grants, 2134
Saginaw Community Foundation YWCA Fund for
    Women and Girls Grants, 2135
Saginaw County Community Foundation Youth
    FORCE Grants, 2136
Saigh Foundation Grants, 2137
Salmon Foundation Grants, 2140
Saltchuk Corporate Giving, 2141
Salt River Project Health and Human Services
    Grants, 2142
Samueli Foundation Education Grants, 2143
Samueli Foundation Youth Services Grants, 2144
Samuel N. and Mary Castle Foundation Grants, 2145
Samuel S. Johnson Foundation Grants, 2146
San Antonio Area Foundation Annual Responsive
    Grants, 2147
San Antonio Area Foundation Capital and Naming
    Rights Grants, 2148
Sands Cares Grants, 2156
San Juan Island Community Foundation Grants, 2158
Sara Elizabeth O'Brien Trust Grants, 2161
Sarah G. McCarthy Memorial Foundation, 2162
Sarkeys Foundation Grants, 2163
Scheumann Foundation Grants, 2166
Schramm Foundation Grants, 2168
Scott County Community Foundation Grants, 2170
Seattle Foundation Arts and Culture Grants, 2174
Seattle Foundation Benjamin N. Phillips Memorial
    Fund Grants, 2176
Seattle Foundation C. Keith Birkenfeld Memorial
    Trust Grants, 2177
Seybert Foundation Grants, 2184
Shell Oil Company Foundation Community
    Development Grants, 2188
Shield-Ayres Foundation Grants, 2189
Shopko Fdn Community Charitable Grants, 2191
Sick Kids Foundation Community Conference
    Grants, 2193
Sick Kids Foundation New Investigator Research
    Grants, 2194
Sidgmore Family Foundation Grants, 2195
Sidney Stern Memorial Trust Grants, 2197
Siebert Lutheran Foundation Grants, 2198
Sierra Health Foundation Responsive Grants, 2199
Singing for Change Foundation Grants, 2202
Sioux Falls Area Community Foundation Community
    Fund Grants, 2203
Sioux Falls Area Community Foundation Spot
    Grants, 2204
Skaggs Foundation Grants, 2207
Skatepark Project Built to Play Skatepark Grant, 2208
Smith Richardson Fdn Direct Service Grants, 2210

Sobrato Family Foundation Grants, 2211
Sobrato Family Fdn Meeting Space Grants, 2212
Sobrato Family Foundation Office Space Grants, 2213
Sorenson Legacy Foundation Grants, 2217
Southern Minnesota Initiative Foundation
    AmeriCorps Leap Grants, 2219
Southern Minnesota Initiative Foundation BookStart
    Grants, 2220
Southern Minnesota Initiative Foundation
    Community Growth Initiative Grants, 2221
Southern Minnesota Initiative Foundation Home
    Visiting Grants, 2222
Southern Minnesota Initiative Foundation Incentive
    Grants, 2223
South Madison Community Foundation - Teacher
    Creativity Mini Grants, 2225
Special Olympics Eunice Kennedy Shriver (EKS)
    Fellowships, 2227
Special Olympics Project UNIFY Grants, 2228
Special Olympics Youth Fan Grants, 2229
Spencer County Community Foundation Recreation
    Grants, 2231
Spencer County Community Foundation Women's
    Fund Grants, 2232
Spencer County Community Foundation Youth
    Development Grants, 2233
Sphinx Competition Awards, 2234
Stan and Sandy Checketts Foundation Grants, 2235
Starr Foundation Grants, 2237
State Farm Good Neighbor Citizenship Company
    Grants, 2238
Stein Family Charitable Trust Grants, 2240
Stella and Charles Guttman Foundation Grants, 2241
Sterling and Shelli Gardner Foundation Grants, 2243
Steven B. Achelis Foundation Grants, 2244
Stillson Foundation Grants, 2245
Stinson Foundation Grants, 2246
Storm Castle Foundation Grants, 2248
Streisand Foundation Grants, 2251
Strong Foundation Grants, 2252
Subaru of America Foundation Grants, 2253
Susan A. and Donald P. Babson Charitable
    Foundation Grants, 2259
Suspended: Community Fdn for Greater Atlanta State
    Farm Education Assist Fund Grants, 2260
Swindells Charitable Foundation Grants, 2261
Sylvia Adams Charitable Trust Grants, 2262
Sylvia Perkin Perpetual Charitable Trust Grants, 2263
TAC Arts Access Grant, 2265
Target Corporation Soccer Grants, 2271
Tata Trust Grant for Certificate Course in Holistic
    inclusion of Learners with Diversities, 2273
Tauck Family Foundation Grants, 2274
Telluride Foundation Community Grants, 2281
Textron Corporate Contributions Grants, 2286
Thelma Braun and Bocklett Family Foundation
    Grants, 2287
Thelma Doelger Charitable Trust Grants, 2288
Thomas and Agnes Carvel Foundation Grants, 2289
Thomas J. Atkins Memorial Trust Fund Grants, 2290
Thomas Sill Foundation Grants, 2292
Thomas W. Bradley Foundation Grants, 2293
Thomas W. Briggs Foundation Grants, 2294
Tides Fdn Friends of the IGF Fund Grants, 2300
TJX Foundation Grants, 2303
Toby Wells Foundation Grants, 2304
Todd Brock Family Foundation Grants, 2305
Tom C. Barnsley Foundation Grants, 2306
Toyota Motor Manufacturing of Indiana Grants, 2310
Toyota Motor Manuf of Kentucky Grants, 2311
Toyota Motor Manuf of Mississippi Grants, 2312
Toyota Motor Manufacturing of Texas Grants, 2313
Toyota Technical Center Grants, 2317
TSYSF Individual Scholarships, 2322
TSYSF Team Grants, 2323
Turner B. Bunn, Jr. and Catherine E. Bunn
    Foundation Grants, 2325
Turtle Bay Foundation Grants, 2327
Twenty-First Century Foundation Grants, 2328

Tyler Aaron Bookman Memorial Foundation Trust
    Grants, 2329
Union Bank, N.A. Corporate Sponsorships and
    Donations, 2333
Union Bank, N.A. Foundation Grants, 2334
Union Labor Health Fdn Angel Fund Grants, 2335
Union Labor Health Foundation Dental Angel Fund
    Grants, 2336
Union Pacific Fdn Community & Civic Grants, 2337
Union Square Award for Social Justice, 2340
United Friends of the Children Scholarships, 2341
UnitedHealthcare Children's Fdn Grants, 2342
United Healthcare Commty Grts in Michigan, 2343
United Methodist Health Ministry Fund Grts, 2345
University of Chicago Chapin Hall Doris Duke
    Fellowships, 2348
UPS Foundation Economic and Global Literacy
    Grants, 2351
USAID Global Development Alliance Grants, 2354
USAID National Governance Project in Yemen
    Grant, 2357
USAID Office of Foreign Disaster Assistance and
    Food for Peace Grants, 2359
USDA Child and Adult Care Food Program, 2362
USDA WIC Nutrition Ed Innovations Grants, 2363
UUA Actions of Public Witness Grants, 2365
UUA Congregation-Based Community Organizing
    Grants, 2366
UUA Fund Grants, 2367
UUA International Fund Grants, 2368
UUA Just Society Fund Grants, 2369
UUA Social Responsibility Grants, 2370
V.V. Cooke Foundation Grants, 2371
Valley-Wide Health Systems Nurse Family
    Partnerships, 2372
Vanderburgh Community Foundation Men's Fund
    Grants, 2373
Vanderburgh Community Foundation Recreation
    Grants, 2374
Vanderburgh Community Foundation Youth
    Development Grants, 2375
Vanderburgh County Community Foundation
    Women's Fund Grants, 2376
Van Kampen Boyer Molinari Charitable Foundation
    Grants, 2377
Victor E. Speas Foundation Grants, 2380
Victoria S. and Bradley L. Geist Foundation
    Enhancement Grants, 2381
Victoria S. and Bradley L. Geist Foundation Grants
    Supporting Foster Care and Their Caregivers, 2382
Victoria S. and Bradley L. Geist Foundation Grants
    Supporting Transitioning Foster Youth, 2383
Vigneron Memorial Fund Grants, 2384
Volkswagen Group of America Corporate
    Contributions Grants, 2389
Volvo Bob the Bunny's Cartoon Competition, 2391
VSA/Metlife Connect All Grants, 2392
VSA/Volkswagen Group of America Exhibition
    Awards, 2393
VSA International Art Program for Children with
    Disabilities, 2394
VSA Playwright Discovery Award, 2396
W.H. and Mary Ellen Cobb Chartbl Trust Grts, 2397
W.M. Keck Fdn Southern California Grants, 2398
W.W. Smith Chartbl Trust Basic Needs Grants, 2400
Walker Area Community Foundation Grants, 2401
Walmart Fdn National Local Giving Grants, 2404
Walter J. and Betty C. Zable Fdn Grants, 2406
Walter S. and Evan C. Jones Testam Trust, 2407
Warrick County Community Foundation Recreation
    Grants, 2410
Warrick County Community Foundation Women's
    Fund, 2411
Warrick County Community Foundation Youth
    Development Grants, 2412
Weaver Foundation Grants, 2420
Weaver Popcorn Foundation Grants, 2421
Welborn Baptist Foundation Promotion of Early
    Childhood Development Grants, 2423

Welborn Foundation Promotion of Healthy
  Adolescent Development Grants, 2425
Wells County Foundation Grants, 2426
Weyerhaeuser Family Fdn Health Grants, 2435
Whitehorse Foundation Grants, 2439
Whiting Foundation Grants, 2440
Whitney Foundation Grants, 2441
WHO Foundation Education/Literacy Grants, 2442
Whole Foods Foundation, 2445
Whole Kids Foundation School Garden Grants, 2446
Widgeon Point Charitable Foundation Grants, 2447
Wild Rivers Community Foundation Holiday
  Partnership Grants, 2448
Wild Rivers Community Foundation Summer Youth
  Mini Grants, 2449
Wilkins Family Foundation Grants, 2450
William A. Badger Foundation Grants, 2451
William A. Cooke Foundation Grants, 2452
William and Flora Hewlett Foundation Education
  Grants, 2454
William B. Stokely Jr. Foundation Grants, 2459
William Bingham Foundation Grants, 2460
William Caspar Graustein Memorial Fund Corinne
  G. Levin Education Grants, 2462
William E. Barth Foundation Grants, 2463
William E. Dean III Charitable Fdn Grants, 2464
William Foulds Family Foundation Grants, 2465
William G. and Helen C. Hoffman Foundation
  Grants, 2466
William J. and Dorothy K. O'Neill Foundation
  Responsive Grants, 2468
William J. Brace Charitable Trust, 2471
William T. Grant Foundation Scholars Program, 2475
Wilton and Effie Hebert Foundation Grants, 2476
Winifred Johnson Clive Foundation Grants, 2478
WinnCompanies Charitable Giving, 2479
Wisconsin Energy Foundation Grants, 2481
Wold Foundation Grants, 2482
Wolfe Associates Grants, 2483
Women's Fund of Hawaii Grants, 2484
Wood-Claeyssens Foundation Grants, 2486
Wood Family Charitable Trust Grants, 2487
World of Children Education Award, 2490
World of Children Youth Award, 2493
WSF Rusty Kanokogi Fund for the Advancement of
  U.S. Judo Grants, 2495
WSF Travel and Training Fund Grants, 2498
WSLBDF Quarterly Grants, 2499
Wyoming Community Fdn General Grants, 2501
Wyoming Community Foundation Hazel Patterson
  Memorial Grants, 2502
Wyomissing Foundation Community Grants, 2504
Yampa Valley Community Foundation Erickson
  Business Week Scholarships, 2508
Yampa Valley Community Foundation Erickson
  Christian Heritage Scholarships, 2509
Yawkey Foundation Grants, 2510
Youths' Friends Association Grants, 2511
YSA National Child Awareness Month Youth
  Ambassador Grants, 2517
YSA NEA Youth Leaders for Literacy Grants, 2518
YSA Radio Disney's Hero for Change Award, 2519
YSA Sodexo Lead Organizer Grants, 2520
YSA UnitedHealth HEROES Service-Learning
  Grants, 2522
Z. Smith Reynolds Foundation Small Grants, 2523
Zane's Foundation Grants, 2524
Zellweger Baby Support Network Grants, 2525
Zollner Foundation Grants, 2526

Children's Literature
ALA Alex Awards, 153
ALA ALSC Distinguished Service Award, 154
ALA Amelia Bloomer Book List Award, 156
ALA Baker and Taylor Summer Reading Program
  Grant, 158
ALA Bookapalooza Grants, 161
ALA Booklist Editors' Choice Books for Youth
  Awards, 162
ALA Bound to Stay Bound Books Scholarships, 163

ALA Children's Literature Legacy Award, 165
ALA Coretta Scott King-John Steptoe Award for
  New Talent, 166
ALA Coretta Scott King-Virginia Hamilton Award
  for Lifetime Achievement, 167
ALA John Newbery Medal, 172
ALA Louise Seaman Bechtel Fellowship, 173
ALA Margaret A. Edwards Award, 175
ALA May Hill Arbuthnot Honor Lecture Award, 176
ALA Mildred L. Batchelder Award, 178
ALA Notable Children's Books Awards, 179
ALA Notable Children's Recordings Awards, 180
ALA Notable Children's Videos Awards, 181
ALA Odyssey Award for Excellence in Audiobook
  Production, 182
ALA Penguin Random House Young Readers Group
  Award, 183
ALA Rainbow Project Book List Award, 187
ALA Randolph Caldecott Medal, 188
ALA Robert F. Sibert Informational Book Medal
  Award, 189
ALA Schneider Family Book Awards, 191
ALA Scholastic Library Publishing Award, 192
ALA Theodor Seuss Geisel Award, 215
Arizona State Library LSTA Learning Grants, 297
Bernard and Audre Rapoport Foundation Arts and
  Culture Grants, 407
Bernard and Audre Rapoport Foundation Education
  Grants, 410
ChLA Article Award, 589
ChLA Book Award, 590
ChLA Carol Gay Award, 591
ChLA Edited Book Award, 592
ChLA Faculty Research Grants, 593
ChLA Graduate Student Essay Awards, 594
ChLA Hannah Beiter Diversity Research Grants, 595
ChLA Hannah Beiter Graduate Student Research
  Grants, 596
ChLA Mentoring Award, 597
ChLA Phoenix Award, 598
ChLA Phoenix Picture Book Award, 599
ILA Arbuthnot Award, 1290
ILA Children's and Young Adults' Book Awds, 1291
National Cowboy and Western Heritage Museum
  Awards, 1722
NCSS Carter G. Woodson Book Awards, 1729
Ontario Arts Foundation Ruth and Sylvia Schwartz
  Children's Book Awards, 1826
PCA Arts Organizations and Arts Programs Grants
  for Literature, 1894
PEN America Phyllis Naylor Grant for Children's and
  Young Adult Novelists, 1928

Children's Museums
Back Home Again Foundation Grants, 344
Ben B. Cheney Foundation Grants, 402
Cabot Corporation Foundation Grants, 490
Chapman Family Charitable Trust Grants, 561
Donald W. Reynolds Foundation Children's
  Discovery Initiative Grants, 841
Francis Beidler Foundation Grants, 1007
Helen E. Ellis Charitable Trust Grants, 1228
Herman P. and Sophia Taubman Fdn Grants, 1247
Hubbard Family Foundation Grants, 1270
Ike and Roz Friedman Foundation Grants, 1289
Jerry L. and Barbara J. Burris Fdn Grants, 1362
LEGO Children's Fund Grants, 1480
Lied Foundation Trust Grants, 1490
Maurice Amado Foundation Grants, 1609
Maurice R. Robinson Fund Grants, 1611
Phoenix Suns Charities Grants, 1964
Richard J. Stern Foundation for the Arts Grants, 2071
Riedman Foundation Grants, 2076
S. Spencer Scott Fund Grants, 2129
Seattle Foundation C. Keith Birkenfeld Memorial
  Trust Grants, 2177
Union Pacific Fdn Community & Civic Grants, 2337
Wilton and Effie Hebert Foundation Grants, 2476

Children's Theater
Bernard and Audre Rapoport Foundation Arts and
  Culture Grants, 407
Illinois Arts Council Theater Program Grants, 1293
LEGO Children's Fund Grants, 1480
NYSCA Arts Education: General Operating Support
  Grants, 1781
NYSCA Theatre: Prof Performances Grants, 1795
Parker Foundation (California) Grants, 1869
PCA Arts Organizations and Arts Programs Grants
  for Theatre, 1896
PCA Entry Track Arts Organizations and Arts
  Programs Grants for Theatre, 1910
Polk County Community Foundation Unrestricted
  Grants, 2001

Chinese Language/Literature
Do Something International Intern, 854

Choreography
PCA Arts Organizations and Arts Programs Grants
  for Dance, 1892
PCA Entry Track Arts Organizations and Arts
  Programs Grants for Dance, 1904
PCA Strategies for Success Grants - Adv Level, 1917
PCA Strategies for Success Grants - Basic Level, 1918
PCA Strategies for Success Grants - Intermediate
  Level, 1919
PennPAT Artist Technical Assistance Grants, 1929
PennPAT Strategic Opportunity Grants, 1933

Chronic Illness
Atkinson Foundation Community Grants, 325
CFF Research Grants, 534
Graham and Carolyn Holloway Family Foundation
  Grants, 1098
Herbert A. and Adrian W. Woods Foundation
  Grants, 1243
Mary Wilmer Covey Charitable Trust Grants, 1600
Medtronic Foundation Strengthening Health Systems
  Grants, 1632
Mid-Iowa Health Foundation Community Response
  Grants, 1667
TJX Foundation Grants, 2303

Churches
ABC Charities Grants, 50
Adams County Community Foundation Grants, 115
Adelaide Christian Home For Children Grants, 124
AHS Foundation Grants, 143
ALA Coretta Scott King Book Donation Grant, 168
Alavi Foundation Education Grants, 216
Albert E. and Birdie W. Einstein Fund Grants, 220
Alvah H. and Wyline P. Chapman Foundation
  Grants, 248
Antone and Edene Vidinha Charitable Grants, 281
Ar-Hale Family Foundation Grants, 290
Austin S. Nelson Foundation Grants, 333
Blue Cross Blue Shield of Minnesota Foundation
  - Healthy Neighborhoods: Connect for Health
  Challenge Grants, 443
Callaway Foundation Grants, 496
Chapman Family Charitable Trust Grants, 561
Chapman Family Foundation, 562
Covenant Foundation of Brentwood Grants, 755
Emerson Kampen Foundation Grants, 911
George Kress Foundation Grants, 1053
HAF Mada Huggins Caldwell Fund Grants, 1147
Harry and Helen Sands Charitable Trust Grants, 1181
James LeVoy Sorenson Foundation Grants, 1343
James M. Collins Foundation Grants, 1344
Jim Blevins Foundation Grants, 1365
John H. and Wilhelmina D. Harland Charitable
  Foundation Children and Youth Grants, 1374
Kathryne Beynon Foundation Grants, 1420
Kawabe Memorial Fund Grants, 1423
Lilly Endowment Summer Youth Grants, 1492
Mervin Bovaird Foundation Grants, 1643
Narragansett Number One Foundation Grants, 1712

Parker Foundation (Virginia) Grants to Support Christian Evangelism, 1870
Perkins Charitable Foundation Grants, 1939
Sioux Falls Area Community Foundation Community Fund Grants, 2203
Sioux Falls Area Community Foundation Spot Grants, 2204
UUA Fund Grants, 2367
Wege Foundation Grants, 2422
Winifred Johnson Clive Foundation Grants, 2478

Circulatory Disease
ACCF of Indiana Angel Funds Grants, 62
Delmarva Power & Light Contributions, 821

Citizenship
Aspen Community Foundation Grants, 316
Bernard and Audre Rapoport Foundation Democracy and Civic Participation Grants, 409
Carnegie Corporation of New York Grants, 511
Chesapeake Bay Trust Mini Grants, 578
Citizens Bank Charitable Foundation Grants, 616
Jacob and Hilda Blaustein Foundation Israel Program Grants, 1335
Kenneth T. and Eileen L. Norris Fdn Grants, 1427
Lubrizol Foundation Grants, 1513
Marsh Corporate Grants, 1580
Mary D. and Walter F. Frear Eleemosynary Trust Grants, 1588
National 4-H Council Grants, 1720
NCSS Award for Global Understanding, 1728
Oregon Community Fdn Community Grants, 1833
Piper Jaffray Foundation Communities Giving Grants, 1974

Civic Affairs
Abbott Fund Global AIDS Care Grants, 47
Adobe Foundation Action Grants, 126
Alaska Airlines Foundation LIFT Grants, 194
Alcatel-Lucent Technologies Foundation Grants, 224
Alliant Energy Foundation Community Giving for Good Sponsorship Grants, 240
Arkema Foundation Grants, 298
Atkinson Foundation Community Grants, 325
Avery Dennison Foundation Education Grants, 337
Bay Area Community Foundation Semiannual Grants, 382
Bernard and Audre Rapoport Foundation Democracy and Civic Participation Grants, 409
Black Hills Corporation Grants, 435
Blumenthal Foundation Grants, 459
Boeing Company Contributions Grants, 462
Bridgestone Americas Trust Fund Grants, 469
Brinker Int Corporation Charitable Giving, 471
Brown Foundation Grants, 476
Burlington Industries Foundation Grants, 481
CCFF Christopher Columbus Awards, 522
CFFVR Basic Needs Giving Partnership Grants, 537
CICF Indianapolis Fdn Community Grants, 606
CIGNA Foundation Grants, 611
Cincinnati Bell Foundation Grants, 612
Clayton Baker Trust Grants, 629
Clinton County Community Foundation Grants, 638
CNCS AmeriCorps NCCC Project Grants, 642
Colgate-Palmolive Company Grants, 652
Colorado Interstate Gas Grants, 661
Community Foundation for Greater Buffalo Competitive Grants, 670
Community Foundation for the National Capital Region Community Leadership Grants, 688
Community Foundation of Eastern Connecticut General Southeast Grants, 696
Community Foundation of Greater Greensboro Community Grants, 708
Community Foundation of Henderson County Community Grants, 711
Community Fdn of Howard County Grants, 712
Community Foundation of Muncie and Delaware County Maxon Grants, 734

Community Foundation of St. Joseph County Special Project Challenge Grants, 738
Community Foundation Serving Riverside and San Bernardino Counties Impact Grants, 742
Con Edison Corporate Giving Civic Grants, 744
Dayton Foundation Grants, 796
Dayton Power and Light Foundation Grants, 802
Decatur County Community Foundation Large Project Grants, 811
Delta Air Lines Foundation Community Enrichment Grants, 823
Dunspaugh-Dalton Foundation Grants, 873
Ella West Freeman Foundation Grants, 904
El Pomar Foundation Anna Keesling Ackerman Fund Grants, 907
El Pomar Foundation Grants, 908
Ethel Sergeant Clark Smith Foundation Grants, 935
F.M. Kirby Foundation Grants, 946
Farmers Insurance Corporate Giving Grants, 948
Fifth Third Foundation Grants, 959
FirstEnergy Foundation Community Grants, 965
Ford Foundation BUILD Grants, 984
Frank S. Flowers Foundation Grants, 1015
Fund for the City of New York Grants, 1029
Georgia-Pacific Fdn Entrepreneurship Grants, 1059
Global Fund for Women Grants, 1073
GNOF IMPACT Grants for Youth Dev, 1084
Greater Tacoma Community Foundation General Operating Grants, 1113
H.A. and Mary K. Chapman Charitable Trust Grants, 1137
Hancock County Community Foundation - Field of Interest Grants, 1161
HLTA Visitor Industry Charity Walk Grant, 1254
HSBC Corporate Giving Grants, 1266
Huntington County Community Foundation Make a Difference Grants, 1280
ING Foundation Grants, 1302
Inland Empire Community Foundation Capacity Building for IE Nonprofits Grants, 1306
Judy and Peter Blum Kovler Foundation Grants, 1396
Kosciusko County Community Fdn Grants, 1452
Kovler Family Foundation Grants, 1454
Laclede Gas Charitable Trust Grants, 1457
Lake County Community Fund Grants, 1463
Land O'Lakes Fdn California Region Grants, 1465
Land O'Lakes Foundation Mid-Atlantic Grants, 1467
Lisa and Douglas Goldman Fund Grants, 1496
Lockheed Martin Corporation Fdn Grants, 1505
Louie M. and Betty M. Phillips Fdn Grants, 1509
Lubrizol Foundation Grants, 1513
Madison County Community Foundation - City of Anderson Quality of Life Grant, 1536
Madison County Community Foundation General Grants, 1537
Marsh Corporate Grants, 1580
Mary D. and Walter F. Frear Eleemosynary Trust Grants, 1588
Mary K. Chapman Foundation Grants, 1590
McCombs Foundation Grants, 1615
Meadows Foundation Grants, 1626
MeadWestvaco Foundation Sustainable Communities Grants, 1627
Meriden Foundation Grants, 1638
Merrick Foundation Grants, 1639
Mertz Gilmore Foundation NYC Communities Grants, 1641
MGM Resorts Foundation Community Grants, 1655
Ms. Foundation for Women Building Democracy Grants, 1706
Narragansett Number One Foundation Grants, 1712
Noble County Community Foundation Grants, 1765
Norcliffe Foundation Grants, 1766
Onan Family Foundation Grants, 1821
Orange County Community Foundation Grants, 1828
Percy B. Ferebee Endowment Grants, 1936
Piedmont Natural Gas Corporate and Charitable Contributions, 1966
Piper Jaffray Foundation Communities Giving Grants, 1974

PMI Foundation Grants, 1982
Powell Family Foundation Grants, 2012
PPCF Community Grants, 2014
Puerto Rico Community Foundation Grants, 2037
Ralph M. Parsons Foundation Grants, 2052
RCF General Community Grants, 2062
RGk Foundation Grants, 2068
Rockwell Collins Charitable Corp Grants, 2098
Rose Hills Foundation Grants, 2106
Ruth and Vernon Taylor Foundation Grants, 2124
Schramm Foundation Grants, 2168
Shell Oil Company Foundation Community Development Grants, 2188
Sony Corporation of America Grants, 2216
Sunoco Foundation Grants, 2256
SunTrust Bank Trusteed Foundations Greene-Sawtell Grants, 2257
SunTrust Bank Trusteed Foundations Nell Warren Elkin and William Simpson Elkin Grants, 2258
TE Foundation Grants, 2279
Tension Envelope Foundation Grants, 2284
Thomas W. Briggs Foundation Grants, 2294
Tides Foundation Grants, 2302
TJX Foundation Grants, 2303
Toyota Motor Manuf of Mississippi Grants, 2312
Toyota Motor Manufacturing of West Virginia Grants, 2314
Toyota Motor North America of NY Grants, 2315
Toyota Motor Sales, USA Grants, 2316
U.S. Cellular Corporation Grants, 2331
United Technologies Corporation Grants, 2347
Vernon K. Krieble Foundation Grants, 2379
Weaver Foundation Grants, 2420
Wells County Foundation Grants, 2426
William Blair and Company Foundation Grants, 2461
William G. and Helen C. Hoffman Foundation Grants, 2466
Williams Comps Homegrown Giving Grants, 2474
Xerox Foundation Grants, 2507
Z. Smith Reynolds Foundation Small Grants, 2523

Civic Engagement
Atwood Foundation General Grants, 330
Ben B. Cheney Foundation Grants, 402
Bernard and Audre Rapoport Foundation Democracy and Civic Participation Grants, 409
Community Foundation for Greater Buffalo Niagara Area Foundation Grants, 673
Community Foundation of Greater Fort Wayne - John S. and James L. Knight Foundation Donor-Advised Grants, 707
Con Edison Corporate Giving Civic Grants, 744
CONSOL Youth Program Grants, 747
Decatur County Community Foundation Small Project Grants, 812
GMFUS Balkan Trust for Democracy Grants, 1075
GNOF Coastal 5 + 1 Grants, 1078
GNOF IMPACT Grants for Youth Dev, 1084
GNOF Stand Up For Our Children Grants, 1092
Mabel Louise Riley Foundation Family Strengthening Small Grants, 1528
Maine Community Foundation People of Color Fund Grants, 1544
Manuel D. and Rhoda Mayerson Fdn Grants, 1550
Maryland State Arts Council Arts in Communities Grants, 1592
Matson Community Giving Grants, 1607
Medtronic Foundation Community Link Arts, Civic, and Culture Grants, 1629
Mertz Gilmore Foundation NYC Communities Grants, 1641
Ms. Foundation for Women Building Democracy Grants, 1706
National 4-H Youth in Action Awards, 1721
Philanthrofund Foundation Grants, 1959
PMI Foundation Grants, 1982
Sioux Falls Area Community Foundation Community Fund Grants, 2203
Sioux Falls Area Community Foundation Spot Grants, 2204

Teaching Tolerance Diverse Democracy Grants, 2275
Threshold Fdn Justice and Democracy Grants, 2298
Union Bank, N.A. Foundation Grants, 2334
USAID Community Livelihoods Project in Yemen
    Grant, 2352
Walmart Foundation State Giving Grants, 2405
YSA MLK Day Lead Organizer Grants, 2516

Civics
Ben B. Cheney Foundation Grants, 402
Bernard and Audre Rapoport Foundation Democracy
    and Civic Participation Grants, 409
Con Edison Corporate Giving Civic Grants, 744
Toyota Motor Manufacturing of Texas Grants, 2313
Toyota Motor Manufacturing of West Virginia
    Grants, 2314
Toyota Motor North America of NY Grants, 2315
Toyota Motor Sales, USA Grants, 2316

Civics Education
Ben B. Cheney Foundation Grants, 402
Bernard and Audre Rapoport Foundation Democracy
    and Civic Participation Grants, 409
CHT Foundation Education Grants, 603
Con Edison Corporate Giving Civic Grants, 744
Daniels Fund Youth Development Grants, 784
Hatton W. Sumners Foundation for the Study and
    Teaching of Self Government Grants, 1196
Teaching Tolerance Diverse Democracy Grants, 2275

Civil Service
CNCS AmeriCorps NCCC Project Grants, 642

Civil Society
Ford Foundation BUILD Grants, 984
OSF Early Childhood Program Grants, 1841
Proteus Fund Grants, 2027
Teaching Tolerance Diverse Democracy Grants, 2275

Civil War
Richard and Caroline T. Gwathmey Memorial Trust
    Grants, 2069

Civil/Human Rights
ALA Coretta Scott King-John Steptoe Award for
    New Talent, 166
Albert W. Cherne Foundation Grants, 222
ALFJ Astraea U.S. and International Emergency
    Fund, 230
Allstate Corporate Giving Grants, 242
Allstate Corp Hometown Commitment Grants, 243
Allstate Foundation Safe and Vital Communities
    Grants, 244
Alvah H. and Wyline P. Chapman Foundation
    Grants, 248
Assisi Fdn of Memphis Capital Project Grants, 317
Assisi Foundation of Memphis General Grants, 318
Assisi Foundation of Memphis Mini Grants, 319
Atlanta Women's Foundation Pathway to Success
    Grants, 327
Bernard and Audre Rapoport Foundation Democracy
    and Civic Participation Grants, 409
Blumenthal Foundation Grants, 459
Clayton Baker Trust Grants, 629
Community Foundation of Greater Chattanooga
    Grants, 704
Community Foundation of Greater Greensboro
    Community Grants, 708
Corina Higginson Trust Grants, 750
Evelyn and Walter Haas, Jr. Fund Gay and Lesbian
    Rights Grants, 940
Evelyn and Walter Haas, Jr. Fund Immigrant Rights
    Grants, 941
FCYO Youth Organizing Grants, 954
Fitzpatrick, Cella, Harper & Scinto Pro Bono
    Services, 976
Ford Foundation BUILD Grants, 984
Global Fund for Women Grants, 1073
Herman Goldman Foundation Grants, 1245
Lisa and Douglas Goldman Fund Grants, 1496

Marriott Int Corporate Giving Grants, 1578
Max and Anna Levinson Foundation Grants, 1612
Mertz Gilmore Foundation NYC Communities
    Grants, 1641
New York Foundation Grants, 1753
Norman Foundation Grants, 1767
NRA Foundation Grants, 1774
OSF Early Childhood Program Grants, 1841
OSF Education Support Program Grants, 1843
OSF Young Feminist Leaders Fellowships, 1845
OSF Youth Action Fund Grants in Kyrgyzstan, 1846
PDF Community Organizing Grants, 1920
PDF Fiscal Sponsorship Grant, 1921
Philanthrofund Foundation Grants, 1959
Proteus Fund Grants, 2027
Public Welfare Foundation Special Opportunities
    Grants, 2035
Samuel S. Johnson Foundation Grants, 2146
Sidney Stern Memorial Trust Grants, 2197
Skaggs Family Foundation Grants, 2206
Skaggs Family Foundation Grants, 2205
Social Justice Fund Northwest Criminal Justice
    Giving Project Grants, 2214
Social Justice Fund Northwest Economic Justice
    Giving Project Grants, 2215
Streisand Foundation Grants, 2251
Teaching Tolerance Diverse Democracy Grants, 2275
Teaching Tolerance Social Justice Educator Grts, 2276
Tides Foundation Grants, 2302
United Methodist Women Brighter Future for
    Children and Youth Grants, 2346
Vernon K. Krieble Foundation Grants, 2379
Weaver Foundation Grants, 2420
YSA MLK Day Lead Organizer Grants, 2516
Z. Smith Reynolds Foundation Small Grants, 2523

Classroom Instruction
100% for Kids - Utah Credit Union Education
    Foundation Major Project Grants, 11
100% for Kids - Utah Credit Union Education
    Foundation Mini Grants, 12
100% for Kids - Utah Credit Union Education
    Foundation School Grants, 13
Arkema Foundation Science Teachers Grants, 299
Community Foundation of Jackson County Classroom
    Education Grants, 713
Community Foundation of Louisville Winston N. and
    Nancy H. Bloch Educational Fund Grants, 729
Delaware Valley Fairness Project Teacher Assistance
    Grants, 818
Foundation for the Mid South Education Grants, 993
Four County Community Foundation 21st Century
    Education Fund Grants, 999
Honeywell Corporation Got 2B Safe Contest, 1256
Huntington County Community Foundation
    Classroom Education Grants, 1279
J. Knox Gholston Foundation Grants, 1321
J. Marion Sims Foundation Teachers' Pet Grant, 1322
Long Island Community Foundation Grants, 1507
Madison Community Foundation Fund for Children
    Grants, 1534
Martha Holden Jennings Foundation Grants-to-
    Educators, 1581
NCSS Award for Global Understanding, 1728
Public Education Power Grants, 2032
Random Acts of Kindness Foundation Lesson Plan
    Contest, 2053
South Madison Community Foundation - Teacher
    Creativity Mini Grants, 2225
Toshiba America Foundation Grades 7-12 Science and
    Math Grants, 2307
Toshiba America Foundation K-6 Science and Math
    Grants, 2308
Toyota USA Foundation Education Grants, 2318
UPS Foundation Economic and Global Literacy
    Grants, 2351

Climate Change
Alaska Conservation Fdn Youth Mini Grants, 210

Climatology
USAID Global Development Alliance Grants, 2354

Clinical Medicine, General
Biogen Foundation General Donations, 432
Piper Trust Healthcare and Med Rsrch Grants, 1978

Clinical Research
Joni Elaine Templeton Foundation Grants, 1384
Marcia and Otto Koehler Foundation Grants, 1553
Marion Gardner Jackson Charitable Trust Grts, 1570
Sara Elizabeth O'Brien Trust Grants, 2161
Sick Kids Foundation New Investigator Research
    Grants, 2194
Victor E. Speas Foundation Grants, 2380

Clinics
Clark and Ruby Baker Foundation Grants, 625
Crystelle Waggoner Charitable Trust Grants, 768
Foundation for Health Enhancement Grants, 990
George E. Hatcher, Jr. and Ann Williams Hatcher
    Foundation Grants, 1045
George W. Wells Foundation Grants, 1057
GNOF IMPACT Gulf States Eye Surg Fund, 1085
Helen Irwin Littauer Educational Trust Grants, 1231
Lumpkin Family Fdn Healthy People Grants, 1518
Marietta McNeill Morgan and Samuel Tate Morgan
    Jr. Trust Grants, 1560
Marin Community Foundation Improving
    Community Health Grants, 1566
Meyer Fdn Healthy Communities Grants, 1650
Mt. Sinai Health Care Foundation Health of the
    Urban Community Grants, 1710
Piper Trust Healthcare and Med Rsrch Grants, 1978
RCF General Community Grants, 2062
Reinberger Foundation Grants, 2066
Shell Deer Park Grants, 2186
Stein Family Charitable Trust Grants, 2240

Coastal Processes
GNOF Bayou Communities Grants, 1077

Cognitive Development/Processes
ACF Head Start and/or Early Head Start Grantee
    - Clay, Randolph, and Talladega Counties,
    Alabama, 82
ACF Head Start and/or Early Head Start Grantee -
    St. Landry Parish, Louisiana, 83
Bay Area Community Foundation Leslie L. Squires
    Foundation Grants, 380
NSF Perception, Action and Cognition (PAC)
    Research Grants, 1775
Peter and Elizabeth C. Tower Foundation Technology
    Initiative Grants, 1949
Peter and Elizabeth C. Tower Foundation Technology
    Planning Grants, 1950

Collaboration
ALA Sara Jaffarian School Library Award for
    Exemplary Humanities Programming, 190
Bill and Melinda Gates Foundation Agricultural
    Development Grants, 425
California Endowment Innovative Ideas Challenge
    Grants, 495
CNCS Social Innovation Grants, 649
Daniels Fund Amateur Sports Grants, 779
GNOF Coastal 5 + 1 Grants, 1078
GNOF IMPACT Grants for Youth Dev, 1084
GNOF Norco Community Grants, 1089
GNOF Organizational Effectiveness Grants and
    Workshops, 1090
GNOF Stand Up For Our Children Grants, 1092
Helen Bader Foundation Grants, 1227
Madison Community Foundation Fund for Children
    Grants, 1534
Maine Community Foundation Edward H. Daveis
    Benevolent Fund Grants, 1540
Piper Trust Arts and Culture Grants, 1975
Teagle Foundation Grants, 2277
Union Square Arts Award, 2339

College Students
Kimball Foundation Grants, 1432

College-Preparatory Education
3M Company Fdn Community Giving Grants, 5
Akron Community Fdn Education Grants, 151
CenturyLink Clarke M. Williams Foundation
    Matching Time Grants, 531
CFGR Ujima Legacy Fund Grants, 555
Chicago Community Trust Arts and Culture Grants:
    Improving Access to Arts Learning, 581
CNCS AmeriCorps State and National Grants, 643
Community Foundation of Louisville Education
    Grants, 724
Foundation for the Mid South Education Grants, 993
Georgia-Pacific Foundation Education Grants, 1058
Marin Community Foundation Closing the Education
    Achievement Gap Grants, 1564
Mary Wilmer Covey Charitable Trust Grants, 1600
Matson Community Giving Grants, 1607
McCune Charitable Foundation Grants, 1617
Meyer Foundation Education Grants, 1649
OMNOVA Solutions Fdn Education Grants, 1820
Piedmont Natural Gas Foundation K-12 Science,
    Technology, Engineering and Math Grant, 1969
Piper Trust Education Grants, 1977
Teagle Foundation Grants, 2277

Communication Systems
Riedman Foundation Grants, 2076

Communications
Abell-Hanger Foundation Grants, 52
American Indian Youth Running Strong Grants, 256
Ann Ludington Sullivan Foundation Grants, 279
Chicago Board of Trade Foundation Grants, 580
Community Foundation for the National Capital
    Region Community Leadership Grants, 688
EPA Children's Health Protection Grants, 923
EQT Fdn Education and Workforce Grants, 927
Klingenstein-Simons Fellowship Awards in the
    Neurosciences, 1441
Kodak Community Relations Grants, 1445
Microsoft Software Donations, 1665
Richard J. Stern Foundation for the Arts Grants, 2071
Tellabs Foundation Grants, 2280
Youths' Friends Association Grants, 2511

Communicative Disorders, Hearing
Alexander Graham Bell Parent and Infant Financial
    Aid Grants, 227
Bay Area Community Foundation Nathalie Awrey
    Memorial Fund Grants, 381
Community Foundation of Jackson County Seymour
    Noon Lions Club Grant, 714
Oticon Focus on People Awards, 1847
Reinberger Foundation Grants, 2066

Communicative Disorders, Speech
Community Foundation of Jackson County Seymour
    Noon Lions Club Grant, 714
Hawaii Community Foundation Oscar and Rosetta
    Fish Fund Grants, 1214

Community Colleges
American Electric Power Corporate Grants, 252
GNOF New Orleans Works Grants, 1088
Kentucky Arts Cncl Access Assistance Grants, 1428
Olive Smith Browning Charitable Trust Grants, 1818
Perry and Sandy Massie Foundation Grants, 1941
Reinberger Foundation Grants, 2066
Suspended: Community Fdn for Greater Atlanta State
    Farm Education Assist Fund Grants, 2260
William and Flora Hewlett Foundation Education
    Grants, 2454

Community Development
2 Depot Square Ipswich Foundation Grants, 3
3M Company Foundation Health and Human
    Services Grants, 6

7-Eleven Corporate Giving Grants, 8
520 Charitable Foundation Grants, 14
A.C. and Penney Hubbard Foundation Grants, 19
A.L. Mailman Family Foundation Grants, 20
A.L. Spencer Foundation Grants, 21
AAUW International Project Grants, 44
Abbott Fund Access to Health Care Grants, 45
Abbott Fund Community Engagement Grants, 46
Abby's Legendary Pizza Foundation Grants, 49
ACCF Dennis and Melanie Bieberich Community
    Enrichment Fund Grants, 59
ACCF John and Kay Boch Fund Grants, 60
ACCF Marlene Bittner Memorial Community
    Enrichment Fund Grants, 61
ACCF of Indiana Anonymous Community
    Enrichment Fund Grants, 63
ACCF of Indiana Bank of Geneva Heritage Fund
    Grants, 64
ACCF of Indiana Berne Ready Mix Community
    Enrichment Fund Grants, 65
ACCF of Indiana First Merchants Bank / Decatur
    Bank and Trust Fund Grants, 66
ACCF of Indiana Michael Basham Community
    Enrichment Fund Grants, 67
ACCF Ralph Biggs Memorial Community
    Enrichment Fund Grants, 69
ACF Marriage Strengthening Research &
    Dissemination Center Grants, 85
ACF Social and Economic Development Strategies
    Grants, 93
Ackerman Foundation Grants, 103
ACL Alternatives to Guardianship Youth Resource
    Center Grants, 104
Adam Don Foundation Grants, 112
Adams Family Fdn of Nora Springs Grants, 118
Adams Family Foundation of Ohio Grants, 119
Adobe Fdn Community Investment Grants, 127
Agnes M. Lindsay Trust Grants, 140
Air Products Foundation Grants, 148
ALA Baker and Taylor Summer Reading Program
    Grant, 158
ALA Bookapalooza Grants, 161
ALA BWI Collection Development Grant, 164
ALA Coretta Scott King-John Steptoe Award for
    New Talent, 166
ALA Coretta Scott King-Virginia Hamilton Award
    for Lifetime Achievement, 167
ALA Scholastic Library Publishing Award, 192
Alaska Airlines Foundation LIFT Grants, 194
Alaska Community Foundation Cordova Community
    Foundation Grants, 201
Alaska Community Foundation Cordova Community
    Foundation Mini-Grants, 202
Alaska Community Foundation Jack and Nona Renn
    Anchorage Football Fund, 204
Alaska Community Foundation Kenai Peninsula
    Foundation Grant, 205
Alaska Community Foundation Ketchikan
    Community Foundation Grant, 206
Alaska Community Foundation Petersburg
    Community Foundation Annual Grant, 207
Alaska Community Foundation Petersburg
    Community Foundation Mini-Grants, 208
Alaska Community Foundation Seward Community
    Foundation Grant, 209
Alaska Conservation Fdn Youth Mini Grants, 210
ALA Sullivan Award for Public Library Admintrs
    Supporting Services to Children, 213
Albert and Ethel Herzstein Charitable Foundation
    Grants, 219
Alden and Vada Dow Fund Grants, 225
Alex Stern Family Foundation Grants, 229
Alfred J Mcallister and Dorothy N Mcallister
    Foundation Grants, 234
Alliance for Strong Families and Communities
    Grants, 239
Alliant Energy Foundation Community Giving for
    Good Sponsorship Grants, 240
Alloy Family Foundation Grants, 241
Ameren Corporation Community Grants, 251

American Indian Youth Running Strong Grants, 256
American Savings Foundation Capital Grants, 260
American Savings Foundation Program Grants, 261
Amerigroup Foundation Grants, 264
AMERIND Community Service Project Grants, 265
Amica Companies Foundation Grants, 266
Amica Insurance Company Sponsorships, 268
Anderson Foundation Grants, 271
Anheuser-Busch Foundation Grants, 273
APAP All-In Grants, 283
Appalachian Community Fund LGBTQ Fund
    Grants, 284
Appalachian Regional Commission Education and
    Training Grants, 286
Arizona State Library LSTA Community Grants, 296
Atlas Insurance Agency Foundation Grants, 329
Atwood Foundation General Grants, 330
Autauga Area Community Foundation Grants, 334
Babcock Charitable Trust Grants, 343
Ball Brothers Foundation Organizational
    Effectiveness/Executive Mentoring Grants, 346
Baltimore Community Foundation Building Stronger
    Neighborhoods Regionwide Grants, 347
Baltimore Community Foundation Mitzvah Fund for
    Good Deeds Grants, 349
Bank of America Charitable Foundation Community
    Development Grants, 355
Bank of America Charitable Foundation Matching
    Gifts, 356
Bank of America Charitable Foundation Student
    Leaders Grants, 357
Bank of America Corporation Sponsorships, 359
Bank of Hawaii Foundation Grants, 360
Barrasso, Usdin, Kupperman, Freeman, and Sarver
    Corporate Grants, 362
Baton Rouge Area Foundation Grants, 365
Batts Foundation Grants, 367
Bay Area Community Foundation Arenac
    Community Fund Grants, 371
Bay Area Community Fdn Auburn Area Chamber of
    Commerce Enrichment Fund Grants, 373
Bay Area Community Foundation Community
    Initiative Fund Grants, 376
Bay Area Community Foundation Human Services
    Fund Grants, 379
Baystate Financial Charitable Foundation Grants, 385
BCBSM Foundation Community Health Matching
    Grants, 392
Beckman Coulter Foundation Grants, 394
Bella Vista Fdn GSS Healthy Living Grants, 396
Ben B. Cheney Foundation Grants, 402
Benwood Foundation Community Grants, 406
Bernard and Audre Rapoport Foundation Arts and
    Culture Grants, 407
Bernard and Audre Rapoport Foundation Democracy
    and Civic Participation Grants, 409
Bernard and Audre Rapoport Foundation Health
    Grants, 411
Best Buy Children's Foundation @15 Community
    Grants , 414
Best Buy Children's Foundation Twin Cities
    Minnesota Capital Grants, 418
Bikes Belong Foundation Paul David Clark Bicycling
    Safety Grants, 422
Bikes Belong Grants, 424
Bill and Melinda Gates Foundation Agricultural
    Development Grants, 425
Biogen Foundation General Donations, 432
Blackford County Community Fdn Grants, 434
Black Hills Corporation Grants, 435
Blandin Foundation Invest Early Grants, 438
Blossom Fund Grants, 441
Blue Cross Blue Shield of Minnesota Fdn - Healthy
    Children: Growing Up Healthy Grants, 442
Blue Cross Blue Shield of Minnesota Foundation
    - Healthy Neighborhoods: Connect for Health
    Challenge Grants, 443
Blue Grass Community Foundation Clark County
    Fund Grants, 444

Blue Grass Community Foundation Fayette County Fund Grants, 446

Blue Grass Community Foundation Franklin County Fund Grants, 447

Blue Grass Community Foundation Harrison County Fund Grants, 448

Blue Grass Community Foundation Hudson-Ellis Grants, 449

Blue Grass Community Foundation Madison County Fund Grants, 450

Blue Grass Community Foundation Magoffin County Fund Grants, 451

Blue Grass Community Foundation Morgan County Fund Grants, 452

Blue Grass Community Foundation Rowan County Fund Grants, 453

Blue Grass Community Foundation Woodford County Fund Grants, 454

Blue Mountain Community Foundation Discretionary Grants, 455

Blumenthal Foundation Grants, 459

Boeing Company Contributions Grants, 462

Bollinger Foundation Grants, 463

BP Foundation Grants, 465

Bradley C. Higgins Foundation Grants, 467

Brian G. Dyson Foundation Grants, 468

Bridgestone Americas Trust Fund Grants, 469

Brinker Int Corporation Charitable Giving, 471

Brunswick Foundation Dollars for Doers Grants, 478

Bryan Adams Foundation Grants, 480

Burlington Industries Foundation Grants, 481

Burton D. Morgan Foundation Hudson Community Grants, 482

Bush Foundation Event Sponsorships, 485

C.F. Adams Charitable Trust Grants, 488

California Endowment Innovative Ideas Challenge Grants, 495

Callaway Foundation Grants, 496

Cal Ripken Sr. Foundation Grants, 497

Campbell Soup Foundation Grants, 501

Caring for Colorado Foundation Sperry S. and Ella Graber Packard Fund for Pueblo Grants, 505

Carl B. and Florence E. King Foundation Grants, 506

Carl M. Freeman Foundation FACES Grants, 507

Carl M. Freeman Foundation Grants, 508

Carroll County Community Foundation Grants, 513

Case Foundation Grants, 514

Cash 4 Clubs Sports Grants, 515

Cass County Community Foundation Grants, 516

Castle Foundation Grants, 517

CCFF Community Grant, 523

CFFVR Basic Needs Giving Partnership Grants, 537

CFFVR Clintonville Area Foundation Grants, 539

CFFVR Clintonville Area Foundation Grants, 538

CFFVR Environmental Stewardship Grants, 540

CFFVR Frank C. Shattuck Community Grants, 541

CFFVR Infant Welfare Circle of Kings Daughters Grants, 542

CFFVR Mielke Family Foundation Grants, 544

CFFVR Myra M. and Robert L. Vandehey Foundation Grants, 545

CFFVR Project Grants, 546

CFFVR Robert and Patricia Endries Family Foundation Grants, 547

CFFVR Schmidt Family G4 Grants, 548

CFFVR Shawano Area Community Foundation Grants, 549

CFFVR Women's Fund for the Fox Valley Region Grants, 550

CFF Winter Park Community Grants, 551

CFGR Community Impact Grants, 552

CFNEM Youth Advisory Council Grants, 558

Charles Delmar Foundation Grants, 564

CHC Foundation Grants, 575

Cheryl Spencer Memorial Foundation Grants, 576

Chesapeake Bay Trust Environmental Education Grants, 577

Chesapeake Bay Trust Outreach and Community Engagement Grants, 579

Chilkat Valley Community Foundation Grants, 588

CICF Summer Youth Grants, 608

Cincinnati Milacron Foundation Grants, 613

Circle K Corporation Contributions Grants, 614

Citizens Savings Foundation Grants, 617

Claremont Savings Bank Foundation Grants, 623

Clarence T.C. Ching Foundation Grants, 624

Clark County Community Foundation Grants, 626

Cleveland Fdn Lake-Geauga Fund Grants, 635

Cleveland Foundation Legacy Village Lyndhurst Community Fund Grants, 636

Clinton County Community Foundation Grants, 638

CNCS AmeriCorps Indian Tribes Plang Grts, 641

CNCS AmeriCorps State and National Grants, 643

CNCS AmeriCorps VISTA Project Grants, 645

CNCS Social Innovation Grants, 649

Colorado Health Foundation Family, Friend and Neighbor Caregiver Supports Grants, 660

Community Foundation for Greater Atlanta Managing For Excellence Award, 665

Community Foundation for Greater Atlanta Metropolitan Extra Wish Grants, 666

Community Foundation for Greater Atlanta Spark Clayton Grants, 667

Community Foundation for Greater Atlanta Spark Newton Grants, 668

Community Foundation for Greater Atlanta Strategic Restructuring Fund Grants, 669

Community Foundation for Greater Buffalo Competitive Grants, 670

Community Foundation for Greater Buffalo Ralph C. Wilson, Jr. Legacy Fund Grants, 674

Community Foundation for Kettering Grants, 676

Community Foundation for San Benito County Grants, 677

Community Foundation for SE Michigan Chelsea Community Fdn Capacity Building Grants, 679

Community Foundation for SE Michigan Chelsea Community Foundation General Grant, 680

Community Foundation for SE Michigan Youth Leadership Grant, 686

Community Foundation for the National Capital Region Community Leadership Grants, 688

Community Foundation of Boone County Grants, 694

Community Foundation of Grant County Grants, 703

Community Foundation of Greater Fort Wayne - John S. and James L. Knight Foundation Donor-Advised Grants, 707

Community Foundation of Greater Greensboro Community Grants, 708

Community Foundation of Greater Greensboro Teen Grantmaking Council Grants, 709

Community Fdn of Howard County Grants, 712

Community Foundation of Jackson Hole Youth Philanthropy Grants, 715

Community Foundation of Louisville Anna Marble Memorial Fund for Princeton Grants, 717

Community Foundation of Louisville Boyette and Edna Edwards Fund Grants, 718

Community Foundation of Louisville We Day Kentucky Grants, 728

Community Foundation of Louisville Youth Philanthropy Council Grants, 730

Community Foundation of Madison and Jefferson County Grants, 731

Community Fdn of Morgan County Grants, 732

Community Foundation of Muncie and Delaware County Maxon Grants, 734

Community Fdn of Randolph County Grants, 735

Community Fdn of Southern Indiana Grants, 736

Community Foundation of St. Joseph County Special Project Challenge Grants, 738

Community Foundation of Switzerland County Grants, 739

Community Fdn of Wabash County Grants, 740

Courtney S. Turner Charitable Trust Grants, 753

Covidien Partnership for Neighborhood Wellness Grants, 759

Cralle Foundation Grants, 760

Crane Fund Grants, 763

D. W. McMillan Foundation Grants, 776

Daniels Fund Amateur Sports Grants, 779

David Alan and Susan Berkman Rahm Foundation Grants, 785

David and Laura Merage Foundation Grants, 789

David M. and Marjorie D. Rosenberg Foundation Grants, 790

Daviess County Community Foundation Recreation Grants, 793

Dayton Power and Light Company Foundation Signature Grants, 801

Deaconess Foundation Advocacy Grants, 804

Dean Foundation Grants, 806

Dearborn Community Foundation City of Lawrenceburg Community Grants, 809

Dearborn Community Foundation City of Lawrenceburg Youth Grants, 810

Decatur County Community Foundation Large Project Grants, 811

Decatur County Community Foundation Small Project Grants, 812

DeKalb County Community Foundation Grants, 815

Delaware Community Foundation Grants, 817

Del Mar Foundation Community Grants, 820

Delta Air Lines Foundation Community Enrichment Grants, 823

Dermody Properties Fdn Capstone Award, 826

DTE Energy Foundation Community Development Grants, 866

DTE Energy Foundation Diversity Grants, 867

DTE Energy Foundation Leadership Grants, 870

Dyson Foundation Mid-Hudson Valley Project Support Grants, 874

E. Clayton and Edith P. Gengras, Jr. Foundation Grants, 875

Eastern Bank Charitable Foundation Partnerships Grants, 881

Eastern Bank Charitable Foundation Targeted Grants, 882

Edward and Ellen Roche Relief Fdn Grants, 887

Edward F. Swinney Trust Grants, 890

Edward W. and Stella C. Van Houten Memorial Fund Grants, 892

Edyth Bush Charitable Foundation Grants, 893

Elkhart County Community Foundation Fund for Elkhart County, 902

Elkhart County Community Foundation Grants, 903

Ella West Freeman Foundation Grants, 904

Ellen Abbott Gilman Trust Grants, 905

Elmer Roe Deaver Foundation Grants, 906

El Pomar Foundation Anna Keesling Ackerman Fund Grants, 907

El Pomar Foundation Grants, 908

Elsie H. Wilcox Foundation Grants, 909

Emily O'Neill Sullivan Foundation Grants, 913

Ensworth Charitable Foundation Grants, 916

Entergy Corporation Micro Grants, 919

Entergy Corporation Open Grants for Arts and Culture, 920

Entergy Corporation Open Grants for Healthy Families, 921

EQT Fdn Community Enrichment Grants, 926

Essex County Community Foundation Greater Lawrence Summer Fund Grants, 932

Essex County Community Foundation Merrimack Valley Municipal Business Development and Recovery Fund Grants, 933

Ethel Sergeant Clark Smith Foundation Grants, 935

Evelyn and Walter Haas, Jr. Fund Nonprofit Leadership Grants, 942

Faye L. and William L. Cowden Charitable Foundation Grants, 950

Fayette County Foundation Grants, 951

Fidelity Foundation Grants, 957

Fifth Third Bank Corporate Giving, 958

Fifth Third Foundation Grants, 959

FirstEnergy Foundation Community Grants, 965

First Hawaiian Bank Foundation Corporate Giving Grants, 967

Florence Foundation Grants, 978

Ford Family Foundation Grants - Positive Youth Development, 982
Ford Family Foundation Grants - Technical Assistance , 983
Forest Foundation Grants, 985
Foundation for Appalachian Ohio Access to Environmental Education Mini-Grants, 989
Foundation of Herkimer and Oneida Counties Youth Sports, Wellness and Recreation Mini-Grants, 994
Foundations of East Chicago Education Grants, 995
Four County Community Foundation General Grants, 1000
Four County Community Foundation Healthy Senior/Healthy Youth Fund Grants, 1001
Fourjay Foundation Grants, 1003
Franklin County Community Fdn Grants, 1010
Franklin H. Wells and Ruth L. Wells Foundation Grants, 1011
Frederick McDonald Trust Grants, 1017
Fremont Area Community Foundation Amazing X Grants, 1019
Fremont Area Community Foundation Community Grants, 1020
Friedman Family Foundation Grants, 1023
Fuller Foundation Youth At Risk Grants, 1028
Fund for the City of New York Grants, 1029
Gamble Foundation Grants, 1032
Gannett Foundation Community Action Grants, 1033
Gardner Foundation Grants, 1034
GCI Corporate Contributions Grants, 1037
Gene Haas Foundation, 1038
George A. & Grace L. Long Fdn Grants, 1041
George A Ohl Jr. Foundation Grants, 1043
George B. Page Foundation Grants, 1044
George Graham and Elizabeth Galloway Smith Foundation Grants, 1047
George H. Sandy Foundation Grants, 1050
George Kress Foundation Grants, 1053
George W.P. Magee Trust Grants, 1056
Gertrude & William C. Wardlaw Grants, 1067
GNOF Bayou Communities Grants, 1077
GNOF Cox Charities of New Orleans Grants, 1079
GNOF Exxon-Mobil Grants, 1080
GNOF Gert Community Fund Grants, 1082
GNOF IMPACT Grants for Arts and Culture, 1083
GNOF New Orleans Works Grants, 1088
GNOF Norco Community Grants, 1089
Graham Foundation Grants, 1101
Greater Milwaukee Foundation Grants, 1109
Greater Saint Louis Community Fdn Grants, 1110
Greater Sitka Legacy Fund Grants, 1111
Green River Area Community Fdn Grants, 1117
Gregory and Helayne Brown Charitable Foundation Grants, 1119
Griffin Family Foundation Grants, 1121
Grundy Foundation Grants, 1124
GTRCF Elk Rapids Area Community Endowment Grants, 1127
GTRCF Joan Rajkovich McGarry Family Education Endowment Grants, 1131
Gulf Coast Foundation of Community Operating Grants, 1134
Gulf Coast Foundation of Community Program Grants, 1135
H.B. Fuller Foundation Grants, 1138
HAF Community Grants, 1141
HAF Don and Bettie Albright Endowment Fund Grants, 1142
HAF Joe Alexandre Mem Family Fund Grants, 1145
HAF Laurence and Elaine Allen Memorial Fund Grants, 1146
HAF Southern Humboldt Grants, 1150
Hampton Roads Community Foundation Community Leadership Partners Grants, 1155
Hannaford Charitable Foundation Grants, 1163
Hannaford Supermarkets Community Giving, 1164
Hardin County Community Foundation Grants, 1167
Harmony Grove Foundation Grants, 1169
Harold and Rebecca H. Gross Fdn Grants, 1171

Harold K.L. Castle Foundation Strengthening Windward Oahu Communities Grants, 1174
Harris Foundation Grants, 1177
Harrison County Community Foundation Signature Grants, 1179
Harry B. and Jane H. Brock Foundation Grants, 1183
Hartford Foundation Regular Grants, 1185
Hattie Mae Lesley Foundation Grants, 1195
Hawai'i Community Foundation Children's Trust Fund Community Awareness: Child Abuse and Neglect Prevention Grants, 1198
Hawai'i Community Foundation East Hawaii Fund Grants, 1199
Hawai'i Community Foundation Ewa Beach Community Trust Fund Grants, 1200
Hawai'i Community Foundation Lana'i Community Benefit Fund, 1203
Hawaiian Electric Industries Charitable Foundation Grants, 1211
Hawaii Community Foundation Omidyar Ohana Fund Grants, 1213
Hawaii Community Foundation Reverend Takie Okumura Family Grants, 1216
Hawaii Community Foundation Sanford Harmony Pillars of Peace Grants, 1217
Hawaii Electric Industries Charitable Foundation Grants, 1218
Hawaii State Legislature Grant-In-Aid, 1219
Helen Bader Foundation Grants, 1227
Hendricks County Community Fdn Grants, 1234
Henry County Community Foundation Grants, 1239
Henry F. Koch Residual Trust Grants, 1241
Highmark Corporate Giving Grants, 1248
Hill Crest Foundation Grants, 1249
Hillsdale County Community Foundation General Grants, 1250
Hillsdale County Community Foundation Love Your Community Grants, 1251
HLTA Visitor Industry Charity Walk Grant, 1254
Honor the Earth Grants, 1259
Horace A. Kimball and S. Ella Kimball Foundation Grants, 1260
HRAMF Community Health Improvement Project Grants in Bowdoin Geneva, 1263
Hubbard Family Foundation Grants, 1271
Humana Foundation Grants, 1275
Huntington Clinical Foundation Grants, 1278
Huntington County Community Foundation Make a Difference Grants, 1280
Iddings Foundation Capital Project Grants, 1283
Iddings Foundation Major Project Grants, 1284
Iddings Foundation Medium Project Grants, 1285
Iddings Foundation Small Project Grants, 1286
Ifuku Family Foundation Grants, 1287
Ike and Roz Friedman Foundation Grants, 1289
Indiana OCRA Quick Impact Placebased (QuIP) Grants, 1300
ING Foundation Grants, 1302
Initiative Foundation Innovation Fund Grants, 1304
Initiative Foundation Minnesota Early Childhood Initiative Grants, 1305
Intel Corporation Community Grants, 1311
Intel Corporation Int Community Grants, 1312
Irving S. Gilmore Foundation Grants, 1314
Isabel Allende Foundation Esperanza Grants, 1315
Island Insurance Foundation Grants, 1316
J. Bulow Campbell Foundation Grants, 1319
J. Edwin Treakle Foundation Grants, 1320
J. Knox Gholston Foundation Grants, 1321
J. Marion Sims Foundation Teachers' Pet Grant, 1322
J.W. Gardner II Foundation Grants, 1323
J.W. Kieckhefer Foundation Grants, 1324
J. Willard and Alice S. Marriott Fdn Grants, 1327
Jack and Dorothy Byrne Foundation Grants, 1329
Jacob G. Schmidlapp Trusts Grants, 1336
James and Abigail Campbell Family Foundation Grants, 1337
James F. and Marion L. Miller Fdn Grants, 1338
James Ford Bell Foundation Grants, 1339
James Graham Brown Foundation Grants, 1340

James Lee Sorenson Family Impact Foundation Grants, 1342
James S. Copley Foundation Grants, 1345
Jane's Trust Grants, 1346
Jane Bradley Pettit Foundation Community and Social Development Grants, 1347
Janet Spencer Weekes Foundation Grants, 1348
Jennings County Community Fdn Grants, 1360
Jessica Stevens Community Foundation Grants, 1363
Joan Bentinck-Smith Charitable Fdn Grants, 1367
John G. Duncan Charitable Trust Grants, 1372
John H. and Wilhelmina D. Harland Charitable Foundation Community Services Grants, 1375
John P. Ellbogen Fdn Community Grants, 1377
Johnson County Community Fdn Grants, 1379
Johnson County Community Foundation Youth Philanthropy Initiative Grants, 1380
John W. Anderson Foundation Grants, 1383
Joseph Henry Edmondson Foundation Grants, 1388
Josephine Schell Russell Chartbl Trust Grants, 1389
Joseph S. Stackpole Charitable Trust Grants, 1390
Journal Gazette Foundation Grants, 1391
JP Morgan Chase Fdn Arts and Culture Grants, 1394
Judith Clark-Morrill Foundation Grants, 1395
KaBOOM! Adventure Courses Grant, 1401
KaBOOM! Build it Grant, 1402
KaBOOM! Creative Play Grant, 1403
KaBOOM! Multi-Sport Courts Grant, 1404
Kalamazoo Community Foundation John E. Fetzer Institute Fund Grants, 1410
Katharine Matthies Foundation Grants, 1418
Katie's Krops Grants, 1421
Kenai Peninsula Foundation Grants, 1425
Ketchikan Community Foundation Grants, 1429
Kind World Foundation Grants, 1438
Koch Family Foundation (Annapolis) Grants, 1444
Kodak Community Relations Grants, 1445
Kodiak Community Foundation Grants, 1446
Kosciusko County Community Fdn Grants, 1452
Kosciusko County Community Foundation REMC Operation Round Up Grants, 1453
Laclede Gas Charitable Trust Grants, 1457
LaGrange Independent Foundation for Endowments (L.I.F.E.), 1459
Laidlaw Foundation Youh Organizing Catalyst Grants, 1461
Laidlaw Foundation Youth Organizaing Initiatives Grants, 1462
Lake County Community Fund Grants, 1463
Land O'Lakes Fdn California Region Grants, 1465
Land O'Lakes Foundation Community Grants, 1466
Lands' End Corporate Giving Program, 1468
Laura Musser Intercultural Harmony Grants, 1472
Lee and Ramona Bass Foundation Grants, 1478
Legler Benbough Foundation Grants, 1479
Leo Niessen Jr., Charitable Trust Grants, 1484
Lewis H. Humphreys Charitable Trust Grants, 1486
LGA Family Foundation Grants, 1487
Liberty Bank Foundation Grants, 1488
LISC Affordable Housing Grants, 1497
LISC Capacity Building Grants, 1498
LISC Community Leadership Operating Grts, 1499
LISC Financial Stability Grants, 1501
Long Island Community Foundation Grants, 1507
Lotus 88 Foundation for Women and Children Grants, 1508
Louie M. and Betty M. Phillips Fdn Grants, 1509
Louis Calder Foundation Grants, 1511
Lubrizol Corporation Community Grants, 1512
Lumpkin Family Foundation Strong Community Leadership Grants, 1519
Mabel A. Horne Fund Grants, 1525
Mabel F. Hoffman Charitable Trust Grants, 1526
Mabel Louise Riley Foundation Family Strengthening Small Grants, 1528
Mabel Louise Riley Foundation Grants, 1529
Mabel Y. Hughes Charitable Trust Grants, 1530
Madison Community Foundation Grants, 1535
Madison County Community Foundation General Grants, 1537

Maine Community Foundation Edward H. Daveis Benevolent Fund Grants, 1540
Maine Community Fdn Peaks Island Grants, 1542
Marathon Petroleum Corporation Grants, 1551
Margaret M. Walker Charitable Fdn Grants, 1556
Marie C. and Joseph C. Wilson Foundation Rochester Small Grants, 1559
Marin Community Foundation Affordable Housing Grants, 1561
Marin Community Foundation Ending the Cycle of Poverty Grants, 1565
Marin Community Foundation Social Justice and Interfaith Understanding Grants, 1567
Marin Community Foundation Stinson Bolinas Community Grants, 1568
Marion Gardner Jackson Charitable Trust Grts, 1570
Marisla Foundation Human Services Grants, 1573
Marquette Bank Neighborhood Commit Grants, 1577
Marshall County Community Fdn Grants, 1579
Marsh Corporate Grants, 1580
Martin Family Foundation Grants, 1583
Mary E. Babcock Foundation, 1589
MassMutual Foundation Edonomic Development Grants, 1603
Matson Adahi I Tano' Grants, 1606
Matson Community Giving Grants, 1607
Matson Ka Ipu 'Aina Grants, 1608
Max and Anna Levinson Foundation Grants, 1612
McConnell Foundation Grants, 1616
McCune Charitable Foundation Grants, 1617
MeadWestvaco Foundation Sustainable Communities Grants, 1627
Medtronic Foundation Community Link Arts, Civic, and Culture Grants, 1629
Merck Family Fund Youth Transforming Urban Communities Grants, 1636
Merrick Foundation Grants, 1639
Merrick Foundation Grants, 1640
Mertz Gilmore Foundation NYC Communities Grants, 1641
Mervin Bovaird Foundation Grants, 1643
Metzger-Price Fund Grants, 1647
Meyer Fdn Management Assistance Grants, 1651
Meyer Memorial Trust Responsive Grants, 1653
MFRI Community Mobilization Grants, 1654
MGM Resorts Foundation Community Grants, 1655
Micron Technology Fdn Community Grants, 1664
Mid-Iowa Health Foundation Community Response Grants, 1667
Middlesex Savings Charitable Foundation Basic Human Needs Grants, 1668
Middlesex Savings Charitable Foundation Educational Opportunities Grants, 1670
MLB Tomorrow Fund Grants, 1679
Montgomery County Community Foundation Health and Human Services Fund Grants, 1689
Moody Foundation Grants, 1692
Motiv8 Foundation Grants, 1702
Ms. Foundation for Women Building Democracy Grants, 1706
Natalie W. Furniss Foundation Grants, 1715
Nathalie and Gladys Dalkowitz Charitable Trust Grants, 1716
NCMCF Youth Advisory Council Grants, 1727
Nestle Purina PetCare Educational Grants, 1738
Nevada Community Foundation Grants, 1741
New Earth Foundation Grants, 1743
New Hampshire Charitable Foundation Community Unrestricted Grants, 1747
New Hampshire Charitable Foundation Neil and Louise Tillotson Fund - Empower Coös Youth Grants, 1748
New York Foundation Grants, 1753
NFL Charities NFL Player Foundation Grants, 1754
Nissan Neighbors Grants, 1762
Noble County Community Foundation Grants, 1765
Northern Chautauqua Community Foundation Community Grants, 1769
NYSCA Arts Education: Community-based Learning Grants, 1780

NYSCA Arts Education: Local Capacity Building Grants (Regrants), 1783
NZDIA Community Org Grants Scheme, 1796
O. Max Gardner Foundation Grants, 1798
OceanFirst Foundation Major Grants, 1803
Office Depot Corporation Community Relations Grants, 1805
Ohio County Community Foundation Board of Directors Grants, 1811
Ohio County Community Foundation Grants, 1812
Ohio County Community Fdn Mini-Grants, 1813
Ohio Valley Foundation Grants, 1814
Olive Smith Browning Charitable Trust Grants, 1818
Olivia R. Gardner Foundation Grants, 1819
Oregon Community Fdn Community Grants, 1833
OSF Baltimore Community Fellowships, 1838
Packard Foundation Local Grants, 1863
Parke County Community Foundation Grants, 1868
Parker Foundation (California) Grants, 1869
Parkersburg Area Community Foundation Action Grants, 1871
Paul and Edith Babson Foundation Grants, 1881
PCA Arts Organizations and Arts Programs Grants for Local Arts, 1895
PCA Entry Track Arts Organizations and Arts Programs Grants for Local Arts, 1907
Pentair Foundation Education and Community Grants, 1934
Percy B. Ferebee Endowment Grants, 1936
Perkins Charitable Foundation Grants, 1939
Petersburg Community Foundation Grants, 1951
Pettus Foundation Grants, 1952
PG&E Community Vitality Grants, 1957
Piedmont Health Foundation Grants, 1965
Piedmont Natural Gas Corporate and Charitable Contributions, 1966
Pinnacle Entertainment Foundation Grants, 1972
Piper Trust Reglious Organizations Grants, 1979
PNC Foundation Community Services Grants, 1984
PNC Foundation Grow Up Great Early Childhood Grants, 1986
Pohlad Family Fdn Large Capital Grants, 1990
Polk County Community Foundation Bradley Breakthrough Community Benefit Grants, 1995
Polk County Community Foundation Free Community Events Grants, 1996
Polk County Community Foundation Marjorie M. and Lawrence R. Bradley Endowment Fund Grants, 1998
Polk County Community Foundation Mary F. Kessler Fund Grants, 1999
Polk County Community Foundation Unrestricted Grants, 2001
Portland General Electric Foundation Grants, 2007
Posey Community Foundation Women's Fund Grants, 2008
PPCF Community Grants, 2014
PPG Industries Foundation Grants, 2017
Priddy Foundation Operating Grants, 2021
Priddy Foundation Organizational Development Grants, 2022
Priddy Foundation Program Grants, 2023
PSEG Corporate Contributions Grants, 2030
Puerto Rico Community Foundation Grants, 2037
Pulaski County Community Foundation Grants, 2038
Putnam County Community Fdn Grants, 2040
Raskob Fdn for Catholic Activities Grants, 2054
Rasmuson Foundation Tier One Grants, 2055
Rasmuson Foundation Tier Two Grants, 2056
RCF General Community Grants, 2062
RCF Individual Assistance Grants, 2063
Ressler-Gertz Foundation Grants, 2067
Richard J. Stern Foundation for the Arts Grants, 2071
Richland County Bank Grants, 2074
Riedman Foundation Grants, 2076
Ripley County Community Foundation Grants, 2077
Ripley County Community Foundation Small Project Grants, 2078
Robbins Charitable Foundation Grants, 2081
Robbins Family Charitable Foundation Grants, 2082

Robert Lee Blaffer Foundation Grants, 2092
Robert R. Meyer Foundation Grants, 2094
Ron and Sanne Higgins Family Fdn Grants, 2101
Roy J. Carver Charitable Trust Youth Services and Recreation Grants, 2117
RR Donnelley Foundation Grants, 2118
Rush County Community Foundation Grants, 2121
Ruth Anderson Foundation Grants, 2122
S. Spencer Scott Fund Grants, 2129
Sabina Dolan and Gladys Saulsbury Foundation Grants, 2130
Saeman Family Fdn A Charitable Grants, 2133
Saginaw Community Foundation Discretionary Grants, 2134
Saginaw County Community Foundation Youth FORCE Grants, 2136
Samuel S. Johnson Foundation Grants, 2146
San Antonio Area Foundation Special and Urgent Needs Funding Grants, 2150
Sand Hill Fdn Small Capital Needs Grants, 2154
Sarkeys Foundation Grants, 2163
Sartain Lanier Family Foundation Grants, 2164
Schramm Foundation Grants, 2168
Scott County Community Foundation Grants, 2170
Seattle Foundation Benjamin N. Phillips Memorial Fund Grants, 2176
Seattle Foundation C. Keith Birkenfeld Memorial Trust Grants, 2177
Seattle Foundation Health and Wellness Grants, 2179
Sensient Technologies Foundation Grants, 2180
Serco Foundation Grants, 2181
Seward Community Foundation Grants, 2182
Seward Community Foundation Mini-Grants, 2183
Shell Deer Park Grants, 2186
Shell Oil Company Foundation Community Development Grants, 2188
Shield-Ayres Foundation Grants, 2189
Shopko Foundation Green Bay Area Community Grants, 2192
Sidgmore Family Foundation Grants, 2195
Sidney Stern Memorial Trust Grants, 2197
Siebert Lutheran Foundation Grants, 2198
Sierra Health Foundation Responsive Grants, 2199
Simpson Lumber Charitable Contributions, 2201
Sioux Falls Area Community Foundation Community Fund Grants, 2203
Sioux Falls Area Community Foundation Spot Grants, 2204
Smith Richardson Fdn Direct Service Grants, 2210
Sobrato Family Foundation Grants, 2211
Sobrato Family Fdn Meeting Space Grants, 2212
Sobrato Family Foundation Office Space Grants, 2213
Sorenson Legacy Foundation Grants, 2217
Southern Minnesota Initiative Foundation AmeriCorps Leap Grants, 2219
Southern Minnesota Initiative Foundation Community Growth Initiative Grants, 2221
Southern Minnesota Initiative Foundation Home Visiting Grants, 2222
Southern Minnesota Initiative Foundation Incentive Grants, 2223
Southwest Initiative Foundation Grants, 2226
Speer Trust Grants, 2230
Spencer County Community Foundation Women's Fund Grants, 2232
Starke County Community Foundation Grants, 2236
Sterling and Shelli Gardner Foundation Grants, 2243
Steven B. Achelis Foundation Grants, 2244
Stillson Foundation Grants, 2245
Stocker Foundation Grants, 2247
Storm Castle Foundation Grants, 2248
Stranahan Foundation Grants, 2250
Strong Foundation Grants, 2252
Summit Foundation Grants, 2255
Suspened: Community Fdn for Greater Atlanta State Farm Education Assist Fund Grants, 2260
Sylvia Perkin Perpetual Charitable Trust Grants, 2263
TAC Arts Access Grant, 2265
Target Foundation Global Grants, 2272
TE Foundation Grants, 2279

Telluride Foundation Community Grants, 2281
Tension Envelope Foundation Grants, 2284
Thelma Braun and Bocklett Family Foundation
  Grants, 2287
Thomas and Agnes Carvel Foundation Grants, 2289
Thomas J. Atkins Memorial Trust Fund Grants, 2290
Threshold Fdn Justice and Democracy Grants, 2298
Toyota Motor Manuf of Alabama Grants, 2309
Toyota Motor Manufacturing of Indiana Grants, 2310
Toyota Motor Manuf of Kentucky Grants, 2311
Toyota Motor Manuf of Mississippi Grants, 2312
Toyota Motor Manufacturing of West Virginia
  Grants, 2314
Toyota Motor North America of NY Grants, 2315
Toyota Motor Sales, USA Grants, 2316
Toyota Technical Center Grants, 2317
Turner Foundation Grants, 2326
Turtle Bay Foundation Grants, 2327
Twenty-First Century Foundation Grants, 2328
U.S. Department of Education Promise
  Neighborhoods Grants, 2332
Union Bank, N.A. Corporate Sponsorships and
  Donations, 2333
Union Bank, N.A. Foundation Grants, 2334
Union Square Award for Social Justice, 2340
UPS Corporate Giving Grants, 2349
UPS Foundation Community Safety Grants, 2350
Vanderburgh Community Foundation Men's Fund
  Grants, 2373
Vanderburgh County Community Foundation
  Women's Fund Grants, 2376
Vermillion County Community Fdn Grants, 2378
Victoria S. and Bradley L. Geist Foundation
  Enhancement Grants, 2381
Victoria S. and Bradley L. Geist Foundation Grants
  Supporting Foster Care and Their Caregivers, 2382
Vigneron Memorial Fund Grants, 2384
Walker Area Community Foundation Grants, 2401
Wallace Foundation Grants, 2402
Walmart Fdn Inclusive Communities Grants, 2403
Walmart Fdn National Local Giving Grants, 2404
Walmart Foundation State Giving Grants, 2405
Walter S. and Evan C. Jones Testam Trust, 2407
Warrick County Community Foundation Women's
  Fund, 2411
Wayne County Foundation Grants, 2419
Wells County Foundation Grants, 2426
Western Indiana Community Fdn Grants, 2428
Western New York Foundation Grants, 2429
West Virginia Commission on the Arts Challenge
  America Partnership Grants, 2430
White County Community Foundation - Women
  Giving Together Grants, 2438
WHO Foundation Education/Literacy Grants, 2442
William A. Badger Foundation Grants, 2451
William A. Miller Foundation Grants, 2453
William Blair and Company Foundation Grants, 2461
William E. Barth Foundation Grants, 2463
William E. Dean III Charitable Fdn Grants, 2464
William Foulds Family Foundation Grants, 2465
William G. and Helen C. Hoffman Grants, 2466
William G. Gilmore Foundation Grants, 2467
William J. and Dorothy K. O'Neill Foundation
  Responsive Grants, 2468
William M. Weaver Foundation Grants, 2472
Williams Comps Homegrown Giving Grants, 2474
WinnCompanies Charitable Giving, 2479
Wiregrass Foundation Grants, 2480
Wood Family Charitable Trust Grants, 2487
Wyoming Community Foundation COVID-19
  Response and Recovery Grants, 2500
Wyoming Community Fdn General Grants, 2501
Wyoming Community Foundation Hazel Patterson
  Memorial Grants, 2502
Wyomissing Foundation Community Grants, 2504
Wyomissing Foundation Thun Family Organizational
  Grants, 2505
Wyomissing Foundation Thun Family Grants, 2506
Xerox Foundation Grants, 2507
YSA MLK Day Lead Organizer Grants, 2516

Community Education
ACCF of Indiana Anonymous Community
  Enrichment Fund Grants, 63
ACF Social and Economic Development Strategies
  Grants, 93
Adams Family Fdn of Nora Springs Grants, 118
AEGON Transamerica Foundation Education and
  Financial Literacy Grants, 132
Akron Community Fdn Education Grants, 151
ALA Sara Jaffarian School Library Award for
  Exemplary Humanities Programming, 190
Alaska Community Foundation Ketchikan
  Community Foundation Grant, 206
Alaska Community Foundation Petersburg
  Community Foundation Annual Grant, 207
Alaska Community Foundation Petersburg
  Community Foundation Mini-Grants, 208
Alaska Community Foundation Seward Community
  Foundation Grant, 209
ALA Sullivan Award for Public Library Admintrs
  Supporting Services to Children, 213
American Indian Youth Running Strong Grants, 256
ATA Local Community Relations Grants, 324
Atlas Insurance Agency Foundation Grants, 329
Autauga Area Community Foundation Grants, 334
Baltimore Community Foundation Mitzvah Fund for
  Good Deeds Grants, 349
Bay Area Community Foundation Arenac
  Community Fund Grants, 371
Beckman Coulter Foundation Grants, 394
Bella Vista Fdn GSS Healthy Living Grants, 396
Ben B. Cheney Foundation Grants, 402
Bernard and Audre Rapoport Foundation Democracy
  and Civic Participation Grants, 409
Best Buy Children's Foundation @15 Community
  Grants , 414
Bill and Melinda Gates Foundation Agricultural
  Development Grants, 425
Blackford County Community Fdn Grants, 434
BP Foundation Grants, 465
Bright Promises Foundation Grants, 470
Brunswick Foundation Dollars for Doers Grants, 478
Bush Foundation Event Sponsorships, 485
California Endowment Innovative Ideas Challenge
  Grants, 495
Camille Beckman Foundation Grants, 499
CCFF Community Grant, 523
CFF Winter Park Community Grants, 551
CFNEM Youth Advisory Council Grants, 558
Citizens Savings Foundation Grants, 617
CJ Fdn for SIDS Program Services Grants, 619
Community Foundation for Greater Atlanta Spark
  Clayton Grants, 667
Community Foundation for Greater Atlanta Spark
  Newton Grants, 668
Community Foundation for SE Michigan Chelsea
  Community Fdn Capacity Building Grants, 679
Community Foundation for SE Michigan Chelsea
  Community Foundation General Grant, 680
Community Foundation of Eastern Connecticut
  Norwich Youth Grants, 699
Community Foundation of Greater Fort Wayne -
  John S. and James L. Knight Foundation Donor-
  Advised Grants, 707
Community Foundation of Louisville Education
  Grants, 724
Community Foundation of Louisville We Day
  Kentucky Grants, 728
Courtney S. Turner Charitable Trust Grants, 753
Crane Fund Grants, 763
David and Laura Merage Foundation Grants, 789
Deaconess Foundation Advocacy Grants, 804
Dean Foundation Grants, 806
Del Mar Foundation Community Grants, 820
Delta Air Lines Foundation Community Enrichment
  Grants, 823
E. Clayton and Edith P. Gengras, Jr. Foundation
  Grants, 875
Edward F. Swinney Trust Grants, 890
Ella West Freeman Foundation Grants, 904

Elmer Roe Deaver Foundation Grants, 906
EQT Fdn Community Enrichment Grants, 926
Essex County Community Foundation Greater
  Lawrence Community Fund Grants, 931
Evelyn and Walter Haas, Jr. Fund Education
  Opportunities Grants, 939
Evelyn and Walter Haas, Jr. Fund Nonprofit
  Leadership Grants, 942
Fifth Third Bank Corporate Giving, 958
First Hawaiian Bank Foundation Corporate Giving
  Grants, 967
Four County Community Foundation General
  Grants, 1000
Four County Community Foundation Healthy
  Senior/Healthy Youth Fund Grants, 1001
Fremont Area Community Foundation Education
  Mini-Grants, 1021
George H. Sandy Foundation Grants, 1050
Georgia-Pacific Foundation Education Grants, 1058
GTRCF Joan Rajkovich McGarry Family Education
  Endowment Grants, 1131
HAF Don and Bettie Albright Endowment Fund
  Grants, 1142
HAF Joe Alexandre Mem Family Fund Grants, 1145
HAF Laurence and Elaine Allen Memorial Fund
  Grants, 1146
Harris Foundation Grants, 1177
Hawaii Electric Industries Charitable Foundation
  Grants, 1218
Hawaii State Legislature Grant-In-Aid, 1219
Helen Bader Foundation Grants, 1227
Henry F. Koch Residual Trust Grants, 1241
Hillsdale County Community Foundation General
  Grants, 1250
HLTA Visitor Industry Charity Walk Grant, 1254
Indiana OCRA Quick Impact Placebased (QuIP)
  Grants, 1300
Initiative Foundation Minnesota Early Childhood
  Initiative Grants, 1305
John P. Ellbogen Fdn Community Grants, 1377
Journal Gazette Foundation Grants, 1391
Kalamazoo Community Foundation John E. Fetzer
  Institute Fund Grants, 1410
Kansas Health Fdn Major Initiatives Grants, 1414
Kenai Peninsula Foundation Grants, 1425
Ketchikan Community Foundation Grants, 1429
Kroger Company Donations, 1456
Laura Musser Intercultural Harmony Grants, 1472
LEGO Children's Fund Grants, 1480
LISC Capacity Building Grants, 1498
LISC Community Leadership Operating Grts, 1499
Marion Gardner Jackson Charitable Trust Grts, 1570
Mary E. Babcock Foundation, 1589
Matson Community Giving Grants, 1607
McCune Charitable Foundation Grants, 1617
Medtronic Foundation Community Link Arts, Civic,
  and Culture Grants, 1629
Mertz Gilmore Foundation NYC Communities
  Grants, 1641
Michael and Susan Dell Foundation Grants, 1657
Michael Reese Health Trust Core Grants, 1658
Michael Reese Health Trust Responsive Grants, 1659
Mt. Sinai Health Care Foundation Health of the
  Urban Community Grants, 1710
Nathalie and Gladys Dalkowitz Charitable Trust
  Grants, 1716
NCMCF Youth Advisory Council Grants, 1727
NFL Charities NFL Player Foundation Grants, 1754
NSTA Distinguished Informal Science Education
  Award, 1777
NYSCA Arts Education: Community-based
  Learning Grants, 1780
NYSCA Arts Education: Local Capacity Building
  Grants (Regrants), 1783
OceanFirst Foundation Major Grants, 1803
Ohio County Community Foundation Board of
  Directors Grants, 1811
Olivia R. Gardner Foundation Grants, 1819
OMNOVA Solutions Fdn Education Grants, 1820

Ontario Arts Council Artists in Communities and
    Schools Project Grants, 1823
Ontario Arts Council Arts Organizations in
    Communities and Schools Operating Grants, 1824
OtterCares Impact Fund Grants, 1849
Parker Foundation (California) Grants, 1869
Philip L. Graham Fund Education Grants, 1962
Piper Trust Education Grants, 1977
Polk County Community Foundation Marjorie M.
    and Lawrence R. Bradley Endowment Fund
    Grants, 1998
Polk County Community Foundation Mary F. Kessler
    Fund Grants, 1999
Polk County Community Foundation Unrestricted
    Grants, 2001
Portland Fdn - Women's Giving Circle Grant, 2006
PPG Industries Foundation Grants, 2017
Rasmuson Foundation Tier Two Grants, 2056
RCF General Community Grants, 2062
RCF Individual Assistance Grants, 2063
Richland County Bank Grants, 2074
Robert Lee Blaffer Foundation Grants, 2092
Saeman Family Fdn A Charitable Grants, 2133
Saginaw Community Foundation Discretionary
    Grants, 2134
Saginaw County Community Foundation Youth
    FORCE Grants, 2136
Seattle Foundation Benjamin N. Phillips Memorial
    Fund Grants, 2176
Seattle Foundation C. Keith Birkenfeld Memorial
    Trust Grants, 2177
Seattle Foundation Education Grants, 2178
Serco Foundation Grants, 2181
Seward Community Foundation Grants, 2182
Seward Community Foundation Mini-Grants, 2183
Shield-Ayres Foundation Grants, 2189
Target Foundation Global Grants, 2272
Turtle Bay Foundation Grants, 2327
Vanderburgh Community Foundation Men's Fund
    Grants, 2373
Vanderburgh County Community Foundation
    Women's Fund Grants, 2376
VSA/Metlife Connect All Grants, 2392
Walker Area Community Foundation Grants, 2401
Walmart Fdn Inclusive Communities Grants, 2403
Walmart Fdn National Local Giving Grants, 2404
Walmart Foundation State Giving Grants, 2405
Warrick County Community Foundation Women's
    Fund, 2411
William A. Miller Foundation Grants, 2453
WinnCompanies Charitable Giving, 2479
Wiregrass Foundation Grants, 2480
Woods Charitable Fund Education Grants, 2488
Wyoming Community Foundation Hazel Patterson
    Memorial Grants, 2502
Wyomissing Foundation Community Grants, 2504
Wyomissing Foundation Thun Family Organizational
    Grants, 2505
Wyomissing Foundation Thun Family Program
    Grants, 2506

Community Outreach
3M Company Fdn Community Giving Grants, 5
ACCF of Indiana Anonymous Community
    Enrichment Fund Grants, 63
ACCF of Indiana Berne Ready Mix Community
    Enrichment Fund Grants, 65
ACF Head Start and/or Early Head Start Grantee
    - Clay, Randolph, and Talladega Counties,
    Alabama, 82
ACF Head Start and/or Early Head Start Grantee -
    St. Landry Parish, Louisiana, 83
Adams Family Fdn of Nora Springs Grants, 118
ALA Sara Jaffarian School Library Award for
    Exemplary Humanities Programming, 190
Alaska Community Foundation Cordova Community
    Foundation Grants, 201
Alaska Community Foundation Cordova Community
    Foundation Mini-Grants, 202

Alaska Community Foundation Jack and Nona Renn
    Anchorage Football Fund, 204
Alaska Community Foundation Kenai Peninsula
    Foundation Grant, 205
Alaska Community Foundation Ketchikan
    Community Foundation Grant, 206
Alaska Conservation Fdn Youth Mini Grants, 210
Albert and Ethel Herzstein Charitable Foundation
    Grants, 219
Alden and Vada Dow Fund Grants, 225
Allstate Corporate Giving Grants, 242
Allstate Corp Hometown Commitment Grants, 243
Allstate Foundation Safe and Vital Communities
    Grants, 244
Anderson Foundation Grants, 271
Ann L. and Carol Green Rhodes Charitable Trust
    Grants, 278
Antone and Edene Vidinha Charitable Grants, 281
Appalachian Community Fund LGBTQ Fund
    Grants, 284
Atlas Insurance Agency Foundation Grants, 329
Autauga Area Community Foundation Grants, 334
Bainum Family Foundation Grants, 345
Bay Area Community Foundation Arenac
    Community Fund Grants, 371
Beckman Coulter Foundation Grants, 394
Ben B. Cheney Foundation Grants, 402
Bernard and Audre Rapoport Foundation Arts and
    Culture Grants, 407
Bernard and Audre Rapoport Foundation Democracy
    and Civic Participation Grants, 409
Bernard and Audre Rapoport Foundation Health
    Grants, 411
Bill and Melinda Gates Foundation Agricultural
    Development Grants, 425
Blandin Foundation Itasca County Area Vitality
    Grants, 439
Blue Cross Blue Shield of Minnesota Foundation
    - Healthy Neighborhoods: Connect for Health
    Challenge Grants, 443
Bright Promises Foundation Grants, 470
Brunswick Foundation Dollars for Doers Grants, 478
Burton D. Morgan Foundation Hudson Community
    Grants, 482
Bush Foundation Event Sponsorships, 485
California Endowment Innovative Ideas Challenge
    Grants, 495
Campbell Soup Foundation Grants, 501
Caring for Colorado Foundation Sperry S. and Ella
    Graber Packard Fund for Pueblo Grants, 505
Carl B. and Florence E. King Foundation Grants, 506
CFFVR Basic Needs Giving Partnership Grants, 537
CFFVR Clintonville Area Foundation Grants, 539
CFFVR Frank C. Shattuck Community Grants, 541
CFFVR Schmidt Family G4 Grants, 548
CFFVR Shawano Area Community Foundation
    Grants, 549
CFFVR Women's Fund for the Fox Valley Region
    Grants, 550
CFF Winter Park Community Grants, 551
Charles Delmar Foundation Grants, 564
Chesapeake Bay Trust Outreach and Community
    Engagement Grants, 579
Citizens Savings Foundation Grants, 617
Claremont Savings Bank Foundation Grants, 623
Columbus Foundation Traditional Grants, 663
Community Foundation for San Benito County
    Grants, 677
Community Foundation for SE Michigan Chelsea
    Community Foundation General Grant, 680
Community Foundation of Greater Fort Wayne -
    John S. and James L. Knight Foundation Donor-
    Advised Grants, 707
Community Foundation of Louisville We Day
    Kentucky Grants, 728
Community Foundation of Madison and Jefferson
    County Grants, 731
Community Fdn of Randolph County Grants, 735
Community Foundation of St. Joseph County African
    American Community Grants, 737

Community Foundation of Switzerland County
    Grants, 739
Cralle Foundation Grants, 760
Crane Fund Grants, 763
D. W. McMillan Foundation Grants, 776
David and Laura Merage Foundation Grants, 789
Deaconess Foundation Advocacy Grants, 804
Delta Air Lines Foundation Community Enrichment
    Grants, 823
E. Clayton and Edith P. Gengras, Jr. Foundation
    Grants, 875
Edward and Ellen Roche Relief Fdn Grants, 887
Edward W. and Stella C. Van Houten Memorial Fund
    Grants, 892
Elkhart County Community Foundation Fund for
    Elkhart County, 902
Ella West Freeman Foundation Grants, 904
El Pomar Foundation Grants, 908
Elsie H. Wilcox Foundation Grants, 909
EPA Children's Health Protection Grants, 923
EQT Fdn Community Enrichment Grants, 926
Essex County Community Foundation Greater
    Lawrence Community Fund Grants, 931
Ethel Sergeant Clark Smith Foundation Grants, 935
Fifth Third Bank Corporate Giving, 958
Florence Foundation Grants, 978
Ford Family Foundation Grants - Technical
    Assistance , 983
Fdn for the Mid South Communities Grants, 992
Foundations of East Chicago Education Grants, 995
Four County Community Foundation General
    Grants, 1000
Four County Community Foundation Healthy
    Senior/Healthy Youth Fund Grants, 1001
Frederick W. Marzahl Memorial Fund Grants, 1018
Fremont Area Community Foundation Amazing X
    Grants, 1019
Fremont Area Community Foundation Youth
    Advisory Committee Grants, 1022
George A Ohl Jr. Foundation Grants, 1043
Greater Sitka Legacy Fund Grants, 1111
Griffin Family Foundation Grants, 1121
GTRCF Elk Rapids Area Community Endowment
    Grants, 1127
Gulf Coast Foundation of Community Operating
    Grants, 1134
Gulf Coast Foundation of Community Program
    Grants, 1135
HAF Don and Bettie Albright Endowment Fund
    Grants, 1142
HAF Joe Alexandre Mem Family Fund Grants, 1145
Hahl Proctor Charitable Trust Grants, 1151
Hardin County Community Foundation Grants, 1167
Harris Foundation Grants, 1177
Hawai'i Community Foundation Children's Trust
    Fund Community Awareness: Child Abuse and
    Neglect Prevention Grants, 1198
Hawai'i Community Foundation Family Literacy and
    Hawaii Pizza Hut Literacy Grants, 1201
Hawaii Community Foundation Omidyar Ohana
    Fund Grants, 1213
Hawaii Community Foundation Sanford Harmony
    Pillars of Peace Grants, 1217
Hawaii Electric Industries Charitable Foundation
    Grants, 1218
Hawaii State Legislature Grant-In-Aid, 1219
Helen Bader Foundation Grants, 1227
Henry County Community Foundation - TASC
    Youth Grants, 1238
Hillsdale County Community Foundation General
    Grants, 1250
HLTA Visitor Industry Charity Walk Grant, 1254
Horace A. Kimball and S. Ella Kimball Foundation
    Grants, 1260
HRAMF Community Health Improvement Project
    Grants in Bowdoin Geneva, 1263
Indiana OCRA Quick Impact Placebased (QuIP)
    Grants, 1300
Jack and Dorothy Byrne Foundation Grants, 1329

James and Abigail Campbell Family Foundation
    Grants, 1337
Jennings County Community Fdn Grants, 1360
John H. and Wilhelmina D. Harland Charitable
    Foundation Community Services Grants, 1375
John P. Ellbogen Fdn Community Grants, 1377
Johnson County Community Fdn Grants, 1379
Johnson Foundation Wingspread Conference Support
    Program, 1381
John W. Anderson Foundation Grants, 1383
Joseph Henry Edmondson Foundation Grants, 1388
Judith Clark-Morrill Foundation Grants, 1395
Kalamazoo Community Foundation John E. Fetzer
    Institute Fund Grants, 1410
Kentucky Arts Cncl Access Assistance Grants, 1428
Ketchikan Community Foundation Grants, 1429
Kosciusko County Community Fdn Grants, 1452
Laclede Gas Charitable Trust Grants, 1457
Land O'Lakes Foundation Community Grants, 1466
Laura Musser Intercultural Harmony Grants, 1472
Lee and Ramona Bass Foundation Grants, 1478
Leo Niessen Jr., Charitable Trust Grants, 1484
LISC Community Leadership Operating Grts, 1499
Lotus 88 Foundation for Women and Children
    Grants, 1508
Mabel F. Hoffman Charitable Trust Grants, 1526
Mabel Louise Riley Foundation Family Strengthening
    Small Grants, 1528
Madison County Community Foundation General
    Grants, 1537
Maine Community Fdn Peaks Island Grants, 1542
Maine Community Foundation Penobscot Valley
    Health Association Grants, 1543
Marion Gardner Jackson Charitable Trust Grts, 1570
Marisla Foundation Human Services Grants, 1573
MassMutual Foundation Edonomic Development
    Grants, 1603
Medtronic Foundation Community Link Arts, Civic,
    and Culture Grants, 1629
Merrick Foundation Grants, 1639
MFRI Community Mobilization Grants, 1654
Michael Reese Health Trust Responsive Grants, 1659
Mid-Iowa Health Foundation Community Response
    Grants, 1667
Ms. Foundation for Women Building Democracy
    Grants, 1706
Mt. Sinai Health Care Foundation Health of the
    Urban Community Grants, 1710
Nathalie and Gladys Dalkowitz Charitable Trust
    Grants, 1716
NEA Student Program Communities Redefining
    Education Advocacy Through Empowerment
    (CREATE) Grants, 1733
New Hampshire Charitable Foundation Community
    Unrestricted Grants, 1747
New Hampshire Charitable Foundation Neil and
    Louise Tillotson Fund - Empower Coös Youth
    Grants, 1748
NFL Charities NFL Player Foundation Grants, 1754
Ohio County Community Foundation Board of
    Directors Grants, 1811
Olivia R. Gardner Foundation Grants, 1819
Parke County Community Foundation Grants, 1868
Parker Foundation (California) Grants, 1869
PCA Arts Organizations and Arts Programs Grants
    for Arts Education Organizations, 1889
PCA Arts Organizations and Arts Programs Grants
    for Crafts, 1891
PCA Arts Organizations and Arts Programs Grants
    for Dance, 1892
PCA Arts Organizations and Arts Programs Grants
    for Literature, 1894
PCA Arts Organizations and Arts Programs Grants
    for Theatre, 1896
PCA Arts Organizations and Arts Programs Grants
    for Traditional and Folk Arts, 1897
PCA Arts Organizations and Arts Programs Grants
    for Visual Arts, 1898

PCA Entry Track Arts Organizations and
    Arts Programs Grants for Arts Education
    Organizations, 1901
PCA Entry Track Arts Organizations and Arts
    Programs Grants for Crafts, 1903
PCA Entry Track Arts Organizations and Arts
    Programs Grants for Dance, 1904
PCA Entry Track Arts Organizations and Arts
    Programs Grants for Theatre, 1910
PCA Entry Track Arts Orgs and Arts Programs
    Grants for Traditional and Folk Arts, 1911
PCA Entry Track Arts Organizations and Arts
    Programs Grants for Visual Arts, 1912
PCA Pennsylvania Partners in the Arts Program
    Stream Grants, 1914
PCA Pennsylvania Partners in the Arts Project
    Stream Grants, 1915
PepsiCo Foundation Grants, 1935
Percy B. Ferebee Endowment Grants, 1936
Petersburg Community Foundation Grants, 1951
Phoenix Coyotes Charities Grants, 1963
Piper Trust Reglious Organizations Grants, 1979
Polk County Community Foundation Bradley
    Breakthrough Community Benefit Grants, 1995
Polk County Community Foundation Free
    Community Events Grants, 1996
Polk County Community Foundation Marjorie M.
    and Lawrence R. Bradley Endowment Fund
    Grants, 1998
Posey Community Foundation Women's Fund
    Grants, 2008
Powell Foundation Grants, 2013
PPG Industries Foundation Grants, 2017
Pulaski County Community Foundation Grants, 2038
Qualcomm Grants, 2042
Rasmuson Foundation Tier One Grants, 2055
Rasmuson Foundation Tier Two Grants, 2056
RCF General Community Grants, 2062
RCF Individual Assistance Grants, 2063
Robbins Family Charitable Foundation Grants, 2082
Robert and Betty Wo Foundation Grants, 2083
Rush County Community Foundation Grants, 2121
Saeman Family Fdn A Charitable Grants, 2133
Saginaw Community Foundation Discretionary
    Grants, 2134
Saginaw County Community Foundation Youth
    FORCE Grants, 2136
Scott County Community Foundation Grants, 2170
Serco Foundation Grants, 2181
Seward Community Foundation Grants, 2182
Seward Community Foundation Mini-Grants, 2183
Shield-Ayres Foundation Grants, 2189
Shopko Foundation Green Bay Area Community
    Grants, 2192
Siebert Lutheran Foundation Grants, 2198
Social Justice Fund Northwest Criminal Justice
    Giving Project Grants, 2214
Sony Corporation of America Grants, 2216
Sorenson Legacy Foundation Grants, 2217
Spencer County Community Foundation Women's
    Fund Grants, 2232
Stocker Foundation Grants, 2247
TAC Arts Education Mini Grants, 2267
Telluride Foundation Community Grants, 2281
Toyota Motor North America of NY Grants, 2315
Turtle Bay Foundation Grants, 2327
Twenty-First Century Foundation Grants, 2328
Valley-Wide Health Systems Nurse Family
    Partnerships, 2372
Vanderburgh Community Foundation Men's Fund
    Grants, 2373
Vanderburgh County Community Foundation
    Women's Fund Grants, 2376
Walker Area Community Foundation Grants, 2401
Walmart Foundation State Giving Grants, 2405
Walter S. and Evan C. Jones Testam Trust, 2407
Warrick County Community Foundation Women's
    Fund, 2411
William Caspar Graustein Memorial Fund Corinne
    G. Levin Education Grants, 2462

William Foulds Family Foundation Grants, 2465
William G. and Helen C. Hoffman Foundation
    Grants, 2466
William G. Gilmore Foundation Grants, 2467
Wiregrass Foundation Grants, 2480
Woods Fund of Chicago Grants, 2489
Wyoming Community Fdn General Grants, 2501
Wyoming Community Foundation Hazel Patterson
    Memorial Grants, 2502

Community Services

3M Company Foundation Health and Human
    Services Grants, 6
A.C. and Penney Hubbard Foundation Grants, 19
A.L. Spencer Foundation Grants, 21
Abbott Fund Community Engagement Grants, 46
Abby's Legendary Pizza Foundation Grants, 49
ACCF Dennis and Melanie Bieberich Community
    Enrichment Fund Grants, 59
ACCF John and Kay Boch Fund Grants, 60
ACCF of Indiana Anonymous Community
    Enrichment Fund Grants, 63
ACCF of Indiana Bank of Geneva Heritage Fund
    Grants, 64
ACCF of Indiana Berne Ready Mix Community
    Enrichment Fund Grants, 65
ACCF of Indiana First Merchants Bank / Decatur
    Bank and Trust Fund Grants, 66
ACCF of Indiana Michael Basham Community
    Enrichment Fund Grants, 67
ACCF Ralph Biggs Memorial Community
    Enrichment Fund Grants, 69
ACF Head Start and/or Early Head Start Grantee
    - Clay, Randolph, and Talladega Counties,
    Alabama, 82
ACF Head Start and/or Early Head Start Grantee -
    St. Landry Parish, Louisiana, 83
ACF Social and Economic Development Strategies
    Grants, 93
ACF Street Outreach Program Grants, 94
Ackerman Foundation Grants, 103
ACL Alternatives to Guardianship Youth Resource
    Center Grants, 104
Adams Family Fdn of Nora Springs Grants, 118
Adams Family Foundation of Ohio Grants, 119
Adelaide Breed Bayrd Foundation Grants, 123
Agnes M. Lindsay Trust Grants, 140
Aid for Starving Children Emerg Aid Grants, 144
Aid for Starving Children Health and Nutrition
    Grants, 145
Aid for Starving Children Homes and Education
    Grants, 146
Aid for Starving Children Water Projects Grants, 147
ALA MAE Award for Best Literature Program for
    Teens, 174
Alaska Community Foundation Cordova Community
    Foundation Grants, 201
Alaska Community Foundation Cordova Community
    Foundation Mini-Grants, 202
Alaska Community Foundation Kenai Peninsula
    Foundation Grant, 205
Alaska Community Foundation Ketchikan
    Community Foundation Grant, 206
Alaska Community Foundation Petersburg
    Community Foundation Annual Grant, 207
Alaska Community Foundation Petersburg
    Community Foundation Mini-Grants, 208
Alaska Community Foundation Seward Community
    Foundation Grant, 209
Alaska Conservation Fdn Youth Mini Grants, 210
ALA Sullivan Award for Public Library Admintrs
    Supporting Services to Children, 213
ALA YALSA Presidential Citation Award, 218
Albert and Ethel Herzstein Charitable Foundation
    Grants, 219
American Indian Youth Running Strong Grants, 256
Amica Insurance Company Community Grants, 267
Anheuser-Busch Foundation Grants, 273
Appalachian Community Fund LGBTQ Fund
    Grants, 284

AT&T Fdn Community Support and Safety, 320
Atlas Insurance Agency Foundation Grants, 329
Austin Community Foundation Grants, 332
Autauga Area Community Foundation Grants, 334
Avery Dennison Foundation Education Grants, 337
Baltimore Community Foundation Mitzvah Fund for
   Good Deeds Grants, 349
Bank of America Charitable Foundation Matching
   Gifts, 356
Bank of Hawaii Foundation Grants, 360
Bay Area Community Foundation Arenac
   Community Fund Grants, 371
Bay Area Community Fdn Auburn Area Chamber of
   Commerce Enrichment Fund Grants, 373
Bay Area Community Foundation Human Services
   Fund Grants, 379
Baystate Financial Charitable Foundation Grants, 385
Beckman Coulter Foundation Grants, 394
Bella Vista Fdn GSS Healthy Living Grants, 396
Ben B. Cheney Foundation Grants, 402
Benwood Foundation Community Grants, 406
Bernard and Audre Rapoport Foundation Democracy
   and Civic Participation Grants, 409
Bernard and Audre Rapoport Foundation Health
   Grants, 411
Best Buy Children's Foundation @15 Community
   Grants , 414
Best Buy Children's Fdn @15 Scholarship , 415
Best Buy Children's Foundation National Grants, 417
Biogen Foundation General Donations, 432
Blackford County Community Fdn Grants, 434
Blandin Foundation Expand Opportunity Grants, 437
Blandin Foundation Invest Early Grants, 438
Blandin Foundation Itasca County Area Vitality
   Grants, 439
Blue Cross Blue Shield of Minnesota Fdn - Healthy
   Children: Growing Up Healthy Grants, 442
Blue Grass Community Foundation Clark County
   Fund Grants, 444
Blue Grass Community Foundation Fayette County
   Fund Grants, 446
Blue Grass Community Foundation Franklin County
   Fund Grants, 447
Blue Grass Community Foundation Harrison County
   Fund Grants, 448
Blue Grass Community Foundation Hudson-Ellis
   Grants, 449
Blue Grass Community Foundation Madison County
   Fund Grants, 450
Blue Grass Community Foundation Magoffin County
   Fund Grants, 451
Blue Grass Community Foundation Morgan County
   Fund Grants, 452
Blue Grass Community Foundation Rowan County
   Fund Grants, 453
Blue Grass Community Foundation Woodford
   County Fund Grants, 454
Blumenthal Foundation Grants, 459
BP Foundation Grants, 465
Bradley C. Higgins Foundation Grants, 467
Bright Promises Foundation Grants, 470
Brinker Int Corporation Charitable Giving, 471
Brown Foundation Grants, 476
Brunswick Foundation Dollars for Doers Grants, 478
Burton D. Morgan Foundation Hudson Community
   Grants, 482
Bush Foundation Event Sponsorships, 485
Byerly Foundation Grants, 487
California Endowment Innovative Ideas Challenge
   Grants, 495
Callaway Foundation Grants, 496
Caring for Colorado Foundation Sperry S. and Ella
   Graber Packard Fund for Pueblo Grants, 505
Carl R. Hendrickson Family Foundation Grants, 509
CFF Winter Park Community Grants, 551
Charles Delmar Foundation Grants, 564
Chilkat Valley Community Foundation Grants, 588
Cisco Systems Foundation San Jose Community
   Grants, 615
Citizens Savings Foundation Grants, 617

Clara Abbott Foundation Need-Based Grants, 620
Claremont Savings Bank Foundation Grants, 623
Clark County Community Foundation Grants, 626
Cleveland Fdn Lake-Geauga Fund Grants, 635
Cleveland Foundation Legacy Village Lyndhurst
   Community Fund Grants, 636
CNCS AmeriCorps NCCC Project Grants, 642
CNCS AmeriCorps State and National Grants, 643
CNCS AmeriCorps State and National Planning
   Grants, 644
Colorado Health Foundation Family, Friend and
   Neighbor Caregiver Supports Grants, 660
Community Foundation for Greater Atlanta
   Metropolitan Extra Wish Grants, 666
Community Foundation for Greater Atlanta Spark
   Clayton Grants, 667
Community Foundation for Greater Atlanta Spark
   Newton Grants, 668
Community Foundation for Greater Atlanta Strategic
   Restructuring Fund Grants, 669
Community Foundation for Greater Buffalo Ralph C.
   Wilson, Jr. Legacy Fund Grants, 674
Community Foundation for Kettering Grants, 676
Community Foundation for San Benito County
   Grants, 677
Community Foundation for SE Michigan Chelsea
   Community Fdn Capacity Building Grants, 679
Community Foundation for SE Michigan Chelsea
   Community Foundation General Grant, 680
Community Foundation of Boone County - Women's
   Grants, 693
Community Foundation of Greater Greensboro Teen
   Grantmaking Council Grants, 709
Community Foundation of Louisville Anna Marble
   Memorial Fund for Princeton Grants, 717
Community Foundation of Louisville We Day
   Kentucky Grants, 728
Community Foundation of Madison and Jefferson
   County Grants, 731
Community Foundation of Muncie and Delaware
   County Maxon Grants, 734
Community Foundation of St. Joseph County African
   American Community Grants, 737
Community Foundation of St. Joseph County Special
   Project Challenge Grants, 738
Community Foundation of Switzerland County
   Grants, 739
Courtney S. Turner Charitable Trust Grants, 753
Cralle Foundation Grants, 760
Crane Fund Grants, 763
D. W. McMillan Foundation Grants, 776
David Alan and Susan Berkman Rahm Foundation
   Grants, 785
David and Laura Merage Foundation Grants, 789
Deaconess Foundation Advocacy Grants, 804
Dean Foundation Grants, 806
Delta Air Lines Foundation Community Enrichment
   Grants, 823
Dominion Foundation Grants, 839
Do Something Awards, 847
DTE Energy Foundation Leadership Grants, 870
E. Clayton and Edith P. Gengras, Jr. Foundation
   Grants, 875
Eastern Bank Charitable Foundation Partnerships
   Grants, 881
Eastern Bank Charitable Foundation Targeted
   Grants, 882
Edward and Ellen Roche Relief Fdn Grants, 887
Edward F. Swinney Trust Grants, 890
Effie and Wofford Cain Foundation Grants, 895
Elkhart County Community Foundation Fund for
   Elkhart County, 902
Ella West Freeman Foundation Grants, 904
Ellen Abbott Gilman Trust Grants, 905
Elmer Roe Deaver Foundation Grants, 906
El Pomar Foundation Grants, 908
Ensworth Charitable Foundation Grants, 916
Entergy Corporation Micro Grants, 919
Environmental Excellence Awards, 922

Essex County Community Foundation Greater
   Lawrence Community Fund Grants, 931
Ethel Sergeant Clark Smith Foundation Grants, 935
Evelyn and Walter Haas, Jr. Fund Nonprofit
   Leadership Grants, 942
Faye L. and William L. Cowden Charitable
   Foundation Grants, 950
Fifth Third Bank Corporate Giving, 958
Florence Foundation Grants, 978
Fdn for the Mid South Communities Grants, 992
Foundation of Herkimer and Oneida Counties Youth
   Sports, Wellness and Recreation Mini-Grants, 994
Foundations of East Chicago Education Grants, 995
Four County Community Foundation General
   Grants, 1000
Four County Community Foundation Healthy
   Senior/Healthy Youth Fund Grants, 1001
Gene Haas Foundation, 1038
George A. & Grace L. Long Fdn Grants, 1041
George A Ohl Jr. Foundation Grants, 1043
George B. Page Foundation Grants, 1044
George Graham and Elizabeth Galloway Smith
   Foundation Grants, 1047
George H. Sandy Foundation Grants, 1050
Gil and Dody Weaver Foundation Grants, 1071
Gloria Barron Prize for Young Heroes, 1074
Graham Family Charitable Foundation Grants, 1099
Graham Foundation Grants, 1101
Greater Sitka Legacy Fund Grants, 1111
Green River Area Community Fdn Grants, 1117
Griffin Family Foundation Grants, 1121
GTRCF Elk Rapids Area Community Endowment
   Grants, 1127
GTRCF Joan Rajkovich McGarry Family Education
   Endowment Grants, 1131
Gulf Coast Foundation of Community Operating
   Grants, 1134
Gulf Coast Foundation of Community Program
   Grants, 1135
HAF Community Grants, 1141
HAF Don and Bettie Albright Endowment Fund
   Grants, 1142
HAF Joe Alexandre Mem Family Fund Grants, 1145
HAF Laurence and Elaine Allen Memorial Fund
   Grants, 1146
HAF Southern Humboldt Grants, 1150
Hahl Proctor Charitable Trust Grants, 1151
Hannaford Charitable Foundation Grants, 1163
Hannaford Supermarkets Community Giving, 1164
Hardin County Community Foundation Grants, 1167
Harmony Grove Foundation Grants, 1169
Harold and Rebecca H. Gross Fdn Grants, 1171
Harold K.L. Castle Foundation Strengthening
   Windward Oahu Communities Grants, 1174
Harold K.L. Castle Foundation Windward Youth
   Leadership Fund Grants, 1175
Harris Foundation Grants, 1177
Harrison County Community Fdn Grants, 1178
Harrison County Community Foundation Signature
   Grants, 1179
Hasbro Corp Gift of Play Holiday Giving, 1190
Hasbro Corporation Gift of Play Hospital and
   Pediatric Health Giving, 1191
Hasbro Corporation Gift of Play Shelter Support
   Giving, 1192
Hawai'i Community Foundation Children's Trust
   Fund Community Awareness: Child Abuse and
   Neglect Prevention Grants, 1198
Hawaii Community Foundation Omidyar Ohana
   Fund Grants, 1213
Hawaii Electric Industries Charitable Foundation
   Grants, 1218
Hawaii State Legislature Grant-In-Aid, 1219
Hazen Foundation Public Education Grants, 1221
Helen Bader Foundation Grants, 1227
Henry County Community Foundation - TASC
   Youth Grants, 1238
Henry F. Koch Residual Trust Grants, 1241
Henry L. Guenther Foundation Grants, 1242

Herbert A. and Adrian W. Woods Foundation Grants, 1243
Hillsdale County Community Foundation Y.O.U.T.H. Grants, 1252
Hispanic Heritage Foundation Youth Awards, 1253
HLTA Visitor Industry Charity Walk Grant, 1254
Horace A. Kimball and S. Ella Kimball Foundation Grants, 1260
HRAMF Community Health Improvement Project Grants in Bowdoin Geneva, 1263
HSFCA Biennium Grants, 1267
Hubbard Family Foundation Grants, 1271
Iddings Foundation Medium Project Grants, 1285
Iddings Foundation Small Project Grants, 1286
Ike and Roz Friedman Foundation Grants, 1289
ING Foundation Grants, 1302
Initiative Foundation Innovation Fund Grants, 1304
J. Knox Gholston Foundation Grants, 1321
Jack and Dorothy Byrne Foundation Grants, 1329
James Lee Sorenson Family Impact Foundation Grants, 1342
James LeVoy Sorenson Foundation Grants, 1343
Jane's Trust Grants, 1346
Janet Spencer Weekes Foundation Grants, 1348
Jennings County Community Fdn Grants, 1360
Jennings County Community Foundation Women's Giving Circle Grant, 1361
Jessica Stevens Community Foundation Grants, 1363
Joan Bentinck-Smith Charitable Fdn Grants, 1367
John Clarke Trust Grants, 1369
John H. and Wilhelmina D. Harland Charitable Foundation Community Services Grants, 1375
John P. Ellbogen Fdn Community Grants, 1377
Johnson County Community Fdn Grants, 1379
John W. Anderson Foundation Grants, 1383
Joseph Henry Edmondson Foundation Grants, 1388
Josephine Schell Russell Chartbl Trust Grants, 1389
Judith Clark-Morrill Foundation Grants, 1395
KaBOOM! Play Everywhere Design Challenge, 1405
Kalamazoo Community Foundation John E. Fetzer Institute Fund Grants, 1410
Kenai Peninsula Foundation Grants, 1425
Ketchikan Community Foundation Grants, 1429
Kevin J Major Youth Sports Scholarships, 1431
KIND Causes Monthly Grants, 1435
Kind World Foundation Grants, 1438
Kodiak Community Foundation Grants, 1446
Koret Foundation Grants, 1449
Kroger Company Donations, 1456
Laclede Gas Charitable Trust Grants, 1457
LaGrange Independent Foundation for Endowments (L.I.F.E.), 1459
Laura Musser Intercultural Harmony Grants, 1472
Lee and Ramona Bass Foundation Grants, 1478
LEGO Children's Fund Grants, 1480
Leo Niessen Jr., Charitable Trust Grants, 1484
Lewis H. Humphreys Charitable Trust Grants, 1486
LGA Family Foundation Grants, 1487
Liberty Bank Foundation Grants, 1488
Lilly Endowment Summer Youth Grants, 1492
LISC Community Leadership Operating Grts, 1499
Louie M. and Betty M. Phillips Fdn Grants, 1509
Mabel A. Horne Fund Grants, 1525
Mabel F. Hoffman Charitable Trust Grants, 1526
Mabel Louise Riley Foundation Family Strengthening Small Grants, 1528
Madison County Community Foundation General Grants, 1537
Maine Community Foundation Penobscot Valley Health Association Grants, 1543
Marathon Petroleum Corporation Grants, 1551
Margaret M. Walker Charitable Fdn Grants, 1556
Marion Gardner Jackson Charitable Trust Grts, 1570
Marisla Foundation Human Services Grants, 1573
Marsh Corporate Grants, 1580
Martin Family Foundation Grants, 1583
Mary A. Crocker Trust Grants, 1584
MassMutual Foundation Edonomic Development Grants, 1603

Matson Community Giving Grants, 1607
McCune Charitable Foundation Grants, 1617
Merrick Foundation Grants, 1640
Mertz Gilmore Foundation NYC Communities Grants, 1641
Metzger-Price Fund Grants, 1647
MFRI Community Mobilization Grants, 1654
Michael Reese Health Trust Core Grants, 1658
Michael Reese Health Trust Responsive Grants, 1659
Microsoft Software Donations, 1665
Middlesex Savings Charitable Foundation Basic Human Needs Grants, 1668
Middlesex Savings Charitable Foundation Capacity Building Grants, 1669
Motiv8 Foundation Grants, 1702
Narragansett Number One Foundation Grants, 1712
Nathalie and Gladys Dalkowitz Charitable Trust Grants, 1716
Nathaniel and Elizabeth P. Stevens Foundation Grants, 1719
New Hampshire Charitable Foundation Community Unrestricted Grants, 1747
New Hampshire Department of Justice Children's Justice Act Coronavirus Emergency Grants, 1749
NFL Charities NFL Player Foundation Grants, 1754
Nissan Neighbors Grants, 1762
NYSCA Arts Education: Community-based Learning Grants, 1780
NZDIA Community Org Grants Scheme, 1796
O. Max Gardner Foundation Grants, 1798
Office Depot Corporation Community Relations Grants, 1805
Ohio County Community Foundation Board of Directors Grants, 1811
Ohio County Community Foundation Grants, 1812
Ohio County Community Fdn Mini-Grants, 1813
Ohio Valley Foundation Grants, 1814
Olga Sipolin Children's Fund Grants, 1815
Olive Smith Browning Charitable Trust Grants, 1818
Oregon Community Fdn Community Grants, 1833
OSF Baltimore Community Fellowships, 1838
Parker Foundation (California) Grants, 1869
Paul and Edith Babson Foundation Grants, 1881
Percy B. Ferebee Endowment Grants, 1936
Petersburg Community Foundation Grants, 1951
Pinnacle Entertainment Foundation Grants, 1972
Pinnacle Foundation Grants, 1973
Piper Trust Healthcare and Med Rsrch Grants, 1978
Piper Trust Reglious Organizations Grants, 1979
PNC Foundation Community Services Grants, 1984
Polk County Community Foundation Bradley Breakthrough Community Benefit Grants, 1995
Polk County Community Foundation Marjorie M. and Lawrence R. Bradley Endowment Fund Grants, 1998
Polk County Community Foundation Unrestricted Grants, 2001
Powell Foundation Grants, 2013
PPCF Esther M. and Freeman E. Everett Charitable Foundation Grants, 2016
PPG Industries Foundation Grants, 2017
Prudential Spirit of Community Awards, 2029
Putnam County Community Fdn Grants, 2040
Radcliffe Institute Carol K. Pforzheimer Student Fellowships, 2048
RCF General Community Grants, 2062
RCF Individual Assistance Grants, 2063
Ressler-Gertz Foundation Grants, 2067
Richland County Bank Grants, 2074
Robert and Betty Wo Foundation Grants, 2083
Rose Hills Foundation Grants, 2106
Sabina Dolan and Gladys Saulsbury Foundation Grants, 2130
Saeman Family Fdn A Charitable Grants, 2133
Saginaw Community Foundation Discretionary Grants, 2134
Saginaw County Community Foundation Youth FORCE Grants, 2136
San Antonio Area Foundation Special and Urgent Needs Funding Grants, 2150

Sand Hill Fdn Small Capital Needs Grants, 2154
Sandy Hill Foundation Grants, 2157
San Juan Island Community Foundation Grants, 2158
Sarkeys Foundation Grants, 2163
Seattle Foundation Basic Needs Grants, 2175
Seattle Foundation Benjamin N. Phillips Memorial Fund Grants, 2176
Seattle Foundation C. Keith Birkenfeld Memorial Trust Grants, 2177
Serco Foundation Grants, 2181
Seward Community Foundation Grants, 2182
Seward Community Foundation Mini-Grants, 2183
Shield-Ayres Foundation Grants, 2189
Shopko Foundation Green Bay Area Community Grants, 2192
Sidgmore Family Foundation Grants, 2195
Sierra Health Foundation Responsive Grants, 2199
Smith Richardson Fdn Direct Service Grants, 2210
Sobrato Family Foundation Grants, 2211
Sobrato Family Fdn Meeting Space Grants, 2212
Sobrato Family Foundation Office Space Grants, 2213
Sorenson Legacy Foundation Grants, 2217
Southern Minnesota Initiative Foundation Community Growth Initiative Grants, 2221
Southern Minnesota Initiative Foundation Home Visiting Grants, 2222
Southwest Initiative Foundation Grants, 2226
Special Olympics Project UNIFY Grants, 2228
Spencer County Community Foundation Women's Fund Grants, 2232
Stan and Sandy Checketts Foundation Grants, 2235
Sterling and Shelli Gardner Foundation Grants, 2243
Steven B. Achelis Foundation Grants, 2244
Stocker Foundation Grants, 2247
Storm Castle Foundation Grants, 2248
Strong Foundation Grants, 2252
Target Foundation Global Grants, 2272
Tauck Family Foundation Grants, 2274
Telluride Foundation Community Grants, 2281
Thelma Braun and Bocklett Family Foundation Grants, 2287
Thomas J. Atkins Memorial Trust Fund Grants, 2290
Toyota Motor Manuf of Alabama Grants, 2309
Toyota Motor Manufacturing of Indiana Grants, 2310
Toyota Motor Manuf of Kentucky Grants, 2311
Toyota Motor Manuf of Mississippi Grants, 2312
Toyota Motor Manufacturing of West Virginia Grants, 2314
Toyota Motor North America of NY Grants, 2315
Toyota Motor Sales, USA Grants, 2316
Tull Charitable Foundation Grants, 2324
Turtle Bay Foundation Grants, 2327
U.S. Cellular Corporation Grants, 2331
Union Pacific Foundation Health and Human Services Grants, 2338
UPS Foundation Community Safety Grants, 2350
Valley-Wide Health Systems Nurse Family Partnerships, 2372
Vanderburgh Community Foundation Men's Fund Grants, 2373
Vanderburgh County Community Foundation Women's Fund Grants, 2376
Vigneron Memorial Fund Grants, 2384
Walker Area Community Foundation Grants, 2401
Walmart Fdn Inclusive Communities Grants, 2403
Walmart Fdn National Local Giving Grants, 2404
Walmart Foundation State Giving Grants, 2405
Walter S. and Evan C. Jones Testam Trust, 2407
Warrick County Community Foundation Women's Fund, 2411
Weaver Popcorn Foundation Grants, 2421
Western New York Foundation Grants, 2429
WHO Foundation Education/Literacy Grants, 2442
Widgeon Point Charitable Foundation Grants, 2447
Wilkins Family Foundation Grants, 2450
William A. Miller Foundation Grants, 2453
William E. Dean III Charitable Fdn Grants, 2464
William G. and Helen C. Hoffman Foundation Grants, 2466
William M. Weaver Foundation Grants, 2472

WinnCompanies Charitable Giving, 2479
Wiregrass Foundation Grants, 2480
Wolfe Associates Grants, 2483
Wood Family Charitable Trust Grants, 2487
WSF GoGirlGo! New York Grants, 2494
Wyoming Community Fdn General Grants, 2501
Wyoming Community Foundation Hazel Patterson
    Memorial Grants, 2502
Wyomissing Foundation Community Grants, 2504
Wyomissing Foundation Thun Family Organizational
    Grants, 2505
Wyomissing Foundation Thun Family Program
    Grants, 2506
YSA ABC Summer of Service Awards, 2512
YSA Get Ur Good On Grants, 2513
YSA Global Youth Service Day Lead Agy Grts, 2514
YSA GYSD Regional Partner Grants, 2515
YSA NEA Youth Leaders for Literacy Grants, 2518
YSA Radio Disney's Hero for Change Award, 2519
YSA Sodexo Lead Organizer Grants, 2520
YSA State Farm Good Neighbor YOUth In The
    Driver Seat Grants, 2521
YSA UnitedHealth HEROES Service-Learning
    Grants, 2522

Community and School Relations
Alaska Community Foundation Anchorage Schools
    Foundation Grant, 197
Delta Air Lines Foundation Community Enrichment
    Grants, 823
F.R. Bigelow Foundation Grants, 947
Farmers Insurance Corporate Giving Grants, 948
HBF Pathways Out of Poverty Grants, 1222
Mt. Sinai Health Care Foundation Health of the
    Urban Community Grants, 1710
NYSCA Arts Education: Local Capacity Building
    Grants (Regrants), 1783
OneFamily Foundation Grants, 1822
Saginaw Community Foundation Discretionary
    Grants, 2134
Teaching Tolerance Social Justice Educator Grts, 2276
West Virginia Commission on the Arts Special
    Projects Grants, 2433

Compensatory Education
Cincinnati Bell Foundation Grants, 612

Complementary Medicine
Bernard and Audre Rapoport Foundation Health
    Grants, 411

Compulsive Behavior
Peter and Elizabeth C. Tower Foundation Mental
    Health Grants, 1946

Computer Applications
SAS Institute Community Relations Donations, 2165

Computer Arts
PCA Arts Organizations and Arts Programs Grants
    for Visual Arts, 1898
PCA Entry Track Arts Organizations and Arts
    Programs Grants for Visual Arts, 1912

Computer Education/Literacy
Achelis and Bodman Foundation Grants, 101
Achelis Foundation Grants, 102
Benton Community Foundation - The Cookie Jar
    Grant, 404
DeKalb County Community Foundation - Literacy
    Grant, 814
Farmers Insurance Corporate Giving Grants, 948
HAF Community Grants, 1141
Hearst Foundations Social Service Grants, 1224
Jane's Trust Grants, 1346
Kodak Community Relations Grants, 1445
LISC Capacity Building Grants, 1498
Robert R. McCormick Tribune Foundation
    Community Grants, 2093
Union Bank, N.A. Foundation Grants, 2334

Computer Music
NYSCA Music: Gen Program Support Grants, 1792

Computer Programming
Foundation for Rural Service Education Grants, 991

Computer Science
Northrop Grumman Foundation Grants, 1773

Computer Science Education
Delta Air Lines Foundation Youth Development
    Grants, 824
Northrop Grumman Foundation Grants, 1773

Computer Software
Armstrong McDonald Foundation Children and
    Youth Grants, 300
Community Foundation of Louisville Winston N. and
    Nancy H. Bloch Educational Fund Grants, 729
McLean Contributionship Grants, 1623
Microsoft Software Donations, 1665
SAS Institute Community Relations Donations, 2165
TAC Arts Access Grant, 2265
TechKnowledgey Community Impact Grants, 2278

Computer Technology
Armstrong McDonald Foundation Children and
    Youth Grants, 300
Best Buy Children's Foundation @15 Community
    Grants , 414
Do Something Back End Developer Intern, 848
Microsoft YouthSpark Grants, 1666
NEH Family and Youth Programs in American
    History Grants, 1734
Peter and Elizabeth C. Tower Foundation Technology
    Initiative Grants, 1949
Peter and Elizabeth C. Tower Foundation Technology
    Planning Grants, 1950
TechKnowledgey Community Impact Grants, 2278

Computer-Aided Instruction
Community Foundation of Jackson County Classroom
    Education Grants, 713
Leonsis Foundation Grants, 1485

Conferences
4imprint One by One Charitable Giving, 7
ALA Penguin Random House Young Readers Group
    Award, 183
Alaska Children's Trust Conference/Training
    Sponsorship, 195
Hatton W. Sumners Foundation for the Study and
    Teaching of Self Government Grants, 1196
Hawai'i Community Foundation Family Literacy and
    Hawaii Pizza Hut Literacy Grants, 1201
IYI Professional Development Grants, 1317
Oppenstein Brothers Foundation Grants, 1827
PAS PASIC International Scholarships, 1875
PCA Professional Development Grants, 1916
Sick Kids Foundation Community Conference
    Grants, 2193
TAC Arts Access Grant, 2265
Virginia Foundation for the Humanities Open
    Grants, 2387

Conferences, Travel to
AACAP Systems of Care Special Program
    Scholarships, 39
ALA Penguin Random House Young Readers Group
    Award, 183
ALFJ International Social Change Opportunity Fund
    Grants, 232
AOCS Thomas H. Smouse Memorial Fellowship, 282
GNOF Organizational Effectiveness Grants and
    Workshops, 1090
IYI Professional Development Grants, 1317
PAS PASIC International Scholarships, 1875
PCA Professional Development Grants, 1916
TAC Arts Education Teacher Incentive Grants, 2268
TSYSF Team Grants, 2323

Conflict/Dispute Resolution
Allstate Corporate Giving Grants, 242
Allstate Corp Hometown Commitment Grants, 243
Chicago Community Trust Arts and Culture Grants:
    Improving Access to Arts Learning, 581
Ford Foundation BUILD Grants, 984
Harry Frank Guggenheim Foundation Research
    Grants, 1184
Honor the Earth Grants, 1259
Laura Musser Intercultural Harmony Grants, 1472
Mary Owen Borden Foundation Grants, 1597
Max and Anna Levinson Foundation Grants, 1612
Sioux Falls Area Community Foundation Spot
    Grants, 2204
Union Square Award for Social Justice, 2340
United Methodist Women Brighter Future for
    Children and Youth Grants, 2346

Connecticut
Anna Fitch Ardenghi Trust Grants, 274
Bodenwein Public Benevolent Foundation Grants, 461
Elizabeth Carse Foundation Grants, 899
Ensworth Charitable Foundation Grants, 916
George A. & Grace L. Long Fdn Grants, 1041
George H.C. Ensworth Memorial Fund Grants, 1049
Lily Palmer Fry Memorial Trust Grants, 1493
Linford & Mildred White Charitable Grants, 1495
Mabel F. Hoffman Charitable Trust Grants, 1526
Olga Sipolin Children's Fund Grants, 1815
R.S. Gernon Trust Grants, 2047
Swindells Charitable Foundation Grants, 2261
Thomas J. Atkins Memorial Trust Fund Grants, 2290
William Foulds Family Foundation Grants, 2465

Conservation
Bee Conservancy Sponsor-A-Hive Grants, 395
Castle Industries Foundation Grants, 519
Dean Foundation Grants, 806
Helen E. Ellis Charitable Trust Grants, 1228
Helen G., Henry F., & Louise Tuechter Dornette
    Foundation Grants, 1229
Lee and Ramona Bass Foundation Grants, 1478
NHSCA Conservation License Plate Grants, 1757
Packard Foundation Local Grants, 1863
Polk County Community Foundation Mary F. Kessler
    Fund Grants, 1999
Sand Hill Foundation Environment and Sustainability
    Grants, 2152
William B. Stokely Jr. Foundation Grants, 2459
Winifred Johnson Clive Foundation Grants, 2478
Wyomissing Foundation Thun Family Organizational
    Grants, 2505
Wyomissing Foundation Thun Family Program
    Grants, 2506

Conservation Education
Bee Conservancy Sponsor-A-Hive Grants, 395
Castle Industries Foundation Grants, 519
Kirkpatrick Foundation Grants, 1440
McCune Charitable Foundation Grants, 1617
NHSCA Conservation License Plate Grants, 1757
Sand Hill Foundation Environment and Sustainability
    Grants, 2152
Wyomissing Foundation Thun Family Organizational
    Grants, 2505
Wyomissing Foundation Thun Family Grants, 2506

Conservation, Agriculture
Dean Foods Community Involvement Grants, 805
Foundation for Appalachian Ohio Access to
    Environmental Education Mini-Grants, 989
Mary A. Crocker Trust Grants, 1584
Norman Foundation Grants, 1767
PepsiCo Foundation Grants, 1935

Conservation, Natural Resources
ACF Social and Economic Development Strategies
    Grants, 93
Alliant Energy Foundation Community Giving for
    Good Sponsorship Grants, 240

Atkinson Foundation Community Grants, 325
Bella Vista Foundation Pre-3 Grants, 397
BMW of North America Charitable Contribs, 460
Boeing Company Contributions Grants, 462
Brunswick Foundation Grants, 479
CFFVR Environmental Stewardship Grants, 540
CHC Foundation Grants, 575
Chesapeake Bay Trust Environmental Education
    Grants, 577
Chesapeake Bay Trust Mini Grants, 578
Chesapeake Bay Trust Outreach and Community
    Engagement Grants, 579
Collins Foundation Grants, 658
Community Foundation of Henderson County
    Community Grants, 711
Dorrance Family Foundation Grants, 845
Dorr Foundation Grants, 846
Earth Island Institute Brower Youth Awards, 879
Edna Wardlaw Charitable Trust Grants, 886
Environmental Excellence Awards, 922
Fidelity Charitable Gift Fund Grants, 956
Gannett Foundation Community Action Grants, 1033
George H. and Jane A. Mifflin Memorial Fund
    Grants, 1048
Greater Milwaukee Foundation Grants, 1109
Harry A. and Margaret D. Towsley Foundation
    Grants, 1180
Helen G., Henry F., & Louise Tuechter Dornette
    Foundation Grants, 1229
Illinois DNR Youth Recreation Corps Grants, 1297
J.W. Kieckhefer Foundation Grants, 1324
Mary Owen Borden Foundation Grants, 1597
McLean Contributionship Grants, 1623
Montana Community Foundation Grants, 1687
New Earth Foundation Grants, 1743
NHSCA Conservation License Plate Grants, 1757
Norcliffe Foundation Grants, 1766
Norman Foundation Grants, 1767
NRA Foundation Grants, 1774
PG&E Bright Ideas Grants, 1956
PG&E Community Vitality Grants, 1957
Piedmont Natural Gas Fdn Envirnmtl Stewardship
    and Energy Sustainability Grant, 1967
PNM Reduce Your Use Grants, 1988
San Juan Island Community Foundation Grants, 2158
Shield-Ayres Foundation Grants, 2189
Singing for Change Foundation Grants, 2202
Skaggs Foundation Grants, 2207
Tides Foundation Grants, 2302
Volvo Adventure Environmental Awards, 2390
Wege Foundation Grants, 2422
Widgeon Point Charitable Foundation Grants, 2447
William A. Cooke Foundation Grants, 2452
Wyomissing Foundation Thun Family Organizational
    Grants, 2505
Wyomissing Foundation Thun Family Program
    Grants, 2506

Constitutional Law
Hatton W. Sumners Foundation for the Study and
    Teaching of Self Government Grants, 1196

Construction Engineering
Barrasso, Usdin, Kupperman, Freeman, and Sarver
    Corporate Grants, 362
GNOF Coastal 5 + 1 Grants, 1078

Consumer Behavior
Achelis and Bodman Foundation Grants, 101

Consumer Education/Information
Achelis and Bodman Foundation Grants, 101
Achelis Foundation Grants, 102
BMW of North America Charitable Contribs, 460
CNCS Senior Corps Retired and Senior Volunteer
    Program Grants, 648
Covidien Partnership for Neighborhood Wellness
    Grants, 759
Progress Energy Foundation Energy Education
    Grants, 2025

Consumer Services
EPA Children's Health Protection Grants, 923

Contraceptives
Lalor Foundation Postdoctoral Fellowships, 1464

Cooperative Education
ACF Head Start and/or Early Head Start Grantee
    - Clay, Randolph, and Talladega Counties,
    Alabama, 82
ACF Head Start and/or Early Head Start Grantee -
    St. Landry Parish, Louisiana, 83

Cooperatives
ACF Head Start and/or Early Head Start Grantee
    - Clay, Randolph, and Talladega Counties,
    Alabama, 82
ACF Head Start and/or Early Head Start Grantee -
    St. Landry Parish, Louisiana, 83
Community Foundation of Western Massachusetts
    Grants, 741
Kentucky Arts Cncl Access Assistance Grants, 1428

Coronavirus
Community Foundation for Greater Buffalo Ralph
    C. Wilson, Jr. Youth Sports COVID-19 Fund
    Grants, 675
New Hampshire Department of Justice Children's
    Justice Act Coronavirus Emergency Grants, 1749
Wyoming Community Foundation COVID-19
    Response and Recovery Grants, 2500

Corporate/Strategic Planning
CNCS AmeriCorps State and National Grants, 643
GNOF Organizational Effectiveness Grants and
    Workshops, 1090
Middlesex Savings Charitable Foundation Capacity
    Building Grants, 1669
PCA Strategies for Success Grants - Adv Level, 1917
Peter and Elizabeth C. Tower Foundation Technology
    Initiative Grants, 1949
Peter and Elizabeth C. Tower Foundation Technology
    Planning Grants, 1950
San Antonio Area Foundation Strengthening
    Nonprofits Grants, 2151

Corporations
GNOF New Orleans Works Grants, 1088

Counseling/Guidance
A Little Hope Grants, 235
Atkinson Foundation Community Grants, 325
Bollinger Foundation Grants, 463
CJ Fdn for SIDS Program Services Grants, 619
DOL Youthbuild Grants, 838
Ford Foundation BUILD Grants, 984
Gulf Coast Foundation of Community Operating
    Grants, 1134
Gulf Coast Foundation of Community Grants, 1135
HRSA Ryan White HIV AIDS Drug Assistance
    Grants, 1265
Kimball International-Habig Foundation Health and
    Human Services Grants, 1434
Leo Niessen Jr., Charitable Trust Grants, 1484
Mary Owen Borden Foundation Grants, 1597
MGM Resorts Foundation Community Grants, 1655
MGN Family Foundation Grants, 1656
Nicole Brown Foundation Grants, 1760
OneFamily Foundation Grants, 1822
Robert R. Meyer Foundation Grants, 2094
Rosenberg Fund for Children Edith and George
    Ziefert Fund Grants, 2110
Rosenberg Fund for Children Grants, 2111
Rosenberg Fund for Children Herman Warsh Fund
    Grant, 2112
Seybert Foundation Grants, 2184
Target Corp Community Engagement Grants, 2270
TE Foundation Grants, 2279
Textron Corporate Contributions Grants, 2286
Z. Smith Reynolds Foundation Small Grants, 2523

Counseling/Guidance Education
Medtronic Foundation Community Link Human
    Services Grants, 1631
Robert R. McCormick Tribune Foundation
    Community Grants, 2093
USDA WIC Nutrition Ed Innovations Grants, 2363

Craft Arts
Crayola Champ Creatively Alive Children Grts, 764
Helen E. Ellis Charitable Trust Grants, 1228
NHSCA Artist Residence Grants, 1756
NHSCA Youth Arts Project Grants: For Extended
    Arts Learning, 1758
NJSCA Artists in Education Residencies, 1763
NJSCA Arts Ed Special Initiative Grants, 1764
PCA-PCD Professional Development for Individual
    Artists Grants, 1883
PCA Arts in Education Residencies, 1885
PCA Arts Organizations and Arts Programs Grants
    for Crafts, 1891
PCA Busing Grants, 1899
PCA Entry Track Arts Organizations and Arts
    Programs Grants for Crafts, 1903
PCA Pennsylvania Partners in the Arts Program
    Stream Grants, 1914
PCA Pennsylvania Partners in the Arts Project
    Stream Grants, 1915
PCA Professional Development Grants, 1916
PCA Strategies for Success Grants - Basic Level, 1918
PCA Strategies for Success Grants - Intermediate
    Level, 1919
TAC Arts Access Grant, 2265
Trinity Trust Summer Youth Mini Grants, 2321
Wild Rivers Community Foundation Summer Youth
    Mini Grants, 2449

Creative Writing
AAAS/Subaru SB&F Prize for Excl in Sci Books, 22
ALA Alex Awards, 153
ALA Amazing Audiobks for Young Adults Awd, 155
ALA Best Fiction for Young Adults Award, 160
ALA Children's Literature Legacy Award, 165
ALA John Newbery Medal, 172
ALA Margaret A. Edwards Award, 175
ALA Notable Children's Books Awards, 179
ALA Randolph Caldecott Medal, 188
Community Foundation of Western Massachusetts
    Grants, 741
Do Something Writing and Journalism Intern, 861
National Cowboy and Western Heritage Museum
    Awards, 1722
Newfoundland and Labrador Arts Council ArtSmarts
    Grants, 1744
NHSCA Artist Residence Grants, 1756
NHSCA Youth Arts Project Grants: For Extended
    Arts Learning, 1758
NJSCA Artists in Education Residencies, 1763
Olive Higgins Prouty Foundation Grants, 1817
PCA Arts Organizations and Arts Programs Grants
    for Literature, 1894
PCA Strategies for Success Grants - Adv Level, 1917
PCA Strategies for Success Grants - Intermediate
    Level, 1919
PEN America Phyllis Naylor Grant for Children's and
    Young Adult Novelists, 1928
Screen Actors Guild PencilPALS Assistance, 2172
Union Square Arts Award, 2339

Creativity
Ezra Jack Keats Foundation Mini-Grants, 944
Hank Aaron Chasing the Dream Fdn Grants, 1162
Meyer Foundation Education Grants, 1649
Phoenix Coyotes Charities Grants, 1963
Rosenberg Fund for Children Ozzy Klate Memorial
    Fund Grants, 2114

Crime Causation
Initiaive Fdn Inside-Out Connections Grants, 1303

Crime Control
George H. and Jane A. Mifflin Memorial Fund
    Grants, 1048

Crime Prevention
A. Alfred Taubman Foundation Grants, 18
American Woodmark Foundation Grants, 263
Austin S. Nelson Foundation Grants, 333
Emily O'Neill Sullivan Foundation Grants, 913
Farmers Insurance Corporate Giving Grants, 948
G.N. Wilcox Trust Grants, 1031
George H. and Jane A. Mifflin Memorial Fund
    Grants, 1048
Herman Goldman Foundation Grants, 1245
Initiaive Fdn Inside-Out Connections Grants, 1303
Ordean Foundation Catalyst Grants, 1830
Ordean Foundation Partnership Grants, 1831
Public Welfare Fdn Juvenile Justice Grants, 2033
R.C. Baker Foundation Grants, 2043
RCF General Community Grants, 2062
Thomas W. Briggs Foundation Grants, 2294
Union Bank, N.A. Foundation Grants, 2334

Crime Victims
Austin S. Nelson Foundation Grants, 333
Cralle Foundation Grants, 760
Initiaive Fdn Inside-Out Connections Grants, 1303

Criminal Behavior
Ordean Foundation Catalyst Grants, 1830
Ordean Foundation Partnership Grants, 1831
OSF Baltimore Criminal and Juve Justice Grts, 1839
Public Welfare Fdn Juvenile Justice Grants, 2033
William J. and Dorothy K. O'Neill Foundation
    Responsive Grants, 2468

Criminal Justice
Bernard F. and Alva B. Gimbel Foundation Criminal
    Justice Grants, 412
Carroll County Community Foundation Grants, 513
Community Foundation of Western Massachusetts
    Grants, 741
Henry County Community Foundation Grants, 1239
Marion I. and Henry J. Knott Foundation Standard
    Grants, 1572
Ms. Foundation for Women Building Democracy
    Grants, 1706
OSF Baltimore Criminal and Juve Justice Grts, 1839
OSF Soros Justice Youth Activist Fellowships, 1844
Public Welfare Fdn Juvenile Justice Grants, 2033
Puerto Rico Community Foundation Grants, 2037
Sioux Falls Area Community Foundation Community
    Fund Grants, 2203
Sioux Falls Area Community Foundation Spot
    Grants, 2204
Social Justice Fund Northwest Criminal Justice
    Giving Project Grants, 2214
Threshold Fdn Justice and Democracy Grants, 2298

Criminology
OSF Soros Justice Youth Activist Fellowships, 1844

Crisis Counseling
Austin S. Nelson Foundation Grants, 333
Charles H. Pearson Foundation Grants, 566
Cleveland Foundation Higley Fund Grants, 634
Community Foundation of Bartholomew County
    Women's Giving Circle, 692
D. W. McMillan Foundation Grants, 776
Edwards Memorial Trust Grants, 891
GNOF Plaquemines Community Grants, 1091
Kimball International-Habig Foundation Health and
    Human Services Grants, 1434
Medtronic Foundation Community Link Human
    Services Grants, 1631
Nationwide Insurance Foundation Grants, 1726
Ordean Foundation Catalyst Grants, 1830
Ordean Foundation Partnership Grants, 1831
Pentair Foundation Education and Community
    Grants, 1934

Perpetual Benevolent Fund, 1940
Sensient Technologies Foundation Grants, 2180
Sierra Health Foundation Responsive Grants, 2199

Critical Care Medicine
E.L. Wiegand Foundation Grants, 877
Herman Goldman Foundation Grants, 1245
Latkin Charitable Foundation Grants, 1469
Piper Trust Healthcare and Med Rsrch Grants, 1978

Cross-Cultural Studies
Nellie Mae Education Foundation District-Level
    Change Grants, 1736
NYSCA Arts Ed: Services to the Field Grants, 1784

Culinary Arts
Adolph Coors Foundation Grants, 129
Carl B. and Florence E. King Foundation Grants, 506
Ifuku Family Foundation Grants, 1287
Radcliffe Institute Carol K. Pforzheimer Student
    Fellowships, 2048

Cultural Activities/Programs
2 Depot Square Ipswich Charitable Foundation
    Grants, 3
Aaron Foundation Grants, 42
Abell-Hanger Foundation Grants, 52
Abington Foundation Grants, 54
Achelis and Bodman Foundation Grants, 101
Achelis Foundation Grants, 102
Adelaide Breed Bayrd Foundation Grants, 123
Adobe Fdn Community Investment Grants, 127
Air Products Foundation Grants, 148
Alaska Airlines Foundation LIFT Grants, 194
Alcatel-Lucent Technologies Foundation Grants, 224
Alex Stern Family Foundation Grants, 229
ALFJ International Fund Grants, 231
Alliant Energy Foundation Community Giving for
    Good Sponsorship Grants, 240
Ama OluKai Foundation Grants, 249
Ameren Corporation Community Grants, 251
American Indian Youth Running Strong Grants, 256
American Savings Foundation Program Grants, 261
Anheuser-Busch Foundation Grants, 273
Anna Fitch Ardenghi Trust Grants, 274
Atlanta Foundation Grants, 326
Austin Community Foundation Grants, 332
Avery Dennison Foundation Education Grants, 337
Batts Foundation Grants, 367
Bay Area Community Foundation Semiannual
    Grants, 382
Benton Community Foundation Grants, 405
Black Hills Corporation Grants, 435
Blandin Foundation Itasca County Area Vitality
    Grants, 439
Blue Cross Blue Shield of Minnesota Foundation
    - Healthy Neighborhoods: Connect for Health
    Challenge Grants, 443
Blue Grass Community Foundation Clark County
    Fund Grants, 444
Blue Grass Community Foundation Fayette County
    Fund Grants, 446
Blue Grass Community Foundation Franklin County
    Fund Grants, 447
Blue Grass Community Foundation Harrison County
    Fund Grants, 448
Blue Grass Community Foundation Hudson-Ellis
    Grants, 449
Blue Grass Community Foundation Madison County
    Fund Grants, 450
Blue Grass Community Foundation Magoffin County
    Fund Grants, 451
Blue Grass Community Foundation Morgan County
    Fund Grants, 452
Blue Grass Community Foundation Rowan County
    Fund Grants, 453
Blue Grass Community Foundation Woodford
    County Fund Grants, 454
Blue River Community Foundation Grants, 458
Boeing Company Contributions Grants, 462

Bradley-Turner Foundation Grants, 466
Brown County Community Foundation Grants, 475
Carl B. and Florence E. King Foundation Grants, 506
Carroll County Community Foundation Grants, 513
Charlotte Martin Foundation Youth Grants, 571
Chicago Board of Trade Foundation Grants, 580
CICF Clare Noyes Grant, 604
CICF Indianapolis Fdn Community Grants, 606
CIGNA Foundation Grants, 611
Cincinnati Bell Foundation Grants, 612
Citizens Bank Charitable Foundation Grants, 616
Claremont Community Foundation Grants, 622
Clark County Community Foundation Grants, 626
Cleveland Browns Foundation Grants, 633
Clinton County Community Foundation Grants, 638
Colgate-Palmolive Company Grants, 652
Collins Foundation Grants, 658
Colorado Interstate Gas Grants, 661
Community Foundation for the National Capital
    Region Community Leadership Grants, 688
Community Foundation of Bartholomew County
    Heritage Fund Grants, 690
Community Foundation of Bartholomew County
    James A. Henderson Award for Fundraising, 691
Community Foundation of Eastern Connecticut
    General Southeast Grants, 696
Community Foundation of Greater Fort Wayne -
    Community Endowment and Clarke Endowment
    Grants, 705
Community Foundation of Greater Fort Wayne -
    John S. and James L. Knight Foundation Donor-
    Advised Grants, 707
Community Foundation of Greater Greensboro
    Community Grants, 708
Community Fdn of Howard County Grants, 712
Community Fdn of Randolph County Grants, 735
Community Foundation Serving Riverside and San
    Bernardino Counties Impact Grants, 742
Cooke Foundation Grants, 748
Cudd Foundation Grants, 769
Dana Brown Charitable Trust Grants, 777
Dayton Foundation Grants, 796
Dayton Power and Light Foundation Grants, 802
Del Mar Foundation Community Grants, 820
Dunspaugh-Dalton Foundation Grants, 873
Edna Wardlaw Charitable Trust Grants, 886
Elkhart County Community Foundation Grants, 903
Entergy Corporation Micro Grants, 919
Ethel Sergeant Clark Smith Foundation Grants, 935
Farmers Insurance Corporate Giving Grants, 948
Faye L. and William L. Cowden Charitable
    Foundation Grants, 950
Fidelity Foundation Grants, 957
FirstEnergy Foundation Community Grants, 965
Foundations of East Chicago Education Grants, 995
Francis L. Abreu Charitable Trust Grants, 1008
Fremont Area Community Foundation Community
    Grants, 1020
G.N. Wilcox Trust Grants, 1031
General Motors Foundation Grants, 1039
George W. Codrington Charitable Foundation
    Grants, 1055
Gertrude & William C. Wardlaw Grants, 1067
GNOF Exxon-Mobil Grants, 1080
Greater Milwaukee Foundation Grants, 1109
Greater Tacoma Community Foundation General
    Operating Grants, 1113
Guy I. Bromley Trust Grants, 1136
H.B. Fuller Foundation Grants, 1138
HAF Ian Chris Mackey Newman Fund Grts, 1143
HAF Laurence and Elaine Allen Memorial Fund
    Grants, 1146
HAF Mada Huggins Caldwell Fund Grants, 1147
Hahl Proctor Charitable Trust Grants, 1151
Hearst Foundations Culture Grants, 1223
Hill Crest Foundation Grants, 1249
HSFCA Folk and Traditional Arts Grants - Culture
    Learning, 1268
Hubbard Family Foundation Grants, 1270
Huffy Foundation Grants, 1273

Humana Foundation Grants, 1275
Huntington County Community Foundation Make a Difference Grants, 1280
Iddings Foundation Capital Project Grants, 1283
Iddings Foundation Major Project Grants, 1284
Island Insurance Foundation Grants, 1316
J.W. Kieckhefer Foundation Grants, 1324
Johnson Controls Foundation Arts and Culture Grants, 1378
JP Morgan Chase Fdn Arts and Culture Grants, 1394
Katharine Matthies Foundation Grants, 1418
Katherine John Murphy Foundation Grants, 1419
Kenneth T. and Eileen L. Norris Fdn Grants, 1427
Kimball Foundation Grants, 1432
Kirby Laing Foundation Grants, 1439
Kirkpatrick Foundation Grants, 1440
Kodak Community Relations Grants, 1445
Kodiak Community Foundation Grants, 1446
Koret Foundation Grants, 1449
Kovler Family Foundation Grants, 1454
Land O'Lakes Foundation Community Grants, 1466
Land O'Lakes Foundation Mid-Atlantic Grants, 1467
Liberty Bank Foundation Grants, 1488
Lied Foundation Trust Grants, 1490
Lockheed Martin Corporation Fdn Grants, 1505
Lotus 88 Foundation for Women and Children Grants, 1508
Mabel Louise Riley Foundation Grants, 1529
Mabel Y. Hughes Charitable Trust Grants, 1530
Madison County Community Foundation General Grants, 1537
Marcia and Otto Koehler Foundation Grants, 1553
Margaret and James A. Elkins Jr. Fdn Grants, 1555
Margaret T. Morris Foundation Grants, 1557
Marin Community Foundation Arts Education Grants, 1562
Marion I. and Henry J. Knott Foundation Discretionary Grants, 1571
Marion I. and Henry J. Knott Foundation Standard Grants, 1572
Marsh Corporate Grants, 1580
Mary K. Chapman Foundation Grants, 1590
Mary Owen Borden Foundation Grants, 1597
Mary S. and David C. Corbin Fdn Grants, 1598
Massachusetts Cultural Council Local Cultural Council (LCC) Grants, 1601
Maurice Amado Foundation Grants, 1609
Maurice J. Masserini Charitable Trust Grants, 1610
McConnell Foundation Grants, 1616
McInerny Foundation Grants, 1622
Meadows Foundation Grants, 1626
Mertz Gilmore Foundation NYC Dance Grants, 1642
Montana Arts Council Cultural and Aesthetic Project Grants, 1685
Montana Community Foundation Grants, 1687
Morris Stulsaft Foundation Early Childhood Education Grants, 1696
Nathaniel and Elizabeth P. Stevens Foundation Grants, 1719
Newfoundland and Labrador Arts Council ArtSmarts Grants, 1744
Noble County Community Foundation Grants, 1765
Norcliffe Foundation Grants, 1766
NYSCA Arts Education: General Program Support Grants, 1782
NYSCA Arts Education: Local Capacity Building Grants (Regrants), 1783
NYSCA Arts Ed: Services to the Field Grants, 1784
NYSCA Special Arts Services: General Program Support Grants, 1793
NYSCA Special Arts Services: Instruction and Training Grants, 1794
Onan Family Foundation Grants, 1821
Oppenstein Brothers Foundation Grants, 1827
Parkersburg Area Community Foundation Action Grants, 1871
PCA Arts Organizations and Arts Programs Grants for Arts Service Organizations, 1890
PCA Arts Organizations and Arts Programs Grants for Local Arts, 1895

PCA Busing Grants, 1899
PCA Entry Track Arts Organizations and Arts Programs Grants for Arts Service Orgs, 1902
PCA Entry Track Arts Organizations and Arts Programs Grants for Local Arts, 1907
PCA Entry Track Arts Organizations and Arts Programs Grants for Theatre, 1910
Percy B. Ferebee Endowment Grants, 1936
Perkins Charitable Foundation Grants, 1939
Peyton Anderson Foundation Grants, 1954
PGE Foundation Grants, 1958
Phoenix Suns Charities Grants, 1964
Piper Jaffray Foundation Communities Giving Grants, 1974
Piper Trust Arts and Culture Grants, 1975
Pohlad Family Fdn Small Capital Grants, 1991
Polk County Community Foundation Unrestricted Grants, 2001
Puerto Rico Community Foundation Grants, 2037
Qualcomm Grants, 2042
R.C. Baker Foundation Grants, 2043
Ralph M. Parsons Foundation Grants, 2052
Rasmuson Foundation Tier One Grants, 2055
RCF General Community Grants, 2062
Reinberger Foundation Grants, 2066
Rockwell Collins Charitable Corp Grants, 2098
Roger L. and Agnes C. Dell Charitable Trust II Grants, 2100
Rosenberg Fund for Children Edith and George Ziefert Fund Grants, 2110
Rosenberg Fund for Children Grants, 2111
Rosenberg Fund for Children Herman Warsh Fund Grant, 2112
Rosenberg Fund for Children Moish and Lillian Antopol Memorial Fund Grants, 2113
Roy and Christine Sturgis Charitable Tr Grts, 2115
Ruth Anderson Foundation Grants, 2122
S. Spencer Scott Fund Grants, 2129
Sarkeys Foundation Grants, 2163
Schlessman Family Foundation Grants, 2167
Scott B. and Annie P. Appleby Charitable Trust Grants, 2169
Scott County Community Foundation Grants, 2170
Seattle Foundation Arts and Culture Grants, 2174
Serco Foundation Grants, 2181
Shell Deer Park Grants, 2186
Shell Oil Company Foundation Community Development Grants, 2188
Skaggs Foundation Grants, 2207
Sony Corporation of America Grants, 2216
Stella and Charles Guttman Foundation Grants, 2241
Strake Foundation Grants, 2249
Stranahan Foundation Grants, 2250
Summit Foundation Grants, 2255
Sunoco Foundation Grants, 2256
SunTrust Bank Trusteed Foundations Greene-Sawtell Grants, 2257
SunTrust Bank Trusteed Foundations Nell Warren Elkin and William Simpson Elkin Grants, 2258
Tauck Family Foundation Grants, 2274
TE Foundation Grants, 2279
Telluride Foundation Community Grants, 2281
Tension Envelope Foundation Grants, 2284
Thomas J. Long Foundation Community Grants, 2291
Thomas W. Briggs Foundation Grants, 2294
Tides Foundation Grants, 2302
TJX Foundation Grants, 2303
U.S. Bank Foundation Grants, 2330
U.S. Cellular Corporation Grants, 2331
Union Bank, N.A. Foundation Grants, 2334
Union Pacific Fdn Community & Civic Grants, 2337
United Technologies Corporation Grants, 2347
Virginia Foundation for the Humanities Open Grants, 2387
Wayne County Foundation Grants, 2419
Western Indiana Community Fdn Grants, 2428
Widgeon Point Charitable Foundation Grants, 2447
Wilkins Family Foundation Grants, 2450
William B. Stokely Jr. Foundation Grants, 2459
William Blair and Company Foundation Grants, 2461

William E. Barth Foundation Grants, 2463
William Foulds Family Foundation Grants, 2465
William J. and Dorothy K. O'Neill Foundation Responsive Grants, 2468
William Ray and Ruth E. Collins Fdn Grants, 2473
Williams Comps Homegrown Giving Grants, 2474
Xerox Foundation Grants, 2507
Z. Smith Reynolds Foundation Small Grants, 2523

Cultural Diversity
Ackerman Foundation Grants, 103
Alaska State Council on the Arts Youth Cultural Heritage Fast Track Grants, 212
American Indian Youth Running Strong Grants, 256
Aspen Community Foundation Grants, 316
ATA Inclusive Learning Communities Grants, 323
Ben Cohen StandUp Foundation Grants, 403
Blossom Fund Grants, 441
Blue Cross Blue Shield of Minnesota Foundation - Healthy Neighborhoods: Connect for Health Challenge Grants, 443
Bodenwein Public Benevolent Foundation Grants, 461
California Arts Cncl Statewide Networks Grants, 493
California Arts Cncl Technical Assistance Grts, 494
California Endowment Innovative Ideas Challenge Grants, 495
Cargill Corporate Giving Grants, 503
Chicago Community Trust Arts and Culture Grants: Improving Access to Arts Learning, 581
Community Foundation of Greater Fort Wayne - John S. and James L. Knight Foundation Donor-Advised Grants, 707
Community Foundation of Greater Greensboro Community Grants, 708
EQT Fdn Community Enrichment Grants, 926
Guy I. Bromley Trust Grants, 1136
Henry County Community Foundation Grants, 1239
Kalamazoo Community Foundation Good Neighbor Grants, 1408
Kirby Laing Foundation Grants, 1439
Kodak Community Relations Grants, 1445
Koret Foundation Grants, 1449
Laidlaw Foundation Youth Organizaing Initiatives Grants, 1462
Laura Musser Intercultural Harmony Grants, 1472
Nathan Cummings Foundation Grants, 1718
NCSS Carter G. Woodson Book Awards, 1729
Nellie Mae Education Foundation District-Level Change Grants, 1736
Noble County Community Foundation Grants, 1765
PCA Arts Organizations and Arts Programs Grants for Arts Education Organizations, 1889
PCA Arts Organizations and Arts Programs Grants for Literature, 1894
PCA Entry Track Arts Organizations and Arts Programs Grants for Arts Education Organizations, 1901
Piper Trust Arts and Culture Grants, 1975
Portland General Electric Foundation Grants, 2007
RISCA Project Grants for Individuals, 2079
Serco Foundation Grants, 2181
Shelley and Donald Rubin Foundation Grants, 2187
Sioux Falls Area Community Foundation Community Fund Grants, 2203
Sioux Falls Area Community Foundation Spot Grants, 2204
Social Justice Fund Northwest Criminal Justice Giving Project Grants, 2214
Subaru of America Foundation Grants, 2253
Teaching Tolerance Diverse Democracy Grants, 2275
Teaching Tolerance Social Justice Educator Grts, 2276
Tides Foundation Girl Rising Fund Grants, 2301
Wallace Foundation Grants, 2402

Cultural Heritage
Adolph Coors Foundation Grants, 129
Albert and Ethel Herzstein Charitable Foundation Grants, 219
American Indian Youth Running Strong Grants, 256
Dayton Foundation Grants, 796

DTE Energy Foundation Diversity Grants, 867
GNOF IMPACT Grants for Arts and Culture, 1083
Greater Sitka Legacy Fund Grants, 1111
Hawai'i SFCA Art Bento Program @ HiSAM
 Grants, 1210
Hawaii Community Foundation Reverend Takie
 Okumura Family Grants, 1216
HSFCA Biennium Grants, 1267
HSFCA Folk and Traditional Arts Grants - Culture
 Learning, 1268
Japan Foundation Los Angeles Mini-Grants for
 Japanese Arts & Culture, 1354
Japan Foundation New York Small Grants for Arts
 and Culture, 1355
Japan Foundation New York World Heritage Photo
 Panel Exhibition, 1356
Kenai Peninsula Foundation Grants, 1425
Ketchikan Community Foundation Grants, 1429
Kirby Laing Foundation Grants, 1439
Kodiak Community Foundation Grants, 1446
Lotus 88 Foundation for Women and Children
 Grants, 1508
Lubrizol Corporation Community Grants, 1512
Mary K. Chapman Foundation Grants, 1590
Massachusetts Cultural Council Local Cultural
 Council (LCC) Grants, 1601
Maurice Amado Foundation Grants, 1609
Nellie Mae Education Foundation District-Level
 Change Grants, 1736
NYSCA Special Arts Services: General Program
 Support Grants, 1793
NYSCA Special Arts Services: Instruction and
 Training Grants, 1794
PCA Arts Organizations and Arts Programs Grants
 for Art Museums, 1888
PCA Entry Track Arts Organizations and Arts
 Programs Grants for Art Museums, 1900
Petersburg Community Foundation Grants, 1951
Shelley and Donald Rubin Foundation Grants, 2187
Virginia Foundation for the Humanities Open
 Grants, 2387
W.M. Keck Fdn Southern California Grants, 2398
West Virginia Commission on the Arts Challenge
 America Partnership Grants, 2430

Cultural Identity
American Indian Youth Running Strong Grants, 256
DTE Energy Foundation Diversity Grants, 867
HSFCA Folk and Traditional Arts Grants - Culture
 Learning, 1268
James and Abigail Campbell Family Fdn Grants, 1337
Laura Musser Intercultural Harmony Grants, 1472
NYSCA Special Arts Services: General Program
 Support Grants, 1793
NYSCA Special Arts Services: Instruction and
 Training Grants, 1794
Shelley and Donald Rubin Foundation Grants, 2187
Tides Foundation Girl Rising Fund Grants, 2301
Virginia Foundation for the Humanities Open
 Grants, 2387
W.M. Keck Fdn Southern California Grants, 2398

Cultural Outreach
2 Depot Square Ipswich Charitable Foundation
 Grants, 3
3M Company Fdn Community Giving Grants, 5
Abney Foundation Grants, 55
American Indian Youth Running Strong Grants, 256
Anheuser-Busch Foundation Grants, 273
Anna Fitch Ardenghi Trust Grants, 274
APAP All-In Grants, 283
ATA Inclusive Learning Communities Grants, 323
Baxter International Foundation Grants, 369
Bernard and Audre Rapoport Foundation Arts and
 Culture Grants, 407
Blandin Foundation Itasca County Area Vitality
 Grants, 439
Blue Cross Blue Shield of Minnesota Foundation
 - Healthy Neighborhoods: Connect for Health
 Challenge Grants, 443

Bodenwein Public Benevolent Foundation Grants, 461
Bridgestone Americas Trust Fund Grants, 469
Carl B. and Florence E. King Foundation Grants, 506
CFFVR Clintonville Area Foundation Grants, 539
Clinton County Community Foundation Grants, 638
Community Foundation of Greater Fort Wayne -
 John S. and James L. Knight Foundation Donor-
 Advised Grants, 707
Community Fdn of Howard County Grants, 712
DTE Energy Foundation Diversity Grants, 867
Essex County Community Foundation Merrimack
 Valley Municipal Business Development and
 Recovery Fund Grants, 933
Gannett Foundation Community Action Grants, 1033
Greater Sitka Legacy Fund Grants, 1111
Greater Tacoma Community Foundation Fund for
 Women and Girls Grants, 1112
Guy I. Bromley Trust Grants, 1136
H.A. and Mary K. Chapman Charitable Trust
 Grants, 1137
HAF Laurence and Elaine Allen Memorial Fund
 Grants, 1146
Hartford Foundation Regular Grants, 1185
Hawai'i Community Foundation East Hawaii Fund
 Grants, 1199
Hawai'i Community Foundation Family Literacy and
 Hawaii Pizza Hut Literacy Grants, 1201
Hawai'i Community Foundation Lana'i Community
 Benefit Fund, 1203
Hawai'i SFCA Art Bento Program @ HiSAM
 Grants, 1210
Hearst Foundations Culture Grants, 1223
Helen Bader Foundation Grants, 1227
Highmark Corporate Giving Grants, 1248
HSFCA Folk and Traditional Arts Grants - Culture
 Learning, 1268
Humana Foundation Grants, 1275
Irving S. Gilmore Foundation Grants, 1314
J. Bulow Campbell Foundation Grants, 1319
Jacob G. Schmidlapp Trusts Grants, 1336
James Ford Bell Foundation Grants, 1339
James S. Copley Foundation Grants, 1345
Katrine Menzing Deakins Chartbl Trust Grants, 1422
Kenai Peninsula Foundation Grants, 1425
Ketchikan Community Foundation Grants, 1429
Kodiak Community Foundation Grants, 1446
Laidlaw Foundation Youh Organizing Catalyst
 Grants, 1461
Land O'Lakes Foundation Community Grants, 1466
Lubrizol Corporation Community Grants, 1512
Ludwick Family Foundation Grants, 1516
M.J. Murdock Charitable Trust General Grants, 1524
Marin Community Foundation Arts Education
 Grants, 1562
Mary K. Chapman Foundation Grants, 1590
Massachusetts Cultural Council Local Cultural
 Council (LCC) Grants, 1601
Max and Anna Levinson Foundation Grants, 1612
McCarthy Family Fdn Charity Fund Grants, 1614
Mertz Gilmore Foundation NYC Dance Grants, 1642
Montana Arts Council Cultural and Aesthetic Project
 Grants, 1685
Nathalie and Gladys Dalkowitz Charitable Trust
 Grants, 1716
Nathan Cummings Foundation Grants, 1718
New Earth Foundation Grants, 1743
NYSCA Arts Education: General Program Support
 Grants, 1782
NYSCA Arts Education: Local Capacity Building
 Grants (Regrants), 1783
NYSCA Arts Ed: Services to the Field Grants, 1784
NYSCA Special Arts Services: General Program
 Support Grants, 1793
NYSCA Special Arts Services: Instruction and
 Training Grants, 1794
PCA Art Organizations and Art Programs Grants for
 Presenting Organizations, 1884
PCA Arts Organizations and Arts Programs Grants
 for Arts Education Organizations, 1889

PCA Arts Organizations and Arts Programs Grants
 for Crafts, 1891
PCA Arts Organizations and Arts Programs Grants
 for Dance, 1892
PCA Arts Organizations and Arts Programs Grants
 for Literature, 1894
PCA Arts Organizations and Arts Programs Grants
 for Local Arts, 1895
PCA Arts Organizations and Arts Programs Grants
 for Theatre, 1896
PCA Arts Organizations and Arts Programs Grants
 for Traditional and Folk Arts, 1897
PCA Arts Organizations and Arts Programs Grants
 for Visual Arts, 1898
PCA Entry Track Arts Organizations and
 Arts Programs Grants for Arts Education
 Organizations, 1901
PCA Entry Track Arts Organizations and Arts
 Programs Grants for Crafts, 1903
PCA Entry Track Arts Organizations and Arts
 Programs Grants for Dance, 1904
PCA Entry Track Arts Organizations and Arts
 Programs Grants for Local Arts, 1907
PCA Entry Track Arts Organizations and Arts
 Programs Grants for Presenting Orgs, 1909
PCA Entry Track Arts Organizations and Arts
 Programs Grants for Theatre, 1910
PCA Entry Track Arts Orgs and Arts Programs
 Grants for Traditional and Folk Arts, 1911
PCA Entry Track Arts Organizations and Arts
 Programs Grants for Visual Arts, 1912
Phoenix Coyotes Charities Grants, 1963
Piper Trust Arts and Culture Grants, 1975
Qualcomm Grants, 2042
Rasmuson Foundation Tier Two Grants, 2056
Samuel N. and Mary Castle Foundation Grants, 2145
Shelley and Donald Rubin Foundation Grants, 2187
Sorenson Legacy Foundation Grants, 2217
TAC Touring Arts and Arts Access Touring Arts
 Grants, 2269
Textron Corporate Contributions Grants, 2286
Thelma Braun and Bocklett Family Foundation
 Grants, 2287
Thomas J. Long Foundation Community Grants, 2291
Virginia Foundation for the Humanities Open
 Grants, 2387
William Ray and Ruth E. Collins Fdn Grants, 2473

Curriculum Development
Adobe Fdn Community Investment Grants, 127
ALA Sara Jaffarian School Library Award for
 Exemplary Humanities Programming, 190
AT&T Foundation Education Grants, 321
Bernard and Audre Rapoport Foundation Education
 Grants, 410
Best Buy Children's Fdn @15 Teach Awards, 416
Bristol-Myers Squibb Foundation Independent
 Medical Education Grants, 472
Brown Rudnick Charitable Foundation Community
 Grants, 477
Calvin Johnson Jr. Foundation Mini Grants, 498
Christensen Fund Regional Grants, 600
Delmarva Power & Light Mini-Grants, 822
Don and May Wilkins Charitable Trust Grants, 842
Dorr Foundation Grants, 846
Foundation for Rural Service Education Grants, 991
Foundation for the Mid South Education Grants, 993
George I. Alden Trust Grants, 1051
Geraldine R. Dodge Fdn Education Grants, 1061
Gray Family Foundation Community Field Trips
 Grants, 1105
Hawai'i Community Foundation Family Literacy and
 Hawaii Pizza Hut Literacy Grants, 1201
Hazel and Walter T. Bales Foundation Grants, 1220
HSFCA Biennium Grants, 1267
Iddings Foundation Major Project Grants, 1284
Indiana OCRA Rural Capacity Grants (RCG), 1301
Jack H. and William M. Light Charitable Trust
 Grants, 1330
Jennings County Community Fdn Grants, 1360

Martha Holden Jennings Foundation Grants-to-Educators, 1581
Mary A. Crocker Trust Grants, 1584
Maurice R. Robinson Fund Grants, 1611
Meadows Foundation Grants, 1626
Meyer Foundation Education Grants, 1649
New Jersey Office of Faith Based Initiatives English as a Second Language Grants, 1751
NJSCA Arts Ed Special Initiative Grants, 1764
Northrop Grumman Foundation Grants, 1773
NRA Foundation Grants, 1774
NYSCA Arts Education: Community-based Learning Grants, 1780
NYSCA Arts Education: General Operating Support Grants, 1781
NYSCA Arts Education: General Program Support Grants, 1782
NYSCA Arts Education: Local Capacity Building Grants (Regrants), 1783
NYSCA Arts Ed: Services to the Field Grants, 1784
Ontario Arts Council Indigenous Culture Fund Indigenous Artists in Communities and Schools Project Grants, 1825
Oregon Community Foundation Edna E. Harrell Community Children's Fund Grants, 1835
Piedmont Natural Gas Fdn Envirnmtl Stewardship and Energy Sustainability Grant, 1967
Progress Energy Foundation Energy Education Grants, 2025
Public Education Power Grants, 2032
Rathmann Family Foundation Grants, 2057
Ruby K. Worner Charitable Trust Grants, 2119
SAS Institute Community Relations Donations, 2165
Silicon Valley Community Foundation Education Grants, 2200
Sorenson Legacy Foundation Grants, 2217
Target Corporation Community Engagement Fund Grants, 2270
Tellabs Foundation Grants, 2280
Toyota USA Foundation Education Grants, 2318
Wege Foundation Grants, 2422
Western Indiana Community Fdn Grants, 2428
West Virginia Commission on the Arts Long-Term Artist Residencies, 2431
YSA State Farm Good Neighbor YOUth In The Driver Seat Grants, 2521

Curriculum Instruction
AT&T Foundation Education Grants, 321
Bernard and Audre Rapoport Foundation Education Grants, 410
Calvin Johnson Jr. Foundation Mini Grants, 498
Don and May Wilkins Charitable Trust Grants, 842
Foundation for the Mid South Education Grants, 993
Gray Family Foundation Community Field Trips Grants, 1105
New Jersey Office of Faith Based Initiatives English as a Second Language Grants, 1751
NJSCA Arts Ed Special Initiative Grants, 1764
Oregon Community Foundation Edna E. Harrell Community Children's Fund Grants, 1835
Ruby K. Worner Charitable Trust Grants, 2119

Cystic Fibrosis
CFF First- and Second-Year Clinical Fellowships, 532
CFF Leroy Matthews Physician-Scientist Awds, 533
CFF Research Grants, 534
CFF Third-, Fourth-, and Fifth-Year Clinical Fellowships, 535
Cystic Fibrosis Lifestyle Foundation Individual Recreation Grants, 772
Cystic Fibrosis Lifestyle Foundation Loretta Morris Memorial Fund Grants, 773
Cystic Fibrosis Lifestyle Foundation Mentored Recreation Grants, 774
Cystic Fibrosis Lifestyle Foundation Peer Support Grants, 775
Robert R. Meyer Foundation Grants, 2094

Dance
Achelis and Bodman Foundation Grants, 101
Achelis Foundation Grants, 102
CICF Clare Noyes Grant, 604
City of Oakland Cultural Funding Grants, 618
Community Foundation of Muncie and Delaware County - Kitselman Grants, 733
Cooke Foundation Grants, 748
Crystelle Waggoner Charitable Trust Grants, 768
Donald G. Gardner Humanities Tr Youth Grts, 840
Georgia Council for the Arts Education Grants, 1060
Hahl Proctor Charitable Trust Grants, 1151
Kenneth T. and Eileen L. Norris Fdn Grants, 1427
Maryland State Arts Council Arts in Communities Grants, 1592
Mertz Gilmore Foundation NYC Dance Grants, 1642
Newfoundland and Labrador Arts Council ArtSmarts Grants, 1744
Newfoundland and Labrador Arts Council School Touring Grants, 1745
NHSCA Artist Residence Grants, 1756
NHSCA Youth Arts Project Grants: For Extended Arts Learning, 1758
NJSCA Artists in Education Residencies, 1763
NJSCA Arts Ed Special Initiative Grants, 1764
Paul and Edith Babson Foundation Grants, 1881
PCA Arts in Education Residencies, 1885
PCA Arts Organizations and Arts Programs Grants for Dance, 1892
PCA Entry Track Arts Organizations and Arts Programs Grants for Dance, 1904
PCA Strategies for Success Grants - Adv Level, 1917
PCA Strategies for Success Grants - Basic Level, 1918
PCA Strategies for Success Grants - Intermediate Level, 1919
PennPAT Artist Technical Assistance Grants, 1929
PennPAT Strategic Opportunity Grants, 1933
Puerto Rico Community Foundation Grants, 2037
Robert R. Meyer Foundation Grants, 2094
Sioux Falls Area Community Foundation Community Fund Grants, 2203
Sioux Falls Area Community Foundation Spot Grants, 2204
Union Square Arts Award, 2339
Wallace Foundation Grants, 2402

Dance Education
CICF Clare Noyes Grant, 604
NHSCA Youth Arts Project Grants: For Extended Arts Learning, 1758

Day Care
Atkinson Foundation Community Grants, 325
Carnegie Corporation of New York Grants, 511
CFFVR Basic Needs Giving Partnership Grants, 537
CFGR Community Impact Grants, 552
Corina Higginson Trust Grants, 750
Daviess County Community Foundation Youth Development Grants, 794
Dermody Properties Foundation Grants, 827
FCD New American Children Grants, 952
Foundations of East Chicago Education Grants, 995
Fred and Gretel Biel Charitable Trust Grants, 1016
Gibson County Community Foundation Youth Development Grants, 1070
Gulf Coast Foundation of Community Operating Grants, 1134
Gulf Coast Foundation of Community Program Grants, 1135
Hasbro Children's Fund Grants, 1189
John Gogian Family Foundation Grants, 1373
Kathryne Beynon Foundation Grants, 1420
Knox County Community Foundation Youth Development Grants, 1443
Kosciusko County Community Foundation REMC Operation Round Up Grants, 1453
Lilly Endowment Summer Youth Grants, 1492
Maryland State Dept of Education Coordinating Entity Services for the Maryland Child Care Res Centers Network Grants, 1594

Mary Owen Borden Foundation Grants, 1597
Montgomery County Community Foundation Youth Services Grants, 1691
Morris Stulsaft Foundation Early Childhood Education Grants, 1696
NSTA Faraday Science Communicator Award, 1778
OneFamily Foundation Grants, 1822
Perry County Community Foundation Youth Development Grants, 1943
Pike County Community Foundation Youth Development Grants, 1971
PMI Foundation Grants, 1982
Porter County Community Foundation Women's Fund Grants, 2005
Posey County Community Foundation Youth Development Grants, 2010
RCF Summertime Kids Grants, 2064
Spencer County Community Foundation Youth Development Grants, 2233
Thomas Sill Foundation Grants, 2292
Union Bank, N.A. Foundation Grants, 2334
USDA Child and Adult Care Food Program, 2362
Vanderburgh Community Foundation Youth Development Grants, 2375
W.H. and Mary Ellen Cobb Chartbl Trust Grts, 2397
Warrick County Community Foundation Youth Development Grants, 2412
William Caspar Graustein Memorial Fund Corinne G. Levin Education Grants, 2462

Death Penalty
Tides Foundation Grants, 2302

Death/Mortality
A Little Hope Grants, 235
Caplow Applied Sci (CappSci) Children's Prize, 502
CIGNA Foundation Grants, 611
Community Foundation of Louisville Children's Memorial Marker Fund Grants, 721
George E. Hatcher, Jr. and Ann Williams Hatcher Foundation Grants, 1045
Tides Fdn Friends of the IGF Fund Grants, 2300

Dementia
ACCF of Indiana Angel Funds Grants, 62
Helen Bader Foundation Grants, 1227
Henrietta Lange Burk Fund Grants, 1235

Democracy
OSF Education Support Program Grants, 1843
OSF Young Feminist Leaders Fellowships, 1845
Proteus Fund Grants, 2027
Susan A. and Donald P. Babson Charitable Foundation Grants, 2259
Teaching Tolerance Social Justice Educator Grts, 2276
Vernon K. Krieble Foundation Grants, 2379

Dental Education
Baxter International Foundation Grants, 369
Community Foundation of Louisville Delta Dental of Kentucky Fund Grants, 722
DeKalb County Community Foundation - Garrett Hospital Aid Foundation Grants, 813
Ford Family Foundation Grants - Access to Health and Dental Services, 980
Pajaro Valley Community Health Health Trust Insurance/Coverage & Education on Using the System Grants, 1864
Pajaro Valley Community Health Trust Oral Health: Prevention & Access Grants, 1866

Dental Health and Hygiene
ADA Foundation Samuel Harris Children's Dental Health Grants, 111
Aetna Foundation Regional Health Grants, 134
CFGR Jenkins Foundation Grants, 553
Community Foundation of Louisville Delta Dental of Kentucky Fund Grants, 722
Elkhart County Community Foundation Fund for Elkhart County, 902

HAF JoAllen K. Twiddy-Wood Memorial Fund
Grants, 1144
Kansas Health Fdn Major Initiatives Grants, 1414
Pajaro Valley Community Health Health Trust
Insurance/Coverage & Education on Using the
System Grants, 1864
Pajaro Valley Community Health Trust Oral Health:
Prevention & Access Grants, 1866
Ruth Camp Campbell Charitable Trust Grants, 2125
Union Labor Health Foundation Dental Angel Fund
Grants, 2336

Dentistry
Foundation for Health Enhancement Grants, 990

Dentistry, Preventive
Ford Family Foundation Grants - Access to Health
and Dental Services, 980
Foundation for Health Enhancement Grants, 990

Depression
Aetna Foundation Regional Health Grants, 134
Nick Traina Foundation Grants, 1759
NIMH Early Identification and Treatment of Mental
Disorders in Children and Adolescents Grts, 1761
Peter and Elizabeth C. Tower Foundation Mental
Health Grants, 1946

Design Arts
Jayne and Leonard Abess Foundation Grants, 1358
NJSCA Artists in Education Residencies, 1763

Developing/Underdeveloped Nations
Bill and Melinda Gates Foundation Agricultural
Development Grants, 425
Bill and Melinda Gates Foundation Emergency
Response Grants, 426
Bill and Melinda Gates Foundation Water, Sanitation
and Hygiene Grants, 428

Developmental Psychology
NSF Social Psychology Grants, 1776

Developmentally Disabled
ACL Alternatives to Guardianship Youth Resource
Center Grants, 104
Amway Corporation Contributions, 269
Armstrong McDonald Foundation Special Needs
Grants, 301
Bay Area Community Foundation Leslie L. Squires
Foundation Grants, 380
Caesars Foundation Grants, 492
CNCS Foster Grandparent Projects Grants, 646
Columbus Foundation Traditional Grants, 663
Community Foundation of Madison and Jefferson
County Grants, 731
George W. Wells Foundation Grants, 1057
Grace Bersted Foundation Grants, 1097
Graham and Carolyn Holloway Family Foundation
Grants, 1098
Hampton Roads Community Foundation
Developmental Disabilities Grants, 1156
J. Willard and Alice S. Marriott Fdn Grants, 1327
John D. and Katherine A. Johnston Foundation
Grants, 1370
John Gogian Family Foundation Grants, 1373
John W. Anderson Foundation Grants, 1383
Lavina Parker Trust Grants, 1477
Leola Osborn Trust Grants, 1483
Lewis H. Humphreys Charitable Trust Grants, 1486
Malone Family Foundation Atypical Development
Initiative Grants, 1549
Marjorie Moore Charitable Foundation Grants, 1574
Moody Foundation Grants, 1692
NZDIA Community Org Grants Scheme, 1796
Peter and Elizabeth C. Tower Foundation Intellectual
Disabilities Grants, 1944
Peter and Elizabeth C. Tower Foundation Small
Grants, 1947

Peter and Elizabeth C. Tower Foundation Technology
Initiative Grants, 1949
Peter and Elizabeth C. Tower Foundation Technology
Planning Grants, 1950
Stein Family Charitable Trust Grants, 2240
Thomas W. Bradley Foundation Grants, 2293
VSA/Metlife Connect All Grants, 2392
VSA International Young Soloists Award, 2395
VSA Playwright Discovery Award, 2396

Diabetes
Abbott Fund Access to Health Care Grants, 45
Abbott Fund Science Education Grants, 48
ACCF of Indiana Angel Funds Grants, 62
Aetna Foundation Regional Health Grants, 134
Austin S. Nelson Foundation Grants, 333
Campbell Soup Foundation Grants, 501
CFFVR Basic Needs Giving Partnership Grants, 537
CFFVR Jewelers Mutual Chartbl Giving Grants, 543
CFFVR Robert and Patricia Endries Family
Foundation Grants, 547
Community Foundation of Jackson County Seymour
Noon Lions Club Grant, 714
Florence Hunt Maxwell Foundation Grants, 979
GNOF IMPACT Kahn-Oppenheim Tr Grts, 1087
Kovler Family Foundation Grants, 1455
Locations Foundation Legacy Grants, 1504
M. Bastian Family Foundation Grants, 1522
Medtronic Foundation Strengthening Health Systems
Grants, 1632
Pajaro Valley Community Health Trust Diabetes and
Contributing Factors Grants, 1865
Premera Blue Cross Grants, 2018
William G. and Helen C. Hoffman Foundation
Grants, 2466

Diabetic Retinopathy
Sara Elizabeth O'Brien Trust Grants, 2161

Diagnosis, Medical
Covidien Partnership for Neighborhood Wellness
Grants, 759
Gerber Fdn Pediatric Health Research Grants, 1063
HRSA Ryan White HIV AIDS Drug Assistance
Grants, 1265
Piper Trust Healthcare and Med Rsrch Grants, 1978

Dietary Supplements
Gerber Foundation Pediatric Nutrition Research
Grants, 1064

Digestive Diseases and Disorders
CFF First- and Second-Year Clinical Fellowships, 532
CFF Research Grants, 534
CFF Third-, Fourth-, and Fifth-Year Clinical
Fellowships, 535

Disabled
Abell-Hanger Foundation Grants, 52
ACL Alternatives to Guardianship Youth Resource
Center Grants, 104
ACL Disability and Rehabilitation Research Projects
(DRRP) Program: Independent Living Transition
Services for Youth and Young Adults Grants, 105
ACL Neonatal Abstinence Syndrome National
Training Initiative Grant, 106
ACL Rehabilitation Research and Training Center
(RRTC) on Employment of Transition-Age Youth
with Disabilities Grants, 107
Adams Rotary Memorial Fund A Grants, 122
Adobe Foundation Action Grants, 126
Albert W. Cherne Foundation Grants, 222
Albert W. Rice Charitable Foundation Grants, 223
ALFJ International Fund Grants, 231
Alfred E. Chase Charitable Foundation Grants, 233
Allan C. and Lelia J. Garden Foundation Grants, 236
Amelia Sillman Rockwell and Carlos Perry Rockwell
Charities Fund Grants, 250
Amerigroup Foundation Grants, 264
Anne J. Caudal Foundation Grants, 276

Armstrong McDonald Foundation Special Needs
Grants, 301
Arthur Ashley Williams Foundation Grants, 302
Atkinson Foundation Community Grants, 325
Austin S. Nelson Foundation Grants, 333
Baxter International Foundation Grants, 369
Bay Area Community Foundation Leslie L. Squires
Foundation Grants, 380
Bothin Foundation Grants, 464
Carl R. Hendrickson Family Foundation Grants, 509
Carl W. and Carrie Mae Joslyn Trust Grants, 510
CFFVR Robert and Patricia Endries Family
Foundation Grants, 547
Charles Delmar Foundation Grants, 564
Charles H. Hall Foundation, 565
Charles Nelson Robinson Fund Grants, 569
Children's Trust Fund of Oregon Fdn Grants, 585
Children's Trust Fund of Oregon Foundation Small
Grants, 586
CICF Indianapolis Fdn Community Grants, 606
Clara Blackford Smith and W. Aubrey Smith
Charitable Foundation Grants, 621
CNCS Foster Grandparent Projects Grants, 646
Colgate-Palmolive Company Grants, 652
Collins Foundation Grants, 658
Columbus Foundation Traditional Grants, 663
Cralle Foundation Grants, 760
Crane Fund for Widows and Children Grants, 762
Crescent Porter Hale Foundation Grants, 767
D. W. McMillan Foundation Grants, 776
Different Needz Foundation Grants, 830
Dolan Children's Foundation Grants, 832
Doree Taylor Charitable Foundation Grants, 843
Dorothea Haus Ross Foundation Grants, 844
Edwards Memorial Trust Grants, 891
Effie and Wofford Cain Foundation Grants, 895
Eide Bailly Resourcefullness Awards, 897
Elsie H. Wilcox Foundation Grants, 909
Fassino Foundation Grants, 949
Fichtenbaum Charitable Trust Grants, 955
Florence Hunt Maxwell Foundation Grants, 979
Foundation Beyond Belief Compassionate Impact
Grants, 986
Foundation Beyond Belief Humanist Grants, 987
Fourjay Foundation Grants, 1003
Fremont Area Community Foundation Amazing X
Grants, 1019
Gannett Foundation Community Action Grants, 1033
George A Ohl Jr. Foundation Grants, 1043
Grace Bersted Foundation Grants, 1097
Graham and Carolyn Holloway Family Foundation
Grants, 1098
Greater Milwaukee Foundation Grants, 1109
Greygates Foundation Grants, 1120
Harold and Rebecca H. Gross Fdn Grants, 1171
Harold Brooks Foundation Grants, 1172
Harry and Jeanette Weinberg Fdn Grants, 1182
Hasbro Children's Fund Grants, 1189
Helen Gertrude Sparks Charitable Trust Grants, 1230
Helen Irwin Littauer Educational Trust Grants, 1231
Henrietta Lange Burk Fund Grants, 1235
Henry E. Niles Foundation Grants, 1240
Herbert A. and Adrian W. Woods Foundation
Grants, 1243
Horace A. Kimball and S. Ella Kimball Foundation
Grants, 1260
HSBC Corporate Giving Grants, 1266
J.W. Kieckhefer Foundation Grants, 1324
J. Walton Bissell Foundation Grants, 1325
J. Willard and Alice S. Marriott Fdn Grants, 1327
Jack Satter Foundation Grants, 1334
James Ford Bell Foundation Grants, 1339
John D. and Katherine A. Johnston Foundation
Grants, 1370
John Gogian Family Foundation Grants, 1373
John H. and Wilhelmina D. Harland Charitable
Foundation Children and Youth Grants, 1374
Johnson Scholarship Foundation Grants, 1382
Kenneth T. and Eileen L. Norris Fdn Grants, 1427
Kentucky Arts Cncl Access Assistance Grants, 1428

Lands' End Corporate Giving Program, 1468
Leola Osborn Trust Grants, 1483
Ludwick Family Foundation Grants, 1516
Luella Kemper Trust Grants, 1517
M.J. Murdock Charitable Trust General Grants, 1524
Mabel H. Flory Charitable Trust Grants, 1527
Manuel D. and Rhoda Mayerson Fdn Grants, 1550
Margaret Wiegand Trust Grants, 1558
Marie C. and Joseph C. Wilson Foundation Rochester
    Small Grants, 1559
Marjorie Moore Charitable Foundation Grants, 1574
Marriott Int Corporate Giving Grants, 1578
Mary Wilmer Covey Charitable Trust Grants, 1600
May and Stanley Smith Charitable Trust Grants, 1613
MGM Resorts Foundation Community Grants, 1655
Mid-Iowa Health Foundation Community Response
    Grants, 1667
Mockingbird Foundation Grants, 1680
Montana Arts Council Cultural and Aesthetic Project
    Grants, 1685
Mt. Sinai Health Care Foundation Health of the
    Jewish Community Grants, 1709
Nell J. Redfield Foundation Grants, 1737
NZDIA Community Org Grants Scheme, 1796
Oppenstein Brothers Foundation Grants, 1827
Ordean Foundation Catalyst Grants, 1830
Ordean Foundation Partnership Grants, 1831
Oticon Focus on People Awards, 1847
Peabody Foundation Grants, 1922
Pentair Foundation Education and Community
    Grants, 1934
Perkins-Ponder Foundation Grants, 1938
Piper Trust Children Grants, 1976
R.C. Baker Foundation Grants, 2043
R.S. Gernon Trust Grants, 2047
Robert R. Meyer Foundation Grants, 2094
Roy and Christine Sturgis Charitable Tr Grts, 2115
Schlessman Family Foundation Grants, 2167
Shell Deer Park Grants, 2186
Shopko Fdn Community Charitable Grants, 2191
Sidney Stern Memorial Trust Grants, 2197
Sioux Falls Area Community Foundation Community
    Fund Grants, 2203
Sioux Falls Area Community Foundation Spot
    Grants, 2204
Starr Foundation Grants, 2237
Stein Family Charitable Trust Grants, 2240
Stella and Charles Guttman Foundation Grants, 2241
Sylvia Adams Charitable Trust Grants, 2262
TAC Touring Arts and Arts Access Touring Arts
    Grants, 2269
Thomas Sill Foundation Grants, 2292
TJX Foundation Grants, 2303
Toby Wells Foundation Grants, 2304
Trinity Trust Summer Youth Mini Grants, 2321
Union Labor Health Fdn Angel Fund Grants, 2335
Victor E. Speas Foundation Grants, 2380
Vigneron Memorial Fund Grants, 2384
VSA/Metlife Connect All Grants, 2392
VSA/Volkswagen Group of America Exhibition
    Awards, 2393
VSA International Art Program for Children with
    Disabilities Grants, 2394
VSA International Young Soloists Award, 2395
VSA Playwright Discovery Award, 2396
W.P. and Bulah Luse Foundation Grants, 2399
William J. and Dorothy K. O'Neill Foundation
    Responsive Grants, 2468

Disabled (Target Groups)
ACL Alternatives to Guardianship Youth Resource
    Center Grants, 104
ACL Disability and Rehabilitation Research Projects
    (DRRP) Program: Independent Living Transition
    Services for Youth and Young Adults Grants, 105
ACL Neonatal Abstinence Syndrome National
    Training Initiative Grant, 106
ACL Rehabilitation Research and Training Center
    (RRTC) on Employment of Transition-Age Youth
    with Disabilities Grants, 107

ALA Baker and Taylor Summer Reading Program
    Grant, 158
ALA Schneider Family Book Awards, 191
Allan C. and Lelia J. Garden Foundation Grants, 236
Anne J. Caudal Foundation Grants, 276
Armstrong McDonald Foundation Special Needs
    Grants, 301
Catherine Holmes Wilkins Foundation Charitable
    Grants, 520
Grifols Community Outreach Grants, 1122
Lavina Parker Trust Grants, 1477
Singing for Change Foundation Grants, 2202
Starr Foundation Grants, 2237
Stein Family Charitable Trust Grants, 2240

Disabled Student Support
ACL Disability and Rehabilitation Research Projects
    (DRRP) Program: Independent Living Transition
    Services for Youth and Young Adults Grants, 105
Allan C. and Lelia J. Garden Foundation Grants, 236
Community Foundation of Madison and Jefferson
    County Grants, 731
Fichtenbaum Charitable Trust Grants, 955
Harold and Rebecca H. Gross Fdn Grants, 1171
Johnson Scholarship Foundation Grants, 1382
Lavina Parker Trust Grants, 1477
Lewis H. Humphreys Charitable Trust Grants, 1486
Peter and Elizabeth C. Tower Foundation Intellectual
    Disabilities Grants, 1944
Stein Family Charitable Trust Grants, 2240
William G. and Helen C. Hoffman Foundation
    Grants, 2466

Disabled, Accessibility for
ACL Rehabilitation Research and Training Center
    (RRTC) on Employment of Transition-Age Youth
    with Disabilities Grants, 107
Adolph Coors Foundation Grants, 129
ALA Baker and Taylor Summer Reading Program
    Grant, 158
Allan C. and Lelia J. Garden Foundation Grants, 236
Anne J. Caudal Foundation Grants, 276
Bay Area Community Foundation Leslie L. Squires
    Foundation Grants, 380
CNCS AmeriCorps State and National Planning
    Grants, 644
Community Foundation of Madison and Jefferson
    County Grants, 731
Fichtenbaum Charitable Trust Grants, 955
Harold and Rebecca H. Gross Fdn Grants, 1171
John F. Kennedy Center for the Performing Arts
    National Rosemary Kennedy Internship, 1371
Johnson Scholarship Foundation Grants, 1382
Lavina Parker Trust Grants, 1477
Leola Osborn Trust Grants, 1483
Lewis H. Humphreys Charitable Trust Grants, 1486
Marietta McNeill Morgan and Samuel Tate Morgan
    Jr. Trust Grants, 1560
Mary Wilmer Covey Charitable Trust Grants, 1600
PCA Art Organizations and Art Programs Grants for
    Presenting Organizations, 1884
PCA Arts Organizations and Arts Program Grants
    for Music, 1887
PCA Arts Organizations and Arts Programs Grants
    for Art Museums, 1888
PCA Arts Organizations and Arts Programs Grants
    for Arts Education Organizations, 1889
PCA Arts Organizations and Arts Programs Grants
    for Arts Service Organizations, 1890
PCA Arts Organizations and Arts Programs Grants
    for Crafts, 1891
PCA Arts Organizations and Arts Programs Grants
    for Dance, 1892
PCA Arts Organizations and Arts Programs Grants
    for Film and Electronic Media, 1893
PCA Arts Organizations and Arts Programs Grants
    for Literature, 1894
PCA Arts Organizations and Arts Programs Grants
    for Local Arts, 1895

PCA Arts Organizations and Arts Programs Grants
    for Theatre, 1896
PCA Arts Organizations and Arts Programs Grants
    for Traditional and Folk Arts, 1897
PCA Arts Organizations and Arts Programs Grants
    for Visual Arts, 1898
PCA Busing Grants, 1899
PCA Entry Track Arts Organizations and Arts
    Programs Grants for Art Museums, 1900
PCA Entry Track Arts Organizations and
    Arts Programs Grants for Arts Education
    Organizations, 1901
PCA Entry Track Arts Organizations and Arts
    Programs Grants for Arts Service Orgs, 1902
PCA Entry Track Arts Organizations and Arts
    Programs Grants for Crafts, 1903
PCA Entry Track Arts Organizations and Arts
    Programs Grants for Dance, 1904
PCA Entry Track Arts Orgs and Arts Programs
    Grants for Film and Electronic Media, 1905
PCA Entry Track Arts Organizations and Arts
    Programs Grants for Local Arts, 1907
PCA Entry Track Arts Organizations and Arts
    Programs Grants for Music, 1908
PCA Entry Track Arts Organizations and Arts
    Programs Grants for Presenting Orgs, 1909
PCA Entry Track Arts Organizations and Arts
    Programs Grants for Theatre, 1910
PCA Entry Track Arts Orgs and Arts Programs
    Grants for Traditional and Folk Arts, 1911
PCA Entry Track Arts Organizations and Arts
    Programs Grants for Visual Arts, 1912
PCA Management/Techl Assistance Grants, 1913
PCA Pennsylvania Partners in the Arts Program
    Stream Grants, 1914
PCA Pennsylvania Partners in the Arts Project
    Stream Grants, 1915
Piper Trust Children Grants, 1976
Stein Family Charitable Trust Grants, 2240
TAC Arts Access Grant, 2265
Vigneron Memorial Fund Grants, 2384
VSA/Metlife Connect All Grants, 2392
William G. and Helen C. Hoffman Foundation
    Grants, 2466

Disabled, Education
ACL Alternatives to Guardianship Youth Resource
    Center Grants, 104
ALA Baker and Taylor Summer Reading Program
    Grant, 158
ALA Schneider Family Book Awards, 191
CEC Clarissa Hug Teacher of the Year Award, 527
CEC J.E. Wallace Wallin Special Education Lifetime
    Achievement Award, 528
CEC Yes I Can! Awards, 529
Charles Lafitte Foundation Grants, 567
Community Foundation of Madison and Jefferson
    County Grants, 731
DeKalb County Community Foundation - Garrett
    Hospital Aid Foundation Grants, 813
Emily Hall Tremaine Foundation Learning
    Disabilities Grants, 912
Fichtenbaum Charitable Trust Grants, 955
Henry and Ruth Blaustein Rosenberg Foundation
    Education Grants, 1236
Johnson Scholarship Foundation Grants, 1382
Lavina Parker Trust Grants, 1477
Leola Osborn Trust Grants, 1483
Marion I. and Henry J. Knott Foundation
    Discretionary Grants, 1571
Marion I. and Henry J. Knott Foundation Standard
    Grants, 1572
Marjorie Moore Charitable Foundation Grants, 1574
Mary Wilmer Covey Charitable Trust Grants, 1600
Roy and Christine Sturgis Charitable Tr Grts, 2115
Singing for Change Foundation Grants, 2202
Stein Family Charitable Trust Grants, 2240
Toby Wells Foundation Grants, 2304
VSA/Metlife Connect All Grants, 2392
VSA Playwright Discovery Award, 2396

Disabled, Higher Education
Greenspun Family Foundation Grants, 1118

Disadvantaged, Economically
ACF Marriage Strengthening Research & Dissemination Center Grants, 85
Achelis and Bodman Foundation Grants, 101
Achelis Foundation Grants, 102
Adobe Foundation Action Grants, 126
Aid for Starving Children Emerg Aid Grants, 144
Aid for Starving Children Health and Nutrition Grants, 145
Aid for Starving Children Homes and Education Grants, 146
Aid for Starving Children Water Projects Grants, 147
ALA Coretta Scott King Book Donation Grant, 168
Alaska Airlines Corporation Career Connections for Youth Grants, 193
Albert W. Rice Charitable Foundation Grants, 223
Alfred E. Chase Charitable Foundation Grants, 233
Allan C. and Lelia J. Garden Foundation Grants, 236
Allegis Group Foundation Grants, 237
Amelia Sillman Rockwell and Carlos Perry Rockwell Charities Fund Grants, 250
Amerigroup Foundation Grants, 264
Andrew Family Foundation Grants, 272
Atkinson Foundation Community Grants, 325
Bainum Family Foundation Grants, 345
BCBSM Foundation Community Health Matching Grants, 392
Bill and Melinda Gates Foundation Emergency Response Grants, 426
Bright Promises Foundation Grants, 470
C.H. Robinson Worldwide Foundation Grants, 489
Cargill Foundation Education Grants, 504
Carl B. and Florence E. King Foundation Grants, 506
Carl R. Hendrickson Family Foundation Grants, 509
Catherine Holmes Wilkins Foundation Grants, 520
Central Pacific Bank Foundation Grants, 530
CFFVR Basic Needs Giving Partnership Grants, 537
CFFVR Jewelers Mutual Chartbl Giving Grants, 543
CFFVR Robert and Patricia Endries Family Foundation Grants, 547
CFFVR Schmidt Family G4 Grants, 548
Charles Delmar Foundation Grants, 564
Charles H. Hall Foundation, 565
Charles H. Pearson Foundation Grants, 566
Charles Nelson Robinson Fund Grants, 569
Clara Blackford Smith and W. Aubrey Smith Charitable Foundation Grants, 621
Clark and Ruby Baker Foundation Grants, 625
Clayton Baker Trust Grants, 629
CNCS AmeriCorps State and National Grants, 643
CNCS AmeriCorps VISTA Project Grants, 645
CNCS Foster Grandparent Projects Grants, 646
Community Foundation for Greater Buffalo Competitive Grants, 670
Community Foundation of Boone County - Women's Grants, 693
Community Foundation of Eastern Connecticut General Southeast Grants, 696
Community Foundation of Louisville CHAMP Fund Grants, 720
Community Foundation of Louisville Madi and Jim Tate Fund Grants, 727
Cone Health Foundation Grants, 745
Corina Higginson Trust Grants, 750
Cralle Foundation Grants, 760
D. W. McMillan Foundation Grants, 776
Daniels Homeless and Disadvantaged Grants, 782
Decatur County Community Foundation Small Project Grants, 812
DOL Youthbuild Grants, 838
Doree Taylor Charitable Foundation Grants, 843
Dorothea Haus Ross Foundation Grants, 844
Dr. and Mrs. Paul Pierce Memorial Foundation Grants, 862
Edward and Ellen Roche Relief Fdn Grants, 887
Edward W. and Stella C. Van Houten Memorial Fund Grants, 892

Elizabeth Carse Foundation Grants, 899
Ensworth Charitable Foundation Grants, 916
Fitzpatrick, Cella, Harper & Scinto Pro Bono Services, 976
Florence Hunt Maxwell Foundation Grants, 979
Fdn for the Mid South Communities Grants, 992
Fourjay Foundation Grants, 1003
Four J Foundation Grants, 1004
Four Lanes Trust Grants, 1005
Frank Reed and Margaret Jane Peters Memorial Fund Grants, 1013
Frank Reed and Margaret Jane Peters Memorial Fund II Grants, 1014
Fred and Gretel Biel Charitable Trust Grants, 1016
Frederick McDonald Trust Grants, 1017
Frederick W. Marzahl Memorial Fund Grants, 1018
Gamble Foundation Grants, 1032
Gannett Foundation Community Action Grants, 1033
George A. & Grace L. Long Fdn Grants, 1041
George A Ohl Jr. Foundation Grants, 1043
George W. Wells Foundation Grants, 1057
Geraldine R. Dodge Fdn Education Grants, 1061
German Protestant Orphan Asylum Foundation Grants, 1066
GNOF IMPACT Gulf States Eye Surg Fund, 1085
Grace Bersted Foundation Grants, 1097
Greygates Foundation Grants, 1120
H.A. and Mary K. Chapman Charitable Trust Grants, 1137
HAF Community Grants, 1141
Hampton Roads Community Foundation Arts and Culture Grants, 1154
Harold Brooks Foundation Grants, 1172
Harry and Jeanette Weinberg Fdn Grants, 1182
Hartley Foundation Grants, 1186
Hasbro Children's Fund Grants, 1189
HBF Pathways Out of Poverty Grants, 1222
Hearst Foundations Social Service Grants, 1224
Helen Gertrude Sparks Charitable Trust Grants, 1230
Helen Irwin Littauer Educational Trust Grants, 1231
Help America Foundation Grants, 1233
Henrietta Lange Burk Fund Grants, 1235
Henry E. Niles Foundation Grants, 1240
Herbert A. and Adrian W. Woods Foundation Grants, 1243
Herman Goldman Foundation Grants, 1245
Horace A. Kimball and S. Ella Kimball Foundation Grants, 1260
Horace A. Moses Charitable Trust Grants, 1261
Hubbard Farms Charitable Foundation Grants, 1272
Hungry for Music Instrument Gifts, 1277
Initiative Foundation Innovation Fund Grants, 1304
James Ford Bell Foundation Grants, 1339
Jane Bradley Pettit Foundation Community and Social Development Grants, 1347
Jaquelin Hume Foundation Grants, 1357
Jeffris Wood Foundation Grants, 1359
Jim Moran Foundation Grants, 1366
John Clarke Trust Grants, 1369
John D. and Katherine A. Johnston Foundation Grants, 1370
Johnson Scholarship Foundation Grants, 1382
Joseph H. and Florence A. Roblee Foundation Education Grants, 1386
Joseph S. Stackpole Charitable Trust Grants, 1390
Katharine Matthies Foundation Grants, 1418
Kawabe Memorial Fund Grants, 1423
Kentucky Arts Cncl Access Assistance Grants, 1428
Kevin J Major Youth Sports Scholarships, 1431
Lands' End Corporate Giving Program, 1468
Legler Benbough Foundation Grants, 1479
LEGO Children's Fund Grants, 1480
Leola Osborn Trust Grants, 1483
Leo Niessen Jr., Charitable Trust Grants, 1484
Lewis H. Humphreys Charitable Trust Grants, 1486
Liberty Bank Foundation Grants, 1488
Lily Palmer Fry Memorial Trust Grants, 1493
Linden Foundation Grants, 1494
Linford & Mildred White Charitable Grants, 1495
LISC Affordable Housing Grants, 1497

LISC Financial Stability Grants, 1501
Lois and Richard England Family Foundation Out-of-School-Time Grants, 1506
Long Island Community Foundation Grants, 1507
Luella Kemper Trust Grants, 1517
M.D. Anderson Foundation Grants, 1523
Mabel A. Horne Fund Grants, 1525
Mabel F. Hoffman Charitable Trust Grants, 1526
Maine Community Foundation People of Color Fund Grants, 1544
Marathon Petroleum Corporation Grants, 1551
Marietta McNeill Morgan and Samuel Tate Morgan Jr. Trust Grants, 1560
Marin Community Foundation Affordable Housing Grants, 1561
Marin Community Foundation Arts in the Community Grants, 1563
Marin Community Foundation Closing the Education Achievement Gap Grants, 1564
Marin Community Foundation Ending the Cycle of Poverty Grants, 1565
Marin Community Foundation Improving Community Health Grants, 1566
Marin Community Foundation Social Justice and Interfaith Understanding Grants, 1567
Mark Wahlberg Youth Foundation Grants, 1576
Marsh Corporate Grants, 1580
Mary K. Chapman Foundation Grants, 1590
Mary Owen Borden Foundation Grants, 1597
May and Stanley Smith Charitable Trust Grants, 1613
Medtronic Foundation Community Link Arts, Civic, and Culture Grants, 1629
Medtronic Foundation CommunityLink Health Grants, 1630
Medtronic Foundation Community Link Human Services Grants, 1631
Mercedes-Benz USA Corporate Contributions, 1634
Meyer Fdn Healthy Communities Grants, 1650
MGM Resorts Foundation Community Grants, 1655
MGN Family Foundation Grants, 1656
Michael and Susan Dell Foundation Grants, 1657
Middlesex Savings Charitable Foundation Basic Human Needs Grants, 1668
Middlesex Savings Charitable Foundation Educational Opportunities Grants, 1670
Minnie M. Jones Trust Grants, 1678
Monsanto United States Grants, 1684
Moody Foundation Grants, 1692
Moran Family Foundation Grants, 1693
Mr. Holland's Opus Foundation Melody Grants, 1703
Nationwide Insurance Foundation Grants, 1726
Nellie Mae Education Foundation District-Level Change Grants, 1736
New York Foundation Grants, 1753
Norman Foundation Grants, 1767
Ober Kaler Community Grants, 1801
Olga Sipolin Children's Fund Grants, 1815
Olive B. Cole Foundation Grants, 1816
Oppenstein Brothers Foundation Grants, 1827
Ordean Foundation Catalyst Grants, 1830
Ordean Foundation Partnership Grants, 1831
OSF Baltimore Community Fellowships, 1838
OSF Soros Justice Youth Activist Fellowships, 1844
OtterCares Champion Fund Grants, 1848
PCA Art Organizations and Art Programs Grants for Presenting Organizations, 1884
PCA Arts Organizations and Arts Program Grants for Music, 1887
PCA Arts Organizations and Arts Programs Grants for Art Museums, 1888
PCA Arts Organizations and Arts Programs Grants for Arts Education Organizations, 1889
PCA Arts Organizations and Arts Programs Grants for Arts Service Organizations, 1890
PCA Arts Organizations and Arts Programs Grants for Crafts, 1891
PCA Arts Organizations and Arts Programs Grants for Dance, 1892
PCA Arts Organizations and Arts Programs Grants for Film and Electronic Media, 1893

PCA Arts Organizations and Arts Programs Grants for Literature, 1894
PCA Arts Organizations and Arts Programs Grants for Local Arts, 1895
PCA Arts Organizations and Arts Programs Grants for Theatre, 1896
PCA Arts Organizations and Arts Programs Grants for Traditional and Folk Arts, 1897
PCA Arts Organizations and Arts Programs Grants for Visual Arts, 1898
PCA Busing Grants, 1899
PCA Entry Track Arts Organizations and Arts Programs Grants for Art Museums, 1900
PCA Entry Track Arts Organizations and Arts Programs Grants for Arts Education Organizations, 1901
PCA Entry Track Arts Organizations and Arts Programs Grants for Arts Service Orgs, 1902
PCA Entry Track Arts Organizations and Arts Programs Grants for Crafts, 1903
PCA Entry Track Arts Organizations and Arts Programs Grants for Dance, 1904
PCA Entry Track Arts Orgs and Arts Programs Grants for Film and Electronic Media, 1905
PCA Entry Track Arts Organizations and Arts Programs Grants for Local Arts, 1907
PCA Entry Track Arts Organizations and Arts Programs Grants for Music, 1908
PCA Entry Track Arts Organizations and Arts Programs Grants for Presenting Orgs, 1909
PCA Entry Track Arts Organizations and Arts Programs Grants for Theatre, 1910
PCA Entry Track Arts Orgs and Arts Programs Grants for Traditional and Folk Arts, 1911
PCA Entry Track Arts Organizations and Arts Programs Grants for Visual Arts, 1912
PCA Pennsylvania Partners in the Arts Program Stream Grants, 1914
PCA Pennsylvania Partners in the Arts Project Stream Grants, 1915
PepsiCo Foundation Grants, 1935
Perkins-Ponder Foundation Grants, 1938
Perpetual Benevolent Fund, 1940
PeyBack Foundation Grants, 1953
Piper Trust Education Grants, 1977
Piper Trust Healthcare and Med Rsrch Grants, 1978
PMI Foundation Grants, 1982
Pohlad Family Foundation Summer Camp Scholarships, 1992
Porter County Community Foundation Women's Fund Grants, 2005
Powell Foundation Grants, 2013
Premera Blue Cross Grants, 2018
Prudential Foundation Education Grants, 2028
Public Education Power Grants, 2032
R.D. Beirne Trust Grants, 2045
R.S. Gernon Trust Grants, 2047
Ralph M. Parsons Foundation Grants, 2052
Raskob Fdn for Catholic Activities Grants, 2054
Ray Charles Foundation Grants, 2058
Richard and Caroline T. Gwathmey Memorial Trust Grants, 2069
Richards Foundation Grants, 2072
Robert R. Meyer Foundation Grants, 2094
Robin Hood Foundation Grants, 2096
Roney-Fitzpatrick Foundation Grants, 2102
Roy and Christine Sturgis Charitable Tr Grts, 2115
Ruddie Memorial Youth Foundation Grants, 2120
Saigh Foundation Grants, 2137
Salt River Project Health and Human Services Grants, 2142
Sands Cares Grants, 2156
Schlessman Family Foundation Grants, 2167
Screen Actors Guild BookPALS Assistance, 2171
Screen Actors Guild PencilPALS Assistance, 2172
Seybert Foundation Grants, 2184
Shopko Fdn Community Charitable Grants, 2191
Singing for Change Foundation Grants, 2202
Sioux Falls Area Community Foundation Community Fund Grants, 2203

Sioux Falls Area Community Foundation Spot Grants, 2204
Social Justice Fund Northwest Economic Justice Giving Project Grants, 2215
Speer Trust Grants, 2230
Steven B. Achelis Foundation Grants, 2244
Swindells Charitable Foundation Grants, 2261
TAC Touring Arts and Arts Access Touring Arts Grants, 2269
Tauck Family Foundation Grants, 2274
Teagle Foundation Grants, 2277
Textron Corporate Contributions Grants, 2286
Thelma Braun and Bocklett Family Foundation Grants, 2287
Thomas J. Atkins Memorial Trust Fund Grants, 2290
Threshold Fdn Justice and Democracy Grants, 2298
Trinity Trust Summer Youth Mini Grants, 2321
TSYSF Individual Scholarships, 2322
TSYSF Team Grants, 2323
Twenty-First Century Foundation Grants, 2328
U.S. Bank Foundation Grants, 2330
Union Bank, N.A. Foundation Grants, 2334
Union Labor Health Fdn Angel Fund Grants, 2335
Union Labor Health Foundation Dental Angel Fund Grants, 2336
USDA WIC Nutrition Ed Innovations Grants, 2363
Volkswagen Group of America Corporate Contributions Grants, 2389
W.P. and Bulah Luse Foundation Grants, 2399
Walter S. and Evan C. Jones Testam Trust, 2407
Washington Area Fuel Fund Grants, 2413
Washington Gas Charitable Contributions, 2417
Weaver Foundation Grants, 2420
Wild Rivers Community Foundation Holiday Partnership Grants, 2448
Wild Rivers Community Foundation Summer Youth Mini Grants, 2449
William Foulds Family Foundation Grants, 2465
William G. and Helen C. Hoffman Foundation Grants, 2466
William J. and Tina Rosenberg Fdn Grants, 2470
William J. Brace Charitable Trust, 2471
Wood Family Charitable Trust Grants, 2487

Disaster Preparedness
3M Company Foundation Health and Human Services Grants, 6
Advance Auto Parts Corporate Giving Grants, 131
Amway Corporation Contributions, 269
Baxter International Corporate Giving Grants, 368
Bill and Melinda Gates Foundation Emergency Response Grants, 426
CNCS AmeriCorps Indian Tribes Plang Grts, 641
CNCS AmeriCorps NCCC Project Grants, 642
CNCS AmeriCorps State and National Grants, 643
Delmarva Power & Light Contributions, 821
Elizabeth Morse Genius Charitable Trust Grants, 901
GNOF Bayou Communities Grants, 1077
GNOF Plaquemines Community Grants, 1091
Honeywell Corp Humanitarian Relief Grants, 1257
Island Insurance Foundation Grants, 1316
Lynn and Foster Friess Family Fdn Grants, 1520
Nationwide Insurance Foundation Grants, 1726
PSEG Fdn Safety and Preparedness Grants, 2031

Disaster Relief
3M Company Foundation Health and Human Services Grants, 6
Advance Auto Parts Corporate Giving Grants, 131
Albertsons Companies Foundation Nourishing Neighbors Grants, 221
Allstate Corporate Giving Grants, 242
Allstate Corp Hometown Commitment Grants, 243
Allstate Foundation Safe and Vital Communities Grants, 244
Anheuser-Busch Foundation Grants, 273
AT&T Fdn Community Support and Safety, 320
Baxter International Corporate Giving Grants, 368
Bill and Melinda Gates Foundation Emergency Response Grants, 426

Blue Mountain Community Foundation Discretionary Grants, 455
Boeing Company Contributions Grants, 462
BP Foundation Grants, 465
California Endowment Innovative Ideas Challenge Grants, 495
Campbell Soup Foundation Grants, 501
Cargill Corporate Giving Grants, 503
Carnegie Corporation of New York Grants, 511
Clark Electric Cooperative Grants, 627
CNCS AmeriCorps Indian Tribes Plang Grts, 641
CNCS AmeriCorps NCCC Project Grants, 642
CNCS AmeriCorps State and National Grants, 643
CNCS AmeriCorps State and National Planning Grants, 644
CNCS AmeriCorps VISTA Project Grants, 645
Community Foundation for the Capital Region Grants, 687
Delmarva Power & Light Contributions, 821
Elizabeth Morse Genius Charitable Trust Grants, 901
Farmers Insurance Corporate Giving Grants, 948
Ford Foundation BUILD Grants, 984
GNOF Bayou Communities Grants, 1077
GNOF Plaquemines Community Grants, 1091
Honeywell Corp Humanitarian Relief Grants, 1257
Humana Foundation Grants, 1275
Island Insurance Foundation Grants, 1316
Kirby Laing Foundation Grants, 1439
Lynn and Foster Friess Family Fdn Grants, 1520
M.J. Murdock Charitable Trust General Grants, 1524
Nationwide Insurance Foundation Grants, 1726
New Covenant Farms Grants, 1742
Noble County Community Foundation Grants, 1765
PSEG Fdn Safety and Preparedness Grants, 2031
Robert R. Meyer Foundation Grants, 2094
San Antonio Area Foundation Capital and Naming Rights Grants, 2148
Shell Deer Park Grants, 2186
Sony Corporation of America Grants, 2216
State Farm Good Neighbor Citizenship Company Grants, 2238
Sunoco Foundation Grants, 2256
Union Bank, N.A. Foundation Grants, 2334
William E. Dean III Charitable Fdn Grants, 2464

Disasters
3M Company Foundation Health and Human Services Grants, 6
Baxter International Corporate Giving Grants, 368
Bill and Melinda Gates Foundation Emergency Response Grants, 426
Clark Electric Cooperative Grants, 627
CNCS AmeriCorps Indian Tribes Plang Grts, 641
CNCS AmeriCorps NCCC Project Grants, 642
CNCS AmeriCorps State and National Grants, 643
Community Foundation for the Capital Region Grants, 687
Delmarva Power & Light Contributions, 821
Elizabeth Morse Genius Charitable Trust Grants, 901
GNOF Bayou Communities Grants, 1077
GNOF Plaquemines Community Grants, 1091
Honeywell Corp Humanitarian Relief Grants, 1257
J. Edwin Treakle Foundation Grants, 1320
PSEG Fdn Safety and Preparedness Grants, 2031
State Farm Good Neighbor Citizenship Company Grants, 2238

Disciples of Christ Church
AHS Foundation Grants, 143
Alvah H. and Wyline P. Chapman Fdn Grants, 248
Chapman Family Foundation, 562
Harry and Helen Sands Charitable Trust Grants, 1181

Discrimination
Allstate Corporate Giving Grants, 242
Allstate Corp Hometown Commitment Grants, 243
Allstate Foundation Safe and Vital Communities Grants, 244
Allstate Foundation Tolerance, Inclusion, and Diversity Grants, 245

Ben Cohen StandUp Foundation Grants, 403
Cheryl Spencer Memorial Foundation Grants, 576
Colin Higgins Foundation Courage Awards, 653
Community Foundation of Greater Chattanooga
Grants, 704
Joseph H. and Florence A. Roblee Foundation
Children and Youth Grants, 1385
OSF Soros Justice Youth Activist Fellowships, 1844
Philanthrofund Foundation Grants, 1959
Sioux Falls Area Community Foundation Spot
Grants, 2204
Social Justice Fund Northwest Criminal Justice
Giving Project Grants, 2214
Teaching Tolerance Diverse Democracy Grants, 2275
Thorman Boyle Foundation Grants, 2295
Threshold Fdn Justice and Democracy Grants, 2298
Tides Foundation Girl Rising Fund Grants, 2301
UUA Actions of Public Witness Grants, 2365
UUA Congregation-Based Community Organizing
Grants, 2366
UUA Fund Grants, 2367
UUA International Fund Grants, 2368
UUA Just Society Fund Grants, 2369
UUA Social Responsibility Grants, 2370
VSA Playwright Discovery Award, 2396

Disease, Chronic
Elizabeth Huth Coates Charitable Foundation
Grants, 900
George E. Hatcher, Jr. and Ann Williams Hatcher
Foundation Grants, 1045
Island Insurance Foundation Grants, 1316
Mary Wilmer Covey Charitable Trust Grants, 1600
Medtronic Foundation Strengthening Health Systems
Grants, 1632
TJX Foundation Grants, 2303

Diseases
A-T Children's Project Grants, 16
A-T Children's Project Post Doctoral Fellowships, 17
A. Alfred Taubman Foundation Grants, 18
Albertsons Companies Foundation Nourishing
Neighbors Grants, 221
Bill and Melinda Gates Foundation Water, Sanitation
and Hygiene Grants, 428
Bushrod H. Campbell and Adah F. Hall Charity
Fund Grants, 486
Clayton Fund Grants, 631
Curtis Foundation Grants, 771
David M. and Marjorie D. Rosenberg Foundation
Grants, 790
Elizabeth Huth Coates Charitable Foundation
Grants, 900
Fidelity Charitable Gift Fund Grants, 956
George E. Hatcher, Jr. and Ann Williams Hatcher
Foundation Grants, 1045
Hawaii Electric Industries Charitable Foundation
Grants, 1218
Herman P. and Sophia Taubman Fdn Grants, 1247
Hubbard Family Foundation Grants, 1270
Ike and Roz Friedman Foundation Grants, 1289
Island Insurance Foundation Grants, 1316
J. Watumull Fund Grants, 1326
Koch Family Foundation (Annapolis) Grants, 1444
Mary Wilmer Covey Charitable Trust Grants, 1600
Perkin Fund Grants, 1937
Premera Blue Cross Grants, 2018
Robert R. Meyer Foundation Grants, 2094
Wilton and Effie Hebert Foundation Grants, 2476
Youths' Friends Association Grants, 2511
Zellweger Baby Support Network Grants, 2525

Distance Learning
Foundation for Rural Service Education Grants, 991

Diversity
ALA Rainbow Project Book List Award, 187
Ben Cohen StandUp Foundation Grants, 403
Benton Community Foundation - The Cookie Jar
Grant, 404

Boeing Company Contributions Grants, 462
Community Foundation of Boone County - Women's
Grants, 693
Community Fdn Of Greater Lafayette Grants, 710
EQT Fdn Community Enrichment Grants, 926
Johnson County Community Foundation Youth
Philanthropy Initiative Grants, 1380
Kalamazoo Community Foundation Good Neighbor
Grants, 1408
Kroger Company Donations, 1456
Maine Community Foundation People of Color Fund
Grants, 1544
PepsiCo Foundation Grants, 1935
Tata Trust Grant for Certificate Course in Holistic
inclusion of Learners with Diversities, 2273
Teaching Tolerance Diverse Democracy Grants, 2275
Teaching Tolerance Social Justice Educator Grts, 2276
Volkswagen Group of America Corporate
Contributions Grants, 2389

Documentaries
National Cowboy and Western Heritage Museum
Awards, 1722
PCA Arts Organizations and Arts Programs Grants
for Film and Electronic Media, 1893
PCA Entry Track Arts Orgs and Arts Programs
Grants for Film and Electronic Media, 1905

Domestic Violence
Amelia Sillman Rockwell and Carlos Perry Rockwell
Charities Fund Grants, 250
American Woodmark Foundation Grants, 263
Anne Arundel Women Giving Together Regular
Grants, 275
Atkinson Foundation Community Grants, 325
Aunt Kate Foundation Grants, 331
Austin S. Nelson Foundation Grants, 333
Baxter International Foundation Grants, 369
Carl M. Freeman Foundation FACES Grants, 507
Charles Nelson Robinson Fund Grants, 569
Children's Trust Fund of Oregon Fdn Grants, 585
Children's Trust Fund of Oregon Foundation Small
Grants, 586
Community Foundation of Eastern Connecticut
Northeast Women and Girls Grants, 697
Community Foundation of Eastern Connecticut
Norwich Women and Girls Grants, 698
Community Foundation of Eastern Connecticut
Southeast Area Women and Girls Grants, 701
Community Foundation of Eastern Connecticut
Windham Area Women and Girls Grants, 702
Covenant for Children Critical Goods Grants, 757
Dolan Media Foundation Grants, 833
Edward and Ellen Roche Relief Fdn Grants, 887
Fremont Area Community Foundation Community
Grants, 1020
Global Fund for Women Grants, 1073
Go Daddy Cares Charitable Contributions, 1093
Harry Frank Guggenheim Foundation Research
Grants, 1184
Hawai'i Community Foundation Children's Trust
Fund Community Awareness: Child Abuse and
Neglect Prevention Grants, 1198
Herbert A. and Adrian W. Woods Foundation
Grants, 1243
Jane Bradley Pettit Foundation Community and
Social Development Grants, 1347
Jeffris Wood Foundation Grants, 1359
Jim Moran Foundation Grants, 1366
John Gogian Family Foundation Grants, 1373
Lucy Downing Nisbet Charitable Fund Grants, 1515
Mabel A. Horne Fund Grants, 1525
Mardag Foundation Grants, 1554
Mertz Gilmore Foundation NYC Communities
Grants, 1641
Meyer Fdn Healthy Communities Grants, 1650
Nicole Brown Foundation Grants, 1760
Northland Foundation Grants, 1771
OneFamily Foundation Grants, 1822

Piper Jaffray Foundation Communities Giving
Grants, 1974
Portland General Electric Foundation Grants, 2007
Posey Community Foundation Women's Fund
Grants, 2008
Public Welfare Foundation Special Initiative to
Advance Civil Legal Aid Grants, 2034
R.S. Gernon Trust Grants, 2047
Reinberger Foundation Grants, 2066
Spencer County Community Foundation Women's
Fund Grants, 2232
Target Corporation Community Engagement Fund
Grants, 2270
TJX Foundation Grants, 2303
Vanderburgh Community Foundation Men's Fund
Grants, 2373
Vanderburgh County Community Foundation
Women's Fund Grants, 2376
Warrick County Community Foundation Women's
Fund, 2411
WHO Foundation Volunteer Service Grants, 2444
Winifred Johnson Clive Foundation Grants, 2478

Drama
Herman Goldman Foundation Grants, 1245
PCA Arts Organizations and Arts Programs Grants
for Theatre, 1896
PCA Entry Track Arts Organizations and Arts
Programs Grants for Theatre, 1910
PCA Strategies for Success Grants - Basic Level, 1918
PCA Strategies for Success Grants - Intermediate
Level, 1919

Dramatic/Theater Arts
Alcatel-Lucent Technologies Foundation Grants, 224
Ann L. and Carol Green Rhodes Charitable Trust
Grants, 278
Blanche and Irving Laurie Foundation Grants, 436
Donald G. Gardner Humanities Tr Youth Grts, 840
F.M. Kirby Foundation Grants, 946
Hearst Foundations Culture Grants, 1223
Huffy Foundation Grants, 1273
Illinois Arts Council Theater Program Grants, 1293
Kenneth T. and Eileen L. Norris Fdn Grants, 1427
Mary D. and Walter F. Frear Eleemosynary Trust
Grants, 1588
Maryland State Arts Council Arts in Communities
Grants, 1592
Morris Stulsaft Foundation Participation in the the
Arts Grants, 1698
NHSCA Artist Residence Grants, 1756
NHSCA Youth Arts Project Grants: For Extended
Arts Learning, 1758
NJSCA Artists in Education Residencies, 1763
NJSCA Arts Ed Special Initiative Grants, 1764
Norcliffe Foundation Grants, 1766
NYSCA Arts Education: General Operating Support
Grants, 1781
NYSCA Arts Education: General Program Support
Grants, 1782
NYSCA Arts Ed: Services to the Field Grants, 1784
NYSCA Special Arts Services: General Program
Support Grants, 1793
NYSCA Special Arts Services: Instruction and
Training Grants, 1794
NYSCA Theatre: Prof Performances Grants, 1795
Parker Foundation (California) Grants, 1869
PCA-PCD Professional Development for Individual
Artists Grants, 1883
PCA Arts in Education Residencies, 1885
PCA Arts Organizations and Arts Programs Grants
for Theatre, 1896
PCA Busing Grants, 1899
PCA Entry Track Arts Organizations and Arts
Programs Grants for Theatre, 1910
PCA Pennsylvania Partners in the Arts Program
Stream Grants, 1914
PCA Pennsylvania Partners in the Arts Project
Stream Grants, 1915
PCA Professional Development Grants, 1916

PCA Strategies for Success Grants - Adv Level, 1917
PCA Strategies for Success Grants - Basic Level, 1918
PCA Strategies for Success Grants - Intermediate Level, 1919
PennPAT Artist Technical Assistance Grants, 1929
PennPAT Strategic Opportunity Grants, 1933
Peyton Anderson Foundation Grants, 1954
TAC Arts Access Grant, 2265
VSA/Volkswagen Group of America Exhibition Awards, 2393
VSA Playwright Discovery Award, 2396
Wallace Foundation Grants, 2402

Driver Education
BMW of North America Charitable Contribs, 460
Four County Community Foundation Kellogg Group Grants, 1002
Matson Community Giving Grants, 1607
State Farm Good Neighbor Citizenship Company Grants, 2238
Toyota USA Foundation Safety Grants, 2320
YSA State Farm Good Neighbor YOUth In The Driver Seat Grants, 2521

Dropouts
CNCS AmeriCorps State and National Grants, 643
CNCS Senior Corps Retired and Senior Volunteer Program Grants, 648
Meyer Foundation Education Grants, 1649
Pacers Foundation Be Educated Grants, 1857
PepsiCo Foundation Grants, 1935

Drug Design
GTRCF Grand Traverse Families in Action for Youth Endowment Grants, 1129

Drug Education
Alcatel-Lucent Technologies Foundation Grants, 224
Appalachian Regional Commission Education and Training Grants, 286
Daniels Drug and Alcohol Addiction Grants, 780
GNOF IMPACT Kahn-Oppenheim Tr Grts, 1087
MetroWest Health Foundation Grants to Reduce the Incidence of High Risk Behaviors Among Adolescents, 1646
SACF Youth Advisory Council Grants, 2131
Weyerhaeuser Family Fdn Health Grants, 2435

Drugs/Drug Abuse
AACAP Jeanne Spurlock Research Fellowship in Substance Abuse and Addiction for Minority Medical Students, 28
Achelis and Bodman Foundation Grants, 101
Achelis Foundation Grants, 102
ACL Neonatal Abstinence Syndrome National Training Initiative Grant, 106
Appalachian Regional Commission Education and Training Grants, 286
Atkinson Foundation Community Grants, 325
Austin S. Nelson Foundation Grants, 333
Benton Community Foundation Grants, 405
Blue River Community Foundation Grants, 458
Brown County Community Foundation Grants, 475
Cleo Foundation Grants, 632
Community Foundation of Bartholomew County Heritage Fund Grants, 690
Community Foundation of Bartholomew County James A. Henderson Award for Fundraising, 691
Community Foundation of Greater Fort Wayne - Community Endowment and Clarke Endowment Grants, 705
Daniels Drug and Alcohol Addiction Grants, 780
Farmers Insurance Corporate Giving Grants, 948
First Nations Development Institute Native Youth and Culture Fund Grants, 974
Foundation for a Healthy Kentucky Grants, 988
Fourjay Foundation Grants, 1003
Fuller Foundation Youth At Risk Grants, 1028
Gerber Foundation Environmental Hazards Research Grants, 1062

GNOF IMPACT Kahn-Oppenheim Tr Grts, 1087
GTRCF Grand Traverse Families in Action for Youth Endowment Grants, 1129
Gulf Coast Foundation of Community Operating Grants, 1134
Gulf Coast Foundation of Community Program Grants, 1135
Harry Frank Guggenheim Foundation Research Grants, 1184
Hasbro Children's Fund Grants, 1189
Hawai'i Community Foundation Kuki'o Community Fund Grants, 1202
Hearst Foundations Social Service Grants, 1224
Huffy Foundation Grants, 1273
March of Dimes Program Grants, 1552
Mary Owen Borden Foundation Grants, 1597
MetroWest Health Foundation Grants to Reduce the Incidence of High Risk Behaviors Among Adolescents, 1646
Mid-Iowa Health Foundation Community Response Grants, 1667
NIMH Early Identification and Treatment of Mental Disorders in Children and Adolescents Grts, 1761
Ordean Foundation Catalyst Grants, 1830
Ordean Foundation Partnership Grants, 1831
OSF Soros Justice Youth Activist Fellowships, 1844
Pacers Foundation Be Drug-Free Grants, 1856
Patrick and Aimee Butler Family Foundation Community Human Services Grants, 1880
Peter and Elizabeth C. Tower Foundation Small Grants, 1947
Peter and Elizabeth C. Tower Foundation Substance Use Disorders Grants, 1948
Phoenix Suns Charities Grants, 1964
Piedmont Natural Gas Foundation Health and Human Services Grants, 1968
Puerto Rico Community Foundation Grants, 2037
Ruth Anderson Foundation Grants, 2122
Sioux Falls Area Community Foundation Community Fund Grants, 2203
Sioux Falls Area Community Foundation Spot Grants, 2204
Stella and Charles Guttman Foundation Grants, 2241
Tides Foundation Grants, 2302
Union Bank, N.A. Foundation Grants, 2334
Whitney Foundation Grants, 2441

Dyslexia
Claremont Community Foundation Grants, 622
Henry and Ruth Blaustein Rosenberg Foundation Education Grants, 1236

Early Childhood Development
ACF Early Care and Education Research Scholars: Head Start Graduate Student Research Grants, 79
ACF Social and Economic Development Strategies Grants, 93
Aldi Corporation Smart Kids Grants, 226
Arthur M. Blank Family Foundation AMB West Community Fund Grants, 304
Bella Vista Fdns GSS Early Literacy Grants, 398
Bernard and Audre Rapoport Foundation Arts and Culture Grants, 407
Bernard and Audre Rapoport Foundation Community Building and Social Service Grants, 408
Bernard and Audre Rapoport Foundation Education Grants, 410
Bernard and Audre Rapoport Foundation Health Grants, 411
Better Way Foundation Grants, 419
Blue Cross Blue Shield of Minnesota Fdn - Healthy Children: Growing Up Healthy Grants, 442
Community Foundation for SE Michigan Youth Leadership Grant, 686
Hawaii Community Foundation Promising Minds Grants, 1215
Hubbard Broadcasting Foundation Grants, 1269
Joseph H. and Florence A. Roblee Foundation Children and Youth Grants, 1385
Linden Foundation Grants, 1494

Malone Family Foundation Atypical Development Initiative Grants, 1549
Maryland State Department of Education Judith P. Hoyer Early Care and Ed Center Grants, 1595
Oregon Community Foundation Edna E. Harrell Community Children's Fund Grants, 1835
Piper Trust Children Grants, 1976
Piper Trust Education Grants, 1977
Piper Trust Healthcare and Med Rsrch Grants, 1978
PNC Foundation Grow Up Great Early Childhood Grants, 1986
Ralph C. Wilson, Jr. Foundation Preparing for Success Grant, 2050
Ralph C. Wilson, Jr. Foundation Youth Sports and Recreation Grant, 2051
TJX Foundation Grants, 2303
Welborn Baptist Foundation Promotion of Early Childhood Development Grants, 2423

Early Childhood Education
ACF American Indian and Alaska Native Early Head Start Expansion Grants, 72
ACF Social and Economic Development Strategies Grants, 93
Adobe Foundation Action Grants, 126
AEGON Transamerica Foundation Education and Financial Literacy Grants, 132
Aetna Foundation Summer Academic Enrichment Grants, 135
Akron Community Fdn Education Grants, 151
ALA Coretta Scott King Book Donation Grant, 168
Aldi Corporation Smart Kids Grants, 226
Arthur M. Blank Family Foundation AMB West Community Fund Grants, 304
Arthur M. Blank Family Foundation Mountain Sky Guest Ranch Fund Grants, 311
Bella Vista Fdns GSS Early Literacy Grants, 398
Bernard and Audre Rapoport Foundation Arts and Culture Grants, 407
Bernard and Audre Rapoport Foundation Education Grants, 410
Better Way Foundation Grants, 419
Blue Grass Community Foundation Early Childhood Education and Literacy Grants, 445
BMW of North America Charitable Contribs, 460
CHT Foundation Education Grants, 603
Community Foundation of Bartholomew County Women's Giving Circle, 692
Community Foundation of Eastern Connecticut Ossen Fund for the Arts Grants, 700
Community Foundation of Louisville Dr. W. Barnett Owen Memorial Fund for the Children of Louisville and Jefferson County Grants, 723
Community Foundation of Louisville Education Grants, 724
Daniels Fund Early Childhood Education Grants, 781
Delta Air Lines Foundation Youth Development Grants, 824
Fichtenbaum Charitable Trust Grants, 955
Fremont Area Community Foundation Education Mini-Grants, 1021
Georgia-Pacific Foundation Education Grants, 1058
Gerber Fdn West Michigan Youth Grants, 1065
German Protestant Orphan Asylum Foundation Grants, 1066
GNOF Stand Up For Our Children Grants, 1092
Harris and Eliza Kempner Fund Ed Grants, 1176
Harry A. and Margaret D. Towsley Foundation Grants, 1180
Hawaii Community Foundation Promising Minds Grants, 1215
Helen E. Ellis Charitable Trust Grants, 1228
Hubbard Broadcasting Foundation Grants, 1269
Joseph H. and Florence A. Roblee Foundation Children and Youth Grants, 1385
Kalamazoo Community Foundation Early Childhood Learning and School Readiness Grants, 1407
LEGO Children's Fund Grants, 1480
Linden Foundation Grants, 1494
Luella Kemper Trust Grants, 1517

Marsh Corporate Grants, 1580
Maryland State Department of Education Judith P. Hoyer Early Care and Ed Center Grants, 1595
McCune Charitable Foundation Grants, 1617
Meyer Foundation Education Grants, 1649
Minnie M. Jones Trust Grants, 1678
Moody Foundation Grants, 1692
Morton K. and Jane Blaustein Foundation Educational Opportunity Grants, 1700
Office Depot Foundation Education Grants, 1806
OMNOVA Solutions Fdn Education Grants, 1820
Oregon Community Foundation Edna E. Harrell Community Children's Fund Grants, 1835
Packard Foundation Local Grants, 1863
Philip L. Graham Fund Education Grants, 1962
Piper Trust Children Grants, 1976
Piper Trust Education Grants, 1977
PNC Foundation Education Grants, 1985
PNC Foundation Grow Up Great Early Childhood Grants, 1986
Ralph C. Wilson, Jr. Foundation Preparing for Success Grant, 2050
Reinberger Foundation Grants, 2066
Robert R. McCormick Tribune Foundation Community Grants, 2093
Robert R. Meyer Foundation Grants, 2094
Samuel N. and Mary Castle Foundation Grants, 2145
San Antonio Area Foundation High School Completion Grants, 2149
Seattle Foundation Education Grants, 2178
Southern California Edison Education Grants, 2218
Stinson Foundation Grants, 2246
Stocker Foundation Grants, 2247
TJX Foundation Grants, 2303
USAID Integrated Youth Development Activity Grants, 2356
VSA/Metlife Connect All Grants, 2392
Welborn Baptist Foundation Promotion of Early Childhood Development Grants, 2423
William Caspar Graustein Memorial Fund Corinne G. Levin Education Grants, 2462
Wiregrass Foundation Grants, 2480

Earth Science Education
Bernard and Audre Rapoport Foundation Education Grants, 410
Northrop Grumman Foundation Grants, 1773
Piedmont Natural Gas Foundation K-12 Science, Technology, Engineering and Math (STEM) Grant, 1969

Earth Sciences
Northrop Grumman Foundation Grants, 1773
PG&E Bright Ideas Grants, 1956

Earthquake Engineering
Honeywell Corp Humanitarian Relief Grants, 1257

Ecology
Illinois DNR Youth Recreation Corps Grants, 1297
Piedmont Natural Gas Corporate and Charitable Contributions, 1966
Union Bank, N.A. Foundation Grants, 2334

Ecology, Environmental Education
Cleo Foundation Grants, 632
GNOF Plaquemines Community Grants, 1091
Gray Family Fdn Camp Maintenance Grants, 1104
Piedmont Natural Gas Fdn Envirnmtl Stewardship and Energy Sustainability Grant, 1967

Economic Development
ACF Social and Economic Development Strategies Grants, 93
Achelis and Bodman Foundation Grants, 101
Achelis Foundation Grants, 102
Air Products Foundation Grants, 148
Alcatel-Lucent Technologies Foundation Grants, 224
Alliance for Strong Families and Communities Grants, 239

Alliant Energy Foundation Community Giving for Good Sponsorship Grants, 240
Alloy Family Foundation Grants, 241
Allstate Corporate Giving Grants, 242
Allstate Corp Hometown Commitment Grants, 243
Allstate Foundation Safe and Vital Communities Grants, 244
American Savings Foundation Program Grants, 261
Anderson Foundation Grants, 271
Appalachian Regional Commission Education and Training Grants, 286
Bank of Hawaii Foundation Grants, 360
Bank of the Orient Community Giving, 361
Bay Area Community Foundation Community Initiative Fund Grants, 376
Blandin Foundation Expand Opportunity Grants, 437
Blossom Fund Grants, 441
Blue Cross Blue Shield of Minnesota Foundation - Healthy Neighborhoods: Connect for Health Challenge Grants, 443
Boeing Company Contributions Grants, 462
Bollinger Foundation Grants, 463
BP Foundation Grants, 465
Byerly Foundation Grants, 487
C.F. Adams Charitable Trust Grants, 488
California Endowment Innovative Ideas Challenge Grants, 495
Campbell Soup Foundation Grants, 501
Carnegie Corporation of New York Grants, 511
Circle K Corporation Contributions Grants, 614
Citizens Savings Foundation Grants, 617
Cleveland Fdn Lake-Geauga Fund Grants, 635
CNCS AmeriCorps Indian Tribes Plang Grts , 641
CNCS Social Innovation Grants, 649
Community Foundation for Greater Atlanta Spark Clayton Grants, 667
Community Foundation for Greater Atlanta Spark Newton Grants, 668
Community Foundation for San Benito County Grants, 677
Community Fdn of Wabash County Grants, 740
Dayton Power and Light Foundation Grants, 802
Dearborn Community Foundation City of Aurora Grants, 808
DTE Energy Foundation Environmental Grants, 868
Emily O'Neill Sullivan Foundation Grants, 913
Ezra M. Cutting Trust Grants, 945
Fayette County Foundation Grants, 951
FCYO Youth Organizing Grants, 954
First Hawaiian Bank Foundation Corporate Giving Grants, 967
Foundation for Appalachian Ohio Access to Environmental Education Mini-Grants, 989
Fdn for the Mid South Communities Grants, 992
Foundations of East Chicago Education Grants, 995
Four County Community Foundation General Grants, 1000
Four Times Foundation Grants, 1006
Franklin H. Wells and Ruth L. Wells Foundation Grants, 1011
Frederick McDonald Trust Grants, 1017
Gannett Foundation Community Action Grants, 1033
Gardner Foundation Grants, 1034
George B. Page Foundation Grants, 1044
GNOF Bayou Communities Grants, 1077
GNOF Gert Community Fund Grants, 1082
GNOF New Orleans Works Grants, 1088
Greater Sitka Legacy Fund Grants, 1111
Greater Tacoma Community Foundation General Operating Grants, 1113
Grotto Foundation Project Grants, 1123
HAF Don and Bettie Albright Endowment Fund Grants, 1142
Harry B. and Jane H. Brock Foundation Grants, 1183
Hartford Foundation Regular Grants, 1185
Hartley Foundation Grants, 1186
Hawai'i Community Foundation East Hawaii Fund Grants, 1199
Hawaii State Legislature Grant-In-Aid, 1219
Hearst Foundations Social Service Grants, 1224

HEI Charitable Foundation Grants, 1226
Helen Bader Foundation Grants, 1227
HSBC Corporate Giving Grants, 1266
Illinois DNR Youth Recreation Corps Grants, 1297
ING Foundation Grants, 1302
Initiative Foundation Innovation Fund Grants, 1304
J. Edwin Treakle Foundation Grants, 1320
J.W. Gardner II Foundation Grants, 1323
Jennings County Community Fdn Grants, 1360
Judith Clark-Morrill Foundation Grants, 1395
Kenai Peninsula Foundation Grants, 1425
Ketchikan Community Foundation Grants, 1429
Kodak Community Relations Grants, 1445
Koret Foundation Grants, 1449
Liberty Bank Foundation Grants, 1488
LISC Affordable Housing Grants, 1497
LISC Capacity Building Grants, 1498
LISC Financial Stability Grants, 1501
Long Island Community Foundation Grants, 1507
M.J. Murdock Charitable Trust General Grants, 1524
Madison County Community Foundation - City of Anderson Quality of Life Grant, 1536
Madison County Community Foundation General Grants, 1537
Marathon Petroleum Corporation Grants, 1551
Marin Community Foundation Affordable Housing Grants, 1561
Marin Community Foundation Ending the Cycle of Poverty Grants, 1565
Mary E. Babcock Foundation, 1589
MassMutual Foundation Edonomic Development Grants, 1603
Max and Anna Levinson Foundation Grants, 1612
McCune Charitable Foundation Grants, 1617
Metzger-Price Fund Grants, 1647
MGM Resorts Foundation Community Grants, 1655
Miller Foundation Grants, 1673
Montana Community Foundation Grants, 1687
Norman Foundation Grants, 1767
Paul and Edith Babson Foundation Grants, 1881
PDF Community Organizing Grants, 1920
Percy B. Ferebee Endowment Grants, 1936
Petersburg Community Foundation Grants, 1951
Pettus Foundation Grants, 1952
Phil Hardin Foundation Grants, 1960
Piedmont Natural Gas Corporate and Charitable Contributions, 1966
PMI Foundation Grants, 1982
Pohlad Family Fdn Large Capital Grants, 1990
Pohlad Family Fdn Small Capital Grants, 1991
Priddy Foundation Organizational Development Grants, 2022
PSEG Corporate Contributions Grants, 2030
Puerto Rico Community Foundation Grants, 2037
Pulaski County Community Foundation Grants, 2038
Putnam County Community Fdn Grants, 2040
RCF General Community Grants, 2062
Riedman Foundation Grants, 2076
Ron and Sanne Higgins Family Fdn Grants, 2101
Sandy Hill Foundation Grants, 2157
Sioux Falls Area Community Foundation Community Fund Grants, 2203
Sioux Falls Area Community Foundation Spot Grants, 2204
Skaggs Family Foundation Grants, 2206
Skaggs Family Foundation Grants, 2205
Sobrato Family Foundation Grants, 2211
Sobrato Family Fdn Meeting Space Grants, 2212
Sobrato Family Foundation Office Space Grants, 2213
Southern Minnesota Initiative Foundation Community Growth Initiative Grants, 2221
Southern Minnesota Initiative Foundation Home Visiting Grants, 2222
Southern Minnesota Initiative Foundation Incentive Grants, 2223
Speer Trust Grants, 2230
Sterling and Shelli Gardner Foundation Grants, 2243
Sunoco Foundation Grants, 2256
SunTrust Bank Trusteed Foundations Greene-Sawtell Grants, 2257

SunTrust Bank Trusteed Foundations Nell Warren Elkin and William Simpson Elkin Grants, 2258
Textron Corporate Contributions Grants, 2286
Twenty-First Century Foundation Grants, 2328
U.S. Bank Foundation Grants, 2330
Union Bank, N.A. Corporate Sponsorships and Donations, 2333
Union Bank, N.A. Foundation Grants, 2334
USAID Global Development Alliance Grants, 2354
Walker Area Community Foundation Grants, 2401
Walmart Fdn National Local Giving Grants, 2404
Weaver Foundation Grants, 2420
Western New York Foundation Grants, 2429
Wilkins Family Foundation Grants, 2450
William M. Weaver Foundation Grants, 2472
Wyomissing Foundation Thun Family Organizational Grants, 2505
Wyomissing Foundation Thun Family Program Grants, 2506
Z. Smith Reynolds Foundation Small Grants, 2523

Economic Justice
Blossom Fund Grants, 441
GNOF Coastal 5 + 1 Grants, 1078
GNOF New Orleans Works Grants, 1088
Maine Women's Fund Econ Security Grants, 1546
Mertz Gilmore Foundation NYC Communities Grants, 1641
New York Foundation Grants, 1753
Oregon Community Foundation Community Recovery Grants, 1834
OSF Baltimore Community Fellowships, 1838
Sapelo Foundation Social Justice Grants, 2160
Skaggs Family Foundation Grants, 2205
Skaggs Family Foundation Grants, 2206
Social Justice Fund Northwest Economic Justice Giving Project Grants, 2215
Target Foundation Global Grants, 2272
Thorman Boyle Foundation Grants, 2295

Economic Opportunities
ACF Social and Economic Development Strategies Grants, 93
Arizona Foundation for Women Deborah G. Carstens Fund Grants, 293
CNCS AmeriCorps Indian Tribes Plang Grts , 641
CNCS AmeriCorps VISTA Project Grants, 645
CNCS Social Innovation Grants, 649
Community Foundation of Louisville Fund 4 Women and Girls Grants, 725
Edward and Ellen Roche Relief Fdn Grants, 887
Ezra M. Cutting Trust Grants, 945
GNOF IMPACT Grants for Arts and Culture, 1083
GNOF New Orleans Works Grants, 1088
Hearst Foundations Social Service Grants, 1224
HEI Charitable Foundation Grants, 1226
Legler Benbough Foundation Grants, 1479
Maine Women's Fund Econ Security Grants, 1546
Mary E. Babcock Foundation, 1589
New York Foundation Grants, 1753
Robin Hood Foundation Grants, 2096
Sobrato Family Foundation Grants, 2211
Sobrato Family Fdn Meeting Space Grants, 2212
Sobrato Family Foundation Office Space Grants, 2213
Target Foundation Global Grants, 2272
U.S. Bank Foundation Grants, 2330
USAID Global Development Alliance Grants, 2354
Walmart Fdn Inclusive Communities Grants, 2403
Walmart Fdn National Local Giving Grants, 2404
Walmart Foundation State Giving Grants, 2405

Economic Self-Sufficiency
Abington Foundation Grants, 54
ACF Marriage Strengthening Research & Dissemination Center Grants, 85
Adolph Coors Foundation Grants, 129
Arizona Foundation for Women Deborah G. Carstens Fund Grants, 293
Aspen Community Foundation Grants, 316
Atkinson Foundation Community Grants, 325

Boeing Company Contributions Grants, 462
CFGR Community Impact Grants, 552
Citizens Bank Charitable Foundation Grants, 616
Community Foundation of Bartholomew County Women's Giving Circle, 692
Community Foundation of Boone County - Women's Grants, 693
Community Foundation of Eastern Connecticut Northeast Women and Girls Grants, 697
Community Foundation of Eastern Connecticut Norwich Women and Girls Grants, 698
Community Foundation of Eastern Connecticut Southeast Area Women and Girls Grants, 701
Community Foundation of Eastern Connecticut Windham Area Women and Girls Grants, 702
Community Foundation of Greater Chattanooga Grants, 704
Community Foundation of Henderson County Community Grants, 711
Dining for Women Grants, 831
Dollar General Family Literacy Grants, 835
Edward and Ellen Roche Relief Fdn Grants, 887
Eileen Fisher Activating Leadership Grants for Women and Girls, 898
Eulalie Bloedel Schneider Foundation Grants, 936
Ewing Marion Kauffman Foundation Grants, 943
Ezra M. Cutting Trust Grants, 945
FCD New American Children Grants, 952
Fdn for the Mid South Communities Grants, 992
Greater Tacoma Community Foundation Fund for Women and Girls Grants, 1112
Hearst Foundations Social Service Grants, 1224
HEI Charitable Foundation Grants, 1226
Henry E. Niles Foundation Grants, 1240
Johnson Scholarship Foundation Grants, 1382
Jovid Foundation Employment Training Grants, 1392
Legler Benbough Foundation Grants, 1479
Madison Community Foundation Altrusa International of Madison Grants, 1533
Maine Women's Fund Econ Security Grants, 1546
Mary D. and Walter F. Frear Eleemosynary Trust Grants, 1588
May and Stanley Smith Charitable Trust Grants, 1613
Medtronic Foundation Community Link Human Services Grants, 1631
Montana Community Fdn Women's Grants, 1688
Ms. Fdn for Women Economic Justice Grants, 1707
New York Foundation Grants, 1753
Northland Foundation Grants, 1771
Olive B. Cole Foundation Grants, 1816
Porter County Community Foundation Women's Fund Grants, 2005
Robin Hood Foundation Grants, 2096
Rose Community Foundation Education Grants, 2104
Salt River Project Health and Human Services Grants, 2142
Samuel S. Johnson Foundation Grants, 2146
Sobrato Family Foundation Grants, 2211
Sobrato Family Fdn Meeting Space Grants, 2212
Sobrato Family Foundation Office Space Grants, 2213
Speer Trust Grants, 2230
TE Foundation Grants, 2279
U.S. Bank Foundation Grants, 2330
Union Bank, N.A. Foundation Grants, 2334
Union Square Award for Social Justice, 2340
Women's Fund of Hawaii Grants, 2485

Economic Stimulus
Ezra M. Cutting Trust Grants, 945
Ms. Fdn for Women Economic Justice Grants, 1707

Economics
ALFJ International Fund Grants, 231
Appalachian Regional Commission Business Development Revolving Loan Fund Grants, 285
AT&T Fdn Community Support and Safety, 320
Atkinson Foundation Community Grants, 325
Atlanta Women's Foundation Pathway to Success Grants, 327
BP Foundation Grants, 465

Burton D. Morgan Foundation Youth Entrepreneurship Grants, 483
Carnegie Corporation of New York Grants, 511
Flinn Foundation Scholarships, 977
Jovid Foundation Employment Training Grants, 1392
Streisand Foundation Grants, 2251
Tides Foundation Grants, 2302
University of Chicago Chapin Hall Doris Duke Fellowships, 2348

Economics Education
3M Company Fdn Community Giving Grants, 5
Air Products Foundation Grants, 148
Allstate Corporate Giving Grants, 242
Allstate Corp Hometown Commitment Grants, 243
Allstate Foundation Safe and Vital Communities Grants, 244
CNO Financial Group Community Grants, 650
Dean Witter Foundation Education Grants, 807
George W. Codrington Charitable Foundation Grants, 1055
HSBC Corporate Giving Grants, 1266
McCune Charitable Foundation Grants, 1617
Michael and Susan Dell Foundation Grants, 1657

Ecosystems
CNCS AmeriCorps State and National Grants, 643
Illinois DNR Youth Recreation Corps Grants, 1297
Washington Gas Charitable Contributions, 2417

Education
1st Source Foundation Community Involvement Grants, 1
2 Depot Square Ipswich Charitable Foundation Grants, 3
7-Eleven Corporate Giving Grants, 8
100% for Kids - Utah Credit Union Education Foundation Major Project Grants, 11
100% for Kids - Utah Credit Union Education Foundation Mini Grants, 12
100% for Kids - Utah Credit Union Education Foundation School Grants, 13
786 Foundation Grants, 15
A.L. Mailman Family Foundation Grants, 20
AAUW International Project Grants, 44
Abbott Fund Community Engagement Grants, 46
Abbott Fund Global AIDS Care Grants, 47
Abeles Foundation Grants, 51
Abell Foundation Education Grants, 53
Abington Foundation Grants, 54
Abney Foundation Grants, 55
ABS Foundation Grants, 56
Abundance Foundation International Grants, 57
Abundance Foundation Local Community Grants, 58
ACCF of Indiana Berne Ready Mix Community Enrichment Fund Grants, 65
Achelis Foundation Grants, 102
Ackerman Foundation Grants, 103
Acuity Charitable Foundation Grants, 110
Adams County Community Foundation Grants, 115
Adams Family Foundation II Grants, 117
Adams Legacy Foundation Grants, 121
Adelaide Breed Bayrd Foundation Grants, 123
Adelaide Christian Home For Children Grants, 124
Adobe Foundation Action Grants, 126
Adobe Fdn Community Investment Grants, 127
Advance Auto Parts Corporate Giving Grants, 131
AEGON Transamerica Foundation Education and Financial Literacy Grants, 132
Aetna Foundation Summer Academic Enrichment Grants, 135
A Friends' Foundation Trust Grants, 136
A Fund for Women Grants, 137
AGFT Pencil Boy Express, 139
Agnes M. Lindsay Trust Grants, 140
AHC R.E.A.C.H. Grants, 141
Aid for Starving Children Homes and Education Grants, 146
Air Products Foundation Grants, 148
ALA Bookapalooza Grants, 161

Alaska Airlines Foundation LIFT Grants, 194
Alaska Community Foundation Anchorage Schools Foundation Grant, 197
Alaska Community Foundation Cordova Community Foundation Grants, 201
Alaska Community Foundation Cordova Community Foundation Mini-Grants, 202
Alaska Community Foundation Kenai Peninsula Foundation Grant, 205
Alaska Community Foundation Petersburg Community Foundation Annual Grant, 207
Alaska Community Foundation Petersburg Community Foundation Mini-Grants, 208
Alaska Community Foundation Seward Community Foundation Grant, 209
Albert and Ethel Herzstein Charitable Foundation Grants, 219
Albert E. and Birdie W. Einstein Fund Grants, 220
Albertsons Companies Foundation Nourishing Neighbors Grants, 221
Albert W. Rice Charitable Foundation Grants, 223
Alden and Vada Dow Fund Grants, 225
Alex Stern Family Foundation Grants, 229
ALFJ International Fund Grants, 231
Alfred E. Chase Charitable Foundation Grants, 233
Alfred J Mcallister and Dorothy N Mcallister Foundation Grants, 234
Allan C. and Lelia J. Garden Foundation Grants, 236
Allegis Group Foundation Grants, 237
Allstate Corporate Giving Grants, 242
Allstate Corp Hometown Commitment Grants, 243
Allstate Foundation Safe and Vital Communities Grants, 244
Alpha Natural Resources Corporate Giving, 246
Altria Group Positive Youth Dev Grants, 247
Alvah H. and Wyline P. Chapman Foundation Grants, 248
American Electric Power Corporate Grants, 252
American Electric Power Foundation Grants, 253
American Honda Foundation Grants, 255
American Psychiatric Fdn Call for Proposals, 257
American Psychiatric Foundation Typical or Troubled School Mental Health Education Grants, 258
American Savings Foundation Program Grants, 261
American Schlafhorst Foundation Grants, 262
American Woodmark Foundation Grants, 263
Amerigroup Foundation Grants, 264
AMERIND Community Service Project Grants, 265
Amica Insurance Company Community Grants, 267
Anchorage Schools Foundation Grants, 270
Anderson Foundation Grants, 271
Andrew Family Foundation Grants, 272
Anheuser-Busch Foundation Grants, 273
Anna Fitch Ardenghi Trust Grants, 274
Anne Arundel Women Giving Together Regular Grants, 275
Ann L. and Carol Green Rhodes Charitable Trust Grants, 278
Antone and Edene Vidinha Charitable Grants, 281
Appalachian Regional Commission Education and Training Grants, 286
Ar-Hale Family Foundation Grants, 290
Arkema Foundation Grants, 298
Arthur Ashley Williams Foundation Grants, 302
Aspen Community Foundation Grants, 316
Assisi Fdn of Memphis Capital Project Grants, 317
Assisi Foundation of Memphis General Grants, 318
Assisi Foundation of Memphis Mini Grants, 319
AT&T Foundation Education Grants, 321
Atlanta Foundation Grants, 326
Austin Community Foundation Grants, 332
Avery Dennison Foundation Education Grants, 337
Avista Foundation Education Grants, 340
Babcock Charitable Trust Grants, 343
Bainum Family Foundation Grants, 345
Ball Brothers Foundation Organizational Effectiveness/Executive Mentoring Grants, 346
Baltimore Community Foundation Children's Fresh Air Society Fund Grants, 348

Bank of America Charitable Foundation Matching Gifts, 356
Bank of America Charitable Foundation Student Leaders Grants, 357
Bank of America Corporation Sponsorships, 359
Barrasso, Usdin, Kupperman, Freeman, and Sarver Corporate Grants, 362
Baton Rouge Area Foundation Community Coffee Fund Grants, 363
Baton Rouge Area Foundation Every Kid a King Fund Grants, 364
Baton Rouge Area Foundation Grants, 365
Batts Foundation Grants, 367
Baxter International Corporate Giving Grants, 368
Bay Area Community Foundation Semiannual Grants, 382
Beacon Society Jan Stauber Grants, 393
Beckman Coulter Foundation Grants, 394
Belvedere Community Foundation Grants, 399
Belvedere Cove Foundation Scholarships, 401
Ben B. Cheney Foundation Grants, 402
Bernard and Audre Rapoport Foundation Education Grants, 410
Best Buy Children's Fdn @15 Teach Awards, 416
BibleLands Grants, 420
Bierhaus Foundation Grants, 421
Bill Graham Memorial Foundation Grants, 429
Blackford County Community Fdn Grants, 434
Black Hills Corporation Grants, 435
Blanche and Irving Laurie Foundation Grants, 436
Blandin Foundation Expand Opportunity Grants, 437
Blossom Fund Grants, 441
Blue Grass Community Foundation Clark County Fund Grants, 444
Blue Grass Community Foundation Fayette County Fund Grants, 446
Blue Grass Community Foundation Franklin County Fund Grants, 447
Blue Grass Community Foundation Harrison County Fund Grants, 448
Blue Grass Community Foundation Hudson-Ellis Grants, 449
Blue Grass Community Foundation Madison County Fund Grants, 450
Blue Grass Community Foundation Magoffin County Fund Grants, 451
Blue Grass Community Foundation Morgan County Fund Grants, 452
Blue Grass Community Foundation Rowan County Fund Grants, 453
Blue Grass Community Foundation Woodford County Fund Grants, 454
Blumenthal Foundation Grants, 459
BMW of North America Charitable Contribs, 460
Bodenwein Public Benevolent Foundation Grants, 461
Bollinger Foundation Grants, 463
Bradley-Turner Foundation Grants, 466
Bradley C. Higgins Foundation Grants, 467
Bridgestone Americas Trust Fund Grants, 469
Bristol-Myers Squibb Foundation Independent Medical Education Grants, 472
Brown Foundation Grants, 476
Brown Rudnick Charitable Foundation Community Grants, 477
Bryan Adams Foundation Grants, 480
Burton D. Morgan Foundation Youth Entrepreneurship Grants, 483
Bush Foundation Event Scholarships, 484
Byerly Foundation Grants, 487
Cabot Corporation Foundation Grants, 490
Callaway Foundation Grants, 496
Campbell Soup Foundation Grants, 501
Cargill Corporate Giving Grants, 503
Cargill Foundation Education Grants, 504
Carl B. and Florence E. King Foundation Grants, 506
Carl M. Freeman Foundation FACES Grants, 507
Carl R. Hendrickson Family Foundation Grants, 509
Carl W. and Carrie Mae Joslyn Trust Grants, 510
Carroll County Community Foundation Grants, 513
Cass County Community Foundation Grants, 516

CCFF Community Grant, 523
Central Pacific Bank Foundation Grants, 530
CenturyLink Clarke M. Williams Foundation Matching Time Grants, 531
CFFVR Appleton Education Foundation Grants, 536
CFFVR Basic Needs Giving Partnership Grants, 537
CFFVR Clintonville Area Foundation Grants, 538
CFFVR Clintonville Area Foundation Grants, 539
CFFVR Frank C. Shattuck Community Grants, 541
CFFVR Jewelers Mutual Chartbl Giving Grants, 543
CFFVR Mielke Family Foundation Grants, 544
CFFVR Myra M. and Robert L. Vandehey Foundation Grants, 545
CFFVR Project Grants, 546
CFFVR Shawano Area Community Foundation Grants, 549
Chapman Charitable Foundation Grants, 560
Chapman Family Foundation, 562
Charles Delmar Foundation Grants, 564
Charles H. Hall Foundation, 565
Charles H. Pearson Foundation Grants, 566
Charles Lafitte Foundation Grants, 567
Charlotte Martin Foundation Youth Grants, 571
Chilkat Valley Community Foundation Grants, 588
Christensen Fund Regional Grants, 600
Christine and Katharina Pauly Charitable Trust Grants, 601
Christopher Ludwick Foundation Grants, 602
CICF Indianapolis Fdn Community Grants, 606
Circle K Corporation Contributions Grants, 614
Cisco Systems Foundation San Jose Community Grants, 615
Citizens Savings Foundation Grants, 617
Clara Blackford Smith and W. Aubrey Smith Charitable Foundation Grants, 621
Clarence T.C. Ching Foundation Grants, 624
Clark County Community Foundation Grants, 626
Clark Electric Cooperative Grants, 627
Clayton Baker Trust Grants, 629
Cleo Foundation Grants, 632
Cleveland Fdn Lake-Geauga Fund Grants, 635
Cleveland H. Dodge Foundation Grants, 637
Clinton County Community Foundation Grants, 638
CNCS AmeriCorps NCCC Project Grants, 642
CNCS AmeriCorps VISTA Project Grants, 645
CNCS School Turnaround AmeriCorps Grants, 647
Coleman Foundation Entrepreneurship Education Grants, 651
Colgate-Palmolive Company Grants, 652
Collins C. Diboll Private Foundation Grants, 657
Collins Foundation Grants, 658
Columbus Foundation Traditional Grants, 663
Community Foundation for Greater Buffalo Competitive Grants, 670
Community Foundation for Greater Buffalo Garman Family Foundation Grants, 671
Community Foundation for Kettering Grants, 676
Community Foundation for San Benito County Grants, 677
Community Foundation for SE Michigan Chelsea Community Fdn Capacity Building Grants, 679
Community Foundation for SE Michigan Chelsea Community Foundation General Grant, 680
Community Foundation for SE Michigan Detroit Auto Dealers Association Charitable Foundation Fund Grants, 681
Community Foundation for the National Capital Region Community Leadership Grants, 688
Community Foundation of Boone County Grants, 694
Community Fdn Of Greater Lafayette Grants, 710
Community Foundation of Henderson County Community Grants, 711
Community Fdn of Howard County Grants, 712
Community Foundation of Louisville Boyette and Edna Edwards Fund Grants, 718

Community Foundation of Louisville Education Grants, 724
Community Foundation of Louisville Madi and Jim Tate Fund Grants, 727
Community Foundation of Louisville Winston N. and Nancy H. Bloch Educational Fund Grants, 729
Community Foundation of Madison and Jefferson County Grants, 731
Community Fdn of Morgan County Grants, 732
Community Foundation of Muncie and Delaware County Maxon Grants, 734
Community Fdn of Randolph County Grants, 735
Community Fdn of Southern Indiana Grants, 736
Community Foundation of St. Joseph County African American Community Grants, 737
Community Foundation of St. Joseph County Special Project Challenge Grants, 738
Community Foundation of Switzerland County Grants, 739
Community Fdn of Wabash County Grants, 740
Community Foundation of Western Massachusetts Grants, 741
Community Memorial Foundation Responsive Grants, 743
Cooke Foundation Grants, 748
Corina Higginson Trust Grants, 750
Courtney S. Turner Charitable Trust Grants, 753
Covenant Foundation of Brentwood Grants, 755
Cralle Foundation Grants, 760
Crane Foundation General Grants, 761
Credit Suisse Foundation Education Grants, 765
Cresap Family Foundation Grants, 766
Cudd Foundation Grants, 769
CUNA Mutual Group Fdn Community Grants, 770
Dana Brown Charitable Trust Grants, 777
Daniel and Nanna Stern Family Fdn Grants, 778
Daniels Fund K-12 Education Reform Grants, 783
David and Barbara B. Hirschhorn Foundation Education and Literacy Grants, 786
David and Betty Sacks Foundation Grants, 788
David and Laura Merage Foundation Grants, 789
David Robinson Foundation Grants, 791
Dayton Foundation Grants, 796
Dayton Foundation Huber Heights Grants, 797
Dayton Foundation Rike Family Scholarships, 798
Dayton Foundation Vandalia-Butler Grants, 799
Dayton Foundation VISIONS Endowment Fund Grants, 800
Dayton Power and Light Company Foundation Signature Grants, 801
Dayton Power and Light Foundation Grants, 802
Deaconess Community Foundation Grants, 803
Dean Foods Community Involvement Grants, 805
Dearborn Community Foundation City of Lawrenceburg Community Grants, 809
Dearborn Community Foundation City of Lawrenceburg Youth Grants, 810
Decatur County Community Foundation Large Project Grants, 811
DeKalb County Community Foundation Grants, 815
Delaware Community Foundation Grants, 817
Delmarva Power & Light Contributions, 821
Delmarva Power & Light Mini-Grants, 822
Delta Air Lines Foundation Community Enrichment Grants, 823
Delta Air Lines Foundation Youth Development Grants, 824
Dermody Properties Fdn Capstone Award, 826
Dermody Properties Foundation Grants, 827
Dining for Women Grants, 831
Dolan Children's Foundation Grants, 832
Dollar General Family Literacy Grants, 835
Dollar General Youth Literacy Grants, 837
Dorrance Family Foundation Grants, 845
Dr. and Mrs. Paul Pierce Memorial Foundation Grants, 862
Dream Weaver Foundation, 865
DTE Energy Foundation Community Development Grants, 866
DTE Energy Foundation Diversity Grants, 867

DTE Energy Foundation Environmental Grants, 868
DTE Energy Foundation Leadership Grants, 870
Dubois County Community Foundation Grants, 871
Dyson Foundation Mid-Hudson Valley Project Support Grants, 874
E.L. Wiegand Foundation Grants, 877
Earl and Maxine Claussen Trust Grants, 878
Eastern Bank Charitable Foundation Partnerships Grants, 881
Eastern Bank Charitable Foundation Targeted Grants, 882
Edward and Helen Bartlett Foundation Grants, 888
Edward F. Swinney Trust Grants, 890
Edward W. and Stella C. Van Houten Memorial Fund Grants, 892
Edyth Bush Charitable Foundation Grants, 893
Elizabeth Carse Foundation Grants, 899
Elizabeth Huth Coates Charitable Foundation Grants, 900
Elizabeth Morse Genius Charitable Trust Grants, 901
Elkhart County Community Foundation Grants, 903
Ellen Abbott Gilman Trust Grants, 905
El Pomar Foundation Anna Keesling Ackerman Fund Grants, 907
El Pomar Foundation Grants, 908
Elsie H. Wilcox Foundation Grants, 909
Emily Hall Tremaine Foundation Learning Disabilities Grants, 912
Ensworth Charitable Foundation Grants, 916
Entergy Charitable Foundation Education and Literacy Grants, 917
Entergy Corporation Micro Grants, 919
Environmental Excellence Awards, 922
EQT Fdn Education and Workforce Grants, 927
Essex County Community Foundation Dee and King Webster Fund for Greater Lawrence Grants, 929
Essex County Community Foundation Greater Lawrence Community Fund Grants, 931
Essex County Community Foundation Greater Lawrence Summer Fund Grants, 932
Essex County Community Foundation Merrimack Valley Municipal Business Development and Recovery Fund Grants, 933
Ethel Sergeant Clark Smith Foundation Grants, 935
Evelyn and Walter Haas, Jr. Fund Education Opportunities Grants, 939
Ezra Jack Keats Foundation Mini-Grants, 944
F.M. Kirby Foundation Grants, 946
F.R. Bigelow Foundation Grants, 947
Farmers Insurance Corporate Giving Grants, 948
Faye L. and William L. Cowden Charitable Foundation Grants, 950
Fayette County Foundation Grants, 951
FCD New American Children Grants, 952
FCYO Youth Organizing Grants, 954
Fichtenbaum Charitable Trust Grants, 955
Fidelity Foundation Grants, 957
Fifth Third Foundation Grants, 959
FirstEnergy Foundation Community Grants, 965
Foundation for Rural Service Education Grants, 991
Foundation for the Mid South Education Grants, 993
Foundations of East Chicago Education Grants, 995
Four County Community Foundation Kellogg Group Grants, 1002
Fourjay Foundation Grants, 1003
Francis Beidler Foundation Grants, 1007
Franklin County Community Fdn Grants, 1010
Franklin H. Wells and Ruth L. Wells Foundation Grants, 1011
Frank Reed and Margaret Jane Peters Memorial Fund Grants, 1013
Frank Reed and Margaret Jane Peters Memorial Fund II Grants, 1014
Frederick W. Marzahl Memorial Fund Grants, 1018
Fremont Area Community Foundation Amazing X Grants, 1019
Fremont Area Community Foundation Community Grants, 1020
Fremont Area Community Foundation Education Mini-Grants, 1021

Fremont Area Community Foundation Youth Advisory Committee Grants, 1022
Fuller E. Callaway Foundation Grants, 1027
Furth Family Foundation Grants, 1030
G.N. Wilcox Trust Grants, 1031
Gannett Foundation Community Action Grants, 1033
Gene Haas Foundation, 1038
General Motors Foundation Grants, 1039
George A. & Grace L. Long Fdn Grants, 1041
George and Ruth Bradford Foundation Grants, 1042
George A Ohl Jr. Foundation Grants, 1043
George Graham and Elizabeth Galloway Smith Foundation Grants, 1047
George H. and Jane A. Mifflin Memorial Fund Grants, 1048
George H.C. Ensworth Memorial Fund Grants, 1049
George I. Alden Trust Grants, 1051
George J. and Effie L. Seay Foundation Grants, 1052
George Kress Foundation Grants, 1053
George P. Davenport Trust Fund Grants, 1054
George W. Codrington Charitable Foundation Grants, 1055
George W.P. Magee Trust Grants, 1056
George W. Wells Foundation Grants, 1057
Georgia-Pacific Foundation Education Grants, 1058
Georgia-Pacific Fdn Entrepreneurship Grants, 1059
Gerber Fdn West Michigan Youth Grants, 1065
Gertrude & William C. Wardlaw Grants, 1067
Gil and Dody Weaver Foundation Grants, 1071
Global Fund for Women Grants, 1073
GNOF Bayou Communities Grants, 1077
GNOF Exxon-Mobil Grants, 1080
GNOF Freeman Challenge Grants, 1081
GNOF Gert Community Fund Grants, 1082
GNOF IMPACT Kahn-Oppenheim Tr Grts, 1087
Good+Foundation Grants, 1096
Grace Bersted Foundation Grants, 1097
Graham Family Charitable Foundation Grants, 1099
Graham Foundation Grants, 1100
Greater Milwaukee Foundation Grants, 1109
Greater Saint Louis Community Fdn Grants, 1110
Greater Sitka Legacy Fund Grants, 1111
Greater Tacoma Community Foundation General Operating Grants, 1113
Griffin Family Foundation Grants, 1121
Grifols Community Outreach Grants, 1122
GTECH After School Advantage Grants, 1125
Gulf Coast Foundation of Community Operating Grants, 1134
Gulf Coast Foundation of Community Program Grants, 1135
Guy I. Bromley Trust Grants, 1136
H.A. and Mary K. Chapman Charitable Trust Grants, 1137
H.B. Fuller Foundation Grants, 1138
HAF Don and Bettie Albright Endowment Fund Grants, 1142
Hahl Proctor Charitable Trust Grants, 1151
Hall-Perrine Foundation Grants, 1152
Hampton Roads Community Foundation Education Grants, 1157
Hampton Roads Community Foundation Nonprofit Facilities Improvement Grants, 1159
Hancock County Community Foundation - Field of Interest Grants, 1161
Hardin County Community Foundation Grants, 1167
Harmony Project Grants, 1170
Harold K.L. Castle Foundation Public Education Redesign and Enhancement Grants, 1173
Harold K.L. Castle Foundation Strengthening Windward Oahu Communities Grants, 1174
Harry A. and Margaret D. Towsley Foundation Grants, 1180
Harry B. and Jane H. Brock Foundation Grants, 1183
Hartford Foundation Regular Grants, 1185
Hawai'i Community Foundation Children's Trust Fund Community Awareness: Child Abuse and Neglect Prevention Grants, 1198
Hawai'i Community Foundation East Hawaii Fund Grants, 1199

Hawai'i Community Foundation Family Literacy and Hawaii Pizza Hut Literacy Grants, 1201
Hawai'i Community Foundation Lana'i Community Benefit Fund, 1203
Hawaiian Electric Industries Charitable Foundation Grants, 1211
HBF Pathways Out of Poverty Grants, 1222
HEI Charitable Foundation Grants, 1226
Helen Bader Foundation Grants, 1227
Helen E. Ellis Charitable Trust Grants, 1228
Helen Gertrude Sparks Charitable Trust Grants, 1230
Helen V. Brach Foundation Grants, 1232
Hendricks County Community Fdn Grants, 1234
Henry County Community Foundation - TASC Youth Grants, 1238
Henry County Community Foundation Grants, 1239
Henry F. Koch Residual Trust Grants, 1241
Herbert Hoover Presidential Library Association Bus Travel Grants, 1244
Highmark Corporate Giving Grants, 1248
Hispanic Heritage Foundation Youth Awards, 1253
HLTA Visitor Industry Charity Walk Grant, 1254
Horace A. Kimball and S. Ella Kimball Foundation Grants, 1260
Horace A. Moses Charitable Trust Grants, 1261
HSBC Corporate Giving Grants, 1266
Hubbard Family Foundation Grants, 1271
Hubbard Family Foundation Grants, 1270
Huffy Foundation Grants, 1273
Human Source Foundation Grants, 1276
Huntington Clinical Foundation Grants, 1278
Huntington County Community Foundation Make a Difference Grants, 1280
Iddings Foundation Capital Project Grants, 1283
Iddings Foundation Major Project Grants, 1284
Iddings Foundation Medium Project Grants, 1285
ILA Grants for Literacy Projects in Countries with Developing Economies, 1292
Illinois Arts Council Youth Employment in the Arts Program Grants, 1294
Illinois DNR School Habitat Action Grants, 1296
Indiana OCRA Rural Capacity Grants (RCG), 1301
Irving S. Gilmore Foundation Grants, 1314
Isabel Allende Foundation Esperanza Grants, 1315
IYI Professional Development Grants, 1317
J. Bulow Campbell Foundation Grants, 1319
J. Edwin Treakle Foundation Grants, 1320
J. Knox Gholston Foundation Grants, 1321
J.W. Gardner II Foundation Grants, 1323
J.W. Kieckhefer Foundation Grants, 1324
J. Willard and Alice S. Marriott Fdn Grants, 1327
Jacob and Hilda Blaustein Foundation Israel Program Grants, 1335
Jacob G. Schmidlapp Trusts Grants, 1336
James and Abigail Campbell Family Foundation Grants, 1337
James F. and Marion L. Miller Fdn Grants, 1338
James Ford Bell Foundation Grants, 1339
James S. Copley Foundation Grants, 1345
Japan Foundation Los Angeles Grants for Japanese-Language Courses, 1352
Jennings County Community Fdn Grants, 1360
Jennings County Community Foundation Women's Giving Circle Grant, 1361
Jessica Stevens Community Foundation Grants, 1363
Jim Moran Foundation Grants, 1366
Joan Bentinck-Smith Charitable Fdn Grants, 1367
John and Marcia Goldman Foundation Youth Development Grants, 1368
John Clarke Trust Grants, 1369
John G. Duncan Charitable Trust Grants, 1372
John M. Weaver Foundation Grants, 1376
Joni Elaine Templeton Foundation Grants, 1384
Joseph Henry Edmondson Foundation Grants, 1388
Joseph S. Stackpole Charitable Trust Grants, 1390
Journal Gazette Foundation Grants, 1391
JP Morgan Chase Fdn Arts and Culture Grants, 1394
Judith Clark-Morrill Foundation Grants, 1395
Julia Temple Davis Brown Foundation Grants, 1399

Kalamazoo Community Foundation Early Childhood Learning and School Readiness Grants, 1407
K and F Baxter Family Foundation Grants, 1413
Katharine Matthies Foundation Grants, 1418
Kathryne Beynon Foundation Grants, 1420
Katrine Menzing Deakins Chartbl Trust Grants, 1422
Kelvin and Eleanor Smith Foundation Grants, 1424
Kenai Peninsula Foundation Grants, 1425
Ketchikan Community Foundation Grants, 1429
Kettering Family Foundation Grants, 1430
Kimball International-Habig Foundation Education Grants, 1433
Kinder Morgan Foundation Grants, 1436
Kindle Project SpiderWeave Flow Fund Grants, 1437
Kind World Foundation Grants, 1438
Kodak Community Relations Grants, 1445
Kodiak Community Foundation Grants, 1446
Koret Foundation Grants, 1449
Kosciusko County Community Fdn Grants, 1452
Kovler Family Foundation Grants, 1455
Kroger Company Donations, 1456
Laclede Gas Charitable Trust Grants, 1457
LaGrange Independent Foundation for Endowments (L.I.F.E.), 1459
Laidlaw Foundation Multi-Year Grants, 1460
Laidlaw Foundation Youh Organizing Catalyst Grants, 1461
Laidlaw Foundation Youth Organizaing Initiatives Grants, 1462
Lake County Community Fund Grants, 1463
Land O'Lakes Foundation Mid-Atlantic Grants, 1467
Lands' End Corporate Giving Program, 1468
Laura B. Vogler Foundation Grants, 1470
Laura Moore Cunningham Foundation Grants, 1474
Laurel Foundation Grants, 1475
Laurie H. Wollmuth Charitable Trust Grants, 1476
Lee and Ramona Bass Foundation Grants, 1478
Legler Benbough Foundation Grants, 1479
Leola Osborn Trust Grants, 1483
Leo Niessen Jr., Charitable Trust Grants, 1484
Leonsis Foundation Grants, 1485
Liberty Bank Foundation Grants, 1488
Lil and Julie Rosenberg Foundation Grants, 1491
Linford & Mildred White Charitable Grants, 1495
Lisa and Douglas Goldman Fund Grants, 1496
Lloyd G. Balfour Foundation Attleboro-Specific Charities Grants, 1502
Long Island Community Foundation Grants, 1507
Lotus 88 Foundation for Women and Children Grants, 1508
Louie M. and Betty M. Phillips Fdn Grants, 1509
Louis Calder Foundation Grants, 1511
Lubrizol Corporation Community Grants, 1512
Lucy Downing Nisbet Charitable Fund Grants, 1515
Ludwick Family Foundation Grants, 1516
Luella Kemper Trust Grants, 1517
Lumpkin Family Foundation Strong Community Leadership Grants, 1519
M.J. Murdock Charitable Trust General Grants, 1524
Mabel A. Horne Fund Grants, 1525
Mabel F. Hoffman Charitable Trust Grants, 1526
Mabel Louise Riley Foundation Grants, 1529
Mabel Y. Hughes Charitable Trust Grants, 1530
Macquarie Bank Foundation Grants, 1532
Madison County Community Foundation - City of Anderson Quality of Life Grant, 1536
Maine Community Foundation Vincent B. and Barbara G. Welch Grants, 1545
Malone Family Foundation Atypical Development Initiative Grants, 1549
Manuel D. and Rhoda Mayerson Fdn Grants, 1550
Marathon Petroleum Corporation Grants, 1551
Marcia and Otto Koehler Foundation Grants, 1553
Mardag Foundation Grants, 1554
Marietta McNeill Morgan and Samuel Tate Morgan Jr. Trust Grants, 1560
Marion and Miriam Rose Fund Grants, 1569
Marion Gardner Jackson Charitable Trust Grts, 1570
Marjorie Moore Charitable Foundation Grants, 1574
Mark W. Coy Foundation Grants, 1575

Marshall County Community Fdn Grants, 1579
Marsh Corporate Grants, 1580
Martin C. Kauffman 100 Club of Alameda County Scholarships, 1582
Mary D. and Walter F. Frear Eleemosynary Trust Grants, 1588
Mary E. Babcock Foundation, 1589
Mary K. Chapman Foundation Grants, 1590
Maryland State Dept of Education 21st Century Community Learning Centers Grants, 1593
Mary Owen Borden Foundation Grants, 1597
Mary Wilmer Covey Charitable Trust Grants, 1600
Maurice Amado Foundation Grants, 1609
McCarthy Family Fdn Charity Fund Grants, 1614
McCombs Foundation Grants, 1615
McCune Charitable Foundation Grants, 1617
McInerny Foundation Grants, 1622
McLean Contributionship Grants, 1623
Meadows Foundation Grants, 1626
Mead Witter Foundation Grants, 1628
Mercedes-Benz USA Corporate Contributions Grants, 1634
Mericos Foundation Grants, 1637
Merrick Foundation Grants, 1639
Mervin Bovaird Foundation Grants, 1643
Metzger-Price Fund Grants, 1647
MGM Resorts Foundation Community Grants, 1655
MGN Family Foundation Grants, 1656
Michelin North America Challenge Education, 1660
Micron Technology Fdn Community Grants, 1664
Middlesex Savings Charitable Foundation Educational Opportunities Grants, 1670
Mile High United Way Stratc Investment Grts, 1671
Milken Family Foundation Grants, 1672
Mimi and Peter Haas Fund Grants, 1677
Minnie M. Jones Trust Grants, 1678
Montana Community Foundation Grants, 1687
Morris Stulsaft Foundation Early Childhood Education Grants, 1696
Morton K. and Jane Blaustein Foundation Educational Opportunity Grants, 1700
Moses Kimball Fund Grants, 1701
Narragansett Number One Foundation Grants, 1712
Natalie W. Furniss Foundation Grants, 1715
Nathaniel and Elizabeth P. Stevens Foundation Grants, 1719
NEA Fdn Read Across America Event Grants, 1731
Nell J. Redfield Foundation Grants, 1737
Nestle Purina PetCare Educational Grants, 1738
Nestle Purina PetCare Youth Grants, 1739
New Earth Foundation Grants, 1743
New York Foundation Grants, 1753
Nissan Neighbors Grants, 1762
Noble County Community Foundation Grants, 1765
Norcliffe Foundation Grants, 1766
Norman Foundation Grants, 1767
NRA Foundation Grants, 1774
O. Max Gardner Foundation Grants, 1798
Ober Kaler Community Grants, 1801
Office Depot Corporation Community Relations Grants, 1805
Office Depot Foundation Education Grants, 1806
OHA Community Grants for Education, 1809
Ohio County Community Foundation Grants, 1812
Ohio County Community Fdn Mini-Grants, 1813
Olga Sipolin Children's Fund Grants, 1815
Olive Smith Browning Charitable Trust Grants, 1818
OMNOVA Solutions Fdn Education Grants, 1820
Onan Family Foundation Grants, 1821
OneFamily Foundation Grants, 1822
Ontario Arts Council Artists in Communities and Schools Project Grants, 1823
Ontario Arts Council Arts Organizations in Communities and Schools Operating Grants, 1824
Ontario Arts Council Indigenous Culture Fund Indigenous Artists in Communities and Schools Project Grants, 1825
Orange County Community Foundation Grants, 1828
Orange County Community Foundation Grants, 1829
Ordean Foundation Catalyst Grants, 1830

Ordean Foundation Partnership Grants, 1831
Oregon Community Fdn Community Grants, 1833
OSF Baltimore Community Fellowships, 1838
OSF Baltimore Education and Youth Development
    Grants, 1840
OSF Education Program Grants in Kyrgyzstan, 1842
OSF Education Support Program Grants, 1843
OtterCares Impact Fund Grants, 1849
OtterCares Inspiration Fund Grants, 1850
P. Buckley Moss Foundation for Children's Education
    Endowed Scholarships, 1854
P. Buckley Moss Foundation for Children's Education
    Teacher Grants, 1855
PacifiCare Foundation Grants, 1861
Palmer Foundation Grants, 1867
Parker Foundation (California) Grants, 1869
Parkersburg Area Community Foundation Action
    Grants, 1871
Paul and Edith Babson Foundation Grants, 1881
PDF Community Organizing Grants, 1920
Peabody Foundation Grants, 1922
Pentair Foundation Education and Community
    Grants, 1934
Percy B. Ferebee Endowment Grants, 1936
Perkins Charitable Foundation Grants, 1939
Petersburg Community Foundation Grants, 1951
Peyton Anderson Scholarships, 1955
PG&E Community Vitality Grants, 1957
PGE Foundation Grants, 1958
Phil Hardin Foundation Grants, 1960
Philip Boyle Foundation Grants, 1961
Philip L. Graham Fund Education Grants, 1962
Piedmont Health Foundation Grants, 1965
Piedmont Natural Gas Corporate and Charitable
    Contributions, 1966
Piedmont Natural Gas Foundation K-12 Science,
    Technology, Engineering and Math (STEM)
    Grant, 1969
Pinnacle Foundation Grants, 1973
Piper Trust Arts and Culture Grants, 1975
PMI Foundation Grants, 1982
PNC Foundation Education Grants, 1985
Pohlad Family Fdn Large Capital Grants, 1990
Pohlad Family Fdn Small Capital Grants, 1991
Pohlad Family Foundation Summer Camp
    Scholarships, 1992
Pokagon Fund Grants, 1994
Polk County Community Foundation Marjorie M.
    and Lawrence R. Bradley Endowment Fund
    Grants, 1998
Polk County Community Foundation Unrestricted
    Grants, 2001
Portland General Electric Foundation Grants, 2007
Powell Foundation Grants, 2013
PPCF Esther M. and Freeman E. Everett Charitable
    Foundation Grants, 2016
PPG Industries Foundation Grants, 2017
Price Chopper's Golub Foundation Grants, 2020
Pride Foundation Grants, 2024
Progress Energy Foundation Energy Education
    Grants, 2025
Prudential Foundation Education Grants, 2028
PSEG Corporate Contributions Grants, 2030
Public Education Power Grants, 2032
Puerto Rico Community Foundation Grants, 2037
Pulaski County Community Foundation Grants, 2038
Putnam County Community Fdn Grants, 2040
Qualcomm Grants, 2042
R.C. Baker Foundation Grants, 2043
R.D. and Joan Dale Hubbard Fdn Grants, 2044
R.J. McElroy Trust Grants, 2046
R.S. Gernon Trust Grants, 2047
Radcliffe Institute Carol K. Pforzheimer Student
    Fellowships, 2048
Rasmuson Foundation Tier One Grants, 2055
Rasmuson Foundation Tier Two Grants, 2056
Rathmann Family Foundation Grants, 2057
Ray Foundation Grants, 2059
RCF General Community Grants, 2062
RCF Summertime Kids Grants, 2064

RGk Foundation Grants, 2068
Richard and Caroline T. Gwathmey Memorial Trust
    Grants, 2069
Richard Davoud Donchian Foundation Grants, 2070
Richard W. Goldman Family Fdn Grants, 2073
Richland County Bank Grants, 2074
Ricks Family Charitable Trust Grants, 2075
Ripley County Community Foundation Grants, 2077
Ripley County Community Foundation Small Project
    Grants, 2078
Robert and Helen Haddad Foundation Grants, 2084
Robert Bowne Foundaion Edmund A. Stanley, Jr.
    Research Grants, 2086
Robert Bowne Foundation Fellowships, 2087
Robert Bowne Foundation Literacy Grants, 2088
Robert Bowne Fdn Youth-Centered Grants, 2089
Robert Lee Blaffer Foundation Grants, 2092
Robert W. Knox, Sr. and Pearl Wallis Knox
    Charitable Foundation, 2095
Robinson Foundation Grants, 2097
Rockwell Collins Charitable Corp Grants, 2098
Roger L. and Agnes C. Dell Charitable Trust II
    Grants, 2100
Roney-Fitzpatrick Foundation Grants, 2102
Rose Community Foundation Education Grants, 2104
Rose Hills Foundation Grants, 2106
Rosenberg Charity Foundation Grants, 2107
Roy and Christine Sturgis Charitable Tr Grts, 2115
RR Donnelley Foundation Grants, 2118
Rush County Community Foundation Grants, 2121
Ruth Anderson Foundation Grants, 2122
Ruth and Vernon Taylor Foundation Grants, 2124
S. D. Bechtel, Jr. Foundation / Stephen Bechtel Fund
    Character and Citizenship Dev Grants, 2128
S. Spencer Scott Fund Grants, 2129
Saigh Foundation Grants, 2137
Saint Louis Rams Foundation Community
    Donations, 2139
Salmon Foundation Grants, 2140
Samueli Foundation Youth Services Grants, 2144
Samuel N. and Mary Castle Foundation Grants, 2145
Samuel S. Johnson Foundation Grants, 2146
SanDisk Corp Community Sharing Grants, 2155
San Juan Island Community Foundation Grants, 2158
Sarah G. McCarthy Memorial Foundation, 2162
Sarkeys Foundation Grants, 2163
SAS Institute Community Relations Donations, 2165
Schlessman Family Foundation Grants, 2167
Scott County Community Foundation Grants, 2170
Screen Actors Guild BookPALS Assistance, 2171
Screen Actors Guild PencilPALS Assistance, 2172
Screen Actors Guild StagePALS Assistance, 2173
Seattle Foundation Arts and Culture Grants, 2174
Seattle Foundation Benjamin N. Phillips Memorial
    Fund Grants, 2176
Seattle Foundation Education Grants, 2178
Sensient Technologies Foundation Grants, 2180
Seward Community Foundation Grants, 2182
Seward Community Foundation Mini-Grants, 2183
Shell Deer Park Grants, 2186
Shield-Ayres Foundation Grants, 2189
Shopko Fdn Community Charitable Grants, 2191
Sidgmore Family Foundation Grants, 2195
Sidney Stern Memorial Trust Grants, 2197
Siebert Lutheran Foundation Grants, 2198
Silicon Valley Community Foundation Education
    Grants, 2200
Simpson Lumber Charitable Contributions, 2201
SME Education Fdn Youth Program Grants, 2209
Sobrato Family Foundation Grants, 2211
Sobrato Family Fdn Meeting Space Grants, 2212
Sobrato Family Foundation Office Space Grants, 2213
Sorenson Legacy Foundation Grants, 2217
Southern California Edison Education Grants, 2218
Southern Minnesota Initiative Foundation BookStart
    Grants, 2220
South Madison Community Foundation - Teacher
    Creativity Mini Grants, 2225
Stella and Charles Guttman Foundation Grants, 2241
Sterling and Shelli Gardner Foundation Grants, 2243

Stinson Foundation Grants, 2246
Stocker Foundation Grants, 2247
Stranahan Foundation Grants, 2250
Subaru of America Foundation Grants, 2253
Subaru of Indiana Automotive Fdn Grants, 2254
Sunoco Foundation Grants, 2256
SunTrust Bank Trusteed Foundations Greene-Sawtell
    Grants, 2257
SunTrust Bank Trusteed Foundations Nell Warren
    Elkin and William Simpson Elkin Grants, 2258
Susan A. and Donald P. Babson Charitable
    Foundation Grants, 2259
Tauck Family Foundation Grants, 2274
TE Foundation Grants, 2279
Tellabs Foundation Grants, 2280
Telluride Foundation Community Grants, 2281
Thelma Braun and Bocklett Family Foundation
    Grants, 2287
Thomas and Agnes Carvel Foundation Grants, 2289
Thomas J. Atkins Memorial Trust Fund Grants, 2290
Thomas J. Long Foundation Community Grants, 2291
Thomas W. Briggs Foundation Grants, 2294
Three Guineas Fund Grants, 2297
Tides Fdn Friends of the IGF Fund Grants, 2300
TJX Foundation Grants, 2303
Toshiba America Foundation Grades 7-12 Science and
    Math Grants, 2307
Toshiba America Foundation K-6 Science and Math
    Grants, 2308
Toyota Motor Manuf of Alabama Grants, 2309
Toyota Motor Manufacturing of Indiana Grants, 2310
Toyota Motor Manuf of Kentucky Grants, 2311
Toyota Motor Manuf of Mississippi Grants, 2312
Toyota Motor Manufacturing of Texas Grants, 2313
Toyota Motor Manufacturing of West Virginia
    Grants, 2314
Toyota Motor North America of NY Grants, 2315
Toyota Motor Sales, USA Grants, 2316
Toyota Technical Center Grants, 2317
Tull Charitable Foundation Grants, 2324
Turner Foundation Grants, 2326
Twenty-First Century Foundation Grants, 2328
U.S. Bank Foundation Grants, 2330
U.S. Cellular Corporation Grants, 2331
Union Bank, N.A. Corporate Sponsorships and
    Donations, 2333
United Technologies Corporation Grants, 2347
University of Chicago Chapin Hall Doris Duke
    Fellowships, 2348
UPS Foundation Economic and Global Literacy
    Grants, 2351
USAID Integrated Youth Development Activity
    Grants, 2356
USAID Nigeria Ed Crisis Response Grants, 2358
USAID School Improvement Program Grants, 2360
V.V. Cooke Foundation Grants, 2371
Victor E. Speas Foundation Grants, 2380
Virginia W. Kettering Foundation Grants, 2388
W.H. and Mary Ellen Cobb Chartbl Trust Grts, 2397
W.P. and Bulah Luse Foundation Grants, 2399
Walker Area Community Foundation Grants, 2401
Wallace Foundation Grants, 2402
Walmart Fdn Inclusive Communities Grants, 2403
Walmart Fdn National Local Giving Grants, 2404
Walter S. and Evan C. Jones Testam Trust, 2407
Walton Family Foundation Education Grants, 2408
Walton Family Foundation Public Charter Startup
    Grants, 2409
Washington County Community Fdn Grants, 2416
Washington Gas Charitable Contributions, 2417
Watson-Brown Foundation Grants, 2418
Wayne County Community Foundation Grants, 2419
Weaver Foundation Grants, 2420
Weaver Popcorn Foundation Grants, 2421
Wege Foundation Grants, 2422
Wells County Foundation Grants, 2426
Western Indiana Community Fdn Grants, 2428
White County Community Foundation - Women
    Giving Together Grants, 2438
Whitney Foundation Grants, 2441

WHO Foundation Education/Literacy Grants, 2442
WHO Foundation General Grants, 2443
Wilkins Family Foundation Grants, 2450
William A. Badger Foundation Grants, 2451
William A. Cooke Foundation Grants, 2452
William and Flora Hewlett Foundation Quality
    Education in Developing Countries Grants, 2456
William Bingham Foundation Grants, 2460
William E. Dean III Charitable Fdn Grants, 2464
William Foulds Family Foundation Grants, 2465
William G. and Helen C. Hoffman Fdn Grants, 2466
William J. and Dorothy K. O'Neill Foundation
    Responsive Grants, 2468
William J. Brace Charitable Trust, 2471
William Ray and Ruth E. Collins Fdn Grants, 2473
Williams Comps Homegrown Giving Grants, 2474
Wood-Claeyssens Foundation Grants, 2486
Wood Family Charitable Trust, 2487
Woods Charitable Fund Education Grants, 2488
World of Children Education Award, 2490
Wyoming Department of Education McKinney-Vento
    Subgrant, 2503
Xerox Foundation Grants, 2507
Yampa Valley Community Foundation Erickson
    Christian Heritage Scholarships, 2509
Yawkey Foundation Grants, 2510
YSA ABC Summer of Service Awards, 2512
YSA Get Ur Good On Grants, 2513
YSA GYSD Regional Partner Grants, 2515
YSA NEA Youth Leaders for Literacy Grants, 2518
YSA Sodexo Lead Organizer Grants, 2520
YSA State Farm Good Neighbor YOUth In The
    Driver Seat Grants, 2521
Z. Smith Reynolds Foundation Small Grants, 2523
Zollner Foundation Grants, 2526

Education Reform
Achelis and Bodman Foundation Grants, 101
Achelis Foundation Grants, 102
Anheuser-Busch Foundation Grants, 273
Bernard and Audre Rapoport Foundation Education
    Grants, 410
Bill and Melinda Gates Foundation Policy and
    Advocacy Grants, 427
Boeing Company Contributions Grants, 462
Carnegie Corporation of New York Grants, 511
CNCS School Turnaround AmeriCorps Grants, 647
Community Foundation of Louisville Education
    Grants, 724
Daniels Fund K-12 Education Reform Grants, 783
Dept of Ed Fund for the Improvement of Education--
    Partnerships in Character Ed Pilot Projects, 825
Foundation for the Mid South Education Grants, 993
Hazen Foundation Public Education Grants, 1221
Joseph H. and Florence A. Roblee Foundation
    Education Grants, 1386
K and F Baxter Family Foundation Grants, 1413
Lewis H. Humphreys Charitable Trust Grants, 1486
Morton K. and Jane Blaustein Foundation
    Educational Opportunity Grants, 1700
OSF Baltimore Education and Youth Development
    Grants, 1840
OSF Education Support Program Grants, 1843
Phil Hardin Foundation Grants, 1960
Piedmont Natural Gas Foundation K-12 Science,
    Technology, Engineering and Math Grant, 1969
Portland General Electric Foundation Grants, 2007
Richard Davoud Donchian Foundation Grants, 2070
Toyota USA Foundation Education Grants, 2318
USAID Nigeria Ed Crisis Response Grants, 2358
William and Flora Hewlett Foundation Education
    Grants, 2454
William Caspar Graustein Memorial Fund Corinne
    G. Levin Education Grants, 2462
William J. Brace Charitable Trust, 2471

Education and Work
Akron Community Fdn Education Grants, 151
Appalachian Regional Commission Education and
    Training Grants, 286

AT&T Foundation Education Grants, 321
Blue Mountain Community Foundation Warren
    Community Action Fund Grants, 457
Community Foundation of Louisville Education
    Grants, 724
Essex County Community Foundation Dee and King
    Webster Fund for Greater Lawrence Grants, 929
Maryland State Dept of Education Coordinating
    Entity Services for the Maryland Child Care Res
    Centers Network Grants, 1594
Morris Stulsaft Foundation Pathways to Work
    Grants, 1699
PepsiCo Foundation Grants, 1935
Philip L. Graham Fund Education Grants, 1962
Radcliffe Institute Carol K. Pforzheimer Student
    Fellowships, 2048
Sobrato Family Foundation Grants, 2211
Sobrato Family Fdn Meeting Space Grants, 2212
Sobrato Family Foundation Office Space Grants, 2213
Toyota Motor Manufacturing of West Virginia
    Grants, 2314
Xerox Foundation Grants, 2507

Educational Administration
ALA May Hill Arbuthnot Honor Lecture Award, 176
CNCS School Turnaround AmeriCorps Grants, 647
George I. Alden Trust Grants, 1051
Meadows Foundation Grants, 1626
Meyer Foundation Education Grants, 1649
Nellie Mae Education Foundation District-Level
    Change Grants, 1736
Piedmont Natural Gas Foundation K-12 Science,
    Technology, Engineering and Math (STEM)
    Grant, 1969
Wallace Foundation Grants, 2402

Educational Evaluation/Assessment
Martha Holden Jennings Foundation Grants-to-
    Educators, 1581
PacifiCare Foundation Grants, 1861
Posse Foundation Scholarships, 2011
Teagle Foundation Grants, 2277
UPS Foundation Economic and Global Literacy
    Grants, 2351
William J. Brace Charitable Trust, 2471

Educational Finance
Allstate Corporate Giving Grants, 242
Allstate Corp Hometown Commitment Grants, 243
Allstate Foundation Safe and Vital Communities
    Grants, 244
Peyton Anderson Scholarships, 1955

Educational Instruction
100% for Kids - Utah Credit Union Education
    Foundation Major Project Grants, 11
100% for Kids - Utah Credit Union Education
    Foundation Mini Grants, 12
100% for Kids - Utah Credit Union Education
    Foundation School Grants, 13
ACF Head Start and/or Early Head Start Grantee
    - Clay, Randolph, and Talladega Counties,
    Alabama, 82
ACF Head Start and/or Early Head Start Grantee -
    St. Landry Parish, Louisiana, 83
ALA May Hill Arbuthnot Honor Lecture Award, 176
Baton Rouge Area Foundation Community Coffee
    Fund Grants, 363
Bernard and Audre Rapoport Foundation Education
    Grants, 410
Bill and Melinda Gates Foundation Policy and
    Advocacy Grants, 427
Carroll County Community Foundation Grants, 513
Charlotte Martin Foundation Youth Grants, 571
Community Foundation of Louisville Education
    Grants, 724
Georgia-Pacific Foundation Education Grants, 1058
Geraldine R. Dodge Fdn Education Grants, 1061
Honeywell Corporation Got 2B Safe Contest, 1256

Kosciusko County Community Foundation
    Endowment Youth Services (KEYS) Grants, 1451
Mary Wilmer Covey Charitable Trust Grants, 1600
OSF Education Program Grants in Kyrgyzstan, 1842
Southern Minnesota Initiative Foundation BookStart
    Grants, 2220
USAID Nigeria Ed Crisis Response Grants, 2358

Educational Planning/Policy
Abell Foundation Education Grants, 53
Achelis and Bodman Foundation Grants, 101
Achelis Foundation Grants, 102
Bill and Melinda Gates Foundation Policy and
    Advocacy Grants, 427
Community Fdn of Louisville Education Grants, 724
Georgia-Pacific Foundation Education Grants, 1058
Hazen Foundation Public Education Grants, 1221
K and F Baxter Family Foundation Grants, 1413
Meyer Foundation Education Grants, 1649
Michael and Susan Dell Foundation Grants, 1657
Nellie Mae Education Foundation District-Level
    Change Grants, 1736
OSF Baltimore Education and Youth Development
    Grants, 1840
Phil Hardin Foundation Grants, 1960
Seattle Foundation Education Grants, 2178
USAID Integrated Youth Development Activity
    Grants, 2356
USAID Nigeria Ed Crisis Response Grants, 2358
Wallace Foundation Grants, 2402

Educational Technology
Adobe Foundation Action Grants, 126
Alcatel-Lucent Technologies Foundation Grants, 224
Bay and Paul Foundations PreK-12 Transformative
    Learning Practices Grants, 370
Foundation for Rural Service Education Grants, 991
Four County Community Foundation Kellogg Group
    Grants, 1002
Leonsis Foundation Grants, 1485
Microsoft YouthSpark Grants, 1666
OSF Education Support Program Grants, 1843
Southern California Edison Education Grants, 2218
Thomas J. Long Foundation Community Grants, 2291
Toshiba America Foundation Grades 7-12 Science and
    Math Grants, 2307
Women's Fund of Hawaii Grants, 2485

Elder Abuse
Austin S. Nelson Foundation Grants, 333
Community Foundation for the Capital Region
    Grants, 687
Curtis Foundation Grants, 771
Hearst Foundations Social Service Grants, 1224
Perkin Fund Grants, 1937
Westerman Foundation Grants, 2427

Elderly
Agnes M. Lindsay Trust Grants, 140
Albert W. Rice Charitable Foundation Grants, 223
Alex Stern Family Foundation Grants, 229
Alfred E. Chase Charitable Foundation Grants, 233
Amelia Sillman Rockwell and Carlos Perry Rockwell
    Charities Fund Grants, 250
Ameren Corporation Community Grants, 251
American Schlafhorst Foundation Grants, 262
Atkinson Foundation Community Grants, 325
Baltimore Community Foundation Mitzvah Fund for
    Good Deeds Grants, 349
Bank of the Orient Community Giving, 361
Ben B. Cheney Foundation Grants, 402
Blackford County Community Fdn Grants, 434
Blanche and Irving Laurie Foundation Grants, 436
Bothin Foundation Grants, 464
Brookdale Fdn Relatives as Parents Grants, 474
Bryan Adams Foundation Grants, 480
Bushrod H. Campbell and Adah F. Hall Charity
    Fund Grants, 486
California Endowment Innovative Ideas Challenge
    Grants, 495

Callaway Foundation Grants, 496
Carl R. Hendrickson Family Foundation Grants, 509
Carl W. and Carrie Mae Joslyn Trust Grants, 510
Carroll County Community Foundation Grants, 513
Central Pacific Bank Foundation Grants, 530
CFFVR Basic Needs Giving Partnership Grants, 537
CFFVR Frank C. Shattuck Community Grants, 541
Charles Nelson Robinson Fund Grants, 569
Christine and Katharina Pauly Charitable Trust
    Grants, 601
CICF Indianapolis Fdn Community Grants, 606
CNCS Foster Grandparent Projects Grants, 646
CNCS Senior Corps Retired and Senior Volunteer
    Program Grants, 648
Community Foundation of Eastern Connecticut
    Northeast Women and Girls Grants, 697
Community Foundation of Eastern Connecticut
    Norwich Women and Girls Grants, 698
Community Foundation of Eastern Connecticut
    Southeast Area Women and Girls Grants, 701
Community Foundation of Eastern Connecticut
    Windham Area Women and Girls Grants, 702
Community Foundation of Louisville CHAMP Fund
    Grants, 720
Community Foundation of Madison and Jefferson
    County Grants, 731
Cooke Foundation Grants, 748
Crescent Porter Hale Foundation Grants, 767
Daniels Homeless and Disadvantaged Grants, 782
Dermody Properties Fdn Capstone Award, 826
Doree Taylor Charitable Foundation Grants, 843
Edward W. and Stella C. Van Houten Memorial Fund
    Grants, 892
Eide Bailly Resourcefullness Awards, 897
Elizabeth Morse Genius Charitable Trust Grants, 901
Ellen Abbott Gilman Trust Grants, 905
Essex County Community Foundation Merrimack
    Valley Municipal Business Development and
    Recovery Fund Grants, 933
Florence Hunt Maxwell Foundation Grants, 979
Fourjay Foundation Grants, 1003
Frank Reed and Margaret Jane Peters Memorial Fund
    Grants, 1013
Frederick McDonald Trust Grants, 1017
Fremont Area Community Foundation Community
    Grants, 1020
G.N. Wilcox Trust Grants, 1031
George A Ohl Jr. Foundation Grants, 1043
George P. Davenport Trust Fund Grants, 1054
GNOF Gert Community Fund Grants, 1082
Golden Heart Community Foundation Grants, 1094
Graham and Carolyn Holloway Family Foundation
    Grants, 1098
Greygates Foundation Grants, 1120
Harold Brooks Foundation Grants, 1172
Hawai'i Community Foundation Ewa Beach
    Community Trust Fund Grants, 1200
Helen Gertrude Sparks Charitable Trust Grants, 1230
Henrietta Lange Burk Fund Grants, 1235
Henry County Community Foundation Grants, 1239
Henry E. Niles Foundation Grants, 1240
J. Walton Bissell Foundation Grants, 1325
Jack Satter Foundation Grants, 1334
Jacob G. Schmidlapp Trusts Grants, 1336
James and Abigail Campbell Family Foundation
    Grants, 1337
Jane Bradley Pettit Foundation Community and
    Social Development Grants, 1347
Jewish Fund Grants, 1364
Jim Moran Foundation Grants, 1366
John W. Anderson Foundation Grants, 1383
Joseph Henry Edmondson Foundation Grants, 1388
Katharine Matthies Foundation Grants, 1418
Kawabe Memorial Fund Grants, 1423
Kentucky Arts Cncl Access Assistance Grants, 1428
Kimball International-Habig Foundation Health and
    Human Services Grants, 1434
Kopp Family Foundation Grants, 1448
Latkin Charitable Foundation Grants, 1469
Laura B. Vogler Foundation Grants, 1470

Leo Niessen Jr., Charitable Trust Grants, 1484
Long Island Community Foundation Grants, 1507
Madison Community Foundation Grants, 1535
Mardag Foundation Grants, 1554
Marie C. and Joseph C. Wilson Foundation Rochester
    Small Grants, 1559
Marjorie Moore Charitable Foundation Grants, 1574
Mary Black Foundation Active Living Grants, 1585
May and Stanley Smith Charitable Trust Grants, 1613
McLean Foundation Grants, 1624
Mericos Foundation Grants, 1637
MGM Resorts Foundation Community Grants, 1655
Michael Reese Health Trust Responsive Grants, 1659
Mid-Iowa Health Foundation Community Response
    Grants, 1667
Montana Arts Council Cultural and Aesthetic Project
    Grants, 1685
Montana Community Foundation Grants, 1687
Mt. Sinai Health Care Foundation Health of the
    Jewish Community Grants, 1709
Nathan B. and Florence R. Burt Fdn Grants, 1717
Nell J. Redfield Foundation Grants, 1737
Norcliffe Foundation Grants, 1766
Northland Foundation Grants, 1771
Oppenstein Brothers Foundation Grants, 1827
PCA Art Organizations and Art Programs Grants for
    Presenting Organizations, 1884
PCA Arts Organizations and Arts Program Grants
    for Music, 1887
PCA Arts Organizations and Arts Programs Grants
    for Art Museums, 1888
PCA Arts Organizations and Arts Programs Grants
    for Arts Education Organizations, 1889
PCA Arts Organizations and Arts Programs Grants
    for Arts Service Organizations, 1890
PCA Arts Organizations and Arts Programs Grants
    for Crafts, 1891
PCA Arts Organizations and Arts Programs Grants
    for Dance, 1892
PCA Arts Organizations and Arts Programs Grants
    for Film and Electronic Media, 1893
PCA Arts Organizations and Arts Programs Grants
    for Literature, 1894
PCA Arts Organizations and Arts Programs Grants
    for Local Arts, 1895
PCA Arts Organizations and Arts Programs Grants
    for Theatre, 1896
PCA Arts Organizations and Arts Programs Grants
    for Traditional and Folk Arts, 1897
PCA Arts Organizations and Arts Programs Grants
    for Visual Arts, 1898
PCA Busing Grants, 1899
PCA Entry Track Arts Organizations and Arts
    Programs Grants for Art Museums, 1900
PCA Entry Track Arts Organizations and
    Arts Programs Grants for Arts Education
    Organizations, 1901
PCA Entry Track Arts Organizations and Arts
    Programs Grants for Arts Service Orgs, 1902
PCA Entry Track Arts Organizations and Arts
    Programs Grants for Crafts, 1903
PCA Entry Track Arts Organizations and Arts
    Programs Grants for Dance, 1904
PCA Entry Track Arts Orgs and Arts Programs
    Grants for Film and Electronic Media, 1905
PCA Entry Track Arts Organizations and Arts
    Programs Grants for Local Arts, 1907
PCA Entry Track Arts Organizations and Arts
    Programs Grants for Music, 1908
PCA Entry Track Arts Organizations and Arts
    Programs Grants for Presenting Orgs, 1909
PCA Entry Track Arts Organizations and Arts
    Programs Grants for Theatre, 1910
PCA Entry Track Arts Orgs and Arts Programs
    Grants for Traditional and Folk Arts, 1911
PCA Entry Track Arts Organizations and Arts
    Programs Grants for Visual Arts, 1912
PCA Pennsylvania Partners in the Arts Program
    Stream Grants, 1914

PCA Pennsylvania Partners in the Arts Project
    Stream Grants, 1915
Perkins-Ponder Foundation Grants, 1938
Perpetual Benevolent Fund, 1940
Piper Trust Education Grants, 1977
Piper Trust Reglious Organizations Grants, 1979
Portland Fdn - Women's Giving Circle Grant, 2006
Powell Foundation Grants, 2013
Puerto Rico Community Foundation Grants, 2037
R.C. Baker Foundation Grants, 2043
R.D. Beirne Trust Grants, 2045
R.S. Gernon Trust Grants, 2047
Ralph M. Parsons Foundation Grants, 2052
Ruth Anderson Foundation Grants, 2122
Schramm Foundation Grants, 2168
Stella and Charles Guttman Foundation Grants, 2241
Susan A. and Donald P. Babson Charitable
    Foundation Grants, 2259
Swindells Charitable Foundation Grants, 2261
TAC Touring Arts and Arts Access Touring Arts
    Grants, 2269
Thelma Braun and Bocklett Family Foundation
    Grants, 2287
Thelma Doelger Charitable Trust Grants, 2288
Union Labor Health Fdn Angel Fund Grants, 2335
Victor E. Speas Foundation Grants, 2380
W.W. Smith Chartbl Trust Basic Needs Grants, 2400
Wild Rivers Community Foundation Holiday
    Partnership Grants, 2448
William Foulds Family Foundation Grants, 2465
William J. Brace Charitable Trust, 2471
Wood-Claeyssens Foundation Grants, 2486

Electoral Systems
Carnegie Corporation of New York Grants, 511
Ford Foundation BUILD Grants, 984

Electric Power
PNM Reduce Your Use Grants, 1988

Electronic Media
NYSCA Electronic Media and Film: Film Festivals
    Grants, 1785
NYSCA Electronic Media and Film: General
    Operating Support, 1786
NYSCA Electronic Media and Film: General
    Program Support, 1787
NYSCA Electronic Media and Film: Screenings
    Grants, 1788
NYSCA Electronic Media and Film: Workspace
    Grants, 1789
PCA Arts Organizations and Arts Programs Grants
    for Film and Electronic Media, 1893
PCA Arts Organizations and Arts Programs Grants
    for Visual Arts, 1898
PCA Entry Track Arts Organizations and Arts
    Programs Grants for Visual Arts, 1912
Reinberger Foundation Grants, 2066

Elementary Education
3M Company Fdn Community Giving Grants, 5
100% for Kids - Utah Credit Union Education
    Foundation Major Project Grants, 11
100% for Kids - Utah Credit Union Education
    Foundation Mini Grants, 12
100% for Kids - Utah Credit Union Education
    Foundation School Grants, 13
A. Alfred Taubman Foundation Grants, 18
A.C. and Penney Hubbard Foundation Grants, 19
A.L. Mailman Family Foundation Grants, 20
AASA Urgent Need Mini-Grants, 43
Abby's Legendary Pizza Foundation Grants, 49
Abeles Foundation Grants, 51
Abell Foundation Education Grants, 53
ACCF John and Kay Boch Fund Grants, 60
ACCF Marlene Bittner Memorial Community
    Enrichment Fund Grants, 61
ACCF of Indiana Bank of Geneva Heritage Fund
    Grants, 64

ACCF of Indiana Berne Ready Mix Community Enrichment Fund Grants, 65
ACCF of Indiana First Merchants Bank / Decatur Bank and Trust Fund Grants, 66
ACCF of Indiana Ron and Susie Ballard Community Enrichment Fund Grants, 68
ACCF Ralph Biggs Memorial Community Enrichment Fund Grants, 69
Acuity Charitable Foundation Grants, 110
Adams Family Foundation I Grants, 116
Adams Legacy Foundation Grants, 121
Adobe Foundation Action Grants, 126
Advance Auto Parts Corporate Giving Grants, 131
AEGON Transamerica Foundation Education and Financial Literacy Grants, 132
Aetna Foundation Summer Academic Enrichment Grants, 135
A Friends' Foundation Trust Grants, 136
AGFT Pencil Boy Express, 139
AHC R.E.A.C.H. Grants, 141
Akron Community Fdn Education Grants, 151
ALA Coretta Scott King Book Donation Grant, 168
ALA Innovative Reading Grant, 171
ALA Sara Jaffarian School Library Award for Exemplary Humanities Programming, 190
Alavi Foundation Education Grants, 216
Albert E. and Birdie W. Einstein Fund Grants, 220
Alcatel-Lucent Technologies Foundation Grants, 224
Alden and Vada Dow Fund Grants, 225
Aldi Corporation Smart Kids Grants, 226
Allegis Group Foundation Grants, 237
Alloy Family Foundation Grants, 241
Alpha Natural Resources Corporate Giving, 246
American Electric Power Corporate Grants, 252
American Electric Power Foundation Grants, 253
American Honda Foundation Grants, 255
American Indian Youth Running Strong Grants, 256
American Schlafhorst Foundation Grants, 262
Amerigroup Foundation Grants, 264
Amica Companies Foundation Grants, 266
Amica Insurance Company Community Grants, 267
Anchorage Schools Foundation Grants, 270
Ann Ludington Sullivan Foundation Grants, 279
Antone and Edene Vidinha Charitable Grants, 281
Arkema Foundation Grants, 298
Arkema Foundation Science Teachers Grants, 299
Arthur M. Blank Family Foundation Art of Change Grants, 306
Arthur M. Blank Family Foundation Mountain Sky Guest Ranch Fund Grants, 311
Arthur M. Blank Family Foundation Pathways to Success Grants, 312
Arthur M. Blank Family Foundation Pipeline Project Grants, 313
Arts Council of Greater Lansing Young Creatives Grants, 314
AT&T Foundation Education Grants, 321
Atlas Insurance Agency Foundation Grants, 329
Aunt Kate Foundation Grants, 331
Avery Family Trust Grants, 338
Avery Foundation Grants, 339
Avista Foundation Education Grants, 340
Bainum Family Foundation Grants, 345
Baltimore Community Foundation Mitzvah Fund for Good Deeds Grants, 349
Baltimore Ravens Corporate Giving, 350
Bank of Hawaii Foundation Grants, 360
Baton Rouge Area Foundation Community Coffee Fund Grants, 363
Baxter International Corporate Giving Grants, 368
Bay and Paul Foundations PreK-12 Transformative Learning Practices Grants, 370
Bay Area Community Foundation Arenac Community Fund Grants, 371
Bay Area Community Fdn Auburn Area Chamber of Commerce Enrichment Fund Grants, 373
Bay Area Community Foundation Community Initiative Fund Grants, 376
Bay Area Community Foundation Dow CommunityGives Youth Service Prog Grants, 377

Bee Conservancy Sponsor-A-Hive Grants, 395
Belvedere Community Foundation Grants, 399
Benton Community Foundation - The Cookie Jar Grant, 404
Bernard and Audre Rapoport Foundation Arts and Culture Grants, 407
Bernard and Audre Rapoport Foundation Education Grants, 410
Bill Graham Memorial Foundation Grants, 429
Blackford County Community Fdn Grants, 434
Blue Grass Community Foundation Clark County Fund Grants, 444
Blue Grass Community Foundation Fayette County Fund Grants, 446
Blue Grass Community Foundation Franklin County Fund Grants, 447
Blue Grass Community Foundation Harrison County Fund Grants, 448
Blue Grass Community Foundation Madison County Fund Grants, 450
Blue Grass Community Foundation Magoffin County Fund Grants, 451
Blue Grass Community Foundation Morgan County Fund Grants, 452
Blue Grass Community Foundation Rowan County Fund Grants, 453
Blue Grass Community Foundation Woodford County Fund Grants, 454
BMW of North America Charitable Contribs, 460
Boeing Company Contributions Grants, 462
BP Foundation Grants, 465
Bridgestone Americas Trust Fund Grants, 469
Bristol-Myers Squibb Foundation Independent Medical Education Grants, 472
Brown Foundation Grants, 476
Brown Rudnick Charitable Foundation Community Grants, 477
Burlington Industries Foundation Grants, 481
Burton D. Morgan Foundation Hudson Community Grants, 482
Burton D. Morgan Foundation Youth Entrepreneurship Grants, 483
Byerly Foundation Grants, 487
C.H. Robinson Worldwide Foundation Grants, 489
Callaway Foundation Grants, 496
Cargill Foundation Education Grants, 504
Carnegie Corporation of New York Grants, 511
Carroll County Community Foundation Grants, 513
Castle Foundation Grants, 518
Castle Foundation Grants, 517
Castle Industries Foundation Grants, 519
CCFF Christopher Columbus Awards, 522
Central Pacific Bank Foundation Grants, 530
CenturyLink Clarke M. Williams Foundation Matching Time Grants, 531
CFFVR Appleton Education Foundation Grants, 536
CFFVR Mielke Family Foundation Grants, 544
CFFVR Shawano Area Community Foundation Grants, 549
CFF Winter Park Community Grants, 551
CFGR Community Impact Grants, 552
CFGR SisterFund Grants, 554
CFGR Ujima Legacy Fund Grants, 555
Chapman Charitable Foundation Grants, 560
Chapman Family Foundation, 562
Charles Lafitte Foundation Grants, 567
Charles N. and Eleanor Knight Leigh Foundation Grants, 568
Cheryl Spencer Memorial Foundation Grants, 576
Chesapeake Bay Trust Mini Grants, 578
Christensen Fund Regional Grants, 600
CHT Foundation Education Grants, 603
Cincinnati Bell Foundation Grants, 612
Cisco Systems Foundation San Jose Community Grants, 615
Clara Blackford Smith and W. Aubrey Smith Charitable Foundation Grants, 621
Claremont Savings Bank Foundation Grants, 623
Clarence T.C. Ching Foundation Grants, 624

Clayton F. and Ruth L. Hawkridge Foundation Grants, 630
Clayton Fund Grants, 631
Cleo Foundation Grants, 632
Cleveland Foundation Higley Fund Grants, 634
Cleveland Foundation Legacy Village Lyndhurst Community Fund Grants, 636
Cleveland H. Dodge Foundation Grants, 637
Clinton County Community Foundation Grants, 638
CNCS AmeriCorps Indian Tribes Plang Grts , 641
CNCS AmeriCorps State and National Grants, 643
CNCS Foster Grandparent Projects Grants, 646
CNCS Senior Corps Retired and Senior Volunteer Program Grants, 648
Colorado Interstate Gas Grants, 661
Community Foundation for Greater Buffalo Niagara Area Foundation Grants, 673
Community Foundation of Crawford County, 695
Community Foundation of Greater Chattanooga Grants, 704
Community Foundation of Jackson County Classroom Education Grants, 713
Community Foundation of Louisville Education Grants, 724
Community Foundation of Louisville Winston N. and Nancy H. Bloch Educational Fund Grants, 729
Community Foundation of Louisville Youth Philanthropy Council Grants, 730
Community Fdn of Morgan County Grants, 732
CONSOL Energy Academic Grants, 746
Cooper Tire and Rubber Foundation Grants, 749
Courtney S. Turner Charitable Trust Grants, 753
Crane Foundation General Grants, 761
Crayola Champ Creatively Alive Children Grts, 764
Credit Suisse Foundation Education Grants, 765
Cresap Family Foundation Grants, 766
Crescent Porter Hale Foundation Grants, 767
Dana Brown Charitable Trust Grants, 777
David M. and Marjorie D. Rosenberg Foundation Grants, 790
David Robinson Foundation Grants, 791
Dayton Foundation VISIONS Endowment Fund Grants, 800
Dean Foods Community Involvement Grants, 805
Dean Foods Community Grants, 806
Dean Witter Foundation Education Grants, 807
Decatur County Community Foundation Large Project Grants, 811
Delaware Community Foundation Grants, 817
Delaware Valley Fairness Project Teacher Assistance Grants, 818
Del Mar Foundation Community Grants, 820
Delmarva Power & Light Mini-Grants, 822
Delta Air Lines Foundation Youth Development Grants, 824
Don and May Wilkins Charitable Trust Grants, 842
Dorrance Family Foundation Grants, 845
Dorr Foundation Grants, 846
Dr. and Mrs. Paul Pierce Memorial Foundation Grants, 862
Dunspaugh-Dalton Foundation Grants, 873
E.J. Grassmann Trust Grants, 876
Earl and Maxine Claussen Trust Grants, 878
Eastern Bank Charitable Foundation Partnerships Grants, 881
Eastern Bank Charitable Foundation Targeted Grants, 882
Effie Allen Little Foundation Grants, 894
Effie and Wofford Cain Foundation Grants, 895
Effie Kuhlman Charitable Trust Grants, 896
Elizabeth Carse Foundation Grants, 899
Elizabeth Huth Coates Charitable Foundation Grants, 900
Ella West Freeman Foundation Grants, 904
El Pomar Foundation Grants, 908
Emily Hall Tremaine Foundation Learning Disabilities Grants, 912
Energy by Design Poster Contest, 915
Entergy Charitable Foundation Education and Literacy Grants, 917

Entergy Corporation Micro Grants, 919
EQT Fdn Education and Workforce Grants, 927
Evelyn and Walter Haas, Jr. Fund Education
  Opportunities Grants, 939
Ezra Jack Keats Foundation Mini-Grants, 944
Faye L. and William L. Cowden Charitable
  Foundation Grants, 950
Fidelity Charitable Gift Fund Grants, 956
Firelight Foundation Grants, 964
FirstEnergy Foundation Science, Technology,
  Engineering, and Mathematics Grants, 966
First Hawaiian Bank Foundation Corporate Giving
  Grants, 967
Florence Foundation Grants, 978
Foundation for Rural Service Education Grants, 991
Foundations of East Chicago Education Grants, 995
Four County Community Foundation 21st Century
  Education Fund Grants, 999
Four County Community Foundation General
  Grants, 1000
Four County Community Foundation Healthy
  Senior/Healthy Youth Fund Grants, 1001
Four County Community Foundation Kellogg Group
  Grants, 1002
Four J Foundation Grants, 1004
Four Lanes Trust Grants, 1005
Frank M. Tait Foundation Grants, 1012
Frank Reed and Margaret Jane Peters Memorial Fund
  II Grants, 1014
Fred and Gretel Biel Charitable Trust Grants, 1016
Fremont Area Community Foundation Education
  Mini-Grants, 1021
Gardner Foundation Grants, 1034
George and Ruth Bradford Foundation Grants, 1042
George F. Baker Trust Grants, 1046
George Graham and Elizabeth Galloway Smith
  Foundation Grants, 1047
George H. and Jane A. Mifflin Memorial Fund
  Grants, 1048
George H. Sandy Foundation Grants, 1050
George J. and Effie L. Seay Foundation Grants, 1052
Georgia-Pacific Foundation Education Grants, 1058
Georgia Council for the Arts Education Grants, 1060
Geraldine R. Dodge Fdn Education Grants, 1061
GNOF Cox Charities of New Orleans Grants, 1079
GNOF Exxon-Mobil Grants, 1080
GNOF Norco Community Grants, 1089
GNOF Plaquemines Community Grants, 1091
Graham Family Charitable Foundation Grants, 1099
Gray Family Foundation Community Field Trips
  Grants, 1105
Gray Family Fdn Outdoor School Grants, 1107
Green River Area Community Fdn Grants, 1117
Greenspun Family Foundation Grants, 1118
Griffin Family Foundation Grants, 1121
Grundy Foundation Grants, 1124
GTRCF Elk Rapids Area Community Endowment
  Grants, 1127
GTRCF Joan Rajkovich McGarry Family Education
  Endowment Grants, 1131
GTRCF Traverse City Track Club Endowment
  Grants, 1132
HAF Joe Alexandre Mem Family Fund Grants, 1145
HAF Laurence and Elaine Allen Memorial Fund
  Grants, 1146
Harold K.L. Castle Foundation Public Education
  Redesign and Enhancement Grants, 1173
Harris and Eliza Kempner Fund Ed Grants, 1176
Harris Foundation Grants, 1177
Harrison County Community Fdn Grants, 1178
Harrison County Community Foundation Signature
  Grants, 1179
Hattie Mae Lesley Foundation Grants, 1195
Hawai'i Community Foundation Richard Smart Fund
  Grants, 1204
Hawai'i Community Foundation Robert E. Black
  Fund Grants, 1205
Hawai'i SFCA Art Bento Program @ HiSAM
  Grants, 1210

Hawaii Community Foundation Omidyar Ohana
  Fund Grants, 1213
Hawaii Community Foundation Sanford Harmony
  Pillars of Peace Grants, 1217
Hawaii Electric Industries Charitable Foundation
  Grants, 1218
Hearst Foundations Culture Grants, 1223
Helen Bader Foundation Grants, 1227
Herbert Hoover Presidential Library Association Bus
  Travel Grants, 1244
Herman Goldman Foundation Grants, 1245
Herman P. and Sophia Taubman Fdn Grants, 1247
Hillsdale County Community Foundation General
  Grants, 1250
HSBC Corporate Giving Grants, 1266
HSFCA Biennium Grants, 1267
Hubbard Broadcasting Foundation Grants, 1269
Hubbard Family Foundation Grants, 1270
Hubbard Family Foundation Grants, 1271
Hubbard Farms Charitable Foundation Grants, 1272
Huisking Foundation Grants, 1274
Iddings Foundation Medium Project Grants, 1285
Iddings Foundation Small Project Grants, 1286
Intel Corporation Community Grants, 1311
Intel Corporation Int Community Grants, 1312
Island Insurance Foundation Grants, 1316
J. Knox Gholston Foundation Grants, 1321
J. Marion Sims Foundation Teachers' Pet Grant, 1322
J. Watumull Fund Grants, 1326
J. William Gholston Foundation Grants, 1328
Jack Kent Cooke Fdn Good Neighbor Grants, 1331
Jack Satter Foundation Grants, 1334
Jacob and Hilda Blaustein Foundation Israel Program
  Grants, 1335
James F. and Marion L. Miller Fdn Grants, 1338
Jaquelin Hume Foundation Grants, 1357
Jessica Stevens Community Foundation Grants, 1363
John and Marcia Goldman Foundation Youth
  Development Grants, 1368
John Clarke Trust Grants, 1369
John H. and Wilhelmina D. Harland Charitable
  Foundation Children and Youth Grants, 1374
John P. Ellbogen Fdn Community Grants, 1377
Joseph H. and Florence A. Roblee Foundation
  Education Grants, 1386
Joseph Henry Edmondson Foundation Grants, 1388
Joseph S. Stackpole Charitable Trust Grants, 1390
Joyce and Randy Seckman Charitable Foundation
  Grants, 1393
JP Morgan Chase Fdn Arts and Culture Grants, 1394
Judy and Peter Blum Kovler Foundation Grants, 1396
Julia Temple Davis Brown Foundation Grants, 1399
Kalamazoo Community Foundation Early Childhood
  Learning and School Readiness Grants, 1407
K and F Baxter Family Foundation Grants, 1413
Katrine Menzing Deakins Chartbl Trust Grants, 1422
Kimball International-Habig Foundation Education
  Grants, 1433
Kinder Morgan Foundation Grants, 1436
Kind World Foundation Grants, 1438
Kirby Laing Foundation Grants, 1439
Koch Family Foundation (Annapolis) Grants, 1444
Kodak Community Relations Grants, 1445
Kopp Family Foundation Grants, 1448
Koret Foundation Grants, 1449
Kosasa Foundation Grants, 1450
Laurie H. Wollmuth Charitable Trust Grants, 1476
LEGO Children's Fund Grants, 1480
Leola Osborn Trust Grants, 1483
Leonsis Foundation Grants, 1485
LGA Family Foundation Grants, 1487
Linford & Mildred White Charitable Grants, 1495
LISC Capacity Building Grants, 1498
LISC Education Grants, 1500
Lloyd G. Balfour Foundation Attleboro-Specific
  Charities Grants, 1502
Locations Foundation Legacy Grants, 1504
Lockheed Martin Corporation Fdn Grants, 1505
Louis and Sandra Berkman Foundation Grants, 1510
Lubrizol Corporation Community Grants, 1512

Luella Kemper Trust Grants, 1517
Lynn and Foster Friess Family Fdn Grants, 1520
M.A. Rikard Charitable Trust Grants, 1521
Mardag Foundation Grants, 1554
Margaret and James A. Elkins Jr. Fdn Grants, 1555
Marin Community Foundation Arts Education
  Grants, 1562
Marion I. and Henry J. Knott Foundation
  Discretionary Grants, 1571
Marion I. and Henry J. Knott Foundation Standard
  Grants, 1572
Marquette Bank Neighborhood Commit Grants, 1577
Marsh Corporate Grants, 1580
Martha Holden Jennings Foundation Grants-to-
  Educators, 1581
Martin Family Foundation Grants, 1583
Mary A. Crocker Trust Grants, 1584
Maryland State Dept of Education 21st Century
  Community Learning Centers Grants, 1593
Maryland State Department of Education Judith P.
  Hoyer Early Care and Ed Center Grants, 1595
Maryland State Department of Education Striving
  Readers Comprehensive Literacy Grants, 1596
Mathile Family Foundation Grants, 1604
Matson Community Giving Grants, 1607
Maurice R. Robinson Fund Grants, 1611
McConnell Foundation Grants, 1616
McGraw-Hill Companies Community Grants, 1620
Mead Family Foundation Grants, 1625
Meadows Foundation Grants, 1626
Memorial Foundation for Children Grants, 1633
Mericos Foundation Grants, 1637
Meta and George Rosenberg Fdn Grants, 1644
Meyer Foundation Education Grants, 1649
Meyer Memorial Trust Responsive Grants, 1653
MGM Resorts Foundation Community Grants, 1655
Micron Technology Fdn Community Grants, 1664
Mile High United Way Stratc Investment Grts, 1671
Miller Foundation Grants, 1673
Mill Spring Foundation Grants, 1674
Milton and Sally Avery Arts Foundation Grants, 1675
Minnie M. Jones Trust Grants, 1678
Moody Foundation Grants, 1692
Mr. Holland's Opus Foundation Melody Grants, 1703
Mr. Holland's Opus Foundation Special Projects
  Grants, 1705
National 4-H Council Grants, 1720
National 4-H Youth in Action Awards, 1721
National Schools of Character Awards Program, 1723
NCSS Award for Global Understanding, 1728
NEH Picturing America Awards, 1735
Nellie Mae Education Foundation District-Level
  Change Grants, 1736
NHSCA Artist Residence Grants, 1756
NHSCA Youth Arts Project Grants: For Extended
  Arts Learning, 1758
NYFA Artists in the School Community Planning
  Grants, 1779
NYSCA Arts Education: Community-based
  Learning Grants, 1780
NYSCA Arts Education: General Operating Support
  Grants, 1781
NYSCA Arts Education: Local Capacity Building
  Grants (Regrants), 1783
NYSCA Arts Ed: Services to the Field Grants, 1784
Ober Kaler Community Grants, 1801
Office Depot Foundation Education Grants, 1806
OHA Community Grants for Education, 1809
Olivia R. Gardner Foundation Grants, 1819
OMNOVA Solutions Fdn Education Grants, 1820
Ontario Arts Council Artists in Communities and
  Schools Project Grants, 1823
Ontario Arts Council Arts Organizations in
  Communities and Schools Operating Grants, 1824
Ontario Arts Council Indigenous Culture Fund
  Indigenous Artists in Communities and Schools
  Project Grants, 1825
Oppenstein Brothers Foundation Grants, 1827
Oregon Community Foundation Community
  Recovery Grants, 1834

P. Buckley Moss Foundation for Children's Education Teacher Grants, 1855
Patricia Kisker Foundation Grants, 1879
Perkin Fund Grants, 1937
Perry and Sandy Massie Foundation Grants, 1941
Pettus Foundation Grants, 1952
Peyton Anderson Foundation Grants, 1954
PG&E Bright Ideas Grants, 1956
PGE Foundation Grants, 1958
Phil Hardin Foundation Grants, 1960
Philip L. Graham Fund Education Grants, 1962
Phoenix Coyotes Charities Grants, 1963
Phoenix Suns Charities Grants, 1964
Piedmont Natural Gas Foundation K-12 Science, Technology, Engineering and Math (STEM) Grant, 1969
Piper Jaffray Foundation Communities Giving Grants, 1974
PMI Foundation Grants, 1982
PNC Foundation Education Grants, 1985
PNC Foundation Grow Up Great Early Childhood Grants, 1986
Polk County Community Foundation Marjorie M. and Lawrence R. Bradley Endowment Fund Grants, 1998
Polk County Community Foundation Mary F. Kessler Fund Grants, 1999
Polk County Community Foundation Grants, 2001
Porter County Community Foundation PCgivingproject Grants, 2003
Powell Foundation Grants, 2013
PPCF Community Grants, 2014
PPCF Edson Foundation Grants, 2015
Public Education Power Grants, 2032
R.D. and Joan Dale Hubbard Fdn Grants, 2044
R.S. Gernon Trust Grants, 2047
Random Acts of Kindness Foundation Lesson Plan Contest, 2053
Raskob Fdn for Catholic Activities Grants, 2054
Ray Charles Foundation Grants, 2058
Reinberger Foundation Grants, 2066
Ressler-Gertz Foundation Grants, 2067
Richard J. Stern Foundation for the Arts Grants, 2071
Richland County Bank Grants, 2074
Riedman Foundation Grants, 2076
Robert and Betty Wo Foundation Grants, 2083
Robert R. McCormick Tribune Foundation Community Grants, 2093
Robert R. Meyer Foundation Grants, 2094
Roger L. and Agnes C. Dell Charitable Trust II Grants, 2100
Ron and Sanne Higgins Family Fdn Grants, 2101
Rose Community Foundation Education Grants, 2104
Rosenberg Charity Foundation Grants, 2107
Ruby K. Worner Charitable Trust Grants, 2119
Ruth and Henry Campbell Foundation Grants, 2123
Ruth Camp Campbell Charitable Trust Grants, 2125
Saigh Foundation Grants, 2137
San Antonio Area Foundation Capital and Naming Rights Grants, 2148
San Antonio Area Foundation High School Completion Grants, 2149
Sand Hill Foundation Environment and Sustainability Grants, 2152
Sand Hill Foundation Health and Opportunity Grants, 2153
San Juan Island Community Foundation Grants, 2158
Sartain Lanier Family Foundation Grants, 2164
Schramm Foundation Grants, 2168
Screen Actors Guild BookPALS Assistance, 2171
Screen Actors Guild PencilPALS Assistance, 2172
Screen Actors Guild StagePALS Assistance, 2173
Seattle Foundation Education Grants, 2178
Serco Foundation Grants, 2181
Seward Community Foundation Grants, 2182
Seward Community Foundation Mini-Grants, 2183
Shopko Fdn Community Charitable Grants, 2191
Sidney and Sandy Brown Foundation Grants, 2196
Silicon Valley Community Foundation Education Grants, 2200

Sioux Falls Area Community Foundation Community Fund Grants, 2203
Sioux Falls Area Community Foundation Spot Grants, 2204
Skaggs Foundation Grants, 2207
Sony Corporation of America Grants, 2216
Sorenson Legacy Foundation Grants, 2217
Southern California Edison Education Grants, 2218
South Madison Community Foundation - Teacher Creativity Mini Grants, 2225
Stillson Foundation Grants, 2245
Stocker Foundation Grants, 2247
Storm Castle Foundation Grants, 2248
Strong Foundation Grants, 2252
Sunoco Foundation Grants, 2256
Sylvia Perkin Perpetual Charitable Trust Grants, 2263
Target Corporation Community Engagement Fund Grants, 2270
Tata Trust Grant for Certificate Course in Holistic inclusion of Learners with Diversities, 2273
Terra Fdn Chicago K–12 Education Grants, 2285
Thelma Braun and Bocklett Family Foundation Grants, 2287
Tom C. Barnsley Foundation Grants, 2306
Toshiba America Foundation K-6 Science and Math Grants, 2308
Toyota USA Foundation Education Grants, 2318
Turtle Bay Foundation Grants, 2327
U.S. Department of Education Promise Neighborhoods Grants, 2332
Union Bank, N.A. Corporate Sponsorships and Donations, 2333
Union Bank, N.A. Foundation Grants, 2334
United Friends of the Children Scholarships, 2341
UPS Foundation Economic and Global Literacy Grants, 2351
USAID Integrated Youth Development Activity Grants, 2356
USAID Nigeria Ed Crisis Response Grants, 2358
USAID School Improvement Program Grants, 2360
USAID U.S.-Egypt Learning Grants, 2361
Victor E. Speas Foundation Grants, 2380
W.H. and Mary Ellen Cobb Chartbl Trust Grts, 2397
Walker Area Community Foundation Grants, 2401
Walter J. and Betty C. Zable Fdn Grants, 2406
Washington Gas Charitable Contributions, 2417
Wege Foundation Grants, 2422
Welborn Baptist Foundation School Based Health Grants, 2424
WHO Foundation General Grants, 2443
Whole Foods Foundation, 2445
William and Flora Hewlett Foundation Education Grants, 2454
William and Flora Hewlett Foundation Quality Education in Developing Countries Grants, 2456
William Blair and Company Foundation Grants, 2461
William Caspar Graustein Memorial Fund Corinne G. Levin Education Grants, 2462
William J. and Dorothy K. O'Neill Foundation Responsive Grants, 2468
William J. and Gertrude R. Casper Foundation Grants, 2469
William J. Brace Charitable Trust, 2471
Williams Comps Homegrown Giving Grants, 2474
Wilton and Effie Hebert Foundation Grants, 2476
Windham Foundation Grants, 2477
Winifred Johnson Clive Foundation Grants, 2478
Wiregrass Foundation Grants, 2480
Wold Foundation Grants, 2482
Woods Charitable Fund Education Grants, 2488
WSLBDF Quarterly Grants, 2499
Wyoming Community Fdn General Grants, 2501
Wyoming Community Foundation Hazel Patterson Memorial Grants, 2502
Wyomissing Foundation Thun Family Organizational Grants, 2505
Wyomissing Foundation Thun Family Program Grants, 2506
Youths' Friends Association Grants, 2511
Zollner Foundation Grants, 2526

Emergency Preparedness
Bill and Melinda Gates Foundation Emergency Response Grants, 426
CNCS AmeriCorps State and National Grants, 643
Delmarva Power & Light Contributions, 821
Elizabeth Morse Genius Charitable Trust Grants, 901
Fidelity Charitable Gift Fund Grants, 956
J. Watumull Fund Grants, 1326
Nationwide Insurance Foundation Grants, 1726
Piedmont Natural Gas Foundation Health and Human Services Grants, 1968
Seattle Foundation Benjamin N. Phillips Memorial Fund Grants, 2176

Emergency Programs
100 Club of Arizona Financial Assistance Grants, 9
A.C. and Penney Hubbard Foundation Grants, 19
AASA Urgent Need Mini-Grants, 43
Aid for Starving Children Emerg Aid Grants, 144
Aid for Starving Children Health and Nutrition Grants, 145
Alcatel-Lucent Technologies Foundation Grants, 224
ALFJ Astraea U.S. and International Emergency Fund, 230
Alliance for Strong Families and Communities Grants, 239
ATA Local Community Relations Grants, 324
Bank of America Charitable Foundation Basic Needs Grants, 354
Bill and Melinda Gates Foundation Emergency Response Grants, 426
BP Foundation Grants, 465
Camille Beckman Foundation Grants, 499
Carl R. Hendrickson Family Foundation Grants, 509
Carrie S. Orleans Trust Grants, 512
Charles H. Hall Foundation, 565
CNCS AmeriCorps State and National Grants, 643
Community Foundation for Greater Atlanta Frances Hollis Brain Foundation Fund Grants, 664
Community Foundation for the Capital Region Grants, 687
Curtis Foundation Grants, 771
Delmarva Power & Light Contributions, 821
Dolan Media Foundation Grants, 833
Doree Taylor Charitable Foundation Grants, 843
Eastern Bank Charitable Foundation Partnerships Grants, 881
Eastern Bank Charitable Foundation Targeted Grants, 882
Effie Allen Little Foundation Grants, 894
Elizabeth Morse Genius Charitable Trust Grants, 901
Emily O'Neill Sullivan Foundation Grants, 913
Episcopal Actors' Guild Actors Florence James Children's Holiday Fund Grant, 925
Fidelity Charitable Gift Fund Grants, 956
Florence Hunt Maxwell Foundation Grants, 979
GNOF Albert N. & Hattie M. McClure Grants, 1076
Harold Brooks Foundation Grants, 1172
Hattie Mae Lesley Foundation Grants, 1195
Helen Irwin Littauer Educational Trust Grants, 1231
Helen V. Brach Foundation Grants, 1232
Henrietta Lange Burk Fund Grants, 1235
Island Insurance Foundation Grants, 1316
J. Watumull Fund Grants, 1326
Jack H. and William M. Light Charitable Trust Grants, 1330
Kalamazoo Community Foundation Individuals and Families Grants, 1409
Kosasa Foundation Grants, 1450
Kosciusko County Community Foundation REMC Operation Round Up Grants, 1453
LGA Family Foundation Grants, 1487
Martin C. Kauffman 100 Club of Alameda County Scholarships, 1582
Meyer Memorial Trust Emergency Grants, 1652
Middlesex Savings Charitable Foundation Basic Human Needs Grants, 1668
Middlesex Savings Charitable Foundation Capacity Building Grants, 1669

Montana Community Foundation Big Sky LIFT Grants, 1686
Montana Community Foundation Grants, 1687
Nationwide Insurance Foundation Grants, 1726
Packard Foundation Local Grants, 1863
Perpetual Benevolent Fund, 1940
PG&E Community Vitality Grants, 1957
Piedmont Natural Gas Foundation Health and Human Services Grants, 1968
Polk County Community Foundation Seasonal Assistance and Cheer Grants for Charitable Programs, 2000
Polk County Community Foundation Unrestricted Grants, 2001
Porter County Community Foundation Women's Fund Grants, 2005
RCF Individual Assistance Grants, 2063
Reinberger Foundation Grants, 2066
Salt River Project Health and Human Services Grants, 2142
San Antonio Area Foundation Special and Urgent Needs Funding Grants, 2150
Seattle Foundation Benjamin N. Phillips Memorial Fund Grants, 2176
Sobrato Family Fdn Meeting Space Grants, 2212
Sobrato Family Foundation Office Space Grants, 2213
Telluride Fdn Emergency Grants, 2282
Union Bank, N.A. Foundation Grants, 2334
Union Labor Health Fdn Angel Fund Grants, 2335
W.H. and Mary Ellen Cobb Chartbl Trust Grts, 2397
Washington Area Fuel Fund Grants, 2413
Widgeon Point Charitable Foundation Grants, 2447
William E. Dean III Charitable Fdn Grants, 2464
Wyoming Community Foundation COVID-19 Response and Recovery Grants, 2500
Youths' Friends Association Grants, 2511

Emergency Services
100 Club of Arizona Financial Assistance Grants, 9
A. Alfred Taubman Foundation Grants, 18
A.C. and Penney Hubbard Foundation Grants, 19
A and B Family Foundation Grants, 40
AASA Urgent Need Mini-Grants, 43
Adams Family Foundation of Tennessee Grants, 120
Aid for Starving Children Emerg Aid Grants, 144
Aid for Starving Children Health and Nutrition Grants, 145
Aid for Starving Children Homes and Education Grants, 146
Aid for Starving Children Water Projects Grants, 147
Albert and Ethel Herzstein Charitable Foundation Grants, 219
ALFJ Astraea U.S. and International Emergency Fund, 230
Alliance for Strong Families and Communities Grants, 239
Austin S. Nelson Foundation Grants, 333
Bank of America Charitable Foundation Basic Needs Grants, 354
Bank of Hawaii Foundation Grants, 360
Bill and Melinda Gates Foundation Emergency Response Grants, 426
BP Foundation Grants, 465
Burlington Industries Foundation Grants, 481
Camille Beckman Foundation Grants, 499
Campbell Soup Foundation Grants, 501
Carrie S. Orleans Trust Grants, 512
Charles H. Hall Foundation, 565
Clara Abbott Foundation Need-Based Grants, 620
CNCS AmeriCorps State and National Grants, 643
Community Foundation for the Capital Region Grants, 687
Community Foundation of Louisville Anna Marble Memorial Fund for Princeton Grants, 717
Curtis Foundation Grants, 771
Dearborn Community Foundation City of Aurora Grants, 808
Delmarva Power & Light Contributions, 821
Eastern Bank Charitable Foundation Targeted Grants, 882

Effie Allen Little Foundation Grants, 894
Elizabeth Morse Genius Charitable Trust Grants, 901
Fayette County Foundation Grants, 951
Fidelity Charitable Gift Fund Grants, 956
Fred and Gretel Biel Charitable Trust Grants, 1016
Gulf Coast Foundation of Community Operating Grants, 1134
Gulf Coast Foundation of Community Program Grants, 1135
Harold Brooks Foundation Grants, 1172
Island Insurance Foundation Grants, 1316
J. Watumull Fund Grants, 1326
Kalamazoo Community Foundation Individuals and Families Grants, 1409
Kopp Family Foundation Grants, 1448
Kosasa Foundation Grants, 1450
Lewis H. Humphreys Charitable Trust Grants, 1486
LGA Family Foundation Grants, 1487
Locations Foundation Legacy Grants, 1504
Martin C. Kauffman 100 Club of Alameda County Scholarships, 1582
Meyer Memorial Trust Emergency Grants, 1652
Middlesex Savings Charitable Foundation Basic Human Needs Grants, 1668
Montana Community Foundation Big Sky LIFT Grants, 1686
Montana Community Foundation Grants, 1687
Nationwide Insurance Foundation Grants, 1726
Olga Sipolin Children's Fund Grants, 1815
Perpetual Benevolent Fund, 1940
Piedmont Natural Gas Foundation Health and Human Services Grants, 1968
Piper Trust Healthcare and Med Rsrch Grants, 1978
Raskob Fdn for Catholic Activities Grants, 2054
RCF Individual Assistance Grants, 2063
Reinberger Foundation Grants, 2066
Robert R. Meyer Foundation Grants, 2094
Salt River Project Health and Human Services Grants, 2142
San Antonio Area Foundation Special and Urgent Needs Funding Grants, 2150
Seattle Foundation Basic Needs Grants, 2175
Sylvia Perkin Perpetual Charitable Trust Grants, 2263
Union Bank, N.A. Corporate Sponsorships and Donations, 2333
Union Bank, N.A. Foundation Grants, 2334
Union Pacific Foundation Health and Human Services Grants, 2338
Wyoming Community Foundation COVID-19 Response and Recovery Grants, 2500
Youths' Friends Association Grants, 2511

Emission Control
New Hampshire Charitable Foundation Neil and Louise Tillotson Fund - Empower Coös Youth Grants, 1748
United Technologies Corporation Grants, 2347

Emotional/Mental Health
Adolph Coors Foundation Grants, 129
ATA Local Community Relations Grants, 324
Bella Vista Foundation Pre-3 Grants, 397
Blue Mountain Community Foundation Garfield County Health Foundation Fund Grants, 456
Charles H. Pearson Foundation Grants, 566
Cigna Civic Affairs Sponsorships, 610
Community Foundation for Greater Buffalo Garman Family Foundation Grants, 671
Community Foundation of Boone County - Women's Grants, 693
Cone Health Foundation Grants, 745
DTE Energy Foundation Health and Human Services Grants, 869
Elizabeth Morse Genius Charitable Trust Grants, 901
HAF Mada Huggins Caldwell Fund Grants, 1147
HAF Phyllis Nilsen Leal Mem Fund Grants, 1149
Hasbro Children's Fund Grants, 1189
Herbert A. and Adrian W. Woods Foundation Grants, 1243
Illinois Children's Healthcare Fdn Grants, 1295

Kansas Health Fdn Major Initiatives Grants, 1414
Long Island Community Foundation Grants, 1507
Moran Family Foundation Grants, 1693
New Jersey Center for Hispanic Policy, Research and Development Innovative Initiatives Grants, 1750
NFL Charities Pro Bowl Community Grants in Hawaii, 1755
Nick Traina Foundation Grants, 1759
Peter and Elizabeth C. Tower Foundation Technology Initiative Grants, 1949
Peter and Elizabeth C. Tower Foundation Technology Planning Grants, 1950
Phoenix Coyotes Charities Grants, 1963
Piedmont Natural Gas Foundation Health and Human Services Grants, 1968
Porter County Community Foundation Women's Fund Grants, 2005
Premera Blue Cross Grants, 2018
Schlessman Family Foundation Grants, 2167
Women's Fund of Hawaii Grants, 2485
Youths' Friends Association Grants, 2511

Emotionally Disturbed
Herbert A. and Adrian W. Woods Foundation Grants, 1243
Marion and Miriam Rose Fund Grants, 1569

Employee Benefits
Ms. Fdn for Women Economic Justice Grants, 1707

Employment Opportunity Programs
ACF Refugee Career Pathways Grants, 90
ACF Voluntary Agencies Matching Grants, 100
Achelis and Bodman Foundation Grants, 101
Achelis Foundation Grants, 102
ACL Rehabilitation Research and Training Center (RRTC) on Employment of Transition-Age Youth with Disabilities Grants, 107
A Fund for Women Grants, 137
Alaska Airlines Corporation Career Connections for Youth Grants, 193
Albert W. Rice Charitable Foundation Grants, 223
Alfred E. Chase Charitable Foundation Grants, 233
AT&T Fdn Community Support and Safety, 320
Autism Speaks Norma and Malcolm Baker Recreation Grants, 335
Baxter International Corporate Giving Grants, 368
BBF Maine Family Literacy Initiative Implementation Grants, 387
BBF Maine Family Literacy Initiative Planning Grants, 388
Bernard and Audre Rapoport Foundation Community Building and Social Service Grants, 408
Blockbuster Corporate Contributions, 440
Blue Mountain Community Foundation Warren Community Action Fund Grants, 457
Charles H. Pearson Foundation Grants, 566
CNCS AmeriCorps State and National Grants, 643
Community Foundation for the Capital Region Grants, 687
Essex County Community Foundation Merrimack Valley Municipal Business Development and Recovery Fund Grants, 933
Essex County Community Foundation Women's Fund Grants, 934
Ewing Marion Kauffman Foundation Grants, 943
Frank Reed and Margaret Jane Peters Memorial Fund II Grants, 1014
Frederick W. Marzahl Memorial Fund Grants, 1018
Gardner Foundation Grants, 1034
George W. Wells Foundation Grants, 1057
GNOF New Orleans Works Grants, 1088
Grifols Community Outreach Grants, 1122
Harold Brooks Foundation Grants, 1172
Helen Bader Foundation Grants, 1227
Henry County Community Foundation Grants, 1239
Henry E. Niles Foundation Grants, 1240
Illinois DNR Youth Recreation Corps Grants, 1297
Initiative Foundation Innovation Fund Grants, 1304
John Gogian Family Foundation Grants, 1373

Jovid Foundation Employment Training Grants, 1392
Lilly Endowment Summer Youth Grants, 1492
M.D. Anderson Foundation Grants, 1523
Mabel Louise Riley Foundation Family Strengthening
    Small Grants, 1528
Mabel Louise Riley Foundation Grants, 1529
Madison Community Foundation Grants, 1535
Marriott Int Corporate Giving Grants, 1578
Meyer Foundation Education Grants, 1649
Moses Kimball Fund Grants, 1701
Ms. Fdn for Women Economic Justice Grants, 1707
Nathaniel and Elizabeth P. Stevens Foundation
    Grants, 1719
Northland Foundation Grants, 1771
Pettus Foundation Grants, 1952
Priddy Foundation Program Grants, 2023
Robbins-de Beaumont Foundation Grants, 2080
Sioux Falls Area Community Foundation Community
    Fund Grants, 2203
Sioux Falls Area Community Foundation Spot
    Grants, 2204
Sobrato Family Foundation Grants, 2211
Stella and Charles Guttman Foundation Grants, 2241
Textron Corporate Contributions Grants, 2286
William J. and Dorothy K. O'Neill Foundation
    Responsive Grants, 2468

Employment/Unemployment Studies
Foundation Beyond Belief Compassionate Impact
    Grants, 986
Foundation Beyond Belief Humanist Grants, 987
Illinois Arts Council Youth Employment in the Arts
    Program Grants, 1294
NZDIA Community Org Grants Scheme, 1796

Endangered Species
Lucy Downing Nisbet Charitable Fund Grants, 1515

Endowments
Clayton Fund Grants, 631
Florence Foundation Grants, 978
GNOF Freeman Challenge Grants, 1081
Hearst Foundations Culture Grants, 1223
Jack H. and William M. Light Charitable Trust
    Grants, 1330
Margaret T. Morris Foundation Grants, 1557
Roy and Christine Sturgis Charitable Tr Grts, 2115
W.P. and Bulah Luse Foundation Grants, 2399

Energy
Delmarva Power & Light Mini-Grants, 822
Dollar Energy Fund Grants, 834
Energy by Design Poster Contest, 915
Entergy Charitable Foundation Low-Income
    Initiatives and Solutions Grants, 918
General Motors Foundation Grants, 1039
Honor the Earth Grants, 1259
McCune Charitable Foundation Grants, 1617
Southwest Initiative Foundation Grants, 2226
USAID Global Development Alliance Grants, 2354
William and Flora Hewlett Foundation
    Environmental Grants, 2455

Energy Assistance
Avista Foundation Vulnerable and Limited Income
    Population Grants, 341
Washington Area Fuel Fund Grants, 2413
Washington Gas Charitable Contributions, 2417

Energy Conservation
CNCS AmeriCorps NCCC Project Grants, 642
CNCS AmeriCorps State and National Grants, 643
CNCS Senior Corps Retired and Senior Volunteer
    Program Grants, 648
Entergy Charitable Foundation Low-Income
    Initiatives and Solutions Grants, 918
Environmental Excellence Awards, 922
PG&E Bright Ideas Grants, 1956
PG&E Community Vitality Grants, 1957
PNM Reduce Your Use Grants, 1988

Sioux Falls Area Community Foundation Community
    Fund Grants, 2203
Sioux Falls Area Community Foundation Spot
    Grants, 2204
Union Bank, N.A. Foundation Grants, 2334
Volvo Adventure Environmental Awards, 2390

Energy Conversion
CNCS AmeriCorps NCCC Project Grants, 642

Energy Economics
GNOF Coastal 5 + 1 Grants, 1078
McCune Charitable Foundation Grants, 1617

Energy Education
Delmarva Power & Light Mini-Grants, 822
Energy by Design Poster Contest, 915
McCune Charitable Foundation Grants, 1617
Piedmont Natural Gas Foundation K-12 Science,
    Technology, Engineering and Math (STEM)
    Grant, 1969
PNM Reduce Your Use Grants, 1988
Progress Energy Foundation Energy Education
    Grants, 2025

Energy Engineering
McCune Charitable Foundation Grants, 1617
Micron Technology Fdn Community Grants, 1664

Energy Utilization
McCune Charitable Foundation Grants, 1617

Energy, Fossil
GNOF Coastal 5 + 1 Grants, 1078
McCune Charitable Foundation Grants, 1617

Energy, Geothermal
McCune Charitable Foundation Grants, 1617

Energy, Hydro
Honor the Earth Grants, 1259

Energy, Solar
McCune Charitable Foundation Grants, 1617
PG&E Bright Ideas Grants, 1956
PG&E Community Vitality Grants, 1957

Energy, Wind
McCune Charitable Foundation Grants, 1617

Engineering
Acuity Charitable Foundation Grants, 110
Arthur M. Blank Family Foundation Pipeline Project
    Grants, 313
Daviess County Community Foundation Advancing
    Out-of-School Learning Grants, 792
FirstEnergy Foundation Science, Technology,
    Engineering, and Mathematics Grants, 966
Flinn Foundation Scholarships, 977
Hearst Foundations Culture Grants, 1223
Hispanic Heritage Foundation Youth Awards, 1253
Honeywell Corporation Leadership Challenge
    Academy, 1258
Meadows Foundation Grants, 1626
Michelin North America Challenge Education, 1660
OSF Baltimore Community Fellowships, 1838
Raytheon Middle School Grants and Schols, 2061

Engineering Education
3M Company Fdn Community Giving Grants, 5
Acuity Charitable Foundation Grants, 110
Alaska Community Foundation Afterschool Network
    Engineering Mindset Mini-Grant, 196
Alcatel-Lucent Technologies Foundation Grants, 224
Bayer Fund STEM Education Grants, 384
Dayton Power and Light Foundation Grants, 802
Northrop Grumman Foundation Grants, 1773
Piedmont Natural Gas Foundation K-12 Science,
    Technology, Engineering and Math (STEM)
    Grant, 1969

Qualcomm Grants, 2042
Ralph M. Parsons Foundation Grants, 2052
Raytheon Middle School Grants and Schols, 2061
Rockwell Collins Charitable Corp Grants, 2098
SAS Institute Community Relations Donations, 2165
Tellabs Foundation Grants, 2280
United Technologies Corporation Grants, 2347
Washington Gas Charitable Contributions, 2417
WSLBDF Quarterly Grants, 2499

English Education
ACF Voluntary Agencies Matching Grants, 100
Bay Area Community Foundation Semiannual
    Grants, 382
Bernard and Audre Rapoport Foundation Education
    Grants, 410
Essex County Community Foundation Greater
    Lawrence Summer Fund Grants, 932
New Jersey Office of Faith Based Initiatives English as
    a Second Language Grants, 1751
Piedmont Natural Gas Foundation K-12 Science,
    Technology, Engineering and Math (STEM)
    Grant, 1969

English as a Second Language
ACF Refugee Career Pathways Grants, 90
ACF Voluntary Agencies Matching Grants, 100
Dollar General Family Literacy Grants, 835
Essex County Community Foundation Greater
    Lawrence Summer Fund Grants, 932
LISC Education Grants, 1500
Luella Kemper Trust Grants, 1517
Marquette Bank Neighborhood Commit Grants, 1577
Middlesex Savings Charitable Foundation
    Educational Opportunities Grants, 1670
New Jersey Office of Faith Based Initiatives English as
    a Second Language Grants, 1751
ProLiteracy National Book Fund Grants, 2026
Robert R. McCormick Tribune Foundation
    Community Grants, 2093
Textron Corporate Contributions Grants, 2286

Enrichment, Student
AASA Urgent Need Mini-Grants, 43
Fdn for the Mid South Communities Grants, 992
Jack Kent Cooke Foundation Summer Enrichment
    Grants, 1332

Entrepreneurship
ACF Sustainable Employment and Economic
    Development Strategies Grants, 95
Achelis and Bodman Foundation Grants, 101
Achelis Foundation Grants, 102
Adolph Coors Foundation Grants, 129
Allstate Corporate Giving Grants, 242
Allstate Corp Hometown Commitment Grants, 243
Allstate Foundation Safe and Vital Communities
    Grants, 244
Appalachian Regional Commission Business
    Development Revolving Loan Fund Grants, 285
Appalachian Regional Commission Entrepreneurship
    and Business Development Grants, 287
California Endowment Innovative Ideas Challenge
    Grants, 495
Carl R. Hendrickson Family Foundation Grants, 509
Coleman Foundation Entrepreneurship Education
    Grants, 651
Community Foundation for SE Michigan Head Start
    Innovation Fund, 682
Draper Richards Kaplan Foundation Grants, 864
Echoing Green Fellowships, 885
Ewing Marion Kauffman Foundation Grants, 943
Georgia-Pacific Fdn Entrepreneurship Grants, 1059
GNOF New Orleans Works Grants, 1088
Hispanic Heritage Foundation Youth Awards, 1253
James Lee Sorenson Family Impact Foundation
    Grants, 1342
Johnson Scholarship Foundation Grants, 1382
Linden Foundation Grants, 1494
Maine Women's Fund Econ Security Grants, 1546

MassMutual Foundation Edonomic Development
    Grants, 1603
NASE Fdn Future Entrepreneur Scholarship, 1713
New Jersey Office of Faith Based Initiatives Services
    to At Risk Youth Grants, 1752
Olive B. Cole Foundation Grants, 1816
OSF Baltimore Community Fellowships, 1838
OtterCares Impact Fund Grants, 1849
OtterCares Inspiration Fund Grants, 1850
OtterCares NoCO Fund Grants, 1851
Paul and Edith Babson Foundation Grants, 1881
PepsiCo Foundation Grants, 1935
Sand Hill Foundation Health and Opportunity
    Grants, 2153
Southwest Initiative Foundation Grants, 2226
Twenty-First Century Foundation Grants, 2328
Union Bank, N.A. Foundation Grants, 2334

Environment
ACCF Dennis and Melanie Bieberich Community
    Enrichment Fund Grants, 59
ACCF John and Kay Boch Fund Grants, 60
ACCF of Indiana Anonymous Community
    Enrichment Fund Grants, 63
ACCF of Indiana Bank of Geneva Heritage Fund
    Grants, 64
ACCF of Indiana Berne Ready Mix Community
    Enrichment Fund Grants, 65
ACCF of Indiana First Merchants Bank / Decatur
    Bank and Trust Fund Grants, 66
ACCF of Indiana Michael Basham Community
    Enrichment Fund Grants, 67
ACCF of Indiana Ron and Susie Ballard Community
    Enrichment Fund Grants, 68
ACCF Ralph Biggs Memorial Community
    Enrichment Fund Grants, 69
Alpha Natural Resources Corporate Giving, 246
Anderson Foundation Grants, 271
Ann Ludington Sullivan Foundation Grants, 279
Atlas Insurance Agency Foundation Grants, 329
Baxter International Corporate Giving Grants, 368
Bay Area Community Fdn Auburn Area Chamber of
    Commerce Enrichment Fund Grants, 373
Bay Area Community Foundation Community
    Initiative Fund Grants, 376
Belvedere Community Foundation Grants, 399
Blue Grass Community Foundation Clark County
    Fund Grants, 444
Blue Grass Community Foundation Fayette County
    Fund Grants, 446
Blue Grass Community Foundation Franklin County
    Fund Grants, 447
Blue Grass Community Foundation Harrison County
    Fund Grants, 448
Blue Grass Community Foundation Madison County
    Fund Grants, 450
Blue Grass Community Foundation Magoffin County
    Fund Grants, 451
Blue Grass Community Foundation Morgan County
    Fund Grants, 452
Blue Grass Community Foundation Rowan County
    Fund Grants, 453
Blue Grass Community Foundation Woodford
    County Fund Grants, 454
Bridgestone Americas Trust Fund Grants, 469
C.F. Adams Charitable Trust Grants, 488
Caesars Foundation Grants, 492
CFF Winter Park Community Grants, 551
Charles N. and Eleanor Knight Leigh Foundation
    Grants, 568
Chilkat Valley Community Foundation Grants, 588
Collective Brands Foundation Grants, 654
Community Foundation for Greater Buffalo Niagara
    Area Foundation Grants, 673
Community Foundation for SE Michigan Detroit
    Auto Dealers Association Charitable Foundation
    Fund Grants, 681
Community Foundation for the Capital Region
    Grants, 687
Community Foundation of Boone County Grants, 694

Community Fdn Of Greater Lafayette Grants, 710
Community Foundation of Louisville Anna Marble
    Memorial Fund for Princeton Grants, 717
Cornell Lab of Ornithology Mini-Grants, 751
Dayton Foundation Vandalia-Butler Grants, 799
Dean Foundation Grants, 806
DeKalb County Community Foundation Grants, 815
Duke Energy Foundation Local Impact Grants, 872
Earl and Maxine Claussen Trust Grants, 878
Eastern Bank Charitable Foundation Neighborhood
    Support Grants, 880
Eastern Bank Charitable Foundation Partnerships
    Grants, 881
Eastern Bank Charitable Foundation Targeted
    Grants, 882
Elmer Roe Deaver Foundation Grants, 906
El Pomar Foundation Anna Keesling Ackerman Fund
    Grants, 907
El Pomar Foundation Grants, 908
Evan Frankel Foundation Grants, 938
Faye L. and William L. Cowden Charitable
    Foundation Grants, 950
Four County Community Foundation General
    Grants, 1000
Gardner Foundation Grants, 1035
George W.P. Magee Trust Grants, 1056
GNOF Norco Community Grants, 1089
Gray Family Fdn Camp Maintenance Grants, 1104
Gray Family Fdn Outdoor School Grants, 1107
Grundy Foundation Grants, 1124
GTRCF Elk Rapids Area Community Endowment
    Grants, 1127
Hampton Roads Community Foundation
    Environment Grants, 1158
Hampton Roads Community Foundation Nonprofit
    Facilities Improvement Grants, 1159
Harry A. and Margaret D. Towsley Foundation
    Grants, 1180
Hawai'i Community Foundation Richard Smart Fund
    Grants, 1204
Hawaii Community Foundation Omidyar Ohana
    Fund Grants, 1213
Hawaii Electric Industries Charitable Foundation
    Grants, 1218
HEI Charitable Foundation Grants, 1226
Helen G., Henry F., & Louise Tuechter Dornette
    Foundation Grants, 1229
Hendricks County Community Fdn Grants, 1234
Hillsdale County Community Foundation General
    Grants, 1250
HSBC Corporate Giving Grants, 1266
Hubbard Family Foundation Grants, 1271
Jane's Trust Grants, 1346
Jennings County Community Foundation Women's
    Giving Circle Grant, 1361
Jessica Stevens Community Foundation Grants, 1363
Julia Temple Davis Brown Foundation Grants, 1399
Laidlaw Foundation Youh Organizing Catalyst
    Grants, 1461
Lake County Community Fund Grants, 1463
Laurel Foundation Grants, 1475
Lily Palmer Fry Memorial Trust Grants, 1493
Louis and Sandra Berkman Foundation Grants, 1510
Madison Community Foundation Grants, 1535
Marathon Petroleum Corporation Grants, 1551
Marriott Int Corporate Giving Grants, 1578
Meadows Foundation Grants, 1626
Mericos Foundation Grants, 1637
Norcliffe Foundation Grants, 1766
North Dakota Community Foundation Grants, 1768
Northrop Grumman Corporation Grants, 1772
Olive Smith Browning Charitable Trust Grants, 1818
Orange County Community Foundation Grants, 1829
Oregon Community Fdn Community Grants, 1833
Parke County Community Foundation Grants, 1868
Parker Foundation (California) Grants, 1869
Paul and Edith Babson Foundation Grants, 1881
PepsiCo Foundation Grants, 1935
Piedmont Natural Gas Fdn Envirnmtl Stewardship
    and Energy Sustainability Grant, 1967

PMI Foundation Grants, 1982
Pokagon Fund Grants, 1994
Polk County Community Foundation Bradley
    Breakthrough Community Benefit Grants, 1995
Polk County Community Foundation Marjorie M.
    and Lawrence R. Bradley Endowment Fund
    Grants, 1998
Polk County Community Foundation Mary F. Kessler
    Fund Grants, 1999
Polk County Community Foundation Unrestricted
    Grants, 2001
PPCF Community Grants, 2014
PSEG Corporate Contributions Grants, 2030
Putnam County Community Fdn Grants, 2040
RCF General Community Grants, 2062
Robbins-de Beaumont Foundation Grants, 2080
Robbins Charitable Foundation Grants, 2081
Sand Hill Foundation Environment and Sustainability
    Grants, 2152
Sartain Lanier Family Foundation Grants, 2164
Seward Community Foundation Grants, 2182
Seward Community Foundation Mini-Grants, 2183
Shield-Ayres Foundation Grants, 2189
Sony Corporation of America Grants, 2216
Starke County Community Foundation Grants, 2236
Three Guineas Fund Grants, 2297
Toyota Motor Manuf of Alabama Grants, 2309
Toyota Motor Manufacturing of Indiana Grants, 2310
Toyota Motor Manuf of Kentucky Grants, 2311
Toyota Motor Manuf of Mississippi Grants, 2312
Toyota Motor Manufacturing of West Virginia
    Grants, 2314
Toyota Motor North America of NY Grants, 2315
Toyota Motor Sales, USA Grants, 2316
Toyota Technical Center Grants, 2317
Toyota USA Foundation Environmental Grants, 2319
Union Bank, N.A. Corporate Sponsorships and
    Donations, 2333
Walker Area Community Foundation Grants, 2401
Walmart Fdn Inclusive Communities Grants, 2403
Wells County Foundation Grants, 2426
Whole Foods Foundation, 2445
William and Flora Hewlett Foundation
    Environmental Grants, 2455
William B. Stokely Jr. Foundation Grants, 2459
William J. and Tina Rosenberg Fdn Grants, 2470
William Ray and Ruth E. Collins Fdn Grants, 2473
Wisconsin Energy Foundation Grants, 2481
Wyoming Community Fdn General Grants, 2501
Wyoming Community Foundation Hazel Patterson
    Memorial Grants, 2502
Wyomissing Foundation Thun Family Organizational
    Grants, 2505
Wyomissing Foundation Thun Family Program
    Grants, 2506
Xerox Foundation Grants, 2507

Environmental Biology
Northrop Grumman Corporation Grants, 1772

Environmental Conservation
ACCF Dennis and Melanie Bieberich Community
    Enrichment Fund Grants, 59
ACCF of Indiana Bank of Geneva Heritage Fund
    Grants, 64
ACCF of Indiana First Merchants Bank / Decatur
    Bank and Trust Fund Grants, 66
ACCF of Indiana Michael Basham Community
    Enrichment Fund Grants, 67
ACCF of Indiana Ron and Susie Ballard Community
    Enrichment Fund Grants, 68
ACCF Ralph Biggs Memorial Community
    Enrichment Fund Grants, 69
Adams Legacy Foundation Grants, 121
Ama OluKai Foundation Grants, 249
Bee Conservancy Sponsor-A-Hive Grants, 395
CNCS AmeriCorps NCCC Project Grants, 642
CNCS AmeriCorps State and National Grants, 643
CNCS AmeriCorps VISTA Project Grants, 645
Collective Brands Foundation Grants, 654

Community Foundation for SE Michigan Livingston County Grants, 683
Dayton Foundation Huber Heights Grants, 797
Dean Foods Community Involvement Grants, 805
Earth Island Institute Brower Youth Awards, 879
Eastern Bank Charitable Foundation Partnerships Grants, 881
Eastern Bank Charitable Foundation Targeted Grants, 882
George H.C. Ensworth Memorial Fund Grants, 1049
GNOF Coastal 5 + 1 Grants, 1078
Hawaii Electric Industries Charitable Foundation Grants, 1218
HEI Charitable Foundation Grants, 1226
Helen E. Ellis Charitable Trust Grants, 1228
Helen G., Henry F., & Louise Tuechter Dornette Foundation Grants, 1229
Jane's Trust Grants, 1346
Kirkpatrick Foundation Grants, 1440
Kroger Company Donations, 1456
Matson Community Giving Grants, 1607
Meadows Foundation Grants, 1626
Meyer Memorial Trust Responsive Grants, 1653
NHSCA Conservation License Plate Grants, 1757
Northrop Grumman Corporation Grants, 1772
Packard Foundation Local Grants, 1863
Piedmont Natural Gas Corporate and Charitable Contributions, 1966
Piedmont Natural Gas Fdn Envirnmtl Stewardship and Energy Sustainability Grant, 1967
Sony Corporation of America Grants, 2216
Tides Fdn Friends of the IGF Fund Grants, 2300
Toyota USA Foundation Environmental Grants, 2319
Union Bank, N.A. Foundation Grants, 2334
Winifred Johnson Clive Foundation Grants, 2478
Wyomissing Foundation Thun Family Organizational Grants, 2505
Wyomissing Foundation Thun Family Program Grants, 2506

Environmental Design

Marin Community Foundation Affordable Housing Grants, 1561
NHSCA Artist Residence Grants, 1756
NHSCA Youth Arts Project Grants: For Extended Arts Learning, 1758
Northrop Grumman Corporation Grants, 1772
Windham Foundation Grants, 2477

Environmental Economics

GNOF New Orleans Works Grants, 1088

Environmental Education

786 Foundation Grants, 15
Abbott Fund Community Engagement Grants, 46
ACCF John and Kay Boch Fund Grants, 60
Adobe Foundation Action Grants, 126
A Friends' Foundation Trust Grants, 136
Allen Foundation Educational Nutrition Grants, 238
Baltimore Community Foundation Children's Fresh Air Society Fund Grants, 348
Bay Area Community Fdn Auburn Area Chamber of Commerce Enrichment Fund Grants, 373
Bernard and Audre Rapoport Foundation Education Grants, 410
Blumenthal Foundation Grants, 459
BMW of North America Charitable Contribs, 460
Boeing Company Contributions Grants, 462
Cabot Corporation Foundation Grants, 490
Cargill Corporate Giving Grants, 503
CFFVR Environmental Stewardship Grants, 540
Chesapeake Bay Trust Environmental Education Grants, 577
Chesapeake Bay Trust Mini Grants, 578
Chesapeake Bay Trust Outreach and Community Engagement Grants, 579
CNCS AmeriCorps State and National Grants, 643
Dean Foods Community Involvement Grants, 805
Dorr Foundation Grants, 846
DTE Energy Foundation Environmental Grants, 868

Dyson Foundation Mid-Hudson Valley Project Support Grants, 874
Eastern Bank Charitable Foundation Neighborhood Support Grants, 880
Elmer Roe Deaver Foundation Grants, 906
Energy by Design Poster Contest, 915
Environmental Excellence Awards, 922
Eulalie Bloedel Schneider Foundation Grants, 936
Foundation for Appalachian Ohio Access to Environmental Education Mini-Grants, 989
Frederick W. Marzahl Memorial Fund Grants, 1018
Gamble Foundation Grants, 1032
Gannett Foundation Community Action Grants, 1033
George and Ruth Bradford Foundation Grants, 1042
George W.P. Magee Trust Grants, 1056
Gray Family Fdn Camp Maintenance Grants, 1104
Gray Family Foundation Community Field Trips Grants, 1105
Gray Family Fdn Outdoor School Grants, 1107
Hampton Roads Community Foundation Environment Grants, 1158
HSBC Corporate Giving Grants, 1266
Illinois DNR School Habitat Action Grants, 1296
Illinois DNR Youth Recreation Corps Grants, 1297
Jessica Stevens Community Foundation Grants, 1363
Johnson Foundation Wingspread Conference Support Program, 1381
Julia Temple Davis Brown Foundation Grants, 1399
Kimball Foundation Grants, 1432
Madison Community Foundation Fund for Children Grants, 1534
Mary A. Crocker Trust Grants, 1584
Matson Community Giving Grants, 1607
McCune Charitable Foundation Grants, 1617
Meadows Foundation Grants, 1626
Northrop Grumman Corporation Grants, 1772
Piedmont Natural Gas Corporate and Charitable Contributions, 1966
Piedmont Natural Gas Fdn Envirnmtl Stewardship and Energy Sustainability Grant, 1967
Piedmont Natural Gas Foundation K-12 Science, Technology, Engineering and Math (STEM) Grant, 1969
Scott County Community Foundation Grants, 2170
Seward Community Foundation Grants, 2182
Seward Community Foundation Mini-Grants, 2183
Skaggs Foundation Grants, 2207
Sorenson Legacy Foundation Grants, 2217
TE Foundation Grants, 2279
Telluride Foundation Community Grants, 2281
Toyota USA Foundation Environmental Grants, 2319
Union Bank, N.A. Foundation Grants, 2334
Volvo Adventure Environmental Awards, 2390
Wyoming Community Foundation Hazel Patterson Memorial Grants, 2502
Wyomissing Foundation Thun Family Organizational Grants, 2505
Wyomissing Foundation Thun Family Program Grants, 2506

Environmental Effects

EPA Children's Health Protection Grants, 923
March of Dimes Program Grants, 1552
Northrop Grumman Corporation Grants, 1772
Piedmont Natural Gas Corporate and Charitable Contributions, 1966
Toyota USA Foundation Environmental Grants, 2319

Environmental Effects, Fossil Fuels

GNOF Coastal 5 + 1 Grants, 1078

Environmental Geography

Gray Family Foundation Geography Education Grants, 1106

Environmental Health

Adobe Foundation Action Grants, 126
Adolph Coors Foundation Grants, 129
Akron Community Foundation Health and Human Services Grants, 152

Allen Foundation Educational Nutrition Grants, 238
Blue Cross Blue Shield of Minnesota Fdn - Healthy Children: Growing Up Healthy Grants, 442
BMW of North America Charitable Contribs, 460
Chesapeake Bay Trust Outreach and Community Engagement Grants, 579
Community Foundation of Switzerland County Grants, 739
DTE Energy Foundation Environmental Grants, 868
Edna Wardlaw Charitable Trust Grants, 886
EPA Children's Health Protection Grants, 923
Fremont Area Community Foundation Community Grants, 1020
Gerber Foundation Environmental Hazards Research Grants, 1062
Hawaii Electric Industries Charitable Foundation Grants, 1218
Max and Anna Levinson Foundation Grants, 1612
Piedmont Natural Gas Fdn Envirnmtl Stewardship and Energy Sustainability Grant, 1967
Powell Foundation Grants, 2013
Pulido Walker Foundation, 2039
Toyota Motor Manufacturing of Texas Grants, 2313
Volvo Bob the Bunny's Cartoon Competition, 2391
Washington Gas Charitable Contributions, 2417
Weaver Foundation Grants, 2420

Environmental Issues

Collective Brands Foundation Grants, 654
Hampton Roads Community Foundation Environment Grants, 1158
Hillsdale County Community Foundation Love Your Community Grants, 1251
Toyota USA Foundation Environmental Grants, 2319
UUA Actions of Public Witness Grants, 2365
UUA Congregation-Based Community Organizing Grants, 2366
UUA International Fund Grants, 2368
UUA Just Society Fund Grants, 2369
UUA Social Responsibility Grants, 2370

Environmental Law

Ann Ludington Sullivan Foundation Grants, 279
Honor the Earth Grants, 1259
Norman Foundation Grants, 1767

Environmental Planning/Policy

Achelis and Bodman Foundation Grants, 101
Achelis Foundation Grants, 102
A Friends' Foundation Trust Grants, 136
American Electric Power Corporate Grants, 252
CFFVR Environmental Stewardship Grants, 540
CFF Winter Park Community Grants, 551
Dyson Foundation Mid-Hudson Valley Project Support Grants, 874
El Pomar Foundation Grants, 908
GNOF Coastal 5 + 1 Grants, 1078
Harrison County Community Foundation Signature Grants, 1179
Hillsdale County Community Foundation General Grants, 1250
Toyota USA Foundation Environmental Grants, 2319
Windham Foundation Grants, 2477

Environmental Programs

3M Company Fdn Community Giving Grants, 5
786 Foundation Grants, 15
Abbott Fund Community Engagement Grants, 46
Abell-Hanger Foundation Grants, 52
ACCF of Indiana Anonymous Community Enrichment Fund Grants, 63
ACCF of Indiana Bank of Geneva Heritage Fund Grants, 64
ACCF of Indiana Ron and Susie Ballard Community Enrichment Fund Grants, 68
Adobe Foundation Action Grants, 126
Air Products Foundation Grants, 148
Alaska Airlines Foundation LIFT Grants, 194
Allen Foundation Educational Nutrition Grants, 238

Alliant Energy Foundation Community Giving for
    Good Sponsorship Grants, 240
Alpha Natural Resources Corporate Giving, 246
Ameren Corporation Community Grants, 251
American Electric Power Corporate Grants, 252
American Electric Power Foundation Grants, 253
American Honda Foundation Grants, 255
Andrew Family Foundation Grants, 272
Anheuser-Busch Foundation Grants, 273
Arthur Ashley Williams Foundation Grants, 302
AT&T Fdn Community Support and Safety, 320
Atlas Insurance Agency Foundation Grants, 329
Austin Community Foundation Grants, 332
Baton Rouge Area Foundation Grants, 365
Baxter International Corporate Giving Grants, 368
Bikes Belong Foundation Paul David Clark Bicycling
    Safety Grants, 422
Bikes Belong Foundation REI Grants, 423
Bikes Belong Grants, 424
Black Hills Corporation Grants, 435
Blue Grass Community Foundation Clark County
    Fund Grants, 444
Blue Grass Community Foundation Fayette County
    Fund Grants, 446
Blue Grass Community Foundation Franklin County
    Fund Grants, 447
Blue Grass Community Foundation Harrison County
    Fund Grants, 448
Blue Grass Community Foundation Madison County
    Fund Grants, 450
Blue Grass Community Foundation Magoffin County
    Fund Grants, 451
Blue Grass Community Foundation Morgan County
    Fund Grants, 452
Blue Grass Community Foundation Rowan County
    Fund Grants, 453
Blue Grass Community Foundation Woodford
    County Fund Grants, 454
BMW of North America Charitable Contribs, 460
Boeing Company Contributions Grants, 462
Bothin Foundation Grants, 464
Brian G. Dyson Foundation Grants, 468
Brunswick Foundation Grants, 479
Caesars Foundation Grants, 492
Callaway Foundation Grants, 496
Carl M. Freeman Foundation FACES Grants, 507
CFFVR Environmental Stewardship Grants, 540
CFFVR Project Grants, 546
CFFVR Shawano Area Community Foundation
    Grants, 549
CFF Winter Park Community Grants, 551
Charles Delmar Foundation Grants, 564
Chesapeake Bay Trust Environmental Education
    Grants, 577
Chesapeake Bay Trust Outreach and Community
    Engagement Grants, 579
Chilkat Valley Community Foundation Grants, 588
CICF Indianapolis Fdn Community Grants, 606
Citizens Bank Charitable Foundation Grants, 616
Clayton Baker Trust Grants, 629
CNCS AmeriCorps NCCC Project Grants, 642
Collective Brands Foundation Grants, 654
Colorado Interstate Gas Grants, 661
Community Foundation for Greater Buffalo
    Competitive Grants, 670
Community Foundation for Greater Buffalo Niagara
    Area Foundation Grants, 673
Community Foundation of Eastern Connecticut
    General Southeast Grants, 696
Community Foundation of Greater Greensboro
    Community Grants, 708
Community Fdn of Randolph County Grants, 735
Community Fdn of Southern Indiana Grants, 736
Community Foundation of St. Joseph County Special
    Project Challenge Grants, 738
Community Fdn of Wabash County Grants, 740
Community Foundation of Western Massachusetts
    Grants, 741
Cooke Foundation Grants, 748
Corina Higginson Trust Grants, 750

Cornell Lab of Ornithology Mini-Grants, 751
Dayton Foundation Grants, 796
Delaware Community Foundation Grants, 817
Dorrance Family Foundation Grants, 845
Do Something Awards, 847
DTE Energy Foundation Community Development
    Grants, 866
DTE Energy Foundation Environmental Grants, 868
Dubois County Community Foundation Grants, 871
Dyson Foundation Mid-Hudson Valley Project
    Support Grants, 874
E.J. Grassmann Trust Grants, 876
Earth Island Institute Brower Youth Awards, 879
Edward and Helen Bartlett Foundation Grants, 888
Elmer Roe Deaver Foundation Grants, 906
Ensworth Charitable Foundation Grants, 916
Environmental Excellence Awards, 922
EPA Children's Health Protection Grants, 923
FirstEnergy Foundation Community Grants, 965
Ford Foundation BUILD Grants, 984
Forest Foundation Grants, 985
Four County Community Foundation General
    Grants, 1000
Franklin County Community Fdn Grants, 1010
Fremont Area Community Foundation Community
    Grants, 1020
G.N. Wilcox Trust Grants, 1031
Gamble Foundation Grants, 1032
Gannett Foundation Community Action Grants, 1033
General Motors Foundation Grants, 1039
George and Ruth Bradford Foundation Grants, 1042
George A Ohl Jr. Foundation Grants, 1043
George H. and Jane A. Mifflin Memorial Fund
    Grants, 1048
George H.C. Ensworth Memorial Fund Grants, 1049
GNOF Bayou Communities Grants, 1077
GNOF Coastal 5 + 1 Grants, 1078
GNOF Exxon-Mobil Grants, 1080
GNOF Gert Community Fund Grants, 1082
Gray Family Fdn Camp Maintenance Grants, 1104
Greater Saint Louis Community Fdn Grants, 1110
Greater Tacoma Community Foundation General
    Operating Grants, 1113
GTRCF Elk Rapids Area Community Endowment
    Grants, 1127
H.A. and Mary K. Chapman Charitable Trust
    Grants, 1137
Harrison County Community Fdn Grants, 1178
Harrison County Community Foundation Signature
    Grants, 1179
Hawai'i Community Foundation East Hawaii Fund
    Grants, 1199
Hawai'i Community Foundation Richard Smart Fund
    Grants, 1204
Hawaiian Electric Industries Charitable Foundation
    Grants, 1211
Hawaii Electric Industries Charitable Foundation
    Grants, 1218
HEI Charitable Foundation Grants, 1226
Hillsdale County Community Foundation General
    Grants, 1250
HLTA Visitor Industry Charity Walk Grant, 1254
Honor the Earth Grants, 1259
Horace A. Kimball and S. Ella Kimball Foundation
    Grants, 1260
Huntington County Community Foundation Make a
    Difference Grants, 1280
Iddings Foundation Major Project Grants, 1284
Illinois DNR School Habitat Action Grants, 1296
Illinois DNR Youth Recreation Corps Grants, 1297
Intel Corporation Community Grants, 1311
Intel Corporation Int Community Grants, 1312
James and Abigail Campbell Family Foundation
    Grants, 1337
James Ford Bell Foundation Grants, 1339
Jane's Trust Grants, 1346
Jennings County Community Fdn Grants, 1360
Jessica Stevens Community Foundation Grants, 1363
Katharine Matthies Foundation Grants, 1418
Kelvin and Eleanor Smith Foundation Grants, 1424

Kenneth T. and Eileen L. Norris Fdn Grants, 1427
Kettering Family Foundation Grants, 1430
Kind World Foundation Grants, 1438
Klingenstein-Simons Fellowship Awards in the
    Neurosciences, 1441
Kosciusko County Community Fdn Grants, 1452
Laidlaw Foundation Youth Organizaing Initiatives
    Grants, 1462
Lands' End Corporate Giving Program, 1468
Lee and Ramona Bass Foundation Grants, 1478
Libra Foundation Grants, 1489
Lisa and Douglas Goldman Fund Grants, 1496
Long Island Community Foundation Grants, 1507
Lotus 88 Foundation for Women and Children
    Grants, 1508
Lubrizol Foundation Grants, 1513
Lumpkin Family Foundation Strong Community
    Leadership Grants, 1519
Macquarie Bank Foundation Grants, 1532
Margaret T. Morris Foundation Grants, 1557
Marie C. and Joseph C. Wilson Foundation Rochester
    Small Grants, 1559
Marshall County Community Fdn Grants, 1579
Mary A. Crocker Trust Grants, 1584
Mary K. Chapman Foundation Grants, 1590
Mary Owen Borden Foundation Grants, 1597
Matson Adahi I Tano' Grants, 1606
Matson Community Giving Grants, 1607
Matson Ka Ipu 'Aina Grants, 1608
Max and Anna Levinson Foundation Grants, 1612
McConnell Foundation Grants, 1616
McGraw-Hill Companies Community Grants, 1620
McInerny Foundation Grants, 1622
McLean Contributionship Grants, 1623
Mead Witter Foundation Grants, 1628
Mervin Bovaird Foundation Grants, 1643
Mimi and Peter Haas Fund Grants, 1677
Natalie W. Furniss Foundation Grants, 1715
Nathan Cummings Foundation Grants, 1718
National Wildlife Federation Craig Tufts Educational
    Scholarship, 1724
New Earth Foundation Grants, 1743
Nissan Neighbors Grants, 1762
Norman Foundation Grants, 1767
North Face Explore Fund, 1770
Northrop Grumman Corporation Grants, 1772
NRA Foundation Grants, 1774
Oregon Community Fdn Community Grants, 1833
Perkins Charitable Foundation Grants, 1939
PG&E Bright Ideas Grants, 1956
PG&E Community Vitality Grants, 1957
PGE Foundation Grants, 1958
Piedmont Natural Gas Corporate and Charitable
    Contributions, 1966
Piedmont Natural Gas Fdn Envirnmtl Stewardship
    and Energy Sustainability Grant, 1967
Pohlad Family Fdn Large Capital Grants, 1990
Pohlad Family Fdn Small Capital Grants, 1991
Polk County Community Foundation Bradley
    Breakthrough Community Benefit Grants, 1995
Polk County Community Foundation Marjorie M.
    and Lawrence R. Bradley Endowment Fund
    Grants, 1998
Polk County Community Foundation Mary F. Kessler
    Fund Grants, 1999
Polk County Community Foundation Unrestricted
    Grants, 2001
Powell Family Foundation Grants, 2012
Powell Foundation Grants, 2013
Pulaski County Community Foundation Grants, 2038
Rathmann Family Foundation Grants, 2057
RCF General Community Grants, 2062
Reinberger Foundation Grants, 2066
Ripley County Community Foundation Grants, 2077
Ripley County Community Foundation Small Project
    Grants, 2078
Robbins-de Beaumont Foundation Grants, 2080
Robbins Charitable Foundation Grants, 2081
Robert R. Meyer Foundation Grants, 2094
Ruth Anderson Foundation Grants, 2122

Ruth and Vernon Taylor Foundation Grants, 2124
Samuel S. Johnson Foundation Grants, 2146
Sand Hill Foundation Environment and Sustainability Grants, 2152
SanDisk Corp Community Sharing Grants, 2155
San Juan Island Community Foundation Grants, 2158
Scott County Community Foundation Grants, 2170
Seward Community Foundation Grants, 2182
Seward Community Foundation Mini-Grants, 2183
Singing for Change Foundation Grants, 2202
Sioux Falls Area Community Foundation Spot Grants, 2204
Skaggs Foundation Grants, 2207
Sony Corporation of America Grants, 2216
Sorenson Legacy Foundation Grants, 2217
Streisand Foundation Grants, 2251
Summit Foundation Grants, 2255
Tellabs Foundation Grants, 2280
Telluride Foundation Community Grants, 2281
Thomas Sill Foundation Grants, 2292
Tides Fdn Friends of the IGF Fund Grants, 2300
Tides Foundation Grants, 2302
Toyota Motor Manuf of Alabama Grants, 2309
Toyota Motor Manuf of Mississippi Grants, 2312
Toyota Motor Manufacturing of West Virginia Grants, 2314
Toyota USA Foundation Environmental Grants, 2319
Turner Foundation Grants, 2326
U.S. Cellular Corporation Grants, 2331
Union Bank, N.A. Corporate Sponsorships and Donations, 2333
Union Pacific Fdn Community & Civic Grants, 2337
United Technologies Corporation Grants, 2347
Virginia W. Kettering Foundation Grants, 2388
Volvo Adventure Environmental Awards, 2390
Walmart Fdn National Local Giving Grants, 2404
Washington County Community Fdn Grants, 2416
Washington Gas Charitable Contributions, 2417
Weaver Foundation Grants, 2420
Wege Foundation Grants, 2422
Widgeon Point Charitable Foundation Grants, 2447
William A. Cooke Foundation Grants, 2452
William G. and Helen C. Hoffman Foundation Grants, 2466
William J. and Dorothy K. O'Neill Foundation Responsive Grants, 2468
William Ray and Ruth E. Collins Fdn Grants, 2473
Wyoming Community Fdn General Grants, 2501
Wyoming Community Foundation Hazel Patterson Memorial Grants, 2502
Wyomissing Foundation Thun Family Organizational Grants, 2505
Wyomissing Foundation Thun Family Program Grants, 2506
YSA Radio Disney's Hero for Change Award, 2519
YSA Sodexo Lead Organizer Grants, 2520
Z. Smith Reynolds Foundation Small Grants, 2523

Environmental Protection
Alpha Natural Resources Corporate Giving, 246
Atlas Insurance Agency Foundation Grants, 329
Caesars Foundation Grants, 492
Collective Brands Foundation Grants, 654
GNOF Coastal 5 + 1 Grants, 1078
Hawaii Electric Industries Charitable Grants, 1218
Meadows Foundation Grants, 1626
Piedmont Natural Gas Corporate and Charitable Contributions, 1966
Piedmont Natural Gas Fdn Envirnmtl Stewardship and Energy Sustainability Grant, 1967
RCF General Community Grants, 2062
Sioux Falls Area Community Foundation Community Fund Grants, 2203
Sioux Falls Area Community Foundation Spot Grants, 2204
Toyota USA Foundation Environmental Grants, 2319
Wyomissing Foundation Thun Family Organizational Grants, 2505
Wyomissing Foundation Thun Family Program Grants, 2506

Environmental Research
Community Foundation of Louisville C. E. and S. Endowment for the Parks Fund Grants, 719
Florence Foundation Grants, 978
Gerber Foundation Environmental Hazards Research Grants, 1062

Environmental Services
ACCF of Indiana Anonymous Community Enrichment Fund Grants, 63
Baxter International Corporate Giving Grants, 368
Bill and Melinda Gates Foundation Emergency Response Grants, 426
Elkhart County Community Foundation Fund for Elkhart County, 902
Toyota USA Foundation Environmental Grants, 2319

Environmental Studies
Collins Foundation Grants, 658
NYSCA Arts Education: Community-based Learning Grants, 1780
NYSCA Arts Education: General Operating Support Grants, 1781
NYSCA Arts Education: Local Capacity Building Grants (Regrants), 1783
NYSCA Arts Ed: Services to the Field Grants, 1784
Piedmont Natural Gas Fdn Envirnmtl Stewardship and Energy Sustainability Grant, 1967

Epidemiology
CDC David J. Sencer Museum Student Field Trip Experience, 524
CDC Disease Detective Camp, 525

Epilepsy
Epilepsy Foundation SUDEP Challenge Initiative Prizes, 924
F.M. Kirby Foundation Grants, 946
Klingenstein-Simons Fellowship Awards in the Neurosciences, 1441

Episcopal Church
AHS Foundation Grants, 143
Alavi Foundation Education Grants, 216
Alvah H. and Wyline P. Chapman Foundation Grants, 248
Chapman Family Foundation, 562
Effie and Wofford Cain Foundation Grants, 895
Harry and Helen Sands Charitable Trust Grants, 1181
Herbert A. and Adrian W. Woods Foundation Grants, 1243

Equal Opportunity
Air Products Foundation Grants, 148
Alaska State Council on the Arts Youth Cultural Heritage Fast Track Grants, 212
Allstate Corporate Giving Grants, 242
Allstate Corp Hometown Commitment Grants, 243
Allstate Foundation Safe and Vital Communities Grants, 244
Ben Cohen StandUp Foundation Grants, 403
Benton Community Foundation - The Cookie Jar Grant, 404
Curtis Foundation Grants, 771
Evelyn and Walter Haas, Jr. Fund Immigrant Rights Grants, 941
HAF Community Grants, 1141
Michigan Women Forward Grants, 1662
OSF Baltimore Education and Youth Development Grants, 1840
Sapelo Foundation Social Justice Grants, 2160
Singing for Change Foundation Grants, 2202

Equine Studies
Bay Area Community Fdn Semiannual Grants, 382

Equipment/Instrumentation
American Honda Foundation Grants, 255
B.F. and Rose H. Perkins Foundation Community Grants, 342

Ben B. Cheney Foundation Grants, 402
Biogen Foundation General Donations, 432
BMW of North America Charitable Contribs, 460
Boeing Company Contributions Grants, 462
Campbell Soup Foundation Grants, 501
Claremont Community Foundation Grants, 622
Collins Foundation Grants, 658
Community Foundation for Greater Atlanta Metropolitan Extra Wish Grants, 666
Community Foundation of Abilene Future Fund Grants, 689
Different Needz Foundation Grants, 830
E.L. Wiegand Foundation Grants, 877
GNOF Albert N. & Hattie M. McClure Grants, 1076
Jack H. & William M. Light Charitable Grants, 1330
Janson Foundation Grants, 1350
Jennings County Community Fdn Grants, 1360
Katharine Matthies Foundation Grants, 1418
Ludwick Family Foundation Grants, 1516
Marion I. and Henry J. Knott Foundation Discretionary Grants, 1571
Marion I. and Henry J. Knott Foundation Standard Grants, 1572
Montgomery County Community Foundation Health and Human Services Fund Grants, 1689
Montgomery County Community Foundation Libby Whitecotton Fund Grants, 1690
Norcliffe Foundation Grants, 1766
Ohio Valley Foundation Grants, 1814
Piper Trust Arts and Culture Grants, 1975
Ralph M. Parsons Foundation Grants, 2052

Ergonomics
BMW of North America Charitable Contribs, 460

Ethics
Cargill Corporate Giving Grants, 503
Elizabeth Morse Genius Charitable Trust Grants, 901
Marion Gardner Jackson Charitable Trust Grts, 1570
National Schools of Character Awards Program, 1723
Richard Davoud Donchian Foundation Grants, 2070

Ethnicity
ACF Ethnic Community Self Help Grants, 80

Europe
Charles Delmar Foundation Grants, 564

Europe, Southern
GMFUS Balkan Trust for Democracy Grants, 1075

Exercise
Air Products Foundation Grants, 148
Bikes Belong Foundation Paul David Clark Bicycling Safety Grants, 422
Bikes Belong Foundation REI Grants, 423
Bikes Belong Grants, 424
Bright Promises Foundation Grants, 470
Elizabeth Morse Genius Charitable Trust Grants, 901
Finish Line Youth Foundation Founder's Grants, 960
Finish Line Youth Foundation Grants, 961
GNOF IMPACT Kahn-Oppenheim Tr Grts, 1087
Linford & Mildred White Charitable Grants, 1495
Paso del Norte Health Foundation Grants, 1874
PepsiCo Foundation Grants, 1935
Phoenix Coyotes Charities Grants, 1963

Exhibitions, Collections, Performances
Alabama Humanities Foundation Major Grants, 159
ALA Booklist Editors' Choice Books for Youth Awards, 162
APAP All-In Grants, 283
Christensen Fund Regional Grants, 600
Crystelle Waggoner Charitable Trust Grants, 768
Daniel and Nanna Stern Family Fdn Grants, 778
Episcopal Actors' Guild Actors Florence James Children's Holiday Fund Grant, 925
HSFCA Biennium Grants, 1267
Japan Foundation Los Angeles Mini-Grants for Japanese Arts & Culture, 1354

Japan Foundation New York Small Grants for Arts and Culture, 1355
Japan Foundation New York World Heritage Photo Panel Exhibition, 1356
Marcia and Otto Koehler Foundation Grants, 1553
Montana Arts Council Cultural and Aesthetic Project Grants, 1685
NYSCA Arts Education: General Program Support Grants, 1782
NYSCA Music: Gen Operating Support Grants, 1791
NYSCA Music: Gen Program Support Grants, 1792
PCA Arts Organizations and Arts Program Grants for Music, 1887
PCA Arts Organizations and Arts Programs Grants for Art Museums, 1888
PCA Arts Organizations and Arts Programs Grants for Dance, 1892
PCA Arts Organizations and Arts Programs Grants for Film and Electronic Media, 1893
PCA Arts Organizations and Arts Programs Grants for Literature, 1894
PCA Arts Organizations and Arts Programs Grants for Visual Arts, 1898
PCA Entry Track Arts Organizations and Arts Programs Grants for Art Museums, 1900
PCA Entry Track Arts Orgs and Arts Programs Grants for Film and Electronic Media, 1905
PCA Entry Track Arts Organizations and Arts Programs Grants for Literature, 1906
PCA Entry Track Arts Organizations and Arts Programs Grants for Music, 1908
PCA Entry Track Arts Organizations and Arts Programs Grants for Visual Arts, 1912
PCA Strategies for Success Grants - Adv Level, 1917
PCA Strategies for Success Grants - Intermediate Level, 1919
R.S. Gernon Trust Grants, 2047
RISCA Project Grants for Individuals, 2079
TAC Arts Access Grant, 2265
TAC Touring Arts and Arts Access Touring Arts Grants, 2269
Virginia Foundation for the Humanities Open Grants, 2387
VSA/Metlife Connect All Grants, 2392
VSA/Volkswagen Group of America Exhibition Awards, 2393
VSA International Art Program for Children with Disabilities Grants, 2394
West Virginia Commission on the Arts Long-Term Artist Residencies, 2431
West Virginia Commission on the Arts Short-Term Artist Residencies, 2432
William Foulds Family Foundation Grants, 2465

Eye Diseases
1st Touch Foundation Grants, 2
Austin S. Nelson Foundation Grants, 333
E.L. Wiegand Foundation Grants, 877
GNOF IMPACT Gulf States Eye Surg Fund, 1085
Margaret Wiegand Trust Grants, 1558
Sara Elizabeth O'Brien Trust Grants, 2161

Facility Support
Easton Foundations Archery Facility Grants, 883
George W.P. Magee Trust Grants, 1056
GNOF Albert N. & Hattie M. McClure Grants, 1076
Marion and Miriam Rose Fund Grants, 1569
Mertz Gilmore Foundation NYC Dance Grants, 1642
Michael Reese Health Trust Core Grants, 1658
Western New York Foundation Grants, 2429

Faculty Development
Aspen Community Foundation Grants, 316
ILA Grants for Literacy Projects in Countries with Developing Economies, 1292
Lee and Ramona Bass Foundation Grants, 1478
San Antonio Area Foundation Strengthening Nonprofits Grants, 2151
Western New York Foundation Grants, 2429

Familial Abuse
ACF Child Abuse Prevention and Treatment Act Discretionary Funds Grants, 74
Anne Arundel Women Giving Together Regular Grants, 275
Austin S. Nelson Foundation Grants, 333
California Endowment Innovative Ideas Challenge Grants, 495
CFNEM Women's Giving Circle Grants, 557
Children's Trust Fund of Oregon Foundation Small Grants, 586
Covenant for Children Critical Goods Grants, 757
Curtis Foundation Grants, 771
Elkhart County Community Foundation Fund for Elkhart County, 902
Hampton Roads Community Foundation Abused People Grants, 1153
Harry and Helen Sands Charitable Trust Grants, 1181
Hawai'i Community Foundation Children's Trust Fund Community Awareness: Child Abuse and Neglect Prevention Grants, 1198
Hearst Foundations Social Service Grants, 1224
Herbert A. and Adrian W. Woods Foundation Grants, 1243
Initiaive Fdn Inside-Out Connections Grants, 1303
Joseph H. and Florence A. Roblee Foundation Family Grants, 1387
Ms. Fdn for Women Ending Violence Grants, 1708
Patrick and Aimee Butler Family Foundation Community Human Services Grants, 1880
Perkin Fund Grants, 1937
Riedman Foundation Grants, 2076
Westerman Foundation Grants, 2427
WHO Foundation Volunteer Service Grants, 2444
Winifred Johnson Clive Foundation Grants, 2478
Women's Fund of Hawaii Grants, 2484

Family
3M Company Fdn Community Giving Grants, 5
100 Club of Dubuque, 10
520 Charitable Foundation Grants, 14
A.L. Mailman Family Foundation Grants, 20
A and B Family Foundation Grants, 40
ACCF Dennis and Melanie Bieberich Community Enrichment Fund Grants, 59
ACCF of Indiana Bank of Geneva Heritage Fund Grants, 64
ACCF of Indiana First Merchants Bank / Decatur Bank and Trust Fund Grants, 66
ACCF of Indiana Michael Basham Community Enrichment Fund Grants, 67
ACCF Ralph Biggs Memorial Community Enrichment Fund Grants, 69
ACF Marriage Strengthening Research & Dissemination Center Grants, 85
ACF Promoting Safe and Stable Families (PSSF) Program Grants, 89
ACF Social and Economic Development Strategies Grants, 93
ACF Tribal Maternal, Infant, and Early Childhood Home Visiting Program: Development and Implementation Grants, 97
ACF Tribal Maternal, Infant, and Early Childhood Home Visiting Program: Implementation and Expansion Grants, 98
Achelis and Bodman Foundation Grants, 101
Achelis Foundation Grants, 102
Active Living Research Grants, 109
Adams Family Foundation of Ohio Grants, 119
Adidas Corporation General Grants, 125
Adobe Foundation Action Grants, 126
AEGON Transamerica Foundation Health and Wellness Grants, 133
Agnes M. Lindsay Trust Grants, 140
Alaska Community Foundation Children's Trust Tier 1 Community Based Child Abuse and Neglect Prevention Grants, 198
Alaska Community Foundation Children's Trust Tier 1 Parenting and Child Development Educational Grants, 199
Alaska Community Foundation Children's Trust Tier 2 Innovation Grants, 200
Alcatel-Lucent Technologies Foundation Grants, 224
Alex Stern Family Foundation Grants, 229
Alliance for Strong Families and Communities Grants, 239
Alpha Natural Resources Corporate Giving, 246
Alvah H. and Wyline P. Chapman Foundation Grants, 248
Amelia Sillman Rockwell and Carlos Perry Rockwell Charities Fund Grants, 250
Ameren Corporation Community Grants, 251
American Savings Foundation Program Grants, 261
Amerigroup Foundation Grants, 264
Andrew Family Foundation Grants, 272
Anne J. Caudal Foundation Grants, 276
Ann Ludington Sullivan Foundation Grants, 279
Appalachian Regl Commission Housing Grants, 289
Ar-Hale Family Foundation Grants, 290
Aspen Community Foundation Grants, 316
AT&T Fdn Community Support and Safety, 320
AT&T Foundation Health and Human Services Grants, 322
Atkinson Foundation Community Grants, 325
Atlanta Foundation Grants, 326
Avery-Fuller-Welch Children's Fdn Grants, 336
Avista Foundation Vulnerable and Limited Income Population Grants, 341
Bank of America Charitable Foundation Basic Needs Grants, 354
Bank of Hawaii Foundation Grants, 360
Bank of the Orient Community Giving, 361
Bay Area Community Foundation Elizabeth Husband Fund Grants, 378
Baystate Financial Charitable Foundation Grants, 385
BBF Florida Family Literacy Initiative Grants, 386
BBF Maine Family Literacy Initiative Implementation Grants, 387
BBF Maine Family Literacy Initiative Planning Grants, 388
BBF Maryland Family Literacy Initiative Implementation Grants, 389
BBF Maryland Family Literacy Initiative Planning Grants, 390
BBF National Grants for Family Literacy, 391
Benton Community Foundation Grants, 405
Better Way Foundation Grants, 419
Bindley Family Foundation Grants, 430
Blockbuster Corporate Contributions, 440
Blue River Community Foundation Grants, 458
Blumenthal Foundation Grants, 459
Bradley-Turner Foundation Grants, 466
Brinker Int Corporation Charitable Giving, 471
Brown County Community Foundation Grants, 475
Brown Foundation Grants, 476
Burlington Industries Foundation Grants, 481
C.H. Robinson Worldwide Foundation Grants, 489
California Endowment Innovative Ideas Challenge Grants, 495
Campbell Soup Foundation Grants, 501
Cargill Corporate Giving Grants, 503
CFFVR Basic Needs Giving Partnership Grants, 537
CFFVR Myra M. and Robert L. Vandehey Foundation Grants, 545
CFF Winter Park Community Grants, 551
CFGR Community Impact Grants, 552
Charles Crane Family Foundation Grants, 563
Children's Trust Fund of Oregon Fdn Grants, 585
Children's Trust Fund of Oregon Foundation Small Grants, 586
CICF Indianapolis Fdn Community Grants, 606
Citizens Bank Charitable Foundation Grants, 616
Clara Abbott Foundation Need-Based Grants, 620
Claremont Savings Bank Foundation Grants, 623
Cleo Foundation Grants, 632
Cleveland Foundation Higley Fund Grants, 634
Colorado Health Foundation Family, Friend and Neighbor Caregiver Supports Grants, 660
Columbus Foundation Traditional Grants, 663

Community Foundation for Greater Atlanta Frances Hollis Brain Foundation Fund Grants, 664
Community Foundation for Greater Buffalo Competitive Grants, 670
Community Foundation for the National Capital Region Community Leadership Grants, 688
Community Foundation of Bartholomew County Heritage Fund Grants, 690
Community Foundation of Bartholomew County James A. Henderson Award for Fundraising, 691
Community Foundation of Crawford County, 695
Community Foundation of Eastern Connecticut General Southeast Grants, 696
Community Foundation of Greater Chattanooga Grants, 704
Community Foundation of Greater Fort Wayne - Community Endowment and Clarke Endowment Grants, 705
Community Foundation of Louisville Boyette and Edna Edwards Fund Grants, 718
Community Foundation of Louisville Human Services Grants, 726
Community Fdn of Southern Indiana Grants, 736
Community Foundation Serving Riverside and San Bernardino Counties Impact Grants, 742
Community Memorial Foundation Responsive Grants, 743
Covenant to Care for Children Crisis Food Pantry Giving, 756
Covenant for Children Critical Goods Grants, 757
Crane Fund Grants, 763
Credit Suisse Foundation Education Grants, 765
Cresap Family Foundation Grants, 766
Daviess County Community Foundation Youth Development Grants, 794
Delta Air Lines Foundation Community Enrichment Grants, 823
Dermody Properties Fdn Capstone Award, 826
Dermody Properties Foundation Grants, 827
Dexter Adams Foundation Grants, 829
Dominion Foundation Grants, 839
Dorrance Family Foundation Grants, 845
Eastern Bank Charitable Foundation Partnerships Grants, 881
Eastern Bank Charitable Foundation Targeted Grants, 882
Effie Allen Little Foundation Grants, 894
El Pomar Foundation Grants, 908
Entergy Charitable Foundation Low-Income Initiatives and Solutions Grants, 918
Entergy Corporation Micro Grants, 919
Entergy Corporation Open Grants for Healthy Families, 921
EPA Children's Health Protection Grants, 923
Eulalie Bloedel Schneider Foundation Grants, 936
Farmers Insurance Corporate Giving Grants, 948
Fassino Foundation Grants, 949
FCD New American Children Grants, 952
Fidelity Foundation Grants, 957
Fifth Third Foundation Grants, 959
First Lady's Family Literacy Initiative for Texas Family Literacy Trailblazer Grants, 968
First Lady's Family Literacy Initiative for Texas Implementation Grants, 969
First Lady's Family Literacy Initiative for Texas Planning Grants, 970
Fdns of East Chicago Family Support Grants, 996
Fremont Area Community Foundation Community Grants, 1020
Friedman Family Foundation Grants, 1023
G.N. Wilcox Trust Grants, 1031
George and Ruth Bradford Foundation Grants, 1042
George Kress Foundation Grants, 1053
George W. Wells Foundation Grants, 1057
Gibson County Community Foundation Youth Development Grants, 1070
GNOF Gert Community Fund Grants, 1082
GNOF Stand Up For Our Children Grants, 1092
Golden Heart Community Foundation Grants, 1094
Good+Foundation Grants, 1096

Greater Sitka Legacy Fund Grants, 1111
Gregory and Helayne Brown Charitable Foundation Grants, 1119
GTRCF Genuine Leelanau Charitable Endowment Grants, 1128
Gulf Coast Foundation of Community Operating Grants, 1134
Gulf Coast Foundation of Community Program Grants, 1135
Hahl Proctor Charitable Trust Grants, 1151
Hampton Roads Community Foundation Abused People Grants, 1153
Hannaford Supermarkets Community Giving, 1164
Harden Foundation Grants, 1166
Harry and Helen Sands Charitable Trust Grants, 1181
Harry and Jeanette Weinberg Fdn Grants, 1182
Harry Frank Guggenheim Foundation Research Grants, 1184
Hasbro Children's Fund Grants, 1189
Hattie Mae Lesley Foundation Grants, 1195
Hawai'i Community Foundation Children's Trust Fund Community Awareness: Child Abuse and Neglect Prevention Grants, 1198
Hawai'i Community Foundation Family Literacy and Hawaii Pizza Hut Literacy Grants, 1201
Hawai'i Community Foundation Kuki'o Community Fund Grants, 1202
Hawai'i Community Foundation Victoria S. and Bradley L. Geist Foundation: Capacity Building Grants, 1206
Hawaiian Electric Industries Charitable Foundation Grants, 1211
Hawaii Community Foundation Oscar and Rosetta Fish Fund Grants, 1214
Hawaii Electric Industries Charitable Foundation Grants, 1218
Helen Bader Foundation Grants, 1227
Help America Foundation Grants, 1233
Herman P. and Sophia Taubman Fdn Grants, 1247
Hillsdale County Community Foundation General Grants, 1250
HLTA Visitor Industry Charity Walk Grant, 1254
HSBC Corporate Giving Grants, 1266
Initiative Foundation Innovation Fund Grants, 1304
Inland Empire Community Foundation Capacity Building for IE Nonprofits Grants, 1306
Island Insurance Foundation Grants, 1316
IYI Responsible Fatherhood Grants, 1318
J. Watumull Fund Grants, 1326
Jack Kent Cooke Fdn Good Neighbor Grants, 1331
Jacob G. Schmidlapp Trusts Grants, 1336
James and Abigail Campbell Family Foundation Grants, 1337
Jane Bradley Pettit Foundation Community and Social Development Grants, 1347
Jim Moran Foundation Grants, 1366
Joseph H. and Florence A. Roblee Foundation Family Grants, 1387
Joseph Henry Edmondson Foundation Grants, 1388
Joseph S. Stackpole Charitable Trust Grants, 1390
Judy and Peter Blum Kovler Foundation Grants, 1396
Kalamazoo Community Foundation Individuals and Families Grants, 1409
Kalamazoo Community Foundation LBGT Equality Fund Grants, 1411
Kansas Health Foundation Recognition Grants, 1415
Kawabe Memorial Fund Grants, 1423
Kenai Peninsula Foundation Grants, 1425
Ketchikan Community Foundation Grants, 1429
Kimball International-Habig Foundation Health and Human Services Grants, 1434
Knox County Community Foundation Youth Development Grants, 1443
Lands' End Corporate Giving Program, 1468
Latkin Charitable Foundation Grants, 1469
Leo Niessen Jr., Charitable Trust Grants, 1484
LGA Family Foundation Grants, 1487
Linden Foundation Grants, 1494
Locations Foundation Legacy Grants, 1504

Lotus 88 Foundation for Women and Children Grants, 1508
Madison Community Foundation Fund for Children Grants, 1534
Maggie Welby Foundation Grants, 1538
Margaret M. Walker Charitable Fdn Grants, 1556
Margaret T. Morris Foundation Grants, 1557
Marie C. and Joseph C. Wilson Foundation Rochester Small Grants, 1559
Marsh Corporate Grants, 1580
Mary Owen Borden Foundation Grants, 1597
Mervin Bovaird Foundation Grants, 1643
MFRI Community Mobilization Grants, 1654
Milton Hicks Wood and Helen Gibbs Wood Charitable Trust Grants, 1676
Mimi and Peter Haas Fund Grants, 1677
Montana Community Foundation Big Sky LIFT Grants, 1686
Montgomery County Community Foundation Youth Services Grants, 1691
Moran Family Foundation Grants, 1693
Moses Kimball Fund Grants, 1701
Nationwide Insurance Foundation Grants, 1726
Northland Foundation Grants, 1771
NZDIA Community Org Grants Scheme, 1796
Ohio County Community Foundation Grants, 1812
Ohio County Community Fdn Mini-Grants, 1813
Ordean Foundation Catalyst Grants, 1830
Ordean Foundation Partnership Grants, 1831
Parkersburg Area Community Foundation Action Grants, 1871
Perpetual Benevolent Fund, 1940
Perry County Community Foundation Youth Development Grants, 1943
Peter and Elizabeth C. Tower Foundation Small Grants, 1947
Petersburg Community Foundation Grants, 1951
Pettus Foundation Grants, 1952
PGE Foundation Grants, 1958
Philip Boyle Foundation Grants, 1961
Phoenix Suns Charities Grants, 1964
Pike County Community Foundation Youth Development Grants, 1971
Pinnacle Foundation Grants, 1973
Piper Jaffray Foundation Communities Giving Grants, 1974
Piper Trust Education Grants, 1977
Pittsburgh Fdn Affordable Housing Grants, 1980
Pittsburgh Foundation Healthy Children and Adults Grants, 1981
PNC Foundation Education Grants, 1985
Portland General Electric Foundation Grants, 2007
Posey Community Foundation Women's Fund Grants, 2008
Posey County Community Foundation Youth Development Grants, 2010
Pride Foundation Grants, 2024
ProLiteracy National Book Fund Grants, 2026
PSEG Corporate Contributions Grants, 2030
Radcliffe Institute Carol K. Pforzheimer Student Fellowships, 2048
Ralph M. Parsons Foundation Grants, 2052
Riedman Foundation Grants, 2076
Robbins Charitable Foundation Grants, 2081
Robbins Family Charitable Foundation Grants, 2082
Robert Bowne Foundaion Edmund A. Stanley, Jr. Research Grants, 2086
Robert Bowne Foundation Fellowships, 2087
Robert Bowne Foundation Literacy Grants, 2088
Robert Bowne Fdn Youth-Centered Grants, 2089
Robert F. Lange Foundation Grants, 2090
Rose Community Foundation Child and Family Development Grants, 2103
Sabina Dolan and Gladys Saulsbury Foundation Grants, 2130
Saginaw Community Foundation YWCA Fund for Women and Girls Grants, 2135
Samueli Foundation Education Grants, 2143
Sand Hill Foundation Health and Opportunity Grants, 2153

SanDisk Corp Community Sharing Grants, 2155
Sarkeys Foundation Grants, 2163
Scott County Community Foundation Grants, 2170
Seattle Foundation Benjamin N. Phillips Memorial
    Fund Grants, 2176
Sensient Technologies Foundation Grants, 2180
Shopko Fdn Community Charitable Grants, 2191
Singing for Change Foundation Grants, 2202
Smith Richardson Fdn Direct Service Grants, 2210
Sobrato Family Foundation Grants, 2211
Sobrato Family Fdn Meeting Space Grants, 2212
Sobrato Family Foundation Office Space Grants, 2213
Sorenson Legacy Foundation Grants, 2217
Spencer County Community Foundation Women's
    Fund Grants, 2232
Spencer County Community Foundation Youth
    Development Grants, 2233
Starr Foundation Grants, 2237
Steven B. Achelis Foundation Grants, 2244
Stinson Foundation Grants, 2246
Susan A. and Donald P. Babson Charitable
    Foundation Grants, 2259
Sylvia Perkin Perpetual Charitable Trust Grants, 2263
Target Corporation Community Engagement Fund
    Grants, 2270
TJX Foundation Grants, 2303
Toyota Motor Manufacturing of Indiana Grants, 2310
Toyota Motor Manuf of Kentucky Grants, 2311
Toyota Technical Center Grants, 2317
Turner Foundation Grants, 2326
University of Chicago Chapin Hall Doris Duke
    Fellowships, 2348
Valley-Wide Health Systems Nurse Family
    Partnerships, 2372
Vanderburgh Community Foundation Men's Fund
    Grants, 2373
Vanderburgh Community Foundation Youth
    Development Grants, 2375
Vanderburgh County Community Foundation
    Women's Fund Grants, 2376
Victoria S. and Bradley L. Geist Foundation Grants
    Supporting Foster Care and Their Caregivers, 2382
Volkswagen Group of America Corporate
    Contributions Grants, 2389
VSA International Art Program for Children with
    Disabilities Grants, 2394
Wallace Foundation Grants, 2402
Warrick County Community Foundation Youth
    Development Grants, 2412
Welborn Foundation Promotion of Healthy
    Adolescent Development Grants, 2425
Westerman Foundation Grants, 2427
Weyerhaeuser Family Fdn Health Grants, 2435
Whitehorse Foundation Grants, 2439
Whole Foods Foundation, 2445
William G. Gilmore Foundation Grants, 2467
William J. and Dorothy K. O'Neill Foundation
    Responsive Grants, 2468
Wilton and Effie Hebert Foundation Grants, 2476
WinnCompanies Charitable Giving, 2479
Wold Foundation Grants, 2482
Youths' Friends Association Grants, 2511
Zane's Foundation Grants, 2524

Family Planning
ACF Promoting Safe and Stable Families (PSSF)
    Program Grants, 89
Albert W. Cherne Foundation Grants, 222
Bushrod H. Campbell and Adah F. Hall Charity
    Fund Grants, 486
Clayton Fund Grants, 631
David Robinson Foundation Grants, 791
J.W. Kieckhefer Foundation Grants, 1324
James Ford Bell Foundation Grants, 1339
Joseph H. and Florence A. Roblee Foundation Family
    Grants, 1387
Klingenstein-Simons Fellowship Awards in the
    Neurosciences, 1441
Mary Owen Borden Foundation Grants, 1597
Oppenstein Brothers Foundation Grants, 1827

Perkins Charitable Foundation Grants, 1939
Portland Fdn - Women's Giving Circle Grant, 2006
Rose Community Foundation Child and Family
    Development Grants, 2103
Samuel S. Johnson Foundation Grants, 2146
Stella and Charles Guttman Foundation Grants, 2241
Valley-Wide Health Systems Nurse Family
    Partnerships, 2372
Widgeon Point Charitable Foundation Grants, 2447

Family Practice
IYI Responsible Fatherhood Grants, 1318

Family/Marriage Counseling
ACF Family Strengthening Scholars Grants, 81
ACF Marriage Strengthening Research &
    Dissemination Center Grants, 85
Adams Family Foundation of Tennessee Grants, 120
Amelia Sillman Rockwell and Carlos Perry Rockwell
    Charities Fund Grants, 250
Charles H. Pearson Foundation Grants, 566
CJ Fdn for SIDS Program Services Grants, 619
Decatur County Community Foundation Small
    Project Grants, 812
Gulf Coast Foundation of Community Operating
    Grants, 1134
Gulf Coast Foundation of Community Program
    Grants, 1135
Hattie Mae Lesley Foundation Grants, 1195
Joseph H. and Florence A. Roblee Foundation Family
    Grants, 1387
Kimball International-Habig Foundation Health and
    Human Services Grants, 1434
Robert R. McCormick Tribune Foundation
    Community Grants, 2093

Farm and Ranch Management
Bill and Melinda Gates Foundation Agricultural
    Development Grants, 425

Farming
Bill and Melinda Gates Foundation Agricultural
    Development Grants, 425
Merck Family Fund Urban Farming and Youth
    Leadership Grants, 1635
Monsanto United States Grants, 1684
Union Bank, N.A. Foundation Grants, 2334

Fellowship Programs, General
A-T Children's Project Post Doctoral Fellowships, 17
AACAP Jeanne Spurlock Research Fellowship in
    Substance Abuse and Addiction for Minority
    Medical Students, 28
AACAP Life Members Mentorship Grants for
    Medical Students, 30
AACAP Summer Medical Student Fellowships, 38
ALA Louise Seaman Bechtel Fellowship, 173
AOCS Thomas H. Smouse Memorial Fellowship, 282
Edward W. and Stella C. Van Houten Memorial Fund
    Grants, 892
Eva Gunther Foundation Fellowships, 937
FCD Young Scholars Program Grants, 953
Kennedy Center National Symphony Orchestra Youth
    Fellowships, 1426
Lubrizol Foundation Grants, 1513
Mericos Foundation Grants, 1637
Phil Hardin Foundation Grants, 1960
Radcliffe Institute Carol K. Pforzheimer Student
    Fellowships, 2048
Sand Hill Foundation Health and Opportunity
    Grants, 2153
Special Olympics Eunice Kennedy Shriver (EKS)
    Fellowships, 2227

Feminism
ALA Amelia Bloomer Book List Award, 156
ALFJ International Fund Grants, 231

Fencing
Perkin Fund Grants, 1937

Fiction
ALA Booklist Editors' Choice Books for Youth
    Awards, 162
ALA Schneider Family Book Awards, 191
National Cowboy and Western Heritage Museum
    Awards, 1722
PCA Arts Organizations and Arts Programs Grants
    for Literature, 1894
PCA Entry Track Arts Organizations and Arts
    Programs Grants for Literature, 1906
PCA Strategies for Success Grants - Adv Level, 1917
PCA Strategies for Success Grants - Basic Level, 1918
PCA Strategies for Success Grants - Intermediate
    Level, 1919
VSA Playwright Discovery Award, 2396

Film Libraries
ALA Fabulous Films for Young Adults Award, 169

Film Production
ALA Fabulous Films for Young Adults Award, 169
Daniel and Nanna Stern Family Fdn Grants, 778
National Cowboy and Western Heritage Museum
    Awards, 1722
NYSCA Electronic Media and Film: General
    Operating Support, 1786
NYSCA Electronic Media and Film: General
    Program Support, 1787
NYSCA Electronic Media and Film: Screenings
    Grants, 1788
NYSCA Electronic Media and Film: Workspace
    Grants, 1789
PCA Arts Organizations and Arts Programs Grants
    for Film and Electronic Media, 1893
PCA Entry Track Arts Orgs and Arts Programs
    Grants for Film and Electronic Media, 1905

Films
ALA Fabulous Films for Young Adults Award, 169
Blockbuster Corporate Contributions, 440
Community Foundation of Greater Greensboro
    Community Grants, 708
Daniel and Nanna Stern Family Fdn Grants, 778
Newfoundland and Labrador Arts Council ArtSmarts
    Grants, 1744
Newfoundland and Labrador Arts Council School
    Touring Grants, 1745
NYSCA Electronic Media and Film: Film Festivals
    Grants, 1785
NYSCA Electronic Media and Film: General
    Operating Support, 1786
NYSCA Electronic Media and Film: General
    Program Support, 1787
NYSCA Electronic Media and Film: Screenings
    Grants, 1788
NYSCA Electronic Media and Film: Workspace
    Grants, 1789

Finance
Colgate-Palmolive Company Grants, 652
Do Something Finance and Human Res Intern, 853
FINRA Smart Investing@Your Library Grants, 963
Social Justice Fund Northwest Criminal Justice
    Giving Project Grants, 2214

Financial Aid (Scholarships and Loans)
ALA Bound to Stay Bound Books Scholarships, 163
Alexander Graham Bell Parent and Infant Financial
    Aid Grants, 227
Alexander Graham Bell Preschool-Age Financial Aid
    Grants, 228
American Express Charitable Fund Scholarships, 254
Arthur E. and Josephine Campbell Beyer Foundation
    Grants, 303
Baltimore Ravens Foundation Scholarships, 352
Barrasso, Usdin, Kupperman, Freeman, and Sarver
    Corporate Grants, 362
Do Something Scholarships, 857
Edward W. and Stella C. Van Houten Memorial Fund
    Grants, 892

Greygates Foundation Grants, 1120
IBCAT Nancy Jaynes Memorial Scholarship, 1281
IIE 911 Armed Forces Scholarships, 1288
James K. and Arlene L. Adams Foundation
　　Scholarships, 1341
Lloyd G. Balfour Foundation Scholarships, 1503
Maggie Welby Foundation Scholarships, 1539
Marathon Petroleum Corporation Grants, 1551
PAS John E. Grimes Timpani Scholarship, 1873
PAS Sabian Larrie London Memorial Schol, 1877
Posse Foundation Scholarships, 2011
Presidio Fencing Club Youth Fencers Assistance
　　Scholarships, 2019
United Friends of the Children Scholarships, 2341
W.P. and Bulah Luse Foundation Grants, 2399

Financial Education

Arizona Foundation for Women Deborah G. Carstens
　　Fund Grants, 293
Bank of Hawaii Foundation Grants, 360
Essex County Community Foundation Women's
　　Fund Grants, 934
FINRA Smart Investing@Your Library Grants, 963
Hawai'i Community Foundation Bernice and Conrad
　　von Hamm Fund Grants, 1197
ING Foundation Grants, 1302
Jack Kent Cooke Fdn Good Neighbor Grants, 1331
Johnson Scholarship Foundation Grants, 1382
Joseph S. Stackpole Charitable Trust Grants, 1390
McCune Charitable Foundation Grants, 1617
McGraw-Hill Companies Community Grants, 1620
Montana Community Fdn Women's Grants, 1688
NZDIA Lottery Minister's Discretionary Fund
　　Grants, 1797
State Farm Good Neighbor Citizenship Company
　　Grants, 2238
Target Foundation Global Grants, 2272

Financial Literacy

Arizona Foundation for Women Deborah G. Carstens
　　Fund Grants, 293
Bank of Hawaii Foundation Grants, 360
Benton Community Foundation - The Cookie Jar
　　Grant, 404
CNCS AmeriCorps State and National Grants, 643
CNCS AmeriCorps VISTA Project Grants, 645
Daniels Fund Youth Development Grants, 784
FINRA Smart Investing@Your Library Grants, 963
GNOF Coastal 5 + 1 Grants, 1078
Hearst Foundations Social Service Grants, 1224
HSBC Corporate Giving Grants, 1266
Johnson Scholarship Foundation Grants, 1382
Joseph S. Stackpole Charitable Trust Grants, 1390
LISC Capacity Building Grants, 1498
Maine Women's Fund Econ Security Grants, 1546
Marin Community Foundation Ending the Cycle of
　　Poverty Grants, 1565
McGraw-Hill Companies Community Grants, 1620
Medtronic Foundation Community Link Human
　　Services Grants, 1631
Middlesex Savings Charitable Foundation
　　Educational Opportunities Grants, 1670
NZDIA Lottery Minister's Discretionary Fund
　　Grants, 1797
Robin Hood Foundation Grants, 2096
Sand Hill Foundation Health and Opportunity
　　Grants, 2153
Union Bank, N.A. Foundation Grants, 2334

Fine Arts

Abell-Hanger Foundation Grants, 52
Achelis and Bodman Foundation Grants, 101
Achelis Foundation Grants, 102
Alliant Energy Foundation Community Giving for
　　Good Sponsorship Grants, 240
Atwood Foundation General Grants, 330
Charles H. Hall Foundation, 565
CICF Clare Noyes Grant, 604
Claremont Community Foundation Grants, 622
Claremont Savings Bank Foundation Grants, 623

Community Foundation of Muncie and Delaware
　　County - Kitselman Grants, 733
Crystelle Waggoner Charitable Trust Grants, 768
E.L. Wiegand Foundation Grants, 877
Elizabeth Morse Genius Charitable Trust Grants, 901
Fichtenbaum Charitable Trust Grants, 955
George A. & Grace L. Long Fdn Grants, 1041
George H.C. Ensworth Memorial Fund Grants, 1049
HAF Joe Alexandre Mem Family Fund Grants, 1145
HAF Laurence and Elaine Allen Memorial Fund
　　Grants, 1146
Hahl Proctor Charitable Trust Grants, 1151
Helen Gertrude Sparks Charitable Trust Grants, 1230
Henrietta Lange Burk Fund Grants, 1235
Hillsdale County Community Foundation General
　　Grants, 1250
Jerry L. and Barbara J. Burris Fdn Grants, 1362
Katrine Menzing Deakins Chartbl Trust Grants, 1422
Lewis H. Humphreys Charitable Trust Grants, 1486
Lied Foundation Trust Grants, 1490
Lumpkin Family Fdn Healthy People Grants, 1518
Marcia and Otto Koehler Foundation Grants, 1553
Marietta McNeill Morgan and Samuel Tate Morgan
　　Jr. Trust Grants, 1560
Marion Gardner Jackson Charitable Trust Grts, 1570
NYSCA Arts Education: Community-based
　　Learning Grants, 1780
NYSCA Arts Education: General Operating Support
　　Grants, 1781
NYSCA Arts Education: General Program Support
　　Grants, 1782
NYSCA Arts Ed: Services to the Field Grants, 1784
PCA-PCD Professional Development for Individual
　　Artists Grants, 1883
PCA Busing Grants, 1899
PCA Pennsylvania Partners in the Arts Program
　　Stream Grants, 1914
PCA Pennsylvania Partners in the Arts Project
　　Stream Grants, 1915
PCA Strategies for Success Grants - Basic Level, 1918
PCA Strategies for Success Grants - Intermediate
　　Level, 1919
PennPAT Artist Technical Assistance Grants, 1929
PennPAT Strategic Opportunity Grants, 1933
Phoenix Coyotes Charities Grants, 1963
Porter County Community Foundation Sparking the
　　Arts Fund Grants, 2004
Puerto Rico Community Foundation Grants, 2037
R.C. Baker Foundation Grants, 2043
Robert R. Meyer Foundation Grants, 2094
Stinson Foundation Grants, 2246
Storm Castle Foundation Grants, 2248
VSA/Volkswagen Group of America Exhibition
　　Awards, 2393

Fire Prevention

100 Club of Arizona Financial Assistance Grants, 9
100 Club of Dubuque, 10
Clark Electric Cooperative Grants, 627
NZDIA Lottery Minister's Discretionary Fund
　　Grants, 1797
RCF General Community Grants, 2062

Firearms

NRA Foundation Grants, 1774

Fish and Fisheries

First Nations Development Institute Native
　　Agriculture and Food Systems Initiative
　　Scholarships, 971
GNOF Bayou Communities Grants, 1077
GNOF Coastal 5 + 1 Grants, 1078
GNOF Plaquemines Community Grants, 1091

Fishing

GNOF Bayou Communities Grants, 1077
Oren Campbell McCleary Chartbl Trust Grants, 1837

Fitness

ACF Social and Economic Development Strategies
　　Grants, 93
Baltimore Ravens Foundation Play 60 Grants, 351
Boeing Company Contributions Grants, 462
Collective Brands Foundation Grants, 654
Collective Brands Foundation Saucony Run for Good
　　Grants, 656
Foundation for a Healthy Kentucky Grants, 988
GNOF IMPACT Kahn-Oppenheim Tr Grts, 1087
Mary Black Foundation Active Living Grants, 1585
Medtronic Foundation CommunityLink Health
　　Grants, 1630
PepsiCo Foundation Grants, 1935
RCF Summertime Kids Grants, 2064
Robert R. Meyer Foundation Grants, 2094
Special Olympics Project UNIFY Grants, 2228
WSF GoGirlGo! New York Grants, 2494

Florida

AGFT A Gift for Music Grants, 138

Folk Medicine

Virginia Foundation for the Humanities Folklife
　　Apprenticeships, 2386
Virginia Foundation for the Humanities Open
　　Grants, 2387

Folk Music

NJSCA Arts Ed Special Initiative Grants, 1764
PennPAT Strategic Opportunity Grants, 1933
Virginia Foundation for the Humanities Folklife
　　Apprenticeships, 2386
Virginia Foundation for the Humanities Open
　　Grants, 2387
VSA International Young Soloists Award, 2395

Folk/Ethnic Arts

First Nations Development Institute Native Arts
　　Initiative Grants, 972
George J. and Effie L. Seay Foundation Grants, 1052
Maryland State Arts Council Arts in Communities
　　Grants, 1592
Montana Arts Council Cultural and Aesthetic Project
　　Grants, 1685
NHSCA Artist Residence Grants, 1756
NHSCA Youth Arts Project Grants: For Extended
　　Arts Learning, 1758
NJSCA Artists in Education Residencies, 1763
NJSCA Arts Ed Special Initiative Grants, 1764
NYSCA Special Arts Services: General Program
　　Support Grants, 1793
NYSCA Special Arts Services: Instruction and
　　Training Grants, 1794
PCA-PCD Professional Development for Individual
　　Artists Grants, 1883
PCA Arts in Education Residencies, 1885
PCA Arts Organizations and Arts Programs Grants
　　for Arts Service Organizations, 1890
PCA Arts Organizations and Arts Programs Grants
　　for Traditional and Folk Arts, 1897
PCA Busing Grants, 1899
PCA Entry Track Arts Organizations and Arts
　　Programs Grants for Arts Service Orgs, 1902
PCA Entry Track Arts Orgs and Arts Programs
　　Grants for Traditional and Folk Arts, 1911
PCA Pennsylvania Partners in the Arts Program
　　Stream Grants, 1914
PCA Pennsylvania Partners in the Arts Project
　　Stream Grants, 1915
PCA Professional Development Grants, 1916
PCA Strategies for Success Grants - Basic Level, 1918
PCA Strategies for Success Grants - Intermediate
　　Level, 1919
PennPAT Artist Technical Assistance Grants, 1929
PennPAT Strategic Opportunity Grants, 1933
Phoenix Coyotes Charities Grants, 1963
Porter County Community Foundation Sparking the
　　Arts Fund Grants, 2004
Shelley and Donald Rubin Foundation Grants, 2187

Southern New England Folk and Traditional Arts
  Apprenticeship Grants, 2224
TAC Arts Access Grant, 2265
Virginia Foundation for the Humanities Folklife
  Apprenticeships, 2386
Virginia Foundation for the Humanities Open
  Grants, 2387

Folklore and Mythology
Montana Arts Council Cultural and Aesthetic Project
  Grants, 1685
Virginia Foundation for the Humanities Open
  Grants, 2387

Food Banks
ACF Voluntary Agencies Matching Grants, 100
Adams Family Foundation of Tennessee Grants, 120
Akron Community Foundation Health and Human
  Services Grants, 152
Albert W. Rice Charitable Foundation Grants, 223
Alfred E. Chase Charitable Foundation Grants, 233
Alpha Natural Resources Corporate Giving, 246
Ann Ludington Sullivan Foundation Grants, 279
Arthur Ashley Williams Foundation Grants, 302
Back Home Again Foundation Grants, 344
Bank of America Charitable Foundation Basic Needs
  Grants, 354
Bank of Hawaii Foundation Grants, 360
C.H. Robinson Worldwide Foundation Grants, 489
Caesars Foundation Grants, 492
Camille Beckman Foundation Grants, 499
Campbell Soup Foundation Grants, 501
Carl M. Freeman Foundation FACES Grants, 507
Carrie S. Orleans Trust Grants, 512
CFFVR Jewelers Mutual Chartbl Giving Grants, 543
Charles H. Pearson Foundation Grants, 566
Charles Nelson Robinson Fund Grants, 569
Clark Electric Cooperative Grants, 627
Cleveland Foundation Higley Fund Grants, 634
Community Foundation for Greater Atlanta Frances
  Hollis Brain Foundation Fund Grants, 664
Community Foundation for Greater Atlanta Spark
  Clayton Grants, 667
Community Foundation for Greater Atlanta Spark
  Newton Grants, 668
Community Foundation of Crawford County, 695
Corina Higginson Trust Grants, 750
Covenant to Care for Children Crisis Food Pantry
  Giving, 756
Doree Taylor Charitable Foundation Grants, 843
Dr. and Mrs. Paul Pierce Memorial Foundation
  Grants, 862
Frank Reed and Margaret Jane Peters Memorial Fund
  II Grants, 1014
George H. Sandy Foundation Grants, 1050
George W. Wells Foundation Grants, 1057
Giving Gardens Challenge Grants, 1072
GTRCF Elk Rapids Area Community Endowment
  Grants, 1127
Harold Brooks Foundation Grants, 1172
Hearst Foundations Social Service Grants, 1224
Helen Gertrude Sparks Charitable Trust Grants, 1230
Janson Foundation Grants, 1349
Kathryne Beynon Foundation Grants, 1420
Kenneth T. and Eileen L. Norris Fdn Grants, 1427
Land O'Lakes Foundation Community Grants, 1466
Marsh Corporate Grants, 1580
Mary Cofer Trigg Trust Fund Grants, 1587
Maurice J. Masserini Charitable Trust Grants, 1610
McCarthy Family Fdn Charity Fund Grants, 1614
McGregor Fund Human Services Grants, 1621
Merck Family Fund Urban Farming and Youth
  Leadership Grants, 1635
Middlesex Savings Charitable Foundation Basic
  Human Needs Grants, 1668
Monsanto United States Grants, 1684
Olga Sipolin Children's Fund Grants, 1815
Ordean Foundation Catalyst Grants, 1830
Ordean Foundation Partnership Grants, 1831
Packard Foundation Local Grants, 1863

Perpetual Benevolent Fund, 1940
Pinnacle Entertainment Foundation Grants, 1972
Reinberger Foundation Grants, 2066
Richard and Caroline T. Gwathmey Memorial Trust
  Grants, 2069
Samuel S. Johnson Foundation Grants, 2146
Sarah G. McCarthy Memorial Foundation, 2162
Shield-Ayres Foundation Grants, 2189
Sierra Health Foundation Responsive Grants, 2199
Skaggs Family Foundation Grants, 2205
Skaggs Family Foundation Grants, 2206
Sobrato Family Foundation Grants, 2211
Sobrato Family Fdn Meeting Space Grants, 2212
Sobrato Family Foundation Office Space Grants, 2213
Swindells Charitable Foundation Grants, 2261
Textron Corporate Contributions Grants, 2286
USAID Office of Foreign Disaster Assistance and
  Food for Peace Grants, 2359
William Blair and Company Foundation Grants, 2461
Wood-Claeyssens Foundation Grants, 2486

Food Consumption
Aetna Foundation Regional Health Grants, 134
USAID Innovations in Feed the Future Monitoring
  and Evaluation Grants, 2355
Windham Foundation Grants, 2477

Food Distribution
Akron Community Foundation Health and Human
  Services Grants, 152
Alaska Conservation Fdn Youth Mini Grants, 210
Albertsons Companies Foundation Nourishing
  Neighbors Grants, 221
Albert W. Rice Charitable Foundation Grants, 223
Annie Gardner Foundation Grants, 277
Bank of America Charitable Foundation Basic Needs
  Grants, 354
Bay Area Community Foundation Elizabeth Husband
  Fund Grants, 378
Benton Community Foundation Grants, 405
Blue River Community Foundation Grants, 458
Brown County Community Foundation Grants, 475
Caesars Foundation Grants, 492
Carrie S. Orleans Trust Grants, 512
Charles H. Pearson Foundation Grants, 566
Christine and Katharina Pauly Charitable Trust
  Grants, 601
Cisco Systems Foundation San Jose Community
  Grants, 615
Community Foundation of Bartholomew County
  Heritage Fund Grants, 690
Community Foundation of Bartholomew County
  James A. Henderson Award for Fundraising, 691
Community Foundation of Greater Fort Wayne -
  Community Endowment and Clarke Endowment
  Grants, 705
Covenant to Care for Children Crisis Food Pantry
  Giving, 756
Florence Hunt Maxwell Foundation Grants, 979
Frank Reed and Margaret Jane Peters Memorial Fund
  II Grants, 1014
George W. Wells Foundation Grants, 1057
Giant Food Charitable Grants, 1068
Harry and Jeanette Weinberg Fdn Grants, 1182
Harvey E. Najim Family Foundation Grants, 1187
Helen Gertrude Sparks Charitable Trust Grants, 1230
Horace A. Moses Charitable Trust Grants, 1261
Land O'Lakes Foundation Community Grants, 1466
Marsh Corporate Grants, 1580
McCarthy Family Fdn Charity Fund Grants, 1614
Merck Family Fund Urban Farming and Youth
  Leadership Grants, 1635
Olga Sipolin Children's Fund Grants, 1815
OneFamily Foundation Grants, 1822
PepsiCo Foundation Grants, 1935
Perpetual Benevolent Fund, 1940
Robert R. Meyer Foundation Grants, 2094
Sarah G. McCarthy Memorial Foundation, 2162
Sensient Technologies Foundation Grants, 2180
Share Our Strength Grants, 2185

Skaggs Family Foundation Grants, 2206
Skaggs Family Foundation Grants, 2205
USAID Innovations in Feed the Future Monitoring
  and Evaluation Grants, 2355
USAID Office of Foreign Disaster Assistance and
  Food for Peace Grants, 2359
USDA Child and Adult Care Food Program, 2362
W.W. Smith Chartbl Trust Basic Needs Grants, 2400

Food Engineering
First Nations Development Institute Native
  Agriculture and Food Systems Initiative
  Scholarships, 971

Food Management
Adolph Coors Foundation Grants, 129
USAID Innovations in Feed the Future Monitoring
  and Evaluation Grants, 2355
Windham Foundation Grants, 2477

Food Preparation
Daniels Homeless and Disadvantaged Grants, 782

Food Production
First Nations Development Institute Native
  Agriculture and Food Systems Initiative
  Scholarships, 971
Giving Gardens Challenge Grants, 1072
USAID Innovations in Feed the Future Monitoring
  and Evaluation Grants, 2355
USAID Office of Foreign Disaster Assistance and
  Food for Peace Grants, 2359

Food Safety
Aetna Foundation Regional Health Grants, 134
Dean Foods Community Involvement Grants, 805
First Nations Development Institute Native
  Agriculture and Food Systems Initiative
  Scholarships, 971
Oren Campbell McCleary Chartbl Trust Grants, 1837
PepsiCo Foundation Grants, 1935
Windham Foundation Grants, 2477

Food Sciences
First Nations Development Institute Native
  Agriculture and Food Systems Initiative
  Scholarships, 971
Ifuku Family Foundation Grants, 1287

Food Service Industry
Circle K Corporation Contributions Grants, 614
Clark Electric Cooperative Grants, 627

Food Technology
USAID Innovations in Feed the Future Monitoring
  and Evaluation Grants, 2355
Windham Foundation Grants, 2477

Foods
Akron Community Foundation Health and Human
  Services Grants, 152
Camille Beckman Foundation Grants, 499
Cleveland Foundation Higley Fund Grants, 634
Columbus Foundation Traditional Grants, 663
Covenant to Care for Children Crisis Food Pantry
  Giving, 756
Dean Foods Community Involvement Grants, 805
Essex County Community Foundation Merrimack
  Valley Municipal Business Development and
  Recovery Fund Grants, 933
Ifuku Family Foundation Grants, 1287
Marriott Int Corporate Giving Grants, 1578
Whole Foods Foundation, 2445

Football
Alaska Community Foundation Jack and Nona Renn
  Anchorage Football Fund, 204
Anthony Munoz Foundation Straight A Student
  Campaign Grants, 280

Arthur M. Blank Family Foundation Atlanta Falcons
   Youth Foundation Grants, 307
Baltimore Ravens Corporate Giving, 350
Baltimore Ravens Fdn Youth Football Grants, 353
Calvin Johnson Jr. Foundation Mini Grants, 498

Foreign Languages
ALA Mildred L. Batchelder Award, 178
Japan Foundation Los Angeles Contests Designed for
   Japanese-Language Learners Grants, 1351
Japan Foundation Los Angeles Grants for Japanese-
   Language Courses, 1352
Japan Foundation Los Angeles Japanese-Language
   Teaching Materials Purchase Grants, 1353

Foreign Languages Education
Alavi Foundation Education Grants, 216
Japan Foundation Los Angeles Contests Designed for
   Japanese-Language Learners Grants, 1351
Japan Foundation Los Angeles Grants for Japanese-
   Language Courses, 1352
Japan Foundation Los Angeles Japanese-Language
   Teaching Materials Purchase Grants, 1353

Forest Ecology
GNOF Plaquemines Community Grants, 1091

Forestry
Oren Campbell McCleary Chartbl Trust Grants, 1837
USAID Global Development Alliance Grants, 2354

Forestry Management
Mary A. Crocker Trust Grants, 1584

Forests and Woodlands
Callaway Foundation Grants, 496

Fossil Fuels
William and Flora Hewlett Foundation
   Environmental Grants, 2455

Fossil Fuels, Petroleum
GNOF Coastal 5 + 1 Grants, 1078

Foster Care
ABC Charities Grants, 50
ACF Child Abuse Prevention and Treatment Act
   Discretionary Funds Grants, 74
ACF Infant Adoption Awareness Training Program
   Grants, 84
Allan C. and Lelia J. Garden Foundation Grants, 236
Brookdale Fdn Relatives as Parents Grants, 474
CNCS Foster Grandparent Projects Grants, 646
Covenant for Children Critical Goods Grants, 757
Dyson Foundation Mid-Hudson Valley Project
   Support Grants, 874
Hawai'i Community Foundation Victoria S. and
   Bradley L. Geist Foundation: Capacity Building
   Grants, 1206
Hawai'i Community Foundation Victoria S. and
   Bradley L. Geist Foundation: Enhancement
   Grants, 1207
Hawai'i Community Foundation Victoria S. and
   Bradley L. Geist Foundation: Supporting Foster
   Children and Their Caregivers, 1208
Hawai'i Community Foundation Victoria S. and
   Bradley L. Geist Foundation: Supporting
   Transitioning Foster Youth Grants, 1209
Joseph H. and Florence A. Roblee Foundation
   Children and Youth Grants, 1385
Joseph H. and Florence A. Roblee Foundation Family
   Grants, 1387
Marion and Miriam Rose Fund Grants, 1569
Mockingbird Foundation Grants, 1680
Morris Stulsaft Foundation Educational Support for
   Children Grants, 1697
Parker Foundation (California) Grants, 1869
Peyton Anderson Foundation Grants, 1954
Samueli Foundation Youth Services Grants, 2144
United Friends of the Children Scholarships, 2341

Victoria S. and Bradley L. Geist Foundation
   Enhancement Grants, 2381
Victoria S. and Bradley L. Geist Foundation Grants
   Supporting Foster Care and Their Caregivers, 2382
Victoria S. and Bradley L. Geist Foundation Grants
   Supporting Transitioning Foster Youth, 2383

Fund-Raising
Ball Brothers Foundation Organizational
   Effectiveness/Executive Mentoring Grants, 346
GNOF Organizational Effectiveness Grants and
   Workshops, 1090
Goldseker Foundation Non-Profit Management
   Assistance Grants, 1095
Hattie Mae Lesley Foundation Grants, 1195
Meyer Foundation Benevon Grants, 1648
Middlesex Savings Charitable Foundation Capacity
   Building Grants, 1669
OtterCares NoCO Fund Grants, 1851
PCA Management/Techl Assistance Grants, 1913
PCA Strategies for Success Grants - Adv Level, 1917
Pohlad Family Fdn Large Capital Grants, 1990
Saint Louis Rams Foundation Community
   Donations, 2139
Social Justice Fund Northwest Criminal Justice
   Giving Project Grants, 2214
Victor E. Speas Foundation Grants, 2380

Gangs
Chicago Community Trust Arts and Culture Grants:
   Improving Access to Arts Learning, 581
New Jersey Office of Faith Based Initiatives Services
   to At Risk Youth Grants, 1752
Piedmont Natural Gas Foundation Health and
   Human Services Grants, 1968
Union Bank, N.A. Foundation Grants, 2334

Gardening
Giving Gardens Challenge Grants, 1072
Katie's Krops Grants, 1421
Robert R. Meyer Foundation Grants, 2094
Whole Foods Foundation, 2445
Whole Kids Foundation School Garden Grants, 2446

Gastroenterology
CFF First- and Second-Year Clinical Fellowships, 532

Gender
Radcliffe Institute Oral History Grants, 2049

Gender Equity
AAUW International Project Grants, 44
ATA Inclusive Learning Communities Grants, 323
Ben Cohen StandUp Foundation Grants, 403
Eileen Fisher Activating Leadership Grants for
   Women and Girls, 898
Essex County Community Foundation Women's
   Fund Grants, 934
Michigan Women Forward Grants, 1662
Ms. Fdn for Women Ending Violence Grants, 1708
Tides Fdn Friends of the IGF Fund Grants, 2300

Gender Studies
Radcliffe Institute Oral History Grants, 2049

Genetics
Dr. John T. Macdonald Foundation Grants, 863
HRAMF Charles H. Hood Foundation Child Health
   Research Awards, 1262
Libra Foundation Grants, 1489
Pediatric Cancer Research Foundation Grants, 1927

Genetics, Molecular
Pediatric Cancer Research Foundation Grants, 1927

Geography
Gray Family Foundation Geography Education
   Grants, 1106

Geography Education
Gray Family Foundation Geography Education
   Grants, 1106

Georgia
J. Knox Gholston Foundation Grants, 1321
J. William Gholston Foundation Grants, 1328
Perkins-Ponder Foundation Grants, 1938
Peyton Anderson Foundation Grants, 1954

Geriatrics
CFGR Jenkins Foundation Grants, 553
Ellen Abbott Gilman Trust Grants, 905
Mt. Sinai Health Care Foundation Health of the
   Jewish Community Grants, 1709
Nell J. Redfield Foundation Grants, 1737

Gifted/Talented Education
CEC Clarissa Hug Teacher of the Year Award, 527
CEC J.E. Wallace Wallin Special Education Lifetime
   Achievement Award, 528
Hattie M. Strong Foundation Grants, 1194
Hearst Foundations Culture Grants, 1223
J. Knox Gholston Foundation Grants, 1321
J. William Gholston Foundation Grants, 1328
Mary Wilmer Covey Charitable Trust Grants, 1600
Meyer Foundation Education Grants, 1649
Posse Foundation Scholarships, 2011

Girls
AAUW International Project Grants, 44
Arizona Foundation for Women Deborah G. Carstens
   Fund Grants, 293
Arizona Foundation for Women General Grants, 294
Benton Community Fdn Cookie Jar Grant, 404
Blossom Fund Grants, 441
CFNEM Women's Giving Circle Grants, 557
Charlotte R. Schmidlapp Fund Grants, 572
CICF Women's Grants , 609
Community Foundation of Eastern Connecticut
   Northeast Women and Girls Grants, 697
Community Foundation of Eastern Connecticut
   Norwich Women and Girls Grants, 698
Community Foundation of Eastern Connecticut
   Southeast Area Women and Girls Grants, 701
Community Foundation of Eastern Connecticut
   Windham Area Women and Girls Grants, 702
Community Foundation of Louisville Fund 4 Women
   and Girls Grants, 725
Dining for Women Grants, 831
Eileen Fisher Activating Leadership Grants for
   Women and Girls, 898
Eva Gunther Foundation Fellowships, 937
Foundation Beyond Belief Compassionate Impact
   Grants, 986
Foundation Beyond Belief Humanist Grants, 987
Frederick McDonald Trust Grants, 1017
Friends of Hawaii Charities Grants, 1024
Global Fund for Women Grants, 1073
Greater Tacoma Community Foundation Fund for
   Women and Girls Grants, 1112
Harmony Project Grants, 1170
Kirby Laing Foundation Grants, 1439
Maine Women's Fund Econ Security Grants, 1546
Maine Women's Fund Girls' Grantmaking Intv, 1547
Make Sense Foundation Grants, 1548
Michigan Women Forward Grants, 1662
Montana Community Fdn Women's Grants, 1688
Pacers Foundation Indiana Fever's Be YOUnique
   Fund Grants, 1860
RCF The Women's Fund Grants, 2065
Spencer County Community Foundation Women's
   Fund Grants, 2232
Tides Foundation Girl Rising Fund Grants, 2301
USAID Family Planning and Reproductive Health
   Methods Grants, 2353
Vanderburgh County Community Foundation
   Women's Fund Grants, 2376
Warrick County Community Foundation Women's
   Fund, 2411

Washington Area Women's Foundation African
   American Women's Giving Circle Grants, 2414
Washington Area Women's Foundation Rainmakers
   Giving Circle Grants, 2415
Women's Fund of Hawaii Grants, 2484
Women's Fund of Hawaii Grants, 2485
WSF GoGirlGo! New York Grants, 2494
WSF Rusty Kanokogi Fund for the Advancement of
   U.S. Judo Grants, 2495
WSF Sports 4 Life Grants, 2496
WSF Sports 4 Life Regional Grants, 2497

Glaucoma
GNOF IMPACT Gulf States Eye Surg Fund, 1085

Global Change
Bill and Melinda Gates Foundation Agricultural
   Development Grants, 425
Bill and Melinda Gates Foundation Emergency
   Response Grants, 426
Bill and Melinda Gates Foundation Policy and
   Advocacy Grants, 427
Bill and Melinda Gates Foundation Water, Sanitation
   and Hygiene Grants, 428
Target Foundation Global Grants, 2272
Tides Fdn Friends of the IGF Fund Grants, 2300

Global Issues
ATA Inclusive Learning Communities Grants, 323
Bill and Melinda Gates Foundation Agricultural
   Development Grants, 425
Bill and Melinda Gates Foundation Emergency
   Response Grants, 426
Bill and Melinda Gates Foundation Policy and
   Advocacy Grants, 427
Bill and Melinda Gates Foundation Water, Sanitation
   and Hygiene Grants, 428
Target Foundation Global Grants, 2272
Tides Fdn Friends of the IGF Fund Grants, 2300

Global Warming
PepsiCo Foundation Grants, 1935
Tides Fdn Friends of the IGF Fund Grants, 2300

Globalization
Boeing Company Contributions Grants, 462

Government
ACF Social and Economic Development Strategies
   Grants, 93
Anderson Foundation Grants, 271
AT&T Fdn Community Support and Safety, 320
Carnegie Corporation of New York Grants, 511
Chesapeake Bay Trust Mini Grants, 578
Community Memorial Foundation Responsive
   Grants, 743
Effie and Wofford Cain Foundation Grants, 895
Ford Foundation BUILD Grants, 984
Hatton W. Sumners Foundation for the Study and
   Teaching of Self Government Grants, 1196
Hearst Foundations United States Senate Youth
   Grants, 1225
Herbert Hoover Presidential Library Association Bus
   Travel Grants, 1244
Nathan Cummings Foundation Grants, 1718
RWJF Childhood Obesity Grants, 2126
Sapelo Foundation Social Justice Grants, 2160
USAID National Governance Project in Yemen
   Grant, 2357

Government Studies
Herbert Hoover Presidential Library Association Bus
   Travel Grants, 1244

Government, Federal
AACAP Mary Crosby Congressional Fellowships, 31
Herbert Hoover Presidential Library Association Bus
   Travel Grants, 1244
Ms. Foundation for Women Building Democracy
   Grants, 1706

Government, Local
Community Foundation of Greater Fort Wayne -
   John S. and James L. Knight Foundation Donor-
   Advised Grants, 707
Cone Health Foundation Grants, 745
Ford Foundation BUILD Grants, 984
HAF Community Grants, 1141
Ms. Foundation for Women Building Democracy
   Grants, 1706
Parke County Community Foundation Grants, 1868
PCA Arts Organizations and Arts Programs Grants
   for Local Arts, 1895
PCA Entry Track Arts Organizations and Arts
   Programs Grants for Local Arts, 1907

Government, Municipal
Bikes Belong Foundation REI Grants, 423
Bikes Belong Grants, 424
Community Foundation for the National Capital
   Region Community Leadership Grants, 688
Four County Community Foundation General
   Grants, 1000
Four County Community Foundation Healthy
   Senior/Healthy Youth Fund Grants, 1001
Widgeon Point Charitable Foundation Grants, 2447

Government, State
Cone Health Foundation Grants, 745
Ford Foundation BUILD Grants, 984
HAF Community Grants, 1141
Kentucky Arts Cncl Access Assistance Grants, 1428
Ms. Foundation for Women Building Democracy
   Grants, 1706

Governmental Functions
Fund for the City of New York Grants, 1029
GMFUS Balkan Trust for Democracy Grants, 1075
Ms. Foundation for Women Building Democracy
   Grants, 1706

Graduate Education
ALA Bound to Stay Bound Books Scholarships, 163
AOCS Thomas H. Smouse Memorial Fellowship, 282
ChLA Graduate Student Essay Awards, 594
Community Foundation for the Capital Region
   Grants, 687
Philip L. Graham Fund Education Grants, 1962

Graphic Design
PCA Arts Organizations and Arts Programs Grants
   for Visual Arts, 1898
PCA Entry Track Arts Organizations and Arts
   Programs Grants for Visual Arts, 1912

Grassroots Leadership
Baltimore Community Foundation Building Stronger
   Neighborhoods Regionwide Grants, 347
Bank of America Charitable Foundation Volunteer
   Grants, 358
Bernard and Audre Rapoport Foundation Community
   Building and Social Service Grants, 408
Bush Foundation Event Scholarships, 484
Community Foundation of Greater Fort Wayne -
   John S. and James L. Knight Foundation Donor-
   Advised Grants, 707
DTE Energy Foundation Leadership Grants, 870
Eileen Fisher Activating Leadership Grants for
   Women and Girls, 898
Eulalie Bloedel Schneider Foundation Grants, 936
Evelyn and Walter Haas, Jr. Fund Nonprofit
   Leadership Grants, 942
GMFUS Balkan Trust for Democracy Grants, 1075
GNOF Coastal 5 + 1 Grants, 1078
GNOF Stand Up For Our Children Grants, 1092
Great Clips Corporate Giving, 1108
Greater Tacoma Community Foundation Spark
   Grants, 1114
Kalamazoo Community Foundation Good Neighbor
   Grants, 1408
KIND Causes Monthly Grants, 1435

Kroger Company Donations, 1456
LISC Community Leadership Operating Grts, 1499
Lumpkin Family Foundation Strong Community
   Leadership Grants, 1519
Merck Family Fund Urban Farming and Youth
   Leadership Grants, 1635
Mertz Gilmore Foundation NYC Communities
   Grants, 1641
Mertz Gilmore Foundation NYC Dance Grants, 1642
Miller Foundation Grants, 1673
Norman Foundation Grants, 1767
OSF Baltimore Criminal and Juve Justice Grts, 1839
OSF Baltimore Education and Youth Development
   Grants, 1840
OSF Soros Justice Youth Activist Fellowships, 1844
OSF Young Feminist Leaders Fellowships, 1845
Paul and Edith Babson Foundation Grants, 1881
PDF Community Organizing Grants, 1920
Philanthrofund Foundation Grants, 1959
Robbins-de Beaumont Foundation Grants, 2080
Rosenberg Foundation Immigrant Rights and
   Integration Grants, 2108
Southwest Initiative Foundation Grants, 2226
Threshold Foundation Queer Youth Grants, 2299
United Methodist Committee on Relief Hunger and
   Poverty Grants, 2344
United Methodist Women Brighter Future for
   Children and Youth Grants, 2346

Grief
A Little Hope Grants, 235
Bollinger Foundation Grants, 463
CJ Fdn for SIDS Program Services Grants, 619
Robert R. Meyer Foundation Grants, 2094

Gun Control
Clayton Baker Trust Grants, 629

HIV
Abbott Fund Science Education Grants, 48
Community Foundation for the Capital Region
   Grants, 687
Community Foundation of Louisville AIDS Project
   Fund Grants, 716
Elton John AIDS Foundation Grants, 910
Firelight Foundation Grants, 964
HRSA Ryan White HIV AIDS Drug Assistance
   Grants, 1265

Habitat Preservation
George H.C. Ensworth Memorial Fund Grants, 1049
Greygates Foundation Grants, 1120
Helen E. Ellis Charitable Trust Grants, 1228
Japan Foundation New York World Heritage Photo
   Panel Exhibition, 1356
Sioux Falls Area Community Foundation Community
   Fund Grants, 2203
Sioux Falls Area Community Foundation Spot
   Grants, 2204
Union Bank, N.A. Foundation Grants, 2334
United Technologies Corporation Grants, 2347

Habitats
Illinois DNR School Habitat Action Grants, 1296
Illinois DNR Youth Recreation Corps Grants, 1297
National Wildlife Federation Craig Tufts Educational
   Scholarship, 1724
PG&E Community Vitality Grants, 1957

Hawaii
Ama OluKai Foundation Grants, 249
Antone and Edene Vidinha Charitable Grants, 281
Clarence T.C. Ching Foundation Grants, 624
Elsie H. Wilcox Foundation Grants, 909
Hawai'i Community Foundation Bernice and Conrad
   von Hamm Fund Grants, 1197
Hawai'i Community Foundation Richard Smart Fund
   Grants, 1204
Hawai'i SFCA Art Bento Program @ HiSAM
   Grants, 1210

Hawaii State Legislature Grant-In-Aid, 1219
OHA 'Ahahui Grants, 1807
OHA Community Grants for Culture, 1808
Ron and Sanne Higgins Family Fdn Grants, 2101

Hawaiian Natives
ACF Native American Social and Economic
    Development Strategies for Alaska Grants, 87
ACF Native Youth Initiative for Leadership,
    Empowerment, and Development Grants, 88
ACF Sustainable Employment and Economic
    Development Strategies Grants, 95
ACF Tribal Maternal, Infant, and Early Childhood
    Home Visiting Program: Development and
    Implementation Grants, 97
ACF Tribal Maternal, Infant, and Early Childhood
    Home Visiting Program: Implementation and
    Expansion Grants, 98
Ama OluKai Foundation Grants, 249
Antone and Edene Vidinha Charitable Grants, 281
Eide Bailly Resourcefullness Awards, 897
Hawai'i Community Foundation Richard Smart Fund
    Grants, 1204
HSFCA Folk and Traditional Arts Grants - Culture
    Learning, 1268
OHA 'Ahahui Grants, 1807
OHA Community Grants for Culture, 1808

Hazardous Waste
Honor the Earth Grants, 1259
Sioux Falls Area Community Foundation Community
    Fund Grants, 2203
Sioux Falls Area Community Foundation Spot
    Grants, 2204

Healing
HAF Mada Huggins Caldwell Fund Grants, 1147

Health
3M Company Fdn Community Giving Grants, 5
7-Eleven Corporate Giving Grants, 8
A.L. Spencer Foundation Grants, 21
Abundance Foundation International Grants, 57
ACCF of Indiana Anonymous Community
    Enrichment Fund Grants, 63
ACCF of Indiana Bank of Geneva Heritage Fund
    Grants, 64
ACCF of Indiana First Merchants Bank / Decatur
    Bank and Trust Fund Grants, 66
ACCF of Indiana Ron and Susie Ballard Community
    Enrichment Fund Grants, 68
Ackerman Foundation Grants, 103
ACL Neonatal Abstinence Syndrome National
    Training Initiative Grant, 106
Active Living Research Grants, 109
Adams and Reese Corporate Giving Grants, 114
Adams Family Fdn of Nora Springs Grants, 118
Advance Auto Parts Corporate Giving Grants, 131
AEGON Transamerica Foundation Health and
    Wellness Grants, 133
Aid for Starving Children Health and Nutrition
    Grants, 145
Alaska Community Foundation Petersburg
    Community Foundation Annual Grant, 207
Alaska Community Foundation Petersburg
    Community Foundation Mini-Grants, 208
Alaska Community Foundation Seward Community
    Foundation Grant, 209
Alaska Conservation Fdn Youth Mini Grants, 210
Allegis Group Foundation Grants, 237
American Electric Power Corporate Grants, 252
American Electric Power Foundation Grants, 253
Amica Insurance Company Sponsorships, 268
Amway Corporation Contributions, 269
Anne Arundel Women Giving Together Regular
    Grants, 275
Appalachian Regional Commission Health Care
    Grants, 288
Arthur M. Blank Family Foundation Inspiring Spaces
    Grants, 309

AT&T Foundation Health and Human Services
    Grants, 322
Avery-Fuller-Welch Children's Fdn Grants, 336
Back Home Again Foundation Grants, 344
Bank of Hawaii Foundation Grants, 360
Bay Area Community Foundation Arenac
    Community Fund Grants, 371
Bay Area Community Foundation Arenac County
    Healthy Youth/Healthy Seniors Fund Grants, 372
Bay Area Community Foundation Bay County
    Healthy Youth/Healthy Seniors Fund Grants, 374
Bay Area Community Foundation Nathalie Awrey
    Memorial Fund Grants, 381
Bernard and Audre Rapoport Foundation Health
    Grants, 411
Bierhaus Foundation Grants, 421
Blue Mountain Community Foundation Garfield
    County Health Foundation Fund Grants, 456
Bradley C. Higgins Foundation Grants, 467
Bright Promises Foundation Grants, 470
Brinker Int Corporation Charitable Giving, 471
C.H. Robinson Worldwide Foundation Grants, 489
Caesars Foundation Grants, 492
Castle Foundation Grants, 518
CFFVR Jewelers Mutual Chartbl Giving Grants, 543
CFFVR Project Grants, 546
CFF Winter Park Community Grants, 551
Chapman Charitable Foundation Grants, 560
Chapman Family Foundation, 562
Chilkat Valley Community Foundation Grants, 588
Cigna Civic Affairs Sponsorships, 610
Claremont Savings Bank Foundation Grants, 623
Cleveland Foundation Higley Fund Grants, 634
CNO Financial Group Community Grants, 650
Collective Brands Foundation Saucony Run for Good
    Grants, 656
Colorado Trust Health Investment Grants, 662
Community Foundation for Greater Buffalo Garman
    Family Foundation Grants, 671
Community Foundation for Greater Buffalo Niagara
    Area Foundation Grants, 673
Community Foundation for San Benito County
    Grants, 677
Community Foundation for SE Michigan Chelsea
    Community Fdn Capacity Building Grants, 679
Community Foundation for SE Michigan Chelsea
    Community Foundation General Grant, 680
Community Foundation for SE Michigan Detroit
    Auto Dealers Association Charitable Foundation
    Fund Grants, 681
Community Foundation for the Capital Region
    Grants, 687
Community Fdn Of Greater Lafayette Grants, 710
Cresap Family Foundation Grants, 766
Dayton Foundation Vandalia-Butler Grants, 799
Dayton Power and Light Company Foundation
    Signature Grants, 801
Dayton Power and Light Foundation Grants, 802
Decatur County Community Foundation Small
    Project Grants, 812
Delmarva Power & Light Contributions, 821
Dining for Women Grants, 831
DTE Energy Foundation Health and Human Services
    Grants, 869
Dyson Foundation Mid-Hudson Valley Project
    Support Grants, 874
Earl and Maxine Claussen Trust Grants, 878
Eastern Bank Charitable Foundation Partnerships
    Grants, 881
Edward and Helen Bartlett Foundation Grants, 888
Edyth Bush Charitable Foundation Grants, 893
Elmer Roe Deaver Foundation Grants, 906
El Pomar Foundation Anna Keesling Ackerman Fund
    Grants, 907
El Pomar Foundation Grants, 908
Emily O'Neill Sullivan Foundation Grants, 913
Evan Frankel Foundation Grants, 938
Fidelity Foundation Grants, 957
Fifth Third Foundation Grants, 959

First Hawaiian Bank Foundation Corporate Giving
    Grants, 967
Foundation of Herkimer and Oneida Counties Youth
    Sports, Wellness and Recreation Mini-Grants, 994
Foundations of East Chicago Health Grants, 997
Four County Community Foundation General
    Grants, 1000
Four County Community Foundation Healthy
    Senior/Healthy Youth Fund Grants, 1001
Four J Foundation Grants, 1004
Frank Reed and Margaret Jane Peters Memorial Fund
    Grants, 1013
Fremont Area Community Foundation Amazing X
    Grants, 1019
George H.C. Ensworth Memorial Fund Grants, 1049
Gerber Foundation Environmental Hazards Research
    Grants, 1062
Gerber Fdn Pediatric Health Research Grants, 1063
Gerber Foundation Pediatric Nutrition Research
    Grants, 1064
Gerber Fdn West Michigan Youth Grants, 1065
Gil and Dody Weaver Foundation Grants, 1071
GNOF Bayou Communities Grants, 1077
Greater Sitka Legacy Fund Grants, 1111
Green River Area Community Fdn Grants, 1117
GTRCF Elk Rapids Area Community Endowment
    Grants, 1127
Guy I. Bromley Trust Grants, 1136
Hampton Roads Community Foundation Nonprofit
    Facilities Improvement Grants, 1159
Hancock County Community Foundation - Field of
    Interest Grants, 1161
Hannaford Charitable Foundation Grants, 1163
Hannaford Supermarkets Community Giving, 1164
Harden Foundation Grants, 1166
Hardin County Community Foundation Grants, 1167
Harris Foundation Grants, 1177
Harrison County Community Fdn Grants, 1178
Harrison County Community Foundation Signature
    Grants, 1179
Hawai'i Community Foundation Robert E. Black
    Fund Grants, 1205
Hawaii Community Foundation Omidyar Ohana
    Fund Grants, 1213
Herbert A. and Adrian W. Woods Foundation
    Grants, 1243
Hill Crest Foundation Grants, 1249
Hillsdale County Community Foundation General
    Grants, 1250
Hillsdale County Community Foundation Love Your
    Community Grants, 1251
HRAMF Community Health Improvement Project
    Grants in Bowdoin Geneva, 1263
HRK Foundation Health Grants, 1264
Hubbard Broadcasting Foundation Grants, 1269
Hubbard Family Foundation Grants, 1270
Hubbard Family Foundation Grants, 1271
Hubbard Farms Charitable Foundation Grants, 1272
Inland Empire Community Foundation Capacity
    Building for IE Nonprofits Grants, 1306
Island Insurance Foundation Grants, 1316
J. Watumull Fund Grants, 1326
Jack Satter Foundation Grants, 1334
Jennings County Community Foundation Women's
    Giving Circle Grant, 1361
Jessica Stevens Community Foundation Grants, 1363
Jim Blevins Foundation Grants, 1365
Joseph Henry Edmondson Foundation Grants, 1388
Judy and Peter Blum Kovler Foundation Grants, 1396
Kenai Peninsula Foundation Grants, 1425
Ketchikan Community Foundation Grants, 1429
Koch Family Foundation (Annapolis) Grants, 1444
Kodiak Community Foundation Grants, 1446
Kosasa Foundation Grants, 1450
Lake County Community Fund Grants, 1463
Legler Benbough Foundation Grants, 1479
LGA Family Foundation Grants, 1487
Libra Foundation Grants, 1489
Lisa and Douglas Goldman Fund Grants, 1496
Louis and Sandra Berkman Foundation Grants, 1510

Lucile Packard Foundation for Children's Health Grants, 1514
Lucy Downing Nisbet Charitable Fund Grants, 1515
Lumpkin Family Fdn Healthy People Grants, 1518
Maine Community Foundation Penobscot Valley Health Association Grants, 1543
Marcia and Otto Koehler Foundation Grants, 1553
Marquette Bank Neighborhood Commit Grants, 1577
Mary Wilmer Covey Charitable Trust Grants, 1600
McCarthy Family Fdn Charity Fund Grants, 1614
Medtronic Foundation CommunityLink Health Grants, 1630
Mercedes-Benz USA Corporate Contributions Grants, 1634
Meyer Memorial Trust Responsive Grants, 1653
MGM Resorts Foundation Community Grants, 1655
Michelin North America Challenge Education, 1660
Montgomery County Community Foundation Health and Human Services Fund Grants, 1689
Moran Family Foundation Grants, 1693
New Jersey Center for Hispanic Policy, Research and Development Innovative Initiatives Grants, 1750
Norcliffe Foundation Grants, 1766
Northrop Grumman Corporation Grants, 1772
OceanFirst Foundation Major Grants, 1803
Orange County Community Foundation Grants, 1829
Oregon Community Fdn Community Grants, 1833
Oregon Community Foundation Community Recovery Grants, 1834
Oren Campbell McCleary Chartbl Trust Grants, 1837
Pajaro Valley Community Health Trust Diabetes and Contributing Factors Grants, 1865
Palmer Foundation Grants, 1867
Perpetual Benevolent Fund, 1940
Petersburg Community Foundation Grants, 1951
Peyton Anderson Foundation Grants, 1954
Pittsburgh Foundation Healthy Children and Adults Grants, 1981
PMI Foundation Grants, 1982
Pokagon Fund Grants, 1994
Polk County Community Foundation Bradley Breakthrough Community Benefit Grants, 1995
Polk County Community Foundation Unrestricted Grants, 2001
Porter County Community Foundation Health and Wellness Grant, 2002
PPCF Community Grants, 2014
PPG Industries Foundation Grants, 2017
Pulido Walker Foundation, 2039
Qualcomm Grants, 2042
R.D. Beirne Trust Grants, 2045
Ripley County Community Foundation Small Project Grants, 2078
Robert and Betty Wo Foundation Grants, 2083
Salt River Project Health and Human Services Grants, 2142
Samuel N. and Mary Castle Foundation Grants, 2145
Sand Hill Foundation Health and Opportunity Grants, 2153
Sarah G. McCarthy Memorial Foundation, 2162
Seattle Foundation Benjamin N. Phillips Memorial Fund Grants, 2176
Seattle Foundation Health and Wellness Grants, 2179
Seward Community Foundation Grants, 2182
Seward Community Foundation Mini-Grants, 2183
Shield-Ayres Foundation Grants, 2189
Sidney and Sandy Brown Foundation Grants, 2196
Simpson Lumber Charitable Contributions, 2201
Sobrato Family Foundation Grants, 2211
Sobrato Family Fdn Meeting Space Grants, 2212
Sobrato Family Foundation Office Space Grants, 2213
Sony Corporation of America Grants, 2216
Special Olympics Project UNIFY Grants, 2228
Textron Corporate Contributions Grants, 2286
Toyota Motor Manuf of Alabama Grants, 2309
Toyota Motor Manuf of Mississippi Grants, 2312
Toyota Motor Manufacturing of Texas Grants, 2313
Toyota Motor Manufacturing of West Virginia Grants, 2314
United Healthcare Commty Grts in Michigan, 2343

United Methodist Health Ministry Fund Grts, 2345
USAID Innovations in Feed the Future Monitoring and Evaluation Grants, 2355
Valley-Wide Health Systems Nurse Family Partnerships, 2372
Walker Area Community Foundation Grants, 2401
Walmart Fdn Inclusive Communities Grants, 2403
Walmart Fdn National Local Giving Grants, 2404
Walter S. and Evan C. Jones Testam Trust, 2407
Wege Foundation Grants, 2422
Welborn Baptist Foundation School Based Health Grants, 2424
Whole Foods Foundation, 2445
William and Sandy Heitz Family Fdn Grants, 2457
William Bingham Foundation Grants, 2460
William Ray and Ruth E. Collins Fdn Grants, 2473
WinnCompanies Charitable Giving, 2479
Wiregrass Foundation Grants, 2480
Wold Foundation Grants, 2482
Wolfe Associates Grants, 2483
Wyoming Community Fdn General Grants, 2501
Wyoming Community Foundation Hazel Patterson Memorial Grants, 2502
Wyomissing Foundation Community Grants, 2504
Wyomissing Foundation Thun Family Organizational Grants, 2505

Health Care

1st Touch Foundation Grants, 2
2 Depot Square Ipswich Charitable Foundation Grants, 3
3M Company Foundation Health and Human Services Grants, 6
A. Alfred Taubman Foundation Grants, 18
A.L. Mailman Family Foundation Grants, 20
A.L. Spencer Foundation Grants, 21
AACAP Jeanne Spurlock Research Fellowship in Substance Abuse and Addiction for Minority Medical Students, 28
AACAP Summer Medical Student Fellowships, 38
Aaron Foundation Grants, 42
Aaron Foundation Grants, 41
Abbott Fund Access to Health Care Grants, 45
Abbott Fund Community Engagement Grants, 46
Abbott Fund Global AIDS Care Grants, 47
Abbott Fund Science Education Grants, 48
Abby's Legendary Pizza Foundation Grants, 49
Abington Foundation Grants, 54
Abney Foundation Grants, 55
ACCF Dennis and Melanie Bieberich Community Enrichment Fund Grants, 59
ACCF of Indiana Anonymous Community Enrichment Fund Grants, 63
ACCF of Indiana Bank of Geneva Heritage Fund Grants, 64
ACCF of Indiana First Merchants Bank / Decatur Bank and Trust Fund Grants, 66
ACCF of Indiana Michael Basham Community Enrichment Fund Grants, 67
ACCF of Indiana Ron and Susie Ballard Community Enrichment Fund Grants, 68
ACCF Ralph Biggs Memorial Community Enrichment Fund Grants, 69
ACF Refugee Health Promotion Grants, 91
ACF Voluntary Agencies Matching Grants, 100
Achelis and Bodman Foundation Grants, 101
Achelis Foundation Grants, 102
ACL Disability and Rehabilitation Research Projects (DRRP) Program: Independent Living Transition Services for Youth and Young Adults Grants, 105
ACL Neonatal Abstinence Syndrome National Training Initiative Grant, 106
ACL Rehabilitation Research and Training Center (RRTC) on Employment of Transition-Age Youth with Disabilities Grants, 107
Acuity Charitable Foundation Grants, 110
Adams and Reese Corporate Giving Grants, 114
Adams County Community Foundation Grants, 115
Adams Family Foundation I Grants, 116
Adams Family Fdn of Nora Springs Grants, 118

Adelaide Breed Bayrd Foundation Grants, 123
Adolph Coors Foundation Grants, 129
Advance Auto Parts Corporate Giving Grants, 131
AEGON Transamerica Foundation Health and Wellness Grants, 133
A Friends' Foundation Trust Grants, 136
Agnes M. Lindsay Trust Grants, 140
Aid for Starving Children Health and Nutrition Grants, 145
Air Products Foundation Grants, 148
AKF Grants for Children, 149
Akron Community Foundation Health and Human Services Grants, 152
Alaska Community Foundation Cordova Community Foundation Grants, 201
Alaska Community Foundation Cordova Community Foundation Mini-Grants, 202
Alaska Community Foundation Kenai Peninsula Foundation Grant, 205
Albertsons Companies Foundation Nourishing Neighbors Grants, 221
Albert W. Rice Charitable Foundation Grants, 223
Alcatel-Lucent Technologies Foundation Grants, 224
Alfred E. Chase Charitable Foundation Grants, 233
Alpha Natural Resources Corporate Giving, 246
Amelia Sillman Rockwell and Carlos Perry Rockwell Charities Fund Grants, 250
American Electric Power Corporate Grants, 252
American Schlafhorst Foundation Grants, 262
Amica Companies Foundation Grants, 266
Amway Corporation Contributions, 269
Anheuser-Busch Foundation Grants, 273
Anna Fitch Ardenghi Trust Grants, 274
Antone and Edene Vidinha Charitable Grants, 281
Appalachian Regional Commission Health Care Grants, 288
Ar-Hale Family Foundation Grants, 290
Aspen Community Foundation Grants, 316
Assisi Fdn of Memphis Capital Project Grants, 317
Assisi Foundation of Memphis General Grants, 318
Assisi Foundation of Memphis Mini Grants, 319
AT&T Foundation Health and Human Services Grants, 322
Atlanta Foundation Grants, 326
Atlas Insurance Agency Foundation Grants, 329
Austin Community Foundation Grants, 332
Avery-Fuller-Welch Children's Fdn Grants, 336
Avery Foundation Grants, 339
Babcock Charitable Trust Grants, 343
Bainum Family Foundation Grants, 345
Bank of Hawaii Foundation Grants, 360
Barrasso, Usdin, Kupperman, Freeman, and Sarver Corporate Grants, 362
Baton Rouge Area Foundation Grants, 365
Baxter International Corporate Giving Grants, 368
Baxter International Foundation Grants, 369
Bay Area Community Foundation Arenac Community Fund Grants, 371
Bay Area Community Foundation Arenac County Healthy Youth/Healthy Seniors Fund Grants, 372
Bay Area Community Fdn Auburn Area Chamber of Commerce Enrichment Fund Grants, 373
Bay Area Community Foundation Bay County Healthy Youth/Healthy Seniors Fund Grants, 374
Bay Area Community Foundation Community Initiative Fund Grants, 376
BCBSM Foundation Community Health Matching Grants, 392
Ben B. Cheney Foundation Grants, 402
Better Way Foundation Grants, 419
Bindley Family Foundation Grants, 430
Blanche and Irving Laurie Foundation Grants, 436
Blue Grass Community Foundation Clark County Fund Grants, 444
Blue Grass Community Foundation Fayette County Fund Grants, 446
Blue Grass Community Foundation Franklin County Fund Grants, 447
Blue Grass Community Foundation Harrison County Fund Grants, 448

Blue Grass Community Foundation Hudson-Ellis Grants, 449

Blue Grass Community Foundation Madison County Fund Grants, 450

Blue Grass Community Foundation Magoffin County Fund Grants, 451

Blue Grass Community Foundation Morgan County Fund Grants, 452

Blue Grass Community Foundation Rowan County Fund Grants, 453

Blue Grass Community Foundation Woodford County Fund Grants, 454

Blue Mountain Community Foundation Garfield County Health Foundation Fund Grants, 456

Bodenwein Public Benevolent Foundation Grants, 461

Boeing Company Contributions Grants, 462

Bothin Foundation Grants, 464

Bradley-Turner Foundation Grants, 466

Bradley C. Higgins Foundation Grants, 467

Brian G. Dyson Foundation Grants, 468

Bridgestone Americas Trust Fund Grants, 469

Brinker Int Corporation Charitable Giving, 471

Burlington Industries Foundation Grants, 481

Bushrod H. Campbell and Adah F. Hall Charity Fund Grants, 486

C.H. Robinson Worldwide Foundation Grants, 489

Caesars Foundation Grants, 492

Callaway Foundation Grants, 496

Camille Beckman Foundation Grants, 499

Campbell Soup Foundation Grants, 501

Carl M. Freeman Foundation FACES Grants, 507

Carl R. Hendrickson Family Foundation Grants, 509

Carl W. and Carrie Mae Joslyn Trust Grants, 510

Carroll County Community Foundation Grants, 513

Castle Foundation Grants, 518

CFFVR Clintonville Area Foundation Grants, 539

CFFVR Clintonville Area Foundation Grants, 538

CFFVR Frank C. Shattuck Community Grants, 541

CFFVR Jewelers Mutual Chartbl Giving Grants, 543

CFFVR Myra M. and Robert L. Vandehey Foundation Grants, 545

CFFVR Robert and Patricia Endries Family Foundation Grants, 547

CFFVR Shawano Area Community Foundation Grants, 549

CFFVR Women's Fund for the Fox Valley Region Grants, 550

CFF Winter Park Community Grants, 551

CFGR Jenkins Foundation Grants, 553

Chapman Charitable Foundation Grants, 560

Chapman Family Foundation, 562

Charles Delmar Foundation Grants, 564

Charles H. Hall Foundation, 565

Charles H. Pearson Foundation Grants, 566

Charles Lafitte Foundation Grants, 567

Charles Nelson Robinson Fund Grants, 569

Chicago Board of Trade Foundation Grants, 580

Children's Brain Tumor Fdn Research Grants, 584

Chilkat Valley Community Foundation Grants, 588

Christine and Katharina Pauly Charitable Trust Grants, 601

CICF Indianapolis Fdn Community Grants, 606

Cigna Civic Affairs Sponsorships, 610

CIGNA Foundation Grants, 611

Cisco Systems Foundation San Jose Community Grants, 615

Citizens Bank Charitable Foundation Grants, 616

Clara Blackford Smith and W. Aubrey Smith Charitable Foundation Grants, 621

Claremont Savings Bank Foundation Grants, 623

Clarence T.C. Ching Foundation Grants, 624

Clark and Ruby Baker Foundation Grants, 625

Clark County Community Foundation Grants, 626

Clark Electric Cooperative Grants, 627

Cleo Foundation Grants, 632

Cleveland Foundation Higley Fund Grants, 634

CNO Financial Group Community Grants, 650

Colgate-Palmolive Company Grants, 652

Collins C. Diboll Private Foundation Grants, 657

Collins Foundation Grants, 658

Colorado Health Foundation Family, Friend and Neighbor Caregiver Supports Grants, 660

Colorado Interstate Gas Grants, 661

Colorado Trust Health Investment Grants, 662

Columbus Foundation Traditional Grants, 663

Community Foundation for Greater Atlanta Frances Hollis Brain Foundation Fund Grants, 664

Community Foundation for Greater Buffalo Competitive Grants, 670

Community Foundation for Greater Buffalo Niagara Area Foundation Grants, 673

Community Foundation for Greater Buffalo Ralph C. Wilson, Jr. Legacy Fund Grants, 674

Community Foundation for SE Michigan Chelsea Community Fdn Capacity Building Grants, 679

Community Foundation for SE Michigan Chelsea Community Foundation General Grant, 680

Community Foundation for the Capital Region Grants, 687

Community Foundation of Crawford County, 695

Community Foundation of Eastern Connecticut General Southeast Grants, 696

Community Foundation of Greater Chattanooga Grants, 704

Community Foundation of Greater Greensboro Community Grants, 708

Community Foundation of Henderson County Community Grants, 711

Community Foundation of Louisville AIDS Project Fund Grants, 716

Community Foundation of Madison and Jefferson County Grants, 731

Community Fdn of Randolph County Grants, 735

Community Fdn of Wabash County Grants, 740

Community Foundation of Western Massachusetts Grants, 741

Community Memorial Foundation Responsive Grants, 743

Cooke Foundation Grants, 748

Cresap Family Foundation Grants, 766

Crystelle Waggoner Charitable Trust Grants, 768

Cudd Foundation Grants, 769

D. W. McMillan Foundation Grants, 776

Dana Brown Charitable Trust Grants, 777

Dayton Foundation Grants, 796

Dayton Power and Light Company Foundation Signature Grants, 801

Dayton Power and Light Foundation Grants, 802

Deaconess Community Foundation Grants, 803

Dean Foods Community Involvement Grants, 805

Delaware Community Foundation Grants, 817

Delmarva Power & Light Contributions, 821

Dolan Children's Foundation Grants, 832

Dominion Foundation Grants, 839

Doree Taylor Charitable Foundation Grants, 843

Dorothea Haus Ross Foundation Grants, 844

Do Something Awards, 847

Dr. and Mrs. Paul Pierce Memorial Foundation Grants, 862

Dr. John T. Macdonald Foundation Grants, 863

DTE Energy Foundation Health and Human Services Grants, 869

Dubois County Community Foundation Grants, 871

Dunspaugh-Dalton Foundation Grants, 873

Dyson Foundation Mid-Hudson Valley Project Support Grants, 874

E. Clayton and Edith P. Gengras, Jr. Foundation Grants, 875

E.J. Grassmann Trust Grants, 876

Earl and Maxine Claussen Trust Grants, 878

Eastern Bank Charitable Foundation Partnerships Grants, 881

Eastern Bank Charitable Foundation Targeted Grants, 882

Edna Wardlaw Charitable Trust Grants, 886

Edward and Ellen Roche Relief Fdn Grants, 887

Edwards Memorial Trust Grants, 891

Edward W. and Stella C. Van Houten Memorial Fund Grants, 892

Effie and Wofford Cain Foundation Grants, 895

Effie Kuhlman Charitable Trust Grants, 896

Elizabeth Morse Genius Charitable Trust Grants, 901

Elkhart County Community Foundation Grants, 903

Elmer Roe Deaver Foundation Grants, 906

El Pomar Foundation Grants, 908

Elsie H. Wilcox Foundation Grants, 909

Emily O'Neill Sullivan Foundation Grants, 913

Ensworth Charitable Foundation Grants, 916

Entergy Corporation Open Grants for Healthy Families, 921

Epilepsy Foundation SUDEP Challenge Initiative Prizes, 924

Erie Chapman Foundation Grants, 928

Essex County Community Foundation Women's Fund Grants, 934

Ethel Sergeant Clark Smith Foundation Grants, 935

Evan Frankel Foundation Grants, 938

F.M. Kirby Foundation Grants, 946

F.R. Bigelow Foundation Grants, 947

Farmers Insurance Corporate Giving Grants, 948

Fayette County Foundation Grants, 951

Fichtenbaum Charitable Trust Grants, 955

Fidelity Foundation Grants, 957

FirstEnergy Foundation Community Grants, 965

First Hawaiian Bank Foundation Corporate Giving Grants, 967

Florence Hunt Maxwell Foundation Grants, 979

Foundation for Health Enhancement Grants, 990

Foundations of East Chicago Health Grants, 997

Four County Community Foundation General Grants, 1000

Four County Community Foundation Healthy Senior/Healthy Youth Fund Grants, 1001

Fourjay Foundation Grants, 1003

Four J Foundation Grants, 1004

Francis L. Abreu Charitable Trust Grants, 1008

Franklin County Community Fdn Grants, 1010

Franklin H. Wells and Ruth L. Wells Foundation Grants, 1011

Frank Reed and Margaret Jane Peters Memorial Fund Grants, 1013

Frank Reed and Margaret Jane Peters Memorial Fund II Grants, 1014

Frank S. Flowers Foundation Grants, 1015

Fred and Gretel Biel Charitable Trust Grants, 1016

Frederick McDonald Trust Grants, 1017

Frederick W. Marzahl Memorial Fund Grants, 1018

Fremont Area Community Foundation Community Grants, 1020

Fuller E. Callaway Foundation Grants, 1027

G.N. Wilcox Trust Grants, 1031

General Motors Foundation Grants, 1039

General Service Foundation Human Rights and Economic Justice Grants, 1040

George A. & Grace L. Long Fdn Grants, 1041

George and Ruth Bradford Foundation Grants, 1042

George A Ohl Jr. Foundation Grants, 1043

George E. Hatcher, Jr. and Ann Williams Hatcher Foundation Grants, 1045

George Kress Foundation Grants, 1053

George P. Davenport Trust Fund Grants, 1054

George W. Wells Foundation Grants, 1057

Gerber Foundation Environmental Hazards Research Grants, 1062

Gerber Fdn Pediatric Health Research Grants, 1063

Gerber Foundation Pediatric Nutrition Research Grants, 1064

Gerber Fdn West Michigan Youth Grants, 1065

Gertrude & William C. Wardlaw Grants, 1067

GNOF IMPACT Harold W. Newman, Jr. Charitable Trust Grants, 1086

GNOF Norco Community Grants, 1089

Grace Bersted Foundation Grants, 1097

Greater Milwaukee Foundation Grants, 1109

Greater Saint Louis Community Fdn Grants, 1110

Greater Sitka Legacy Fund Grants, 1111

Greater Tacoma Community Foundation General Operating Grants, 1113

Green Foundation Human Services Grants, 1116

Green River Area Community Fdn Grants, 1117

Grotto Foundation Project Grants, 1123
GTRCF Elk Rapids Area Community Endowment
    Grants, 1127
GTRCF Joan Rajkovich McGarry Family Education
    Endowment Grants, 1131
Guy I. Bromley Trust Grants, 1136
H.A. and Mary K. Chapman Charitable Trust
    Grants, 1137
Hall-Perrine Foundation Grants, 1152
Hannaford Charitable Foundation Grants, 1163
Hardin County Community Foundation Grants, 1167
Harris Foundation Grants, 1177
Harrison County Community Foundation Signature
    Grants, 1179
Hartford Foundation Regular Grants, 1185
Hattie Mae Lesley Foundation Grants, 1195
Hawai'i Community Foundation East Hawaii Fund
    Grants, 1199
Hawai'i Community Foundation Robert E. Black
    Fund Grants, 1205
Hawaii Community Foundation Omidyar Ohana
    Fund Grants, 1213
Hawaii Community Foundation Reverend Takie
    Okumura Family Grants, 1216
Helen Gertrude Sparks Charitable Trust Grants, 1230
Helen Irwin Littauer Educational Trust Grants, 1231
Helen V. Brach Foundation Grants, 1232
Henrietta Lange Burk Fund Grants, 1235
Henry County Community Foundation Grants, 1239
Herman Goldman Foundation Grants, 1245
Highmark Corporate Giving Grants, 1248
Hillsdale County Community Foundation General
    Grants, 1250
Hispanic Heritage Foundation Youth Awards, 1253
HLTA Visitor Industry Charity Walk Grant, 1254
Horace A. Kimball and S. Ella Kimball Foundation
    Grants, 1260
Horace A. Moses Charitable Trust Grants, 1261
HRAMF Community Health Improvement Project
    Grants in Bowdoin Geneva, 1263
HRK Foundation Health Grants, 1264
HSBC Corporate Giving Grants, 1266
Hubbard Broadcasting Foundation Grants, 1269
Hubbard Family Foundation Grants, 1270
Hubbard Family Foundation Grants, 1271
Hubbard Farms Charitable Foundation Grants, 1272
Huffy Foundation Grants, 1273
Huntington Clinical Foundation Grants, 1278
Huntington County Community Foundation Make a
    Difference Grants, 1280
Iddings Foundation Capital Project Grants, 1283
Iddings Foundation Major Project Grants, 1284
Iddings Foundation Medium Project Grants, 1285
Iddings Foundation Small Project Grants, 1286
Illinois Children's Healthcare Fdn Grants, 1295
Irving S. Gilmore Foundation Grants, 1314
Isabel Allende Foundation Esperanza Grants, 1315
Island Insurance Foundation Grants, 1316
J. Edwin Treakle Foundation Grants, 1320
J.W. Kieckhefer Foundation Grants, 1324
J. Watumull Fund Grants, 1326
Jack Satter Foundation Grants, 1334
Jacob G. Schmidlapp Trusts Grants, 1336
James and Abigail Campbell Family Foundation
    Grants, 1337
James Ford Bell Foundation Grants, 1339
James Graham Brown Foundation Grants, 1340
James M. Collins Foundation Grants, 1344
James S. Copley Foundation Grants, 1345
Jennings County Community Fdn Grants, 1360
Jessica Stevens Community Foundation Grants, 1363
Jewish Fund Grants, 1364
Jim Blevins Foundation Grants, 1365
John Clarke Trust Grants, 1369
John G. Duncan Charitable Trust Grants, 1372
Johnson County Community Fdn Grants, 1379
John W. Anderson Foundation Grants, 1383
Joseph Henry Edmondson Foundation Grants, 1388
Josephine Schell Russell Chartbl Trust Grants, 1389
Judy and Peter Blum Kovler Foundation Grants, 1396

Julia Temple Davis Brown Foundation Grants, 1399
Kate B. Reynolds Charitable Trust Health Care
    Grants, 1416
Kate B. Reynolds Charitable Trust Poor and Needy
    Grants, 1417
Katharine Matthies Foundation Grants, 1418
Katherine John Murphy Foundation Grants, 1419
Katrine Menzing Deakins Chartbl Trust Grants, 1422
Kelvin and Eleanor Smith Foundation Grants, 1424
Kenai Peninsula Foundation Grants, 1425
Ketchikan Community Foundation Grants, 1429
Kettering Family Foundation Grants, 1430
Kimball International-Habig Foundation Health and
    Human Services Grants, 1434
Klingenstein-Simons Fellowship Awards in the
    Neurosciences, 1441
Koch Family Foundation (Annapolis) Grants, 1444
Kodak Community Relations Grants, 1445
Kodiak Community Foundation Grants, 1446
Kosasa Foundation Grants, 1450
Kovler Family Foundation Grants, 1454
Laidlaw Foundation Youth Organizaing Initiatives
    Grants, 1462
Land O'Lakes Foundation Mid-Atlantic Grants, 1467
Lands' End Corporate Giving Program, 1468
Latkin Charitable Foundation Grants, 1469
Laura B. Vogler Foundation Grants, 1470
Laura Moore Cunningham Foundation Grants, 1474
Lee and Ramona Bass Foundation Grants, 1478
Leola Osborn Trust Grants, 1483
Leo Niessen Jr., Charitable Trust Grants, 1484
LGA Family Foundation Grants, 1487
Liberty Bank Foundation Grants, 1488
Linford & Mildred White Charitable Grants, 1495
Lisa and Douglas Goldman Fund Grants, 1496
Lockheed Martin Corporation Fdn Grants, 1505
Louie M. and Betty M. Phillips Fdn Grants, 1509
Louis and Sandra Berkman Foundation Grants, 1510
Lubrizol Foundation Grants, 1513
Lucile Packard Foundation for Children's Health
    Grants, 1514
Lucy Downing Nisbet Charitable Fund Grants, 1515
Ludwick Family Foundation Grants, 1516
Lumpkin Family Fdn Healthy People Grants, 1518
M. Bastian Family Foundation Grants, 1522
Mabel A. Horne Fund Grants, 1525
Mabel F. Hoffman Charitable Trust Grants, 1526
Mabel H. Flory Charitable Trust Grants, 1527
Mabel Y. Hughes Charitable Trust Grants, 1530
Macquarie Bank Foundation Grants, 1532
Maine Community Foundation Vincent B. and
    Barbara G. Welch Grants, 1545
Marathon Petroleum Corporation Grants, 1551
Marcia and Otto Koehler Foundation Grants, 1553
Marie C. and Joseph C. Wilson Foundation Rochester
    Small Grants, 1559
Marion Gardner Jackson Charitable Trust Grts, 1570
Marion I. and Henry J. Knott Foundation
    Discretionary Grants, 1571
Marion I. and Henry J. Knott Foundation Standard
    Grants, 1572
Marjorie Moore Charitable Foundation Grants, 1574
Marquette Bank Neighborhood Commit Grants, 1577
Mary K. Chapman Foundation Grants, 1590
Mary Owen Borden Foundation Grants, 1597
Mary S. and David C. Corbin Fdn Grants, 1598
Mary Wilmer Covey Charitable Trust Grants, 1600
Max and Anna Levinson Foundation Grants, 1612
McCarthy Family Fdn Charity Fund Grants, 1614
McConnell Foundation Grants, 1616
McInerny Foundation Grants, 1622
McLean Contributionship Grants, 1623
Meadows Foundation Grants, 1626
MeadWestvaco Foundation Sustainable Communities
    Grants, 1627
Mead Witter Foundation Grants, 1628
Mericos Foundation Grants, 1637
Meriden Foundation Grants, 1638
Mervin Bovaird Foundation Grants, 1643
Metzger-Price Fund Grants, 1647

Meyer Fdn Healthy Communities Grants, 1650
MGN Family Foundation Grants, 1656
Michael Reese Health Trust Core Grants, 1658
Michelin North America Challenge Education, 1660
Milton Hicks Wood and Helen Gibbs Wood
    Charitable Trust Grants, 1676
Mimi and Peter Haas Fund Grants, 1677
Montgomery County Community Foundation Health
    and Human Services Fund Grants, 1689
Mt. Sinai Health Care Foundation Health of the
    Jewish Community Grants, 1709
Nathan Cummings Foundation Grants, 1718
Nell J. Redfield Foundation Grants, 1737
Nicole Brown Foundation Grants, 1760
Noble County Community Foundation Grants, 1765
Northrop Grumman Corporation Grants, 1772
OceanFirst Foundation Major Grants, 1803
Ohio County Community Foundation Grants, 1812
Ohio County Community Fdn Mini-Grants, 1813
Olga Sipolin Children's Fund Grants, 1815
Olive Higgins Prouty Foundation Grants, 1817
Olive Smith Browning Charitable Trust Grants, 1818
Oppenstein Brothers Foundation Grants, 1827
Ordean Foundation Catalyst Grants, 1830
Ordean Foundation Partnership Grants, 1831
Oregon Community Fdn Community Grants, 1833
Oregon Community Foundation Community
    Recovery Grants, 1834
Oren Campbell McCleary Chartbl Trust Grants, 1837
OSF Youth Action Fund Grants in Kyrgyzstan, 1846
Pajaro Valley Community Health Health Trust
    Insurance/Coverage & Education on Using the
    System Grants, 1864
Pajaro Valley Community Health Trust Oral Health:
    Prevention & Access Grants, 1866
Parkersburg Area Community Foundation Action
    Grants, 1871
Peabody Foundation Grants, 1922
Pediatric Brain Tumor Foundation Early Career
    Development Grants, 1924
Pediatric Brain Tumor Foundation Early Career
    Development Grants, 1923
Pediatric Brain Tumor Fdn Institute Grants, 1925
Pediatric Brain Tumor Foundation Opportunity
    Grants, 1926
Percy B. Ferebee Endowment Grants, 1936
Perkin Fund Grants, 1937
Perkins Charitable Foundation Grants, 1939
Petersburg Community Foundation Grants, 1951
Peyton Anderson Foundation Grants, 1954
Phoenix Coyotes Charities Grants, 1963
Piedmont Health Foundation Grants, 1965
Piedmont Natural Gas Foundation Health and
    Human Services Grants, 1968
Pinnacle Entertainment Foundation Grants, 1972
Pinnacle Foundation Grants, 1973
Pittsburgh Foundation Healthy Children and Adults
    Grants, 1981
Pohlad Family Fdn Large Capital Grants, 1990
Pohlad Family Fdn Small Capital Grants, 1991
Polk County Community Foundation Bradley
    Breakthrough Community Benefit Grants, 1995
Polk County Community Foundation Marjorie M.
    and Lawrence R. Bradley Endowment Fund
    Grants, 1998
Polk County Community Foundation Unrestricted
    Grants, 2001
Posey Community Foundation Women's Fund
    Grants, 2008
Powell Foundation Grants, 2013
PPCF Community Grants, 2014
Price Chopper's Golub Foundation Grants, 2020
Priddy Foundation Program Grants, 2023
Pride Foundation Grants, 2024
Puerto Rico Community Foundation Grants, 2037
Pulaski County Community Foundation Grants, 2038
Pulido Walker Foundation, 2039
Putnam County Community Fdn Grants, 2040
Qualcomm Grants, 2042
R.C. Baker Foundation Grants, 2043

R.D. Beirne Trust Grants, 2045
R.S. Gernon Trust Grants, 2047
Ralph M. Parsons Foundation Grants, 2052
Raskob Fdn for Catholic Activities Grants, 2054
Rasmuson Foundation Tier One Grants, 2055
Rasmuson Foundation Tier Two Grants, 2056
Rathmann Family Foundation Grants, 2057
Ressler-Gertz Foundation Grants, 2067
Richard and Caroline T. Gwathmey Memorial Trust
    Grants, 2069
Ricks Family Charitable Trust Grants, 2075
Riedman Foundation Grants, 2076
Ripley County Community Foundation Grants, 2077
Ripley County Community Foundation Small Project
    Grants, 2078
Robert and Betty Wo Foundation Grants, 2083
Robert and Helen Haddad Foundation Grants, 2084
Robert F. Lange Foundation Grants, 2090
Rockwell Collins Charitable Corp Grants, 2098
Rose Community Foundation Health Grants, 2105
Rose Hills Foundation Grants, 2106
Roy and Christine Sturgis Charitable Tr Grts, 2115
Rush County Community Foundation Grants, 2121
Ruth Anderson Foundation Grants, 2122
Ruth and Vernon Taylor Foundation Grants, 2124
Ruth Camp Campbell Charitable Trust Grants, 2125
Saigh Foundation Grants, 2137
Saint Louis Rams Foundation Community
    Donations, 2139
Samuel S. Johnson Foundation Grants, 2146
San Antonio Area Foundation Annual Responsive
    Grants, 2147
San Antonio Area Foundation Capital and Naming
    Rights Grants, 2148
Sand Hill Foundation Health and Opportunity
    Grants, 2153
Sands Cares Grants, 2156
San Juan Island Community Foundation Grants, 2158
Sarah G. McCarthy Memorial Foundation, 2162
Sarkeys Foundation Grants, 2163
Schramm Foundation Grants, 2168
Scott County Community Foundation Grants, 2170
Seattle Foundation Benjamin N. Phillips Memorial
    Fund Grants, 2176
Seattle Foundation Health and Wellness Grants, 2179
Seward Community Foundation Grants, 2182
Seward Community Foundation Mini-Grants, 2183
Shell Deer Park Grants, 2186
Shell Oil Company Foundation Community
    Development Grants, 2188
Shield-Ayres Foundation Grants, 2189
Sidney and Sandy Brown Foundation Grants, 2196
Sidney Stern Memorial Trust Grants, 2197
Siebert Lutheran Foundation Grants, 2198
Singing for Change Foundation Grants, 2202
Sioux Falls Area Community Foundation Community
    Fund Grants, 2203
Sioux Falls Area Community Foundation Spot
    Grants, 2204
Skaggs Family Foundation Grants, 2206
Skaggs Family Foundation Grants, 2205
Spencer County Community Foundation Women's
    Fund Grants, 2232
Stan and Sandy Checketts Foundation Grants, 2235
Subaru of Indiana Automotive Fdn Grants, 2254
Summit Foundation Grants, 2255
Sunoco Foundation Grants, 2256
SunTrust Bank Trusteed Foundations Greene-Sawtell
    Grants, 2257
SunTrust Bank Trusteed Foundations Nell Warren
    Elkin and William Simpson Elkin Grants, 2258
Swindells Charitable Foundation Grants, 2261
Tellabs Foundation Grants, 2280
Telluride Foundation Community Grants, 2281
Tension Envelope Foundation Grants, 2284
Textron Corporate Contributions Grants, 2286
Thelma Braun and Bocklett Family Foundation
    Grants, 2287
Thomas J. Atkins Memorial Trust Fund Grants, 2290
Thomas J. Long Foundation Community Grants, 2291

Thomas Sill Foundation Grants, 2292
TJX Foundation Grants, 2303
Todd Brock Family Foundation Grants, 2305
Toyota Motor Manuf of Alabama Grants, 2309
Toyota Motor Manuf of Mississippi Grants, 2312
Toyota Motor Manufacturing of Texas Grants, 2313
Toyota Motor Manufacturing of West Virginia
    Grants, 2314
Tull Charitable Foundation Grants, 2324
Turner Foundation Grants, 2326
Union Bank, N.A. Corporate Sponsorships and
    Donations, 2333
Union Bank, N.A. Foundation Grants, 2334
United Healthcare Commty Grts in Michigan, 2343
United Technologies Corporation Grants, 2347
USAID Office of Foreign Disaster Assistance and
    Food for Peace Grants, 2359
Valley-Wide Health Systems Nurse Family
    Partnerships, 2372
Vanderburgh Community Foundation Men's Fund
    Grants, 2373
Vanderburgh County Community Foundation
    Women's Fund Grants, 2376
Victor E. Speas Foundation Grants, 2380
Vigneron Memorial Fund Grants, 2384
Virginia W. Kettering Foundation Grants, 2388
Volkswagen Group of America Corporate
    Contributions Grants, 2389
W.H. and Mary Ellen Cobb Chartbl Trust Grts, 2397
W.M. Keck Fdn Southern California Grants, 2398
W.P. and Bulah Luse Foundation Grants, 2399
Walker Area Community Foundation Grants, 2401
Walter S. and Evan C. Jones Testam Trust, 2407
Washington Gas Charitable Contributions, 2417
Wayne County Foundation Grants, 2419
Weaver Popcorn Foundation Grants, 2421
Western Indiana Community Fdn Grants, 2428
Weyerhaeuser Family Fdn Health Grants, 2435
WHO Foundation General Grants, 2443
WHO Foundation Volunteer Service Grants, 2444
Wilkins Family Foundation Grants, 2450
William A. Badger Foundation Grants, 2451
William B. Stokely Jr. Foundation Grants, 2459
William Blair and Company Foundation Grants, 2461
William G. and Helen C. Hoffman Foundation
    Grants, 2466
William G. Gilmore Foundation Grants, 2467
William J. and Dorothy K. O'Neill Foundation
    Responsive Grants, 2468
William J. and Tina Rosenberg Fdn Grants, 2470
William J. Brace Charitable Trust, 2471
William Ray and Ruth E. Collins Fdn Grants, 2473
Williams Comps Homegrown Giving Grants, 2474
WinnCompanies Charitable Giving, 2479
Wiregrass Foundation Grants, 2480
Wold Foundation Grants, 2482
Wolfe Associates Grants, 2483
Wood-Claeyssens Foundation Grants, 2486
Wood Family Charitable Trust Grants, 2487
World of Children Health Award, 2491
Wyoming Community Fdn General Grants, 2501
Wyoming Community Foundation Hazel Patterson
    Memorial Grants, 2502
Wyomissing Foundation Community Grants, 2504
Wyomissing Foundation Thun Family Organizational
    Grants, 2505
Wyomissing Foundation Thun Family Program
    Grants, 2506
Yawkey Foundation Grants, 2510
Youths' Friends Association Grants, 2511
ZYTL Foundation Grants, 2528

Health Care Access
2 Depot Square Ipswich Charitable Foundation
    Grants, 3
3M Company Foundation Health and Human
    Services Grants, 6
A. Alfred Taubman Foundation Grants, 18
Abbott Fund Community Engagement Grants, 46
Abundance Foundation International Grants, 57

ACCF Dennis and Melanie Bieberich Community
    Enrichment Fund Grants, 59
ACCF of Indiana Anonymous Community
    Enrichment Fund Grants, 63
ACCF of Indiana Bank of Geneva Heritage Fund
    Grants, 64
ACCF of Indiana First Merchants Bank / Decatur
    Bank and Trust Fund Grants, 66
ACCF of Indiana Michael Basham Community
    Enrichment Fund Grants, 67
ACCF of Indiana Ron and Susie Ballard Community
    Enrichment Fund Grants, 68
ACCF Ralph Biggs Memorial Community
    Enrichment Fund Grants, 69
ACF Refugee Health Promotion Grants, 91
ACF Voluntary Agencies Matching Grants, 100
Achelis and Bodman Foundation Grants, 101
Achelis Foundation Grants, 102
Adams and Reese Corporate Giving Grants, 114
Adams Family Fdn of Nora Springs Grants, 118
Advance Auto Parts Corporate Giving Grants, 131
AEGON Transamerica Foundation Health and
    Wellness Grants, 133
A Friends' Foundation Trust Grants, 136
Agnes M. Lindsay Trust Grants, 140
AKF Grants for Children, 149
Akron Community Foundation Health and Human
    Services Grants, 152
Albert W. Rice Charitable Foundation Grants, 223
Alfred E. Chase Charitable Foundation Grants, 233
Allan C. and Lelia J. Garden Foundation Grants, 236
Alpha Natural Resources Corporate Giving, 246
Amelia Sillman Rockwell and Carlos Perry Rockwell
    Charities Fund Grants, 250
Amica Companies Foundation Grants, 266
Anheuser-Busch Foundation Grants, 273
Appalachian Regional Commission Health Care
    Grants, 288
Ar-Hale Family Foundation Grants, 290
AT&T Foundation Health and Human Services
    Grants, 322
Atlas Insurance Agency Foundation Grants, 329
Avery-Fuller-Welch Children's Fdn Grants, 336
Avery Foundation Grants, 339
Babcock Charitable Trust Grants, 343
Bank of Hawaii Foundation Grants, 360
Barrasso, Usdin, Kupperman, Freeman, and Sarver
    Corporate Grants, 362
Baxter International Corporate Giving Grants, 368
Baxter International Foundation Grants, 369
Bay Area Community Foundation Arenac County
    Healthy Youth/Healthy Seniors Fund Grants, 372
Bay Area Community Fdn Auburn Area Chamber of
    Commerce Enrichment Fund Grants, 373
Bay Area Community Foundation Bay County
    Healthy Youth/Healthy Seniors Fund Grants, 374
Bay Area Community Foundation Community
    Initiative Fund Grants, 376
BCBSM Foundation Community Health Matching
    Grants, 392
Benton Community Fdn Cookie Jar Grant, 404
Bernard and Audre Rapoport Foundation Health
    Grants, 411
Better Way Foundation Grants, 419
Blue Cross Blue Shield of Minnesota Fdn - Healthy
    Children: Growing Up Healthy Grants, 442
Blue Grass Community Foundation Clark County
    Fund Grants, 444
Blue Grass Community Foundation Fayette County
    Fund Grants, 446
Blue Grass Community Foundation Franklin County
    Fund Grants, 447
Blue Grass Community Foundation Harrison County
    Fund Grants, 448
Blue Grass Community Foundation Madison County
    Fund Grants, 450
Blue Grass Community Foundation Magoffin County
    Fund Grants, 451
Blue Grass Community Foundation Morgan County
    Fund Grants, 452

Blue Grass Community Foundation Rowan County Fund Grants, 453
Blue Grass Community Foundation Woodford County Fund Grants, 454
Blue Mountain Community Foundation Garfield County Health Foundation Fund Grants, 456
Bodenwein Public Benevolent Foundation Grants, 461
Brian G. Dyson Foundation Grants, 468
Brinker Int Corporation Charitable Giving, 471
C.H. Robinson Worldwide Foundation Grants, 489
Caesars Foundation Grants, 492
California Endowment Innovative Ideas Challenge Grants, 495
Camille Beckman Foundation Grants, 499
Cargill Corporate Giving Grants, 503
Carl B. and Florence E. King Foundation Grants, 506
Carl R. Hendrickson Family Foundation Grants, 509
Castle Foundation Grants, 518
CFFVR Jewelers Mutual Chartbl Giving Grants, 543
CFF Winter Park Community Grants, 551
Chapman Charitable Foundation Grants, 560
Chapman Family Foundation, 562
Charles H. Hall Foundation, 565
Charles H. Pearson Foundation Grants, 566
Charles Nelson Robinson Fund Grants, 569
Chilkat Valley Community Foundation Grants, 588
Cigna Civic Affairs Sponsorships, 610
Claremont Savings Bank Foundation Grants, 623
Clark and Ruby Baker Foundation Grants, 625
Clark Electric Cooperative Grants, 627
CNCS AmeriCorps Indian Tribes Plang Grts , 641
CNCS Social Innovation Grants, 649
Colorado Health Foundation Family, Friend and Neighbor Caregiver Supports Grants, 660
Colorado Trust Health Investment Grants, 662
Community Foundation for Greater Atlanta Frances Hollis Brain Foundation Fund Grants, 664
Community Foundation for Greater Buffalo Niagara Area Foundation Grants, 673
Community Foundation for Greater Buffalo Ralph C. Wilson, Jr. Legacy Fund Grants, 674
Community Foundation for SE Michigan Chelsea Community Foundation General Grant, 680
Community Foundation for the Capital Region Grants, 687
Community Foundation of Boone County - Women's Grants, 693
Community Foundation of Crawford County, 695
Community Foundation of Greater Chattanooga Grants, 704
Community Fdn of Howard County Grants, 712
Community Foundation of Louisville AIDS Project Fund Grants, 716
Community Fdn of Southern Indiana Grants, 736
Community Foundation of Switzerland County Grants, 739
Community Foundation Serving Riverside and San Bernardino Counties Impact Grants, 742
Community Memorial Foundation Responsive Grants, 743
Covidien Partnership for Neighborhood Wellness Grants, 759
Cresap Family Foundation Grants, 766
D. W. McMillan Foundation Grants, 776
Dana Brown Charitable Trust Grants, 777
Daniels Homeless and Disadvantaged Grants, 782
Dayton Power and Light Foundation Grants, 802
Delmarva Power & Light Contributions, 821
Dining for Women Grants, 831
Dominion Foundation Grants, 839
Doree Taylor Charitable Foundation Grants, 843
Dr. and Mrs. Paul Pierce Memorial Foundation Grants, 862
DTE Energy Foundation Health and Human Services Grants, 869
Dyson Foundation Mid-Hudson Valley Project Support Grants, 874
E. Clayton and Edith P. Gengras, Jr. Foundation Grants, 875
Earl and Maxine Claussen Trust Grants, 878

Eastern Bank Charitable Foundation Partnerships Grants, 881
Eastern Bank Charitable Foundation Targeted Grants, 882
Edward and Ellen Roche Relief Fdn Grants, 887
Effie Kuhlman Charitable Trust Grants, 896
Elkhart County Community Foundation Fund for Elkhart County, 902
Elmer Roe Deaver Foundation Grants, 906
El Pomar Foundation Grants, 908
Ensworth Charitable Foundation Grants, 916
Erie Chapman Foundation Grants, 928
Essex County Community Foundation Merrimack Valley Municipal Business Development and Recovery Fund Grants, 933
Evan Frankel Foundation Grants, 938
FCD New American Children Grants, 952
First Hawaiian Bank Foundation Corporate Giving Grants, 967
Ford Family Foundation Grants - Access to Health and Dental Services, 980
Foundation for a Healthy Kentucky Grants, 988
Fdn for the Mid South Communities Grants, 992
Foundations of East Chicago Health Grants, 997
Four County Community Foundation General Grants, 1000
Four County Community Foundation Healthy Senior/Healthy Youth Fund Grants, 1001
Frank Reed and Margaret Jane Peters Memorial Fund II Grants, 1014
Frederick McDonald Trust Grants, 1017
Frederick W. Marzahl Memorial Fund Grants, 1018
General Service Foundation Human Rights and Economic Justice Grants, 1040
George A. & Grace L. Long Fdn Grants, 1041
George E. Hatcher, Jr. and Ann Williams Hatcher Foundation Grants, 1045
George W. Wells Foundation Grants, 1057
German Protestant Orphan Asylum Foundation Grants, 1066
GNOF Bayou Communities Grants, 1077
GNOF IMPACT Gulf States Eye Surg Fund, 1085
GNOF IMPACT Harold W. Newman, Jr. Charitable Trust Grants, 1086
GNOF Norco Community Grants, 1089
Grace Bersted Foundation Grants, 1097
Greater Sitka Legacy Fund Grants, 1111
Green Foundation Human Services Grants, 1116
Green River Area Community Fdn Grants, 1117
GTRCF Elk Rapids Area Community Endowment Grants, 1127
GTRCF Joan Rajkovich McGarry Family Education Endowment Grants, 1131
Guy I. Bromley Trust Grants, 1136
HAF Barry F. Phelps Leukemia Fund Grants, 1140
HAF JoAllen K. Twiddy-Wood Memorial Fund Grants, 1144
Hannaford Charitable Foundation Grants, 1163
Hardin County Community Foundation Grants, 1167
Harold Brooks Foundation Grants, 1172
Harrison County Community Foundation Signature Grants, 1179
Hattie Mae Lesley Foundation Grants, 1195
Hawai'i Community Foundation Robert E. Black Fund Grants, 1205
Helen Irwin Littauer Educational Trust Grants, 1231
Henrietta Lange Burk Fund Grants, 1235
Henry E. Niles Foundation Grants, 1240
Hill Crest Foundation Grants, 1249
Hillsdale County Community Foundation General Grants, 1261
Horace A. Moses Charitable Trust Grants, 1261
HRAMF Community Health Improvement Project Grants in Bowdoin Geneva, 1263
HRK Foundation Health Grants, 1264
Hubbard Broadcasting Foundation Grants, 1269
Hubbard Family Foundation Grants, 1271
Hubbard Farms Charitable Foundation Grants, 1272
Huntington Clinical Foundation Grants, 1278

Huntington County Community Foundation Make a Difference Grants, 1280
Iddings Foundation Capital Project Grants, 1283
Iddings Foundation Major Project Grants, 1284
Iddings Foundation Medium Project Grants, 1285
Iddings Foundation Small Project Grants, 1286
J. Edwin Treakle Foundation Grants, 1320
Jessica Stevens Community Foundation Grants, 1363
Jewish Fund Grants, 1364
John Clarke Trust Grants, 1369
Joseph Henry Edmondson Foundation Grants, 1388
Josephine Schell Russell Chartbl Trust Grants, 1389
Judy and Peter Blum Kovler Foundation Grants, 1396
Kansas Health Fdn Major Initiatives Grants, 1414
Kate B. Reynolds Charitable Trust Poor and Needy Grants, 1417
Kenai Peninsula Foundation Grants, 1425
Kenneth T. and Eileen L. Norris Fdn Grants, 1427
Ketchikan Community Foundation Grants, 1429
Kimball International-Habig Foundation Health and Human Services Grants, 1434
Koch Family Foundation (Annapolis) Grants, 1444
Kodiak Community Foundation Grants, 1446
Locations Foundation Legacy Grants, 1504
Louie M. and Betty M. Phillips Fdn Grants, 1509
Lumpkin Family Fdn Healthy People Grants, 1518
M.A. Rikard Charitable Trust Grants, 1521
Macquarie Bank Foundation Grants, 1532
Marathon Petroleum Corporation Grants, 1551
Marion Gardner Jackson Charitable Trust Grts, 1570
Marquette Bank Neighborhood Commit Grants, 1577
Marshall County Community Fdn Grants, 1579
Mary K. Chapman Foundation Grants, 1590
Mary Wilmer Covey Charitable Trust Grants, 1600
McCarthy Family Fdn Charity Fund Grants, 1614
Medtronic Foundation CommunityLink Health Grants, 1630
Medtronic Foundation Strengthening Health Systems Grants, 1632
Metzger-Price Fund Grants, 1647
Meyer Fdn Healthy Communities Grants, 1650
MGM Resorts Foundation Community Grants, 1655
Michael and Susan Dell Foundation Grants, 1657
Michael Reese Health Trust Responsive Grants, 1659
Mid-Iowa Health Foundation Community Response Grants, 1667
Montgomery County Community Foundation Health and Human Services Fund Grants, 1689
Mt. Sinai Health Care Foundation Health of the Jewish Community Grants, 1709
Mt. Sinai Health Care Foundation Health of the Urban Community Grants, 1710
OceanFirst Foundation Major Grants, 1803
Ohio County Community Foundation Grants, 1812
Ohio County Community Fdn Mini-Grants, 1813
Olga Sipolin Children's Fund Grants, 1815
Olive Smith Browning Charitable Trust Grants, 1818
Orange County Community Foundation Grants, 1828
Ordean Foundation Partnership Grants, 1831
Oregon Community Fdn Community Grants, 1833
Oregon Community Foundation Community Recovery Grants, 1834
Oren Campbell McCleary Chartbl Trust Grants, 1837
OSF Youth Action Fund Grants in Kyrgyzstan, 1846
Pajaro Valley Community Health Health Trust Insurance/Coverage & Education on Using the System Grants, 1864
Pajaro Valley Community Health Trust Oral Health: Prevention & Access Grants, 1866
Perkin Fund Grants, 1937
Petersburg Community Foundation Grants, 1951
Peyton Anderson Foundation Grants, 1954
Philanthrofund Foundation Grants, 1959
Piedmont Natural Gas Foundation Health and Human Services Grants, 1968
Pinnacle Entertainment Foundation Grants, 1972
Piper Trust Healthcare and Med Rsrch Grants, 1978
Piper Trust Reglious Organizations Grants, 1979
Pittsburgh Foundation Healthy Children and Adults Grants, 1981

Pohlad Family Fdn Large Capital Grants, 1990
Polk County Community Foundation Marjorie M. &
    Lawrence R. Bradley Endowment Grants, 1998
Polk County Community Foundation Unrestricted
    Grants, 2001
Porter County Community Foundation Health and
    Wellness Grant, 2002
Portland Fdn - Women's Giving Circle Grant, 2006
PPCF Community Grants, 2014
Price Chopper's Golub Foundation Grants, 2020
Pulido Walker Foundation, 2039
Qualcomm Grants, 2042
Ralph M. Parsons Foundation Grants, 2052
Rasmuson Foundation Tier Two Grants, 2056
Richard & Caroline T. Gwathmey Trust Grants, 2069
Ricks Family Charitable Trust Grants, 2075
Riedman Foundation Grants, 2076
Robert F. Lange Foundation Grants, 2090
Robert R. Meyer Foundation Grants, 2094
Rose Community Foundation Health Grants, 2105
San Antonio Area Foundation Annual Responsive
    Grants, 2147
San Antonio Area Foundation Capital and Naming
    Rights Grants, 2148
Sand Hill Fdn Health and Opportunity Grants, 2153
Sands Cares Grants, 2156
Santa Fe Community Foundation Seasonal Grants-
    Fall Cycle, 2159
Seattle Foundation Benjamin N. Phillips Memorial
    Fund Grants, 2176
Seattle Foundation Health and Wellness Grants, 2179
Seward Community Foundation Grants, 2182
Seward Community Foundation Mini-Grants, 2183
Shelley and Donald Rubin Foundation Grants, 2187
Shield-Ayres Foundation Grants, 2189
Sierra Health Foundation Responsive Grants, 2199
Skaggs Family Foundation Grants, 2206
Skaggs Family Foundation Grants, 2205
Spencer County Community Foundation Women's
    Fund Grants, 2232
SunTrust Bank Trusteed Foundations Greene-Sawtell
    Grants, 2257
SunTrust Bank Trusteed Foundations Nell Warren
    Elkin and William Simpson Elkin Grants, 2258
Thelma Braun and Bocklett Family Foundation
    Grants, 2287
Thomas J. Long Foundation Community Grants, 2291
Toyota Motor Manufacturing of West Virginia
    Grants, 2314
Union Labor Health Fdn Angel Fund Grants, 2335
USAID Office of Foreign Disaster Assistance and
    Food for Peace Grants, 2359
Valley-Wide Health Systems Nurse Family
    Partnerships, 2372
Vanderburgh Community Foundation Men's Fund
    Grants, 2373
Vanderburgh County Community Foundation
    Women's Fund Grants, 2376
W.H. and Mary Ellen Cobb Chartbl Trust Grts, 2397
W.M. Keck Fdn Southern California Grants, 2398
W.P. and Bulah Luse Foundation Grants, 2399
Walker Area Community Foundation Grants, 2401
Warrick County Community Foundation Women's
    Fund, 2411
Weaver Popcorn Foundation Grants, 2421
Weyerhaeuser Family Fdn Health Grants, 2435
WHO Foundation General Grants, 2443
Whole Foods Foundation, 2445
William J. and Tina Rosenberg Fdn Grants, 2470
William J. Brace Charitable Trust, 2471
William Ray and Ruth E. Collins Fdn Grants, 2473
Wiregrass Foundation Grants, 2480
Wold Foundation Grants, 2482
Wolfe Associates Grants, 2483
Wyoming Community Fdn General Grants, 2501
Wyoming Community Foundation Hazel Patterson
    Memorial Grants, 2502
Wyomissing Foundation Community Grants, 2504
Wyomissing Foundation Thun Family Organizational
    Grants, 2505

Wyomissing Foundation Thun Family Program
    Grants, 2506
Youths' Friends Association Grants, 2511
ZYTL Foundation Grants, 2528

Health Care Administration
Beckman Coulter Foundation Grants, 394
CMS Historically Black Colleges and Universities
    (HBCU) Health Services Research Grants, 639
Covenant Educational Foundation Grants, 754
Michael Reese Health Trust Core Grants, 1658

Health Care Assessment
AACAP Jeanne Spurlock Research Fellowship in
    Substance Abuse and Addiction for Minority
    Medical Students, 28
AACAP Summer Medical Student Fellowships, 38
Colorado Health Foundation Family, Friend and
    Neighbor Caregiver Supports Grants, 660
Community Foundation for the National Capital
    Region Community Leadership Grants, 688
Covidien Partnership for Neighborhood Wellness
    Grants, 759
Illinois Children's Healthcare Fdn Grants, 1295
Kansas Health Fdn Major Initiatives Grants, 1414
Kansas Health Foundation Recognition Grants, 1415
Piedmont Natural Gas Foundation Health and
    Human Services Grants, 1968

Health Care Economics
Percy B. Ferebee Endowment Grants, 1936

Health Care Financing
AKF Grants for Children, 149
Colorado Trust Health Investment Grants, 662
Covidien Partnership for Neighborhood Wellness
    Grants, 759

Health Care Personnel
Covidien Partnership for Neighborhood Wellness
    Grants, 759

Health Care Promotion
ACF Refugee Health Promotion Grants, 91
Albert W. Rice Charitable Foundation Grants, 223
AT&T Foundation Health and Human Services
    Grants, 322
Cigna Civic Affairs Sponsorships, 610
CNCS AmeriCorps Indian Tribes Plang Grts , 641
Colorado Health Foundation Family, Friend and
    Neighbor Caregiver Supports Grants, 660
Colorado Trust Health Investment Grants, 662
Covidien Partnership for Neighborhood Wellness
    Grants, 759
Fdn for the Mid South Communities Grants, 992
George E. Hatcher, Jr. and Ann Williams Hatcher
    Foundation Grants, 1045
GNOF IMPACT Kahn-Oppenheim Tr Grts, 1087
Hill Crest Foundation Grants, 1249
HRK Foundation Health Grants, 1264
Kansas Health Fdn Major Initiatives Grants, 1414
Medtronic Foundation Strengthening Health Systems
    Grants, 1632
Meyer Fdn Healthy Communities Grants, 1650
Michael Reese Health Trust Responsive Grants, 1659
Mt. Sinai Health Care Foundation Health of the
    Urban Community Grants, 1710
Porter County Community Foundation Health and
    Wellness Grant, 2002
United Healthcare Commty Grts in Michigan, 2343
Wyomissing Foundation Thun Family Program
    Grants, 2506

Health Disparities
Appalachian Regional Commission Health Care
    Grants, 288
California Endowment Innovative Ideas Challenge
    Grants, 495
Guy I. Bromley Trust Grants, 1136

Maine Community Foundation Penobscot Valley
    Health Association Grants, 1543
Medtronic Foundation CommunityLink Health
    Grants, 1630
Michael and Susan Dell Foundation Grants, 1657
Porter County Community Foundation Health and
    Wellness Grant, 2002

Health Insurance
CMS Research and Demonstration Grants, 640
Edwards Memorial Trust Grants, 891
Foundation for a Healthy Kentucky Grants, 988
Michael Reese Health Trust Responsive Grants, 1659
Mid-Iowa Health Foundation Community Response
    Grants, 1667
Packard Foundation Children, Families, and
    Communities Grants, 1862
Public Welfare Foundation Special Initiative to
    Advance Civil Legal Aid Grants, 2034

Health Planning/Policy
3M Company Foundation Health and Human
    Services Grants, 6
Akron Community Foundation Health and Human
    Services Grants, 152
Appalachian Regional Commission Health Care
    Grants, 288
Baxter International Corporate Giving Grants, 368
Cigna Civic Affairs Sponsorships, 610
Entergy Corporation Open Grants for Healthy
    Families, 921
Foundation for a Healthy Kentucky Grants, 988
General Service Foundation Human Rights and
    Economic Justice Grants, 1040
Grifols Community Outreach Grants, 1122
Kansas Health Foundation Recognition Grants, 1415
Meyer Fdn Healthy Communities Grants, 1650
Rose Community Foundation Health Grants, 2105
Seattle Foundation Health and Wellness Grants, 2179
USAID Innovations in Feed the Future Monitoring
    and Evaluation Grants, 2355

Health Promotion
Abington Foundation Grants, 54
Adolph Coors Foundation Grants, 129
AEGON Transamerica Foundation Health and
    Wellness Grants, 133
Air Products Foundation Grants, 148
Albertsons Companies Foundation Nourishing
    Neighbors Grants, 221
Allen Foundation Educational Nutrition Grants, 238
Anheuser-Busch Foundation Grants, 273
Appalachian Regional Commission Health Care
    Grants, 288
Atkinson Foundation Community Grants, 325
Bikes Belong Foundation Paul David Clark Bicycling
    Safety Grants, 422
Bikes Belong Foundation REI Grants, 423
Bikes Belong Grants, 424
Bright Promises Foundation Grants, 470
California Endowment Innovative Ideas Challenge
    Grants, 495
Charles H. Pearson Foundation Grants, 566
Cigna Civic Affairs Sponsorships, 610
CJ Fdn for SIDS Program Services Grants, 619
CNCS AmeriCorps Indian Tribes Plang Grts , 641
CNCS AmeriCorps State and National Grants, 643
CNCS AmeriCorps VISTA Project Grants, 645
CNCS Social Innovation Grants, 649
Finish Line Youth Foundation Founder's Grants, 960
Finish Line Youth Foundation Grants, 961
Finish Line Youth Foundation Legacy Grants, 962
Foundation for a Healthy Kentucky Grants, 988
Frank Reed and Margaret Jane Peters Memorial Fund
    II Grants, 1014
George E. Hatcher, Jr. and Ann Williams Hatcher
    Foundation Grants, 1045
Global Fund for Women Grants, 1073
GNOF IMPACT Kahn-Oppenheim Tr Grts, 1087
GNOF Norco Community Grants, 1089

GNOF Stand Up For Our Children Grants, 1092
Hasbro Children's Fund Grants, 1189
HRAMF Charles H. Hood Foundation Child Health
  Research Awards, 1262
Jewish Fund Grants, 1364
Kansas Health Foundation Recognition Grants, 1415
Linford & Mildred White Charitable Grants, 1495
Louie M. and Betty M. Phillips Fdn Grants, 1509
Mary Black Foundation Active Living Grants, 1585
Mary Wilmer Covey Charitable Trust Grants, 1600
Medtronic Foundation CommunityLink Health
  Grants, 1630
Michael Reese Health Trust Responsive Grants, 1659
Nell J. Redfield Foundation Grants, 1737
Paso del Norte Health Foundation Grants, 1874
PepsiCo Foundation Grants, 1935
Phoenix Coyotes Charities Grants, 1963
Piedmont Health Foundation Grants, 1965
Pinnacle Foundation Grants, 1973
Pittsburgh Foundation Healthy Children and Adults
  Grants, 1981
Premera Blue Cross Grants, 2018
RGk Foundation Grants, 2068
Robert R. McCormick Tribune Foundation
  Community Grants, 2093
Robert R. Meyer Foundation Grants, 2094
Roney-Fitzpatrick Foundation Grants, 2102
RWJF Healthy Eating Research Grants, 2127
Saigh Foundation Grants, 2137
San Juan Island Community Foundation Grants, 2158
Scott County Community Foundation Grants, 2170
Sunoco Foundation Grants, 2256
Tellabs Foundation Grants, 2280
Textron Corporate Contributions Grants, 2286
TJX Foundation Grants, 2303
USAID Innovations in Feed the Future Monitoring
  and Evaluation Grants, 2355
Washington Gas Charitable Contributions, 2417
Whitney Foundation Grants, 2441
World of Children Humanitarian Award, 2492

Health Research
ACL Rehabilitation Research and Training Center
  (RRTC) on Employment of Transition-Age Youth
  with Disabilities Grants, 107
Active Living Research Grants, 109
Catherine Holmes Wilkins Foundation Charitable
  Grants, 520
Fichtenbaum Charitable Trust Grants, 955
Joni Elaine Templeton Foundation Grants, 1384
Marcia and Otto Koehler Foundation Grants, 1553
Sara Elizabeth O'Brien Trust Grants, 2161
Special Olympics Youth Fan Grants, 2229

Health Sciences
CFFVR Jewelers Mutual Chartbl Giving Grants, 543
Harry A. and Margaret D. Towsley Foundation
  Grants, 1180

Health Services Delivery
3M Company Foundation Health and Human
  Services Grants, 6
Abbott Fund Access to Health Care Grants, 45
Abell-Hanger Foundation Grants, 52
Abington Foundation Grants, 54
Ackerman Foundation Grants, 103
Albertsons Companies Foundation Nourishing
  Neighbors Grants, 221
Allan C. and Lelia J. Garden Foundation Grants, 236
Amica Insurance Company Community Grants, 267
Appalachian Regional Commission Health Care
  Grants, 288
Back Home Again Foundation Grants, 344
Blackford County Community Fdn Grants, 434
Burlington Industries Foundation Grants, 481
California Endowment Innovative Ideas Challenge
  Grants, 495
Carl B. and Florence E. King Foundation Grants, 506
Charles H. Pearson Foundation Grants, 566

Christine and Katharina Pauly Charitable Trust
  Grants, 601
Clinton County Community Foundation Grants, 638
CMS Historically Black Colleges and Universities
  (HBCU) Health Services Research Grants, 639
Community Foundation of Boone County Grants, 694
Community Foundation of Grant County Grants, 703
Community Foundation of Louisville Anna Marble
  Memorial Fund for Princeton Grants, 717
Community Foundation of St. Joseph County Special
  Project Challenge Grants, 738
Community Foundation Serving Riverside and San
  Bernardino Counties Impact Grants, 742
Cone Health Foundation Grants, 745
Daniels Homeless and Disadvantaged Grants, 782
Dearborn Community Foundation City of
  Lawrenceburg Community Grants, 809
Decatur County Community Foundation Large
  Project Grants, 811
DeKalb County Community Foundation Grants, 815
DTE Energy Foundation Health and Human Services
  Grants, 869
Entergy Corporation Open Grants for Healthy
  Families, 921
Foundation for a Healthy Kentucky Grants, 988
Foundation for Health Enhancement Grants, 990
Foundations of East Chicago Health Grants, 997
George E. Hatcher, Jr. and Ann Williams Hatcher
  Foundation Grants, 1045
Gil and Dody Weaver Foundation Grants, 1071
Grundy Foundation Grants, 1124
HAF Phyllis Nilsen Leal Mem Fund Grants, 1149
Hall-Perrine Foundation Grants, 1152
Hasbro Children's Fund Grants, 1189
Hendricks County Community Fdn Grants, 1234
Herman P. and Sophia Taubman Fdn Grants, 1247
Hill Crest Foundation Grants, 1249
Horace A. Kimball and S. Ella Kimball Foundation
  Grants, 1260
HRSA Ryan White HIV AIDS Drug Assistance
  Grants, 1265
Illinois Children's Healthcare Fdn Grants, 1295
Inland Empire Community Foundation Capacity
  Building for IE Nonprofits Grants, 1306
Jewish Fund Grants, 1364
Johnson County Community Fdn Grants, 1379
Kodak Community Relations Grants, 1445
LaGrange County Community Fdn Grants, 1458
Liberty Bank Foundation Grants, 1488
M.D. Anderson Foundation Grants, 1523
M.J. Murdock Charitable Trust General Grants, 1524
Madison County Community Foundation - City of
  Anderson Quality of Life Grant, 1536
Marie C. and Joseph C. Wilson Foundation Rochester
  Small Grants, 1559
Marin Community Foundation Improving
  Community Health Grants, 1566
McGraw-Hill Companies Community Grants, 1620
McLean Foundation Grants, 1624
Medtronic Foundation CommunityLink Health
  Grants, 1630
Medtronic Foundation Strengthening Health Systems
  Grants, 1632
Michael Reese Health Trust Core Grants, 1658
Michael Reese Health Trust Responsive Grants, 1659
Mid-Iowa Health Foundation Community Response
  Grants, 1667
Miller Foundation Grants, 1673
Northrop Grumman Corporation Grants, 1772
Office Depot Corporation Community Relations
  Grants, 1805
Piedmont Natural Gas Foundation Health and
  Human Services Grants, 1968
Porter County Community Foundation Health and
  Wellness Grant, 2002
Premera Blue Cross Grants, 2018
Priddy Foundation Program Grants, 2023
Qualcomm Grants, 2042
RCF General Community Grants, 2062

Robert R. McCormick Tribune Foundation
  Community Grants, 2093
Robert R. Meyer Foundation Grants, 2094
Saigh Foundation Grants, 2137
Samuel S. Johnson Foundation Grants, 2146
Santa Fe Community Foundation Seasonal Grants-
  Fall Cycle, 2159
Sartain Lanier Family Foundation Grants, 2164
Seattle Foundation Benjamin N. Phillips Memorial
  Fund Grants, 2176
Shell Oil Company Foundation Community
  Development Grants, 2188
Sierra Health Foundation Responsive Grants, 2199
Sony Corporation of America Grants, 2216
Starke County Community Foundation Grants, 2236
Sunoco Foundation Grants, 2256
TE Foundation Grants, 2279
Textron Corporate Contributions Grants, 2286
Thomas J. Long Foundation Community Grants, 2291
U.S. Cellular Corporation Grants, 2331
Union Bank, N.A. Corporate Sponsorships and
  Donations, 2333
Union Pacific Foundation Health and Human
  Services Grants, 2338
Washington County Community Fdn Grants, 2416
Wells County Foundation Grants, 2426
William B. Stokely Jr. Foundation Grants, 2459
ZYTL Foundation Grants, 2528

Health and Safety Education
7-Eleven Corporate Giving Grants, 8
ACCF Dennis and Melanie Bieberich Community
  Enrichment Fund Grants, 59
ACCF of Indiana Michael Basham Community
  Enrichment Fund Grants, 67
Active Living Research Grants, 109
Aetna Foundation Regional Health Grants, 134
Atkinson Foundation Community Grants, 325
Baxter International Foundation Grants, 369
CFGR SisterFund Grants, 554
Charles Lafitte Foundation Grants, 567
Cigna Civic Affairs Sponsorships, 610
CJ Fdn for SIDS Program Services Grants, 619
Community Foundation of Greater Chattanooga
  Grants, 704
Dayton Foundation Vandalia-Butler Grants, 799
Dearborn Community Foundation City of
  Lawrenceburg Community Grants, 809
Dr. John T. Macdonald Foundation Grants, 863
Foundation for a Healthy Kentucky Grants, 988
Foundations of East Chicago Health Grants, 997
Fremont Area Community Foundation Youth
  Advisory Committee Grants, 1022
Gerber Fdn West Michigan Youth Grants, 1065
GNOF IMPACT Kahn-Oppenheim Tr Grts, 1087
Golden Heart Community Foundation Grants, 1094
Greater Sitka Legacy Fund Grants, 1111
Grifols Community Outreach Grants, 1122
Hannaford Charitable Foundation Grants, 1163
Hillsdale County Community Foundation General
  Grants, 1250
Honeywell Corporation Family Safety and Security
  Grants, 1255
Johnson County Community Fdn Grants, 1379
Kansas Health Foundation Recognition Grants, 1415
Kenai Peninsula Foundation Grants, 1425
Ketchikan Community Foundation Grants, 1429
Mary Black Foundation Active Living Grants, 1585
Matson Community Giving Grants, 1607
New Jersey Center for Hispanic Policy, Research and
  Development Innovative Initiatives Grants, 1750
Northrop Grumman Corporation Grants, 1772
NRA Foundation Grants, 1774
Oregon Community Fdn Community Grants, 1833
Pajaro Valley Community Health Trust Diabetes and
  Contributing Factors Grants, 1865
Petersburg Community Foundation Grants, 1951
Phoenix Suns Charities Grants, 1964
Pittsburgh Foundation Healthy Children and Adults
  Grants, 1981

PMI Foundation Grants, 1982
Posey Community Foundation Women's Fund
    Grants, 2008
PPG Industries Foundation Grants, 2017
PSEG Fdn Safety and Preparedness Grants, 2031
Salt River Project Health and Human Services
    Grants, 2142
Skaggs Family Foundation Grants, 2206
Skaggs Family Foundation Grants, 2205
Spencer County Community Foundation Women's
    Fund Grants, 2232
Tellabs Foundation Grants, 2280
United Healthcare Commty Grts in Michigan, 2343
Vanderburgh Community Foundation Men's Fund
    Grants, 2373
Vanderburgh County Community Foundation
    Women's Fund Grants, 2376
Warrick County Community Foundation Women's
    Fund, 2411
Welborn Baptist Foundation School Based Health
    Grants, 2424
Whole Foods Foundation, 2445

Hearing
Alexander Graham Bell Parent and Infant Financial
    Aid Grants, 227
Alexander Graham Bell Preschool-Age Financial Aid
    Grants, 228
Bay Area Community Foundation Nathalie Awrey
    Memorial Fund Grants, 381
Oticon Focus on People Awards, 1847
Reinberger Foundation Grants, 2066
William and Sandy Heitz Family Fdn Grants, 2457

Hearing Impairments
Alexander Graham Bell Parent and Infant Financial
    Aid Grants, 227
Alexander Graham Bell Preschool-Age Financial Aid
    Grants, 228
Bay Area Community Foundation Nathalie Awrey
    Memorial Fund Grants, 381
Bushrod H. Campbell and Adah F. Hall Charity
    Fund Grants, 486
Carl W. and Carrie Mae Joslyn Trust Grants, 510
Charles Delmar Foundation Grants, 564
Community Foundation of Jackson County Seymour
    Noon Lions Club Grant, 714
Cralle Foundation Grants, 760
Herbert A. and Adrian W. Woods Foundation
    Grants, 1243
Johnson Scholarship Foundation Grants, 1382
Mabel H. Flory Charitable Trust Grants, 1527
Oticon Focus on People Awards, 1847
Ray Charles Foundation Grants, 2058

Hematology
Grifols Community Outreach Grants, 1122

Hemophilia
Baxter International Corporate Giving Grants, 368

Heroism
OceanFirst Foundation Home Runs for Heroes
    Grants, 1802
OceanFirst Foundation Major Grants, 1803

Higher Education
3M Company Fdn Community Giving Grants, 5
A. Alfred Taubman Foundation Grants, 18
A.C. and Penney Hubbard Foundation Grants, 19
Aaron Foundation Grants, 42
Abbott Fund Global AIDS Care Grants, 47
Abeles Foundation Grants, 51
Abell-Hanger Foundation Grants, 52
Abell Foundation Education Grants, 53
Abney Foundation Grants, 55
Achelis and Bodman Foundation Grants, 101
Achelis Foundation Grants, 102
Acuity Charitable Foundation Grants, 110
Adams-Mastrovich Family Foundation Grants, 113

Adams Family Foundation II Grants, 117
Adolph Coors Foundation Grants, 129
A Friends' Foundation Trust Grants, 136
Agnes M. Lindsay Trust Grants, 140
Air Products Foundation Grants, 148
ALA Coretta Scott King Book Donation Grant, 168
Alavi Foundation Education Grants, 216
Albert E. and Birdie W. Einstein Fund Grants, 220
Albertsons Companies Foundation Nourishing
    Neighbors Grants, 221
Alloy Family Foundation Grants, 241
Alpha Natural Resources Corporate Giving, 246
American Electric Power Corporate Grants, 252
American Electric Power Foundation Grants, 253
American Honda Foundation Grants, 255
American Indian Youth Running Strong Grants, 256
American Schlafhorst Foundation Grants, 262
American Woodmark Foundation Grants, 263
Amerigroup Foundation Grants, 264
Amica Insurance Company Community Grants, 267
Anderson Foundation Grants, 271
Andrew Family Foundation Grants, 272
Ann Ludington Sullivan Foundation Grants, 279
Antone and Edene Vidinha Charitable Grants, 281
Ar-Hale Family Foundation Grants, 290
Arkema Foundation Grants, 298
Atkinson Foundation Community Grants, 325
Atlanta Foundation Grants, 326
Avery Foundation Grants, 339
Avista Foundation Education Grants, 340
Babcock Charitable Trust Grants, 343
Back Home Again Foundation Grants, 344
Bank of Hawaii Foundation Grants, 360
Batts Foundation Grants, 367
Bay Area Community Fdn Auburn Area Chamber of
    Commerce Enrichment Fund Grants, 373
Bay Area Community Foundation Community
    Initiative Fund Grants, 376
Better Way Foundation Grants, 419
Blumenthal Foundation Grants, 459
BMW of North America Charitable Contribs, 460
Boeing Company Contributions Grants, 462
BP Foundation Grants, 465
Bradley-Turner Foundation Grants, 466
Brian G. Dyson Foundation Grants, 468
Bridgestone Americas Trust Fund Grants, 469
Brinker Int Corporation Charitable Giving, 471
Brown Foundation Grants, 476
Brunswick Foundation Grants, 479
Burlington Industries Foundation Grants, 481
C.H. Robinson Worldwide Foundation Grants, 489
Cadillac Products Packaging Company Foundation
    Grants, 491
Caesars Foundation Grants, 492
Callaway Foundation Grants, 496
Campbell Foundation Grants, 500
Campbell Soup Foundation Grants, 501
Cargill Corporate Giving Grants, 503
Cargill Foundation Education Grants, 504
Carl B. and Florence E. King Foundation Grants, 506
Carnegie Corporation of New York Grants, 511
Castle Foundation Grants, 518
Castle Foundation Grants, 517
CFFVR Appleton Education Foundation Grants, 536
CFFVR Clintonville Area Foundation Grants, 539
CFFVR Clintonville Area Foundation Grants, 538
CFFVR Shawano Area Community Foundation
    Grants, 549
CFGR SisterFund Grants, 554
Chapman Charitable Foundation Grants, 560
Charles Delmar Foundation Grants, 564
Cheryl Spencer Memorial Foundation Grants, 576
Chicago Board of Trade Foundation Grants, 580
Chicago Community Trust Arts and Culture Grants:
    Improving Access to Arts Learning, 581
Christensen Fund Regional Grants, 600
CIGNA Foundation Grants, 611
Cincinnati Bell Foundation Grants, 612
Cincinnati Milacron Foundation Grants, 613
Citizens Savings Foundation Grants, 617

Clark and Ruby Baker Foundation Grants, 625
Clayton Fund Grants, 631
CNCS AmeriCorps State and National Grants, 643
Collins C. Diboll Private Foundation Grants, 657
Collins Foundation Grants, 658
Colorado Interstate Gas Grants, 661
Community Foundation of Louisville Education
    Grants, 724
Community Foundation of Madison and Jefferson
    County Grants, 731
Community Fdn of Morgan County Grants, 732
Community Fdn of Wabash County Grants, 740
CONSOL Energy Academic Grants, 746
Cooper Tire and Rubber Foundation Grants, 749
Cralle Foundation Grants, 760
Crane Foundation General Grants, 761
Crane Fund for Widows and Children Grants, 762
Crescent Porter Hale Foundation Grants, 767
Curtis Foundation Grants, 771
David M. and Marjorie D. Rosenberg Foundation
    Grants, 790
David Robinson Foundation Grants, 791
Dean Foundation Grants, 806
Decatur County Community Foundation Large
    Project Grants, 811
Dolan Children's Foundation Grants, 832
Doree Taylor Charitable Foundation Grants, 843
Dorrance Family Foundation Grants, 845
Dorr Foundation Grants, 846
DTE Energy Foundation Environmental Grants, 868
Dunspaugh-Dalton Foundation Grants, 873
E.J. Grassmann Trust Grants, 876
E.L. Wiegand Foundation Grants, 877
Earl and Maxine Claussen Trust Grants, 878
Edward and Helen Bartlett Foundation Grants, 888
Effie Allen Little Foundation Grants, 894
Elizabeth Huth Coates Charitable Foundation
    Grants, 900
El Pomar Foundation Grants, 908
Elsie H. Wilcox Foundation Grants, 909
Emerson Kampen Foundation Grants, 911
Emily O'Neill Sullivan Foundation Grants, 913
Faye L. and William L. Cowden Charitable
    Foundation Grants, 950
Fidelity Charitable Gift Fund Grants, 956
FirstEnergy Foundation Community Grants, 965
First Hawaiian Bank Foundation Corporate Giving
    Grants, 967
Florence Foundation Grants, 978
Foundation for Rural Service Education Grants, 991
Four County Community Foundation General
    Grants, 1000
Four County Community Foundation Healthy
    Senior/Healthy Youth Fund Grants, 1001
Four J Foundation Grants, 1004
Francis Beidler Foundation Grants, 1007
Francis L. Abreu Charitable Trust Grants, 1008
Fuller E. Callaway Foundation Grants, 1027
Gardner W. and Joan G. Heidrick, Jr. Foundation
    Grants, 1036
George and Ruth Bradford Foundation Grants, 1042
George F. Baker Trust Grants, 1046
George Graham and Elizabeth Galloway Smith
    Foundation Grants, 1047
George I. Alden Trust Grants, 1051
George Kress Foundation Grants, 1053
George P. Davenport Trust Fund Grants, 1054
George W. Codrington Charitable Foundation
    Grants, 1055
Georgia-Pacific Foundation Education Grants, 1058
Georgia-Pacific Fdn Entrepreneurship Grants, 1059
Geraldine R. Dodge Fdn Education Grants, 1061
Gertrude & William C. Wardlaw Grants, 1067
GNOF Exxon-Mobil Grants, 1080
GNOF New Orleans Works Grants, 1088
GNOF Norco Community Grants, 1089
Greater Milwaukee Foundation Grants, 1109
Green River Area Community Fdn Grants, 1117
Greenspun Family Foundation Grants, 1118
Griffin Family Foundation Grants, 1121

Grifols Community Outreach Grants, 1122
Haddad Foundation Grants, 1139
Hall-Perrine Foundation Grants, 1152
Harris and Eliza Kempner Fund Ed Grants, 1176
Harris Foundation Grants, 1177
Harry B. and Jane H. Brock Foundation Grants, 1183
Harvey Randall Wickes Foundation Grants, 1188
Hawaii Electric Industries Charitable Foundation
    Grants, 1218
Helen Irwin Littauer Educational Trust Grants, 1231
Herman P. and Sophia Taubman Fdn Grants, 1247
Hill Crest Foundation Grants, 1249
Hubbard Broadcasting Foundation Grants, 1269
Huffy Foundation Grants, 1273
Humana Foundation Grants, 1275
Ike and Roz Friedman Foundation Grants, 1289
Intel Corporation Community Grants, 1311
Island Insurance Foundation Grants, 1316
J.W. Kieckhefer Foundation Grants, 1324
J. Walton Bissell Foundation Grants, 1325
J. Watumull Fund Grants, 1326
J. Willard and Alice S. Marriott Fdn Grants, 1327
James F. and Marion L. Miller Fdn Grants, 1338
James Ford Bell Foundation Grants, 1339
James M. Collins Foundation Grants, 1344
Jennings County Community Fdn Grants, 1360
Jim Blevins Foundation Grants, 1365
John H. and Wilhelmina D. Harland Charitable
    Foundation Children and Youth Grants, 1374
John P. Ellbogen Fdn Community Grants, 1377
John W. Anderson Foundation Grants, 1383
Joseph Henry Edmondson Foundation Grants, 1388
Journal Gazette Foundation Grants, 1391
Julia Richardson Brown Foundation Grants, 1398
Julius N. Frankel Foundation Grants, 1400
Katherine John Murphy Foundation Grants, 1419
Kathryne Beynon Foundation Grants, 1420
Kentucky Arts Cncl Access Assistance Grants, 1428
Kinder Morgan Foundation Grants, 1436
Kind World Foundation Grants, 1438
Koch Family Foundation (Annapolis) Grants, 1444
Kodak Community Relations Grants, 1445
Kopp Family Foundation Grants, 1448
Koret Foundation Grants, 1449
Kosasa Foundation Grants, 1450
Kovler Family Foundation Grants, 1455
Kovler Family Foundation Grants, 1454
Lee and Ramona Bass Foundation Grants, 1478
Leo Niessen Jr., Charitable Trust Grants, 1484
LGA Family Foundation Grants, 1487
Libra Foundation Grants, 1489
Lied Foundation Trust Grants, 1490
LISC Capacity Building Grants, 1498
Lloyd G. Balfour Foundation Attleboro-Specific
    Charities Grants, 1502
Lloyd G. Balfour Foundation Scholarships, 1503
Lockheed Martin Corporation Fdn Grants, 1505
Long Island Community Foundation Grants, 1507
Louis and Sandra Berkman Foundation Grants, 1510
Lubrizol Foundation Grants, 1513
Lumpkin Family Fdn Healthy People Grants, 1518
M.A. Rikard Charitable Trust Grants, 1521
M. Bastian Family Foundation Grants, 1522
M.J. Murdock Charitable Trust General Grants, 1524
Madison County Community Foundation General
    Grants, 1537
Manuel D. and Rhoda Mayerson Fdn Grants, 1550
Margaret and James A. Elkins Jr. Fdn Grants, 1555
Margaret T. Morris Foundation Grants, 1557
Marion Gardner Jackson Charitable Trust Grts, 1570
Martin Family Foundation Grants, 1583
Maryland State Arts Council Arts in Communities
    Grants, 1592
Mary S. and David C. Corbin Fdn Grants, 1598
Matilda R. Wilson Fund Grants, 1605
Maurice J. Masserini Charitable Trust Grants, 1610
Maurice R. Robinson Fund Grants, 1611
McCombs Foundation Grants, 1615
McCune Foundation Education Grants, 1618
McGraw-Hill Companies Community Grants, 1620

Mead Witter Foundation Grants, 1628
Mericos Foundation Grants, 1637
Meriden Foundation Grants, 1638
Merrick Foundation Grants, 1640
Meyer Foundation Education Grants, 1649
Meyer Memorial Trust Responsive Grants, 1653
MGM Resorts Foundation Community Grants, 1655
MGN Family Foundation Grants, 1656
Milton and Sally Avery Arts Foundation Grants, 1675
Nellie Mae Education Foundation District-Level
    Change Grants, 1736
Nell J. Redfield Foundation Grants, 1737
NFL Charities Pro Bowl Community Grants in
    Hawaii, 1755
Norcliffe Foundation Grants, 1766
Olive Higgins Prouty Foundation Grants, 1817
Olivia R. Gardner Foundation Grants, 1819
Oppenstein Brothers Foundation Grants, 1827
Oregon Community Foundation Community
    Recovery Grants, 1834
Parkersburg Area Community Foundation Action
    Grants, 1871
PepsiCo Foundation Grants, 1935
Percy B. Ferebee Endowment Grants, 1936
Perkin Fund Grants, 1937
Perkins Charitable Foundation Grants, 1939
Perry and Sandy Massie Foundation Grants, 1941
Pettus Foundation Grants, 1952
Peyton Anderson Foundation Grants, 1954
Peyton Anderson Scholarships, 1955
PGE Foundation Grants, 1958
Phil Hardin Foundation Grants, 1960
Philip L. Graham Fund Education Grants, 1962
Pinnacle Entertainment Foundation Grants, 1972
Piper Jaffray Foundation Communities Giving
    Grants, 1974
PMI Foundation Grants, 1982
Polk County Community Foundation Marjorie M.
    and Lawrence R. Bradley Endowment Fund
    Grants, 1998
Posse Foundation Scholarships, 2011
Powell Foundation Grants, 2013
Price Chopper's Golub Foundation Grants, 2020
Pulaski County Community Foundation Grants, 2038
Pulido Walker Foundation, 2039
R.C. Baker Foundation Grants, 2043
R.D. and Joan Dale Hubbard Fdn Grants, 2044
Ralph M. Parsons Foundation Grants, 2052
Rasmuson Foundation Tier Two Grants, 2056
RCF General Community Grants, 2062
Reinberger Foundation Grants, 2066
RGk Foundation Grants, 2068
Richard J. Stern Foundation for the Arts Grants, 2071
Richard W. Goldman Family Fdn Grants, 2073
Richland County Bank Grants, 2074
Riedman Foundation Grants, 2076
Ripley County Community Foundation Grants, 2077
Ripley County Community Foundation Small Project
    Grants, 2078
Robert and Betty Wo Foundation Grants, 2083
Roger L. and Agnes C. Dell Charitable Trust I
    Grants, 2099
Roney-Fitzpatrick Foundation Grants, 2102
Rush County Community Foundation Grants, 2121
Ruth Camp Campbell Charitable Trust Grants, 2125
Saltchuk Corporate Giving, 2141
Samueli Foundation Education Grants, 2143
San Antonio Area Foundation Capital and Naming
    Rights Grants, 2148
Sand Hill Foundation Environment and Sustainability
    Grants, 2152
Sand Hill Foundation Health and Opportunity
    Grants, 2153
Sandy Hill Foundation Grants, 2157
Sarkeys Foundation Grants, 2163
Sartain Lanier Family Foundation Grants, 2164
Schramm Foundation Grants, 2168
Scott B. and Annie P. Appleby Charitable Trust
    Grants, 2169
Scott County Community Foundation Grants, 2170

Seattle Foundation Education Grants, 2178
Sensient Technologies Foundation Grants, 2180
Serco Foundation Grants, 2181
Shell Deer Park Grants, 2186
Shield-Ayres Foundation Grants, 2189
Sidney and Sandy Brown Foundation Grants, 2196
Sioux Falls Area Community Foundation Community
    Fund Grants, 2203
Sioux Falls Area Community Foundation Spot
    Grants, 2204
SME Education Fdn Youth Program Grants, 2209
Sony Corporation of America Grants, 2216
Sorenson Legacy Foundation Grants, 2217
Stranahan Foundation Grants, 2250
Sunoco Foundation Grants, 2256
SunTrust Bank Trusteed Foundations Greene-Sawtell
    Grants, 2257
SunTrust Bank Trusteed Foundations Nell Warren
    Elkin and William Simpson Elkin Grants, 2258
Suspened: Community Fdn for Greater Atlanta State
    Farm Education Assist Fund Grants, 2260
Sylvia Perkin Perpetual Charitable Trust Grants, 2263
Tata Trust Grant for Certificate Course in Holistic
    inclusion of Learners with Diversities, 2273
Teagle Foundation Grants, 2277
TE Foundation Grants, 2279
Tension Envelope Foundation Grants, 2284
Textron Corporate Contributions Grants, 2286
Thelma Doelger Charitable Trust Grants, 2288
Thomas J. Long Foundation Community Grants, 2291
Thomas Sill Foundation Grants, 2292
Thomas W. Briggs Foundation Grants, 2294
Toyota USA Foundation Education Grants, 2318
Union Bank, N.A. Corporate Sponsorships and
    Donations, 2333
Union Bank, N.A. Foundation Grants, 2334
United Technologies Corporation Grants, 2347
USDEd Gaining Early Awareness and Readiness for
    Undergrad Programs (GEAR UP) Grants, 2364
V.V. Cooke Foundation Grants, 2371
Vermillion County Community Fdn Grants, 2378
Virginia Foundation for the Humanities Open
    Grants, 2387
W.P. and Bulah Luse Foundation Grants, 2399
Walker Area Community Foundation Grants, 2401
Wallace Foundation Grants, 2402
Watson-Brown Foundation Grants, 2418
Weaver Popcorn Foundation Grants, 2421
Wege Foundation Grants, 2422
Whitney Foundation Grants, 2441
Widgeon Point Charitable Foundation Grants, 2447
William and Sandy Heitz Family Fdn Grants, 2457
William B. Stokely Jr. Foundation Grants, 2459
William Blair and Company Foundation Grants, 2461
William G. and Helen C. Hoffman Foundation
    Grants, 2466
William G. Gilmore Foundation Grants, 2467
William J. and Gertrude R. Casper Foundation
    Grants, 2469
Wilton and Effie Hebert Foundation Grants, 2476
Windham Foundation Grants, 2477
Winifred Johnson Clive Foundation Grants, 2478
Wiregrass Foundation Grants, 2480
Wold Foundation Grants, 2482
Wyoming Community Fdn General Grants, 2501
Wyoming Community Foundation Hazel Patterson
    Memorial Grants, 2502
Wyomissing Foundation Community Grants, 2504
Wyomissing Foundation Thun Family Organizational
    Grants, 2505
Wyomissing Foundation Thun Family Program
    Grants, 2506
Yawkey Foundation Grants, 2510
Youths' Friends Association Grants, 2511
Zollner Foundation Grants, 2526

Higher Education Studies

White County Community Foundation - Landis
    Memorial Scholarship, 2437

Higher Education, Private
Abell-Hanger Foundation Grants, 52
ACF Family Strengthening Scholars Grants, 81
Cadillac Products Packaging Company Foundation
Grants, 491
Dayton Foundation VISIONS Endowment Fund
Grants, 800
Francis Beidler Foundation Grants, 1007
Georgia-Pacific Foundation Education Grants, 1058
Geraldine R. Dodge Fdn Education Grants, 1061
Haddad Foundation Grants, 1139
Hall-Perrine Foundation Grants, 1152
Huisking Foundation Grants, 1274
Kenneth T. and Eileen L. Norris Fdn Grants, 1427
Marion I. and Henry J. Knott Foundation
Discretionary Grants, 1571
Marion I. and Henry J. Knott Foundation Standard
Grants, 1572
Philip L. Graham Fund Education Grants, 1962
Sandy Hill Foundation Grants, 2157
Strake Foundation Grants, 2249
Suspened: Community Fdn for Greater Atlanta State
Farm Education Assist Fund Grants, 2260

Higher Education, Public
ACF Family Strengthening Scholars Grants, 81
Cadillac Products Packaging Company Foundation
Grants, 491
Dayton Foundation VISIONS Endowment Fund
Grants, 800
Francis Beidler Foundation Grants, 1007
Georgia-Pacific Foundation Education Grants, 1058
Geraldine R. Dodge Fdn Education Grants, 1061
Philip L. Graham Fund Education Grants, 1962
Sandy Hill Foundation Grants, 2157
Suspened: Community Fdn for Greater Atlanta State
Farm Education Assist Fund Grants, 2260
William J. and Tina Rosenberg Fdn Grants, 2470

Hispanic Education
General Motors Foundation Grants, 1039
McCune Charitable Foundation Grants, 1617
New Jersey Center for Hispanic Policy, Research and
Development Innovative Initiatives Grants, 1750
Target Corporation Community Engagement Fund
Grants, 2270

Hispanics
BBF Florida Family Literacy Initiative Grants, 386
BBF Maine Family Literacy Initiative Implementation
Grants, 387
BBF Maine Family Literacy Initiative Planning
Grants, 388
Charles Delmar Foundation Grants, 564
Effie and Wofford Cain Foundation Grants, 895
Eide Bailly Resourcefullness Awards, 897
Foundation Beyond Belief Compassionate Impact
Grants, 986
Foundation Beyond Belief Humanist Grants, 987
Kalamazoo Community Foundation Early Childhood
Learning and School Readiness Grants, 1407
New Jersey Center for Hispanic Policy, Research and
Development Innovative Initiatives Grants, 1750
Robert R. Meyer Foundation Grants, 2094

Historical Preservation
Alabama Humanities Foundation Major Grants, 159
Albert W. Cherne Foundation Grants, 222
Ama OluKai Foundation Grants, 249
C.F. Adams Charitable Trust Grants, 488
Collins C. Diboll Private Foundation Grants, 657
Decatur County Community Foundation Large
Project Grants, 811
Effie Allen Little Foundation Grants, 894
Elkhart County Community Foundation Fund for
Elkhart County, 902
First Hawaiian Bank Foundation Corporate Giving
Grants, 967
Fdn for the Mid South Communities Grants, 992
Frank M. Tait Foundation Grants, 1012

George J. and Effie L. Seay Foundation Grants, 1052
George Kress Foundation Grants, 1053
Hawaii Electric Industries Charitable Foundation
Grants, 1218
Helen E. Ellis Charitable Trust Grants, 1228
HSFCA Biennium Grants, 1267
HSFCA Folk and Traditional Arts Grants - Culture
Learning, 1268
Island Insurance Foundation Grants, 1316
Kovler Family Foundation Grants, 1454
LGA Family Foundation Grants, 1487
M.A. Rikard Charitable Trust Grants, 1521
McCombs Foundation Grants, 1615
McLean Contributionship Grants, 1623
Norcliffe Foundation Grants, 1766
Orange County Community Foundation Grants, 1828
Parke County Community Foundation Grants, 1868
Richard and Caroline T. Gwathmey Memorial Trust
Grants, 2069
Richard J. Stern Foundation for the Arts Grants, 2071
Samuel N. and Mary Castle Foundation Grants, 2145
Sioux Falls Area Community Foundation Community
Fund Grants, 2203
Sioux Falls Area Community Foundation Spot
Grants, 2204
Sylvia Perkin Perpetual Charitable Trust Grants, 2263
Turner Foundation Grants, 2326
Virginia Foundation for the Humanities Folklife
Apprenticeships, 2386
Virginia Foundation for the Humanities Open
Grants, 2387
Widgeon Point Charitable Foundation Grants, 2447
Windham Foundation Grants, 2477

History
Alabama Humanities Foundation Major Grants, 159
ALA May Hill Arbuthnot Honor Lecture Award, 176
Atwood Foundation General Grants, 330
Blanche and Irving Laurie Foundation Grants, 436
Cooke Foundation Grants, 748
Dayton Foundation Grants, 796
Dean Foundation Grants, 806
E.J. Grassmann Trust Grants, 876
George I. Alden Trust Grants, 1051
Hawai'i SFCA Art Bento Program @ HiSAM
Grants, 1210
Montana Arts Council Cultural and Aesthetic Project
Grants, 1685
NCSS Award for Global Understanding, 1728
NEH Family and Youth Programs in American
History Grants, 1734
Richard and Caroline T. Gwathmey Memorial Trust
Grants, 2069
Sarah G. McCarthy Memorial Foundation, 2162
Turner Foundation Grants, 2326
University of Chicago Chapin Hall Doris Duke
Fellowships, 2348
Virginia Foundation for the Humanities Open
Grants, 2387
Watson-Brown Foundation Grants, 2418

History Education
Alabama Humanities Foundation Major Grants, 159
CHT Foundation Education Grants, 603
NEH Family and Youth Programs in American
History Grants, 1734

Homeland Security
CNCS AmeriCorps NCCC Project Grants, 642

Homeless Shelters
ACF Basic Center Program Grants, 73
ACF Child Welfare Training Grants, 75
Adams Family Foundation of Tennessee Grants, 120
Adobe Fdn Hunger and Homelessness Grants, 128
AEGON Transamerica Foundation Health and
Wellness Grants, 133
Akron Community Foundation Health and Human
Services Grants, 152
ALA Coretta Scott King Book Donation Grant, 168

Alliance for Strong Families and Communities
Grants, 239
Alloy Family Foundation Grants, 241
Alpha Natural Resources Corporate Giving, 246
Alvah H. and Wyline P. Chapman Foundation
Grants, 248
ATA Local Community Relations Grants, 324
Bank of Hawaii Foundation Grants, 360
Bushrod H. Campbell and Adah F. Hall Charity
Fund Grants, 486
C.H. Robinson Worldwide Foundation Grants, 489
Carl B. and Florence E. King Foundation Grants, 506
Carl M. Freeman Foundation FACES Grants, 507
Carrie S. Orleans Trust Grants, 512
Charles H. Hall Foundation, 565
Circle K Corporation Contributions Grants, 614
Citizens Savings Foundation Grants, 617
Clara Blackford Smith and W. Aubrey Smith
Charitable Foundation Grants, 621
Community Foundation for Greater Atlanta Frances
Hollis Brain Foundation Fund Grants, 664
Community Foundation of Crawford County, 695
Community Foundation of Muncie and Delaware
County Maxon Grants, 734
Community Foundation of Switzerland County
Grants, 739
Daniels Homeless and Disadvantaged Grants, 782
Dominion Foundation Grants, 839
Emily O'Neill Sullivan Foundation Grants, 913
Emma J. Adams Memorial Fund Grants, 914
Essex County Community Foundation Greater
Lawrence Community Fund Grants, 931
Fitzpatrick, Cella, Harper & Scinto Pro Bono
Services, 976
Frank Reed and Margaret Jane Peters Memorial Fund
II Grants, 1014
Gardner Foundation Grants, 1034
George E. Hatcher, Jr. and Ann Williams Hatcher
Foundation Grants, 1045
George H. Sandy Foundation Grants, 1050
Green Foundation Human Services Grants, 1116
Harold Brooks Foundation Grants, 1172
Hattie Mae Lesley Foundation Grants, 1195
Helen Irwin Littauer Educational Trust Grants, 1231
Henrietta Lange Burk Fund Grants, 1235
Herman P. and Sophia Taubman Fdn Grants, 1247
Horace A. Kimball and S. Ella Kimball Foundation
Grants, 1260
J. Watumull Fund Grants, 1326
Jeffris Wood Foundation Grants, 1359
Joseph Henry Edmondson Foundation Grants, 1388
Judy and Peter Blum Kovler Foundation Grants, 1396
Kate B. Reynolds Charitable Trust Poor and Needy
Grants, 1417
Leo Niessen Jr., Charitable Trust Grants, 1484
LISC Affordable Housing Grants, 1497
Marietta McNeill Morgan and Samuel Tate Morgan
Jr. Trust Grants, 1560
Marquette Bank Neighborhood Commit Grants, 1577
Marriott Int Corporate Giving Grants, 1578
McCarthy Family Fdn Charity Fund Grants, 1614
McGregor Fund Human Services Grants, 1621
Medtronic Foundation Community Link Human
Services Grants, 1631
Meyer Fdn Healthy Communities Grants, 1650
Narragansett Number One Foundation Grants, 1712
Oak Fdn Housing and Homelessness Grants, 1800
Ordean Foundation Catalyst Grants, 1830
Ordean Foundation Partnership Grants, 1831
Packard Foundation Local Grants, 1863
Perkins-Ponder Foundation Grants, 1938
Perpetual Benevolent Fund, 1940
Pinnacle Foundation Grants, 1973
Reinberger Foundation Grants, 2066
Robert and Betty Wo Foundation Grants, 2083
Robert R. Meyer Foundation Grants, 2094
Robinson Foundation Grants, 2097
Sarah G. McCarthy Memorial Foundation, 2162
Sierra Health Foundation Responsive Grants, 2199
Swindells Charitable Foundation Grants, 2261

Sylvia Adams Charitable Trust Grants, 2262
Textron Corporate Contributions Grants, 2286
Union Bank, N.A. Foundation Grants, 2334
Union Square Award for Social Justice, 2340
Whitehorse Foundation Grants, 2439
WHO Foundation Volunteer Service Grants, 2444
Wold Foundation Grants, 2482
Women's Fund of Hawaii Grants, 2484

Homelessness

ACF Basic Center Program Grants, 73
ACF Child Welfare Training Grants, 75
Achelis and Bodman Foundation Grants, 101
Achelis Foundation Grants, 102
Adobe Foundation Action Grants, 126
Adobe Fdn Hunger and Homelessness Grants, 128
AEGON Transamerica Foundation Health and
    Wellness Grants, 133
Alloy Family Foundation Grants, 241
Alvah H. and Wyline P. Chapman Foundation
    Grants, 248
Atkinson Foundation Community Grants, 325
Atlanta Women's Foundation Pathway to Success
    Grants, 327
Baxter International Foundation Grants, 369
Bushrod H. Campbell and Adah F. Hall Charity
    Fund Grants, 486
C.H. Robinson Worldwide Foundation Grants, 489
Carl B. and Florence E. King Foundation Grants, 506
CFFVR Robert and Patricia Endries Family
    Foundation Grants, 547
Charles Delmar Foundation Grants, 564
Community Foundation for the Capital Region
    Grants, 687
Cralle Foundation Grants, 760
Crane Fund for Widows and Children Grants, 762
D. W. McMillan Foundation Grants, 776
Daniels Homeless and Disadvantaged Grants, 782
Delaware Community Foundation Grants, 817
Dominion Foundation Grants, 839
Edna Wardlaw Charitable Trust Grants, 886
Effie and Wofford Cain Foundation Grants, 895
El Pomar Foundation Anna Keesling Ackerman Fund
    Grants, 907
El Pomar Foundation Grants, 908
Emma J. Adams Memorial Fund Grants, 914
Ensworth Charitable Foundation Grants, 916
Essex County Community Foundation Merrimack
    Valley Municipal Business Development and
    Recovery Fund Grants, 933
Fassino Foundation Grants, 949
Fourjay Foundation Grants, 1003
Friends of Hawaii Charities Grants, 1024
Gardner Foundation Grants, 1034
George A Ohl Jr. Foundation Grants, 1043
Giant Food Charitable Grants, 1068
Green Foundation Human Services Grants, 1116
Greenspun Family Foundation Grants, 1118
H.B. Fuller Foundation Grants, 1138
Hasbro Children's Fund Grants, 1189
Helen V. Brach Foundation Grants, 1232
Horace A. Kimball and S. Ella Kimball Foundation
    Grants, 1260
Horace A. Moses Charitable Trust Grants, 1261
Jacob G. Schmidlapp Trusts Grants, 1336
John Gogian Family Foundation Grants, 1373
Joseph Henry Edmondson Foundation Grants, 1388
Judy and Peter Blum Kovler Foundation Grants, 1396
Kate B. Reynolds Charitable Trust Poor and Needy
    Grants, 1417
Lands' End Corporate Giving Program, 1468
Laura B. Vogler Foundation Grants, 1470
Leo Niessen Jr., Charitable Trust Grants, 1484
Linden Foundation Grants, 1494
LISC Affordable Housing Grants, 1497
M.J. Murdock Charitable Trust General Grants, 1524
Manuel D. and Rhoda Mayerson Fdn Grants, 1550
Marietta McNeill Morgan and Samuel Tate Morgan
    Jr. Trust Grants, 1560

Marin Community Foundation Affordable Housing
    Grants, 1561
McGregor Fund Human Services Grants, 1621
Mervin Bovaird Foundation Grants, 1643
Meyer Fdn Healthy Communities Grants, 1650
Moody Foundation Grants, 1692
Morris Stulsaft Foundation Pathways to Work
    Grants, 1699
Narragansett Number One Foundation Grants, 1712
Northland Foundation Grants, 1771
Oak Fdn Housing and Homelessness Grants, 1800
Oppenstein Brothers Foundation Grants, 1827
Ordean Foundation Catalyst Grants, 1830
Ordean Foundation Partnership Grants, 1831
OSF Soros Justice Youth Activist Fellowships, 1844
Perpetual Benevolent Fund, 1940
Pinnacle Foundation Grants, 1973
Portland General Electric Foundation Grants, 2007
Public Welfare Foundation Special Initiative to
    Advance Civil Legal Aid Grants, 2034
Publix Super Markets Charities Local Grants, 2036
Puerto Rico Community Foundation Grants, 2037
Reinberger Foundation Grants, 2066
Robert R. Meyer Foundation Grants, 2094
Robin Hood Foundation Grants, 2096
Robinson Foundation Grants, 2097
Ruth Anderson Foundation Grants, 2122
Schlessman Family Foundation Grants, 2167
Sensient Technologies Foundation Grants, 2180
Singing for Change Foundation Grants, 2202
Swindells Charitable Foundation Grants, 2261
Sylvia Adams Charitable Trust Grants, 2262
Union Bank, N.A. Foundation Grants, 2334
Union Square Award for Social Justice, 2340
USDA Child and Adult Care Food Program, 2362
Whitehorse Foundation Grants, 2439
WHO Foundation Volunteer Service Grants, 2444
William G. and Helen C. Hoffman Foundation
    Grants, 2466
William J. and Dorothy K. O'Neill Foundation
    Responsive Grants, 2468
Women's Fund of Hawaii Grants, 2485
Women's Fund of Hawaii Grants, 2484
Wyoming Department of Education McKinney-Vento
    Subgrant, 2503
Xerox Foundation Grants, 2507

Homeownership

ACF Marriage Strengthening Research &
    Dissemination Center Grants, 85
Bank of America Charitable Foundation Community
    Development Grants, 355
Community Foundation of Western Massachusetts
    Grants, 741
Dolan Media Foundation Grants, 833
Entergy Charitable Foundation Low-Income
    Initiatives and Solutions Grants, 918
Joseph S. Stackpole Charitable Trust Grants, 1390
Middlesex Savings Charitable Foundation
    Educational Opportunities Grants, 1670
PMI Foundation Grants, 1982
Public Welfare Foundation Special Initiative to
    Advance Civil Legal Aid Grants, 2034
Speer Trust Grants, 2230
Union Bank, N.A. Foundation Grants, 2334

Homosexuals, Female

ACF Runaway and Homeless Youth Training and
    Technical Assistance Center Grants, 92
ALA Rainbow Project Book List Award, 187
ALFJ International Fund Grants, 231
Appalachian Community Fund LGBTQ Fund
    Grants, 284
California Endowment Innovative Ideas Challenge
    Grants, 495
Colin Higgins Foundation Courage Awards, 653
Community Foundation for the National Capital
    Region Community Leadership Grants, 688
Eide Bailly Resourcefullness Awards, 897

Evelyn and Walter Haas, Jr. Fund Gay and Lesbian
    Rights Grants, 940
FCYO Youth Organizing Grants, 954
Foundation Beyond Belief Compassionate Impact
    Grants, 986
Foundation Beyond Belief Humanist Grants, 987
Joseph H. and Florence A. Roblee Foundation
    Children and Youth Grants, 1385
Kalamazoo Community Foundation LBGT Equality
    Fund Grants, 1411
Maine Community Foundation Equity Grants, 1541
Ms. Foundation for Women Building Democracy
    Grants, 1706
Ms. Fdn for Women Ending Violence Grants, 1708
New York Foundation Grants, 1753
Philanthrofund Foundation Grants, 1959
Pride Foundation Grants, 2024
Proteus Fund Grants, 2027
Streisand Foundation Grants, 2251
Susan A. and Donald P. Babson Charitable
    Foundation Grants, 2259
Threshold Foundation Queer Youth Grants, 2299
Tides Foundation Grants, 2302
Women's Fund of Hawaii Grants, 2485
Xerox Foundation Grants, 2507

Homosexuals, Male

ACF Runaway and Homeless Youth Training and
    Technical Assistance Center Grants, 92
ALA Rainbow Project Book List Award, 187
ALFJ International Fund Grants, 231
Appalachian Community Fund LGBTQ Fund
    Grants, 284
California Endowment Innovative Ideas Challenge
    Grants, 495
Colin Higgins Foundation Courage Awards, 653
Community Foundation for the National Capital
    Region Community Leadership Grants, 688
Eide Bailly Resourcefullness Awards, 897
Evelyn and Walter Haas, Jr. Fund Gay and Lesbian
    Rights Grants, 940
FCYO Youth Organizing Grants, 954
Foundation Beyond Belief Compassionate Impact
    Grants, 986
Foundation Beyond Belief Humanist Grants, 987
Joseph H. and Florence A. Roblee Foundation
    Children and Youth Grants, 1385
Kalamazoo Community Foundation LBGT Equality
    Fund Grants, 1411
Maine Community Foundation Equity Grants, 1541
Ms. Foundation for Women Building Democracy
    Grants, 1706
Ms. Fdn for Women Ending Violence Grants, 1708
New York Foundation Grants, 1753
Philanthrofund Foundation Grants, 1959
Pride Foundation Grants, 2024
Proteus Fund Grants, 2027
Streisand Foundation Grants, 2251
Susan A. and Donald P. Babson Charitable
    Foundation Grants, 2259
Threshold Foundation Queer Youth Grants, 2299
Tides Foundation Grants, 2302
Women's Fund of Hawaii Grants, 2485
Xerox Foundation Grants, 2507

Horticulture

First Nations Development Institute Native
    Agriculture and Food Systems Initiative
    Scholarships, 971
Frederick W. Marzahl Memorial Fund Grants, 1018

Hospice Care

ACCF of Indiana Angel Funds Grants, 62
Adelaide Breed Bayrd Foundation Grants, 123
Alex Stern Family Foundation Grants, 229
Burlington Industries Foundation Grants, 481
Carl B. and Florence E. King Foundation Grants, 506
Carl W. and Carrie Mae Joslyn Trust Grants, 510
Citizens Savings Foundation Grants, 617
Cleo Foundation Grants, 632

D. W. McMillan Foundation Grants, 776
Dunspaugh-Dalton Foundation Grants, 873
Edward W. and Stella C. Van Houten Memorial Fund
    Grants, 892
First Hawaiian Bank Foundation Corporate Giving
    Grants, 967
Gardner Foundation Grants, 1034
George E. Hatcher, Jr. and Ann Williams Hatcher
    Foundation Grants, 1045
Hasbro Corporation Gift of Play Hospital and
    Pediatric Health Giving, 1191
J.W. Kieckhefer Foundation Grants, 1324
Margaret T. Morris Foundation Grants, 1557
MGN Family Foundation Grants, 1656
Samuel S. Johnson Foundation Grants, 2146
Sensient Technologies Foundation Grants, 2180

Hospitals
1st Source Foundation Community Involvement
    Grants, 1
A.L. Spencer Foundation Grants, 21
Adams-Mastrovich Family Foundation Grants, 113
Adelaide Breed Bayrd Foundation Grants, 123
Alavi Foundation Education Grants, 216
Andrew Family Foundation Grants, 272
Antone and Edene Vidinha Charitable Grants, 281
Avery Foundation Grants, 339
Bank of Hawaii Foundation Grants, 360
Beckman Coulter Foundation Grants, 394
BibleLands Grants, 420
Blumenthal Foundation Grants, 459
Burlington Industries Foundation Grants, 481
Bushrod H. Campbell and Adah F. Hall Charity
    Fund Grants, 486
C.H. Robinson Worldwide Foundation Grants, 489
Caesars Foundation Grants, 492
Callaway Foundation Grants, 496
Carl B. and Florence E. King Foundation Grants, 506
Charles Delmar Foundation Grants, 564
Cheryl Spencer Memorial Foundation Grants, 576
Clark and Ruby Baker Foundation Grants, 625
Crystelle Waggoner Charitable Trust Grants, 768
Dana Brown Charitable Trust Grants, 777
Daniel and Nanna Stern Family Fdn Grants, 778
David M. and Marjorie D. Rosenberg Foundation
    Grants, 790
Dolan Children's Foundation Grants, 832
Dunspaugh-Dalton Foundation Grants, 873
E.J. Grassmann Trust Grants, 876
Edwards Memorial Trust Grants, 891
Effie and Wofford Cain Foundation Grants, 895
Effie Kuhlman Charitable Trust Grants, 896
Elsie H. Wilcox Foundation Grants, 909
F.M. Kirby Foundation Grants, 946
FirstEnergy Foundation Community Grants, 965
First Hawaiian Bank Foundation Corporate Giving
    Grants, 967
Foundation for Health Enhancement Grants, 990
Four J Foundation Grants, 1004
Frank S. Flowers Foundation Grants, 1015
G.N. Wilcox Trust Grants, 1031
George E. Hatcher, Jr. and Ann Williams Hatcher
    Foundation Grants, 1045
George F. Baker Trust Grants, 1046
George Kress Foundation Grants, 1053
George W. Codrington Charitable Foundation
    Grants, 1055
Gertrude & William C. Wardlaw Grants, 1067
GNOF IMPACT Gulf States Eye Surg Fund, 1085
Harvey Randall Wickes Foundation Grants, 1188
Helen Irwin Littauer Educational Trust Grants, 1231
Henry County Community Foundation Grants, 1239
Henry L. Guenther Foundation Grants, 1242
HLTA Visitor Industry Charity Walk Grant, 1254
Hubbard Broadcasting Foundation Grants, 1269
Huffy Foundation Grants, 1273
Huisking Foundation Grants, 1274
J. Walton Bissell Foundation Grants, 1325
John Clarke Trust Grants, 1369
Journal Gazette Foundation Grants, 1391

Joyce and Randy Seckman Charitable Foundation
    Grants, 1393
Katherine John Murphy Foundation Grants, 1419
Kathryne Beynon Foundation Grants, 1420
Kovler Family Foundation Grants, 1454
Lumpkin Family Fdn Healthy People Grants, 1518
Mabel Y. Hughes Charitable Trust Grants, 1530
Margaret and James A. Elkins Jr. Fdn Grants, 1555
Mary S. and David C. Corbin Fdn Grants, 1598
Matilda R. Wilson Fund Grants, 1605
McLean Contributionship Grants, 1623
Meadows Foundation Grants, 1626
Mericos Foundation Grants, 1637
Meriden Foundation Grants, 1638
Mervin Bovaird Foundation Grants, 1643
Mockingbird Foundation Grants, 1680
Norcliffe Foundation Grants, 1766
Olive Higgins Prouty Foundation Grants, 1817
Oppenstein Brothers Foundation Grants, 1827
Pinnacle Entertainment Foundation Grants, 1972
Piper Jaffray Foundation Communities Giving
    Grants, 1974
R.C. Baker Foundation Grants, 2043
Raskob Fdn for Catholic Activities Grants, 2054
Reinberger Foundation Grants, 2066
Riedman Foundation Grants, 2076
Robert R. Meyer Foundation Grants, 2094
Sara Elizabeth O'Brien Trust Grants, 2161
Scott County Community Foundation Grants, 2170
Sensient Technologies Foundation Grants, 2180
Shell Deer Park Grants, 2186
Shell Oil Company Foundation Community
    Development Grants, 2188
Strake Foundation Grants, 2249
SunTrust Bank Trusteed Foundations Greene-Sawtell
    Grants, 2257
SunTrust Bank Trusteed Foundations Nell Warren
    Elkin and William Simpson Elkin Grants, 2258
Swindells Charitable Foundation Grants, 2261
Tellabs Foundation Grants, 2280
Thelma Doelger Charitable Trust Grants, 2288
Victor E. Speas Foundation Grants, 2380
Wege Foundation Grants, 2422
William B. Stokely Jr. Foundation Grants, 2459
Wilton and Effie Hebert Foundation Grants, 2476
Wyomissing Foundation Community Grants, 2504

Housing
786 Foundation Grants, 15
ACF Voluntary Agencies Matching Grants, 100
Adobe Fdn Hunger and Homelessness Grants, 128
Agnes M. Lindsay Trust Grants, 140
Aid for Starving Children Homes and Education
    Grants, 146
Alliant Energy Foundation Community Giving for
    Good Sponsorship Grants, 240
Alloy Family Foundation Grants, 241
Alpha Natural Resources Corporate Giving, 246
American Electric Power Foundation Grants, 253
American Woodmark Foundation Grants, 263
AMERIND Community Service Project Grants, 265
Annie Gardner Foundation Grants, 277
Appalachian Regl Commission Housing Grants, 289
Arthur Ashley Williams Foundation Grants, 302
Atkinson Foundation Community Grants, 325
Atlanta Foundation Grants, 326
Bank of America Charitable Foundation Basic Needs
    Grants, 354
Bank of America Charitable Foundation Community
    Development Grants, 355
Bank of Hawaii Foundation Grants, 360
Bank of the Orient Community Giving, 361
Bollinger Foundation Grants, 463
C.H. Robinson Worldwide Foundation Grants, 489
Camille Beckman Foundation Grants, 499
Campbell Soup Foundation Grants, 501
Carl B. and Florence E. King Foundation Grants, 506
Carl M. Freeman Foundation FACES Grants, 507
Carrie S. Orleans Trust Grants, 512

CFFVR Robert and Patricia Endries Family
    Foundation Grants, 547
CFGR Community Impact Grants, 552
Circle K Corporation Contributions Grants, 614
Citizens Bank Charitable Foundation Grants, 616
Citizens Savings Foundation Grants, 617
Cleo Foundation Grants, 632
Cleveland Foundation Higley Fund Grants, 634
CNCS AmeriCorps State and National Grants, 643
CNCS AmeriCorps VISTA Project Grants, 645
Community Foundation of Western Massachusetts
    Grants, 741
Dearborn Community Foundation City of Aurora
    Grants, 808
Delaware Community Foundation Grants, 817
Delmarva Power & Light Contributions, 821
DOL Youthbuild Grants, 838
Dominion Foundation Grants, 839
Doree Taylor Charitable Foundation Grants, 843
DTE Energy Foundation Community Development
    Grants, 866
Eastern Bank Charitable Foundation Partnerships
    Grants, 881
Eastern Bank Charitable Foundation Targeted
    Grants, 882
Edward and Ellen Roche Relief Fdn Grants, 887
Ensworth Charitable Foundation Grants, 916
Entergy Charitable Foundation Low-Income
    Initiatives and Solutions Grants, 918
First Hawaiian Bank Foundation Corporate Giving
    Grants, 967
Fitzpatrick, Cella, Harper & Scinto Pro Bono
    Services, 976
Fdns of East Chicago Family Support Grants, 996
Fourjay Foundation Grants, 1003
Frank Reed and Margaret Jane Peters Memorial Fund
    II Grants, 1014
Fund for the City of New York Grants, 1029
George and Ruth Bradford Foundation Grants, 1042
George A Ohl Jr. Foundation Grants, 1043
GNOF Coastal 5 + 1 Grants, 1078
GNOF Gert Community Fund Grants, 1082
Gregory and Helayne Brown Charitable Foundation
    Grants, 1119
GTRCF Elk Rapids Area Community Endowment
    Grants, 1127
Hartford Foundation Regular Grants, 1185
Hearst Foundations Social Service Grants, 1224
HSBC Corporate Giving Grants, 1266
J.W. Gardner II Foundation Grants, 1323
Jacob G. Schmidlapp Trusts Grants, 1336
Janson Foundation Grants, 1349
Joan Bentinck-Smith Charitable Fdn Grants, 1367
Kalamazoo Community Foundation Individuals and
    Families Grants, 1409
Kate B. Reynolds Charitable Trust Poor and Needy
    Grants, 1417
Katharine Matthies Foundation Grants, 1418
Kathryne Beynon Foundation Grants, 1420
Koch Family Foundation (Annapolis) Grants, 1444
Liberty Bank Foundation Grants, 1488
Linden Foundation Grants, 1494
LISC Affordable Housing Grants, 1497
LISC Capacity Building Grants, 1498
LISC Community Leadership Operating Grts, 1499
Locations Foundation Legacy Grants, 1504
M.A. Rikard Charitable Trust Grants, 1521
Mabel Louise Riley Foundation Grants, 1529
Madison Community Foundation Grants, 1535
Manuel D. and Rhoda Mayerson Fdn Grants, 1550
Marietta McNeill Morgan and Samuel Tate Morgan
    Jr. Trust Grants, 1560
Marquette Bank Neighborhood Commit Grants, 1577
Marriott Int Corporate Giving Grants, 1578
Mary Owen Borden Foundation Grants, 1597
Mary S. and David C. Corbin Fdn Grants, 1598
McCarthy Family Fdn Charity Fund Grants, 1614
McGregor Fund Human Services Grants, 1621
Mericos Foundation Grants, 1637
Meyer Fdn Healthy Communities Grants, 1650

Moses Kimball Fund Grants, 1701
Nicole Brown Foundation Grants, 1760
Oak Fdn Housing and Homelessness Grants, 1800
Olga Sipolin Children's Fund Grants, 1815
Ordean Foundation Catalyst Grants, 1830
Ordean Foundation Partnership Grants, 1831
OSF Youth Action Fund Grants in Kyrgyzstan, 1846
Parker Foundation (California) Grants, 1869
Patrick and Aimee Butler Family Foundation
    Community Human Services Grants, 1880
Perkins-Ponder Foundation Grants, 1938
Perpetual Benevolent Fund, 1940
Peyton Anderson Foundation Grants, 1954
Piper Jaffray Foundation Communities Giving
    Grants, 1974
Piper Trust Reglious Organizations Grants, 1979
Pittsburgh Fdn Affordable Housing Grants, 1980
PMI Foundation Grants, 1982
PNC Foundation Affordable Housing Grants, 1983
PNC Foundation Revitalization and Stabilization
    Grants, 1987
Pohlad Family Fdn Small Capital Grants, 1991
Puerto Rico Community Foundation Grants, 2037
Reinberger Foundation Grants, 2066
Ruth Anderson Foundation Grants, 2122
Sarah G. McCarthy Memorial Foundation, 2162
Schramm Foundation Grants, 2168
Sobrato Family Foundation Grants, 2211
Textron Corporate Contributions Grants, 2286
TJX Foundation Grants, 2303
U.S. Bank Foundation Grants, 2330
Union Bank, N.A. Corporate Sponsorships and
    Donations, 2333
Union Bank, N.A. Foundation Grants, 2334
Wayne County Foundation Grants, 2419
Whitehorse Foundation Grants, 2439
Whole Foods Foundation, 2445
William J. and Dorothy K. O'Neill Foundation
    Responsive Grants, 2468
Women's Fund of Hawaii Grants, 2484

Human Development
Bank of Hawaii Foundation Grants, 360
University of Chicago Chapin Hall Doris Duke
    Fellowships, 2348

Human Learning and Memory
Helen Bader Foundation Grants, 1227
NSF Perception, Action and Cognition (PAC)
    Research Grants, 1775
Wallace Foundation Grants, 2402

Human Reproduction/Fertility
A. Alfred Taubman Foundation Grants, 18
Edna Wardlaw Charitable Trust Grants, 886
Gardner Foundation Grants, 1034
General Service Foundation Human Rights and
    Economic Justice Grants, 1040
Packard Foundation Local Grants, 1863
USAID Family Planning and Reproductive Health
    Methods Grants, 2353
WestWind Foundation Reproductive Health and
    Rights Grants, 2434

Human Resources
Bill and Melinda Gates Foundation Emergency
    Response Grants, 426
Bill and Melinda Gates Foundation Water, Sanitation
    and Hygiene Grants, 428
Do Something Finance and Human Res Intern, 853
Ella West Freeman Foundation Grants, 904
LGA Family Foundation Grants, 1487
Middlesex Savings Charitable Foundation Capacity
    Building Grants, 1669

Human Services
3M Company Fdn Community Giving Grants, 5
3M Company Foundation Health and Human
    Services Grants, 6
A.C. and Penney Hubbard Foundation Grants, 19

A.L. Spencer Foundation Grants, 21
Abbott Fund Global AIDS Care Grants, 47
ABS Foundation Grants, 56
ACCF of Indiana Bank of Geneva Heritage Fund
    Grants, 64
ACCF of Indiana First Merchants Bank / Decatur
    Bank and Trust Fund Grants, 66
ACF Social and Economic Development Strategies
    Grants, 93
Ackerman Foundation Grants, 103
Adams-Mastrovich Family Foundation Grants, 113
Adams and Reese Corporate Giving Grants, 114
Adams Family Foundation of Ohio Grants, 119
Adelaide Breed Bayrd Foundation Grants, 123
Adelaide Christian Home For Children Grants, 124
AHS Foundation Grants, 143
Albert E. and Birdie W. Einstein Fund Grants, 220
Albert W. Cherne Foundation Grants, 222
Albert W. Rice Charitable Foundation Grants, 223
Alfred E. Chase Charitable Foundation Grants, 233
Alfred J Mcallister and Dorothy N Mcallister
    Foundation Grants, 234
Allan C. and Lelia J. Garden Foundation Grants, 236
Allegis Group Foundation Grants, 237
Alliance for Strong Families and Communities
    Grants, 239
Alloy Family Foundation Grants, 241
Alpha Natural Resources Corporate Giving, 246
Amelia Sillman Rockwell and Carlos Perry Rockwell
    Charities Fund Grants, 250
American Electric Power Corporate Grants, 252
American Electric Power Foundation Grants, 253
American Indian Youth Running Strong Grants, 256
American Woodmark Foundation Grants, 263
Anderson Foundation Grants, 271
Anna Fitch Ardenghi Trust Grants, 274
Anne J. Caudal Foundation Grants, 276
Annie Gardner Foundation Grants, 277
Ann L. and Carol Green Rhodes Charitable Trust
    Grants, 278
Ann Ludington Sullivan Foundation Grants, 279
Ar-Hale Family Foundation Grants, 290
Assisi Fdn of Memphis Capital Project Grants, 317
Assisi Foundation of Memphis General Grants, 318
Assisi Foundation of Memphis Mini Grants, 319
Atlas Insurance Agency Foundation Grants, 329
Aunt Kate Foundation Grants, 331
Avery-Fuller-Welch Children's Fdn Grants, 336
Avery Foundation Grants, 339
Back Home Again Foundation Grants, 344
Bank of Hawaii Foundation Grants, 360
Bay Area Community Fdn Auburn Area Chamber of
    Commerce Enrichment Fund Grants, 373
Bay Area Community Foundation Community
    Initiative Fund Grants, 376
Bay Area Community Foundation Human Services
    Fund Grants, 379
Belvedere Community Foundation Grants, 399
Benwood Foundation Community Grants, 406
Better Way Foundation Grants, 419
Bierhaus Foundation Grants, 421
Blackford County Community Fdn Grants, 434
Blandin Foundation Itasca County Area Vitality
    Grants, 439
Bodenwein Public Benevolent Foundation Grants, 461
Boeing Company Contributions Grants, 462
BP Foundation Grants, 465
Bradley C. Higgins Foundation Grants, 467
Brown Foundation Grants, 476
Burton D. Morgan Foundation Hudson Community
    Grants, 482
Bushrod H. Campbell and Adah F. Hall Charity
    Fund Grants, 486
C.F. Adams Charitable Trust Grants, 488
C.H. Robinson Worldwide Foundation Grants, 489
Caesars Foundation Grants, 492
Camille Beckman Foundation Grants, 499
Campbell Foundation Grants, 500
Carl R. Hendrickson Family Foundation Grants, 509
Cass County Community Foundation Grants, 516

Castle Foundation Grants, 518
Castle Foundation Grants, 517
Central Pacific Bank Foundation Grants, 530
CFFVR Project Grants, 546
Chapman Family Foundation, 562
Charles H. Hall Foundation, 565
Charles H. Pearson Foundation Grants, 566
Charles Nelson Robinson Fund Grants, 569
Charlotte and Joseph Gardner Fdn Grants, 570
Chilkat Valley Community Foundation Grants, 588
Christine and Katharina Pauly Charitable Trust
    Grants, 601
Citizens Savings Foundation Grants, 617
Clara Blackford Smith and W. Aubrey Smith
    Charitable Foundation Grants, 621
Clarence T.C. Ching Foundation Grants, 624
Clark Electric Cooperative Grants, 627
Claude A. and Blanche McCubbin Abbott Charitable
    Trust Grants, 628
Clayton F. and Ruth L. Hawkridge Foundation
    Grants, 630
Clayton Fund Grants, 631
Clinton County Community Foundation Grants, 638
CNCS Foster Grandparent Projects Grants, 646
CNO Financial Group Community Grants, 650
Community Foundation for Greater Atlanta Spark
    Clayton Grants, 667
Community Foundation for Greater Atlanta Spark
    Newton Grants, 668
Community Foundation for Greater Buffalo Niagara
    Area Foundation Grants, 673
Community Foundation for Kettering Grants, 676
Community Foundation for SE Michigan Detroit
    Auto Dealers Association Charitable Foundation
    Fund Grants, 681
Community Foundation of Boone County Grants, 694
Community Foundation of Crawford County, 695
Community Foundation of Grant County Grants, 703
Community Foundation of Louisville Human
    Services Grants, 726
Community Foundation of Muncie and Delaware
    County Maxon Grants, 734
Community Fdn of Southern Indiana Grants, 736
Community Foundation of St. Joseph County Special
    Project Challenge Grants, 738
Community Foundation Serving Riverside and San
    Bernardino Counties Impact Grants, 742
Covenant Educational Foundation Grants, 754
Covenant Foundation of Brentwood Grants, 755
Curtis Foundation Grants, 771
Dana Brown Charitable Trust Grants, 777
David and Betty Sacks Foundation Grants, 788
David M. and Marjorie D. Rosenberg Foundation
    Grants, 790
David Robinson Foundation Grants, 791
Dayton Power and Light Foundation Grants, 802
Decatur County Community Foundation Large
    Project Grants, 811
DeKalb County Community Foundation Grants, 815
Dominion Foundation Grants, 839
Dr. and Mrs. Paul Pierce Memorial Foundation
    Grants, 862
Dream Weaver Foundation, 865
DTE Energy Foundation Health and Human Services
    Grants, 869
Earl and Maxine Claussen Trust Grants, 878
Eastern Bank Charitable Foundation Partnerships
    Grants, 881
Eastern Bank Charitable Foundation Targeted
    Grants, 882
Edward and Ellen Roche Relief Fdn Grants, 887
Edward and Helen Bartlett Foundation Grants, 888
Effie Allen Little Foundation Grants, 894
Effie Kuhlman Charitable Trust Grants, 896
Elizabeth Morse Genius Charitable Trust Grants, 901
Emily O'Neill Sullivan Foundation Grants, 913
Ensworth Charitable Foundation Grants, 916
Faye L. and William L. Cowden Charitable
    Foundation Grants, 950
Fidelity Charitable Gift Fund Grants, 956

Fifth Third Foundation Grants, 959
First Hawaiian Bank Foundation Corporate Giving Grants, 967
Fitzpatrick, Cella, Harper & Scinto Pro Bono Services, 976
Four County Community Foundation General Grants, 1000
Four County Community Foundation Healthy Senior/Healthy Youth Fund Grants, 1001
Francis Beidler Foundation Grants, 1007
Frankel Brothers Foundation Grants, 1009
Franklin H. Wells and Ruth L. Wells Foundation Grants, 1011
Frank Reed and Margaret Jane Peters Memorial Fund Grants, 1013
Frank Reed and Margaret Jane Peters Memorial Fund II Grants, 1014
Fred and Gretel Biel Charitable Trust Grants, 1016
Frederick McDonald Trust Grants, 1017
Frederick W. Marzahl Memorial Fund Grants, 1018
Furth Family Foundation Grants, 1030
Gardner Foundation Grants, 1034
Gardner W. and Joan G. Heidrick, Jr. Foundation Grants, 1036
Gene Haas Foundation, 1038
George A. & Grace L. Long Fdn Grants, 1041
George B. Page Foundation Grants, 1044
George F. Baker Trust Grants, 1046
George Graham and Elizabeth Galloway Smith Foundation Grants, 1047
George H.C. Ensworth Memorial Fund Grants, 1049
George J. and Effie L. Seay Foundation Grants, 1052
George Kress Foundation Grants, 1053
George W. Wells Foundation Grants, 1057
Gil and Dody Weaver Foundation Grants, 1071
GNOF Bayou Communities Grants, 1077
GNOF Freeman Challenge Grants, 1081
GNOF Norco Community Grants, 1089
Grace Bersted Foundation Grants, 1097
Graham Family Charitable Foundation Grants, 1099
Graham Foundation Grants, 1100
Green Foundation Human Services Grants, 1116
Green River Area Community Fdn Grants, 1117
Grundy Foundation Grants, 1124
Guy I. Bromley Trust Grants, 1136
Haddad Foundation Grants, 1139
Hahl Proctor Charitable Trust Grants, 1151
Hampton Roads Community Foundation Nonprofit Facilities Improvement Grants, 1159
Hancock County Community Foundation - Field of Interest Grants, 1161
Harmony Grove Foundation Grants, 1169
Harris Foundation Grants, 1177
Harry and Helen Sands Charitable Trust Grants, 1181
Harry B. and Jane H. Brock Foundation Grants, 1183
Harvey Randall Wickes Foundation Grants, 1188
Hattie Mae Lesley Foundation Grants, 1195
Hawaii Community Foundation Omidyar Ohana Fund Grants, 1213
Hawaii Electric Industries Charitable Foundation Grants, 1218
Helen Irwin Littauer Educational Trust Grants, 1231
Hendricks County Community Fdn Grants, 1234
Henrietta Lange Burk Fund Grants, 1235
Herbert A. and Adrian W. Woods Foundation Grants, 1243
Herman P. and Sophia Taubman Fdn Grants, 1247
Hill Crest Foundation Grants, 1249
Horace A. Moses Charitable Trust Grants, 1261
Hubbard Broadcasting Foundation Grants, 1269
Hubbard Family Foundation Grants, 1270
Hubbard Family Foundation Grants, 1271
Hubbard Farms Charitable Foundation Grants, 1272
Human Source Foundation Grants, 1276
Huntington County Community Foundation Make a Difference Grants, 1280
Ike and Roz Friedman Foundation Grants, 1289
Inland Empire Community Foundation Capacity Building for IE Nonprofits Grants, 1306
Irving S. Gilmore Foundation Grants, 1314

Island Insurance Foundation Grants, 1316
J. Edwin Treakle Foundation Grants, 1320
J.W. Gardner II Foundation Grants, 1323
Jack H. and William M. Light Charitable Trust Grants, 1330
Jacob G. Schmidlapp Trusts Grants, 1336
James Ford Bell Foundation Grants, 1339
Jane's Trust Grants, 1346
Jayne and Leonard Abess Foundation Grants, 1358
Jessica Stevens Community Foundation Grants, 1363
Jim Blevins Foundation Grants, 1365
Joan Bentinck-Smith Charitable Fdn Grants, 1367
John M. Weaver Foundation Grants, 1376
Josephine Schell Russell Chartbl Trust Grants, 1389
Joseph S. Stackpole Charitable Trust Grants, 1390
Julius N. Frankel Foundation Grants, 1400
Katharine Matthies Foundation Grants, 1418
Katrine Menzing Deakins Chartbl Trust Grants, 1422
Kawabe Memorial Fund Grants, 1423
Kettering Family Foundation Grants, 1430
Kimball International-Habig Foundation Health and Human Services Grants, 1434
Kosasa Foundation Grants, 1450
Kovler Family Foundation Grants, 1455
Laclede Gas Charitable Trust Grants, 1457
Lake County Community Fund Grants, 1463
Land O'Lakes Foundation Community Grants, 1466
Lewis H. Humphreys Charitable Trust Grants, 1486
Liberty Bank Foundation Grants, 1488
Libra Foundation Grants, 1489
Lil and Julie Rosenberg Foundation Grants, 1491
Linford & Mildred White Charitable Grants, 1495
Lisa and Douglas Goldman Fund Grants, 1496
Locations Foundation Legacy Grants, 1504
Lucy Downing Nisbet Charitable Fund Grants, 1515
Luella Kemper Trust Grants, 1517
M.A. Rikard Charitable Trust Grants, 1521
M.D. Anderson Foundation Grants, 1523
Mabel A. Horne Fund Grants, 1525
Mabel F. Hoffman Charitable Trust Grants, 1526
Madison County Community Foundation - City of Anderson Quality of Life Grant, 1536
Marathon Petroleum Corporation Grants, 1551
Margaret M. Walker Charitable Fdn Grants, 1556
Marietta McNeill Morgan and Samuel Tate Morgan Jr. Trust Grants, 1560
Marion and Miriam Rose Fund Grants, 1569
Marion Gardner Jackson Charitable Trust Grts, 1570
Marion I. and Henry J. Knott Foundation Discretionary Grants, 1571
Marion I. and Henry J. Knott Foundation Standard Grants, 1572
Marisla Foundation Human Services Grants, 1573
Marjorie Moore Charitable Foundation Grants, 1574
Mark W. Coy Foundation Community Grants, 1575
Marshall County Community Fdn Grants, 1579
Marsh Corporate Grants, 1580
Mary Wilmer Covey Charitable Trust Grants, 1600
McGraw-Hill Companies Community Grants, 1620
Mercedes-Benz USA Corporate Contributions Grants, 1634
Merrick Foundation Grants, 1639
Meta and George Rosenberg Fdn Grants, 1644
Metzger-Price Fund Grants, 1647
Meyer Memorial Trust Responsive Grants, 1653
Michelin North America Challenge Education, 1660
Middlesex Savings Charitable Foundation Basic Human Needs Grants, 1668
Miller Foundation Grants, 1673
Milton Hicks Wood and Helen Gibbs Wood Charitable Trust Grants, 1676
Moses Kimball Fund Grants, 1701
Nell J. Redfield Foundation Grants, 1737
Northrop Grumman Corporation Grants, 1772
Olga Sipolin Children's Fund Grants, 1815
Olive Smith Browning Charitable Trust Grants, 1818
Olivia R. Gardner Foundation Grants, 1819
Oppenstein Brothers Foundation Grants, 1827
Orange County Community Foundation Grants, 1829
Orange County Community Foundation Grants, 1828

Oregon Community Foundation Community Recovery Grants, 1834
Oren Campbell McCleary Chartbl Trust Grants, 1837
Palmer Foundation Grants, 1867
PDF Fiscal Sponsorship Grant, 1921
Perkin Fund Grants, 1937
Perkins-Ponder Foundation Grants, 1938
Perpetual Benevolent Fund, 1940
Pettus Foundation Grants, 1952
Piedmont Natural Gas Corporate and Charitable Contributions, 1966
PMI Foundation Grants, 1982
PNC Foundation Community Services Grants, 1984
Pokagon Fund Grants, 1994
Polk County Community Foundation Bradley Breakthrough Community Benefit Grants, 1995
Polk County Community Foundation Unrestricted Grants, 2001
PPCF Community Grants, 2014
PPCF Esther M. and Freeman E. Everett Charitable Foundation Grants, 2016
PPG Industries Foundation Grants, 2017
Priddy Foundation Program Grants, 2023
Pulido Walker Foundation, 2039
Putnam County Community Fdn Grants, 2040
R.D. Beirne Trust Grants, 2045
R.S. Gernon Trust Grants, 2047
RCF General Community Grants, 2062
Reinberger Foundation Grants, 2066
Richard J. Stern Foundation for the Arts Grants, 2071
Richard W. Goldman Family Fdn Grants, 2073
Robert and Betty Wo Foundation Grants, 2083
Robert F. Lange Foundation Grants, 2090
Robert Lee Adams Foundation Grants, 2091
Robert R. Meyer Foundation Grants, 2094
Robert W. Knox, Sr. and Pearl Wallis Knox Charitable Foundation, 2095
Roger L. and Agnes C. Dell Charitable Trust II Grants, 2100
Ruth and Henry Campbell Foundation Grants, 2123
Sandy Hill Foundation Grants, 2157
San Juan Island Community Foundation Grants, 2158
Santa Fe Community Foundation Seasonal Grants-Fall Cycle, 2159
Sarkeys Foundation Grants, 2163
Sartain Lanier Family Foundation Grants, 2164
Schlessman Family Foundation Grants, 2167
Seattle Foundation Basic Needs Grants, 2175
Seward Community Foundation Grants, 2182
Seward Community Foundation Mini-Grants, 2183
Shell Oil Company Foundation Community Development Grants, 2188
Simpson Lumber Charitable Contributions, 2201
Sioux Falls Area Community Foundation Community Fund Grants, 2203
Sioux Falls Area Community Foundation Spot Grants, 2204
Skaggs Family Foundation Grants, 2206
Skaggs Family Foundation Grants, 2205
Sony Corporation of America Grants, 2216
Stan and Sandy Checketts Foundation Grants, 2235
Starke County Community Foundation Grants, 2236
Stein Family Charitable Trust Grants, 2240
Sterling and Shelli Gardner Foundation Grants, 2243
Sunoco Foundation Grants, 2256
Swindells Charitable Foundation Grants, 2261
Sylvia Perkin Perpetual Charitable Trust Grants, 2263
Textron Corporate Contributions Grants, 2286
Thelma Braun and Bocklett Family Foundation Grants, 2287
Thelma Doelger Charitable Trust Grants, 2288
Thomas J. Atkins Memorial Trust Fund Grants, 2290
Thomas J. Long Foundation Community Grants, 2291
Thorman Boyle Foundation Grants, 2295
Toyota Motor Manuf of Alabama Grants, 2309
Toyota Motor Manufacturing of Indiana Grants, 2310
Toyota Motor Manuf of Mississippi Grants, 2312
Toyota Motor Manufacturing of Texas Grants, 2313
Toyota Motor Manufacturing of West Virginia Grants, 2314

Turner B. Bunn, Jr. and Catherine E. Bunn
Foundation Grants, 2325
U.S. Bank Foundation Grants, 2330
Union Bank, N.A. Corporate Sponsorships and
Donations, 2333
Union Pacific Foundation Health and Human
Services Grants, 2338
United Technologies Corporation Grants, 2347
Victor E. Speas Foundation Grants, 2380
Vigneron Memorial Fund Grants, 2384
Virginia W. Kettering Foundation Grants, 2388
W.H. and Mary Ellen Cobb Chartbl Trust Grts, 2397
W.P. and Bulah Luse Foundation Grants, 2399
Walker Area Community Foundation Grants, 2401
Walter S. and Evan C. Jones Testam Trust, 2407
Washington County Community Fdn Grants, 2416
Weaver Popcorn Foundation Grants, 2421
Wege Foundation Grants, 2422
Wells County Foundation Grants, 2426
Western New York Foundation Grants, 2429
White County Community Foundation - Women
Giving Together Grants, 2438
WHO Foundation Volunteer Service Grants, 2444
Whole Foods Foundation, 2445
William Bingham Foundation Grants, 2460
William Foulds Family Foundation Grants, 2465
William J. and Gertrude R. Casper Foundation
Grants, 2469
William Ray and Ruth E. Collins Fdn Grants, 2473
Wilton and Effie Hebert Foundation Grants, 2476
Windham Foundation Grants, 2477
Wold Foundation Grants, 2482
Wood Family Charitable Trust Grants, 2487
Wyomissing Foundation Thun Family Organizational
Grants, 2505
Wyomissing Foundation Thun Family Program
Grants, 2506
Yawkey Foundation Grants, 2510
Youths' Friends Association Grants, 2511
ZYTL Foundation Grants, 2528

Human Trafficking
ACF Basic Center Program Grants, 73
ACF Infant Adoption Awareness Training Program
Grants, 84
ACF National Human Trafficking Hotline Grants, 86
ACF Street Outreach Program Grants, 94
ACF Transitional Living Program and Maternity
Group Homes Grants, 96
ACF Unaccompanied Refugee Children Grants, 99
Women's Fund of Hawaii Grants, 2485

Humanitarianism
Bill and Melinda Gates Foundation Emergency
Response Grants, 426
Catherine Holmes Wilkins Foundation Charitable
Grants, 520
Cisco Systems Foundation San Jose Community
Grants, 615
Harris Foundation Grants, 1177
Inland Empire Community Foundation Capacity
Building for IE Nonprofits Grants, 1306
Island Insurance Foundation Grants, 1316
Jane's Trust Grants, 1346
OSF Early Childhood Program Grants, 1841
UUA Fund Grants, 2367

Humanities
ACCF John and Kay Boch Fund Grants, 60
ACCF of Indiana Bank of Geneva Heritage Fund
Grants, 64
ACCF of Indiana Ron and Susie Ballard Community
Enrichment Fund Grants, 68
AHC R.E.A.C.H. Grants, 141
Alabama Humanities Foundation Major Grants, 159
ALA Booklist Editors' Choice Books for Youth
Awards, 162
Albert W. Cherne Foundation Grants, 222
Baton Rouge Area Foundation Grants, 365

Blue Grass Community Foundation Clark County
Fund Grants, 444
Blue Grass Community Foundation Fayette County
Fund Grants, 446
Blue Grass Community Foundation Franklin County
Fund Grants, 447
Blue Grass Community Foundation Harrison County
Fund Grants, 448
Blue Grass Community Foundation Hudson-Ellis
Grants, 449
Blue Grass Community Foundation Madison County
Fund Grants, 450
Blue Grass Community Foundation Magoffin County
Fund Grants, 451
Blue Grass Community Foundation Morgan County
Fund Grants, 452
Blue Grass Community Foundation Rowan County
Fund Grants, 453
Blue Grass Community Foundation Woodford
County Fund Grants, 454
Callaway Foundation Grants, 496
Cisco Systems Foundation San Jose Community
Grants, 615
Clark County Community Foundation Grants, 626
CNO Financial Group Community Grants, 650
Collins Foundation Grants, 658
Community Foundation for Greater Atlanta Spark
Clayton Grants, 667
Community Foundation for Greater Atlanta Spark
Newton Grants, 668
Community Foundation of Crawford County, 695
Community Foundation of Henderson County
Community Grants, 711
Community Foundation of Louisville Anna Marble
Memorial Fund for Princeton Grants, 717
Community Foundation of Madison and Jefferson
County Grants, 731
Community Fdn of Randolph County Grants, 735
Cooke Foundation Grants, 748
Cresap Family Foundation Grants, 766
David and Betty Sacks Foundation Grants, 788
Dayton Foundation Huber Heights Grants, 797
Delaware Community Foundation Grants, 817
Dubois County Community Foundation Grants, 871
Earl and Maxine Claussen Trust Grants, 878
El Pomar Foundation Anna Keesling Ackerman Fund
Grants, 907
Evan Frankel Foundation Grants, 938
F.M. Kirby Foundation Grants, 946
F.R. Bigelow Foundation Grants, 947
Flinn Foundation Scholarships, 977
George J. and Effie L. Seay Foundation Grants, 1052
GNOF Freeman Challenge Grants, 1081
GNOF Norco Community Grants, 1089
Graham Foundation Grants, 1101
Graham Foundation Grants, 1100
GTRCF Elk Rapids Area Community Endowment
Grants, 1127
HAF Joe Alexandre Mem Family Fund Grants, 1145
HAF Laurence and Elaine Allen Memorial Fund
Grants, 1146
Harris Foundation Grants, 1177
Hawai'i SFCA Art Bento Program @ HiSAM
Grants, 1210
HLTA Visitor Industry Charity Walk Grant, 1254
Hubbard Family Foundation Grants, 1271
Inland Empire Community Foundation Capacity
Building for IE Nonprofits Grants, 1306
Inland Empire Community Foundation Coachella
Valley Youth Grants, 1307
Inland Empire Community Foundation Native Youth
Grants, 1308
Inland Empire Community Foundation Riverside
Youth Grants, 1309
Inland Empire Community Foundation San
Bernardino Youth Grants, 1310
Island Insurance Foundation Grants, 1316
Japan Foundation Los Angeles Mini-Grants for
Japanese Arts & Culture, 1354

Japan Foundation New York World Heritage Photo
Panel Exhibition, 1356
Johnson County Community Fdn Grants, 1379
John W. Anderson Foundation Grants, 1383
Katharine Matthies Foundation Grants, 1418
Land O'Lakes Foundation Mid-Atlantic Grants, 1467
Libra Foundation Grants, 1489
Marietta McNeill Morgan and Samuel Tate Morgan
Jr. Trust Grants, 1560
Marion Gardner Jackson Charitable Trust Grts, 1570
Marion I. and Henry J. Knott Foundation
Discretionary Grants, 1571
Marion I. and Henry J. Knott Foundation Standard
Grants, 1572
Martha Holden Jennings Foundation Grants-to-
Educators, 1581
McCune Foundation Humanities Grants, 1619
Mimi and Peter Haas Fund Grants, 1677
NEH Family and Youth Programs in American
History Grants, 1734
Noble County Community Foundation Grants, 1765
Olive Smith Browning Charitable Trust Grants, 1818
Perkin Fund Grants, 1937
Pinnacle Entertainment Foundation Grants, 1972
Polk County Community Foundation Bradley
Breakthrough Community Benefit Grants, 1995
Powell Family Foundation Grants, 2012
Pulaski County Community Foundation Grants, 2038
R.D. and Joan Dale Hubbard Fdn Grants, 2044
Richard J. Stern Foundation for the Arts Grants, 2071
Ripley County Community Foundation Grants, 2077
Ripley County Community Foundation Small Project
Grants, 2078
Robert R. Meyer Foundation Grants, 2094
Rush County Community Foundation Grants, 2121
Ruth and Vernon Taylor Foundation Grants, 2124
Schramm Foundation Grants, 2168
Virginia Foundation for the Humanities Folklife
Apprenticeships, 2386
Walker Area Community Foundation Grants, 2401
Watson-Brown Foundation Grants, 2418
Western New York Foundation Grants, 2429
William Ray and Ruth E. Collins Fdn Grants, 2473

Humanities Education
AHC R.E.A.C.H. Grants, 141
Alabama Humanities Foundation Major Grants, 159
ALA Sara Jaffarian School Library Award for
Exemplary Humanities Programming, 190
Harry Frank Guggenheim Foundation Research
Grants, 1184
Lewis H. Humphreys Charitable Trust Grants, 1486
Martha Holden Jennings Foundation Grants-to-
Educators, 1581
McCune Foundation Humananities Grants, 1619
Natalie W. Furniss Foundation Grants, 1715
NEH Family and Youth Programs in American
History Grants, 1734
Virginia Foundation for the Humanities Folklife
Apprenticeships, 2386
Virginia Foundation for the Humanities Open
Grants, 2387

Hunger
Adobe Fdn Hunger and Homelessness Grants, 128
Aid for Starving Children Emerg Aid Grants, 144
Aid for Starving Children Health and Nutrition
Grants, 145
Aid for Starving Children Water Projects Grants, 147
Albertsons Companies Foundation Nourishing
Neighbors Grants, 221
American Electric Power Corporate Grants, 252
American Electric Power Foundation Grants, 253
Bank of America Charitable Foundation Basic Needs
Grants, 354
Bill and Melinda Gates Foundation Emergency
Response Grants, 426
Bill and Melinda Gates Foundation Policy and
Advocacy Grants, 427
Campbell Soup Foundation Grants, 501

Cisco Systems Foundation San Jose Community Grants, 615
Dominion Foundation Grants, 839
Essex County Community Foundation Greater Lawrence Community Fund Grants, 931
Farmers Insurance Corporate Giving Grants, 948
Fourjay Foundation Grants, 1003
Giant Food Charitable Grants, 1068
Good+Foundation Grants, 1096
Green Foundation Human Services Grants, 1116
Hannaford Supermarkets Community Giving, 1164
Katie's Krops Grants, 1421
Kroger Company Donations, 1456
Land O'Lakes Fdn California Region Grants, 1465
Land O'Lakes Foundation Community Grants, 1466
Land O'Lakes Foundation Mid-Atlantic Grants, 1467
Marquette Bank Neighborhood Commit Grants, 1577
McGregor Fund Human Services Grants, 1621
Meyer Fdn Healthy Communities Grants, 1650
PepsiCo Foundation Grants, 1935
Publix Super Markets Charities Local Grants, 2036
Quaker Oats Company Kids Care Clubs Grants, 2041
R.C. Baker Foundation Grants, 2043
Robert R. McCormick Tribune Foundation Community Grants, 2093
Share Our Strength Grants, 2185
Tides Fdn Friends of the IGF Fund Grants, 2300
United Methodist Committee on Relief Hunger and Poverty Grants, 2344
USAID Office of Foreign Disaster Assistance and Food for Peace Grants, 2359
WHO Foundation Volunteer Service Grants, 2444
YSA Sodexo Lead Organizer Grants, 2520

Hurricanes
GNOF Coastal 5 + 1 Grants, 1078
Honeywell Corp Humanitarian Relief Grants, 1257

Hypertension
Premera Blue Cross Grants, 2018

Illustration
ALA Children's Literature Legacy Award, 165
ALA Coretta Scott King-John Steptoe Award for New Talent, 166
ALA Coretta Scott King-Virginia Hamilton Award for Lifetime Achievement, 167
ALA Randolph Caldecott Medal, 188
ALA Robert F. Sibert Informational Book Medal Award, 189
ALA Schneider Family Book Awards, 191

Immigrants
ACF Unaccompanied Refugee Children Grants, 99
Atkinson Foundation Community Grants, 325
BBF Florida Family Literacy Initiative Grants, 386
BBF Maine Family Literacy Initiative Implementation Grants, 387
BBF Maine Family Literacy Initiative Planning Grants, 388
Blue Cross Blue Shield of Minnesota Foundation - Healthy Neighborhoods: Connect for Health Challenge Grants, 443
Cisco Systems Foundation San Jose Community Grants, 615
Community Foundation for SE Michigan Southeast Michigan Immigrant and Refugee Funder Collaborative Grant, 685
Cralle Foundation Grants, 760
Edward and Ellen Roche Relief Fdn Grants, 887
Eide Bailly Resourcefullness Awards, 897
Eulalie Bloedel Schneider Foundation Grants, 936
Evelyn and Walter Haas, Jr. Fund Immigrant Rights Grants, 941
FCD Young Scholars Program Grants, 953
Grotto Foundation Project Grants, 1123
Jacob and Hilda Blaustein Foundation Israel Program Grants, 1335
Jaquelin Hume Foundation Grants, 1357
Margaret M. Walker Charitable Fdn Grants, 1556

Marie C. and Joseph C. Wilson Foundation Rochester Small Grants, 1559
Marin Community Foundation Arts in the Community Grants, 1563
Michael Reese Health Trust Responsive Grants, 1659
Morton K. and Jane Blaustein Foundation Educational Opportunity Grants, 1700
New York Foundation Grants, 1753
Norman Foundation Grants, 1767
Rosenberg Foundation Immigrant Rights and Integration Grants, 2108
UUA Actions of Public Witness Grants, 2365
UUA Congregation-Based Community Organizing Grants, 2366
UUA Fund Grants, 2367
UUA International Fund Grants, 2368
UUA Just Society Fund Grants, 2369
UUA Social Responsibility Grants, 2370
Women's Fund of Hawaii Grants, 2485

Immigration Law
Ms. Foundation for Women Building Democracy Grants, 1706
OSF Soros Justice Youth Activist Fellowships, 1844
Rosenberg Foundation Immigrant Rights and Integration Grants, 2108
UUA Actions of Public Witness Grants, 2365
UUA Congregation-Based Community Organizing Grants, 2366
UUA Fund Grants, 2367
UUA International Fund Grants, 2368
UUA Just Society Fund Grants, 2369
UUA Social Responsibility Grants, 2370

Immune System Disorders
HRSA Ryan White HIV AIDS Drug Assistance Grants, 1265

Immunization Programs
Bernard and Audre Rapoport Foundation Health Grants, 411
CDC David J. Sencer Museum Student Field Trip Experience, 524
German Protestant Orphan Asylum Foundation Grants, 1066
Grifols Community Outreach Grants, 1122
Premera Blue Cross Grants, 2018

Immunology
Baxter International Corporate Giving Grants, 368

Incarceration
Initiaive Fdn Inside-Out Connections Grants, 1303
Mabel Louise Riley Foundation Family Strengthening Small Grants, 1528
New York Foundation Grants, 1753
OSF Baltimore Criminal and Juve Justice Grts, 1839
OSF Soros Justice Youth Activist Fellowships, 1844
Threshold Fdn Justice and Democracy Grants, 2298
Women's Fund of Hawaii Grants, 2485

Independent Living Programs
ACL Disability and Rehabilitation Research Projects (DRRP) Program: Independent Living Transition Services for Youth and Young Adults Grants, 105
Clark and Ruby Baker Foundation Grants, 625
CNCS AmeriCorps State and National Grants, 643
CNCS Senior Corps Retired and Senior Volunteer Program Grants, 648
Daniels Homeless and Disadvantaged Grants, 782
Florence Hunt Maxwell Foundation Grants, 979
Marietta McNeill Morgan and Samuel Tate Morgan Jr. Trust Grants, 1560
May and Stanley Smith Charitable Trust Grants, 1613
McLean Contributionship Grants, 1623
Mericos Foundation Grants, 1637
Peter and Elizabeth C. Tower Foundation Intellectual Disabilities Grants, 1944
Piper Trust Reglious Organizations Grants, 1979
Priddy Foundation Program Grants, 2023

Reinberger Foundation Grants, 2066
Sara Elizabeth O'Brien Trust Grants, 2161
Union Bank, N.A. Foundation Grants, 2334
W.P. and Bulah Luse Foundation Grants, 2399

India
Robert R. Meyer Foundation Grants, 2094

Indiana
Community Foundation of Grant County Grants, 703
Community Foundation of Madison and Jefferson County Grants, 731
Dearborn Community Foundation City of Aurora Grants, 808
Dearborn Community Foundation City of Lawrenceburg Community Grants, 809
Decatur County Community Foundation Large Project Grants, 811
Fayette County Foundation Grants, 951
Henry County Community Foundation Grants, 1239
Johnson County Community Fdn Grants, 1379
Johnson County Community Foundation Youth Philanthropy Initiative Grants, 1380
Marshall County Community Fdn Grants, 1579

Indigenous Cultures
Ama OluKai Foundation Grants, 249
American Indian Youth Running Strong Grants, 256
Hawai'i Community Foundation Robert E. Black Fund Grants, 1205
Honor the Earth Grants, 1259
Matson Community Giving Grants, 1607
OHA Community Grants for Culture, 1808
Ontario Arts Council Indigenous Culture Fund Indigenous Artists in Communities and Schools Project Grants, 1825

Industry
ACF Social and Economic Development Strategies Grants, 93
Collective Brands Foundation Grants, 654

Infants
ACF Head Start and/or Early Head Start Grantee - Clay, Randolph, and Talladega Counties, Alabama, 82
ACF Head Start and/or Early Head Start Grantee - St. Landry Parish, Louisiana, 83
Alexander Graham Bell Parent and Infant Financial Aid Grants, 227
Bernard and Audre Rapoport Foundation Health Grants, 411
CIGNA Foundation Grants, 611
CNCS Foster Grandparent Projects Grants, 646
Gerber Foundation Environmental Hazards Research Grants, 1062
Gerber Fdn Pediatric Health Research Grants, 1063
Gerber Foundation Pediatric Nutrition Research Grants, 1064
Initiative Foundation Minnesota Early Childhood Initiative Grants, 1305
Kimball International-Habig Foundation Health and Human Services Grants, 1434
March of Dimes Program Grants, 1552
Milton Hicks Wood and Helen Gibbs Wood Charitable Trust Grants, 1676

Infectious Diseases/Agents
CDC David J. Sencer Museum Student Field Trip Experience, 524
Grifols Community Outreach Grants, 1122
March of Dimes Program Grants, 1552

Information Dissemination
ALA Robert F. Sibert Informational Book Medal Award, 189
Community Foundation of Greater Fort Wayne - John S. and James L. Knight Foundation Donor-Advised Grants, 707

Information Science/Systems
Cisco Systems Foundation San Jose Community Grants, 615
McLean Contributionship Grants, 1623
Xerox Foundation Grants, 2507

Information Technology
Do Something Digital Content Intern, 851
Do Something Digital Member Exp Intern, 852
Go Daddy Cares Charitable Contributions, 1093
Goldseker Foundation Non-Profit Management Assistance Grants, 1095
GTECH After School Advantage Grants, 1125
Peter and Elizabeth C. Tower Foundation Technology Initiative Grants, 1949
Peter and Elizabeth C. Tower Foundation Technology Planning Grants, 1950
TechKnowledgey Community Impact Grants, 2278

Infrastructure
Jack H. and William M. Light Charitable Trust Grants, 1330
MassMutual Foundation Edonomic Development Grants, 1603
San Juan Island Community Foundation Grants, 2158
State Farm Good Neighbor Citizenship Company Grants, 2238

Injury
Dorothea Haus Ross Foundation Grants, 844
George E. Hatcher, Jr. and Ann Williams Hatcher Foundation Grants, 1045

Injury, Spinal Cord
Toby Wells Foundation Grants, 2304

Inner Cities
Abell Foundation Education Grants, 53
Adolph Coors Foundation Grants, 129
Credit Suisse Foundation Education Grants, 765
GTECH After School Advantage Grants, 1125
J. Willard and Alice S. Marriott Fdn Grants, 1327
Marie C. and Joseph C. Wilson Foundation Rochester Small Grants, 1559
Mark Wahlberg Youth Foundation Grants, 1576
Mercedes-Benz USA Corp Contributions, 1634
OSF Baltimore Community Fellowships, 1838

Instruction/Curriculum Development
ACF Head Start and/or Early Head Start Grantee - Clay, Randolph, and Talladega Counties, Alabama, 82
ACF Head Start and/or Early Head Start Grantee - St. Landry Parish, Louisiana, 83
ALA Sara Jaffarian School Library Award for Exemplary Humanities Programming, 190
AT&T Foundation Education Grants, 321
Brown Rudnick Charitable Foundation Community Grants, 477
Calvin Johnson Jr. Foundation Mini Grants, 498
Community Foundation of Jackson County Classroom Education Grants, 713
Energy by Design Poster Contest, 915
Honeywell Corporation Got 2B Safe Contest, 1256
Huntington County Community Foundation Classroom Education Grants, 1279
J. Knox Gholston Foundation Grants, 1321
J. William Gholston Foundation Grants, 1328
Meyer Foundation Education Grants, 1649
NCSS Award for Global Understanding, 1728
New Jersey Office of Faith Based Initiatives English as a Second Language Grants, 1751
Oregon Community Foundation Edna E. Harrell Community Children's Fund Grants, 1835
OtterCares Impact Fund Grants, 1849
Piper Trust Reglious Organizations Grants, 1979
Toshiba America Foundation Grades 7-12 Science and Math Grants, 2307
Toshiba America Foundation K-6 Science and Math Grants, 2308

Instructional Materials and Practices
ALA PRIME TIME Family Reading Time Grts, 185
Hatton W. Sumners Foundation for the Study and Teaching of Self Government Grants, 1196
Japan Foundation Los Angeles Japanese-Language Teaching Materials Purchase Grants, 1353
Toshiba America Foundation Grades 7-12 Science and Math Grants, 2307
Toshiba America Foundation K-6 Science and Math Grants, 2308

Instrumentation, Medical
Covidien Partnership for Neighborhood Wellness Grants, 759

Intercultural Studies
ATA Inclusive Learning Communities Grants, 323
BMW of North America Charitable Contribs, 460

Interdisciplinary Arts
NJSCA Artists in Education Residencies, 1763
NYSCA Electronic Media and Film: Screenings Grants, 1788
PCA-PCD Professional Development for Individual Artists Grants, 1883
PCA Arts in Education Residencies, 1885
PCA Arts Organizations and Arts Programs Grants for Arts Education Organizations, 1889
PCA Arts Organizations and Arts Programs Grants for Visual Arts, 1898
PCA Busing Grants, 1899
PCA Entry Track Arts Organizations and Arts Programs Grants for Arts Education Organizations, 1901
PCA Entry Track Arts Organizations and Arts Programs Grants for Visual Arts, 1912
PCA Pennsylvania Partners in the Arts Program Stream Grants, 1914
PCA Pennsylvania Partners in the Arts Project Stream Grants, 1915
PCA Professional Development Grants, 1916
PCA Strategies for Success Grants - Basic Level, 1918
PCA Strategies for Success Grants - Intermediate Level, 1919
PennPAT Artist Technical Assistance Grants, 1929
PennPAT Strategic Opportunity Grants, 1933

International Affairs
Bill and Melinda Gates Foundation Policy and Advocacy Grants, 427
Cisco Systems Foundation San Jose Community Grants, 615
Do Something International Intern, 854

International Agriculture
Bill and Melinda Gates Foundation Agricultural Development Grants, 425
Bill and Melinda Gates Foundation Policy and Advocacy Grants, 427
Michael and Susan Dell Foundation Grants, 1657
PepsiCo Foundation Grants, 1935

International Economics
Bill and Melinda Gates Foundation Policy and Advocacy Grants, 427
BP Foundation Grants, 465
Curtis Foundation Grants, 771
GMFUS Balkan Trust for Democracy Grants, 1075
Michael and Susan Dell Foundation Grants, 1657

International Education/Training
AAUW International Project Grants, 44
Abundance Foundation International Grants, 57
Bill and Melinda Gates Foundation Agricultural Development Grants, 425
Bill and Melinda Gates Foundation Policy and Advocacy Grants, 427
Cisco Systems Foundation San Jose Community Grants, 615
H.B. Fuller Foundation Grants, 1138

ILA Grants for Literacy Projects in Countries with Developing Economies, 1292
Medtronic Foundation Strengthening Health Systems Grants, 1632
Michael and Susan Dell Foundation Grants, 1657
USAID Integrated Youth Development Activity Grants, 2356

International Exchange Programs
HLTA Visitor Industry Charity Walk Grant, 1254
Mertz Gilmore Foundation NYC Dance Grants, 1642

International Justice
Abundance Foundation International Grants, 57
ALFJ Astraea U.S. and International Emergency Fund, 230
Bill and Melinda Gates Foundation Policy and Advocacy Grants, 427
Cisco Systems Foundation San Jose Community Grants, 615
PDF Fiscal Sponsorship Grant, 1921

International Organizations
Bill and Melinda Gates Foundation Policy and Advocacy Grants, 427
Gannett Foundation Community Action Grants, 1033
Medtronic Foundation CommunityLink Health Grants, 1630
OSF Early Childhood Program Grants, 1841
OSF Education Program Grants in Kyrgyzstan, 1842
OSF Education Support Program Grants, 1843
OSF Soros Justice Youth Activist Fellowships, 1844
OSF Youth Action Fund Grants in Kyrgyzstan, 1846
Raskob Fdn for Catholic Activities Grants, 2054

International Planning/Policy
Bill and Melinda Gates Foundation Policy and Advocacy Grants, 427
Youths' Friends Association Grants, 2511

International Programs
AAUW International Project Grants, 44
Abundance Foundation International Grants, 57
Ann Ludington Sullivan Foundation Grants, 279
Atkinson Foundation Community Grants, 325
Baxter International Foundation Grants, 369
Bill and Melinda Gates Foundation Agricultural Development Grants, 425
Bill and Melinda Gates Foundation Emergency Response Grants, 426
Bill and Melinda Gates Foundation Policy and Advocacy Grants, 427
Bill and Melinda Gates Foundation Water, Sanitation and Hygiene Grants, 428
Brinker Int Corporation Charitable Giving, 471
Cargill Corporate Giving Grants, 503
Charles Delmar Foundation Grants, 564
CIGNA Foundation Grants, 611
Cisco Systems Foundation San Jose Community Grants, 615
Curtis Foundation Grants, 771
Fidelity Charitable Gift Fund Grants, 956
Helen Bader Foundation Grants, 1227
Japan Foundation Los Angeles Mini-Grants for Japanese Arts & Culture, 1354
Ludwick Family Foundation Grants, 1516
Max and Anna Levinson Foundation Grants, 1612
OSF Early Childhood Program Grants, 1841
OSF Education Program Grants in Kyrgyzstan, 1842
OSF Education Support Program Grants, 1843
OSF Youth Action Fund Grants in Kyrgyzstan, 1846
PDF Fiscal Sponsorship Grant, 1921
Rockwell Collins Charitable Corp Grants, 2098
SanDisk Corp Community Sharing Grants, 2155
United Technologies Corporation Grants, 2347
Volvo Adventure Environmental Awards, 2390
YSA GYSD Regional Partner Grants, 2515

International Relations

Do Something International Intern, 854
Ford Foundation BUILD Grants, 984
GMFUS Balkan Trust for Democracy Grants, 1075
Japan Foundation Los Angeles Mini-Grants for
   Japanese Arts & Culture, 1354
Japan Foundation New York World Heritage Photo
   Panel Exhibition, 1356
PDF Community Organizing Grants, 1920
PDF Fiscal Sponsorship Grant, 1921
Stella and Charles Guttman Foundation Grants, 2241
Tides Foundation Grants, 2302

International Students

VSA International Art Program for Children with
   Disabilities Grants, 2394
VSA International Young Soloists Award, 2395

International and Comparative Law

Bill and Melinda Gates Foundation Policy and
   Advocacy Grants, 427
Ford Foundation BUILD Grants, 984

Internet

Leonsis Foundation Grants, 1485
Microsoft Software Donations, 1665
NSTA Faraday Science Communicator Award, 1778
Shelley and Donald Rubin Foundation Grants, 2187
VSA International Art Program for Children with
   Disabilities Grants, 2394

Internship Programs

Bank of America Charitable Foundation Student
   Leaders Grants, 357
Do Something Back End Developer Intern, 848
Do Something Business Development Intern, 849
Do Something Campaigns Intern, 850
Do Something Digital Content Intern, 851
Do Something Digital Member Exp Intern, 852
Do Something Finance and Human Res Intern, 853
Do Something International Intern, 854
Do Something Intern of Fun, 855
Do Something Partnerships and Public Relations
   Intern, 856
Do Something TMI Intern, 858
Do Something User Experience Research Intern, 859
Do Something Web Developer Intern, 860
Do Something Writing and Journalism Intern, 861
Maurice R. Robinson Fund Grants, 1611
PCA Arts Management Internship, 1886
Sand Hill Foundation Health and Opportunity
   Grants, 2153
Skaggs Foundation Grants, 2207
TAC Arts Access Grant, 2265
William Blair and Company Foundation Grants, 2461

Intervention Programs

Achelis and Bodman Foundation Grants, 101
Ford Family Foundation Grants - Child Abuse
   Prevention and Intervention, 981
Hasbro Children's Fund Grants, 1189
Nicole Brown Foundation Grants, 1760
Peter and Elizabeth C. Tower Foundation Mental
   Health Grants, 1946
Priddy Foundation Program Grants, 2023
Union Bank, N.A. Foundation Grants, 2334

Invention and Innovation

Coleman Foundation Entrepreneurship Education
   Grants, 651
Community Foundation for SE Michigan Head Start
   Innovation Fund, 682
GNOF Coastal 5 + 1 Grants, 1078
GNOF New Orleans Works Grants, 1088
Lemelson-MIT InvenTeam Grants, 1481
PPCF Edson Foundation Grants, 2015

Investments and Securities

Bill and Melinda Gates Foundation Policy and
   Advocacy Grants, 427

Islamic Studies

Alavi Foundation Education Grants, 216

Israel

Helen Bader Foundation Grants, 1227
Jacob and Hilda Blaustein Foundation Israel Program
   Grants, 1335
Koret Foundation Grants, 1449
Max and Anna Levinson Foundation Grants, 1612
Stella and Charles Guttman Foundation Grants, 2241
USAID School Improvement Program Grants, 2360

Japan

Japan Foundation Los Angeles Contests Designed for
   Japanese-Language Learners Grants, 1351
Japan Foundation Los Angeles Grants for Japanese-
   Language Courses, 1352
Japan Foundation Los Angeles Japanese-Language
   Teaching Materials Purchase Grants, 1353
Japan Foundation Los Angeles Mini-Grants for
   Japanese Arts & Culture, 1354
Japan Foundation New York World Heritage Photo
   Panel Exhibition, 1356

Japanese Americans

California Endowment Innovative Ideas Challenge
   Grants, 495

Japanese Art

Japan Foundation Los Angeles Mini-Grants for
   Japanese Arts & Culture, 1354
Japan Foundation New York Small Grants for Arts
   and Culture, 1355

Japanese Language/Literature

Japan Foundation Los Angeles Contests Designed for
   Japanese-Language Learners Grants, 1351
Japan Foundation Los Angeles Grants for Japanese-
   Language Courses, 1352
Japan Foundation Los Angeles Japanese-Language
   Teaching Materials Purchase Grants, 1353

Jazz

NYSCA Music: Commty Music Schools Grants, 1790
PAS Freddie Gruber Scholarship, 1872
PAS John E. Grimes Timpani Scholarship, 1873
PAS PASIC International Scholarships, 1875
PAS SABIAN/PASIC Scholarship, 1876
PAS Sabian Larrie London Memorial Schol, 1877

Jewish Culture

Arthur M. Blank Family Foundation Molly Blank
   Fund Grants, 310
Charles Crane Family Foundation Grants, 563
Frankel Brothers Foundation Grants, 1009
Jack Satter Foundation Grants, 1334
Maurice Amado Foundation Grants, 1609
Nathalie and Gladys Dalkowitz Charitable Trust
   Grants, 1716

Jewish Services

Aaron Foundation Grants, 42
Adolph Coors Foundation Grants, 129
Albert E. and Birdie W. Einstein Fund Grants, 220
Ameren Corporation Community Grants, 251
Blanche and Irving Laurie Foundation Grants, 436
Blumenthal Foundation Grants, 459
Charles Crane Family Foundation Grants, 563
Cheryl Spencer Memorial Foundation Grants, 576
David and Barbara B. Hirschhorn Foundation
   Education and Literacy Grants, 786
David and Laura Merage Foundation Grants, 789
Frankel Brothers Foundation Grants, 1009
Frank M. Tait Foundation Grants, 1012
Friedman Family Foundation Grants, 1023
George B. Page Foundation Grants, 1044
Greenspun Family Foundation Grants, 1118
Herman P. and Sophia Taubman Fdn Grants, 1247
Jewish Fund Grants, 1364
Koret Foundation Grants, 1449

Kovler Family Foundation Grants, 1455
Lisa and Douglas Goldman Fund Grants, 1496
Manuel D. and Rhoda Mayerson Fdn Grants, 1550
Max and Anna Levinson Foundation Grants, 1612
Michael Reese Health Trust Responsive Grants, 1659
Mt. Sinai Health Care Foundation Health of the
   Jewish Community Grants, 1709
Nathalie and Gladys Dalkowitz Charitable Trust
   Grants, 1716
Oppenstein Brothers Foundation Grants, 1827
Roger L. and Agnes C. Dell Charitable Trust II
   Grants, 2100
Tension Envelope Foundation Grants, 2284

Jewish Studies

Blanche and Irving Laurie Foundation Grants, 436
Blumenthal Foundation Grants, 459
Charles Crane Family Foundation Grants, 563
Cheryl Spencer Memorial Foundation Grants, 576
Helen Bader Foundation Grants, 1227
Maurice Amado Foundation Grants, 1609
Nathan Cummings Foundation Grants, 1718
Oppenstein Brothers Foundation Grants, 1827
Rosenberg Charity Foundation Grants, 2107

Job Training Programs

3M Company Fdn Community Giving Grants, 5
ACF Refugee Career Pathways Grants, 90
ACF Social and Economic Development Strategies
   Grants, 93
ACF Sustainable Employment and Economic
   Development Strategies Grants, 95
Achelis and Bodman Foundation Grants, 101
Achelis Foundation Grants, 102
Alaska Airlines Foundation LIFT Grants, 194
Alliant Energy Foundation Community Giving for
   Good Sponsorship Grants, 240
AT&T Foundation Education Grants, 321
Atkinson Foundation Community Grants, 325
Bank of America Charitable Foundation Student
   Leaders Grants, 357
Bernard and Audre Rapoport Foundation Community
   Building and Social Service Grants, 408
Blockbuster Corporate Contributions, 440
Blue Mountain Community Foundation Warren
   Community Action Fund Grants, 457
Boeing Company Contributions Grants, 462
BP Foundation Grants, 465
CFFVR Jewelers Mutual Chartbl Giving Grants, 543
CFFVR Schmidt Family G4 Grants, 548
Citizens Bank Charitable Foundation Grants, 616
Cleveland Foundation Higley Fund Grants, 634
CNCS AmeriCorps State and National Grants, 643
Coleman Foundation Entrepreneurship Education
   Grants, 651
DeKalb County Community Foundation - Garrett
   Hospital Aid Foundation Grants, 813
DOL Youthbuild Grants, 838
Edward and Ellen Roche Relief Fdn Grants, 887
Emily O'Neill Sullivan Foundation Grants, 913
Essex County Community Foundation F1rst Jobs
   Fund Grants, 930
Ford Family Foundation Grants - Access to Health
   and Dental Services, 980
GNOF New Orleans Works Grants, 1088
Grifols Community Outreach Grants, 1122
Harold Brooks Foundation Grants, 1172
Harold K.L. Castle Foundation Public Education
   Redesign and Enhancement Grants, 1173
Hattie M. Strong Foundation Grants, 1194
HBF Pathways Out of Poverty Grants, 1222
Hearst Foundations Social Service Grants, 1224
Helen Bader Foundation Grants, 1227
Helen V. Brach Foundation Grants, 1232
Henry E. Niles Foundation Grants, 1240
Highmark Corporate Giving Grants, 1248
HSBC Corporate Giving Grants, 1266
Initiative Foundation Innovation Fund Grants, 1304
Liberty Bank Foundation Grants, 1488
Linden Foundation Grants, 1494

May and Stanley Smith Charitable Trust Grants, 1613
MGM Resorts Foundation Community Grants, 1655
Middlesex Savings Charitable Foundation
   Educational Opportunities Grants, 1670
Morris Stulsaft Foundation Pathways to Work
   Grants, 1699
Moses Kimball Fund Grants, 1701
Ms. Fdn for Women Economic Justice Grants, 1707
Northland Foundation Grants, 1771
Olive B. Cole Foundation Grants, 1816
OneFamily Foundation Grants, 1822
Oregon Community Foundation Community
   Recovery Grants, 1834
Paul and Edith Babson Foundation Grants, 1881
Pentair Foundation Education and Community
   Grants, 1934
Piper Jaffray Foundation Communities Giving
   Grants, 1974
PMI Foundation Grants, 1982
Portland General Electric Foundation Grants, 2007
PPCF Edson Foundation Grants, 2015
Priddy Foundation Program Grants, 2023
Robin Hood Foundation Grants, 2096
Sierra Health Foundation Responsive Grants, 2199
Sioux Falls Area Community Foundation Community
   Fund Grants, 2203
Sioux Falls Area Community Foundation Spot
   Grants, 2204
Skaggs Family Foundation Grants, 2205
Skaggs Family Foundation Grants, 2206
Sobrato Family Foundation Grants, 2211
Sobrato Family Fdn Meeting Space Grants, 2212
Sobrato Family Foundation Office Space Grants, 2213
Textron Corporate Contributions Grants, 2286
TJX Foundation Grants, 2303
Union Bank, N.A. Foundation Grants, 2334
Youths' Friends Association Grants, 2511

Journalism
Akron Community Foundation Arts and Culture
   Grants, 150
Atwood Foundation General Grants, 330
Bodenwein Public Benevolent Foundation Grants, 461
Do Something Writing and Journalism Intern, 861
Helen Irwin Littauer Educational Trust Grants, 1231
Hispanic Heritage Foundation Youth Awards, 1253
Klingenstein-Simons Fellowship Awards in the
   Neurosciences, 1441
NAA Foundation High Five Grants, 1711
PCA Arts Organizations and Arts Programs Grants
   for Film and Electronic Media, 1893
PCA Entry Track Arts Orgs and Arts Programs
   Grants for Film and Electronic Media, 1905
Prudential Foundation Education Grants, 2028

Journalism Education
Helen Irwin Littauer Educational Trust Grants, 1231

Judaism
A. Alfred Taubman Foundation Grants, 18
David M. & Marjorie D. Rosenberg Fdn Grants, 790
Herman P. and Sophia Taubman Fdn Grants, 1247
Ike and Roz Friedman Foundation Grants, 1289
Jack Satter Foundation Grants, 1334
Lil and Julie Rosenberg Foundation Grants, 1491
Rosenberg Charity Foundation Grants, 2107
Sylvia Perkin Perpetual Charitable Trust Grants, 2263

Junior High School Education
ALA Coretta Scott King Book Donation Grant, 168
Alaska Community Foundation Anchorage Schools
   Foundation Grant, 197
CDC David J. Sencer Museum Student Field Trip
   Experience, 524
Central Pacific Bank Foundation Grants, 530
CFFVR Appleton Education Foundation Grants, 536
CFFVR Mielke Family Foundation Grants, 544
CFFVR Shawano Area Community Fdn Grants, 549
Community Foundation of Jackson County Classroom
   Education Grants, 713

Community Foundation of Louisville Education
   Grants, 724
Dr. and Mrs. Paul Pierce Memorial Foundation
   Grants, 862
Elizabeth Carse Foundation Grants, 899
Energy by Design Poster Contest, 915
Fred and Gretel Biel Charitable Trust Grants, 1016
Fremont Area Community Foundation Education
   Mini-Grants, 1021
George J. and Effie L. Seay Foundation Grants, 1052
Helen Bader Foundation Grants, 1227
J. Knox Gholston Foundation Grants, 1321
J. William Gholston Foundation Grants, 1328
Jack Kent Cooke Foundation Summer Enrichment
   Grants, 1332
John Clarke Trust Grants, 1369
Joseph S. Stackpole Charitable Trust Grants, 1390
Katrine Menzing Deakins Chartbl Trust Grants, 1422
LEGO Children's Fund Grants, 1480
Linford & Mildred White Charitable Grants, 1495
Luella Kemper Trust Grants, 1517
Marin Community Foundation Closing the Education
   Achievement Gap Grants, 1564
Phoenix Coyotes Charities Grants, 1963
R.S. Gernon Trust Grants, 2047
Southern California Edison Education Grants, 2218
Toshiba America Foundation Grades 7-12 Science and
   Math Grants, 2307
USDEd Gaining Early Awareness and Readiness for
   Undergrad Programs (GEAR UP) Grants, 2364
W.H. and Mary Ellen Cobb Chartbl Trust Grts, 2397
West Virginia Commission on the Arts Special
   Projects Grants, 2433
William J. Brace Charitable Trust, 2471

Junior and Community Colleges
American Electric Power Corporate Grants, 252
American Electric Power Foundation Grants, 253
American Honda Foundation Grants, 255
CFFVR Appleton Education Foundation Grants, 536
Cisco Systems Foundation San Jose Community
   Grants, 615
CNCS AmeriCorps State and National Grants, 643
Doree Taylor Charitable Foundation Grants, 843
FirstEnergy Foundation Community Grants, 965
GNOF New Orleans Works Grants, 1088
Harvey Randall Wickes Foundation Grants, 1188
Laurel Foundation Grants, 1475
Marion Gardner Jackson Charitable Trust Grts, 1570
McGraw-Hill Companies Community Grants, 1620
PMI Foundation Grants, 1982
Sidgmore Family Foundation Grants, 2195
Virginia Foundation for the Humanities Open
   Grants, 2387
White County Community Foundation - Landis
   Memorial Scholarship, 2437
Windham Foundation Grants, 2477

Justice
OSF Baltimore Criminal and Juve Justice Grts, 1839
OSF Young Feminist Leaders Fellowships, 1845
OSF Youth Action Fund Grants in Kyrgyzstan, 1846
Sapelo Foundation Social Justice Grants, 2160
Thorman Boyle Foundation Grants, 2295

Juvenile Correctional Facilities
Bernard F. and Alva B. Gimbel Foundation Criminal
   Justice Grants, 412
CNCS Foster Grandparent Projects Grants, 646
Countess Moira Charitable Foundation Grants, 752
Public Welfare Fdn Juvenile Justice Grants, 2033

Juvenile Delinquency
Adidas Corporation General Grants, 125
Bernard F. and Alva B. Gimbel Foundation Criminal
   Justice Grants, 412
G.N. Wilcox Trust Grants, 1031
Mary Owen Borden Foundation Grants, 1597
Oppenstein Brothers Foundation Grants, 1827
Public Welfare Fdn Juvenile Justice Grants, 2033

Juvenile Law
Bernard F. and Alva B. Gimbel Foundation Criminal
   Justice Grants, 412
OSF Baltimore Criminal and Juve Justice Grts, 1839
Public Welfare Fdn Juvenile Justice Grants, 2033

Kayaking
Outrigger Duke Kahanamoku Foundation Athletic
   Event Grants, 1852
Outrigger Duke Kahanamoku Foundation Athletic
   Team Grants, 1853

Kenya
Aid for Starving Children Water Projects Grants, 147

Kidney Diseases and Disorders
ACCF of Indiana Angel Funds Grants, 62
AKF Grants for Children, 149
Austin S. Nelson Foundation Grants, 333
Baxter International Corporate Giving Grants, 368
CFFVR Robert and Patricia Endries Family
   Foundation Grants, 547
Collins C. Diboll Private Foundation Grants, 657

Kyrgyzstan
OSF Education Program Grants in Kyrgyzstan, 1842
OSF Youth Action Fund Grants in Kyrgyzstan, 1846

Land Management
Fremont Area Community Foundation Community
   Grants, 1020
Illinois DNR Youth Recreation Corps Grants, 1297
Mary A. Crocker Trust Grants, 1584
Samuel S. Johnson Foundation Grants, 2146
Union Pacific Fdn Community & Civic Grants, 2337
Washington Gas Charitable Contributions, 2417
William and Flora Hewlett Foundation
   Environmental Grants, 2455

Land Use Planning/Policy
ACF Social and Economic Development Strategies
   Grants, 93
Adams Legacy Foundation Grants, 121
GNOF Coastal 5 + 1 Grants, 1078
Washington Gas Charitable Contributions, 2417

Landscape Architecture/Design
Community Foundation of Western Massachusetts
   Grants, 741
GNOF Gert Community Fund Grants, 1082

Language
AHC R.E.A.C.H. Grants, 141
Akron Community Foundation Arts and Culture
   Grants, 150
Community Memorial Foundation Responsive
   Grants, 743
Japan Foundation Los Angeles Contests Designed for
   Japanese-Language Learners Grants, 1351

Language Acquisition and Development
AHC R.E.A.C.H. Grants, 141
Robert Bowne Foundaion Edmund A. Stanley, Jr.
   Research Grants, 2086
Robert Bowne Foundation Literacy Grants, 2088
Robert Bowne Fdn Youth-Centered Grants, 2089

Language Arts Education
McCune Charitable Foundation Grants, 1617

Latin America
Atkinson Foundation Community Grants, 325
Charles Delmar Foundation Grants, 564
Foundation Beyond Belief Compassionate Impact
   Grants, 986
Foundation Beyond Belief Humanist Grants, 987
OSF Young Feminist Leaders Fellowships, 1845

Law
E.L. Wiegand Foundation Grants, 877
Hearst Foundations United States Senate Youth
   Grants, 1225
OSF Baltimore Community Fellowships, 1838
Prudential Foundation Education Grants, 2028
University of Chicago Chapin Hall Doris Duke
   Fellowships, 2348
Wallace Foundation Grants, 2402
Watson-Brown Foundation Grants, 2418

Law Enforcement
Kenneth T. and Eileen L. Norris Fdn Grants, 1427
LISC Affordable Housing Grants, 1497
LISC Financial Stability Grants, 1501
NRA Foundation Grants, 1774
Robert R. Meyer Foundation Grants, 2094
William J. and Dorothy K. O'Neill Foundation
   Responsive Grants, 2468

Law and Social Change
ALFJ International Social Change Opportunity Fund
   Grants, 232
OSF Soros Justice Youth Activist Fellowships, 1844

Law and Society
Hatton W. Sumners Foundation for the Study and
   Teaching of Self Government Grants, 1196

Law, History of
Bernard and Audre Rapoport Foundation Democracy
   and Civic Participation Grants, 409

Leadership
ACF Native Youth Initiative for Leadership,
   Empowerment, and Development Grants, 88
Achelis and Bodman Foundation Grants, 101
Arthur M. Blank Family Foundation American
   Explorers Grants, 305
Arthur M. Blank Family Foundation Atlanta Falcons
   Youth Foundation Grants, 307
Baltimore Community Foundation Building Stronger
   Neighborhoods Regionwide Grants, 347
Bank of America Charitable Foundation Community
   Development Grants, 355
Bank of America Charitable Foundation Volunteer
   Grants, 358
Bernard and Audre Rapoport Foundation Democracy
   and Civic Participation Grants, 409
Best Buy Children's Foundation National Grants, 417
Boeing Company Contributions Grants, 462
Bush Foundation Event Scholarships, 484
Carroll County Community Foundation Grants, 513
CFGR SisterFund Grants, 554
Charles Lafitte Foundation Grants, 567
Community Foundation for SE Michigan Youth
   Leadership Grant, 686
Community Foundation for the National Capital
   Region Community Leadership Grants, 688
Community Foundation of St. Joseph County African
   American Community Grants, 737
Dayton Foundation Dayton Youth Enrichment Fund
   Grant, 795
Dean Witter Foundation Education Grants, 807
DOL Youthbuild Grants, 838
DTE Energy Foundation Leadership Grants, 870
Eileen Fisher Activating Leadership Grants for
   Women and Girls, 898
Essex County Community Foundation Women's
   Fund Grants, 934
Evelyn and Walter Haas, Jr. Fund Nonprofit
   Leadership Grants, 942
Ewing Marion Kauffman Foundation Grants, 943
FCD New American Children Grants, 952
FCYO Youth Organizing Grants, 954
Finish Line Youth Foundation Founder's Grants, 960
Finish Line Youth Foundation Grants, 961
Finish Line Youth Foundation Legacy Grants, 962
Ford Family Foundation Grants - Technical
   Assistance , 983

Frank Reed and Margaret Jane Peters Memorial Fund
   II Grants, 1014
From the Top Alumni Leadership Grants, 1025
Fuller Foundation Youth At Risk Grants, 1028
GMFUS Balkan Trust for Democracy Grants, 1075
Greater Tacoma Community Foundation Spark
   Grants, 1114
HAF Community Grants, 1141
Hampton Roads Community Foundation Community
   Leadership Partners Grants, 1155
Harmony Project Grants, 1170
Harold K.L. Castle Foundation Windward Youth
   Leadership Fund Grants, 1175
Hazen Foundation Public Education Grants, 1221
Hubbard Broadcasting Foundation Grants, 1269
ING Foundation Grants, 1302
James Lee Sorenson Family Impact Foundation
   Grants, 1342
Kalamazoo Community Foundation Good Neighbor
   Grants, 1408
Kalamazoo Community Foundation LBGT Equality
   Fund Grants, 1411
KIND Causes Monthly Grants, 1435
Lumpkin Family Foundation Strong Community
   Leadership Grants, 1519
Maine Community Foundation Edward H. Daveis
   Benevolent Fund Grants, 1540
Maine Community Foundation People of Color Fund
   Grants, 1544
Maine Women's Fund Econ Security Grants, 1546
Maine Women's Fund Girls' Grantmaking Intv, 1547
Merck Family Fund Urban Farming and Youth
   Leadership Grants, 1635
MetLife Fdn Preparing Young People Grants, 1645
Meyer Fdn Management Assistance Grants, 1651
Miller Foundation Grants, 1673
Morris Stulsaft Foundation Educational Support for
   Children Grants, 1697
NASE Fdn Future Entrepreneur Scholarship, 1713
National Schools of Character Awards Program, 1723
Nestle Very Best in Youth Competition, 1740
Paso del Norte Health Foundation Grants, 1874
Paul and Edith Babson Foundation Grants, 1881
PepsiCo Foundation Grants, 1935
PeyBack Foundation Grants, 1953
Philanthrofund Foundation Grants, 1959
Phil Hardin Foundation Grants, 1960
Portland General Electric Foundation Grants, 2007
Posse Foundation Scholarships, 2011
PPCF Edson Foundation Grants, 2015
Prudential Foundation Education Grants, 2028
Prudential Spirit of Community Awards, 2029
Quaker Oats Company Kids Care Clubs Grants, 2041
Richard Davoud Donchian Foundation Grants, 2070
Robert R. Meyer Foundation Grants, 2094
Roney-Fitzpatrick Foundation Grants, 2102
S. D. Bechtel, Jr. Foundation / Stephen Bechtel Fund
   Character and Citizenship Dev Grants, 2128
Saint Louis Rams Foundation Community
   Donations, 2139
San Antonio Area Foundation Strengthening
   Nonprofits Grants, 2151
Seybert Foundation Grants, 2184
Social Justice Fund Northwest Criminal Justice
   Giving Project Grants, 2214
Southwest Initiative Foundation Grants, 2226
Target Foundation Global Grants, 2272
Teaching Tolerance Social Justice Educator Grts, 2276
Twenty-First Century Foundation Grants, 2328
University of Chicago Chapin Hall Doris Duke
   Fellowships, 2348
USAID Community Livelihoods Project in Yemen
   Grant, 2352
USAID Global Development Alliance Grants, 2354
Wallace Foundation Grants, 2402
Xerox Foundation Grants, 2507
YSA NEA Youth Leaders for Literacy Grants, 2518
Zonta International Foundation Young Women in
   Public Affairs Award, 2527

Learning Disabilities
AACAP Sidney Berman Award for the School-Based
   Study and Intervention for Learning Disorders and
   Mental Illness, 36
ACL Alternatives to Guardianship Youth Resource
   Center Grants, 104
Adams Rotary Memorial Fund A Grants, 122
Armstrong McDonald Foundation Special Needs
   Grants, 301
Bay Area Community Foundation Leslie L. Squires
   Foundation Grants, 380
CICF Howard Intermill and Marion Intermill
   Fenstermaker Grants, 605
Dollar General Summer Reading Grants, 836
Elsie H. Wilcox Foundation Grants, 909
Graham and Carolyn Holloway Family Foundation
   Grants, 1098
Henry and Ruth Blaustein Rosenberg Foundation
   Education Grants, 1236
Johnson Scholarship Foundation Grants, 1382
Lavina Parker Trust Grants, 1477
Leola Osborn Trust Grants, 1483
NYFA Artists in the School Community Planning
   Grants, 1779
NZDIA Community Org Grants Scheme, 1796
OSF Education Program Grants in Kyrgyzstan, 1842
Peter and Elizabeth C. Tower Foundation Intellectual
   Disabilities Grants, 1944
Peter and Elizabeth C. Tower Foundation Learning
   Disability Grants, 1945
Peter and Elizabeth C. Tower Foundation Mental
   Health Grants, 1946
Peter and Elizabeth C. Tower Foundation Technology
   Initiative Grants, 1949
Peter and Elizabeth C. Tower Foundation Technology
   Planning Grants, 1950
Roy and Christine Sturgis Charitable Tr Grts, 2115
Stein Family Charitable Trust Grants, 2240
Thomas Sill Foundation Grants, 2292
VSA/Metlife Connect All Grants, 2392
VSA International Young Soloists Award, 2395
VSA Playwright Discovery Award, 2396
Women's Fund of Hawaii Grants, 2485

Learning Disabled, Education for
Community Foundation of Madison and Jefferson
   County Grants, 731
DeKalb County Community Foundation - Garrett
   Hospital Aid Foundation Grants, 813
Emily Hall Tremaine Foundation Learning
   Disabilities Grants, 912
Johnson Scholarship Foundation Grants, 1382
Lavina Parker Trust Grants, 1477
Leola Osborn Trust Grants, 1483
Peter and Elizabeth C. Tower Foundation Intellectual
   Disabilities Grants, 1944
VSA/Metlife Connect All Grants, 2392

Learning Motivation
ACF Head Start and/or Early Head Start Grantee
   - Clay, Randolph, and Talladega Counties,
   Alabama, 82
ACF Head Start and/or Early Head Start Grantee -
   St. Landry Parish, Louisiana, 83
Community Foundation of Jackson County Classroom
   Education Grants, 713
Dayton Foundation Dayton Youth Enrichment Fund
   Grant, 795
Huntington County Community Foundation
   Classroom Education Grants, 1279
Meyer Foundation Education Grants, 1649
Nellie Mae Education Foundation District-Level
   Change Grants, 1736
San Antonio Area Foundation Strengthening
   Nonprofits Grants, 2151
Subaru of America Foundation Grants, 2253

Lectureships
ALA May Hill Arbuthnot Honor Lecture Award, 176

Legal Education
CICF Indianapolis Fdn Community Grants, 606
Widgeon Point Charitable Foundation Grants, 2447

Legal Procedure
Bernard F. and Alva B. Gimbel Foundation Criminal
Justice Grants, 412

Legal Redress
Bernard F. and Alva B. Gimbel Foundation Criminal
Justice Grants, 412

Legal Reform
Public Welfare Foundation Special Initiative to
Advance Civil Legal Aid Grants, 2034
Threshold Fdn Justice and Democracy Grants, 2298

Legal Services
Akron Community Foundation Health and Human
Services Grants, 152
Altria Group Positive Youth Dev Grants, 247
Ann Ludington Sullivan Foundation Grants, 279
Barrasso, Usdin, Kupperman, Freeman, and Sarver
Corporate Grants, 362
Bernard F. and Alva B. Gimbel Foundation Criminal
Justice Grants, 412
Bingham McHale LLP Pro Bono Services, 431
Charles H. Pearson Foundation Grants, 566
Fitzpatrick, Cella, Harper & Scinto Pro Bono
Services, 976
Fred and Gretel Biel Charitable Trust Grants, 1016
George H. and Jane A. Mifflin Memorial Fund
Grants, 1048
Hattie Mae Lesley Foundation Grants, 1195
Marie C. and Joseph C. Wilson Foundation Rochester
Small Grants, 1559
Public Welfare Foundation Special Initiative to
Advance Civil Legal Aid Grants, 2034
Sobrato Family Foundation Grants, 2211
Wilton and Effie Hebert Foundation Grants, 2476

Legal Systems
Bernard F. and Alva B. Gimbel Foundation Criminal
Justice Grants, 412

Leukemia
Austin S. Nelson Foundation Grants, 333
Dexter Adams Foundation Grants, 829
HAF Barry F. Phelps Leukemia Fund Grants, 1140

Liberal Arts Education
Lee and Ramona Bass Foundation Grants, 1478
McCune Charitable Foundation Grants, 1617

Liberty
Ann Ludington Sullivan Foundation Grants, 279
Thorman Boyle Foundation Grants, 2295

Libraries
Air Products Foundation Grants, 148
ALA Alex Awards, 153
ALA ALSC Distinguished Service Award, 154
ALA Amazing Audiobks for Young Adults Awd, 155
ALA Amelia Bloomer Book List Award, 156
ALA Baker and Taylor Summer Reading Program
Grant, 158
ALA Best Fiction for Young Adults Award, 160
ALA Bookapalooza Grants, 161
ALA Booklist Editors' Choice Books for Youth
Awards, 162
ALA Bound to Stay Bound Books Scholarships, 163
ALA BWI Collection Development Grant, 164
ALA Coretta Scott King-John Steptoe Award for
New Talent, 166
ALA Coretta Scott King-Virginia Hamilton Award
for Lifetime Achievement, 167
ALA Fabulous Films for Young Adults Award, 169
ALA Great Books Giveaway Competition, 170
ALA Innovative Reading Grant, 171
ALA John Newbery Medal, 172

ALA Louise Seaman Bechtel Fellowship, 173
ALA MAE Award for Best Literature Program for
Teens, 174
ALA Margaret A. Edwards Award, 175
ALA May Hill Arbuthnot Honor Lecture Award, 176
ALA Michael L. Printz Award, 177
ALA Notable Children's Videos Awards, 181
ALA Penguin Random House Young Readers Group
Award, 183
ALA Popular Paperbacks for Young Adults Awds, 184
ALA PRIME TIME Family Reading Time Grts, 185
ALA Quick Picks for Reluctant Young Adult Readers
Award, 186
ALA Rainbow Project Book List Award, 187
ALA Randolph Caldecott Medal, 188
ALA Robert F. Sibert Informational Book Medal
Award, 189
ALA Sara Jaffarian School Library Award for
Exemplary Humanities Programming, 190
ALA Schneider Family Book Awards, 191
ALA Sullivan Award for Public Library Admintrs
Supporting Services to Children, 213
ALA Teen's Top Ten Awards, 214
ALA Theodor Seuss Geisel Award, 215
ALA YALSA Presidential Citation Award, 218
Alcatel-Lucent Technologies Foundation Grants, 224
Arizona State Library LSTA Collections Grants, 295
Arizona State Library LSTA Community Grants, 296
Arizona State Library LSTA Learning Grants, 297
ATA Local Community Relations Grants, 324
Bay and Paul Foundations PreK-12 Transformative
Learning Practices Grants, 370
Callaway Foundation Grants, 496
Chicago Board of Trade Foundation Grants, 580
Clark and Ruby Baker Foundation Grants, 625
Community Foundation of Eastern Connecticut
General Southeast Grants, 696
Community Fdn of Randolph County Grants, 735
Del Mar Foundation Community Grants, 820
FINRA Smart Investing@Your Library Grants, 963
George I. Alden Trust Grants, 1051
George Kress Foundation Grants, 1053
Greater Sitka Legacy Fund Grants, 1111
Hall-Perrine Foundation Grants, 1152
Harmony Grove Foundation Grants, 1169
Harvey Randall Wickes Foundation Grants, 1188
Hatton W. Sumners Foundation for the Study and
Teaching of Self Government Grants, 1196
Hearst Foundations Culture Grants, 1223
IMLS Grants to State Library Administrative
Agencies, 1298
James F. and Marion L. Miller Fdn Grants, 1338
Kenai Peninsula Foundation Grants, 1425
Ketchikan Community Foundation Grants, 1429
Laura Bush Foundation for America's Libraries
Grants, 1471
Maryland State Arts Council Arts in Communities
Grants, 1592
McLean Contributionship Grants, 1623
Narragansett Number One Foundation Grants, 1712
Parkersburg Area Community Foundation Action
Grants, 1871
PCA Art Organizations and Art Programs Grants for
Presenting Organizations, 1884
PCA Entry Track Arts Organizations and Arts
Programs Grants for Presenting Orgs, 1909
Portland General Electric Foundation Grants, 2007
Reinberger Foundation Grants, 2066
Richard J. Stern Foundation for the Arts Grants, 2071
Riedman Foundation Grants, 2076
San Antonio Area Foundation Capital and Naming
Rights Grants, 2148
Schlessman Family Foundation Grants, 2167
Shell Deer Park Grants, 2186
Sioux Falls Area Community Foundation Community
Fund Grants, 2203
Sioux Falls Area Community Foundation Spot
Grants, 2204
Thomas J. Long Foundation Community Grants, 2291
Thomas Sill Foundation Grants, 2292

Union Pacific Fdn Community & Civic Grants, 2337
Virginia Foundation for the Humanities Open
Grants, 2387
Widgeon Point Charitable Foundation Grants, 2447

Libraries, Academic
ALA Louise Seaman Bechtel Fellowship, 173
ALA May Hill Arbuthnot Honor Lecture Award, 176
ALA YALSA Presidential Citation Award, 218
Arizona State Library LSTA Collections Grants, 295
Arizona State Library LSTA Community Grants, 296
Arizona State Library LSTA Learning Grants, 297
Humana Foundation Grants, 1275
IMLS Grants to State Library Administrative
Agencies, 1298
IMLS National Leadership Grants for Libraries, 1299
Kelvin and Eleanor Smith Foundation Grants, 1424

Libraries, Art
IMLS Grants to State Library Administrative
Agencies, 1298
IMLS National Leadership Grants for Libraries, 1299

Libraries, Law
IMLS Grants to State Library Administrative
Agencies, 1298
IMLS National Leadership Grants for Libraries, 1299

Libraries, Medical
IMLS Grants to State Library Administrative
Agencies, 1298
IMLS National Leadership Grants for Libraries, 1299

Libraries, Presidential
Herbert Hoover Presidential Library Association Bus
Travel Grants, 1244
IMLS National Leadership Grants for Libraries, 1299

Libraries, Public
Adelaide Breed Bayrd Foundation Grants, 123
ALA Baker and Taylor/YALSA Collection
Development Grants, 157
ALA Baker and Taylor Summer Reading Program
Grant, 158
ALA Bookapalooza Grants, 161
ALA Booklist Editors' Choice Books for Youth
Awards, 162
ALA Bound to Stay Bound Books Scholarships, 163
ALA BWI Collection Development Grant, 164
ALA Great Books Giveaway Competition, 170
ALA MAE Award for Best Literature Program for
Teens, 174
ALA May Hill Arbuthnot Honor Lecture Award, 176
ALA Penguin Random House Young Readers Group
Award, 183
ALA Scholastic Library Publishing Award, 192
ALA Sullivan Award for Public Library Admintrs
Supporting Services to Children, 213
ALA YALSA Presidential Citation Award, 218
Arizona State Library LSTA Collections Grants, 295
Arizona State Library LSTA Community Grants, 296
Arizona State Library LSTA Learning Grants, 297
Clark Electric Cooperative Grants, 627
FINRA Smart Investing@Your Library Grants, 963
IMLS Grants to State Library Administrative
Agencies, 1298
IMLS National Leadership Grants for Libraries, 1299
J. Edwin Treakle Foundation Grants, 1320
Kentucky Arts Cncl Access Assistance Grants, 1428
NEH Picturing America Awards, 1735
Piedmont Natural Gas Corporate and Charitable
Contributions, 1966
Union Pacific Fdn Community & Civic Grants, 2337

Libraries, Research
IMLS Grants to State Library Administrative
Agencies, 1298
IMLS National Leadership Grants for Libraries, 1299

Libraries, School
ALA ALSC Distinguished Service Award, 154
ALA Bookapalooza Grants, 161
ALA Bound to Stay Bound Books Scholarships, 163
ALA Great Books Giveaway Competition, 170
ALA Innovative Reading Grant, 171
ALA MAE Award for Best Literature Program for Teens, 174
ALA May Hill Arbuthnot Honor Lecture Award, 176
ALA Penguin Random House Young Readers Group Award, 183
ALA Sara Jaffarian School Library Award for Exemplary Humanities Programming, 190
ALA Scholastic Library Publishing Award, 192
ALA YALSA Presidential Citation Award, 218
Arizona State Library LSTA Community Grants, 296
Arizona State Library LSTA Learning Grants, 297
Ezra Jack Keats Foundation Mini-Grants, 944
IMLS Grants to State Library Administrative Agencies, 1298
IMLS National Leadership Grants for Libraries, 1299
NEA Foundation Read Across America Library Books Awards, 1732

Libraries, Special
Arizona State Library LSTA Collections Grants, 295
Arizona State Library LSTA Learning Grants, 297
IMLS Grants to State Library Administrative Agencies, 1298
IMLS National Leadership Grants for Libraries, 1299

Libraries, State
Arizona State Library LSTA Community Grants, 296
Arizona State Library LSTA Learning Grants, 297
IMLS Grants to State Library Admin Agencies, 1298
IMLS National Leadership Grants for Libraries, 1299

Library Administration
ALA ALSC Distinguished Service Award, 154
ALA Louise Seaman Bechtel Fellowship, 173
ALA Penguin Random House Young Readers Group Award, 183
ALA Sullivan Award for Public Library Admintrs Supporting Services to Children, 213
IMLS Grants to State Library Administrative Agencies, 1298
IMLS National Leadership Grants for Libraries, 1299
Petersburg Community Foundation Grants, 1951

Library Automation
Arizona State Library LSTA Collections Grants, 295
IMLS Grants to State Library Administrative Agencies, 1298
IMLS National Leadership Grants for Libraries, 1299

Library History
ALA ALSC Distinguished Service Award, 154
IMLS Grants to State Library Administrative Agencies, 1298
IMLS National Leadership Grants for Libraries, 1299

Library Science
ALA ALSC Distinguished Service Award, 154
ALA Coretta Scott King-Virginia Hamilton Award for Lifetime Achievement, 167
ALA Penguin Random House Young Readers Group Award, 183
ALA PRIME TIME Family Reading Time Grts, 185
ALA Sara Jaffarian School Library Award for Exemplary Humanities Programming, 190
ALA Sullivan Award for Public Library Admintrs Supporting Services to Children, 213
Arizona State Library LSTA Collections Grants, 295
IMLS National Leadership Grants for Libraries, 1299
Thomas J. Long Foundation Community Grants, 2291

Library Science Education
ALA Bound to Stay Bound Books Scholarships, 163
ALA Louise Seaman Bechtel Fellowship, 173
IMLS National Leadership Grants for Libraries, 1299

Life Skills Training
ACF Head Start and/or Early Head Start Grantee - Clay, Randolph, and Talladega Counties, Alabama, 82
ACF Head Start and/or Early Head Start Grantee - St. Landry Parish, Louisiana, 83
Albert W. Rice Charitable Foundation Grants, 223
Alfred E. Chase Charitable Foundation Grants, 233
Cargill Corporate Giving Grants, 503
Collective Brands Foundation Saucony Run for Good Grants, 656
Countess Moira Charitable Foundation Grants, 752
Frank Reed and Margaret Jane Peters Memorial Fund II Grants, 1014
John Gogian Family Foundation Grants, 1373
May and Stanley Smith Charitable Trust Grants, 1613
Middlesex Savings Charitable Foundation Educational Opportunities Grants, 1670
PPCF Edson Foundation Grants, 2015
Robbins-de Beaumont Foundation Grants, 2080
Robert R. Meyer Foundation Grants, 2094
Union Bank, N.A. Foundation Grants, 2334

Literacy
7-Eleven Corporate Giving Grants, 8
ACCF of Indiana Berne Ready Mix Community Enrichment Fund Grants, 65
Achelis and Bodman Foundation Grants, 101
Adobe Foundation Action Grants, 126
AEGON Transamerica Foundation Education and Financial Literacy Grants, 132
ALA PRIME TIME Family Reading Time Grts, 185
Albert W. Cherne Foundation Grants, 222
Alcatel-Lucent Technologies Foundation Grants, 224
American Savings Foundation Program Grants, 261
Arizona State Library LSTA Learning Grants, 297
Assisi Fdn of Memphis Capital Project Grants, 317
Assisi Foundation of Memphis General Grants, 318
Atkinson Foundation Community Grants, 325
Atlanta Foundation Grants, 326
Bainum Family Foundation Grants, 345
Bank of Hawaii Foundation Grants, 360
Bank of the Orient Community Giving, 361
BBF Florida Family Literacy Initiative Grants, 386
BBF Maine Family Literacy Initiative Implementation Grants, 387
BBF Maine Family Literacy Initiative Planning Grants, 388
BBF Maryland Family Literacy Initiative Implementation Grants, 389
BBF Maryland Family Literacy Initiative Planning Grants, 390
BBF National Grants for Family Literacy, 391
Benton Community Foundation Grants, 405
Blue Grass Community Foundation Early Childhood Education and Literacy Grants, 445
Blue River Community Foundation Grants, 458
Bridgestone Americas Trust Fund Grants, 469
Brown County Community Foundation Grants, 475
Cabot Corporation Foundation Grants, 490
CFFVR Jewelers Mutual Chartbl Giving Grants, 543
CFFVR Schmidt Family G4 Grants, 548
Charles Lafitte Foundation Grants, 567
Chicago Board of Trade Foundation Grants, 580
CHT Foundation Education Grants, 603
CIGNA Foundation Grants, 611
Clarence T.C. Ching Foundation Grants, 624
CNO Financial Group Community Grants, 650
Community Foundation of Bartholomew County Heritage Fund Grants, 690
Community Foundation of Bartholomew County James A. Henderson Award for Fundraising, 691
Community Foundation of Greater Chattanooga Grants, 704
Community Foundation of Greater Fort Wayne - Community Endowment and Clarke Endowment Grants, 705
Community Foundation of Western Massachusetts Grants, 741
Covenant Educational Foundation Grants, 754

David and Barbara B. Hirschhorn Foundation Education and Literacy Grants, 786
Dayton Power and Light Foundation Grants, 802
Deaconess Community Foundation Grants, 803
Decatur County Community Foundation Large Project Grants, 811
DeKalb County Community Foundation - Literacy Grant, 814
DeKalb County Community Foundation VOICE Grant, 816
Delta Air Lines Foundation Community Enrichment Grants, 823
Dollar General Family Literacy Grants, 835
Dollar General Summer Reading Grants, 836
Dollar General Youth Literacy Grants, 837
Dorrance Family Foundation Grants, 845
Edyth Bush Charitable Foundation Grants, 893
Entergy Charitable Foundation Education and Literacy Grants, 917
Entergy Corporation Micro Grants, 919
Essex County Community Foundation Merrimack Valley Municipal Business Development and Recovery Fund Grants, 933
Ezra Jack Keats Foundation Mini-Grants, 944
F.R. Bigelow Foundation Grants, 947
Farmers Insurance Corporate Giving Grants, 948
Fidelity Charitable Gift Fund Grants, 956
Fidelity Foundation Grants, 957
First Hawaiian Bank Foundation Corporate Giving Grants, 967
First Lady's Family Literacy Initiative for Texas Family Literacy Trailblazer Grants, 968
First Lady's Family Literacy Initiative for Texas Implementation Grants, 969
First Lady's Family Literacy Initiative for Texas Planning Grants, 970
Fourjay Foundation Grants, 1003
Fremont Area Community Foundation Amazing X Grants, 1019
G.N. Wilcox Trust Grants, 1031
George I. Alden Trust Grants, 1051
Gerber Fdn West Michigan Youth Grants, 1065
German Protestant Orphan Asylum Foundation Grants, 1066
H.B. Fuller Foundation Grants, 1138
Hall-Perrine Foundation Grants, 1152
Harris and Eliza Kempner Fund Ed Grants, 1176
Harris Foundation Grants, 1177
Hartley Foundation Grants, 1186
Hasbro Children's Fund Grants, 1189
Hattie M. Strong Foundation Grants, 1194
Hawai'i Community Foundation Family Literacy and Hawaii Pizza Hut Literacy Grants, 1201
Hawaii State Legislature Grant-In-Aid, 1219
HBF Pathways Out of Poverty Grants, 1222
Hearst Foundations Social Service Grants, 1224
Henry and Ruth Blaustein Rosenberg Foundation Education Grants, 1236
Henry E. Niles Foundation Grants, 1240
Herbert A. and Adrian W. Woods Foundation Grants, 1243
Highmark Corporate Giving Grants, 1248
Humana Foundation Grants, 1275
Iddings Foundation Major Project Grants, 1284
Iddings Foundation Medium Project Grants, 1285
Iddings Foundation Small Project Grants, 1286
ILA Grants for Literacy Projects in Countries with Developing Economies, 1292
Indiana OCRA Rural Capacity Grants (RCG), 1301
Initiative Foundation Minnesota Early Childhood Initiative Grants, 1305
Jacob and Hilda Blaustein Foundation Israel Program Grants, 1335
James S. Copley Foundation Grants, 1345
Jane's Trust Grants, 1346
Jim Moran Foundation Grants, 1366
John H. and Wilhelmina D. Harland Charitable Foundation Children and Youth Grants, 1374
Joseph H. and Florence A. Roblee Foundation Education Grants, 1386

Kirkpatrick Foundation Grants, 1440
Kodak Community Relations Grants, 1445
Kosasa Foundation Grants, 1450
Kosciusko County Community Foundation REMC
    Operation Round Up Grants, 1453
Laura Bush Foundation for America's Libraries
    Grants, 1471
Leo Goodwin Foundation Grants, 1482
Leo Niessen Jr., Charitable Trust Grants, 1484
LGA Family Foundation Grants, 1487
Lisa and Douglas Goldman Fund Grants, 1496
LISC Capacity Building Grants, 1498
LISC Community Leadership Operating Grts, 1499
LISC Education Grants, 1500
Locations Foundation Legacy Grants, 1504
Louis Calder Foundation Grants, 1511
Lubrizol Foundation Grants, 1513
M.A. Rikard Charitable Trust Grants, 1521
Mardag Foundation Grants, 1554
Marie C. and Joseph C. Wilson Foundation Rochester
    Small Grants, 1559
Marin Community Foundation Stinson Bolinas
    Community Grants, 1568
Maryland State Department of Education Striving
    Readers Comprehensive Literacy Grants, 1596
Mary W.B. Curtis Trust Grants, 1599
May and Stanley Smith Charitable Trust Grants, 1613
McCune Foundation Education Grants, 1618
Mile High United Way Stratc Investment Grts, 1671
Moses Kimball Fund Grants, 1701
Motiv8 Foundation Grants, 1702
NEA Fdn Read Across America Event Grants, 1731
NEA Foundation Read Across America Library
    Books Awards, 1732
NFL Charities Pro Bowl Community Grants in
    Hawaii, 1755
Norcliffe Foundation Grants, 1766
OHA Community Grants for Education, 1809
Parkersburg Area Community Foundation Action
    Grants, 1871
PepsiCo Foundation Grants, 1935
Percy B. Ferebee Endowment Grants, 1936
Peyton Anderson Foundation Grants, 1954
PMI Foundation Grants, 1982
Portland General Electric Foundation Grants, 2007
Progress Energy Foundation Energy Education
    Grants, 2025
ProLiteracy National Book Fund Grants, 2026
Public Education Power Grants, 2032
Publix Super Markets Charities Local Grants, 2036
Quaker Oats Company Kids Care Clubs Grants, 2041
Reinberger Foundation Grants, 2066
RGk Foundation Grants, 2068
Richard Davoud Donchian Foundation Grants, 2070
Robert and Betty Wo Foundation Grants, 2083
Robert Bowne Foundaion Edmund A. Stanley, Jr.
    Research Grants, 2086
Robert Bowne Foundation Fellowships, 2087
Robert Bowne Foundation Literacy Grants, 2088
Robert Bowne Fdn Youth-Centered Grants, 2089
Robert F. Lange Foundation Grants, 2090
Robert R. Meyer Foundation Grants, 2094
RR Donnelley Foundation Grants, 2118
Saint Louis Rams Foundation Community
    Donations, 2139
Samuel N. and Mary Castle Foundation Grants, 2145
Samuel S. Johnson Foundation Grants, 2146
Sony Corporation of America Grants, 2216
Southern Minnesota Initiative Foundation BookStart
    Grants, 2220
Stocker Foundation Grants, 2247
Strake Foundation Grants, 2249
Textron Corporate Contributions Grants, 2286
Thomas Sill Foundation Grants, 2292
Toyota USA Foundation Education Grants, 2318
Union Bank, N.A. Foundation Grants, 2334
UPS Foundation Economic and Global Literacy
    Grants, 2351
Virginia Foundation for the Humanities Open
    Grants, 2387

Wayne County Foundation Grants, 2419
WHO Foundation Education/Literacy Grants, 2442
WHO Foundation Volunteer Service Grants, 2444
Whole Foods Foundation, 2445
William G. and Helen C. Hoffman Foundation
    Grants, 2466
William J. and Dorothy K. O'Neill Foundation
    Responsive Grants, 2468
WinnCompanies Charitable Giving, 2479
YSA NEA Youth Leaders for Literacy Grants, 2518

Literary Arts
ChLA Faculty Research Grants, 593
Donald G. Gardner Humanities Tr Youth Grts, 840
Lil and Julie Rosenberg Foundation Grants, 1491
Marion Gardner Jackson Charitable Trust Grts, 1570
NJSCA Arts Ed Special Initiative Grants, 1764
NYSCA Special Arts Services: General Program
    Support Grants, 1793
PCA-PCD Professional Development for Individual
    Artists Grants, 1883
PCA Arts in Education Residencies, 1885
PCA Arts Organizations and Arts Programs Grants
    for Literature, 1894
PCA Busing Grants, 1899
PCA Entry Track Arts Organizations and Arts
    Programs Grants for Literature, 1906
PCA Pennsylvania Partners in the Arts Program
    Stream Grants, 1914
PCA Pennsylvania Partners in the Arts Project
    Stream Grants, 1915
PCA Professional Development Grants, 1916
PCA Strategies for Success Grants - Basic Level, 1918
PCA Strategies for Success Grants - Intermediate
    Level, 1919
PennPAT Artist Technical Assistance Grants, 1929
PennPAT Strategic Opportunity Grants, 1933
TAC Arts Access Grant, 2265

Literary Criticism
ChLA Article Award, 589
ChLA Faculty Research Grants, 593
ChLA Hannah Beiter Diversity Research Grants, 595
ChLA Hannah Beiter Graduate Student Research
    Grants, 596

Literary Magazines
PCA Arts Organizations and Arts Programs Grants
    for Literature, 1894
PCA Entry Track Arts Organizations and Arts
    Programs Grants for Literature, 1906

Literature
ALA Alex Awards, 153
ALA Amelia Bloomer Book List Award, 156
ALA Best Fiction for Young Adults Award, 160
ALA Bookapalooza Grants, 161
ALA Booklist Editors' Choice Books for Youth
    Awards, 162
ALA MAE Award for Best Literature Program for
    Teens, 174
ALA Michael L. Printz Award, 177
ALA Notable Children's Books Awards, 179
ALA Notable Children's Recordings Awards, 180
ALA Notable Children's Videos Awards, 181
ALA Odyssey Award for Excellence in Audiobook
    Production, 182
Alvah H. and Wyline P. Chapman Foundation
    Grants, 248
Arthur Ashley Williams Foundation Grants, 302
Assisi Foundation of Memphis Mini Grants, 319
Beacon Society Jan Stauber Grants, 393
Helen V. Brach Foundation Grants, 1232
Hispanic Heritage Foundation Youth Awards, 1253
ILA Arbuthnot Award, 1290
Joni Elaine Templeton Foundation Grants, 1384
Mary D. and Walter F. Frear Eleemosynary Trust
    Grants, 1588
Maryland State Arts Council Arts in Communities
    Grants, 1592

Mercedes-Benz USA Corporate Contributions
    Grants, 1634
Montana Arts Council Cultural and Aesthetic Project
    Grants, 1685
NEH Family and Youth Programs in American
    History Grants, 1734
Ontario Arts Foundation Ruth and Sylvia Schwartz
    Children's Book Awards, 1826
PCA Arts Organizations and Arts Programs Grants
    for Literature, 1894
PCA Entry Track Arts Organizations and Arts
    Programs Grants for Literature, 1906
PCA Strategies for Success Grants - Basic Level, 1918
PEN America Phyllis Naylor Grant for Children's and
    Young Adult Novelists, 1928
Richard and Caroline T. Gwathmey Memorial Trust
    Grants, 2069
Robert W. Knox, Sr. and Pearl Wallis Knox
    Charitable Foundation, 2095
SunTrust Bank Trusteed Foundations Greene-Sawtell
    Grants, 2257
SunTrust Bank Trusteed Foundations Nell Warren
    Elkin and William Simpson Elkin Grants, 2258
Watson-Brown Foundation Grants, 2418

Literature, Media Arts
PCA-PCD Professional Development for Individual
    Artists Grants, 1883
PCA Arts in Education Residencies, 1885
PCA Arts Organizations and Arts Programs Grants
    for Film and Electronic Media, 1893
PCA Busing Grants, 1899
PCA Entry Track Arts Orgs and Arts Programs
    Grants for Film and Electronic Media, 1905
PCA Pennsylvania Partners in the Arts Program
    Stream Grants, 1914
PCA Pennsylvania Partners in the Arts Project
    Stream Grants, 1915
PCA Professional Development Grants, 1916
PCA Strategies for Success Grants - Basic Level, 1918
PCA Strategies for Success Grants - Intermediate
    Level, 1919
PennPAT Artist Technical Assistance Grants, 1929
PennPAT Strategic Opportunity Grants, 1933
Richard J. Stern Foundation for the Arts Grants, 2071

Literature, Translation
ALA Mildred L. Batchelder Award, 178

Livestock
Michigan Youth Livestock Scholarship and State-
    Wide Scholarship, 1663

Local History
Alabama Humanities Foundation Major Grants, 159
Community Foundation of Muncie and Delaware
    County - Kitselman Grants, 733
Parke County Community Foundation Grants, 1868
Sarkeys Foundation Grants, 2163
Turner Foundation Grants, 2326
Virginia Foundation for the Humanities Open
    Grants, 2387

Long-Term Care
Blanche and Irving Laurie Foundation Grants, 436
George E. Hatcher, Jr. and Ann Williams Hatcher
    Foundation Grants, 1045
Sensient Technologies Foundation Grants, 2180

Loss-Prevention Programs
Priddy Foundation Program Grants, 2023
RCF General Community Grants, 2062

Lung Disease
ACCF of Indiana Angel Funds Grants, 62
Austin S. Nelson Foundation Grants, 333
Medtronic Foundation Strengthening Health Systems
    Grants, 1632

Lutheran Church
AHS Foundation Grants, 143
Alvah H. and Wyline P. Chapman Fdn Grants, 248
Chapman Family Foundation, 562
Harry and Helen Sands Charitable Trust Grants, 1181

Maine
Doree Taylor Charitable Foundation Grants, 843

Malaria
Tides Fdn Friends of the IGF Fund Grants, 2300

Mammalogy
Lalor Foundation Postdoctoral Fellowships, 1464

Managed Care
CMS Research and Demonstration Grants, 640
Community Foundation for the National Capital
    Region Community Leadership Grants, 688
Piper Trust Reglious Organizations Grants, 1979

Management
Benton Community Foundation Grants, 405
Blue River Community Foundation Grants, 458
Brown County Community Foundation Grants, 475
Cause Populi Worthy Cause Grants, 521
Community Foundation for Greater Atlanta
    Managing For Excellence Award, 665
Community Foundation of Bartholomew County
    Heritage Fund Grants, 690
Community Foundation of Bartholomew County
    James A. Henderson Award for Fundraising, 691
Community Foundation of Greater Fort Wayne -
    Community Endowment and Clarke Endowment
    Grants, 705
GNOF Organizational Effectiveness Grants and
    Workshops, 1090
Goldseker Foundation Non-Profit Management
    Assistance Grants, 1095
Hawai'i Community Foundation Bernice and Conrad
    von Hamm Fund Grants, 1197
OSF Baltimore Community Fellowships, 1838
Social Justice Fund Northwest Criminal Justice
    Giving Project Grants, 2214
Target Corporation Community Engagement Fund
    Grants, 2270

Management Planning/Policy
Lewis H. Humphreys Charitable Trust Grants, 1486
San Antonio Area Foundation Strengthening
    Nonprofits Grants, 2151

Management Sciences
General Motors Foundation Grants, 1039
Xerox Foundation Grants, 2507

Manufacturing
SME Education Fdn Youth Program Grants, 2209

Manufacturing Processes
SME Education Fdn Youth Program Grants, 2209

Manuscripts/Books/Music Scores
AAAS/Subaru SB&F Prize for Excl in Sci Books, 22
ALA Notable Children's Recordings Awards, 180
Laura Bush Foundation for America's Libraries
    Grants, 1471

Marine Resources
Janet Spencer Weekes Foundation Grants, 1348
Matson Community Giving Grants, 1607
Perkin Fund Grants, 1937

Marine Sciences
Chapman Family Foundation, 562
Margaret T. Morris Foundation Grants, 1557
Matson Community Giving Grants, 1607
Maurice J. Masserini Charitable Trust Grants, 1610
Perkin Fund Grants, 1937
Skaggs Foundation Grants, 2207

Maritime Industry
Matson Community Giving Grants, 1607

Marketing/Public Relations
4imprint One by One Charitable Giving, 7
Cause Populi Worthy Cause Grants, 521
Curtis Foundation Grants, 771
Kodak Community Relations Grants, 1445
PCA Arts Organizations and Arts Programs Grants
    for Literature, 1894
PCA Entry Track Arts Organizations and Arts
    Programs Grants for Literature, 1906
PCA Management/Techl Assistance Grants, 1913
TAC Arts Access Grant, 2265
Western New York Foundation Grants, 2429

Mass Communication
Ann Ludington Sullivan Foundation Grants, 279
Virginia Foundation for the Humanities Open
    Grants, 2387

Mass Media
Akron Community Foundation Arts and Culture
    Grants, 150
Chicago Board of Trade Foundation Grants, 580
NYSCA Electronic Media and Film: Screenings
    Grants, 1788

Massachusetts
Alfred E. Chase Charitable Foundation Grants, 233
Ezra M. Cutting Trust Grants, 945
Frank Reed and Margaret Jane Peters Memorial Fund
    Grants, 1013
George W.P. Magee Trust Grants, 1056
George W. Wells Foundation Grants, 1057
Harold Brooks Foundation Grants, 1172
Helen E. Ellis Charitable Trust Grants, 1228
Lloyd G. Balfour Foundation Attleboro-Specific
    Charities Grants, 1502
Lloyd G. Balfour Foundation Scholarships, 1503
Mabel A. Horne Fund Grants, 1525
McCarthy Family Fdn Charity Fund Grants, 1614
Perpetual Benevolent Fund, 1940
Sara Elizabeth O'Brien Trust Grants, 2161
Sarah G. McCarthy Memorial Foundation, 2162

Materials Acquisition (Books, Tapes, etc.)
AGFT A Gift for Music Grants, 138
AGFT Pencil Boy Express, 139
ALA Bookapalooza Grants, 161
ALA BWI Collection Development Grant, 164
ALA Coretta Scott King Book Donation Grant, 168
ALA Great Books Giveaway Competition, 170
ALA PRIME TIME Family Reading Time Grts, 185
Arizona State Library LSTA Collections Grants, 295
Armstrong McDonald Foundation Special Needs
    Grants, 301
HAF Phyllis Nilsen Leal Mem Fund Grants, 1149
Hungry for Music Instrument Gifts, 1277
Janson Foundation Grants, 1350
Japan Foundation Los Angeles Japanese-Language
    Teaching Materials Purchase Grants, 1353
OSF Education Support Program Grants, 1843
Porter County Community Foundation Health and
    Wellness Grant, 2002
ProLiteracy National Book Fund Grants, 2026
Vermillion County Community Fdn Grants, 2378

Materials Sciences
Northrop Grumman Foundation Grants, 1773

Mathematics
Arthur M. Blank Family Foundation Pipeline Project
    Grants, 313
Baxter International Corporate Giving Grants, 368
BP Foundation Grants, 465
Daviess County Community Foundation Advancing
    Out-of-School Learning Grants, 792
EQT Fdn Education and Workforce Grants, 927

FirstEnergy Foundation Science, Technology,
    Engineering, and Mathematics Grants, 966
Hearst Foundations Culture Grants, 1223
Hispanic Heritage Foundation Youth Awards, 1253
Honeywell Corporation Leadership Challenge
    Academy, 1258
Intel Corporation Community Grants, 1311
Intel Corporation Int Community Grants, 1312
Michelin North America Challenge Education, 1660
Micron Technology Fdn Community Grants, 1664
Northrop Grumman Foundation Grants, 1773
Qualcomm Grants, 2042
Raytheon Middle School Grants and Schols, 2061
Toyota Motor Manuf of Kentucky Grants, 2311
Toyota Technical Center Grants, 2317
USAID U.S.-Egypt Learning Grants, 2361

Mathematics Education
3M Company Fdn Community Giving Grants, 5
AAUW International Project Grants, 44
American Electric Power Corporate Grants, 252
American Electric Power Foundation Grants, 253
Avista Foundation Education Grants, 340
Bay and Paul Foundations PreK-12 Transformative
    Learning Practices Grants, 370
Bay Area Community Foundation Semiannual
    Grants, 382
Bayer Fund STEM Education Grants, 384
Essex County Community Foundation Greater
    Lawrence Summer Fund Grants, 932
Ewing Marion Kauffman Foundation Grants, 943
Grifols Community Outreach Grants, 1122
H.B. Fuller Foundation Grants, 1138
Lockheed Martin Corporation Fdn Grants, 1505
McCune Charitable Foundation Grants, 1617
Michelin North America Challenge Education, 1660
Micron Technology Fdn Community Grants, 1664
Northrop Grumman Foundation Grants, 1773
Piedmont Natural Gas Foundation K-12 Science,
    Technology, Engineering and Math Grant, 1969
Qualcomm Grants, 2042
Rathmann Family Foundation Grants, 2057
Raytheon Middle School Grants and Schols, 2061
RGk Foundation Grants, 2068
Rockwell Collins Charitable Corp Grants, 2098
SAS Institute Community Relations Donations, 2165
TE Foundation Community Grants, 2279
Tellabs Foundation Grants, 2280
Toshiba America Foundation Grades 7-12 Science and
    Math Grants, 2307
Toshiba America Foundation K-6 Science and Math
    Grants, 2308
Toyota USA Foundation Education Grants, 2318
United Technologies Corporation Grants, 2347
Washington Gas Charitable Contributions, 2417
WSLBDF Quarterly Grants, 2499

Mathematics, Applied
Northrop Grumman Foundation Grants, 1773

Mechanical Engineering
Lubrizol Foundation Grants, 1513

Mechanics
BMW of North America Charitable Contribs, 460

Media
A.C. and Penney Hubbard Foundation Grants, 19
First Hawaiian Bank Foundation Corporate Giving
    Grants, 967
NYSCA Electronic Media and Film: General
    Operating Support, 1786
Reinberger Foundation Grants, 2066
Richard J. Stern Foundation for the Arts Grants, 2071
Virginia Foundation for the Humanities Open
    Grants, 2387

Media Arts
Akron Community Foundation Arts and Culture
    Grants, 150

Donald G. Gardner Humanities Tr Youth Grts, 840
Japan Foundation Los Angeles Mini-Grants for
    Japanese Arts & Culture, 1354
Japan Foundation New York Small Grants for Arts
    and Culture, 1355
Maryland State Arts Council Arts in Communities
    Grants, 1592
Montana Arts Council Cultural and Aesthetic Project
    Grants, 1685
Morris Stulsaft Foundation Participation in the the
    Arts Grants, 1698
NEH Family and Youth Programs in American
    History Grants, 1734
Newfoundland and Labrador Arts Council ArtSmarts
    Grants, 1744
NHSCA Artist Residence Grants, 1756
NHSCA Conservation License Plate Grants, 1757
NHSCA Youth Arts Project Grants: For Extended
    Arts Learning, 1758
NJSCA Artists in Education Residencies, 1763
NJSCA Arts Ed Special Initiative Grants, 1764
NYSCA Electronic Media and Film: Film Festivals
    Grants, 1785
NYSCA Electronic Media and Film: General
    Operating Support, 1786
NYSCA Electronic Media and Film: General
    Program Support, 1787
NYSCA Electronic Media and Film: Screenings
    Grants, 1788
NYSCA Electronic Media and Film: Workspace
    Grants, 1789
PAS John E. Grimes Timpani Scholarship, 1873
PCA-PCD Professional Development for Individual
    Artists Grants, 1883
PCA Arts in Education Residencies, 1885
PCA Arts Organizations and Arts Programs Grants
    for Film and Electronic Media, 1893
PCA Arts Organizations and Arts Programs Grants
    for Visual Arts, 1898
PCA Busing Grants, 1899
PCA Entry Track Arts Orgs and Arts Programs
    Grants for Film and Electronic Media, 1905
PCA Entry Track Arts Organizations and Arts
    Programs Grants for Visual Arts, 1912
PCA Pennsylvania Partners in the Arts Program
    Stream Grants, 1914
PCA Pennsylvania Partners in the Arts Project
    Stream Grants, 1915
PCA Professional Development Grants, 1916
PCA Strategies for Success Grants - Adv Level, 1917
PCA Strategies for Success Grants Basic Level, 1918
PCA Strategies for Success Grants - Intermediate
    Level, 1919
PennPAT Artist Technical Assistance Grants, 1929
PennPAT Strategic Opportunity Grants, 1933
Reinberger Foundation Grants, 2066
TAC Arts Access Grant, 2265
Union Square Arts Award, 2339

Medical Education
1st Source Foundation Community Involvement
    Grants, 1
AACAP Jeanne Spurlock Research Fellowship in
    Substance Abuse and Addiction for Minority
    Medical Students, 28
AACAP Life Members Mentorship Grants for
    Medical Students, 30
AACAP Summer Medical Student Fellowships, 38
Catherine Holmes Wilkins Foundation Charitable
    Grants, 520
Community Foundation for the Capital Region
    Grants, 687
Effie and Wofford Cain Foundation Grants, 895
Harry A. and Margaret D. Towsley Foundation
    Grants, 1180
Herman Goldman Foundation Grants, 1245
J.W. Kieckhefer Foundation Grants, 1324
James M. Collins Foundation Grants, 1344
Julius N. Frankel Foundation Grants, 1400
Margaret and James A. Elkins Jr. Fdn Grants, 1555

Mt. Sinai Health Care Foundation Health of the
    Jewish Community Grants, 1709
Paso del Norte Health Foundation Grants, 1874
Piper Trust Healthcare and Med Rsrch Grants, 1978
Rathmann Family Foundation Grants, 2057
V.V. Cooke Foundation Grants, 2371
Widgeon Point Charitable Foundation Grants, 2447

Medical Informatics
Covidien Partnership for Neighborhood Wellness
    Grants, 759

Medical Physics
Piedmont Natural Gas Foundation Health and
    Human Services Grants, 1968

Medical Programs
A.L. Spencer Foundation Grants, 21
AASA Urgent Need Mini-Grants, 43
Alvah H. and Wyline P. Chapman Foundation
    Grants, 248
Armstrong McDonald Foundation Special Needs
    Grants, 301
B.F. and Rose H. Perkins Foundation Community
    Grants, 342
Baton Rouge Area Foundation Grants, 365
Bernard and Audre Rapoport Foundation Health
    Grants, 411
Carl R. Hendrickson Family Foundation Grants, 509
Carroll County Community Foundation Grants, 513
Clark and Ruby Baker Foundation Grants, 625
DeKalb County Community Foundation - Garrett
    Hospital Aid Foundation Grants, 813
Different Needz Foundation Grants, 830
Emily O'Neill Sullivan Foundation Grants, 913
Florence Hunt Maxwell Foundation Grants, 979
Ford Family Foundation Grants - Access to Health
    and Dental Services, 980
Frederick McDonald Trust Grants, 1017
Frederick W. Marzahl Memorial Fund Grants, 1018
Green River Area Community Fdn Grants, 1117
Henrietta Lange Burk Fund Grants, 1235
Henry L. Guenther Foundation Grants, 1242
Horace A. Moses Charitable Trust Grants, 1261
HRK Foundation Health Grants, 1264
James M. Collins Foundation Grants, 1344
Kimball International-Habig Foundation Health and
    Human Services Grants, 1434
Kirby Laing Foundation Grants, 1439
Koch Family Foundation (Annapolis) Grants, 1444
Lucile Packard Foundation for Children's Health
    Grants, 1514
M.D. Anderson Foundation Grants, 1523
Mabel A. Horne Fund Grants, 1525
Marcia and Otto Koehler Foundation Grants, 1553
Marjorie Moore Charitable Foundation Grants, 1574
Milken Family Foundation Grants, 1672
OSF Youth Action Fund Grants in Kyrgyzstan, 1846
Parker Foundation (California) Grants, 1869
Polk County Community Foundation Marjorie M.
    and Lawrence R. Bradley Endowment Fund
    Grants, 1998
San Antonio Area Foundation Annual Responsive
    Grants, 2147
Sick Kids Fdn Community Conference Grants, 2193
Sorenson Legacy Foundation Grants, 2217
UnitedHealthcare Children's Fdn Grants, 2342
Volkswagen Group of America Corporate
    Contributions Grants, 2389
Walter J. and Betty C. Zable Fdn Grants, 2406
Walter S. and Evan C. Jones Testam Trust, 2407
WHO Foundation Volunteer Service Grants, 2444

Medical Research
A.L. Mailman Family Foundation Grants, 20
AACAP Life Members Mentorship Grants for
    Medical Students, 30
ACL Rehabilitation Research and Training Center
    (RRTC) on Employment of Transition-Age Youth
    with Disabilities Grants, 107

Adams Family Foundation II Grants, 117
Avery Foundation Grants, 339
Catherine Holmes Wilkins Foundation Charitable
    Grants, 520
Children's Tumor Foundation Young Investigator
    Awards, 587
Community Foundation of Louisville Dr. W.
    Barnett Owen Memorial Fund for the Children of
    Louisville and Jefferson County Grants, 723
Elizabeth Morse Genius Charitable Trust Grants, 901
Fichtenbaum Charitable Trust Grants, 955
Florence Foundation Grants, 978
Frank Reed and Margaret Jane Peters Memorial Fund
    II Grants, 1014
Gerber Foundation Environmental Hazards Research
    Grants, 1062
Gerber Fdn Pediatric Health Research Grants, 1063
Gerber Foundation Pediatric Nutrition Research
    Grants, 1064
Giant Food Charitable Grants, 1068
HRK Foundation Health Grants, 1264
Kirby Laing Foundation Grants, 1439
Kovler Family Foundation Grants, 1455
Leo Goodwin Foundation Grants, 1482
LGA Family Foundation Grants, 1487
Louis and Sandra Berkman Foundation Grants, 1510
Marcia and Otto Koehler Foundation Grants, 1553
Margaret and James A. Elkins Jr. Fdn Grants, 1555
Marion Gardner Jackson Charitable Trust Grts, 1570
Mericos Foundation Grants, 1637
Merrick Foundation Grants, 1640
Milken Family Foundation Grants, 1672
Nash Avery Foundation Grants, 1714
Reinberger Foundation Grants, 2066
San Antonio Area Foundation Capital and Naming
    Rights Grants, 2148
Sara Elizabeth O'Brien Trust Grants, 2161
Schramm Foundation Grants, 2168
Sick Kids Foundation New Investigator Research
    Grants, 2194
Sioux Falls Area Community Foundation Community
    Fund Grants, 2203
Sioux Falls Area Community Foundation Spot
    Grants, 2204
Victor E. Speas Foundation Grants, 2380
William and Sandy Heitz Family Fdn Grants, 2457

Medical Sciences
Gerber Foundation Environmental Hazards Research
    Grants, 1062
Gerber Fdn Pediatric Health Research Grants, 1063
Gerber Foundation Pediatric Nutrition Research
    Grants, 1064
Harmony Project Grants, 1170
Leola Osborn Trust Grants, 1483

Medical Technology
Armstrong McDonald Foundation Special Needs
    Grants, 301
Bernard and Audre Rapoport Foundation Health
    Grants, 411
Piedmont Natural Gas Foundation Health and
    Human Services Grants, 1968

Medical/Diagnostics Imaging
Piper Trust Healthcare and Med Rsrch Grants, 1978

Medicine
OSF Baltimore Community Fellowships, 1838
Piper Trust Healthcare and Med Rsrch Grants, 1978
Union Labor Health Fdn Angel Fund Grants, 2335
Wolfe Associates Grants, 2483

Medicine, Internal
CFF First- and Second-Year Clinical Fellowships, 532
CFF Leroy Matthews Physician-Scientist Awds, 533

Medicine, Palliative
Daniels Homeless and Disadvantaged Grants, 782

Men

Charles Delmar Foundation Grants, 564
Foundation Beyond Belief Compassionate Impact
    Grants, 986
Foundation Beyond Belief Humanist Grants, 987
Vanderburgh Community Foundation Men's Fund
    Grants, 2373

Mental Disorders

AACAP Rieger Service Program Award for
    Excellence, 34
AACAP Sidney Berman Award for the School-Based
    Study and Intervention for Learning Disorders and
    Mental Ilness, 36
Adolph Coors Foundation Grants, 129
ALFJ International Fund Grants, 231
American Psychiatric Fdn Call for Proposals, 257
American Psychiatric Foundation Typical or Troubled
    School Mental Health Education Grants, 258
Atkinson Foundation Community Grants, 325
Ben B. Cheney Foundation Grants, 402
Bothin Foundation Grants, 464
Catherine Holmes Wilkins Foundation Charitable
    Grants, 520
Collins Foundation Grants, 658
Cralle Foundation Grants, 760
Crane Fund for Widows and Children Grants, 762
Elizabeth Morse Genius Charitable Trust Grants, 901
Elkhart County Community Foundation Fund for
    Elkhart County, 902
Lavina Parker Trust Grants, 1477
Luella Kemper Trust Grants, 1517
Montgomery County Community Foundation Libby
    Whitecotton Fund Grants, 1690
NIMH Early Identification and Treatment of Mental
    Disorders in Children and Adolescents Grts, 1761
Oppenstein Brothers Foundation Grants, 1827
Pentair Foundation Education and Community
    Grants, 1934
Peter and Elizabeth C. Tower Foundation Mental
    Health Grants, 1946
Peter and Elizabeth C. Tower Foundation Small
    Grants, 1947
Peter and Elizabeth C. Tower Foundation Technology
    Initiative Grants, 1949
Peter and Elizabeth C. Tower Foundation Technology
    Planning Grants, 1950
Piedmont Natural Gas Foundation Health and
    Human Services Grants, 1968
San Antonio Area Foundation Capital and Naming
    Rights Grants, 2148
Staunton Farm Foundation Grants, 2239
Stein Family Charitable Trust Grants, 2240
Weyerhaeuser Family Fdn Health Grants, 2435

Mental Health

AACAP Sidney Berman Award for the School-Based
    Study and Intervention for Learning Disorders and
    Mental Ilness, 36
Abbott Fund Science Education Grants, 48
Adolph Coors Foundation Grants, 129
Alliance for Strong Families and Communities
    Grants, 239
American Psychiatric Fdn Call for Proposals, 257
American Psychiatric Foundation Typical or Troubled
    School Mental Health Education Grants, 258
Atlanta Women's Foundation Pathway to Success
    Grants, 327
Austin S. Nelson Foundation Grants, 333
Avery-Fuller-Welch Children's Fdn Grants, 336
Baxter International Foundation Grants, 369
Bella Vista Fdn GSS Healthy Living Grants, 396
Ben B. Cheney Foundation Grants, 402
Caesars Foundation Grants, 492
California Endowment Innovative Ideas Challenge
    Grants, 495
CFFVR Jewelers Mutual Chartbl Giving Grants, 543
CFFVR Robert and Patricia Endries Family
    Foundation Grants, 547
CFFVR Schmidt Family G4 Grants, 548

Charles H. Pearson Foundation Grants, 566
Chicago Board of Trade Foundation Grants, 580
Community Foundation for Greater Buffalo Garman
    Family Foundation Grants, 671
D. W. McMillan Foundation Grants, 776
Dolan Children's Foundation Grants, 832
Edwards Memorial Trust Grants, 891
Elizabeth Morse Genius Charitable Trust Grants, 901
First Nations Development Institute Native Youth
    and Culture Fund Grants, 974
Foundation for a Healthy Kentucky Grants, 988
Fourjay Foundation Grants, 1003
Gardner Foundation Grants, 1034
George H.C. Ensworth Memorial Fund Grants, 1049
Gulf Coast Foundation of Community Operating
    Grants, 1134
Gulf Coast Foundation of Community Program
    Grants, 1135
Harold Brooks Foundation Grants, 1172
Hasbro Children's Fund Grants, 1189
Hattie Mae Lesley Foundation Grants, 1195
Iddings Foundation Capital Project Grants, 1283
Iddings Foundation Major Project Grants, 1284
Iddings Foundation Medium Project Grants, 1285
Iddings Foundation Small Project Grants, 1286
J. Watumull Fund Grants, 1326
Koch Family Foundation (Annapolis) Grants, 1444
Lavina Parker Trust Grants, 1477
M.J. Murdock Charitable Trust General Grants, 1524
Margaret T. Morris Foundation Grants, 1557
Meadows Foundation Grants, 1626
Montgomery County Community Foundation Libby
    Whitecotton Fund Grants, 1690
Nick Traina Foundation Grants, 1759
North Dakota Community Foundation Grants, 1768
Ordean Foundation Catalyst Grants, 1830
Ordean Foundation Partnership Grants, 1831
Paso del Norte Health Foundation Grants, 1874
Perpetual Benevolent Fund, 1940
Peter and Elizabeth C. Tower Foundation Mental
    Health Grants, 1946
Peter and Elizabeth C. Tower Foundation Small
    Grants, 1947
Peter and Elizabeth C. Tower Foundation Technology
    Initiative Grants, 1949
Peter and Elizabeth C. Tower Foundation Technology
    Planning Grants, 1950
Piedmont Natural Gas Foundation Health and
    Human Services Grants, 1968
Posey Community Foundation Women's Grants, 2008
Ruth Camp Campbell Charitable Trust Grants, 2125
San Antonio Area Foundation Capital and Naming
    Rights Grants, 2148
Sand Hill Foundation Health and Opportunity
    Grants, 2153
Sensient Technologies Foundation Grants, 2180
Sidgmore Family Foundation Grants, 2195
Sierra Health Foundation Responsive Grants, 2199
Sioux Falls Area Community Foundation Community
    Fund Grants, 2203
Sioux Falls Area Community Foundation Spot
    Grants, 2204
Spencer County Community Foundation Women's
    Fund Grants, 2232
Staunton Farm Foundation Grants, 2239
Stella and Charles Guttman Foundation Grants, 2241
Thomas W. Bradley Foundation Grants, 2293
Vanderburgh Community Foundation Men's Fund
    Grants, 2373
Vanderburgh County Community Foundation
    Women's Fund Grants, 2376
Warrick County Community Foundation Women's
    Fund, 2411
Weyerhaeuser Family Fdn Health Grants, 2435
Whatcom Community Foundation Grants, 2436
Women's Fund of Hawaii Grants, 2484

Mental Retardation

Ben B. Cheney Foundation Grants, 402
Benton Community Foundation Grants, 405

Blue River Community Foundation Grants, 458
Brown County Community Foundation Grants, 475
Community Foundation of Bartholomew County
    Heritage Fund Grants, 690
Community Foundation of Bartholomew County
    James A. Henderson Award for Fundraising, 691
Community Foundation of Greater Fort Wayne -
    Community Endowment and Clarke Endowment
    Grants, 705
Peter and Elizabeth C. Tower Foundation Mental
    Health Grants, 1946
Saint Louis Rams Foundation Community
    Donations, 2139
Stein Family Charitable Trust Grants, 2240
Thomas Sill Foundation Grants, 2292

Mentoring Programs

Alaska Airlines Foundation LIFT Grants, 194
Alliant Energy Foundation Community Giving for
    Good Sponsorship Grants, 240
American Savings Foundation Program Grants, 261
Andrew Family Foundation Grants, 272
Ball Brothers Foundation Organizational
    Effectiveness/Executive Mentoring Grants, 346
Boeing Company Contributions Grants, 462
Calvin Johnson Jr. Foundation Mini Grants, 498
ChLA Mentoring Award, 597
Cincinnati Bell Foundation Grants, 612
CNCS Foster Grandparent Projects Grants, 646
CNCS Senior Corps Retired and Senior Volunteer
    Program Grants, 648
Covenant for Children Critical Goods Grants, 757
Cystic Fibrosis Lifestyle Foundation Mentored
    Recreation Grants, 774
Dollar General Family Literacy Grants, 835
Essex County Community Foundation Women's
    Fund Grants, 934
Farmers Insurance Corporate Giving Grants, 948
Ford Family Foundation Grants - Positive Youth
    Development, 982
Foundation for the Mid South Education Grants, 993
German Protestant Orphan Asylum Foundation
    Grants, 1066
GNOF IMPACT Grants for Youth Dev, 1084
Greater Milwaukee Foundation Grants, 1109
Hawai'i Community Foundation Kuki'o Community
    Fund Grants, 1202
HBF Pathways Out of Poverty Grants, 1222
Henry E. Niles Foundation Grants, 1240
Highmark Corporate Giving Grants, 1248
Initiative Foundation Innovation Fund Grants, 1304
J.W. Gardner II Foundation Grants, 1323
Kansas Health Foundation Recognition Grants, 1415
Kosciusko County Community Foundation REMC
    Operation Round Up Grants, 1453
Leonsis Foundation Grants, 1485
Liberty Bank Foundation Grants, 1488
Locations Foundation Legacy Grants, 1504
Luella Kemper Trust Grants, 1517
Mark Wahlberg Youth Foundation Grants, 1576
Mary W.B. Curtis Trust Grants, 1599
Maurice R. Robinson Fund Grants, 1611
Mericos Foundation Grants, 1637
Morris K. Udall and Stewart L. Udall Foundation
    Parks in Focus Program, 1695
New Jersey Office of Faith Based Initiatives Services
    to At Risk Youth Grants, 1752
NFL Charities Pro Bowl Community Grants in
    Hawaii, 1755
NYSCA Electronic Media and Film: Workspace
    Grants, 1789
OneFamily Foundation Grants, 1822
Oren Campbell McCleary Chartbl Trust Grants, 1837
OSF Baltimore Community Fellowships, 1838
OSF Early Childhood Program Grants, 1841
Pacers Foundation Be Educated Grants, 1857
Perry and Sandy Massie Foundation Grants, 1941
Peyton Anderson Foundation Grants, 1954
Phoenix Coyotes Charities Grants, 1963

Piedmont Natural Gas Foundation Health and
    Human Services Grants, 1968
Piper Trust Education Grants, 1977
PPCF Edson Foundation Grants, 2015
Priddy Foundation Program Grants, 2023
Prudential Foundation Education Grants, 2028
Robert R. Meyer Foundation Grants, 2094
Saint Louis Rams Foundation Community
    Donations, 2139
Samuel S. Johnson Foundation Grants, 2146
Schlessman Family Foundation Grants, 2167
Sidgmore Family Foundation Grants, 2195
U.S. Bank Foundation Grants, 2330
UPS Foundation Economic and Global Literacy
    Grants, 2351
Welborn Foundation Promotion of Healthy
    Adolescent Development Grants, 2425
Whole Foods Foundation, 2445
YSA MLK Day Lead Organizer Grants, 2516

Metabolic Diseases
CFF Research Grants, 534
Zellweger Baby Support Network Grants, 2525

Metabolism
CFF Research Grants, 534

Metallurgy
Dorr Foundation Grants, 846

Methodist Church
AHS Foundation Grants, 143
Alvah H. and Wyline P. Chapman Foundation
    Grants, 248
Bradley-Turner Foundation Grants, 466
Chapman Family Foundation, 562
Clark and Ruby Baker Foundation Grants, 625
Curtis Foundation Grants, 771
Effie and Wofford Cain Foundation Grants, 895
Harry and Helen Sands Charitable Trust Grants, 1181
United Methodist Committee on Relief Hunger and
    Poverty Grants, 2344

Microeconomics
McCune Charitable Foundation Grants, 1617

Microenterprises
Union Bank, N.A. Foundation Grants, 2334

Microfilming and Microforms
Claremont Community Foundation Grants, 622

Middle East
Alavi Foundation Education Grants, 216

Middle School
ALA Coretta Scott King Book Donation Grant, 168
Alaska Community Foundation Anchorage Schools
    Foundation Grant, 197
CDC David J. Sencer Museum Student Field Trip
    Experience, 524
CNCS AmeriCorps State and National Grants, 643
NAA Foundation High Five Grants, 1711
Oregon Community Foundation K-12 Student
    Success: Out-of-School Grants, 1836
Public Education Power Grants, 2032
SME Education Fdn Youth Program Grants, 2209
VSA/Metlife Connect All Grants, 2392
W.H. and Mary Ellen Cobb Chartbl Trust Grts, 2397
West Virginia Commission on the Arts Special
    Projects Grants, 2433

Middle School Education
Akron Community Fdn Education Grants, 151
ALA Innovative Reading Grant, 171
ALA Sara Jaffarian School Library Award for
    Exemplary Humanities Programming, 190
Alaska Community Foundation Anchorage Schools
    Foundation Grant, 197
American Electric Power Corporate Grants, 252

American Electric Power Foundation Grants, 253
Carnegie Corporation of New York Grants, 511
Central Pacific Bank Foundation Grants, 530
CNCS AmeriCorps State and National Grants, 643
Community Foundation of Jackson County Classroom
    Education Grants, 713
Community Foundation of Louisville Education
    Grants, 724
Cooper Tire and Rubber Foundation Grants, 749
Dr. and Mrs. Paul Pierce Memorial Foundation
    Grants, 862
Elizabeth Carse Foundation Grants, 899
Energy by Design Poster Contest, 915
Evelyn and Walter Haas, Jr. Fund Education
    Opportunities Grants, 939
Fred and Gretel Biel Charitable Trust Grants, 1016
George J. and Effie L. Seay Foundation Grants, 1052
Helen Bader Foundation Grants, 1227
Intel Corporation Community Grants, 1311
Intel Corporation Int Community Grants, 1312
J. Knox Gholston Foundation Grants, 1321
J. Marion Sims Foundation Teachers' Pet Grant, 1322
J. William Gholston Foundation Grants, 1328
Jack Kent Cooke Fdn Good Neighbor Grants, 1331
Jack Kent Cooke Foundation Summer Enrichment
    Grants, 1332
John Clarke Trust Grants, 1369
Joseph S. Stackpole Charitable Trust Grants, 1390
Katrine Menzing Deakins Chartbl Trust Grants, 1422
LEGO Children's Fund Grants, 1480
Linford & Mildred White Charitable Grants, 1495
Luella Kemper Trust Grants, 1517
Marin Community Foundation Closing the Education
    Achievement Gap Grants, 1564
Marjorie Moore Charitable Foundation Grants, 1574
McCune Charitable Foundation Grants, 1617
Meyer Foundation Education Grants, 1649
Miller Foundation Grants, 1673
Minnie M. Jones Trust Grants, 1678
Nellie Mae Education Foundation District-Level
    Change Grants, 1736
Ober Kaler Community Grants, 1801
Oregon Community Foundation K-12 Student
    Success: Out-of-School Grants, 1836
PG&E Bright Ideas Grants, 1956
Piedmont Natural Gas Foundation K-12 Science,
    Technology, Engineering and Math (STEM)
    Grant, 1969
Public Education Power Grants, 2032
R.S. Gernon Trust Grants, 2047
Raskob Fdn for Catholic Activities Grants, 2054
Reinberger Foundation Grants, 2066
Thelma Braun and Bocklett Family Foundation
    Grants, 2287
USAID Integrated Youth Development Activity
    Grants, 2356
USDEd Gaining Early Awareness and Readiness for
    Undergrad Programs (GEAR UP) Grants, 2364
West Virginia Commission on the Arts Special
    Projects Grants, 2433
William J. Brace Charitable Trust, 2471
Wisconsin Energy Foundation Grants, 2481

Migrant Labor
Charles Delmar Foundation Grants, 564
Union Bank, N.A. Foundation Grants, 2334

Migrants
BBF Florida Family Literacy Initiative Grants, 386
BBF Maine Family Literacy Initiative Planning
    Grants, 388
California Endowment Innovative Ideas Challenge
    Grants, 495
Eide Bailly Resourcefullness Awards, 897
Farmers Insurance Corporate Giving Grants, 948
Foundation Beyond Belief Compassionate Impact
    Grants, 986
Foundation Beyond Belief Humanist Grants, 987
Union Bank, N.A. Foundation Grants, 2334

Migratory Animals and Birds
Chick and Sophie Major Memorial Duck Calling
    Contest Scholarships, 583
Cornell Lab of Ornithology Mini-Grants, 751
Herman H. Nettelroth Fund Grants, 1246

Military Personnel
Anne J. Caudal Foundation Grants, 276
IIE 911 Armed Forces Scholarships, 1288
Northrop Grumman Corporation Grants, 1772
OceanFirst Foundation Home Runs for Heroes
    Grants, 1802
William E. Dean III Charitable Fdn Grants, 2464

Military Sciences
MFRI Community Mobilization Grants, 1654
Northrop Grumman Corporation Grants, 1772

Military Training
Gulf Coast Foundation of Community Operating
    Grants, 1134
Gulf Coast Foundation of Community Program
    Grants, 1135
Northrop Grumman Corporation Grants, 1772

Mime
NHSCA Artist Residence Grants, 1756

Ministry
Chapman Charitable Foundation Grants, 560
Chapman Family Charitable Trust Grants, 561
Covenant Foundation of Brentwood Grants, 755

Minorities
ACL Disability and Rehabilitation Research Projects
    (DRRP) Program: Independent Living Transition
    Services for Youth and Young Adults Grants, 105
Active Living Research Grants, 109
Adolph Coors Foundation Grants, 129
Alex Stern Family Foundation Grants, 229
ALFJ International Fund Grants, 231
Alliant Energy Foundation Community Giving for
    Good Sponsorship Grants, 240
Anheuser-Busch Foundation Grants, 273
Bee Conservancy Sponsor-A-Hive Grants, 395
Benton Community Foundation Grants, 405
Blue River Community Foundation Grants, 458
BMW of North America Charitable Contribs, 460
Bodenwein Public Benevolent Foundation Grants, 461
Bothin Foundation Grants, 464
Brown County Community Foundation Grants, 475
California Arts Cncl Technical Assistance Grts, 494
Carnegie Corporation of New York Grants, 511
Charles Delmar Foundation Grants, 564
Chesapeake Bay Trust Outreach and Community
    Engagement Grants, 579
Chicago Board of Trade Foundation Grants, 580
Claremont Savings Bank Foundation Grants, 623
Colgate-Palmolive Company Grants, 652
Colorado Interstate Gas Grants, 661
Community Foundation of Bartholomew County
    Heritage Fund Grants, 690
Community Foundation of Bartholomew County
    James A. Henderson Award for Fundraising, 691
Community Foundation of Greater Fort Wayne -
    Community Endowment and Clarke Endowment
    Grants, 705
Community Foundation of St. Joseph County African
    American Community Grants, 737
Cralle Foundation Grants, 760
Edward W. and Stella C. Van Houten Memorial Fund
    Grants, 892
Eide Bailly Resourcefullness Awards, 897
Farmers Insurance Corporate Giving Grants, 948
Frederick McDonald Trust Grants, 1017
General Service Foundation Human Rights and
    Economic Justice Grants, 1040
George A. & Grace L. Long Fdn Grants, 1041
George W. Wells Foundation Grants, 1057
Georgia-Pacific Fdn Entrepreneurship Grants, 1059

Grotto Foundation Project Grants, 1123
HAF Community Grants, 1141
Harold Brooks Foundation Grants, 1172
Hubbard Farms Charitable Foundation Grants, 1272
ING Foundation Grants, 1302
Jacob G. Schmidlapp Trusts Grants, 1336
James Ford Bell Foundation Grants, 1339
John Clarke Trust Grants, 1369
Joseph H. and Florence A. Roblee Foundation
    Education Grants, 1386
Joseph S. Stackpole Charitable Trust Grants, 1390
Katharine Matthies Foundation Grants, 1418
Marriott Int Corporate Giving Grants, 1578
Maryland State Dept of Education Coordinating
    Entity Services for the Maryland Child Care Res
    Centers Network Grants, 1594
Montana Arts Council Cultural and Aesthetic Project
    Grants, 1685
Moses Kimball Fund Grants, 1701
NCSS Carter G. Woodson Book Awards, 1729
Oppenstein Brothers Foundation Grants, 1827
Oregon Community Foundation Black Student
    Success Community Network Grants, 1832
OSF Baltimore Community Fellowships, 1838
PCA-PCD Organizational Short-Term Professional
    Development and Consulting Grants, 1882
PCA Arts Management Internship, 1886
PCA Arts Organizations and Arts Programs Grants
    for Dance, 1892
PCA Entry Track Arts Organizations and Arts
    Programs Grants for Dance, 1904
PCA Strategies for Success Grants - Adv Level, 1917
PDF Community Organizing Grants, 1920
Portland General Electric Foundation Grants, 2007
Powell Foundation Grants, 2013
Prudential Foundation Education Grants, 2028
Robert R. Meyer Foundation Grants, 2094
Samueli Foundation Youth Services Grants, 2144
Sensient Technologies Foundation Grants, 2180
Shell Oil Company Foundation Community
    Development Grants, 2188
Sony Corporation of America Grants, 2216
Textron Corporate Contributions Grants, 2286
Thelma Braun and Bocklett Family Foundation
    Grants, 2287
Union Bank, N.A. Foundation Grants, 2334
Virginia Foundation for the Humanities Open
    Grants, 2387
Volkswagen Group of America Corporate
    Contributions Grants, 2389
Woods Fund of Chicago Grants, 2489
Z. Smith Reynolds Foundation Small Grants, 2523

Minorities, Ethnic
ACF Ethnic Community Self Help Grants, 80
Bee Conservancy Sponsor-A-Hive Grants, 395
BMW of North America Charitable Contribs, 460
California Arts Cncl Technical Assistance Grts, 494
Eide Bailly Resourcefullness Awards, 897
Foundation Beyond Belief Compassionate Impact
    Grants, 986
Foundation Beyond Belief Humanist Grants, 987
Four Lanes Trust Grants, 1005
Hartley Foundation Grants, 1186
Kentucky Arts Cncl Access Assistance Grants, 1428
Maine Community Foundation People of Color Fund
    Grants, 1544
Margaret M. Walker Charitable Fdn Grants, 1556
NZDIA Community Org Grants Scheme, 1796
Robert R. Meyer Foundation Grants, 2094
Samueli Foundation Youth Services Grants, 2144
Starr Foundation Grants, 2237
TAC Touring Arts and Arts Access Touring Arts
    Grants, 2269

Minority Education
3M Company Fdn Community Giving Grants, 5
ACF Head Start and/or Early Head Start Grantee
    - Clay, Randolph, and Talladega Counties,
    Alabama, 82

ACF Head Start and/or Early Head Start Grantee -
    St. Landry Parish, Louisiana, 83
ACL Disability and Rehabilitation Research Projects
    (DRRP) Program: Independent Living Transition
    Services for Youth and Young Adults Grants, 105
Air Products Foundation Grants, 148
ALA Coretta Scott King Book Donation Grant, 168
Anheuser-Busch Foundation Grants, 273
BMW of North America Charitable Contribs, 460
California Arts Cncl Technical Assistance Grts, 494
CIGNA Foundation Grants, 611
CMS Historically Black Colleges and Universities
    (HBCU) Health Services Research Grants, 639
Colgate-Palmolive Company Grants, 652
Edward W. and Stella C. Van Houten Memorial Fund
    Grants, 892
Eide Bailly Resourcefullness Awards, 897
Evelyn and Walter Haas, Jr. Fund Education
    Opportunities Grants, 939
Grand Circle Foundation Associates Grants, 1102
Grifols Community Outreach Grants, 1122
HAF Community Grants, 1141
HLTA Visitor Industry Charity Walk Grant, 1254
Kodak Community Relations Grants, 1445
Lloyd G. Balfour Foundation Attleboro-Specific
    Charities Grants, 1502
McCune Charitable Foundation Grants, 1617
Michael and Susan Dell Foundation Grants, 1657
Posse Foundation Scholarships, 2011
RGk Foundation Grants, 2068
Southern California Edison Education Grants, 2218
William J. Brace Charitable Trust, 2471
Xerox Foundation Grants, 2507

Minority Employment
Albert W. Rice Charitable Foundation Grants, 223
Charles H. Pearson Foundation Grants, 566
Eide Bailly Resourcefullness Awards, 897
GNOF New Orleans Works Grants, 1088
M.D. Anderson Foundation Grants, 1523
Mabel Louise Riley Foundation Family Strengthening
    Small Grants, 1528
Marriott Int Corporate Giving Grants, 1578
Meyer Foundation Education Grants, 1649
Moses Kimball Fund Grants, 1701
Oregon Community Foundation Black Student
    Success Community Network Grants, 1832
Pettus Foundation Grants, 1952
Public Welfare Foundation Special Initiative to
    Advance Civil Legal Aid Grants, 2034
Textron Corporate Contributions Grants, 2286

Minority Health
Aid for Starving Children Emerg Aid Grants, 144
Aid for Starving Children Health and Nutrition
    Grants, 145
Aid for Starving Children Water Projects Grants, 147
Anheuser-Busch Foundation Grants, 273
California Endowment Innovative Ideas Challenge
    Grants, 495
Cigna Civic Affairs Sponsorships, 610
Community Foundation for the National Capital
    Region Community Leadership Grants, 688
Foundations of East Chicago Health Grants, 997
Moses Kimball Fund Grants, 1701
Oregon Community Foundation Black Student
    Success Community Network Grants, 1832
Portland General Electric Foundation Grants, 2007
Seattle Foundation Health and Wellness Grants, 2179

Minority Schools
Alaska Community Foundation Anchorage Schools
    Foundation Grant, 197
Bee Conservancy Sponsor-A-Hive Grants, 395
Bush Foundation Event Scholarships, 484
California Arts Cncl Technical Assistance Grts, 494
Meyer Foundation Education Grants, 1649
Nellie Mae Education Foundation District-Level
    Change Grants, 1736

Oregon Community Foundation Black Student
    Success Community Network Grants, 1832
VSA/Metlife Connect All Grants, 2392

Minority/Woman-Owned Business
ACF Sustainable Employment and Economic
    Development Strategies Grants, 95
Dining for Women Grants, 831
ING Foundation Grants, 1302
NZDIA Community Org Grants Scheme, 1796

Missouri
Christine and Katharina Pauly Charitable Trust
    Grants, 601
Edward F. Swinney Trust Grants, 890
Guy I. Bromley Trust Grants, 1136
Herbert A. and Adrian W. Woods Foundation
    Grants, 1243
Victor E. Speas Foundation Grants, 2380
William J. Brace Charitable Trust, 2471

Multiculturalism
Laura Musser Intercultural Harmony Grants, 1472
NYSCA Special Arts Services: Instruction and
    Training Grants, 1794
OSF Education Program Grants in Kyrgyzstan, 1842
Posse Foundation Scholarships, 2011

Multidisciplinary Arts
Maryland State Arts Council Arts in Communities
    Grants, 1592
NJSCA Arts Ed Special Initiative Grants, 1764
NYSCA Electronic Media and Film: General
    Operating Support, 1786
NYSCA Electronic Media and Film: Workspace
    Grants, 1789
PCA-PCD Professional Development for Individual
    Artists Grants, 1883
PCA Arts in Education Residencies, 1885
PCA Arts Organizations and Arts Programs Grants
    for Local Arts, 1895
PCA Busing Grants, 1899
PCA Entry Track Arts Organizations and Arts
    Programs Grants for Local Arts, 1907
PCA Pennsylvania Partners in the Arts Program
    Stream Grants, 1914
PCA Pennsylvania Partners in the Arts Project
    Stream Grants, 1915
PCA Professional Development Grants, 1916
PCA Strategies for Success Grants - Basic Level, 1918
PCA Strategies for Success Grants - Intermediate
    Level, 1919
PennPAT Artist Technical Assistance Grants, 1929
PennPAT Strategic Opportunity Grants, 1933

Multiple Sclerosis
Austin S. Nelson Foundation Grants, 333

Muscular Dystrophy
Nash Avery Foundation Grants, 1714
Wilton and Effie Hebert Foundation Grants, 2476

Musculoskeletal Disorders
CDI Interdisciplinary Research Intvs Grants, 526

Musculoskeletal System
CDI Interdisciplinary Research Intvs Grants, 526

Museum Education
3 Dog Garage Museum Tours, 4
George Graham and Elizabeth Galloway Smith
    Foundation Grants, 1047
George J. and Effie L. Seay Foundation Grants, 1052
Hubbard Broadcasting Foundation Grants, 1269
McCune Charitable Foundation Grants, 1617
NSTA Distinguished Informal Science Education
    Award, 1777
NSTA Faraday Science Communicator Award, 1778
Shield-Ayres Foundation Grants, 2189

Museums

1st Source Foundation Community Involvement Grants, 1
3M Company Fdn Community Giving Grants, 5
A. Alfred Taubman Foundation Grants, 18
A.C. and Penney Hubbard Foundation Grants, 19
Air Products Foundation Grants, 148
Akron Community Foundation Arts and Culture Grants, 150
Andrew Family Foundation Grants, 272
Ann L. and Carol Green Rhodes Charitable Trust Grants, 278
Arthur Ashley Williams Foundation Grants, 302
Back Home Again Foundation Grants, 344
Ben B. Cheney Foundation Grants, 402
Bothin Foundation Grants, 464
Bradley C. Higgins Foundation Grants, 467
Burlington Industries Foundation Grants, 481
Campbell Foundation Grants, 500
Chapman Family Charitable Trust Grants, 561
Chicago Board of Trade Foundation Grants, 580
Christensen Fund Regional Grants, 600
Collins C. Diboll Private Foundation Grants, 657
Community Foundation of Eastern Connecticut General Southeast Grants, 696
Cooper Tire and Rubber Foundation Grants, 749
Cralle Foundation Grants, 760
Crystelle Waggoner Charitable Trust Grants, 768
Donald W. Reynolds Foundation Children's Discovery Initiative Grants, 841
Dorrance Family Foundation Grants, 845
Edyth Bush Charitable Foundation Grants, 893
Elizabeth Huth Coates Foundation Grants, 900
Ellen Abbott Gilman Trust Grants, 905
FirstEnergy Foundation Community Grants, 965
First Hawaiian Bank Foundation Corporate Giving Grants, 967
Gardner Foundation Grants, 1034
George and Ruth Bradford Foundation Grants, 1042
George Graham and Elizabeth Galloway Smith Foundation Grants, 1047
George I. Alden Trust Grants, 1051
George J. and Effie L. Seay Foundation Grants, 1052
George W. Codrington Charitable Foundation Grants, 1055
Greenspun Family Foundation Grants, 1118
Hawai'i SFCA Art Bento Program @ HiSAM Grants, 1210
Hubbard Broadcasting Foundation Grants, 1269
Hubbard Family Foundation Grants, 1270
Huffy Foundation Grants, 1273
Ike and Roz Friedman Foundation Grants, 1289
J.W. Gardner II Foundation Grants, 1323
James F. and Marion L. Miller Fdn Grants, 1338
Jerry L. and Barbara J. Burris Fdn Grants, 1362
JP Morgan Chase Fdn Arts and Culture Grants, 1394
Kenneth T. and Eileen L. Norris Fdn Grants, 1427
Kirkpatrick Foundation Grants, 1440
Lee and Ramona Bass Foundation Grants, 1478
LGA Family Foundation Grants, 1487
Louis and Sandra Berkman Foundation Grants, 1510
Mabel Y. Hughes Charitable Trust Grants, 1530
Marcia and Otto Koehler Foundation Grants, 1553
Marin Community Foundation Stinson Bolinas Community Grants, 1568
Maryland State Arts Council Arts in Communities Grants, 1592
Maurice Amado Foundation Grants, 1609
Maurice J. Masserini Charitable Trust Grants, 1610
Maurice R. Robinson Fund Grants, 1611
McConnell Foundation Grants, 1616
McLean Contributionship Grants, 1623
Mericos Foundation Grants, 1637
Narragansett Number One Foundation Grants, 1712
Oppenstein Brothers Foundation Grants, 1827
Parker Foundation (California) Grants, 1869
Parkersburg Area Community Foundation Action Grants, 1871
PCA Art Organizations and Art Programs Grants for Presenting Organizations, 1884

PCA Arts Organizations and Arts Programs Grants for Art Museums, 1888
PCA Entry Track Arts Organizations and Arts Programs Grants for Art Museums, 1900
PCA Entry Track Arts Organizations and Arts Programs Grants for Presenting Orgs, 1909
Perkin Fund Grants, 1937
Perkins Charitable Foundation Grants, 1939
Piedmont Natural Gas Corporate and Charitable Contributions, 1966
PMI Foundation Grants, 1982
R.C. Baker Foundation Grants, 2043
R.D. and Joan Dale Hubbard Fdn Grants, 2044
Reinberger Foundation Grants, 2066
Richard J. Stern Foundation for the Arts Grants, 2071
Riedman Foundation Grants, 2076
Robert and Betty Wo Foundation Grants, 2083
S. Spencer Scott Fund Grants, 2129
Samuel S. Johnson Foundation Grants, 2146
San Antonio Area Foundation Capital and Naming Rights Grants, 2148
Schlessman Family Foundation Grants, 2167
Seattle Foundation C. Keith Birkenfeld Memorial Trust Grants, 2177
Shell Deer Park Grants, 2186
Shield-Ayres Foundation Grants, 2189
Sioux Falls Area Community Foundation Community Fund Grants, 2203
Sioux Falls Area Community Foundation Spot Grants, 2204
Starr Foundation Grants, 2237
Storm Castle Foundation Grants, 2248
Strake Foundation Grants, 2249
Stranahan Foundation Grants, 2250
SunTrust Bank Trusteed Foundations Greene-Sawtell Grants, 2257
SunTrust Bank Trusteed Foundations Nell Warren Elkin and William Simpson Elkin Grants, 2258
Textron Corporate Contributions Grants, 2286
Thelma Doelger Charitable Trust Grants, 2288
Thomas Sill Foundation Grants, 2292
Thomas W. Briggs Foundation Grants, 2294
Union Bank, N.A. Foundation Grants, 2334
Union Pacific Fdn Community & Civic Grants, 2337
Virginia Foundation for the Humanities Open Grants, 2387
VSA/Metlife Connect All Grants, 2392
Wayne County Foundation Grants, 2419
Wege Foundation Grants, 2422
Widgeon Point Charitable Foundation Grants, 2447
William B. Dietrich Foundation Grants, 2458
William B. Stokely Jr. Foundation Grants, 2459
William E. Barth Foundation Grants, 2463
William G. Gilmore Foundation Grants, 2467
William J. and Tina Rosenberg Fdn Grants, 2470
Wilton and Effie Hebert Foundation Grants, 2476
Wold Foundation Grants, 2482

Music

A.C. and Penney Hubbard Foundation Grants, 19
Adams-Mastrovich Family Foundation Grants, 113
AGFT A Gift for Music Grants, 138
ASCAP Foundation Grants, 315
Avery Family Trust Grants, 338
Bill Graham Memorial Foundation Grants, 429
Blanche and Irving Laurie Foundation Grants, 436
City of Oakland Cultural Funding Grants, 618
Community Foundation for the Capital Region Grants, 687
Community Foundation of Muncie and Delaware County - Kitselman Grants, 733
Covenant to Care for Children Enrichment Fund Grants, 758
Cudd Foundation Grants, 769
David and Betty Sacks Foundation Grants, 788
Donald G. Gardner Humanities Tr Youth Grts, 840
Ensworth Charitable Foundation Grants, 916
FirstEnergy Foundation Community Grants, 965
From the Top Alumni Leadership Grants, 1025

From the Top Jack Kent Cooke Young Artist Scholarships, 1026
George Graham and Elizabeth Galloway Smith Foundation Grants, 1047
Greater Milwaukee Foundation Grants, 1109
Hahl Proctor Charitable Trust Grants, 1151
Hampton Roads Community Foundation Arts and Culture Grants, 1154
Helen E. Ellis Charitable Trust Grants, 1228
Hungry for Music Instrument Gifts, 1277
Jack Kent Cooke Fdn Young Artist Awards, 1333
Julia and Tunnicliff Fox Chartbl Trust Grants, 1397
Katharine Matthies Foundation Grants, 1418
Kennedy Center National Symphony Orchestra Youth Fellowships, 1426
Long Island Community Foundation Grants, 1507
M. Bastian Family Foundation Grants, 1522
Margaret T. Morris Foundation Grants, 1557
Mary D. and Walter F. Frear Eleemosynary Trust Grants, 1588
Maryland State Arts Council Arts in Communities Grants, 1592
Maurice Amado Foundation Grants, 1609
Maurice J. Masserini Charitable Trust Grants, 1610
National Cowboy and Western Heritage Museum Awards, 1722
Newfoundland and Labrador Arts Council ArtSmarts Grants, 1744
Newfoundland and Labrador Arts Council School Touring Grants, 1745
NHSCA Artist Residence Grants, 1756
NHSCA Youth Arts Project Grants: For Extended Arts Learning, 1758
NJSCA Artists in Education Residencies, 1763
NJSCA Arts Ed Special Initiative Grants, 1764
NYSCA Music: Commty Music Schools Grants, 1790
NYSCA Music: Gen Operating Support Grants, 1791
NYSCA Music: Gen Program Support Grants, 1792
Olive Higgins Prouty Foundation Grants, 1817
Oren Campbell McCleary Chartbl Trust Grants, 1837
PAS Freddie Gruber Scholarship, 1872
PAS John E. Grimes Timpani Scholarship, 1873
PAS PASIC International Scholarships, 1875
PAS SABIAN/PASIC Scholarship, 1876
PAS Sabian Larrie London Memorial Schol, 1877
PAS Zildjian Family Opportunity Fund Grants, 1878
Paul and Edith Babson Foundation Grants, 1881
PCA-PCD Professional Development for Individual Artists Grants, 1883
PCA Arts in Education Residencies, 1885
PCA Arts Organizations and Arts Program Grants for Music, 1887
PCA Entry Track Arts Organizations and Arts Programs Grants for Music, 1908
PCA Professional Development Grants, 1916
PCA Strategies for Success Grants - Adv Level, 1917
PCA Strategies for Success Grants - Basic Level, 1918
PCA Strategies for Success Grants - Intermediate Level, 1919
PennPAT Artist Technical Assistance Grants, 1929
PennPAT Strategic Opportunity Grants, 1933
Raymond Austin Hagen Family Fdn Grants, 2060
Richard and Caroline T. Gwathmey Memorial Trust Grants, 2069
Seattle Foundation C. Keith Birkenfeld Memorial Trust Grants, 2177
South Madison Community Foundation - Teacher Creativity Mini Grants, 2225
TAC Arts Access Grant, 2265
Thelma Braun and Bocklett Family Foundation Grants, 2287
Union Square Arts Award, 2339
VSA International Young Soloists Award, 2395
Whiting Foundation Grants, 2440

Music Appreciation

A.C. and Penney Hubbard Foundation Grants, 19
Dayton Foundation Dayton Youth Enrichment Fund Grant, 795
Helen E. Ellis Charitable Trust Grants, 1228

NYSCA Music: Gen Operating Support Grants, 1791
NYSCA Music: Gen Program Support Grants, 1792
PAS Zildjian Family Opportunity Fund Grants, 1878
Raymond Austin Hagen Family Fdn Grants, 2060

Music Composition
ASCAP Foundation Grants, 315
Mockingbird Foundation Grants, 1680
NYSCA Music: Gen Operating Support Grants, 1791
NYSCA Music: Gen Program Support Grants, 1792
PCA-PCD Professional Development for Individual
    Artists Grants, 1883
PCA Strategies for Success Grants - Adv Level, 1917
PCA Strategies for Success Grants - Basic Level, 1918
PCA Strategies for Success Grants - Intermediate
    Level, 1919
Seattle Foundation C. Keith Birkenfeld Memorial
    Trust Grants, 2177

Music Education
AGFT A Gift for Music Grants, 138
ASCAP Foundation Grants, 315
Bill Graham Memorial Foundation Grants, 429
CFKF Instrument Matching Grants, 556
Crescent Porter Hale Foundation Grants, 767
From the Top Alumni Leadership Grants, 1025
From the Top Jack Kent Cooke Young Artist
    Scholarships, 1026
George A. & Grace L. Long Fdn Grants, 1041
Hungry for Music Instrument Gifts, 1277
Jack Kent Cooke Fdn Young Artist Awards, 1333
Kennedy Center National Symphony Orchestra Youth
    Fellowships, 1426
Mockingbird Foundation Grants, 1680
Mr. Holland's Opus Foundation Melody Grants, 1703
Mr. Holland's Opus Foundation Michael Kamen Solo
    Award, 1704
Mr. Holland's Opus Special Projects Grants, 1705
NYSCA Music: Commty Music Schools Grants, 1790
NYSCA Music: Gen Operating Support Grants, 1791
NYSCA Music: Gen Program Support Grants, 1792
PAS John E. Grimes Timpani Scholarship, 1873
PAS SABIAN/PASIC Scholarship, 1876
Piper Trust Arts and Culture Grants, 1975
Portland General Electric Foundation Grants, 2007
Raymond Austin Hagen Family Fdn Grants, 2060

Music Recording
NYSCA Music: Gen Operating Support Grants, 1791
NYSCA Music: Gen Program Support Grants, 1792

Music Therapy
Community Fdn for the Capital Region Grants, 687
Oren Campbell McCleary Chartbl Trust Grants, 1837

Music Video Industry
Daniel and Nanna Stern Family Fdn Grants, 778

Music, Composition
NYSCA Music: Gen Operating Support Grants, 1791
NYSCA Music: Gen Program Support Grants, 1792
PCA Professional Development Grants, 1916

Music, Experimental
NYSCA Music: Commty Music Schools Grants, 1790
NYSCA Music: Gen Program Support Grants, 1792
VSA International Young Soloists Award, 2395

Music, Instrumental
ACMP Foundation Community Music Grants, 108
AGFT A Gift for Music Grants, 138
David and Betty Sacks Foundation Grants, 788
Jack Kent Cooke Fdn Young Artist Awards, 1333
Kennedy Center National Symphony Orchestra Youth
    Fellowships, 1426
Mockingbird Foundation Grants, 1680
NYSCA Music: Gen Operating Support Grants, 1791
NYSCA Music: Gen Program Support Grants, 1792
PAS Freddie Gruber Scholarship, 1872
PAS PASIC International Scholarships, 1875

PAS SABIAN/PASIC Scholarship, 1876
Sphinx Competition Awards, 2234
VSA International Young Soloists Award, 2395

Music, Vocal
ACMP Foundation Community Music Grants, 108
David and Betty Sacks Foundation Grants, 788
Mockingbird Foundation Grants, 1680
NYSCA Music: Commty Music Schools Grants, 1790
NYSCA Music: Gen Operating Support Grants, 1791
Peyton Anderson Foundation Grants, 1954
VSA International Young Soloists Award, 2395

Musical Instruments
CFKF Instrument Matching Grants, 556
Covenant to Care for Children Enrichment Fund
    Grants, 758
David and Betty Sacks Foundation Grants, 788
From the Top Jack Kent Cooke Young Artist
    Scholarships, 1026
Hampton Roads Community Foundation Arts and
    Culture Grants, 1154
Hungry for Music Instrument Gifts, 1277
Mockingbird Foundation Grants, 1680
Mr. Holland's Opus Foundation Melody Grants, 1703
Mr. Holland's Opus Foundation Michael Kamen Solo
    Award, 1704
Mr. Holland's Opus Foundation Special Projects
    Grants, 1705
PAS John E. Grimes Timpani Scholarship, 1873
PAS Sabian Larrie London Memorial Schol, 1877
Raymond Austin Hagen Family Fdn Grants, 2060
VSA International Young Soloists Award, 2395

Musicians in Residence
NYSCA Music: Commty Music Schools Grants, 1790
NYSCA Music: Gen Operating Support Grants, 1791
NYSCA Music: Gen Program Support Grants, 1792
TAC Arts Access Grant, 2265

National Disease Organizations
Alcatel-Lucent Technologies Foundation Grants, 224
Lockheed Martin Corporation Fdn Grants, 1505

National Security
Carnegie Corporation of New York Grants, 511
Gulf Coast Foundation of Community Operating
    Grants, 1134
Gulf Coast Foundation of Community Program
    Grants, 1135

Native American Education
ACF Native American Social and Economic
    Development Strategies for Alaska Grants, 87
ACF Native Youth Initiative for Leadership,
    Empowerment, and Development Grants, 88
ACF Sustainable Employment and Economic
    Development Strategies Grants, 95
ACF Tribal Maternal, Infant, and Early Childhood
    Home Visiting Program: Development and
    Implementation Grants, 97
ACF Tribal Maternal, Infant, and Early Childhood
    Home Visiting Program: Implementation and
    Expansion Grants, 98
AMERIND Community Service Project Grants, 265
Dorothea Haus Ross Foundation Grants, 844
Evelyn and Walter Haas, Jr. Fund Education
    Opportunities Grants, 939
First Nations Development Institute Native Arts
    Initiative Grants, 972
First Nations Development Institute Native Language
    Immersion Initiative Grants, 973
First Nations Development Institute Native Youth
    and Culture Fund Grants, 974
General Motors Foundation Grants, 1039
HAF Community Grants, 1141
HAF Native Cultures Fund Grants, 1148
Kindle Project SpiderWeave Flow Fund Grants, 1437
Target Corporation Community Engagement Fund
    Grants, 2270

Native American Languages
ACF Native American Social and Economic
    Development Strategies for Alaska Grants, 87
ACF Native Youth Initiative for Leadership,
    Empowerment, and Development Grants, 88
First Nations Development Institute Native Language
    Immersion Initiative Grants, 973
HAF Native Cultures Fund Grants, 1148
Kindle Project SpiderWeave Flow Fund Grants, 1437

Native American Studies
ACF Native American Social and Economic
    Development Strategies for Alaska Grants, 87
First Nations Development Institute Native Arts
    Initiative Grants, 972
First Nations Development Institute Native Language
    Immersion Initiative Grants, 973
First Nations Development Institute Native Youth
    and Culture Fund Grants, 974
HAF Native Cultures Fund Grants, 1148

Native Americans
ACF Abandoned Infants Assistance Grants, 70
ACF Community-Based Child Abuse
    Prevention (CBCAP) Tribal and Migrant
    DiscretionaryGrants, 77
ACF Native American Social and Economic
    Development Strategies for Alaska Grants, 87
ACF Native Youth Initiative for Leadership,
    Empowerment, and Development Grants, 88
ACF Sustainable Employment and Economic
    Development Strategies Grants, 95
ACF Tribal Maternal, Infant, and Early Childhood
    Home Visiting Program: Development and
    Implementation Grants, 97
ACF Tribal Maternal, Infant, and Early Childhood
    Home Visiting Program: Implementation and
    Expansion Grants, 98
AMERIND Community Service Project Grants, 265
Bush Foundation Event Scholarships, 484
Charles Delmar Foundation Grants, 564
CNCS AmeriCorps State and National Grants, 643
First Nations Development Institute Native Arts
    Initiative Grants, 972
First Nations Development Institute Nourishing
    Native Children: Feeding Our Future Project
    Grants, 975
Four Times Foundation Grants, 1006
GNOF Bayou Communities Grants, 1077
Grotto Foundation Project Grants, 1123
HAF Native Cultures Fund Grants, 1148
Honor the Earth Grants, 1259
Kindle Project SpiderWeave Flow Fund Grants, 1437
Lotus 88 Foundation for Women and Children
    Grants, 1508
Percy B. Ferebee Endowment Grants, 1936
Susan A. and Donald P. Babson Charitable
    Foundation Grants, 2259
Tides Foundation Grants, 2302

Natural Products
Dean Foods Community Involvement Grants, 805
Maurice R. Robinson Fund Grants, 1611

Natural Resources
786 Foundation Grants, 15
A. Alfred Taubman Foundation Grants, 18
A.C. and Penney Hubbard Foundation Grants, 19
Ann Ludington Sullivan Foundation Grants, 279
BP Foundation Grants, 465
CFFVR Environmental Stewardship Grants, 540
Charles Delmar Foundation Grants, 564
Clayton Fund Grants, 631
Community Foundation for Greater Buffalo
    Competitive Grants, 670
Dorrance Family Foundation Grants, 845
Fidelity Charitable Gift Fund Grants, 956
Fremont Area Community Foundation Community
    Grants, 1020
George and Ruth Bradford Foundation Grants, 1042

H.A. and Mary K. Chapman Charitable Trust
    Grants, 1137
Hawaii Electric Industries Charitable Foundation
    Grants, 1218
Horace A. Kimball and S. Ella Kimball Foundation
    Grants, 1260
James Ford Bell Foundation Grants, 1339
Jane's Trust Grants, 1346
Kosasa Foundation Grants, 1450
Kosciusko County Community Fdn Grants, 1452
LGA Family Foundation Grants, 1487
Mary K. Chapman Foundation Grants, 1590
Perkin Fund Grants, 1937
Perkins Charitable Foundation Grants, 1939
Pettus Foundation Grants, 1952
Piedmont Natural Gas Fdn Envirnmtl Stewardship
    and Energy Sustainability Grant, 1967
Pulaski County Community Foundation Grants, 2038
Ripley County Community Foundation Grants, 2077
Ripley County Community Foundation Small Project
    Grants, 2078
Samuel S. Johnson Foundation Grants, 2146

Natural Sciences
Harry Frank Guggenheim Foundation Research
    Grants, 1184
Reinberger Foundation Grants, 2066

Nature Centers
NSTA Faraday Science Communicator Award, 1778
Shield-Ayres Foundation Grants, 2189
Union Bank, N.A. Foundation Grants, 2334

Neighborhood Revitalization
7-Eleven Corporate Giving Grants, 8
520 Charitable Foundation Grants, 14
ACCF of Indiana First Merchants Bank / Decatur
    Bank and Trust Fund Grants, 66
Alloy Family Foundation Grants, 241
Appalachian Regl Commission Housing Grants, 289
AT&T Foundation Health and Human Services
    Grants, 322
Bank of America Charitable Foundation Community
    Development Grants, 355
Bay Area Community Fdn Auburn Area Chamber of
    Commerce Enrichment Fund Grants, 373
Blackford County Community Fdn Grants, 434
Blue Cross Blue Shield of Minnesota Fdn - Healthy
    Children: Growing Up Healthy Grants, 442
Blue Cross Blue Shield of Minnesota Foundation
    - Healthy Neighborhoods: Connect for Health
    Challenge Grants, 443
CFF Winter Park Community Grants, 551
Eastern Bank Charitable Foundation Neighborhood
    Support Grants, 880
Eastern Bank Charitable Foundation Partnerships
    Grants, 881
Eastern Bank Charitable Foundation Targeted
    Grants, 882
El Pomar Foundation Grants, 908
George A. & Grace L. Long Fdn Grants, 1041
GNOF Gert Community Fund Grants, 1082
GTRCF Elk Rapids Area Community Endowment
    Grants, 1127
Hardin County Community Foundation Grants, 1167
LISC Financial Stability Grants, 1501
Mabel F. Hoffman Charitable Trust Grants, 1526
Mabel Louise Riley Foundation Family Strengthening
    Small Grants, 1528
Marquette Bank Neighborhood Commit Grants, 1577
MassMutual Foundation Edonomic Development
    Grants, 1603
Mertz Gilmore Foundation NYC Communities
    Grants, 1641
MGM Resorts Foundation Community Grants, 1655
Miller Foundation Grants, 1673
Northland Foundation Grants, 1771
Pittsburgh Fdn Affordable Housing Grants, 1980
PNC Foundation Revitalization and Stabilization
    Grants, 1987

Robbins Family Charitable Foundation Grants, 2082
Textron Corporate Contributions Grants, 2286
U.S. Department of Education Promise
    Neighborhoods Grants, 2332

Neighborhoods
ACCF of Indiana Bank of Geneva Heritage Fund
    Grants, 64
ACCF of Indiana First Merchants Bank / Decatur
    Bank and Trust Fund Grants, 66
Adobe Foundation Action Grants, 126
Allstate Corporate Giving Grants, 242
Allstate Corp Hometown Commitment Grants, 243
Allstate Foundation Safe and Vital Communities
    Grants, 244
Amerigroup Foundation Grants, 264
Appalachian Regl Commission Housing Grants, 289
Baltimore Community Foundation Building Stronger
    Neighborhoods Regionwide Grants, 347
Bank of America Charitable Foundation Community
    Development Grants, 355
Blue Cross Blue Shield of Minnesota Foundation
    - Healthy Neighborhoods: Connect for Health
    Challenge Grants, 443
Carnegie Corporation of New York Grants, 511
CFGR Community Impact Grants, 552
Citizens Bank Charitable Foundation Grants, 616
Colorado Health Foundation Family, Friend and
    Neighbor Caregiver Supports Grants, 660
Community Foundation for the National Capital
    Region Community Leadership Grants, 688
Community Foundation of Greater Chattanooga
    Grants, 704
Deuce McAllister Catch 22 Foundation Grants, 828
Eastern Bank Charitable Foundation Neighborhood
    Support Grants, 880
EQT Fdn Community Enrichment Grants, 926
F.R. Bigelow Foundation Grants, 947
Farmers Insurance Corporate Giving Grants, 948
Four County Community Foundation General
    Grants, 1000
Gannett Foundation Community Action Grants, 1033
Giant Food Charitable Grants, 1068
Greater Milwaukee Foundation Grants, 1109
GTRCF Elk Rapids Area Community Endowment
    Grants, 1127
Hasbro Children's Fund Grants, 1189
Helen Bader Foundation Grants, 1227
Herbert A. and Adrian W. Woods Foundation
    Grants, 1243
Hillsdale County Community Foundation General
    Grants, 1250
ING Foundation Grants, 1302
Kalamazoo Community Foundation Good Neighbor
    Grants, 1408
Liberty Bank Foundation Grants, 1488
LISC Affordable Housing Grants, 1497
LISC Financial Stability Grants, 1501
Mabel Louise Riley Foundation Grants, 1529
Marquette Bank Neighborhood Commit Grants, 1577
Marsh Corporate Grants, 1580
Mertz Gilmore Foundation NYC Communities
    Grants, 1641
MGM Resorts Foundation Community Grants, 1655
OSF Baltimore Community Fellowships, 1838
Piper Trust Education Grants, 1977
Pittsburgh Fdn Affordable Housing Grants, 1980
PNC Foundation Revitalization and Stabilization
    Grants, 1987
Powell Family Foundation Grants, 2012
Robbins Family Charitable Foundation Grants, 2082
Speer Trust Grants, 2230
U.S. Bank Foundation Grants, 2330
U.S. Department of Education Promise
    Neighborhoods Grants, 2332
UPS Corporate Giving Grants, 2349

Neonatal Disorders
ACL Neonatal Abstinence Syndrome National
    Training Initiative Grant, 106

Nervous System
A-T Children's Project Grants, 16
A-T Children's Project Post Doctoral Fellowships, 17

Networking (Computers)
Cause Populi Worthy Cause Grants, 521
TechKnowledgey Community Impact Grants, 2278

Neuroendocrinology
HRAMF Charles H. Hood Foundation Child Health
    Research Awards, 1262

Neuroscience
Klingenstein-Simons Fellowship Awards in the
    Neurosciences, 1441

New York
Edward and Ellen Roche Relief Fdn Grants, 887
Frederick McDonald Trust Grants, 1017
Lily Palmer Fry Memorial Trust Grants, 1493
Northern Chautauqua Community Foundation
    Community Grants, 1769

Nigeria
USAID Nigeria Ed Crisis Response Grants, 2358

Nonfiction
ALA Booklist Editors' Choice Books for Youth
    Awards, 162
ALA Schneider Family Book Awards, 191
PCA Arts Organizations and Arts Programs Grants
    for Literature, 1894
PCA Entry Track Arts Organizations and Arts
    Programs Grants for Literature, 1906
PCA Strategies for Success Grants - Adv Level, 1917
PCA Strategies for Success Grants - Basic Level, 1918
PCA Strategies for Success Grants - Intermediate
    Level, 1919

Nonprofit Organizations
4imprint One by One Charitable Giving, 7
A. Alfred Taubman Foundation Grants, 18
Abby's Legendary Pizza Foundation Grants, 49
ADA Foundation Samuel Harris Children's Dental
    Health Grants, 111
Alaska Community Foundation Ketchikan
    Community Foundation Grant, 206
Albert and Ethel Herzstein Charitable Foundation
    Grants, 219
Alfred E. Chase Charitable Foundation Grants, 233
Anna Fitch Ardenghi Trust Grants, 274
Ann L. and Carol Green Rhodes Charitable Trust
    Grants, 278
Antone and Edene Vidinha Charitable Grants, 281
Bikes Belong Grants, 424
Blue Cross Blue Shield of Minnesota Fdn - Healthy
    Children: Growing Up Healthy Grants, 442
Blue Cross Blue Shield of Minnesota Foundation
    - Healthy Neighborhoods: Connect for Health
    Challenge Grants, 443
Blumenthal Foundation Grants, 459
Bodenwein Public Benevolent Foundation Grants, 461
C.H. Robinson Worldwide Foundation Grants, 489
Carl M. Freeman Foundation Grants, 508
Carl R. Hendrickson Family Foundation Grants, 509
Carrie S. Orleans Trust Grants, 512
Catherine Holmes Wilkins Foundation Charitable
    Grants, 520
CFFVR Clintonville Area Foundation Grants, 539
CFFVR Frank C. Shattuck Community Grants, 541
CFFVR Infant Welfare Circle of Kings Daughters
    Grants, 542
CFFVR Shawano Area Community Foundation
    Grants, 549
CFFVR Women's Fund for the Fox Valley Region
    Grants, 550
Charles Nelson Robinson Fund Grants, 569
Christine and Katharina Pauly Charitable Trust
    Grants, 601
CICF Summer Youth Grants, 608

Clara Blackford Smith and W. Aubrey Smith Charitable Foundation Grants, 621
Clarence T.C. Ching Foundation Grants, 624
Clark and Ruby Baker Foundation Grants, 625
Cleveland Foundation Legacy Village Lyndhurst Community Fund Grants, 636
CNCS AmeriCorps NCCC Project Grants, 642
CNCS Social Innovation Grants, 649
Community Foundation of Abilene Future Fund Grants, 689
Community Foundation of Bartholomew County Women's Giving Circle, 692
Community Foundation of Jackson County Seymour Noon Lions Club Grant, 714
Community Fdn of Morgan County Grants, 732
Community Foundation of Muncie and Delaware County Maxon Grants, 734
Community Foundation of St. Joseph County Special Project Challenge Grants, 738
Community Memorial Foundation Responsive Grants, 743
Cone Health Foundation Grants, 745
Courtney S. Turner Charitable Trust Grants, 753
Covenant to Care for Children Enrichment Fund Grants, 758
Crystelle Waggoner Charitable Trust Grants, 768
Curtis Foundation Grants, 771
David and Betty Sacks Foundation Grants, 788
David M. and Marjorie D. Rosenberg Foundation Grants, 790
Daviess County Community Foundation Recreation Grants, 793
Daviess County Community Foundation Youth Development Grants, 794
Decatur County Community Foundation Small Project Grants, 812
Doree Taylor Charitable Foundation Grants, 843
Dr. and Mrs. Paul Pierce Memorial Foundation Grants, 862
Draper Richards Kaplan Foundation Grants, 864
DTE Energy Foundation Leadership Grants, 870
Dubois County Community Foundation Grants, 871
Dyson Foundation Mid-Hudson Valley Project Support Grants, 874
Edward and Ellen Roche Relief Fdn Grants, 887
Edward F. Swinney Trust Grants, 890
Elizabeth Carse Foundation Grants, 899
Elizabeth Morse Genius Charitable Trust Grants, 901
Ensworth Charitable Foundation Grants, 916
Ezra M. Cutting Trust Grants, 945
F.R. Bigelow Foundation Grants, 947
FCYO Youth Organizing Grants, 954
Fichtenbaum Charitable Trust Grants, 955
First Hawaiian Bank Foundation Corporate Giving Grants, 967
Florence Foundation Grants, 978
Forest Foundation Grants, 985
Franklin H. Wells and Ruth L. Wells Foundation Grants, 1011
Frank Reed and Margaret Jane Peters Memorial Fund Grants, 1013
Frederick McDonald Trust Grants, 1017
Fund for the City of New York Grants, 1029
Furth Family Foundation Grants, 1030
George A. & Grace L. Long Fdn Grants, 1041
George H.C. Ensworth Memorial Fund Grants, 1049
George J. and Effie L. Seay Foundation Grants, 1052
George W. Wells Foundation Grants, 1057
Gibson County Community Foundation Recreation Grants, 1069
Gibson County Community Foundation Youth Development Grants, 1070
GNOF Exxon-Mobil Grants, 1080
GNOF Freeman Challenge Grants, 1081
GNOF IMPACT Grants for Youth Dev, 1084
GNOF New Orleans Works Grants, 1088
GNOF Norco Community Grants, 1089
GNOF Organizational Effectiveness Grants and Workshops, 1090
GNOF Stand Up For Our Children Grants, 1092

Goldseker Foundation Non-Profit Management Assistance Grants, 1095
Grace Bersted Foundation Grants, 1097
Grand Circle Foundation Associates Grants, 1102
Great Clips Corporate Giving, 1108
Grundy Foundation Grants, 1124
Guy I. Bromley Trust Grants, 1136
HAF Community Grants, 1141
HAF Southern Humboldt Grants, 1150
Hahl Proctor Charitable Trust Grants, 1151
Harden Foundation Grants, 1166
Harold and Rebecca H. Gross Fdn Grants, 1171
Harold Brooks Foundation Grants, 1172
Harvey Randall Wickes Foundation Grants, 1188
Helen Bader Foundation Grants, 1227
Helen E. Ellis Charitable Trust Grants, 1228
Helen Gertrude Sparks Charitable Trust Grants, 1230
Helen Irwin Littauer Educational Trust Grants, 1231
Henrietta Lange Burk Fund Grants, 1235
Herbert A. and Adrian W. Woods Foundation Grants, 1243
Horace A. Moses Charitable Trust Grants, 1261
Hubbard Family Foundation Grants, 1270
Human Source Foundation Grants, 1276
J. Knox Gholston Foundation Grants, 1321
J. William Gholston Foundation Grants, 1328
Janson Foundation Grants, 1350
Jaquelin Hume Foundation Grants, 1357
Jeffris Wood Foundation Grants, 1359
John Clarke Trust Grants, 1369
John D. and Katherine A. Johnston Foundation Grants, 1370
John F. Kennedy Center for the Performing Arts National Rosemary Kennedy Internship, 1371
Johnson County Community Foundation Youth Philanthropy Initiative Grants, 1380
Johnson Foundation Wingspread Conference Support Program, 1381
Joni Elaine Templeton Foundation Grants, 1384
Katharine Matthies Foundation Grants, 1418
Katrine Menzing Deakins Chartbl Trust Grants, 1422
Kawabe Memorial Fund Grants, 1423
Knox County Community Foundation Recreation Grants, 1442
Knox County Community Foundation Youth Development Grants, 1443
Land O'Lakes Fdn California Region Grants, 1465
Leola Osborn Trust Grants, 1483
Lewis H. Humphreys Charitable Trust Grants, 1486
Libra Foundation Grants, 1489
Lily Palmer Fry Memorial Trust Grants, 1493
Linford & Mildred White Charitable Grants, 1495
Lloyd G. Balfour Foundation Attleboro-Specific Charities Grants, 1502
Locations Foundation Legacy Grants, 1504
Lucy Downing Nisbet Charitable Fund Grants, 1515
Luella Kemper Trust Grants, 1517
M.A. Rikard Charitable Trust Grants, 1521
M.J. Murdock Charitable Trust General Grants, 1524
Mabel A. Horne Fund Grants, 1525
Mabel F. Hoffman Charitable Trust Grants, 1526
MacLellan Foundation Grants, 1531
Maine Women's Fund Girls' Grantmaking Intv, 1547
Manuel D. and Rhoda Mayerson Fdn Grants, 1550
Marcia and Otto Koehler Foundation Grants, 1553
Marietta McNeill Morgan and Samuel Tate Morgan Jr. Trust Grants, 1560
Marin Community Foundation Arts in the Community Grants, 1563
Marin Community Foundation Closing the Education Achievement Gap Grants, 1564
Marin Community Foundation Ending the Cycle of Poverty Grants, 1565
Marin Community Foundation Social Justice and Interfaith Understanding Grants, 1567
Marin Community Foundation Stinson Bolinas Community Grants, 1568
Marion and Miriam Rose Fund Grants, 1569
Marion Gardner Jackson Charitable Trust Grts, 1570
Marjorie Moore Charitable Foundation Grants, 1574

Maryland State Arts Council Arts in Communities Grants, 1592
Mary S. and David C. Corbin Fdn Grants, 1598
Mathile Family Foundation Grants, 1604
McCarthy Family Fdn Charity Fund Grants, 1614
McConnell Foundation Grants, 1616
McLean Foundation Grants, 1624
Medtronic Foundation Community Link Arts, Civic, and Culture Grants, 1629
Medtronic Foundation CommunityLink Health Grants, 1630
Memorial Foundation for Children Grants, 1633
Meyer Foundation Benevon Grants, 1648
Meyer Fdn Management Assistance Grants, 1651
MGN Family Foundation Grants, 1656
Michael and Susan Dell Foundation Grants, 1657
Microsoft Software Donations, 1665
Middlesex Savings Charitable Foundation Capacity Building Grants, 1669
Miller Foundation Grants, 1673
Milton Hicks Wood and Helen Gibbs Wood Charitable Trust Grants, 1676
Minnie M. Jones Trust Grants, 1678
Montgomery County Community Foundation Health and Human Services Fund Grants, 1689
Montgomery County Community Foundation Youth Services Grants, 1691
Ms. Foundation for Women Building Democracy Grants, 1706
Ms. Fdn for Women Economic Justice Grants, 1707
Ms. Fdn for Women Ending Violence Grants, 1708
Nathalie and Gladys Dalkowitz Charitable Trust Grants, 1716
Nellie Mae Education Foundation District-Level Change Grants, 1736
New Earth Foundation Grants, 1743
Northern Chautauqua Community Foundation Community Grants, 1769
Ohio Arts Council Artist in Residence Grants for Sponsors, 1810
Olga Sipolin Children's Fund Grants, 1815
OSF Baltimore Criminal and Juve Justice Grts, 1839
OSF Baltimore Education and Youth Development Grants, 1840
OSF Young Feminist Leaders Fellowships, 1845
PCA-PCD Organizational Short-Term Professional Development and Consulting Grants, 1882
PCA Management/Techl Assistance Grants, 1913
PCA Strategies for Success Grants - Adv Level, 1917
Percy B. Ferebee Endowment Grants, 1936
Perkins-Ponder Foundation Grants, 1938
Perpetual Benevolent Fund, 1940
Perry County Community Foundation Youth Development Grants, 1943
Peter and Elizabeth C. Tower Foundation Technology Initiative Grants, 1949
Peter and Elizabeth C. Tower Foundation Technology Planning Grants, 1950
Phoenix Suns Charities Grants, 1964
Piedmont Health Foundation Grants, 1965
Pike County Community Foundation Youth Development Grants, 1971
PNM Reduce Your Use Grants, 1988
Posey County Community Foundation Youth Development Grants, 2010
Priddy Foundation Program Grants, 2023
R.D. Beirne Trust Grants, 2045
R.S. Gernon Trust Grants, 2047
Richard and Caroline T. Gwathmey Memorial Trust Grants, 2069
Robert and Betty Wo Foundation Grants, 2083
Robert W. Knox, Sr. and Pearl Wallis Knox Charitable Foundation, 2095
Rose Hills Foundation Grants, 2106
Roy and Christine Sturgis Charitable Tr Grts, 2115
Sara Elizabeth O'Brien Trust Grants, 2161
Sarah G. McCarthy Memorial Foundation, 2162
Share Our Strength Grants, 2185
Spencer County Community Foundation Youth Development Grants, 2233

Stein Family Charitable Trust Grants, 2240
Stinson Foundation Grants, 2246
Stranahan Foundation Grants, 2250
Swindells Charitable Foundation Grants, 2261
TechKnowledgey Community Impact Grants, 2278
Telluride Fdn Emergency Grants, 2282
Thelma Braun and Bocklett Family Foundation
    Grants, 2287
Threshold Foundation Queer Youth Grants, 2299
Toby Wells Foundation Grants, 2304
Trinity Trust Summer Youth Mini Grants, 2321
Union Square Arts Award, 2339
Union Square Award for Social Justice, 2340
Vanderburgh Community Foundation Youth
    Development Grants, 2375
Victor E. Speas Foundation Grants, 2380
Vigneron Memorial Fund Grants, 2384
VSA/Metlife Connect All Grants, 2392
W.H. and Mary Ellen Cobb Chartbl Trust Grts, 2397
W.P. and Bulah Luse Foundation Grants, 2399
Walter S. and Evan C. Jones Testam Trust, 2407
Warren County Community Foundation Youth
    Development Grants, 2412
Wege Foundation Grants, 2422
Wild Rivers Community Foundation Holiday
    Partnership Grants, 2448
William A. Badger Foundation Grants, 2451
William E. Dean III Charitable Fdn Grants, 2464
William Foulds Family Foundation Grants, 2465
William J. Brace Charitable Trust, 2471
Wood Family Charitable Trust Grants, 2487
Z. Smith Reynolds Foundation Small Grants, 2523

Nuclear/Radioactive Waste Disposal
Honor the Earth Grants, 1259

Nursing
Abington Foundation Grants, 54
CFGR Jenkins Foundation Grants, 553
Foundation for Health Enhancement Grants, 990
Kaiser Permanente Hawaii Region Community
    Grants, 1406
Koch Family Foundation (Annapolis) Grants, 1444
LGA Family Foundation Grants, 1487
Lucy Downing Nisbet Charitable Fund Grants, 1515

Nursing Education
Abell-Hanger Foundation Grants, 52
Burlington Industries Foundation Grants, 481
Edward W. and Stella C. Van Houten Memorial Fund
    Grants, 892
Effie and Wofford Cain Foundation Grants, 895
LGA Family Foundation Grants, 1487
Samuel S. Johnson Foundation Grants, 2146

Nursing Homes
Community Foundation for the Capital Region
    Grants, 687
Kentucky Arts Cncl Access Assistance Grants, 1428
McLean Contributionship Grants, 1623
Mervin Bovaird Foundation Grants, 1643
Reinberger Foundation Grants, 2066
Union Bank, N.A. Foundation Grants, 2334

Nutrition Education
Abbott Fund Access to Health Care Grants, 45
Abbott Fund Science Education Grants, 48
ACF Social and Economic Development Strategies
    Grants, 93
Allen Foundation Educational Nutrition Grants, 238
Amway Corporation Contributions, 269
Baltimore Ravens Foundation Play 60 Grants, 351
Caesars Foundation Grants, 492
Campbell Soup Foundation Grants, 501
CNCS AmeriCorps State and National Grants, 643
Fremont Area Community Foundation Youth
    Advisory Committee Grants, 1022
George H. Sandy Foundation Grants, 1050
Gerber Fdn West Michigan Youth Grants, 1065

Medtronic Foundation CommunityLink Health
    Grants, 1630
Milton Hicks Wood and Helen Gibbs Wood
    Charitable Trust Grants, 1676
Mt. Sinai Health Care Foundation Health of the
    Jewish Community Grants, 1709
Mt. Sinai Health Care Foundation Health of the
    Urban Community Grants, 1710
NFL Charities Pro Bowl Community Grants in
    Hawaii, 1755
Paso del Norte Health Foundation Grants, 1874
PepsiCo Foundation Grants, 1935
Posey Community Foundation Women's Fund
    Grants, 2008
Robert R. Meyer Foundation Grants, 2094
Sierra Health Foundation Responsive Grants, 2199
Spencer County Community Foundation Women's
    Fund Grants, 2232
USDA WIC Nutrition Ed Innovations Grants, 2363
Vanderburgh Community Foundation Men's Fund
    Grants, 2373
Vanderburgh County Community Foundation
    Women's Fund Grants, 2376
Warrick County Community Foundation Women's
    Fund, 2411

Nutrition/Dietetics
Abbott Fund Science Education Grants, 48
Aid for Starving Children Health and Nutrition
    Grants, 145
Albertsons Companies Foundation Nourishing
    Neighbors Grants, 221
Allen Foundation Educational Nutrition Grants, 238
Amway Corporation Contributions, 269
Atkinson Foundation Community Grants, 325
Better Way Foundation Grants, 419
Boeing Company Contributions Grants, 462
Caesars Foundation Grants, 492
First Nations Development Institute Nourishing
    Native Children: Feeding Our Future Project
    Grants, 975
Foundation for a Healthy Kentucky Grants, 988
Gerber Foundation Pediatric Nutrition Research
    Grants, 1064
Gerber Fdn West Michigan Youth Grants, 1065
March of Dimes Program Grants, 1552
McCarthy Family Fdn Charity Fund Grants, 1614
Meyer Fdn Healthy Communities Grants, 1650
NFL Charities Pro Bowl Community Grants in
    Hawaii, 1755
Paso del Norte Health Foundation Grants, 1874
Sensient Technologies Foundation Grants, 2180
Thomas and Agnes Carvel Foundation Grants, 2289
USDA Child and Adult Care Food Program, 2362

Nutritional Diseases and Disorders
Abbott Fund Science Education Grants, 48
Gerber Foundation Pediatric Nutrition Research
    Grants, 1064

Obesity
Active Living Research Grants, 109
Bright Promises Foundation Grants, 470
Campbell Soup Foundation Grants, 501
CDC David J. Sencer Museum Student Field Trip
    Experience, 524
CNCS AmeriCorps State and National Grants, 643
Collective Brands Foundation Saucony Run for Good
    Grants, 656
GNOF IMPACT Kahn-Oppenheim Tr Grts, 1087
HRAMF Charles H. Hood Foundation Child Health
    Research Awards, 1262
Mt. Sinai Health Care Foundation Health of the
    Jewish Community Grants, 1709
Pacers Foundation Be Healthy and Fit Grants, 1858
Pajaro Valley Community Health Trust Diabetes and
    Contributing Factors Grants, 1865
PepsiCo Foundation Grants, 1935
Piedmont Health Foundation Grants, 1965
RCF The Women's Fund Grants, 2065

RWJF Childhood Obesity Grants, 2126
RWJF Healthy Eating Research Grants, 2127
YSA UnitedHealth HEROES Service-Learning
    Grants, 2522

Obstetrics-Gynecology
Blanche and Irving Laurie Foundation Grants, 436
HRAMF Charles H. Hood Foundation Child Health
    Research Awards, 1262

Oceanography
Environmental Excellence Awards, 922

Oceans and Seas
Ama OluKai Foundation Grants, 249
Matson Adahi I Tano' Grants, 1606
Matson Community Giving Grants, 1607

Oncology
Abbott Fund Science Education Grants, 48
Pediatric Cancer Research Foundation Grants, 1927

Opera/Musical Theater
Avery Family Trust Grants, 338
Hahl Proctor Charitable Trust Grants, 1151
Hattie Mae Lesley Foundation Grants, 1195
Henrietta Lange Burk Fund Grants, 1235
Mabel Y. Hughes Charitable Trust Grants, 1530
NJSCA Artists in Education Residencies, 1763
NJSCA Arts Ed Special Initiative Grants, 1764
NYSCA Arts Education: General Operating Support
    Grants, 1781
NYSCA Music: Commty Music Schools Grants, 1790
NYSCA Theatre: Prof Performances Grants, 1795
PennPAT Artist Technical Assistance Grants, 1929
PennPAT Strategic Opportunity Grants, 1933
Piper Trust Arts and Culture Grants, 1975

Operating Support
Abby's Legendary Pizza Foundation Grants, 49
Adam Don Foundation Grants, 112
Adams Family Foundation I Grants, 116
A Friends' Foundation Trust Grants, 136
Albert and Ethel Herzstein Charitable Foundation
    Grants, 219
Albert W. Cherne Foundation Grants, 222
Alex Stern Family Foundation Grants, 229
Alfred E. Chase Charitable Foundation Grants, 233
Alliance for Strong Families and Communities
    Grants, 239
Anne J. Caudal Foundation Grants, 276
Arthur E. and Josephine Campbell Beyer Foundation
    Grants, 303
Blue Grass Community Foundation Clark County
    Fund Grants, 444
Blumenthal Foundation Grants, 459
Bodenwein Public Benevolent Foundation Grants, 461
Burton D. Morgan Foundation Youth
    Entrepreneurship Grants, 483
Cadillac Products Packaging Company Foundation
    Grants, 491
Caring for Colorado Foundation Sperry S. and Ella
    Graber Packard Fund for Pueblo Grants, 505
Carl R. Hendrickson Family Foundation Grants, 509
CJ Fdn for SIDS Program Services Grants, 619
Community Foundation for Greater Atlanta
    Metropolitan Extra Wish Grants, 666
Community Foundation for Greater Atlanta Spark
    Clayton Grants, 667
Community Foundation for Greater Atlanta Spark
    Newton Grants, 668
David and Barbara B. Hirschhorn Foundation
    Summer Camping Grants, 787
Dean Foundation Grants, 806
Dream Weaver Foundation, 865
E. Clayton and Edith P. Gengras, Jr. Foundation
    Grants, 875
Edward and Romell Ackley Foundation Grants, 889
Edward F. Swinney Trust Grants, 890
Florence Hunt Maxwell Foundation Grants, 979

Ford Family Foundation Grants - Technical Assistance , 983
Fred and Gretel Biel Charitable Trust Grants, 1016
Frederick McDonald Trust Grants, 1017
George E. Hatcher, Jr. and Ann Williams Hatcher Foundation Grants, 1045
George H.C. Ensworth Memorial Fund Grants, 1049
GNOF IMPACT Grants for Arts and Culture, 1083
GNOF IMPACT Grants for Youth Dev, 1084
Grace Bersted Foundation Grants, 1097
Greater Tacoma Community Foundation General Operating Grants, 1113
Green River Area Community Fdn Grants, 1117
Guy I. Bromley Trust Grants, 1136
Hahl Proctor Charitable Trust Grants, 1151
Hardin County Community Foundation Grants, 1167
Harmony Grove Foundation Grants, 1169
Harold and Rebecca H. Gross Fdn Grants, 1171
Hawaii State Legislature Grant-In-Aid, 1219
Hazel and Walter T. Bales Foundation Grants, 1220
Hearst Foundations Culture Grants, 1223
Hearst Foundations Social Service Grants, 1224
Helen Gertrude Sparks Charitable Trust Grants, 1230
Henry and Ruth Blaustein Rosenberg Foundation Education Grants, 1236
Horace A. Moses Charitable Trust Grants, 1261
Hubbard Broadcasting Foundation Grants, 1269
Hubbard Family Foundation Grants, 1271
Hubbard Family Foundation Grants, 1270
Island Insurance Foundation Grants, 1316
J. Knox Gholston Foundation Grants, 1321
J. William Gholston Foundation Grants, 1328
Jack and Dorothy Byrne Foundation Grants, 1329
Jack H. and William M. Light Charitable Trust Grants, 1330
Janet Spencer Weekes Foundation Grants, 1348
Jayne and Leonard Abess Foundation Grants, 1358
John Clarke Trust Grants, 1369
John D. and Katherine A. Johnston Foundation Grants, 1370
John P. Ellbogen Fdn Community Grants, 1377
Joni Elaine Templeton Foundation Grants, 1384
Joseph Henry Edmondson Foundation Grants, 1388
Katharine Matthies Foundation Grants, 1418
Katrine Menzing Deakins Chartbl Trust Grants, 1422
Kawabe Memorial Fund Grants, 1423
Kimball International-Habig Foundation Education Grants, 1433
Kind World Foundation Grants, 1438
Laclede Gas Charitable Trust Grants, 1457
Laura L. Adams Foundation Grants, 1473
Lavina Parker Trust Grants, 1477
Leola Osborn Trust Grants, 1483
Lewis H. Humphreys Charitable Trust Grants, 1486
Linford & Mildred White Charitable Grants, 1495
Lloyd G. Balfour Foundation Attleboro-Specific Charities Grants, 1502
Lucy Downing Nisbet Charitable Fund Grants, 1515
Mabel A. Horne Fund Grants, 1525
Marcia and Otto Koehler Foundation Grants, 1553
Marion and Miriam Rose Fund Grants, 1569
Marion Gardner Jackson Charitable Trust Grts, 1570
Marion I. and Henry J. Knott Foundation Discretionary Grants, 1571
Marion I. and Henry J. Knott Foundation Standard Grants, 1572
Marjorie Moore Charitable Foundation Grants, 1574
Mary Wilmer Covey Charitable Trust Grants, 1600
Maurice R. Robinson Fund Grants, 1611
May and Stanley Smith Charitable Trust Grants, 1613
McCarthy Family Fdn Charity Fund Grants, 1614
Meyer Foundation Education Grants, 1649
Michael Reese Health Trust Core Grants, 1658
Milton Hicks Wood and Helen Gibbs Wood Charitable Trust Grants, 1676
Montana Community Foundation Grants, 1687
Nell J. Redfield Foundation Grants, 1737
New Hampshire Charitable Foundation Community Unrestricted Grants, 1747

NYSCA Arts Education: General Operating Support Grants, 1781
Olive Higgins Prouty Foundation Grants, 1817
OMNOVA Solutions Fdn Education Grants, 1820
Perkins-Ponder Foundation Grants, 1938
Perpetual Benevolent Fund, 1940
PPCF Esther M. and Freeman E. Everett Charitable Foundation Grants, 2016
Priddy Foundation Operating Grants, 2021
R.D. Beirne Trust Grants, 2045
R.S. Gernon Trust Grants, 2047
Richard and Caroline T. Gwathmey Memorial Trust Grants, 2069
Richard W. Goldman Family Fdn Grants, 2073
Robert Lee Adams Foundation Grants, 2091
Robert Lee Blaffer Foundation Grants, 2092
Robert R. Meyer Foundation Grants, 2094
Robert W. Knox, Sr. and Pearl Wallis Knox Charitable Foundation, 2095
Roger L. and Agnes C. Dell Charitable Trust I Grants, 2099
Roy and Christine Sturgis Charitable Tr Grts, 2115
Sadler Family Foundation Grants, 2132
Saeman Family Fdn A Charitable Grants, 2133
Sara Elizabeth O'Brien Trust Grants, 2161
Sarah G. McCarthy Memorial Foundation, 2162
Shield-Ayres Foundation Grants, 2189
Sidney and Sandy Brown Foundation Grants, 2196
Stan and Sandy Checketts Foundation Grants, 2235
Stein Family Charitable Trust Grants, 2240
Stinson Foundation Grants, 2246
Swindells Charitable Foundation Grants, 2261
Sylvia Perkin Perpetual Charitable Trust Grants, 2263
Thelma Braun and Bocklett Family Foundation Grants, 2287
Thomas J. Atkins Memorial Trust Fund Grants, 2290
Tides Foundation Girl Rising Fund Grants, 2301
Tom C. Barnsley Foundation Grants, 2306
Victor E. Speas Foundation Grants, 2380
Vigneron Memorial Fund Grants, 2384
W.P. and Bulah Luse Foundation Grants, 2399
Walter J. and Betty C. Zable Fdn Grants, 2406
Walter S. and Evan C. Jones Testam Trust, 2407
William E. Dean III Charitable Fdn Grants, 2464
William J. Brace Charitable Trust, 2471
Wood Family Charitable Trust Grants, 2487
Wyoming Community Fdn General Grants, 2501
Wyoming Community Foundation Hazel Patterson Memorial Grants, 2502
ZYTL Foundation Grants, 2528

Oral Diseases
Pajaro Valley Community Health Trust Oral Health: Prevention & Access Grants, 1866

Oral Health and Hygiene
ADA Foundation Samuel Harris Children's Dental Health Grants, 111
Aetna Foundation Regional Health Grants, 134
Illinois Children's Healthcare Fdn Grants, 1295
Pajaro Valley Community Health Trust Oral Health: Prevention & Access Grants, 1866

Oral History
Alabama Humanities Foundation Major Grants, 159
Radcliffe Institute Oral History Grants, 2049
Turner Foundation Grants, 2326
Virginia Foundation for the Humanities Open Grants, 2387

Orchestras
Alcatel-Lucent Technologies Foundation Grants, 224
Ar-Hale Family Foundation Grants, 290
Avery Family Trust Grants, 338
Fremont Area Community Foundation Community Grants, 1020
George Graham and Elizabeth Galloway Smith Foundation Grants, 1047
George W. Codrington Charitable Foundation Grants, 1055

Hattie Mae Lesley Foundation Grants, 1195
Helen E. Ellis Charitable Trust Grants, 1228
Henrietta Lange Burk Fund Grants, 1235
Hubbard Broadcasting Foundation Grants, 1269
Katrine Menzing Deakins Chartbl Trust Grants, 1422
Kenneth T. and Eileen L. Norris Fdn Grants, 1427
Kirkpatrick Foundation Grants, 1440
NJSCA Arts Ed Special Initiative Grants, 1764
NYSCA Music: Commty Music Schools Grants, 1790
Sphinx Competition Awards, 2234
Wayne County Foundation Grants, 2419
William Foulds Family Foundation Grants, 2465

Organic Farming
Merck Family Fund Urban Farming and Youth Leadership Grants, 1635

Organizational Development
California Endowment Innovative Ideas Challenge Grants, 495
CNCS AmeriCorps Indian Tribes Plang Grts , 641
CNCS AmeriCorps State and National Grants, 643
CNCS Social Innovation Grants, 649
Easton Foundations Archery Facility Grants, 883
GNOF Organizational Effectiveness Grants and Workshops, 1090
Goldseker Foundation Non-Profit Management Assistance Grants, 1095
Lisa and Douglas Goldman Fund Grants, 1496
Meyer Foundation Benevon Grants, 1648
Meyer Foundation Education Grants, 1649
Meyer Fdn Management Assistance Grants, 1651
Middlesex Savings Charitable Foundation Capacity Building Grants, 1669
Oren Campbell McCleary Chartbl Trust Grants, 1837
PCA-PCD Organizational Short-Term Professional Development and Consulting Grants, 1882
PCA Arts Management Internship, 1886
PCA Management/Techl Assistance Grants, 1913
PCA Strategies for Success Grants - Adv Level, 1917
PCA Strategies for Success Grants - Basic Level, 1918
PCA Strategies for Success Grants - Intermediate Level, 1919
Priddy Foundation Organizational Development Grants, 2022
Saginaw Community Foundation Discretionary Grants, 2134
Telluride Fdn Technical Assistance Grants, 2283
Union Bank, N.A. Foundation Grants, 2334
Union Square Award for Social Justice, 2340

Organizational Theory and Behavior
PDF Community Organizing Grants, 1920
PDF Fiscal Sponsorship Grant, 1921
Social Justice Fund Northwest Criminal Justice Giving Project Grants, 2214

Ornithology
Cornell Lab of Ornithology Mini-Grants, 751

Orthopedics
Union Labor Health Fdn Angel Fund Grants, 2335

Osteoporosis
Premera Blue Cross Grants, 2018

Otology
Oticon Focus on People Awards, 1847

Outpatient Care
Alliance for Strong Families and Communities Grants, 239
Camille Beckman Foundation Grants, 499
J. Watumull Fund Grants, 1326
Pinnacle Entertainment Foundation Grants, 1972

Ovarian Cancer
GNOF IMPACT Harold W. Newman, Jr. Charitable Trust Grants, 1086

Pacific Islanders
Ama OluKai Foundation Grants, 249
Eide Bailly Resourcefullness Awards, 897
NZDIA Community Org Grants Scheme, 1796

Pacific Islands
Ama OluKai Foundation Grants, 249
Matson Adahi I Tano' Grants, 1606

Painting
PCA Arts Organizations and Arts Programs Grants
for Visual Arts, 1898
PCA Entry Track Arts Organizations and Arts
Programs Grants for Visual Arts, 1912

Palestine
USAID School Improvement Program Grants, 2360

Palliative Care
Aetna Foundation Regional Health Grants, 134
Austin S. Nelson Foundation Grants, 333
Daniels Homeless and Disadvantaged Grants, 782
Piper Trust Healthcare and Med Rsrch Grants, 1978
Sara Elizabeth O'Brien Trust Grants, 2161

Pancreatic Cancer
Camille Beckman Foundation Grants, 499
GNOF IMPACT Harold W. Newman, Jr. Charitable
Trust Grants, 1086

Parent Education
3M Company Fdn Community Giving Grants, 5
ACF Abandoned Infants Assistance Grants, 70
Achelis and Bodman Foundation Grants, 101
A Fund for Women Grants, 137
Alaska Community Foundation Children's Trust Tier
1 Parenting and Child Development Educational
Grants, 199
Allen Foundation Educational Nutrition Grants, 238
BBF Florida Family Literacy Initiative Grants, 386
BBF Maine Family Literacy Initiative Implementation
Grants, 387
BBF Maine Family Literacy Initiative Planning
Grants, 388
BBF Maryland Family Literacy Initiative
Implementation Grants, 389
BBF National Grants for Family Literacy, 391
CFGR Community Impact Grants, 552
Children's Trust Fund of Oregon Fdn Grants, 585
Children's Trust Fund of Oregon Foundation Small
Grants, 586
CJ Fdn for SIDS Program Services Grants, 619
Community Foundation for Greater Atlanta Spark
Clayton Grants, 667
Community Foundation for Greater Atlanta Spark
Newton Grants, 668
Community Foundation of Bartholomew County
Women's Giving Circle, 692
FCD New American Children Grants, 952
First Lady's Family Literacy Initiative for Texas
Family Literacy Trailblazer Grants, 968
First Lady's Family Literacy Initiative for Texas
Implementation Grants, 969
First Lady's Family Literacy Initiative for Texas
Planning Grants, 970
Ford Family Foundation Grants - Child Abuse
Prevention and Intervention, 981
Gerber Fdn West Michigan Youth Grants, 1065
German Protestant Orphan Asylum Foundation
Grants, 1066
Helen V. Brach Foundation Grants, 1232
Initiative Foundation Minnesota Early Childhood
Initiative Grants, 1305
Joseph H. and Florence A. Roblee Foundation Family
Grants, 1387
Linden Foundation Grants, 1494
Marin Community Foundation Stinson Bolinas
Community Grants, 1568
Mary Black Foundation Early Childhood
Development Grants, 1586

Medtronic Foundation Community Link Human
Services Grants, 1631
MFRI Community Mobilization Grants, 1654
MGM Resorts Foundation Community Grants, 1655
Nellie Mae Education Foundation District-Level
Change Grants, 1736
Olga Sipolin Children's Fund Grants, 1815
OneFamily Foundation Grants, 1822
Piper Jaffray Foundation Communities Giving
Grants, 1974
Robbins-de Beaumont Foundation Grants, 2080
Rose Community Foundation Education Grants, 2104
Seattle Foundation Benjamin N. Phillips Memorial
Fund Grants, 2176
Target Corporation Community Engagement Fund
Grants, 2270
Union Bank, N.A. Foundation Grants, 2334
USDA WIC Nutrition Ed Innovations Grants, 2363
Wood-Claeyssens Foundation Grants, 2486

Parent Involvement
ACF Family Strengthening Scholars Grants, 81
Achelis and Bodman Foundation Grants, 101
Alaska Community Foundation Children's Trust Tier
1 Parenting and Child Development Educational
Grants, 199
BBF Florida Family Literacy Initiative Grants, 386
BBF Maine Family Literacy Initiative Implementation
Grants, 387
BBF Maine Family Literacy Initiative Planning
Grants, 388
BBF Maryland Family Literacy Initiative
Implementation Grants, 389
BBF Maryland Family Literacy Initiative Planning
Grants, 390
BBF National Grants for Family Literacy, 391
Bella Vista Foundation Pre-3 Grants, 397
Daniels Fund Early Childhood Education Grants, 781
First Lady's Family Literacy Initiative for Texas
Family Literacy Trailblazer Grants, 968
First Lady's Family Literacy Initiative for Texas
Implementation Grants, 969
First Lady's Family Literacy Initiative for Texas
Planning Grants, 970
GNOF Stand Up For Our Children Grants, 1092
Harmony Project Grants, 1170
Joseph H. and Florence A. Roblee Foundation Family
Grants, 1387
Mary Black Foundation Early Childhood
Development Grants, 1586
National Wildlife Federation Craig Tufts Educational
Scholarship, 1724
Northland Foundation Grants, 1771
Pulaski County Community Foundation Grants, 2038
Twenty-First Century Foundation Grants, 2328
United Methodist Women Brighter Future for
Children and Youth Grants, 2346
William Caspar Graustein Memorial Fund Corinne
G. Levin Education Grants, 2462

Parks
ACCF of Indiana Berne Ready Mix Community
Enrichment Fund Grants, 65
Arthur M. Blank Family Foundation Inspiring Spaces
Grants, 309
Bikes Belong Grants, 424
Blackford County Community Fdn Grants, 434
BMW of North America Charitable Contribs, 460
Brunswick Foundation Grants, 479
Clara Blackford Smith and W. Aubrey Smith
Charitable Foundation Grants, 621
Community Foundation of Louisville C. E. and S.
Endowment for the Parks Fund Grants, 719
Community Foundation of St. Joseph County Special
Project Challenge Grants, 738
Daniels Fund Amateur Sports Grants, 779
Dayton Foundation Grants, 796
Del Mar Foundation Community Grants, 820
Fdn for the Mid South Communities Grants, 992
Harry and Helen Sands Charitable Trust Grants, 1181

Janson Foundation Grants, 1349
KaBOOM! Adventure Courses Grant, 1401
KaBOOM! Build it Grant, 1402
KaBOOM! Creative Play Grant, 1403
KaBOOM! Multi-Sport Courts Grant, 1404
Mary D. and Walter F. Frear Eleemosynary Trust
Grants, 1588
Merrick Foundation Grants, 1639
Morris K. Udall and Stewart L. Udall Foundation
Parks in Focus Program, 1695
Narragansett Number One Foundation Grants, 1712
NSTA Faraday Science Communicator Award, 1778
Pike County Community Foundation Recreation
Grants, 1970
Posey County Community Foundation Recreation
Grants, 2009
Pulaski County Community Foundation Grants, 2038
San Antonio Area Foundation Capital and Naming
Rights Grants, 2148
Sioux Falls Area Community Foundation Community
Fund Grants, 2203
Sioux Falls Area Community Foundation Spot
Grants, 2204
Skatepark Project Built to Play Skatepark Grant, 2208
Spencer County Community Foundation Recreation
Grants, 2231
Union Bank, N.A. Foundation Grants, 2334
Vanderburgh Community Foundation Recreation
Grants, 2374
Warrick County Community Foundation Recreation
Grants, 2410
Weaver Foundation Grants, 2420
William and Flora Hewlett Foundation
Environmental Grants, 2455

Patient Care and Education
C.H. Robinson Worldwide Foundation Grants, 489
Camille Beckman Foundation Grants, 499
Four J Foundation Grants, 1004
Mary Wilmer Covey Charitable Trust Grants, 1600
Mt. Sinai Health Care Foundation Health of the
Jewish Community Grants, 1709
Pinnacle Entertainment Foundation Grants, 1972
Piper Trust Reglious Organizations Grants, 1979
Rathmann Family Foundation Grants, 2057

Peace/Disarmament
Edna Wardlaw Charitable Trust Grants, 886
Elizabeth Morse Genius Charitable Trust Grants, 901
Ford Foundation BUILD Grants, 984
Global Fund for Women Grants, 1073
PDF Community Organizing Grants, 1920
PDF Fiscal Sponsorship Grant, 1921
Streisand Foundation Grants, 2251

Pedagogy
Bay and Paul Foundations PreK-12 Transformative
Learning Practices Grants, 370

Pediatric Cancer
CDI Interdisciplinary Research Intvs Grants, 526
Central Pacific Bank Foundation Grants, 530
GNOF IMPACT Harold W. Newman, Jr. Charitable
Trust Grants, 1086
Michelle O'Neill Foundation Grants, 1661
Pediatric Brain Tumor Foundation Early Career
Development Grants, 1924
Pediatric Brain Tumor Foundation Early Career
Development Grants, 1923
Pediatric Brain Tumor Foundation Opportunity
Grants, 1926
Sara Elizabeth O'Brien Trust Grants, 2161
William and Sandy Heitz Family Fdn Grants, 2457

Pediatrics
AACAP Robert Cancro Academic Leadership
Award, 35
Austin S. Nelson Foundation Grants, 333
CDI Interdisciplinary Research Intvs Grants, 526
CFF First- and Second-Year Clinical Fellowships, 532

CFF Leroy Matthews Physician-Scientist Awds, 533
Children's Brain Tumor Fdn Research Grants, 584
Epilepsy Foundation SUDEP Challenge Initiative
  Prizes, 924
Gerber Foundation Environmental Hazards Research
  Grants, 1062
Gerber Fdn Pediatric Health Research Grants, 1063
Gerber Foundation Pediatric Nutrition Research
  Grants, 1064
HRAMF Charles H. Hood Foundation Child Health
  Research Awards, 1262
Lucile Packard Foundation for Children's Health
  Grants, 1514
M. Bastian Family Foundation Grants, 1522
Mary S. and David C. Corbin Fdn Grants, 1598
Peabody Foundation Grants, 1922
Pediatric Brain Tumor Foundation Early Career
  Development Grants, 1923
Pediatric Brain Tumor Foundation Early Career
  Development Grants, 1924
Pediatric Brain Tumor Fdn Institute Grants, 1925
Pediatric Brain Tumor Foundation Opportunity
  Grants, 1926
Pediatric Cancer Research Foundation Grants, 1927
Piper Trust Healthcare and Med Rsrch Grants, 1978
Ralph M. Parsons Foundation Grants, 2052
Victor E. Speas Foundation Grants, 2380

Performance Art

Crystelle Waggoner Charitable Trust Grants, 768
Episcopal Actors' Guild Actors Florence James
  Children's Holiday Fund Grant, 925
NYSCA Arts Education: General Operating Support
  Grants, 1781
NYSCA Arts Education: General Program Support
  Grants, 1782
NYSCA Arts Ed: Services to the Field Grants, 1784
NYSCA Special Arts Services: General Program
  Support Grants, 1793
NYSCA Special Arts Services: Instruction and
  Training Grants, 1794
NYSCA Theatre: Prof Performances Grants, 1795
PCA Arts Organizations and Arts Programs Grants
  for Literature, 1894
PCA Entry Track Arts Organizations and Arts
  Programs Grants for Literature, 1906
PCA Strategies for Success Grants - Adv Level, 1917
PCA Strategies for Success Grants - Basic Level, 1918

Performing Arts

A. Alfred Taubman Foundation Grants, 18
A.C. and Penney Hubbard Foundation Grants, 19
Adams-Mastrovich Family Foundation Grants, 113
AHS Foundation Grants, 143
Akron Community Foundation Arts and Culture
  Grants, 150
Alcatel-Lucent Technologies Foundation Grants, 224
Alden and Vada Dow Fund Grants, 225
Alvah H. and Wyline P. Chapman Fdn Grants, 248
Ann L. and Carol Green Rhodes Trust Grants, 278
APAP All-In Grants, 283
Ar-Hale Family Foundation Grants, 290
Atlanta Foundation Grants, 326
Avery Family Trust Grants, 338
Back Home Again Foundation Grants, 344
Bank of Hawaii Foundation Grants, 360
Bayer Fund Community Development Grants, 383
Bill Graham Memorial Foundation Grants, 429
Blanche and Irving Laurie Foundation Grants, 436
Boeing Company Contributions Grants, 462
Brown Foundation Grants, 476
Charles Delmar Foundation Grants, 564
City of Oakland Cultural Funding Grants, 618
Cudd Foundation Grants, 769
Daniel and Nanna Stern Family Fdn Grants, 778
Delta Air Lines Foundation Community Enrichment
  Grants, 823
Donald G. Gardner Humanities Tr Youth Grts, 840
Elizabeth Morse Genius Charitable Trust Grants, 901
Elsie H. Wilcox Foundation Grants, 909

Entergy Corporation Open Grants for Arts and
  Culture, 920
Episcopal Actors' Guild Actors Florence James
  Children's Holiday Fund Grant, 925
Fidelity Charitable Gift Fund Grants, 956
FirstEnergy Foundation Community Grants, 965
G.N. Wilcox Trust Grants, 1031
Gardner Foundation Grants, 1034
George A. & Grace L. Long Fdn Grants, 1041
George Graham and Elizabeth Galloway Smith
  Foundation Grants, 1047
George W. Codrington Charitable Fdn Grants, 1055
GNOF IMPACT Grants for Arts and Culture, 1083
Hahl Proctor Charitable Trust Grants, 1151
Hampton Roads Community Foundation Arts and
  Culture Grants, 1154
Hattie Mae Lesley Foundation Grants, 1195
Hawaii Electric Industries Foundation Grants, 1218
Helen Gertrude Sparks Charitable Trust Grants, 1230
Henrietta Lange Burk Fund Grants, 1235
Herman Goldman Foundation Grants, 1245
Herman P. and Sophia Taubman Fdn Grants, 1247
Horace A. Moses Charitable Trust Grants, 1261
HSFCA Biennium Grants, 1267
Island Insurance Foundation Grants, 1316
J. Watumull Fund Grants, 1326
James S. Copley Foundation Grants, 1345
Japan Foundation Los Angeles Mini-Grants for
  Japanese Arts & Culture, 1354
Japan Foundation New York Small Grants for Arts
  and Culture, 1355
John F. Kennedy Center for the Performing Arts
  National Rosemary Kennedy Internship, 1371
Julius N. Frankel Foundation Grants, 1400
Katharine Matthies Foundation Grants, 1418
Kelvin and Eleanor Smith Foundation Grants, 1424
Kennedy Center National Symphony Orchestra Youth
  Fellowships, 1426
Kirkpatrick Foundation Grants, 1440
Kosasa Foundation Grants, 1450
Laidlaw Foundation Youth Organizaing Initiatives
  Grants, 1462
Leo Goodwin Foundation Grants, 1482
Lewis H. Humphreys Charitable Trust Grants, 1486
Lied Foundation Trust Grants, 1490
Linford & Mildred White Charitable Grants, 1495
Lubrizol Foundation Grants, 1513
Mabel Y. Hughes Charitable Trust Grants, 1530
Marcia and Otto Koehler Foundation Grants, 1553
Margaret T. Morris Foundation Grants, 1557
Marjorie Moore Charitable Foundation Grants, 1574
McLean Contributionship Grants, 1623
Mertz Gilmore Foundation NYC Dance Grants, 1642
Montana Arts Council Cultural and Aesthetic Project
  Grants, 1685
Morris Stulsaft Foundation Participation in the the
  Arts Grants, 1698
NJSCA Arts Ed Special Initiative Grants, 1764
NYSCA Arts Education: Community-based
  Learning Grants, 1780
NYSCA Arts Education: General Operating Support
  Grants, 1781
NYSCA Arts Education: General Program Support
  Grants, 1782
NYSCA Arts Ed: Services to the Field Grants, 1784
NYSCA Music: Gen Operating Support Grants, 1791
NYSCA Music: Gen Program Support Grants, 1792
NYSCA Special Arts Services: General Program
  Support Grants, 1793
NYSCA Special Arts Services: Instruction and
  Training Grants, 1794
NYSCA Theatre: Prof Performances Grants, 1795
Oppenstein Brothers Foundation Grants, 1827
Oren Campbell McCleary Chartbl Trust Grants, 1837
PAS Freddie Gruber Scholarship, 1872
PAS John E. Grimes Timpani Scholarship, 1873
PAS PASIC International Scholarships, 1875
PAS Zildjian Family Opportunity Fund Grants, 1878
PCA-PCD Professional Development for Individual
  Artists Grants, 1883

PCA Art Organizations and Art Programs Grants for
  Presenting Organizations, 1884
PCA Arts in Education Residencies, 1885
PCA Arts Organizations and Arts Program Grants
  for Music, 1887
PCA Arts Organizations and Arts Programs Grants
  for Arts Service Organizations, 1890
PCA Arts Organizations and Arts Programs Grants
  for Dance, 1892
PCA Busing Grants, 1899
PCA Entry Track Arts Organizations and Arts
  Programs Grants for Arts Service Orgs, 1902
PCA Entry Track Arts Organizations and Arts
  Programs Grants for Music, 1908
PCA Entry Track Arts Organizations and Arts
  Programs Grants for Presenting Orgs, 1909
PCA Pennsylvania Partners in the Arts Program
  Stream Grants, 1914
PCA Pennsylvania Partners in the Arts Project
  Stream Grants, 1915
PCA Professional Development Grants, 1916
PCA Strategies for Success Grants - Adv Level, 1917
PCA Strategies for Success Grants - Basic Level, 1918
PCA Strategies for Success Grants - Intermediate
  Level, 1919
PennPAT Artist Technical Assistance Grants, 1929
PennPAT Fee-Support Grants for Presenters, 1930
PennPAT New Directions Grants for Presenters, 1931
PennPAT Presenter Travel Grants, 1932
PennPAT Strategic Opportunity Grants, 1933
Perkin Fund Grants, 1937
Phil Hardin Foundation Grants, 1960
Piedmont Natural Gas Corporate and Charitable
  Contributions, 1966
Pinnacle Entertainment Foundation Grants, 1972
Piper Trust Arts and Culture Grants, 1975
Powell Foundation Grants, 2013
R.S. Gernon Trust Grants, 2047
Raymond Austin Hagen Family Fdn Grants, 2060
Reinberger Foundation Grants, 2066
Richard J. Stern Foundation for the Arts Grants, 2071
Riedman Foundation Grants, 2076
Robbins-de Beaumont Foundation Grants, 2080
Robert and Betty Wo Foundation Grants, 2083
San Juan Island Community Foundation Grants, 2158
Screen Actors Guild StagePALS Assistance, 2173
Seattle Foundation Arts and Culture Grants, 2174
Sensient Technologies Foundation Grants, 2180
Shell Deer Park Grants, 2186
SunTrust Bank Trusteed Foundations Greene-Sawtell
  Grants, 2257
SunTrust Bank Trusteed Foundations Nell Warren
  Elkin and William Simpson Elkin Grants, 2258
TAC Touring Arts and Arts Access Touring Arts
  Grants, 2269
Textron Corporate Contributions Grants, 2286
Thomas Sill Foundation Grants, 2292
Union Bank, N.A. Foundation Grants, 2334
Virginia Commission for the Arts Artists in
  Education Residency Grants, 2385
VSA/Metlife Connect All Grants, 2392
VSA/Volkswagen Group of America Exhibition
  Awards, 2393
Wege Foundation Grants, 2422
William Foulds Family Foundation Grants, 2465
William G. Gilmore Foundation Grants, 2467
Wilton and Effie Hebert Foundation Grants, 2476
Xerox Foundation Grants, 2507
Youths' Friends Association Grants, 2511

Perinatal Disorders

HRAMF Charles H. Hood Foundation Child Health
  Research Awards, 1262

Personnel Training and Development

Piper Trust Healthcare and Med Rsrch Grants, 1978
PPCF Edson Foundation Grants, 2015
Priddy Foundation Organizational Development
  Grants, 2022
Union Bank, N.A. Foundation Grants, 2334

Pharmaceuticals
Ruth Camp Campbell Charitable Trust Grants, 2125

Philanthropy
C.F. Adams Charitable Trust Grants, 488
CICF Indianapolis Fdn Community Grants, 606
Community Foundation of Eastern Connecticut
General Southeast Grants, 696
Community Foundation of Jackson Hole Youth
Philanthropy Grants, 715
Ewing Marion Kauffman Foundation Grants, 943
Fidelity Charitable Gift Fund Grants, 956
First Hawaiian Bank Foundation Corporate Giving
Grants, 967
George W. Codrington Charitable Foundation
Grants, 1055
Global Fund for Women Grants, 1073
Hampton Roads Community Foundation Community
Leadership Partners Grants, 1155
Harry and Helen Sands Charitable Trust Grants, 1181
Helen V. Brach Foundation Grants, 1232
Hillsdale County Community Foundation Love Your
Community Grants, 1251
Hillsdale County Community Foundation
Y.O.U.T.H. Grants, 1252
Huffy Foundation Grants, 1273
Johnson County Community Foundation Youth
Philanthropy Initiative Grants, 1380
Kansas Health Fdn Major Initiatives Grants, 1414
Leo Goodwin Foundation Grants, 1482
Libra Foundation Grants, 1489
Maine Women's Fund Girls' Grantmaking Intv, 1547
Mary D. and Walter F. Frear Eleemosynary Trust
Grants, 1588
McCombs Foundation Grants, 1615
OneFamily Foundation Grants, 1822
OtterCares Impact Fund Grants, 1849
OtterCares Inspiration Fund Grants, 1850
OtterCares NoCO Fund Grants, 1851
Parkersburg Area Community Foundation Action
Grants, 1871
PGE Foundation Grants, 1958
Philanthrofund Foundation Grants, 1959
Polk County Community Foundation Unrestricted
Grants, 2001
Ruth Anderson Foundation Grants, 2122
Saginaw Community Foundation Discretionary
Grants, 2134
Sioux Falls Area Community Foundation Spot
Grants, 2204

Philosophy
NEH Family and Youth Programs in American
History Grants, 1734

Photography
Japan Foundation New York World Heritage Photo
Panel Exhibition, 1356
Meta and George Rosenberg Fdn Grants, 1644
Morris K. Udall and Stewart L. Udall Foundation
Parks in Focus Program, 1695
NJSCA Artists in Education Residencies, 1763
PCA Arts Organizations and Arts Programs Grants
for Visual Arts, 1898
PCA Entry Track Arts Organizations and Arts
Programs Grants for Visual Arts, 1912

Physical Activity
Active Living Research Grants, 109
Autism Speaks Norma and Malcolm Baker Recreation
Grants, 335
Baltimore Ravens Foundation Play 60 Grants, 351
CNCS AmeriCorps State and National Grants, 643
Collective Brands Foundation Grants, 654
Collective Brands Foundation Saucony Run for Good
Grants, 656
HAF Mada Huggins Caldwell Fund Grants, 1147
North Face Explore Fund, 1770
Phoenix Coyotes Charities Grants, 1963

Physical Disability
Adams Rotary Memorial Fund A Grants, 122
ALA Baker and Taylor Summer Reading Program
Grant, 158
Allan C. and Lelia J. Garden Foundation Grants, 236
Armstrong McDonald Foundation Special Needs
Grants, 301
Bay Area Community Foundation Leslie L. Squires
Foundation Grants, 380
Bay Area Community Foundation Nathalie Awrey
Memorial Fund Grants, 381
CICF Howard Intermill and Marion Intermill
Fenstermaker Grants, 605
Different Needz Foundation Grants, 830
Elkhart County Community Foundation Fund for
Elkhart County, 902
Fichtenbaum Charitable Trust Grants, 955
George E. Hatcher, Jr. and Ann Williams Hatcher
Foundation Grants, 1045
Grace Bersted Foundation Grants, 1097
HAF Ian Chris Mackey Newman Fund Grts, 1143
Harold and Rebecca H. Gross Fdn Grants, 1171
Jack Satter Foundation Grants, 1334
John D. and Katherine A. Johnston Fdn Grants, 1370
Johnson Scholarship Foundation Grants, 1382
Margaret Wiegand Trust Grants, 1558
Mill Spring Foundation Grants, 1674
Montgomery County Community Foundation Libby
Whitecotton Fund Grants, 1690
Northland Foundation Grants, 1771
NZDIA Community Org Grants Scheme, 1796
OSF Education Program Grants in Kyrgyzstan, 1842
OSF Youth Action Fund Grants in Kyrgyzstan, 1846
San Antonio Area Foundation Capital and Naming
Rights Grants, 2148
Sara Elizabeth O'Brien Trust Grants, 2161
Sobrato Family Foundation Grants, 2211
Sobrato Family Fdn Meeting Space Grants, 2212
Sobrato Family Foundation Office Space Grants, 2213
Stein Family Charitable Trust Grants, 2240
Sylvia Adams Charitable Trust Grants, 2262
Thomas W. Bradley Foundation Grants, 2293
VSA Playwright Discovery Award, 2396
Women's Fund of Hawaii Grants, 2485

Physical Education
Baltimore Ravens Foundation Play 60 Grants, 351
CNCS AmeriCorps State and National Grants, 643
Fremont Area Community Foundation Youth
Advisory Committee Grants, 1022
WSF GoGirlGo! New York Grants, 2494

Physical Growth/Retardation
Columbus Foundation Traditional Grants, 663

Physical Medicine and Rehabilitation
Montgomery County Community Foundation Libby
Whitecotton Fund Grants, 1690

Physical Sciences
Marion I. and Henry J. Knott Foundation Standard
Grants, 1572
Northrop Grumman Foundation Grants, 1773

Physical Sciences Education
Northrop Grumman Foundation Grants, 1773

Physics
Marion I. and Henry J. Knott Foundation Standard
Grants, 1572

Physics Education
George I. Alden Trust Grants, 1051

Physiology
Lalor Foundation Postdoctoral Fellowships, 1464

Planetariums
Maurice R. Robinson Fund Grants, 1611
NSTA Faraday Science Communicator Award, 1778

Planning/Policy Studies
Ball Brothers Foundation Organizational
Effectiveness/Executive Mentoring Grants, 346
Meyer Fdn Healthy Communities Grants, 1650

Plant Genetics
First Nations Development Institute Native
Agriculture and Food Systems Scholarships, 971
Louis and Sandra Berkman Foundation Grants, 1510

Plant Sciences
Louis and Sandra Berkman Foundation Grants, 1510

Playgrounds
Clara Blackford Smith and W. Aubrey Smith
Charitable Foundation Grants, 621
Community Foundation of Louisville C. E. and S.
Endowment for the Parks Fund Grants, 719
Hasbro Children's Fund Grants, 1189
Herman H. Nettelroth Fund Grants, 1246
KaBOOM! Play Everywhere Design Challenge, 1405
William Blair and Company Foundation Grants, 2461

Poetry
Alabama Humanities Foundation Major Grants, 159
National Cowboy and Western Heritage Museum
Awards, 1722
NJSCA Arts Ed Special Initiative Grants, 1764
Olive Higgins Prouty Foundation Grants, 1817
PCA Arts Organizations and Arts Programs Grants
for Literature, 1894
PCA Entry Track Arts Organizations and Arts
Programs Grants for Literature, 1906
PCA Strategies for Success Grants - Adv Level, 1917
PCA Strategies for Success Grants - Basic Level, 1918
PCA Strategies for Success Grants - Intermediate
Level, 1919
Poetry Fdn Young People's Poet Laureate, 1989

Political Behavior
Carnegie Corporation of New York Grants, 511
Harry Frank Guggenheim Foundation Grants, 1184
NEA Student Program Communities Redefining
Education Advocacy Through Empowerment
(CREATE) Grants, 1733
PDF Community Organizing Grants, 1920
PDF Fiscal Sponsorship Grant, 1921
Proteus Fund Grants, 2027
Rosenberg Fund for Children Edith and George
Ziefert Fund Grants, 2110
Rosenberg Fund for Children Grants, 2111
Rosenberg Fund for Children Herman Warsh Fund
Grant, 2112
Rosenberg Fund for Children Moish and Lillian
Antopol Memorial Fund Grants, 2113
USAID Community Livelihoods Project in Yemen
Grant, 2352

Political Parties
Hearst Foundations United States Senate Youth
Grants, 1225

Political Science
ALFJ International Fund Grants, 231
Hearst Foundations United States Senate Youth
Grants, 1225

Political Science Education
Hatton W. Sumners Foundation for the Study and
Teaching of Self Government Grants, 1196

Political Theory
Bernard and Audre Rapoport Foundation Democracy
and Civic Participation Grants, 409

Politics
Bernard and Audre Rapoport Foundation Democracy
and Civic Participation Grants, 409
USAID Community Livelihoods Project in Yemen
Grant, 2352

Pollution
Gamble Foundation Grants, 1032

Pollution Control
Sioux Falls Area Community Foundation Spot
Grants, 2204

Pollution, Air
Colorado Interstate Gas Grants, 661
Washington Gas Charitable Contributions, 2417

Pollution, Land
Matson Adahi I Tano' Grants, 1606
Matson Ka Ipu 'Aina Grants, 1608

Pollution, Water
Chesapeake Bay Trust Environmental Education
Grants, 577
Chesapeake Bay Trust Outreach and Community
Engagement Grants, 579
Mary A. Crocker Trust Grants, 1584
Matson Adahi I Tano' Grants, 1606
Matson Ka Ipu 'Aina Grants, 1608
PepsiCo Foundation Grants, 1935
Washington Gas Charitable Contributions, 2417
William Bingham Foundation Grants, 2460

Population Control
Bushrod H. Campbell and Adah F. Hall Charity
Fund Grants, 486
Clayton Baker Trust Grants, 629
Cleveland H. Dodge Foundation Grants, 637
General Service Foundation Human Rights and
Economic Justice Grants, 1040
Klingenstein-Simons Fellowship Awards in the
Neurosciences, 1441
Lumpkin Family Fdn Healthy People Grants, 1518
Mary A. Crocker Trust Grants, 1584
Packard Foundation Local Grants, 1863

Poverty and the Poor
ACF Marriage Strengthening Research &
Dissemination Center Grants, 85
Achelis and Bodman Foundation Grants, 101
Achelis Foundation Grants, 102
Aid for Starving Children Emerg Aid Grants, 144
Aid for Starving Children Health and Nutrition
Grants, 145
Aid for Starving Children Homes and Education
Grants, 146
Aid for Starving Children Water Projects Grants, 147
ALA PRIME TIME Family Reading Time Grts, 185
Allen Foundation Educational Nutrition Grants, 238
Annie Gardner Foundation Grants, 277
ATA Inclusive Learning Communities Grants, 323
Atlanta Women's Foundation Pathway to Success
Grants, 327
Austin S. Nelson Foundation Grants, 333
Avista Foundation Vulnerable and Limited Income
Population Grants, 341
Bank of the Orient Community Giving, 361
Bernard and Audre Rapoport Foundation Arts and
Culture Grants, 407
Bernard and Audre Rapoport Foundation Community
Building and Social Service Grants, 408
Bernard and Audre Rapoport Foundation Democracy
and Civic Participation Grants, 409
Bernard and Audre Rapoport Foundation Education
Grants, 410
Bernard and Audre Rapoport Foundation Health
Grants, 411
Bill and Melinda Gates Foundation Agricultural
Development Grants, 425
Bill and Melinda Gates Foundation Emergency
Response Grants, 426
Bill and Melinda Gates Foundation Policy and
Advocacy Grants, 427
Bill and Melinda Gates Foundation Water, Sanitation
and Hygiene Grants, 428
Bodenwein Public Benevolent Foundation Grants, 461

Carnegie Corporation of New York Grants, 511
Central Pacific Bank Foundation Grants, 530
CFFVR Basic Needs Giving Partnership Grants, 537
CFFVR Jewelers Mutual Chartbl Giving Grants, 543
CFGR Community Impact Grants, 552
CFGR Jenkins Foundation Grants, 553
CICF Indianapolis Fdn Community Grants, 606
CNCS AmeriCorps VISTA Project Grants, 645
Community Foundation for Greater Buffalo Josephine
Goodyear Foundation Grants, 672
Community Foundation of Western Massachusetts
Grants, 741
Crane Fund for Widows and Children Grants, 762
David Alan and Susan Berkman Rahm Foundation
Grants, 785
Edyth Bush Charitable Foundation Grants, 893
Eide Bailly Resourcefullness Awards, 897
Farmers Insurance Corporate Giving Grants, 948
Fitzpatrick, Cella, Harper & Scinto Pro Bono
Services, 976
Foundation Beyond Belief Compassionate Impact
Grants, 986
Foundation Beyond Belief Humanist Grants, 987
Four J Foundation Grants, 1004
Four Lanes Trust Grants, 1005
Friedman Family Foundation Grants, 1023
Friends of Hawaii Charities Grants, 1024
General Service Foundation Human Rights and
Economic Justice Grants, 1040
George H. Sandy Foundation Grants, 1050
George P. Davenport Trust Fund Grants, 1054
GNOF Stand Up For Our Children Grants, 1092
Good+Foundation Grants, 1096
Greater Milwaukee Foundation Grants, 1109
H.B. Fuller Foundation Grants, 1138
Hartley Foundation Grants, 1186
Hasbro Children's Fund Grants, 1189
Hawai'i Community Foundation Bernice and Conrad
von Hamm Fund Grants, 1197
HBF Pathways Out of Poverty Grants, 1222
Hearst Foundations Social Service Grants, 1224
Help America Foundation Grants, 1233
Henry E. Niles Foundation Grants, 1240
Jack Kent Cooke Fdn Good Neighbor Grants, 1331
Jacob G. Schmidlapp Trusts Grants, 1336
Jane's Trust Grants, 1346
Janson Foundation Grants, 1349
John H. and Wilhelmina D. Harland Charitable
Foundation Community Services Grants, 1375
Jovid Foundation Employment Training Grants, 1392
Kate B. Reynolds Charitable Trust Poor and Needy
Grants, 1417
Kroger Company Donations, 1456
Linden Foundation Grants, 1494
LISC Community Leadership Operating Grts, 1499
Marie C. and Joseph C. Wilson Foundation Rochester
Small Grants, 1559
Marin Community Foundation Ending the Cycle of
Poverty Grants, 1565
May and Stanley Smith Charitable Trust Grants, 1613
McGregor Fund Human Services Grants, 1621
Meyer Fdn Healthy Communities Grants, 1650
Michael Reese Health Trust Core Grants, 1658
Michael Reese Health Trust Responsive Grants, 1659
Michigan Women Forward Grants, 1662
Mid-Iowa Health Foundation Community Response
Grants, 1667
Mill Spring Foundation Grants, 1674
Mockingbird Foundation Grants, 1680
Moran Family Foundation Grants, 1693
Morris Stulsaft Foundation Early Childhood
Education Grants, 1696
Morris Stulsaft Foundation Educational Support for
Children Grants, 1697
Morris Stulsaft Foundation Participation in the the
Arts Grants, 1698
Nathan Cummings Foundation Grants, 1718
Nationwide Insurance Foundation Grants, 1726
New Covenant Farms Grants, 1742
OneFamily Foundation Grants, 1822

Oregon Community Foundation K-12 Student
Success: Out-of-School Grants, 1836
Packard Foundation Children, Families, and
Communities Grants, 1862
Paso del Norte Health Foundation Grants, 1874
PepsiCo Foundation Grants, 1935
Piper Trust Children Grants, 1976
PNC Foundation Affordable Housing Grants, 1983
Quaker Oats Company Kids Care Clubs Grants, 2041
Robin Hood Foundation Grants, 2096
Robinson Foundation Grants, 2097
Rosenberg Charity Foundation Grants, 2107
Sand Hill Foundation Health and Opportunity
Grants, 2153
SanDisk Corp Community Sharing Grants, 2155
Shield-Ayres Foundation Grants, 2189
Sidgmore Family Foundation Grants, 2195
Sioux Falls Area Community Fdn Spot Grants, 2204
Speer Trust Grants, 2230
Starr Foundation Grants, 2237
Susan A. and Donald P. Babson Charitable
Foundation Grants, 2259
Sylvia Adams Charitable Trust Grants, 2262
Thomas Sill Foundation Grants, 2292
Tides Fdn Friends of the IGF Fund Grants, 2300
TJX Foundation Grants, 2303
United Methodist Committee on Relief Hunger and
Poverty Grants, 2344
USDA WIC Nutrition Ed Innovations Grants, 2363
USDEd Gaining Early Awareness and Readiness for
Undergrad Programs (GEAR UP) Grants, 2364
W.W. Smith Chartbl Trust Basic Needs Grants, 2400
Walter J. and Betty C. Zable Fdn Grants, 2406
Weaver Foundation Grants, 2420
Westerman Foundation Grants, 2427
William J. and Dorothy K. O'Neill Foundation
Responsive Grants, 2468
Women's Fund of Hawaii Grants, 2484

Pregnancy
ACF Transitional Living Program and Maternity
Group Homes Grants, 96
Adams Family Foundation of Tennessee Grants, 120
Allen Foundation Educational Nutrition Grants, 238
General Service Foundation Human Rights and
Economic Justice Grants, 1040
Portland Fdn - Women's Giving Circle Grant, 2006
USAID Family Planning and Reproductive Health
Methods Grants, 2353
USDA WIC Nutrition Ed Innovations Grants, 2363
W.P. and Bulah Luse Foundation Grants, 2399

Prenatal Factors
Ford Family Foundation Grants - Access to Health
and Dental Services, 980
TJX Foundation Grants, 2303

Presbyterian Church
AHS Foundation Grants, 143
Alvah H. and Wyline P. Chapman Foundation
Grants, 248
Aunt Kate Foundation Grants, 331
Bradley-Turner Foundation Grants, 466
Chapman Family Foundation, 562
Effie and Wofford Cain Foundation Grants, 895
Harry and Helen Sands Charitable Trust Grants, 1181
Speer Trust Grants, 2230

Preschool Education
ACCF of Indiana Bank of Geneva Heritage Fund
Grants, 64
ACCF of Indiana First Merchants Bank / Decatur
Bank and Trust Fund Grants, 66
ACCF of Indiana Ron and Susie Ballard Community
Enrichment Fund Grants, 68
ACF Head Start and/or Early Head Start Grantee
- Clay, Randolph, and Talladega Counties,
Alabama, 82
ACF Head Start and/or Early Head Start Grantee -
St. Landry Parish, Louisiana, 83

Akron Community Fdn Education Grants, 151
ALA Coretta Scott King Book Donation Grant, 168
Albert E. and Birdie W. Einstein Fund Grants, 220
Aldi Corporation Smart Kids Grants, 226
Alexander Graham Bell Preschool-Age Financial Aid
    Grants, 228
Allegis Group Foundation Grants, 237
American Electric Power Corporate Grants, 252
American Electric Power Foundation Grants, 253
Anchorage Schools Foundation Grants, 270
Arts Council of Greater Lansing Young Creatives
    Grants, 314
AT&T Foundation Education Grants, 321
Aunt Kate Foundation Grants, 331
Avery Foundation Grants, 339
Baltimore Community Foundation Mitzvah Fund for
    Good Deeds Grants, 349
Baton Rouge Area Foundation Community Coffee
    Fund Grants, 363
Benton Community Foundation Grants, 405
Blackford County Community Fdn Grants, 434
Blue Grass Community Foundation Clark County
    Fund Grants, 444
Blue Grass Community Foundation Early Childhood
    Education and Literacy Grants, 445
Blue Grass Community Foundation Fayette County
    Fund Grants, 446
Blue Grass Community Foundation Franklin County
    Fund Grants, 447
Blue Grass Community Foundation Harrison County
    Fund Grants, 448
Blue Grass Community Foundation Madison County
    Fund Grants, 450
Blue Grass Community Foundation Magoffin County
    Fund Grants, 451
Blue Grass Community Foundation Morgan County
    Fund Grants, 452
Blue Grass Community Foundation Rowan County
    Fund Grants, 453
Blue Grass Community Foundation Woodford
    County Fund Grants, 454
Blue River Community Foundation Grants, 458
Brown County Community Foundation Grants, 475
Byerly Foundation Grants, 487
Carnegie Corporation of New York Grants, 511
CFFVR Basic Needs Giving Partnership Grants, 537
CFF Winter Park Community Grants, 551
CFGR Community Impact Grants, 552
Chapman Family Foundation, 562
CHT Foundation Education Grants, 603
Claremont Savings Bank Foundation Grants, 623
Cleveland Foundation Legacy Village Lyndhurst
    Community Fund Grants, 636
Cleveland H. Dodge Foundation Grants, 637
Clinton County Community Foundation Grants, 638
CNCS Foster Grandparent Projects Grants, 646
CNO Financial Group Community Grants, 650
Community Foundation of Bartholomew County
    Heritage Fund Grants, 690
Community Foundation of Bartholomew County
    James A. Henderson Award for Fundraising, 691
Community Foundation of Crawford County, 695
Community Foundation of Greater Chattanooga
    Grants, 704
Community Foundation of Greater Fort Wayne -
    Community Endowment and Clarke Endowment
    Grants, 705
Community Foundation of Jackson County Classroom
    Education Grants, 713
Community Foundation of Louisville Education
    Grants, 724
Community Fdn of Southern Indiana Grants, 736
Delaware Valley Fairness Project Teacher Assistance
    Grants, 818
Eastern Bank Charitable Foundation Partnerships
    Grants, 881
Eastern Bank Charitable Foundation Targeted
    Grants, 882
Effie and Wofford Cain Foundation Grants, 895
FCD New American Children Grants, 952

Foundations of East Chicago Education Grants, 995
Four County Community Fdn General Grants, 1000
GTRCF Elk Rapids Area Community Endowment
    Grants, 1127
GTRCF Joan Rajkovich McGarry Family Education
    Endowment Grants, 1131
Harris and Eliza Kempner Fund Ed Grants, 1176
Harris Foundation Grants, 1177
Hawai'i Community Foundation Richard Smart Fund
    Grants, 1204
Hawaii Community Foundation Omidyar Ohana
    Fund Grants, 1213
Hawaii Community Foundation Sanford Harmony
    Pillars of Peace Grants, 1217
Henry and Ruth Blaustein Rosenberg Foundation
    Education Grants, 1236
Hillsdale County Community Foundation General
    Grants, 1250
Iddings Foundation Medium Project Grants, 1285
Iddings Foundation Small Project Grants, 1286
Island Insurance Foundation Grants, 1316
Joseph H. and Florence A. Roblee Foundation
    Education Grants, 1386
Kodak Community Relations Grants, 1445
Laura B. Vogler Foundation Grants, 1470
Marie C. and Joseph C. Wilson Foundation Rochester
    Small Grants, 1559
Marin Community Foundation Arts Education
    Grants, 1562
Marin Community Foundation Stinson Bolinas
    Community Grants, 1568
Marquette Bank Neighborhood Commit Grants, 1577
Maryland State Department of Education Judith P.
    Hoyer Early Care and Ed Center Grants, 1595
Meyer Foundation Education Grants, 1649
Mile High United Way Stratc Investment Grts, 1671
Miller Foundation Grants, 1673
Mimi and Peter Haas Fund Grants, 1677
NYSCA Arts Education: Community-based
    Learning Grants, 1780
NYSCA Arts Education: Local Capacity Building
    Grants (Regrants), 1783
NYSCA Arts Ed: Services to the Field Grants, 1784
Office Depot Foundation Education Grants, 1806
OMNOVA Solutions Fdn Education Grants, 1820
Oppenstein Brothers Foundation Grants, 1827
Packard Foundation Children, Families, and
    Communities Grants, 1862
Phoenix Suns Charities Grants, 1964
Piper Trust Arts and Culture Grants, 1975
Piper Trust Children Grants, 1976
Piper Trust Education Grants, 1977
Piper Trust Reglious Organizations Grants, 1979
PNC Foundation Grow Up Great Early Childhood
    Grants, 1986
Polk County Community Foundation Marjorie M.
    and Lawrence R. Bradley Endowment Fund
    Grants, 1998
Polk County Community Foundation Unrestricted
    Grants, 2001
Portland General Electric Foundation Grants, 2007
R.D. and Joan Dale Hubbard Fdn Grants, 2044
Riedman Foundation Grants, 2076
Robert and Betty Wo Foundation Grants, 2083
Ruth and Henry Campbell Foundation Grants, 2123
San Antonio Area Foundation Capital and Naming
    Rights Grants, 2148
San Antonio Area Foundation High School
    Completion Grants, 2149
Turtle Bay Foundation Grants, 2327
U.S. Department of Education Promise
    Neighborhoods Grants, 2332
Union Bank, N.A. Foundation Grants, 2334
Wayne County Foundation Grants, 2419
William Caspar Graustein Memorial Fund Corinne
    G. Levin Education Grants, 2462
Windham Foundation Grants, 2477
Wiregrass Foundation Grants, 2480
Woods Charitable Fund Education Grants, 2488
Wyoming Community Fdn General Grants, 2501

Preventive Medicine

Akron Community Foundation Health and Human
    Services Grants, 152
California Endowment Innovative Ideas Challenge
    Grants, 495
Dr. John T. Macdonald Foundation Grants, 863
Edwards Memorial Trust Grants, 891
Foundation for Health Enhancement Grants, 990
Kansas Health Foundation Recognition Grants, 1415
Mary Black Foundation Active Living Grants, 1585
Michael Reese Health Trust Responsive Grants, 1659
Paso del Norte Health Foundation Grants, 1874
Premera Blue Cross Grants, 2018

Primary Care Services

Kansas Health Foundation Recognition Grants, 1415
Union Pacific Foundation Health and Human
    Services Grants, 2338

Print Media

Akron Community Foundation Arts and Culture
    Grants, 150

Prison Reform

OSF Baltimore Criminal and Juve Justice Grts, 1839
OSF Soros Justice Youth Activist Fellowships, 1844
Threshold Fdn Justice and Democracy Grants, 2298

Prisoners

Achelis and Bodman Foundation Grants, 101
Achelis Foundation Grants, 102
John Gogian Family Foundation Grants, 1373
Mockingbird Foundation Grants, 1680
Rosenberg Fund for Children Clinton and Muriel
    Jencks Memorial Fund Grants, 2109

Prisons

ALA Coretta Scott King Book Donation Grant, 168
Kentucky Arts Cncl Access Assistance Grants, 1428
OSF Soros Justice Youth Activist Fellowships, 1844
Rosenberg Fund for Children Clinton and Muriel
    Jencks Memorial Fund Grants, 2109

Private and Parochial Education

Abell Foundation Education Grants, 53
Brown Foundation Grants, 476
Community Foundation of Louisville Education
    Grants, 724
Dayton Foundation Rike Family Scholarships, 798
Foundations of East Chicago Education Grants, 995
Frank Reed and Margaret Jane Peters Memorial Fund
    II Grants, 1014
Hawai'i Community Foundation Robert E. Black
    Fund Grants, 1205
Huisking Foundation Grants, 1274
Huntington County Community Foundation
    Classroom Education Grants, 1279
Kenneth T. and Eileen L. Norris Fdn Grants, 1427
Klingenstein-Simons Fellowship Awards in the
    Neurosciences, 1441
Lubrizol Foundation Grants, 1513
Marion I. and Henry J. Knott Foundation
    Discretionary Grants, 1571
Marion I. and Henry J. Knott Foundation Standard
    Grants, 1572
Mathile Family Foundation Grants, 1604
Mervin Bovaird Foundation Grants, 1643
MGN Family Foundation Grants, 1656
NEH Picturing America Awards, 1735
Ober Kaler Community Grants, 1801
Office Depot Foundation Education Grants, 1806
Piper Jaffray Foundation Communities Giving
    Grants, 1974
Piper Trust Reglious Organizations Grants, 1979
Sidney and Sandy Brown Foundation Grants, 2196
Strake Foundation Grants, 2249
Target Corporation Community Engagement Fund
    Grants, 2270
Toshiba America Foundation Grades 7-12 Science and
    Math Grants, 2307

Toshiba America Foundation K-6 Science and Math
  Grants, 2308
Turner B. Bunn, Jr. and Catherine E. Bunn
  Foundation Grants, 2325

Problem Solving
Aspen Community Foundation Grants, 316
Land O'Lakes Foundation Community Grants, 1466
NSF Perception, Action and Cognition (PAC)
  Research Grants, 1775

Professional Associations
ALA Louise Seaman Bechtel Fellowship, 173
ALA MAE Award for Best Literature Program for
  Teens, 174
ALA PRIME TIME Family Reading Time Grts, 185
ALA Scholastic Library Publishing Award, 192
ALA Sullivan Award for Public Library Admintrs
  Supporting Services to Children, 213
ALA YALSA Presidential Citation Award, 218
AOCS Thomas H. Smouse Memorial Fellowship, 282
ILA Arbuthnot Award, 1290
ILA Grants for Literacy Projects in Countries with
  Developing Economies, 1292
PCA Art Organizations and Art Programs Grants for
  Presenting Organizations, 1884
PCA Entry Track Arts Organizations and Arts
  Programs Grants for Presenting Orgs, 1909

Professional Development
ALA ALSC Distinguished Service Award, 154
ALA Louise Seaman Bechtel Fellowship, 173
ALA William C. Morris Debut YA Award, 217
AOCS Thomas H. Smouse Memorial Fellowship, 282
Arizona Commission on the Arts Learning
  Collaboration Grant, 291
CICF Summer Youth Grants, 608
Community Fdn for the Capital Region Grants, 687
GNOF IMPACT Grants for Youth Dev, 1084
ILA Grants for Literacy Projects in Countries with
  Developing Economies, 1292
John F. Kennedy Center for the Performing Arts
  National Rosemary Kennedy Internship, 1371
NJSCA Artists in Education Residencies, 1763
NYSCA Arts Education: Local Capacity Building
  Grants (Regrants), 1783
NYSCA Music: Gen Operating Support Grants, 1791
NYSCA Special Arts Services: Instruction and
  Training Grants, 1794
PCA-PCD Professional Development for Individual
  Artists Grants, 1883
PCA Arts Organizations and Arts Programs Grants
  for Crafts, 1891
PCA Entry Track Arts Organizations and Arts
  Programs Grants for Crafts, 1903
PCA Professional Development Grants, 1916
PennPAT New Directions Grants for Presenters, 1931
Piedmont Natural Gas Fdn Envirnmtl Stewardship
  and Energy Sustainability Grant, 1967
Priddy Foundation Organizational Development
  Grants, 2022
Public Education Power Grants, 2032
RISCA Project Grants for Individuals, 2079
San Antonio Area Foundation Strengthening
  Nonprofits Grants, 2151
TAC Arts Education Teacher Incentive Grants, 2268
VSA/Volkswagen Group of America Exhibition
  Awards, 2393

Professorship
Cabot Corporation Foundation Grants, 490
Roy and Christine Sturgis Charitable Tr Grts, 2115

Program Evaluation
Goldseker Foundation Non-Profit Management
  Assistance Grants, 1095
Priddy Foundation Program Grants, 2023

Project Management
Cause Populi Worthy Cause Grants, 521

Protestant Church
ABC Charities Grants, 50
AHS Foundation Grants, 143
Alvah H. and Wyline P. Chapman Foundation
  Grants, 248
Aunt Kate Foundation Grants, 331
Bierhaus Foundation Grants, 421
Chapman Family Foundation, 562
Charles Delmar Foundation Grants, 564
Clark and Ruby Baker Foundation Grants, 625
Collins C. Diboll Private Foundation Grants, 657
Elizabeth Huth Coates Charitable Foundation
  Grants, 900
G.N. Wilcox Trust Grants, 1031
Harry and Helen Sands Charitable Trust Grants, 1181
Henrietta Lange Burk Fund Grants, 1235
J. Edwin Treakle Foundation Grants, 1320
Jim Blevins Foundation Grants, 1365
William M. Weaver Foundation Grants, 2472

Psychiatry
AACAP Educational Outreach Program for Child
  and Adolescent Psychiatry Residents, 23
AACAP Educational Outreach Program for General
  Psychiatry Residents, 24
AACAP George Tarjan Award for Contributions in
  Developmental Disabilities, 25
AACAP Irving Philips Award for Prevention, 26
AACAP Jeanne Spurlock Lecture and Award on
  Diversity and Culture, 27
AACAP Rieger Psychodyn Psychotherapy Award, 33
AACAP Rieger Service Program Award for
  Excellence, 34
AACAP Robert Cancro Academic Leadership
  Award, 35
AACAP Sidney Berman Award for the School-Based
  Study and Intervention for Learning Disorders and
  Mental Ilness, 36
AACAP Simon Wile Leadership in Consultation
  Award, 37
AACAP Systems of Care Special Program
  Scholarships, 39
American Psychiatric Fdn Call for Proposals, 257
American Psychiatric Foundation Typical or Troubled
  School Mental Health Education Grants, 258
Lavina Parker Trust Grants, 1477

Psychodynamics
AACAP Rieger Psychodyn Psychotherapy Award, 33

Psychology
George I. Alden Trust Grants, 1051
NSF Social Psychology Grants, 1776
University of Chicago Chapin Hall Doris Duke
  Fellowships, 2348

Psychotherapy
AACAP Rieger Psychodyn Psychotherapy Award, 33
Avery-Fuller-Welch Children's Fdn Grants, 336
WHO Foundation Volunteer Service Grants, 2444

Public Administration
Anderson Foundation Grants, 271
Community Foundation for the National Capital
  Region Community Leadership Grants, 688
Effie and Wofford Cain Foundation Grants, 895
Huffy Foundation Grants, 1273
M.D. Anderson Foundation Grants, 1523

Public Affairs
1st Source Foundation Community Involvement
  Grants, 1
Amica Companies Foundation Grants, 266
Bernard and Audre Rapoport Foundation Democracy
  and Civic Participation Grants, 409
Blue Grass Community Foundation Clark County
  Fund Grants, 444
Blue Grass Community Foundation Fayette County
  Fund Grants, 446

Blue Grass Community Foundation Franklin County
  Fund Grants, 447
Blue Grass Community Foundation Harrison County
  Fund Grants, 448
Blue Grass Community Foundation Hudson-Ellis
  Grants, 449
Blue Grass Community Foundation Madison County
  Fund Grants, 450
Blue Grass Community Foundation Magoffin County
  Fund Grants, 451
Blue Grass Community Foundation Morgan County
  Fund Grants, 452
Blue Grass Community Foundation Rowan County
  Fund Grants, 453
Blue Grass Community Foundation Woodford
  County Fund Grants, 454
Brown Foundation Grants, 476
Caesars Foundation Grants, 492
Clark County Community Foundation Grants, 626
Community Foundation for SE Michigan Detroit
  Auto Dealers Association Charitable Foundation
  Fund Grants, 681
Earl and Maxine Claussen Trust Grants, 878
F.M. Kirby Foundation Grants, 946
FirstEnergy Foundation Community Grants, 965
Francis Beidler Foundation Grants, 1007
Furth Family Foundation Grants, 1030
HLTA Visitor Industry Charity Walk Grant, 1254
Katharine Matthies Foundation Grants, 1418
Land O'Lakes Foundation Mid-Atlantic Grants, 1467
Libra Foundation Grants, 1489
Lockheed Martin Corporation Fdn Grants, 1505
Marathon Petroleum Corporation Grants, 1551
Marjorie Moore Charitable Foundation Grants, 1574
Meadows Foundation Grants, 1626
Meyer Memorial Trust Responsive Grants, 1653
Mimi and Peter Haas Fund Grants, 1677
New York Foundation Grants, 1753
Noble County Community Foundation Grants, 1765
OSF Early Childhood Program Grants, 1841
Putnam County Community Fdn Grants, 2040
Robert R. Meyer Foundation Grants, 2094
Ruth and Vernon Taylor Foundation Grants, 2124
Schramm Foundation Grants, 2168
Shell Deer Park Grants, 2186
Shell Oil Company Foundation Community
  Development Grants, 2188
Social Justice Fund Northwest Economic Justice
  Giving Project Grants, 2215
Vernon K. Krieble Foundation Grants, 2379
William B. Stokely Jr. Foundation Grants, 2459
William Blair and Company Foundation Grants, 2461
Z. Smith Reynolds Foundation Small Grants, 2523
Zonta International Foundation Young Women in
  Public Affairs Award, 2527

Public Broadcasting
Air Products Foundation Grants, 148
Doree Taylor Charitable Foundation Grants, 843
G.N. Wilcox Trust Grants, 1031
PMI Foundation Grants, 1982
Rasmuson Foundation Tier One Grants, 2055
Rasmuson Foundation Tier Two Grants, 2056
Textron Corporate Contributions Grants, 2286

Public Education
Abell Foundation Education Grants, 53
Baton Rouge Area Foundation Community Coffee
  Fund Grants, 363
Brown Foundation Grants, 476
Bush Foundation Event Sponsorships, 485
Collective Brands Foundation Saucony Run for Good
  Grants, 656
Community Foundation of Greater Fort Wayne -
  John S. and James L. Knight Foundation Donor-
  Advised Grants, 707
Community Foundation of Louisville Education
  Grants, 724
Evelyn and Walter Haas, Jr. Fund Education
  Opportunities Grants, 939

HAF Community Grants, 1141
Harold K.L. Castle Foundation Public Education
Redesign and Enhancement Grants, 1173
Huntington County Community Foundation
Classroom Education Grants, 1279
JP Morgan Chase Fdn Arts and Culture Grants, 1394
NEA Foundation Read Across America Library
Books Awards, 1732
Ober Kaler Community Grants, 1801
PG&E Community Vitality Grants, 1957
Piedmont Natural Gas Foundation K-12 Science,
Technology, Engineering and Math (STEM)
Grant, 1969
Rasmuson Foundation Tier Two Grants, 2056
Southern California Edison Education Grants, 2218
USAID Integrated Youth Development Activity
Grants, 2356
William J. and Tina Rosenberg Fdn Grants, 2470

Public Health
Akron Community Foundation Health and Human
Services Grants, 152
Appalachian Regional Commission Health Care
Grants, 288
Baxter International Foundation Grants, 369
CDC David J. Sencer Museum Student Field Trip
Experience, 524
Cigna Civic Affairs Sponsorships, 610
Colgate-Palmolive Company Grants, 652
Collective Brands Foundation Saucony Run for Good
Grants, 656
Deaconess Community Foundation Grants, 803
Edward and Helen Bartlett Foundation Grants, 888
George W. Wells Foundation Grants, 1057
GNOF IMPACT Kahn-Oppenheim Tr Grts, 1087
Kansas Health Foundation Recognition Grants, 1415
Michael Reese Health Trust Responsive Grants, 1659
Norman Foundation Grants, 1767
Piedmont Natural Gas Foundation Health and
Human Services Grants, 1968
Premera Blue Cross Grants, 2018
Seattle Foundation Health and Wellness Grants, 2179
William and Sandy Heitz Family Fdn Grants, 2457

Public Planning/Policy
Achelis and Bodman Foundation Grants, 101
Achelis Foundation Grants, 102
Adolph Coors Foundation Grants, 129
Amerigroup Foundation Grants, 264
AT&T Fdn Community Support and Safety, 320
Carnegie Corporation of New York Grants, 511
CIGNA Foundation Grants, 611
Community Foundation of Eastern Connecticut
General Southeast Grants, 696
Curtis Foundation Grants, 771
E.L. Wiegand Foundation Grants, 877
Ewing Marion Kauffman Foundation Grants, 943
F.M. Kirby Foundation Grants, 946
FCD New American Children Grants, 952
Ford Foundation BUILD Grants, 984
General Motors Foundation Grants, 1039
Greenspun Family Foundation Grants, 1118
Hatton W. Sumners Foundation for the Study and
Teaching of Self Government Grants, 1196
Inland Empire Community Foundation Capacity
Building for IE Nonprofits Grants, 1306
J.W. Kieckhefer Foundation Grants, 1324
Jaquelin Hume Foundation Grants, 1357
Klingenstein-Simons Fellowship Awards in the
Neurosciences, 1441
Koret Foundation Grants, 1449
Laurel Foundation Grants, 1475
M.D. Anderson Foundation Grants, 1523
Marin Community Foundation Affordable Housing
Grants, 1561
Meyer Fdn Healthy Communities Grants, 1650
Mimi and Peter Haas Fund Grants, 1677
Norman Foundation Grants, 1767
OSF Early Childhood Program Grants, 1841
PMI Foundation Grants, 1982

Sapelo Foundation Social Justice Grants, 2160
Sensient Technologies Foundation Grants, 2180
Social Justice Fund Northwest Criminal Justice
Giving Project Grants, 2214
Streisand Foundation Grants, 2251
Tides Foundation Grants, 2302
University of Chicago Chapin Hall Doris Duke
Fellowships, 2348
Vernon K. Krieble Foundation Grants, 2379
William T. Grant Foundation Scholars Program, 2475
Windham Foundation Grants, 2477
Woods Fund of Chicago Grants, 2489
Z. Smith Reynolds Foundation Small Grants, 2523

Public Policy Systems Analysis
Marin Community Foundation Affordable Housing
Grants, 1561
USAID National Governance Project in Yemen
Grant, 2357

Public Relations
Do Something Partnerships and Public Relations
Intern, 856

Public Safety
100 Club of Dubuque, 10
ACF Social and Economic Development Strategies
Grants, 93
Ameren Corporation Community Grants, 251
American Woodmark Foundation Grants, 263
Bayer Fund Community Development Grants, 383
Bikes Belong Foundation Paul David Clark Bicycling
Safety Grants, 422
Caesars Foundation Grants, 492
California Endowment Innovative Ideas Challenge
Grants, 495
CNCS AmeriCorps NCCC Project Grants, 642
Francis Beidler Foundation Grants, 1007
General Motors Foundation Grants, 1039
Greater Sitka Legacy Fund Grants, 1111
Harrison County Community Foundation Signature
Grants, 1179
Harry and Helen Sands Charitable Trust Grants, 1181
Honeywell Corporation Family Safety and Security
Grants, 1255
Kenai Peninsula Foundation Grants, 1425
Ketchikan Community Foundation Grants, 1429
Kodiak Community Foundation Grants, 1446
Lil and Julie Rosenberg Foundation Grants, 1491
LISC Affordable Housing Grants, 1497
LISC Financial Stability Grants, 1501
Meyer Fdn Healthy Communities Grants, 1650
Michelin North America Challenge Education, 1660
Narragansett Number One Foundation Grants, 1712
Petersburg Community Foundation Grants, 1951
PSEG Fdn Safety and Preparedness Grants, 2031
Skaggs Family Foundation Grants, 2206
Skaggs Family Foundation Grants, 2205
State Farm Good Neighbor Citizenship Company
Grants, 2238
Toyota Motor Manufacturing of Indiana Grants, 2310
Toyota Motor Manuf of Kentucky Grants, 2311
Toyota USA Foundation Safety Grants, 2320

Publication
George A Ohl Jr. Foundation Grants, 1043
HSFCA Biennium Grants, 1267
Maurice Amado Foundation Grants, 1609
NEH Family and Youth Programs in American
History Grants, 1734

Publication Education
NEH Picturing America Awards, 1735
Office Depot Foundation Education Grants, 1806
Seattle Foundation Education Grants, 2178

Publishing Industry
Hubbard Broadcasting Foundation Grants, 1269
PCA Arts Organizations and Arts Programs Grants
for Literature, 1894

PCA Entry Track Arts Organizations and Arts
Programs Grants for Literature, 1906
PEN America Phyllis Naylor Grant for Children's and
Young Adult Novelists, 1928

Pulmonary Diseases
CDI Interdisciplinary Research Intvs Grants, 526
CFF First- and Second-Year Clinical Fellowships, 532
CFF Research Grants, 534
CFF Third-, Fourth-, and Fifth-Year Clinical
Fellowships, 535
M. Bastian Family Foundation Grants, 1522
William and Sandy Heitz Family Fdn Grants, 2457

Puppetry
NHSCA Artist Residence Grants, 1756

Quality of Life
Alliant Energy Foundation Community Giving for
Good Sponsorship Grants, 240
Bernard and Audre Rapoport Foundation Arts and
Culture Grants, 407
Bernard and Audre Rapoport Foundation Community
Building and Social Service Grants, 408
Bernard and Audre Rapoport Foundation Democracy
and Civic Participation Grants, 409
Bernard and Audre Rapoport Foundation Education
Grants, 410
Bernard and Audre Rapoport Foundation Health
Grants, 411
Bikes Belong Foundation Paul David Clark Bicycling
Safety Grants, 422
Bikes Belong Foundation REI Grants, 423
Bikes Belong Grants, 424
Collective Brands Foundation Payless Gives Shoes 4
Kids Grants, 655
Countess Moira Charitable Foundation Grants, 752
Elizabeth Carse Foundation Grants, 899
Ezra M. Cutting Trust Grants, 945
Fifth Third Foundation Grants, 959
GNOF IMPACT Grants for Arts and Culture, 1083
Granger Foundation Grants, 1103
Hall-Perrine Foundation Grants, 1152
Jim Moran Foundation Grants, 1366
Johnson Scholarship Foundation Grants, 1382
Mary Wilmer Covey Charitable Trust Grants, 1600
May and Stanley Smith Charitable Trust Grants, 1613
Middlesex Savings Charitable Foundation Basic
Human Needs Grants, 1668
Schlessman Family Foundation Grants, 2167
Simpson Lumber Charitable Contributions, 2201
Singing for Change Foundation Grants, 2202
Turner Foundation Grants, 2326
Volvo Bob the Bunny's Cartoon Competition, 2391
Weaver Foundation Grants, 2420

Race Relations
Public Welfare Foundation Special Opportunities
Grants, 2035
UUA Actions of Public Witness Grants, 2365
UUA Fund Grants, 2367
Weaver Foundation Grants, 2420

Racial Equality
Alaska State Council on the Arts Youth Cultural
Heritage Fast Track Grants, 212
ATA Inclusive Learning Communities Grants, 323
Ben Cohen StandUp Foundation Grants, 403
Evelyn and Walter Haas, Jr. Fund Immigrant Rights
Grants, 941
HAF Community Grants, 1141
Hartley Foundation Grants, 1186
Maine Community Foundation People of Color Fund
Grants, 1544
OSF Baltimore Criminal and Juve Justice Grts, 1839
PDF Fiscal Sponsorship Grant, 1921
Public Welfare Foundation Special Opportunities
Grants, 2035
UUA Actions of Public Witness Grants, 2365

UUA Congregation-Based Community Organizing Grants, 2366
UUA Fund Grants, 2367
UUA International Fund Grants, 2368
UUA Just Society Fund Grants, 2369
UUA Social Responsibility Grants, 2370
Women's Fund of Hawaii Grants, 2484
Women's Fund of Hawaii Grants, 2485

Racism
ALFJ International Fund Grants, 231
Allstate Corporate Giving Grants, 242
Allstate Corp Hometown Commitment Grants, 243
Allstate Foundation Safe and Vital Communities Grants, 244
Community Foundation of Greater Chattanooga Grants, 704
FCYO Youth Organizing Grants, 954
Joseph H. and Florence A. Roblee Foundation Education Grants, 1386
Mabel Louise Riley Foundation Grants, 1529
Meadows Foundation Grants, 1626
NCSS Carter G. Woodson Book Awards, 1729
PDF Community Organizing Grants, 1920
PDF Fiscal Sponsorship Grant, 1921
Public Welfare Foundation Special Opportunities Grants, 2035
Saginaw Community Foundation YWCA Fund for Women and Girls Grants, 2135
Sioux Falls Area Community Foundation Spot Grants, 2204
Teaching Tolerance Diverse Democracy Grants, 2275
Teaching Tolerance Social Justice Educator Grts, 2276
Women's Fund of Hawaii Grants, 2485

Radio
Alabama Humanities Foundation Major Grants, 159
Doree Taylor Charitable Foundation Grants, 843
G.N. Wilcox Trust Grants, 1031
Island Insurance Foundation Grants, 1316
NEH Family and Youth Programs in American History Grants, 1734
NSTA Faraday Science Communicator Award, 1778
PCA Arts Organizations and Arts Programs Grants for Film and Electronic Media, 1893
PCA Entry Track Arts Orgs and Arts Programs Grants for Film and Electronic Media, 1905
San Antonio Area Foundation Capital and Naming Rights Grants, 2148
TE Foundation Grants, 2279
Union Pacific Fdn Community & Civic Grants, 2337

Rape/Sexual Assault
Atlanta Women's Foundation Pathway to Success Grants, 327
Meyer Fdn Healthy Communities Grants, 1650
Pacers Foundation Indiana Fever's Be YOUnique Fund Grants, 1860

Reading
7-Eleven Corporate Giving Grants, 8
ALA Baker and Taylor Summer Reading Program Grant, 158
ALA Innovative Reading Grant, 171
ALA MAE Award for Best Literature Program for Teens, 174
ALA Popular Paperbacks for Young Adults Awds, 184
ALA PRIME TIME Family Reading Time Grts, 185
ALA Quick Picks for Reluctant Young Adult Readers Award, 186
ALA Scholastic Library Publishing Award, 192
ALA Teen's Top Ten Awards, 214
ALA Theodor Seuss Geisel Award, 215
American Savings Foundation Program Grants, 261
Bank of Hawaii Foundation Grants, 360
Bank of the Orient Community Giving, 361
BBF Florida Family Literacy Initiative Grants, 386
BBF Maine Family Literacy Initiative Implementation Grants, 387

BBF Maine Family Literacy Initiative Planning Grants, 388
BBF Maryland Family Literacy Initiative Implementation Grants, 389
BBF Maryland Family Literacy Initiative Planning Grants, 390
BBF National Grants for Family Literacy, 391
Blue Grass Community Foundation Early Childhood Education and Literacy Grants, 445
Bridgestone Americas Trust Fund Grants, 469
CHT Foundation Education Grants, 603
Clarence T.C. Ching Foundation Grants, 624
David and Barbara B. Hirschhorn Foundation Education and Literacy Grants, 786
DeKalb County Community Foundation - Literacy Grant, 814
Dollar General Family Literacy Grants, 835
Dollar General Summer Reading Grants, 836
EQT Fdn Education and Workforce Grants, 927
Fidelity Charitable Gift Fund Grants, 956
First Hawaiian Bank Foundation Corporate Giving Grants, 967
First Lady's Family Literacy Initiative for Texas Family Literacy Trailblazer Grants, 968
First Lady's Family Literacy Initiative for Texas Implementation Grants, 969
First Lady's Family Literacy Initiative for Texas Planning Grants, 970
Harris Foundation Grants, 1177
Hattie M. Strong Foundation Grants, 1194
Hawaii State Legislature Grant-In-Aid, 1219
Jane's Trust Grants, 1346
Kalamazoo Community Foundation Early Childhood Learning and School Readiness Grants, 1407
Laura Bush Foundation for America's Libraries Grants, 1471
LGA Family Foundation Grants, 1487
LISC Community Leadership Operating Grts, 1499
LISC Education Grants, 1500
Locations Foundation Legacy Grants, 1504
Louis Calder Foundation Grants, 1511
M.A. Rikard Charitable Trust Grants, 1521
Madison Community Foundation Grants, 1535
Mary D. and Walter F. Frear Eleemosynary Trust Grants, 1588
Maryland State Department of Education Striving Readers Comprehensive Literacy Grants, 1596
NEA Fdn Read Across America Event Grants, 1731
NEA Foundation Read Across America Library Books Awards, 1732
NSF Perception, Action and Cognition (PAC) Research Grants, 1775
OHA Community Grants for Education, 1809
Piper Trust Children Grants, 1976
ProLiteracy National Book Fund Grants, 2026
Robert Bowne Foundaion Edmund A. Stanley, Jr. Research Grants, 2086
Robert Bowne Foundation Fellowships, 2087
Robert Bowne Foundation Literacy Grants, 2088
Robert Bowne Fdn Youth-Centered Grants, 2089
Robert R. Meyer Foundation Grants, 2094
Screen Actors Guild BookPALS Assistance, 2171
Stocker Foundation Grants, 2247
Target Corporation Community Engagement Fund Grants, 2270
USAID U.S.-Egypt Learning Grants, 2361
William and Flora Hewlett Foundation Quality Education in Developing Countries Grants, 2456
WinnCompanies Charitable Giving, 2479

Reading Education
ACF Head Start and/or Early Head Start Grantee - Clay, Randolph, and Talladega Counties, Alabama, 82
ACF Head Start and/or Early Head Start Grantee - St. Landry Parish, Louisiana, 83
ALA Baker and Taylor Summer Reading Program Grant, 158
ALA Coretta Scott King Book Donation Grant, 168
ALA Innovative Reading Grant, 171

ALA PRIME TIME Family Reading Time Grts, 185
ALA Theodor Seuss Geisel Award, 215
Bank of Hawaii Foundation Grants, 360
Bank of the Orient Community Giving, 361
BBF Florida Family Literacy Initiative Grants, 386
BBF Maine Family Literacy Initiative Implementation Grants, 387
BBF Maine Family Literacy Initiative Planning Grants, 388
BBF Maryland Family Literacy Initiative Implementation Grants, 389
BBF Maryland Family Literacy Initiative Planning Grants, 390
BBF National Grants for Family Literacy, 391
Bernau Family Foundation Grants, 413
Blue Grass Community Foundation Early Childhood Education and Literacy Grants, 445
Clarence T.C. Ching Foundation Grants, 624
David and Barbara B. Hirschhorn Foundation Education and Literacy Grants, 786
DeKalb County Community Foundation - Literacy Grant, 814
Dollar General Family Literacy Grants, 835
EQT Fdn Education and Workforce Grants, 927
Essex County Community Foundation Greater Lawrence Summer Fund Grants, 932
Fidelity Charitable Gift Fund Grants, 956
First Hawaiian Bank Foundation Corporate Giving Grants, 967
First Lady's Family Literacy Initiative for Texas Family Literacy Trailblazer Grants, 968
First Lady's Family Literacy Initiative for Texas Implementation Grants, 969
First Lady's Family Literacy Initiative for Texas Planning Grants, 970
HBF Pathways Out of Poverty Grants, 1222
Laura Bush Foundation for America's Libraries Grants, 1471
LISC Education Grants, 1500
Locations Foundation Legacy Grants, 1504
M.A. Rikard Charitable Trust Grants, 1521
Maryland State Department of Education Striving Readers Comprehensive Literacy Grants, 1596
NEA Fdn Read Across America Event Grants, 1731
NEA Foundation Read Across America Library Books Awards, 1732
OHA Community Grants for Education, 1809
Piedmont Natural Gas Foundation K-12 Science, Technology, Engineering and Math (STEM) Grant, 1969
Piper Trust Children Grants, 1976
Public Education Power Grants, 2032
Screen Actors Guild BookPALS Assistance, 2171
Stocker Foundation Grants, 2247
Target Corporation Community Engagement Fund Grants, 2270
USAID U.S.-Egypt Learning Grants, 2361
WinnCompanies Charitable Giving, 2479

Recidivism
OSF Baltimore Criminal and Juve Justice Grts, 1839

Recreation and Leisure
A.L. Spencer Foundation Grants, 21
ACCF of Indiana Berne Ready Mix Community Enrichment Fund Grants, 65
Agnes M. Lindsay Trust Grants, 140
Alden and Vada Dow Fund Grants, 225
Arthur M. Blank Family Foundation Inspiring Spaces Grants, 309
Atlanta Foundation Grants, 326
Austin Community Foundation Grants, 332
Autism Speaks Norma and Malcolm Baker Recreation Grants, 335
Back Home Again Foundation Grants, 344
Batters Up USA Equipment Grants, 366
Bay Area Community Fdn Auburn Area Chamber of Commerce Enrichment Fund Grants, 373
Bay Area Community Foundation Community Initiative Fund Grants, 376

Belvedere Community Foundation Grants, 399
Belvedere Cove Foundation Grants, 400
Belvedere Cove Foundation Scholarships, 401
Ben B. Cheney Foundation Grants, 402
Bikes Belong Foundation Paul David Clark Bicycling
    Safety Grants, 422
Bikes Belong Foundation REI Grants, 423
Bikes Belong Grants, 424
Brunswick Foundation Grants, 479
Campbell Soup Foundation Grants, 501
CFFVR Shawano Area Community Foundation
    Grants, 549
Charlotte and Joseph Gardner Fdn Grants, 570
Clara Blackford Smith and W. Aubrey Smith
    Charitable Foundation Grants, 621
Clark Electric Cooperative Grants, 627
Community Foundation for SE Michigan Detroit
    Auto Dealers Association Charitable Foundation
    Fund Grants, 681
Community Foundation of Boone County Grants, 694
Community Foundation of Muncie and Delaware
    County - Kitselman Grants, 733
Community Fdn of Southern Indiana Grants, 736
Community Foundation of St. Joseph County Special
    Project Challenge Grants, 738
Community Fdn of Wabash County Grants, 740
Cystic Fibrosis Lifestyle Foundation Individual
    Recreation Grants, 772
Cystic Fibrosis Lifestyle Foundation Loretta Morris
    Memorial Fund Grants, 773
Cystic Fibrosis Lifestyle Foundation Mentored
    Recreation Grants, 774
Cystic Fibrosis Lifestyle Foundation Peer Support
    Grants, 775
Daniels Fund Amateur Sports Grants, 779
Daviess County Community Foundation Recreation
    Grants, 793
Dayton Foundation Vandalia-Butler Grants, 799
Decatur County Community Foundation Large
    Project Grants, 811
Decatur County Community Foundation Small
    Project Grants, 812
Del Mar Foundation Community Grants, 820
Dubois County Community Foundation Grants, 871
Florence Foundation Grants, 978
Florence Hunt Maxwell Foundation Grants, 979
Frederick W. Marzahl Memorial Fund Grants, 1018
Fremont Area Community Foundation Community
    Grants, 1020
Fremont Area Community Foundation Youth
    Advisory Committee Grants, 1022
Gardner W. and Joan G. Heidrick, Jr. Foundation
    Grants, 1036
George A. & Grace L. Long Fdn Grants, 1041
George and Ruth Bradford Foundation Grants, 1042
George A Ohl Jr. Foundation Grants, 1043
George Kress Foundation Grants, 1053
Gibson County Community Foundation Recreation
    Grants, 1069
Gil and Dody Weaver Foundation Grants, 1071
Golden Heart Community Foundation Grants, 1094
Greater Sitka Legacy Fund Grants, 1111
Greenspun Family Foundation Grants, 1118
Hardin County Community Foundation Grants, 1167
Harmony Foundation for Children Grants, 1168
Harrison County Community Fdn Grants, 1178
Harrison County Community Foundation Signature
    Grants, 1179
Harry and Helen Sands Charitable Trust Grants, 1181
Harvey Randall Wickes Foundation Grants, 1188
Hasbro Children's Fund Grants, 1189
Hawai'i Community Foundation Lana'i Community
    Benefit Fund, 1203
Hillsdale County Community Foundation General
    Grants, 1250
Hubbard Farms Charitable Foundation Grants, 1272
ICCF Youth Advisory Council Grants, 1282
Illinois DNR Youth Recreation Corps Grants, 1297
James LeVoy Sorenson Foundation Grants, 1343
James S. Copley Foundation Grants, 1345

Janet Spencer Weekes Foundation Grants, 1348
Kenai Peninsula Foundation Grants, 1425
Knox County Community Foundation Recreation
    Grants, 1442
Kosciusko County Community Fdn Grants, 1452
LaGrange Independent Foundation for Endowments
    (L.I.F.E.), 1459
Lily Palmer Fry Memorial Trust Grants, 1493
Lisa and Douglas Goldman Fund Grants, 1496
LISC Capacity Building Grants, 1498
Lubrizol Foundation Grants, 1513
Marjorie Moore Charitable Foundation Grants, 1574
Mark Wahlberg Youth Foundation Grants, 1576
Marshall County Community Fdn Grants, 1579
McCombs Foundation Grants, 1615
McConnell Foundation Grants, 1616
Miller Foundation Grants, 1673
Narragansett Number One Foundation Grants, 1712
NCMCF Youth Advisory Council Grants, 1727
North Dakota Community Foundation Grants, 1768
North Face Explore Fund, 1770
Orange County Community Foundation Grants, 1828
Perkin Fund Grants, 1937
Perry County Community Foundation Recreation
    Grants, 1942
Petersburg Community Foundation Grants, 1951
Phoenix Suns Charities Grants, 1964
Pike County Community Foundation Recreation
    Grants, 1970
Pinnacle Entertainment Foundation Grants, 1972
Pohlad Family Foundation Summer Camp
    Scholarships, 1992
Pokagon Fund Grants, 1994
Posey County Community Foundation Recreation
    Grants, 2009
Pride Foundation Grants, 2024
Putnam County Community Fdn Grants, 2040
Reinberger Foundation Grants, 2066
Roney-Fitzpatrick Foundation Grants, 2102
Rosenberg Fund for Children Edith and George
    Ziefert Fund Grants, 2110
Rosenberg Fund for Children Grants, 2111
Rosenberg Fund for Children Herman Warsh Fund
    Grant, 2112
Rosenberg Fund for Children Moish and Lillian
    Antopol Memorial Fund Grants, 2113
Roy J. Carver Charitable Trust Youth Services and
    Recreation Grants, 2117
SACF Youth Advisory Council Grants, 2131
Saint Louis Rams Foundation Community
    Donations, 2139
Scheumann Foundation Grants, 2166
Scott County Community Foundation Grants, 2170
Sidgmore Family Foundation Grants, 2195
Sioux Falls Area Community Foundation Community
    Fund Grants, 2203
Sioux Falls Area Community Foundation Spot
    Grants, 2204
Skatepark Project Built to Play Skatepark Grant, 2208
Spencer County Community Foundation Recreation
    Grants, 2231
Starke County Community Foundation Grants, 2236
Turner B. Bunn, Jr. and Catherine E. Bunn
    Foundation Grants, 2325
Turner Foundation Grants, 2326
Vanderburgh Community Foundation Recreation
    Grants, 2374
Walker Area Community Foundation Grants, 2401
Warrick County Community Foundation Recreation
    Grants, 2410
Washington County Community Fdn Grants, 2416
Weaver Foundation Grants, 2420
Wells County Foundation Grants, 2426
William Foulds Family Foundation Grants, 2465
William M. Weaver Foundation Grants, 2472
WSF Sports 4 Life Grants, 2496
WSF Sports 4 Life Regional Grants, 2497
Yawkey Foundation Grants, 2510

Recreation and Leisure Studies
Huntington County Community Foundation Make a
    Difference Grants, 1280

Recycling
Giant Food Charitable Grants, 1068
Union Bank, N.A. Foundation Grants, 2334

Reference Materials
ALA BWI Collection Development Grant, 164
Japan Foundation Los Angeles Japanese-Language
    Teaching Materials Purchase Grants, 1353
OSF Education Support Program Grants, 1843

Refugees
ACF Ethnic Community Self Help Grants, 80
ACF Refugee Career Pathways Grants, 90
ACF Refugee Health Promotion Grants, 91
ACF Unaccompanied Refugee Children Grants, 99
ACF Voluntary Agencies Matching Grants, 100
Blumenthal Foundation Grants, 459
Community Foundation for SE Michigan Southeast
    Michigan Immigrant and Refugee Funder
    Collaborative Grant, 685
Edward and Ellen Roche Relief Fdn Grants, 887
IRC Community Collaboratives for Refugee Women
    and Youth Grants, 1313
Jaquelin Hume Foundation Grants, 1357
Laura Musser Intercultural Harmony Grants, 1472
Michael Reese Health Trust Responsive Grants, 1659
Nathan Cummings Foundation Grants, 1718
New York Foundation Grants, 1753
ProLiteracy National Book Fund Grants, 2026

Regional Economics
GNOF Coastal 5 + 1 Grants, 1078
Walmart Foundation State Giving Grants, 2405

Regional Planning/Policy
Community Foundation for the National Capital
    Region Community Leadership Grants, 688
GNOF Coastal 5 + 1 Grants, 1078
Lockheed Martin Corporation Fdn Grants, 1505
Sarkeys Foundation Grants, 2163

Regional/Urban Design
Mary A. Crocker Trust Grants, 1584
United Technologies Corporation Grants, 2347

Rehabilitation/Therapy
ACL Disability and Rehabilitation Research Projects
    (DRRP) Program: Independent Living Transition
    Services for Youth and Young Adults Grants, 105
Alvah H. and Wyline P. Chapman Fdn Grants, 248
Carl W. and Carrie Mae Joslyn Trust Grants, 510
Chicago Board of Trade Foundation Grants, 580
Dolan Children's Foundation Grants, 832
Dr. John T. Macdonald Foundation Grants, 863
Edward W. and Stella C. Van Houten Memorial Fund
    Grants, 892
Emily O'Neill Sullivan Foundation Grants, 913
Fremont Area Community Foundation Amazing X
    Grants, 1019
Henry County Community Foundation Grants, 1239
Koch Family Foundation (Annapolis) Grants, 1444
Lubrizol Foundation Grants, 1513
Ordean Foundation Catalyst Grants, 1830
Ordean Foundation Partnership Grants, 1831
Peabody Foundation Grants, 1922
Phoenix Suns Charities Grants, 1964
Robert R. Meyer Foundation Grants, 2094
Sara Elizabeth O'Brien Trust Grants, 2161
Shell Deer Park Grants, 2186
WHO Foundation Volunteer Service Grants, 2444

Rehabilitation/Therapy, Emotional/Social
Different Needz Foundation Grants, 830
Fourjay Foundation Grants, 1003
NFL Charities Pro Bowl Community Grants in
    Hawaii, 1755

Sobrato Family Foundation Grants, 2211
Sobrato Family Fdn Meeting Space Grants, 2212
Sobrato Family Foundation Office Space Grants, 2213
Threshold Fdn Justice and Democracy Grants, 2298
WHO Foundation Volunteer Service Grants, 2444

Rehabilitation/Therapy, Occupational/Vocational
Achelis and Bodman Foundation Grants, 101
Achelis Foundation Grants, 102
Atkinson Foundation Community Grants, 325
Different Needz Foundation Grants, 830
Robert R. Meyer Foundation Grants, 2094
WHO Foundation Volunteer Service Grants, 2444

Rehabilitation/Therapy, Physical
Alvah H. and Wyline P. Chapman Foundation
    Grants, 248
Different Needz Foundation Grants, 830
Robert R. Meyer Foundation Grants, 2094
WHO Foundation Volunteer Service Grants, 2444

Religion
Aaron Foundation Grants, 42
ABC Charities Grants, 50
Abell-Hanger Foundation Grants, 52
Achelis and Bodman Foundation Grants, 101
Adams-Mastrovich Family Foundation Grants, 113
Adams County Community Foundation Grants, 115
Adams Family Foundation I Grants, 116
Adams Family Foundation II Grants, 117
Adelaide Christian Home For Children Grants, 124
A Friends' Foundation Trust Grants, 136
Alaska Community Foundation Kenai Peninsula
    Foundation Grant, 205
Amelia Sillman Rockwell and Carlos Perry Rockwell
    Charities Fund Grants, 250
Amerigroup Foundation Grants, 264
Anderson Foundation Grants, 271
Ann Ludington Sullivan Foundation Grants, 279
Antone and Edene Vidinha Charitable Grants, 281
Arthur Ashley Williams Foundation Grants, 302
Arthur M. Blank Family Foundation Molly Blank
    Fund Grants, 310
Atkinson Foundation Community Grants, 325
Aunt Kate Foundation Grants, 331
Babcock Charitable Trust Grants, 343
Baton Rouge Area Foundation Grants, 365
BibleLands Grants, 420
Blumenthal Foundation Grants, 459
Bradley-Turner Foundation Grants, 466
Callaway Foundation Grants, 496
Carl R. Hendrickson Family Foundation Grants, 509
Castle Industries Foundation Grants, 519
CFFVR Robert and Patricia Endries Family
    Foundation Grants, 547
Chapman Charitable Foundation Grants, 560
Chapman Family Charitable Trust Grants, 561
Cincinnati Milacron Foundation Grants, 613
Clark and Ruby Baker Foundation Grants, 625
Collins Foundation Grants, 658
Community Foundation of Madison and Jefferson
    County Grants, 731
Covenant Foundation of Brentwood Grants, 755
Crane Foundation General Grants, 761
Curtis Foundation Grants, 771
David Alan and Susan Berkman Rahm Foundation
    Grants, 785
David and Barbara B. Hirschhorn Foundation
    Education and Literacy Grants, 786
David Robinson Foundation Grants, 791
Deaconess Community Foundation Grants, 803
Earl and Maxine Claussen Trust Grants, 878
Effie Allen Little Foundation Grants, 894
Effie and Wofford Cain Foundation Grants, 895
Effie Kuhlman Charitable Trust Grants, 896
Elsie H. Wilcox Foundation Grants, 909
Ensworth Charitable Foundation Grants, 916
Erie Chapman Foundation Grants, 928
F.M. Kirby Foundation Grants, 946
Fidelity Charitable Gift Fund Grants, 956

First Hawaiian Bank Foundation Corporate Giving
    Grants, 967
Florence Foundation Grants, 978
Franklin County Community Fdn Grants, 1010
Frank S. Flowers Foundation Grants, 1015
Fuller E. Callaway Foundation Grants, 1027
G.N. Wilcox Trust Grants, 1031
Gardner Foundation Grants, 1035
George H.C. Ensworth Memorial Fund Grants, 1049
George I. Alden Trust Grants, 1051
George Kress Foundation Grants, 1053
George P. Davenport Trust Fund Grants, 1054
Granger Foundation Grants, 1103
Greater Saint Louis Community Fdn Grants, 1110
HAF Joe Alexandre Mem Family Fund Grants, 1145
Harris Foundation Grants, 1177
Harry Frank Guggenheim Foundation Research
    Grants, 1184
Hattie Mae Lesley Foundation Grants, 1195
Hawai'i Community Foundation Victoria S. and
    Bradley L. Geist Foundation: Enhancement
    Grants, 1207
Hawai'i Community Foundation Victoria S. and
    Bradley L. Geist Foundation: Supporting Foster
    Children and Their Caregivers, 1208
Hawai'i Community Foundation Victoria S. and
    Bradley L. Geist Foundation: Supporting
    Transitioning Foster Youth Grants, 1209
Helen Bader Foundation Grants, 1227
Helen V. Brach Foundation Grants, 1232
J. Bulow Campbell Foundation Grants, 1319
James M. Collins Foundation Grants, 1344
Jayne and Leonard Abess Foundation Grants, 1358
John G. Duncan Charitable Trust Grants, 1372
John H. and Wilhelmina D. Harland Charitable
    Foundation Children and Youth Grants, 1374
Joni Elaine Templeton Foundation Grants, 1384
Joseph H. and Florence A. Roblee Foundation
    Education Grants, 1386
Katharine Matthies Foundation Grants, 1418
Kathryne Beynon Foundation Grants, 1420
Kawabe Memorial Fund Grants, 1423
Kirby Laing Foundation Grants, 1439
Klingenstein-Simons Fellowship Awards in the
    Neurosciences, 1441
Koret Foundation Grants, 1449
Leo Niessen Jr., Charitable Trust Grants, 1484
Libra Foundation Grants, 1489
Locations Foundation Legacy Grants, 1504
Lotus 88 Foundation for Women and Children
    Grants, 1508
Louis and Sandra Berkman Foundation Grants, 1510
Louis Calder Foundation Grants, 1511
Lumpkin Family Fdn Healthy People Grants, 1518
Lynn and Foster Friess Family Fdn Grants, 1520
M. Bastian Family Foundation Grants, 1522
MacLellan Foundation Grants, 1531
Marion I. and Henry J. Knott Foundation
    Discretionary Grants, 1571
Marion I. and Henry J. Knott Foundation Standard
    Grants, 1572
Mark W. Coy Foundation Grants, 1575
Martin Family Foundation Grants, 1583
Mary D. and Walter F. Frear Eleemosynary Trust
    Grants, 1588
McCombs Foundation Grants, 1615
Meriden Foundation Grants, 1638
Mervin Bovaird Foundation Grants, 1643
MGN Family Foundation Grants, 1656
Narragansett Number One Foundation Grants, 1712
Nathalie and Gladys Dalkowitz Charitable Trust
    Grants, 1716
Nathan Cummings Foundation Grants, 1718
Nell J. Redfield Foundation Grants, 1737
Norcliffe Foundation Grants, 1766
O. Max Gardner Foundation Grants, 1798
Olive Smith Browning Charitable Trust Grants, 1818
Onan Family Foundation Grants, 1821
Parker Foundation (Virginia) Grants to Support
    Christian Evangelism, 1870

Perkins Charitable Foundation Grants, 1939
Philip Boyle Foundation Grants, 1961
R.C. Baker Foundation Grants, 2043
Richard and Caroline T. Gwathmey Memorial Trust
    Grants, 2069
Ricks Family Charitable Trust Grants, 2075
Robbins Family Charitable Foundation Grants, 2082
Robert and Helen Haddad Foundation Grants, 2084
Robert W. Knox, Sr. and Pearl Wallis Knox
    Charitable Foundation, 2095
Roger L. and Agnes C. Dell Charitable Trust I
    Grants, 2099
Rush County Community Foundation Grants, 2121
Sadler Family Foundation Grants, 2132
Saint Ann Legacy Grants, 2138
Sidney and Sandy Brown Foundation Grants, 2196
Siebert Lutheran Foundation Grants, 2198
Sioux Falls Area Community Foundation Community
    Fund Grants, 2203
Sioux Falls Area Community Foundation Spot
    Grants, 2204
Todd Brock Family Foundation Grants, 2305
Turner B. Bunn, Jr. and Catherine E. Bunn
    Foundation Grants, 2325
UUA Actions of Public Witness Grants, 2365
UUA Congregation-Based Community Organizing
    Grants, 2366
UUA Fund Grants, 2367
UUA International Fund Grants, 2368
UUA Just Society Fund Grants, 2369
UUA Social Responsibility Grants, 2370
V.V. Cooke Foundation Grants, 2371
Victoria S. and Bradley L. Geist Foundation Grants
    Supporting Foster Care and Their Caregivers, 2382
Victoria S. and Bradley L. Geist Foundation Grants
    Supporting Transitioning Foster Youth, 2383
Widgeon Point Charitable Foundation Grants, 2447
William B. Stokely Jr. Foundation Grants, 2459
William G. and Helen C. Hoffman Foundation
    Grants, 2466
William Ray and Ruth E. Collins Fdn Grants, 2473
Wold Foundation Grants, 2482
Youths' Friends Association Grants, 2511

Religious Studies
Alavi Foundation Education Grants, 216
Blumenthal Foundation Grants, 459
Covenant Foundation of Brentwood Grants, 755
FirstEnergy Foundation Community Grants, 965
Jayne and Leonard Abess Foundation Grants, 1358
Kawabe Memorial Fund Grants, 1423
Maurice Amado Foundation Grants, 1609
Minnie M. Jones Trust Grants, 1678
Nathalie and Gladys Dalkowitz Charitable Trust
    Grants, 1716
Nathan Cummings Foundation Grants, 1718
Saint Ann Legacy Grants, 2138
Siebert Lutheran Foundation Grants, 2198
Turner B. Bunn, Jr. and Catherine E. Bunn
    Foundation Grants, 2325
UUA Fund Grants, 2367

Religious Welfare Programs
Adams County Community Foundation Grants, 115
Adelaide Christian Home For Children Grants, 124
Alavi Foundation Education Grants, 216
Anne Arundel Women Giving Together Regular
    Grants, 275
Aunt Kate Foundation Grants, 331
Babcock Charitable Trust Grants, 343
Baton Rouge Area Foundation Every Kid a King
    Fund Grants, 364
Blue Cross Blue Shield of Minnesota Fdn - Healthy
    Children: Growing Up Healthy Grants, 442
Blue Cross Blue Shield of Minnesota Foundation
    - Healthy Neighborhoods: Connect for Health
    Challenge Grants, 443
Carl R. Hendrickson Family Foundation Grants, 509
Charles H. Hall Foundation, 565
Clark and Ruby Baker Foundation Grants, 625

Covenant Foundation of Brentwood Grants, 755
Crane Foundation General Grants, 761
Curtis Foundation Grants, 771
Earl and Maxine Claussen Trust Grants, 878
Effie Allen Little Foundation Grants, 894
Effie Kuhlman Charitable Trust Grants, 896
Ensworth Charitable Foundation Grants, 916
Fidelity Charitable Gift Fund Grants, 956
Florence Foundation Grants, 978
Frederick W. Marzahl Memorial Fund Grants, 1018
George A. & Grace L. Long Fdn Grants, 1041
George E. Hatcher, Jr. and Ann Williams Hatcher
    Foundation Grants, 1045
Greenspun Family Foundation Grants, 1118
HAF Joe Alexandre Mem Family Fund Grants, 1145
HAF Laurence and Elaine Allen Memorial Fund
    Grants, 1146
Harold Brooks Foundation Grants, 1172
Harris Foundation Grants, 1177
Harvey Randall Wickes Foundation Grants, 1188
Hattie Mae Lesley Foundation Grants, 1195
Hawai'i Community Foundation Victoria S. and
    Bradley L. Geist Foundation: Capacity Building
    Grants, 1206
Hawai'i Community Foundation Victoria S. and
    Bradley L. Geist Foundation: Enhancement
    Grants, 1207
Hawai'i Community Foundation Victoria S. and
    Bradley L. Geist Foundation: Supporting
    Transitioning Foster Youth Grants, 1209
Helen Irwin Littauer Educational Trust Grants, 1231
Henrietta Lange Burk Fund Grants, 1235
Herbert A. and Adrian W. Woods Foundation
    Grants, 1243
Horace A. Moses Charitable Trust Grants, 1261
Huisking Foundation Grants, 1274
Janson Foundation Grants, 1350
Jayne and Leonard Abess Foundation Grants, 1358
Joni Elaine Templeton Foundation Grants, 1384
Joyce and Randy Seckman Fdn Grants, 1393
Kawabe Memorial Fund Grants, 1423
Laura Musser Intercultural Harmony Grants, 1472
Lilly Endowment Summer Youth Grants, 1492
Locations Foundation Legacy Grants, 1504
MacLellan Foundation Grants, 1531
Margaret and James A. Elkins Jr. Fdn Grants, 1555
Margaret M. Walker Charitable Fdn Grants, 1556
Mark W. Coy Foundation Grants, 1575
Martin Family Foundation Grants, 1583
Mathile Family Foundation Grants, 1604
Meriden Foundation Grants, 1638
Nathalie and Gladys Dalkowitz Trust Grants, 1716
Parke County Community Foundation Grants, 1868
Perkins-Ponder Foundation Grants, 1938
Pettus Foundation Grants, 1952
Philip Boyle Foundation Grants, 1961
Priddy Foundation Program Grants, 2023
Robbins Charitable Foundation Grants, 2081
Robbins Family Charitable Foundation Grants, 2082
Robert R. McCormick Tribune Foundation
    Community Grants, 2093
Robert W. Knox, Sr. and Pearl Wallis Knox
    Charitable Foundation, 2095
Robinson Foundation Grants, 2097
Saint Ann Legacy Grants, 2138
Sierra Health Foundation Responsive Grants, 2199
Swindells Charitable Foundation Grants, 2261
Todd Brock Family Foundation Grants, 2305
UUA Actions of Public Witness Grants, 2365
UUA Congregation-Based Community Organizing
    Grants, 2366
UUA Fund Grants, 2367
UUA International Fund Grants, 2368
UUA Just Society Fund Grants, 2369
UUA Social Responsibility Grants, 2370
William E. Dean III Charitable Fdn Grants, 2464
William J. and Tina Rosenberg Fdn Grants, 2470
William Ray and Ruth E. Collins Fdn Grants, 2473
Youths' Friends Association Grants, 2511
ZYTL Foundation Grants, 2528

Remedial Education
Albert W. Rice Charitable Foundation Grants, 223
Charles H. Pearson Foundation Grants, 566
Community Foundation for the Capital Region
    Grants, 687
Foundation for the Mid South Education Grants, 993
Frank Reed and Margaret Jane Peters Memorial Fund
    II Grants, 1014
GNOF IMPACT Grants for Youth Dev, 1084
Harold Brooks Foundation Grants, 1172
Hattie M. Strong Foundation Grants, 1194
J. Knox Gholston Foundation Grants, 1321
J. William Gholston Foundation Grants, 1328
Luella Kemper Trust Grants, 1517
Mary Wilmer Covey Charitable Trust Grants, 1600
Piper Trust Education Grants, 1977

Renewable Energy Sources
GNOF Coastal 5 + 1 Grants, 1078
Southwest Initiative Foundation Grants, 2226
Union Bank, N.A. Foundation Grants, 2334
William and Flora Hewlett Foundation
    Environmental Grants, 2455

Renovation
Chatham Athletic Foundation Grants, 574
Courtney S. Turner Charitable Trust Grants, 753
GNOF Albert N. & Hattie M. McClure Grants, 1076
GNOF Exxon-Mobil Grants, 1080
GNOF Norco Community Grants, 1089
Hazel and Walter T. Bales Foundation Grants, 1220
Iddings Foundation Capital Project Grants, 1283
J. William Gholston Foundation Grants, 1328
Janson Foundation Grants, 1350
Katharine Matthies Foundation Grants, 1418
Marietta McNeill Morgan and Samuel Tate Morgan
    Jr. Trust Grants, 1560
Marjorie Moore Charitable Foundation Grants, 1574
Montana Community Foundation Grants, 1687
Perkins-Ponder Foundation Grants, 1938
Richard and Caroline T. Gwathmey Memorial Trust
    Grants, 2069
UUA Fund Grants, 2367
Vigneron Memorial Fund Grants, 2384

Reproduction
Gardner Foundation Grants, 1034
Packard Foundation Local Grants, 1863
USAID Family Planning and Reproductive Health
    Methods Grants, 2353
WestWind Foundation Reproductive Health and
    Rights Grants, 2434

Reproductive Disorders
USAID Family Planning and Reproductive Health
    Methods Grants, 2353

Reproductive Rights
Baxter International Corporate Giving Grants, 368
Curtis Foundation Grants, 771
Global Fund for Women Grants, 1073
USAID Family Planning and Reproductive Health
    Methods Grants, 2353
WestWind Foundation Reproductive Health and
    Rights Grants, 2434
Women's Fund of Hawaii Grants, 2485

Research Participation
ACF Early Care and Education Research Scholars:
    Child Care Research Scholars, 78
Do Something User Experience Research Intern, 859
Edward W. and Stella C. Van Houten Memorial Fund
    Grants, 892
George A Ohl Jr. Foundation Grants, 1043
John G. Duncan Charitable Trust Grants, 1372
John W. Anderson Foundation Grants, 1383
Mabel H. Flory Charitable Trust Grants, 1527
NRA Foundation Grants, 1774
NSF Perception, Action and Cognition (PAC)
    Research Grants, 1775

Percy B. Ferebee Endowment Grants, 1936
R.C. Baker Foundation Grants, 2043
Skaggs Foundation Grants, 2207

Research Resources (Health/Safety/Medical)
Catherine Holmes Wilkins Foundation Charitable
    Grants, 520
Gerber Foundation Environmental Hazards Research
    Grants, 1062
Gerber Fdn Pediatric Health Research Grants, 1063
Gerber Foundation Pediatric Nutrition Research
    Grants, 1064
John W. Anderson Foundation Grants, 1383
PSEG Fdn Safety and Preparedness Grants, 2031
Sorenson Legacy Foundation Grants, 2217

Respiratory Diseases
Medtronic Foundation Strengthening Health Systems
    Grants, 1632

Restoration and Preservation
Boeing Company Contributions Grants, 462
Callaway Foundation Grants, 496
Cudd Foundation Grants, 769
Fayette County Foundation Grants, 951
FirstEnergy Foundation Community Grants, 965
Fdn for the Mid South Communities Grants, 992
Foundations of East Chicago Education Grants, 995
GNOF Bayou Communities Grants, 1077
GNOF Exxon-Mobil Grants, 1080
Greater Milwaukee Foundation Grants, 1109
Helen E. Ellis Charitable Trust Grants, 1228
HSFCA Folk and Traditional Arts Grants - Culture
    Learning, 1268
Illinois DNR Youth Recreation Corps Grants, 1297
Jennings County Community Fdn Grants, 1360
Kirkpatrick Foundation Grants, 1440
Lumpkin Family Foundation Strong Community
    Leadership Grants, 1519
Mary Black Foundation Active Living Grants, 1585
McLean Contributionship Grants, 1623
Montana Arts Council Cultural and Aesthetic Project
    Grants, 1685
Norcliffe Foundation Grants, 1766
NYSCA Electronic Media and Film: Film Festivals
    Grants, 1785
Parkersburg Area Community Foundation Action
    Grants, 1871
Perkins Charitable Foundation Grants, 1939
Polk County Community Foundation Mary F. Kessler
    Fund Grants, 1999
Richard and Caroline T. Gwathmey Memorial Trust
    Grants, 2069
Ripley County Community Foundation Small Project
    Grants, 2078
Roy and Christine Sturgis Charitable Tr Grts, 2115
Saginaw Community Foundation Discretionary
    Grants, 2134
Shelley and Donald Rubin Foundation Grants, 2187
SunTrust Bank Trusteed Foundations Greene-Sawtell
    Grants, 2257
SunTrust Bank Trusteed Foundations Nell Warren
    Elkin and William Simpson Elkin Grants, 2258
Union Bank, N.A. Foundation Grants, 2334
Watson-Brown Foundation Grants, 2418
Wayne County Foundation Grants, 2419
Widgeon Point Charitable Foundation Grants, 2447

Restoration and Preservation, Art Works/Artifacts
HSFCA Biennium Grants, 1267
HSFCA Folk and Traditional Arts Grants - Culture
    Learning, 1268
PCA Arts Organizations and Arts Programs Grants
    for Art Museums, 1888
PCA Entry Track Arts Organizations and Arts
    Programs Grants for Art Museums, 1900
Robert R. Meyer Foundation Grants, 2094

Restoration and Preservation, Manuscripts/Books/Music Scores
HSFCA Biennium Grants, 1267
PCA Arts Organizations and Arts Programs Grants for Art Museums, 1888
PCA Entry Track Arts Organizations and Arts Programs Grants for Art Museums, 1900

Restoration and Preservation, Structural/Architectural
Benton Community Foundation Grants, 405
Blue River Community Foundation Grants, 458
Brown County Community Foundation Grants, 475
Community Foundation of Bartholomew County Heritage Fund Grants, 690
Community Foundation of Bartholomew County James A. Henderson Award for Fundraising, 691
Community Foundation of Greater Fort Wayne - Community Endowment and Clarke Endowment Grants, 705
Delaware Community Foundation Grants, 817
GNOF Exxon-Mobil Grants, 1080
Kosciusko County Community Foundation REMC Operation Round Up Grants, 1453
Ripley County Community Foundation Grants, 2077
Ripley County Community Foundation Small Project Grants, 2078
Robert R. Meyer Foundation Grants, 2094
Textron Corporate Contributions Grants, 2286
Watson-Brown Foundation Grants, 2418

Retirement
CNCS Senior Corps Retired and Senior Volunteer Program Grants, 648

Rhode Island
John Clarke Trust Grants, 1369
John D. and Katherine A. Johnston Foundation Grants, 1370
Vigneron Memorial Fund Grants, 2384

Risk Factors/Analysis
Ford Family Foundation Grants - Child Abuse Prevention and Intervention, 981

Roma
OSF Early Childhood Program Grants, 1841

Roman Catholic Church
Adams-Mastrovich Family Foundation Grants, 113
AHS Foundation Grants, 143
Alvah H. and Wyline P. Chapman Foundation Grants, 248
Ar-Hale Family Foundation Grants, 290
Avery Foundation Grants, 339
Chapman Family Foundation, 562
Claude A. and Blanche McCubbin Abbott Charitable Trust Grants, 628
Dolan Children's Foundation Grants, 832
Elizabeth Huth Coates Charitable Foundation Grants, 900
Graham Family Charitable Foundation Grants, 1099
Harry and Helen Sands Charitable Trust Grants, 1181
Huisking Foundation Grants, 1274
Kopp Family Foundation Grants, 1448
Robinson Foundation Grants, 2097
Saeman Family Fdn A Charitable Grants, 2133
Westerman Foundation Grants, 2427

Runaway Youth
ACF Abandoned Infants Assistance Grants, 70
ACF Basic Center Program Grants, 73
ACF Child Welfare Training Grants, 75
ACF Infant Adoption Awareness Training Program Grants, 84
ACF National Human Trafficking Hotline Grants, 86
ACF Street Outreach Program Grants, 94
ACF Transitional Living Program and Maternity Group Homes Grants, 96
ACF Unaccompanied Refugee Children Grants, 99

Christine and Katharina Pauly Charitable Trust Grants, 601
Crane Fund for Widows and Children Grants, 762
Fidelity Charitable Gift Fund Grants, 956
First Nations Development Institute Native Youth and Culture Fund Grants, 974
Foundations of East Chicago Youth Development Grants, 998
Fuller Foundation Youth At Risk Grants, 1028
GTRCF Boys and Girls Club of Grand Traverse Endowment Grants, 1126
Joseph H. and Florence A. Roblee Foundation Children and Youth Grants, 1385
New Jersey Office of Faith Based Initiatives Services to At Risk Youth Grants, 1752
Public Welfare Fdn Juvenile Justice Grants, 2033

Rural Areas
Agnes M. Lindsay Trust Grants, 140
ALFJ International Fund Grants, 231
Blandin Foundation Expand Opportunity Grants, 437
CNCS AmeriCorps NCCC Project Grants, 642
Dean Foods Community Involvement Grants, 805
Donald W. Reynolds Foundation Children's Discovery Initiative Grants, 841
Land O'Lakes Foundation Mid-Atlantic Grants, 1467
Montana Arts Council Cultural and Aesthetic Project Grants, 1685
NHSCA Conservation License Plate Grants, 1757
NZDIA Community Org Grants Scheme, 1796
PCA Art Organizations and Art Programs Grants for Presenting Organizations, 1884
PCA Arts in Education Residencies, 1885
PCA Arts Organizations and Arts Program Grants for Music, 1887
PCA Arts Organizations and Arts Programs Grants for Art Museums, 1888
PCA Arts Organizations and Arts Programs Grants for Arts Education Organizations, 1889
PCA Arts Organizations and Arts Programs Grants for Arts Service Organizations, 1890
PCA Arts Organizations and Arts Programs Grants for Crafts, 1891
PCA Arts Organizations and Arts Programs Grants for Dance, 1892
PCA Arts Organizations and Arts Programs Grants for Film and Electronic Media, 1893
PCA Arts Organizations and Arts Programs Grants for Literature, 1894
PCA Arts Organizations and Arts Programs Grants for Local Arts, 1895
PCA Arts Organizations and Arts Programs Grants for Theatre, 1896
PCA Arts Organizations and Arts Programs Grants for Traditional and Folk Arts, 1897
PCA Arts Organizations and Arts Programs Grants for Visual Arts, 1898
PCA Busing Grants, 1899
PCA Entry Track Arts Organizations and Arts Programs Grants for Art Museums, 1900
PCA Entry Track Arts Organizations and Arts Programs Grants for Arts Education Organizations, 1901
PCA Entry Track Arts Organizations and Arts Programs Grants for Arts Service Orgs, 1902
PCA Entry Track Arts Organizations and Arts Programs Grants for Crafts, 1903
PCA Entry Track Arts Organizations and Arts Programs Grants for Dance, 1904
PCA Entry Track Arts Orgs and Arts Programs Grants for Film and Electronic Media, 1905
PCA Entry Track Arts Organizations and Arts Programs Grants for Literature, 1906
PCA Entry Track Arts Organizations and Arts Programs Grants for Local Arts, 1907
PCA Entry Track Arts Organizations and Arts Programs Grants for Music, 1908
PCA Entry Track Arts Organizations and Arts Programs Grants for Presenting Orgs, 1909

PCA Entry Track Arts Organizations and Arts Programs Grants for Theatre, 1910
PCA Entry Track Arts Orgs and Arts Programs Grants for Traditional and Folk Arts, 1911
PCA Entry Track Arts Organizations and Arts Programs Grants for Visual Arts, 1912
ProLiteracy National Book Fund Grants, 2026
Samuel S. Johnson Foundation Grants, 2146
Virginia Foundation for the Humanities Open Grants, 2387
West Virginia Commission on the Arts Long-Term Artist Residencies, 2431

Rural Development
Bay Area Community Foundation Community Initiative Fund Grants, 376
Cleveland Fdn Lake-Geauga Fund Grants, 635
CNCS AmeriCorps NCCC Project Grants, 642
Donald W. Reynolds Foundation Children's Discovery Initiative Grants, 841
HAF Don and Bettie Albright Endowment Fund Grants, 1142
Indiana OCRA Rural Capacity Grants (RCG), 1301
Marin Community Foundation Arts in the Community Grants, 1563
Priddy Foundation Organizational Development Grants, 2022
WinnCompanies Charitable Giving, 2479

Rural Education
BBF Florida Family Literacy Initiative Grants, 386
BBF Maine Family Literacy Initiative Implementation Grants, 387
BBF Maine Family Literacy Initiative Planning Grants, 388
Indiana OCRA Rural Capacity Grants (RCG), 1301
Marin Community Foundation Arts in the Community Grants, 1563
Oregon Community Foundation K-12 Student Success: Out-of-School Grants, 1836

Rural Health Care
Appalachian Regional Commission Health Care Grants, 288
CFGR Jenkins Foundation Grants, 553
Kansas Health Foundation Recognition Grants, 1415
Marathon Petroleum Corporation Grants, 1551

Rural Planning/Policy
Indiana OCRA Rural Capacity Grants (RCG), 1301
Virginia Foundation for the Humanities Open Grants, 2387

Russia
Carnegie Corporation of New York Grants, 511

Safety
7-Eleven Corporate Giving Grants, 8
100 Club of Arizona Financial Assistance Grants, 9
100 Club of Dubuque, 10
ACCF Dennis and Melanie Bieberich Community Enrichment Fund Grants, 59
ACCF of Indiana Michael Basham Community Enrichment Fund Grants, 67
ACF Social and Economic Development Strategies Grants, 93
Air Products Foundation Grants, 148
Alcatel-Lucent Technologies Foundation Grants, 224
Allstate Corporate Giving Grants, 242
Allstate Corp Hometown Commitment Grants, 243
Allstate Foundation Safe and Vital Communities Grants, 244
American Electric Power Corporate Grants, 252
American Electric Power Foundation Grants, 253
Autism Speaks Norma and Malcolm Baker Recreation Grants, 335
Bikes Belong Foundation Paul David Clark Bicycling Safety Grants, 422
Bikes Belong Foundation REI Grants, 423
Bikes Belong Grants, 424

BMW of North America Charitable Contribs, 460
Decatur County Community Foundation Large
    Project Grants, 811
EPA Children's Health Protection Grants, 923
Essex County Community Foundation Women's
    Fund Grants, 934
Farmers Insurance Corporate Giving Grants, 948
General Motors Foundation Grants, 1039
Golden Heart Community Foundation Grants, 1094
Greater Sitka Legacy Fund Grants, 1111
Harrison County Community Fdn Grants, 1178
Harrison County Community Foundation Signature
    Grants, 1179
Helen V. Brach Foundation Grants, 1232
Honeywell Corporation Family Safety and Security
    Grants, 1255
Honeywell Corporation Got 2B Safe Contest, 1256
Kenai Peninsula Foundation Grants, 1425
Ketchikan Community Foundation Grants, 1429
Kodiak Community Foundation Grants, 1446
LISC Affordable Housing Grants, 1497
LISC Capacity Building Grants, 1498
LISC Financial Stability Grants, 1501
Mabel Louise Riley Foundation Grants, 1529
Michelin North America Challenge Education, 1660
Monsanto United States Grants, 1684
Noble County Community Foundation Grants, 1765
NRA Foundation Grants, 1774
Petersburg Community Foundation Grants, 1951
PG&E Community Vitality Grants, 1957
Philanthrofund Foundation Grants, 1959
PPCF Edson Foundation Grants, 2015
PPG Industries Foundation Grants, 2017
PSEG Fdn Safety and Preparedness Grants, 2031
Robert R. Meyer Foundation Grants, 2094
Salt River Project Health and Human Services
    Grants, 2142
State Farm Good Neighbor Citizenship Company
    Grants, 2238
Toyota Motor Manuf of Alabama Grants, 2309
Toyota Motor Manufacturing of Indiana Grants, 2310
Toyota Motor Manuf of Kentucky Grants, 2311
Toyota Motor North America of NY Grants, 2315
Toyota Motor Sales, USA Grants, 2316
Toyota Technical Center Grants, 2317
Toyota USA Foundation Safety Grants, 2320
UPS Foundation Community Safety Grants, 2350
Volvo Bob the Bunny's Cartoon Competition, 2391

Safety Engineering
BMW of North America Charitable Contribs, 460

Sanitary Engineering
Bill and Melinda Gates Foundation Water, Sanitation
    and Hygiene Grants, 428
Dorr Foundation Grants, 846

Schizophrenia
NIMH Early Identification and Treatment of Mental
    Disorders in Children and Adolescents Grts, 1761
Peter and Elizabeth C. Tower Foundation Mental
    Health Grants, 1946
Peter and Elizabeth C. Tower Foundation Small
    Grants, 1947

Scholarship Programs, General
Abell-Hanger Foundation Grants, 52
Abney Foundation Grants, 55
Achelis and Bodman Foundation Grants, 101
Achelis Foundation Grants, 102
Agnes M. Lindsay Trust Grants, 140
ALA Bound to Stay Bound Books Scholarships, 163
American Express Charitable Fund Scholarships, 254
Andrew Family Foundation Grants, 272
Antone and Edene Vidinha Charitable Grants, 281
Arthur E. and Josephine Campbell Beyer Foundation
    Grants, 303
Arts Council of Greater Lansing Young Creatives
    Grants, 314
Atwood Foundation General Grants, 330

Baltimore Ravens Foundation Scholarships, 352
Batts Foundation Grants, 367
Belvedere Cove Foundation Scholarships, 401
Ben B. Cheney Foundation Grants, 402
Best Buy Children's Fdn @15 Scholarship , 415
Bindley Family Foundation Grants, 430
Burlington Industries Foundation Grants, 481
C.H. Robinson Worldwide Foundation Grants, 489
Campbell Soup Foundation Grants, 501
Cargill Foundation Education Grants, 504
CFFVR Appleton Education Foundation Grants, 536
CFFVR Shawano Area Community Foundation
    Grants, 549
CFFVR Women's Fund for the Fox Valley Region
    Grants, 550
CFGR Community Impact Grants, 552
Chick and Sophie Major Memorial Duck Calling
    Contest Scholarships, 583
Clarence T.C. Ching Foundation Grants, 624
Cleveland Fdn Lake-Geauga Fund Grants, 635
Clinton County Community Foundation Grants, 638
Collins Foundation Grants, 658
Community Foundation for Greater Buffalo
    Competitive Grants, 670
Community Foundation for SE Michigan Renaissance
    of Values Scholarships, 684
Community Foundation of Madison and Jefferson
    County Grants, 731
Community Fdn of Randolph County Grants, 735
Community Foundation of Western Massachusetts
    Grants, 741
Crane Fund for Widows and Children Grants, 762
Crescent Porter Hale Foundation Grants, 767
Dayton Foundation Rike Family Scholarships, 798
Dell Scholars Program Scholarships, 819
Dorr Foundation Grants, 846
Do Something Scholarships, 857
Dubois County Community Foundation Grants, 871
Edward W. and Stella C. Van Houten Memorial Fund
    Grants, 892
Elsie H. Wilcox Foundation Grants, 909
Florence Foundation Grants, 978
Fourjay Foundation Grants, 1003
Franklin County Community Fdn Grants, 1010
Frank S. Flowers Foundation Grants, 1015
George and Ruth Bradford Foundation Grants, 1042
George I. Alden Trust Grants, 1051
Georgia-Pacific Fdn Entrepreneurship Grants, 1059
Gil and Dody Weaver Foundation Grants, 1071
Greater Saint Louis Community Fdn Grants, 1110
Gregory and Helayne Brown Charitable Foundation
    Grants, 1119
Hank Aaron Chasing the Dream Fdn Grants, 1162
Hearst Foundations United States Senate Youth
    Grants, 1225
Helen Irwin Littauer Educational Trust Grants, 1231
Helen V. Brach Foundation Grants, 1232
Henry County Community Foundation Grants, 1239
Herman H. Nettelroth Fund Grants, 1246
Hubbard Farms Charitable Foundation Grants, 1272
Huisking Foundation Grants, 1274
Humana Foundation Grants, 1275
IBCAT Nancy Jaynes Memorial Scholarship, 1281
Iddings Foundation Major Project Grants, 1284
Ifuku Family Foundation Grants, 1287
IIE 911 Armed Forces Scholarships, 1288
Intel Corporation Community Grants, 1311
Intel Corporation Int Community Grants, 1312
Isabel Allende Foundation Esperanza Grants, 1315
J. Willard and Alice S. Marriott Fdn Grants, 1327
Jack Kent Cooke Fdn Young Artist Awards, 1333
Jacob G. Schmidlapp Trusts Grants, 1336
James and Abigail Campbell Family Foundation
    Grants, 1337
James K. and Arlene L. Adams Foundation
    Scholarships, 1341
John W. Anderson Foundation Grants, 1383
Kathryne Beynon Foundation Grants, 1420
Kawabe Memorial Fund Grants, 1423

Kodak Community Relations Grants, 1445
Kohl's Cares Scholarships, 1447
Kopp Family Foundation Grants, 1448
Laura L. Adams Foundation Grants, 1473
Leo Goodwin Foundation Grants, 1482
Lloyd G. Balfour Foundation Attleboro-Specific
    Charities Grants, 1502
Lloyd G. Balfour Foundation Scholarships, 1503
Louis Calder Foundation Grants, 1511
Lubrizol Foundation Grants, 1513
Lumpkin Family Fdn Healthy People Grants, 1518
M. Bastian Family Foundation Grants, 1522
Maggie Welby Foundation Scholarships, 1539
Martin C. Kauffman 100 Club of Alameda County
    Scholarships, 1582
Maurice R. Robinson Fund Grants, 1611
McInerny Foundation Grants, 1622
Mead Witter Foundation Grants, 1628
MGN Family Foundation Grants, 1656
NASE Fdn Future Entrepreneur Scholarship, 1713
National Wildlife Federation Craig Tufts Educational
    Scholarship, 1724
National YoungArts Foundation Awards, 1725
OceanFirst Foundation Summer Camp Grants, 1804
Ordean Foundation Catalyst Grants, 1830
P. Buckley Moss Foundation for Children's Education
    Endowed Scholarships, 1854
Parkersburg Area Community Foundation Action
    Grants, 1871
PAS Freddie Gruber Scholarship, 1872
PAS John E. Grimes Timpani Scholarship, 1873
PAS SABIAN/PASIC Scholarship, 1876
PAS Sabian Larrie London Memorial Schol, 1877
Percy B. Ferebee Endowment Grants, 1936
Peyton Anderson Scholarships, 1955
Polk County Community Foundation Grants, 2001
Posse Foundation Scholarships, 2011
Puerto Rico Community Foundation Grants, 2037
R.D. and Joan Dale Hubbard Fdn Grants, 2044
Rathmann Family Foundation Grants, 2057
Rosenberg Fund for Children Edith and George
    Ziefert Fund Grants, 2110
Rosenberg Fund for Children Grants, 2111
Rosenberg Fund for Children Herman Warsh Fund
    Grant, 2112
Roy J. Carver Trust Statewide Scholarships, 2116
Samuel S. Johnson Foundation Grants, 2146
San Antonio Area Foundation Capital and Naming
    Rights Grants, 2148
Sand Hill Foundation Health and Opportunity
    Grants, 2153
Sandy Hill Foundation Grants, 2157
Shimizu Foundation Scholarships, 2190
Target Corporation Community Engagement Fund
    Grants, 2270
United Friends of the Children Scholarships, 2341
USDEd Gaining Early Awareness and Readiness for
    Undergrad Programs (GEAR UP) Grants, 2364
Watson-Brown Foundation Grants, 2418
White County Community Foundation - Landis
    Memorial Scholarship, 2437
William B. Stokely Jr. Foundation Grants, 2459
William G. and Helen C. Hoffman Fdn Grants, 2466
William G. Gilmore Foundation Grants, 2467
Wood-Claeyssens Foundation Grants, 2486
Xerox Foundation Grants, 2507
Z. Smith Reynolds Foundation Small Grants, 2523

School Dental Programs
ADA Foundation Samuel Harris Children's Dental
    Health Grants, 111
Community Foundation of Louisville Delta Dental of
    Kentucky Fund Grants, 722

School Food Programs
Bank of America Charitable Foundation Basic Needs
    Grants, 354
C.H. Robinson Worldwide Foundation Grants, 489
Giving Gardens Challenge Grants, 1072
Share Our Strength Grants, 2185

School Health Programs

Appalachian Regional Commission Health Care Grants, 288
Cigna Civic Affairs Sponsorships, 610
Circle K Corporation Contributions Grants, 614
Collective Brands Foundation Saucony Run for Good Grants, 656
Cone Health Foundation Grants, 745
Dr. John T. Macdonald Foundation Grants, 863
Foundations of East Chicago Health Grants, 997
Frank Reed and Margaret Jane Peters Memorial Fund Grants, 1013
Mt. Sinai Health Care Foundation Health of the Urban Community Grants, 1710
Piedmont Health Foundation Grants, 1965
Seattle Foundation Health and Wellness Grants, 2179
United Methodist Health Ministry Fund Grts, 2345

School Libraries

ALA ALSC Distinguished Service Award, 154
ALA Bookapalooza Grants, 161
ALA Bound to Stay Bound Books Scholarships, 163
ALA Coretta Scott King Book Donation Grant, 168
ALA Great Books Giveaway Competition, 170
ALA Innovative Reading Grant, 171
ALA MAE Award for Best Literature Program for Teens, 174
ALA Sara Jaffarian School Library Award for Exemplary Humanities Programming, 190
Arizona State Library LSTA Collections Grants, 295
Arizona State Library LSTA Community Grants, 296
Laura Bush Foundation for America's Libraries Grants, 1471

School-to-Work Transition

Alliant Energy Foundation Community Giving for Good Sponsorship Grants, 240
American Honda Foundation Grants, 255
Blue Mountain Community Foundation Warren Community Action Fund Grants, 457
Ewing Marion Kauffman Foundation Grants, 943
Georgia-Pacific Fdn Entrepreneurship Grants, 1059
Hawaiian Electric Industries Charitable Foundation Grants, 1211
J. Willard and Alice S. Marriott Fdn Grants, 1327
Liberty Bank Foundation Education Grants, 1488
Meyer Foundation Education Grants, 1649
Nevada Community Foundation Grants, 1741
Pentair Foundation Education and Community Grants, 1934
Peter and Elizabeth C. Tower Foundation Intellectual Disabilities Grants, 1944
Textron Corporate Contributions Grants, 2286

Science

AAAS/Subaru SB&F Prize for Excl in Sci Books, 22
Alvah H. and Wyline P. Chapman Foundation Grants, 248
American Schlafhorst Foundation Grants, 262
Arkema Foundation Science Teachers Grants, 299
Arthur Ashley Williams Foundation Grants, 302
Arthur M. Blank Family Foundation Pipeline Project Grants, 313
Baxter International Corporate Giving Grants, 368
Bay Area Community Foundation Semiannual Grants, 382
Blumenthal Foundation Grants, 459
BP Foundation Grants, 465
Bristol-Myers Squibb Foundation Independent Medical Education Grants, 472
Cabot Corporation Foundation Grants, 490
Crane Foundation General Grants, 761
Daviess County Community Foundation Advancing Out-of-School Learning Grants, 792
Dolan Children's Foundation Grants, 832
E.L. Wiegand Foundation Grants, 877
EQT Fdn Education and Workforce Grants, 927
FirstEnergy Foundation Science, Technology, Engineering, and Mathematics Grants, 966
Flinn Foundation Scholarships, 977

George A Ohl Jr. Foundation Grants, 1043
H.B. Fuller Foundation Grants, 1138
Hearst Foundations Culture Grants, 1223
Helen V. Brach Foundation Grants, 1232
Hispanic Heritage Foundation Youth Awards, 1253
Honeywell Corporation Leadership Challenge Academy, 1258
Intel Corporation Community Grants, 1311
Intel Corporation Int Community Grants, 1312
Joni Elaine Templeton Foundation Grants, 1384
Kenneth T. and Eileen L. Norris Fdn Grants, 1427
Kodak Community Relations Grants, 1445
Land O'Lakes Foundation Mid-Atlantic Grants, 1467
Lil and Julie Rosenberg Foundation Grants, 1491
M.J. Murdock Charitable Trust General Grants, 1524
Marion Gardner Jackson Charitable Trust Grts, 1570
Martha Holden Jennings Foundation Grants-to-Educators, 1581
Mary D. and Walter F. Frear Eleemosynary Trust Grants, 1588
Meadows Foundation Grants, 1626
Mercedes-Benz USA Corporate Contributions Grants, 1634
Micron Technology Fdn Community Grants, 1664
National 4-H Council Grants, 1720
NEH Family and Youth Programs in American History Grants, 1734
Northrop Grumman Foundation Grants, 1773
Perkin Fund Grants, 1937
Phoenix Suns Charities Grants, 1964
Puerto Rico Community Foundation Grants, 2037
Qualcomm Grants, 2042
R.C. Baker Foundation Grants, 2043
Raytheon Middle School Grants and Schols, 2061
Robert W. Knox, Sr. and Pearl Wallis Knox Charitable Foundation, 2095
Saint Louis Rams Foundation Community Donations, 2139
Schramm Foundation Grants, 2168
Sidney Stern Memorial Trust Grants, 2197
Sorenson Legacy Foundation Grants, 2217
Stella and Charles Guttman Foundation Grants, 2241
Toyota Technical Center Grants, 2317
Xerox Foundation Grants, 2507

Science Education

3M Company Fdn Community Giving Grants, 5
AAUW International Project Grants, 44
Abbott Fund Global AIDS Care Grants, 47
Abell-Hanger Foundation Grants, 52
Achelis and Bodman Foundation Grants, 101
American Electric Power Corporate Grants, 252
American Electric Power Foundation Grants, 253
American Honda Foundation Grants, 255
Arkema Foundation Grants, 298
Arkema Foundation Science Teachers Grants, 299
Avista Foundation Education Grants, 340
Bay and Paul Foundations PreK-12 Transformative Learning Practices Grants, 370
Bayer Fund STEM Education Grants, 384
Beckman Coulter Foundation Grants, 394
Bill and Melinda Gates Foundation Agricultural Development Grants, 425
Bristol-Myers Squibb Foundation Independent Medical Education Grants, 472
Cabot Corporation Foundation Grants, 490
CCFF Christopher Columbus Awards, 522
CDC David J. Sencer Museum Student Field Trip Experience, 524
CDC Disease Detective Camp, 525
Chicago Board of Trade Foundation Grants, 580
Delta Air Lines Foundation Youth Development Grants, 824
Dorr Foundation Grants, 846
Duke Energy Foundation Local Impact Grants, 872
Essex County Community Foundation Greater Lawrence Summer Fund Grants, 932
Ewing Marion Kauffman Foundation Grants, 943
Gerber Fdn West Michigan Youth Grants, 1065
Grifols Community Outreach Grants, 1122

Lockheed Martin Corporation Fdn Grants, 1505
Martha Holden Jennings Foundation Grants-to-Educators, 1581
Mary A. Crocker Trust Grants, 1584
McCune Charitable Foundation Grants, 1617
Mercedes-Benz USA Corporate Contributions Grants, 1634
Michelin North America Challenge Education, 1660
Micron Technology Fdn Community Grants, 1664
Monsanto Science and Math K-12 Grants, 1683
Northrop Grumman Foundation Grants, 1773
NSTA Distinguished Informal Science Education Award, 1777
PG&E Bright Ideas Grants, 1956
Piedmont Natural Gas Foundation K-12 Science, Technology, Engineering and Math (STEM) Grant, 1969
Qualcomm Grants, 2042
Rathmann Family Foundation Grants, 2057
Raytheon Middle School Grants and Schols, 2061
RGk Foundation Grants, 2068
Rockwell Collins Charitable Corp Grants, 2098
Sand Hill Foundation Environment and Sustainability Grants, 2152
SAS Institute Community Relations Donations, 2165
TE Foundation Grants, 2279
Tellabs Foundation Grants, 2280
Toshiba America Foundation Grades 7-12 Science and Math Grants, 2307
Toshiba America Foundation K-6 Science and Math Grants, 2308
Toyota USA Foundation Education Grants, 2318
United Technologies Corporation Grants, 2347
Washington Gas Charitable Contributions, 2417
WSLBDF Quarterly Grants, 2499
Xerox Foundation Grants, 2507

Science Fiction

ChLA Hannah Beiter Graduate Student Research Grants, 596

Science and Technology

Ameren Corporation Community Grants, 251
Beckman Coulter Foundation Grants, 394
Bill and Melinda Gates Foundation Agricultural Development Grants, 425
BP Foundation Grants, 465
CCFF Christopher Columbus Awards, 522
Florence Foundation Grants, 978
Hearst Foundations Culture Grants, 1223
Hispanic Heritage Foundation Youth Awards, 1253
Joni Elaine Templeton Foundation Grants, 1384
Michelin North America Challenge Education, 1660
Northrop Grumman Foundation Grants, 1773
SAS Institute Community Relations Donations, 2165
William Bingham Foundation Grants, 2460

Science and Technology Centers

Marion Gardner Jackson Charitable Trust Grts, 1570
NSTA Distinguished Informal Science Education Award, 1777

Scouting

Effie Allen Little Foundation Grants, 894
Effie Kuhlman Charitable Trust Grants, 896
George W.P. Magee Trust Grants, 1056
Harry and Helen Sands Charitable Trust Grants, 1181

Scriptwriting

PCA Arts Organizations and Arts Programs Grants for Literature, 1894
PCA Entry Track Arts Organizations and Arts Programs Grants for Literature, 1906
PCA Strategies for Success Grants - Adv Level, 1917
PCA Strategies for Success Grants - Basic Level, 1918
PCA Strategies for Success Grants - Intermediate Level, 1919
VSA Playwright Discovery Award, 2396

Sculpture
PCA Arts Organizations and Arts Programs Grants
for Visual Arts, 1898
PCA Entry Track Arts Organizations and Arts
Programs Grants for Visual Arts, 1912

Secondary Education
3M Company Fdn Community Giving Grants, 5
100% for Kids - Utah Credit Union Education
Foundation Major Project Grants, 11
100% for Kids - Utah Credit Union Education
Foundation Mini Grants, 12
100% for Kids - Utah Credit Union Education
Foundation School Grants, 13
A. Alfred Taubman Foundation Grants, 18
A.C. and Penney Hubbard Foundation Grants, 19
AASA Urgent Need Mini-Grants, 43
AAUW International Project Grants, 44
Abby's Legendary Pizza Foundation Grants, 49
Abeles Foundation Grants, 51
Abell Foundation Education Grants, 53
ACCF John and Kay Boch Fund Grants, 60
ACCF Marlene Bittner Memorial Community
Enrichment Fund Grants, 61
ACCF of Indiana Bank of Geneva Heritage Fund
Grants, 64
ACCF of Indiana Berne Ready Mix Community
Enrichment Fund Grants, 65
ACCF of Indiana First Merchants Bank / Decatur
Bank and Trust Fund Grants, 66
ACCF of Indiana Ron and Susie Ballard Community
Enrichment Fund Grants, 68
ACCF Ralph Biggs Memorial Community
Enrichment Fund Grants, 69
Acuity Charitable Foundation Grants, 110
Adams Family Foundation I Grants, 116
Adams Legacy Foundation Grants, 121
Adobe Foundation Action Grants, 126
Adolph Coors Foundation Grants, 129
Advance Auto Parts Corporate Giving Grants, 131
AEGON Transamerica Foundation Education and
Financial Literacy Grants, 132
Aetna Foundation Summer Academic Enrichment
Grants, 135
A Friends' Foundation Trust Grants, 136
A Fund for Women Grants, 137
AGFT Pencil Boy Express, 139
AHC R.E.A.C.H. Grants, 141
Akron Community Fdn Education Grants, 151
Alavi Foundation Education Grants, 216
Albert E. and Birdie W. Einstein Fund Grants, 220
Alcatel-Lucent Technologies Foundation Grants, 224
Alden and Vada Dow Fund Grants, 225
Aldi Corporation Smart Kids Grants, 226
Allegis Group Foundation Grants, 237
Alloy Family Foundation Grants, 241
Alpha Natural Resources Corporate Giving, 246
American Electric Power Corporate Grants, 252
American Electric Power Foundation Grants, 253
American Honda Foundation Grants, 255
American Indian Youth Running Strong Grants, 256
American Schlafhorst Foundation Grants, 262
Amerigroup Foundation Grants, 264
Amica Companies Foundation Grants, 266
Amica Insurance Company Community Grants, 267
Anchorage Schools Foundation Grants, 270
Anderson Foundation Grants, 271
Andrew Family Foundation Grants, 272
Ann Ludington Sullivan Foundation Grants, 279
Anthony Munoz Foundation Straight A Student
Campaign Grants, 280
Antone and Edene Vidinha Charitable Grants, 281
Ar-Hale Family Foundation Grants, 290
Arkema Foundation Grants, 298
Arthur M. Blank Family Foundation Art of Change
Grants, 306
Arthur M. Blank Family Foundation Mountain Sky
Guest Ranch Fund Grants, 311
Arthur M. Blank Family Foundation Pathways to
Success Grants, 312

Arthur M. Blank Family Foundation Pipeline Project
Grants, 313
Arts Council of Greater Lansing Young Creatives
Grants, 314
AT&T Foundation Education Grants, 321
Atkinson Foundation Community Grants, 325
Atlas Insurance Agency Foundation Grants, 329
Aunt Kate Foundation Grants, 331
Avery Family Trust Grants, 338
Avery Foundation Grants, 339
Avista Foundation Education Grants, 340
Baltimore Community Foundation Mitzvah Fund for
Good Deeds Grants, 349
Baltimore Ravens Corporate Giving, 350
Bank of Hawaii Foundation Grants, 360
Baton Rouge Area Foundation Community Coffee
Fund Grants, 363
Baxter International Corporate Giving Grants, 368
Bay and Paul Foundations PreK-12 Transformative
Learning Practices Grants, 370
Bay Area Community Foundation Arenac
Community Fund Grants, 371
Bay Area Community Fdn Auburn Area Chamber of
Commerce Enrichment Fund Grants, 373
Bay Area Community Foundation Community
Initiative Fund Grants, 376
Bay Area Community Foundation Dow
CommunityGives Youth Service Prog Grants, 377
Bee Conservancy Sponsor-A-Hive Grants, 395
Belvedere Community Foundation Grants, 399
Bill Graham Memorial Foundation Grants, 429
Blackford County Community Fdn Grants, 434
Blue Grass Community Foundation Clark County
Fund Grants, 444
Blue Grass Community Foundation Fayette County
Fund Grants, 446
Blue Grass Community Foundation Franklin County
Fund Grants, 447
Blue Grass Community Foundation Harrison County
Fund Grants, 448
Blue Grass Community Foundation Madison County
Fund Grants, 450
Blue Grass Community Foundation Magoffin County
Fund Grants, 451
Blue Grass Community Foundation Morgan County
Fund Grants, 452
Blue Grass Community Foundation Rowan County
Fund Grants, 453
Blue Grass Community Foundation Woodford
County Fund Grants, 454
BMW of North America Charitable Contribs, 460
Boeing Company Contributions Grants, 462
BP Foundation Grants, 465
Bridgestone Americas Trust Fund Grants, 469
Bristol-Myers Squibb Foundation Independent
Medical Education Grants, 472
Brown Foundation Grants, 476
Brown Rudnick Charitable Foundation Community
Grants, 477
Burlington Industries Foundation Grants, 481
Burton D. Morgan Foundation Hudson Community
Grants, 482
Burton D. Morgan Foundation Youth
Entrepreneurship Grants, 483
Byerly Foundation Grants, 487
C.H. Robinson Worldwide Foundation Grants, 489
Callaway Foundation Grants, 496
Cargill Foundation Education Grants, 504
Carnegie Corporation of New York Grants, 511
Carroll County Community Foundation Grants, 513
Castle Foundation Grants, 518
Castle Foundation Grants, 517
Castle Industries Foundation Grants, 519
CCFF Christopher Columbus Awards, 522
CDC David J. Sencer Museum Student Field Trip
Experience, 524
Central Pacific Bank Foundation Grants, 530
CenturyLink Clarke M. Williams Foundation
Matching Time Grants, 531
CFFVR Appleton Education Foundation Grants, 536

CFFVR Mielke Family Foundation Grants, 544
CFF Winter Park Community Grants, 551
CFGR Community Impact Grants, 552
CFGR SisterFund Grants, 554
CFGR Ujima Legacy Fund Grants, 555
Chapman Charitable Foundation Grants, 560
Chapman Family Foundation, 562
Charles H. Pearson Foundation Grants, 566
Charles N. and Eleanor Knight Leigh Foundation
Grants, 568
Charles Nelson Robinson Fund Grants, 569
Cheryl Spencer Memorial Foundation Grants, 576
Chesapeake Bay Trust Mini Grants, 578
Chick and Sophie Major Memorial Duck Calling
Contest Scholarships, 583
CIGNA Foundation Grants, 611
Cincinnati Bell Foundation Grants, 612
Cisco Systems Foundation San Jose Community
Grants, 615
Citizens Savings Foundation Grants, 617
Clara Blackford Smith and W. Aubrey Smith
Charitable Foundation Grants, 621
Claremont Savings Bank Foundation Grants, 623
Clarence T.C. Ching Foundation Grants, 624
Clayton F. and Ruth L. Hawkridge Foundation
Grants, 630
Clayton Fund Grants, 631
Cleo Foundation Grants, 632
Cleveland Foundation Higley Fund Grants, 634
Cleveland Foundation Legacy Village Lyndhurst
Community Fund Grants, 636
Cleveland H. Dodge Foundation Grants, 637
Clinton County Community Foundation Grants, 638
CMS Historically Black Colleges and Universities
(HBCU) Health Services Research Grants, 639
CNCS AmeriCorps Indian Tribes Plang Grts , 641
CNCS AmeriCorps State and National Grants, 643
CNCS Foster Grandparent Projects Grants, 646
CNCS Senior Corps Retired and Senior Volunteer
Program Grants, 648
Colonel Stanley R. McNeil Foundation Grants, 659
Colorado Interstate Gas Grants, 661
Community Foundation for Greater Buffalo Niagara
Area Foundation Grants, 673
Community Foundation of Crawford County, 695
Community Foundation of Greater Chattanooga
Grants, 704
Community Foundation of Jackson County Classroom
Education Grants, 713
Community Foundation of Louisville Education
Grants, 724
Community Foundation of Louisville Winston N. and
Nancy H. Bloch Educational Fund Grants, 729
Community Foundation of Louisville Youth
Philanthropy Council Grants, 730
Community Fdn of Morgan County Grants, 732
Community Fdn of Southern Indiana Grants, 736
CONSOL Energy Academic Grants, 746
Cooper Tire and Rubber Foundation Grants, 749
Courtney S. Turner Charitable Trust Grants, 753
Crane Foundation General Grants, 761
Crayola Champ Creatively Alive Children Grts, 764
Credit Suisse Foundation Education Grants, 765
Cresap Family Foundation Grants, 766
Crescent Porter Hale Foundation Grants, 767
Dana Brown Charitable Trust Grants, 777
David M. and Marjorie D. Rosenberg Foundation
Grants, 790
David Robinson Foundation Grants, 791
Dean Foods Community Involvement Grants, 805
Dean Foundation Grants, 806
Dean Witter Foundation Education Grants, 807
Decatur County Community Foundation Large
Project Grants, 811
Delaware Community Foundation Grants, 817
Delaware Valley Fairness Project Teacher Assistance
Grants, 818
Del Mar Foundation Community Grants, 820
Delmarva Power & Light Mini-Grants, 822

Delta Air Lines Foundation Youth Development Grants, 824
Don and May Wilkins Charitable Trust Grants, 842
Dorrance Family Foundation Grants, 845
Dorr Foundation Grants, 846
Dr. and Mrs. Paul Pierce Memorial Foundation Grants, 862
Duke Energy Foundation Local Impact Grants, 872
Dunspaugh-Dalton Foundation Grants, 873
E.J. Grassmann Trust Grants, 876
Earl and Maxine Claussen Trust Grants, 878
Eastern Bank Charitable Foundation Partnerships Grants, 881
Eastern Bank Charitable Foundation Targeted Grants, 882
Effie Allen Little Foundation Grants, 894
Effie and Wofford Cain Foundation Grants, 895
Effie Kuhlman Charitable Trust Grants, 896
Elizabeth Carse Foundation Grants, 899
Elizabeth Huth Coates Charitable Foundation Grants, 900
Ella West Freeman Foundation Grants, 904
El Pomar Foundation Grants, 908
Emily Hall Tremaine Foundation Learning Disabilities Grants, 912
Entergy Charitable Foundation Education and Literacy Grants, 917
EQT Fdn Education and Workforce Grants, 927
Essex County Community Foundation Dee and King Webster Fund for Greater Lawrence Grants, 929
Evelyn and Walter Haas, Jr. Fund Education Opportunities Grants, 939
Ezra Jack Keats Foundation Mini-Grants, 944
Faye L. and William L. Cowden Charitable Foundation Grants, 950
Fidelity Charitable Gift Fund Grants, 956
Firelight Foundation Grants, 964
FirstEnergy Foundation Community Grants, 965
FirstEnergy Foundation Science, Technology, Engineering, and Mathematics Grants, 966
First Hawaiian Bank Foundation Corporate Giving Grants, 967
Florence Foundation Grants, 978
Foundation for Rural Service Education Grants, 991
Foundations of East Chicago Education Grants, 995
Four County Community Foundation 21st Century Education Fund Grants, 999
Four County Community Foundation General Grants, 1000
Four County Community Foundation Healthy Senior/Healthy Youth Fund Grants, 1001
Four County Community Foundation Kellogg Group Grants, 1002
Four J Foundation Grants, 1004
Four Lanes Trust Grants, 1005
Francis L. Abreu Charitable Trust Grants, 1008
Frank M. Tait Foundation Grants, 1012
Frank Reed and Margaret Jane Peters Memorial Fund II Grants, 1014
Fred and Gretel Biel Charitable Trust Grants, 1016
Fremont Area Community Foundation Education Mini-Grants, 1021
Gardner Foundation Grants, 1034
George and Ruth Bradford Foundation Grants, 1042
George A Ohl Jr. Foundation Grants, 1043
George F. Baker Trust Grants, 1046
George Graham and Elizabeth Galloway Smith Foundation Grants, 1047
George H. and Jane A. Mifflin Memorial Fund Grants, 1048
George H. Sandy Foundation Grants, 1050
George I. Alden Trust Grants, 1051
George J. and Effie L. Seay Foundation Grants, 1052
Georgia-Pacific Foundation Education Grants, 1058
Georgia Council for the Arts Education Grants, 1060
Geraldine R. Dodge Fdn Education Grants, 1061
GNOF Cox Charities of New Orleans Grants, 1079
GNOF Exxon-Mobil Grants, 1080
GNOF New Orleans Works Grants, 1088
GNOF Norco Community Grants, 1089

GNOF Plaquemines Community Grants, 1091
Graham Family Charitable Foundation Grants, 1099
Greater Milwaukee Foundation Grants, 1109
Green River Area Community Fdn Grants, 1117
Greenspun Family Foundation Grants, 1118
Griffin Family Foundation Grants, 1121
Grundy Foundation Grants, 1124
GTRCF Elk Rapids Area Community Endowment Grants, 1127
GTRCF Joan Rajkovich McGarry Family Education Endowment Grants, 1131
GTRCF Traverse City Track Club Endowment Grants, 1132
HAF Joe Alexandre Mem Family Fund Grants, 1145
HAF Laurence and Elaine Allen Memorial Fund Grants, 1146
Harold K.L. Castle Foundation Public Education Redesign and Enhancement Grants, 1173
Harris and Eliza Kempner Fund Ed Grants, 1176
Harris Foundation Grants, 1177
Harrison County Community Fdn Grants, 1178
Harrison County Community Foundation Signature Grants, 1179
Hattie Mae Lesley Foundation Grants, 1195
Hawai'i Community Foundation Richard Smart Fund Grants, 1204
Hawai'i Community Foundation Robert E. Black Fund Grants, 1205
Hawaii Community Foundation Omidyar Ohana Fund Grants, 1213
Hawaii Electric Industries Charitable Foundation Grants, 1218
HBF Pathways Out of Poverty Grants, 1222
Hearst Foundations Culture Grants, 1223
Helen Bader Foundation Grants, 1227
Helen Gertrude Sparks Charitable Trust Grants, 1230
Herbert Hoover Presidential Library Association Bus Travel Grants, 1244
Herman P. and Sophia Taubman Fdn Grants, 1247
Hillsdale County Community Foundation General Grants, 1250
Honeywell Corporation Leadership Challenge Academy, 1258
Horace A. Kimball and S. Ella Kimball Foundation Grants, 1260
HSBC Corporate Giving Grants, 1266
HSFCA Biennium Grants, 1267
Hubbard Broadcasting Foundation Grants, 1269
Hubbard Family Foundation Grants, 1270
Hubbard Family Foundation Grants, 1271
Hubbard Farms Charitable Foundation Grants, 1272
Huisking Foundation Grants, 1274
Iddings Foundation Medium Project Grants, 1285
Iddings Foundation Small Project Grants, 1286
Intel Corporation Community Grants, 1311
Intel Corporation Int Community Grants, 1312
Island Insurance Foundation Grants, 1316
J. Knox Gholston Foundation Grants, 1321
J. Marion Sims Foundation Teachers' Pet Grant, 1322
J. Walton Bissell Foundation Grants, 1325
J. Watumull Fund Grants, 1326
J. William Gholston Foundation Grants, 1328
Jack Kent Cooke Fdn Good Neighbor Grants, 1331
Jack Kent Cooke Foundation Summer Enrichment Grants, 1332
Jack Satter Foundation Grants, 1334
Jacob and Hilda Blaustein Foundation Israel Program Grants, 1335
James F. and Marion L. Miller Fdn Grants, 1338
Jessica Stevens Community Foundation Grants, 1363
John and Marcia Goldman Foundation Youth Development Grants, 1368
John Clarke Trust Grants, 1369
John H. and Wilhelmina D. Harland Charitable Foundation Children and Youth Grants, 1374
John P. Ellbogen Fdn Community Grants, 1377
Joseph H. and Florence A. Roblee Foundation Education Grants, 1386
Joseph Henry Edmondson Foundation Grants, 1388
Joseph S. Stackpole Charitable Trust Grants, 1390

Joyce and Randy Seckman Charitable Foundation Grants, 1393
JP Morgan Chase Fdn Arts and Culture Grants, 1394
Judy and Peter Blum Kovler Foundation Grants, 1396
Julia Temple Davis Brown Foundation Grants, 1399
K and F Baxter Family Foundation Grants, 1413
Katrine Menzing Deakins Chartbl Trust Grants, 1422
Kenneth T. and Eileen L. Norris Fdn Grants, 1427
Kimball International-Habig Foundation Education Grants, 1433
Kinder Morgan Foundation Grants, 1436
Kind World Foundation Grants, 1438
Kirby Laing Foundation Grants, 1439
Klingenstein-Simons Fellowship Awards in the Neurosciences, 1441
Koch Family Foundation (Annapolis) Grants, 1444
Kodak Community Relations Grants, 1445
Kopp Family Foundation Grants, 1448
Koret Foundation Grants, 1449
Kosasa Foundation Grants, 1450
Laurie H. Wollmuth Charitable Trust Grants, 1476
Lee and Ramona Bass Foundation Grants, 1478
Lemelson-MIT InvenTeam Grants, 1481
LGA Family Foundation Grants, 1487
Linford & Mildred White Charitable Grants, 1495
LISC Capacity Building Grants, 1498
LISC Education Grants, 1500
Lloyd G. Balfour Foundation Attleboro-Specific Charities Grants, 1502
Lloyd G. Balfour Foundation Scholarships, 1503
Locations Foundation Legacy Grants, 1504
Lockheed Martin Corporation Fdn Grants, 1505
Louis and Sandra Berkman Foundation Grants, 1510
Lubrizol Corporation Community Grants, 1512
Lubrizol Foundation Grants, 1513
Luella Kemper Trust Grants, 1517
Lumpkin Family Fdn Healthy People Grants, 1518
Lynn and Foster Friess Family Fdn Grants, 1520
M.A. Rikard Charitable Trust Grants, 1521
Maine Women's Fund Girls' Grantmaking Intv, 1547
Margaret and James A. Elkins Jr. Fdn Grants, 1555
Marin Community Foundation Arts Education Grants, 1562
Marion I. and Henry J. Knott Foundation Discretionary Grants, 1571
Marion I. and Henry J. Knott Foundation Standard Grants, 1572
Marquette Bank Neighborhood Commit Grants, 1577
Martha Holden Jennings Foundation Grants-to-Educators, 1581
Martin Family Foundation Grants, 1583
Mary A. Crocker Trust Grants, 1584
Maryland State Dept of Education 21st Century Community Learning Centers Grants, 1593
Maryland State Department of Education Striving Readers Comprehensive Literacy Grants, 1596
Mathile Family Foundation Grants, 1604
Matson Community Giving Grants, 1607
Maurice R. Robinson Fund Grants, 1611
McConnell Foundation Grants, 1616
McCune Charitable Foundation Grants, 1617
McGraw-Hill Companies Community Grants, 1620
Mead Family Foundation Grants, 1625
Mead Witter Foundation Grants, 1628
Mericos Foundation Grants, 1637
Meta and George Rosenberg Fdn Grants, 1644
Meyer Foundation Education Grants, 1649
Meyer Memorial Trust Responsive Grants, 1653
MGM Resorts Foundation Community Grants, 1655
Micron Technology Fdn Community Grants, 1664
Mile High United Way Stratc Investment Grts, 1671
Mill Spring Foundation Grants, 1674
Milton and Sally Avery Arts Foundation Grants, 1675
Moody Foundation Grants, 1692
Morris Stulsaft Foundation Pathways to Work Grants, 1699
Mr. Holland's Opus Foundation Melody Grants, 1703
Mr. Holland's Opus Foundation Michael Kamen Solo Award, 1704

Mr. Holland's Opus Foundation Special Projects Grants, 1705
National 4-H Council Grants, 1720
National 4-H Youth in Action Awards, 1721
National Schools of Character Awards Program, 1723
NEH Picturing America Awards, 1735
Nellie Mae Education Foundation District-Level Change Grants, 1736
NHSCA Artist Residence Grants, 1756
NHSCA Youth Arts Project Grants: For Extended Arts Learning, 1758
Norcliffe Foundation Grants, 1766
NYFA Artists in the School Community Planning Grants, 1779
NYSCA Arts Education: Community-based Learning Grants, 1780
NYSCA Arts Education: Local Capacity Building Grants (Regrants), 1783
NYSCA Arts Ed: Services to the Field Grants, 1784
Ober Kaler Community Grants, 1801
Office Depot Foundation Education Grants, 1806
OHA Community Grants for Education, 1809
Olga Sipolin Children's Fund Grants, 1815
Olive Higgins Prouty Foundation Grants, 1817
Olivia R. Gardner Foundation Grants, 1819
OMNOVA Solutions Fdn Education Grants, 1820
Ontario Arts Council Artists in Communities and Schools Project Grants, 1823
Ontario Arts Council Arts Organizations in Communities and Schools Operating Grants, 1824
Ontario Arts Council Indigenous Culture Fund Indigenous Artists in Communities and Schools Project Grants, 1825
Oppenstein Brothers Foundation Grants, 1827
Oregon Community Foundation Community Recovery Grants, 1834
P. Buckley Moss Foundation for Children's Education Endowed Scholarships, 1854
P. Buckley Moss Foundation for Children's Education Teacher Grants, 1855
Parkersburg Area Community Foundation Action Grants, 1871
Patricia Kisker Foundation Grants, 1879
Perkin Fund Grants, 1937
Perry and Sandy Massie Foundation Grants, 1941
Pettus Foundation Grants, 1952
PG&E Bright Ideas Grants, 1956
PGE Foundation Grants, 1958
Phil Hardin Foundation Grants, 1960
Philip L. Graham Fund Education Grants, 1962
Phoenix Coyotes Charities Grants, 1963
Phoenix Suns Charities Grants, 1964
Piedmont Natural Gas Foundation K-12 Science, Technology, Engineering and Math (STEM) Grant, 1969
Piper Jaffray Foundation Communities Giving Grants, 1974
PMI Foundation Grants, 1982
PNC Foundation Education Grants, 1985
Polk County Community Foundation Marjorie M. and Lawrence R. Bradley Endowment Fund Grants, 1998
Polk County Community Foundation Mary F. Kessler Fund Grants, 1999
Polk County Community Foundation Unrestricted Grants, 2001
Porter County Community Foundation PCgivingproject Grants, 2003
PPCF Community Grants, 2014
PPCF Edson Foundation Grants, 2015
Public Education Power Grants, 2032
R.D. and Joan Dale Hubbard Fdn Grants, 2044
R.S. Gernon Trust Grants, 2047
Random Acts of Kindness Foundation Lesson Plan Contest, 2053
Raskob Fdn for Catholic Activities Grants, 2054
Ray Charles Foundation Grants, 2058
Reinberger Foundation Grants, 2066
Ressler-Gertz Foundation Grants, 2067
Richard J. Stern Foundation for the Arts Grants, 2071

Richland County Bank Grants, 2074
Riedman Foundation Grants, 2076
Robert and Betty Wo Foundation Grants, 2083
Robert R. McCormick Tribune Foundation Community Grants, 2093
Robert R. Meyer Foundation Grants, 2094
Roger L. and Agnes C. Dell Charitable Trust II Grants, 2100
Ron and Sanne Higgins Family Fdn Grants, 2101
Rose Community Foundation Education Grants, 2104
Rosenberg Charity Foundation Grants, 2107
Roy and Christine Sturgis Charitable Tr Grts, 2115
Ruby K. Worner Charitable Trust Grants, 2119
Ruth and Henry Campbell Foundation Grants, 2123
Ruth Camp Campbell Charitable Trust Grants, 2125
Saigh Foundation Grants, 2137
San Antonio Area Foundation Capital and Naming Rights Grants, 2148
San Antonio Area Foundation High School Completion Grants, 2149
Sand Hill Foundation Environment and Sustainability Grants, 2152
Sand Hill Foundation Health and Opportunity Grants, 2153
San Juan Island Community Foundation Grants, 2158
Sartain Lanier Family Foundation Grants, 2164
Scott County Community Foundation Grants, 2170
Screen Actors Guild StagePALS Assistance, 2173
Seattle Foundation Education Grants, 2178
Serco Foundation Grants, 2181
Seward Community Foundation Grants, 2182
Seward Community Foundation Mini-Grants, 2183
Shopko Fdn Community Charitable Grants, 2191
Sidney and Sandy Brown Foundation Grants, 2196
Silicon Valley Community Foundation Education Grants, 2200
Sioux Falls Area Community Foundation Community Fund Grants, 2203
Sioux Falls Area Community Foundation Spot Grants, 2204
Skaggs Foundation Grants, 2207
SME Education Fdn Youth Program Grants, 2209
Sony Corporation of America Grants, 2216
Sorenson Legacy Foundation Grants, 2217
Southern California Edison Education Grants, 2218
Stillson Foundation Grants, 2245
Storm Castle Foundation Grants, 2248
Strake Foundation Grants, 2249
Strong Foundation Grants, 2252
Sunoco Foundation Grants, 2256
Sylvia Perkin Perpetual Charitable Trust Grants, 2263
Tata Trust Grant for Certificate Course in Holistic inclusion of Learners with Diversities, 2273
TE Foundation Grants, 2279
Terra Fdn Chicago K–12 Education Grants, 2285
Thelma Braun and Bocklett Family Foundation Grants, 2287
Tom C. Barnsley Foundation Grants, 2306
Toshiba America Foundation Grades 7-12 Science and Math Grants, 2307
Toyota USA Foundation Education Grants, 2318
Turtle Bay Foundation Grants, 2327
U.S. Department of Education Promise Neighborhoods Grants, 2332
Union Bank, N.A. Corporate Sponsorships and Donations, 2333
Union Bank, N.A. Foundation Grants, 2334
United Friends of the Children Scholarships, 2341
UPS Foundation Economic and Global Literacy Grants, 2351
USAID Integrated Youth Development Activity Grants, 2356
USAID Nigeria Ed Crisis Response Grants, 2358
USAID School Improvement Program Grants, 2360
USAID U.S.-Egypt Learning Grants, 2361
W.H. and Mary Ellen Cobb Chartbl Trust Grts, 2397
Walker Area Community Foundation Grants, 2401
Walter J. and Betty C. Zable Fdn Grants, 2406
Washington Gas Charitable Contributions, 2417
Weaver Popcorn Foundation Grants, 2421

Wege Foundation Grants, 2422
Welborn Baptist Foundation School Based Health Grants, 2424
Whole Foods Foundation, 2445
Widgeon Point Charitable Foundation Grants, 2447
William J. and Dorothy K. O'Neill Foundation Responsive Grants, 2468
William J. and Gertrude R. Casper Foundation Grants, 2469
William J. Brace Charitable Trust, 2471
Williams Comps Homegrown Giving Grants, 2474
Wilton and Effie Hebert Foundation Grants, 2476
Windham Foundation Grants, 2477
Winifred Johnson Clive Foundation Grants, 2478
Wiregrass Foundation Grants, 2480
Wold Foundation Grants, 2482
Woods Charitable Fund Education Grants, 2488
Wyoming Community Fdn General Grants, 2501
Wyoming Community Foundation Hazel Patterson Memorial Grants, 2502
Wyomissing Foundation Thun Family Organizational Grants, 2505
Wyomissing Foundation Thun Family Program Grants, 2506
Youths' Friends Association Grants, 2511
Z. Smith Reynolds Foundation Small Grants, 2523
Zollner Foundation Grants, 2526

Security
Honeywell Corporation Family Safety and Security Grants, 1255
Koret Foundation Grants, 1449
Philanthrofund Foundation Grants, 1959

Seminars
Alavi Foundation Education Grants, 216
GNOF Organizational Effectiveness Grants and Workshops, 1090
Meyer Foundation Benevon Grants, 1648
Oppenstein Brothers Foundation Grants, 1827
Virginia Foundation for the Humanities Open Grants, 2387

Senile Dementia
Helen Bader Foundation Grants, 1227

Senior Citizen Programs and Services
Adelaide Breed Bayrd Foundation Grants, 123
Amelia Sillman Rockwell and Carlos Perry Rockwell Charities Fund Grants, 250
Avista Foundation Vulnerable and Limited Income Population Grants, 341
Baltimore Community Foundation Mitzvah Fund for Good Deeds Grants, 349
Bay Area Community Foundation Arenac County Healthy Youth/Healthy Seniors Fund Grants, 372
Bushrod H. Campbell and Adah F. Hall Charity Fund Grants, 486
California Endowment Innovative Ideas Challenge Grants, 495
Central Pacific Bank Foundation Grants, 530
Christine and Katharina Pauly Charitable Trust Grants, 601
Citizens Savings Foundation Grants, 617
Clark and Ruby Baker Foundation Grants, 625
CNCS AmeriCorps Indian Tribes Plang Grts , 641
CNCS Foster Grandparent Projects Grants, 646
CNCS Senior Corps Retired and Senior Volunteer Program Grants, 648
Community Foundation for the Capital Region Grants, 687
Community Foundation of Boone County Grants, 694
Corina Higginson Trust Grants, 750
Dermody Properties Foundation Grants, 827
Florence Hunt Maxwell Foundation Grants, 979
Foundations of East Chicago Education Grants, 995
Frank Reed and Margaret Jane Peters Memorial Fund Grants, 1013
Frederick McDonald Trust Grants, 1017
George H. Sandy Foundation Grants, 1050

GNOF Gert Community Fund Grants, 1082
GTRCF Healthy Youth and Healthy Seniors
    Endowment Grants, 1130
Harden Foundation Grants, 1166
Hawai'i Community Foundation Lana'i Community
    Benefit Fund, 1203
Helen Bader Foundation Grants, 1227
Henrietta Lange Burk Fund Grants, 1235
Jim Moran Foundation Grants, 1366
Kansas Health Foundation Recognition Grants, 1415
M.D. Anderson Foundation Grants, 1523
Marin Community Foundation Stinson Bolinas
    Community Grants, 1568
Marjorie Moore Charitable Foundation Grants, 1574
McLean Foundation Grants, 1624
Mericos Foundation Grants, 1637
Nell J. Redfield Foundation Grants, 1737
New Jersey Center for Hispanic Policy, Research and
    Development Innovative Initiatives Grants, 1750
Oregon Community Fdn Community Grants, 1833
PCA Busing Grants, 1899
PCA Pennsylvania Partners in the Arts Program
    Stream Grants, 1914
PCA Pennsylvania Partners in the Arts Project
    Stream Grants, 1915
Piper Trust Reglious Organizations Grants, 1979
PMI Foundation Grants, 1982
Portland General Electric Foundation Grants, 2007
Priddy Foundation Program Grants, 2023
San Antonio Area Foundation Annual Responsive
    Grants, 2147
San Antonio Area Foundation Capital and Naming
    Rights Grants, 2148
Scott County Community Foundation Grants, 2170
Seattle Foundation Basic Needs Grants, 2175
Sierra Health Foundation Responsive Grants, 2199
Union Bank, N.A. Foundation Grants, 2334
Vigneron Memorial Fund Grants, 2384

Service Delivery Programs
Carl R. Hendrickson Family Foundation Grants, 509
CFGR Jenkins Foundation Grants, 553
Clark and Ruby Baker Foundation Grants, 625
CMS Research and Demonstration Grants, 640
Community Foundation of Louisville Anna Marble
    Memorial Fund for Princeton Grants, 717
Community Memorial Foundation Responsive
    Grants, 743
DOL Youthbuild Grants, 838
Florence Hunt Maxwell Foundation Grants, 979
Goldseker Foundation Non-Profit Management
    Assistance Grants, 1095
Harold and Rebecca H. Gross Fdn Grants, 1171
Hasbro Children's Fund Grants, 1189
Hawai'i Community Foundation Children's Trust
    Fund Community Awareness: Child Abuse and
    Neglect Prevention Grants, 1198
Hearst Foundations Social Service Grants, 1224
Henry L. Guenther Foundation Grants, 1242
IRC Community Collaboratives for Refugee Women
    and Youth Grants, 1313
Marin Community Foundation Stinson Bolinas
    Community Grants, 1568
Mericos Foundation Grants, 1637
Middlesex Savings Charitable Foundation Basic
    Human Needs Grants, 1668
Middlesex Savings Charitable Foundation Capacity
    Building Grants, 1669
PCA Arts Organizations and Arts Programs Grants
    for Arts Service Organizations, 1890
PCA Entry Track Arts Organizations and Arts
    Programs Grants for Arts Service Orgs, 1902
Qualcomm Grants, 2042
Roger L. and Agnes C. Dell Charitable Trust I
    Grants, 2099
Seattle Foundation Basic Needs Grants, 2175
Singing for Change Foundation Grants, 2202
Sunoco Foundation Grants, 2256
Union Pacific Foundation Health and Human
    Services Grants, 2338

United Methodist Women Brighter Future for
    Children and Youth Grants, 2346
YSA UnitedHealth HEROES Service-Learning
    Grants, 2522

Service Learning
Countess Moira Charitable Foundation Grants, 752
Harold K.L. Castle Foundation Windward Youth
    Leadership Fund Grants, 1175
TAC Arts Education Mini Grants, 2267
YSA ABC Summer of Service Awards, 2512
YSA GYSD Regional Partner Grants, 2515
YSA NEA Youth Leaders for Literacy Grants, 2518
YSA Sodexo Lead Organizer Grants, 2520

Sex Education
Ms. Fdn for Women Ending Violence Grants, 1708
Susan A. and Donald P. Babson Charitable
    Foundation Grants, 2259

Sex Roles
FCYO Youth Organizing Grants, 954
Ford Foundation BUILD Grants, 984
Susan A. and Donald P. Babson Charitable
    Foundation Grants, 2259

Sexism
ALFJ International Fund Grants, 231
Ms. Fdn for Women Ending Violence Grants, 1708
PDF Community Organizing Grants, 1920
Saginaw Community Foundation YWCA Fund for
    Women and Girls Grants, 2135
Sioux Falls Area Community Fdn Spot Grants, 2204
Teaching Tolerance Social Justice Educator Grts, 2276

Sexual Abuse
Austin S. Nelson Foundation Grants, 333
Baxter International Foundation Grants, 369
CFFVR Schmidt Family G4 Grants, 548
CFNEM Women's Giving Circle Grants, 557
Community Foundation of Eastern Connecticut
    Southeast Area Women and Girls Grants, 701
Curtis Foundation Grants, 771
Fassino Foundation Grants, 949
Ford Foundation BUILD Grants, 984
Global Fund for Women Grants, 1073
Hearst Foundations Social Service Grants, 1224
Initiaive Fdn Inside-Out Connections Grants, 1303
OneFamily Foundation Grants, 1822
Perkin Fund Grants, 1937
Riedman Foundation Grants, 2076
Westerman Foundation Grants, 2427
WHO Foundation Volunteer Service Grants, 2444
Women's Fund of Hawaii Grants, 2484
Women's Fund of Hawaii Grants, 2485

Sexual Behavior
Community Foundation of Eastern Connecticut
    Northeast Women and Girls Grants, 697
Community Foundation of Eastern Connecticut
    Norwich Women and Girls Grants, 698
Community Foundation of Eastern Connecticut
    Windham Area Women and Girls Grants, 702
Pride Foundation Grants, 2024

Sexuality
ALA Rainbow Project Book List Award, 187

Sexually Transmitted Diseases
Community Foundation of Eastern Connecticut
    Northeast Women and Girls Grants, 697
Community Foundation of Eastern Connecticut
    Norwich Women and Girls Grants, 698
Community Foundation of Eastern Connecticut
    Southeast Area Women and Girls Grants, 701
Community Foundation of Eastern Connecticut
    Windham Area Women and Girls Grants, 702
Cone Health Foundation Grants, 745
Kate B. Reynolds Charitable Trust Health Care
    Grants, 1416

Shelters
ACF Basic Center Program Grants, 73
Akron Community Foundation Health and Human
    Services Grants, 152
Alliance for Strong Families and Communities
    Grants, 239
Alloy Family Foundation Grants, 241
Alpha Natural Resources Corporate Giving, 246
Amelia Sillman Rockwell and Carlos Perry Rockwell
    Charities Fund Grants, 250
Annie Gardner Foundation Grants, 277
Aspen Community Foundation Grants, 316
Atkinson Foundation Community Grants, 325
Aunt Kate Foundation Grants, 331
Bank of Hawaii Foundation Grants, 360
Campbell Soup Foundation Grants, 501
Carrie S. Orleans Trust Grants, 512
CFFVR Jewelers Mutual Chartbl Giving Grants, 543
CFFVR Schmidt Family G4 Grants, 548
Charles H. Hall Foundation, 565
Charles Nelson Robinson Fund Grants, 569
Cisco Systems Foundation San Jose Community
    Grants, 615
Clara Blackford Smith and W. Aubrey Smith
    Charitable Foundation Grants, 621
Columbus Foundation Traditional Grants, 663
Community Foundation for Greater Atlanta Frances
    Hollis Brain Foundation Fund Grants, 664
Curtis Foundation Grants, 771
Doree Taylor Charitable Foundation Grants, 843
Emily O'Neill Sullivan Foundation Grants, 913
Essex County Community Foundation Greater
    Lawrence Community Fund Grants, 931
Frank Reed and Margaret Jane Peters Memorial Fund
    II Grants, 1014
George and Ruth Bradford Foundation Grants, 1042
George E. Hatcher, Jr. and Ann Williams Hatcher
    Foundation Grants, 1045
HAF Community Grants, 1141
Hahl Proctor Charitable Trust Grants, 1151
Harold Brooks Foundation Grants, 1172
Harry and Helen Sands Charitable Trust Grants, 1181
Harvey E. Najim Family Foundation Grants, 1187
Hattie Mae Lesley Foundation Grants, 1195
Helen Irwin Littauer Educational Trust Grants, 1231
Helen V. Brach Foundation Grants, 1232
Herman P. and Sophia Taubman Fdn Grants, 1247
HSBC Corporate Giving Grants, 1266
J. Watumull Fund Grants, 1326
Jacob G. Schmidlapp Trusts Grants, 1336
Jeffris Wood Foundation Grants, 1359
Joseph S. Stackpole Charitable Trust Grants, 1390
Kosasa Foundation Grants, 1450
Laura B. Vogler Foundation Grants, 1470
Lied Foundation Trust Grants, 1490
Mardag Foundation Grants, 1554
Marietta McNeill Morgan and Samuel Tate Morgan
    Jr. Trust Grants, 1560
Marquette Bank Neighborhood Commit Grants, 1577
Marriott Int Corporate Giving Grants, 1578
Mary Kay Foundation Domestic Violence Shelter
    Grants, 1591
Maurice J. Masserini Charitable Trust Grants, 1610
McCarthy Family Fdn Charity Fund Grants, 1614
McGregor Fund Human Services Grants, 1621
Mericos Foundation Grants, 1637
Mervin Bovaird Foundation Grants, 1643
MGN Family Foundation Grants, 1656
Middlesex Savings Charitable Foundation Basic
    Human Needs Grants, 1668
Olga Sipolin Children's Fund Grants, 1815
OneFamily Foundation Grants, 1822
Packard Foundation Local Grants, 1863
Perkins-Ponder Foundation Grants, 1938
Perpetual Benevolent Fund, 1940
Porter County Community Foundation Women's
    Fund Grants, 2005
R.S. Gernon Trust Grants, 2047
Richard and Caroline T. Gwathmey Memorial Trust
    Grants, 2069

Robert and Betty Wo Foundation Grants, 2083
Samuel S. Johnson Foundation Grants, 2146
Sarah G. McCarthy Memorial Foundation, 2162
Swindells Charitable Foundation Grants, 2261
Target Corporation Community Engagement Fund
  Grants, 2270
Textron Corporate Contributions Grants, 2286
Thomas Sill Foundation Grants, 2292
TJX Foundation Grants, 2303
USDA Child and Adult Care Food Program, 2362
W.W. Smith Chartbl Trust Basic Needs Grants, 2400
Wilton and Effie Hebert Foundation Grants, 2476
Wold Foundation Grants, 2482
Youths' Friends Association Grants, 2511

Single-Parent Families
ACF Promoting Safe and Stable Families (PSSF)
  Program Grants, 89
ACF Tribal Maternal, Infant, and Early Childhood
  Home Visiting Program: Development and
  Implementation Grants, 97
ACF Tribal Maternal, Infant, and Early Childhood
  Home Visiting Program: Implementation and
  Expansion Grants, 98
Baystate Financial Charitable Foundation Grants, 385
CFFVR Robert and Patricia Endries Family
  Foundation Grants, 547
CFF Winter Park Community Grants, 551
Community Foundation for Greater Atlanta Spark
  Clayton Grants, 667
Community Foundation for Greater Atlanta Spark
  Newton Grants, 668
Community Foundation of Bartholomew County
  Women's Giving Circle, 692
Community Foundation of Louisville Human
  Services Grants, 726
Cralle Foundation Grants, 760
David Robinson Foundation Grants, 791
Fdns of East Chicago Family Support Grants, 996
Joseph H. and Florence A. Roblee Foundation Family
  Grants, 1387
Kalamazoo Community Foundation Individuals and
  Families Grants, 1409
Mabel Louise Riley Foundation Family Strengthening
  Small Grants, 1528
Mary Black Foundation Early Childhood
  Development Grants, 1586
Medtronic Foundation Community Link Human
  Services Grants, 1631
Morris Stulsaft Foundation Educational Support for
  Children Grants, 1697
Pittsburgh Foundation Healthy Children and Adults
  Grants, 1981
Robin Hood Foundation Grants, 2096
Rose Community Foundation Education Grants, 2104
Seattle Foundation Benjamin N. Phillips Memorial
  Fund Grants, 2176
Smith Richardson Fdn Direct Service Grants, 2210
USDA WIC Nutrition Ed Innovations Grants, 2363
Warrick County Community Foundation Women's
  Fund, 2411
Whitehorse Foundation Grants, 2439

Skin Diseases
Hubbard Broadcasting Foundation Grants, 1269

Sleep Disorders
CJ Fdn for SIDS Program Services Grants, 619

Small Businesses
ACF Sustainable Employment and Economic
  Development Strategies Grants, 95
Appalachian Regional Commission Business
  Development Revolving Loan Fund Grants, 285
Appalachian Regional Commission Entrepreneurship
  and Business Development Grants, 287
Dayton Foundation Vandalia-Butler Grants, 799
Draper Richards Kaplan Foundation Grants, 864
Frederick McDonald Trust Grants, 1017
McCune Charitable Foundation Grants, 1617

TechKnowledgey Community Impact Grants, 2278
Union Bank, N.A. Foundation Grants, 2334

Smoking Behavior
Foundation for a Healthy Kentucky Grants, 988
GNOF IMPACT Kahn-Oppenheim Tr Grts, 1087
Premera Blue Cross Grants, 2018

Soccer
Arthur M. Blank Family Foundation Atlanta United
  Foundation Grants, 308
Henry and Ruth Blaustein Rosenberg Foundation
  Youth Development Grants, 1237
Susan A. and Donald P. Babson Charitable
  Foundation Grants, 2259
Target Corporation Soccer Grants, 2271

Social Change
ALFJ International Social Change Opportunity Fund
  Grants, 232
Appalachian Community Fund LGBTQ Fund
  Grants, 284
Blue Cross Blue Shield of Minnesota Foundation
  - Healthy Neighborhoods: Connect for Health
  Challenge Grants, 443
Changemakers Innovation Awards, 559
Community Foundation of Greater Fort Wayne -
  John S. and James L. Knight Foundation Donor-
  Advised Grants, 707
Earth Island Institute Brower Youth Awards, 879
Echoing Green Fellowships, 885
FCYO Youth Organizing Grants, 954
Global Fund for Women Grants, 1073
Maine Women's Fund Econ Security Grants, 1546
McCune Charitable Foundation Grants, 1617
Michigan Women Forward Grants, 1662
Norman Foundation Grants, 1767
PDF Community Organizing Grants, 1920
PDF Fiscal Sponsorship Grant, 1921
Philanthrofund Foundation Grants, 1959
Rosenberg Foundation Immigrant Rights and
  Integration Grants, 2108
Shelley and Donald Rubin Foundation Grants, 2187
Singing for Change Foundation Grants, 2202
Social Justice Fund Northwest Criminal Justice
  Giving Project Grants, 2214
Social Justice Fund Northwest Economic Justice
  Giving Project Grants, 2215
Teaching Tolerance Social Justice Educator Grts, 2276
Union Square Arts Award, 2339
United Methodist Women Brighter Future for
  Children and Youth Grants, 2346
USAID Global Development Alliance Grants, 2354
UUA Just Society Fund Grants, 2369
Wyomissing Foundation Thun Family Organizational
  Grants, 2505
Wyomissing Foundation Thun Family Program
  Grants, 2506

Social History
Radcliffe Institute Carol K. Pforzheimer Student
  Fellowships, 2048
Turner Foundation Grants, 2326

Social Justice
ALA Coretta Scott King-John Steptoe Award for
  New Talent, 166
ALFJ Astraea U.S. and International Emergency
  Fund, 230
Marin Community Foundation Social Justice and
  Interfaith Understanding Grants, 1567
McCune Charitable Foundation Grants, 1617
Mertz Gilmore Foundation NYC Communities
  Grants, 1641
Meyer Fdn Healthy Communities Grants, 1650
Northland Foundation Grants, 1771
Oregon Community Foundation Community
  Recovery Grants, 1834
OSF Baltimore Community Fellowships, 1838
OSF Baltimore Criminal and Juve Justice Grts, 1839

OSF Youth Action Fund Grants in Kyrgyzstan, 1846
PDF Fiscal Sponsorship Grant, 1921
Rosenberg Foundation Immigrant Rights and
  Integration Grants, 2108
Sapelo Foundation Social Justice Grants, 2160
Skaggs Family Foundation Grants, 2206
Skaggs Family Foundation Grants, 2205
Thorman Boyle Foundation Grants, 2295
UUA Actions of Public Witness Grants, 2365
UUA Congregation-Based Community Organizing
  Grants, 2366
UUA International Fund Grants, 2368
UUA Just Society Fund Grants, 2369
UUA Social Responsibility Grants, 2370
Woods Fund of Chicago Grants, 2489
Wyomissing Foundation Thun Family Organizational
  Grants, 2505
Wyomissing Foundation Thun Family Program
  Grants, 2506

Social Movements
PDF Fiscal Sponsorship Grant, 1921
Teaching Tolerance Social Justice Educator Grts, 2276

Social Psychology
NSF Social Psychology Grants, 1776

Social Science Education
McCune Charitable Foundation Grants, 1617
NCSS Award for Global Understanding, 1728
NCSS Christa McA Reach for the Stars Awd, 1730

Social Sciences
Community Fdn of Wabash County Grants, 740
Harry Frank Guggenheim Foundation Research
  Grants, 1184
NCSS Award for Global Understanding, 1728
NCSS Carter G. Woodson Book Awards, 1729
Radcliffe Institute Oral History Grants, 2049
Thomas Sill Foundation Grants, 2292

Social Services
1st Source Foundation Community Involvement
  Grants, 1
786 Foundation Grants, 15
Aaron Foundation Grants, 41
Aaron Foundation Grants, 42
Abbott Fund Community Engagement Grants, 46
ABC Charities Grants, 50
Abney Foundation Grants, 55
ACF Marriage Strengthening Research &
  Dissemination Center Grants, 85
Achelis and Bodman Foundation Grants, 101
Adams and Reese Corporate Giving Grants, 114
Adams Family Foundation I Grants, 116
Adidas Corporation General Grants, 125
A Friends' Foundation Trust Grants, 136
Air Products Foundation Grants, 148
Akron Community Foundation Health and Human
  Services Grants, 152
ALA Coretta Scott King Book Donation Grant, 168
Albertsons Companies Foundation Nourishing
  Neighbors Grants, 221
Albert W. Cherne Foundation Grants, 222
Alcatel-Lucent Technologies Foundation Grants, 224
Alex Stern Family Foundation Grants, 229
Alliant Energy Foundation Community Giving for
  Good Sponsorship Grants, 240
Alloy Family Foundation Grants, 241
Amerigroup Foundation Grants, 264
Andrew Family Foundation Grants, 272
Anheuser-Busch Foundation Grants, 273
Anna Fitch Ardenghi Trust Grants, 274
Arthur Ashley Williams Foundation Grants, 302
Aspen Community Foundation Grants, 316
AT&T Fdn Community Support and Safety, 320
Atkinson Foundation Community Grants, 325
Atlanta Foundation Grants, 326
Austin Community Foundation Grants, 332
Avery Dennison Foundation Education Grants, 337

Baton Rouge Area Foundation Grants, 365
Batts Foundation Grants, 367
Baxter International Foundation Grants, 369
Ben B. Cheney Foundation Grants, 402
Benton Community Foundation Grants, 405
Benwood Foundation Community Grants, 406
Blanche and Irving Laurie Foundation Grants, 436
Blandin Foundation Itasca County Area Vitality
    Grants, 439
Blue Grass Community Foundation Clark County
    Fund Grants, 444
Blue Grass Community Foundation Fayette County
    Fund Grants, 446
Blue Grass Community Foundation Franklin County
    Fund Grants, 447
Blue Grass Community Foundation Harrison County
    Fund Grants, 448
Blue Grass Community Foundation Hudson-Ellis
    Grants, 449
Blue Grass Community Foundation Madison County
    Fund Grants, 450
Blue Grass Community Foundation Magoffin County
    Fund Grants, 451
Blue Grass Community Foundation Morgan County
    Fund Grants, 452
Blue Grass Community Foundation Rowan County
    Fund Grants, 453
Blue Grass Community Foundation Woodford
    County Fund Grants, 454
Blue River Community Foundation Grants, 458
Blumenthal Foundation Grants, 459
Boeing Company Contributions Grants, 462
Bothin Foundation Grants, 464
Bridgestone Americas Trust Fund Grants, 469
Brown County Community Foundation Grants, 475
Burlington Industries Foundation Grants, 481
Campbell Soup Foundation Grants, 501
Carl B. and Florence E. King Foundation Grants, 506
Carl M. Freeman Foundation FACES Grants, 507
Carl R. Hendrickson Family Foundation Grants, 509
Central Pacific Bank Foundation Grants, 530
CFFVR Clintonville Area Foundation Grants, 538
CFFVR Frank C. Shattuck Community Grants, 541
CFFVR Project Grants, 546
CFFVR Robert and Patricia Endries Family
    Foundation Grants, 547
CFFVR Shawano Area Community Foundation
    Grants, 549
Charles Delmar Foundation Grants, 564
Charles N. and Eleanor Knight Leigh Foundation
    Grants, 568
CHC Foundation Grants, 575
CICF Indianapolis Fdn Community Grants, 606
CIGNA Foundation Grants, 611
Cincinnati Bell Foundation Grants, 612
Claremont Community Foundation Grants, 622
Clark County Community Foundation Grants, 626
Colgate-Palmolive Company Grants, 652
Collins Foundation Grants, 658
Colorado Interstate Gas Grants, 661
Columbus Foundation Traditional Grants, 663
Community Foundation for Kettering Grants, 676
Community Foundation for San Benito County
    Grants, 677
Community Foundation of Bartholomew County
    Heritage Fund Grants, 690
Community Foundation of Bartholomew County
    James A. Henderson Award for Fundraising, 691
Community Foundation of Eastern Connecticut
    General Southeast Grants, 696
Community Foundation of Greater Fort Wayne -
    Community Endowment and Clarke Endowment
    Grants, 705
Community Foundation of Greater Fort Wayne -
    Edna Foundation Grants, 706
Community Foundation of Greater Greensboro
    Community Grants, 708
Community Foundation of Henderson County
    Community Grants, 711
Community Fdn of Howard County Grants, 712

Community Foundation of Louisville Anna Marble
    Memorial Fund for Princeton Grants, 717
Community Foundation of Louisville Human
    Services Grants, 726
Community Fdn of Wabash County Grants, 740
Community Foundation of Western Massachusetts
    Grants, 741
Cooke Foundation Grants, 748
Corina Higginson Trust Grants, 750
Cralle Foundation Grants, 760
Crescent Porter Hale Foundation Grants, 767
Crystelle Waggoner Charitable Trust Grants, 768
CUNA Mutual Group Fdn Community Grants, 770
D. W. McMillan Foundation Grants, 776
Dayton Foundation Grants, 796
Dayton Foundation Vandalia-Butler Grants, 799
Dayton Power and Light Foundation Grants, 802
Delaware Community Foundation Grants, 817
Delta Air Lines Foundation Community Enrichment
    Grants, 823
Dunspaugh-Dalton Foundation Grants, 873
E.J. Grassmann Trust Grants, 876
Earl and Maxine Claussen Trust Grants, 878
Edna Wardlaw Charitable Trust Grants, 886
Edwards Memorial Trust Grants, 891
Effie Allen Little Foundation Grants, 894
Effie Kuhlman Charitable Trust Grants, 896
Elizabeth Carse Foundation Grants, 899
Elizabeth Morse Genius Charitable Trust Grants, 901
Elkhart County Community Foundation Grants, 903
Elsie H. Wilcox Foundation Grants, 909
Ensworth Charitable Foundation Grants, 916
Ethel Sergeant Clark Smith Foundation Grants, 935
Evan Frankel Foundation Grants, 938
F.M. Kirby Foundation Grants, 946
F.R. Bigelow Foundation Grants, 947
Farmers Insurance Corporate Giving Grants, 948
FirstEnergy Foundation Community Grants, 965
Fourjay Foundation Grants, 1003
Frankel Brothers Foundation Grants, 1009
Frank S. Flowers Foundation Grants, 1015
Fremont Area Community Foundation Community
    Grants, 1020
Fuller E. Callaway Foundation Grants, 1027
G.N. Wilcox Trust Grants, 1031
George and Ruth Bradford Foundation Grants, 1042
George A Ohl Jr. Foundation Grants, 1043
George H. and Jane A. Mifflin Memorial Fund
    Grants, 1048
GNOF IMPACT Grants for Youth Dev, 1084
GNOF Norco Community Grants, 1089
Greater Milwaukee Foundation Grants, 1109
Greater Saint Louis Community Fdn Grants, 1110
Greater Tacoma Community Foundation General
    Operating Grants, 1113
Green Foundation Human Services Grants, 1116
Grotto Foundation Project Grants, 1123
H.A. and Mary K. Chapman Charitable Trust
    Grants, 1137
H.B. Fuller Foundation Grants, 1138
Hall-Perrine Foundation Grants, 1152
Hannaford Charitable Foundation Grants, 1163
Harrison County Community Fdn Grants, 1178
Harrison County Community Foundation Signature
    Grants, 1179
Harry A. and Margaret D. Towsley Foundation
    Grants, 1180
Hartford Foundation Regular Grants, 1185
Hawai'i Community Foundation Lana'i Community
    Benefit Fund, 1203
Hawai'i Community Foundation Victoria S. and
    Bradley L. Geist Foundation: Capacity Building
    Grants, 1206
Hawai'i Community Foundation Victoria S. and
    Bradley L. Geist Foundation: Enhancement
    Grants, 1207
Hawai'i Community Foundation Victoria S. and
    Bradley L. Geist Foundation: Supporting Foster
    Children and Their Caregivers, 1208

Hawai'i Community Foundation Victoria S. and
    Bradley L. Geist Foundation: Supporting
    Transitioning Foster Youth Grants, 1209
Hearst Foundations Social Service Grants, 1224
Henry L. Guenther Foundation Grants, 1242
Highmark Corporate Giving Grants, 1248
Hillsdale County Community Foundation General
    Grants, 1250
HLTA Visitor Industry Charity Walk Grant, 1254
Horace A. Kimball and S. Ella Kimball Foundation
    Grants, 1260
HRSA Ryan White HIV AIDS Drug Assistance
    Grants, 1265
HSBC Corporate Giving Grants, 1266
Huffy Foundation Grants, 1273
Humana Foundation Grants, 1275
Iddings Foundation Major Project Grants, 1284
Iddings Foundation Medium Project Grants, 1285
Iddings Foundation Small Project Grants, 1286
J.W. Kieckhefer Foundation Grants, 1324
Jacob G. Schmidlapp Trusts Grants, 1336
James Graham Brown Foundation Grants, 1340
James M. Collins Foundation Grants, 1344
James S. Copley Foundation Grants, 1345
John G. Duncan Charitable Trust Grants, 1372
John H. and Wilhelmina D. Harland Charitable
    Foundation Children and Youth Grants, 1374
Journal Gazette Foundation Grants, 1391
Judy and Peter Blum Kovler Foundation Grants, 1396
Katharine Matthies Foundation Grants, 1418
Kathryne Beynon Foundation Grants, 1420
Kentucky Arts Cncl Access Assistance Grants, 1428
Kimball International-Habig Foundation Health and
    Human Services Grants, 1434
Kind World Foundation Grants, 1438
Kodak Community Relations Grants, 1445
Kopp Family Foundation Grants, 1448
Kovler Family Foundation Grants, 1454
Laclede Gas Charitable Trust Grants, 1457
Land O'Lakes Foundation Mid-Atlantic Grants, 1467
Lands' End Corporate Giving Program, 1468
Latkin Charitable Foundation Grants, 1469
Laura B. Vogler Foundation Grants, 1470
Laura Moore Cunningham Foundation Grants, 1474
Lisa and Douglas Goldman Fund Grants, 1496
Lockheed Martin Corporation Fdn Grants, 1505
Lotus 88 Foundation for Women and Children
    Grants, 1508
Louie M. and Betty M. Phillips Fdn Grants, 1509
Lubrizol Foundation Grants, 1513
M. Bastian Family Foundation Grants, 1522
Mabel Louise Riley Foundation Grants, 1529
Mabel Y. Hughes Charitable Trust Grants, 1530
Marcia and Otto Koehler Foundation Grants, 1553
Margaret and James A. Elkins Jr. Fdn Grants, 1555
Margaret T. Morris Foundation Grants, 1557
Mark W. Coy Foundation Grants, 1575
Mary K. Chapman Foundation Grants, 1590
Mary S. and David C. Corbin Fdn Grants, 1598
Matilda R. Wilson Fund Grants, 1605
McConnell Foundation Grants, 1616
McCune Charitable Foundation Grants, 1617
McInerny Foundation Grants, 1622
McLean Foundation Grants, 1624
Meadows Foundation Grants, 1626
Mead Witter Foundation Grants, 1628
Meriden Foundation Grants, 1638
Merrick Foundation Grants, 1639
Mervin Bovaird Foundation Grants, 1643
Meyer Fdn Healthy Communities Grants, 1650
MGN Family Foundation Grants, 1656
Mimi and Peter Haas Fund Grants, 1677
Monsanto United States Grants, 1684
Montana Community Foundation Grants, 1687
Morris Stulsaft Foundation Early Childhood
    Education Grants, 1696
New Covenant Farms Grants, 1742
New Earth Foundation Grants, 1743
Norcliffe Foundation Grants, 1766
Onan Family Foundation Grants, 1821

Oppenstein Brothers Foundation Grants, 1827
Ordean Foundation Catalyst Grants, 1830
Ordean Foundation Partnership Grants, 1831
Parkersburg Area Community Foundation Action
    Grants, 1871
PCA Arts Organizations and Arts Programs Grants
    for Local Arts, 1895
PCA Entry Track Arts Organizations and Arts
    Programs Grants for Local Arts, 1907
Percy B. Ferebee Endowment Grants, 1936
Peyton Anderson Foundation Grants, 1954
Phoenix Suns Charities Grants, 1964
PNC Foundation Community Services Grants, 1984
Pohlad Family Fdn Large Capital Grants, 1990
Pohlad Family Fdn Small Capital Grants, 1991
Powell Foundation Grants, 2013
PPCF Esther M. and Freeman E. Everett Charitable
    Foundation Grants, 2016
Pride Foundation Grants, 2024
Puerto Rico Community Foundation Grants, 2037
R.C. Baker Foundation Grants, 2043
Raskob Fdn for Catholic Activities Grants, 2054
Rasmuson Foundation Tier One Grants, 2055
Rasmuson Foundation Tier Two Grants, 2056
RCF General Community Grants, 2062
RCF Individual Assistance Grants, 2063
Reinberger Foundation Grants, 2066
Richards Foundation Grants, 2072
Ripley County Community Foundation Grants, 2077
Ripley County Community Foundation Small Project
    Grants, 2078
Robert R. Meyer Foundation Grants, 2094
Roy and Christine Sturgis Charitable Tr Grts, 2115
Ruth Anderson Foundation Grants, 2122
Ruth and Vernon Taylor Foundation Grants, 2124
Samuel S. Johnson Foundation Grants, 2146
Sandy Hill Foundation Grants, 2157
Santa Fe Community Foundation Seasonal Grants-
    Fall Cycle, 2159
Sarkeys Foundation Grants, 2163
Schlessman Family Foundation Grants, 2167
Seattle Foundation Basic Needs Grants, 2175
Sensient Technologies Foundation Grants, 2180
Serco Foundation Grants, 2181
Shell Deer Park Grants, 2186
Sidney Stern Memorial Trust Grants, 2197
Siebert Lutheran Foundation Grants, 2198
Sioux Falls Area Community Foundation Community
    Fund Grants, 2203
Sioux Falls Area Community Foundation Spot
    Grants, 2204
Sobrato Family Foundation Grants, 2211
Sobrato Family Fdn Meeting Space Grants, 2212
Sobrato Family Foundation Office Space Grants, 2213
Southern Minnesota Initiative Foundation
    AmeriCorps Leap Grants, 2219
Sunoco Foundation Grants, 2256
SunTrust Bank Trusteed Foundations Greene-Sawtell
    Grants, 2257
SunTrust Bank Trusteed Foundations Nell Warren
    Elkin and William Simpson Elkin Grants, 2258
Sylvia Adams Charitable Trust Grants, 2262
Target Corporation Community Engagement Fund
    Grants, 2270
Tauck Family Foundation Grants, 2274
Tellabs Foundation Grants, 2280
Textron Corporate Contributions Grants, 2286
Thomas J. Atkins Memorial Trust Fund Grants, 2290
Thomas J. Long Foundation Community Grants, 2291
Thomas W. Briggs Foundation Grants, 2294
TJX Foundation Grants, 2303
Tull Charitable Foundation Grants, 2324
U.S. Cellular Corporation Grants, 2331
Union Bank, N.A. Foundation Grants, 2334
Union Pacific Fdn Community & Civic Grants, 2337
Union Pacific Foundation Health and Human
    Services Grants, 2338
United Technologies Corporation Grants, 2347
Victoria S. and Bradley L. Geist Foundation Grants
    Supporting Foster Care and Their Caregivers, 2382

Victoria S. and Bradley L. Geist Foundation Grants
    Supporting Transitioning Foster Youth, 2383
W.H. and Mary Ellen Cobb Chartbl Trust Grts, 2397
Washington County Community Fdn Grants, 2416
Wayne County Foundation Grants, 2419
Whiting Foundation Grants, 2440
WHO Foundation General Grants, 2443
William G. and Helen C. Hoffman Foundation
    Grants, 2466
William G. Gilmore Foundation Grants, 2467
William J. and Tina Rosenberg Fdn Grants, 2470
Williams Comps Homegrown Giving Grants, 2474
Wilton and Effie Hebert Foundation Grants, 2476
Wood-Claeyssens Foundation Grants, 2486
Wyomissing Foundation Community Grants, 2504
Z. Smith Reynolds Foundation Small Grants, 2523

Social Services Delivery
Aaron Foundation Grants, 42
Abbott Fund Community Engagement Grants, 46
ACF Social and Economic Development Strategies
    Grants, 93
Adobe Foundation Action Grants, 126
Albert E. and Birdie W. Einstein Fund Grants, 220
Alliant Energy Foundation Community Giving for
    Good Sponsorship Grants, 240
Ameren Corporation Community Grants, 251
American Savings Foundation Program Grants, 261
American Schlafhorst Foundation Grants, 262
Amica Insurance Company Community Grants, 267
Anheuser-Busch Foundation Grants, 273
Blackford County Community Fdn Grants, 434
Blue Grass Community Foundation Clark County
    Fund Grants, 444
Blue Grass Community Foundation Fayette County
    Fund Grants, 446
Blue Grass Community Foundation Franklin County
    Fund Grants, 447
Blue Grass Community Foundation Harrison County
    Fund Grants, 448
Blue Grass Community Foundation Madison County
    Fund Grants, 450
Blue Grass Community Foundation Magoffin County
    Fund Grants, 451
Blue Grass Community Foundation Morgan County
    Fund Grants, 452
Blue Grass Community Foundation Rowan County
    Fund Grants, 453
Blue Grass Community Foundation Woodford
    County Fund Grants, 454
Catherine Holmes Wilkins Foundation Charitable
    Grants, 520
Central Pacific Bank Foundation Grants, 530
Charles H. Hall Foundation, 565
Charles Lafitte Foundation Grants, 567
Clinton County Community Foundation Grants, 638
CNCS AmeriCorps NCCC Project Grants, 642
Community Foundation of Louisville Anna Marble
    Memorial Fund for Princeton Grants, 717
Community Foundation of Louisville Human
    Services Grants, 726
Community Foundation of St. Joseph County Special
    Project Challenge Grants, 738
Crystelle Waggoner Charitable Trust Grants, 768
Cudd Foundation Grants, 769
David Robinson Foundation Grants, 791
Deaconess Community Foundation Grants, 803
Earl and Maxine Claussen Trust Grants, 878
Edna Wardlaw Charitable Trust Grants, 886
Effie Kuhlman Charitable Trust Grants, 896
Evan Frankel Foundation Grants, 938
First Nations Development Institute Native Youth
    and Culture Fund Grants, 974
Francis L. Abreu Charitable Trust Grants, 1008
Frankel Brothers Foundation Grants, 1009
Goldseker Foundation Non-Profit Management
    Assistance Grants, 1095
Graham Foundation Grants, 1101
Green Foundation Human Services Grants, 1116
Grifols Community Outreach Grants, 1122

Hall-Perrine Foundation Grants, 1152
Hampton Roads Community Foundation Nonprofit
    Facilities Improvement Grants, 1159
Harrison County Community Fdn Grants, 1178
Harrison County Community Foundation Signature
    Grants, 1179
Harry and Jeanette Weinberg Fdn Grants, 1182
Hasbro Children's Fund Grants, 1189
Hawai'i Community Foundation Victoria S. and
    Bradley L. Geist Foundation: Capacity Building
    Grants, 1206
Hawai'i Community Foundation Victoria S. and
    Bradley L. Geist Foundation: Supporting
    Transitioning Foster Youth Grants, 1209
Hearst Foundations Social Service Grants, 1224
Henry L. Guenther Foundation Grants, 1242
Hillsdale County Community Foundation General
    Grants, 1250
Iddings Foundation Small Project Grants, 1286
James M. Collins Foundation Grants, 1344
Jane Bradley Pettit Foundation Community and
    Social Development Grants, 1347
Jennings County Community Foundation Women's
    Giving Circle Grant, 1361
Kettering Family Foundation Grants, 1430
Laclede Gas Charitable Trust Grants, 1457
Laura Moore Cunningham Foundation Grants, 1474
Louie M. and Betty M. Phillips Fdn Grants, 1509
Ludwick Family Foundation Grants, 1516
Mabel Louise Riley Foundation Family Strengthening
    Small Grants, 1528
Marie C. and Joseph C. Wilson Foundation Rochester
    Small Grants, 1559
Marion I. and Henry J. Knott Foundation
    Discretionary Grants, 1571
Marion I. and Henry J. Knott Foundation Standard
    Grants, 1572
Mary K. Chapman Foundation Grants, 1590
McCune Charitable Foundation Grants, 1617
MeadWestvaco Foundation Sustainable Communities
    Grants, 1627
Meriden Foundation Grants, 1638
Monsanto United States Grants, 1684
Ohio Valley Foundation Grants, 1814
Parke County Community Foundation Grants, 1868
PNC Foundation Community Services Grants, 1984
Portland Fdn - Women's Giving Circle Grant, 2006
Powell Foundation Grants, 2013
Priddy Foundation Program Grants, 2023
Rasmuson Foundation Tier One Grants, 2055
Rasmuson Foundation Tier Two Grants, 2056
Ripley County Community Foundation Small Project
    Grants, 2078
Robert R. Meyer Foundation Grants, 2094
Sandy Hill Foundation Grants, 2157
San Juan Island Community Foundation Grants, 2158
Santa Fe Community Foundation Seasonal Grants-
    Fall Cycle, 2159
Sarkeys Foundation Grants, 2163
Sartain Lanier Family Foundation Grants, 2164
Schramm Foundation Grants, 2168
Seattle Foundation Basic Needs Grants, 2175
Shell Oil Company Foundation Community
    Development Grants, 2188
Sierra Health Foundation Responsive Grants, 2199
Sony Corporation of America Grants, 2216
Southern Minnesota Initiative Foundation
    AmeriCorps Leap Grants, 2219
Stella and Charles Guttman Foundation Grants, 2241
Summit Foundation Grants, 2255
Thomas J. Atkins Memorial Trust Fund Grants, 2290
Thomas J. Long Foundation Community Grants, 2291
U.S. Bank Foundation Grants, 2330
U.S. Cellular Corporation Grants, 2331
Virginia W. Kettering Foundation Grants, 2388
Volkswagen Group of America Corporate
    Contributions Grants, 2389
White County Community Foundation - Women
    Giving Together Grants, 2438
Whiting Foundation Grants, 2440

Whitney Foundation Grants, 2441
WHO Foundation General Grants, 2443
Wild Rivers Community Foundation Holiday
Partnership Grants, 2448
William J. and Dorothy K. O'Neill Foundation
Responsive Grants, 2468
Wilton and Effie Hebert Foundation Grants, 2476

Social Stratification/Mobility
ALFJ International Fund Grants, 231
FCYO Youth Organizing Grants, 954
PDF Fiscal Sponsorship Grant, 1921

Social Work
Elizabeth Morse Genius Charitable Trust Grants, 901
GNOF IMPACT Grants for Youth Dev, 1084
University of Chicago Chapin Hall Doris Duke
Fellowships, 2348

Sociology
University of Chicago Chapin Hall Doris Duke
Fellowships, 2348

Software
TechKnowledgey Community Impact Grants, 2278

Soil Sciences, Soil Genesis
Land O'Lakes Foundation Mid-Atlantic Grants, 1467

Solid Waste Disposal
Fremont Area Community Foundation Community
Grants, 1020

Special Education
Air Products Foundation Grants, 148
Blackford County Community Fdn Grants, 434
Carroll County Community Foundation Grants, 513
CEC Yes I Can! Awards, 529
Clayton F. and Ruth L. Hawkridge Foundation
Grants, 630
Clinton County Community Foundation Grants, 638
Dorr Foundation Grants, 846
Hasbro Children's Fund Grants, 1189
Henry County Community Foundation Grants, 1239
Henry E. Niles Foundation Grants, 1240
Herbert A. and Adrian W. Woods Foundation
Grants, 1243
HLTA Visitor Industry Charity Walk Grant, 1254
Marjorie Moore Charitable Foundation Grants, 1574
OSF Education Program Grants in Kyrgyzstan, 1842
P. Buckley Moss Foundation for Children's Education
Teacher Grants, 1855
Parke County Community Foundation Grants, 1868
Peter and Elizabeth C. Tower Foundation Intellectual
Disabilities Grants, 1944
Roy and Christine Sturgis Charitable Tr Grts, 2115
Scott County Community Foundation Grants, 2170
Skaggs Foundation Grants, 2207
Southern California Edison Education Grants, 2218
Special Olympics Youth Fan Grants, 2229
Thomas Sill Foundation Grants, 2292

Special Populations
Active Living Research Grants, 109
Alfred E. Chase Charitable Foundation Grants, 233
Bill and Melinda Gates Foundation Policy and
Advocacy Grants, 427
Bodenwein Public Benevolent Foundation Grants, 461
Carl R. Hendrickson Family Foundation Grants, 509
Charles H. Hall Foundation, 565
Christine and Katharina Pauly Charitable Trust
Grants, 601
Clara Blackford Smith and W. Aubrey Smith
Charitable Foundation Grants, 621
Curtis Foundation Grants, 771
Florence Hunt Maxwell Foundation Grants, 979
Helen Irwin Littauer Educational Trust Grants, 1231
Henrietta Lange Burk Fund Grants, 1235
Herbert A. and Adrian W. Woods Foundation
Grants, 1243

John Clarke Trust Grants, 1369
Kosasa Foundation Grants, 1450
Michelle O'Neill Foundation Grants, 1661
Ms. Foundation for Women Building Democracy
Grants, 1706
NYSCA Special Arts Services: Instruction and
Training Grants, 1794
PAS Zildjian Family Opportunity Fund Grants, 1878
PCA Pennsylvania Partners in the Arts Program
Stream Grants, 1914
PCA Pennsylvania Partners in the Arts Project
Stream Grants, 1915
Philip Boyle Foundation Grants, 1961
Piper Trust Children Grants, 1976
Roy and Christine Sturgis Charitable Tr Grts, 2115
TAC Arts Access Grant, 2265
Vigneron Memorial Fund Grants, 2384

Specialized Museums
Bradley C. Higgins Foundation Grants, 467
Donald W. Reynolds Foundation Children's
Discovery Initiative Grants, 841
George Graham and Elizabeth Galloway Smith
Foundation Grants, 1047
George J. and Effie L. Seay Foundation Grants, 1052
Hattie Mae Lesley Foundation Grants, 1195
Hubbard Family Foundation Grants, 1270
Jerry L. and Barbara J. Burris Fdn Grants, 1362
S. Spencer Scott Fund Grants, 2129
Seattle Foundation C. Keith Birkenfeld Memorial
Trust Grants, 2177
Union Pacific Fdn Community & Civic Grants, 2337

Speech
Hawaii Community Foundation Oscar and Rosetta
Fish Fund Grants, 1214
Reinberger Foundation Grants, 2066

Speech Pathology
Community Memorial Foundation Responsive
Grants, 743
Edward W. and Stella C. Van Houten Memorial Fund
Grants, 892
German Protestant Orphan Asylum Foundation
Grants, 1066
Hawaii Community Foundation Oscar and Rosetta
Fish Fund Grants, 1214
Mabel H. Flory Charitable Trust Grants, 1527

Speech/Communication Education
Hawaii Community Foundation Oscar and Rosetta
Fish Fund Grants, 1214
Mabel H. Flory Charitable Trust Grants, 1527

Spirituality
Parker Foundation (Virginia) Grants to Support
Christian Evangelism, 1870

Sports
A.C. and Penney Hubbard Foundation Grants, 19
A.L. Spencer Foundation Grants, 21
Abby's Legendary Pizza Foundation Grants, 49
Adam Don Foundation Grants, 112
Adidas Corporation General Grants, 125
Adray Foundation, 130
Alaska Community Foundation Jack and Nona Renn
Anchorage Football Fund, 204
Amica Insurance Company Sponsorships, 268
Anthony Munoz Foundation Straight A Student
Campaign Grants, 280
Arthur M. Blank Family Foundation Atlanta United
Foundation Grants, 308
Autism Speaks Norma and Malcolm Baker Recreation
Grants, 335
Baltimore Community Foundation Mitzvah Fund for
Good Deeds Grants, 349
Baltimore Ravens Corporate Giving, 350
Baltimore Ravens Fdn Youth Football Grants, 353
Bank of America Corporation Sponsorships, 359

Barrasso, Usdin, Kupperman, Freeman, and Sarver
Corporate Grants, 362
Batters Up USA Equipment Grants, 366
Belvedere Community Foundation Grants, 399
Belvedere Cove Foundation Grants, 400
Belvedere Cove Foundation Scholarships, 401
Ben Cohen StandUp Foundation Grants, 403
Bikes Belong Foundation REI Grants, 423
Cal Ripken Sr. Foundation Grants, 497
CFFVR Robert and Patricia Endries Family
Foundation Grants, 547
Charlotte and Joseph Gardner Fdn Grants, 570
Charlotte Martin Foundation Youth Grants, 571
Chatham Athletic Foundation Grants, 574
Cleveland Browns Foundation Grants, 633
Collins C. Diboll Private Foundation Grants, 657
Community Foundation for Greater Buffalo Ralph C.
Wilson, Jr. Legacy Fund Grants, 674
Community Foundation for Greater Buffalo Ralph
C. Wilson, Jr. Youth Sports COVID-19 Fund
Grants, 675
Community Foundation of Louisville CHAMP Fund
Grants, 720
CONSOL Youth Program Grants, 747
David and Betty Sacks Foundation Grants, 788
Daviess County Community Foundation Recreation
Grants, 793
Daviess County Community Foundation Youth
Development Grants, 794
Dearborn Community Foundation City of Aurora
Grants, 808
Dearborn Community Foundation City of
Lawrenceburg Youth Grants, 810
Easton Foundations Archery Facility Grants, 883
Easton Sports Development Foundation National
Archery in the Schools Grants, 884
Elizabeth Morse Genius Charitable Trust Grants, 901
El Pomar Foundation Anna Keesling Ackerman Fund
Grants, 907
El Pomar Foundation Grants, 908
Finish Line Youth Foundation Founder's Grants, 960
Finish Line Youth Foundation Grants, 961
Finish Line Youth Foundation Legacy Grants, 962
First Hawaiian Bank Foundation Corporate Giving
Grants, 967
Foundation of Herkimer and Oneida Counties Youth
Sports, Wellness and Recreation Mini-Grants, 994
Foundations of East Chicago Education Grants, 995
Four County Community Foundation General
Grants, 1000
Gardner W. and Joan G. Heidrick, Jr. Foundation
Grants, 1036
George Kress Foundation Grants, 1053
Gibson County Community Foundation Recreation
Grants, 1069
Gibson County Community Foundation Youth
Development Grants, 1070
GNOF IMPACT Grants for Youth Dev, 1084
GTRCF Traverse City Track Club Endowment
Grants, 1132
Hampton Roads Community Foundation Youth
Baseball and Softball Program Grants, 1160
Harmony Foundation for Children Grants, 1168
Harry and Helen Sands Charitable Trust Grants, 1181
Helen Bader Foundation Grants, 1227
Hubbard Broadcasting Foundation Grants, 1269
ICCF Youth Advisory Council Grants, 1282
Island Insurance Foundation Grants, 1316
John and Marcia Goldman Foundation Youth
Development Grants, 1368
John M. Weaver Foundation Grants, 1376
Kalamazoo Community Foundation Youth
Development Grants, 1412
Kevin J Major Youth Sports Scholarships, 1431
Knox County Community Foundation Recreation
Grants, 1442
Knox County Community Foundation Youth
Development Grants, 1443
Laura L. Adams Foundation Grants, 1473
Laurie H. Wollmuth Charitable Trust Grants, 1476

Lisa and Douglas Goldman Fund Grants, 1496
LISC Capacity Building Grants, 1498
Locations Foundation Legacy Grants, 1504
Marion I. and Henry J. Knott Foundation Standard
    Grants, 1572
McCombs Foundation Grants, 1615
MLB Tomorrow Fund Grants, 1679
Montgomery County Community Foundation Youth
    Services Grants, 1691
Motiv8 Foundation Grants, 1702
NCMCF Youth Advisory Council Grants, 1727
NRA Foundation Grants, 1774
OtterCares Champion Fund Grants, 1848
Outrigger Duke Kahanamoku Foundation Athletic
    Event Grants, 1852
Outrigger Duke Kahanamoku Foundation Athletic
    Team Grants, 1853
Paul and Edith Babson Foundation Grants, 1881
Perkin Fund Grants, 1937
Perry County Community Foundation Recreation
    Grants, 1942
Perry County Community Foundation Youth
    Development Grants, 1943
Phoenix Coyotes Charities Grants, 1963
Pike County Community Foundation Recreation
    Grants, 1970
Pike County Community Foundation Youth
    Development Grants, 1971
Pohlad Family Fdn Small Capital Grants, 1991
Polk County Community Foundation Kirby Harmon
    Field Fund Grants, 1997
Posey County Community Foundation Recreation
    Grants, 2009
Posey County Community Foundation Youth
    Development Grants, 2010
Presidio Fencing Club Youth Fencers Assistance
    Scholarships, 2019
PSEG Corporate Contributions Grants, 2030
Robert R. Meyer Foundation Grants, 2094
Roney-Fitzpatrick Foundation Grants, 2102
SACF Youth Advisory Council Grants, 2131
Sadler Family Foundation Grants, 2132
Saint Louis Rams Foundation Community
    Donations, 2139
SanDisk Corp Community Sharing Grants, 2155
Scheumann Foundation Grants, 2166
Sidgmore Family Foundation Grants, 2195
Special Olympics Eunice Kennedy Shriver (EKS)
    Fellowships, 2227
Spencer County Community Foundation Recreation
    Grants, 2231
Spencer County Community Foundation Youth
    Development Grants, 2233
Stein Family Charitable Trust Grants, 2240
Summit Foundation Grants, 2255
Susan A. and Donald P. Babson Charitable
    Foundation Grants, 2259
Telluride Foundation Community Grants, 2281
TSYSF Individual Scholarships, 2322
TSYSF Team Grants, 2323
UPS Corporate Giving Grants, 2349
Vanderburgh Community Foundation Recreation
    Grants, 2374
Vanderburgh Community Foundation Youth
    Development Grants, 2375
Walter J. and Betty C. Zable Fdn Grants, 2406
Warrick County Community Foundation Recreation
    Grants, 2410
Warrick County Community Foundation Youth
    Development Grants, 2412
William J. and Gertrude R. Casper Foundation
    Grants, 2469
Wold Foundation Grants, 2482
Women's Fund of Hawaii Grants, 2485
WSF GoGirlGo! New York Grants, 2494
WSF Rusty Kanokogi Fund for the Advancement of
    U.S. Judo Grants, 2495
WSF Sports 4 Life Grants, 2496
WSF Sports 4 Life Regional Grants, 2497
WSF Travel and Training Fund Grants, 2498

Sports Equipment
1st Touch Foundation Grants, 2
Abby's Legendary Pizza Foundation Grants, 49
Adidas Corporation General Grants, 125
Adray Foundation, 130
Alaska Community Foundation Jack and Nona Renn
    Anchorage Football Fund, 204
American Savings Fdn After School Grants, 259
Armstrong McDonald Foundation Children and
    Youth Grants, 300
Arthur M. Blank Family Foundation Atlanta Falcons
    Youth Foundation Grants, 307
Arthur M. Blank Family Foundation Atlanta United
    Foundation Grants, 308
Baltimore Community Foundation Mitzvah Fund for
    Good Deeds Grants, 349
Baltimore Ravens Corporate Giving, 350
Baltimore Ravens Fdn Youth Football Grants, 353
Bank of America Corporation Sponsorships, 359
Batters Up USA Equipment Grants, 366
Chassé Youth Leaders Fund Grants, 573
Chatham Athletic Foundation Grants, 574
Community Foundation for Greater Buffalo Ralph C.
    Wilson, Jr. Legacy Fund Grants, 674
Community Foundation for Greater Buffalo Ralph
    C. Wilson, Jr. Youth Sports COVID-19 Fund
    Grants, 675
CONSOL Youth Program Grants, 747
Covenant to Care for Children Enrichment Fund
    Grants, 758
David and Betty Sacks Foundation Grants, 788
Easton Foundations Archery Facility Grants, 883
Easton Sports Development Foundation National
    Archery in the Schools Grants, 884
El Pomar Foundation Grants, 908
Finish Line Youth Foundation Founder's Grants, 960
Finish Line Youth Foundation Legacy Grants, 962
First Hawaiian Bank Foundation Corporate Giving
    Grants, 967
Foundation of Herkimer and Oneida Counties Youth
    Sports, Wellness and Recreation Mini-Grants, 994
Gibson County Community Foundation Recreation
    Grants, 1069
Gibson County Community Foundation Youth
    Development Grants, 1070
Hampton Roads Community Foundation Youth
    Baseball and Softball Program Grants, 1160
Harmony Foundation for Children Grants, 1168
Hubbard Broadcasting Foundation Grants, 1269
ICCF Youth Advisory Council Grants, 1282
Island Insurance Foundation Grants, 1316
John and Marcia Goldman Foundation Youth
    Development Grants, 1368
Kalamazoo Community Foundation Youth
    Development Grants, 1412
Kevin J Major Youth Sports Scholarships, 1431
Knox County Community Foundation Recreation
    Grants, 1442
Knox County Community Foundation Youth
    Development Grants, 1443
Montgomery County Community Foundation Youth
    Services Grants, 1691
Motiv8 Foundation Grants, 1702
OtterCares Champion Fund Grants, 1848
Perkin Fund Grants, 1937
Perry County Community Foundation Recreation
    Grants, 1942
Perry County Community Foundation Youth
    Development Grants, 1943
Pike County Community Foundation Recreation
    Grants, 1970
Pike County Community Foundation Youth
    Development Grants, 1971
Polk County Community Foundation Kirby Harmon
    Field Fund Grants, 1997
Posey County Community Foundation Recreation
    Grants, 2009
Posey County Community Foundation Youth
    Development Grants, 2010
SACF Youth Advisory Council Grants, 2131

Scheumann Foundation Grants, 2166
Spencer County Community Foundation Recreation
    Grants, 2231
Spencer County Community Foundation Youth
    Development Grants, 2233
Trinity Trust Summer Youth Mini Grants, 2321
TSYSF Individual Scholarships, 2322
TSYSF Team Grants, 2323
Vanderburgh Community Foundation Recreation
    Grants, 2374
Vanderburgh Community Foundation Youth
    Development Grants, 2375
Van Kampen Boyer Molinari Charitable Foundation
    Grants, 2377
Walter J. and Betty C. Zable Fdn Grants, 2406
Warrick County Community Foundation Recreation
    Grants, 2410
Warrick County Community Foundation Youth
    Development Grants, 2412
Wild Rivers Community Foundation Summer Youth
    Mini Grants, 2449
William J. and Gertrude R. Casper Foundation
    Grants, 2469
Wold Foundation Grants, 2482
WSF Sports 4 Life Grants, 2496
WSF Sports 4 Life Regional Grants, 2497

Sports, Amateur
A.C. and Penney Hubbard Foundation Grants, 19
A.L. Spencer Foundation Grants, 21
Abby's Legendary Pizza Foundation Grants, 49
Adidas Corporation General Grants, 125
Adray Foundation, 130
American Savings Fdn After School Grants, 259
Amica Insurance Company Sponsorships, 268
Arthur M. Blank Family Foundation Atlanta United
    Foundation Grants, 308
Bank of America Corporation Sponsorships, 359
Batters Up USA Equipment Grants, 366
Belvedere Community Foundation Grants, 399
Ben Cohen StandUp Foundation Grants, 403
Charlotte and Joseph Gardner Fdn Grants, 570
Chatham Athletic Foundation Grants, 574
Community Foundation for Greater Buffalo Ralph C.
    Wilson, Jr. Legacy Fund Grants, 674
Community Foundation for Greater Buffalo Ralph
    C. Wilson, Jr. Youth Sports COVID-19 Fund
    Grants, 675
Community Foundation of Louisville CHAMP Fund
    Grants, 720
Daniels Fund Amateur Sports Grants, 779
Easton Foundations Archery Facility Grants, 883
First Hawaiian Bank Foundation Corporate Giving
    Grants, 967
Foundation of Herkimer and Oneida Counties Youth
    Sports, Wellness and Recreation Mini-Grants, 994
Gibson County Community Foundation Recreation
    Grants, 1069
Gibson County Community Foundation Youth
    Development Grants, 1070
GTRCF Traverse City Track Club Endowment
    Grants, 1132
Harmony Foundation for Children Grants, 1168
Island Insurance Foundation Grants, 1316
John M. Weaver Foundation Grants, 1376
Kevin J Major Youth Sports Scholarships, 1431
Knox County Community Foundation Recreation
    Grants, 1442
Knox County Community Foundation Youth
    Development Grants, 1443
Laura L. Adams Foundation Grants, 1473
Laurie H. Wollmuth Charitable Trust Grants, 1476
Lil and Julie Rosenberg Foundation Grants, 1491
LISC Capacity Building Grants, 1498
Locations Foundation Legacy Grants, 1504
Montgomery County Community Foundation Youth
    Services Grants, 1691
Motiv8 Foundation Grants, 1702
OtterCares Champion Fund Grants, 1848
Perkin Fund Grants, 1937

Perry County Community Foundation Recreation Grants, 1942
Perry County Community Foundation Youth Development Grants, 1943
Pike County Community Foundation Recreation Grants, 1970
Pike County Community Foundation Youth Development Grants, 1971
Polk County Community Foundation Kirby Harmon Field Fund Grants, 1997
Posey County Community Foundation Recreation Grants, 2009
Posey County Community Foundation Youth Development Grants, 2010
Presidio Fencing Club Youth Fencers Assistance Scholarships, 2019
Spencer County Community Foundation Recreation Grants, 2231
Spencer County Community Foundation Youth Development Grants, 2233
Telluride Foundation Community Grants, 2281
TSYSF Individual Scholarships, 2322
TSYSF Team Grants, 2323
Vanderburgh Community Recreation Grants, 2374
Vanderburgh Community Foundation Youth Development Grants, 2375
Walter J. and Betty C. Zable Fdn Grants, 2406
Warrick County Community Foundation Recreation Grants, 2410
Warrick County Community Foundation Youth Development Grants, 2412
William J. and Gertrude R. Casper Foundation Grants, 2469
WSF Rusty Kanokogi Fund for the Advancement of U.S. Judo Grants, 2495
WSF Sports 4 Life Grants, 2496
WSF Sports 4 Life Regional Grants, 2497

Stem Cell Therapy
Pediatric Cancer Research Foundation Grants, 1927

Stem Cell Transplantation
Pediatric Cancer Research Foundation Grants, 1927

Storytelling
ACF Head Start and/or Early Head Start Grantee - Clay, Randolph, and Talladega Counties, Alabama, 82
ACF Head Start and/or Early Head Start Grantee - St. Landry Parish, Louisiana, 83
NHSCA Artist Residence Grants, 1756

Strategic Planning
CNCS AmeriCorps State and National Grants, 643
GNOF Organizational Effectiveness Grants and Workshops, 1090
Goldseker Foundation Non-Profit Management Assistance Grants, 1095
Meyer Fdn Management Assistance Grants, 1651
Middlesex Savings Charitable Foundation Capacity Building Grants, 1669
PCA-PCD Organizational Short-Term Professional Development and Consulting Grants, 1882
PCA Management/Techl Assistance Grants, 1913
Peter and Elizabeth C. Tower Foundation Technology Initiative Grants, 1949
Peter and Elizabeth C. Tower Foundation Technology Planning Grants, 1950
San Antonio Area Foundation Strengthening Nonprofits Grants, 2151
TAC Arts Access Grant, 2265

Stress
Peter and Elizabeth C. Tower Foundation Mental Health Grants, 1946
Premera Blue Cross Grants, 2018

Stroke
Premera Blue Cross Grants, 2018

Substance Abuse
ACF Community-Based Child Abuse Prevention (CBCAP) Grants, 76
ACF Community-Based Child Abuse Prevention (CBCAP) Tribal and Migrant DiscretionaryGrants, 77
Akron Community Foundation Health and Human Services Grants, 152
Alpha Natural Resources Corporate Giving, 246
Altria Group Positive Youth Dev Grants, 247
Alvah H. and Wyline P. Chapman Foundation Grants, 248
Austin S. Nelson Foundation Grants, 333
Children's Trust Fund of Oregon Fdn Grants, 585
Children's Trust Fund of Oregon Foundation Small Grants, 586
Cone Health Foundation Grants, 745
Cralle Foundation Grants, 760
Gamble Foundation Grants, 1032
George H.C. Ensworth Memorial Fund Grants, 1049
GTRCF Grand Traverse Families in Action for Youth Endowment Grants, 1129
Hearst Foundations Social Service Grants, 1224
Initiaive Fdn Inside-Out Connections Grants, 1303
Joseph H. and Florence A. Roblee Foundation Children and Youth Grants, 1385
May and Stanley Smith Charitable Trust Grants, 1613
MetroWest Health Foundation Grants to Reduce the Incidence of High Risk Behaviors Among Adolescents, 1646
New Jersey Office of Faith Based Initiatives Services to At Risk Youth Grants, 1752
Pacers Foundation Be Drug-Free Grants, 1856
Paso del Norte Health Foundation Grants, 1874
Patrick and Aimee Butler Family Foundation Community Human Services Grants, 1880
Peter and Elizabeth C. Tower Foundation Small Grants, 1947
Peter and Elizabeth C. Tower Foundation Substance Use Disorders Grants, 1948
Peter and Elizabeth C. Tower Foundation Technology Initiative Grants, 1949
Peter and Elizabeth C. Tower Foundation Technology Planning Grants, 1950
Piedmont Natural Gas Foundation Health and Human Services Grants, 1968
Reinberger Foundation Grants, 2066
Riedman Foundation Grants, 2076
Robbins-de Beaumont Foundation Grants, 2080
Sierra Health Foundation Responsive Grants, 2199
Sioux Falls Area Community Foundation Community Fund Grants, 2203
Sioux Falls Area Community Foundation Spot Grants, 2204
T.L.L. Temple Foundation Grants, 2264
Union Bank, N.A. Foundation Grants, 2334
Wilton and Effie Hebert Foundation Grants, 2476
Women's Fund of Hawaii Grants, 2485

Sudden Infant Death Syndrome
CJ Fdn for SIDS Program Services Grants, 619

Suicide
Alaska Community Foundation GCI Suicide Prevention Grant, 203

Suicide Prevention
ACF Social and Economic Development Strategies Grants, 93
Alaska Community Foundation GCI Suicide Prevention Grant, 203
Arthur M. Blank Family Foundation AMB West Community Fund Grants, 304
Gulf Coast Foundation of Community Operating Grants, 1134
Gulf Coast Foundation of Community Program Grants, 1135
Nick Traina Foundation Grants, 1759
RCF General Community Grants, 2062

Summer Camp
A.L. Spencer Foundation Grants, 21
AKF Grants for Children, 149
Autism Speaks Norma and Malcolm Baker Recreation Grants, 335
Back Home Again Foundation Grants, 344
Baltimore Community Foundation Children's Fresh Air Society Fund Grants, 348
CDC Disease Detective Camp, 525
Covenant to Care for Children Enrichment Fund Grants, 758
David and Barbara B. Hirschhorn Foundation Summer Camping Grants, 787
Dayton Foundation Dayton Youth Enrichment Fund Grant, 795
Florence Hunt Maxwell Foundation Grants, 979
Frederick W. Marzahl Memorial Fund Grants, 1018
George W.P. Magee Trust Grants, 1056
Gerber Fdn West Michigan Youth Grants, 1065
German Protestant Orphan Asylum Foundation Grants, 1066
Gil and Dody Weaver Foundation Grants, 1071
Gray Family Fdn Outdoor School Grants, 1107
HAF Mada Huggins Caldwell Fund Grants, 1147
Hasbro Corporation Gift of Play Summer Camp Support, 1193
Lily Palmer Fry Memorial Trust Grants, 1493
Marin Community Foundation Stinson Bolinas Community Grants, 1568
National Wildlife Federation Craig Tufts Educational Scholarship, 1724
OceanFirst Foundation Summer Camp Grants, 1804
Oregon Community Foundation K-12 Student Success: Out-of-School Grants, 1836
RCF Summertime Kids Grants, 2064
Robert and Helen Harmony Fund for Needy Children Grants, 2085
Robert Lee Adams Foundation Grants, 2091
Wild Rivers Community Foundation Summer Youth Mini Grants, 2449
Zane's Foundation Grants, 2524

Supportive Housing Programs
Adelaide Breed Bayrd Foundation Grants, 123
Aid for Starving Children Homes and Education Grants, 146
Aunt Kate Foundation Grants, 331
Bank of America Charitable Foundation Basic Needs Grants, 354
Bank of America Charitable Foundation Community Development Grants, 355
Bill and Melinda Gates Foundation Emergency Response Grants, 426
Blue Cross Blue Shield of Minnesota Fdn - Healthy Children: Growing Up Healthy Grants, 442
Citizens Savings Foundation Grants, 617
Cleveland Foundation Higley Fund Grants, 634
Dominion Foundation Grants, 839
First Hawaiian Bank Foundation Corporate Giving Grants, 967
Fitzpatrick, Cella, Harper & Scinto Pro Bono Services, 976
Fdns of East Chicago Family Support Grants, 996
Hearst Foundations Social Service Grants, 1224
Herman P. and Sophia Taubman Fdn Grants, 1247
Koch Family Foundation (Annapolis) Grants, 1444
Linden Foundation Grants, 1494
LISC Affordable Housing Grants, 1497
LISC Capacity Building Grants, 1498
Madison Community Foundation Grants, 1535
Marin Community Foundation Affordable Housing Grants, 1561
May and Stanley Smith Charitable Trust Grants, 1613
McCarthy Family Fdn Charity Fund Grants, 1614
Mericos Foundation Grants, 1637
Mertz Gilmore Foundation NYC Communities Grants, 1641
Meyer Memorial Trust Responsive Grants, 1653
MGM Resorts Foundation Community Grants, 1655

Nathaniel and Elizabeth P. Stevens Foundation
    Grants, 1719
Northland Foundation Grants, 1771
Parker Foundation (California) Grants, 1869
Perkins-Ponder Foundation Grants, 1938
Perpetual Benevolent Fund, 1940
Piedmont Natural Gas Foundation Health and
    Human Services Grants, 1968
Piper Trust Reglious Organizations Grants, 1979
Pittsburgh Fdn Affordable Housing Grants, 1980
PNC Foundation Affordable Housing Grants, 1983
Polk County Community Foundation Seasonal
    Assistance and Cheer Grants for Charitable
    Programs, 2000
Priddy Foundation Program Grants, 2023
Reinberger Foundation Grants, 2066
Robert R. McCormick Tribune Foundation
    Community Grants, 2093
Sarah G. McCarthy Memorial Foundation, 2162
U.S. Bank Foundation Grants, 2330
Union Bank, N.A. Corporate Sponsorships and
    Donations, 2333
Union Bank, N.A. Foundation Grants, 2334
Whitehorse Foundation Grants, 2439
Women's Fund of Hawaii Grants, 2485

Surfing
Outrigger Duke Kahanamoku Foundation Athletic
    Event Grants, 1852
Outrigger Duke Kahanamoku Foundation Athletic
    Team Grants, 1853

Surgery
E.L. Wiegand Foundation Grants, 877
Foundation for Health Enhancement Grants, 990
HRAMF Charles H. Hood Foundation Child Health
    Research Awards, 1262

Surrogate Parenting
Brookdale Fdn Relatives as Parents Grants, 474
Joseph H. and Florence A. Roblee Foundation Family
    Grants, 1387

Sustainable Development
ATA Inclusive Learning Communities Grants, 323
Bill and Melinda Gates Foundation Agricultural
    Development Grants, 425
Boeing Company Contributions Grants, 462
Draper Richards Kaplan Foundation Grants, 864
GNOF Coastal 5 + 1 Grants, 1078
HAF Community Grants, 1141
Honor the Earth Grants, 1259
McCune Charitable Foundation Grants, 1617
McGraw-Hill Companies Community Grants, 1620
Michael Reese Health Trust Core Grants, 1658
Nellie Mae Education Foundation District-Level
    Change Grants, 1736
Oren Campbell McCleary Chartbl Trust Grants, 1837
PepsiCo Foundation Grants, 1935
Priddy Foundation Organizational Development
    Grants, 2022
Threshold Fdn Justice and Democracy Grants, 2298
United Technologies Corporation Grants, 2347

Swimming
Autism Speaks Norma and Malcolm Baker Recreation
    Grants, 335
Daniels Fund Amateur Sports Grants, 779
Outrigger Duke Kahanamoku Foundation Athletic
    Event Grants, 1852
Outrigger Duke Kahanamoku Foundation Athletic
    Team Grants, 1853

Teacher Attitudes
CEC Clarissa Hug Teacher of the Year Award, 527
Elizabeth Carse Foundation Grants, 899
Meyer Foundation Education Grants, 1649
NCSS Christa McA Reach for the Stars Awd, 1730

Teacher Certification
Bernard and Audre Rapoport Foundation Education
    Grants, 410
Morris Stulsaft Foundation Early Childhood
    Education Grants, 1696
Piper Trust Reglious Organizations Grants, 1979
R.D. and Joan Dale Hubbard Fdn Grants, 2044

Teacher Education
Abell-Hanger Foundation Grants, 52
Alabama Humanities Foundation Major Grants, 159
Allen Foundation Educational Nutrition Grants, 238
ATA Local Community Relations Grants, 324
Baxter International Corporate Giving Grants, 368
Bernard and Audre Rapoport Foundation Education
    Grants, 410
Calvin Johnson Jr. Foundation Mini Grants, 498
Carnegie Corporation of New York Grants, 511
Elizabeth Carse Foundation Grants, 899
Foundation for the Mid South Education Grants, 993
Hatton W. Sumners Foundation for the Study and
    Teaching of Self Government Grants, 1196
Joseph H. and Florence A. Roblee Foundation
    Education Grants, 1386
Kawabe Memorial Fund Grants, 1423
Lavina Parker Trust Grants, 1477
Lied Foundation Trust Grants, 1490
Meadows Foundation Grants, 1626
Micron Technology Fdn Community Grants, 1664
Morris Stulsaft Foundation Early Childhood
    Education Grants, 1696
NEA Student Program Communities Redefining
    Education Advocacy Through Empowerment
    (CREATE) Grants, 1733
NYSCA Arts Education: Community-based
    Learning Grants, 1780
NYSCA Arts Education: Local Capacity Building
    Grants (Regrants), 1783
NYSCA Arts Ed: Services to the Field Grants, 1784
Piedmont Natural Gas Foundation K-12 Science,
    Technology, Engineering and Math (STEM)
    Grant, 1969
Piper Trust Reglious Organizations Grants, 1979
Progress Energy Foundation Energy Education
    Grants, 2025
SAS Institute Community Relations Donations, 2165
Subaru of America Foundation Grants, 2253
Virginia Foundation for the Humanities Open
    Grants, 2387
Wallace Foundation Grants, 2402

Teacher Education, Inservice
Alabama Humanities Foundation Major Grants, 159
Baxter International Corporate Giving Grants, 368
Bernard and Audre Rapoport Foundation Education
    Grants, 410
Elizabeth Carse Foundation Grants, 899
Foundation for the Mid South Education Grants, 993
Mary A. Crocker Trust Grants, 1584
Meyer Foundation Education Grants, 1649
Micron Technology Fdn Community Grants, 1664
Morris Stulsaft Foundation Early Childhood
    Education Grants, 1696
PCA Arts in Education Residencies, 1885
Piedmont Natural Gas Foundation K-12 Science,
    Technology, Engineering and Math (STEM)
    Grant, 1969
Public Education Power Grants, 2032
Southern California Edison Education Grants, 2218
TAC Arts Education Mini Grants, 2267
Toyota USA Foundation Education Grants, 2318
West Virginia Commission on the Arts Long-Term
    Artist Residencies, 2431

Teacher Training
ALA Innovative Reading Grant, 171
Aldi Corporation Smart Kids Grants, 226
Baxter International Corporate Giving Grants, 368
Bernard and Audre Rapoport Foundation Education
    Grants, 410

Calvin Johnson Jr. Foundation Mini Grants, 498
Daniels Fund K-12 Education Reform Grants, 783
Elizabeth Carse Foundation Grants, 899
George J. and Effie L. Seay Foundation Grants, 1052
Grifols Community Outreach Grants, 1122
Hampton Roads Community Foundation Education
    Grants, 1157
Kawabe Memorial Fund Grants, 1423
Lavina Parker Trust Grants, 1477
Meyer Foundation Education Grants, 1649
Morris Stulsaft Foundation Early Childhood
    Education Grants, 1696
Nellie Mae Education Foundation District-Level
    Change Grants, 1736
NJSCA Artists in Education Residencies, 1763
OSF Education Program Grants in Kyrgyzstan, 1842
Piedmont Natural Gas Fdn Envirnmtl Stewardship
    and Energy Sustainability Grant, 1967
Piedmont Natural Gas Foundation K-12 Science,
    Technology, Engineering and Math (STEM)
    Grant, 1969
Piper Trust Reglious Organizations Grants, 1979
Progress Energy Foundation Energy Education
    Grants, 2025
Public Education Power Grants, 2032
Sidgmore Family Foundation Grants, 2195
TAC Arts Education Mini Grants, 2267
Virginia Foundation for the Humanities Open
    Grants, 2387
W.H. and Mary Ellen Cobb Chartbl Trust Grts, 2397

Technological Change
Best Buy Children's Foundation National Grants, 417
Best Buy Children's Foundation Twin Cities
    Minnesota Capital Grants, 418
Bill and Melinda Gates Foundation Agricultural
    Development Grants, 425

Technology
Adobe Foundation Action Grants, 126
American Honda Foundation Grants, 255
Arthur M. Blank Family Foundation Pipeline Project
    Grants, 313
AT&T Fdn Community Support and Safety, 320
Best Buy Children's Foundation @15 Community
    Grants , 414
Best Buy Children's Fdn @15 Teach Awards, 416
Best Buy Children's Foundation National Grants, 417
Best Buy Children's Foundation Twin Cities
    Minnesota Capital Grants, 418
BP Foundation Grants, 465
Cabot Corporation Foundation Grants, 490
Cause Populi Worthy Cause Grants, 521
Daviess County Community Foundation Advancing
    Out-of-School Learning Grants, 792
Dolan Children's Foundation Grants, 832
Do Something Back End Developer Intern, 848
Do Something Digital Content Intern, 851
Do Something TMI Intern, 858
Do Something Web Developer Intern, 860
EQT Fdn Education and Workforce Grants, 927
FirstEnergy Foundation Science, Technology,
    Engineering, and Mathematics Grants, 966
Foundation for Rural Service Education Grants, 991
GNOF Coastal 5 + 1 Grants, 1078
GNOF New Orleans Works Grants, 1088
Go Daddy Cares Charitable Contributions, 1093
GTECH After School Advantage Grants, 1125
H.B. Fuller Foundation Grants, 1138
Hawai'i Community Foundation Family Literacy and
    Hawaii Pizza Hut Literacy Grants, 1201
Honeywell Corporation Leadership Challenge
    Academy, 1258
Intel Corporation Community Grants, 1311
Intel Corporation Int Community Grants, 1312
Kodak Community Relations Grants, 1445
Leonsis Foundation Grants, 1485
Marion I. and Henry J. Knott Foundation
    Discretionary Grants, 1571

Marion I. and Henry J. Knott Foundation Standard
Grants, 1572
Meadows Foundation Grants, 1626
Mericos Foundation Grants, 1637
Michelin North America Challenge Education, 1660
Micron Technology Fdn Community Grants, 1664
Microsoft Software Donations, 1665
Microsoft YouthSpark Grants, 1666
NEH Family and Youth Programs in American
History Grants, 1734
Northrop Grumman Foundation Grants, 1773
PCA Arts Organizations and Arts Programs Grants
for Arts Education Organizations, 1889
PCA Entry Track Arts Organizations and
Arts Programs Grants for Arts Education
Organizations, 1901
Puerto Rico Community Foundation Grants, 2037
Raytheon Middle School Grants and Schols, 2061
Roney-Fitzpatrick Foundation Grants, 2102
SAS Institute Community Relations Donations, 2165
Schramm Foundation Grants, 2168
Tellabs Foundation Grants, 2280
Western New York Foundation Grants, 2429
Xerox Foundation Grants, 2507

Technology Education
AAUW International Project Grants, 44
American Electric Power Corporate Grants, 252
American Electric Power Foundation Grants, 253
Avista Foundation Education Grants, 340
Bayer Fund STEM Education Grants, 384
Bernard and Audre Rapoport Foundation Education
Grants, 410
Best Buy Children's Foundation @15 Community
Grants , 414
Best Buy Children's Fdn @15 Teach Awards, 416
Best Buy Children's Foundation National Grants, 417
Best Buy Children's Foundation Twin Cities
Minnesota Capital Grants, 418
Bill and Melinda Gates Foundation Agricultural
Development Grants, 425
Boeing Company Contributions Grants, 462
Charles Lafitte Foundation Grants, 567
Chicago Board of Trade Foundation Grants, 580
Dayton Foundation Dayton Youth Enrichment Fund
Grant, 795
Ewing Marion Kauffman Foundation Grants, 943
Foundation for Rural Service Education Grants, 991
Marie C. and Joseph C. Wilson Foundation Rochester
Small Grants, 1559
Michelin North America Challenge Education, 1660
Micron Technology Fdn Community Grants, 1664
Microsoft YouthSpark Grants, 1666
Northrop Grumman Foundation Grants, 1773
Qualcomm Grants, 2042
Raytheon Middle School Grants and Schols, 2061
RGk Foundation Grants, 2068
Roney-Fitzpatrick Foundation Grants, 2102
SAS Institute Community Relations Donations, 2165
Sony Corporation of America Grants, 2216
Toshiba America Foundation Grades 7-12 Science and
Math Grants, 2307
Toshiba America Foundation K-6 Science and Math
Grants, 2308
United Technologies Corporation Grants, 2347
Washington Gas Charitable Contributions, 2417
Women's Fund of Hawaii Grants, 2485
WSLBDF Quarterly Grants, 2499
Xerox Foundation Grants, 2507

Technology Education Translation
NEH Family and Youth Programs in American
History Grants, 1734
Northrop Grumman Foundation Grants, 1773

Technology Planning/Policy
ALFJ International Social Change Opportunity Fund
Grants, 232
Cause Populi Worthy Cause Grants, 521

Peter and Elizabeth C. Tower Foundation Technology
Initiative Grants, 1949
Peter and Elizabeth C. Tower Foundation Technology
Planning Grants, 1950

Technology Transfer
Boeing Company Contributions Grants, 462
Northrop Grumman Foundation Grants, 1773

Technology, Hardware and Software
E.L. Wiegand Foundation Grants, 877
GTECH After School Advantage Grants, 1125
Northrop Grumman Foundation Grants, 1773
Peter and Elizabeth C. Tower Foundation Technology
Initiative Grants, 1949
Peter and Elizabeth C. Tower Foundation Technology
Planning Grants, 1950
Puerto Rico Community Foundation Grants, 2037
TechKnowledgey Community Impact Grants, 2278
Western New York Foundation Grants, 2429

Teen Pregnancy
ACF Transitional Living Program and Maternity
Group Homes Grants, 96
Adams Family Foundation of Tennessee Grants, 120
Community Foundation of Eastern Connecticut
Northeast Women and Girls Grants, 697
Community Foundation of Eastern Connecticut
Norwich Women and Girls Grants, 698
Community Foundation of Eastern Connecticut
Southeast Area Women and Girls Grants, 701
Community Foundation of Eastern Connecticut
Windham Area Women and Girls Grants, 702
Cone Health Foundation Grants, 745
First Nations Development Institute Native Youth
and Culture Fund Grants, 974
Helen V. Brach Foundation Grants, 1232
Joseph H. and Florence A. Roblee Foundation
Children and Youth Grants, 1385
Mary Black Foundation Early Childhood
Development Grants, 1586
MetroWest Health Foundation Grants to Reduce
the Incidence of High Risk Behaviors Among
Adolescents, 1646
OneFamily Foundation Grants, 1822
Puerto Rico Community Foundation Grants, 2037
SACF Youth Advisory Council Grants, 2131
USAID Family Planning and Reproductive Health
Methods Grants, 2353
Women's Fund of Hawaii Grants, 2485

Television
1st Source Foundation Community Involvement
Grants, 1
Daniel and Nanna Stern Family Fdn Grants, 778
National Cowboy and Western Heritage Museum
Awards, 1722
NEH Family and Youth Programs in American
History Grants, 1734
NSTA Faraday Science Communicator Award, 1778
PCA Arts Organizations and Arts Programs Grants
for Film and Electronic Media, 1893
PCA Entry Track Arts Orgs and Arts Programs
Grants for Film and Electronic Media, 1905
San Antonio Area Foundation Capital and Naming
Rights Grants, 2148
Shelley and Donald Rubin Foundation Grants, 2187
Wyomissing Foundation Community Grants, 2504

Television, Children's
Farmers Insurance Corporate Giving Grants, 948
Union Pacific Fdn Community & Civic Grants, 2337

Television, Public
Air Products Foundation Grants, 148
Doree Taylor Charitable Foundation Grants, 843
Farmers Insurance Corporate Giving Grants, 948
George W. Codrington Charitable Foundation
Grants, 1055

Hawaiian Electric Industries Charitable Foundation
Grants, 1211
Martha Holden Jennings Foundation Grants-to-
Educators, 1581
Onan Family Foundation Grants, 1821
PMI Foundation Grants, 1982
TE Foundation Grants, 2279
Union Pacific Fdn Community & Civic Grants, 2337

Terminally Ill
Cralle Foundation Grants, 760
Florence Hunt Maxwell Foundation Grants, 979
Graham and Carolyn Holloway Family Foundation
Grants, 1098
Herbert A. and Adrian W. Woods Foundation
Grants, 1243
May and Stanley Smith Charitable Trust Grants, 1613

Texas
Albert and Ethel Herzstein Charitable Foundation
Grants, 219
Carrie S. Orleans Trust Grants, 512
Crystelle Waggoner Charitable Trust Grants, 768
David and Betty Sacks Foundation Grants, 788
Dr. and Mrs. Paul Pierce Memorial Foundation
Grants, 862
Fichtenbaum Charitable Trust Grants, 955
Florence Foundation Grants, 978
Hahl Proctor Charitable Trust Grants, 1151
Helen Gertrude Sparks Charitable Trust Grants, 1230
Helen Irwin Littauer Educational Trust Grants, 1231
Katrine Menzing Deakins Chartbl Trust Grants, 1422
Lee and Ramona Bass Foundation Grants, 1478
Luella Kemper Trust Grants, 1517
Marcia and Otto Koehler Foundation Grants, 1553
Milton Hicks Wood and Helen Gibbs Wood
Charitable Trust Grants, 1676
Minnie M. Jones Trust Grants, 1678
Nathalie and Gladys Dalkowitz Charitable Trust
Grants, 1716
R.D. Beirne Trust Grants, 2045
Robert W. Knox, Sr. and Pearl Wallis Knox
Charitable Foundation, 2095
Roy and Christine Sturgis Charitable Tr Grts, 2115
Stinson Foundation Grants, 2246
Thelma Braun and Bocklett Family Foundation
Grants, 2287
W.H. and Mary Ellen Cobb Chartbl Trust Grts, 2397
W.P. and Bulah Luse Foundation Grants, 2399

Theater
Ann L. and Carol Green Rhodes Charitable Trust
Grants, 278
City of Oakland Cultural Funding Grants, 618
Community Foundation of Muncie and Delaware
County - Kitselman Grants, 733
Donald G. Gardner Humanities Tr Youth Grts, 840
Horace A. Moses Charitable Trust Grants, 1261
Hubbard Broadcasting Foundation Grants, 1269
Newfoundland and Labrador Arts Council ArtSmarts
Grants, 1744
Newfoundland and Labrador Arts Council School
Touring Grants, 1745
NJSCA Artists in Education Residencies, 1763
NYSCA Theatre: Prof Performances Grants, 1795
Parker Foundation (California) Grants, 1869
Paul and Edith Babson Foundation Grants, 1881
Richard J. Stern Foundation for the Arts Grants, 2071
Robert R. Meyer Foundation Grants, 2094
Sioux Falls Area Community Foundation Spot
Grants, 2204
Union Square Arts Award, 2339
Whitney Foundation Grants, 2441

Theology
Cheryl Spencer Memorial Foundation Grants, 576
FirstEnergy Foundation Community Grants, 965
MacLellan Foundation Grants, 1531

Therapy/Rehabilitation
Avery-Fuller-Welch Children's Fdn Grants, 336
Different Needz Foundation Grants, 830
Koch Family Foundation (Annapolis) Grants, 1444
Oren Campbell McCleary Chartbl Trust Grants, 1837

Third World Nations
Dorothea Haus Ross Foundation Grants, 844
PepsiCo Foundation Grants, 1935

Tobacco
Altria Group Positive Youth Dev Grants, 247
Fuller Foundation Youth At Risk Grants, 1028
Paso del Norte Health Foundation Grants, 1874

Tolerance
Allstate Foundation Tolerance, Inclusion, and
    Diversity Grants, 245
Elizabeth Morse Genius Charitable Trust Grants, 901
Pacers Foundation Be Tolerant Grants, 1859
UUA Actions of Public Witness Grants, 2365
UUA Congregation-Based Community Organizing
    Grants, 2366
UUA Fund Grants, 2367
UUA International Fund Grants, 2368
UUA Just Society Fund Grants, 2369
UUA Social Responsibility Grants, 2370

Tolerance, Ethnic
ACF Ethnic Community Self Help Grants, 80
Allstate Foundation Tolerance, Inclusion, and
    Diversity Grants, 245
Elizabeth Morse Genius Charitable Trust Grants, 901
Foundation Beyond Belief Compassionate Impact
    Grants, 986
Foundation Beyond Belief Humanist Grants, 987
Pacers Foundation Be Tolerant Grants, 1859
UUA Actions of Public Witness Grants, 2365
UUA Congregation-Based Community Organizing
    Grants, 2366
UUA Fund Grants, 2367
UUA International Fund Grants, 2368
UUA Just Society Fund Grants, 2369
UUA Social Responsibility Grants, 2370

Tolerance, Religious
Allstate Foundation Tolerance, Inclusion, and
    Diversity Grants, 245
Elizabeth Morse Genius Charitable Trust Grants, 901
Kawabe Memorial Fund Grants, 1423
Laura Musser Intercultural Harmony Grants, 1472
Marin Community Foundation Social Justice and
    Interfaith Understanding Grants, 1567
Nathalie and Gladys Dalkowitz Charitable Trust
    Grants, 1716
Pacers Foundation Be Tolerant Grants, 1859
Sadler Family Foundation Grants, 2132
UUA Actions of Public Witness Grants, 2365
UUA Congregation-Based Community Organizing
    Grants, 2366
UUA Fund Grants, 2367
UUA International Fund Grants, 2368
UUA Just Society Fund Grants, 2369
UUA Social Responsibility Grants, 2370

Touring Arts Programs
APAP All-In Grants, 283
Japan Foundation Los Angeles Mini-Grants for
    Japanese Arts & Culture, 1354
Japan Foundation New York Small Grants for Arts
    and Culture, 1355
NYSCA Arts Ed: Services to the Field Grants, 1784
NYSCA Electronic Media and Film: Film Festivals
    Grants, 1785
NYSCA Electronic Media and Film: General
    Operating Support, 1786
NYSCA Electronic Media and Film: Screenings
    Grants, 1788
PCA-PCD Professional Development for Individual
    Artists Grants, 1883

PCA Art Organizations and Art Programs Grants for
    Presenting Organizations, 1884
PCA Arts Organizations and Arts Programs Grants
    for Art Museums, 1888
PCA Arts Organizations and Arts Programs Grants
    for Arts Service Organizations, 1890
PCA Arts Organizations and Arts Programs Grants
    for Dance, 1892
PCA Arts Organizations and Arts Programs Grants
    for Local Arts, 1895
PCA Arts Organizations and Arts Programs Grants
    for Theatre, 1896
PCA Arts Organizations and Arts Programs Grants
    for Traditional and Folk Arts, 1897
PCA Arts Organizations and Arts Programs Grants
    for Visual Arts, 1898
PCA Busing Grants, 1899
PCA Entry Track Arts Organizations and Arts
    Programs Grants for Art Museums, 1900
PCA Entry Track Arts Organizations and Arts
    Programs Grants for Arts Service Orgs, 1902
PCA Entry Track Arts Organizations and Arts
    Programs Grants for Dance, 1904
PCA Entry Track Arts Organizations and Arts
    Programs Grants for Local Arts, 1907
PCA Entry Track Arts Organizations and Arts
    Programs Grants for Presenting Orgs, 1909
PCA Entry Track Arts Organizations and Arts
    Programs Grants for Theatre, 1910
PCA Entry Track Arts Orgs and Arts Programs
    Grants for Traditional and Folk Arts, 1911
PCA Entry Track Arts Organizations and Arts
    Programs Grants for Visual Arts, 1912
PCA Pennsylvania Partners in the Arts Program
    Stream Grants, 1914
PCA Pennsylvania Partners in the Arts Project
    Stream Grants, 1915
PCA Strategies for Success Grants - Basic Level, 1918
PCA Strategies for Success Grants - Intermediate
    Level, 1919
PennPAT Artist Technical Assistance Grants, 1929
PennPAT Fee-Support Grants for Presenters, 1930
PennPAT New Directions Grants for Presenters, 1931
PennPAT Presenter Travel Grants, 1932
PennPAT Strategic Opportunity Grants, 1933
TAC Arts Access Grant, 2265
TAC Touring Arts and Arts Access Touring Arts
    Grants, 2269

Tourism
Miller Foundation Grants, 1673

Training and Development
ACF Social and Economic Development Strategies
    Grants, 93
Adobe Foundation Action Grants, 126
Alaska Children's Trust Conference/Training
    Sponsorship, 195
Aldi Corporation Smart Kids Grants, 226
Allen Foundation Educational Nutrition Grants, 238
Boeing Company Contributions Grants, 462
Cleveland Foundation Higley Fund Grants, 634
Cleveland H. Dodge Foundation Grants, 637
Community Foundation of Western Massachusetts
    Grants, 741
DOL Youthbuild Grants, 838
Entergy Charitable Foundation Low-Income
    Initiatives and Solutions Grants, 918
Fremont Area Community Foundation Amazing X
    Grants, 1019
GNOF Organizational Effectiveness Grants and
    Workshops, 1090
Greater Milwaukee Foundation Grants, 1109
Harmony Project Grants, 1170
Hawai'i Community Foundation Victoria S. and
    Bradley L. Geist Foundation: Capacity Building
    Grants, 1206
Hawai'i Community Foundation Victoria S. and
    Bradley L. Geist Foundation: Supporting Foster
    Children and Their Caregivers, 1208

Indiana OCRA Rural Capacity Grants (RCG), 1301
Jovid Foundation Employment Training Grants, 1392
Koret Foundation Grants, 1449
Lilly Endowment Summer Youth Grants, 1492
Mary Wilmer Covey Charitable Trust Grants, 1600
OneFamily Foundation Grants, 1822
Priddy Foundation Organizational Development
    Grants, 2022
Progress Energy Foundation Energy Education
    Grants, 2025
Prudential Foundation Education Grants, 2028
Raskob Fdn for Catholic Activities Grants, 2054
Scott County Community Foundation Grants, 2170
Sioux Falls Area Community Foundation Community
    Fund Grants, 2203
Sioux Falls Area Community Foundation Spot
    Grants, 2204
Social Justice Fund Northwest Criminal Justice
    Giving Project Grants, 2214
Southern New England Folk and Traditional Arts
    Apprenticeship Grants, 2224
TAC Arts Education Teacher Incentive Grants, 2268
Union Bank, N.A. Foundation Grants, 2334
Victoria S. and Bradley L. Geist Foundation Grants
    Supporting Foster Care and Their Caregivers, 2382
Victoria S. and Bradley L. Geist Foundation Grants
    Supporting Transitioning Foster Youth, 2383

Transexuals
ACF Runaway and Homeless Youth Training and
    Technical Assistance Center Grants, 92
Appalachian Community LGBTQ Fund Grants, 284
Maine Community Foundation Equity Grants, 1541
Ms. Fdn for Women Ending Violence Grants, 1708
New York Foundation Grants, 1753
Philanthrofund Foundation Grants, 1959
Threshold Foundation Queer Youth Grants, 2299

Transitional Students
ACL Disability and Rehabilitation Research Projects
    (DRRP) Program: Independent Living Transition
    Services for Youth and Young Adults Grants, 105
ACL Rehabilitation Research and Training Center
    (RRTC) on Employment of Transition-Age Youth
    with Disabilities Grants, 107
Meyer Foundation Education Grants, 1649

Translation
ALA Mildred L. Batchelder Award, 178

Transportation
ACF Voluntary Agencies Matching Grants, 100
Community Foundation of Louisville CHAMP Fund
    Grants, 720
Dearborn Community Foundation City of Aurora
    Grants, 808
Elizabeth Morse Genius Charitable Trust Grants, 901
Farmers Insurance Corporate Giving Grants, 948
Fremont Area Community Foundation Amazing X
    Grants, 1019
Vigneron Memorial Fund Grants, 2384

Transportation Engineering
Elizabeth Morse Genius Charitable Trust Grants, 901

Transportation Planning/Policy
Bikes Belong Foundation Paul David Clark Bicycling
    Safety Grants, 422
Bikes Belong Foundation REI Grants, 423
Bikes Belong Grants, 424
Elizabeth Morse Genius Charitable Trust Grants, 901
Volvo Adventure Environmental Awards, 2390
William and Flora Hewlett Foundation
    Environmental Grants, 2455

Trauma
ACL Neonatal Abstinence Syndrome National
    Training Initiative Grant, 106
Peter and Elizabeth C. Tower Foundation Mental
    Health Grants, 1946

Travel
AACAP Educational Outreach Program for Child and Adolescent Psychiatry Residents, 23
AACAP Educational Outreach Program for General Psychiatry Residents, 24
AACAP Systems of Care Special Program Scholarships, 39
ALA Penguin Random House Young Readers Group Award, 183
ALFJ International Social Change Opportunity Fund Grants, 232
HAF Ian Chris Mackey Newman Fund Grts, 1143
Hearst Foundations United States Senate Youth Grants, 1225
Herbert Hoover Presidential Library Association Bus Travel Grants, 1244
IYI Professional Development Grants, 1317
Newfoundland and Labrador Arts Council Visiting Artists Grants, 1746
NZDIA Lottery Minister's Discretionary Fund Grants, 1797
PCA Busing Grants, 1899
PennPAT Presenter Travel Grants, 1932
Robert R. Meyer Foundation Grants, 2094
TAC Arts Education Teacher Incentive Grants, 2268
Union Labor Health Fdn Angel Fund Grants, 2335

Trees
GNOF Gert Community Fund Grants, 1082

Tumor Immunology
Children's Brain Tumor Fdn Research Grants, 584
Children's Tumor Foundation Young Investigator Awards, 587

Undergraduate Education
BMW of North America Charitable Contribs, 460
Maurice R. Robinson Fund Grants, 1611

Unitarian Church
AHS Foundation Grants, 143
Alvah H. and Wyline P. Chapman Fdn Grants, 248
Chapman Family Foundation, 562
Harry and Helen Sands Charitable Trust Grants, 1181
UUA Actions of Public Witness Grants, 2365
UUA Congregation-Based Community Organizing Grants, 2366
UUA Fund Grants, 2367
UUA International Fund Grants, 2368
UUA Just Society Fund Grants, 2369
UUA Social Responsibility Grants, 2370

United States History
CDC David J. Sencer Museum Student Field Trip Experience, 524
NEH Family and Youth Programs in American History Grants, 1734
Virginia Foundation for the Humanities Folklife Apprenticeships, 2386
Virginia Fdn for Humanities Open Grants, 2387

United States, Northwest
National Cowboy and Western Heritage Museum Awards, 1722

United States, Southwest
National Cowboy and Western Heritage Museum Awards, 1722

University/Industry Cooperative Activities
Shell Deer Park Grants, 2186

Urban Affairs
Community Foundation for the National Capital Region Community Leadership Grants, 688
Community Foundation of St. Joseph County Special Project Challenge Grants, 738
Nellie Mae Education Foundation District-Level Change Grants, 1736
Paul and Edith Babson Foundation Grants, 1881

Urban Areas
Achelis and Bodman Foundation Grants, 101
Achelis Foundation Grants, 102
AT&T Foundation Health and Human Services Grants, 322
CNCS AmeriCorps NCCC Project Grants, 642
CUNA Mutual Group Fdn Community Grants, 770
E.L. Wiegand Foundation Grants, 877
Fund for the City of New York Grants, 1029
Hasbro Children's Fund Grants, 1189
Mark Wahlberg Youth Foundation Grants, 1576
Merck Family Fund Urban Farming and Youth Leadership Grants, 1635
Merck Family Fund Youth Transforming Urban Communities Grants, 1636
Paul and Edith Babson Foundation Grants, 1881
ProLiteracy National Book Fund Grants, 2026
William and Flora Hewlett Foundation Environmental Grants, 2455

Urban Education
ALA Coretta Scott King Book Donation Grant, 168
Carnegie Corporation of New York Grants, 511
Martha Holden Jennings Foundation Grants-to-Educators, 1581
Merck Family Fund Youth Transforming Urban Communities Grants, 1636
Michael and Susan Dell Foundation Grants, 1657
Nellie Mae Education Foundation District-Level Change Grants, 1736

Urban Planning/Policy
Air Products Foundation Grants, 148
Merck Family Fund Youth Transforming Urban Communities Grants, 1636
Meyer Fdn Healthy Communities Grants, 1650
Michael and Susan Dell Foundation Grants, 1657
Paul and Edith Babson Foundation Grants, 1881
Sensient Technologies Foundation Grants, 2180
Western New York Foundation Grants, 2429

Urban Sociology
Michael and Susan Dell Foundation Grants, 1657

Utilities
ACF Voluntary Agencies Matching Grants, 100
Avista Foundation Vulnerable and Limited Income Population Grants, 341
Delmarva Power & Light Contributions, 821
Dollar Energy Fund Grants, 834
Entergy Charitable Foundation Low-Income Initiatives and Solutions Grants, 918
MGM Resorts Foundation Community Grants, 1655
Polk County Community Foundation Seasonal Assistance and Cheer Grants for Charitable Programs, 2000

Vaccines
Grifols Community Outreach Grants, 1122
Thrasher Research Fund Grants, 2296

Values/Moral Education
Cargill Corporate Giving Grants, 503
CICF John Harrison Brown and Rob Burse Grt, 607
McCune Foundation Humananities Grants, 1619
Moran Family Foundation Grants, 1693
National Schools of Character Awards Program, 1723
Quaker Oats Company Kids Care Clubs Grants, 2041
S. D. Bechtel, Jr. Foundation / Stephen Bechtel Fund Character and Citizenship Dev Grants, 2128

Venture Capital
Draper Richards Kaplan Foundation Grants, 864
Union Bank, N.A. Foundation Grants, 2334

Veterans
Anne J. Caudal Foundation Grants, 276
Charles Delmar Foundation Grants, 564
CNCS AmeriCorps Indian Tribes Plang Grts, 641
CNCS AmeriCorps State and National Grants, 643

CNCS AmeriCorps VISTA Project Grants, 645
CNCS Senior Corps Retired and Senior Volunteer Program Grants, 648
David Robinson Foundation Grants, 791
Fitzpatrick, Cella, Harper & Scinto Pro Bono Services, 976
Help America Foundation Grants, 1233
MGN Family Foundation Grants, 1656
Northrop Grumman Corporation Grants, 1772
OceanFirst Foundation Home Runs for Heroes Grants, 1802
OceanFirst Foundation Major Grants, 1803
Walter J. and Betty C. Zable Fdn Grants, 2406

Veterinary Medicine
Achelis and Bodman Foundation Grants, 101
Natalie W. Furniss Foundation Grants, 1715

Video Production
ALA Notable Children's Videos Awards, 181
Daniel and Nanna Stern Family Fdn Grants, 778
PCA Arts Organizations and Arts Programs Grants for Film and Electronic Media, 1893
PCA Entry Track Arts Orgs and Arts Programs Grants for Film and Electronic Media, 1905

Videos
ALA Bookapalooza Grants, 161
ALA Notable Children's Videos Awards, 181
Blockbuster Corporate Contributions, 440
Cincinnati Bell Foundation Grants, 612
Newfoundland and Labrador Arts Council ArtSmarts Grants, 1744

Violence
Allstate Corporate Giving Grants, 242
Allstate Corp Hometown Commitment Grants, 243
Anne Arundel Women Giving Together Regular Grants, 275
Atkinson Foundation Community Grants, 325
Atlanta Women's Foundation Pathway to Success Grants, 327
California Endowment Innovative Ideas Challenge Grants, 495
Charles Crane Family Foundation Grants, 563
Community Foundation for the National Capital Region Community Leadership Grants, 688
Global Fund for Women Grants, 1073
Harry Frank Guggenheim Foundation Research Grants, 1184
Hasbro Children's Fund Grants, 1189
Initiaive Fdn Inside-Out Connections Grants, 1303
Isabel Allende Foundation Esperanza Grants, 1315
Joseph H. and Florence A. Roblee Foundation Children and Youth Grants, 1385
Nicole Brown Foundation Grants, 1760
Target Corporation Community Engagement Fund Grants, 2270
United Methodist Women Brighter Future for Children and Youth Grants, 2346
Virginia Foundation for the Humanities Open Grants, 2387
Women's Fund of Hawaii Grants, 2485

Violence Prevention
Albert W. Rice Charitable Foundation Grants, 223
Alfred E. Chase Charitable Foundation Grants, 233
Anne Arundel Women Giving Together Regular Grants, 275
ATA Inclusive Learning Communities Grants, 323
Atlanta Women's Foundation Pathway to Success Grants, 327
Ben Cohen StandUp Foundation Grants, 403
Charles Crane Family Foundation Grants, 563
Charles H. Pearson Foundation Grants, 566
Eastern Bank Charitable Foundation Partnerships Grants, 881
Eastern Bank Charitable Foundation Targeted Grants, 882
Edward and Ellen Roche Relief Fdn Grants, 887

Ford Family Foundation Grants - Child Abuse
    Prevention and Intervention, 981
Frank Reed and Margaret Jane Peters Memorial Fund
    II Grants, 1014
Go Daddy Cares Charitable Contributions, 1093
Initiaive Fdn Inside-Out Connections Grants, 1303
Joseph H. and Florence A. Roblee Foundation
    Children and Youth Grants, 1385
Linford & Mildred White Charitable Grants, 1495
Maine Women's Fund Econ Security Grants, 1546
Meyer Fdn Healthy Communities Grants, 1650
Moody Foundation Grants, 1692
Ms. Fdn for Women Ending Violence Grants, 1708
Philanthrofund Foundation Grants, 1959
RCF General Community Grants, 2062
Robert R. McCormick Tribune Foundation
    Community Grants, 2093
Union Bank, N.A. Foundation Grants, 2334
Virginia Foundation for the Humanities Open
    Grants, 2387

Violence in Schools
Teaching Tolerance Social Justice Educator Grts, 2276

Violent Crime
Allstate Corporate Giving Grants, 242
Allstate Corp Hometown Commitment Grants, 243
HAF Mada Huggins Caldwell Fund Grants, 1147
Initiaive Fdn Inside-Out Connections Grants, 1303
Max and Anna Levinson Foundation Grants, 1612

Violin Music
AGFT A Gift for Music Grants, 138
CFKF Instrument Matching Grants, 556
Sphinx Competition Awards, 2234

Virginia
George J. and Effie L. Seay Foundation Grants, 1052
Marietta McNeill Morgan and Samuel Tate Morgan
    Jr. Trust Grants, 1560
Richard and Caroline T. Gwathmey Memorial Trust
    Grants, 2069

Vision
1st Touch Foundation Grants, 2
Bay Area Community Foundation Nathalie Awrey
    Memorial Fund Grants, 381
Fichtenbaum Charitable Trust Grants, 955
HAF JoAllen K. Twiddy-Wood Memorial Fund
    Grants, 1144
Meyer Fdn Management Assistance Grants, 1651
Ray Charles Foundation Grants, 2058
William and Sandy Heitz Family Fdn Grants, 2457

Visual Arts
ALA Children's Literature Legacy Award, 165
ALA Randolph Caldecott Medal, 188
Brown Foundation Grants, 476
Camille Beckman Foundation Grants, 499
Christensen Fund Regional Grants, 600
Delta Air Lines Foundation Community Enrichment
    Grants, 823
Donald G. Gardner Humanities Tr Youth Grts, 840
Entergy Corporation Open Grants for Arts and
    Culture, 920
Georgia Council for the Arts Education Grants, 1060
GNOF IMPACT Grants for Arts and Culture, 1083
Hampton Roads Community Foundation Arts and
    Culture Grants, 1154
Helen E. Ellis Charitable Trust Grants, 1228
Helen Gertrude Sparks Charitable Trust Grants, 1230
JP Morgan Chase Fdn Arts and Culture Grants, 1394
Kelvin and Eleanor Smith Foundation Grants, 1424
Kirkpatrick Foundation Grants, 1440
Maryland State Arts Council Arts in Communities
    Grants, 1592
Milton and Sally Avery Arts Foundation Grants, 1675
Montana Arts Council Cultural and Aesthetic Project
    Grants, 1685

Morris Stulsaft Foundation Participation in the the
    Arts Grants, 1698
Newfoundland and Labrador Arts Council ArtSmarts
    Grants, 1744
Newfoundland and Labrador Arts Council School
    Touring Grants, 1745
NHSCA Artist Residence Grants, 1756
NHSCA Conservation License Plate Grants, 1757
NHSCA Youth Arts Project Grants: For Extended
    Arts Learning, 1758
NJSCA Artists in Education Residencies, 1763
NJSCA Arts Ed Special Initiative Grants, 1764
NYSCA Arts Education: Community-based
    Learning Grants, 1780
NYSCA Arts Education: General Operating Support
    Grants, 1781
NYSCA Arts Education: General Program Support
    Grants, 1782
NYSCA Arts Ed: Services to the Field Grants, 1784
NYSCA Electronic Media and Film: Film Festivals
    Grants, 1785
NYSCA Electronic Media and Film: General
    Operating Support, 1786
NYSCA Electronic Media and Film: General
    Program Support, 1787
NYSCA Electronic Media and Film: Screenings
    Grants, 1788
NYSCA Electronic Media and Film: Workspace
    Grants, 1789
NYSCA Special Arts Services: General Program
    Support Grants, 1793
NYSCA Special Arts Services: Instruction and
    Training Grants, 1794
NYSCA Theatre: Prof Performances Grants, 1795
Oren Campbell McCleary Chartbl Trust Grants, 1837
Parker Foundation (California) Grants, 1869
PCA-PCD Professional Development for Individual
    Artists Grants, 1883
PCA Arts in Education Residencies, 1885
PCA Arts Organizations and Arts Programs Grants
    for Arts Service Organizations, 1890
PCA Arts Organizations and Arts Programs Grants
    for Visual Arts, 1898
PCA Busing Grants, 1899
PCA Entry Track Arts Organizations and Arts
    Programs Grants for Arts Service Orgs, 1902
PCA Entry Track Arts Organizations and Arts
    Programs Grants for Visual Arts, 1912
PCA Pennsylvania Partners in the Arts Program
    Stream Grants, 1914
PCA Pennsylvania Partners in the Arts Project
    Stream Grants, 1915
PCA Professional Development Grants, 1916
PCA Strategies for Success Grants - Adv Level, 1917
PCA Strategies for Success Grants - Basic Level, 1918
PCA Strategies for Success Grants - Intermediate
    Level, 1919
Phoenix Coyotes Charities Grants, 1963
Piedmont Natural Gas Corporate Contributions, 1966
Powell Foundation Grants, 2013
Reinberger Foundation Grants, 2066
Robbins-de Beaumont Foundation Grants, 2080
Shell Deer Park Grants, 2186
TAC Arts Access Grant, 2265
Textron Corporate Contributions Grants, 2286
Thomas Sill Foundation Grants, 2292
Union Square Arts Award, 2339
Wold Foundation Grants, 2482
Wood-Claeyssens Foundation Grants, 2486

Visual Impairments
Agnes M. Lindsay Trust Grants, 140
Bushrod H. Campbell and Adah F. Hall Charity
    Fund Grants, 486
Carl W. and Carrie Mae Joslyn Trust Grants, 510
Charles Delmar Foundation Grants, 564
Chicago Board of Trade Foundation Grants, 580
Claremont Community Foundation Grants, 622
Cralle Foundation Grants, 760
Florence Hunt Maxwell Foundation Grants, 979

J. Walton Bissell Foundation Grants, 1325
Mabel H. Flory Charitable Trust Grants, 1527
Mericos Foundation Grants, 1637
Mill Spring Foundation Grants, 1674
R.D. Beirne Trust Grants, 2045
Sara Elizabeth O'Brien Trust Grants, 2161
Shell Deer Park Grants, 2186
Thomas Sill Foundation Grants, 2292
W.P. and Bulah Luse Foundation Grants, 2399
William G. and Helen C. Hoffman Foundation
    Grants, 2466

Vocational Counseling
Achelis and Bodman Foundation Grants, 101
Achelis Foundation Grants, 102
GNOF New Orleans Works Grants, 1088

Vocational Education
Bernard and Audre Rapoport Foundation Community
    Building and Social Service Grants, 408
BMW of North America Charitable Contribs, 460
Charles Nelson Robinson Fund Grants, 569
Edward F. Swinney Trust Grants, 890
GNOF New Orleans Works Grants, 1088
Kimball Foundation Grants, 1432
OMNOVA Solutions Fdn Education Grants, 1820
Southern California Edison Education Grants, 2218

Vocational Services
Bernard and Audre Rapoport Foundation Community
    Building and Social Service Grants, 408
GNOF New Orleans Works Grants, 1088

Vocational Training
Alfred E. Chase Charitable Foundation Grants, 233
Bernard and Audre Rapoport Foundation Community
    Building and Social Service Grants, 408
Charles Nelson Robinson Fund Grants, 569
Cleveland Foundation Higley Fund Grants, 634
DOL Youthbuild Grants, 838
Gamble Foundation Grants, 1032
George W. Wells Foundation Grants, 1057
GNOF New Orleans Works Grants, 1088
Kimball Foundation Grants, 1432
MGM Resorts Foundation Community Grants, 1655
Middlesex Savings Charitable Foundation
    Educational Opportunities Grants, 1670
Morris Stulsaft Foundation Pathways to Work
    Grants, 1699
PMI Foundation Grants, 1982
Sand Hill Foundation Health and Opportunity
    Grants, 2153
Sioux Falls Area Community Foundation Community
    Fund Grants, 2203
Sioux Falls Area Community Fdn Spot Grants, 2204
Union Bank, N.A. Foundation Grants, 2334

Vocational/Technical Education
Alaska Airlines Foundation LIFT Grants, 194
Atkinson Foundation Community Grants, 325
Burlington Industries Foundation Grants, 481
Charles Nelson Robinson Fund Grants, 569
FirstEnergy Foundation Community Grants, 965
Georgia-Pacific Fdn Entrepreneurship Grants, 1059
GNOF New Orleans Works Grants, 1088
Hattie M. Strong Foundation Grants, 1194
HLTA Visitor Industry Charity Walk Grant, 1254
Mabel Louise Riley Foundation Grants, 1529
McCune Charitable Foundation Grants, 1617
Norcliffe Foundation Grants, 1766
OMNOVA Solutions Fdn Education Grants, 1820
Oppenstein Brothers Foundation Grants, 1827
Samuel S. Johnson Foundation Grants, 2146
United Technologies Corporation Grants, 2347

Volleyball
Outrigger Duke Kahanamoku Foundation Athletic
    Event Grants, 1852
Outrigger Duke Kahanamoku Foundation Athletic
    Team Grants, 1853

Volunteers

Achelis and Bodman Foundation Grants, 101

Aspen Community Foundation Grants, 316

Ball Brothers Foundation Organizational
Effectiveness/Executive Mentoring Grants, 346

Bank of America Charitable Foundation Volunteer
Grants, 358

Benton Community Foundation Grants, 405

Blue River Community Foundation Grants, 458

Brown County Community Foundation Grants, 475

Brunswick Foundation Dollars for Doers Grants, 478

Brunswick Foundation Grants, 479

C.F. Adams Charitable Trust Grants, 488

Campbell Soup Foundation Grants, 501

Chesapeake Bay Trust Mini Grants, 578

CNCS AmeriCorps Indian Tribes Plang Grts , 641

CNCS AmeriCorps NCCC Project Grants, 642

CNCS AmeriCorps State and National Grants, 643

CNCS Foster Grandparent Projects Grants, 646

CNCS Senior Corps Retired and Senior Volunteer
Program Grants, 648

CNCS Social Innovation Grants, 649

Colorado Interstate Gas Grants, 661

Community Foundation of Bartholomew County
Heritage Fund Grants, 690

Community Foundation of Bartholomew County
James A. Henderson Award for Fundraising, 691

Community Foundation of Greater Fort Wayne -
Community Endowment and Clarke Endowment
Grants, 705

Community Foundation of Henderson County
Community Grants, 711

Eastern Bank Charitable Foundation Partnerships
Grants, 881

Eastern Bank Charitable Fdn Targeted Grants, 882

FCYO Youth Organizing Grants, 954

Fidelity Foundation Grants, 957

G.N. Wilcox Trust Grants, 1031

Harry B. and Jane H. Brock Foundation Grants, 1183

Help America Foundation Grants, 1233

Hillsdale County Community Foundation
Y.O.U.T.H. Grants, 1252

Katie's Krops Grants, 1421

KIND Causes Monthly Grants, 1435

Kinder Morgan Foundation Grants, 1436

Lewis H. Humphreys Charitable Trust Grants, 1486

Lockheed Martin Corporation Fdn Grants, 1505

McCombs Foundation Grants, 1615

MetLife Fdn Preparing Young People Grants, 1645

Oppenstein Brothers Foundation Grants, 1827

PepsiCo Foundation Grants, 1935

PGE Foundation Grants, 1958

PNM Reduce Your Use Grants, 1988

Prudential Foundation Education Grants, 2028

Prudential Spirit of Community Awards, 2029

Quaker Oats Company Kids Care Clubs Grants, 2041

Radcliffe Institute Carol K. Pforzheimer Student
Fellowships, 2048

Robbins-de Beaumont Foundation Grants, 2080

Sensient Technologies Foundation Grants, 2180

Sony Corporation of America Grants, 2216

Special Olympics Eunice Kennedy Shriver (EKS)
Fellowships, 2227

United Technologies Corporation Grants, 2347

UPS Foundation Economic and Global Literacy
Grants, 2351

Xerox Foundation Grants, 2507

YSA ABC Summer of Service Awards, 2512

YSA GYSD Regional Partner Grants, 2515

YSA MLK Day Lead Organizer Grants, 2516

YSA National Child Awareness Month Youth
Ambassador Grants, 2517

YSA Sodexo Lead Organizer Grants, 2520

YSA UnitedHealth HEROES Service-Learning
Grants, 2522

Volunteers (Education)

ACF Head Start and/or Early Head Start Grantee
- Clay, Randolph, and Talladega Counties,
Alabama, 82

ACF Head Start and/or Early Head Start Grantee -
St. Landry Parish, Louisiana, 83

ATA Local Community Relations Grants, 324

C.F. Adams Charitable Trust Grants, 488

Daniels Homeless and Disadvantaged Grants, 782

Harry B. and Jane H. Brock Foundation Grants, 1183

Hillsdale County Community Foundation
Y.O.U.T.H. Grants, 1252

Piper Trust Education Grants, 1977

Prudential Spirit of Community Awards, 2029

Radcliffe Institute Carol K. Pforzheimer Student
Fellowships, 2048

Samuel S. Johnson Foundation Grants, 2146

YSA ABC Summer of Service Awards, 2512

YSA GYSD Regional Partner Grants, 2515

YSA Sodexo Lead Organizer Grants, 2520

Voter Educational Programs

Clayton Baker Trust Grants, 629

Farmers Insurance Corporate Giving Grants, 948

Streisand Foundation Grants, 2251

Teaching Tolerance Diverse Democracy Grants, 2275

Voter Registration Programs

Clayton Baker Trust Grants, 629

Wage and Salary Administration

NYSCA Theatre: Prof Performances Grants, 1795

Waste Management

Bill and Melinda Gates Foundation Water, Sanitation
and Hygiene Grants, 428

Volvo Adventure Environmental Awards, 2390

Waste Management/Fossil Energy

Honor the Earth Grants, 1259

Mary A. Crocker Trust Grants, 1584

Wastewater Treatment

Bill and Melinda Gates Foundation Water, Sanitation
and Hygiene Grants, 428

Water Polo

Outrigger Duke Kahanamoku Foundation Athletic
Event Grants, 1852

Outrigger Duke Kahanamoku Foundation Athletic
Team Grants, 1853

Water Resources

Aid for Starving Children Water Projects Grants, 147

Bill and Melinda Gates Foundation Water, Sanitation
and Hygiene Grants, 428

Brunswick Foundation Grants, 479

Chesapeake Bay Trust Environmental Education
Grants, 577

Chesapeake Bay Trust Mini Grants, 578

Chesapeake Bay Trust Outreach and Community
Engagement Grants, 579

CNCS AmeriCorps State and National Grants, 643

Fremont Area Community Foundation Community
Grants, 1020

GNOF Coastal 5 + 1 Grants, 1078

Greater Milwaukee Foundation Grants, 1109

Mary A. Crocker Trust Grants, 1584

PepsiCo Foundation Grants, 1935

Union Bank, N.A. Foundation Grants, 2334

William Bingham Foundation Grants, 2460

Water Resources, Environmental Impacts

Bill and Melinda Gates Foundation Water, Sanitation
and Hygiene Grants, 428

Chesapeake Bay Trust Environmental Education
Grants, 577

Chesapeake Bay Trust Outreach and Community
Engagement Grants, 579

GNOF Bayou Communities Grants, 1077

GNOF Coastal 5 + 1 Grants, 1078

HSBC Corporate Giving Grants, 1266

Land O'Lakes Foundation Mid-Atlantic Grants, 1467

Matson Community Giving Grants, 1607

Meadows Foundation Grants, 1626

PepsiCo Foundation Grants, 1935

Sioux Falls Area Community Foundation Community
Fund Grants, 2203

Sioux Falls Area Community Foundation Spot
Grants, 2204

Water Resources, Management/Planning

Bill and Melinda Gates Foundation Water, Sanitation
and Hygiene Grants, 428

GNOF Coastal 5 + 1 Grants, 1078

Illinois DNR Youth Recreation Corps Grants, 1297

PepsiCo Foundation Grants, 1935

Union Pacific Fdn Community & Civic Grants, 2337

Volvo Adventure Environmental Awards, 2390

Water Supply

Aid for Starving Children Water Projects Grants, 147

Bill and Melinda Gates Foundation Water, Sanitation
and Hygiene Grants, 428

Monsanto United States Grants, 1684

PepsiCo Foundation Grants, 1935

William and Flora Hewlett Foundation
Environmental Grants, 2455

William Bingham Foundation Grants, 2460

Water Treatment

Bill and Melinda Gates Foundation Water, Sanitation
and Hygiene Grants, 428

Waterways and Harbors

BMW of North America Charitable Contribs, 460

GNOF Coastal 5 + 1 Grants, 1078

Welfare Reform

Baton Rouge Area Foundation Every Kid a King
Fund Grants, 364

Legler Benbough Foundation Grants, 1479

Macquarie Bank Foundation Grants, 1532

William J. and Tina Rosenberg Fdn Grants, 2470

Welfare-to-Work Programs

AT&T Foundation Health and Human Services
Grants, 322

Blue Mountain Community Foundation Warren
Community Action Fund Grants, 457

CNCS AmeriCorps State and National Grants, 643

D. W. McMillan Foundation Grants, 776

Elizabeth Carse Foundation Grants, 899

Elizabeth Morse Genius Charitable Trust Grants, 901

Helen Bader Foundation Grants, 1227

Joseph Henry Edmondson Foundation Grants, 1388

Mabel Louise Riley Foundation Family Strengthening
Small Grants, 1528

Marin Community Foundation Ending the Cycle of
Poverty Grants, 1565

Morris Stulsaft Foundation Pathways to Work
Grants, 1699

Pettus Foundation Grants, 1952

Priddy Foundation Program Grants, 2023

Prudential Foundation Education Grants, 2028

Robert R. McCormick Tribune Foundation
Community Grants, 2093

Textron Corporate Contributions Grants, 2286

U.S. Bank Foundation Grants, 2330

Union Bank, N.A. Foundation Grants, 2334

Wellness

7-Eleven Corporate Giving Grants, 8

Alaska Conservation Fdn Youth Mini Grants, 210

Arthur M. Blank Family Foundation AMB West
Community Fund Grants, 304

Bay Area Community Foundation Community
Initiative Fund Grants, 376

Blue Mountain Community Foundation Garfield
County Health Foundation Fund Grants, 456

CDC David J. Sencer Museum Student Field Trip
Experience, 524

CFFVR Jewelers Mutual Chartbl Giving Grants, 543

Cigna Civic Affairs Sponsorships, 610

Community Foundation for Greater Buffalo Garman Family Foundation Grants, 671
Cresap Family Foundation Grants, 766
Finish Line Youth Foundation Founder's Grants, 960
Finish Line Youth Foundation Grants, 961
Finish Line Youth Foundation Legacy Grants, 962
Foundation of Herkimer and Oneida Counties Youth Sports, Wellness and Recreation Mini-Grants, 994
Giant Food Charitable Grants, 1068
Hannaford Supermarkets Community Giving, 1164
Hillsdale County Community Foundation General Grants, 1250
Hillsdale County Community Foundation Love Your Community Grants, 1251
Jane's Trust Grants, 1346
Manuel D. and Rhoda Mayerson Fdn Grants, 1550
Marquette Bank Neighborhood Commit Grants, 1577
Mary Wilmer Covey Charitable Trust Grants, 1600
Mt. Sinai Health Care Foundation Health of the Urban Community Grants, 1710
Oregon Community Fdn Community Grants, 1833
Robert R. McCormick Tribune Foundation Community Grants, 2093
San Antonio Area Foundation Capital and Naming Rights Grants, 2148
Seattle Foundation Health and Wellness Grants, 2179
Walmart Fdn Inclusive Communities Grants, 2403
Walmart Fdn National Local Giving Grants, 2404
Washington Gas Charitable Contributions, 2417

Wetlands
Chesapeake Bay Trust Environmental Education Grants, 577
Chesapeake Bay Trust Mini Grants, 578
GNOF Coastal 5 + 1 Grants, 1078

Wildlife
Alfred J Mcallister and Dorothy N Mcallister Foundation Grants, 234
Ann L. and Carol Green Rhodes Charitable Trust Grants, 278
Arthur Ashley Williams Foundation Grants, 302
Chicago Board of Trade Foundation Grants, 580
Collins Foundation Grants, 658
Dream Weaver Foundation, 865
Elkhart County Community Foundation Fund for Elkhart County, 902
Environmental Excellence Awards, 922
First Nations Development Institute Native Agriculture and Food Systems Initiative Scholarships, 971
George and Ruth Bradford Foundation Grants, 1042
Greygates Foundation Grants, 1120
H.A. and Mary K. Chapman Charitable Trust Grants, 1137
Helen E. Ellis Charitable Trust Grants, 1228
Illinois DNR School Habitat Action Grants, 1296
James Ford Bell Foundation Grants, 1339
James S. Copley Foundation Grants, 1345
John M. Weaver Foundation Grants, 1376
M. Bastian Family Foundation Grants, 1522
Mary K. Chapman Foundation Grants, 1590
Mericos Foundation Grants, 1637
Natalie W. Furniss Foundation Grants, 1715
National Wildlife Federation Craig Tufts Educational Scholarship, 1724
North Dakota Community Foundation Grants, 1768
Perkins Charitable Foundation Grants, 1939
Sioux Falls Area Community Foundation Community Fund Grants, 2203
Sioux Falls Area Community Foundation Spot Grants, 2204
Skaggs Foundation Grants, 2207
Thorman Boyle Foundation Grants, 2295
Union Bank, N.A. Foundation Grants, 2334
William A. Cooke Foundation Grants, 2452
William and Flora Hewlett Foundation Environmental Grants, 2455
Winifred Johnson Clive Foundation Grants, 2478
Yawkey Foundation Grants, 2510

Women
A Fund for Women Grants, 137
Aid for Starving Children Water Projects Grants, 147
ALA Amelia Bloomer Book List Award, 156
Alden and Vada Dow Fund Grants, 225
ALFJ International Fund Grants, 231
Allstate Corporate Giving Grants, 242
Allstate Corp Hometown Commitment Grants, 243
Arizona Foundation for Women Deborah G. Carstens Fund Grants, 293
Arizona Foundation for Women General Grants, 294
Atlanta Women's Foundation Pathway to Success Grants, 327
Atlanta Women's Foundation Sue Wieland Embracing Possibility Award, 328
Bay Area Community Foundation Civic League Endowment Fund Grants, 375
Benton Community Foundation - The Cookie Jar Grant, 404
Bill and Melinda Gates Foundation Agricultural Development Grants, 425
Blossom Fund Grants, 441
BMW of North America Charitable Contribs, 460
Bothin Foundation Grants, 464
Carnegie Corporation of New York Grants, 511
Catherine Holmes Wilkins Foundation Charitable Grants, 520
Central Pacific Bank Foundation Grants, 530
CFFVR Schmidt Family G4 Grants, 548
CFFVR Women's Fund for the Fox Valley Region Grants, 550
CFNEM Women's Giving Circle Grants, 557
Charles Delmar Foundation Grants, 564
Charlotte R. Schmidlapp Fund Grants, 572
CICF Women's Grants , 609
Colgate-Palmolive Company Grants, 652
Community Foundation for Greater Buffalo Josephine Goodyear Foundation Grants, 672
Community Foundation of Bartholomew County Women's Giving Circle, 692
Community Foundation of Eastern Connecticut Northeast Women and Girls Grants, 697
Community Foundation of Eastern Connecticut Norwich Women and Girls Grants, 698
Community Foundation of Eastern Connecticut Southeast Area Women and Girls Grants, 701
Community Foundation of Eastern Connecticut Windham Area Women and Girls Grants, 702
Community Foundation of Louisville Fund 4 Women and Girls Grants, 725
Corina Higginson Trust Grants, 750
Cralle Foundation Grants, 760
Dining for Women Grants, 831
Edward and Ellen Roche Relief Fdn Grants, 887
Eide Bailly Resourcefulness Awards, 897
Eileen Fisher Activating Leadership Grants for Women and Girls, 898
Essex County Community Foundation Women's Fund Grants, 934
Eulalie Bloedel Schneider Foundation Grants, 936
Fassino Foundation Grants, 949
Ford Foundation BUILD Grants, 984
Foundation Beyond Belief Compassionate Impact Grants, 986
Foundation Beyond Belief Humanist Grants, 987
Fourjay Foundation Grants, 1003
Frederick McDonald Trust Grants, 1017
Fremont Area Community Foundation Community Grants, 1020
Friends of Hawaii Charities Grants, 1024
General Service Foundation Human Rights and Economic Justice Grants, 1040
Georgia-Pacific Fdn Entrepreneurship Grants, 1059
Global Fund for Women Grants, 1073
Go Daddy Cares Charitable Contributions, 1093
Greater Tacoma Community Foundation Fund for Women and Girls Grants, 1112
Harry B. and Jane H. Brock Foundation Grants, 1183
Helen V. Brach Foundation Grants, 1232
Huffy Foundation Grants, 1273

ING Foundation Grants, 1302
Intel Corporation Community Grants, 1311
Intel Corporation Int Community Grants, 1312
IRC Community Collaboratives for Refugee Women and Youth Grants, 1313
Isabel Allende Foundation Esperanza Grants, 1315
James Ford Bell Foundation Grants, 1339
Katharine Matthies Foundation Grants, 1418
Kimball International-Habig Foundation Health and Human Services Grants, 1434
Kirby Laing Foundation Grants, 1439
Kopp Family Foundation Grants, 1448
Kosciusko County Community Fdn Grants, 1452
Kroger Company Donations, 1456
Laura B. Vogler Foundation Grants, 1470
Long Island Community Foundation Grants, 1507
Lotus 88 Foundation for Women and Children Grants, 1508
Maine Women's Fund Econ Security Grants, 1546
Maine Women's Fund Girls' Grantmaking Intv, 1547
Make Sense Foundation Grants, 1548
Mardag Foundation Grants, 1554
Margaret M. Walker Charitable Fdn Grants, 1556
Mary Kay Foundation Domestic Violence Shelter Grants, 1591
Mercedes-Benz USA Corporate Contributions Grants, 1634
Michigan Women Forward Grants, 1662
Montana Arts Council Cultural and Aesthetic Project Grants, 1685
Montana Community Fdn Women's Grants, 1688
Nell J. Redfield Foundation Grants, 1737
New York Foundation Grants, 1753
NRA Foundation Grants, 1774
NZDIA Community Org Grants Scheme, 1796
OneFamily Foundation Grants, 1822
OSF Young Feminist Leaders Fellowships, 1845
Patrick and Aimee Butler Family Foundation Community Human Services Grants, 1880
PDF Community Organizing Grants, 1920
PDF Fiscal Sponsorship Grant, 1921
Posey Community Foundation Women's Fund Grants, 2008
ProLiteracy National Book Fund Grants, 2026
R.S. Gernon Trust Grants, 2047
Radcliffe Institute Oral History Grants, 2049
RCF The Women's Fund Grants, 2065
Robert R. Meyer Foundation Grants, 2094
Saginaw Community Foundation YWCA Fund for Women and Girls Grants, 2135
Saint Ann Legacy Grants, 2138
Schramm Foundation Grants, 2168
Spencer County Community Foundation Women's Fund Grants, 2232
Streisand Foundation Grants, 2251
Textron Corporate Contributions Grants, 2286
Thomas Sill Foundation Grants, 2292
Tides Foundation Girl Rising Fund Grants, 2301
Tides Foundation Grants, 2302
United Methodist Women Brighter Future for Children and Youth Grants, 2346
USAID Family Planning and Reproductive Health Methods Grants, 2353
USAID Global Development Alliance Grants, 2354
Vanderburgh County Community Foundation Women's Fund Grants, 2376
Victor E. Speas Foundation Grants, 2380
Washington Area Women's Foundation African American Women's Giving Circle Grants, 2414
Washington Area Women's Foundation Rainmakers Giving Circle Grants, 2415
WHO Foundation Education/Literacy Grants, 2442
WHO Foundation General Grants, 2443
Women's Fund of Hawaii Grants, 2485
Women's Fund of Hawaii Grants, 2484
WSF GoGirlGo! New York Grants, 2494
WSF Rusty Kanokogi Fund for the Advancement of U.S. Judo Grants, 2495
WSF Sports 4 Life Regional Grants, 2497
WSF Travel and Training Fund Grants, 2498

Z. Smith Reynolds Foundation Small Grants, 2523
Zonta International Foundation Young Women in
Public Affairs Award, 2527

Women's Education
AAUW International Project Grants, 44
A Fund for Women Grants, 137
Arizona Foundation for Women Deborah G. Carstens
Fund Grants, 293
Arizona Foundation for Women General Grants, 294
Bay Area Community Foundation Civic League
Endowment Fund Grants, 375
Benton Community Foundation - The Cookie Jar
Grant, 404
Blackford County Community Foundation - WOW
Grants, 433
Blossom Fund Grants, 441
CFFVR Schmidt Family G4 Grants, 548
CFNEM Women's Giving Circle Grants, 557
Charlotte R. Schmidlapp Fund Grants, 572
CICF Women's Grants , 609
Community Foundation of Bartholomew County
Women's Giving Circle, 692
Community Foundation of Boone County - Women's
Grants, 693
Community Foundation of Eastern Connecticut
Northeast Women and Girls Grants, 697
Community Foundation of Eastern Connecticut
Norwich Women and Girls Grants, 698
Community Foundation of Eastern Connecticut
Southeast Area Women and Girls Grants, 701
Community Foundation of Eastern Connecticut
Windham Area Women and Girls Grants, 702
Community Foundation of Louisville Fund 4 Women
and Girls Grants, 725
Community Foundation of Western Massachusetts
Grants, 741
Dining for Women Grants, 831
Essex County Community Foundation Women's
Fund Grants, 934
Greater Tacoma Community Foundation Fund for
Women and Girls Grants, 1112
Make Sense Foundation Grants, 1548
NZDIA Community Org Grants Scheme, 1796
OSF Young Feminist Leaders Fellowships, 1845
PepsiCo Foundation Grants, 1935
Porter County Community Foundation Women's
Fund Grants, 2005
Posey Community Foundation Women's Fund
Grants, 2008
RCF The Women's Fund Grants, 2065
RGk Foundation Grants, 2068
Saginaw Community Foundation YWCA Fund for
Women and Girls Grants, 2135
Spencer County Community Foundation Women's
Fund Grants, 2232
Three Guineas Fund Grants, 2297
Tides Foundation Girl Rising Fund Grants, 2301
USAID Global Development Alliance Grants, 2354
Vanderburgh County Community Foundation
Women's Fund Grants, 2376
Warrick County Community Foundation Women's
Fund, 2411
Washington Area Women's Foundation African
American Women's Giving Circle Grants, 2414
Washington Area Women's Foundation Rainmakers
Giving Circle Grants, 2415
WestWind Foundation Reproductive Health and
Rights Grants, 2434
WHO Foundation General Grants, 2443
Women's Fund of Hawaii Grants, 2484
Women's Fund of Hawaii Grants, 2485

Women's Employment
Albert W. Rice Charitable Foundation Grants, 223
Arizona Foundation for Women Deborah G. Carstens
Fund Grants, 293
Arizona Foundation for Women General Grants, 294
Atlanta Women's Foundation Pathway to Success
Grants, 327

Bay Area Community Foundation Civic League
Endowment Fund Grants, 375
Benton Community Foundation - The Cookie Jar
Grant, 404
Bernard and Audre Rapoport Foundation Community
Building and Social Service Grants, 408
Bill and Melinda Gates Foundation Agricultural
Development Grants, 425
Blossom Fund Grants, 441
Blue Mountain Community Foundation Warren
Community Action Fund Grants, 457
CFFVR Schmidt Family G4 Grants, 548
Charles H. Pearson Foundation Grants, 566
Charlotte R. Schmidlapp Fund Grants, 572
CICF Women's Grants , 609
Community Foundation of Bartholomew County
Women's Giving Circle, 692
Community Foundation of Eastern Connecticut
Northeast Women and Girls Grants, 697
Community Foundation of Eastern Connecticut
Southeast Area Women and Girls Grants, 701
Community Foundation of Eastern Connecticut
Windham Area Women and Girls Grants, 702
Essex County Community Foundation Women's
Fund Grants, 934
George W. Wells Foundation Grants, 1057
Global Fund for Women Grants, 1073
Greater Tacoma Community Foundation Fund for
Women and Girls Grants, 1112
Herman P. and Sophia Taubman Fdn Grants, 1247
M.D. Anderson Foundation Grants, 1523
Maine Women's Fund Econ Security Grants, 1546
Make Sense Foundation Grants, 1548
Moses Kimball Fund Grants, 1701
Ms. Fdn for Women Economic Justice Grants, 1707
NZDIA Community Org Grants Scheme, 1796
OSF Young Feminist Leaders Fellowships, 1845
Pettus Foundation Grants, 1952
Posey Community Foundation Women's Fund
Grants, 2008
RCF The Women's Fund Grants, 2065
Spencer County Community Foundation Women's
Fund Grants, 2232
Textron Corporate Contributions Grants, 2286
Three Guineas Fund Grants, 2297
USAID Global Development Alliance Grants, 2354
Vanderburgh County Community Foundation
Women's Fund Grants, 2376
Washington Area Women's Foundation African
American Women's Giving Circle Grants, 2414
Washington Area Women's Foundation Rainmakers
Giving Circle Grants, 2415
Women's Fund of Hawaii Grants, 2485
Women's Fund of Hawaii Grants, 2484

Women's Health
A Fund for Women Grants, 137
Appalachian Regional Commission Health Care
Grants, 288
Arizona Foundation for Women General Grants, 294
Atlanta Women's Foundation Pathway to Success
Grants, 327
Bay Area Community Foundation Civic League
Endowment Fund Grants, 375
Benton Community Foundation - The Cookie Jar
Grant, 404
Bernard and Audre Rapoport Foundation Health
Grants, 411
Blackford County Community Foundation - WOW
Grants, 433
Blanche and Irving Laurie Foundation Grants, 436
Blossom Fund Grants, 441
California Endowment Innovative Ideas Challenge
Grants, 495
CFFVR Schmidt Family G4 Grants, 548
CFNEM Women's Giving Circle Grants, 557
Charlotte R. Schmidlapp Fund Grants, 572
CICF Women's Grants , 609
Collective Brands Foundation Grants, 654

Community Foundation of Boone County - Women's
Grants, 693
Community Foundation of Eastern Connecticut
Northeast Women and Girls Grants, 697
Community Foundation of Eastern Connecticut
Norwich Women and Girls Grants, 698
Community Foundation of Eastern Connecticut
Southeast Area Women and Girls Grants, 701
Community Foundation of Eastern Connecticut
Windham Area Women and Girls Grants, 702
Dining for Women Grants, 831
Essex County Community Foundation Women's
Fund Grants, 934
Foundations of East Chicago Health Grants, 997
Global Fund for Women Grants, 1073
Greater Tacoma Community Foundation Fund for
Women and Girls Grants, 1112
Harry B. and Jane H. Brock Foundation Grants, 1183
Herman P. and Sophia Taubman Fdn Grants, 1247
Jennings County Community Foundation Women's
Giving Circle Grant, 1361
Kate B. Reynolds Charitable Trust Health Care
Grants, 1416
Kosciusko County Community Foundation REMC
Operation Round Up Grants, 1453
Lisa and Douglas Goldman Fund Grants, 1496
Maine Women's Fund Econ Security Grants, 1546
Porter County Community Foundation Health and
Wellness Grant, 2002
Porter County Community Foundation Women's
Fund Grants, 2005
Posey Community Foundation Women's Fund
Grants, 2008
Pride Foundation Grants, 2024
Radcliffe Institute Carol K. Pforzheimer Student
Fellowships, 2048
Ralph M. Parsons Foundation Grants, 2052
RCF The Women's Fund Grants, 2065
Robert R. Meyer Foundation Grants, 2094
Saginaw Community Foundation YWCA Fund for
Women and Girls Grants, 2135
Seattle Foundation Health and Wellness Grants, 2179
Spencer County Community Foundation Women's
Fund Grants, 2232
Stella and Charles Guttman Foundation Grants, 2241
USAID Family Planning and Reproductive Health
Methods Grants, 2353
USDA WIC Nutrition Ed Innovations Grants, 2363
Vanderburgh County Community Foundation
Women's Fund Grants, 2376
W.P. and Bulah Luse Foundation Grants, 2399
Warrick County Community Foundation Women's
Fund, 2411
Washington Area Women's Foundation African
American Women's Giving Circle Grants, 2414
Washington Area Women's Foundation Rainmakers
Giving Circle Grants, 2415
WHO Foundation General Grants, 2443
Women's Fund of Hawaii Grants, 2485
Women's Fund of Hawaii Grants, 2484

Women's Rights
ALA Amelia Bloomer Book List Award, 156
Arizona Foundation for Women General Grants, 294
Baxter International Corporate Giving Grants, 368
Benton Community Foundation - The Cookie Jar
Grant, 404
Bernard and Audre Rapoport Foundation Democracy
and Civic Participation Grants, 409
Bill and Melinda Gates Foundation Agricultural
Development Grants, 425
Blackford County Community Foundation - WOW
Grants, 433
Blossom Fund Grants, 441
CFNEM Women's Giving Circle Grants, 557
Charlotte R. Schmidlapp Fund Grants, 572
Community Foundation of Bartholomew County
Women's Giving Circle, 692
Community Foundation of Boone County - Women's
Grants, 693

Community Foundation of Eastern Connecticut
    Norwich Women and Girls Grants, 698
Community Foundation of Eastern Connecticut
    Southeast Area Women and Girls Grants, 701
Community Foundation of Eastern Connecticut
    Windham Area Women and Girls Grants, 702
Community Foundation of Louisville Fund 4 Women
    and Girls Grants, 725
Dining for Women Grants, 831
Elkhart County Community Foundation Fund for
    Elkhart County, 902
Global Fund for Women Grants, 1073
Kimball International-Habig Foundation Health and
    Human Services Grants, 1434
Margaret M. Walker Charitable Fdn Grants, 1556
Mary Kay Foundation Domestic Violence Shelter
    Grants, 1591
Ms. Fdn for Women Economic Justice Grants, 1707
New York Foundation Grants, 1753
NZDIA Community Org Grants Scheme, 1796
OSF Young Feminist Leaders Fellowships, 1845
OSF Youth Action Fund Grants in Kyrgyzstan, 1846
Patrick and Aimee Butler Family Foundation
    Community Human Services Grants, 1880
PDF Fiscal Sponsorship Grant, 1921
Porter County Community Foundation Women's
    Fund Grants, 2005
RCF The Women's Fund Grants, 2065
Saginaw Community Foundation YWCA Fund for
    Women and Girls Grants, 2135
Tides Foundation Girl Rising Fund Grants, 2301
Warrick County Community Foundation Women's
    Fund, 2411
Washington Area Women's Foundation African
    American Women's Giving Circle Grants, 2414
Washington Area Women's Foundation Rainmakers
    Giving Circle Grants, 2415
WestWind Foundation Reproductive Health and
    Rights Grants, 2434
Women's Fund of Hawaii Grants, 2485
Women's Fund of Hawaii Grants, 2484

Women's Studies
Greater Tacoma Community Foundation Fund for
    Women and Girls Grants, 1112
Radcliffe Institute Oral History Grants, 2049
Saginaw Community Foundation YWCA Fund for
    Women and Girls Grants, 2135

Work Motivation
Blue Mountain Community Foundation Warren
    Community Action Fund Grants, 457
Elizabeth Morse Genius Charitable Trust Grants, 901

Workforce Development
Alfred E. Chase Charitable Foundation Grants, 233
Bernard and Audre Rapoport Foundation Community
    Building and Social Service Grants, 408
Blue Mountain Community Foundation Warren
    Community Action Fund Grants, 457
Boeing Company Contributions Grants, 462
CFGR SisterFund Grants, 554
CNCS AmeriCorps State and National Grants, 643
Elizabeth Morse Genius Charitable Trust Grants, 901
Fdn for the Mid South Communities Grants, 992
Frederick W. Marzahl Memorial Fund Grants, 1018
GNOF Coastal 5 + 1 Grants, 1078
GNOF New Orleans Works Grants, 1088
HAF Don and Bettie Albright Endowment Fund
    Grants, 1142
Harold Brooks Foundation Grants, 1172
Helen Bader Foundation Grants, 1227
Indiana OCRA Rural Capacity Grants (RCG), 1301
Linden Foundation Grants, 1494
Marin Community Foundation Ending the Cycle of
    Poverty Grants, 1565
Mertz Gilmore Foundation NYC Communities
    Grants, 1641
Meyer Foundation Education Grants, 1649

Middlesex Savings Charitable Foundation
    Educational Opportunities Grants, 1670
Morris Stulsaft Foundation Pathways to Work
    Grants, 1699
Nevada Community Foundation Grants, 1741
New York Foundation Grants, 1753
PG&E Community Vitality Grants, 1957
PMI Foundation Grants, 1982
Priddy Foundation Organizational Development
    Grants, 2022
RCF General Community Grants, 2062
Reinberger Foundation Grants, 2066
Richard and Caroline T. Gwathmey Memorial Trust
    Grants, 2069
Robert R. McCormick Tribune Foundation
    Community Grants, 2093
Suspened: Community Fdn for Greater Atlanta State
    Farm Education Assist Fund Grants, 2260
U.S. Bank Foundation Grants, 2330
Union Bank, N.A. Foundation Grants, 2334
USAID Global Development Alliance Grants, 2354
Walmart Fdn Inclusive Communities Grants, 2403
Walmart Fdn National Local Giving Grants, 2404

Workshops
CJ Fdn for SIDS Program Services Grants, 619
GNOF Organizational Effectiveness Grants and
    Workshops, 1090
Hawai'i Community Foundation Family Literacy and
    Hawaii Pizza Hut Literacy Grants, 1201
IYI Professional Development Grants, 1317
Mabel Louise Riley Foundation Family Strengthening
    Small Grants, 1528
Meyer Foundation Benevon Grants, 1648
Middlesex Savings Charitable Foundation
    Educational Opportunities Grants, 1670
NYSCA Electronic Media and Film: Workspace
    Grants, 1789
PCA Arts Organizations and Arts Programs Grants
    for Arts Education Organizations, 1889
PCA Entry Track Arts Organizations and
    Arts Programs Grants for Arts Education
    Organizations, 1901
PCA Professional Development Grants, 1916
RISCA Project Grants for Individuals, 2079
TAC Arts Access Grant, 2265
Virginia Foundation for the Humanities Open
    Grants, 2387
William Caspar Graustein Memorial Fund Corinne
    G. Levin Education Grants, 2462

Writers in Residence
TAC Arts Access Grant, 2265

Writing
AAAS/Subaru SB&F Prize for Excl in Sci Books, 22
ALA Coretta Scott King-John Steptoe Award for
    New Talent, 166
ALA Coretta Scott King-Virginia Hamilton Award
    for Lifetime Achievement, 167
ALA Notable Children's Books Awards, 179
ALA Robert F. Sibert Informational Book Medal
    Award, 189
CHT Foundation Education Grants, 603
Do Something Writing and Journalism Intern, 861
EQT Fdn Education and Workforce Grants, 927
Jayne and Leonard Abess Foundation Grants, 1358
Newfoundland and Labrador Arts Council School
    Touring Grants, 1745
Olive Higgins Prouty Foundation Grants, 1817
PCA Arts Organizations and Arts Programs Grants
    for Literature, 1894
PCA Entry Track Arts Organizations and Arts
    Programs Grants for Literature, 1906
PEN America Phyllis Naylor Grant for Children's and
    Young Adult Novelists, 1928
Robert Bowne Foundation Fellowships, 2087
Screen Actors Guild PencilPALS Assistance, 2172

Writing/Composition Education
Bay and Paul Foundations PreK-12 Transformative
    Learning Practices Grants, 370
Beacon Society Jan Stauber Grants, 393
Entergy Charitable Foundation Low-Income
    Initiatives and Solutions Grants, 918
Robert Bowne Foundaion Edmund A. Stanley, Jr.
    Research Grants, 2086
Robert Bowne Foundation Literacy Grants, 2088
Robert Bowne Fdn Youth-Centered Grants, 2089

Yemen
USAID Community Livelihoods Project in Yemen
    Grant, 2352
USAID National Governance Project in Yemen
    Grant, 2357

Young Adult Literature
ALA Alex Awards, 153
ALA Amazing Audiobks for Young Adults Awd, 155
ALA Amelia Bloomer Book List Award, 156
ALA Best Fiction for Young Adults Award, 160
ALA Bookapalooza Grants, 161
ALA BWI Collection Development Grant, 164
ALA Coretta Scott King-John Steptoe Award for
    New Talent, 166
ALA Coretta Scott King-Virginia Hamilton Award
    for Lifetime Achievement, 167
ALA Fabulous Films for Young Adults Award, 169
ALA Great Books Giveaway Competition, 170
ALA MAE Award for Best Literature Program for
    Teens, 174
ALA Margaret A. Edwards Award, 175
ALA Michael L. Printz Award, 177
ALA Notable Children's Books Awards, 179
ALA Notable Children's Recordings Awards, 180
ALA Notable Children's Videos Awards, 181
ALA Odyssey Award for Excellence in Audiobook
    Production, 182
ALA Popular Paperbacks for Young Adults Awds, 184
ALA Quick Picks for Reluctant Young Adult Readers
    Award, 186
ALA Schneider Family Book Awards, 191
ALA Scholastic Library Publishing Award, 192
ALA Teen's Top Ten Awards, 214
ALA William C. Morris Debut YA Award, 217
ALA YALSA Presidential Citation Award, 218
ChLA Article Award, 589
ChLA Book Award, 590
ChLA Carol Gay Award, 591
ChLA Edited Book Award, 592
ChLA Faculty Research Grants, 593
ChLA Graduate Student Essay Awards, 594
ChLA Hannah Beiter Diversity Research Grants, 595
ChLA Hannah Beiter Graduate Student Research
    Grants, 596
ChLA Phoenix Award, 598
ChLA Phoenix Picture Book Award, 599
NCSS Carter G. Woodson Book Awards, 1729
PEN America Phyllis Naylor Grant for Children's and
    Young Adult Novelists, 1928

Youth Programs
3M Company Fdn Community Giving Grants, 5
520 Charitable Foundation Grants, 14
A.L. Mailman Family Foundation Grants, 20
A.L. Spencer Foundation Grants, 21
A and B Family Foundation Grants, 40
Aaron Foundation Grants, 42
ABC Charities Grants, 50
Abell-Hanger Foundation Grants, 52
ABS Foundation Grants, 56
Abundance Foundation Local Community Grants, 58
ACCF Dennis and Melanie Bieberich Community
    Enrichment Fund Grants, 59
ACCF John and Kay Boch Fund Grants, 60
ACCF Marlene Bittner Memorial Community
    Enrichment Fund Grants, 61
ACCF of Indiana Anonymous Community
    Enrichment Fund Grants, 63

ACCF of Indiana Bank of Geneva Heritage Fund Grants, 64

ACCF of Indiana Berne Ready Mix Community Enrichment Fund Grants, 65

ACCF of Indiana First Merchants Bank / Decatur Bank and Trust Fund Grants, 66

ACCF of Indiana Michael Basham Community Enrichment Fund Grants, 67

ACCF of Indiana Ron and Susie Ballard Community Enrichment Fund Grants, 68

ACCF Ralph Biggs Memorial Community Enrichment Fund Grants, 69

ACF Abandoned Infants Assistance Grants, 70

ACF Adoption Opportunities Grants, 71

ACF American Indian and Alaska Native Early Head Start Expansion Grants, 72

ACF Basic Center Program Grants, 73

ACF Child Abuse Prevention and Treatment Act Discretionary Funds Grants, 74

ACF Child Welfare Training Grants, 75

ACF Community-Based Child Abuse Prevention (CBCAP) Grants, 76

ACF Community-Based Child Abuse Prevention (CBCAP) Tribal and Migrant DiscretionaryGrants, 77

ACF Infant Adoption Awareness Training Program Grants, 84

ACF National Human Trafficking Hotline Grants, 86

ACF Native Youth Initiative for Leadership, Empowerment, and Development Grants, 88

ACF Promoting Safe and Stable Families (PSSF) Program Grants, 89

ACF Runaway and Homeless Youth Training and Technical Assistance Center Grants, 92

ACF Social and Economic Development Strategies Grants, 93

ACF Street Outreach Program Grants, 94

ACF Transitional Living Program and Maternity Group Homes Grants, 96

ACF Tribal Maternal, Infant, and Early Childhood Home Visiting Program: Development and Implementation Grants, 97

ACF Tribal Maternal, Infant, and Early Childhood Home Visiting Program: Implementation and Expansion Grants, 98

ACF Unaccompanied Refugee Children Grants, 99

ACF Voluntary Agencies Matching Grants, 100

Achelis and Bodman Foundation Grants, 101

ACMP Foundation Community Music Grants, 108

Acuity Charitable Foundation Grants, 110

Adam Don Foundation Grants, 112

Adams and Reese Corporate Giving Grants, 114

Adams Family Fdn of Nora Springs Grants, 118

Adelaide Breed Bayrd Foundation Grants, 123

Adelaide Christian Home For Children Grants, 124

Adobe Foundation Action Grants, 126

Adolph Coors Foundation Grants, 129

Agnes M. Lindsay Trust Grants, 140

ALA BWI Collection Development Grant, 164

ALA MAE Award for Best Literature Program for Teens, 174

ALA Scholastic Library Publishing Award, 192

Alaska Airlines Corporation Career Connections for Youth Grants, 193

Alaska Community Foundation Children's Trust Tier 1 Community Based Child Abuse and Neglect Prevention Grants, 198

Alaska Community Foundation Children's Trust Tier 1 Parenting and Child Development Educational Grants, 199

Alaska Community Foundation Children's Trust Tier 2 Innovation Grants, 200

Alaska Community Foundation Ketchikan Community Foundation Grant, 206

Alaska State Council on the Arts Youth Cultural Heritage Fast Track Grants, 212

Albertsons Companies Foundation Nourishing Neighbors Grants, 221

Albert W. Rice Charitable Foundation Grants, 223

Alcatel-Lucent Technologies Foundation Grants, 224

Alden and Vada Dow Fund Grants, 225

Allen Foundation Educational Nutrition Grants, 238

Alliance for Strong Families and Communities Grants, 239

Alliant Energy Foundation Community Giving for Good Sponsorship Grants, 240

Alloy Family Foundation Grants, 241

Alpha Natural Resources Corporate Giving, 246

Amelia Sillman Rockwell and Carlos Perry Rockwell Charities Fund Grants, 250

American Honda Foundation Grants, 255

American Indian Youth Running Strong Grants, 256

American Savings Fdn After School Grants, 259

Amway Corporation Contributions, 269

Anderson Foundation Grants, 271

Andrew Family Foundation Grants, 272

Ann L. and Carol Green Rhodes Charitable Trust Grants, 278

Antone and Edene Vidinha Charitable Grants, 281

Appalachian Regional Commission Business Development Revolving Loan Fund Grants, 285

Arkema Foundation Science Teachers Grants, 299

Armstrong McDonald Foundation Children and Youth Grants, 300

Arthur M. Blank Family Foundation AMB West Community Fund Grants, 304

Arthur M. Blank Family Foundation American Explorers Grants, 305

Arthur M. Blank Family Foundation Atlanta Falcons Youth Foundation Grants, 307

Arthur M. Blank Family Foundation Atlanta United Foundation Grants, 308

Arthur M. Blank Family Foundation Molly Blank Fund Grants, 310

Arthur M. Blank Family Foundation Mountain Sky Guest Ranch Fund Grants, 311

Arthur M. Blank Family Foundation Pathways to Success Grants, 312

Arthur M. Blank Family Foundation Pipeline Project Grants, 313

AT&T Fdn Community Support and Safety, 320

ATA Local Community Relations Grants, 324

Atlanta Foundation Grants, 326

Aunt Kate Foundation Grants, 331

Avery-Fuller-Welch Children's Fdn Grants, 336

Avery Family Trust Grants, 338

Back Home Again Foundation Grants, 344

Ball Brothers Foundation Organizational Effectiveness/Executive Mentoring Grants, 346

Baltimore Community Foundation Building Stronger Neighborhoods Regionwide Grants, 347

Baltimore Community Foundation Mitzvah Fund for Good Deeds Grants, 349

Baltimore Ravens Corporate Giving, 350

Baltimore Ravens Foundation Play 60 Grants, 351

Baltimore Ravens Fdn Youth Football Grants, 353

Bank of Hawaii Foundation Grants, 360

Bank of the Orient Community Giving, 361

Baton Rouge Area Foundation Every Kid a King Fund Grants, 364

Batters Up USA Equipment Grants, 366

Bay Area Community Foundation Arenac County Healthy Youth/Healthy Seniors Fund Grants, 372

Bay Area Community Fdn Auburn Area Chamber of Commerce Enrichment Fund Grants, 373

Bay Area Community Foundation Bay County Healthy Youth/Healthy Seniors Fund Grants, 374

Bay Area Community Foundation Civic League Endowment Fund Grants, 375

Bay Area Community Foundation Dow CommunityGives Youth Service Prog Grants, 377

Bay Area Community Foundation Human Services Fund Grants, 379

Bay Area Community Foundation Nathalie Awrey Memorial Fund Grants, 381

Bay Area Community Foundation Semiannual Grants, 382

Bayer Fund Community Development Grants, 383

Baystate Financial Charitable Foundation Grants, 385

Ben B. Cheney Foundation Grants, 402

Ben Cohen StandUp Foundation Grants, 403

Benton Community Foundation Grants, 405

Bernard and Audre Rapoport Foundation Arts and Culture Grants, 407

Bernard and Audre Rapoport Foundation Community Building and Social Service Grants, 408

Bernard and Audre Rapoport Foundation Democracy and Civic Participation Grants, 409

Bernard and Audre Rapoport Foundation Education Grants, 410

Best Buy Children's Foundation @15 Community Grants , 414

Best Buy Children's Fdn @15 Teach Awards, 416

Bierhaus Foundation Grants, 421

Blossom Fund Grants, 441

Blue Grass Community Foundation Hudson-Ellis Grants, 449

Blue Mountain Community Foundation Warren Community Action Fund Grants, 457

Blue River Community Foundation Grants, 458

Blumenthal Foundation Grants, 459

Bothin Foundation Grants, 464

Bridgestone Americas Trust Fund Grants, 469

British Columbia Arts Council Youth Engagement Program Grants, 473

Brown County Community Foundation Grants, 475

Burlington Industries Foundation Grants, 481

Bushrod H. Campbell and Adah F. Hall Charity Fund Grants, 486

C.F. Adams Charitable Trust Grants, 488

Campbell Foundation Grants, 500

Cargill Corporate Giving Grants, 503

Cargill Foundation Education Grants, 504

Carl B. and Florence E. King Foundation Grants, 506

Carnegie Corporation of New York Grants, 511

Carroll County Community Foundation Grants, 513

CFFVR Clintonville Area Foundation Grants, 538

CFFVR Infant Welfare Circle of Kings Daughters Grants, 542

CFFVR Jewelers Mutual Chartbl Giving Grants, 543

CFFVR Myra M. and Robert L. Vandehey Foundation Grants, 545

CFFVR Robert and Patricia Endries Family Foundation Grants, 547

CFFVR Schmidt Family G4 Grants, 548

CFFVR Shawano Area Community Foundation Grants, 549

CFF Winter Park Community Grants, 551

CFGR SisterFund Grants, 554

CFGR Ujima Legacy Fund Grants, 555

CFNEM Youth Advisory Council Grants, 558

Chapman Family Foundation, 562

Charles N. and Eleanor Knight Leigh Foundation Grants, 568

Charlotte Martin Foundation Youth Grants, 571

Chassé Youth Leaders Fund Grants, 573

Chesapeake Bay Trust Environmental Education Grants, 577

Christine and Katharina Pauly Charitable Trust Grants, 601

Christopher Ludwick Foundation Grants, 602

CICF Clare Noyes Grant, 604

CICF Howard Intermill and Marion Intermill Fenstermaker Grants, 605

CICF Summer Youth Grants, 608

Cincinnati Bell Foundation Grants, 612

Cincinnati Milacron Foundation Grants, 613

Circle K Corporation Contributions Grants, 614

Citizens Savings Foundation Grants, 617

Claremont Community Foundation Grants, 622

Claremont Savings Bank Foundation Grants, 623

Clark and Ruby Baker Foundation Grants, 625

Cleveland Foundation Higley Fund Grants, 634

Cleveland Foundation Legacy Village Lyndhurst Community Fund Grants, 636

Cleveland H. Dodge Foundation Grants, 637

CMS Research and Demonstration Grants, 640

CNCS Foster Grandparent Projects Grants, 646

CNCS Senior Corps Retired and Senior Volunteer Program Grants, 648

Coleman Foundation Entrepreneurship Education Grants, 651
Colgate-Palmolive Company Grants, 652
Collective Brands Foundation Payless Gives Shoes 4 Kids Grants, 655
Collins C. Diboll Private Foundation Grants, 657
Collins Foundation Grants, 658
Colorado Interstate Gas Grants, 661
Community Foundation for Greater Buffalo Ralph C. Wilson, Jr. Legacy Fund Grants, 674
Community Foundation for Greater Buffalo Ralph C. Wilson, Jr. Youth Sports COVID-19 Fund Grants, 675
Community Foundation for Kettering Grants, 676
Community Foundation for San Benito County Grants, 677
Community Foundation of Abilene Future Fund Grants, 689
Community Foundation of Bartholomew County Heritage Fund Grants, 690
Community Foundation of Bartholomew County James A. Henderson Award for Fundraising, 691
Community Foundation of Boone County Grants, 694
Community Foundation of Crawford County, 695
Community Foundation of Eastern Connecticut General Southeast Grants, 696
Community Foundation of Eastern Connecticut Norwich Youth Grants, 699
Community Foundation of Greater Fort Wayne - Community Endowment and Clarke Endowment Grants, 705
Community Foundation of Greater Greensboro Teen Grantmaking Council Grants, 709
Community Foundation of Jackson County Seymour Noon Lions Club Grant, 714
Community Foundation of Jackson Hole Youth Philanthropy Grants, 715
Community Foundation of Louisville Boyette and Edna Edwards Fund Grants, 718
Community Foundation of Louisville C. E. and S. Endowment for the Parks Fund Grants, 719
Community Foundation of Louisville Dr. W. Barnett Owen Memorial Fund for the Children of Louisville and Jefferson County Grants, 723
Community Foundation of Louisville Human Services Grants, 726
Community Foundation of Madison and Jefferson County Grants, 731
Community Fdn of Randolph County Grants, 735
Community Fdn of Southern Indiana Grants, 736
Community Foundation of St. Joseph County Special Project Challenge Grants, 738
Community Foundation of Switzerland County Grants, 739
Community Foundation of Western Massachusetts Grants, 741
Community Foundation Serving Riverside and San Bernardino Counties Impact Grants, 742
Community Memorial Foundation Responsive Grants, 743
Cooke Foundation Grants, 748
Cooper Tire and Rubber Foundation Grants, 749
Countess Moira Charitable Foundation Grants, 752
Covenant to Care for Children Enrichment Fund Grants, 758
Cralle Foundation Grants, 760
Cresap Family Foundation Grants, 766
Crescent Porter Hale Foundation Grants, 767
Cudd Foundation Grants, 769
CUNA Mutual Group Fdn Community Grants, 770
Curtis Foundation Grants, 771
D. W. McMillan Foundation Grants, 776
Dana Brown Charitable Trust Grants, 777
Daniels Fund K-12 Education Reform Grants, 783
Daniels Fund Youth Development Grants, 784
Dayton Foundation Grants, 796
Dayton Power and Light Company Foundation Signature Grants, 801
Deaconess Foundation Advocacy Grants, 804
Dean Foods Community Involvement Grants, 805

Dean Foundation Grants, 806
Dearborn Community Foundation City of Aurora Grants, 808
Dearborn Community Foundation City of Lawrenceburg Community Grants, 809
Dearborn Community Foundation City of Lawrenceburg Youth Grants, 810
Decatur County Community Foundation Large Project Grants, 811
Decatur County Community Foundation Small Project Grants, 812
DeKalb County Community Foundation - Garrett Hospital Aid Foundation Grants, 813
DeKalb County Community Foundation Grants, 815
Delaware Community Foundation Grants, 817
Del Mar Foundation Community Grants, 820
Delmarva Power & Light Contributions, 821
Delta Air Lines Foundation Youth Development Grants, 824
Deuce McAllister Catch 22 Foundation Grants, 828
Dollar General Family Literacy Grants, 835
Dollar General Summer Reading Grants, 836
Dollar General Youth Literacy Grants, 837
DOL Youthbuild Grants, 838
Don and May Wilkins Charitable Trust Grants, 842
Dorrance Family Foundation Grants, 845
Dorr Foundation Grants, 846
Do Something Awards, 847
Do Something Scholarships, 857
Dubois County Community Foundation Grants, 871
Dunspaugh-Dalton Foundation Grants, 873
Earth Island Institute Brower Youth Awards, 879
Eastern Bank Charitable Foundation Neighborhood Support Grants, 880
Eastern Bank Charitable Foundation Partnerships Grants, 881
Eastern Bank Charitable Foundation Targeted Grants, 882
Easton Foundations Archery Facility Grants, 883
Easton Sports Development Foundation National Archery in the Schools Grants, 884
Edna Wardlaw Charitable Trust Grants, 886
Edward and Romell Ackley Foundation Grants, 889
Effie Allen Little Foundation Grants, 894
Effie Kuhlman Charitable Trust Grants, 896
Eide Bailly Resourcefullness Awards, 897
Elmer Roe Deaver Foundation Grants, 906
Emerson Kampen Foundation Grants, 911
Emily O'Neill Sullivan Foundation Grants, 913
Ensworth Charitable Foundation Grants, 916
Essex County Community Foundation F1rst Jobs Fund Grants, 930
Essex County Community Foundation Greater Lawrence Summer Fund Grants, 932
Eva Gunther Foundation Fellowships, 937
F.M. Kirby Foundation Grants, 946
Farmers Insurance Corporate Giving Grants, 948
Fayette County Foundation Grants, 951
FCYO Youth Organizing Grants, 954
Fidelity Charitable Gift Fund Grants, 956
Fidelity Foundation Grants, 957
Finish Line Youth Foundation Founder's Grants, 960
Finish Line Youth Foundation Legacy Grants, 962
FINRA Smart Investing@Your Library Grants, 963
FirstEnergy Foundation Community Grants, 965
First Hawaiian Bank Foundation Corporate Giving Grants, 967
First Nations Development Institute Native Youth and Culture Fund Grants, 974
First Nations Development Institute Nourishing Native Children: Feeding Our Future Project Grants, 975
Florence Foundation Grants, 978
Florence Hunt Maxwell Foundation Grants, 979
Ford Family Foundation Grants - Positive Youth Development, 982
Ford Family Foundation Grants - Technical Assistance , 983
Foundation for Appalachian Ohio Access to Environmental Education Mini-Grants, 989

Foundations of East Chicago Education Grants, 995
Foundations of East Chicago Youth Development Grants, 998
Four County Community Foundation General Grants, 1000
Four County Community Foundation Healthy Senior/Healthy Youth Fund Grants, 1001
Four Lanes Trust Grants, 1005
Frank Reed and Margaret Jane Peters Memorial Fund Grants, 1013
Frederick W. Marzahl Memorial Fund Grants, 1018
Fremont Area Community Foundation Amazing X Grants, 1019
Fremont Area Community Foundation Community Grants, 1020
Fremont Area Community Foundation Youth Advisory Committee Grants, 1022
Friends of Hawaii Charities Grants, 1024
Fuller E. Callaway Foundation Grants, 1027
Fuller Foundation Youth At Risk Grants, 1028
G.N. Wilcox Trust Grants, 1031
Gamble Foundation Grants, 1032
Gannett Foundation Community Action Grants, 1033
Gardner Foundation Grants, 1035
General Motors Foundation Grants, 1039
George A. & Grace L. Long Fdn Grants, 1041
George and Ruth Bradford Foundation Grants, 1042
George I. Alden Trust Grants, 1051
Georgia-Pacific Fdn Entrepreneurship Grants, 1059
Gertrude & William C. Wardlaw Grants, 1067
Gibson County Community Foundation Recreation Grants, 1069
Gibson County Community Foundation Youth Development Grants, 1070
Gil and Dody Weaver Foundation Grants, 1071
GMFUS Balkan Trust for Democracy Grants, 1075
GNOF Coastal 5 + 1 Grants, 1078
GNOF Cox Charities of New Orleans Grants, 1079
GNOF Gert Community Fund Grants, 1082
GNOF IMPACT Grants for Youth Dev, 1084
GNOF Norco Community Grants, 1089
Go Daddy Cares Charitable Contributions, 1093
Golden Heart Community Foundation Grants, 1094
Greater Milwaukee Foundation Grants, 1109
Greater Tacoma Community Foundation General Operating Grants, 1113
Greater Tacoma Community Foundation Spark Grants, 1114
Greater Tacoma Community Foundation Youth Program Grants, 1115
Green River Area Community Fdn Grants, 1117
GTRCF Boys and Girls Club of Grand Traverse Endowment Grants, 1126
GTRCF Elk Rapids Area Community Endowment Grants, 1127
GTRCF Grand Traverse Families in Action for Youth Endowment Grants, 1129
GTRCF Healthy Youth and Healthy Seniors Endowment Grants, 1130
GTRCF Youth Endowment Grants, 1133
H.B. Fuller Foundation Grants, 1138
HAF Community Grants, 1141
Hahl Proctor Charitable Trust Grants, 1151
Hampton Roads Community Foundation Community Leadership Partners Grants, 1155
Hannah's Helping Hands Grants, 1165
Harmony Foundation for Children Grants, 1168
Harold K.L. Castle Foundation Windward Youth Leadership Fund Grants, 1175
Harry and Helen Sands Charitable Trust Grants, 1181
Harry and Jeanette Weinberg Fdn Grants, 1182
Hartley Foundation Grants, 1186
Hasbro Corp Gift of Play Holiday Giving, 1190
Hasbro Corporation Gift of Play Hospital and Pediatric Health Giving, 1191
Hasbro Corporation Gift of Play Shelter Support Giving, 1192
Hasbro Corporation Gift of Play Summer Camp Support, 1193
Hattie Mae Lesley Foundation Grants, 1195

Hatton W. Sumners Foundation for the Study and Teaching of Self Government Grants, 1196
Hawai'i Community Foundation Bernice and Conrad von Hamm Fund Grants, 1197
Hawai'i Community Foundation Ewa Beach Community Trust Fund Grants, 1200
Hawai'i Community Foundation Kuki'o Community Fund Grants, 1202
Hawai'i Community Foundation Lana'i Community Benefit Fund, 1203
Hawai'i Community Foundation Richard Smart Fund Grants, 1204
Hawai'i Community Foundation Victoria S. and Bradley L. Geist Foundation: Capacity Building Grants, 1206
Hawai'i Community Foundation Victoria S. and Bradley L. Geist Foundation: Enhancement Grants, 1207
Hawai'i Community Foundation Victoria S. and Bradley L. Geist Foundation: Supporting Foster Children and Their Caregivers, 1208
Hawai'i Community Foundation Victoria S. and Bradley L. Geist Foundation: Supporting Transitioning Foster Youth Grants, 1209
Hawaii Community Foundation Omidyar Ohana Fund Grants, 1213
Hawaii Community Foundation Reverend Takie Okumura Family Grants, 1216
Hawaii Community Foundation Sanford Harmony Pillars of Peace Grants, 1217
Hawaii Electric Industries Charitable Foundation Grants, 1218
Hearst Foundations Social Service Grants, 1224
Hearst Foundations United States Senate Youth Grants, 1225
Helen G., Henry F., & Louise Tuechter Dornette Foundation Grants, 1229
Helen Irwin Littauer Educational Trust Grants, 1231
Hendricks County Community Fdn Grants, 1234
Henry and Ruth Blaustein Rosenberg Foundation Education Grants, 1236
Henry and Ruth Blaustein Rosenberg Foundation Youth Development Grants, 1237
Henry County Community Foundation - TASC Youth Grants, 1238
Henry F. Koch Residual Trust Grants, 1241
Hill Crest Foundation Grants, 1249
Hillsdale County Community Foundation General Grants, 1250
Hillsdale County Community Foundation Y.O.U.T.H. Grants, 1252
Horace A. Kimball and S. Ella Kimball Foundation Grants, 1260
Horace A. Moses Charitable Trust Grants, 1261
Hubbard Farms Charitable Foundation Grants, 1272
Huffy Foundation Grants, 1273
Humana Foundation Grants, 1275
Human Source Foundation Grants, 1276
ICCF Youth Advisory Council Grants, 1282
Iddings Foundation Capital Project Grants, 1283
Iddings Foundation Major Project Grants, 1284
Iddings Foundation Medium Project Grants, 1285
Iddings Foundation Small Project Grants, 1286
Initiaive Fdn Inside-Out Connections Grants, 1303
Inland Empire Community Foundation Capacity Building for IE Nonprofits Grants, 1306
Inland Empire Community Foundation Coachella Valley Youth Grants, 1307
Inland Empire Community Foundation Native Youth Grants, 1308
Inland Empire Community Foundation Riverside Youth Grants, 1309
Inland Empire Community Foundation San Bernardino Youth Grants, 1310
Island Insurance Foundation Grants, 1316
J.W. Gardner II Foundation Grants, 1323
J.W. Kieckhefer Foundation Grants, 1324
J. Walton Bissell Foundation Grants, 1325
J. Willard and Alice S. Marriott Fdn Grants, 1327

Jack H. and William M. Light Charitable Trust Grants, 1330
Jack Kent Cooke Fdn Good Neighbor Grants, 1331
James and Abigail Campbell Family Foundation Grants, 1337
James Graham Brown Foundation Grants, 1340
James LeVoy Sorenson Foundation Grants, 1343
James S. Copley Foundation Grants, 1345
Janet Spencer Weekes Foundation Grants, 1348
Jeffris Wood Foundation Grants, 1359
Jim Blevins Foundation Grants, 1365
John and Marcia Goldman Foundation Youth Development Grants, 1368
John F. Kennedy Center for the Performing Arts National Rosemary Kennedy Internship, 1371
John H. and Wilhelmina D. Harland Charitable Foundation Children and Youth Grants, 1374
John P. Ellbogen Fdn Community Grants, 1377
Johnson County Community Foundation Youth Philanthropy Initiative Grants, 1380
John W. Anderson Foundation Grants, 1383
Joseph H. and Florence A. Roblee Foundation Children and Youth Grants, 1385
Josephine Schell Russell Chartbl Trust Grants, 1389
Joyce and Randy Seckman Charitable Foundation Grants, 1393
JP Morgan Chase Fdn Arts and Culture Grants, 1394
Judith Clark-Morrill Foundation Grants, 1395
Judy and Peter Blum Kovler Foundation Grants, 1396
Julia and Tunnicliff Fox Chartbl Trust Grants, 1397
Julia Richardson Brown Foundation Grants, 1398
Julius N. Frankel Foundation Grants, 1400
Kalamazoo Community Foundation LBGT Equality Fund Grants, 1411
Kate B. Reynolds Charitable Trust Poor and Needy Grants, 1417
Katharine Matthies Foundation Grants, 1418
Katherine John Murphy Foundation Grants, 1419
Kathryne Beynon Foundation Grants, 1420
Kenneth T. and Eileen L. Norris Fdn Grants, 1427
Kimball Foundation Grants, 1432
Kimball International-Habig Foundation Health and Human Services Grants, 1434
Kinder Morgan Foundation Grants, 1436
Kirby Laing Foundation Grants, 1439
Knox County Community Foundation Youth Development Grants, 1443
Koch Family Foundation (Annapolis) Grants, 1444
Kopp Family Foundation Grants, 1448
Koret Foundation Grants, 1449
Kosasa Foundation Grants, 1450
Kosciusko County Community Fdn Grants, 1452
Kosciusko County Community Foundation REMC Operation Round Up Grants, 1453
Land O'Lakes Fdn California Region Grants, 1465
Land O'Lakes Foundation Community Grants, 1466
Land O'Lakes Foundation Mid-Atlantic Grants, 1467
LEGO Children's Fund Grants, 1480
Leo Goodwin Foundation Grants, 1482
Liberty Bank Foundation Grants, 1488
Libra Foundation Grants, 1489
Lied Foundation Trust Grants, 1490
Lilly Endowment Summer Youth Grants, 1492
Lily Palmer Fry Memorial Trust Grants, 1493
Linden Foundation Grants, 1494
Linford & Mildred White Charitable Grants, 1495
Lloyd G. Balfour Foundation Attleboro-Specific Charities Grants, 1502
Locations Foundation Legacy Grants, 1504
Lois and Richard England Family Foundation Out-of-School-Time Grants, 1506
Louis Calder Foundation Grants, 1511
Lubrizol Foundation Grants, 1513
Luella Kemper Trust Grants, 1517
Lumpkin Family Fdn Healthy People Grants, 1518
Lynn and Foster Friess Family Fdn Grants, 1520
M.J. Murdock Charitable Trust General Grants, 1524
Mabel A. Horne Fund Grants, 1525
Mabel F. Hoffman Charitable Trust Grants, 1526
Mabel Y. Hughes Charitable Trust Grants, 1530

Madison Community Foundation Grants, 1535
Maine Community Foundation Edward H. Daveis Benevolent Fund Grants, 1540
Maine Community Foundation Vincent B. and Barbara G. Welch Grants, 1545
Make Sense Foundation Grants, 1548
Mardag Foundation Grants, 1554
Margaret and James A. Elkins Jr. Fdn Grants, 1555
Marie C. and Joseph C. Wilson Foundation Rochester Small Grants, 1559
Mark Wahlberg Youth Foundation Grants, 1576
Marsh Corporate Grants, 1580
Martin Family Foundation Grants, 1583
Mary Black Foundation Early Childhood Development Grants, 1586
Mary Cofer Trigg Trust Fund Grants, 1587
Mary D. and Walter F. Frear Eleemosynary Trust Grants, 1588
Mary Owen Borden Foundation Grants, 1597
Mary S. and David C. Corbin Fdn Grants, 1598
Mary W.B. Curtis Trust Grants, 1599
Mathile Family Foundation Grants, 1604
Matilda R. Wilson Fund Grants, 1605
Max and Anna Levinson Foundation Grants, 1612
McCombs Foundation Grants, 1615
McCune Foundation Education Grants, 1618
McInerny Foundation Grants, 1622
McLean Contributionship Grants, 1623
Mead Family Foundation Grants, 1625
Mead Witter Foundation Grants, 1628
Merck Family Fund Urban Farming and Youth Leadership Grants, 1635
Merck Family Fund Youth Transforming Urban Communities Grants, 1636
Mericos Foundation Grants, 1637
Meriden Foundation Grants, 1638
Merrick Foundation Grants, 1640
Mervin Bovaird Foundation Grants, 1643
MetLife Fdn Preparing Young People Grants, 1645
MGN Family Foundation Grants, 1656
Microsoft Software Donations, 1665
Microsoft YouthSpark Grants, 1666
Mid-Iowa Health Foundation Community Response Grants, 1667
Middlesex Savings Charitable Foundation Capacity Building Grants, 1669
Middlesex Savings Charitable Foundation Educational Opportunities Grants, 1670
Mill Spring Foundation Grants, 1674
Minnie M. Jones Trust Grants, 1678
Monsanto Access to the Arts Grants, 1681
Monsanto Kids Garden Fresh Grants, 1682
Monsanto United States Grants, 1684
Montana Community Foundation Grants, 1687
Montgomery County Community Foundation Youth Services Grants, 1691
Moody Foundation Grants, 1692
Morris K. Udall and Stewart L. Udall Foundation Parks in Focus Program, 1695
Morris Stulsaft Foundation Early Childhood Education Grants, 1696
Morris Stulsaft Foundation Educational Support for Children Grants, 1697
Morris Stulsaft Foundation Participation in the the Arts Grants, 1698
Morris Stulsaft Foundation Pathways to Work Grants, 1699
Morton K. and Jane Blaustein Foundation Educational Opportunity Grants, 1700
Moses Kimball Fund Grants, 1701
Motiv8 Foundation Grants, 1702
Nathaniel and Elizabeth P. Stevens Foundation Grants, 1719
National 4-H Council Grants, 1720
National 4-H Youth in Action Awards, 1721
NCMCF Youth Advisory Council Grants, 1727
Nestle Purina PetCare Educational Grants, 1738
Nestle Purina PetCare Youth Grants, 1739
Nevada Community Foundation Grants, 1741

Newfoundland and Labrador Arts Council ArtSmarts Grants, 1744
New Hampshire Charitable Foundation Neil and Louise Tillotson Fund - Empower Coös Youth Grants, 1748
New Hampshire Department of Justice Children's Justice Act Coronavirus Emergency Grants, 1749
New Jersey Office of Faith Based Initiatives Services to At Risk Youth Grants, 1752
New York Foundation Grants, 1753
NFL Charities NFL Player Foundation Grants, 1754
NFL Charities Pro Bowl Community Grants in Hawaii, 1755
Noble County Community Foundation Grants, 1765
Norcliffe Foundation Grants, 1766
North Dakota Community Foundation Grants, 1768
Northland Foundation Grants, 1771
NRA Foundation Grants, 1774
NSTA Faraday Science Communicator Award, 1778
NZDIA Community Org Grants Scheme, 1796
OceanFirst Foundation Summer Camp Grants, 1804
Ohio Valley Foundation Grants, 1814
Olive B. Cole Foundation Grants, 1816
Onan Family Foundation Grants, 1821
OneFamily Foundation Grants, 1822
Oppenstein Brothers Foundation Grants, 1827
Orange County Community Foundation Grants, 1828
Ordean Foundation Catalyst Grants, 1830
Ordean Foundation Partnership Grants, 1831
Oren Campbell McCleary Chartbl Trust Grants, 1837
OSF Early Childhood Program Grants, 1841
OSF Youth Action Fund Grants in Kyrgyzstan, 1846
OtterCares Champion Fund Grants, 1848
OtterCares Impact Fund Grants, 1849
OtterCares Inspiration Fund Grants, 1850
OtterCares NoCO Fund Grants, 1851
Pacers Foundation Be Drug-Free Grants, 1856
Pacers Foundation Be Educated Grants, 1857
Pacers Foundation Be Healthy and Fit Grants, 1858
Pacers Foundation Be Tolerant Grants, 1859
Pacers Foundation Indiana Fever's Be YOUnique Fund Grants, 1860
Parke County Community Foundation Grants, 1868
Parker Foundation (California) Grants, 1869
Patricia Kisker Foundation Grants, 1879
Paul and Edith Babson Foundation Grants, 1881
PCA Arts Organizations and Arts Programs Grants for Arts Education Organizations, 1889
PCA Busing Grants, 1899
PCA Entry Track Arts Organizations and Arts Programs Grants for Arts Education Organizations, 1901
PCA Pennsylvania Partners in the Arts Program Stream Grants, 1914
PCA Pennsylvania Partners in the Arts Project Stream Grants, 1915
PDF Community Organizing Grants, 1920
Pentair Foundation Education and Community Grants, 1934
Perkin Fund Grants, 1937
Perkins-Ponder Foundation Grants, 1938
Perkins Charitable Foundation Grants, 1939
Perry and Sandy Massie Foundation Grants, 1941
Perry County Community Foundation Youth Development Grants, 1943
Peter and Elizabeth C. Tower Foundation Intellectual Disabilities Grants, 1944
Peter and Elizabeth C. Tower Foundation Learning Disability Grants, 1945
Peter and Elizabeth C. Tower Foundation Mental Health Grants, 1946
Peter and Elizabeth C. Tower Foundation Small Grants, 1947
Peter and Elizabeth C. Tower Foundation Substance Use Disorders Grants, 1948
Peter and Elizabeth C. Tower Foundation Technology Initiative Grants, 1949
Peter and Elizabeth C. Tower Foundation Technology Planning Grants, 1950
Pettus Foundation Grants, 1952

PeyBack Foundation Grants, 1953
Philip Boyle Foundation Grants, 1961
Phoenix Coyotes Charities Grants, 1963
Piedmont Natural Gas Corporate and Charitable Contributions, 1966
Piedmont Natural Gas Foundation Health and Human Services Grants, 1968
Pike County Community Foundation Youth Development Grants, 1971
Pinnacle Entertainment Foundation Grants, 1972
Pinnacle Foundation Grants, 1973
Piper Jaffray Foundation Communities Giving Grants, 1974
Pittsburgh Foundation Healthy Children and Adults Grants, 1981
PMI Foundation Grants, 1982
PNC Foundation Education Grants, 1985
Poetry Fdn Young People's Poet Laureate, 1989
Pohlad Family Fdn Large Capital Grants, 1990
Pohlad Family Fdn Small Capital Grants, 1991
Pohlad Family Foundation Summer Camp Scholarships, 1992
Pohlad Family Foundation Youth Advancement Grants, 1993
Polk County Community Foundation Bradley Breakthrough Community Benefit Grants, 1995
Polk County Community Foundation Kirby Harmon Field Fund Grants, 1997
Polk County Community Foundation Marjorie M. and Lawrence R. Bradley Endowment Fund Grants, 1998
Polk County Community Foundation Seasonal Assistance and Cheer Grants for Charitable Programs, 2000
Porter County Community Foundation Health and Wellness Grant, 2002
Porter County Community Foundation PCgivingproject Grants, 2003
Portland Fdn - Women's Giving Circle Grant, 2006
Posey Community Foundation Women's Fund Grants, 2008
Posey County Community Foundation Youth Development Grants, 2010
PPCF Edson Foundation Grants, 2015
PPCF Esther M. and Freeman E. Everett Charitable Foundation Grants, 2016
Price Chopper's Golub Foundation Grants, 2020
Priddy Foundation Program Grants, 2023
Pride Foundation Grants, 2024
Prudential Foundation Education Grants, 2028
Prudential Spirit of Community Awards, 2029
Public Welfare Fdn Juvenile Justice Grants, 2033
Publix Super Markets Charities Local Grants, 2036
R.C. Baker Foundation Grants, 2043
R.S. Gernon Trust Grants, 2047
Ralph M. Parsons Foundation Grants, 2052
Raskob Fdn for Catholic Activities Grants, 2054
Ray Foundation Grants, 2059
Robert and Betty Wo Foundation Grants, 2083
Robert and Helen Harmony Fund for Needy Children Grants, 2085
Robert Bowne Foundaion Edmund A. Stanley, Jr. Research Grants, 2086
Robert Bowne Foundation Fellowships, 2087
Robert Bowne Foundation Literacy Grants, 2088
Robert Bowne Fdn Youth-Centered Grants, 2089
Robert F. Lange Foundation Grants, 2090
Robert R. McCormick Tribune Foundation Community Grants, 2093
Rockwell Collins Charitable Corp Grants, 2098
Roger L. and Agnes C. Dell Charitable Trust II Grants, 2100
Rose Hills Foundation Grants, 2106
Rosenberg Fund for Children Ozzy Klate Memorial Fund Grants, 2114
Roy and Christine Sturgis Charitable Tr Grts, 2115
Roy J. Carver Charitable Trust Youth Services and Recreation Grants, 2117
Ruddie Memorial Youth Foundation Grants, 2120
Rush County Community Foundation Grants, 2121

Ruth Camp Campbell Charitable Trust Grants, 2125
SACF Youth Advisory Council Grants, 2131
Saginaw County Community Foundation Youth FORCE Grants, 2136
Saint Louis Rams Foundation Community Donations, 2139
Salmon Foundation Grants, 2140
Saltchuk Corporate Giving, 2141
Samuel S. Johnson Foundation Grants, 2146
San Antonio Area Foundation Annual Responsive Grants, 2147
San Antonio Area Foundation Capital and Naming Rights Grants, 2148
Sand Hill Foundation Environment and Sustainability Grants, 2152
Sand Hill Foundation Health and Opportunity Grants, 2153
SanDisk Corp Community Sharing Grants, 2155
Sands Cares Grants, 2156
Scheumann Foundation Grants, 2166
Schlessman Family Foundation Grants, 2167
Scott County Community Foundation Grants, 2170
Seattle Foundation Benjamin N. Phillips Memorial Fund Grants, 2176
Seybert Foundation Grants, 2184
Sierra Health Foundation Responsive Grants, 2199
Skaggs Foundation Grants, 2207
Sobrato Family Foundation Grants, 2211
Sobrato Family Fdn Meeting Space Grants, 2212
Sobrato Family Foundation Office Space Grants, 2213
Sorenson Legacy Foundation Grants, 2217
Special Olympics Project UNIFY Grants, 2228
Spencer County Community Foundation Women's Fund Grants, 2232
Spencer County Community Foundation Youth Development Grants, 2233
Stan and Sandy Checketts Foundation Grants, 2235
State Farm Good Neighbor Citizenship Company Grants, 2238
Sterling and Shelli Gardner Foundation Grants, 2243
Stillson Foundation Grants, 2245
Streisand Foundation Grants, 2251
Strong Foundation Grants, 2252
SunTrust Bank Trusteed Foundations Greene-Sawtell Grants, 2257
SunTrust Bank Trusteed Foundations Nell Warren Elkin and William Simpson Elkin Grants, 2258
Susan A. and Donald P. Babson Charitable Foundation Grants, 2259
Suspened: Community Fdn for Greater Atlanta State Farm Education Assist Fund Grants, 2260
Sylvia Perkin Perpetual Charitable Trust Grants, 2263
Target Corporation Soccer Grants, 2271
Tata Trust Grant for Certificate Course in Holistic inclusion of Learners with Diversities, 2273
Tauck Family Foundation Grants, 2274
Teaching Tolerance Social Justice Educator Grts, 2276
Teagle Foundation Grants, 2277
Tension Envelope Foundation Grants, 2284
Thomas and Agnes Carvel Foundation Grants, 2289
Thomas J. Long Foundation Community Grants, 2291
Thomas W. Briggs Foundation Grants, 2294
Thorman Boyle Foundation Grants, 2295
Threshold Fdn Justice and Democracy Grants, 2298
Threshold Foundation Queer Youth Grants, 2299
Toby Wells Foundation Grants, 2304
Tom C. Barnsley Foundation Grants, 2306
Toyota Motor Manuf of Mississippi Grants, 2312
Toyota USA Foundation Safety Grants, 2320
Trinity Trust Summer Youth Mini Grants, 2321
TSYSF Team Grants, 2323
Tull Charitable Foundation Grants, 2324
Turtle Bay Foundation Grants, 2327
Twenty-First Century Foundation Grants, 2328
Union Bank, N.A. Foundation Grants, 2334
Union Labor Health Foundation Dental Angel Fund Grants, 2336
Union Pacific Fdn Community & Civic Grants, 2337
United Friends of the Children Scholarships, 2341
United Healthcare Commty Grts in Michigan, 2343

University of Chicago Chapin Hall Doris Duke Fellowships, 2348
USAID Office of Foreign Disaster Assistance and Food for Peace Grants, 2359
Vanderburgh Community Foundation Men's Fund Grants, 2373
Vanderburgh Community Foundation Youth Development Grants, 2375
Vanderburgh County Community Foundation Women's Fund Grants, 2376
Van Kampen Boyer Molinari Charitable Foundation Grants, 2377
Victor E. Speas Foundation Grants, 2380
Victoria S. and Bradley L. Geist Foundation Grants Supporting Foster Care and Their Caregivers, 2382
Victoria S. and Bradley L. Geist Foundation Grants Supporting Transitioning Foster Youth, 2383
Volkswagen Group of America Corporate Contributions Grants, 2389
Volvo Adventure Environmental Awards, 2390
Walker Area Community Foundation Grants, 2401
Walmart Fdn National Local Giving Grants, 2404
Walter J. and Betty C. Zable Fdn Grants, 2406
Warrick County Community Foundation Youth Development Grants, 2412
Washington County Community Fdn Grants, 2416
Weaver Popcorn Foundation Grants, 2421
Wege Foundation Grants, 2422
West Virginia Commission on the Arts Challenge America Partnership Grants, 2430
WestWind Foundation Reproductive Health and Rights Grants, 2434
Whole Foods Foundation, 2445
Widgeon Point Charitable Foundation Grants, 2447
William A. Cooke Foundation Grants, 2452
William B. Stokely Jr. Foundation Grants, 2459
William Blair and Company Foundation Grants, 2461
William G. Gilmore Foundation Grants, 2467
Wilton and Effie Hebert Foundation Grants, 2476
Winifred Johnson Clive Foundation Grants, 2478
WinnCompanies Charitable Giving, 2479
Wisconsin Energy Foundation Grants, 2481
Wold Foundation Grants, 2482
Women's Fund of Hawaii Grants, 2484
Wood-Claeyssens Foundation Grants, 2486
World of Children Youth Award, 2493
Wyoming Community Fdn General Grants, 2501
Wyoming Community Foundation Hazel Patterson Memorial Grants, 2502
Wyomissing Foundation Community Grants, 2504
Yawkey Foundation Grants, 2510
Youths' Friends Association Grants, 2511
YSA Get Ur Good On Grants, 2513
YSA Global Youth Service Day Lead Agy Grts, 2514
YSA MLK Day Lead Organizer Grants, 2516
YSA National Child Awareness Month Youth Ambassador Grants, 2517
YSA NEA Youth Leaders for Literacy Grants, 2518
YSA Radio Disney's Hero for Change Award, 2519
YSA State Farm Good Neighbor YOUth In The Driver Seat Grants, 2521
Zollner Foundation Grants, 2526
Zonta International Foundation Young Women in Public Affairs Award, 2527

Youth Services

520 Charitable Foundation Grants, 14
A and B Family Foundation Grants, 40
ABS Foundation Grants, 56
Abundance Foundation Local Community Grants, 58
ACCF Dennis and Melanie Bieberich Community Enrichment Fund Grants, 59
ACCF of Indiana Angel Funds Grants, 62
ACCF of Indiana Anonymous Community Enrichment Fund Grants, 63
ACCF of Indiana Bank of Geneva Heritage Fund Grants, 64
ACCF of Indiana First Merchants Bank / Decatur Bank and Trust Fund Grants, 66

ACCF of Indiana Michael Basham Community Enrichment Fund Grants, 67
ACCF of Indiana Ron and Susie Ballard Community Enrichment Fund Grants, 68
ACCF Ralph Biggs Memorial Community Enrichment Fund Grants, 69
ACF Abandoned Infants Assistance Grants, 70
ACF Adoption Opportunities Grants, 71
ACF American Indian and Alaska Native Early Head Start Expansion Grants, 72
ACF Basic Center Program Grants, 73
ACF Child Abuse Prevention and Treatment Act Discretionary Funds Grants, 74
ACF Child Welfare Training Grants, 75
ACF Community-Based Child Abuse Prevention (CBCAP) Grants, 76
ACF Community-Based Child Abuse Prevention (CBCAP) Tribal and Migrant DiscretionaryGrants, 77
ACF Ethnic Community Self Help Grants, 80
ACF Infant Adoption Awareness Training Program Grants, 84
ACF National Human Trafficking Hotline Grants, 86
ACF Promoting Safe and Stable Families (PSSF) Program Grants, 89
ACF Social and Economic Development Strategies Grants, 93
ACF Street Outreach Program Grants, 94
ACF Transitional Living Program and Maternity Group Homes Grants, 96
ACF Tribal Maternal, Infant, and Early Childhood Home Visiting Program: Development and Implementation Grants, 97
ACF Tribal Maternal, Infant, and Early Childhood Home Visiting Program: Implementation and Expansion Grants, 98
ACF Unaccompanied Refugee Children Grants, 99
ACF Voluntary Agencies Matching Grants, 100
ACL Rehabilitation Research and Training Center (RRTC) on Employment of Transition-Age Youth with Disabilities Grants, 107
Acuity Charitable Foundation Grants, 110
Adams and Reese Corporate Giving Grants, 114
Adams Family Fdn of Nora Springs Grants, 118
Adelaide Christian Home For Children Grants, 124
ALA Penguin Random House Young Readers Group Award, 183
Alaska Airlines Corporation Career Connections for Youth Grants, 193
Alaska Community Foundation Children's Trust Tier 1 Community Based Child Abuse and Neglect Prevention Grants, 198
Alaska Community Foundation Children's Trust Tier 1 Parenting and Child Development Educational Grants, 199
Alaska Community Foundation Children's Trust Tier 2 Innovation Grants, 200
Alaska Community Foundation Ketchikan Community Foundation Grant, 206
Allan C. and Lelia J. Garden Foundation Grants, 236
Allen Foundation Educational Nutrition Grants, 238
Alliance for Strong Families and Communities Grants, 239
Alloy Family Foundation Grants, 241
Amelia Sillman Rockwell and Carlos Perry Rockwell Charities Fund Grants, 250
American Indian Youth Running Strong Grants, 256
Amway Corporation Contributions, 269
Anderson Foundation Grants, 271
Armstrong McDonald Foundation Children and Youth Grants, 300
Arthur M. Blank Family Foundation AMB West Community Fund Grants, 304
Arthur M. Blank Family Foundation American Explorers Grants, 305
Arthur M. Blank Family Foundation Molly Blank Fund Grants, 310
Arthur M. Blank Family Foundation Mountain Sky Guest Ranch Fund Grants, 311

Arthur M. Blank Family Foundation Pathways to Success Grants, 312
ATA Local Community Relations Grants, 324
Aunt Kate Foundation Grants, 331
Avery-Fuller-Welch Children's Fdn Grants, 336
Avery Foundation Grants, 339
Back Home Again Foundation Grants, 344
Baltimore Community Foundation Mitzvah Fund for Good Deeds Grants, 349
Baltimore Ravens Corporate Giving, 350
Bank of Hawaii Foundation Grants, 360
Bank of the Orient Community Giving, 361
Baton Rouge Area Foundation Every Kid a King Fund Grants, 364
Baxter International Corporate Giving Grants, 368
Bay Area Community Foundation Arenac County Healthy Youth/Healthy Seniors Fund Grants, 372
Bay Area Community Fdn Auburn Area Chamber of Commerce Enrichment Fund Grants, 373
Bay Area Community Foundation Bay County Healthy Youth/Healthy Seniors Fund Grants, 374
Bay Area Community Foundation Civic League Endowment Fund Grants, 375
Bay Area Community Foundation Dow CommunityGives Youth Service Prog Grants, 377
Bay Area Community Foundation Nathalie Awrey Memorial Fund Grants, 381
Bayer Fund Community Development Grants, 383
Baystate Financial Charitable Foundation Grants, 385
Ben B. Cheney Foundation Grants, 402
Ben Cohen StandUp Foundation Grants, 403
Bernard and Audre Rapoport Foundation Arts and Culture Grants, 407
Bernard and Audre Rapoport Foundation Community Building and Social Service Grants, 408
Bernard and Audre Rapoport Foundation Democracy and Civic Participation Grants, 409
Bernard and Audre Rapoport Foundation Education Grants, 410
Best Buy Children's Foundation @15 Community Grants , 414
Bierhaus Foundation Grants, 421
Blue Grass Community Foundation Hudson-Ellis Grants, 449
Bridgestone Americas Trust Fund Grants, 469
Bushrod H. Campbell and Adah F. Hall Charity Fund Grants, 486
C.F. Adams Charitable Trust Grants, 488
Caesars Foundation Grants, 492
Campbell Foundation Grants, 500
CFFVR Jewelers Mutual Chartbl Giving Grants, 543
CFF Winter Park Community Grants, 551
CFGR SisterFund Grants, 554
CFGR Ujima Legacy Fund Grants, 555
CFNEM Youth Advisory Council Grants, 558
Chapman Family Foundation, 562
Charles H. Pearson Foundation Grants, 566
Charles N. and Eleanor Knight Leigh Foundation Grants, 568
Cheryl Spencer Memorial Foundation Grants, 576
Christine and Katharina Pauly Charitable Trust Grants, 601
CICF Howard Intermill and Marion Intermill Fenstermaker Grants, 605
Citizens Savings Foundation Grants, 617
Claremont Savings Bank Foundation Grants, 623
Cleveland Foundation Higley Fund Grants, 634
Cleveland Foundation Legacy Village Lyndhurst Community Fund Grants, 636
Cleveland H. Dodge Foundation Grants, 637
CMS Historically Black Colleges and Universities (HBCU) Health Services Research Grants, 639
CNCS AmeriCorps State and National Grants, 643
CNCS Foster Grandparent Projects Grants, 646
Collective Brands Foundation Payless Gives Shoes 4 Kids Grants, 655
Community Foundation for Kettering Grants, 676
Community Foundation for San Benito County Grants, 677

Community Foundation of Abilene Future Fund Grants, 689
Community Foundation of Crawford County, 695
Community Foundation of Louisville Boyette and Edna Edwards Fund Grants, 718
Community Foundation of Louisville Dr. W. Barnett Owen Memorial Fund for the Children of Louisville and Jefferson County Grants, 723
Community Foundation of Louisville Human Services Grants, 726
Community Fdn of Southern Indiana Grants, 736
Community Foundation of Western Massachusetts Grants, 741
Countess Moira Charitable Foundation Grants, 752
Covenant to Care for Children Enrichment Fund Grants, 758
Crane Fund Grants, 763
CUNA Mutual Group Fdn Community Grants, 770
Curtis Foundation Grants, 771
Daniels Fund Youth Development Grants, 784
David Alan and Susan Berkman Rahm Foundation Grants, 785
David and Laura Merage Foundation Grants, 789
Deaconess Foundation Advocacy Grants, 804
Decatur County Community Foundation Large Project Grants, 811
Decatur County Community Foundation Small Project Grants, 812
Delaware Community Foundation Grants, 817
Del Mar Foundation Community Grants, 820
Delmarva Power & Light Contributions, 821
Delta Air Lines Foundation Youth Development Grants, 824
Deuce McAllister Catch 22 Foundation Grants, 828
Dollar General Youth Literacy Grants, 837
Don and May Wilkins Charitable Trust Grants, 842
Dorrance Family Foundation Grants, 845
Eastern Bank Charitable Foundation Partnerships Grants, 881
Eastern Bank Charitable Foundation Targeted Grants, 882
Edward and Romell Ackley Foundation Grants, 889
Effie Allen Little Foundation Grants, 894
Effie Kuhlman Charitable Trust Grants, 896
Eide Bailly Resourcefullness Awards, 897
Elmer Roe Deaver Foundation Grants, 906
Emerson Kampen Foundation Grants, 911
Essex County Community Foundation F1rst Jobs Fund Grants, 930
Ezra M. Cutting Trust Grants, 945
Fidelity Charitable Gift Fund Grants, 956
Fidelity Foundation Grants, 957
Finish Line Youth Foundation Legacy Grants, 962
First Hawaiian Bank Foundation Corporate Giving Grants, 967
First Nations Development Institute Native Youth and Culture Fund Grants, 974
First Nations Development Institute Nourishing Native Children: Feeding Our Future Project Grants, 975
Florence Foundation Grants, 978
Foundations of East Chicago Youth Development Grants, 998
Four County Community Foundation General Grants, 1000
Four County Community Foundation Healthy Senior/Healthy Youth Fund Grants, 1001
Four Lanes Trust Grants, 1005
Frederick McDonald Trust Grants, 1017
Friends of Hawaii Charities Grants, 1024
Fuller Foundation Youth At Risk Grants, 1028
Gardner Foundation Grants, 1035
George B. Page Foundation Grants, 1044
George H.C. Ensworth Memorial Fund Grants, 1049
George W. Wells Foundation Grants, 1057
Gil and Dody Weaver Foundation Grants, 1071
GNOF Norco Community Grants, 1089
Go Daddy Cares Charitable Contributions, 1093
Golden Heart Community Foundation Grants, 1094

Greater Tacoma Community Foundation Spark Grants, 1114
Greater Tacoma Community Foundation Youth Program Grants, 1115
Green River Area Community Fdn Grants, 1117
Greenspun Family Foundation Grants, 1118
GTRCF Boys and Girls Club of Grand Traverse Endowment Grants, 1126
GTRCF Elk Rapids Area Community Endowment Grants, 1127
GTRCF Grand Traverse Families in Action for Youth Endowment Grants, 1129
GTRCF Healthy Youth and Healthy Seniors Endowment Grants, 1130
GTRCF Youth Endowment Grants, 1133
Haddad Foundation Grants, 1139
Hannah's Helping Hands Grants, 1165
Harry and Helen Sands Charitable Trust Grants, 1181
Harry and Jeanette Weinberg Fdn Grants, 1182
Hartley Foundation Grants, 1186
Harvey E. Najim Family Foundation Grants, 1187
Hattie Mae Lesley Foundation Grants, 1195
Hawai'i Community Foundation Richard Smart Fund Grants, 1204
Hawai'i Community Foundation Victoria S. and Bradley L. Geist Foundation: Capacity Building Grants, 1206
Hawai'i Community Foundation Victoria S. and Bradley L. Geist Foundation: Enhancement Grants, 1207
Hawai'i Community Foundation Victoria S. and Bradley L. Geist Foundation: Supporting Transitioning Foster Youth Grants, 1209
Hawaii Children's Cancer Fdn Contributions, 1212
Hawaii Community Foundation Omidyar Ohana Fund Grants, 1213
Hawaii Community Foundation Oscar and Rosetta Fish Fund Grants, 1214
Hawaii Community Foundation Sanford Harmony Pillars of Peace Grants, 1217
Hawaii Electric Industries Charitable Foundation Grants, 1218
Hearst Foundations Social Service Grants, 1224
Helen G., Henry F., & Louise Tuechter Dornette Foundation Grants, 1229
Henry and Ruth Blaustein Rosenberg Foundation Youth Development Grants, 1237
Henry F. Koch Residual Trust Grants, 1241
Herman P. and Sophia Taubman Fdn Grants, 1247
Hillsdale County Community Foundation General Grants, 1250
Hillsdale County Community Foundation Y.O.U.T.H. Grants, 1252
Hubbard Farms Charitable Foundation Grants, 1272
ICCF Youth Advisory Council Grants, 1282
Iddings Foundation Capital Project Grants, 1283
Iddings Foundation Major Project Grants, 1284
Iddings Foundation Medium Project Grants, 1285
Iddings Foundation Small Project Grants, 1286
Initiaive Fdn Inside-Out Connections Grants, 1303
Inland Empire Community Foundation Coachella Valley Youth Grants, 1307
Inland Empire Community Foundation Native Youth Grants, 1308
Inland Empire Community Foundation Riverside Youth Grants, 1309
Inland Empire Community Foundation San Bernardino Youth Grants, 1310
Island Insurance Foundation Grants, 1316
Jack H. and William M. Light Charitable Trust Grants, 1330
Jack Kent Cooke Fdn Good Neighbor Grants, 1331
Jack Satter Foundation Grants, 1334
Janet Spencer Weekes Foundation Grants, 1348
Jim Blevins Foundation Grants, 1365
John and Marcia Goldman Foundation Youth Development Grants, 1368
John P. Ellbogen Fdn Community Grants, 1377
Johnson County Community Foundation Youth Philanthropy Initiative Grants, 1380

Joseph H. and Florence A. Roblee Foundation Children and Youth Grants, 1385
Josephine Schell Russell Chartbl Trust Grants, 1389
Joseph S. Stackpole Charitable Trust Grants, 1390
Joyce and Randy Seckman Charitable Foundation Grants, 1393
Judith Clark-Morrill Foundation Grants, 1395
Judy and Peter Blum Kovler Foundation Grants, 1396
Julia and Tunnicliff Fox Chartbl Trust Grants, 1397
Julius N. Frankel Foundation Grants, 1400
Kate B. Reynolds Charitable Trust Poor and Needy Grants, 1417
Kimball Foundation Grants, 1432
Kimball International-Habig Foundation Health and Human Services Grants, 1434
Kirby Laing Foundation Grants, 1439
Koch Family Foundation (Annapolis) Grants, 1444
Kosasa Foundation Grants, 1450
Kovler Family Foundation Grants, 1455
Lake County Community Fund Grants, 1463
Land O'Lakes Fdn California Region Grants, 1465
Land O'Lakes Foundation Community Grants, 1466
LEGO Children's Fund Grants, 1480
Lilly Endowment Summer Youth Grants, 1492
Lily Palmer Fry Memorial Trust Grants, 1493
Locations Foundation Legacy Grants, 1504
Lois and Richard England Family Foundation Out-of-School-Time Grants, 1506
Lynn and Foster Friess Family Fdn Grants, 1520
M.D. Anderson Foundation Grants, 1523
Madison Community Foundation Grants, 1535
Make Sense Foundation Grants, 1548
Marion and Miriam Rose Fund Grants, 1569
Mary Black Foundation Early Childhood Development Grants, 1586
Mary Cofer Trigg Trust Fund Grants, 1587
Mary W.B. Curtis Trust Grants, 1599
Mathile Family Foundation Grants, 1604
May and Stanley Smith Charitable Trust Grants, 1613
Mead Family Foundation Grants, 1625
Merrick Foundation Grants, 1640
MetLife Fdn Preparing Young People Grants, 1645
Middlesex Savings Charitable Foundation Capacity Building Grants, 1669
Mill Spring Foundation Grants, 1674
Milton Hicks Wood and Helen Gibbs Wood Charitable Trust Grants, 1676
Minnie M. Jones Trust Grants, 1678
Monsanto Kids Garden Fresh Grants, 1682
Monsanto United States Grants, 1684
Montgomery County Community Foundation Youth Services Grants, 1691
Moody Foundation Grants, 1692
Morris Stulsaft Foundation Educational Support for Children Grants, 1697
Morris Stulsaft Foundation Participation in the the Arts Grants, 1698
Morton K. and Jane Blaustein Foundation Educational Opportunity Grants, 1700
Moses Kimball Fund Grants, 1701
Motiv8 Foundation Grants, 1702
NCMCF Youth Advisory Council Grants, 1727
New Hampshire Department of Justice Children's Justice Act Coronavirus Emergency Grants, 1749
New Jersey Office of Faith Based Initiatives Services to At Risk Grants, 1752
NFL Charities NFL Player Foundation Grants, 1754
NSTA Faraday Science Communicator Award, 1778
NZDIA Community Org Grants Scheme, 1796
Olga Sipolin Children's Fund Grants, 1815
Olive B. Cole Foundation Grants, 1816
Oppenstein Brothers Foundation Grants, 1827
Orange County Community Foundation Grants, 1828
Ordean Foundation Partnership Grants, 1831
OSF Early Childhood Program Grants, 1841
OSF Youth Action Fund Grants in Kyrgyzstan, 1846
Pacers Foundation Be Drug-Free Grants, 1856
Pacers Foundation Be Educated Grants, 1857
Pacers Foundation Be Tolerant Grants, 1859

Pacers Foundation Indiana Fever's Be YOUnique Fund Grants, 1860
Parker Foundation (California) Grants, 1869
Patricia Kisker Foundation Grants, 1879
Paul and Edith Babson Foundation Grants, 1881
Perkin Fund Grants, 1937
Perry and Sandy Massie Foundation Grants, 1941
Perry County Community Foundation Youth Development Grants, 1943
Peter and Elizabeth C. Tower Foundation Intellectual Disabilities Grants, 1944
Peter and Elizabeth C. Tower Foundation Learning Disability Grants, 1945
Peter and Elizabeth C. Tower Foundation Mental Health Grants, 1946
Peter and Elizabeth C. Tower Foundation Small Grants, 1947
Peter and Elizabeth C. Tower Foundation Substance Use Disorders Grants, 1948
Peter and Elizabeth C. Tower Foundation Technology Initiative Grants, 1949
Peter and Elizabeth C. Tower Foundation Technology Planning Grants, 1950
Pettus Foundation Grants, 1952
Philip Boyle Foundation Grants, 1961
Piedmont Natural Gas Foundation Health and Human Services Grants, 1968
Pike County Community Foundation Youth Development Grants, 1971
Pinnacle Entertainment Foundation Grants, 1972
Piper Trust Education Grants, 1977
Pittsburgh Foundation Healthy Children and Adults Grants, 1981
PMI Foundation Grants, 1982
Pohlad Family Fdn Large Capital Grants, 1990
Pohlad Family Foundation Youth Advancement Grants, 1993
Polk County Community Foundation Bradley Breakthrough Community Benefit Grants, 1995
Porter County Community Foundation Health and Wellness Grant, 2002
Porter County Community Foundation PCgivingproject Grants, 2003
Portland Fdn - Women's Giving Circle Grant, 2006
Posey County Community Foundation Youth Development Grants, 2010
PPCF Edson Foundation Grants, 2015
PPCF Esther M. and Freeman E. Everett Charitable Foundation Grants, 2016
Presidio Fencing Club Youth Fencers Assistance Scholarships, 2019
Price Chopper's Golub Foundation Grants, 2020
Public Welfare Fdn Juvenile Justice Grants, 2033
R.S. Gernon Trust Grants, 2047
Reinberger Foundation Grants, 2066
Richard Davoud Donchian Foundation Grants, 2070
Robert and Betty Wo Foundation Grants, 2083
Robert F. Lange Foundation Grants, 2090
Rosenberg Fund for Children Clinton and Muriel Jencks Memorial Fund Grants, 2109
Roy J. Carver Charitable Trust Youth Services and Recreation Grants, 2117
Ruth Camp Campbell Charitable Trust Grants, 2125
RWJF Childhood Obesity Grants, 2126
SACF Youth Advisory Council Grants, 2131
Saginaw County Community Foundation Youth FORCE Grants, 2136
Saltchuk Corporate Giving, 2141
San Antonio Area Foundation Annual Responsive Grants, 2147
Sand Hill Foundation Health and Opportunity Grants, 2153
Sandy Hill Foundation Grants, 2157
Scheumann Foundation Grants, 2166
Seattle Foundation Basic Needs Grants, 2175
Seattle Foundation Benjamin N. Phillips Memorial Fund Grants, 2176
Seybert Foundation Grants, 2184
Sobrato Family Foundation Grants, 2211
Sobrato Family Fdn Meeting Space Grants, 2212

Sobrato Family Foundation Office Space Grants, 2213
Southwest Initiative Foundation Grants, 2226
Spencer County Community Foundation Youth Development Grants, 2233
Stein Family Charitable Trust Grants, 2240
Sterling and Shelli Gardner Foundation Grants, 2243
Stillson Foundation Grants, 2245
Strong Foundation Grants, 2252
Suspened: Community Fdn for Greater Atlanta State Farm Education Assist Fund Grants, 2260
Sylvia Perkin Perpetual Charitable Trust Grants, 2263
Thomas and Agnes Carvel Foundation Grants, 2289
Thorman Boyle Foundation Grants, 2295
Tom C. Barnsley Foundation Grants, 2306
Toyota Motor Manuf of Mississippi Grants, 2312
Toyota Motor Manufacturing of Texas Grants, 2313
Toyota USA Foundation Safety Grants, 2320
Trinity Trust Summer Youth Mini Grants, 2321
Turtle Bay Foundation Grants, 2327
Union Labor Health Foundation Dental Angel Fund Grants, 2336
Union Pacific Foundation Health and Human Services Grants, 2338
United Friends of the Children Scholarships, 2341
United Healthcare Commty Grts in Michigan, 2343
Valley-Wide Health Systems Nurse Family Partnerships, 2372
Vanderburgh Community Foundation Youth Development Grants, 2375
Volkswagen Group of America Corporate Contributions Grants, 2389
Walker Area Community Foundation Grants, 2401
Walmart Fdn National Local Giving Grants, 2404
Warrick County Community Foundation Youth Development Grants, 2412
Washington County Community Fdn Grants, 2416
Weaver Popcorn Foundation Grants, 2421
Whole Foods Foundation, 2445
Wilton and Effie Hebert Foundation Grants, 2476
Winifred Johnson Clive Foundation Grants, 2478
WinnCompanies Charitable Giving, 2479
Wold Foundation Grants, 2482
Wolfe Associates Grants, 2483
Women's Fund of Hawaii Grants, 2484
Wood-Claeyssens Foundation Grants, 2486
World of Children Youth Award, 2493
Wyoming Community Fdn General Grants, 2501
Wyoming Community Foundation Hazel Patterson Memorial Grants, 2502
Wyomissing Foundation Community Grants, 2504
Youths' Friends Association Grants, 2511
Zollner Foundation Grants, 2526

Youth Violence

Alaska Community Foundation Children's Trust Tier 1 Community Based Child Abuse and Neglect Prevention Grants, 198
Alaska Community Foundation Children's Trust Tier 1 Parenting and Child Development Educational Grants, 199
Alaska Community Foundation Children's Trust Tier 2 Innovation Grants, 200
Alaska Community Foundation Ketchikan Community Foundation Grant, 206
Allstate Foundation Tolerance, Inclusion, and Diversity Grants, 245
Ben Cohen StandUp Foundation Grants, 403
Bernard and Audre Rapoport Foundation Community Building and Social Service Grants, 408
Deuce McAllister Catch 22 Foundation Grants, 828
First Nations Development Institute Native Youth and Culture Fund Grants, 974
Foundations of East Chicago Youth Development Grants, 998
Fuller Foundation Youth At Risk Grants, 1028
Gamble Foundation Grants, 1032
Go Daddy Cares Charitable Contributions, 1093
Greater Tacoma Community Foundation Youth Program Grants, 1115

GTRCF Boys and Girls Club of Grand Traverse Endowment Grants, 1126
Hawai'i Community Foundation Kuki'o Community Fund Grants, 1202
Joseph H. and Florence A. Roblee Foundation Children and Youth Grants, 1385
Kansas Health Foundation Recognition Grants, 1415
Ms. Fdn for Women Ending Violence Grants, 1708
New Jersey Office of Faith Based Initiatives Services to At Risk Youth Grants, 1752
NFL Charities Pro Bowl Community Grants in Hawaii, 1755
Ordean Foundation Catalyst Grants, 1830
Ordean Foundation Partnership Grants, 1831
Piedmont Natural Gas Foundation Health and Human Services Grants, 1968
Public Welfare Fdn Juvenile Justice Grants, 2033
Sorenson Legacy Foundation Grants, 2217
United Methodist Women Brighter Future for Children and Youth Grants, 2346
Winifred Johnson Clive Foundation Grants, 2478

Zoology

Jerry L. and Barbara J. Burris Fdn Grants, 1362

Zoos

Chesapeake Bay Trust Mini Grants, 578
Elizabeth Huth Coates Charitable Foundation Grants, 900
FirstEnergy Foundation Community Grants, 965
George F. Baker Trust Grants, 1046
Hubbard Broadcasting Foundation Grants, 1269
Jerry L. and Barbara J. Burris Fdn Grants, 1362
Katherine John Murphy Foundation Grants, 1419
Kovler Family Foundation Grants, 1454
Lee and Ramona Bass Foundation Grants, 1478
Mill Spring Foundation Grants, 1674
NSTA Faraday Science Communicator Award, 1778
Parker Foundation (California) Grants, 1869
PMI Foundation Grants, 1982
Reinberger Foundation Grants, 2066
Riedman Foundation Grants, 2076
Saint Louis Rams Foundation Community Donations, 2139
Schlessman Family Foundation Grants, 2167
Shell Deer Park Grants, 2186
Thelma Doelger Charitable Trust Grants, 2288
Union Pacific Fdn Community & Civic Grants, 2337
Widgeon Point Charitable Foundation Grants, 2447

PROGRAM TYPE INDEX

NOTE: Numbers refer to entry numbers

Adult Basic Education
7-Eleven Corporate Giving Grants, 8
Abell Foundation Education Grants, 53
ACCF of Indiana Bank of Geneva Heritage Fund
    Grants, 64
ACCF of Indiana First Merchants Bank / Decatur
    Bank and Trust Fund Grants, 66
ACF Refugee Career Pathways Grants, 90
ACF Voluntary Agencies Matching Grants, 100
Achelis and Bodman Foundation Grants, 101
Achelis Foundation Grants, 102
Adolph Coors Foundation Grants, 129
AEGON Transamerica Foundation Education and
    Financial Literacy Grants, 132
Akron Community Fdn Education Grants, 151
Albert W. Cherne Foundation Grants, 222
Alliance for Strong Families and Communities
    Grants, 239
Ar-Hale Family Foundation Grants, 290
Atkinson Foundation Community Grants, 325
Atlanta Foundation Grants, 326
Atlas Insurance Agency Foundation Grants, 329
Autauga Area Community Foundation Grants, 334
Bank of the Orient Community Giving, 361
BBF Maine Family Literacy Initiative Planning
    Grants, 388
Beckman Coulter Foundation Grants, 394
Benton Community Foundation Grants, 405
Bernard and Audre Rapoport Foundation Education
    Grants, 410
Blandin Foundation Invest Early Grants, 438
Blue Mountain Community Foundation Warren
    Community Action Fund Grants, 457
Blue River Community Foundation Grants, 458
Bridgestone Americas Trust Fund Grants, 469
Brown County Community Foundation Grants, 475
Camille Beckman Foundation Grants, 499
Carl R. Hendrickson Family Foundation Grants, 509
Cass County Community Foundation Grants, 516
CFGR SisterFund Grants, 554
Charles Nelson Robinson Fund Grants, 569
Chicago Board of Trade Foundation Grants, 580
Chilkat Valley Community Foundation Grants, 588
CIGNA Foundation Grants, 611
Claremont Savings Bank Foundation Grants, 623
Clinton County Community Foundation Grants, 638
CNCS AmeriCorps State and National Grants, 643
CNCS AmeriCorps VISTA Project Grants, 645
Community Foundation for the Capital Region
    Grants, 687
Community Foundation of Bartholomew County
    Heritage Fund Grants, 690
Community Foundation of Boone County Grants, 694
Community Foundation of Crawford County, 695
Community Foundation of Eastern Connecticut
    General Southeast Grants, 696
Community Foundation of Greater Fort Wayne -
    Community Endowment and Clarke Endowment
    Grants, 705
Community Foundation of Louisville Education
    Grants, 724
Community Foundation of Western Massachusetts
    Grants, 741
David and Barbara B. Hirschhorn Foundation
    Education and Literacy Grants, 786
Dayton Power and Light Foundation Grants, 802
Dean Foods Community Involvement Grants, 805
DeKalb County Community Foundation - Literacy
    Grant, 814
Del Mar Foundation Community Grants, 820
Dollar General Family Literacy Grants, 835
DOL Youthbuild Grants, 838
Eastern Bank Charitable Foundation Partnerships
    Grants, 881
Eastern Bank Charitable Foundation Targeted
    Grants, 882
Edward and Ellen Roche Relief Fdn Grants, 887
Edward F. Swinney Trust Grants, 890

Edward W. and Stella C. Van Houten Memorial Fund
    Grants, 892
Eide Bailly Resourcefulness Awards, 897
Elizabeth Morse Genius Charitable Trust Grants, 901
El Pomar Foundation Anna Keesling Ackerman Fund
    Grants, 907
El Pomar Foundation Grants, 908
Eulalie Bloedel Schneider Foundation Grants, 936
F.R. Bigelow Foundation Grants, 947
Fidelity Charitable Gift Fund Grants, 956
First Hawaiian Bank Foundation Corporate Giving
    Grants, 967
First Lady's Family Literacy Initiative for Texas
    Family Literacy Trailblazer Grants, 968
First Lady's Family Literacy Initiative for Texas
    Implementation Grants, 969
First Lady's Family Literacy Initiative for Texas
    Planning Grants, 970
Foundation Beyond Belief Compassionate Impact
    Grants, 986
Foundation Beyond Belief Humanist Grants, 987
Foundation for Rural Service Education Grants, 991
Four County Community Foundation General
    Grants, 1000
Frank Reed and Margaret Jane Peters Memorial Fund
    II Grants, 1014
G.N. Wilcox Trust Grants, 1031
Gannett Foundation Community Action Grants, 1033
George W. Wells Foundation Grants, 1057
Greater Sitka Legacy Fund Grants, 1111
Greygates Foundation Grants, 1120
H.B. Fuller Foundation Grants, 1138
HAF Community Grants, 1141
Hannaford Supermarkets Community Giving, 1164
Harden Foundation Grants, 1166
Harold Brooks Foundation Grants, 1172
Harris and Eliza Kempner Fund Ed Grants, 1176
Hawaii Electric Industries Charitable Foundation
    Grants, 1218
Hawaii State Legislature Grant-In-Aid, 1219
HBF Pathways Out of Poverty Grants, 1222
Helen Gertrude Sparks Charitable Trust Grants, 1230
HLTA Visitor Industry Charity Walk Grant, 1254
Iddings Foundation Medium Project Grants, 1285
Island Insurance Foundation Grants, 1316
J.W. Gardner II Foundation Grants, 1323
J. Watumull Fund Grants, 1326
James Ford Bell Foundation Grants, 1339
James S. Copley Foundation Grants, 1345
Jessica Stevens Community Foundation Grants, 1363
John H. and Wilhelmina D. Harland Charitable
    Foundation Children and Youth Grants, 1374
Joseph H. and Florence A. Roblee Foundation
    Education Grants, 1386
Joseph Henry Edmondson Foundation Grants, 1388
Joseph S. Stackpole Charitable Trust Grants, 1390
Ketchikan Community Foundation Grants, 1429
Kodiak Community Foundation Grants, 1446
Leo Niessen Jr., Charitable Trust Grants, 1484
Liberty Bank Foundation Grants, 1488
Lubrizol Foundation Grants, 1513
Luella Kemper Trust Grants, 1517
M.A. Rikard Charitable Trust Grants, 1521
Mabel Louise Riley Foundation Family Strengthening
    Small Grants, 1528
Mardag Foundation Grants, 1554
Margaret M. Walker Charitable Fdn Grants, 1556
Marin Community Foundation Social Justice and
    Interfaith Understanding Grants, 1567
Marquette Bank Neighborhood Commit Grants, 1577
Mary Wilmer Covey Charitable Trust Grants, 1600
May and Stanley Smith Charitable Trust Grants, 1613
McCune Charitable Foundation Grants, 1617
McCune Foundation Education Grants, 1618
Middlesex Savings Charitable Foundation
    Educational Opportunities Grants, 1670
Norcliffe Foundation Grants, 1766
Oak Fdn Housing and Homelessness Grants, 1800

OMNOVA Solutions Fdn Education Grants, 1820
Oppenstein Brothers Foundation Grants, 1827
Oregon Community Fdn Community Grants, 1833
Parkersburg Area Community Foundation Action
    Grants, 1871
PepsiCo Foundation Grants, 1935
Pettus Foundation Grants, 1952
Peyton Anderson Foundation Grants, 1954
Philip L. Graham Fund Education Grants, 1962
Piper Jaffray Foundation Communities Giving
    Grants, 1974
PMI Foundation Grants, 1982
Polk County Community Foundation Marjorie M.
    and Lawrence R. Bradley Endowment Fund
    Grants, 1998
Polk County Community Foundation Unrestricted
    Grants, 2001
Portland General Electric Foundation Grants, 2007
ProLiteracy National Book Fund Grants, 2026
Putnam County Community Fdn Grants, 2040
RCF Individual Assistance Grants, 2063
Reinberger Foundation Grants, 2066
Robbins-de Beaumont Foundation Grants, 2080
Robert and Betty Wo Foundation Grants, 2083
Robert R. McCormick Tribune Foundation
    Community Grants, 2093
Robert R. Meyer Foundation Grants, 2094
Rose Community Foundation Child and Family
    Development Grants, 2103
Rose Hills Foundation Grants, 2106
Saltchuk Corporate Giving, 2141
Sand Hill Foundation Health and Opportunity
    Grants, 2153
Serco Foundation Grants, 2181
Seward Community Foundation Grants, 2182
Seward Community Foundation Mini-Grants, 2183
Shield-Ayres Foundation Grants, 2189
Sony Corporation of America Grants, 2216
Sorenson Legacy Foundation Grants, 2217
Southern California Edison Education Grants, 2218
Sylvia Perkin Perpetual Charitable Trust Grants, 2263
Thomas Sill Foundation Grants, 2292
TJX Foundation Grants, 2303
UPS Foundation Economic and Global Literacy
    Grants, 2351
UUA Actions of Public Witness Grants, 2365
UUA Congregation-Based Community Organizing
    Grants, 2366
UUA Fund Grants, 2367
UUA International Fund Grants, 2368
UUA Just Society Fund Grants, 2369
UUA Social Responsibility Grants, 2370
Vanderburgh Community Foundation Men's Fund
    Grants, 2373
Vanderburgh County Community Foundation
    Women's Fund Grants, 2376
Walker Area Community Foundation Grants, 2401
Walter J. and Betty C. Zable Fdn Grants, 2406
Warrick County Community Foundation Women's
    Fund, 2411
Wayne County Foundation Grants, 2419
WHO Foundation General Grants, 2443
WHO Foundation Volunteer Service Grants, 2444
WinnCompanies Charitable Giving, 2479
Women's Fund of Hawaii Grants, 2484
Woods Charitable Fund Education Grants, 2488
Xerox Foundation Grants, 2507

Adult/Family Literacy Training
7-Eleven Corporate Giving Grants, 8
ACCF of Indiana Bank of Geneva Heritage Fund
    Grants, 64
ACCF of Indiana Berne Ready Mix Community
    Enrichment Fund Grants, 65
ACCF of Indiana First Merchants Bank / Decatur
    Bank and Trust Fund Grants, 66
ACF Refugee Career Pathways Grants, 90
ACF Voluntary Agencies Matching Grants, 100

Achelis and Bodman Foundation Grants, 101
Achelis Foundation Grants, 102
Adolph Coors Foundation Grants, 129
AEGON Transamerica Foundation Education and
    Financial Literacy Grants, 132
Akron Community Fdn Education Grants, 151
Albert W. Cherne Foundation Grants, 222
Alcatel-Lucent Technologies Foundation Grants, 224
Alliance for Strong Families and Communities
    Grants, 239
Alliant Energy Foundation Community Giving for
    Good Sponsorship Grants, 240
Alpha Natural Resources Corporate Giving, 246
American Indian Youth Running Strong Grants, 256
American Savings Foundation Program Grants, 261
Assisi Foundation of Memphis General Grants, 318
Assisi Foundation of Memphis Mini Grants, 319
Atkinson Foundation Community Grants, 325
Atlanta Foundation Grants, 326
Atlas Insurance Agency Foundation Grants, 329
Autauga Area Community Foundation Grants, 334
Bank of Hawaii Foundation Grants, 360
Bank of the Orient Community Giving, 361
Bay Area Community Foundation Civic League
    Endowment Fund Grants, 375
BBF Florida Family Literacy Initiative Grants, 386
BBF Maine Family Literacy Initiative Implementation
    Grants, 387
BBF Maine Family Literacy Planning Grants, 388
BBF Maryland Family Literacy Initiative
    Implementation Grants, 389
BBF Maryland Family Literacy Initiative Planning
    Grants, 390
BBF National Grants for Family Literacy, 391
Beckman Coulter Foundation Grants, 394
Benton Community Foundation Grants, 405
Bernard and Audre Rapoport Foundation Education
    Grants, 410
Best Buy Children's Fdn @15 Teach Awards, 416
Blue Grass Community Foundation Early Childhood
    Education and Literacy Grants, 445
Blue Mountain Community Foundation Warren
    Community Action Fund Grants, 457
Blue River Community Foundation Grants, 458
Brown County Community Foundation Grants, 475
Cabot Corporation Foundation Grants, 490
Caesars Foundation Grants, 492
Camille Beckman Foundation Grants, 499
Carl B. and Florence E. King Foundation Grants, 506
Cass County Community Foundation Grants, 516
CFFVR Basic Needs Giving Partnership Grants, 537
CFFVR Schmidt Family G4 Grants, 548
CFGR SisterFund Grants, 554
CFGR Ujima Legacy Fund Grants, 555
Charles Delmar Foundation Grants, 564
Chicago Board of Trade Foundation Grants, 580
Chilkat Valley Community Foundation Grants, 588
CIGNA Foundation Grants, 611
Claremont Savings Bank Foundation Grants, 623
Clinton County Community Foundation Grants, 638
CNCS AmeriCorps State and National Grants, 643
CNCS AmeriCorps VISTA Project Grants, 645
CNO Financial Group Community Grants, 650
Community Foundation for Greater Buffalo Niagara
    Area Foundation Grants, 673
Community Foundation for the Capital Region
    Grants, 687
Community Foundation for the National Capital
    Region Community Leadership Grants, 688
Community Foundation of Bartholomew County
    Heritage Fund Grants, 690
Community Foundation of Boone County Grants, 694
Community Foundation of Crawford County, 695
Community Foundation of Eastern Connecticut
    General Southeast Grants, 696
Community Foundation of Greater Chattanooga
    Grants, 704
Community Foundation of Greater Fort Wayne -
    Community Endowment and Clarke Endowment
    Grants, 705

Community Foundation of Louisville Education
    Grants, 724
Community Foundation of Muncie and Delaware
    County Maxon Grants, 734
Community Foundation of Western Massachusetts
    Grants, 741
David and Barbara B. Hirschhorn Foundation
    Education and Literacy Grants, 786
Dayton Power and Light Foundation Grants, 802
Deaconess Community Foundation Grants, 803
Dean Foundation Grants, 806
Del Mar Foundation Community Grants, 820
Delta Air Lines Foundation Community Enrichment
    Grants, 823
Dollar General Family Literacy Grants, 835
Edward and Ellen Roche Relief Fdn Grants, 887
Edward W. and Stella C. Van Houten Memorial Fund
    Grants, 892
Elizabeth Morse Genius Charitable Trust Grants, 901
Entergy Charitable Foundation Education and
    Literacy Grants, 917
Entergy Charitable Foundation Low-Income
    Initiatives and Solutions Grants, 918
Entergy Corporation Micro Grants, 919
Essex County Community Foundation Merrimack
    Valley Municipal Business Development and
    Recovery Fund Grants, 933
Ezra Jack Keats Foundation Mini-Grants, 944
F.R. Bigelow Foundation Grants, 947
Farmers Insurance Corporate Giving Grants, 948
Fidelity Charitable Gift Fund Grants, 956
First Hawaiian Bank Foundation Corporate Giving
    Grants, 967
First Lady's Family Literacy Initiative for Texas
    Family Literacy Trailblazer Grants, 968
First Lady's Family Literacy Initiative for Texas
    Implementation Grants, 969
First Lady's Family Literacy Initiative for Texas
    Planning Grants, 970
Foundation Beyond Belief Compassionate Impact
    Grants, 986
Foundation Beyond Belief Humanist Grants, 987
Foundation for Rural Service Education Grants, 991
Four County Community Foundation General
    Grants, 1000
Fourjay Foundation Grants, 1003
Frank Reed and Margaret Jane Peters Memorial Fund
    II Grants, 1014
Fred and Gretel Biel Charitable Trust Grants, 1016
Fremont Area Community Foundation Amazing X
    Grants, 1019
G.N. Wilcox Trust Grants, 1031
Gannett Foundation Community Action Grants, 1033
George I. Alden Trust Grants, 1051
George W. Wells Foundation Grants, 1057
Greater Sitka Legacy Fund Grants, 1111
H.B. Fuller Foundation Grants, 1138
HAF Community Grants, 1141
Hancock County Community Foundation - Field of
    Interest Grants, 1161
Hannaford Supermarkets Community Giving, 1164
Harold Brooks Foundation Grants, 1172
Harris and Eliza Kempner Fund Ed Grants, 1176
Hartley Foundation Grants, 1186
Hasbro Children's Fund Grants, 1189
Hattie M. Strong Foundation Grants, 1194
Hawai'i Community Foundation Family Literacy and
    Hawaii Pizza Hut Literacy Grants, 1201
Hawaii State Legislature Grant-In-Aid, 1219
HBF Pathways Out of Poverty Grants, 1222
Hearst Foundations Social Service Grants, 1224
Helen Bader Foundation Grants, 1227
Henry E. Niles Foundation Grants, 1240
Highmark Corporate Giving Grants, 1248
HLTA Visitor Industry Charity Walk Grant, 1254
Humana Foundation Grants, 1275
Iddings Foundation Major Project Grants, 1284
Iddings Foundation Medium Project Grants, 1285
ILA Grants for Literacy Projects in Countries with
    Developing Economies, 1292

Island Insurance Foundation Grants, 1316
IYI Responsible Fatherhood Grants, 1318
J.W. Gardner II Foundation Grants, 1323
J. Watumull Fund Grants, 1326
James and Abigail Campbell Family Fdn Grants, 1337
James LeVoy Sorenson Foundation Grants, 1343
James S. Copley Foundation Grants, 1345
Jane's Trust Grants, 1346
Jessica Stevens Community Foundation Grants, 1363
Jim Moran Foundation Grants, 1366
John H. and Wilhelmina D. Harland Charitable
    Foundation Children and Youth Grants, 1374
Johnson Scholarship Foundation Grants, 1382
Joseph H. and Florence A. Roblee Foundation
    Education Grants, 1386
Joseph H. and Florence A. Roblee Foundation Family
    Grants, 1387
Joseph Henry Edmondson Foundation Grants, 1388
Joseph S. Stackpole Charitable Trust Grants, 1390
Kenai Peninsula Foundation Grants, 1425
Ketchikan Community Foundation Grants, 1429
Kodiak Community Foundation Grants, 1446
Leo Goodwin Foundation Grants, 1482
Leo Niessen Jr., Charitable Trust Grants, 1484
LGA Family Foundation Grants, 1487
Linden Foundation Grants, 1494
LISC Capacity Building Grants, 1498
Locations Foundation Legacy Grants, 1504
Louis Calder Foundation Grants, 1511
Lubrizol Foundation Grants, 1513
M.A. Rikard Charitable Trust Grants, 1521
Mabel Louise Riley Foundation Family Strengthening
    Small Grants, 1528
Macquarie Bank Foundation Grants, 1532
Mardag Foundation Grants, 1554
Marie C. and Joseph C. Wilson Foundation Rochester
    Small Grants, 1559
Marin Community Foundation Social Justice and
    Interfaith Understanding Grants, 1567
Marquette Bank Neighborhood Commit Grants, 1577
Mary D. and Walter F. Frear Eleemosynary Trust
    Grants, 1588
Maryland State Department of Education Striving
    Readers Comprehensive Literacy Grants, 1596
Mary Wilmer Covey Charitable Trust Grants, 1600
May and Stanley Smith Charitable Trust Grants, 1613
McCune Charitable Foundation Grants, 1617
McCune Foundation Education Grants, 1618
McGraw-Hill Companies Community Grants, 1620
MFRI Community Mobilization Grants, 1654
Michigan Women Forward Grants, 1662
Middlesex Savings Charitable Foundation
    Educational Opportunities Grants, 1670
Moses Kimball Fund Grants, 1701
National 4-H Council Grants, 1720
Nationwide Insurance Foundation Grants, 1726
Norcliffe Foundation Grants, 1766
Northern Chautauqua Community Foundation
    Community Grants, 1769
OMNOVA Solutions Fdn Education Grants, 1820
Oregon Community Fdn Community Grants, 1833
Oregon Community Foundation Edna E. Harrell
    Community Children's Fund Grants, 1835
PacifiCare Foundation Grants, 1861
Parkersburg Area Community Foundation Action
    Grants, 1871
PepsiCo Foundation Grants, 1935
Percy B. Ferebee Endowment Grants, 1936
Petersburg Community Foundation Grants, 1951
Pettus Foundation Grants, 1952
Peyton Anderson Foundation Grants, 1954
Philip L. Graham Fund Education Grants, 1962
Piper Trust Children Grants, 1976
Piper Trust Education Grants, 1977
PMI Foundation Grants, 1982
Polk County Community Foundation Marjorie M.
    and Lawrence R. Bradley Endowment Fund
    Grants, 1998
Polk County Community Foundation Unrestricted
    Grants, 2001

Price Chopper's Golub Foundation Grants, 2020
ProLiteracy National Book Fund Grants, 2026
RCF Individual Assistance Grants, 2063
Reinberger Foundation Grants, 2066
RGk Foundation Grants, 2068
Richard Davoud Donchian Foundation Grants, 2070
Robbins-de Beaumont Foundation Grants, 2080
Robert Bowne Foundaion Edmund A. Stanley, Jr.
    Research Grants, 2086
Robert Bowne Foundation Fellowships, 2087
Robert Bowne Foundation Literacy Grants, 2088
Robert Bowne Fdn Youth-Centered Grants, 2089
Robert R. McCormick Tribune Foundation
    Community Grants, 2093
Robert R. Meyer Foundation Grants, 2094
Rose Hills Foundation Grants, 2106
RR Donnelley Foundation Grants, 2118
Saint Louis Rams Foundation Community
    Donations, 2139
Samuel S. Johnson Foundation Grants, 2146
San Antonio Area Foundation Annual Responsive
    Grants, 2147
Sand Hill Foundation Health and Opportunity
    Grants, 2153
Seattle Foundation Benjamin N. Phillips Memorial
    Fund Grants, 2176
Serco Foundation Grants, 2181
Seward Community Foundation Grants, 2182
Seward Community Foundation Mini-Grants, 2183
Shield-Ayres Foundation Grants, 2189
Sidney Stern Memorial Trust Grants, 2197
Sierra Health Foundation Responsive Grants, 2199
Sony Corporation of America Grants, 2216
Sorenson Legacy Foundation Grants, 2217
Southern California Edison Education Grants, 2218
Sterling-Turner Charitable Foundation Grants, 2242
Stocker Foundation Grants, 2247
Target Corporation Community Engagement Fund
    Grants, 2270
Textron Corporate Contributions Grants, 2286
Thomas Sill Foundation Grants, 2292
TJX Foundation Grants, 2303
Todd Brock Family Foundation Grants, 2305
Toyota USA Foundation Education Grants, 2318
Turtle Bay Foundation Grants, 2327
U.S. Bank Foundation Grants, 2330
Union Bank, N.A. Foundation Grants, 2334
UPS Foundation Economic and Global Literacy
    Grants, 2351
Vanderburgh Community Foundation Men's Fund
    Grants, 2373
Vanderburgh County Community Foundation
    Women's Fund Grants, 2376
Walker Area Community Foundation Grants, 2401
Wallace Foundation Grants, 2402
Warrick County Community Foundation Women's
    Fund, 2411
Wayne County Foundation Grants, 2419
Western New York Foundation Grants, 2429
WHO Foundation Education/Literacy Grants, 2442
WHO Foundation General Grants, 2443
WHO Foundation Volunteer Service Grants, 2444
Whole Foods Foundation, 2445
WinnCompanies Charitable Giving, 2479
Wiregrass Foundation Grants, 2480
Women's Fund of Hawaii Grants, 2484
Woods Charitable Fund Education Grants, 2488
Xerox Foundation Grants, 2507
YSA NEA Youth Leaders for Literacy Grants, 2518

Awards/Prizes

AAAS/Subaru SB&F Prize for Excl in Sci Books, 22
AACAP George Tarjan Award for Contributions in
    Developmental Disabilities, 25
AACAP Irving Philips Award for Prevention, 26
AACAP Jeanne Spurlock Lecture and Award on
    Diversity and Culture, 27
AACAP Rieger Psychodyn Psychotherapy Award, 33
AACAP Rieger Service Program Award for
    Excellence, 34

AACAP Robert Cancro Academic Leadership
    Award, 35
AACAP Sidney Berman Award for the School-Based
    Study and Intervention for Learning Disorders and
    Mental Ilness, 36
AACAP Simon Wile Leadership in Consultation
    Award, 37
ALA Alex Awards, 153
ALA ALSC Distinguished Service Award, 154
ALA Amazing Audiobks for Young Adults Awd, 155
ALA Amelia Bloomer Book List Award, 156
ALA Baker and Taylor/YALSA Collection
    Development Grants, 157
ALA Best Fiction for Young Adults Award, 160
ALA Booklist Editors' Choice Books for Youth
    Awards, 162
ALA Children's Literature Legacy Award, 165
ALA Coretta Scott King-John Steptoe Award for
    New Talent, 166
ALA Coretta Scott King-Virginia Hamilton Award
    for Lifetime Achievement, 167
ALA Coretta Scott King Book Donation Grant, 168
ALA Fabulous Films for Young Adults Award, 169
ALA Great Books Giveaway Competition, 170
ALA John Newbery Medal, 172
ALA MAE Award for Best Literature Program for
    Teens, 174
ALA Margaret A. Edwards Award, 175
ALA May Hill Arbuthnot Honor Lecture Award, 176
ALA Michael L. Printz Award, 177
ALA Mildred L. Batchelder Award, 178
ALA Notable Children's Books Awards, 179
ALA Notable Children's Recordings Awards, 180
ALA Notable Children's Videos Awards, 181
ALA Odyssey Award for Excellence in Audiobook
    Production, 182
ALA Penguin Random House Young Readers Group
    Award, 183
ALA Popular Paperbacks for Young Adults Awds, 184
ALA Quick Picks for Reluctant Young Adult Readers
    Award, 186
ALA Rainbow Project Book List Award, 187
ALA Randolph Caldecott Medal, 188
ALA Robert F. Sibert Informational Book Medal
    Award, 189
ALA Sara Jaffarian School Library Award for
    Exemplary Humanities Programming, 190
ALA Schneider Family Book Awards, 191
ALA Scholastic Library Publishing Award, 192
ALA Sullivan Award for Public Library Admintrs
    Supporting Services to Children, 213
ALA Teen's Top Ten Awards, 214
ALA Theodor Seuss Geisel Award, 215
ALA William C. Morris Debut YA Award, 217
ALA YALSA Presidential Citation Award, 218
Anne J. Caudal Foundation Grants, 276
Anthony Munoz Foundation Straight A Student
    Campaign Grants, 280
Atlanta Women's Foundation Sue Wieland Embracing
    Possibility Award, 328
Caplow Applied Sci (CappSci) Children's Prize, 502
CCFF Christopher Columbus Awards, 522
CEC Clarissa Hug Teacher of the Year Award, 527
CEC J.E. Wallace Wallin Special Education Lifetime
    Achievement Award, 528
CEC Yes I Can! Awards, 529
Changemakers Innovation Awards, 559
Chick and Sophie Major Memorial Duck Calling
    Contest Scholarships, 583
ChLA Book Award, 590
ChLA Carol Gay Award, 591
ChLA Edited Book Award, 592
ChLA Graduate Student Essay Awards, 594
ChLA Mentoring Award, 597
ChLA Phoenix Award, 598
ChLA Phoenix Picture Book Award, 599
Colin Higgins Foundation Courage Awards, 653
Community Foundation for Greater Atlanta
    Managing For Excellence Award, 665

Community Foundation of Bartholomew County
    James A. Henderson Award for Fundraising, 691
Do Something Awards, 847
Eide Bailly Resourcefullness Awards, 897
El Pomar Foundation Anna Keesling Ackerman Fund
    Grants, 907
Energy by Design Poster Contest, 915
Environmental Excellence Awards, 922
Epilepsy Foundation SUDEP Challenge Initiative
    Prizes, 924
Gloria Barron Prize for Young Heroes, 1074
Great Clips Corporate Giving, 1108
Hispanic Heritage Foundation Youth Awards, 1253
Honeywell Corporation Got 2B Safe Contest, 1256
ILA Arbuthnot Award, 1290
ILA Children's and Young Adults' Book Awds, 1291
J. Marion Sims Foundation Teachers' Pet Grant, 1322
Japan Foundation Los Angeles Contests Designed for
    Japanese-Language Learners Grants, 1351
KIND Causes Monthly Grants, 1435
Kohl's Cares Scholarships, 1447
Koret Foundation Grants, 1449
Lemelson-MIT InvenTeam Grants, 1481
Mr. Holland's Opus Foundation Michael Kamen Solo
    Award, 1704
National Cowboy and Western Heritage Museum
    Awards, 1722
National YoungArts Foundation Awards, 1725
NCSS Award for Global Understanding, 1728
NCSS Carter G. Woodson Book Awards, 1729
NCSS Christa McA Reach for the Stars Awd, 1730
Nestle Very Best in Youth Competition, 1740
NSTA Distinguished Informal Science Education
    Award, 1777
NSTA Faraday Science Communicator Award, 1778
Ontario Arts Foundation Ruth and Sylvia Schwartz
    Children's Book Awards, 1826
Oticon Focus on People Awards, 1847
P. Buckley Moss Foundation for Children's Education
    Teacher Grants, 1855
Poetry Fdn Young People's Poet Laureate, 1989
Portland General Electric Foundation Grants, 2007
Prudential Spirit of Community Awards, 2029
Random Acts of Kindness Foundation Lesson Plan
    Contest, 2053
Raytheon Middle School Grants and Schols, 2061
Sphinx Competition Awards, 2234
Union Square Arts Award, 2339
Union Square Award for Social Justice, 2340
Volvo Adventure Environmental Awards, 2390
Volvo Bob the Bunny's Cartoon Competition, 2391
VSA/Volkswagen Group of America Exhibition
    Awards, 2393
VSA International Young Soloists Award, 2395
VSA Playwright Discovery Award, 2396
World of Children Education Award, 2490
World of Children Health Award, 2491
World of Children Humanitarian Award, 2492
World of Children Youth Award, 2493
Yampa Valley Community Foundation Erickson
    Christian Heritage Scholarships, 2509
YSA Get Ur Good On Grants, 2513
Zonta International Foundation Young Women in
    Public Affairs Award, 2527

Basic Research

1st Touch Foundation Grants, 2
A-T Children's Project Grants, 16
A-T Children's Project Post Doctoral Fellowships, 17
A.L. Mailman Family Foundation Grants, 20
AACAP Educational Outreach Program for General
    Psychiatry Residents, 24
AACAP George Tarjan Award for Contributions in
    Developmental Disabilities, 25
AACAP Irving Philips Award for Prevention, 26
AACAP Jeanne Spurlock Lecture and Award on
    Diversity and Culture, 27
AACAP Jeanne Spurlock Research Fellowship in
    Substance Abuse and Addiction for Minority
    Medical Students, 28

AACAP Junior Investigator Awards, 29
AACAP Life Members Mentorship Grants for Medical Students, 30
AACAP Mary Crosby Congressional Fellowships, 31
AACAP Pilot Rsrch Awd for Att-Deficit Disorder, 32
AACAP Rieger Psychodyn Psychotherapy Award, 33
AACAP Rieger Service Program Award for Excellence, 34
AACAP Robert Cancro Academic Leadership Award, 35
AACAP Sidney Berman Award for the School-Based Study and Intervention for Learning Disorders and Mental Ilness, 36
AACAP Summer Medical Student Fellowships, 38
Abbott Fund Access to Health Care Grants, 45
Abbott Fund Science Education Grants, 48
Abell-Hanger Foundation Grants, 52
Abington Foundation Grants, 54
ACF Early Care and Education Research Scholars: Child Care Research Scholars, 78
ACF Early Care and Education Research Scholars: Head Start Graduate Student Research Grants, 79
ACF Family Strengthening Scholars Grants, 81
Achelis and Bodman Foundation Grants, 101
Achelis Foundation Grants, 102
ACL Disability and Rehabilitation Research Projects (DRRP) Program: Independent Living Transition Services for Youth and Young Adults Grants, 105
ACL Rehabilitation Research and Training Center (RRTC) on Employment of Transition-Age Youth with Disabilities Grants, 107
Active Living Research Grants, 109
Adams County Community Foundation Grants, 115
Alex Stern Family Foundation Grants, 229
Ameren Corporation Community Grants, 251
American Psychiatric Fdn Call for Proposals, 257
American Schlafhorst Foundation Grants, 262
AMERIND Community Service Project Grants, 265
Andrew Family Foundation Grants, 272
Arthur Ashley Williams Foundation Grants, 302
Assisi Foundation of Memphis General Grants, 318
Avery Foundation Grants, 339
Bainum Family Foundation Grants, 345
Batts Foundation Grants, 367
Baxter International Foundation Grants, 369
Beckman Coulter Foundation Grants, 394
Benton Community Foundation Grants, 405
Better Way Foundation Grants, 419
Bill and Melinda Gates Foundation Agricultural Development Grants, 425
Bill and Melinda Gates Foundation Policy and Advocacy Grants, 427
Bill and Melinda Gates Foundation Water, Sanitation and Hygiene Grants, 428
Blandin Foundation Expand Opportunity Grants, 437
BMW of North America Charitable Contribs, 460
Bridgestone Americas Trust Fund Grants, 469
Bryan Adams Foundation Grants, 480
Burlington Industries Foundation Grants, 481
Bushrod H. Campbell and Adah F. Hall Charity Fund Grants, 486
Cabot Corporation Foundation Grants, 490
Caesars Foundation Grants, 492
Camille Beckman Foundation Grants, 499
Campbell Soup Foundation Grants, 501
Cargill Corporate Giving Grants, 503
Carl M. Freeman Foundation Grants, 508
Carl W. and Carrie Mae Joslyn Trust Grants, 510
Carnegie Corporation of New York Grants, 511
Catherine Holmes Wilkins Foundation Charitable Grants, 520
CDI Interdisciplinary Research Intvs Grants, 526
CFF Research Grants, 534
Chapman Charitable Foundation Grants, 560
Charles Lafitte Foundation Grants, 567
Children's Brain Tumor Fdn Research Grants, 584
Children's Tumor Foundation Young Investigator Awards, 587
ChLA Faculty Research Grants, 593
ChLA Hannah Beiter Diversity Research Grants, 595

ChLA Hannah Beiter Graduate Student Research Grants, 596
CICF Indianapolis Fdn Community Grants, 606
CICF Women's Grants , 609
Cincinnati Milacron Foundation Grants, 613
CMS Historically Black Colleges and Universities (HBCU) Health Services Research Grants, 639
CMS Research and Demonstration Grants, 640
Colonel Stanley R. McNeil Foundation Grants, 659
Community Foundation for Greater Buffalo Competitive Grants, 670
Community Foundation of Boone County Grants, 694
Community Foundation of Greater Fort Wayne - Community Endowment and Clarke Endowment Grants, 705
Community Foundation of Louisville C. E. and S. Endowment for the Parks Fund Grants, 719
Community Foundation of Louisville Dr. W. Barnett Owen Memorial Fund for the Children of Louisville and Jefferson County Grants, 723
Community Foundation of St. Joseph County African American Community Grants, 737
Community Fdn of Wabash County Grants, 740
Corina Higginson Trust Grants, 750
Crane Foundation General Grants, 761
Cudd Foundation Grants, 769
David Alan and Susan Berkman Rahm Foundation Grants, 785
Dorothea Haus Ross Foundation Grants, 844
Dorr Foundation Grants, 846
Edward W. and Stella C. Van Houten Memorial Fund Grants, 892
Elizabeth Huth Coates Foundation Grants, 900
Elizabeth Morse Genius Charitable Trust Grants, 901
Elton John AIDS Foundation Grants, 910
Epilepsy Foundation SUDEP Challenge Initiative Prizes, 924
F.M. Kirby Foundation Grants, 946
Farmers Insurance Corporate Giving Grants, 948
FCD New American Children Grants, 952
Fichtenbaum Charitable Trust Grants, 955
Fidelity Foundation Grants, 957
FirstEnergy Foundation Community Grants, 965
Ford Foundation BUILD Grants, 984
Forest Foundation Grants, 985
Francis L. Abreu Charitable Trust Grants, 1008
Frank M. Tait Foundation Grants, 1012
Frank Reed and Margaret Jane Peters Memorial Fund II Grants, 1014
General Motors Foundation Grants, 1039
George W. Codrington Charitable Foundation Grants, 1055
Gerber Foundation Environmental Hazards Research Grants, 1062
Gerber Fdn Pediatric Health Research Grants, 1063
Gerber Foundation Pediatric Nutrition Research Grants, 1064
Gil and Dody Weaver Foundation Grants, 1071
Grifols Community Outreach Grants, 1122
H.A. and Mary K. Chapman Charitable Trust Grants, 1137
Harmony Project Grants, 1170
Harry A. and Margaret D. Towsley Foundation Grants, 1180
Harry Frank Guggenheim Foundation Research Grants, 1184
Hawaii Children's Cancer Fdn Contributions, 1212
Helen Bader Foundation Grants, 1227
Helen V. Brach Foundation Grants, 1232
Henrietta Lange Burk Fund Grants, 1235
Henry L. Guenther Foundation Grants, 1242
Herbert A. and Adrian W. Woods Foundation Grants, 1243
Herman Goldman Foundation Grants, 1245
Herman P. and Sophia Taubman Fdn Grants, 1247
Hill Crest Foundation Grants, 1249
HRAMF Charles H. Hood Foundation Child Health Research Awards, 1262
Huffy Foundation Grants, 1273
Huisking Foundation Grants, 1274

Huntington County Community Foundation Make a Difference Grants, 1280
IMLS Grants to State Library Administrative Agencies, 1298
J.W. Kieckhefer Foundation Grants, 1324
Jack H. and William M. Light Charitable Trust Grants, 1330
James M. Collins Foundation Grants, 1344
James S. Copley Foundation Grants, 1345
Jaquelin Hume Foundation Grants, 1357
Joni Elaine Templeton Foundation Grants, 1384
Kathryne Beynon Foundation Grants, 1420
Kenneth T. and Eileen L. Norris Fdn Grants, 1427
Kind World Foundation Grants, 1438
Klingenstein-Simons Fellowship Awards in the Neurosciences, 1441
Koret Foundation Grants, 1449
Kovler Family Foundation Grants, 1455
Kovler Family Foundation Grants, 1454
Lalor Foundation Postdoctoral Fellowships, 1464
Land O'Lakes Fdn California Region Grants, 1465
Land O'Lakes Foundation Mid-Atlantic Grants, 1467
Laurel Foundation Grants, 1475
Leo Goodwin Foundation Grants, 1482
LGA Family Foundation Grants, 1487
Libra Foundation Grants, 1489
Lotus 88 Foundation for Women and Children Grants, 1508
Louis and Sandra Berkman Foundation Grants, 1510
Louis Calder Foundation Grants, 1511
Lubrizol Foundation Grants, 1513
Lumpkin Family Fdn Healthy People Grants, 1518
M. Bastian Family Foundation Grants, 1522
M.J. Murdock Charitable Trust General Grants, 1524
Mabel H. Flory Charitable Trust Grants, 1527
Mabel Louise Riley Foundation Grants, 1529
Mabel Y. Hughes Charitable Trust Grants, 1530
Marcia and Otto Koehler Foundation Grants, 1553
Margaret and James A. Elkins Jr. Fdn Grants, 1555
Margaret T. Morris Foundation Grants, 1557
Marion Gardner Jackson Charitable Trust Grts, 1570
Mary K. Chapman Foundation Grants, 1590
Mary S. and David C. Corbin Fdn Grants, 1598
Matilda R. Wilson Fund Grants, 1605
McCombs Foundation Grants, 1615
McCune Charitable Foundation Grants, 1617
McGraw-Hill Companies Community Grants, 1620
McLean Contributionship Grants, 1623
Meadows Foundation Grants, 1626
Mead Witter Foundation Grants, 1628
Mericos Foundation Grants, 1637
Merrick Foundation Grants, 1640
Mervin Bovaird Foundation Grants, 1643
Meta and George Rosenberg Fdn Grants, 1644
Meyer Memorial Trust Responsive Grants, 1653
MGM Resorts Foundation Community Grants, 1655
MGN Family Foundation Grants, 1656
Milken Family Foundation Grants, 1672
Mimi and Peter Haas Fund Grants, 1677
Morgan Adams Foundation Research Grants, 1694
Nash Avery Foundation Grants, 1714
Nellie Mae Education Foundation District-Level Change Grants, 1736
NIMH Early Identification and Treatment of Mental Disorders in Children and Adolescents Grts, 1761
Noble County Community Foundation Grants, 1765
Norcliffe Foundation Grants, 1766
Northrop Grumman Foundation Grants, 1773
NRA Foundation Grants, 1774
NSF Perception, Action and Cognition (PAC) Research Grants, 1775
NSF Social Psychology Grants, 1776
OneFamily Foundation Grants, 1822
Oppenstein Brothers Foundation Grants, 1827
OSF Soros Justice Youth Activist Fellowships, 1844
OSF Young Feminist Leaders Fellowships, 1845
Peabody Foundation Grants, 1922
Pediatric Brain Tumor Foundation Early Career Development Grants, 1923

Pediatric Brain Tumor Foundation Early Career
    Development Grants, 1924
Pediatric Brain Tumor Fdn Institute Grants, 1925
Pediatric Brain Tumor Foundation Opportunity
    Grants, 1926
Pediatric Cancer Research Foundation Grants, 1927
Percy B. Ferebee Endowment Grants, 1936
Perkin Fund Grants, 1937
Peyton Anderson Foundation Grants, 1954
Phil Hardin Foundation Grants, 1960
Phoenix Suns Charities Grants, 1964
Piper Jaffray Foundation Communities Giving
    Grants, 1974
Piper Trust Healthcare and Med Rsrch Grants, 1978
Powell Family Foundation Grants, 2012
PPG Industries Foundation Grants, 2017
ProLiteracy National Book Fund Grants, 2026
Prudential Foundation Education Grants, 2028
R.C. Baker Foundation Grants, 2043
Ralph M. Parsons Foundation Grants, 2052
Reinberger Foundation Grants, 2066
RGk Foundation Grants, 2068
Richard Davoud Donchian Foundation Grants, 2070
Richard W. Goldman Family Fdn Grants, 2073
RWJF Childhood Obesity Grants, 2126
RWJF Healthy Eating Research Grants, 2127
Sara Elizabeth O'Brien Trust Grants, 2161
Sarkeys Foundation Grants, 2163
Schramm Foundation Grants, 2168
Sensient Technologies Foundation Grants, 2180
Sick Kids Foundation New Investigator Research
    Grants, 2194
Sidgmore Family Foundation Grants, 2195
Sioux Falls Area Community Foundation Community
    Fund Grants, 2203
Sioux Falls Area Community Foundation Spot
    Grants, 2204
Skaggs Foundation Grants, 2207
Sony Corporation of America Grants, 2216
Sorenson Legacy Foundation Grants, 2217
Special Olympics Youth Fan Grants, 2229
State Farm Good Neighbor Citizenship Company
    Grants, 2238
Strake Foundation Grants, 2249
Tellabs Foundation Grants, 2280
Thomas and Agnes Carvel Foundation Grants, 2289
Thomas W. Bradley Foundation Grants, 2293
Thrasher Research Fund Grants, 2296
Union Pacific Fdn Community & Civic Grants, 2337
Union Pacific Foundation Health and Human
    Services Grants, 2338
University of Chicago Chapin Hall Doris Duke
    Fellowships, 2348
USAID Family Planning and Reproductive Health
    Methods Grants, 2353
Victor E. Speas Foundation Grants, 2380
Virginia Foundation for the Humanities Open
    Grants, 2387
Virginia W. Kettering Foundation Grants, 2388
W.W. Smith Chartbl Trust Basic Needs Grants, 2400
Wallace Foundation Grants, 2402
Watson-Brown Foundation Grants, 2418
William and Sandy Heitz Family Fdn Grants, 2457
William Blair and Company Foundation Grants, 2461
William G. and Helen C. Hoffman Foundation
    Grants, 2466
William T. Grant Foundation Scholars Program, 2475
Wilton and Effie Hebert Foundation Grants, 2476
Xerox Foundation Grants, 2507

Building Construction and/or Renovation
Abbott Fund Global AIDS Care Grants, 47
Achelis and Bodman Foundation Grants, 101
Achelis Foundation Grants, 102
Adams County Community Foundation Grants, 115
Adelaide Breed Bayrd Foundation Grants, 123
Adolph Coors Foundation Grants, 129
Agnes M. Lindsay Trust Grants, 140
Air Products Foundation Grants, 148

Albertsons Companies Foundation Nourishing
    Neighbors Grants, 221
Albert W. Cherne Foundation Grants, 222
Alex Stern Family Foundation Grants, 229
Alloy Family Foundation Grants, 241
Alvah H. and Wyline P. Chapman Foundation
    Grants, 248
Ameren Corporation Community Grants, 251
American Savings Foundation Program Grants, 261
American Schlafhorst Foundation Grants, 262
American Woodmark Foundation Grants, 263
Amerigroup Foundation Grants, 264
Anderson Foundation Grants, 271
Anheuser-Busch Foundation Grants, 273
Antone and Edene Vidinha Charitable Grants, 281
Appalachian Regl Commission Housing Grants, 289
Ar-Hale Family Foundation Grants, 290
Arkema Foundation Grants, 298
Armstrong McDonald Foundation Children and
    Youth Grants, 300
Aspen Community Foundation Grants, 316
Assisi Foundation of Memphis General Grants, 318
Atkinson Foundation Community Grants, 325
Atlanta Foundation Grants, 326
Babcock Charitable Trust Grants, 343
Bank of America Charitable Foundation Volunteer
    Grants, 358
Barrasso, Usdin, Kupperman, Freeman, and Sarver
    Corporate Grants, 362
Ben B. Cheney Foundation Grants, 402
Best Buy Children's Foundation Twin Cities
    Minnesota Capital Grants, 418
Bikes Belong Foundation Paul David Clark Bicycling
    Safety Grants, 422
Bikes Belong Foundation REI Grants, 423
Bikes Belong Grants, 424
Bill and Melinda Gates Foundation Emergency
    Response Grants, 426
Bill and Melinda Gates Foundation Water, Sanitation
    and Hygiene Grants, 428
Blanche and Irving Laurie Foundation Grants, 436
Blue Grass Community Foundation Clark County
    Fund Grants, 444
Blue Grass Community Foundation Fayette County
    Fund Grants, 446
Blue Grass Community Foundation Franklin County
    Fund Grants, 447
Blue Grass Community Foundation Harrison County
    Fund Grants, 448
Blue Grass Community Foundation Hudson-Ellis
    Grants, 449
Blue Grass Community Foundation Madison County
    Fund Grants, 450
Blue Grass Community Foundation Magoffin County
    Fund Grants, 451
Blue Grass Community Foundation Morgan County
    Fund Grants, 452
Blue Grass Community Foundation Rowan County
    Fund Grants, 453
Blue Grass Community Foundation Woodford
    County Fund Grants, 454
Blue River Community Foundation Grants, 458
Blumenthal Foundation Grants, 459
Bodenwein Public Benevolent Foundation Grants, 461
Boeing Company Contributions Grants, 462
Bothin Foundation Grants, 464
Brunswick Foundation Grants, 479
Bryan Adams Foundation Grants, 480
Bushrod H. Campbell and Adah F. Hall Charity
    Fund Grants, 486
Cabot Corporation Foundation Grants, 490
Callaway Foundation Grants, 496
Campbell Soup Foundation Grants, 501
Cargill Corporate Giving Grants, 503
Carl M. Freeman Foundation FACES Grants, 507
Carl M. Freeman Foundation Grants, 508
CFGR Community Impact Grants, 552
CFGR Jenkins Foundation Grants, 553
Charles Delmar Foundation Grants, 564
Chatham Athletic Foundation Grants, 574

CHC Foundation Grants, 575
Christensen Fund Regional Grants, 600
Cincinnati Bell Foundation Grants, 612
Citizens Bank Charitable Foundation Grants, 616
Citizens Savings Foundation Grants, 617
Clara Blackford Smith and W. Aubrey Smith
    Charitable Foundation Grants, 621
Clarence T.C. Ching Foundation Grants, 624
Clark and Ruby Baker Foundation Grants, 625
Clark County Community Foundation Grants, 626
Clayton Baker Trust Grants, 629
Clayton Fund Grants, 631
Cleo Foundation Grants, 632
Cleveland H. Dodge Foundation Grants, 637
Collins C. Diboll Private Foundation Grants, 657
Collins Foundation Grants, 658
Colonel Stanley R. McNeil Foundation Grants, 659
Community Foundation for Greater Buffalo
    Competitive Grants, 670
Community Foundation for Greater Buffalo Niagara
    Area Foundation Grants, 673
Community Foundation of Bartholomew County
    Heritage Fund Grants, 690
Community Foundation of Eastern Connecticut
    General Southeast Grants, 696
Community Foundation of Western Massachusetts
    Grants, 741
Community Memorial Foundation Responsive
    Grants, 743
Cooke Foundation Grants, 748
Courtney S. Turner Charitable Trust Grants, 753
Crystelle Waggoner Charitable Trust Grants, 768
Cudd Foundation Grants, 769
Dayton Foundation Grants, 796
Dayton Power and Light Company Foundation
    Signature Grants, 801
Delaware Community Foundation Grants, 817
Dolan Children's Foundation Grants, 832
DOL Youthbuild Grants, 838
Doree Taylor Charitable Foundation Grants, 843
Dorothea Haus Ross Foundation Grants, 844
Dr. John T. Macdonald Foundation Grants, 863
DTE Energy Foundation Community Development
    Grants, 866
E.J. Grassmann Trust Grants, 876
E.L. Wiegand Foundation Grants, 877
Eastern Bank Charitable Foundation Partnerships
    Grants, 881
Eastern Bank Charitable Foundation Targeted
    Grants, 882
Easton Foundations Archery Facility Grants, 883
Edwards Memorial Trust Grants, 891
Edward W. and Stella C. Van Houten Memorial Fund
    Grants, 892
Edyth Bush Charitable Foundation Grants, 893
Effie and Wofford Cain Foundation Grants, 895
El Pomar Foundation Anna Keesling Ackerman Fund
    Grants, 907
El Pomar Foundation Grants, 908
Elsie H. Wilcox Foundation Grants, 909
Evan Frankel Foundation Grants, 938
F.R. Bigelow Foundation Grants, 947
Fayette County Foundation Grants, 951
Fidelity Foundation Grants, 957
Fifth Third Foundation Grants, 959
Finish Line Youth Foundation Legacy Grants, 962
Ford Family Foundation Grants - Access to Health
    and Dental Services, 980
Foundation Beyond Belief Compassionate Impact
    Grants, 986
Foundation Beyond Belief Humanist Grants, 987
Foundations of East Chicago Education Grants, 995
Four County Community Foundation General
    Grants, 1000
Four County Community Foundation Healthy
    Senior/Healthy Youth Fund Grants, 1001
Francis Beidler Foundation Grants, 1007
Fremont Area Community Foundation Amazing X
    Grants, 1019

Fremont Area Community Foundation Community Grants, 1020
Fuller E. Callaway Foundation Grants, 1027
G.N. Wilcox Trust Grants, 1031
General Motors Foundation Grants, 1039
George and Ruth Bradford Foundation Grants, 1042
George H. and Jane A. Mifflin Memorial Fund Grants, 1048
George I. Alden Trust Grants, 1051
George Kress Foundation Grants, 1053
George W. Codrington Charitable Foundation Grants, 1055
George W.P. Magee Trust Grants, 1056
Gil and Dody Weaver Foundation Grants, 1071
GNOF Albert N. & Hattie M. McClure Grants, 1076
GNOF Bayou Communities Grants, 1077
GNOF Coastal 5 + 1 Grants, 1078
GNOF Exxon-Mobil Grants, 1080
GNOF Gert Community Fund Grants, 1082
GNOF Norco Community Grants, 1089
GNOF Plaquemines Community Grants, 1091
Graham Foundation Grants, 1101
Greater Saint Louis Community Fdn Grants, 1110
Greater Tacoma Community Foundation General Operating Grants, 1113
Greenspun Family Foundation Grants, 1118
GTRCF Elk Rapids Area Community Endowment Grants, 1127
Guy I. Bromley Trust Grants, 1136
H.A. and Mary K. Chapman Charitable Trust Grants, 1137
Hampton Roads Community Foundation Nonprofit Facilities Improvement Grants, 1159
Harold K.L. Castle Foundation Strengthening Windward Oahu Communities Grants, 1174
Harry A. and Margaret D. Towsley Foundation Grants, 1180
Harry and Jeanette Weinberg Fdn Grants, 1182
Hartford Foundation Regular Grants, 1185
Harvey Randall Wickes Foundation Grants, 1188
Hazel and Walter T. Bales Foundation Grants, 1220
HEI Charitable Foundation Grants, 1226
Helen Bader Foundation Grants, 1227
Helen V. Brach Foundation Grants, 1232
Henry L. Guenther Foundation Grants, 1242
Herman P. and Sophia Taubman Fdn Grants, 1247
Hill Crest Foundation Grants, 1249
Honeywell Corporation Family Safety and Security Grants, 1255
Honeywell Corp Humanitarian Relief Grants, 1257
Horace A. Kimball and S. Ella Kimball Foundation Grants, 1260
Hubbard Family Foundation Grants, 1271
Huisking Foundation Grants, 1274
Iddings Foundation Capital Project Grants, 1283
Iddings Foundation Major Project Grants, 1284
J. Bulow Campbell Foundation Grants, 1319
J. Edwin Treakle Foundation Grants, 1320
J. Knox Gholston Foundation Grants, 1321
J.W. Kieckhefer Foundation Grants, 1324
J. William Gholston Foundation Grants, 1328
James and Abigail Campbell Family Foundation Grants, 1337
James Graham Brown Foundation Grants, 1340
James Lee Sorenson Family Impact Foundation Grants, 1342
James LeVoy Sorenson Foundation Grants, 1343
Janson Foundation Grants, 1350
Jennings County Community Fdn Grants, 1360
Jessica Stevens Community Foundation Grants, 1363
John D. and Katherine A. Johnston Foundation Grants, 1370
John G. Duncan Charitable Trust Grants, 1372
John H. and Wilhelmina D. Harland Charitable Foundation Children and Youth Grants, 1374
John H. and Wilhelmina D. Harland Charitable Foundation Community Services Grants, 1375
Joseph H. and Florence A. Roblee Foundation Education Grants, 1386

Joseph H. and Florence A. Roblee Foundation Family Grants, 1387
Joseph Henry Edmondson Foundation Grants, 1388
Josephine Schell Russell Chartbl Trust Grants, 1389
KaBOOM! Adventure Courses Grant, 1401
Katharine Matthies Foundation Grants, 1418
Katherine John Murphy Foundation Grants, 1419
Kelvin and Eleanor Smith Foundation Grants, 1424
Kenneth T. and Eileen L. Norris Fdn Grants, 1427
Kind World Foundation Grants, 1438
Koch Family Foundation (Annapolis) Grants, 1444
Kodak Community Relations Grants, 1445
Kosciusko County Community Foundation Endowment Youth Services (KEYS) Grants, 1451
Laura B. Vogler Foundation Grants, 1470
Lewis H. Humphreys Charitable Trust Grants, 1486
Lied Foundation Trust Grants, 1490
Louie M. and Betty M. Phillips Fdn Grants, 1509
Lubrizol Foundation Grants, 1513
Ludwick Family Foundation Grants, 1516
Lynn and Foster Friess Family Fdn Grants, 1520
M.D. Anderson Foundation Grants, 1523
M.J. Murdock Charitable Trust General Grants, 1524
Mabel Y. Hughes Charitable Trust Grants, 1530
Macquarie Bank Foundation Grants, 1532
Margaret and James A. Elkins Jr. Fdn Grants, 1555
Margaret M. Walker Charitable Fdn Grants, 1556
Margaret T. Morris Foundation Grants, 1557
Marietta McNeill Morgan and Samuel Tate Morgan Jr. Trust Grants, 1560
Marin Community Foundation Affordable Housing Grants, 1561
Marion Gardner Jackson Charitable Trust Grts, 1570
Marion I. and Henry J. Knott Foundation Discretionary Grants, 1571
Marion I. and Henry J. Knott Foundation Standard Grants, 1572
Marjorie Moore Charitable Foundation Grants, 1574
Marquette Bank Neighborhood Commit Grants, 1577
Marsh Corporate Grants, 1580
Mary Black Foundation Active Living Grants, 1585
Mary D. and Walter F. Frear Eleemosynary Trust Grants, 1588
Mary K. Chapman Foundation Grants, 1590
Mary S. and David C. Corbin Fdn Grants, 1598
Mathile Family Foundation Grants, 1604
Matilda R. Wilson Fund Grants, 1605
Maurice J. Masserini Charitable Trust Grants, 1610
McInerny Foundation Grants, 1622
McLean Contributionship Grants, 1623
Mericos Foundation Grants, 1637
Mervin Bovaird Foundation Grants, 1643
Meyer Memorial Trust Responsive Grants, 1653
MLB Tomorrow Fund Grants, 1679
Montana Arts Council Cultural and Aesthetic Project Grants, 1685
Moses Kimball Fund Grants, 1701
Mt. Sinai Health Care Foundation Health of the Jewish Community Grants, 1709
Mt. Sinai Health Care Foundation Health of the Urban Community Grants, 1710
Narragansett Number One Foundation Grants, 1712
Nell J. Redfield Foundation Grants, 1737
Norcliffe Foundation Grants, 1766
Ohio Valley Foundation Grants, 1814
Oppenstein Brothers Foundation Grants, 1827
Oregon Community Fdn Community Grants, 1833
Parkersburg Area Community Foundation Action Grants, 1871
PCA Entry Track Arts Organizations and Arts Programs Grants for Dance, 1904
Peter and Elizabeth C. Tower Foundation Technology Initiative Grants, 1949
Phil Hardin Foundation Grants, 1960
Piper Trust Healthcare and Med Rsrch Grants, 1978
Piper Trust Reglious Organizations Grants, 1979
Pittsburgh Fdn Affordable Housing Grants, 1980
PNC Foundation Affordable Housing Grants, 1983
PNC Foundation Revitalization and Stabilization Grants, 1987

Pohlad Family Fdn Large Capital Grants, 1990
Pohlad Family Fdn Small Capital Grants, 1991
Polk County Community Foundation Bradley Breakthrough Community Benefit Grants, 1995
Polk County Community Foundation Unrestricted Grants, 2001
Porter County Community Foundation Health and Wellness Grant, 2002
PPG Industries Foundation Grants, 2017
Price Chopper's Golub Foundation Grants, 2020
Puerto Rico Community Foundation Grants, 2037
R.C. Baker Foundation Grants, 2043
R.D. and Joan Dale Hubbard Fdn Grants, 2044
Ralph M. Parsons Foundation Grants, 2052
Rathmann Family Foundation Grants, 2057
RCF General Community Grants, 2062
Reinberger Foundation Grants, 2066
Richard and Caroline T. Gwathmey Memorial Trust Grants, 2069
Robert Lee Blaffer Foundation Grants, 2092
Robert R. Meyer Foundation Grants, 2094
Robin Hood Foundation Grants, 2096
Ron and Sanne Higgins Family Fdn Grants, 2101
Rose Community Foundation Health Grants, 2105
Rose Hills Foundation Grants, 2106
Roy J. Carver Charitable Trust Youth Services and Recreation Grants, 2117
Rush County Community Foundation Grants, 2121
Ruth Anderson Foundation Grants, 2122
Saginaw Community Foundation Discretionary Grants, 2134
Samuel N. and Mary Castle Foundation Grants, 2145
Samuel S. Johnson Foundation Grants, 2146
San Juan Island Community Foundation Grants, 2158
Sarkeys Foundation Grants, 2163
Sartain Lanier Family Foundation Grants, 2164
Schramm Foundation Grants, 2168
Scott B. and Annie P. Appleby Charitable Trust Grants, 2169
Seattle Foundation Arts and Culture Grants, 2174
Seattle Foundation C. Keith Birkenfeld Memorial Trust Grants, 2177
Sensient Technologies Foundation Grants, 2180
Seward Community Foundation Grants, 2182
Seward Community Foundation Mini-Grants, 2183
Shell Deer Park Grants, 2186
Shield-Ayres Foundation Grants, 2189
Sidney Stern Memorial Trust Grants, 2197
Siebert Lutheran Foundation Grants, 2198
Skatepark Project Built to Play Skatepark Grant, 2208
Sony Corporation of America Grants, 2216
Sorenson Legacy Foundation Grants, 2217
Strake Foundation Grants, 2249
Stranahan Foundation Grants, 2250
Subaru of Indiana Automotive Fdn Grants, 2254
Summit Foundation Grants, 2255
Sunoco Foundation Grants, 2256
SunTrust Bank Trusteed Foundations Greene-Sawtell Grants, 2257
SunTrust Bank Trusteed Foundations Nell Warren Elkin and William Simpson Elkin Grants, 2258
T.L.L. Temple Foundation Grants, 2264
TE Foundation Grants, 2279
Tellabs Foundation Grants, 2280
Textron Corporate Contributions Grants, 2286
Thomas and Agnes Carvel Foundation Grants, 2289
Thomas W. Briggs Foundation Grants, 2294
Tull Charitable Foundation Grants, 2324
Turner Foundation Grants, 2326
Union Bank, N.A. Foundation Grants, 2334
Union Pacific Foundation Health and Human Services Grants, 2338
United Technologies Corporation Grants, 2347
UUA Congregation-Based Community Organizing Grants, 2366
UUA Fund Grants, 2367
V.V. Cooke Foundation Grants, 2371
Victor E. Speas Foundation Grants, 2380
Vigneron Memorial Fund Grants, 2384
W.W. Smith Chartbl Trust Basic Needs Grants, 2400

Walker Area Community Foundation Grants, 2401
Walter S. and Evan C. Jones Testam Trust, 2407
Widgeon Point Charitable Foundation Grants, 2447
William Blair and Company Foundation Grants, 2461
William E. Barth Foundation Grants, 2463
William G. Gilmore Foundation Grants, 2467
Windham Foundation Grants, 2477
Wyomissing Foundation Community Grants, 2504
Wyomissing Foundation Thun Family Organizational
    Grants, 2505
Wyomissing Foundation Thun Family Program
    Grants, 2506
Xerox Foundation Grants, 2507
Z. Smith Reynolds Foundation Small Grants, 2523
Zollner Foundation Grants, 2526

Capital Campaigns
A.C. and Penney Hubbard Foundation Grants, 19
A.L. Spencer Foundation Grants, 21
Aaron Foundation Grants, 42
Abbott Fund Global AIDS Care Grants, 47
Abell-Hanger Foundation Grants, 52
Achelis and Bodman Foundation Grants, 101
Achelis Foundation Grants, 102
Ackerman Foundation Grants, 103
Adams Community Foundation Community Grants, 115
Adelaide Breed Bayrd Foundation Grants, 123
Adolph Coors Foundation Grants, 129
Agnes M. Lindsay Trust Grants, 140
Air Products Foundation Grants, 148
Alavi Foundation Education Grants, 216
Albert W. Cherne Foundation Grants, 222
Albert W. Rice Charitable Foundation Grants, 223
Alex Stern Family Foundation Grants, 229
Alliant Energy Foundation Community Giving for
    Good Sponsorship Grants, 240
Alpha Natural Resources Corporate Giving, 246
Alvah H. and Wyline P. Chapman Foundation
    Grants, 248
Ameren Corporation Community Grants, 251
American Electric Power Corporate Grants, 252
American Electric Power Foundation Grants, 253
American Savings Foundation Capital Grants, 260
American Schlafhorst Foundation Grants, 262
Anderson Foundation Grants, 271
Andrew Family Foundation Grants, 272
Anheuser-Busch Foundation Grants, 273
Ar-Hale Family Foundation Grants, 290
Arthur Ashley Williams Foundation Grants, 302
Assisi Fdn of Memphis Capital Project Grants, 317
Barrasso, Usdin, Kupperman, Freeman, and Sarver
    Corporate Grants, 362
Baton Rouge Area Foundation Grants, 365
Batts Foundation Grants, 367
Ben B. Cheney Foundation Grants, 402
Benton Community Foundation Grants, 405
Benwood Foundation Community Grants, 406
Bill and Melinda Gates Foundation Emergency
    Response Grants, 426
Bill and Melinda Gates Foundation Water, Sanitation
    and Hygiene Grants, 428
Blanche and Irving Laurie Foundation Grants, 436
Blue River Community Foundation Grants, 458
Blumenthal Foundation Grants, 459
BMW of North America Charitable Contribs, 460
Bodenwein Public Benevolent Foundation Grants, 461
Boeing Company Contributions Grants, 462
Bothin Foundation Grants, 464
Bradley-Turner Foundation Grants, 466
Brown County Community Foundation Grants, 475
Brunswick Foundation Grants, 479
Burlington Industries Foundation Grants, 481
Burton D. Morgan Foundation Hudson Community
    Grants, 482
Burton D. Morgan Foundation Youth
    Entrepreneurship Grants, 483
C.H. Robinson Worldwide Foundation Grants, 489
Cabot Corporation Foundation Grants, 490
Callaway Foundation Grants, 496
Cargill Corporate Giving Grants, 503

Carl B. and Florence E. King Foundation Grants, 506
Carl M. Freeman Foundation Grants, 508
Carl W. and Carrie Mae Joslyn Trust Grants, 510
Central Pacific Bank Foundation Grants, 530
CFFVR Basic Needs Giving Partnership Grants, 537
CFFVR Clintonville Area Foundation Grants, 539
CFFVR Clintonville Area Foundation Grants, 538
CFFVR Frank C. Shattuck Community Grants, 541
CFFVR Robert and Patricia Endries Family
    Foundation Grants, 547
CFFVR Schmidt Family G4 Grants, 548
CFGR Jenkins Foundation Grants, 553
Chapman Charitable Foundation Grants, 560
Chapman Family Charitable Trust Grants, 561
Charles Delmar Foundation Grants, 564
CHC Foundation Grants, 575
Chicago Board of Trade Foundation Grants, 580
CHT Foundation Education Grants, 603
CICF Indianapolis Fdn Community Grants, 606
Cincinnati Milacron Foundation Grants, 613
Clark and Ruby Baker Foundation Grants, 625
Clayton Fund Grants, 631
Cleo Foundation Grants, 632
Collins C. Diboll Private Foundation Grants, 657
Colonel Stanley R. McNeil Foundation Grants, 659
Colorado Interstate Gas Grants, 661
Community Foundation for Greater Buffalo
    Competitive Grants, 670
Community Foundation for the Capital Region
    Grants, 687
Community Foundation of Bartholomew County
    Heritage Fund Grants, 690
Community Foundation of Boone County Grants, 694
Community Foundation of Greater Fort Wayne -
    Community Endowment and Clarke Endowment
    Grants, 705
Community Fdn Of Greater Lafayette Grants, 710
Community Foundation of St. Joseph County Special
    Project Challenge Grants, 738
Community Foundation of Western Massachusetts
    Grants, 741
Cooke Foundation Grants, 748
Countess Moira Charitable Foundation Grants, 752
Courtney S. Turner Charitable Trust Grants, 753
Covidien Partnership for Neighborhood Wellness
    Grants, 759
Cralle Foundation Grants, 760
Crescent Porter Hale Foundation Grants, 767
Crystelle Waggoner Charitable Trust Grants, 768
Cudd Foundation Grants, 769
Daniel and Nanna Stern Family Fdn Grants, 778
Daniels Homeless and Disadvantaged Grants, 782
Deaconess Community Foundation Grants, 803
Delaware Community Foundation Grants, 817
Del Mar Foundation Community Grants, 820
Dermody Properties Foundation Grants, 827
Dolan Children's Foundation Grants, 832
Don and May Wilkins Charitable Trust Grants, 842
Dorrance Family Foundation Grants, 845
Dunspaugh-Dalton Foundation Grants, 873
Dyson Foundation Mid-Hudson Valley Project
    Support Grants, 874
E. Clayton and Edith P. Gengras, Jr. Foundation
    Grants, 875
E.J. Grassmann Trust Grants, 876
Eastern Bank Charitable Foundation Partnerships
    Grants, 881
Eastern Bank Charitable Foundation Targeted
    Grants, 882
Easton Foundations Archery Facility Grants, 883
Edwards Memorial Trust Grants, 891
Edward W. and Stella C. Van Houten Memorial Fund
    Grants, 892
Edyth Bush Charitable Foundation Grants, 893
Effie and Wofford Cain Foundation Grants, 895
Elizabeth Huth Coates Charitable Foundation
    Grants, 900
Ella West Freeman Foundation Grants, 904
Ethel Sergeant Clark Smith Foundation Grants, 935

Evelyn and Walter Haas, Jr. Fund Gay and Lesbian
    Rights Grants, 940
Ewing Marion Kauffman Foundation Grants, 943
Ezra M. Cutting Trust Grants, 945
F.R. Bigelow Foundation Grants, 947
Fichtenbaum Charitable Trust Grants, 955
Fidelity Foundation Grants, 957
FirstEnergy Foundation Community Grants, 965
First Hawaiian Bank Foundation Corporate Giving
    Grants, 967
Forest Foundation Grants, 985
Four County Community Foundation General
    Grants, 1000
Four County Community Foundation Healthy
    Senior/Healthy Youth Fund Grants, 1001
Fourjay Foundation Grants, 1003
Francis L. Abreu Charitable Trust Grants, 1008
Franklin County Community Fdn Grants, 1010
Frank M. Tait Foundation Grants, 1012
Frederick McDonald Trust Grants, 1017
Fuller E. Callaway Foundation Grants, 1027
G.N. Wilcox Trust Grants, 1031
Gardner Foundation Grants, 1034
George B. Page Foundation Grants, 1044
George Graham and Elizabeth Galloway Smith
    Foundation Grants, 1047
George H. and Jane A. Mifflin Memorial Fund
    Grants, 1048
George I. Alden Trust Grants, 1051
George Kress Foundation Grants, 1053
George W. Codrington Charitable Foundation
    Grants, 1055
George W.P. Magee Trust Grants, 1056
George W. Wells Foundation Grants, 1057
Georgia-Pacific Fdn Entrepreneurship Grants, 1059
Gil and Dody Weaver Foundation Grants, 1071
GNOF Exxon-Mobil Grants, 1080
GNOF Norco Community Grants, 1089
Graham Foundation Grants, 1100
Greater Tacoma Community Foundation General
    Operating Grants, 1113
Grundy Foundation Grants, 1124
H.A. and Mary K. Chapman Charitable Trust
    Grants, 1137
Hampton Roads Community Foundation Nonprofit
    Facilities Improvement Grants, 1159
Hannaford Charitable Foundation Grants, 1163
Harry A. and Margaret D. Towsley Foundation
    Grants, 1180
Harry and Jeanette Weinberg Fdn Grants, 1182
Harry B. and Jane H. Brock Foundation Grants, 1183
Hartford Foundation Regular Grants, 1185
Hattie Mae Lesley Foundation Grants, 1195
Hawaii Electric Industries Charitable Foundation
    Grants, 1218
Hazel and Walter T. Bales Foundation Grants, 1220
Hearst Foundations Culture Grants, 1223
Hearst Foundations Social Service Grants, 1224
HEI Charitable Foundation Grants, 1226
Helen Bader Foundation Grants, 1227
Herbert A. and Adrian W. Woods Foundation
    Grants, 1243
Hill Crest Foundation Grants, 1249
Honor the Earth Grants, 1259
Horace A. Kimball and S. Ella Kimball Foundation
    Grants, 1260
HRK Foundation Health Grants, 1264
Hubbard Broadcasting Foundation Grants, 1269
Huffy Foundation Grants, 1273
Huisking Foundation Grants, 1274
Huntington County Community Foundation Make a
    Difference Grants, 1280
Iddings Foundation Capital Project Grants, 1283
Iddings Foundation Major Project Grants, 1284
Irving S. Gilmore Foundation Grants, 1314
J. Bulow Campbell Foundation Grants, 1319
J. Edwin Treakle Foundation Grants, 1320
J. William Gholston Foundation Grants, 1328
Jack H. and William M. Light Charitable Trust
    Grants, 1330

Jacob G. Schmidlapp Trusts Grants, 1336
James F. and Marion L. Miller Fdn Grants, 1338
James Graham Brown Foundation Grants, 1340
James LeVoy Sorenson Foundation Grants, 1343
James S. Copley Foundation Grants, 1345
Jane's Trust Grants, 1346
Janson Foundation Grants, 1350
John H. and Wilhelmina D. Harland Charitable
    Foundation Children and Youth Grants, 1374
John W. Anderson Foundation Grants, 1383
Joseph H. and Florence A. Roblee Foundation
    Children and Youth Grants, 1385
Joseph H. and Florence A. Roblee Foundation
    Education Grants, 1386
Joseph H. and Florence A. Roblee Foundation Family
    Grants, 1387
Joseph Henry Edmondson Foundation Grants, 1388
Josephine Schell Russell Chartbl Trust Grants, 1389
Journal Gazette Foundation Grants, 1391
JP Morgan Chase Fdn Arts and Culture Grants, 1394
Judy and Peter Blum Kovler Foundation Grants, 1396
Kansas Health Foundation Recognition Grants, 1415
Kate B. Reynolds Charitable Trust Poor and Needy
    Grants, 1417
Katharine Matthies Foundation Grants, 1418
Katherine John Murphy Foundation Grants, 1419
Kathryne Beynon Foundation Grants, 1420
Kawabe Memorial Fund Grants, 1423
Kelvin and Eleanor Smith Foundation Grants, 1424
Kenneth T. and Eileen L. Norris Fdn Grants, 1427
Kinder Morgan Foundation Grants, 1436
Kind World Foundation Grants, 1438
Kodak Community Relations Grants, 1445
Kopp Family Foundation Grants, 1448
Land O'Lakes Foundation Mid-Atlantic Grants, 1467
Laurel Foundation Grants, 1475
Lavina Parker Trust Grants, 1477
Leo Goodwin Foundation Grants, 1482
Lewis H. Humphreys Charitable Trust Grants, 1486
LGA Family Foundation Grants, 1487
Lied Foundation Trust Grants, 1490
Louie M. and Betty M. Phillips Fdn Grants, 1509
Louis Calder Foundation Grants, 1511
Lubrizol Corporation Community Grants, 1512
Lubrizol Foundation Grants, 1513
Lumpkin Family Fdn Healthy People Grants, 1518
Lynn and Foster Friess Family Fdn Grants, 1520
Mabel Y. Hughes Charitable Trust Grants, 1530
Macquarie Bank Foundation Grants, 1532
Mardag Foundation Grants, 1554
Margaret and James A. Elkins Jr. Fdn Grants, 1555
Margaret M. Walker Charitable Fdn Grants, 1556
Margaret T. Morris Foundation Grants, 1557
Marietta McNeill Morgan and Samuel Tate Morgan
    Jr. Trust Grants, 1560
Marion Gardner Jackson Charitable Trust Grts, 1570
Marion I. and Henry J. Knott Foundation
    Discretionary Grants, 1571
Marion I. and Henry J. Knott Foundation Standard
    Grants, 1572
Marjorie Moore Charitable Foundation Grants, 1574
Marsh Corporate Grants, 1580
Mary D. and Walter F. Frear Eleemosynary Trust
    Grants, 1588
Mary K. Chapman Foundation Grants, 1590
Mary Owen Borden Foundation Grants, 1597
Mathile Family Foundation Grants, 1604
Matilda R. Wilson Fund Grants, 1605
Maurice R. Robinson Fund Grants, 1611
McCarthy Family Fdn Charity Fund Grants, 1614
McGregor Fund Human Services Grants, 1621
McInerny Foundation Grants, 1622
McLean Contributionship Grants, 1623
Mead Witter Foundation Grants, 1628
Meyer Foundation Education Grants, 1649
Meyer Fdn Healthy Communities Grants, 1650
Mill Spring Foundation Grants, 1674
Mimi and Peter Haas Fund Grants, 1677
Montana Arts Council Cultural and Aesthetic Project
    Grants, 1685

Narragansett Number One Foundation Grants, 1712
Nathaniel and Elizabeth P. Stevens Foundation
    Grants, 1719
Nationwide Insurance Foundation Grants, 1726
Nell J. Redfield Foundation Grants, 1737
Noble County Community Foundation Grants, 1765
Norcliffe Foundation Grants, 1766
Northern Chautauqua Community Foundation
    Community Grants, 1769
Oak Foundation Child Abuse Grants, 1799
Ohio Valley Foundation Grants, 1814
Olive Higgins Prouty Foundation Grants, 1817
OneFamily Foundation Grants, 1822
Oppenstein Brothers Foundation Grants, 1827
Oregon Community Fdn Community Grants, 1833
Parkersburg Area Community Foundation Action
    Grants, 1871
Perkin Fund Grants, 1937
Peter and Elizabeth C. Tower Foundation Technology
    Initiative Grants, 1949
Phil Hardin Foundation Grants, 1960
Phoenix Suns Charities Grants, 1964
Piper Jaffray Foundation Communities Giving
    Grants, 1974
Piper Trust Arts and Culture Grants, 1975
Piper Trust Healthcare and Med Rsrch Grants, 1978
Pohlad Family Fdn Large Capital Grants, 1990
Pohlad Family Fdn Small Capital Grants, 1991
Polk County Community Foundation Bradley
    Breakthrough Community Benefit Grants, 1995
Polk County Community Foundation Unrestricted
    Grants, 2001
Powell Family Foundation Grants, 2012
Powell Foundation Grants, 2013
PPG Industries Foundation Grants, 2017
Price Chopper's Golub Foundation Grants, 2020
Prudential Foundation Education Grants, 2028
R.C. Baker Foundation Grants, 2043
R.D. and Joan Dale Hubbard Fdn Grants, 2044
Raskob Fdn for Catholic Activities Grants, 2054
Rasmuson Foundation Tier One Grants, 2055
Rasmuson Foundation Tier Two Grants, 2056
Rathmann Family Foundation Grants, 2057
RCF General Community Grants, 2062
Reinberger Foundation Grants, 2066
Richard W. Goldman Family Fdn Grants, 2073
Robinson Foundation Grants, 2097
Ron and Sanne Higgins Family Fdn Grants, 2101
Ruth and Vernon Taylor Foundation Grants, 2124
Salmon Foundation Grants, 2140
San Antonio Area Foundation Capital and Naming
    Rights Grants, 2148
Sand Hill Fdn Small Capital Needs Grants, 2154
San Juan Island Community Foundation Grants, 2158
Sarkeys Foundation Grants, 2163
Sartain Lanier Family Foundation Grants, 2164
Schlessman Family Foundation Grants, 2167
Scott B. and Annie P. Appleby Charitable Trust
    Grants, 2169
Seattle Foundation C. Keith Birkenfeld Memorial
    Trust Grants, 2177
Sensient Technologies Foundation Grants, 2180
Shell Deer Park Grants, 2186
Shield-Ayres Foundation Grants, 2189
Simpson Lumber Charitable Contributions, 2201
Sony Corporation of America Grants, 2216
Starr Foundation Grants, 2237
Strake Foundation Grants, 2249
Stranahan Foundation Grants, 2250
Strong Foundation Grants, 2252
Subaru of Indiana Automotive Fdn Grants, 2254
Summit Foundation Grants, 2255
SunTrust Bank Trusteed Foundations Greene-Sawtell
    Grants, 2257
SunTrust Bank Trusteed Foundations Nell Warren
    Elkin and William Simpson Elkin Grants, 2258
T.L.L. Temple Foundation Grants, 2264
TE Foundation Grants, 2279
Tension Envelope Foundation Grants, 2284
Textron Corporate Contributions Grants, 2286

Thomas Sill Foundation Grants, 2292
Thomas W. Briggs Foundation Grants, 2294
Tull Charitable Foundation Grants, 2324
U.S. Bank Foundation Grants, 2330
Union Bank, N.A. Foundation Grants, 2334
Union Pacific Fdn Community & Civic Grants, 2337
Union Pacific Foundation Health and Human
    Services Grants, 2338
V.V. Cooke Foundation Grants, 2371
Vanderburgh County Community Foundation
    Women's Fund Grants, 2376
Walker Area Community Foundation Grants, 2401
Watson-Brown Foundation Grants, 2418
Widgeon Point Charitable Foundation Grants, 2447
William A. Badger Foundation Grants, 2451
William G. and Helen C. Hoffman Foundation
    Grants, 2466
William G. Gilmore Foundation Grants, 2467
William J. and Gertrude R. Casper Foundation
    Grants, 2469
Wilton and Effie Hebert Foundation Grants, 2476
Wyomissing Foundation Community Grants, 2504
Wyomissing Foundation Thun Family Organizational
    Grants, 2505
Wyomissing Foundation Thun Family Program
    Grants, 2506

Centers: Research/Demonstration/Service

ACF Adoption Opportunities Grants, 71
ACF Basic Center Program Grants, 73
ACF Child Welfare Training Grants, 75
ACF National Human Trafficking Hotline Grants, 86
ACF Promoting Safe and Stable Families (PSSF)
    Program Grants, 89
ACF Street Outreach Program Grants, 94
ACL Alternatives to Guardianship Youth Resource
    Center Grants, 104
ACL Disability and Rehabilitation Research Projects
    (DRRP) Program: Independent Living Transition
    Services for Youth and Young Adults Grants, 105
ACL Rehabilitation Research and Training Center
    (RRTC) on Employment of Transition-Age Youth
    with Disabilities Grants, 107
Akron Community Foundation Health and human
    services Grants, 152
Armstrong McDonald Foundation Special Needs
    Grants, 301
Autism Speaks Norma and Malcolm Baker Recreation
    Grants, 335
Ben Cohen StandUp Foundation Grants, 403
Carrie S. Orleans Trust Grants, 512
CDI Interdisciplinary Research Intvs Grants, 526
CMS Historically Black Colleges and Universities
    (HBCU) Health Services Research Grants, 639
CMS Research and Demonstration Grants, 640
Collins C. Diboll Private Foundation Grants, 657
Colonel Stanley R. McNeil Foundation Grants, 659
Dayton Foundation Vandalia-Butler Grants, 799
Dr. John T. Macdonald Foundation Grants, 863
Easton Foundations Archery Facility Grants, 883
Fdn for the Mid South Communities Grants, 992
Foundation for the Mid South Education Grants, 993
Frederick McDonald Trust Grants, 1017
George W.P. Magee Trust Grants, 1056
George W. Wells Foundation Grants, 1057
Giving Gardens Challenge Grants, 1072
Goldseker Foundation Non-Profit Management
    Assistance Grants, 1095
Guy I. Bromley Trust Grants, 1136
Herbert A. and Adrian W. Woods Fdn Grants, 1243
HSBC Corporate Giving Grants, 1266
Katharine Matthies Foundation Grants, 1418
LEGO Children's Fund Grants, 1480
Leo Goodwin Foundation Grants, 1482
Lied Foundation Trust Grants, 1490
Marjorie Moore Charitable Foundation Grants, 1574
McGraw-Hill Companies Community Grants, 1620
Mertz Gilmore Foundation NYC Dance Grants, 1642
MGN Family Foundation Grants, 1656
Michael Reese Health Trust Core Grants, 1658

Michael Reese Health Trust Responsive Grants, 1659
Michigan Women Forward Grants, 1662
Mid-Iowa Health Foundation Community Response Grants, 1667
Morris Stulsaft Foundation Early Childhood Education Grants, 1696
Morris Stulsaft Foundation Educational Support for Children Grants, 1697
Morris Stulsaft Foundation Pathways to Work Grants, 1699
Mt. Sinai Health Care Foundation Health of the Jewish Community Grants, 1709
Mt. Sinai Health Care Foundation Health of the Urban Community Grants, 1710
Narragansett Number One Foundation Grants, 1712
Northrop Grumman Foundation Grants, 1773
NSTA Faraday Science Communicator Award, 1778
PCA Arts Organizations and Arts Programs Grants for Local Arts, 1895
PCA Entry Track Arts Organizations and Arts Programs Grants for Local Arts, 1907
Piper Trust Arts and Culture Grants, 1975
Piper Trust Education Grants, 1977
Piper Trust Healthcare and Med Rsrch Grants, 1978
Piper Trust Reglious Organizations Grants, 1979
Richard Davoud Donchian Foundation Grants, 2070
Robin Hood Foundation Grants, 2096
Sapelo Foundation Social Justice Grants, 2160
Shell Deer Park Grants, 2186
Sidgmore Family Foundation Grants, 2195
Stocker Foundation Grants, 2247
T.L.L. Temple Foundation Grants, 2264
Target Foundation Global Grants, 2272
Telluride Fdn Emergency Grants, 2282
Telluride Fdn Technical Assistance Grants, 2283
Vigneron Memorial Fund Grants, 2384
W.P. and Bulah Luse Foundation Grants, 2399

Citizenship Instruction
ACF Voluntary Agencies Matching Grants, 100
Adolph Coors Foundation Grants, 129
Bank of Hawaii Foundation Grants, 360
Bernard and Audre Rapoport Foundation Democracy and Civic Participation Grants, 409
Brookdale Fdn Relatives as Parents Grants, 474
Dearborn Community Foundation City of Lawrenceburg Youth Grants, 810
Foundation Beyond Belief Compassionate Impact Grants, 986
Foundation Beyond Belief Humanist Grants, 987
HAF Community Grants, 1141
Hearst Foundations United States Senate Youth Grants, 1225
Helen Irwin Littauer Educational Trust Grants, 1231
HLTA Visitor Industry Charity Walk Grant, 1254
Jacob and Hilda Blaustein Foundation Israel Program Grants, 1335
Koret Foundation Grants, 1449
Mardag Foundation Grants, 1554
Marin Community Foundation Social Justice and Interfaith Understanding Grants, 1567
Marsh Corporate Grants, 1580
Polk County Community Foundation Unrestricted Grants, 2001
Teaching Tolerance Diverse Democracy Grants, 2275
TJX Foundation Grants, 2303
UUA Actions of Public Witness Grants, 2365
UUA Congregation-Based Community Organizing Grants, 2366
UUA Fund Grants, 2367
UUA International Fund Grants, 2368
UUA Just Society Fund Grants, 2369
UUA Social Responsibility Grants, 2370
Vanderburgh Community Foundation Men's Fund Grants, 2373
Vanderburgh County Community Foundation Women's Fund Grants, 2376
Warrick County Community Foundation Women's Fund, 2411
Women's Fund of Hawaii Grants, 2484

Community Development
1st Source Foundation Community Involvement Grants, 1
1st Touch Foundation Grants, 2
2 Depot Square Ipswich Charitable Foundation Grants, 3
3 Dog Garage Museum Tours, 4
3M Company Fdn Community Giving Grants, 5
3M Company Foundation Health and Human Services Grants, 6
4imprint One by One Charitable Giving, 7
520 Charitable Foundation Grants, 14
786 Foundation Grants, 15
A. Alfred Taubman Foundation Grants, 18
A.C. and Penney Hubbard Foundation Grants, 19
A.L. Mailman Family Foundation Grants, 20
A.L. Spencer Foundation Grants, 21
A and B Family Foundation Grants, 40
Aaron Foundation Grants, 42
Aaron Foundation Grants, 41
AAUW International Project Grants, 44
Abbott Fund Access to Health Care Grants, 45
Abbott Fund Community Engagement Grants, 46
Abbott Fund Global AIDS Care Grants, 47
Abbott Fund Science Education Grants, 48
Abby's Legendary Pizza Foundation Grants, 49
ABC Charities Grants, 50
Abell-Hanger Foundation Grants, 52
Abington Foundation Grants, 54
Abney Foundation Grants, 55
ABS Foundation Grants, 56
Abundance Foundation International Grants, 57
Abundance Foundation Local Community Grants, 58
ACCF Dennis and Melanie Bieberich Community Enrichment Fund Grants, 59
ACCF John and Kay Boch Fund Grants, 60
ACCF Marlene Bittner Memorial Community Enrichment Fund Grants, 61
ACCF of Indiana Angel Funds Grants, 62
ACCF of Indiana Anonymous Community Enrichment Fund Grants, 63
ACCF of Indiana Bank of Geneva Heritage Fund Grants, 64
ACCF of Indiana Berne Ready Mix Community Enrichment Fund Grants, 65
ACCF of Indiana First Merchants Bank / Decatur Bank and Trust Fund Grants, 66
ACCF of Indiana Michael Basham Community Enrichment Fund Grants, 67
ACCF of Indiana Ron and Susie Ballard Community Enrichment Fund Grants, 68
ACCF Ralph Biggs Memorial Community Enrichment Fund Grants, 69
ACF Abandoned Infants Assistance Grants, 70
ACF Adoption Opportunities Grants, 71
ACF American Indian and Alaska Native Early Head Start Expansion Grants, 72
ACF Basic Center Program Grants, 73
ACF Child Abuse Prevention and Treatment Act Discretionary Funds Grants, 74
ACF Child Welfare Training Grants, 75
ACF Community-Based Child Abuse Prevention (CBCAP) Grants, 76
ACF Community-Based Child Abuse Prevention (CBCAP) Tribal and Migrant DiscretionaryGrants, 77
ACF Head Start and/or Early Head Start Grantee - Clay, Randolph, and Talladega Counties, Alabama, 82
ACF Head Start and/or Early Head Start Grantee - St. Landry Parish, Louisiana, 83
ACF Infant Adoption Awareness Training Program Grants, 84
ACF Marriage Strengthening Research & Dissemination Center Grants, 85
ACF Native American Social and Economic Development Strategies for Alaska Grants, 87
ACF Native Youth Initiative for Leadership, Empowerment, and Development Grants, 88

ACF Promoting Safe and Stable Families (PSSF) Program Grants, 89
ACF Refugee Career Pathways Grants, 90
ACF Refugee Health Promotion Grants, 91
ACF Runaway and Homeless Youth Training and Technical Assistance Center Grants, 92
ACF Social and Economic Development Strategies Grants, 93
ACF Street Outreach Program Grants, 94
ACF Sustainable Employment and Economic Development Strategies Grants, 95
ACF Transitional Living Program and Maternity Group Homes Grants, 96
ACF Tribal Maternal, Infant, and Early Childhood Home Visiting Program: Development and Implementation Grants, 97
ACF Tribal Maternal, Infant, and Early Childhood Home Visiting Program: Implementation and Expansion Grants, 98
ACF Voluntary Agencies Matching Grants, 100
Achelis and Bodman Foundation Grants, 101
Achelis Foundation Grants, 102
Ackerman Foundation Grants, 103
ACL Alternatives to Guardianship Youth Resource Center Grants, 104
ACL Neonatal Abstinence Syndrome National Training Initiative Grant, 106
ACL Rehabilitation Research and Training Center (RRTC) on Employment of Transition-Age Youth with Disabilities Grants, 107
Acuity Charitable Foundation Grants, 110
Adam Don Foundation Grants, 112
Adams-Mastrovich Family Foundation Grants, 113
Adams and Reese Corporate Giving Grants, 114
Adams Family Foundation I Grants, 116
Adams Family Fdn of Nora Springs Grants, 118
Adams Family Foundation of Ohio Grants, 119
Adelaide Breed Bayrd Foundation Grants, 123
Adelaide Christian Home For Children Grants, 124
Adobe Fdn Community Investment Grants, 127
Adobe Fdn Hunger and Homelessness Grants, 128
Adolph Coors Foundation Grants, 129
Advance Auto Parts Corporate Giving Grants, 131
AEGON Transamerica Foundation Health and Wellness Grants, 133
A Friends' Foundation Trust Grants, 136
A Fund for Women Grants, 137
AGFT Pencil Boy Express, 139
Agnes M. Lindsay Trust Grants, 140
AHC R.E.A.C.H. Grants, 141
Ahearn Family Foundation Grants, 142
AHS Foundation Grants, 143
Aid for Starving Children Emerg Aid Grants, 144
Aid for Starving Children Health and Nutrition Grants, 145
Aid for Starving Children Homes and Education Grants, 146
Air Products Foundation Grants, 148
Akron Community Foundation Arts and Culture Grants, 150
Akron Community Foundation Health and human services Grants, 152
ALA Baker and Taylor Summer Reading Program Grant, 158
Alabama Humanities Foundation Major Grants, 159
ALA Bookapalooza Grants, 161
ALA BWI Collection Development Grant, 164
ALA Coretta Scott King-Virginia Hamilton Award for Lifetime Achievement, 167
ALA Coretta Scott King Book Donation Grant, 168
ALA Great Books Giveaway Competition, 170
ALA Penguin Random House Young Readers Group Award, 183
ALA Sara Jaffarian School Library Award for Exemplary Humanities Programming, 190
ALA Schneider Family Book Awards, 191
ALA Scholastic Library Publishing Award, 192
Alaska Airlines Corporation Career Connections for Youth Grants, 193
Alaska Airlines Foundation LIFT Grants, 194

Alaska Community Foundation Afterschool Network Engineering Mindset Mini-Grant, 196

Alaska Community Foundation Children's Trust Tier 1 Community Based Child Abuse and Neglect Prevention Grants, 198

Alaska Community Foundation Children's Trust Tier 1 Parenting and Child Development Educational Grants, 199

Alaska Community Foundation Children's Trust Tier 2 Innovation Grants, 200

Alaska Community Foundation Cordova Community Foundation Grants, 201

Alaska Community Foundation Cordova Community Foundation Mini-Grants, 202

Alaska Community Foundation GCI Suicide Prevention Grant, 203

Alaska Community Foundation Jack and Nona Renn Anchorage Football Fund, 204

Alaska Community Foundation Kenai Peninsula Foundation Grant, 205

Alaska Community Foundation Ketchikan Community Foundation Grant, 206

Alaska Community Foundation Petersburg Community Foundation Annual Grant, 207

Alaska Community Foundation Petersburg Community Foundation Mini-Grants, 208

Alaska Community Foundation Seward Community Foundation Grant, 209

Alaska Conservation Fdn Youth Mini Grants, 210

Alaska State Council on the Arts Youth Cultural Heritage Fast Track Grants, 212

ALA Sullivan Award for Public Library Admintrs Supporting Services to Children, 213

Albert and Ethel Herzstein Charitable Foundation Grants, 219

Albertsons Companies Foundation Nourishing Neighbors Grants, 221

Albert W. Rice Charitable Foundation Grants, 223

Alcatel-Lucent Technologies Foundation Grants, 224

Alden and Vada Dow Fund Grants, 225

Alex Stern Family Foundation Grants, 229

ALFJ International Fund Grants, 231

Alfred E. Chase Charitable Foundation Grants, 233

Alfred J Mcallister and Dorothy N Mcallister Foundation Grants, 234

A Little Hope Grants, 235

Allan C. and Lelia J. Garden Foundation Grants, 236

Alliance for Strong Families and Communities Grants, 239

Alliant Energy Foundation Community Giving for Good Sponsorship Grants, 240

Alloy Family Foundation Grants, 241

Allstate Corporate Giving Grants, 242

Allstate Corp Hometown Commitment Grants, 243

Allstate Foundation Safe and Vital Communities Grants, 244

Allstate Foundation Tolerance, Inclusion, and Diversity Grants, 245

Alpha Natural Resources Corporate Giving, 246

Alvah H. and Wyline P. Chapman Foundation Grants, 248

Ama OluKai Foundation Grants, 249

Amelia Sillman Rockwell and Carlos Perry Rockwell Charities Fund Grants, 250

Ameren Corporation Community Grants, 251

American Electric Power Corporate Grants, 252

American Electric Power Foundation Grants, 253

American Honda Foundation Grants, 255

American Indian Youth Running Strong Grants, 256

American Schlafhorst Foundation Grants, 262

American Woodmark Foundation Grants, 263

Amerigroup Foundation Grants, 264

AMERIND Community Service Project Grants, 265

Amica Companies Foundation Grants, 266

Amica Insurance Company Sponsorships, 268

Amway Corporation Contributions, 269

Anderson Foundation Grants, 271

Andrew Family Foundation Grants, 272

Anheuser-Busch Foundation Grants, 273

Anna Fitch Ardenghi Trust Grants, 274

Anne Arundel Women Giving Together Regular Grants, 275

Anne J. Caudal Foundation Grants, 276

Ann L. and Carol Green Rhodes Charitable Trust Grants, 278

Ann Ludington Sullivan Foundation Grants, 279

Antone and Edene Vidinha Charitable Grants, 281

APAP All-In Grants, 283

Appalachian Community Fund LGBTQ Fund Grants, 284

Appalachian Regional Commission Business Development Revolving Loan Fund Grants, 285

Appalachian Regional Commission Education and Training Grants, 286

Appalachian Regional Commission Entrepreneurship and Business Development Grants, 287

Appalachian Regional Commission Health Care Grants, 288

Appalachian Regl Commission Housing Grants, 289

Ar-Hale Family Foundation Grants, 290

Arizona Commission on the Arts Learning Collaboration Grant, 291

Arizona Foundation for Women Deborah G. Carstens Fund Grants, 293

Arizona Foundation for Women General Grants, 294

Arizona State Library LSTA Collections Grants, 295

Arizona State Library LSTA Community Grants, 296

Arizona State Library LSTA Learning Grants, 297

Arkema Foundation Grants, 298

Arthur Ashley Williams Foundation Grants, 302

Arthur E. and Josephine Campbell Beyer Foundation Grants, 303

Arthur M. Blank Family Foundation AMB West Community Fund Grants, 304

Arthur M. Blank Family Foundation American Explorers Grants, 305

Arthur M. Blank Family Foundation Art of Change Grants, 306

Arthur M. Blank Family Foundation Atlanta United Foundation Grants, 308

Arthur M. Blank Family Foundation Inspiring Spaces Grants, 309

Arthur M. Blank Family Foundation Molly Blank Fund Grants, 310

Arthur M. Blank Family Foundation Pathways to Success Grants, 312

Arts Council of Greater Lansing Young Creatives Grants, 314

Aspen Community Foundation Grants, 316

Assisi Foundation of Memphis General Grants, 318

Assisi Foundation of Memphis Mini Grants, 319

AT&T Fdn Community Support and Safety, 320

AT&T Foundation Education Grants, 321

AT&T Foundation Health and Human Services Grants, 322

ATA Local Community Relations Grants, 324

Atkinson Foundation Community Grants, 325

Atlanta Foundation Grants, 326

Atlanta Women's Foundation Pathway to Success Grants, 327

Atlas Insurance Agency Foundation Grants, 329

Atwood Foundation General Grants, 330

Aunt Kate Foundation Grants, 331

Austin Community Foundation Grants, 332

Austin S. Nelson Foundation Grants, 333

Autauga Area Community Foundation Grants, 334

Autism Speaks Norma and Malcolm Baker Recreation Grants, 335

Avery Dennison Foundation Education Grants, 337

Avery Foundation Grants, 339

Avista Foundation Vulnerable and Limited Income Population Grants, 341

Babcock Charitable Trust Grants, 343

Back Home Again Foundation Grants, 344

Bainum Family Foundation Grants, 345

Ball Brothers Foundation Organizational Effectiveness/Executive Mentoring Grants, 346

Baltimore Community Foundation Building Stronger Neighborhoods Regionwide Grants, 347

Baltimore Community Foundation Children's Fresh Air Society Fund Grants, 348

Baltimore Community Foundation Mitzvah Fund for Good Deeds Grants, 349

Bank of America Charitable Foundation Basic Needs Grants, 354

Bank of America Charitable Foundation Community Development Grants, 355

Bank of America Charitable Foundation Matching Gifts, 356

Bank of America Charitable Foundation Student Leaders Grants, 357

Bank of America Charitable Foundation Volunteer Grants, 358

Bank of America Corporation Sponsorships, 359

Bank of Hawaii Foundation Grants, 360

Bank of the Orient Community Giving, 361

Barrasso, Usdin, Kupperman, Freeman, and Sarver Corporate Grants, 362

Baton Rouge Area Foundation Grants, 365

Batts Foundation Grants, 367

Baxter International Corporate Giving Grants, 368

Baxter International Foundation Grants, 369

Bay and Paul Foundations PreK-12 Transformative Learning Practices Grants, 370

Bay Area Community Foundation Arenac Community Fund Grants, 371

Bay Area Community Foundation Arenac County Healthy Youth/Healthy Seniors Fund Grants, 372

Bay Area Community Fdn Auburn Area Chamber of Commerce Enrichment Fund Grants, 373

Bay Area Community Foundation Bay County Healthy Youth/Healthy Seniors Fund Grants, 374

Bay Area Community Foundation Civic League Endowment Fund Grants, 375

Bay Area Community Foundation Community Initiative Fund Grants, 376

Bay Area Community Foundation Elizabeth Husband Fund Grants, 378

Bay Area Community Foundation Human Services Fund Grants, 379

Bay Area Community Foundation Leslie L. Squires Foundation Grants, 380

Bay Area Community Foundation Nathalie Awrey Memorial Fund Grants, 381

Bayer Fund Community Development Grants, 383

Bayer Fund STEM Education Grants, 384

Baystate Financial Charitable Foundation Grants, 385

BBF Maine Family Literacy Initiative Planning Grants, 388

BBF Maryland Family Literacy Initiative Implementation Grants, 389

BBF Maryland Family Literacy Initiative Planning Grants, 390

BBF National Grants for Family Literacy, 391

BCBSM Foundation Community Health Matching Grants, 392

Beckman Coulter Foundation Grants, 394

Bee Conservancy Sponsor-A-Hive Grants, 395

Bella Vista Fdn GSS Healthy Living Grants, 396

Bella Vista Foundation Pre-3 Grants, 397

Bella Vista Fdns GSS Early Literacy Grants, 398

Belvedere Community Foundation Grants, 399

Belvedere Cove Foundation Grants, 400

Ben B. Cheney Foundation Grants, 402

Ben Cohen StandUp Foundation Grants, 403

Benton Community Foundation - The Cookie Jar Grant, 404

Benton Community Foundation Grants, 405

Benwood Foundation Community Grants, 406

Bernard and Audre Rapoport Foundation Arts and Culture Grants, 407

Bernard and Audre Rapoport Foundation Community Building and Social Service Grants, 408

Bernard and Audre Rapoport Foundation Democracy and Civic Participation Grants, 409

Bernard and Audre Rapoport Foundation Education Grants, 410

Bernard and Audre Rapoport Foundation Health Grants, 411

Bernard F. and Alva B. Gimbel Foundation Criminal Justice Grants, 412
Bernau Family Foundation Grants, 413
Best Buy Children's Foundation @15 Community Grants , 414
Best Buy Children's Fdn @15 Scholarship , 415
Best Buy Children's Fdn @15 Teach Awards, 416
Best Buy Children's Foundation National Grants, 417
Best Buy Children's Foundation Twin Cities Minnesota Capital Grants, 418
Better Way Foundation Grants, 419
Bikes Belong Foundation Paul David Clark Bicycling Safety Grants, 422
Bikes Belong Foundation REI Grants, 423
Bikes Belong Grants, 424
Bill and Melinda Gates Foundation Agricultural Development Grants, 425
Bill and Melinda Gates Foundation Emergency Response Grants, 426
Bill and Melinda Gates Foundation Policy and Advocacy Grants, 427
Bill and Melinda Gates Foundation Water, Sanitation and Hygiene Grants, 428
Bingham McHale LLP Pro Bono Services, 431
Biogen Foundation General Donations, 432
Blackford County Community Fdn Grants, 434
Black Hills Corporation Grants, 435
Blanche and Irving Laurie Foundation Grants, 436
Blandin Foundation Expand Opportunity Grants, 437
Blandin Foundation Invest Early Grants, 438
Blandin Foundation Itasca County Area Vitality Grants, 439
Blockbuster Corporate Contributions, 440
Blossom Fund Grants, 441
Blue Cross Blue Shield of Minnesota Foundation - Healthy Neighborhoods: Connect for Health Challenge Grants, 443
Blue Grass Community Foundation Clark County Fund Grants, 444
Blue Grass Community Foundation Fayette County Fund Grants, 446
Blue Grass Community Foundation Franklin County Fund Grants, 447
Blue Grass Community Foundation Harrison County Fund Grants, 448
Blue Grass Community Foundation Hudson-Ellis Grants, 449
Blue Grass Community Foundation Madison County Fund Grants, 450
Blue Grass Community Foundation Magoffin County Fund Grants, 451
Blue Grass Community Foundation Morgan County Fund Grants, 452
Blue Grass Community Foundation Rowan County Fund Grants, 453
Blue Grass Community Foundation Woodford County Fund Grants, 454
Blue Mountain Community Foundation Discretionary Grants, 455
Blue Mountain Community Foundation Garfield County Health Foundation Fund Grants, 456
Blue Mountain Community Foundation Warren Community Action Fund Grants, 457
Blue River Community Foundation Grants, 458
Blumenthal Foundation Grants, 459
Bodenwein Public Benevolent Foundation Grants, 461
Boeing Company Contributions Grants, 462
BP Foundation Grants, 465
Bradley-Turner Foundation Grants, 466
Bradley C. Higgins Foundation Grants, 467
Brian G. Dyson Foundation Grants, 468
Bridgestone Americas Trust Fund Grants, 469
Bright Promises Foundation Grants, 470
British Columbia Arts Council Youth Engagement Program Grants, 473
Brookdale Fdn Relatives as Parents Grants, 474
Brown County Community Foundation Grants, 475
Brown Foundation Grants, 476
Brunswick Foundation Dollars for Doers Grants, 478
Bryan Adams Foundation Grants, 480

Burlington Industries Foundation Grants, 481
Burton D. Morgan Foundation Hudson Community Grants, 482
Burton D. Morgan Foundation Youth Entrepreneurship Grants, 483
Bush Foundation Event Scholarships, 484
Bush Foundation Event Sponsorships, 485
Bushrod H. Campbell and Adah F. Hall Charity Fund Grants, 486
Byerly Foundation Grants, 487
C.H. Robinson Worldwide Foundation Grants, 489
Cabot Corporation Foundation Grants, 490
Caesars Foundation Grants, 492
California Arts Cncl Statewide Networks Grants, 493
California Arts Cncl Technical Assistance Grts, 494
California Endowment Innovative Ideas Challenge Grants, 495
Callaway Foundation Grants, 496
Cal Ripken Sr. Foundation Grants, 497
Camille Beckman Foundation Grants, 499
Campbell Foundation Grants, 500
Campbell Soup Foundation Grants, 501
Cargill Corporate Giving Grants, 503
Caring for Colorado Foundation Sperry S. and Ella Graber Packard Fund for Pueblo Grants, 505
Carl B. and Florence E. King Foundation Grants, 506
Carl M. Freeman Foundation FACES Grants, 507
Carl M. Freeman Foundation Grants, 508
Carl R. Hendrickson Family Foundation Grants, 509
Carl W. and Carrie Mae Joslyn Trust Grants, 510
Carnegie Corporation of New York Grants, 511
Carrie S. Orleans Trust Grants, 512
Carroll County Community Foundation Grants, 513
Case Foundation Grants, 514
Cash 4 Clubs Sports Grants, 515
Cass County Community Foundation Grants, 516
Castle Foundation Grants, 517
Castle Foundation Grants, 518
Castle Industries Foundation Grants, 519
Cause Populi Worthy Cause Grants, 521
CCFF Community Grant, 523
Central Pacific Bank Foundation Grants, 530
CenturyLink Clarke M. Williams Foundation Matching Time Grants, 531
CFFVR Appleton Education Foundation Grants, 536
CFFVR Basic Needs Giving Partnership Grants, 537
CFFVR Clintonville Area Foundation Grants, 538
CFFVR Clintonville Area Foundation Grants, 539
CFFVR Environmental Stewardship Grants, 540
CFFVR Frank C. Shattuck Community Grants, 541
CFFVR Infant Welfare Circle of Kings Daughters Grants, 542
CFFVR Jewelers Mutual Chartbl Giving Grants, 543
CFFVR Mielke Family Foundation Grants, 544
CFFVR Myra M. and Robert L. Vandehey Foundation Grants, 545
CFFVR Project Grants, 546
CFFVR Robert and Patricia Endries Family Foundation Grants, 547
CFFVR Schmidt Family G4 Grants, 548
CFFVR Shawano Area Community Foundation Grants, 549
CFFVR Women's Fund for the Fox Valley Region Grants, 550
CFF Winter Park Community Grants, 551
CFGR Community Impact Grants, 552
CFGR Jenkins Foundation Grants, 553
CFGR SisterFund Grants, 554
CFNEM Women's Giving Circle Grants, 557
CFNEM Youth Advisory Council Grants, 558
Chapman Charitable Foundation Grants, 560
Chapman Family Foundation, 562
Charles Crane Family Foundation Grants, 563
Charles Delmar Foundation Grants, 564
Charles H. Hall Foundation, 565
Charles H. Pearson Foundation Grants, 566
Charles Lafitte Foundation Grants, 567
Charles N. and Eleanor Knight Leigh Foundation Grants, 568
Charles Nelson Robinson Fund Grants, 569

Charlotte and Joseph Gardner Fdn Grants, 570
Charlotte Martin Foundation Youth Grants, 571
Charlotte R. Schmidlapp Fund Grants, 572
Chatham Athletic Foundation Grants, 574
CHC Foundation Grants, 575
Cheryl Spencer Memorial Foundation Grants, 576
Chesapeake Bay Trust Environmental Education Grants, 577
Chesapeake Bay Trust Mini Grants, 578
Chesapeake Bay Trust Outreach and Community Engagement Grants, 579
Chicago Board of Trade Foundation Grants, 580
Chicago Community Trust Arts and Culture Grants: Improving Access to Arts Learning, 581
Chicago Neighborhood Arts Program Grants, 582
Children's Trust Fund of Oregon Fdn Grants, 585
Children's Trust Fund of Oregon Foundation Small Grants, 586
Chilkat Valley Community Foundation Grants, 588
Christine and Katharina Pauly Charitable Trust Grants, 601
CICF Clare Noyes Grant, 604
CICF Howard Intermill and Marion Intermill Fenstermaker Grants, 605
CICF Indianapolis Fdn Community Grants, 606
CICF John Harrison Brown and Rob Burse Grt, 607
CICF Summer Youth Grants, 608
CICF Women's Grants , 609
Cigna Civic Affairs Sponsorships, 610
Cincinnati Bell Foundation Grants, 612
Cincinnati Milacron Foundation Grants, 613
Circle K Corporation Contributions Grants, 614
Cisco Systems Foundation San Jose Community Grants, 615
Citizens Bank Charitable Foundation Grants, 616
Clara Abbott Foundation Need-Based Grants, 620
Clara Blackford Smith and W. Aubrey Smith Charitable Foundation Grants, 621
Claremont Community Foundation Grants, 622
Claremont Savings Bank Foundation Grants, 623
Clarence T.C. Ching Foundation Grants, 624
Clark and Ruby Baker Foundation Grants, 625
Clark County Community Foundation Grants, 626
Clark Electric Cooperative Grants, 627
Claude A. and Blanche McCubbin Abbott Charitable Trust Grants, 628
Clayton Baker Trust Grants, 629
Clayton Fund Grants, 631
Cleo Foundation Grants, 632
Cleveland Foundation Higley Fund Grants, 634
Cleveland Fdn Lake-Geauga Fund Grants, 635
Cleveland Foundation Legacy Village Lyndhurst Community Fund Grants, 636
Cleveland H. Dodge Foundation Grants, 637
Clinton County Community Foundation Grants, 638
CNCS AmeriCorps Indian Tribes Plang Grts , 641
CNCS AmeriCorps NCCC Project Grants, 642
CNCS AmeriCorps State and National Grants, 643
CNCS AmeriCorps State and National Planning Grants, 644
CNCS AmeriCorps VISTA Project Grants, 645
CNCS Foster Grandparent Projects Grants, 646
CNCS School Turnaround AmeriCorps Grants, 647
CNCS Senior Corps Retired and Senior Volunteer Program Grants, 648
CNCS Social Innovation Grants, 649
CNO Financial Group Community Grants, 650
Colgate-Palmolive Company Grants, 652
Collective Brands Foundation Grants, 654
Collective Brands Foundation Payless Gives Shoes 4 Kids Grants, 655
Collective Brands Foundation Saucony Run for Good Grants, 656
Collins C. Diboll Private Foundation Grants, 657
Collins Foundation Grants, 658
Colonel Stanley R. McNeil Foundation Grants, 659
Colorado Health Foundation Family, Friend and Neighbor Caregiver Supports Grants, 660
Colorado Interstate Gas Grants, 661
Colorado Trust Health Investment Grants, 662

Columbus Foundation Traditional Grants, 663
Community Foundation for Greater Atlanta Frances Hollis Brain Foundation Fund Grants, 664
Community Foundation for Greater Atlanta Managing For Excellence Award, 665
Community Foundation for Greater Atlanta Metropolitan Extra Wish Grants, 666
Community Foundation for Greater Atlanta Spark Clayton Grants, 667
Community Foundation for Greater Atlanta Spark Newton Grants, 668
Community Foundation for Greater Atlanta Strategic Restructuring Fund Grants, 669
Community Foundation for Greater Buffalo Competitive Grants, 670
Community Foundation for Greater Buffalo Garman Family Foundation Grants, 671
Community Foundation for Greater Buffalo Josephine Goodyear Foundation Grants, 672
Community Foundation for Greater Buffalo Niagara Area Foundation Grants, 673
Community Foundation for Greater Buffalo Ralph C. Wilson, Jr. Legacy Fund Grants, 674
Community Foundation for Kettering Grants, 676
Community Foundation for San Benito County Grants, 677
Community Foundation for SE Michigan Chelsea Community Fdn Capacity Building Grants, 679
Community Foundation for SE Michigan Chelsea Community Foundation General Grant, 680
Community Foundation for SE Michigan Detroit Auto Dealers Association Charitable Foundation Fund Grants, 681
Community Foundation for SE Michigan Head Start Innovation Fund, 682
Community Foundation for SE Michigan Southeast Michigan Immigrant and Refugee Funder Collaborative Grant, 685
Community Foundation for SE Michigan Youth Leadership Grant, 686
Community Foundation for the Capital Region Grants, 687
Community Foundation for the National Capital Region Community Leadership Grants, 688
Community Foundation of Abilene Future Fund Grants, 689
Community Foundation of Bartholomew County Heritage Fund Grants, 690
Community Foundation of Bartholomew County Women's Giving Circle, 692
Community Foundation of Boone County Grants, 694
Community Foundation of Crawford County, 695
Community Foundation of Eastern Connecticut General Southeast Grants, 696
Community Foundation of Eastern Connecticut Northeast Women and Girls Grants, 697
Community Foundation of Eastern Connecticut Norwich Women and Girls Grants, 698
Community Foundation of Eastern Connecticut Norwich Youth Grants, 699
Community Foundation of Eastern Connecticut Ossen Fund for the Arts Grants, 700
Community Foundation of Eastern Connecticut Southeast Area Women and Girls Grants, 701
Community Foundation of Eastern Connecticut Windham Area Women and Girls Grants, 702
Community Foundation of Grant County Grants, 703
Community Foundation of Greater Chattanooga Grants, 704
Community Foundation of Greater Fort Wayne - Community Endowment and Clarke Endowment Grants, 705
Community Foundation of Greater Fort Wayne - Edna Foundation Grants, 706
Community Foundation of Greater Fort Wayne - John S. and James L. Knight Foundation Donor-Advised Grants, 707
Community Foundation of Greater Greensboro Community Grants, 708

Community Foundation of Greater Greensboro Teen Grantmaking Council Grants, 709
Community Fdn Of Greater Lafayette Grants, 710
Community Foundation of Henderson County Community Grants, 711
Community Fdn of Howard County Grants, 712
Community Foundation of Jackson Hole Youth Philanthropy Grants, 715
Community Foundation of Louisville AIDS Project Fund Grants, 716
Community Foundation of Louisville Anna Marble Memorial Fund for Princeton Grants, 717
Community Foundation of Louisville Boyette and Edna Edwards Fund Grants, 718
Community Foundation of Louisville C. E. and S. Endowment for the Parks Fund Grants, 719
Community Foundation of Louisville CHAMP Fund Grants, 720
Community Foundation of Louisville Children's Memorial Marker Fund Grants, 721
Community Foundation of Louisville Delta Dental of Kentucky Fund Grants, 722
Community Foundation of Louisville Dr. W. Barnett Owen Memorial Fund for the Children of Louisville and Jefferson County Grants, 723
Community Foundation of Louisville Fund 4 Women and Girls Grants, 725
Community Foundation of Louisville Human Services Grants, 726
Community Foundation of Louisville We Day Kentucky Grants, 728
Community Foundation of Louisville Youth Philanthropy Council Grants, 730
Community Fdn of Morgan County Grants, 732
Community Foundation of Muncie and Delaware County Maxon Grants, 734
Community Fdn of Randolph County Grants, 735
Community Fdn of Southern Indiana Grants, 736
Community Foundation of St. Joseph County African American Community Grants, 737
Community Foundation of St. Joseph County Special Project Challenge Grants, 738
Community Foundation of Switzerland County Grants, 739
Community Foundation of Western Massachusetts Grants, 741
Community Foundation Serving Riverside and San Bernardino Counties Impact Grants, 742
Community Memorial Foundation Responsive Grants, 743
Con Edison Corporate Giving Civic Grants, 744
Cone Health Foundation Grants, 745
CONSOL Youth Program Grants, 747
Cooke Foundation Grants, 748
Corina Higginson Trust Grants, 750
Cornell Lab of Ornithology Mini-Grants, 751
Countess Moira Charitable Foundation Grants, 752
Courtney S. Turner Charitable Trust Grants, 753
Covenant Educational Foundation Grants, 754
Covenant to Care for Children Crisis Food Pantry Giving, 756
Covenant to Care for Children Enrichment Fund Grants, 758
Covidien Partnership for Neighborhood Wellness Grants, 759
Cralle Foundation Grants, 760
Crane Foundation General Grants, 761
Crane Fund Grants, 763
Cresap Family Foundation Grants, 766
Crescent Porter Hale Foundation Grants, 767
Crystelle Waggoner Charitable Trust Grants, 768
CUNA Mutual Group Fdn Community Grants, 770
Curtis Foundation Grants, 771
D. W. McMillan Foundation Grants, 776
Dana Brown Charitable Trust Grants, 777
Daniel and Nanna Stern Family Fdn Grants, 778
Daniels Fund Amateur Sports Grants, 779
Daniels Drug and Alcohol Addiction Grants, 780
Daniels Homeless and Disadvantaged Grants, 782
Daniels Fund Youth Development Grants, 784

David Alan and Susan Berkman Rahm Foundation Grants, 785
David and Betty Sacks Foundation Grants, 788
David and Laura Merage Foundation Grants, 789
David M. and Marjorie D. Rosenberg Foundation Grants, 790
Daviess County Community Foundation Recreation Grants, 793
Daviess County Community Foundation Youth Development Grants, 794
Dayton Foundation Dayton Youth Enrichment Fund Grant, 795
Dayton Foundation Grants, 796
Dayton Foundation Huber Heights Grants, 797
Dayton Foundation Rike Family Scholarships, 798
Dayton Foundation Vandalia-Butler Grants, 799
Dayton Foundation VISIONS Endowment Fund Grants, 800
Dayton Power and Light Company Foundation Signature Grants, 801
Dayton Power and Light Foundation Grants, 802
Deaconess Community Foundation Grants, 803
Deaconess Foundation Advocacy Grants, 804
Dean Foods Community Involvement Grants, 805
Dean Foundation Grants, 806
Dearborn Community Foundation City of Aurora Grants, 808
Dearborn Community Foundation City of Lawrenceburg Community Grants, 809
Decatur County Community Foundation Large Project Grants, 811
Decatur County Community Foundation Small Project Grants, 812
DeKalb County Community Foundation - Garrett Hospital Aid Foundation Grants, 813
DeKalb County Community Foundation - Literacy Grant, 814
DeKalb County Community Foundation Grants, 815
DeKalb County Community Foundation VOICE Grant, 816
Delaware Community Foundation Grants, 817
Del Mar Foundation Community Grants, 820
Delmarva Power & Light Contributions, 821
Delta Air Lines Foundation Community Enrichment Grants, 823
Dermody Properties Fdn Capstone Award, 826
Dermody Properties Foundation Grants, 827
Deuce McAllister Catch 22 Foundation Grants, 828
Dining for Women Grants, 831
Dollar Energy Fund Grants, 834
Dollar General Family Literacy Grants, 835
Dollar General Youth Literacy Grants, 837
DOL Youthbuild Grants, 838
Dominion Foundation Grants, 839
Donald W. Reynolds Foundation Children's Discovery Initiative Grants, 841
Don and May Wilkins Charitable Trust Grants, 842
Doree Taylor Charitable Foundation Grants, 843
Dorothea Haus Ross Foundation Grants, 844
Dorrance Family Foundation Grants, 845
Dorr Foundation Grants, 846
Do Something Awards, 847
Dr. and Mrs. Paul Pierce Memorial Foundation Grants, 862
Dr. John T. Macdonald Foundation Grants, 863
Dream Weaver Foundation, 865
DTE Energy Foundation Community Development Grants, 866
DTE Energy Foundation Diversity Grants, 867
DTE Energy Foundation Health and Human Services Grants, 869
DTE Energy Foundation Leadership Grants, 870
Dubois County Community Foundation Grants, 871
Duke Energy Foundation Local Impact Grants, 872
Dunspaugh-Dalton Foundation Grants, 873
Dyson Foundation Mid-Hudson Valley Project Support Grants, 874
E. Clayton and Edith P. Gengras, Jr. Foundation Grants, 875
E.J. Grassmann Trust Grants, 876

E.L. Wiegand Foundation Grants, 877
Earl and Maxine Claussen Trust Grants, 878
Eastern Bank Charitable Foundation Neighborhood
    Support Grants, 880
Eastern Bank Charitable Foundation Partnerships
    Grants, 881
Eastern Bank Charitable Foundation Targeted
    Grants, 882
Easton Foundations Archery Facility Grants, 883
Edna Wardlaw Charitable Trust Grants, 886
Edward and Ellen Roche Relief Fdn Grants, 887
Edward and Helen Bartlett Foundation Grants, 888
Edward and Romell Ackley Foundation Grants, 889
Edward F. Swinney Trust Grants, 890
Edwards Memorial Trust Grants, 891
Edward W. and Stella C. Van Houten Memorial Fund
    Grants, 892
Edyth Bush Charitable Foundation Grants, 893
Effie Allen Little Foundation Grants, 894
Effie and Wofford Cain Foundation Grants, 895
Effie Kuhlman Charitable Trust Grants, 896
Eide Bailly Resourcefullness Awards, 897
Eileen Fisher Activating Leadership Grants for
    Women and Girls, 898
Elizabeth Carse Foundation Grants, 899
Elizabeth Huth Coates Charitable Foundation
    Grants, 900
Elizabeth Morse Genius Charitable Trust Grants, 901
Elkhart County Community Foundation Fund for
    Elkhart County, 902
Elkhart County Community Foundation Grants, 903
Ella West Freeman Foundation Grants, 904
Elmer Roe Deaver Foundation Grants, 906
El Pomar Foundation Anna Keesling Ackerman Fund
    Grants, 907
El Pomar Foundation Grants, 908
Elsie H. Wilcox Foundation Grants, 909
Emerson Kampen Foundation Grants, 911
Emily Hall Tremaine Foundation Learning
    Disabilities Grants, 912
Emily O'Neill Sullivan Foundation Grants, 913
Emma J. Adams Memorial Fund Grants, 914
Energy by Design Poster Contest, 915
Ensworth Charitable Foundation Grants, 916
Entergy Charitable Foundation Low-Income
    Initiatives and Solutions Grants, 918
Entergy Corporation Micro Grants, 919
Entergy Corporation Open Grants for Arts and
    Culture, 920
Entergy Corporation Open Grants for Healthy
    Families, 921
EPA Children's Health Protection Grants, 923
Episcopal Actors' Guild Actors Florence James
    Children's Holiday Fund Grant, 925
EQT Fdn Community Enrichment Grants, 926
EQT Fdn Education and Workforce Grants, 927
Erie Chapman Foundation Grants, 928
Essex County Community Foundation F1rst Jobs
    Fund Grants, 930
Essex County Community Foundation Greater
    Lawrence Community Fund Grants, 931
Essex County Community Foundation Greater
    Lawrence Summer Fund Grants, 932
Essex County Community Foundation Merrimack
    Valley Municipal Business Development and
    Recovery Fund Grants, 933
Essex County Community Foundation Women's
    Fund Grants, 934
Ethel Sergeant Clark Smith Foundation Grants, 935
Evan Frankel Foundation Grants, 938
Evelyn and Walter Haas, Jr. Fund Immigrant Rights
    Grants, 941
Evelyn and Walter Haas, Jr. Fund Nonprofit
    Leadership Grants, 942
Ewing Marion Kauffman Foundation Grants, 943
Ezra M. Cutting Trust Grants, 945
F.M. Kirby Foundation Grants, 946
F.R. Bigelow Foundation Grants, 947
Farmers Insurance Corporate Giving Grants, 948
Fassino Foundation Grants, 949

Faye L. and William L. Cowden Charitable
    Foundation Grants, 950
Fayette County Foundation Grants, 951
FCYO Youth Organizing Grants, 954
Fichtenbaum Charitable Trust Grants, 955
Fidelity Charitable Gift Fund Grants, 956
Fidelity Foundation Grants, 957
Fifth Third Bank Corporate Giving, 958
Fifth Third Foundation Grants, 959
Finish Line Youth Foundation Founder's Grants, 960
Finish Line Youth Foundation Grants, 961
Finish Line Youth Foundation Legacy Grants, 962
FINRA Smart Investing@Your Library Grants, 963
FirstEnergy Foundation Community Grants, 965
First Hawaiian Bank Foundation Corporate Giving
    Grants, 967
First Nations Development Institute Native Youth
    and Culture Fund Grants, 974
Florence Foundation Grants, 978
Florence Hunt Maxwell Foundation Grants, 979
Ford Family Foundation Grants - Access to Health
    and Dental Services, 980
Ford Family Foundation Grants - Positive Youth
    Development, 982
Ford Family Foundation Grants - Technical
    Assistance , 983
Forest Foundation Grants, 985
Foundation Beyond Belief Compassionate Impact
    Grants, 986
Foundation Beyond Belief Humanist Grants, 987
Foundation for Appalachian Ohio Access to
    Environmental Education Mini-Grants, 989
Foundation for Health Enhancement Grants, 990
Fdn for the Mid South Communities Grants, 992
Foundation of Herkimer and Oneida Counties Youth
    Sports, Wellness and Recreation Mini-Grants, 994
Foundations of East Chicago Education Grants, 995
Fdns of East Chicago Family Support Grants, 996
Foundations of East Chicago Health Grants, 997
Foundations of East Chicago Youth Development
    Grants, 998
Four County Community Foundation General
    Grants, 1000
Four County Community Foundation Healthy
    Senior/Healthy Youth Fund Grants, 1001
Fourjay Foundation Grants, 1003
Four J Foundation Grants, 1004
Four Lanes Trust Grants, 1005
Four Times Foundation Grants, 1006
Francis Beidler Foundation Grants, 1007
Francis L. Abreu Charitable Trust Grants, 1008
Frankel Brothers Foundation Grants, 1009
Franklin County Community Fdn Grants, 1010
Franklin H. Wells and Ruth L. Wells Foundation
    Grants, 1011
Frank M. Tait Foundation Grants, 1012
Frank Reed and Margaret Jane Peters Memorial Fund
    Grants, 1013
Frank Reed and Margaret Jane Peters Memorial Fund
    II Grants, 1014
Fred and Gretel Biel Charitable Trust Grants, 1016
Frederick McDonald Trust Grants, 1017
Frederick W. Marzahl Memorial Fund Grants, 1018
Fremont Area Community Foundation Amazing X
    Grants, 1019
Fremont Area Community Foundation Community
    Grants, 1020
Fremont Area Community Foundation Youth
    Advisory Committee Grants, 1022
Friedman Family Foundation Grants, 1023
Friends of Hawaii Charities Grants, 1024
Fuller E. Callaway Foundation Grants, 1027
Fuller Foundation Youth At Risk Grants, 1028
Fund for the City of New York Grants, 1029
Furth Family Foundation Grants, 1030
Gamble Foundation Grants, 1032
Gannett Foundation Community Action Grants, 1033
Gardner Foundation Grants, 1035
Gardner Foundation Grants, 1034
GCI Corporate Contributions Grants, 1037

Gene Haas Foundation, 1038
General Motors Foundation Grants, 1039
General Service Foundation Human Rights and
    Economic Justice Grants, 1040
George A. & Grace L. Long Fdn Grants, 1041
George and Ruth Bradford Foundation Grants, 1042
George A Ohl Jr. Foundation Grants, 1043
George B. Page Foundation Grants, 1044
George F. Baker Trust Grants, 1046
George Graham and Elizabeth Galloway Smith
    Foundation Grants, 1047
George H. and Jane A. Mifflin Memorial Fund
    Grants, 1048
George H.C. Ensworth Memorial Fund Grants, 1049
George H. Sandy Foundation Grants, 1050
George I. Alden Trust Grants, 1051
George J. and Effie L. Seay Foundation Grants, 1052
George P. Davenport Trust Fund Grants, 1054
George W. Codrington Charitable Foundation
    Grants, 1055
George W.P. Magee Trust Grants, 1056
George W. Wells Foundation Grants, 1057
Georgia-Pacific Fdn Entrepreneurship Grants, 1059
Geraldine R. Dodge Fdn Education Grants, 1061
Gerber Fdn West Michigan Youth Grants, 1065
German Protestant Orphan Asylum Foundation
    Grants, 1066
Gertrude & William C. Wardlaw Grants, 1067
Giant Food Charitable Grants, 1068
Gibson County Community Foundation Recreation
    Grants, 1069
Gibson County Community Foundation Youth
    Development Grants, 1070
Gil and Dody Weaver Foundation Grants, 1071
Giving Gardens Challenge Grants, 1072
Global Fund for Women Grants, 1073
GMFUS Balkan Trust for Democracy Grants, 1075
GNOF Albert N. & Hattie M. McClure Grants, 1076
GNOF Bayou Communities Grants, 1077
GNOF Coastal 5 + 1 Grants, 1078
GNOF Cox Charities of New Orleans Grants, 1079
GNOF Exxon-Mobil Grants, 1080
GNOF Gert Community Fund Grants, 1082
GNOF IMPACT Grants for Arts and Culture, 1083
GNOF IMPACT Grants for Youth Dev, 1084
GNOF IMPACT Gulf States Eye Surg Fund, 1085
GNOF IMPACT Harold W. Newman, Jr. Charitable
    Trust Grants, 1086
GNOF IMPACT Kahn-Oppenheim Tr Grts, 1087
GNOF New Orleans Works Grants, 1088
GNOF Norco Community Grants, 1089
GNOF Organizational Effectiveness Grants and
    Workshops, 1090
GNOF Plaquemines Community Grants, 1091
GNOF Stand Up For Our Children Grants, 1092
Go Daddy Cares Charitable Contributions, 1093
Golden Heart Community Foundation Grants, 1094
Goldseker Foundation Non-Profit Management
    Assistance Grants, 1095
Good+Foundation Grants, 1096
Grace Bersted Foundation Grants, 1097
Graham and Carolyn Holloway Family Foundation
    Grants, 1098
Graham Family Charitable Foundation Grants, 1099
Graham Foundation Grants, 1101
Graham Foundation Grants, 1100
Grand Circle Foundation Associates Grants, 1102
Gray Family Fdn Camp Maintenance Grants, 1104
Great Clips Corporate Giving, 1108
Greater Milwaukee Foundation Grants, 1109
Greater Saint Louis Community Fdn Grants, 1110
Greater Sitka Legacy Fund Grants, 1111
Greater Tacoma Community Foundation General
    Operating Grants, 1113
Greater Tacoma Community Foundation Youth
    Program Grants, 1115
Green Foundation Human Services Grants, 1116
Green River Area Community Fdn Grants, 1117
Gregory and Helayne Brown Charitable Foundation
    Grants, 1119

Greygates Foundation Grants, 1120
Griffin Family Foundation Grants, 1121
Grotto Foundation Project Grants, 1123
Grundy Foundation Grants, 1124
GTRCF Boys and Girls Club of Grand Traverse
    Endowment Grants, 1126
GTRCF Elk Rapids Area Community Endowment
    Grants, 1127
GTRCF Genuine Leelanau Charitable Endowment
    Grants, 1128
GTRCF Healthy Youth and Healthy Seniors
    Endowment Grants, 1130
GTRCF Joan Rajkovich McGarry Family Education
    Endowment Grants, 1131
GTRCF Traverse City Track Club Endowment
    Grants, 1132
GTRCF Youth Endowment Grants, 1133
Gulf Coast Foundation of Community Operating
    Grants, 1134
Gulf Coast Foundation of Community Program
    Grants, 1135
Guy I. Bromley Trust Grants, 1136
H.A. and Mary K. Chapman Charitable Trust
    Grants, 1137
H.B. Fuller Foundation Grants, 1138
Haddad Foundation Grants, 1139
HAF Community Grants, 1141
HAF Don and Bettie Albright Endowment Fund
    Grants, 1142
HAF Joe Alexandre Mem Family Fund Grants, 1145
HAF Laurence and Elaine Allen Memorial Fund
    Grants, 1146
HAF Mada Huggins Caldwell Fund Grants, 1147
HAF Native Cultures Fund Grants, 1148
HAF Southern Humboldt Grants, 1150
Hahl Proctor Charitable Trust Grants, 1151
Hall-Perrine Foundation Grants, 1152
Hampton Roads Community Foundation Abused
    People Grants, 1153
Hampton Roads Community Foundation Community
    Leadership Partners Grants, 1155
Hampton Roads Community Foundation Nonprofit
    Facilities Improvement Grants, 1159
Hampton Roads Community Foundation Youth
    Baseball and Softball Program Grants, 1160
Hancock County Community Foundation - Field of
    Interest Grants, 1161
Hannaford Charitable Foundation Grants, 1163
Hannaford Supermarkets Community Giving, 1164
Hannah's Helping Hands Grants, 1165
Harden Foundation Grants, 1166
Hardin County Community Foundation Grants, 1167
Harmony Grove Foundation Grants, 1169
Harmony Project Grants, 1170
Harold and Rebecca H. Gross Fdn Grants, 1171
Harold Brooks Foundation Grants, 1172
Harold K.L. Castle Foundation Public Education
    Redesign and Enhancement Grants, 1173
Harold K.L. Castle Foundation Strengthening
    Windward Oahu Communities Grants, 1174
Harold K.L. Castle Foundation Windward Youth
    Leadership Fund Grants, 1175
Harris Foundation Grants, 1177
Harrison County Community Fdn Grants, 1178
Harrison County Community Foundation Signature
    Grants, 1179
Harry and Jeanette Weinberg Fdn Grants, 1182
Harry B. and Jane H. Brock Foundation Grants, 1183
Hartford Foundation Regular Grants, 1185
Hartley Foundation Grants, 1186
Harvey E. Najim Family Foundation Grants, 1187
Harvey Randall Wickes Foundation Grants, 1188
Hasbro Children's Fund Grants, 1189
Hattie Mae Lesley Foundation Grants, 1195
Hatton W. Sumners Foundation for the Study and
    Teaching of Self Government Grants, 1196
Hawai'i Community Foundation Children's Trust
    Fund Community Awareness: Child Abuse and
    Neglect Prevention Grants, 1198

Hawai'i Community Foundation East Hawaii Fund
    Grants, 1199
Hawai'i Community Foundation Ewa Beach
    Community Trust Fund Grants, 1200
Hawai'i Community Foundation Family Literacy and
    Hawaii Pizza Hut Literacy Grants, 1201
Hawai'i Community Foundation Lana'i Community
    Benefit Fund, 1203
Hawai'i Community Foundation Richard Smart Fund
    Grants, 1204
Hawai'i Community Foundation Robert E. Black
    Fund Grants, 1205
Hawai'i Community Foundation Victoria S. and
    Bradley L. Geist Foundation: Capacity Building
    Grants, 1206
Hawai'i Community Foundation Victoria S. and
    Bradley L. Geist Foundation: Enhancement
    Grants, 1207
Hawai'i Community Foundation Victoria S. and
    Bradley L. Geist Foundation: Supporting
    Transitioning Foster Youth Grants, 1209
Hawaiian Electric Industries Charitable Foundation
    Grants, 1211
Hawaii Community Foundation Omidyar Ohana
    Fund Grants, 1213
Hawaii Community Foundation Promising Minds
    Grants, 1215
Hawaii Community Foundation Reverend Takie
    Okumura Family Grants, 1216
Hawaii Community Foundation Sanford Harmony
    Pillars of Peace Grants, 1217
Hawaii Electric Industries Charitable Foundation
    Grants, 1218
Hawaii State Legislature Grant-In-Aid, 1219
Hazel and Walter T. Bales Foundation Grants, 1220
Hazen Foundation Public Education Grants, 1221
HBF Pathways Out of Poverty Grants, 1222
Hearst Foundations Culture Grants, 1223
Hearst Foundations Social Service Grants, 1224
HEI Charitable Foundation Grants, 1226
Helen Bader Foundation Grants, 1227
Helen E. Ellis Charitable Trust Grants, 1228
Helen G., Henry F., & Louise Tuechter Dornette
    Foundation Grants, 1229
Helen Gertrude Sparks Charitable Trust Grants, 1230
Helen Irwin Littauer Educational Trust Grants, 1231
Helen V. Brach Foundation Grants, 1232
Hendricks County Community Fdn Grants, 1234
Henrietta Lange Burk Fund Grants, 1235
Henry and Ruth Blaustein Rosenberg Foundation
    Youth Development Grants, 1237
Henry County Community Foundation - TASC
    Youth Grants, 1238
Henry County Community Foundation Grants, 1239
Henry E. Niles Foundation Grants, 1240
Henry F. Koch Residual Trust Grants, 1241
Henry L. Guenther Foundation Grants, 1242
Herbert A. and Adrian W. Woods Foundation
    Grants, 1243
Herman Goldman Foundation Grants, 1245
Herman H. Nettelroth Fund Grants, 1246
Herman P. and Sophia Taubman Fdn Grants, 1247
Highmark Corporate Giving Grants, 1248
Hill Crest Foundation Grants, 1249
Hillsdale County Community Foundation General
    Grants, 1250
Hillsdale County Community Foundation Love Your
    Community Grants, 1251
Hillsdale County Community Foundation
    Y.O.U.T.H. Grants, 1252
HLTA Visitor Industry Charity Walk Grant, 1254
Honeywell Corporation Family Safety and Security
    Grants, 1255
Honeywell Corporation Leadership Challenge
    Academy, 1258
Honor the Earth Grants, 1259
Horace A. Kimball and S. Ella Kimball Foundation
    Grants, 1260
Horace A. Moses Charitable Trust Grants, 1261

HRAMF Community Health Improvement Project
    Grants in Bowdoin Geneva, 1263
HRK Foundation Health Grants, 1264
HRSA Ryan White HIV AIDS Drug Assistance
    Grants, 1265
HSBC Corporate Giving Grants, 1266
HSFCA Biennium Grants, 1267
HSFCA Folk and Traditional Arts Grants - Culture
    Learning, 1268
Hubbard Family Foundation Grants, 1271
Hubbard Family Foundation Grants, 1270
Huffy Foundation Grants, 1273
Humana Foundation Grants, 1275
Huntington Clinical Foundation Grants, 1278
Huntington County Community Foundation Make a
    Difference Grants, 1280
ICCF Youth Advisory Council Grants, 1282
Iddings Foundation Capital Project Grants, 1283
Iddings Foundation Major Project Grants, 1284
Iddings Foundation Medium Project Grants, 1285
Iddings Foundation Small Project Grants, 1286
Ifuku Family Foundation Grants, 1287
Ike and Roz Friedman Foundation Grants, 1289
Illinois DNR School Habitat Action Grants, 1296
Illinois DNR Youth Recreation Corps Grants, 1297
IMLS National Leadership Grants for Libraries, 1299
Indiana OCRA Quick Impact Placebased (QuIP)
    Grants, 1300
Indiana OCRA Rural Capacity Grants (RCG), 1301
ING Foundation Grants, 1302
Initiaive Fdn Inside-Out Connections Grants, 1303
Initiative Foundation Innovation Fund Grants, 1304
Initiative Foundation Minnesota Early Childhood
    Initiative Grants, 1305
Inland Empire Community Foundation Capacity
    Building for IE Nonprofits Grants, 1306
Inland Empire Community Foundation Coachella
    Valley Youth Grants, 1307
Inland Empire Community Foundation Native Youth
    Grants, 1308
Intel Corporation Community Grants, 1311
Intel Corporation Int Community Grants, 1312
IRC Community Collaboratives for Refugee Women
    and Youth Grants, 1313
Irving S. Gilmore Foundation Grants, 1314
Isabel Allende Foundation Esperanza Grants, 1315
Island Insurance Foundation Grants, 1316
IYI Responsible Fatherhood Grants, 1318
J. Bulow Campbell Foundation Grants, 1319
J. Edwin Treakle Foundation Grants, 1320
J. Knox Gholston Foundation Grants, 1321
J. Marion Sims Foundation Teachers' Pet Grant, 1322
J.W. Gardner II Foundation Grants, 1323
J.W. Kieckhefer Foundation Grants, 1324
J. Walton Bissell Foundation Grants, 1325
J. Watumull Fund Grants, 1326
J. Willard and Alice S. Marriott Fdn Grants, 1327
Jack and Dorothy Byrne Foundation Grants, 1329
Jack H. and William M. Light Charitable Trust
    Grants, 1330
Jack Kent Cooke Fdn Good Neighbor Grants, 1331
Jack Satter Foundation Grants, 1334
Jacob and Hilda Blaustein Foundation Israel Program
    Grants, 1335
Jacob G. Schmidlapp Trusts Grants, 1336
James and Abigail Campbell Family Foundation
    Grants, 1337
James F. and Marion L. Miller Fdn Grants, 1338
James Ford Bell Foundation Grants, 1339
James Graham Brown Foundation Grants, 1340
James Lee Sorenson Family Impact Foundation
    Grants, 1342
James LeVoy Sorenson Foundation Grants, 1343
James M. Collins Foundation Grants, 1344
James S. Copley Foundation Grants, 1345
Jane's Trust Grants, 1346
Jane Bradley Pettit Foundation Community and
    Social Development Grants, 1347
Janet Spencer Weekes Foundation Grants, 1348
Janson Foundation Grants, 1350

Janson Foundation Grants, 1349
Japan Foundation Los Angeles Mini-Grants for
    Japanese Arts & Culture, 1354
Japan Foundation New York Small Grants for Arts
    and Culture, 1355
Jaquelin Hume Foundation Grants, 1357
Jeffris Wood Foundation Grants, 1359
Jennings County Community Fdn Grants, 1360
Jennings County Community Foundation Women's
    Giving Circle Grant, 1361
Jerry L. and Barbara J. Burris Fdn Grants, 1362
Jessica Stevens Community Foundation Grants, 1363
Jewish Fund Grants, 1364
Jim Blevins Foundation Grants, 1365
Jim Moran Foundation Grants, 1366
Joan Bentinck-Smith Charitable Fdn Grants, 1367
John and Marcia Goldman Foundation Youth
    Development Grants, 1368
John Clarke Trust Grants, 1369
John D. and Katherine A. Johnston Foundation
    Grants, 1370
John F. Kennedy Center for the Performing Arts
    National Rosemary Kennedy Internship, 1371
John G. Duncan Charitable Trust Grants, 1372
John H. and Wilhelmina D. Harland Charitable
    Foundation Community Services Grants, 1375
John M. Weaver Foundation Grants, 1376
John P. Ellbogen Fdn Community Grants, 1377
Johnson Controls Foundation Arts and Culture
    Grants, 1378
Johnson County Community Fdn Grants, 1379
Johnson County Community Foundation Youth
    Philanthropy Initiative Grants, 1380
Johnson Scholarship Foundation Grants, 1382
John W. Anderson Foundation Grants, 1383
Joni Elaine Templeton Foundation Grants, 1384
Joseph H. and Florence A. Roblee Foundation
    Children and Youth Grants, 1385
Joseph H. and Florence A. Roblee Foundation Family
    Grants, 1387
Joseph Henry Edmondson Foundation Grants, 1388
Josephine Schell Russell Chartbl Trust Grants, 1389
Joseph S. Stackpole Charitable Trust Grants, 1390
Journal Gazette Foundation Grants, 1391
Jovid Foundation Employment Training Grants, 1392
Joyce and Randy Seckman Charitable Foundation
    Grants, 1393
JP Morgan Chase Fdn Arts and Culture Grants, 1394
Judith Clark-Morrill Foundation Grants, 1395
Judy and Peter Blum Kovler Foundation Grants, 1396
Julia and Tunnicliff Fox Chartbl Trust Grants, 1397
Julia Richardson Brown Foundation Grants, 1398
Julius N. Frankel Foundation Grants, 1400
KaBOOM! Adventure Courses Grant, 1401
KaBOOM! Build it Grant, 1402
KaBOOM! Creative Play Grant, 1403
KaBOOM! Multi-Sport Courts Grant, 1404
KaBOOM! Play Everywhere Design Challenge, 1405
Kalamazoo Community Foundation Good Neighbor
    Grants, 1408
Kalamazoo Community Foundation Individuals and
    Families Grants, 1409
Kalamazoo Community Foundation John E. Fetzer
    Institute Fund Grants, 1410
Kalamazoo Community Foundation LBGT Equality
    Fund Grants, 1411
Kalamazoo Community Foundation Youth
    Development Grants, 1412
Kansas Health Fdn Major Initiatives Grants, 1414
Kansas Health Foundation Recognition Grants, 1415
Kate B. Reynolds Charitable Trust Health Care
    Grants, 1416
Kate B. Reynolds Charitable Trust Poor and Needy
    Grants, 1417
Katharine Matthies Foundation Grants, 1418
Kathryne Beynon Foundation Grants, 1420
Katie's Krops Grants, 1421
Katrine Menzing Deakins Chartbl Trust Grants, 1422
Kawabe Memorial Fund Grants, 1423
Kelvin and Eleanor Smith Foundation Grants, 1424

Kenai Peninsula Foundation Grants, 1425
Kentucky Arts Cncl Access Assistance Grants, 1428
Ketchikan Community Foundation Grants, 1429
Kimball Foundation Grants, 1432
Kimball International-Habig Foundation Health and
    Human Services Grants, 1434
KIND Causes Monthly Grants, 1435
Kinder Morgan Foundation Grants, 1436
Kirby Laing Foundation Grants, 1439
Kirkpatrick Foundation Grants, 1440
Klingenstein-Simons Fellowship Awards in the
    Neurosciences, 1441
Knox County Community Foundation Recreation
    Grants, 1442
Knox County Community Foundation Youth
    Development Grants, 1443
Koch Family Foundation (Annapolis) Grants, 1444
Kodiak Community Foundation Grants, 1446
Koret Foundation Grants, 1449
Kosasa Foundation Grants, 1450
Kosciusko County Community Foundation
    Endowment Youth Services (KEYS) Grants, 1451
Kosciusko County Community Fdn Grants, 1452
Kosciusko County Community Foundation REMC
    Operation Round Up Grants, 1453
Kovler Family Foundation Grants, 1454
Kovler Family Foundation Grants, 1455
Kroger Company Donations, 1456
Laclede Gas Charitable Trust Grants, 1457
LaGrange County Community Fdn Grants, 1458
LaGrange Independent Foundation for Endowments
    (L.I.F.E.), 1459
Laidlaw Foundation Multi-Year Grants, 1460
Laidlaw Foundation Youh Organizing Catalyst
    Grants, 1461
Laidlaw Foundation Youth Organizaing Initiatives
    Grants, 1462
Lake County Community Fund Grants, 1463
Land O'Lakes Fdn California Region Grants, 1465
Land O'Lakes Foundation Community Grants, 1466
Land O'Lakes Foundation Mid-Atlantic Grants, 1467
Lands' End Corporate Giving Program, 1468
Latkin Charitable Foundation Grants, 1469
Laura B. Vogler Foundation Grants, 1470
Laura Musser Intercultural Harmony Grants, 1472
Laura Moore Cunningham Foundation Grants, 1474
Laurel Foundation Grants, 1475
Laurie H. Wollmuth Charitable Trust Grants, 1476
Lee and Ramona Bass Foundation Grants, 1478
Legler Benbough Foundation Grants, 1479
LEGO Children's Fund Grants, 1480
Leo Goodwin Foundation Grants, 1482
Leo Niessen Jr., Charitable Trust Grants, 1484
Lewis H. Humphreys Charitable Trust Grants, 1486
LGA Family Foundation Grants, 1487
Liberty Bank Foundation Grants, 1488
Libra Foundation Grants, 1489
Lied Foundation Trust Grants, 1490
Lil and Julie Rosenberg Foundation Grants, 1491
Lilly Endowment Summer Youth Grants, 1492
Lily Palmer Fry Memorial Trust Grants, 1493
Linden Foundation Grants, 1494
Linford & Mildred White Charitable Grants, 1495
Lisa and Douglas Goldman Fund Grants, 1496
LISC Affordable Housing Grants, 1497
LISC Capacity Building Grants, 1498
LISC Community Leadership Operating Grts, 1499
LISC Education Grants, 1500
LISC Financial Stability Grants, 1501
Lloyd G. Balfour Foundation Attleboro-Specific
    Charities Grants, 1502
Locations Foundation Legacy Grants, 1504
Lockheed Martin Corporation Fdn Grants, 1505
Long Island Community Foundation Grants, 1507
Lotus 88 Foundation for Women and Children
    Grants, 1508
Louie M. and Betty M. Phillips Fdn Grants, 1509
Louis and Sandra Berkman Foundation Grants, 1510
Louis Calder Foundation Grants, 1511
Lubrizol Corporation Community Grants, 1512

Lubrizol Foundation Grants, 1513
Lucile Packard Foundation for Children's Health
    Grants, 1514
Lucy Downing Nisbet Charitable Fund Grants, 1515
Luella Kemper Trust Grants, 1517
Lumpkin Family Fdn Healthy People Grants, 1518
Lumpkin Family Foundation Strong Community
    Leadership Grants, 1519
Lynn and Foster Friess Family Fdn Grants, 1520
M.A. Rikard Charitable Trust Grants, 1521
M. Bastian Family Foundation Grants, 1522
M.J. Murdock Charitable Trust General Grants, 1524
Mabel A. Horne Fund Grants, 1525
Mabel F. Hoffman Charitable Trust Grants, 1526
Mabel Louise Riley Foundation Family Strengthening
    Small Grants, 1528
Mabel Louise Riley Foundation Grants, 1529
Macquarie Bank Foundation Grants, 1532
Madison Community Foundation Altrusa
    International of Madison Grants, 1533
Madison Community Foundation Grants, 1535
Madison County Community Foundation - City of
    Anderson Quality of Life Grant, 1536
Madison County Community Foundation General
    Grants, 1537
Maine Community Foundation Edward H. Daveis
    Benevolent Fund Grants, 1540
Maine Community Foundation Equity Grants, 1541
Maine Community Fdn Peaks Island Grants, 1542
Maine Community Foundation Penobscot Valley
    Health Association Grants, 1543
Maine Community Foundation People of Color Fund
    Grants, 1544
Maine Community Foundation Vincent B. and
    Barbara G. Welch Grants, 1545
Maine Women's Fund Econ Security Grants, 1546
Maine Women's Fund Girls' Grantmaking Intv, 1547
Make Sense Foundation Grants, 1548
Manuel D. and Rhoda Mayerson Fdn Grants, 1550
Marathon Petroleum Corporation Grants, 1551
March of Dimes Program Grants, 1552
Marcia and Otto Koehler Foundation Grants, 1553
Mardag Foundation Grants, 1554
Margaret and James A. Elkins Jr. Fdn Grants, 1555
Margaret M. Walker Charitable Fdn Grants, 1556
Margaret T. Morris Foundation Grants, 1557
Marie C. and Joseph C. Wilson Foundation Rochester
    Small Grants, 1559
Marietta McNeill Morgan and Samuel Tate Morgan
    Jr. Trust Grants, 1560
Marin Community Foundation Affordable Housing
    Grants, 1561
Marin Community Foundation Arts in the
    Community Grants, 1563
Marin Community Foundation Ending the Cycle of
    Poverty Grants, 1565
Marin Community Foundation Improving
    Community Health Grants, 1566
Marin Community Foundation Social Justice and
    Interfaith Understanding Grants, 1567
Marin Community Foundation Stinson Bolinas
    Community Grants, 1568
Marion and Miriam Rose Fund Grants, 1569
Marion Gardner Jackson Charitable Trust Grts, 1570
Marion I. and Henry J. Knott Foundation
    Discretionary Grants, 1571
Marion I. and Henry J. Knott Foundation Standard
    Grants, 1572
Marisla Foundation Human Services Grants, 1573
Marjorie Moore Charitable Foundation Grants, 1574
Mark W. Coy Foundation Grants, 1575
Mark Wahlberg Youth Foundation Grants, 1576
Marquette Bank Neighborhood Commit Grants, 1577
Marriott Int Corporate Giving Grants, 1578
Marshall County Community Fdn Grants, 1579
Marsh Corporate Grants, 1580
Martin Family Foundation Grants, 1583
Mary A. Crocker Trust Grants, 1584
Mary Black Foundation Active Living Grants, 1585

Mary Black Foundation Early Childhood Development Grants, 1586
Mary Cofer Trigg Trust Fund Grants, 1587
Mary D. and Walter F. Frear Eleemosynary Trust Grants, 1588
Mary E. Babcock Foundation, 1589
Mary K. Chapman Foundation Grants, 1590
Mary Kay Foundation Domestic Violence Shelter Grants, 1591
Maryland State Dept of Education 21st Century Community Learning Centers Grants, 1593
Mary Owen Borden Foundation Grants, 1597
Mary S. and David C. Corbin Fdn Grants, 1598
Mary W.B. Curtis Trust Grants, 1599
Massachusetts Cultural Council Local Cultural Council (LCC) Grants, 1601
MassMutual Foundation Edonomic Development Grants, 1603
Mathile Family Foundation Grants, 1604
Matson Adahi I Tano' Grants, 1606
Matson Community Giving Grants, 1607
Matson Ka Ipu 'Aina Grants, 1608
Maurice Amado Foundation Grants, 1609
Maurice J. Masserini Charitable Trust Grants, 1610
Maurice R. Robinson Fund Grants, 1611
Max and Anna Levinson Foundation Grants, 1612
May and Stanley Smith Charitable Trust Grants, 1613
McCarthy Family Fdn Charity Fund Grants, 1614
McConnell Foundation Grants, 1616
McCune Charitable Foundation Grants, 1617
McCune Foundation Humananities Grants, 1619
McGraw-Hill Companies Community Grants, 1620
McGregor Fund Human Services Grants, 1621
McInerny Foundation Grants, 1622
McLean Contributionship Grants, 1623
McLean Foundation Grants, 1624
Mead Family Foundation Grants, 1625
Meadows Foundation Grants, 1626
Mead Witter Foundation Grants, 1628
Medtronic Foundation Community Link Arts, Civic, and Culture Grants, 1629
Medtronic Foundation CommunityLink Health Grants, 1630
Memorial Foundation for Children Grants, 1633
Merck Family Fund Urban Farming and Youth Leadership Grants, 1635
Merck Family Fund Youth Transforming Urban Communities Grants, 1636
Mericos Foundation Grants, 1637
Meriden Foundation Grants, 1638
Merrick Foundation Grants, 1640
Merrick Foundation Grants, 1639
Mertz Gilmore Foundation NYC Communities Grants, 1641
Mertz Gilmore Foundation NYC Dance Grants, 1642
Mervin Bovaird Foundation Grants, 1643
Meta and George Rosenberg Fdn Grants, 1644
MetLife Fdn Preparing Young People Grants, 1645
MetroWest Health Foundation Grants to Reduce the Incidence of High Risk Behaviors Among Adolescents, 1646
Metzger-Price Fund Grants, 1647
Meyer Foundation Benevon Grants, 1648
Meyer Foundation Education Grants, 1649
Meyer Fdn Healthy Communities Grants, 1650
Meyer Fdn Management Assistance Grants, 1651
Meyer Memorial Trust Responsive Grants, 1653
MFRI Community Mobilization Grants, 1654
MGM Resorts Foundation Community Grants, 1655
MGN Family Foundation Grants, 1656
Michael and Susan Dell Foundation Grants, 1657
Michael Reese Health Trust Core Grants, 1658
Michael Reese Health Trust Responsive Grants, 1659
Michelin North America Challenge Education, 1660
Michigan Women Forward Grants, 1662
Microsoft Software Donations, 1665
Microsoft YouthSpark Grants, 1666
Mid-Iowa Health Foundation Community Response Grants, 1667

Middlesex Savings Charitable Foundation Basic Human Needs Grants, 1668
Middlesex Savings Charitable Foundation Capacity Building Grants, 1669
Middlesex Savings Charitable Foundation Educational Opportunities Grants, 1670
Mile High United Way Stratc Investment Grts, 1671
Milken Family Foundation Grants, 1672
Miller Foundation Grants, 1673
Mill Spring Foundation Grants, 1674
Milton and Sally Avery Arts Foundation Grants, 1675
Milton Hicks Wood and Helen Gibbs Wood Charitable Trust Grants, 1676
Mimi and Peter Haas Fund Grants, 1677
Minnie M. Jones Trust Grants, 1678
MLB Tomorrow Fund Grants, 1679
Monsanto Kids Garden Fresh Grants, 1682
Monsanto United States Grants, 1684
Montana Arts Council Cultural and Aesthetic Project Grants, 1685
Montana Community Foundation Grants, 1687
Montana Community Fdn Women's Grants, 1688
Montgomery County Community Foundation Health and Human Services Fund Grants, 1689
Montgomery County Community Foundation Youth Services Grants, 1691
Moody Foundation Grants, 1692
Moran Family Foundation Grants, 1693
Morris Stulsaft Foundation Early Childhood Education Grants, 1696
Morris Stulsaft Foundation Educational Support for Children Grants, 1697
Morris Stulsaft Foundation Participation in the the Arts Grants, 1698
Morris Stulsaft Foundation Pathways to Work Grants, 1699
Moses Kimball Fund Grants, 1701
Motiv8 Foundation Grants, 1702
Ms. Foundation for Women Building Democracy Grants, 1706
Ms. Fdn for Women Economic Justice Grants, 1707
Ms. Fdn for Women Ending Violence Grants, 1708
Mt. Sinai Health Care Foundation Health of the Jewish Community Grants, 1709
Mt. Sinai Health Care Foundation Health of the Urban Community Grants, 1710
Narragansett Number One Foundation Grants, 1712
NASE Fdn Future Entrepreneur Scholarship, 1713
Natalie W. Furniss Foundation Grants, 1715
Nathalie and Gladys Dalkowitz Charitable Trust Grants, 1716
Nathaniel and Elizabeth P. Stevens Foundation Grants, 1719
Nationwide Insurance Foundation Grants, 1726
NCMCF Youth Advisory Council Grants, 1727
Nellie Mae Education Foundation District-Level Change Grants, 1736
Nell J. Redfield Foundation Grants, 1737
Nevada Community Foundation Grants, 1741
New Earth Foundation Grants, 1743
Newfoundland and Labrador Arts Council ArtSmarts Grants, 1744
Newfoundland and Labrador Arts Council School Touring Grants, 1745
Newfoundland and Labrador Arts Council Visiting Artists Grants, 1746
New Hampshire Charitable Foundation Community Unrestricted Grants, 1747
New Hampshire Charitable Foundation Neil and Louise Tillotson Fund - Empower Coös Youth Grants, 1748
New Hampshire Department of Justice Children's Justice Act Coronavirus Emergency Grants, 1749
New Jersey Center for Hispanic Policy, Research and Development Innovative Initiatives Grants, 1750
New York Foundation Grants, 1753
NFL Charities NFL Player Foundation Grants, 1754
NFL Charities Pro Bowl Community Grants in Hawaii, 1755
Nick Traina Foundation Grants, 1759

Nissan Neighbors Grants, 1762
Noble County Community Foundation Grants, 1765
Norcliffe Foundation Grants, 1766
Norman Foundation Grants, 1767
North Dakota Community Foundation Grants, 1768
Northern Chautauqua Community Foundation Community Grants, 1769
North Face Explore Fund, 1770
NRA Foundation Grants, 1774
NSTA Distinguished Informal Science Education Award, 1777
NYFA Artists in the School Community Planning Grants, 1779
NYSCA Arts Education: General Operating Support Grants, 1781
NYSCA Arts Education: General Program Support Grants, 1782
NYSCA Arts Education: Local Capacity Building Grants (Regrants), 1783
NYSCA Electronic Media and Film: Film Festivals Grants, 1785
NYSCA Electronic Media and Film: General Operating Support, 1786
NYSCA Electronic Media and Film: General Program Support, 1787
NYSCA Electronic Media and Film: Screenings Grants, 1788
NYSCA Music: Commty Music Schools Grants, 1790
NYSCA Music: Gen Operating Support Grants, 1791
NYSCA Music: Gen Program Support Grants, 1792
NYSCA Special Arts Services: General Program Support Grants, 1793
NYSCA Special Arts Services: Instruction and Training Grants, 1794
NYSCA Theatre: Prof Performances Grants, 1795
NZDIA Community Org Grants Scheme, 1796
O. Max Gardner Foundation Grants, 1798
Oak Foundation Child Abuse Grants, 1799
Oak Fdn Housing and Homelessness Grants, 1800
OceanFirst Foundation Home Runs for Heroes Grants, 1802
OceanFirst Foundation Major Grants, 1803
Office Depot Corporation Community Relations Grants, 1805
OHA 'Ahahui Grants, 1807
OHA Community Grants for Culture, 1808
OHA Community Grants for Education, 1809
Ohio Arts Council Artist in Residence Grants for Sponsors, 1810
Ohio County Community Foundation Board of Directors Grants, 1811
Ohio County Community Foundation Grants, 1812
Olga Sipolin Children's Fund Grants, 1815
Olive B. Cole Foundation Grants, 1816
Olive Higgins Prouty Foundation Grants, 1817
Olive Smith Browning Charitable Trust Grants, 1818
Olivia R. Gardner Foundation Grants, 1819
Onan Family Foundation Grants, 1821
OneFamily Foundation Grants, 1822
Ontario Arts Council Arts Organizations in Communities and Schools Operating Grants, 1824
Ontario Arts Council Indigenous Culture Fund Indigenous Artists in Communities and Schools Project Grants, 1825
Oppenstein Brothers Foundation Grants, 1827
Orange County Community Foundation Grants, 1829
Orange County Community Foundation Grants, 1828
Ordean Foundation Catalyst Grants, 1830
Ordean Foundation Partnership Grants, 1831
Oregon Community Foundation Black Student Success Community Network Grants, 1832
Oregon Community Fdn Community Grants, 1833
Oregon Community Foundation Community Recovery Grants, 1834
Oregon Community Foundation Edna E. Harrell Community Children's Fund Grants, 1835
Oren Campbell McCleary Chartbl Trust Grants, 1837
OSF Baltimore Community Fellowships, 1838
OSF Baltimore Criminal and Juve Justice Grts, 1839

OSF Baltimore Education and Youth Development Grants, 1840
OSF Early Childhood Program Grants, 1841
OSF Education Program Grants in Kyrgyzstan, 1842
OSF Young Feminist Leaders Fellowships, 1845
OSF Youth Action Fund Grants in Kyrgyzstan, 1846
OtterCares Champion Fund Grants, 1848
OtterCares Impact Fund Grants, 1849
OtterCares Inspiration Fund Grants, 1850
OtterCares NoCO Fund Grants, 1851
Outrigger Duke Kahanamoku Foundation Athletic Event Grants, 1852
Outrigger Duke Kahanamoku Foundation Athletic Team Grants, 1853
Pacers Foundation Be Drug-Free Grants, 1856
Pacers Foundation Be Educated Grants, 1857
Pacers Foundation Indiana Fever's Be YOUnique Fund Grants, 1860
PacifiCare Foundation Grants, 1861
Packard Foundation Children, Families, and Communities Grants, 1862
Packard Foundation Local Grants, 1863
Pajaro Valley Community Health Health Trust Insurance/Coverage & Education on Using the System Grants, 1864
Pajaro Valley Community Health Trust Diabetes and Contributing Factors Grants, 1865
Parke County Community Foundation Grants, 1868
Parker Foundation (California) Grants, 1869
Parker Foundation (Virginia) Grants to Support Christian Evangelism, 1870
Parkersburg Area Community Foundation Action Grants, 1871
Paso del Norte Health Foundation Grants, 1874
PAS Zildjian Family Opportunity Fund Grants, 1878
Patricia Kisker Foundation Grants, 1879
Patrick and Aimee Butler Family Foundation Community Human Services Grants, 1880
Paul and Edith Babson Foundation Grants, 1881
PCA-PCD Organizational Short-Term Professional Development and Consulting Grants, 1882
PCA-PCD Professional Development for Individual Artists Grants, 1883
PCA Art Organizations and Art Programs Grants for Presenting Organizations, 1884
PCA Arts Management Internship, 1886
PCA Arts Organizations and Arts Program Grants for Music, 1887
PCA Arts Organizations and Arts Programs Grants for Arts Education Organizations, 1889
PCA Arts Organizations and Arts Programs Grants for Arts Service Organizations, 1890
PCA Arts Organizations and Arts Programs Grants for Crafts, 1891
PCA Arts Organizations and Arts Programs Grants for Local Arts, 1895
PCA Arts Organizations and Arts Programs Grants for Visual Arts, 1898
PCA Entry Track Arts Organizations and Arts Programs Grants for Art Museums, 1900
PCA Entry Track Arts Organizations and Arts Programs Grants for Arts Education Organizations, 1901
PCA Entry Track Arts Organizations and Arts Programs Grants for Arts Service Orgs, 1902
PCA Entry Track Arts Organizations and Arts Programs Grants for Crafts, 1903
PCA Entry Track Arts Organizations and Arts Programs Grants for Local Arts, 1907
PCA Entry Track Arts Organizations and Arts Programs Grants for Music, 1908
PCA Entry Track Arts Organizations and Arts Programs Grants for Presenting Orgs, 1909
PCA Entry Track Arts Organizations and Arts Programs Grants for Theatre, 1910
PCA Entry Track Arts Organizations and Arts Programs Grants for Visual Arts, 1912
PCA Management/Techl Assistance Grants, 1913
PCA Pennsylvania Partners in the Arts Program Stream Grants, 1914

PCA Pennsylvania Partners in the Arts Project Stream Grants, 1915
PCA Strategies for Success Grants - Adv Level, 1917
PCA Strategies for Success Grants - Basic Level, 1918
PCA Strategies for Success Grants - Intermediate Level, 1919
PDF Fiscal Sponsorship Grant, 1921
PennPAT Fee-Support Grants for Presenters, 1930
Pentair Foundation Education and Community Grants, 1934
PepsiCo Foundation Grants, 1935
Percy B. Ferebee Endowment Grants, 1936
Perkin Fund Grants, 1937
Perkins-Ponder Foundation Grants, 1938
Perkins Charitable Foundation Grants, 1939
Perpetual Benevolent Fund, 1940
Perry County Community Foundation Recreation Grants, 1942
Perry County Community Foundation Youth Development Grants, 1943
Peter and Elizabeth C. Tower Foundation Intellectual Disabilities Grants, 1944
Peter and Elizabeth C. Tower Foundation Learning Disability Grants, 1945
Peter and Elizabeth C. Tower Foundation Mental Health Grants, 1946
Peter and Elizabeth C. Tower Foundation Small Grants, 1947
Peter and Elizabeth C. Tower Foundation Substance Use Disorders Grants, 1948
Peter and Elizabeth C. Tower Foundation Technology Initiative Grants, 1949
Peter and Elizabeth C. Tower Foundation Technology Planning Grants, 1950
Petersburg Community Foundation Grants, 1951
Pettus Foundation Grants, 1952
Peyton Anderson Foundation Grants, 1954
PG&E Community Vitality Grants, 1957
PGE Foundation Grants, 1958
Philanthrofund Foundation Grants, 1959
Phoenix Coyotes Charities Grants, 1963
Phoenix Suns Charities Grants, 1964
Piedmont Health Foundation Grants, 1965
Piedmont Natural Gas Corporate and Charitable Contributions, 1966
Piedmont Natural Gas Fdn Envirnmtl Stewardship and Energy Sustainability Grant, 1967
Piedmont Natural Gas Foundation Health and Human Services Grants, 1968
Pike County Community Foundation Recreation Grants, 1970
Pike County Community Foundation Youth Development Grants, 1971
Pinnacle Entertainment Foundation Grants, 1972
Pinnacle Foundation Grants, 1973
Piper Jaffray Foundation Communities Giving Grants, 1974
Piper Trust Arts and Culture Grants, 1975
Piper Trust Children Grants, 1976
Piper Trust Education Grants, 1977
Piper Trust Healthcare and Med Rsrch Grants, 1978
Piper Trust Reglious Organizations Grants, 1979
Pittsburgh Fdn Affordable Housing Grants, 1980
Pittsburgh Foundation Healthy Children and Adults Grants, 1981
PMI Foundation Grants, 1982
PNC Foundation Affordable Housing Grants, 1983
PNC Foundation Community Services Grants, 1984
PNC Foundation Grow Up Great Early Childhood Grants, 1986
PNC Foundation Revitalization and Stabilization Grants, 1987
PNM Reduce Your Use Grants, 1988
Pohlad Family Fdn Large Capital Grants, 1990
Pohlad Family Fdn Small Capital Grants, 1991
Pohlad Family Foundation Youth Advancement Grants, 1993
Pokagon Fund Grants, 1994
Polk County Community Foundation Bradley Breakthrough Community Benefit Grants, 1995

Polk County Community Foundation Free Community Events Grants, 1996
Polk County Community Foundation Kirby Harmon Field Fund Grants, 1997
Polk County Community Foundation Marjorie M. and Lawrence R. Bradley Endowment Fund Grants, 1998
Polk County Community Foundation Mary F. Kessler Fund Grants, 1999
Polk County Community Foundation Seasonal Assistance and Cheer Grants for Charitable Programs, 2000
Polk County Community Foundation Unrestricted Grants, 2001
Porter County Community Foundation Health and Wellness Grant, 2002
Porter County Community Foundation PCgivingproject Grants, 2003
Porter County Community Foundation Sparking the Arts Fund Grants, 2004
Porter County Community Foundation Women's Fund Grants, 2005
Portland Fdn - Women's Giving Circle Grant, 2006
Portland General Electric Foundation Grants, 2007
Posey Community Foundation Women's Fund Grants, 2008
Posey County Community Foundation Recreation Grants, 2009
Posey County Community Foundation Youth Development Grants, 2010
Powell Family Foundation Grants, 2012
Powell Foundation Grants, 2013
PPCF Community Grants, 2014
PPCF Esther M. and Freeman E. Everett Charitable Foundation Grants, 2016
PPG Industries Foundation Grants, 2017
Premera Blue Cross Grants, 2018
Presidio Fencing Club Youth Fencers Assistance Scholarships, 2019
Price Chopper's Golub Foundation Grants, 2020
Priddy Foundation Organizational Development Grants, 2022
Pride Foundation Grants, 2024
Proteus Fund Grants, 2027
PSEG Corporate Contributions Grants, 2030
PSEG Fdn Safety and Preparedness Grants, 2031
Public Education Power Grants, 2032
Public Welfare Fdn Juvenile Justice Grants, 2033
Public Welfare Foundation Special Initiative to Advance Civil Legal Aid Grants, 2034
Publix Super Markets Charities Local Grants, 2036
Puerto Rico Community Foundation Grants, 2037
Pulaski County Community Foundation Grants, 2038
Pulido Walker Foundation, 2039
Putnam County Community Fdn Grants, 2040
Quaker Oats Company Kids Care Clubs Grants, 2041
R.C. Baker Foundation Grants, 2043
R.D. Beirne Trust Grants, 2045
R.J. McElroy Trust Grants, 2046
R.S. Gernon Trust Grants, 2047
Radcliffe Institute Oral History Grants, 2049
Ralph C. Wilson, Jr. Foundation Youth Sports and Recreation Grant, 2051
Raskob Fdn for Catholic Activities Grants, 2054
Rasmuson Foundation Tier One Grants, 2055
Rasmuson Foundation Tier Two Grants, 2056
Rathmann Family Foundation Grants, 2057
Ray Foundation Grants, 2059
RCF General Community Grants, 2062
RCF Individual Assistance Grants, 2063
RCF Summertime Kids Grants, 2064
RCF The Women's Fund Grants, 2065
Reinberger Foundation Grants, 2066
Ressler-Gertz Foundation Grants, 2067
Richard and Caroline T. Gwathmey Memorial Trust Grants, 2069
Richard Davoud Donchian Foundation Grants, 2070
Richard J. Stern Foundation for the Arts Grants, 2071
Richards Foundation Grants, 2072
Richard W. Goldman Family Fdn Grants, 2073

Richland County Bank Grants, 2074
Riedman Foundation Grants, 2076
Ripley County Community Foundation Grants, 2077
Robbins-de Beaumont Foundation Grants, 2080
Robbins Charitable Foundation Grants, 2081
Robbins Family Charitable Foundation Grants, 2082
Robert and Betty Wo Foundation Grants, 2083
Robert and Helen Haddad Foundation Grants, 2084
Robert Bowne Foundaion Edmund A. Stanley, Jr.
    Research Grants, 2086
Robert Bowne Foundation Fellowships, 2087
Robert Bowne Foundation Literacy Grants, 2088
Robert Bowne Fdn Youth-Centered Grants, 2089
Robert F. Lange Foundation Grants, 2090
Robert Lee Adams Foundation Grants, 2091
Robert Lee Blaffer Foundation Grants, 2092
Robert R. McCormick Tribune Foundation
    Community Grants, 2093
Robert R. Meyer Foundation Grants, 2094
Robert W. Knox, Sr. and Pearl Wallis Knox
    Charitable Foundation, 2095
Robin Hood Foundation Grants, 2096
Robinson Foundation Grants, 2097
Ron and Sanne Higgins Family Fdn Grants, 2101
Roney-Fitzpatrick Foundation Grants, 2102
Rose Community Foundation Child and Family
    Development Grants, 2103
Rose Community Foundation Health Grants, 2105
Rose Hills Foundation Grants, 2106
Rosenberg Foundation Immigrant Rights and
    Integration Grants, 2108
Roy and Christine Sturgis Charitable Tr Grts, 2115
Roy J. Carver Charitable Trust Youth Services and
    Recreation Grants, 2117
RR Donnelley Foundation Grants, 2118
Rush County Community Foundation Grants, 2121
Ruth Anderson Foundation Grants, 2122
Ruth and Henry Campbell Foundation Grants, 2123
Ruth and Vernon Taylor Foundation Grants, 2124
Ruth Camp Campbell Charitable Trust Grants, 2125
RWJF Healthy Eating Research Grants, 2127
S. D. Bechtel, Jr. Foundation / Stephen Bechtel Fund
    Character and Citizenship Dev Grants, 2128
S. Spencer Scott Fund Grants, 2129
Sabina Dolan and Gladys Saulsbury Foundation
    Grants, 2130
SACF Youth Advisory Council Grants, 2131
Saeman Family Fdn A Charitable Grants, 2133
Saginaw Community Foundation Discretionary
    Grants, 2134
Saginaw Community Foundation YWCA Fund for
    Women and Girls Grants, 2135
Saginaw County Community Foundation Youth
    FORCE Grants, 2136
Saigh Foundation Grants, 2137
Saint Ann Legacy Grants, 2138
Saint Louis Rams Foundation Community
    Donations, 2139
Salmon Foundation Grants, 2140
Saltchuk Corporate Giving, 2141
Salt River Project Health and Human Services
    Grants, 2142
Samueli Foundation Youth Services Grants, 2144
Samuel N. and Mary Castle Foundation Grants, 2145
Samuel S. Johnson Foundation Grants, 2146
San Antonio Area Foundation Annual Responsive
    Grants, 2147
San Antonio Area Foundation Capital and Naming
    Rights Grants, 2148
San Antonio Area Foundation High School
    Completion Grants, 2149
San Antonio Area Foundation Special and Urgent
    Needs Funding Grants, 2150
San Antonio Area Foundation Strengthening
    Nonprofits Grants, 2151
Sand Hill Foundation Environment and Sustainability
    Grants, 2152
Sand Hill Foundation Health and Opportunity
    Grants, 2153
Sand Hill Fdn Small Capital Needs Grants, 2154

SanDisk Corp Community Sharing Grants, 2155
Sands Cares Grants, 2156
Sandy Hill Foundation Grants, 2157
San Juan Island Community Foundation Grants, 2158
Santa Fe Community Foundation Seasonal Grants-
    Fall Cycle, 2159
Sapelo Foundation Social Justice Grants, 2160
Sarah G. McCarthy Memorial Foundation, 2162
Sarkeys Foundation Grants, 2163
Sartain Lanier Family Foundation Grants, 2164
Scheumann Foundation Grants, 2166
Schlessman Family Foundation Grants, 2167
Schramm Foundation Grants, 2168
Scott B. and Annie P. Appleby Charitable Trust
    Grants, 2169
Scott County Community Foundation Grants, 2170
Seattle Foundation Arts and Culture Grants, 2174
Seattle Foundation Basic Needs Grants, 2175
Seattle Foundation Benjamin N. Phillips Memorial
    Fund Grants, 2176
Seattle Foundation C. Keith Birkenfeld Memorial
    Trust Grants, 2177
Seattle Foundation Education Grants, 2178
Seattle Foundation Health and Wellness Grants, 2179
Sensient Technologies Foundation Grants, 2180
Serco Foundation Grants, 2181
Seward Community Foundation Grants, 2182
Seward Community Foundation Mini-Grants, 2183
Seybert Foundation Grants, 2184
Share Our Strength Grants, 2185
Shell Deer Park Grants, 2186
Shell Oil Company Foundation Community
    Development Grants, 2188
Shield-Ayres Foundation Grants, 2189
Shopko Fdn Community Charitable Grants, 2191
Shopko Foundation Green Bay Area Community
    Grants, 2192
Sidgmore Family Foundation Grants, 2195
Sidney Stern Memorial Trust Grants, 2197
Siebert Lutheran Foundation Grants, 2198
Sierra Health Foundation Responsive Grants, 2199
Simpson Lumber Charitable Contributions, 2201
Singing for Change Foundation Grants, 2202
Sioux Falls Area Community Foundation Community
    Fund Grants, 2203
Sioux Falls Area Community Foundation Spot
    Grants, 2204
Skaggs Family Foundation Grants, 2205
Skaggs Family Foundation Grants, 2206
Skaggs Foundation Grants, 2207
Smith Richardson Fdn Direct Service Grants, 2210
Sobrato Family Foundation Grants, 2211
Sobrato Family Fdn Meeting Space Grants, 2212
Sobrato Family Foundation Office Space Grants, 2213
Social Justice Fund Northwest Economic Justice
    Giving Project Grants, 2215
Sony Corporation of America Grants, 2216
Sorenson Legacy Foundation Grants, 2217
Southern Minnesota Initiative Foundation
    AmeriCorps Leap Grants, 2219
Southern Minnesota Initiative Foundation BookStart
    Grants, 2220
Southern Minnesota Initiative Foundation
    Community Growth Initiative Grants, 2221
Southern Minnesota Initiative Foundation Incentive
    Grants, 2223
Southern New England Folk and Traditional Arts
    Apprenticeship Grants, 2224
Southwest Initiative Foundation Grants, 2226
Special Olympics Eunice Kennedy Shriver (EKS)
    Fellowships, 2227
Special Olympics Project UNIFY Grants, 2228
Speer Trust Grants, 2230
Spencer County Community Foundation Recreation
    Grants, 2231
Spencer County Community Foundation Women's
    Fund Grants, 2232
Spencer County Community Foundation Youth
    Development Grants, 2233
Stan and Sandy Checketts Foundation Grants, 2235

Starke County Community Foundation Grants, 2236
State Farm Good Neighbor Citizenship Company
    Grants, 2238
Stella and Charles Guttman Foundation Grants, 2241
Sterling-Turner Charitable Foundation Grants, 2242
Sterling and Shelli Gardner Foundation Grants, 2243
Steven B. Achelis Foundation Grants, 2244
Stillson Foundation Grants, 2245
Stinson Foundation Grants, 2246
Stocker Foundation Grants, 2247
Storm Castle Foundation Grants, 2248
Strake Foundation Grants, 2249
Stranahan Foundation Grants, 2250
Streisand Foundation Grants, 2251
Subaru of Indiana Automotive Fdn Grants, 2254
Summit Foundation Grants, 2255
Sunoco Foundation Grants, 2256
SunTrust Bank Trusteed Foundations Greene-Sawtell
    Grants, 2257
SunTrust Bank Trusteed Foundations Nell Warren
    Elkin and William Simpson Elkin Grants, 2258
Susan A. and Donald P. Babson Charitable
    Foundation Grants, 2259
Suspened: Community Fdn for Greater Atlanta State
    Farm Education Assist Fund Grants, 2260
Swindells Charitable Foundation Grants, 2261
Sylvia Adams Charitable Trust Grants, 2262
Sylvia Perkin Perpetual Charitable Trust Grants, 2263
T.L.L. Temple Foundation Grants, 2264
TAC Arts Access Grant, 2265
TAC Touring Arts and Arts Access Touring Arts
    Grants, 2269
Target Corporation Community Engagement Fund
    Grants, 2270
Target Corporation Soccer Grants, 2271
Target Foundation Global Grants, 2272
Tata Trust Grant for Certificate Course in Holistic
    inclusion of Learners with Diversities, 2273
Tauck Family Foundation Grants, 2274
Teaching Tolerance Diverse Democracy Grants, 2275
TechKnowledgey Community Impact Grants, 2278
TE Foundation Grants, 2279
Telluride Foundation Community Grants, 2281
Telluride Fdn Emergency Grants, 2282
Telluride Fdn Technical Assistance Grants, 2283
Tension Envelope Foundation Grants, 2284
Textron Corporate Contributions Grants, 2286
Thelma Braun and Bocklett Family Foundation
    Grants, 2287
Thelma Doelger Charitable Trust Grants, 2288
Thomas J. Atkins Memorial Trust Fund Grants, 2290
Thomas J. Long Foundation Community Grants, 2291
Thomas Sill Foundation Grants, 2292
Thomas W. Bradley Foundation Grants, 2293
Thomas W. Briggs Foundation Grants, 2294
Thorman Boyle Foundation Grants, 2295
Threshold Fdn Justice and Democracy Grants, 2298
Threshold Foundation Queer Youth Grants, 2299
Tides Fdn Friends of the IGF Fund Grants, 2300
Tides Foundation Girl Rising Fund Grants, 2301
Tides Foundation Grants, 2302
TJX Foundation Grants, 2303
Toby Wells Foundation Grants, 2304
Todd Brock Family Foundation Grants, 2305
Toyota Motor Manuf of Alabama Grants, 2309
Toyota Motor Manufacturing of Indiana Grants, 2310
Toyota Motor Manuf of Kentucky Grants, 2311
Toyota Motor Manuf of Mississippi Grants, 2312
Toyota Motor Manufacturing of Texas Grants, 2313
Toyota Motor Manufacturing of West Virginia
    Grants, 2314
Toyota Motor North America of NY Grants, 2315
Toyota Motor Sales, USA Grants, 2316
Toyota Technical Center Grants, 2317
Toyota USA Foundation Environmental Grants, 2319
Trinity Trust Summer Youth Mini Grants, 2321
TSYSF Individual Scholarships, 2322
TSYSF Team Grants, 2323
Tull Charitable Foundation Grants, 2324

Turner B. Bunn, Jr. and Catherine E. Bunn Foundation Grants, 2325
Turner Foundation Grants, 2326
Turtle Bay Foundation Grants, 2327
Twenty-First Century Foundation Grants, 2328
U.S. Bank Foundation Grants, 2330
U.S. Cellular Corporation Grants, 2331
U.S. Department of Education Promise Neighborhoods Grants, 2332
Union Bank, N.A. Corporate Sponsorships and Donations, 2333
Union Bank, N.A. Foundation Grants, 2334
Union Pacific Fdn Community & Civic Grants, 2337
Union Pacific Foundation Health and Human Services Grants, 2338
Union Square Arts Award, 2339
Union Square Award for Social Justice, 2340
United Healthcare Commty Grts in Michigan, 2343
United Methodist Committee on Relief Hunger and Poverty Grants, 2344
United Methodist Health Ministry Fund Grts, 2345
United Methodist Women Brighter Future for Children and Youth Grants, 2346
United Technologies Corporation Grants, 2347
UPS Corporate Giving Grants, 2349
UPS Foundation Community Safety Grants, 2350
USAID Community Livelihoods Project in Yemen Grant, 2352
USAID Global Development Alliance Grants, 2354
USAID Innovations in Feed the Future Monitoring and Evaluation Grants, 2355
USAID Integrated Youth Development Activity Grants, 2356
USAID National Governance Project in Yemen Grant, 2357
USAID Nigeria Ed Crisis Response Grants, 2358
USAID Office of Foreign Disaster Assistance and Food for Peace Grants, 2359
USDA Child and Adult Care Food Program, 2362
UUA Actions of Public Witness Grants, 2365
UUA Congregation-Based Community Organizing Grants, 2366
UUA Fund Grants, 2367
UUA International Fund Grants, 2368
UUA Just Society Fund Grants, 2369
UUA Social Responsibility Grants, 2370
V.V. Cooke Foundation Grants, 2371
Valley-Wide Health Systems Nurse Family Partnerships, 2372
Vanderburgh Community Foundation Men's Fund Grants, 2373
Vanderburgh Community Foundation Recreation Grants, 2374
Vanderburgh Community Foundation Youth Development Grants, 2375
Vanderburgh County Community Foundation Women's Fund Grants, 2376
Van Kampen Boyer Molinari Charitable Foundation Grants, 2377
Vermillion County Community Fdn Grants, 2378
Vernon K. Krieble Foundation Grants, 2379
Victor E. Speas Foundation Grants, 2380
Victoria S. and Bradley L. Geist Foundation Enhancement Grants, 2381
Victoria S. and Bradley L. Geist Foundation Grants Supporting Foster Care and Their Caregivers, 2382
Victoria S. and Bradley L. Geist Foundation Grants Supporting Transitioning Foster Youth, 2383
Vigneron Memorial Fund Grants, 2384
Virginia Foundation for the Humanities Folklife Apprenticeships, 2386
Virginia Foundation for the Humanities Open Grants, 2387
Virginia W. Kettering Foundation Grants, 2388
Volkswagen Group of America Corporate Contributions Grants, 2389
Volvo Adventure Environmental Awards, 2390
VSA/Metlife Connect All Grants, 2392
VSA International Art Program for Children with Disabilities Grants, 2394

W.H. and Mary Ellen Cobb Chartbl Trust Grts, 2397
W.M. Keck Fdn Southern California Grants, 2398
W.P. and Bulah Luse Foundation Grants, 2399
W.W. Smith Chartbl Trust Basic Needs Grants, 2400
Walker Area Community Foundation Grants, 2401
Wallace Foundation Grants, 2402
Walmart Fdn Inclusive Communities Grants, 2403
Walmart Fdn National Local Giving Grants, 2404
Walmart Foundation State Giving Grants, 2405
Walter J. and Betty C. Zable Fdn Grants, 2406
Walter S. and Evan C. Jones Testam Trust, 2407
Warrick County Community Foundation Recreation Grants, 2410
Warrick County Community Foundation Women's Fund, 2411
Warrick County Community Foundation Youth Development Grants, 2412
Washington Area Fuel Fund Grants, 2413
Washington Area Women's Foundation African American Women's Giving Circle Grants, 2414
Washington Area Women's Foundation Rainmakers Giving Circle Grants, 2415
Washington County Community Fdn Grants, 2416
Washington Gas Charitable Contributions, 2417
Watson-Brown Foundation Grants, 2418
Wayne County Foundation Grants, 2419
Weaver Foundation Grants, 2420
Weaver Popcorn Foundation Grants, 2421
Wells County Foundation Grants, 2426
Westerman Foundation Grants, 2427
Western Indiana Community Fdn Grants, 2428
Western New York Foundation Grants, 2429
West Virginia Commission on the Arts Challenge America Partnership Grants, 2430
Weyerhaeuser Family Fdn Health Grants, 2435
Whatcom Community Foundation Grants, 2436
White County Community Foundation - Women Giving Together Grants, 2438
Whitehorse Foundation Grants, 2439
Whiting Foundation Grants, 2440
Whitney Foundation Grants, 2441
WHO Foundation Education/Literacy Grants, 2442
WHO Foundation General Grants, 2443
WHO Foundation Volunteer Service Grants, 2444
Whole Foods Foundation, 2445
Whole Kids Foundation School Garden Grants, 2446
Widgeon Point Charitable Foundation Grants, 2447
Wild Rivers Community Foundation Holiday Partnership Grants, 2448
Wild Rivers Community Foundation Summer Youth Mini Grants, 2449
Wilkins Family Foundation Grants, 2450
William A. Badger Foundation Grants, 2451
William A. Cooke Foundation Grants, 2452
William A. Miller Foundation Grants, 2453
William B. Dietrich Foundation Grants, 2458
William B. Stokely Jr. Foundation Grants, 2459
William Blair and Company Foundation Grants, 2461
William E. Barth Foundation Grants, 2463
William E. Dean III Charitable Fdn Grants, 2464
William Foulds Family Foundation Grants, 2465
William G. and Helen C. Hoffman Foundation Grants, 2466
William G. Gilmore Foundation Grants, 2467
William J. and Dorothy K. O'Neill Foundation Responsive Grants, 2468
William J. and Gertrude R. Casper Foundation Grants, 2469
William J. and Tina Rosenberg Fdn Grants, 2470
William J. Brace Charitable Trust, 2471
William M. Weaver Foundation Grants, 2472
William Ray and Ruth E. Collins Fdn Grants, 2473
Williams Comps Homegrown Giving Grants, 2474
Wilton and Effie Hebert Foundation Grants, 2476
Windham Foundation Grants, 2477
Winifred Johnson Clive Foundation Grants, 2478
WinnCompanies Charitable Giving, 2479
Wiregrass Foundation Grants, 2480
Wisconsin Energy Foundation Grants, 2481
Wold Foundation Grants, 2482

Wolfe Associates Grants, 2483
Women's Fund of Hawaii Grants, 2485
Women's Fund of Hawaii Grants, 2484
Wood-Claeyssens Foundation Grants, 2486
Wood Family Charitable Trust Grants, 2487
Woods Fund of Chicago Grants, 2489
World of Children Youth Award, 2493
WSF GoGirlGo! New York Grants, 2494
WSF Rusty Kanokogi Fund for the Advancement of U.S. Judo Grants, 2495
WSF Sports 4 Life Grants, 2496
WSF Sports 4 Life Regional Grants, 2497
WSF Travel and Training Fund Grants, 2498
Wyoming Community Foundation COVID-19 Response and Recovery Grants, 2500
Wyoming Community Fdn General Grants, 2501
Wyoming Community Foundation Hazel Patterson Memorial Grants, 2502
Wyomissing Foundation Community Grants, 2504
Wyomissing Foundation Thun Family Organizational Grants, 2505
Wyomissing Foundation Thun Family Program Grants, 2506
Xerox Foundation Grants, 2507
Yampa Valley Community Foundation Erickson Business Week Scholarships, 2508
Yawkey Foundation Grants, 2510
Youths' Friends Association Grants, 2511
YSA ABC Summer of Service Awards, 2512
YSA Global Youth Service Day Lead Agy Grts, 2514
YSA GYSD Regional Partner Grants, 2515
YSA MLK Day Lead Organizer Grants, 2516
YSA National Child Awareness Month Youth Ambassador Grants, 2517
YSA NEA Youth Leaders for Literacy Grants, 2518
YSA Sodexo Lead Organizer Grants, 2520
YSA State Farm Good Neighbor YOUth In The Driver Seat Grants, 2521
YSA UnitedHealth HEROES Service-Learning Grants, 2522
Z. Smith Reynolds Foundation Small Grants, 2523
Zollner Foundation Grants, 2526
ZYTL Foundation Grants, 2528

Consulting/Visiting Personnel
Abbott Fund Access to Health Care Grants, 45
Abbott Fund Global AIDS Care Grants, 47
ALFJ International Social Change Opportunity Fund Grants, 232
Atkinson Foundation Community Grants, 325
California Arts Cncl Statewide Networks Grants, 493
City of Oakland Cultural Funding Grants, 618
CJ Fdn for SIDS Program Services Grants, 619
Columbus Foundation Traditional Grants, 663
Community Foundation for Greater Buffalo Competitive Grants, 670
Community Foundation of Greater Fort Wayne - Community Endowment and Clarke Endowment Grants, 705
D. W. McMillan Foundation Grants, 776
Ewing Marion Kauffman Foundation Grants, 943
Foundations of East Chicago Education Grants, 995
Fremont Area Community Foundation Amazing X Grants, 1019
Fremont Area Community Foundation Community Grants, 1020
Fund for the City of New York Grants, 1029
GNOF Plaquemines Community Grants, 1091
Goldseker Foundation Non-Profit Management Assistance Grants, 1095
Gulf Coast Foundation of Community Operating Grants, 1134
Gulf Coast Foundation of Community Program Grants, 1135
James and Abigail Campbell Family Foundation Grants, 1337
Jennings County Community Fdn Grants, 1360
Kind World Foundation Grants, 1438
LaGrange Independent Foundation for Endowments (L.I.F.E.), 1459

Leo Niessen Jr., Charitable Trust Grants, 1484
Meyer Fdn Management Assistance Grants, 1651
NHSCA Artist Residence Grants, 1756
NJSCA Artists in Education Residencies, 1763
Noble County Community Foundation Grants, 1765
NYSCA Arts Education: Community-based
   Learning Grants, 1780
NYSCA Arts Ed: Services to the Field Grants, 1784
NYSCA Electronic Media and Film: Workspace
   Grants, 1789
NYSCA Music: Commty Music Schools Grants, 1790
NYSCA Special Arts Services: Instruction and
   Training Grants, 1794
Ohio Arts Council Artist in Residence Grants for
   Sponsors, 1810
OneFamily Foundation Grants, 1822
Ontario Arts Council Artists in Communities and
   Schools Project Grants, 1823
Ordean Foundation Catalyst Grants, 1830
PCA-PCD Organizational Short-Term Professional
   Development and Consulting Grants, 1882
PCA Arts in Education Residencies, 1885
PCA Arts Organizations and Arts Programs Grants
   for Crafts, 1891
PCA Arts Organizations and Arts Programs Grants
   for Visual Arts, 1898
PCA Entry Track Arts Organizations and Arts
   Programs Grants for Crafts, 1903
PCA Entry Track Arts Organizations and Arts
   Programs Grants for Visual Arts, 1912
PCA Management/Techl Assistance Grants, 1913
PCA Pennsylvania Partners in the Arts Project
   Stream Grants, 1915
PennPAT Artist Technical Assistance Grants, 1929
Prudential Foundation Education Grants, 2028
Puerto Rico Community Foundation Grants, 2037
Ruddie Memorial Youth Foundation Grants, 2120
Samuel S. Johnson Foundation Grants, 2146
Shell Oil Company Foundation Community
   Development Grants, 2188
TAC Arts Access Grant, 2265
TAC Arts Education Mini Grants, 2267
Telluride Foundation Community Grants, 2281
Telluride Fdn Technical Assistance Grants, 2283
West Virginia Commission on the Arts Long-Term
   Artist Residencies, 2431
West Virginia Commission on the Arts Short-Term
   Artist Residencies, 2432
WSF GoGirlGo! New York Grants, 2494
WSF Travel and Training Fund Grants, 2498

Cultural Outreach
3M Company Fdn Community Giving Grants, 5
A.C. and Penney Hubbard Foundation Grants, 19
Aaron Foundation Grants, 42
Abbott Fund Community Engagement Grants, 46
Abby's Legendary Pizza Foundation Grants, 49
Abell-Hanger Foundation Grants, 52
Abington Foundation Grants, 54
ABS Foundation Grants, 56
ACCF Dennis and Melanie Bieberich Community
   Enrichment Fund Grants, 59
ACCF John and Kay Boch Fund Grants, 60
ACCF of Indiana Anonymous Community
   Enrichment Fund Grants, 63
ACCF of Indiana Bank of Geneva Heritage Fund
   Grants, 64
ACCF of Indiana Berne Ready Mix Community
   Enrichment Fund Grants, 65
ACCF of Indiana First Merchants Bank / Decatur
   Bank and Trust Fund Grants, 66
ACCF of Indiana Michael Basham Community
   Enrichment Fund Grants, 67
ACCF of Indiana Ron and Susie Ballard Community
   Enrichment Fund Grants, 68
ACCF Ralph Biggs Memorial Community
   Enrichment Fund Grants, 69
ACF Native American Social and Economic
   Development Strategies for Alaska Grants, 87

ACF Native Youth Initiative for Leadership,
   Empowerment, and Development Grants, 88
ACF Tribal Maternal, Infant, and Early Childhood
   Home Visiting Program: Development and
   Implementation Grants, 97
ACF Tribal Maternal, Infant, and Early Childhood
   Home Visiting Program: Implementation and
   Expansion Grants, 98
Achelis and Bodman Foundation Grants, 101
Achelis Foundation Grants, 102
Ackerman Foundation Grants, 103
Acuity Charitable Foundation Grants, 110
Adams-Mastrovich Family Foundation Grants, 113
Adams Family Fdn of Nora Springs Grants, 118
Adelaide Breed Bayrd Foundation Grants, 123
Adolph Coors Foundation Grants, 129
A Friends' Foundation Trust Grants, 136
Air Products Foundation Grants, 148
Akron Community Foundation Arts and Culture
   Grants, 150
Alabama Humanities Foundation Major Grants, 159
ALA Coretta Scott King Book Donation Grant, 168
ALA John Newbery Medal, 172
Alaska State Council on the Arts Cultural
   Collaboration Project Grants, 211
Alaska State Council on the Arts Youth Cultural
   Heritage Fast Track Grants, 212
Albert E. and Birdie W. Einstein Fund Grants, 220
Albertsons Companies Foundation Nourishing
   Neighbors Grants, 221
Alcatel-Lucent Technologies Foundation Grants, 224
Alden and Vada Dow Fund Grants, 225
Alex Stern Family Foundation Grants, 229
ALFJ International Fund Grants, 231
ALFJ International Social Change Opportunity Fund
   Grants, 232
Alliant Energy Foundation Community Giving for
   Good Sponsorship Grants, 240
Alloy Family Foundation Grants, 241
Allstate Corp Hometown Commitment Grants, 243
Allstate Foundation Tolerance, Inclusion, and
   Diversity Grants, 245
Alpha Natural Resources Corporate Giving, 246
Ama OluKai Foundation Grants, 249
Ameren Corporation Community Grants, 251
American Electric Power Foundation Grants, 253
American Indian Youth Running Strong Grants, 256
American Savings Fdn After School Grants, 259
American Savings Foundation Program Grants, 261
Amerigroup Foundation Grants, 264
Amica Insurance Company Community Grants, 267
Anderson Foundation Grants, 271
Anheuser-Busch Foundation Grants, 273
Anna Fitch Ardenghi Trust Grants, 274
Ann L. and Carol Green Rhodes Charitable Trust
   Grants, 278
APAP All-In Grants, 283
Ar-Hale Family Foundation Grants, 290
Arizona Commission on the Arts Learning
   Collaboration Grant, 291
Arizona State Library LSTA Learning Grants, 297
Arkema Foundation Grants, 298
Arthur Ashley Williams Foundation Grants, 302
Arthur M. Blank Family Foundation Molly Blank
   Fund Grants, 310
Arts Council of Greater Lansing Young Creatives
   Grants, 314
Assisi Foundation of Memphis General Grants, 318
Assisi Foundation of Memphis Mini Grants, 319
AT&T Fdn Community Support and Safety, 320
ATA Inclusive Learning Communities Grants, 323
Atlanta Foundation Grants, 326
Atlas Insurance Agency Foundation Grants, 329
Austin Community Foundation Grants, 332
Autauga Area Community Foundation Grants, 334
Avery Dennison Foundation Education Grants, 337
Avery Family Trust Grants, 338
Avery Foundation Grants, 339
Babcock Charitable Trust Grants, 343
Back Home Again Foundation Grants, 344

Baltimore Community Foundation Mitzvah Fund for
   Good Deeds Grants, 349
Bank of America Charitable Foundation Matching
   Gifts, 356
Bank of America Charitable Foundation Volunteer
   Grants, 358
Bank of America Corporation Sponsorships, 359
Bank of Hawaii Foundation Grants, 360
Barrasso, Usdin, Kupperman, Freeman, and Sarver
   Corporate Grants, 362
Baton Rouge Area Foundation Grants, 365
Batts Foundation Grants, 367
Baxter International Corporate Giving Grants, 368
Baxter International Foundation Grants, 369
Bay and Paul Foundations PreK-12 Transformative
   Learning Practices Grants, 370
Bay Area Community Fdn Auburn Area Chamber of
   Commerce Enrichment Fund Grants, 373
Bay Area Community Foundation Semiannual
   Grants, 382
Bayer Fund Community Development Grants, 383
Beckman Coulter Foundation Grants, 394
Ben Cohen StandUp Foundation Grants, 403
Bernard and Audre Rapoport Foundation Arts and
   Culture Grants, 407
Bernau Family Foundation Grants, 413
Bill and Melinda Gates Foundation Agricultural
   Development Grants, 425
Bill and Melinda Gates Foundation Emergency
   Response Grants, 426
Bill and Melinda Gates Foundation Policy and
   Advocacy Grants, 427
Bill Graham Memorial Foundation Grants, 429
Blackford County Community Fdn Grants, 434
Black Hills Corporation Grants, 435
Blanche and Irving Laurie Foundation Grants, 436
Blandin Foundation Itasca County Area Vitality
   Grants, 439
Blockbuster Corporate Contributions, 440
Blue Cross Blue Shield of Minnesota Foundation
   - Healthy Neighborhoods: Connect for Health
   Challenge Grants, 443
Blue Grass Community Foundation Clark County
   Fund Grants, 444
Blue Grass Community Foundation Fayette County
   Fund Grants, 446
Blue Grass Community Foundation Franklin County
   Fund Grants, 447
Blue Grass Community Foundation Harrison County
   Fund Grants, 448
Blue Grass Community Foundation Hudson-Ellis
   Grants, 449
Blue Grass Community Foundation Madison County
   Fund Grants, 450
Blue Grass Community Foundation Magoffin County
   Fund Grants, 451
Blue Grass Community Foundation Morgan County
   Fund Grants, 452
Blue Grass Community Foundation Rowan County
   Fund Grants, 453
Blue Grass Community Foundation Woodford
   County Fund Grants, 454
Blumenthal Foundation Grants, 459
Bodenwein Public Benevolent Foundation Grants, 461
Boeing Company Contributions Grants, 462
Bothin Foundation Grants, 464
Bradley-Turner Foundation Grants, 466
Bradley C. Higgins Foundation Grants, 467
Bridgestone Americas Trust Fund Grants, 469
Brinker Int Corporation Charitable Giving, 471
British Columbia Arts Council Youth Engagement
   Program Grants, 473
Brown Foundation Grants, 476
Burlington Industries Foundation Grants, 481
Caesars Foundation Grants, 492
California Arts Cncl Statewide Networks Grants, 493
California Arts Cncl Technical Assistance Grts, 494
Campbell Soup Foundation Grants, 501
Carl B. and Florence E. King Foundation Grants, 506
Carl M. Freeman Foundation FACES Grants, 507

Carl M. Freeman Foundation Grants, 508
Carnegie Corporation of New York Grants, 511
Carroll County Community Foundation Grants, 513
Castle Foundation Grants, 518
Castle Foundation Grants, 517
Central Pacific Bank Foundation Grants, 530
CFFVR Clintonville Area Foundation Grants, 539
CFFVR Jewelers Mutual Chartbl Giving Grants, 543
CFFVR Project Grants, 546
CFFVR Shawano Area Community Foundation
    Grants, 549
CFF Winter Park Community Grants, 551
CFGR Community Impact Grants, 552
Chapman Family Charitable Trust Grants, 561
Charles H. Hall Foundation, 565
Charles Lafitte Foundation Grants, 567
Charlotte Martin Foundation Youth Grants, 571
Chicago Board of Trade Foundation Grants, 580
Chicago Neighborhood Arts Program Grants, 582
Chilkat Valley Community Foundation Grants, 588
ChLA Article Award, 589
CICF Clare Noyes Grant, 604
CICF Indianapolis Fdn Community Grants, 606
CIGNA Foundation Grants, 611
Circle K Corporation Contributions Grants, 614
Citizens Bank Charitable Foundation Grants, 616
Claremont Community Foundation Grants, 622
Claremont Savings Bank Foundation Grants, 623
Clayton F. and Ruth L. Hawkridge Foundation
    Grants, 630
Cleveland Browns Foundation Grants, 633
CNO Financial Group Community Grants, 650
Collins Foundation Grants, 658
Colonel Stanley R. McNeil Foundation Grants, 659
Community Foundation for Greater Atlanta Spark
    Clayton Grants, 667
Community Foundation for Greater Atlanta Spark
    Newton Grants, 668
Community Foundation for Greater Buffalo Niagara
    Area Foundation Grants, 673
Community Foundation for Greater Buffalo Ralph C.
    Wilson, Jr. Legacy Fund Grants, 674
Community Foundation for Kettering Grants, 676
Community Foundation for San Benito County
    Grants, 677
Community Foundation for SE Michigan Chelsea
    Community Foundation General Grant, 680
Community Foundation for the Capital Region
    Grants, 687
Community Foundation for the National Capital
    Region Community Leadership Grants, 688
Community Foundation of Bartholomew County
    Heritage Fund Grants, 690
Community Foundation of Eastern Connecticut
    General Southeast Grants, 696
Community Foundation of Grant County Grants, 703
Community Foundation of Greater Chattanooga
    Grants, 704
Community Foundation of Greater Fort Wayne -
    Community Endowment and Clarke Endowment
    Grants, 705
Community Foundation of Greater Fort Wayne -
    John S. and James L. Knight Foundation Donor-
    Advised Grants, 707
Community Foundation of Greater Greensboro
    Community Grants, 708
Community Foundation of Henderson County
    Community Grants, 711
Community Fdn of Howard County Grants, 712
Community Fdn of Morgan County Grants, 732
Community Foundation of Muncie and Delaware
    County - Kitselman Grants, 733
Community Foundation of Muncie and Delaware
    County Maxon Grants, 734
Community Fdn of Randolph County Grants, 735
Community Foundation of Western Massachusetts
    Grants, 741
Community Foundation Serving Riverside and San
    Bernardino Counties Impact Grants, 742
Cooke Foundation Grants, 748

Cooper Tire and Rubber Foundation Grants, 749
Covenant Educational Foundation Grants, 754
Crane Foundation General Grants, 761
Crane Fund Grants, 763
Cresap Family Foundation Grants, 766
Crescent Porter Hale Foundation Grants, 767
Crystelle Waggoner Charitable Trust Grants, 768
Cudd Foundation Grants, 769
CUNA Mutual Group Fdn Community Grants, 770
Dana Brown Charitable Trust Grants, 777
Daniel and Nanna Stern Family Fdn Grants, 778
David and Betty Sacks Foundation Grants, 788
Dayton Foundation Grants, 796
Dayton Foundation Huber Heights Grants, 797
Dayton Power and Light Foundation Grants, 802
Dean Foundation Grants, 806
DeKalb County Community Foundation - Literacy
    Grant, 814
Delaware Community Foundation Grants, 817
Del Mar Foundation Community Grants, 820
Dermody Properties Foundation Grants, 827
Dorrance Family Foundation Grants, 845
Dorr Foundation Grants, 846
Draper Richards Kaplan Foundation Grants, 864
DTE Energy Foundation Diversity Grants, 867
Dunspaugh-Dalton Foundation Grants, 873
E. Clayton and Edith P. Gengras, Jr. Foundation
    Grants, 875
E.L. Wiegand Foundation Grants, 877
Earl and Maxine Claussen Trust Grants, 878
Eastern Bank Charitable Foundation Partnerships
    Grants, 881
Eastern Bank Charitable Foundation Targeted
    Grants, 882
Edyth Bush Charitable Foundation Grants, 893
Effie Allen Little Foundation Grants, 894
Elizabeth Carse Foundation Grants, 899
Elizabeth Morse Genius Charitable Trust Grants, 901
Elkhart County Community Foundation Grants, 903
Ella West Freeman Foundation Grants, 904
Elmer Roe Deaver Foundation Grants, 906
El Pomar Foundation Anna Keesling Ackerman Fund
    Grants, 907
El Pomar Foundation Grants, 908
Elsie H. Wilcox Foundation Grants, 909
Ensworth Charitable Foundation Grants, 916
Entergy Charitable Foundation Low-Income
    Initiatives and Solutions Grants, 918
Entergy Corporation Micro Grants, 919
Entergy Corporation Open Grants for Arts and
    Culture, 920
EQT Fdn Community Enrichment Grants, 926
Essex County Community Foundation Dee and King
    Webster Fund for Greater Lawrence Grants, 929
Essex County Community Foundation Merrimack
    Valley Municipal Business Development and
    Recovery Fund Grants, 933
Ethel Sergeant Clark Smith Foundation Grants, 935
Eulalie Bloedel Schneider Foundation Grants, 936
Evan Frankel Foundation Grants, 938
F.M. Kirby Foundation Grants, 946
F.R. Bigelow Foundation Grants, 947
Farmers Insurance Corporate Giving Grants, 948
Faye L. and William L. Cowden Charitable
    Foundation Grants, 950
Fidelity Charitable Gift Fund Grants, 956
Fifth Third Bank Corporate Giving, 958
First Hawaiian Bank Foundation Corporate Giving
    Grants, 967
First Nations Development Institute Native Arts
    Initiative Grants, 972
Foundation Beyond Belief Compassionate Impact
    Grants, 986
Foundation Beyond Belief Humanist Grants, 987
Fdn for the Mid South Communities, 992
Foundations of East Chicago Education Grants, 995
Four County Community Foundation General
    Grants, 1000
Four J Foundation Grants, 1004
Francis Beidler Foundation Grants, 1007

Francis L. Abreu Charitable Trust Grants, 1008
Frank M. Tait Foundation Grants, 1012
Frederick W. Marzahl Memorial Fund Grants, 1018
Fremont Area Community Foundation Amazing X
    Grants, 1019
Fremont Area Community Foundation Community
    Grants, 1020
Fremont Area Community Foundation Youth
    Advisory Committee Grants, 1022
Friends of Hawaii Charities Grants, 1024
From the Top Alumni Leadership Grants, 1025
G.N. Wilcox Trust Grants, 1031
Gannett Foundation Community Action Grants, 1033
Gene Haas Foundation, 1038
General Motors Foundation Grants, 1039
George A. & Grace L. Long Fdn Grants, 1041
George and Ruth Bradford Foundation Grants, 1042
George A Ohl Jr. Foundation Grants, 1043
George Graham and Elizabeth Galloway Smith
    Foundation Grants, 1047
George H.C. Ensworth Memorial Fund Grants, 1049
George I. Alden Trust Grants, 1051
George J. and Effie L. Seay Foundation Grants, 1052
George Kress Foundation Grants, 1053
George W.P. Magee Trust Grants, 1056
Georgia-Pacific Foundation Education Grants, 1058
Gertrude & William C. Wardlaw Grants, 1067
Giant Food Charitable Grants, 1068
Gil and Dody Weaver Foundation Grants, 1071
GNOF Exxon-Mobil Grants, 1080
GNOF IMPACT Grants for Arts and Culture, 1083
GNOF Norco Community Grants, 1089
Golden Heart Community Foundation Grants, 1094
Graham Foundation Grants, 1100
Graham Foundation Grants, 1101
Grand Circle Foundation Associates Grants, 1102
Greater Milwaukee Foundation Grants, 1109
Greater Saint Louis Community Fdn Grants, 1110
Greater Sitka Legacy Fund Grants, 1111
Greater Tacoma Community Foundation Fund for
    Women and Girls Grants, 1112
Greater Tacoma Community Foundation General
    Operating Grants, 1113
Green River Area Community Fdn Grants, 1117
Grundy Foundation Grants, 1124
GTRCF Elk Rapids Area Community Endowment
    Grants, 1127
GTRCF Genuine Leelanau Charitable Endowment
    Grants, 1128
Guy I. Bromley Trust Grants, 1136
H.A. and Mary K. Chapman Charitable Trust
    Grants, 1137
H.B. Fuller Foundation Grants, 1138
HAF Community Grants, 1141
HAF Joe Alexandre Mem Family Fund Grants, 1145
HAF Laurence and Elaine Allen Memorial Fund
    Grants, 1146
HAF Native Cultures Fund Grants, 1148
HAF Southern Humboldt Grants, 1150
Hahl Proctor Charitable Trust Grants, 1151
Hampton Roads Community Foundation Arts and
    Culture Grants, 1154
Hampton Roads Community Foundation Nonprofit
    Facilities Improvement Grants, 1159
Hardin County Community Foundation Grants, 1167
Harmony Grove Foundation Grants, 1169
Harold K.L. Castle Foundation Strengthening
    Windward Oahu Communities Grants, 1174
Harris Foundation Grants, 1177
Harrison County Community Fdn Grants, 1178
Harrison County Community Foundation Signature
    Grants, 1179
Harry Frank Guggenheim Foundation Research
    Grants, 1184
Hartford Foundation Regular Grants, 1185
Hattie Mae Lesley Foundation Grants, 1195
Hawai'i Community Foundation East Hawaii Fund
    Grants, 1199
Hawai'i Community Foundation Family Literacy and
    Hawaii Pizza Hut Literacy Grants, 1201

Hawai'i Community Foundation Lana'i Community Benefit Fund, 1203
Hawai'i Community Foundation Robert E. Black Fund Grants, 1205
Hawai'i SFCA Art Bento Program @ HiSAM Grants, 1210
Hawaiian Electric Industries Charitable Foundation Grants, 1211
Hawaii Community Foundation Reverend Takie Okumura Family Grants, 1216
Hawaii Electric Industries Charitable Foundation Grants, 1218
Hawaii State Legislature Grant-In-Aid, 1219
Hazel and Walter T. Bales Foundation Grants, 1220
Hearst Foundations Culture Grants, 1223
HEI Charitable Foundation Grants, 1226
Helen Bader Foundation Grants, 1227
Helen E. Ellis Charitable Trust Grants, 1228
Helen Gertrude Sparks Charitable Trust Grants, 1230
Helen Irwin Littauer Educational Trust Grants, 1231
Helen V. Brach Foundation Grants, 1232
Henrietta Lange Burk Fund Grants, 1235
Henry E. Niles Foundation Grants, 1240
Herbert A. and Adrian W. Woods Foundation Grants, 1243
Herman Goldman Foundation Grants, 1245
Highmark Corporate Giving Grants, 1248
Hill Crest Foundation Grants, 1249
Hillsdale County Community Foundation General Grants, 1250
Hillsdale County Community Foundation Love Your Community Grants, 1251
HLTA Visitor Industry Charity Walk Grant, 1254
Honor the Earth Grants, 1259
Horace A. Kimball and S. Ella Kimball Foundation Grants, 1260
Horace A. Moses Charitable Trust Grants, 1261
HSBC Corporate Giving Grants, 1266
HSFCA Biennium Grants, 1267
HSFCA Folk and Traditional Arts Grants - Culture Learning, 1268
Huffy Foundation Grants, 1273
Humana Foundation Grants, 1275
Iddings Foundation Major Project Grants, 1284
Iddings Foundation Medium Project Grants, 1285
Iddings Foundation Small Project Grants, 1286
Ike and Roz Friedman Foundation Grants, 1289
IMLS Grants to State Library Administrative Agencies, 1298
IMLS National Leadership Grants for Libraries, 1299
ING Foundation Grants, 1302
Inland Empire Community Foundation Capacity Building for IE Nonprofits Grants, 1306
Inland Empire Community Foundation Coachella Valley Youth Grants, 1307
Inland Empire Community Foundation Native Youth Grants, 1308
Inland Empire Community Foundation Riverside Youth Grants, 1309
Inland Empire Community Foundation San Bernardino Youth Grants, 1310
IRC Community Collaboratives for Refugee Women and Youth Grants, 1313
Irving S. Gilmore Foundation Grants, 1314
J. Bulow Campbell Foundation Grants, 1319
J. Edwin Treakle Foundation Grants, 1320
J.W. Gardner II Foundation Grants, 1323
J. Walton Bissell Foundation Grants, 1325
J. Watumull Fund Grants, 1326
Jacob G. Schmidlapp Trusts Grants, 1336
James and Abigail Campbell Family Foundation Grants, 1337
James F. and Marion L. Miller Fdn Grants, 1338
James Ford Bell Foundation Grants, 1339
James Graham Brown Foundation Grants, 1340
James Lee Sorenson Family Impact Foundation Grants, 1342
James LeVoy Sorenson Foundation Grants, 1343
James M. Collins Foundation Grants, 1344
James S. Copley Foundation Grants, 1345

Jane's Trust Grants, 1346
Japan Foundation Los Angeles Mini-Grants for Japanese Arts & Culture, 1354
Japan Foundation New York Small Grants for Arts and Culture, 1355
Japan Foundation New York World Heritage Photo Panel Exhibition, 1356
Jayne and Leonard Abess Foundation Grants, 1358
Jennings County Community Foundation Women's Giving Circle Grant, 1361
Jessica Stevens Community Foundation Grants, 1363
Jim Moran Foundation Grants, 1366
John G. Duncan Charitable Trust Grants, 1372
Joseph Henry Edmondson Foundation Grants, 1388
JP Morgan Chase Fdn Arts and Culture Grants, 1394
Julia and Tunnicliff Fox Charitable Trust Grants, 1397
Julia Richardson Brown Foundation Grants, 1398
Julia Temple Davis Brown Foundation Grants, 1399
Julius N. Frankel Foundation Grants, 1400
Kalamazoo Community Foundation Good Neighbor Grants, 1408
Kalamazoo Community Foundation John E. Fetzer Institute Fund Grants, 1410
Katharine Matthies Foundation Grants, 1418
Katrine Menzing Deakins Chartbl Trust Grants, 1422
Kawabe Memorial Fund Grants, 1423
Kelvin and Eleanor Smith Foundation Grants, 1424
Kenai Peninsula Foundation Grants, 1425
Kenneth T. and Eileen L. Norris Fdn Grants, 1427
Kentucky Arts Cncl Access Assistance Grants, 1428
Ketchikan Community Foundation Grants, 1429
Kettering Family Foundation Grants, 1430
Kimball Foundation Grants, 1432
Kindle Project SpiderWeave Flow Fund Grants, 1437
Kind World Foundation Grants, 1438
Kirby Laing Foundation Grants, 1443
Koch Family Foundation (Annapolis) Grants, 1444
Kodak Community Relations Grants, 1445
Kodiak Community Foundation Grants, 1446
Koret Foundation Grants, 1449
Kosasa Foundation Grants, 1450
Kovler Family Foundation Grants, 1455
Kovler Family Foundation Grants, 1454
Laclede Gas Charitable Trust Grants, 1457
Laidlaw Foundation Multi-Year Grants, 1460
Laidlaw Foundation Youth Organizaing Initiatives Grants, 1462
Land O'Lakes Fdn California Region Grants, 1465
Land O'Lakes Foundation Mid-Atlantic Grants, 1467
Laura Musser Intercultural Harmony Grants, 1472
Laurel Foundation Grants, 1475
Lee and Ramona Bass Foundation Grants, 1478
Legler Benbough Foundation Grants, 1479
Leo Goodwin Foundation Grants, 1482
Leola Osborn Trust Grants, 1483
Leo Niessen Jr., Charitable Trust Grants, 1484
Lewis H. Humphreys Charitable Trust Grants, 1486
Liberty Bank Foundation Grants, 1488
Libra Foundation Grants, 1489
Lied Foundation Trust Grants, 1490
Lisa and Douglas Goldman Fund Grants, 1496
Lotus 88 Foundation for Women and Children Grants, 1508
Louie M. and Betty M. Phillips Fdn Grants, 1509
Louis and Sandra Berkman Foundation Grants, 1510
Louis Calder Foundation Grants, 1511
Lubrizol Corporation Community Grants, 1512
Lubrizol Foundation Grants, 1513
Lucy Downing Nisbet Charitable Fund Grants, 1515
Ludwick Family Foundation Grants, 1516
M. Bastian Family Foundation Grants, 1522
M.J. Murdock Charitable Trust General Grants, 1524
Mabel Louise Riley Foundation Family Strengthening Small Grants, 1528
Mabel Louise Riley Foundation Grants, 1529
Mabel Y. Hughes Charitable Trust Grants, 1530
Macquarie Bank Foundation Grants, 1532
Madison Community Foundation Fund for Children Grants, 1534

Madison County Community Foundation General Grants, 1537
Maine Community Fdn Peaks Island Grants, 1542
Maine Community Foundation Vincent B. and Barbara G. Welch Grants, 1545
Manuel D. and Rhoda Mayerson Fdn Grants, 1550
Marcia and Otto Koehler Foundation Grants, 1553
Margaret and James A. Elkins Jr. Fdn Grants, 1555
Margaret T. Morris Foundation Grants, 1557
Marin Community Foundation Arts Education Grants, 1562
Marin Community Foundation Arts in the Community Grants, 1563
Marin Community Foundation Social Justice and Interfaith Understanding Grants, 1567
Marion I. and Henry J. Knott Foundation Discretionary Grants, 1571
Marion I. and Henry J. Knott Foundation Standard Grants, 1572
Marquette Bank Neighborhood Commit Grants, 1577
Marsh Corporate Grants, 1580
Mary D. and Walter F. Frear Eleemosynary Trust Grants, 1588
Mary K. Chapman Foundation Grants, 1590
Maryland State Arts Council Arts in Communities Grants, 1592
Mary Owen Borden Foundation Grants, 1597
Massachusetts Cultural Council Local Cultural Council (LCC) Grants, 1601
MassMutual Foundation Edonomic Development Grants, 1603
Matilda R. Wilson Fund Grants, 1605
Matson Community Giving Grants, 1607
Maurice Amado Foundation Grants, 1609
Maurice J. Masserini Charitable Trust Grants, 1610
Maurice R. Robinson Fund Grants, 1611
McCune Charitable Foundation Grants, 1617
McCune Foundation Humananities Grants, 1619
McGraw-Hill Companies Community Grants, 1620
McInerny Foundation Grants, 1622
McLean Contributionship Grants, 1623
Meadows Foundation Grants, 1626
MeadWestvaco Foundation Sustainable Communities Grants, 1627
Mead Witter Foundation Grants, 1628
Medtronic Foundation Community Link Arts, Civic, and Culture Grants, 1629
Medtronic Foundation CommunityLink Health Grants, 1630
Memorial Foundation for Children Grants, 1633
Mercedes-Benz USA Corporate Contributions Grants, 1634
Mericos Foundation Grants, 1637
Meriden Foundation Grants, 1638
Merrick Foundation Grants, 1639
Mertz Gilmore Foundation NYC Dance Grants, 1642
Meyer Memorial Trust Responsive Grants, 1653
MGN Family Foundation Grants, 1656
Microsoft Software Donations, 1665
Mimi and Peter Haas Fund Grants, 1677
Mockingbird Foundation Grants, 1680
Monsanto Access to the Arts Grants, 1681
Montana Arts Council Cultural and Aesthetic Project Grants, 1685
Montana Community Foundation Grants, 1687
Morris Stulsaft Foundation Participation in the the Arts Grants, 1698
Mr. Holland's Opus Foundation Melody Grants, 1703
Narragansett Number One Foundation Grants, 1712
Nathalie and Gladys Dalkowitz Charitable Trust Grants, 1716
Nathan Cummings Foundation Grants, 1718
Nathaniel and Elizabeth P. Stevens Foundation Grants, 1719
Nell J. Redfield Foundation Grants, 1737
New Earth Foundation Grants, 1743
Newfoundland and Labrador Arts Council ArtSmarts Grants, 1744
Newfoundland and Labrador Arts Council School Touring Grants, 1745

Newfoundland and Labrador Arts Council Visiting Artists Grants, 1746
New Hampshire Charitable Foundation Community Unrestricted Grants, 1747
New York Foundation Grants, 1753
NFL Charities NFL Player Foundation Grants, 1754
NHSCA Conservation License Plate Grants, 1757
NHSCA Youth Arts Project Grants: For Extended Arts Learning, 1758
Nissan Neighbors Grants, 1762
NJSCA Arts Ed Special Initiative Grants, 1764
Noble County Community Foundation Grants, 1765
Norcliffe Foundation Grants, 1766
Norman Foundation Grants, 1767
North Dakota Community Foundation Grants, 1768
Northern Chautauqua Community Foundation Community Grants, 1769
NYSCA Arts Education: General Operating Support Grants, 1781
NYSCA Arts Education: General Program Support Grants, 1782
NYSCA Arts Education: Local Capacity Building Grants (Regrants), 1783
NYSCA Electronic Media and Film: Film Festivals Grants, 1785
NYSCA Electronic Media and Film: General Operating Support, 1786
NYSCA Electronic Media and Film: General Program Support, 1787
NYSCA Electronic Media and Film: Screenings Grants, 1788
NYSCA Electronic Media and Film: Workspace Grants, 1789
NYSCA Music: Commty Music Schools Grants, 1790
NYSCA Music: Gen Operating Support Grants, 1791
NYSCA Music: Gen Program Support Grants, 1792
NYSCA Special Arts Services: General Program Support Grants, 1793
NYSCA Special Arts Services: Instruction and Training Grants, 1794
NYSCA Theatre: Prof Performances Grants, 1795
OceanFirst Foundation Major Grants, 1803
OHA 'Ahahui Grants, 1807
OHA Community Grants for Culture, 1808
Olive B. Cole Foundation Grants, 1816
Olive Higgins Prouty Foundation Grants, 1817
Olive Smith Browning Charitable Trust Grants, 1818
Olivia R. Gardner Foundation Grants, 1819
Ontario Arts Council Artists in Communities and Schools Project Grants, 1823
Ontario Arts Council Arts Organizations in Communities and Schools Operating Grants, 1824
Ontario Arts Council Indigenous Culture Fund Indigenous Artists in Communities and Schools Project Grants, 1825
Oppenstein Brothers Foundation Grants, 1827
Orange County Community Foundation Grants, 1829
Orange County Community Foundation Grants, 1828
Ordean Foundation Catalyst Grants, 1830
Ordean Foundation Partnership Grants, 1831
Oregon Community Fdn Community Grants, 1833
Oren Campbell McCleary Chartbl Trust Grants, 1837
Packard Foundation Local Grants, 1863
Palmer Foundation Grants, 1867
Parker Foundation (California) Grants, 1869
Parkersburg Area Community Foundation Action Grants, 1871
PAS Zildjian Family Opportunity Fund Grants, 1878
Patricia Kisker Foundation Grants, 1879
Paul and Edith Babson Foundation Grants, 1881
PCA-PCD Organizational Short-Term Professional Development and Consulting Grants, 1882
PCA Art Organizations and Art Programs Grants for Presenting Organizations, 1884
PCA Arts in Education Residencies, 1885
PCA Arts Management Internship, 1886
PCA Arts Organizations and Arts Program Grants for Music, 1887
PCA Arts Organizations and Arts Programs Grants for Arts Education Organizations, 1889

PCA Arts Organizations and Arts Programs Grants for Crafts, 1891
PCA Arts Organizations and Arts Programs Grants for Literature, 1894
PCA Arts Organizations and Arts Programs Grants for Local Arts, 1895
PCA Arts Organizations and Arts Programs Grants for Theatre, 1896
PCA Arts Organizations and Arts Programs Grants for Traditional and Folk Arts, 1897
PCA Arts Organizations and Arts Programs Grants for Visual Arts, 1898
PCA Busing Grants, 1899
PCA Entry Track Arts Organizations and Arts Programs Grants for Art Museums, 1900
PCA Entry Track Arts Organizations and Arts Programs Grants for Arts Education Organizations, 1901
PCA Entry Track Arts Organizations and Arts Programs Grants for Crafts, 1903
PCA Entry Track Arts Organizations and Arts Programs Grants for Literature, 1906
PCA Entry Track Arts Organizations and Arts Programs Grants for Local Arts, 1907
PCA Entry Track Arts Organizations and Arts Programs Grants for Music, 1908
PCA Entry Track Arts Organizations and Arts Programs Grants for Presenting Orgs, 1909
PCA Entry Track Arts Organizations and Arts Programs Grants for Theatre, 1910
PCA Entry Track Arts Orgs and Arts Programs Grants for Traditional and Folk Arts, 1911
PCA Entry Track Arts Organizations and Arts Programs Grants for Visual Arts, 1912
PCA Management/Techl Assistance Grants, 1913
PCA Pennsylvania Partners in the Arts Program Stream Grants, 1914
PCA Pennsylvania Partners in the Arts Project Stream Grants, 1915
PCA Strategies for Success Grants - Adv Level, 1917
PCA Strategies for Success Grants - Basic Level, 1918
PCA Strategies for Success Grants - Intermediate Level, 1919
PDF Community Organizing Grants, 1920
PennPAT Artist Technical Assistance Grants, 1929
PennPAT Fee-Support Grants for Presenters, 1930
PennPAT New Directions Grants for Presenters, 1931
PennPAT Presenter Travel Grants, 1932
PennPAT Strategic Opportunity Grants, 1933
Percy B. Ferebee Endowment Grants, 1936
Perkin Fund Grants, 1937
Perkins Charitable Foundation Grants, 1939
Petersburg Community Foundation Grants, 1951
Pettus Foundation Grants, 1952
Peyton Anderson Foundation Grants, 1954
PGE Foundation Grants, 1958
Philanthrofund Foundation Grants, 1959
Phil Hardin Foundation Grants, 1960
Phoenix Coyotes Charities Grants, 1963
Phoenix Suns Charities Grants, 1964
Piedmont Natural Gas Corporate and Charitable Contributions, 1966
Pinnacle Entertainment Foundation Grants, 1972
Piper Trust Arts and Culture Grants, 1975
Piper Trust Reglious Organizations Grants, 1979
PMI Foundation Grants, 1982
PNC Foundation Affordable Housing Grants, 1983
PNM Reduce Your Use Grants, 1988
Pohlad Family Fdn Small Capital Grants, 1991
Pokagon Fund Grants, 1994
Polk County Community Foundation Free Community Events Grants, 1996
Polk County Community Foundation Marjorie M. and Lawrence R. Bradley Endowment Fund Grants, 1998
Polk County Community Foundation Mary F. Kessler Fund Grants, 1999
Polk County Community Foundation Unrestricted Grants, 2001
Portland General Electric Foundation Grants, 2007

Posey Community Foundation Women's Fund Grants, 2008
Powell Foundation Grants, 2013
PPCF Community Grants, 2014
PPCF Esther M. and Freeman E. Everett Charitable Foundation Grants, 2016
PPG Industries Foundation Grants, 2017
Price Chopper's Golub Foundation Grants, 2020
Priddy Foundation Program Grants, 2023
Pride Foundation Grants, 2024
Puerto Rico Community Foundation Grants, 2037
Pulido Walker Foundation, 2039
Putnam County Community Fdn Grants, 2040
Qualcomm Grants, 2042
R.C. Baker Foundation Grants, 2043
Radcliffe Institute Oral History Grants, 2049
Ralph M. Parsons Foundation Grants, 2052
Rasmuson Foundation Tier One Grants, 2055
Rasmuson Foundation Tier Two Grants, 2056
Rathmann Family Foundation Grants, 2057
Raymond Austin Hagen Family Fdn Grants, 2060
RCF General Community Grants, 2062
Reinberger Foundation Grants, 2066
Ressler-Gertz Foundation Grants, 2067
Richard and Caroline T. Gwathmey Memorial Trust Grants, 2069
Richard J. Stern Foundation for the Arts Grants, 2071
Richland County Bank Grants, 2074
Riedman Foundation Grants, 2076
Ripley County Community Foundation Grants, 2077
Ripley County Community Foundation Small Project Grants, 2078
RISCA Project Grants for Individuals, 2079
Robbins Charitable Foundation Grants, 2081
Robert and Betty Wo Foundation Grants, 2083
Robert and Helen Haddad Foundation Grants, 2084
Robert F. Lange Foundation Grants, 2090
Robert Lee Blaffer Foundation Grants, 2092
Robert R. Meyer Foundation Grants, 2094
Roger L. and Agnes C. Dell Charitable Trust II Grants, 2100
Rose Hills Foundation Grants, 2106
Rosenberg Fund for Children Edith and George Ziefert Fund Grants, 2110
Rosenberg Fund for Children Grants, 2111
Rosenberg Fund for Children Moish and Lillian Antopol Memorial Fund Grants, 2113
Ruth and Vernon Taylor Foundation Grants, 2124
Ruth Camp Campbell Charitable Trust Grants, 2125
S. Spencer Scott Fund Grants, 2129
Saginaw Community Foundation Discretionary Grants, 2134
Saginaw Community Foundation YWCA Fund for Women and Girls Grants, 2135
Saigh Foundation Grants, 2137
Samuel N. and Mary Castle Foundation Grants, 2145
Samuel S. Johnson Foundation Grants, 2146
San Antonio Area Foundation Annual Responsive Grants, 2147
San Juan Island Community Foundation Grants, 2158
Santa Fe Community Foundation Seasonal Grants-Fall Cycle, 2159
Sarkeys Foundation Grants, 2163
Sartain Lanier Family Foundation Grants, 2164
Schlessman Family Foundation Grants, 2167
Schramm Foundation Grants, 2168
Scott B. and Annie P. Appleby Charitable Trust Grants, 2169
Scott County Community Foundation Grants, 2170
Seattle Foundation Arts and Culture Grants, 2174
Sensient Technologies Foundation Grants, 2180
Serco Foundation Grants, 2181
Seward Community Foundation Grants, 2182
Seward Community Foundation Mini-Grants, 2183
Shell Deer Park Grants, 2186
Shield-Ayres Foundation Grants, 2189
Shopko Fdn Community Charitable Grants, 2191
Shopko Foundation Green Bay Area Community Grants, 2192
Siebert Lutheran Foundation Grants, 2198

Sioux Falls Area Community Foundation Community Fund Grants, 2203
Sioux Falls Area Community Foundation Spot Grants, 2204
Skaggs Foundation Grants, 2207
Social Justice Fund Northwest Economic Justice Giving Project Grants, 2215
Sony Corporation of America Grants, 2216
Sorenson Legacy Foundation Grants, 2217
Spencer County Community Foundation Women's Fund Grants, 2232
Stella and Charles Guttman Foundation Grants, 2241
Sterling-Turner Charitable Foundation Grants, 2242
Sterling and Shelli Gardner Foundation Grants, 2243
Stinson Foundation Grants, 2246
Storm Castle Foundation Grants, 2248
Strake Foundation Grants, 2249
Stranahan Foundation Grants, 2250
Subaru of Indiana Automotive Fdn Grants, 2254
Summit Foundation Grants, 2255
SunTrust Bank Trusteed Foundations Greene-Sawtell Grants, 2257
SunTrust Bank Trusteed Foundations Nell Warren Elkin and William Simpson Elkin Grants, 2258
Sylvia Perkin Perpetual Charitable Trust Grants, 2263
T.L.L. Temple Foundation Grants, 2264
TAC Arts Access Grant, 2265
TAC Arts Education Mini Grants, 2267
TAC Touring Arts and Arts Access Touring Arts Grants, 2269
Target Corporation Community Engagement Fund Grants, 2270
Tauck Family Foundation Grants, 2274
Teaching Tolerance Social Justice Educator Grts, 2276
TE Foundation Grants, 2279
Telluride Fdn Emergency Grants, 2282
Tension Envelope Foundation Grants, 2284
Terra Fdn Chicago K–12 Education Grants, 2285
Textron Corporate Contributions Grants, 2286
Thelma Braun and Bocklett Family Foundation Grants, 2287
Thomas J. Long Foundation Community Grants, 2291
Thomas Sill Foundation Grants, 2292
Thomas W. Briggs Foundation Grants, 2294
Threshold Foundation Queer Youth Grants, 2299
Tides Foundation Grants, 2302
Toyota Motor Manuf of Mississippi Grants, 2312
Toyota Motor Manufacturing of Texas Grants, 2313
Toyota Motor Manufacturing of West Virginia Grants, 2314
Toyota Motor Sales, USA Grants, 2316
Tull Charitable Foundation Grants, 2324
U.S. Bank Foundation Grants, 2330
U.S. Cellular Corporation Grants, 2331
Union Bank, N.A. Corporate Sponsorships and Donations, 2333
Union Bank, N.A. Foundation Grants, 2334
Union Pacific Fdn Community & Civic Grants, 2337
Union Square Arts Award, 2339
United Technologies Corporation Grants, 2347
UPS Corporate Giving Grants, 2349
UUA Actions of Public Witness Grants, 2365
UUA Congregation-Based Community Organizing Grants, 2366
UUA Fund Grants, 2367
UUA International Fund Grants, 2368
UUA Just Society Fund Grants, 2369
UUA Social Responsibility Grants, 2370
Vanderburgh Community Foundation Men's Fund Grants, 2373
Vanderburgh County Community Foundation Women's Fund Grants, 2376
Vigneron Memorial Fund Grants, 2384
Virginia Commission for the Arts Artists in Education Residency Grants, 2385
Virginia Foundation for the Humanities Folklife Apprenticeships, 2386
Virginia Foundation for the Humanities Open Grants, 2387
Virginia W. Kettering Foundation Grants, 2388

Volkswagen Group of America Corporate Contributions Grants, 2389
VSA/Volkswagen Group of America Exhibition Awards, 2393
VSA International Art Program for Children with Disabilities Grants, 2394
W.M. Keck Fdn Southern California Grants, 2398
Walker Area Community Foundation Grants, 2401
Wallace Foundation Grants, 2402
Warrick County Community Foundation Women's Fund, 2411
Washington County Community Fdn Grants, 2416
Wayne County Foundation Grants, 2419
Western Indiana Community Fdn Grants, 2428
Western New York Foundation Grants, 2429
West Virginia Commission on the Arts Challenge America Partnership Grants, 2430
West Virginia Commission on the Arts Special Projects Grants, 2433
Whatcom Community Foundation Grants, 2436
White County Community Foundation - Women Giving Together Grants, 2438
Whiting Foundation Grants, 2440
Whitney Foundation Grants, 2441
Widgeon Point Charitable Foundation Grants, 2447
Wilkins Family Foundation Grants, 2450
William B. Dietrich Foundation Grants, 2458
William B. Stokely Jr. Foundation Grants, 2459
William Bingham Foundation Grants, 2460
William Blair and Company Foundation Grants, 2461
William E. Barth Foundation Grants, 2463
William Foulds Family Foundation Grants, 2465
William G. Gilmore Foundation Grants, 2467
William J. and Dorothy K. O'Neill Foundation Responsive Grants, 2468
William J. and Gertrude R. Casper Foundation Grants, 2469
William J. and Tina Rosenberg Fdn Grants, 2470
William Ray and Ruth E. Collins Fdn Grants, 2473
Williams Comps Homegrown Giving Grants, 2474
Windham Foundation Grants, 2477
WinnCompanies Charitable Giving, 2479
Wisconsin Energy Foundation Grants, 2481
Wolfe Associates Grants, 2483
Women's Fund of Hawaii Grants, 2484
Wood-Claeyssens Foundation Grants, 2486
Woods Fund of Chicago Grants, 2489
Wyomissing Foundation Community Grants, 2504
Wyomissing Foundation Thun Family Organizational Grants, 2505
Wyomissing Foundation Thun Family Program Grants, 2506
Xerox Foundation Grants, 2507
Youths' Friends Association Grants, 2511
Z. Smith Reynolds Foundation Small Grants, 2523

Curriculum Development/Teacher Training

3M Company Fdn Community Giving Grants, 5
100% for Kids - Utah Credit Union Education Foundation Major Project Grants, 11
100% for Kids - Utah Credit Union Education Foundation Mini Grants, 12
100% for Kids - Utah Credit Union Education Foundation School Grants, 13
A.C. and Penney Hubbard Foundation Grants, 19
Abbott Fund Science Education Grants, 48
Abell Foundation Education Grants, 53
Abington Foundation Grants, 54
ACCF John and Kay Boch Fund Grants, 60
ACCF of Indiana First Merchants Bank / Decatur Bank and Trust Fund Grants, 66
Adams Legacy Foundation Grants, 121
Adobe Foundation Action Grants, 126
Advance Auto Parts Corporate Giving Grants, 131
A Fund for Women Grants, 137
Ahearn Family Foundation Grants, 142
ALA Innovative Reading Grant, 171
Albertsons Companies Foundation Nourishing Neighbors Grants, 221
Alden and Vada Dow Fund Grants, 225

Aldi Corporation Smart Kids Grants, 226
Alliant Energy Foundation Community Giving for Good Sponsorship Grants, 240
Alpha Natural Resources Corporate Giving, 246
American Electric Power Corporate Grants, 252
American Electric Power Foundation Grants, 253
American Psychiatric Foundation Typical or Troubled School Mental Health Education Grants, 258
American Woodmark Foundation Grants, 263
Amerigroup Foundation Grants, 264
Anchorage Schools Foundation Grants, 270
Anderson Foundation Grants, 271
Ann Ludington Sullivan Foundation Grants, 279
Ar-Hale Family Foundation Grants, 290
Arizona Commission on the Arts Learning Collaboration Grant, 291
Arizona Commission on the Arts Youth Arts Engagement Grant, 292
Arkema Foundation Grants, 298
Arkema Foundation Science Teachers Grants, 299
Arthur M. Blank Family Foundation Pipeline Project Grants, 313
AT&T Foundation Education Grants, 321
Autauga Area Community Foundation Grants, 334
Avista Foundation Education Grants, 340
Babcock Charitable Trust Grants, 343
Baltimore Community Foundation Mitzvah Fund for Good Deeds Grants, 349
Bank of Hawaii Foundation Grants, 360
Baton Rouge Area Foundation Community Coffee Fund Grants, 363
Baxter International Corporate Giving Grants, 368
Bayer Fund STEM Education Grants, 384
Beckman Coulter Foundation Grants, 394
Benton Community Foundation Grants, 405
Bernard and Audre Rapoport Foundation Education Grants, 410
Best Buy Children's Fdn @15 Teach Awards, 416
Blue River Community Foundation Grants, 458
Boeing Company Contributions Grants, 462
BP Foundation Grants, 465
Bristol-Myers Squibb Foundation Independent Medical Education Grants, 472
Brown County Community Foundation Grants, 475
Brown Rudnick Charitable Foundation Community Grants, 477
Cabot Corporation Foundation Grants, 490
California Arts Cncl Statewide Networks Grants, 493
Calvin Johnson Jr. Foundation Mini Grants, 498
Camille Beckman Foundation Grants, 499
Carl M. Freeman Foundation Grants, 508
Carnegie Corporation of New York Grants, 511
Central Pacific Bank Foundation Grants, 530
CFFVR Clintonville Area Foundation Grants, 539
Chapman Charitable Foundation Grants, 560
Chapman Family Foundation, 562
Chesapeake Bay Trust Environmental Education Grants, 577
Chilkat Valley Community Foundation Grants, 588
Christensen Fund Regional Grants, 600
CHT Foundation Education Grants, 603
Circle K Corporation Contributions Grants, 614
Claremont Savings Bank Foundation Grants, 623
Clark County Community Foundation Grants, 626
Clinton County Community Foundation Grants, 638
Coleman Foundation Entrepreneurship Education Grants, 651
Community Foundation for Kettering Grants, 676
Community Foundation for the Capital Region Grants, 687
Community Foundation of Bartholomew County Heritage Fund Grants, 690
Community Foundation of Boone County Grants, 694
Community Foundation of Crawford County, 695
Community Foundation of Eastern Connecticut Ossen Fund for the Arts Grants, 700
Community Foundation of Louisville Boyette and Edna Edwards Fund Grants, 718
Community Foundation of Louisville Education Grants, 724

Community Foundation of Louisville Madi and Jim Tate Fund Grants, 727
Community Foundation of Louisville Winston N. and Nancy H. Bloch Educational Fund Grants, 729
Community Fdn of Morgan County Grants, 732
Community Fdn of Wabash County Grants, 740
CONSOL Energy Academic Grants, 746
Corina Higginson Trust Grants, 750
Cudd Foundation Grants, 769
David and Barbara B. Hirschhorn Foundation Education and Literacy Grants, 786
Dayton Foundation VISIONS Endowment Fund Grants, 800
Dayton Power and Light Foundation Grants, 802
Dean Foods Community Involvement Grants, 805
Dean Witter Foundation Education Grants, 807
Delaware Valley Fairness Project Teacher Assistance Grants, 818
Del Mar Foundation Community Grants, 820
Delmarva Power & Light Mini-Grants, 822
Dollar General Family Literacy Grants, 835
Dollar General Youth Literacy Grants, 837
Don and May Wilkins Charitable Trust Grants, 842
Dorr Foundation Grants, 846
Dubois County Community Foundation Grants, 871
Earl and Maxine Claussen Trust Grants, 878
Eastern Bank Charitable Foundation Targeted Grants, 882
Easton Sports Development Foundation National Archery in the Schools Grants, 884
Edward W. and Stella C. Van Houten Memorial Fund Grants, 892
Effie Allen Little Foundation Grants, 894
Effie and Wofford Cain Foundation Grants, 895
Elizabeth Carse Foundation Grants, 899
Elizabeth Huth Coates Charitable Foundation Grants, 900
Ella West Freeman Foundation Grants, 904
Ellen Abbott Gilman Trust Grants, 905
Entergy Charitable Foundation Education and Literacy Grants, 917
Evelyn and Walter Haas, Jr. Fund Education Opportunities Grants, 939
Faye L. and William L. Cowden Charitable Foundation Grants, 950
FirstEnergy Foundation Science, Technology, Engineering, and Mathematics Grants, 966
First Hawaiian Bank Foundation Corporate Giving Grants, 967
First Nations Development Institute Native Language Immersion Initiative Grants, 973
First Nations Development Institute Native Youth and Culture Fund Grants, 974
Florence Foundation Grants, 978
Foundation for Rural Service Education Grants, 991
Fdn for the Mid South Communities Grants, 992
Foundation for the Mid South Education Grants, 993
Four County Community Foundation 21st Century Education Fund Grants, 999
Four County Community Foundation General Grants, 1000
Four Lanes Trust Grants, 1005
Fremont Area Community Foundation Community Grants, 1020
Friends of Hawaii Charities Grants, 1024
Fuller Foundation Youth At Risk Grants, 1028
George Graham and Elizabeth Galloway Smith Foundation Grants, 1047
Georgia Council for the Arts Education Grants, 1060
Geraldine R. Dodge Fdn Education Grants, 1061
GNOF Exxon-Mobil Grants, 1080
GNOF IMPACT Kahn-Oppenheim Tr Grts, 1087
Golden Heart Community Foundation Grants, 1094
Graham Foundation Grants, 1100
Gray Family Foundation Community Field Trips Grants, 1105
Gray Family Foundation Geography Education Grants, 1106
Gray Family Fdn Outdoor School Grants, 1107
Greater Sitka Legacy Fund Grants, 1111

Green River Area Community Fdn Grants, 1117
Grifols Community Outreach Grants, 1122
HAF Joe Alexandre Mem Family Fund Grants, 1145
HAF Laurence and Elaine Allen Memorial Fund Grants, 1146
HAF Native Cultures Fund Grants, 1148
Hampton Roads Community Foundation Education Grants, 1157
Hardin County Community Foundation Grants, 1167
Harmony Project Grants, 1170
Harold K.L. Castle Foundation Public Education Redesign and Enhancement Grants, 1173
Harris and Eliza Kempner Fund Ed Grants, 1176
Harris Foundation Grants, 1177
Harrison County Community Foundation Signature Grants, 1179
Hattie M. Strong Foundation Grants, 1194
Hawai'i Community Foundation Family Literacy and Hawaii Pizza Hut Literacy Grants, 1201
Hazel and Walter T. Bales Foundation Grants, 1220
Henry and Ruth Blaustein Rosenberg Foundation Education Grants, 1236
Hillsdale County Community Foundation General Grants, 1250
Hillsdale County Community Foundation Love Your Community Grants, 1251
HLTA Visitor Industry Charity Walk Grant, 1254
Hubbard Family Foundation Grants, 1271
Huntington County Community Foundation Classroom Education Grants, 1279
Huntington County Community Foundation Make a Difference Grants, 1280
ILA Grants for Literacy Projects in Countries with Developing Economies, 1292
Illinois DNR School Habitat Action Grants, 1296
Indiana OCRA Rural Capacity Grants (RCG), 1301
J. Edwin Treakle Foundation Grants, 1320
Jack H. and William M. Light Charitable Trust Grants, 1330
James and Abigail Campbell Family Foundation Grants, 1337
James Lee Sorenson Family Impact Foundation Grants, 1342
Japan Foundation Los Angeles Contests Designed for Japanese-Language Learners Grants, 1351
Japan Foundation Los Angeles Grants for Japanese-Language Courses, 1352
Jennings County Community Fdn Grants, 1360
Jessica Stevens Community Foundation Grants, 1363
John M. Weaver Foundation Grants, 1376
Joseph H. and Florence A. Roblee Foundation Education Grants, 1386
Joseph Henry Edmondson Foundation Grants, 1388
Kalamazoo Community Foundation Early Childhood Learning and School Readiness Grants, 1407
K and F Baxter Family Foundation Grants, 1413
Kenai Peninsula Foundation Grants, 1425
Ketchikan Community Foundation Grants, 1429
Kimball International-Habig Foundation Education Grants, 1433
Kodiak Community Foundation Grants, 1446
LaGrange Independent Foundation for Endowments (L.I.F.E.), 1459
Laurel Foundation Grants, 1475
LGA Family Foundation Grants, 1487
LISC Education Grants, 1500
Lotus 88 Foundation for Women and Children Grants, 1508
Louis Calder Foundation Grants, 1511
Marin Community Foundation Arts Education Grants, 1562
Martha Holden Jennings Foundation Grants-to-Educators, 1581
Mary A. Crocker Trust Grants, 1584
Massachusetts Cultural Council Local Cultural Council (LCC) Grants, 1601
Massachusetts Cultural Cncl YouthReach Grts, 1602
Maurice R. Robinson Fund Grants, 1611
Meadows Foundation Grants, 1626
Meyer Foundation Education Grants, 1649

Meyer Memorial Trust Responsive Grants, 1653
Michelin North America Challenge Education, 1660
Mid-Iowa Health Foundation Community Response Grants, 1667
Mile High United Way Stratc Investment Grts, 1671
Mimi and Peter Haas Fund Grants, 1677
Mockingbird Foundation Grants, 1680
Morris Stulsaft Foundation Early Childhood Education Grants, 1696
Narragansett Number One Foundation Grants, 1712
NCSS Award for Global Understanding, 1728
NCSS Christa McA Reach for the Stars Awd, 1730
NEH Picturing America Awards, 1735
New Earth Foundation Grants, 1743
New Jersey Office of Faith Based Initiatives English as a Second Language Grants, 1751
New Jersey Office of Faith Based Initiatives Services to At Risk Youth Grants, 1752
NHSCA Youth Arts Project Grants: For Extended Arts Learning, 1758
NJSCA Artists in Education Residencies, 1763
Northern Chautauqua Community Foundation Community Grants, 1769
Northrop Grumman Foundation Grants, 1773
NRA Foundation Grants, 1774
NYSCA Arts Education: Community-based Learning Grants, 1780
NYSCA Arts Education: Local Capacity Building Grants (Regrants), 1783
NYSCA Arts Ed: Services to the Field Grants, 1784
NYSCA Music: Commty Music Schools Grants, 1790
NYSCA Special Arts Services: Instruction and Training Grants, 1794
Office Depot Foundation Education Grants, 1806
Ohio County Community Foundation Board of Directors Grants, 1811
OMNOVA Solutions Fdn Education Grants, 1820
Ontario Arts Council Indigenous Culture Fund Indigenous Artists in Communities and Schools Project Grants, 1825
Oppenstein Brothers Foundation Grants, 1827
Oregon Community Fdn Community Grants, 1833
Oregon Community Foundation Edna E. Harrell Community Children's Fund Grants, 1835
OSF Education Program Grants in Kyrgyzstan, 1842
OSF Education Support Program Grants, 1843
P. Buckley Moss Foundation for Children's Education Teacher Grants, 1855
PacifiCare Foundation Grants, 1861
Patricia Kisker Foundation Grants, 1879
Perkin Fund Grants, 1937
Petersburg Community Foundation Grants, 1951
Pettus Foundation Grants, 1952
Philip L. Graham Fund Education Grants, 1962
Piedmont Natural Gas Fdn Envirnmtl Stewardship and Energy Sustainability Grant, 1967
Piedmont Natural Gas Foundation K-12 Science, Technology, Engineering and Math (STEM) Grant, 1969
Piper Trust Education Grants, 1977
PNC Foundation Education Grants, 1985
Pokagon Fund Grants, 1994
Polk County Community Foundation Marjorie M. and Lawrence R. Bradley Endowment Fund Grants, 1998
Polk County Community Foundation Unrestricted Grants, 2001
Progress Energy Foundation Energy Education Grants, 2025
Public Education Power Grants, 2032
Rathmann Family Foundation Grants, 2057
Richard Davoud Donchian Foundation Grants, 2070
Richland County Bank Grants, 2074
Ripley County Community Foundation Small Project Grants, 2078
Robbins-de Beaumont Foundation Grants, 2080
Robert Lee Blaffer Foundation Grants, 2092
Robert R. Meyer Foundation Grants, 2094
Ron and Sanne Higgins Family Fdn Grants, 2101
Rose Community Foundation Education Grants, 2104

Ruby K. Worner Charitable Trust Grants, 2119
Samueli Foundation Education Grants, 2143
Samuel N. and Mary Castle Foundation Grants, 2145
Sand Hill Foundation Health and Opportunity
  Grants, 2153
SAS Institute Community Relations Donations, 2165
Schlessman Family Foundation Grants, 2167
Seattle Foundation Arts and Culture Grants, 2174
Seattle Foundation Education Grants, 2178
Seattle Foundation Health and Wellness Grants, 2179
Seward Community Foundation Grants, 2182
Seward Community Foundation Mini-Grants, 2183
Shell Oil Company Foundation Community
  Development Grants, 2188
Shield-Ayres Foundation Grants, 2189
Sidgmore Family Foundation Grants, 2195
Silicon Valley Community Foundation Education
  Grants, 2200
Sony Corporation of America Grants, 2216
Sorenson Legacy Foundation Grants, 2217
Southern California Edison Education Grants, 2218
Summit Foundation Grants, 2255
TAC Arts Education Mini Grants, 2267
TAC Arts Education Teacher Incentive Grants, 2268
Teaching Tolerance Diverse Democracy Grants, 2275
Tellabs Foundation Grants, 2280
Thomas Sill Foundation Grants, 2292
Toshiba America Foundation Grades 7-12 Science and
  Math Grants, 2307
Toshiba America Foundation K-6 Science and Math
  Grants, 2308
Toyota Motor Manuf of Alabama Grants, 2309
Toyota Motor Manufacturing of Indiana Grants, 2310
Toyota Motor Manuf of Mississippi Grants, 2312
Toyota Motor Manufacturing of Texas Grants, 2313
Toyota Motor Manufacturing of West Virginia
  Grants, 2314
Toyota Motor Sales, USA Grants, 2316
Toyota Technical Center Grants, 2317
Toyota USA Foundation Education Grants, 2318
Toyota USA Foundation Safety Grants, 2320
Turtle Bay Foundation Grants, 2327
Union Bank, N.A. Foundation Grants, 2334
UPS Foundation Economic and Global Literacy
  Grants, 2351
Virginia Commission for the Arts Artists in
  Education Residency Grants, 2385
Virginia Foundation for the Humanities Open
  Grants, 2387
W.H. and Mary Ellen Cobb Chartbl Trust Grts, 2397
Weaver Popcorn Foundation Grants, 2421
Western Indiana Community Fdn Grants, 2428
William Ray and Ruth E. Collins Fdn Grants, 2473
Wilton and Effie Hebert Foundation Grants, 2476
Wiregrass Foundation Grants, 2480
WSF GoGirlGo! New York Grants, 2494
WSF Sports 4 Life Regional Grants, 2497
WSLBDF Quarterly Grants, 2499
Xerox Foundation Grants, 2507
Youths' Friends Association Grants, 2511
YSA State Farm Good Neighbor YOUth In The
  Driver Seat Grants, 2521
YSA UnitedHealth HEROES Service-Learning
  Grants, 2522

Demonstration Grants

ACF Child Abuse Prevention and Treatment Act
  Discretionary Funds Grants, 74
ACF National Human Trafficking Hotline Grants, 86
ACF Runaway and Homeless Youth Training and
  Technical Assistance Center Grants, 92
ACF Social and Economic Development Strategies
  Grants, 93
ACF Unaccompanied Refugee Children Grants, 99
Alaska Community Foundation GCI Suicide
  Prevention Grant, 203
ALFJ International Fund Grants, 231
American Woodmark Foundation Grants, 263
Bank of America Charitable Foundation Matching
  Gifts, 356

Bikes Belong Grants, 424
Burton D. Morgan Foundation Hudson Community
  Grants, 482
Caesars Foundation Grants, 492
Cause Populi Worthy Cause Grants, 521
Cigna Civic Affairs Sponsorships, 610
Circle K Corporation Contributions Grants, 614
Clayton Fund Grants, 631
CNCS AmeriCorps State and National Planning
  Grants, 644
CNCS School Turnaround AmeriCorps Grants, 647
CNCS Social Innovation Grants, 649
Community Foundation for Greater Atlanta
  Metropolitan Extra Wish Grants, 666
Community Foundation for Greater Buffalo Ralph
  C. Wilson, Jr. Youth Sports COVID-19 Fund
  Grants, 675
Community Foundation of Greater Fort Wayne -
  Community Endowment and Clarke Endowment
  Grants, 705
Community Foundation of Louisville Anna Marble
  Memorial Fund for Princeton Grants, 717
Curtis Foundation Grants, 771
Del Mar Foundation Community Grants, 820
Dyson Foundation Mid-Hudson Valley Project
  Support Grants, 874
Eastern Bank Charitable Foundation Partnerships
  Grants, 881
Eastern Bank Charitable Foundation Targeted
  Grants, 882
Eide Bailly Resourcefullness Awards, 897
Evelyn and Walter Haas, Jr. Fund Immigrant Rights
  Grants, 941
Foundation Beyond Belief Compassionate Impact
  Grants, 986
Foundation Beyond Belief Humanist Grants, 987
GMFUS Balkan Trust for Democracy Grants, 1075
Iddings Foundation Major Project Grants, 1284
Iddings Foundation Medium Project Grants, 1285
IMLS Grants to State Library Administrative
  Agencies, 1298
Indiana OCRA Rural Capacity Grants (RCG), 1301
Laidlaw Foundation Youh Organizing Catalyst
  Grants, 1461
Laidlaw Foundation Youth Organizaing Initiatives
  Grants, 1462
Laura Musser Intercultural Harmony Grants, 1472
Marin Community Foundation Arts Education
  Grants, 1562
Merck Family Fund Youth Transforming Urban
  Communities Grants, 1636
Mt. Sinai Health Care Foundation Health of the
  Jewish Community Grants, 1709
New Hampshire Charitable Foundation Community
  Unrestricted Grants, 1747
Northern Chautauqua Community Foundation
  Community Grants, 1769
OceanFirst Foundation Major Grants, 1803
OHA Community Grants for Culture, 1808
Oregon Community Fdn Community Grants, 1833
PEN America Phyllis Naylor Grant for Children's and
  Young Adult Novelists, 1928
Polk County Community Foundation Unrestricted
  Grants, 2001
Ruth Camp Campbell Charitable Trust Grants, 2125
San Antonio Area Foundation Annual Responsive
  Grants, 2147
San Antonio Area Foundation Capital and Naming
  Rights Grants, 2148
Sand Hill Foundation Environment and Sustainability
  Grants, 2152
Sand Hill Foundation Health and Opportunity
  Grants, 2153
Sapelo Foundation Social Justice Grants, 2160
Seattle Foundation Benjamin N. Phillips Memorial
  Fund Grants, 2176
Union Bank, N.A. Foundation Grants, 2334
Union Square Award for Social Justice, 2340
USAID Nigeria Ed Crisis Response Grants, 2358

UUA Congregation-Based Community Organizing
  Grants, 2366
UUA Fund Grants, 2367
UUA International Fund Grants, 2368
UUA Just Society Fund Grants, 2369
UUA Social Responsibility Grants, 2370
Weyerhaeuser Family Fdn Health Grants, 2435
Whitehorse Foundation Grants, 2439
Wiregrass Foundation Grants, 2480
Xerox Foundation Grants, 2507

Development (Institutional/Departmental)

ACF Marriage Strengthening Research &
  Dissemination Center Grants, 85
ACF Social and Economic Development Strategies
  Grants, 93
Acuity Charitable Foundation Grants, 110
Amerigroup Foundation Grants, 264
AMERIND Community Service Project Grants, 265
Anheuser-Busch Foundation Grants, 273
Anna Fitch Ardenghi Trust Grants, 274
Ar-Hale Family Foundation Grants, 290
Arthur M. Blank Family Foundation Atlanta Falcons
  Youth Foundation Grants, 307
Assisi Foundation of Memphis General Grants, 318
Assisi Foundation of Memphis Mini Grants, 319
Autism Speaks Norma and Malcolm Baker Recreation
  Grants, 335
Bank of America Charitable Foundation Volunteer
  Grants, 358
Baxter International Foundation Grants, 369
Bernard and Audre Rapoport Foundation Education
  Grants, 410
Best Buy Children's Foundation @15 Community
  Grants , 414
Best Buy Children's Foundation National Grants, 417
Best Buy Children's Foundation Twin Cities
  Minnesota Capital Grants, 418
Bill and Melinda Gates Foundation Policy and
  Advocacy Grants, 427
Blandin Foundation Expand Opportunity Grants, 437
Blue Cross Blue Shield of Minnesota Fdn - Healthy
  Children: Growing Up Healthy Grants, 442
Blumenthal Foundation Grants, 459
Burlington Industries Foundation Grants, 481
C.F. Adams Charitable Trust Grants, 488
California Endowment Innovative Ideas Challenge
  Grants, 495
Carl M. Freeman Foundation Grants, 508
Carnegie Corporation of New York Grants, 511
Cash 4 Clubs Sports Grants, 515
CFFVR Clintonville Area Foundation Grants, 539
Cincinnati Bell Foundation Grants, 612
Cincinnati Milacron Foundation Grants, 613
Circle K Corporation Contributions Grants, 614
CNCS AmeriCorps Indian Tribes Plang Grts , 641
CNCS AmeriCorps NCCC Project Grants, 642
CNCS AmeriCorps State and National Grants, 643
CNCS Social Innovation Grants, 649
Community Foundation for Greater Atlanta Strategic
  Restructuring Fund Grants, 669
Community Foundation for SE Michigan Chelsea
  Community Fdn Capacity Building Grants, 679
Community Foundation of St. Joseph County Special
  Project Challenge Grants, 738
Daniels Homeless and Disadvantaged Grants, 782
Dubois County Community Foundation Grants, 871
Eastern Bank Charitable Foundation Partnerships
  Grants, 881
Eastern Bank Charitable Foundation Targeted
  Grants, 882
Eileen Fisher Activating Leadership Grants for
  Women and Girls, 898
Emerson Kampen Foundation Grants, 911
Eulalie Bloedel Schneider Foundation Grants, 936
Evelyn and Walter Haas, Jr. Fund Immigrant Rights
  Grants, 941
F.R. Bigelow Foundation Grants, 947
Farmers Insurance Corporate Giving Grants, 948
Fidelity Foundation Grants, 957

Fifth Third Bank Corporate Giving, 958
Fifth Third Foundation Grants, 959
Finish Line Youth Foundation Legacy Grants, 962
Fdn for the Mid South Communities Grants, 992
Foundation for the Mid South Education Grants, 993
Fund for the City of New York Grants, 1029
George B. Page Foundation Grants, 1044
George I. Alden Trust Grants, 1051
GNOF Bayou Communities Grants, 1077
GNOF New Orleans Works Grants, 1088
GNOF Organizational Effectiveness Grants and
    Workshops, 1090
GNOF Stand Up For Our Children Grants, 1092
Goldseker Foundation Non-Profit Management
    Assistance Grants, 1095
Graham Foundation Grants, 1101
Greater Saint Louis Community Fdn Grants, 1110
Greygates Foundation Grants, 1120
Harry A. and Margaret D. Towsley Foundation
    Grants, 1180
Hawai'i Community Foundation Victoria S. and
    Bradley L. Geist Foundation: Capacity Building
    Grants, 1206
Honor the Earth Grants, 1259
Iddings Foundation Major Project Grants, 1284
Iddings Foundation Medium Project Grants, 1285
James Ford Bell Foundation Grants, 1339
Japan Foundation Los Angeles Grants for Japanese-
    Language Courses, 1352
Joan Bentinck-Smith Charitable Fdn Grants, 1367
Johnson Controls Foundation Arts and Culture
    Grants, 1378
Johnson Scholarship Foundation Grants, 1382
Jovid Foundation Employment Training Grants, 1392
LISC Capacity Building Grants, 1498
Long Island Community Foundation Grants, 1507
Lotus 88 Foundation for Women and Children
    Grants, 1508
Malone Family Foundation Atypical Development
    Initiative Grants, 1549
Margaret M. Walker Charitable Fdn Grants, 1556
Marion I. and Henry J. Knott Foundation
    Discretionary Grants, 1571
Marion I. and Henry J. Knott Foundation Standard
    Grants, 1572
Marquette Bank Neighborhood Commit Grants, 1577
Mary E. Babcock Foundation, 1589
Maurice J. Masserini Charitable Trust Grants, 1610
May and Stanley Smith Charitable Trust Grants, 1613
Mertz Gilmore Foundation NYC Communities
    Grants, 1641
Mertz Gilmore Foundation NYC Dance Grants, 1642
Meyer Foundation Benevon Grants, 1648
Meyer Foundation Education Grants, 1649
Meyer Fdn Healthy Communities Grants, 1650
Meyer Fdn Management Assistance Grants, 1651
Michael Reese Health Trust Core Grants, 1658
Michigan Women Forward Grants, 1662
Mid-Iowa Health Foundation Community Response
    Grants, 1667
Middlesex Savings Charitable Foundation Capacity
    Building Grants, 1669
Montana Arts Council Cultural and Aesthetic Project
    Grants, 1685
Mt. Sinai Health Care Foundation Health of the
    Jewish Community Grants, 1709
Mt. Sinai Health Care Foundation Health of the
    Urban Community Grants, 1710
New York Foundation Grants, 1753
Noble County Community Foundation Grants, 1765
Norman Foundation Grants, 1767
NYSCA Arts Education: General Program Support
    Grants, 1782
NYSCA Music: Gen Program Support Grants, 1792
Pajaro Valley Community Health Health Trust
    Insurance/Coverage & Education on Using the
    System Grants, 1864
Pajaro Valley Community Health Trust Diabetes and
    Contributing Factors Grants, 1865

Pajaro Valley Community Health Trust Oral Health:
    Prevention & Access Grants, 1866
PCA-PCD Organizational Short-Term Professional
    Development and Consulting Grants, 1882
PCA Arts Management Internship, 1886
PCA Management/Techl Assistance Grants, 1913
PCA Strategies for Success Grants - Adv Level, 1917
PCA Strategies for Success Grants - Basic Level, 1918
PCA Strategies for Success Grants - Intermediate
    Level, 1919
Peter and Elizabeth C. Tower Foundation Intellectual
    Disabilities Grants, 1944
Peter and Elizabeth C. Tower Foundation Mental
    Health Grants, 1946
Peter and Elizabeth C. Tower Foundation Small
    Grants, 1947
Peter and Elizabeth C. Tower Foundation Technology
    Initiative Grants, 1949
Peter and Elizabeth C. Tower Foundation Technology
    Planning Grants, 1950
Philanthrofund Foundation Grants, 1959
Piper Trust Education Grants, 1977
Piper Trust Healthcare and Med Rsrch Grants, 1978
Piper Trust Reglious Organizations Grants, 1979
Price Chopper's Golub Foundation Grants, 2020
Priddy Foundation Organizational Development
    Grants, 2022
Richard Davoud Donchian Foundation Grants, 2070
Ruddie Memorial Youth Foundation Grants, 2120
Saginaw Community Foundation Discretionary
    Grants, 2134
San Antonio Area Foundation Strengthening
    Nonprofits Grants, 2151
Sapelo Foundation Social Justice Grants, 2160
Sartain Lanier Family Foundation Grants, 2164
Seattle Foundation Health and Wellness Grants, 2179
Sensient Technologies Foundation Grants, 2180
Serco Foundation Grants, 2181
Sierra Health Foundation Responsive Grants, 2199
Sioux Falls Area Community Foundation Community
    Fund Grants, 2203
Sioux Falls Area Community Foundation Spot
    Grants, 2204
Social Justice Fund Northwest Criminal Justice
    Giving Project Grants, 2214
Telluride Fdn Technical Assistance Grants, 2283
TJX Foundation Grants, 2303
Union Bank, N.A. Foundation Grants, 2334
Wallace Foundation Grants, 2402
William J. and Dorothy K. O'Neill Foundation
    Responsive Grants, 2468
WSF Sports 4 Life Grants, 2496
Wyomissing Foundation Community Grants, 2504
Z. Smith Reynolds Foundation Small Grants, 2523

Dissertation/Thesis Research Support
Gerber Foundation Environmental Hazards Research
    Grants, 1062
Gerber Fdn Pediatric Health Research Grants, 1063
Gerber Foundation Pediatric Nutrition Research
    Grants, 1064

Educational Programs
1st Source Foundation Community Involvement
    Grants, 1
2 Depot Square Ipswich Charitable Foundation
    Grants, 3
3 Dog Garage Museum Tours, 4
3M Company Fdn Community Giving Grants, 5
3M Company Foundation Health and Human
    Services Grants, 6
4imprint One by One Charitable Giving, 7
100% for Kids - Utah Credit Union Education
    Foundation Major Project Grants, 11
100% for Kids - Utah Credit Union Education
    Foundation Mini Grants, 12
100% for Kids - Utah Credit Union Education
    Foundation School Grants, 13
520 Charitable Foundation Grants, 14
786 Foundation Grants, 15

A. Alfred Taubman Foundation Grants, 18
A.C. and Penney Hubbard Foundation Grants, 19
A.L. Mailman Family Foundation Grants, 20
A.L. Spencer Foundation Grants, 21
Aaron Foundation Grants, 42
AASA Urgent Need Mini-Grants, 43
AAUW International Project Grants, 44
Abbott Fund Access to Health Care Grants, 45
Abbott Fund Community Engagement Grants, 46
Abbott Fund Global AIDS Care Grants, 47
Abbott Fund Science Education Grants, 48
Abby's Legendary Pizza Foundation Grants, 49
Abeles Foundation Grants, 51
Abell-Hanger Foundation Grants, 52
Abell Foundation Education Grants, 53
Abington Foundation Grants, 54
Abney Foundation Grants, 55
ABS Foundation Grants, 56
Abundance Foundation International Grants, 57
Abundance Foundation Local Community Grants, 58
ACCF Dennis and Melanie Bieberich Community
    Enrichment Fund Grants, 59
ACCF John and Kay Boch Fund Grants, 60
ACCF Marlene Bittner Memorial Community
    Enrichment Fund Grants, 61
ACCF of Indiana Anonymous Community
    Enrichment Fund Grants, 63
ACCF of Indiana Bank of Geneva Heritage Fund
    Grants, 64
ACCF of Indiana Berne Ready Mix Community
    Enrichment Fund Grants, 65
ACCF of Indiana First Merchants Bank / Decatur
    Bank and Trust Fund Grants, 66
ACCF of Indiana Michael Basham Community
    Enrichment Fund Grants, 67
ACCF of Indiana Ron and Susie Ballard Community
    Enrichment Fund Grants, 68
ACCF Ralph Biggs Memorial Community
    Enrichment Fund Grants, 69
ACF Abandoned Infants Assistance Grants, 70
ACF Adoption Opportunities Grants, 71
ACF American Indian and Alaska Native Early Head
    Start Expansion Grants, 72
ACF Basic Center Program Grants, 73
ACF Child Welfare Training Grants, 75
ACF Community-Based Child Abuse Prevention
    (CBCAP) Grants, 76
ACF Community-Based Child Abuse
    Prevention (CBCAP) Tribal and Migrant
    DiscretionaryGrants, 77
ACF Head Start and/or Early Head Start Grantee
    - Clay, Randolph, and Talladega Counties,
    Alabama, 82
ACF Head Start and/or Early Head Start Grantee -
    St. Landry Parish, Louisiana, 83
ACF Infant Adoption Awareness Training Program
    Grants, 84
ACF Marriage Strengthening Research &
    Dissemination Center Grants, 85
ACF Native American Social and Economic
    Development Strategies for Alaska Grants, 87
ACF Native Youth Initiative for Leadership,
    Empowerment, and Development Grants, 88
ACF Promoting Safe and Stable Families (PSSF)
    Program Grants, 89
ACF Refugee Career Pathways Grants, 90
ACF Refugee Health Promotion Grants, 91
ACF Runaway and Homeless Youth Training and
    Technical Assistance Center Grants, 92
ACF Social and Economic Development Strategies
    Grants, 93
ACF Street Outreach Program Grants, 94
ACF Tribal Maternal, Infant, and Early Childhood
    Home Visiting Program: Development and
    Implementation Grants, 97
ACF Tribal Maternal, Infant, and Early Childhood
    Home Visiting Program: Implementation and
    Expansion Grants, 98
ACF Unaccompanied Refugee Children Grants, 99
ACF Voluntary Agencies Matching Grants, 100

Achelis and Bodman Foundation Grants, 101
Achelis Foundation Grants, 102
Ackerman Foundation Grants, 103
ACL Alternatives to Guardianship Youth Resource Center Grants, 104
ACL Disability and Rehabilitation Research Projects (DRRP) Program: Independent Living Transition Services for Youth and Young Adults Grants, 105
ACMP Foundation Community Music Grants, 108
Active Living Research Grants, 109
Acuity Charitable Foundation Grants, 110
Adams-Mastrovich Family Foundation Grants, 113
Adams and Reese Corporate Giving Grants, 114
Adams County Community Foundation Grants, 115
Adams Family Foundation I Grants, 116
Adams Family Foundation II Grants, 117
Adams Family Fdn of Nora Springs Grants, 118
Adams Family Foundation of Ohio Grants, 119
Adams Legacy Foundation Grants, 121
Adelaide Breed Bayrd Foundation Grants, 123
Adobe Foundation Action Grants, 126
Adobe Fdn Community Investment Grants, 127
Adolph Coors Foundation Grants, 129
Advance Auto Parts Corporate Giving Grants, 131
AEGON Transamerica Foundation Education and Financial Literacy Grants, 132
AEGON Transamerica Foundation Health and Wellness Grants, 133
Aetna Foundation Summer Academic Enrichment Grants, 135
A Friends' Foundation Trust Grants, 136
A Fund for Women Grants, 137
AGFT A Gift for Music Grants, 138
AGFT Pencil Boy Express, 139
Agnes M. Lindsay Trust Grants, 140
Ahearn Family Foundation Grants, 142
AHS Foundation Grants, 143
Aid for Starving Children Homes and Education Grants, 146
Air Products Foundation Grants, 148
Akron Community Foundation Arts and Culture Grants, 150
Akron Community Fdn Education Grants, 151
Akron Community Foundation Health and human services Grants, 152
ALA Baker and Taylor Summer Reading Program Grant, 158
Alabama Humanities Foundation Major Grants, 159
ALA Innovative Reading Grant, 171
ALA MAE Award for Best Literature Program for Teens, 174
ALA Sara Jaffarian School Library Award for Exemplary Humanities Programming, 190
Alaska Airlines Corporation Career Connections for Youth Grants, 193
Alaska Airlines Foundation LIFT Grants, 194
Alaska Community Foundation Afterschool Network Engineering Mindset Mini-Grant, 196
Alaska Community Foundation Anchorage Schools Foundation Grant, 197
Alaska Community Foundation GCI Suicide Prevention Grant, 203
Alaska State Council on the Arts Cultural Collaboration Project Grants, 211
Albert and Ethel Herzstein Charitable Foundation Grants, 219
Albert E. and Birdie W. Einstein Fund Grants, 220
Albertsons Companies Foundation Nourishing Neighbors Grants, 221
Albert W. Cherne Foundation Grants, 222
Albert W. Rice Charitable Foundation Grants, 223
Alcatel-Lucent Technologies Foundation Grants, 224
Alden and Vada Dow Fund Grants, 225
Aldi Corporation Smart Kids Grants, 226
Alexander Graham Bell Preschool-Age Financial Aid Grants, 228
Alex Stern Family Foundation Grants, 229
ALFJ International Fund Grants, 231
Alfred E. Chase Charitable Foundation Grants, 233

Alfred J Mcallister and Dorothy N Mcallister Foundation Grants, 234
Allan C. and Lelia J. Garden Foundation Grants, 236
Allegis Group Foundation Grants, 237
Allen Foundation Educational Nutrition Grants, 238
Alliance for Strong Families and Communities Grants, 239
Alliant Energy Foundation Community Giving for Good Sponsorship Grants, 240
Alloy Family Foundation Grants, 241
Allstate Corporate Giving Grants, 242
Allstate Corp Hometown Commitment Grants, 243
Allstate Foundation Safe and Vital Communities Grants, 244
Allstate Foundation Tolerance, Inclusion, and Diversity Grants, 245
Alpha Natural Resources Corporate Giving, 246
Altria Group Positive Youth Dev Grants, 247
Ama OluKai Foundation Grants, 249
Amelia Sillman Rockwell and Carlos Perry Rockwell Charities Fund Grants, 250
Ameren Corporation Community Grants, 251
American Electric Power Corporate Grants, 252
American Electric Power Foundation Grants, 253
American Honda Foundation Grants, 255
American Psychiatric Fdn Call for Proposals, 257
American Psychiatric Foundation Typical or Troubled School Mental Health Education Grants, 258
American Savings Fdn After School Grants, 259
American Savings Foundation Program Grants, 261
American Woodmark Foundation Grants, 263
Amerigroup Foundation Grants, 264
Amica Companies Foundation Grants, 266
Amica Insurance Company Community Grants, 267
Amway Corporation Contributions, 269
Anchorage Schools Foundation Grants, 270
Anderson Foundation Grants, 271
Andrew Family Foundation Grants, 272
Anheuser-Busch Foundation Grants, 273
Anne Arundel Women Giving Together Regular Grants, 275
Anne J. Caudal Foundation Grants, 276
Ann L. and Carol Green Rhodes Charitable Trust Grants, 278
Ann Ludington Sullivan Foundation Grants, 279
Anthony Munoz Foundation Straight A Student Campaign Grants, 280
Antone and Edene Vidinha Charitable Grants, 281
APAP All-In Grants, 283
Appalachian Regional Commission Business Development Revolving Loan Fund Grants, 285
Appalachian Regional Commission Education and Training Grants, 286
Appalachian Regional Commission Entrepreneurship and Business Development Grants, 287
Appalachian Regional Commission Health Care Grants, 288
Ar-Hale Family Foundation Grants, 290
Arizona Commission on the Arts Learning Collaboration Grant, 291
Arizona Commission on the Arts Youth Arts Engagement Grant, 292
Arizona Foundation for Women Deborah G. Carstens Fund Grants, 293
Arizona Foundation for Women General Grants, 294
Arizona State Library LSTA Collections Grants, 295
Arizona State Library LSTA Community Grants, 296
Arizona State Library LSTA Learning Grants, 297
Arkema Foundation Grants, 298
Arkema Foundation Science Teachers Grants, 299
Arthur Ashley Williams Foundation Grants, 302
Arthur E. and Josephine Campbell Beyer Foundation Grants, 303
Arthur M. Blank Family Foundation AMB West Community Fund Grants, 304
Arthur M. Blank Family Foundation Art of Change Grants, 306
Arthur M. Blank Family Foundation Atlanta Falcons Youth Foundation Grants, 307

Arthur M. Blank Family Foundation Mountain Sky Guest Ranch Fund Grants, 311
Arthur M. Blank Family Foundation Pathways to Success Grants, 312
Arthur M. Blank Family Foundation Pipeline Project Grants, 313
Arts Council of Greater Lansing Young Creatives Grants, 314
ASCAP Foundation Grants, 315
Aspen Community Foundation Grants, 316
Assisi Foundation of Memphis General Grants, 318
Assisi Foundation of Memphis Mini Grants, 319
AT&T Foundation Education Grants, 321
ATA Inclusive Learning Communities Grants, 323
ATA Local Community Relations Grants, 324
Atkinson Foundation Community Grants, 325
Atlanta Foundation Grants, 326
Atlanta Women's Foundation Pathway to Success Grants, 327
Atlas Insurance Agency Foundation Grants, 329
Aunt Kate Foundation Grants, 331
Austin Community Foundation Grants, 332
Austin S. Nelson Foundation Grants, 333
Autauga Area Community Foundation Grants, 334
Avery Dennison Foundation Education Grants, 337
Avery Family Trust Grants, 338
Avery Foundation Grants, 339
Avista Foundation Education Grants, 340
Avista Foundation Vulnerable and Limited Income Population Grants, 341
B.F. and Rose H. Perkins Foundation Community Grants, 342
Babcock Charitable Trust Grants, 343
Back Home Again Foundation Grants, 344
Bainum Family Foundation Grants, 345
Ball Brothers Foundation Organizational Effectiveness/Executive Mentoring Grants, 346
Baltimore Community Foundation Building Stronger Neighborhoods Regionwide Grants, 347
Baltimore Community Foundation Children's Fresh Air Society Fund Grants, 348
Baltimore Community Foundation Mitzvah Fund for Good Deeds Grants, 349
Baltimore Ravens Corporate Giving, 350
Baltimore Ravens Foundation Play 60 Grants, 351
Bank of America Charitable Foundation Matching Gifts, 356
Bank of America Charitable Foundation Student Leaders Grants, 357
Bank of America Charitable Foundation Volunteer Grants, 358
Bank of America Corporation Sponsorships, 359
Bank of Hawaii Foundation Grants, 360
Baton Rouge Area Foundation Community Coffee Fund Grants, 363
Baton Rouge Area Foundation Every Kid a King Fund Grants, 364
Baton Rouge Area Foundation Grants, 365
Batters Up USA Equipment Grants, 366
Batts Foundation Grants, 367
Baxter International Corporate Giving Grants, 368
Baxter International Foundation Grants, 369
Bay and Paul Foundations PreK-12 Transformative Learning Practices Grants, 370
Bay Area Community Fdn Auburn Area Chamber of Commerce Enrichment Fund Grants, 373
Bay Area Community Foundation Community Initiative Fund Grants, 376
Bay Area Community Foundation Dow CommunityGives Youth Service Prog Grants, 377
Bay Area Community Foundation Semiannual Grants, 382
Bayer Fund Community Development Grants, 383
Bayer Fund STEM Education Grants, 384
BBF Florida Family Literacy Initiative Grants, 386
BBF Maine Family Literacy Initiative Planning Grants, 388
BBF Maryland Family Literacy Initiative Planning Grants, 390
BBF National Grants for Family Literacy, 391

Beacon Society Jan Stauber Grants, 393
Beckman Coulter Foundation Grants, 394
Bee Conservancy Sponsor-A-Hive Grants, 395
Bella Vista Fdn GSS Healthy Living Grants, 396
Bella Vista Fdns GSS Early Literacy Grants, 398
Belvedere Community Foundation Grants, 399
Belvedere Cove Foundation Grants, 400
Belvedere Cove Foundation Scholarships, 401
Ben B. Cheney Foundation Grants, 402
Ben Cohen StandUp Foundation Grants, 403
Benton Community Foundation - The Cookie Jar Grant, 404
Benton Community Foundation Grants, 405
Bernard and Audre Rapoport Foundation Democracy and Civic Participation Grants, 409
Bernard and Audre Rapoport Foundation Education Grants, 410
Bernau Family Foundation Grants, 413
Best Buy Children's Foundation @15 Community Grants , 414
Best Buy Children's Fdn @15 Teach Awards, 416
Best Buy Children's Foundation Twin Cities Minnesota Capital Grants, 418
Better Way Foundation Grants, 419
Bierhaus Foundation Grants, 421
Bikes Belong Foundation Paul David Clark Bicycling Safety Grants, 422
Bill and Melinda Gates Foundation Agricultural Development Grants, 425
Bill and Melinda Gates Foundation Policy and Advocacy Grants, 427
Bill and Melinda Gates Foundation Water, Sanitation and Hygiene Grants, 428
Bill Graham Memorial Foundation Grants, 429
Bindley Family Foundation Grants, 430
Blackford County Community Foundation - WOW Grants, 433
Blackford County Community Fdn Grants, 434
Black Hills Corporation Grants, 435
Blanche and Irving Laurie Foundation Grants, 436
Blandin Foundation Expand Opportunity Grants, 437
Blandin Foundation Invest Early Grants, 438
Blockbuster Corporate Contributions, 440
Blossom Fund Grants, 441
Blue Grass Community Foundation Clark County Fund Grants, 444
Blue Grass Community Foundation Early Childhood Education and Literacy Grants, 445
Blue Grass Community Foundation Fayette County Fund Grants, 446
Blue Grass Community Foundation Franklin County Fund Grants, 447
Blue Grass Community Foundation Harrison County Fund Grants, 448
Blue Grass Community Foundation Madison County Fund Grants, 450
Blue Grass Community Foundation Magoffin County Fund Grants, 451
Blue Grass Community Foundation Morgan County Fund Grants, 452
Blue Grass Community Foundation Rowan County Fund Grants, 453
Blue Grass Community Foundation Woodford County Fund Grants, 454
Blue Mountain Community Foundation Warren Community Action Fund Grants, 457
Blue River Community Foundation Grants, 458
Blumenthal Foundation Grants, 459
BMW of North America Charitable Contribs, 460
Bodenwein Public Benevolent Foundation Grants, 461
Boeing Company Contributions Grants, 462
Bollinger Foundation Grants, 463
BP Foundation Grants, 465
Bradley-Turner Foundation Grants, 466
Bradley C. Higgins Foundation Grants, 467
Brian G. Dyson Foundation Grants, 468
Bridgestone Americas Trust Fund Grants, 469
Bright Promises Foundation Grants, 470
Brinker Int Corporation Charitable Giving, 471

Bristol-Myers Squibb Foundation Independent Medical Education Grants, 472
Brookdale Fdn Relatives as Parents Grants, 474
Brown County Community Foundation Grants, 475
Brown Foundation Grants, 476
Brown Rudnick Charitable Foundation Community Grants, 477
Brunswick Foundation Dollars for Doers Grants, 478
Brunswick Foundation Grants, 479
Bryan Adams Foundation Grants, 480
Burlington Industries Foundation Grants, 481
Burton D. Morgan Foundation Hudson Community Grants, 482
Burton D. Morgan Foundation Youth Entrepreneurship Grants, 483
Bush Foundation Event Sponsorships, 485
Byerly Foundation Grants, 487
C.H. Robinson Worldwide Foundation Grants, 489
Cadillac Products Packaging Company Foundation Grants, 491
Caesars Foundation Grants, 492
California Arts Cncl Statewide Networks Grants, 493
California Endowment Innovative Ideas Challenge Grants, 495
Callaway Foundation Grants, 496
Calvin Johnson Jr. Foundation Mini Grants, 498
Camille Beckman Foundation Grants, 499
Campbell Foundation Grants, 500
Campbell Soup Foundation Grants, 501
Cargill Corporate Giving Grants, 503
Cargill Foundation Education Grants, 504
Carl B. and Florence E. King Foundation Grants, 506
Carl M. Freeman Foundation FACES Grants, 507
Carl M. Freeman Foundation Grants, 508
Carl R. Hendrickson Family Foundation Grants, 509
Carnegie Corporation of New York Grants, 511
Carroll County Community Foundation Grants, 513
Cass County Community Foundation Grants, 516
Castle Foundation Grants, 518
Castle Foundation Grants, 517
Castle Industries Foundation Grants, 519
Catherine Holmes Wilkins Foundation Charitable Grants, 520
CCFF Christopher Columbus Awards, 522
CCFF Community Grant, 523
CDC David J. Sencer Museum Student Field Trip Experience, 524
CDC Disease Detective Camp, 525
Central Pacific Bank Foundation Grants, 530
CenturyLink Clarke M. Williams Foundation Matching Time Grants, 531
CFFVR Appleton Education Foundation Grants, 536
CFFVR Basic Needs Giving Partnership Grants, 537
CFFVR Clintonville Area Foundation Grants, 538
CFFVR Clintonville Area Foundation Grants, 539
CFFVR Environmental Stewardship Grants, 540
CFFVR Frank C. Shattuck Community Grants, 541
CFFVR Jewelers Mutual Chartbl Giving Grants, 543
CFFVR Mielke Family Foundation Grants, 544
CFFVR Myra M. and Robert L. Vandehey Foundation Grants, 545
CFFVR Project Grants, 546
CFFVR Robert and Patricia Endries Family Foundation Grants, 547
CFFVR Schmidt Family G4 Grants, 548
CFFVR Shawano Area Community Foundation Grants, 549
CFFVR Women's Fund for the Fox Valley Region Grants, 550
CFF Winter Park Community Grants, 551
CFGR Community Impact Grants, 552
CFGR Jenkins Foundation Grants, 553
CFGR SisterFund Grants, 554
CFGR Ujima Legacy Fund Grants, 555
CFKF Instrument Matching Grants, 556
CFNEM Women's Giving Circle Grants, 557
CFNEM Youth Advisory Council Grants, 558
Chapman Charitable Foundation Grants, 560
Chapman Family Charitable Trust Grants, 561
Chapman Family Foundation, 562

Charles Crane Family Foundation Grants, 563
Charles Delmar Foundation Grants, 564
Charles H. Hall Foundation, 565
Charles H. Pearson Foundation Grants, 566
Charles Lafitte Foundation Grants, 567
Charles Nelson Robinson Fund Grants, 569
Charlotte Martin Foundation Youth Grants, 571
Charlotte R. Schmidlapp Fund Grants, 572
Chatham Athletic Foundation Grants, 574
Cheryl Spencer Memorial Foundation Grants, 576
Chesapeake Bay Trust Environmental Education Grants, 577
Chesapeake Bay Trust Mini Grants, 578
Chesapeake Bay Trust Outreach and Community Engagement Grants, 579
Chicago Board of Trade Foundation Grants, 580
Chicago Community Trust Arts and Culture Grants: Improving Access to Arts Learning, 581
Chicago Neighborhood Arts Program Grants, 582
Chilkat Valley Community Foundation Grants, 588
Christensen Fund Regional Grants, 600
Christine and Katharina Pauly Charitable Trust Grants, 601
Christopher Ludwick Foundation Grants, 602
CHT Foundation Education Grants, 603
CICF Clare Noyes Grant, 604
CICF Indianapolis Fdn Community Grants, 606
CICF John Harrison Brown and Rob Burse Grt, 607
CICF Summer Youth Grants, 608
CICF Women's Grants , 609
Cigna Civic Affairs Sponsorships, 610
CIGNA Foundation Grants, 611
Cincinnati Bell Foundation Grants, 612
Cincinnati Milacron Foundation Grants, 613
Circle K Corporation Contributions Grants, 614
Citizens Bank Charitable Foundation Grants, 616
City of Oakland Cultural Funding Grants, 618
CJ Fdn for SIDS Program Services Grants, 619
Clara Blackford Smith and W. Aubrey Smith Charitable Foundation Grants, 621
Claremont Savings Bank Foundation Grants, 623
Clarence T.C. Ching Foundation Grants, 624
Clark and Ruby Baker Foundation Grants, 625
Clark County Community Foundation Grants, 626
Clark Electric Cooperative Grants, 627
Clayton Baker Trust Grants, 629
Clayton F. and Ruth L. Hawkridge Foundation Grants, 630
Clayton Fund Grants, 631
Cleo Foundation Grants, 632
Cleveland Browns Foundation Grants, 633
Cleveland Foundation Higley Fund Grants, 634
Cleveland Fdn Lake-Geauga Fund Grants, 635
Cleveland Foundation Legacy Village Lyndhurst Community Fund Grants, 636
Cleveland H. Dodge Foundation Grants, 637
Clinton County Community Foundation Grants, 638
CNCS AmeriCorps Indian Tribes Plang Grts , 641
CNCS AmeriCorps NCCC Project Grants, 642
CNCS AmeriCorps State and National Grants, 643
CNCS School Turnaround AmeriCorps Grants, 647
CNCS Senior Corps Retired and Senior Volunteer Program Grants, 648
CNO Financial Group Community Grants, 650
Coleman Foundation Entrepreneurship Education Grants, 651
Colgate-Palmolive Company Grants, 652
Collective Brands Foundation Saucony Run for Good Grants, 656
Collins C. Diboll Private Foundation Grants, 657
Collins Foundation Grants, 658
Colonel Stanley R. McNeil Foundation Grants, 659
Colorado Interstate Gas Grants, 661
Columbus Foundation Traditional Grants, 663
Community Foundation for Greater Atlanta Metropolitan Extra Wish Grants, 666
Community Foundation for Greater Atlanta Spark Clayton Grants, 667
Community Foundation for Greater Atlanta Spark Newton Grants, 668

Community Foundation for Greater Buffalo Competitive Grants, 670

Community Foundation for Greater Buffalo Niagara Area Foundation Grants, 673

Community Foundation for Kettering Grants, 676

Community Foundation for San Benito County Grants, 677

Community Foundation for SE Michigan Chelsea Community Foundation General Grant, 680

Community Foundation for the Capital Region Grants, 687

Community Foundation for the National Capital Region Community Leadership Grants, 688

Community Foundation of Bartholomew County Heritage Fund Grants, 690

Community Foundation of Boone County - Women's Grants, 693

Community Foundation of Boone County Grants, 694

Community Foundation of Crawford County, 695

Community Foundation of Eastern Connecticut General Southeast Grants, 696

Community Foundation of Eastern Connecticut Northeast Women and Girls Grants, 697

Community Foundation of Eastern Connecticut Norwich Youth Grants, 699

Community Foundation of Eastern Connecticut Southeast Area Women and Girls Grants, 701

Community Foundation of Grant County Grants, 703

Community Foundation of Greater Chattanooga Grants, 704

Community Foundation of Greater Fort Wayne - Community Endowment and Clarke Endowment Grants, 705

Community Foundation of Greater Fort Wayne - Edna Foundation Grants, 706

Community Foundation of Greater Fort Wayne - John S. and James L. Knight Foundation Donor-Advised Grants, 707

Community Foundation of Greater Greensboro Teen Grantmaking Council Grants, 709

Community Foundation of Henderson County Community Grants, 711

Community Fdn of Howard County Grants, 712

Community Foundation of Jackson County Classroom Education Grants, 713

Community Foundation of Louisville AIDS Project Fund Grants, 716

Community Foundation of Louisville Anna Marble Memorial Fund for Princeton Grants, 717

Community Foundation of Louisville Boyette and Edna Edwards Fund Grants, 718

Community Foundation of Louisville C. E. and S. Endowment for the Parks Fund Grants, 719

Community Foundation of Louisville Delta Dental of Kentucky Fund Grants, 722

Community Foundation of Louisville Dr. W. Barnett Owen Memorial Fund for the Children of Louisville and Jefferson County Grants, 723

Community Foundation of Louisville Education Grants, 724

Community Foundation of Louisville Fund 4 Women and Girls Grants, 725

Community Foundation of Louisville Madi and Jim Tate Fund Grants, 727

Community Foundation of Louisville Winston N. and Nancy H. Bloch Educational Fund Grants, 729

Community Foundation of Louisville Youth Philanthropy Council Grants, 730

Community Fdn of Morgan County Grants, 732

Community Foundation of Muncie and Delaware County Maxon Grants, 734

Community Fdn of Randolph County Grants, 735

Community Fdn of Southern Indiana Grants, 736

Community Foundation of St. Joseph County African American Community Grants, 737

Community Foundation of St. Joseph County Special Project Challenge Grants, 738

Community Foundation of Switzerland County Grants, 739

Community Foundation of Western Massachusetts Grants, 741

Community Foundation Serving Riverside and San Bernardino Counties Impact Grants, 742

Community Memorial Foundation Responsive Grants, 743

Con Edison Corporate Giving Civic Grants, 744

Cone Health Foundation Grants, 745

CONSOL Energy Academic Grants, 746

CONSOL Youth Program Grants, 747

Cooper Tire and Rubber Foundation Grants, 749

Corina Higginson Trust Grants, 750

Cornell Lab of Ornithology Mini-Grants, 751

Countess Moira Charitable Foundation Grants, 752

Courtney S. Turner Charitable Trust Grants, 753

Covidien Partnership for Neighborhood Wellness Grants, 759

Cralle Foundation Grants, 760

Crane Foundation General Grants, 761

Crane Fund Grants, 763

Crayola Champ Creatively Alive Children Grts, 764

Credit Suisse Foundation Education Grants, 765

Cresap Family Foundation Grants, 766

Crescent Porter Hale Foundation Grants, 767

Crystelle Waggoner Charitable Trust Grants, 768

Cudd Foundation Grants, 769

CUNA Mutual Group Fdn Community Grants, 770

Curtis Foundation Grants, 771

Daniel and Nanna Stern Family Fdn Grants, 778

Daniels Fund Early Childhood Education Grants, 781

Daniels Fund K-12 Education Reform Grants, 783

Daniels Fund Youth Development Grants, 784

David Alan and Susan Berkman Rahm Foundation Grants, 785

David and Barbara B. Hirschhorn Foundation Education and Literacy Grants, 786

David and Betty Sacks Foundation Grants, 788

David and Laura Merage Foundation Grants, 789

David M. and Marjorie D. Rosenberg Foundation Grants, 790

David Robinson Foundation Grants, 791

Daviess County Community Foundation Advancing Out-of-School Learning Grants, 792

Dayton Foundation Dayton Youth Enrichment Fund Grant, 795

Dayton Foundation Grants, 796

Dayton Foundation Huber Heights Grants, 797

Dayton Foundation Vandalia-Butler Grants, 799

Dayton Power and Light Company Foundation Signature Grants, 801

Dayton Power and Light Foundation Grants, 802

Deaconess Community Foundation Grants, 803

Dean Foods Community Involvement Grants, 805

Dean Foundation Grants, 806

Dean Witter Foundation Education Grants, 807

Dearborn Community Foundation City of Aurora Grants, 808

DeKalb County Community Foundation - Literacy Grant, 814

DeKalb County Community Foundation Grants, 815

DeKalb County Community Foundation VOICE Grant, 816

Delaware Community Foundation Grants, 817

Delaware Valley Fairness Project Teacher Assistance Grants, 818

Del Mar Foundation Community Grants, 820

Delmarva Power & Light Contributions, 821

Delmarva Power & Light Mini-Grants, 822

Delta Air Lines Foundation Community Enrichment Grants, 823

Delta Air Lines Foundation Youth Development Grants, 824

Dept of Ed Fund for the Improvement of Education-- Partnerships in Character Ed Pilot Projects, 825

Dermody Properties Foundation Grants, 827

Deuce McAllister Catch 22 Foundation Grants, 828

Dining for Women Grants, 831

Dollar General Family Literacy Grants, 835

Dollar General Summer Reading Grants, 836

Dollar General Youth Literacy Grants, 837

DOL Youthbuild Grants, 838

Donald G. Gardner Humanities Tr Youth Grts, 840

Donald W. Reynolds Foundation Children's Discovery Initiative Grants, 841

Don and May Wilkins Charitable Trust Grants, 842

Doree Taylor Charitable Foundation Grants, 843

Dorothea Haus Ross Foundation Grants, 844

Dorrance Family Foundation Grants, 845

Dorr Foundation Grants, 846

Do Something Awards, 847

Dr. and Mrs. Paul Pierce Memorial Foundation Grants, 862

Draper Richards Kaplan Foundation Grants, 864

Dream Weaver Foundation, 865

DTE Energy Foundation Community Development Grants, 866

DTE Energy Foundation Diversity Grants, 867

DTE Energy Foundation Environmental Grants, 868

DTE Energy Foundation Health and Human Services Grants, 869

DTE Energy Foundation Leadership Grants, 870

Dubois County Community Foundation Grants, 871

Duke Energy Foundation Local Impact Grants, 872

Dunspaugh-Dalton Foundation Grants, 873

Dyson Foundation Mid-Hudson Valley Project Support Grants, 874

E. Clayton and Edith P. Gengras, Jr. Foundation Grants, 875

E.J. Grassmann Trust Grants, 876

E.L. Wiegand Foundation Grants, 877

Earl and Maxine Claussen Trust Grants, 878

Eastern Bank Charitable Foundation Partnerships Grants, 881

Eastern Bank Charitable Foundation Targeted Grants, 882

Easton Foundations Archery Facility Grants, 883

Easton Sports Development Foundation National Archery in the Schools Grants, 884

Edward and Helen Bartlett Foundation Grants, 888

Edward F. Swinney Trust Grants, 890

Edward W. and Stella C. Van Houten Memorial Fund Grants, 892

Edyth Bush Charitable Foundation Grants, 893

Effie Allen Little Foundation Grants, 894

Effie and Wofford Cain Foundation Grants, 895

Eide Bailly Resourcefullness Awards, 897

Eileen Fisher Activating Leadership Grants for Women and Girls, 898

Elizabeth Carse Foundation Grants, 899

Elizabeth Huth Coates Charitable Foundation Grants, 900

Elizabeth Morse Genius Charitable Trust Grants, 901

Elkhart County Community Foundation Grants, 903

Ella West Freeman Foundation Grants, 904

Ellen Abbott Gilman Trust Grants, 905

Elmer Roe Deaver Foundation Grants, 906

El Pomar Foundation Anna Keesling Ackerman Fund Grants, 907

El Pomar Foundation Grants, 908

Elsie H. Wilcox Foundation Grants, 909

Emerson Kampen Foundation Grants, 911

Emily Hall Tremaine Foundation Learning Disabilities Grants, 912

Emily O'Neill Sullivan Foundation Grants, 913

Energy by Design Poster Contest, 915

Ensworth Charitable Foundation Grants, 916

Entergy Charitable Foundation Education and Literacy Grants, 917

Entergy Charitable Foundation Low-Income Initiatives and Solutions Grants, 918

Entergy Corporation Micro Grants, 919

Entergy Corporation Open Grants for Arts and Culture, 920

Entergy Corporation Open Grants for Healthy Families, 921

EPA Children's Health Protection Grants, 923

EQT Fdn Education and Workforce Grants, 927

Essex County Community Foundation Dee and King Webster Fund for Greater Lawrence Grants, 929

Essex County Community Foundation Greater
  Lawrence Summer Fund Grants, 932
Essex County Community Foundation Merrimack
  Valley Municipal Business Development and
  Recovery Fund Grants, 933
Essex County Community Foundation Women's
  Fund Grants, 934
Ethel Sergeant Clark Smith Foundation Grants, 935
Eulalie Bloedel Schneider Foundation Grants, 936
Eva Gunther Foundation Fellowships, 937
Evan Frankel Foundation Grants, 938
Evelyn and Walter Haas, Jr. Fund Education
  Opportunities Grants, 939
Evelyn and Walter Haas, Jr. Fund Gay and Lesbian
  Rights Grants, 940
Evelyn and Walter Haas, Jr. Fund Immigrant Rights
  Grants, 941
Evelyn and Walter Haas, Jr. Fund Nonprofit
  Leadership Grants, 942
Ewing Marion Kauffman Foundation Grants, 943
Ezra Jack Keats Foundation Mini-Grants, 944
Ezra M. Cutting Trust Grants, 945
F.M. Kirby Foundation Grants, 946
F.R. Bigelow Foundation Grants, 947
Farmers Insurance Corporate Giving Grants, 948
Faye L. and William L. Cowden Charitable
  Foundation Grants, 950
Fayette County Foundation Grants, 951
FCD New American Children Grants, 952
FCD Young Scholars Program Grants, 953
Fichtenbaum Charitable Trust Grants, 955
Fidelity Charitable Gift Fund Grants, 956
Fidelity Foundation Grants, 957
Fifth Third Bank Corporate Giving, 958
Fifth Third Foundation Grants, 959
FINRA Smart Investing@Your Library Grants, 963
Firelight Foundation Grants, 964
FirstEnergy Foundation Community Grants, 965
FirstEnergy Foundation Science, Technology,
  Engineering, and Mathematics Grants, 966
First Hawaiian Bank Foundation Corporate Giving
  Grants, 967
First Lady's Family Literacy Initiative for Texas
  Family Literacy Trailblazer Grants, 968
First Lady's Family Literacy Initiative for Texas
  Implementation Grants, 969
First Lady's Family Literacy Initiative for Texas
  Planning Grants, 970
First Nations Development Institute Native Arts
  Initiative Grants, 972
First Nations Development Institute Native Language
  Immersion Initiative Grants, 973
First Nations Development Institute Native Youth
  and Culture Fund Grants, 974
Flinn Foundation Scholarships, 977
Florence Foundation Grants, 978
Foundation Beyond Belief Compassionate Impact
  Grants, 986
Foundation Beyond Belief Humanist Grants, 987
Foundation for a Healthy Kentucky Grants, 988
Foundation for Health Enhancement Grants, 990
Foundation for Rural Service Education Grants, 991
Fdn for the Mid South Communities Grants, 992
Foundation for the Mid South Education Grants, 993
Foundation of Herkimer and Oneida Counties Youth
  Sports, Wellness and Recreation Mini-Grants, 994
Foundations of East Chicago Education Grants, 995
Foundations of East Chicago Health Grants, 997
Foundations of East Chicago Youth Development
  Grants, 998
Four County Community Foundation 21st Century
  Education Fund Grants, 999
Four County Community Foundation General
  Grants, 1000
Four County Community Foundation Healthy
  Senior/Healthy Youth Fund Grants, 1001
Four County Community Foundation Kellogg Group
  Grants, 1002
Fourjay Foundation Grants, 1003
Four J Foundation Grants, 1004

Four Lanes Trust Grants, 1005
Francis Beidler Foundation Grants, 1007
Francis L. Abreu Charitable Trust Grants, 1008
Franklin County Community Fdn Grants, 1010
Franklin H. Wells and Ruth L. Wells Foundation
  Grants, 1011
Frank Reed and Margaret Jane Peters Memorial Fund
  Grants, 1013
Frank Reed and Margaret Jane Peters Memorial Fund
  II Grants, 1014
Frank S. Flowers Foundation Grants, 1015
Fred and Gretel Biel Charitable Trust Grants, 1016
Frederick McDonald Trust Grants, 1017
Frederick W. Marzahl Memorial Fund Grants, 1018
Fremont Area Community Foundation Amazing X
  Grants, 1019
Fremont Area Community Foundation Community
  Grants, 1020
Fremont Area Community Foundation Education
  Mini-Grants, 1021
Fremont Area Community Foundation Youth
  Advisory Committee Grants, 1022
Friends of Hawaii Charities Grants, 1024
Fuller Foundation Youth At Risk Grants, 1028
G.N. Wilcox Trust Grants, 1031
Gamble Foundation Grants, 1032
Gannett Foundation Community Action Grants, 1033
Gardner Foundation Grants, 1035
Gardner W. and Joan G. Heidrick, Jr. Foundation
  Grants, 1036
Gene Haas Foundation, 1038
General Motors Foundation Grants, 1039
George A. & Grace L. Long Fdn Grants, 1041
George and Ruth Bradford Foundation Grants, 1042
George A Ohl Jr. Foundation Grants, 1043
George F. Baker Trust Grants, 1046
George Graham and Elizabeth Galloway Smith
  Foundation Grants, 1047
George H. and Jane A. Mifflin Memorial Fund
  Grants, 1048
George H.C. Ensworth Memorial Fund Grants, 1049
George H. Sandy Foundation Grants, 1050
George I. Alden Trust Grants, 1051
George J. and Effie L. Seay Foundation Grants, 1052
George Kress Foundation Grants, 1053
George P. Davenport Trust Fund Grants, 1054
George W. Codrington Charitable Foundation
  Grants, 1055
George W.P. Magee Trust Grants, 1056
George W. Wells Foundation Grants, 1057
Georgia Pacific Fdn Entrepreneurship Grants, 1059
Georgia Council for the Arts Education Grants, 1060
Geraldine R. Dodge Fdn Education Grants, 1061
Gerber Fdn West Michigan Youth Grants, 1065
Gertrude & William C. Wardlaw Grants, 1067
Gil and Dody Weaver Foundation Grants, 1071
Giving Gardens Challenge Grants, 1072
Global Fund for Women Grants, 1073
GMFUS Balkan Trust for Democracy Grants, 1075
GNOF Cox Charities of New Orleans Grants, 1079
GNOF Exxon-Mobil Grants, 1080
GNOF Gert Community Fund Grants, 1082
GNOF IMPACT Grants for Arts and Culture, 1083
GNOF IMPACT Grants for Youth Dev, 1084
GNOF IMPACT Kahn-Oppenheim Tr Grts, 1087
GNOF New Orleans Works Grants, 1088
GNOF Norco Community Grants, 1089
GNOF Organizational Effectiveness Grants and
  Workshops, 1090
GNOF Plaquemines Community Grants, 1091
GNOF Stand Up For Our Children Grants, 1092
Go Daddy Cares Charitable Contributions, 1093
Golden Heart Community Foundation Grants, 1094
Grace Bersted Foundation Grants, 1097
Graham Family Charitable Foundation Grants, 1099
Gray Family Fdn Camp Maintenance Grants, 1104
Gray Family Foundation Community Field Trips
  Grants, 1105
Gray Family Foundation Geography Education
  Grants, 1106

Gray Family Fdn Outdoor School Grants, 1107
Greater Milwaukee Foundation Grants, 1109
Greater Saint Louis Community Fdn Grants, 1110
Greater Sitka Legacy Fund Grants, 1111
Greater Tacoma Community Foundation Fund for
  Women and Girls Grants, 1112
Greater Tacoma Community Foundation General
  Operating Grants, 1113
Greater Tacoma Community Foundation Youth
  Program Grants, 1115
Green River Area Community Fdn Grants, 1117
Greenspun Family Foundation Grants, 1118
Grifols Community Outreach Grants, 1122
Grotto Foundation Project Grants, 1123
Grundy Foundation Grants, 1124
GTECH After School Advantage Grants, 1125
GTRCF Boys and Girls Club of Grand Traverse
  Endowment Grants, 1126
GTRCF Elk Rapids Area Community Endowment
  Grants, 1127
GTRCF Healthy Youth and Healthy Seniors
  Endowment Grants, 1130
GTRCF Joan Rajkovich McGarry Family Education
  Endowment Grants, 1131
GTRCF Youth Endowment Grants, 1133
Gulf Coast Foundation of Community Operating
  Grants, 1134
Gulf Coast Foundation of Community Program
  Grants, 1135
Guy I. Bromley Trust Grants, 1136
H.A. and Mary K. Chapman Charitable Trust
  Grants, 1137
H.B. Fuller Foundation Grants, 1138
Haddad Foundation Grants, 1139
HAF Community Grants, 1141
HAF Don and Bettie Albright Endowment Fund
  Grants, 1142
HAF Joe Alexandre Mem Family Fund Grants, 1145
HAF Laurence and Elaine Allen Memorial Fund
  Grants, 1146
HAF Native Cultures Fund Grants, 1148
HAF Southern Humboldt Grants, 1150
Hahl Proctor Charitable Trust Grants, 1151
Hall-Perrine Foundation Grants, 1152
Hampton Roads Community Foundation Abused
  People Grants, 1153
Hampton Roads Community Foundation Education
  Grants, 1157
Hampton Roads Community Foundation
  Environment Grants, 1158
Hampton Roads Community Foundation Nonprofit
  Facilities Improvement Grants, 1159
Hancock County Community Foundation - Field of
  Interest Grants, 1161
Hank Aaron Chasing the Dream Fdn Grants, 1162
Hannaford Charitable Foundation Grants, 1163
Hannaford Supermarkets Community Giving, 1164
Hardin County Community Foundation Grants, 1167
Harmony Grove Foundation Grants, 1169
Harmony Project Grants, 1170
Harold Brooks Foundation Grants, 1172
Harold K.L. Castle Foundation Public Education
  Redesign and Enhancement Grants, 1173
Harold K.L. Castle Foundation Strengthening
  Windward Oahu Communities Grants, 1174
Harold K.L. Castle Foundation Windward Youth
  Leadership Fund Grants, 1175
Harris and Eliza Kempner Fund Ed Grants, 1176
Harris Foundation Grants, 1177
Harrison County Community Fdn Grants, 1178
Harrison County Community Foundation Signature
  Grants, 1179
Harry and Jeanette Weinberg Fdn Grants, 1182
Harry B. and Jane H. Brock Foundation Grants, 1183
Harry Frank Guggenheim Foundation Research
  Grants, 1184
Hartford Foundation Regular Grants, 1185
Hartley Foundation Grants, 1186
Harvey Randall Wickes Foundation Grants, 1188
Hasbro Children's Fund Grants, 1189

Hattie M. Strong Foundation Grants, 1194
Hatton W. Sumners Foundation for the Study and Teaching of Self Government Grants, 1196
Hawai'i Community Foundation Bernice and Conrad von Hamm Fund Grants, 1197
Hawai'i Community Foundation Children's Trust Fund Community Awareness: Child Abuse and Neglect Prevention Grants, 1198
Hawai'i Community Foundation East Hawaii Fund Grants, 1199
Hawai'i Community Foundation Family Literacy and Hawaii Pizza Hut Literacy Grants, 1201
Hawai'i Community Foundation Kuki'o Community Fund Grants, 1202
Hawai'i Community Foundation Lana'i Community Benefit Fund, 1203
Hawai'i Community Foundation Richard Smart Fund Grants, 1204
Hawai'i Community Foundation Robert E. Black Fund Grants, 1205
Hawai'i SFCA Art Bento Program @ HiSAM Grants, 1210
Hawaiian Electric Industries Charitable Foundation Grants, 1211
Hawaii Community Foundation Omidyar Ohana Fund Grants, 1213
Hawaii Community Foundation Promising Minds Grants, 1215
Hawaii Community Foundation Reverend Takie Okumura Family Grants, 1216
Hawaii Community Foundation Sanford Harmony Pillars of Peace Grants, 1217
Hawaii Electric Industries Charitable Foundation Grants, 1218
Hazel and Walter T. Bales Foundation Grants, 1220
Hazen Foundation Public Education Grants, 1221
HBF Pathways Out of Poverty Grants, 1222
Hearst Foundations Culture Grants, 1223
Hearst Foundations Social Service Grants, 1224
Hearst Foundations United States Senate Youth Grants, 1225
HEI Charitable Foundation Grants, 1226
Helen Bader Foundation Grants, 1227
Helen E. Ellis Charitable Trust Grants, 1228
Helen Gertrude Sparks Charitable Trust Grants, 1230
Helen Irwin Littauer Educational Trust Grants, 1231
Helen V. Brach Foundation Grants, 1232
Hendricks County Community Fdn Grants, 1234
Henry and Ruth Blaustein Rosenberg Foundation Education Grants, 1236
Henry and Ruth Blaustein Rosenberg Foundation Youth Development Grants, 1237
Henry County Community Foundation - TASC Youth Grants, 1238
Henry E. Niles Foundation Grants, 1240
Henry F. Koch Residual Trust Grants, 1241
Herbert A. and Adrian W. Woods Foundation Grants, 1243
Herbert Hoover Presidential Library Association Bus Travel Grants, 1244
Herman P. and Sophia Taubman Fdn Grants, 1247
Highmark Corporate Giving Grants, 1248
Hill Crest Foundation Grants, 1249
Hillsdale County Community Foundation General Grants, 1250
Hillsdale County Community Foundation Love Your Community Grants, 1251
HLTA Visitor Industry Charity Walk Grant, 1254
Honeywell Corporation Got 2B Safe Contest, 1256
Honeywell Corporation Leadership Challenge Academy, 1258
Horace A. Kimball and S. Ella Kimball Foundation Grants, 1260
Horace A. Moses Charitable Trust Grants, 1261
HSBC Corporate Giving Grants, 1266
HSFCA Biennium Grants, 1267
HSFCA Folk and Traditional Arts Grants - Culture Learning, 1268
Hubbard Broadcasting Foundation Grants, 1269
Hubbard Family Foundation Grants, 1270

Hubbard Family Foundation Grants, 1271
Hubbard Farms Charitable Foundation Grants, 1272
Huisking Foundation Grants, 1274
Humana Foundation Grants, 1275
Human Source Foundation Grants, 1276
Hungry for Music Instrument Gifts, 1277
Huntington Clinical Foundation Grants, 1278
Huntington County Community Foundation Classroom Education Grants, 1279
Huntington County Community Foundation Make a Difference Grants, 1280
ICCF Youth Advisory Council Grants, 1282
Iddings Foundation Major Project Grants, 1284
Iddings Foundation Medium Project Grants, 1285
Iddings Foundation Small Project Grants, 1286
Ifuku Family Foundation Grants, 1287
IIE 911 Armed Forces Scholarships, 1288
Ike and Roz Friedman Foundation Grants, 1289
ILA Grants for Literacy Projects in Countries with Developing Economies, 1292
Illinois Arts Council Youth Employment in the Arts Program Grants, 1294
Illinois DNR School Habitat Action Grants, 1296
Illinois DNR Youth Recreation Corps Grants, 1297
IMLS National Leadership Grants for Libraries, 1299
Indiana OCRA Rural Capacity Grants (RCG), 1301
ING Foundation Grants, 1302
Inland Empire Community Foundation Capacity Building for IE Nonprofits Grants, 1306
Inland Empire Community Foundation Coachella Valley Youth Grants, 1307
Inland Empire Community Foundation Native Youth Grants, 1308
Inland Empire Community Foundation Riverside Youth Grants, 1309
Inland Empire Community Foundation San Bernardino Youth Grants, 1310
Intel Corporation Community Grants, 1311
Intel Corporation Int Community Grants, 1312
IRC Community Collaboratives for Refugee Women and Youth Grants, 1313
Irving S. Gilmore Foundation Grants, 1314
Isabel Allende Foundation Esperanza Grants, 1315
Island Insurance Foundation Grants, 1316
J. Bulow Campbell Foundation Grants, 1319
J. Edwin Treakle Foundation Grants, 1320
J. Knox Gholston Foundation Grants, 1321
J. Marion Sims Foundation Teachers' Pet Grant, 1322
J.W. Gardner II Foundation Grants, 1323
J. Walton Bissell Foundation Grants, 1325
J. Watumull Fund Grants, 1326
J. Willard and Alice S. Marriott Fdn Grants, 1327
J. William Gholston Foundation Grants, 1328
Jack and Dorothy Byrne Foundation Grants, 1329
Jack H. and William M. Light Charitable Trust Grants, 1330
Jack Kent Cooke Fdn Good Neighbor Grants, 1331
Jack Kent Cooke Foundation Summer Enrichment Grants, 1332
Jack Kent Cooke Fdn Young Artist Awards, 1333
Jack Satter Foundation Grants, 1334
Jacob and Hilda Blaustein Foundation Israel Program Grants, 1335
Jacob G. Schmidlapp Trusts Grants, 1336
James and Abigail Campbell Family Foundation Grants, 1337
James F. and Marion L. Miller Fdn Grants, 1338
James Ford Bell Foundation Grants, 1339
James Graham Brown Foundation Grants, 1340
James Lee Sorenson Family Impact Foundation Grants, 1342
James LeVoy Sorenson Foundation Grants, 1343
James M. Collins Foundation Grants, 1344
James S. Copley Foundation Grants, 1345
Jane's Trust Grants, 1346
Jane Bradley Pettit Foundation Community and Social Development Grants, 1347
Janet Spencer Weekes Foundation Grants, 1348
Janson Foundation Grants, 1350

Japan Foundation Los Angeles Contests Designed for Japanese-Language Learners Grants, 1351
Japan Foundation Los Angeles Grants for Japanese-Language Courses, 1352
Japan Foundation Los Angeles Japanese-Language Teaching Materials Purchase Grants, 1353
Japan Foundation Los Angeles Mini-Grants for Japanese Arts & Culture, 1354
Japan Foundation New York Small Grants for Arts and Culture, 1355
Japan Foundation New York World Heritage Photo Panel Exhibition, 1356
Jaquelin Hume Foundation Grants, 1357
Jayne and Leonard Abess Foundation Grants, 1358
Jeffris Wood Foundation Grants, 1359
Jennings County Community Fdn Grants, 1360
Jennings County Community Foundation Women's Giving Circle Grant, 1361
Jessica Stevens Community Foundation Grants, 1363
Jim Blevins Foundation Grants, 1365
Jim Moran Foundation Grants, 1366
Joan Bentinck-Smith Charitable Fdn Grants, 1367
John and Marcia Goldman Foundation Youth Development Grants, 1368
John Clarke Trust Grants, 1369
John D. and Katherine A. Johnston Foundation Grants, 1370
John F. Kennedy Center for the Performing Arts National Rosemary Kennedy Internship, 1371
John G. Duncan Charitable Trust Grants, 1372
John H. and Wilhelmina D. Harland Charitable Foundation Children and Youth Grants, 1374
John M. Weaver Foundation Grants, 1376
John P. Ellbogen Fdn Community Grants, 1377
Johnson Controls Foundation Arts and Culture Grants, 1378
Johnson Foundation Wingspread Conference Support Program, 1381
Johnson Scholarship Foundation Grants, 1382
John W. Anderson Foundation Grants, 1383
Joni Elaine Templeton Foundation Grants, 1384
Joseph H. and Florence A. Roblee Foundation Children and Youth Grants, 1385
Joseph H. and Florence A. Roblee Foundation Education Grants, 1386
Joseph H. and Florence A. Roblee Foundation Family Grants, 1387
Joseph Henry Edmondson Foundation Grants, 1388
Joseph S. Stackpole Charitable Trust Grants, 1390
Journal Gazette Foundation Grants, 1391
Jovid Foundation Employment Training Grants, 1392
Joyce and Randy Seckman Charitable Foundation Grants, 1393
JP Morgan Chase Fdn Arts and Culture Grants, 1394
Julia and Tunnicliff Fox Chartbl Trust Grants, 1397
Julia Richardson Brown Foundation Grants, 1398
Julia Temple Davis Brown Foundation Grants, 1399
Julius N. Frankel Foundation Grants, 1400
Kaiser Permanente Hawaii Region Community Grants, 1406
Kalamazoo Community Foundation Early Childhood Learning and School Readiness Grants, 1407
Kalamazoo Community Foundation Good Neighbor Grants, 1408
Kalamazoo Community Foundation John E. Fetzer Institute Fund Grants, 1410
Kalamazoo Community Foundation LBGT Equality Fund Grants, 1411
Kalamazoo Community Foundation Youth Development Grants, 1412
K and F Baxter Family Foundation Grants, 1413
Kansas Health Fdn Major Initiatives Grants, 1414
Kate B. Reynolds Charitable Trust Poor and Needy Grants, 1417
Katharine Matthies Foundation Grants, 1418
Kathryne Beynon Foundation Grants, 1420
Katrine Menzing Deakins Chartbl Trust Grants, 1422
Kawabe Memorial Fund Grants, 1423
Kelvin and Eleanor Smith Foundation Grants, 1424
Kenai Peninsula Foundation Grants, 1425

Kenneth T. and Eileen L. Norris Fdn Grants, 1427
Kentucky Arts Cncl Access Assistance Grants, 1428
Ketchikan Community Foundation Grants, 1429
Kettering Family Foundation Grants, 1430
Kimball Foundation Grants, 1432
Kimball International-Habig Foundation Education
    Grants, 1433
Kinder Morgan Foundation Grants, 1436
Kindle Project SpiderWeave Flow Fund Grants, 1437
Kind World Foundation Grants, 1438
Kirby Laing Foundation Grants, 1439
Koch Family Foundation (Annapolis) Grants, 1444
Kodak Community Relations Grants, 1445
Kodiak Community Foundation Grants, 1446
Kohl's Cares Scholarships, 1447
Kopp Family Foundation Grants, 1448
Koret Foundation Grants, 1449
Kosasa Foundation Grants, 1450
Kosciusko County Community Foundation
    Endowment Youth Services (KEYS) Grants, 1451
Kosciusko County Community Fdn Grants, 1452
Kovler Family Foundation Grants, 1455
Kovler Family Foundation Grants, 1454
Kroger Company Donations, 1456
Laclede Gas Charitable Trust Grants, 1457
LaGrange County Community Fdn Grants, 1458
LaGrange Independent Foundation for Endowments
    (L.I.F.E.), 1459
Laidlaw Foundation Youth Organizaing Initiatives
    Grants, 1462
Lalor Foundation Postdoctoral Fellowships, 1464
Land O'Lakes Fdn California Region Grants, 1465
Land O'Lakes Foundation Mid-Atlantic Grants, 1467
Lands' End Corporate Giving Program, 1468
Laura B. Vogler Foundation Grants, 1470
Laura Bush Foundation for America's Libraries
    Grants, 1471
Laura Musser Intercultural Harmony Grants, 1472
Laura L. Adams Foundation Grants, 1473
Laura Moore Cunningham Foundation Grants, 1474
Laurie H. Wollmuth Charitable Trust Grants, 1476
Lavina Parker Trust Grants, 1477
Lee and Ramona Bass Foundation Grants, 1478
LEGO Children's Fund Grants, 1480
Leo Goodwin Foundation Grants, 1482
Leola Osborn Trust Grants, 1483
Leo Niessen Jr., Charitable Trust Grants, 1484
Leonsis Foundation Grants, 1485
Lewis H. Humphreys Charitable Trust Grants, 1486
LGA Family Foundation Grants, 1487
Liberty Bank Foundation Grants, 1488
Libra Foundation Grants, 1489
Lied Foundation Trust Grants, 1490
Lilly Endowment Summer Youth Grants, 1492
Lily Palmer Fry Memorial Trust Grants, 1493
Linden Foundation Grants, 1494
Linford & Mildred White Charitable Grants, 1495
Lisa and Douglas Goldman Fund Grants, 1496
LISC Affordable Housing Grants, 1497
LISC Capacity Building Grants, 1498
LISC Education Grants, 1500
LISC Financial Stability Grants, 1501
Lloyd G. Balfour Foundation Attleboro-Specific
    Charities Grants, 1502
Lloyd G. Balfour Foundation Scholarships, 1503
Locations Foundation Legacy Grants, 1504
Long Island Community Foundation Grants, 1507
Lotus 88 Foundation for Women and Children
    Grants, 1508
Louie M. and Betty M. Phillips Fdn Grants, 1509
Louis and Sandra Berkman Foundation Grants, 1510
Louis Calder Foundation Grants, 1511
Lubrizol Corporation Community Grants, 1512
Lubrizol Foundation Grants, 1513
Lucy Downing Nisbet Charitable Fund Grants, 1515
Luella Kemper Trust Grants, 1517
Lumpkin Family Foundation Strong Community
    Leadership Grants, 1519
M.A. Rikard Charitable Trust Grants, 1521
M. Bastian Family Foundation Grants, 1522

M.J. Murdock Charitable Trust General Grants, 1524
Mabel A. Horne Fund Grants, 1525
Mabel F. Hoffman Charitable Trust Grants, 1526
Mabel Louise Riley Foundation Grants, 1529
Mabel Y. Hughes Charitable Trust Grants, 1530
Macquarie Bank Foundation Grants, 1532
Madison Community Foundation Altrusa
    International of Madison Grants, 1533
Madison Community Foundation Fund for Children
    Grants, 1534
Madison Community Foundation Grants, 1535
Madison County Community Foundation General
    Grants, 1537
Maine Women's Fund Econ Security Grants, 1546
Maine Women's Fund Girls' Grantmaking Intv, 1547
Make Sense Foundation Grants, 1548
Malone Family Foundation Atypical Development
    Initiative Grants, 1549
Manuel D. and Rhoda Mayerson Fdn Grants, 1550
March of Dimes Program Grants, 1552
Marcia and Otto Koehler Foundation Grants, 1553
Mardag Foundation Grants, 1554
Margaret and James A. Elkins Jr. Fdn Grants, 1555
Margaret T. Morris Foundation Grants, 1557
Marie C. and Joseph C. Wilson Foundation Rochester
    Small Grants, 1559
Marietta McNeill Morgan and Samuel Tate Morgan
    Jr. Trust Grants, 1560
Marin Community Foundation Arts Education
    Grants, 1562
Marin Community Foundation Arts in the
    Community Grants, 1563
Marin Community Foundation Closing the Education
    Achievement Gap Grants, 1564
Marin Community Foundation Ending the Cycle of
    Poverty Grants, 1565
Marin Community Foundation Improving
    Community Health Grants, 1566
Marin Community Foundation Social Justice and
    Interfaith Understanding Grants, 1567
Marion and Miriam Rose Fund Grants, 1569
Marion Gardner Jackson Charitable Trust Grts, 1570
Marion I. and Henry J. Knott Foundation
    Discretionary Grants, 1571
Marion I. and Henry J. Knott Foundation Standard
    Grants, 1572
Marisla Foundation Human Services Grants, 1573
Marjorie Moore Charitable Foundation Grants, 1574
Mark W. Coy Foundation Grants, 1575
Marquette Bank Neighborhood Commit Grants, 1577
Marshall County Community Fdn Grants, 1579
Marsh Corporate Grants, 1580
Martha Holden Jennings Foundation Grants-to-
    Educators, 1581
Martin Family Foundation Grants, 1583
Mary A. Crocker Trust Grants, 1584
Mary Black Foundation Active Living Grants, 1585
Mary Black Foundation Early Childhood
    Development Grants, 1586
Mary D. and Walter F. Frear Eleemosynary Trust
    Grants, 1588
Mary E. Babcock Foundation, 1589
Mary K. Chapman Foundation Grants, 1590
Maryland State Dept of Education 21st Century
    Community Learning Centers Grants, 1593
Maryland State Dept of Education Coordinating
    Entity Services for the Maryland Child Care Res
    Centers Network Grants, 1594
Maryland State Department of Education Judith P.
    Hoyer Early Care and Ed Center Grants, 1595
Maryland State Department of Education Striving
    Readers Comprehensive Literacy Grants, 1596
Mary Owen Borden Foundation Grants, 1597
Mary S. and David C. Corbin Fdn Grants, 1598
Mary W.B. Curtis Trust Grants, 1599
Mary Wilmer Covey Charitable Trust Grants, 1600
Massachusetts Cultural Council Local Cultural
    Council (LCC) Grants, 1601
Massachusetts Cultural Cncl YouthReach Grts, 1602
Mathile Family Foundation Grants, 1604

Matilda R. Wilson Fund Grants, 1605
Matson Adahi I Tano' Grants, 1606
Matson Community Giving Grants, 1607
Maurice Amado Foundation Grants, 1609
Maurice J. Masserini Charitable Trust Grants, 1610
Maurice R. Robinson Fund Grants, 1611
May and Stanley Smith Charitable Trust Grants, 1613
McCarthy Family Fdn Charity Fund Grants, 1614
McCombs Foundation Grants, 1615
McConnell Foundation Grants, 1616
McCune Charitable Foundation Grants, 1617
McCune Foundation Education Grants, 1618
McCune Foundation Humananities Grants, 1619
McGraw-Hill Companies Community Grants, 1620
McInerny Foundation Grants, 1622
McLean Contributionship Grants, 1623
McLean Foundation Grants, 1624
Mead Family Foundation Grants, 1625
Meadows Foundation Grants, 1626
Mead Witter Foundation Grants, 1628
Medtronic Foundation Community Link Arts, Civic,
    and Culture Grants, 1629
Medtronic Foundation CommunityLink Health
    Grants, 1630
Medtronic Foundation Strengthening Health Systems
    Grants, 1632
Memorial Foundation for Children Grants, 1633
Mercedes-Benz USA Corporate Contributions
    Grants, 1634
Merck Family Fund Youth Transforming Urban
    Communities Grants, 1636
Mericos Foundation Grants, 1637
Meriden Foundation Grants, 1638
Merrick Foundation Grants, 1640
Merrick Foundation Grants, 1639
Meta and George Rosenberg Fdn Grants, 1644
MetLife Fdn Preparing Young People Grants, 1645
MetroWest Health Foundation Grants to Reduce
    the Incidence of High Risk Behaviors Among
    Adolescents, 1646
Metzger-Price Fund Grants, 1647
Meyer Foundation Education Grants, 1649
Meyer Fdn Healthy Communities Grants, 1650
Meyer Memorial Trust Responsive Grants, 1653
MFRI Community Mobilization Grants, 1654
MGM Resorts Foundation Community Grants, 1655
MGN Family Foundation Grants, 1656
Michael and Susan Dell Foundation Grants, 1657
Michelin North America Challenge Education, 1660
Micron Technology Fdn Community Grants, 1664
Microsoft Software Donations, 1665
Microsoft YouthSpark Grants, 1666
Middlesex Savings Charitable Foundation
    Educational Opportunities Grants, 1670
Mile High United Way Stratc Investment Grts, 1671
Milken Family Foundation Grants, 1672
Miller Foundation Grants, 1673
Mill Spring Foundation Grants, 1674
Milton and Sally Avery Arts Foundation Grants, 1675
Mimi and Peter Haas Fund Grants, 1677
Minnie M. Jones Trust Grants, 1678
Mockingbird Foundation Grants, 1680
Monsanto Science and Math K-12 Grants, 1683
Montana Community Foundation Grants, 1687
Montana Community Fdn Women's Grants, 1688
Montgomery County Community Foundation Health
    and Human Services Fund Grants, 1689
Moody Foundation Grants, 1692
Moran Family Foundation Grants, 1693
Morris Stulsaft Foundation Early Childhood
    Education Grants, 1696
Morris Stulsaft Foundation Educational Support for
    Children Grants, 1697
Morris Stulsaft Foundation Participation in the the
    Arts Grants, 1698
Morris Stulsaft Foundation Pathways to Work
    Grants, 1699
Morton K. and Jane Blaustein Foundation
    Educational Opportunity Grants, 1700
Moses Kimball Fund Grants, 1701

Motiv8 Foundation Grants, 1702
Mr. Holland's Opus Foundation Melody Grants, 1703
Mr. Holland's Opus Foundation Special Projects Grants, 1705
Ms. Foundation for Women Building Democracy Grants, 1706
Ms. Fdn for Women Economic Justice Grants, 1707
Ms. Fdn for Women Ending Violence Grants, 1708
Mt. Sinai Health Care Foundation Health of the Urban Community Grants, 1710
NAA Foundation High Five Grants, 1711
Narragansett Number One Foundation Grants, 1712
Natalie W. Furniss Foundation Grants, 1715
Nathalie and Gladys Dalkowitz Charitable Trust Grants, 1716
Nathan B. and Florence R. Burt Fdn Grants, 1717
Nathan Cummings Foundation Grants, 1718
Nathaniel and Elizabeth P. Stevens Foundation Grants, 1719
National 4-H Council Grants, 1720
National 4-H Youth in Action Awards, 1721
National Schools of Character Awards Program, 1723
National Wildlife Federation Craig Tufts Educational Scholarship, 1724
NCMCF Youth Advisory Council Grants, 1727
NCSS Award for Global Understanding, 1728
NCSS Christa McA Reach for the Stars Awd, 1730
NEA Fdn Read Across America Event Grants, 1731
NEA Student Program Communities Redefining Education Advocacy Through Empowerment (CREATE) Grants, 1733
NEH Family and Youth Programs in American History Grants, 1734
NEH Picturing America Awards, 1735
Nellie Mae Education Foundation District-Level Change Grants, 1736
Nell J. Redfield Foundation Grants, 1737
Nevada Community Foundation Grants, 1741
New Earth Foundation Grants, 1743
Newfoundland and Labrador Arts Council ArtSmarts Grants, 1744
New Hampshire Charitable Foundation Neil and Louise Tillotson Fund - Empower Coös Youth Grants, 1748
New Jersey Center for Hispanic Policy, Research and Development Innovative Initiatives Grants, 1750
New Jersey Office of Faith Based Initiatives English as a Second Language Grants, 1751
New Jersey Office of Faith Based Initiatives Services to At Risk Youth Grants, 1752
NFL Charities NFL Player Foundation Grants, 1754
NFL Charities Pro Bowl Community Grants in Hawaii, 1755
NHSCA Artist Residence Grants, 1756
NHSCA Conservation License Plate Grants, 1757
NHSCA Youth Arts Project Grants: For Extended Arts Learning, 1758
Nissan Neighbors Grants, 1762
NJSCA Artists in Education Residencies, 1763
NJSCA Arts Ed Special Initiative Grants, 1764
Noble County Community Foundation Grants, 1765
Norcliffe Foundation Grants, 1766
Norman Foundation Grants, 1767
North Dakota Community Foundation Grants, 1768
Northern Chautauqua Community Foundation Community Grants, 1769
Northrop Grumman Corporation Grants, 1772
Northrop Grumman Foundation Grants, 1773
NRA Foundation Grants, 1774
NSTA Distinguished Informal Science Education Award, 1777
NSTA Faraday Science Communicator Award, 1778
NYFA Artists in the School Community Planning Grants, 1779
NYSCA Arts Education: Community-based Learning Grants, 1780
NYSCA Arts Education: General Operating Support Grants, 1781
NYSCA Arts Education: General Program Support Grants, 1782

NYSCA Arts Education: Local Capacity Building Grants (Regrants), 1783
NYSCA Arts Ed: Services to the Field Grants, 1784
NYSCA Electronic Media and Film: General Program Support, 1787
NYSCA Electronic Media and Film: Workspace Grants, 1789
NYSCA Music: Commty Music Schools Grants, 1790
NYSCA Music: Gen Operating Support Grants, 1791
NYSCA Music: Gen Program Support Grants, 1792
NYSCA Special Arts Services: General Program Support Grants, 1793
NYSCA Special Arts Services: Instruction and Training Grants, 1794
NYSCA Theatre: Prof Performances Grants, 1795
NZDIA Community Org Grants Scheme, 1796
NZDIA Lottery Minister's Discretionary Fund Grants, 1797
O. Max Gardner Foundation Grants, 1798
Oak Foundation Child Abuse Grants, 1799
Ober Kaler Community Grants, 1801
OceanFirst Foundation Summer Camp Grants, 1804
Office Depot Corporation Community Relations Grants, 1805
Office Depot Foundation Education Grants, 1806
OHA Community Grants for Culture, 1808
OHA Community Grants for Education, 1809
Ohio County Community Foundation Board of Directors Grants, 1811
Ohio County Community Foundation Grants, 1812
Ohio County Community Fdn Mini-Grants, 1813
Olga Sipolin Children's Fund Grants, 1815
Olive B. Cole Foundation Grants, 1816
Olive Higgins Prouty Foundation Grants, 1817
Olive Smith Browning Charitable Trust Grants, 1818
Olivia R. Gardner Foundation Grants, 1819
OMNOVA Solutions Fdn Education Grants, 1820
Onan Family Foundation Grants, 1821
OneFamily Foundation Grants, 1822
Ontario Arts Council Artists in Communities and Schools Project Grants, 1823
Ontario Arts Council Arts Organizations in Communities and Schools Operating Grants, 1824
Ontario Arts Council Indigenous Culture Fund Indigenous Artists in Communities and Schools Project Grants, 1825
Oppenstein Brothers Foundation Grants, 1827
Orange County Community Foundation Grants, 1829
Orange County Community Foundation Grants, 1828
Ordean Foundation Catalyst Grants, 1830
Ordean Foundation Partnership Grants, 1831
Oregon Community Fdn Community Grants, 1833
Oregon Community Foundation Community Recovery Grants, 1834
Oregon Community Foundation Edna E. Harrell Community Children's Fund Grants, 1835
Oregon Community Foundation K-12 Student Success: Out-of-School Grants, 1836
OSF Baltimore Community Fellowships, 1838
OSF Baltimore Criminal and Juve Justice Grts, 1839
OSF Baltimore Education and Youth Development Grants, 1840
OSF Early Childhood Program Grants, 1841
OSF Education Program Grants in Kyrgyzstan, 1842
OSF Education Support Program Grants, 1843
OSF Youth Action Fund Grants in Kyrgyzstan, 1846
OtterCares Impact Fund Grants, 1849
OtterCares Inspiration Fund Grants, 1850
OtterCares NoCO Fund Grants, 1851
P. Buckley Moss Foundation for Children's Education Endowed Scholarships, 1854
P. Buckley Moss Foundation for Children's Education Teacher Grants, 1855
Pacers Foundation Be Drug-Free Grants, 1856
Pacers Foundation Be Educated Grants, 1857
Pacers Foundation Be Healthy and Fit Grants, 1858
Pacers Foundation Be Tolerant Grants, 1859
Pacers Foundation Indiana Fever's Be YOUnique Fund Grants, 1860
PacifiCare Foundation Grants, 1861

Packard Foundation Children, Families, and Communities Grants, 1862
Packard Foundation Local Grants, 1863
Pajaro Valley Community Health Trust Oral Health: Prevention & Access Grants, 1866
Parkersburg Area Community Foundation Action Grants, 1871
Paso del Norte Health Foundation Grants, 1874
PAS Sabian Larrie London Memorial Schol, 1877
PAS Zildjian Family Opportunity Fund Grants, 1878
Patricia Kisker Foundation Grants, 1879
Paul and Edith Babson Foundation Grants, 1881
PCA Arts in Education Residencies, 1885
PCA Arts Organizations and Arts Programs Grants for Art Museums, 1888
PCA Arts Organizations and Arts Programs Grants for Arts Education Organizations, 1889
PCA Arts Organizations and Arts Programs Grants for Crafts, 1891
PCA Arts Organizations and Arts Programs Grants for Visual Arts, 1898
PCA Entry Track Arts Organizations and Arts Programs Grants for Art Museums, 1900
PCA Entry Track Arts Organizations and Arts Programs Grants for Arts Education Organizations, 1901
PCA Entry Track Arts Organizations and Arts Programs Grants for Crafts, 1903
PCA Entry Track Arts Organizations and Arts Programs Grants for Visual Arts, 1912
PCA Pennsylvania Partners in the Arts Program Stream Grants, 1914
PCA Pennsylvania Partners in the Arts Project Stream Grants, 1915
PDF Community Organizing Grants, 1920
PDF Fiscal Sponsorship Grant, 1921
Pentair Foundation Education and Community Grants, 1934
PepsiCo Foundation Grants, 1935
Percy B. Ferebee Endowment Grants, 1936
Perkin Fund Grants, 1937
Perkins Charitable Foundation Grants, 1939
Perry and Sandy Massie Foundation Grants, 1941
Peter and Elizabeth C. Tower Foundation Intellectual Disabilities Grants, 1944
Peter and Elizabeth C. Tower Foundation Learning Disability Grants, 1945
Peter and Elizabeth C. Tower Foundation Mental Health Grants, 1946
Peter and Elizabeth C. Tower Foundation Small Grants, 1947
Peter and Elizabeth C. Tower Foundation Substance Use Disorders Grants, 1948
Peter and Elizabeth C. Tower Foundation Technology Initiative Grants, 1949
Peter and Elizabeth C. Tower Foundation Technology Planning Grants, 1950
Petersburg Community Foundation Grants, 1951
Pettus Foundation Grants, 1952
PeyBack Foundation Grants, 1953
Peyton Anderson Foundation Grants, 1954
PG&E Bright Ideas Grants, 1956
PG&E Community Vitality Grants, 1957
PGE Foundation Grants, 1958
Philanthrofund Foundation Grants, 1959
Phil Hardin Foundation Grants, 1960
Philip Boyle Foundation Grants, 1961
Philip L. Graham Fund Education Grants, 1962
Phoenix Coyotes Charities Grants, 1963
Phoenix Suns Charities Grants, 1964
Piedmont Health Foundation Grants, 1965
Piedmont Natural Gas Corporate and Charitable Contributions, 1966
Piedmont Natural Gas Fdn Envirnmtl Stewardship and Energy Sustainability Grant, 1967
Piedmont Natural Gas Foundation K-12 Science, Technology, Engineering and Math (STEM) Grant, 1969
Pinnacle Entertainment Foundation Grants, 1972
Pinnacle Foundation Grants, 1973

Piper Trust Arts and Culture Grants, 1975
Piper Trust Children Grants, 1976
Piper Trust Education Grants, 1977
Piper Trust Reglious Organizations Grants, 1979
Pittsburgh Foundation Healthy Children and Adults
    Grants, 1981
PMI Foundation Grants, 1982
PNC Foundation Community Services Grants, 1984
PNC Foundation Education Grants, 1985
PNC Foundation Grow Up Great Early Childhood
    Grants, 1986
PNC Foundation Revitalization and Stabilization
    Grants, 1987
PNM Reduce Your Use Grants, 1988
Pohlad Family Fdn Large Capital Grants, 1990
Pohlad Family Fdn Small Capital Grants, 1991
Pohlad Family Foundation Summer Camp
    Scholarships, 1992
Pohlad Family Foundation Youth Advancement
    Grants, 1993
Pokagon Fund Grants, 1994
Polk County Community Foundation Bradley
    Breakthrough Community Benefit Grants, 1995
Polk County Community Foundation Free
    Community Events Grants, 1996
Polk County Community Foundation Marjorie M.
    and Lawrence R. Bradley Endowment Fund
    Grants, 1998
Polk County Community Foundation Mary F. Kessler
    Fund Grants, 1999
Polk County Community Foundation Unrestricted
    Grants, 2001
Porter County Community Foundation Health and
    Wellness Grant, 2002
Porter County Community Foundation
    PCgivingproject Grants, 2003
Porter County Community Foundation Women's
    Fund Grants, 2005
Portland Fdn - Women's Giving Circle Grant, 2006
Portland General Electric Foundation Grants, 2007
Posey Community Foundation Women's Fund
    Grants, 2008
Powell Family Foundation Grants, 2012
Powell Foundation Grants, 2013
PPCF Community Grants, 2014
PPCF Edson Foundation Grants, 2015
PPCF Esther M. and Freeman E. Everett Charitable
    Foundation Grants, 2016
PPG Industries Foundation Grants, 2017
Premera Blue Cross Grants, 2018
Price Chopper's Golub Foundation Grants, 2020
Priddy Foundation Program Grants, 2023
Pride Foundation Grants, 2024
Progress Energy Foundation Energy Education
    Grants, 2025
ProLiteracy National Book Fund Grants, 2026
Proteus Fund Grants, 2027
Prudential Foundation Education Grants, 2028
PSEG Corporate Contributions Grants, 2030
Public Education Power Grants, 2032
Public Welfare Fdn Juvenile Justice Grants, 2033
Public Welfare Foundation Special Initiative to
    Advance Civil Legal Aid Grants, 2034
Public Welfare Foundation Special Opportunities
    Grants, 2035
Publix Super Markets Charities Local Grants, 2036
Puerto Rico Community Foundation Grants, 2037
Pulaski County Community Foundation Grants, 2038
Pulido Walker Foundation, 2039
Putnam County Community Fdn Grants, 2040
Quaker Oats Company Kids Care Clubs Grants, 2041
Qualcomm Grants, 2042
R.C. Baker Foundation Grants, 2043
R.D. and Joan Dale Hubbard Fdn Grants, 2044
R.D. Beirne Trust Grants, 2045
R.J. McElroy Trust Grants, 2046
R.S. Gernon Trust Grants, 2047
Radcliffe Institute Oral History Grants, 2049
Ralph C. Wilson, Jr. Foundation Preparing for
    Success Grant, 2050

Ralph C. Wilson, Jr. Foundation Youth Sports and
    Recreation Grant, 2051
Raskob Fdn for Catholic Activities Grants, 2054
Rasmuson Foundation Tier One Grants, 2055
Rasmuson Foundation Tier Two Grants, 2056
Rathmann Family Foundation Grants, 2057
Ray Charles Foundation Grants, 2058
Ray Foundation Grants, 2059
Raymond Austin Hagen Family Fdn Grants, 2060
RCF General Community Grants, 2062
RCF Individual Assistance Grants, 2063
RCF Summertime Kids Grants, 2064
RCF The Women's Fund Grants, 2065
Reinberger Foundation Grants, 2066
Ressler-Gertz Foundation Grants, 2067
RGk Foundation Grants, 2068
Richard and Caroline T. Gwathmey Memorial Trust
    Grants, 2069
Richard Davoud Donchian Foundation Grants, 2070
Richard J. Stern Foundation for the Arts Grants, 2071
Richard W. Goldman Family Fdn Grants, 2073
Richland County Bank Grants, 2074
Ricks Family Charitable Trust Grants, 2075
Riedman Foundation Grants, 2076
Ripley County Community Foundation Grants, 2077
Ripley County Community Foundation Small Project
    Grants, 2078
RISCA Project Grants for Individuals, 2079
Robbins-de Beaumont Foundation Grants, 2080
Robbins Family Charitable Foundation Grants, 2082
Robert and Betty Wo Foundation Grants, 2083
Robert and Helen Haddad Foundation Grants, 2084
Robert and Helen Harmony Fund for Needy Children
    Grants, 2085
Robert Bowne Foundation Fellowships, 2087
Robert F. Lange Foundation Grants, 2090
Robert Lee Blaffer Foundation Grants, 2092
Robert R. McCormick Tribune Foundation
    Community Grants, 2093
Robert R. Meyer Foundation Grants, 2094
Robert W. Knox, Sr. and Pearl Wallis Knox
    Charitable Foundation, 2095
Rockwell Collins Charitable Corp Grants, 2098
Roger L. and Agnes C. Dell Charitable Trust II
    Grants, 2100
Ron and Sanne Higgins Family Fdn Grants, 2101
Roney-Fitzpatrick Foundation Grants, 2102
Rose Community Foundation Child and Family
    Development Grants, 2103
Rose Community Foundation Education Grants, 2104
Rose Hills Foundation Grants, 2106
Rosenberg Charity Foundation Grants, 2107
Rosenberg Fund for Children Ozzy Klate Memorial
    Fund Grants, 2114
Roy and Christine Sturgis Charitable Tr Grts, 2115
RR Donnelley Foundation Grants, 2118
Ruby K. Worner Charitable Trust Grants, 2119
Rush County Community Foundation Grants, 2121
Ruth Anderson Foundation Grants, 2122
Ruth and Henry Campbell Foundation Grants, 2123
Ruth and Vernon Taylor Foundation Grants, 2124
S. D. Bechtel, Jr. Foundation / Stephen Bechtel
    Fund Character and Citizenship Dev Grants, 2128
S. Spencer Scott Fund Grants, 2129
Sabina Dolan and Gladys Saulsbury Foundation
    Grants, 2130
SACF Youth Advisory Council Grants, 2131
Saginaw Community Foundation Discretionary
    Grants, 2134
Saigh Foundation Grants, 2137
Salmon Foundation Grants, 2140
Saltchuk Corporate Giving, 2141
Samueli Foundation Education Grants, 2143
Samueli Foundation Youth Services Grants, 2144
Samuel N. and Mary Castle Foundation Grants, 2145
Samuel S. Johnson Foundation Grants, 2146
San Antonio Area Foundation High School
    Completion Grants, 2149
San Antonio Area Foundation Special and Urgent
    Needs Funding Grants, 2150

Sand Hill Foundation Environment and Sustainability
    Grants, 2152
Sand Hill Foundation Health and Opportunity
    Grants, 2153
SanDisk Corp Community Sharing Grants, 2155
Sandy Hill Foundation Grants, 2157
San Juan Island Community Foundation Grants, 2158
Santa Fe Community Foundation Seasonal Grants-
    Fall Cycle, 2159
Sarah G. McCarthy Memorial Foundation, 2162
Sarkeys Foundation Grants, 2163
Sartain Lanier Family Foundation Grants, 2164
SAS Institute Community Relations Donations, 2165
Schlessman Family Foundation Grants, 2167
Schramm Foundation Grants, 2168
Scott B. and Annie P. Appleby Charitable Trust
    Grants, 2169
Scott County Community Foundation Grants, 2170
Screen Actors Guild BookPALS Assistance, 2171
Screen Actors Guild PencilPALS Assistance, 2172
Screen Actors Guild StagePALS Assistance, 2173
Seattle Foundation Arts and Culture Grants, 2174
Seattle Foundation Benjamin N. Phillips Memorial
    Fund Grants, 2176
Seattle Foundation C. Keith Birkenfeld Memorial
    Trust Grants, 2177
Seattle Foundation Education Grants, 2178
Sensient Technologies Foundation Grants, 2180
Serco Foundation Grants, 2181
Seward Community Foundation Grants, 2182
Seward Community Foundation Mini-Grants, 2183
Shell Deer Park Grants, 2186
Shelley and Donald Rubin Foundation Grants, 2187
Shell Oil Company Foundation Community
    Development Grants, 2188
Shield-Ayres Foundation Grants, 2189
Shopko Fdn Community Charitable Grants, 2191
Shopko Foundation Green Bay Area Community
    Grants, 2192
Sidgmore Family Foundation Grants, 2195
Sidney and Sandy Brown Foundation Grants, 2196
Sidney Stern Memorial Trust Grants, 2197
Siebert Lutheran Foundation Grants, 2198
Sierra Health Foundation Responsive Grants, 2199
Silicon Valley Community Foundation Education
    Grants, 2200
Simpson Lumber Charitable Contributions, 2201
Singing for Change Foundation Grants, 2202
Sioux Falls Area Community Foundation Community
    Fund Grants, 2203
Sioux Falls Area Community Foundation Spot
    Grants, 2204
Skaggs Family Foundation Grants, 2206
Skaggs Family Foundation Grants, 2205
Skaggs Foundation Grants, 2207
SME Education Fdn Youth Program Grants, 2209
Sobrato Family Foundation Grants, 2211
Sobrato Family Fdn Meeting Space Grants, 2212
Sobrato Family Foundation Office Space Grants, 2213
Social Justice Fund Northwest Criminal Justice
    Giving Project Grants, 2214
Social Justice Fund Northwest Economic Justice
    Giving Project Grants, 2215
Sony Corporation of America Grants, 2216
Sorenson Legacy Foundation Grants, 2217
Southern California Edison Education Grants, 2218
Southern Minnesota Initiative Foundation BookStart
    Grants, 2220
Southern Minnesota Initiative Foundation Home
    Visiting Grants, 2222
South Madison Community Foundation - Teacher
    Creativity Mini Grants, 2225
Special Olympics Project UNIFY Grants, 2228
Special Olympics Youth Fan Grants, 2229
Speer Trust Grants, 2230
Spencer County Community Foundation Recreation
    Grants, 2231
Spencer County Community Foundation Women's
    Fund Grants, 2232
Sphinx Competition Awards, 2234

State Farm Good Neighbor Citizenship Company Grants, 2238
Staunton Farm Foundation Grants, 2239
Stein Family Charitable Trust Grants, 2240
Sterling-Turner Charitable Foundation Grants, 2242
Sterling and Shelli Gardner Foundation Grants, 2243
Steven B. Achelis Foundation Grants, 2244
Stillson Foundation Grants, 2245
Stinson Foundation Grants, 2246
Stocker Foundation Grants, 2247
Storm Castle Foundation Grants, 2248
Strake Foundation Grants, 2249
Stranahan Foundation Grants, 2250
Strong Foundation Grants, 2252
Subaru of America Foundation Grants, 2253
Subaru of Indiana Automotive Fdn Grants, 2254
Summit Foundation Grants, 2255
Sunoco Foundation Grants, 2256
SunTrust Bank Trusteed Foundations Greene-Sawtell Grants, 2257
SunTrust Bank Trusteed Foundations Nell Warren Elkin and William Simpson Elkin Grants, 2258
Suspened: Community Fdn for Greater Atlanta State Farm Education Assist Fund Grants, 2260
Sylvia Perkin Perpetual Charitable Trust Grants, 2263
T.L.L. Temple Foundation Grants, 2264
TAC Arts Education Funds for At-Risk Youth, 2266
TAC Arts Education Mini Grants, 2267
Target Corporation Community Engagement Fund Grants, 2270
Target Foundation Global Grants, 2272
Tata Trust Grant for Certificate Course in Holistic inclusion of Learners with Diversities, 2273
Tauck Family Foundation Grants, 2274
Teaching Tolerance Diverse Democracy Grants, 2275
Teaching Tolerance Social Justice Educator Grts, 2276
Teagle Foundation Grants, 2277
TE Foundation Grants, 2279
Tellabs Foundation Grants, 2280
Telluride Foundation Community Grants, 2281
Telluride Fdn Emergency Grants, 2282
Telluride Fdn Technical Assistance Grants, 2283
Tension Envelope Foundation Grants, 2284
Terra Fdn Chicago K–12 Education Grants, 2285
Textron Corporate Contributions Grants, 2286
Thelma Braun and Bocklett Family Foundation Grants, 2287
Thelma Doelger Charitable Trust Grants, 2288
Thomas J. Atkins Memorial Trust Fund Grants, 2290
Thomas J. Long Foundation Community Grants, 2291
Thomas Sill Foundation Grants, 2292
Thomas W. Briggs Foundation Grants, 2294
Three Guineas Fund Grants, 2297
Threshold Fdn Justice and Democracy Grants, 2298
Threshold Foundation Queer Youth Grants, 2299
Tides Foundation Girl Rising Fund Grants, 2301
TJX Foundation Grants, 2303
Toby Wells Foundation Grants, 2304
Todd Brock Family Foundation Grants, 2305
Tom C. Barnsley Foundation Grants, 2306
Toshiba America Foundation Grades 7-12 Science and Math Grants, 2307
Toshiba America Foundation K-6 Science and Math Grants, 2308
Toyota Motor Manuf of Alabama Grants, 2309
Toyota Motor Manufacturing of Indiana Grants, 2310
Toyota Motor Manuf of Kentucky Grants, 2311
Toyota Motor Manuf of Mississippi Grants, 2312
Toyota Motor Manufacturing of Texas Grants, 2313
Toyota Motor Manufacturing of West Virginia Grants, 2314
Toyota Motor North America of NY Grants, 2315
Toyota Motor Sales, USA Grants, 2316
Toyota Technical Center Grants, 2317
Toyota USA Foundation Education Grants, 2318
Toyota USA Foundation Safety Grants, 2320
Tull Charitable Foundation Grants, 2324
Turner B. Bunn, Jr. and Catherine E. Bunn Foundation Grants, 2325
Turner Foundation Grants, 2326

Turtle Bay Foundation Grants, 2327
Twenty-First Century Foundation Grants, 2328
U.S. Bank Foundation Grants, 2330
U.S. Cellular Corporation Grants, 2331
U.S. Department of Education Promise Neighborhoods Grants, 2332
Union Bank, N.A. Corporate Sponsorships and Donations, 2333
Union Bank, N.A. Foundation Grants, 2334
Union Square Arts Award, 2339
Union Square Award for Social Justice, 2340
United Friends of the Children Scholarships, 2341
United Methodist Health Ministry Fund Grts, 2345
United Technologies Corporation Grants, 2347
UPS Corporate Giving Grants, 2349
UPS Foundation Community Safety Grants, 2350
UPS Foundation Economic and Global Literacy Grants, 2351
USAID Global Development Alliance Grants, 2354
USAID Integrated Youth Development Activity Grants, 2356
USAID Nigeria Ed Crisis Response Grants, 2358
USAID School Improvement Program Grants, 2360
USAID U.S.-Egypt Learning Grants, 2361
USDEd Gaining Early Awareness and Readiness for Undergrad Programs (GEAR UP) Grants, 2364
UUA Actions of Public Witness Grants, 2365
UUA Congregation-Based Community Organizing Grants, 2366
UUA Fund Grants, 2367
UUA International Fund Grants, 2368
UUA Just Society Fund Grants, 2369
UUA Social Responsibility Grants, 2370
V.V. Cooke Foundation Grants, 2371
Vanderburgh Community Foundation Men's Fund Grants, 2373
Vanderburgh Community Foundation Recreation Grants, 2374
Vanderburgh County Community Foundation Women's Fund Grants, 2376
Van Kampen Boyer Molinari Charitable Foundation Grants, 2377
Victor E. Speas Foundation Grants, 2380
Virginia Commission for the Arts Artists in Education Residency Grants, 2385
Virginia Foundation for the Humanities Folklife Apprenticeships, 2386
Virginia Foundation for the Humanities Open Grants, 2387
Virginia W. Kettering Foundation Grants, 2388
Volkswagen Group of America Corporate Contributions Grants, 2389
Volvo Adventure Environmental Awards, 2390
Volvo Bob the Bunny's Cartoon Competition, 2391
VSA/Metlife Connect All Grants, 2392
VSA/Volkswagen Group of America Exhibition Awards, 2393
VSA International Art Program for Children with Disabilities Grants, 2394
W.H. and Mary Ellen Cobb Chartbl Trust Grts, 2397
W.M. Keck Fdn Southern California Grants, 2398
W.P. and Bulah Luse Foundation Grants, 2399
Walker Area Community Foundation Grants, 2401
Wallace Foundation Grants, 2402
Walmart Fdn Inclusive Communities Grants, 2403
Walmart Fdn National Local Giving Grants, 2404
Walmart Foundation State Giving Grants, 2405
Walter J. and Betty C. Zable Fdn Grants, 2406
Walton Family Foundation Education Grants, 2408
Walton Family Foundation Public Charter Startup Grants, 2409
Warrick County Community Foundation Recreation Grants, 2410
Warrick County Community Foundation Women's Fund, 2411
Washington Area Women's Foundation African American Women's Giving Circle Grants, 2414
Washington Area Women's Foundation Rainmakers Giving Circle Grants, 2415
Washington County Community Fdn Grants, 2416

Washington Gas Charitable Contributions, 2417
Watson-Brown Foundation Grants, 2418
Wayne County Foundation Grants, 2419
Weaver Foundation Grants, 2420
Weaver Popcorn Foundation Grants, 2421
Welborn Baptist Foundation Promotion of Early Childhood Development Grants, 2423
Welborn Baptist Foundation School Based Health Grants, 2424
Welborn Foundation Promotion of Healthy Adolescent Development Grants, 2425
Wells County Foundation Grants, 2426
Western Indiana Community Fdn Grants, 2428
Western New York Foundation Grants, 2429
West Virginia Commission on the Arts Long-Term Artist Residencies, 2431
West Virginia Commission on the Arts Special Projects Grants, 2433
WestWind Foundation Reproductive Health and Rights Grants, 2434
White County Community Foundation - Women Giving Together Grants, 2438
Whitney Foundation Grants, 2441
WHO Foundation Education/Literacy Grants, 2442
WHO Foundation General Grants, 2443
WHO Foundation Volunteer Service Grants, 2444
Whole Foods Foundation, 2445
Widgeon Point Charitable Foundation Grants, 2447
Wilkins Family Foundation Grants, 2450
William A. Badger Foundation Grants, 2451
William A. Cooke Foundation Grants, 2452
William and Flora Hewlett Foundation Education Grants, 2454
William and Flora Hewlett Foundation Quality Education in Developing Countries Grants, 2456
William and Sandy Heitz Family Fdn Grants, 2457
William B. Stokely Jr. Foundation Grants, 2459
William Bingham Foundation Grants, 2460
William Blair and Company Foundation Grants, 2461
William Caspar Graustein Memorial Fund Corinne G. Levin Education Grants, 2462
William E. Barth Foundation Grants, 2463
William E. Dean III Charitable Fdn Grants, 2464
William Foulds Family Foundation Grants, 2465
William G. and Helen C. Hoffman Foundation Grants, 2466
William G. Gilmore Foundation Grants, 2467
William J. and Dorothy K. O'Neill Foundation Responsive Grants, 2468
William J. and Gertrude R. Casper Foundation Grants, 2469
William J. and Tina Rosenberg Fdn Grants, 2470
William J. Brace Charitable Trust, 2471
William Ray and Ruth E. Collins Fdn Grants, 2473
Williams Comps Homegrown Giving Grants, 2474
William T. Grant Foundation Scholars Program, 2475
Wilton and Effie Hebert Foundation Grants, 2476
Windham Foundation Grants, 2477
Winifred Johnson Clive Foundation Grants, 2478
WinnCompanies Charitable Giving, 2479
Wiregrass Foundation Grants, 2480
Wisconsin Energy Foundation Grants, 2481
Wold Foundation Grants, 2482
Wolfe Associates Grants, 2483
Women's Fund of Hawaii Grants, 2484
Women's Fund of Hawaii Grants, 2485
Wood-Claeyssens Foundation Grants, 2486
Wood Family Charitable Trust Grants, 2487
Woods Charitable Fund Education Grants, 2488
World of Children Education Award, 2490
WSF GoGirlGo! New York Grants, 2494
WSF Sports 4 Life Grants, 2496
WSF Sports 4 Life Regional Grants, 2497
WSLBDF Quarterly Grants, 2499
Wyoming Community Fdn General Grants, 2501
Wyoming Community Foundation Hazel Patterson Memorial Grants, 2502
Wyoming Department of Education McKinney-Vento Subgrant, 2503
Wyomissing Foundation Community Grants, 2504

Wyomissing Foundation Thun Family Organizational Grants, 2505
Wyomissing Foundation Thun Family Program Grants, 2506
Xerox Foundation Grants, 2507
Yampa Valley Community Foundation Erickson Business Week Scholarships, 2508
Yampa Valley Community Foundation Erickson Christian Heritage Scholarships, 2509
Yawkey Foundation Grants, 2510
Youths' Friends Association Grants, 2511
YSA ABC Summer of Service Awards, 2512
YSA Get Ur Good On Grants, 2513
YSA MLK Day Lead Organizer Grants, 2516
YSA National Child Awareness Month Youth Ambassador Grants, 2517
YSA NEA Youth Leaders for Literacy Grants, 2518
YSA Sodexo Lead Organizer Grants, 2520
YSA State Farm Good Neighbor YOUth In The Driver Seat Grants, 2521
YSA UnitedHealth HEROES Service-Learning Grants, 2522
Z. Smith Reynolds Foundation Small Grants, 2523
Zollner Foundation Grants, 2526

Emergency Programs
100 Club of Dubuque, 10
A. Alfred Taubman Foundation Grants, 18
A.C. and Penney Hubbard Foundation Grants, 19
AASA Urgent Need Mini-Grants, 43
Abundance Foundation International Grants, 57
ACCF of Indiana Angel Funds Grants, 62
ACF Family Strengthening Scholars Grants, 81
Adams Family Foundation of Tennessee Grants, 120
Adelaide Breed Bayrd Foundation Grants, 123
Advance Auto Parts Corporate Giving Grants, 131
AEGON Transamerica Foundation Health and Wellness Grants, 133
Ahearn Family Foundation Grants, 142
Aid for Starving Children Emerg Aid Grants, 144
Aid for Starving Children Health and Nutrition Grants, 145
Aid for Starving Children Homes and Education Grants, 146
Akron Community Foundation Health and human services Grants, 152
Albert and Ethel Herzstein Charitable Foundation Grants, 219
Alcatel-Lucent Technologies Foundation Grants, 224
Alex Stern Family Foundation Grants, 229
ALFJ Astraea U.S. and International Emergency Fund, 230
Allan C. and Lelia J. Garden Foundation Grants, 236
Alliance for Strong Families and Communities Grants, 239
Alloy Family Foundation Grants, 241
Alvah H. and Wyline P. Chapman Foundation Grants, 248
Anheuser-Busch Foundation Grants, 273
Annie Gardner Foundation Grants, 277
Arizona Foundation for Women General Grants, 294
Arthur E. and Josephine Campbell Beyer Foundation Grants, 303
AT&T Foundation Health and Human Services Grants, 322
Austin S. Nelson Foundation Grants, 333
Avista Foundation Vulnerable and Limited Income Population Grants, 341
B.F. and Rose H. Perkins Foundation Community Grants, 342
Bank of America Charitable Foundation Basic Needs Grants, 354
Bank of America Charitable Foundation Matching Gifts, 356
Bank of America Charitable Foundation Volunteer Grants, 358
Bank of Hawaii Foundation Grants, 360
Baton Rouge Area Foundation Every Kid a King Fund Grants, 364
Baxter International Corporate Giving Grants, 368

Beckman Coulter Foundation Grants, 394
Bill and Melinda Gates Foundation Emergency Response Grants, 426
Biogen Foundation General Donations, 432
Blumenthal Foundation Grants, 459
Boeing Company Contributions Grants, 462
BP Foundation Grants, 465
C.H. Robinson Worldwide Foundation Grants, 489
Camille Beckman Foundation Grants, 499
Campbell Soup Foundation Grants, 501
Cargill Corporate Giving Grants, 503
Carl R. Hendrickson Family Foundation Grants, 509
Carrie S. Orleans Trust Grants, 512
Castle Foundation Grants, 518
Catherine Holmes Wilkins Foundation Charitable Grants, 520
CFNEM Women's Giving Circle Grants, 557
Charles Crane Family Foundation Grants, 563
Charles H. Hall Foundation, 565
Charles Nelson Robinson Fund Grants, 569
Christine and Katharina Pauly Charitable Trust Grants, 601
Clara Blackford Smith and W. Aubrey Smith Charitable Foundation Grants, 621
Clark and Ruby Baker Foundation Grants, 625
Clark Electric Cooperative Grants, 627
Cleveland Foundation Higley Fund Grants, 634
CNCS AmeriCorps Indian Tribes Plang Grts, 641
CNCS AmeriCorps NCCC Project Grants, 642
CNCS AmeriCorps State and National Grants, 643
CNCS AmeriCorps VISTA Project Grants, 645
Community Foundation for Greater Atlanta Frances Hollis Brain Foundation Fund Grants, 664
Community Foundation for Greater Buffalo Niagara Area Foundation Grants, 673
Community Foundation for SE Michigan Chelsea Community Foundation General Grant, 680
Community Foundation of Eastern Connecticut General Southeast Grants, 696
Community Foundation of Eastern Connecticut Norwich Women and Girls Grants, 698
Community Foundation of Greater Fort Wayne - Community Endowment and Clarke Endowment Grants, 705
Community Foundation of Louisville Anna Marble Memorial Fund for Princeton Grants, 717
Community Foundation of Louisville Human Services Grants, 726
Covenant to Care for Children Crisis Food Pantry Giving, 756
Cudd Foundation Grants, 769
Curtis Foundation Grants, 771
Daniels Homeless and Disadvantaged Grants, 782
Dearborn Community Foundation City of Aurora Grants, 808
Dermody Properties Fdn Capstone Award, 826
Dexter Adams Foundation Grants, 829
Dining for Women Grants, 831
Dolan Media Foundation Grants, 833
Dollar Energy Fund Grants, 834
Dominion Foundation Grants, 839
Doree Taylor Charitable Foundation Grants, 843
Dr. and Mrs. Paul Pierce Memorial Foundation Grants, 862
Eastern Bank Charitable Foundation Partnerships Grants, 881
Eastern Bank Charitable Foundation Targeted Grants, 882
Edward and Ellen Roche Relief Fdn Grants, 887
Edyth Bush Charitable Foundation Grants, 893
Effie Allen Little Foundation Grants, 894
Eide Bailly Resourcefullness Awards, 897
Emma J. Adams Memorial Fund Grants, 914
Ensworth Charitable Foundation Grants, 916
Episcopal Actors' Guild Actors Florence James Children's Holiday Fund Grant, 925
Erie Chapman Foundation Grants, 928
Fidelity Charitable Gift Fund Grants, 956
Fifth Third Bank Corporate Giving, 958
Finish Line Youth Foundation Founder's Grants, 960

First Hawaiian Bank Foundation Corporate Giving Grants, 967
Franklin H. Wells and Ruth L. Wells Foundation Grants, 1011
Fremont Area Community Foundation Community Grants, 1020
Gardner Foundation Grants, 1034
Gene Haas Foundation, 1038
George B. Page Foundation Grants, 1044
George H.C. Ensworth Memorial Fund Grants, 1049
George H. Sandy Foundation Grants, 1050
GNOF Albert N. & Hattie M. McClure Grants, 1076
GNOF Bayou Communities Grants, 1077
GNOF IMPACT Harold W. Newman, Jr. Charitable Trust Grants, 1086
GNOF Plaquemines Community Grants, 1091
Grace Bersted Foundation Grants, 1097
Graham Foundation Grants, 1101
Green Foundation Human Services Grants, 1116
Green River Area Community Fdn Grants, 1117
GTRCF Elk Rapids Area Community Endowment Grants, 1127
GTRCF Healthy Youth and Healthy Seniors Endowment Grants, 1130
Gulf Coast Foundation of Community Operating Grants, 1134
Gulf Coast Foundation of Community Program Grants, 1135
HAF Don and Bettie Albright Endowment Fund Grants, 1142
Hahl Proctor Charitable Trust Grants, 1151
Hannaford Supermarkets Community Giving, 1164
Hardin County Community Foundation Grants, 1167
Harold Brooks Foundation Grants, 1172
Harrison County Community Foundation Signature Grants, 1179
Hartley Foundation Grants, 1186
Harvey E. Najim Family Foundation Grants, 1187
Hattie Mae Lesley Foundation Grants, 1195
Hawaii Community Foundation Oscar and Rosetta Fish Fund Grants, 1214
Hawaii Electric Industries Charitable Foundation Grants, 1218
Hearst Foundations Social Service Grants, 1224
Helen G., Henry F., & Louise Tuechter Dornette Foundation Grants, 1229
Helen V. Brach Foundation Grants, 1232
Henrietta Lange Burk Fund Grants, 1235
Herbert A. and Adrian W. Woods Foundation Grants, 1243
Honeywell Corporation Family Safety and Security Grants, 1255
Honeywell Corp Humanitarian Relief Grants, 1257
Horace A. Moses Charitable Trust Grants, 1261
Hubbard Farms Charitable Foundation Grants, 1272
Humana Foundation Grants, 1275
Ike and Roz Friedman Foundation Grants, 1289
Island Insurance Foundation Grants, 1316
J. Watumull Fund Grants, 1326
James and Abigail Campbell Family Foundation Grants, 1337
James Graham Brown Foundation Grants, 1340
Janson Foundation Grants, 1349
Jim Blevins Foundation Grants, 1365
John and Marcia Goldman Foundation Youth Development Grants, 1368
John G. Duncan Charitable Trust Grants, 1372
John H. and Wilhelmina D. Harland Charitable Foundation Community Services Grants, 1375
Joni Elaine Templeton Foundation Grants, 1384
Joseph H. and Florence A. Roblee Foundation Children and Youth Grants, 1385
Joseph S. Stackpole Charitable Trust Grants, 1390
Judith Clark-Morrill Foundation Grants, 1395
Kalamazoo Community Foundation Individuals and Families Grants, 1409
Kate B. Reynolds Charitable Trust Poor and Needy Grants, 1417
Kimball International-Habig Foundation Health and Human Services Grants, 1434

Kopp Family Foundation Grants, 1448
Kosasa Foundation Grants, 1450
Kovler Family Foundation Grants, 1454
LGA Family Foundation Grants, 1487
Linford & Mildred White Charitable Grants, 1495
LISC Capacity Building Grants, 1498
Lucy Downing Nisbet Charitable Fund Grants, 1515
Make Sense Foundation Grants, 1548
Margaret M. Walker Charitable Fdn Grants, 1556
Marion and Miriam Rose Fund Grants, 1569
Marion I. and Henry J. Knott Foundation
    Discretionary Grants, 1571
Marriott Int Corporate Giving Grants, 1578
Mary Cofer Trigg Trust Fund Grants, 1587
McCarthy Family Fdn Charity Fund Grants, 1614
McGregor Fund Human Services Grants, 1621
Mertz Gilmore Foundation NYC Communities
    Grants, 1641
Meyer Fdn Healthy Communities Grants, 1650
Meyer Memorial Trust Emergency Grants, 1652
Michelle O'Neill Foundation Grants, 1661
Middlesex Savings Charitable Foundation Basic
    Human Needs Grants, 1668
Montana Community Foundation Big Sky LIFT
    Grants, 1686
Nathaniel and Elizabeth P. Stevens Foundation
    Grants, 1719
Nationwide Insurance Foundation Grants, 1726
New Covenant Farms Grants, 1742
New Hampshire Department of Justice Children's
    Justice Act Coronavirus Emergency Grants, 1749
Oak Fdn Housing and Homelessness Grants, 1800
Olga Sipolin Children's Fund Grants, 1815
Oppenstein Brothers Foundation Grants, 1827
Oregon Community Fdn Community Grants, 1833
Oregon Community Foundation Community
    Recovery Grants, 1834
Packard Foundation Local Grants, 1863
Patrick and Aimee Butler Family Foundation
    Community Human Services Grants, 1880
Perkins-Ponder Foundation Grants, 1938
Perpetual Benevolent Fund, 1940
PG&E Community Vitality Grants, 1957
Piedmont Natural Gas Foundation Health and
    Human Services Grants, 1968
PMI Foundation Grants, 1982
Polk County Community Foundation Seasonal
    Assistance and Cheer Grants for Charitable
    Programs, 2000
Polk County Community Foundation Unrestricted
    Grants, 2001
PSEG Fdn Safety and Preparedness Grants, 2031
Public Welfare Foundation Special Initiative to
    Advance Civil Legal Aid Grants, 2034
Puerto Rico Community Foundation Grants, 2037
R.D. Beirne Trust Grants, 2045
R.S. Gernon Trust Grants, 2047
RCF Individual Assistance Grants, 2063
Reinberger Foundation Grants, 2066
Richard and Caroline T. Gwathmey Memorial Trust
    Grants, 2069
Robbins Family Charitable Foundation Grants, 2082
Robert R. Meyer Foundation Grants, 2094
Robinson Foundation Grants, 2097
Saltchuk Corporate Giving, 2141
Salt River Project Health and Human Services
    Grants, 2142
Samuel S. Johnson Foundation Grants, 2146
San Antonio Area Foundation Special and Urgent
    Needs Grants, 2150
Sapelo Foundation Social Justice Grants, 2160
Sara Elizabeth O'Brien Trust Grants, 2161
Sarah G. McCarthy Memorial Foundation, 2162
Seattle Foundation Basic Needs Grants, 2175
Seattle Foundation C. Keith Birkenfeld Memorial
    Trust Grants, 2177
Serco Foundation Grants, 2181
Shield-Ayres Foundation Grants, 2189

Sioux Falls Area Community Foundation Community
    Fund Grants, 2203
Sioux Falls Area Community Foundation Spot
    Grants, 2204
Skaggs Family Foundation Grants, 2206
Skaggs Family Foundation Grants, 2205
Sobrato Family Foundation Grants, 2211
Sobrato Family Fdn Meeting Space Grants, 2212
Sobrato Family Foundation Office Space Grants, 2213
Sony Corporation of America Grants, 2216
Sunoco Foundation Grants, 2256
Swindells Charitable Foundation Grants, 2261
Sylvia Adams Charitable Trust Grants, 2262
Target Foundation Global Grants, 2272
Telluride Fdn Emergency Grants, 2282
Textron Corporate Contributions Grants, 2286
TJX Foundation Grants, 2303
Todd Brock Family Foundation Grants, 2305
Union Bank, N.A. Corporate Sponsorships and
    Donations, 2333
Union Bank, N.A. Foundation Grants, 2334
Union Labor Health Foundation Dental Angel Fund
    Grants, 2336
Union Pacific Foundation Health and Human
    Services Grants, 2338
UnitedHealthcare Children's Fdn Grants, 2342
USDA Child and Adult Care Food Program, 2362
UUA Actions of Public Witness Grants, 2365
UUA Congregation-Based Community Organizing
    Grants, 2366
UUA Fund Grants, 2367
UUA International Fund Grants, 2368
UUA Just Society Fund Grants, 2369
UUA Social Responsibility Grants, 2370
Victor E. Speas Foundation Grants, 2380
W.H. and Mary Ellen Cobb Chartbl Trust Grts, 2397
Walker Area Community Foundation Grants, 2401
Walter J. and Betty C. Zable Fdn Grants, 2406
Washington Area Fuel Fund Grants, 2413
Washington Gas Charitable Contributions, 2417
William and Flora Hewlett Foundation
    Environmental Grants, 2455
William B. Stokely Jr. Foundation Grants, 2459
William E. Dean III Charitable Fdn Grants, 2464
WinnCompanies Charitable Giving, 2479
Women's Fund of Hawaii Grants, 2484
Wyoming Community Foundation COVID-19
    Response and Recovery Grants, 2500
Youths' Friends Association Grants, 2511
Zellweger Baby Support Network Grants, 2525
ZYTL Foundation Grants, 2528

Endowments

Achelis and Bodman Foundation Grants, 101
Achelis Foundation Grants, 102
AHS Foundation Grants, 143
Alvah H. and Wyline P. Chapman Foundation
    Grants, 248
Ar-Hale Family Foundation Grants, 290
Bierhaus Foundation Grants, 421
Blanche and Irving Laurie Foundation Grants, 436
Blandin Foundation Itasca County Area Vitality
    Grants, 439
Blumenthal Foundation Grants, 459
BMW of North America Charitable Contribs, 460
Caesars Foundation Grants, 492
Clayton Fund Grants, 631
Community Foundation for SE Michigan Livingston
    County Grants, 683
Countess Moira Charitable Foundation Grants, 752
Cralle Foundation Grants, 760
Florence Foundation Grants, 978
George Graham and Elizabeth Galloway Smith
    Foundation Grants, 1047
GNOF Freeman Challenge Grants, 1081
Graham Foundation Grants, 1100
Hearst Foundations Culture Grants, 1223
Herman P. and Sophia Taubman Fdn Grants, 1247
J.W. Kieckhefer Foundation Grants, 1324

Jack H. and William M. Light Charitable Trust
    Grants, 1330
Johnson Scholarship Foundation Grants, 1382
Kovler Family Foundation Grants, 1454
Kovler Family Foundation Grants, 1455
Leonsis Foundation Grants, 1485
Lied Foundation Trust Grants, 1490
Margaret T. Morris Foundation Grants, 1557
McLean Contributionship Grants, 1623
Norcliffe Foundation Grants, 1766
Paso del Norte Health Foundation Grants, 1874
PMI Foundation Grants, 1982
RCF The Women's Fund Grants, 2065
Reinberger Foundation Grants, 2066
Robert R. Meyer Foundation Grants, 2094
Roy and Christine Sturgis Charitable Tr Grts, 2115
Saigh Foundation Grants, 2137
Shield-Ayres Foundation Grants, 2189
Sony Corporation of America Grants, 2216
Textron Corporate Contributions Grants, 2286
Union Bank, N.A. Foundation Grants, 2334
W.P. and Bulah Luse Foundation Grants, 2399
William Blair and Company Foundation Grants, 2461

Environmental Programs

3M Company Fdn Community Giving Grants, 5
A.C. and Penney Hubbard Foundation Grants, 19
Abbott Fund Community Engagement Grants, 46
Abell-Hanger Foundation Grants, 52
ACCF Dennis and Melanie Bieberich Community
    Enrichment Fund Grants, 59
ACCF John and Kay Boch Fund Grants, 60
ACCF of Indiana Anonymous Community
    Enrichment Fund Grants, 63
ACCF of Indiana Bank of Geneva Heritage Fund
    Grants, 64
ACCF of Indiana First Merchants Bank / Decatur
    Bank and Trust Fund Grants, 66
ACCF of Indiana Michael Basham Community
    Enrichment Fund Grants, 67
ACCF of Indiana Ron and Susie Ballard Community
    Enrichment Fund Grants, 68
ACCF Ralph Biggs Memorial Community
    Enrichment Fund Grants, 69
ACF Social and Economic Development Strategies
    Grants, 93
Achelis and Bodman Foundation Grants, 101
Achelis Foundation Grants, 102
Adams Family Fdn of Nora Springs Grants, 118
Adobe Foundation Action Grants, 126
Adobe Fdn Community Investment Grants, 127
Air Products Foundation Grants, 148
Alaska Airlines Foundation LIFT Grants, 194
Alaska Conservation Fdn Youth Mini Grants, 210
Alfred J Mcallister and Dorothy N Mcallister
    Foundation Grants, 234
Allen Foundation Educational Nutrition Grants, 238
Alliant Energy Foundation Community Giving for
    Good Sponsorship Grants, 240
Allstate Corporate Giving Grants, 242
Allstate Corp Hometown Commitment Grants, 243
Alpha Natural Resources Corporate Giving, 246
Ama OluKai Foundation Grants, 249
Ameren Corporation Community Grants, 251
American Electric Power Corporate Grants, 252
American Electric Power Foundation Grants, 253
American Honda Foundation Grants, 255
American Savings Fdn After School Grants, 259
Anderson Foundation Grants, 271
Andrew Family Foundation Grants, 272
Anheuser-Busch Foundation Grants, 273
Ann L. and Carol Green Rhodes Charitable Trust
    Grants, 278
Ann Ludington Sullivan Foundation Grants, 279
Arthur Ashley Williams Foundation Grants, 302
AT&T Fdn Community Support and Safety, 320
Atkinson Foundation Community Grants, 325
Austin Community Foundation Grants, 332
Autauga Area Community Foundation Grants, 334

Avista Foundation Vulnerable and Limited Income Population Grants, 341
Babcock Charitable Trust Grants, 343
Baltimore Community Foundation Children's Fresh Air Society Fund Grants, 348
Baltimore Community Foundation Mitzvah Fund for Good Deeds Grants, 349
Bank of America Charitable Foundation Matching Gifts, 356
Bank of America Charitable Foundation Volunteer Grants, 358
Bank of Hawaii Foundation Grants, 360
Barrasso, Usdin, Kupperman, Freeman, and Sarver Corporate Grants, 362
Baton Rouge Area Foundation Grants, 365
Baxter International Corporate Giving Grants, 368
Bay and Paul Foundations PreK-12 Transformative Learning Practices Grants, 370
Bay Area Community Fdn Auburn Area Chamber of Commerce Enrichment Fund Grants, 373
Bay Area Community Foundation Community Initiative Fund Grants, 376
Beckman Coulter Foundation Grants, 394
Belvedere Community Foundation Grants, 399
Benton Community Foundation Grants, 405
Bikes Belong Foundation REI Grants, 423
Bikes Belong Grants, 424
Bill and Melinda Gates Foundation Agricultural Development Grants, 425
Bill and Melinda Gates Foundation Emergency Response Grants, 426
Bill and Melinda Gates Foundation Policy and Advocacy Grants, 427
Black Hills Corporation Grants, 435
Blue Grass Community Foundation Clark County Fund Grants, 444
Blue Grass Community Foundation Fayette County Fund Grants, 446
Blue Grass Community Foundation Franklin County Fund Grants, 447
Blue Grass Community Foundation Harrison County Fund Grants, 448
Blue Grass Community Foundation Madison County Fund Grants, 450
Blue Grass Community Foundation Magoffin County Fund Grants, 451
Blue Grass Community Foundation Morgan County Fund Grants, 452
Blue Grass Community Foundation Rowan County Fund Grants, 453
Blue Grass Community Foundation Woodford County Fund Grants, 454
Blue River Community Foundation Grants, 458
Blumenthal Foundation Grants, 459
Boeing Company Contributions Grants, 462
Bothin Foundation Grants, 464
BP Foundation Grants, 465
Brian G. Dyson Foundation Grants, 468
Bridgestone Americas Trust Fund Grants, 469
Brown County Community Foundation Grants, 475
Brunswick Foundation Dollars for Doers Grants, 478
Brunswick Foundation Grants, 479
Burton D. Morgan Foundation Hudson Community Grants, 482
Bush Foundation Event Sponsorships, 485
Cabot Corporation Foundation Grants, 490
Callaway Foundation Grants, 496
Camille Beckman Foundation Grants, 499
Cargill Corporate Giving Grants, 503
Carl M. Freeman Foundation FACES Grants, 507
Carl M. Freeman Foundation Grants, 508
Cass County Community Foundation Grants, 516
Castle Industries Foundation Grants, 519
CFFVR Environmental Stewardship Grants, 540
CFFVR Project Grants, 546
CFFVR Shawano Area Community Foundation Grants, 549
CFNEM Youth Advisory Council Grants, 558
Chapman Charitable Foundation Grants, 560
Charles Delmar Foundation Grants, 564

Charles H. Hall Foundation, 565
CHC Foundation Grants, 575
Cheryl Spencer Memorial Foundation Grants, 576
Chesapeake Bay Trust Environmental Education Grants, 577
Chesapeake Bay Trust Mini Grants, 578
Chesapeake Bay Trust Outreach and Community Engagement Grants, 579
Chicago Board of Trade Foundation Grants, 580
Chilkat Valley Community Foundation Grants, 588
Christensen Fund Regional Grants, 600
CICF Indianapolis Fdn Community Grants, 606
Circle K Corporation Contributions Grants, 614
Citizens Bank Charitable Foundation Grants, 616
Claremont Savings Bank Foundation Grants, 623
Clark County Community Foundation Grants, 626
Clayton Baker Trust Grants, 629
Cleo Foundation Grants, 632
Clinton County Community Foundation Grants, 638
CNCS AmeriCorps Indian Tribes Plang Grts, 641
CNCS AmeriCorps NCCC Project Grants, 642
CNCS AmeriCorps State and National Grants, 643
CNCS AmeriCorps VISTA Project Grants, 645
CNCS Senior Corps Retired and Senior Volunteer Program Grants, 648
Collective Brands Foundation Grants, 654
Collins Foundation Grants, 658
Colorado Interstate Gas Grants, 661
Community Foundation for Greater Atlanta Metropolitan Extra Wish Grants, 666
Community Foundation for Greater Buffalo Competitive Grants, 670
Community Foundation for Greater Buffalo Niagara Area Foundation Grants, 673
Community Foundation for San Benito County Grants, 677
Community Foundation for the Capital Region Grants, 687
Community Foundation for the National Capital Region Community Leadership Grants, 688
Community Foundation of Bartholomew County Heritage Fund Grants, 690
Community Foundation of Boone County Grants, 694
Community Foundation of Eastern Connecticut General Southeast Grants, 696
Community Foundation of Greater Chattanooga Grants, 704
Community Foundation of Greater Greensboro Community Grants, 708
Community Foundation of Henderson County Community Grants, 711
Community Foundation of Muncie and Delaware County Maxon Grants, 734
Community Fdn of Randolph County Grants, 735
Community Fdn of Southern Indiana Grants, 736
Community Foundation of Switzerland County Grants, 739
Community Foundation of Western Massachusetts Grants, 741
Cooke Foundation Grants, 748
Corina Higginson Trust Grants, 750
Cornell Lab of Ornithology Mini-Grants, 751
Cresap Family Foundation Grants, 766
Crystelle Waggoner Charitable Trust Grants, 768
Cudd Foundation Grants, 769
David Robinson Foundation Grants, 791
Dayton Foundation Grants, 796
Dayton Foundation Huber Heights Grants, 797
Dayton Power and Light Company Foundation Signature Grants, 801
Dean Foods Community Involvement Grants, 805
Dean Foundation Grants, 806
DeKalb County Community Foundation Grants, 815
Delaware Community Foundation Grants, 817
Del Mar Foundation Community Grants, 820
Delmarva Power & Light Contributions, 821
Doree Taylor Charitable Foundation Grants, 843
Do Something Awards, 847
Draper Richards Kaplan Foundation Grants, 864
DTE Energy Foundation Environmental Grants, 868

Dubois County Community Foundation Grants, 871
Dyson Foundation Mid-Hudson Valley Project Support Grants, 874
E. Clayton and Edith P. Gengras, Jr. Foundation Grants, 875
E.J. Grassmann Trust Grants, 876
Earl and Maxine Claussen Trust Grants, 878
Earth Island Institute Brower Youth Awards, 879
Eastern Bank Charitable Foundation Neighborhood Support Grants, 880
Eastern Bank Charitable Foundation Partnerships Grants, 881
Eastern Bank Charitable Foundation Targeted Grants, 882
Edna Wardlaw Charitable Trust Grants, 886
Edward and Helen Bartlett Foundation Grants, 888
Elmer Roe Deaver Foundation Grants, 906
El Pomar Foundation Anna Keesling Ackerman Fund Grants, 907
El Pomar Foundation Grants, 908
Energy by Design Poster Contest, 915
Environmental Excellence Awards, 922
EPA Children's Health Protection Grants, 923
Eulalie Bloedel Schneider Foundation Grants, 936
Evan Frankel Foundation Grants, 938
Faye L. and William L. Cowden Charitable Foundation Grants, 950
Fidelity Charitable Gift Fund Grants, 956
FirstEnergy Foundation Community Grants, 965
First Hawaiian Bank Foundation Corporate Giving Grants, 967
Ford Foundation BUILD Grants, 984
Forest Foundation Grants, 985
Foundation Beyond Belief Compassionate Impact Grants, 986
Foundation Beyond Belief Humanist Grants, 987
Foundation for Appalachian Ohio Access to Environmental Education Mini-Grants, 989
Fdn for the Mid South Communities Grants, 992
Four County Community Foundation General Grants, 1000
Franklin County Community Fdn Grants, 1010
Frederick W. Marzahl Memorial Fund Grants, 1018
Fremont Area Community Foundation Community Grants, 1020
Friends of Hawaii Charities Grants, 1024
G.N. Wilcox Trust Grants, 1031
Gamble Foundation Grants, 1032
Gannett Foundation Community Action Grants, 1033
Gene Haas Foundation, 1038
General Motors Foundation Grants, 1039
George and Ruth Bradford Foundation Grants, 1042
George A Ohl Jr. Foundation Grants, 1043
George H. and Jane A. Mifflin Memorial Fund Grants, 1048
George H.C. Ensworth Memorial Fund Grants, 1049
George W.P. Magee Trust Grants, 1056
Gerber Foundation Environmental Hazards Research Grants, 1062
Giving Gardens Challenge Grants, 1072
Global Fund for Women Grants, 1073
GNOF Bayou Communities Grants, 1077
GNOF Coastal 5 + 1 Grants, 1078
GNOF Exxon-Mobil Grants, 1080
GNOF Gert Community Fund Grants, 1082
GNOF Norco Community Grants, 1089
GNOF Plaquemines Community Grants, 1091
Gray Family Fdn Camp Maintenance Grants, 1104
Gray Family Foundation Community Field Trips Grants, 1105
Gray Family Foundation Geography Education Grants, 1106
Gray Family Fdn Outdoor School Grants, 1107
Greater Milwaukee Foundation Grants, 1109
Greater Saint Louis Community Fdn Grants, 1110
Greater Sitka Legacy Fund Grants, 1111
Greater Tacoma Community Foundation General Operating Grants, 1113
Green River Area Community Fdn Grants, 1117
Greygates Foundation Grants, 1120

Grundy Foundation Grants, 1124
GTRCF Elk Rapids Area Community Endowment Grants, 1127
H.A. and Mary K. Chapman Charitable Trust Grants, 1137
HAF Don and Bettie Albright Endowment Fund Grants, 1142
HAF Joe Alexandre Mem Family Fund Grants, 1145
HAF Laurence and Elaine Allen Memorial Fund Grants, 1146
HAF Southern Humboldt Grants, 1150
Hampton Roads Community Foundation Environment Grants, 1158
Hampton Roads Community Foundation Nonprofit Facilities Improvement Grants, 1159
Hannaford Charitable Foundation Grants, 1163
Hannaford Supermarkets Community Giving, 1164
Harden Foundation Grants, 1166
Hardin County Community Foundation Grants, 1167
Harmony Grove Foundation Grants, 1169
Harold K.L. Castle Foundation Windward Youth Leadership Fund Grants, 1175
Harrison County Community Fdn Grants, 1178
Harrison County Community Foundation Signature Grants, 1179
Harry A. and Margaret D. Towsley Foundation Grants, 1180
Harry Frank Guggenheim Foundation Research Grants, 1184
Hawai'i Community Foundation East Hawaii Fund Grants, 1199
Hawai'i Community Foundation Richard Smart Fund Grants, 1204
Hawai'i Community Foundation Robert E. Black Fund Grants, 1205
Hawaiian Electric Industries Charitable Foundation Grants, 1211
Hawaii Community Foundation Omidyar Ohana Fund Grants, 1213
Hawaii Electric Industries Charitable Foundation Grants, 1218
Helen E. Ellis Charitable Trust Grants, 1228
Helen G., Henry F., & Louise Tuechter Dornette Foundation Grants, 1229
Hendricks County Community Fdn Grants, 1234
Herbert A. and Adrian W. Woods Foundation Grants, 1243
Hillsdale County Community Foundation Love Your Community Grants, 1251
Honor the Earth Grants, 1259
Horace A. Kimball and S. Ella Kimball Foundation Grants, 1260
HSBC Corporate Giving Grants, 1266
Hubbard Family Foundation Grants, 1271
Huntington County Community Foundation Make a Difference Grants, 1280
Iddings Foundation Major Project Grants, 1284
Iddings Foundation Medium Project Grants, 1285
Illinois DNR School Habitat Action Grants, 1296
Illinois DNR Youth Recreation Corps Grants, 1297
Intel Corporation Community Grants, 1311
Intel Corporation Int Community Grants, 1312
J.W. Gardner II Foundation Grants, 1323
J.W. Kieckhefer Foundation Grants, 1324
J. Watumull Fund Grants, 1326
Jack and Dorothy Byrne Foundation Grants, 1329
James and Abigail Campbell Family Foundation Grants, 1337
James Ford Bell Foundation Grants, 1339
James S. Copley Foundation Grants, 1345
Jane's Trust Grants, 1346
Janet Spencer Weekes Foundation Grants, 1348
Janson Foundation Grants, 1349
Japan Foundation New York World Heritage Photo Panel Exhibition, 1356
Jeffris Wood Foundation Grants, 1359
Jennings County Community Fdn Grants, 1360
Jennings County Community Foundation Women's Giving Circle Grant, 1361
Jessica Stevens Community Foundation Grants, 1363

Joni Elaine Templeton Foundation Grants, 1384
Joseph Henry Edmondson Foundation Grants, 1388
Julia Temple Davis Brown Foundation Grants, 1399
Katharine Matthies Foundation Grants, 1418
Katie's Krops Grants, 1421
Kelvin and Eleanor Smith Foundation Grants, 1424
Kenai Peninsula Foundation Grants, 1425
Ketchikan Community Foundation Grants, 1429
Kettering Family Foundation Grants, 1430
Kimball Foundation Grants, 1432
Kind World Foundation Grants, 1438
Kirby Laing Foundation Grants, 1439
Kirkpatrick Foundation Grants, 1440
Kodiak Community Foundation Grants, 1446
Kosasa Foundation Grants, 1450
Kosciusko County Community Fdn Grants, 1452
Kovler Family Foundation Grants, 1454
LaGrange County Community Fdn Grants, 1458
LaGrange Independent Foundation for Endowments (L.I.F.E.), 1459
Laidlaw Foundation Youth Organizaing Initiatives Grants, 1462
Land O'Lakes Foundation Mid-Atlantic Grants, 1467
Lands' End Corporate Giving Program, 1468
Laurel Foundation Grants, 1475
Libra Foundation Grants, 1489
Lily Palmer Fry Memorial Trust Grants, 1493
Lisa and Douglas Goldman Fund Grants, 1496
LISC Affordable Housing Grants, 1497
LISC Financial Stability Grants, 1501
Long Island Community Foundation Grants, 1507
Lotus 88 Foundation for Women and Children Grants, 1508
Louis and Sandra Berkman Foundation Grants, 1510
Louis Calder Foundation Grants, 1511
Lubrizol Foundation Grants, 1513
Lucy Downing Nisbet Charitable Fund Grants, 1515
Macquarie Bank Foundation Grants, 1532
Madison Community Foundation Grants, 1535
Margaret and James A. Elkins Jr. Fdn Grants, 1555
Margaret T. Morris Foundation Grants, 1557
Marie C. and Joseph C. Wilson Foundation Rochester Small Grants, 1559
Marjorie Moore Charitable Foundation Grants, 1574
Marquette Bank Neighborhood Commit Grants, 1577
Marriott Int Corporate Giving Grants, 1578
Marshall County Community Fdn Grants, 1579
Mary A. Crocker Trust Grants, 1584
Mary K. Chapman Foundation Grants, 1590
Mary Owen Borden Foundation Grants, 1597
MassMutual Foundation Edonomic Development Grants, 1603
Matson Adahi I Tano' Grants, 1606
Matson Community Giving Grants, 1607
Matson Ka Ipu 'Aina Grants, 1608
Max and Anna Levinson Foundation Grants, 1612
McConnell Foundation Grants, 1616
McCune Charitable Foundation Grants, 1617
McInerny Foundation Grants, 1622
McLean Contributionship Grants, 1623
MeadWestvaco Foundation Sustainable Communities Grants, 1627
Mead Witter Foundation Grants, 1628
Merrick Foundation Grants, 1639
Meyer Memorial Trust Responsive Grants, 1653
Michelin North America Challenge Education, 1660
Mimi and Peter Haas Fund Grants, 1677
Montgomery County Community Foundation Health and Human Services Fund Grants, 1689
Morris K. Udall and Stewart L. Udall Foundation Parks in Focus Program, 1695
Natalie W. Furniss Foundation Grants, 1715
Nathan Cummings Foundation Grants, 1718
National Wildlife Federation Craig Tufts Educational Scholarship, 1724
New Earth Grants, 1743
New Hampshire Charitable Foundation Neil and Louise Tillotson Fund - Empower Coös Youth Grants, 1748
NHSCA Conservation License Plate Grants, 1757

Nissan Neighbors Grants, 1762
Norcliffe Foundation Grants, 1766
Norman Foundation Grants, 1767
North Dakota Community Foundation Grants, 1768
Northern Chautauqua Community Foundation Community Grants, 1769
North Face Explore Fund, 1770
Northrop Grumman Corporation Grants, 1772
NRA Foundation Grants, 1774
NZDIA Lottery Minister's Discretionary Fund Grants, 1797
Ohio County Community Foundation Board of Directors Grants, 1811
Ohio County Community Foundation Grants, 1812
OMNOVA Solutions Fdn Education Grants, 1820
Oppenstein Brothers Foundation Grants, 1827
Orange County Community Foundation Grants, 1828
Oregon Community Fdn Community Grants, 1833
Packard Foundation Local Grants, 1863
Parker Foundation (California) Grants, 1869
Paul and Edith Babson Foundation Grants, 1881
PepsiCo Foundation Grants, 1935
Perkins Charitable Foundation Grants, 1939
Petersburg Community Foundation Grants, 1951
Pettus Foundation Grants, 1952
PG&E Bright Ideas Grants, 1956
PG&E Community Vitality Grants, 1957
PGE Foundation Grants, 1958
Piedmont Natural Gas Corporate and Charitable Contributions, 1966
Piedmont Natural Gas Fdn Envirnmtl Stewardship and Energy Sustainability Grant, 1967
Piedmont Natural Gas Foundation K-12 Science, Technology, Engineering and Math (STEM) Grant, 1969
PNM Reduce Your Use Grants, 1988
Pohlad Family Fdn Large Capital Grants, 1990
Pohlad Family Fdn Small Capital Grants, 1991
Pokagon Fund Grants, 1994
Polk County Community Foundation Bradley Breakthrough Community Benefit Grants, 1995
Polk County Community Foundation Marjorie M. and Lawrence R. Bradley Endowment Fund Grants, 1998
Polk County Community Foundation Mary F. Kessler Fund Grants, 1999
Polk County Community Foundation Unrestricted Grants, 2001
Powell Foundation Grants, 2013
PPCF Community Grants, 2014
PPCF Esther M. and Freeman E. Everett Charitable Foundation Grants, 2016
Premera Blue Cross Grants, 2018
Pulaski County Community Foundation Grants, 2038
Putnam County Community Fdn Grants, 2040
Rathmann Family Foundation Grants, 2057
RCF General Community Grants, 2062
Richland County Bank Grants, 2074
Ripley County Community Foundation Grants, 2077
Ripley County Community Foundation Small Project Grants, 2078
Robbins-de Beaumont Foundation Grants, 2080
Robbins Charitable Foundation Grants, 2081
Robert and Helen Harmony Fund for Needy Children Grants, 2085
Robert R. Meyer Foundation Grants, 2094
Robert W. Knox, Sr. and Pearl Wallis Knox Charitable Foundation, 2095
Ruth Anderson Foundation Grants, 2122
Ruth and Vernon Taylor Foundation Grants, 2124
Saginaw Community Foundation Discretionary Grants, 2134
Samuel S. Johnson Foundation Grants, 2146
San Antonio Area Foundation Special and Urgent Needs Funding Grants, 2150
Sand Hill Foundation Environment and Sustainability Grants, 2152
SanDisk Corp Community Sharing Grants, 2155
San Juan Island Community Foundation Grants, 2158
Sartain Lanier Family Foundation Grants, 2164

Scott County Community Foundation Grants, 2170
Serco Foundation Grants, 2181
Seward Community Foundation Grants, 2182
Seward Community Foundation Mini-Grants, 2183
Shell Deer Park Grants, 2186
Shell Oil Company Foundation Community
    Development Grants, 2188
Singing for Change Foundation Grants, 2202
Sioux Falls Area Community Foundation Community
    Fund Grants, 2203
Sioux Falls Area Community Foundation Spot
    Grants, 2204
Skaggs Foundation Grants, 2207
Sony Corporation of America Grants, 2216
Sorenson Legacy Foundation Grants, 2217
Spencer County Community Foundation Recreation
    Grants, 2231
Streisand Foundation Grants, 2251
Summit Foundation Grants, 2255
Sunoco Foundation Grants, 2256
T.L.L. Temple Foundation Grants, 2264
Tata Trust Grant for Certificate Course in Holistic
    inclusion of Learners with Diversities, 2273
Tellabs Foundation Grants, 2280
Telluride Foundation Community Grants, 2281
Telluride Fdn Technical Assistance Grants, 2283
Thomas J. Long Foundation Community Grants, 2291
Thomas Sill Foundation Grants, 2292
Thorman Boyle Foundation Grants, 2295
Three Guineas Fund Grants, 2297
Tides Foundation Grants, 2302
Toyota Motor Manuf of Alabama Grants, 2309
Toyota Motor Manufacturing of Indiana Grants, 2310
Toyota Motor Manuf of Kentucky Grants, 2311
Toyota Motor Manuf of Mississippi Grants, 2312
Toyota Motor Manufacturing of Texas Grants, 2313
Toyota Motor Manufacturing of West Virginia
    Grants, 2314
Toyota Motor North America of NY Grants, 2315
Toyota Motor Sales, USA Grants, 2316
Toyota Technical Center Grants, 2317
Toyota USA Foundation Environmental Grants, 2319
Turner Foundation Grants, 2326
U.S. Cellular Corporation Grants, 2331
Union Bank, N.A. Corporate Sponsorships and
    Donations, 2333
Union Bank, N.A. Foundation Grants, 2334
Union Pacific Fdn Community & Civic Grants, 2337
United Technologies Corporation Grants, 2347
Vanderburgh Community Foundation Men's Fund
    Grants, 2373
Vanderburgh Community Foundation Recreation
    Grants, 2374
Vanderburgh County Community Foundation
    Women's Fund Grants, 2376
Virginia W. Kettering Foundation Grants, 2388
Volvo Adventure Environmental Awards, 2390
Volvo Bob the Bunny's Cartoon Competition, 2391
Walker Area Community Foundation Grants, 2401
Walmart Fdn Inclusive Communities Grants, 2403
Walmart Fdn National Local Giving Grants, 2404
Walmart Foundation State Giving Grants, 2405
Warrick County Community Foundation Recreation
    Grants, 2410
Washington County Community Fdn Grants, 2416
Washington Gas Charitable Contributions, 2417
Weaver Foundation Grants, 2420
Wells County Foundation Grants, 2426
Western Indiana Community Fdn Grants, 2428
Whatcom Community Foundation Grants, 2436
Whole Foods Foundation, 2445
Widgeon Point Charitable Foundation Grants, 2447
William A. Cooke Foundation Grants, 2452
William B. Stokely Jr. Foundation Grants, 2459
William E. Dean III Charitable Fdn Grants, 2464
William G. and Helen C. Hoffman Foundation
    Grants, 2466
William Ray and Ruth E. Collins Fdn Grants, 2473
Windham Foundation Grants, 2477
Winifred Johnson Clive Foundation Grants, 2478

WinnCompanies Charitable Giving, 2479
Wisconsin Energy Foundation Grants, 2481
Wyomissing Foundation Thun Family Organizational
    Grants, 2505
Wyomissing Foundation Thun Family Program
    Grants, 2506
Xerox Foundation Grants, 2507
Youths' Friends Association Grants, 2511
Z. Smith Reynolds Foundation Small Grants, 2523

Exchange Programs
Laura Musser Intercultural Harmony Grants, 1472

**Exhibitions, Collections, Performances, Video/
Film Production**
3M Company Fdn Community Giving Grants, 5
A.L. Mailman Family Foundation Grants, 20
Aaron Foundation Grants, 42
Abell-Hanger Foundation Grants, 52
ACCF of Indiana Ron and Susie Ballard Community
    Enrichment Fund Grants, 68
ACMP Foundation Community Music Grants, 108
Akron Community Foundation Arts and Culture
    Grants, 150
ALA Baker and Taylor/YALSA Collection
    Development Grants, 157
Alabama Humanities Foundation Major Grants, 159
Albert E. and Birdie W. Einstein Fund Grants, 220
Alcatel-Lucent Technologies Foundation Grants, 224
Amica Insurance Company Sponsorships, 268
Anne J. Caudal Foundation Grants, 276
Ann L. and Carol Green Rhodes Charitable Trust
    Grants, 278
APAP All-In Grants, 283
Arthur Ashley Williams Foundation Grants, 302
ASCAP Foundation Grants, 315
Atlanta Women's Foundation Pathway to Success
    Grants, 327
Autauga Area Community Foundation Grants, 334
Bank of America Charitable Foundation Matching
    Gifts, 356
Bank of Hawaii Foundation Grants, 360
Bayer Fund Community Development Grants, 383
Beckman Coulter Foundation Grants, 394
Benton Community Foundation Grants, 405
Blue River Community Foundation Grants, 458
Boeing Company Contributions Grants, 462
Burton D. Morgan Foundation Hudson Community
    Grants, 482
Caesars Foundation Grants, 492
California Arts Cncl Statewide Networks Grants, 493
Carl M. Freeman Foundation FACES Grants, 507
Carl M. Freeman Foundation Grants, 508
CDC David J. Sencer Museum Student Field Trip
    Experience, 524
CFFVR Project Grants, 546
CFGR Community Impact Grants, 552
Chicago Neighborhood Arts Program Grants, 582
Chilkat Valley Community Foundation Grants, 588
CICF Clare Noyes Grant, 604
City of Oakland Cultural Funding Grants, 618
Collins Foundation Grants, 658
Community Foundation for Greater Buffalo Niagara
    Area Foundation Grants, 673
Community Foundation for the Capital Region
    Grants, 687
Community Foundation of Eastern Connecticut
    General Southeast Grants, 696
Community Foundation of Muncie and Delaware
    County - Kitselman Grants, 733
Community Foundation of Western Massachusetts
    Grants, 741
Cralle Foundation Grants, 760
Crayola Champ Creatively Alive Children Grts, 764
Cresap Family Foundation Grants, 766
Crystelle Waggoner Charitable Trust Grants, 768
Daniel and Nanna Stern Family Fdn Grants, 778
Dayton Foundation Grants, 796
Dean Foundation Grants, 806
Del Mar Foundation Community Grants, 820

Dorrance Family Foundation Grants, 845
Earl and Maxine Claussen Trust Grants, 878
Edyth Bush Charitable Foundation Grants, 893
Ensworth Charitable Foundation Grants, 916
Episcopal Actors' Guild Actors Florence James
    Children's Holiday Fund Grant, 925
Fidelity Charitable Gift Fund Grants, 956
Fifth Third Foundation Grants, 959
Four County Community Foundation General
    Grants, 1000
George A Ohl Jr. Foundation Grants, 1043
George Graham and Elizabeth Galloway Smith
    Foundation Grants, 1047
Georgia-Pacific Foundation Education Grants, 1058
Gil and Dody Weaver Foundation Grants, 1071
GNOF Exxon-Mobil Grants, 1080
GNOF IMPACT Grants for Arts and Culture, 1083
Golden Heart Community Foundation Grants, 1094
Greater Sitka Legacy Fund Grants, 1111
Hahl Proctor Charitable Trust Grants, 1151
Harris Foundation Grants, 1177
Hearst Foundations Culture Grants, 1223
Helen E. Ellis Charitable Trust Grants, 1228
Helen Gertrude Sparks Charitable Trust Grants, 1230
Horace A. Moses Charitable Trust Grants, 1261
HSFCA Biennium Grants, 1267
Inland Empire Community Foundation Capacity
    Building for IE Nonprofits Grants, 1306
James F. and Marion L. Miller Fdn Grants, 1338
Japan Foundation Los Angeles Mini-Grants for
    Japanese Arts & Culture, 1354
Japan Foundation New York Small Grants for Arts
    and Culture, 1355
Japan Foundation New York World Heritage Photo
    Panel Exhibition, 1356
Jessica Stevens Community Foundation Grants, 1363
Joseph Henry Edmondson Foundation Grants, 1388
JP Morgan Chase Fdn Arts and Culture Grants, 1394
Kenai Peninsula Foundation Grants, 1425
Kentucky Arts Cncl Access Assistance Grants, 1428
Ketchikan Community Foundation Grants, 1429
Kodiak Community Foundation Grants, 1446
Leo Goodwin Foundation Grants, 1482
LGA Family Foundation Grants, 1487
Libra Foundation Grants, 1489
Marcia and Otto Koehler Foundation Grants, 1553
Massachusetts Cultural Council Local Cultural
    Council (LCC) Grants, 1601
McCombs Foundation Grants, 1615
Meriden Foundation Grants, 1638
Mertz Gilmore Foundation NYC Dance Grants, 1642
Michelin North America Challenge Education, 1660
Milton and Sally Avery Arts Foundation Grants, 1675
NJSCA Arts Ed Special Initiative Grants, 1764
Norcliffe Foundation Grants, 1766
NYSCA Arts Education: General Operating Support
    Grants, 1781
NYSCA Arts Education: General Program Support
    Grants, 1782
NYSCA Electronic Media and Film: Film Festivals
    Grants, 1785
NYSCA Electronic Media and Film: General
    Operating Support, 1786
NYSCA Electronic Media and Film: General
    Program Support, 1787
NYSCA Electronic Media and Film: Screenings
    Grants, 1788
NYSCA Electronic Media and Film: Workspace
    Grants, 1789
NYSCA Music: Gen Operating Support Grants, 1791
NYSCA Music: Gen Program Support Grants, 1792
NYSCA Special Arts Services: General Program
    Support Grants, 1793
NYSCA Special Arts Services: Instruction and
    Training Grants, 1794
NYSCA Theatre: Prof Performances Grants, 1795
OceanFirst Foundation Major Grants, 1803
OceanFirst Foundation Summer Camp Grants, 1804
OHA 'Ahahui Grants, 1807

Ohio Arts Council Artist in Residence Grants for
    Sponsors, 1810
Olivia R. Gardner Foundation Grants, 1819
Oppenstein Brothers Foundation Grants, 1827
Oregon Community Fdn Community Grants, 1833
Oren Campbell McCleary Chartbl Trust Grants, 1837
Outrigger Duke Kahanamoku Foundation Athletic
    Event Grants, 1852
Outrigger Duke Kahanamoku Foundation Athletic
    Team Grants, 1853
Parker Foundation (California) Grants, 1869
PAS Zildjian Family Opportunity Fund Grants, 1878
PCA Art Organizations and Art Programs Grants for
    Presenting Organizations, 1884
PCA Arts Organizations and Arts Program Grants
    for Music, 1887
PCA Arts Organizations and Arts Programs Grants
    for Art Museums, 1888
PCA Arts Organizations and Arts Programs Grants
    for Crafts, 1891
PCA Arts Organizations and Arts Programs Grants
    for Dance, 1892
PCA Arts Organizations and Arts Programs Grants
    for Film and Electronic Media, 1893
PCA Arts Organizations and Arts Programs Grants
    for Literature, 1894
PCA Arts Organizations and Arts Programs Grants
    for Local Arts, 1895
PCA Arts Organizations and Arts Programs Grants
    for Theatre, 1896
PCA Arts Organizations and Arts Programs Grants
    for Visual Arts, 1898
PCA Busing Grants, 1899
PCA Entry Track Arts Organizations and Arts
    Programs Grants for Art Museums, 1900
PCA Entry Track Arts Organizations and Arts
    Programs Grants for Crafts, 1903
PCA Entry Track Arts Organizations and Arts
    Programs Grants for Dance, 1904
PCA Entry Track Arts Orgs and Arts Programs
    Grants for Film and Electronic Media, 1905
PCA Entry Track Arts Organizations and Arts
    Programs Grants for Literature, 1906
PCA Entry Track Arts Organizations and Arts
    Programs Grants for Local Arts, 1907
PCA Entry Track Arts Organizations and Arts
    Programs Grants for Music, 1908
PCA Entry Track Arts Organizations and Arts
    Programs Grants for Presenting Orgs, 1909
PCA Entry Track Arts Organizations and Arts
    Programs Grants for Theatre, 1910
PCA Entry Track Arts Organizations and Arts
    Programs Grants for Visual Arts, 1912
PCA Pennsylvania Partners in the Arts Program
    Stream Grants, 1914
PCA Pennsylvania Partners in the Arts Project
    Stream Grants, 1915
PCA Strategies for Success Grants - Adv Level, 1917
PCA Strategies for Success Grants - Basic Level, 1918
PCA Strategies for Success Grants - Intermediate
    Level, 1919
PennPAT Artist Technical Assistance Grants, 1929
PennPAT Fee-Support Grants for Presenters, 1930
PennPAT New Directions Grants for Presenters, 1931
PennPAT Presenter Travel Grants, 1932
PennPAT Strategic Opportunity Grants, 1933
Petersburg Community Foundation Grants, 1951
Piedmont Natural Gas Corporate and Charitable
    Contributions, 1966
Polk County Community Foundation Marjorie M.
    and Lawrence R. Bradley Endowment Fund
    Grants, 1998
Polk County Community Foundation Mary F. Kessler
    Fund Grants, 1999
PPCF Community Grants, 2014
Price Chopper's Golub Foundation Grants, 2020
R.S. Gernon Trust Grants, 2047
Rasmuson Foundation Tier Two Grants, 2056
Raymond Austin Hagen Family Fdn Grants, 2060
Reinberger Foundation Grants, 2066

Richard and Caroline T. Gwathmey Memorial Trust
    Grants, 2069
RISCA Project Grants for Individuals, 2079
Robbins-de Beaumont Foundation Grants, 2080
Robbins Charitable Foundation Grants, 2081
Robert R. Meyer Foundation Grants, 2094
Rockwell Collins Charitable Corp Grants, 2098
Santa Fe Community Foundation Seasonal Grants-
    Fall Cycle, 2159
Scott B. and Annie P. Appleby Charitable Trust
    Grants, 2169
Screen Actors Guild StagePALS Assistance, 2173
Seattle Foundation Arts and Culture Grants, 2174
Seward Community Foundation Grants, 2182
Seward Community Foundation Mini-Grants, 2183
Shelley and Donald Rubin Foundation Grants, 2187
Shield-Ayres Foundation Grants, 2189
Sioux Falls Area Community Foundation Community
    Fund Grants, 2203
Sioux Falls Area Community Foundation Spot
    Grants, 2204
Sony Corporation of America Grants, 2216
Sphinx Competition Awards, 2234
SunTrust Bank Trusteed Foundations Greene-Sawtell
    Grants, 2257
SunTrust Bank Trusteed Foundations Nell Warren
    Elkin and William Simpson Elkin Grants, 2258
TAC Arts Access Grant, 2265
TAC Touring Arts and Arts Access Touring Arts
    Grants, 2269
Thomas J. Long Foundation Community Grants, 2291
Union Bank, N.A. Foundation Grants, 2334
United Technologies Corporation Grants, 2347
Virginia Commission for the Arts Artists in
    Education Residency Grants, 2385
Virginia Foundation for the Humanities Open
    Grants, 2387
VSA International Art Program for Children with
    Disabilities Grants, 2394
W.M. Keck Fdn Southern California Grants, 2398
Walker Area Community Foundation Grants, 2401
William Foulds Family Foundation Grants, 2465
William Ray and Ruth E. Collins Fdn Grants, 2473
Wyomissing Foundation Thun Family Program
    Grants, 2506

Faculty/Professional Development
A.C. and Penney Hubbard Foundation Grants, 19
ALA ALSC Distinguished Service Award, 154
Amerigroup Foundation Grants, 264
Anheuser-Busch Foundation Grants, 273
Arizona Commission on the Arts Learning
    Collaboration Grant, 291
Assisi Foundation of Memphis General Grants, 318
Assisi Foundation of Memphis Mini Grants, 319
Baxter International Foundation Grants, 369
Bernard and Audre Rapoport Foundation Education
    Grants, 410
Boeing Company Contributions Grants, 462
Cabot Corporation Foundation Grants, 490
Carl B. and Florence E. King Foundation Grants, 506
Carl M. Freeman Foundation Grants, 508
CFF Leroy Matthews Physician-Scientist Awds, 533
CFF Research Grants, 534
CFFVR Basic Needs Giving Partnership Grants, 537
CFFVR Environmental Stewardship Grants, 540
CFFVR Mielke Family Foundation Grants, 544
Chesapeake Bay Trust Environmental Education
    Grants, 577
Christensen Fund Regional Grants, 600
Community Foundation of St. Joseph County African
    American Community Grants, 737
Daniels Fund Youth Development Grants, 784
Dubois County Community Foundation Grants, 871
Dunspaugh-Dalton Foundation Grants, 873
Edward W. and Stella C. Van Houten Memorial Fund
    Grants, 892
Effie and Wofford Cain Foundation Grants, 895
Fremont Area Community Foundation Amazing X
    Grants, 1019

Fremont Area Community Foundation Community
    Grants, 1020
George A Ohl Jr. Foundation Grants, 1043
George Kress Foundation Grants, 1053
GNOF IMPACT Grants for Youth Dev, 1084
Goldseker Foundation Non-Profit Management
    Assistance Grants, 1095
Grifols Community Outreach Grants, 1122
Hampton Roads Community Foundation Education
    Grants, 1157
Harry A. and Margaret D. Towsley Foundation
    Grants, 1180
Harry Frank Guggenheim Foundation Research
    Grants, 1184
Hawai'i Community Foundation Victoria S. and
    Bradley L. Geist Foundation: Capacity Building
    Grants, 1206
Hill Crest Foundation Grants, 1249
ILA Grants for Literacy Projects in Countries with
    Developing Economies, 1292
Kenneth T. and Eileen L. Norris Fdn Grants, 1427
Kosciusko County Community Fdn Grants, 1452
Lilly Endowment Summer Youth Grants, 1492
Margaret and James A. Elkins Jr. Fdn Grants, 1555
Martha Holden Jennings Foundation Grants-to-
    Educators, 1581
Meadows Foundation Grants, 1626
Mead Witter Foundation Grants, 1628
Micron Technology Fdn Community Grants, 1664
Morris Stulsaft Foundation Early Childhood
    Education Grants, 1696
New Earth Foundation Grants, 1743
Noble County Community Foundation Grants, 1765
Northern Chautauqua Community Foundation
    Community Grants, 1769
NRA Foundation Grants, 1774
NSTA Distinguished Informal Science Education
    Award, 1777
NYSCA Arts Education: Local Capacity Building
    Grants (Regrants), 1783
NYSCA Electronic Media and Film: General
    Operating Support, 1786
NYSCA Electronic Media and Film: Workspace
    Grants, 1789
NYSCA Special Arts Services: General Program
    Support Grants, 1793
NYSCA Special Arts Services: Instruction and
    Training Grants, 1794
NYSCA Theatre: Prof Performances Grants, 1795
P. Buckley Moss Foundation for Children's Education
    Teacher Grants, 1855
PCA-PCD Professional Development for Individual
    Artists Grants, 1883
PCA Arts in Education Residencies, 1885
PCA Arts Organizations and Arts Programs Grants
    for Visual Arts, 1898
PCA Entry Track Arts Organizations and Arts
    Programs Grants for Crafts, 1903
PCA Entry Track Arts Organizations and Arts
    Programs Grants for Visual Arts, 1912
PCA Pennsylvania Partners in the Arts Project
    Stream Grants, 1915
PCA Professional Development Grants, 1916
Philip L. Graham Fund Education Grants, 1962
Polk County Community Foundation Unrestricted
    Grants, 2001
Public Education Power Grants, 2032
Puerto Rico Community Foundation Grants, 2037
Pulaski County Community Foundation Grants, 2038
R.D. and Joan Dale Hubbard Fdn Grants, 2044
Roney-Fitzpatrick Foundation Grants, 2102
Samuel N. and Mary Castle Foundation Grants, 2145
San Antonio Area Foundation Strengthening
    Nonprofits Grants, 2151
Sarkeys Foundation Grants, 2163
SAS Institute Community Relations Donations, 2165
Skaggs Foundation Grants, 2207
Subaru of America Foundation Grants, 2253
TAC Arts Education Teacher Incentive Grants, 2268
V.V. Cooke Foundation Grants, 2371

VSA International Young Soloists Award, 2395
Watson-Brown Foundation Grants, 2418
World of Children Humanitarian Award, 2492
WSF Sports 4 Life Grants, 2496
Xerox Foundation Grants, 2507

Fellowships
3M Company Fdn Community Giving Grants, 5
A-T Children's Project Post Doctoral Fellowships, 17
AACAP Jeanne Spurlock Research Fellowship in
 Substance Abuse and Addiction for Minority
 Medical Students, 28
AACAP Life Members Mentorship Grants for
 Medical Students, 30
AACAP Mary Crosby Congressional Fellowships, 31
AACAP Summer Medical Student Fellowships, 38
Abbott Fund Science Education Grants, 48
Abell-Hanger Foundation Grants, 52
Abney Foundation Grants, 55
ALA Louise Seaman Bechtel Fellowship, 173
Alliant Energy Foundation Community Giving for
 Good Sponsorship Grants, 240
AOCS Thomas H. Smouse Memorial Fellowship, 282
Ar-Hale Family Foundation Grants, 290
Boeing Company Contributions Grants, 462
Cabot Corporation Foundation Grants, 490
Caesars Foundation Grants, 492
Carroll County Community Foundation Grants, 513
CFF First- and Second-Year Clinical Fellowships, 532
CFF Third-, Fourth-, and Fifth-Year Clinical
 Fellowships, 535
Christensen Fund Regional Grants, 600
CIGNA Foundation Grants, 611
Community Foundation of Western Massachusetts
 Grants, 741
Echoing Green Fellowships, 885
Edward W. and Stella C. Van Houten Memorial Fund
 Grants, 892
Effie and Wofford Cain Foundation Grants, 895
Eva Gunther Foundation Fellowships, 937
Evan Frankel Foundation Grants, 938
FCD Young Scholars Program Grants, 953
Ford Foundation BUILD Grants, 984
H.A. and Mary K. Chapman Charitable Trust
 Grants, 1137
Kansas Health Foundation Recognition Grants, 1415
Kennedy Center National Symphony Orchestra Youth
 Fellowships, 1426
Klingenstein-Simons Fellowship Awards in the
 Neurosciences, 1441
Kodak Community Relations Grants, 1445
Lalor Foundation Postdoctoral Fellowships, 1464
Lubrizol Foundation Grants, 1513
Mary K. Chapman Foundation Grants, 1590
Mericos Foundation Grants, 1637
Norcliffe Foundation Grants, 1766
NYSCA Music: Commty Music Schools Grants, 1790
OSF Baltimore Community Fellowships, 1838
OSF Soros Justice Youth Activist Fellowships, 1844
OSF Young Feminist Leaders Fellowships, 1845
PCA Arts Organizations and Arts Programs Grants
 for Crafts, 1891
Pediatric Brain Tumor Foundation Early Career
 Development Grants, 1923
Pediatric Brain Tumor Foundation Early Career
 Development Grants, 1924
Pediatric Brain Tumor Fdn Institute Grants, 1925
Pediatric Brain Tumor Foundation Opportunity
 Grants, 1926
Perkin Fund Grants, 1937
Phil Hardin Foundation Grants, 1960
R.C. Baker Foundation Grants, 2043
Radcliffe Institute Carol K. Pforzheimer Student
 Fellowships, 2048
Ralph M. Parsons Foundation Grants, 2052
Rathmann Family Foundation Grants, 2057
Shell Oil Company Foundation Community
 Development Grants, 2188
Special Olympics Eunice Kennedy Shriver (EKS)
 Fellowships, 2227

University of Chicago Chapin Hall Doris Duke
 Fellowships, 2348
Wallace Foundation Grants, 2402
William T. Grant Foundation Scholars Program, 2475
Xerox Foundation Grants, 2507

General Operating Support
1st Source Foundation Community Involvement
 Grants, 1
520 Charitable Foundation Grants, 14
786 Foundation Grants, 15
A. Alfred Taubman Foundation Grants, 18
A.C. and Penney Hubbard Foundation Grants, 19
A.L. Mailman Family Foundation Grants, 20
A.L. Spencer Foundation Grants, 21
Abbott Fund Access to Health Care Grants, 45
Abbott Fund Community Engagement Grants, 46
Abbott Fund Global AIDS Care Grants, 47
Abbott Fund Science Education Grants, 48
Abby's Legendary Pizza Foundation Grants, 49
Abeles Foundation Grants, 51
Abell-Hanger Foundation Grants, 52
Abundance Foundation International Grants, 57
ACCF Dennis and Melanie Bieberich Community
 Enrichment Fund Grants, 59
ACCF of Indiana Bank of Geneva Heritage Fund
 Grants, 64
ACCF of Indiana First Merchants Bank / Decatur
 Bank and Trust Fund Grants, 66
ACCF of Indiana Michael Basham Community
 Enrichment Fund Grants, 67
ACCF Ralph Biggs Memorial Community
 Enrichment Fund Grants, 69
ACF Adoption Opportunities Grants, 71
ACF American Indian and Alaska Native Early Head
 Start Expansion Grants, 72
ACF Child Welfare Training Grants, 75
ACF Head Start and/or Early Head Start Grantee
 - Clay, Randolph, and Talladega Counties,
 Alabama, 82
ACF Head Start and/or Early Head Start Grantee -
 St. Landry Parish, Louisiana, 83
ACF Infant Adoption Awareness Training Program
 Grants, 84
ACF Promoting Safe and Stable Families (PSSF)
 Program Grants, 89
ACF Transitional Living Program and Maternity
 Group Homes Grants, 96
ACF Unaccompanied Refugee Children Grants, 99
ACF Voluntary Agencies Matching Grants, 100
Achelis and Bodman Foundation Grants, 101
Achelis Foundation Grants, 102
Ackerman Foundation Grants, 103
ACL Alternatives to Guardianship Youth Resource
 Center Grants, 104
ACL Neonatal Abstinence Syndrome National
 Training Initiative Grant, 106
Acuity Charitable Foundation Grants, 110
Adam Don Foundation Grants, 112
Adams-Mastrovich Family Foundation Grants, 113
Adams and Reese Corporate Giving Grants, 114
Adams County Community Foundation Grants, 115
Adams Family Foundation I Grants, 116
Adams Family Foundation II Grants, 117
Adams Family Fdn of Nora Springs Grants, 118
Adams Family Foundation of Ohio Grants, 119
Adams Family Foundation of Tennessee Grants, 120
Adobe Foundation Action Grants, 126
Adolph Coors Foundation Grants, 129
Adray Foundation, 130
Advance Auto Parts Corporate Giving Grants, 131
AEGON Transamerica Foundation Education and
 Financial Literacy Grants, 132
AEGON Transamerica Foundation Health and
 Wellness Grants, 133
AHS Foundation Grants, 143
Air Products Foundation Grants, 148
Akron Community Fdn Education Grants, 151
Akron Community Foundation Health and human
 services Grants, 152

Alaska Community Foundation Children's Trust Tier
 1 Community Based Child Abuse and Neglect
 Prevention Grants, 198
Alaska Community Foundation Children's Trust Tier
 2 Innovation Grants, 200
Albert and Ethel Herzstein Charitable Foundation
 Grants, 219
Albertsons Companies Foundation Nourishing
 Neighbors Grants, 221
Albert W. Cherne Foundation Grants, 222
Albert W. Rice Charitable Foundation Grants, 223
Alcatel-Lucent Technologies Foundation Grants, 224
Alden and Vada Dow Fund Grants, 225
Alex Stern Family Foundation Grants, 229
ALFJ International Fund Grants, 231
ALFJ International Social Change Opportunity Fund
 Grants, 232
Alfred E. Chase Charitable Foundation Grants, 233
A Little Hope Grants, 235
Allan C. and Lelia J. Garden Foundation Grants, 236
Allegis Group Foundation Grants, 237
Alliance for Strong Families and Communities
 Grants, 239
Alliant Energy Foundation Community Giving for
 Good Sponsorship Grants, 240
Alloy Family Foundation Grants, 241
Alpha Natural Resources Corporate Giving, 246
Alvah H. and Wyline P. Chapman Foundation
 Grants, 248
Amelia Sillman Rockwell and Carlos Perry Rockwell
 Charities Fund Grants, 250
Ameren Corporation Community Grants, 251
American Schlafhorst Foundation Grants, 262
American Woodmark Foundation Grants, 263
Amerigroup Foundation Grants, 264
AMERIND Community Service Project Grants, 265
Anderson Foundation Grants, 271
Andrew Family Foundation Grants, 272
Anheuser-Busch Foundation Grants, 273
Anna Fitch Ardenghi Trust Grants, 274
Anne J. Caudal Foundation Grants, 276
Ann L. and Carol Green Rhodes Charitable Trust
 Grants, 278
Ann Ludington Sullivan Foundation Grants, 279
Antone and Edene Vidinha Charitable Grants, 281
Ar-Hale Family Foundation Grants, 290
Arkema Foundation Grants, 298
Arthur E. and Josephine Campbell Beyer Foundation
 Grants, 303
Aspen Community Foundation Grants, 316
Atkinson Foundation Community Grants, 325
Atlanta Foundation Grants, 326
Atlanta Women's Foundation Pathway to Success
 Grants, 327
Atlas Insurance Agency Foundation Grants, 329
Aunt Kate Foundation Grants, 331
Austin S. Nelson Foundation Grants, 333
Autauga Area Community Foundation Grants, 334
Avery Family Trust Grants, 338
Avery Foundation Grants, 339
Babcock Charitable Trust Grants, 343
Back Home Again Foundation Grants, 344
Bank of America Charitable Foundation Matching
 Gifts, 356
Bank of America Charitable Foundation Volunteer
 Grants, 358
Bank of America Corporation Sponsorships, 359
Bank of Hawaii Foundation Grants, 360
Bank of the Orient Community Giving, 361
Barrasso, Usdin, Kupperman, Freeman, and Sarver
 Corporate Grants, 362
Batts Foundation Grants, 367
Baxter International Corporate Giving Grants, 368
Baxter International Foundation Grants, 369
Bay and Paul Foundations PreK-12 Transformative
 Learning Practices Grants, 386
BBF Florida Family Literacy Initiative Grants, 386
Belvedere Community Foundation Grants, 399
Bernard F. and Alva B. Gimbel Foundation Criminal
 Justice Grants, 412

Bernau Family Foundation Grants, 413
Bierhaus Foundation Grants, 421
Bill and Melinda Gates Foundation Agricultural Development Grants, 425
Bill and Melinda Gates Foundation Emergency Response Grants, 426
Bill and Melinda Gates Foundation Water, Sanitation and Hygiene Grants, 428
Bill Graham Memorial Foundation Grants, 429
Bindley Family Foundation Grants, 430
Blanche and Irving Laurie Foundation Grants, 436
Blandin Foundation Expand Opportunity Grants, 437
Blandin Foundation Itasca County Area Vitality Grants, 439
Blue Grass Community Foundation Clark County Fund Grants, 444
Blue Grass Community Foundation Fayette County Fund Grants, 446
Blue Grass Community Foundation Franklin County Fund Grants, 447
Blue Grass Community Foundation Harrison County Fund Grants, 448
Blue Grass Community Foundation Madison County Fund Grants, 450
Blue Grass Community Foundation Magoffin County Fund Grants, 451
Blue Grass Community Foundation Morgan County Fund Grants, 452
Blue Grass Community Foundation Rowan County Fund Grants, 453
Blue Grass Community Foundation Woodford County Fund Grants, 454
Blue Mountain Community Foundation Warren Community Action Fund Grants, 457
Blumenthal Foundation Grants, 459
BMW of North America Charitable Contribs, 460
Bodenwein Public Benevolent Foundation Grants, 461
Boeing Company Contributions Grants, 462
Bradley-Turner Foundation Grants, 466
Bradley C. Higgins Foundation Grants, 467
Bright Promises Foundation Grants, 470
Brown Foundation Grants, 476
Brunswick Foundation Dollars for Doers Grants, 478
Brunswick Foundation Grants, 479
Burton D. Morgan Foundation Hudson Community Grants, 482
Burton D. Morgan Foundation Youth Entrepreneurship Grants, 483
Bushrod H. Campbell and Adah F. Hall Charity Fund Grants, 486
C.F. Adams Charitable Trust Grants, 488
C.H. Robinson Worldwide Foundation Grants, 489
Cabot Corporation Foundation Grants, 490
Cadillac Products Packaging Company Foundation Grants, 491
Caesars Foundation Grants, 492
Callaway Foundation Grants, 496
Camille Beckman Foundation Grants, 499
Campbell Foundation Grants, 500
Campbell Soup Foundation Grants, 501
Cargill Corporate Giving Grants, 503
Carl M. Freeman Foundation FACES Grants, 507
Carl M. Freeman Foundation Grants, 508
Carl R. Hendrickson Family Foundation Grants, 509
Carl W. and Carrie Mae Joslyn Trust Grants, 510
Carnegie Corporation of New York Grants, 511
Castle Foundation Grants, 518
Castle Foundation Grants, 517
Castle Industries Foundation Grants, 519
Catherine Holmes Wilkins Foundation Charitable Grants, 520
CFFVR Appleton Education Foundation Grants, 536
CFFVR Basic Needs Giving Partnership Grants, 537
CFFVR Clintonville Area Foundation Grants, 538
CFFVR Clintonville Area Foundation Grants, 539
CFFVR Environmental Stewardship Grants, 540
CFFVR Frank C. Shattuck Community Grants, 541
CFFVR Schmidt Family G4 Grants, 548
CFFVR Shawano Area Community Foundation Grants, 549

CFFVR Women's Fund for the Fox Valley Region Grants, 550
CFF Winter Park Community Grants, 551
CFGR Community Impact Grants, 552
CFGR Jenkins Foundation Grants, 553
Chapman Charitable Foundation Grants, 560
Chapman Family Foundation, 562
Charles Crane Family Foundation Grants, 563
Charles Delmar Foundation Grants, 564
Charles H. Hall Foundation, 565
Charles H. Pearson Foundation Grants, 566
Charles N. and Eleanor Knight Leigh Foundation Grants, 568
Charles Nelson Robinson Fund Grants, 569
CHC Foundation Grants, 575
Chesapeake Bay Trust Environmental Education Grants, 577
Chesapeake Bay Trust Outreach and Community Engagement Grants, 579
Chicago Neighborhood Arts Program Grants, 582
Chilkat Valley Community Foundation Grants, 588
Christensen Fund Regional Grants, 600
Christine and Katharina Pauly Charitable Trust Grants, 601
CHT Foundation Education Grants, 603
CICF Indianapolis Fdn Community Grants, 606
CICF John Harrison Brown and Rob Burse Grt, 607
CIGNA Foundation Grants, 611
Cincinnati Bell Foundation Grants, 612
Cincinnati Milacron Foundation Grants, 613
Circle K Corporation Contributions Grants, 614
Citizens Savings Foundation Grants, 617
City of Oakland Cultural Funding Grants, 618
CJ Fdn for SIDS Program Services Grants, 619
Clara Blackford Smith and W. Aubrey Smith Charitable Foundation Grants, 621
Clarence T.C. Ching Foundation Grants, 624
Clark and Ruby Baker Foundation Grants, 625
Claude A. and Blanche McCubbin Abbott Charitable Trust Grants, 628
Clayton Baker Trust Grants, 629
Cleveland Foundation Higley Fund Grants, 634
CNCS Foster Grandparent Projects Grants, 646
CNCS Senior Corps Retired and Senior Volunteer Program Grants, 648
Colgate-Palmolive Company Grants, 652
Collins C. Diboll Private Foundation Grants, 657
Collins Foundation Grants, 658
Colonel Stanley R. McNeil Foundation Grants, 659
Colorado Interstate Gas Grants, 661
Colorado Trust Health Investment Grants, 662
Columbus Foundation Traditional Grants, 663
Community Foundation for Greater Atlanta Spark Clayton Grants, 667
Community Foundation for Greater Atlanta Spark Newton Grants, 668
Community Foundation for Greater Buffalo Competitive Grants, 670
Community Foundation for Greater Buffalo Niagara Area Foundation Grants, 673
Community Foundation for Greater Buffalo Ralph C. Wilson, Jr. Legacy Fund Grants, 674
Community Foundation for SE Michigan Chelsea Community Foundation General Grant, 680
Community Foundation for the Capital Region Grants, 687
Community Foundation for the National Capital Region Community Leadership Grants, 688
Community Foundation of Bartholomew County Heritage Fund Grants, 690
Community Foundation of Crawford County, 695
Community Foundation of Grant County Grants, 703
Community Foundation of Greater Greensboro Community Grants, 708
Community Foundation of Madison and Jefferson County Grants, 731
Community Foundation of St. Joseph County Special Project Challenge Grants, 738
Community Foundation of Switzerland County Grants, 739

Community Fdn of Wabash County Grants, 740
Community Memorial Foundation Responsive Grants, 743
Cooke Foundation Grants, 748
Corina Higginson Trust Grants, 750
Countess Moira Charitable Foundation Grants, 752
Courtney S. Turner Charitable Trust Grants, 753
Cralle Foundation Grants, 760
Crane Foundation General Grants, 761
Crane Fund Grants, 763
Cresap Family Foundation Grants, 766
Crescent Porter Hale Foundation Grants, 767
Curtis Foundation Grants, 771
D. W. McMillan Foundation Grants, 776
Daniel and Nanna Stern Family Fdn Grants, 778
Daniels Fund Amateur Sports Grants, 779
Daniels Drug and Alcohol Addiction Grants, 780
Daniels Homeless and Disadvantaged Grants, 782
David Alan and Susan Berkman Rahm Foundation Grants, 785
David and Barbara B. Hirschhorn Foundation Education and Literacy Grants, 786
David and Barbara B. Hirschhorn Foundation Summer Camping Grants, 787
David and Betty Sacks Foundation Grants, 788
David M. and Marjorie D. Rosenberg Foundation Grants, 790
Dayton Foundation Grants, 796
Dayton Foundation Huber Heights Grants, 797
Dayton Foundation Vandalia-Butler Grants, 799
Dayton Power and Light Foundation Grants, 802
Deaconess Community Foundation Grants, 803
Dean Foundation Grants, 806
DeKalb County Community Foundation Grants, 815
Del Mar Foundation Community Grants, 820
Delmarva Power & Light Contributions, 821
Dining for Women Grants, 831
Dolan Children's Foundation Grants, 832
Don and May Wilkins Charitable Trust Grants, 842
Doree Taylor Charitable Foundation Grants, 843
Dorrance Family Foundation Grants, 845
Dorr Foundation Grants, 846
Dream Weaver Foundation, 865
DTE Energy Foundation Community Development Grants, 866
DTE Energy Foundation Health and Human Services Grants, 869
DTE Energy Foundation Leadership Grants, 870
Dubois County Community Foundation Grants, 871
Dunspaugh-Dalton Foundation Grants, 873
Eastern Bank Charitable Foundation Partnerships Grants, 881
Eastern Bank Charitable Foundation Targeted Grants, 882
Edna Wardlaw Charitable Trust Grants, 886
Edward and Ellen Roche Relief Fdn Grants, 887
Edward and Romell Ackley Foundation Grants, 889
Edward F. Swinney Trust Grants, 890
Edwards Memorial Trust Grants, 891
Edward W. and Stella C. Van Houten Memorial Fund Grants, 892
Effie Allen Little Foundation Grants, 894
Effie and Wofford Cain Foundation Grants, 895
Effie Kuhlman Charitable Trust Grants, 896
Eileen Fisher Activating Leadership Grants for Women and Girls, 898
Elizabeth Huth Coates Charitable Foundation Grants, 900
Elizabeth Morse Genius Charitable Trust Grants, 901
Ella West Freeman Foundation Grants, 904
Ellen Abbott Gilman Trust Grants, 905
El Pomar Foundation Anna Keesling Ackerman Fund Grants, 907
El Pomar Foundation Grants, 908
Elsie H. Wilcox Foundation Grants, 909
Emily Hall Tremaine Foundation Learning Disabilities Grants, 912
Ethel Sergeant Clark Smith Foundation Grants, 935
Eulalie Bloedel Schneider Foundation Grants, 936
Evan Frankel Foundation Grants, 938

Evelyn and Walter Haas, Jr. Fund Gay and Lesbian Rights Grants, 940

Evelyn and Walter Haas, Jr. Fund Immigrant Rights Grants, 941

Evelyn and Walter Haas, Jr. Fund Nonprofit Leadership Grants, 942

Ewing Marion Kauffman Foundation Grants, 943

Faye L. and William L. Cowden Charitable Foundation Grants, 950

Fidelity Charitable Gift Fund Grants, 956

Fifth Third Bank Corporate Giving, 958

Finish Line Youth Foundation Founder's Grants, 960

FirstEnergy Foundation Community Grants, 965

Florence Foundation Grants, 978

Florence Hunt Maxwell Foundation Grants, 979

Ford Family Foundation Grants - Access to Health and Dental Services, 980

Ford Family Foundation Grants - Technical Assistance , 983

Forest Foundation Grants, 985

Foundations of East Chicago Education Grants, 995

Four County Community Foundation General Grants, 1000

Four County Community Foundation Healthy Senior/Healthy Youth Fund Grants, 1001

Fourjay Foundation Grants, 1003

Four Lanes Trust Grants, 1005

Francis Beidler Foundation Grants, 1007

Francis L. Abreu Charitable Trust Grants, 1008

Franklin County Community Fdn Grants, 1010

Frank Reed and Margaret Jane Peters Memorial Fund Grants, 1013

Frank Reed and Margaret Jane Peters Memorial Fund II Grants, 1014

Fred and Gretel Biel Charitable Trust Grants, 1016

Frederick McDonald Trust Grants, 1017

Frederick W. Marzahl Memorial Fund Grants, 1018

Fremont Area Community Foundation Amazing X Grants, 1019

Fremont Area Community Foundation Community Grants, 1020

Fremont Area Community Foundation Youth Advisory Committee Grants, 1022

Friedman Family Foundation Grants, 1023

Fuller E. Callaway Foundation Grants, 1027

Fuller Foundation Youth At Risk Grants, 1028

Fund for the City of New York Grants, 1029

G.N. Wilcox Trust Grants, 1031

Gamble Foundation Grants, 1032

Gardner Foundation Grants, 1035

Gardner Foundation Grants, 1034

Gardner W. and Joan G. Heidrick, Jr. Foundation Grants, 1036

Gene Haas Foundation, 1038

General Motors Foundation Grants, 1039

George and Ruth Bradford Foundation Grants, 1042

George A Ohl Jr. Foundation Grants, 1043

George B. Page Foundation Grants, 1044

George E. Hatcher, Jr. and Ann Williams Hatcher Foundation Grants, 1045

George F. Baker Trust Grants, 1046

George Graham and Elizabeth Galloway Smith Foundation Grants, 1047

George H. and Jane A. Mifflin Memorial Fund Grants, 1048

George H.C. Ensworth Memorial Fund Grants, 1049

George H. Sandy Foundation Grants, 1050

George Kress Foundation Grants, 1053

George P. Davenport Trust Fund Grants, 1054

George W. Codrington Charitable Foundation Grants, 1055

George W. Wells Foundation Grants, 1057

Georgia-Pacific Fdn Entrepreneurship Grants, 1059

Geraldine R. Dodge Fdn Education Grants, 1061

German Protestant Orphan Asylum Foundation Grants, 1066

Gertrude & William C. Wardlaw Grants, 1067

Gil and Dody Weaver Foundation Grants, 1071

Global Fund for Women Grants, 1073

GNOF Bayou Communities Grants, 1077

GNOF IMPACT Grants for Arts and Culture, 1083

GNOF IMPACT Grants for Youth Dev, 1084

GNOF IMPACT Harold W. Newman, Jr. Charitable Trust Grants, 1086

GNOF Plaquemines Community Grants, 1091

Golden Heart Community Foundation Grants, 1094

Good+Foundation Grants, 1096

Grace Bersted Foundation Grants, 1097

Graham and Carolyn Holloway Family Foundation Grants, 1098

Graham Family Charitable Foundation Grants, 1099

Graham Foundation Grants, 1100

Greater Saint Louis Community Fdn Grants, 1110

Greater Tacoma Community Foundation Fund for Women and Girls Grants, 1112

Greater Tacoma Community Foundation General Operating Grants, 1113

Green River Area Community Fdn Grants, 1117

Greenspun Family Foundation Grants, 1118

Gregory and Helayne Brown Charitable Foundation Grants, 1119

Greygates Foundation Grants, 1120

Grotto Foundation Project Grants, 1123

Grundy Foundation Grants, 1124

GTRCF Boys and Girls Club of Grand Traverse Endowment Grants, 1126

GTRCF Elk Rapids Area Community Endowment Grants, 1127

GTRCF Joan Rajkovich McGarry Family Education Endowment Grants, 1131

Gulf Coast Foundation of Community Operating Grants, 1134

Guy I. Bromley Trust Grants, 1136

H.A. and Mary K. Chapman Charitable Trust Grants, 1137

Hahl Proctor Charitable Trust Grants, 1151

Harden Foundation Grants, 1166

Hardin County Community Foundation Grants, 1167

Harmony Foundation for Children Grants, 1168

Harmony Grove Foundation Grants, 1169

Harold and Rebecca H. Gross Fdn Grants, 1171

Harold Brooks Foundation Grants, 1172

Harold K.L. Castle Foundation Windward Youth Leadership Fund Grants, 1175

Harris and Eliza Kempner Fund Ed Grants, 1176

Harris Foundation Grants, 1177

Harry and Helen Sands Charitable Trust Grants, 1181

Harry and Jeanette Weinberg Fdn Grants, 1182

Harry B. and Jane H. Brock Foundation Grants, 1183

Harry Frank Guggenheim Foundation Research Grants, 1184

Hartford Foundation Regular Grants, 1185

Hattie M. Strong Foundation Grants, 1194

Hawai'i Community Foundation Richard Smart Fund Grants, 1204

Hawai'i Community Foundation Robert E. Black Fund Grants, 1205

Hawaii Community Foundation Omidyar Ohana Fund Grants, 1213

Hawaii Electric Industries Charitable Foundation Grants, 1218

Hawaii State Legislature Grant-In-Aid, 1219

Hazel and Walter T. Bales Foundation Grants, 1220

Hearst Foundations Culture Grants, 1223

Hearst Foundations Social Service Grants, 1224

Helen Bader Foundation Grants, 1227

Helen Gertrude Sparks Charitable Trust Grants, 1230

Helen Irwin Littauer Educational Trust Grants, 1231

Helen V. Brach Foundation Grants, 1232

Henrietta Lange Burk Fund Grants, 1235

Henry and Ruth Blaustein Rosenberg Foundation Education Grants, 1236

Henry and Ruth Blaustein Rosenberg Foundation Youth Development Grants, 1237

Henry F. Koch Residual Trust Grants, 1241

Herbert A. and Adrian W. Woods Foundation Grants, 1243

Herman Goldman Foundation Grants, 1245

Hillsdale County Community Foundation General Grants, 1250

Hillsdale County Community Foundation Y.O.U.T.H. Grants, 1252

Honor the Earth Grants, 1259

Horace A. Kimball and S. Ella Kimball Foundation Grants, 1260

Horace A. Moses Charitable Trust Grants, 1261

HRK Foundation Health Grants, 1264

Hubbard Broadcasting Foundation Grants, 1269

Hubbard Family Foundation Grants, 1271

Hubbard Family Foundation Grants, 1270

Hubbard Farms Charitable Foundation Grants, 1272

Huffy Foundation Grants, 1273

Huisking Foundation Grants, 1274

Human Source Foundation Grants, 1276

Huntington Clinical Foundation Grants, 1278

Iddings Foundation Major Project Grants, 1284

Iddings Foundation Medium Project Grants, 1285

Iddings Foundation Small Project Grants, 1286

Ike and Roz Friedman Foundation Grants, 1289

Illinois Arts Council Theater Program Grants, 1293

Indiana OCRA Rural Capacity Grants (RCG), 1301

Irving S. Gilmore Foundation Grants, 1314

Island Insurance Foundation Grants, 1316

J. Knox Gholston Foundation Grants, 1321

J.W. Gardner II Foundation Grants, 1323

J.W. Kieckhefer Foundation Grants, 1324

J. Walton Bissell Foundation Grants, 1325

J. Watumull Fund Grants, 1326

J. Willard and Alice S. Marriott Fdn Grants, 1327

J. William Gholston Foundation Grants, 1328

Jack and Dorothy Byrne Foundation Grants, 1329

Jack H. and William M. Light Charitable Trust Grants, 1330

Jacob and Hilda Blaustein Foundation Israel Program Grants, 1335

James and Abigail Campbell Family Foundation Grants, 1337

James Ford Bell Foundation Grants, 1339

James LeVoy Sorenson Foundation Grants, 1343

Jane's Trust Grants, 1346

Jane Bradley Pettit Foundation Community and Social Development Grants, 1347

Janet Spencer Weekes Foundation Grants, 1348

Jaquelin Hume Foundation Grants, 1357

Jayne and Leonard Abess Foundation Grants, 1358

Jeffris Wood Foundation Grants, 1359

Jerry L. and Barbara J. Burris Fdn Grants, 1362

Jewish Fund Grants, 1364

Jim Moran Foundation Grants, 1366

Joan Bentinck-Smith Charitable Fdn Grants, 1367

John and Marcia Goldman Foundation Youth Development Grants, 1368

John Clarke Trust Grants, 1369

John D. and Katherine A. Johnston Foundation Grants, 1370

John H. and Wilhelmina D. Harland Charitable Foundation Children and Youth Grants, 1374

John H. and Wilhelmina D. Harland Charitable Foundation Community Services Grants, 1375

John M. Weaver Foundation Grants, 1376

John P. Ellbogen Fdn Community Grants, 1377

John W. Anderson Foundation Grants, 1383

Joni Elaine Templeton Foundation Grants, 1384

Joseph H. and Florence A. Roblee Foundation Children and Youth Grants, 1385

Joseph H. and Florence A. Roblee Foundation Education Grants, 1386

Joseph H. and Florence A. Roblee Foundation Family Grants, 1387

Joseph Henry Edmondson Foundation Grants, 1388

Joseph S. Stackpole Charitable Trust Grants, 1390

Journal Gazette Foundation Grants, 1391

Joyce and Randy Seckman Charitable Foundation Grants, 1393

JP Morgan Chase Fdn Arts and Culture Grants, 1394

Judy and Peter Blum Kovler Foundation Grants, 1396

Julius N. Frankel Foundation Grants, 1400

K and F Baxter Family Foundation Grants, 1413

Kansas Health Foundation Recognition Grants, 1415

Kate B. Reynolds Charitable Trust Health Care Grants, 1416
Kate B. Reynolds Charitable Trust Poor and Needy Grants, 1417
Katharine Matthies Foundation Grants, 1418
Kathryne Beynon Foundation Grants, 1420
Kawabe Memorial Fund Grants, 1423
Kelvin and Eleanor Smith Foundation Grants, 1424
Kenneth T. and Eileen L. Norris Fdn Grants, 1427
Kimball International-Habig Foundation Education Grants, 1433
Kimball International-Habig Foundation Health and Human Services Grants, 1434
Kind World Foundation Grants, 1438
Kirkpatrick Foundation Grants, 1440
Klingenstein-Simons Fellowship Awards in the Neurosciences, 1441
Kopp Family Foundation Grants, 1448
Koret Foundation Grants, 1449
Kovler Family Foundation Grants, 1454
Kovler Family Foundation Grants, 1455
Laclede Gas Charitable Trust Grants, 1457
Land O'Lakes Foundation Mid-Atlantic Grants, 1467
Latkin Charitable Foundation Grants, 1469
Laura L. Adams Foundation Grants, 1473
Laurel Foundation Grants, 1475
Lavina Parker Trust Grants, 1477
Leola Osborn Trust Grants, 1483
Leo Niessen Jr., Charitable Trust Grants, 1484
Leonsis Foundation Grants, 1485
Lewis H. Humphreys Charitable Trust Grants, 1486
LGA Family Foundation Grants, 1487
Lil and Julie Rosenberg Foundation Grants, 1491
Lilly Endowment Summer Youth Grants, 1492
Linford & Mildred White Charitable Grants, 1495
Lloyd G. Balfour Foundation Attleboro-Specific Charities Grants, 1502
Locations Foundation Legacy Grants, 1504
Lotus 88 Foundation for Women and Children Grants, 1508
Louie M. and Betty M. Phillips Fdn Grants, 1509
Louis and Sandra Berkman Foundation Grants, 1510
Louis Calder Foundation Grants, 1511
Lubrizol Corporation Community Grants, 1512
Lubrizol Foundation Grants, 1513
Lucy Downing Nisbet Charitable Fund Grants, 1515
Lumpkin Family Fdn Healthy People Grants, 1518
Lynn and Foster Friess Family Fdn Grants, 1520
M.A. Rikard Charitable Trust Grants, 1521
M. Bastian Family Foundation Grants, 1522
Mabel A. Horne Fund Grants, 1525
Mabel F. Hoffman Charitable Trust Grants, 1526
Mabel Y. Hughes Charitable Trust Grants, 1530
Macquarie Bank Foundation Grants, 1532
Madison County Community Foundation General Grants, 1537
Maine Women's Fund Econ Security Grants, 1546
Manuel D. and Rhoda Mayerson Fdn Grants, 1550
Marathon Petroleum Corporation Grants, 1551
Marcia and Otto Koehler Foundation Grants, 1553
Mardag Foundation Grants, 1554
Margaret M. Walker Charitable Fdn Grants, 1556
Margaret T. Morris Foundation Grants, 1557
Marie C. and Joseph C. Wilson Foundation Rochester Small Grants, 1559
Marin Community Foundation Social Justice and Interfaith Understanding Grants, 1567
Marion and Miriam Rose Fund Grants, 1569
Marion Gardner Jackson Charitable Trust Grts, 1570
Marion I. and Henry J. Knott Foundation Discretionary Grants, 1571
Marion I. and Henry J. Knott Foundation Standard Grants, 1572
Marisla Foundation Human Services Grants, 1573
Marjorie Moore Charitable Foundation Grants, 1574
Marquette Bank Neighborhood Commit Grants, 1577
Marsh Corporate Grants, 1580
Martin Family Foundation Grants, 1583
Mary Black Foundation Active Living Grants, 1585

Mary D. and Walter F. Frear Eleemosynary Trust Grants, 1588
Mary K. Chapman Foundation Grants, 1590
Mary Owen Borden Foundation Grants, 1597
Mary W.B. Curtis Trust Grants, 1599
Mary Wilmer Covey Charitable Trust Grants, 1600
Mathile Family Foundation Grants, 1604
Matilda R. Wilson Fund Grants, 1605
Maurice J. Masserini Charitable Trust Grants, 1610
Maurice R. Robinson Fund Grants, 1611
Max and Anna Levinson Foundation Grants, 1612
May and Stanley Smith Charitable Trust Grants, 1613
McCarthy Family Fdn Charity Fund Grants, 1614
McCune Charitable Foundation Grants, 1617
McGregor Fund Human Services Grants, 1621
McInerny Foundation Grants, 1622
Mead Family Foundation Grants, 1625
MeadWestvaco Foundation Sustainable Communities Grants, 1627
Mead Witter Foundation Grants, 1628
Memorial Foundation for Children Grants, 1633
Merck Family Fund Urban Farming and Youth Leadership Grants, 1635
Merck Family Fund Youth Transforming Urban Communities Grants, 1636
Mericos Foundation Grants, 1637
Meriden Foundation Grants, 1638
Merrick Foundation Grants, 1640
Merrick Foundation Grants, 1639
Mertz Gilmore Foundation NYC Communities Grants, 1641
Mervin Bovaird Foundation Grants, 1643
Meta and George Rosenberg Fdn Grants, 1644
Metzger-Price Fund Grants, 1647
Meyer Foundation Education Grants, 1649
Meyer Fdn Healthy Communities Grants, 1650
Meyer Memorial Trust Responsive Grants, 1653
MGN Family Foundation Grants, 1656
Michael Reese Health Trust Core Grants, 1658
Michael Reese Health Trust Responsive Grants, 1659
Milton Hicks Wood and Helen Gibbs Wood Charitable Trust Grants, 1676
Mimi and Peter Haas Fund Grants, 1677
Montana Arts Council Cultural and Aesthetic Project Grants, 1685
Montana Community Foundation Grants, 1687
Montgomery County Community Foundation Health and Human Services Fund Grants, 1689
Morris Stulsaft Foundation Early Childhood Education Grants, 1696
Morris Stulsaft Foundation Educational Support for Children Grants, 1697
Morris Stulsaft Foundation Participation in the the Arts Grants, 1698
Morris Stulsaft Foundation Pathways to Work Grants, 1699
Moses Kimball Fund Grants, 1701
Ms. Fdn for Women Economic Justice Grants, 1707
Mt. Sinai Health Care Foundation Health of the Urban Community Grants, 1710
Narragansett Number One Foundation Grants, 1712
Natalie W. Furniss Foundation Grants, 1715
Nathaniel and Elizabeth P. Stevens Foundation Grants, 1719
Nationwide Insurance Foundation Grants, 1726
Nellie Mae Education Foundation District-Level Change Grants, 1736
Nell J. Redfield Foundation Grants, 1737
New Covenant Farms Grants, 1742
New Earth Foundation Grants, 1743
New Hampshire Charitable Foundation Community Unrestricted Grants, 1747
New York Foundation Grants, 1753
Noble County Community Foundation Grants, 1765
Norcliffe Foundation Grants, 1766
Norman Foundation Grants, 1767
Northern Chautauqua Community Foundation Community Grants, 1769
NYFA Artists in the School Community Planning Grants, 1779

NYSCA Arts Education: General Operating Support Grants, 1781
NYSCA Arts Education: Local Capacity Building Grants (Regrants), 1783
NYSCA Electronic Media and Film: General Operating Support, 1786
NYSCA Music: Gen Operating Support Grants, 1791
O. Max Gardner Foundation Grants, 1798
OceanFirst Foundation Major Grants, 1803
OceanFirst Foundation Summer Camp Grants, 1804
Olive B. Cole Foundation Grants, 1816
Olive Higgins Prouty Foundation Grants, 1817
Olive Smith Browning Charitable Trust Grants, 1818
Olivia R. Gardner Foundation Grants, 1819
OMNOVA Solutions Fdn Education Grants, 1820
OneFamily Foundation Grants, 1822
Ontario Arts Council Arts Organizations in Communities and Schools Operating Grants, 1824
Oppenstein Brothers Foundation Grants, 1827
Ordean Foundation Catalyst Grants, 1830
Ordean Foundation Partnership Grants, 1831
Oren Campbell McCleary Chartbl Trust Grants, 1837
Pacers Foundation Be Drug-Free Grants, 1856
Pacers Foundation Be Educated Grants, 1857
Pacers Foundation Be Healthy and Fit Grants, 1858
Pacers Foundation Be Tolerant Grants, 1859
Pacers Foundation Indiana Fever's Be YOUnique Fund Grants, 1860
PacifiCare Foundation Grants, 1861
Packard Foundation Local Grants, 1863
Pajaro Valley Community Health Trust Insurance/Coverage & Education on Using the System Grants, 1864
Pajaro Valley Community Health Trust Diabetes and Contributing Factors Grants, 1865
Pajaro Valley Community Health Trust Oral Health: Prevention & Access Grants, 1866
Palmer Foundation Grants, 1867
Parker Foundation (California) Grants, 1869
Patrick and Aimee Butler Family Foundation Community Human Services Grants, 1880
Paul and Edith Babson Foundation Grants, 1881
PCA Arts Organizations and Arts Programs Grants for Art Museums, 1888
PCA Entry Track Arts Organizations and Arts Programs Grants for Art Museums, 1900
PDF Community Organizing Grants, 1920
Pentair Foundation Education and Community Grants, 1934
Percy B. Ferebee Endowment Grants, 1936
Perkin Fund Grants, 1937
Perkins-Ponder Foundation Grants, 1938
Perkins Charitable Foundation Grants, 1939
Perpetual Benevolent Fund, 1940
Perry and Sandy Massie Foundation Grants, 1941
Pettus Foundation Grants, 1952
Philanthrofund Foundation Grants, 1959
Phil Hardin Foundation Grants, 1960
Philip L. Graham Fund Education Grants, 1962
Phoenix Suns Charities Grants, 1964
Piedmont Health Foundation Grants, 1965
Piedmont Natural Gas Foundation Health and Human Services Grants, 1968
Pinnacle Entertainment Foundation Grants, 1972
Piper Jaffray Foundation Communities Giving Grants, 1974
Piper Trust Arts and Culture Grants, 1975
Piper Trust Children Grants, 1976
Piper Trust Education Grants, 1977
Pittsburgh Fdn Affordable Housing Grants, 1980
Pittsburgh Foundation Healthy Children and Adults Grants, 1981
PMI Foundation Grants, 1982
Polk County Community Foundation Marjorie M. and Lawrence R. Bradley Endowment Fund Grants, 1998
Porter County Community Foundation Health and Wellness Grant, 2002
Porter County Community Foundation PCgivingproject Grants, 2003

Porter County Community Foundation Sparking the
Arts Fund Grants, 2004
Powell Family Foundation Grants, 2012
Powell Foundation Grants, 2013
PPCF Esther M. and Freeman E. Everett Charitable
Foundation Grants, 2016
PPG Industries Foundation Grants, 2017
Price Chopper's Golub Foundation Grants, 2020
Priddy Foundation Operating Grants, 2021
Proteus Fund Grants, 2027
Prudential Foundation Education Grants, 2028
Public Welfare Fdn Juvenile Justice Grants, 2033
Public Welfare Foundation Special Initiative to
Advance Civil Legal Aid Grants, 2034
Public Welfare Foundation Special Opportunities
Grants, 2035
Publix Super Markets Charities Local Grants, 2036
Puerto Rico Community Foundation Grants, 2037
Pulido Walker Foundation, 2039
Putnam County Community Fdn Grants, 2040
R.C. Baker Foundation Grants, 2043
R.D. Beirne Trust Grants, 2045
R.S. Gernon Trust Grants, 2047
Ralph M. Parsons Foundation Grants, 2052
Raskob Fdn for Catholic Activities Grants, 2054
Rathmann Family Foundation Grants, 2057
RCF General Community Grants, 2062
Reinberger Foundation Grants, 2066
Ressler-Gertz Foundation Grants, 2067
Richard and Caroline T. Gwathmey Memorial Trust
Grants, 2069
Richard J. Stern Foundation for the Arts Grants, 2071
Richard W. Goldman Family Fdn Grants, 2073
Richland County Bank Grants, 2074
Ricks Family Charitable Trust Grants, 2075
Riedman Foundation Grants, 2076
Ripley County Community Foundation Grants, 2077
Robbins-de Beaumont Foundation Grants, 2080
Robbins Charitable Foundation Grants, 2081
Robbins Family Charitable Foundation Grants, 2082
Robert and Betty Wo Foundation Grants, 2083
Robert and Helen Haddad Foundation Grants, 2084
Robert F. Lange Foundation Grants, 2090
Robert Lee Adams Foundation Grants, 2091
Robert Lee Blaffer Foundation Grants, 2092
Robert R. Meyer Foundation Grants, 2094
Robert W. Knox, Sr. and Pearl Wallis Knox
Charitable Foundation, 2095
Robin Hood Foundation Grants, 2096
Robinson Foundation Grants, 2097
Roger L. and Agnes C. Dell Charitable Trust I
Grants, 2099
Roger L. and Agnes C. Dell Charitable Trust II
Grants, 2100
Ron and Sanne Higgins Family Fdn Grants, 2101
Roney-Fitzpatrick Foundation Grants, 2102
Rose Hills Foundation Grants, 2106
Rosenberg Charity Foundation Grants, 2107
Roy and Christine Sturgis Charitable Tr Grts, 2115
Ruth Anderson Foundation Grants, 2122
Ruth and Henry Campbell Foundation Grants, 2123
Ruth and Vernon Taylor Foundation Grants, 2124
Ruth Camp Campbell Charitable Trust Grants, 2125
Sabina Dolan and Gladys Saulsbury Foundation
Grants, 2130
Sadler Family Foundation Grants, 2132
Saeman Family Fdn A Charitable Grants, 2133
Saint Louis Rams Foundation Community
Donations, 2139
Salmon Foundation Grants, 2140
Saltchuk Corporate Giving, 2141
Samuel N. and Mary Castle Foundation Grants, 2145
Samuel S. Johnson Foundation Grants, 2146
San Antonio Area Foundation Annual Responsive
Grants, 2147
Sand Hill Foundation Environment and Sustainability
Grants, 2152
Sand Hill Foundation Health and Opportunity
Grants, 2153

Santa Fe Community Foundation Seasonal Grants-
Fall Cycle, 2159
Sapelo Foundation Social Justice Grants, 2160
Sara Elizabeth O'Brien Trust Grants, 2161
Sarah G. McCarthy Memorial Foundation, 2162
Sartain Lanier Family Foundation Grants, 2164
Scheumann Foundation Grants, 2166
Schlessman Family Foundation Grants, 2167
Schramm Foundation Grants, 2168
Scott B. and Annie P. Appleby Charitable Trust
Grants, 2169
Seattle Foundation Arts and Culture Grants, 2174
Seattle Foundation Basic Needs Grants, 2175
Seattle Foundation Benjamin N. Phillips Memorial
Fund Grants, 2176
Seattle Foundation Health and Wellness Grants, 2179
Sensient Technologies Foundation Grants, 2180
Serco Foundation Grants, 2181
Seybert Foundation Grants, 2184
Shield-Ayres Foundation Grants, 2189
Sidgmore Family Foundation Grants, 2195
Sidney and Sandy Brown Foundation Grants, 2196
Sidney Stern Memorial Trust Grants, 2197
Siebert Lutheran Foundation Grants, 2198
Sioux Falls Area Community Foundation Community
Fund Grants, 2203
Sioux Falls Area Community Foundation Spot
Grants, 2204
Skaggs Family Foundation Grants, 2205
Skaggs Family Foundation Grants, 2206
Skaggs Foundation Grants, 2207
Social Justice Fund Northwest Economic Justice
Giving Project Grants, 2215
Sony Corporation of America Grants, 2216
Sorenson Legacy Foundation Grants, 2217
Stan and Sandy Checketts Foundation Grants, 2235
Starr Foundation Grants, 2237
State Farm Good Neighbor Citizenship Company
Grants, 2238
Staunton Farm Foundation Grants, 2239
Stein Family Charitable Trust Grants, 2240
Stella and Charles Guttman Foundation Grants, 2241
Sterling-Turner Charitable Foundation Grants, 2242
Sterling and Shelli Gardner Foundation Grants, 2243
Steven B. Achelis Foundation Grants, 2244
Stinson Foundation Grants, 2246
Storm Castle Foundation Grants, 2248
Strake Foundation Grants, 2249
Stranahan Foundation Grants, 2250
Streisand Foundation Grants, 2251
Swindells Charitable Foundation Grants, 2261
Sylvia Perkin Perpetual Charitable Trust Grants, 2263
TE Foundation Grants, 2279
Telluride Foundation Community Grants, 2281
Telluride Fdn Emergency Grants, 2282
Textron Corporate Contributions Grants, 2286
Thelma Braun and Bocklett Family Foundation
Grants, 2287
Thelma Doelger Charitable Trust Grants, 2288
Thomas and Agnes Carvel Foundation Grants, 2289
Thomas J. Atkins Memorial Trust Fund Grants, 2290
Thomas Sill Foundation Grants, 2292
Thomas W. Bradley Foundation Grants, 2293
Thomas W. Briggs Foundation Grants, 2294
Thorman Boyle Foundation Grants, 2295
Three Guineas Fund Grants, 2297
Tides Fdn Friends of the IGF Fund Grants, 2300
Tides Foundation Girl Rising Fund Grants, 2301
Tides Foundation Grants, 2302
Todd Brock Family Foundation Grants, 2305
Tom C. Barnsley Foundation Grants, 2306
Toyota Motor North America of NY Grants, 2315
TSYSF Team Grants, 2323
U.S. Bank Foundation Grants, 2330
Union Bank, N.A. Foundation Grants, 2334
Union Pacific Fdn Community & Civic Grants, 2337
Union Pacific Foundation Health and Human
Services Grants, 2338
Union Square Arts Award, 2339
Union Square Award for Social Justice, 2340

United Technologies Corporation Grants, 2347
V.V. Cooke Foundation Grants, 2371
Victor E. Speas Foundation Grants, 2380
Victoria S. and Bradley L. Geist Foundation
Enhancement Grants, 2381
Vigneron Memorial Fund Grants, 2384
Volkswagen Group of America Corporate
Contributions Grants, 2389
W.P. and Bulah Luse Foundation Grants, 2399
W.W. Smith Chartbl Trust Basic Needs Grants, 2400
Walter J. and Betty C. Zable Fdn Grants, 2406
Walter S. and Evan C. Jones Testam Trust, 2407
Watson-Brown Foundation Grants, 2418
Weaver Foundation Grants, 2420
Weaver Popcorn Foundation Grants, 2421
WestWind Foundation Reproductive Health and
Rights Grants, 2434
Whitehorse Foundation Grants, 2439
Whole Foods Foundation, 2445
Widgeon Point Charitable Foundation Grants, 2447
William A. Badger Foundation Grants, 2451
William Blair and Company Foundation Grants, 2461
William E. Dean III Charitable Fdn Grants, 2464
William G. and Helen C. Hoffman Foundation
Grants, 2466
William G. Gilmore Foundation Grants, 2467
William J. and Gertrude R. Casper Foundation
Grants, 2469
William J. and Tina Rosenberg Fdn Grants, 2470
William J. Brace Charitable Trust, 2471
William M. Weaver Foundation Grants, 2472
William Ray and Ruth E. Collins Fdn Grants, 2473
Williams Comps Homegrown Giving Grants, 2474
Wilton and Effie Hebert Foundation Grants, 2476
Wold Foundation Grants, 2482
Wolfe Associates Grants, 2483
Women's Fund of Hawaii Grants, 2485
Wood Family Charitable Trust Grants, 2487
Woods Fund of Chicago Grants, 2489
WSF Travel and Training Fund Grants, 2498
Wyoming Community Fdn General Grants, 2501
Wyoming Community Foundation Hazel Patterson
Memorial Grants, 2502
Xerox Foundation Grants, 2507
Youths' Friends Association Grants, 2511
YSA Global Youth Service Day Lead Agy Grts, 2514
YSA National Child Awareness Month Youth
Ambassador Grants, 2517
Z. Smith Reynolds Foundation Small Grants, 2523
Zollner Foundation Grants, 2526
ZYTL Foundation Grants, 2528

Graduate Assistantships
Abbott Fund Science Education Grants, 48
Xerox Foundation Grants, 2507

Grants to Individuals
ACCF of Indiana Angel Funds Grants, 62
Adams Family Foundation of Tennessee Grants, 120
Adams Rotary Memorial Fund A Grants, 122
AKF Grants for Children, 149
ALA Innovative Reading Grant, 171
Annie Gardner Foundation Grants, 277
Avista Foundation Vulnerable and Limited Income
Population Grants, 341
Bank of America Charitable Foundation Basic Needs
Grants, 354
Bingham McHale LLP Pro Bono Services, 431
CDC Disease Detective Camp, 525
Charlotte and Joseph Gardner Fdn Grants, 570
Clara Abbott Foundation Need-Based Grants, 620
Community Foundation for San Benito County
Martin Rajkovich Children's Fund Grants, 678
Community Foundation of Louisville CHAMP Fund
Grants, 720
Cystic Fibrosis Lifestyle Foundation Individual
Recreation Grants, 772
Cystic Fibrosis Lifestyle Foundation Loretta Morris
Memorial Fund Grants, 773

Cystic Fibrosis Lifestyle Foundation Mentored Recreation Grants, 774
Cystic Fibrosis Lifestyle Foundation Peer Support Grants, 775
Delmarva Power & Light Contributions, 821
Dexter Adams Foundation Grants, 829
Different Needz Foundation Grants, 830
Dolan Media Foundation Grants, 833
Dollar Energy Fund Grants, 834
Donald G. Gardner Humanities Tr Youth Grts, 840
Do Something Back End Developer Intern, 848
Do Something Business Development Intern, 849
Do Something Campaigns Intern, 850
Do Something Digital Content Intern, 851
Do Something Digital Member Exp Intern, 852
Do Something Finance and Human Res Intern, 853
Do Something International Intern, 854
Do Something Intern of Fun, 855
Do Something Partnerships and Public Relations Intern, 856
Do Something TMI Intern, 858
Do Something User Experience Research Intern, 859
Do Something Web Developer Intern, 860
Do Something Writing and Journalism Intern, 861
Eastern Bank Charitable Foundation Neighborhood Support Grants, 880
Emily O'Neill Sullivan Foundation Grants, 913
Emma J. Adams Memorial Fund Grants, 914
Eva Gunther Foundation Fellowships, 937
Fitzpatrick, Cella, Harper & Scinto Pro Bono Services, 976
From the Top Alumni Leadership Grants, 1025
Greater Tacoma Community Foundation Spark Grants, 1114
HAF Barry F. Phelps Leukemia Fund Grants, 1140
HAF Ian Chris Mackey Newman Fund Grts, 1143
HAF Phyllis Nilsen Leal Mem Fund Grants, 1149
Hannah's Helping Hands Grants, 1165
Hawaii Community Foundation Oscar and Rosetta Fish Fund Grants, 1214
Hearst Foundations United States Senate Youth Grants, 1225
James K. and Arlene L. Adams Foundation Scholarships, 1341
Kalamazoo Community Foundation Individuals and Families Grants, 1409
Katie's Krops Grants, 1421
Kevin J Major Youth Sports Scholarships, 1431
KIND Causes Monthly Grants, 1435
Maggie Welby Foundation Grants, 1538
Maggie Welby Foundation Scholarships, 1539
Margaret Wiegand Trust Grants, 1558
Marin Community Foundation Stinson Bolinas Community Grants, 1568
Mark W. Coy Foundation Grants, 1575
Michelle O'Neill Foundation Grants, 1661
Montana Arts Council Cultural and Aesthetic Project Grants, 1685
Montana Community Foundation Big Sky LIFT Grants, 1686
Montgomery County Community Foundation Libby Whitecotton Fund Grants, 1690
New Covenant Farms Grants, 1742
OSF Soros Justice Youth Activist Fellowships, 1844
PCA-PCD Professional Development for Individual Artists Grants, 1883
PCA Arts Management Internship, 1886
PCA Pennsylvania Partners in the Arts Project Stream Grants, 1915
PCA Professional Development Grants, 1916
PennPAT Artist Technical Assistance Grants, 1929
PennPAT Strategic Opportunity Grants, 1933
Presidio Fencing Club Youth Fencers Assistance Scholarships, 2019
Quaker Oats Company Kids Care Clubs Grants, 2041
RISCA Project Grants for Individuals, 2079
Sabina Dolan and Gladys Saulsbury Foundation Grants, 2130
Sphinx Competition Awards, 2234
Stan and Sandy Checketts Foundation Grants, 2235

TSYSF Individual Scholarships, 2322
Union Labor Health Fdn Angel Fund Grants, 2335
Union Labor Health Foundation Dental Angel Fund Grants, 2336
UnitedHealthcare Children's Fdn Grants, 2342
Virginia Foundation for the Humanities Folklife Apprenticeships, 2386
Washington Area Fuel Fund Grants, 2413
WSF Rusty Kanokogi Fund for the Advancement of U.S. Judo Grants, 2495
WSF Travel and Training Fund Grants, 2498
Zane's Foundation Grants, 2524
Zellweger Baby Support Network Grants, 2525

International Exchange Programs
Shell Deer Park Grants, 2186
Summit Foundation Grants, 2255

International Grants
AAUW International Project Grants, 44
Abbott Fund Global AIDS Care Grants, 47
Abundance Foundation International Grants, 57
Adobe Foundation Action Grants, 126
Aid for Starving Children Emerg Aid Grants, 144
Aid for Starving Children Health and Nutrition Grants, 145
Aid for Starving Children Homes and Education Grants, 146
Air Products Foundation Grants, 148
ALFJ Astraea U.S. and International Emergency Fund, 230
ALFJ International Fund Grants, 231
Arthur M. Blank Family Foundation American Explorers Grants, 305
Bank of America Charitable Foundation Matching Gifts, 356
Baxter International Corporate Giving Grants, 368
Baxter International Foundation Grants, 369
Bay and Paul Foundations PreK-12 Transformative Learning Practices Grants, 370
Best Buy Children's Fdn @15 Scholarship , 415
BibleLands Grants, 420
Bill and Melinda Gates Foundation Agricultural Development Grants, 425
Bill and Melinda Gates Foundation Emergency Response Grants, 426
Bill and Melinda Gates Foundation Policy and Advocacy Grants, 427
Bill and Melinda Gates Foundation Water, Sanitation and Hygiene Grants, 428
Blossom Fund Grants, 441
BP Foundation Grants, 465
Brinker Int Corporation Charitable Giving, 471
Cabot Corporation Foundation Grants, 490
Caesars Foundation Grants, 492
Cargill Corporate Giving Grants, 503
Carnegie Corporation of New York Grants, 511
Changemakers Innovation Awards, 559
Charles Delmar Foundation Grants, 564
Christensen Fund Regional Grants, 600
CIGNA Foundation Grants, 611
Cisco Systems Foundation San Jose Community Grants, 615
Collective Brands Foundation Payless Gives Shoes 4 Kids Grants, 655
Curtis Foundation Grants, 771
Echoing Green Fellowships, 885
Elton John AIDS Foundation Grants, 910
Firelight Foundation Grants, 964
Ford Foundation BUILD Grants, 984
Foundation Beyond Belief Compassionate Impact Grants, 986
Foundation Beyond Belief Humanist Grants, 987
Giving Gardens Challenge Grants, 1072
Global Fund for Women Grants, 1073
GMFUS Balkan Trust for Democracy Grants, 1075
Greater Saint Louis Community Fdn Grants, 1110
Greygates Foundation Grants, 1120
H.B. Fuller Foundation Grants, 1138

Harry Frank Guggenheim Foundation Research Grants, 1184
Helen Bader Foundation Grants, 1227
IIE 911 Armed Forces Scholarships, 1288
ILA Grants for Literacy Projects in Countries with Developing Economies, 1292
Isabel Allende Foundation Esperanza Grants, 1315
Jacob and Hilda Blaustein Foundation Israel Program Grants, 1335
Japan Foundation Los Angeles Grants for Japanese-Language Courses, 1352
Japan Foundation Los Angeles Japanese-Language Teaching Materials Purchase Grants, 1353
Japan Foundation New York World Heritage Photo Panel Exhibition, 1356
Kodak Community Relations Grants, 1445
Ludwick Family Foundation Grants, 1516
May and Stanley Smith Charitable Trust Grants, 1613
NIMH Early Identification and Treatment of Mental Disorders in Children and Adolescents Grts, 1761
Norman Foundation Grants, 1767
Oak Foundation Child Abuse Grants, 1799
OSF Early Childhood Program Grants, 1841
OSF Education Program Grants in Kyrgyzstan, 1842
OSF Education Support Program Grants, 1843
OSF Young Feminist Leaders Fellowships, 1845
OSF Youth Action Fund Grants in Kyrgyzstan, 1846
Palmer Foundation Grants, 1867
PDF Community Organizing Grants, 1920
PDF Fiscal Sponsorship Grant, 1921
Pentair Foundation Education and Community Grants, 1934
PepsiCo Foundation Grants, 1935
Pettus Foundation Grants, 1952
Radcliffe Institute Carol K. Pforzheimer Student Fellowships, 2048
Radcliffe Institute Oral History Grants, 2049
Raskob Fdn for Catholic Activities Grants, 2054
Rockwell Collins Charitable Corp Grants, 2098
SanDisk Corp Community Sharing Grants, 2155
Stella and Charles Guttman Foundation Grants, 2241
Sylvia Adams Charitable Trust Grants, 2262
Tata Trust Grant for Certificate Course in Holistic inclusion of Learners with Diversities, 2273
TE Foundation Grants, 2279
Thrasher Research Fund Grants, 2296
Tides Fdn Friends of the IGF Fund Grants, 2300
United Methodist Committee on Relief Hunger and Poverty Grants, 2344
United Technologies Corporation Grants, 2347
UPS Foundation Economic and Global Literacy Grants, 2351
USAID Innovations in Feed the Future Monitoring and Evaluation Grants, 2355
USAID Integrated Youth Development Activity Grants, 2356
USAID Nigeria Ed Crisis Response Grants, 2358
USAID School Improvement Program Grants, 2360
USAID U.S.-Egypt Learning Grants, 2361
Volvo Adventure Environmental Awards, 2390
WestWind Foundation Reproductive Health and Rights Grants, 2434
World of Children Humanitarian Award, 2492
Xerox Foundation Grants, 2507
Youths' Friends Association Grants, 2511
YSA GYSD Regional Partner Grants, 2515

Job Training/Adult Vocational Programs
3M Company Fdn Community Giving Grants, 5
ACCF of Indiana Bank of Geneva Heritage Fund Grants, 64
ACCF of Indiana First Merchants Bank / Decatur Bank and Trust Fund Grants, 66
ACF Refugee Career Pathways Grants, 90
ACF Social and Economic Development Strategies Grants, 93
ACF Sustainable Employment and Economic Development Strategies Grants, 95
ACF Voluntary Agencies Matching Grants, 100
Achelis and Bodman Foundation Grants, 101

Achelis Foundation Grants, 102
Adolph Coors Foundation Grants, 129
A Fund for Women Grants, 137
Akron Community Fdn Education Grants, 151
Alaska Airlines Foundation LIFT Grants, 194
Allstate Corporate Giving Grants, 242
Allstate Foundation Safe and Vital Communities
    Grants, 244
Alpha Natural Resources Corporate Giving, 246
Ama OluKai Foundation Grants, 249
Anderson Foundation Grants, 271
Arizona Foundation for Women Deborah G. Carstens
    Fund Grants, 293
Assisi Foundation of Memphis General Grants, 318
Assisi Foundation of Memphis Mini Grants, 319
AT&T Foundation Education Grants, 321
Atkinson Foundation Community Grants, 325
Autauga Area Community Foundation Grants, 334
Baltimore Community Foundation Mitzvah Fund for
    Good Deeds Grants, 349
Bank of America Charitable Foundation Student
    Leaders Grants, 357
Bank of Hawaii Foundation Grants, 360
BBF Maine Family Literacy Initiative Planning
    Grants, 388
Beckman Coulter Foundation Grants, 394
Benton Community Foundation Grants, 405
Bernard and Audre Rapoport Foundation Education
    Grants, 410
Blue Mountain Community Foundation Warren
    Community Action Fund Grants, 457
Blue River Community Foundation Grants, 458
Boeing Company Contributions Grants, 462
BP Foundation Grants, 465
Bridgestone Americas Trust Fund Grants, 469
Brown County Community Foundation Grants, 475
Burlington Industries Foundation Grants, 481
Burton D. Morgan Foundation Youth
    Entrepreneurship Grants, 483
Camille Beckman Foundation Grants, 499
Cargill Corporate Giving Grants, 503
Carl M. Freeman Foundation Grants, 508
CenturyLink Clarke M. Williams Foundation
    Matching Time Grants, 531
CFFVR Jewelers Mutual Chartbl Giving Grants, 543
CFFVR Schmidt Family G4 Grants, 548
CICF Women's Grants , 609
Citizens Bank Charitable Foundation Grants, 616
Claremont Savings Bank Foundation Grants, 623
Cleveland Browns Foundation Grants, 633
Community Foundation for the Capital Region
    Grants, 687
Community Foundation of Bartholomew County
    Heritage Fund Grants, 690
Community Foundation of Crawford County, 695
Community Foundation of Eastern Connecticut
    Northeast Women and Girls Grants, 697
Community Foundation of Louisville Anna Marble
    Memorial Fund for Princeton Grants, 717
Community Foundation of Louisville Education
    Grants, 724
Community Foundation of Louisville Human
    Services Grants, 726
Community Foundation of Muncie and Delaware
    County Maxon Grants, 734
Daniels Fund Youth Development Grants, 784
Del Mar Foundation Community Grants, 820
DOL Youthbuild Grants, 838
Eastern Bank Charitable Foundation Targeted
    Grants, 882
Edward and Ellen Roche Relief Fdn Grants, 887
Edward F. Swinney Trust Grants, 890
Eide Bailly Resourcefullness Awards, 897
Essex County Community Foundation F1rst Jobs
    Fund Grants, 930
Essex County Community Foundation Women's
    Fund Grants, 934
Eulalie Bloedel Schneider Foundation Grants, 936
Evelyn and Walter Haas, Jr. Fund Immigrant Rights
    Grants, 941

Fidelity Charitable Gift Fund Grants, 956
First Hawaiian Bank Foundation Corporate Giving
    Grants, 967
Foundation Beyond Belief Compassionate Impact
    Grants, 986
Foundation Beyond Belief Humanist Grants, 987
Four County Community Foundation General
    Grants, 1000
Four Lanes Trust Grants, 1005
Friends of Hawaii Charities Grants, 1024
Gannett Foundation Community Action Grants, 1033
Georgia-Pacific Fdn Entrepreneurship Grants, 1059
GNOF New Orleans Works Grants, 1088
Go Daddy Cares Charitable Contributions, 1093
Greater Milwaukee Foundation Grants, 1109
Greater Sitka Legacy Fund Grants, 1111
Greater Tacoma Community Foundation Fund for
    Women and Girls Grants, 1112
Green River Area Community Fdn Grants, 1117
Grifols Community Outreach Grants, 1122
GTRCF Elk Rapids Area Community Endowment
    Grants, 1127
HAF Community Grants, 1141
HAF Joe Alexandre Mem Family Fund Grants, 1145
HAF Laurence and Elaine Allen Memorial Fund
    Grants, 1146
Hannaford Supermarkets Community Giving, 1164
Harold K.L. Castle Foundation Strengthening
    Windward Oahu Communities Grants, 1174
Harris Foundation Grants, 1177
Harry and Jeanette Weinberg Fdn Grants, 1182
Hattie M. Strong Foundation Grants, 1194
HBF Pathways Out of Poverty Grants, 1222
Hearst Foundations Social Service Grants, 1224
Helen Bader Foundation Grants, 1227
Helen V. Brach Foundation Grants, 1232
Highmark Corporate Giving Grants, 1248
HLTA Visitor Industry Charity Walk Grant, 1254
Intel Corporation Community Grants, 1311
Isabel Allende Foundation Esperanza Grants, 1315
Jane Bradley Pettit Foundation Community and
    Social Development Grants, 1347
Jessica Stevens Community Foundation Grants, 1363
John F. Kennedy Center for the Performing Arts
    National Rosemary Kennedy Internship, 1371
Joseph H. and Florence A. Roblee Foundation Family
    Grants, 1387
Joseph Henry Edmondson Foundation Grants, 1388
Jovid Foundation Employment Training Grants, 1392
Ketchikan Community Foundation Grants, 1429
Kodak Community Relations Grants, 1445
Kodiak Community Foundation Grants, 1446
Liberty Bank Foundation Grants, 1488
Linden Foundation Grants, 1494
Mabel Louise Riley Foundation Family Strengthening
    Small Grants, 1528
Make Sense Foundation Grants, 1548
Margaret M. Walker Charitable Fdn Grants, 1556
Marquette Bank Neighborhood Commit Grants, 1577
Marriott Int Corporate Giving Grants, 1578
Matson Community Giving Grants, 1607
May and Stanley Smith Charitable Trust Grants, 1613
McCune Charitable Foundation Grants, 1617
Merrick Foundation Grants, 1639
Middlesex Savings Charitable Foundation
    Educational Opportunities Grants, 1670
Miller Foundation Grants, 1673
Ms. Fdn for Women Economic Justice Grants, 1707
Norcliffe Foundation Grants, 1766
Norman Foundation Grants, 1767
NZDIA Lottery Minister's Discretionary Fund
    Grants, 1797
OMNOVA Solutions Fdn Education Grants, 1820
OneFamily Foundation Grants, 1822
Oppenstein Brothers Foundation Grants, 1827
Oregon Community Fdn Community Grants, 1833
PacifiCare Foundation Grants, 1861
Pentair Foundation Education and Community
    Grants, 1934
PG&E Community Vitality Grants, 1957

PGE Foundation Grants, 1958
Philip L. Graham Fund Education Grants, 1962
Piedmont Natural Gas Corporate and Charitable
    Contributions, 1966
Piper Jaffray Foundation Communities Giving
    Grants, 1974
Polk County Community Foundation Marjorie M.
    and Lawrence R. Bradley Endowment Fund
    Grants, 1998
Polk County Community Foundation Unrestricted
    Grants, 2001
Portland General Electric Foundation Grants, 2007
Price Chopper's Golub Foundation Grants, 2020
Pulaski County Community Foundation Grants, 2038
Reinberger Foundation Grants, 2066
Robbins-de Beaumont Foundation Grants, 2080
Salmon Foundation Grants, 2140
Samuel S. Johnson Foundation Grants, 2146
Sand Hill Foundation Environment and Sustainability
    Grants, 2152
Sand Hill Foundation Health and Opportunity
    Grants, 2153
Seward Community Foundation Grants, 2182
Seward Community Foundation Mini-Grants, 2183
Shield-Ayres Foundation Grants, 2189
Sierra Health Foundation Responsive Grants, 2199
Sioux Falls Area Community Foundation Community
    Fund Grants, 2203
Sioux Falls Area Community Fdn Spot Grants, 2204
Sobrato Family Foundation Grants, 2211
Sobrato Family Fdn Meeting Space Grants, 2212
Sobrato Family Foundation Office Space Grants, 2213
Sorenson Legacy Foundation Grants, 2217
Speer Trust Grants, 2230
Strake Foundation Grants, 2249
Textron Corporate Contributions Grants, 2286
Thomas Sill Foundation Grants, 2292
Toyota Motor Manuf of Mississippi Grants, 2312
Toyota Motor Manufacturing of West Virginia
    Grants, 2314
Toyota USA Foundation Education Grants, 2318
U.S. Bank Foundation Grants, 2330
Union Bank, N.A. Foundation Grants, 2334
UPS Foundation Economic and Global Literacy
    Grants, 2351
USAID Community Livelihoods Project in Yemen
    Grant, 2352
Vanderburgh Community Foundation Men's Fund
    Grants, 2373
Vanderburgh County Community Foundation
    Women's Fund Grants, 2376
Walker Area Community Foundation Grants, 2401
Women's Fund of Hawaii Grants, 2485
Wyomissing Foundation Thun Family Organizational
    Grants, 2505
Wyomissing Foundation Thun Family Program
    Grants, 2506
Xerox Foundation Grants, 2507

Land Acquisition
Ar-Hale Family Foundation Grants, 290
Arkema Foundation Grants, 298
Eastern Bank Charitable Foundation Partnerships
    Grants, 881
Harrison County Community Foundation Signature
    Grants, 1179
Janson Foundation Grants, 1350
Lynn and Foster Friess Family Fdn Grants, 1520
Norcliffe Foundation Grants, 1766
Oregon Community Fdn Community Grants, 1833
Polk County Community Foundation Bradley
    Breakthrough Community Benefit Grants, 1995
Robert R. Meyer Foundation Grants, 2094
Seattle Foundation C. Keith Birkenfeld Memorial
    Trust Grants, 2177
Shield-Ayres Foundation Grants, 2189
Van Kampen Boyer Molinari Charitable Foundation
    Grants, 2377
William J. and Gertrude R. Casper Foundation
    Grants, 2469

Matching/Challenge Funds
3M Company Fdn Community Giving Grants, 5
A.L. Mailman Family Foundation Grants, 20
Abbott Fund Global AIDS Care Grants, 47
Abell-Hanger Foundation Grants, 52
ACCF John and Kay Boch Fund Grants, 60
ACF Marriage Strengthening Research &
    Dissemination Center Grants, 85
ACF Social and Economic Development Strategies
    Grants, 93
ACF Voluntary Agencies Matching Grants, 100
AEGON Transamerica Foundation Education and
    Financial Literacy Grants, 132
Agnes M. Lindsay Trust Grants, 140
Air Products Foundation Grants, 148
Alabama Humanities Foundation Major Grants, 159
Alaska State Council on the Arts Cultural
    Collaboration Project Grants, 211
Albertsons Companies Foundation Nourishing
    Neighbors Grants, 221
Alex Stern Family Foundation Grants, 229
Allstate Corporate Giving Grants, 242
Allstate Corp Hometown Commitment Grants, 243
Allstate Foundation Safe and Vital Communities
    Grants, 244
Alpha Natural Resources Corporate Giving, 246
American Woodmark Foundation Grants, 263
Amica Insurance Company Community Grants, 267
Anheuser-Busch Foundation Grants, 273
Appalachian Regional Commission Business
    Development Revolving Loan Fund Grants, 285
Appalachian Regional Commission Education and
    Training Grants, 286
Appalachian Regional Commission Health Care
    Grants, 288
Ar-Hale Family Foundation Grants, 290
Arizona Commission on the Arts Youth Arts
    Engagement Grant, 292
Arthur Ashley Williams Foundation Grants, 302
Aspen Community Foundation Grants, 316
Assisi Fdn of Memphis Capital Project Grants, 317
Austin Community Foundation Grants, 332
Bank of America Charitable Foundation Matching
    Gifts, 356
Baton Rouge Area Foundation Grants, 365
Batts Foundation Grants, 367
Baxter International Corporate Giving Grants, 368
Baxter International Foundation Grants, 369
Bay and Paul Foundations PreK-12 Transformative
    Learning Practices Grants, 370
BCBSM Foundation Community Health Matching
    Grants, 392
Benton Community Foundation Grants, 405
Bikes Belong Grants, 424
Blandin Foundation Itasca County Area Vitality
    Grants, 439
Blue Grass Community Foundation Clark County
    Fund Grants, 444
Blue Grass Community Foundation Fayette County
    Fund Grants, 446
Blue Grass Community Foundation Franklin County
    Fund Grants, 447
Blue Grass Community Foundation Harrison County
    Fund Grants, 448
Blue Grass Community Foundation Hudson-Ellis
    Grants, 449
Blue Grass Community Foundation Magoffin County
    Fund Grants, 451
Blue Grass Community Foundation Morgan County
    Fund Grants, 452
Blue Grass Community Foundation Rowan County
    Fund Grants, 453
Blue Grass Community Foundation Woodford
    County Fund Grants, 454
Blue River Community Foundation Grants, 458
Blumenthal Foundation Grants, 459
Boeing Company Contributions Grants, 462
Bridgestone Americas Trust Fund Grants, 469
Brookdale Fdn Relatives as Parents Grants, 474
Brown Foundation Grants, 476

Brunswick Foundation Dollars for Doers Grants, 478
Brunswick Foundation Grants, 479
Burlington Industries Foundation Grants, 481
C.H. Robinson Worldwide Foundation Grants, 489
Cabot Corporation Foundation Grants, 490
California Arts Cncl Statewide Networks Grants, 493
Callaway Foundation Grants, 496
Campbell Soup Foundation Grants, 501
Cargill Corporate Giving Grants, 503
Carl M. Freeman Foundation Grants, 508
Cass County Community Foundation Grants, 516
Cause Populi Worthy Cause Grants, 521
CenturyLink Clarke M. Williams Foundation
    Matching Time Grants, 531
CFFVR Clintonville Area Foundation Grants, 539
CFFVR Robert and Patricia Endries Family
    Foundation Grants, 547
CFFVR Women's Fund for the Fox Valley Region
    Grants, 550
CFF Winter Park Community Grants, 551
CFKF Instrument Matching Grants, 556
Chassé Youth Leaders Fund Grants, 573
CHC Foundation Grants, 575
Chesapeake Bay Trust Mini Grants, 578
Chilkat Valley Community Foundation Grants, 588
Christensen Fund Regional Grants, 600
CIGNA Foundation Grants, 611
Cincinnati Bell Foundation Grants, 612
Circle K Corporation Contributions Grants, 614
Cleveland H. Dodge Foundation Grants, 637
CNCS AmeriCorps Indian Tribes Plang Grts , 641
CNCS AmeriCorps State and National Grants, 643
CNCS AmeriCorps State and National Planning
    Grants, 644
CNCS Foster Grandparent Projects Grants, 646
CNCS Senior Corps Retired and Senior Volunteer
    Program Grants, 648
CNCS Social Innovation Grants, 649
Colgate-Palmolive Company Grants, 652
Collins Foundation Grants, 658
Colonel Stanley R. McNeil Foundation Grants, 659
Community Foundation for Greater Buffalo
    Competitive Grants, 670
Community Foundation for the Capital Region
    Grants, 687
Community Foundation of Bartholomew County
    Heritage Fund Grants, 690
Community Foundation of Boone County Grants, 694
Community Foundation of Greater Fort Wayne -
    Community Endowment and Clarke Endowment
    Grants, 705
Community Fdn Of Greater Lafayette Grants, 710
Community Fdn of Morgan County Grants, 732
Community Foundation of St. Joseph County African
    American Community Grants, 737
Community Foundation of St. Joseph County Special
    Project Challenge Grants, 738
Community Fdn of Wabash County Grants, 740
Community Foundation of Western Massachusetts
    Grants, 741
Cooke Foundation Grants, 748
Corina Higginson Trust Grants, 750
Cralle Foundation Grants, 760
Crescent Porter Hale Foundation Grants, 767
Daniels Homeless and Disadvantaged Grants, 782
Decatur County Community Foundation Large
    Project Grants, 811
Del Mar Foundation Community Grants, 820
Delmarva Power & Light Contributions, 821
Dolan Children's Foundation Grants, 832
DOL Youthbuild Grants, 838
Dorothea Haus Ross Foundation Grants, 844
Dr. John T. Macdonald Foundation Grants, 863
Dunspaugh-Dalton Foundation Grants, 873
Dyson Foundation Mid-Hudson Valley Project
    Support Grants, 874
Edward W. and Stella C. Van Houten Memorial Fund
    Grants, 892
Edyth Bush Charitable Foundation Grants, 893
Effie and Wofford Cain Foundation Grants, 895

Elizabeth Morse Genius Charitable Trust Grants, 901
Elkhart County Community Foundation Grants, 903
Evan Frankel Foundation Grants, 938
Evelyn and Walter Haas, Jr. Fund Gay and Lesbian
    Rights Grants, 940
Evelyn and Walter Haas, Jr. Fund Immigrant Rights
    Grants, 941
F.R. Bigelow Foundation Grants, 947
Farmers Insurance Corporate Giving Grants, 948
Fayette County Foundation Grants, 951
Fichtenbaum Charitable Trust Grants, 955
Fidelity Foundation Grants, 957
FirstEnergy Foundation Community Grants, 965
Forest Foundation Grants, 985
Francis L. Abreu Charitable Trust Grants, 1008
Franklin County Community Fdn Grants, 1010
Frank M. Tait Foundation Grants, 1012
Fremont Area Community Foundation Community
    Grants, 1020
Fuller E. Callaway Foundation Grants, 1027
Fuller Foundation Youth At Risk Grants, 1028
G.N. Wilcox Trust Grants, 1031
Gene Haas Foundation, 1038
George F. Baker Trust Grants, 1046
George H. and Jane A. Mifflin Memorial Fund
    Grants, 1048
George I. Alden Trust Grants, 1051
George P. Davenport Trust Fund Grants, 1054
Georgia-Pacific Fdn Entrepreneurship Grants, 1059
Georgia Council for the Arts Education Grants, 1060
Geraldine R. Dodge Fdn Education Grants, 1061
German Protestant Orphan Asylum Foundation
    Grants, 1066
GNOF Freeman Challenge Grants, 1081
Golden Heart Community Foundation Grants, 1094
Goldseker Foundation Non-Profit Management
    Assistance Grants, 1095
Graham Foundation Grants, 1101
Green River Area Community Fdn Grants, 1117
H.A. and Mary K. Chapman Charitable Trust
    Grants, 1137
HAF Laurence and Elaine Allen Memorial Fund
    Grants, 1146
Hardin County Community Foundation Grants, 1167
Harry A. and Margaret D. Towsley Foundation
    Grants, 1180
Harry and Jeanette Weinberg Fdn Grants, 1182
Hartford Foundation Regular Grants, 1185
Harvey Randall Wickes Foundation Grants, 1188
Hatton W. Sumners Foundation for the Study and
    Teaching of Self Government Grants, 1196
Hawai'i Community Foundation Bernice and Conrad
    von Hamm Fund Grants, 1197
Hazel and Walter T. Bales Foundation Grants, 1220
Herbert A. and Adrian W. Woods Foundation
    Grants, 1243
Hill Crest Foundation Grants, 1249
Horace A. Kimball and S. Ella Kimball Foundation
    Grants, 1260
HRK Foundation Health Grants, 1264
HSFCA Biennium Grants, 1267
Huffy Foundation Grants, 1273
Humana Foundation Grants, 1275
Iddings Foundation Major Project Grants, 1284
Iddings Foundation Medium Project Grants, 1285
Iddings Foundation Small Project Grants, 1286
IMLS National Leadership Grants for Libraries, 1299
Indiana OCRA Quick Impact Placebased (QuIP)
    Grants, 1300
ING Foundation Grants, 1302
J. Bulow Campbell Foundation Grants, 1319
J.W. Kieckhefer Foundation Grants, 1324
James S. Copley Foundation Grants, 1345
Jennings County Community Fdn Grants, 1360
Jessica Stevens Community Foundation Grants, 1363
John H. and Wilhelmina D. Harland Charitable
    Foundation Community Services Grants, 1375
KaBOOM! Play Everywhere Design Challenge, 1405
Kalamazoo Community Foundation Early Childhood
    Learning and School Readiness Grants, 1407

Kenneth T. and Eileen L. Norris Fdn Grants, 1427
Kentucky Arts Cncl Access Assistance Grants, 1428
Kind World Foundation Grants, 1438
Kopp Family Foundation Grants, 1448
Land O'Lakes Foundation Mid-Atlantic Grants, 1467
Laurel Foundation Grants, 1475
LEGO Children's Fund Grants, 1480
Lied Foundation Trust Grants, 1490
Lloyd G. Balfour Foundation Attleboro-Specific
    Charities Grants, 1502
Lotus 88 Foundation for Women and Children
    Grants, 1508
Louis Calder Foundation Grants, 1511
Lubrizol Corporation Community Grants, 1512
Lubrizol Foundation Grants, 1513
Lucy Downing Nisbet Charitable Fund Grants, 1515
Lumpkin Family Fdn Healthy People Grants, 1518
M.D. Anderson Foundation Grants, 1523
Mabel Louise Riley Foundation Grants, 1529
Madison Community Foundation Fund for Children
    Grants, 1534
Manuel D. and Rhoda Mayerson Fdn Grants, 1550
Mardag Foundation Grants, 1554
Margaret and James A. Elkins Jr. Fdn Grants, 1555
Margaret T. Morris Foundation Grants, 1557
Marietta McNeill Morgan and Samuel Tate Morgan
    Jr. Trust Grants, 1560
Martha Holden Jennings Foundation Grants-to-
    Educators, 1581
Mary A. Crocker Trust Grants, 1584
Mary D. and Walter F. Frear Eleemosynary Trust
    Grants, 1588
Mary K. Chapman Foundation Grants, 1590
Mary Owen Borden Foundation Grants, 1597
Mary S. and David C. Corbin Fdn Grants, 1598
Mathile Family Foundation Grants, 1604
Matilda R. Wilson Fund Grants, 1605
Maurice J. Masserini Charitable Trust Grants, 1610
McCarthy Family Fdn Charity Fund Grants, 1614
McConnell Foundation Grants, 1616
McCune Charitable Foundation Grants, 1617
McCune Foundation Education Grants, 1618
McGraw-Hill Companies Community Grants, 1620
Mead Witter Foundation Grants, 1628
Mercedes-Benz USA Corporate Contributions
    Grants, 1634
Mericos Foundation Grants, 1637
Mertz Gilmore Foundation NYC Communities
    Grants, 1641
Mertz Gilmore Foundation NYC Dance Grants, 1642
Mervin Bovaird Foundation Grants, 1643
Meyer Fdn Management Assistance Grants, 1651
Meyer Memorial Trust Responsive Grants, 1653
Mill Spring Foundation Grants, 1674
Mimi and Peter Haas Fund Grants, 1677
Montana Arts Council Cultural and Aesthetic Project
    Grants, 1685
NEH Family and Youth Programs in American
    History Grants, 1734
NHSCA Artist Residence Grants, 1756
NHSCA Conservation License Plate Grants, 1757
NHSCA Youth Arts Project Grants: For Extended
    Arts Learning, 1758
NJSCA Artists in Education Residencies, 1763
NJSCA Arts Ed Special Initiative Grants, 1764
Noble County Community Foundation Grants, 1765
Norcliffe Foundation Grants, 1766
Northern Chautauqua Community Foundation
    Community Grants, 1769
North Face Explore Fund, 1770
NYFA Artists in the School Community Planning
    Grants, 1779
Office Depot Foundation Education Grants, 1806
OHA 'Ahahui Grants, 1807
Ohio Arts Council Artist in Residence Grants for
    Sponsors, 1810
Oppenstein Brothers Foundation Grants, 1827
Ordean Foundation Catalyst Grants, 1830
Oregon Community Fdn Community Grants, 1833
Pacers Foundation Be Drug-Free Grants, 1856

Pacers Foundation Be Educated Grants, 1857
Pacers Foundation Be Healthy and Fit Grants, 1858
Pacers Foundation Be Tolerant Grants, 1859
Pacers Foundation Indiana Fever's Be YOUnique
    Fund Grants, 1860
Palmer Foundation Grants, 1867
Parkersburg Area Community Foundation Action
    Grants, 1871
PCA Art Organizations and Art Programs Grants for
    Presenting Organizations, 1884
PCA Arts in Education Residencies, 1885
PCA Arts Organizations and Arts Program Grants
    for Music, 1887
PCA Arts Organizations and Arts Programs Grants
    for Art Museums, 1888
PCA Arts Organizations and Arts Programs Grants
    for Arts Education Organizations, 1889
PCA Arts Organizations and Arts Programs Grants
    for Arts Service Organizations, 1890
PCA Arts Organizations and Arts Programs Grants
    for Crafts, 1891
PCA Arts Organizations and Arts Programs Grants
    for Dance, 1892
PCA Arts Organizations and Arts Programs Grants
    for Film and Electronic Media, 1893
PCA Arts Organizations and Arts Programs Grants
    for Literature, 1894
PCA Arts Organizations and Arts Programs Grants
    for Local Arts, 1895
PCA Arts Organizations and Arts Programs Grants
    for Theatre, 1896
PCA Arts Organizations and Arts Programs Grants
    for Traditional and Folk Arts, 1897
PCA Entry Track Arts Organizations and Arts
    Programs Grants for Art Museums, 1900
PCA Entry Track Arts Organizations and
    Arts Programs Grants for Arts Education
    Organizations, 1901
PCA Entry Track Arts Organizations and Arts
    Programs Grants for Arts Service Orgs, 1902
PCA Entry Track Arts Organizations and Arts
    Programs Grants for Crafts, 1903
PCA Entry Track Arts Organizations and Arts
    Programs Grants for Dance, 1904
PCA Entry Track Arts Orgs and Arts Programs
    Grants for Film and Electronic Media, 1905
PCA Entry Track Arts Organizations and Arts
    Programs Grants for Literature, 1906
PCA Entry Track Arts Organizations and Arts
    Programs Grants for Local Arts, 1907
PCA Entry Track Arts Organizations and Arts
    Programs Grants for Music, 1908
PCA Entry Track Arts Organizations and Arts
    Programs Grants for Presenting Orgs, 1909
PCA Entry Track Arts Organizations and Arts
    Programs Grants for Theatre, 1910
PCA Entry Track Arts Orgs and Arts Programs
    Grants for Traditional and Folk Arts, 1911
PCA Pennsylvania Partners in the Arts Project
    Stream Grants, 1915
PCA Strategies for Success Grants - Adv Level, 1917
PCA Strategies for Success Grants - Intermediate
    Level, 1919
PennPAT Artist Technical Assistance Grants, 1929
PennPAT Strategic Opportunity Grants, 1933
PeyBack Foundation Grants, 1953
Phil Hardin Foundation Grants, 1960
Phoenix Suns Charities Grants, 1964
Piedmont Natural Gas Corporate and Charitable
    Contributions, 1966
Piper Jaffray Foundation Communities Giving
    Grants, 1974
PMI Foundation Grants, 1982
Pohlad Family Fdn Large Capital Grants, 1990
Pohlad Family Fdn Small Capital Grants, 1991
Polk County Community Foundation Unrestricted
    Grants, 2001
Price Chopper's Golub Foundation Grants, 2020
Prudential Foundation Education Grants, 2028
Public Welfare Fdn Juvenile Justice Grants, 2033

Public Welfare Foundation Special Initiative to
    Advance Civil Legal Aid Grants, 2034
Public Welfare Foundation Special Opportunities
    Grants, 2035
Puerto Rico Community Foundation Grants, 2037
Pulaski County Community Foundation Grants, 2038
Putnam County Community Fdn Grants, 2040
R.C. Baker Foundation Grants, 2043
R.D. and Joan Dale Hubbard Fdn Grants, 2044
Ralph M. Parsons Foundation Grants, 2052
Raskob Fdn for Catholic Activities Grants, 2054
Rathmann Family Foundation Grants, 2057
RCF General Community Grants, 2062
RCF Individual Assistance Grants, 2063
Reinberger Foundation Grants, 2066
Richard and Caroline T. Gwathmey Memorial Trust
    Grants, 2069
Ripley County Community Foundation Grants, 2077
Rose Community Foundation Child and Family
    Development Grants, 2103
Rose Community Foundation Education Grants, 2104
Rose Hills Foundation Grants, 2106
Rush County Community Foundation Grants, 2121
Ruth Anderson Foundation Grants, 2122
Samuel S. Johnson Foundation Grants, 2146
San Juan Island Community Foundation Grants, 2158
Sara Elizabeth O'Brien Trust Grants, 2161
Sarkeys Foundation Grants, 2163
Schlessman Family Foundation Grants, 2167
Schramm Foundation Grants, 2168
Scott County Community Foundation Grants, 2170
Seward Community Foundation Grants, 2182
Seward Community Foundation Mini-Grants, 2183
Shell Deer Park Grants, 2186
Shell Oil Company Foundation Community
    Development Grants, 2188
Skaggs Foundation Grants, 2207
Sony Corporation of America Grants, 2216
Stella and Charles Guttman Foundation Grants, 2241
Strake Foundation Grants, 2249
Summit Foundation Grants, 2255
TAC Arts Access Grant, 2265
TAC Touring Arts and Arts Access Touring Arts
    Grants, 2269
TE Foundation Grants, 2279
Telluride Foundation Community Grants, 2281
Textron Corporate Contributions Grants, 2286
Thomas and Agnes Carvel Foundation Grants, 2289
Toyota Motor Manufacturing of West Virginia
    Grants, 2314
Toyota Motor North America of NY Grants, 2315
Union Bank, N.A. Foundation Grants, 2334
Union Pacific Fdn Community & Civic Grants, 2337
Union Pacific Foundation Health and Human
    Services Grants, 2338
United Technologies Corporation Grants, 2347
UPS Foundation Economic and Global Literacy
    Grants, 2351
UUA Actions of Public Witness Grants, 2365
UUA Congregation-Based Community Organizing
    Grants, 2366
UUA Fund Grants, 2367
UUA International Fund Grants, 2368
UUA Just Society Fund Grants, 2369
UUA Social Responsibility Grants, 2370
Victor E. Speas Foundation Grants, 2380
Virginia Commission for the Arts Artists in
    Education Residency Grants, 2385
Virginia Foundation for the Humanities Open
    Grants, 2387
W.W. Smith Chartbl Trust Basic Needs Grants, 2400
Walker Area Community Foundation Grants, 2401
Washington County Community Fdn Grants, 2416
Watson-Brown Foundation Grants, 2418
William J. and Dorothy K. O'Neill Foundation
    Responsive Grants, 2468
Wyomissing Foundation Community Grants, 2504
Xerox Foundation Grants, 2507
Z. Smith Reynolds Foundation Small Grants, 2523

Materials/Equipment Acquisition (Computers, Books, Videos, etc.)
1st Touch Foundation Grants, 2
4imprint One by One Charitable Giving, 7
Abell-Hanger Foundation Grants, 52
Abington Foundation Grants, 54
ACCF of Indiana Bank of Geneva Heritage Fund Grants, 64
ACF Unaccompanied Refugee Children Grants, 99
Achelis and Bodman Foundation Grants, 101
Achelis Foundation Grants, 102
Adams County Community Foundation Grants, 115
Adelaide Breed Bayrd Foundation Grants, 123
Advance Auto Parts Corporate Giving Grants, 131
AGFT A Gift for Music Grants, 138
AGFT Pencil Boy Express, 139
Agnes M. Lindsay Trust Grants, 140
Ahearn Family Foundation Grants, 142
Air Products Foundation Grants, 148
Akron Community Fdn Education Grants, 151
ALA Bookapalooza Grants, 161
ALA BWI Collection Development Grant, 164
ALA Coretta Scott King Book Donation Grant, 168
ALA Great Books Giveaway Competition, 170
ALA PRIME TIME Family Reading Time Grts, 185
ALA Theodor Seuss Geisel Award, 215
Albert W. Rice Charitable Foundation Grants, 223
Alex Stern Family Foundation Grants, 229
ALFJ International Social Change Opportunity Fund Grants, 232
Alliant Energy Foundation Community Giving for Good Sponsorship Grants, 240
Alloy Family Foundation Grants, 241
Amelia Sillman Rockwell and Carlos Perry Rockwell Charities Fund Grants, 250
Ameren Corporation Community Grants, 251
American Savings Foundation Program Grants, 261
American Schlafhorst Foundation Grants, 262
Anchorage Schools Foundation Grants, 270
Anheuser-Busch Foundation Grants, 273
Antone and Edene Vidinha Charitable Grants, 281
Arizona State Library LSTA Collections Grants, 295
Arizona State Library LSTA Learning Grants, 297
Armstrong McDonald Foundation Children and Youth Grants, 300
Armstrong McDonald Foundation Special Needs Grants, 301
Arthur M. Blank Family Foundation Atlanta Falcons Youth Foundation Grants, 307
Aspen Community Foundation Grants, 316
Assisi Fdn of Memphis Capital Project Grants, 317
Assisi Foundation of Memphis General Grants, 318
Assisi Foundation of Memphis Mini Grants, 319
AT&T Fdn Community Support and Safety, 320
Atlanta Foundation Grants, 326
Atlanta Women's Foundation Pathway to Success Grants, 327
Autauga Area Community Foundation Grants, 334
Back Home Again Foundation Grants, 344
Baltimore Community Foundation Mitzvah Fund for Good Deeds Grants, 349
Baltimore Ravens Corporate Giving, 350
Baltimore Ravens Fdn Youth Football Grants, 353
Bank of Hawaii Foundation Grants, 360
Barrasso, Usdin, Kupperman, Freeman, and Sarver Corporate Grants, 362
Batters Up USA Equipment Grants, 366
Beckman Coulter Foundation Grants, 394
Bee Conservancy Sponsor-A-Hive Grants, 395
Ben B. Cheney Foundation Grants, 402
Benton Community Foundation Grants, 405
Best Buy Children's Fdn @15 Teach Awards, 416
Bill and Melinda Gates Foundation Agricultural Development Grants, 425
Biogen Foundation General Donations, 432
Blanche and Irving Laurie Foundation Grants, 436
Blandin Foundation Expand Opportunity Grants, 437
Blockbuster Corporate Contributions, 440
Blue Grass Community Foundation Hudson-Ellis Grants, 449

Blue River Community Foundation Grants, 458
Blumenthal Foundation Grants, 459
BMW of North America Charitable Contribs, 460
Bodenwein Public Benevolent Foundation Grants, 461
Boeing Company Contributions Grants, 462
Bollinger Foundation Grants, 463
Bothin Foundation Grants, 464
Brown County Community Foundation Grants, 475
Brown Rudnick Charitable Foundation Community Grants, 477
Brunswick Foundation Dollars for Doers Grants, 478
Bushrod H. Campbell and Adah F. Hall Charity Fund Grants, 486
Cabot Corporation Foundation Grants, 490
Caesars Foundation Grants, 492
California Endowment Innovative Ideas Challenge Grants, 495
Callaway Foundation Grants, 496
Camille Beckman Foundation Grants, 499
Campbell Soup Foundation Grants, 501
Cargill Corporate Giving Grants, 503
Carl M. Freeman Foundation FACES Grants, 507
Carl M. Freeman Foundation Grants, 508
Carl W. and Carrie Mae Joslyn Trust Grants, 510
Cash 4 Clubs Sports Grants, 515
CFFVR Appleton Education Foundation Grants, 536
CFFVR Basic Needs Giving Partnership Grants, 537
CFFVR Clintonville Area Foundation Grants, 538
CFFVR Clintonville Area Foundation Grants, 539
CFFVR Environmental Stewardship Grants, 540
CFFVR Mielke Family Foundation Grants, 544
CFFVR Shawano Area Community Foundation Grants, 549
CFGR Community Impact Grants, 552
CFGR Jenkins Foundation Grants, 553
CFKF Instrument Matching Grants, 556
Charles H. Pearson Foundation Grants, 566
Chassé Youth Leaders Fund Grants, 573
Chatham Athletic Foundation Grants, 574
Chesapeake Bay Trust Environmental Education Grants, 577
Chesapeake Bay Trust Mini Grants, 578
Chesapeake Bay Trust Outreach and Community Engagement Grants, 579
Chilkat Valley Community Foundation Grants, 588
CICF Indianapolis Fdn Community Grants, 606
Cincinnati Bell Foundation Grants, 612
Cisco Systems Foundation San Jose Community Grants, 615
Citizens Savings Foundation Grants, 617
Clara Blackford Smith and W. Aubrey Smith Charitable Foundation Grants, 621
Claremont Community Foundation Grants, 622
Clarence T.C. Ching Foundation Grants, 624
Clark County Community Foundation Grants, 626
Cleveland H. Dodge Foundation Grants, 637
CNCS Foster Grandparent Projects Grants, 646
CNCS Senior Corps Retired and Senior Volunteer Program Grants, 648
Collins Foundation Grants, 658
Colorado Interstate Gas Grants, 661
Community Foundation for Greater Atlanta Metropolitan Extra Wish Grants, 666
Community Foundation for Greater Buffalo Competitive Grants, 670
Community Foundation for Greater Buffalo Niagara Area Foundation Grants, 673
Community Foundation for Greater Buffalo Ralph C. Wilson, Jr. Youth Sports COVID-19 Fund Grants, 675
Community Foundation of Abilene Future Fund Grants, 689
Community Foundation of Bartholomew County Heritage Fund Grants, 690
Community Foundation of Boone County Grants, 694
Community Foundation of Eastern Connecticut General Southeast Grants, 696
Community Foundation of Eastern Connecticut Norwich Youth Grants, 699

Community Foundation of Greater Fort Wayne - Community Endowment and Clarke Endowment Grants, 705
Community Foundation of Henderson County Community Grants, 711
Community Foundation of Louisville Boyette and Edna Edwards Fund Grants, 718
Community Foundation of Louisville Education Grants, 724
Community Foundation of Louisville Winston N. and Nancy H. Bloch Educational Fund Grants, 729
Community Fdn of Southern Indiana Grants, 736
Community Fdn of Wabash County Grants, 740
Community Foundation of Western Massachusetts Grants, 741
Corina Higginson Trust Grants, 750
Cralle Foundation Grants, 760
Cresap Family Foundation Grants, 766
Cudd Foundation Grants, 769
Dayton Foundation Grants, 796
Dayton Foundation VISIONS Endowment Fund Grants, 800
Deaconess Community Foundation Grants, 803
Dean Witter Foundation Education Grants, 807
DeKalb County Community Foundation VOICE Grant, 816
Delaware Community Foundation Grants, 817
Del Mar Foundation Community Grants, 820
Delta Air Lines Foundation Youth Development Grants, 824
Different Needz Foundation Grants, 830
Dolan Children's Foundation Grants, 832
Dollar General Family Literacy Grants, 835
Doree Taylor Charitable Foundation Grants, 843
Dorothea Haus Ross Foundation Grants, 844
Dubois County Community Foundation Grants, 871
E.J. Grassmann Trust Grants, 876
E.L. Wiegand Foundation Grants, 877
Eastern Bank Charitable Foundation Partnerships Grants, 881
Eastern Bank Charitable Foundation Targeted Grants, 882
Easton Sports Development Foundation National Archery in the Schools Grants, 884
Edwards Memorial Trust Grants, 891
Edward W. and Stella C. Van Houten Memorial Fund Grants, 892
Edyth Bush Charitable Foundation Grants, 893
Effie and Wofford Cain Foundation Grants, 895
El Pomar Foundation Anna Keesling Ackerman Fund Grants, 907
El Pomar Foundation Grants, 908
Elsie H. Wilcox Foundation Grants, 909
Energy by Design Poster Contest, 915
Evelyn and Walter Haas, Jr. Fund Immigrant Rights Grants, 941
F.M. Kirby Foundation Grants, 946
Fifth Third Bank Corporate Giving, 958
Finish Line Youth Foundation Founder's Grants, 960
FirstEnergy Foundation Community Grants, 965
First Hawaiian Bank Foundation Corporate Giving Grants, 967
Ford Family Foundation Grants - Access to Health and Dental Services, 980
Four County Community Foundation General Grants, 1000
Four County Community Foundation Healthy Senior/Healthy Youth Fund Grants, 1001
Four County Community Foundation Kellogg Group Grants, 1002
Francis L. Abreu Charitable Trust Grants, 1008
Frank Reed and Margaret Jane Peters Memorial Fund Grants, 1013
Frank Reed and Margaret Jane Peters Memorial Fund II Grants, 1014
Frederick McDonald Trust Grants, 1017
Fremont Area Community Foundation Amazing X Grants, 1019
Fremont Area Community Foundation Community Grants, 1020

Fremont Area Community Foundation Youth Advisory Committee Grants, 1022
From the Top Jack Kent Cooke Young Artist Scholarships, 1026
Fuller E. Callaway Foundation Grants, 1027
G.N. Wilcox Trust Grants, 1031
Gamble Foundation Grants, 1032
General Motors Foundation Grants, 1039
George A Ohl Jr. Foundation Grants, 1043
George I. Alden Trust Grants, 1051
George Kress Foundation Grants, 1053
George W. Codrington Charitable Foundation Grants, 1055
George W.P. Magee Trust Grants, 1056
George W. Wells Foundation Grants, 1057
Georgia-Pacific Fdn Entrepreneurship Grants, 1059
Gil and Dody Weaver Foundation Grants, 1071
Giving Gardens Challenge Grants, 1072
GNOF Albert N. & Hattie M. McClure Grants, 1076
Go Daddy Cares Charitable Contributions, 1093
Graham Foundation Grants, 1100
Greater Saint Louis Community Fdn Grants, 1110
Greater Sitka Legacy Fund Grants, 1111
Greater Tacoma Community Foundation Fund for Women and Girls Grants, 1112
Greater Tacoma Community Foundation General Operating Grants, 1113
Green River Area Community Fdn Grants, 1117
Greygates Foundation Grants, 1120
Grundy Foundation Grants, 1124
GTECH After School Advantage Grants, 1125
GTRCF Elk Rapids Area Community Endowment Grants, 1127
GTRCF Traverse City Track Club Endowment Grants, 1132
Guy I. Bromley Trust Grants, 1136
H.A. and Mary K. Chapman Charitable Trust Grants, 1137
HAF Phyllis Nilsen Leal Mem Fund Grants, 1149
Hannaford Supermarkets Community Giving, 1164
Harmony Foundation for Children Grants, 1168
Harold K.L. Castle Foundation Windward Youth Leadership Fund Grants, 1175
Harrison County Community Fdn Grants, 1178
Harrison County Community Foundation Signature Grants, 1179
Harry and Jeanette Weinberg Fdn Grants, 1182
Hartford Foundation Regular Grants, 1185
Hawai'i Community Foundation Lana'i Community Benefit Fund, 1203
Hawai'i Community Foundation Victoria S. and Bradley L. Geist Foundation: Enhancement Grants, 1207
Hawaii Community Foundation Omidyar Ohana Fund Grants, 1213
Hearst Foundations Social Service Grants, 1224
HEI Charitable Foundation Grants, 1226
Helen Bader Foundation Grants, 1227
Helen Irwin Littauer Educational Trust Grants, 1231
Helen V. Brach Foundation Grants, 1232
Henry E. Niles Foundation Grants, 1240
Henry L. Guenther Foundation Grants, 1242
Hill Crest Foundation Grants, 1249
Honeywell Corporation Got 2B Safe Contest, 1256
Honor the Earth Grants, 1259
Horace A. Moses Charitable Trust Grants, 1261
HRK Foundation Health Grants, 1264
Hubbard Family Foundation Grants, 1270
Hubbard Family Foundation Grants, 1271
Hungry for Music Instrument Gifts, 1277
Huntington Clinical Foundation Grants, 1278
Iddings Foundation Major Project Grants, 1284
Iddings Foundation Medium Project Grants, 1285
IMLS Grants to State Library Administrative Agencies, 1298
Inland Empire Community Foundation Capacity Building for IE Nonprofits Grants, 1306
J. Edwin Treakle Foundation Grants, 1320
J. Knox Gholston Foundation Grants, 1321
J.W. Kieckhefer Foundation Grants, 1324

J. William Gholston Foundation Grants, 1328
Jack H. and William M. Light Charitable Trust Grants, 1330
Jacob G. Schmidlapp Trusts Grants, 1336
James and Abigail Campbell Family Foundation Grants, 1337
James Graham Brown Foundation Grants, 1340
James S. Copley Foundation Grants, 1345
Janson Foundation Grants, 1350
Japan Foundation Los Angeles Japanese-Language Teaching Materials Purchase Grants, 1353
Jaquelin Hume Foundation Grants, 1357
Jennings County Community Fdn Grants, 1360
John D. and Katherine A. Johnston Foundation Grants, 1370
John G. Duncan Charitable Trust Grants, 1372
John H. and Wilhelmina D. Harland Charitable Foundation Children and Youth Grants, 1374
John M. Weaver Foundation Grants, 1376
Joseph H. and Florence A. Roblee Foundation Education Grants, 1386
Joseph Henry Edmondson Foundation Grants, 1388
Josephine Schell Russell Chartbl Trust Grants, 1389
JP Morgan Chase Fdn Arts and Culture Grants, 1394
KaBOOM! Play Everywhere Design Challenge, 1405
Katharine Matthies Foundation Grants, 1418
Katherine John Murphy Foundation Grants, 1419
Katie's Krops Grants, 1421
Kawabe Memorial Fund Grants, 1423
Kelvin and Eleanor Smith Foundation Grants, 1424
Kenai Peninsula Foundation Grants, 1425
Kenneth T. and Eileen L. Norris Fdn Grants, 1427
Ketchikan Community Foundation Grants, 1429
Kind World Foundation Grants, 1438
Kodak Community Relations Grants, 1445
Kodiak Community Foundation Grants, 1446
Koret Foundation Grants, 1449
LaGrange Independent Foundation for Endowments (L.I.F.E.), 1459
Land O'Lakes Foundation Mid-Atlantic Grants, 1467
Latkin Charitable Foundation Grants, 1469
Lavina Parker Trust Grants, 1477
Lewis H. Humphreys Charitable Trust Grants, 1486
Lied Foundation Trust Grants, 1490
Lilly Endowment Summer Youth Grants, 1492
Linford & Mildred White Charitable Grants, 1495
Lotus 88 Foundation for Women and Children Grants, 1508
Louie M. and Betty M. Phillips Fdn Grants, 1509
Louis Calder Foundation Grants, 1511
Lubrizol Corporation Community Grants, 1512
Lubrizol Foundation Grants, 1513
Lucy Downing Nisbet Charitable Fund Grants, 1515
Ludwick Family Foundation Grants, 1516
Lumpkin Family Fdn Healthy People Grants, 1518
Lynn and Foster Friess Family Fdn Grants, 1520
M.D. Anderson Foundation Grants, 1523
M.J. Murdock Charitable Trust General Grants, 1524
Mabel A. Horne Fund Grants, 1525
Mabel Louise Riley Foundation Grants, 1529
Mabel Y. Hughes Charitable Trust Grants, 1530
Macquarie Bank Foundation Grants, 1532
Marcia and Otto Koehler Foundation Grants, 1553
Mardag Foundation Grants, 1554
Margaret and James A. Elkins Jr. Fdn Grants, 1555
Marie C. and Joseph C. Wilson Foundation Rochester Small Grants, 1559
Marin Community Foundation Social Justice and Interfaith Understanding Grants, 1567
Marion Gardner Jackson Charitable Trust Grts, 1570
Marion I. and Henry J. Knott Foundation Discretionary Grants, 1571
Marion I. and Henry J. Knott Foundation Standard Grants, 1572
Marjorie Moore Charitable Foundation Grants, 1574
Mary Black Foundation Active Living Grants, 1585
Mary D. and Walter F. Frear Eleemosynary Trust Grants, 1588
Mary K. Chapman Foundation Grants, 1590
Mary Owen Borden Foundation Grants, 1597

Mary S. and David C. Corbin Fdn Grants, 1598
Matilda R. Wilson Fund Grants, 1605
Matson Community Giving Grants, 1607
Maurice J. Masserini Charitable Trust Grants, 1610
Max and Anna Levinson Foundation Grants, 1612
May and Stanley Smith Charitable Trust Grants, 1613
McCarthy Family Fdn Charity Fund Grants, 1614
McConnell Foundation Grants, 1616
McCune Charitable Foundation Grants, 1617
McCune Foundation Education Grants, 1618
McInerny Foundation Grants, 1622
McLean Contributionship Grants, 1623
Meadows Foundation Grants, 1626
Mead Witter Foundation Grants, 1628
Mericos Foundation Grants, 1637
Meriden Foundation Grants, 1638
Merrick Foundation Grants, 1639
Meyer Foundation Education Grants, 1649
Meyer Memorial Trust Responsive Grants, 1653
MFRI Community Mobilization Grants, 1654
MGN Family Foundation Grants, 1656
Michael and Susan Dell Foundation Grants, 1657
Michigan Women Forward Grants, 1662
Microsoft Software Donations, 1665
Mimi and Peter Haas Fund Grants, 1677
MLB Tomorrow Fund Grants, 1679
Mockingbird Foundation Grants, 1680
Montgomery County Community Foundation Health and Human Services Fund Grants, 1689
Montgomery County Community Foundation Libby Whitecotton Fund Grants, 1690
Moran Family Foundation Grants, 1693
Morris Stulsaft Foundation Early Childhood Education Grants, 1696
Morris Stulsaft Foundation Participation in the the Arts Grants, 1698
Moses Kimball Fund Grants, 1701
Mr. Holland's Opus Foundation Melody Grants, 1703
Mr. Holland's Opus Foundation Michael Kamen Solo Award, 1704
Mr. Holland's Opus Foundation Special Projects Grants, 1705
Narragansett Number One Foundation Grants, 1712
Natalie W. Furniss Foundation Grants, 1715
NEA Foundation Read Across America Library Books Awards, 1732
Nell J. Redfield Foundation Grants, 1737
New Covenant Farms Grants, 1742
New Earth Foundation Grants, 1743
Noble County Community Foundation Grants, 1765
Norcliffe Foundation Grants, 1766
Northern Chautauqua Community Foundation Community Grants, 1769
NYSCA Electronic Media and Film: Workspace Grants, 1789
OceanFirst Foundation Major Grants, 1803
Ohio County Community Foundation Board of Directors Grants, 1811
Ohio Valley Foundation Grants, 1814
Olga Sipolin Children's Fund Grants, 1815
OMNOVA Solutions Fdn Education Grants, 1820
OneFamily Foundation Grants, 1822
Oppenstein Brothers Foundation Grants, 1827
Oregon Community Fdn Community Grants, 1833
Oregon Community Foundation K-12 Student Success: Out-of-School Grants, 1836
OtterCares Champion Fund Grants, 1848
Parker Foundation (California) Grants, 1869
Parkersburg Area Community Foundation Action Grants, 1871
Perpetual Benevolent Fund, 1940
Perry County Community Foundation Recreation Grants, 1942
Peter and Elizabeth C. Tower Foundation Technology Initiative Grants, 1949
Petersburg Community Foundation Grants, 1951
Phil Hardin Foundation Grants, 1960
Piper Trust Arts and Culture Grants, 1975
Piper Trust Children Grants, 1976
Piper Trust Education Grants, 1977

Piper Trust Healthcare and Med Rsrch Grants, 1978
Piper Trust Reglious Organizations Grants, 1979
PNC Foundation Revitalization and Stabilization Grants, 1987
Pokagon Fund Grants, 1994
Polk County Community Foundation Marjorie M. and Lawrence R. Bradley Endowment Fund Grants, 1998
Polk County Community Foundation Unrestricted Grants, 2001
Portland General Electric Foundation Grants, 2007
Posey Community Foundation Women's Fund Grants, 2008
Powell Family Foundation Grants, 2012
PPCF Community Grants, 2014
PPG Industries Foundation Grants, 2017
Prudential Foundation Education Grants, 2028
Puerto Rico Community Foundation Grants, 2037
R.C. Baker Foundation Grants, 2043
Ralph M. Parsons Foundation Grants, 2052
Raskob Fdn for Catholic Activities Grants, 2054
Rasmuson Foundation Tier One Grants, 2055
Rasmuson Foundation Tier Two Grants, 2056
Rathmann Family Foundation Grants, 2057
RCF General Community Grants, 2062
Reinberger Foundation Grants, 2066
Richard J. Stern Foundation for the Arts Grants, 2071
Ripley County Community Foundation Grants, 2077
Ripley County Community Foundation Small Project Grants, 2078
Robbins-de Beaumont Foundation Grants, 2080
Robert R. Meyer Foundation Grants, 2094
Rush County Community Foundation Grants, 2121
Ruth Camp Campbell Charitable Trust Grants, 2125
Saginaw Community Foundation Discretionary Grants, 2134
Samuel S. Johnson Foundation Grants, 2146
Sand Hill Foundation Health and Opportunity Grants, 2153
San Juan Island Community Foundation Grants, 2158
Santa Fe Community Foundation Seasonal Grants- Fall Cycle, 2159
Sarkeys Foundation Grants, 2163
SAS Institute Community Relations Donations, 2165
Schlessman Family Foundation Grants, 2167
Schramm Foundation Grants, 2168
Seattle Foundation Arts and Culture Grants, 2174
Seattle Foundation C. Keith Birkenfeld Memorial Trust Grants, 2177
Sensient Technologies Foundation Grants, 2180
Shell Deer Park Grants, 2186
Shield-Ayres Foundation Grants, 2189
Shopko Foundation Green Bay Area Community Grants, 2192
Sidney Stern Memorial Trust Grants, 2197
Siebert Lutheran Foundation Grants, 2198
Sierra Health Foundation Responsive Grants, 2199
Sioux Falls Area Community Foundation Community Fund Grants, 2203
Sioux Falls Area Community Foundation Spot Grants, 2204
Skaggs Foundation Grants, 2207
Sony Corporation of America Grants, 2216
Sorenson Legacy Foundation Grants, 2217
Southern California Edison Education Grants, 2218
South Madison Community Foundation - Teacher Creativity Mini Grants, 2225
Spencer County Community Foundation Women's Fund Grants, 2232
Stein Family Charitable Trust Grants, 2240
Sterling-Turner Charitable Foundation Grants, 2242
Stinson Foundation Grants, 2246
Stocker Foundation Grants, 2247
Strake Foundation Grants, 2249
Subaru of Indiana Automotive Fdn Grants, 2254
Summit Foundation Grants, 2255
Sunoco Foundation Grants, 2256
T.L.L. Temple Foundation Grants, 2264
TechKnowledgey Community Impact Grants, 2278
TE Foundation Grants, 2279

Telluride Foundation Community Grants, 2281
Textron Corporate Contributions Grants, 2286
Thomas and Agnes Carvel Foundation Grants, 2289
Thomas J. Long Foundation Community Grants, 2291
Thomas Sill Foundation Grants, 2292
TJX Foundation Grants, 2303
Toshiba America Foundation Grades 7-12 Science and Math Grants, 2307
Toshiba America Foundation K-6 Science and Math Grants, 2308
Toyota Motor Manuf of Alabama Grants, 2309
Toyota Motor Manufacturing of West Virginia Grants, 2314
Toyota Motor Sales, USA Grants, 2316
Toyota USA Foundation Education Grants, 2318
TSYSF Individual Scholarships, 2322
TSYSF Team Grants, 2323
U.S. Bank Foundation Grants, 2330
Union Bank, N.A. Foundation Grants, 2334
Union Pacific Fdn Community & Civic Grants, 2337
United Technologies Corporation Grants, 2347
UPS Foundation Economic and Global Literacy Grants, 2351
V.V. Cooke Foundation Grants, 2371
Van Kampen Boyer Molinari Charitable Foundation Grants, 2377
Vermillion County Community Fdn Grants, 2378
Victor E. Speas Foundation Grants, 2380
Vigneron Memorial Fund Grants, 2384
W.M. Keck Fdn Southern California Grants, 2398
W.W. Smith Chartbl Trust Basic Needs Grants, 2400
Walker Area Community Foundation Grants, 2401
Wayne County Foundation Grants, 2419
Wege Foundation Grants, 2422
Western Indiana Community Fdn Grants, 2428
Western New York Foundation Grants, 2429
Widgeon Point Charitable Foundation Grants, 2447
William A. Cooke Foundation Grants, 2452
William Foulds Family Foundation Grants, 2465
William G. and Helen C. Hoffman Foundation Grants, 2466
William G. Gilmore Foundation Grants, 2467
Wilton and Effie Hebert Foundation Grants, 2476
Wiregrass Foundation Grants, 2480
Wood Family Charitable Trust Grants, 2487
WSF GoGirlGo! New York Grants, 2494
WSF Sports 4 Life Grants, 2496
WSF Sports 4 Life Regional Grants, 2497
WSF Travel and Training Fund Grants, 2498
Wyomissing Foundation Community Grants, 2504
Z. Smith Reynolds Foundation Small Grants, 2523
Zollner Foundation Grants, 2526

Preservation/Restoration

A. Alfred Taubman Foundation Grants, 18
Abell-Hanger Foundation Grants, 52
ACCF of Indiana Ron and Susie Ballard Community Enrichment Fund Grants, 68
Ahearn Family Foundation Grants, 142
AHS Foundation Grants, 143
Akron Community Foundation Arts and Culture Grants, 150
Alabama Humanities Foundation Major Grants, 159
Albert W. Cherne Foundation Grants, 222
Alloy Family Foundation Grants, 241
Alpha Natural Resources Corporate Giving, 246
Ama OluKai Foundation Grants, 249
American Woodmark Foundation Grants, 263
Anderson Foundation Grants, 271
Anne J. Caudal Foundation Grants, 276
Ar-Hale Family Foundation Grants, 290
Bank of America Charitable Foundation Matching Gifts, 356
Bay and Paul Foundations PreK-12 Transformative Learning Practices Grants, 370
Beckman Coulter Foundation Grants, 394
Blue River Community Foundation Grants, 458
Callaway Foundation Grants, 496
Carl M. Freeman Foundation Grants, 508
CFFVR Environmental Stewardship Grants, 540

Chesapeake Bay Trust Environmental Education Grants, 577
Chesapeake Bay Trust Mini Grants, 578
Circle K Corporation Contributions Grants, 614
Community Foundation for Greater Buffalo Competitive Grants, 670
Community Foundation for Greater Buffalo Niagara Area Foundation Grants, 673
Community Foundation of Western Massachusetts Grants, 741
Cudd Foundation Grants, 769
Daniel and Nanna Stern Family Fdn Grants, 778
Dearborn Community Foundation City of Aurora Grants, 808
Del Mar Foundation Community Grants, 820
Donald W. Reynolds Foundation Children's Discovery Initiative Grants, 841
Earl and Maxine Claussen Trust Grants, 878
Earth Island Institute Brower Youth Awards, 879
Eastern Bank Charitable Foundation Neighborhood Support Grants, 880
El Pomar Foundation Anna Keesling Ackerman Fund Grants, 907
El Pomar Foundation Grants, 908
Fifth Third Bank Corporate Giving, 958
First Hawaiian Bank Foundation Corporate Giving Grants, 967
Foundations of East Chicago Education Grants, 995
Four County Community Foundation General Grants, 1000
Friends of Hawaii Charities Grants, 1024
George Graham and Elizabeth Galloway Smith Foundation Grants, 1047
George Kress Foundation Grants, 1053
GNOF Coastal 5 + 1 Grants, 1078
GNOF Exxon-Mobil Grants, 1080
GNOF Gert Community Fund Grants, 1082
Greater Milwaukee Foundation Grants, 1109
Greater Tacoma Community Foundation General Operating Grants, 1113
Green River Area Community Fdn Grants, 1117
HAF Don and Bettie Albright Endowment Fund Grants, 1142
HAF Joe Alexandre Mem Family Fund Grants, 1145
HAF Laurence and Elaine Allen Memorial Fund Grants, 1146
HAF Native Cultures Fund Grants, 1148
Harris Foundation Grants, 1177
Harrison County Community Fdn Grants, 1178
Harrison County Community Foundation Signature Grants, 1179
Hawai'i Community Foundation Robert E. Black Fund Grants, 1205
Hawaii Electric Industries Charitable Foundation Grants, 1218
Helen E. Ellis Charitable Trust Grants, 1228
HSFCA Folk and Traditional Arts Grants - Culture Learning, 1268
Hubbard Family Foundation Grants, 1271
Huntington County Community Foundation Make a Difference Grants, 1280
IMLS Grants to State Library Administrative Agencies, 1298
J.W. Kieckhefer Foundation Grants, 1324
Jennings County Community Fdn Grants, 1360
Jessica Stevens Community Foundation Grants, 1363
Joseph Henry Edmondson Foundation Grants, 1388
Klingenstein-Simons Fellowship Awards in the Neurosciences, 1441
LGA Family Foundation Grants, 1487
Lotus 88 Foundation for Women and Children Grants, 1508
Marcia and Otto Koehler Foundation Grants, 1553
Margaret and James A. Elkins Jr. Fdn Grants, 1555
Mary Black Foundation Active Living Grants, 1585
MassMutual Foundation Edonomic Development Grants, 1603
Matson Community Giving Grants, 1607
McCombs Foundation Grants, 1615
McCune Charitable Foundation Grants, 1617

McLean Contributionship Grants, 1623
Merrick Foundation Grants, 1639
MLB Tomorrow Fund Grants, 1679
Montana Arts Council Cultural and Aesthetic Project
    Grants, 1685
Norcliffe Foundation Grants, 1766
NYSCA Arts Education: General Program Support
    Grants, 1782
NYSCA Electronic Media and Film: General
    Program Support, 1787
NYSCA Electronic Media and Film: Screenings
    Grants, 1788
NYSCA Special Arts Services: General Program
    Support Grants, 1793
NYSCA Special Arts Services: Instruction and
    Training Grants, 1794
OceanFirst Foundation Major Grants, 1803
Oregon Community Fdn Community Grants, 1833
Parkersburg Area Community Foundation Action
    Grants, 1871
Perkins Charitable Foundation Grants, 1939
Pittsburgh Fdn Affordable Housing Grants, 1980
Pokagon Fund Grants, 1994
Polk County Community Foundation Mary F. Kessler
    Fund Grants, 1999
Polk County Community Foundation Unrestricted
    Grants, 2001
Putnam County Community Fdn Grants, 2040
Rasmuson Foundation Tier Two Grants, 2056
Richard and Caroline T. Gwathmey Memorial Trust
    Grants, 2069
Ripley County Community Foundation Grants, 2077
Ripley County Community Foundation Small Project
    Grants, 2078
Robert R. Meyer Foundation Grants, 2094
Saginaw Community Foundation Discretionary
    Grants, 2134
Seward Community Foundation Grants, 2182
Seward Community Foundation Mini-Grants, 2183
Shield-Ayres Foundation Grants, 2189
Sioux Falls Area Community Foundation Community
    Fund Grants, 2203
Sioux Falls Area Community Foundation Spot
    Grants, 2204
Strake Foundation Grants, 2249
Textron Corporate Contributions Grants, 2286
Toyota Motor Manuf of Mississippi Grants, 2312
Turner Foundation Grants, 2326
Union Bank, N.A. Foundation Grants, 2334
Vanderburgh Community Foundation Men's Fund
    Grants, 2373
Vanderburgh County Community Foundation
    Women's Fund Grants, 2376
Virginia Foundation for the Humanities Open
    Grants, 2387
Walker Area Community Foundation Grants, 2401
Washington County Community Fdn Grants, 2416
Watson-Brown Foundation Grants, 2418
Western Indiana Community Fdn Grants, 2428
Widgeon Point Charitable Foundation Grants, 2447
William J. and Gertrude R. Casper Foundation
    Grants, 2469
Wyomissing Foundation Thun Family Organizational
    Grants, 2505
Wyomissing Foundation Thun Family Program
    Grants, 2506

Publishing/Editing/Translating
A.L. Mailman Family Foundation Grants, 20
Akron Community Foundation Arts and Culture
    Grants, 150
Anderson Foundation Grants, 271
Bay and Paul Foundations PreK-12 Transformative
    Learning Practices Grants, 370
Chesapeake Bay Trust Outreach and Community
    Engagement Grants, 579
ChLA Article Award, 589
ChLA Book Award, 590
ChLA Carol Gay Award, 591
ChLA Edited Book Award, 592

ChLA Faculty Research Grants, 593
ChLA Graduate Student Essay Awards, 594
ChLA Hannah Beiter Diversity Research Grants, 595
ChLA Hannah Beiter Graduate Student Research
    Grants, 596
ChLA Mentoring Award, 597
ChLA Phoenix Award, 598
ChLA Phoenix Picture Book Award, 599
CJ Fdn for SIDS Program Services Grants, 619
Claremont Community Foundation Grants, 622
Community Foundation of Eastern Connecticut
    General Southeast Grants, 696
Community Foundation of Henderson County
    Community Grants, 711
Community Foundation of Western Massachusetts
    Grants, 741
Corina Higginson Trust Grants, 750
Dyson Foundation Mid-Hudson Valley Project
    Support Grants, 874
Ford Foundation BUILD Grants, 984
General Motors Foundation Grants, 1039
George A Ohl Jr. Foundation Grants, 1043
Helen V. Brach Foundation Grants, 1232
Hill Crest Foundation Grants, 1249
ILA Children's and Young Adults' Book Awds, 1291
J.W. Kieckhefer Foundation Grants, 1324
Jaquelin Hume Foundation Grants, 1357
Koret Foundation Grants, 1449
Laurel Foundation Grants, 1475
Max and Anna Levinson Foundation Grants, 1612
McLean Contributionship Grants, 1623
NAA Foundation High Five Grants, 1711
Norcliffe Foundation Grants, 1766
NYSCA Electronic Media and Film: General
    Program Support, 1787
Ohio County Community Foundation Board of
    Directors Grants, 1811
PCA Arts Organizations and Arts Programs Grants
    for Literature, 1894
PCA Arts Organizations and Arts Programs Grants
    for Visual Arts, 1898
PCA Entry Track Arts Organizations and Arts
    Programs Grants for Literature, 1906
PCA Entry Track Arts Organizations and Arts
    Programs Grants for Visual Arts, 1912
PEN America Phyllis Naylor Grant for Children's and
    Young Adult Novelists, 1928
Phil Hardin Foundation Grants, 1960
Puerto Rico Community Foundation Grants, 2037
Reinberger Foundation Grants, 2066
Richard J. Stern Foundation for the Arts Grants, 2071
Ruddie Memorial Youth Foundation Grants, 2120
Shell Oil Company Foundation Community
    Development Grants, 2188
TAC Arts Access Grant, 2265
Textron Corporate Contributions Grants, 2286
Virginia Foundation for the Humanities Open
    Grants, 2387
VSA Playwright Discovery Award, 2396
Watson-Brown Foundation Grants, 2418
Wayne County Foundation Grants, 2419

Religious Programs
Aaron Foundation Grants, 42
ABC Charities Grants, 50
Abell-Hanger Foundation Grants, 52
Abell Foundation Education Grants, 53
ACF Street Outreach Program Grants, 94
ACF Transitional Living Program and Maternity
    Group Homes Grants, 96
ACF Voluntary Agencies Matching Grants, 100
Achelis and Bodman Foundation Grants, 101
Achelis Foundation Grants, 102
Adams-Mastrovich Family Foundation Grants, 113
Adams Family Foundation of Ohio Grants, 119
Adelaide Christian Home For Children Grants, 124
Aetna Foundation Regional Health Grants, 134
A Friends' Foundation Trust Grants, 136
AHS Foundation Grants, 143
Alavi Foundation Education Grants, 216

Albertsons Companies Foundation Nourishing
    Neighbors Grants, 221
Albert W. Cherne Foundation Grants, 222
Allan C. and Lelia J. Garden Foundation Grants, 236
Alloy Family Foundation Grants, 241
Ameren Corporation Community Grants, 251
American Savings Foundation Program Grants, 261
Amerigroup Foundation Grants, 264
Anderson Foundation Grants, 271
Anheuser-Busch Foundation Grants, 273
Ann Ludington Sullivan Foundation Grants, 279
Antone and Edene Vidinha Charitable Grants, 281
Ar-Hale Family Foundation Grants, 290
Armstrong McDonald Foundation Special Needs
    Grants, 301
Arthur Ashley Williams Foundation Grants, 302
Arthur M. Blank Family Foundation Molly Blank
    Fund Grants, 310
Assisi Foundation of Memphis General Grants, 318
Assisi Foundation of Memphis Mini Grants, 319
Atkinson Foundation Community Grants, 325
Babcock Charitable Trust Grants, 343
Baton Rouge Area Foundation Every Kid a King
    Fund Grants, 364
Baton Rouge Area Foundation Grants, 365
Bay and Paul Foundations PreK-12 Transformative
    Learning Practices Grants, 370
Bernau Family Foundation Grants, 413
BibleLands Grants, 420
Blanche and Irving Laurie Foundation Grants, 436
Blue Cross Blue Shield of Minnesota Foundation
    - Healthy Neighborhoods: Connect for Health
    Challenge Grants, 443
Blumenthal Foundation Grants, 459
Bodenwein Public Benevolent Foundation Grants, 461
Bradley-Turner Foundation Grants, 466
Bright Promises Foundation Grants, 470
Brunswick Foundation Grants, 479
Cabot Corporation Foundation Grants, 490
Callaway Foundation Grants, 496
Cargill Corporate Giving Grants, 503
Carl R. Hendrickson Family Foundation Grants, 509
CenturyLink Clarke M. Williams Foundation
    Matching Time Grants, 531
CFFVR Basic Needs Giving Partnership Grants, 537
CFFVR Myra M. and Robert L. Vandehey
    Foundation Grants, 545
CFFVR Robert and Patricia Endries Family
    Foundation Grants, 547
Chapman Charitable Foundation Grants, 560
Chapman Family Charitable Trust Grants, 561
Chapman Family Foundation, 562
Charles Crane Family Foundation Grants, 563
Charles Delmar Foundation Grants, 564
Charles H. Hall Foundation, 565
Charles Nelson Robinson Fund Grants, 569
Cheryl Spencer Memorial Foundation Grants, 576
Cincinnati Milacron Foundation Grants, 613
Citizens Bank Charitable Foundation Grants, 616
Clark and Ruby Baker Foundation Grants, 625
Claude A. and Blanche McCubbin Abbott Charitable
    Trust Grants, 628
Cleveland Browns Foundation Grants, 633
CNCS AmeriCorps NCCC Project Grants, 642
CNCS Foster Grandparent Projects Grants, 646
Collins C. Diboll Private Foundation Grants, 657
Collins Foundation Grants, 658
Community Foundation for Greater Buffalo
    Competitive Grants, 670
Community Foundation of Bartholomew County
    Women's Giving Circle, 692
Community Foundation of Greater Fort Wayne -
    Community Endowment and Clarke Endowment
    Grants, 705
Covenant Foundation of Brentwood Grants, 755
Covidien Partnership for Neighborhood Wellness
    Grants, 759
Crane Foundation General Grants, 761
Crane Fund for Widows and Children Grants, 762
Crescent Porter Hale Foundation Grants, 767

CUNA Mutual Group Fdn Community Grants, 770
Curtis Foundation Grants, 771
David Alan and Susan Berkman Rahm Foundation Grants, 785
David and Barbara B. Hirschhorn Foundation Education and Literacy Grants, 786
David and Laura Merage Foundation Grants, 789
David M. and Marjorie D. Rosenberg Foundation Grants, 790
David Robinson Foundation Grants, 791
Delaware Community Foundation Grants, 817
Dolan Children's Foundation Grants, 832
Don and May Wilkins Charitable Trust Grants, 842
Dorrance Family Foundation Grants, 845
E. Clayton and Edith P. Gengras, Jr. Foundation Grants, 875
Earl and Maxine Claussen Trust Grants, 878
Eastern Bank Charitable Foundation Partnerships Grants, 881
Eastern Bank Charitable Foundation Targeted Grants, 882
Edyth Bush Charitable Foundation Grants, 893
Effie Allen Little Foundation Grants, 894
Effie and Wofford Cain Foundation Grants, 895
El Pomar Foundation Anna Keesling Ackerman Fund Grants, 907
El Pomar Foundation Grants, 908
Elsie H. Wilcox Foundation Grants, 909
Emerson Kampen Foundation Grants, 911
Emma J. Adams Memorial Fund Grants, 914
Ensworth Charitable Foundation Grants, 916
Entergy Charitable Foundation Education and Literacy Grants, 917
Entergy Corporation Micro Grants, 919
Erie Chapman Foundation Grants, 928
Evan Frankel Foundation Grants, 938
F.M. Kirby Foundation Grants, 946
FirstEnergy Foundation Community Grants, 965
Florence Foundation Grants, 978
Forest Foundation Grants, 985
Foundation for a Healthy Kentucky Grants, 988
Francis Beidler Foundation Grants, 1007
Frankel Brothers Foundation Grants, 1009
Franklin County Community Fdn Grants, 1010
Frank M. Tait Foundation Grants, 1012
Frank Reed and Margaret Jane Peters Memorial Fund II Grants, 1014
Friedman Family Foundation Grants, 1023
Fuller E. Callaway Foundation Grants, 1027
Fuller Foundation Youth At Risk Grants, 1028
Furth Family Foundation Grants, 1030
G.N. Wilcox Trust Grants, 1031
Gardner Foundation Grants, 1035
George A. & Grace L. Long Fdn Grants, 1041
George E. Hatcher, Jr. and Ann Williams Hatcher Foundation Grants, 1045
George H.C. Ensworth Memorial Fund Grants, 1049
George H. Sandy Foundation Grants, 1050
George I. Alden Trust Grants, 1051
George J. and Effie L. Seay Foundation Grants, 1052
George Kress Foundation Grants, 1053
George P. Davenport Trust Fund Grants, 1054
Gerber Fdn West Michigan Youth Grants, 1065
Giant Food Charitable Grants, 1068
Grace Bersted Foundation Grants, 1097
Graham Family Charitable Foundation Grants, 1099
Graham Foundation Grants, 1101
Granger Foundation Grants, 1103
Greater Saint Louis Community Fdn Grants, 1110
Greater Tacoma Community Foundation General Operating Grants, 1113
Greenspun Family Foundation Grants, 1118
HAF Joe Alexandre Mem Family Fund Grants, 1145
HAF Laurence and Elaine Allen Memorial Fund Grants, 1146
Hahl Proctor Charitable Trust Grants, 1151
Harold Brooks Foundation Grants, 1172
Harris Foundation Grants, 1177
Harrison County Community Fdn Grants, 1178

Harrison County Community Foundation Signature Grants, 1179
Harry and Helen Sands Charitable Trust Grants, 1181
Harry Frank Guggenheim Foundation Research Grants, 1184
Harvey Randall Wickes Foundation Grants, 1188
Hawai'i Community Foundation Children's Trust Fund Community Awareness: Child Abuse and Neglect Prevention Grants, 1198
Hawai'i Community Foundation Victoria S. and Bradley L. Geist Foundation: Supporting Foster Children and Their Caregivers, 1208
Hawai'i Community Foundation Victoria S. and Bradley L. Geist Foundation: Supporting Transitioning Foster Youth Grants, 1209
Hawaii Community Foundation Reverend Takie Okumura Family Grants, 1216
HBF Pathways Out of Poverty Grants, 1222
Helen Bader Foundation Grants, 1227
Helen V. Brach Foundation Grants, 1232
Henrietta Lange Burk Fund Grants, 1235
Henry E. Niles Foundation Grants, 1240
Henry L. Guenther Foundation Grants, 1242
Herbert A. and Adrian W. Woods Foundation Grants, 1243
Highmark Corporate Giving Grants, 1248
Honeywell Corporation Family Safety and Security Grants, 1255
Huffy Foundation Grants, 1273
Huisking Foundation Grants, 1274
Ike and Roz Friedman Foundation Grants, 1289
ING Foundation Grants, 1302
J. Bulow Campbell Foundation Grants, 1319
J. Knox Gholston Foundation Grants, 1321
James LeVoy Sorenson Foundation Grants, 1343
James M. Collins Foundation Grants, 1344
Jayne and Leonard Abess Foundation Grants, 1358
Jeffris Wood Foundation Grants, 1359
Jewish Fund Grants, 1364
Jim Blevins Foundation Grants, 1365
John Clarke Trust Grants, 1369
John G. Duncan Charitable Trust Grants, 1372
John H. and Wilhelmina D. Harland Charitable Foundation Children and Youth Grants, 1374
John M. Weaver Foundation Grants, 1376
Johnson Scholarship Foundation Grants, 1382
Joni Elaine Templeton Foundation Grants, 1384
Joseph H. and Florence A. Roblee Foundation Education Grants, 1386
Joyce and Randy Seckman Charitable Foundation Grants, 1393
Judith Clark-Morrill Foundation Grants, 1395
Judy and Peter Blum Kovler Foundation Grants, 1396
Julia and Tunnicliff Fox Chartbl Trust Grants, 1397
Kaiser Permanente Hawaii Region Community Grants, 1406
Katharine Matthies Foundation Grants, 1418
Katrine Menzing Deakins Chartbl Trust Grants, 1422
Kawabe Memorial Fund Grants, 1423
Kimball International-Habig Foundation Health and Human Services Grants, 1434
Klingenstein-Simons Fellowship Awards in the Neurosciences, 1441
Kodak Community Relations Grants, 1445
Kopp Family Foundation Grants, 1448
Koret Foundation Grants, 1449
Kovler Family Foundation Grants, 1454
Kovler Family Foundation Grants, 1455
Lands' End Corporate Giving Program, 1468
Laura Musser Intercultural Harmony Grants, 1472
Laurie H. Wollmuth Charitable Trust Grants, 1476
Leo Niessen Jr., Charitable Trust Grants, 1484
Lewis H. Humphreys Charitable Trust Grants, 1486
Liberty Bank Foundation Grants, 1488
Libra Foundation Grants, 1489
Lil and Julie Rosenberg Foundation Grants, 1491
Lilly Endowment Summer Youth Grants, 1492
Linford & Mildred White Charitable Grants, 1495
Locations Foundation Legacy Grants, 1504

Lotus 88 Foundation for Women and Children Grants, 1508
Louis and Sandra Berkman Foundation Grants, 1510
Louis Calder Foundation Grants, 1511
Lumpkin Family Fdn Healthy People Grants, 1518
Lumpkin Family Foundation Strong Community Leadership Grants, 1519
M.A. Rikard Charitable Trust Grants, 1521
M. Bastian Family Foundation Grants, 1522
M.J. Murdock Charitable Trust General Grants, 1524
Mabel F. Hoffman Charitable Trust Grants, 1526
MacLellan Foundation Grants, 1531
Manuel D. and Rhoda Mayerson Fdn Grants, 1550
Mardag Foundation Grants, 1554
Margaret and James A. Elkins Jr. Fdn Grants, 1555
Margaret M. Walker Charitable Fdn Grants, 1556
Marin Community Foundation Social Justice and Interfaith Understanding Grants, 1567
Marion Gardner Jackson Charitable Trust Grts, 1570
Marion I. and Henry J. Knott Foundation Discretionary Grants, 1571
Marion I. and Henry J. Knott Foundation Standard Grants, 1572
Marjorie Moore Charitable Foundation Grants, 1574
Mark W. Coy Foundation Grants, 1575
Martin Family Foundation Grants, 1583
Mary Black Foundation Active Living Grants, 1585
Mary D. and Walter F. Frear Eleemosynary Trust Grants, 1588
Maryland State Arts Council Arts in Communities Grants, 1592
Mathile Family Foundation Grants, 1604
Maurice Amado Foundation Grants, 1609
Maurice J. Masserini Charitable Trust Grants, 1610
Max and Anna Levinson Foundation Grants, 1612
McCune Foundation Humananities Grants, 1619
Mead Witter Foundation Grants, 1628
Medtronic Foundation CommunityLink Health Grants, 1630
Meriden Foundation Grants, 1638
Mertz Gilmore Foundation NYC Dance Grants, 1642
Mervin Bovaird Foundation Grants, 1643
MGN Family Foundation Grants, 1656
Michael and Susan Dell Foundation Grants, 1657
Michael Reese Health Trust Core Grants, 1658
Michael Reese Health Trust Responsive Grants, 1659
Minnie M. Jones Trust Grants, 1678
Moody Foundation Grants, 1692
Moran Family Foundation Grants, 1693
Morris Stulsaft Foundation Early Childhood Education Grants, 1696
Mt. Sinai Health Care Foundation Health of the Jewish Community Grants, 1709
Mt. Sinai Health Care Foundation Health of the Urban Community Grants, 1710
Narragansett Number One Foundation Grants, 1712
Nathalie and Gladys Dalkowitz Charitable Trust Grants, 1716
Nathan Cummings Foundation Grants, 1718
Nathaniel and Elizabeth P. Stevens Foundation Grants, 1719
Nell J. Redfield Foundation Grants, 1737
New Jersey Office of Faith Based Initiatives Services to At Risk Youth Grants, 1752
Norcliffe Foundation Grants, 1766
Olga Sipolin Children's Fund Grants, 1815
Onan Family Foundation Grants, 1821
Oppenstein Brothers Foundation Grants, 1827
PacifiCare Foundation Grants, 1861
Perkins-Ponder Foundation Grants, 1938
Perkins Charitable Foundation Grants, 1939
PG&E Community Vitality Grants, 1957
PGE Foundation Grants, 1958
Philip Boyle Foundation Grants, 1961
Piper Trust Reglious Organizations Grants, 1979
Pohlad Family Foundation Youth Advancement Grants, 1993
Powell Foundation Grants, 2013
Premera Blue Cross Grants, 2018

Priddy Foundation Organizational Development
  Grants, 2022
Priddy Foundation Program Grants, 2023
R.C. Baker Foundation Grants, 2043
R.S. Gernon Trust Grants, 2047
Raskob Fdn for Catholic Activities Grants, 2054
Rathmann Family Foundation Grants, 2057
RGk Foundation Grants, 2068
Richard and Caroline T. Gwathmey Memorial Trust
  Grants, 2069
Ricks Family Charitable Trust Grants, 2075
Robbins Charitable Foundation Grants, 2081
Robbins Family Charitable Foundation Grants, 2082
Robert and Helen Haddad Foundation Grants, 2084
Robert R. McCormick Tribune Foundation
  Community Grants, 2093
Robert W. Knox, Sr. and Pearl Wallis Knox
  Charitable Foundation, 2095
Rockwell Collins Charitable Corp Grants, 2098
Roger L. and Agnes C. Dell Charitable Trust I
  Grants, 2099
Rosenberg Charity Foundation Grants, 2107
Roy and Christine Sturgis Charitable Tr Grts, 2115
Ruth Camp Campbell Charitable Trust Grants, 2125
S. Spencer Scott Fund Grants, 2129
Sadler Family Foundation Grants, 2132
Saeman Family Fdn A Charitable Grants, 2133
Saint Ann Legacy Grants, 2138
Sandy Hill Foundation Grants, 2157
Sarah G. McCarthy Memorial Foundation, 2162
Schlessman Family Foundation Grants, 2167
Scott B. and Annie P. Appleby Charitable Trust
  Grants, 2169
Shell Deer Park Grants, 2186
Sidney Stern Memorial Trust Grants, 2197
Siebert Lutheran Foundation Grants, 2198
Sierra Health Foundation Responsive Grants, 2199
Sioux Falls Area Community Foundation Community
  Fund Grants, 2203
Sioux Falls Area Community Foundation Spot
  Grants, 2204
Sorenson Legacy Foundation Grants, 2217
Speer Trust Grants, 2230
Stan and Sandy Checketts Foundation Grants, 2235
Stella and Charles Guttman Foundation Grants, 2241
Strake Foundation Grants, 2249
SunTrust Bank Trusteed Foundations Greene-Sawtell
  Grants, 2257
SunTrust Bank Trusteed Foundations Nell Warren
  Elkin and William Simpson Elkin Grants, 2258
Sylvia Perkin Perpetual Charitable Trust Grants, 2263
T.L.L. Temple Foundation Grants, 2264
Tension Envelope Foundation Grants, 2284
Thomas and Agnes Carvel Foundation Grants, 2289
Todd Brock Family Foundation Grants, 2305
Turner B. Bunn, Jr. and Catherine E. Bunn
  Foundation Grants, 2325
Tyler Aaron Bookman Memorial Foundation Trust
  Grants, 2329
U.S. Cellular Corporation Grants, 2331
United Methodist Committee on Relief Hunger and
  Poverty Grants, 2344
United Methodist Health Ministry Fund Grts, 2345
USAID Nigeria Ed Crisis Response Grants, 2358
USDEd Gaining Early Awareness and Readiness for
  Undergrad Programs (GEAR UP) Grants, 2364
UUA Actions of Public Witness Grants, 2365
UUA Congregation-Based Community Organizing
  Grants, 2366
UUA Fund Grants, 2367
UUA International Fund Grants, 2368
UUA Just Society Fund Grants, 2369
UUA Social Responsibility Grants, 2370
V.V. Cooke Foundation Grants, 2371
Vanderburgh Community Foundation Men's Fund
  Grants, 2373
Vanderburgh County Community Foundation
  Women's Fund Grants, 2376
Victoria S. and Bradley L. Geist Foundation Grants
  Supporting Foster Care and Their Caregivers, 2382

Victoria S. and Bradley L. Geist Foundation Grants
  Supporting Transitioning Foster Youth, 2383
W.H. and Mary Ellen Cobb Chartbl Trust Grts, 2397
W.P. and Bulah Luse Foundation Grants, 2399
Warrick County Community Foundation Women's
  Fund, 2411
Washington Area Fuel Fund Grants, 2413
Washington Gas Charitable Contributions, 2417
Welborn Baptist Foundation Promotion of Early
  Childhood Development Grants, 2423
Welborn Foundation Promotion of Healthy
  Adolescent Development Grants, 2425
Widgeon Point Charitable Foundation Grants, 2447
William Foulds Family Foundation Grants, 2465
William G. and Helen C. Hoffman Foundation
  Grants, 2466
William M. Weaver Foundation Grants, 2472
William Ray and Ruth E. Collins Fdn Grants, 2473
Winifred Johnson Clive Foundation Grants, 2478
Youths' Friends Association Grants, 2511
ZYTL Foundation Grants, 2528

Scholarships
A.C. and Penney Hubbard Foundation Grants, 19
Abbott Fund Science Education Grants, 48
Abell-Hanger Foundation Grants, 52
Abell Foundation Education Grants, 53
ACCF of Indiana Berne Ready Mix Community
  Enrichment Fund Grants, 65
Achelis and Bodman Foundation Grants, 101
Achelis Foundation Grants, 102
Adams County Community Foundation Grants, 115
Adray Foundation, 130
Agnes M. Lindsay Trust Grants, 140
Akron Community Fdn Education Grants, 151
ALA Bound to Stay Bound Books Scholarships, 163
Alavi Foundation Education Grants, 216
Alcatel-Lucent Technologies Foundation Grants, 224
Alexander Graham Bell Parent and Infant Financial
  Aid Grants, 227
Alex Stern Family Foundation Grants, 229
ALFJ International Fund Grants, 231
Alpha Natural Resources Corporate Giving, 246
American Express Charitable Fund Scholarships, 254
American Savings Foundation Program Grants, 261
American Schlafhorst Foundation Grants, 262
Andrew Family Foundation Grants, 272
Anheuser-Busch Foundation Grants, 273
Antone and Edene Vidinha Charitable Grants, 281
Ar-Hale Family Foundation Grants, 290
Arthur E. and Josephine Campbell Beyer Foundation
  Grants, 303
Arthur M. Blank Family Foundation Molly Blank
  Fund Grants, 310
Arts Council of Greater Lansing Young Creatives
  Grants, 314
Atkinson Foundation Community Grants, 325
Atwood Foundation General Grants, 330
B.F. and Rose H. Perkins Foundation Community
  Grants, 342
Baltimore Ravens Foundation Scholarships, 352
Batts Foundation Grants, 367
Bay Area Community Foundation Semiannual
  Grants, 382
Belvedere Cove Foundation Scholarships, 401
Ben B. Cheney Foundation Grants, 402
Best Buy Children's Fdn @15 Scholarship , 415
Bindley Family Foundation Grants, 430
Blanche and Irving Laurie Foundation Grants, 436
Blue Grass Community Foundation Hudson-Ellis
  Grants, 449
Boeing Company Contributions Grants, 462
Bollinger Foundation Grants, 463
Brunswick Foundation Grants, 479
C.H. Robinson Worldwide Foundation Grants, 489
Cabot Corporation Foundation Grants, 490
Campbell Soup Foundation Grants, 501
Cargill Corporate Giving Grants, 503
Carroll County Community Foundation Grants, 513
Central Pacific Bank Foundation Grants, 530

CFFVR Appleton Education Foundation Grants, 536
CFFVR Shawano Area Community Foundation
  Grants, 549
CFFVR Women's Fund for the Fox Valley Region
  Grants, 550
Charles Delmar Foundation Grants, 564
Chick and Sophie Major Memorial Duck Calling
  Contest Scholarships, 583
Christensen Fund Regional Grants, 600
CIGNA Foundation Grants, 611
Citizens Savings Foundation Grants, 617
Clarence T.C. Ching Foundation Grants, 624
Colgate-Palmolive Company Grants, 652
Collins Foundation Grants, 658
Colorado Interstate Gas Grants, 661
Community Foundation for Greater Buffalo
  Competitive Grants, 670
Community Foundation for SE Michigan Renaissance
  of Values Scholarships, 684
Community Foundation of Crawford County, 695
Community Foundation of Greater Fort Wayne -
  Community Endowment and Clarke Endowment
  Grants, 705
Community Foundation of Henderson County
  Community Grants, 711
Community Foundation of Madison and Jefferson
  County Grants, 731
Community Fdn of Randolph County Grants, 735
Community Fdn of Wabash County Grants, 740
Community Foundation of Western Massachusetts
  Grants, 741
Cralle Foundation Grants, 760
Crescent Porter Hale Foundation Grants, 767
Cudd Foundation Grants, 769
Dayton Foundation Rike Family Scholarships, 798
Dell Scholars Program Scholarships, 819
Do Something Awards, 847
Do Something Scholarships, 857
Edward W. and Stella C. Van Houten Memorial Fund
  Grants, 892
Effie and Wofford Cain Foundation Grants, 895
Elsie H. Wilcox Foundation Grants, 909
Evan Frankel Foundation Grants, 938
Fichtenbaum Charitable Trust Grants, 955
Finish Line Youth Foundation Grants, 961
First Nations Development Institute Native
  Agriculture and Food Systems Initiative
  Scholarships, 971
Flinn Foundation Scholarships, 977
Florence Foundation Grants, 978
Four J Foundation Grants, 1004
Fremont Area Community Foundation Community
  Grants, 1020
From the Top Jack Kent Cooke Young Artist
  Scholarships, 1026
Fuller E. Callaway Foundation Grants, 1027
G.N. Wilcox Trust Grants, 1031
Gene Haas Foundation, 1038
George and Ruth Bradford Foundation Grants, 1042
George H. and Jane A. Mifflin Memorial Fund
  Grants, 1048
George I. Alden Trust Grants, 1051
Georgia-Pacific Fdn Entrepreneurship Grants, 1059
Greater Saint Louis Community Fdn Grants, 1110
Gregory and Helayne Brown Charitable Foundation
  Grants, 1119
Hank Aaron Chasing the Dream Fdn Grants, 1162
Harold K.L. Castle Foundation Public Education
  Redesign and Enhancement Grants, 1173
Harrison County Community Fdn Grants, 1178
Hearst Foundations United States Senate Youth
  Grants, 1225
Helen Bader Foundation Grants, 1227
Helen Irwin Littauer Educational Trust Grants, 1231
Helen V. Brach Foundation Grants, 1232
Hillsdale County Community Foundation Love Your
  Community Grants, 1251
Huisking Foundation Grants, 1274
Humana Foundation Grants, 1275
IBCAT Nancy Jaynes Memorial Scholarship, 1281

Iddings Foundation Major Project Grants, 1284
Ifuku Family Foundation Grants, 1287
IIE 911 Armed Forces Scholarships, 1288
Intel Corporation Int Community Grants, 1312
Isabel Allende Foundation Esperanza Grants, 1315
J. Watumull Fund Grants, 1326
J. Willard and Alice S. Marriott Fdn Grants, 1327
Jack Kent Cooke Fdn Young Artist Awards, 1333
James and Abigail Campbell Family Foundation
    Grants, 1337
James K. and Arlene L. Adams Foundation
    Scholarships, 1341
James S. Copley Foundation Grants, 1345
Jerry L. and Barbara J. Burris Fdn Grants, 1362
John H. and Wilhelmina D. Harland Charitable
    Foundation Children and Youth Grants, 1374
John W. Anderson Foundation Grants, 1383
Julia Temple Davis Brown Foundation Grants, 1399
Kathryne Beynon Foundation Grants, 1420
Kawabe Memorial Fund Grants, 1423
Kenneth T. and Eileen L. Norris Fdn Grants, 1427
Kevin J Major Youth Sports Scholarships, 1431
Kind World Foundation Grants, 1438
Kodak Community Relations Grants, 1445
Kohl's Cares Scholarships, 1447
Kopp Family Foundation Grants, 1448
Latkin Charitable Foundation Grants, 1469
Laura L. Adams Foundation Grants, 1473
Leo Goodwin Foundation Grants, 1482
Lily Palmer Fry Memorial Trust Grants, 1493
Lloyd G. Balfour Foundation Attleboro-Specific
    Charities Grants, 1502
Lloyd G. Balfour Foundation Scholarships, 1503
Louis Calder Foundation Grants, 1511
Lubrizol Foundation Grants, 1513
M. Bastian Family Foundation Grants, 1522
Maggie Welby Foundation Scholarships, 1539
Marathon Petroleum Corporation Grants, 1551
Margaret T. Morris Foundation Grants, 1557
Martin C. Kauffman 100 Club of Alameda County
    Scholarships, 1582
Mary D. and Walter F. Frear Eleemosynary Trust
    Grants, 1588
Matilda R. Wilson Fund Grants, 1605
Maurice R. Robinson Fund Grants, 1611
McCune Charitable Foundation Grants, 1617
McGraw-Hill Companies Community Grants, 1620
McInerny Foundation Grants, 1622
Mead Witter Foundation Grants, 1628
Meriden Foundation Grants, 1638
Mervin Bovaird Foundation Grants, 1643
MGN Family Foundation Grants, 1656
Michigan Youth Livestock Scholarship and State-
    Wide Scholarship, 1663
NASE Fdn Future Entrepreneur Scholarship, 1713
National 4-H Youth in Action Awards, 1721
National YoungArts Foundation Awards, 1725
Nell J. Redfield Foundation Grants, 1737
Norcliffe Foundation Grants, 1766
Ordean Foundation Catalyst Grants, 1830
Oregon Community Foundation Edna E. Harrell
    Community Children's Fund Grants, 1835
OtterCares Champion Fund Grants, 1848
P. Buckley Moss Foundation for Children's Education
    Endowed Scholarships, 1854
PAS Freddie Gruber Scholarship, 1872
PAS John E. Grimes Timpani Scholarship, 1873
PAS PASIC International Scholarships, 1875
PAS SABIAN/PASIC Scholarship, 1876
PAS Sabian Larrie London Memorial Schol, 1877
Percy B. Ferebee Endowment Grants, 1936
Pettus Foundation Grants, 1952
Peyton Anderson Foundation Grants, 1954
Peyton Anderson Scholarships, 1955
PG&E Community Vitality Grants, 1957
PGE Foundation Grants, 1958
Phil Hardin Foundation Grants, 1960
Piper Jaffray Foundation Communities Giving
    Grants, 1974

Pohlad Family Foundation Summer Camp
    Scholarships, 1992
Portland General Electric Foundation Grants, 2007
Posse Foundation Scholarships, 2011
PPG Industries Foundation Grants, 2017
Presidio Fencing Club Youth Fencers Assistance
    Scholarships, 2019
Price Chopper's Golub Foundation Grants, 2020
ProLiteracy National Book Fund Grants, 2026
Prudential Foundation Education Grants, 2028
PSEG Corporate Contributions Grants, 2030
Putnam County Community Fdn Grants, 2040
R.C. Baker Foundation Grants, 2043
R.D. and Joan Dale Hubbard Fdn Grants, 2044
Ralph M. Parsons Foundation Grants, 2052
Rathmann Family Foundation Grants, 2057
Reinberger Foundation Grants, 2066
Richland County Bank Grants, 2074
Robert R. Meyer Foundation Grants, 2094
Roger L. and Agnes C. Dell Charitable Trust I
    Grants, 2099
Roger L. and Agnes C. Dell Charitable Trust II
    Grants, 2100
Roy J. Carver Trust Statewide Scholarships, 2116
Samuel S. Johnson Foundation Grants, 2146
San Juan Island Community Foundation Grants, 2158
Sartain Lanier Family Foundation Grants, 2164
Schramm Foundation Grants, 2168
Scott B. and Annie P. Appleby Charitable Trust
    Grants, 2169
Shell Oil Company Foundation Community
    Development Grants, 2188
Shimizu Foundation Scholarships, 2190
Sony Corporation of America Grants, 2216
Strake Foundation Grants, 2249
Stranahan Foundation Grants, 2250
Summit Foundation Grants, 2255
Target Corporation Community Engagement Fund
    Grants, 2270
Telluride Foundation Community Grants, 2281
TSYSF Individual Scholarships, 2322
Tull Charitable Foundation Grants, 2324
Turtle Bay Foundation Grants, 2327
Union Bank, N.A. Foundation Grants, 2334
Union Pacific Fdn Community & Civic Grants, 2337
United Friends of the Children Scholarships, 2341
USAID U.S.-Egypt Learning Grants, 2361
VSA Playwright Discovery Award, 2396
W.P. and Bulah Luse Foundation Grants, 2399
W.W. Smith Chartbl Trust Basic Needs Grants, 2400
Wayne County Community Grants, 2419
White County Community Foundation - Landis
    Memorial Scholarship, 2437
William Blair and Company Foundation Grants, 2461
William G. and Helen C. Hoffman Foundation
    Grants, 2466
William G. Gilmore Foundation Grants, 2467
William J. and Gertrude R. Casper Foundation
    Grants, 2469
Wilton and Effie Hebert Foundation Grants, 2476
WinnCompanies Charitable Giving, 2479
Wolfe Associates Grants, 2483
Xerox Foundation Grants, 2507
Z. Smith Reynolds Foundation Small Grants, 2523

Seed Grants
3M Company Foundation Health and Human
    Services Grants, 6
A.L. Mailman Family Foundation Grants, 20
A.L. Spencer Foundation Grants, 21
Abbott Fund Community Engagement Grants, 46
Abby's Legendary Pizza Foundation Grants, 49
Abell-Hanger Foundation Grants, 52
ACCF John and Kay Boch Fund Grants, 60
ACCF of Indiana Anonymous Community
    Enrichment Fund Grants, 63
ACCF of Indiana Bank of Geneva Heritage Fund
    Grants, 64
ACCF of Indiana First Merchants Bank / Decatur
    Bank and Trust Fund Grants, 66

ACCF of Indiana Ron and Susie Ballard Community
    Enrichment Fund Grants, 68
ACF Abandoned Infants Assistance Grants, 70
ACF American Indian and Alaska Native Early Head
    Start Expansion Grants, 72
ACF Infant Adoption Awareness Training Program
    Grants, 84
ACF National Human Trafficking Hotline Grants, 86
ACF Street Outreach Program Grants, 94
Achelis and Bodman Foundation Grants, 101
Achelis Foundation Grants, 102
Adams County Community Foundation Grants, 115
Adams Family Fdn of Nora Springs Grants, 118
Adelaide Breed Bayrd Foundation Grants, 123
Adolph Coors Foundation Grants, 129
A Friends' Foundation Trust Grants, 136
Agnes M. Lindsay Trust Grants, 140
Air Products Foundation Grants, 148
Akron Community Foundation Health and human
    services Grants, 152
Alabama Humanities Foundation Major Grants, 159
Albert W. Cherne Foundation Grants, 222
Alliance for Strong Families and Communities
    Grants, 239
Alliant Energy Foundation Community Giving for
    Good Sponsorship Grants, 240
Allstate Corporate Giving Grants, 242
Allstate Corp Hometown Commitment Grants, 243
Alpha Natural Resources Corporate Giving, 246
Ameren Corporation Community Grants, 251
American Indian Youth Running Strong Grants, 256
American Schlafhorst Foundation Grants, 262
American Woodmark Foundation Grants, 263
Amway Corporation Contributions, 269
Anderson Foundation Grants, 271
Ann Ludington Sullivan Foundation Grants, 279
Appalachian Regional Commission Entrepreneurship
    and Business Development Grants, 287
Ar-Hale Family Foundation Grants, 290
Arizona Foundation for Women General Grants, 294
Arthur Ashley Williams Foundation Grants, 302
Arthur M. Blank Family Foundation Inspiring Spaces
    Grants, 309
Arthur M. Blank Family Foundation Mountain Sky
    Guest Ranch Fund Grants, 311
Aspen Community Foundation Grants, 316
AT&T Fdn Community Support and Safety, 320
Atkinson Foundation Community Grants, 325
Atlanta Foundation Grants, 326
Atlas Insurance Agency Foundation Grants, 329
Austin Community Foundation Grants, 332
Austin S. Nelson Foundation Grants, 333
Autauga Area Community Foundation Grants, 334
Babcock Charitable Trust Grants, 343
Baltimore Community Foundation Building Stronger
    Neighborhoods Regionwide Grants, 347
Bank of America Charitable Foundation Community
    Development Grants, 355
Bank of America Charitable Foundation Matching
    Gifts, 356
Bank of America Charitable Foundation Volunteer
    Grants, 358
Bank of Hawaii Foundation Grants, 360
Baton Rouge Area Foundation Grants, 365
Baxter International Corporate Giving Grants, 368
Baxter International Foundation Grants, 369
Bay and Paul Foundations PreK-12 Transformative
    Learning Practices Grants, 370
Bay Area Community Foundation Arenac
    Community Fund Grants, 371
Bay Area Community Fdn Auburn Area Chamber of
    Commerce Enrichment Fund Grants, 373
Bay Area Community Foundation Community
    Initiative Fund Grants, 376
Bay Area Community Foundation Dow
    CommunityGives Youth Service Prog Grants, 377
Beckman Coulter Foundation Grants, 394
Bernard and Audre Rapoport Foundation Education
    Grants, 410
Better Way Foundation Grants, 419

Bikes Belong Grants, 424
Bill and Melinda Gates Foundation Agricultural Development Grants, 425
Blandin Foundation Expand Opportunity Grants, 437
Blue Grass Community Foundation Clark County Fund Grants, 444
Blue Grass Community Foundation Fayette County Fund Grants, 446
Blue Grass Community Foundation Franklin County Fund Grants, 447
Blue Grass Community Foundation Harrison County Fund Grants, 448
Blue Grass Community Foundation Hudson-Ellis Grants, 449
Blue Grass Community Foundation Madison County Fund Grants, 450
Blue Grass Community Foundation Magoffin County Fund Grants, 451
Blue Grass Community Foundation Morgan County Fund Grants, 452
Blue Grass Community Foundation Rowan County Fund Grants, 453
Blue Grass Community Foundation Woodford County Fund Grants, 454
Blue Mountain Community Foundation Warren Community Action Fund Grants, 457
Blue River Community Foundation Grants, 458
Blumenthal Foundation Grants, 459
Boeing Company Contributions Grants, 462
BP Foundation Grants, 465
Brookdale Fdn Relatives as Parents Grants, 474
Brunswick Foundation Dollars for Doers Grants, 478
Bushrod H. Campbell and Adah F. Hall Charity Fund Grants, 486
C.H. Robinson Worldwide Foundation Grants, 489
Cabot Corporation Foundation Grants, 490
Caesars Foundation Grants, 492
California Arts Cncl Statewide Networks Grants, 493
Campbell Soup Foundation Grants, 501
Carl M. Freeman Foundation Grants, 508
Castle Foundation Grants, 518
CenturyLink Clarke M. Williams Foundation Matching Time Grants, 531
CFFVR Clintonville Area Foundation Grants, 539
CFFVR Clintonville Area Foundation Grants, 538
CFFVR Mielke Family Foundation Grants, 544
CFFVR Schmidt Family G4 Grants, 548
CFFVR Women's Fund for the Fox Valley Region Grants, 550
CFGR SisterFund Grants, 554
Chapman Charltable Foundation Grants, 560
Charles Delmar Foundation Grants, 564
Cheryl Spencer Memorial Foundation Grants, 576
Chesapeake Bay Trust Mini Grants, 578
Chilkat Valley Community Foundation Grants, 588
Christensen Fund Regional Grants, 600
Cigna Civic Affairs Sponsorships, 610
Cincinnati Milacron Foundation Grants, 613
Circle K Corporation Contributions Grants, 614
Clark County Community Foundation Grants, 626
Clayton Baker Trust Grants, 629
Cleveland Foundation Higley Fund Grants, 634
CNCS AmeriCorps State and National Grants, 643
Collins C. Diboll Private Foundation Grants, 657
Columbus Foundation Traditional Grants, 663
Community Foundation for Greater Atlanta Metropolitan Extra Wish Grants, 666
Community Foundation for Greater Atlanta Spark Clayton Grants, 667
Community Foundation for Greater Atlanta Spark Newton Grants, 668
Community Foundation for Greater Atlanta Strategic Restructuring Fund Grants, 669
Community Foundation for Greater Buffalo Competitive Grants, 670
Community Foundation for Greater Buffalo Ralph C. Wilson, Jr. Legacy Fund Grants, 674
Community Foundation for Kettering Grants, 676
Community Foundation for SE Michigan Head Start Innovation Fund, 682

Community Foundation for the Capital Region Grants, 687
Community Foundation of Bartholomew County Heritage Fund Grants, 690
Community Foundation of Boone County Grants, 694
Community Foundation of Eastern Connecticut General Southeast Grants, 696
Community Foundation of Greater Chattanooga Grants, 704
Community Foundation of Greater Fort Wayne - Community Endowment and Clarke Endowment Grants, 705
Community Foundation of Greater Greensboro Community Grants, 708
Community Foundation of Henderson County Community Grants, 711
Community Fdn of Howard County Grants, 712
Community Foundation of Louisville Anna Marble Memorial Fund for Princeton Grants, 717
Community Fdn of Randolph County Grants, 735
Community Fdn of Wabash County Grants, 740
Community Foundation of Western Massachusetts Grants, 741
Community Memorial Foundation Responsive Grants, 743
CONSOL Youth Program Grants, 747
Cooke Foundation Grants, 748
Corina Higginson Trust Grants, 750
Countess Moira Charitable Foundation Grants, 752
Cralle Foundation Grants, 760
Crane Fund Grants, 763
Curtis Foundation Grants, 771
Daniels Homeless and Disadvantaged Grants, 782
Dayton Power and Light Company Foundation Signature Grants, 801
Deaconess Foundation Advocacy Grants, 804
Dearborn Community Foundation City of Aurora Grants, 808
Decatur County Community Foundation Large Project Grants, 811
Del Mar Foundation Community Grants, 820
Dermody Properties Foundation Grants, 827
Don and May Wilkins Charitable Trust Grants, 842
Dorothea Haus Ross Foundation Grants, 844
Dorr Foundation Grants, 846
Dr. John T. Macdonald Foundation Grants, 863
Dyson Foundation Mid-Hudson Valley Project Support Grants, 874
E. Clayton and Edith P. Gengras, Jr. Foundation Grants, 875
Eastern Bank Charitable Foundation Neighborhood Support Grants, 880
Eastern Bank Charitable Foundation Partnerships Grants, 881
Eastern Bank Charitable Foundation Targeted Grants, 882
Echoing Green Fellowships, 885
Edyth Bush Charitable Foundation Grants, 893
Effie Allen Little Foundation Grants, 894
Effie and Wofford Cain Foundation Grants, 895
Eileen Fisher Activating Leadership Grants for Women and Girls, 898
Elizabeth Morse Genius Charitable Trust Grants, 901
Ella West Freeman Foundation Grants, 904
Elmer Roe Deaver Foundation Grants, 906
El Pomar Foundation Anna Keesling Ackerman Fund Grants, 907
El Pomar Foundation Grants, 908
Elton John AIDS Foundation Grants, 910
Emerson Kampen Foundation Grants, 911
Evelyn and Walter Haas, Jr. Fund Immigrant Rights Grants, 941
Evelyn and Walter Haas, Jr. Fund Nonprofit Leadership Grants, 942
Ewing Marion Kauffman Foundation Grants, 943
F.M. Kirby Foundation Grants, 946
F.R. Bigelow Foundation Grants, 947
Fidelity Charitable Gift Fund Grants, 956
Fifth Third Bank Corporate Giving, 958

First Hawaiian Bank Foundation Corporate Giving Grants, 967
Florence Foundation Grants, 978
Foundation Beyond Belief Compassionate Impact Grants, 986
Foundation Beyond Belief Humanist Grants, 987
Foundation of Herkimer and Oneida Counties Youth Sports, Wellness and Recreation Mini-Grants, 994
Four County Community Foundation General Grants, 1000
Four County Community Foundation Healthy Senior/Healthy Youth Fund Grants, 1001
Four J Foundation Grants, 1004
Francis Beidler Foundation Grants, 1007
Francis L. Abreu Charitable Trust Grants, 1008
Franklin H. Wells and Ruth L. Wells Foundation Grants, 1011
Frank M. Tait Foundation Grants, 1012
Fremont Area Community Foundation Community Grants, 1020
Furth Family Foundation Grants, 1030
G.N. Wilcox Trust Grants, 1031
Gene Haas Foundation, 1038
General Motors Foundation Grants, 1039
George B. Page Foundation Grants, 1044
George Graham and Elizabeth Galloway Smith Foundation Grants, 1047
George P. Davenport Trust Fund Grants, 1054
George W. Wells Foundation Grants, 1057
German Protestant Orphan Asylum Foundation Grants, 1066
Gil and Dody Weaver Foundation Grants, 1071
GNOF Exxon-Mobil Grants, 1080
GNOF Norco Community Grants, 1089
Golden Heart Community Foundation Grants, 1094
Good+Foundation Grants, 1096
Graham Foundation Grants, 1100
Graham Foundation Grants, 1101
Greater Saint Louis Community Fdn Grants, 1110
Greater Sitka Legacy Fund Grants, 1111
Greater Tacoma Community Foundation General Operating Grants, 1113
Green Foundation Human Services Grants, 1116
Green River Area Community Fdn Grants, 1117
GTRCF Elk Rapids Area Community Endowment Grants, 1127
GTRCF Grand Traverse Families in Action for Youth Endowment Grants, 1129
Gulf Coast Foundation of Community Program Grants, 1135
HAF Joe Alexandre Mem Family Fund Grants, 1145
HAF Laurence and Elaine Allen Memorial Fund Grants, 1146
Hannaford Supermarkets Community Giving, 1164
Hardin County Community Foundation Grants, 1167
Harmony Grove Foundation Grants, 1169
Harold K.L. Castle Foundation Windward Youth Leadership Fund Grants, 1175
Harris Foundation Grants, 1177
Harry A. and Margaret D. Towsley Foundation Grants, 1180
Hartford Foundation Regular Grants, 1185
Harvey Randall Wickes Foundation Grants, 1188
Hasbro Children's Fund Grants, 1189
Hawaii Children's Cancer Fdn Contributions, 1212
Hawaii Community Foundation Sanford Harmony Pillars of Peace Grants, 1217
Hawaii Electric Industries Charitable Foundation Grants, 1218
Hawaii State Legislature Grant-In-Aid, 1219
Hazel and Walter T. Bales Foundation Grants, 1220
HEI Charitable Foundation Grants, 1226
Henry and Ruth Blaustein Rosenberg Foundation Youth Development Grants, 1237
Herman Goldman Foundation Grants, 1245
Herman P. and Sophia Taubman Fdn Grants, 1247
Hill Crest Foundation Grants, 1249
Honor the Earth Grants, 1259
Horace A. Kimball and S. Ella Kimball Foundation Grants, 1260

HRAMF Charles H. Hood Foundation Child Health Research Awards, 1262
HRK Foundation Health Grants, 1264
Hubbard Family Foundation Grants, 1271
Huffy Foundation Grants, 1273
ICCF Youth Advisory Council Grants, 1282
Iddings Foundation Major Project Grants, 1284
Iddings Foundation Medium Project Grants, 1285
Ike and Roz Friedman Foundation Grants, 1289
IMLS National Leadership Grants for Libraries, 1299
Inland Empire Community Foundation Coachella Valley Youth Grants, 1307
Inland Empire Community Foundation Native Youth Grants, 1308
Inland Empire Community Foundation Riverside Youth Grants, 1309
Inland Empire Community Foundation San Bernardino Youth Grants, 1310
Island Insurance Foundation Grants, 1316
J. Edwin Treakle Foundation Grants, 1320
J. Walton Bissell Foundation Grants, 1325
J. Watumull Fund Grants, 1326
Jack H. and William M. Light Charitable Trust Grants, 1330
Jack Kent Cooke Foundation Summer Enrichment Grants, 1332
Jacob G. Schmidlapp Trusts Grants, 1336
James Ford Bell Foundation Grants, 1339
James Lee Sorenson Family Impact Foundation Grants, 1342
Jessica Stevens Community Foundation Grants, 1363
Jewish Fund Grants, 1364
John G. Duncan Charitable Trust Grants, 1372
John H. and Wilhelmina D. Harland Charitable Foundation Community Services Grants, 1375
Johnson County Community Fdn Grants, 1379
Josephine Schell Russell Chartbl Trust Grants, 1389
Judith Clark-Morrill Foundation Grants, 1395
Kalamazoo Community Foundation Early Childhood Learning and School Readiness Grants, 1407
Kalamazoo Community Foundation LBGT Equality Fund Grants, 1411
Kalamazoo Community Foundation Youth Development Grants, 1412
Kate B. Reynolds Charitable Trust Health Care Grants, 1416
Kate B. Reynolds Charitable Trust Poor and Needy Grants, 1417
Katherine John Murphy Foundation Grants, 1419
Kenai Peninsula Foundation Grants, 1425
Ketchikan Community Foundation Grants, 1429
KIND Causes Monthly Grants, 1435
Kind World Foundation Grants, 1438
Kodiak Community Foundation Grants, 1446
Koret Foundation Grants, 1449
Kosasa Foundation Grants, 1450
Kosciusko County Community Fdn Grants, 1452
Land O'Lakes Foundation Mid-Atlantic Grants, 1467
Laura B. Vogler Foundation Grants, 1470
LGA Family Foundation Grants, 1487
Lied Foundation Trust Grants, 1490
LISC Capacity Building Grants, 1498
LISC Community Leadership Operating Grts, 1499
Lloyd G. Balfour Foundation Attleboro-Specific Charities Grants, 1502
Louis and Sandra Berkman Foundation Grants, 1510
Lubrizol Corporation Community Grants, 1512
M.A. Rikard Charitable Trust Grants, 1521
M.D. Anderson Foundation Grants, 1523
Mabel Louise Riley Foundation Grants, 1529
Mabel Y. Hughes Charitable Trust Grants, 1530
Macquarie Bank Foundation Grants, 1532
Maine Women's Fund Econ Security Grants, 1546
Malone Family Foundation Atypical Development Initiative Grants, 1549
Manuel D. and Rhoda Mayerson Fdn Grants, 1550
Marathon Petroleum Corporation Grants, 1551
Mardag Foundation Grants, 1554
Margaret M. Walker Charitable Fdn Grants, 1556

Marie C. and Joseph C. Wilson Foundation Rochester Small Grants, 1559
Marquette Bank Neighborhood Commit Grants, 1577
Martha Holden Jennings Foundation Grants-to-Educators, 1581
Mary A. Crocker Trust Grants, 1584
Mary D. and Walter F. Frear Eleemosynary Trust Grants, 1588
Mary E. Babcock Foundation, 1589
Mary Owen Borden Foundation Grants, 1597
MassMutual Foundation Edonomic Development Grants, 1603
Maurice R. Robinson Fund Grants, 1611
Max and Anna Levinson Foundation Grants, 1612
McConnell Foundation Grants, 1616
McCune Charitable Foundation Grants, 1617
McInerny Foundation Grants, 1622
McLean Contributionship Grants, 1623
Meadows Foundation Grants, 1626
MeadWestvaco Foundation Sustainable Communities Grants, 1627
Mead Witter Foundation Grants, 1628
Memorial Foundation for Children Grants, 1633
Merck Family Fund Urban Farming and Youth Leadership Grants, 1635
Merck Family Fund Youth Transforming Urban Communities Grants, 1636
Merrick Foundation Grants, 1639
Meyer Memorial Trust Responsive Grants, 1653
Michelin North America Challenge Education, 1660
Morton K. and Jane Blaustein Foundation Educational Opportunity Grants, 1700
Motiv8 Foundation Grants, 1702
Narragansett Number One Foundation Grants, 1712
NCMCF Youth Advisory Council Grants, 1727
Nellie Mae Education Foundation District-Level Change Grants, 1736
New Hampshire Charitable Foundation Community Unrestricted Grants, 1747
New Hampshire Charitable Foundation Neil and Louise Tillotson Fund - Empower Coös Youth Grants, 1748
New York Foundation Grants, 1753
Noble County Community Foundation Grants, 1765
Norcliffe Foundation Grants, 1766
Northern Chautauqua Community Foundation Community Grants, 1769
Oak Foundation Child Abuse Grants, 1799
Oppenstein Brothers Foundation Grants, 1827
Oregon Community Fdn Community Grants, 1833
Oregon Community Foundation K-12 Student Success: Out-of-School Grants, 1836
PacifiCare Foundation Grants, 1861
Patrick and Aimee Butler Family Foundation Community Human Services Grants, 1880
PDF Community Organizing Grants, 1920
Pediatric Brain Tumor Foundation Early Career Development Grants, 1923
Pediatric Brain Tumor Foundation Early Career Development Grants, 1924
Pediatric Brain Tumor Fdn Institute Grants, 1925
Pediatric Brain Tumor Foundation Opportunity Grants, 1926
Perkin Fund Grants, 1937
Petersburg Community Foundation Grants, 1951
Pettus Foundation Grants, 1952
Peyton Anderson Foundation Grants, 1954
Phil Hardin Foundation Grants, 1960
Piedmont Health Foundation Grants, 1965
Pinnacle Entertainment Foundation Grants, 1972
PNC Foundation Revitalization and Stabilization Grants, 1987
Pokagon Fund Grants, 1994
Polk County Community Foundation Bradley Breakthrough Community Benefit Grants, 1995
Polk County Community Foundation Kirby Harmon Field Fund Grants, 1997
Polk County Community Foundation Marjorie M. and Lawrence R. Bradley Endowment Fund Grants, 1998

Polk County Community Foundation Mary F. Kessler Fund Grants, 1999
Polk County Community Foundation Unrestricted Grants, 2001
Price Chopper's Golub Foundation Grants, 2020
Priddy Foundation Organizational Development Grants, 2022
Proteus Fund Grants, 2027
Prudential Foundation Education Grants, 2028
Public Welfare Fdn Juvenile Justice Grants, 2033
R.J. McElroy Trust Grants, 2046
Ralph M. Parsons Foundation Grants, 2052
Raskob Fdn for Catholic Activities Grants, 2054
Rathmann Family Foundation Grants, 2057
RCF General Community Grants, 2062
Ressler-Gertz Foundation Grants, 2067
Richland County Bank Grants, 2074
Ripley County Community Foundation Grants, 2077
Ripley County Community Foundation Small Project Grants, 2078
Robert Lee Blaffer Foundation Grants, 2092
Robert R. Meyer Foundation Grants, 2094
Robin Hood Foundation Grants, 2096
Rosenberg Foundation Immigrant Rights and Integration Grants, 2108
Ruth Anderson Foundation Grants, 2122
S. Spencer Scott Fund Grants, 2129
SACF Youth Advisory Council Grants, 2131
Saigh Foundation Grants, 2137
Samuel S. Johnson Foundation Grants, 2146
Sand Hill Foundation Health and Opportunity Grants, 2153
Sartain Lanier Family Foundation Grants, 2164
Scott County Community Foundation Grants, 2170
Seattle Foundation Health and Wellness Grants, 2179
Sensient Technologies Foundation Grants, 2180
Serco Foundation Grants, 2181
Seward Community Foundation Grants, 2182
Seward Community Foundation Mini-Grants, 2183
Shield-Ayres Foundation Grants, 2189
Sidney Stern Memorial Trust Grants, 2197
Siebert Lutheran Foundation Grants, 2198
Sioux Falls Area Community Foundation Community Fund Grants, 2203
Sioux Falls Area Community Foundation Spot Grants, 2204
Smith Richardson Fdn Direct Service Grants, 2210
Sony Corporation of America Grants, 2216
Stranahan Foundation Grants, 2250
Summit Foundation Grants, 2255
Sunoco Foundation Grants, 2256
Target Corporation Soccer Grants, 2271
Telluride Foundation Community Grants, 2281
Textron Corporate Contributions Grants, 2286
Thomas and Agnes Carvel Foundation Grants, 2289
Three Guineas Fund Grants, 2297
Todd Brock Family Foundation Grants, 2305
Toyota Motor Manuf of Alabama Grants, 2309
Toyota Motor Manufacturing of Indiana Grants, 2310
Toyota Motor Manuf of Kentucky Grants, 2311
Toyota Motor Manuf of Mississippi Grants, 2312
Toyota Motor Manufacturing of Texas Grants, 2313
Toyota Motor Manufacturing of West Virginia Grants, 2314
Toyota Motor North America of NY Grants, 2315
Toyota Technical Center Grants, 2317
Toyota USA Foundation Environmental Grants, 2319
Toyota USA Foundation Safety Grants, 2320
Turtle Bay Foundation Grants, 2327
United Healthcare Commty Grts in Michigan, 2343
UUA Actions of Public Witness Grants, 2365
UUA Congregation-Based Community Organizing Grants, 2366
UUA Fund Grants, 2367
UUA International Fund Grants, 2368
UUA Just Society Fund Grants, 2369
UUA Social Responsibility Grants, 2370
Van Kampen Boyer Molinari Charitable Foundation Grants, 2377
Victor E. Speas Foundation Grants, 2380

Virginia W. Kettering Foundation Grants, 2388
W.M. Keck Fdn Southern California Grants, 2398
Walker Area Community Foundation Grants, 2401
Wayne County Foundation Grants, 2419
Westerman Foundation Grants, 2427
Whole Foods Foundation, 2445
William J. and Dorothy K. O'Neill Foundation
    Responsive Grants, 2468
William J. and Gertrude R. Casper Foundation
    Grants, 2469
William J. and Tina Rosenberg Fdn Grants, 2470
William Ray and Ruth E. Collins Fdn Grants, 2473
Wilton and Effie Hebert Foundation Grants, 2476
Winifred Johnson Clive Foundation Grants, 2478
WinnCompanies Charitable Giving, 2479
Wiregrass Foundation Grants, 2480
Women's Fund of Hawaii Grants, 2484
Wyomissing Foundation Community Grants, 2504
Wyomissing Foundation Thun Family Organizational
    Grants, 2505
Wyomissing Foundation Thun Family Program
    Grants, 2506
Youths' Friends Association Grants, 2511
YSA Get Ur Good On Grants, 2513
YSA Radio Disney's Hero for Change Award, 2519
Z. Smith Reynolds Foundation Small Grants, 2523

Service Delivery Programs
1st Source Foundation Community Involvement
    Grants, 1
2 Depot Square Ipswich Charitable Foundation
    Grants, 3
3M Company Fdn Community Giving Grants, 5
3M Company Foundation Health and Human
    Services Grants, 6
4imprint One by One Charitable Giving, 7
100 Club of Arizona Financial Assistance Grants, 9
100 Club of Dubuque, 10
786 Foundation Grants, 15
A. Alfred Taubman Foundation Grants, 18
A.C. and Penney Hubbard Foundation Grants, 19
A.L. Mailman Family Foundation Grants, 20
A.L. Spencer Foundation Grants, 21
A and B Family Foundation Grants, 40
Aaron Foundation Grants, 41
Aaron Foundation Grants, 42
Abbott Fund Access to Health Care Grants, 45
Abbott Fund Community Engagement Grants, 46
Abbott Fund Global AIDS Care Grants, 47
Abbott Fund Science Education Grants, 48
ABC Charities Grants, 50
Abell-Hanger Foundation Grants, 52
Abington Foundation Grants, 54
ABS Foundation Grants, 56
ACCF Dennis and Melanie Bieberich Community
    Enrichment Fund Grants, 59
ACCF John and Kay Boch Fund Grants, 60
ACCF of Indiana Angel Funds Grants, 62
ACCF of Indiana Anonymous Community
    Enrichment Fund Grants, 63
ACCF of Indiana Bank of Geneva Heritage Fund
    Grants, 64
ACCF of Indiana Berne Ready Mix Community
    Enrichment Fund Grants, 65
ACCF of Indiana First Merchants Bank / Decatur
    Bank and Trust Fund Grants, 66
ACCF of Indiana Michael Basham Community
    Enrichment Fund Grants, 67
ACCF of Indiana Ron and Susie Ballard Community
    Enrichment Fund Grants, 68
ACCF Ralph Biggs Memorial Community
    Enrichment Fund Grants, 69
ACF Child Abuse Prevention and Treatment Act
    Discretionary Funds Grants, 74
ACF Community-Based Child Abuse Prevention
    (CBCAP) Grants, 76
ACF Community-Based Child Abuse
    Prevention (CBCAP) Tribal and Migrant
    DiscretionaryGrants, 77
ACF Ethnic Community Self Help Grants, 80

ACF Marriage Strengthening Research &
    Dissemination Center Grants, 85
ACF National Human Trafficking Hotline Grants, 86
ACF Refugee Health Promotion Grants, 91
ACF Social and Economic Development Strategies
    Grants, 93
ACF Street Outreach Program Grants, 94
ACF Transitional Living Program and Maternity
    Group Homes Grants, 96
ACF Tribal Maternal, Infant, and Early Childhood
    Home Visiting Program: Development and
    Implementation Grants, 97
ACF Tribal Maternal, Infant, and Early Childhood
    Home Visiting Program: Implementation and
    Expansion Grants, 98
ACF Voluntary Agencies Matching Grants, 100
Achelis and Bodman Foundation Grants, 101
Achelis Foundation Grants, 102
ADA Foundation Samuel Harris Children's Dental
    Health Grants, 111
Adams County Community Foundation Grants, 115
Adams Family Fdn of Nora Springs Grants, 118
Adams Family Foundation of Tennessee Grants, 120
Adams Rotary Memorial Fund A Grants, 122
Adelaide Breed Bayrd Foundation Grants, 123
Adelaide Christian Home For Children Grants, 124
Adidas Corporation General Grants, 125
Adobe Foundation Action Grants, 126
Adobe Fdn Community Investment Grants, 127
Adobe Fdn Hunger and Homelessness Grants, 128
Advance Auto Parts Corporate Giving Grants, 131
AEGON Transamerica Foundation Health and
    Wellness Grants, 133
Aetna Foundation Regional Health Grants, 134
A Friends' Foundation Trust Grants, 136
A Fund for Women Grants, 137
Agnes M. Lindsay Trust Grants, 140
AHS Foundation Grants, 143
Aid for Starving Children Emerg Aid Grants, 144
Aid for Starving Children Health and Nutrition
    Grants, 145
Aid for Starving Children Homes and Education
    Grants, 146
Aid for Starving Children Water Projects Grants, 147
Air Products Foundation Grants, 148
Akron Community Foundation Health and human
    services grants, 152
Alaska Airlines Foundation LIFT Grants, 194
Alaska Community Foundation Children's Trust Tier
    1 Community Based Child Abuse and Neglect
    Prevention Grants, 198
Alaska Community Foundation Children's Trust Tier
    2 Innovation Grants, 200
Alaska Community Foundation GCI Suicide
    Prevention Grant, 203
Albert and Ethel Herzstein Charitable Foundation
    Grants, 219
Albert E. and Birdie W. Einstein Fund Grants, 220
Albertsons Companies Foundation Nourishing
    Neighbors Grants, 221
Albert W. Cherne Foundation Grants, 222
Albert W. Rice Charitable Foundation Grants, 223
Alcatel-Lucent Technologies Foundation Grants, 224
Alex Stern Family Foundation Grants, 229
ALFJ Astraea U.S. and International Emergency
    Fund, 230
Alfred E. Chase Charitable Foundation Grants, 233
Alfred J Mcallister and Dorothy N Mcallister
    Foundation Grants, 234
Allan C. and Lelia J. Garden Foundation Grants, 236
Allegis Group Foundation Grants, 237
Alliance for Strong Families and Communities
    Grants, 239
Alliant Energy Foundation Community Giving for
    Good Sponsorship Grants, 240
Alloy Family Foundation Grants, 241
Allstate Corporate Giving Grants, 242
Allstate Corp Hometown Commitment Grants, 243
Allstate Foundation Safe and Vital Communities
    Grants, 244

Alpha Natural Resources Corporate Giving, 246
Altria Group Positive Youth Dev Grants, 247
Ama OluKai Foundation Grants, 249
Amelia Sillman Rockwell and Carlos Perry Rockwell
    Charities Fund Grants, 250
American Electric Power Corporate Grants, 252
American Electric Power Foundation Grants, 253
American Honda Foundation Grants, 255
American Indian Youth Running Strong Grants, 256
American Psychiatric Fdn Call for Proposals, 257
American Savings Foundation Program Grants, 261
American Woodmark Foundation Grants, 263
Amerigroup Foundation Grants, 264
Amica Companies Foundation Grants, 266
Amica Insurance Company Community Grants, 267
Amway Corporation Contributions, 269
Anderson Foundation Grants, 271
Anheuser-Busch Foundation Grants, 273
Anna Fitch Ardenghi Trust Grants, 274
Anne Arundel Women Giving Together Regular
    Grants, 275
Anne J. Caudal Foundation Grants, 276
Ann L. and Carol Green Rhodes Charitable Trust
    Grants, 278
Ann Ludington Sullivan Foundation Grants, 279
Appalachian Regional Commission Health Care
    Grants, 288
Ar-Hale Family Foundation Grants, 290
Arizona Foundation for Women Deborah G. Carstens
    Fund Grants, 293
Arizona Foundation for Women General Grants, 294
Armstrong McDonald Foundation Special Needs
    Grants, 301
Arthur Ashley Williams Foundation Grants, 302
Arthur M. Blank Family Foundation Molly Blank
    Fund Grants, 310
Aspen Community Foundation Grants, 316
Assisi Foundation of Memphis General Grants, 318
Assisi Foundation of Memphis Mini Grants, 319
AT&T Fdn Community Support and Safety, 320
AT&T Foundation Health and Human Services
    Grants, 322
Atkinson Foundation Community Grants, 325
Atlanta Foundation Grants, 326
Atlanta Women's Foundation Pathway to Success
    Grants, 327
Atlas Insurance Agency Foundation Grants, 329
Aunt Kate Foundation Grants, 331
Austin Community Foundation Grants, 332
Austin S. Nelson Foundation Grants, 333
Autauga Area Community Foundation Grants, 334
Autism Speaks Norma and Malcolm Baker Recreation
    Grants, 335
Avery-Fuller-Welch Children's Fdn Grants, 336
Avery Dennison Foundation Education Grants, 337
Avery Foundation Grants, 339
Avista Foundation Vulnerable and Limited Income
    Population Grants, 341
Babcock Charitable Trust Grants, 343
Back Home Again Foundation Grants, 344
Bainum Family Foundation Grants, 345
Baltimore Community Foundation Mitzvah Fund for
    Good Deeds Grants, 349
Bank of America Charitable Foundation Basic Needs
    Grants, 354
Bank of America Charitable Foundation Matching
    Gifts, 356
Bank of Hawaii Foundation Grants, 360
Bank of the Orient Community Giving, 361
Baton Rouge Area Foundation Every Kid a King
    Fund Grants, 364
Baton Rouge Area Foundation Grants, 365
Batters Up USA Equipment Grants, 366
Baxter International Corporate Giving Grants, 368
Baxter International Foundation Grants, 369
Bay Area Community Foundation Arenac
    Community Fund Grants, 371
Bay Area Community Fdn Auburn Area Chamber of
    Commerce Enrichment Fund Grants, 373

Bay Area Community Foundation Bay County Healthy Youth/Healthy Seniors Fund Grants, 374

Bay Area Community Foundation Civic League Endowment Fund Grants, 375

Bay Area Community Foundation Community Initiative Fund Grants, 376

Bay Area Community Foundation Elizabeth Husband Fund Grants, 378

Bay Area Community Foundation Leslie L. Squires Foundation Grants, 380

Bay Area Community Foundation Nathalie Awrey Memorial Fund Grants, 381

Baystate Financial Charitable Foundation Grants, 385

BCBSM Foundation Community Health Matching Grants, 392

Beckman Coulter Foundation Grants, 394

Belvedere Community Foundation Grants, 399

Ben B. Cheney Foundation Grants, 402

Ben Cohen StandUp Foundation Grants, 403

Benton Community Foundation Grants, 405

Benwood Foundation Community Grants, 406

Bernard F. and Alva B. Gimbel Foundation Criminal Justice Grants, 412

Bernau Family Foundation Grants, 413

Better Way Foundation Grants, 419

BibleLands Grants, 420

Bikes Belong Grants, 424

Bill and Melinda Gates Foundation Agricultural Development Grants, 425

Blanche and Irving Laurie Foundation Grants, 436

Blandin Foundation Expand Opportunity Grants, 437

Blandin Foundation Invest Early Grants, 438

Blandin Foundation Itasca County Area Vitality Grants, 439

Blockbuster Corporate Contributions, 440

Blue Cross Blue Shield of Minnesota Fdn - Healthy Children: Growing Up Healthy Grants, 442

Blue Grass Community Foundation Clark County Fund Grants, 444

Blue Grass Community Foundation Fayette County Fund Grants, 446

Blue Grass Community Foundation Franklin County Fund Grants, 447

Blue Grass Community Foundation Harrison County Fund Grants, 448

Blue Grass Community Foundation Hudson-Ellis Grants, 449

Blue Grass Community Foundation Madison County Fund Grants, 450

Blue Grass Community Foundation Magoffin County Fund Grants, 451

Blue Grass Community Foundation Morgan County Fund Grants, 452

Blue Grass Community Foundation Rowan County Fund Grants, 453

Blue Grass Community Foundation Woodford County Fund Grants, 454

Blue Mountain Community Foundation Garfield County Health Foundation Fund Grants, 456

Blue River Community Foundation Grants, 458

Blumenthal Foundation Grants, 459

Bodenwein Public Benevolent Foundation Grants, 461

Bothin Foundation Grants, 464

BP Foundation Grants, 465

Bradley-Turner Foundation Grants, 466

Bradley C. Higgins Foundation Grants, 467

Brian G. Dyson Foundation Grants, 468

Bridgestone Americas Trust Fund Grants, 469

Bright Promises Foundation Grants, 470

Brookdale Fdn Relatives as Parents Grants, 474

Brown County Community Foundation Grants, 475

Brown Foundation Grants, 476

Brunswick Foundation Dollars for Doers Grants, 478

Burton D. Morgan Foundation Hudson Community Grants, 482

Bushrod H. Campbell and Adah F. Hall Charity Fund Grants, 486

C.H. Robinson Worldwide Foundation Grants, 489

Caesars Foundation Grants, 492

California Endowment Innovative Ideas Challenge Grants, 495

Camille Beckman Foundation Grants, 499

Campbell Foundation Grants, 500

Cargill Corporate Giving Grants, 503

Caring for Colorado Foundation Sperry S. and Ella Graber Packard Fund for Pueblo Grants, 505

Carl M. Freeman Foundation FACES Grants, 507

Carl M. Freeman Foundation Grants, 508

Carl R. Hendrickson Family Foundation Grants, 509

Carl W. and Carrie Mae Joslyn Trust Grants, 510

Carrie S. Orleans Trust Grants, 512

Cass County Community Foundation Grants, 516

Castle Foundation Grants, 518

Castle Foundation Grants, 517

Catherine Holmes Wilkins Foundation Charitable Grants, 520

Central Pacific Bank Foundation Grants, 530

CFFVR Basic Needs Giving Partnership Grants, 537

CFFVR Project Grants, 546

CFFVR Shawano Area Community Foundation Grants, 549

CFGR Community Impact Grants, 552

CFGR Jenkins Foundation Grants, 553

Chapman Charitable Foundation Grants, 560

Chapman Family Charitable Trust Grants, 561

Chapman Family Foundation, 562

Charles Crane Family Foundation Grants, 563

Charles H. Hall Foundation, 565

Charles H. Pearson Foundation Grants, 566

Charles Lafitte Foundation Grants, 567

Charles Nelson Robinson Fund Grants, 569

Charlotte Martin Foundation Youth Grants, 571

Chatham Athletic Foundation Grants, 574

CHC Foundation Grants, 575

Cheryl Spencer Memorial Foundation Grants, 576

Chicago Board of Trade Foundation Grants, 580

Chicago Community Trust Arts and Culture Grants: Improving Access to Arts Learning, 581

Children's Trust Fund of Oregon Fdn Grants, 585

Children's Trust Fund of Oregon Foundation Small Grants, 586

Chilkat Valley Community Foundation Grants, 588

Christine and Katharina Pauly Charitable Trust Grants, 601

CICF Indianapolis Fdn Community Grants, 606

CICF John Harrison Brown and Rob Burse Grt, 607

Cigna Civic Affairs Sponsorships, 610

CIGNA Foundation Grants, 611

Circle K Corporation Contributions Grants, 614

Cisco Systems Foundation San Jose Community Grants, 615

Citizens Bank Charitable Foundation Grants, 616

CJ Fdn for SIDS Program Services Grants, 619

Clara Abbott Foundation Need-Based Grants, 620

Clara Blackford Smith and W. Aubrey Smith Charitable Foundation Grants, 621

Claremont Community Foundation Grants, 622

Claremont Savings Bank Foundation Grants, 623

Clark and Ruby Baker Foundation Grants, 625

Clark County Community Foundation Grants, 626

Clark Electric Cooperative Grants, 627

Claude A. and Blanche McCubbin Abbott Charitable Trust Grants, 628

Clayton Baker Trust Grants, 629

Clayton F. and Ruth L. Hawkridge Foundation Grants, 630

Clayton Fund Grants, 631

Cleo Foundation Grants, 632

Cleveland Browns Foundation Grants, 633

Cleveland Foundation Higley Fund Grants, 634

Cleveland Fdn Lake-Geauga Fund Grants, 635

Cleveland Foundation Legacy Village Lyndhurst Community Fund Grants, 636

Cleveland H. Dodge Foundation Grants, 637

Clinton County Community Foundation Grants, 638

CMS Research and Demonstration Grants, 640

CNCS AmeriCorps Indian Tribes Plang Grts , 641

CNCS AmeriCorps NCCC Project Grants, 642

CNCS AmeriCorps State and National Grants, 643

CNCS AmeriCorps State and National Planning Grants, 644

CNCS Foster Grandparent Projects Grants, 646

CNCS Senior Corps Retired and Senior Volunteer Program Grants, 648

CNCS Social Innovation Grants, 649

CNO Financial Group Community Grants, 650

Coleman Foundation Entrepreneurship Education Grants, 651

Colgate-Palmolive Company Grants, 652

Collective Brands Foundation Saucony Run for Good Grants, 656

Collins Foundation Grants, 658

Colonel Stanley R. McNeil Foundation Grants, 659

Colorado Interstate Gas Grants, 661

Colorado Trust Health Investment Grants, 662

Columbus Foundation Traditional Grants, 663

Community Foundation for Greater Atlanta Frances Hollis Brain Foundation Fund Grants, 664

Community Foundation for Greater Atlanta Spark Clayton Grants, 667

Community Foundation for Greater Atlanta Spark Newton Grants, 668

Community Foundation for Greater Buffalo Garman Family Foundation Grants, 671

Community Foundation for Greater Buffalo Josephine Goodyear Foundation Grants, 672

Community Foundation for Greater Buffalo Niagara Area Foundation Grants, 673

Community Foundation for Kettering Grants, 676

Community Foundation for SE Michigan Chelsea Community Foundation General Grant, 680

Community Foundation for the Capital Region Grants, 687

Community Foundation of Bartholomew County Heritage Fund Grants, 690

Community Foundation of Boone County Grants, 694

Community Foundation of Crawford County, 695

Community Foundation of Eastern Connecticut General Southeast Grants, 696

Community Foundation of Eastern Connecticut Northeast Women and Girls Grants, 697

Community Foundation of Eastern Connecticut Norwich Women and Girls Grants, 698

Community Foundation of Eastern Connecticut Southeast Area Women and Girls Grants, 701

Community Foundation of Eastern Connecticut Windham Area Women and Girls Grants, 702

Community Foundation of Greater Chattanooga Grants, 704

Community Foundation of Greater Fort Wayne - Community Endowment and Clarke Endowment Grants, 705

Community Foundation of Greater Fort Wayne - Edna Foundation Grants, 706

Community Foundation of Greater Greensboro Community Grants, 708

Community Foundation of Henderson County Community Grants, 711

Community Foundation of Jackson County Seymour Noon Lions Club Grant, 714

Community Foundation of Louisville AIDS Project Fund Grants, 716

Community Foundation of Louisville Anna Marble Memorial Fund for Princeton Grants, 717

Community Foundation of Louisville Children's Memorial Marker Fund Grants, 721

Community Foundation of Louisville Human Services Grants, 726

Community Foundation of Muncie and Delaware County Maxon Grants, 734

Community Foundation of St. Joseph County African American Community Grants, 737

Community Foundation of St. Joseph County Special Project Challenge Grants, 738

Community Foundation of Western Massachusetts Grants, 741

Community Foundation Serving Riverside and San Bernardino Counties Impact Grants, 742

Community Memorial Foundation Responsive Grants, 743
Cone Health Foundation Grants, 745
Cooke Foundation Grants, 748
Cooper Tire and Rubber Foundation Grants, 749
Corina Higginson Trust Grants, 750
Countess Moira Charitable Foundation Grants, 752
Courtney S. Turner Charitable Trust Grants, 753
Covenant Educational Foundation Grants, 754
Covenant Foundation of Brentwood Grants, 755
Covenant to Care for Children Crisis Food Pantry Giving, 756
Covenant for Children Critical Goods Grants, 757
Covenant to Care for Children Enrichment Fund Grants, 758
Covidien Partnership for Neighborhood Wellness Grants, 759
Cralle Foundation Grants, 760
Crane Fund for Widows and Children Grants, 762
Crane Fund Grants, 763
Credit Suisse Foundation Education Grants, 765
Cresap Family Foundation Grants, 766
Crescent Porter Hale Foundation Grants, 767
Crystelle Waggoner Charitable Trust Grants, 768
Cudd Foundation Grants, 769
CUNA Mutual Group Fdn Community Grants, 770
Curtis Foundation Grants, 771
Dana Brown Charitable Trust Grants, 777
Daniels Homeless and Disadvantaged Grants, 782
David Alan and Susan Berkman Rahm Foundation Grants, 785
David and Betty Sacks Foundation Grants, 788
David and Laura Merage Foundation Grants, 789
David M. and Marjorie D. Rosenberg Foundation Grants, 790
David Robinson Foundation Grants, 791
Dayton Power and Light Company Foundation Signature Grants, 801
Dayton Power and Light Foundation Grants, 802
Deaconess Community Foundation Grants, 803
Deaconess Foundation Advocacy Grants, 804
Dean Foods Community Involvement Grants, 805
Dean Foundation Grants, 806
Delaware Community Foundation Grants, 817
Del Mar Foundation Community Grants, 820
Delmarva Power & Light Contributions, 821
Delta Air Lines Foundation Community Enrichment Grants, 823
Dermody Properties Fdn Capstone Award, 826
Deuce McAllister Catch 22 Foundation Grants, 828
Dining for Women Grants, 831
Dolan Children's Foundation Grants, 832
Dollar Energy Fund Grants, 834
Dollar General Family Literacy Grants, 835
DOL Youthbuild Grants, 838
Dominion Foundation Grants, 839
Don and May Wilkins Charitable Trust Grants, 842
Doree Taylor Charitable Foundation Grants, 843
Dorrance Family Foundation Grants, 845
Do Something Awards, 847
Do Something User Experience Research Intern, 859
Dr. and Mrs. Paul Pierce Memorial Foundation Grants, 862
Dr. John T. Macdonald Foundation Grants, 863
Draper Richards Kaplan Foundation Grants, 864
DTE Energy Foundation Community Development Grants, 866
DTE Energy Foundation Health and Human Services Grants, 869
Dunspaugh-Dalton Foundation Grants, 873
E. Clayton and Edith P. Gengras, Jr. Foundation Grants, 875
E.J. Grassmann Trust Grants, 876
Earl and Maxine Claussen Trust Grants, 878
Eastern Bank Charitable Foundation Partnerships Grants, 881
Eastern Bank Charitable Foundation Targeted Grants, 882
Easton Foundations Archery Facility Grants, 883
Edna Wardlaw Charitable Trust Grants, 886

Edward and Ellen Roche Relief Fdn Grants, 887
Edward and Helen Bartlett Foundation Grants, 888
Edward and Romell Ackley Foundation Grants, 889
Edwards Memorial Trust Grants, 891
Edyth Bush Charitable Foundation Grants, 893
Effie Allen Little Foundation Grants, 894
Effie and Wofford Cain Foundation Grants, 895
Eide Bailly Resourcefullness Awards, 897
Eileen Fisher Activating Leadership Grants for Women and Girls, 898
Elizabeth Carse Foundation Grants, 899
Elizabeth Huth Coates Charitable Foundation Grants, 900
Elizabeth Morse Genius Charitable Trust Grants, 901
Elkhart County Community Foundation Grants, 903
Ella West Freeman Foundation Grants, 904
Ellen Abbott Gilman Trust Grants, 905
Elmer Roe Deaver Foundation Grants, 906
El Pomar Foundation Anna Keesling Ackerman Fund Grants, 907
El Pomar Foundation Grants, 908
Elsie H. Wilcox Foundation Grants, 909
Emma J. Adams Memorial Fund Grants, 914
Energy by Design Poster Contest, 915
Entergy Charitable Foundation Low-Income Initiatives and Solutions Grants, 918
Entergy Corporation Micro Grants, 919
Entergy Corporation Open Grants for Healthy Families, 921
EPA Children's Health Protection Grants, 923
Erie Chapman Foundation Grants, 928
Essex County Community Foundation Greater Lawrence Community Fund Grants, 931
Essex County Community Foundation Merrimack Valley Municipal Business Development and Recovery Fund Grants, 933
Essex County Community Foundation Women's Fund Grants, 934
Ethel Sergeant Clark Smith Foundation Grants, 935
Evan Frankel Foundation Grants, 938
Evelyn and Walter Haas, Jr. Fund Immigrant Rights Grants, 941
F.M. Kirby Foundation Grants, 946
F.R. Bigelow Foundation Grants, 947
Farmers Insurance Corporate Giving Grants, 948
Fassino Foundation Grants, 949
Faye L. and William L. Cowden Charitable Foundation Grants, 950
FCD New American Children Grants, 952
FCYO Youth Organizing Grants, 954
Fichtenbaum Charitable Trust Grants, 955
Fidelity Charitable Gift Fund Grants, 956
Fidelity Foundation Grants, 957
Fifth Third Bank Corporate Giving, 958
Fifth Third Foundation Grants, 959
Finish Line Youth Foundation Founder's Grants, 960
Finish Line Youth Foundation Grants, 961
Finish Line Youth Foundation Legacy Grants, 962
Firelight Foundation Grants, 964
FirstEnergy Foundation Community Grants, 965
First Hawaiian Bank Foundation Corporate Giving Grants, 967
First Nations Development Institute Nourishing Native Children: Feeding Our Future Project Grants, 975
Fitzpatrick, Cella, Harper & Scinto Pro Bono Services, 976
Florence Foundation Grants, 978
Florence Hunt Maxwell Foundation Grants, 979
Ford Family Foundation Grants - Access to Health and Dental Services, 980
Ford Family Foundation Grants - Child Abuse Prevention and Intervention, 981
Ford Foundation BUILD Grants, 984
Forest Foundation Grants, 985
Foundation Beyond Belief Compassionate Impact Grants, 986
Foundation Beyond Belief Humanist Grants, 987
Foundation for a Healthy Kentucky Grants, 988
Foundation for Health Enhancement Grants, 990

Fdn for the Mid South Communities Grants, 992
Foundation for the Mid South Education Grants, 993
Foundation of Herkimer and Oneida Counties Youth Sports, Wellness and Recreation Mini-Grants, 994
Foundations of East Chicago Education Grants, 995
Foundations of East Chicago Health Grants, 997
Four County Community Foundation General Grants, 1000
Four County Community Foundation Healthy Senior/Healthy Youth Fund Grants, 1001
Fourjay Foundation Grants, 1003
Four J Foundation Grants, 1004
Four Lanes Trust Grants, 1005
Four Times Foundation Grants, 1006
Francis Beidler Foundation Grants, 1007
Francis L. Abreu Charitable Trust Grants, 1008
Frankel Brothers Foundation Grants, 1009
Franklin H. Wells and Ruth L. Wells Foundation Grants, 1011
Frank Reed and Margaret Jane Peters Memorial Fund Grants, 1013
Frank Reed and Margaret Jane Peters Memorial Fund II Grants, 1014
Fred and Gretel Biel Charitable Trust Grants, 1016
Frederick McDonald Trust Grants, 1017
Fremont Area Community Foundation Amazing X Grants, 1019
Fremont Area Community Foundation Community Grants, 1020
Friends of Hawaii Charities Grants, 1024
Fuller E. Callaway Foundation Grants, 1027
Fund for the City of New York Grants, 1029
Furth Family Foundation Grants, 1030
G.N. Wilcox Trust Grants, 1031
Gannett Foundation Community Action Grants, 1033
Gardner Foundation Grants, 1035
Gardner W. and Joan G. Heidrick, Jr. Foundation Grants, 1036
GCI Corporate Contributions Grants, 1037
Gene Haas Foundation, 1038
George A. & Grace L. Long Fdn Grants, 1041
George and Ruth Bradford Foundation Grants, 1042
George E. Hatcher, Jr. and Ann Williams Hatcher Foundation Grants, 1045
George F. Baker Trust Grants, 1046
George Graham and Elizabeth Galloway Smith Foundation Grants, 1047
George H. and Jane A. Mifflin Memorial Fund Grants, 1048
George H.C. Ensworth Memorial Fund Grants, 1049
George H. Sandy Foundation Grants, 1050
George J. and Effie L. Seay Foundation Grants, 1052
George Kress Foundation Grants, 1053
George P. Davenport Trust Fund Grants, 1054
George W. Codrington Charitable Foundation Grants, 1055
George W. Wells Foundation Grants, 1057
German Protestant Orphan Asylum Foundation Grants, 1066
Giant Food Charitable Grants, 1068
Gil and Dody Weaver Foundation Grants, 1071
Giving Gardens Challenge Grants, 1072
GNOF Albert N. & Hattie M. McClure Grants, 1076
GNOF Bayou Communities Grants, 1077
GNOF Exxon-Mobil Grants, 1080
GNOF Gert Community Fund Grants, 1082
GNOF IMPACT Grants for Youth Dev, 1084
GNOF IMPACT Gulf States Eye Surg Fund, 1085
GNOF IMPACT Harold W. Newman, Jr. Charitable Trust Grants, 1086
GNOF Norco Community Grants, 1089
GNOF Organizational Effectiveness Grants and Workshops, 1090
GNOF Plaquemines Community Grants, 1091
GNOF Stand Up For Our Children Grants, 1092
Go Daddy Cares Charitable Contributions, 1093
Golden Heart Community Foundation Grants, 1094
Goldseker Foundation Non-Profit Management Assistance Grants, 1095
Good+Foundation Grants, 1096

Grace Bersted Foundation Grants, 1097
Graham and Carolyn Holloway Family Foundation Grants, 1098
Graham Family Charitable Foundation Grants, 1099
Graham Foundation Grants, 1100
Graham Foundation Grants, 1101
Granger Foundation Grants, 1103
Great Clips Corporate Giving, 1108
Greater Milwaukee Foundation Grants, 1109
Greater Saint Louis Community Fdn Grants, 1110
Greater Sitka Legacy Fund Grants, 1111
Greater Tacoma Community Foundation Fund for Women and Girls Grants, 1112
Greater Tacoma Community Foundation General Operating Grants, 1113
Greater Tacoma Community Foundation Youth Program Grants, 1115
Green Foundation Human Services Grants, 1116
Green River Area Community Fdn Grants, 1117
Greenspun Family Foundation Grants, 1118
Griffin Family Foundation Grants, 1121
Grifols Community Outreach Grants, 1122
Grotto Foundation Project Grants, 1123
Grundy Foundation Grants, 1124
GTECH After School Advantage Grants, 1125
GTRCF Boys and Girls Club of Grand Traverse Endowment Grants, 1126
GTRCF Elk Rapids Area Community Endowment Grants, 1127
GTRCF Grand Traverse Families in Action for Youth Endowment Grants, 1129
GTRCF Healthy Youth and Healthy Seniors Endowment Grants, 1130
GTRCF Joan Rajkovich McGarry Family Education Endowment Grants, 1131
Gulf Coast Foundation of Community Program Grants, 1135
Guy I. Bromley Trust Grants, 1136
H.A. and Mary K. Chapman Charitable Trust Grants, 1137
H.B. Fuller Foundation Grants, 1138
Haddad Foundation Grants, 1139
HAF Community Grants, 1141
HAF Don and Bettie Albright Endowment Fund Grants, 1142
HAF JoAllen K. Twiddy-Wood Memorial Fund Grants, 1144
HAF Joe Alexandre Mem Family Fund Grants, 1145
HAF Laurence and Elaine Allen Memorial Fund Grants, 1146
HAF Mada Huggins Caldwell Fund Grants, 1147
HAF Native Cultures Fund Grants, 1148
HAF Phyllis Nilsen Leal Mem Fund Grants, 1149
HAF Southern Humboldt Grants, 1150
Hahl Proctor Charitable Trust Grants, 1151
Hall-Perrine Foundation Grants, 1152
Hampton Roads Community Foundation Abused People Grants, 1153
Hampton Roads Community Foundation Developmental Disabilities Grants, 1156
Hampton Roads Community Foundation Nonprofit Facilities Improvement Grants, 1159
Hancock County Community Foundation - Field of Interest Grants, 1161
Hannaford Charitable Foundation Grants, 1163
Hannaford Supermarkets Community Giving, 1164
Hardin County Community Foundation Grants, 1167
Harold and Rebecca H. Gross Fdn Grants, 1171
Harold Brooks Foundation Grants, 1172
Harold K.L. Castle Foundation Public Education Redesign and Enhancement Grants, 1173
Harold K.L. Castle Foundation Strengthening Windward Oahu Communities Grants, 1174
Harold K.L. Castle Foundation Windward Youth Leadership Fund Grants, 1175
Harris Foundation Grants, 1177
Harrison County Community Fdn Grants, 1178
Harrison County Community Foundation Signature Grants, 1179
Harry and Jeanette Weinberg Fdn Grants, 1182

Hartford Foundation Regular Grants, 1185
Hartley Foundation Grants, 1186
Harvey E. Najim Family Foundation Grants, 1187
Harvey Randall Wickes Foundation Grants, 1188
Hasbro Children's Fund Grants, 1189
Hasbro Corp Gift of Play Holiday Giving, 1190
Hasbro Corporation Gift of Play Hospital and Pediatric Health Giving, 1191
Hasbro Corporation Gift of Play Shelter Support Giving, 1192
Hasbro Corporation Gift of Play Summer Camp Support, 1193
Hawai'i Community Foundation Children's Trust Fund Community Awareness: Child Abuse and Neglect Prevention Grants, 1198
Hawai'i Community Foundation East Hawaii Fund Grants, 1199
Hawai'i Community Foundation Ewa Beach Community Trust Fund Grants, 1200
Hawai'i Community Foundation Family Literacy and Hawaii Pizza Hut Literacy Grants, 1201
Hawai'i Community Foundation Kuki'o Community Fund Grants, 1202
Hawai'i Community Foundation Lana'i Community Benefit Fund, 1203
Hawai'i Community Foundation Richard Smart Fund Grants, 1204
Hawai'i Community Foundation Robert E. Black Fund Grants, 1205
Hawai'i Community Foundation Victoria S. and Bradley L. Geist Foundation: Capacity Building Grants, 1206
Hawai'i Community Foundation Victoria S. and Bradley L. Geist Foundation: Enhancement Grants, 1207
Hawai'i Community Foundation Victoria S. and Bradley L. Geist Foundation: Supporting Foster Children and Their Caregivers, 1208
Hawai'i Community Foundation Victoria S. and Bradley L. Geist Foundation: Supporting Transitioning Foster Youth Grants, 1209
Hawaiian Electric Industries Charitable Foundation Grants, 1211
Hawaii Children's Cancer Fdn Contributions, 1212
Hawaii Community Foundation Omidyar Ohana Fund Grants, 1213
Hawaii Community Foundation Reverend Takie Okumura Family Grants, 1216
Hawaii Electric Industries Charitable Foundation Grants, 1218
Hawaii State Legislature Grant-In-Aid, 1219
Hazel and Walter T. Bales Foundation Grants, 1220
Hazen Foundation Public Education Grants, 1221
Hearst Foundations Social Service Grants, 1224
Helen Bader Foundation Grants, 1227
Helen Gertrude Sparks Charitable Trust Grants, 1230
Helen Irwin Littauer Educational Trust Grants, 1231
Helen V. Brach Foundation Grants, 1232
Help America Foundation Grants, 1233
Henrietta Lange Burk Fund Grants, 1235
Henry E. Niles Foundation Grants, 1240
Henry F. Koch Residual Trust Grants, 1241
Henry L. Guenther Foundation Grants, 1242
Herbert A. and Adrian W. Woods Foundation Grants, 1243
Herman Goldman Foundation Grants, 1245
Herman P. and Sophia Taubman Fdn Grants, 1247
Highmark Corporate Giving Grants, 1248
Hill Crest Foundation Grants, 1249
Hillsdale County Community Foundation General Grants, 1250
Hillsdale County Community Foundation Love Your Community Grants, 1251
Hillsdale County Community Foundation Y.O.U.T.H. Grants, 1252
HLTA Visitor Industry Charity Walk Grant, 1254
Horace A. Moses Charitable Trust Grants, 1261
HRAMF Community Health Improvement Project Grants in Bowdoin Geneva, 1263

HRSA Ryan White HIV AIDS Drug Assistance Grants, 1265
HSBC Corporate Giving Grants, 1266
HSFCA Biennium Grants, 1267
HSFCA Folk and Traditional Arts Grants - Culture Learning, 1268
Hubbard Broadcasting Foundation Grants, 1269
Hubbard Family Foundation Grants, 1270
Hubbard Family Foundation Grants, 1271
Hubbard Farms Charitable Foundation Grants, 1272
Huffy Foundation Grants, 1273
Humana Foundation Grants, 1275
Human Source Foundation Grants, 1276
Huntington County Community Foundation Make a Difference Grants, 1280
Iddings Foundation Medium Project Grants, 1285
Iddings Foundation Small Project Grants, 1286
Ike and Roz Friedman Foundation Grants, 1289
Illinois Children's Healthcare Fdn Grants, 1295
Indiana OCRA Rural Capacity Grants (RCG), 1301
ING Foundation Grants, 1302
Inland Empire Community Foundation Capacity Building for IE Nonprofits Grants, 1306
Inland Empire Community Foundation Coachella Valley Youth Grants, 1307
Inland Empire Community Foundation Native Youth Grants, 1308
Inland Empire Community Foundation Riverside Youth Grants, 1309
Inland Empire Community Foundation San Bernardino Youth Grants, 1310
Intel Corporation Community Grants, 1311
Intel Corporation Int Community Grants, 1312
Irving S. Gilmore Foundation Grants, 1314
Isabel Allende Foundation Esperanza Grants, 1315
Island Insurance Foundation Grants, 1316
J. Bulow Campbell Foundation Grants, 1319
J. Edwin Treakle Foundation Grants, 1320
J.W. Gardner II Foundation Grants, 1323
J.W. Kieckhefer Foundation Grants, 1324
J. Walton Bissell Foundation Grants, 1325
J. Watumull Fund Grants, 1326
J. Willard and Alice S. Marriott Fdn Grants, 1327
Jack and Dorothy Byrne Foundation Grants, 1329
Jack H. and William M. Light Charitable Trust Grants, 1330
Jack Kent Cooke Fdn Good Neighbor Grants, 1331
Jack Satter Foundation Grants, 1334
Jacob G. Schmidlapp Trusts Grants, 1336
James and Abigail Campbell Family Foundation Grants, 1337
James Ford Bell Foundation Grants, 1339
James Lee Sorenson Family Impact Foundation Grants, 1342
James LeVoy Sorenson Foundation Grants, 1343
James M. Collins Foundation Grants, 1344
James S. Copley Foundation Grants, 1345
Jane's Trust Grants, 1346
Jane Bradley Pettit Foundation Community and Social Development Grants, 1347
Jayne and Leonard Abess Foundation Grants, 1358
Jeffris Wood Foundation Grants, 1359
Jennings County Community Foundation Women's Giving Circle Grant, 1361
Jessica Stevens Community Foundation Grants, 1363
Jewish Fund Grants, 1364
Jim Blevins Foundation Grants, 1365
Jim Moran Foundation Grants, 1366
Joan Bentinck-Smith Charitable Fdn Grants, 1367
John and Marcia Goldman Foundation Youth Development Grants, 1368
John Clarke Trust Grants, 1369
John D. and Katherine A. Johnston Foundation Grants, 1370
John Gogian Family Foundation Grants, 1373
John H. and Wilhelmina D. Harland Charitable Foundation Community Services Grants, 1375
John M. Weaver Foundation Grants, 1376
Joni Elaine Templeton Foundation Grants, 1384

Joseph H. and Florence A. Roblee Foundation Children and Youth Grants, 1385
Joseph H. and Florence A. Roblee Foundation Family Grants, 1387
Joseph Henry Edmondson Foundation Grants, 1388
Josephine Schell Russell Chartbl Trust Grants, 1389
Joseph S. Stackpole Charitable Trust Grants, 1390
Joyce and Randy Seckman Charitable Foundation Grants, 1393
Judith Clark-Morrill Foundation Grants, 1395
Judy and Peter Blum Kovler Foundation Grants, 1396
Julia and Tunnicliff Fox Chartbl Trust Grants, 1397
Julius N. Frankel Foundation Grants, 1400
Kaiser Permanente Hawaii Region Community Grants, 1406
Kalamazoo Community Foundation Individuals and Families Grants, 1409
Kansas Health Foundation Recognition Grants, 1415
Kate B. Reynolds Charitable Trust Health Care Grants, 1416
Kate B. Reynolds Charitable Trust Poor and Needy Grants, 1417
Katharine Matthies Foundation Grants, 1418
Kathryne Beynon Foundation Grants, 1420
Katrine Menzing Deakins Chartbl Trust Grants, 1422
Kawabe Memorial Fund Grants, 1423
Kelvin and Eleanor Smith Foundation Grants, 1424
Kenai Peninsula Foundation Grants, 1425
Kenneth T. and Eileen L. Norris Fdn Grants, 1427
Ketchikan Community Foundation Grants, 1429
Kettering Family Foundation Grants, 1430
Kimball Foundation Grants, 1432
Kimball International-Habig Foundation Health and Human Services Grants, 1434
Kinder Morgan Foundation Grants, 1436
Kind World Foundation Grants, 1438
Kirby Laing Foundation Grants, 1439
Klingenstein-Simons Fellowship Awards in the Neurosciences, 1441
Koch Family Foundation (Annapolis) Grants, 1444
Kodak Community Relations Grants, 1445
Kodiak Community Foundation Grants, 1446
Koret Foundation Grants, 1449
Kosasa Foundation Grants, 1450
Kovler Family Foundation Grants, 1455
Kovler Family Foundation Grants, 1454
Kroger Company Donations, 1456
Laclede Gas Charitable Trust Grants, 1457
LaGrange County Community Fdn Grants, 1458
LaGrange Independent Foundation for Endowments (L.I.F.E.), 1459
Land O'Lakes Foundation Mid-Atlantic Grants, 1467
Lands' End Corporate Giving Program, 1468
Latkin Charitable Foundation Grants, 1469
Laura B. Vogler Foundation Grants, 1470
Laura Musser Intercultural Harmony Grants, 1472
Laurel Foundation Grants, 1475
LEGO Children's Fund Grants, 1480
Leo Goodwin Foundation Grants, 1482
Leola Osborn Trust Grants, 1483
Leo Niessen Jr., Charitable Trust Grants, 1484
Leonsis Foundation Grants, 1485
LGA Family Foundation Grants, 1487
Liberty Bank Foundation Grants, 1488
Libra Foundation Grants, 1489
Lied Foundation Trust Grants, 1490
Lil and Julie Rosenberg Foundation Grants, 1491
Linden Foundation Grants, 1494
LISC Affordable Housing Grants, 1497
LISC Capacity Building Grants, 1498
LISC Financial Stability Grants, 1501
Locations Foundation Legacy Grants, 1504
Lois and Richard England Family Foundation Out-of-School-Time Grants, 1506
Louie M. and Betty M. Phillips Fdn Grants, 1509
Louis and Sandra Berkman Foundation Grants, 1510
Louis Calder Foundation Grants, 1511
Lubrizol Corporation Community Grants, 1512
Ludwick Family Foundation Grants, 1516
Luella Kemper Trust Grants, 1517

Lumpkin Family Foundation Strong Community Leadership Grants, 1519
M.A. Rikard Charitable Trust Grants, 1521
M. Bastian Family Foundation Grants, 1522
Mabel A. Horne Fund Grants, 1525
Mabel F. Hoffman Charitable Trust Grants, 1526
Mabel Louise Riley Foundation Grants, 1529
Mabel Y. Hughes Charitable Trust Grants, 1530
Macquarie Bank Foundation Grants, 1532
Madison Community Foundation Grants, 1535
Maggie Welby Foundation Grants, 1538
Make Sense Foundation Grants, 1548
Manuel D. and Rhoda Mayerson Fdn Grants, 1550
Marathon Petroleum Corporation Grants, 1551
March of Dimes Program Grants, 1552
Marcia and Otto Koehler Foundation Grants, 1553
Margaret and James A. Elkins Jr. Fdn Grants, 1555
Margaret M. Walker Charitable Fdn Grants, 1556
Margaret T. Morris Foundation Grants, 1557
Marie C. and Joseph C. Wilson Foundation Rochester Small Grants, 1559
Marin Community Foundation Improving Community Health Grants, 1566
Marion and Miriam Rose Fund Grants, 1569
Marion Gardner Jackson Charitable Trust Grts, 1570
Marion I. and Henry J. Knott Foundation Discretionary Grants, 1571
Marion I. and Henry J. Knott Foundation Standard Grants, 1572
Marisla Foundation Human Services Grants, 1573
Mark Wahlberg Youth Foundation Grants, 1576
Marquette Bank Neighborhood Commit Grants, 1577
Marshall County Community Fdn Grants, 1579
Marsh Corporate Grants, 1580
Martin Family Foundation Grants, 1583
Mary A. Crocker Trust Grants, 1584
Mary Black Foundation Active Living Grants, 1585
Mary Black Foundation Early Childhood Development Grants, 1586
Mary Cofer Trigg Trust Fund Grants, 1587
Mary E. Babcock Foundation Grants, 1589
Mary K. Chapman Foundation Grants, 1590
Mary Kay Foundation Domestic Violence Shelter Grants, 1591
Maryland State Dept of Education Coordinating Entity Services for the Maryland Child Care Res Centers Network Grants, 1594
Mary Owen Borden Foundation Grants, 1597
Mary S. and David C. Corbin Fdn Grants, 1598
Mary Wilmer Covey Charitable Trust Grants, 1600
MassMutual Foundation Economic Development Grants, 1603
Mathile Family Foundation Grants, 1604
Matilda R. Wilson Fund Grants, 1605
Matson Community Giving Grants, 1607
Maurice J. Masserini Charitable Trust Grants, 1610
May and Stanley Smith Charitable Trust Grants, 1613
McCarthy Family Fdn Charity Fund Grants, 1614
McCombs Foundation Grants, 1615
McConnell Foundation Grants, 1616
McCune Charitable Foundation Grants, 1617
McGraw-Hill Companies Community Grants, 1620
McInerny Foundation Grants, 1622
McLean Contributionship Grants, 1623
McLean Foundation Grants, 1624
Mead Family Foundation Grants, 1625
Meadows Foundation Grants, 1626
MeadWestvaco Foundation Sustainable Communities Grants, 1627
Mead Witter Foundation Grants, 1628
Medtronic Foundation CommunityLink Health Grants, 1630
Medtronic Foundation Community Link Human Services Grants, 1631
Medtronic Foundation Strengthening Health Systems Grants, 1632
Mercedes-Benz USA Corporate Contributions Grants, 1634
Mericos Foundation Grants, 1637
Meriden Foundation Grants, 1638

Merrick Foundation Grants, 1639
Merrick Foundation Grants, 1640
Mertz Gilmore Foundation NYC Communities Grants, 1641
Mertz Gilmore Foundation NYC Dance Grants, 1642
Mervin Bovaird Foundation Grants, 1643
Meta and George Rosenberg Fdn Grants, 1644
MetroWest Health Foundation Grants to Reduce the Incidence of High Risk Behaviors Among Adolescents, 1646
Metzger-Price Fund Grants, 1647
Meyer Fdn Healthy Communities Grants, 1650
Meyer Memorial Trust Responsive Grants, 1653
MFRI Community Mobilization Grants, 1654
MGM Resorts Foundation Community Grants, 1655
MGN Family Foundation Grants, 1656
Michael Reese Health Trust Core Grants, 1658
Michael Reese Health Trust Responsive Grants, 1659
Michelin North America Challenge Education, 1660
Michigan Women Forward Grants, 1662
Mid-Iowa Health Foundation Community Response Grants, 1667
Middlesex Savings Charitable Foundation Basic Human Needs Grants, 1668
Middlesex Savings Charitable Foundation Capacity Building Grants, 1669
Miller Foundation Grants, 1673
Mill Spring Foundation Grants, 1674
Milton Hicks Wood and Helen Gibbs Wood Charitable Trust Grants, 1676
Mimi and Peter Haas Fund Grants, 1677
Monsanto United States Grants, 1684
Montana Arts Council Cultural and Aesthetic Project Grants, 1685
Montana Community Foundation Grants, 1687
Montana Community Fdn Women's Grants, 1688
Montgomery County Community Foundation Health and Human Services Fund Grants, 1689
Montgomery County Community Foundation Libby Whitecotton Fund Grants, 1690
Moody Foundation Grants, 1692
Moran Family Foundation Grants, 1693
Morris Stulsaft Foundation Early Childhood Education Grants, 1696
Morris Stulsaft Foundation Educational Support for Children Grants, 1697
Morris Stulsaft Foundation Participation in the the Arts Grants, 1698
Morris Stulsaft Foundation Pathways to Work Grants, 1699
Moses Kimball Fund Grants, 1701
Ms. Fdn for Women Ending Violence Grants, 1708
Mt. Sinai Health Care Foundation Health of the Jewish Community Grants, 1709
Mt. Sinai Health Care Foundation Health of the Urban Community Grants, 1710
Narragansett Number One Foundation Grants, 1712
Nathan B. and Florence R. Burt Fdn Grants, 1717
Nathan Cummings Foundation Grants, 1718
Nathaniel and Elizabeth P. Stevens Foundation Grants, 1719
Nationwide Insurance Foundation Grants, 1726
NCMCF Youth Advisory Council Grants, 1727
Nell J. Redfield Foundation Grants, 1737
Nestle Purina PetCare Educational Grants, 1738
Nestle Purina PetCare Youth Grants, 1739
New Covenant Farms Grants, 1742
New Earth Foundation Grants, 1743
New Hampshire Charitable Foundation Neil and Louise Tillotson Fund - Empower Coös Youth Grants, 1748
New Jersey Center for Hispanic Policy, Research and Development Innovative Initiatives Grants, 1750
Nicole Brown Foundation Grants, 1760
Norcliffe Foundation Grants, 1766
Northern Chautauqua Community Foundation Community Grants, 1769
North Face Explore Fund, 1770
Northland Foundation Grants, 1771
NZDIA Community Org Grants Scheme, 1796

Oak Foundation Child Abuse Grants, 1799
Oak Fdn Housing and Homelessness Grants, 1800
OceanFirst Foundation Home Runs for Heroes Grants, 1802
OceanFirst Foundation Major Grants, 1803
Office Depot Corporation Community Relations Grants, 1805
Ohio County Community Foundation Board of Directors Grants, 1811
Ohio County Community Foundation Grants, 1812
Ohio Valley Foundation Grants, 1814
Olga Sipolin Children's Fund Grants, 1815
Olive B. Cole Foundation Grants, 1816
Olive Higgins Prouty Foundation Grants, 1817
Olive Smith Browning Charitable Trust Grants, 1818
Olivia R. Gardner Foundation Grants, 1819
Onan Family Foundation Grants, 1821
OneFamily Foundation Grants, 1822
Oppenstein Brothers Foundation Grants, 1827
Orange County Community Foundation Grants, 1829
Orange County Community Foundation Grants, 1828
Ordean Foundation Catalyst Grants, 1830
Ordean Foundation Partnership Grants, 1831
Oregon Community Foundation Black Student Success Community Network Grants, 1832
Oregon Community Fdn Community Grants, 1833
Oregon Community Foundation Community Recovery Grants, 1834
Oren Campbell McCleary Chartbl Trust Grants, 1837
OSF Youth Action Fund Grants in Kyrgyzstan, 1846
OtterCares Champion Fund Grants, 1848
OtterCares Impact Fund Grants, 1849
OtterCares Inspiration Fund Grants, 1850
Pacers Foundation Be Drug-Free Grants, 1856
Pacers Foundation Be Educated Grants, 1857
Pacers Foundation Be Healthy and Fit Grants, 1858
Pacers Foundation Be Tolerant Grants, 1859
Pacers Foundation Indiana Fever's Be YOUnique Fund Grants, 1860
PacifiCare Foundation Grants, 1861
Packard Foundation Local Grants, 1863
Pajaro Valley Community Health Health Trust Insurance/Coverage & Education on Using the System Grants, 1864
Pajaro Valley Community Health Trust Diabetes and Contributing Factors Grants, 1865
Pajaro Valley Community Health Trust Oral Health: Prevention & Access Grants, 1866
Palmer Foundation Grants, 1867
Parker Foundation (California) Grants, 1869
Parkersburg Area Community Foundation Action Grants, 1871
Paso del Norte Health Foundation Grants, 1874
Patrick and Aimee Butler Family Foundation Community Human Services Grants, 1880
Paul and Edith Babson Foundation Grants, 1881
PCA Arts Organizations and Arts Programs Grants for Arts Service Organizations, 1890
PCA Arts Organizations and Arts Programs Grants for Local Arts, 1895
PCA Busing Grants, 1899
PCA Entry Track Arts Organizations and Arts Programs Grants for Arts Service Orgs, 1902
PCA Entry Track Arts Organizations and Arts Programs Grants for Local Arts, 1907
PCA Entry Track Arts Orgs and Arts Programs Grants for Traditional and Folk Arts, 1911
PCA Pennsylvania Partners in the Arts Program Stream Grants, 1914
PCA Pennsylvania Partners in the Arts Project Stream Grants, 1915
PDF Fiscal Sponsorship Grant, 1921
Peabody Foundation Grants, 1922
Percy B. Ferebee Endowment Grants, 1936
Perkin Fund Grants, 1937
Perkins-Ponder Foundation Grants, 1938
Perpetual Benevolent Fund, 1940
Perry and Sandy Massie Foundation Grants, 1941
Peter and Elizabeth C. Tower Foundation Intellectual Disabilities Grants, 1944

Peter and Elizabeth C. Tower Foundation Learning Disability Grants, 1945
Peter and Elizabeth C. Tower Foundation Mental Health Grants, 1946
Peter and Elizabeth C. Tower Foundation Small Grants, 1947
Peter and Elizabeth C. Tower Foundation Substance Use Disorders Grants, 1948
Peter and Elizabeth C. Tower Foundation Technology Initiative Grants, 1949
Peter and Elizabeth C. Tower Foundation Technology Planning Grants, 1950
Petersburg Community Foundation Grants, 1951
Pettus Foundation Grants, 1952
PeyBack Foundation Grants, 1953
Peyton Anderson Foundation Grants, 1954
PG&E Community Vitality Grants, 1957
Philanthrofund Foundation Grants, 1959
Philip Boyle Foundation Grants, 1961
Phoenix Coyotes Charities Grants, 1963
Phoenix Suns Charities Grants, 1964
Piedmont Health Foundation Grants, 1965
Piedmont Natural Gas Corporate and Charitable Contributions, 1966
Piedmont Natural Gas Foundation Health and Human Services Grants, 1968
Pinnacle Foundation Grants, 1973
Piper Jaffray Foundation Communities Giving Grants, 1974
Piper Trust Arts and Culture Grants, 1975
Piper Trust Children Grants, 1976
Piper Trust Education Grants, 1977
Piper Trust Healthcare and Med Rsrch Grants, 1978
Piper Trust Reglious Organizations Grants, 1979
Pittsburgh Fdn Affordable Housing Grants, 1980
Pittsburgh Foundation Healthy Children and Adults Grants, 1981
PMI Foundation Grants, 1982
PNC Foundation Affordable Housing Grants, 1983
PNC Foundation Community Services Grants, 1984
PNC Foundation Grow Up Great Early Childhood Grants, 1986
PNM Reduce Your Use Grants, 1988
Pohlad Family Fdn Large Capital Grants, 1990
Pohlad Family Fdn Small Capital Grants, 1991
Pokagon Fund Grants, 1994
Polk County Community Foundation Bradley Breakthrough Community Benefit Grants, 1995
Polk County Community Foundation Marjorie M. and Lawrence R. Bradley Endowment Fund Grants, 1998
Polk County Community Foundation Seasonal Assistance and Cheer Grants for Charitable Programs, 2000
Polk County Community Foundation Unrestricted Grants, 2001
Porter County Community Foundation Sparking the Arts Fund Grants, 2004
Portland General Electric Foundation Grants, 2007
PPCF Community Grants, 2014
PPG Industries Foundation Grants, 2017
Premera Blue Cross Grants, 2018
Price Chopper's Golub Foundation Grants, 2020
Priddy Foundation Program Grants, 2023
ProLiteracy National Book Fund Grants, 2026
PSEG Fdn Safety and Preparedness Grants, 2031
Public Education Power Grants, 2032
Public Welfare Fdn Juvenile Justice Grants, 2033
Public Welfare Foundation Special Initiative to Advance Civil Legal Aid Grants, 2034
Public Welfare Foundation Special Opportunities Grants, 2035
Publix Super Markets Charities Local Grants, 2036
Puerto Rico Community Foundation Grants, 2037
Putnam County Community Fdn Grants, 2040
Qualcomm Grants, 2042
R.C. Baker Foundation Grants, 2043
R.D. Beirne Trust Grants, 2045
R.S. Gernon Trust Grants, 2047
Ralph M. Parsons Foundation Grants, 2052

Raskob Fdn for Catholic Activities Grants, 2054
Rathmann Family Foundation Grants, 2057
Ray Charles Foundation Grants, 2058
RCF General Community Grants, 2062
RCF Individual Assistance Grants, 2063
Reinberger Foundation Grants, 2066
Ressler-Gertz Foundation Grants, 2067
RGk Foundation Grants, 2068
Richard Davoud Donchian Foundation Grants, 2070
Richard W. Goldman Family Fdn Grants, 2073
Richland County Bank Grants, 2074
Ricks Family Charitable Trust Grants, 2075
Robbins-de Beaumont Foundation Grants, 2080
Robbins Charitable Foundation Grants, 2081
Robbins Family Charitable Foundation Grants, 2082
Robert and Betty Wo Foundation Grants, 2083
Robert and Helen Haddad Foundation Grants, 2084
Robert F. Lange Foundation Grants, 2090
Robert Lee Adams Foundation Grants, 2091
Robert Lee Blaffer Foundation Grants, 2092
Robert R. McCormick Tribune Foundation Community Grants, 2093
Robert R. Meyer Foundation Grants, 2094
Robin Hood Foundation Grants, 2096
Robinson Foundation Grants, 2097
Rockwell Collins Charitable Corp Grants, 2098
Roger L. and Agnes C. Dell Charitable Trust I Grants, 2099
Rose Community Foundation Child and Family Development Grants, 2103
Rose Community Foundation Health Grants, 2105
Rose Hills Foundation Grants, 2106
Rosenberg Charity Foundation Grants, 2107
Rosenberg Foundation Immigrant Rights and Integration Grants, 2108
Rosenberg Fund for Children Clinton and Muriel Jencks Memorial Fund Grants, 2109
Rosenberg Fund for Children Edith and George Ziefert Fund Grants, 2110
Rosenberg Fund for Children Grants, 2111
Rosenberg Fund for Children Herman Warsh Fund Grant, 2112
Rosenberg Fund for Children Moish and Lillian Antopol Memorial Fund Grants, 2113
Rosenberg Fund for Children Ozzy Klate Memorial Fund Grants, 2114
Roy and Christine Sturgis Charitable Tr Grts, 2115
Ruddie Memorial Youth Foundation Grants, 2120
Ruth Anderson Foundation Grants, 2122
Ruth and Vernon Taylor Foundation Grants, 2124
Ruth Camp Campbell Charitable Trust Grants, 2125
Saigh Foundation Grants, 2137
Saint Louis Rams Foundation Community Donations, 2139
Salmon Foundation Grants, 2140
Samuel S. Johnson Foundation Grants, 2146
San Antonio Area Foundation Annual Responsive Grants, 2147
San Antonio Area Foundation Special and Urgent Needs Funding Grants, 2150
Sand Hill Fdn Small Capital Needs Grants, 2154
Sands Cares Grants, 2156
San Juan Island Community Foundation Grants, 2158
Santa Fe Community Foundation Seasonal Grants-Fall Cycle, 2159
Sapelo Foundation Social Justice Grants, 2160
Sara Elizabeth O'Brien Trust Grants, 2161
Sarah G. McCarthy Memorial Foundation, 2162
Sarkeys Foundation Grants, 2163
Sartain Lanier Family Foundation Grants, 2164
Schlessman Family Foundation Grants, 2167
Schramm Foundation Grants, 2168
Scott B. and Annie P. Appleby Charitable Trust Grants, 2169
Screen Actors Guild BookPALS Assistance, 2171
Screen Actors Guild PencilPALS Assistance, 2172
Seattle Foundation Arts and Culture Grants, 2174
Seattle Foundation Basic Needs Grants, 2175
Seattle Foundation Benjamin N. Phillips Memorial Fund Grants, 2176

Seattle Foundation C. Keith Birkenfeld Memorial Trust Grants, 2177
Sensient Technologies Foundation Grants, 2180
Serco Foundation Grants, 2181
Seward Community Foundation Grants, 2182
Seward Community Foundation Mini-Grants, 2183
Seybert Foundation Grants, 2184
Share Our Strength Grants, 2185
Shell Oil Company Foundation Community Development Grants, 2188
Shield-Ayres Foundation Grants, 2189
Shopko Fdn Community Charitable Grants, 2191
Shopko Foundation Green Bay Area Community Grants, 2192
Sidgmore Family Foundation Grants, 2195
Sidney Stern Memorial Trust Grants, 2197
Siebert Lutheran Foundation Grants, 2198
Sierra Health Foundation Responsive Grants, 2199
Simpson Lumber Charitable Contributions, 2201
Singing for Change Foundation Grants, 2202
Sioux Falls Area Community Foundation Community Fund Grants, 2203
Sioux Falls Area Community Foundation Spot Grants, 2204
Skaggs Family Foundation Grants, 2205
Skaggs Family Foundation Grants, 2206
Smith Richardson Fdn Direct Service Grants, 2210
Sobrato Family Foundation Grants, 2211
Sobrato Family Fdn Meeting Space Grants, 2212
Sobrato Family Foundation Office Space Grants, 2213
Sony Corporation of America Grants, 2216
Sorenson Legacy Foundation Grants, 2217
Southern Minnesota Initiative Foundation BookStart Grants, 2220
Southern Minnesota Initiative Foundation Community Growth Initiative Grants, 2221
Southern Minnesota Initiative Foundation Incentive Grants, 2223
Special Olympics Eunice Kennedy Shriver (EKS) Fellowships, 2227
Special Olympics Project UNIFY Grants, 2228
Speer Trust Grants, 2230
Stan and Sandy Checketts Foundation Grants, 2235
Staunton Farm Foundation Grants, 2239
Stein Family Charitable Trust Grants, 2240
Stella and Charles Guttman Foundation Grants, 2241
Sterling-Turner Charitable Foundation Grants, 2242
Sterling and Shelli Gardner Foundation Grants, 2243
Steven B. Achelis Foundation Grants, 2244
Stocker Foundation Grants, 2247
Strake Foundation Grants, 2249
Stranahan Foundation Grants, 2250
Streisand Foundation Grants, 2251
Subaru of Indiana Automotive Fdn Grants, 2254
Summit Foundation Grants, 2255
Sunoco Foundation Grants, 2256
SunTrust Bank Trusteed Foundations Greene-Sawtell Grants, 2257
SunTrust Bank Trusteed Foundations Nell Warren Elkin and William Simpson Elkin Grants, 2258
Suspened: Community Fdn for Greater Atlanta State Farm Education Assist Fund Grants, 2260
Swindells Charitable Foundation Grants, 2261
Sylvia Adams Charitable Trust Grants, 2262
Sylvia Perkin Perpetual Charitable Trust Grants, 2263
T.L.L. Temple Foundation Grants, 2264
Target Corporation Community Engagement Fund Grants, 2270
Target Foundation Global Grants, 2272
Tata Trust Grant for Certificate Course in Holistic inclusion of Learners with Diversities, 2273
Tauck Family Foundation Grants, 2274
Teaching Tolerance Diverse Democracy Grants, 2275
Teaching Tolerance Social Justice Educator Grts, 2276
TechKnowledgey Community Impact Grants, 2278
TE Foundation Grants, 2279
Tellabs Foundation Grants, 2280
Telluride Fdn Emergency Grants, 2282
Telluride Fdn Technical Assistance Grants, 2283
Tension Envelope Foundation Grants, 2284

Textron Corporate Contributions Grants, 2286
Thelma Doelger Charitable Trust Grants, 2288
Thomas and Agnes Carvel Foundation Grants, 2289
Thomas J. Atkins Memorial Trust Fund Grants, 2290
Thomas J. Long Foundation Community Grants, 2291
Thomas Sill Foundation Grants, 2292
Thomas W. Briggs Foundation Grants, 2294
Tides Fdn Friends of the IGF Fund Grants, 2300
Tides Foundation Girl Rising Fund Grants, 2301
TJX Foundation Grants, 2303
Todd Brock Family Foundation Grants, 2305
Toyota Motor Manuf of Alabama Grants, 2309
Toyota Motor Manufacturing of Indiana Grants, 2310
Toyota Motor Manuf of Kentucky Grants, 2311
Toyota Motor Manuf of Mississippi Grants, 2312
Toyota Motor Manufacturing of Texas Grants, 2313
Toyota Motor Manufacturing of West Virginia Grants, 2314
Toyota Motor North America of NY Grants, 2315
Toyota Motor Sales, USA Grants, 2316
Toyota Technical Center Grants, 2317
Trinity Trust Summer Youth Mini-Grants, 2321
TSYSF Team Grants, 2323
Tull Charitable Foundation Grants, 2324
Twenty-First Century Foundation Grants, 2328
U.S. Bank Foundation Grants, 2330
U.S. Cellular Corporation Grants, 2331
Union Bank, N.A. Corporate Sponsorships and Donations, 2333
Union Bank, N.A. Foundation Grants, 2334
Union Pacific Fdn Community & Civic Grants, 2337
Union Pacific Foundation Health and Human Services Grants, 2338
Union Square Award for Social Justice, 2340
UnitedHealthcare Children's Fdn Grants, 2342
United Healthcare Commty Grts in Michigan, 2343
United Methodist Committee on Relief Hunger and Poverty Grants, 2344
United Methodist Women Brighter Future for Children and Youth Grants, 2346
United Technologies Corporation Grants, 2347
UPS Foundation Community Safety Grants, 2350
USAID Office of Foreign Disaster Assistance and Food for Peace Grants, 2359
USDA WIC Nutrition Ed Innovations Grants, 2363
UUA Actions of Public Witness Grants, 2365
UUA Congregation-Based Community Organizing Grants, 2366
UUA Fund Grants, 2367
UUA International Fund Grants, 2368
UUA Just Society Fund Grants, 2369
UUA Social Responsibility Grants, 2370
Valley-Wide Health Systems Nurse Family Partnerships, 2372
Vanderburgh Community Foundation Men's Fund Grants, 2373
Vanderburgh County Community Foundation Women's Fund Grants, 2376
Victor E. Speas Foundation Grants, 2380
Victoria S. and Bradley L. Geist Foundation Grants Supporting Foster Care and Their Caregivers, 2382
Victoria S. and Bradley L. Geist Foundation Grants Supporting Transitioning Foster Youth, 2383
Vigneron Memorial Fund Grants, 2384
Virginia W. Kettering Foundation Grants, 2388
Volkswagen Group of America Corporate Contributions Grants, 2389
W.H. and Mary Ellen Cobb Chartbl Trust Grts, 2397
W.M. Keck Fdn Southern California Grants, 2398
W.P. and Bulah Luse Foundation Grants, 2399
W.W. Smith Chartbl Trust Basic Needs Grants, 2400
Walker Area Community Foundation Grants, 2401
Wallace Foundation Grants, 2402
Walter J. and Betty C. Zable Fdn Grants, 2406
Walter S. and Evan C. Jones Testam Trust, 2407
Warrick County Community Foundation Women's Fund, 2411
Washington Area Fuel Fund Grants, 2413
Washington Gas Charitable Contributions, 2417
Wayne County Foundation Grants, 2419

Weaver Popcorn Foundation Grants, 2421
Westerman Foundation Grants, 2427
Western Indiana Community Fdn Grants, 2428
WestWind Foundation Reproductive Health and Rights Grants, 2434
Weyerhaeuser Family Fdn Health Grants, 2435
Whitehorse Foundation Grants, 2439
Whiting Foundation Grants, 2440
WHO Foundation Education/Literacy Grants, 2442
WHO Foundation General Grants, 2443
WHO Foundation Volunteer Service Grants, 2444
Whole Foods Foundation, 2445
Widgeon Point Charitable Foundation Grants, 2447
Wilkins Family Foundation Grants, 2450
William B. Stokely Jr. Foundation Grants, 2459
William Blair and Company Foundation Grants, 2461
William J. and Dorothy K. O'Neill Foundation Responsive Grants, 2468
William J. and Gertrude R. Casper Foundation Grants, 2469
William J. and Tina Rosenberg Fdn Grants, 2470
William J. Brace Charitable Trust, 2471
William M. Weaver Foundation Grants, 2472
William Ray and Ruth E. Collins Fdn Grants, 2473
Williams Comps Homegrown Giving Grants, 2474
Wilton and Effie Hebert Foundation Grants, 2476
Windham Foundation Grants, 2477
Winifred Johnson Clive Foundation Grants, 2478
WinnCompanies Charitable Giving, 2479
Wiregrass Foundation Grants, 2480
Wolfe Associates Grants, 2483
Women's Fund of Hawaii Grants, 2485
Women's Fund of Hawaii Grants, 2484
Wood Family Charitable Trust Grants, 2487
Woods Fund of Chicago Grants, 2489
World of Children Youth Award, 2493
WSF GoGirlGo! New York Grants, 2494
WSF Sports 4 Life Grants, 2496
WSF Sports 4 Life Regional Grants, 2497
WSLBDF Quarterly Grants, 2499
Wyomissing Foundation Community Grants, 2504
Wyomissing Foundation Thun Family Organizational Grants, 2505
Wyomissing Foundation Thun Family Program Grants, 2506
Xerox Foundation Grants, 2507
Youths' Friends Association Grants, 2511
YSA ABC Summer of Service Awards, 2512
YSA Get Ur Good On Grants, 2513
YSA Global Youth Service Day Lead Agy Grts, 2514
YSA MLK Day Lead Organizer Grants, 2516
YSA NEA Youth Leaders for Literacy Grants, 2518
YSA Radio Disney's Hero for Change Award, 2519
YSA State Farm Good Neighbor YOUth In The Driver Seat Grants, 2521
YSA UnitedHealth HEROES Service-Learning Grants, 2522
Z. Smith Reynolds Foundation Small Grants, 2523
Zane's Foundation Grants, 2524
ZYTL Foundation Grants, 2528

Symposiums, Conferences, Workshops, Seminars

AACAP Systems of Care Special Program Scholarships, 39
ALA Penguin Random House Young Readers Group Award, 183
Alaska Children's Trust Conference/Training Sponsorship, 195
ALFJ International Fund Grants, 231
ALFJ International Social Change Opportunity Fund Grants, 232
Ameren Corporation Community Grants, 251
Atlanta Women's Foundation Pathway to Success Grants, 327
Bayer Fund Community Development Grants, 383
Blue Cross Blue Shield of Minnesota Foundation - Healthy Neighborhoods: Connect for Health Challenge Grants, 443
Blumenthal Foundation Grants, 459
Boeing Company Contributions Grants, 462

California Arts Cncl Statewide Networks Grants, 493
Carl M. Freeman Foundation Grants, 508
Cash 4 Clubs Sports Grants, 515
CFFVR Environmental Stewardship Grants, 540
CFFVR Mielke Family Foundation Grants, 544
Charles Delmar Foundation Grants, 564
Charles Lafitte Foundation Grants, 567
Chesapeake Bay Trust Outreach and Community
   Engagement Grants, 579
CIGNA Foundation Grants, 611
City of Oakland Cultural Funding Grants, 618
CJ Fdn for SIDS Program Services Grants, 619
Community Foundation for Greater Buffalo
   Competitive Grants, 670
Community Foundation of Eastern Connecticut
   General Southeast Grants, 696
Community Foundation of Greater Fort Wayne -
   John S. and James L. Knight Foundation Donor-
   Advised Grants, 707
Community Foundation of Louisville Education
   Grants, 724
Community Foundation of Western Massachusetts
   Grants, 741
Corina Higginson Trust Grants, 750
Covidien Partnership for Neighborhood Wellness
   Grants, 759
DeKalb County Community Foundation - Literacy
   Grant, 814
Dubois County Community Foundation Grants, 871
Dyson Foundation Mid-Hudson Valley Project
   Support Grants, 874
Ewing Marion Kauffman Foundation Grants, 943
Fayette County Foundation Grants, 951
FINRA Smart Investing@Your Library Grants, 963
Ford Foundation BUILD Grants, 984
Fremont Area Community Foundation Community
   Grants, 1020
Geraldine R. Dodge Fdn Education Grants, 1061
Global Fund for Women Grants, 1073
GNOF IMPACT Grants for Youth Dev, 1084
GNOF Organizational Effectiveness Grants and
   Workshops, 1090
Greater Saint Louis Community Fdn Grants, 1110
HAF Community Grants, 1141
HAF Southern Humboldt Grants, 1150
Hatton W. Sumners Foundation for the Study and
   Teaching of Self Government Grants, 1196
Hawai'i Community Foundation Family Literacy and
   Hawaii Pizza Hut Literacy Grants, 1201
Hawai'i Community Foundation Victoria S. and
   Bradley L. Geist Foundation: Capacity Building
   Grants, 1206
Hawai'i SFCA Art Bento Program @ HiSAM
   Grants, 1210
Hearst Foundations United States Senate Youth
   Grants, 1225
Helen Bader Foundation Grants, 1227
Honeywell Corporation Leadership Challenge
   Academy, 1258
Honor the Earth Grants, 1259
HSFCA Biennium Grants, 1267
HSFCA Folk and Traditional Arts Grants - Culture
   Learning, 1268
Indiana OCRA Rural Capacity Grants (RCG), 1301
IYI Professional Development Grants, 1317
J.W. Kieckhefer Foundation Grants, 1324
Japan Foundation Los Angeles Mini-Grants for
   Japanese Arts & Culture, 1354
Japan Foundation New York Small Grants for Arts
   and Culture, 1355
Johnson Foundation Wingspread Conference Support
   Program, 1381
Kentucky Arts Cncl Access Assistance Grants, 1428
Klingenstein-Simons Fellowship Awards in the
   Neurosciences, 1441
Kodak Community Relations Grants, 1445
Koret Foundation Grants, 1449
Laurel Foundation Grants, 1475
LEGO Children's Fund Grants, 1480
Louis Calder Foundation Grants, 1511

Manuel D. and Rhoda Mayerson Fdn Grants, 1550
Marie C. and Joseph C. Wilson Foundation Rochester
   Small Grants, 1559
Martha Holden Jennings Foundation Grants-to-
   Educators, 1581
Mary Black Foundation Active Living Grants, 1585
Mary D. and Walter F. Frear Eleemosynary Trust
   Grants, 1588
Maurice Amado Foundation Grants, 1609
Max and Anna Levinson Foundation Grants, 1612
McCune Charitable Foundation Grants, 1617
McLean Contributionship Grants, 1623
Mertz Gilmore Foundation NYC Dance Grants, 1642
Meyer Foundation Benevon Grants, 1648
MFRI Community Mobilization Grants, 1654
MGN Family Foundation Grants, 1656
Michigan Women Forward Grants, 1662
NEA Fdn Read Across America Event Grants, 1731
NEH Picturing America Awards, 1735
Nellie Mae Education Foundation District-Level
   Change Grants, 1736
Noble County Community Foundation Grants, 1765
Norcliffe Foundation Grants, 1766
NYSCA Arts Education: Community-based
   Learning Grants, 1780
NYSCA Electronic Media and Film: Workspace
   Grants, 1789
NYSCA Special Arts Services: General Program
   Support Grants, 1793
OHA 'Ahahui Grants, 1807
Oppenstein Brothers Foundation Grants, 1827
Oregon Community Fdn Community Grants, 1833
OtterCares NoCO Fund Grants, 1851
PAS PASIC International Scholarships, 1875
PCA-PCD Professional Development for Individual
   Artists Grants, 1883
PCA Arts in Education Residencies, 1885
PCA Arts Organizations and Arts Programs Grants
   for Arts Education Organizations, 1889
PCA Entry Track Arts Organizations and
   Arts Programs Grants for Arts Education
   Organizations, 1901
PCA Entry Track Arts Organizations and Arts
   Programs Grants for Crafts, 1903
PCA Professional Development Grants, 1916
PennPAT Artist Technical Assistance Grants, 1929
Phil Hardin Foundation Grants, 1960
Philip L. Graham Fund Education Grants, 1962
Polk County Community Foundation Unrestricted
   Grants, 2001
Prudential Foundation Education Grants, 2028
Public Education Power Grants, 2032
Puerto Rico Community Foundation Grants, 2037
Raskob Fdn for Catholic Activities Grants, 2054
Rathmann Family Foundation Grants, 2057
RGk Foundation Grants, 2068
Ruddie Memorial Youth Foundation Grants, 2120
SAS Institute Community Relations Donations, 2165
Screen Actors Guild BookPALS Assistance, 2171
Shelley and Donald Rubin Foundation Grants, 2187
Sick Kids Foundation Community Conference
   Grants, 2193
Social Justice Fund Northwest Criminal Justice
   Giving Project Grants, 2214
Summit Foundation Grants, 2255
TAC Arts Access Grant, 2265
TAC Arts Education Teacher Incentive Grants, 2268
Telluride Foundation Community Grants, 2281
Textron Corporate Contributions Grants, 2286
Wayne County Foundation Grants, 2419
YSA National Child Awareness Month Youth
   Ambassador Grants, 2517
Z. Smith Reynolds Foundation Small Grants, 2523

Technical Assistance
A.L. Mailman Family Foundation Grants, 20
Abbott Fund Access to Health Care Grants, 45
Abbott Fund Global AIDS Care Grants, 47
ACCF of Indiana Bank of Geneva Heritage Fund
   Grants, 64

ACCF of Indiana First Merchants Bank / Decatur
   Bank and Trust Fund Grants, 66
ACF Adoption Opportunities Grants, 71
ACF Basic Center Program Grants, 73
ACF Ethnic Community Self Help Grants, 80
ACF National Human Trafficking Hotline Grants, 86
ACF Promoting Safe and Stable Families (PSSF)
   Program Grants, 89
ACF Refugee Career Pathways Grants, 90
ACF Sustainable Employment and Economic
   Development Strategies Grants, 95
ACL Neonatal Abstinence Syndrome National
   Training Initiative Grant, 106
ACL Rehabilitation Research and Training Center
   (RRTC) on Employment of Transition-Age Youth
   with Disabilities Grants, 107
Ahearn Family Foundation Grants, 142
Akron Community Foundation Arts and Culture
   Grants, 150
Akron Community Fdn Education Grants, 151
Akron Community Foundation Health and human
   services Grants, 152
Alex Stern Family Foundation Grants, 229
ALFJ International Social Change Opportunity Fund
   Grants, 232
Allstate Corporate Giving Grants, 242
Alpha Natural Resources Corporate Giving, 246
American Woodmark Foundation Grants, 263
Anderson Foundation Grants, 271
Appalachian Regional Commission Entrepreneurship
   and Business Development Grants, 287
Appalachian Regl Commission Housing Grants, 289
Ar-Hale Family Foundation Grants, 290
Arizona Foundation for Women Deborah G. Carstens
   Fund Grants, 293
Arkema Foundation Grants, 298
Aspen Community Foundation Grants, 316
Assisi Foundation of Memphis General Grants, 318
Assisi Foundation of Memphis Mini Grants, 319
Atkinson Foundation Community Grants, 325
Autauga Area Community Foundation Grants, 334
Baxter International Corporate Giving Grants, 368
Beckman Coulter Foundation Grants, 394
Best Buy Children's Fdn @15 Teach Awards, 416
Best Buy Children's Foundation National Grants, 417
Bill and Melinda Gates Foundation Agricultural
   Development Grants, 425
Blandin Foundation Expand Opportunity Grants, 437
Blue River Community Foundation Grants, 458
Boeing Company Contributions Grants, 462
BP Foundation Grants, 465
Brookdale Fdn Relatives as Parents Grants, 474
Burlington Industries Foundation Grants, 481
C.H. Robinson Worldwide Foundation Grants, 489
Caesars Foundation Grants, 492
California Arts Cncl Technical Assistance Grts, 494
Carl M. Freeman Foundation Grants, 508
Cash 4 Clubs Sports Grants, 515
Cass County Community Foundation Grants, 516
Cause Populi Worthy Cause Grants, 521
CenturyLink Clarke M. Williams Foundation
   Matching Time Grants, 531
CFFVR Basic Needs Giving Partnership Grants, 537
CFFVR Environmental Stewardship Grants, 540
CFF Winter Park Community Grants, 551
Chicago Community Trust Arts and Culture Grants:
   Improving Access to Arts Learning, 581
Chilkat Valley Community Foundation Grants, 588
Circle K Corporation Contributions Grants, 614
CNCS Foster Grandparent Projects Grants, 646
CNCS School Turnaround AmeriCorps Grants, 647
CNCS Senior Corps Retired and Senior Volunteer
   Program Grants, 648
Colorado Trust Health Investment Grants, 662
Columbus Foundation Traditional Grants, 663
Community Foundation for Greater Atlanta
   Metropolitan Extra Wish Grants, 666
Community Foundation for Greater Atlanta Strategic
   Restructuring Fund Grants, 669

Community Foundation for Greater Buffalo
    Competitive Grants, 670
Community Foundation for Greater Buffalo Niagara
    Area Foundation Grants, 673
Community Foundation for the Capital Region
    Grants, 687
Community Foundation for the National Capital
    Region Community Leadership Grants, 688
Community Foundation of Boone County Grants, 694
Community Foundation of Eastern Connecticut
    General Southeast Grants, 696
Community Foundation of Greater Fort Wayne -
    Community Endowment and Clarke Endowment
    Grants, 705
Community Foundation of Greater Greensboro
    Community Grants, 708
Community Foundation of Henderson County
    Community Grants, 711
Community Fdn of Wabash County Grants, 740
Community Foundation of Western Massachusetts
    Grants, 741
Cooke Foundation Grants, 748
Del Mar Foundation Community Grants, 820
Dorothea Haus Ross Foundation Grants, 844
DTE Energy Foundation Community Development
    Grants, 866
Dyson Foundation Mid-Hudson Valley Project
    Support Grants, 874
Echoing Green Fellowships, 885
Edyth Bush Charitable Foundation Grants, 893
Elizabeth Morse Genius Charitable Trust Grants, 901
Elkhart County Community Foundation Grants, 903
Entergy Charitable Foundation Low-Income
    Initiatives and Solutions Grants, 918
Eulalie Bloedel Schneider Foundation Grants, 936
Evelyn and Walter Haas, Jr. Fund Nonprofit
    Leadership Grants, 942
Ewing Marion Kauffman Foundation Grants, 943
Fidelity Foundation Grants, 957
FINRA Smart Investing@Your Library Grants, 963
First Hawaiian Bank Foundation Corporate Giving
    Grants, 967
Ford Family Foundation Grants - Technical
    Assistance , 983
Foundation Beyond Belief Compassionate Impact
    Grants, 986
Foundation Beyond Belief Humanist Grants, 987
Four County Community Foundation General
    Grants, 1000
Four County Community Foundation Healthy
    Senior/Healthy Youth Fund Grants, 1001
Frederick McDonald Trust Grants, 1017
Fremont Area Community Foundation Community
    Grants, 1020
Gene Haas Foundation, 1038
General Motors Foundation Grants, 1039
Gerber Foundation Environmental Hazards Research
    Grants, 1062
Gerber Fdn Pediatric Health Research Grants, 1063
Gerber Foundation Pediatric Nutrition Research
    Grants, 1064
GNOF IMPACT Grants for Youth Dev, 1084
GNOF Organizational Effectiveness Grants and
    Workshops, 1090
Goldseker Foundation Non-Profit Management
    Assistance Grants, 1095
Greater Tacoma Community Foundation General
    Operating Grants, 1113
Green River Area Community Fdn Grants, 1117
GTECH After School Advantage Grants, 1125
Gulf Coast Foundation of Community Operating
    Grants, 1134
Gulf Coast Foundation of Community Program
    Grants, 1135
HAF Don and Bettie Albright Endowment Fund
    Grants, 1142
Hannaford Supermarkets Community Giving, 1164
Hardin County Community Foundation Grants, 1167
Harold K.L. Castle Foundation Strengthening
    Windward Oahu Communities Grants, 1174

Harris and Eliza Kempner Fund Ed Grants, 1176
Harris Foundation Grants, 1177
Hawai'i Community Foundation Victoria S. and
    Bradley L. Geist Foundation: Capacity Building
    Grants, 1206
Hill Crest Foundation Grants, 1249
Honor the Earth Grants, 1259
HRSA Ryan White HIV AIDS Drug Assistance
    Grants, 1265
Iddings Foundation Medium Project Grants, 1285
Inland Empire Community Foundation Capacity
    Building for IE Nonprofits Grants, 1306
Island Insurance Foundation Grants, 1316
IYI Responsible Fatherhood Grants, 1318
Jacob G. Schmidlapp Trusts Grants, 1336
Jessica Stevens Community Foundation Grants, 1363
Joseph Henry Edmondson Foundation Grants, 1388
KaBOOM! Play Everywhere Design Challenge, 1405
Kalamazoo Community Foundation Early Childhood
    Learning and School Readiness Grants, 1407
Kansas Health Foundation Recognition Grants, 1415
Katie's Krops Grants, 1421
Lewis H. Humphreys Charitable Trust Grants, 1486
LGA Family Foundation Grants, 1487
Linford & Mildred White Charitable Grants, 1495
Lubrizol Corporation Community Grants, 1512
Manuel D. and Rhoda Mayerson Fdn Grants, 1550
Marquette Bank Neighborhood Commit Grants, 1577
McCune Charitable Foundation Grants, 1617
Merrick Foundation Grants, 1639
Mertz Gilmore Foundation NYC Communities
    Grants, 1641
Mertz Gilmore Foundation NYC Dance Grants, 1642
MGN Family Foundation Grants, 1656
Michael Reese Health Trust Core Grants, 1658
Michigan Women Forward Grants, 1662
Mimi and Peter Haas Fund Grants, 1677
Montgomery County Community Foundation Health
    and Human Services Fund Grants, 1689
New Earth Foundation Grants, 1743
New Jersey Office of Faith Based Initiatives Services
    to At Risk Youth Grants, 1752
New York Foundation Grants, 1753
Norcliffe Foundation Grants, 1766
NYFA Artists in the School Community Planning
    Grants, 1779
NYSCA Electronic Media and Film: Workspace
    Grants, 1789
Ohio County Community Foundation Board of
    Directors Grants, 1811
OneFamily Foundation Grants, 1822
Oregon Community Fdn Community Grants, 1833
Paso del Norte Health Foundation Grants, 1874
PCA-PCD Organizational Short-Term Professional
    Development and Consulting Grants, 1882
PCA Management/Techl Assistance Grants, 1913
PDF Community Organizing Grants, 1920
PennPAT Artist Technical Assistance Grants, 1929
Peter and Elizabeth C. Tower Foundation Technology
    Initiative Grants, 1949
Peter and Elizabeth C. Tower Foundation Technology
    Planning Grants, 1950
Pettus Foundation Grants, 1952
PNC Foundation Community Services Grants, 1984
Pokagon Fund Grants, 1994
Polk County Community Foundation Marjorie M.
    and Lawrence R. Bradley Endowment Fund
    Grants, 1998
PPCF Community Grants, 2014
ProLiteracy National Book Fund Grants, 2026
Proteus Fund Grants, 2027
Prudential Foundation Education Grants, 2028
Puerto Rico Community Foundation Grants, 2037
Putnam County Community Fdn Grants, 2040
San Antonio Area Foundation Capital and Naming
    Rights Grants, 2148
Sand Hill Foundation Health and Opportunity
    Grants, 2153
Seattle Foundation Arts and Culture Grants, 2174
Seattle Foundation Education Grants, 2178

Seattle Foundation Health and Wellness Grants, 2179
Seward Community Foundation Grants, 2182
Seward Community Foundation Mini-Grants, 2183
Shield-Ayres Foundation Grants, 2189
Skaggs Foundation Grants, 2207
Skatepark Project Built to Play Skatepark Grant, 2208
Social Justice Fund Northwest Criminal Justice
    Giving Project Grants, 2214
Streisand Foundation Grants, 2251
Target Foundation Global Grants, 2272
TechKnowledgey Community Impact Grants, 2278
Telluride Foundation Community Grants, 2281
Telluride Fdn Emergency Grants, 2282
Telluride Fdn Technical Assistance Grants, 2283
Textron Corporate Contributions Grants, 2286
Tides Foundation Grants, 2302
Toyota Motor Manufacturing of West Virginia
    Grants, 2314
Toyota Motor North America of NY Grants, 2315
Toyota Motor Sales, USA Grants, 2316
Union Bank, N.A. Foundation Grants, 2334
Union Pacific Foundation Health and Human
    Services Grants, 2338
Union Square Award for Social Justice, 2340
USAID Integrated Youth Development Activity
    Grants, 2356
Virginia Commission for the Arts Artists in
    Education Residency Grants, 2385
W.M. Keck Fdn Southern California Grants, 2398
Walker Area Community Foundation Grants, 2401
Washington Area Women's Foundation African
    American Women's Giving Circle Grants, 2414
Washington Area Women's Foundation Rainmakers
    Giving Circle Grants, 2415
Western Indiana Community Fdn Grants, 2428
Whitehorse Foundation Grants, 2439
William G. Gilmore Foundation Grants, 2467
William Ray and Ruth E. Collins Fdn Grants, 2473
Wiregrass Foundation Grants, 2480
Women's Fund of Hawaii Grants, 2484
WSF Rusty Kanokogi Fund for the Advancement of
    U.S. Judo Grants, 2495
WSF Sports 4 Life Regional Grants, 2497
Wyomissing Foundation Thun Family Organizational
    Grants, 2505
Wyomissing Foundation Thun Family Program
    Grants, 2506
Xerox Foundation Grants, 2507
YSA ABC Summer of Service Awards, 2512
YSA Global Youth Service Day Lead Agy Grts, 2514
YSA MLK Day Lead Organizer Grants, 2516
YSA National Child Awareness Month Youth
    Ambassador Grants, 2517

Training Programs/Internships
ACF Child Welfare Training Grants, 75
ACF Social and Economic Development Strategies
    Grants, 93
Achelis and Bodman Foundation Grants, 101
Achelis Foundation Grants, 102
ACL Neonatal Abstinence Syndrome National
    Training Initiative Grant, 106
Adolph Coors Foundation Grants, 129
Alaska Airlines Corporation Career Connections for
    Youth Grants, 193
Allen Foundation Educational Nutrition Grants, 238
Bank of America Charitable Foundation Student
    Leaders Grants, 357
Baxter International Corporate Giving Grants, 368
Cash 4 Clubs Sports Grants, 515
Charles Delmar Foundation Grants, 564
Circle K Corporation Contributions Grants, 614
CNCS AmeriCorps State and National Planning
    Grants, 644
CNCS Social Innovation Grants, 649
Collins Foundation Grants, 658
Community Foundation for Greater Buffalo
    Competitive Grants, 670
Community Foundation of Louisville Education
    Grants, 724

Corina Higginson Trust Grants, 750
Donald W. Reynolds Foundation Children's Discovery Initiative Grants, 841
Do Something Back End Developer Intern, 848
Do Something Business Development Intern, 849
Do Something Campaigns Intern, 850
Do Something Digital Content Intern, 851
Do Something Digital Member Exp Intern, 852
Do Something Finance and Human Res Intern, 853
Do Something International Intern, 854
Do Something Intern of Fun, 855
Do Something Partnerships and Public Relations Intern, 856
Do Something TMI Intern, 858
Do Something Web Developer Intern, 860
Do Something Writing and Journalism Intern, 861
Dr. John T. Macdonald Foundation Grants, 863
E.L. Wiegand Foundation Grants, 877
Earl and Maxine Claussen Trust Grants, 878
Effie and Wofford Cain Foundation Grants, 895
Essex County Community Foundation Merrimack Valley Municipal Business Development and Recovery Fund Grants, 933
Essex County Community Foundation Women's Fund Grants, 934
Eulalie Bloedel Schneider Foundation Grants, 936
F.R. Bigelow Foundation Grants, 947
FCD New American Children Grants, 952
Ford Foundation BUILD Grants, 984
Fdn for the Mid South Communities Grants, 992
Frederick W. Marzahl Memorial Fund Grants, 1018
GNOF New Orleans Works Grants, 1088
HAF Community Grants, 1141
Hattie M. Strong Foundation Grants, 1194
Hatton W. Sumners Foundation for the Study and Teaching of Self Government Grants, 1196
Hawai'i Community Foundation Bernice and Conrad von Hamm Fund Grants, 1197
Hawai'i Community Foundation Victoria S. and Bradley L. Geist Foundation: Supporting Foster Children and Their Caregivers, 1208
Hawai'i Community Foundation Victoria S. and Bradley L. Geist Foundation: Supporting Transitioning Foster Youth Grants, 1209
Hearst Foundations Social Service Grants, 1224
Helen Bader Foundation Grants, 1227
Indiana OCRA Rural Capacity Grants (RCG), 1301
Intel Corporation Int Community Grants, 1312
John F. Kennedy Center for the Performing Arts National Rosemary Kennedy Internship, 1371
Kind World Foundation Grants, 1438
Lilly Endowment Summer Youth Grants, 1492
Linden Foundation Grants, 1494
Macquarie Bank Foundation Grants, 1532
Maine Women's Fund Econ Security Grants, 1546
Marin Community Foundation Social Justice and Interfaith Understanding Grants, 1567
Maurice R. Robinson Fund Grants, 1611
May and Stanley Smith Charitable Trust Grants, 1613
McLean Contributionship Grants, 1623
Meadows Foundation Grants, 1626
Meyer Foundation Education Grants, 1649
Middlesex Savings Charitable Foundation Educational Opportunities Grants, 1670
Morris Stulsaft Foundation Pathways to Work Grants, 1699
Ms. Fdn for Women Economic Justice Grants, 1707
NRA Foundation Grants, 1774
NYSCA Electronic Media and Film: Workspace Grants, 1789
PCA Arts Management Internship, 1886
PCA Arts Organizations and Arts Programs Grants for Crafts, 1891
PCA Entry Track Arts Organizations and Arts Programs Grants for Crafts, 1903
Polk County Community Foundation Unrestricted Grants, 2001
PPG Industries Foundation Grants, 2017
ProLiteracy National Book Fund Grants, 2026
Prudential Foundation Education Grants, 2028

Ralph M. Parsons Foundation Grants, 2052
Raskob Fdn for Catholic Activities Grants, 2054
Rathmann Family Foundation Grants, 2057
Rose Community Foundation Child and Family Development Grants, 2103
Salmon Foundation Grants, 2140
San Antonio Area Foundation Strengthening Nonprofits Grants, 2151
Sand Hill Foundation Health and Opportunity Grants, 2153
Sidgmore Family Foundation Grants, 2195
Sierra Health Foundation Responsive Grants, 2199
Sioux Falls Area Community Foundation Community Fund Grants, 2203
Sioux Falls Area Community Foundation Spot Grants, 2204
Skaggs Foundation Grants, 2207
Sony Corporation of America Grants, 2216
Sorenson Legacy Foundation Grants, 2217
Southern New England Folk and Traditional Arts Apprenticeship Grants, 2224
TAC Arts Access Grant, 2265
TE Foundation Grants, 2279
Textron Corporate Contributions Grants, 2286
Toyota USA Foundation Education Grants, 2318
Union Bank, N.A. Foundation Grants, 2334
USAID Global Development Alliance Grants, 2354
Walker Area Community Foundation Grants, 2401
Woods Charitable Fund Education Grants, 2488
Wyomissing Foundation Thun Family Organizational Grants, 2505
Wyomissing Foundation Thun Family Program Grants, 2506
Xerox Foundation Grants, 2507

Travel Grants

AACAP Educational Outreach Program for Child and Adolescent Psychiatry Residents, 23
AACAP Educational Outreach Program for General Psychiatry Residents, 24
AACAP Life Members Mentorship Grants for Medical Students, 30
AACAP Systems of Care Special Program Scholarships, 39
ALA Penguin Random House Young Readers Group Award, 183
ALFJ International Social Change Opportunity Fund Grants, 232
Carl M. Freeman Foundation Grants, 508
CJ Fdn for SIDS Program Services Grants, 619
Colin Higgins Foundation Courage Awards, 653
Community Foundation of Louisville CHAMP Fund Grants, 720
Decatur County Community Foundation Large Project Grants, 811
Global Fund for Women Grants, 1073
GNOF Organizational Effectiveness Grants and Workshops, 1090
Gray Family Foundation Community Field Trips Grants, 1105
Hearst Foundations United States Senate Youth Grants, 1225
Herbert Hoover Presidential Library Association Bus Travel Grants, 1244
IYI Professional Development Grants, 1317
LaGrange Independent Foundation for Endowments (L.I.F.E.), 1459
Meyer Foundation Benevon Grants, 1648
MFRI Community Mobilization Grants, 1654
Newfoundland and Labrador Arts Council Visiting Artists Grants, 1746
NZDIA Lottery Minister's Discretionary Fund Grants, 1797
Oregon Community Fdn Community Grants, 1833
PAS PASIC International Scholarships, 1875
PCA-PCD Professional Development for Individual Artists Grants, 1883
PCA Busing Grants, 1899
PCA Professional Development Grants, 1916
PennPAT Artist Technical Assistance Grants, 1929

PennPAT Presenter Travel Grants, 1932
PennPAT Strategic Opportunity Grants, 1933
Pokagon Fund Grants, 1994
TAC Arts Education Teacher Incentive Grants, 2268
TSYSF Team Grants, 2323
Walker Area Community Foundation Grants, 2401
WSF Sports 4 Life Grants, 2496
WSF Travel and Training Fund Grants, 2498
YSA Global Youth Service Day Lead Agy Grts, 2514
YSA National Child Awareness Month Youth Ambassador Grants, 2517

Vocational Education

ACCF of Indiana Bank of Geneva Heritage Fund Grants, 64
ACF Refugee Career Pathways Grants, 90
ACF Voluntary Agencies Matching Grants, 100
Achelis and Bodman Foundation Grants, 101
Achelis Foundation Grants, 102
Adams Family Fdn of Nora Springs Grants, 118
Adolph Coors Foundation Grants, 129
Akron Community Fdn Education Grants, 151
Alaska Airlines Foundation LIFT Grants, 194
Alliant Energy Foundation Community Giving for Good Sponsorship Grants, 240
Alpha Natural Resources Corporate Giving, 246
Arizona Foundation for Women Deborah G. Carstens Fund Grants, 293
Autism Speaks Norma and Malcolm Baker Recreation Grants, 335
Bank of Hawaii Foundation Grants, 360
Blue Mountain Community Foundation Warren Community Action Fund Grants, 457
BP Foundation Grants, 465
Camille Beckman Foundation Grants, 499
Carl M. Freeman Foundation Grants, 508
CFGR SisterFund Grants, 554
Chilkat Valley Community Foundation Grants, 588
Claremont Savings Bank Foundation Grants, 623
Cleveland Browns Foundation Grants, 633
CNCS AmeriCorps State and National Grants, 643
Community Foundation for Greater Buffalo Niagara Area Foundation Grants, 673
Community Foundation of Crawford County, 695
Community Foundation of Louisville Education Grants, 724
Daniels Fund Youth Development Grants, 784
Del Mar Foundation Community Grants, 820
DOL Youthbuild Grants, 838
Eide Bailly Resourcefullness Awards, 897
Elizabeth Morse Genius Charitable Trust Grants, 901
Eulalie Bloedel Schneider Foundation Grants, 936
First Hawaiian Bank Foundation Corporate Giving Grants, 967
Foundation for Rural Service Education Grants, 991
Four County Community Foundation General Grants, 1000
Frank Reed and Margaret Jane Peters Memorial Fund II Grants, 1014
Gamble Foundation Grants, 1032
George W. Wells Foundation Grants, 1057
GNOF New Orleans Works Grants, 1088
Greater Sitka Legacy Fund Grants, 1111
GTRCF Elk Rapids Area Community Endowment Grants, 1127
HAF Community Grants, 1141
Harold K.L. Castle Foundation Public Education Redesign and Enhancement Grants, 1173
Harold K.L. Castle Foundation Strengthening Windward Oahu Communities Grants, 1174
Harris and Eliza Kempner Fund Ed Grants, 1176
Harris Foundation Grants, 1177
HBF Pathways Out of Poverty Grants, 1222
Hearst Foundations Social Service Grants, 1224
HLTA Visitor Industry Charity Walk Grant, 1254
Iddings Foundation Small Project Grants, 1286
Intel Corporation Community Grants, 1311
Jane Bradley Pettit Foundation Community and Social Development Grants, 1347
Jessica Stevens Community Foundation Grants, 1363

John Gogian Family Foundation Grants, 1373
Johnson Scholarship Foundation Grants, 1382
Joseph Henry Edmondson Foundation Grants, 1388
Ketchikan Community Foundation Grants, 1429
Kodiak Community Foundation Grants, 1446
Leo Goodwin Foundation Grants, 1482
Mabel Louise Riley Foundation Grants, 1529
Marquette Bank Neighborhood Commit Grants, 1577
May and Stanley Smith Charitable Trust Grants, 1613
Meyer Foundation Education Grants, 1649
Middlesex Savings Charitable Foundation
    Educational Opportunities Grants, 1670
OMNOVA Solutions Fdn Education Grants, 1820
Oppenstein Brothers Foundation Grants, 1827
Oregon Community Fdn Community Grants, 1833
Pentair Foundation Education and Community
    Grants, 1934
Pettus Foundation Grants, 1952
PG&E Community Vitality Grants, 1957
Philip L. Graham Fund Education Grants, 1962
Polk County Community Foundation Marjorie M.
    and Lawrence R. Bradley Endowment Fund
    Grants, 1998
Reinberger Foundation Grants, 2066
Robbins-de Beaumont Foundation Grants, 2080
Robert R. Meyer Foundation Grants, 2094
Samuel S. Johnson Foundation Grants, 2146
Sand Hill Foundation Environment and Sustainability
    Grants, 2152
Sand Hill Foundation Health and Opportunity
    Grants, 2153
Serco Foundation Grants, 2181
Seward Community Foundation Grants, 2182
Seward Community Foundation Mini-Grants, 2183
Shield-Ayres Foundation Grants, 2189
SME Education Fdn Youth Program Grants, 2209
Southern California Edison Education Grants, 2218
Textron Corporate Contributions Grants, 2286
Thomas Sill Foundation Grants, 2292
Union Bank, N.A. Foundation Grants, 2334
Walker Area Community Foundation Grants, 2401
Walter J. and Betty C. Zable Fdn Grants, 2406
Wiregrass Foundation Grants, 2480
Women's Fund of Hawaii Grants, 2484
Woods Charitable Fund Education Grants, 2488
Wyomissing Foundation Thun Family Organizational
    Grants, 2505
Wyomissing Foundation Thun Family Program
    Grants, 2506
Xerox Foundation Grants, 2507Carl R. Hendrickson
    Family Foundation Grants, 509
Cass County Community Foundation Grants, 516
CFGR SisterFund Grants, 554
Charles Nelson Robinson Fund Grants, 569
Chicago Board of Trade Foundation Grants, 580
Chilkat Valley Community Foundation Grants, 588
CIGNA Foundation Grants, 611
Claremont Savings Bank Foundation Grants, 623
Clinton County Community Foundation Grants, 638
CNCS AmeriCorps State and National Grants, 643
CNCS AmeriCorps VISTA Project Grants, 645
Community Foundation for the Capital Region
    Grants, 687
Community Foundation of Bartholomew County
    Heritage Fund Grants, 690
Community Foundation of Boone County Grants, 694
Community Foundation of Crawford County, 695
Community Foundation of Eastern Connecticut
    General Southeast Grants, 696
Community Foundation of Greater Fort Wayne -
    Community Endowment and Clarke Endowment
    Grants, 705
Community Foundation of Louisville Education
    Grants, 724
Community Foundation of Western Massachusetts
    Grants, 741
David and Barbara B. Hirschhorn Foundation
    Education and Literacy Grants, 786
Dayton Power and Light Foundation Grants, 802
Dean Foods Community Involvement Grants, 805

DeKalb County Community Foundation - Literacy
    Grant, 814
Del Mar Foundation Community Grants, 820
Dollar General Family Literacy Grants, 835
DOL Youthbuild Grants, 838
Eastern Bank Charitable Foundation Partnerships
    Grants, 881
Eastern Bank Charitable Foundation Targeted
    Grants, 882
Edward and Ellen Roche Relief Fdn Grants, 887
Edward F. Swinney Trust Grants, 890
Edward W. and Stella C. Van Houten Memorial Fund
    Grants, 892
Eide Bailly Resourcefullness Awards, 897
Elizabeth Morse Genius Charitable Trust Grants, 901
El Pomar Foundation Anna Keesling Ackerman Fund
    Grants, 907
El Pomar Foundation Grants, 908
Eulalie Bloedel Schneider Foundation Grants, 936
F.R. Bigelow Foundation Grants, 947
Fidelity Charitable Gift Fund Grants, 956
First Hawaiian Bank Foundation Corporate Giving
    Grants, 967
First Lady's Family Literacy Initiative for Texas
    Family Literacy Trailblazer Grants, 968
First Lady's Family Literacy Initiative for Texas
    Implementation Grants, 969
First Lady's Family Literacy Initiative for Texas
    Planning Grants, 970
Foundation Beyond Belief Compassionate Impact
    Grants, 986
Foundation Beyond Belief Humanist Grants, 987
Foundation for Rural Service Education Grants, 991
Four County Community Foundation General
    Grants, 1000
Frank Reed and Margaret Jane Peters Memorial Fund
    II Grants, 1014
G.N. Wilcox Trust Grants, 1031
Gannett Foundation Community Action Grants, 1033
George W. Wells Foundation Grants, 1057
Greater Sitka Legacy Fund Grants, 1111
Greygates Foundation Grants, 1120
H.B. Fuller Foundation Grants, 1138
HAF Community Grants, 1141
Hannaford Supermarkets Community Giving, 1164
Harden Foundation Grants, 1166
Harold Brooks Foundation Grants, 1172
Harris and Eliza Kempner Fund Ed Grants, 1176
Hawaii Electric Industries Charitable Foundation
    Grants, 1218
Hawaii State Legislature Grant-In-Aid, 1219
HBF Pathways Out of Poverty Grants, 1222
Helen Gertrude Sparks Charitable Trust Grants, 1230
HLTA Visitor Industry Charity Walk Grant, 1254
Iddings Foundation Medium Project Grants, 1285
Island Insurance Foundation Grants, 1316
J.W. Gardner II Foundation Grants, 1323
J. Watumull Fund Grants, 1326
James Ford Bell Foundation Grants, 1339
James S. Copley Foundation Grants, 1345
Jessica Stevens Community Foundation Grants, 1363
John H. and Wilhelmina D. Harland Charitable
    Foundation Children and Youth Grants, 1374
Joseph H. and Florence A. Roblee Foundation
    Education Grants, 1386
Joseph Henry Edmondson Foundation Grants, 1388
Joseph S. Stackpole Charitable Trust Grants, 1390
Ketchikan Community Foundation Grants, 1429
Kodiak Community Foundation Grants, 1446
Leo Niessen Jr., Charitable Trust Grants, 1484
Liberty Bank Foundation Grants, 1488
Lubrizol Foundation Grants, 1513
Luella Kemper Trust Grants, 1517
M.A. Rikard Charitable Trust Grants, 1521
Mabel Louise Riley Foundation Family Strengthening
    Small Grants, 1528
Mardag Foundation Grants, 1554
Margaret M. Walker Charitable Fdn Grants, 1556
Marin Community Foundation Social Justice and
    Interfaith Understanding Grants, 1567

Marquette Bank Neighborhood Commit Grants, 1577
Mary Wilmer Covey Charitable Trust Grants, 1600
May and Stanley Smith Charitable Trust Grants, 1613
McCune Charitable Foundation Grants, 1617
McCune Foundation Education Grants, 1618
Middlesex Savings Charitable Foundation
    Educational Opportunities Grants, 1670
Norcliffe Foundation Grants, 1766
Oak Fdn Housing and Homelessness Grants, 1800
OMNOVA Solutions Fdn Education Grants, 1820
Oppenstein Brothers Foundation Grants, 1827
Oregon Community Fdn Community Grants, 1833
Parkersburg Area Community Foundation Action
    Grants, 1871
PepsiCo Foundation Grants, 1935
Pettus Foundation Grants, 1952
Peyton Anderson Foundation Grants, 1954
Philip L. Graham Fund Education Grants, 1962
Piper Jaffray Foundation Communities Giving
    Grants, 1974
PMI Foundation Grants, 1982
Polk County Community Foundation Marjorie M.
    and Lawrence R. Bradley Endowment Fund
    Grants, 1998
Polk County Community Foundation Unrestricted
    Grants, 2001
Portland General Electric Foundation Grants, 2007
ProLiteracy National Book Fund Grants, 2026
Putnam County Community Fdn Grants, 2040
RCF Individual Assistance Grants, 2063
Reinberger Foundation Grants, 2066
Robbins-de Beaumont Foundation Grants, 2080
Robert and Betty Wo Foundation Grants, 2083
Robert R. McCormick Tribune Foundation
    Community Grants, 2093
Robert R. Meyer Foundation Grants, 2094
Rose Community Foundation Child and Family
    Development Grants, 2103
Rose Hills Foundation Grants, 2106
Saltchuk Corporate Giving, 2141
Sand Hill Foundation Health and Opportunity
    Grants, 2153
Serco Foundation Grants, 2181
Seward Community Foundation Grants, 2182
Seward Community Foundation Mini-Grants, 2183
Shield-Ayres Foundation Grants, 2189
Sony Corporation of America Grants, 2216
Sorenson Legacy Foundation Grants, 2217
Southern California Edison Education Grants, 2218
Sylvia Perkin Perpetual Charitable Trust Grants, 2263
Thomas Sill Foundation Grants, 2292
TJX Foundation Grants, 2303
UPS Foundation Economic and Global Literacy
    Grants, 2351
UUA Actions of Public Witness Grants, 2365
UUA Congregation-Based Community Organizing
    Grants, 2366
UUA Fund Grants, 2367
UUA International Fund Grants, 2368
UUA Just Society Fund Grants, 2369
UUA Social Responsibility Grants, 2370
Vanderburgh Community Foundation Men's Fund
    Grants, 2373
Vanderburgh County Community Foundation
    Women's Fund Grants, 2376
Walker Area Community Foundation Grants, 2401
Walter J. and Betty C. Zable Fdn Grants, 2406
Warrick County Community Foundation Women's
    Fund, 2411
Wayne County Foundation Grants, 2419
WHO Foundation General Grants, 2443
WHO Foundation Volunteer Service Grants, 2444
WinnCompanies Charitable Giving, 2479
Women's Fund of Hawaii Grants, 2484
Woods Charitable Fund Education Grants, 2488
Xerox Foundation Grants, 2507

GEOGRAPHIC INDEX

Note: This index lists grants for which applicants must be residents of or located in a specific geographic area. Numbers refer to entry numbers.

United States

All States

1st Touch Foundation Grants, 2
3 Dog Garage Museum Tours, 4
4imprint One by One Charitable Giving, 7
7-Eleven Corporate Giving Grants, 8
786 Foundation Grants, 15
A-T Children's Project Grants, 16
A-T Children's Project Post Doctoral Fellowships, 17
A.L. Mailman Family Foundation Grants, 20
AAAS/Subaru SB&F Prize for Excl in Sci Books, 22
AACAP Educational Outreach Program for Child and Adolescent Psychiatry Residents, 23
AACAP Educational Outreach Program for General Psychiatry Residents, 24
AACAP George Tarjan Award for Contributions in Developmental Disabilities, 25
AACAP Irving Philips Award for Prevention, 26
AACAP Jeanne Spurlock Lecture and Award on Diversity and Culture, 27
AACAP Jeanne Spurlock Research Fellowship in Substance Abuse and Addiction for Minority Medical Students, 28
AACAP Junior Investigator Awards, 29
AACAP Life Members Mentorship Grants for Medical Students, 30
AACAP Mary Crosby Congressional Fellowships, 31
AACAP Pilot Rsrch Awd for Att-Deficit Disorder, 32
AACAP Rieger Psychodyn Psychotherapy Award, 33
AACAP Rieger Service Program Award for Excellence, 34
AACAP Robert Cancro Academic Leadership Award, 35
AACAP Sidney Berman Award for the School-Based Study and Intervention for Learning Disorders and Mental Ilness, 36
AACAP Simon Wile Leadership in Consultation Award, 37
AACAP Summer Medical Student Fellowships, 38
AACAP Systems of Care Special Program Scholarships, 39
AASA Urgent Need Mini-Grants, 43
Abundance Foundation International Grants, 57
ACF Abandoned Infants Assistance Grants, 70
ACF Adoption Opportunities Grants, 71
ACF American Indian and Alaska Native Early Head Start Expansion Grants, 72
ACF Basic Center Program Grants, 73
ACF Child Abuse Prevention and Treatment Act Discretionary Funds Grants, 74
ACF Child Welfare Training Grants, 75
ACF Community-Based Child Abuse Prevention (CBCAP) Grants, 76
ACF Community-Based Child Abuse Prevention (CBCAP) Tribal and Migrant Discretionary Grants, 77
ACF Early Care and Education Research Scholars: Child Care Research Scholars, 78
ACF Early Care and Education Research Scholars: Head Start Graduate Student Research Grants, 79
ACF Ethnic Community Self Help Grants, 80
ACF Family Strengthening Scholars Grants, 81
ACF Infant Adoption Awareness Training Program Grants, 84
ACF Marriage Strengthening Research & Dissemination Center Grants, 85
ACF National Human Trafficking Hotline Grants, 86
ACF Native American Social and Economic Development Strategies for Alaska Grants, 87
ACF Native Youth Initiative for Leadership, Empowerment, and Development Grants, 88
ACF Promoting Safe and Stable Families (PSSF) Program Grants, 89
ACF Refugee Career Pathways Grants, 90
ACF Refugee Health Promotion Grants, 91
ACF Runaway and Homeless Youth Training and Technical Assistance Center Grants, 92

ACF Social and Economic Development Strategies Grants, 93
ACF Street Outreach Program Grants, 94
ACF Sustainable Employment and Economic Development Strategies Grants, 95
ACF Transitional Living Program and Maternity Group Homes Grants, 96
ACF Tribal Maternal, Infant, and Early Childhood Home Visiting Program: Development and Implementation Grants, 97
ACF Tribal Maternal, Infant, and Early Childhood Home Visiting Program: Implementation and Expansion Grants, 98
ACF Unaccompanied Refugee Children Grants, 99
ACF Voluntary Agencies Matching Grants, 100
ACL Alternatives to Guardianship Youth Resource Center Grants, 104
ACL Disability and Rehabilitation Research Projects (DRRP) Program: Independent Living Transition Services for Youth and Young Adults Grants, 105
ACL Neonatal Abstinence Syndrome National Training Initiative Grant, 106
ACL Rehabilitation Research and Training Center (RRTC) on Employment of Transition-Age Youth with Disabilities Grants, 107
ACMP Foundation Community Music Grants, 108
Active Living Research Grants, 109
ADA Foundation Samuel Harris Children's Dental Health Grants, 111
Adidas Corporation General Grants, 125
Adobe Foundation Action Grants, 126
Adolph Coors Foundation Grants, 129
Advance Auto Parts Corporate Giving Grants, 131
Air Products Foundation Grants, 148
AKF Grants for Children, 149
ALA Alex Awards, 153
ALA ALSC Distinguished Service Award, 154
ALA Amazing Audiobks for Young Adults Awd, 155
ALA Amelia Bloomer Book List Award, 156
ALA Baker and Taylor/YALSA Collection Development Grants, 157
ALA Baker and Taylor Summer Reading Program Grant, 158
ALA Best Fiction for Young Adults Award, 160
ALA Bookapalooza Grants, 161
ALA Booklist Editors' Choice Books for Youth Awards, 162
ALA Bound to Stay Bound Books Scholarships, 163
ALA BWI Collection Development Grant, 164
ALA Children's Literature Legacy Award, 165
ALA Coretta Scott King-John Steptoe Award for New Talent, 166
ALA Coretta Scott King-Virginia Hamilton Award for Lifetime Achievement, 167
ALA Coretta Scott King Book Donation Grant, 168
ALA Fabulous Films for Young Adults Award, 169
ALA Great Books Giveaway Competition, 170
ALA Innovative Reading Grant, 171
ALA John Newbery Medal, 172
ALA Louise Seaman Bechtel Fellowship, 173
ALA MAE Award for Best Literature Program for Teens, 174
ALA Margaret A. Edwards Award, 175
ALA May Hill Arbuthnot Honor Lecture Award, 176
ALA Michael L. Printz Award, 177
ALA Mildred L. Batchelder Award, 178
ALA Notable Children's Books Awards, 179
ALA Notable Children's Recordings Awards, 180
ALA Notable Children's Videos Awards, 181
ALA Odyssey Award for Excellence in Audiobook Production, 182
ALA Penguin Random House Young Readers Group Award, 183
ALA Popular Paperbacks for Young Adults Awds, 184
ALA PRIME TIME Family Reading Time Grts, 185
ALA Quick Picks for Reluctant Young Adult Readers Award, 186
ALA Rainbow Project Book List Award, 187

ALA Randolph Caldecott Medal, 188
ALA Robert F. Sibert Informational Book Medal Award, 189
ALA Sara Jaffarian School Library Award for Exemplary Humanities Programming, 190
ALA Schneider Family Book Awards, 191
ALA Scholastic Library Publishing Award, 192
ALA Sullivan Award for Public Library Admintrs Supporting Services to Children, 213
ALA Teen's Top Ten Awards, 214
ALA Theodor Seuss Geisel Award, 215
Alavi Foundation Education Grants, 216
ALA William C. Morris Debut YA Award, 217
ALA YALSA Presidential Citation Award, 218
Albert W. Cherne Foundation Grants, 222
Alcatel-Lucent Technologies Foundation Grants, 224
Alexander Graham Bell Parent and Infant Financial Aid Grants, 227
Alexander Graham Bell Preschool-Age Financial Aid Grants, 228
ALFJ Astraea U.S. and International Emergency Fund, 230
ALFJ International Fund Grants, 231
ALFJ International Social Change Opportunity Fund Grants, 232
A Little Hope Grants, 235
Allegis Group Foundation Grants, 237
Allen Foundation Educational Nutrition Grants, 238
Alliance for Strong Families and Communities Grants, 239
Allstate Corporate Giving Grants, 242
Allstate Foundation Safe and Vital Communities Grants, 244
Allstate Foundation Tolerance, Inclusion, and Diversity Grants, 245
Altria Group Positive Youth Dev Grants, 247
American Honda Foundation Grants, 255
American Indian Youth Running Strong Grants, 256
American Psychiatric Fdn Call for Proposals, 257
American Psychiatric Foundation Typical or Troubled School Mental Health Education Grants, 258
AMERIND Community Service Project Grants, 265
Amway Corporation Contributions, 269
Anne J. Caudal Foundation Grants, 276
Ann Ludington Sullivan Foundation Grants, 279
AOCS Thomas H. Smouse Memorial Fellowship, 282
APAP All-In Grants, 283
Arthur Ashley Williams Foundation Grants, 302
Arthur M. Blank Family Foundation Atlanta United Foundation Grants, 308
Arthur M. Blank Family Foundation Molly Blank Fund Grants, 310
ASCAP Foundation Grants, 315
AT&T Fdn Community Support and Safety, 320
AT&T Foundation Education Grants, 321
AT&T Foundation Health and Human Services Grants, 322
Autism Speaks Norma and Malcolm Baker Recreation Grants, 335
Avery Dennison Foundation Education Grants, 337
Bank of America Charitable Foundation Basic Needs Grants, 354
Bank of America Charitable Foundation Community Development Grants, 355
Bank of America Charitable Foundation Matching Gifts, 356
Bank of America Charitable Foundation Student Leaders Grants, 357
Bank of America Charitable Foundation Volunteer Grants, 358
Bank of America Corporation Sponsorships, 359
Batters Up USA Equipment Grants, 366
Baxter International Corporate Giving Grants, 368
Baxter International Foundation Grants, 369
BBF National Grants for Family Literacy, 391
Beacon Society Jan Stauber Grants, 393
Beckman Coulter Foundation Grants, 394
Bee Conservancy Sponsor-A-Hive Grants, 395

Ben Cohen StandUp Foundation Grants, 403
Bernard and Audre Rapoport Foundation Arts and
Culture Grants, 407
Bernard and Audre Rapoport Foundation Community
Building and Social Service Grants, 408
Bernard and Audre Rapoport Foundation Democracy
and Civic Participation Grants, 409
Bernard and Audre Rapoport Foundation Education
Grants, 410
Bernard and Audre Rapoport Foundation Health
Grants, 411
Best Buy Children's Foundation @15 Community
Grants , 414
Best Buy Children's Fdn @15 Scholarship , 415
Best Buy Children's Fdn @15 Teach Awards, 416
Best Buy Children's Foundation National Grants, 417
Bikes Belong Foundation Paul David Clark Bicycling
Safety Grants, 422
Bikes Belong Foundation REI Grants, 423
Bikes Belong Grants, 424
Bill and Melinda Gates Foundation Water, Sanitation
and Hygiene Grants, 428
Biogen Foundation General Donations, 432
Blanche and Irving Laurie Foundation Grants, 436
Blockbuster Corporate Contributions, 440
BMW of North America Charitable Contribs, 460
Bollinger Foundation Grants, 463
BP Foundation Grants, 465
Bridgestone Americas Trust Fund Grants, 469
Brinker Int Corporation Charitable Giving, 471
Bristol-Myers Squibb Foundation Independent
Medical Education Grants, 472
Brookdale Fdn Relatives as Parents Grants, 474
Bryan Adams Foundation Grants, 480
Cal Ripken Sr. Foundation Grants, 497
Campbell Foundation Grants, 500
Caplow Applied Sci (CappSci) Children's Prize, 502
Cargill Corporate Giving Grants, 503
Carnegie Corporation of New York Grants, 511
Case Foundation Grants, 514
Cause Populi Worthy Cause Grants, 521
CCFF Christopher Columbus Awards, 522
CCFF Community Grant, 523
CDC David J. Sencer Museum Student Field Trip
Experience, 524
CDC Disease Detective Camp, 525
CEC Clarissa Hug Teacher of the Year Award, 527
CEC J.E. Wallace Wallin Special Education Lifetime
Achievement Award, 528
CEC Yes I Can! Awards, 529
CFF First- and Second-Year Clinical Fellowships, 532
CFF Leroy Matthews Physician-Scientist Awds, 533
CFF Research Grants, 534
CFF Third-, Fourth-, and Fifth-Year Clinical
Fellowships, 535
CFKF Instrument Matching Grants, 556
Changemakers Innovation Awards, 559
Charles Lafitte Foundation Grants, 567
Chassé Youth Leaders Fund Grants, 573
Chick and Sophie Major Memorial Duck Calling
Contest Scholarships, 583
Children's Brain Tumor Fdn Research Grants, 584
Children's Tumor Foundation Young Investigator
Awards, 587
ChLA Article Award, 589
ChLA Book Award, 590
ChLA Carol Gay Award, 591
ChLA Edited Book Award, 592
ChLA Faculty Research Grants, 593
ChLA Graduate Student Essay Awards, 594
ChLA Hannah Beiter Diversity Research Grants, 595
ChLA Hannah Beiter Graduate Student Research
Grants, 596
ChLA Mentoring Award, 597
ChLA Phoenix Award, 598
ChLA Phoenix Picture Book Award, 599
Christensen Fund Regional Grants, 600
Cigna Civic Affairs Sponsorships, 610
CIGNA Foundation Grants, 611
Cisco Systems Fdn San Jose Community Grants, 615

CJ Fdn for SIDS Program Services Grants, 619
Clara Abbott Foundation Need-Based Grants, 620
Cleveland H. Dodge Foundation Grants, 637
CMS Historically Black Colleges and Universities
(HBCU) Health Services Research Grants, 639
CMS Research and Demonstration Grants, 640
CNCS AmeriCorps Indian Tribes Plang Grts , 641
CNCS AmeriCorps NCCC Project Grants, 642
CNCS AmeriCorps State and National Grants, 643
CNCS AmeriCorps State and National Planning
Grants, 644
CNCS AmeriCorps VISTA Project Grants, 645
CNCS Foster Grandparent Projects Grants, 646
CNCS School Turnaround AmeriCorps Grants, 647
CNCS Senior Corps Retired and Senior Volunteer
Program Grants, 648
CNCS Social Innovation Grants, 649
CNO Financial Group Community Grants, 650
Colgate-Palmolive Company Grants, 652
Colin Higgins Foundation Courage Awards, 653
Collective Brands Foundation Grants, 654
Collective Brands Foundation Payless Gives Shoes 4
Kids Grants, 655
Collective Brands Foundation Saucony Run for Good
Grants, 656
Community Foundation of Western Massachusetts
Grants, 741
Cooper Tire and Rubber Foundation Grants, 749
Cornell Lab of Ornithology Mini-Grants, 751
Covidien Partnership for Neighborhood Wellness
Grants, 759
Crane Foundation General Grants, 761
Crane Fund for Widows and Children Grants, 762
Crane Fund Grants, 763
Crayola Champ Creatively Alive Children Grts, 764
Credit Suisse Foundation Education Grants, 765
Cystic Fibrosis Lifestyle Foundation Individual
Recreation Grants, 772
Cystic Fibrosis Lifestyle Foundation Loretta Morris
Memorial Fund Grants, 773
Cystic Fibrosis Lifestyle Foundation Mentored
Recreation Grants, 774
Cystic Fibrosis Lifestyle Foundation Peer Support
Grants, 775
David and Laura Merage Foundation Grants, 789
Dean Foods Community Involvement Grants, 805
Dell Scholars Program Scholarships, 819
Delta Air Lines Foundation Community Enrichment
Grants, 823
Delta Air Lines Foundation Youth Development
Grants, 824
Dept of Ed Fund for the Improvement of Education--
Partnerships in Character Ed Pilot Projects, 825
Dexter Adams Foundation Grants, 829
Different Needz Foundation Grants, 830
Dining for Women Grants, 831
DOL Youthbuild Grants, 838
Doree Taylor Charitable Foundation Grants, 843
Dorothea Haus Ross Foundation Grants, 844
Do Something Awards, 847
Do Something Back End Developer Intern, 848
Do Something Business Development Intern, 849
Do Something Campaigns Intern, 850
Do Something Digital Content Intern, 851
Do Something Digital Member Exp Intern, 852
Do Something Finance and Human Res Intern, 853
Do Something International Intern, 854
Do Something Intern of Fun, 855
Do Something Partnerships and Public Relations
Intern, 856
Do Something Scholarships, 857
Do Something TMI Intern, 858
Do Something User Experience Research Intern, 859
Do Something Web Developer Intern, 860
Do Something Writing and Journalism Intern, 861
Draper Richards Kaplan Foundation Grants, 864
E. Clayton and Edith P. Gengras, Jr. Foundation
Grants, 875
Earth Island Institute Brower Youth Awards, 879
Easton Foundations Archery Facility Grants, 883

Easton Sports Development Foundation National
Archery in the Schools Grants, 884
Echoing Green Fellowships, 885
Edna Wardlaw Charitable Trust Grants, 886
Eileen Fisher Activating Leadership Grants for
Women and Girls, 898
Elmer Roe Deaver Foundation Grants, 906
Elton John AIDS Foundation Grants, 910
Emily Hall Tremaine Foundation Learning
Disabilities Grants, 912
Emily O'Neill Sullivan Foundation Grants, 913
Environmental Excellence Awards, 922
EPA Children's Health Protection Grants, 923
Epilepsy Foundation SUDEP Challenge Initiative
Prizes, 924
Evan Frankel Foundation Grants, 938
Evelyn and Walter Haas, Jr. Fund Gay and Lesbian
Rights Grants, 940
Ewing Marion Kauffman Foundation Grants, 943
Ezra Jack Keats Foundation Mini-Grants, 944
Farmers Insurance Corporate Giving Grants, 948
FCD New American Children Grants, 952
FCD Young Scholars Program Grants, 953
FCYO Youth Organizing Grants, 954
Fidelity Charitable Gift Fund Grants, 956
Fidelity Foundation Grants, 957
Finish Line Youth Foundation Founder's Grants, 960
Finish Line Youth Foundation Grants, 961
Finish Line Youth Foundation Legacy Grants, 962
FINRA Smart Investing@Your Library Grants, 963
First Nations Development Institute Native
Agriculture and Food Systems Initiative
Scholarships, 971
First Nations Development Institute Native Arts
Initiative Grants, 972
First Nations Development Institute Native Language
Immersion Initiative Grants, 973
First Nations Development Institute Native Youth
and Culture Fund Grants, 974
First Nations Development Institute Nourishing
Native Children: Feeding Our Future Project
Grants, 975
Ford Foundation BUILD Grants, 984
Foundation Beyond Belief Compassionate Impact
Grants, 986
Foundation Beyond Belief Humanist Grants, 987
Foundation for Rural Service Education Grants, 991
From the Top Alumni Leadership Grants, 1025
From the Top Jack Kent Cooke Young Artist
Scholarships, 1026
General Motors Foundation Grants, 1039
General Service Foundation Human Rights and
Economic Justice Grants, 1040
George Graham and Elizabeth Galloway Smith
Foundation Grants, 1047
Gerber Foundation Environmental Hazards Research
Grants, 1062
Gerber Fdn Pediatric Health Research Grants, 1063
Gerber Foundation Pediatric Nutrition Research
Grants, 1064
Giving Gardens Challenge Grants, 1072
Gloria Barron Prize for Young Heroes, 1074
GMFUS Balkan Trust for Democracy Grants, 1075
GNOF Coastal 5 + 1 Grants, 1078
GNOF Gert Community Fund Grants, 1082
GNOF IMPACT Grants for Arts and Culture, 1083
GNOF IMPACT Grants for Youth Dev, 1084
GNOF IMPACT Gulf States Eye Surg Fund, 1085
GNOF IMPACT Harold W. Newman, Jr. Charitable
Trust Grants, 1086
GNOF IMPACT Kahn-Oppenheim Tr Grts, 1087
GNOF New Orleans Works Grants, 1088
Good+Foundation Grants, 1096
Graham Family Charitable Foundation Grants, 1099
Great Clips Corporate Giving, 1108
Green Foundation Human Services Grants, 1116
Greygates Foundation Grants, 1120
GTECH After School Advantage Grants, 1125
Hank Aaron Chasing the Dream Fdn Grants, 1162
Harold and Rebecca H. Gross Fdn Grants, 1171

Harry and Jeanette Weinberg Fdn Grants, 1182
Harry Frank Guggenheim Foundation Research Grants, 1184
Hearst Foundations Culture Grants, 1223
Hearst Foundations Social Service Grants, 1224
Hearst Foundations United States Senate Youth Grants, 1225
Helen Bader Foundation Grants, 1227
Helen V. Brach Foundation Grants, 1232
Help America Foundation Grants, 1233
Henry and Ruth Blaustein Rosenberg Foundation Education Grants, 1236
Henry E. Niles Foundation Grants, 1240
Herbert Hoover Presidential Library Association Bus Travel Grants, 1244
Honeywell Corporation Family Safety and Security Grants, 1255
Honeywell Corporation Got 2B Safe Contest, 1256
Honeywell Corp Humanitarian Relief Grants, 1257
Honeywell Corporation Leadership Challenge Academy, 1258
Honor the Earth Grants, 1259
HRSA Ryan White HIV AIDS Drug Assistance Grants, 1265
HSBC Corporate Giving Grants, 1266
Hubbard Broadcasting Foundation Grants, 1269
Huisking Foundation Grants, 1274
Hungry for Music Instrument Gifts, 1277
IIE 911 Armed Forces Scholarships, 1288
ILA Arbuthnot Award, 1290
ILA Children's and Young Adults' Book Awds, 1291
ILA Grants for Literacy Projects in Countries with Developing Economies, 1292
IMLS Grants to State Library Administrative Agencies, 1298
IMLS National Leadership Grants for Libraries, 1299
ING Foundation Grants, 1302
IRC Community Collaboratives for Refugee Women and Youth Grants, 1313
Island Insurance Foundation Grants, 1316
J.W. Kieckhefer Foundation Grants, 1324
Jack Kent Cooke Foundation Summer Enrichment Grants, 1332
Jack Kent Cooke Fdn Young Artist Awards, 1333
James Lee Sorenson Family Impact Foundation Grants, 1342
Jane's Trust Grants, 1346
Japan Foundation Los Angeles Contests Designed for Japanese-Language Learners Grants, 1351
Japan Foundation Los Angeles Grants for Japanese-Language Courses, 1352
Japan Foundation Los Angeles Japanese-Language Teaching Materials Purchase Grants, 1353
Japan Foundation Los Angeles Mini-Grants for Japanese Arts & Culture, 1354
Japan Foundation New York Small Grants for Arts and Culture, 1355
Japan Foundation New York World Heritage Photo Panel Exhibition, 1356
Jaquelin Hume Foundation Grants, 1357
Jayne and Leonard Abess Foundation Grants, 1358
John F. Kennedy Center for the Performing Arts National Rosemary Kennedy Internship, 1371
Johnson Controls Foundation Arts and Culture Grants, 1378
Johnson Foundation Wingspread Conference Support Program, 1381
Johnson Scholarship Foundation Grants, 1382
Joseph H. and Florence A. Roblee Foundation Family Grants, 1387
Judy and Peter Blum Kovler Foundation Grants, 1396
KaBOOM! Adventure Courses Grant, 1401
KaBOOM! Creative Play Grant, 1403
KaBOOM! Multi-Sport Courts Grant, 1404
K and F Baxter Family Foundation Grants, 1413
Katie's Krops Grants, 1421
Kenai Peninsula Foundation Grants, 1425
Kettering Family Foundation Grants, 1430
KIND Causes Monthly Grants, 1435
Kindle Project SpiderWeave Flow Fund Grants, 1437

Kirby Laing Foundation Grants, 1439
Klingenstein-Simons Fellowship Awards in the Neurosciences, 1441
Koch Family Foundation (Annapolis) Grants, 1444
Kodak Community Relations Grants, 1445
Kohl's Cares Scholarships, 1447
Koret Foundation Grants, 1449
Kovler Family Foundation Grants, 1454
Kroger Company Donations, 1456
Lalor Foundation Postdoctoral Fellowships, 1464
Laura Bush Foundation for America's Libraries Grants, 1471
Lee and Ramona Bass Foundation Grants, 1478
LEGO Children's Fund Grants, 1480
Lemelson-MIT InvenTeam Grants, 1481
Lisa and Douglas Goldman Fund Grants, 1496
LISC Affordable Housing Grants, 1497
LISC Capacity Building Grants, 1498
LISC Community Leadership Operating Grts, 1499
LISC Education Grants, 1500
Lotus 88 Fdn for Women and Children Grants, 1508
Louis and Sandra Berkman Foundation Grants, 1510
Louis Calder Foundation Grants, 1511
Ludwick Family Foundation Grants, 1516
Lumpkin Family Fdn Healthy People Grants, 1518
M. Bastian Family Foundation Grants, 1522
MacLellan Foundation Grants, 1531
Macquarie Bank Foundation Grants, 1532
Maggie Welby Foundation Grants, 1538
Maggie Welby Foundation Scholarships, 1539
Make Sense Foundation Grants, 1548
Malone Family Foundation Atypical Development Initiative Grants, 1549
March of Dimes Program Grants, 1552
Marion Gardner Jackson Charitable Trust Grts, 1570
Mark Wahlberg Youth Foundation Grants, 1576
Marriott Int Corporate Giving Grants, 1578
Martin Family Foundation Grants, 1583
Mary Kay Foundation Domestic Violence Shelter Grants, 1591
Maurice Amado Foundation Grants, 1609
Max and Anna Levinson Foundation Grants, 1612
May and Stanley Smith Charitable Trust Grants, 1613
McCune Foundation Education Grants, 1618
McCune Foundation Humananities Grants, 1619
McGraw-Hill Companies Community Grants, 1620
Merck Family Fund Youth Transforming Urban Communities Grants, 1636
MetLife Fdn Preparing Young People Grants, 1645
Meyer Fdn Healthy Communities Grants, 1650
MGN Family Foundation Grants, 1656
Michelle O'Neill Foundation Grants, 1661
Microsoft Software Donations, 1665
Microsoft YouthSpark Grants, 1666
Mile High United Way Stratc Investment Grts, 1671
Milken Family Foundation Grants, 1672
MLB Tomorrow Fund Grants, 1679
Mockingbird Foundation Grants, 1680
Monsanto United States Grants, 1684
Morgan Adams Foundation Research Grants, 1694
Mr. Holland's Opus Foundation Melody Grants, 1703
Mr. Holland's Opus Foundation Michael Kamen Solo Award, 1704
Mr. Holland's Opus Foundation Special Projects Grants, 1705
Ms. Foundn for Women Building Democracy Grants, 1706
Ms. Fdn for Women Economic Justice Grants, 1707
Ms. Fdn for Women Ending Violence Grants, 1708
NAA Foundation High Five Grants, 1711
NASE Fdn Future Entrepreneur Scholarship, 1713
Nash Avery Foundation Grants, 1714
Nathan Cummings Foundation Grants, 1718
National 4-H Council Grants, 1720
National 4-H Youth in Action Awards, 1721
National Cowboy and Western Heritage Museum Awards, 1722
National Schools of Character Awards Program, 1723
National Wildlife Federation Craig Tufts Educational Scholarship, 1724

National YoungArts Foundation Awards, 1725
NCSS Award for Global Understanding, 1728
NCSS Carter G. Woodson Book Awards, 1729
NCSS Christa McA Reach for the Stars Awd, 1730
NEA Fdn Read Across America Event Grants, 1731
NEA Foundation Read Across America Library Books Awards, 1732
NEA Student Program Communities Redefining Education Advocacy Through Empowerment (CREATE) Grants, 1733
NEH Family and Youth Programs in American History Grants, 1734
NEH Picturing America Awards, 1735
Nestle Very Best in Youth Competition, 1740
New Earth Foundation Grants, 1743
NFL Charities NFL Player Foundation Grants, 1754
Nicole Brown Foundation Grants, 1760
NIMH Early Identification and Treatment of Mental Disorders in Children and Adolescents Grts, 1761
Norman Foundation Grants, 1767
North Face Explore Fund, 1770
Northrop Grumman Corporation Grants, 1772
Northrop Grumman Foundation Grants, 1773
NRA Foundation Grants, 1774
NSF Perception, Action and Cognition (PAC) Research Grants, 1775
NSF Social Psychology Grants, 1776
NSTA Distinguished Informal Science Education Award, 1777
NSTA Faraday Science Communicator Award, 1778
Oak Foundation Child Abuse Grants, 1799
Oak Fdn Housing and Homelessness Grants, 1800
Office Depot Corporation Community Relations Grants, 1805
Office Depot Foundation Education Grants, 1806
Olive Higgins Prouty Foundation Grants, 1817
OSF Baltimore Community Fellowships, 1838
OSF Early Childhood Program Grants, 1841
OSF Soros Justice Youth Activist Fellowships, 1844
Oticon Focus on People Awards, 1847
P. Buckley Moss Foundation for Children's Education Endowed Scholarships, 1854
P. Buckley Moss Foundation for Children's Education Teacher Grants, 1855
Pacers Foundation Be Drug-Free Grants, 1856
Pacers Foundation Be Educated Grants, 1857
Pacers Foundation Be Healthy and Fit Grants, 1858
Pacers Foundation Be Tolerant Grants, 1859
Pacers Foundation Indiana Fever's Be YOUnique Fund Grants, 1860
Packard Foundation Children, Families, and Communities Grants, 1862
Palmer Foundation Grants, 1867
Parker Foundation (Virginia) Grants to Support Christian Evangelism, 1870
PAS Freddie Gruber Scholarship, 1872
PAS John E. Grimes Timpani Scholarship, 1873
PAS PASIC International Scholarships, 1875
PAS SABIAN/PASIC Scholarship, 1876
PAS Sabian Larrie London Memorial Schol, 1877
PAS Zildjian Family Opportunity Fund Grants, 1878
Patricia Kisker Foundation Grants, 1879
PDF Community Organizing Grants, 1920
PDF Fiscal Sponsorship Grant, 1921
Pediatric Brain Tumor Foundation Early Career Development Grants, 1923
Pediatric Brain Tumor Foundation Early Career Development Grants, 1924
Pediatric Brain Tumor Fdn Institute Grants, 1925
Pediatric Brain Tumor Foundation Opportunity Grants, 1926
Pediatric Cancer Research Foundation Grants, 1927
PEN America Phyllis Naylor Grant for Children's and Young Adult Novelists, 1928
PennPAT Presenter Travel Grants, 1932
PepsiCo Foundation Grants, 1935
Perkins Charitable Foundation Grants, 1939
Pettus Foundation Grants, 1952
Pinnacle Foundation Grants, 1973
PMI Foundation Grants, 1982

Poetry Fdn Young People's Poet Laureate, 1989
PPG Industries Foundation Grants, 2017
Presidio Fencing Club Youth Fencers Assistance
    Scholarships, 2019
ProLiteracy National Book Fund Grants, 2026
Proteus Fund Grants, 2027
Prudential Spirit of Community Awards, 2029
Public Welfare Fdn Juvenile Justice Grants, 2033
Public Welfare Foundation Special Initiative to
    Advance Civil Legal Aid Grants, 2034
Public Welfare Foundation Special Opportunities
    Grants, 2035
Quaker Oats Company Kids Care Clubs Grants, 2041
R.C. Baker Foundation Grants, 2043
Radcliffe Institute Carol K. Pforzheimer Student
    Fellowships, 2048
Radcliffe Institute Oral History Grants, 2049
Random Acts of Kindness Foundation Lesson Plan
    Contest, 2053
Raskob Fdn for Catholic Activities Grants, 2054
Ray Charles Foundation Grants, 2058
Ray Foundation Grants, 2059
Raytheon Middle School Grants and Schols, 2061
Ressler-Gertz Foundation Grants, 2067
RGk Foundation Grants, 2068
Richards Foundation Grants, 2072
Robbins-de Beaumont Foundation Grants, 2080
Robert Bowne Foundaion Edmund A. Stanley, Jr.
    Research Grants, 2086
Robert W. Knox, Sr. and Pearl Wallis Knox
    Charitable Foundation, 2095
Rockwell Collins Charitable Corp Grants, 2098
Roney-Fitzpatrick Foundation Grants, 2102
Rosenberg Charity Foundation Grants, 2107
Rosenberg Fund for Children Clinton and Muriel
    Jencks Memorial Fund Grants, 2109
Rosenberg Fund for Children Edith and George
    Ziefert Fund Grants, 2110
Rosenberg Fund for Children Grants, 2111
Rosenberg Fund for Children Herman Warsh Fund
    Grant, 2112
Rosenberg Fund for Children Moish and Lillian
    Antopol Memorial Fund Grants, 2113
Rosenberg Fund for Children Ozzy Klate Memorial
    Fund Grants, 2114
RR Donnelley Foundation Grants, 2118
RWJF Childhood Obesity Grants, 2126
RWJF Healthy Eating Research Grants, 2127
Samueli Foundation Education Grants, 2143
SanDisk Corp Community Sharing Grants, 2155
Scott B. & Annie P. Appleby Charitable Grants, 2169
Share Our Strength Grants, 2185
Shell Oil Company Foundation Community
    Development Grants, 2188
Sidgmore Family Foundation Grants, 2195
Sidney Stern Memorial Trust Grants, 2197
Singing for Change Foundation Grants, 2202
Skaggs Family Foundation Grants, 2205
Skaggs Family Foundation Grants, 2206
SME Education Fdn Youth Program Grants, 2209
Sony Corporation of America Grants, 2216
Sorenson Legacy Foundation Grants, 2217
Special Olympics Eunice Kennedy Shriver (EKS)
    Fellowships, 2227
Special Olympics Project UNIFY Grants, 2228
Special Olympics Youth Fan Grants, 2229
Sphinx Competition Awards, 2234
State Farm Good Neighbor Citizenship Company
    Grants, 2238
Steven B. Achelis Foundation Grants, 2244
Storm Castle Foundation Grants, 2248
Strake Foundation Grants, 2249
Stranahan Foundation Grants, 2250
Streisand Foundation Grants, 2251
SunTrust Bank Trusteed Foundations Nell Warren
    Elkin and William Simpson Elkin Grants, 2258
Susan A. and Donald P. Babson Charitable
    Foundation Grants, 2259
Target Corporation Community Engagement Fund
    Grants, 2270

Target Corporation Soccer Grants, 2271
Target Foundation Global Grants, 2272
Teaching Tolerance Diverse Democracy Grants, 2275
Teaching Tolerance Social Justice Educator Grts, 2276
Teagle Foundation Grants, 2277
Thorman Boyle Foundation Grants, 2295
Thrasher Research Fund Grants, 2296
Three Guineas Fund Grants, 2297
Threshold Fdn Justice and Democracy Grants, 2298
Threshold Foundation Queer Youth Grants, 2299
Tides Fdn Friends of the IGF Fund Grants, 2300
Tides Foundation Grants, 2302
TJX Foundation Grants, 2303
Toshiba America Foundation Grades 7-12 Science and
    Math Grants, 2307
Toshiba America Foundation K-6 Science and Math
    Grants, 2308
Toyota Motor Manuf of Mississippi Grants, 2312
Toyota Motor North America of NY Grants, 2315
Toyota USA Foundation Education Grants, 2318
Toyota USA Foundation Environmental Grants, 2319
Toyota USA Foundation Safety Grants, 2320
TSYSF Individual Scholarships, 2322
TSYSF Team Grants, 2323
Twenty-First Century Foundation Grants, 2328
U.S. Department of Education Promise
    Neighborhoods Grants, 2332
UnitedHealthcare Children's Fdn Grants, 2342
United Healthcare Commty Grts in Michigan, 2343
United Methodist Committee on Relief Hunger and
    Poverty Grants, 2344
United Methodist Women Brighter Future for
    Children and Youth Grants, 2346
United Technologies Corporation Grants, 2347
University of Chicago Chapin Hall Doris Duke
    Fellowships, 2348
UPS Corporate Giving Grants, 2349
UPS Foundation Community Safety Grants, 2350
UPS Foundation Economic and Global Literacy
    Grants, 2351
USAID Community Livelihoods Project in Yemen
    Grant, 2352
USAID Family Planning and Reproductive Health
    Methods Grants, 2353
USAID Global Development Alliance Grants, 2354
USAID Innovations in Feed the Future Monitoring
    and Evaluation Grants, 2355
USAID Integrated Youth Development Activity
    Grants, 2356
USAID National Governance Project in Yemen
    Grant, 2357
USAID Nigeria Ed Crisis Response Grants, 2358
USAID Office of Foreign Disaster Assistance and
    Food for Peace Grants, 2359
USAID School Improvement Program Grants, 2360
USAID U.S.-Egypt Learning Grants, 2361
USDA Child and Adult Care Food Program, 2362
USDA WIC Nutrition Ed Innovations Grants, 2363
USDEd Gaining Early Awareness and Readiness for
    Undergrad Programs (GEAR UP) Grants, 2364
UUA Actions of Public Witness Grants, 2365
UUA Congregation-Based Community Organizing
    Grants, 2366
UUA Fund Grants, 2367
UUA International Fund Grants, 2368
UUA Just Society Fund Grants, 2369
UUA Social Responsibility Grants, 2370
Van Kampen Boyer Molinari Charitable Foundation
    Grants, 2377
Vernon K. Krieble Foundation Grants, 2379
Virginia Foundation for the Humanities Open
    Grants, 2387
Volvo Adventure Environmental Awards, 2390
Volvo Bob the Bunny's Cartoon Competition, 2391
VSA/Volkswagen Group of America Exhibition
    Awards, 2393
VSA International Art Program for Children with
    Disabilities Grants, 2394
VSA International Young Soloists Award, 2395
VSA Playwright Discovery Award, 2396

Wallace Foundation Grants, 2402
Walmart Fdn Inclusive Communities Grants, 2403
Walmart Fdn National Local Giving Grants, 2404
Walmart Foundation State Giving Grants, 2405
Walton Family Foundation Education Grants, 2408
Westerman Foundation Grants, 2427
WestWind Foundation Reproductive Health and
    Rights Grants, 2434
Weyerhaeuser Family Fdn Health Grants, 2435
WHO Foundation Education/Literacy Grants, 2442
WHO Foundation General Grants, 2443
WHO Foundation Volunteer Service Grants, 2444
Whole Kids Foundation School Garden Grants, 2446
Wilkins Family Foundation Grants, 2450
William A. Badger Foundation Grants, 2451
William and Flora Hewlett Foundation Education
    Grants, 2454
William and Flora Hewlett Foundation
    Environmental Grants, 2455
William and Sandy Heitz Family Fdn Grants, 2457
William B. Dietrich Foundation Grants, 2458
William Bingham Foundation Grants, 2460
William E. Dean III Charitable Fdn Grants, 2464
William G. and Helen C. Hoffman Foundation
    Grants, 2466
William T. Grant Foundation Scholars Program, 2475
Winifred Johnson Clive Foundation Grants, 2478
World of Children Education Award, 2490
World of Children Health Award, 2491
World of Children Humanitarian Award, 2492
World of Children Youth Award, 2493
WSF Rusty Kanokogi Fund for the Advancement of
    U.S. Judo Grants, 2495
WSF Sports 4 Life Grants, 2496
WSF Sports 4 Life Regional Grants, 2497
WSF Travel and Training Fund Grants, 2498
Wyomissing Foundation Thun Family Program
    Grants, 2506
Xerox Foundation Grants, 2507
Youths' Friends Association Grants, 2511
YSA ABC Summer of Service Awards, 2512
YSA Get Ur Good On Grants, 2513
YSA Global Youth Service Day Lead Agy Grts, 2514
YSA MLK Day Lead Organizer Grants, 2516
YSA National Child Awareness Month Youth
    Ambassador Grants, 2517
YSA NEA Youth Leaders for Literacy Grants, 2518
YSA Radio Disney's Hero for Change Award, 2519
YSA Sodexo Lead Organizer Grants, 2520
YSA State Farm Good Neighbor YOUth In The
    Driver Seat Grants, 2521
YSA UnitedHealth HEROES Service-Learning
    Grants, 2522
Zellweger Baby Support Network Grants, 2525
Zonta International Foundation Young Women in
    Public Affairs Award, 2527
ZYTL Foundation Grants, 2528

Alabama
3M Company Fdn Community Giving Grants, 5
3M Company Foundation Health and Human
    Services Grants, 6
ABC Charities Grants, 50
ACF Head Start and/or Early Head Start Grantee
    - Clay, Randolph, and Talladega Counties,
    Alabama, 82
Adams and Reese Corporate Giving Grants, 114
A Friends' Foundation Trust Grants, 136
Alabama Humanities Foundation Major Grants, 159
Aldi Corporation Smart Kids Grants, 226
Appalachian Regional Commission Business
    Development Revolving Loan Fund Grants, 285
Appalachian Regional Commission Education and
    Training Grants, 286
Appalachian Regional Commission Entrepreneurship
    and Business Development Grants, 287
Appalachian Regional Commission Health Care
    Grants, 288
Appalachian Regl Commission Housing Grants, 289
Arkema Foundation Grants, 298

Arkema Foundation Science Teachers Grants, 299
Assisi Foundation of Memphis Mini Grants, 319
Autauga Area Community Foundation Grants, 334
Boeing Company Contributions Grants, 462
Brunswick Foundation Dollars for Doers Grants, 478
Brunswick Foundation Grants, 479
Circle K Corporation Contributions Grants, 614
D. W. McMillan Foundation Grants, 776
Dollar General Family Literacy Grants, 835
Dollar General Summer Reading Grants, 836
Dollar General Youth Literacy Grants, 837
Gannett Foundation Community Action Grants, 1033
Georgia-Pacific Foundation Education Grants, 1058
Georgia-Pacific Fdn Entrepreneurship Grants, 1059
Harry B. and Jane H. Brock Foundation Grants, 1183
Hill Crest Foundation Grants, 1249
J. Bulow Campbell Foundation Grants, 1319
Joyce and Randy Seckman Charitable Foundation
    Grants, 1393
Kinder Morgan Foundation Grants, 1436
M.A. Rikard Charitable Trust Grants, 1521
MeadWestvaco Foundation Sustainable Communities
    Grants, 1627
Mercedes-Benz USA Corporate Contributions, 1634
Michelin North America Challenge Education, 1660
PNC Foundation Affordable Housing Grants, 1983
PNC Foundation Community Services Grants, 1984
PNC Foundation Education Grants, 1985
PNC Foundation Grow Up Great Early Childhood
    Grants, 1986
PNC Foundation Revitalization and Stabilization
    Grants, 1987
Publix Super Markets Charities Local Grants, 2036
Robert R. Meyer Foundation Grants, 2094
Salmon Foundation Grants, 2140
Sunoco Foundation Grants, 2256
TAC Arts Education Funds for At-Risk Youth, 2266
TAC Arts Education Mini Grants, 2267
TAC Touring Arts and Arts Access Touring Arts
    Grants, 2269
Toyota Motor Manuf of Alabama Grants, 2309
Walker Area Community Foundation Grants, 2401
Watson-Brown Foundation Grants, 2418
Whole Foods Foundation, 2445
Williams Comps Homegrown Giving Grants, 2474
Wiregrass Foundation Grants, 2480

Alaska
3M Company Fdn Community Giving Grants, 5
3M Company Foundation Health and Human
    Services Grants, 6
Alaska Airlines Corporation Career Connections for
    Youth Grants, 193
Alaska Airlines Foundation LIFT Grants, 194
Alaska Children's Trust Conference/Training
    Sponsorship, 195
Alaska Community Foundation Afterschool Network
    Engineering Mindset Mini-Grant, 196
Alaska Community Foundation Anchorage Schools
    Foundation Grant, 197
Alaska Community Foundation Children's Trust Tier
    1 Community Based Child Abuse and Neglect
    Prevention Grants, 198
Alaska Community Foundation Children's Trust Tier
    1 Parenting and Child Development Educational
    Grants, 199
Alaska Community Foundation Children's Trust Tier
    2 Innovation Grants, 200
Alaska Community Foundation Cordova Community
    Foundation Grants, 201
Alaska Community Foundation Cordova Community
    Foundation Mini-Grants, 202
Alaska Community Foundation GCI Suicide
    Prevention Grant, 203
Alaska Community Foundation Jack and Nona Renn
    Anchorage Football Fund, 204
Alaska Community Foundation Kenai Peninsula
    Foundation Grant, 205
Alaska Community Foundation Ketchikan
    Community Foundation Grant, 206

Alaska Community Foundation Petersburg
    Community Foundation Annual Grant, 207
Alaska Community Foundation Petersburg
    Community Foundation Mini-Grants, 208
Alaska Community Foundation Seward Community
    Foundation Grant, 209
Alaska Conservation Fdn Youth Mini Grants, 210
Alaska State Council on the Arts Cultural
    Collaboration Project Grants, 211
Alaska State Council on the Arts Youth Cultural
    Heritage Fast Track Grants, 212
Anchorage Schools Foundation Grants, 270
Atwood Foundation General Grants, 330
Avista Foundation Education Grants, 340
Avista Foundation Vulnerable and Limited Income
    Population Grants, 341
Charlotte Martin Foundation Youth Grants, 571
Chilkat Valley Community Foundation Grants, 588
GCI Corporate Contributions Grants, 1037
Golden Heart Community Foundation Grants, 1094
Greater Sitka Legacy Fund Grants, 1111
Jessica Stevens Community Foundation Grants, 1363
Ketchikan Community Foundation Grants, 1429
Kodiak Community Foundation Grants, 1446
M.J. Murdock Charitable Trust General Grants, 1524
Matson Community Giving Grants, 1607
Petersburg Community Foundation Grants, 1951
Pride Foundation Grants, 2024
Rasmuson Foundation Tier One Grants, 2055
Rasmuson Foundation Tier Two Grants, 2056
Saltchuk Corporate Giving, 2141
Seward Community Foundation Grants, 2182
Seward Community Foundation Mini-Grants, 2183
Skaggs Foundation Grants, 2207
WinnCompanies Charitable Giving, 2479

American Samoa
7-Eleven Corporate Giving Grants, 8
AAAS/Subaru SB&F Prize for Excl in Sci Books, 22
AASA Urgent Need Mini-Grants, 43
ACF Social and Economic Development Strategies
    Grants, 93
Adidas Corporation General Grants, 125
A Little Hope Grants, 235
Bank of America Charitable Foundation Matching
    Gifts, 356
Bank of America Charitable Foundation Volunteer
    Grants, 358
Beacon Society Jan Stauber Grants, 393
Beckman Coulter Foundation Grants, 394
Bee Conservancy Sponsor-A-Hive Grants, 395
Brinker Int Corporation Charitable Giving, 471
Brookdale Fdn Relatives as Parents Grants, 474
Fidelity Charitable Gift Fund Grants, 956
First Nations Development Institute Native
    Agriculture and Food Systems Scholarships, 971
First Nations Development Institute Native Arts
    Initiative Grants, 972
First Nations Development Institute Native Language
    Immersion Initiative Grants, 973
First Nations Development Institute Native Youth
    and Culture Fund Grants, 974
First Nations Development Institute Nourishing
    Native Children: Feeding Our Future Project
    Grants, 975
Ford Foundation BUILD Grants, 984
From the Top Alumni Leadership Grants, 1025
From the Top Jack Kent Cooke Young Artist
    Scholarships, 1026
Good+Foundation Grants, 1096
IMLS Grants to State Library Administrative
    Agencies, 1298
IMLS National Leadership Grants for Libraries, 1299
Jack Kent Cooke Fdn Young Artist Awards, 1333
Judy and Peter Blum Kovler Foundation Grants, 1396
NEA Student Program Communities Redefining
    Education Advocacy Through Empowerment
    (CREATE) Grants, 1733
NSF Perception, Action and Cognition (PAC)
    Research Grants, 1775

NZDIA Community Org Grants Scheme, 1796
Ray Charles Foundation Grants, 2058
Target Corporation Soccer Grants, 2271
U.S. Department of Education Promise
    Neighborhoods Grants, 2332
USAID Community Livelihoods Project in Yemen
    Grant, 2352
USAID Family Planning and Reproductive Health
    Methods Grants, 2353
USAID Global Development Alliance Grants, 2354
USAID National Governance Project in Yemen
    Grant, 2357
USAID Office of Foreign Disaster Assistance and
    Food for Peace Grants, 2359
USAID School Improvement Program Grants, 2360
USAID U.S.-Egypt Learning Grants, 2361
WHO Foundation Education/Literacy Grants, 2442
WSF Rusty Kanokogi Fund for the Advancement of
    U.S. Judo Grants, 2495
WSF Sports 4 Life Grants, 2496
WSF Sports 4 Life Regional Grants, 2497
WSF Travel and Training Fund Grants, 2498

Arizona
100 Club of Arizona Financial Assistance Grants, 9
Abbott Fund Access to Health Care Grants, 45
Abbott Fund Community Engagement Grants, 46
Abbott Fund Global AIDS Care Grants, 47
Abbott Fund Science Education Grants, 48
ABC Charities Grants, 50
Aetna Foundation Regional Health Grants, 134
Albertsons Companies Foundation Nourishing
    Neighbors Grants, 221
American Express Charitable Fund Scholarships, 254
American Woodmark Foundation Grants, 263
Amerigroup Foundation Grants, 264
Amica Insurance Company Community Grants, 267
Amica Insurance Company Sponsorships, 268
Arizona Commission on the Arts Learning
    Collaboration Grant, 291
Arizona Commission on the Arts Youth Arts
    Engagement Grant, 292
Arizona Foundation for Women Deborah G. Carstens
    Fund Grants, 293
Arizona Foundation for Women General Grants, 294
Arizona State Library LSTA Collections Grants, 295
Arizona State Library LSTA Community Grants, 296
Arizona State Library LSTA Learning Grants, 297
Armstrong McDonald Foundation Children and
    Youth Grants, 300
Armstrong McDonald Foundation Special Needs
    Grants, 301
Bayer Fund Community Development Grants, 383
Bayer Fund STEM Education Grants, 384
Boeing Company Contributions Grants, 462
Brunswick Foundation Dollars for Doers Grants, 478
Brunswick Foundation Grants, 479
Cadillac Products Packaging Company Foundation
    Grants, 491
Caesars Foundation Grants, 492
Campbell Soup Foundation Grants, 501
Charlotte Martin Foundation Youth Grants, 571
Circle K Corporation Contributions Grants, 614
Dean Foundation Grants, 806
Dollar General Family Literacy Grants, 835
Dollar General Summer Reading Grants, 836
Dollar General Youth Literacy Grants, 837
Dorrance Family Foundation Grants, 845
E.L. Wiegand Foundation Grants, 877
Eide Bailly Resourcefullness Awards, 897
Flinn Foundation Scholarships, 977
Gannett Foundation Community Action Grants, 1033
Go Daddy Cares Charitable Contributions, 1093
Hispanic Heritage Foundation Youth Awards, 1253
Humana Foundation Grants, 1275
Intel Corporation Community Grants, 1311
JP Morgan Chase Fdn Arts and Culture Grants, 1394
KaBOOM! Build it Grant, 1402
Kinder Morgan Foundation Grants, 1436
Lynn and Foster Friess Family Fdn Grants, 1520

Margaret T. Morris Foundation Grants, 1557
Medtronic Foundation Community Link Arts, Civic, and Culture Grants, 1629
Medtronic Foundation CommunityLink Health Grants, 1630
Medtronic Foundation Community Link Human Services Grants, 1631
Morris K. Udall and Stewart L. Udall Foundation Parks in Focus Program, 1695
Nationwide Insurance Foundation Grants, 1726
Nestle Purina PetCare Educational Grants, 1738
Nestle Purina PetCare Youth Grants, 1739
PacifiCare Foundation Grants, 1861
Perry and Sandy Massie Foundation Grants, 1941
Phoenix Coyotes Charities Grants, 1963
Phoenix Suns Charities Grants, 1964
Piper Jaffray Foundation Communities Giving Grants, 1974
Piper Trust Arts and Culture Grants, 1975
Piper Trust Children Grants, 1976
Piper Trust Education Grants, 1977
Piper Trust Healthcare and Med Rsrch Grants, 1978
Piper Trust Reglious Organizations Grants, 1979
PNC Foundation Affordable Housing Grants, 1983
PNC Foundation Community Services Grants, 1984
PNC Foundation Education Grants, 1985
PNC Foundation Grow Up Great Early Childhood Grants, 1986
PNC Foundation Revitalization and Stabilization Grants, 1987
Prudential Foundation Education Grants, 2028
Salt River Project Health and Human Services Grants, 2142
Screen Actors Guild BookPALS Assistance, 2171
Screen Actors Guild PencilPALS Assistance, 2172
Screen Actors Guild StagePALS Assistance, 2173
Stocker Foundation Grants, 2247
Toyota Technical Center Grants, 2317
U.S. Bank Foundation Grants, 2330
Union Pacific Fdn Community & Civic Grants, 2337
Union Pacific Foundation Health and Human Services Grants, 2338
VSA/Metlife Connect All Grants, 2392
Walton Family Foundation Public Charter Startup Grants, 2409
Whole Foods Foundation, 2445
Wold Foundation Grants, 2482

Arkansas
3M Company Fdn Community Giving Grants, 5
3M Company Foundation Health and Human Services Grants, 6
AEGON Transamerica Foundation Education and Financial Literacy Grants, 132
AEGON Transamerica Foundation Health and Wellness Grants, 133
AHC R.E.A.C.H. Grants, 141
Albertsons Companies Foundation Nourishing Neighbors Grants, 221
Aldi Corporation Smart Kids Grants, 226
American Electric Power Corporate Grants, 252
American Electric Power Foundation Grants, 253
Assisi Fdn of Memphis Capital Project Grants, 317
Assisi Foundation of Memphis General Grants, 318
Campbell Soup Foundation Grants, 501
Carl B. and Florence E. King Foundation Grants, 506
Circle K Corporation Contributions Grants, 614
Dollar General Family Literacy Grants, 835
Dollar General Summer Reading Grants, 836
Dollar General Youth Literacy Grants, 837
Donald W. Reynolds Foundation Children's Discovery Initiative Grants, 841
Entergy Charitable Foundation Education and Literacy Grants, 917
Entergy Charitable Foundation Low-Income Initiatives and Solutions Grants, 918
Entergy Corporation Micro Grants, 919
Entergy Corporation Open Grants for Arts and Culture, 920

Entergy Corporation Open Grants for Healthy Families, 921
Fdn for the Mid South Communities Grants, 992
Foundation for the Mid South Education Grants, 993
Gannett Foundation Community Action Grants, 1033
Georgia-Pacific Foundation Education Grants, 1058
Georgia-Pacific Fdn Entrepreneurship Grants, 1059
Hatton W. Sumners Foundation for the Study and Teaching of Self Government Grants, 1196
Hubbard Farms Charitable Foundation Grants, 1272
Land O'Lakes Foundation Community Grants, 1466
Marion and Miriam Rose Fund Grants, 1569
MeadWestvaco Foundation Sustainable Communities Grants, 1627
Piper Jaffray Foundation Communities Giving Grants, 1974
Roy and Christine Sturgis Charitable Tr Grts, 2115
Starr Foundation Grants, 2237
T.L.L. Temple Foundation Grants, 2264
TAC Arts Education Funds for At-Risk Youth, 2266
TAC Arts Education Mini Grants, 2267
TAC Touring Arts and Arts Access Touring Arts Grants, 2269
U.S. Bank Foundation Grants, 2330
Union Pacific Fdn Community & Civic Grants, 2337
Union Pacific Foundation Health and Human Services Grants, 2338
Walton Family Foundation Public Charter Startup Grants, 2409
Watson-Brown Foundation Grants, 2418
Whole Foods Foundation, 2445

California
3M Company Fdn Community Giving Grants, 5
3M Company Foundation Health and Human Services Grants, 6
Aaron Foundation Grants, 41
Abbott Fund Access to Health Care Grants, 45
Abbott Fund Community Engagement Grants, 46
Abbott Fund Global AIDS Care Grants, 47
Abbott Fund Science Education Grants, 48
ABS Foundation Grants, 56
Abundance Foundation Local Community Grants, 58
Adams-Mastrovich Family Foundation Grants, 113
Adams Legacy Foundation Grants, 121
Adelaide Christian Home For Children Grants, 124
Adobe Fdn Community Investment Grants, 127
Adobe Fdn Hunger and Homelessness Grants, 128
AEGON Transamerica Foundation Education and Financial Literacy Grants, 132
AEGON Transamerica Foundation Health and Wellness Grants, 133
Aetna Foundation Regional Health Grants, 134
A Friends' Foundation Trust Grants, 136
AHS Foundation Grants, 143
Alaska Airlines Foundation LIFT Grants, 194
Albertsons Companies Foundation Nourishing Neighbors Grants, 221
Aldi Corporation Smart Kids Grants, 226
American Express Charitable Fund Scholarships, 254
Amerigroup Foundation Grants, 264
Amica Insurance Company Community Grants, 267
Amica Insurance Company Sponsorships, 268
Anheuser-Busch Foundation Grants, 273
Atkinson Foundation Community Grants, 325
Avery-Fuller-Welch Children's Fdn Grants, 336
Avista Foundation Education Grants, 340
Avista Foundation Vulnerable and Limited Income Population Grants, 341
Bank of the Orient Community Giving, 361
Bayer Fund Community Development Grants, 383
Bayer Fund STEM Education Grants, 384
Bella Vista Fdn GSS Healthy Living Grants, 396
Bella Vista Foundation Pre-3 Grants, 397
Bella Vista Fdns GSS Early Literacy Grants, 398
Belvedere Community Foundation Grants, 399
Belvedere Cove Foundation Grants, 400
Belvedere Cove Foundation Scholarships, 401
Ben B. Cheney Foundation Grants, 402
Better Way Foundation Grants, 419

Bill Graham Memorial Foundation Grants, 429
Boeing Company Contributions Grants, 462
Bothin Foundation Grants, 464
Brown Rudnick Charitable Foundation Community Grants, 477
Caesars Foundation Grants, 492
California Arts Cncl Statewide Networks Grants, 493
California Arts Cncl Technical Assistance Grts, 494
California Endowment Innovative Ideas Challenge Grants, 495
Campbell Soup Foundation Grants, 501
Chapman Charitable Foundation Grants, 560
Circle K Corporation Contributions Grants, 614
City of Oakland Cultural Funding Grants, 618
Claremont Community Foundation Grants, 622
Cleo Foundation Grants, 632
Community Foundation for San Benito County Grants, 677
Community Foundation for San Benito County Martin Rajkovich Children's Fund Grants, 678
Community Foundation Serving Riverside and San Bernardino Counties Impact Grants, 742
Crescent Porter Hale Foundation Grants, 767
Cudd Foundation Grants, 769
David M. and Marjorie D. Rosenberg Foundation Grants, 790
Dean Witter Foundation Education Grants, 807
Del Mar Foundation Community Grants, 820
Dorrance Family Foundation Grants, 845
Dunspaugh-Dalton Foundation Grants, 873
E.L. Wiegand Foundation Grants, 877
Eva Gunther Foundation Fellowships, 937
Evelyn and Walter Haas, Jr. Fund Education Opportunities Grants, 939
Evelyn and Walter Haas, Jr. Fund Immigrant Rights Grants, 941
Evelyn and Walter Haas, Jr. Fund Nonprofit Leadership Grants, 942
Fitzpatrick, Cella, Harper & Scinto Pro Bono Services, 976
Ford Family Foundation Grants - Access to Health and Dental Services, 980
Ford Family Foundation Grants - Child Abuse Prevention and Intervention, 981
Ford Family Foundation Grants - Positive Youth Development, 982
Ford Family Foundation Grants - Technical Assistance , 983
Friedman Family Foundation Grants, 1023
Furth Family Foundation Grants, 1030
Gamble Foundation Grants, 1032
Gannett Foundation Community Action Grants, 1033
Gene Haas Foundation, 1038
George and Ruth Bradford Foundation Grants, 1042
George B. Page Foundation Grants, 1044
George H. Sandy Foundation Grants, 1050
Georgia-Pacific Foundation Education Grants, 1058
Georgia-Pacific Fdn Entrepreneurship Grants, 1059
Gil and Dody Weaver Foundation Grants, 1071
Go Daddy Cares Charitable Contributions, 1093
Grifols Community Outreach Grants, 1122
HAF Barry F. Phelps Leukemia Fund Grants, 1140
HAF Community Grants, 1141
HAF Don and Bettie Albright Endowment Fund Grants, 1142
HAF Ian Chris Mackey Newman Fund Grts, 1143
HAF JoAllen K. Twiddy-Wood Memorial Fund Grants, 1144
HAF Joe Alexandre Mem Family Fund Grants, 1145
HAF Laurence and Elaine Allen Memorial Fund Grants, 1146
HAF Mada Huggins Caldwell Fund Grants, 1147
HAF Native Cultures Fund Grants, 1148
HAF Phyllis Nilsen Leal Mem Fund Grants, 1149
HAF Southern Humboldt Grants, 1150
Harden Foundation Grants, 1166
Harmony Foundation for Children Grants, 1168
Hasbro Children's Fund Grants, 1189
Hasbro Corp Gift of Play Holiday Giving, 1190

Hasbro Corporation Gift of Play Hospital and Pediatric Health Giving, 1191
Hasbro Corporation Gift of Play Shelter Support Giving, 1192
Hasbro Corporation Gift of Play Summer Camp Support, 1193
Hazen Foundation Public Education Grants, 1221
Henry L. Guenther Foundation Grants, 1242
Herman P. and Sophia Taubman Fdn Grants, 1247
Hispanic Heritage Foundation Youth Awards, 1253
Huffy Foundation Grants, 1273
Inland Empire Community Foundation Capacity Building for IE Nonprofits Grants, 1306
Inland Empire Community Foundation Coachella Valley Youth Grants, 1307
Inland Empire Community Foundation Native Youth Grants, 1308
Inland Empire Community Foundation Riverside Youth Grants, 1309
Inland Empire Community Foundation San Bernardino Youth Grants, 1310
Intel Corporation Community Grants, 1311
Isabel Allende Foundation Esperanza Grants, 1315
James S. Copley Foundation Grants, 1345
John and Marcia Goldman Foundation Youth Development Grants, 1368
John Gogian Family Foundation Grants, 1373
John M. Weaver Foundation Grants, 1376
JP Morgan Chase Fdn Arts and Culture Grants, 1394
Julia Richardson Brown Foundation Grants, 1398
KaBOOM! Build it Grant, 1402
Kathryne Beynon Foundation Grants, 1420
Kenneth T. and Eileen L. Norris Fdn Grants, 1427
Kimball Foundation Grants, 1432
Kimball International-Habig Foundation Education Grants, 1433
Kimball International-Habig Foundation Health and Human Services Grants, 1434
Kinder Morgan Foundation Grants, 1436
Kind World Foundation Grants, 1438
Land O'Lakes Fdn California Region Grants, 1465
Land O'Lakes Foundation Community Grants, 1466
Latkin Charitable Foundation Grants, 1469
Legler Benbough Foundation Grants, 1479
LGA Family Foundation Grants, 1487
LISC Financial Stability Grants, 1501
Lockheed Martin Corporation Fdn Grants, 1505
Lucile Packard Foundation for Children's Health Grants, 1514
Lumpkin Family Foundation Strong Community Leadership Grants, 1519
Manuel D. and Rhoda Mayerson Fdn Grants, 1550
Marin Community Foundation Affordable Housing Grants, 1561
Marin Community Foundation Arts Education Grants, 1562
Marin Community Foundation Arts in the Community Grants, 1563
Marin Community Foundation Closing the Education Achievement Gap Grants, 1564
Marin Community Foundation Ending the Cycle of Poverty Grants, 1565
Marin Community Foundation Improving Community Health Grants, 1566
Marin Community Foundation Social Justice and Interfaith Understanding Grants, 1567
Marin Community Foundation Stinson Bolinas Community Grants, 1568
Marisla Foundation Human Services Grants, 1573
Martin C. Kauffman 100 Club of Alameda County Scholarships, 1582
Mary A. Crocker Trust Grants, 1584
Matson Community Giving Grants, 1607
Maurice J. Masserini Charitable Trust Grants, 1610
McConnell Foundation Grants, 1616
McLean Foundation Grants, 1624
MeadWestvaco Foundation Sustainable Communities Grants, 1627
Medtronic Foundation Community Link Arts, Civic, and Culture Grants, 1629

Medtronic Foundation CommunityLink Health Grants, 1630
Medtronic Foundation Community Link Human Services Grants, 1631
Mercedes-Benz USA Corporate Contributions Grants, 1634
Mericos Foundation Grants, 1637
Meta and George Rosenberg Fdn Grants, 1644
Mimi and Peter Haas Fund Grants, 1677
Morris K. Udall and Stewart L. Udall Foundation Parks in Focus Program, 1695
Morris Stulsaft Foundation Early Childhood Education Grants, 1696
Morris Stulsaft Foundation Educational Support for Children Grants, 1697
Morris Stulsaft Foundation Participation in the the Arts Grants, 1698
Morris Stulsaft Foundation Pathways to Work Grants, 1699
Nationwide Insurance Foundation Grants, 1726
Nestle Purina PetCare Educational Grants, 1738
Nestle Purina PetCare Youth Grants, 1739
Nick Traina Foundation Grants, 1759
Nissan Neighbors Grants, 1762
Orange County Community Foundation Grants, 1829
OtterCares Inspiration Fund Grants, 1850
PacifiCare Foundation Grants, 1861
Packard Foundation Local Grants, 1863
Pajaro Valley Community Health Health Trust Insurance/Coverage & Education on Using the System Grants, 1864
Pajaro Valley Community Health Trust Diabetes and Contributing Factors Grants, 1865
Pajaro Valley Community Health Trust Oral Health: Prevention & Access Grants, 1866
Parker Foundation (California) Grants, 1869
Perkins Charitable Foundation Grants, 1939
PG&E Bright Ideas Grants, 1956
PG&E Community Vitality Grants, 1957
Piper Jaffray Foundation Communities Giving Grants, 1974
Posse Foundation Scholarships, 2011
Presidio Fencing Club Youth Fencers Assistance Scholarships, 2019
Prudential Foundation Education Grants, 2028
Pulido Walker Foundation, 2039
Qualcomm Grants, 2042
R.D. and Joan Dale Hubbard Fdn Grants, 2044
Ralph M. Parsons Foundation Grants, 2052
Rathmann Family Foundation Grants, 2057
Raymond Austin Hagen Family Fdn Grants, 2060
Richard W. Goldman Family Fdn Grants, 2073
Robert and Betty Wo Foundation Grants, 2083
Robert Lee Adams Foundation Grants, 2091
Robert R. McCormick Tribune Foundation Community Grants, 2093
Rose Hills Foundation Grants, 2106
Rosenberg Foundation Immigrant Rights and Integration Grants, 2108
Ruddie Memorial Youth Foundation Grants, 2120
S. D. Bechtel, Jr. Foundation / Stephen Bechtel Fund Character and Citizenship Dev Grants, 2128
Salmon Foundation Grants, 2140
Samueli Foundation Youth Services Grants, 2144
Sand Hill Foundation Environment and Sustainability Grants, 2152
Sand Hill Foundation Health and Opportunity Grants, 2153
Sand Hill Fdn Small Capital Needs Grants, 2154
Screen Actors Guild BookPALS Assistance, 2171
Screen Actors Guild PencilPALS Assistance, 2172
Screen Actors Guild StagePALS Assistance, 2173
Shopko Fdn Community Charitable Grants, 2191
Sierra Health Foundation Responsive Grants, 2199
Silicon Valley Community Foundation Education Grants, 2200
Sobrato Family Foundation Grants, 2211
Sobrato Family Fdn Meeting Space Grants, 2212
Sobrato Family Foundation Office Space Grants, 2213
Southern California Edison Education Grants, 2218

Stocker Foundation Grants, 2247
Storm Castle Foundation Grants, 2248
TE Foundation Grants, 2279
Tellabs Foundation Grants, 2280
Tension Envelope Foundation Grants, 2284
Thelma Doelger Charitable Trust Grants, 2288
Thomas J. Long Foundation Community Grants, 2291
Toby Wells Foundation Grants, 2304
Toyota Motor Sales, USA Grants, 2316
Toyota Technical Center Grants, 2317
Trinity Trust Summer Youth Mini Grants, 2321
U.S. Bank Foundation Grants, 2330
U.S. Cellular Corporation Grants, 2331
Union Bank, N.A. Corporate Sponsorships and Donations, 2333
Union Bank, N.A. Foundation Grants, 2334
Union Labor Health Fdn Angel Fund Grants, 2335
Union Labor Health Foundation Dental Angel Fund Grants, 2336
Union Pacific Fdn Community & Civic Grants, 2337
Union Pacific Foundation Health and Human Services Grants, 2338
United Friends of the Children Scholarships, 2341
VSA/Metlife Connect All Grants, 2392
W.M. Keck Fdn Southern California Grants, 2398
Walter J. and Betty C. Zable Fdn Grants, 2406
Walton Family Foundation Public Charter Startup Grants, 2409
Whole Foods Foundation, 2445
Wild Rivers Community Foundation Holiday Partnership Grants, 2448
Wild Rivers Community Foundation Summer Youth Mini Grants, 2449
William G. Gilmore Foundation Grants, 2467
Wood-Claeyssens Foundation Grants, 2486

Colorado

ABS Foundation Grants, 56
Albertsons Companies Foundation Nourishing Neighbors Grants, 221
Amerigroup Foundation Grants, 264
Amica Insurance Company Community Grants, 267
Amica Insurance Company Sponsorships, 268
Anheuser-Busch Foundation Grants, 273
Aspen Community Foundation Grants, 316
Boeing Company Contributions Grants, 462
Caring for Colorado Foundation Sperry S. and Ella Graber Packard Fund for Pueblo Grants, 505
Carl W. and Carrie Mae Joslyn Trust Grants, 510
Circle K Corporation Contributions Grants, 614
Colorado Health Foundation Family, Friend and Neighbor Caregiver Supports Grants, 660
Colorado Interstate Gas Grants, 661
Colorado Trust Health Investment Grants, 662
Daniels Fund Amateur Sports Grants, 779
Daniels Fund Drug and Alcohol Addiction Grants, 780
Daniels Fund Early Childhood Education Grants, 781
Daniels Homeless and Disadvantaged Grants, 782
Daniels Fund K-12 Education Reform Grants, 783
Daniels Fund Youth Development Grants, 784
Dean Foundation Grants, 806
Dean Witter Foundation Education Grants, 807
Dollar General Family Literacy Grants, 835
Dollar General Summer Reading Grants, 836
Dollar General Youth Literacy Grants, 837
Don and May Wilkins Charitable Trust Grants, 842
Eide Bailly Resourcefulness Awards, 897
El Pomar Foundation Anna Keesling Ackerman Fund Grants, 907
El Pomar Foundation Grants, 908
Gannett Foundation Community Action Grants, 1033
Gil and Dody Weaver Foundation Grants, 1071
Go Daddy Cares Charitable Contributions, 1093
Humana Foundation Grants, 1275
Intel Corporation Community Grants, 1311
John G. Duncan Charitable Trust Grants, 1372
Joseph Henry Edmondson Foundation Grants, 1388
JP Morgan Chase Fdn Arts and Culture Grants, 1394
KaBOOM! Build it Grant, 1402
Kinder Morgan Foundation Grants, 1436

Laura Musser Intercultural Harmony Grants, 1472
Lockheed Martin Corporation Fdn Grants, 1505
Mabel Y. Hughes Charitable Trust Grants, 1530
Medtronic Foundation Community Link Arts, Civic, and Culture Grants, 1629
Medtronic Foundation CommunityLink Health Grants, 1630
Medtronic Foundation Community Link Human Services Grants, 1631
Nathan B. and Florence R. Burt Fdn Grants, 1717
Nationwide Insurance Foundation Grants, 1726
Nestle Purina PetCare Educational Grants, 1738
Nestle Purina PetCare Youth Grants, 1739
OtterCares Champion Fund Grants, 1848
OtterCares Impact Fund Grants, 1849
OtterCares NoCO Fund Grants, 1851
PacifiCare Foundation Grants, 1861
Packard Foundation Local Grants, 1863
PeyBack Foundation Grants, 1953
Piper Jaffray Foundation Communities Giving Grants, 1974
PNC Foundation Affordable Housing Grants, 1983
PNC Foundation Community Services Grants, 1984
PNC Foundation Education Grants, 1985
PNC Foundation Grow Up Great Early Childhood Grants, 1986
PNC Foundation Revitalization and Stabilization Grants, 1987
PPCF Community Grants, 2014
PPCF Edson Foundation Grants, 2015
PPCF Esther M. and Freeman E. Everett Charitable Foundation Grants, 2016
Qualcomm Grants, 2042
Robert R. McCormick Tribune Foundation Community Grants, 2093
Rose Community Foundation Child and Family Development Grants, 2103
Rose Community Foundation Education Grants, 2104
Rose Community Foundation Health Grants, 2105
Ruth and Vernon Taylor Foundation Grants, 2124
Saeman Family Fdn A Charitable Grants, 2133
Salmon Foundation Grants, 2140
Schlessman Family Foundation Grants, 2167
Schramm Foundation Grants, 2168
Subaru of America Foundation Grants, 2253
Summit Foundation Grants, 2255
Telluride Foundation Community Grants, 2281
Telluride Fdn Emergency Grants, 2282
Telluride Fdn Technical Assistance Grants, 2283
U.S. Bank Foundation Grants, 2330
Union Pacific Fdn Community & Civic Grants, 2337
Union Pacific Foundation Health and Human Services Grants, 2338
Valley-Wide Health Systems Nurse Family Partnerships, 2372
VSA/Metlife Connect All Grants, 2392
Walton Family Foundation Public Charter Startup Grants, 2409
Whole Foods Foundation, 2445
William G. Gilmore Foundation Grants, 2467
William Ray and Ruth E. Collins Fdn Grants, 2473
Wold Foundation Grants, 2482
Yampa Valley Community Foundation Erickson Business Week Scholarships, 2508
Yampa Valley Community Foundation Erickson Christian Heritage Scholarships, 2509

Connecticut
3M Company Fdn Community Giving Grants, 5
3M Company Foundation Health and Human Services Grants, 6
Aaron Foundation Grants, 42
Aetna Foundation Regional Health Grants, 134
Aetna Foundation Summer Academic Enrichment Grants, 135
Ahearn Family Foundation Grants, 142
Aldi Corporation Smart Kids Grants, 226
American Savings Fdn After School Grants, 259
American Savings Foundation Capital Grants, 260
American Savings Foundation Program Grants, 261

Amerigroup Foundation Grants, 264
Amica Insurance Company Community Grants, 267
Amica Insurance Company Sponsorships, 268
Anna Fitch Ardenghi Trust Grants, 274
Bay and Paul Foundations PreK-12 Transformative Learning Practices Grants, 370
Baystate Financial Charitable Foundation Grants, 385
Bernau Family Foundation Grants, 413
Bodenwein Public Benevolent Foundation Grants, 461
Brown Rudnick Charitable Foundation Community Grants, 477
Brunswick Foundation Dollars for Doers Grants, 478
Brunswick Foundation Grants, 479
Campbell Soup Foundation Grants, 501
Charles Nelson Robinson Fund Grants, 569
Citizens Bank Charitable Foundation Grants, 616
Clayton F. and Ruth L. Hawkridge Foundation Grants, 630
Community Foundation of Eastern Connecticut General Southeast Grants, 696
Community Foundation of Eastern Connecticut Northeast Women and Girls Grants, 697
Community Foundation of Eastern Connecticut Norwich Women and Girls Grants, 698
Community Foundation of Eastern Connecticut Norwich Youth Grants, 699
Community Foundation of Eastern Connecticut Ossen Fund for the Arts Grants, 700
Community Foundation of Eastern Connecticut Southeast Area Women and Girls Grants, 701
Community Foundation of Eastern Connecticut Windham Area Women and Girls Grants, 702
Countess Moira Charitable Foundation Grants, 752
Covenant to Care for Children Crisis Food Pantry Giving, 756
Covenant for Children Critical Goods Grants, 757
Covenant to Care for Children Enrichment Fund Grants, 758
Dominion Foundation Grants, 839
Dorr Foundation Grants, 846
Elizabeth Carse Foundation Grants, 899
Ensworth Charitable Foundation Grants, 916
Frederick W. Marzahl Memorial Fund Grants, 1018
George A. & Grace L. Long Fdn Grants, 1041
George F. Baker Trust Grants, 1046
George H.C. Ensworth Memorial Fund Grants, 1049
George I. Alden Trust Grants, 1051
Hartford Foundation Regular Grants, 1185
HRAMF Charles H. Hood Foundation Child Health Research Awards, 1262
J. Walton Bissell Foundation Grants, 1325
Jack and Dorothy Byrne Foundation Grants, 1329
Joseph S. Stackpole Charitable Trust Grants, 1390
JP Morgan Chase Fdn Arts and Culture Grants, 1394
Katharine Matthies Foundation Grants, 1418
Leola Osborn Trust Grants, 1483
Liberty Bank Foundation Grants, 1488
Lil and Julie Rosenberg Foundation Grants, 1491
Lily Palmer Fry Memorial Trust Grants, 1493
Linford & Mildred White Charitable Grants, 1495
Lumpkin Family Foundation Strong Community Leadership Grants, 1519
Mabel F. Hoffman Charitable Trust Grants, 1526
Marjorie Moore Charitable Foundation Grants, 1574
MassMutual Foundation Edonomic Development Grants, 1603
Maurice R. Robinson Fund Grants, 1611
Meriden Foundation Grants, 1638
Nellie Mae Education Foundation District-Level Change Grants, 1736
Olga Sipolin Children's Fund Grants, 1815
Perkin Fund Grants, 1937
Perkins Charitable Foundation Grants, 1939
Price Chopper's Golub Foundation Grants, 2020
Prudential Education Foundation Grants, 2028
PSEG Corporate Contributions Grants, 2030
PSEG Fdn Safety and Preparedness Grants, 2031
R.S. Gernon Trust Grants, 2047
Richard Davoud Donchian Foundation Grants, 2070
Richard W. Goldman Family Fdn Grants, 2073

S. Spencer Scott Fund Grants, 2129
Sabina Dolan and Gladys Saulsbury Foundation Grants, 2130
Salmon Foundation Grants, 2140
Smith Richardson Fdn Direct Service Grants, 2210
Southern New England Folk and Traditional Arts Apprenticeship Grants, 2224
Stocker Foundation Grants, 2247
Sunoco Foundation Grants, 2256
Swindells Charitable Foundation Grants, 2261
Tauck Family Foundation Grants, 2274
Thomas and Agnes Carvel Foundation Grants, 2289
Thomas J. Atkins Memorial Trust Fund Grants, 2290
VSA/Metlife Connect All Grants, 2392
Whole Foods Foundation, 2445
Widgeon Point Charitable Foundation Grants, 2447
William Caspar Graustein Memorial Fund Corinne G. Levin Education Grants, 2462
William Foulds Family Foundation Grants, 2465
Yawkey Foundation Grants, 2510

Delaware
Albertsons Companies Foundation Nourishing Neighbors Grants, 221
Aldi Corporation Smart Kids Grants, 226
Carl M. Freeman Foundation FACES Grants, 507
Carl M. Freeman Foundation Grants, 508
Citizens Bank Charitable Foundation Grants, 616
Dean Foundation Grants, 806
Delaware Community Foundation Grants, 817
Delmarva Power & Light Contributions, 821
Delmarva Power & Light Mini-Grants, 822
Dollar General Family Literacy Grants, 835
Dollar General Summer Reading Grants, 836
Dollar General Youth Literacy Grants, 837
Gannett Foundation Community Action Grants, 1033
Giant Food Charitable Grants, 1068
Highmark Corporate Giving Grants, 1248
JP Morgan Chase Fdn Arts and Culture Grants, 1394
Merck Family Fund Urban Farming and Youth Leadership Grants, 1635
PennPAT Fee-Support Grants for Presenters, 1930
PennPAT New Directions Grants for Presenters, 1931
PNC Foundation Affordable Housing Grants, 1983
PNC Foundation Community Services Grants, 1984
PNC Foundation Education Grants, 1985
PNC Foundation Grow Up Great Early Childhood Grants, 1986
PNC Foundation Revitalization and Stabilization Grants, 1987
Richard Davoud Donchian Foundation Grants, 2070
Speer Trust Grants, 2230
Sunoco Foundation Grants, 2256

District of Columbia
7-Eleven Corporate Giving Grants, 8
AAAS/Subaru SB&F Prize for Excl in Sci Books, 22
AASA Urgent Need Mini-Grants, 43
Adams and Reese Corporate Giving Grants, 114
Adidas Corporation General Grants, 125
Aetna Foundation Regional Health Grants, 134
Aldi Corporation Smart Kids Grants, 226
A Little Hope Grants, 235
Alloy Family Foundation Grants, 241
American Express Charitable Fund Scholarships, 254
Autism Speaks Norma and Malcolm Baker Recreation Grants, 335
Bainum Family Foundation Grants, 345
Bank of America Charitable Foundation Matching Gifts, 356
Bank of America Charitable Foundation Volunteer Grants, 358
Beckman Coulter Foundation Grants, 394
Bee Conservancy Sponsor-A-Hive Grants, 395
Boeing Company Contributions Grants, 462
Brinker Int Corporation Charitable Giving, 471
Brookdale Fdn Relatives as Parents Grants, 474
Brown Rudnick Charitable Foundation Community Grants, 477
Case Foundation Grants, 514

CFKF Instrument Matching Grants, 556
Charles Delmar Foundation Grants, 564
Community Foundation for the National Capital
    Region Community Leadership Grants, 688
Corina Higginson Trust Grants, 750
David M. and Marjorie D. Rosenberg Foundation
    Grants, 790
E.L. Wiegand Foundation Grants, 877
Fidelity Charitable Gift Fund Grants, 956
First Nations Development Institute Native Arts
    Initiative Grants, 972
First Nations Development Institute Native Language
    Immersion Initiative Grants, 973
First Nations Development Institute Native Youth
    and Culture Fund Grants, 974
First Nations Development Institute Nourishing
    Native Children: Feeding Our Future Project
    Grants, 975
Fitzpatrick, Cella, Harper & Scinto Pro Bono
    Services, 976
Ford Foundation BUILD Grants, 984
Four Lanes Trust Grants, 1005
From the Top Alumni Leadership Grants, 1025
From the Top Jack Kent Cooke Young Artist
    Scholarships, 1026
Gannett Foundation Community Action Grants, 1033
Giant Food Charitable Grants, 1068
Good+Foundation Grants, 1096
Hattie M. Strong Foundation Grants, 1194
HBF Pathways Out of Poverty Grants, 1222
Hispanic Heritage Foundation Youth Awards, 1253
IMLS Grants to State Library Administrative
    Agencies, 1298
IMLS National Leadership Grants for Libraries, 1299
J. Willard and Alice S. Marriott Fdn Grants, 1327
Jack Kent Cooke Fdn Good Neighbor Grants, 1331
Jack Kent Cooke Fdn Young Artist Awards, 1333
Jovid Foundation Employment Training Grants, 1392
Judy and Peter Blum Kovler Foundation Grants, 1396
KaBOOM! Build it Grant, 1402
Kennedy Center National Symphony Orchestra Youth
    Fellowships, 1426
Kovler Family Foundation Grants, 1454
Leonsis Foundation Grants, 1485
Lois and Richard England Family Foundation Out-
    of-School-Time Grants, 1506
Lynn and Foster Friess Family Fdn Grants, 1520
Mabel H. Flory Charitable Trust Grants, 1527
Maurice R. Robinson Fund Grants, 1611
Mead Family Foundation Grants, 1625
MeadWestvaco Foundation Sustainable Communities
    Grants, 1627
Meyer Foundation Benevon Grants, 1648
Meyer Foundation Education Grants, 1649
Meyer Fdn Management Assistance Grants, 1651
Moran Family Foundation Grants, 1693
Morton K. and Jane Blaustein Foundation
    Educational Opportunity Grants, 1700
NEA Student Program Communities Redefining
    Education Advocacy Through Empowerment
    (CREATE) Grants, 1733
NSF Perception, Action and Cognition (PAC)
    Research Grants, 1775
Ober Kaler Community Grants, 1801
PennPAT Fee-Support Grants for Presenters, 1930
PennPAT New Directions Grants for Presenters, 1931
Philip L. Graham Fund Education Grants, 1962
PNC Foundation Affordable Housing Grants, 1983
PNC Foundation Community Services Grants, 1984
PNC Foundation Education Grants, 1985
PNC Foundation Grow Up Great Early Childhood
    Grants, 1986
PNC Foundation Revitalization and Stabilization
    Grants, 1987
Posse Foundation Scholarships, 2011
Ray Charles Foundation Grants, 2058
Richard Davoud Donchian Foundation Grants, 2070
Richard W. Goldman Family Fdn Grants, 2073
Robert R. McCormick Tribune Foundation
    Community Grants, 2093

Ruddie Memorial Youth Foundation Grants, 2120
Salmon Foundation Grants, 2140
Screen Actors Guild BookPALS Assistance, 2171
Screen Actors Guild PencilPALS Assistance, 2172
Screen Actors Guild StagePALS Assistance, 2173
Sidney and Sandy Brown Foundation Grants, 2196
Sunoco Foundation Grants, 2256
Target Corporation Soccer Grants, 2271
U.S. Department of Education Promise
    Neighborhoods Grants, 2332
USAID Community Livelihoods Project in Yemen
    Grant, 2352
USAID Family Planning and Reproductive Health
    Methods Grants, 2353
USAID Global Development Alliance Grants, 2354
USAID National Governance Project in Yemen
    Grant, 2357
USAID Office of Foreign Disaster Assistance and
    Food for Peace Grants, 2359
USAID School Improvement Program Grants, 2360
USAID U.S.-Egypt Learning Grants, 2361
USDEd Gaining Early Awareness and Readiness for
    Undergrad Programs (GEAR UP) Grants, 2364
Volkswagen Group of America Corporate
    Contributions Grants, 2389
Walton Family Foundation Public Charter Startup
    Grants, 2409
Washington Area Fuel Fund Grants, 2413
Washington Area Women's Foundation African
    American Women's Giving Circle Grants, 2414
Washington Area Women's Foundation Rainmakers
    Giving Circle Grants, 2415
Washington Gas Charitable Contributions, 2417
Whole Foods Foundation, 2445
William J. and Dorothy K. O'Neill Foundation
    Responsive Grants, 2468
WSF Rusty Kanokogi Fund for the Advancement of
    U.S. Judo Grants, 2495
WSF Sports 4 Life Grants, 2496
WSF Sports 4 Life Regional Grants, 2497
WSF Travel and Training Fund Grants, 2498

Florida
A.L. Spencer Foundation Grants, 21
ABC Charities Grants, 50
Adams and Reese Corporate Giving Grants, 114
AEGON Transamerica Foundation Education and
    Financial Literacy Grants, 132
AEGON Transamerica Foundation Health and
    Wellness Grants, 133
Aetna Foundation Regional Health Grants, 134
A Friends' Foundation Trust Grants, 136
AGFT A Gift for Music Grants, 138
AGFT Pencil Boy Express, 139
Albert E. and Birdie W. Einstein Fund Grants, 220
Albertsons Companies Foundation Nourishing
    Neighbors Grants, 221
Aldi Corporation Smart Kids Grants, 226
Alvah H. and Wyline P. Chapman Foundation
    Grants, 248
American Express Charitable Fund Scholarships, 254
Amerigroup Foundation Grants, 264
Anheuser-Busch Foundation Grants, 273
Babcock Charitable Trust Grants, 343
BBF Florida Family Literacy Initiative Grants, 386
Boeing Company Contributions Grants, 462
Brunswick Foundation Dollars for Doers Grants, 478
Brunswick Foundation Grants, 479
Campbell Soup Foundation Grants, 501
CFF Winter Park Community Grants, 551
Chapman Family Foundation, 562
Charles N. and Eleanor Knight Leigh Foundation
    Grants, 568
Cheryl Spencer Memorial Foundation Grants, 576
Circle K Corporation Contributions Grants, 614
Claude A. and Blanche McCubbin Abbott Charitable
    Trust Grants, 628
D. W. McMillan Foundation Grants, 776
Dollar General Family Literacy Grants, 835
Dollar General Summer Reading Grants, 836

Dollar General Youth Literacy Grants, 837
Dr. John T. Macdonald Foundation Grants, 863
Dream Weaver Foundation, 865
Duke Energy Foundation Local Impact Grants, 872
Dunspaugh-Dalton Foundation Grants, 873
Edyth Bush Charitable Foundation Grants, 893
Erie Chapman Foundation Grants, 928
Fifth Third Bank Corporate Giving, 958
Fifth Third Foundation Grants, 959
Gannett Foundation Community Action Grants, 1033
George F. Baker Trust Grants, 1046
Georgia-Pacific Foundation Education Grants, 1058
Georgia-Pacific Fdn Entrepreneurship Grants, 1059
Gulf Coast Foundation of Community Operating
    Grants, 1134
Gulf Coast Foundation of Community Program
    Grants, 1135
Hannah's Helping Hands Grants, 1165
Hazen Foundation Public Education Grants, 1221
Hispanic Heritage Foundation Youth Awards, 1253
Humana Foundation Grants, 1275
J. Bulow Campbell Foundation Grants, 1319
Jack and Dorothy Byrne Foundation Grants, 1329
Jerry L. and Barbara J. Burris Fdn Grants, 1362
Jim Moran Foundation Grants, 1366
Joseph H. and Florence A. Roblee Foundation
    Children and Youth Grants, 1385
Joseph H. and Florence A. Roblee Foundation
    Education Grants, 1386
Joseph H. and Florence A. Roblee Foundation Family
    Grants, 1387
Joyce and Randy Seckman Charitable Foundation
    Grants, 1393
JP Morgan Chase Fdn Arts and Culture Grants, 1394
KaBOOM! Build it Grant, 1402
Kimball International-Habig Foundation Education
    Grants, 1433
Kimball International-Habig Foundation Health and
    Human Services Grants, 1434
Kinder Morgan Foundation Grants, 1436
Leo Goodwin Foundation Grants, 1482
Lockheed Martin Corporation Fdn Grants, 1505
M.A. Rikard Charitable Trust Grants, 1521
Manuel D. and Rhoda Mayerson Fdn Grants, 1550
McLean Contributionship Grants, 1623
MeadWestvaco Foundation Sustainable Communities
    Grants, 1627
Medtronic Foundation Community Link Arts, Civic,
    and Culture Grants, 1629
Medtronic Foundation CommunityLink Health
    Grants, 1630
Medtronic Foundation Community Link Human
    Services Grants, 1631
Mercedes-Benz USA Corporate Contributions
    Grants, 1634
Nationwide Insurance Foundation Grants, 1726
Olivia R. Gardner Foundation Grants, 1819
Perkins Charitable Foundation Grants, 1939
PNC Foundation Affordable Housing Grants, 1983
PNC Foundation Community Services Grants, 1984
PNC Foundation Education Grants, 1985
PNC Foundation Grow Up Great Early Childhood
    Grants, 1986
PNC Foundation Revitalization and Stabilization
    Grants, 1987
Posse Foundation Scholarships, 2011
Progress Energy Foundation Energy Education
    Grants, 2025
Prudential Foundation Education Grants, 2028
Public Education Power Grants, 2032
Publix Super Markets Charities Local Grants, 2036
Richard Davoud Donchian Foundation Grants, 2070
Robert R. McCormick Tribune Foundation
    Community Grants, 2093
Ruth Anderson Foundation Grants, 2122
Saltchuk Corporate Giving, 2141
Screen Actors Guild BookPALS Assistance, 2171
Screen Actors Guild PencilPALS Assistance, 2172
Screen Actors Guild StagePALS Assistance, 2173
Sunoco Foundation Grants, 2256

VSA/Metlife Connect All Grants, 2392
Walton Family Foundation Public Charter Startup
    Grants, 2409
Watson-Brown Foundation Grants, 2418
Whole Foods Foundation, 2445
William J. and Dorothy K. O'Neill Foundation
    Responsive Grants, 2468
William J. and Tina Rosenberg Fdn Grants, 2470
Zollner Foundation Grants, 2526

Georgia
3M Company Fdn Community Giving Grants, 5
3M Company Foundation Health and Human
    Services Grants, 6
ABS Foundation Grants, 56
AEGON Transamerica Foundation Education and
    Financial Literacy Grants, 132
AEGON Transamerica Foundation Health and
    Wellness Grants, 133
Aetna Foundation Regional Health Grants, 134
Albertsons Companies Foundation Nourishing
    Neighbors Grants, 221
Aldi Corporation Smart Kids Grants, 226
Allan C. and Lelia J. Garden Foundation Grants, 236
American Express Charitable Fund Scholarships, 254
American Woodmark Foundation Grants, 263
Amerigroup Foundation Grants, 264
Amica Insurance Company Community Grants, 267
Amica Insurance Company Sponsorships, 268
Anheuser-Busch Foundation Grants, 273
Appalachian Regional Commission Business
    Development Revolving Loan Fund Grants, 285
Appalachian Regional Commission Education and
    Training Grants, 286
Appalachian Regional Commission Entrepreneurship
    and Business Development Grants, 287
Appalachian Regional Commission Health Care
    Grants, 288
Appalachian Regl Commission Housing Grants, 289
Arthur M. Blank Family Foundation American
    Explorers Grants, 305
Arthur M. Blank Family Foundation Art of Change
    Grants, 306
Arthur M. Blank Family Foundation Atlanta Falcons
    Youth Foundation Grants, 307
Arthur M. Blank Family Foundation Inspiring Spaces
    Grants, 309
Arthur M. Blank Family Foundation Pathways to
    Success Grants, 312
Arthur M. Blank Family Foundation Pipeline Project
    Grants, 313
Atlanta Foundation Grants, 326
Atlanta Women's Foundation Pathway to Success
    Grants, 327
Atlanta Women's Foundation Sue Wieland Embracing
    Possibility Award, 328
Boeing Company Contributions Grants, 462
Bradley-Turner Foundation Grants, 466
Brian G. Dyson Foundation Grants, 468
Brunswick Foundation Dollars for Doers Grants, 478
Brunswick Foundation Grants, 479
Cabot Corporation Foundation Grants, 490
Callaway Foundation Grants, 496
Calvin Johnson Jr. Foundation Mini Grants, 498
Campbell Soup Foundation Grants, 501
Circle K Corporation Contributions Grants, 614
Clark and Ruby Baker Foundation Grants, 625
Community Foundation for Greater Atlanta Frances
    Hollis Brain Foundation Fund Grants, 664
Community Foundation for Greater Atlanta
    Managing For Excellence Award, 665
Community Foundation for Greater Atlanta
    Metropolitan Extra Wish Grants, 666
Community Foundation for Greater Atlanta Spark
    Clayton Grants, 667
Community Foundation for Greater Atlanta Spark
    Newton Grants, 668
Community Foundation for Greater Atlanta Strategic
    Restructuring Fund Grants, 669
Dermody Properties Foundation Grants, 827

Dollar General Family Literacy Grants, 835
Dollar General Summer Reading Grants, 836
Dollar General Youth Literacy Grants, 837
Dream Weaver Foundation, 865
E.J. Grassmann Trust Grants, 876
Florence Hunt Maxwell Foundation Grants, 979
Francis L. Abreu Charitable Trust Grants, 1008
Fuller E. Callaway Foundation Grants, 1027
Gannett Foundation Community Action Grants, 1033
George E. Hatcher, Jr. and Ann Williams Hatcher
    Foundation Grants, 1045
Georgia-Pacific Foundation Education Grants, 1058
Georgia-Pacific Fdn Entrepreneurship Grants, 1059
Georgia Council for the Arts Education Grants, 1060
Gertrude & William C. Wardlaw Grants, 1067
H.B. Fuller Foundation Grants, 1138
Harmony Grove Foundation Grants, 1169
Humana Foundation Grants, 1275
J. Bulow Campbell Foundation Grants, 1319
J. Knox Gholston Foundation Grants, 1321
J. William Gholston Foundation Grants, 1328
John H. and Wilhelmina D. Harland Charitable
    Foundation Children and Youth Grants, 1374
John H. and Wilhelmina D. Harland Charitable
    Foundation Community Services Grants, 1375
Joyce and Randy Seckman Charitable Foundation
    Grants, 1393
KaBOOM! Build it Grant, 1402
Katherine John Murphy Foundation Grants, 1419
Kinder Morgan Foundation Grants, 1436
Lockheed Martin Corporation Fdn Grants, 1505
Lynn and Foster Friess Family Fdn Grants, 1520
M.A. Rikard Charitable Trust Grants, 1521
Mary Wilmer Covey Charitable Trust Grants, 1600
MeadWestvaco Foundation Sustainable Communities
    Grants, 1627
Nationwide Insurance Foundation Grants, 1726
Nestle Purina PetCare Educational Grants, 1738
Nestle Purina PetCare Youth Grants, 1739
Olivia R. Gardner Foundation Grants, 1819
OMNOVA Solutions Fdn Education Grants, 1820
Perkins-Ponder Foundation Grants, 1938
Peyton Anderson Foundation Grants, 1954
Peyton Anderson Scholarships, 1955
PNC Foundation Affordable Housing Grants, 1983
PNC Foundation Community Services Grants, 1984
PNC Foundation Education Grants, 1985
PNC Foundation Grow Up Great Early Childhood
    Grants, 1986
PNC Foundation Revitalization and Stabilization
    Grants, 1987
Posse Foundation Scholarships, 2011
Prudential Foundation Education Grants, 2028
Publix Super Markets Charities Local Grants, 2036
Qualcomm Grants, 2042
Sapelo Foundation Social Justice Grants, 2160
Sartain Lanier Family Foundation Grants, 2164
Screen Actors Guild BookPALS Assistance, 2171
Screen Actors Guild PencilPALS Assistance, 2172
Screen Actors Guild StagePALS Assistance, 2173
Storm Castle Foundation Grants, 2248
Subaru of America Foundation Grants, 2253
Sunoco Foundation Grants, 2256
SunTrust Bank Trusteed Foundations Greene-Sawtell
    Grants, 2257
SunTrust Bank Trusteed Foundations Nell Warren
    Elkin and William Simpson Elkin Grants, 2258
Suspened: Community Fdn for Greater Atlanta State
    Farm Education Assist Fund Grants, 2260
TAC Arts Education Funds for At-Risk Youth, 2266
TAC Arts Education Mini Grants, 2267
TAC Touring Arts and Arts Access Touring Arts
    Grants, 2269
Textron Corporate Contributions Grants, 2286
Tull Charitable Foundation Grants, 2324
VSA/Metlife Connect All Grants, 2392
Walton Family Foundation Public Charter Startup
    Grants, 2409
Watson-Brown Foundation Grants, 2418
Whole Foods Foundation, 2445

Guam
7-Eleven Corporate Giving Grants, 8
AAAS/Subaru SB&F Prize for Excl in Sci Books, 22
AASA Urgent Need Mini-Grants, 43
ACF Social and Economic Development Strategies
    Grants, 93
Adidas Corporation General Grants, 125
A Little Hope Grants, 235
Bank of America Charitable Foundation Matching
    Gifts, 356
Bank of America Charitable Foundation Volunteer
    Grants, 358
Beacon Society Jan Stauber Grants, 393
Beckman Coulter Foundation Grants, 394
Bee Conservancy Sponsor-A-Hive Grants, 395
Brinker Int Corporation Charitable Giving, 471
Brookdale Fdn Relatives as Parents Grants, 474
Fidelity Charitable Gift Fund Grants, 956
First Nations Development Institute Native
    Agriculture and Food Systems Initiative
    Scholarships, 971
First Nations Development Institute Native Arts
    Initiative Grants, 972
First Nations Development Institute Native Language
    Immersion Initiative Grants, 973
First Nations Development Institute Native Youth
    and Culture Fund Grants, 974
First Nations Development Institute Nourishing
    Native Children: Feeding Our Future Project
    Grants, 975
Ford Foundation BUILD Grants, 984
From the Top Alumni Leadership Grants, 1025
From the Top Jack Kent Cooke Young Artist
    Scholarships, 1026
Gannett Foundation Community Action Grants, 1033
Good+Foundation Grants, 1096
IMLS Grants to State Library Administrative
    Agencies, 1298
IMLS National Leadership Grants for Libraries, 1299
Jack Kent Cooke Fdn Young Artist Awards, 1333
Judy and Peter Blum Kovler Foundation Grants, 1396
Matson Adahi I Tano' Grants, 1606
Matson Community Giving Grants, 1607
NEA Student Program Communities Redefining
    Education Advocacy Through Empowerment
    (CREATE) Grants, 1733
NSF Perception, Action and Cognition (PAC)
    Research Grants, 1775
NZDIA Community Org Grants Scheme, 1796
Ray Charles Foundation Grants, 2058
Target Corporation Soccer Grants, 2271
U.S. Department of Education Promise
    Neighborhoods Grants, 2332
USAID Community Livelihoods Project in Yemen
    Grant, 2352
USAID Family Planning and Reproductive Health
    Methods Grants, 2353
USAID Global Development Alliance Grants, 2354
USAID National Governance Project in Yemen
    Grant, 2357
USAID Office of Foreign Disaster Assistance and
    Food for Peace Grants, 2359
USAID School Improvement Program Grants, 2360
USAID U.S.-Egypt Learning Grants, 2361
WHO Foundation Education/Literacy Grants, 2442
WSF Rusty Kanokogi Fund for the Advancement of
    U.S. Judo Grants, 2495
WSF Sports 4 Life Grants, 2496
WSF Sports 4 Life Regional Grants, 2497
WSF Travel and Training Fund Grants, 2498

Hawaii
3M Company Fdn Community Giving Grants, 5
3M Company Foundation Health and Human
    Services Grants, 6
ABS Foundation Grants, 56
AHS Foundation Grants, 143
Alaska Airlines Foundation LIFT Grants, 194
Ama OluKai Foundation Grants, 249
Anheuser-Busch Foundation Grants, 273

Antone and Edene Vidinha Charitable Grants, 281
Atlas Insurance Agency Foundation Grants, 329
Bank of Hawaii Foundation Grants, 360
Bank of the Orient Community Giving, 361
Bayer Fund Community Development Grants, 383
Bayer Fund STEM Education Grants, 384
Boeing Company Contributions Grants, 462
Central Pacific Bank Foundation Grants, 530
Clarence T.C. Ching Foundation Grants, 624
Cooke Foundation Grants, 748
Dorrance Family Foundation Grants, 845
Elsie H. Wilcox Foundation Grants, 909
First Hawaiian Bank Foundation Corporate Giving
  Grants, 967
Friends of Hawaii Charities Grants, 1024
G.N. Wilcox Trust Grants, 1031
Gannett Foundation Community Action Grants, 1033
Harold K.L. Castle Foundation Public Education
  Redesign and Enhancement Grants, 1173
Harold K.L. Castle Foundation Strengthening
  Windward Oahu Communities Grants, 1174
Harold K.L. Castle Foundation Windward Youth
  Leadership Fund Grants, 1175
Hartley Foundation Grants, 1186
Hawai'i Community Foundation Bernice and Conrad
  von Hamm Fund Grants, 1197
Hawai'i Community Foundation Children's Trust
  Fund Community Awareness: Child Abuse and
  Neglect Prevention Grants, 1198
Hawai'i Community Foundation East Hawaii Fund
  Grants, 1199
Hawai'i Community Foundation Ewa Beach
  Community Trust Fund Grants, 1200
Hawai'i Community Foundation Family Literacy and
  Hawaii Pizza Hut Literacy Grants, 1201
Hawai'i Community Foundation Kuki'o Community
  Fund Grants, 1202
Hawai'i Community Foundation Lana'i Community
  Benefit Fund, 1203
Hawai'i Community Foundation Richard Smart Fund
  Grants, 1204
Hawai'i Community Foundation Robert E. Black
  Fund Grants, 1205
Hawai'i Community Foundation Victoria S. and
  Bradley L. Geist Foundation: Capacity Building
  Grants, 1206
Hawai'i Community Foundation Victoria S. and
  Bradley L. Geist Foundation: Enhancement
  Grants, 1207
Hawai'i Community Foundation Victoria S. and
  Bradley L. Geist Foundation: Supporting Foster
  Children and Their Caregivers, 1208
Hawai'i Community Foundation Victoria S. and
  Bradley L. Geist Foundation: Supporting
  Transitioning Foster Youth Grants, 1209
Hawai'i SFCA Art Bento Program @ HiSAM
  Grants, 1210
Hawaiian Electric Industries Charitable Foundation
  Grants, 1211
Hawaii Children's Cancer Fdn Contributions, 1212
Hawaii Community Foundation Omidyar Ohana
  Fund Grants, 1213
Hawaii Community Foundation Oscar and Rosetta
  Fish Fund Grants, 1214
Hawaii Community Foundation Promising Minds
  Grants, 1215
Hawaii Community Foundation Reverend Takie
  Okumura Family Grants, 1216
Hawaii Community Foundation Sanford Harmony
  Pillars of Peace Grants, 1217
Hawaii Electric Industries Charitable Foundation
  Grants, 1218
Hawaii State Legislature Grant-In-Aid, 1219
HEI Charitable Foundation Grants, 1226
Herman P. and Sophia Taubman Fdn Grants, 1247
HLTA Visitor Industry Charity Walk Grant, 1254
HSFCA Biennium Grants, 1267
HSFCA Folk and Traditional Arts Grants - Culture
  Learning, 1268
Ifuku Family Foundation Grants, 1287

Island Insurance Foundation Grants, 1316
J. Watumull Fund Grants, 1326
James and Abigail Campbell Family Foundation
  Grants, 1337
Julia Temple Davis Brown Foundation Grants, 1399
Kaiser Permanente Hawaii Region Community
  Grants, 1406
Kosasa Foundation Grants, 1450
Laura Musser Intercultural Harmony Grants, 1472
LGA Family Foundation Grants, 1487
Locations Foundation Legacy Grants, 1504
M.A. Rikard Charitable Trust Grants, 1521
Mary D. and Walter F. Frear Eleemosynary Trust
  Grants, 1588
Matson Community Giving Grants, 1607
Matson Ka Ipu 'Aina Grants, 1608
McInerny Foundation Grants, 1622
Motiv8 Foundation Grants, 1702
NFL Charities Pro Bowl Community Grants in
  Hawaii, 1755
OHA 'Ahahui Grants, 1807
OHA Community Grants for Culture, 1808
OHA Community Grants for Education, 1809
Outrigger Duke Kahanamoku Foundation Athletic
  Event Grants, 1852
Outrigger Duke Kahanamoku Foundation Athletic
  Team Grants, 1853
Prudential Foundation Education Grants, 2028
Robert and Betty Wo Foundation Grants, 2083
Robert F. Lange Foundation Grants, 2090
Ron and Sanne Higgins Family Fdn Grants, 2101
Saltchuk Corporate Giving, 2141
Samuel N. and Mary Castle Foundation Grants, 2145
Serco Foundation Grants, 2181
Shimizu Foundation Scholarships, 2190
Strong Community Grants, 2252
Turtle Bay Foundation Grants, 2327
Victoria S. and Bradley L. Geist Foundation
  Enhancement Grants, 2381
Victoria S. and Bradley L. Geist Foundation Grants
  Supporting Foster Care and Their Caregivers, 2382
Victoria S. and Bradley L. Geist Foundation Grants
  Supporting Transitioning Foster Youth, 2383
Whole Foods Foundation, 2445
William J. and Dorothy K. O'Neill Foundation
  Responsive Grants, 2468
WinnCompanies Charitable Giving, 2479
Women's Fund of Hawaii Grants, 2485
Women's Fund of Hawaii Grants, 2484

Idaho
Albertsons Companies Foundation Nourishing
  Neighbors Grants, 221
Avista Foundation Education Grants, 340
Avista Foundation Vulnerable and Limited Income
  Population Grants, 341
Bayer Fund Community Development Grants, 383
Bayer Fund STEM Education Grants, 384
Camille Beckman Foundation Grants, 499
Charlotte Martin Foundation Youth Grants, 571
CHC Foundation Grants, 575
E.L. Wiegand Foundation Grants, 877
Four J Foundation Grants, 1004
Kimball International-Habig Foundation Education
  Grants, 1433
Kimball International-Habig Foundation Health and
  Human Services Grants, 1434
Land O'Lakes Foundation Community Grants, 1466
Laura Moore Cunningham Foundation Grants, 1474
M.J. Murdock Charitable Trust General Grants, 1524
Micron Technology Fdn Community Grants, 1664
Olive Smith Browning Charitable Trust Grants, 1818
Piper Jaffray Foundation Communities Giving
  Grants, 1974
Pride Foundation Grants, 2024
Shopko Fdn Community Charitable Grants, 2191
Social Justice Fund Northwest Criminal Justice
  Giving Project Grants, 2214
Social Justice Fund Northwest Economic Justice
  Giving Project Grants, 2215

U.S. Bank Foundation Grants, 2330
Union Pacific Fdn Community & Civic Grants, 2337
Union Pacific Foundation Health and Human
  Services Grants, 2338

Illinois
3M Company Fdn Community Giving Grants, 5
3M Company Foundation Health and Human
  Services Grants, 6
A and B Family Foundation Grants, 40
Abbott Fund Access to Health Care Grants, 45
Abbott Fund Community Engagement Grants, 46
Abbott Fund Global AIDS Care Grants, 47
Abbott Fund Science Education Grants, 48
Adam Don Foundation Grants, 112
Aetna Foundation Regional Health Grants, 134
Albertsons Companies Foundation Nourishing
  Neighbors Grants, 221
Aldi Corporation Smart Kids Grants, 226
Allstate Corp Hometown Commitment Grants, 243
Alpha Natural Resources Corporate Giving, 246
Ameren Corporation Community Grants, 251
American Express Charitable Fund Scholarships, 254
Amica Insurance Company Community Grants, 267
Amica Insurance Company Sponsorships, 268
Anderson Foundation Grants, 271
Andrew Family Foundation Grants, 272
Baxter International Foundation Grants, 369
Bayer Fund Community Development Grants, 383
Bayer Fund STEM Education Grants, 384
Bernau Family Foundation Grants, 413
Bindley Family Foundation Grants, 430
Boeing Company Contributions Grants, 462
Bright Promises Foundation Grants, 470
Brunswick Foundation Dollars for Doers Grants, 478
Brunswick Foundation Grants, 479
C.H. Robinson Worldwide Foundation Grants, 489
Cabot Corporation Foundation Grants, 490
Caesars Foundation Grants, 492
Campbell Soup Foundation Grants, 501
Carl R. Hendrickson Family Foundation Grants, 509
Castle Foundation Grants, 517
Chicago Board of Trade Foundation Grants, 580
Chicago Community Trust Arts and Culture Grants:
  Improving Access to Arts Learning, 581
Chicago Neighborhood Arts Program Grants, 582
Circle K Corporation Contributions Grants, 614
Citizens Savings Foundation Grants, 617
Coleman Foundation Entrepreneurship Education
  Grants, 651
Colonel Stanley R. McNeil Foundation Grants, 659
Community Memorial Foundation Responsive
  Grants, 743
Deaconess Foundation Advocacy Grants, 804
Dermody Properties Foundation Grants, 827
Dollar General Family Literacy Grants, 835
Dollar General Summer Reading Grants, 836
Dollar General Youth Literacy Grants, 837
Dominion Foundation Grants, 839
Elizabeth Morse Genius Charitable Trust Grants, 901
Emerson Kampen Foundation Grants, 911
Energy by Design Poster Contest, 915
Fifth Third Bank Corporate Giving, 958
Fifth Third Foundation Grants, 959
Foundation for Health Enhancement Grants, 990
Francis Beidler Foundation Grants, 1007
Gardner W. and Joan G. Heidrick, Jr. Foundation
  Grants, 1036
Georgia-Pacific Foundation Education Grants, 1058
Georgia-Pacific Fdn Entrepreneurship Grants, 1059
Grace Bersted Foundation Grants, 1097
Greater Saint Louis Community Fdn Grants, 1110
H.B. Fuller Foundation Grants, 1138
Henrietta Lange Burk Fund Grants, 1235
Hispanic Heritage Foundation Youth Awards, 1253
Humana Foundation Grants, 1275
Illinois Arts Council Theater Program Grants, 1293
Illinois Arts Council Youth Employment in the Arts
  Program Grants, 1294
Illinois Children's Healthcare Fdn Grants, 1295

Illinois DNR School Habitat Action Grants, 1296
Illinois DNR Youth Recreation Corps Grants, 1297
J.W. Gardner II Foundation Grants, 1323
James S. Copley Foundation Grants, 1345
JP Morgan Chase Fdn Arts and Culture Grants, 1394
Julius N. Frankel Foundation Grants, 1400
KaBOOM! Build it Grant, 1402
Kinder Morgan Foundation Grants, 1436
Kovler Family Foundation Grants, 1454
Kovler Family Foundation Grants, 1455
Land O'Lakes Foundation Community Grants, 1466
LISC Financial Stability Grants, 1501
Lumpkin Family Foundation Strong Community
    Leadership Grants, 1519
Marathon Petroleum Corporation Grants, 1551
Marion Gardner Jackson Charitable Trust Grts, 1570
Marquette Bank Neighborhood Commit Grants, 1577
MeadWestvaco Foundation Sustainable Communities
    Grants, 1627
Mercedes-Benz USA Corporate Contributions
    Grants, 1634
Michael Reese Health Trust Core Grants, 1658
Michael Reese Health Trust Responsive Grants, 1659
Piper Jaffray Foundation Communities Giving
    Grants, 1974
PNC Foundation Affordable Housing Grants, 1983
PNC Foundation Community Services Grants, 1984
PNC Foundation Education Grants, 1985
PNC Foundation Grow Up Great Early Childhood
    Grants, 1986
PNC Foundation Revitalization and Stabilization
    Grants, 1987
Posse Foundation Scholarships, 2011
Prudential Foundation Education Grants, 2028
Robert R. McCormick Tribune Foundation
    Community Grants, 2093
Roy J. Carver Trust Statewide Scholarships, 2116
Roy J. Carver Charitable Trust Youth Services and
    Recreation Grants, 2117
Ruby K. Worner Charitable Trust Grants, 2119
Ruth and Vernon Taylor Foundation Grants, 2124
Shopko Fdn Community Charitable Grants, 2191
Subaru of America Foundation Grants, 2253
Tellabs Foundation Grants, 2280
Terra Fdn Chicago K–12 Education Grants, 2285
Textron Corporate Contributions Grants, 2286
Toyota Motor Manufacturing of Indiana Grants, 2310
U.S. Bank Foundation Grants, 2330
U.S. Cellular Corporation Grants, 2331
Union Pacific Fdn Community & Civic Grants, 2337
Walton Family Foundation Public Charter Startup
    Grants, 2409
Welborn Baptist Foundation Promotion of Early
    Childhood Development Grants, 2423
Welborn Baptist Foundation School Based Health
    Grants, 2424
Welborn Foundation Promotion of Healthy
    Adolescent Development Grants, 2425
Whole Foods Foundation, 2445
William Blair and Company Foundation Grants, 2461
Woods Fund of Chicago Grants, 2489
WSLBDF Quarterly Grants, 2499

Indiana
1st Source Foundation Community Involvement
    Grants, 1
3M Company Fdn Community Giving Grants, 5
3M Company Foundation Health and Human
    Services Grants, 6
ABC Charities Grants, 50
ACCF Dennis and Melanie Bieberich Community
    Enrichment Fund Grants, 59
ACCF John and Kay Boch Fund Grants, 60
ACCF Marlene Bittner Memorial Community
    Enrichment Fund Grants, 61
ACCF of Indiana Angel Funds Grants, 62
ACCF of Indiana Anonymous Community
    Enrichment Fund Grants, 63
ACCF of Indiana Bank of Geneva Heritage Fund
    Grants, 64

ACCF of Indiana Berne Ready Mix Community
    Enrichment Fund Grants, 65
ACCF of Indiana First Merchants Bank / Decatur
    Bank and Trust Fund Grants, 66
ACCF of Indiana Michael Basham Community
    Enrichment Fund Grants, 67
ACCF of Indiana Ron and Susie Ballard Community
    Enrichment Fund Grants, 68
ACCF Ralph Biggs Memorial Community
    Enrichment Fund Grants, 69
Ackerman Foundation Grants, 103
Adams Rotary Memorial Fund A Grants, 122
Albertsons Companies Foundation Nourishing
    Neighbors Grants, 221
Aldi Corporation Smart Kids Grants, 226
Alfred J Mcallister and Dorothy N Mcallister
    Foundation Grants, 234
Allstate Corp Hometown Commitment Grants, 243
American Electric Power Corporate Grants, 252
American Electric Power Foundation Grants, 253
American Woodmark Foundation Grants, 263
Amerigroup Foundation Grants, 264
Anderson Foundation Grants, 271
Anthony Munoz Foundation Straight A Student
    Campaign Grants, 280
Arthur E. and Josephine Campbell Beyer Foundation
    Grants, 303
Back Home Again Foundation Grants, 344
Ball Brothers Foundation Organizational
    Effectiveness/Executive Mentoring Grants, 346
Bayer Fund Community Development Grants, 383
Bayer Fund STEM Education Grants, 384
Benton Community Foundation - The Cookie Jar
    Grant, 404
Benton Community Foundation Grants, 405
Better Way Foundation Grants, 419
Bierhaus Foundation Grants, 421
Bindley Family Foundation Grants, 430
Bingham McHale LLP Pro Bono Services, 431
Blackford County Community Foundation - WOW
    Grants, 433
Blackford County Community Fdn Grants, 434
Blue River Community Foundation Grants, 458
Brown County Community Foundation Grants, 475
Brunswick Foundation Dollars for Doers Grants, 478
Brunswick Foundation Grants, 479
C.H. Robinson Worldwide Foundation Grants, 489
Cadillac Products Packaging Company Foundation
    Grants, 491
Caesars Foundation Grants, 492
Campbell Soup Foundation Grants, 501
Carroll County Community Foundation Grants, 513
Cass County Community Foundation Grants, 516
Castle Foundation Grants, 517
CICF Clare Noyes Grants, 604
CICF Howard Intermill and Marion Intermill
    Fenstermaker Grants, 605
CICF Indianapolis Fdn Community Grants, 606
CICF John Harrison Brown and Rob Burse Grt, 607
CICF Summer Youth Grants, 608
CICF Women's Grants , 609
Circle K Corporation Contributions Grants, 614
Citizens Savings Foundation Grants, 617
Clinton County Community Foundation Grants, 638
Coleman Foundation Entrepreneurship Education
    Grants, 651
Community Foundation of Bartholomew County
    Heritage Fund Grants, 690
Community Foundation of Bartholomew County
    James A. Henderson Award for Fundraising, 691
Community Foundation of Bartholomew County
    Women's Giving Circle, 692
Community Foundation of Boone County - Women's
    Grants, 693
Community Foundation of Boone County Grants, 694
Community Foundation of Crawford County, 695
Community Foundation of Grant County Grants, 703
Community Foundation of Greater Fort Wayne -
    Community Endowment and Clarke Endowment
    Grants, 705

Community Foundation of Greater Fort Wayne -
    Edna Foundation Grants, 706
Community Foundation of Greater Fort Wayne -
    John S. and James L. Knight Foundation Donor-
    Advised Grants, 707
Community Fdn Of Greater Lafayette Grants, 710
Community Fdn of Howard County Grants, 712
Community Foundation of Jackson County Classroom
    Education Grants, 713
Community Foundation of Jackson County Seymour
    Noon Lions Club Grant, 714
Community Foundation of Madison and Jefferson
    County Grants, 731
Community Fdn of Morgan County Grants, 732
Community Foundation of Muncie and Delaware
    County - Kitselman Grants, 733
Community Foundation of Muncie and Delaware
    County Maxon Grants, 734
Community Fdn of Randolph County Grants, 735
Community Fdn of Southern Indiana Grants, 736
Community Foundation of St. Joseph County African
    American Community Grants, 737
Community Foundation of St. Joseph County Special
    Project Challenge Grants, 738
Community Foundation of Switzerland County
    Grants, 739
Community Fdn of Wabash County Grants, 740
Daviess County Community Foundation Advancing
    Out-of-School Learning Grants, 792
Daviess County Community Foundation Recreation
    Grants, 793
Daviess County Community Foundation Youth
    Development Grants, 794
Dearborn Community Foundation City of Aurora
    Grants, 808
Dearborn Community Foundation City of
    Lawrenceburg Community Grants, 809
Dearborn Community Foundation City of
    Lawrenceburg Youth Grants, 810
Decatur County Community Foundation Large
    Project Grants, 811
Decatur County Community Foundation Small
    Project Grants, 812
DeKalb County Community Foundation - Garrett
    Hospital Aid Foundation Grants, 813
DeKalb County Community Foundation - Literacy
    Grant, 814
DeKalb County Community Foundation Grants, 815
DeKalb County Community Foundation VOICE
    Grant, 816
Dollar General Family Literacy Grants, 835
Dollar General Summer Reading Grants, 836
Dollar General Youth Literacy Grants, 837
Dominion Foundation Grants, 839
Dubois County Community Foundation Grants, 871
Duke Energy Foundation Local Impact Grants, 872
Effie Kuhlman Charitable Trust Grants, 896
Elkhart County Community Foundation Fund for
    Elkhart County, 902
Elkhart County Community Foundation Grants, 903
Emerson Kampen Foundation Grants, 911
Fayette County Foundation Grants, 951
Fifth Third Bank Corporate Giving, 958
Fifth Third Foundation Grants, 959
Foundations of East Chicago Education Grants, 995
Fdns of East Chicago Family Support Grants, 996
Foundations of East Chicago Health Grants, 997
Foundations of East Chicago Youth Development
    Grants, 998
Franklin County Community Fdn Grants, 1010
Gannett Foundation Community Action Grants, 1033
Georgia-Pacific Foundation Education Grants, 1058
Georgia-Pacific Fdn Entrepreneurship Grants, 1059
Gibson County Community Foundation Recreation
    Grants, 1069
Gibson County Community Foundation Youth
    Development Grants, 1070
Hancock County Community Foundation - Field of
    Interest Grants, 1161
Hannah's Helping Hands Grants, 1165

Harrison County Community Fdn Grants, 1178
Harrison County Community Foundation Signature
    Grants, 1179
Hazel and Walter T. Bales Foundation Grants, 1220
Hendricks County Community Fdn Grants, 1234
Henry County Community Foundation - TASC
    Youth Grants, 1238
Henry County Community Foundation Grants, 1239
Henry F. Koch Residual Trust Grants, 1241
Humana Foundation Grants, 1275
Huntington County Community Foundation
    Classroom Education Grants, 1279
Huntington County Community Foundation Make a
    Difference Grants, 1280
IBCAT Nancy Jaynes Memorial Scholarship, 1281
Indiana OCRA Quick Impact Placebased (QuIP)
    Grants, 1300
Indiana OCRA Rural Capacity Grants (RCG), 1301
IYI Professional Development Grants, 1317
IYI Responsible Fatherhood Grants, 1318
Jacob G. Schmidlapp Trusts Grants, 1336
Jennings County Community Fdn Grants, 1360
Jennings County Community Foundation Women's
    Giving Circle Grant, 1361
Jerry L. and Barbara J. Burris Fdn Grants, 1362
Johnson County Community Fdn Grants, 1379
Johnson County Community Foundation Youth
    Philanthropy Initiative Grants, 1380
John W. Anderson Foundation Grants, 1383
Journal Gazette Foundation Grants, 1391
JP Morgan Chase Fdn Arts and Culture Grants, 1394
Judith Clark-Morrill Foundation Grants, 1395
KaBOOM! Build it Grant, 1402
Kimball International-Habig Foundation Education
    Grants, 1433
Kimball International-Habig Foundation Health and
    Human Services Grants, 1434
Knox County Community Foundation Recreation
    Grants, 1442
Knox County Community Foundation Youth
    Development Grants, 1443
Kosciusko County Community Foundation
    Endowment Youth Services (KEYS) Grants, 1451
Kosciusko County Community Fdn Grants, 1452
Kosciusko County Community Foundation REMC
    Operation Round Up Grants, 1453
LaGrange County Community Fdn Grants, 1458
LaGrange Independent Foundation for Endowments
    (L.I.F.E.), 1459
Lake County Community Fund Grants, 1463
Land O'Lakes Foundation Community Grants, 1466
Lilly Endowment Summer Youth Grants, 1492
LISC Financial Stability Grants, 1501
Lumpkin Family Foundation Strong Community
    Leadership Grants, 1519
Madison County Community Foundation - City of
    Anderson Quality of Life Grant, 1536
Madison County Community Foundation General
    Grants, 1537
Marathon Petroleum Corporation Grants, 1551
Mark W. Coy Foundation Grants, 1575
Marshall County Community Fdn Grants, 1579
Marsh Corporate Grants, 1580
Medtronic Foundation Community Link Arts, Civic,
    and Culture Grants, 1629
Medtronic Foundation CommunityLink Health
    Grants, 1630
Medtronic Foundation Community Link Human
    Services Grants, 1631
MFRI Community Mobilization Grants, 1654
Michelin North America Challenge Education, 1660
Montgomery County Community Foundation Health
    and Human Services Fund Grants, 1689
Montgomery County Community Foundation Libby
    Whitecotton Fund Grants, 1690
Montgomery County Community Foundation Youth
    Services Grants, 1691
Noble County Community Foundation Grants, 1765
Ohio County Community Foundation Board of
    Directors Grants, 1811

Ohio County Community Foundation Grants, 1812
Ohio County Community Fdn Mini-Grants, 1813
Olive B. Cole Foundation Grants, 1816
Orange County Community Foundation Grants, 1828
Parke County Community Foundation Grants, 1868
Perry County Community Foundation Recreation
    Grants, 1942
Perry County Community Foundation Youth
    Development Grants, 1943
PeyBack Foundation Grants, 1953
Pike County Community Foundation Recreation
    Grants, 1970
Pike County Community Foundation Youth
    Development Grants, 1971
PNC Foundation Affordable Housing Grants, 1983
PNC Foundation Community Services Grants, 1984
PNC Foundation Education Grants, 1985
PNC Foundation Grow Up Great Early Childhood
    Grants, 1986
PNC Foundation Revitalization and Stabilization
    Grants, 1987
Porter County Community Foundation Health and
    Wellness Grant, 2002
Porter County Community Foundation
    PCgivingproject Grants, 2003
Porter County Community Foundation Sparking the
    Arts Fund Grants, 2004
Porter County Community Foundation Women's
    Fund Grants, 2005
Portland Fdn - Women's Giving Circle Grant, 2006
Posey Community Foundation Women's Fund
    Grants, 2008
Posey County Community Foundation Recreation
    Grants, 2009
Posey County Community Foundation Youth
    Development Grants, 2010
Pulaski County Community Foundation Grants, 2038
Putnam County Community Fdn Grants, 2040
Ripley County Community Foundation Grants, 2077
Ripley County Community Foundation Small Project
    Grants, 2078
Robert and Helen Haddad Foundation Grants, 2084
Robert Lee Blaffer Foundation Grants, 2092
Rush County Community Foundation Grants, 2121
Scheumann Foundation Grants, 2166
Scott County Community Foundation Grants, 2170
Sensient Technologies Foundation Grants, 2180
Shopko Fdn Community Charitable Grants, 2191
South Madison Community Foundation - Teacher
    Creativity Mini Grants, 2225
Spencer County Community Foundation Recreation
    Grants, 2231
Spencer County Community Foundation Women's
    Fund Grants, 2232
Spencer County Community Foundation Youth
    Development Grants, 2233
Starke County Community Foundation Grants, 2236
Subaru of Indiana Automotive Fdn Grants, 2254
Sunoco Foundation Grants, 2256
TechKnowledgey Community Impact Grants, 2278
Toyota Motor Manufacturing of Indiana Grants, 2310
U.S. Cellular Corporation Grants, 2331
Vanderburgh Community Foundation Men's Fund
    Grants, 2373
Vanderburgh Community Foundation Recreation
    Grants, 2374
Vanderburgh Community Foundation Youth
    Development Grants, 2375
Vanderburgh County Community Foundation
    Women's Fund Grants, 2376
Vermillion County Community Fdn Grants, 2378
Walton Family Foundation Public Charter Startup
    Grants, 2409
Warrick County Community Foundation Recreation
    Grants, 2410
Warrick County Community Foundation Women's
    Fund, 2411
Warrick County Community Foundation Youth
    Development Grants, 2412
Washington County Community Fdn Grants, 2416

Wayne County Foundation Grants, 2419
Weaver Popcorn Foundation Grants, 2421
Welborn Baptist Foundation Promotion of Early
    Childhood Development Grants, 2423
Welborn Baptist Foundation School Based Health
    Grants, 2424
Welborn Foundation Promotion of Healthy
    Adolescent Development Grants, 2425
Wells County Foundation Grants, 2426
Western Indiana Community Fdn Grants, 2428
White County Community Foundation - Landis
    Memorial Scholarship, 2437
White County Community Foundation - Women
    Giving Together Grants, 2438
Whole Foods Foundation, 2445
William A. Miller Foundation Grants, 2453
Zollner Foundation Grants, 2526

Iowa
3M Company Fdn Community Giving Grants, 5
3M Company Foundation Health and Human
    Services Grants, 6
100 Club of Dubuque, 10
Adams Family Fdn of Nora Springs Grants, 118
AEGON Transamerica Foundation Education and
    Financial Literacy Grants, 132
AEGON Transamerica Foundation Health and
    Wellness Grants, 133
Albertsons Companies Foundation Nourishing
    Neighbors Grants, 221
Aldi Corporation Smart Kids Grants, 226
Alliant Energy Foundation Community Giving for
    Good Sponsorship Grants, 240
Bayer Fund Community Development Grants, 383
Bayer Fund STEM Education Grants, 384
C.H. Robinson Worldwide Foundation Grants, 489
Caesars Foundation Grants, 492
Circle K Corporation Contributions Grants, 614
Coleman Foundation Entrepreneurship Education
    Grants, 651
CUNA Mutual Group Fdn Community Grants, 770
Dollar General Family Literacy Grants, 835
Dollar General Summer Reading Grants, 836
Dollar General Youth Literacy Grants, 837
Gannett Foundation Community Action Grants, 1033
Georgia-Pacific Foundation Education Grants, 1058
Georgia-Pacific Fdn Entrepreneurship Grants, 1059
Go Daddy Cares Charitable Contributions, 1093
Hall-Perrine Foundation Grants, 1152
Kind World Foundation Grants, 1438
Land O'Lakes Foundation Community Grants, 1466
Lied Foundation Trust Grants, 1490
Meta and George Rosenberg Fdn Grants, 1644
Mid-Iowa Health Foundation Community Response
    Grants, 1667
Nationwide Insurance Foundation Grants, 1726
Nestle Purina PetCare Educational Grants, 1738
Nestle Purina PetCare Youth Grants, 1739
Philanthrofund Foundation Grants, 1959
Piper Jaffray Foundation Communities Giving
    Grants, 1974
Prudential Foundation Education Grants, 2028
R.J. McElroy Trust Grants, 2046
Robert and Betty Wo Foundation Grants, 2083
Roy J. Carver Trust Statewide Scholarships, 2116
Roy J. Carver Charitable Trust Youth Services and
    Recreation Grants, 2117
Shopko Fdn Community Charitable Grants, 2191
Tension Envelope Foundation Grants, 2284
U.S. Bank Foundation Grants, 2330
U.S. Cellular Corporation Grants, 2331
Union Pacific Fdn Community & Civic Grants, 2337
Union Pacific Foundation Health and Human
    Services Grants, 2338

Kansas
Abbott Fund Access to Health Care Grants, 45
Abbott Fund Community Engagement Grants, 46
Abbott Fund Global AIDS Care Grants, 47
Abbott Fund Science Education Grants, 48

Albertsons Companies Foundation Nourishing
    Neighbors Grants, 221
Aldi Corporation Smart Kids Grants, 226
Amerigroup Foundation Grants, 264
Boeing Company Contributions Grants, 462
Colorado Interstate Gas Grants, 661
Courtney S. Turner Charitable Trust Grants, 753
Dollar General Family Literacy Grants, 835
Dollar General Summer Reading Grants, 836
Dollar General Youth Literacy Grants, 837
Guy I. Bromley Trust Grants, 1136
Hatton W. Sumners Foundation for the Study and
    Teaching of Self Government Grants, 1196
Humana Foundation Grants, 1275
Kansas Health Fdn Major Initiatives Grants, 1414
Kansas Health Foundation Recognition Grants, 1415
Land O'Lakes Foundation Community Grants, 1466
Lewis H. Humphreys Charitable Trust Grants, 1486
Lied Foundation Trust Grants, 1490
MeadWestvaco Foundation Sustainable Communities
    Grants, 1627
Piper Jaffray Foundation Communities Giving
    Grants, 1974
PNC Foundation Affordable Housing Grants, 1983
PNC Foundation Community Services Grants, 1984
PNC Foundation Education Grants, 1985
PNC Foundation Grow Up Great Early Childhood
    Grants, 1986
PNC Foundation Revitalization and Stabilization
    Grants, 1987
R.D. and Joan Dale Hubbard Fdn Grants, 2044
Richard J. Stern Foundation for the Arts Grants, 2071
Shopko Fdn Community Charitable Grants, 2191
Tension Envelope Foundation Grants, 2284
Textron Corporate Contributions Grants, 2286
U.S. Bank Foundation Grants, 2330
Union Pacific Fdn Community & Civic Grants, 2337
Union Pacific Foundation Health and Human
    Services Grants, 2338
United Methodist Health Ministry Fund Grts, 2345
Walter S. and Evan C. Jones Testam Trust, 2407
Whole Foods Foundation, 2445

Kentucky
3M Company Fdn Community Giving Grants, 5
3M Company Foundation Health and Human
    Services Grants, 6
AEGON Transamerica Foundation Education and
    Financial Literacy Grants, 132
AEGON Transamerica Foundation Health and
    Wellness Grants, 133
Aldi Corporation Smart Kids Grants, 226
Alpha Natural Resources Corporate Giving, 246
American Electric Power Corporate Grants, 252
American Electric Power Foundation Grants, 253
American Woodmark Foundation Grants, 263
Amerigroup Foundation Grants, 264
Anheuser-Busch Foundation Grants, 273
Annie Gardner Foundation Grants, 277
Anthony Munoz Foundation Straight A Student
    Campaign Grants, 280
Appalachian Community Fund LGBTQ Fund
    Grants, 284
Appalachian Regional Commission Business
    Development Revolving Loan Fund Grants, 285
Appalachian Regional Commission Education and
    Training Grants, 286
Appalachian Regional Commission Entrepreneurship
    and Business Development Grants, 287
Appalachian Regional Commission Health Care
    Grants, 288
Appalachian Regl Commission Housing Grants, 289
Ar-Hale Family Foundation Grants, 290
Arkema Foundation Grants, 298
Arkema Foundation Science Teachers Grants, 299
Blue Grass Community Foundation Clark County
    Fund Grants, 444
Blue Grass Community Foundation Early Childhood
    Education and Literacy Grants, 445

Blue Grass Community Foundation Fayette County
    Fund Grants, 446
Blue Grass Community Foundation Franklin County
    Fund Grants, 447
Blue Grass Community Foundation Harrison County
    Fund Grants, 448
Blue Grass Community Foundation Hudson-Ellis
    Grants, 449
Blue Grass Community Foundation Madison County
    Fund Grants, 450
Blue Grass Community Foundation Magoffin County
    Fund Grants, 451
Blue Grass Community Foundation Morgan County
    Fund Grants, 452
Blue Grass Community Foundation Rowan County
    Fund Grants, 453
Blue Grass Community Foundation Woodford
    County Fund Grants, 454
Brunswick Foundation Dollars for Doers Grants, 478
Brunswick Foundation Grants, 479
C.H. Robinson Worldwide Foundation Grants, 489
Cincinnati Bell Foundation Grants, 612
Circle K Corporation Contributions Grants, 614
Clark County Community Foundation Grants, 626
Community Foundation of Louisville AIDS Project
    Fund Grants, 716
Community Foundation of Louisville Anna Marble
    Memorial Fund for Princeton Grants, 717
Community Foundation of Louisville Boyette and
    Edna Edwards Fund Grants, 718
Community Foundation of Louisville C. E. and S.
    Endowment for the Parks Fund Grants, 719
Community Foundation of Louisville CHAMP Fund
    Grants, 720
Community Foundation of Louisville Children's
    Memorial Marker Fund Grants, 721
Community Foundation of Louisville Delta Dental of
    Kentucky Fund Grants, 722
Community Foundation of Louisville Dr. W.
    Barnett Owen Memorial Fund for the Children of
    Louisville and Jefferson County Grants, 723
Community Foundation of Louisville Education
    Grants, 724
Community Foundation of Louisville Fund 4 Women
    and Girls Grants, 725
Community Foundation of Louisville Human
    Services Grants, 726
Community Foundation of Louisville Madi and Jim
    Tate Fund Grants, 727
Community Foundation of Louisville We Day
    Kentucky Grants, 728
Community Foundation of Louisville Winston N. and
    Nancy H. Bloch Educational Fund Grants, 729
Community Foundation of Louisville Youth
    Philanthropy Council Grants, 730
Cralle Foundation Grants, 760
Dollar General Family Literacy Grants, 835
Dollar General Summer Reading Grants, 836
Dollar General Youth Literacy Grants, 837
Duke Energy Foundation Local Impact Grants, 872
Effie Kuhlman Charitable Trust Grants, 896
Fifth Third Bank Corporate Giving, 958
Fifth Third Foundation Grants, 959
Foundation for a Healthy Kentucky Grants, 988
Gannett Foundation Community Action Grants, 1033
Gardner Foundation Grants, 1035
George and Ruth Bradford Foundation Grants, 1042
Georgia-Pacific Foundation Education Grants, 1058
Georgia-Pacific Fdn Entrepreneurship Grants, 1059
Green River Area Community Fdn Grants, 1117
H.B. Fuller Foundation Grants, 1138
Harmony Project Grants, 1170
Hazel and Walter T. Bales Foundation Grants, 1220
Herman H. Nettelroth Fund Grants, 1246
Humana Foundation Grants, 1275
Jacob G. Schmidlapp Trusts Grants, 1336
James Graham Brown Foundation Grants, 1340
Josephine Schell Russell Chartbl Trust Grants, 1389
Joyce and Randy Seckman Charitable Foundation
    Grants, 1393

JP Morgan Chase Fdn Arts and Culture Grants, 1394
Kentucky Arts Cncl Access Assistance Grants, 1428
Kimball International-Habig Foundation Education
    Grants, 1433
Kimball International-Habig Foundation Health and
    Human Services Grants, 1434
LISC Financial Stability Grants, 1501
Marathon Petroleum Corporation Grants, 1551
Mary Cofer Trigg Trust Fund Grants, 1587
Michelin North America Challenge Education, 1660
Piper Jaffray Foundation Communities Giving
    Grants, 1974
PNC Foundation Affordable Housing Grants, 1983
PNC Foundation Community Services Grants, 1984
PNC Foundation Education Grants, 1985
PNC Foundation Grow Up Great Early Childhood
    Grants, 1986
PNC Foundation Revitalization and Stabilization
    Grants, 1987
Shopko Fdn Community Charitable Grants, 2191
Sunoco Foundation Grants, 2256
TAC Arts Education Funds for At-Risk Youth, 2266
TAC Arts Education Mini Grants, 2267
TAC Touring Arts and Arts Access Touring Arts
    Grants, 2269
Toyota Motor Manufacturing of Indiana Grants, 2310
Toyota Motor Manuf of Kentucky Grants, 2311
U.S. Bank Foundation Grants, 2330
V.V. Cooke Foundation Grants, 2371
Watson-Brown Foundation Grants, 2418
Welborn Baptist Foundation Promotion of Early
    Childhood Development Grants, 2423
Welborn Baptist Foundation School Based Health
    Grants, 2424
Welborn Foundation Promotion of Healthy
    Adolescent Development Grants, 2425
Whole Foods Foundation, 2445
William E. Barth Foundation Grants, 2463
WinnCompanies Charitable Giving, 2479

Louisiana
ACF Head Start and/or Early Head Start Grantee -
    St. Landry Parish, Louisiana, 83
Adams and Reese Corporate Giving Grants, 114
Albertsons Companies Foundation Nourishing
    Neighbors Grants, 221
Aldi Corporation Smart Kids Grants, 226
American Electric Power Corporate Grants, 252
American Electric Power Foundation Grants, 253
Amerigroup Foundation Grants, 264
Barrasso, Usdin, Kupperman, Freeman, and Sarver
    Corporate Grants, 362
Baton Rouge Area Foundation Community Coffee
    Fund Grants, 363
Baton Rouge Area Foundation Every Kid a King
    Fund Grants, 364
Baton Rouge Area Foundation Grants, 365
Bayer Fund Community Development Grants, 383
Bayer Fund STEM Education Grants, 384
Brunswick Foundation Dollars for Doers Grants, 478
Brunswick Foundation Grants, 479
Cabot Corporation Foundation Grants, 490
Caesars Foundation Grants, 492
Collins C. Diboll Private Foundation Grants, 657
Cudd Foundation Grants, 769
Deuce McAllister Catch 22 Foundation Grants, 828
Dollar Energy Fund Grants, 834
Dollar General Family Literacy Grants, 835
Dollar General Summer Reading Grants, 836
Dollar General Youth Literacy Grants, 837
Ella West Freeman Foundation Grants, 904
Entergy Charitable Foundation Education and
    Literacy Grants, 917
Entergy Charitable Foundation Low-Income
    Initiatives and Solutions Grants, 918
Entergy Corporation Micro Grants, 919
Entergy Corporation Open Grants for Arts and
    Culture, 920
Entergy Corporation Open Grants for Healthy
    Families, 921

Fdn for the Mid South Communities Grants, 992
Foundation for the Mid South Education Grants, 993
Gannett Foundation Community Action Grants, 1033
Georgia-Pacific Foundation Education Grants, 1058
Georgia-Pacific Fdn Entrepreneurship Grants, 1059
German Protestant Orphan Asylum Foundation
    Grants, 1066
Gil and Dody Weaver Foundation Grants, 1071
GNOF Albert N. & Hattie M. McClure Grants, 1076
GNOF Bayou Communities Grants, 1077
GNOF Cox Charities of New Orleans Grants, 1079
GNOF Exxon-Mobil Grants, 1080
GNOF Freeman Challenge Grants, 1081
GNOF Norco Community Grants, 1089
GNOF Organizational Effectiveness Grants and
    Workshops, 1090
GNOF Plaquemines Community Grants, 1091
GNOF Stand Up For Our Children Grants, 1092
Hatton W. Sumners Foundation for the Study and
    Teaching of Self Government Grants, 1196
Hazen Foundation Public Education Grants, 1221
Humana Foundation Grants, 1275
JP Morgan Chase Fdn Arts and Culture Grants, 1394
KaBOOM! Build it Grant, 1402
Kinder Morgan Foundation Grants, 1436
Lockheed Martin Corporation Fdn Grants, 1505
Marathon Petroleum Corporation Grants, 1551
MeadWestvaco Foundation Sustainable Communities
    Grants, 1627
PeyBack Foundation Grants, 1953
Pinnacle Entertainment Foundation Grants, 1972
Posse Foundation Scholarships, 2011
Prudential Foundation Education Grants, 2028
Textron Corporate Contributions Grants, 2286
Union Pacific Fdn Community & Civic Grants, 2337
Union Pacific Foundation Health and Human
    Services Grants, 2338
Walton Family Foundation Public Charter Startup
    Grants, 2409
Watson-Brown Foundation Grants, 2418
Whole Foods Foundation, 2445
Williams Comps Homegrown Giving Grants, 2474

Maine
Aetna Foundation Regional Health Grants, 134
Agnes M. Lindsay Trust Grants, 140
Albertsons Companies Foundation Nourishing
    Neighbors Grants, 221
Amerigroup Foundation Grants, 264
Amica Insurance Company Community Grants, 267
Amica Insurance Company Sponsorships, 268
Bay and Paul Foundations PreK-12 Transformative
    Learning Practices Grants, 370
Baystate Financial Charitable Foundation Grants, 385
BBF Maine Family Literacy Initiative Implementation
    Grants, 387
BBF Maine Family Literacy Initiative Planning
    Grants, 388
C.F. Adams Charitable Trust Grants, 488
Clayton F. and Ruth L. Hawkridge Foundation
    Grants, 630
Doree Taylor Charitable Foundation Grants, 843
Dorr Foundation Grants, 846
Four Lanes Trust Grants, 1005
Gannett Foundation Community Action Grants, 1033
George I. Alden Trust Grants, 1051
George P. Davenport Trust Fund Grants, 1054
Hannaford Charitable Foundation Grants, 1163
Hannaford Supermarkets Community Giving, 1164
HRAMF Charles H. Hood Foundation Child Health
    Research Awards, 1262
Jack and Dorothy Byrne Foundation Grants, 1329
Libra Foundation Grants, 1489
Maine Community Foundation Edward H. Daveis
    Benevolent Fund Grants, 1540
Maine Community Foundation Equity Grants, 1541
Maine Community Fdn Peaks Island Grants, 1542
Maine Community Foundation Penobscot Valley
    Health Association Grants, 1543

Maine Community Foundation People of Color Fund
    Grants, 1544
Maine Community Foundation Vincent B. and
    Barbara G. Welch Grants, 1545
Maine Women's Fund Econ Security Grants, 1546
Maine Women's Fund Girls' Grantmaking Intv, 1547
Merck Family Fund Urban Farming and Youth
    Leadership Grants, 1635
Narragansett Number One Foundation Grants, 1712
Richard Davoud Donchian Foundation Grants, 2070
S. Spencer Scott Fund Grants, 2129
Sunoco Foundation Grants, 2256
Whole Foods Foundation, 2445
Yawkey Foundation Grants, 2510

Marshall Islands
7-Eleven Corporate Giving Grants, 8
AAAS/Subaru SB&F Prize for Excl in Sci Books, 22
AASA Urgent Need Mini-Grants, 43
ACF Social and Economic Development Strategies
    Grants, 93
Adidas Corporation General Grants, 125
A Little Hope Grants, 235
Bank of America Charitable Foundation Matching
    Gifts, 356
Bank of America Charitable Foundation Volunteer
    Grants, 358
Beckman Coulter Foundation Grants, 394
Bee Conservancy Sponsor-A-Hive Grants, 395
Brinker Int Corporation Charitable Giving, 471
Brookdale Fdn Relatives as Parents Grants, 474
Fidelity Charitable Gift Fund Grants, 956
First Nations Development Institute Native
    Agriculture and Food Systems Initiative
    Scholarships, 971
First Nations Development Institute Native Arts
    Initiative Grants, 972
First Nations Development Institute Native Language
    Immersion Initiative Grants, 973
First Nations Development Institute Native Youth
    and Culture Fund Grants, 974
First Nations Development Institute Nourishing
    Native Children: Feeding Our Future Project
    Grants, 975
Ford Foundation BUILD Grants, 984
From the Top Alumni Leadership Grants, 1025
From the Top Jack Kent Cooke Young Artist
    Scholarships, 1026
Good+Foundation Grants, 1096
IMLS Grants to State Library Administrative
    Agencies, 1298
IMLS National Leadership Grants for Libraries, 1299
Jack Kent Cooke Fdn Young Artist Awards, 1333
Judy and Peter Blum Kovler Foundation Grants, 1396
NEA Student Program Communities Redefining
    Education Advocacy Through Empowerment
    (CREATE) Grants, 1733
NSF Perception, Action and Cognition (PAC)
    Research Grants, 1775
NZDIA Community Org Grants Scheme, 1796
Ray Charles Foundation Grants, 2058
Target Corporation Soccer Grants, 2271
U.S. Department of Education Promise
    Neighborhoods Grants, 2332
USAID Community Livelihoods Project in Yemen
    Grant, 2352
USAID Family Planning and Reproductive Health
    Methods Grants, 2353
USAID Global Development Alliance Grants, 2354
USAID National Governance Project in Yemen
    Grant, 2357
USAID School Improvement Program Grants, 2360
USAID U.S.-Egypt Learning Grants, 2361
WHO Foundation Education/Literacy Grants, 2442
WSF Rusty Kanokogi Fund for the Advancement of
    U.S. Judo Grants, 2495
WSF Sports 4 Life Grants, 2496
WSF Sports 4 Life Regional Grants, 2497
WSF Travel and Training Fund Grants, 2498

Maryland
A.C. and Penney Hubbard Foundation Grants, 19
Abell Foundation Education Grants, 53
AEGON Transamerica Foundation Education and
    Financial Literacy Grants, 132
AEGON Transamerica Foundation Health and
    Wellness Grants, 133
Aetna Foundation Regional Health Grants, 134
Albertsons Companies Foundation Nourishing
    Neighbors Grants, 221
Aldi Corporation Smart Kids Grants, 226
Alloy Family Foundation Grants, 241
American Woodmark Foundation Grants, 263
Amerigroup Foundation Grants, 264
Amica Insurance Company Community Grants, 267
Amica Insurance Company Sponsorships, 268
Anne Arundel Women Giving Together Regular
    Grants, 275
Appalachian Regional Commission Business
    Development Revolving Loan Fund Grants, 285
Appalachian Regional Commission Education and
    Training Grants, 286
Appalachian Regional Commission Entrepreneurship
    and Business Development Grants, 287
Appalachian Regional Commission Health Care
    Grants, 288
Appalachian Regl Commission Housing Grants, 289
Aunt Kate Foundation Grants, 331
Babcock Charitable Trust Grants, 343
Bainum Family Foundation Grants, 345
Baltimore Community Foundation Building Stronger
    Neighborhoods Regionwide Grants, 347
Baltimore Community Foundation Children's Fresh
    Air Society Fund Grants, 348
Baltimore Community Foundation Mitzvah Fund for
    Good Deeds Grants, 349
Baltimore Ravens Corporate Giving, 350
Baltimore Ravens Foundation Play 60 Grants, 351
Baltimore Ravens Foundation Scholarships, 352
Baltimore Ravens Fdn Youth Football Grants, 353
BBF Maryland Family Literacy Initiative
    Implementation Grants, 389
BBF Maryland Family Literacy Initiative Planning
    Grants, 390
Bernau Family Foundation Grants, 413
Boeing Company Contributions Grants, 462
Brunswick Foundation Dollars for Doers Grants, 478
Brunswick Foundation Grants, 479
Carl M. Freeman Foundation FACES Grants, 507
Carl M. Freeman Foundation Grants, 508
Charles Crane Family Foundation Grants, 563
Charles Delmar Foundation Grants, 564
Chesapeake Bay Trust Environmental Education
    Grants, 577
Chesapeake Bay Trust Mini Grants, 578
Chesapeake Bay Trust Outreach and Community
    Engagement Grants, 579
Claude A. and Blanche McCubbin Abbott Charitable
    Trust Grants, 628
Clayton Baker Trust Grants, 629
Clayton Fund Grants, 631
Community Foundation for the National Capital
    Region Community Leadership Grants, 688
Corina Higginson Trust Grants, 750
David and Barbara B. Hirschhorn Foundation
    Education and Literacy Grants, 786
David and Barbara B. Hirschhorn Foundation
    Summer Camping Grants, 787
Delmarva Power & Light Contributions, 821
Delmarva Power & Light Mini-Grants, 822
Dollar Energy Fund Grants, 834
Dollar General Family Literacy Grants, 835
Dollar General Summer Reading Grants, 836
Dollar General Youth Literacy Grants, 837
Dominion Foundation Grants, 839
FirstEnergy Foundation Community Grants, 965
FirstEnergy Foundation Science, Technology,
    Engineering, and Mathematics Grants, 966
Four Lanes Trust Grants, 1005
Gannett Foundation Community Action Grants, 1033

Giant Food Charitable Grants, 1068
Goldseker Foundation Non-Profit Management
  Assistance Grants, 1095
HBF Pathways Out of Poverty Grants, 1222
Henry and Ruth Blaustein Rosenberg Foundation
  Youth Development Grants, 1237
J. Willard and Alice S. Marriott Fdn Grants, 1327
Jack Kent Cooke Fdn Good Neighbor Grants, 1331
KaBOOM! Build it Grant, 1402
Kennedy Center National Symphony Orchestra Youth
  Fellowships, 1426
Land O'Lakes Foundation Mid-Atlantic Grants, 1467
Leonsis Foundation Grants, 1485
Lockheed Martin Corporation Fdn Grants, 1505
Mabel H. Flory Charitable Trust Grants, 1527
Marion I. and Henry J. Knott Foundation
  Discretionary Grants, 1571
Marion I. and Henry J. Knott Fdn Grants, 1572
Maryland State Arts Council Arts in Communities
  Grants, 1592
Maryland State Dept of Education 21st Century
  Community Learning Centers Grants, 1593
Maryland State Dept of Education Coordinating
  Entity Services for the Maryland Child Care Res
  Centers Network Grants, 1594
Maryland State Department of Education Judith P.
  Hoyer Early Care and Ed Center Grants, 1595
Maryland State Department of Education Striving
  Readers Comprehensive Literacy Grants, 1596
Maurice R. Robinson Fund Grants, 1611
Mead Family Foundation Grants, 1625
Mercedes-Benz USA Corporate Contributions, 1634
Merck Family Fund Urban Farming and Youth
  Leadership Grants, 1635
Meyer Foundation Benevon Grants, 1648
Meyer Foundation Education Grants, 1649
Meyer Fdn Management Assistance Grants, 1651
Morton K. and Jane Blaustein Foundation
  Educational Opportunity Grants, 1700
Nationwide Insurance Foundation Grants, 1726
Ober Kaler Community Grants, 1801
OSF Baltimore Criminal and Juve Justice Grts, 1839
OSF Baltimore Education and Youth Development
  Grants, 1840
PennPAT Fee-Support Grants for Presenters, 1930
PennPAT New Directions Grants for Presenters, 1931
Philip L. Graham Fund Education Grants, 1962
PNC Foundation Affordable Housing Grants, 1983
PNC Foundation Community Services Grants, 1984
PNC Foundation Education Grants, 1985
PNC Foundation Grow Up Great Early Childhood
  Grants, 1986
PNC Foundation Revitalization and Stabilization
  Grants, 1987
Rathmann Family Foundation Grants, 2057
Richard Davoud Donchian Foundation Grants, 2070
Ruddie Memorial Youth Foundation Grants, 2120
S. Spencer Scott Fund Grants, 2129
Salmon Foundation Grants, 2140
Screen Actors Guild BookPALS Assistance, 2171
Screen Actors Guild PencilPALS Assistance, 2172
Screen Actors Guild StagePALS Assistance, 2173
Speer Trust Grants, 2230
Sunoco Foundation Grants, 2256
Textron Corporate Contributions Grants, 2286
Thomas W. Bradley Foundation Grants, 2293
U.S. Cellular Corporation Grants, 2331
VSA/Metlife Connect All Grants, 2392
Washington Area Fuel Fund Grants, 2413
Washington Gas Charitable Contributions, 2417
Whole Foods Foundation, 2445
William J. and Dorothy K. O'Neill Foundation
  Responsive Grants, 2468

Massachusetts
2 Depot Square Ipswich Charitable Foundation
  Grants, 3
3M Company Fdn Community Giving Grants, 5
3M Company Foundation Health and Human
  Services Grants, 6

Aaron Foundation Grants, 42
Abbott Fund Access to Health Care Grants, 45
Abbott Fund Community Engagement Grants, 46
Abbott Fund Global AIDS Care Grants, 47
Abbott Fund Science Education Grants, 48
Adelaide Breed Bayrd Foundation Grants, 123
Agnes M. Lindsay Trust Grants, 140
Albertsons Companies Foundation Nourishing
  Neighbors Grants, 221
Albert W. Rice Charitable Foundation Grants, 223
Aldi Corporation Smart Kids Grants, 226
Alfred E. Chase Charitable Foundation Grants, 233
Amelia Sillman Rockwell and Carlos Perry Rockwell
  Charities Fund Grants, 250
American Express Charitable Fund Scholarships, 254
Amerigroup Foundation Grants, 264
Amica Insurance Company Community Grants, 267
Amica Insurance Company Sponsorships, 268
Anheuser-Busch Foundation Grants, 273
Babcock Charitable Trust Grants, 343
Bay and Paul Foundations PreK-12 Transformative
  Learning Practices Grants, 370
Bayer Fund Community Development Grants, 383
Bayer Fund STEM Education Grants, 384
Baystate Financial Charitable Foundation Grants, 385
Blossom Fund Grants, 441
Bradley C. Higgins Foundation Grants, 467
Brown Rudnick Charitable Foundation Community
  Grants, 477
Bushrod H. Campbell and Adah F. Hall Charity
  Fund Grants, 486
C.F. Adams Charitable Trust Grants, 488
Cabot Corporation Foundation Grants, 490
Campbell Soup Foundation Grants, 501
Charles H. Hall Foundation, 565
Charles H. Pearson Foundation Grants, 566
Cheryl Spencer Memorial Foundation Grants, 576
CHT Foundation Education Grants, 603
Citizens Bank Charitable Foundation Grants, 616
Clayton F. and Ruth L. Hawkridge Foundation
  Grants, 630
Dominion Foundation Grants, 839
Dorr Foundation Grants, 846
Eastern Bank Charitable Foundation Neighborhood
  Support Grants, 880
Eastern Bank Charitable Foundation Partnerships
  Grants, 881
Eastern Bank Charitable Foundation Targeted
  Grants, 882
Ellen Abbott Gilman Trust Grants, 905
Entergy Charitable Foundation Education and
  Literacy Grants, 917
Entergy Charitable Foundation Low-Income
  Initiatives and Solutions Grants, 918
Entergy Corporation Micro Grants, 919
Entergy Corporation Open Grants for Arts and
  Culture, 920
Entergy Corporation Open Grants for Healthy
  Families, 921
Essex County Community Foundation Dee and King
  Webster Fund for Greater Lawrence Grants, 929
Essex County Community Foundation F1rst Jobs
  Fund Grants, 930
Essex County Community Foundation Greater
  Lawrence Community Fund Grants, 931
Essex County Community Foundation Greater
  Lawrence Summer Fund Grants, 932
Essex County Community Foundation Merrimack
  Valley Municipal Business Development and
  Recovery Fund Grants, 933
Essex County Community Foundation Women's
  Fund Grants, 934
Ezra M. Cutting Trust Grants, 945
Fassino Foundation Grants, 949
Four Lanes Trust Grants, 1005
Frank Reed and Margaret Jane Peters Memorial Fund
  Grants, 1013
Frank Reed and Margaret Jane Peters Memorial Fund
  II Grants, 1014
Fuller Foundation Youth At Risk Grants, 1028

George F. Baker Trust Grants, 1046
George H. and Jane A. Mifflin Memorial Fund
  Grants, 1048
George I. Alden Trust Grants, 1051
George W.P. Magee Trust Grants, 1056
George W. Wells Foundation Grants, 1057
Georgia-Pacific Foundation Education Grants, 1058
Georgia-Pacific Fdn Entrepreneurship Grants, 1059
Grand Circle Foundation Associates Grants, 1102
Hannaford Charitable Foundation Grants, 1163
Hannaford Supermarkets Community Giving, 1164
Harold Brooks Foundation Grants, 1172
Hasbro Children's Fund Grants, 1189
Hasbro Corp Gift of Play Holiday Giving, 1190
Hasbro Corporation Gift of Play Hospital and
  Pediatric Health Giving, 1191
Hasbro Corporation Gift of Play Shelter Support
  Giving, 1192
Hasbro Corporation Gift of Play Summer Camp
  Support, 1193
Helen E. Ellis Charitable Trust Grants, 1228
Horace A. Moses Charitable Trust Grants, 1261
HRAMF Charles H. Hood Foundation Child Health
  Research Awards, 1262
HRAMF Community Health Improvement Project
  Grants in Bowdoin Geneva, 1263
Intel Corporation Community Grants, 1311
Jack and Dorothy Byrne Foundation Grants, 1329
Jack Satter Foundation Grants, 1334
Joan Bentinck-Smith Charitable Fdn Grants, 1367
Julia Richardson Brown Foundation Grants, 1398
Kevin J Major Youth Sports Scholarships, 1431
Linden Foundation Grants, 1494
Lloyd G. Balfour Foundation Attleboro-Specific
  Charities Grants, 1502
Lloyd G. Balfour Foundation Scholarships, 1503
Mabel A. Horne Fund Grants, 1525
Mabel Louise Riley Foundation Family Strengthening
  Small Grants, 1528
Mabel Louise Riley Foundation Grants, 1529
Mary W.B. Curtis Trust Grants, 1599
Massachusetts Cultural Council Local Cultural
  Council (LCC) Grants, 1601
Massachusetts Cultural Cncl YouthReach Grts, 1602
MassMutual Foundation Edonomic Development
  Grants, 1603
Maurice R. Robinson Fund Grants, 1611
McCarthy Family Fdn Charity Fund Grants, 1614
Medtronic Foundation Community Link Arts, Civic,
  and Culture Grants, 1629
Medtronic Foundation CommunityLink Health
  Grants, 1630
Medtronic Foundation Community Link Human
  Services Grants, 1631
Merck Family Fund Urban Farming and Youth
  Leadership Grants, 1635
MetroWest Health Foundation Grants to Reduce
  the Incidence of High Risk Behaviors Among
  Adolescents, 1646
Middlesex Savings Charitable Foundation Basic
  Human Needs Grants, 1668
Middlesex Savings Charitable Foundation Capacity
  Building Grants, 1669
Middlesex Savings Charitable Foundation
  Educational Opportunities Grants, 1670
Moses Kimball Fund Grants, 1701
Nathaniel and Elizabeth P. Stevens Foundation
  Grants, 1719
Nellie Mae Education Foundation District-Level
  Change Grants, 1736
OMNOVA Solutions Fdn Education Grants, 1820
Oren Campbell McCleary Chartbl Trust Grants, 1837
OtterCares Inspiration Fund Grants, 1850
Paul and Edith Babson Foundation Grants, 1881
Peabody Foundation Grants, 1922
Perkin Fund Grants, 1937
Perkins Charitable Foundation Grants, 1939
Perpetual Benevolent Fund, 1940
Peter and Elizabeth C. Tower Foundation Intellectual
  Disabilities Grants, 1944

Peter and Elizabeth C. Tower Foundation Learning
    Disability Grants, 1945
Peter and Elizabeth C. Tower Foundation Mental
    Health Grants, 1946
Peter and Elizabeth C. Tower Foundation Small
    Grants, 1947
Peter and Elizabeth C. Tower Foundation Substance
    Use Disorders Grants, 1948
Peter and Elizabeth C. Tower Foundation Technology
    Initiative Grants, 1949
Peter and Elizabeth C. Tower Foundation Technology
    Planning Grants, 1950
PNC Foundation Affordable Housing Grants, 1983
PNC Foundation Community Services Grants, 1984
PNC Foundation Education Grants, 1985
PNC Foundation Grow Up Great Early Childhood
    Grants, 1986
PNC Foundation Revitalization and Stabilization
    Grants, 1987
Posse Foundation Scholarships, 2011
Price Chopper's Golub Foundation Grants, 2020
Robbins Charitable Foundation Grants, 2081
Ruddie Memorial Youth Foundation Grants, 2120
S. Spencer Scott Fund Grants, 2129
Sara Elizabeth O'Brien Trust Grants, 2161
Sarah G. McCarthy Memorial Foundation, 2162
Screen Actors Guild BookPALS Assistance, 2171
Screen Actors Guild PencilPALS Assistance, 2172
Screen Actors Guild StagePALS Assistance, 2173
Southern New England Folk and Traditional Arts
    Apprenticeship Grants, 2224
Sunoco Foundation Grants, 2256
TE Foundation Grants, 2279
Textron Corporate Contributions Grants, 2286
VSA/Metlife Connect All Grants, 2392
Whole Foods Foundation, 2445
WinnCompanies Charitable Giving, 2479
Yawkey Foundation Grants, 2510

Michigan

3M Company Fdn Community Giving Grants, 5
3M Company Foundation Health and Human
    Services Grants, 6
A. Alfred Taubman Foundation Grants, 18
Abbott Fund Access to Health Care Grants, 45
Abbott Fund Community Engagement Grants, 46
Abbott Fund Global AIDS Care Grants, 47
Abbott Fund Science Education Grants, 48
Adray Foundation, 130
Albertsons Companies Foundation Nourishing
    Neighbors Grants, 221
Alden and Vada Dow Fund Grants, 225
Aldi Corporation Smart Kids Grants, 226
American Electric Power Corporate Grants, 252
American Electric Power Foundation Grants, 253
Amica Insurance Company Community Grants, 267
Amica Insurance Company Sponsorships, 268
Anderson Foundation Grants, 271
Ann Ludington Sullivan Foundation Grants, 279
Arkema Foundation Grants, 298
Arkema Foundation Science Teachers Grants, 299
Arts Council of Greater Lansing Young Creatives
    Grants, 314
Batts Foundation Grants, 367
Bay Area Community Foundation Arenac
    Community Fund Grants, 371
Bay Area Community Foundation Arenac County
    Healthy Youth/Healthy Seniors Fund Grants, 372
Bay Area Community Fdn Auburn Area Chamber of
    Commerce Enrichment Fund Grants, 373
Bay Area Community Foundation Bay County
    Healthy Youth/Healthy Seniors Fund Grants, 374
Bay Area Community Foundation Civic League
    Endowment Fund Grants, 375
Bay Area Community Foundation Community
    Initiative Fund Grants, 376
Bay Area Community Foundation Dow
    CommunityGives Youth Service Prog Grants, 377
Bay Area Community Foundation Elizabeth Husband
    Fund Grants, 378

Bay Area Community Foundation Human Services
    Fund Grants, 379
Bay Area Community Foundation Leslie L. Squires
    Foundation Grants, 380
Bay Area Community Foundation Nathalie Awrey
    Memorial Fund Grants, 381
Bay Area Community Foundation Semiannual
    Grants, 382
Bayer Fund Community Development Grants, 383
Bayer Fund STEM Education Grants, 384
BCBSM Foundation Community Health Matching
    Grants, 392
Brunswick Foundation Dollars for Doers Grants, 478
Brunswick Foundation Grants, 479
C.H. Robinson Worldwide Foundation Grants, 489
Calvin Johnson Jr. Foundation Mini Grants, 498
Castle Foundation Grants, 517
CFNEM Women's Giving Circle Grants, 557
CFNEM Youth Advisory Council Grants, 558
Cincinnati Milacron Foundation Grants, 613
Circle K Corporation Contributions Grants, 614
Coleman Foundation Entrepreneurship Education
    Grants, 651
Community Foundation for SE Michigan Chelsea
    Community Fdn Capacity Building Grants, 679
Community Foundation for SE Michigan Chelsea
    Community Foundation General Grant, 680
Community Foundation for SE Michigan Detroit
    Auto Dealers Association Charitable Foundation
    Fund Grants, 681
Community Foundation for SE Michigan Head Start
    Innovation Fund, 682
Community Foundation for SE Michigan Livingston
    County Grants, 683
Community Foundation for SE Michigan Renaissance
    of Values Scholarships, 684
Community Foundation for SE Michigan Southeast
    Michigan Immigrant and Refugee Funder
    Collaborative Grant, 685
Community Foundation for SE Michigan Youth
    Leadership Grant, 686
Dollar General Family Literacy Grants, 835
Dollar General Summer Reading Grants, 836
Dollar General Youth Literacy Grants, 837
DTE Energy Foundation Community Development
    Grants, 866
DTE Energy Foundation Diversity Grants, 867
DTE Energy Foundation Environmental Grants, 868
DTE Energy Foundation Health and Human Services
    Grants, 869
DTE Energy Foundation Leadership Grants, 870
Entergy Charitable Foundation Education and
    Literacy Grants, 917
Entergy Charitable Foundation Low-Income
    Initiatives and Solutions Grants, 918
Entergy Corporation Micro Grants, 919
Entergy Corporation Open Grants for Arts and
    Culture, 920
Entergy Corporation Open Grants for Healthy
    Families, 921
Fifth Third Bank Corporate Giving, 958
Fifth Third Foundation Grants, 959
Four County Community Foundation 21st Century
    Education Fund Grants, 999
Four County Community Foundation General
    Grants, 1000
Four County Community Foundation Healthy
    Senior/Healthy Youth Fund Grants, 1001
Four County Community Foundation Kellogg Group
    Grants, 1002
Fremont Area Community Foundation Amazing X
    Grants, 1019
Fremont Area Community Foundation Community
    Grants, 1020
Fremont Area Community Foundation Education
    Mini-Grants, 1021
Fremont Area Community Foundation Youth
    Advisory Committee Grants, 1022
Gannett Foundation Community Action Grants, 1033
George and Ruth Bradford Foundation Grants, 1042

Georgia-Pacific Foundation Education Grants, 1058
Georgia-Pacific Fdn Entrepreneurship Grants, 1059
Gerber Fdn West Michigan Youth Grants, 1065
Granger Foundation Grants, 1103
Gregory and Helayne Brown Charitable Foundation
    Grants, 1119
GTRCF Boys and Girls Club of Grand Traverse
    Endowment Grants, 1126
GTRCF Elk Rapids Area Community Endowment
    Grants, 1127
GTRCF Genuine Leelanau Charitable Endowment
    Grants, 1128
GTRCF Grand Traverse Families in Action for Youth
    Endowment Grants, 1129
GTRCF Healthy Youth and Healthy Seniors
    Endowment Grants, 1130
GTRCF Joan Rajkovich McGarry Family Education
    Endowment Grants, 1131
GTRCF Traverse City Track Club Endowment
    Grants, 1132
GTRCF Youth Endowment Grants, 1133
H.B. Fuller Foundation Grants, 1138
Harry A. and Margaret D. Towsley Foundation
    Grants, 1180
Harvey Randall Wickes Foundation Grants, 1188
Hillsdale County Community Foundation General
    Grants, 1250
Hillsdale County Community Foundation Love Your
    Community Grants, 1251
Hillsdale County Community Foundation
    Y.O.U.T.H. Grants, 1252
Humana Foundation Grants, 1275
ICCF Youth Advisory Council Grants, 1282
Irving S. Gilmore Foundation Grants, 1314
Jacob G. Schmidlapp Trusts Grants, 1336
Jewish Fund Grants, 1364
JP Morgan Chase Fdn Arts and Culture Grants, 1394
KaBOOM! Build it Grant, 1402
KaBOOM! Play Everywhere Design Challenge, 1405
Kalamazoo Community Foundation Early Childhood
    Learning and School Readiness Grants, 1407
Kalamazoo Community Foundation Good Neighbor
    Grants, 1408
Kalamazoo Community Foundation Individuals and
    Families Grants, 1409
Kalamazoo Community Foundation John E. Fetzer
    Institute Fund Grants, 1410
Kalamazoo Community Foundation LBGT Equality
    Fund Grants, 1411
Kalamazoo Community Foundation Youth
    Development Grants, 1412
Land O'Lakes Foundation Community Grants, 1466
Laura Musser Intercultural Harmony Grants, 1472
LISC Financial Stability Grants, 1501
Marathon Petroleum Corporation Grants, 1551
Matilda R. Wilson Fund Grants, 1605
McGregor Fund Human Services Grants, 1621
MGM Resorts Foundation Community Grants, 1655
Michigan Women Forward Grants, 1662
Michigan Youth Livestock Scholarship and State-
    Wide Scholarship, 1663
Miller Foundation Grants, 1673
Morris K. Udall and Stewart L. Udall Foundation
    Parks in Focus Program, 1695
NCMCF Youth Advisory Council Grants, 1727
Nissan Neighbors Grants, 1762
PNC Foundation Affordable Housing Grants, 1983
PNC Foundation Community Services Grants, 1984
PNC Foundation Education Grants, 1985
PNC Foundation Grow Up Great Early Childhood
    Grants, 1986
PNC Foundation Revitalization and Stabilization
    Grants, 1987
Pokagon Fund Grants, 1994
Ralph C. Wilson, Jr. Foundation Preparing for
    Success Grant, 2050
Ralph C. Wilson, Jr. Foundation Youth Sports and
    Recreation Grant, 2051
SACF Youth Advisory Council Grants, 2131

Saginaw Community Foundation Discretionary Grants, 2134
Saginaw Community Foundation YWCA Fund for Women and Girls Grants, 2135
Saginaw County Community Foundation Youth FORCE Grants, 2136
Shopko Fdn Community Charitable Grants, 2191
Skatepark Project Built to Play Skatepark Grant, 2208
Sunoco Foundation Grants, 2256
TE Foundation Grants, 2279
Toyota Technical Center Grants, 2317
VSA/Metlife Connect All Grants, 2392
Walton Family Foundation Public Charter Startup Grants, 2409
Wege Foundation Grants, 2422
Whiting Foundation Grants, 2440
Whole Foods Foundation, 2445
Wisconsin Energy Foundation Grants, 2481

Minnesota

3M Company Fdn Community Giving Grants, 5
3M Company Foundation Health and Human Services Grants, 6
AHS Foundation Grants, 143
Albertsons Companies Foundation Nourishing Neighbors Grants, 221
Aldi Corporation Smart Kids Grants, 226
Alex Stern Family Foundation Grants, 229
Amica Insurance Company Community Grants, 267
Amica Insurance Company Sponsorships, 268
Arkema Foundation Grants, 298
Arkema Foundation Science Teachers Grants, 299
Bayer Fund Community Development Grants, 383
Bayer Fund STEM Education Grants, 384
Best Buy Children's Foundation Twin Cities Minnesota Capital Grants, 418
Better Way Foundation Grants, 419
Blandin Foundation Expand Opportunity Grants, 437
Blandin Foundation Invest Early Grants, 438
Blandin Foundation Itasca County Area Vitality Grants, 439
Blue Cross Blue Shield of Minnesota Fdn - Healthy Children: Growing Up Healthy Grants, 442
Blue Cross Blue Shield of Minnesota Foundation - Healthy Neighborhoods: Connect for Health Challenge Grants, 443
Brunswick Foundation Dollars for Doers Grants, 478
Brunswick Foundation Grants, 479
Bush Foundation Event Scholarships, 484
Bush Foundation Event Sponsorships, 485
C.H. Robinson Worldwide Foundation Grants, 489
Campbell Soup Foundation Grants, 501
Cargill Foundation Education Grants, 504
Dolan Media Foundation Grants, 833
Dollar General Family Literacy Grants, 835
Dollar General Summer Reading Grants, 836
Dollar General Youth Literacy Grants, 837
Donald G. Gardner Humanities Tr Youth Grts, 840
Edwards Memorial Trust Grants, 891
Eide Bailly Resourcefullness Awards, 897
F.R. Bigelow Foundation Grants, 947
Four Times Foundation Grants, 1006
Gannett Foundation Community Action Grants, 1033
Grotto Foundation Project Grants, 1123
H.B. Fuller Foundation Grants, 1138
HRK Foundation Health Grants, 1264
Hubbard Broadcasting Foundation Grants, 1269
Initiaive Fdn Inside-Out Connections Grants, 1303
Initiative Foundation Innovation Fund Grants, 1304
Initiative Foundation Minnesota Early Childhood Initiative Grants, 1305
James Ford Bell Foundation Grants, 1339
KaBOOM! Build it Grant, 1402
Kopp Family Foundation Grants, 1448
Land O'Lakes Foundation Community Grants, 1466
Laura Musser Intercultural Harmony Grants, 1472
LISC Financial Stability Grants, 1501
Lockheed Martin Corporation Fdn Grants, 1505
Mardag Foundation Grants, 1554

MeadWestvaco Foundation Sustainable Communities Grants, 1627
Medtronic Foundation Community Link Arts, Civic, and Culture Grants, 1629
Medtronic Foundation CommunityLink Health Grants, 1630
Medtronic Foundation Community Link Human Services Grants, 1631
Northland Foundation Grants, 1771
Onan Family Foundation Grants, 1821
Ordean Foundation Catalyst Grants, 1830
Ordean Foundation Partnership Grants, 1831
Patrick and Aimee Butler Family Foundation Community Human Services Grants, 1880
Philanthrofund Foundation Grants, 1959
Piper Jaffray Foundation Communities Giving Grants, 1974
PNC Foundation Affordable Housing Grants, 1983
PNC Foundation Community Services Grants, 1984
PNC Foundation Education Grants, 1985
PNC Foundation Grow Up Great Early Childhood Grants, 1986
PNC Foundation Revitalization and Stabilization Grants, 1987
Pohlad Family Fdn Large Capital Grants, 1990
Pohlad Family Fdn Small Capital Grants, 1991
Pohlad Family Foundation Summer Camp Scholarships, 1992
Pohlad Family Foundation Youth Advancement Grants, 1993
Prudential Foundation Education Grants, 2028
Rathmann Family Foundation Grants, 2057
Roger L. and Agnes C. Dell Charitable Trust I Grants, 2099
Roger L. and Agnes C. Dell Charitable Trust II Grants, 2100
Screen Actors Guild BookPALS Assistance, 2171
Screen Actors Guild PencilPALS Assistance, 2172
Screen Actors Guild StagePALS Assistance, 2173
Shopko Fdn Community Charitable Grants, 2191
Southern Minnesota Initiative Foundation AmeriCorps Leap Grants, 2219
Southern Minnesota Initiative Foundation BookStart Grants, 2220
Southern Minnesota Initiative Foundation Community Growth Initiative Grants, 2221
Southern Minnesota Initiative Foundation Home Visiting Grants, 2222
Southern Minnesota Initiative Foundation Incentive Grants, 2223
Southwest Initiative Foundation Grants, 2226
Tata Trust Grant for Certificate Course in Holistic inclusion of Learners with Diversities, 2273
Tension Envelope Foundation Grants, 2284
U.S. Bank Foundation Grants, 2330
Union Pacific Fdn Community & Civic Grants, 2337
Union Pacific Foundation Health and Human Services Grants, 2338
VSA/Metlife Connect All Grants, 2392
Walton Family Foundation Public Charter Startup Grants, 2409
Whitney Foundation Grants, 2441
Whole Foods Foundation, 2445

Mississippi

Adams and Reese Corporate Giving Grants, 114
Albertsons Companies Foundation Nourishing Neighbors Grants, 221
Aldi Corporation Smart Kids Grants, 226
Appalachian Regional Commission Business Development Revolving Loan Fund Grants, 285
Appalachian Regional Commission Education and Training Grants, 286
Appalachian Regional Commission Health Care Grants, 288
Assisi Fdn of Memphis Capital Project Grants, 317
Assisi Foundation of Memphis General Grants, 318
Assisi Foundation of Memphis Mini Grants, 319
Bayer Fund Community Development Grants, 383
Bayer Fund STEM Education Grants, 384

Brunswick Foundation Dollars for Doers Grants, 478
Brunswick Foundation Grants, 479
Caesars Foundation Grants, 492
Circle K Corporation Contributions Grants, 614
Deuce McAllister Catch 22 Foundation Grants, 828
Dollar General Family Literacy Grants, 835
Dollar General Summer Reading Grants, 836
Dollar General Youth Literacy Grants, 837
Entergy Charitable Foundation Education and Literacy Grants, 917
Entergy Charitable Foundation Low-Income Initiatives and Solutions Grants, 918
Entergy Corporation Micro Grants, 919
Entergy Corporation Open Grants for Arts and Culture, 920
Entergy Corporation Open Grants for Healthy Families, 921
Fdn for the Mid South Communities Grants, 992
Foundation for the Mid South Education Grants, 993
Gannett Foundation Community Action Grants, 1033
Georgia-Pacific Foundation Education Grants, 1058
Georgia-Pacific Fdn Entrepreneurship Grants, 1059
Gil and Dody Weaver Foundation Grants, 1071
Hazen Foundation Public Education Grants, 1221
Land O'Lakes Foundation Community Grants, 1466
Lockheed Martin Corporation Fdn Grants, 1505
MGM Resorts Foundation Community Grants, 1655
Nissan Neighbors Grants, 1762
OMNOVA Solutions Fdn Education Grants, 1820
Phil Hardin Foundation Grants, 1960
TAC Arts Education Funds for At-Risk Youth, 2266
TAC Arts Education Mini Grants, 2267
TAC Touring Arts and Arts Access Touring Arts Grants, 2269
Watson-Brown Foundation Grants, 2418

Missouri

3M Company Fdn Community Giving Grants, 5
3M Company Foundation Health and Human Services Grants, 6
A Friends' Foundation Trust Grants, 136
Albertsons Companies Foundation Nourishing Neighbors Grants, 221
Aldi Corporation Smart Kids Grants, 226
Ameren Corporation Community Grants, 251
Amerigroup Foundation Grants, 264
Anheuser-Busch Foundation Grants, 273
Aunt Kate Foundation Grants, 331
Bayer Fund Community Development Grants, 383
Bayer Fund STEM Education Grants, 384
Boeing Company Contributions Grants, 462
Caesars Foundation Grants, 492
Castle Foundation Grants, 517
CDI Interdisciplinary Research Intvs Grants, 526
Christine and Katharina Pauly Charitable Trust Grants, 601
Dana Brown Charitable Trust Grants, 777
Deaconess Foundation Advocacy Grants, 804
Dollar General Family Literacy Grants, 835
Dollar General Summer Reading Grants, 836
Dollar General Youth Literacy Grants, 837
Edward F. Swinney Trust Grants, 890
Gannett Foundation Community Action Grants, 1033
Greater Saint Louis Community Fdn Grants, 1110
Griffin Family Foundation Grants, 1121
Guy I. Bromley Trust Grants, 1136
Hatton W. Sumners Foundation for the Study and Teaching of Self Government Grants, 1196
Herbert A. and Adrian W. Woods Foundation Grants, 1243
Joseph H. and Florence A. Roblee Foundation Children and Youth Grants, 1385
Joseph H. and Florence A. Roblee Foundation Education Grants, 1386
Joseph H. and Florence A. Roblee Foundation Family Grants, 1387
Laclede Gas Charitable Trust Grants, 1457
Land O'Lakes Foundation Community Grants, 1466
Lumpkin Family Foundation Strong Community Leadership Grants, 1519

Monsanto Access to the Arts Grants, 1681
Monsanto Kids Garden Fresh Grants, 1682
Monsanto Science and Math K-12 Grants, 1683
Nestle Purina PetCare Educational Grants, 1738
Nestle Purina PetCare Youth Grants, 1739
Oppenstein Brothers Foundation Grants, 1827
Piper Jaffray Foundation Communities Giving
    Grants, 1974
PNC Foundation Affordable Housing Grants, 1983
PNC Foundation Community Services Grants, 1984
PNC Foundation Education Grants, 1985
PNC Foundation Grow Up Great Early Childhood
    Grants, 1986
PNC Foundation Revitalization and Stabilization
    Grants, 1987
Powell Family Foundation Grants, 2012
Richard J. Stern Foundation for the Arts Grants, 2071
Saigh Foundation Grants, 2137
Saint Louis Rams Fdn Community Donations, 2139
Sensient Technologies Foundation Grants, 2180
Shopko Fdn Community Charitable Grants, 2191
TAC Arts Education Funds for At-Risk Youth, 2266
TAC Arts Education Mini Grants, 2267
TAC Touring Arts and Arts Access Touring Arts
    Grants, 2269
Tension Envelope Foundation Grants, 2284
U.S. Bank Foundation Grants, 2330
U.S. Cellular Corporation Grants, 2331
Union Pacific Fdn Community & Civic Grants, 2337
Union Pacific Foundation Health and Human
    Services Grants, 2338
Victor E. Speas Foundation Grants, 2380
VSA/Metlife Connect All Grants, 2392
Walton Family Foundation Public Charter Startup
    Grants, 2409
Watson-Brown Foundation Grants, 2418
Whole Foods Foundation, 2445
William J. Brace Charitable Trust, 2471

Montana
Albertsons Companies Foundation Nourishing
    Neighbors Grants, 221
Arthur M. Blank Family Foundation AMB West
    Community Fund Grants, 304
Arthur M. Blank Family Foundation Mountain Sky
    Guest Ranch Fund Grants, 311
Avista Foundation Education Grants, 340
Avista Foundation Vulnerable and Limited Income
    Population Grants, 341
Charlotte Martin Foundation Youth Grants, 571
Four Times Foundation Grants, 1006
Gannett Foundation Community Action Grants, 1033
M.J. Murdock Charitable Trust General Grants, 1524
Montana Arts Council Cultural and Aesthetic Project
    Grants, 1685
Montana Community Big Sky LIFT Grants, 1686
Montana Community Foundation Grants, 1687
Montana Community Fdn Women's Grants, 1688
Morris K. Udall and Stewart L. Udall Foundation
    Parks in Focus Program, 1695
Piper Jaffray Foundation Communities Giving
    Grants, 1974
Pride Foundation Grants, 2024
Ruth and Vernon Taylor Foundation Grants, 2124
Shopko Fdn Community Charitable Grants, 2191
Social Justice Fund Northwest Criminal Justice
    Giving Project Grants, 2214
Social Justice Fund Northwest Economic Justice
    Giving Project Grants, 2215
U.S. Bank Foundation Grants, 2330
Union Pacific Fdn Community & Civic Grants, 2337
Union Pacific Foundation Health and Human
    Services Grants, 2338

Nebraska
3M Company Fdn Community Giving Grants, 5
3M Company Foundation Health and Human
    Services Grants, 6
Albertsons Companies Foundation Nourishing
    Neighbors Grants, 221

Aldi Corporation Smart Kids Grants, 226
Armstrong McDonald Foundation Children and
    Youth Grants, 300
Armstrong McDonald Foundation Special Needs
    Grants, 301
Bayer Fund Community Development Grants, 383
Bayer Fund STEM Education Grants, 384
Brunswick Foundation Dollars for Doers Grants, 478
Brunswick Foundation Grants, 479
Dollar General Family Literacy Grants, 835
Dollar General Summer Reading Grants, 836
Dollar General Youth Literacy Grants, 837
Earl and Maxine Claussen Trust Grants, 878
Hatton W. Sumners Foundation for the Study and
    Teaching of Self Government Grants, 1196
Ike and Roz Friedman Foundation Grants, 1289
KaBOOM! Build it Grant, 1402
Land O'Lakes Foundation Community Grants, 1466
Lied Foundation Trust Grants, 1490
Merrick Foundation Grants, 1639
Nationwide Insurance Foundation Grants, 1726
Nestle Purina PetCare Educational Grants, 1738
Nestle Purina PetCare Youth Grants, 1739
Piper Jaffray Foundation Communities Giving
    Grants, 1974
Robbins Family Charitable Foundation Grants, 2082
Shopko Fdn Community Charitable Grants, 2191
U.S. Bank Foundation Grants, 2330
U.S. Cellular Corporation Grants, 2331
Union Pacific Fdn Community & Civic Grants, 2337
Union Pacific Foundation Health and Human
    Services Grants, 2338
Whole Foods Foundation, 2445
Woods Charitable Fund Education Grants, 2488

Nevada
Albertsons Companies Foundation Nourishing
    Neighbors Grants, 221
Amerigroup Foundation Grants, 264
Amica Insurance Company Community Grants, 267
Amica Insurance Company Sponsorships, 268
Boeing Company Contributions Grants, 462
Caesars Foundation Grants, 492
Circle K Corporation Contributions Grants, 614
Dermody Properties Fdn Capstone Award, 826
Dermody Properties Foundation Grants, 827
Donald W. Reynolds Foundation Children's
    Discovery Initiative Grants, 841
E.L. Wiegand Foundation Grants, 877
Gannett Foundation Community Action Grants, 1033
Greenspun Family Foundation Grants, 1118
Lied Foundation Trust Grants, 1490
MeadWestvaco Foundation Sustainable Communities
    Grants, 1627
MGM Resorts Foundation Community Grants, 1655
Nell J. Redfield Foundation Grants, 1737
Nevada Community Foundation Grants, 1741
PacifiCare Foundation Grants, 1861
Pinnacle Entertainment Foundation Grants, 1972
Piper Jaffray Foundation Communities Giving
    Grants, 1974
Sands Cares Grants, 2156
Screen Actors Guild BookPALS Assistance, 2171
Screen Actors Guild PencilPALS Assistance, 2172
U.S. Bank Foundation Grants, 2330
Union Pacific Fdn Community & Civic Grants, 2337
Union Pacific Foundation Health and Human
    Services Grants, 2338
Whole Foods Foundation, 2445

New Hampshire
520 Charitable Foundation Grants, 14
Agnes M. Lindsay Trust Grants, 140
Albertsons Companies Foundation Nourishing
    Neighbors Grants, 221
Aldi Corporation Smart Kids Grants, 226
Amerigroup Foundation Grants, 264
Amica Insurance Company Community Grants, 267
Amica Insurance Company Sponsorships, 268
Anheuser-Busch Foundation Grants, 273

Bay and Paul Foundations PreK-12 Transformative
    Learning Practices Grants, 370
Baystate Financial Charitable Foundation Grants, 385
Citizens Bank Charitable Foundation Grants, 616
Claremont Savings Bank Foundation Grants, 623
Clayton F. and Ruth L. Hawkridge Foundation
    Grants, 630
Dorr Foundation Grants, 846
Entergy Charitable Foundation Education and
    Literacy Grants, 917
Entergy Charitable Foundation Low-Income
    Initiatives and Solutions Grants, 918
Entergy Corporation Micro Grants, 919
Entergy Corporation Open Grants for Arts and
    Culture, 920
Entergy Corporation Open Grants for Healthy
    Families, 921
Fuller Foundation Youth At Risk Grants, 1028
George I. Alden Trust Grants, 1051
Hannaford Charitable Foundation Grants, 1163
Hannaford Supermarkets Community Giving, 1164
HRAMF Charles H. Hood Foundation Child Health
    Research Awards, 1262
Hubbard Farms Charitable Foundation Grants, 1272
Jack and Dorothy Byrne Foundation Grants, 1329
Linden Foundation Grants, 1494
McLean Contributionship Grants, 1623
Merck Family Fund Urban Farming and Youth
    Leadership Grants, 1635
New Hampshire Charitable Foundation Community
    Unrestricted Grants, 1747
New Hampshire Charitable Foundation Neil and
    Louise Tillotson Fund - Empower Coös Youth
    Grants, 1748
New Hampshire Department of Justice Children's
    Justice Act Coronavirus Emergency Grants, 1749
NHSCA Artist Residence Grants, 1756
NHSCA Conservation License Plate Grants, 1757
NHSCA Youth Arts Project Grants: For Extended
    Arts Learning, 1758
OMNOVA Solutions Fdn Education Grants, 1820
Price Chopper's Golub Foundation Grants, 2020
S. Spencer Scott Fund Grants, 2129
Salmon Foundation Grants, 2140
Sunoco Foundation Grants, 2256
Yawkey Foundation Grants, 2510

New Jersey
3M Company Foundation Health and Human
    Services Grants, 6
Abbott Fund Access to Health Care Grants, 45
Abbott Fund Community Engagement Grants, 46
Abbott Fund Global AIDS Care Grants, 47
Abbott Fund Science Education Grants, 48
Achelis and Bodman Foundation Grants, 101
Aetna Foundation Regional Health Grants, 134
AHS Foundation Grants, 143
Albertsons Companies Foundation Nourishing
    Neighbors Grants, 221
Aldi Corporation Smart Kids Grants, 226
Amerigroup Foundation Grants, 264
Amica Insurance Company Community Grants, 267
Amica Insurance Company Sponsorships, 268
Anheuser-Busch Foundation Grants, 273
Arkema Foundation Grants, 298
Arkema Foundation Science Teachers Grants, 299
Bay and Paul Foundations PreK-12 Transformative
    Learning Practices Grants, 370
Bayer Fund Community Development Grants, 383
Bayer Fund STEM Education Grants, 384
Blanche and Irving Laurie Foundation Grants, 436
Caesars Foundation Grants, 492
Campbell Soup Foundation Grants, 501
Chatham Athletic Foundation Grants, 574
Citizens Bank Charitable Foundation Grants, 616
Countess Moira Charitable Foundation Grants, 752
Dean Foundation Grants, 806
Dollar General Family Literacy Grants, 835
Dollar General Summer Reading Grants, 836
Dollar General Youth Literacy Grants, 837

E.J. Grassmann Trust Grants, 876
Edward W. and Stella C. Van Houten Memorial Fund
    Grants, 892
Emerson Kampen Foundation Grants, 911
F.M. Kirby Foundation Grants, 946
FirstEnergy Foundation Community Grants, 965
FirstEnergy Foundation Science, Technology,
    Engineering, and Mathematics Grants, 966
Frank S. Flowers Foundation Grants, 1015
Gannett Foundation Community Action Grants, 1033
George A Ohl Jr. Foundation Grants, 1043
George I. Alden Trust Grants, 1051
Georgia-Pacific Foundation Education Grants, 1058
Georgia-Pacific Fdn Entrepreneurship Grants, 1059
Geraldine R. Dodge Fdn Education Grants, 1061
Hannah's Helping Hands Grants, 1165
JP Morgan Chase Fdn Arts and Culture Grants, 1394
Kinder Morgan Foundation Grants, 1436
Land O'Lakes Foundation Mid-Atlantic Grants, 1467
Laurie H. Wollmuth Charitable Trust Grants, 1476
Lockheed Martin Corporation Fdn Grants, 1505
Mary Owen Borden Foundation Grants, 1597
MeadWestvaco Foundation Sustainable Communities
    Grants, 1627
Mercedes-Benz USA Corporate Contributions
    Grants, 1634
Merck Family Fund Urban Farming and Youth
    Leadership Grants, 1635
Natalie W. Furniss Foundation Grants, 1715
New Jersey Center for Hispanic Policy, Research and
    Development Innovative Initiatives Grants, 1750
New Jersey Office of Faith Based Initiatives English as
    a Second Language Grants, 1751
New Jersey Office of Faith Based Initiatives Services
    to At Risk Youth Grants, 1752
NJSCA Artists in Education Residencies, 1763
NJSCA Arts Ed Special Initiative Grants, 1764
OceanFirst Foundation Home Runs for Heroes
    Grants, 1802
OceanFirst Foundation Major Grants, 1803
OceanFirst Foundation Summer Camp Grants, 1804
OMNOVA Solutions Fdn Education Grants, 1820
PennPAT Fee-Support Grants for Presenters, 1930
PennPAT New Directions Grants for Presenters, 1931
PNC Foundation Affordable Housing Grants, 1983
PNC Foundation Community Services Grants, 1984
PNC Foundation Education Grants, 1985
PNC Foundation Grow Up Great Early Childhood
    Grants, 1986
PNC Foundation Revitalization and Stabilization
    Grants, 1987
Prudential Foundation Education Grants, 2028
PSEG Corporate Contributions Grants, 2030
PSEG Fdn Safety and Preparedness Grants, 2031
Qualcomm Grants, 2042
Richard Davoud Donchian Foundation Grants, 2070
Ruth and Vernon Taylor Foundation Grants, 2124
Sidney and Sandy Brown Foundation Grants, 2196
Subaru of America Foundation Grants, 2253
Sunoco Foundation Grants, 2256
Thomas and Agnes Carvel Foundation Grants, 2289
Tyler Aaron Bookman Memorial Foundation Trust
    Grants, 2329
Whole Foods Foundation, 2445
Williams Comps Homegrown Giving Grants, 2474

New Mexico
Abeles Foundation Grants, 51
Albertsons Companies Foundation Nourishing
    Neighbors Grants, 221
Amerigroup Foundation Grants, 264
Boeing Company Contributions Grants, 462
Cabot Corporation Foundation Grants, 490
Circle K Corporation Contributions Grants, 614
Cudd Foundation, 769
Daniels Fund Amateur Sports Grants, 779
Daniels Drug and Alcohol Addiction Grants, 780
Daniels Fund Early Childhood Education Grants, 781
Daniels Homeless and Disadvantaged Grants, 782
Daniels Fund K-12 Education Reform Grants, 783

Daniels Fund Youth Development Grants, 784
Dollar General Family Literacy Grants, 835
Dollar General Summer Reading Grants, 836
Dollar General Youth Literacy Grants, 837
Four Times Foundation Grants, 1006
George and Ruth Bradford Foundation Grants, 1042
Gil and Dody Weaver Foundation Grants, 1071
Hattie Mae Lesley Foundation Grants, 1195
Hatton W. Sumners Foundation for the Study and
    Teaching of Self Government Grants, 1196
Intel Corporation Community Grants, 1311
Lockheed Martin Corporation Fdn Grants, 1505
Lumpkin Family Foundation Strong Community
    Leadership Grants, 1519
McCune Charitable Foundation Grants, 1617
PNM Reduce Your Use Grants, 1988
R.D. and Joan Dale Hubbard Fdn Grants, 2044
Sadler Family Foundation Grants, 2132
Santa Fe Community Foundation Seasonal Grants-
    Fall Cycle, 2159
Stocker Foundation Grants, 2247
U.S. Bank Foundation Grants, 2330
Union Pacific Fdn Community & Civic Grants, 2337
Union Pacific Foundation Health and Human
    Services Grants, 2338
Whole Foods Foundation, 2445
WinnCompanies Charitable Giving, 2479

New York
3M Company Fdn Community Giving Grants, 5
3M Company Foundation Health and Human
    Services Grants, 6
A. Alfred Taubman Foundation Grants, 18
Abbott Fund Access to Health Care Grants, 45
Abbott Fund Community Engagement Grants, 46
Abbott Fund Global AIDS Care Grants, 47
Abbott Fund Science Education Grants, 48
Achelis and Bodman Foundation Grants, 101
Achelis Foundation Grants, 102
AEGON Transamerica Foundation Education and
    Financial Literacy Grants, 132
AEGON Transamerica Foundation Health and
    Wellness Grants, 133
Aetna Foundation Regional Health Grants, 134
Aldi Corporation Smart Kids Grants, 226
American Express Charitable Fund Scholarships, 254
Amerigroup Foundation Grants, 264
Amica Insurance Company Community Grants, 267
Amica Insurance Company Sponsorships, 268
Anheuser-Busch Foundation Grants, 273
Appalachian Regional Commission Business
    Development Revolving Loan Fund Grants, 285
Appalachian Regional Commission Education and
    Training Grants, 286
Appalachian Regional Commission Entrepreneurship
    and Business Development Grants, 287
Appalachian Regional Commission Health Care
    Grants, 288
Appalachian Regl Commission Housing Grants, 289
Arkema Foundation Grants, 298
Arkema Foundation Science Teachers Grants, 299
Arthur M. Blank Family Foundation Inspiring Spaces
    Grants, 309
Babcock Charitable Trust Grants, 343
Bay and Paul Foundations PreK-12 Transformative
    Learning Practices Grants, 370
Bernard F. and Alva B. Gimbel Foundation Criminal
    Justice Grants, 412
Bernau Family Foundation Grants, 413
Blanche and Irving Laurie Foundation Grants, 436
Brown Rudnick Charitable Foundation Community
    Grants, 477
Chapman Family Charitable Trust Grants, 561
Charlotte and Joseph Gardner Fdn Grants, 570
Cheryl Spencer Memorial Foundation Grants, 576
Citizens Bank Charitable Foundation Grants, 616
Clayton F. and Ruth L. Hawkridge Foundation
    Grants, 630
Clayton Fund Grants, 631

Community Foundation for Greater Buffalo
    Competitive Grants, 670
Community Foundation for Greater Buffalo Garman
    Family Foundation Grants, 671
Community Foundation for Greater Buffalo Josephine
    Goodyear Foundation Grants, 672
Community Foundation for Greater Buffalo Niagara
    Area Foundation Grants, 673
Community Foundation for Greater Buffalo Ralph C.
    Wilson, Jr. Legacy Fund Grants, 674
Community Foundation for Greater Buffalo Ralph
    C. Wilson, Jr. Youth Sports COVID-19 Fund
    Grants, 675
Community Foundation for the Capital Region
    Grants, 687
Con Edison Corporate Giving Civic Grants, 744
Countess Moira Charitable Foundation Grants, 752
Daniel and Nanna Stern Family Fdn Grants, 778
David Alan and Susan Berkman Rahm Foundation
    Grants, 785
Dean Foundation Grants, 806
Dolan Children's Foundation Grants, 832
Dollar General Family Literacy Grants, 835
Dollar General Summer Reading Grants, 836
Dollar General Youth Literacy Grants, 837
Dorr Foundation Grants, 846
Dyson Foundation Mid-Hudson Valley Project
    Support Grants, 874
E.L. Wiegand Foundation Grants, 877
Edward and Ellen Roche Relief Fdn Grants, 887
Emma J. Adams Memorial Fund Grants, 914
Entergy Charitable Foundation Education and
    Literacy Grants, 917
Entergy Charitable Foundation Low-Income
    Initiatives and Solutions Grants, 918
Entergy Corporation Micro Grants, 919
Entergy Corporation Open Grants for Arts and
    Culture, 920
Entergy Corporation Open Grants for Healthy
    Families, 921
Episcopal Actors' Guild Actors Florence James
    Children's Holiday Fund Grant, 925
F.M. Kirby Foundation Grants, 946
Fitzpatrick, Cella, Harper & Scinto Pro Bono
    Services, 976
Foundation of Herkimer and Oneida Counties Youth
    Sports, Wellness and Recreation Mini-Grants, 994
Frankel Brothers Foundation Grants, 1009
Frederick McDonald Trust Grants, 1017
Fund for the City of New York Grants, 1029
Gannett Foundation Community Action Grants, 1033
George F. Baker Trust Grants, 1046
George I. Alden Trust Grants, 1051
Georgia-Pacific Foundation Education Grants, 1058
Georgia-Pacific Fdn Entrepreneurship Grants, 1059
Hannaford Charitable Foundation Grants, 1163
Hannaford Supermarkets Community Giving, 1164
Hannah's Helping Hands Grants, 1165
Hazen Foundation Public Education Grants, 1221
Herman Goldman Foundation Grants, 1245
Herman P. and Sophia Taubman Fdn Grants, 1247
Hispanic Heritage Foundation Youth Awards, 1253
Jack and Dorothy Byrne Foundation Grants, 1329
Jacob and Hilda Blaustein Foundation Israel Program
    Grants, 1335
JP Morgan Chase Fdn Arts and Culture Grants, 1394
KaBOOM! Build it Grant, 1402
KaBOOM! Play Everywhere Design Challenge, 1405
Land O'Lakes Foundation Mid-Atlantic Grants, 1467
Laura B. Vogler Foundation Grants, 1470
Laura Musser Intercultural Harmony Grants, 1472
Laura L. Adams Foundation Grants, 1473
Lily Palmer Fry Memorial Trust Grants, 1493
Lockheed Martin Corporation Fdn Grants, 1505
Long Island Community Foundation Grants, 1507
Lumpkin Family Foundation Strong Community
    Leadership Grants, 1519
Marie C. and Joseph C. Wilson Foundation Rochester
    Small Grants, 1559
Maurice R. Robinson Fund Grants, 1611

MeadWestvaco Foundation Sustainable Communities Grants, 1627
Merck Family Fund Urban Farming and Youth Leadership Grants, 1635
Mertz Gilmore Foundation NYC Communities Grants, 1641
Mertz Gilmore Foundation NYC Dance Grants, 1642
Metzger-Price Fund Grants, 1647
Milton and Sally Avery Arts Foundation Grants, 1675
Morton K. and Jane Blaustein Foundation Educational Opportunity Grants, 1700
Nationwide Insurance Foundation Grants, 1726
Nestle Purina PetCare Educational Grants, 1738
Nestle Purina PetCare Youth Grants, 1739
New York Foundation Grants, 1753
Northern Chautauqua Community Foundation Community Grants, 1769
NYFA Artists in the School Community Planning Grants, 1779
NYSCA Arts Education: Community-based Learning Grants, 1780
NYSCA Arts Education: General Operating Support Grants, 1781
NYSCA Arts Education: General Program Support Grants, 1782
NYSCA Arts Education: Local Capacity Building Grants (Regrants), 1783
NYSCA Arts Ed: Services to the Field Grants, 1784
NYSCA Electronic Media and Film: Film Festivals Grants, 1785
NYSCA Electronic Media and Film: General Operating Support, 1786
NYSCA Electronic Media and Film: General Program Support, 1787
NYSCA Electronic Media and Film: Screenings Grants, 1788
NYSCA Electronic Media and Film: Workspace Grants, 1789
NYSCA Music: Commty Music Schools Grants, 1790
NYSCA Music: Gen Operating Support Grants, 1791
NYSCA Music: Gen Program Support Grants, 1792
NYSCA Special Arts Services: General Program Support Grants, 1793
NYSCA Special Arts Services: Instruction and Training Grants, 1794
NYSCA Theatre: Prof Performances Grants, 1795
OMNOVA Solutions Fdn Education Grants, 1820
PennPAT Fee-Support Grants for Presenters, 1930
PennPAT New Directions Grants for Presenters, 1931
Perkin Fund Grants, 1937
Peter and Elizabeth C. Tower Foundation Intellectual Disabilities Grants, 1944
Peter and Elizabeth C. Tower Foundation Learning Disability Grants, 1945
Peter and Elizabeth C. Tower Foundation Mental Health Grants, 1946
Peter and Elizabeth C. Tower Foundation Small Grants, 1947
Peter and Elizabeth C. Tower Foundation Substance Use Disorders Grants, 1948
Peter and Elizabeth C. Tower Foundation Technology Initiative Grants, 1949
Peter and Elizabeth C. Tower Foundation Technology Planning Grants, 1950
Posse Foundation Scholarships, 2011
Price Chopper's Golub Foundation Grants, 2020
Prudential Foundation Education Grants, 2028
PSEG Corporate Contributions Grants, 2030
PSEG Fdn Safety and Preparedness Grants, 2031
Ralph C. Wilson, Jr. Foundation Preparing for Success Grant, 2050
Ralph C. Wilson, Jr. Foundation Youth Sports and Recreation Grant, 2051
Richard Davoud Donchian Foundation Grants, 2070
Richard W. Goldman Family Fdn Grants, 2073
Riedman Foundation Grants, 2076
Robert Bowne Foundation Fellowships, 2087
Robert Bowne Foundation Literacy Grants, 2088
Robert Bowne Fdn Youth-Centered Grants, 2089

Robert R. McCormick Tribune Foundation Community Grants, 2093
Robin Hood Foundation Grants, 2096
Ruth and Vernon Taylor Foundation Grants, 2124
S. Spencer Scott Fund Grants, 2129
Sandy Hill Foundation Grants, 2157
Screen Actors Guild BookPALS Assistance, 2171
Screen Actors Guild PencilPALS Assistance, 2172
Screen Actors Guild StagePALS Assistance, 2173
Shelley and Donald Rubin Foundation Grants, 2187
Skatepark Project Built to Play Skatepark Grant, 2208
Stella and Charles Guttman Foundation Grants, 2241
Sunoco Foundation Grants, 2256
SunTrust Bank Trusteed Foundations Nell Warren Elkin and William Simpson Elkin Grants, 2258
Textron Corporate Contributions Grants, 2286
Thomas and Agnes Carvel Foundation Grants, 2289
Union Square Arts Award, 2339
Union Square Award for Social Justice, 2340
Walton Family Foundation Public Charter Startup Grants, 2409
Western New York Foundation Grants, 2429
Whole Foods Foundation, 2445
Widgeon Point Charitable Foundation Grants, 2447
William J. and Dorothy K. O'Neill Foundation Responsive Grants, 2468
WSF GoGirlGo! New York Grants, 2494

North Carolina
Abbott Fund Access to Health Care Grants, 45
Abbott Fund Community Engagement Grants, 46
Abbott Fund Global AIDS Care Grants, 47
Abbott Fund Science Education Grants, 48
Aetna Foundation Regional Health Grants, 134
A Friends' Foundation Trust Grants, 136
Aldi Corporation Smart Kids Grants, 226
American Express Charitable Fund Scholarships, 254
American Schlafhorst Foundation Grants, 262
Amica Insurance Company Community Grants, 267
Amica Insurance Company Sponsorships, 268
Ann Ludington Sullivan Foundation Grants, 279
Appalachian Regional Commission Business Development Revolving Loan Fund Grants, 285
Appalachian Regional Commission Education and Training Grants, 286
Appalachian Regional Commission Entrepreneurship and Business Development Grants, 287
Appalachian Regional Commission Health Care Grants, 288
Appalachian Regl Commission Housing Grants, 289
Arthur M. Blank Family Foundation American Explorers Grants, 305
Bayer Fund Community Development Grants, 383
Bayer Fund STEM Education Grants, 384
Blumenthal Foundation Grants, 459
Brunswick Foundation Dollars for Doers Grants, 478
Brunswick Foundation Grants, 479
Burlington Industries Foundation Grants, 481
Caesars Foundation Grants, 492
Campbell Soup Foundation Grants, 501
Charles N. and Eleanor Knight Leigh Foundation Grants, 568
Circle K Corporation Contributions Grants, 614
Community Foundation of Greater Greensboro Community Grants, 708
Community Foundation of Greater Greensboro Teen Grantmaking Council Grants, 709
Community Foundation of Henderson County Community Grants, 711
Cone Health Foundation Grants, 745
Covenant Educational Foundation Grants, 754
Curtis Foundation Grants, 771
Dean Foundation Grants, 806
Dollar General Family Literacy Grants, 835
Dollar General Summer Reading Grants, 836
Dollar General Youth Literacy Grants, 837
Dominion Foundation Grants, 839
Duke Energy Foundation Local Impact Grants, 872
Dunspaugh-Dalton Foundation Grants, 873
Effie Allen Little Foundation Grants, 894

F.M. Kirby Foundation Grants, 946
Gannett Foundation Community Action Grants, 1033
Gardner W. and Joan G. Heidrick, Jr. Foundation Grants, 1036
Georgia-Pacific Foundation Education Grants, 1058
Georgia-Pacific Fdn Entrepreneurship Grants, 1059
Graham and Carolyn Holloway Family Foundation Grants, 1098
Hubbard Farms Charitable Foundation Grants, 1272
J. Bulow Campbell Foundation Grants, 1319
Joyce and Randy Seckman Charitable Foundation Grants, 1393
KaBOOM! Build it Grant, 1402
Kate B. Reynolds Charitable Trust Health Care Grants, 1416
Kate B. Reynolds Charitable Trust Poor and Needy Grants, 1417
Mead Family Foundation Grants, 1625
MeadWestvaco Foundation Sustainable Communities Grants, 1627
Michelin North America Challenge Education, 1660
Nationwide Insurance Foundation Grants, 1726
O. Max Gardner Foundation Grants, 1798
Olivia R. Gardner Foundation Grants, 1819
OMNOVA Solutions Fdn Education Grants, 1820
Percy B. Ferebee Endowment Grants, 1936
Piedmont Natural Gas Corporate and Charitable Contributions, 1966
Piedmont Natural Gas Fdn Envirnmtl Stewardship and Energy Sustainability Grant, 1967
Piedmont Natural Gas Foundation Health and Human Services Grants, 1968
Piedmont Natural Gas Foundation K-12 Science, Technology, Engineering and Math (STEM) Grant, 1969
PNC Foundation Affordable Housing Grants, 1983
PNC Foundation Community Services Grants, 1984
PNC Foundation Education Grants, 1985
PNC Foundation Grow Up Great Early Childhood Grants, 1986
PNC Foundation Revitalization and Stabilization Grants, 1987
Polk County Community Foundation Bradley Breakthrough Community Benefit Grants, 1995
Polk County Community Foundation Free Community Events Grants, 1996
Polk County Community Foundation Kirby Harmon Field Fund Grants, 1997
Polk County Community Foundation Marjorie M. and Lawrence R. Bradley Endowment Fund Grants, 1998
Polk County Community Foundation Mary F. Kessler Fund Grants, 1999
Polk County Community Foundation Seasonal Assistance and Cheer Grants for Charitable Programs, 2000
Polk County Community Foundation Unrestricted Grants, 2001
Progress Energy Foundation Energy Education Grants, 2025
Qualcomm Grants, 2042
Richard Davoud Donchian Foundation Grants, 2070
Ricks Family Charitable Trust Grants, 2075
SAS Institute Community Relations Donations, 2165
Smith Richardson Fdn Direct Service Grants, 2210
Sunoco Foundation Grants, 2256
TAC Arts Education Funds for At-Risk Youth, 2266
TAC Arts Education Mini Grants, 2267
TAC Touring Arts and Arts Access Touring Arts Grants, 2269
TE Foundation Grants, 2279
Tension Envelope Foundation Grants, 2284
Textron Corporate Contributions Grants, 2286
Turner B. Bunn, Jr. and Catherine E. Bunn Foundation Grants, 2325
Tyler Aaron Bookman Memorial Foundation Trust Grants, 2329
U.S. Cellular Corporation Grants, 2331
VSA/Metlife Connect All Grants, 2392
Watson-Brown Foundation Grants, 2418

Weaver Foundation Grants, 2420
Whole Foods Foundation, 2445
Williams Comps Homegrown Giving Grants, 2474
WinnCompanies Charitable Giving, 2479
Z. Smith Reynolds Foundation Small Grants, 2523

North Dakota
Albertsons Companies Foundation Nourishing
    Neighbors Grants, 221
Alex Stern Family Foundation Grants, 229
Bayer Fund Community Development Grants, 383
Bayer Fund STEM Education Grants, 384
Bush Foundation Event Scholarships, 484
Bush Foundation Event Sponsorships, 485
Kinder Morgan Foundation Grants, 1436
Land O'Lakes Foundation Community Grants, 1466
North Dakota Community Foundation Grants, 1768
Philanthrofund Foundation Grants, 1959
Piper Jaffray Foundation Communities Giving
    Grants, 1974
Shopko Fdn Community Charitable Grants, 2191
U.S. Bank Foundation Grants, 2330

Northern Mariana Islands
7-Eleven Corporate Giving Grants, 8
AAAS/Subaru SB&F Prize for Excl in Sci Books, 22
AASA Urgent Need Mini-Grants, 43
ACF Social and Economic Development Strategies
    Grants, 93
Adidas Corporation General Grants, 125
A Little Hope Grants, 235
Bank of America Charitable Foundation Matching
    Gifts, 356
Bank of America Charitable Foundation Volunteer
    Grants, 358
Beacon Society Jan Stauber Grants, 393
Beckman Coulter Foundation Grants, 394
Bee Conservancy Sponsor-A-Hive Grants, 395
Brinker Int Corporation Charitable Giving, 471
Brookdale Fdn Relatives as Parents Grants, 474
Fidelity Charitable Gift Fund Grants, 956
First Nations Development Institute Native
    Agriculture and Food Systems Initiative
    Scholarships, 971
First Nations Development Institute Native Arts
    Initiative Grants, 972
First Nations Development Institute Native Language
    Immersion Initiative Grants, 973
First Nations Development Institute Native Youth
    and Culture Fund Grants, 974
First Nations Development Institute Nourishing
    Native Children: Feeding Our Future Project
    Grants, 975
Ford Foundation BUILD Grants, 984
From the Top Alumni Leadership Grants, 1025
From the Top Jack Kent Cooke Young Artist
    Scholarships, 1026
Good+Foundation Grants, 1096
IMLS Grants to State Library Administrative
    Agencies, 1298
IMLS National Leadership Grants for Libraries, 1299
Jack Kent Cooke Fdn Young Artist Awards, 1333
Judy and Peter Blum Kovler Foundation Grants, 1396
NEA Student Program Communities Redefining
    Education Advocacy Through Empowerment
    (CREATE) Grants, 1733
NSF Perception, Action and Cognition (PAC)
    Research Grants, 1775
NZDIA Community Org Grants Scheme, 1796
Ray Charles Foundation Grants, 2058
Target Corporation Soccer Grants, 2271
U.S. Department of Education Promise
    Neighborhoods Grants, 2332
USAID Community Livelihoods Project in Yemen
    Grant, 2352
USAID Family Planning and Reproductive Health
    Methods Grants, 2353
USAID Global Development Alliance Grants, 2354
USAID National Governance Project in Yemen
    Grant, 2357

USAID Office of Foreign Disaster Assistance and
    Food for Peace Grants, 2359
USAID School Improvement Program Grants, 2360
USAID U.S.-Egypt Learning Grants, 2361
WHO Foundation Education/Literacy Grants, 2442
WSF Rusty Kanokogi Fund for the Advancement of
    U.S. Judo Grants, 2495
WSF Sports 4 Life Grants, 2496
WSF Sports 4 Life Regional Grants, 2497
WSF Travel and Training Fund Grants, 2498

Ohio
3M Company Fdn Community Giving Grants, 5
3M Company Foundation Health and Human
    Services Grants, 6
Abbott Fund Access to Health Care Grants, 45
Abbott Fund Community Engagement Grants, 46
Abbott Fund Global AIDS Care Grants, 47
Abbott Fund Science Education Grants, 48
ABC Charities Grants, 50
Abington Foundation Grants, 54
Adams Family Foundation of Ohio Grants, 119
Adams Legacy Foundation Grants, 121
Aetna Foundation Regional Health Grants, 134
AHS Foundation Grants, 143
Akron Community Foundation Arts and Culture
    Grants, 150
Akron Community Fdn Education Grants, 151
Akron Community Foundation Health and human
    services Grants, 152
Aldi Corporation Smart Kids Grants, 226
American Electric Power Corporate Grants, 252
American Electric Power Foundation Grants, 253
Amerigroup Foundation Grants, 264
Amica Insurance Company Community Grants, 267
Amica Insurance Company Sponsorships, 268
Anderson Foundation Grants, 271
Anheuser-Busch Foundation Grants, 273
Anthony Munoz Foundation Straight A Student
    Campaign Grants, 280
Appalachian Regional Commission Business
    Development Revolving Loan Fund Grants, 285
Appalachian Regional Commission Education and
    Training Grants, 286
Appalachian Regional Commission Entrepreneurship
    and Business Development Grants, 287
Appalachian Regional Commission Health Care
    Grants, 288
Appalachian Regl Commission Housing Grants, 289
Ar-Hale Family Foundation Grants, 290
Boeing Company Contributions Grants, 462
Burton D. Morgan Foundation Hudson Community
    Grants, 482
Burton D. Morgan Foundation Youth
    Entrepreneurship Grants, 483
C.H. Robinson Worldwide Foundation Grants, 489
Campbell Soup Foundation Grants, 501
Castle Foundation Grants, 517
Charlotte R. Schmidlapp Fund Grants, 572
Cincinnati Bell Foundation Grants, 612
Cincinnati Milacron Foundation Grants, 613
Circle K Corporation Contributions Grants, 614
Cleveland Browns Foundation Grants, 633
Cleveland Foundation Higley Fund Grants, 634
Cleveland Fdn Lake-Geauga Fund Grants, 635
Cleveland Foundation Legacy Village Lyndhurst
    Community Fund Grants, 636
Coleman Foundation Entrepreneurship Education
    Grants, 651
Columbus Foundation Traditional Grants, 663
Community Foundation for Kettering Grants, 676
CONSOL Energy Academic Grants, 746
CONSOL Youth Program Grants, 747
Dayton Foundation Dayton Youth Enrichment Fund
    Grant, 795
Dayton Foundation Grants, 796
Dayton Foundation Huber Heights Grants, 797
Dayton Foundation Rike Family Scholarships, 798
Dayton Foundation Vandalia-Butler Grants, 799

Dayton Foundation VISIONS Endowment Fund
    Grants, 800
Dayton Power and Light Company Foundation
    Signature Grants, 801
Dayton Power and Light Foundation Grants, 802
Deaconess Community Foundation Grants, 803
Dean Foundation Grants, 806
Dollar Energy Fund Grants, 834
Dollar General Family Literacy Grants, 835
Dollar General Summer Reading Grants, 836
Dollar General Youth Literacy Grants, 837
Dominion Foundation Grants, 839
Duke Energy Foundation Local Impact Grants, 872
EQT Fdn Community Enrichment Grants, 926
EQT Fdn Education and Workforce Grants, 927
Fifth Third Bank Corporate Giving, 958
Fifth Third Foundation Grants, 959
FirstEnergy Foundation Community Grants, 965
FirstEnergy Foundation Science, Technology,
    Engineering, and Mathematics Grants, 966
Foundation for Appalachian Ohio Access to
    Environmental Education Mini-Grants, 989
Frank M. Tait Foundation Grants, 1012
Gannett Foundation Community Action Grants, 1033
George W. Codrington Charitable Foundation
    Grants, 1055
Georgia-Pacific Foundation Education Grants, 1058
Georgia-Pacific Fdn Entrepreneurship Grants, 1059
Hardin County Community Foundation Grants, 1167
Harmony Project Grants, 1170
Helen G., Henry F., & Louise Tuechter Dornette
    Foundation Grants, 1229
Huffy Foundation Grants, 1273
Humana Foundation Grants, 1275
Iddings Foundation Capital Project Grants, 1283
Iddings Foundation Major Project Grants, 1284
Iddings Foundation Medium Project Grants, 1285
Iddings Foundation Small Project Grants, 1286
Jacob G. Schmidlapp Trusts Grants, 1336
James S. Copley Foundation Grants, 1345
Josephine Schell Russell Chartbl Trust Grants, 1389
Joyce and Randy Seckman Charitable Foundation
    Grants, 1393
JP Morgan Chase Fdn Arts and Culture Grants, 1394
KaBOOM! Build it Grant, 1402
Kelvin and Eleanor Smith Foundation Grants, 1424
Land O'Lakes Foundation Community Grants, 1466
LISC Financial Stability Grants, 1501
Lockheed Martin Corporation Fdn Grants, 1505
Lubrizol Corporation Community Grants, 1512
Lubrizol Foundation Grants, 1513
Manuel D. and Rhoda Mayerson Fdn Grants, 1550
Marathon Petroleum Corporation Grants, 1551
Marsh Corporate Grants, 1580
Martha Holden Jennings Foundation Grants-to-
    Educators, 1581
Mary E. Babcock Foundation, 1589
Mary S. and David C. Corbin Fdn Grants, 1598
Mathile Family Foundation Grants, 1604
MeadWestvaco Foundation Sustainable Communities
    Grants, 1627
Moran Family Foundation Grants, 1693
Mt. Sinai Health Care Foundation Health of the
    Jewish Community Grants, 1709
Mt. Sinai Health Care Foundation Health of the
    Urban Community Grants, 1710
Nationwide Insurance Foundation Grants, 1726
Nestle Purina PetCare Educational Grants, 1738
Nestle Purina PetCare Youth Grants, 1739
Ohio Arts Council Artist in Residence Grants for
    Sponsors, 1810
Ohio Valley Foundation Grants, 1814
OMNOVA Solutions Fdn Education Grants, 1820
Parkersburg Area Community Foundation Action
    Grants, 1871
PennPAT Fee-Support Grants for Presenters, 1930
PennPAT New Directions Grants for Presenters, 1931
Perkins Charitable Foundation Grants, 1939
Piper Jaffray Foundation Communities Giving
    Grants, 1974

PNC Foundation Affordable Housing Grants, 1983
PNC Foundation Community Services Grants, 1984
PNC Foundation Education Grants, 1985
PNC Foundation Grow Up Great Early Childhood Grants, 1986
PNC Foundation Revitalization and Stabilization Grants, 1987
RCF General Community Grants, 2062
RCF Individual Assistance Grants, 2063
RCF Summertime Kids Grants, 2064
RCF The Women's Fund Grants, 2065
Reinberger Foundation Grants, 2066
Robert and Helen Harmony Fund for Needy Children Grants, 2085
Saint Ann Legacy Grants, 2138
Shopko Fdn Community Charitable Grants, 2191
Stillson Foundation Grants, 2245
Stocker Foundation Grants, 2247
Sunoco Foundation Grants, 2256
Turner Foundation Grants, 2326
U.S. Bank Foundation Grants, 2330
Virginia W. Kettering Foundation Grants, 2388
Walton Family Foundation Public Charter Startup Grants, 2409
Whole Foods Foundation, 2445
William J. and Dorothy K. O'Neill Foundation Responsive Grants, 2468
Wolfe Associates Grants, 2483
Zane's Foundation Grants, 2524

Oklahoma
Albertsons Companies Foundation Nourishing Neighbors Grants, 221
Aldi Corporation Smart Kids Grants, 226
American Electric Power Corporate Grants, 252
American Electric Power Foundation Grants, 253
American Woodmark Foundation Grants, 263
Anheuser-Busch Foundation Grants, 273
Ar-Hale Family Foundation Grants, 290
Avery Family Trust Grants, 338
Boeing Company Contributions Grants, 462
Brunswick Foundation Dollars for Doers Grants, 478
Brunswick Foundation Grants, 479
Circle K Corporation Contributions Grants, 614
Cresap Family Foundation Grants, 766
Cudd Foundation Grants, 769
Dollar General Family Literacy Grants, 835
Dollar General Summer Reading Grants, 836
Dollar General Youth Literacy Grants, 837
Donald W. Reynolds Foundation Children's Discovery Initiative Grants, 841
Edward and Helen Bartlett Foundation Grants, 888
Georgia-Pacific Foundation Education Grants, 1058
Georgia-Pacific Fdn Entrepreneurship Grants, 1059
Gil and Dody Weaver Foundation Grants, 1071
H.A. and Mary K. Chapman Charitable Trust Grants, 1137
Harris Foundation Grants, 1177
Hatton W. Sumners Foundation for the Study and Teaching of Self Government Grants, 1196
JP Morgan Chase Fdn Arts and Culture Grants, 1394
Kinder Morgan Foundation Grants, 1436
Kirkpatrick Foundation Grants, 1440
Lavina Parker Trust Grants, 1477
Mary K. Chapman Foundation Grants, 1590
Merrick Foundation Grants, 1640
Mervin Bovaird Foundation Grants, 1643
Michelin North America Challenge Education, 1660
Nestle Purina PetCare Educational Grants, 1738
Nestle Purina PetCare Youth Grants, 1739
PacifiCare Foundation Grants, 1861
Philip Boyle Foundation Grants, 1961
Priddy Foundation Operating Grants, 2021
Priddy Foundation Organizational Development Grants, 2022
Priddy Foundation Program Grants, 2023
R.D. and Joan Dale Hubbard Fdn Grants, 2044
Robinson Foundation Grants, 2097
Sarkeys Foundation Grants, 2163
U.S. Cellular Corporation Grants, 2331

Union Pacific Fdn Community & Civic Grants, 2337
Union Pacific Foundation Health and Human Services Grants, 2338
VSA/Metlife Connect All Grants, 2392
Whole Foods Foundation, 2445
Williams Comps Homegrown Giving Grants, 2474

Oregon
Abby's Legendary Pizza Foundation Grants, 49
Alaska Airlines Corporation Career Connections for Youth Grants, 193
Alaska Airlines Foundation LIFT Grants, 194
Albertsons Companies Foundation Nourishing Neighbors Grants, 221
Amica Insurance Company Community Grants, 267
Amica Insurance Company Sponsorships, 268
Avista Foundation Education Grants, 340
Avista Foundation Vulnerable and Limited Income Population Grants, 341
Bella Vista Foundation Pre-3 Grants, 397
Bella Vista Fdns GSS Early Literacy Grants, 398
Ben B. Cheney Foundation Grants, 402
Blue Mountain Community Foundation Discretionary Grants, 455
Blue Mountain Community Foundation Garfield County Health Foundation Fund Grants, 456
Blue Mountain Community Foundation Warren Community Action Fund Grants, 457
Boeing Company Contributions Grants, 462
Brunswick Foundation Dollars for Doers Grants, 478
Brunswick Foundation Grants, 479
Campbell Soup Foundation Grants, 501
Charlotte Martin Foundation Youth Grants, 571
Children's Trust Fund of Oregon Fdn Grants, 585
Children's Trust Fund of Oregon Foundation Small Grants, 586
Circle K Corporation Contributions Grants, 614
Collins Foundation Grants, 658
E.L. Wiegand Foundation Grants, 877
Edward and Romell Ackley Foundation Grants, 889
Ford Family Foundation Grants - Access to Health and Dental Services, 980
Ford Family Foundation Grants - Child Abuse Prevention and Intervention, 981
Ford Family Foundation Grants - Positive Youth Development, 982
Ford Family Foundation Grants - Technical Assistance , 983
Gannett Foundation Community Action Grants, 1033
George and Ruth Bradford Foundation Grants, 1042
Georgia-Pacific Foundation Education Grants, 1058
Georgia-Pacific Fdn Entrepreneurship Grants, 1059
Gray Family Fdn Camp Maintenance Grants, 1104
Gray Family Foundation Community Field Trips Grants, 1105
Gray Family Foundation Geography Education Grants, 1106
Gray Family Fdn Outdoor School Grants, 1107
Intel Corporation Community Grants, 1311
James F. and Marion L. Miller Fdn Grants, 1338
Janet Spencer Weekes Foundation Grants, 1348
KaBOOM! Build it Grant, 1402
Land O'Lakes Foundation Community Grants, 1466
M.J. Murdock Charitable Trust General Grants, 1524
Meyer Memorial Trust Emergency Grants, 1652
Meyer Memorial Trust Responsive Grants, 1653
Motiv8 Foundation Grants, 1702
Oregon Community Foundation Black Student Success Community Network Grants, 1832
Oregon Community Fdn Community Grants, 1833
Oregon Community Foundation Community Recovery Grants, 1834
Oregon Community Foundation Edna E. Harrell Community Children's Fund Grants, 1835
Oregon Community Foundation K-12 Student Success: Out-of-School Grants, 1836
PacifiCare Foundation Grants, 1861
PGE Foundation Grants, 1958
Piper Jaffray Foundation Communities Giving Grants, 1974

Portland General Electric Foundation Grants, 2007
Pride Foundation Grants, 2024
Samuel S. Johnson Foundation Grants, 2146
Shopko Fdn Community Charitable Grants, 2191
Social Justice Fund Northwest Criminal Justice Giving Project Grants, 2214
Social Justice Fund Northwest Economic Justice Giving Project Grants, 2215
U.S. Bank Foundation Grants, 2330
U.S. Cellular Corporation Grants, 2331
Union Bank, N.A. Corporate Sponsorships and Donations, 2333
Union Bank, N.A. Foundation Grants, 2334
Union Pacific Fdn Community & Civic Grants, 2337
Union Pacific Foundation Health and Human Services Grants, 2338
VSA/Metlife Connect All Grants, 2392
Whole Foods Foundation, 2445
William G. Gilmore Foundation Grants, 2467
Wold Foundation Grants, 2482
Wood Family Charitable Trust Grants, 2487

Pennsylvania
A.L. Spencer Foundation Grants, 21
Adams County Community Foundation Grants, 115
AEGON Transamerica Foundation Education and Financial Literacy Grants, 132
AEGON Transamerica Foundation Health and Wellness Grants, 133
Aetna Foundation Regional Health Grants, 134
Albertsons Companies Foundation Nourishing Neighbors Grants, 221
Aldi Corporation Smart Kids Grants, 226
Alpha Natural Resources Corporate Giving, 246
American Express Charitable Fund Scholarships, 254
Amica Insurance Company Community Grants, 267
Amica Insurance Company Sponsorships, 268
Appalachian Regional Commission Business Development Revolving Loan Fund Grants, 285
Appalachian Regional Commission Education and Training Grants, 286
Appalachian Regional Commission Entrepreneurship and Business Development Grants, 287
Appalachian Regional Commission Health Care Grants, 288
Appalachian Regl Commission Housing Grants, 289
Ar-Hale Family Foundation Grants, 290
Arkema Foundation Grants, 298
Arkema Foundation Science Teachers Grants, 299
Avery Family Foundation Grants, 339
Babcock Charitable Trust Grants, 343
Bayer Fund Community Development Grants, 383
Bayer Fund STEM Education Grants, 384
Boeing Company Contributions Grants, 462
C.H. Robinson Worldwide Foundation Grants, 489
Cabot Corporation Foundation Grants, 490
Caesars Foundation Grants, 492
Campbell Soup Foundation Grants, 501
Christopher Ludwick Foundation Grants, 602
Circle K Corporation Contributions Grants, 614
Citizens Bank Charitable Foundation Grants, 616
CONSOL Energy Academic Grants, 746
CONSOL Youth Program Grants, 747
David M. and Marjorie D. Rosenberg Foundation Grants, 790
Delaware Valley Fairness Project Teacher Assistance Grants, 818
Dermody Properties Foundation Grants, 827
Dollar Energy Fund Grants, 834
Dollar General Family Literacy Grants, 835
Dollar General Summer Reading Grants, 836
Dollar General Youth Literacy Grants, 837
Dominion Foundation Grants, 839
EQT Fdn Community Enrichment Grants, 926
EQT Fdn Education and Workforce Grants, 927
Ethel Sergeant Clark Smith Foundation Grants, 935
F.M. Kirby Foundation Grants, 946
FirstEnergy Foundation Community Grants, 965
FirstEnergy Foundation Science, Technology, Engineering, and Mathematics Grants, 966

Fourjay Foundation Grants, 1003
Franklin H. Wells and Ruth L. Wells Foundation Grants, 1011
Frank S. Flowers Foundation Grants, 1015
George I. Alden Trust Grants, 1051
Georgia-Pacific Foundation Education Grants, 1058
Georgia-Pacific Fdn Entrepreneurship Grants, 1059
Graham Foundation Grants, 1100
Grifols Community Outreach Grants, 1122
Grundy Foundation Grants, 1124
Highmark Corporate Giving Grants, 1248
Hispanic Heritage Foundation Youth Awards, 1253
Huffy Foundation Grants, 1273
James K. and Arlene L. Adams Foundation Scholarships, 1341
Janson Foundation Grants, 1349
Land O'Lakes Foundation Community Grants, 1466
Land O'Lakes Foundation Mid-Atlantic Grants, 1467
Laurel Foundation Grants, 1475
Leo Niessen Jr., Charitable Trust Grants, 1484
Lockheed Martin Corporation Fdn Grants, 1505
Margaret M. Walker Charitable Fdn Grants, 1556
McLean Contributionship Grants, 1623
Merck Family Fund Urban Farming and Youth Leadership Grants, 1635
Mill Spring Foundation Grants, 1674
Nationwide Insurance Foundation Grants, 1726
Nestle Purina PetCare Educational Grants, 1738
Nestle Purina PetCare Youth Grants, 1739
OMNOVA Solutions Fdn Education Grants, 1820
PCA-PCD Organizational Short-Term Professional Development and Consulting Grants, 1882
PCA-PCD Professional Development for Individual Artists Grants, 1883
PCA Art Organizations and Art Programs Grants for Presenting Organizations, 1884
PCA Arts in Education Residencies, 1885
PCA Arts Management Internship, 1886
PCA Arts Organizations and Arts Program Grants for Music, 1887
PCA Arts Organizations and Arts Programs Grants for Art Museums, 1888
PCA Arts Organizations and Arts Programs Grants for Arts Education Organizations, 1889
PCA Arts Organizations and Arts Programs Grants for Arts Service Organizations, 1890
PCA Arts Organizations and Arts Programs Grants for Crafts, 1891
PCA Arts Organizations and Arts Programs Grants for Dance, 1892
PCA Arts Organizations and Arts Programs Grants for Film and Electronic Media, 1893
PCA Arts Organizations and Arts Programs Grants for Literature, 1894
PCA Arts Organizations and Arts Programs Grants for Local Arts, 1895
PCA Arts Organizations and Arts Programs Grants for Theatre, 1896
PCA Arts Organizations and Arts Programs Grants for Traditional and Folk Arts, 1897
PCA Arts Organizations and Arts Programs Grants for Visual Arts, 1898
PCA Busing Grants, 1899
PCA Entry Track Arts Organizations and Arts Programs Grants for Art Museums, 1900
PCA Entry Track Arts Organizations and Arts Programs Grants for Arts Education Organizations, 1901
PCA Entry Track Arts Organizations and Arts Programs Grants for Arts Service Orgs, 1902
PCA Entry Track Arts Organizations and Arts Programs Grants for Crafts, 1903
PCA Entry Track Arts Organizations and Arts Programs Grants for Dance, 1904
PCA Entry Track Arts Orgs and Arts Programs Grants for Film and Electronic Media, 1905
PCA Entry Track Arts Organizations and Arts Programs Grants for Literature, 1906
PCA Entry Track Arts Organizations and Arts Programs Grants for Local Arts, 1907

PCA Entry Track Arts Organizations and Arts Programs Grants for Music, 1908
PCA Entry Track Arts Organizations and Arts Programs Grants for Presenting Orgs, 1909
PCA Entry Track Arts Organizations and Arts Programs Grants for Theatre, 1910
PCA Entry Track Arts Orgs and Arts Programs Grants for Traditional and Folk Arts, 1911
PCA Entry Track Arts Organizations and Arts Programs Grants for Visual Arts, 1912
PCA Management/Techl Assistance Grants, 1913
PCA Pennsylvania Partners in the Arts Program Stream Grants, 1914
PCA Pennsylvania Partners in the Arts Project Stream Grants, 1915
PCA Professional Development Grants, 1916
PCA Strategies for Success Grants - Adv Level, 1917
PCA Strategies for Success Grants - Basic Level, 1918
PCA Strategies for Success Grants - Intermediate Level, 1919
PennPAT Artist Technical Assistance Grants, 1929
PennPAT Fee-Support Grants for Presenters, 1930
PennPAT New Directions Grants for Presenters, 1931
PennPAT Strategic Opportunity Grants, 1933
Pittsburgh Fdn Affordable Housing Grants, 1980
Pittsburgh Foundation Healthy Children and Adults Grants, 1981
PNC Foundation Affordable Housing Grants, 1983
PNC Foundation Community Services Grants, 1984
PNC Foundation Education Grants, 1985
PNC Foundation Grow Up Great Early Childhood Grants, 1986
PNC Foundation Revitalization and Stabilization Grants, 1987
PPG Industries Foundation Grants, 2017
Price Chopper's Golub Foundation Grants, 2020
Prudential Foundation Education Grants, 2028
Rathmann Family Foundation Grants, 2057
Ruddie Memorial Youth Foundation Grants, 2120
Ruth and Vernon Taylor Foundation Grants, 2124
S. Spencer Scott Fund Grants, 2129
Salmon Foundation Grants, 2140
Sands Cares Grants, 2156
Seybert Foundation Grants, 2184
Sidney and Sandy Brown Foundation Grants, 2196
Staunton Farm Foundation Grants, 2239
Storm Castle Foundation Grants, 2248
Sunoco Foundation Grants, 2256
SunTrust Bank Trusteed Foundations Nell Warren Elkin and William Simpson Elkin Grants, 2258
Sylvia Perkin Perpetual Charitable Trust Grants, 2263
TE Foundation Grants, 2279
Textron Corporate Contributions Grants, 2286
Tyler Aaron Bookman Memorial Foundation Trust Grants, 2329
VSA/Metlife Connect All Grants, 2392
W.W. Smith Chartbl Trust Basic Needs Grants, 2400
Whole Foods Foundation, 2445
Williams Comps Homegrown Giving Grants, 2474
Wyomissing Foundation Community Grants, 2504
Wyomissing Foundation Thun Family Organizational Grants, 2505

Puerto Rico
7-Eleven Corporate Giving Grants, 8
AASA Urgent Need Mini-Grants, 43
Abbott Fund Access to Health Care Grants, 45
Abbott Fund Community Engagement Grants, 46
Abbott Fund Global AIDS Care Grants, 47
Abbott Fund Science Education Grants, 48
Adidas Corporation General Grants, 125
A Friends' Foundation Trust Grants, 136
A Little Hope Grants, 235
Bank of America Charitable Foundation Matching Gifts, 356
Bank of America Charitable Foundation Volunteer Grants, 358
Bayer Fund Community Development Grants, 383
Bayer Fund STEM Education Grants, 384
Beacon Society Jan Stauber Grants, 393

Beckman Coulter Foundation Grants, 394
Bee Conservancy Sponsor-A-Hive Grants, 395
Best Buy Children's Fdn @15 Scholarship , 415
Brinker Int Corporation Charitable Giving, 471
Brookdale Fdn Relatives as Parents Grants, 474
Case Foundation Grants, 514
Elton John AIDS Foundation Grants, 910
Fidelity Charitable Gift Fund Grants, 956
First Nations Development Institute Native Agriculture and Food Systems Initiative Scholarships, 971
First Nations Development Institute Native Arts Initiative Grants, 972
First Nations Development Institute Native Language Immersion Initiative Grants, 973
First Nations Development Institute Native Youth and Culture Fund Grants, 974
First Nations Development Institute Nourishing Native Children: Feeding Our Future Project Grants, 975
Ford Foundation BUILD Grants, 984
From the Top Alumni Leadership Grants, 1025
From the Top Jack Kent Cooke Young Artist Scholarships, 1026
Good+Foundation Grants, 1096
IMLS Grants to State Library Administrative Agencies, 1298
IMLS National Leadership Grants for Libraries, 1299
Jack Kent Cooke Fdn Young Artist Awards, 1333
Judy and Peter Blum Kovler Foundation Grants, 1396
Laura Bush Foundation for America's Libraries Grants, 1471
Medtronic Foundation CommunityLink Health Grants, 1630
NEA Student Program Communities Redefining Education Advocacy Through Empowerment (CREATE) Grants, 1733
NSF Perception, Action and Cognition (PAC) Research Grants, 1775
OSF Young Feminist Leaders Fellowships, 1845
PDF Community Organizing Grants, 1920
PDF Fiscal Sponsorship Grant, 1921
Puerto Rico Community Foundation Grants, 2037
Ray Charles Foundation Grants, 2058
Saltchuk Corporate Giving, 2141
Target Corporation Soccer Grants, 2271
U.S. Department of Education Promise Neighborhoods Grants, 2332
USAID Community Livelihoods Project in Yemen Grant, 2352
USAID Family Planning and Reproductive Health Methods Grants, 2353
USAID Global Development Alliance Grants, 2354
USAID National Governance Project in Yemen Grant, 2357
USAID Office of Foreign Disaster Assistance and Food for Peace Grants, 2359
USAID School Improvement Program Grants, 2360
USAID U.S.-Egypt Learning Grants, 2361
WHO Foundation Education/Literacy Grants, 2442
WHO Foundation General Grants, 2443
WHO Foundation Volunteer Service Grants, 2444
WSF Rusty Kanokogi Fund for the Advancement of U.S. Judo Grants, 2495
WSF Sports 4 Life Grants, 2496
WSF Sports 4 Life Regional Grants, 2497
WSF Travel and Training Fund Grants, 2498

Rhode Island
AAAS/Subaru SB&F Prize for Excl in Sci Books, 22
Aaron Foundation Grants, 42
Aldi Corporation Smart Kids Grants, 226
Amica Companies Foundation Grants, 266
Amica Insurance Company Community Grants, 267
Amica Insurance Company Sponsorships, 268
Bay and Paul Foundations PreK-12 Transformative Learning Practices Grants, 370
Baystate Financial Charitable Foundation Grants, 385
Brown Rudnick Charitable Foundation Community Grants, 477

Citizens Bank Charitable Foundation Grants, 616
Clayton F. and Ruth L. Hawkridge Foundation
    Grants, 630
Dominion Foundation Grants, 839
George I. Alden Trust Grants, 1051
Hannah's Helping Hands Grants, 1165
Hasbro Children's Fund Grants, 1189
Hasbro Corp Gift of Play Holiday Giving, 1190
Hasbro Corporation Gift of Play Hospital and
    Pediatric Health Giving, 1191
Hasbro Corporation Gift of Play Shelter Support
    Giving, 1192
Hasbro Corporation Gift of Play Summer Camp
    Support, 1193
Horace A. Kimball and S. Ella Kimball Foundation
    Grants, 1260
HRAMF Charles H. Hood Foundation Child Health
    Research Awards, 1262
John Clarke Trust Grants, 1369
John D. and Katherine A. Johnston Foundation
    Grants, 1370
LISC Financial Stability Grants, 1501
Maurice R. Robinson Fund Grants, 1611
Merck Family Fund Urban Farming and Youth
    Leadership Grants, 1635
Nellie Mae Education Foundation District-Level
    Change Grants, 1736
Perkins Charitable Foundation Grants, 1939
RISCA Project Grants for Individuals, 2079
S. Spencer Scott Fund Grants, 2129
Southern New England Folk and Traditional Arts
    Apprenticeship Grants, 2224
Sunoco Foundation Grants, 2256
Textron Corporate Contributions Grants, 2286
Vigneron Memorial Fund Grants, 2384
VSA/Metlife Connect All Grants, 2392
Whole Foods Foundation, 2445
Yawkey Foundation Grants, 2510

South Carolina
3M Company Fdn Community Giving Grants, 5
3M Company Foundation Health and Human
    Services Grants, 6
Abney Foundation Grants, 55
Adams and Reese Corporate Giving Grants, 114
Aldi Corporation Smart Kids Grants, 226
Amerigroup Foundation Grants, 264
Amica Insurance Company Community Grants, 267
Amica Insurance Company Sponsorships, 268
Appalachian Regional Commission Business
    Development Revolving Loan Fund Grants, 285
Appalachian Regional Commission Education and
    Training Grants, 286
Appalachian Regional Commission Entrepreneurship
    and Business Development Grants, 287
Appalachian Regional Commission Health Care
    Grants, 288
Appalachian Regl Commission Housing Grants, 289
Boeing Company Contributions Grants, 462
Brunswick Foundation Dollars for Doers Grants, 478
Brunswick Foundation Grants, 479
Burlington Industries Foundation Grants, 481
Byerly Foundation Grants, 487
Chapman Family Charitable Trust Grants, 561
Circle K Corporation Contributions Grants, 614
Dollar General Family Literacy Grants, 835
Dollar General Summer Reading Grants, 836
Dollar General Youth Literacy Grants, 837
Duke Energy Foundation Local Impact Grants, 872
Gannett Foundation Community Action Grants, 1033
Georgia-Pacific Foundation Education Grants, 1058
Georgia-Pacific Fdn Entrepreneurship Grants, 1059
Graham Foundation Grants, 1101
J. Bulow Campbell Foundation Grants, 1319
J. Marion Sims Foundation Teachers' Pet Grant, 1322
Joyce and Randy Seckman Charitable Foundation
    Grants, 1393
Lockheed Martin Corporation Fdn Grants, 1505
Mary Black Foundation Active Living Grants, 1585

Mary Black Foundation Early Childhood
    Development Grants, 1586
MeadWestvaco Foundation Sustainable Communities
    Grants, 1627
Michelin North America Challenge Education, 1660
OMNOVA Solutions Fdn Education Grants, 1820
Piedmont Health Foundation Grants, 1965
Piedmont Natural Gas Corporate and Charitable
    Contributions, 1966
Piedmont Natural Gas Fdn Envirnmtl Stewardship
    and Energy Sustainability Grant, 1967
Piedmont Natural Gas Foundation Health and
    Human Services Grants, 1968
Piedmont Natural Gas Foundation K-12 Science,
    Technology, Engineering and Math (STEM)
    Grant, 1969
PNC Foundation Affordable Housing Grants, 1983
PNC Foundation Community Services Grants, 1984
PNC Foundation Education Grants, 1985
PNC Foundation Grow Up Great Early Childhood
    Grants, 1986
PNC Foundation Revitalization and Stabilization
    Grants, 1987
Progress Energy Foundation Energy Education
    Grants, 2025
Publix Super Markets Charities Local Grants, 2036
Pulido Walker Foundation, 2039
Richard Davoud Donchian Foundation Grants, 2070
Sunoco Foundation Grants, 2256
TE Foundation Grants, 2279
Watson-Brown Foundation Grants, 2418
Whole Foods Foundation, 2445
Williams Comps Homegrown Giving Grants, 2474
WinnCompanies Charitable Giving, 2479
Yawkey Foundation Grants, 2510

South Dakota
3M Company Fdn Community Giving Grants, 5
3M Company Foundation Health and Human
    Services Grants, 6
Adams-Mastrovich Family Foundation Grants, 113
A Friends' Foundation Trust Grants, 136
Albertsons Companies Foundation Nourishing
    Neighbors Grants, 221
Black Hills Corporation Grants, 435
Bush Foundation Event Scholarships, 484
Bush Foundation Event Sponsorships, 485
Dollar General Family Literacy Grants, 835
Dollar General Summer Reading Grants, 836
Dollar General Youth Literacy Grants, 837
Four Times Foundation Grants, 1006
Gannett Foundation Community Action Grants, 1033
Land O'Lakes Foundation Community Grants, 1466
Philanthrofund Foundation Grants, 1959
Piper Jaffray Foundation Communities Giving
    Grants, 1974
Shopko Fdn Community Charitable Grants, 2191
Sioux Falls Area Community Foundation Community
    Fund Grants, 2203
Sioux Falls Area Community Foundation Spot
    Grants, 2204
U.S. Bank Foundation Grants, 2330

Tennessee
ABC Charities Grants, 50
Adams and Reese Corporate Giving Grants, 114
Adams Family Foundation I Grants, 116
Adams Family Foundation II Grants, 117
Adams Family Foundation of Tennessee Grants, 120
Aetna Foundation Regional Health Grants, 134
A Friends' Foundation Trust Grants, 136
Albertsons Companies Foundation Nourishing
    Neighbors Grants, 221
Aldi Corporation Smart Kids Grants, 226
American Electric Power Corporate Grants, 252
American Electric Power Foundation Grants, 253
American Woodmark Foundation Grants, 263
Amerigroup Foundation Grants, 264
Amica Insurance Company Community Grants, 267
Amica Insurance Company Sponsorships, 268

Appalachian Community Fund LGBTQ Fund
    Grants, 284
Appalachian Regional Commission Business
    Development Revolving Loan Fund Grants, 285
Appalachian Regional Commission Education and
    Training Grants, 286
Appalachian Regional Commission Entrepreneurship
    and Business Development Grants, 287
Appalachian Regional Commission Health Care
    Grants, 288
Appalachian Regl Commission Housing Grants, 289
Arkema Foundation Grants, 298
Arkema Foundation Science Teachers Grants, 299
Assisi Fdn of Memphis Capital Project Grants, 317
Assisi Foundation of Memphis General Grants, 318
Assisi Foundation of Memphis Mini Grants, 319
Benwood Foundation Community Grants, 406
Bernau Family Foundation Grants, 413
Brunswick Foundation Dollars for Doers Grants, 478
Brunswick Foundation Grants, 479
Circle K Corporation Contributions Grants, 614
Community Foundation of Greater Chattanooga
    Grants, 704
Covenant Foundation of Brentwood Grants, 755
Dollar Energy Fund Grants, 834
Dollar General Family Literacy Grants, 835
Dollar General Summer Reading Grants, 836
Dollar General Youth Literacy Grants, 837
Erie Chapman Foundation Grants, 928
Fifth Third Bank Corporate Giving, 958
Fifth Third Foundation Grants, 959
Gannett Foundation Community Action Grants, 1033
Georgia-Pacific Foundation Education Grants, 1058
Georgia-Pacific Fdn Entrepreneurship Grants, 1059
Graham and Carolyn Holloway Family Foundation
    Grants, 1098
Hubbard Farms Charitable Foundation Grants, 1272
Humana Foundation Grants, 1275
J. Bulow Campbell Foundation Grants, 1319
Jim Blevins Foundation Grants, 1365
KaBOOM! Build it Grant, 1402
Louie M. and Betty M. Phillips Fdn Grants, 1509
M.A. Rikard Charitable Trust Grants, 1521
Medtronic Foundation Community Link Arts, Civic,
    and Culture Grants, 1629
Medtronic Foundation CommunityLink Health
    Grants, 1630
Medtronic Foundation Community Link Human
    Services Grants, 1631
Motiv8 Foundation Grants, 1702
Nationwide Insurance Foundation Grants, 1726
Nissan Neighbors Grants, 1762
PeyBack Foundation Grants, 1953
Piedmont Natural Gas Corporate and Charitable
    Contributions, 1966
Piedmont Natural Gas Fdn Envirnmtl Stewardship
    and Energy Sustainability Grant, 1967
Piedmont Natural Gas Foundation Health and
    Human Services Grants, 1968
Piedmont Natural Gas Foundation K-12 Science,
    Technology, Engineering and Math (STEM)
    Grant, 1969
Piper Jaffray Foundation Communities Giving
    Grants, 1974
PNC Foundation Affordable Housing Grants, 1983
PNC Foundation Community Services Grants, 1984
PNC Foundation Education Grants, 1985
PNC Foundation Grow Up Great Early Childhood
    Grants, 1986
PNC Foundation Revitalization and Stabilization
    Grants, 1987
Publix Super Markets Charities Local Grants, 2036
Salmon Foundation Grants, 2140
Sunoco Foundation Grants, 2256
TAC Arts Access Grant, 2265
TAC Arts Education Funds for At-Risk Youth, 2266
TAC Arts Education Mini Grants, 2267
TAC Arts Education Teacher Incentive Grants, 2268
TAC Touring Arts and Arts Access Touring Arts
    Grants, 2269

Tension Envelope Foundation Grants, 2284
Thomas W. Briggs Foundation Grants, 2294
U.S. Bank Foundation Grants, 2330
U.S. Cellular Corporation Grants, 2331
Union Pacific Fdn Community & Civic Grants, 2337
Union Pacific Foundation Health and Human
    Services Grants, 2338
Volkswagen Group of America Corporate
    Contributions Grants, 2389
VSA/Metlife Connect All Grants, 2392
Watson-Brown Foundation Grants, 2418
Whole Foods Foundation, 2445
William B. Stokely Jr. Foundation Grants, 2459

Texas
3M Company Fdn Community Giving Grants, 5
3M Company Foundation Health and Human
    Services Grants, 6
Abbott Fund Access to Health Care Grants, 45
Abbott Fund Community Engagement Grants, 46
Abbott Fund Global AIDS Care Grants, 47
Abbott Fund Science Education Grants, 48
ABC Charities Grants, 50
Abell-Hanger Foundation Grants, 52
Adams and Reese Corporate Giving Grants, 114
AEGON Transamerica Foundation Education and
    Financial Literacy Grants, 132
AEGON Transamerica Foundation Health and
    Wellness Grants, 133
Aetna Foundation Regional Health Grants, 134
Albert and Ethel Herzstein Charitable Foundation
    Grants, 219
Albertsons Companies Foundation Nourishing
    Neighbors Grants, 221
Aldi Corporation Smart Kids Grants, 226
American Electric Power Corporate Grants, 252
American Electric Power Foundation Grants, 253
American Express Charitable Fund Scholarships, 254
Amerigroup Foundation Grants, 264
Amica Insurance Company Community Grants, 267
Amica Insurance Company Sponsorships, 268
Anheuser-Busch Foundation Grants, 273
Ann L. and Carol Green Rhodes Grants, 278
Arkema Foundation Grants, 298
Arkema Foundation Science Teachers Grants, 299
Austin Community Foundation Grants, 332
Bayer Fund Community Development Grants, 383
Bayer Fund STEM Education Grants, 384
Bernau Family Foundation Grants, 413
Boeing Company Contributions Grants, 462
Brown Foundation Grants, 476
Brunswick Foundation Dollars for Doers Grants, 478
Brunswick Foundation Grants, 479
Cabot Corporation Foundation Grants, 490
Campbell Soup Foundation Grants, 501
Carl B. and Florence E. King Foundation Grants, 506
Carrie S. Orleans Trust Grants, 512
Circle K Corporation Contributions Grants, 614
Clara Blackford Smith and W. Aubrey Smith
    Charitable Foundation Grants, 621
Clayton Fund Grants, 631
Colorado Interstate Gas Grants, 661
Community Foundation of Abilene Future Fund
    Grants, 689
Crystelle Waggoner Charitable Trust Grants, 768
CUNA Mutual Group Fdn Community Grants, 770
David and Betty Sacks Foundation Grants, 788
David Robinson Foundation Grants, 791
Dollar Energy Fund Grants, 834
Dollar General Family Literacy Grants, 835
Dollar General Summer Reading Grants, 836
Dollar General Youth Literacy Grants, 837
Dominion Foundation Grants, 839
Dr. and Mrs. Paul Pierce Memorial Foundation
    Grants, 862
Effie and Wofford Cain Foundation Grants, 895
Elizabeth Huth Coates Charitable Foundation
    Grants, 900
Entergy Charitable Foundation Low-Income
    Initiatives and Solutions Grants, 918

Entergy Corporation Micro Grants, 919
Entergy Corporation Open Grants for Arts and
    Culture, 920
Entergy Corporation Open Grants for Healthy
    Families, 921
Faye L. and William L. Cowden Charitable
    Foundation Grants, 950
Fichtenbaum Charitable Trust Grants, 955
First Lady's Family Literacy Initiative for Texas
    Family Literacy Trailblazer Grants, 968
First Lady's Family Literacy Initiative for Texas
    Implementation Grants, 969
First Lady's Family Literacy Initiative for Texas
    Planning Grants, 970
Florence Foundation Grants, 978
Gardner W. and Joan G. Heidrick, Jr. Foundation
    Grants, 1036
Georgia-Pacific Foundation Education Grants, 1058
Georgia-Pacific Fdn Entrepreneurship Grants, 1059
Gil and Dody Weaver Foundation Grants, 1071
Graham and Carolyn Holloway Family Foundation
    Grants, 1098
Hahl Proctor Charitable Trust Grants, 1151
Harris and Eliza Kempner Fund Ed Grants, 1176
Harvey E. Najim Family Foundation Grants, 1187
Hattie Mae Lesley Foundation Grants, 1195
Hatton W. Sumners Foundation for the Study and
    Teaching of Self Government Grants, 1196
Helen Gertrude Sparks Charitable Trust Grants, 1230
Helen Irwin Littauer Educational Trust Grants, 1231
Herman P. and Sophia Taubman Fdn Grants, 1247
Hispanic Heritage Foundation Youth Awards, 1253
Humana Foundation Grants, 1275
Human Source Foundation Grants, 1276
Intel Foundation Community Grants, 1311
Jack H. and William M. Light Charitable Trust
    Grants, 1330
James M. Collins Foundation Grants, 1344
Joni Elaine Templeton Foundation Grants, 1384
JP Morgan Chase Fdn Arts and Culture Grants, 1394
KaBOOM! Build it Grant, 1402
Katrine Menzing Deakins Chartbl Trust Grants, 1422
Kinder Morgan Foundation Grants, 1436
Land O'Lakes Foundation Community Grants, 1466
Laura Musser Intercultural Harmony Grants, 1472
LISC Financial Stability Grants, 1501
Lockheed Martin Corporation Fdn Grants, 1505
Lubrizol Foundation Grants, 1513
Luella Kemper Trust Grants, 1517
M.D. Anderson Foundation Grants, 1523
Marathon Petroleum Corporation Grants, 1551
Marcia and Otto Koehler Foundation Grants, 1553
Margaret and James A. Elkins Jr. Fdn Grants, 1555
McCombs Foundation Grants, 1615
Meadows Foundation Grants, 1626
MeadWestvaco Foundation Sustainable Communities
    Grants, 1627
Medtronic Foundation Community Link Arts, Civic,
    and Culture Grants, 1629
Medtronic Foundation CommunityLink Health
    Grants, 1630
Medtronic Foundation Community Link Human
    Services Grants, 1631
Mercedes-Benz USA Corporate Contributions
    Grants, 1634
Michael and Susan Dell Foundation Grants, 1657
Milton Hicks Wood and Helen Gibbs Wood
    Charitable Trust Grants, 1676
Minnie M. Jones Trust Grants, 1678
Moody Foundation Grants, 1692
Nathalie and Gladys Dalkowitz Charitable Trust
    Grants, 1716
Nationwide Insurance Foundation Grants, 1726
New Covenant Farms Grants, 1742
Nissan Neighbors Grants, 1762
OMNOVA Solutions Fdn Education Grants, 1820
PacifiCare Foundation Grants, 1861
Paso del Norte Health Foundation Grants, 1874
PNC Foundation Affordable Housing Grants, 1983
PNC Foundation Community Services Grants, 1984

PNC Foundation Education Grants, 1985
PNC Foundation Grow Up Great Early Childhood
    Grants, 1986
PNC Foundation Revitalization and Stabilization
    Grants, 1987
Posse Foundation Scholarships, 2011
Powell Foundation Grants, 2013
Priddy Foundation Operating Grants, 2021
Priddy Foundation Organizational Development
    Grants, 2022
Priddy Foundation Program Grants, 2023
Prudential Foundation Education Grants, 2028
Qualcomm Grants, 2042
R.D. and Joan Dale Hubbard Fdn Grants, 2044
R.D. Beirne Trust Grants, 2045
Robert W. Knox, Sr. and Pearl Wallis Knox
    Charitable Foundation, 2095
Roy and Christine Sturgis Charitable Tr Grts, 2115
Ruth and Vernon Taylor Foundation Grants, 2124
Sadler Family Foundation Grants, 2132
San Antonio Area Foundation Annual Responsive
    Grants, 2147
San Antonio Area Foundation Capital and Naming
    Rights Grants, 2148
San Antonio Area Foundation High School
    Completion Grants, 2149
San Antonio Area Foundation Special and Urgent
    Needs Funding Grants, 2150
San Antonio Area Foundation Strengthening
    Nonprofits Grants, 2151
Shell Deer Park Grants, 2186
Shield-Ayres Foundation Grants, 2189
Stein Family Charitable Trust Grants, 2240
Sterling-Turner Charitable Foundation Grants, 2242
Stinson Foundation Grants, 2246
T.L.L. Temple Foundation Grants, 2264
TE Foundation Grants, 2279
Tellabs Foundation Grants, 2280
Tension Envelope Foundation Grants, 2284
Textron Corporate Contributions Grants, 2286
Thelma Braun and Bocklett Family Foundation
    Grants, 2287
Todd Brock Family Foundation Grants, 2305
Tom C. Barnsley Foundation Grants, 2306
Toyota Motor Manufacturing of Texas Grants, 2313
U.S. Cellular Corporation Grants, 2331
Union Pacific Fdn Community & Civic Grants, 2337
Union Pacific Foundation Health and Human
    Services Grants, 2338
VSA/Metlife Connect All Grants, 2392
W.H. and Mary Ellen Cobb Chartbl Trust Grts, 2397
W.P. and Bulah Luse Foundation Grants, 2399
Whole Foods Foundation, 2445
William J. and Dorothy K. O'Neill Foundation
    Responsive Grants, 2468
William M. Weaver Foundation Grants, 2472
Williams Comps Homegrown Giving Grants, 2474
Wilton and Effie Hebert Foundation Grants, 2476
WinnCompanies Charitable Giving, 2479

US Virgin Islands
7-Eleven Corporate Giving Grants, 8
AAAS/Subaru SB&F Prize for Excl in Sci Books, 22
AASA Urgent Need Mini-Grants, 43
Adidas Corporation General Grants, 125
A Little Hope Grants, 235
Bank of America Charitable Foundation Matching
    Gifts, 356
Bank of America Charitable Foundation Volunteer
    Grants, 358
Beacon Society Jan Stauber Grants, 393
Beckman Coulter Foundation Grants, 394
Bee Conservancy Sponsor-A-Hive Grants, 395
Brinker Int Corporation Charitable Giving, 471
Brookdale Fdn Relatives as Parents Grants, 474
Elton John AIDS Foundation Grants, 910
Fidelity Charitable Gift Fund Grants, 956
First Nations Development Institute Native
    Agriculture and Food Systems Initiative
    Scholarships, 971

First Nations Development Institute Native Arts
Initiative Grants, 972
First Nations Development Institute Native Language
Immersion Initiative Grants, 973
First Nations Development Institute Native Youth
and Culture Fund Grants, 974
First Nations Development Institute Nourishing
Native Children: Feeding Our Future Project
Grants, 975
Ford Foundation BUILD Grants, 984
From the Top Alumni Leadership Grants, 1025
From the Top Jack Kent Cooke Young Artist
Scholarships, 1026
Good+Foundation Grants, 1096
IMLS Grants to State Library Administrative
Agencies, 1298
IMLS National Leadership Grants for Libraries, 1299
Jack Kent Cooke Fdn Young Artist Awards, 1333
Judy and Peter Blum Kovler Foundation Grants, 1396
Laura Bush Foundation for America's Libraries
Grants, 1471
NEA Student Program Communities Redefining
Education Advocacy Through Empowerment
(CREATE) Grants, 1733
NSF Perception, Action and Cognition (PAC)
Research Grants, 1775
PDF Fiscal Sponsorship Grant, 1921
PennPAT Fee-Support Grants for Presenters, 1930
PennPAT New Directions Grants for Presenters, 1931
Ray Charles Foundation Grants, 2058
Target Corporation Soccer Grants, 2271
U.S. Department of Education Promise
Neighborhoods Grants, 2332
USAID Community Livelihoods Project in Yemen
Grant, 2352
USAID Family Planning and Reproductive Health
Methods Grants, 2353
USAID Global Development Alliance Grants, 2354
USAID National Governance Project in Yemen
Grant, 2357
USAID Office of Foreign Disaster Assistance and
Food for Peace Grants, 2359
USAID School Improvement Program Grants, 2360
USAID U.S.-Egypt Learning Grants, 2361
WHO Foundation Education/Literacy Grants, 2442
WSF Rusty Kanokogi Fund for the Advancement of
U.S. Judo Grants, 2495
WSF Sports 4 Life Grants, 2496
WSF Sports 4 Life Regional Grants, 2497
WSF Travel and Training Fund Grants, 2498

Utah
3M Company Fdn Community Giving Grants, 5
3M Company Foundation Health and Human
Services Grants, 6
100% for Kids - Utah Credit Union Education
Foundation Major Project Grants, 11
100% for Kids - Utah Credit Union Education
Foundation Mini Grants, 12
100% for Kids - Utah Credit Union Education
Foundation School Grants, 13
Abbott Fund Access to Health Care Grants, 45
Abbott Fund Community Engagement Grants, 46
Abbott Fund Global AIDS Care Grants, 47
Abbott Fund Science Education Grants, 48
Albertsons Companies Foundation Nourishing
Neighbors Grants, 221
American Express Charitable Fund Scholarships, 254
Bernau Family Foundation Grants, 413
Boeing Company Contributions Grants, 462
Campbell Soup Foundation Grants, 501
Castle Foundation Grants, 518
Colorado Interstate Gas Grants, 661
Daniels Fund Amateur Sports Grants, 779
Daniels Drug and Alcohol Addiction Grants, 780
Daniels Fund Early Childhood Education Grants, 781
Daniels Fund Homeless and Disadvantaged Grants, 782
Daniels Fund K-12 Education Reform Grants, 783
Daniels Fund Youth Development Grants, 784
Dollar General Family Literacy Grants, 835

Dollar General Summer Reading Grants, 836
Dollar General Youth Literacy Grants, 837
E.L. Wiegand Foundation Grants, 877
Eide Bailly Resourcefulness Awards, 897
Gannett Foundation Community Action Grants, 1033
Humana Foundation Grants, 1275
Intel Corporation Community Grants, 1311
James LeVoy Sorenson Foundation Grants, 1343
JP Morgan Chase Fdn Arts and Culture Grants, 1394
Julia Richardson Brown Foundation Grants, 1398
KaBOOM! Build it Grant, 1402
Piper Jaffray Foundation Communities Giving
Grants, 1974
Shopko Fdn Community Charitable Grants, 2191
Stan and Sandy Checketts Foundation Grants, 2235
Sterling and Shelli Gardner Foundation Grants, 2243
U.S. Bank Foundation Grants, 2330
Union Pacific Fdn Community & Civic Grants, 2337
Union Pacific Foundation Health and Human
Services Grants, 2338
Whole Foods Foundation, 2445

Vermont
Agnes M. Lindsay Trust Grants, 140
Albertsons Companies Foundation Nourishing
Neighbors Grants, 221
Aldi Corporation Smart Kids Grants, 226
Bay and Paul Foundations PreK-12 Transformative
Learning Practices Grants, 370
Baystate Financial Charitable Foundation Grants, 385
Citizens Bank Charitable Foundation Grants, 616
Claremont Savings Bank Foundation Grants, 623
Clayton F. and Ruth L. Hawkridge Foundation
Grants, 630
Dollar General Family Literacy Grants, 835
Dollar General Summer Reading Grants, 836
Dollar General Youth Literacy Grants, 837
Dorr Foundation Grants, 846
Entergy Charitable Foundation Education and
Literacy Grants, 917
Entergy Corporation Micro Grants, 919
Entergy Corporation Open Grants for Arts and
Culture, 920
Entergy Corporation Open Grants for Healthy
Families, 921
Gannett Foundation Community Action Grants, 1033
George I. Alden Trust Grants, 1051
Hannaford Charitable Foundation Grants, 1163
Hannaford Supermarkets Community Giving, 1164
HRAMF Charles H. Hood Foundation Child Health
Research Awards, 1262
Hubbard Farms Charitable Foundation Grants, 1272
Jack and Dorothy Byrne Foundation Grants, 1329
Lucy Downing Nisbet Charitable Fund Grants, 1515
Merck Family Fund Urban Farming and Youth
Leadership Grants, 1635
New Hampshire Charitable Foundation Neil and
Louise Tillotson Fund - Empower Coös Youth
Grants, 1748
Perkins Charitable Foundation Grants, 1939
Price Chopper's Golub Foundation Grants, 2020
Richard Davoud Donchian Foundation Grants, 2070
S. Spencer Scott Fund Grants, 2129
Sunoco Foundation Grants, 2256
Windham Foundation Grants, 2477
Yawkey Foundation Grants, 2510

Virginia
Abbott Fund Access to Health Care Grants, 45
Abbott Fund Community Engagement Grants, 46
Abbott Fund Global AIDS Care Grants, 47
Abbott Fund Science Education Grants, 48
Aetna Foundation Regional Health Grants, 134
Aldi Corporation Smart Kids Grants, 226
Alloy Family Foundation Grants, 241
Alpha Natural Resources Corporate Giving, 246
American Electric Power Corporate Grants, 252
American Electric Power Foundation Grants, 253
American Woodmark Foundation Grants, 263
Amerigroup Foundation Grants, 264

Amica Insurance Company Community Grants, 267
Amica Insurance Company Sponsorships, 268
Anheuser-Busch Foundation Grants, 273
Appalachian Community Fund LGBTQ Fund
Grants, 284
Appalachian Regional Commission Business
Development Revolving Loan Fund Grants, 285
Appalachian Regional Commission Education and
Training Grants, 286
Appalachian Regional Commission Entrepreneurship
and Business Development Grants, 287
Appalachian Regional Commission Health Care
Grants, 288
Appalachian Regl Commission Housing Grants, 289
Bainum Family Foundation Grants, 345
Bernau Family Foundation Grants, 413
Burlington Industries Foundation Grants, 481
CFGR Community Impact Grants, 552
CFGR Jenkins Foundation Grants, 553
CFGR SisterFund Grants, 554
CFGR Ujima Legacy Fund Grants, 555
Charles Delmar Foundation Grants, 564
Community Foundation for the National Capital
Region Community Leadership Grants, 688
CONSOL Energy Academic Grants, 746
CONSOL Youth Program Grants, 747
Corina Higginson Trust Grants, 750
Dollar Energy Fund Grants, 834
Dollar General Family Literacy Grants, 835
Dollar General Summer Reading Grants, 836
Dollar General Youth Literacy Grants, 837
Dominion Foundation Grants, 839
Four Lanes Trust Grants, 1005
Gannett Foundation Community Action Grants, 1033
George J. and Effie L. Seay Foundation Grants, 1052
Georgia-Pacific Foundation Education Grants, 1058
Georgia-Pacific Fdn Entrepreneurship Grants, 1059
Giant Food Charitable Grants, 1068
Hampton Roads Community Foundation Abused
People Grants, 1153
Hampton Roads Community Foundation Arts and
Culture Grants, 1154
Hampton Roads Community Foundation Community
Leadership Partners Grants, 1155
Hampton Roads Community Foundation
Developmental Disabilities Grants, 1156
Hampton Roads Community Foundation Education
Grants, 1157
Hampton Roads Community Foundation
Environment Grants, 1158
Hampton Roads Community Foundation Nonprofit
Facilities Improvement Grants, 1159
Hampton Roads Community Foundation Youth
Baseball and Softball Program Grants, 1160
HBF Pathways Out of Poverty Grants, 1222
J. Edwin Treakle Foundation Grants, 1320
J. Willard and Alice S. Marriott Fdn Grants, 1327
Jack Kent Cooke Fdn Good Neighbor Grants, 1331
Julia and Tunnicliff Fox Chartbl Trust Grants, 1397
KaBOOM! Build it Grant, 1402
Kennedy Center National Symphony Orchestra Youth
Fellowships, 1426
Kinder Morgan Foundation Grants, 1436
Land O'Lakes Foundation Mid-Atlantic Grants, 1467
Leonsis Foundation Grants, 1485
Lockheed Martin Corporation Fdn Grants, 1505
Marietta McNeill Morgan and Samuel Tate Morgan
Jr. Trust Grants, 1560
Mary Wilmer Covey Charitable Trust Grants, 1600
Maurice R. Robinson Fund Grants, 1611
MeadWestvaco Foundation Sustainable Communities
Grants, 1627
Memorial Foundation for Children Grants, 1633
Meyer Foundation Benevon Grants, 1648
Meyer Foundation Education Grants, 1649
Meyer Fdn Management Assistance Grants, 1651
Micron Technology Fdn Community Grants, 1664
Moran Family Foundation Grants, 1693
Nationwide Insurance Foundation Grants, 1726
Nestle Purina PetCare Educational Grants, 1738

Nestle Purina PetCare Youth Grants, 1739
PennPAT Fee-Support Grants for Presenters, 1930
PennPAT New Directions Grants for Presenters, 1931
Perkins Charitable Foundation Grants, 1939
Philip L. Graham Fund Education Grants, 1962
PNC Foundation Affordable Housing Grants, 1983
PNC Foundation Community Services Grants, 1984
PNC Foundation Education Grants, 1985
PNC Foundation Grow Up Great Early Childhood
    Grants, 1986
PNC Foundation Revitalization and Stabilization
    Grants, 1987
Richard and Caroline T. Gwathmey Memorial Trust
    Grants, 2069
Richard Davoud Donchian Foundation Grants, 2070
Ruth and Henry Campbell Foundation Grants, 2123
Ruth Camp Campbell Charitable Trust Grants, 2125
Salmon Foundation Grants, 2140
Sunoco Foundation Grants, 2256
TAC Arts Education Funds for At-Risk Youth, 2266
TAC Arts Education Mini Grants, 2267
TAC Touring Arts and Arts Access Touring Arts
    Grants, 2269
TE Foundation Grants, 2279
U.S. Cellular Corporation Grants, 2331
Virginia Commission for the Arts Artists in
    Education Residency Grants, 2385
Virginia Foundation for the Humanities Folklife
    Apprenticeships, 2386
Volkswagen Group of America Corporate
    Contributions Grants, 2389
Washington Area Fuel Fund Grants, 2413
Washington Gas Charitable Contributions, 2417
Watson-Brown Foundation Grants, 2418
Whole Foods Foundation, 2445
William A. Cooke Foundation Grants, 2452
William J. and Dorothy K. O'Neill Foundation
    Responsive Grants, 2468
Williams Comps Homegrown Giving Grants, 2474
WinnCompanies Charitable Giving, 2479

Washington
Abby's Legendary Pizza Foundation Grants, 49
Adobe Fdn Community Investment Grants, 127
Adobe Fdn Hunger and Homelessness Grants, 128
Aetna Foundation Regional Health Grants, 134
Alaska Airlines Corporation Career Connections for
    Youth Grants, 193
Alaska Airlines Foundation LIFT Grants, 194
Albertsons Companies Foundation Nourishing
    Neighbors Grants, 221
Amerigroup Foundation Grants, 264
Amica Insurance Company Community Grants, 267
Amica Insurance Company Sponsorships, 268
Avista Foundation Education Grants, 340
Avista Foundation Vulnerable and Limited Income
    Population Grants, 341
Bayer Fund Community Development Grants, 383
Bayer Fund STEM Education Grants, 384
Ben B. Cheney Foundation Grants, 402
Better Way Foundation Grants, 419
Blue Mountain Community Foundation Discretionary
    Grants, 455
Blue Mountain Community Foundation Garfield
    County Health Foundation Fund Grants, 456
Blue Mountain Community Foundation Warren
    Community Action Fund Grants, 457
Boeing Company Contributions Grants, 462
Brunswick Foundation Dollars for Doers Grants, 478
Brunswick Foundation Grants, 479
Catherine Holmes Wilkins Fdn Charitable Grts, 520
Charlotte Martin Foundation Youth Grants, 571
Circle K Corporation Contributions Grants, 614
Dean Foundation Grants, 806
Dean Witter Foundation Education Grants, 807
E.L. Wiegand Foundation Grants, 877
Eulalie Bloedel Schneider Foundation Grants, 936
Forest Foundation Grants, 985
Fred and Gretel Biel Charitable Trust Grants, 1016
Georgia-Pacific Foundation Education Grants, 1058

Georgia-Pacific Fdn Entrepreneurship Grants, 1059
Greater Tacoma Community Foundation Fund for
    Women and Girls Grants, 1112
Greater Tacoma Community Foundation General
    Operating Grants, 1113
Greater Tacoma Community Fdn Spark Grants, 1114
Greater Tacoma Community Foundation Youth
    Program Grants, 1115
Grifols Community Outreach Grants, 1122
H.B. Fuller Foundation Grants, 1138
Hasbro Children's Fund Grants, 1189
Hasbro Corp Gift of Play Holiday Giving, 1190
Hasbro Corporation Gift of Play Hospital and
    Pediatric Health Giving, 1191
Hasbro Corporation Gift of Play Shelter Support
    Giving, 1192
Hasbro Corporation Gift of Play Summer Camp
    Support, 1193
Herman P. and Sophia Taubman Fdn Grants, 1247
Hubbard Family Foundation Grants, 1271
Hubbard Family Foundation Grants, 1270
Intel Corporation Community Grants, 1311
Janson Foundation Grants, 1350
Jeffris Wood Foundation Grants, 1359
KaBOOM! Build it Grant, 1402
Kawabe Memorial Fund Grants, 1423
Kinder Morgan Foundation Grants, 1436
Land O'Lakes Foundation Community Grants, 1466
M.A. Rikard Charitable Trust Grants, 1521
M.J. Murdock Charitable Trust General Grants, 1524
Medtronic Foundation Community Link Arts, Civic,
    and Culture Grants, 1629
Medtronic Foundation CommunityLink Health
    Grants, 1630
Medtronic Foundation Community Link Human
    Services Grants, 1631
Norcliffe Foundation Grants, 1766
OneFamily Foundation Grants, 1822
PacifiCare Foundation Grants, 1861
Piper Jaffray Foundation Communities Giving
    Grants, 1974
PNC Foundation Revitalization and Stabilization
    Grants, 1987
Premera Blue Cross Grants, 2018
Pride Foundation Grants, 2024
Rathmann Family Foundation Grants, 2057
Saltchuk Corporate Giving, 2141
Samuel S. Johnson Foundation Grants, 2146
San Juan Island Community Foundation Grants, 2158
Seattle Foundation Arts and Culture Grants, 2174
Seattle Foundation Basic Needs Grants, 2175
Seattle Foundation Benjamin N. Phillips Memorial
    Fund Grants, 2176
Seattle Foundation C. Keith Birkenfeld Memorial
    Trust Grants, 2177
Seattle Foundation Education Grants, 2178
Seattle Foundation Health and Wellness Grants, 2179
Shopko Fdn Community Charitable Grants, 2191
Simpson Lumber Charitable Contributions, 2201
Social Justice Fund Northwest Criminal Justice
    Giving Project Grants, 2214
Social Justice Fund Northwest Economic Justice
    Giving Project Grants, 2215
Stocker Foundation Grants, 2247
U.S. Bank Foundation Grants, 2330
U.S. Cellular Corporation Grants, 2331
Union Bank, N.A. Corporate Sponsorships and
    Donations, 2333
Union Bank, N.A. Foundation Grants, 2334
Union Pacific Fdn Community & Civic Grants, 2337
Union Pacific Foundation Health and Human
    Services Grants, 2338
VSA/Metlife Connect All Grants, 2392
Whatcom Community Foundation Grants, 2436
Whitehorse Foundation Grants, 2439
Whole Foods Foundation, 2445

West Virginia
Aldi Corporation Smart Kids Grants, 226
Alpha Natural Resources Corporate Giving, 246

American Electric Power Corporate Grants, 252
American Electric Power Foundation Grants, 253
American Woodmark Foundation Grants, 263
Amerigroup Foundation Grants, 264
Appalachian Community Fund LGBTQ Fund
    Grants, 284
Appalachian Regional Commission Business
    Development Revolving Loan Fund Grants, 285
Appalachian Regional Commission Education and
    Training Grants, 286
Appalachian Regional Commission Entrepreneurship
    and Business Development Grants, 287
Appalachian Regional Commission Health Care
    Grants, 288
Appalachian Regl Commission Housing Grants, 289
Cabot Corporation Foundation Grants, 490
Carl M. Freeman Foundation FACES Grants, 507
Carl M. Freeman Foundation Grants, 508
Charles Delmar Foundation Grants, 564
CONSOL Energy Academic Grants, 746
CONSOL Youth Program Grants, 747
Dollar Energy Fund Grants, 834
Dollar General Family Literacy Grants, 835
Dollar General Summer Reading Grants, 836
Dollar General Youth Literacy Grants, 837
Dominion Foundation Grants, 839
EQT Fdn Community Enrichment Grants, 926
EQT Fdn Education and Workforce Grants, 927
Fifth Third Bank Corporate Giving, 958
Fifth Third Foundation Grants, 959
FirstEnergy Foundation Community Grants, 965
FirstEnergy Foundation Science, Technology,
    Engineering, and Mathematics Grants, 966
Georgia-Pacific Foundation Education Grants, 1058
Georgia-Pacific Fdn Entrepreneurship Grants, 1059
Haddad Foundation Grants, 1139
Harry and Helen Sands Charitable Trust Grants, 1181
Highmark Corporate Giving Grants, 1248
Huntington Clinical Foundation Grants, 1278
JP Morgan Chase Fdn Arts and Culture Grants, 1394
Marathon Petroleum Corporation Grants, 1551
MeadWestvaco Foundation Sustainable Communities
    Grants, 1627
Nestle Purina PetCare Educational Grants, 1738
Nestle Purina PetCare Youth Grants, 1739
Parkersburg Area Community Foundation Action
    Grants, 1871
PennPAT Fee-Support Grants for Presenters, 1930
PennPAT New Directions Grants for Presenters, 1931
Sunoco Foundation Grants, 2256
Toyota Motor Manufacturing of West Virginia
    Grants, 2314
U.S. Cellular Corporation Grants, 2331
Watson-Brown Foundation Grants, 2418
West Virginia Commission on the Arts Challenge
    America Partnership Grants, 2430
West Virginia Commission on the Arts Long-Term
    Artist Residencies, 2431
West Virginia Commission on the Arts Short-Term
    Artist Residencies, 2432
West Virginia Commission on the Arts Special
    Projects Grants, 2433

Wisconsin
3M Company Fdn Community Giving Grants, 5
3M Company Foundation Health and Human
    Services Grants, 6
Acuity Charitable Foundation Grants, 110
A Fund for Women Grants, 137
Albertsons Companies Foundation Nourishing
    Neighbors Grants, 221
Aldi Corporation Smart Kids Grants, 226
Alliant Energy Foundation Community Giving for
    Good Sponsorship Grants, 240
Amerigroup Foundation Grants, 264
Amica Insurance Company Community Grants, 267
Amica Insurance Company Sponsorships, 268
Babcock Charitable Trust Grants, 343
Brunswick Foundation Dollars for Doers Grants, 478
Brunswick Foundation Grants, 479

C.H. Robinson Worldwide Foundation Grants, 489
Campbell Soup Foundation Grants, 501
Castle Foundation Grants, 517
Castle Industries Foundation Grants, 519
CFFVR Appleton Education Foundation Grants, 536
CFFVR Basic Needs Giving Partnership Grants, 537
CFFVR Clintonville Area Foundation Grants, 538
CFFVR Clintonville Area Foundation Grants, 539
CFFVR Environmental Stewardship Grants, 540
CFFVR Frank C. Shattuck Community Grants, 541
CFFVR Infant Welfare Circle of Kings Daughters
   Grants, 542
CFFVR Jewelers Mutual Chartbl Giving Grants, 543
CFFVR Mielke Family Foundation Grants, 544
CFFVR Myra M. and Robert L. Vandehey
   Foundation Grants, 545
CFFVR Project Grants, 546
CFFVR Robert and Patricia Endries Family
   Foundation Grants, 547
CFFVR Schmidt Family G4 Grants, 548
CFFVR Shawano Area Community Foundation
   Grants, 549
CFFVR Women's Fund for the Fox Valley Region
   Grants, 550
Clark Electric Cooperative Grants, 627
Coleman Foundation Entrepreneurship Education
   Grants, 651
CUNA Mutual Group Fdn Community Grants, 770
Dollar General Family Literacy Grants, 835
Dollar General Summer Reading Grants, 836
Dollar General Youth Literacy Grants, 837
Gannett Foundation Community Action Grants, 1033
Gardner Foundation Grants, 1034
George Kress Foundation Grants, 1053
Georgia-Pacific Foundation Education Grants, 1058
Georgia-Pacific Fdn Entrepreneurship Grants, 1059
Greater Milwaukee Foundation Grants, 1109
HRK Foundation Health Grants, 1264
Huffy Foundation Grants, 1273
Humana Foundation Grants, 1275
Jane Bradley Pettit Foundation Community and
   Social Development Grants, 1347
JP Morgan Chase Fdn Arts and Culture Grants, 1394
Land O'Lakes Foundation Community Grants, 1466
Lands' End Corporate Giving Program, 1468
Lumpkin Family Foundation Strong Community
   Leadership Grants, 1519
Madison Community Foundation Altrusa
   International of Madison Grants, 1533
Madison Community Foundation Fund for Children
   Grants, 1534
Madison Community Foundation Grants, 1535
Margaret Wiegand Trust Grants, 1558
Mead Witter Foundation Grants, 1628
Nationwide Insurance Foundation Grants, 1726
Nestle Purina PetCare Educational Grants, 1738
Nestle Purina PetCare Youth Grants, 1739
OMNOVA Solutions Fdn Education Grants, 1820
Pentair Foundation Education and Community
   Grants, 1934
Philanthrofund Foundation Grants, 1959
Piper Jaffray Foundation Communities Giving
   Grants, 1974
PNC Foundation Affordable Housing Grants, 1983
PNC Foundation Community Services Grants, 1984
PNC Foundation Education Grants, 1985
PNC Foundation Grow Up Great Early Childhood
   Grants, 1986
PNC Foundation Revitalization and Stabilization
   Grants, 1987
PPCF Esther M. and Freeman E. Everett Charitable
   Foundation Grants, 2016
Richland County Bank Grants, 2074
Ruddie Memorial Youth Foundation Grants, 2120
Sensient Technologies Foundation Grants, 2180
Shopko Fdn Community Charitable Grants, 2191
Shopko Foundation Green Bay Area Community
   Grants, 2192
Siebert Lutheran Foundation Grants, 2198
U.S. Bank Foundation Grants, 2330

U.S. Cellular Corporation Grants, 2331
Union Pacific Fdn Community & Civic Grants, 2337
Union Pacific Foundation Health and Human
   Services Grants, 2338
Walton Family Foundation Public Charter Startup
   Grants, 2409
Whole Foods Foundation, 2445
William J. and Gertrude R. Casper Foundation
   Grants, 2469
Wisconsin Energy Foundation Grants, 2481

Wyoming
A.C. and Penney Hubbard Foundation Grants, 19
Albertsons Companies Foundation Nourishing
   Neighbors Grants, 221
B.F. and Rose H. Perkins Foundation Community
   Grants, 342
CenturyLink Clarke M. Williams Foundation
   Matching Time Grants, 531
Colorado Interstate Gas Grants, 661
Community Foundation of Jackson Hole Youth
   Philanthropy Grants, 715
Daniels Fund Amateur Sports Grants, 779
Daniels Drug and Alcohol Addiction Grants, 780
Daniels Fund Early Childhood Education Grants, 781
Daniels Homeless and Disadvantaged Grants, 782
Daniels Fund K-12 Education Reform Grants, 783
Daniels Fund Youth Development Grants, 784
John P. Ellbogen Fdn Community Grants, 1377
Laura Musser Intercultural Harmony Grants, 1472
Lynn and Foster Friess Family Fdn Grants, 1520
Piper Jaffray Foundation Communities Giving
   Grants, 1974
Ruth and Vernon Taylor Foundation Grants, 2124
Shopko Fdn Community Charitable Grants, 2191
Social Justice Fund Northwest Criminal Justice
   Giving Project Grants, 2214
Social Justice Fund Northwest Economic Justice
   Giving Project Grants, 2215
U.S. Bank Foundation Grants, 2330
Union Pacific Fdn Community & Civic Grants, 2337
Union Pacific Foundation Health and Human
   Services Grants, 2338
Wold Foundation Grants, 2482
Wyoming Community Foundation COVID-19
   Response and Recovery Grants, 2500
Wyoming Community Fdn General Grants, 2501
Wyoming Community Foundation Hazel Patterson
   Memorial Grants, 2502
Wyoming Department of Education McKinney-Vento
   Subgrant, 2503

Outside of the United States

All Countries
AAUW International Project Grants, 44
ACMP Foundation Community Music Grants, 108
Adobe Foundation Action Grants, 126
Air Products Foundation Grants, 148
ALA Alex Awards, 153
ALA Amazing Audiobks for Young Adults Awd, 155
ALA Children's Literature Legacy Award, 165
ALA May Hill Arbuthnot Honor Lecture Award, 176
ALA Michael L. Printz Award, 177
Alcatel-Lucent Technologies Foundation Grants, 224
ALFJ Astraea U.S. and International Emergency
   Fund, 230
ALFJ International Social Change Opportunity Fund
   Grants, 232
AOCS Thomas H. Smouse Memorial Fellowship, 282
Baxter International Corporate Giving Grants, 368
Baxter International Foundation Grants, 369
Bill and Melinda Gates Foundation Agricultural
   Development Grants, 425
Bill and Melinda Gates Foundation Emergency
   Response Grants, 426
Bill and Melinda Gates Foundation Policy and
   Advocacy Grants, 427
Bill and Melinda Gates Foundation Water, Sanitation
   and Hygiene Grants, 428

Bryan Adams Foundation Grants, 480
Cause Populi Worthy Cause Grants, 521
Changemakers Innovation Awards, 559
Cisco Systems Foundation San Jose Community
   Grants, 615
Credit Suisse Foundation Education Grants, 765
Foundation Beyond Belief Compassionate Impact
   Grants, 986
Foundation Beyond Belief Humanist Grants, 987
Giving Gardens Challenge Grants, 1072
Global Fund for Women Grants, 1073
Greygates Foundation Grants, 1120
Harry Frank Guggenheim Foundation Research
   Grants, 1184
Helen Bader Foundation Grants, 1227
Honeywell Corp Humanitarian Relief Grants, 1257
ILA Arbuthnot Award, 1290
ILA Children's and Young Adults' Book Awds, 1291
ILA Grants for Literacy Projects in Countries with
   Developing Economies, 1292
Kirby Laing Foundation Grants, 1439
MacLellan Foundation Grants, 1531
Macquarie Bank Foundation Grants, 1532
MeadWestvaco Foundation Sustainable Communities
   Grants, 1627
Microsoft YouthSpark Grants, 1666
NSF Social Psychology Grants, 1776
OSF Early Childhood Program Grants, 1841
OSF Education Support Program Grants, 1843
PepsiCo Foundation Grants, 1935
Radcliffe Institute Oral History Grants, 2049
Raskob Fdn for Catholic Activities Grants, 2054
Target Foundation Global Grants, 2272
Thrasher Research Fund Grants, 2296
Tides Fdn Friends of the IGF Fund Grants, 2300
Tides Foundation Girl Rising Fund Grants, 2301
Tides Foundation Grants, 2302
United Methodist Committee on Relief Hunger and
   Poverty Grants, 2344
United Technologies Corporation Grants, 2347
USAID Community Livelihoods Project in Yemen
   Grant, 2352
USAID Family Planning and Reproductive Health
   Methods Grants, 2353
USAID Global Development Alliance Grants, 2354
USAID Innovations in Feed the Future Monitoring
   and Evaluation Grants, 2355
USAID Integrated Youth Development Activity
   Grants, 2356
USAID National Governance Project in Yemen
   Grant, 2357
USAID School Improvement Program Grants, 2360
USAID U.S.-Egypt Learning Grants, 2361
Volvo Adventure Environmental Awards, 2390
VSA International Art Program for Children with
   Disabilities Grants, 2394
VSA International Young Soloists Award, 2395
YSA GYSD Regional Partner Grants, 2515
Zonta International Foundation Young Women in
   Public Affairs Award, 2527

Abkhazia
H.B. Fuller Foundation Grants, 1138

Afghanistan
H.B. Fuller Foundation Grants, 1138

Albania
Cargill Corporate Giving Grants, 503
Charles Delmar Foundation Grants, 564
GMFUS Balkan Trust for Democracy Grants, 1075

Algeria
Cargill Corporate Giving Grants, 503

Andorra
Cargill Corporate Giving Grants, 503
Charles Delmar Foundation Grants, 564

Angola
Cargill Corporate Giving Grants, 503

Anguilla
Elton John AIDS Foundation Grants, 910

Antigua & Barbuda
Atkinson Foundation Community Grants, 325
Elton John AIDS Foundation Grants, 910
SME Education Fdn Youth Program Grants, 2209

Argentina
Charles Delmar Foundation Grants, 564
Elton John AIDS Foundation Grants, 910
Katherine John Murphy Foundation Grants, 1419
OSF Young Feminist Leaders Fellowships, 1845

Armenia
Cargill Corporate Giving Grants, 503
Charles Delmar Foundation Grants, 564
H.B. Fuller Foundation Grants, 1138

Aruba
Elton John AIDS Foundation Grants, 910

Australia
Boeing Company Contributions Grants, 462
May and Stanley Smith Charitable Trust Grants, 1613
NZDIA Community Org Grants Scheme, 1796
Pediatric Brain Tumor Foundation Early Career
    Development Grants, 1924
Pediatric Brain Tumor Fdn Institute Grants, 1925
Pediatric Brain Tumor Fdn Opportunity Grants, 1926
Serco Foundation Grants, 2181

Austria
BP Foundation Grants, 465
Cargill Corporate Giving Grants, 503
Charles Delmar Foundation Grants, 564
Medtronic Foundation Strengthening Health Systems
    Grants, 1632

Azerbaijan
Cargill Corporate Giving Grants, 503
Charles Delmar Foundation Grants, 564
H.B. Fuller Foundation Grants, 1138

Bahamas
Atkinson Foundation Community Grants, 325
Elton John AIDS Foundation Grants, 910
May and Stanley Smith Charitable Trust Grants, 1613
SME Education Fdn Youth Program Grants, 2209

Bahrain
H.B. Fuller Foundation Grants, 1138

Bangladesh
H.B. Fuller Foundation Grants, 1138

Barbados
Atkinson Foundation Community Grants, 325
Elton John AIDS Foundation Grants, 910
SME Education Fdn Youth Program Grants, 2209

Belarus
Cargill Corporate Giving Grants, 503
Charles Delmar Foundation Grants, 564
Medtronic Foundation Strengthening Health Systems
    Grants, 1632

Belgium
BP Foundation Grants, 465
Cabot Corporation Foundation Grants, 490
Cargill Corporate Giving Grants, 503
Charles Delmar Foundation Grants, 564
Lubrizol Corporation Community Grants, 1512

Belize
Atkinson Foundation Community Grants, 325
Blossom Fund Grants, 441

Elton John AIDS Foundation Grants, 910
SME Education Fdn Youth Program Grants, 2209

Benin
Cargill Corporate Giving Grants, 503

Bhutan
H.B. Fuller Foundation Grants, 1138

Bolivia
Charles Delmar Foundation Grants, 564
Elton John AIDS Foundation Grants, 910
Katherine John Murphy Foundation Grants, 1419
OSF Young Feminist Leaders Fellowships, 1845

Bosnia & Herzegovina
Cargill Corporate Giving Grants, 503
Charles Delmar Foundation Grants, 564
GMFUS Balkan Trust for Democracy Grants, 1075

Botswana
Cargill Corporate Giving Grants, 503

Brazil
Abbott Fund Community Engagement Grants, 46
Abbott Fund Science Education Grants, 48
Avery Dennison Foundation Education Grants, 337
Charles Delmar Foundation Grants, 564
Elton John AIDS Foundation Grants, 910
Katherine John Murphy Foundation Grants, 1419
Medtronic Foundation Strengthening Health Systems
    Grants, 1632
Oak Foundation Child Abuse Grants, 1799
OSF Young Feminist Leaders Fellowships, 1845

British Indian Ocean Territory
H.B. Fuller Foundation Grants, 1138

British Virgin Islands
Elton John AIDS Foundation Grants, 910

Brunei
H.B. Fuller Foundation Grants, 1138

Bulgaria
Cargill Corporate Giving Grants, 503
Charles Delmar Foundation Grants, 564
GMFUS Balkan Trust for Democracy Grants, 1075
Medtronic Foundation Strengthening Health Systems
    Grants, 1632
Oak Foundation Child Abuse Grants, 1799

Burkina Faso
Cargill Corporate Giving Grants, 503

Burundi
Cargill Corporate Giving Grants, 503

Cambodia
H.B. Fuller Foundation Grants, 1138

Cameroon
Cargill Corporate Giving Grants, 503

Canada
4imprint One by One Charitable Giving, 7
Abbott Fund Community Engagement Grants, 46
Abbott Fund Science Education Grants, 48
Adobe Fdn Community Investment Grants, 127
Adobe Fdn Hunger and Homelessness Grants, 128
ALA Baker and Taylor/YALSA Collection
    Development Grants, 157
ALA Booklist Editors' Choice Books for Youth
    Awards, 162
ALA Bound to Stay Bound Books Scholarships, 163
ALA Louise Seaman Bechtel Fellowship, 173
Alaska Airlines Corporation Career Connections for
    Youth Grants, 193
ATA Inclusive Learning Communities Grants, 323
ATA Local Community Relations Grants, 324

Austin S. Nelson Foundation Grants, 333
Bank of America Charitable Foundation Matching
    Gifts, 356
Bank of America Charitable Foundation Volunteer
    Grants, 358
Beacon Society Jan Stauber Grants, 393
Boeing Company Contributions Grants, 462
BP Foundation Grants, 465
British Columbia Arts Council Youth Engagement
    Program Grants, 473
Cabot Corporation Foundation Grants, 490
CEC Clarissa Hug Teacher of the Year Award, 527
CEC J.E. Wallace Wallin Special Education Lifetime
    Achievement Award, 528
CEC Yes I Can! Awards, 529
Crayola Champ Creatively Alive Children Grts, 764
Elton John AIDS Foundation Grants, 910
Gloria Barron Prize for Young Heroes, 1074
Honor the Earth Grants, 1259
Johnson Scholarship Foundation Grants, 1382
KaBOOM! Build it Grant, 1402
KIND Causes Monthly Grants, 1435
Laidlaw Foundation Multi-Year Grants, 1460
Laidlaw Foundation Youh Organizing Catalyst
    Grants, 1461
Laidlaw Foundation Youth Organizaing Initiatives
    Grants, 1462
Lockheed Martin Corporation Fdn Grants, 1505
May and Stanley Smith Charitable Trust Grants, 1613
Medtronic Foundation CommunityLink Health
    Grants, 1630
Michelin North America Challenge Education, 1660
MLB Tomorrow Fund Grants, 1679
Newfoundland and Labrador Arts Council ArtSmarts
    Grants, 1744
Newfoundland and Labrador Arts Council School
    Touring Grants, 1745
Newfoundland and Labrador Arts Council Visiting
    Artists Grants, 1746
Oak Foundation Child Abuse Grants, 1799
Ontario Arts Council Artists in Communities and
    Schools Project Grants, 1823
Ontario Arts Council Arts Organizations in
    Communities and Schools Operating Grants, 1824
Ontario Arts Council Indigenous Culture Fund
    Indigenous Artists in Communities and Schools
    Project Grants, 1825
Ontario Arts Foundation Ruth and Sylvia Schwartz
    Children's Book Awards, 1826
Pediatric Brain Tumor Foundation Early Career
    Development Grants, 1924
Pediatric Brain Tumor Fdn Institute Grants, 1925
Pediatric Brain Tumor Foundation Opportunity
    Grants, 1926
Sick Kids Foundation Community Conference
    Grants, 2193
Sick Kids Foundation New Investigator Research
    Grants, 2194
Thomas Sill Foundation Grants, 2292
UUA Actions of Public Witness Grants, 2365
UUA Congregation-Based Community Organizing
    Grants, 2366
UUA Fund Grants, 2367
UUA International Fund Grants, 2368
UUA Just Society Fund Grants, 2369
UUA Social Responsibility Grants, 2370
Virginia Foundation for the Humanities Open
    Grants, 2387
Whole Foods Foundation, 2445
Whole Kids Foundation School Garden Grants, 2446
William and Flora Hewlett Foundation
    Environmental Grants, 2455
YSA Global Youth Service Day Lead Agy Grts, 2514

Cape Verde
Cargill Corporate Giving Grants, 503

Cayman Islands
Elton John AIDS Foundation Grants, 910

Central African Republic
Cargill Corporate Giving Grants, 503

Chad
Cargill Corporate Giving Grants, 503

Chile
Charles Delmar Foundation Grants, 564
Elton John AIDS Foundation Grants, 910
Isabel Allende Foundation Esperanza Grants, 1315
Katherine John Murphy Foundation Grants, 1419
OSF Young Feminist Leaders Fellowships, 1845

China
Avery Dennison Foundation Education Grants, 337
BP Foundation Grants, 465
Cabot Corporation Foundation Grants, 490
H.B. Fuller Foundation Grants, 1138
Intel Corporation Int Community Grants, 1312
Kimball International-Habig Foundation Education
    Grants, 1433
Kimball International-Habig Foundation Health and
    Human Services Grants, 1434
Medtronic Foundation Strengthening Health Systems
    Grants, 1632

Christmas Island
H.B. Fuller Foundation Grants, 1138

Cocos
H.B. Fuller Foundation Grants, 1138

Colombia
Charles Delmar Foundation Grants, 564
Elton John AIDS Foundation Grants, 910
Katherine John Murphy Foundation Grants, 1419
OSF Young Feminist Leaders Fellowships, 1845

Comoros
Cargill Corporate Giving Grants, 503

Congo, Democratic Republic of
Cargill Corporate Giving Grants, 503

Congo, Republic of the
Cargill Corporate Giving Grants, 503

Cook Islands
NZDIA Community Org Grants Scheme, 1796

Costa Rica
Atkinson Foundation Community Grants, 325
Blossom Fund Grants, 441
Elton John AIDS Foundation Grants, 910
Intel Corporation Int Community Grants, 1312
Katherine John Murphy Foundation Grants, 1419
OSF Young Feminist Leaders Fellowships, 1845
SME Education Fdn Youth Program Grants, 2209

Cote d' Ivoire (Ivory Coast)
Cargill Corporate Giving Grants, 503

Croatia
Cargill Corporate Giving Grants, 503
Charles Delmar Foundation Grants, 564
GMFUS Balkan Trust for Democracy Grants, 1075
Medtronic Foundation Strengthening Health Systems
    Grants, 1632

Cuba
Atkinson Foundation Community Grants, 325
Elton John AIDS Foundation Grants, 910
Katherine John Murphy Foundation Grants, 1419
OSF Young Feminist Leaders Fellowships, 1845
SME Education Fdn Youth Program Grants, 2209

Cyprus
Cargill Corporate Giving Grants, 503
Charles Delmar Foundation Grants, 564
H.B. Fuller Foundation Grants, 1138

Czech Republic (Czechia)
Cargill Corporate Giving Grants, 503
Charles Delmar Foundation Grants, 564
Medtronic Foundation Strengthening Health Systems
    Grants, 1632

Denmark
BP Foundation Grants, 465
Cargill Corporate Giving Grants, 503
Charles Delmar Foundation Grants, 564

Djibouti
Cargill Corporate Giving Grants, 503

Dominica
Atkinson Foundation Community Grants, 325
Elton John AIDS Foundation Grants, 910
SME Education Fdn Youth Program Grants, 2209

Dominican Republic
Atkinson Foundation Community Grants, 325
Elton John AIDS Foundation Grants, 910
Katherine John Murphy Foundation Grants, 1419
OSF Young Feminist Leaders Fellowships, 1845
SME Education Fdn Youth Program Grants, 2209

Ecuador
Charles Delmar Foundation Grants, 564
Elton John AIDS Foundation Grants, 910
Katherine John Murphy Foundation Grants, 1419
OSF Young Feminist Leaders Fellowships, 1845

Egypt
BibleLands Grants, 420
Cargill Corporate Giving Grants, 503

El Salvador
Atkinson Foundation Community Grants, 325
Blossom Fund Grants, 441
Elton John AIDS Foundation Grants, 910
Katherine John Murphy Foundation Grants, 1419
OSF Young Feminist Leaders Fellowships, 1845
SME Education Fdn Youth Program Grants, 2209

Equatorial Guinea
Cargill Corporate Giving Grants, 503

Eritrea
Cargill Corporate Giving Grants, 503

Estonia
BP Foundation Grants, 465
Cargill Corporate Giving Grants, 503
Charles Delmar Foundation Grants, 564

Eswatini (Swaziland)
Cargill Corporate Giving Grants, 503

Ethiopia
Aid for Starving Children Emerg Aid Grants, 144
Cargill Corporate Giving Grants, 503
Firelight Foundation Grants, 964
Oak Foundation Child Abuse Grants, 1799

Fiji
NZDIA Community Org Grants Scheme, 1796

Finland
BP Foundation Grants, 465
Cargill Corporate Giving Grants, 503
Charles Delmar Foundation Grants, 564

France
BP Foundation Grants, 465
Cargill Corporate Giving Grants, 503
Charles Delmar Foundation Grants, 564

French Guiana
OSF Young Feminist Leaders Fellowships, 1845

French Polynesia
NZDIA Community Org Grants Scheme, 1796

Gabon
Cargill Corporate Giving Grants, 503

Gambia
Cargill Corporate Giving Grants, 503

Georgia
Cargill Corporate Giving Grants, 503
Charles Delmar Foundation Grants, 564

Germany
Abbott Fund Community Engagement Grants, 46
Abbott Fund Science Education Grants, 48
BP Foundation Grants, 465
Cargill Corporate Giving Grants, 503
Charles Delmar Foundation Grants, 564
Medtronic Foundation Strengthening Health Systems
    Grants, 1632
Pediatric Brain Tumor Foundation Early Career
    Development Grants, 1924
Textron Corporate Contributions Grants, 2286

Ghana
Cargill Corporate Giving Grants, 503
William and Flora Hewlett Foundation Quality
    Education in Developing Countries Grants, 2456

Greece
BP Foundation Grants, 465
Cargill Corporate Giving Grants, 503
Charles Delmar Foundation Grants, 564

Grenada
Atkinson Foundation Community Grants, 325
Elton John AIDS Foundation Grants, 910
SME Education Fdn Youth Program Grants, 2209

Guadeloupe
Elton John AIDS Foundation Grants, 910
OSF Young Feminist Leaders Fellowships, 1845

Guatemala
Atkinson Foundation Community Grants, 325
Blossom Fund Grants, 441
Elton John AIDS Foundation Grants, 910
Katherine John Murphy Foundation Grants, 1419
OSF Young Feminist Leaders Fellowships, 1845
SME Education Fdn Youth Program Grants, 2209

Guinea
Cargill Corporate Giving Grants, 503

Guinea-Bissau
Cargill Corporate Giving Grants, 503

Guyana
Charles Delmar Foundation Grants, 564
Elton John AIDS Foundation Grants, 910

Haiti
Abundance Foundation International Grants, 57
Aid for Starving Children Health and Nutrition
    Grants, 145
Atkinson Foundation Community Grants, 325
Elton John AIDS Foundation Grants, 910
Katherine John Murphy Foundation Grants, 1419
OSF Young Feminist Leaders Fellowships, 1845
PDF Community Organizing Grants, 1920
PDF Fiscal Sponsorship Grant, 1921
SME Education Fdn Youth Program Grants, 2209

Holy See (Vatican City State)
Cargill Corporate Giving Grants, 503
Charles Delmar Foundation Grants, 564

Honduras
Atkinson Foundation Community Grants, 325
Blossom Fund Grants, 441
Elton John AIDS Foundation Grants, 910
Katherine John Murphy Foundation Grants, 1419
OSF Young Feminist Leaders Fellowships, 1845
SME Education Fdn Youth Program Grants, 2209

Hong Kong
BP Foundation Grants, 465
H.B. Fuller Foundation Grants, 1138
Lubrizol Corporation Community Grants, 1512
May and Stanley Smith Charitable Trust Grants, 1613

Hungary
Cargill Corporate Giving Grants, 503
Charles Delmar Foundation Grants, 564
Medtronic Foundation Strengthening Health Systems
    Grants, 1632

Iceland
Cargill Corporate Giving Grants, 503
Charles Delmar Foundation Grants, 564

India
Avery Dennison Foundation Education Grants, 337
H.B. Fuller Foundation Grants, 1138
Intel Corporation Int Community Grants, 1312
J. Watumull Fund Grants, 1326
Medtronic Foundation Strengthening Health Systems
    Grants, 1632
Michael and Susan Dell Foundation Grants, 1657
Oak Fdn Housing and Homelessness Grants, 1800
Prudential Spirit of Community Awards, 2029
William and Flora Hewlett Foundation Quality
    Education in Developing Countries Grants, 2456

Indonesia
H.B. Fuller Foundation Grants, 1138

Iran
H.B. Fuller Foundation Grants, 1138

Iraq
H.B. Fuller Foundation Grants, 1138

Ireland
Abbott Fund Community Engagement Grants, 46
Abbott Fund Science Education Grants, 48
BP Foundation Grants, 465
Cargill Corporate Giving Grants, 503
Charles Delmar Foundation Grants, 564
Intel Corporation Int Community Grants, 1312
Medtronic Foundation CommunityLink Health
    Grants, 1630
Prudential Spirit of Community Awards, 2029

Israel
BibleLands Grants, 420
H.B. Fuller Foundation Grants, 1138
Intel Corporation Int Community Grants, 1312
Jacob and Hilda Blaustein Foundation Israel Program
    Grants, 1335
Koret Foundation Grants, 1449
Manuel D. and Rhoda Mayerson Fdn Grants, 1550

Italy
Abbott Fund Community Engagement Grants, 46
Abbott Fund Science Education Grants, 48
BP Foundation Grants, 465
Cargill Corporate Giving Grants, 503
Charles Delmar Foundation Grants, 564
Micron Technology Fdn Community Grants, 1664

Jamaica
Atkinson Foundation Community Grants, 325
Elton John AIDS Foundation Grants, 910
SME Education Fdn Youth Program Grants, 2209

Japan
Abbott Fund Community Engagement Grants, 46
Abbott Fund Science Education Grants, 48
BP Foundation Grants, 465
H.B. Fuller Foundation Grants, 1138
Medtronic Foundation CommunityLink Health
    Grants, 1630
Micron Technology Fdn Community Grants, 1664
Prudential Spirit of Community Awards, 2029

Jordan
H.B. Fuller Foundation Grants, 1138

Kazakhstan
H.B. Fuller Foundation Grants, 1138

Kenya
Aid for Starving Children Homes and Ed Grants, 146
Aid for Starving Children Water Projects Grants, 147
Cargill Corporate Giving Grants, 503
Firelight Foundation Grants, 964
William and Flora Hewlett Foundation Quality
    Education in Developing Countries Grants, 2456

Kiribati
NZDIA Community Org Grants Scheme, 1796

Kosovo
Cargill Corporate Giving Grants, 503
Charles Delmar Foundation Grants, 564
GMFUS Balkan Trust for Democracy Grants, 1075

Kuwait
H.B. Fuller Foundation Grants, 1138

Kyrgyz Republic (Kyrgystan)
H.B. Fuller Foundation Grants, 1138
OSF Education Program Grants in Kyrgyzstan, 1842
OSF Youth Action Fund Grants in Kyrgyzstan, 1846

Laos
H.B. Fuller Foundation Grants, 1138

Latvia
Cargill Corporate Giving Grants, 503
Charles Delmar Foundation Grants, 564
Oak Foundation Child Abuse Grants, 1799

Lebanon
BibleLands Grants, 420
H.B. Fuller Foundation Grants, 1138

Lesotho
Cargill Corporate Giving Grants, 503
Firelight Foundation Grants, 964

Liberia
Cargill Corporate Giving Grants, 503

Libya
Cargill Corporate Giving Grants, 503

Liechtenstein
Cargill Corporate Giving Grants, 503
Charles Delmar Foundation Grants, 564
Medtronic Foundation Strengthening Health Systems
    Grants, 1632

Lithuania
Cargill Corporate Giving Grants, 503
Charles Delmar Foundation Grants, 564

Luxembourg
BP Foundation Grants, 465
Cargill Corporate Giving Grants, 503
Charles Delmar Foundation Grants, 564

Macau
H.B. Fuller Foundation Grants, 1138
Sands Cares Grants, 2156

Madagascar
Cargill Corporate Giving Grants, 503

Malawi
Aid for Starving Children Emerg Aid Grants, 144
Cargill Corporate Giving Grants, 503
Firelight Foundation Grants, 964

Malaysia
H.B. Fuller Foundation Grants, 1138
Intel Corporation Int Community Grants, 1312

Maldives
H.B. Fuller Foundation Grants, 1138

Mali
Cargill Corporate Giving Grants, 503
William and Flora Hewlett Foundation Quality
    Education in Developing Countries Grants, 2456

Malta
Cargill Corporate Giving Grants, 503
Charles Delmar Foundation Grants, 564

Martinique
Elton John AIDS Foundation Grants, 910
OSF Young Feminist Leaders Fellowships, 1845

Mauritania
Cargill Corporate Giving Grants, 503

Mauritius
Cargill Corporate Giving Grants, 503

Mexico
Alaska Airlines Corporation Career Connections for
    Youth Grants, 193
Atkinson Foundation Community Grants, 325
Blossom Fund Grants, 441
BP Foundation Grants, 465
Elton John AIDS Foundation Grants, 910
General Service Foundation Human Rights and
    Economic Justice Grants, 1040
Katherine John Murphy Foundation Grants, 1419
Kimball International-Habig Foundation Education
    Grants, 1433
Kimball International-Habig Foundation Health and
    Human Services Grants, 1434
New Covenant Farms Grants, 1742
Oak Foundation Child Abuse Grants, 1799
OSF Young Feminist Leaders Fellowships, 1845
Paso del Norte Health Foundation Grants, 1874
PDF Community Organizing Grants, 1920
PDF Fiscal Sponsorship Grant, 1921
SME Education Fdn Youth Program Grants, 2209
UUA Actions of Public Witness Grants, 2365
UUA Congregation-Based Community Organizing
    Grants, 2366
UUA Fund Grants, 2367
UUA International Fund Grants, 2368
UUA Social Responsibility Grants, 2370

Micronesia
NZDIA Community Org Grants Scheme, 1796

Moldova
Cargill Corporate Giving Grants, 503
Charles Delmar Foundation Grants, 564
Medtronic Foundation Strengthening Health Systems
    Grants, 1632
Oak Foundation Child Abuse Grants, 1799

Monaco
Cargill Corporate Giving Grants, 503
Charles Delmar Foundation Grants, 564

Mongolia
H.B. Fuller Foundation Grants, 1138

Montenegro
Cargill Corporate Giving Grants, 503
Charles Delmar Foundation Grants, 564
GMFUS Balkan Trust for Democracy Grants, 1075

Montserrat
Elton John AIDS Foundation Grants, 910

Morocco
Cargill Corporate Giving Grants, 503

Mozambique
Cargill Corporate Giving Grants, 503

Myanmar (Burma)
H.B. Fuller Foundation Grants, 1138

Nagorno-Karabakh
H.B. Fuller Foundation Grants, 1138

Namibia
Cargill Corporate Giving Grants, 503

Nauru
NZDIA Community Org Grants Scheme, 1796

Nepal
H.B. Fuller Foundation Grants, 1138

Netherlands
Abbott Fund Community Engagement Grants, 46
Abbott Fund Science Education Grants, 48
BP Foundation Grants, 465
Cargill Corporate Giving Grants, 503
Charles Delmar Foundation Grants, 564
Medtronic Foundation CommunityLink Health
    Grants, 1630
Oak Foundation Child Abuse Grants, 1799

New Caledonia
NZDIA Community Org Grants Scheme, 1796

New Zealand
NZDIA Community Org Grants Scheme, 1796
NZDIA Lottery Minister's Discretionary Fund
    Grants, 1797

Nicaragua
Aid for Starving Children Health and Nutrition
    Grants, 145
Atkinson Foundation Community Grants, 325
Blossom Fund Grants, 441
Elton John AIDS Foundation Grants, 910
Katherine John Murphy Foundation Grants, 1419
OSF Young Feminist Leaders Fellowships, 1845
SME Education Fdn Youth Program Grants, 2209

Niger
Cargill Corporate Giving Grants, 503

Nigeria
Cargill Corporate Giving Grants, 503
USAID Nigeria Ed Crisis Response Grants, 2358

Niue
NZDIA Community Org Grants Scheme, 1796

North Korea
H.B. Fuller Foundation Grants, 1138

North Macedonia
Cargill Corporate Giving Grants, 503
Charles Delmar Foundation Grants, 564
GMFUS Balkan Trust for Democracy Grants, 1075

Northern Cyprus
H.B. Fuller Foundation Grants, 1138

Norway
BP Foundation Grants, 465
Cargill Corporate Giving Grants, 503
Charles Delmar Foundation Grants, 564

Oman
H.B. Fuller Foundation Grants, 1138
Pakistan
H.B. Fuller Foundation Grants, 1138

Palau
NZDIA Community Org Grants Scheme, 1796

Palestinian Authority
BibleLands Grants, 420
H.B. Fuller Foundation Grants, 1138

Palestinian Territory
BibleLands Grants, 420

Panama
Blossom Fund Grants, 441
Elton John AIDS Foundation Grants, 910
Katherine John Murphy Foundation Grants, 1419
OSF Young Feminist Leaders Fellowships, 1845

Papua New Guinea
NZDIA Community Org Grants Scheme, 1796

Paraguay
Charles Delmar Foundation Grants, 564
Elton John AIDS Foundation Grants, 910
Katherine John Murphy Foundation Grants, 1419
OSF Young Feminist Leaders Fellowships, 1845

Peru
Charles Delmar Foundation Grants, 564
Elton John AIDS Foundation Grants, 910
Katherine John Murphy Foundation Grants, 1419
OSF Young Feminist Leaders Fellowships, 1845

Philippines
Aid for Starving Children Health and Nutrition
    Grants, 145
BP Foundation Grants, 465
H.B. Fuller Foundation Grants, 1138
Intel Corporation Int Community Grants, 1312

Pitcairn
NZDIA Community Org Grants Scheme, 1796

Poland
BP Foundation Grants, 465
Cargill Corporate Giving Grants, 503
Charles Delmar Foundation Grants, 564
Kimball International-Habig Foundation Education
    Grants, 1433
Kimball International-Habig Foundation Health and
    Human Services Grants, 1434
Medtronic Foundation Strengthening Health Systems
    Grants, 1632

Portugal
BP Foundation Grants, 465
Cargill Corporate Giving Grants, 503
Charles Delmar Foundation Grants, 564

Qatar
H.B. Fuller Foundation Grants, 1138

Romania
Cargill Corporate Giving Grants, 503
Charles Delmar Foundation Grants, 564
GMFUS Balkan Trust for Democracy Grants, 1075
Medtronic Foundation Strengthening Health Systems
    Grants, 1632

Russia
BP Foundation Grants, 465
Cargill Corporate Giving Grants, 503

Charles Delmar Foundation Grants, 564
H.B. Fuller Foundation Grants, 1138
Intel Corporation Int Community Grants, 1312
Medtronic Foundation Strengthening Health Systems
    Grants, 1632

Rwanda
Cargill Corporate Giving Grants, 503
Firelight Foundation Grants, 964

Saint Kitts And Nevis
Elton John AIDS Foundation Grants, 910

Saint Lucia
Elton John AIDS Foundation Grants, 910

Saint Vincent and the Grenadines
Elton John AIDS Foundation Grants, 910

San Marino
Cargill Corporate Giving Grants, 503
Charles Delmar Foundation Grants, 564

Sao Tome & Principe
Cargill Corporate Giving Grants, 503

Saudi Arabia
H.B. Fuller Foundation Grants, 1138

Senegal
Cargill Corporate Giving Grants, 503
William and Flora Hewlett Foundation Quality
    Education in Developing Countries Grants, 2456

Serbia
Cargill Corporate Giving Grants, 503
Charles Delmar Foundation Grants, 564
GMFUS Balkan Trust for Democracy Grants, 1075
Medtronic Foundation Strengthening Health Systems
    Grants, 1632

Seychelles
Cargill Corporate Giving Grants, 503

Sierra Leone
Cargill Corporate Giving Grants, 503

Singapore
BP Foundation Grants, 465
H.B. Fuller Foundation Grants, 1138
Micron Technology Fdn Community Grants, 1664
Sands Cares Grants, 2156

Slovakia
Cargill Corporate Giving Grants, 503
Charles Delmar Foundation Grants, 564
Medtronic Foundation Strengthening Health Systems
    Grants, 1632

Slovenia
Cargill Corporate Giving Grants, 503
Charles Delmar Foundation Grants, 564
Medtronic Foundation Strengthening Health Systems
    Grants, 1632

Solomon Islands
NZDIA Community Org Grants Scheme, 1796

Somalia
Aid for Starving Children Emerg Aid Grants, 144
Cargill Corporate Giving Grants, 503

South Africa
Cargill Corporate Giving Grants, 503
Firelight Foundation Grants, 964
Medtronic Foundation Strengthening Health Systems
    Grants, 1632
Michael and Susan Dell Foundation Grants, 1657
Oak Foundation Child Abuse Grants, 1799

South Korea
H.B. Fuller Foundation Grants, 1138
Prudential Spirit of Community Awards, 2029

South Ossetia
H.B. Fuller Foundation Grants, 1138

South Sudan
Aid for Starving Children Emerg Aid Grants, 144

Spain
BP Foundation Grants, 465
Cargill Corporate Giving Grants, 503
Charles Delmar Foundation Grants, 564

Sri Lanka
H.B. Fuller Foundation Grants, 1138

Sudan
Cargill Corporate Giving Grants, 503

Suriname
Elton John AIDS Foundation Grants, 910

Sweden
BP Foundation Grants, 465
Cargill Corporate Giving Grants, 503
Charles Delmar Foundation Grants, 564

Switzerland
BP Foundation Grants, 465
Cabot Corporation Foundation Grants, 490
Cargill Corporate Giving Grants, 503
Charles Delmar Foundation Grants, 564
Medtronic Foundation CommunityLink Health
    Grants, 1630
Medtronic Foundation Strengthening Health Systems
    Grants, 1632
Oak Foundation Child Abuse Grants, 1799

Syrian Arab Republic
H.B. Fuller Foundation Grants, 1138

Taiwan
H.B. Fuller Foundation Grants, 1138
Prudential Spirit of Community Awards, 2029

Tajikistan
H.B. Fuller Foundation Grants, 1138

Tanzania
Better Way Foundation Grants, 419
Firelight Foundation Grants, 964
Oak Foundation Child Abuse Grants, 1799
William and Flora Hewlett Foundation Quality
    Education in Developing Countries Grants, 2456

Thailand
H.B. Fuller Foundation Grants, 1138

Timor-Lester
H.B. Fuller Foundation Grants, 1138

Tokelau
NZDIA Community Org Grants Scheme, 1796

Tonga
NZDIA Community Org Grants Scheme, 1796

Trinidad and Tobago
Elton John AIDS Foundation Grants, 910

Turkey
Cargill Corporate Giving Grants, 503
Charles Delmar Foundation Grants, 564
H.B. Fuller Foundation Grants, 1138

Turkmenistan
H.B. Fuller Foundation Grants, 1138

Turks and Caicos Islands
Elton John AIDS Foundation Grants, 910

Tuvalu
NZDIA Community Org Grants Scheme, 1796

Uganda
Aid for Starving Children Homes and Education
    Grants, 146
Firelight Foundation Grants, 964
Oak Foundation Child Abuse Grants, 1799
William and Flora Hewlett Foundation Quality
    Education in Developing Countries Grants, 2456

Ukraine
Cargill Corporate Giving Grants, 503
Charles Delmar Foundation Grants, 564
Medtronic Foundation Strengthening Health Systems
    Grants, 1632

United Arab Emirates
H.B. Fuller Foundation Grants, 1138

United Kingdom
Abbott Fund Community Engagement Grants, 46
Abbott Fund Science Education Grants, 48
Bank of America Charitable Foundation Matching
    Gifts, 356
Bank of America Charitable Foundation Volunteer
    Grants, 358
Ben Cohen StandUp Foundation Grants, 403
BP Foundation Grants, 465
Cabot Corporation Foundation Grants, 490
Cargill Corporate Giving Grants, 503
Cash 4 Clubs Sports Grants, 515
Charles Delmar Foundation Grants, 564
Gannett Foundation Community Action Grants, 1033
May and Stanley Smith Charitable Trust Grants, 1613
Oak Foundation Child Abuse Grants, 1799
Oak Fdn Housing and Homelessness Grants, 1800
Sylvia Adams Charitable Trust Grants, 2262
Textron Corporate Contributions Grants, 2286
Whole Foods Foundation, 2445
Whole Kids Foundation School Garden Grants, 2446

Uruguay
Elton John AIDS Foundation Grants, 910
Katherine John Murphy Foundation Grants, 1419
OSF Young Feminist Leaders Fellowships, 1845

Uzbekistan
H.B. Fuller Foundation Grants, 1138

Vanuatu
NZDIA Community Org Grants Scheme, 1796

Venezuela
Elton John AIDS Foundation Grants, 910
Katherine John Murphy Foundation Grants, 1419
OSF Young Feminist Leaders Fellowships, 1845

Vietnam
H.B. Fuller Foundation Grants, 1138

Wallis and Furuna Islands
NZDIA Community Org Grants Scheme, 1796

Yemen
H.B. Fuller Foundation Grants, 1138

Zambia
Aid for Starving Children Homes and Education
    Grants, 146
Firelight Foundation Grants, 964

Zimbabwe
Firelight Foundation Grants, 964

CPSIA information can be obtained
at www.ICGtesting.com
Printed in the USA
LVHW021147150323
741648LV00006B/126